TITLES OF UNITED STATES CODE

*1. General Provisions.

2. The Congress.

*3. The President.

*4. Flag and Seal, Seat of Government, and the States.

*5. Government Organization and Employees; and Appendix.

†6. [Surety Bonds.]

7. Agriculture.

8. Aliens and Nationality.

*9. Arbitration.

*10. Armed Forces; and Appendix.

*11. Bankruptcy; and Appendix.

12. Banks and Banking.

*13. Census.

*14. Coast Guard.

15. Commerce and Trade.

16. Conservation.

*17. Copyrights.

*18. Crimes and Criminal Procedure; and Appendix.

19. Customs Duties.

20. Education.

21. Food and Drugs.

22. Foreign Relations and Intercourse.

*23. Highways.

24. Hospitals and Asylums.

25. Indians.

26. Internal Revenue Code; and Appendix.

27. Intoxicating Liquors.

*28. Judiciary and Judicial Procedure; and Appendix.

29. Labor.

30. Mineral Lands and Mining.

*31. Money and Finance.

*32. National Guard.

33. Navigation and Navigable Waters.

‡34. [Navy.]

*35. Patents.

*36. Patriotic and National Observances, Ceremonies, and Organizations.

*37. Pay and Allowances of the Uniformed Services.

*38. Veterans' Benefits; and Appendix.

*39. Postal Service.

40. Public Buildings, Property, and Works; and Appendix.

41. Public Contracts.

42. The Public Health and Welfare.

43. Public Lands.

*44. Public Printing and Documents.

45. Railroads.

*46. Shipping; and Appendix.

47. Telegraphs, Telephones, and Radiotelegraphs.

48. Territories and Insular Possessions.

*49. Transportation.

50. War and National Defense; and Appendix.

---

*This title has been enacted as positive law. However, any Appendix to this title has not been enacted as positive law.
†This title was repealed by the enactment of Title 31.
‡This title was eliminated by the enactment of Title 10.

CONTENTS

Page V

CONTENTS

PREFACE—2000 EDITION

The 2000 edition of the United States Code represents the 75th anniversary of the Code. It is the thirteenth edition of the Code, first published in 1926 with a new edition published every six years since 1934. This edition is a consolidation and codification of the general and permanent laws of the United States in force on January 2, 2001. The only basic differences between this edition and the 1994 edition of the Code are the changes required to incorporate the legislation enacted subsequent to the 1994 edition. This edition was prepared and published under the supervision of John R. Miller, Law Revision Counsel of the House of Representatives, pursuant to section 285b of Title 2 of the Code, and may be cited "U.S.C. 2000 ed."

As adopted in 1926, the Code establishes prima facie the general and permanent laws of the United States. Since that time, the Office of the Law Revision Counsel and its predecessors have been engaged in an ongoing effort to revise and codify for enactment into positive law specific titles of the Code. Upon enactment into positive law, those titles became legal evidence of the law contained therein, and provide an updated statement of the law with the elimination of inconsistent, redundant, and obsolete provisions. As indicated in the table of titles, about half of the titles of the Code have been enacted into positive law. When the entire Code is enacted, there will be no need to resort to the numerous volumes of the United States Statutes at Large for general and permanent law.

Speaker of the House of Representatives

WASHINGTON, D.C., *January 2, 2001.*

TABLE OF TITLES AND CHAPTERS

THE ORGANIC LAWS
OF
THE UNITED STATES OF AMERICA

THE DECLARATION OF INDEPENDENCE—1776 [1]

IN CONGRESS, JULY 4, 1776

The unanimous Declaration of the thirteen united States of America

WHEN in the Course of human events, it becomes necessary for one people to dissolve the political bands which have connected them with another, and to assume among the powers of the earth, the separate and equal station to which the Laws of Nature and of Nature's God entitle them, a decent respect to the opinions of mankind requires that they should declare the causes which impel them to the separation.

[1] The delegates of the United Colonies of New Hampshire; Massachusetts Bay; Rhode Island and Providence Plantations; Connecticut; New York; New Jersey; Pennsylvania; New Castle, Kent, and Sussex, in Delaware; Maryland; Virginia; North Carolina, and South Carolina, In Congress assembled at Philadelphia, *Resolved* on the 10th of May, 1776, to recommend to the respective assemblies and conventions of the United Colonies, where no government sufficient to the exigencies of their affairs had been established, to adopt such a government as should, in the opinion of the representatives of the people, best conduce to the happiness and safety of their constituents in particular, and of America in general. A preamble to this resolution, agreed to on the 15th of May, stated the intention to be totally to suppress the exercise of every kind of authority under the British crown. On the 7th of June, certain resolutions respecting independency were moved and seconded. On the 10th of June it was resolved, that a committee should be appointed to prepare a declaration to the following effect: "That the United Colonies are, and of right ought to be, free and independent States; that they are absolved from all allegiance to the British crown; and that all political connection between them and the State of Great Britain is, and ought to be, totally dissolved." On the preceding day it was determined that the committee for preparing the declaration should consist of five, and they were chosen accordingly, in the following order: Mr. Jefferson, Mr. J. Adams, Mr. Franklin, Mr. Sherman, Mr. R. R. Livingston. On the 11th of June a resolution was passed to appoint a committee to prepare and digest the form of a confederation to be entered into between the colonies, and another committee to prepare a plan of treaties to be proposed to foreign powers. On the 12th of June, it was resolved, that a committee of Congress should be appointed by the name of a board of war and ordnance, to consist of five members. On the 25th of June, a declaration of the deputies of Pennsylvania, met in provincial conference, expressing their willingness to concur in a vote declaring the United Colonies free and independent States, was laid before Congress and read. On the 28th of June, the committee appointed to prepare a declaration of independence brought in a draught, which was read, and ordered to lie on the table. On the 1st of July, a resolution of the convention of Maryland, passed the 28th of June, authorizing the deputies of that colony to concur in declaring the United Colonies free and independent States, was laid before Congress and read. On the same day Congress resolved itself into a committee of the whole, to take into consideration the resolution respecting independency. On the 2d of July, a resolution declaring the colonies free and independent States, was adopted. A declaration to that effect was, on the same and the following days, taken into further consideration. Finally, on the 4th of July, the Declaration of Independence was agreed to, engrossed on paper, signed by John Hancock as president, and directed to be sent to the several assemblies, conventions, and committees, or councils of safety, and to the several commanding officers of the continental troops, and to be proclaimed in each of the United States, and at the head of the Army. It was also ordered to be entered upon the Journals of Congress, and on the 2d of August, a copy engrossed on parchment was signed by all but one of the fifty-six signers whose names are appended to it. That one was Matthew Thornton, of New Hampshire, who on taking his seat in November asked and obtained the privilege of signing it. Several who signed it on the 2d of August were absent when it was adopt-

We hold these truths to be self-evident, that all men are created equal, that they are endowed by their Creator with certain unalienable Rights, that among these are Life, Liberty and the pursuit of Happiness. That to secure these rights, Governments are instituted among Men, deriving their just powers from the consent of the governed,—That whenever any Form of Government becomes destructive of these ends, it is the Right of the People to alter or to abolish it, and to institute new Government, laying its foundation on such principles and organizing its powers in such form, as to them shall seem most likely to effect their Safety and Happiness. Prudence, indeed, will dictate that Governments long established should not be changed for light and transient causes; and accordingly all experience hath shewn, that mankind are more disposed to suffer, while evils are sufferable, than to right themselves by abolishing the forms to which they are accustomed. But when a long train of abuses and usurpations, pursuing invariably the same Object evinces a design to reduce them under absolute Despotism, it is their right, it is their duty, to throw off such Government, and to provide new Guards for their future security.—Such has been the patient sufferance of these Colonies; and such is now the necessity which constrains them to alter their former Systems of Government. The history of the present King of Great Britain is a history of repeated injuries and usurpations, all having in direct object the establishment of an absolute Tyranny over these States. To prove this, let Facts be submitted to a candid world.

He has refused his Assent to Laws, the most wholesome and necessary for the public good.

He has forbidden his Governors to pass Laws of immediate and pressing importance, unless suspended in their operation till his Assent should be obtained; and when so suspended, he has utterly neglected to attend to them.

He has refused to pass other Laws for the accommodation of large districts of people, unless those people would relinquish the right of Representation in the Legislature, a right inestimable to them and formidable to tyrants only.

He has called together legislative bodies at places unusual, uncomfortable, and distance

ed on the 4th of July, but, approving of it, they thus signified their approbation.

NOTE.—The proof of this document, as published above, was read by Mr. Ferdinand Jefferson, the Keeper of the Rolls at the Department of State, at Washington, who compared it with the fac-simile of the original in his custody. He says: "In the fac-simile, as in the original, the whole instrument runs on without a break, but dashes are mostly inserted. I have, in this copy, followed the arrangement of paragraphs adopted in the publication of the Declaration in the newspaper of John Dunlap, and as printed by him for the Congress, which printed copy is inserted in the original Journal of the old Congress. The same paragraphs are also made by the author, in the original draught preserved in the Department of State."

from the depository of their public Records, for the sole purpose of fatiguing them into compliance with his measures.

He has dissolved Representative Houses repeatedly, for opposing with manly firmness his invasions on the rights of the people.

He has refused for a long time, after such dissolutions, to cause others to be elected; whereby the Legislative powers, incapable of Annihilation, have returned to the People at large for their exercise; the State remaining in the mean time exposed to all the dangers of invasion from without, and convulsions within.

He has endeavoured to prevent the population of these States; for that purpose obstructing the Laws for Naturalization of Foreigners; refusing to pass others to encourage their migrations hither, and raising the conditions of new Appropriations of Lands.

He has obstructed the Administration of Justice, by refusing his Assent to Laws for establishing Judiciary powers.

He has made Judges dependent on his Will alone, for the tenure of their offices, and the amount and payment of their salaries.

He has erected a multitude of New Offices, and sent hither swarms of Officers to harass our people, and eat out their substance.

He has kept among us, in times of peace, Standing Armies without the Consent of our legislatures.

He has affected to render the Military independent of and superior to the Civil power.

He has combined with others to subject us to a jurisdiction foreign to our constitution, and unacknowledged by our laws; giving his Assent to their acts of pretended Legislation:

For quartering large bodies of armed troops among us:

For protecting them, by a mock Trial, from punishment for any Murders which they should commit on the Inhabitants of these States:

For cutting off our Trade with all parts of the world:

For imposing Taxes on us without our Consent:

For depriving us in many cases, of the benefits of Trial by Jury:

For transporting us beyond Seas to be tried for pretended offenses:

For abolishing the free System of English Laws in a neighbouring Province, establishing therein an Arbitrary government, and enlarging its Boundaries so as to render it at once an example and fit instrument for introducing the same absolute rule into these Colonies:

For taking away our Charters, abolishing our most valuable Laws, and altering fundamentally the Forms of our Governments:

For suspending our own Legislatures, and declaring themselves invested with power to legislate for us in all cases whatsoever.

He has abdicated Government here, by declaring us out of his Protection and waging War against us.

He has plundered our seas, ravaged our Coasts, burnt our towns, and destroyed the lives of our people.

He is at this time transporting large Armies of foreign Mercenaries to compleat the works of death, desolation and tyranny, already begun with circumstances of Cruelty & perfidy scarcely paralleled in the most barbarous ages, and totally unworthy the Head of a civilized nation.

He has constrained our fellow Citizens taken Captive on the high Seas to bear Arms against their Country, to become the executioners of their friends and Brethren, or to fall themselves by their Hands.

He has excited domestic insurrections amongst us, and has endeavoured to bring on the inhabitants of our frontiers, the merciless Indian Savages, whose known rule of warfare, is an undistinguished destruction of all ages, sexes and conditions.

In every stage of these Oppressions We have Petitioned for Redress in the most humble terms: Our repeated Petitions have been answered only by repeated injury. A Prince, whose character is thus marked by every act which may define a Tyrant, is unfit to be the ruler of a free people.

Nor have We been wanting in attentions to our Brittish brethren. We have warned them from time to time of attempts by their legislature to extend an unwarrantable jurisdiction over us. We have reminded them of the circumstances of our emigration and settlement here. We have appealed to their native justice and magnanimity, and we have conjured them by the ties of our common kindred to disavow these usurpations, which, would inevitably interrupt our connections and correspondence. They too have been deaf to the voice of justice and of consanguinity. We must, therefore, acquiesce in the necessity, which denounces our Separation, and hold them, as we hold the rest of mankind, Enemies in War, in Peace Friends.

WE, THEREFORE, the Representatives of the UNITED STATES OF AMERICA, in General Congress, Assembled, appealing to the Supreme Judge of the world for the rectitude of our intentions, do, in the Name, and by Authority of the good People of these Colonies, solemnly publish and declare, That these United Colonies are, and of Right ought to be FREE AND INDEPENDENT STATES; that they are Absolved from all Allegiance to the British Crown, and that all political connection between them and the State of Great Britain, is and ought to be totally dissolved; and that as Free and Independent States, they have full Power to levy War, conclude Peace, contract Alliances, establish Commerce, and to do all other Acts and Things which Independent States may of right do. And for the support of this Declaration, with a firm reliance on the protection of divine Providence, we mutually pledge to each other our Lives, our Fortunes and our sacred Honor.

JOHN HANCOCK.

New Hampshire

JOSIAH BARTLETT,   MATTHEW THORNTON.
WM. WHIPPLE,

Massachusetts Bay

SAML. ADAMS,   ROBT. TREAT PAINE,
JOHN ADAMS,   ELBRIDGE GERRY.

Rhode Island

STEP. HOPKINS,   WILLIAM ELLERY.

Connecticut

ROGER SHERMAN,   WM. WILLIAMS,
SAM'EL HUNTINGTON,   OLIVER WOLCOTT.

New York

WM. FLOYD,   FRANS. LEWIS,
PHIL. LIVINGSTON,   LEWIS MORRIS.

New Jersey

RICHD. STOCKTON,   JOHN HART,
JNO. WITHERSPOON,   ABRA. CLARK.
FRAS. HOPKINSON,

Pennsylvania

ROBT. MORRIS,   JAS. SMITH,
BENJAMIN RUSH,   GEO. TAYLOR,
BENJA. FRANKLIN,   JAMES WILSON,
JOHN MORTON,   GEO. ROSS.
GEO. CLYMER,

Delaware

CAESAR RODNEY,   THO. M'KEAN.
GEO. READ,

Maryland

SAMUEL CHASE,   CHARLES CARROLL OF
WM. PACA,   Carrollton.
THOS. STONE,

Virginia

GEORGE WYTHE,   THOS. NELSON, jr.,
RICHARD HENRY LEE,   FRANCIS LIGHTFOOT
TH. JEFFERSON,   LEE,
BENJA. HARRISON,   CARTER BRAXTON.

North Carolina

WM. HOOPER,   JOHN PENN.
JOSEPH HEWES,

South Carolina

THOS. HEYWARD,   THOMAS LYNCH, Junr.,
  Junr.,   ARTHUR MIDDLETON.
EDWARD RUTLEDGE,

Georgia

BUTTON GWINNETT,   GEO. WALTON.
LYMAN HALL,

NOTE.—Mr. Ferdinand Jefferson, Keeper of the Rolls in the Department of State, at Washington, says: "The names of the signers are spelt above as in the fac-simile of the original, but the punctuation of them is not always the same; neither do the names of the States appear in the fac-simile of the original. The names of the signers of each State are grouped together in the fac-simile of the original, except the name of Matthew Thornton, which follows that of Oliver Wolcott."

ARTICLES OF CONFEDERATION—1777[1]

To all to whom these Presents shall come, we the undersigned Delegates of the States affixed to our Names send greeting

Whereas the Delegates of the United States of America in Congress assembled did on the fifteenth day of November in the Year of our Lord One Thousand Seven Hundred and Seventyseven, and in the Second Year of the Independence of America agree to certain articles of Confederation and perpetual Union between the States of Newhampshire, Massachusetts-bay, Rhodeisland and Providence Plantations, Connecticut, New York, New Jersey, Pennsylvania, Delaware, Maryland, Virginia, North-Carolina, South-Carolina and Georgia in the Words following, viz.

"Articles of Confederation and perpetual Union between the States of Newhampshire, Massachusettsbay, Rhodeisland and Providence Plantations, Connecticut, New-York, New-Jersey, Pennsylvania, Delaware, Maryland, Virginia, North-Carolina, South-Carolina and Georgia.

---

[1] Congress *Resolved*, on the 11th of June, 1776, that a committee should be appointed to prepare and digest the form of a confederation to be entered into between the Colonies; and on the day following, after it had been determined that the committee should consist of a member from each Colony, the following persons were appointed to perform that duty, to wit: Mr. Bartlett, Mr. S. Adams, Mr. Hopkins, Mr. Sherman, Mr. R. R. Livingston, Mr. Dickinson, Mr. M'Kean, Mr. Stone, Mr. Nelson, Mr. Hewes, Mr. E. Rutledge, and Mr. Gwinnett. Upon the report of this committee, the subject was, from time to time, debated, until the 15th of November, 1777, when a copy of the confederation being made out, and sundry amendments made in the diction, without altering the sense, the same was finally agreed to. Congress, at the same time, directed that the articles should be proposed to the legislatures of all the United States, to be considered, and if approved of by them, they were advised to authorize their delegates to ratify the same in the Congress of the United States; which being done, the same should become conclusive. Three hundred copies of the Articles of Confederation were ordered to be printed for the use of Congress; and on the 17th of November, the form of a circular letter to accompany them was brought in by a committee appointed to prepare it, and being agreed to, thirteen copies of it were ordered to be made out, to be signed by the president and forwarded to the several States, with copies of the confederation. On the 29th of November ensuing, a committee of three was appointed, to procure a translation of the articles to be made into the French language, and to report an address to the inhabitants of Canada, &c. On the 26th of June, 1778, the form of a ratification of the Articles of Confederation was adopted, and, it having been engrossed on parchment, it was signed on the 9th of July on the part and in behalf of their respective States, by the delegates of New Hampshire, Massachusetts Bay, Rhode Island and Providence Plantations, Connecticut, New York, Pennsylvania, Virginia, and South Carolina, agreeably to the powers vested in them. The delegates of North Carolina signed on the 21st of July, those of Georgia on the 24th of July, and those of New Jersey on the 26th of November following. On the 5th of May, 1779, Mr. Dickinson and Mr. Van Dyke signed in behalf of the State of Delaware, Mr. M'Kean having previously signed in February, at which time he produced a power to that effect. Maryland did not ratify until the year 1781. She had instructed her delegates, on the 15th of December, 1778, not to agree to the confederation until matters respecting the western lands should be settled on principles of equity and sound policy; but, on the 30th of January, 1781, finding that the enemies of the country took advantage of the circumstance to disseminate opinions of an ultimate dissolution of the Union, the

ARTICLE I. The stile of this confederacy shall be "The United States of America."

ARTICLE II. Each State retains its sovereignty, freedom and independence, and every power, jurisdiction and right, which is not by this confederation expressly delegated to the United States, in Congress assembled.

ARTICLE III. The said States hereby severally enter into a firm league of friendship with each other, for their common defence, the security of their liberties, and their mutual and general welfare, binding themselves to assist each other, against all force offered to, or attacks made upon them, or any of them, on account of religion, sovereignty, trade, or any other pretence whatever.

ARTICLE IV. The better to secure and perpetuate mutual friendship and intercourse among the people of the different States in this Union, the free inhabitants of each of these States, paupers, vagabonds and fugitives from justice excepted, shall be entitled to all privileges and immunities of free citizens in the several States; and the people of each State shall have free ingress and regress to and from any other State, and shall enjoy therein all the privileges of trade and commerce, subject to the same duties, impositions and restrictions as the inhabitants thereof respectively, provided that such restrictions shall not extend so far as to prevent the removal of property imported into any State, to any other State of which the owner is an inhabitant; provided also that no imposition, duties or restriction shall be laid by any State, on the property of the United States, or either of them.

If any person guilty of, or charged with treason, felony, or other high misdemeanor in any State, shall flee from justice, and be found in any of the United States, he shall upon demand of the Governor or Executive power, of the State from which he fled, be delivered up and removed to the State having jurisdiction of his offence.

Full faith and credit shall be given in each of these States to the records, acts and judicial proceedings of the courts and magistrats of every other State.

ARTICLE V. For the more convenient management of the general interests of the United

---

legislature of the State passed an act to empower their delegates to subscribe and ratify the articles, which was accordingly done by Mr. Hanson and Mr. Carroll, on the 1st of March of that year, which completed the ratifications of the act; and Congress assembled on the 2d of March under the new powers.

NOTE.—The proof of this document, as published above, was read by Mr. Ferdinand Jefferson, the Keeper of the Rolls of the Department of State, at Washington, who compared it with the original in his custody. He says: "The initial letters of many of the words in the original of this instrument are capitals, but as no system appears to have been observed, the same words sometimes beginning with a capital and sometimes with a small letter, I have thought it best not to undertake to follow the original in this particular. Moreover, there are three forms of the letter s: the capital S, the small s and the long s, the last being used indiscriminately to words that should begin with a capital and those that should begin with a small s."

States, delegates shall be annually appointed in such manner as the legislature of each State shall direct, to meet in Congress on the first Monday in November, in every year, with a power reserved to each State, to recall its delegates, or any of them, at any time within the year, and to send others in their stead, for the remainder of the year.

No State shall be represented in Congress by less than two, nor by more than seven members; and no person shall be capable of being a delegate for more than three years in any term of six years; nor shall any person, being a delegate, be capable of holding any office under the United States, for which he, or another for his benefit receives any salary, fees or emolument of any kind.

Each State shall maintain its own delegates in a meeting of the States, and while they act as members of the committee of the States.

In determining questions in the United States, in Congress assembled, each State shall have one vote.

Freedom of speech and debate in Congress shall not be impeached or questioned in any court, or place out of Congress, and the members of Congress shall be protected in their persons from arrests and imprisonments, during the time of their going to and from, and attendance on Congress, except for treason, felony, or breach of the peace.

ARTICLE VI. No State without the consent of the United States in Congress assembled, shall send any embassy to, or receive any embassy from, or enter into any conference, agreement, alliance or treaty with any king, prince or state; nor shall any person holding any office of profit or trust under the United States, or any of them, accept of any present, emolument, office or title of any kind whatever from any king, prince or foreign state; nor shall the United States in Congress assembled, or any of them, grant any title of nobility.

No two or more States shall enter into any treaty, confederation or alliance whatever between them, without the consent of the United States in Congress assembled, specifying accurately the purposes for which the same is to be entered into, and how long it shall continue.

No State shall lay any imposts or duties, which may interfere with any stipulations in treaties, entered into by the United States in Congress assembled, with any king, prince or state, in pursuance of any treaties already proposed by Congress, to the courts of France and Spain.

No vessels of war shall be kept up in time of peace by any State, except such number only, as shall be deemed necessary by the United States in Congress assembled, for the defence of such State, or its trade; nor shall any body of forces be kept up by any State, in time of peace, except such number only, as in the judgment of the United States, in Congress assembled, shall be deemed requisite to garrison the forts necessary for the defence of such State; but every State shall always keep up a well regulated and disciplined militia, sufficiently armed and accoutered, and shall provide and constantly have ready for use, in public stores, a due number of field pieces and tents, and a proper quantity of arms, ammunition and camp equipage.

No State shall engage in any war without the consent of the United States in Congress assembled, unless such State be actually invaded by enemies, or shall have received certain advice of a resolution being formed by some nation of Indians to invade such State, and the danger is so imminent as not to admit of a delay, till the United States in Congress assembled can be consulted: nor shall any State grant commissions to any ships or vessels of war, nor letters of marque or reprisal, except it be after a declaration of war by the United States in Congress assembled, and then only against the kingdom or state and the subjects thereof, against which war has been so declared, and under such regulations as shall be established by the United States in Congress assembled, unless such State be infested by pirates, in which case vessels of war may be fitted out for that occasion, and kept so long as the danger shall continue or until the United States in Congress assembled shall determine otherwise.

ARTICLE VII. When land-forces are raised by any State for the common defence, all officers of or under the rank of colonel, shall be appointed by the Legislature of each State respectively by whom such forces shall be raised, or in such manner as such State shall direct, and all vacancies shall be filled up by the State which first made the appointment.

ARTICLE VIII. All charges of war, and all other expenses that shall be incurred for the common defence or general welfare, and allowed by the United States in Congress assembled, shall be defrayed out of a common treasury, which shall be supplied by the several States, in proportion to the value of all land within each State, granted to or surveyed for any person, as such land and the buildings and improvements thereon shall be estimated according to such mode as the United States in Congress assembled, shall from time to time direct and appoint.

The taxes for paying that proportion shall be laid and levied by the authority and direction of the Legislatures of the several States within the time agreed upon by the United States in Congress assembled.

ARTICLE IX. The United States in Congress assembled, shall have the sole and exclusive right and power of determining on peace and war, except in the cases mentioned in the sixth article—of sending and receiving ambassadors—entering into treaties and alliances, provided that no treaty of commerce shall be made whereby the legislative power of the respective States shall be restrained from imposing such imposts and duties on foreigners, as their own people are subjected to, or from prohibiting the exportation or importation of any species of goods or commodities whatsoever—of establishing rules for deciding in all cases, what captures on land or water shall be legal, and in what manner prizes taken by land or naval forces in the service of the United States shall be divided or appropriated—of granting letters of marque and reprisal in times of peace—appointing courts for the trial of piracies and felonies committed on the high seas and establishing courts for receiving and determining finally appeals in all cases of captures, provided that no member of Congress shall be appointed a judge of any of the said courts.

The United States in Congress assembled shall also be the last resort on appeal in all disputes and differences now subsisting or that hereafter may arise between two or more States concerning boundary, jurisdiction or any other cause whatever; which authority shall always be exercised in the manner following. Whenever the legislative or executive authority or lawful agent of any State in controversy with another shall present a petition to Congress, stating the matter in question and praying for a hearing, notice thereof shall be given by order of Congress to the legislative or executive authority of the other State in controversy, and a day assigned for the appearance of the parties by their lawful agents, who shall then be directed to appoint by joint consent, commissioners or judges to constitute a court for hearing and determining the matter in question: but if they cannot agree, Congress shall name three persons out of each of the United States, and from the list of such persons each party shall alternately strike out one, the petitioners beginning, until the number shall be reduced to thirteen; and from that number not less than seven, nor more than nine names as Congress shall direct, shall in the presence of Congress be drawn out by lot, and the persons whose names shall be so drawn or any five of them, shall be commissioners or judges, to hear and finally determine the controversy, so always as a major part of the judges who shall hear the cause shall agree in the determination: and if either party shall neglect to attend at the day appointed, without showing reasons, which Congress shall judge sufficient, or being present shall refuse to strike, the Congress shall proceed to nominate three persons out of each State, and the Secretary of Congress shall strike in behalf of such party absent or refusing; and the judgment and sentence of the court to be appointed, in the manner before prescribed, shall be final and conclusive; and if any of the parties shall refuse to submit to the authority of such court, or to appear or defend their claim or cause, the court shall nevertheless proceed to pronounce sentence, or judgment, which shall in like manner be final and decisive, the judgment or sentence and other proceedings being in either case transmitted to Congress, and lodged among the acts of Congress for the security of the parties concerned: provided that every commissioner, before he sits in judgment, shall take an oath to be administered by one of the judges of the supreme or superior court of the State where the cause shall be tried, "well and truly to hear and determine the matter in question, according to the best of his judgment, without favour, affection or hope of reward:" provided also that no State shall be deprived of territory for the benefit of the United States.

All controversies concerning the private right of soil claimed under different grants of two or more States, whose jurisdiction as they may respect such lands, and the States which passed such grants are adjusted, the said grants or either of them being at the same time claimed to have originated antecedent to such settlement of jurisdiction, shall on the petition of either party to the Congress of the United States, be finally determined as near as may be in the same manner as is before prescribed for deciding disputes respecting territorial jurisdiction between different States.

The United States in Congress assembled shall also have the sole and exclusive right and power of regulating the alloy and value of coin struck by their own authority, or by that of the respective States.—fixing the standard of weights and measures throughout the United States.—regulating the trade and managing all affairs with the Indians, not members of any of the States, provided that the legislative right of any State within its own limits be not infringed or violated—establishing and regulating post-offices from one State to another, throughout all the United States, and exacting such postage on the papers passing thro' the same as may be requisite to defray the expenses of the said office—appointing all officers of the land forces, in the service of the United States, excepting regimental officers—appointing all the officers of the naval forces, and commissioning all officers whatever in the service of the United States—making rules for the government and regulation of the said land and naval forces, and directing their operations.

The United States in Congress assembled shall have authority to appoint a committee, to sit in the recess of Congress, to be denominated "a Committee of the States", and to consist of one delegate from each State; and to appoint such other committees and civil officers as may be necessary for managing the general affairs of the United States under their direction—to appoint one of their number to preside, provided that no person be allowed to serve in the office of president more than one year in any term of three years; to ascertain the necessary sums of money to be raised for the service of the United States, and to appropriate and apply the same for defraying the public expenses—to borrow money, or emit bills on the credit of the United States, transmitting every half year to the respective States an account of the sums of money so borrowed or emitted,—to build and equip a navy—to agree upon the number of land forces, and to make requisitions from each State for its quota, in proportion to the number of white inhabitants in such State; which requisition shall be binding, and thereupon the Legislature of each State shall appoint the regimental officers, raise the men and cloath, arm and equip them in a soldier like manner, at the expense of the United States; and the officers and men so cloathed, armed and equipped shall march to the place appointed, and within the time agreed on by the United States in Congress assembled: but if the United States in Congress assembled shall, on consideration of circumstances judge proper that any State should not raise men, or should raise a smaller number than its quota, and that any other State should raise a greater number of men than the quota thereof, such extra number shall be raised, officered, cloathed, armed and equipped in the same manner as the quota of such State, unless the legislature of such State shall judge that such extra number cannot be safely spared out of the same, in which case they shall raise, officer, cloath, arm and equip as many of such extra number as they judge can be safely spared. And the officers and men so cloathed, armed and equipped, shall march to the place appointed, and within the time agreed on by the United States in Congress assembled.

The United States in Congress assembled shall never engage in a war, nor grant letters of marque and reprisal in time of peace, nor enter into any treaties or alliances, nor coin money, nor regulate the value thereof, nor ascertain the sums and expenses necessary for the defence and welfare of the United States, or any of them, nor emit bills, nor borrow money on the credit of the United States, nor appropriate money, nor agree upon the number of vessels of war, to be built or purchased, or the number of land or sea forces to be raised, nor appoint a commander in chief of the army or navy, unless nine States assent to the same; nor shall a question on any other point, except for adjourning from day to day be determined, unless by the votes of a majority of the United States in Congress assembled.

The Congress of the United States shall have power to adjourn to any time within the year, and to any place within the United States, so that no period of adjournment be for a longer duration than the space of six months, and shall publish the journal of their proceedings monthly, except such parts thereof relating to treaties, alliances or military operations, as in their judgment require secresy; and the yeas and nays of the delegates of each State on any question shall be entered on the journal, when it is desired by any delegate; and the delegates of a State, or any of them, at his or their request shall be furnished with a transcript of the said journal, except such parts as are above excepted, to lay before the Legislatures of the several States.

ARTICLE X. The committee of the States, or any nine of them, shall be authorized to execute, in the recess of Congress, such of the powers of Congress as the United States in Congress assembled, by the consent of nine States, shall from time to time think expedient to vest them with; provided that no power be delegated to the said committee, for the exercise of which, by the articles of confederation, the voice of nine States in the Congress of the United States assembled is requisite.

ARTICLE XI. Canada acceding to this confederation, and joining in the measures of the United States, shall be admitted into, and entitled to all the advantages of this Union: but no other colony shall be admitted into the same, unless such admission be agreed to by nine States.

ARTICLE XII. All bills of credit emitted, monies borrowed and debts contracted by, or under the authority of Congress, before the assembling of the United States, in pursuance of the present confederation, shall be deemed and considered as a charge against the United States, for payment and satisfaction whereof the said United States, and the public faith are hereby solemnly pledged.

ARTICLE XIII. Every State shall abide by the determinations of the United States in Congress assembled, on all questions which by this confederation are submitted to them. And the articles of this confederation shall be inviolably observed by every State, and the Union shall be perpetual; nor shall any alteration at any time hereafter be made in any of them; unless such alteration be agreed to in a Congress of the United States, and be afterwards confirmed by the Legislatures of every State.

And whereas it has pleased the Great Governor of the world to incline the hearts of the Legislatures we respectively represent in Congress, to approve of, and to authorize us to ratify the said articles of confederation and perpetual union. Know ye that we the undersigned delegates, by virtue of the power and authority to us given for that purpose, do by these presents, in the name and in behalf of our respective constituents, fully and entirely ratify and confirm each and every of the said articles of confederation and perpetual union, and all and singular the matters and things therein contained: and we do further solemnly plight and engage the faith of our respective constituents, that they shall abide by the determinations of the United States in Congress assembled, on all questions, which by the said confederation are submitted to them. And that the articles thereof shall be inviolably observed by the States we re[s]pectively represent, and that the Union shall be perpetual.

In witness whereof we have hereunto set our hands in Congress. Done at Philadelphia in the State of Pennsylvania the ninth day of July in the year of our Lord one thousand seven hundred and seventy-eight, and in the third year of the independence of America.[2]

On the part & behalf of the State of New Hampshire

JOSIAH BARTLETT,   JOHN WENTWORTH, Junr., August 8th, 1778.

On the part and behalf of the State of Massachusetts Bay

JOHN HANCOCK,   FRANCIS DANA,
SAMUEL ADAMS,   JAMES LOVELL,
ELBRIDGE GERRY,   SAMUEL HOLTEN.

On the part and behalf of the State of Rhode Island and Providence Plantations

WILLIAM ELLERY,   JOHN COLLINS.
HENRY MARCHANT,

On the part and behalf of the State of Connecticut

ROGER SHERMAN,   TITUS HOSMER,
SAMUEL   ANDREW ADAMS.
HUNTINGTON,
OLIVER WOLCOTT,

On the part and behalf of the State of New York

JAS. DUANE,   WM. DUER,
FRA. LEWIS,   GOUV. MORRIS.

On the part and in behalf of the State of New Jersey, Novr. 26, 1778

JNO. WITHERSPOON.   NATHL. SCUDDER.

On the part and behalf of the State of Pennsylvania

[2] From the circumstances of delegates from the same State having signed the Articles of Confederation at different times, as appears by the dates, it is probable they affixed their names as they happened to be present in Congress, after they had been authorized by their constituents.

ROBT. MORRIS,
DANIEL ROBERDEAU,
JONA. BAYARD
  SMITH,

WILLIAM CLINGAN,
JOSEPH REED, 22d
  July, 1778.

On the part & behalf of the State of Delaware

THO. M'KEAN, Feby.
  12, 1779.
JOHN DICKINSON,
  May 5th, 1779.

NICHOLAS VAN DYKE.

On the part and behalf of the State of Maryland

JOHN HANSON,
  March 1, 1781.

DANIEL CARROLL,
  Mar. 1, 1781.

On the part and behalf of the State of Virginia

RICHARD HENRY LEE,

JNO. HARVIE,

JOHN BANISTER,
THOMAS ADAMS,

FRANCIS LIGHTFOOT
  LEE.

On the part and behalf of the State of No. Carolina

JOHN PENN,
  July 21st, 1778.

CORNS. HARNETT,
JNO. WILLIAMS.

On the part & behalf of the State of South Carolina

HENRY LAURENS,
WILLIAM HENRY
  DRAYTON,
JNO. MATHEWS,

RICHD. HUTSON,
THOS. HEYWARD, Junr.

On the part & behalf of the State of Georgia

JNO. WALTON, 24th
  July, 1778.

EDWD. TELFAIR,
EDWD. LANGWORTHY.

ORDINANCE OF 1787: THE NORTHWEST TERRITORIAL GOVERNMENT

[THE CONFEDERATE CONGRESS, JULY 13, 1787]

An Ordinance for the government of the territory of the United States northwest of the river Ohio

SECTION 1. *Be it ordained by the United States in Congress assembled*, That the said territory, for the purpose of temporary government, be one district, subject, however, to be divided into two districts, as future circumstances may, in the opinion of Congress, make it expedient.

SEC. 2. *Be it ordained by the authority aforesaid*, That the estates both of resident and non-resident proprietors in the said territory, dying intestate, shall descent to, and be distributed among, their children and the descendants of a deceased child in equal parts, the descendants of a deceased child or grandchild to take the share of their deceased parent in equal parts among them; and where there shall be no children or descendants, then in equal parts to the next of kin, in equal degree; and among collaterals, the children of a deceased brother or sister of the intestate shall have, in equal parts among them, their deceased parent's share; and there shall, in no case, be a distinction between kindred of the whole and half blood; saving in all cases to the widow of the intestate, her third part of the real estate for life, and one-third part of the personal estate; and this law relative to descents and dower, shall remain in full force until altered by the legislature of the district. And until the governor and judges shall adopt laws as hereinafter mentioned, estates in the said territory may be devised or bequeathed by wills in writing, signed and sealed by him or her in whom the estate may be, (being of full age,) and attested by three witnesses; and real estates may be conveyed by lease and release, or bargain and sale, signed, sealed, and delivered by the person, being of full age, in whom the estate may be, and attested by two witnesses, provided such wills be duly proved, and such conveyances be acknowledged, or the execution thereof duly proved, and be recorded within one year after proper magistrates, courts, and registers, shall be appointed for that purpose; and personal property may be transferred by delivery, saving, however, to the French and Canadian inhabitants, and other settlers of the Kaskaskies, Saint Vincents, and the neighboring villages, who have heretofore professed themselves citizens of Virginia, their laws and customs now in force among them, relative to the descent and conveyance of property.

SEC. 3. *Be it ordained by the authority aforesaid*, That there shall be appointed, from time to time, by Congress, a governor, whose commission shall continue in force for the term of three years, unless sooner revoked by Congress; he shall reside in the district, and have a freehold estate therein, in one thousand acres of land, while in the exercise of his office.

SEC. 4. There shall be appointed from time to time, by Congress, a secretary, whose commission shall continue in force for four years, unless sooner revoked; he shall reside in the district, and have a freehold estate therein, in five hundred acres of land, while in the exercise of his office. It shall be his duty to keep and preserve the acts and laws passed by the legislature, and the public records of the district, and the proceedings of the governor in his executive department, and transmit authentic copies of such acts and proceedings every six months to the Secretary of Congress. There shall also be appointed a court, to consist of three judges, any two of whom to form a court, who shall have a common-law jurisdiction, and reside in the district, and have each therein a freehold estate, in five hundred acres of land, while in the exercise of their offices; and their commissions shall continue in force during good behavior.

SEC. 5. The governor and judges, or a majority of them, shall adopt and publish in the district such laws of the original States, criminal and civil, as may be necessary, and best suited to the circumstances of the district, and report them to Congress from time to time, which laws shall be in force in the district until the organization of the general assembly therein, unless disapproved of by Congress; but afterwards the legislature shall have authority to alter them as they shall think fit.

SEC. 6. The governor, for the time being, shall be commander-in-chief of the militia, appoint and commission all officers in the same below the rank of general officers; all general officers shall be appointed and commissioned by Congress.

SEC. 7. Previous to the organization of the general assembly the governor shall appoint such magistrates, and other civil officers, in each county or township, as he shall find necessary for the preservation of the peace and good order in the same. After the general assembly shall be organized the powers and duties of magistrates and other civil officers shall be regulated and defined by the said assembly; but all magistrates and other civil officers, not herein otherwise directed, shall, during the continuance of this temporary government, be appointed by the governor.

SEC. 8. For the prevention of crimes and injuries, the laws to be adopted or made shall have force in all parts of the district, and for the execution of process, criminal and civil, the governor shall make proper divisions thereof; and he shall proceed, from time to time, as circumstances may require, to lay out the parts of the district in which the Indian titles shall have been extinguished, into counties and townships, subject, however, to such alterations as may thereafter be made by the legislature.

SEC. 9. So soon as there shall be five thousand free male inhabitants, of full age, in the district, upon giving proof thereof to the governor, they shall receive authority, with time and place, to elect representatives from their counties or townships, to represent them in the general assembly: *Provided*, That for every five hundred free male inhabitants there shall be one representative, and so on, progressively, with the number of free male inhabitants, shall the right of representation increase, until the number of representatives shall amount to twenty-five; after which the number and proportion of representatives shall be regulated by the legislature: *Provided*, That no person be eligible or qualified to act as a representative, unless he shall have been a citizen of one of the United States three years, and be a resident in the district, or unless he shall have resided in the district three years; and, in either case, shall likewise hold in his own right, in fee-simple, two hundred acres of land within the same: *Provided also*, That a freehold in fifty acres of land in the district, having been a citizen of one of the States, and being resident in the district, or the like freehold and two years' residence in the district, shall be necessary to qualify a man as an elector of a representative.

SEC. 10. The representatives thus elected shall serve for the term of two years; and in case of the death of a representative, or removal from office, the governor shall issue a writ to the county or township, for which he was a member, to elect another in his stead, to serve for the residue of the term.

SEC. 11. The general assembly or legislature, shall consist of the governor, legislative counsel, and a house of representatives. The legislative council shall consist of five members, to continue in office five years, unless sooner removed by Congress; any three of whom to be a quorum; and the members of the council shall be nominated and appointed in the following manner, to wit: As soon as representatives shall be elected the governor shall appoint a time and place for them to meet together, and when met they shall nominate ten persons, resident in the district, and each possessed of a freehold in five hundred acres of land, and return their names to Congress, five of whom Congress shall appoint and commission to serve as aforesaid; and whenever a vacancy shall happen in the council, by death or removal from office, the house of representatives shall nominate two persons, qualified as aforesaid, for each vacancy, and return their names to Congress, one of whom Congress shall appoint and commission for the residue of the term; and every five years, four months at least before the expiration of the time of service of the members of the council, the said house shall nominate ten persons, qualified as aforesaid, and return their names to Congress, five of whom Congress shall appoint and commission to serve as members of the council five years, unless sooner removed. And the governor, legislative council, and house of representatives shall have authority to make laws in all cases for the good government of the district, not repugnant to the principles and articles in this ordinance established and declared. And all bills, having passed by a majority in the house, and by a majority in the council, shall be referred to the governor for his assent; but no bill, or legislative act whatever, shall be of any force without his assent. The governor shall have power to convene, prorogue, and dissolve the general assembly when, in his opinion, it shall be expedient.

SEC. 12. The governor, judges, legislative council, secretary, and such other officers as Congress shall appoint in the district, shall take an oath or affirmation of fidelity, and of office; the governor before the President of Congress, and all other officers before the governor. As soon as a legislature shall be formed in the district, the council and house assembled, in one room, shall have authority, by joint ballot, to elect a delegate to Congress, who shall have a seat in Congress with a right of debating, but not of voting, during this temporary government.

SEC. 13. And for extending the fundamental principles of civil and religious liberty, which form the basis whereon these republics, their laws and constitutions, are erected; to fix and establish those principles as the basis of all laws, constitutions, and governments, which forever hereafter shall be formed in the said territory; to provide, also, for the establishment of States, and permanent government therein, and for their admission to a share in the Federal councils on an equal footing with the original States, at as early periods as may be consistent with the general interest:

SEC. 14. It is hereby ordained and declared, by the authority aforesaid, that the following articles shall be considered as articles of compact, between the original States and the people and States in the said territory, and forever remain unalterable, unless by common consent, to wit:

ARTICLE I

No person, demeaning himself in a peaceable and orderly manner, shall ever be molested on account of his mode of worship, or religious sentiments, in the said territories.

ARTICLE II

The inhabitants of the said territory shall always be entitled to the benefits of the writs of *habeas corpus*, and of the trial by jury; of a proportionate representation of the people in the legislature, and of judicial proceedings according to the course of the common law. All persons shall be bailable, unless for capital offences, where the proof shall be evident, or the presumption great. All fines shall be moderate; and no cruel or unusual punishments shall be inflicted. No man shall be deprived of his liberty or property, but by the judgment of his peers, or the law of the land, and should the public exigencies make it necessary, for the common preservation, to take any person's property, or to demand his particular services, full compensation shall be paid for the same. And, in the just preservation of rights and property, it is understood and declared, that no law ought ever to be made or have force in the said territory, that shall, in any manner whatever, interfere with or affect private contracts, or engagements, *bona fide*, and without fraud previously formed.

ARTICLE III

Religion, morality, and knowledge being necessary to good government and the happiness of mankind, schools and the means of education shall forever be encouraged. The utmost good faith shall always be observed towards the Indians; their lands and property shall never be taken from them without their consent; and in their property, rights, and liberty they never shall be invaded or disturbed, unless in just and lawful wars authorized by Congress; but laws founded in justice and humanity shall, from time to time, be made, for preventing wrongs being done to them, and for preserving peace and friendship with them.

ARTICLE IV

The said territory, and the States which may be formed therein, shall forever remain a part of this confederacy of the United States of America, subject to the Articles of Confederation, and to such alterations therein as shall be constitutionally made; and to all the acts and ordinances of the United States in Congress assembled, conformable thereto. The inhabitants and settlers in the said territory shall be subject to pay a part of the Federal debts, contracted, or to be contracted, and a proportional part of the expenses of government to be apportioned on them by Congress, according to the same common rule and measure by which apportionments thereof shall be made on the other States; and the taxes for paying their proportion shall be laid and levied by the authority and direction of the legislatures of the district, or districts, or new States, as in the original States, within the time agreed upon by the United States in Congress assembled. The legislatures of those districts, or new States, shall never interfere with the primary disposal of the soil by the United States in Congress assembled, nor with any regulations Congress may find necessary for securing the title in such soil to the *bona fide* purchasers. No tax shall be imposed on lands the property of the United States; and in no case shall non-resident proprietors be taxed higher than residents. The navigable waters leading into the Mississippi and Saint Lawrence, and the carrying places between the same, shall be common highways, and forever free, as well to the inhabitants of the said territory as to the citizens of the United States, and those of any other States that may be admitted into the confederacy, without any tax, impost, or duty therefor.

ARTICLE V

There shall be formed in the said territory not less than three nor more than five States; and the boundaries of the States, as soon as Virginia shall alter her act of cession and consent to the same, shall become fixed and established as follows, to wit: The western State, in the said territory, shall be bounded by the Mississippi, the Ohio, and the Wabash Rivers; a direct line drawn from the Wabash and Post Vincents, due north, to the territorial line between the United States and Canada; and by the said territorial line to the Lake of the Woods and Mississippi. The middle State shall be bounded by the said direct line, the Wabash from Post Vincents to the Ohio, by the Ohio, by a direct line drawn due north from the mouth of the Great Miami to the said territorial line, and by the said territorial line. The eastern State shall be bounded by the last-mentioned direct line, the Ohio, Pennsylvania, and the said territorial line: *Provided, however,* And it is further understood and declared, that the boundaries of these three States shall be subject so far to be altered, that, if Congress shall hereafter find it expedient, they shall have authority to form one or two States in that part of the said territory which lies north of an east and west line drawn through the southerly bend or extreme of Lake Michigan. And whenever any of the said States shall have sixty thousand free inhabitants therein, such State shall be admitted, by its delegates, into the Congress of the United States, on an equal footing with the original States, in all respects whatever; and shall be at liberty to form a permanent constitution and State government: *Provided,* The constitution and government, so to be formed, shall be republican, and in conformity to the principles contained in these articles, and, so far as it can be consistent with the general interest of the confederacy, such admission shall be allowed at an earlier period, and when there may be a less number of free inhabitants in the State than sixty thousand.

ARTICLE VI

There shall be neither slavery nor involuntary servitude in the said territory, otherwise than in the punishment of crimes, whereof the party shall have been duly convicted: *Provided always,* That any person escaping into the same, from whom labor or service is lawfully claimed in any one of the original States, such fugitive may be lawfully reclaimed, and conveyed to the person claiming his or her labor or service as aforesaid.

Be it ordained by the authority aforesaid, That the resolutions of the 23d of April, 1784, relative to the subject of this ordinance, be, and the same are hereby, repealed, and declared null and void.

Done by the United States, in Congress assembled, the 13th day of July, in the year of our Lord 1787, and of their sovereignty and independence the twelfth.

CONSTITUTION OF THE UNITED STATES OF AMERICA—1787[1]

WE THE PEOPLE of the United States, in Order to form a more perfect Union, establish Justice, insure domestic Tranquility, provide for the common defence, promote the general Welfare, and secure the Blessings of Liberty to ourselves and our Posterity, do ordain and establish this Constitution for the United States of America.

ARTICLE. I.

SECTION 1. All legislative Powers herein granted shall be vested in a Congress of the United States, which shall consist of a Senate and House of Representatives.

[1] This text of the Constitution follows the engrossed copy signed by Gen. Washington and the deputies from 12 States. The small superior figures preceding the paragraphs designate clauses, and were not in the original and have no reference to footnotes.

In May 1785, a committee of Congress made a report recommending an alteration in the Articles of Confederation, but no action was taken on it, and it was left to the State Legislatures to proceed in the matter. In January 1786, the Legislature of Virginia passed a resolution providing for the appointment of five commissioners, who, or any three of them, should meet such commissioners as might be appointed in the other States of the Union, at a time and place to be agreed upon, to take into consideration the trade of the United States; to consider how far a uniform system in their commercial regulations may be necessary to their common interest and their permanent harmony; and to report to the several States such an act, relative to this great object, as, when ratified by them, will enable the United States in Congress effectually to provide for the same. The Virginia commissioners, after some correspondence, fixed the first Monday in September as the time, and the city of Annapolis as the place for the meeting, but only four other States were represented, viz: Delaware, New York, New Jersey, and Pennsylvania; the commissioners appointed by Massachusetts, New Hampshire, North Carolina, and Rhode Island failed to attend. Under the circumstances of so partial a representation, the commissioners present agreed upon a report, (drawn by Mr. Hamilton, of New York,) expressing their unanimous conviction that it might essentially tend to advance the interests of the Union if the States by which they were respectively delegated would concur, and use their endeavors to procure the concurrence of the other States, in the appointment of commissioners to meet at Philadelphia on the Second Monday of May following, to take into consideration the situation of the United States; to devise such further provisions as should appear to them necessary to render the Constitution of the Federal Government adequate to the exigencies of the Union; and to report such an act for that purpose to the United States in Congress assembled as, when agreed to by them and afterwards confirmed by the Legislatures of every State, would effectually provide for the same.

Congress, on the 21st of February, 1787, adopted a resolution in favor of a convention, and the Legislatures of those States which had not already done so (with the exception of Rhode Island) promptly appointed delegates. On the 25th of May, seven States having convened, George Washington, of Virginia, was unanimously elected President, and the consideration of the proposed constitution was commenced. On the 17th of September, 1787, the Constitution as engrossed and agreed upon was signed by all the members present, except Mr. Gerry of Massachusetts, and Messrs. Mason and Randolph, of Virginia. The president of the convention transmitted it to Congress, with a resolution stating how the proposed Federal Government should be put in operation, and an explanatory letter. Congress, on the 28th of September, 1787, directed the Constitution so framed, with the resolutions and letter concerning the same, to "be transmitted to the several Legislatures in order to be submitted to a convention of delegates chosen in each State by the people thereof, in conformity to the resolves of the convention."

On the 4th of March, 1789, the day which had been fixed for commencing the operations of Government under the new Con-

SECTION. 2. [1] The House of Representatives shall be composed of Members chosen every second Year by the People of the several States, and the Electors in each State shall have the Qualifications requisite for Electors of the most numerous Branch of the State Legislature.

[2] No Person shall be a Representative who shall not have attained to the Age of twenty five Years, and been seven Years a Citizen of the United States, and who shall not, when elected, be an Inhabitant of that State in which he shall be chosen.

[3] Representatives and direct Taxes shall be apportioned among the several States which may be included within this Union, according to their respective Numbers, which shall be determined by adding to the whole Number of free Persons, including those bound to Service for a Term of Years, and excluding Indians not taxed, three fifths of all other Persons.[2] The actual Enumeration shall be made within three Years after the first Meeting of the Congress of the United States, and within every subsequent Term of ten Years, in such Manner as they shall by Law direct. The Number of Representatives shall not exceed one for every thirty Thousand, but each State shall have at Least one Representative; and until such enumeration shall be made, the State of New Hampshire shall be entitled to chuse three, Massachusetts eight, Rhode-Island and Providence Plantations one, Connecticut five, New-York six, New Jersey four, Pennsylvania eight, Delaware one, Maryland six, Virginia ten, North Carolina five, South Carolina five, and Georgia three.

[4] When vacancies happen in the Representation from any State, the Executive Authority thereof shall issue Writs of Election to fill such Vacancies.

[5] The House of Representatives shall chuse their Speaker and other Officers; and shall have the sole Power of Impeachment.

SECTION. 3. [1] The Senate of the United States shall be composed of two Senators from each State, chosen by the Legislature thereof,[3] for six Years; and each Senator shall have one Vote.

stitution, it had been ratified by the conventions chosen in each State to consider it, as follows: Delaware, December 7, 1787; Pennsylvania, December 12, 1787; New Jersey, December 18, 1787; Georgia, January 2, 1788; Connecticut, January 9, 1788; Massachusetts, February 6, 1788; Maryland, April 28, 1788; South Carolina, May 23, 1788; New Hampshire, June 21, 1788; Virginia, June 25, 1788; and New York, July 26, 1788.

The President informed Congress, on the 28th of January, 1790, that North Carolina had ratified the Constitution November 21, 1789; and he informed Congress on the 1st of June, 1790, that Rhode Island had ratified the Constitution May 29, 1790. Vermont, in convention, ratified the Constitution January 10, 1791, and was, by an act of Congress approved February 18, 1791, "received and admitted into this Union as a new and entire member of the United States."

[2] The part of this clause relating to the mode of apportionment of representatives among the several States has been affected by section 2 of amendment XIV, and as to taxes on incomes without apportionment by amendment XVI.

[3] This clause has been affected by clause 1 of amendment XVII.

2 Immediately after they shall be assembled in Consequence of the first Election, they shall be divided as equally as may be into three Classes. The Seats of the Senators of the first Class shall be vacated at the Expiration of the second Year, of the second Class at the Expiration of the fourth Year, and of the third Class at the Expiration of the sixth Year, so that one third may be chosen every second Year; and if Vacancies happen by Resignation, or otherwise, during the Recess of the Legislature of any State, the Executive thereof may make temporary Appointments until the next Meeting of the Legislature, which shall then fill such Vacancies.4

3 No Person shall be a Senator who shall not have attained to the Age of thirty Years, and been nine Years a Citizen of the United States, and who shall not, when elected, be an Inhabitant of that State for which he shall be chosen.

4 The Vice President of the United States shall be President of the Senate, but shall have no Vote, unless they be equally divided.

5 The Senate shall chuse their other Officers, and also a President pro tempore, in the Absence of the Vice President, or when he shall exercise the Office of President of the United States.

6 The Senate shall have the sole Power to try all Impeachments. When sitting for that Purpose, they shall be on Oath or Affirmation. When the President of the United States is tried, the Chief Justice shall preside: And no Person shall be convicted without the Concurrence of two thirds of the Members present.

7 Judgment in Cases of Impeachment shall not extend further than to removal from Office, and disqualification to hold and enjoy any Office of honor, Trust or Profit under the United States: but the Party convicted shall nevertheless be liable and subject to Indictment, Trial, Judgment and Punishment, according to Law.

SECTION. 4. 1 The Times, Places and Manner of holding Elections for Senators and Representatives, shall be prescribed in each State by the Legislature thereof; but the Congress may at any time by Law make or alter such Regulations, except as to the Places of chusing Senators.

2 The Congress shall assemble at least once in every Year, and such Meeting shall be on the first Monday in December,5 unless they shall by Law appoint a different Day.

SECTION. 5. 1 Each House shall be the Judge of the Elections, Returns and Qualifications of its own Members, and a Majority of each shall constitute a Quorum to do Business; but a smaller Number may adjourn from day to day, and may be authorized to compel the Attendance of absent Members, in such Manner, and under such Penalties as each House may provide.

2 Each House may determine the Rules of its Proceedings, punish its Members for disorderly Behaviour, and, with the Concurrence of two thirds, expel a Member.

3 Each House shall keep a Journal of its Proceedings, and from time to time publish the same, excepting such Parts as may in their

Judgment require Secrecy; and the Yeas and Nays of the Members of either House on any question shall, at the Desire of one fifth of those Present, be entered on the Journal.

4 Neither House, during the Session of Congress, shall, without the Consent of the other, adjourn for more than three days, nor to any other Place than that in which the two Houses shall be sitting.

SECTION. 6. 1 The Senators and Representatives shall receive a Compensation for their Services, to be ascertained by Law, and paid out of the Treasury of the United States.6 They shall in all Cases, except Treason, Felony and Breach of the Peace, be privileged from Arrest during their Attendance at the Session of their respective Houses, and in going to and returning from the same; and for any Speech or Debate in either House, they shall not be questioned in any other Place.

2 No Senator or Representative shall, during the Time for which he was elected, be appointed to any civil Office under the Authority of the United States, which shall have been created, or the Emoluments whereof shall have been encreased during such time; and no Person holding any Office under the United States, shall be a Member of either House during his Continuance in Office.

SECTION. 7. 1 All Bills for raising Revenue shall originate in the House of Representatives; but the Senate may propose or concur with Amendments as on other Bills.

2 Every Bill which shall have passed the House of Representatives and the Senate, shall, before it become a Law, be presented to the President of the United States; If he approve he shall sign it, but if not he shall return it, with his Objections to that House in which it shall have originated, who shall enter the Objections at large on their Journal, and proceed to reconsider it. If after such Reconsideration two thirds of that House shall agree to pass the Bill, it shall be sent, together with the Objections, to the other House, by which it shall likewise be reconsidered, and if approved by two thirds of that House, it shall become a Law. But in all such Cases the Votes of both Houses shall be determined by yeas and Nays, and the Names of the Persons voting for and against the Bill shall be entered on the Journal of each House respectively. If any Bill shall not be returned by the President within ten Days (Sundays excepted) after it shall have been presented to him, the Same shall be a Law, in like Manner as if he had signed it, unless the Congress by their Adjournment prevent its Return, in which Case it shall not be a Law.

3 Every Order, Resolution, or Vote to which the Concurrence of the Senate and House of Representatives may be necessary (except on a question of Adjournment) shall be presented to the President of the United States; and before the Same shall take Effect, shall be approved by him, or being disapproved by him, shall be repassed by two thirds of the Senate and House of Representatives, according to the Rules and Limitations prescribed in the Case of a Bill.

SECTION. 8. 1 The Congress shall have Power To lay and collect Taxes, Duties, Imposts and Ex-

---

4 This clause has been affected by clause 2 of amendment XVIII.

5 This clause has been affected by amendment XX.

6 This clause has been affected by amendment XXVII.

cises, to pay the Debts and provide for the common Defence and general Welfare of the United States; but all Duties, Imposts and Excises shall be uniform throughout the United States;

²To borrow Money on the credit of the United States;

³To regulate Commerce with foreign Nations, and among the several States, and with the Indian Tribes;

⁴To establish an uniform Rule of Naturalization, and uniform Laws on the subject of Bankruptcies throughout the United States;

⁵To coin Money, regulate the Value thereof, and of foreign Coin, and fix the Standard of Weights and Measures;

⁶To provide for the Punishment of counterfeiting the Securities and current Coin of the United States;

⁷To establish Post Offices and post Roads;

⁸To promote the Progress of Science and useful Arts, by securing for limited Times to Authors and Inventors the exclusive Right to their respective Writings and Discoveries;

⁹To constitute Tribunals inferior to the supreme Court;

¹⁰To define and punish Piracies and Felonies committed on the high Seas, and Offences against the Law of Nations;

¹¹To declare War, grant Letters of Marque and Reprisal, and make Rules concerning Captures on Land and Water;

¹²To raise and support Armies, but no Appropriation of Money to that Use shall be for a longer Term than two Years;

¹³To provide and maintain a Navy;

¹⁴To make Rules for the Government and Regulation of the land and naval Forces;

¹⁵To provide for calling forth the Militia to execute the Laws of the Union, suppress Insurrections and repel Invasions;

¹⁶To provide for organizing, arming, and disciplining, the Militia, and for governing such Part of them as may be employed in the Service of the United States, reserving to the States respectively, the Appointment of the Officers, and the Authority of training the Militia according to the discipline prescribed by Congress;

¹⁷To exercise exclusive Legislation in all Cases whatsoever, over such District (not exceeding ten Miles square) as may, by Cession of particular States, and the Acceptance of Congress, become the Seat of the Government of the United States, and to exercise like Authority over all Places purchased by the Consent of the Legislature of the State in which the Same shall be, for the Erection of Forts, Magazines, Arsenals, dock-Yards, and other needful Buildings;—And

¹⁸To make all Laws which shall be necessary and proper for carrying into Execution the foregoing Powers, and all other Powers vested by this Constitution in the Government of the United States, or in any Department or Officer thereof.

SECTION. 9. ¹The Migration or Importation of such Persons as any of the States now existing shall think proper to admit, shall not be prohibited by the Congress prior to the Year one thousand eight hundred and eight, but a Tax or duty may be imposed on such Importation, not exceeding ten dollars for each Person.

²The Privilege of the Writ of Habeas Corpus shall not be suspended, unless when in Cases of Rebellion or Invasion the public Safety may require it.

³No Bill of Attainder or ex post facto Law shall be passed.

⁴No Capitation, or other direct, Tax shall be laid, unless in Proportion to the Census or Enumeration herein before directed to be taken.⁷

⁵No Tax or Duty shall be laid on Articles exported from any State.

⁶No Preference shall be given by any Regulation of Commerce or Revenue to the Ports of one State over those of another: nor shall Vessels bound to, or from, one State, be obliged to enter, clear, or pay Duties in another.

⁷No Money shall be drawn from the Treasury, but in Consequence of Appropriations made by Law; and a regular Statement and Account of the Receipts and Expenditures of all public Money shall be published from time to time.

⁸No Title of Nobility shall be granted by the United States: And no Person holding any Office of Profit or Trust under them, shall, without the Consent of the Congress, accept of any present, Emolument, Office, or Title, of any kind whatever, from any King, Prince, or foreign State.

SECTION. 10. ¹No State shall enter into any Treaty, Alliance, or Confederation; grant Letters of Marque and Reprisal; coin Money; emit Bills of Credit; make any Thing but gold and silver Coin a Tender in Payment of Debts; pass any Bill of Attainder, ex post facto Law, or Law impairing the Obligation of Contracts, or grant any Title of Nobility.

²No State shall, without the Consent of the Congress, lay any Imposts or Duties on Imports or Exports, except what may be absolutely necessary for executing it's inspection Laws: and the net Produce of all Duties and Imposts, laid by any State on Imports or Exports, shall be for the Use of the Treasury of the United States; and all such Laws shall be subject to the Revision and Controul of the Congress.

³No State shall, without the Consent of Congress, lay any Duty of Tonnage, keep Troops, or Ships of War in time of Peace, enter into any Agreement or Compact with another State, or with a foreign Power, or engage in War, unless actually invaded, or in such imminent Danger as will not admit of delay.

ARTICLE. II.

SECTION. 1. ¹The executive Power shall be vested in a President of the United States of America. He shall hold his Office during the Term of four Years, and, together with the Vice President, chosen for the same Term, be elected, as follows

²Each State shall appoint, in such Manner as the Legislature thereof may direct, a Number of Electors, equal to the whole Number of Senators and Representatives to which the State may be entitled in the Congress: but no Senator or Representative, or Person holding an Office of Trust or Profit under the United States, shall be appointed an Elector.

³The Electors shall meet in their respective States, and vote by Ballot for two Persons, of whom one at least shall not be an Inhabitant of the same State with themselves. And they shall

---

⁷This clause has been affected by amendment XVI.

make a List of all the Persons voted for, and of the Number of Votes for each; which List they shall sign and certify, and transmit sealed to the Seat of the Government of the United States, directed to the President of the Senate. The President of the Senate shall, in the Presence of the Senate and House of Representatives, open all the Certificates, and the Votes shall then be counted. The Person having the greatest Number of Votes shall be the President, if such Number be a Majority of the whole Number of Electors appointed; and if there be more than one who have such Majority, and have an equal Number of Votes, then the House of Representatives shall immediately chuse by Ballot one of them for President; and if no Person have a Majority, then from the five highest on the List the said House shall in like Manner chuse the President. But in chusing the President, the Votes shall be taken by States, the Representation from each State having one Vote; A quorum for this Purpose shall consist of a Member or Members from two thirds of the States, and a Majority of all the States shall be necessary to a Choice. In every Case, after the Choice of the President, the Person having the greatest Number of Votes of the Electors shall be the Vice President. But if there should remain two or more who have equal Votes, the Senate shall chuse from them by Ballot the Vice President.[8]

[4] The Congress may determine the Time of chusing the Electors, and the Day on which they shall give their Votes; which Day shall be the same throughout the United States.

[5] No Person except a natural born Citizen, or a Citizen of the United States, at the time of the Adoption of this Constitution, shall be eligible to the Office of President; neither shall any Person be eligible to that Office who shall not have attained to the Age of thirty five Years, and been fourteen Years a Resident within the United States.

[6] In Case of the Removal of the President from Office, or of his Death, Resignation, or Inability to discharge the Powers and Duties of the said Office,[9] the Same shall devolve on the Vice President, and the Congress may by Law provide for the Case of Removal, Death, Resignation or Inability, both of the President and Vice President, declaring what Officer shall then act as President, and such Officer shall act accordingly, until the Disability be removed, or a President shall be elected.

[7] The President shall, at stated Times, receive for his Services, a Compensation, which shall neither be encreased nor diminished during the Period for which he shall have been elected, and he shall not receive within that Period any other Emolument from the United States, or any of them.

[8] Before he enter on the Execution of his Office, he shall take the following Oath or Affirmation:—"I do solemnly swear (or affirm) that I will faithfully execute the Office of President of the United States, and will to the best of my Ability, preserve, protect and defend the Constitution of the United States."

SECTION. 2. [1] The President shall be Commander in Chief of the Army and Navy of the United States, and of the Militia of the several States, when called into the actual Service of the United States; he may require the Opinion, in writing, of the principal Officer in each of the executive Departments, upon any Subject relating to the Duties of their respective Offices, and he shall have Power to grant Reprieves and Pardons for Offences against the United States, except in Cases of Impeachment.

[2] He shall have Power, by and with the Advice and Consent of the Senate, to make Treaties, provided two thirds of the Senators present concur; and he shall nominate, and by and with the Advice and Consent of the Senate, shall appoint Ambassadors, other public Ministers and Consuls, Judges of the supreme Court, and all other Officers of the United States, whose Appointments are not herein otherwise provided for, and which shall be established by Law: but the Congress may by Law vest the Appointment of such inferior Officers, as they think proper, in the President alone, in the Courts of Law, or in the Heads of Departments.

[3] The President shall have Power to fill up all Vacancies that may happen during the Recess of the Senate, by granting Commissions which shall expire at the End of their next Session.

SECTION. 3. He shall from time to time give to the Congress Information of the State of the Union, and recommend to their Consideration such Measures as he shall judge necessary and expedient; he may, on extraordinary Occasions, convene both Houses, or either of them, and in Case of Disagreement between them, with Respect to the Time of Adjournment, he may adjourn them to such Time as he shall think proper; he shall receive Ambassadors and other public Ministers; he shall take Care that the Laws be faithfully executed, and shall Commission all the Officers of the United States.

SECTION. 4. The President, Vice President and all civil Officers of the United States, shall be removed from Office on Impeachment for, and Conviction of, Treason, Bribery, or other high Crimes and Misdemeanors.

ARTICLE. III.

SECTION. 1. The judicial Power of the United States, shall be vested in one supreme Court, and in such inferior Courts as the Congress may from time to time ordain and establish. The Judges, both of the supreme and inferior Courts, shall hold their Offices during good Behaviour, and shall, at stated Times, receive for their Services, a Compensation, which shall not be diminished during their Continuance in Office.

SECTION. 2. [1] The judicial Power shall extend to all Cases, in Law and Equity, arising under this Constitution, the Laws of the United States, and Treaties made, or which shall be made, under their Authority;—to all Cases affecting Ambassadors, other public Ministers and Consuls;—to all Cases of admiralty and maritime Jurisdiction;—to Controversies to which the United States shall be a Party;—to Controversies between two or more States;—between a State and Citizens of another State; [10]—between Citizens of different States,—between Citizens of the same State claiming Lands under Grants of different

---

[8] This clause has been superseded by amendment XII.

[9] This clause has been affected by amendment XXV.

[10] This clause has been affected by amendment XI.

States, and between a State, or the Citizens thereof, and foreign States, Citizens or Subjects.

²In all Cases affecting Ambassadors, other public Ministers and Consuls, and those in which a State shall be Party, the supreme Court shall have original Jurisdiction. In all the other Cases before mentioned, the supreme Court shall have appellate Jurisdiction, both as to Law and Fact, with such Exceptions, and under such Regulations as the Congress shall make.

³The Trial of all Crimes, except in Cases of Impeachment, shall be by Jury; and such Trial shall be held in the State where the said Crimes shall have been committed; but when not committed within any State, the Trial shall be at such Place or Places as the Congress may by Law have directed.

SECTION. 3. ¹Treason against the United States, shall consist only in levying War against them, or in adhering to their Enemies, giving them Aid and Comfort. No Person shall be convicted of Treason unless on the Testimony of two Witnesses to the same overt Act, or on Confession in open Court.

²The Congress shall have Power to declare the Punishment of Treason, but no Attainder of Treason shall work Corruption of Blood, or Forfeiture except during the Life of the Person attainted.

ARTICLE. IV.

SECTION. 1. Full Faith and Credit shall be given in each State to the public Acts, Records, and judicial Proceedings of every other State. And the Congress may by general Laws prescribe the Manner in which such Acts, Records and Proceedings shall be proved, and the Effect thereof.

SECTION. 2. ¹The Citizens of each State shall be entitled to all Privileges and Immunities of Citizens in the several States.

²A Person charged in any State with Treason, Felony, or other Crime, who shall flee from Justice, and be found in another State, shall on Demand of the executive Authority of the State from which he fled, be delivered up, to be removed to the State having Jurisdiction of the Crime.

³No Person held to Service or Labour in one State, under the Laws thereof, escaping into another, shall, in Consequence of any Law or Regulation therein, be discharged from such Service or Labour, but shall be delivered up on Claim of the Party to whom such Service or Labour may be due.¹¹

SECTION. 3. ¹New States may be admitted by the Congress into this Union; but no new State shall be formed or erected within the Jurisdiction of any other State; nor any State be formed by the Junction of two or more States, or Parts of States, without the Consent of the Legislatures of the States concerned as well as of the Congress.

²The Congress shall have Power to dispose of and make all needful Rules and Regulations respecting the Territory or other Property belonging to the United States; and nothing in this Constitution shall be so construed as to Prejudice any Claims of the United States, or of any particular State.

SECTION. 4. The United States shall guarantee to every State in this Union a Republican Form of Government, and shall protect each of them against Invasion; and on Application of the Legislature, or of the Executive (when the Legislature cannot be convened) against domestic Violence.

ARTICLE. V.

The Congress, whenever two thirds of both Houses shall deem it necessary, shall propose Amendments to this Constitution, or, on the Application of the Legislatures of two thirds of the several States, shall call a Convention for proposing Amendments, which, in either Case, shall be valid to all Intents and Purposes, as Part of this Constitution, when ratified by the Legislatures of three fourths of the several States, or by Conventions in three fourths thereof, as the one or the other Mode of Ratification may be proposed by the Congress; Provided that no Amendment which may be made prior to the Year One thousand eight hundred and eight shall in any Manner affect the first and fourth Clauses in the Ninth Section of the first Article; and that no State, without its Consent, shall be deprived of its equal Suffrage in the Senate.

ARTICLE. VI.

¹All Debts contracted and Engagements entered into, before the Adoption of this Constitution, shall be as valid against the United States under this Constitution, as under the Confederation.

²This Constitution, and the Laws of the United States which shall be made in Pursuance thereof; and all Treaties made, or which shall be made, under the Authority of the United States, shall be the supreme Law of the Land; and the Judges in every State shall be bound thereby, any Thing in the Constitution or Laws of any State to the Contrary notwithstanding.

³The Senators and Representatives before mentioned, and the Members of the several State Legislatures, and all executive and judicial Officers, both of the United States and of the several States, shall be bound by Oath or Affirmation, to support this Constitution; but no religious Test shall ever be required as a Qualification to any Office or public Trust under the United States.

ARTICLE. VII.

The Ratification of the Conventions of nine States, shall be sufficient for the Establishment of this Constitution between the States so ratifying the Same.

DONE in Convention by the Unanimous Consent of the States present the Seventeenth Day of September in the Year of our Lord one thousand seven hundred and Eighty seven and of the Independence of the United States of America the Twelfth   IN WITNESS whereof We have hereunto subscribed our Names,

G⁰. WASHINGTON—*Presidᵗ*.

and deputy from Virginia

[Signed also by the deputies of twelve States.]
New Hampshire
JOHN LANGDON

---

¹¹ This clause has been affected by amendment XIII.

NICHOLAS GILMAN

Massachusetts

NATHANIEL GORHAM
RUFUS KING

Connecticut

WM. SAML. JOHNSON
ROGER SHERMAN

New York

ALEXANDER HAMILTON

New Jersey

WIL: LIVINGSTON
DAVID BREARLEY.
WM. PATERSON.
JONA: DAYTON

Pennsylvania

B FRANKLIN
THOMAS MIFFLIN
ROBT MORRIS
GEO. CLYMER
THOS. FITZSIMONS
JARED INGERSOLL
JAMES WILSON.
GOUV MORRIS

Delaware

GEO: READ
GUNNING BEDFORD jun
JOHN DICKINSON
RICHARD BASSETT
JACO: BROOM

Maryland

JAMES MCHENRY
DAN OF ST THOS. JENIFER
DANL CARROLL.

Virginia

JOHN BLAIR—
JAMES MADISON Jr.

North Carolina

WM BLOUNT
RICHD. DOBBS SPAIGHT.
HU WILLIAMSON

South Carolina

J. RUTLEDGE
CHARLES COTESWORTH PINCKNEY
CHARLES PINCKNEY
PIERCE BUTLER.

Georgia

WILLIAM FEW
ABR BALDWIN

Attest   WILLIAM JACKSON *Secretary*

ARTICLES IN ADDITION TO, AND AMEND-
MENT OF, THE CONSTITUTION OF THE
UNITED STATES OF AMERICA, PROPOSED
BY CONGRESS, AND RATIFIED BY THE
LEGISLATURES OF THE SEVERAL
STATES, PURSUANT TO THE FIFTH ARTI-
CLE OF THE ORIGINAL CONSTITUTION [12]

---

[12] The first ten amendments to the Constitution of the United
States (and two others, one of which failed of ratification and
the other which later became the 27th amendment) were proposed to the legislatures of the several States by the First Congress on September 25, 1789. The first ten amendments were rati-

ARTICLE [I.] [13]

Congress shall make no law respecting an establishment of religion, or prohibiting the free
exercise thereof; or abridging the freedom of
speech, or of the press; or the right of the people
peaceably to assemble, and to petition the Government for a redress of grievances.

ARTICLE [II.]

A well regulated Militia, being necessary to
the security of a free State, the right of the people to keep and bear Arms, shall not be infringed.

ARTICLE [III.]

No Soldier shall, in time of peace be quartered
in any house, without the consent of the Owner,
nor in time of war, but in a manner to be prescribed by law.

ARTICLE [IV.]

The right of the people to be secure in their
persons, houses, papers, and effects, against unreasonable searches and seizures, shall not be
violated, and no Warrants shall issue, but upon
probable cause, supported by Oath or affirmation, and particularly describing the place to be
searched, and the persons or things to be seized.

ARTICLE [V.]

No person shall be held to answer for a capital,
or otherwise infamous crime, unless on a presentment or indictment of a Grand Jury, except
in cases arising in the land or naval forces, or in
the Militia, when in actual service in time of
War or public danger; nor shall any person be
subject for the same offence to be twice put in
jeopardy of life or limb; nor shall be compelled
in any criminal case to be a witness against
himself, nor be deprived of life, liberty, or property, without due process of law; nor shall private property be taken for public use, without
just compensation.

ARTICLE [VI.]

In all criminal prosecutions, the accused shall
enjoy the right to a speedy and public trial, by
an impartial jury of the State and district
wherein the crime shall have been committed,
which district shall have been previously ascertained by law, and to be informed of the nature
and cause of the accusation; to be confronted
with the witnesses against him; to have compulsory process for obtaining witnesses in his favor,
and to have the Assistance of Counsel for his defence.

---

fied by the following States, and the notifications of ratification
by the Governors thereof were successively communicated by
the President to Congress: New Jersey, November 20, 1789; Maryland, December 19, 1789; North Carolina, December 22, 1789; South
Carolina, January 19, 1790; New Hampshire, January 25, 1790;
Delaware, January 28, 1790; New York, February 24, 1790; Pennsylvania, March 10, 1790; Rhode Island, June 7, 1790; Vermont,
November 3, 1791; and Virginia, December 15, 1791.

Ratification was completed on December 15, 1791.

The amendments were subsequently ratified by the legislatures of Massachusetts, March 2, 1939; Georgia, March 18, 1939;
and Connecticut, April 19, 1939.

[13] Only the 13th, 14th, 15th, and 16th articles of amendment had
numbers assigned to them at the time of ratification.

ARTICLE [VII.]

In Suits at common law, where the value in controversy shall exceed twenty dollars, the right of trial by jury shall be preserved, and no fact tried by a jury, shall be otherwise re-examined in any Court of the United States, than according to the rules of the common law.

ARTICLE [VIII.]

Excessive bail shall not be required, nor excessive fines imposed, nor cruel and unusual punishments inflicted.

ARTICLE [IX.]

The enumeration in the Constitution, of certain rights, shall not be construed to deny or disparage others retained by the people.

ARTICLE [X.]

The powers not delegated to the United States by the Constitution, nor prohibited by it to the States, are reserved to the States respectively, or to the people.

[ARTICLE XI.]

The Judicial power of the United States shall not be construed to extend to any suit in law or equity, commenced or prosecuted against one of the United States by Citizens of another State, or by Citizens or Subjects of any Foreign State.

PROPOSAL AND RATIFICATION

The eleventh amendment to the Constitution of the United States was proposed to the legislatures of the several States by the Third Congress, on the 4th of March 1794; and was declared in a message from the President to Congress, dated the 8th of January, 1798, to have been ratified by the legislatures of three-fourths of the States. The dates of ratification were: New York, March 27, 1794; Rhode Island, March 31, 1794; Connecticut, May 8, 1794; New Hampshire, June 16, 1794; Massachusetts, June 26, 1794; Vermont, between October 9, 1794 and November 9, 1794; Virginia, November 18, 1794; Georgia, November 29, 1794; Kentucky, December 7, 1794; Maryland, December 26, 1794; Delaware, January 23, 1795; North Carolina, February 7, 1795.

Ratification was completed on February 7, 1795.

The amendment was subsequently ratified by South Carolina on December 4, 1797. New Jersey and Pennsylvania did not take action on the amendment.

[ARTICLE XII.]

The Electors shall meet in their respective states, and vote by ballot for President and Vice-President, one of whom, at least, shall not be an inhabitant of the same state with themselves; they shall name in their ballots the person voted for as President, and in distinct ballots the person voted for as Vice-President, and they shall make distinct lists of all persons voted for as President, and of all persons voted for as Vice-President, and of the number of votes for each, which lists they shall sign and certify, and transmit sealed to the seat of the government of the United States, directed to the President of the Senate;—The President of the Senate shall, in the presence of the Senate and House of Representatives, open all the certificates and the votes shall then be counted;—The person having the greatest number of votes for President, shall be the President, if such number

be a majority of the whole number of Electors appointed; and if no person have such majority, then from the persons having the highest numbers not exceeding three on the list of those voted for as President, the House of Representatives shall choose immediately, by ballot, the President. But in choosing the President, the votes shall be taken by states, the representation from each state having one vote; a quorum for this purpose shall consist of a member or members from two-thirds of the states, and a majority of all the states shall be necessary to a choice. And if the House of Representatives shall not choose a President whenever the right of choice shall devolve upon them, before the fourth day of March next following, then the Vice-President shall act as President, as in the case of the death or other constitutional disability of the President.[14]—The person having the greatest number of votes as Vice-President, shall be the Vice-President, if such number be a majority of the whole number of Electors appointed, and if no person have a majority, then from the two highest numbers on the list, the Senate shall choose the Vice-President; a quorum for the purpose shall consist of two-thirds of the whole number of Senators, and a majority of the whole number shall be necessary to a choice. But no person constitutionally ineligible to the office of President shall be eligible to that of Vice-President of the United States.

PROPOSAL AND RATIFICATION

The twelfth amendment to the Constitution of the United States was proposed to the legislatures of the several States by the Eighth Congress, on the 9th of December, 1803, in lieu of the original third paragraph of the first section of the second article; and was declared in a proclamation of the Secretary of State, dated the 25th of September, 1804, to have been ratified by the legislatures of 13 of the 17 States. The dates of ratification were: North Carolina, December 21, 1803; Maryland, December 24, 1803; Kentucky, December 27, 1803; Ohio, December 30, 1803; Pennsylvania, January 5, 1804; Vermont, January 30, 1804; Virginia, February 3, 1804; New York, February 10, 1804; New Jersey, February 22, 1804; Rhode Island, March 12, 1804; South Carolina, May 15, 1804; Georgia, May 19, 1804; New Hampshire, June 15, 1804.

Ratification was completed on June 15, 1804.

The amendment was subsequently ratified by Tennessee, July 27, 1804.

The amendment was rejected by Delaware, January 18, 1804; Massachusetts, February 3, 1804; Connecticut, at its session begun May 10, 1804.

ARTICLE XIII.

SECTION 1. Neither slavery nor involuntary servitude, except as a punishment for crime whereof the party shall have been duly convicted, shall exist within the United States, or any place subject to their jurisdiction.

SECTION 2. Congress shall have power to enforce this article by appropriate legislation.

PROPOSAL AND RATIFICATION

The thirteenth amendment to the Constitution of the United States was proposed to the legislatures of the several States by the Thirty-eighth Congress, on the 31st day of January, 1865, and was declared, in a procla-

---

[14] This sentence has been superseded by section 3 of amendment XX.

mation of the Secretary of State, dated the 18th of December, 1865, to have been ratified by the legislatures of twenty-seven of the thirty-six States. The dates of ratification were: Illinois, February 1, 1865; Rhode Island, February 2, 1865; Michigan, February 2, 1865; Maryland, February 3, 1865; New York, February 3, 1865; Pennsylvania, February 3, 1865; West Virginia, February 3, 1865; Missouri, February 6, 1865; Maine, February 7, 1865; Kansas, February 7, 1865; Massachusetts, February 7, 1865; Virginia, February 9, 1865; Ohio, February 10, 1865; Indiana, February 13, 1865; Nevada, February 16, 1865; Louisiana, February 17, 1865; Minnesota, February 23, 1865; Wisconsin, February 24, 1865; Vermont, March 9, 1865; Tennessee, April 7, 1865; Arkansas, April 14, 1865; Connecticut, May 4, 1865; New Hampshire, July 1, 1865; South Carolina, November 13, 1865; Alabama, December 2, 1865; North Carolina, December 4, 1865; Georgia, December 6, 1865.

Ratification was completed on December 6, 1865.

The amendment was subsequently ratified by Oregon, December 8, 1865; California, December 19, 1865; Florida, December 28, 1865 (Florida again ratified on June 9, 1868, upon its adoption of a new constitution); Iowa, January 15, 1866; New Jersey, January 23, 1866 (after having rejected the amendment on March 16, 1865); Texas, February 18, 1870; Delaware, February 12, 1901 (after having rejected the amendment on February 8, 1865); Kentucky, March 18, 1976 (after having rejected it on February 24, 1865).

The amendment was rejected (and not subsequently ratified) by Mississippi, December 4, 1865.

ARTICLE XIV.

SECTION 1. All persons born or naturalized in the United States, and subject to the jurisdiction thereof, are citizens of the United States and of the State wherein they reside. No State shall make or enforce any law which shall abridge the privileges or immunities of citizens of the United States; nor shall any State deprive any person of life, liberty, or property, without due process of law; nor deny to any person within its jurisdiction the equal protection of the laws.

SECTION 2. Representatives shall be apportioned among the several States according to their respective numbers, counting the whole number of persons in each State, excluding Indians not taxed. But when the right to vote at any election for the choice of electors for President and Vice President of the United States, Representatives in Congress, the Executive and Judicial officers of a State, or the members of the Legislature thereof, is denied to any of the male inhabitants of such State, being twenty-one years of age,[15] and citizens of the United States, or in any way abridged, except for participation in rebellion, or other crime, the basis of representation therein shall be reduced in the proportion which the number of such male citizens shall bear to the whole number of male citizens twenty-one years of age in such State.

SECTION 3. No person shall be a Senator or Representative in Congress, or elector of President and Vice President, or hold any office, civil or military, under the United States, or under any State, who, having previously taken an oath, as a member of Congress, or as an officer of the United States, or as a member of any State legislature, or as an executive or judicial officer of any State, to support the Constitution of the United States, shall have engaged in in-

---

[15] See amendment XIX and section 1 of amendment XXVI.

surrection or rebellion against the same, or given aid or comfort to the enemies thereof. But Congress may by a vote of two-thirds of each House, remove such disability.

SECTION 4. The validity of the public debt of the United States, authorized by law, including debts incurred for payment of pensions and bounties for services in suppressing insurrection or rebellion, shall not be questioned. But neither the United States nor any State shall assume or pay any debt or obligation incurred in aid of insurrection or rebellion against the United States, or any claim for the loss or emancipation of any slave; but all such debts, obligations and claims shall be held illegal and void.

SECTION 5. The Congress shall have power to enforce, by appropriate legislation, the provisions of this article.

PROPOSAL AND RATIFICATION

The fourteenth amendment to the Constitution of the United States was proposed to the legislatures of the several States by the Thirty-ninth Congress, on the 13th of June, 1866. It was declared, in a certificate of the Secretary of State dated July 28, 1868 to have been ratified by the legislatures of 28 of the 37 States. The dates of ratification were: Connecticut, June 25, 1866; New Hampshire, July 6, 1866; Tennessee, July 19, 1866; New Jersey, September 11, 1866 (subsequently the legislature rescinded its ratification, and on March 24, 1868, readopted its resolution of rescission over the Governor's veto, and on Nov. 12, 1980, expressed support for the amendment); Oregon, September 19, 1866 (and rescinded its ratification on October 15, 1868); Vermont, October 30, 1866; Ohio, January 4, 1867 (and rescinded its ratification on January 15, 1868); New York, January 10, 1867; Kansas, January 11, 1867; Illinois, January 15, 1867; West Virginia, January 16, 1867; Michigan, January 16, 1867; Minnesota, January 16, 1867; Maine, January 19, 1867; Nevada, January 22, 1867; Indiana, January 23, 1867; Missouri, January 25, 1867; Rhode Island, February 7, 1867; Wisconsin, February 7, 1867; Pennsylvania, February 12, 1867; Massachusetts, March 20, 1867; Nebraska, June 15, 1867; Iowa, March 16, 1868; Arkansas, April 6, 1868; Florida, June 9, 1868; North Carolina, July 4, 1868 (after having rejected it on December 14, 1866); Louisiana, July 9, 1868 (after having rejected it on February 6, 1867); South Carolina, July 9, 1868 (after having rejected it on December 20, 1866).

Ratification was completed on July 9, 1868.

The amendment was subsequently ratified by Alabama, July 13, 1868; Georgia, July 21, 1868 (after having rejected it on November 9, 1866); Virginia, October 8, 1869 (after having rejected it on January 9, 1867); Mississippi, January 17, 1870; Texas, February 18, 1870 (after having rejected it on October 27, 1866); Delaware, February 12, 1901 (after having rejected it on February 8, 1867); Maryland, April 4, 1959 (after having rejected it on March 23, 1867); California, May 6, 1959; Kentucky, March 18, 1976 (after having rejected it on January 8, 1867).

ARTICLE XV.

SECTION 1. The right of citizens of the United States to vote shall not be denied or abridged by the United States or by any State on account of race, color, or previous condition of servitude.

SECTION 2. The Congress shall have power to enforce this article by appropriate legislation.

PROPOSAL AND RATIFICATION

The fifteenth amendment to the Constitution of the United States was proposed to the legislatures of the several States by the Fortieth Congress, on the 26th of February, 1869, and was declared, in a proclamation of the Secretary of State, dated March 30, 1870, to have been ratified by the legislatures of twenty-nine of the thirty-seven States. The dates of ratification were: Nevada, March 1, 1869; West Virginia, March 3, 1869; Illinois, March 5, 1869; Louisiana, March 5, 1869; North Carolina, March 5, 1869; Michigan, March 8, 1869; Wisconsin, March 9, 1869; Maine, March 11, 1869; Massachusetts, March 12, 1869; Arkansas, March 15, 1869; South Carolina, March 15, 1869; Pennsylvania, March 25, 1869; New York, April 14, 1869 (and the legislature of the same State passed a resolution January 5, 1870, to withdraw its consent to it, which action it rescinded on March 30, 1970); Indiana, May 14, 1869; Connecticut, May 19, 1869; Florida, June 14, 1869; New Hampshire, July 1, 1869; Virginia, October 8, 1869; Vermont, October 20, 1869; Missouri, January 7, 1870; Minnesota, January 13, 1870; Mississippi, January 17, 1870; Rhode Island, January 18, 1870; Kansas, January 19, 1870; Ohio, January 27, 1870 (after having rejected it on April 30, 1869); Georgia, February 2, 1870; Iowa, February 3, 1870; Tennessee, April 2, 1997 (after having rejected it on November 16, 1869).

Ratification was completed on February 3, 1870, unless the withdrawal of ratification by New York was effective; in which event ratification was completed on February 17, 1870, when Nebraska ratified.

The amendment was subsequently ratified by Texas, February 18, 1870; New Jersey, February 15, 1871 (after having rejected it on February 7, 1870); Delaware, February 12, 1901 (after having rejected it on March 18, 1869); Oregon, February 24, 1959; California, April 3, 1962 (after having rejected it on January 28, 1870); Kentucky, March 18, 1976 (after having rejected it on March 12, 1869).

The amendment was approved by the Governor of Maryland, May 7, 1973; Maryland having previously rejected it on February 26, 1870.

ARTICLE XVI.

The Congress shall have power to lay and collect taxes on incomes, from whatever source derived, without apportionment among the several States, and without regard to any census or enumeration.

PROPOSAL AND RATIFICATION

The sixteenth amendment to the Constitution of the United States was proposed to the legislatures of the several States by the Sixty-first Congress on the 12th of July, 1909, and was declared, in a proclamation of the Secretary of State, dated the 25th of February, 1913, to have been ratified by 36 of the 48 States. The dates of ratification were: Alabama, August 10, 1909; Kentucky, February 8, 1910; South Carolina, February 19, 1910; Illinois, March 1, 1910; Mississippi, March 7, 1910; Oklahoma, March 10, 1910; Maryland, April 8, 1910; Georgia, August 3, 1910; Texas, August 16, 1910; Ohio, January 19, 1911; Idaho, January 20, 1911; Oregon, January 23, 1911; Washington, January 26, 1911; Montana, January 30, 1911; Indiana, January 30, 1911; California, January 31, 1911; Nevada, January 31, 1911; South Dakota, February 3, 1911; Nebraska, February 9, 1911; North Carolina, February 11, 1911; Colorado, February 15, 1911; North Dakota, February 17, 1911; Kansas, February 18, 1911; Michigan, February 23, 1911; Iowa, February 24, 1911; Missouri, March 16, 1911; Maine, March 31, 1911; Tennessee, April 7, 1911; Arkansas, April 22, 1911 (after having rejected it earlier); Wisconsin, May 26, 1911; New York, July 12, 1911; Arizona, April 6, 1912; Minnesota, June 11, 1912; Louisiana, June 28, 1912; West Virginia, January 31, 1913; New Mexico, February 3, 1913.

Ratification was completed on February 3, 1913.

The amendment was subsequently ratified by Massachusetts, March 4, 1913; New Hampshire, March 7, 1913 (after having rejected it on March 2, 1911).

The amendment was rejected (and not subsequently ratified) by Connecticut, Rhode Island, and Utah.

[ARTICLE XVII.]

The Senate of the United States shall be composed of two Senators from each State, elected by the people thereof, for six years; and each Senator shall have one vote. The electors in each State shall have the qualifications requisite for electors of the most numerous branch of the State legislatures.

When vacancies happen in the representation of any State in the Senate, the executive authority of such State shall issue writs of election to fill such vacancies: *Provided*, That the legislature of any State may empower the executive thereof to make temporary appointments until the people fill the vacancies by election as the legislature may direct.

This amendment shall not be so construed as to affect the election or term of any Senator chosen before it becomes valid as part of the Constitution.

PROPOSAL AND RATIFICATION

The seventeenth amendment to the Constitution of the United States was proposed to the legislatures of the several States by the Sixty-second Congress on the 13th of May, 1912, and was declared, in a proclamation of the Secretary of State, dated the 31st of May, 1913, to have been ratified by the legislatures of 36 of the 48 States. The dates of ratification were: Massachusetts, May 22, 1912; Arizona, June 3, 1912; Minnesota, June 10, 1912; New York, January 15, 1913; Kansas, January 17, 1913; Oregon, January 23, 1913; North Carolina, January 25, 1913; California, January 28, 1913; Michigan, January 28, 1913; Iowa, January 30, 1913; Montana, January 30, 1913; Idaho, January 31, 1913; West Virginia, February 4, 1913; Colorado, February 5, 1913; Nevada, February 6, 1913; Texas, February 7, 1913; Washington, February 7, 1913; Wyoming, February 8, 1913; Arkansas, February 11, 1913; Maine, February 11, 1913; Illinois, February 13, 1913; North Dakota, February 14, 1913; Wisconsin, February 18, 1913; Indiana, February 19, 1913; New Hampshire, February 19, 1913; Vermont, February 19, 1913; South Dakota, February 19, 1913; Oklahoma, February 24, 1913; Ohio, February 25, 1913; Missouri, March 7, 1913; New Mexico, March 13, 1913; Nebraska, March 14, 1913; New Jersey, March 17, 1913; Tennessee, April 1, 1913; Pennsylvania, April 2, 1913; Connecticut, April 8, 1913.

Ratification was completed on April 8, 1913.

The amendment was subsequently ratified by Louisiana, June 11, 1914.

The amendment was rejected by Utah (and not subsequently ratified) on February 26, 1913.

ARTICLE [XVIII].[16]

SECTION 1. After one year from the ratification of this article the manufacture, sale, or transportation of intoxicating liquors within, the importation thereof into, or the exportation thereof from the United States and all territory subject to the jurisdiction thereof for beverage purposes is hereby prohibited.

SEC. 2. The Congress and the several States shall have concurrent power to enforce this article by appropriate legislation.

SEC. 3. This article shall be inoperative unless it shall have been ratified as an amendment to the Constitution by the legislatures of the several States, as provided in the Constitution, within seven years from the date of the submission hereof to the States by the Congress.

PROPOSAL AND RATIFICATION

The eighteenth amendment to the Constitution of the United States was proposed to the legislatures of the several States by the Sixty-fifth Congress, on the 18th

---

[16] Repealed by section 1 of amendment XXI.

of December, 1917, and was declared, in a proclamation of the Secretary of State, dated the 29th of January, 1919, to have been ratified by the legislatures of 36 of the 48 States. The dates of ratification were: Mississippi, January 8, 1918; Virginia, January 11, 1918; Kentucky, January 14, 1918; North Dakota, January 25, 1918; South Carolina, January 29, 1918; Maryland, February 13, 1918; Montana, February 19, 1918; Texas, March 4, 1918; Delaware, March 18, 1918; South Dakota, March 20, 1918; Massachusetts, April 2, 1918; Arizona, May 24, 1918; Georgia, June 26, 1918; Louisiana, August 3, 1918; Florida, December 3, 1918; Michigan, January 2, 1919; Ohio, January 7, 1919; Oklahoma, January 7, 1919; Idaho, January 8, 1919; Maine, January 8, 1919; West Virginia, January 9, 1919; California, January 13, 1919; Tennessee, January 13, 1919; Washington, January 13, 1919; Arkansas, January 14, 1919; Kansas, January 14, 1919; Alabama, January 15, 1919; Colorado, January 15, 1919; Iowa, January 15, 1919; New Hampshire, January 15, 1919; Oregon, January 15, 1919; Nebraska, January 16, 1919; North Carolina, January 16, 1919; Utah, January 16, 1919; Missouri, January 16, 1919; Wyoming, January 16, 1919.

Ratification was completed on January 16, 1919. See *Dillon v. Gloss*, 256 U.S. 368, 376 (1921).

The amendment was subsequently ratified by Minnesota on January 17, 1919; Wisconsin, January 17, 1919; New Mexico, January 20, 1919; Nevada, January 21, 1919; New York, January 29, 1919; Vermont, January 29, 1919; Pennsylvania, February 25, 1919; Connecticut, May 6, 1919; and New Jersey, March 9, 1922.

The amendment was rejected (and not subsequently ratified) by Rhode Island.

Article [XIX].

The right of citizens of the United States to vote shall not be denied or abridged by the United States or by any State on account of sex.

Congress shall have power to enforce this article by appropriate legislation.

Proposal and Ratification

The nineteenth amendment to the Constitution of the United States was proposed to the legislatures of the several States by the Sixty-sixth Congress, on the 4th of June, 1919, and was declared, in a proclamation of the Secretary of State, dated the 26th of August, 1920, to have been ratified by the legislatures of 36 of the 48 States. The dates of ratification were: Illinois, June 10, 1919 (and that State readopted its resolution of ratification June 17, 1919); Michigan, June 10, 1919; Wisconsin, June 10, 1919; Kansas, June 16, 1919; New York, June 16, 1919; Ohio, June 16, 1919; Pennsylvania, June 24, 1919; Massachusetts, June 25, 1919; Texas, June 28, 1919; Iowa, July 2, 1919; Missouri, July 3, 1919; Arkansas, July 28, 1919; Montana, August 2, 1919; Nebraska, August 2, 1919; Minnesota, September 8, 1919; New Hampshire, September 10, 1919; Utah, October 2, 1919; California, November 1, 1919; Maine, November 5, 1919; North Dakota, December 1, 1919; South Dakota, December 4, 1919; Colorado, December 15, 1919; Kentucky, January 6, 1920; Rhode Island, January 6, 1920; Oregon, January 13, 1920; Indiana, January 16, 1920; Wyoming, January 27, 1920; Nevada, February 7, 1920; New Jersey, February 9, 1920; Idaho, February 11, 1920; Arizona, February 12, 1920; New Mexico, February 21, 1920; Oklahoma, February 28, 1920; West Virginia, March 10, 1920; Washington, March 22, 1920; Tennessee, August 18, 1920.

Ratification was completed on August 18, 1920.

The amendment was subsequently ratified by Connecticut on September 14, 1920 (and that State reaffirmed on September 21, 1920); Vermont, February 8, 1921; Delaware, March 6, 1923 (after having rejected it on June 2, 1920); Maryland, March 29, 1941 (after having rejected it on February 24, 1920, ratification certified on February 25, 1958); Virginia, February 21, 1952 (after having rejected it on February 12, 1920); Alabama, September 8, 1953 (after having rejected it on September 22,

1919); Florida, May 13, 1969; South Carolina, July 1, 1969 (after having rejected it on January 28, 1920, ratification certified on August 22, 1973); Georgia, February 20, 1970 (after having rejected it on July 24, 1919); Louisiana, June 11, 1970 (after having rejected it on July 1, 1920); North Carolina, May 6, 1971; Mississippi, March 22, 1984 (after having rejected it on March 29, 1920).

Article [XX.]

Section 1. The terms of the President and Vice President shall end at noon on the 20th day of January, and the terms of Senators and Representatives at noon on the 3d day of January, of the years in which such terms would have ended if this article had not been ratified; and the terms of their successors shall then begin.

Sec. 2. The Congress shall assemble at least once in every year, and such meeting shall begin at noon on the 3d day of January, unless they shall by law appoint a different day.

Sec. 3. If, at the time fixed for the beginning of the term of the President, the President elect shall have died, the Vice President elect shall become President. If a President shall not have been chosen before the time fixed for the beginning of his term, or if the President elect shall have failed to qualify, then the Vice President elect shall act as President until a President shall have qualified; and the Congress may by law provide for the case wherein neither a President elect nor a Vice President elect shall have qualified, declaring who shall then act as President, or the manner in which one who is to act shall be selected, and such person shall act accordingly until a President or Vice President shall have qualified.

Sec. 4. The Congress may by law provide for the case of the death of any of the persons from whom the House of Representatives may choose a President whenever the right of choice shall have devolved upon them, and for the case of the death of any of the persons from whom the Senate may choose a Vice President whenever the right of choice shall have devolved upon them.

Sec. 5. Sections 1 and 2 shall take effect on the 15th day of October following the ratification of this article.

Sec. 6. This article shall be inoperative unless it shall have been ratified as an amendment to the Constitution by the legislatures of three-fourths of the several States within seven years from the date of its submission.

Proposal and Ratification

The twentieth amendment to the Constitution was proposed to the legislatures of the several states by the Seventy-Second Congress, on the 2d day of March, 1932, and was declared, in a proclamation by the Secretary of State, dated on the 6th day of February, 1933, to have been ratified by the legislatures of 36 of the 48 States. The dates of ratification were: Virginia, March 4, 1932; New York, March 11, 1932; Mississippi, March 16, 1932; Arkansas, March 17, 1932; Kentucky, March 17, 1932; New Jersey, March 21, 1932; South Carolina, March 25, 1932; Michigan, March 31, 1932; Maine, April 1, 1932; Rhode Island, April 14, 1932; Illinois, April 21, 1932; Louisiana, June 22, 1932; West Virginia, July 30, 1932; Pennsylvania, August 11, 1932; Indiana, August 15, 1932; Texas, September 7, 1932; Alabama, September 13, 1932; California, January 4, 1933; North Carolina, January 5, 1933; North Dakota, January 9, 1933; Minnesota, January 12, 1933; Arizona, January 13, 1933; Montana, January 13, 1933; Nebraska, January 13, 1933; Oklahoma, January 13, 1933; Kansas, January 16, 1933; Oregon, January

16, 1933; Delaware, January 19, 1933; Washington, January 19, 1933; Wyoming, January 19, 1933; Iowa, January 20, 1933; South Dakota, January 20, 1933; Tennessee, January 20, 1933; Idaho, January 21, 1933; New Mexico, January 21, 1933; Georgia, January 23, 1933; Missouri, January 23, 1933; Ohio, January 23, 1933; Utah, January 23, 1933.

Ratification was completed on January 23, 1933.

The amendment was subsequently ratified by Massachusetts on January 24, 1933; Wisconsin, January 24, 1933; Colorado, January 24, 1933; Nevada, January 26, 1933; Connecticut, January 27, 1933; New Hampshire, January 31, 1933; Vermont, February 2, 1933; Maryland, March 24, 1933; Florida, April 26, 1933.

ARTICLE [XXI.]

SECTION 1. The eighteenth article of amendment to the Constitution of the United States is hereby repealed.

SECTION 2. The transportation or importation into any State, Territory, or possession of the United States for delivery or use therein of intoxicating liquors, in violation of the laws thereof, is hereby prohibited.

SECTION 3. This article shall be inoperative unless it shall have been ratified as an amendment to the Constitution by conventions in the several States, as provided in the Constitution, within seven years from the date of the submission hereof to the States by the Congress.

PROPOSAL AND RATIFICATION

The twenty-first amendment to the Constitution was proposed to the several states by the Seventy-Second Congress, on the 20th day of February, 1933, and was declared, in a proclamation by the Secretary of State, dated on the 5th day of December, 1933, to have been ratified by 36 of the 48 States. The dates of ratification were: Michigan, April 10, 1933; Wisconsin, April 25, 1933; Rhode Island, May 8, 1933; Wyoming, May 25, 1933; New Jersey, June 1, 1933; Delaware, June 24, 1933; Indiana, June 26, 1933; Massachusetts, June 26, 1933; New York, June 27, 1933; Illinois, July 10, 1933; Iowa, July 10, 1933; Connecticut, July 11, 1933; New Hampshire, July 11, 1933; California, July 24, 1933; West Virginia, July 25, 1933; Arkansas, August 1, 1933; Oregon, August 7, 1933; Alabama, August 8, 1933; Tennessee, August 11, 1933; Missouri, August 29, 1933; Arizona, September 5, 1933; Nevada, September 5, 1933; Vermont, September 23, 1933; Colorado, September 26, 1933; Washington, October 3, 1933; Minnesota, October 10, 1933; Idaho, October 17, 1933; Maryland, October 18, 1933; Virginia, October 25, 1933; New Mexico, November 2, 1933; Florida, November 14, 1933; Texas, November 24, 1933; Kentucky, November 27, 1933; Ohio, December 5, 1933; Pennsylvania, December 5, 1933; Utah, December 5, 1933.

Ratification was completed on December 5, 1933.

The amendment was subsequently ratified by Maine, on December 6, 1933, and by Montana, on August 6, 1934.

The amendment was rejected (and not subsequently ratified) by South Carolina, on December 4, 1933.

ARTICLE [XXII.]

SECTION 1. No person shall be elected to the office of the President more than twice, and no person who has held the office of President, or acted as President, for more than two years of a term to which some other person was elected President shall be elected to the office of the President more than once. But this Article shall not apply to any person holding the office of President when this Article was proposed by the Congress, and shall not prevent any person who may be holding the office of President, or acting as President, during the term within which this Article becomes operative from holding the office of President or acting as President during the remainder of such term.

SEC. 2. This article shall be inoperative unless it shall have been ratified as an amendment to the Constitution by the legislatures of three-fourths of the several States within seven years from the date of its submission to the States by the Congress.

PROPOSAL AND RATIFICATION

This amendment was proposed to the legislatures of the several States by the Eightieth Congress on Mar. 21, 1947 by House Joint Res. No. 27, and was declared by the Administrator of General Services, on Mar. 1, 1951, to have been ratified by the legislatures of 36 of the 48 States. The dates of ratification were: Maine, March 31, 1947; Michigan, March 31, 1947; Iowa, April 1, 1947; Kansas, April 1, 1947; New Hampshire, April 1, 1947; Delaware, April 2, 1947; Illinois, April 3, 1947; Oregon, April 3, 1947; Colorado, April 12, 1947; California, April 15, 1947; New Jersey, April 15, 1947; Vermont, April 15, 1947; Ohio, April 16, 1947; Wisconsin, April 16, 1947; Pennsylvania, April 29, 1947; Connecticut, May 21, 1947; Missouri, May 22, 1947; Nebraska, May 23, 1947; Virginia, January 28, 1948; Mississippi, February 12, 1948; New York, March 9, 1948; South Dakota, January 21, 1949; North Dakota, February 25, 1949; Louisiana, May 17, 1950; Montana, January 25, 1951; Indiana, January 29, 1951; Idaho, January 30, 1951; New Mexico, February 12, 1951; Wyoming, February 12, 1951; Arkansas, February 15, 1951; Georgia, February 17, 1951; Tennessee, February 20, 1951; Texas, February 22, 1951; Nevada, February 26, 1951; Utah, February 26, 1951; Minnesota, February 27, 1951.

Ratification was completed on February 27, 1951.

The amendment was subsequently ratified by North Carolina on February 28, 1951; South Carolina, March 13, 1951; Maryland, March 14, 1951; Florida, April 16, 1951; Alabama, May 4, 1951.

The amendment was rejected (and not subsequently ratified) by Oklahoma in June 1947, and Massachusetts on June 9, 1949.

CERTIFICATION OF VALIDITY

Publication of the certifying statement of the Administrator of General Services that the amendment had become valid was made on Mar. 1, 1951, F.R. Doc. 51–2940, 16 F.R. 2019.

ARTICLE [XXIII.]

SECTION 1. The District constituting the seat of Government of the United States shall appoint in such manner as the Congress may direct:

A number of electors of President and Vice President equal to the whole number of Senators and Representatives in Congress to which the District would be entitled if it were a State, but in no event more than the least populous State; they shall be in addition to those appointed by the States, but they shall be considered, for the purposes of the election of President and Vice President, to be electors appointed by a State; and they shall meet in the District and perform such duties as provided by the twelfth article of amendment.

SEC. 2. The Congress shall have power to enforce this article by appropriate legislation.

PROPOSAL AND RATIFICATION

This amendment was proposed by the Eighty-sixth Congress on June 17, 1960 and was declared by the Administrator of General Services on Apr. 3, 1961, to have been ratified by 38 of the 50 States. The dates of ratification were: Hawaii, June 23, 1960 (and that State made a technical correction to its resolution on June 30, 1960); Massachusetts, August 22, 1960; New Jersey, December 19, 1960; New York, January 17, 1961; California, January 19, 1961; Oregon, January 27, 1961; Maryland, January 30, 1961; Idaho, January 31, 1961; Maine, January 31, 1961; Minnesota, January 31, 1961; New Mexico, February 1, 1961; Nevada, February 2, 1961; Montana, February 6, 1961; South Dakota, February 6, 1961; Colorado, February 8, 1961; Washington, February 9, 1961; West Virginia, February 9, 1961; Alaska, February 10, 1961; Wyoming, February 13, 1961; Delaware, February 20, 1961; Utah, February 21, 1961; Wisconsin, February 21, 1961; Pennsylvania, February 28, 1961; Indiana, March 3, 1961; North Dakota, March 3, 1961; Tennessee, March 6, 1961; Michigan, March 8, 1961; Connecticut, March 9, 1961; Arizona, March 10, 1961; Illinois, March 14, 1961; Nebraska, March 15, 1961; Vermont, March 15, 1961; Iowa, March 16, 1961; Missouri, March 20, 1961; Oklahoma, March 21, 1961; Rhode Island, March 22, 1961; Kansas, March 29, 1961; Ohio, March 29, 1961.

Ratification was completed on March 29, 1961.

The amendment was subsequently ratified by New Hampshire on March 30, 1961 (when that State annulled and then repeated its ratification of March 29, 1961).

The amendment was rejected (and not subsequently ratified) by Arkansas on January 24, 1961.

CERTIFICATION OF VALIDITY

Publication of the certifying statement of the Administrator of General Services that the amendment had become valid was made on Apr. 3, 1961, F.R. Doc. 61–3017, 26 F.R. 2808.

ARTICLE [XXIV.]

SECTION 1. The right of citizens of the United States to vote in any primary or other election for President or Vice President, for electors for President or Vice President, or for Senator or Representative in Congress, shall not be denied or abridged by the United States or any State by reason of failure to pay any poll tax or other tax.

SEC. 2. The Congress shall have power to enforce this article by appropriate legislation.

PROPOSAL AND RATIFICATION

This amendment was proposed by the Eighty-seventh Congress by Senate Joint Resolution No. 29, which was approved by the Senate on Mar. 27, 1962, and by the House of Representatives on Aug. 27, 1962. It was declared by the Administrator of General Services on Feb. 4, 1964, to have been ratified by the legislatures of 38 of the 50 States.

This amendment was ratified by the following States: Illinois, November 14, 1962; New Jersey, December 3, 1962; Oregon, January 25, 1963; Montana, January 28, 1963; West Virginia, February 1, 1963; New York, February 4, 1963; Maryland, February 6, 1963; California, February 7, 1963; Alaska, February 11, 1963; Rhode Island, February 14, 1963; Indiana, February 19, 1963; Utah, February 20, 1963; Michigan, February 20, 1963; Colorado, February 21, 1963; Ohio, February 27, 1963; Minnesota, February 27, 1963; New Mexico, March 5, 1963; Hawaii, March 6, 1963; North Dakota, March 7, 1963; Idaho, March 8, 1963; Washington, March 14, 1963; Vermont, March 15, 1963; Nevada, March 19, 1963; Connecticut, March 20, 1963; Tennessee, March 21, 1963; Pennsylvania, March 25, 1963; Wisconsin, March 26, 1963; Kansas, March 28, 1963; Massachusetts, March 28, 1963; Nebraska, April 4, 1963; Florida, April 18, 1963; Iowa, April 24, 1963; Delaware, May 1, 1963; Missouri, May 13, 1963; New Hampshire, June 12, 1963; Kentucky, June 27, 1963; Maine, January 16, 1964; South Dakota, January 23, 1964; Virginia, February 25, 1977.

Ratification was completed on January 23, 1964.

The amendment was subsequently ratified by North Carolina on May 3, 1989.

The amendment was rejected by Mississippi (and not subsequently ratified) on December 20, 1962.

CERTIFICATION OF VALIDITY

Publication of the certifying statement of the Administrator of General Services that the amendment had become valid was made on Feb. 5, 1964, F.R. Doc. 64–1229, 29 F.R. 1715.

ARTICLE [XXV.]

SECTION 1. In case of the removal of the President from office or of his death or resignation, the Vice President shall become President.

SEC. 2. Whenever there is a vacancy in the office of the Vice President, the President shall nominate a Vice President who shall take office upon confirmation by a majority vote of both Houses of Congress.

SEC. 3. Whenever the President transmits to the President pro tempore of the Senate and the Speaker of the House of Representatives his written declaration that he is unable to discharge the powers and duties of his office, and until he transmits to them a written declaration to the contrary, such powers and duties shall be discharged by the Vice President as Acting President.

SEC. 4. Whenever the Vice President and a majority of either the principal officers of the executive departments or of such other body as Congress may by law provide, transmit to the President pro tempore of the Senate and the Speaker of the House of Representatives their written declaration that the President is unable to discharge the powers and duties of his office, the Vice President shall immediately assume the powers and duties of the office as Acting President.

Thereafter, when the President transmits to the President pro tempore of the Senate and the Speaker of the House of Representatives his written declaration that no inability exists, he shall resume the powers and duties of his office unless the Vice President and a majority of either the principal officers of the executive department[17] or of such other body as Congress may by law provide, transmit within four days to the President pro tempore of the Senate and the Speaker of the House of Representatives their written declaration that the President is unable to discharge the powers and duties of his office. Thereupon Congress shall decide the issue, assembling within forty-eight hours for that purpose if not in session. If the Congress, within twenty-one days after receipt of the latter written declaration, or, if Congress is not in session, within twenty-one days after Congress is required to assemble, determines by two-thirds vote of both Houses that the President is unable to discharge the powers and duties of his office, the Vice President shall continue to discharge the same as Acting President; otherwise, the President shall resume the powers and duties of his office.

PROPOSAL AND RATIFICATION

This amendment was proposed by the Eighty-ninth Congress by Senate Joint Resolution No. 1, which was approved by the Senate on Feb. 19, 1965, and by the House of Representatives, in amended form, on Apr. 13,

---

[17] So in original. Probably should be "departments".

1965. The House of Representatives agreed to a Conference Report on June 30, 1965, and the Senate agreed to the Conference Report on July 6, 1965. It was declared by the Administrator of General Services, on Feb. 23, 1967, to have been ratified by the legislatures of 39 of the 50 States.

This amendment was ratified by the following States: Nebraska, July 12, 1965; Wisconsin, July 13, 1965; Oklahoma, July 16, 1965; Massachusetts, August 9, 1965; Pennsylvania, August 18, 1965; Kentucky, September 15, 1965; Arizona, September 22, 1965; Michigan, October 5, 1965; Indiana, October 20, 1965; California, October 21, 1965; Arkansas, November 4, 1965; New Jersey, November 29, 1965; Delaware, December 7, 1965; Utah, January 17, 1966; West Virginia, January 20, 1966; Maine, January 24, 1966; Rhode Island, January 28, 1966; Colorado, February 3, 1966; New Mexico, February 3, 1966; Kansas, February 8, 1966; Vermont, February 10, 1966; Alaska, February 18, 1966; Idaho, March 2, 1966; Hawaii, March 3, 1966; Virginia, March 8, 1966; Mississippi, March 10, 1966; New York, March 14, 1966; Maryland, March 23, 1966; Missouri, March 30, 1966; New Hampshire, June 13, 1966; Louisiana, July 5, 1966; Tennessee, January 12, 1967; Wyoming, January 25, 1967; Washington, January 26, 1967; Iowa, January 26, 1967; Oregon, February 2, 1967; Minnesota, February 10, 1967; Nevada, February 10, 1967.

Ratification was completed on February 10, 1967.

The amendment was subsequently ratified by Connecticut, February 14, 1967; Montana, February 15, 1967; South Dakota, March 6, 1967; Ohio, March 7, 1967; Alabama, March 14, 1967; North Carolina, March 22, 1967; Illinois, March 22, 1967; Texas, April 25, 1967; Florida, May 25, 1967.

CERTIFICATION OF VALIDITY

Publication of the certifying statement of the Administrator of General Services that the amendment had become valid was made on Feb. 25, 1967, F.R. Doc. 67-2208, 32 F.R. 3287.

ARTICLE [XXVI.]

SECTION 1. The right of citizens of the United States, who are eighteen years of age or older, to vote shall not be denied or abridged by the United States or by any State on account of age.

SEC. 2. The Congress shall have power to enforce this article by appropriate legislation.

PROPOSAL AND RATIFICATION

This amendment was proposed by the Ninety-second Congress by Senate Joint Resolution No. 7, which was approved by the Senate on Mar. 10, 1971, and by the House of Representatives on Mar. 23, 1971. It was declared by the Administrator of General Services on July 5, 1971, to have been ratified by the legislatures of 39 of the 50 States.

This amendment was ratified by the following States: Connecticut, March 23, 1971; Delaware, March 23, 1971; Minnesota, March 23, 1971; Tennessee, March 23, 1971; Washington, March 23, 1971; Hawaii, March 24, 1971; Massachusetts, March 24, 1971; Montana, March 29, 1971; Arkansas, March 30, 1971; Idaho, March 30, 1971; Iowa, March 30, 1971; Nebraska, April 2, 1971; New Jersey, April 3, 1971; Kansas, April 7, 1971; Michigan, April 7, 1971; Alaska, April 8, 1971; Maryland, April 8, 1971; Indiana, April 8, 1971; Maine, April 9, 1971; Vermont, April 16, 1971; Louisiana, April 17, 1971; California, April 19, 1971; Colorado, April 27, 1971; Pennsylvania, April 27, 1971; Texas, April 27, 1971; South Carolina, April 28, 1971; West Virginia, April 28, 1971; New Hampshire, May 13, 1971; Arizona, May 14, 1971; Rhode Island, May 27, 1971; New York, June 2, 1971; Oregon, June 4, 1971; Missouri, June 14, 1971; Wisconsin, June 22, 1971; Illinois, June 29, 1971; Alabama, June 30, 1971; Ohio, June 30, 1971; North Carolina, July 1, 1971; Oklahoma, July 1, 1971.

Ratification was completed on July 1, 1971.

The amendment was subsequently ratified by Virginia, July 8, 1971; Wyoming, July 8, 1971; Georgia, October 4, 1971.

CERTIFICATION OF VALIDITY

Publication of the certifying statement of the Administrator of General Services that the amendment had become valid was made on July 7, 1971, F.R. Doc. 71-9691, 36 F.R. 12725.

ARTICLE [XXVII.]

No law, varying the compensation for the services of the Senators and Representatives, shall take effect, until an election of Representatives shall have intervened.

PROPOSAL AND RATIFICATION

This amendment, being the second of twelve articles proposed by the First Congress on Sept. 25, 1789, was declared by the Archivist of the United States on May 18, 1992, to have been ratified by the legislatures of 40 of the 50 States.

This amendment was ratified by the following States: Maryland, December 19, 1789; North Carolina, December 22, 1789; South Carolina, January 19, 1790; Delaware, January 28, 1790; Vermont, November 3, 1791; Virginia, December 15, 1791; Ohio, May 6, 1873; Wyoming, March 6, 1978; Maine, April 27, 1983; Colorado, April 22, 1984; South Dakota, February 21, 1985; New Hampshire, March 7, 1985; Arizona, April 3, 1985; Tennessee, May 23, 1985; Oklahoma, July 10, 1985; New Mexico, February 14, 1986; Indiana, February 24, 1986; Utah, February 25, 1986; Arkansas, March 6, 1987; Montana, March 17, 1987; Connecticut, May 13, 1987; Wisconsin, July 15, 1987; Georgia, February 2, 1988; West Virginia, March 10, 1988; Louisiana, July 7, 1988; Iowa, February 9, 1989; Idaho, March 23, 1989; Nevada, April 26, 1989; Alaska, May 6, 1989; Oregon, May 19, 1989; Minnesota, May 22, 1989; Texas, May 25, 1989; Kansas, April 5, 1990; Florida, May 31, 1990; North Dakota, March 25, 1991; Alabama, May 5, 1992; Missouri, May 5, 1992; Michigan, May 7, 1992; New Jersey, May 7, 1992.

Ratification was completed on May 7, 1992.

The amendment was subsequently ratified by Illinois on May 12, 1992; California, June 26, 1992; Rhode Island, June 10, 1993.

CERTIFICATION OF VALIDITY

Publication of the certifying statement of the Archivist of the United States that the amendment had become valid was made on May 18, 1992, F.R. Doc. 92-11951, 57 F.R. 21187.

PROPOSED AMENDMENTS TO THE CONSTITUTION NOT RATIFIED BY THE STATES

In addition to the 27 amendments that have been ratified by the required three-fourths of the States, six other amendments have been submitted to the States but have not been ratified by them.

Beginning with the proposed Eighteenth Amendment, Congress has customarily included a provision requiring ratification within seven years from the time of the submission to the States. The Supreme Court in *Coleman* v. *Miller*, 307 U.S. 433 (1939), declared that the question of the reasonableness of the time within which a sufficient number of States must act is a political question to be determined by the Congress.

In 1789, twelve proposed articles of amendment were submitted to the States. Of these, Articles III–XII were ratified and became the first ten amendments to the Constitution, popularly known as the Bill of Rights. In 1992, proposed Article II was ratified and became the 27th amendment to the Constitution. Proposed Article I which was not ratified is as follows:

"ARTICLE THE FIRST

"After the first enumeration required by the first article of the Constitution, there shall be one Representative for every thirty thousand, until the number shall amount to one hundred, after which the proportion shall be so regulated by Congress, that there shall be not less than one hundred Representatives, nor less than one Representative for every forty thousand persons, until the number of Representatives shall amount to two hundred; after which the proportion shall be so regulated by Congress, that there shall not be less than two hundred Representatives, nor more than one Representative for every fifty thousand persons."

Thereafter, in the 2d session of the Eleventh Congress, the Congress proposed the following article of amendment to the Constitution relating to acceptance by citizens of the United States of titles of nobility from any foreign government.

The proposed amendment, which was not ratified by three-fourths of the States, is as follows:

Resolved by the Senate and House of Representatives of the United States of America, in Congress assembled, Two thirds of both Houses concurring, that the following section be submitted to the legislatures of the several states, which when ratified by the legislatures of three fourths of the states, shall be valid and binding, as a part of the constitution of the United States:

If any citizen of the United States shall accept, claim, receive or retain any title of nobility or honor, or shall, without the consent of Congress, accept and retain any present, pension, office or emolument of any kind whatever, from any emperor, king, prince or foreign power, such person shall cease to be a citizen of the United States, and shall be incapable of holding any office of trust or profit under them, or either of them.

The following amendment to the Constitution relating to slavery was proposed by the 2d session of the Thirty-sixth Congress on March 2, 1861, when it passed the Senate, having previously passed the House on February 28, 1861. It is interesting to note in this connection that this is the only proposed (and not ratified) amendment to the Constitution to have been signed by the President. The President's signature is considered unnecessary because of the constitutional provision that on the concurrence of two-thirds of both Houses of Congress the proposal shall be submitted to the States for ratification.

Resolved by the Senate and House of Representatives of the United States of America in Congress assembled, That the following article be proposed to the Legislatures of the several States as an amendment to the Constitution of the United States, which, when ratified by three-fourths of said Legislatures, shall be valid, to all intents and purposes, as part of the said Constitution, viz:

"ARTICLE THIRTEEN

"No amendment shall be made to the Constitution which will authorize or give to Congress the power to abolish or interfere, within any State, with the domestic institutions thereof, including that of persons held to labor or service by the laws of said State."

A child labor amendment was proposed by the 1st session of the Sixty-eighth Congress on June

2, 1926, when it passed the Senate, having previously passed the House on April 26, 1926. The proposed amendment, which has been ratified by 28 States, to date, is as follows:

JOINT RESOLUTION PROPOSING AN AMENDMENT TO THE CONSTITUTION OF THE UNITED STATES

Resolved by the Senate and House of Representatives of the United States of America in Congress assembled (two-thirds of each House concurring therein), That the following article is proposed as an amendment to the Constitution of the United States, which, when ratified by the legislatures of three-fourths of the several States, shall be valid to all intents and purposes as a part of the Constitution:

"ARTICLE—.

"SECTION 1. The Congress shall have power to limit, regulate, and prohibit the labor of persons under eighteen years of age.

"SECTION 2. The power of the several States is unimpaired by this article except that the operation of State laws shall be suspended to the extent necessary to give effect to legislation enacted by the Congress."

An amendment relative to equal rights for men and women was proposed by the 2d session of the Ninety-second Congress on March 22, 1972, when it passed the Senate, having previously passed the House on October 12, 1971. The seven-year deadline for ratification of the proposed amendment was extended to June 30, 1982, by the 2d session of the Ninety-fifth Congress. The proposed amendment, which was not ratified by three-fourths of the States by June 30, 1982, is as follows:

JOINT RESOLUTION PROPOSING AN AMENDMENT TO THE CONSTITUTION OF THE UNITED STATES RELATIVE TO EQUAL RIGHTS FOR MEN AND WOMEN

Resolved by the Senate and House of Representatives of the United States of America in Congress assembled (two-thirds of each House concurring therein), That the following article is proposed as an amendment to the Constitution of the United States, which shall be valid to all intents and purposes as part of the Constitution when ratified by the legislatures of three-fourths of the several States within seven years from the date of its submission by the Congress:

"ARTICLE—

"SECTION 1. Equality of rights under the law shall not be denied or abridged by the United States or by any State on account of sex.

"SEC. 2. The Congress shall have the power to enforce, by appropriate legislation, the provisions of this article.

"SEC. 3. This amendment shall take effect two years after the date of ratification."

An amendment relative to voting rights for the District of Columbia was proposed by the 2d session of the Ninety-fifth Congress on August 22, 1978, when it passed the Senate, having previously passed the House on March 2, 1978. The proposed amendment, which was not ratified by three-fourths of the States within the specified seven-year period, is as follows:

JOINT RESOLUTION PROPOSING AN AMENDMENT TO THE CONSTITUTION TO PROVIDE FOR REPRESENTATION OF THE DISTRICT OF COLUMBIA IN THE CONGRESS.

Resolved by the Senate and House of Representatives of the United States of America in Congress assembled (two-

thirds of each House concurring therein), That the following article is proposed as an amendment to the Constitution of the United States, which shall be valid to all intents and purposes as part of the Constitution when ratified by the legislatures of three-fourths of the several States within seven years from the date of its submission by the Congress:

"ARTICLE—

"SECTION 1. For purposes of representation in the Congress, election of the President and Vice President, and article V of this Constitution, the District constituting the seat of government of the United States shall be treated as though it were a State.

"SEC. 2. The exercise of the rights and powers conferred under this article shall be by the people of the District constituting the seat of government, and as shall be provided by the Congress.

"SEC. 3. The twenty-third article of amendment to the Constitution of the United States is hereby repealed.

"SEC. 4. This article shall be inoperative, unless it shall have been ratified as an amendment to the Constitution by the legislatures of three-fourths of the several States within seven years from the date of its submission."

ANALYTICAL INDEX TO THE CONSTITUTION OF THE UNITED STATES AND THE AMENDMENTS THERETO

THE CODE OF LAWS

OF THE

UNITED STATES OF AMERICA

OF A GENERAL AND PERMANENT CHARACTER IN FORCE JANUARY
SECOND, TWO THOUSAND AND ONE

2000 EDITION

CONSOLIDATED, CODIFIED, SET FORTH, AND PUBLISHED IN TWO THOUSAND AND ONE, IN THE TWO
HUNDRED AND TWENTY-FIFTH YEAR OF THE REPUBLIC, UNDER THE SUPERVISION OF THE OFFICE
OF THE LAW REVISION COUNSEL OF THE HOUSE OF REPRESENTATIVES, PURSUANT TO THE DUTY
AND AUTHORITY IMPOSED UPON IT BY SECTION TWO HUNDRED AND EIGHTY-FIVE-B OF TITLE TWO

THE CODE OF THE LAWS OF THE UNITED STATES
OF AMERICA, 1925 EDITION

JUNE 30, 1926
[H. R. 10000]
[PUBLIC, No. 440]
Chapter 712

AN ACT To consolidate, codify, and set forth the general and permanent laws of the United States in force December seventh, one thousand nine hundred and twenty-five

Be it enacted by the Senate and House of Representatives of the United States of America in Congress assembled, That the fifty titles hereinafter set forth are intended to embrace the laws of the United States, general and permanent in their nature, in force on the 7th day of December, 1925, compiled into a single volume under the authority of Congress, and designated "The Code of the Laws of the United States of America."

SEC. 2. In all courts, tribunals, and public offices of the United States, at home or abroad, of the District of Columbia, and of each State, Territory, or insular possession of the United States—

(a) The matter set forth in the Code, evidenced as hereinafter in this section provided, shall establish prima facie [1] the laws of the United States, general and permanent in their nature, in force on the 7th day of December, 1925; but nothing in this Act shall be construed as repealing or amending any such law, or as enacting as new law any matter contained in the Code. In case of any inconsistency arising through omission or otherwise between the provisions of any section of this Code and the corresponding portion of legislation heretofore enacted effect shall be given for all purposes whatsoever to such enactments.

(b) Copies of this Act printed at the Government Printing Office and bearing its imprint shall be conclusive evidence of the original of the Code in the custody of the Secretary of State.

(c) The Code may be cited as "U.S.C."

---

[1] See section 204(a) of Title 1 regarding titles that are legal evidence of the law.

THE CODE OF LAWS OF THE UNITED STATES OF AMERICA

TITLE 1—GENERAL PROVISIONS

This title was enacted by act July 30, 1947, ch. 388, §1, 61 Stat. 633

POSITIVE LAW; CITATION

This title has been made positive law by section 1 of act July 30, 1947, ch. 388, 61 Stat. 633, which provided in part that: "Title 1 of the United States Code entitled 'General Provisions', is codified and enacted into positive law and may be cited as '1 U. S. C., §——.'"

REPEALS

Section 2 of act July 30, 1947, provided that the sections or parts thereof of the Statutes at Large or the Revised Statutes covering provisions codified in this Act are repealed insofar as the provisions appeared in former Title 1, and provided that any rights or liabilities now existing under the repealed sections or parts thereof shall not be affected by the repeal.

WRITS OF ERROR

Section 23 of act June 25, 1948, ch. 646, 62 Stat. 990, provided that: "All Acts of Congress referring to writs of error shall be construed as amended to the extent necessary to substitute appeal for writ of error."

TABLE SHOWING DISPOSITION OF ALL SECTIONS OF FORMER TITLE 1

Title 1 Former Sections	Revised Statutes Statutes at Large	Title 1 New Sections
1	R.S., §1	1
2	R.S., §2	2
3	R.S., §3	3
4	R.S., §4	4
5	R.S., §5	5
6	June 11, 1940, ch. 325, §1, 54 Stat. 305	6
21	R.S., §7	101
22	R.S., §8	102
23	R.S., §9	103
24	R.S., §10	104
25	R.S., §11	105
26	Nov. 1, 1893, 28 Stat. App. 5	106
	Mar. 2, 1895, ch. 177, §1, 28 Stat. 769.	
27	Mar. 6, 1920, ch. 94, §1, 41 Stat. 520	107
28	R.S., §12	108
29	R.S., §13	109
	Mar. 22, 1944, ch. 123, 58 Stat. 118.	
29a	R.S., §5599	110
29b	Mar. 3, 1933, ch. 202, §3, 47 Stat. 1431	111
30	Jan. 12, 1895, ch. 23, §73, 28 Stat. 615	112
	June 20, 1936, ch. 630, §9, 49 Stat. 1551.	
	June 16, 1938, ch. 477, §1, 52 Stat. 760.	

TABLE SHOWING DISPOSITION OF ALL SECTIONS OF FORMER TITLE 1—Continued

Title 1 Former Sections	Revised Statutes Statutes at Large	Title 1 New Sections
30a	R.S., §908	113
31	R.S., §6	114
51a	Mar. 2, 1929, ch. 586, §1, 45 Stat. 1540	201
52	May 29, 1928, ch. 910, §2, 45 Stat. 1007	202
	Mar. 2, 1929, ch. 586, §2, 45 Stat. 1541.	
53	May 29, 1928, ch. 910, §3, 45 Stat. 1007	203
54	May 29, 1928, ch. 910, §4, 45 Stat. 1007	204
	Mar. 2, 1929, ch. 586, §3, 45 Stat. 1541.	
54a	Mar. 2, 1929, ch. 586, §4, 45 Stat. 1542	205
	Mar. 4, 1933, ch. 282, §1, 47 Stat. 1603.	
	June 13, 1934, ch. 483, §§1, 2, 48 Stat. 948.	
54b	Mar. 2, 1929, ch. 586, §5, 45 Stat. 1542	206
	Mar. 4, 1933, ch. 282, §1, 47 Stat. 1603.	
	June 13, 1934, ch. 483, §§1, 2, 48 Stat. 948.	
54c	Mar. 2, 1929, ch. 586, §6, 45 Stat. 1542	207
54d	Mar. 2, 1929, ch. 586, §7, 45 Stat. 1542	208
55	May 29, 1928, ch. 910, §5, 45 Stat. 1007	209
56	May 29, 1928, ch. 910, §6, 45 Stat. 1007	210
57	May 29, 1928, ch. 910, §7, 45 Stat. 1008	211
58	May 29, 1928, ch. 910, §8, 45 Stat. 1008	212
59	May 29, 1928, ch. 910, §10, 45 Stat. 1008	213
60	Mar. 3, 1933, ch. 202, §2, 47 Stat. 1431	Rep.

TITLE REFERRED TO IN OTHER SECTIONS

This title is referred to in title 46 App. section 1279e.

CHAPTER 1—RULES OF CONSTRUCTION

AMENDMENTS

1996—Pub. L. 104–199, §3(b), Sept. 21, 1996, 110 Stat. 2420, added item 7.

§1. Words denoting number, gender, and so forth

In determining the meaning of any Act of Congress, unless the context indicates otherwise—

words importing the singular include and apply to several persons, parties, or things;

---

[1] So in original. Does not conform to section catchline.

words importing the plural include the singular;

words importing the masculine gender include the feminine as well;

words used in the present tense include the future as well as the present;

the words "insane" and "insane person" and "lunatic" shall include every idiot, lunatic, insane person, and person non compos mentis;

the words "person" and "whoever" include corporations, companies, associations, firms, partnerships, societies, and joint stock companies, as well as individuals;

"officer" includes any person authorized by law to perform the duties of the office;

"signature" or "subscription" includes a mark when the person making the same intended it as such;

"oath" includes affirmation, and "sworn" includes affirmed;

"writing" includes printing and typewriting and reproductions of visual symbols by photographing, multigraphing, mimeographing, manifolding, or otherwise.

(July 30, 1947, ch. 388, 61 Stat. 633; June 25, 1948, ch. 645, §6, 62 Stat. 859; Oct. 31, 1951, ch. 655, §1, 65 Stat. 710.)

AMENDMENTS

1951—Act Oct. 31, 1951, substituted, in fourth clause after opening clause, "used" for "use".

1948—Act June 25, 1948, included "tense", "whoever", "signature", "subscription", "writing" and a broader definition of "person".

SHORT TITLE OF 1996 AMENDMENT

Pub. L. 104–199, §1, Sept. 21, 1996, 110 Stat. 2419, provided that: "This Act [enacting section 7 of this title and section 1738C of Title 28, Judiciary and Judicial Procedure] may be cited as the 'Defense of Marriage Act'."

CONTINENTAL UNITED STATES

Section 48 of Pub. L. 86–70, June 25, 1959, 73 Stat. 154, provided that: "Whenever the phrase 'continental United States' is used in any law of the United States enacted after the date of enactment of this Act [June 25, 1959], it shall mean the 49 States on the North American Continent and the District of Columbia, unless otherwise expressly provided."

SECTION REFERRED TO IN OTHER SECTIONS

This section is referred to in title 7 section 241; title 10 section 101; title 16 section 2402; title 20 section 5607b; title 28 section 3701; title 30 sections 1511, 1531; title 31 section 5312; title 32 section 101; title 37 section 101; title 39 section 5215; title 49 sections 5102, 10102, 13102, 40102, 60101.

§ 2. "County" as including "parish", and so forth

The word "county" includes a parish, or any other equivalent subdivision of a State or Territory of the United States.

(July 30, 1947, ch. 388, 61 Stat. 633.)

SECTION REFERRED TO IN OTHER SECTIONS

This section is referred to in title 10 section 101; title 12 sections 3702, 3752; title 32 section 101; title 37 section 101.

§ 3. "Vessel" as including all means of water transportation

The word "vessel" includes every description of watercraft or other artificial contrivance used, or capable of being used, as a means of transportation on water.

(July 30, 1947, ch. 388, 61 Stat. 633.)

SECTION REFERRED TO IN OTHER SECTIONS

This section is referred to in title 10 section 101; title 32 section 101; title 37 section 101; title 46 section 2101; title 46 App. section 1241o.

§ 4. "Vehicle" as including all means of land transportation

The word "vehicle" includes every description of carriage or other artificial contrivance used, or capable of being used, as a means of transportation on land.

(July 30, 1947, ch. 388, 61 Stat. 633.)

SECTION REFERRED TO IN OTHER SECTIONS

This section is referred to in title 10 section 101; title 32 section 101; title 37 section 101.

§ 5. "Company" or "association" as including successors and assigns

The word "company" or "association", when used in reference to a corporation, shall be deemed to embrace the words "successors and assigns of such company or association", in like manner as if these last-named words, or words of similar import, were expressed.

(July 30, 1947, ch. 388, 61 Stat. 633.)

SECTION REFERRED TO IN OTHER SECTIONS

This section is referred to in title 10 section 101; title 32 section 101; title 37 section 101.

§ 6. Limitation of term "products of American fisheries"

Wherever, in the statutes of the United States or in the rulings, regulations, or interpretations of various administrative bureaus and agencies of the United States there appears or may appear the term "products of American fisheries" said term shall not include fresh or frozen fish fillets, fresh or frozen fish steaks, or fresh or frozen slices of fish substantially free of bone (including any of the foregoing divided into sections), produced in a foreign country or its territorial waters, in whole or in part with the use of the labor of persons who are not residents of the United States.

(July 30, 1947, ch. 388, 61 Stat. 634.)

§ 7. Definition of "marriage" and "spouse"

In determining the meaning of any Act of Congress, or of any ruling, regulation, or interpretation of the various administrative bureaus and agencies of the United States, the word "marriage" means only a legal union between one man and one woman as husband and wife, and the word "spouse" refers only to a person of the opposite sex who is a husband or a wife.

(Added Pub. L. 104–199, §3(a), Sept. 21, 1996, 110 Stat. 2419.)

CHAPTER 2—ACTS AND RESOLUTIONS; FORMALITIES OF ENACTMENT; REPEALS; SEALING OF INSTRUMENTS

Sec.
101.   Enacting clause.

AMENDMENTS

1972—Pub. L. 92–403, §2, Aug. 22, 1972, 86 Stat. 619, added item 112b.

1966—Pub. L. 89–497, §2, July 8, 1966, 80 Stat. 271, inserted "slip laws; Treaties and Other International Acts Series;" in item 113.

1951—Act Oct. 31, 1951, ch. 655, §2(a), 65 Stat. 710, added items 106a and 106b.

1950—Act Sept. 23, 1950, ch. 1001, §3, 64 Stat. 980, added item 112a.

§ 101. Enacting clause

The enacting clause of all Acts of Congress shall be in the following form: "Be it enacted by the Senate and House of Representatives of the United States of America in Congress assembled."

(July 30, 1947, ch. 388, 61 Stat. 634.)

§ 102. Resolving clause

The resolving clause of all joint resolutions shall be in the following form: "Resolved by the Senate and House of Representatives of the United States of America in Congress assembled."

(July 30, 1947, ch. 388, 61 Stat. 634.)

§ 103. Enacting or resolving words after first section

No enacting or resolving words shall be used in any section of an Act or resolution of Congress except in the first.

(July 30, 1947, ch. 388, 61 Stat. 634.)

§ 104. Numbering of sections; single proposition

Each section shall be numbered, and shall contain, as nearly as may be, a single proposition of enactment.

(July 30, 1947, ch. 388, 61 Stat. 634.)

§ 105. Title of appropriation Acts

The style and title of all Acts making appropriations for the support of Government shall be

---

[1] So in original. Does not conform to section catchline.

as follows: "An Act making appropriations (here insert the object) for the year ending September 30 (here insert the calendar year)."

(July 30, 1947, ch. 388, 61 Stat. 634; Pub. L. 93–344, title V, §506(a), July 12, 1974, 88 Stat. 322.)

AMENDMENTS

1974—Pub. L. 93–344 substituted "September 30" for "June 30".

EFFECTIVE DATE OF 1974 AMENDMENT

Section 506(b) of Pub. L. 93–344, which provided that the amendment of this section by Pub. L. 93–344 was effective with respect to Acts making appropriations for the support of the Government for any fiscal year commencing on or after Oct. 1, 1976, was omitted in the complete revision of title V of Pub. L. 93–344 by Pub. L. 101–508, title XIII, §13201(a), Nov. 5, 1990, 104 Stat. 1388–609.

SECTION REFERRED TO IN OTHER SECTIONS

This section is referred to in title 2 sections 622, 691e.

§ 106. Printing bills and joint resolutions

Every bill or joint resolution in each House of Congress shall, when such bill or resolution passes either House, be printed, and such printed copy shall be called the engrossed bill or resolution as the case may be. Said engrossed bill or resolution shall be signed by the Clerk of the House or the Secretary of the Senate, and shall be sent to the other House, and in that form shall be dealt with by that House and its officers, and, if passed, returned signed by said Clerk or Secretary. When such bill, or joint resolution shall have passed both Houses, it shall be printed and shall then be called the enrolled bill, or joint resolution, as the case may be, and shall be signed by the presiding officers of both Houses and sent to the President of the United States. During the last six days of a session such engrossing and enrolling of bills and joint resolutions may be done otherwise than as above prescribed, upon the order of Congress by concurrent resolution.

(July 30, 1947, ch. 388, 61 Stat. 634.)

REFERENCE TO OBRA; EFFECTIVE DATE; RATIFICATION OF ENROLLMENT CORRECTIONS AND PRINTED ENROLLMENT

Pub. L. 100–360, title IV, §411(a), July 1, 1988, 102 Stat. 768, provided that:

"(1) REFERENCE.—In this section, the term 'OBRA' refers to the Omnibus Budget Reconciliation Act of 1987 (Public Law 100–203) [Pub. L. 100–203, Dec. 22, 1987, 101 Stat. 1330, see Tables for classification].

"(2) EFFECTIVE DATE.—Except as specifically provided in this section, the amendments made by this section [amending sections 254o, 294f, 300aa–12, 300aa–15, 300aa–21, 426, 704, 912, 1320a–7, 1320a–7a, 1320a–7b, 1320b–5, 1320b–7, 1320b–8, 1320c–3, 1320c–5, 1320c–9, 1395e, 1395h, 1395i–2, 1395i–3, 1395k, 1395l, 1395m, 1395u, 1395w–1, 1395w–2, 1395x, 1395y, 1395aa, 1395bb, 1395cc, 1395dd, 1395gg, 1395mm, 1395ss, 1395tt, 1395ww, 1395aaa, 1395bbb, 1395ccc, 1396a, 1396b, 1396d, 1396j, 1396n, 1396o, 1396p, 1396r, 1396r–1, 1396r–3, 1396r–4, 1396s, and 1397d of Title 42, The Public Health and Welfare, amending provisions set out as notes under sections 426, 1320a–7a, 1320c–2, 1320c–3, 1395b–1, 1395h, 1395i–3, 1395l, 1395m, 1395n, 1395u, 1395w–1, 1395x, 1395aa, 1395dd, 1395mm, 1395ss, 1395ww, 1395bbb, 1396a, 1396b, and 1396r of Title 42, and repealing provisions set out as notes under section 1395l of Title 42], as they relate to a provision in OBRA, shall be effective as if they were included in the enactment of that provision in OBRA.

"(3) RATIFICATION OF ENROLLMENT CORRECTIONS AND PRINTED ENROLLMENT.—

"(A) IN GENERAL.—Except as provided in subparagraph (B), the enrollment corrections noted in footnotes numbered 9 through 72 of OBRA are hereby ratified and shall be considered to have been enacted as part of OBRA. The printed enrollment of title IV of OBRA [Pub. L. 100–203, title IV, Dec. 22, 1987, 101 Stat. 1330–39], as prepared and printed under section 8004 of OBRA [section 8004 of Pub. L. 100–203, set out below] (including the footnote corrections described in subparagraph (B) and as incorporating the clarifications described in subparagraph (C)), shall be deemed to constitute title IV of OBRA as enacted.

"(B) FOOTNOTE CORRECTIONS.—(i) With respect to the reference to which footnote 28 relates (101 Stat. 1330–81), the reference shall be deemed to have read '1320a–7b)'.

"(ii) With respect to the word to which footnote 30 relates (101 Stat. 1330–91), the word shall be deemed to have read 'the'.

"(iii) With respect to the designation to which footnote 52 relates (101 Stat. 1330–151), the designation shall be deemed to have read '(F)'.

"(C) CLARIFICATIONS OF ILLEGIBLE MATTER.—(i) Section 1842(n)(1)(A) of the Social Security Act, as added by section 4051(a) of OBRA (101 Stat. 1330–93) [42 U.S.C. 1395m(n)(1)(A)], is deemed to have the phrase 'the supplier's reasonable charge to individuals enrolled under this part for the test' immediately after 'or, if lower, the'.

"(ii) Section 1834(a)(7)(B)(i) of the Social Security Act, as inserted by section 4062(b) of OBRA (101 Stat. 1330–103) [42 U.S.C. 1395m(a)(7)(B)(i)], is deemed to have a reference to '1987' immediately after 'December'."

PRINTED ENROLLMENTS PREPARED AFTER ENACTMENT

Pub. L. 106–93, Nov. 10, 1999, 113 Stat. 1310, provided: "That the provisions of sections 106 and 107 of title 1, United States Code, are waived for the remainder of the first session of the One Hundred Sixth Congress with respect to the printing (on parchment or otherwise) of the enrollment of any bill or joint resolution making general appropriations or continuing appropriations for the fiscal year ending September 30, 2000. The enrollment of any such bill or joint resolution shall be in such form as the Committee on House Administration of the House of Representatives certifies to be a true enrollment."

Pub. L. 105–253, Oct. 12, 1998, 112 Stat. 1887, provided: "That the provisions of sections 106 and 107 of title 1, United States Code, are waived for the remainder of the One Hundred Fifth Congress with respect to the printing (on parchment or otherwise) of the enrollment of any bill or joint resolution making general appropriations or continuing appropriations for the fiscal year ending September 30, 1999. The enrollment of any such bill or joint resolution shall be in such form as the Committee on House Oversight of the House of Representatives certifies to be a true enrollment."

Pub. L. 105–120, Nov. 26, 1997, 111 Stat. 2527, provided: "That the provisions of sections 106 and 107 of title 1, United States Code, are waived for the balance of the first session of the One Hundred Fifth Congress with respect to the printing (on parchment or otherwise) of the enrollment of any bill or joint resolution making general appropriations for the fiscal year ending on September 30, 1998, or continuing appropriations for the fiscal year ending on September 30, 1998. The enrollment of any such bill or joint resolution shall be in such form as the Committee on House Oversight of the House of Representatives certifies to be a true enrollment."

Pub. L. 105–32, Aug. 1, 1997, 111 Stat. 250, provided: "That the provisions of sections 106 and 107 of title 1, United States Code, are waived with respect to the printing (on parchment or otherwise) of the enrollment of H.R. 2014 [Pub. L. 105–34, Aug. 5, 1997, 111 Stat. 788] and of H.R. 2015 [Pub. L. 105–33, Aug. 5, 1997, 111 Stat.

251] of the One Hundred Fifth Congress. The enrollment of each of those bills shall be in such form as the Committee on House Oversight of the House of Representatives certifies to be a true enrollment."

Pub. L. 104–207, Sept. 30, 1996, 110 Stat. 3008, provided that:

"SECTION 1. WAIVER OF REQUIREMENT FOR PARCHMENT PRINTING.

"(a) WAIVER.—The provisions of sections 106 and 107 of title 1, United States Code, are waived with respect to the printing (on parchment or otherwise) of the enrollment of any appropriation measure of the One Hundred Fourth Congress presented to the President after the enactment of this joint resolution [Sept. 30, 1996].

"(b) CERTIFICATION OF ENROLLMENT BY COMMITTEE ON HOUSE OVERSIGHT.—The enrollment of any such measure shall be in such form as the Committee on House Oversight of the House of Representatives certifies to be a true enrollment.

"SEC. 2. APPROPRIATION MEASURE DEFINED.

"For purposes of this joint resolution, the term 'appropriation measure' means a bill or joint resolution that includes provisions making general or continuing appropriations for the fiscal year ending September 30, 1997."

Pub. L. 104–129, Apr. 9, 1996, 110 Stat. 1199, provided: "That the provisions of sections 106 and 107 of title 1, United States Code, are waived with respect to the printing (on parchment or otherwise) of the enrollment of H.R. 3019 [Pub. L. 104–134, Apr. 26, 1996, 110 Stat. 1321] and the enrollment of H.R. 3136 [Pub. L. 104–121, Mar. 29, 1996, 110 Stat. 847], each of the One Hundred Fourth Congress. The enrollment of either such bill shall be in such form as the Committee on House Oversight of the House of Representatives certifies to be a true enrollment."

Pub. L. 104–56, title II, §§ 201, 202, Nov. 20, 1995, 109 Stat. 553, provided that:

"SEC. 201. WAIVER OF REQUIREMENT FOR PARCHMENT PRINTING.

"(a) WAIVER.—The provisions of sections 106 and 107 of title 1, United States Code, are waived with respect to the printing (on parchment or otherwise) of the enrollment of any of the following measures of the first session of the One Hundred Fourth Congress presented to the President after the enactment of this joint resolution [Nov. 20, 1995]:

"(1) A continuing resolution.

"(2) A debt limit extension measure.

"(3) A reconciliation bill.

"(b) CERTIFICATION BY COMMITTEE ON HOUSE OVERSIGHT.—The enrollment of a measure to which subsection (a) applies shall be in such form as the Committee on House Oversight of the House of Representatives certifies to be a true enrollment.

"SEC. 202. DEFINITIONS.

"As used in this joint resolution:

"(1) CONTINUING RESOLUTION.—The term 'continuing resolution' means a bill or joint resolution that includes provisions making further continuing appropriations for fiscal year 1996.

"(2) DEBT LIMIT EXTENSION MEASURE.—The term 'debt limit extension measure' means a bill or joint resolution that includes provisions increasing or waiving (for a temporary period or otherwise) the public debt limit under section 3101(b) of title 31, United States Code.

"(3) RECONCILIATION BILL.—The term 'reconciliation bill' means a bill that is a reconciliation bill within the meaning of section 310 of the Congressional Budget Act of 1974 [2 U.S.C. 641]."

Identical provisions were contained in Pub. L. 104–54, title II, §§ 201, 202, Nov. 19, 1995, 109 Stat. 545.

Pub. L. 102–387, Oct. 6, 1992, 106 Stat. 1519, provided: "That the provisions of sections 106 and 107 of title 1, United States Code, are waived with respect to the printing (on parchment or otherwise) of the enrollment of any appropriation bill of the One Hundred Second Congress hereafter to be presented to the President. Such an enrollment shall be in such form as the Committee on House Administration of the House of Representatives certifies to be a true enrollment. As used in this resolution, the term 'appropriation bill' means a bill or joint resolution making or continuing appropriations for the fiscal year ending September 30, 1993.''

Pub. L. 102–260, Mar. 20, 1992, 106 Stat. 85, provided that:

"SECTION 1. WAIVER OF REQUIREMENT FOR PARCHMENT PRINTING.

"The provisions of sections 106 and 107 of title 1, United States Code, are waived with respect to the printing (on parchment or otherwise) of the enrollment of H.R. 4210 of the 102d Congress [H.R. 4210 was vetoed by the President on Mar. 20, 1992].

"SEC. 2. CERTIFICATION BY COMMITTEE ON HOUSE ADMINISTRATION.

"The enrollment of H.R. 4210 of the 102d Congress shall be in such form as the Committee on House Administration of the House of Representatives certifies to be a true enrollment.''

Pub. L. 101–497, Oct. 31, 1990, 104 Stat. 1205, provided that:

"SECTION 1. WAIVER OF REQUIREMENT FOR PARCHMENT PRINTING OF ENROLLMENT OF CERTAIN MEASURES.

"(a) WAIVER.—The provisions of sections 106 and 107 of title 1, United States Code, are waived with respect to the printing (on parchment or otherwise) of the enrollment of S. 2830 [Pub. L. 101–624, Nov. 28, 1990, 104 Stat. 3359].

"(b) CERTIFICATION OF ENROLLMENT BY THE SECRETARY OF THE SENATE.—The enrollment of S. 2830 shall be in such form as the Secretary of the Senate certifies to be a true enrollment.

"SEC. 2. SUBSEQUENT PREPARATION AND CERTIFICATION OF PRINTED ENROLLMENT.

"(a) PREPARATION.—

"(1) IN GENERAL.—If S. 2830 is presented to the President in the form of a hand enrollment pursuant to the authority of section 1, then upon the enactment of that bill the Secretary of the Senate shall prepare a printed enrollment of the bill as in the case of a bill to which sections 106 and 107 of title 1, United States Code, apply.

"(2) TYPOGRAPHICAL CORRECTIONS.—A printed enrollment prepared pursuant to paragraph (1) may, in order to conform to customary style for printed laws, include corrections in indentation, type face, and type size and may include notations (in the margins or as otherwise appropriate) of obvious errors in spelling or punctuation in the hand enrollment.

"(b) TRANSMITTAL TO PRESIDENT.—A printed enrollment prepared pursuant to subsection (a), after being certified by the Secretary of the Senate to be a correct printing of the hand enrollment, shall be signed by the presiding officer of each House of Congress and transmitted to the President.

"(c) CERTIFICATION BY PRESIDENT; PRESERVATION IN ARCHIVES.—Upon certification by the President that a printed enrollment transmitted pursuant to subsection (b) is a correct printing of the hand enrollment, such printed enrollment shall be transmitted to the Archivist of the United States, who shall preserve it with the hand enrollment.

"(d) PUBLICATION OF LAW.—In preparing the bill or joint resolution for publication in slip form and in the United States Statutes at Large pursuant to section 112 of title 1, United States Code, the Archivist of the United States shall use the printed enrollment certified by the President under subsection (c) in lieu of the hand enrollment.

"SEC. 3. DEFINITIONS.

"As used in this resolution:

"(1) [sic] HAND ENROLLMENT.—The term 'hand enrollment' means the enrollment, as authorized by section 1, of a bill or joint resolution for presentment to the President in a form other than the printed form required by sections 106 and 107 of title 1, United States Code.''

Pub. L. 101–466, Oct. 27, 1990, 104 Stat. 1084, provided that:

"SECTION 1. WAIVER OF REQUIREMENT FOR PARCHMENT PRINTING OF ENROLLMENT OF CERTAIN MEASURES.

"(a) WAIVER.—The provisions of sections 106 and 107 of title 1, United States Code, are waived with respect to the printing (on parchment or otherwise) of the enrollment of any reconciliation bill, appropriation bill, or continuing resolution of the One Hundred First Congress presented to the President after the enactment of this joint resolution [Oct. 27, 1990].

"(b) CERTIFICATION OF ENROLLMENT BY COMMITTEE ON HOUSE ADMINISTRATION.—The enrollment of any such bill or joint resolution shall be in such form as the Committee on House Administration of the House of Representatives certifies to be a true enrollment.

"SEC. 2. SUBSEQUENT PREPARATION AND CERTIFICATION OF PRINTED ENROLLMENT.

"(a) PREPARATION.—

"(1) IN GENERAL.—If a reconciliation bill, appropriation bill, or continuing resolution is presented to the President in the form of a hand enrollment pursuant to the authority of section 1, then upon the enactment of that bill or joint resolution the Clerk of the House of Representatives shall prepare a printed enrollment of the bill or joint resolution as in the case of a bill or joint resolution to which sections 106 and 107 of title 1, United States Code, apply.

"(2) TYPOGRAPHICAL CORRECTIONS.—A printed enrollment prepared pursuant to paragraph (1) may, in order to conform to customary style for printed laws, include corrections in indentation, type face, and type size and may include notations (in the margins or as otherwise appropriate) of obvious errors in spelling or punctuation in the hand enrollment.

"(b) TRANSMITTAL TO PRESIDENT.—A printed enrollment prepared pursuant to subsection (a), after being certified by the Committee on House Administration of the House of Representatives to be a correct printing of the hand enrollment, shall be signed by the presiding officer of each House of Congress and transmitted to the President.

"(c) CERTIFICATION BY PRESIDENT; PRESERVATION IN ARCHIVES.—Upon certification by the President that a printed enrollment transmitted pursuant to subsection (b) is a correct printing of the hand enrollment, such printed enrollment shall be transmitted to the Archivist of the United States, who shall preserve it with the hand enrollment.

"(d) PUBLICATION OF LAW.—In preparing the bill or joint resolution for publication in slip form and in the United States Statutes at Large pursuant to section 112 of title 1, United States Code, the Archivist of the United States shall use the printed enrollment certified by the President under subsection (c) in lieu of the hand enrollment.

"SEC. 3. DEFINITIONS.

"As used in this resolution:

"(1) RECONCILIATION BILL.—The term 'reconciliation bill' means a bill to provide for reconciliation pursuant to section 4 of the concurrent resolution on the budget for fiscal year 1991.

"(2) APPROPRIATION BILL.—The term 'appropriation bill' means a general appropriation bill making appropriations for the fiscal year ending September 30, 1991.

"(3) CONTINUING RESOLUTION.—The term 'continuing resolution' means a joint resolution making continuing appropriations for the fiscal year 1991.

"(4) HAND ENROLLMENT.—The term 'hand enrollment' means the enrollment, as authorized by section

1, of a bill or joint resolution for presentment to the President in a form other than the printed form required by sections 106 and 107 of title 1, United States Code.''

Pub. L. 100–454, Sept. 29, 1988, 102 Stat. 1914, provided that:

"SECTION 1. HAND ENROLLMENT AUTHORIZED FOR GENERAL APPROPRIATIONS BILLS.

"(a) WAIVER OF CERTAIN LAWS WITH RESPECT TO PRINTING OF ENROLLED BILLS.—During the remainder of the second session of the One Hundredth Congress, the provisions of sections 106 and 107 of title 1, United States Code, are waived with respect to the printing (on parchment or otherwise) of the enrollment of any general appropriations bill making appropriations for the fiscal year ending September 30, 1989.

"(b) CERTIFICATION BY COMMITTEE ON HOUSE ADMINISTRATION.—The enrollment of any such bill shall be in such form as the Committee on House Administration of the House of Representatives certifies to be a true enrollment.

"SEC. 2. SUBSEQUENT PREPARATION AND CERTIFICATION OF PRINTED ENROLLMENTS.

"(a) PREPARATION.—

"(1) IN GENERAL.—Upon the enactment of a bill following presentment of such bill to the President in the form of a hand enrollment pursuant to the authority of section 1 of this resolution, the Clerk of the House of Representatives shall prepare a printed enrollment of that bill as in the case of a bill to which sections 106 and 107 of title 1, United States Code, apply.

"(2) LIMITED STYLISTIC CORRECTIONS.—A printed enrollment prepared pursuant to paragraph (1) may, in order to conform to customary style for printed laws, include corrections in spelling, punctuation, indentation, type face, and type size and other necessary stylistic corrections to the hand enrollment. Such a printed enrollment shall include notations (in the margins or as otherwise appropriate) of all such corrections.

"(b) TRANSMITTAL TO PRESIDENT.—A printed enrollment prepared pursuant to subsection (a) shall be signed by the presiding officer of each House of Congress as a correct printing of the hand enrollment and shall be transmitted to the President.

"(c) CERTIFICATION BY PRESIDENT; LEGAL EFFECT.— Upon certification by the President that a printed enrollment transmitted pursuant to subsection (b) is a correct printing of the hand enrollment, such printed enrollment shall be considered for all purposes as the original enrollment of the bill concerned and as valid evidence of the enactment of that bill.

"(d) ARCHIVES.—A printed enrollment certified by the President under subsection (c) shall be transmitted to the Archivist of the United States, who shall preserve it with the hand enrollment. In preparing the bill concerned for publication in slip form and in the United States Statutes at Large pursuant to section 112 of title 1, United States Code, the Archivist of the United States shall use the printed enrollment certified by the President under subsection (c) in lieu of the hand enrollment.

"(e) HAND ENROLLMENT DEFINED.—As used in this section, the term 'hand enrollment' means the enrollment, as authorized by section 1, of a bill for presentment to the President in a form other than the printed form required by sections 106 and 107 of title 1, United States Code.''

Pub. L. 100–203, title VIII, § 8004, Dec. 22, 1987, 101 Stat. 1330–282, provided that:

"(a) PREPARATION OF PRINTED ENROLLMENT.—(1) Upon the enactment of this Act enrolled as a hand enrollment, the Clerk of the House of Representatives shall prepare a printed enrollment of this Act as in the case of a bill or joint resolution to which sections 106 and 107 of title 1, United States Code, apply. Such enrollment shall be a correct enrollment of this Act as enrolled in the hand enrollment.

"(2) A printed enrollment prepared pursuant to paragraph (1) may, in order to conform to customary style for printed laws, include corrections in spelling, punctuation, indentation, type face, and type size and other necessary stylistic corrections to the hand enrollment. Such a printed enrollment shall include notations (in the margins or as otherwise appropriate) of all such corrections.

"(b) TRANSMITTAL TO PRESIDENT.—A printed enrollment prepared pursuant to subsection (a) shall be signed by the presiding officers of both Houses of Congress as a correct printing of the hand enrollment of this Act and shall be transmitted to the President.

"(c) CERTIFICATION BY PRESIDENT; LEGAL EFFECT.— Upon certification by the President that a printed enrollment transmitted pursuant to subsection (b) is a correct printing of the hand enrollment of this Act, such printed enrollment shall be considered for all purposes as the original enrollment of this Act and as valid evidence of the enactment of this Act.

"(d) ARCHIVES.—A printed enrollment certified by the President under subsection (c) shall be transmitted to the Archivist of the United States, who shall preserve it with the hand enrollment. In preparing this Act for publication in slip form and in the United States Statutes at Large pursuant to section 112 of title 1, United States Code, the Archivist of the United States shall use the printed enrollment certified by the President under subsection (c) in lieu of the hand enrollment.

"(e) HAND ENROLLMENT DEFINED.—As used in this section, the term 'hand enrollment' means enrollment in a form other than the printed form required by sections 106 and 107 of title 1, United States Code, as authorized by the joint resolution entitled 'Joint resolution authorizing the hand enrollment of the budget reconciliation bill and of the full-year continuing resolution for fiscal year 1988', approved December 1987 (H.J. Res. 426 of the 100th Congress) [Pub. L. 100–199, Dec. 21, 1987, 101 Stat. 1326].''

Pub. L. 100–202, § 101(n), Dec. 22, 1987, 101 Stat. 1329–432, provided that:

"(1) Upon the enactment of this resolution enrolled as a hand enrollment, the Clerk of the House of Representatives shall prepare a printed enrollment of this resolution as in the case of a bill or joint resolution to which sections 106 and 107 of title 1, United States Code, apply. Such enrollment shall be a correct enrollment of this resolution as enrolled in the hand enrollment.

"(2) A printed enrollment prepared pursuant to subsection (n)(1) may, in order to conform to customary style for printed laws, include corrections in spelling, punctuation, indentation, type face, and type size and other necessary stylistic corrections to the hand enrollment. Such a printed enrollment shall include notations (in the margins or as otherwise appropriate) of all such corrections.

"(3) A printed enrollment prepared pursuant to subsection (n)(1) shall be signed by the presiding officers of both Houses of Congress as a correct printing of the hand enrollment of this resolution and shall be transmitted to the President.

"(4) Upon certification by the President that a printed enrollment transmitted pursuant to subsection (n)(3) is a correct printing of the hand enrollment of this resolution, such printed enrollment shall be considered for all purposes as the original enrollment of this resolution and as valid evidence of the enactment of this resolution.

"(5) A printed enrollment certified by the President under subsection (n)(4) shall be transmitted to the Archivist of the United States, who shall preserve it with the hand enrollment. In preparing this resolution for publication in slip form and in the United States Statutes at Large pursuant to section 112 of title 1, United States Code, the Archivist of the United States shall use the printed enrollment certified by the President under subsection (n)(4) in lieu of the hand enrollment.

"(6) As used in this section, the term 'hand enrollment' means enrollment in a form other than the printed form required by sections 106 and 107 of title 1, United States Code, as authorized by the joint resolution entitled 'Joint resolution authorizing the hand enrollment of the budget reconciliation bill and of the full-year continuing resolution for fiscal year 1988', approved December 1987 (H.J. Res. 426 of the 100th Congress) [Pub. L. 100–199, Dec. 21, 1987, 101 Stat. 1326].''

CERTIFICATION OF PRINTED ENROLLMENTS OF CERTAIN PUBLIC LAWS

Memorandum of the President of the United States, Jan. 10, 1991, 56 F.R. 1481, provided:

Memorandum for the Archivist of the United States

By the authority vested in me as President by the Constitution and laws of the United States, including Section 301 of Title 3 of the United States Code, I hereby authorize you to ascertain whether the printed enrollment of H.R. 5835, the Omnibus Budget Reconciliation Act of 1990 (Public Law 101–508), approved on November 5, 1990, is a correct printing of the hand enrollment and if so to make on my behalf the certification specified in Section 2(c) of H.J. Res. 682 (Public Law 101–466) [set out as a note above].

Attached is the printed enrollment that was received at the White House on January 7, 1991.

This memorandum shall be published in the Federal Register.

GEORGE BUSH.

Memorandum of the President of the United States, Dec. 12, 1988, 53 F.R. 50373, provided:

Memorandum for the Archivist of the United States

By the authority vested in me as President by the Constitution and laws of the United States, including Section 301 of Title 3 of the United States Code, I hereby authorize you to ascertain whether the printed enrollments of H.R. 4637, the Foreign Operations, Export Financing, and Related Programs Appropriations Act, 1989 (Public Law 100–461), H.R. 4776, the District of Columbia Appropriations Act, 1989 (Public Law 100–462), and H.R. 4781, the Department of Defense Appropriations Act, 1989 (Public Law 100–463), are correct printings of the hand enrollments, which were approved on October 1, 1988, and if so to make on my behalf the certifications required by Section 2(c) of H.J. Res. 665 (Public Law 100–454) [set out as a note above].

Attached are the printed enrollments of H.R. 4637, H.R. 4776, and H.R. 4781, which were received at the White House on December 1, 1988.

This memorandum shall be published in the Federal Register.

RONALD REAGAN.

Memorandum of the President of the United States, Jan. 28, 1988, 53 F.R. 2816, provided:

Memorandum for the Archivist of the United States

By the authority vested in me as President by the Constitution and laws of the United States, including Section 301 of Title 3 of the United States Code, I hereby authorize you to ascertain whether the printed enrollments of H.J. Res. 395, Joint Resolution making further continuing appropriations for the fiscal year 1988 (Public Law 100–202), and H.R. 3545, the Omnibus Budget Reconciliation Act of 1987 (Public Law 100–203), are correct printings of the hand enrollments, which were approved on December 22, 1987, and if so to make on my behalf the certifications required by Section 101(n)(4) of H.J. Res. 395 and Section 8004(c) of H.R. 3545 [set out as notes above].

Attached are the printed enrollments of H.J. Res. 395 and H.R. 3545, which were received at the White House on January 27, 1988.

This memorandum shall be published in the Federal Register.

RONALD REAGAN.

§ 106a. Promulgation of laws

Whenever a bill, order, resolution, or vote of the Senate and House of Representatives, having been approved by the President, or not having been returned by him with his objections, becomes a law or takes effect, it shall forthwith be received by the Archivist of the United States from the President; and whenever a bill, order, resolution, or vote is returned by the President with his objections, and, on being reconsidered, is agreed to be passed, and is approved by two-thirds of both Houses of Congress, and thereby becomes a law or takes effect, it shall be received by the Archivist of the United States from the President of the Senate, or Speaker of the House of Representatives in whichsoever House it shall last have been so approved, and he shall carefully preserve the originals.

(Added Oct. 31, 1951, ch. 655, § 2(b), 65 Stat. 710; amended Pub. L. 98–497, title I, § 107(d), Oct. 19, 1984, 98 Stat. 2291.)

AMENDMENTS

1984—Pub. L. 98–497 substituted "Archivist of the United States" for "Administrator of General Services" in two places.

EFFECTIVE DATE OF 1984 AMENDMENT

Amendment by Pub. L. 98–497 effective Apr. 1, 1985, see section 301 of Pub. L. 98–497, set out as a note under section 2102 of Title 44, Public Printing and Documents.

SIMILAR PROVISIONS; REPEAL; SAVING CLAUSE; DELEGATION OF FUNCTIONS; TRANSFER OF PROPERTY AND PERSONNEL

Similar provisions were contained in R.S. § 204; act Dec. 28, 1874, ch. 9, § 2, 18 Stat. 294; 1950 Reorg. Plan No. 20, § 1, eff. May 24, 1950, 15 F.R. 3178, 64 Stat. 1272, which with the exception of the reorganization plan, were repealed by section 56(h) of act Oct. 31, 1951. Subsec. (l) of that section 56 provided that the repeal should not affect any rights or liabilities existing under those statutes on the effective date of the repeal (Oct. 31, 1951). For delegation of functions under the repealed statutes, and transfer of records, property, personnel, and funds, see sections 3 and 4 of 1950 Reorg. Plan No. 20, set out in the Appendix to Title 5, Government Organization and Employees.

§ 106b. Amendments to Constitution

Whenever official notice is received at the National Archives and Records Administration that any amendment proposed to the Constitution of the United States has been adopted, according to the provisions of the Constitution, the Archivist of the United States shall forthwith cause the amendment to be published, with his certificate, specifying the States by which the same may have been adopted, and that the same has become valid, to all intents and purposes, as a part of the Constitution of the United States.

(Added Oct. 31, 1951, ch. 655, § 2(b), 65 Stat. 710; amended Pub. L. 98–497, title I, § 107(d), Oct. 19, 1984, 98 Stat. 2291.)

AMENDMENTS

1984—Pub. L. 98–497 substituted "National Archives and Records Administration" and "Archivist of the United States" for "General Services Administration" and "Administrator of General Services", respectively.

EFFECTIVE DATE OF 1984 AMENDMENT

Amendment by Pub. L. 98–497 effective Apr. 1, 1985, see section 301 of Pub. L. 98–497, set out as a note under section 2102 of Title 44, Public Printing and Documents.

SIMILAR PROVISIONS; REPEAL; SAVING CLAUSE; DELEGATION OF FUNCTIONS; TRANSFER OF PROPERTY AND PERSONNEL

Similar provisions were contained in R.S. § 205; 1950 Reorg. Plan No. 20, § 1, eff. May 24, 1950, 15 F.R. 3178, 64 Stat. 1272. R.S. § 205 was repealed by section 56(h) of act Oct. 31, 1951. Subsec. (*l*) of section 56 provided that the repeal should not affect any rights or liabilities existing under the repealed statute on the effective date of the repeal (Oct. 31, 1951). For delegation of functions under the repealed statute, and transfer of records, property, personnel, and funds, see sections 3 and 4 of 1950 Reorg. Plan No. 20, set out in the Appendix to Title 5, Government Organization and Employees.

SECTION REFERRED TO IN OTHER SECTIONS

This section is referred to in section 112 of this title.

§ 107. Parchment or paper for printing enrolled bills or resolutions

Enrolled bills and resolutions of either House of Congress shall be printed on parchment or paper of suitable quality as shall be determined by the Joint Committee on Printing.

(July 30, 1947, ch. 388, 61 Stat. 635.)

§ 108. Repeal of repealing act

Whenever an Act is repealed, which repealed a former Act, such former Act shall not thereby be revived, unless it shall be expressly so provided.

(July 30, 1947, ch. 388, 61 Stat. 635.)

§ 109. Repeal of statutes as affecting existing liabilities

The repeal of any statute shall not have the effect to release or extinguish any penalty, forfeiture, or liability incurred under such statute, unless the repealing Act shall so expressly provide, and such statute shall be treated as still remaining in force for the purpose of sustaining any proper action or prosecution for the enforcement of such penalty, forfeiture, or liability. The expiration of a temporary statute shall not have the effect to release or extinguish any penalty, forfeiture, or liability incurred under such statute, unless the temporary statute shall so expressly provide, and such statute shall be treated as still remaining in force for the purpose of sustaining any proper action or prosecution for the enforcement of such penalty, forfeiture, or liability.

(July 30, 1947, ch. 388, 61 Stat. 635.)

§ 110. Saving clause of Revised Statutes

All acts of limitation, whether applicable to civil causes and proceedings, or to the prosecution of offenses, or for the recovery of penalties or forfeitures, embraced in the Revised Statutes and covered by the repeal contained therein, shall not be affected thereby, but all suits, proceedings, or prosecutions, whether civil or criminal, for causes arising, or acts done or committed prior to said repeal, may be commenced and prosecuted within the same time as if said repeal had not been made.

(July 30, 1947, ch. 388, 61 Stat. 635.)

§ 111. Repeals as evidence of prior effectiveness

No inference shall be raised by the enactment of the Act of March 3, 1933 (ch. 202, 47 Stat. 1431), that the sections of the Revised Statutes repealed by such Act were in force or effect at the time of such enactment: *Provided, however,* That any rights or liabilities existing under such repealed sections shall not be affected by their repeal.

(July 30, 1947, ch. 388, 61 Stat. 635.)

REFERENCES IN TEXT

Act of March 3, 1933, referred to in text, was repealed by section 2 of act July 30, 1947, section 1 of which enacted this title.

§ 112. Statutes at Large; contents; admissibility in evidence

The Archivist of the United States shall cause to be compiled, edited, indexed, and published, the United States Statutes at Large, which shall contain all the laws and concurrent resolutions enacted during each regular session of Congress; all proclamations by the President in the numbered series issued since the date of the adjournment of the regular session of Congress next preceding; and also any amendments to the Constitution of the United States proposed or ratified pursuant to article V thereof since that date, together with the certificate of the Archivist of the United States issued in compliance with the provision contained in section 106b of this title. In the event of an extra session of Congress, the Archivist of the United States shall cause all the laws and concurrent resolutions enacted during said extra session to be consolidated with, and published as part of, the contents of the volume for the next regular session. The United States Statutes at Large shall be legal evidence of laws, concurrent resolutions, treaties, international agreements other than treaties, proclamations by the President, and proposed or ratified amendments to the Constitution of the United States therein contained, in all the courts of the United States, the several States, and the Territories and insular possessions of the United States.

(July 30, 1947, ch. 388, 61 Stat. 636; Sept. 23, 1950, ch. 1001, § 1, 64 Stat. 979; Oct. 31, 1951, ch. 655, § 3, 65 Stat. 710; Pub. L. 98–497, title I, § 107(d), Oct. 19, 1984, 98 Stat. 2291.)

AMENDMENTS

1984—Pub. L. 98–497 substituted "Archivist of the United States" for "Administrator of General Services" in three places.

1951—Act Oct. 31, 1951, substituted "106b of this title" for "205 of the Revised Statutes" in first sentence.

1950—Act Sept. 23, 1950, amended section generally to implement 1950 Reorg. Plan No. 20, § 1, eff. May 24, 1950, 15 F.R. 3178, 64 Stat. 1272, which transferred to the Administrator of General Services certain duties formerly performed by the Secretary of State.

EFFECTIVE DATE OF 1984 AMENDMENT

Amendment by Pub. L. 98–497 effective Apr. 1, 1985, see section 301 of Pub. L. 98–497, set out as a note under section 2102 of Title 44, Public Printing and Documents.

PUBLICATION OF CERTAIN LAWS OF 106TH CONGRESS

Pub. L. 106–554, § 1(b), Dec. 21, 2000, 114 Stat. 2763, provided that: "In publishing this Act in slip form and in the United States Statutes at Large pursuant to section 112 of title 1, United States Code, the Archivist of the United States shall include after the date of approval at the end appendixes setting forth the texts of the bills referred to in subsection (a) of this section [enacting into law H.R. 5656, H.R. 5657, H.R. 5658, H.R. 5660, H.R. 5661, H.R. 5662, and H.R. 5663 of the 106th Congress, as introduced on Dec. 14, 2000, and H.R. 5666 and H.R. 5667 of the 106th Congress, as introduced on Dec. 15, 2000, except that the text of H.R. 5666, as so enacted, shall not include section 123] and the text of any other bill enacted into law by reference by reason of the enactment of this Act.''

Pub. L. 106–553, §1(b), Dec. 21, 2000, 114 Stat. 2762, provided that: ''In publishing this Act in slip form and in the United States Statutes at Large pursuant to section 112 of title 1, United States Code, the Archivist of the United States shall include after the date of approval at the end appendixes setting forth the texts of the bills referred to in subsection (a) of this section [enacting into law H.R. 5547 and H.R. 5548 of the 106th Congress, as introduced on Oct. 25, 2000].''

Pub. L. 106–429, §101(a) [title V, §595(b)], Nov. 6, 2000, 114 Stat. 1900, 1900A–60, provided that: ''In publishing the Act in slip form and in the United States Statutes at Large pursuant to section 112, of title 1, United States Code, the Archivist of the United States shall include after the date of approval at the end appendixes setting forth the texts of the bill referred to in subsection (a) of this section [enacting into law S. 3140 of the 106th Congress, as introduced on Sept. 28, 2000].''

Pub. L. 106–429, §101(b), Nov. 6, 2000, 114 Stat. 1900, provided that: ''In publishing this Act in slip form and in the United States Statutes at Large pursuant to section 112 of title 1, United States Code, the Archivist of the United States shall include after the date of approval at the end an appendix setting forth the text of the bill referred to in subsection (a) of this section [enacting into law H.R. 5526 of the 106th Congress, as introduced on Oct. 24, 2000].''

Pub. L. 106–398, §2, Oct. 30, 2000, 114 Stat. 1654, provided that: ''In publishing this Act in slip form and in the United States Statutes at Large pursuant to section 112 of title 1, United States Code, the Archivist of the United States shall include after the date of approval an appendix setting forth the text of the bill referred to in section 1 [enacting into law H.R. 5408 of the 106th Congress, as introduced on Oct. 6, 2000].''

Pub. L. 106–387, §1(b), Oct. 28, 2000, 114 Stat. 1549, provided that: ''In publishing this Act in slip form and in the United States Statutes at Large pursuant to section 112 of title 1, United States Code, the Archivist of the United States shall include after the date of approval at the end an appendix setting forth the text of the bill referred to in subsection (a) of this section [enacting into law H.R. 5426 of the 106th Congress, as introduced on Oct. 6, 2000].''

Pub. L. 106–377, §1(b), Oct. 27, 2000, 114 Stat. 1441, provided that: ''In publishing this Act in slip form and in the United States Statutes at Large pursuant to section 112 of title 1, United States Code, the Archivist of the United States shall include after the date of approval at the end appendixes setting forth the texts of the bills referred to in subsection (a) of this section [enacting into law H.R. 5482 and 5483 of the 106th Congress, as introduced on Oct. 18, 2000].''

Pub. L. 106–346, §101(b), Oct. 23, 2000, 114 Stat. 1356, provided that: ''In publishing the Act in slip form and in the United States Statutes at Large pursuant to section 112 of title 1, United States Code, the Archivist of the United States shall include after the date of approval at the end an appendix setting forth the text of the bill referred to in subsection (a) of this section [enacting into law H.R. 5394 of the 106th Congress, as introduced on Oct. 5, 2000].''

Pub. L. 106–113, div. B, §1000(b), Nov. 29, 1999, 113 Stat. 1536, provided that: ''In publishing the Act in slip form and in the United States Statutes at Large pursuant to section 112, of title 1, United States Code, the Archivist

of the United States shall include after the date of approval at the end appendixes setting forth the texts of the bills referred to in subsection (a) of this section [enacting into law H.R. 3421, H.R. 3422, H.R. 3423, H.R. 3424, H.R. 3425, H.R. 3426, H.R. 3427 (as amended), H.R. 3428, and S. 1948 of the 106th Congress, as introduced on Nov. 17, 1999].''

EFFECT OF REPEAL OF SECTION 73 OF ACT JAN. 12, 1895

This section and section 112a of this title as not affected by the repeal of section 73 of act Jan. 12, 1895, ch. 23, 28 Stat. 615, which related to the same subject matter, see section 56(i) of act Oct. 31, 1951, ch. 655, 65 Stat. 729.

§112a. United States Treaties and Other International Agreements; contents; admissibility in evidence

(a) The Secretary of State shall cause to be compiled, edited, indexed, and published, beginning as of January 1, 1950, a compilation entitled ''United States Treaties and Other International Agreements,'' which shall contain all treaties to which the United States is a party that have been proclaimed during each calendar year, and all international agreements other than treaties to which the United States is a party that have been signed, proclaimed, or with reference to which any other final formality has been executed, during each calendar year. The said United States Treaties and Other International Agreements shall be legal evidence of the treaties, international agreements other than treaties, and proclamations by the President of such treaties and agreements, therein contained, in all the courts of the United States, the several States, and the Territories and insular possessions of the United States.

(b) The Secretary of State may determine that publication of certain categories of agreements is not required, if the following criteria are met:

(1) such agreements are not treaties which have been brought into force for the United States after having received Senate advice and consent pursuant to section 2(2) of Article II of the Constitution of the United States;

(2) the public interest in such agreements is insufficient to justify their publication, because (A) as of the date of enactment of the Foreign Relations Authorization Act, Fiscal Years 1994 and 1995, the agreements are no longer in force,[1] (B) the agreements do not create private rights or duties, or establish standards intended to govern government action in the treatment of private individuals; (C) in view of the limited or specialized nature of the public interest in such agreements, such interest can adequately be satisfied by an alternative means; or (D) the public disclosure of the text of the agreement would, in the opinion of the President, be prejudicial to the national security of the United States; and

(3) copies of such agreements (other than those in paragraph (2)(D)), including certified copies where necessary for litigation or similar purposes, will be made available by the Department of State upon request.

(c) Any determination pursuant to subsection (b) shall be published in the Federal Register.

---

[1] So in original. The comma probably should be a semicolon.

(Added Sept. 23, 1950, ch. 1001, §2, 64 Stat. 980; amended Pub. L. 103–236, title I, §138, Apr. 30, 1994, 108 Stat. 397.)

The date of enactment of the Foreign Relations Authorization Act, Fiscal Years 1994 and 1995, referred to in subsec. (b)(2)(A), is the date of enactment of Pub. L. 103–236, which was approved Apr. 30, 1994.

AMENDMENTS

1994—Pub. L. 103–236 designated existing provisions as subsec. (a) and added subsecs. (b) and (c).

EFFECT OF REPEAL OF SECTION 73 OF ACT JAN. 12, 1895

This section and section 112 of this title as not affected by the repeal of section 73 of act Jan. 12, 1895, ch. 23, 28 Stat. 615, which related to the same subject matter, see section 56(i) of act Oct. 31, 1951, ch. 655, 65 Stat. 729.

WRITTEN REQUESTS FOR DOCUMENTS

Copies of United States Treaties and Other International Agreements not available to Senators or Representatives unless specifically requested by them, in writing, see Pub. L. 94–59, title VIII, §801, July 25, 1975, 89 Stat. 296, set out as a note under section 1317 of Title 44, Public Printing and Documents.

§ 112b. United States international agreements; transmission to Congress

(a) The Secretary of State shall transmit to the Congress the text of any international agreement (including the text of any oral international agreement, which agreement shall be reduced to writing), other than a treaty, to which the United States is a party as soon as practicable after such agreement has entered into force with respect to the United States but in no event later than sixty days thereafter. However, any such agreement the immediate public disclosure of which would, in the opinion of the President, be prejudicial to the national security of the United States shall not be so transmitted to the Congress but shall be transmitted to the Committee on Foreign Relations of the Senate and the Committee on Foreign Affairs of the House of Representatives under an appropriate injunction of secrecy to be removed only upon due notice from the President. Any department or agency of the United States Government which enters into any international agreement on behalf of the United States shall transmit to the Department of State the text of such agreement not later than twenty days after such agreement has been signed.

(b) Not later than March 1, 1979, and at yearly intervals thereafter, the President shall, under his own signature, transmit to the Speaker of the House of Representatives and the chairman of the Committee on Foreign Relations of the Senate a report with respect to each international agreement which, during the preceding year, was transmitted to the Congress after the expiration of the 60-day period referred to in the first sentence of subsection (a), describing fully and completely the reasons for the late transmittal.

(c) Notwithstanding any other provision of law, an international agreement may not be signed or otherwise concluded on behalf of the United States without prior consultation with the Secretary of State. Such consultation may encompass a class of agreements rather than a particular agreement.

(d) The Secretary of State shall determine for and within the executive branch whether an arrangement constitutes an international agreement within the meaning of this section.

(e) The President shall, through the Secretary of State, promulgate such rules and regulations as may be necessary to carry out this section.

(Added Pub. L. 92–403, §1, Aug. 22, 1972, 86 Stat. 619; amended Pub. L. 95–45, §5, June 15, 1977, 91 Stat. 224; Pub. L. 95–426, title VII, §708, Oct. 7, 1978, 92 Stat. 993; Pub. L. 103–437, §1, Nov. 2, 1994, 108 Stat. 4581.)

AMENDMENTS

1994—Subsec. (a). Pub. L. 103–437 substituted "Committee on Foreign Affairs" for "Committee on International Relations".

1978—Pub. L. 95–426 designated existing provisions as subsec. (a), inserted "(including the text of any oral international agreement, which agreement shall be reduced to writing)", and added subsecs. (b) to (e).

1977—Pub. L. 95–45 substituted "Committee on International Relations of the House of Representatives" for "Committee on Foreign Affairs of the House of Representatives" and inserted requirement that any department or agency of the United States Government which enters into any international agreement on behalf of the United States transmit to the Department of State the text of such agreement not later than twenty days after the agreement has been signed.

CHANGE OF NAME

Committee on Foreign Affairs of House of Representatives treated as referring to Committee on International Relations of House of Representatives by section 1(a) of Pub. L. 104–14, set out as a note preceding section 21 of Title 2, The Congress.

SHORT TITLE

This section is popularly known as the Case-Zablocki Act.

TERMINATION OF REPORTING REQUIREMENTS

For termination, effective May 15, 2000, of provisions of law requiring submittal to Congress of any annual, semiannual, or other regular periodic report listed in House Document No. 103–7 (in which the report required by subsec. (b) of this section is listed on page 38), see section 3003 of Pub. L. 104–66, as amended, set out as a note under section 1113 of Title 31, Money and Finance.

ENFORCEMENT

Pub. L. 100–204, title I, §139, Dec. 22, 1987, 101 Stat. 1347, provided that:

"(a) RESTRICTION ON USE OF FUNDS.—If any international agreement, whose text is required to be transmitted to the Congress pursuant to the first sentence of subsection (a) of section 112b of title 1, United States Code (commonly referred to as the 'Case-Zablocki Act'), is not so transmitted within the 60-day period specified in that sentence, then no funds authorized to be appropriated by this or any other Act shall be available after the end of that 60-day period to implement that agreement until the text of that agreement has been so transmitted.

"(b) EFFECTIVE DATE.—Subsection (a) shall take effect 60 days after the date of enactment of this Act [Dec. 22, 1987] and shall apply during fiscal years 1988 and 1989."

§ 113. "Little and Brown's" edition of laws and treaties; slip laws; Treaties and Other International Acts Series; admissibility in evidence

The edition of the laws and treaties of the United States, published by Little and Brown, and the publications in slip or pamphlet form of the laws of the United States issued under the authority of the Archivist of the United States, and the Treaties and Other International Acts Series issued under the authority of the Secretary of State shall be competent evidence of the several public and private Acts of Congress, and of the treaties, international agreements other than treaties, and proclamations by the President of such treaties and international agreements other than treaties, as the case may be, therein contained, in all the courts of law and equity and of maritime jurisdiction, and in all the tribunals and public offices of the United States, and of the several States, without any further proof or authentication thereof.

(July 30, 1947, ch. 388, 61 Stat. 636; Pub. L. 89–497, §1, July 8, 1966, 80 Stat. 271; Pub. L. 98–497, title I, §107(d), Oct. 19, 1984, 98 Stat. 2291.)

AMENDMENTS

1984—Pub. L. 98–497 substituted "Archivist of the United States" for "Administrator of General Services".

1966—Pub. L. 89–497 made slip laws and the Treaties and Other International Acts Series competent legal evidence of the several acts of Congress and the treaties and other international agreements contained therein.

EFFECTIVE DATE OF 1984 AMENDMENT

Amendment by Pub. L. 98–497 effective Apr. 1, 1985, see section 301 of Pub. L. 98–497, set out as a note under section 2102 of Title 44, Public Printing and Documents.

§ 114. Sealing of instruments

In all cases where a seal is necessary by law to any commission, process, or other instrument provided for by the laws of Congress, it shall be lawful to affix the proper seal by making an impression therewith directly on the paper to which such seal is necessary; which shall be as valid as if made on wax or other adhesive substance.

(July 30, 1947, ch. 388, 61 Stat. 636.)

CHAPTER 3—CODE OF LAWS OF UNITED STATES AND SUPPLEMENTS; DISTRICT OF COLUMBIA CODE AND SUPPLEMENTS

§ 201. Publication and distribution of Code of Laws of United States and Supplements and District of Columbia Code and Supplements

In order to avoid duplication and waste—

(a) Publishing in slip or pamphlet form or in Statutes at Large.—Publication in slip or pamphlet form or in the Statutes at Large of any of the volumes or publications enumerated in sections 202 and 203 of this title, shall, in event of enactment, be dispensed with whenever the Committee on the Judiciary of the House of Representatives so directs the Archivist of the United States;

(b) Curtailing number of copies published.— Curtailment of the number provided by law to be printed and distributed of the volumes or publications enumerated in sections 202 and 203 of this title may be directed by such committee, except that the Public Printer shall print such numbers as are necessary for depository library distribution and for sale; and

(c) Dispensing with publication of more than one Supplement for each Congress.—Such committee may direct that the printing and distribution of any supplement to the Code of Laws of the United States or to the Code of the District of Columbia be dispensed with entirely, except that there shall be printed and distributed for each Congress at least one supplement to each such code, containing the legislation of such Congress.

(July 30, 1947, ch. 388, 61 Stat. 637; Sept. 3, 1954, ch. 1263, §1, 68 Stat. 1226; Pub. L. 98–497, title I, §107(d), Oct. 19, 1984, 98 Stat. 2291.)

AMENDMENTS

1984—Subsec. (a). Pub. L. 98–497 substituted "Archivist of the United States" for "Administrator of General Services".

1954—Subsec. (a). Act Sept. 3, 1954, substituted "Administrator of General Services" for "Secretary of State".

------

[1] So in original. Does not conform to section catchline.

EFFECTIVE DATE OF 1984 AMENDMENT

Amendment by Pub. L. 98–497 effective Apr. 1, 1985, see section 301 of Pub. L. 98–497, set out as a note under section 2102 of Title 44, Public Printing and Documents.

SECTION REFERRED TO IN OTHER SECTIONS

This section is referred to in section 208 of this title.

§ 202. Preparation and publication of Codes and Supplements

There shall be prepared and published under the supervision of the Committee on the Judiciary of the House of Representatives—

(a) Cumulative Supplements to Code of Laws of United States for each session of Congress.— A supplement for each session of the Congress to the then current edition of the Code of Laws of the United States, cumulatively embracing the legislation of the then current supplement, and correcting errors in such edition and supplement;

(b) Cumulative Supplement to District of Columbia Code for each session of Congress.—A supplement for each session of the Congress to the then current edition of the Code of the District of Columbia, cumulatively embracing the legislation of the then current supplement, and correcting errors in such edition and supplement;

(c) New editions of Codes and Supplements.— New editions of the Code of Laws of the United States and of the Code of the District of Columbia, correcting errors and incorporating the then current supplement. In the case of each code new editions shall not be published oftener than once in each five years. Copies of each such edition shall be distributed in the same manner as provided in the case of supplements to the code of which it is a new edition. Supplements published after any new edition shall not contain the legislation of supplements published before such new edition.

(July 30, 1947, ch. 388, 61 Stat. 637.)

CROSS REFERENCES

Council of the District of Columbia, functions respecting, see section 2 of Pub. L. 94–386, Aug. 14, 1976, 90 Stat. 1170, set out as a note under section 285b of Title 2, The Congress.

Office of the Law Revision Counsel, functions respecting preparation, revision, publication, etc., see section 285b of Title 2.

SECTION REFERRED TO IN OTHER SECTIONS

This section is referred to in sections 201, 205, 208, 209, 210, 211, 213 of this title.

§ 203. District of Columbia Code; preparation and publication; cumulative supplements

The Committee on the Judiciary of the House of Representatives is authorized to print bills to codify, revise, and reenact the general and permanent laws relating to the District of Columbia and cumulative supplements thereto, similar in style, respectively, to the Code of Laws of the United States, and supplements thereto, and to so continue until final enactment thereof in both Houses of the Congress of the United States.

(July 30, 1947, ch. 388, 61 Stat. 638.)

COMMISSION ON REVISION OF THE CRIMINAL LAWS OF THE DISTRICT OF COLUMBIA

Pub. L. 90–226, title X, Dec. 27, 1967, 81 Stat. 742, provided for creation and operation of a commission to study and make recommendations with reference to a revised code of criminal law and procedure for the District of Columbia, prior to repeal by Pub. L. 91–358, title VI, § 601, July 29, 1970, 84 Stat. 667, as amended by Pub. L. 91–530, § 2(b)(1), Dec. 7, 1970, 84 Stat. 1390.

CROSS REFERENCES

Council of the District of Columbia, functions respecting, see section 2 of Pub. L. 94–386, Aug. 14, 1976, 90 Stat. 1170, set out as a note under section 285b of Title 2, The Congress.

Office of the Law Revision Counsel, functions respecting, see section 285b of Title 2.

SECTION REFERRED TO IN OTHER SECTIONS

This section is referred to in sections 201, 205, 208, 209, 210, 211, 213 of this title.

§ 204. Codes and Supplements as evidence of the laws of United States and District of Columbia; citation of Codes and Supplements

In all courts, tribunals, and public offices of the United States, at home or abroad, of the District of Columbia, and of each State, Territory, or insular possession of the United States—

(a) United States Code.—The matter set forth in the edition of the Code of Laws of the United States current at any time shall, together with the then current supplement, if any, establish prima facie the laws of the United States, general and permanent in their nature, in force on the day preceding the commencement of the session following the last session the legislation of which is included: *Provided, however*, That whenever titles of such Code shall have been enacted into positive law the text thereof shall be legal evidence of the laws therein contained, in all the courts of the United States, the several States, and the Territories and insular possessions of the United States.

(b) District of Columbia Code.—The matter set forth in the edition of the Code of the District of Columbia current at any time shall, together with the then current supplement, if any, establish prima facie the laws, general and permanent in their nature, relating to or in force in the District of Columbia on the day preceding the commencement of the session following the last session the legislation of which is included, except such laws as are of application in the District of Columbia by reason of being laws of the United States general and permanent in their nature.

(c) District of Columbia Code; citation.—The Code of the District of Columbia may be cited as "D.C. Code".

(d) Supplements to Codes; citation.—Supplements to the Code of Laws of the United States and to the Code of the District of Columbia may be cited, respectively, as "U.S.C., Sup.   ", and "D.C. Code, Sup.   ", the blank in each case being filled with Roman figures denoting the number of the supplement.

(e) New edition of Codes; citation.—New editions of each of such codes may be cited, respectively, as "U.S.C.,   ed.", and "D.C. Code,   ed.", the blank in each case being filled with figures denoting the last year the legislation of which is included in whole or in part.

(July 30, 1947, ch. 388, 61 Stat. 638.)

TITLE 26, INTERNAL REVENUE CODE

The Internal Revenue Code of 1954 was enacted in the form of a separate code by act Aug. 16, 1954, ch. 736, 68A Stat. 1. Pub. L. 99–514, §2(a), Oct. 22, 1986, 100 Stat. 2095, provided that the Internal Revenue Title enacted Aug. 16, 1954, as heretofore, hereby, or hereafter amended, may be cited as the "Internal Revenue Code of 1986". The sections of Title 26, United States Code, are identical to the sections of the Internal Revenue Code.

SECTION REFERRED TO IN OTHER SECTIONS

This section is referred to in section 208 of this title.

§ 205. Codes and Supplement; where printed; form and style; ancillaries

The publications provided for in sections 202, 203 of this title shall be printed at the Government Printing Office and shall be in such form and style and with such ancillaries as may be prescribed by the Committee on the Judiciary of the House of Representatives. The Librarian of Congress is directed to cooperate with such committee in the preparation of such ancillaries. Such publications shall be furnished with such thumb insets[1] and other devices to distinguish parts, with such facilities for the insertion of additional matter, and with such explanatory and advertising slips, and shall be printed on such paper and bound in such material, as may be prescribed by such committee.

(July 30, 1947, ch. 388, 61 Stat. 639.)

SECTION REFERRED TO IN OTHER SECTIONS

This section is referred to in section 208 of this title; title 44 section 707.

§ 206. Bills and resolutions of Committee on the Judiciary of House of Representatives; form and style; ancillaries; curtailment of copies

All bills and resolutions relating to the revision of the laws referred to or reported by the Committee on the Judiciary of the House of Representatives shall be printed in such form and style, and with such ancillaries, as such committee may prescribe as being economical and suitable, to so continue until final enactment thereof in both Houses of Congress; and such committee may also curtail the number of copies of such bills to be printed in the various parliamentary stages in the House of Representatives.

(July 30, 1947, ch. 388, 61 Stat. 639.)

SECTION REFERRED TO IN OTHER SECTIONS

This section is referred to in section 208 of this title; title 44 section 707.

§ 207. Copies of acts and resolutions in slip form; additional number printed for Committee on the Judiciary of House of Representatives

The Public Printer is directed to print, in addition to the number provided by existing law, and, as soon as printed, to distribute in such manner as the Committee on the Judiciary of the House of Representatives shall determine, twenty copies in slip form of each public Act and joint resolution.

(July 30, 1947, ch. 388, 61 Stat. 639.)

SECTION REFERRED TO IN OTHER SECTIONS

This section is referred to in section 208 of this title.

§ 208. Delegation of function of Committee on the Judiciary to other agencies; printing, and so forth, under direction of Joint Committee on Printing

The functions vested by sections 201, 202, 204–207 of this title in the Committee on the Judiciary of the House of Representatives may from time to time be vested in such other agency as the Congress may by concurrent resolution provide: *Provided*, That the printing, binding, and distribution of the volumes and publications enumerated in sections 202, 203 of this title shall

---

[1] So in original. Probably should be "inserts".

be done under the direction of the Joint Committee on Printing.

(July 30, 1947, ch. 388, 61 Stat. 639.)

§ 209. Copies of Supplements to Code of Laws of United States and of District of Columbia Code and Supplements; conclusive evidence of original

Copies of the Code of Laws relating to the District of Columbia and copies of the supplements provided for by sections 202 and 203 of this title printed at the Government Printing Office and bearing its imprint, shall be conclusive evidence of the original of such code and supplements in the custody of the Administrator of General Services.

(July 30, 1947, ch. 388, 61 Stat. 639; Sept. 3, 1954, ch. 1263, § 2, 68 Stat. 1226.)

AMENDMENTS

1954—Act Sept. 3, 1954, substituted "Administrator of General Services" for "Secretary of State".

§ 210. Distribution of Supplements to Code of Laws of United States and of District of Columbia Code and Supplements; slip and pamphlet copies

Copies of the Code of Laws relating to the District of Columbia, and of the supplements provided for by sections 202, 203 of this title shall be distributed by the Superintendent of Documents in the same manner as bound volumes of the Statutes at Large: *Provided*, That no slip or pamphlet copies of the Code of Laws relating to the District of Columbia, and of the supplements provided for by sections 202, 203 of this title need be printed or distributed.

(July 30, 1947, ch. 388, 61 Stat. 640.)

CROSS REFERENCES

Distribution of Statutes at Large, see section 728 of Title 44, Public Printing and Documents.

SECTION REFERRED TO IN OTHER SECTIONS

This section is referred to in section 211 of this title.

§ 211. Copies to Members of Congress

In addition to quotas provided for by section 210 of this title there shall be printed, published, and distributed of the Code of Laws relating to the District of Columbia with tables, index, and other ancillaries, suitably bound and with thumb inserts and other convenient devices to distinguish the parts, and of the supplements to both codes as provided for by sections 202, 203 of this title, ten copies of each for each Member of the Senate and House of Representatives of the Congress in which the original authorized publication is made, for his use and distribution, and in addition for the Committee on the Judiciary of the House of Representatives and the Committee on the Judiciary of the Senate a number of bound copies of each equal to ten times the number of members of such committees, and one bound copy of each for the use of each committee of the Senate and House of Representatives.

(July 30, 1947, ch. 388, 61 Stat. 640.)

LIMITATION ON COPIES OF NEW EDITIONS FOR HOUSE OF REPRESENTATIVES

Pub. L. 92–342, § 101, July 10, 1972, 86 Stat. 447, provided that: "Hereafter, appropriations for authorized printing and binding for the Congress shall not be available under the authority of the Act of July 30, 1947 (1 U.S.C. 211) for the printing, publication, and distribution of more than two copies of new editions of the Code of Laws of the United States and of the Code of the District of Columbia for each Member of the House of Representatives."

WRITTEN REQUESTS FOR DOCUMENTS

Copies of District of Columbia Code and Supplements not available to Senators or Representatives unless specifically requested by them, in writing, see Pub. L. 94–59, title VIII, § 801, July 25, 1975, 89 Stat. 296, set out as a note under section 1317 of Title 44, Public Printing and Documents.

§ 212. Additional distribution at each new Congress

In addition the Superintendent of Documents shall, at the beginning of the first session of each Congress, supply to each Senator and Representative in such Congress, who may in writing apply for the same, one copy each of the Code of Laws of the United States, the Code of Laws relating to the District of Columbia, and the latest supplement to each code: *Provided*, That such applicant shall certify in his written application for the same that the volume or volumes for which he applies is intended for his personal use exclusively: *And provided further*, That no Senator or Representative during his term of service shall receive under this section more than one copy each of the volumes enumerated herein.

(July 30, 1947, ch. 388, 61 Stat. 640.)

SECTION REFERRED TO IN OTHER SECTIONS

This section is referred to in title 2 sections 54, 55.

§ 213. Appropriation for preparing and editing supplements

For preparation and editing an annual appropriation of $6,500 is authorized to carry out the purposes of sections 202 and 203 of this title.

(July 30, 1947, ch. 388, 61 Stat. 640.)

TITLE 2—THE CONGRESS

CHAPTER 1—ELECTION OF SENATORS AND REPRESENTATIVES

§ 1. Time for election of Senators

At the regular election held in any State next preceding the expiration of the term for which any Senator was elected to represent such State in Congress, at which election a Representative to Congress is regularly by law to be chosen, a United States Senator from said State shall be elected by the people thereof for the term commencing on the 3d day of January next thereafter.

(June 4, 1914, ch. 103, § 1, 38 Stat. 384; June 5, 1934, ch. 390, § 3, 48 Stat. 879.)

AMENDMENTS

1934—Act June 5, 1934, substituted "3d day of January" for "fourth day of March".

CONSTITUTIONAL PROVISIONS

The first section of Amendment XX to the Constitution provides in part: "* * * the terms of Senators and Representatives [shall end] at noon on the 3d day of January, of the years in which such terms would have ended if this article had not been ratified; and the terms of their successors shall then begin."

Time for election of Senators, see Const. Art. I, § 4, cl. 1.

Vacancies in the Senate, see Const. Amend. XVII.

§ 1a. Election to be certified by governor

It shall be the duty of the executive of the State from which any Senator has been chosen to certify his election, under the seal of the State, to the President of the Senate of the United States.

(R.S. § 18.)

CODIFICATION

R.S. § 18 derived from act July 25, 1866, ch. 245, § 3, 14 Stat. 244.

SECTION REFERRED TO IN OTHER SECTIONS

This section is referred to in section 1b of this title.

§ 1b. Countersignature of certificate of election

The certificate mentioned in section 1a of this title shall be countersigned by the secretary of state of the State.

(R.S. § 19.)

CODIFICATION

R.S. § 19 derived from act July 25, 1866, ch. 245, § 3, 14 Stat. 244.

§ 2. Omitted

CODIFICATION

Section, act Aug. 8, 1911, ch. 5, §§ 1, 2, 37 Stat. 13, 14, fixed composition of House of Representatives at 435 Members, to be apportioned to the States therein enumerated. For provisions dealing with reapportionment of Representatives and manner of election, etc., see sections 2a and 2b of this title.

§ 2a. Reapportionment of Representatives; time and manner; existing decennial census figures as basis; statement by President; duty of clerk

(a) On the first day, or within one week thereafter, of the first regular session of the Eighty-second Congress and of each fifth Congress thereafter, the President shall transmit to the Congress a statement showing the whole number of persons in each State, excluding Indians not taxed, as ascertained under the seventeenth and each subsequent decennial census of the population, and the number of Representatives to which each State would be entitled under an apportionment of the then existing number of Representatives by the method known as the method of equal proportions, no State to receive less than one Member.

(b) Each State shall be entitled, in the Eighty-third Congress and in each Congress thereafter until the taking effect of a reapportionment under this section or subsequent statute, to the number of Representatives shown in the statement required by subsection (a) of this section, no State to receive less than one Member. It shall be the duty of the Clerk of the House of Representatives, within fifteen calendar days after the receipt of such statement, to send to the executive of each State a certificate of the number of Representatives to which such State is entitled under this section. In case of a vacancy in the office of Clerk, or of his absence or inability to discharge this duty, then such duty shall devolve upon the Sergeant at Arms of the House of Representatives.

(c) Until a State is redistricted in the manner provided by the law thereof after any apportionment, the Representatives to which such State is entitled under such apportionment shall be elected in the following manner: (1) If there is no change in the number of Representatives, they shall be elected from the districts then prescribed by the law of such State, and if any of them are elected from the State at large they shall continue to be so elected; (2) if there is an increase in the number of Representatives, such additional Representative or Representatives shall be elected from the State at large and the other Representatives from the districts then prescribed by the law of such State; (3) if there is a decrease in the number of Representatives but the number of districts in such State is equal to such decreased number of Representatives, they shall be elected from the districts then prescribed by the law of such State; (4) if there is a decrease in the number of Representatives but the number of districts in such State is less than such number of Representatives, the number of Representatives by which such number of districts is exceeded shall be elected from the State at large and the other Representatives from the districts then prescribed by the law of such State; or (5) if there is a decrease in the number of Representatives and the number of districts in such State exceeds such decreased number of Representatives, they shall be elected from the State at large.

(June 18, 1929, ch. 28, § 22, 46 Stat. 26; Apr. 25, 1940, ch. 152, 54 Stat. 162; Nov. 15, 1941, ch. 470, § 1, 55 Stat. 761; Pub. L. 104–186, title II, § 201, Aug. 20, 1996, 110 Stat. 1724.)

AMENDMENTS

1996—Subsec. (b). Pub. L. 104–186 struck out at end "; and in case of vacancies in the offices of both the Clerk and the Sergeant at Arms, or the absence or inability of both to act, such duty shall devolve upon the Doorkeeper of the House of Representatives".
1941—Act Nov. 15, 1941, provided for reapportionment based on seventeenth and subsequent decennial censuses.
1940—Act Apr. 25, 1940, provided for reapportionment based on sixteenth decennial census.

TERMINATION OF REPORTING REQUIREMENTS

For termination, effective May 15, 2000, of provisions of law requiring submittal to Congress of any annual, semiannual, or other regular periodic report listed in House Document No. 103–7 (in which the report required by subsec. (a) of this section is listed on page 17), see section 3003 of Pub. L. 104–66, as amended, set out as a note under section 1113 of Title 31, Money and Finance.

CONSTITUTIONAL PROVISIONS

Apportionment of Representatives among the several States, see Const. Art. I, § 2, cl. 3, and Amend. XIV, § 2.

TEMPORARY INCREASE IN MEMBERSHIP

Representation of States of Alaska and Hawaii in House of Representatives as not affecting basis of apportionment established by this section, see section 9 of Pub. L. 85–508, July 7, 1958, 72 Stat. 339, set out as a note preceding section 21 of Title 48, Territories and Insular Possessions, and section 8 of Pub. L. 86–3, Mar. 18, 1959, 73 Stat. 4, set out as a note preceding section 491 of Title 48.

SECTION REFERRED TO IN OTHER SECTIONS

This section is referred to in sections 2b, 2c of this title.

§ 2b. Number of Representatives from each State in 78th and subsequent Congresses

Each State shall be entitled, in the Seventy-eighth and in each Congress thereafter until the taking effect of a reapportionment under a subsequent statute or section 2a of this title, to the number of Representatives shown in the statement transmitted to the Congress on January 8, 1941, based upon the method known as the method of equal proportions, no State to receive less than one Member.

(Nov. 15, 1941, ch. 470, §2(a), 55 Stat. 762.)

CERTIFICATES TO EXECUTIVES OF STATES

Section 2(b) of act Nov. 15, 1941, required Clerk of House of Representatives, within 15 days of Nov. 15, 1941, to send a new certificate of entitlement of a State to Representatives, if such a certificate had been sent prior to Nov. 15, 1941, under provisions of section 2a of this title.

§2c. Number of Congressional Districts; number of Representatives from each District

In each State entitled in the Ninety-first Congress or in any subsequent Congress thereafter to more than one Representative under an apportionment made pursuant to the provisions of section 2a(a) of this title, there shall be established by law a number of districts equal to the number of Representatives to which such State is so entitled, and Representatives shall be elected only from districts so established, no district to elect more than one Representative (except that a State which is entitled to more than one Representative and which has in all previous elections elected its Representatives at Large may elect its Representatives at Large to the Ninety-first Congress).

(Pub. L. 90–196, Dec. 14, 1967, 81 Stat. 581.)

§§3, 4. Omitted

CODIFICATION

Section 3, act Aug. 8, 1911, ch. 5, §3, 37 Stat. 14, which related to election by districts, expired by its own limitation on enactment of Reapportionment Act of June 18, 1929, ch. 28, §22, 46 Stat. 21 (section 2a of this title). It was not restated in act June 18, 1929, providing for reapportionment under Fifteenth Census, and hence it was not applicable thereto. See *Wood v. Brown*, 1932 (53 S. Ct. 1, 287 U.S. 1, 77 L. Ed. 131).

Section 4, act Aug. 8, 1911, ch. 5, §4, 37 Stat. 14, which related to additional Representatives at large, expired by its own limitation on enactment of Reapportionment Act of June 18, 1929, ch. 28, §22, 46 Stat. 21 (section 2a of this title). It was not restated in act June 18, 1929, providing for reapportionment under Fifteenth Census, and hence it was not applicable thereto. See *Wood v. Brown*, 1932 (53 S. Ct. 1, 287 U.S. 1, 77 L. Ed. 131).

§5. Nominations for Representatives at large

Candidates for Representative or Representatives to be elected at large in any State shall be nominated in the same manner as candidates for governor, unless otherwise provided by the laws of such State.

(Aug. 8, 1911, ch. 5, §5, 37 Stat. 14.)

§6. Reduction of representation

Should any State deny or abridge the right of any of the male inhabitants thereof, being twenty-one years of age, and citizens of the United States, to vote at any election named in the amendment to the Constitution, article 14, section 2, except for participation in the rebellion or other crime, the number of Representatives apportioned to such State shall be reduced in the proportion which the number of such male citizens shall have to the whole number of male citizens twenty-one years of age in such State.

(R.S. §22.)

CODIFICATION

R.S. §22 derived from act Feb. 2, 1872, ch. 11, §6, 17 Stat. 29.

§7. Time of election

The Tuesday next after the 1st Monday in November, in every even numbered year, is established as the day for the election, in each of the States and Territories of the United States, of Representatives and Delegates to the Congress commencing on the 3d day of January next thereafter.

(R.S. §25; Mar. 3, 1875, ch. 130, §6, 18 Stat. 400; June 5, 1934, ch. 390, §2, 48 Stat. 879.)

CODIFICATION

R.S. §25 derived from act Feb. 2, 1872, ch. 11, §3, 17 Stat. 28.

The second sentence of this section, which was based on section 6 of the act Mar. 3, 1875 and made this section inapplicable to any State that had not yet changed its day of election and whose constitution required an amendment to change the day of election of its State officers, was omitted.

AMENDMENTS

1934—Act June 5, 1934, substituted "3d day of January" for "fourth day of March".

CONSTITUTIONAL PROVISIONS

The first section of Amendment XX to the Constitution provides: "The terms of Senators and Representatives [shall end] at noon on the 3d day of January, of the years in which such terms would have ended if this article had not been ratified; and the terms of their successors shall then begin."

Time for election of Representatives, see Const. Art. I, §4, cl. 1.

§8. Vacancies

The time for holding elections in any State, District, or Territory for a Representative or Delegate to fill a vacancy, whether such vacancy is caused by a failure to elect at the time prescribed by law, or by the death, resignation, or incapacity of a person elected, may be prescribed by the laws of the several States and Territories respectively.

(R.S. §26.)

CODIFICATION

R.S. §26 derived from act Feb. 2, 1872, ch. 11, §4, 17 Stat. 28.

CONSTITUTIONAL PROVISIONS

Vacancies in the House of Representatives, see Const. Art. I, §2, cl. 4.

§9. Voting for Representatives

All votes for Representatives in Congress must be by written or printed ballot, or voting machine the use of which has been duly authorized by the State law; and all votes received or recorded contrary to this section shall be of no effect.

(R.S. § 27; Feb. 14, 1899, ch. 154, 30 Stat. 836.)

CODIFICATION

R.S. § 27 derived from acts Feb. 28, 1871, ch. 99, § 19, 16 Stat. 440, and May 30, 1872, ch. 239, 17 Stat. 192.

CHAPTER 2—ORGANIZATION OF CONGRESS

CHANGE OF NAME AND TRANSFER OF FUNCTIONS OF COMMITTEES AND OFFICERS OF HOUSE OF REPRESENTATIVES

Pub. L. 104–14, June 3, 1995, 109 Stat. 186, provided that:

"SECTION 1. REFERENCES IN LAW TO COMMITTEES OF THE HOUSE OF REPRESENTATIVES.

"(a) REFERENCES TO COMMITTEES WITH NEW NAMES.—Except as provided in subsection (c), any reference in any provision of law enacted before January 4, 1995, to—

"(1) the Committee on Armed Services of the House of Representatives shall be treated as referring to the Committee on National Security of the House of Representatives;

"(2) the Committee on Banking, Finance and Urban Affairs of the House of Representatives shall be treated as referring to the Committee on Banking and Financial Services of the House of Representatives;

"(3) the Committee on Education and Labor of the House of Representatives shall be treated as referring to the Committee on Economic and Educational Opportunities of the House of Representatives;

"(4) the Committee on Energy and Commerce of the House of Representatives shall be treated as referring to the Committee on Commerce of the House of Representatives;

"(5) the Committee on Foreign Affairs of the House of Representatives shall be treated as referring to the Committee on International Relations of the House of Representatives;

"(6) the Committee on Government Operations of the House of Representatives shall be treated as referring to the Committee on Government Reform and Oversight of the House of Representatives;

"(7) the Committee on House Administration of the House of Representatives shall be treated as referring to the Committee on House Oversight of the House of Representatives;

"(8) the Committee on Natural Resources of the House of Representatives shall be treated as referring to the Committee on Resources of the House of Representatives;

"(9) the Committee on Public Works and Transportation of the House of Representatives shall be treated as referring to the Committee on Transportation and Infrastructure of the House of Representatives; and

"(10) the Committee on Science, Space, and Technology of the House of Representatives shall be treated as referring to the Committee on Science of the House of Representatives.

"(b) REFERENCES TO ABOLISHED COMMITTEES.—Any reference in any provision of law enacted before January 4, 1995, to—

"(1) the Committee on District of Columbia of the House of Representatives shall be treated as referring to the Committee on Government Reform and Oversight of the House of Representatives;

"(2) the Committee on Post Office and Civil Service of the House of Representatives shall be treated as referring to the Committee on Government Reform and Oversight of the House of Representatives, except that a reference with respect to the House Commission on Congressional Mailings [probably should be "Mailing"] Standards (the 'Franking Commission') shall be treated as referring to the Committee on House Oversight of the House of Representatives; and

"(3) the Committee on Merchant Marine and Fisheries of the House of Representatives shall be treated as referring to—

"(A) the Committee on Agriculture of the House of Representatives, in the case of a provision of law relating to inspection of seafood or seafood products;

"(B) the Committee on National Security of the House of Representatives, in the case of a provision of law relating to interoceanic canals, the Merchant Marine Academy and State Maritime Academies, or national security aspects of merchant marine;

"(C) the Committee on Resources of the House of Representatives, in the case of a provision of law relating to fisheries, wildlife, international fishing agreements, marine affairs (including coastal zone management) except for measures relating to oil and other pollution of navigable waters, or oceanography;

"(D) the Committee on Science of the House of Representatives, in the case of a provision of law relating to marine research; and

"(E) the Committee on Transportation and Infrastructure of the House of Representatives, in the case of a provision of law relating to a matter other than a matter described in any of subparagraphs (A) through (D).

"(c) REFERENCES TO COMMITTEES WITH JURISDICTION CHANGES.—Any reference in any provision of law enacted before January 4, 1995, to—

"(1) the Committee on Energy and Commerce of the House of Representatives shall be treated as referring to—

"(A) the Committee on Agriculture of the House of Representatives, in the case of a provision of law relating to inspection of seafood or seafood products;

"(B) the Committee on Banking and Financial Services of the House of Representatives, in the case of a provision of law relating to bank capital markets activities generally or to depository institution securities activities generally; and

"(C) the Committee on Transportation and Infrastructure of the House of Representatives, in the case of a provision of law relating to railroads, railway labor, or railroad retirement and unemployment (except revenue measures related thereto); and

"(2) the Committee on Government Operations of the House of Representatives shall be treated as referring to the Committee on the Budget of the House of Representatives in the case of a provision of law relating to the establishment, extension, and enforcement of special controls over the Federal budget.

"SEC. 2. REFERENCES IN LAW TO OFFICERS OF THE HOUSE OF REPRESENTATIVES.

"Any reference in any provision of law enacted before January 4, 1995, to a function, duty, or authority—

"(1) of the Clerk of the House of Representatives shall be treated as referring, with respect to that function, duty, or authority, to the officer of the House of Representatives exercising that function, duty, or authority, as determined by the Committee on House Oversight of the House of Representatives;

"(2) of the Doorkeeper of the House of Representatives shall be treated as referring, with respect to that function, duty, or authority, to the officer of the House of Representatives exercising that function, duty, or authority, as determined by the Committee on House Oversight of the House of Representatives;

"(3) of the Postmaster of the House of Representatives shall be treated as referring, with respect to that function, duty, or authority, to the officer of the House of Representatives exercising that function, duty, or authority, as determined by the Committee on House Oversight of the House of Representatives; and

"(4) of the Director of Non-legislative and Financial Services of the House of Representatives shall be

treated as referring, with respect to that function, duty, or authority, to the officer of the House of Representatives exercising that function, duty, or authority, as determined by the Committee on House Oversight of the House of Representatives."

§ 21. Oath of Senators

The oath of office shall be administered by the President of the Senate to each Senator who shall be elected, previous to his taking his seat.

(R.S. § 28.)

CODIFICATION

R.S. § 28 derived from act June 1, 1789, ch. 1, § 2, 1 Stat. 23.

§ 22. Oath of President of Senate

When a President of the Senate has not taken the oath of office, it shall be administered to him by any Member of the Senate.

(R.S. § 29.)

CODIFICATION

R.S. § 29 derived from act June 1, 1789, ch. 1, § 2, 1 Stat. 23.

§ 23. Presiding officer of Senate may administer oaths

The presiding officer, for the time being, of the Senate of the United States, shall have power to administer all oaths and affirmations that are or may be required by the Constitution, or by law, to be taken by any Senator, officer of the Senate, witness, or other person, in respect to any matter within the jurisdiction of the Senate.

(Apr. 18, 1876, ch. 66, § 1, 19 Stat. 34.)

§ 24. Secretary of Senate or assistant secretary may administer oaths

The Secretary of the Senate, and the assistant secretary thereof, shall, respectively, have power to administer any oath or affirmation required by law, or by the rules or orders of the Senate, to be taken by any officer of the Senate, and to any witness produced before it.

(Apr. 18, 1876, ch. 66, § 2, 19 Stat. 34; Pub. L. 92–51, July 9, 1971, 85 Stat. 125.)

CHANGE OF NAME

Assistant secretary of the Senate deemed successor in references to chief clerk of the Senate in all laws, rules, resolutions, and orders, effective July 1, 1971, under provisions of Pub. L. 92–51, July 9, 1971, 85 Stat. 125.

§ 25. Oath of Speaker, Members, and Delegates

At the first session of Congress after every general election of Representatives, the oath of office shall be administered by any Member of the House of Representatives to the Speaker; and by the Speaker to all the Members and Delegates present, and to the Clerk, previous to entering on any other business; and to the Members and Delegates who afterward appear, previous to their taking their seats.

The Clerk of the House of Representatives of the Eightieth and each succeeding Congress shall cause the oath of office to be printed, furnishing two copies to each Member and Delegate who has taken the oath of office in accordance with law, which shall be subscribed in person by the Member or Delegate, who shall thereupon deliver them to the Clerk, one to be filed in the records of the House of Representatives, and the other to be recorded in the Journal of the House and in the Congressional Record; and such signed copies, or certified copies thereof, or of either of such records thereof, shall be admissible in evidence in any court of the United States, and shall be held conclusive proof of the fact that the signer duly took the oath of office in accordance with law.

(R.S. § 30; Feb. 18, 1948, ch. 53, 62 Stat. 20.)

CODIFICATION

R.S. § 30 derived from act June 1, 1789, ch. 1, § 2, 1 Stat. 23.

The last paragraph of this section, which permitted Members and Delegates of the House of Representatives of the Eightieth Congress to subscribe and deliver two signed copies of the printed oath of office at any time before the expiration of the Eightieth Congress, was omitted.

AMENDMENTS

1948—Act Feb. 18, 1948, added last two paragraphs to provide a way by which any Member of House of Representatives can establish by record evidence the fact that the Member took the oath of office and so became a Member.

§ 25a. Delegate to House of Representatives from District of Columbia

(a) The people of the District of Columbia shall be represented in the House of Representatives by a Delegate, to be known as the "Delegate to the House of Representatives from the District of Columbia", who shall be elected by the voters of the District of Columbia in accordance with the District of Columbia Election Act. The Delegate shall have a seat in the House of Representatives, with the right of debate, but not of voting, shall have all the privileges granted a Representative by section 6 of Article I of the Constitution, and shall be subject to the same restrictions and regulations as are imposed by law or rules on Representatives. The Delegate shall be elected to serve during each Congress.

(b) No individual may hold the office of Delegate to the House of Representatives from the District of Columbia unless on the date of his election—

(1) he is a qualified elector (as that term is defined in section 2(2) of the District of Columbia Election Act) of the District of Columbia;

(2) he is at least twenty-five years of age;

(3) he holds no other paid public office; and

(4) he has resided in the District of Columbia continuously since the beginning of the three-year period ending on such date.

He shall forfeit his office upon failure to maintain the qualifications required by this subsection.

(Pub. L. 91–405, title II, § 202, Sept. 22, 1970, 84 Stat. 848.)

REFERENCES IN TEXT

The District of Columbia Election Act, referred to in subsecs. (a) and (b)(1), is act Aug. 12, 1955, ch. 862, 69 Stat. 699, as amended, which is not classified to the Code.

EFFECTIVE DATE

Section 206(b) of title II of Pub. L. 91–405 provided that: "This title and the amendments made by this title [enacting this section and section 25b of this title and amending section 2106 of Title 5, Government Organization and Employees, sections 4342, 6954, and 9342 of Title 10, Armed Forces, sections 201, 203, 204, 591, 594, and 595 of Title 18, Crimes and Criminal Procedure, and section 1973i of Title 42, The Public Health and Welfare] shall take effect on the date of its enactment [Sept. 22, 1970]."

§ 25b. Repealed. Pub. L. 104–186, title II, § 202(1), Aug. 20, 1996. 110 Stat. 1724

Section, Pub. L. 91–405, title II, § 204(a), Sept. 22, 1970, 84 Stat. 852, related to application of certain Federal laws to Delegate to House of Representatives from District of Columbia.

§ 26. Roll of Representatives-elect

Before the first meeting of each Congress the Clerk of the next preceding House of Representatives shall make a roll of the Representatives-elect, and place thereon the names of those persons, and of such persons only, whose credentials show that they were regularly elected in accordance with the laws of their States respectively, or the laws of the United States. In case of a vacancy in the office of Clerk of the House of Representatives, or of the absence or inability of the Clerk to discharge the duties imposed on him by law or custom relative to the preparation of the roll of Representatives or the organization of the House, those duties shall devolve on the Sergeant at Arms of the next preceding House of Representatives.

(R.S. §§ 31–33; Pub. L. 104–186, title II, § 202(2), Aug. 20, 1996, 110 Stat. 1724.)

CODIFICATION

R.S. § 31 derived from acts Feb. 21, 1867, ch. 56, § 1, 14 Stat. 397 and Mar. 3, 1863, ch. 108, 12 Stat. 804.

R.S. §§ 32 and 33 derived from act Feb. 21, 1867, ch. 56, § 2, 14 Stat. 397.

R.S. § 31 constitutes first sentence; R.S. § 32 constitutes second sentence; and R.S. § 33 constituted the third sentence, prior to repeal by Pub. L. 104–186. See 1996 Amendment note below.

AMENDMENTS

1996—Pub. L. 104–186 struck out third sentence which read as follows: "In case of vacancies in the offices of both the Clerk and the Sergeant at Arms, or of the absence or inability of both to act, the duties of the Clerk relative to the preparation of the roll of the House of Representatives or the organization of the House shall be performed by the Doorkeeper of the next preceding House of Representatives." See Codification note above.

SECTION REFERRED TO IN OTHER SECTIONS

This section is referred to in section 34 of this title.

§ 27. Change of place of meeting

Whenever Congress is about to convene, and from the prevalence of contagious sickness, or the existence of other circumstances, it would, in the opinion of the President, be hazardous to the lives or health of the members to meet at the seat of Government, the President is authorized, by proclamation, to convene Congress at such other place as he may judge proper.

(R.S. § 34.)

CODIFICATION

R.S. § 34 derived from act Apr. 3, 1794, ch. 17, 1 Stat. 353.

§ 28. Parliamentary precedents of House of Representatives

(a) Periodic compilation; other useful materials; index digest; date of completion

The Parliamentarian of the House of Representatives, at the beginning of the fifth fiscal year following the completion and publication of the parliamentary precedents of the House authorized by the Legislative Branch Appropriation Act, 1966 (79 Stat. 270; Public Law 89–90), and at the beginning of each fifth fiscal year thereafter, shall commence the compilation and preparation for printing of the parliamentary precedents of the House of Representatives, together with such other materials as may be useful in connection therewith, and an index digest of such precedents and other materials. Each such compilation and preparation for printing of the parliamentary precedents of the House shall be completed by the close of the fiscal year immediately following the fiscal year in which such work is commenced.

(b) Form, number, and distribution of compilation

As so compiled and prepared, such precedents and other materials and index digest shall be printed on pages of such size, and in such type and format, as the Parliamentarian may determine and shall be printed in such numbers and for such distribution as may be provided by law enacted prior to printing.

(c) Appointment and compensation of personnel; utilization of services of personnel of Federal agencies

For the purpose of carrying out each such compilation and preparation, the Parliamentarian may—

(1) subject to the approval of the Speaker, appoint (as employees of the House of Representatives) clerical and other personnel and fix their respective rates of pay; and

(2) utilize the services of personnel of the Library of Congress and the Government Printing Office.

(Pub. L. 91–510, title III, § 331, Oct. 26, 1970, 84 Stat. 1186.)

REFERENCES IN TEXT

The Legislative Branch Appropriation Act, 1966, referred to in subsec. (a), is Pub. L. 89–90, July 27, 1965, 79 Stat. 265. For complete classification of this Act to the Code, see Tables.

EFFECTIVE DATE

Section effective immediately prior to noon on Jan. 3, 1971, see section 601(1) of Pub. L. 91–510, set out as an Effective Date of 1970 Amendment note under section 72a of this title.

§ 28a. Compilation of the Precedents of House of Representatives; date of completion; biennial update; printing and availability of copies

The Speaker is authorized and directed to complete the Compilation of the Precedents of the House of Representatives by January 1, 1977, and prepare an updated compilation of such precedents every two years thereafter. Copies of the Compilation of Precedents shall be printed in sufficient quantity to be available to every Member and the standing committees of the House of Representatives.

(Pub. L. 93–554, title I, ch. III, Dec. 27, 1974, 88 Stat. 1777.)

CODIFICATION

Section is based on section 208 of House Resolution No. 988, Ninety-third Congress, Oct. 8, 1974, which was enacted into permanent law by Pub. L. 93–554.

EFFECTIVE DATE

Pub. L. 93–554 provided that the enactment of House Resolution No. 988, Ninety-third Congress, into permanent law is effective Jan. 2, 1975.

§ 28b. Printing and binding as public document of Precedents of House of Representatives; number of sets authorized

(a) There shall be printed and bound as a public document two thousand sets of the Precedents of the House of Representatives compiled and prepared by Lewis Deschler (hereinafter in sections 28b to 28e of this title referred to as the "Precedents") in accordance with the provisions of the Legislative Branch Appropriation Act, 1966 (Public Law 89–90; 79 Stat. 265).

(b) The number of sets authorized to be printed and bound by or pursuant to sections 28b to 28e of this title shall be in lieu of the usual number of copies for binding and distribution required by section 701 of title 44.

(Pub. L. 94–551, § 1, Oct. 18, 1976, 90 Stat. 2537.)

REFERENCES IN TEXT

The Legislative Branch Appropriation Act, 1966, referred to in text, is Pub. L. 89–90, July 27, 1965, 79 Stat. 265. For complete classification of this Act to the Code, see Tables.

SECTION REFERRED TO IN OTHER SECTIONS

This section is referred to in section 28e of this title.

§ 28c. Distribution of Precedents by Public Printer

(a) Delivery to Members of Ninety-fifth Congress; marking of volumes

The Public Printer shall deliver one set of the Precedents to each Senator or Representative in, or Delegate or Resident Commissioner to, the Ninety-fifth Congress. The name of the Member to whom the set is delivered shall be legibly stamped on the front cover of each volume of the set.

(b) Members of Congress following Ninety-fifth Congress not already having sets of Precedents; necessity of written request to Superintendent of Documents for set

Each Senator or Representative in, or Delegate or Resident Commissioner to, each Congress following the Ninety-fifth Congress who has not theretofore received a set of the Precedents shall be entitled to receive one set of the Precedents, upon transmitting a written request for such set to the Superintendent of Documents.

(c) Additional distribution of sets

The Public Printer shall make the following distribution of sets of the Precedents:

(1) to the office of the Vice President, to the office of the speaker of the House of Representatives, and to the office of the President pro tempore of the Senate, each, five sets;

(2) to the office of the majority leader of the House of Representatives and to the office of the minority leader of the House of Representatives, each, three sets;

(3) to the Parliamentarian of the House of Representatives, sixty sets;

(4) to the Parliamentarian of the Senate, five sets;

(5) to the Clerk of the House of Representatives and to the Sergeant at Arms of the House of Representatives, each[1] two sets;

(6) to the Secretary of the Senate and to the Sergeant at Arms of the Senate, each, two sets;

(7) to the superintendent of the House document room, two sets;

(8) to the superintendent of the Senate document room, two sets;

(9) to the Library of Congress, for international exchange and for official use in Washington, District of Columbia, one hundred and fifty sets;

(10) to the National Archives, three sets;

(11) to the government of the District of Columbia, twelve sets;

(12) to the Smithsonian Institute, two sets;

(13) to the library of each legislative branch of each State, territory, and possession of the United States, one set; and

(14) to the Superintendent of Documents, eight hundred and sixteen sets for distribution to the depository library system.

(Pub. L. 94–551, § 2, Oct. 18, 1976, 90 Stat. 2537; Pub. L. 104–186, title II, § 202(3), Aug. 20, 1996, 110 Stat. 1724.)

AMENDMENTS

1996—Subsec. (c)(2). Pub. L. 104–186, § 202(3)(A), substituted "Representatives, each" for "Representives, each".

Subsec. (c)(5). Pub. L. 104–186, § 202(3)(B), substituted "and to the Sergeant at Arms of the House of Representatives, each two sets" for ", to the Sergeant at Arms of the House of Representatives, and to the Doorkeeper of the House of Representatives, each, two sets".

SECTION REFERRED TO IN OTHER SECTIONS

This section is referred to in sections 28b, 28e of this title.

§ 28d. Distribution of Precedents by Public Printer for official use; particular distribution; marking and ownership of sets

(a) The Public Printer shall make the following distribution of sets of the Precedents;

[1] So in original. Probably should be followed by a comma.

(1) to each standing or joint committee of the Congress which is in existence on October 18, 1976, or which is established after October 18, 1976, four sets;

(2) to the office of the Legislative Counsel of the House of Representatives, five sets;

(3) to the office of the Legislative Counsel of the Senate, five sets;

(4) to the library of the House of Representatives, four sets;

(5) to the library of the Senate, two sets;

(6) to the library of the Supreme Court of the United States, nine sets;

(7) to the office of the Official Reporter of Debates of the House of Representatives, three sets; and

(8) to the office of the Official Reporter of Debates of the Senate, three sets.

(b) Each set of Precedents distributed by the Public Printer under subsection (a) of this section shall be for official use. Each such set shall be legibly stamped on the front cover "Property of the United States Government." Each such set, upon delivery, shall become and remain the property of the United States, and may not be removed from the building in which is located the designated library or office, as the case may be.

(Pub. L. 94–551, § 3, Oct. 18, 1976, 90 Stat. 2538.)

SECTION REFERRED TO IN OTHER SECTIONS

This section is referred to in sections 28b, 28e of this title.

§ 28e. Distribution of Precedents by Joint Committee on Printing of surplus sets; additional printing, etc., of sets under authority of Joint Committee

(a) Any set of the Precedents printed and bound pursuant to subsection (a) of section 28b of this title, not needed to carry out the distributions required by sections 28b to 28e of this title, shall be distributed under the direction of the Joint Committee on Printing.

(b) The Joint Committee on Printing may from time to time authorize and direct that additional sets of the Precedents, be printed, bound, and distributed in such manner as the Joint Committee determines will best carry out the purposes of sections 28b to 28e of this title.

(Pub. L. 94–551, § 4, Oct. 18, 1976, 90 Stat. 2538.)

SECTION REFERRED TO IN OTHER SECTIONS

This section is referred to in section 28b of this title.

§ 29. Condensed and simplified versions of House precedents; other useful materials in summary form; form and distribution to Members of Congress, Resident Commissioner from Puerto Rico, and others; appointment and compensation of personnel; utilization of services of personnel of Federal agencies

The Parliamentarian of the House of Representatives shall prepare, compile, and maintain on a current basis and in cumulative form, for each Congress commencing with the Ninety-third Congress a condensed and, insofar as practicable, up-to-date version of all of the parliamentary precedents of the House of Representatives which have current use and application in the House, together with informative text prepared by the Parliamentarian and other useful related material in summary form. The Parliamentarian shall have such matter printed for each Congress on pages of such size and in such type and format as he considers advisable to promote the usefulness of such matter to the Members of the House and shall provide a printed copy thereof to each Member in each Congress, including the Resident Commissioner from Puerto Rico, and may make such other distribution of such printed copies as he considers advisable. In carrying out this section, the Parliamentarian may appoint and fix the pay of personnel and utilize the services of personnel of the Library of Congress and the Government Printing Office.

(Pub. L. 91–510, title III, § 332, Oct. 26, 1970, 84 Stat. 1186.)

EFFECTIVE DATE

Section effective immediately prior to noon on Jan. 3, 1971, see section 601(1) of Pub. L. 91–510, set out as an Effective Date of 1970 Amendment note under section 72a of this title.

§ 29a. Early organization of House of Representatives

(a) Caucus or conference for incumbent Members reelected to and Members-elect of ensuing Congress; time and procedure for calling

(1) The majority leader or minority leader of the House of Representatives after consultation with the Speaker may at any time during any even-numbered year call a caucus or conference, to begin on or after the first day of December and conclude on or before the twentieth day of December in such year and to be attended by all incumbent Members of his or her political party who have been reelected to the ensuing Congress and all other Members-elect of such party, for the purpose of taking all steps necessary to achieve the prompt organization of the Members and Members-elect of such party for the ensuing Congress.

(2) If the majority leader or minority leader calls an organizational caucus or conference under paragraph (1), he or she shall file with the Clerk of the House a written notice designating the date upon which the caucus or conference is to convene. As soon as possible after the election of Members to the ensuing Congress, the Clerk shall furnish each Member-elect of the party involved with appropriate written notification of the caucus or conference.

(3) If a vacancy occurs in the office of majority leader or minority leader during any even-numbered year (and has not been filled), the chairman of the caucus or conference of the party involved for the current Congress may call an organizational caucus or conference under paragraph (1) by filing written notice thereof as provided by paragraph (2).

(b) Payment and reimbursement for travel and per diem expenses for Members attending caucus or conference; exceptions; regulations governing payments and reimbursements; reimbursement vouchers

(1)(A) Each Member-elect (other than an incumbent Member reelected to the ensuing Congress) who attends a caucus or conference called under subsection (a) of this section, and each incumbent Member reelected to the ensuing Congress who attends any such caucus or conference convening after the adjournment sine die of the Congress in the year involved, shall be paid for one round trip between his or her place of residence in the district which he or she represents and Washington, District of Columbia, for the purpose of attending such caucus or conference. Payment shall be made through the issuance of a transportation request form to each such Member-elect or incumbent Member by the Finance Office of the House before such caucus or conference.

(B) Each Member-elect (other than an incumbent Member reelected to the ensuing Congress) who attends a caucus or conference called under subsection (a) of this section shall in addition be reimbursed on a per diem or other basis for expenses incurred in connection with his or her attendance at such caucus or conference for a period not to exceed the shorter of the following—

(i) the period beginning with the day before the designated date upon which such caucus or conference is to convene and ending with the day after the date of the final adjournment of such caucus or conference; or

(ii) fourteen days.

(2) Payments and reimbursements to Members-elect under paragraph (1) shall be made as provided (with respect to Members) in the regulations prescribed by the Committee on House Oversight with respect to travel and other expenses of committees and Members. Reimbursements shall be paid on special voucher forms prescribed by the Committee on House Oversight.

(c) Availability of applicable accounts of House

The applicable accounts of the House of Representatives are made available to carry out the purposes of this section.

(Pub. L. 93–554, title I, ch. III, Dec. 27, 1974, 88 Stat. 1777; Pub. L. 104–186, title II, § 202(4), Aug. 20, 1996, 110 Stat. 1725.)

CODIFICATION

Section is based on section 202 of House Resolution No. 988, Ninety-third Congress, Oct. 8, 1974, which was enacted into permanent law by Pub. L. 93–554.

AMENDMENTS

1996—Subsec. (b)(2). Pub. L. 104–186, § 202(4)(A), substituted "House Oversight" for "House Administration" in two places.

Subsec. (c). Pub. L. 104–186, § 202(4)(B), substituted "applicable accounts of the House of Representatives are" for "contingent fund of the House is".

CHANGE OF NAME

Committee on House Oversight of House of Representatives changed to Committee on House Administration of House of Representatives by House Resolution No. 5, One Hundred Sixth Congress, Jan. 6, 1999.

EFFECTIVE DATE

Pub. L. 93–554 provided that the enactment of House Resolution No. 988, Ninety-third Congress, into permanent law is effective Jan. 2, 1975.

SECTION REFERRED TO IN OTHER SECTIONS

This section is referred to in section 43b–2 of this title.

§§ 29b, 29c. Omitted

CODIFICATION

Section 29b, based on section 204 of House Resolution No. 988, Ninety-third Congress, Oct. 8, 1974, which was enacted into permanent law, effective Jan. 2, 1975, by Pub. L. 93–554, title I, ch. III, Dec. 27, 1974, 88 Stat. 1777, established a Commission on Information and Facilities in House of Representatives to be composed of nine members of the House appointed by Speaker, required Speaker to appoint an Advisory Council to assist Commission in carrying out its functions, required Commission to conduct study of informational problems, facilities and space, and House legislative counsel requirements, provided for the scope of study of informational problems, and required Commission to make an annual progress report to Speaker, to complete study of House legislative counsel requirements by Jan. 1, 1976, and to submit a final report by Jan. 2, 1977.

Section 29c, based on clause 10, rule I, of the Rules of the House of Representatives as in effect before July 17, 1984, relating to the Office for the Bicentennial for the House of Representatives, established by House Resolution No. 621, Ninety-seventh Congress, Dec. 17, 1982, which was enacted into permanent law by Pub. L. 98–367, title I, §102, July 17, 1984, 98 Stat. 479, established in House of Representatives an Office for the Bicentennial of the House of Representatives to coordinate planning of commemoration of two-hundredth anniversary of House of Representatives and to be staffed by a professional historian appointed by Speaker without regard to political affiliation and solely on basis of fitness to perform duties of the position and to serve at pleasure of Speaker, and provided that the Office cease to exist not later than Sept. 30, 1989, unless otherwise provided by law or resolution. Office of the Historian of the House of Representatives was established by clause 10, rule I, of the Rules of the House of Representatives, as added on Jan. 3, 1989 (H. Res. 5, 101st Congress).

§ 29d. Committee on Standards of Official Conduct of House of Representatives

(a) Omitted

(b) Committee composition

The respective party caucus or conference of the House of Representatives shall each nominate to the House of Representatives at the beginning of each Congress 7 members to serve on the Committee on Standards of Official Conduct.

(c) Investigative subcommittees

The Committee on Standards of Official Conduct shall adopt rules providing—

(1) for the establishment of a 4 or 6-member investigative subcommittee (with equal representation from the majority and minority parties) whenever the committee votes to undertake any investigation;

(2) that the senior majority and minority members on an investigative subcommittee shall serve as the chairman and ranking minority member of the subcommittee; and

(3) that the chairman and ranking minority member of the full committee may only serve as non-voting, ex officio members on an investigative subcommittee.

Clause 5(d) of rule XI[1] of the Rules of the House of Representatives shall not apply to any investigative subcommittee.

(d) Adjudicatory subcommittees

The Committee on Standards of Official Conduct shall adopt rules providing—

(1) that upon the completion of an investigation, an investigative subcommittee shall report its findings and recommendations to the committee;

(2) that, if an investigative subcommittee by majority vote of its membership adopts a statement of alleged violation, the remaining members of the committee shall comprise an adjudicatory subcommittee to hold a disciplinary hearing on the violation alleged in the statement;

(3) that any statement of alleged violation and any written response thereto shall be made public at the first meeting or hearing on the matter which is open to the public after the respondent has been given full opportunity to respond to the statement in accordance with committee rules, but, if no public hearing or meeting is held on the matter, the statement of alleged violation and any written response thereto shall be included in the committee's final report to the House of Representatives as required by clause 4(e)(1)(B) of rule X[1] of the Rules of the House of Representatives;

(4) that a quorum for an adjudicatory subcommittee for the purpose of taking testimony and conducting any business shall consist of a majority of the membership of the subcommittee plus one; and

(5) that an adjudicatory subcommittee shall determine, after receiving evidence, whether the counts in the statement have been proved and shall report its findings to the committee.

Clause 5(d) of rule XI[1] of the Rules of the House of Representatives shall not apply to any adjudicatory subcommittee.

(e) to (h) Omitted

(i) Advice and education

(1) The Committee on Standards of Official Conduct shall establish within the committee an Office on Advice and Education (hereinafter in this subsection referred to as the "Office") under the supervision of the chairman.

(2) The Office shall be headed by a director who shall be appointed by the chairman, in consultation with the ranking minority member, and shall be comprised of such staff as the chairman determines is necessary to carry out the responsibilities of the Office.

(3) The primary responsibilities of the Office shall include:

(A) Providing information and guidance to Members, officers and employees of the House regarding any laws, rules, regulations, and other standards of conduct applicable to such individuals in their official capacities, and any interpretations and advisory opinions of the committee.

(B) Submitting to the chairman and ranking minority member of the committee any written request from any such Member, officer or employee for an interpretation of applicable laws, rules, regulations, or other standards of conduct, together with any recommendations thereon.

(C) Recommending to the committee for its consideration formal advisory opinions of general applicability.

---

[1] See References in Text note below.

(D) Developing and carrying out, subject to the approval of the chairman, periodic educational briefings for Members, officers and employees of the House on those laws, rules, regulations, or other standards of conduct applicable to them.

(4) No information provided to the Committee on Standards of Official Conduct by a Member, officer or employee of the House of Representatives when seeking advice regarding prospective conduct of such Member, officer or employee may be used as the basis for initiating an investigation under clause 4(e)(1)(B) of rule X [1] of the Rules of the House of Representatives, if such Member, officer or employee acts in accordance with the written advice of the committee.

(j) Effective date

This section shall take effect immediately before noon January 3, 1991, except that subsections (g), (h), and (i) shall take effect on January 1, 1990.

(Pub. L. 101–194, title VIII, §803, Nov. 30, 1989, 103 Stat. 1774.)

REFERENCES IN TEXT

The Rules of the House of Representatives for the One Hundred Sixth Congress were adopted and amended generally by House Resolution No. 5, One Hundred Sixth Congress, Jan. 6, 1999. Provisions formerly appearing in clause 5(d) of rule XI, referred to in subsecs. (c) and (d), are now contained in clause 6(d) of rule X. Provisions formerly appearing in clause 4(e)(1)(B) of rule X, referred to in subsecs. (d)(3) and (i)(4), are now contained in clause 3(a)(2) of rule XI.

CODIFICATION

Section is comprised of section 803 of Pub. L. 101–194. Subsecs. (a) and (e) to (h) of section 803 amended the Rules of the House of Representatives which are not classified to the Code.

ACCEPTANCE OF GIFTS; AMENDMENTS TO ADVISORY OPINIONS

Section 801(e) of Pub. L. 101–194 provided that: "The Committee on Standards of Official Conduct of the House of Representatives shall amend its advisory opinions relating to the acceptance of gifts (1) to prohibit lodging received as personal hospitality in excess of 30 days in any calendar year from any individual unless a written waiver is granted by the committee and (2) to exempt gifts of food and beverages consumed not in connection with gifts of lodging from coverage under clause 4 of rule XLIII [now clause 4 of rule XXIII] of the Rules of the House of Representatives."

NONCAMPAIGN USE OF CAMPAIGN VEHICLES

Section 802(e) of Pub. L. 101–194 provided that: "The Committee on Standards of Official Conduct of the House of Representatives shall issue an advisory opinion to provide for appropriate conditions for the incidental noncampaign use of vehicles owned or leased by a campaign committee of a Member of the House of Representatives."

RESTRICTIONS ON REIMBURSABLE TRAVEL EXPENSES

Section 805 of Pub. L. 101–194 provided that:
"(a) RESTRICTIONS.—The Committee on Standards of Official Conduct of the House of Representatives shall amend its advisory opinions relating to the acceptance of necessary travel expenses incurred on or after January 1, 1990, in connection with speaking engagements and similar events to—
"(1) prohibit the acceptance of such expenses for more than 4 consecutive days in the case of domestic travel and 7 consecutive days (excluding travel days) in the case of foreign travel; and
"(2) permit the acceptance of travel expenses for the spouse or other family member in connection with any substantial participation event or fact-finding activity.
"(b) EXEMPTION AUTHORITY.—The Committee on Standards of Official Conduct of the House of Representatives is authorized to grant prior written exemptions from the limitations contained in subsection (a)(1) in exceptional circumstances."

§30. Term of service of Members of Congress as trustees or directors of corporations or institutions appropriated for

In all cases where Members of Congress or Senators are appointed to represent Congress on any board of trustees or board of directors of any corporation or institution to which Congress makes any appropriation, the term of said Members or Senators, as such trustee or director, shall continue until the expiration of two months after the first meeting of the Congress chosen next after their appointment.

(Mar. 3, 1893, ch. 199, §1, 27 Stat. 553.)

CODIFICATION

Section was formerly classified to section 722 of Title 31 prior to the general revision and enactment of Title 31, Money and Finance, by Pub. L. 97–258, §1, Sept. 13, 1982, 96 Stat. 877.

§30a. Jury duty exemption of elected officials of legislative branch

(a) Notwithstanding any other provision of Federal, State or local law, no elected official of the legislative branch of the United States Government shall be required to serve on a grand or petit jury, convened by any Federal, State or local court, whether such service is requested by judicial summons or by some other means of compulsion.

(b) "Elected official of the legislative branch" shall mean each Member of the United States House of Representatives, the Delegates from the District of Columbia, Guam, the American Virgin Islands, and American Samoa, and the Resident Commissioner from Puerto Rico, and each United States Senator.

(Pub. L. 101–520, title III, §310, Nov. 5, 1990, 104 Stat. 2278.)

CODIFICATION

Section is from the Legislative Branch Appropriations Act, 1991.

CHAPTER 3—COMPENSATION AND ALLOWANCES OF MEMBERS

§ 31. Compensation of Members of Congress

(1) The annual rate of pay for—

(A) each Senator, Member of the House of Representatives, and Delegate to the House of Representatives, and the Resident Commissioner from Puerto Rico,

(B) the President pro tempore of the Senate, the majority leader and the minority leader of the Senate, and the majority leader and the minority leader of the House of Representatives, and

(C) the Speaker of the House of Representatives,

shall be the rate determined for such positions under chapter 11 of this title, as adjusted by paragraph (2) of this section.

(2)(A) Subject to subparagraph (B), effective at the beginning of the first applicable pay period commencing on or after the first day of the month in which an adjustment takes effect under section 5303 of title 5 in the rates of pay under the General Schedule, each annual rate referred to in paragraph (1) shall be adjusted by an amount, rounded to the nearest multiple of $100 (or if midway between multiples of $100, to the next higher multiple of $100), equal to the percentage of such annual rate which corresponds to the most recent percentage change in the ECI (relative to the date described in the next sentence), as determined under section 704(a)(1) of the Ethics Reform Act of 1989. The appropriate date under this sentence is the first day of the fiscal year in which such adjustment in the rates of pay under the General Schedule takes effect.

(B) In no event shall the percentage adjustment taking effect under subparagraph (A) in any calendar year (before rounding), in any rate of pay, exceed the percentage adjustment taking effect in such calendar year under section 5303 of title 5 in the rates of pay under the General Schedule.

(Aug. 2, 1946, ch. 753, title VI, §601(a), 60 Stat. 850; Jan. 19, 1949, ch. 2, §1(d), 63 Stat. 4; Mar. 2, 1955, ch. 9, §4(a), 69 Stat. 11; Pub. L. 88–426, title II, §204, Aug. 14, 1964, 78 Stat. 415; Pub. L. 89–301, §11(e), Oct. 29, 1965, 79 Stat. 1120; Pub. L. 91–67, §2, Sept. 15, 1969, 83 Stat. 107; Pub. L. 94–82, title II, §204(a), Aug. 9, 1975, 89 Stat. 421; Pub. L. 101–194, title VII, §704(a)(2)(B), Nov. 30, 1989, 103 Stat. 1769; Pub. L. 101–509, title V, §529 [title I, §101(b)(4)(D)], Nov. 5, 1990, 104 Stat. 1427, 1439; Pub. L. 103–356, title I, §101(1), Oct. 13, 1994, 108 Stat. 3410.)

References in Text

The General Schedule, referred to in par. (2), is set out under section 5332 of Title 5, Government Organization and Employees.

Section 704(a)(1) of the Ethics Reform Act of 1989, referred to in par. (2)(A), is section 704(a)(1) of Pub. L. 101–194, which is set out as a note under section 5318 of Title 5.

Prior Provisions

A prior section 31, acts Feb. 26, 1907, ch. 1635, §4, 34 Stat. 993; Mar. 4, 1925, ch. 549, §4, 43 Stat. 1301; May 17, 1932, ch. 190, 47 Stat. 158, related to compensation of Members of Congress, prior to enactment of act Aug. 2, 1946.

Amendments

1994—Par. (2). Pub. L. 103–356 designated existing provisions as subpar. (A), substituted "Subject to subparagraph (B), effective" for "Effective", and added subpar. (B).

1990—Par. (2). Pub. L. 101–509 substituted "5303" for "5305".

1989—Par. (2). Pub. L. 101–194 substituted "the most recent percentage change in the ECI (relative to the date described in the next sentence), as determined under section 704(a)(1) of the Ethics Reform Act of 1989. The appropriate date under this sentence is the first day of the fiscal year in which such adjustment in the rates of pay under the General Schedule takes effect" for "the overall average percentage (as set forth in the report transmitted to the Congress under such section 5305) of the adjustment in the rates of pay under the General Schedule".

1975—Pub. L. 94–82 designated existing provisions as par. (1), substituted provisions that rate of pay of the specified parties shall be determined under section 351 et seq. of this title, as adjusted by par. (2) for provisions setting rate of compensation at $42,500 for Senators, Representatives, Delegates, and Resident Commissioner, $62,500 for Speaker, and $49,500 for President pro tempore of Senate and Majority and Minority Leaders of House and Senate, and added par. (2).

1969—Pub. L. 91–67 increased compensation of Speaker from $43,000 to $62,500 per annum and compensation of Majority and Minority Leaders of both Houses of Congress from $35,000 to $49,500 per annum, and fixed compensation of President pro tempore of Senate at $49,500 per annum.

1965—Pub. L. 89–301 inserted provisions setting rate of compensation of Majority and Minority Leaders of Senate and House of Representatives at $35,000 per annum each.

1964—Pub. L. 88–426 increased compensation of Senators, Representatives and Resident Commissioner from $22,500 to $30,000 per annum and that of Speaker from $35,000 to $43,000 per annum, and eliminated provisions which related to Delegates from the Territories.

1955—Act Mar. 2, 1955, increased salaries of Senators, Representatives, Delegates, and Resident Commissioner from $12,500 a year to $22,500 and compensation of Speaker from $30,000 to $35,000 a year.

1949—Act Jan. 19, 1949, increased Speaker's salary from $20,000 per year to $30,000.

Effective Date of 1994 Amendment

Section 101 of Pub. L. 103–356 provided that the amendment made by that section is effective Dec. 31, 1994.

Effective Date of 1990 Amendment

Amendment by Pub. L. 101–509 effective on such date as the President shall determine, but not earlier than 90 days, and not later than 180 days, after Nov. 5, 1990, see section 529 [title III, §305] of Pub. L. 101–509, set out as a note under section 5301 of Title 5, Government Organization and Employees.

Effective Date of 1989 Amendment

Amendment by Pub. L. 101–194 effective Jan. 1, 1991, see section 704(b) of Pub. L. 101–194, set out as a note under section 5318 of Title 5, Government Organization and Employees.

Effective Date of 1969 Amendment

Amendment by Pub. L. 91–67 effective Mar. 1, 1969, see section 3 of Pub. L. 91–67, set out as a note under section 104 of Title 3, The President.

Effective Date of 1965 Amendment

Amendment by Pub. L. 89–301 effective on first day of first pay period which begins on or after October 1, 1965, see section 17 of Pub. L. 89–301.

Effective Date of 1964 Amendment

Amendment by Pub. L. 88–426 effective at noon, Jan. 3, 1965, see section 501(b) of Pub. L. 88–426.

Effective Date of 1955 Amendment

Section 5 of act Mar. 2, 1955, provided that: "The provisions of this Act [amending this section, section 104 of Title 3, The President, section 7443 of Title 26, Internal Revenue Code, sections 5, 44, 135, 173, 213, 252, and 508 of Title 28, Judiciary and Judicial Procedure, section 101 of Title 48, Territories and Insular Possessions, and section 654 of Title 50, War and National Defense, and repealing section 31a of this title] shall take effect Mar. 1, 1955."

Effective Date of 1949 Amendment

Amendment by act Jan. 19, 1949, effective at noon, Jan. 20, 1949, see section 3 of act Jan. 19, 1949.

Effective Date

Section 601(a) of act Aug. 2, 1946, provided that the salary rates provided by such section 601(a) are effective Jan. 3, 1947.

Short Title of 1996 Amendment

Pub. L. 104–186, §1(a), Aug. 20, 1996, 110 Stat. 1718, provided that: "This Act [see Tables for classification] may be cited as the 'House of Representatives Administrative Reform Technical Corrections Act'."

SHORT TITLE OF 1964 AMENDMENT

Section 201 of title II of Pub. L. 88–426 provided that: "This title [enacting sections 61a, 61a–2, 61d, 61e, 60e–11, 84–2, 136a, 136b, and 273 of this title, sections 42a and 51a of former Title 31, Money and Finance, sections 162a, 166b, and 166b–1 of Title 40, Public Buildings, Property, and Works, and section 39a of former Title 44, Public Printing and Documents, amending this section and section 72a of this title, and enacting provisions set out as notes under this section and sections 60a–1 and 60f of this title] may be cited as the 'Federal Legislative Salary Act of 1964'."

APPROPRIATION OF FUNDS FOR COMPENSATION OF MEMBERS OF CONGRESS AND FOR ADMINISTRATIVE EXPENSES AT LEVELS AUTHORIZED BY LAW AND RECOMMENDED BY THE PRESIDENT FOR FEDERAL EMPLOYEES

Pub. L. 97–51, § 130(c), Oct. 1, 1981, 95 Stat. 966, provided that: "Effective beginning with fiscal year 1983, and continuing each year thereafter, such sums as hereafter may be necessary for 'Compensation of Members' (and administrative expenses related thereto), as authorized by law and at such level recommended by the President for Federal employees for that fiscal year are hereby appropriated from money in the Treasury not otherwise appropriated. Such sums when paid shall be in lieu of any sums accrued in prior years but not paid. For purposes of this subsection, the term 'Member' means each Member of the Senate and the House of Representatives, the Resident Commissioner from Puerto Rico, the Delegates from the District of Columbia, Guam, Virgin Islands, and American Samoa, and the Vice President."

SALARY INCREASES

2001—Ex. Ord. No. 13182, Dec. 23, 2000, 65 F.R. 82879, 66 F.R. 10057, set out as a note under section 5332 of Title 5, Government Organization and Employees, provided for the adjustment of pay rates effective Jan. 1, 2001.

2000—Ex. Ord. No. 13144, Dec. 21, 1999, 64 F.R. 72237, which provided for the adjustment of pay rates effective Jan. 1, 2000, was superseded by Ex. Ord. No. 13182, Dec. 23, 2000, 65 F.R. 82879, set out as a note under section 5332 of Title 5.

1999—Ex. Ord. No. 13106, Dec. 7, 1998, 63 F.R. 68151, which provided for the adjustment of pay rates effective Jan. 1, 1999, was substantially superseded by Ex. Ord. No. 13144, Dec. 21, 1999, 64 F.R. 72237, formerly set out as a note under section 5332 of Title 5.

1998—Ex. Ord. No. 13071, Dec. 29, 1997, 62 F.R. 68521, which provided for the adjustment of pay rates effective Jan. 1, 1998, was superseded by Ex. Ord. No. 13106, Dec. 7, 1998, 63 F.R. 68151, formerly set out as a note under section 5332 of Title 5.

1997—Ex. Ord. No. 13033, Dec. 27, 1996, 61 F.R. 68987, which provided for the adjustment of pay rates effective Jan. 1, 1997, was superseded by Ex. Ord. No. 13071, Dec. 29, 1997, 62 F.R. 68521, formerly set out as a note under section 5332 of Title 5.

1996—Ex. Ord. No. 12984, Dec. 28, 1995, 61 F.R. 237, which provided for the adjustment of pay rates effective Jan. 1, 1996, was superseded by Ex. Ord. No. 13033, Dec. 27, 1996, 61 F.R. 68987, formerly set out as a note under section 5332 of Title 5.

1995—Ex. Ord. No. 12944, Dec. 28, 1994, 60 F.R. 309, which provided for the adjustment of pay rates effective Jan. 1, 1995, was superseded by Ex. Ord. No. 12984, Dec. 28, 1995, 61 F.R. 237, formerly set out as a note under section 5332 of Title 5.

1994—Pub. L. 103–6, § 7, Mar. 4, 1993, 107 Stat. 35, provided that:

"(a) COST OF LIVING ADJUSTMENT.—Notwithstanding section 601(a)(2) of the Legislative Reorganization Act of 1946 (2 U.S.C. 31(2)), the cost of living adjustment (relating to pay for Members of Congress) which would become effective under such provision of law during calendar year 1994 shall not take effect.

"(b) SEVERABILITY.—If any provision of this Act [enacting provisions set out as notes under sections 1 and 3304 of Title 26, Internal Revenue Code, and section 352 of Title 45, Railroads, and amending provisions set out as notes under section 3304 of Title 26 and section 352 of Title 45], or an amendment made by this Act, or the application of such provision to any person or circumstance, is held to be invalid, the remainder of this Act, or an amendment made by this Act, or the application of such provision to other persons or circumstances, shall not be affected."

1993—Ex. Ord. No. 12826, Dec. 30, 1992, 57 F.R. 62909, which provided for the adjustment of pay rates effective Jan. 1, 1993, was superseded by Ex. Ord. No. 12944, Dec. 28, 1994, 60 F.R. 309, formerly set out as a note under section 5332 of Title 5, Government Organization and Employees.

1992—Ex. Ord. No. 12786, Dec. 26, 1991, 56 F.R. 67453, which provided for the adjustment of pay rates effective Jan. 1, 1992, was superseded by Ex. Ord. No. 12826, Dec. 30, 1992, 57 F.R. 62909, formerly set out as a note under section 5332 of Title 5.

1991—Ex. Ord. No. 12736, Dec. 12, 1990, 55 F.R. 51385, which provided for the adjustment of pay rates effective Jan. 1, 1991, was superseded by Ex. Ord. No. 12786, Dec. 26, 1991, 56 F.R. 67453, formerly set out as a note under section 5332 of Title 5.

1990—Ex. Ord. No. 12698, Dec. 23, 1989, 54 F.R. 53473, which provided for adjustments of pay rates effective Jan. 1, 1990, and Jan. 31, 1990, was superseded by Ex. Ord. No. 12736, Dec. 12, 1990, 55 F.R. 51385, formerly set out as a note under section 5332 of Title 5.

1989—Pub. L. 101–194, title VII, § 703(a)(2), Nov. 30, 1989, 103 Stat. 1768, set out as a note under section 5318 of Title 5, provided that effective Jan. 1, 1991, the rate of basic pay for the offices and positions under 2 U.S.C. 356(A) and (B) shall be increased in the amount of 25 percent of their respective rates (as last in effect before the increase), except that this shall not affect the rate of basic pay for a Senator, the President pro tempore of the Senate, or the majority leader or the minority leader of the Senate.

Ex. Ord. No. 12663, Jan. 6, 1989, 54 F.R. 791, which provided for the adjustment of pay rates effective Jan. 1, 1989, was superseded by Ex. Ord. No. 12698, Dec. 23, 1989, 54 F.R. 53473, formerly set out as a note under section 5332 of Title 5.

1988—Ex. Ord. No. 12622, Dec. 31, 1987, 53 F.R. 222, which provided for the adjustment of pay rates effective Jan. 1, 1988, was superseded by Ex. Ord. No. 12663, Jan. 6, 1989, 54 F.R. 791, formerly set out as a note under section 5332 of Title 5.

1987—Salary of Speaker of House of Representatives increased to $115,000 per annum; salaries of President pro tempore of Senate, majority leader and minority leader of Senate, and majority leader and minority leader of House of Representatives increased to $99,500 per annum; and salaries of Senators, Members of House of Representatives, Delegates to House of Representatives, and Resident Commissioner from Puerto Rico increased to $89,500 per annum, on recommendation of the President of the United States, effective Mar. 1, 1987, set out as a note under section 358 of this title.

Ex. Ord. No. 12578, Dec. 31, 1986, 52 F.R. 505, which provided for the adjustment of pay rates effective Jan. 1, 1987, was superseded by Ex. Ord. No. 12622, Dec. 31, 1987, 53 F.R. 222, formerly set out as a note under section 5332 of Title 5, Government Organization and Employees.

1985—Ex. Ord. No. 12496, Dec. 28, 1984, 50 F.R. 211, as amended by Ex. Ord. No. 12540, Dec. 30, 1985, 51 F.R. 577, which provided for the adjustment of pay rates effective Jan. 1, 1985, was superseded by Ex. Ord. No. 12578, Dec. 31, 1986, 52 F.R. 505, formerly set out as a note under section 5332 of Title 5.

1984—Ex. Ord. No. 12456, Dec. 30, 1983, 49 F.R. 347, as amended by Ex. Ord. No. 12477, May 23, 1984, 49 F.R. 22041; Ex. Ord. No. 12487, Sept. 14, 1984, 49 F.R. 36493, which provided for the adjustment of pay rates effective Jan. 1, 1984, was superseded by Ex. Ord. No. 12496, Dec. 28, 1984, 50 F.R. 211, as amended by Ex. Ord. No. 12540, Dec. 30, 1985, 51 F.R. 577, formerly set out as a note under section 5332 of Title 5.

1983—Pub. L. 98–63, title I, §908(d), (f), July 30, 1983, 97 Stat. 338, which provided that, effective with respect to service as a Member performed on or after July 1, 1983, and notwithstanding any other provision of law, in the case of a Member serving in office or position of Senator, President pro tempore of Senate, Majority Leader of Senate, or Minority Leader of Senate during a calendar year, the annual rate of pay paid to such Member for such service would not be less than the annual rate of pay payable for such position on Dec. 17, 1982, increased by 15 percent and rounded in accordance with section 5318 of Title 5, was repealed by Pub. L. 102–90, title I, §6(c), Aug. 14, 1991, 105 Stat. 451.

1982—Ex. Ord. No. 12387, Oct. 8, 1982, 47 F.R. 44981, which provided for the adjustment of pay rates effective Oct. 1, 1982, was superseded by Ex. Ord. No. 12456, Dec. 30, 1983, 49 F.R. 347, as amended by Ex. Ord. No. 12477, May 23, 1984, 49 F.R. 22041; Ex. Ord. No. 12487, Sept. 14, 1984, 49 F.R. 36493, formerly set out as a note under section 5332 of Title 5.

Maximum rates payable after Dec. 17, 1982, increased from $60,662.50, $68,575.00, and $79,125.00 to $69,800.00, $78,900.00, and $91,000.00, respectively, except for Senators, see Pub. L. 97–377, title I, §129(b)–(d), Dec. 21, 1982, 96 Stat. 1914, set out as a note under section 5318 of Title 5.

Limitations on use of funds for fiscal year ending Sept. 30, 1983, appropriated by any Act to pay the salary or pay of any individual in legislative, executive, or judicial branch in position equal to or above level V of the Executive Schedule, see section 101(e) of Pub. L. 97–276, as amended, set out as a note under section 5318 of Title 5.

1981—Ex. Ord. No. 12330, Oct. 15, 1981, 46 F.R. 50921, which provided for the adjustment of pay rates effective Oct. 1, 1981, was superseded by Ex. Ord. No. 12387, Oct. 8, 1982, 47 F.R. 44981, formerly set out as a note under section 5332 of Title 5.

Limitations on use of funds for fiscal year ending Sept. 30, 1982, appropriated by any Act to pay the salary or pay of any individual in legislative, executive, or judicial branch in position equal to or above level V of the Executive Schedule, see sections 101(g) and 141 of Pub. L. 97–92, set out as a note under section 5318 of Title 5.

1980—Ex. Ord. No. 12248, Oct. 16, 1980, 45 F.R. 69199, which provided for the adjustment of pay rates effective Oct. 1, 1980, was superseded by Ex. Ord. No. 12330, Oct. 15, 1981, 46 F.R. 50921, formerly set out as a note under section 5332 of Title 5.

Limitations on use of funds for fiscal year ending Sept. 30, 1981, appropriated by any Act to pay the salary or pay of any individual in legislative, executive, or judicial branch in position equal to or above Level V of the Executive Schedule, see section 101(c) of Pub. L. 96–536, as amended, set out as a note under section 5318 of Title 5.

1979—Ex. Ord. No. 12165, Oct. 9, 1979, 44 F.R. 58761, as amended by Ex. Ord. No. 12200, Mar. 12, 1980, 45 F.R. 16443, which provided for the adjustment of pay rates effective Oct. 1, 1979, was superseded by Ex. Ord. No. 12248, Oct. 16, 1980, 45 F.R. 69199, formerly set out as a note under section 5332 of Title 5.

Applicability to funds appropriated by any Act for fiscal year ending Sept. 30, 1980, of limitation of section 304 of Pub. L. 95–391 on use of funds to pay the salary or pay of any individual in legislative, executive, or judicial branch in position equal to or above Level V of the Executive Schedule, see section 101 of Pub. L. 96–86, set out as a note under section 5318 of Title 5.

1978—Ex. Ord. No. 12087, Oct. 7, 1978, 43 F.R. 46823, which provided for the adjustment of pay rates effective Oct. 1, 1978, was superseded by Ex. Ord. No. 12165, Oct. 9, 1979, 44 F.R. 58671, formerly set out as a note under section 5332 of Title 5.

Limitations on use of funds for fiscal year ending Sept. 30, 1979, appropriated by any Act to pay the salary or pay of any individual in legislative, executive, or judicial branch in position equal or above Level V of the Executive Schedule, see section 304 of Pub. L. 95–391

and section 613 of Pub. L. 95–429, set out as a note under section 5318 of Title 5.

1977—Salary of Speaker of House of Representatives increased to $75,000 per annum; salaries of President pro tempore of Senate, majority leader and minority leader of Senate, and majority leader and minority leader of House of Representatives increased to $65,000 per annum; and salaries of Senators, Members of House of Representatives, Delegate to House of Representatives and Resident Commissioner from Puerto Rico increased to $57,500 per annum, on recommendation of the President of the United States effective at the beginning of the first pay period beginning after the 30th day following Jan. 17, 1977, set out as a note under section 358 of this title.

Pub. L. 95–66, §1(2), July 11, 1977, 91 Stat. 270, set out as a note under section 5318 of Title 5, Government Organization and Employees, provided that the first adjustment which, but for the enactment of Pub. L. 95–66, would have been made in the annual rate of pay for Members of Congress under paragraph (2) of this section after July 11, 1977, would not take effect.

1976—Ex. Ord. No. 11941, Oct. 1, 1976, 41 F.R. 43899, as amended by Ex. Ord. No. 11943, Oct. 25, 1976, 41 F.R. 47213, which provided for the adjustment of pay rates effective Oct. 1, 1976, was superseded by Ex. Ord. No. 12010, Sept. 28, 1977, 42 F.R. 52365, formerly set out as a note under section 5332 of Title 5.

1975—Ex. Ord. No. 11883, Oct. 6, 1975, 40 F.R. 47091, which provided for the adjustment of pay rates effective Oct. 1, 1975, was superseded by Ex. Ord. No. 11941, Oct. 1, 1976, 41 F.R. 43899, as amended by Ex. Ord. No. 11943, Oct. 25, 1976, 41 F.R. 47213, formerly set out as a note under section 5332 of Title 5.

1969—Salaries of Senators, Members of House of Representatives, and Resident Commissioner from Puerto Rico increased to $42,500, on recommendation of the President of the United States, effective at beginning of first pay period beginning after the 30th day following Jan. 15, 1969, set out as a note under section 358 of this title.

COMMISSION ON JUDICIAL AND CONGRESSIONAL SALARIES

Act Aug. 7, 1953, ch. 353, 67 Stat. 485, which established a Commission to determine appropriate rates of salaries for justices and judges of courts of United States and for Vice President, Speaker of House of Representatives, and Members of Congress, was repealed by Pub. L. 89–554, §8(a), Sept. 6, 1966, 80 Stat. 657.

§ 31–1. Repealed. Pub. L. 102–90, title I, § 6(c), Aug. 14, 1991, 105 Stat. 451

Section, Pub. L. 98–63, title I, §908(a)–(c), July 30, 1983, 97 Stat. 337, 338; Pub. L. 99–190, §137, Dec. 19, 1985, 99 Stat. 1323; Pub. L. 101–194, title VI, §601(b)(2), title XI, §1101(b), Nov. 30, 1989, 103 Stat. 1762, 1782; Pub. L. 101–280, §7(b)(2)[(d)(2)], May 4, 1990, 104 Stat. 161, related to maximum amount of honoraria which could be accepted by Members of Congress.

§ 31–2. Gifts and travel

(a) Gifts

(1) No Member, officer, or employee of the Senate, or the spouse or dependent thereof, shall knowingly accept, directly or indirectly, any gift or gifts in any calendar year aggregating more than the minimal value as established by section 7342(a)(5) of title 5 or $250, whichever is greater[1] from any person, organization, or corporation unless, in an unusual case, a waiver is granted by the Select Committee on Ethics.

(2) The prohibitions of this subsection do not apply to gifts—

    (A) from relatives;

---

[1] So in original. Probably should be followed by a comma.

(B) with a value of $100 or less, as adjusted under section 102(a)(2)(A) of the Ethics in Government Act of 1978; or

(C) of personal hospitality of an individual.

(3) For purposes of this subsection—

(A) the term "gift" means a payment, subscription, advance, forbearance, rendering, or deposit of money, services, or anything of value, including food, lodging, transportation, or entertainment, and reimbursement for other than necessary expenses, unless consideration of equal or greater value is received, but does not include (1) a political contribution otherwise reported as required by law, (2) a loan made in a commercially reasonable manner (including requirements that the loan be repaid and that a reasonable rate of interest be paid), (3) a bequest, inheritance, or other transfer at death, (4) a bona fide award presented in recognition of public service and available to the general public, (5) a reception at which the Member, officer, or employee is to be honored, provided such individual receives no other gifts that exceed the restrictions in this rule, other than a suitable memento, (6) meals or beverages consumed or enjoyed, provided the meals or beverages are not consumed or enjoyed in connection with a gift of overnight lodging, or (7) anything of value given to a spouse or dependent of a reporting individual by the employer of such spouse or dependent in recognition of the service provided by such spouse or dependent; and

(B) the term "relative" has the same meaning given to such term in section 107(2) of title I of the Ethics in Government Act of 1978 (Public Law 95–521).[2]

(4) If a Member, officer, or employee, after exercising reasonable diligence to obtain the information necessary to comply with this rule, unknowingly accepts a gift described in paragraph (1) such Member, officer, or employee shall, upon learning of the nature of the gift and its source, return the gift or, if it is not possible to return the gift, reimburse the donor for the value of the gift.

(5)(A) Notwithstanding the provisions of this subsection, a Member, officer, or employee of the Senate may participate in a program, the principal objective of which is educational, sponsored by a foreign government or a foreign educational or charitable organization involving travel to a foreign country paid for by that foreign government or organization if such participation is not in violation of any law and if the select[3] Committee on Ethics has determined that participation in such program by Members, officers, or employees of the Senate is in the interests of the Senate and the United States.

(B) Any Member who accepts an invitation to participate in any such program shall notify the Select Committee in writing of his acceptance. A Member shall also notify the Select Committee in writing whenever he has permitted any officer or employee whom he supervises to participate in any such program. The chairman of the Select Committee shall place in the Congressional Record a list of all individuals,[4] participating, the supervisors of such individuals where applicable;[5] and the nature and itinerary of such program.

(C) No Member, officer, or employee may accept funds in connection with participation in a program permitted under subparagraph (A) if such funds are not used for necessary food, lodging, transportation, and related expenses of the Member, officer, or employee.

(b) Limits on domestic and foreign travel by Members and staff of Senate

The term "necessary expenses", with respect to limits on domestic and foreign travel by Members and staff of the Senate, means reasonable expenses for food, lodging, or transportation which are incurred by a Member, officer, or employee of the Senate in connection with services provided to (or participation in an event sponsored by) the organization which provides reimbursement for such expenses or which provides the food, lodging, or transportation directly. Necessary expenses do not include the provision of food, lodging, or transportation, or the payment for such expenses, for a continuous period in excess of 3 days exclusive of travel time within the United States or 7 days exclusive of travel time outside of the United States unless such travel is approved by the Committee on Ethics as necessary for participation in a conference, seminar, meeting or similar matter. Necessary expenses do not include the provision of food, lodging, or transportation, or the payment for such expenses, for anyone accompanying a Member, officer, or employee of the Senate, other than the spouse or child of such Member, officer, or employee of the Senate or one Senate employee acting as an aide to a Member.

(Pub. L. 101–194, title IX, § 901, Nov. 30, 1989, 103 Stat. 1778; Pub. L. 101–280, § 8, May 4, 1990, 104 Stat. 162; Pub. L. 102–90, title III, § 314(c), Aug. 14, 1991, 105 Stat. 470.)

REFERENCES IN TEXT

Section 102(a)(2)(A) of the Ethics in Government Act of 1978, referred to in subsec. (a)(2)(B), is section 102(a)(2)(A) of title I of Pub. L. 95–521, as amended. Section 102 was classified to section 702 of this title prior to the general amendment of title I of Pub. L. 95–521 by Pub. L. 101–194, title II, § 202, Nov. 30, 1989, 103 Stat. 1724. Title I of Pub. L. 95–521, as so amended, is set out in the Appendix to Title 5, Government Organization and Employees.

Section 107(2) of title I of the Ethics in Government Act of 1978 (Public Law 95–521), referred to in subsec. (a)(3)(B), was classified to section 707(2) of this title prior to the general amendment of title I of Pub. L. 95–521 by Pub. L. 101–194, title II, § 202, Nov. 30, 1989, 103 Stat. 1724. Title I of Pub. L. 95–521, as so amended, is set out in the Appendix to Title 5, and the definition of "relative" is contained in section 109(16) of Pub. L. 95–521.

AMENDMENTS

1991—Subsec. (a)(1). Pub. L. 102–90, § 314(c)(1)–(3), redesignated par. (2) as (1), substituted "in any calendar year aggregating more than the minimal value as established by section 7342(a)(5) of title 5 or $250, whichever is greater" for "having an aggregate value exceed-

---

[2] See References in Text note below.
[3] So in original. Probably should be capitalized.

[4] So in original. The comma probably should not appear.
[5] So in original. The semicolon probably should be a comma.

ing $300 during a calendar year", and struck out former par. (1) which read as follows: "No Member, officer, or employee of the Senate, or the spouse or dependent thereof, shall knowingly accept, directly or indirectly, any gift or gifts having an aggregate value exceeding $100 during a calendar year directly or indirectly from any person, organization, or corporation having a direct interest in legislation before the Congress or from any foreign national unless, in an unusual case, a waiver is granted by the Select Committee on Ethics."

Subsec. (a)(2). Pub. L. 102–90, §314(c)(2), (4), redesignated par. (5) as (2) and, in subpar. (B), substituted "$100 or less, as adjusted under section 102(a)(2)(A) of the Ethics in Government Act of 1978" for "less than $75". Former par. (2) redesignated (1).

Subsec. (a)(3). Pub. L. 102–90, §314(c)(5), redesignated subpars. (B) and (C) as (A) and (B), respectively, and struck out former subpar. (A) which read as follows: "the term 'foreign national' means a person acting directly or indirectly on behalf of a foreign corporation, partnership, or business enterprise, a foreign trade, cultural, educational, or other association, a foreign political party, or a foreign government;".

Pub. L. 102–90, §314(c)(1), (2), redesignated par. (6) as (3) and struck out former par. (3) which read as follows: "In determining the aggregate value of any gift or gifts accepted by an individual during a calendar year from any person, organization, or corporation, there may be deducted the aggregate value of gifts (other than gifts described in paragraph (5)) given by such individual to such person, organization, or corporation during that calendar year."

Subsec. (a)(4). Pub. L. 102–90, §314(c)(1), (2), redesignated par. (7) as (4) and struck out former par. (4) which read as follows: "For purposes of this subsection, only the following shall be deemed to have a direct interest in legislation before the Congress:

"(A) a person, organization, or corporation registered under the Federal Regulation of Lobbying Act of 1946, or any successor statute, a person who is an officer or director of such a registered lobbyist, or a person who has been employed or retained by such a registered lobbyist for the purpose of influencing legislation before the Congress; or

"(B) a corporation, labor organization, or other organization which maintains a separate segregated fund for political purposes (within the meaning of section 441b of this title), a person who is an officer or director of such corporation, labor organization, or other organization, or a person who has been employed or retained by such corporation, labor organization, or other organization for the purpose of influencing legislation before the Congress."

Subsec. (a)(5) to (8). Pub. L. 102–90, §314(c)(2), redesignated pars. (5) to (8) as (2) to (5), respectively.

1990—Subsec. (a)(5)(D). Pub. L. 101–280, §8(1)(A), struck out subpar. (D) which read as follows: "from an individual who is a foreign national if that individual is not acting; directly or indirectly, on behalf of a foreign corporation, partnership or business enterprise, a foreign trade, cultural, educational or other association, a foreign political party or a foreign government."

Subsec. (a)(6)(A) to (C). Pub. L. 101–280, §8(1)(B), added subpar. (A) and redesignated former subpars. (A) and (B) as (B) and (C), respectively.

Subsec. (b). Pub. L. 101–280, §8(2), substituted "or child of such Member" for "of a Member" and struck out "(and 2 nights)" after "of 3 days" and "(and 6 nights)" after "or 7 days".

EFFECTIVE DATE OF 1991 AMENDMENT

Section 314(g) of Pub. L. 102–90, as amended by Pub. L. 102–378, §4(c), Oct. 2, 1992, 106 Stat. 1358, provided that:

"(1) The amendments made by subsections (b) through (f) [amending this section, section 505 of the Ethics in Government Act of 1978, Pub. L. 95–521, set out in the Appendix to Title 5, Government Organization and Employees, and section 7701 of Title 26, Internal Revenue Code] shall take effect on January 1, 1992.

"(2) The amendment made by subsection (a) [amending section 102 of the Ethics in Government Act of 1978, Pub. L. 95–521, set out in the Appendix to Title 5] shall take effect on January 1, 1993."

[Amendment by Pub. L. 102–378 to section 314(g) of Pub. L. 102–90, set out above, effective Dec. 31, 1991, see section 9(b)(1) of Pub. L. 102–378, set out as an Effective Date of 1992 Amendment note under section 6303 of Title 5.]

§ 31a. Repealed. Mar. 2, 1955, ch. 9, § 4(b), 69 Stat. 11, eff. Mar. 1, 1955

Section, acts Aug. 2, 1946, ch. 753, title VI, §601(b), 60 Stat. 850; Oct. 20, 1951, ch. 521, title VI, §619(d), 65 Stat. 570, related to expense allowance for Senators, Representatives, Delegates, and Resident Commissioner.

§ 31a–1. Expense allowance of Majority and Minority Leaders of Senate; expense allowance of Majority and Minority Whips; methods of payment; taxability

Effective fiscal year 1978 and each fiscal year thereafter, the expense allowances of the Majority and Minority Leaders of the Senate are increased to $10,000 each fiscal year for each leader: *Provided*, That, effective with the fiscal year 1983 and each fiscal year thereafter, the expense allowance of the Majority and Minority Whips of the Senate shall not exceed $5,000 each fiscal year for each Whip: *Provided further*, That, during the period beginning on January 3, 1977, and ending September 30, 1977, and during each fiscal year thereafter, the Vice President, the Majority Leader, the Minority Leader, the Majority Whip, and the Minority Whip may receive the expense allowance (a) as reimbursement for actual expenses incurred upon certification and documentation of such expenses by the Vice President, the respective Leader or the respective Whip, or (b) in equal monthly payments: *Provided further*, That effective January 3, 1977, the amounts paid to the Vice President, the Majority or Minority Leader of the Senate, or the Majority or Minority Whip of the Senate as reimbursement of actual expenses incurred upon certification and documentation pursuant to the second proviso of this section shall not be reported as income, and the expenses so reimbursed shall not be allowed as a deduction, under title 26.

(Pub. L. 95–26, title I, May 4, 1977, 91 Stat. 79; Pub. L. 95–94, title I, §109, Aug. 5, 1977, 91 Stat. 661; Pub. L. 95–355, title I, Sept. 8, 1978, 92 Stat. 532; Pub. L. 98–63, title I, §101, July 30, 1983, 97 Stat. 333; Pub. L. 99–514, §2, Oct. 22, 1986, 100 Stat. 2095.)

CODIFICATION

Section is based on the three provisos in paragraph under heading "Expense Allowances of the Vice President, Majority and Minority Leaders and Majority and Minority Whips" in the appropriation for the Senate in the Supplemental Appropriations Act, 1977 (Pub. L. 95–26), and section 109 of the Congressional Operations Appropriation Act, 1978, which is title I of the Legislative Branch Appropriation Act, 1978 (Pub. L. 95–94), and subsequent acts cited in the credits to this section.

AMENDMENTS

1986—Pub. L. 99–514 substituted "Internal Revenue Code of 1986" for "Internal Revenue Code of 1954", which for purposes of codification was translated as "title 26" thus requiring no change in text.

1983—Pub. L. 98–63 substituted provisions increasing allowances for each Whip to $5,000 each fiscal year, effective fiscal year 1983 and each fiscal year thereafter, for provisions authorizing not to exceed $2,500 each fiscal year for each Whip, effective Apr. 1, 1977.

1978—Pub. L. 95–355 substituted provisions increasing allowances for each leader to $10,000 each fiscal year, effective fiscal year 1978 and each fiscal year thereafter, for provisions authorizing not to exceed $5,000 each fiscal year for each leader, effective with fiscal year 1977 and each fiscal year thereafter.

§ 31a–2. Representation Allowance Account for Majority and Minority Leaders of Senate

(a) Establishment; purpose

There is hereby established an account, within the Senate, to be known as the "Representation Allowance Account for the Majority and Minority Leaders". Such Allowance Account shall be used by the Majority and Minority Leaders of the Senate to assist them properly to discharge their appropriate responsibilities in the United States to members of foreign legislative bodies and prominent officials of foreign governments and intergovernmental organizations.

(b) Payments; allotment; reimbursement for actual expenses; taxability

Payments authorized to be made under this section shall be paid by the Secretary of the Senate. Of the funds available for expenditure from such Allowance Account for any fiscal year, one-half shall be allotted to the Majority Leader and one-half shall be allotted to the Minority Leader. Amounts paid from such Allowance Account to the Majority or Minority Leader shall be paid to him from his allotment and shall be paid to him only as reimbursement for actual expenses incurred by him and upon certification and documentation of such expenses. Amounts paid to the Majority or Minority Leader pursuant to this section shall not be reported as income and shall not be allowed as a deduction under title 26.

(c) Authorization of appropriations

There are authorized to be appropriated for each fiscal year (commencing with the fiscal year ending September 30, 1985) not more than $20,000 to the Allowance Account established by this section.

(Pub. L. 99–88, title I, §197, Aug. 15, 1985, 99 Stat. 350.)

CODIFICATION

Section is from the Supplemental Appropriations Act, 1985.

SECTION REFERRED TO IN OTHER SECTIONS

This section is referred to in section 31a–2a of this title.

§ 31a–2a. Transfer of funds from representation allowance of Majority and Minority Leaders of Senate to expense allowance; availability; definitions

(a) The Secretary of the Senate shall, upon the written request of the Majority or Minority Leader of the Senate, transfer from any available funds in such Leader's allotment in the Leader's Representation Allowance (as defined in subsection (b)(1) of this section) for any fiscal year (commencing with the fiscal year ending September 30, 1985) to such Leader's Expense Allowance (as defined in subsection (b)(2) of this section) to such year such amount as is specified in the request. Any funds so transferred for any fiscal year at the request of either such Leader shall be available to such Leader for such year for the same purposes as, and in like manner and subject to the same conditions as, are other funds which are available to him for such year as his expense allowance as Majority or Minority Leader.

(b)(1) The term "Leader's Representation Allowance" means the Representation Allowance Account for the Majority and Minority Leaders established by section 31a–2 of this title.

(2) The term "Leader's Expense Allowance", when used in reference to the Majority or Minority Leader of the Senate, refers to such Leader as an expense allowance and the appropriation account from which such moneys are funded.

(Pub. L. 100–71, title I, §1, July 11, 1987, 101 Stat. 422.)

CODIFICATION

Section is from the Supplemental Appropriations Act, 1987.

§ 31a–2b. Transfer of funds from appropriations account of Majority and Minority Leaders of Senate to appropriations account, Miscellaneous Items, within Senate contingent fund

(a) Requests for transfers

Upon the written request of the Majority or Minority Leader of the Senate, the Secretary of the Senate shall transfer during any fiscal year, from the appropriations account appropriated under the headings "Salaries, Officers and Employees" and "Offices of the Majority and Minority Leaders", such amount as either Leader shall specify to the appropriations account, within the contingent fund of the Senate, "Miscellaneous Items".

(b) Authority to incur expenses

The Majority and Minority Leaders of the Senate are each authorized to incur such expenses as may be necessary or appropriate. Expenses incurred by either such leader shall be paid from the amount transferred pursuant to subsection (a) of this section by such leader and upon vouchers approved by such leader.

(c) Authority to advance sums

The Secretary of the Senate is authorized to advance such sums as may be necessary to defray expenses incurred in carrying out subsections (a) and (b) of this section.

(Pub. L. 102–27, title II, Apr. 10, 1991, 105 Stat. 144.)

CODIFICATION

Section is from the Dire Emergency Supplemental Appropriations for Consequences of Operation Desert Shield/Desert Storm, Food Stamps, Unemployment Compensation Administration, Veterans Compensation and Pensions, and Other Urgent Needs Act of 1991.

§ 31a–2c. Transfer of funds from appropriations account of Majority and Minority Whips of Senate to appropriations account, Miscellaneous Items, within Senate contingent fund

(a) Requests for transfers

Upon the written request of the Majority or Minority Whip of the Senate, the Secretary of the Senate shall transfer during any fiscal year, from the appropriations account appropriated under the headings "SALARIES, OFFICERS AND EMPLOYEES" and "OFFICES OF THE MAJORITY AND MINORITY WHIPS", such amount as either whip shall specify to the appropriations account, within the contingent fund of the Senate, "MISCELLANEOUS ITEMS".

(b) Authority to incur expenses

The Majority and Minority Whips of the Senate are each authorized to incur such expenses as may be necessary or appropriate. Expenses incurred by either such whip shall be paid from the amount transferred pursuant to subsection (a) of this section by such whip and upon vouchers approved by such whip.

(c) Authority to advance sums

The Secretary of the Senate is authorized to advance such sums as may be necessary to defray expenses incurred in carrying out subsections (a) and (b) of this section.

(Pub. L. 105–55, title I, § 2, Oct. 7, 1997, 111 Stat. 1180.)

CODIFICATION

Section is from the Congressional Operations Appropriations Act, 1998, which is title I of the Legislative Branch Appropriations Act, 1998.

§ 31a–3. Expense allowance for Chairmen of Majority and Minority Conference Committees of Senate; method of payment; taxability

For each fiscal year (commencing with the fiscal year ending September 30, 1985), there is hereby authorized an expense allowance for the Chairmen of the Majority and Minority Conference Committees which shall not exceed $3,000 each fiscal year for each such Chairman; and amounts from such allowance shall be paid to either of such Chairmen only as reimbursement for actual expenses incurred by him and upon certification and documentation of such expenses, and amounts so paid shall not be reported as income and shall not be allowed as a deduction under title 26.

(Pub. L. 99–88, title I, Aug. 15, 1985, 99 Stat. 348.)

CODIFICATION

Section is from the Supplemental Appropriations Act, 1985.

§ 31a–4. Expense allowance for Chairmen of Majority and Minority Policy Committees of Senate; method of payment; taxability

For each fiscal year (commencing with the fiscal year ending September 30, 2001), there is authorized an expense allowance for the Chairmen of the Majority and Minority Policy Committees which shall not exceed $3,000 each fiscal year for each such Chairman; and amounts from such allowance shall be paid to either of such Chairmen only as reimbursement for actual expenses incurred by him and upon certification and documentation of such expenses, and amounts so paid shall not be reported as income and shall not be allowed as a deduction under title 26.

(Pub. L. 106–554, § 1(a)(2) [title I, § 5], Dec. 21, 2000, 114 Stat. 2763, 2763A–97.)

CODIFICATION

Section is from the Congressional Operations Appropriations Act, 2001, which is title I of the Legislative Branch Appropriations Act, 2001.

§ 31b. Expense allowance of Speaker of House of Representatives

There shall be paid to the Speaker of the House of Representatives in equal monthly installments an expense allowance of $10,000 per annum to assist in defraying expenses relating to or resulting from the discharge of his official duties, for which no accounting, other than for income tax purposes, shall be made by him.

(Jan. 19, 1949, ch. 2, § 1(e), 63 Stat. 4; Oct. 20, 1951, ch. 521, title VI, § 619(c), 65 Stat. 570; Pub. L. 104–186, title II, § 203(1), Aug. 20, 1996, 110 Stat. 1725.)

AMENDMENTS

1996—Pub. L. 104–186 struck out "(which shall be in lieu of the allowance provided by section 601(b) of the Legislative Reorganization Act of 1946, as amended)" after "per annum".

1951—Act Oct. 20, 1951, made Speaker's expense allowance taxable.

EFFECTIVE DATE OF 1951 AMENDMENT

Amendment by act Oct. 20, 1951, effective at noon, Jan. 3, 1953, see section 619(e) of act Oct. 20, 1951, set out as a note under section 102 of Title 3, The President.

EFFECTIVE DATE

Section effective at noon, Jan. 20, 1949, see section 3 of act Jan. 19, 1949.

§ 31b–1. Former Speakers of House of Representatives; retention of office, furniture, etc., in Congressional district following expiration of term as Representative; exceptions

(a) Each former Speaker of the House of Representatives (hereafter referred to in sections 31b–1 to 31b–7 of this title as the "Speaker") is entitled to retain, for as long as he determines there is need therefor, commencing at the expiration of his term of office as a Representative in Congress the complete and exclusive use of one office selected by him in order to facilitate the administration, settlement, and conclusion of matters pertaining to or arising out of his incumbency in office as a Representative in Congress and as Speaker of the House of Representatives. Such office shall be located in the United States and shall be furnished and maintained by the Government in a condition appropriate for his use.

(b) Sections 31b–1 to 31b–7 of this title shall not apply with respect to any former Speaker of the House of Representatives for any period during which such former Speaker holds an appointive or elective office or position in or under the Federal Government or the government of the District of Columbia to which is attached a rate of pay other than a nominal rate or to any former Speaker separated from the service by reason of expulsion from the House.

(Pub. L. 91–665, ch. VIII, Jan. 8, 1971, 84 Stat. 1989; Pub. L. 93–532, § 1, Dec. 22, 1974, 88 Stat. 1723; Pub. L. 99–225, Dec. 28, 1985, 99 Stat. 1743.)

CODIFICATION

Subsection (a) of this section is based on section 1 of House Resolution No. 1238, Ninety-first Congress, Dec. 23, 1970, which was enacted into permanent law by Pub. L. 91–665.

Subsection (b) of this section is based on section 1(b) of Pub. L. 93–532.

As originally enacted into permanent law, section applied to Speaker of House of Representatives in 91st Congress and has been extended to apply to each former Speaker of House of Representatives. See section 1(a) of Pub. L. 93–532, set out as a note under this section.

AMENDMENTS

1985—Subsec. (a). Pub. L. 99–225 substituted "one office selected by him in order to facilitate the administration, settlement, and conclusion of matters pertaining to or arising out of his incumbency in office as a Representative in Congress and as Speaker of the House of Representatives. Such office shall be located in the United States and shall be furnished and maintained by the Government in a condition appropriate for his use" for "the Federal office space which is currently made available for his use in the congressional district represented by him and which shall be maintained by the Government in a condition appropriate for his use as he may request, together with all furniture, equipment, and furnishings currently made available by the Government for his use in connection with such office space, including any necessary replacements of such office furniture, equipment, and furnishings, in order to facilitate the administration, settlement, and conclusion of matters pertaining to or arising out of his incumbency in office as a Representative in Congress and as Speaker of the House of Representatives".

EFFECTIVE DATE

Section 7 of House Resolution No. 1238, Ninety-first Congress, Dec. 23, 1970, as enacted into permanent law by Pub. L. 91–665, provided that: "The foregoing provisions of this resolution [enacting sections 31b–1 to 31b–6 of this title] shall become effective on the date of the enactment of this resolution as permanent law [Jan. 8, 1971]."

EXTENSION OF HOUSE RESOLUTION NO. 1238, 91ST CONGRESS, TO FORMER SPEAKERS OF HOUSE OF REPRESENTATIVES

Section 1(a) of Pub. L. 93–532 provided that: "The provisions of H. Res. 1238, Ninety-first Congress, as enacted into permanent law by the Supplemental Appropriations Act, 1971 (84 Stat. 1989) [enacting sections 31b–1 to 31b–6 of this title and provision set out as a note under this section], are hereby extended to, and made applicable with respect to, each former Speaker of the House of Representatives, as long as he determines there is need therefor, commencing at the expiration of his term of office as Representative in Congress."

SECTION REFERRED TO IN OTHER SECTIONS

This section is referred to in section 31b–7 of this title.

§ 31b–2. Allowance available to former Speaker for payment of office and other expenses for administration, etc., of matters pertaining to incumbency in office as Representative and Speaker

The Speaker is entitled to have the applicable accounts of the House of Representatives be available for payment of, for as long as he determines there is need therefor, commencing at the expiration of his term of office as a Representative in Congress, an allowance equal to the Members' Representational Allowance (to be paid in the same manner as such Allowance) for office and other expenses incurred in connection with the administration, settlement, and conclusion of matters pertaining to or arising out of his incumbency in office as a Representative in Congress and as Speaker of the House of Representatives.

(Pub. L. 91–665, ch. VIII, Jan. 8, 1971, 84 Stat. 1989; Pub. L. 93–532, § 1(a), Dec. 22, 1974, 88 Stat. 1723; Pub. L. 99–151, title I, § 102(b), Nov. 13, 1985, 99 Stat. 797; Pub. L. 104–186, title II, § 203(2), Aug. 20, 1996, 110 Stat. 1725.)

CODIFICATION

Section is based on section 2 of House Resolution No. 1238, Ninety-first Congress, Dec. 23, 1970, which was enacted into permanent law by Pub. L. 91–665.

As originally enacted into permanent law, section applied to Speaker of House of Representatives in 91st Congress and has been extended to apply to each former Speaker of House of Representatives. See section 1(a) of Pub. L. 93–532, set out as a note under section 31b–1 of this title.

AMENDMENTS

1996—Pub. L. 104–186 substituted "applicable accounts of the House of Representatives" for "contingent fund of the House" and "Members' Representational Allowance" for "base allowance component of the Official Expenses Allowance then currently in effect for each Member of the House".

1985—Pub. L. 99–151 substituted "have the contingent fund of the House be available for payment of" for "reimbursement, from the contingent fund of the House" and "an allowance equal to the base allowance component of the Official Expenses Allowance then currently in effect for each Member of the House (to be paid in the same manner as such Allowance)" for "in the manner provided by applicable provisions of the Legislative Appropriation Act, 1955, as amended by the Act of June 13, 1957 (71 Stat. 82; Public Law 85–54), and by the provisions of House Resolution 831, Eighty-eighth Congress, adopted August 14, 1964, enacted as permanent law by section 103 of the Legislative Branch Appropriation Act, 1966 (79 Stat. 281; Public Law 89–90; 2 U.S.C. 122a), in an aggregate quarterly amount equal to the aggregate quarterly amount to which a Member of the House of Representatives is entitled under such provisions of law as in effect on January 8, 1971, or as amended or supplemented after such date,".

EFFECTIVE DATE

Section effective Jan. 8, 1971, see Effective Date note set out under section 31b–1 of this title.

CROSS REFERENCES

For establishment of Members' Representational Allowance, see section 57b of this title.

SECTION REFERRED TO IN OTHER SECTIONS

This section is referred to in sections 31b–1, 31b–7 of this title.

§ 31b–3. Repealed. Pub. L. 99–151, title I, § 102(b), Nov. 13, 1985, 99 Stat. 797

Section, based on H. Res. No. 1238, § 3, Dec. 23, 1970, enacted into permanent law by Pub. L. 91–665, ch. VIII, Jan. 8, 1971, 84 Stat. 1989; Pub. L. 93–532, § 1(a), Dec. 22, 1974, 88 Stat. 1723, provided for reimbursement of former Speaker of House for telephone service charges for administration, etc., of matters pertaining to incumbency in office as Representative and Speaker.

§ 31b–4. Franked mail and printing privileges of former Speaker

(a) The Speaker may send mail as franked mail under sections 3210 and 3213 of title 39, and send and receive mail as franked mail under section 3211 of that title, for as long as he determines there is need therefor, commencing at the close of the period specified in those sections following the expiration of his term of office as a Representative in Congress. The postage on such mail, including registry fees if registration is required, shall be paid and credited as provided by section 3216(a) of title 39.

(b) For as long as he determines there is need therefor, commencing at the expiration of his term of office as a Representative in Congress, the Speaker shall be entitled to the benefits afforded by section 733 of title 44.

(Pub. L. 91–665, ch. VIII, Jan. 8, 1971, 84 Stat. 1989; Pub. L. 93–532, § 1(a), Dec. 22, 1974, 88 Stat. 1723.)

CODIFICATION

Section is based on section 4 of House Resolution No. 1238, Ninety-first Congress, Dec. 23, 1970, which was enacted into permanent law by Pub. L. 91–665.

As originally enacted into permanent law, section applied to Speaker of House of Representatives in 91st Congress and has been extended to apply to each former Speaker of House of Representatives. See section 1(a) of Pub. L. 93–532, set out as a note under section 31b–1 of this title.

References to sections of Title 39, Postal Service, have been substituted for references to obsolete sections of Title 39, The Postal Service, in view of revision and reenactment of such Title by the Postal Reorganization Act, Pub. L. 91–375, Aug. 12, 1970, 84 Stat. 719.

EFFECTIVE DATE

Section effective Jan. 8, 1971, see Effective Date note set out under section 31b–1 of this title.

SECTION REFERRED TO IN OTHER SECTIONS

This section is referred to in sections 31b–1, 31b–7 of this title.

§ 31b–5. Staff assistance to former Speaker for administration, etc., of matters pertaining to incumbency in office as Representative and Speaker; compensation and status of staff

In order to provide staff assistance to the Speaker in connection with the administration, settlement, and conclusion of matters pertaining to or arising out of his incumbency in office as a Representative in Congress and as Speaker of the House of Representatives, the contingent fund of the House is hereby made available, for as long as he determines there is need therefor, commencing at the expiration of the term of office of the Speaker as a Representative in Congress for payment of the salaries of an Administrative Assistant, who shall be paid at a basic

per annum rate of not to exceed the then current rate for step 5 of level 11 of the House Employees Schedule, as determined by the Speaker, a Secretary, who shall be paid at a basic per annum rate of not to exceed the then current rate for step 9 of level 8 of such Schedule, as determined by the Speaker, and an additional Secretary, who shall be paid at a gross per annum rate of not to exceed the then current rate for step 1 of level 6 of such Schedule as determined by the Speaker, designated and appointed by the Speaker to serve as members of his office staff in such period. Each person so designated and appointed shall be held and considered, for the duration of such appointment, as—

(1) an "employee" for the purposes of subchapter I of chapter 81 (relating to compensation for work injuries) of title 5, and

(2) a "congressional employee" within the meaning of section 2107 of title 5, for the purposes of—

(A) subchapter III (relating to civil service retirement) of chapter 83 of such title,

(B) chapter 87 (relating to Federal employees group life insurance) of such title, and

(C) chapter 89 (relating to Federal employees group health insurance) of such title.

(Pub. L. 91–665, ch. VIII, Jan. 8, 1971, 84 Stat. 1989; Pub. L. 93–532, § 1(a), Dec. 22, 1974, 88 Stat. 1723; Pub. L. 95–94, title I, § 115, Aug. 5, 1977, 91 Stat. 668; Pub. L. 99–151, title I, § 102(a), Nov. 13, 1985, 99 Stat. 797; Pub. L. 104–186, title II, § 203(3), Aug. 20, 1996, 110 Stat. 1725.)

CODIFICATION

Section is based on section 5 of House Resolution No. 1238, Ninety-first Congress, Dec. 23, 1970, which was enacted into permanent law by Pub. L. 91–665.

Amendment by Pub. L. 95–94 is based on section 2 of House Resolution No. 1576, Ninety-fourth Congress, Sept. 30, 1976, which was enacted into permanent law by Pub. L. 95–94.

As originally enacted into permanent law, section applied to Speaker of House of Representatives in 91st Congress and has been extended to apply to each former Speaker of House of Representatives. See section 1(a) of Pub. L. 93–532, set out as a note under section 31b–1 of this title.

AMENDMENTS

1996—Pub. L. 104–186 substituted "for payment of" for "to enable the Clerk of the House to pay".

1985—Pub. L. 99–151 substituted "not to exceed the then current rate for step 5 of level 11 of the House Employees Schedule" for "not to exceed $3,000" the first place it appeared, "not to exceed the then current rate for step 9 of level 8 of such Schedule" for "not to exceed $3,000" the second place it appeared, and "not to exceed the then current rate for step 1 of level 6 of such Schedule" for "not to exceed $9,000".

1977—Pub. L. 95–94 inserted reference to an additional Secretary paid at a gross per annum of not to exceed $9,000 as determined by the Speaker and struck out "as Administrative Assistant or Secretary" after "Each person so designated and appointed".

EFFECTIVE DATE OF 1977 AMENDMENT

Section 2 of H. Res. 1576 provided that amendment is effective on the date of enactment of such section 2 into permanent law, Aug. 5, 1977, the date of approval of Pub. L. 95–94. See Codification note above.

Section effective Jan. 8, 1971, see Effective Date note set out under section 31b–1 of this title.

SECTION REFERRED TO IN OTHER SECTIONS

This section is referred to in sections 31b–1, 31b–7 of this title.

§ 31b–6. Repealed. Pub. L. 99–151, title I, § 102(b), Nov. 13, 1985, 99 Stat. 797

Section, based on H. Res. No. 1238, § 6, Dec. 23, 1970, enacted into permanent law by Pub. L. 91–665, ch. VIII, Jan. 8, 1971, 84 Stat. 1989; Pub. L. 93–532, § 1(a), Dec. 22, 1974, 88 Stat. 1723, provided for an allowance to the former Speaker of the House for stationery and other office supplies.

§ 31b–7. Availability of entitlements of former Speaker for 5 years

The entitlements of a former Speaker of the House of Representatives under sections 31b–1 to 31b–7 of this title shall be available—

　(1) in the case of an individual who is a former Speaker on October 1, 1993, for 5 years, commencing on October 1, 1993; and

　(2) in the case of an individual who becomes a former Speaker after October 1, 1993, for 5 years, commencing at the expiration of the term of office of the individual as a Representative in Congress.

(Pub. L. 103–69, title I, § 101A(a), Aug. 11, 1993, 107 Stat. 699.)

CODIFICATION

Section is based on section 8 of House Resolution No. 1238, Ninety-first Congress, Dec. 23, 1970, as added by Pub. L. 103–69. House Resolution No. 1238 was enacted into permanent law by Pub. L. 91–665, ch. VIII, Jan. 8, 1971, 84 Stat. 1989.

EFFECTIVE DATE

Section 101A(b) of Pub. L. 103–69 provided that: "The amendment made by subsection (a) [enacting this section] shall take effect on October 1, 1993."

SECTION REFERRED TO IN OTHER SECTIONS

This section is referred to in section 31b–1 of this title.

§ 31c. Repealed. Pub. L. 97–51, § 139(b)(2), Oct. 1, 1981, 95 Stat. 967

Section, acts July 9, 1952, ch. 598, 66 Stat. 467; Aug. 1, 1953, ch. 304, title I, 67 Stat. 322, provided that, for taxable years beginning after Dec. 31, 1953, the place of residence of a Member of Congress (including any Delegate and Resident Commissioner) within the State, congressional district, Territory, or possession which he represented in Congress would be considered his home for the purposes of tax provisions making deductible certain living expenses away from home, but that amounts expended by such Member within each taxable year for living expenses could not be deducted for income tax purposes in excess of $3,000.

EFFECTIVE DATE OF REPEAL

Repeal applicable to taxable years beginning after Dec. 31, 1980, see section 139(b)(3) of Pub. L. 97–51, as amended, set out as an Effective Date of 1981 Amendment note under section 162 of Title 26, Internal Revenue Code.

§ 32. Compensation of President pro tempore of Senate

Whenever there is no Vice President, the President of the Senate for the time being is en-

titled to the compensation provided by law for the Vice President.

(R.S. § 36.)

CODIFICATION

R.S. § 36 derived from act Aug. 16, 1856, ch. 123, § 2, 11 Stat. 48.

CROSS REFERENCES

Compensation of Vice President, see section 104 of Title 3, The President.

§ 32a. Compensation of Deputy President pro tempore of Senate

Effective January 5, 1977, the compensation of a Deputy President pro tempore of the Senate shall be at a rate equal to the rate of annual compensation of the President pro tempore and the Majority and Minority Leaders of the Senate.

(Pub. L. 95–26, title I, May 4, 1977, 91 Stat. 79.)

CODIFICATION

Section is from the Supplemental Appropriations Act, 1977.

§ 32b. Expense allowance of President pro tempore of Senate; methods of payment; taxability

Effective with fiscal year 1978 and each fiscal year thereafter, there is hereby authorized an expense allowance for the President Pro Tempore which shall not exceed $10,000 each fiscal year. The President Pro Tempore may receive the expense allowance (1) as reimbursement for actual expenses incurred upon certification and documentation of such expenses by the President Pro Tempore, or (2) in equal monthly payments. Such amounts paid to the President Pro Tempore as reimbursement of actual expenses incurred upon certification and documentation pursuant to this provision, shall not be reported as income, and the expenses so reimbursed shall not be allowed as a deduction, under title 26.

(Pub. L. 95–355, title I, Sept. 8, 1978, 92 Stat. 532; Pub. L. 99–514, § 2, Oct. 22, 1986, 100 Stat. 2095.)

AMENDMENTS

1986—Pub. L. 99–514 substituted "Internal Revenue Code of 1986" for "Internal Revenue Code of 1954", which for purposes of codification was translated as "title 26" thus requiring no change in text.

§ 33. Senators' salaries

Senators elected, whose term of office begins on the 3d day of January, and whose credentials in due form of law shall have been presented in the Senate, may receive their compensation from the beginning of their term.

(June 19, 1934, ch. 648, title I, § 1, 48 Stat. 1022; Pub. L. 97–51, § 112(b)(2), Oct. 1, 1981, 95 Stat. 963.)

PRIOR PROVISIONS

A prior section 33, act Mar. 3, 1883, ch. 143, 22 Stat. 632, entitled Senators to receive their compensation monthly, from the beginning of their term, prior to repeal by section 112(b)(1) of Pub. L. 97–51.

AMENDMENTS

1981—Pub. L. 97–51 struck out "monthly" after "may receive their compensation".

EFFECTIVE DATE OF 1981 AMENDMENT

Section 112(e) of Pub. L. 97–51 provided that: "The amendments and repeals made by this section [enacting section 35a of this title and amending this section and sections 39 and 60c–1 of this title] shall be effective in the case of compensation payable for months after December 1981."

§ 34. Representatives' and Delegates' salaries payable monthly

Representatives and Delegates-elect to Congress, whose credentials in due form of law have been duly filed with the Clerk of the House of Representatives, in accordance with the provisions of section 26 of this title, may receive their compensation monthly, from the beginning of their term until the beginning of the first session of each Congress, upon a certificate in the form now in use to be signed by the Clerk of the House, which certificate shall have the like force and effect as is given to the certificate of the Speaker.

(R.S. § 38; Mar. 3, 1875, ch. 130, § 1, 18 Stat. 389.)

CODIFICATION

R.S. § 38 derived from act Mar. 3, 1873, ch. 226, § 1, 17 Stat. 488.

§ 35. Salaries payable monthly after taking oath

Each Member and Delegate, after he has taken and subscribed the required oath, is entitled to receive his salary at the end of each month.

(R.S. § 39.)

CODIFICATION

R.S. § 39 derived from Res. Mar. 29, 1867, No. 18, 15 Stat. 24.

SECTION REFERRED TO IN OTHER SECTIONS

This section is referred to in section 35a of this title.

§ 35a. End-of-the-month salary payment schedule inapplicable to Senators

Section 35 of this title shall not be construed as being applicable to a Senator.

(Pub. L. 97–51, § 112(c), Oct. 1, 1981, 95 Stat. 963.)

CODIFICATION

Provisions of subsec. (c) of section 112 of Pub. L. 97–51 that such subsec. (c) would apply on and after the effective date of the amendments and repeals made by section 112 of Pub. L. 97–51 were omitted in the codification of this section since their impact was identical to that of the effective date provisions of subsec. (e) of section 112 of Pub. L. 97–51, set out as an Effective Date of 1981 Amendment note under section 33 of this title. See Effective Date note below.

EFFECTIVE DATE

Section effective in the case of compensation payable for months after December 1981, see section 112(e) of Pub. L. 97–51, set out as an Effective Date of 1981 Amendment note under section 33 of this title.

§ 36. Salaries of Senators

Salaries of Senators appointed to fill vacancies in the Senate shall commence on the day of their appointment and continue until their successors are elected and qualified: *Provided*, That when Senators have been elected during a sine die adjournment of the Senate to succeed appointees, the salaries of Senators so elected shall commence on the day following their election.

Salaries of Senators elected during a session to succeed appointees shall commence on the day they qualify: *Provided*, That when Senators have been elected during a session to succeed appointees, but have not qualified, the salaries of Senators so elected shall commence on the day following the sine die adjournment of the Senate.

When no appointments have been made the salaries of Senators elected to fill such vacancies shall commence on the day following their election.

(Feb. 10, 1923, ch. 68, 42 Stat. 1225; Feb. 6, 1931, ch. 111, 46 Stat. 1065; June 19, 1934, ch. 648, title I, § 1, 48 Stat. 1022; Feb. 13, 1935, ch. 6, § 1, 49 Stat. 22, 23.)

PRIOR PROVISIONS

July 31, 1894, ch. 174, 28 Stat. 162.
R.S. § 51.

AMENDMENTS

1935—Act Feb. 13, 1935, inserted proviso as to commencement of salaries of Senators elected during a sine die adjournment on day following their election and provision as to commencement of salaries of Senators elected during a session to succeed appointees on day they qualify but that upon failure to qualify their salaries are to commence on day following sine die adjournment of Senate and struck out provision that salaries of Senators elected to fill vacancies are to commence on day they qualify.

1934—Act June 19, 1934, made nonsubstantive changes in grammar and punctuation.

1931—Act Feb. 6, 1931, made nonsubstantive changes in grammar and punctuation and struck out "to fill such vacancies" after "When no appointments have been made".

CONSTITUTIONAL PROVISIONS

The first section of amendment XX to the Constitution provides in part: "* * * the terms of Senators and Representatives [shall end] at noon on the 3d day of January, of the years in which such terms would have ended if this article had not been ratified; and the terms of their successors shall then begin."

§ 36a. Payment of sums due deceased Senators and Senate personnel

Under regulations prescribed by the Secretary of the Senate, a person serving as a Senator or officer or employee whose compensation is disbursed by the Secretary of the Senate may designate a beneficiary or beneficiaries to be paid any unpaid balance of salary or other sums due such person at the time of his death. When any person dies while so serving, any such unpaid balance shall be paid by the disbursing officer of the Senate to the designated beneficiary or beneficiaries. If no designation has been made, such unpaid balance shall be paid to the widow or widower of that person, or if there is no widow or widower, to the next of kin or heirs at law of that person.

Section 50 of the Revised Statutes [1] shall not be effective as to persons included within the foregoing.

(Jan. 6, 1951, ch. 1213, Ch. I, § 1, 64 Stat. 1224; Pub. L. 92–607, ch. V, § 503, Oct. 31, 1972, 86 Stat. 1505.)

_____
[1] See References in Text note below.

REFERENCES IN TEXT

Section 50 of the Revised Statutes, referred to in text, was classified to section 38 of this title and was repealed by Pub. L. 104–186, title II, § 203(4), Aug. 20, 1996, 110 Stat. 1725. See section 38a of this title.

AMENDMENTS

1972—Pub. L. 92–607 inserted provisions for designation of a beneficiary by Senators and officers and employees whose compensation is disbursed by Secretary of Senate to whom shall be paid any unpaid balance of salary or other sums due such person at time of death.

SECTION REFERRED TO IN OTHER SECTIONS

This section is referred to in title 5 section 5581.

§ 37. Salaries of Representatives, Delegates, and Resident Commissioners elected for unexpired terms

The salaries of Representatives in Congress, Delegates from Territories, and Resident Commissioners, elected for unexpired terms, shall commence on the date of their election and not before.

(July 16, 1914, ch. 141, § 1, 38 Stat. 458.)

§ 38. Repealed. Pub. L. 104–186, title II, § 203(4), Aug. 20, 1996, 110 Stat. 1725

Section, R.S. §§ 49, 50; acts Jan. 20, 1874, ch. 11, 18 Stat. 4; Mar. 4, 1925, ch. 549, § 4, 43 Stat. 1301, related to pay of member dying after commencement of Congress. See section 38a of this title.

§ 38a. Disposition of unpaid salary and other sums on death of Representative or Resident Commissioner

When any individual who has been elected a Member of, or Resident Commissioner to, the House of Representatives dies after the commencement of the Congress to which he has been elected, any unpaid balance of salary and other sums due such individual shall be paid to the person or persons surviving at the date of death, in the following order of precedence, and such payment shall be a bar to the recovery by any other person of amounts so paid:

First, to the beneficiary or beneficiaries designated by such individual in writing to receive such unpaid balance and other sums due filed with the Chief Administrative Officer of the House of Representatives and received by the Chief Administrative Officer prior to such individual's death;

Second, if there be no such beneficiary, to the widow or widower of such individual;

Third, if there be no beneficiary or surviving spouse, to the child or children of such individual, and descendants of deceased children, by representation;

Fourth, if none of the above, to the parents of such individual, or the survivor of them;

Fifth, if there be none of the above, to the duly appointed legal representative of the estate of the deceased individual, or if there be none, to the person or persons determined to be entitled thereto under the laws of the domicile of the deceased individual.

(July 2, 1954, ch. 455, title I, § 105, 68 Stat. 409; Pub. L. 86–102, July 23, 1959, 73 Stat. 224; Pub. L. 104–186, title II, § 203(5), Aug. 20, 1996, 110 Stat. 1725.)

AMENDMENTS

1996—Pub. L. 104–186 struck out "(including amounts held in the trust fund account in the office of the Sergeant at Arms)" after "due such individual" in first undesignated par. and substituted "Chief Administrative Officer of the House of Representatives and received by the Chief Administrative Officer" for "Sergeant at Arms, and received by the Sergeant at Arms" in second undesignated par.

1959—Pub. L. 86–102 inserted provisions including amounts held in trust fund account, authorizing an individual to designate a beneficiary or beneficiaries, and prescribing order of precedence in cases where no designation of beneficiary has been made.

§ 38b. Death gratuity payments as gifts

Any death gratuity payment at any time specifically appropriated by any Act of Congress or at any time made out of the applicable accounts of the House of Representatives or the contingent fund of the Senate shall be held to have been a gift.

(June 5, 1952, ch. 369, Ch. I, 66 Stat. 101; Pub. L. 104–186, title II, § 203(6), Aug. 20, 1996, 110 Stat. 1725.)

CODIFICATION

Section is also set out as section 125a of this title.

AMENDMENTS

1996—Pub. L. 104–186 substituted "applicable accounts of the House of Representatives or the contingent fund" for "contingent fund of the House of Representatives or".

§ 39. Deductions for absence

The Secretary of the Senate and the Chief Administrative Officer of the House of Representatives (upon certification by the Clerk of the House of Representatives), respectively, shall deduct from the monthly payments (or other periodic payments authorized by law) of each Member or Delegate the amount of his salary for each day that he has been absent from the Senate or House, respectively, unless such Member or Delegate assigns as the reason for such absence the sickness of himself or of some member of his family.

(R.S. § 40; Pub. L. 97–51, § 112(d), Oct. 1, 1981, 95 Stat. 963; Pub. L. 104–186, title II, § 203(7), Aug. 20, 1996, 110 Stat. 1726.)

CODIFICATION

R.S. § 40 derived from act Aug. 16, 1856, ch. 123, § 6, 11 Stat. 49.

AMENDMENTS

1996—Pub. L. 104–186 substituted "the Chief Administrative Officer of the House of Representatives (upon certification by the Clerk of the House of Representatives)" for "Sergeant-at-Arms of the House".

1981—Pub. L. 97–51 substituted "from the monthly payments (or other periodic payments authorized by law)" for "from the monthly payments".

EFFECTIVE DATE OF 1981 AMENDMENT

Amendment by Pub. L. 97–51 effective in the case of compensation payable for months after December 1981, see section 112(e) of Pub. L. 97–51, set out as a note under section 33 of this title.

§ 40. Deductions for withdrawal

When any Member or Delegate withdraws from his seat and does not return before the adjournment of Congress, he shall, in addition to the sum deducted for each day, forfeit a sum equal to the amount which would have been allowed by law for his mileage in returning home; and such sum shall be deducted from his compensation, unless the withdrawal is with the leave of the Senate or House of Representatives respectively.

(R.S. § 41.)

CODIFICATION

R.S. § 41 derived from Res. July 17, 1862, No. 68, § 2, 12 Stat. 628.

§ 40a. Deductions for delinquent indebtedness

Whenever a Representative, Delegate, Resident Commissioner, or a United States Senator, shall fail to pay any sum or sums due from such person to the House of Representatives or Senate, respectively, the appropriate committee or officer of the House of Representatives or Senate, as the case may be, having jurisdiction of the activity under which such debt arose, shall certify such delinquent sum or sums to the Chief Administrative Officer of the House of Representatives in the case of an indebtedness to the House of Representatives and to the Secretary of the Senate in the case of an indebtedness to the Senate, and such latter officials are authorized and directed, respectively, to deduct from any salary, mileage, or expense money due to any such delinquent such certified amounts or so much thereof as the balance or balances due such delinquent may cover. Sums so deducted by the Secretary of the Senate shall be disposed of by him in accordance with existing law, and sums so deducted by the Chief Administrative Officer of the House of Representatives shall be disposed of by him in accordance with existing law.

(June 19, 1934, ch. 648, title I, § 1, 48 Stat. 1024; Pub. L. 104–186, title II, § 203(8), Aug. 20, 1996, 110 Stat. 1726.)

AMENDMENTS

1996—Pub. L. 104–186 substituted "Chief Administrative Officer of the House of Representatives in" for "Sergeant at Arms of the House in" and "Chief Administrative Officer of the House of Representatives shall be" for "Sergeant at Arms of the House shall be paid to the Clerk of the House and".

§§ 41, 42. Repealed. Pub. L. 104–186, title II, § 203(9)(A), (10), Aug. 20, 1996, 110 Stat. 1726

Section 41, R.S. § 43, provided that no Member or Delegate was entitled to any allowance for newspapers.

Section 42, based on H. Res. No. 420, Ninety-second Congress, May 18, 1971, enacted into permanent law by Pub. L. 92–184, ch. IV, Dec. 15, 1971, 85 Stat. 636, related to furnishing of postage stamps to Members, committees, and officers of House of Representatives.

A prior section 42, R.S. § 44, which proscribed compensation or allowance to Senators, Representatives, or Delegates for postage, was repealed by Pub. L. 104–186, title II, § 203(11), Aug. 20, 1996, 110 Stat. 1726. See sections 42a and 46a of this title.

APPLICABILITY OF PROHIBITION DURING NINETY-FIFTH CONGRESS

Section 302(c) of H. Res. No. 287, Ninety-fifth Congress, Mar. 2, 1977, enacted into permanent law by Pub. L. 95–94, title I, § 115, Aug. 5, 1977, 91 Stat. 668, which

provided that former section 41 of this title was to have no effect during the Ninety-fifth Congress, was repealed by Pub. L. 104–186, title II, § 203(9)(B), Aug. 20, 1996, 110 Stat. 1726.

§ 42a. Special delivery postage allowance for President of Senate

The Secretary of the Senate is authorized and directed to procure and furnish each fiscal year (commencing with the fiscal year ending September 30, 1982) to the President of the Senate, upon request by such person, United States special delivery postage stamps in such amount as may be necessary for the mailing of postal matters arising in connection with his official business.

(Pub. L. 97–51, § 127(a)(1), Oct. 1, 1981, 95 Stat. 965.)

PRIOR PROVISIONS

A prior section 42a, acts July 1, 1941, ch. 268, 55 Stat. 450; June 26, 1944, ch. 277, title I, 58 Stat. 339; June 13, 1945, ch. 189, 59 Stat. 243; Oct. 11, 1951, ch. 485, 65 Stat. 391; July 2, 1954, ch. 455, title I, 68 Stat. 402; Aug. 5, 1955, ch. 568, 69 Stat. 503; June 27, 1956, ch. 453, 70 Stat. 359; July 31, 1958, Pub. L. 85–570, 72 Stat. 442; July 12, 1960, Pub. L. 86–628, 74 Stat. 449; Dec. 30, 1963, Pub. L. 88–248, 77 Stat. 805; July 27, 1965, Pub. L. 89–90, 79 Stat. 268; July 23, 1968, Pub. L. 90–417, 82 Stat. 400; Dec. 12, 1969, Pub. L. 91–145, 83 Stat. 342; July 9, 1971, Pub. L. 92–51, 85 Stat. 128; Oct. 31, 1972, Pub. L. 92–607, ch. V, § 506(k)(1), formerly § 506(h)(1), 86 Stat. 1508, redesignated § 506(i)(1) by Pub. L. 95–391, title I, Sept. 30, 1978, 92 Stat. 773, redesignated § 506(j)(1) by Pub. L. 96–304, title I, § 101, July 8, 1980, 94 Stat. 889, and redesignated § 506(k)(1) by Pub. L. 97–276, § 101(e), Oct. 2, 1982, 96 Stat. 1189, provided for an airmail and special-delivery postage allowance for President of the Senate, prior to repeal by section 127(a)(2) of Pub. L. 97–51.

§§ 42a–1, 42b. Omitted

CODIFICATION

Section 42a–1, act July 2, 1954, ch. 455, title I, 68 Stat. 402, prescribed airmail and special-delivery postage allowances for Speaker and House majority and minority leaders and whips, and was omitted from the Code as superseded by former section 42d of this title.

Section 42b, acts June 22, 1949, ch. 235, 63 Stat. 222; July 2, 1954, ch. 455, title I, 68 Stat. 402, prescribed airmail and special-delivery postage allowances for each House standing committee, and was omitted from the Code as superseded by former section 42c of this title.

§§ 42c, 42d. Repealed. Pub. L. 104–186, title II, § 203(12), Aug. 20, 1996, 110 Stat. 1726

Section 42c, Pub. L. 85–778, § 1, Aug. 27, 1958, 72 Stat. 934; H. Res. No. 532, Eighty-eighth Congress, Oct. 2, 1963, enacted into permanent law by Pub. L. 88–454, § 103, Aug. 20, 1964, 78 Stat. 550; H. Res. No. 1003, Ninetieth Congress, Dec. 14, 1967, enacted into permanent law by Pub. L. 90–392, title I, July 9, 1968, 82 Stat. 318, related to airmail and special delivery stamps for House Members and standing committees.

Section 42d, Pub. L. 85–778, § 2, Aug. 27, 1958, 72 Stat. 934; H. Res. No. 532, Eighty-eighth Congress, Oct. 2, 1963, enacted into permanent law by Pub. L. 88–454, § 103, Aug. 20, 1964, 78 Stat. 550; H. Res. No. 1003, Ninetieth Congress, Dec. 14, 1967, enacted into permanent law by Pub. L. 90–392, title I, July 9, 1968, 82 Stat. 318, related to airmail and special delivery stamps for House Speaker, leaders, whips, and officers.

EXISTING ENTITLEMENTS

Sections 3 and 4 of Pub. L. 85–778, which provided that Members, committees, and officers of the House of Representatives retained their existing entitlements to airmail and special delivery postage stamps until June 30, 1959, and thereafter the airmail and special delivery stamps made available under former sections 42c and 42d of this title were to be in lieu of any made available under any other law, were repealed by Pub. L. 104–186, title II, §203(12), Aug. 20, 1996, 110 Stat. 1726.

§§43, 43a. Omitted

CODIFICATION

Section 43, acts July 28, 1866, ch. 296, §17, 14 Stat. 323; Aug. 11, 1993, Pub. L. 103–69, title III, §310(a), 107 Stat. 712, provided for Senators to receive mileage for travel to and from regular sessions, and was omitted from the Code in view of the termination of mileage under this section for Senators by section 1(a) of Pub. L. 104–53, set out below.

Section 43a, acts July 8, 1935, ch. 374, 49 Stat. 459; Aug. 11, 1993, Pub. L. 103–69, title III, §310(b), 107 Stat. 712, provided for President of Senate to be paid mileage, and was omitted from the Code in view of the termination of mileage under this section for President of Senate by section 1(b) of Pub. L. 104–53, set out below.

TERMINATION OF MILEAGE FOR SENATORS AND PRESIDENT OF SENATE

Pub. L. 104–53, title I, §1, Nov. 19, 1995, 109 Stat. 517, provided that:

"(a) On and after October 1, 1995, no Senator shall receive mileage under section 17 of the Act of July 28, 1866 (2 U.S.C. 43).

"(b) On and after October 1, 1995, the President of the Senate shall not receive mileage under the first section of the Act of July 8, 1935 (2 U.S.C. 43a)."

§§43b, 43b–1. Repealed. Pub. L. 104–186, title II, §203(13), (14), Aug. 20, 1996, 110 Stat. 1726

Section 43b, Pub. L. 85–570, July 31, 1958, 72 Stat. 443; Pub. L. 86–176, Aug. 21, 1959, 73 Stat. 401; Pub. L. 88–70, July 19, 1963, 77 Stat. 82; Pub. L. 89–90, July 27, 1965, 79 Stat. 269; Pub. L. 89–147, §1, Aug. 28, 1965, 79 Stat. 583; Pub. L. 89–545, Aug. 27, 1966, 80 Stat. 358; Pub. L. 90–86, §1, Sept. 17, 1967, 81 Stat. 226; Pub. L. 91–145, Dec. 12, 1969, 83 Stat. 343; Pub. L. 92–51, July 9, 1971, 85 Stat. 128; Pub. L. 92–607, ch. V, §§502, 506(k)(2), formerly §506(h)(2), Oct. 31, 1972, 86 Stat. 1504, 1508, renumbered §506(i)(2), Pub. L. 95–391, title I, §108(a), Sept. 30, 1978, 92 Stat. 773, renumbered §506(j)(2), Pub. L. 96–304, title I, §101, July 8, 1980, 94 Stat. 889, renumbered §506(k)(2), Pub. L. 97–276, §101(e), Oct. 2, 1982, 96 Stat. 1189, provided for reimbursement of House Members for additional transportation expenses.

Section 43b–1, Pub. L. 89–147, §2, Aug. 28, 1965, 79 Stat. 583; Pub. L. 90–86, §2, Sept. 17, 1967, 81 Stat. 226, authorized election by House Members of lump sum transportation payments in lieu of reimbursement of transportation expenses.

§43b–2. Staff expenses for House Members attending organizational caucus or conference

(a) Each Member-elect (other than an incumbent Member reelected to the ensuing Congress) who attends a caucus or conference called under section 29a(a) of this title, and each incumbent Member reelected to the ensuing Congress who attends any such caucus or conference convening after the adjournment sine die of the Congress in the year involved, shall be entitled to designate one staff person to be paid for one round trip between that person's place of residence, provided such place of residence is in the district which the Member-elect or incumbent Member represents, and Washington, District of Columbia, for the purpose of accompanying that Member-elect or incumbent Member to such caucus or conference.

(b) Each Member-elect (other than an incumbent Member reelected to the ensuing Congress) who attends a caucus or conference called under such section 29a(a) of this title shall be entitled to designate one staff person who shall in addition be reimbursed on a per diem or other basis for expenses incurred in accompanying the Member-elect at the time of such caucus or conference for a period not to exceed the shorter of the following—

(i) the period beginning with the day before the designated date upon which such caucus or conference is to convene and ending with the day after the date of the final adjournment of such caucus or conference; or

(ii) fourteen days.

(Pub. L. 94–59, title II, July 25, 1975, 89 Stat. 282.)

CODIFICATION

Section is based on section 1 of House Resolution No. 10, Ninety-fourth Congress, Jan. 14, 1975, which was enacted into permanent law by Pub. L. 94–59.

SECTION REFERRED TO IN OTHER SECTIONS

This section is referred to in section 43b–3 of this title.

§43b–3. Payments and reimbursements for certain House staff expenses

(a) Payments and reimbursements to staff persons under section 43b–2 of this title shall be made as provided (with respect to staff) in the regulations prescribed by the Committee on House Oversight with respect to travel and other expenses of staff. Reimbursements shall be paid on special voucher forms prescribed by the Committee on House Oversight.

(b) Additional funds, if any, for staff allowances and office space for use by Members-elect (other than an incumbent Member reelected to the ensuing Congress) shall be authorized by the Committee on House Oversight.

(Pub. L. 94–59, title II, July 25, 1975, 89 Stat. 282; Pub. L. 104–186, title II, §203(15), Aug. 20, 1996, 110 Stat. 1727.)

CODIFICATION

Section is based on section 2 of House Resolution No. 10, Ninety-fourth Congress, Jan. 14, 1975, which was enacted into permanent law by Pub. L. 94–59.

AMENDMENTS

1996—Pub. L. 104–186 substituted "House Oversight" for "House Administration" wherever appearing.

CHANGE OF NAME

Committee on House Oversight of House of Representatives changed to Committee on House Administration of House of Representatives by House Resolution No. 5, One Hundred Sixth Congress, Jan. 6, 1999.

§43c. Repealed. Pub. L. 89–147, §4, Aug. 28, 1965, 79 Stat. 584

Section, Pub. L. 86–628, §105(c), July 12, 1960, 74 Stat. 461, restricted payment of travel or subsistence expenses of Senators and Representatives to specifically authorized trips, official participation in funeral services of deceased Members, and official trips originating in Senator's State or Representative's district when Congress was not in session.

§ 43d. Organizational expenses of Senator-elect

(a) Appointment of employees by Secretary of Senate to assist; termination of employment

Upon the recommendation of a Senator-elect (other than an incumbent Senator or a Senator elected to fill a vacancy), the Secretary of the Senate shall appoint two employees to assist such Senator-elect. Any employee so appointed shall serve through the day before the date on which the Senator-elect recommending his appointment commences his service as a Senator, except that his employment may be terminated before such day upon recommendation of such Senator-elect.

(b) Payment of salaries of appointed employees; funding; maximum amount

(1) Salaries of employees appointed under subsection (a) of this section shall be paid from the appropriation for "Administrative, Clerical, and Legislative Assistance to Senators".

(2) Salaries paid to employees appointed upon recommendation of a Senator-elect under subsection (a) of this section shall be charged against the amount of compensation which may be paid to employees in his office under section 61–1(d) of this title (hereinafter referred to as the "clerk-hire allowance"), for the fiscal year in which his service as a Senator commences. The total amount of salaries paid to employees so appointed upon recommendation of a Senator-elect shall be charged against his clerk-hire allowance for each month in such fiscal year beginning with the month in which his service as a Senator commences (until the total amount has been charged) by whichever of the following amounts is greater: (1) one-ninth of the amount of salaries so paid, or (2) the amount by which the aggregate amount of his clerk-hire allowance which may be paid as of the close of such month under section 61–1(d)(1)(B) of this title exceeds the aggregate amount of his clerk-hire allowance actually paid as of the close of such month.

(c) Payment of transportation and per diem expenses of Senator-elect and appointed employees for one round trip from home State to Washington, D.C. for business of impending Congress; funding; maximum amount

Each Senator-elect and each employee appointed under subsection (a) of this section is authorized one round trip from the home State of the Senator-elect to Washington, D.C., and return, for the purposes of attending conferences, caucuses, or organizational meetings, or for any other official business connected with the impending Congress. In addition, each Senator-elect and each such employee is authorized per diem for not more than seven days while en route to and from Washington, D.C., and while in Washington, D.C. Such transportation and per diem expenses shall be in the same amounts as are payable to Senators and employees in the office of a Senator under section 58(e) of this title, and shall be paid from the contingent fund of the Senate upon itemized vouchers certified by the Senator-elect concerned and approved by the Secretary of the Senate.

(d) Payment of telegrams, telephone services, and stationery expenses

(1) Each Senator-elect is authorized to be reimbursed for expenses incurred for telegrams, telephone services, and stationery related to his position as a Senator-elect in an amount not exceeding one-twelfth of the total amount of expenses authorized to be paid to or on behalf of a Senator from the State which he will represent under section 58 of this title. Reimbursement to a Senator-elect under this subsection shall be paid from the contingent fund of the Senate upon itemized vouchers certified by such Senator-elect and approved by the Secretary of the Senate.

(2) Amounts reimbursed to a Senator-elect under this subsection shall be charged against the amount of expenses which are authorized to be paid to him or on his behalf under section 58 of this title, for each of the twelve months beginning with the month in which his service as a Senator commences (until all of such amounts have been charged) by whichever of the following amounts is greater: (1) one-twelfth of the amounts so reimbursed, or (2) the amount by which the aggregate amount authorized to be so paid under section 58(c) of this title as of the close of such month exceeds the aggregate amount actually paid under such section 58 as of the close of such month.

(e) Effective Date

This section shall take effect on October 1, 1978.

(Pub. L. 95–355, title I, § 105, Sept. 8, 1978, 92 Stat. 534; Pub. L. 104–197, title I, § 2, Sept. 16, 1996, 110 Stat. 2397.)

AMENDMENTS

1996—Subsec. (d)(1). Pub. L. 104–197 substituted ", telephone services, and stationery" for "and telephone services".

SENATORS' OFFICIAL PERSONNEL AND OFFICE EXPENSE ACCOUNT

References in any law, rule, regulation, or order to Senate appropriation account for Administrative, Clerical, and Legislative Assistance Allowance to Senators deemed references to the "Senators' Official Personnel and Office Expense Account", see section 58c(2) of this title.

§§ 44 to 46. Omitted

CODIFICATION

Section 44, act May 7, 1906, ch. 2083, § 1, 34 Stat. 170, authorized a mileage allowance to Delegate from Alaska, and was omitted from the Code as obsolete because Alaska was admitted into the Union with membership of one Representative in Congress on Jan. 3, 1959, upon issuance of Proc. No. 3269, Jan. 3, 1959, 24 F.R. 81, 73 Stat. c16, as required by sections 1, 7 and 8 of Pub. L. 85–508, July 7, 1958, 72 Stat. 339, set out as notes preceding section 21 of Title 48, Territories and Insular Possessions.

Section 45, acts July 1, 1902, ch. 1369, § 8, 32 Stat. 694; Aug. 29, 1916, ch. 416, § 20, 39 Stat. 552, which authorized a mileage allowance to Resident Commissioners from Philippine Islands, and was formerly covered by section 1237 of Title 48, Territories and Insular Possessions, is no longer in force in view of the independence of the Philippine Islands effected by section 1394 of Title 22, Foreign Relations and Intercourse, and proclaimed by the President of the United States in Proc. No. 2695,

July 4, 1946, 11 F.R. 7517, 60 Stat. 1352, set out as note under section 1394 of Title 22. Act Aug. 29, 1916, ch. 416, § 20, 39 Stat. 552, from which section 45 of this title was derived, was repealed by Pub. L. 89–554, § 8(a), Sept. 6, 1966, 80 Stat. 643.

Section 46, acts Mar. 2, 1917, ch. 145, § 36, 39 Stat. 963; May 17, 1932, ch. 190, 47 Stat. 158, allowed sum of $500 as mileage for each session to Resident Commissioner, and was omitted from the Code as superseded by former section 43b–1 of this title.

§ 46a. Stationery allowance for President of Senate

Effective April 1, 1975, and each fiscal year thereafter, the annual allowance for stationery for the President of the Senate shall be $4,500.

(July 1, 1941, ch. 268, 55 Stat. 450; June 13, 1945, ch. 189, 59 Stat. 244; June 14, 1948, ch. 467, 62 Stat. 425; Oct. 11, 1951, ch. 485, 65 Stat. 391; Aug. 1, 1953, ch. 304, title I, 67 Stat. 320; Aug. 5, 1955, ch. 568, 69 Stat. 504; Pub. L. 88–258, title IV, Jan. 6, 1964, 77 Stat. 864; Pub. L. 90–21, title I, May 29, 1967, 81 Stat. 38; Pub. L. 91–145, Dec. 12, 1969, 83 Stat. 342; Pub. L. 92–51, July 9, 1971, 85 Stat. 128; Pub. L. 92–184, ch. IV, Dec. 15, 1971, 85 Stat. 635; Pub. L. 92–607, ch. V, § 506(k)(3), formerly § 506(h)(3), Oct. 31, 1972, 86 Stat. 1508, renumbered § 506(i)(3), Pub. L. 95–391, title I, § 108(a), Sept. 30, 1978, 92 Stat. 773, renumbered § 506(j)(3), Pub. L. 96–304, title I, § 101(e), July 8, 1980, 94 Stat. 889, renumbered § 506(k)(3), Pub. L. 97–276, § 101(e), Oct. 2, 1982, 96 Stat. 1189; Pub. L. 94–32, title I, June 12, 1975, 89 Stat. 182.)

Codification

Section is from Legislative Branch Appropriation Act, 1942, and subsequent Legislative Branch Appropriation Acts.

Amendments

1975—Pub. L. 94–32 substituted "Effective April 1, 1975, and each fiscal year thereafter" for "Effective with the fiscal year 1972 and thereafter" and "$4,500" for "$3,600".

1972—Pub. L. 92–607 repealed this section insofar as it related to Senators. For purposes of codification this entailed substituting a period for a comma following "President of the Senate shall be $3,600" and striking out provisions which allowed Senators from $3,600 to $5,000 annually depending on the population of the Senator's home State. See section 58 of this title.

1971—Pub. L. 92–184 inserted provision for an increased allowance for Senators from more populous States ranging from $3,800 for Senators from States of from 3,000,000 to 4,999,999 population to $5,000 for Senators from States of 17,000,000 population and over.

Pub. L. 92–51 provided allowance for Senators from States having population of ten million or more inhabitants of $4,000 per annum effective fiscal year 1972 and thereafter.

1969—Pub. L. 91–145 increased allowance from $3,000 to $3,600 effective with fiscal year 1970.

1967—Pub. L. 90–21 increased allowance from $2,400 to $3,000 effective with fiscal year 1967.

1964—Pub. L. 88–258 increased allowance from $1,800 to $2,400 effective with fiscal year 1964.

1955—Act Aug. 5, 1955, increased allowance from $1,200 to $1,800.

1953—Act Aug. 1, 1953, increased allowance from $800 to $1,200 effective with fiscal year 1954.

1951—Act Oct. 11, 1951, increased allowance from $500 to $800.

1948—Act June 14, 1948, increased allowance from $400 to $500.

1945—Act June 13, 1945, increased allowance from $200 to $400.

Effective Date of 1972 Amendment

Section 506(k), formerly § 506(h), of Pub. L. 92–607, renumbered § 506(i) by Pub. L. 95–391, title I, § 108(a), Sept. 30, 1978, 92 Stat. 773, renumbered § 506(j) by Pub. L. 96–304, title I, § 101, July 8, 1980, 94 Stat. 889, and renumbered § 506(k) by Pub. L. 97–276, § 101(e), Oct. 2, 1982, 96 Stat. 1189, provided that the amendment made by that section is effective Jan. 1, 1973.

Additional Allowances

The following acts authorized additional stationery allowances for each Senator and the President of the Senate:

July 15, 1952, ch. 758, Ch. II, 66 Stat. 639.
Sept. 27, 1950, ch. 1052, Ch. II, 64 Stat. 1047.
Oct. 10, 1949, ch. 662, title I, 63 Stat. 738.
May 10, 1948, ch. 270, 62 Stat. 213.
May 1, 1947, ch. 49, title I, 61 Stat. 58.
July 23, 1946, ch. 591, title I, 60 Stat. 602.
Dec. 28, 1945, ch. 589, title I, 59 Stat. 633.

§ 46a–1. Senate revolving fund for stationery allowances; availability of unexpended balances; withdrawals

There is established within the Contingent Fund of the Senate a revolving fund which shall consist of (1) the unexpended balance of the appropriation "Contingent Expenses, Senate, Stationery, fiscal year 1957", (2) any amounts hereafter appropriated for stationery allowances of the President of the Senate, and for stationery for use of officers of the Senate and the Conference of the Majority and the Conference of the Minority of the Senate, and (3) any undeposited amounts heretofore received, and any amounts hereafter received as proceeds of sales by the stationery room of the Senate. Any moneys in the fund shall be available until expended for use in the same manner and for the same purposes as funds heretofore appropriated to the Contingent Fund of the Senate for stationery, except that (1) the balance of any amount appropriated for stationery for use of committees and officers of the Senate which remains unexpended at the end of any fiscal year and (2) allowances which are not available for obligation due to vacancies or waiver of entitlement thereto, shall be withdrawn from the revolving fund. Disbursements from the fund shall be made upon vouchers approved by the Secretary of the Senate, or his designee.

(Pub. L. 85–58, ch. XI, June 21, 1957, 71 Stat. 188; Pub. L. 92–607, ch. V, § 506(l), formerly § 506(i), Oct. 31, 1972, 86 Stat. 1508, renumbered § 506(j), Pub. L. 95–391, title I, § 108(a), Sept. 30, 1978, 92 Stat. 773, renumbered § 506(k) and amended Pub. L. 96–304, title I, §§ 101, 112(b)(3), July 8, 1980, 94 Stat. 889, 892, renumbered § 506(l), Pub. L. 97–276, § 101(e), Oct. 2, 1982, 96 Stat. 1189; Pub. L. 105–55, title I, § 7, Oct. 7, 1997, 111 Stat. 1181.)

Amendments

1997—Pub. L. 105–55, which directed the amendment of section 1101 of Pub. L. 85–58 by inserting at end "Disbursements from the fund shall be made upon vouchers approved by the Secretary of the Senate, or his designee.", was executed by making the insertion at the end of this section which is second par. under heading "CONTINGENT EXPENSES OF THE SENATE" to reflect the probable intent of Congress.

1980—Pub. L. 96–304, § 112(b)(3), substituted in cl. (2), "officers of the Senate and the Conference of the Majority and the Conference of the Minority of the Senate" for "committees and officers of the Senate".

1972—Pub. L. 92–607 struck out "and of Senators" after "the President of the Senate".

EFFECTIVE DATE OF 1980 AMENDMENT

Section 112(b) of Pub. L. 96–304 provided that the amendment made by section 112(b)(3) of Pub. L. 96–304 is effective as of the close of Feb. 28, 1981.

EFFECTIVE DATE OF 1972 AMENDMENT

Section 506(l), formerly § 506(i), of Pub. L. 92–607, renumbered § 506(j) by Pub. L. 95–391, title I, § 108(a), Sept. 30, 1978, 92 Stat. 773, renumbered § 506(k) by Pub. L. 96–304, title I, § 101, July 8, 1980, 94 Stat. 889, and renumbered § 506(l) by Pub. L. 97–276, § 101(e), Oct. 2, 1982, 96 Stat. 1189, provided that the amendment made by that section is effective Jan. 1, 1973.

TRANSFER OF MONEYS TO FUND BY SECRETARY OF THE SENATE

Pub. L. 101–163, title I, § 6, Nov. 21, 1989, 103 Stat. 1045, provided that: "On and after the date this Act becomes law [Nov. 21, 1989], the Secretary of the Senate, subject to the approval of the Committee on Appropriations of the Senate, is authorized to provide up to $1,000,000 for capitalization purposes to the revolving fund established by the last paragraph under the heading 'Contingent Expenses of the Senate' appearing under the heading 'SENATE' in chapter XI of the Third Supplemental Appropriation Act, 1957 (2 U.S.C. 46a–1), by transferring to such revolving fund any funds available from any Senate appropriation account, with respect to which he has disbursement authority, for the fiscal year in which the transfer is made (or for any preceding fiscal year) or which have been made available until expended; and any moneys so transferred shall be available for use in like manner and to the same extent as the moneys in such revolving fund which were not transferred thereto pursuant to this section."

§ 46a–2. Omitted

CODIFICATION

Section, Pub. L. 89–545, § 101, Aug. 27, 1966, 80 Stat. 356, provided, effective fiscal year 1967 and thereafter, for stationery allowance of $3,000 per annum for Senators from States having population of 10 million or more inhabitants. See amendment by Pub. L. 90–21 to section 46a of this title providing such an allowance to all Senators effective fiscal year 1967 and thereafter.

§ 46a–3. Repealed. Pub. L. 92–607, ch. V, § 506(k)(4), formerly § 506(h)(4), Oct. 31, 1972, 86 Stat. 1508, renumbered § 506(i)(4), Pub. L. 95–391, title I, § 108(a), Sept. 30, 1978, 92 Stat. 773, renumbered § 506(j)(4), Pub. L. 96–304, title I, § 101, July 8, 1980, 94 Stat. 889, renumbered § 506(k)(4), Pub. L. 97–276, § 101(e), Oct. 2, 1982, 96 Stat. 1189

Section, Pub. L. 90–417, § 106, July 23, 1968, 82 Stat. 413, placed limits on the availability of the stationery allowance for Senators. See section 58 of this title.

EFFECTIVE DATE OF REPEAL

Section 506(k), formerly § 506(h), of Pub. L. 92–607, as amended by Pub. L. 93–145, § 101, Nov. 1, 1973, 87 Stat. 532, and renumbered § 506(i) by Pub. L. 95–391, title I, § 108(a), Sept. 30, 1978, 92 Stat. 773, renumbered § 506(j) by Pub. L. 96–304, title I, § 101, July 8, 1980, 94 Stat. 889, and renumbered § 506(k) by Pub. L. 97–276, § 101(e), Oct. 2, 1982, 96 Stat. 1189, provided that, insofar as this section has application to Senators, the repeal is effective Jan. 1, 1973.

§ 46a–4. Omitted

CODIFICATION

Section, Pub. L. 91–145, Dec. 12, 1969, 83 Stat. 342, made section 46a–3 of this title applicable to President of Senate, and was omitted from the Code in view of the repeal of section 46a–3.

§ 46b. Repealed. Pub. L. 104–186, title II, § 203(16), Aug. 20, 1996, 110 Stat. 1727

Section, acts July 2, 1954, ch. 455, title I, 68 Stat. 402; July 12, 1960, Pub. L. 86–628, 74 Stat. 452; H. Res. No. 533, Eighty-eighth Congress, Oct. 2, 1963, enacted into permanent law by act Aug. 20, 1964, Pub. L. 88–454, § 103, 78 Stat. 550; H. Res. No. 1029, Eighty-ninth Congress, Oct. 5, 1966; H. Res. No. 112, Ninetieth Congress, Mar. 8, 1967, enacted into permanent law by act May 29, 1967, Pub. L. 90–21, title I, 81 Stat. 38, related to stationery allowance for House Members.

Provisions similar to those in this section were contained in the following prior acts:

Aug. 1, 1953, ch. 304, title I, 67 Stat. 324.
July 9, 1952, ch. 598, 66 Stat. 469.
Oct. 11, 1951, ch. 486, 65 Stat. 394.
Sept. 6, 1950, ch. 896, Ch. II, 64 Stat. 600.
June 22, 1949, ch. 235, 63 Stat. 221.
June 14, 1948, ch. 467, 62 Stat. 428.
July 17, 1947, ch. 262, 61 Stat. 366.
June 16, 1939, ch. 208, 53 Stat. 830.

§ 46b–1. House revolving fund for stationery allowances; disposition of moneys from stationery sales; availability of unexpended balances

There is established a revolving fund for the purpose of administering the funds appropriated for stationery allowances to each Representative, Delegate, the Resident Commissioner from Puerto Rico; and stationery for use of the committees, departments, and officers of the House. All moneys hereafter received by the stationery room of the House of Representatives from the sale of stationery supplies and other equipment shall be deposited in the revolving fund and shall be available for disbursement from the fund in the same manner as other sums that may be appropriated by the Congress for this purpose. The unexpended balance of all moneys heretofore received by the stationery room of the House of Representatives from the sale of stationery supplies and equipment shall be deposited in the Treasury of the United States to the credit of the fund: *Provided*, That the unexpended balances in the appropriations "Contingent expenses, House of Representatives, stationery, 1945–1946"; "Contingent expenses, House of Representatives, stationery, 1946"; "Contingent expenses, House of Representatives, stationery, 1947–48", as of June 30, 1947, shall be transferred to and made available for expenditure out of the fund, together with appropriations herein or hereafter made therefor, to remain available until expended.

(July 17, 1947, ch. 262, 61 Stat. 366.)

CHANGE OF NAME

Stationery room of House of Representatives redesignated Office Supply Service.

§ 46b–2. Repealed. Pub. L. 104–186, title II, § 203(17), Aug. 20, 1996, 110 Stat. 1727

Section, act Feb. 27, 1956, ch. 73, 70 Stat. 31, provided for prorated stationery allowance for House Members.

§§ 46c, 46d. Repealed. Pub. L. 90–57, July 28, 1967, 81 Stat. 129

Section 46c, acts June 13, 1945, ch. 189, 59 Stat. 244; July 1, 1946, ch. 530, 60 Stat. 392; Aug. 2, 1946, ch. 753, title I, § 102, 60 Stat. 814; Nov. 1, 1951, ch. 665, Ch. 1, 65 Stat. 760; Aug. 1, 1953, ch. 304, title I, 67 Stat. 321; June 27, 1956, ch. 453, 70 Stat. 360; Jan. 6, 1964, Pub. L. 88–258, title IV, 77 Stat. 863; July 27, 1965, Pub. L. 89–90, 79 Stat. 268; Aug. 27, 1966, Pub. L. 89–545, 80 Stat. 357, provided for payment of long-distance telephone calls for Senators and Vice President made to and from Washington, D.C. See section 58 of this title.

Section 46d, acts June 13, 1945, ch. 189, 59 Stat. 244; July 1, 1946, ch. 530, 60 Stat. 392; Aug. 2, 1946, ch. 753, title I, § 102, 60 Stat. 814; Aug. 1, 1953, ch. 304, title I, 67 Stat. 321; July 2, 1954, ch. 455, title I, 68 Stat. 400; July 31, 1958, Pub. L. 85–570, 72 Stat. 442; July 27, 1965, Pub. L. 89–90, 79 Stat. 268, provided for payment from contingent fund of Senate of long-distance telephone calls for Senators, originating and terminating outside Washington, D.C., and additional payments for calls to or from Washington, D.C. See section 58 of this title.

EFFECTIVE DATE OF REPEAL

Pub. L. 90–57 provided that the repeal is effective Jan. 1, 1968.

§ 46d–1. Long-distance telephone calls for Vice President

Commencing January 20, 1949, the provisions of existing law relating to long-distance telephone calls for Senators shall be equally applicable to the Vice President of the United States.

(May 24, 1949, ch. 138, title I, 63 Stat. 77.)

§ 46d–2. Repealed. Pub. L. 90–57, July 28, 1967, 81 Stat. 130

Section, Pub. L. 89–90, § 101, July 27, 1965, 79 Stat. 268, provided for computation of long-distance telephone calls for Senators, wide area telephone service contracts, and effective date of changes. See section 58 of this title.

EFFECTIVE DATE OF REPEAL

Pub. L. 90–57 provided that the repeal is effective Jan. 1, 1968.

§ 46d–3. Repealed. Pub. L. 92–184, ch. IV, Dec. 15, 1971, 85 Stat. 635

Section, Pub. L. 90–21, title I, May 29, 1967, 81 Stat. 38, made contingent fund of Senate available for reimbursement of each Senator of strictly official telephone service charges incurred outside District of Columbia up to $300 in each fiscal quarter. See section 58 of this title.

EFFECTIVE DATE OF REPEAL

Pub. L. 92–184 provided that the repeal is effective Jan. 1, 1972.

§ 46d–4. Repealed. Pub. L. 92–607, ch. V, § 506(k)(5), formerly § 506(h)(5), Oct. 31, 1972, 86 Stat. 1508, renumbered § 506(i)(5), Pub. L. 95–391, title I, § 108(a), Sept. 30, 1978, 92 Stat. 773, renumbered § 506(j)(5), Pub. L. 96–304, title I, § 101, July 8, 1980, 94 Stat. 889, renumbered § 506(k)(5), Pub. L. 97–276, § 101(e), Oct. 2, 1982, 96 Stat. 1189

Section, Pub. L. 90–57, July 28, 1967, 81 Stat. 130, authorized payment from contingent fund of Senate of charges for long distance telephone calls by Senators. See section 58 of this title.

EFFECTIVE DATE OF REPEAL

Section 506(k), formerly § 506(h), of Pub. L. 92–607, renumbered § 506(i) by Pub. L. 95–391, title I, § 108(a), Sept. 30, 1978, 92 Stat. 773, renumbered § 506(j) by Pub. L. 96–304 title I, § 101, July 8, 1980, 94 Stat. 889, and renum-

bered § 506(k) by Pub. L. 97–276, § 101(e), Oct. 2, 1982, 96 Stat. 1189, provided that the repeal is effective Jan. 1, 1973.

§ 46d–5. Repealed. Pub. L. 92–342, July 10, 1972, 86 Stat. 435

Section, Pub. L. 91–382, Aug. 18, 1970, 84 Stat. 810, related to reimbursement to Senators and President of Senate of official telephone and telegraph communications charges incurred by them or on their behalf out of contingent fund of Senate up to a maximum of $150 per annum.

EFFECTIVE DATE OF REPEAL

Pub. L. 92–342 provided that the repeal is effective July 1, 1972.

§ 46e. Repealed. Pub. L. 92–607, ch. V, § 506(k)(6), formerly § 506(h)(6), Oct. 31, 1972, 86 Stat. 1508, renumbered § 506(i)(6), Pub. L. 95–391, title I, § 108(a), Sept. 30, 1978, 92 Stat. 773, renumbered § 506(j)(6), Pub. L. 96–304, title I, § 101, July 8, 1980, 94 Stat. 889, renumbered § 506(k)(6), Pub. L. 97–276, § 101(e), Oct. 2, 1982, 96 Stat. 1189

Section, acts July 1, 1946, ch. 530, 60 Stat. 392; Aug. 2, 1946, ch. 753, title I, § 102, 60 Stat. 814, authorized the payment of charges for telegrams by Senators. See section 58 of this title.

EFFECTIVE DATE OF REPEAL

Section 506(k), formerly § 506(h), of Pub. L. 92–607, renumbered § 506(i) by Pub. L. 95–391, title I, § 108(a), Sept. 30, 1978, 92 Stat. 773, renumbered § 506(j) by Pub. L. 96–304, title I, § 101, July 8, 1980, 94 Stat. 889, and renumbered § 506(k) by Pub. L. 97–276, § 101(e), Oct. 2, 1982, 96 Stat. 1189, provided that the repeal is effective Jan. 1, 1973.

§ 46f. Repealed. Pub. L. 104–186, title II, § 203(18)(A), Aug. 20, 1996, 110 Stat. 1727

Section, acts June 23, 1949, ch. 238, § 1, 63 Stat. 264; May 29, 1951, ch. 117, § 1, 65 Stat. 47; Mar. 10, 1953, ch. 6, § 1, 67 Stat. 5; Feb. 27, 1956, ch. 74, § 1, 70 Stat. 31; Sept. 21, 1959, Pub. L. 86–340, § 1, 73 Stat. 605, related to telephone, telegraph, and radiotelegraph allowances for Representatives, Delegates, and Resident Commissioner.

§ 46f–1. Repealed. Feb. 27, 1956, ch. 74, § 2(b), 70 Stat. 32

Section, act July 2, 1954, ch. 455, title I, 68 Stat. 402, fixed maximum minute allowance on long distance telephone calls of House Members, Delegates, and Resident Commissioner.

EFFECTIVE DATE OF REPEAL

Section 3 of act Feb. 27, 1956, provided that: "The amendments made by this Act [amending sections 46f and 46g of this title and repealing this section] shall take effect as of noon on January 3, 1956."

§§ 46g, 46g–1. Repealed. Pub. L. 104–186, title II, § 203(18)(B), (19), Aug. 20, 1996, 110 Stat. 1727, 1728

Section 46g, acts June 23, 1949, ch. 238, § 2, 63 Stat. 265; May 29, 1951, ch. 117, § 1, 65 Stat. 47; July 8, 1952, ch. 590, § 1, 66 Stat. 443; Mar. 10, 1953, ch. 6, § 1, 67 Stat. 5; Feb. 27, 1956, ch. 74, § 2(a), (c), 70 Stat. 32; Sept. 4, 1957, Pub. L. 85–289, § 1, 71 Stat. 614; Sept. 21, 1959, Pub. L. 86–340, § 2, 73 Stat. 605; H. Res. No. 735, Eighty-seventh Congress, July 25, 1962, enacted into permanent law by act Dec. 30, 1963, Pub. L. 88–248, § 103, 77 Stat. 817; H. Res. No. 531, Eighty-eighth Congress, Oct. 2, 1963, enacted into permanent law by act Aug. 20, 1964, Pub. L. 88–454, § 103, 78 Stat. 550; Aug. 21, 1965, Pub. L. 89–131, § 1, 79 Stat. 544; H. Res. No. 901, Eighty-ninth Congress, July 29, 1966, enacted into permanent law by act Oct. 27, 1966, Pub. L. 89–697, ch. VI, 80 Stat. 1064, related to telephone, telegraph, and radiotelegraph allowances for House Members.

Section 46g–1, based on H. Res. No. 418, § 1, Ninety-second Congress, May 18, 1971, enacted into permanent law by Pub. L. 92–184, ch. IV, Dec. 15, 1971, 85 Stat. 636, related to telephone allowances for House Members for strictly official telephone service.

A prior section 46g–1, based on H. Res. No. 161, Ninetieth Congress, May 11, 1967, enacted into permanent law by Pub. L. 90–392, title I, July 9, 1968, 82 Stat. 318, was repealed by H. Res. No. 418, § 3, Ninety-second Congress, May 18, 1971, enacted into permanent law by Pub. L. 92–184, ch. IV, Dec. 15, 1971, 85 Stat. 636, effective Dec. 15, 1971.

§ 46h. Repealed. May 29, 1951, ch. 117, § 2, 65 Stat. 47, eff. July 1, 1951

Section, act June 23, 1949, ch. 238, § 3, 63 Stat. 265, related to limitation on charging telegrams to official business of the House.

§ 46i. Repealed. Pub. L. 104–186, title II, § 203(18)(C), Aug. 20, 1996, 110 Stat. 1728

Section, acts June 23, 1949, ch. 238, § 6, 63 Stat. 265; May 29, 1951, ch. 117, § 3, 65 Stat. 47, defined terms used in former section 46g of this title.

§ 47. Mode of payment

The compensation of Members and Delegates shall be passed as public accounts, and paid out of the public Treasury.

(R.S. § 46.)

CODIFICATION

R.S. § 46 derived from acts Jan. 22, 1818, ch. 5, § 3, 3 Stat. 404, and Feb. 10, 1854, ch. 11, § 1, 10 Stat. 267.

§ 48. Certification of salary and mileage accounts

Salary and mileage accounts of Senators shall be certified by the President of the Senate, and those of Representatives and Delegates by the Speaker of the House of Representatives; and such certificates shall be conclusive upon all the departments and officers of the Government.

(R.S. §§ 47, 48; July 28, 1866, ch. 296, § 17, 14 Stat. 323; Jan. 20, 1874, ch. 11, 18 Stat. 4.)

CODIFICATION

R.S. § 47 derived from acts July 28, 1866, ch. 296, § 17, 14 Stat. 323, and Jan. 22, 1818, ch. 5, § 3, 3 Stat. 404.

R.S. § 48 derived from act Sept. 30, 1850, ch. 90, § 1, 9 Stat. 523.

R.S. § 47 constitutes first clause and R.S. § 48 constitutes remainder.

SECTION REFERRED TO IN OTHER SECTIONS

This section is referred to in section 50 of this title.

§ 49. Certificate of salary during recess

The Clerk of the House of Representatives is authorized and directed to sign, during the recess of Congress after the first session and until the first day of the second session, the certificates for the monthly compensation of Members and Delegates in Congress, which certificate shall be in the form in use on August 15, 1876, and shall have the like force and effect as is given to the certificate of the Speaker.

(Aug. 15, 1876, ch. 287, § 1, 19 Stat. 145.)

§ 50. Substitute to sign certificates for salary and accounts

The Speaker is authorized to designate from time to time some one from among those appointed by him and appropriated for and employed in his office, whose duty it shall be under the direction of the Speaker to sign in his name and for him all certificates required by section 48 of this title for salary and accounts for traveling expenses in going to and returning from Congress of Representatives and Delegates.

(Nov. 12, 1903, P. Res. No. 1, 33 Stat. 1.)

§ 51. Monuments to deceased Senators or House Members

Whenever any deceased Senator or Member of the House of Representatives shall be actually interred in the Congressional Cemetery, so-called, it shall be the duty of the Sergeant at Arms of the Senate, in the case of a Senator, and of the Sergeant at Arms of the House of Representatives, in the case of a Member of the House, to have a monument erected, of granite, with suitable inscriptions, and the cost of the same shall be a charge upon and paid out either from the contingent funds of the Senate or of the House of Representatives, to whichever the deceased may have belonged, and any existing omissions of monuments or inscriptions, as aforesaid, are directed and authorized to be supplied in like manner.

(May 23, 1876, ch. 103, 19 Stat. 54.)

NATIONAL TRUST ENDOWMENT FOR CARE AND MAINTENANCE OF CONGRESSIONAL CEMETERY

Pub. L. 105–275, title II, § 209, Oct. 21, 1998, 112 Stat. 2448, provided that:

"(a) GRANT FOR CARE AND MAINTENANCE OF CONGRESSIONAL CEMETERY.—In order to assist in the perpetual care and maintenance of the historic Congressional Cemetery, the Architect of the Capitol shall make a grant to the National Trust for Historic Preservation (hereafter in this section referred to as the 'National Trust') in accordance with an agreement entered into by the Architect of the Capitol with the National Trust and the Association for the Preservation of Historic Congressional Cemetery (hereafter in this section referred to as the 'Association') which contains the terms and conditions described in subsection (b) and such other provisions as the Architect may deem necessary or desirable for the implementation of this section or for the protection of the interests of the Federal Government.

"(b) TERMS AND CONDITIONS OF AGREEMENT.—The terms and conditions described in this subsection are as follows:

"(1) Upon receipt of the amounts provided under the grant made under subsection (a), the National Trust shall deposit the amounts in a permanently restricted account in its endowment and shall administer, invest, and manage such grant funds in the same manner as other National Trust endowment funds.

"(2) The National Trust shall make distributions to the Association from the amounts deposited in the endowment pursuant to paragraph (1), in accordance with its regularly established spending rate, for the care and maintenance of the Cemetery (other than the cost of personnel), except that the National Trust may only make such distributions incrementally and proportionately upon receipt by the National Trust of contributions from the Association which incrementally match the amounts provided under the grant made under subsection (a) and which are to be added to the permanently restricted account described in paragraph (1).

"(3) The Association shall use such distributions from the endowment and the match for the care and maintenance of Congressional Cemetery, except that the Association may not use such distributions for nonroutine restoration or capital projects.

"(4) The Association, or any successor thereto, shall maintain adequate records and accounts of all financial transactions and operations carried out with such distributions, and such records shall be available at all times for audit and investigation by the Architect of the Capitol and the Comptroller General.

"(c) NO TITLE IN UNITED STATES.—Nothing in this section shall be construed to vest title to the Congressional Cemetery in the United States."

CONGRESSIONAL CEMETERY; RESTORATION AND PRESERVATION; GRANTS TO THE ASSOCIATION FOR THE PRESERVATION OF HISTORIC CONGRESSIONAL CEMETERY

Pub. L. 97–245, Aug. 26, 1982, 96 Stat. 313, provided: "That the Congress finds and declares that—

"(1) sections of the Congressional Cemetery in the District of Columbia are of national historic significance, including those areas in which John Philip Sousa, Matthew Brady, J. Edgar Hoover, several former Members of the United States Senate and House of Representatives, and many other persons of historical importance and interest are buried; and

"(2) the physical condition of these areas and related portions of the cemetery has deteriorated to the extent that restoration is necessary to protect and preserve the historical values of these areas.

"SEC. 2. In order to assist in the restoration and preservation of the historic values of the Congressional Cemetery, the Architect of the Capitol is authorized and directed to make grants to the Association for the Preservation of Historic Congressional Cemetery, Washington, District of Columbia, to be used for a program of restoration and preservation (but not routine maintenance) of the cemetery to be carried out under terms and conditions to be prescribed by the Architect of the Capitol. The Association shall maintain adequate records and accounts of all financial transactions and operations carried out under such program, and such records shall be available at all times for audit and investigation by the Architect or the Comptroller General of the United States. Nothing in this Act [this note] shall be construed to vest title to the Congressional Cemetery in the United States.

"SEC. 3. There is authorized to be appropriated $300,000 for grants to be made under section 2 of this Act, such sums to remain available until expended.

"SEC. 4. No authority under this Act [this note] to make payments shall be effective except to the extent and in such amounts as provided in advance in appropriations Acts."

§§ 52, 53. Repealed. Pub. L. 92–607, ch. V, § 506(k)(7), formerly § 506(h)(7), Oct. 31, 1972, 86 Stat. 1508, redesignated § 506(i)(7), Pub. L. 95–391, title I, § 108(a), Sept. 30, 1978, 92 Stat. 773, redesignated § 506(j)(7), Pub. L. 96–304, title I, § 101, July 8, 1980, 94 Stat. 889, redesignated § 506(k)(7), Pub. L. 97–276, § 101(e), Oct. 2, 1982, 96 Stat. 1189

Section 52, Pub. L. 92–184, ch. IV, Dec. 15, 1971, 85 Stat. 634, provided for office space for Senators in their home states. See section 58 of this title.

Similar provisions were contained in the following prior appropriations acts:

June 27, 1956, ch. 453, 70 Stat. 359, as amended Pub. L. 89–211, § 1(b), Sept. 29, 1965, 79 Stat. 857.

Aug. 5, 1955, ch. 568, 69 Stat. 504.

July 2, 1954, ch. 455, title I, 68 Stat. 399.

Aug. 1, 1953, ch. 304, title I, 67 Stat. 321.

July 9, 1952, ch. 598, 66 Stat. 466.

Oct. 11, 1951, ch. 485, 65 Stat. 391.

Sept. 6, 1950, ch. 896, Ch. II, 64 Stat. 597.

June 22, 1949, ch. 235, 63 Stat. 219.

June 14, 1948, ch. 467, 62 Stat. 425.

Section 53, Pub. L. 92–184, ch. IV, Dec. 15, 1971, 85 Stat. 634, provided for payment of office expenses of Senators in their home states. See section 58 of this title.

Similar provisions were contained in the following prior appropriations acts:

June 27, 1956, ch. 453, 70 Stat. 359, as amended Pub. L. 89–90, July 27, 1965, 79 Stat. 269; Pub. L. 91–145, Dec. 12, 1969, 83 Stat. 343.

Aug. 5, 1955, ch. 568, 69 Stat. 504.

July 2, 1954, ch. 455, title I, 68 Stat. 399.

EFFECTIVE DATE OF REPEAL

Section 506(k), formerly § 506(h), of Pub. L. 92–607, redesignated § 506(i) by Pub. L. 95–391, title I, § 108(a), Sept. 30, 1978, 92 Stat. 773, redesignated § 506(j) by Pub. L. 96–304, title I, § 101, July 8, 1980, 94 Stat. 889, and redesignated § 506(k) by Pub. L. 97–276, § 101(e), Oct. 2, 1982, 96 Stat. 1189, provided that the repeal is effective Jan. 1, 1973.

§ 54. Annotated United States Code for Members of House of Representatives to be paid for from Members' Representational Allowance

(a) In general

The Clerk of the House of Representatives shall, at the request of a Member of the House of Representatives, furnish to the Member, for official use only, one set of a privately published annotated version of the United States Code, including supplements and pocket parts. The furnishing of a set of the United States Code under this section shall be in lieu of any distribution under section 212 of title 1 and shall be paid for from the Members' Representational Allowance.

(b) "Member of the House of Representatives" defined

As used in this section, the term "Member of the House of Representatives" means a Representative in, or a Delegate or Resident Commissioner to, the Congress.

(c) Regulations

The Committee on House Oversight of the House of Representatives shall have authority to prescribe regulations to carry out this section.

(Pub. L. 104–186, title I, § 107, Aug. 20, 1996, 110 Stat. 1723.)

CODIFICATION

Section is comprised of section 107 of Pub. L. 104–186. Subsec. (d) of section 107 of Pub. L. 104–186 repealed former section 54 of this title. See Prior Provisions note below.

PRIOR PROVISIONS

A prior section 54, based on H. Res. No. 506, Ninetieth Congress, Aug. 21, 1967, enacted into permanent law by Pub. L. 90–392, title I, July 9, 1968, 82 Stat. 318, related to procurement for House Members of sets of United States Code Annotated or Federal Code Annotated, prior to repeal by Pub. L. 104–186, title I, § 107(d), Aug. 20, 1996, 110 Stat. 1723.

CHANGE OF NAME

Committee on House Oversight of House of Representatives changed to Committee on House Administration of House of Representatives by House Resolution No. 5, One Hundred Sixth Congress, Jan. 6, 1999.

§ 55. United States Code Annotated or United States Code Service; procurement for Senators

In lieu of the volumes of the Code of Laws of the United States, and the supplements thereto, supplied a Senator under section 212 of title 1, the Secretary of the Senate is authorized and directed to supply to a Senator upon written request of, and as specified by, that Senator—

(1) one copy of each of the volumes of the United States Code Annotated being published at the time the Senator takes office, and, as long as that Senator holds office, one copy of each replacement volume, each annual pocket part, and each pamphlet supplementing each such pocket part to the United States Code Annotated; or

(2) one copy of each of the volumes of the United States Code Service being published at the time the Senator takes office, and, as long as the Senator holds office, one copy of each replacement volume and each pocket supplement to the United States Code Service.

A Senator is entitled to make a written request under this paragraph and be supplied such volumes, pocket parts, and supplements the first time he takes office as a Senator and each time thereafter he takes office as a Senator after a period of time during which he has not been a Senator. In submitting such written request, the Senator shall certify that the volumes, pocket parts, or supplements he is to be supplied are to be for his exclusive, personal use. A Senator holding office on July 9, 1971, shall be entitled to file a written request and receive the volumes, pocket parts, and supplements, as the case may be, referred to in this paragraph if such request is filed within 60 days after July 9, 1971. Expenses incurred under this authorization shall be paid from the contingent fund of the Senate.

(Pub. L. 92–51, July 9, 1971, 85 Stat. 129; Pub. L. 92–607, ch. V, § 501, Oct. 31, 1972, 86 Stat. 1504.)

AMENDMENTS

1972—Pub. L. 92–607 substituted "United States Code Service" for "Federal Code Annotated" in two places.

§ 56. Repealed. Pub. L. 104–186, title II, § 203(20)(A), Aug. 20, 1996, 110 Stat. 1728

Section, based on H. Res. No. 418, § 2, Ninety-second Congress, May 18, 1971, enacted into permanent law by Pub. L. 92–184, ch. IV, Dec. 15, 1971, 85 Stat. 636, related to office expenses within District of Columbia of Delegate from District of Columbia.

REIMBURSEMENT OF EXPENSES OF HOUSE MEMBERS; MEMBER OF HOUSE OF REPRESENTATIVES AND MEMBER DEFINED

Section 302(a), (b), and (d) of H. Res. No. 287, Ninety-fifth Congress, Mar. 2, 1977, enacted into permanent law by Pub. L. 95–94, title I, § 115, Aug. 5, 1977, 91 Stat. 668, which related to reimbursement to Members of House of Representatives for official expenses incurred in the United States, was repealed by Pub. L. 104–186, title II, § 203(20)(B), Aug. 20, 1996, 110 Stat. 1728.

§ 57. Adjustment of House of Representatives allowances by Committee on House Oversight

(a) In general

Subject to the provision of law specified in subsection (b) of this section, the Committee on House Oversight of the House of Representatives may, by order of the Committee, fix and adjust the amounts, terms, and conditions of, and other matters relating to, allowances of the House of Representatives within the following categories:

(1) For Members of the House of Representatives, the Members' Representational Allowance, including all aspects of official mail within the jurisdiction of the Committee under section 59e of this title.

(2) For committees, the Speaker, the Majority and Minority Leaders, the Clerk, the Sergeant at Arms, and the Chief Administrative Officer, allowances for official mail (including all aspects of official mail within the jurisdiction of the Committee under section 59e of this title), stationery, and telephone and telegraph and other communications.

(b) Provision specified

The provision of law referred to in subsection (a) of this section is section 57a of this title.

(c) "Member of the House of Representatives" defined

As used in this section, the term "Member of the House of Representatives" means a Representative in, or a Delegate or Resident Commissioner to, the Congress.

(Pub. L. 92–184, ch. IV, Dec. 15, 1971, 85 Stat. 636; Pub. L. 104–186, title I, § 102, Aug. 20, 1996, 110 Stat. 1719; Pub. L. 106–57, title I, § 103(a)(4)(A), Sept. 29, 1999, 113 Stat. 415.)

CODIFICATION

Section is based on House Resolution No. 457, Ninety-second Congress, July 21, 1971, which was enacted into permanent law by Pub. L. 92–184.

AMENDMENTS

1999—Subsec. (a)(1), (2). Pub. L. 106–57 substituted "all aspects of official mail" for "all aspects of the Official Mail Allowance".

1996—Pub. L. 104–186 amended section generally. Prior to amendment, section consisted of subsecs. (a) and (b) authorizing Committee on House Administration to adjust certain allowances for Members, committees, and officers of House of Representatives.

CHANGE OF NAME

Committee on House Oversight of House of Representatives changed to Committee on House Administration of House of Representatives by House Resolution No. 5, One Hundred Sixth Congress, Jan. 6, 1999.

EFFECTIVE DATE OF 1999 AMENDMENT

Pub. L. 106–57, title I, § 103(c), Sept. 29, 1999, 113 Stat. 416, provided that: "The amendments made by this section [amending this section and sections 59e and 92 of this title] shall apply with respect to the first session of the One Hundred Sixth Congress and each succeeding session of Congress."

CLERK HIRE ALLOWANCE; INCREASE

Pub. L. 101–520, title I, § 104, Nov. 5, 1990, 104 Stat. 2262, effective for 102d Congress, increased authorization for the Clerk Hire Allowance by $50,000.

COMMITTEE ORDER NO. 1 (REVISED)[1]

Resolved, that effective January 25, 1972, each Member of the House of Representatives shall be entitled to office space suitable for his use in the district he represents at such places designated by him in such district. The Sergeant at Arms shall secure office space satisfactory to the Member in post offices or Federal buildings at not more than two (2) locations if such space is available. Office space to which a Member is entitled under this resolution which is not secured by the Sergeant at Arms may be secured by the Member, and the Clerk shall approve for payment from the contingent fund of the House of Representatives vouchers covering bona fide statements of amounts due for office space not exceeding a total allowance to each Member of $200 per month; but if a Member certifies to the Committee on House Administration that he is unable to obtain suitable space in his district for $200 per month due to high rental rates or other factors, the Committee on House Administration may, as the Committee considers appropriate, direct the Clerk to approve for payment from the contingent fund of the House of Representatives vouchers covering bona fide statements of amounts due for suitable office space not exceeding a total allowance to each Member of $350 per month. Members shall be entitled to have no more than three (3) district offices outfitted with office equipment, carpeting, and draperies at the expense of the General Services Administration.

As used in this resolution the term "Member" means any Member of the House of Representatives, the Resident Commissioner of Puerto Rico, and the Delegate of the District of Columbia.

COMMITTEE ORDER NO. 2 (REVISED)

Resolved, that effective January 3, 1973, until otherwise provided by order of the Committee on House Administration:

(a) The contingent fund of the House of Representatives is made available for reimbursement of transportation expenses incurred by Members (including the Resident Commissioner from Puerto Rico) in traveling on official business, by the nearest usual route, between Washington, District of Columbia, and any point in the district which he represents, for not more than 36 round trips during each Congress, such reimbursement to be made in accordance with rules and regulations established by the Committee on House Administration of the House of Representatives.

(b) The contingent fund of the House of Representatives is made available for reimbursement of transportation expenses incurred by employees in the office of a Member (including the Resident Commissioner from Puerto Rico) for not more than 6 round trips during any Congress between Washington, District of Columbia and any point in the Congressional district represented by the Member. Such payment shall be made only upon vouchers approved by the Member, containing a certification by him that such travel was performed on official duty. The Committee on House Administration shall make such rules and regulations as may be necessary to carry out this section.

(c) A Member of the House of Representatives (including the Resident Commissioner from Puerto Rico) may elect to receive in any Congress, in lieu of reimbursement of transportation expenses for such Congress is authorized in paragraph (a) above, a lump sum transportation payment of $2,250 for each Congress. The Committee on House Administration of the House of Representatives shall make such rules and regulations as may be necessary to carry out this section.

(d) This order shall not affect any allowance for travel of Members of the House of Representatives (including the Resident Commissioner from Puerto Rico) which is authorized to be paid from funds other than the contingent fund of the House of Representatives.

COMMITTEE ORDER NO. 3

Resolved, that effective March 1, 1972, until otherwise provided by order of the Committee on House Administration, each Member of the House of Representatives, the Resident Commissioner from Puerto Rico, and the Delegate from the District of Columbia shall be entitled to an annual clerk hire allowance of $157,092 for not to exceed 16 clerks. There shall be paid out of the contingent fund of the House of Representatives such sums as may be necessary to carry out this order until otherwise provided by law.

COMMITTEE ORDER NO. 4

Resolved, that effective January 3, 1973, until otherwise provided by order of the Committee on House Administration; the allowance for stationery for each Member of the House of Representatives, Delegates, and Resident Commissioner shall be $4,250 per regular session.

COMMITTEE ORDER NO. 5

Resolved, that effective May 1, 1973, until otherwise provided by order of the Committee on House Administration upon written request to the Committee on House Administration, a Member, the Resident Commissioner from Puerto Rico, or a Delegate to the House of Representatives may employ in lieu of 1 of the 16 clerks allowed under his clerk hire allowance, a research assistant at such salary as the Member may designate. The Member's annual clerk hire allowance will then be increased at the rate of $20,000.

There shall be paid out of the contingent fund of the House of Representatives such sums as may be necessary to carry out this order until otherwise provided by law.

COMMITTEE ORDER NO. 6

Resolved, that effective May 1, 1973, until otherwise provided by order of the Committee on House Administration, upon written request to the Committee on House Administration, a Member, the Resident Commissioner from Puerto Rico or a Delegate to the House of Representatives may allocate up to $250 a month of any unused portion of his clerk hire allowance for the leasing of equipment necessary for the conduct of his office.

There shall be paid out of the contingent fund of the House of Representatives such sums as may be necessary to carry out this order until otherwise provided by law.

COMMITTEE ORDER NO. 7

Resolved, that effective October 1, 1973, until otherwise provided by Order of the Committee on House Administration the quarterly allowance for official telephone service outside the District of Columbia for Members, Delegates, and the Resident Commissioner from Puerto Rico is increased from $450 quarterly to $600 quarterly.

COMMITTEE ORDER NO. 8

Resolved, that effective October 1, 1973, until otherwise provided by Order of the Committee on House Administration the quarterly allowance for official office expenses incurred outside the District of Columbia by Members, Delegates, and the Resident Commissioner from Puerto Rico has been increased from $300 quarterly to $500 quarterly.

COMMITTEE ORDER NO. 9

Resolved, that effective October 1, 1973, until otherwise provided by Order of the Committee on House Administration the number of units provided for official telephone calls, telegrams, cablegrams, and radiograms made or sent by on or behalf of a Member, Delegate, or the Resident Commissioner of Puerto Rico has been increased from 80,000 units to 100,000 units for each regular session of Congress. Such units shall accumulate

---

[1] Rescinded. See Committee Order No. 12.

and be available for use until the aggregate number of such units in the close of each session is not more than 200,000. Unused units in excess of 200,000 at the close of session may not be carried forward for use in a succeeding session.

COMMITTEE ORDER NO. 10

Resolved, that until otherwise provided by the Committee on House Administration, there shall be paid from the contingent fund of the House of Representatives to each Member, Resident Commissioner, or Delegate to the House of Representatives an additional allowance of $1,000 for stationery. Such payment shall be effective each session beginning with the 2nd Session of the 93d Congress.

Effective date: 2d Session of the 93d Congress.

COMMITTEE ORDER NO. 11

Resolved, that effective January 1, 1974, until otherwise provided by the Committee on House Administration, one word of a telegram, cablegram, or radiogram, shall be charged as two (2) units, except that one word of a night letter shall be charged as one (1) unit. In addition, twelve (12) units shall be charged for physical delivery of any telegram, cablegram, or radiogram, by the Telegraph Company.

COMMITTEE ORDER NO. 12

Resolved, that effective March 1, 1974, each Member of the House of Representatives shall be entitled to office space suitable for his use in the district he represents at such places designated by him in such district. The Sergeant at Arms shall secure office space satisfactory to the Member in post offices or Federal buildings at not more than three (3) locations if such space is available. Office space to which a Member is entitled under this resolution which is not secured by the Sergeant At Arms may be secured by the Member, and the Clerk shall approve for payment from the contingent fund of the House of Representatives vouchers covering bona fide statements of amounts due for office space not exceeding a total allowance to each Member of $200 per month; but if a Member certifies to the Committee on House Administration that he is unable to obtain suitable space in his district for $200 per month due to high rental rates or other factors, the Committee on House Administration may, as the Committee considers appropriate, direct the Clerk to approve for payment from the contingent fund of the House of Representatives vouchers covering bona fide statements of amounts due for suitable office space not exceeding a total allowance to each Member of $500 per month. In the event suitable office space is not available in post offices or other Federal buildings and the Member certifies to the Committee on House Administration that he is unable to obtain suitable private space in his district for $500.00 per month due to high rental rates or other factors, the Committee on House Administration may direct the Clerk to approve for payment from the contingent fund of the House of Representatives vouchers covering bona fide statements of amounts due for suitable office space not exceeding approximately 1,500 square feet at rates not to exceed the highest applicable rate charged to Federal agencies in the district established by regulations issued by the Administrator of General Services pursuant to Section 210(j) of the Federal Property and Administrative Services Act of 1949, as amended (40 U.S.C. 490(j)). Members shall be entitled to have no more than three (3) district offices outfitted with office equipment, carpeting, and draperies at the expense of the General Services Administration.

As used in this resolution the term "Member" means any Member of the House of Representatives, the Resident Commissioner from Puerto Rico, and the Delegates from the District of Columbia, Guam, and the Virgin Islands.

Committee Order No. 12 rescinds the provisions of Committee Order No. 1 revised.

COMMITTEE ORDER NO. 13

Resolved, that in addition to postage stamps authorized to be furnished under any other provision of law, until otherwise provided by order of the Committee on House Administration, the Clerk of the House of Representatives shall for each regular session of Congress procure and furnish United States postage stamps to each Representative, the Resident Commissioner of Puerto Rico, and the Delegates from the District of Columbia, Guam, and the Virgin Islands in an amount not exceeding $230, and to each standing committee of the House of Representatives upon request of the chairman thereof, in an amount not exceeding $140. In addition to postage stamps authorized under any other provision of law, until otherwise provided by order of the Committee on House Administration, the Speaker, the majority and minority leaders, and the majority and minority whips of the House of Representatives shall each be allowed United States postage stamps in an amount not exceeding $205.

Effective date: August 20, 1974.

COMMITTEE ORDER NO. 14

Resolved, that until otherwise provided by order of the Committee on House Administration; the allowance for Stationery for each Member of the House of Representatives, Delegate, and Resident Commissioner, shall be $6,500 per regular session. Such payment shall be made to each Member, Delegate, and the Resident Commissioner serving as such on or after the date of adoption of this resolution.

Effective date: August 20, 1974.

COMMITTEE ORDER NO. 15

Resolved, the Clerk of the House is authorized and directed to pay each Member, the Resident Commissioner from Puerto Rico, and the Delegates to the House of Representatives from the contingent fund of the House the amount of $500 quarterly upon the certification of each such Member, Resident Commissioner and Delegate for official expenses incurred outside the District of Columbia; effective with the beginning of the 94th Congress.

Effective date: December 18, 1974.

COMMITTEE ORDER NO. 16

Resolved, that effective this date, until otherwise provided by order of the Committee on House Administration, each Member, the Resident Commissioner from Puerto Rico, and the Delegate from the District of Columbia to the House of Representatives shall be entitled to an annual clerk hire allowance for the employment of not to exceed 18 clerks, and the Delegates from Guam and the Virgin Islands to the House of Representatives shall be entitled to an annual clerk hire allowance for the employment of not to exceed 11 clerks.

Effective date: March 6, 1975.

COMMITTEE ORDER NO. 17

Resolved, that effective March 1, 1975, until otherwise provided by order of the Committee on House Administration, upon written request to the Committee on House Administration, a Member, the Resident Commissioner from Puerto Rico or a Delegate to the House of Representatives may allocate an amount not to exceed $250 a month of any unused portion of his or her clerk hire allowance for the leasing of equipment necessary for the conduct of his or her office or for the leasing of computer and related services in connection with his or her official duties.

COMMITTEE ORDER NO. 18

Resolved, that effective this date, until otherwise provided by order of the Committee on House Administration, each Member, the Resident Commissioner from Puerto Rico or a Delegate to the House of Representatives is authorized a $650 per month allowance to lease office equipment, and upon written request to the Committee on House Administration, a Member, the Resident Commissioner from Puerto Rico or a Delegate to the House of Representatives may allocate an amount not to exceed $250 a month of any unused portion of his or her clerk hire allowance for the leasing of equipment necessary for the conduct of his or her office or for the leasing of computer and related services in connection with his or her official duties. The said monthly allowances are not cumulative.

Effective date: April 23, 1975.

COMMITTEE ORDER NO. 19

Resolved, that effective this date [June 2, 1975], until otherwise provided by order of the Committee on House Administration:

(a) The contingent fund of the House of Representatives is made available for reimbursement of transportation expenses incurred by Members (including the Resident Commissioner from Puerto Rico, the Delegates from the District of Columbia, the Virgin Islands, and Guam) in traveling, on official business, by the nearest usual route, between Washington, District of Columbia, and any point in the district which he represents, for not more than 26-round trips during each session of Congress (at the discretion of the Member, Resident Commissioner and Delegates no more than 6 of the 26-round trips may be allocated to the employees of their offices, such reimbursement to be made in accordance with rules and regulations established by the Committee on House Administration of the House of Representatives.

(b) The contingent fund of the House of Representatives is made available for reimbursement of transportation expenses incurred by employees in the office of a Member (including the Resident Commissioner from Puerto Rico, the Delegates from the District of Columbia, the Virgin Islands, and Guam) in traveling, on official business, by the nearest usual route, between Washington, District of Columbia, and any point in the Congressional district represented by the Member, for not more than 6-round trips during each session of Congress. Such payment shall be made only upon the receipt of a voucher approved by the Member, containing a certification by him stating that such travel was performed on official business. The Committee on House Administration shall make such rules and regulations as may be necessary to carry out this section.

(c) A Member of the House of Representatives (including the Resident Commissioner from Puerto Rico, the Delegates from the District of Columbia, the Virgin Islands, and Guam) may elect to receive in each session of Congress, in lieu of reimbursement of transportation expenses for each session of Congress as authorized in paragraph (a) above, a lump sum transportation payment of $2,250 for each session of Congress. The Committee on House Administration of the House of Representatives shall make such rules and regulations as may be necessary to carry out this section.

(d) This order shall not affect any allowance for travel of Members of the House of Representatives (including the Resident Commissioner from Puerto Rico, the Delegates from the District of Columbia, the Virgin Islands, and Guam) which is authorized to be paid from funds other than the contingent fund of the House of Representatives.

COMMITTEE ORDER NO. 20

Resolved, that effective June 1, 1975, until otherwise provided by order of the Committee on House Administration, each Member of the House of Representatives, the Resident Commissioner from Puerto Rico, and the Delegates from the District of Columbia, the Virgin Islands, and Guam shall be entitled to an additional annual clerk hire allowance of $22,500. There shall be paid out of the contingent fund of the House of Representatives such sums as may be necessary to carry out this order until otherwise provided by law.

COMMITTEE ORDER NO. 21

Resolved, that effective June 1, 1975, until otherwise provided by order of the Committee on House Administration, each Member of the House of Representatives, Delegate and Resident Commissioner shall be entitled to a constituent communication's allowance equivalent to the fair market value of the printing and production costs of two standard 11 x 17 inch Congressional district-wide constituent reports per annum for use in production and printing of newsletters, questionnaires or similar correspondence eligible to be mailed under the frank. The Committee on House Administration shall make such rules and regulations as may be necessary to establish the fair market value of the cost of printing and production of two standard 11 x 17 inch Congressional district-wide constituent report. There shall be paid out of the contingent fund of the House of Representatives such sums as may be necessary until otherwise provided by law.

COMMITTEE ORDER NO. 22

Resolved, that effective for the 94th Congress, until otherwise provided by Order of the Committee on House Administration, that in addition to the basic installation and service charges not to exceed the cost of three telephone lines at each of three district offices, the number of units provided for official telephone calls, telegrams, cablegrams, and radiograms made or sent by on or behalf of a Member, Delegate, or the Resident Commissioner of Puerto Rico is hereby changed to an overall allowance of 125,000 units for each regular session of Congress. These units shall be transferable among the Washington, D.C. and district offices. In addition, payment for the use of a WATS line is authorized, but the charges for such WATS line shall be calculated and deducted at a rate of 11 cents per unit. Such units shall accumulate and be available for use until the aggregate number of such units at the close of each session or Congress is not more than 250,000. Unused units in excess of 250,000 at the close of a session may not be carried forward for use in a succeeding session or Congress.

COMMITTEE ORDER NO. 23

Resolved, that effective this date [July 29, 1975], until otherwise provided by order of the Committee on House Administration, each Member, the Resident Commissioner from Puerto Rico or a Delegate to the House of Representatives is authorized upon written request to the Committee on House Administration, to allocate an amount not to exceed $1000 a month of any unused portion of his or her clerk hire allowance for the leasing of computer and related services in connection with his or her official duties. The said monthly allowance is not cumulative.

COMMITTEE ORDER NO. 24

Resolved, that effective October 1, 1975, until otherwise provided by order of the Committee on House Administration, each Member, the Resident Commissioner from Puerto Rico or a Delegate to the House of Representatives is authorized a $750.00 per month allowance to lease office equipment, and upon written request to the Committee on House Administration, a Member, the Resident Commissioner from Puerto Rico or a Delegate to the House of Representatives may allocate an amount not to exceed $250.00 a month of any unused portion of his or her clerk hire allowance for the leasing of equipment necessary for the conduct of his or her office in connection with his or her official duties. The said monthly allowances are not cumulative.

COMMITTEE ORDER NO. 25

Resolved, that effective immediately prior to noon on January 3, 1977, until otherwise provided by order of the Committee on House Administration, the allowance for airmail and special delivery stamps authorized by 2 U.S.C. 42c and 42d shall be reduced from its existing level to one dollar per session.

COMMITTEE ORDER No. 26

Resolved, that effective immediately prior to noon, January 3, 1977, until otherwise provided by Order of the Committee on House Administration, each Member of the House of Representatives shall be entitled to annual clerk-hire allowance of $238,584.00 for not to exceed 18 clerks. The amount of this allowance may be adjusted by the Committee on House Administration subsequent to the adoption of this order to reflect any adjustment to federal salary levels that occur under the Federal Pay Comparability Act of 1971.

The Committee on House Administration of the House of Representatives shall promulgate such regulations as may be necessary to carry out the provisions of this resolution.

"Member" means each Representative in, or Delegate or Resident Commissioner to, the House of Representatives.

COMMITTEE ORDER No. 27

Resolved, that effective September 1, 1976, until otherwise provided by order of the Committee on House Administration, reimbursements to Members for authorized expenditures shall be made only as prescribed by regulations of, and on forms issued by the Committee on House Administration.

"Member" means each Representative in, or Delegate or Resident Commissioner to, the House of Representatives.

COMMITTEE ORDER No. 28

Resolved, that effective immediately prior to noon on January 3, 1977, until otherwise provided by Order of the Committee on House Administration, if a Member elects to utilize WATS or similar service in his or her office in the District of Columbia, the Telecommunications Allowance shall be reduced by one-half. The Committee on House Administration shall promulgate regulations to implement this order and ensure adequate telecommunications service for Members representing districts where WATS or similar service is not available.

"Member" means each Representative in, or Delegate or Resident Commissioner to, the House of Representatives.

COMMITTEE ORDER No. 29

Resolved, that effective immediately prior to noon on January 3, 1977, until otherwise provided by Order of the Committee on House Administration, a Member may at any time during a session of Congress:

1—Receive in lieu of transportation authorized under 2 U.S.C. 43b a lump sum payment not to exceed $1.00 per session.

2—Withdraw a sum not to exceed $1.00 per session from his or her stationery account.

3—Receive under the provisions of 2 U.S.C. 122a an amount not to exceed $1.00 per session for official expenses outside the District of Columbia unless such Member submits an itemization of the expenses for which such Member seeks reimbursement.

The Committee on House Administration of the House of Representatives shall promulgate such regulations as may be necessary to carry out the provisions of this resolution.

"Member" means each Representative in, or Delegate or Resident Commissioner to, the House of Representatives.

COMMITTEE ORDER No. 30

Resolved, that effective immediately prior to noon on January 3, 1977, until otherwise provided by Order of the Committee on House Administration, Members may elect to transfer the authorization to expend funds among the following allowances.

1. Constituent Communication Allowance.

2. Official Expenses Outside the District of Columbia Allowance.

3. Stationery Allowance.

4. Equipment Lease Allowance.

5. Travel Allowance for Members and Designated Employees. The maximum amount transferable will be limited to an amount computed as follows:

64 times the rate per mile between the District of Columbia and the furthest point in the Member's District, according to the Rand McNally Standard Highway Mileage Guide. In no case shall this amount be less than $2,250. The following rates per mile apply:

Under 500 miles	$.15/mile
At least 500 but under 750 miles	.14/mile
At least 750 but under 1000 miles	.13/mile
At least 1000 but under 1750 miles	.12/mile
At least 1750 but under 2250 miles	.11/mile
At least 2250 but under 2500 miles	.10/mile
At least 2500 but under 3000 miles	.09/mile
3000 miles or over	.08/mile

6. Telephone and Telegraph Allowance. The maximum amount transferable will be limited to an amount computed as follows:

15,000 minutes times the highest long-distance telephone rate from the District of Columbia to the Member's District.

If the Member has elected to utilize WATS or similar service in his or her office in the District of Columbia, the amount will be reduced by one-half.

7. District Office Rental Allowance. The maximum amount transferable will be computed as follows:

1500 times the highest allowable GSA rental cost per square foot for office space in the Member's District.

Additionally, a Member may transfer a maximum of $12,000 per regular session of Congress for computer and related services and a maximum of $3,000 per regular session of Congress for Office Equipment leasing for his or her clerk-hire allowance.

All transfers made under this order shall be among the several above-stated categories and for the necessary and official expenses incurred by the Member in the conduct of his or her duties as a Member of the House of Representatives.

In the event the House precludes the use of the contingent fund of the House for implementation of this committee order, the status quo anti shall be restored as respects the individual accounts and allowances heretofore established by committee order or regulation prior to the adoption of this committee order.

The Committee on House Administration of the House of Representatives shall promulgate such regulations as may be necessary to carry out the provisions of this resolution.

"Member" means each Representative in, or Delegate or Resident Commissioner to, the House of Representatives.

COMMITTEE ORDER No. 31

Resolved, that effective April 1, 1977, until otherwise provided by order of the Committee on House Administration, each Member, Delegate or Resident Commissioner of the House of Representatives may compensate employees from the clerk-hire allowance at a per annum rate equivalent to, and not to exceed, the highest per annum rate of basic pay, as in effect from time to time, authorized for Level V of the Executive Schedule (5 U.S.C. 5316).

To Accompany Committee Order No. 31

This order will tie the maximum annual rate of compensation which may be paid from the clerk-hire allowance to the Executive Schedule, and will reestablish the previously existing parity between the maximum which may be paid a committee employee, and the maximum which may be paid a clerk-hire employee.

The Order raises the ceiling from its present level of $39,600 to $47,500, which corresponds to a Level V position, but provides no additional funds to the clerk-hire allowance. If a Member desires to raise an employee's salary, it must be done from the existing allowance.

This action is clearly within the Committee's authority under 2 U.S.C. 57 as modified by H.Res. 1372 (P.L. 94–440) [2 U.S.C. 57a], because it sets a "term or condition" of an allowance, and does not fix or adjust the amount of an allowance, which action would require a vote on the House floor.

COMMITTEE ORDER NO. 32

Resolved, That effective October 1, 1977, until otherwise provided by order of the Committee on House Administration, reimbursement for travel by members and employees by privately owned conveyance shall be at the rate of 17 cents per mile for automobile, 15 cents per mile for motorcycle, 36 cents per mile for aircraft, and that such reimbursement shall be made in accordance with rules and regulations established by the Committee on House Administration.

COMMITTEE ORDER NO. 33

Resolved, That effective May 1, 1981, until otherwise provided by the Committee on House Administration, the Allowance for Official Expenses and the Inventory Allowance for District Office Equipment and Furnishings are adjusted as follows:

1. The base allowance for Official expenses is increased to $47,300.
2. The Travel Allowance is increased to a base of $4,950, and the multiplier in the formula used to compute the variable for travel is increased to a range of 18 to 30 cents.
3. The Inventory Allowance for District Office Equipment and Furnishing is increased to $35,000.

Expenditures of these funds shall be made in accordance with rules and regulations established by the Committee on House Administration.

COMMITTEE ORDER NO. 34

Resolved, that effective January 3, 1983, until otherwise provided by the Committee on House Administration, the Allowance for Official Expenses is as follows:

1. The base allowance for Official Expenses is increased to $52,000.
2. The Travel Allowance is increased to a minimum of $5,700, and the multiplier in the formula used to compute the variable for travel is increased to a range of 21 to 35 cents.

Expenditures of these funds shall be made in accordance with rules and regulations established by the Committee on House Administration.

COMMITTEE ORDER NO. 35

Resolved, That effective May 1, 1983, until otherwise provided by the Committee on House Administration, the Clerk-Hire Allowance and the Official Expenses Allowance are adjusted as follows:

1. The base allowance for Official Expenses is increased by $15,000.
2. Each session a Member may allocate not to exceed $30,000 from the basic Clerk-Hire Allowance which may be used to supplement the Official Expenses Allowance, and may allocate not to exceed $30,000 from the Official Expenses Allowance to supplement the basic Clerk-Hire Allowance, provided however that monthly Clerk-Hire disbursements may not exceed 10 percent of the basic Clerk-Hire Allowance.

All disbursements and allocations shall be made in accordance with rules and regulations established by the Committee on House Administration.

COMMITTEE ORDER NO. 36

Resolved, That effective January 3, 1984, until otherwise provided by the Committee on House Administration, the Allowance for Official Expenses is adjusted as follows:

(1) The Travel Allowance is increased to reflect a cost per mile variable ranging from $.23 to $.39, with a minimum of $6,200.

Expenditures of these funds shall be made in accordance with rules and regulations established by the Committee on House Administration.

COMMITTEE ORDER NO. 37

Resolved, That effective October 1, 1985, until otherwise provided by order of the Committee on House Administration, each Member is entitled to three FTS lines for use in district office(s) without charge to the official expenses allowance.

COMMITTEE ORDER NO. 38

Resolved, That effective August 1, 1985, until otherwise provided by the Committee on House Administration, the Clerk-Hire Allowance and the Official Expenses Allowance are adjusted as follows:

Each session a member may allocate not to exceed $40,000 from the basic Clerk-Hire Allowance which may be used to supplement the Official Expenses Allowance, and may allocate not to exceed $40,000 from the Official Expenses Allowance to supplement the basic Clerk-Hire Allowance, provided however that monthly Clerk-Hire disbursements may not exceed 10% of the basic Clerk-Hire Allowance.

All disbursements and allocations shall be made in accordance with rules and regulations established by the Committee on House Administration.

COMMITTEE ORDER NO. 39

Resolved, that effective March 15, 1990, until otherwise provided by the Committee on House Administration, the Clerk-Hire Allowance and the Official Expenses Allowance are adjusted as follows:

Each session a Member may allocate not to exceed $50,000 from the basic Clerk-Hire Allowance which may be used to supplement the Official Expenses Allowance, and may allocate not to exceed $50,000 from the Official Expenses Allowance to supplement the basic Clerk-Hire Allowance, provided however that monthly Clerk-Hire disbursements may not exceed 10% of the basic Clerk-Hire Allowance.

All disbursements and allocations shall be made in accordance with rules and regulations established by the Committee on House Administration.

COMMITTEE ORDER NO. 40

Resolved, That effective May 8, 1991, until otherwise provided by the Committee on House Administration, the Clerk-Hire Allowance and the Official Expenses Allowance are adjusted as follows: Each session a Member may allocate not to exceed $75,000 from the basic Clerk-Hire Allowance which may be used to supplement the Official Expenses Allowance, and may allocate not to exceed $75,000 from the Official Expenses Allowance to supplement the basic Clerk-Hire Allowance, provided however that monthly Clerk Hire disbursements may not exceed 10 percent of the basic Clerk-Hire Allowance.

All disbursements and allocations shall be made in accordance with rules and regulations established by the Committee on House Administration.

COMMITTEE ORDER NO. 41

Resolved, That (a) effective September 1, 1995, and subject to subsection (b), the Clerk Hire Allowance, the Official Expenses Allowance, and the Official Mail Allowance shall cease to exist and the functions formerly carried out under such allowances shall be carried out under a single allowance, to be known as the "Members' Representational Allowance".

(b) Under the Members' Representational Allowance, the amount that shall be available to a Member for franked mail with respect to a session of Congress shall be the amount allocated for that purpose by the Committee on House Oversight under paragraphs (1)(A) and

(2)(B) of subsection (e) of section 311 of the Legislative Branch Appropriations Act, 1991 [2 U.S.C. 59e(e)(1)(A), (2)(B)], plus an amount equal to the amount permitted to be transferred to the former Official Mail Allowance under paragraph (3) of that subsection.

SEC. 2. The Committee on House Oversight shall have authority to prescribe regulations to carry out this resolution.

COMMITTEE ORDER NO. 42

Resolved, that pursuant to 2 U.S.C. § 57 and 2 U.S.C. § 59e, the Committee hereby orders that:

Sec. 1 Effective January 3, 1999 the amount available within the Members' Representational Allowance for franked mail with respect to a session of Congress shall not be limited by subsection (b) of Committee Order No. 41.

Sec. 2 The Committee on House Oversight shall have the authority to prescribe regulations to carry out this resolution.

SECTION REFERRED TO IN OTHER SECTIONS

This section is referred to in section 57a of this title.

§ 57a. Limitation on allowance authority of Committee on House Oversight

(a) In general

An order under the provision of law specified in subsection (c) of this section may fix or adjust the allowances of the House of Representatives only by reason of—

(1) a change in the price of materials, services, or office space;

(2) a technological change or other improvement in office equipment; or

(3) an increase under section 5303 of title 5 in rates of pay under the General Schedule.

(b) Resolution requirement

In the case of reasons other than the reasons specified in paragraph (1), (2), or (3) of subsection (a) of this section, the fixing and adjustment of the allowances of the House of Representatives in the categories described in the provision of law specified in subsection (c) of this section may be carried out only by resolution of the House of Representatives.

(c) Provision specified

The provision of law referred to in subsections (a) and (b) of this section is section 57 of this title.

(Pub. L. 94–440, title II, § 101, Oct. 1, 1976, 90 Stat. 1448; Pub. L. 104–186, title I, § 103, Aug. 20, 1996, 110 Stat. 1720.)

REFERENCES IN TEXT

The General Schedule, referred to in subsec. (a)(3), is set out under section 5332 of Title 5, Government Organization and Employees.

CODIFICATION

Section is based on House Resolution No. 1372, § 1, Ninety-fourth Congress, July 1, 1976, which was enacted into permanent law by Pub. L. 94–440.

AMENDMENTS

1996—Pub. L. 104–186 amended section generally. Prior to amendment, section consisted of subsecs. (a) and (b) relating to limitations on authority of the Committee on House Administration to fix and adjust allowances.

CHANGE OF NAME

Committee on House Oversight of House of Representatives changed to Committee on House Administration of House of Representatives by House Resolution No. 5, One Hundred Sixth Congress, Jan. 6, 1999.

SECTION REFERRED TO IN OTHER SECTIONS

This section is referred to in section 57 of this title.

§ 57b. Representational allowance for Members of House of Representatives

(a) In general

There is established for the House of Representatives a single allowance, to be known as the "Members' Representational Allowance", which shall be available to support the conduct of the official and representational duties of a Member of the House of Representatives with respect to the district from which the Member is elected.

(b) Merger

The Clerk Hire Allowance, the Official Expenses Allowance, and the Official Mail Allowance, as in effect on the day before September 1, 1995, are merged into the Members' Representational Allowance.

(c) "Member of the House of Representatives" defined

As used in this section, the term "Member of the House of Representatives" means a Representative in, or a Delegate or Resident Commissioner to, the Congress.

(d) Regulations

The Committee on House Oversight of the House of Representatives shall have authority to prescribe regulations to carry out this section.

(e) Effective date

This section shall take effect on September 1, 1995 and shall apply with respect to official and representational duties carried out on or after that date.

(Pub. L. 104–186, title I, § 101, Aug. 20, 1996, 110 Stat. 1719.)

PRIOR PROVISIONS

A prior section 57b, Pub. L. 104–53, title III, § 314, Nov. 19, 1995, 109 Stat. 538, provided that, effective Sept. 1, 1995, Committee on House Oversight of House of Representatives had authority to combine House of Representatives Clerk Hire Allowance, Official Expenses Allowance, and Official Mail Allowance into single allowance, to be known as the "Members' Representational Allowance" and to prescribe regulations relating to allocations, expenditures, and other matters with respect to Members' Representational Allowance.

CHANGE OF NAME

Committee on House Oversight of House of Representatives changed to Committee on House Administration of House of Representatives by House Resolution No. 5, One Hundred Sixth Congress, Jan. 6, 1999.

§ 58. Mail, telegraph, telephone, stationery, office supplies, and home State office and travel expenses for Senators

(a) Authorization for payment from Senate contingent fund

The contingent fund of the Senate is made available for payment (including reimbursement) to or on behalf of each Senator, upon certification of the Senator, for the following expenses incurred by the Senator and his staff:

(1) telecommunications equipment and services subject to such regulations as may be promulgated by the Committee on Rules and Administration of the Senate;

(2)(A) stationery and other office supplies procured for use for official business, and

(B) metered charges for use of copying equipment provided by the Sergeant at Arms and Doorkeeper of the Senate;

(3)[(A) Repealed. Pub. L. 101–520, title I, § 11, Nov. 5, 1990, 104 Stat. 2260] (B) postage on, and fees and charges in connection with official mail matter sent through the mail other than the franking privilege upon certification by the Senate Sergeant at Arms and subject to such regulations as may be promulgated by the Committee on Rules and Administration, and (C) costs incurred in the preparation of required official reports, and the acquisition of mailing lists to be used for official purposes, and in the mailing, delivery, or transmitting of matters relating to official business;

(4) official office expenses incurred (other than for equipment and furniture and expenses described in paragraphs (1) through (3)) for an office in his home State;

(5) expenses incurred for publications printed or recorded in any way for auditory and visual use (including subscriptions to books, newspapers, magazines, clipping, and other information services);

(6) subject to the provisions of subsection (e) of this section, reimbursement of travel expenses incurred by the Senator and employees in his office;

(7) expenses incurred for additional office equipment and services related thereto (but not including personal services), in accordance with regulations promulgated by the Committee on Rules and Administration of the Senate;

(8) charges officially incurred for recording and photographic services and products; and

(9) such other official expenses as the Senator determines to be necessary.

Payment under this section shall be made only upon presentation of itemized vouchers for expenses incurred and, in the case of expenses paid or reimbursed under paragraphs (6) and (9), only upon presentation of detailed itemized vouchers for such expenses. Vouchers presented for payment under this section shall be accompanied by such documentation as is required under regulations promulgated by the Committee on Rules and Administration of the Senate. No payment shall be made under paragraph (4) or (9) for any expense incurred for entertainment or meals.

(b) Limits for authorized expenses; recalculation formula

(1)(A) Except as is otherwise provided in the succeeding paragraphs of this subsection and subject to subparagraph (B) of this paragraph, the total amount of expenses authorized to be paid to or on behalf of a Senator under this section shall not exceed for calendar year 1977 or any calendar year thereafter an amount equal to one-half of the sum of the amounts authorized to be paid under this section on the day before

August 5, 1977, to or on behalf of both of the Senators from the State which he represents, increased by an amount equal to twenty percent thereof and rounded to the next higher multiple of $1,000.

(B) In the event that the term of office of a Senator begins after the first month of any such calendar year or ends (except by reason of death, resignation, or expulsion) before the last month of any such calendar year, the aggregate amount available to such Senator for such year shall be the aggregate amount computed under paragraph (1) of this subsection, divided by 12, and multiplied by the number of months in such year which are included in the Senator's term of office, counting any fraction of a month as a full month.

(2)(A) In the case of the period which commences January 1, 1988, and ends September 30, 1988, the total of—

(i) the expenses paid to or on behalf of a Senator under this section for such period, plus

(ii) the aggregate amount of gross compensation which is paid to employees in the office of such Senator for such period (as determined for purposes of section 61–1(d) of this title),

shall not exceed the aggregate of—

(iii) subject to subparagraph (B), an amount equal to 75 percent of the amount of the authorized expenses under this section for the calendar year ending December 31, 1987, as determined in the case of a Senator, who represents the State which such Senator represents, whose term of office included all of such calendar year, plus

(iv) the amount by which (I) the aggregate of the gross compensation which may be paid to employees in the office of such Senator for the fiscal year ending September 30, 1988, pursuant to the limitations imposed by section 61–1(d) of this title (as determined without regard to paragraph (1)(B) thereof), exceeds (II) the aggregate amount of gross compensation which is paid to employees in the office of such Senator for that part of such fiscal year which precedes January 1, 1988.

(B) In the event that the term of office of a Senator begins after the first month of the period which commences January 1, 1988, and ends September 30, 1988, or ends (except by reason of death, resignation, or expulsion) before the last month of such period, the amount computed pursuant to subparagraph (A)(iii) of this paragraph (but before application of this subparagraph) shall be recalculated as follows: such amount, as computed under subparagraph (A)(iii) of this paragraph, shall be divided by 9, and multiplied by the number of months in such period which are included in the Senator's term of office, counting any fraction of a month as a full month.

(3)(A) In the case of the fiscal year beginning October 1, 1988, or any fiscal year thereafter, the total of—

(i) the expenses paid to or on behalf of a Senator under this section for such fiscal year, plus

(ii) the aggregate amount of gross compensation which is paid to employees in the office of such Senator for such fiscal year (as determined for purposes of section 61–1(d) of this title),

shall not exceed the aggregate of—
    (iii) subject to subparagraph (B)—
        (I) in case the Senator represents Alabama, $116,300, Alaska, $221,600, Arizona, $128,975, Arkansas, $118,250, California, $168,950, Colorado, $124,100, Connecticut, $105,575, Delaware, $95,825, Florida, $120,200, Georgia, $116,300, Hawaii, $245,000, Idaho, $128,000, Illinois, $138,725, Indiana, $116,300, Iowa, $119,225, Kansas, $119,225, Kentucky, $115,325, Louisiana, $120,200, Maine, $110,450, Maryland, $100,700, Massachusetts, $114,350, Michigan, $124,100, Minnesota, $120,200, Mississippi, $118,250, Missouri, $121,175, Montana, $128,000, Nebraska, $120,200, Nevada, $129,950, New Hampshire, $106,550, New Jersey, $110,450, New Mexico, $125,075, New York, $145,550, North Carolina, $112,400, North Dakota, $119,225, Ohio, $129,950, Oklahoma, $123,125, Oregon, $132,875, Pennsylvania, $128,975, Rhode Island, $104,600, South Carolina, $110,450, South Dakota, $120,200, Tennessee, $116,300, Texas, $149,450, Utah, $128,000, Vermont, $105,575, Virginia, $106,550, Washington, $135,800, West Virginia, $105,575, Wisconsin, $119,225, Wyoming, $123,125, plus
        (II) the amount that is equal to the Senator's share for the fiscal year, as determined in accordance with regulations of the Committee on Rules and Administration, of the amount made available within the Senators' Official Personnel and Office Expense Account in the contingent fund of the Senate for official mail expenses of Senators, plus

    (iv) the aggregate of the gross compensation which may be paid to employees in the office of such Senator for such fiscal year, under the limitations imposed by section 61–1(d) of this title, but without regard to the provisions of paragraph (1)(C)(iv) thereof.

(B) In the event that the term of office of a Senator begins after the first month of any such fiscal year or ends (except by reason of death, resignation, or expulsion) before the last month of any such fiscal year, the amount referred to in subparagraph (A)(iii)(I) shall be recalculated as follows: such amount, as computed under subparagraph (iii), shall be divided by 12, and multiplied by the number of months in such year which are included in the Senator's term of office, counting any fraction of a month as a full month; and the amount referred to in subparagraph (A)(iii)(II) shall be recalculated in accordance with regulations of the Committee on Rules and Administration.

(c) Repealed. Pub. L. 97–51, § 122, Oct. 1, 1981, 95 Stat. 965

(d) Repealed. Pub. L. 93–371, § 101(3)(e), Aug. 13, 1974, 88 Stat. 429

(e) Transportation, essential travel-related expenses, and per diem expenses; coverage; limitations; amounts

Subject to and in accordance with regulations promulgated by the Committee on Rules and Administration of the Senate, a Senator and the employees in his office shall be reimbursed under this section for travel expenses incurred by the Senator or employee while traveling on official business within the United States. The term "travel expenses" includes actual transportation expenses, essential travel-related expenses, and, where applicable, per diem expenses (but not in excess of actual expenses). A Senator or an employee of the Senator shall not be reimbursed for any travel expenses (other than actual transportation expenses) for any travel occurring during the sixty days immediately before the date of any primary or general election (whether regular, special, or runoff) in which the Senator is a candidate for public office (within the meaning of section 431(b)[1] of this title, unless his candidacy in such election is uncontested. For purposes of this subsection and subsection (a)(6) of this section, an employee in the Office of the President pro tempore, Deputy President pro tempore, Majority Leader, Minority Leader, Majority Whip, Minority Whip, Secretary of the Conference of the Majority, or Secretary of the Conference of the Minority shall be considered to be an employee in the office of the Senator holding such office.

(f) Omitted

(g) Closing of deceased Senator's State offices

In the case of the death of any Senator, the chairman of the Committee on Rules and Administration may certify for such deceased Senator for any portion of such sum already obligated but not certified to at the time of such Senator's death, and for any additional amount which may be reasonably needed for the purpose of closing such deceased Senator's State offices, for payment to the person or persons designated as entitled to such payment by such chairman.

(h) Individuals serving on panels or other bodies recommending nominees for Federal judgeships, service academies, United States Attorneys, or United States Marshals

For purposes of subsections (a) and (e) of this section, an individual who is selected by a Senator to serve on a panel or other body to make recommendations for nominees to one or more Federal judgeships or to one or more service academies or one or more positions of United States Attorney or United States Marshal shall be considered to be an employee in the office of that Senator with respect to travel and official expenses incurred in performing duties as a member of such panel or other body, and shall be reimbursed (A) for actual transportation expenses and per diem expenses (but not exceeding actual travel expenses) incurred while traveling in performing such duties within the Senator's home State or between that State and Washington, District of Columbia, and each of the service academies, (B) for official expenses incurred in performing such duties. For purposes of this subsection and subsection (a) of this section, "official expenses" means expenses of the type for which reimbursement may be made to an employee in the office of a Senator when traveling on business of a committee of which that

---

[1] So in original. Probably should be section "431(2)".

Senator is a member, and, for accounting purposes, such expenses shall be treated as expenses for which reimbursement may be made under subsection (a)(4) of this section.

(i) Authorization of Secretary of Senate to pay reimbursable expenses

Whenever a Senator or an employee in his office has incurred an expense for which reimbursement may be made under this section, the Secretary of the Senate is authorized to make payment to that Senator or employee for the expense incurred, subject to the same terms and conditions as apply to reimbursement of the expense under this section.

(j) Advances from Senate contingent fund for travel expenses for official business trips; vouchers; settlement

Whenever a Senator or employee of his office plans an official business trip with respect to which reimbursement for travel expenses is authorized under the preceding provisions of section (a), the Senator (or such an employee who has been designated by the Senator to do so) may, prior to the commencement of such trip and in accordance with applicable regulations of the Senate Committee on Rules and Administration, obtain from any moneys in the contingent fund of the Senate which are available to him for purposes specified in subsection (a)(6) of this section, such advance sum as he shall certify (and be accountable for), to the Secretary of the Senate, to be necessary to defray some or all of the expenses to be incurred on such trip which expenses are reimbursable under the preceding provisions of this section. The receipt by any Senator for any sum so advanced to him or his order out of the contingent fund of the Senate by the Secretary of the Senate shall be taken and passed by the accounting officers of the Government as a full and sufficient voucher; but it shall be the duty of such Senator (or employee of his office, as the case may be), as soon as practicable, to furnish to the Secretary of the Senate a detailed voucher of the expenses incurred for the travel with respect to which the sum was so advanced, and make settlement with respect to such sum.

(Pub. L. 92–607, ch. V, § 506(a)–(j), Oct. 31, 1972, 86 Stat. 1505–1507; Pub. L. 93–145, Nov. 1, 1973, 87 Stat. 532; Pub. L. 93–371, § 3(e), Aug. 13, 1974, 88 Stat. 429; Pub. L. 94–59, title I, § 103, July 25, 1975, 89 Stat. 274; Pub. L. 95–94, title I, § 112(a)–(c), Aug. 5, 1977, 91 Stat. 663, 664; Pub. L. 95–240, title II, § 208, Mar. 7, 1978, 92 Stat. 117; Pub. L. 95–391, title I, § 108(a), Sept. 30, 1978, 92 Stat. 773; Pub. L. 96–304, title I, §§ 101, 102(a), 103, 104, July 8, 1980, 94 Stat. 889; Pub. L. 97–19, July 6, 1981, 95 Stat. 103; Pub. L. 97–51, § 122, Oct. 1, 1981, 95 Stat. 965; Pub. L. 97–257, title I, § 104(a), Sept. 10, 1982, 96 Stat. 849; Pub. L. 97–276, Oct. 2, 1982, § 101(e), 96 Stat. 1189; Pub. L. 98–51, title I, § 102, July 14, 1983, 97 Stat. 266; Pub. L. 98–181, title I, § 1204(a), Nov. 30, 1983, 97 Stat. 1290; Pub. L. 99–65, § 1(a), July 12, 1985, 99 Stat. 163; Pub. L. 100–137, § 1(b), Oct. 21, 1987, 101 Stat. 815; Pub. L. 100–458, title I, §§ 8(a), 13, 14(a), Oct. 1, 1988, 102 Stat. 2162, 2163; Pub. L. 101–163, title I, § 5(a), Nov. 21, 1989, 103 Stat. 1045; Pub. L. 101–520, title I, §§ 4(c), 8, 9(a), 11, title III, § 311(h)(2), Nov. 5, 1990, 104 Stat.

2258–2260, 2280; Pub. L. 102–90, title I, § 7(a), Aug. 14, 1991, 105 Stat. 451; Pub. L. 105–55, title I, § 3(a), Oct. 7, 1997, 111 Stat. 1180; Pub. L. 105–275, title I, § 1, Oct. 21, 1998, 112 Stat. 2432; Pub. L. 106–57, title I, § 1[(a)], (b), Sept. 29, 1999, 113 Stat. 410, 411.)

CODIFICATION

Section consists of subsecs. (a) to (j) of section 506 of Pub. L. 92–607, as amended. Original subsecs. (h) and (i) which made certain amendments and repeals to sections of this title that contained the provisions now covered by this section, and subsec. (j) which amended earlier appropriations not classified to the Code, were redesignated as subsecs. (i) to (k) by Pub. L. 95–391, title I, § 108(a), Sept. 30, 1978, 92 Stat. 773, further redesignated as subsecs. (j) to (*l*) by Pub. L. 96–304, title I, § 101, July 8, 1980, 94 Stat. 889, and subsequently redesignated as subsecs. (k) to (m) by Pub. L. 97–276, § 101(e), Oct. 2, 1982, 96 Stat. 1189.

Subsec. (f) related to a reduction of allowances for fiscal year 1973.

The 1982 amendments by Pub. L. 97–276 are based on sections 103 and 106(a) of S. 2939, Ninety-seventh Congress, 2d Session, as reported Sept. 22, 1982, as incorporated by reference in section 101(e) of Pub. L. 97–276, to be effective as if enacted into law.

AMENDMENTS

1999—Subsec. (b)(3)(A)(iii). Pub. L. 106–57, § 1[(a)], amended cl. (iii) generally. Prior to amendment, cl. (iii) read as follows: "subject to subparagraph (B), in case the Senator represents Alabama, $183,565, Alaska, $252,505, Arizona, $197,409, Arkansas, $168,535, California, $470,272, Colorado, $187,366, Connecticut, $161,691, Delaware, $127,384, Florida, $302,307, Georgia, $211,784, Hawaii, $279,648, Idaho, $163,841, Illinois, $267,000, Indiana, $195,391, Iowa, $171,340, Kansas, $168,912, Kentucky, $176,975, Louisiana, $186,714, Maine, $148,205, Maryland, $172,455, Massachusetts, $196,819, Michigan, $235,846, Minnesota, $187,742, Mississippi, $168,587, Missouri, $198,365, Montana, $161,857, Nebraska, $160,550, Nevada, $171,208, New Hampshire, $142,497, New Jersey, $207,754, New Mexico, $166,721, New York, $328,586, North Carolina, $212,711, North Dakota, $150,225, Ohio, $262,252, Oklahoma, $181,913, Oregon, $189,258, Pennsylvania, $267,240, Rhode Island, $138,637, South Carolina, $171,731, South Dakota, $151,838, Tennessee, $192,508, Texas, $353,911, Utah, $168,959, Vermont, $136,315, Virginia, $193,935, Washington, $213,887, West Virginia, $149,135, Wisconsin, $191,314, Wyoming, $153,016, plus".

Subsec. (b)(3)(B). Pub. L. 106–57, § 1(b), substituted "the amount referred to in subparagraph (A)(iii)(I)" for "that part of the amount referred to in subparagraph (A)(iii) that is not specifically allocated for official mail expenses" and "the amount referred to in subparagraph (A)(iii)(II)" for "the part of the amount referred to in subparagraph (A)(iii) that is allocated for official mail expenses".

1998—Subsec. (b)(3)(A)(iii). Pub. L. 105–275, § 1(a), amended cl. (iii) generally. Prior to amendment, cl. (iii) read as follows: "subject to subparagraph (B), in case the Senator represents Alabama, $182,567, Alaska, $251,901, Arizona, $197,079, Arkansas, $168,282, California, $468,724, Colorado, $186,350, Connecticut, $160,903, Delaware, $127,198, Florida, $299,746, Georgia, $210,214, Hawaii, $279,512, Idaho, $163,335, Illinois, $266,248, Indiana, $194,770, Iowa, $170,565, Kansas, $168,177, Kentucky, $177,338, Louisiana, $185,647, Maine, $147,746, Maryland, $173,020, Massachusetts, $195,799, Michigan, $236,459, Minnesota, $187,702, Mississippi, $168,103, Missouri, $197,941, Montana, $161,725, Nebraska, $160,361, Nevada, $171,096, New Hampshire, $142,394, New Jersey, $206,260, New Mexico, $166,140, New York, $327,955, North Carolina, $210,946, North Dakota, $149,824, Ohio, $259,452, Oklahoma, $181,761, Oregon, $189,345, Pennsylvania, $266,148, Rhode Island, $138,582, South Carolina, $170,451, South Dakota, $151,450, Tennessee, $191,954, Texas, $348,681, Utah, $168,632, Vermont, $135,925, Virginia,

$193,467, Washington, $214,694, West Virginia, $147,772, Wisconsin, $191,569, Wyoming, $152,438, plus''.

Subsec. (b)(3)(B). Pub. L. 105–275, §1(b), substituted "that part of the amount referred to in subparagraph (A)(iii) that is not specifically allocated for official mail expenses" for "the amount referred to in subparagraph (A)(iii)" and inserted before period at end "; and the part of the amount referred to in subparagraph (A)(iii) that is allocated for official mail expenses shall be recalculated in accordance with regulations of the Committee on Rules and Administration".

1997—Subsec. (b)(3)(A)(iii). Pub. L. 105–55 amended cl. (iii) generally. Prior to amendment, cl. (iii) read as follows: "subject to subparagraph (B), in case the Senator represents Alabama, $68,000, Alaska, $176,000, Arizona, $81,000, Arkansas, $70,000, California, $122,000, Colorado, $76,000, Connecticut, $57,000, Delaware, $47,000, Florida, $72,000, Georgia, $68,000, Hawaii, $200,000, Idaho, $80,000, Illinois, $91,000, Indiana, $68,000, Iowa, $71,000, Kansas, $71,000, Kentucky, $67,000, Louisiana, $72,000, Maine, $62,000, Maryland, $52,000, Massachusetts, $66,000, Michigan, $76,000, Minnesota, $72,000, Mississippi, $70,000, Missouri, $73,000, Montana, $80,000, Nebraska, $72,000, Nevada, $82,000, New Hampshire, $58,000, New Jersey, $62,000, New Mexico, $77,000, New York, $98,000, North Carolina, $64,000, North Dakota, $71,000, Ohio, $82,000, Oklahoma, $75,000, Oregon, $85,000, Pennsylvania, $81,000, Rhode Island, $56,000, South Carolina, $62,000, South Dakota, $72,000, Tennessee, $68,000, Texas, $102,000, Utah, $80,000, Vermont, $57,000, Virginia, $58,000, Washington, $88,000, West Virginia, $57,000, Wisconsin, $71,000, Wyoming, $75,000, plus''.

1991—Subsec. (a). Pub. L. 102–90, §7(a)(1), (3)–(5), substituted "payment (including reimbursement)" for "payment" in introductory provisions, substituted "Payment" for "Reimbursement to a Senator and his employees" and "paid or reimbursed" for "reimbursed" in second sentence, and substituted "payment" for "reimbursement" in last sentence.

Subsec. (a)(3) to (5), (7) to (9). Pub. L. 102–90, §7(a)(2), struck out "reimbursement to each Senator for" at beginning of pars. (3), (4), and (7) to (9) and in par. (5) direction to strike such language was executed by striking out "reimbursements to each Senator for" to reflect the probable intent of Congress.

1990—Subsec. (a)(2). Pub. L. 101–520, §4(c), amended par. (2) generally. Prior to amendment, par. (2) read as follows: "stationery and other office supplies procured for use for official business;".

Subsec. (a)(3). Pub. L. 101–520, §311(h)(2), which directed that par. (3) be amended by striking out "postage on," and all that follows through "Senate, and", could not be executed because those words do not appear in par. (3) as amended generally by Pub. L. 101–163 which in part restated provisions directed to be stricken by Pub. L. 101–520, §311(h)(2), as subpar. (A). See 1990 and 1989 Amendment notes below.

Pub. L. 101–520, §11, struck out subpar. (A) which read as follows: "postage on, and fees and charges in connection with, mail matter sent through the mail under the franking privilege in excess of amounts provided from the appropriation for official mail costs, upon certification by the Senate Sergeant at Arms and subject to such regulations as may be promulgated by the Committee on Rules and Administration,".

Subsec. (b)(3)(A)(iii). Pub. L. 101–520, §8, amended cl. (iii) generally. Prior to amendment, cl. (iii) read as follows: "subject to subparagraph (B), in case the Senator represents Alabama, $53,000, Alaska, $137,000, Arizona, $63,000, Arkansas, $54,000, California, $95,000, Colorado, $59,000, Connecticut, $44,000, Delaware, $36,000, Florida, $56,000, Georgia, $53,000, Hawaii, $156,000, Idaho, $62,000, Illinois, $71,000, Indiana, $53,000, Iowa, $55,000, Kansas, $55,000, Kentucky, $52,000, Louisiana, $56,000, Maine, $48,000, Maryland, $40,000, Massachusetts, $51,000, Michigan, $59,000, Minnesota, $56,000, Mississippi, $54,000, Missouri, $57,000, Montana, $62,000, Nebraska, $56,000, Nevada, $64,000, New Hampshire, $45,000, New Jersey, $48,000, New Mexico, $60,000, New York, $76,000, North Carolina, $50,000, North Dakota, $55,000, Ohio, $64,000,

Oklahoma, $58,000, Oregon, $66,000, Pennsylvania, $63,000, Rhode Island, $43,000, South Carolina, $48,000, South Dakota, $56,000, Tennessee, $53,000, Texas, $79,000, Utah, $62,000, Vermont, $44,000, Virginia, $45,000, Washington, $68,000, West Virginia $44,000, Wisconsin, $55,000, Wyoming, $58,000, plus''.

Subsec. (h). Pub. L. 101–520, §9(a), inserted "or one or more positions of United States Attorney or United States Marshal" after "one or more service academies".

1989—Subsec. (a)(3). Pub. L. 101–163 amended par. (3) generally. Prior to amendment, par. (3) read as follows: "postage on, and fees and charges in connection with, mail matter sent through the mail under the franking privilege in excess of amounts provided from the appropriation for official mail costs, upon certification by the Senate Sergeant at Arms and subject to such regulations as may be promulgated by the Committee on Rules and Administration of the Senate, and reimbursement to each Senator for costs incurred in the preparation of required official reports, and the acquisition of mailing lists to be used for official purposes, and in the mailing, delivery, or transmitting of matters relating to official business;".

1988—Subsec. (a)(3). Pub. L. 100–458, §13, inserted "postage on, and fees and charges in connection with, mail matter sent through the mail under the franking privilege in excess of amounts provided from the appropriation for official mail costs, upon certification by the Senate Sergeant at Arms and subject to such regulations as may be promulgated by the Committee on Rules and Administration of the Senate, and" before "reimbursement".

Subsec. (a)(9). Pub. L. 100–458, §§8(a), 14(a), made identical amendments, striking out ", but only (A) in the case of expenses for the period commencing January 1, 1988, and ending with the close of September 30, 1988, to the extent that such expenses do not exceed ten percent of the total amount of expenses authorized to be paid to or on behalf of such Senator under this section (excluding any amount so authorized by subsection (b)(2)(A)(iv) of this section), and (B) in the case of expenditures for periods commencing on or after October 1, 1988, to the extent such expenses do not exceed ten percent of the total amount of expenses authorized to be paid to or on behalf of such Senator under this section (excluding any amount so authorized by subsection (b)(3)(A)(iv) of this section for the fiscal year involved)" after "necessary".

1987—Subsec. (a). Pub. L. 100–137, §1(b)(1), amended subsec. (a) generally, substituting provisions authorizing payments from the Senate contingent fund for former provisions authorizing such payments.

Subsec. (b). Pub. L. 100–137, §1(b)(2), designated existing provisions of par. (1) as subpar. (A) of par. (1), substituted "Except as is otherwise provided in the succeeding paragraphs of this subsection and subject to subparagraph (B) of this paragraph," for "Except as otherwise provided in paragraph (2) of this subsection,", added pars. (2) and (3), and redesignated former par. (2) as subpar. (B) of par. (1).

Subsec. (e). Pub. L. 100–137, §1(b)(4), amended subsection (e) generally, substituting provisions relating to reimbursement for travel expenses incurred by Senators and employees for former provisions relating to reimbursement of those expenses.

Subsec. (h). Pub. L. 100–137, §1(b)(3), struck out "(1)" after "(h)", substituted "(a)(4)" for "(a)(5)", and struck out par. (2) which read as follows: "The amount of official expenses incurred by individuals selected by a Senator for which reimbursement may be made under this subsection shall not exceed $500 each calendar year, and the total amount of expenses incurred by such individuals for which reimbursement may be made under this subsection shall not exceed $3,000 each calendar year."

Subsec. (j). Pub. L. 100–137, §1(b)(5), substituted "(a)(6)" for "(a)(8)".

1985—Subsec. (a)(6). Pub. L. 99–65 amended par. (6) generally, substituting "for telephone service charges officially incurred outside Washington, District of Columbia, which are based on the amount of time the service is used" for "reimbursement to each Senator for telephone service charges officially incurred outside Washington, District of Columbia".

1983—Subsec. (e). Pub. L. 98–181 inserted references to Secretary of Conference of Majority and Secretary of Conference of Minority.

Pub. L. 98–51 inserted provisions authorizing reimbursement for essential travel-related expenses and defined those expenses for purposes of this subsection.

1982—Subsec. (b)(1). Pub. L. 97–276 substituted "equal to twenty percent thereof" for "equal to ten percent thereof". See Codification note above.

Subsec. (b)(2). Pub. L. 97–257 substituted "(2) In the event that the term of office of a Senator begins after the first month of any such calendar year or ends (except by reason of death, resignation, or expulsion) before the last month of any such calendar year, the aggregate amount available to such Senator for such year shall be the aggregate amount computed under paragraph (1) of this subsection, divided by 12, and multiplied by the number of months in such year which are included in the Senator's term of office, counting any fraction of a month as a full month." for "(2) In any such calendar year in which a Senator does not hold the office of Senator at least part of each month of that year, the aggregate amount available to the Senator shall be the aggregate amount, computed under paragraph (1) of this subsection, divided by 12, and multiplied by the number of months the Senator holds such office during that year, counting any fraction of a month as a full month."

Subsec. (j). Pub. L. 97–276 added subsec. (j). See Codification note above.

1981—Subsec. (a)(9). Pub. L. 97–19 inserted provisions which authorized reimbursement out of contingent fund of Senate to each Senator for expenses for additional office equipment.

Subsec. (c). Pub. L. 97–51 struck out subsec. (c) which provided that aggregate of payments made to or on behalf of a Senator under this section not exceed at any time during each calendar year one-twelfth of the amount computed under subsection (b)(1) of this section multiplied by the number of months (counting a fraction of a month as a month) elapsing from the first month in that calendar year in which the Senator held the office of Senator through the date of payment.

1980—Subsec. (a)(3). Pub. L. 96–304, § 103, substituted "costs incurred in the mailing or delivery of" for "air mail and special delivery postage for expenses incurred in the mailing of postal".

Subsec. (e). Pub. L. 96–304, § 102(a), substituted "prescribed by the Committee on Rules and Administration" for "in effect under section 5702 of title 5 for employees of agencies".

Subsec. (h)(1). Pub. L. 96–304, § 104, substituted "to an employee in the office of a Senator when traveling on business of a committee of which that Senator is a member" for "under subsection (a)(9) when such expenses are incurred by or on behalf of a Senator".

Subsec. (i). Pub. L. 96–304, § 101, added subsec. (i).

1978—Subsec. (e). Pub. L. 95–240 inserted reference to President pro tempore and Deputy President pro tempore.

Subsec. (h). Pub. L. 95–391 added subsec. (h).

1977—Subsec. (a). Pub. L. 95–94, § 112(a), in par. (1) struck out provision requiring authorization by the Committee on Rules and Administration in the manner prescribed by such Committee, in par. (7) struck out "and" at end thereof, in par. (8) substituted provisions requiring reimbursement of travel expenses incurred by the Senator and employees in his office subject to the provisions of subsec. (e) of this section, for provisions authorizing reimbursement of actual travel expenses incurred by the Senator in travel-on official business between Washington, D.C. and the State he represents and within such State, and travel expenses incurred by employees in the Senator's office subject to the provisions of subsec. (e) of this section, added par. (9), and in text following par. (9) inserted provisions relating to reimbursement of expenses incurred under par. (9).

Subsec. (b)(1). Pub. L. 95–94, § 112(b), substituted provisions setting forth criteria for determination of total amount of expenses authorized to be paid to or on behalf of a Senator under this section for calendar year 1977 or any calendar year thereafter, for provisions setting forth criteria for determination of total amount of expenses authorized to be paid to or on behalf of a Senator under this section for calendar year 1973 or any calendar year thereafter.

Subsec. (e). Pub. L. 95–94, § 112(c), substituted provisions setting forth prerequisites, conditions, and amounts of reimbursement for actual transportation expenses and per diem expenses, but not exceeding actual travel expenses, incurred by a Senator or employee in his office while traveling on official business within the United States, for provisions setting forth prerequisites, conditions, and amounts of reimbursement for per diem and actual transportation expenses incurred, or actual travel expenses incurred, by an employee in a Senator's office, including employees authorized by Senate Resolution 60, 94th Congress, and former section 72a–1c of this title, for round trips made by the employee on official business by the nearest usual route between Washington, D.C. and the home State of the Senator involved, and in traveling within the State.

1975—Subsec. (a)(8). Pub. L. 94–59, § 103(1), substituted "travel expenses incurred by employees" for "actual transportation expenses incurred by employees".

Subsec. (e). Pub. L. 94–59, § 103(2), inserted new administrative provisions covering the payment of travel expenses of employees in Senators' offices for round trips between Washington, D.C., and the Senators' home States, inserted references to Senate Resolution 60, 94th Congress, agreed to June 12, 1975, and to sections 68b and 72a–1c of this title, and inserted limiting provisions prohibiting reimbursement for travel during the 60-day period immediately preceding any election in which the Senator is a candidate.

1974—Subsec. (a)(4). Pub. L. 93–371 struck out par. (4) which related to rental charges for office space at not more than three places designated by the Senator in the State he represents. See section 59 of this title.

Subsec. (c). Pub. L. 93–371 struck out provisions setting forth the maximum allowable amount for rental payments for office space occupied by the Senator in State he represents. See section 59 of this title.

Subsec. (d). Pub. L. 93–371 struck out subsec. (d) which authorized the Sergeant at Arms to secure for each Senator home State office space at not more than three places designated by the Senator in such home State. See section 59 of this title.

1973—Subsec. (a)(7). Pub. L. 93–145 inserted "newspapers," after "subscriptions to".

EFFECTIVE DATE OF 1999 AMENDMENT

Pub. L. 106–57, title I, § 1[(a)], Sept. 29, 1999, 113 Stat. 410, provided that the amendment made by section 1[(a)] is effective in the case of any fiscal year which begins on or after Oct. 1, 1999.

Pub. L. 106–57, title I, § 1(c), Sept. 29, 1999, 113 Stat. 411, provided that: "The amendments made by this section [amending this section] shall apply to any fiscal year which begins on or after October 1, 1999."

EFFECTIVE DATE OF 1998 AMENDMENT

Pub. L. 105–275, title I, § 1(a), Oct. 21, 1998, 112 Stat. 2432, provided that the amendment made by section 1(a) is effective in the case of any fiscal year which begins on or after Oct. 1, 1998.

EFFECTIVE DATE OF 1997 AMENDMENT

Section 3(a) of Pub. L. 105–55 provided that the amendment made by that section is effective in the case of any fiscal year beginning on or after Oct. 1, 1997.

EFFECTIVE DATE OF 1991 AMENDMENT

Section 7(c) of Pub. L. 102–90 provided that: "The amendments made by subsections (a) and (b) [amending this section and section 59 of this title] shall take effect October 1, 1991.''

EFFECTIVE DATE OF 1990 AMENDMENT

Section 4(d) of Pub. L. 101–520 provided that: "The provisions of subsections (a) and (b) [enacting section 58a–4 of this title], and the amendment made by subsection (c) [amending this section] shall take effect on October 1, 1990.''

Section 8 of Pub. L. 101–520 provided that the amendment made by that section is effective in the case of any fiscal year which begins on or after October 1, 1990.

Section 9(b) of Pub. L. 101–520 provided that: "The amendment made by subsection (a) [amending this section] shall be effective in the case of expenses incurred after September 30, 1989.''

Amendment by section 311(h)(2) of Pub. L. 101–520 applicable with respect to sessions of Congress beginning with the first session of the One Hundred Second Congress, see section 59e(i) of this title.

EFFECTIVE DATE OF 1988 AMENDMENT

Sections 8(b) and 14(b) of Pub. L. 100–458 provided that: "The amendment made by subsection (a) [amending this section] shall be effective only in the case of expenses incurred on or after October 1, 1988.''

EFFECTIVE DATE OF 1987 AMENDMENT

Section 1(b)(1)–(5) of Pub. L. 100–137 provided that the amendments made by that section are effective Jan. 1, 1988.

EFFECTIVE DATE OF 1985 AMENDMENT

Section 2 of Pub. L. 99–65 provided that: "The amendments made by this Act [amending this section and section 58a of this title] shall take effect on the first day of the first calendar month which begins more than sixty days after the date of enactment of this Act [July 12, 1985].''

EFFECTIVE DATE OF 1983 AMENDMENT

Section 1204(b) of Pub. L. 98–181 provided that: "The amendment made by subsection (a) [amending this section] shall be effective in the case of expenses incurred or charges imposed on or after October 1, 1983.''

EFFECTIVE DATE OF 1982 AMENDMENTS

Section 103(b) of S. 2939, as reported Sept. 22, 1982, and enacted into permanent law by section 101(e) of Pub. L. 97–276 provided that: "The amendment made by subsection (a) [amending this section] shall be effective with respect to calendar years after the calendar year 1982.''

Section 106(b) of S. 2939, as reported Sept. 22, 1982, and enacted into permanent law by section 101(e) of Pub. L. 97–276 provided that: "The amendments made by subsection (a) of this section [amending this section] shall take effect January 1, 1983.''

Section 104(b) of Pub. L. 97–257 provided that: "The amendment made by subsection (a) of this section [amending this section] shall be effective on and after January 1, 1982.''

EFFECTIVE DATE OF 1981 AMENDMENT

Section 122 of Pub. L. 97–51 provided that the amendment made by that section is effective Jan. 1, 1982.

EFFECTIVE DATE OF 1980 AMENDMENT

Section 101 of Pub. L. 96–304 provided that the amendment made by that section is effective Oct. 1, 1979.

Section 103 of Pub. L. 96–304 provided that the amendment made by that section is effective Feb. 1, 1980.

Section 104 of Pub. L. 96–304 provided that the amendment made by that section is effective Jan. 1, 1980.

EFFECTIVE DATE OF 1978 AMENDMENTS

Section 108(b) of Pub. L. 95–391 provided that: "The amendment made by subsection (a) [amending this section] shall take effect on January 1, 1978.''

Section 208 of Pub. L. 95–240 provided that the amendment made by that section is effective Aug. 5, 1977.

EFFECTIVE DATE OF 1977 AMENDMENT

Section 112(f) of Pub. L. 95–94 provided that: "The amendments made by subsections (a), (c), (d), and (e) [amending this section and sections 59 and 68b of this title] shall take effect on the date of the enactment of this Act [Aug. 5, 1977]. The amendment made by subsection (b) [amending this section] shall take effect as of January 1, 1977.''

EFFECTIVE DATE OF 1974 AMENDMENT

Amendment by Pub. L. 93–371 effective on and after July 1, 1974, see section 59(g) of this title.

EFFECTIVE DATE OF 1973 AMENDMENT

Section 101 of Pub. L. 93–145 provided that the amendment made by that section is effective Jan. 1, 1973.

INCREASE IN CERTAIN AUTHORIZED EXPENSE LIMITS EFFECTIVE OCTOBER 1, 1994

For provisions increasing each of the figures contained in subsec. (b)(3)(A)(iii) of this section by $50,000 effective Oct. 1, 1994, see section 5 of Pub. L. 103–283, set out as a Mass Mailings by Senators note under section 3210 of Title 39, Postal Service.

DECREASE IN CERTAIN AUTHORIZED EXPENSE LIMITS EFFECTIVE OCTOBER 1, 1993

Pub. L. 103–69, title I, § 2, Aug. 11, 1993, 107 Stat. 695, provided that: "Effective on and after October 1, 1993, the aggregate of each of the sums determined under clauses (iii) and (iv) of section 506(b)(3)(A) of the Supplemental Appropriations Act, 1973 (2 U.S.C. 58(b)(3)(A)(iii) and (iv)), shall be deemed decreased by 2.5 percent.''

PAYMENT TO UNITED STATES POSTAL SERVICE FOR POSTAGE, FEES, AND CHARGES

Section 5(b) of Pub. L. 101–163 provided that: "Receipts paid to the Sergeant at Arms from sales of postage on, and fees and charges in connection with mail matter sent through the mail by Senators, Senate committees, or other Senate offices (including joint committees and commissions funded from the contingent fund of the Senate), other than under the franking privilege, as cash or check payments directly from such Senators, committees, or offices, or as reimbursement from the Financial Clerk of the Senate pursuant to certification by the Sergeant at Arms of charges to be made to such funds available to such Senators, committees, or offices for such postage, fees and charges shall be used by the Sergeant at Arms for payment to the United States Postal Service for such postage, fees, and charges.''

SECTION REFERRED TO IN OTHER SECTIONS

This section is referred to in sections 43d, 61–1, 68b of this title.

§ 58a. Telecommunications services for Senators; payment of costs out of contingent fund

The Sergeant at Arms and Doorkeeper of the Senate shall furnish each Senator local and long-distance telecommunications services in Washington, District of Columbia, and in such Senator's State in accordance with regulations prescribed by the Senate Committee on Rules and Administration; and the costs of such service shall be paid out of the contingent fund of the Senate from moneys made available to him for that purpose.

(Pub. L. 98–181, title I, § 1205(a), Nov. 30, 1983, 97 Stat. 1290; Pub. L. 99–65, § 1(b), July 12, 1985, 99

Stat. 163; Pub. L. 99–439, Oct. 2, 1986, 100 Stat. 1085.)

CODIFICATION

Section is from the Supplemental Appropriations Act, 1984.

PRIOR PROVISIONS

A prior section 58a, Pub. L. 95–94, title I, § 112(g), Aug. 5, 1977, 91 Stat. 665, directed Sergeant at Arms and Doorkeeper of Senate to furnish not more than two WATS lines to any Senator requesting them, with the cost of such service to be paid out of contingent fund of Senate, prior to repeal by section 1205(b) of Pub. L. 98–181, effective first day of first calendar month which begins more than thirty days after Nov. 30, 1983.

AMENDMENTS

1986—Pub. L. 99–439 struck out "(except services for which the charge is based on the amount of time the service is used)" after "Senator's State".

1985—Pub. L. 99–65 inserted "and in such Senator's State (except services for which the charge is based on the amount of time the service is used)".

EFFECTIVE DATE OF 1985 AMENDMENT

Amendment by Pub. L. 99–65 effective on first day of first calendar month beginning more than 60 days after July 12, 1985, see section 2 of Pub. L. 99–65, set out as a note under section 58 of this title.

PAYMENT FOR TELECOMMUNICATIONS SERVICE

Pub. L. 104–53, title I, § 5, Nov. 19, 1995, 109 Stat. 517, as amended by Pub. L. 104–197, title I, § 4(a), Sept. 16, 1996, 110 Stat. 2397, provided that:

"(a) Any payment for local and long distance telecommunications service provided to any user shall cover the total invoiced amount, including any amount relating to separately identified toll calls, and shall be charged to the appropriation for the fiscal year in which the underlying base service period covered by the invoice ends.

"(b) As used in subsection (a), the term 'user' means a Senator, an Officer of the Senate, and any office, committee, or other entity the funds of which are disbursed by the Secretary of the Senate."

[Pub. L. 104–197, title I, § 4(b), Sept. 16, 1996, 110 Stat. 2397, provided that: "The amendments made by subsection (a) [amending section 5 of Pub. L. 104–53, set out above] shall take effect on October 1, 1996, and shall apply to all payments made on or after such date for local and long distance telecommunications service."]

§ 58a–1. Payment for telecommunications equipment and services; definitions

As used in sections 58a–1 to 58a–3 of this title, the term—

(1) "Sergeant at Arms" means the Sergeant at Arms and Doorkeeper of the United States Senate; and

(2) "user" means any Senator, Officer of the Senate, Committee, office, or entity provided telephone equipment and services by the Sergeant at Arms.

(Pub. L. 100–123, § 1, Oct. 5, 1987, 101 Stat. 794.)

EFFECTIVE DATE

Section 4 of Pub. L. 100–123 provided that: "This Act [enacting this section and sections 58a–2 and 58a–3 of this title] shall take effect on October 1, 1987."

SECTION REFERRED TO IN OTHER SECTIONS

This section is referred to in sections 58a–2, 58a–3 of this title.

§ 58a–2. Certification of telecommunications equipment and services as official

(a) Regulations issued by Committee on Rules and Administration

Subject to such regulations as may hereafter be issued by the Committee on Rules and Administration of the Senate, the Sergeant at Arms shall have the authority, with respect to telephone equipment and services provided to any user on a reimbursable basis (including repair or replacement), solely for the purposes of this section, to make such certification as may be necessary to establish such services and equipment as official, issue invoices in conjunction therewith, and receive payment for such services and equipment by certification, voucher, or otherwise.

(b) Equipment and services provided on reimbursable basis

For purposes of sections 58a–1 to 58a–3 of this title, telephone equipment and services provided to any user for which payment, prior to October 1, 1987, was not authorized from the contingent fund of the Senate shall, on and after October 1, 1987, be considered telephone equipment and services provided on a reimbursable basis for which payment may be obtained from such fund in accordance with subsection (a) of this section.

(c) Establishment of reasonable charges

Subject to the approval of the Committee on Rules and Administration, the Sergeant at Arms may establish reasonable charges for telephone equipment and services provided to any user which may be in addition to that regularly authorized by the Committee.

(d) Disposition of moneys received

All moneys, derived from payments for telephone equipment and services provided from funds from the Appropriation Account within the contingent fund of the Senate for "Contingent Expenses, Sergeant at Arms and Doorkeeper of the Senate" under the line item for Telecommunications (including receipts from carriers and others for loss or damage to such services or equipment for which repair or replacement has been provided by the Sergeant at Arms), and all other moneys received by the Sergeant at Arms as charges or commissions for telephone services, shall be deposited in and made a part of such Appropriation Account and under such line item, and shall be available for expenditure or obligation, or both, in like manner and subject to the same limitations as any other moneys in such account and under such line item.

(e) Committee authority to classify or reclassify equipment and services

Nothing in sections 58a–1 to 58a–3 of this title shall be construed as limiting or otherwise affecting the authority of the Committee on Rules and Administration of the Senate to classify or reclassify telephone equipment and services provided to any user as equipment or services for which reimbursement may or may not be required.

(Pub. L. 100–123, § 2, Oct. 5, 1987, 101 Stat. 794; Pub. L. 101–163, title I, § 3, Nov. 21, 1989, 103 Stat. 1044.)

AMENDMENTS

1989—Subsec. (d). Pub. L. 101–163 inserted "and all other moneys received by the Sergeant at Arms as charges or commissions for telephone services," after "by the Sergeant at Arms),".

EFFECTIVE DATE

Section effective Oct. 1, 1987, see section 4 of Pub. L. 100–123, set out as a note under section 58a–1 of this title.

SECTION REFERRED TO IN OTHER SECTIONS

This section is referred to in sections 58a–1, 58a–3 of this title.

§ 58a–3. Report on telecommunications to Committee on Rules and Administration

The Sergeant at Arms shall report to the Committee on Rules and Administration of the Senate, at such time or times, and in such form and manner, as the Committee may direct, on expenditures made, and revenues received, pursuant to sections 58a–1 to 58a–3 of this title. It shall be the function of the Sergeant at Arms to advise the Committee, as soon as possible, of any dispute regarding payments to and from such Appropriation Account as related to the line item for Telecommunications, including any amounts due and unpaid by any user, if any such dispute has remained unresolved for a period of at least 60 days.

(Pub. L. 100–123, § 3, Oct. 5, 1987, 101 Stat. 795.)

EFFECTIVE DATE

Section effective Oct. 1, 1987, see section 4 of Pub. L. 100–123, set out as a note under section 58a–1 of this title.

SECTION REFERRED TO IN OTHER SECTIONS

This section is referred to in sections 58a–1, 58a–2 of this title.

§ 58a–4. Metered charges on copiers; "Sergeant at Arms" and "user" defined; certification of services and equipment as official; deposit of payments; availability for expenditure

(a) As used in this section, the term—

(1) "Sergeant at Arms" means the Sergeant at Arms and Doorkeeper of the United States Senate; and

(2) "user" means any Senator, Officer of the Senate, Committee, office, or entity provided copiers by the Sergeant at Arms.

(b)(1) Subject to such regulations as may on and after November 5, 1990, be issued by the Committee on Rules and Administration of the Senate, the Sergeant at Arms shall have the authority, with respect to metered charges on copying equipment provided by the Sergeant at Arms, solely for the purposes of this section, to make such certification as may be necessary to establish such services and equipment as official, issue invoices in conjunction therewith, and receive payment for such services and equipment by certification, voucher, or otherwise.

(2) All moneys, derived from the payment of metered charges on copying equipment provided from funds from the Appropriation Account within the contingent fund of the Senate for "Contingent Expenses, Sergeant at Arms and Doorkeeper of the Senate" under the line item

for the Service Department, shall be deposited in and made a part of such Appropriation Account and under such line item, and shall be available for expenditure or obligation, or both, in like manner and subject to the same limitations as any other moneys in such account and under such line item.

(Pub. L. 101–520, title I, § 4(a), (b), Nov. 5, 1990, 104 Stat. 2257.)

REFERENCES IN TEXT

This section, referred to in text, means section 4 of Pub. L. 101–520, which enacted this section, amended section 58 of this title, and enacted provisions set out as a note under section 58 of this title.

CODIFICATION

Section is from the Congressional Operations Appropriations Act, 1991, which is title I of the Legislative Branch Appropriations Act, 1991.

EFFECTIVE DATE

Section effective Oct. 1, 1990, see section 4(d) of Pub. L. 101–520, set out as an Effective Date of 1990 Amendment note under section 58 of this title.

§ 58b. Repealed. Pub. L. 100–137, § 2, Oct. 21, 1987, 101 Stat. 819

Section, Pub. L. 97–12, title I, § 110, June 5, 1981, 95 Stat. 62; Pub. L. 97–51, § 125, Oct. 1, 1981, 95 Stat. 965; Pub. L. 98–367, title I, § 11(a), July 17, 1984, 98 Stat. 476; Pub. L. 99–349, title I, § 2(a), (b), July 2, 1986, 100 Stat. 741, 742, provided for transfer to a Senator's Official Office Expense Account of that Senator's clerk hire allowance funds remaining at end of fiscal year. See section 58c of this title.

EFFECTIVE DATE OF REPEAL

Section 2 of Pub. L. 100–137 provided that the repeal is effective Jan. 1, 1988.

§ 58c. Senators' Official Personnel and Office Expense Account

(1) Effective January 1, 1988, there shall be, within the contingent fund of the Senate, a separate appropriation account to be known as the "Senators' Official Personnel and Office Expense Account" (hereinafter in this section referred to as the "Senators' Account").

(2) The Senators' Account shall be used for the funding of all items, activities, and expenses which, immediately prior to January 1, 1988, were funded under either (A) the Senate appropriation account for "Administrative, Clerical, and Legislative Assistance Allowance to Senators" (hereinafter in this section referred to as the "Senators' Clerk Hire Allowance Account") under the headings "SENATE" and "Salaries, Officers and Employees", or (B) that part of the account, within the contingent fund of the Senate, for "Miscellaneous Items" (hereinafter in this section referred to as the "Senators' Official Office Expense Account") which is available for allocation to Senatorial Official Office Expense Accounts. In addition, the Senators' Account shall be used for the funding of agency contributions payable with respect to compensation payable by such account, but moneys appropriated to such account for this purpose shall not be available for any other purpose. The account, which in clause (A) of the first sentence of this paragraph is identified as the "Senators'

Clerk Hire Allowance Account" and the account, which in clause (B) of such sentence is identified as the "Senators' Official Office Expense Account" shall, when referred to in other law, rule, regulation, or order (whether referred to by such name or any other) shall on and after January 1, 1988, be deemed to refer to the "Senators' Official Personnel and Office Expense Account".

(3)(A) Effective on January 1, 1988, there shall be transferred to the Senators' Account from the Senators' Clerk Hire Allowance Account all funds therein which were available for expenditure or obligation during the fiscal year ending September 30, 1988, and from the Senators' Official Office Expense Account so much of the funds therein as was available for expenditure or obligation for the period commencing January 1, 1988, and ending September 30, 1988; except that the Senators' Official Office Expense Account shall remain in being solely for the purpose of being available to pay for any authorized item, activity, or expense, for which funds therein had been obligated, but not paid, prior to such transfer.

(B) Any of the funds transferred to the Senators' Account from the Senators' Clerk Hire Allowance Account pursuant to subparagraph (A) which, prior to such transfer, had been obligated, but not expended, for any authorized item, activity, or expense, shall be available to pay for such item, activity, or expense in like manner as if such transfer had not been made.

(4) On January 1, 1988, there shall be transferred to the Senators' Account, from the appropriation account for "Agency Contributions", under the headings "SENATE" and "Salaries, Officers and Employees", so much of the moneys in such account as was appropriated for the purpose of making agency contributions for administrative, clerical, and legislative assistance to Senators with respect to compensation payable for the period commencing January 1, 1988, and ending September 30, 1988; and the moneys so transferred shall be available only for the payment of such agency contributions with respect to such compensation.

(5) Vouchers shall not be required for the disbursement, from the Senators' Account, of salaries of employees in the office of a Senator.

(6) Effective on and after October 1, 1997, the Senators' Account shall be available for the payment of franked mail expenses of Senators.

(Pub. L. 100–137, § 1(a), Oct. 21, 1987, 101 Stat. 814; Pub. L. 105–55, title I, § 3(b), Oct. 7, 1997, 111 Stat. 1180.)

REFERENCES IN TEXT

This section, referred to in pars. (1) and (2), means section 1 of Pub. L. 100–137, Oct. 21, 1987, 101 Stat. 814, which enacted this section, amended sections 58 and 61–1 of this title, and enacted provisions set out as notes under sections 58 and 61–1 of this title.

AMENDMENTS

1997—Par. (6). Pub. L. 105–55 added par. (6).

CONSTRUCTION OF 1997 AMENDMENT

Section 3(d) of Pub. L. 105–55 provided that: "Nothing in this section [amending this section and section 58 of this title, repealing section 58c–1 of this title, and enacting provisions set out as notes under sections 58 and 58c–1 of this title] affects the authority of the Committee on Rules and Administration of the Senate to prescribe regulations relating to the frank by Senators and officers of the Senate."

§ 58c–1. Repealed. Pub. L. 105–55, title I, § 3(c)(1), Oct. 7, 1997, 111 Stat. 1180

Section, Pub. L. 101–520, title I, § 12, Nov. 5, 1990, 104 Stat. 2260; Pub. L. 102–392, title III, § 313, Oct. 6, 1992, 106 Stat. 1723; Pub. L. 103–69, title I, § 3, Aug. 11, 1993, 107 Stat. 695, related to transfer of funds by Members of Senate from Senate Official Mail Costs Account to Senators' Official Personnel and Office Expense Account.

EFFECTIVE DATE OF REPEAL

Section 3(c)(2) of Pub. L. 105–55 provided that: "The amendment made by paragraph (1) [repealing this section] shall be effective on and after October 1, 1997."

§ 59. Home State office space for Senators; lease of office space

(a) Procurement by Sergeant at Arms of Senate in places designated by Senator; places subject to use; lease of office space

(1) The Sergeant at Arms of the Senate shall secure for each Senator office space suitable for the Senator's official use in places designated by the Senator in the State he represents. That space shall be secured in post offices or other Federal buildings at such places. In the event suitable office space is not available in post offices or other Federal buildings, the Sergeant at Arms shall secure other office space in those places.

(2) The Senator may lease, on behalf of the United States Senate, the office space so secured for a term not extending beyond the term of office which he is serving on the first day of such lease, except that, in the case of a Senator whose term of office is expiring and who has been elected for another term, such lease may extend until the end of the term for which he has been so elected. Each such lease shall contain a provision permitting its cancellation upon sixty days written notice by the Sergeant at Arms and Doorkeeper of the Senate, in the event of the death or resignation of the Senator. A copy of each such lease shall be furnished to the Sergeant at Arms. Nothing in this paragraph shall be construed to require the Sergeant at Arms to enter into or execute any lease for or on behalf of a Senator.

(b) Maximum amount of aggregate square feet for each Senator

The aggregate square feet of office space secured for Senator shall not at any time exceed—

(1) 5,000 square feet if the population of the State of the Senator is less than 3,000,000;

(2) 5,200 square feet if such population is 3,000,000 but less than 4,000,000;

(3) 5,400 square feet if such population is 4,000,000 but less than 5,000,000;

(4) 5,800 square feet if such population is 5,000,000 but less than 7,000,000;

(5) 6,200 square feet if such population is 7,000,000 but less than 9,000,000;

(6) 6,400 square feet if such population is 9,000,000 but less than 10,000,000;

(7) 6,600 square feet if such population is 10,000,000 but less than 11,000,000;

(8) 6,800 square feet if such population is 11,000,000 but less than 12,000,000;

(9) 7,000 square feet if such population is 12,000,000 but less than 13,000,000;

(10) 7,400 square feet if such population is 13,000,000 but less than 15,000,000;

(11) 7,800 square feet if such population is 15,000,000 but less than 17,000,000; or

(12) 8,200 square feet if such population is 17,000,000 or more.

(c) Maximum annual rental rate; maximum aggregate amount for acquisition of furniture, equipment, and other office furnishings

(1) The maximum annual rate that may be paid for the rental of an office secured for a Senator not in a post office or other Federal building shall not exceed the highest rate per square foot charged Federal agencies on the first day of the lease of such office by the Administrator of General Services, based upon a 100 percent building quality rating, for office space located in the place in which the Senator's office is located, multiplied by the number of square feet contained in that office used by the Senator and his employees to perform their duties.

(2) The aggregate amount that may be paid for the acquisition of furniture, equipment, and other office furnishings heretofore provided by the Administrator of General Services for one or more offices secured for the Senator is $40,000 if the aggregate square feet of office space is not in excess of 5,000 square feet. Such amount is increased by $1,000 for each authorized additional incremental increase in office space of 200 square feet. Effective beginning with the 106th Congress, the aggregate amount in effect under this paragraph for any Congress shall be increased by the inflation adjustment factor for the calendar year in which the Congress begins. For purposes of the preceding sentence, the inflation adjustment factor for any calendar year is a fraction the numerator of which is the implicit price deflator for the gross domestic product as computed and published by the Department of Commerce for the preceding calendar year and the denominator of which is such deflator for the calendar year 1998.

(d) Senators subject to maximum amount of aggregate square feet and maximum annual rental rate

(1) Notwithstanding subsection (b) of this section, the aggregate square feet of office space secured for a Senator who is a Senator on July 1, 1974, shall not at any time exceed, as long as he continuously serves as a Senator, the greater of—

(A) the applicable square footage limitation of such subsection; or

(B) the total square footage of those offices that the Senator has on such date and which are continuously maintained in the same buildings in which such offices were located on such date.

(2) The provisions of subsection (c) of this section do not apply to any office that a Senator has on July 1, 1974, not in a post office or other Federal building, as long as—

(A) that Senator continuously serves as a Senator; and

(B) that office is maintained in the same building in which it was located on such date

and contains not more than the same number of square feet it contained in such date.

(e) Omitted

(f) Mobile office

(1) Subject to the provisions of paragraphs (2), (3), (4), and (5), a Senator may lease one mobile office for use only in the State he represents and the contingent fund of the Senate is available for the rental payments (including by way of reimbursement) made under such lease together with the actual nonpersonnel cost of operating such mobile office. The term of any such lease shall not exceed 3 years. A copy of each such lease shall be furnished to the Sergeant at Arms of the Senate.

(2) The maximum aggregate annual rental payments and operating costs (except furniture, equipment, and furnishings) that may be paid to a Senator under paragraph (1) shall not at any time exceed an amount determined by multiplying (A) the highest applicable rate per square foot charged Federal agencies by the Administrator of General Services in the State which that Senator represents, based upon a 100 percent building quality rating, by (B) the maximum aggregate square feet of office space to which that Senator is entitled under subsection (b) of this section reduced by the number of square feet contained in offices secured for that Senator under subsection (a) of this section and used by that Senator and his employees to perform their duties.

(3) No payment shall be made under paragraph (1) for rental payments and operating costs of a mobile office of a Senator unless the following provisions are included in its lease:

(A) Liability insurance in the amount of $1,000,000 shall be provided with respect to the operation and use of such mobile office.

(B) Either of the following inscriptions shall be clearly visible on three sides of such mobile office in letters not less than three inches high:

"UNITED STATES GOVERNMENT VEHICLE

"FOR OFFICIAL USE ONLY";

OR

"MOBILE OFFICE OF SENATOR _____

"FOR OFFICIAL USE ONLY".

(4) No payment shall be made under paragraph (1) for rental payments and operating costs of a mobile office of a Senator which are attributable to or incurred during the 60-day period ending with the date of any primary or general election (whether regular, special, or runoff) in which that Senator is a candidate for public office, unless his candidacy in such election is uncontested.

(5) Payment under paragraph (1) shall be made on a monthly basis and shall be paid upon vouchers approved by the Sergeant at Arms of the Senate.

(g) Effective date

This section is effective on and after July 1, 1974.

(Pub. L. 93–371, §3, Aug. 13, 1974, 88 Stat. 428; Pub. L. 94–32, title I, §4, June 12, 1975, 89 Stat. 183; Pub. L. 94–59, title I, §§106(a), 107, July 25, 1975, 89 Stat. 276; Pub. L. 95–26, title I, §105, May 4, 1977, 91 Stat. 83; Pub. L. 95–94, title I, §112(d), Aug. 5, 1977, 91 Stat. 664; Pub. L. 96–304, title I, §109, July 8, 1980, 94 Stat. 890; Pub. L. 99–88, title I, §194, Aug. 15, 1985, 99 Stat. 349; Pub. L. 102–27, title II, Apr. 10, 1991, 105 Stat. 144; Pub. L. 102–90, title I, §7(b), Aug. 14, 1991, 105 Stat. 451; Pub. L. 104–197, title I, §3, Sept. 16, 1996, 110 Stat. 2397; Pub. L. 106–57, title I, §3, Sept. 29, 1999, 113 Stat. 411.)

CODIFICATION

Section is comprised of section 3 of Pub. L. 93–371. Subsec. (e) of section 3 of Pub. L. 93–371 amended section 58 of this title.

AMENDMENTS

1999—Subsec. (b)(1). Pub. L. 106–57, §3(1)(A), added par. (1) and struck out former par. (1) which read as follows: "4,800 square feet if the population of his State is less than 2,000,000;".

Subsec. (b)(2). Pub. L. 106–57, §3(1)(A), (C), redesignated par. (3) as (2) and struck out former par. (2) which read as follows: "5,000 square feet if such population is 2,000,000 but less than 3,000,000;".

Subsec. (b)(3) to (12). Pub. L. 106–57, §3(1)(C), redesignated pars. (4) to (13) as (3) to (12), respectively. Former par. (3) redesignated (2).

Subsec. (b)(13). Pub. L. 106–57, §3(1)(C), redesignated par. (13) as (12).

Pub. L. 106–57, §3(1)(B), substituted "8,200" for "8,000".

Subsec. (c)(2). Pub. L. 106–57, §3(2), substituted "$40,000" for "$30,000", "5,000 square feet" for "4,800 square feet", and "$1,000" for "$734" and inserted at end "Effective beginning with the 106th Congress, the aggregate amount in effect under this paragraph for any Congress shall be increased by the inflation adjustment factor for the calendar year in which the Congress begins. For purposes of the preceding sentence, the inflation adjustment factor for any calendar year is a fraction the numerator of which is the implicit price deflator for the gross domestic product as computed and published by the Department of Commerce for the preceding calendar year and the denominator of which is such deflator for the calendar year 1998."

1996—Subsec. (f)(1). Pub. L. 104–197 substituted "3 years" for "one year" in second sentence.

1991—Subsec. (f)(1). Pub. L. 102–90, §7(b)(1), substituted "the contingent fund of the Senate is available for the rental payments (including by way of reimbursement)" for "shall be reimbursed from the contingent fund of the Senate for the rental payments".

Subsec. (f)(2). Pub. L. 102–90, §7(b)(2), substituted "paid" for "reimbursed".

Subsec. (f)(3). Pub. L. 102–90, §7(b)(3), substituted "payment" for "reimbursement".

Subsec. (f)(3)(B). Pub. L. 102–27 added subpar. (B) and struck out former subpar. (B) which read as follows: "The following inscription shall be clearly visible on three sides of such mobile office in letters not less than four inches high:

"'Mobile Office of Senator (name of Senator)

"'FOR OFFICIAL OFFICE USE ONLY'."

Subsec. (f)(4). Pub. L. 102–90, §7(b)(4), substituted "payment" for "reimbursement".

Subsec. (f)(5). Pub. L. 102–90, §7(b)(5), substituted "Payment" for "Reimbursement".

1985—Subsec. (c)(2). Pub. L. 99–88 substituted "$30,000" for "$22,550" and "$734" for "$550".

1980—Subsec. (a)(2). Pub. L. 96–304, §109(1), substituted provision limiting term of a lease of office space to a term not extending beyond the term of office which Senator is serving on first day of such lease, except in case of a Senator whose term is expiring and who has been elected to another term, to end of term for which he has been so elected, for provision limiting term of a lease of office space to a term of not to exceed one year and inserted provision requiring each lease to contain a provision permitting cancellation upon sixty days written notification by Sergeant at Arms and Doorkeeper of Senate, in event of death or resignation of Senator.

Subsec. (c). Pub. L. 96–304, §109(2), substituted "shall not exceed the highest rate per square foot charged Federal agencies on the first day of the lease of such office" for "shall not at any time exceed the applicable rate per square foot charged Federal agencies".

1977—Subsec. (c)(2). Pub. L. 95–94 substituted "$22,550" for "$20,500" and "$550" for "$500".

Subsec. (f)(5). Pub. L. 95–26 substituted "monthly" for "quarterly".

1975—Subsec. (a). Pub. L. 94–59, §107, designated existing provisions as par. (1) and added par. (2).

Subsec. (c). Pub. L. 94–59, §106(a), designated existing provisions as par. (1) and added par. (2).

Subsecs. (f), (g). Pub. L. 94–32 added subsec. (f) and redesignated former subsec. (f) as (g).

EFFECTIVE DATE OF 1991 AMENDMENT

Amendment by Pub. L. 102–90 effective Oct. 1, 1991, see section 7(c) of Pub. L. 102–90, set out as a note under section 58 of this title.

EFFECTIVE DATE OF 1980 AMENDMENT

Section 109 of Pub. L. 96–304 provided that the amendment made by that section is effective Jan. 1, 1980.

EFFECTIVE DATE OF 1977 AMENDMENT

Amendment by Pub. L. 95–94 effective Aug. 5, 1977, see section 112(f) of Pub. L. 95–94, set out as a note under section 58 of this title.

EFFECTIVE DATE OF 1975 AMENDMENT

Section 106(b) of Pub. L. 94–59 provided that: "The amendment made by subsection (a) of this section [amending this section] is effective on and after July 1, 1975."

§ 59–1. Additional home State office space for Senators; declaration of disaster or emergency

(a) Notwithstanding any other provision of law or regulation, with the approval of the Committee on Rules and Administration of the Senate, the Sergeant at Arms and Doorkeeper of the Senate is authorized to provide additional facilities, services, equipment, and office space for use by a Senator in that Senator's State in connection with a disaster or emergency declared by the President under the Robert T. Stafford Disaster Relief and Emergency Assistance Act [42 U.S.C. 5121 et seq.]. Expenses incurred by the Sergeant at Arms and Doorkeeper of the Senate under this section shall be paid from the appropriation account, within the contingent fund of the Senate, for expenses of the Office of the Sergeant at Arms and Doorkeeper of the Senate, upon vouchers signed by the Sergeant at Arms and Doorkeeper of the Senate with the approval of the Committee on Rules and Administration of the Senate.

(b) This section is effective on and after June 12, 1997.

(Pub. L. 105–18, title II, §7002, June 12, 1997, 111 Stat. 192.)

REFERENCES IN TEXT

The Robert T. Stafford Disaster Relief and Emergency Assistance Act, referred to in subsec. (a), is Pub.

L. 93–288, May 22, 1974, 88 Stat. 143, as amended, which is classified principally to chapter 68 (§ 5121 et seq.) of Title 42, The Public Health and Welfare. For complete classification of this Act to the Code, see Short Title note set out under section 5121 of Title 42 and Tables.

§ 59a. Repealed. Pub. L. 101–163, title I, § 103(b), Nov. 21, 1989, 103 Stat. 1050

Section, Pub. L. 93–462, § 1, Oct. 20, 1974, 88 Stat. 1388, related to purchase of office equipment or furnishings by House Members.

Effective Date of Repeal

Repeal effective Oct. 1, 1989, see section 103(c) of Pub. L. 101–163, set out as an Effective Date of 1989 Amendment note under section 117e of this title.

§ 59b. Purchase of office equipment or furnishings by Senators

(a) Authorization; conditions

Notwithstanding any other provision of law, a United States Senator may purchase, upon leaving office or otherwise ceasing to be a Senator (except by expulsion), any item or items of office equipment or office furnishings provided by the General Services Administration and then currently located and in use in an office of such Senator in the State then represented by such Senator.

(b) Request by Senator and arrangement for purchase by Sergeant at Arms of Senate; regulations governing purchase; price

At the request of any United States Senator, the Sergeant at Arms of the Senate shall arrange for and make the purchase of equipment and furnishings under subsection (a) of this section on behalf of such Senator. Each such purchase shall be—

(1) in accordance with regulations which shall be prescribed by the Committee on Rules and Administration of the Senate, after consultation with the General Services Administration; and

(2) at a price equal to the acquisition cost to the Federal Government of the equipment or furnishings so purchased, less allowance for depreciation determined under such regulations, but in no instance less than the fair market value of such items.

(c) Remittance of amounts received to General Services Administration; disposition

Amounts received by the Federal Government from the sale of items of office equipment or office furnishings under this section shall be remitted to the General Services Administration and credited to the appropriate account or accounts.

(Pub. L. 93–462, § 2, Oct. 20, 1974, 88 Stat. 1388.)

§ 59c. Transferred

Codification

Section, Pub. L. 95–94, title I, § 103, Aug. 5, 1977, 91 Stat. 660; Pub. L. 97–51, § 118, Oct. 1, 1981, 95 Stat. 964, which related to disposal of used or surplus furniture and equipment by Sergeant at Arms and Doorkeeper of Senate, and procedure with respect to deposit of receipts from sale of such furniture and equipment, was transferred to section 117b of this title.

§ 59d. Transportation of official records and papers to House Member's district

(a) Payment of reasonable expenses from applicable accounts of House; rules and regulations

Effective August 16, 1978, notwithstanding any provision of law and until otherwise provided by law, the applicable accounts of the House shall be available to pay the reasonable expenses of sending or transporting the official records and papers of any Member of the House of Representatives from the District of Columbia to any location designated by such Member in the district represented by the Member.

The Chief Administrative Officer of the House of Representatives is authorized and directed to provide for the most economical means of sending or transporting such documents to insure the orderly and timely delivery to the specified location. The Committee on House Oversight shall have the authority to issue rules and regulations to carry out the provisions of this section.

(b) "Member of the House of Representatives" and "official records and papers" defined

As used in this section—

(1) the term "Member of the House of Representatives" means a Representative in, or a Delegate or Resident Commissioner to, the Congress; and

(2) the term "official records and papers" means books, records, papers, and official files which could be sent as franked mail.

(Pub. L. 98–51, title I, § 111(1), July 14, 1983, 97 Stat. 269; Pub. L. 104–186, title II, § 203(21), Aug. 20, 1996, 110 Stat. 1728.)

Codification

In subsec. (a), "August 16, 1978" substituted for "upon the date of adoption of this resolution" meaning the date of adoption of House Resolution No. 1297, which was agreed to Aug. 16, 1978.

Section is based on House Resolution No. 1297, Ninety-fifth Congress, Aug. 16, 1978, which was enacted into permanent law by Pub. L. 98–51.

Sections 1 and 2 of House Resolution No. 1297 were redesignated subsecs. (a) and (b) of this section, respectively, for purposes of codification.

Amendments

1996—Subsec. (a). Pub. L. 104–186, § 203(21)(A)–(C), substituted "applicable accounts" for "contingent fund" in first par. and "Chief Administrative Officer of the House of Representatives" for "Clerk of the House of Representatives" and "House Oversight" for "House Administration" in second par.

Subsec. (b)(1). Pub. L. 104–186, § 203(21)(D), amended par. (1) generally. Prior to amendment, par. (1) read as follows: "the term 'Member' means a Representative, a Resident Commissioner in the House, and a Delegate to the House; and".

Change of Name

Committee on House Oversight of House of Representatives changed to Committee on House Administration of House of Representatives by House Resolution No. 5, One Hundred Sixth Congress, Jan. 6, 1999.

§ 59e. Official mail of persons entitled to use congressional frank

(a) Congressional committee regulations for expenditure of appropriations for official mail

Except as otherwise provided in this section, funds appropriated by this Act or any other Act for expenses of official mail of any person entitled to use the congressional frank may be expended only in accordance with regulations prescribed by the Committee on Rules and Administration of the Senate or the Committee on House Oversight of the House of Representatives, as applicable. Such regulations shall require—

(1) individual accountability for use of official mail by each person entitled to use the congressional frank;

(2)(A) with respect to the House of Representatives, allocation of funds for official mail to be made to each such person with respect to each session of Congress (with no transfer to any other session or to any other such person); and

(B) with respect to the Senate, allocation of funds for official mail to be made to each such person with respect to each session of Congress (with no transfer to any other session, other than transfers from the first session of a Congress to the second session of that Congress, or to any other such person); and

(3) with respect to the House of Representatives, that in addition to any other report or information made available to the public (through the House Commission on Congressional Mailing Standards or otherwise) regarding the use of the frank, the Chief Administrative Officer of the House of Representatives shall include in the quarterly report of receipts and expenditures submitted to the House of Representatives a statement (based solely on data provided for that purpose by the Committee on House Oversight of the House of Representatives and the House Commission on Congressional Mailing Standards) of costs incurred for official mail by each person entitled to use the congressional frank.

(b) Postmaster General functions

The Postmaster General, in consultation with the Committee on Rules and Administration of the Senate and the Committee on House Oversight of the House of Representatives—

(1) shall monitor use of official mail by each person entitled to use the congressional frank;

(2) at least monthly, shall notify any person with an allocation under subsection (a)(2)(A) of this section as to the amount that has been used and any person with an allocation under subsection (a)(2)(B) of this section as to the percentage of the allocation that has been used; and

(3) may not carry or deliver official mail the cost of which is in excess of an allocation under subsection (a)(2) of this section.

(c) Source of funds for expenses of official mail

Expenses of official mail of the Senate and the House of Representatives may be paid only from funds specifically appropriated for that purpose and funds so appropriated—

(1) may be supplemented by other appropriated funds only if such supplementation is provided for by law or by regulation under subsection (a) of this section; and

(2) may not be supplemented by funds from any other source, public or private.

(d) Maintenance or use of unofficial office accounts or defrayal of official expenses from certain funds prohibited

No Senator or Member of the House of Representatives may maintain or use, directly or indirectly, an unofficial office account or defray official expenses from—

(1) funds received from a political committee or derived from a contribution or expenditure (as such terms are defined in section 431 of this title);

(2) funds received as reimbursement for expenses incurred by the Senator or Member in connection with personal services provided by the Senator or Member to the person making the reimbursement; or

(3) any other funds that are not specifically appropriated for official expenses.

(e) Official Mail Allowance in House of Representatives

(1) The use of funds of the House of Representatives which are made available for official mail of Members, officers, and employees of the House of Representatives who are persons entitled to use the congressional frank shall be governed by regulations promulgated—

(A) by the Committee on House Oversight of the House of Representatives, with respect to allocation and expenditures relating to official mail (except as provided in subparagraph (B)); and

(B) by the House Commission on Congressional Mailing Standards, with respect to matters under section 3210(a)(6)(D) of title 39.

(2) Funds used for official mail—

(A) with respect to a Member of the House of Representatives, shall be available, in a session of Congress, in a total amount, as determined under paragraph (1)(A), of not more than the product of (i) 3 times the single-piece rate applicable to first class mail, and (ii) the number (as determined by the Postmaster General) of addresses (other than business possible delivery stops) in the congressional district, as such addresses are described in section 3210(d)(7)(B) of title 39; and

(B) with respect to any other person entitled to use the congressional frank in the House of Representatives (including any Member of the House of Representatives who receives an allocation under subsection (a)(2) of this section with respect to duties as an elected officer of, or holder of another position in, the House of Representatives), shall be available, in a session of Congress, in a total amount determined under paragraph (1)(A).

(f) Mass mailing; submission of samples or description of proposed mail matter; advisory opinion

A Member of the House of Representatives shall, before making any mass mailing, submit a sample or description of the mail matter involved to the House Commission on Congressional Mailing Standards for an advisory opinion as to whether such proposed mailing is in compliance with applicable provisions of law, rule, or regulation.

(g) "Member of the House of Representatives" and "person entitled to use the congressional frank" defined

As used in subsections (a) through (f) of this section—

(1) the term "Member of the House of Representatives" means a Representative in, or a Delegate or Resident Commissioner to, the Congress; and

(2) the term "person entitled to use the congressional frank" means a Senator, Member of the House of Representatives, or other person authorized to use the frank under section 3210(b) of title 39.

(h) Omitted

(i) Effective date

This section and the amendments made by this section shall apply with respect to sessions of Congress beginning with the first session of the One Hundred Second Congress, except that, with respect to the Senate, subsection (d) of this section shall apply beginning on May 1, 1992, and the funds referred to in paragraph (3) of such subsection shall not include personal funds of a Senator or Member of the House of Representatives.

(Pub. L. 101–520, title III, § 311, Nov. 5, 1990, 104 Stat. 2278; Pub. L. 102–229, title II, § 211, Dec. 12, 1991, 105 Stat. 1718; Pub. L. 104–186, title II, § 203(22), Aug. 20, 1996, 110 Stat. 1728; Pub. L. 105–275, title I, § 104, Oct. 21, 1998, 112 Stat. 2439; Pub. L. 106–19, § 1(a), Apr. 8, 1999, 113 Stat. 29; Pub. L. 106–57, title I, §§ 102, 103(a)(1)–(3), (4)(B), Sept. 29, 1999, 113 Stat. 415.)

References in Text

The amendments made by this section, referred to in subsec. (i), means the amendments made by section 311(h) of Pub. L. 101–520, which amended section 58 of this title and sections 3210 and 3216 of Title 39, Postal Service, and amended provisions set out as notes under sections 3210 and 3216 of Title 39.

Codification

Section is from the Legislative Branch Appropriations Act, 1991.

Subsec. (h) of this section made the amendments specified in the References in Text note above.

Amendments

1999—Subsec. (a)(3). Pub. L. 106–57, § 103(a)(4)(B), substituted "costs incurred for official mail by" for "costs charged against the Official Mail Allowance for".

Subsec. (b)(2). Pub. L. 106–19 substituted "any person with an allocation under subsection (a)(2)(A) as to the amount that has been used and any person with an allocation under subsection (a)(2)(B)" for "any person with an allocation under subsection (a)(2)".

Subsec. (e)(1). Pub. L. 106–57, § 103(a)(1)(A), in introductory provisions, substituted "The use of funds of the House of Representatives which are made available for official mail of Members, officers, and employees of the House of Representatives who are persons entitled to use the congressional frank shall be governed by regulations promulgated—" for "There is established in the House of Representatives an Official Mail Allowance for Members, officers, and employees of the House of Representatives who are persons entitled to use the congressional frank. Regulations for use of the Official Mail Allowance shall be prescribed—".

Subsec. (e)(1)(A). Pub. L. 106–57, § 103(a)(1)(B), substituted "official mail (except as provided in subparagraph (B))" for "the Allowance".

Subsec. (e)(2). Pub. L. 106–57, § 103(a)(2)(A), substituted "Funds used for official mail—" for "The Official Mail Allowance—" in introductory provisions.

Pub. L. 106–57, § 102, made technical correction to directory language of Pub. L. 105–275, § 104(a). See 1998 Amendment note below.

Subsec. (e)(2)(A) to (C). Pub. L. 106–57, § 103(a)(2)(B), (C), redesignated subpars. (B) and (C) as (A) and (B), respectively, and struck out former subpar. (A) which read as follows: "shall be available for postage for franked mail sent at a first class, third class, or fourth class rate;".

Subsec. (e)(3). Pub. L. 106–57, § 103(a)(3), struck out par. (3) which read as follows:

"(3)(A) Subject to subparagraph (B), each Member of the House of Representatives may transfer amounts from the Members' Representational Allowance of the Member to the Official Mail Allowance of the Member.

"(B) The total amount a Member may so transfer with respect to a session of Congress may not exceed $25,000."

1998—Subsec. (e)(2). Pub. L. 105–275, § 104(a), as amended by Pub. L. 106–57, § 102, inserted "and" at end of subpar. (B), substituted a period for "; and" at end of subpar. (C), and struck out subpar. (D) which read as follows: "shall not be available for payment of any nonpostage fee or charge, including any fee or charge for express mail, express mail drop shipment, certified mail, registered mail, return receipt, address correction, or postal insurance."

Subsec. (e)(4). Pub. L. 105–275, § 104(b), struck out par. (4) which read as follows: "The Members' Representational Allowance shall be available to a Member of the House of Representatives for the payment of nonpostage fees and charges referred to in paragraph (2)(D) and for postage for mail for official business sent outside the United States."

1996—Subsec. (a). Pub. L. 104–186, § 203(22)(B)(i), substituted "House Oversight" for "House Administration" in introductory provisions.

Subsec. (a)(3). Pub. L. 104–186, § 203(22)(A), (B)(ii), substituted "Chief Administrative Officer of the House of Representatives" for "Clerk of the House of Representatives" and "House Oversight" for "House Administration".

Subsec. (b). Pub. L. 104–186, § 203(22)(B)(iii), substituted "House Oversight" for "House Administration" in introductory provisions.

Subsec. (e)(1)(A). Pub. L. 104–186, § 203(22)(B)(iv), substituted "House Oversight" for "House Administration".

Subsec. (e)(2)(A). Pub. L. 104–186, § 203(22)(B)(v), struck out "only" after "available".

Subsec. (e)(3)(A). Pub. L. 104–186, § 203(22)(B)(vi), substituted "Members' Representational Allowance" for "Official Expenses Allowance and the Clerk Hire Allowance".

Subsec. (e)(4). Pub. L. 104–186, § 203(22)(B)(vii), substituted "Members' Representational Allowance" for "Official Expenses Allowance".

1991—Subsec. (i). Pub. L. 102–229 substituted "beginning on May 1, 1992," for "with respect to sessions of Congress beginning with the second session of the One Hundred Second Congress,".

Change of Name

Committee on House Oversight of House of Representatives changed to Committee on House Administration of House of Representatives by House Resolution No. 5, One Hundred Sixth Congress, Jan. 6, 1999.

Effective Date of 1999 Amendments

Amendment by section 103(a)(1)–(3), (4)(B) of Pub. L. 106–57 applicable with respect to the first session of the One Hundred Sixth Congress and each succeeding session of Congress, see section 103(c) of Pub. L. 106–57, set out as a note under section 57 of this title.

Pub. L. 106–19, § 1(b), Apr. 8, 1999, 113 Stat. 29, provided that: "The amendment made by subsection (a) [amending this section] shall apply with respect to January 1999 and each succeeding month.''

SECTION REFERRED TO IN OTHER SECTIONS

This section is referred to in section 57 of this title.

§ 59f. Mass mailings by Senate offices; quarterly statements; publication of summary tabulations

Two weeks after the close of each calendar quarter, or as soon as practicable thereafter, the Sergeant at Arms and Doorkeeper of the Senate shall send to each Senate office a statement of the cost of postage and paper and of the other operating expenses incurred as a result of mass mailings processed for such Senate office during such quarter. The statement shall separately identify the cost of postage and paper and other costs, and shall distinguish the costs attributable to newsletters and all other mass mailings. The statement shall also include the total cost per capita in the State. A compilation of all such statements shall be sent to the Senate Committee on Rules and Administration. A summary tabulation of such information shall be published quarterly in the Congressional Record and included in the semiannual report of the Secretary of the Senate. Such summary tabulation shall set forth for each Senate office the following information: the Senate office's name, the total number of pieces of mass mail mailed during the quarter, the total cost of such mail, and, in the case of Senators, the cost of such mail divided by the total population of the State from which the Senator was elected, and the total number of pieces of mass mail divided by the total population of the State from which the Senator was elected, and in the case of each Senator, the allocation made to such Senator from the appropriation for official mail expenses.

(Pub. L. 101–520, title III, § 318, Nov. 5, 1990, 104 Stat. 2283; Pub. L. 103–283, title I, § 3(b), July 22, 1994, 108 Stat. 1427.)

CODIFICATION

Section is from the Legislative Branch Appropriations Act, 1991.

AMENDMENTS

1994—Pub. L. 103–283 inserted before period at end '', and in the case of each Senator, the allocation made to such Senator from the appropriation for official mail expenses''.

EFFECTIVE DATE OF 1994 AMENDMENT

Section 3(c) of Pub. L. 103–283 provided that: ''The amendments made by this section [amending this section and section 104a of this title] shall be effective with respect to—

''(1) reports and statements covering periods beginning on and after October 1, 1994; and

''(2) appropriations made and obligations incurred on and after such date.''

§ 59g. Mass mailing of information by Senators under frank; quarterly registration with Secretary of Senate

In fiscal year 1991 and thereafter, when a Senator disseminates information under the frank by a mass mailing (as defined in section 3210(a)(6)(E) of title 39), the Senator shall register quarterly with the Secretary of the Senate such mass mailings. Such registration shall be made by filing with the Secretary a copy of the matter mailed and providing, on a form supplied by the Secretary, a description of the group or groups of persons to whom the mass mailing was mailed and the number of pieces mailed.

(Pub. L. 101–520, title III, § 320, Nov. 5, 1990, 104 Stat. 2285.)

CODIFICATION

Section is from the Legislative Branch Appropriations Act, 1991.

§ 59h. Mass mailing sent by House Members

(a) Notice that mailing is at taxpayer expense

Each mass mailing sent by a Member of the House of Representatives shall bear in a prominent place on its face, or on the envelope or outside cover or wrapper in which the mail matter is sent, the following notice: "THIS MAILING WAS PREPARED, PUBLISHED, AND MAILED AT TAXPAYER EXPENSE.", or a notice to the same effect in words which may be prescribed under subsection (c) of this section. The notice shall be printed in a type size not smaller than 7-point.

(b) Publication of each Member's total expense and amount

(1) There shall be published in the itemized report of disbursements of the House of Representatives as required by law, a summary tabulation setting forth, for the office of each Member of the House of Representatives, the total number of pieces of mass mail mailed during the period involved and the total cost of those mass mailings.

(2) Each such tabulation shall also include—

(A) the total cost (as referred to in paragraph (1)) divided by the number (as determined by the Postmaster General) of addresses (other than business possible delivery stops) in the Congressional district from which the Member was elected (as such addresses are described in section 3210(d)(7)(B) of title 39); and

(B) the total number of pieces of mass mail (as referred to in paragraph (1)) divided by the number (as determined by the Postmaster General) of addresses (other than business possible delivery stops) in the Congressional district from which the Member was elected (as such addresses are described in section 3210(d)(7)(B) of title 39).

(c) Regulations

The Committee on House Oversight shall prescribe such rules and regulations and shall take such other action as the Committee considers necessary and proper for Members to conform to the provisions of this subsection and applicable rules and regulations.

(d) Definitions

For purposes of this section—

(1) the term "Member of the House of Representatives" means a Representative in, or a Delegate or Resident Commissioner to, the Congress; and

(2) the term "mass mailing" has the meaning given such term by section 3210(a)(6)(E) of title 39.

(e) Applicability

This section shall apply with respect to sessions of Congress beginning after September 16, 1996.

(Pub. L. 104–197, title III, § 311, Sept. 16, 1996, 110 Stat. 2414.)

CODIFICATION

Section is from the Legislative Branch Appropriations Act, 1997.

CHANGE OF NAME

Committee on House Oversight of House of Representatives changed to Committee on House Administration of House of Representatives by House Resolution No. 5, One Hundred Sixth Congress, Jan. 6, 1999.

CHAPTER 4—OFFICERS AND EMPLOYEES OF SENATE AND HOUSE OF REPRESENTATIVES

Sec.
130b.   Jury and witness service by Senate and House
            employees.
            (a) Definitions.
            (b) Service as juror or witness in connec-
                  tion with a judicial proceeding; pro-
                  hibition against reduction of pay.
            (c) Official duty.
            (d) Prohibition on receipt of jury or wit-
                  ness fees.
            (e) Travel expenses.
            (f) Rules and regulations.
            (g) Congressional consent not conferred
                  for production of official records or
                  to testimony concerning activities
                  related to employment.
130c.   Waiver by Secretary of Senate of claims of
            United States arising out of erroneous pay-
            ments to Vice President, Senator, or Senate
            employee paid by Secretary of Senate.
            (a) Waiver of claim for erroneous pay-
                  ment of pay or allowances.
            (b) Prohibition of waiver.
            (c) Credit for waiver.
            (d) Effect of waiver.
            (e) Construction with other laws.
            (f) Rules and regulations.
130d.   Waiver by Speaker of House of claims of
            United States arising out of erroneous pay-
            ments to officers or employees paid by
            Chief Administrative Officer of House.
            (a) Waiver of claim for erroneous pay-
                  ment of pay or allowances.
            (b) Investigation and report.
            (c) Prohibition of waiver.
            (d) Credit for waiver.
            (e) Effect of waiver.
            (f) Construction with other laws.
            (g) Rules and regulations.
130e.   Special Services Office.
130f.   Office of General Counsel of House; administra-
            trative provisions.
            (a) Compliance with admission require-
                  ments.
            (b) Notification by Attorney General.
            (c) General Counsel definition.
            (d) Effective date.

§ 60. Repealed. June 20, 1929, ch. 33, § 6, 46 Stat. 39

Section, acts May 24, 1924, ch. 183, § 1, 43 Stat. 146;
May 29, 1928, ch. 853, § 1, 45 Stat. 885, related to rates of
pay for various officers and employees of Government.
See notes set out under section 60a–1 and section 60c–1
et seq. of this title.

§ 60–1. Authority of officers of Congress over Congressional employees

(a) Qualifications determinations; removal and discipline

Each officer of the Congress having responsibility for the supervision of employees, including employees appointed upon recommendation
of Members of Congress, shall have authority—
    (1) to determine, before the appointment of
any individual as an employee under the supervision of that officer of the Congress,
whether that individual possesses the qualifications necessary for the satisfactory performance of the duties and responsibilities to
be assigned to him; and
    (2) to remove or otherwise discipline any em-
ployee under his supervision.

(b) "Officer of the Congress" defined

As used in this section, the term "officer of
the Congress" means—

    (1) an elected officer of the Senate or House
of Representatives who is not a Member of the
Senate or House; and
    (2) The Architect of the Capitol.

(Pub. L. 91–510, title IV, § 431, Oct. 26, 1970, 84
Stat. 1190.)

Section effective immediately prior to noon on Jan.
3, 1971, see section 601(1) of Pub. L. 91–510, set out as an
Effective Date of 1970 Amendment note under section
72a of this title.

REDUCTION IN NUMBER OF EMPLOYEE POSITIONS;
REPORTS

Pub. L. 103–69, title III, § 307, Aug. 11, 1993, 107 Stat.
710, as amended by Pub. L. 103–283, title III, § 305, July
22, 1994, 108 Stat. 1441; Pub. L. 104–316, title I, § 102(a),
Oct. 19, 1996, 110 Stat. 3827, provided for reduction in
number of employee positions on full-time equivalent
basis, other than those supported by gift and trust
funds, for each entity of legislative branch with more
than 100 employee positions, on full-time equivalent
basis, as of Sept. 30, 1992, by at least 4 percent from
level as of such date, provided that such reduction was
to be completed not later than Sept. 30, 1995, with at
least 62.5 percent of reduction for each entity to be
achieved by Sept. 30, 1994, and defined "entity of legislative branch".

SECTION REFERRED TO IN OTHER SECTIONS

This section is referred to in title 40 section 212a–2.

§ 60–2. Amendment to Senate conflict of interest rule

(a) Except as provided by subsection (b) of this
section, any employee of the Senate who is required to file a report pursuant to Senate rules
shall refrain from participating personally and
substantially as an employee of the Senate in
any contact with any agency of the executive or
judicial branch of Government with respect to
non-legislative matters affecting any non-governmental person in which the employee has a
significant financial interest.

(b) Subsection (a) of this section shall not
apply if an employee first advises his supervisor
of his significant financial interest and obtains
from such supervisor a written waiver stating
that the participation of the employee is necessary. A copy of each such waiver shall be filed
with the Select Committee.

(Pub. L. 101–194, title IX, § 903, Nov. 30, 1989, 103
Stat. 1781.)

§ 60a. Omitted

CODIFICATION

Present provisions relating to personnel and compensation of Congressional officers and employees may
be found elsewhere in this chapter and in Acts and Resolutions cited in notes hereunder. Section was based on
the following acts:

1949—Jan. 19, 1949, ch. 2, § 1(d), (f), 63 Stat. 4.
        May 24, 1949, ch. 138, title I, 63 Stat. 76.
        Oct. 10, 1949, ch. 662, title I, 63 Stat. 738.
        Oct. 14, 1949, ch. 694, title I, 63 Stat. 869.
1948—June 14, 1948, ch. 467, §§ 101, 105, 62 Stat. 423, 437.
        June 25, 1948, ch. 658, title I, 62 Stat. 1027.
1947—Jan. 31, 1947, ch. 1, 61 Stat. 1.
        Feb. 19, 1947, ch. 3, 61 Stat. 4.
        July 17, 1947, ch. 262, §§ 101, 105, 61 Stat. 361, 377.
        July 30, 1947, ch. 361, 61 Stat. 610.
        July 31, 1947, ch. 414, 61 Stat. 695.

1946—July 1, 1946, ch. 530, §§ 101, 105, 60 Stat. 387, 407.
 July 23, 1946, ch. 591, title I, 60 Stat. 600.
 Aug. 2, 1946, ch. 753, title II, § 201(a), 60 Stat. 834.
 Aug. 8, 1946, ch. 870, title I, 60 Stat. 910.
1945—Apr. 25, 1945, ch. 95, title I, 59 Stat. 77.
 June 13, 1945, ch. 189, §§ 101, 105, 59 Stat. 238, 259.
 July 5, 1945, ch. 271, title I, 59 Stat. 412.
 Dec. 28, 1945, ch. 589, title I, 59 Stat. 632.
1944—June 26, 1944, ch. 277, title I, §§ 101, 104, 58 Stat. 334, 354.
 June 28, 1944, ch. 304, title I, 58 Stat. 597.
 Dec. 22, 1944, ch. 660, title I, 58 Stat. 853.
1943—June 28, 1943, ch. 173, title I, §§ 101, 104, 57 Stat. 220, 239.
1942—June 8, 1942, ch. 396, §§ 1, 4, 56 Stat. 330, 349.
1941—Mar. 1, 1941, ch. 9, 55 Stat. 14.
 July 1, 1941, ch. 268, §§ 1, 4, 55 Stat. 446, 465.
1940—June 18, 1940, ch. 396, §§ 1, 4, 54 Stat. 462, 480.
 Oct. 9, 1940, ch. 780, title I, 54 Stat. 1030.
1939—June 16, 1939, ch. 208, §§ 1, 4, 53 Stat. 822, 839.
 July 25, 1939, ch. 352, § 2, 53 Stat. 1080.
1938—May 17, 1938, ch. 236, §§ 1, 4, 52 Stat. 381, 398.
 June 25, 1938, ch. 681, 52 Stat. 1114.
1937—May 18, 1937, ch. 223, 50 Stat. 169.
1934—May 30, 1934, ch. 372, 48 Stat. 817.
1933—Feb. 28, 1933, ch. 134, 47 Stat. 1350.
1929—June 20, 1929, ch. 33, 46 Stat. 32.

In addition to these acts the following House Resolutions affected the salary of certain employees and were made permanent law by section 105 of act July 17, 1947, ch. 262, 61 Stat. 377: House Resolutions 628, 691, and 693 of the Seventy-ninth Congress and House Resolutions 42, 54, 74, 78, 96, 113, and 183 [which related to Office of Coordinator of Information of the House and which was repealed by Pub. L. 91–510, title III, § 322, Oct. 26, 1970, 84 Stat. 1185] of the Eightieth Congress. House Resolutions 281 and 336 of the Eightieth Congress were made permanent law by act June 14, 1948, ch. 467, § 105, 62 Stat. 437. House Resolutions No. 653 of the Eightieth Congress, and 6, 39, 45, 62, 84, 103, 172, and 188 of the 81st Congress were made permanent law by act June 22, 1949, ch. 235, § 105, 63 Stat. 230.

LEGISLATIVE BRANCH APPROPRIATION ACTS

The following acts have provided for funds for the operation of Congress:
Pub. L. 106–554, § 1(a)(2) [title I], Dec. 21, 2000, 114 Stat. 2763, 2763A–93.
Pub. L. 106–57, title I, Sept. 29, 1999, 113 Stat. 408.
Pub. L. 105–275, title I, Oct. 21, 1998, 112 Stat. 2430.
Pub. L. 105–55, title I, Oct. 7, 1997, 111 Stat. 1177.
Pub. L. 104–197, title I, Sept. 16, 1996, 110 Stat. 2394.
Pub. L. 104–53, title I, Nov. 19, 1995, 109 Stat. 514.
Pub. L. 103–283, title I, July 22, 1994, 108 Stat. 1423.
Pub. L. 103–69, title I, Aug. 11, 1993, 107 Stat. 692.
Pub. L. 102–392, title I, Oct. 6, 1992, 106 Stat. 1703.
Pub. L. 102–90, title I, Aug. 14, 1991, 105 Stat. 447.
Pub. L. 101–520, title I, Nov. 5, 1990, 104 Stat. 2254.
Pub. L. 101–163, title I, Nov. 21, 1989, 103 Stat. 1041.
Pub. L. 100–458, title I, Oct. 1, 1988, 102 Stat. 2158.
Pub. L. 100–202, § 101(i) [title I], Dec. 22, 1987, 101 Stat. 1329–290.
Pub. L. 99–500, § 101(j), Oct. 18, 1986, 100 Stat. 1783–287, and Pub. L. 99–591, § 101(j), Oct. 30, 1986, 100 Stat. 3341–287.
Pub. L. 99–151, title I, Nov. 13, 1985, 99 Stat. 792.
Pub. L. 98–367, title I, July 17, 1984, 98 Stat. 472.
Pub. L. 98–51, title I, July 14, 1983, 97 Stat. 263.
Pub. L. 97–276, § 101(e), Oct. 2, 1982, 96 Stat. 1189.
Pub. L. 97–51, § 101(c), Oct. 1, 1981, 95 Stat. 959.
Pub. L. 96–536, § 101(c), (d), Dec. 16, 1980, 94 Stat. 3167.
Pub. L. 96–369, § 101(c), (d), Oct. 1, 1980, 94 Stat. 1352, 1353.
Pub. L. 96–86, § 101(c), Oct. 12, 1979, 93 Stat. 657.
Pub. L. 95–391, title I, Sept. 30, 1978, 92 Stat. 763.
Pub. L. 95–94, title I, Aug. 5, 1977, 91 Stat. 653.
Pub. L. 94–440, title I, Oct. 1, 1976, 90 Stat. 1439.
Pub. L. 94–59, title I, July 25, 1975, 89 Stat. 269.
Pub. L. 93–371, Aug. 13, 1974, 88 Stat. 424.

Pub. L. 93–145, Nov. 1, 1973, 87 Stat. 527.
Pub. L. 92–342, July 10, 1972, 86 Stat. 432.
Pub. L. 92–51, July 9, 1971, 85 Stat. 125.
Pub. L. 91–382, Aug. 18, 1970, 84 Stat. 807.
Pub. L. 91–145, Dec. 12, 1969, 83 Stat. 339.
Pub. L. 90–417, July 23, 1968, 82 Stat. 398.
Pub. L. 90–57, July 28, 1967, 81 Stat. 127.
Pub. L. 89–545, Aug. 27, 1966, 80 Stat. 354.
Pub. L. 89–90, July 27, 1965, 79 Stat. 265.
Pub. L. 88–454, Aug. 20, 1964, 78 Stat. 535.
Pub. L. 88–248, Dec. 30, 1963, 77 Stat. 803.
Pub. L. 87–730, Oct. 2, 1962, 76 Stat. 680.
Pub. L. 87–130, Aug. 10, 1961, 75 Stat. 320.
Pub. L. 86–628, July 12, 1960, 74 Stat. 446.
Pub. L. 86–176, Aug. 21, 1959, 73 Stat. 398.
Pub. L. 85–570, July 31, 1958, 72 Stat. 439.
Pub. L. 85–75, July 1, 1957, 71 Stat. 244.
June 27, 1956, ch. 453, 70 Stat. 356.
Aug. 5, 1955, ch. 568, 69 Stat. 499.
July 2, 1954, ch. 455, title I, 68 Stat. 396.
Aug. 1, 1953, ch. 304, title I, 67 Stat. 318.
July 9, 1952, ch. 598, 66 Stat. 464.
Oct. 11, 1951, ch. 485, 65 Stat. 388.
Sept. 6, 1950, ch. 896, Ch. II, 64 Stat. 595.
June 22, 1949, ch. 235, 63 Stat. 216.

LIMITATION ON FUNDS AVAILABLE TO SENATE FOR FISCAL YEAR BEGINNING OCTOBER 1, 1980

Pub. L. 96–508, § 10, Dec. 8, 1980, 94 Stat. 2749, provided that in the fiscal year beginning October 1, 1980, the aggregate amount of funds made available to the Senate shall not exceed 90 per centum of the aggregate amount of the funds made available for such purposes for the fiscal year beginning on October 1, 1979.

SENATE AND HOUSE COMMITTEE EMPLOYEES

Senate and House committee employees, formerly provided for by this section, are covered by section 72a of this title.

§ 60a–1. Senate pay adjustments; action by President pro tempore of Senate

(a) Each time the President adjusts the rates of pay of employees under section 5303 of title 5 (or section 5304 or 5304a of such title, as applied to employees employed in the pay locality of the Washington, D.C.-Baltimore, Maryland consolidated metropolitan statistical area) the President pro tempore of the Senate shall, as he considers appropriate—

(1)(A) adjust the rates of pay of personnel whose pay is disbursed by the Secretary of the Senate, and any minimum or maximum rate applicable to any such personnel; or

(B) in the case of such personnel whose rates of pay are fixed by or pursuant to law at specific rates, adjust such rates (including the adjustment of such specific rates to maximum pay rates) and, in the case of all other personnel whose pay is disbursed by the Secretary of the Senate, adjust only the minimum or maximum rates applicable to such other personnel; and

(2) adjust any limitation or allowance applicable to such personnel;

by percentages which are equal or equivalent, insofar as practicable and with such exceptions as may be necessary to provide for appropriate pay relationships between positions, to the percentages of the adjustments made by the President under such section 5303 (and, as the case may be, section 5304 or 5304a of such title, as applied to employees employed in the pay locality of the Washington, D.C.-Baltimore, Maryland consolidated metropolitan statistical area) for corresponding rates of pay for employees subject to the General Schedule contained in section 5332 of such title and adjust the rates of such personnel by such amounts as necessary to restore the same pay relationships that existed on December 31, 1986, between personnel and Senators and between positions. Such rates, limitations, and allowances adjusted by the President pro tempore shall become effective on the first day of the month in which any adjustment becomes effective under such section 5303 or section 3(c) of this Act.

(b) The adjustments made by the President pro tempore shall be made in such manner as he considers advisable and shall have the force and effect of law.

(c) Nothing in this section shall impair any authority pursuant to which rates of pay may be fixed by administrative action.

(d) No rate of pay shall be adjusted under the provisions of this section to an amount in excess of the rate of basic pay for level III of the Executive Schedule contained in section 5314 of title 5, except in cases in which it is necessary to restore and maintain the same pay relationships that existed on December 31, 1986, between personnel and Senators and between positions.

(e) Any percentage used in any statute specifically providing for an adjustment in rates of pay in lieu of an adjustment made under section 5303 of title 5 and, as the case may be, section 5304 or 5304a of such title for any calendar year shall be treated as the percentage used in an adjustment made under such section 5303, 5304, or 5304a, as applicable, for purposes of subsection (a) of this section.

(f) For purposes of this section, the term "personnel" does not include any Senator.

(Pub. L. 91–656, § 4, Jan. 8, 1971, 84 Stat. 1952; Pub. L. 92–298, § 3(a), May 17, 1972, 86 Stat. 146; Pub. L. 92–392, § 14(a), Aug. 19, 1972, 86 Stat. 575; Pub. L. 94–82, title II, § 204(d), Aug. 9, 1975, 89 Stat. 422; Pub. L. 100–202, § 101(i) [title III, § 311(a), (b)], Dec. 22, 1987, 101 Stat. 1329–290, 1329–310; Pub. L. 101–509, title V, § 529 [title I, § 101(b)(4)(E)], Nov. 5, 1990, 104 Stat. 1427, 1440; Pub. L. 106–554, § 1(a)(2) [title I, § 2], Dec. 21, 2000, 114 Stat. 2763, 2763A–96.)

REFERENCES IN TEXT

Section 3(c) of this Act, referred to in subsec. (a), is section 3(c) of Pub. L. 91–656, which is set out as a note under section 5303 of Title 5, Government Organization and Employees.

AMENDMENTS

2000—Subsec. (a). Pub. L. 106–554, § 1(a)(2) [title I, § 2(1)], in introductory provisions, inserted "(or section 5304 or 5304a of such title, as applied to employees employed in the pay locality of the Washington, D.C.-Baltimore, Maryland consolidated metropolitan statistical area)" after "employees under section 5303 of title 5" and in concluding provisions, inserted "(and, as the case may be, section 5304 or 5304a of such title, as applied to employees employed in the pay locality of the Washington, D.C.-Baltimore, Maryland consolidated metropolitan statistical area)" after "the President under such section 5303".

Subsecs. (e), (f). Pub. L. 106–554, § 1(a)(2) [title I, § 2(2), (3)], added subsec. (e) and redesignated former subsec. (e) as (f).

1990—Subsec. (a). Pub. L. 101–509 substituted "5303" for "5305" wherever appearing.

1987—Subsec. (a). Pub. L. 100–202, § 101(i) [title III, § 311(a)], inserted requirement that rates of personnel be adjusted by such amounts as necessary to restore same pay relationships that existed on Dec. 31, 1986, between personnel and Senators and between positions.

Subsec. (d). Pub. L. 100–202, § 101(i) [title III, § 311(b)], inserted exception for cases in which it is necessary to restore and maintain same pay relationships that existed on Dec. 31, 1986, between personnel and Senators and between positions.

1975—Subsec. (d). Pub. L. 94–82 substituted "level III" for "level V", and "section 5314 of title 5" for "section 5316 of title 5."

1972—Subsec. (a). Pub. L. 92–298 and Pub. L. 92–392 made identical amendments by substituting "first day of the month in which any adjustment becomes effective" for "first day of the first pay period which begins on or after the day on which any adjustment becomes effective" in last sentence.

EFFECTIVE DATE OF 1990 AMENDMENT

Amendment by Pub. L. 101–509 effective on such date as the President shall determine, but not earlier than 90 days, and not later than 180 days, after Nov. 5, 1990, see section 529 [title III, § 305] of Pub. L. 101–509, set out as a note under section 5301 of Title 5, Government Organization and Employees.

EFFECTIVE DATE OF 1987 AMENDMENT

Section 101(i) [title III, § 311(c)] of Pub. L. 100–202 provided that: "Notwithstanding any other provision of this Act [see Tables for classification] or any other provision of law, subsections (a) and (b) of this section [amending this section] shall be effective in the case of pay orders issued by the President pro tempore of the Senate on or after January 1, 1988."

EFFECTIVE DATE OF 1972 AMENDMENT

Amendment by Pub. L. 92–392 effective on first day of first applicable pay period beginning on or after 90th day after Aug. 19, 1972, see section 15(a) of Pub. L. 92–392, set out as an Effective Date note under section 5341 of Title 5, Government Organization and Employees.

ORDER OF THE PRESIDENT PRO TEMPORE OF THE UNITED STATES SENATE

DECEMBER 20, 2000

By virtue of the authority vested in me by section 4 of the Federal Pay Comparability Act of 1970 (2 U.S.C. 60a–1) in order—

(1) to provide (subject to the provisions of section 704 of the Ethics Reform Act of 1989 (5 U.S.C. 5318 note; Public Law 101–194) and the amendments made by such section [amending section 31 of this title, section 104 of Title 3, The President, section 5318 of Title 5, Government Organization and Employees, and section 461 of Title 28, Judiciary and Judicial Procedure]) increases in the annual rates of compensation for officers and employees of the Senate that are comparable to the increases in rates of pay under the General Schedule taking effect on January 1, 2001, pursuant to sections 5303 and 5304 or 5304a of title 5, United States Code, and

(2) to provide (subject to such provisions of law) for the restoration of, and to maintain in effect, the same pay relationships that existed on December 31, 1986, between personnel and Senators and between Senate positions,
it is hereby—
Ordered,

DEFINITION

SECTION 1. For purposes of this Order, the term "employee" includes an officer (other than a United States Senator).

RATE INCREASES FOR SPECIFIED POSITIONS

SEC. 2. (a) The annual rates of compensation of the Secretary of the Senate, the Sergeant at Arms and

Doorkeeper, and the Legislative Counsel shall each be $143,600.

(b) The annual rates of compensation of the Secretary for the Majority and the Secretary for the Minority shall each be $143,034.

(c) The annual rates of compensation of the Deputy Legislative Counsel and the Senior Counsels in the Office of the Legislative Counsel and the maximum annual rates of compensation for the Assistant Secretary of the Senate, the Parliamentarian, the Financial Clerk, the Assistant to the Majority Leader for Floor Operations, the Assistant to the Minority Leader for Floor Operations, the Chief of Staff for the Majority Leader, and the Chief of Staff for the Minority Leader shall each be $142,415.

(d) The maximum annual rates of compensation for the positions authorized for the Capitol Guide Service by the Capitol Guide Board shall each be increased by 3.81 percent.

CHAPLAIN'S OFFICE

SEC. 3. The annual rate of compensation of the Chaplain is equal to the annual rate of pay provided for level IV of the Executive Schedule under section 5315 of title 5, United States Code, except that such annual rate of compensation may not at any time exceed the rate equal to the difference between the annual rate of compensation for a position referred to in section 2(a) and $11,713.

OFFICES OF SENATE

SEC. 4. (a) The following individuals are authorized to increase the annual rates of compensation of the employees specified, subject to applicable limitations adjusted by this Order:

(1) The Vice President, for any employee under his jurisdiction.

(2) The President pro tempore, for any employee under his jurisdiction.

(3) The Deputy President pro tempore, for any employee under his jurisdiction.

(4) The Majority Leader and the Minority Leader, for any employee under their respective jurisdictions (subject, in the case of the Assistant to the Majority Leader for Floor Operations, the Assistant to the Minority Leader for Floor Operations, the Chief of Staff for the Majority Leader, and the Chief of Staff for the Minority Leader, respectively, to the provisions of section 2(c) of this Order).

(5) The Majority Whip and the Minority Whip, for any employee under their respective jurisdictions.

(6) The Secretary of the Conference of the Majority and the Secretary of the Conference of the Minority, for any employee under their respective jurisdictions.

(7) The Secretary of the Senate, for any employee under his jurisdiction (subject to the provisions of section 2(c) of this Order).

(8) The Sergeant at Arms and Doorkeeper, for any employee under his jurisdiction.

(9) The Chaplain, for any employee under his jurisdiction.

(10) The Legislative Counsel, subject to the approval of the President pro tempore, for any employee under his jurisdiction (other than the Deputy Legislative Counsel and the Senior Counsels).

(11) The Senate Legal Counsel, for any employee under his jurisdiction (subject to the provisions of section 701(b) of the Ethics in Government Act of 1978 (2 U.S.C. 288(b))).

(12) The Secretary for the Majority and the Secretary for the Minority, for any employee under their respective jurisdictions.

(13) The Capitol Guide Board, for any employee under the jurisdiction of the Board.

(14) The appointing authority of any Senate entity not referred to under paragraphs (1) through (13) for any employee under its jurisdiction.

(b) Except for those officers and employees referred to in section 2 of this Order, no officer or employee within the Office of the Secretary of the Senate and no officer or employee within the Office of the Sergeant at Arms and Doorkeeper shall, for any period of time, be paid gross compensation at an annual rate which is in excess of the maximum prescribed in section 105(f) of the Legislative Branch Appropriation Act, 1968 (2 U.S.C. 61–1(f)) (as such rate is adjusted in section 7(b) of the Order of the President pro tempore of December 12, 1999).

COMMITTEE STAFFS

SEC. 5. (a) Subject to the provisions of section 105 of the Legislative Branch Appropriation Act, 1968 (2 U.S.C. 61–1) (as modified by this Order), and to the other provisions of this Order, the chairman of any standing, special, or select committee of the Senate (including the majority and minority policy committees and the conference majority and the conference minority of the Senate), and the chairman of any joint committee of the Congress whose funds are disbursed by the Secretary of the Senate, are each authorized to increase the annual rate of compensation of any employee of the committee, or any subcommittee thereof, of which he is chairman, subject to applicable limitations adjusted by this Order.

(b) The maximum annual rates of "$136,264", "$136,759", and "$138,615" referred to in section 105(e) of the Legislative Branch Appropriation Act, 1968 (2 U.S.C. 61–1(e)) (as provided for in section 5(b) of the Order of the President pro tempore of December 12, 1999) shall be deemed to be the figures "$140,064", "$140,559", and "$142,415", respectively.

SENATORS' OFFICES

SEC. 6. (a) Subject to the provisions of section 105 of the Legislative Branch Appropriation Act, 1968 (2 U.S.C. 61–1), as modified by this Order, and to the other provisions of this Order, each Senator is authorized to increase the annual rate of compensation of any employee in his office, subject to applicable limitations adjusted by this Order.

(b) The table contained in section 105(d)(1) of such Act shall be deemed to read as follows:

"$1,399,205 if the population of the State is less than 5,000,000;

"$1,451,667 if such population is 5,000,000 but less than 6,000,000;

"$1,504,132 if such population is 6,000,000 but less than 7,000,000;

"$1,556,595 if such population is 7,000,000 but less than 8,000,000;

"$1,609,059 if such population is 8,000,000 but less than 9,000,000;

"$1,661,521 if such population is 9,000,000 but less than 10,000,000;

"$1,713,987 if such population is 10,000,000 but less than 11,000,000;

"$1,766,451 if such population is 11,000,000 but less than 12,000,000;

"$1,818,913 if such population is 12,000,000 but less than 13,000,000;

"$1,871,377 if such population is 13,000,000 but less than 14,000,000;

"$1,923,841 if such population is 14,000,000 but less than 15,000,000;

"$1,976,305 if such population is 15,000,000 but less than 16,000,000;

"$2,028,770 if such population is 16,000,000 but less than 17,000,000;

"$2,081,234 if such population is 17,000,000 but less than 18,000,000;

"$2,114,796 if such population is 18,000,000 but less than 19,000,000;

"$2,148,362 if such population is 19,000,000 but less than 20,000,000;

"$2,181,928 if such population is 20,000,000 but less than 21,000,000;

"$2,215,493 if such population is 21,000,000 but less than 22,000,000;

"$2,249,059 if such population is 22,000,000 but less than 23,000,000;

"$2,282,624 if such population is 23,000,000 but less than 24,000,000;

"$2,316,186 if such population is 24,000,000 but less than 25,000,000;

"$2,349,749 if such population is 25,000,000 but less than 26,000,000;

"$2,383,317 if such population is 26,000,000 but less than 27,000,000;

"$2,416,881 if such population is 27,000,000 but less than 28,000,000; and

"$2,450,448 if such population is 28,000,000 or more.".

(c) The figures "$1,893" and "$136,759" referred to in the second sentence of section 105(d)(2) of the Legislative Branch Appropriation Act, 1968 (2 U.S.C. 61–1(d)(2)) (as provided in section 6(c) of the Order of the President pro tempore of December 12, 1999) shall be deemed to be the figures "$1,966" and "$140,559", respectively.

(d) The amount referred to under section 111(a) of the Legislative Branch Appropriation Act, 1978 (2 U.S.C. 61–1 note), as amended by section 1 of the Legislative Branch Appropriations Act, 1993 (Public Law 102–392; 106 Stat. 1706) shall be $421,677.

GENERAL LIMITATION

SEC. 7. (a) The figure "$1,893" referred to in section 105(f) of the Legislative Branch Appropriation Act, 1968 (2 U.S.C. 61–1(f)) (as provided in section 7(a) of the Order of the President pro tempore of December 12, 1999) shall be deemed to be the figure "$1,966".

(b) The maximum annual rate of compensation of "$136,759" appearing in section 105(f) of the Legislative Branch Appropriation Act, 1968 (2 U.S.C. 61–1(f)) (as provided for in section 7(b) of the Order of the President pro tempore of December 12, 1999) shall be deemed to be the figure "$140,559".

NOTIFYING DISBURSING OFFICE OF INCREASES

SEC. 8. In order for an employee to receive the increase in his annual rate of compensation pursuant to section 4, 5, or 6, the individual designated to authorize such increases for that employee shall notify the Disbursing Office of the Senate in writing that he authorizes such increase for that employee and the date (prescribed in accordance with section 105(a)(2) of the Legislative Branch Appropriation Act, 1968 (2 U.S.C. 61–1(a)(2))) on which such increase is to be effective. Such increase shall become effective as provided in section 105(a)(2) of the Legislative Branch Appropriation Act, 1968 (2 U.S.C. 61–1(a)(2)), except that if the notice required by the preceding sentence is given within five days (not counting Saturdays, Sundays, or holidays) after the date on which this Order is issued, such increase may become effective on January 1, 2001.

DUAL COMPENSATION

SEC. 9. The figure "$25,362" referred to in section 5533(c)(1) of title 5, United States Code (as provided in section 9 of the Order of the President pro tempore of December 12, 1999) shall be deemed to be the figure "$26,329".

OFFICE OF THE SENATE LEGAL COUNSEL

SEC. 10. (a) The annual rate of compensation of the Senate Legal Counsel shall be $143,600.

(b) The annual rate of compensation of the Deputy Senate Legal Counsel shall be $142,300.

(c) The maximum annual rate of compensation of each Assistant Senate Legal Counsel may not at any time exceed the rate equal to the difference between the annual rate of compensation for a position referred to in section 2(a) and $4,900.

EFFECTIVE DATE

SEC. 11. Sections 1 through 10 of this Order are effective January 1, 2001.

STROM THURMOND
President pro tempore

Prior Orders of the President pro tempore of the Senate were issued on the following dates:

Dec. 12, 1999, eff. Jan. 1, 2000.
Dec. 16, 1998, eff. Jan. 1, 1999.
Dec. 19, 1997, eff. Jan. 1, 1998.
Dec. 18, 1996, eff. Jan. 1, 1997.
Dec. 28, 1994, eff. Jan. 1, 1995.
Dec. 17, 1992, eff. Jan. 1, 1993.
Dec. 18, 1991, eff. Jan. 1, 1992.
Dec. 20, 1990, eff. Jan. 1, 1991.
Dec. 21, 1989, eff. Jan. 1, 1990.
Dec. 9, 1988, eff. Jan. 1, 1989.
Jan. 4, 1988, eff. Jan. 1, 1988.
Dec. 19, 1986, eff. Jan. 1, 1987.
Jan. 4, 1985, eff. Jan. 1, 1985.
Dec. 20, 1983, amended May 2, 1987, eff. Jan. 1, 1984.
Oct. 1, 1982, eff. Oct. 1, 1982; Cong. Rec., vol. 128, pt. 20, p. 26968.
Oct. 5, 1981, amended Dec. 15, 1981, eff. Jan. 1, 1981; Cong. Rec., vol. 127, pt. 19, p. 24991.
Oct. 1, 1980, eff. Oct. 1, 1980; Cong. Rec., vol. 126, pt. 25, p. 34376.
Oct. 13, 1979, eff. Oct. 1, 1979; Cong. Rec., vol. 125, pt. 22, p. 28404.
Oct. 9, 1978, eff. Oct. 1, 1978; Cong. Rec., vol. 124, pt. 28, p. 37837.
Sept. 29, 1977, eff. Oct. 1, 1977.
Oct. 8, 1976, eff. Oct. 1, 1976; Cong. Rec., vol. 123, pt. 3, p. 3784.
Oct. 2, 1975, eff. Oct. 1, 1975; Cong. Rec., vol. 121, pt. 27, p. 34398.
Oct. 7, 1974, eff. Oct. 1, 1975; Cong. Rec., vol. 120, pt. 27, p. 36717.
Oct. 4, 1973, eff. Oct. 1, 1973.
Dec. 16, 1972, eff. Jan. 1, 1973; Cong. Rec., vol. 119, pt. 1, p. 674.
Dec. 23, 1971, eff. Jan. 1, 1972; Cong. Rec., vol. 118, pt. 1, p. 235.
Jan. 15, 1971, eff. Feb. 1, 1971; Cong. Rec., vol. 117, pt. 1, p. 770.
Apr. 15, 1970, eff. Jan. 1, and May 1, 1970; Cong. Rec., vol. 116, pt. 9, p. 11860.
June 17, 1969, eff. July 1, 1969; Cong. Rec., vol. 115, pt. 12, p. 16103.
June 12, 1968, eff. July 1, 1968; Cong. Rec., vol. 114, pt. 13, p. 16890.

INCREASE IN COMPENSATION OF OFFICERS OF SENATE; LIMITATIONS ON BASIC AND GROSS COMPENSATION—1966

Pub. L. 89–504, title III, § 302(g), (h), July 18, 1966, 80 Stat. 295, provided that:

"(g) Notwithstanding the provision referred to in subsection (h), the rates of gross compensation of the Secretary for the Majority of the Senate, the Secretary for the Minority of the Senate, the Chief Reporter of Debates of the Senate, the Parliamentarian of the Senate, the Senior Counsel in the Office of the Legislative Counsel of the Senate, the Chief Clerk of the Senate, the Chaplain of the Senate, and the Postmaster and Assistant Postmaster of the Senate are hereby increased by 2.9 per centum.

"(h) The paragraph imposing limitations on basic and gross compensation of officers and employees of the Senate appearing under the heading 'SENATE' in the Legislative Appropriation Act, 1956, as amended (74 Stat. 304; Public Law 86–568), is amended by striking out '$23,770' and inserting in lieu thereof '$24,460'." [The paragraph in the Legislative Appropriation Act, 1956, referred to above, was repealed by Pub. L. 90–57, § 105(i)(3), July 28, 1967, 81 Stat. 144, eff. Aug. 1, 1967.]

INCREASE IN COMPENSATION OF OFFICERS OF SENATE; LIMITATIONS ON BASIC AND GROSS COMPENSATION—1965

Pub. L. 89–301, § 11(g), (h), Oct. 29, 1965, 79 Stat. 1121, provided that:

"(g) Notwithstanding the provision referred to in subsection (h), the rates of gross compensation of the Secretary for the Majority of the Senate, the Secretary for the Minority of the Senate, the Chief Reporter of Debates of the Senate, the Parliamentarian of the Senate, the Senior Counsel in the Office of the Legislative Counsel of the Senate, the Chief Clerk of the Senate, the Chaplain of the Senate, and the Postmaster and Assistant Postmaster of the Senate are hereby increased by 3.6 per centum.

"(h) The paragraph imposing limitations on basic and gross compensation of officers and employees of the Senate appearing under the heading 'SENATE' in the Legislative Appropriation Act, 1956, as amended (74 Stat. 304; Public Law 86–568), is amended by striking out '$22,945' and inserting in lieu thereof '$23,770'." [The paragraph in the Legislative Appropriation Act, 1956, referred to above, was repealed by Pub. L. 90–57, §105(i)(3), July 28, 1967, 81 Stat. 144, eff. Aug. 1, 1967.]

INCREASE IN COMPENSATION OF OFFICERS OF SENATE; LIMITATIONS ON BASIC AND GROSS COMPENSATION—1964

Pub. L. 88–426, title II, §202(f), (g), Aug. 14, 1964, 78 Stat. 414, provided that:

"(f) Notwithstanding the provision referred to in subsection (g), the rates of gross compensation of the Secretary for the Majority of the Senate, the Secretary for the Minority of the Senate, the Official Reporters of Debates of the Senate, the Parliamentarian of the Senate, the Senior Counsel in the Office of the Legislative Counsel of the Senate, and the Chief Clerk of the Senate are hereby increased by an amount which is equal to the amount of the increase which would be provided by subsection (a) of this section [section 60e–11 of this title] in that gross rate determined without regard to the provisions referred to in subsection (g) of this section which is nearest in amount to the total annual compensation of such officer or employee.

"(g) The paragraph imposing limitations on basic and gross compensation of officers and employees of the Senate appearing under the heading 'SENATE' in the Legislative Appropriation Act, 1956, as amended (74 Stat. 304; Public Law 86–568), is amended by striking out '$18,880' and inserting in lieu thereof '$22,945'." [The paragraph in the Legislative Appropriation Act, 1956, referred to above, was repealed by Pub. L. 90–57, §105(i)(3), July 28, 1967, 81 Stat. 144, eff. Aug. 1, 1967.]

INCREASE IN COMPENSATION OF OFFICERS OF SENATE; LIMITATIONS ON BASIC AND GROSS COMPENSATION—1962

Pub. L. 87–793, §1005(c), (d), Oct. 11, 1962, 76 Stat. 867, provided that:

"(c) Notwithstanding the provision referred to in subsection (d), the rates of gross compensation of the elected officers of the Senate (except the Presiding Officer of the Senate), the Legislative Counsel of the Senate, the Official Reporters of Debates of the Senate, the Parliamentarian of the Senate, the Senior Counsel in the Office of the Legislative Counsel of the Senate, and the Chief Clerk of the Senate are hereby increased by 7 per centum.

"(d) The paragraph imposing limitations on basic and gross compensation of officers and employees of the Senate appearing under the heading 'SENATE' in the Legislative Appropriation Act, 1956, as amended (74 Stat. 304; Public Law 86–568), is amended to read as follows:

"'No officer or employee whose compensation is disbursed by the Secretary of the Senate shall be paid basic compensation at a rate in excess of $8,880 per annum, or gross compensation at a rate in excess of $18,880 per annum, unless expressly authorized by law.'" [The paragraph in the Legislative Appropriation Act, 1956, referred to above, was repealed by Pub. L. 90–57, §105(i)(3), July 28, 1967, 81 Stat. 144, eff. Aug. 1, 1967.]

INCREASE IN COMPENSATION OF OFFICERS OF SENATE; LIMITATIONS ON BASIC AND GROSS COMPENSATION—1960

Pub. L. 86–568, title I, §117(c), (d), July 1, 1960, 74 Stat. 303, provided that:

"(c) Notwithstanding the provision referred to in subsection (d), the rates of gross compensation of each of the elected officers of the Senate (except the Presiding Officer of the Senate), the Parliamentarian of the Senate, the Legislative Counsel of the Senate, the Senior Counsel in the Office of the Legislative Counsel of the Senate, and the Chief Clerk of the Senate are hereby increased by 7.5 per centum.

"(d) The paragraph imposing limitations on basic and gross compensation of officers and employees of the Senate appearing under the heading 'SENATE' in the Legislative Appropriation Act, 1956 (69 Stat. 510; Public Law 242, Eighty-fourth Congress), is amended to read as follows:

"'No officer or employee whose compensation is disbursed by the Secretary of the Senate shall be paid basic compensation at a rate in excess of $8,880 per annum, or gross compensation at a rate in excess of $17,525 per annum, unless expressly authorized by law.'" [Prior to this amendment "$8,880" and "$17,525" were, respectively, "$8,880" and "$16,300" per annum.] [The paragraph in the Legislative Appropriation Act, 1956, referred to above was repealed by Pub. L. 90–57, §105(i)(3), July 28, 1967, 81 Stat. 144, eff. Aug. 1, 1967.]

INCREASE IN COMPENSATION OF OFFICERS OF SENATE; LIMITATIONS ON BASIC AND GROSS COMPENSATION—1958

Pub. L. 85–462, §4(c), (d), June 20, 1958, 72 Stat. 208, provided that:

"(c) Notwithstanding the provision referred to in subsection (d), the rates of gross compensation of each of the elected officers of the Senate (except the presiding officer of the Senate), the Parliamentarian of the Senate, the Legislative Counsel of the Senate, the Senior Counsel in the Office of the Legislative Counsel of the Senate, and the Chief Clerk of the Senate are hereby increased by 10 per centum.

"(d) The paragraph imposing limitations on basic and gross compensation of officers and employees of the Senate appearing under the heading 'SENATE' in the Legislative Appropriation Act, 1956 (69 Stat. 510; Public Law 242, Eighty-fourth Congress), is amended to read as follows:

"'No officer or employee, whose compensation is disbursed by the Secretary of the Senate shall be paid basic compensation at a rate in excess of $8,880 per annum, or gross compensation at a rate in excess of $16,300 per annum, unless expressly authorized by law.'" [Prior to this amendment "$8,880" and "$16,300" were, respectively, "$8,820" and "$14,800" per annum.] [The paragraph in the Legislative Appropriation Act, 1956, referred to above, was repealed by Pub. L. 90–57, §105(i) (3), July 28, 1967, 81 Stat. 144, eff. Aug. 1, 1967.]

INCREASE IN COMPENSATION OF OFFICERS OF SENATE AND HOUSE—1955

Act June 28, 1955, ch. 189, §4(c), 69 Stat. 176, provided that: "The rates of basic compensation of each of the elected officers of the Senate and the House of Representatives (not including the presiding officers of the two Houses), the Parliamentarian of the Senate, the Parliamentarian of the House of Representatives, the Legislative Counsel of the Senate, the Legislative Counsel of the House of Representatives, and the Coordinator of Information of the House of Representatives are hereby increased by 7.5 per centum."

INCREASE IN COMPENSATION OF OFFICERS OF SENATE AND HOUSE—1951

Act Oct. 24, 1951, ch. 554, §2(e), 65 Stat. 614, provided that: "The rates of basic compensation of each of the elected officers of the Senate and the House of Representatives (not including the presiding officers of the two Houses), the Parliamentarian of the Senate, the Parliamentarian of the House of Representatives, the legislative counsel of the Senate, the legislative counsel of the House of Representatives, and the Coordinator of Information of the House of Representatives are hereby increased by 10 per centum, except that in no case shall any such rate be increased by less than $300 per annum or by more than $800 per annum."

INCREASE IN COMPENSATION OF OFFICERS OF SENATE
AND HOUSE—1949

Act Oct. 28, 1949, ch. 783, title I, § 101(d), 63 Stat. 974, provided that: "The rates of basic compensation of each of the elected officers of the Senate and the House of Representatives (not including the presiding officers of the two Houses) are hereby increased by 5 per centum."

SECTION REFERRED TO IN OTHER SECTIONS

This section is referred to in section 60a-1a of this title.

§ 60a-1a. Rates of compensation paid by Secretary of Senate; applicability of Senate pay adjustments by President pro tempore of Senate

No provision of this Act or of any Act enacted after October 1, 1976, which specifies a rate of compensation (including a maximum rate) for any position or employee whose compensation is disbursed by the Secretary of the Senate shall, unless otherwise specifically provided therein, be construed to affect the applicability of section 60a-1 of this title to such rate.

(Pub. L. 94-440, title I, § 107, Oct. 1, 1976, 90 Stat. 1444.)

REFERENCES IN TEXT

This Act, referred to in text, means the Legislative Branch Appropriation Act, 1977, Pub. L. 94-440, Oct. 1, 1976, 90 Stat. 1439, as amended. For complete classification of this Act to the Code, see Tables.

§ 60a-1b. Senate pay adjustments; action by President pro tempore of Senate

(a) Whenever, after November 5, 1990, there is an adjustment in rates of pay for Senators (other than an adjustment which occurs by virtue of an adjustment under section 5303 of title 5 in rates of pay under the General Schedule), the President pro tempore of the Senate may, notwithstanding any other provision of law, rule, or regulation, adjust the rate of pay (and any minimum or maximum rate, limitation, or allowance) applicable to personnel whose pay is disbursed by the Secretary of the Senate to the extent necessary to maintain the same pay relationships that existed on December 31, 1986, between personnel and Senators and between positions.

(b) Adjustments made by the President pro tempore under this section shall be made in such manner as he considers advisable and shall have the force and effect of law.

(Pub. L. 101-520, title III, § 315, Nov. 5, 1990, 104 Stat. 2283; Pub. L. 102-90, title III, § 308, Aug. 14, 1991, 105 Stat. 466.)

REFERENCES IN TEXT

The General Schedule, referred to in subsec. (a), is set out under section 5332 of Title 5, Government Organization and Employees.

CODIFICATION

Section is from the Legislative Branch Appropriations Act, 1991.

AMENDMENTS

1991—Subsec. (a). Pub. L. 102-90 substituted "5303" for "5305".

§ 60a-2. House of Representatives pay adjustments; action by Chief Administrative Officer of House

(a) Whenever an adjustment under section 5303 of title 5 becomes effective with respect to rates of pay under the General Schedule, the Chief Administrative Officer of the House of Representatives, in such manner as he considers advisable—

(1) effective on the first day of the month in which such pay adjustment by the President is made effective as described above, shall adjust—

(A) each minimum and maximum rate of pay applicable to any employee or class of employees whose pay is disbursed by the Chief Administrative Officer (other than a maximum rate equal to or greater than the maximum rate then currently being paid under the General Schedule of section 5332 of title 5 as a result of such adjustment); and

(B) each monetary limitation on or monetary allowance for pay applicable to any such employee or class of employees;

by an amount rounded to the nearest $100 and computed on the basis of a percentage equal or equivalent, insofar as practicable and with such variations as the Chief Administrative Officer considers appropriate, to the percentage of the adjustment under such section 5303;

(2) shall determine, with respect to the employees and classes of employees within the purview of this section whose pay is disbursed by the Chief Administrative Officer, the respective amounts of pay adjustments which are equal or equivalent, insofar as practicable and with such exceptions and modifications as may be necessary to provide for appropriate pay relationships between positions, to corresponding increases in pay, as determined by the Chief Administrative Officer, made by the pay adjustment by the President; and

(3) shall transmit to the appropriate pay-fixing authority concerned in the House of Representatives a copy of his determinations with respect to the pay of those employees whose pay is fixed and adjusted by that authority.

(b) After consideration of the pay determinations transmitted by the Chief Administrative Officer, the pay-fixing authority concerned may adjust, notwithstanding the provisions contained in sections 1341, 1342, and 1349-1351 and subchapter II of chapter 15 of title 31, the rates of pay concerned in such manner as that authority considers appropriate.

(c) Nothing in this section shall impair any authority pursuant to which rates of pay may be fixed by administrative action.

(d) This section shall not be deemed to authorize any adjustment in the rates of pay of employees whose rates of pay are disbursed by the Chief Administrative Officer and are fixed and adjusted from time to time as nearly as is consistent with the public interest in accordance with prevailing rates or practices, including employees subject to the House Wage Schedule.

(e) No rate of pay shall be adjusted under this section to an amount in excess of the rate of basic pay of level V of the Executive Schedule contained in section 5316 of title 5.

(Pub. L. 91–656, §5, Jan. 8, 1971, 84 Stat. 1952; Pub. L. 92–298, §3(b), May 17, 1972, 86 Stat. 146; Pub. L. 92–392, §14(b), Aug. 19, 1972, 86 Stat. 575; Pub. L. 101–509, title V, §529 [title I, §101(b)(4)(F), (10)], Nov. 5, 1990, 104 Stat. 1427, 1440, 1442; Pub. L. 102–378, §5(b), Oct. 2, 1992, 106 Stat. 1358; Pub. L. 104–186, title II, §204(1), Aug. 20, 1996, 110 Stat. 1729.)

CODIFICATION

In subsec. (b), "sections 1341, 1342, and 1349–1351 and subchapter II of chapter 15 of title 31" substituted for "section 665 of title 31, United States Code" on authority of Pub. L. 97–258, §4(b), Sept. 13, 1982, 96 Stat. 1067, the first section of which enacted Title 31, Money and Finance.

AMENDMENTS

1996—Subsec. (a). Pub. L. 104–186, §204(1)(A), substituted "Chief Administrative Officer of the House of Representatives" for "Clerk of the House of Representatives" in introductory provisions.

Subsec. (a)(1). Pub. L. 104–186, §204(1)(D), substituted "Chief Administrative Officer" for "Clerk" in concluding provisions.

Subsec. (a)(1)(A). Pub. L. 104–186, §204(1)(B), substituted "Chief Administrative Officer" for "Clerk of the House".

Subsec. (a)(1)(B). Pub. L. 104–186, §204(1)(C), struck out ", including but not limited to—

"(i) the clerk hire allowance for each Member of the House of Representatives and the Resident Commissioner from Puerto Rico; and

"(ii) the allowances for additional office personnel in the offices of the Speaker, the majority leader, the minority leader, the majority whip, and the minority whip, of the House of Representatives" after "class of employees".

Subsec. (a)(2). Pub. L. 104–186, §204(1)(E), substituted "Chief Administrative Officer" for "Clerk" in two places.

Subsec. (b). Pub. L. 104–186, §204(1)(F), substituted "Chief Administrative Officer" for "Clerk of the House".

Subsec. (d). Pub. L. 104–186, §204(1)(G), substituted "Chief Administrative Officer" for "Clerk of the House of Representatives".

1992—Subsec. (a). Pub. L. 102–378 inserted "of title 5" after "section 5303".

1990—Subsec. (a). Pub. L. 101–509, §529 [title I, §101(b)(4)(F)(i)], substituted "(a) Whenever an adjustment under section 5303 becomes effective with respect to rates of pay under the General Schedule," for "(a) Whenever a pay adjustment by the President under section 5305 of title 5 is made effective pursuant to subsection (a)(2), or subsections (c) to (m), inclusive, as the case may be, of such section 5305, or section 3(c) of this Act, then".

Subsec. (a)(1). Pub. L. 101–509, §529 [title I, §101(b)(10)], made technical correction to Pub. L. 92–298 and Pub. L. 92–392, see 1972 Amendment note below.

Pub. L. 101–509, §529 [title I, §101(b)(4)(F)(iii)], in closing provisions, substituted "adjustment under such section 5303;" for "pay adjustment made by the President;".

Subsec. (a)(1)(A). Pub. L. 101–509, §529 [title I, §101(b)(4)(F)(ii)], substituted "adjustment)" for "pay adjustment by the President)".

1972—Subsec. (a)(1). Pub. L. 92–298 and Pub. L. 92–392, as amended by Pub. L. 101–509, §529 [title I, §101(b)(10)], made identical substitutions in introductory provisions of "effective on the first day of the month in which such pay adjustments by the President" for "effective at the beginning of the first pay period commencing on or after the day on which such pay adjustment by the President".

EFFECTIVE DATE OF 1990 AMENDMENT

Amendment by Pub. L. 101–509 effective on such date as the President shall determine, but not earlier than 90 days, and not later than 180 days, after Nov. 5, 1990, see section 529 [title III, §305] of Pub. L. 101–509, set out as a note under section 5301 of Title 5, Government Organization and Employees.

EFFECTIVE DATE OF 1972 AMENDMENT

Amendment by Pub. L. 92–392 effective on first day of first applicable pay period beginning on or after 90th day after Aug. 19, 1972, see section 15(a) of Pub. L. 92–392, set out as an Effective Date note under section 5341 of Title 5, Government Organization and Employees.

DIRECTIVE OF THE SPEAKER OF THE HOUSE OF REPRESENTATIVES IMPLEMENTING THE SALARY COMPARABILITY POLICY IN 1969 FOR OFFICERS AND EMPLOYEES OF THE HOUSE OF REPRESENTATIVES REQUIRED BY SECTION 212 OF THE FEDERAL SALARY ACT OF 1967 [5 U.S.C. 5304 NOTE]

Salary Directives of the Speaker of the House of Representatives were issued on the following dates:

June 17, 1969, increases eff. July 1, 1969, Cong. Rec., vol. 115, pt. 12, p. 16196.

June 11, 1968, increases eff. July 1, 1968, Cong. Rec., vol. 114, pt. 13, p. 16717.

INCREASES IN COMPENSATION

The following acts provided increases in compensation for elected officers and certain employees of the House of Representatives:

June 20, 1958, Pub. L. 85–462, §4(k), (l), 72 Stat. 209.

June 28, 1955, ch. 189, §4(c), 69 Stat. 176.

Oct. 24, 1951, ch. 554, §2(e), 65 Stat. 614.

Oct. 28, 1949, ch. 783, title I, §101(d), 63 Stat. 974.

§ 60a–2a. Rates of compensation disbursed by Chief Administrative Officer of House; adjustments by Speaker; "Member of the House of Representatives" defined

(1) Notwithstanding any other provision of this Act, or any other provision of law, rule, or regulation, on and after December 22, 1987, each time the President pro tempore of the Senate exercises any authority pursuant to any of the amendments made by this section with respect to rates of pay or any other matter relating to personnel whose pay is disbursed by the Secretary of the Senate, or whenever any of the events described in paragraph (2) occurs, the Speaker of the House of Representatives may adjust the rates of pay (and any minimum or maximum rate, limitation, or allowance) applicable to personnel whose pay is disbursed by the Chief Administrative Officer of the House of Representatives to the extent necessary to ensure—

(A) appropriate pay levels and relationships between and among positions held by personnel of the House of Representatives; and

(B) appropriate pay relationships between—

(i) positions referred to in subparagraph (A); and

(ii)(I) positions under subparagraphs (A) through (D) of section 356 of this title;

(II) positions held by personnel whose pay is disbursed by the Secretary of the Senate; and

(III) positions to which the General Schedule applies.

(2) The other events permitting an exercise of authority under this section are either—

(A) an adjustment under section 5303 of title 5 in rates of pay under the General Schedule; or

(B) an adjustment in rates of pay for Members of the House of Representatives (other than an adjustment which occurs by virtue of an adjustment described in subparagraph (A)).

(3) For the purpose of this section, the term "Member of the House of Representatives" means a Member of the House of Representatives, a Delegate to the House of Representatives, and the Resident Commissioner from Puerto Rico.

(Pub. L. 100–202, §101(i) [title III, §311(d)], Dec. 22, 1987, 101 Stat. 1329–290, 1329–310; Pub. L. 101–520, title III, §308, Nov. 5, 1990, 104 Stat. 2277; Pub. L. 102–90, title III, §308, Aug. 14, 1991, 105 Stat. 466; Pub. L. 104–186, title II, §204(2), Aug. 20, 1996, 110 Stat. 1729.)

REFERENCES IN TEXT

This Act, referred to in par. (1), probably means the Legislative Branch Appropriations Act, 1988, Pub. L. 100–202, §101(i), Dec. 22, 1987, 101 Stat. 1329–290. For complete classification of this Act to the Code, see Tables.

The amendments made by this section, referred to in par. (1), means the amendments made by section 101(i) [title III, §311] of Pub. L. 100–202, Dec. 22, 1987, 101 Stat. 1329–290, 1329–310, which enacted this section, amended section 60a–1 of this title, and enacted provisions set out as a note under section 60a–1 of this title.

The General Schedule, referred to in pars. (1)(B)(i)(III) and (2)(A), is set out under section 5332 of Title 5, Government Organization and Employees.

CODIFICATION

Section is from the Congressional Operations Appropriations Act, 1988, which is title I of the Legislative Branch Appropriations Act, 1988.

AMENDMENTS

1996—Par. (1). Pub. L. 104–186 substituted "Chief Administrative Officer of the House of Representatives" for "Clerk of the House of Representatives".

1991—Par. (2)(A). Pub. L. 102–90 substituted "5303" for "5305".

1990—Pub. L. 101–520 designated existing provisions as par. (1), inserted "or whenever any of the events described in par. (2) occurs," after "Secretary of the Senate,", substituted "may adjust the rates of pay (and any minimum or maximum rate, limitation, or allowance) applicable to personnel whose pay is disbursed by the Clerk of the House of Representatives to the extent necessary to ensure—" and subpars. (A) and (B) for "may, with respect to personnel whose pay is disbursed by the Clerk of the House of Representatives, exercise the same authority to the extent necessary to ensure parity of treatment between personnel of the respective Houses of Congress having comparable duties and responsibilities.", and added pars. (2) and (3).

ORDER OF THE SPEAKER OF THE HOUSE OF REPRESENTATIVES

JANUARY 5, 2001

Pursuant to the authority vested in the Speaker by section 311(d) of the Legislative Branch Appropriations Act, 1988 (2 U.S.C. 60a–2a), in order to ensure parity of treatment between employees of the House of Representatives and certain other employees of the Government, it is hereby—

Ordered,

PAY FOR SPECIFIED POSITIONS

SECTION 1. (a) The annual rate of pay for the Clerk, the Sergeant-at-Arms, the Chief Administrative Officer, the Chaplain, the Parliamentarian, the Legislative Counsel, the Law Revision Counsel, the General Counsel to the House, and the Inspector General is $143,600.

(b) Subject to the approval of the Speaker, the Clerk, the Sergeant-at-Arms, the General Counsel to the House, and the Law Revision Counsel may establish the pay for the Deputy Clerk, the Deputy Sergeant-at-Arms, the Deputy General Counsel, and, notwithstanding section 2(b)(2), the Deputy Law Revision Counsel, respectively, at a maximum annual rate of $142,357.

PAY FOR CERTAIN OTHER POSITIONS

SEC. 2. (a) Subject to the maximums under subsection (b), the following Members, officers, and employees are authorized to establish annual rates of pay for their respective employees:

(1) The Speaker.

(2) The majority and minority leaders, including with respect to the majority leader, for the Republican employee under subsection (b)(1)(B)(i).

(3) The majority and minority whips.

(4) The chief deputy majority and minority whips.

(5) The Chairman of the Republican Steering Committee and the Chairman of the Republican Conference, other than for the Republican employee referred to in paragraph (2).

(6) The Chairman of the Democratic Steering and Policy Committee and the Chairman of the Democratic Caucus.

(7) The Parliamentarian, subject to the approval of the Speaker.

(8) The Legislative Counsel, subject to the approval of the Speaker.

(9) The Law Revision Counsel, subject to the approval of the Speaker.

(b)(1) The maximum annual rate under subsection (a) is $143,600 for—

(A) any employee whose maximum annual rate of pay, but for the pay authority of the Speaker under section 311(d) of the Legislative Branch Appropriations Act, 1988 (2 U.S.C. 60a–2a), would be subject to a maximum equal to the rate payable for level III or IV of the Executive Schedule; and

(B)(i) one employee of the Republican Conference and one employee of the Democratic Steering and Policy Committee, (ii) any employee in a position under 77 Stat. 817, (iii) 6 minority employees, (iv) the employee in the position in the Office of the Speaker created in 1967, (v) 3 employees in the Speaker's Office for Legislative Floor Activities, and (vi) 3 further minority employees.

(2) The maximum annual rate under subsection (a) is $140,451 for any employee whose maximum annual rate of pay, but for the pay authority of the Speaker referred to in paragraph (1), would be subject to a maximum equal to the rate payable for level V of the Executive Schedule.

PAY FOR EMPLOYEES OF COMMITTEES

SEC. 3. (a) Except as provided in subsection (b), the chairman of a standing, special, or select committee of the House or of a joint committee of Congress, if applicable, may establish the pay for employees of the committee at a maximum annual rate of $140,451.

(b)(1) Each chairman may establish the pay for 3 employees at a maximum annual rate of $143,600, with one such employee to be designated by the ranking minority party member.

(2) Each chairman may establish the pay for 9 employees at a maximum annual rate of $142,357, with 3 such employees to be designated by the ranking minority party member, except that the Chairman of the Committee on Appropriations may so establish pay for 24 employees, with 7 such employees to be designated by the ranking minority party member.

PAY FOR EMPLOYEES OF MEMBERS

SEC. 4. Each Member of the House may establish the pay for employees in the office of the Member at a maximum annual rate of $140,451.

MISCELLANEOUS PAY PROVISIONS

SEC. 5. (a) Subject to the approval of the Speaker, the Clerk may establish the pay for 3 employees at a maximum annual rate of $140,451.

(b) Subject to the approval of the Speaker, the Sergeant-at-Arms may establish the pay—

(1) for one employee at a maximum annual rate of $140,451; and

(2) for 3 employees at a maximum annual rate equal to 75 percent of the maximum under paragraph (1).

(c) Subject to the approval of the Speaker, the Chief Administrative Officer may establish the pay—

(1) for 2 employees at a maximum annual rate of $140,451; and

(2) for 3 employees at a maximum annual rate of $142,357.

GENERAL LIMITATION

SEC. 6. The maximum annual rate of pay is $140,451 for any employee whose pay is disbursed by the Chief Administrative Officer and is not otherwise provided for in this Order or otherwise limited by law, rule, or regulation.

SHARED EMPLOYEES

SEC. 7. An employee who, under applicable rules and regulations, is paid from 2 or more House sources may receive pay totaling the highest limitation applicable to any of the positions the employee occupies.

EFFECTIVE DATE

SEC. 8. The provisions of this Order shall take effect on January 1, 2001.

J. DENNIS HASTERT
Speaker

Prior Orders of the Speaker of the House of Representatives were issued on the following dates:

Jan. 5, 2000, eff. Jan. 1, 2000.
Feb. 3, 1999, eff. Feb. 1, 1999.
Jan. 24, 1997, eff. Feb. 1, 1997.
Jan. 17, 1995, eff. Jan. 4, 1995.
May 11, 1993, eff. May 1, 1993, as amended.
Feb. 27, 1992, eff. Jan. 1, 1992.
Jan. 28, 1991, eff. Jan. 1, 1991.
Feb. 8, 1990, eff. Feb. 1, 1990.
Jan. 20, 1988, eff. Jan. 1, 1988.

SECTION REFERRED TO IN OTHER SECTIONS

This section is referred to in section 74d of this title.

§§ 60b, 60c. Omitted

CODIFICATION

Section 60b, acts June 20, 1929, ch. 33, § 2, 46 Stat. 38; July 25, 1939, ch. 352, § 3, 53 Stat. 1080, which provided that clerk hire should be at rate of $6,500 per annum and limited individual salaries to $3,900 per annum, was superseded by former section 60g of this title.

Section 60c, R.S. § 55, related to payment of salaries of chaplains.

§ 60c–1. Vice President, Senators, officers, and employees paid by Secretary of Senate; payment of salary; advance payment

The compensation of the Vice President, Senators, and officers and employees, whose compensation is disbursed by the Secretary of the Senate, shall be payable on the fifth day of the month following the month in which such compensation accrued, except that—

(1) Repealed. Pub. L. 97–51, § 111(a)(1), Oct. 1, 1981, 95 Stat. 962;

(2) when such fifth or twentieth day falls on Saturday, Sunday, or on a legal holiday (including any holiday on which the banks of the District of Columbia are closed pursuant to law) such compensation shall be payable on the next preceding workday; and

(3) any part of such compensation accrued for any month may, in the discretion of the Secretary of the Senate, be paid prior to the day specified in the preceding provisions of this section.

For purposes of title 26 and for accounting and reporting purposes, disbursements made in accordance with this section on the fifth day of a month, or on the next preceding workday if such fifth day falls on Saturday, Sunday, or a legal holiday, shall be considered to have been made on the last day of the preceding month.

(Pub. L. 86–426, § 1, Apr. 20, 1960, 74 Stat. 53; Pub. L. 92–136, § 6, Oct. 11, 1971, 85 Stat. 378; Pub. L. 96–38, title I, § 108(a), July 25, 1979, 93 Stat. 113; Pub. L. 97–51, §§ 111(a), 112(a), Oct. 1, 1981, 95 Stat. 962; Pub. L. 97–257, title I, § 105(a), Sept. 10, 1982, 96 Stat. 849; Pub. L. 99–514, § 2, Oct. 22, 1986, 100 Stat. 2095.)

AMENDMENTS

1986—Pub. L. 99–514 substituted "Internal Revenue Code of 1986" for "Internal Revenue Code of 1954", which for purposes of codification was translated as "title 26" thus requiring no change in text.

1982—Pub. L. 97–257 inserted reference to the Vice President.

1981—Pub. L. 97–51 substituted "Senators and officers and employees" for "officers (other than Senators) and employees", struck out cl. (1) which provided that all compensation for the month of December be payable on the twentieth day of December, inserted "purposes of title 26 and for" after "For" in second sentence, and struck out provisions that, in cases in which officers or employees of the Senate died during the month of December and the full compensation of that officer or employee for that month had been disbursed by the Secretary of the Senate before the Secretary received notice of the death, no recovery could be made of any portion of the compensation so disbursed.

1979—Pub. L. 96–38 provided that, in cases in which officers or employees of the Senate die during the month of December and the full compensation of that officer or employee for that month has been disbursed by the Secretary of the Senate before the Secretary receives notice of the death, no recovery shall be made of any portion of the compensation so disbursed.

1971—Cl. (2). Pub. L. 92–136 inserted "(including any holiday on which the banks of the District of Columbia are closed pursuant to law)" after "holiday".

EFFECTIVE DATE OF 1982 AMENDMENT

Section 105(c) of Pub. L. 97–257 provided that: "Amendments and repeals made by the preceding provisions of this section [amending this section and section 104 of Title 3, The President] shall be effective in the case of compensation payable for months after December 1981."

EFFECTIVE DATE OF 1981 AMENDMENT

Section 111(b) of Pub. L. 97–51 provided that: "The amendments made by subsection (a) [amending this section] shall be effective in the case of compensation payable for months after December 1982."

Amendment by section 112(a) of Pub. L. 97–51 effective in the case of compensation payable for months after December 1981, see section 112(e) of Pub. L. 97–51, set out as an Effective Date of 1981 Amendment note under section 33 of this title.

EFFECTIVE DATE OF 1979 AMENDMENT

Section 108(b) of Pub. L. 96–38 provided that: "The amendment made by subsection (a) [amending this section] shall take effect on October 1, 1978."

EFFECTIVE DATE OF 1971 AMENDMENT

Section 9(b) of Pub. L. 92–136 provided that: "Sections 4 and 6 of this Act [enacting section 60c–2 of this title and amending this section] shall become effective as of July 1, 1971.''

EFFECTIVE DATE

Section 3 of Pub. L. 86–426 provided that: "This joint resolution [enacting this section and amending sections 60d to 60e–1 of this title] shall be effective with respect to compensation accruing on or after the first day of the month following the month in which it is enacted [Apr. 1, 1960].''

§ 60c–2. Repealed. Pub. L. 97–258, § 5(b), Sept. 13, 1982, 96 Stat. 1068

Section, Pub. L. 92–136, § 4, Oct. 11, 1971, 85 Stat. 377, authorized and directed Secretary of Senate, if requested by an individual paid by Secretary, to pay compensation by sending a check to a financial organization designated by the individual. See section 3332 of Title 31, Money and Finance.

§ 60c–2a. Banking and financial transactions of Secretary of Senate

(a) Reimbursement of banks for costs of clearing items for Senate

The Secretary of the Senate is authorized to reimburse any bank which clears items for the United States Senate for the costs incurred therein. Such reimbursements shall be made from the contingent fund of the Senate.

(b) Check cashing regulations for Disbursing Office of Senate

The Secretary of the Senate is authorized to prescribe such regulations as he deems necessary to govern the cashing of personal checks by the Disbursing Office of the Senate.

(c) Amounts withheld from disbursements for employee indebtedness

Whenever an employee whose compensation is disbursed by the Secretary of the Senate becomes indebted to the Senate and such employee fails to pay such indebtedness, the Secretary of the Senate is authorized to withhold the amount of the indebtedness from any amount which is disbursed by him and which is due to, or on behalf of, such employee. Whenever an amount is withheld under this section, the appropriate account shall be credited in an amount equal to the amount so withheld.

(Pub. L. 94–440, title I, § 104, Oct. 1, 1976, 90 Stat. 1443.)

§ 60c–3. Withholding and remittance of State income tax by Secretary of Senate

(a) Agreement by Secretary with appropriate State official; covered individuals

Whenever—

(1) the law of any State provides for the collection of an income tax by imposing upon employers generally the duty of withholding sums from the compensation of employees and remitting such sums to the authorities of such State; and

(2) such duty to withhold is imposed generally with respect to the compensation of employees who are residents of such State;

then the Secretary of the Senate is authorized, in accordance with the provisions of this section to enter into an agreement with the appropriate official of that State to provide for the withholding and remittance of sums for individuals—

(A) whose pay is disbursed by the Secretary; and

(B) who request the Secretary to make such withholdings for remittance to that State.

(b) Number of remittances authorized

Any agreement entered into under subsection (a) of this section shall not require the Secretary to remit such sums more often than once each calendar quarter.

(c) Requests by individuals of Secretary for withholding and remittance; amount of withholding; number and effective date of requests; change of designated State; revocation of request; rules and regulations

(1) An individual whose pay is disbursed by the Secretary may request the Secretary to withhold sums from his pay for remittance to the appropriate authorities of the State that he designates. Amounts of withholdings shall be made in accordance with those provisions of the law of that State which apply generally to withholding by employers.

(2) An individual may have in effect at any time only one request for withholdings, and he may not have more than two such requests in effect with respect to different States during any one calendar year. The request for withholdings is effective on the first day of the first month commencing after the day on which the request is received in the Disbursing Office of the Senate, except that—

(A) when the Secretary first enters into an agreement with a State, a request for withholdings shall be effective on such date as the Secretary may determine; and

(B) when an individual first receives an appointment, the request shall be effective on the day of appointment, if the individual makes the request at the time of appointment.

(3) An individual may change the State designated by him for the purposes of having withholdings made and request that the withholdings be remitted in accordance with such change, and he may also revoke his request for withholdings. Any change in the State designated or revocation is effective on the first day of the first month commencing after the day on which the request for change or the revocation is received in the Disbursing Office.

(4) The Secretary is authorized to issue rules and regulations he considers appropriate in carrying out this subsection.

(d) Time or times of agreements by Secretary

The Secretary may enter into agreements under subsection (a) of this section at such time or times as he considers appropriate.

(e) Provisions as not imposing duty, burden, requirement or penalty on United States, Senate, or any officer or employee of United States; effect of filing paper, form, or document with Secretary

This section imposes no duty, burden, or requirement upon the United States, the Senate, or any officer or employee of the United States, except as specifically provided in this section. Nothing in this section shall be deemed to consent to the application of any provision of law which has the effect of subjecting the United

States, the Senate, or any officer or employee of the United States to any penalty or liability by reason of the provisions of this section. Any paper, form, or document filed with the Secretary under this section is a paper of the Senate within the provisions of rule XXX of the Standing Rules of the Senate.

(f) "State" defined

For the purposes of this section, "State" means any of the States of the United States and the District of Columbia.

(Pub. L. 93–371, § 2, Aug. 13, 1974, 88 Stat. 427.)

REFERENCES IN TEXT

The Standing Rules of the Senate, referred to in subsec. (e), were revised generally in 1979. Provisions relating to withdrawal of papers from the files of the Senate which were formerly contained in Rule XXX of the Standing Rules of the Senate are contained in Rule XI of the Standing Rules of the Senate.

§ 60c–4. Withholding of charitable contributions from salaries paid by Secretary of Senate and from employees of Architect of Capitol

(a) Definitions

For purposes of this section, the term—

(1) "Secretary" means the Secretary of the Senate; and

(2) "Architect" means the Architect of the Capitol.

(b) Notice; deduction and transmission

(1) The Secretary and the Architect shall notify individuals whose pay is disbursed by the Secretary or who are employees of the Architect, including employees of the Botanic Garden or the Senate Restaurants of the opportunity to have amounts withheld from their pay pursuant to this section for contribution to national voluntary health and welfare agencies designated by the Director of the Office of Personnel Management pursuant to Executive Order 10927, dated March 18, 1961.

(2) Upon request by such an individual specifying the amount to be withheld and one Combined Federal Campaign Center in the Washington metropolitan area to receive such amount, the Secretary, the Architect, or any other officer who disburses the pay of such individual, as the case may be, shall—

(A) withhold such amount from the pay of such individual; and

(B) transmit (not less than once each calendar quarter) the amount so withheld to the Combined Federal Campaign Center as specified in such request.

(c) Time of withholding and transmission

The Secretary and the Architect shall, to the extent practicable, carry out subsection (b) of this section at or about the time of the Combined Federal Campaign and other fundraising in the executive branch of the Federal Government conducted pursuant to Executive Order 10927, dated March 18, 1961, and at such other times as each such officer deems appropriate.

(d) Amount

(1) No amount shall be withheld under subsection (b) of this section from the pay of any individual for any pay period if the amount of such pay for such period is less than the sum of—

(A) the amount specified to be withheld from such pay under subsection (b) of this section for such period; plus

(B) the amount of all other withholdings from such pay for such period.

(2) No amount may be specified by an individual to be withheld for any pay period under subsection (b) of this section which is less than—

(A) 50 cents, if the pay period of such individual is biweekly or semimonthly; or

(B) $1, if the pay period of such individual is monthly.

(e) Provisions as not imposing duty, burden, requirement or penalty on United States, Senate, or any officer or employee of United States; effect of filing paper

This section imposes no duty, burden, or requirement upon the United States, the Senate, or any officer or employee of the United States, except as specifically provided in this section. Nothing in this section shall be deemed to consent to the application of any provision of law which has the effect of subjecting the United States, the Senate, or any officer or employee of the United States to any penalty or liability by reason of the provisions of this section. Any paper, form, document, or any other item filed with the Secretary under this section is a paper of the Senate within the provisions of rule XXX of the Standing Rules of the Senate.

(f) Rules and regulations

The Secretary and the Architect are authorized to issue rules and regulations they consider appropriate in carrying out their duties under this section.

(Pub. L. 95–470, Oct. 17, 1978, 92 Stat. 1323; 1978 Reorg. Plan No. 2, § 102, eff. Jan. 1, 1979, 43 F.R. 36037, 92 Stat. 3783.)

REFERENCES IN TEXT

Executive Order 10927, dated March 18, 1961, referred to in subsecs. (b)(1) and (c), was revoked by, and is covered by, Ex. Ord. No. 12353, Mar. 23, 1982, 47 F.R. 12785.

The Standing Rules of the Senate, referred to in subsec. (e), were revised generally in 1979. Provisions relating to withdrawal of papers from the files of the Senate which were formerly contained in Rule XXX of the Standing Rules of the Senate are contained in Rule XI of the Standing Rules of the Senate.

TRANSFER OF FUNCTIONS

"Director of the Office of Personnel Management" substituted for "Chairman of the Civil Service Commission" in subsec. (b)(1) pursuant to Reorg. Plan No. 2 of 1978, § 102, 43 F.R. 36037, 92 Stat. 3783, set out under section 1101 of Title 5, Government Organization and Employees, which transferred functions vested by statute in United States Civil Service Commission and Chairman thereof to Director of Office of Personnel Management (except as otherwise specified), effective Jan. 1, 1979, as provided by section 1–102 of Ex. Ord. No. 12107, Dec. 28, 1978, 44 F.R. 1055, set out under section 1101 of Title 5.

§ 60d. Officers and employees paid by Chief Administrative Officer of House; payment of December salary

The Chief Administrative Officer of the House of Representatives is authorized and directed to

pay to the officers and employees of the House
of Representatives, including the Capitol Police
and Office of Legislative Counsel, and employees
paid on vouchers under authority of resolutions,
their respective salaries for the month of December on the 20th day of that month, each
year, except when the 20th of the month falls on
Sunday, in which case the said salaries shall be
paid on the 19th of December.

(May 21, 1937, ch. 236, §1, 50 Stat. 199; Pub. L.
86–426, §2(a), Apr. 20, 1960, 74 Stat. 53; Pub. L.
104–186, title II, §204(3), Aug. 20, 1996, 110 Stat.
1729.)

Amendments

1996—Pub. L. 104–186 substituted "Chief Administrative Officer" for "Clerk".
1960—Pub. L. 86–426 struck out provisions which related to officers and employees of the Senate. See section
60c–1 of this title.

Effective Date of 1960 Amendment

Amendment by Pub. L. 86–426 effective with respect
to compensation accruing on or after first day of
month following April 1960, see section 3 of Pub. L.
86–426, set out as an Effective Date note under section
60c–1 of this title.

§ 60e. Payment of salary for months other than December by Chief Administrative Officer of House to officers and employees

The Chief Administrative Officer of the House
of Representatives is authorized and directed to
pay to the officers and employees of the House
of Representatives, including the Capitol Police
and Office of Legislative Counsel, and employees
paid on voucher under authority of resolutions,
their respective salaries on the first workday
preceding the last day of any month (except the
month of December) when the last day of such
month falls on a Sunday or a legal holiday.

(May 21, 1937, ch. 236, §2, as added June 2, 1939,
ch. 171, 53 Stat. 802; amended Pub. L. 86–426,
§2(b), Apr. 20, 1960, 74 Stat. 54; Pub. L. 104–186,
title II, §204(3), Aug. 20, 1996, 110 Stat. 1729.)

Amendments

1996—Pub. L. 104–186 substituted "Chief Administrative Officer" for "Clerk".
1960—Pub. L. 86–426 struck out provisions which related to officers and employees of the Senate. See section
60c–1 of this title.

Effective Date of 1960 Amendment

Amendment by Pub. L. 86–426 effective with respect
to compensation accruing on or after first day of
month following April 1960, see section 3 of Pub. L.
86–426, set out as an Effective Date note under section
60c–1 of this title.

§ 60e–1. Payment of salaries in or under House when payday falls on Saturday

Whenever the usual day for paying salaries in
or under the House of Representatives falls on
Saturday, such salaries may be paid on the preceding workday.

(Dec. 28, 1945, ch. 589, title I, 59 Stat. 633; Pub. L.
86–426, §2(c), Apr. 20, 1960, 74 Stat. 54.)

Amendments

1960—Pub. L. 86–426 struck out provisions which related to payment of salaries in Senate. See section 60c–1
of this title.

Effective Date of 1960 Amendment

Amendment by Pub. L. 86–426 effective with respect
to compensation accruing on or after first day of
month following April 1960, see section 3 of Pub. L.
86–426, set out as an Effective Date note under section
60c–1 of this title.

§ 60e–1a. Withholding of State income tax by Chief Administrative Officer of House

(a) Agreement with proper State official; covered individuals

Until otherwise provided by law, the Chief Administrative Officer of the House of Representatives shall, in accordance with subsections (b),
(c), and (d) of this section enter into an agreement with any State, at the request for agreement from the proper State official. The agreement shall provide that the Chief Administrative Officer shall withhold State income tax in
the case of each Member and employee who is
subject to such income tax and who voluntarily
requests such withholding.

(b) Number of remittances authorized

Any agreement entered into under subsection
(a) of this section shall not require the Chief Administrative Officer to remit sums withheld pursuant to any such agreement more often than
once each calendar quarter.

(c) Acceptance or disapproval of proposed agreement by Committee on House Administration

(1) The Chief Administrative Officer shall, before entering into any agreement under subsection (a) of this section, transmit a statement
with respect to the proposed agreement to the
Committee on House Administration of the
House of Representatives (hereinafter in this
section and section 60e–1b of this title referred
to as the "committee"). Such statement shall
set forth a detailed description of the proposed
agreement, together with any other information
which the committee may require.

(2) If the committee does not disapprove,
through appropriate action, any proposed agreement transmitted to the committee under paragraph (1) no later than ten legislative days after
receiving such proposed agreement, then the
Chief Administrative Officer may enter into
such proposed agreement. The Chief Administrative Officer may not enter into any proposed
agreement if such proposed agreement is disapproved by the committee under this paragraph.

(d) Number and effective date of requests for withholding; change of designated State; revocation of request

(1) A Member or employee may have in effect
at any time only one request for withholding
under subsection (a) of this section, and such
Member or employee may not have more than
two such requests in effect with respect to different States during any one calendar year. The
request for withholding is effective on the first
day of the month in which the request is processed by the Chief Administrative Officer, but in
no event later than on the first day of the first
month beginning after the day on which such request is received by the Chief Administrative Officer, except that—

(A) when the Chief Administrative Officer
first enters into an agreement with a State

under subsection (a) of this section, a request for withholding shall be effective on such date as the Chief Administrative Officer may determine;

(B) when an individual first receives an appointment as an employee, the request shall be effective on the day of appointment, if the individual makes the request at the time of appointment; and

(C) when an individual first becomes a Member, the request shall be effective on the day such individual takes the oath of office as a Member, if the individual makes the request at such time.

(2) A Member or employee may change the State designated by such Member or employee for purposes of having withholdings made, and may request that the withholdings be remitted in accordance with such change. A Member or employee also may revoke any request of such Member or employee for withholding. Any change in the State designated or revocation is effective on the first day of the month in which the request or the revocation is processed by the Chief Administrative Officer, but in no event later than on the first day of the first month beginning after the day on which such request or revocation is received by the Chief Administrative Officer.

(e) Provisions as not imposing duty, burden, requirement or penalty on United States, House, or any officer or employee of United States; effect of filing paper, form, or document with Chief Administrative Officer

This section and section 60e–1b of this title impose no duty, burden, or requirement upon the United States, the House of Representatives, or any officer or employee of the United States, except as specifically provided in this section and section 60e–1b of this title. Nothing in this section and section 60e–1b of this title shall be deemed to consent to the application of any provision of law which has the effect of subjecting the United States, the House of Representatives, or any officer or employee of the United States to any penalty or liability by reason of the provisions of this section and section 60e–1b of this title. Any paper, form, document, or any other item filed with, or submitted to, the Chief Administrative Officer under this section and section 60e–1b of this title is considered to be a paper of the House of Representatives within the provisions of the Rules of the House of Representatives.

(Pub. L. 94–440, title II, §101, Oct. 1, 1976, 90 Stat. 1448; Pub. L. 104–186, title II, §204(4), Aug. 20, 1996, 110 Stat. 1730.)

CODIFICATION

Section is based on section 1 of House Resolution No. 732, Ninety-fourth Congress, Nov. 4, 1975, which was enacted into permanent law by Pub. L. 94–440.

AMENDMENTS

1996—Subsec. (a). Pub. L. 104–186, §204(4)(B), substituted "provide that the Chief Administrative Officer shall withhold" for "provide that—

"(1) the Clerk, in the case of employees whose compensation is disbursed by the Clerk; and

"(2) the Sergeant at Arms, in the case of Members of the House of Representatives;

shall withhold".

Pub. L. 104–186, §204(4)(A), substituted "Chief Administrative Officer of the House of Representatives shall, in accordance with" for "Clerk of the House of Representatives (hereinafter in this section and section 60e–1b of this title referred to as the 'Clerk') and the Sergeant at Arms of the House of Representatives (hereinafter in this section and section 60e–1b of this title referred to as the 'Sergeant at Arms') shall, in accordance with the provisions of".

Subsec. (b). Pub. L. 104–186, §204(4)(C), substituted "Chief Administrative Officer" for "Clerk or the Sergeant at Arms".

Subsec. (c)(1). Pub. L. 104–186, §204(4)(D), substituted "Chief Administrative Officer" for "Clerk and the Sergeant at Arms".

Subsec. (c)(2). Pub. L. 104–186, §204(4)(E), substituted "Chief Administrative Officer" for "Clerk or the Sergeant at Arms, as the case may be," in two places.

Subsecs. (d), (e). Pub. L. 104–186, §204(4)(F), substituted "Chief Administrative Officer" for "Clerk or the Sergeant at Arms" wherever appearing.

SECTION REFERRED TO IN OTHER SECTIONS

This section is referred to in section 60e–1b of this title.

§ 60e–1b. State income tax withholding; definitions

For purposes of section 60e–1a of this title and this section—

(1) the term "State" means any of the several States, the District of Columbia, the Commonwealth of Puerto Rico, or any other territory or possession of the United States;

(2) the term "Member" means a Member of the House of Representatives, the Delegates from the District of Columbia, Guam, and the Virgin Islands, and the Resident Commissioner from Puerto Rico; and

(3) the term "legislative days" does not include any calendar day on which the House of Representatives is not in session.

(Pub. L. 94–440, title II, §101, Oct. 1, 1976, 90 Stat. 1448.)

CODIFICATION

Section is based on section 2 of House Resolution No. 732, Ninety-fourth Congress, Nov. 4, 1975, which was enacted into permanent law by Pub. L. 94–440.

SECTION REFERRED TO IN OTHER SECTIONS

This section is referred to in section 60e–1a of this title.

§ 60e–1c. Withholding of charitable contributions by Chief Administrative Officer of House

(a) Authority

Until otherwise provided by law and except as provided in subsection (c) of this section, the Chief Administrative Officer of the House of Representatives shall—

(1) notify employees of the opportunity to have amounts withheld from their compensation for contribution to charitable organizations; and

(2) if an employee files with such officer a voluntary request specifying the amount to be withheld and one Combined Federal Campaign Center in the Washington metropolitan area to receive such amount—

(A) withhold such amount from the compensation of such employee, and

(B) transmit (not less than once each calendar quarter) the amount so withheld to the Combined Federal Campaign Center as specified in such request.

(b) Time of fundraising activities

The Chief Administrative Officer of the House of Representatives shall, to the extent practicable, carry out subsection (a) of this section at or about the time of the Combined Federal Campaign and other fundraising in the executive branch of the Federal Government conducted pursuant to Executive Order 10927, dated March 18, 1961, and at such other times as such officer deems appropriate.

(c) Minimum amounts withheld

(1) No amount shall be withheld under subsection (a) of this section from the compensation of any employee for any pay period if the amount of such compensation for such period is less than the sum of—

(A) the amount specified to be withheld from such compensation under subsection (a) of this section for such period, plus

(B) the amount of all other withholdings from such compensation for such period.

(2) No amount may be specified by an employee to be withheld for any pay period under subsection (a) of this section which is less than—

(A) 50 cents, if the pay period of such individual is biweekly or semimonthly; or

(B) $1, if the pay period of such individual is monthly.

(d) Duty, burden, or requirement not imposed

This section imposes no duty, burden, or requirement upon the United States, the House of Representatives, or any officer or employee of the United States, except as specifically provided in this section. Nothing in this section shall be deemed to consent to the application of any provision of law which has the effect of subjecting the United States, the House of Representatives, or any officer or employee of the United States to any penalty or liability by reason of the provisions of this section. Any paper, form, document, or any other item filed with, or submitted to, the Chief Administrative Officer of the House of Representatives under this section is considered to be a paper of the House of Representatives within the provisions of the Rules of the House of Representatives.

(Pub. L. 95–391, title I, § 111, Sept. 30, 1978, 92 Stat. 777; Pub. L. 104–186, title II, § 204(5)(A), Aug. 20, 1996, 110 Stat. 1730.)

References in Text

Executive Order 10927, dated March 18, 1961, referred to in subsec. (b), was revoked, and is covered, by Ex. Ord. No. 12353, Mar. 23, 1982, 47 F.R. 12785.

Codification

Section is based on section 1 of House Resolution No. 12, Ninety-fifth Congress, August 5, 1977, which was enacted into permanent law by Pub. L. 95–391.

Amendments

1996—Subsec. (a). Pub. L. 104–186, § 204(5)(A)(i), substituted "Chief Administrative Officer" for "Clerk" in introductory provisions.

Subsecs. (b), (d). Pub. L. 104–186, § 204(5)(A)(ii), substituted "Chief Administrative Officer of the House of Representatives" for "Clerk".

Section Referred to in Other Sections

This section is referred to in section 60e–1d of this title.

§ 60e–1d. Withholding of charitable contributions; definitions

For purposes of section 60e–1c of this title—

(1) the term "charitable organizations" means national voluntary health and welfare agencies designated by the Director of the Office of Personnel Management pursuant to Executive Order 10927, dated March 19, 1961; and

(2) the term "employee" means any employee of the House of Representatives whose compensation is disbursed by the Chief Administrative Officer of the House of Representatives.

(Pub. L. 95–391, title I, § 111, Sept. 30, 1978, 92 Stat. 777; 1978 Reorg. Plan No. 2, § 102, eff. Jan. 1, 1979, 43 F.R. 36037, 92 Stat. 3783; Pub. L. 104–186, title II, § 204(5)(B), Aug. 20, 1996, 110 Stat. 1730.)

References in Text

Executive Order 10927, dated March 18, 1961, referred to in par. (1), was revoked, and is covered, by Ex. Ord. No. 12353, Mar. 23, 1982, 47 F.R. 12785.

Codification

Section is based on section 2 of House Resolution No. 12, Ninety-fifth Congress, August 5, 1977, which was enacted into permanent law by Pub. L. 95–391.

Amendments

1996—Par. (1). Pub. L. 104–186, § 204(5)(B)(i), inserted "and" at end.

Par. (2). Pub. L. 104–186, § 204(5)(B)(ii), (iv), redesignated par. (3) as (2) and struck out former par. (2) which read as follows: "the term 'Clerk' means the Clerk of the House of Representatives;".

Par. (3). Pub. L. 104–186, § 204(5)(B)(iii), (iv), substituted "Chief Administrative Officer of the House of Representatives" for "Clerk" and redesignated par. (3) as (2).

Transfer of Functions

"Director of the Office of Personnel Management" substituted for "Chairman of the Civil Service Commission" in par. (1) pursuant to Reorg. Plan No. 2 of 1978, § 102, 43 F.R. 36037, 92 Stat. 3783, set out under section 1101 of Title 5, Government Organization and Employees, which transferred functions vested by statute in United States Civil Service Commission and Chairman thereof to Director of Office of Personnel Management (except as otherwise provided), effective Jan. 1, 1979, as provided by section 1–102 of Ex. Ord. No. 12107, Dec. 28, 1978, 44 F.R. 1055, set out under section 1101 of Title 5.

§ 60e–2. Omitted

Section, acts June 30, 1945, ch. 212, title I, §§ 101(c), 102(a), 59 Stat. 295, 296; Oct. 28, 1949, ch. 782, title XI, § 1106(a), 63 Stat. 972; Sept. 6, 1966, Pub. L. 89–554, § 8(a), 80 Stat. 653, which related to coverage of officers and employees of legislative branch under act June 30, 1945, known as Federal Employees Pay Act of 1945, was omitted in view of repeal or omission from the Code of provisions of act June 30, 1945, with exception of section 60e–2b of this title which was expressly exempted from the provisions involved.

§ 60e–2a. Exemption of officers and employees of Architect of Capitol from certain Federal pay provisions

The classes of employees whose compensation is authorized by section 3 of the Legislative Pay Act of 1929, as amended (46 Stat. 38; 55 Stat. 615), to be fixed by the Architect of the Capitol without regard to the Classification Act of 1923, as amended, are authorized to be compensated without regard to chapter 51 and subchapter III of chapter 53 of title 5.

(Oct. 28, 1949, ch. 782, title II, § 204(a), 63 Stat. 957.)

REFERENCES IN TEXT

Section 3 of the Legislative Pay Act of 1929, as amended (40 Stat. 38; 55 Stat. 615), referred to in text, which was an amendment of the Classification Act of 1923 and which was classified to section 662 of former Title 5, Executive Departments and Government Officers and Employees, was repealed by section 1202 of the Classification Act of 1949, Oct. 28, 1949, ch. 782, 63 Stat. 972.

The Classification Act of 1923, as amended, referred to in text, is act Mar. 4, 1923, ch. 265, 42 Stat. 1488, as amended, which was classified to section 661 et seq. of such former Title 5, and was repealed by section 1202 of the Classification Act of 1949.

CODIFICATION

Section is comprised of section 204(a) of act Oct. 28, 1949. Subsections (b) and (c) of such section were repealed by Pub. L. 89–554, § 8, Sept. 6, 1966, 80 Stat. 655, and reenacted as sections 5102(d) and 5103 of Title 5, Government Organization and Employees.

Section was classified to section 1084(a) of Title 5 prior to the general revision and enactment of Title 5 by Pub. L. 89–554, § 1, Sept. 6, 1966, 80 Stat. 378.

"Chapter 51 and subchapter III of chapter 53 of title 5" substituted in text for "this Act", referring to the Classification Act of 1949, on authority of section 7(b) of Pub. L. 89–554, Sept. 6, 1966, 80 Stat. 631, section 1 of which enacted Title 5.

§ 60e–2b. Overtime compensation for certain employees of Architect of Capitol

For overtime pay purposes, per diem and per hour employees under the Office of the Architect of the Capitol not subject to chapter 51 and subchapter III of chapter 53 of title 5, shall be regarded as subject to the provisions of sections 5544(a) and 6102 of title 5, and sections 60e–3 and 60e–4 of this title shall not be applicable to such employees.

(June 30, 1945, ch. 212, title V, § 503, 59 Stat. 301; Oct. 28, 1949, ch. 782, title XI, § 1106(a), 63 Stat. 972.)

REFERENCES IN TEXT

Section 6102 of title 5, referred to in text, was repealed by Pub. L. 92–392, § 7(a), Aug. 19, 1972, 86 Stat. 573, and reenacted as section 6101(a)(1) of Title 5, Government Organization and Employees.

Sections 60e–3 and 60e–4 of this title, referred to in text, were omitted from the Code.

CODIFICATION

Section was classified to section 933 of Title 5 prior to the general revision and enactment of Title 5, Government Organization and Employees, by Pub. L. 89–554, § 1, Sept. 6, 1966, 80 Stat. 378.

"Chapter 51 and subchapter III of chapter 53 of title 5" substituted in text for "the Classification Act of 1949, as amended", and "sections 5544(a) and 6102 of title 5" substituted for "section 23 of the Act of March 28, 1934 (U.S.C., 1940 edition, title 5, sec. 673c)", on authority of section 7(b) of Pub. L. 89–554, Sept. 6, 1966, 80 Stat. 631, section 1 of which enacted Title 5.

AMENDMENTS

1949—Act Oct. 28, 1949, substituted "Classification Act of 1949" for "Classification Act of 1923".

REPEALS

Act Oct. 28, 1949, ch. 782, cited as a credit to this section, was repealed (subject to a savings clause) by Pub. L. 89–554, Sept. 6, 1966, § 8, 80 Stat. 632, 655.

§§ 60e–3 to 60e–14. Omitted

CODIFICATION

Sections were omitted as obsolete and superseded. See section 61–1 of this title and chapter 10A (§ 331 et seq.) of this title.

Section 60e–3, acts June 30, 1945, ch. 212, title V, § 501, 59 Stat. 301; May 24, 1946, ch. 270, § 5(a), (b), 60 Stat. 217; June 23, 1949, ch. 238, § 5, 63 Stat. 265, provided for payment of additional compensation to legislative branch employees.

Section 60e–4, acts June 30, 1945, ch. 212, title V, § 502, 59 Stat. 301; May 24, 1946, ch. 270, § 5(c), 60 Stat. 217, provided for payment of additional compensation to legislative branch employees.

Section 60e–4a, act July 3, 1948, ch. 830, title III, § 301, 62 Stat. 1267, provided for payment of additional compensation to employees of the Federal Government and the District of Columbia government.

Section 60e–5, acts Oct. 28, 1949, ch. 783, title I, § 101(a), (b), 63 Stat. 974; June 28, 1955, ch. 189, § 4(e)(1), 69 Stat. 177, provided for payment of additional compensation to and an annual limit on compensation for legislative branch employees.

Section 60e–6, acts Oct. 24, 1951, ch. 554, § 2(a), (b), (d), 65 Stat. 613; June 28, 1955, ch. 189, § 4(b), (e)(1), 69 Stat. 176, 177, provided for payment of additional compensation to and an annual limit on compensation for legislative branch employees.

Section 60e–7, acts June 28, 1955, ch. 189, § 4(a), (e)(1), (g), (h), 69 Stat. 176–178; June 27, 1956, ch. 453, § 101, 70 Stat. 363, provided for payment of additional compensation to legislative branch employees.

Section 60e–8, Pub. L. 85–462, § 4(a), (e), (f), (r), June 20, 1958, 72 Stat. 207–209, provided for payment of additional compensation to legislative branch employees.

Section 60e–9, Pub. L. 86–568, title I, § 117(a), (e)–(h), July 1, 1960, 74 Stat. 303, provided for payment of additional compensation to legislative branch employees.

Section 60e–10, Pub. L. 87–793, § 1005(a), (e)–(g), (i), Oct. 11, 1962, 76 Stat. 866, provided for payment of additional compensation to and an annual limit on compensation for legislative branch employees.

Section 60e–11, Pub. L. 88–426, title II, § 202(a)–(c), (h), Aug. 14, 1964, 78 Stat. 413, 414, provided for payment of additional compensation to legislative branch employees.

Section 60e–12, Pub. L. 89–301, § 11(a), (b), (i), Oct. 29, 1965, 79 Stat. 1120, 1121, provided for payment of additional compensation to legislative branch employees.

Section 60e–13, Pub. L. 89–504, title III, § 302(a), (b), (e), (i), July 18, 1966, 80 Stat. 294, provided for payment of additional compensation to legislative branch employees.

Section 60e–14, Pub. L. 90–206, title II, § 214(a), (b), (f), (m), Dec. 16, 1967, 81 Stat. 635–637, provided for payment of additional compensation to legislative branch employees.

§ 60f. Repealed. Pub. L. 90–57, § 105(i)(2), July 28, 1967, 81 Stat. 144

Section, acts July 1, 1941, ch. 268, 55 Stat. 448; June 8, 1942, ch. 396, 56 Stat. 333; June 28, 1943, ch. 173, title I,

57 Stat. 222; June 26, 1944, ch. 277, title I, 58 Stat. 337; Dec. 20, 1944, ch. 617, § 2(a), 58 Stat. 832; June 13, 1945, ch. 189, 59 Stat. 241; July 1, 1946, ch. 530, 60 Stat. 390; Oct. 28, 1949, ch. 783, title I, § 101(c)(3), 63 Stat. 974; Oct. 24, 1951, ch. 554, § 2(c)(2), 65 Stat. 614; June 28, 1955, ch. 189, § 4(e)(3), 69 Stat. 177; May 19, 1956, ch. 313, Ch. XII, 70 Stat. 175; Sept. 1, 1959, Pub. L. 86-213, § 1(a), (b), 73 Stat. 443; Aug. 10, 1961, Pub. L. 87-130, 75 Stat. 323, authorized Senators and committee chairmen to change employees' salaries, required certifications, and provided for designation of titles for positions. See section 61-1(a), (d), (e) of this title.

EFFECTIVE DATE OF REPEAL

Repeal effective Aug. 1, 1967, see section 105(k) of Pub. L. 90-57, set out as an Effective Date note under section 61-1 of this title.

§ 60f-1. Repealed. Pub. L. 86-213, § 1(c), Sept. 1, 1959, 73 Stat. 444

Section, act June 27, 1956, ch. 453, 70 Stat. 359, authorized Senators to fix basic compensation of one employee at a rate not to exceed $8,040 per annum.

§§ 60g, 60g-1. Repealed. Pub. L. 91-510, title IV, § 477(a)(1), (2), Oct. 26, 1970, 84 Stat. 1195

Section 60g, acts Dec. 20, 1944, ch. 617, § 1, 58 Stat. 831; June 23, 1949, ch. 238, § 4, 63 Stat. 265, related to clerk hire for Members and Resident Commissioner, rearrangements or changes in salaries and number of employees, maximum and minimum salaries, prohibition against increase in aggregate amount of salaries, required compensation rate to be in multiples of five, and certification of rearrangements or changes of salary schedules.

Section 60g-1, acts July 2, 1954, ch. 455, title I, 68 Stat. 401; Aug. 5, 1955, ch. 568, § 11(a), 69 Stat. 509; Aug. 3, 1956, ch. 938, § 1(a), 70 Stat. 990; Aug. 10, 1961, Pub. L. 87-130, § 103, 75 Stat. 334; July 27, 1965, Pub. L. 89-90, § 103, 79 Stat. 81; Aug. 27, 1966, Pub. L. 89- 545, § 103, 80 Stat. 369, related to increase in basic rates for clerk hire for House Members and Resident Commissioner, including the case of a constituency having a population of five hundred thousand or more, limited basic rate to $7,500 per annum and to one person at any one time.

EFFECTIVE DATE OF REPEAL

Repeal effective immediately prior to noon on Jan. 3, 1971, see section 601(1) of Pub. L. 91-510, set out as an Effective Date of 1970 Amendment note under section 72a of this title.

§ 60g-2. Lyndon Baines Johnson congressional interns

(a) Hiring authority of House Members, Delegates, and Resident Commissioners; allowance for payment of compensation

Until otherwise provided by law and notwithstanding any other provision of law, each Member of, Delegate to, and Resident Commissioner in, the House of Representatives is authorized to hire for two months in any year one additional employee to be known as a Lyndon Baines Johnson congressional intern in honor of the former President. Each such intern shall be a student or a teacher and certified as such under subsection (b) of this section. Each such Member, Delegate, or Resident Commissioner shall have available for payment of compensation to such intern a total allowance of $1,000, to be payable to such intern at a rate not to exceed $500 per month, out of the applicable accounts of the House of Representatives. Such intern and such allowance shall be in addition to all personnel and allowances made available to such Member, Delegate, or Resident Commissioner under other provisions of law or other authority.

(b) Certification of intern status; filing

No person shall be paid compensation as a Lyndon Baines Johnson congressional intern who does not have on file with the Chief Administrative Officer of the House of Representatives, at all times during the period of his employment as such intern, an appropriate certificate which is applicable to his intern status, as described below:

(1) if the intern is a student, a certificate that such intern was during the academic year immediately preceding his employment, a bona fide student at a college, university, or similar institution of higher learning; or

(2) if the intern is a teacher, a certificate that such intern was, in the year immediately preceding his employment, a bona fide teacher in government or social studies at a secondary school or a postsecondary school.

(c) Regulations by Committee on House Oversight

The Committee on House Oversight shall prescribe such regulations as may be necessary to carry out this section.

(Pub. L. 93-245, ch. VI, Jan. 3, 1974, 87 Stat. 1079; Pub. L. 104-186, title II, § 204(6), (7), Aug. 20, 1996, 110 Stat. 1730.)

CODIFICATION

Section is based on section 1 of House Resolution No. 420, Ninety-third Congress, Sept. 18, 1973, which was enacted into permanent law by Pub. L. 93-245.

PRIOR PROVISIONS

A prior section 60g-2, based on House Resolution No. 416, Eighty-ninth Congress, June 16, 1965, as enacted into permanent law by Pub. L. 89-545, § 103, Aug. 27, 1966, 80 Stat. 369, which related to employment of student congressional interns by Members of the House of Representatives and the Resident Commissioner from Puerto Rico, was repealed by section 2 of House Resolution No. 420, Ninety-third Congress, Sept. 18, 1973, as enacted into permanent law by Pub. L. 93-245, ch. VI, § 600, Jan. 3, 1974, 87 Stat. 1079, which provided that: "H. Res. 416, Eighty-ninth Congress, adopted June 16, 1965, and enacted as permanent law by section 103 of the Legislative Branch Appropriation Act, 1967 (80 Stat. 369; Public Law 89-545; 2 U.S.C. 60g-2), shall not be effective in the Ninety-third Congress on and after the effective date specified in section 3 of this resolution; and, effective on the date of enactment of the provisions of this resolution as permanent law, such H. Res. 416, Eighty-ninth Congress, is repealed."

AMENDMENTS

1996—Subsec. (a). Pub. L. 104-186, § 204(7)(A), substituted "applicable accounts of the House of Representatives" for "contingent fund of the House".

Subsec. (b). Pub. L. 104-186, § 204(6), substituted "Chief Administrative Officer" for "Clerk".

Subsec. (c). Pub. L. 104-186, § 204(7)(B), substituted "House Oversight" for "House Administration".

CHANGE OF NAME

Committee on House Oversight of House of Representatives changed to Committee on House Administration of House of Representatives by House Resolution No. 5, One Hundred Sixth Congress, Jan. 6, 1999.

EFFECTIVE DATE

Section 3 of House Resolution No. 420, Ninety-third Congress, as enacted into permanent law by Pub. L.

93–245, provided that: "The provisions of this resolution [enacting this section and repealing House Resolution No. 416, Eighty-ninth Congress, formerly classified to this section] shall become effective on January 1, 1974."

§ 60h. Omitted

CODIFICATION

Section, act Apr. 25, 1945, ch. 95, title I, 59 Stat. 78, limited salary increases under section 60g of this title of standing committee clerks.

§ 60i. Repealed. Pub. L. 87–730, § 106(c), Oct. 2, 1962, 76 Stat. 695

Section, act Feb. 13, 1945, ch. 2, § 1, 59 Stat. 4, prescribed basic rates of compensation of telephone operators on the United States Capitol telephone exchange and authorized certain longevity increases. See section 60j of this title.

EFFECTIVE DATE OF REPEAL

Repeal effective Sept. 1, 1962, see section 106(e) of Pub. L. 87–730, set out as an Effective Date note under section 60j of this title.

PROHIBITION AGAINST PAYMENT OF LONGEVITY INCREASE AFTER SEPTEMBER 1, 1962

Section 106(c) of Pub. L. 87–730 provided in part that no longevity increase payable under authority of this section prior to Sept. 1, 1962, shall be payable on or after Sept. 1, 1962.

§ 60j. Longevity compensation

(a) Eligible employees

This section shall apply to—

(1) each employee of the Senate whose compensation is paid from the appropriation for Salaries, Officers and Employees under the following headings:

(A) Office of the Secretary, including individuals employed under authority of section 74b of this title;

(B) Office of the Sergeant at Arms and Doorkeeper, except employees designated as "special employees"; and

(C) Offices of the Secretaries for the Majority and the Minority;

(2) each employee of the Senate authorized by Senate resolution to be appointed by the Secretary of the Senate or the Sergeant at Arms and Doorkeeper, except employees designated as "special employees"; and

(3) each employee of the Capitol Guide Service established under section 851 of title 40.

(b) Rate of compensation; limitation on increases; computation of service; effective date of payment

(1) Except as provided in paragraph (2), an employee to whom this section applies shall be paid, during any period of continuous creditable service, additional annual compensation (hereinafter referred to as "longevity compensation") at the rate of $482 for (A) each year of creditable service performed for the first five years and (B) each two years of creditable service performed during the twenty-year period following the first five years.

(2) The amount of longevity compensation which may be paid to an employee, when added to his regular annual compensation, shall not exceed the maximum annual compensation which may be paid to Senate employees generally as prescribed by law or orders of the President pro tempore issued under authority of section 60a–1 of this title.

(3) For purposes of this section—

(A) creditable service includes (i) service performed as an employee described in subsection (a) of this section, (ii) service performed as a member of the Capitol Police or as an employee of the United States Capitol Telephone Exchange while compensation therefor is disbursed by the Clerk of the House of Representatives, and (iii) service which is creditable for purposes of this section as in effect on September 30, 1978;

(B) in computing length of continuous creditable service, only creditable service performed subsequent to August 31, 1957, shall be taken into account, except that, in the case of service as an employee employed under authority of section 74b of this title, only creditable service performed subsequent to January 2, 1971, shall be taken into account; and

(C) continuity of creditable service shall not be deemed to be broken by separations from service of not more than thirty days, by the performance of service as an employee (other than an employee subject to the provisions of this section) whose compensation is disbursed by the Secretary of the Senate or the Clerk of the House of Representatives, or by the performance of active military service in the armed forces of the United States, but periods of such separations and service shall not be creditable service.

(4) Longevity compensation shall be payable on and after the first day of the first month following completion of each period of creditable service upon which such compensation is based.

(Pub. L. 87–730, § 106(a), (b), (d), Oct. 2, 1962, 76 Stat. 694, 695; Pub. L. 88–454, § 104(b), Aug. 20, 1964, 78 Stat. 550; Pub. L. 90–57, § 105(g), July 28, 1967, 81 Stat. 143; Pub. L. 90–206, title II, § 214(n), Dec. 16, 1967, 81 Stat. 637; Pub. L. 91–656, § 4, Jan. 8, 1971, 84 Stat. 1952; Pub. L. 93–371, Aug. 13, 1974, 88 Stat. 436; Pub. L. 95–240, title II, § 205, Mar. 7, 1978, 92 Stat. 117; Pub. L. 95–391, title I, § 110(a), Sept. 30, 1978, 92 Stat. 774; Pub. L. 96–304, title I, § 107(b), July 8, 1980, 94 Stat. 890.)

INAPPLICABILITY OF SECTION TO CERTAIN EMPLOYEES ON AND AFTER OCTOBER 1, 1983

This section not to apply, on or after Oct. 1, 1983, to any individual whose pay is disbursed by the Secretary of the Senate except for individuals entitled to longevity compensation prior to Oct. 1, 1983, on the basis of service performed prior to such date, see section 60j–4 of this title.

CODIFICATION

Subsecs. (a) and (b) of this section are from subsecs. (a) and (b) of section 106 of the Legislative Branch Appropriation Act, 1963 (Pub. L. 87–730). Subsec. (c) of this section was the second sentence of subsec. (d) of section 106, and was repealed by section 104(b) of Pub. L. 88–454. Subsec. (c) of section 106 repealed section 60i of this title, and the first sentence of subsec. (d) of section 106 repealed section 105 of the Legislative Branch Appropriation Act, 1959.

AMENDMENTS

1982—Subsec. (b)(1). Figure "463" deemed to refer to the figure "482", effective Oct. 1, 1982, pursuant to Pub.

L. 91–656, § 4, see section 10 of Salary Directive of President pro tempore of the Senate, Oct. 1, 1982, set out as a note under section 60a–1 of this title.

1981—Subsec. (b)(1). Figure "$441" deemed to refer to the figure "$463", effective Oct. 1, 1981, pursuant to Pub. L. 91–656, § 4, see section 9 of Salary Directive of President pro tempore of the Senate, Oct. 5, 1981, set out as a note under section 60a–1 of this title.

1980—Subsec. (b)(1). Figure "404" deemed to refer to the figure "441", effective Oct. 1, 1980, pursuant to Pub. L. 91–656, § 4, see section 10 of Salary Directive of President pro tempore of the Senate, Oct. 1, 1980, set out as a note under section 60a–1 of this title.

Pub. L. 96–304 substituted "$404" for "two times the multiple contained in section 1(a) of the applicable Order of the President Pro Tempore of the Senate issued under authority of section 60a–1 of this title".

1978—Subsec. (a). Pub. L. 95–391 in par. (1) substituted cls. (A) to (C) for provisions respecting heading "Office of the Secretary", except the Assistant to the Majority and the Assistant to the Minority, in par. (2) substituted provisions relating to employees appointed by the Secretary of the Senate or the Sergeant at Arms and Doorkeeper, under a Senate resolution, for provisions relating to employees under the heading "Office of Sergeant at Arms and Doorkeeper", in par. (3) substituted provisions relating to employees of the Capitol Guide Service for provisions relating to employees under the heading "Official Reporters of Debates", and struck out pars. (4) to (8) relating to, respectively, employees under heading "Offices of the Secretaries for the Majority and the Minority", employees appointed by the Secretary or Sergeant at Arms, telephone operators on the United States Capitol exchange, members of the Capitol Police, and the Chief Guide, etc., of the Capitol Guide Service.

Pub. L. 95–240 inserted reference to Deputy Chief Guide in par. (8).

Subsec. (b). Pub. L. 95–391 substituted provisions setting forth requirements respecting the computation, except as provided in par. (2), of additional annual compensation for any employee to whom this section applies during any period of continuous creditable service, for provisions setting forth requirements respecting the computation of additional gross compensation for any employee to whom this section applies during any period of continuous service.

1977—Subsec. (b). Figure "1,002" deemed to refer to the figure "1,074", effective Oct. 1, 1977, pursuant to Pub. L. 91–656, § 4, see section 4(c) of Salary Directive of President pro tempore of the Senate, Sept. 29, 1977, set out as a note under section 60a–1 of this title.

1976—Subsec. (b). Figure "954" deemed to refer to the figure "1,002", effective Oct. 1, 1976, pursuant to Pub. L. 91–656, § 4, see section 4(d) of Salary Directive of President pro tempore of the Senate, Oct. 8, 1976, set out as a note under section 60a–1 of this title.

1975—Subsec. (b). Figure "906" deemed to refer to the figure "954", effective Oct. 1, 1975, pursuant to Pub. L. 91–656, § 4, see section 4(d) of Salary Directive of President pro tempore of the Senate, Oct. 2, 1975, set out as a note under section 60a–1 of this title.

1974—Subsec. (a)(8). Pub. L. 93–371 added par. (8).

Subsec. (b). Figure "855" deemed to refer to the figure "906", effective Oct. 1, 1974, pursuant to Pub. L. 91–656, § 4, see section 4(d) of Salary Directive of President pro tempore of the Senate, Oct. 7, 1974, set out as a note under section 60a–1 of this title.

1973—Subsec. (b). Figure "816" deemed to refer to the figure "855", effective Oct. 1, 1973, pursuant to Pub. L. 91–656, § 4, see section 4(d) of Salary Directive of President pro tempore of the Senate, Oct. 4, 1973, set out as a note under section 60a–1 of this title.

1972—Subsec. (b). Figure "777" deemed to refer to the figure "816" pursuant to Pub. L. 91–656, § 4, see section 4(d) of Salary Directive of President pro tempore of the Senate, Dec. 16, 1972, set out as a note under section 60a–1 of this title.

1971—Subsec. (b). Figure "738" deemed to refer to the figure "777", effective Jan. 1, 1972, pursuant to Pub. L.

91–656, § 4, see section 4(d) of Salary Directive of President pro tempore of the Senate, Dec. 23, 1971, set out as a note under section 60a–1 of this title.

Figure "696" deemed to refer to the figure "738", effective Feb. 1, 1971, pursuant to Pub. L. 91–656, see section 4(d) of Salary Directive of President pro tempore of the Senate, Jan. 15, 1971, set out as a note under section 60a–1 of this title.

1969—Subsec. (b). Figure "597", as increased by Order of June 12, 1968, deemed, on and after July 1, 1969, to refer to the figure "657", pursuant to Pub. L. 90–206, § 225(h), see section 4(c) of Salary Directive of President pro tempore of the Senate, June 17, 1969, set out as a note under section 60a–1 of this title.

1968—Subsec. (b). Figure "564", deemed, on and after July 1, 1968, to refer to the figure "597", pursuant to Pub. L. 90–206, § 225(h), see section 1(h) of Salary Directive of President pro tempore of the Senate, June 12, 1968, set out as a note under section 60a–1 of this title.

1967—Subsec. (b). Pub. L. 90–206, § 214(n), substituted "$564" for "540".

Pub. L. 90–57 substituted in first sentence "gross compensation" and "$540 per annum" for "basic compensation" and "$120 per annum" and struck out "if at the time of such payment the annual rate of basic compensation (exclusive of longevity compensation) of the position in which employed is less than $1,800, or $180 per annum if at such time such rate is $1,800 or more," before "for each five years of service".

1964—Subsec. (c). Pub. L. 88–454 repealed subsec. (c) which related to increases for members of Capitol Police. See section 60j–1 of this title.

EFFECTIVE DATE OF 1980 AMENDMENT

Section 107(d) of Pub. L. 96–304 provided that: "The amendments made by this section [amending this section and sections 60j–3 and 61–1 of this title] shall take effect on October 1, 1980."

EFFECTIVE DATE OF 1978 AMENDMENTS

Section 110(b) of Pub. L. 95–391 provided that: "The amendment made by subsection (a) [amending this section] shall take effect on the first day of the first month which begins after the date of the enactment of this Act [Sept. 30, 1978]. The gross compensation of employees entitled to longevity compensation on such first day under section 106 of the Legislative Branch Appropriation Act, 1963 [this section], shall be adjusted in accordance with the provisions of such section as amended by subsection (a). No increase in compensation by reason of such amendment shall take effect for any pay period beginning before such first day, and no monetary benefit by reason of such amendment shall accrue for any period before such first day."

Section 205 of Pub. L. 95–240 provided that the amendment made by that section is effective Oct. 1, 1977.

EFFECTIVE DATE OF 1967 AMENDMENTS

Amendment by Pub. L. 90–206 effective at beginning of first pay period which begins on or after Dec. 16, 1967, see section 220(a)(3) of Pub. L. 90–206, set out as a note under section 603 of Title 28, Judiciary and Judicial Procedure.

Amendment by Pub. L. 90–57 effective Aug. 1, 1967, see section 105(k) of Pub. L. 90–57, set out as an Effective Date note under section 61–1 of this title.

EFFECTIVE DATE OF 1964 AMENDMENT

Amendment by Pub. L. 88–454 effective Sept. 1, 1964, see section 104(d) of Pub. L. 88–454, set out as an Effective Date note under section 60j–1 of this title.

EFFECTIVE DATE

Section 106(e) of Pub. L. 87–730 provided that: "This section [enacting this section and amending section 60i of this title] shall become effective on September 1, 1962."

TRANSFER OF FUNCTIONS

Certain functions of Clerk of House of Representatives transferred to Director of Non-legislative and Financial Services by section 7 of House Resolution No. 423, One Hundred Second Congress, Apr. 9, 1992. Director of Non-legislative and Financial Services replaced by Chief Administrative Officer of House of Representatives by House Resolution No. 6, One Hundred Fourth Congress, Jan. 4, 1995.

SECTION REFERRED TO IN OTHER SECTIONS

This section is referred to in sections 60j-1, 60j-2, 60j-4, 61-1 of this title.

§ 60j-1. Capitol Police longevity compensation

Any member of the Capitol Police who by reason of the provision repealed by subsection (b) was receiving immediately prior to September 1, 1964, longevity compensation provided by section 105[1] of the Legislative Branch Appropriation Act, 1959, shall, on and after September 1, 1964, receive in lieu thereof a longevity increase under section 60j(b) of this title, in addition to any other such increases (not to exceed three) to which he may otherwise be entitled under such section. In computing the length of service of such member for the purpose of such other increases, only service performed subsequent to the date on which he began receiving longevity compensation in accordance with such section 105[1] shall be counted.

(Pub. L. 88-454, § 104(c), Aug. 20, 1964, 78 Stat. 550.)

INAPPLICABILITY OF SECTION TO CERTAIN EMPLOYEES ON AND AFTER OCTOBER 1, 1983

Section 60j of this title, referred to in text, not to apply, on or after Oct. 1, 1983, to any individual whose pay is disbursed by the Secretary of the Senate except for individuals entitled to longevity compensation prior to Oct. 1, 1983, on the basis of service performed prior to such date, see section 60j-4 of this title.

REFERENCES IN TEXT

The provision repealed by subsection (b), referred to in text, means subsec. (c) of section 60j of this title.

Section 105 of the Legislative Branch Appropriation Act, 1959, referred to in text, is section 105 of Pub. L. 85-570, July 31, 1958, 72 Stat. 453, which was repealed by Pub. L. 87-730, § 106(d), Oct. 2, 1962, 76 Stat. 695.

EFFECTIVE DATE

Section 104(d) of Pub. L. 88-454 provided that: "This section [enacting this section and amending section 60j of this title] shall become effective on the first day of the month following the date of enactment of this Act [Aug. 20, 1964]."

§ 60j-2. Longevity compensation for telephone operators on United States telephone exchange and members of Capitol Police paid by Chief Administrative Officer of House

The provisions of subsections (a) and (b) of section 60j of this title (as amended by section 110 of Pub. L. 95-391), shall apply to telephone operators (including the chief operator and assistant chief operators) on the United States Capitol telephone exchange and members of the Capitol Police whose compensation is disbursed by the Chief Administrative Officer of the House of Representatives in the same manner and to the same extent as such provisions apply to in-

dividuals whose compensation is disbursed by the Secretary of the Senate. For purposes of so applying such subsections, creditable service shall include service performed as an employee of the United States Capitol telephone exchange or a member of the Capitol Police whether compensation therefor is disbursed by the Chief Administrative Officer of the House of Representatives or the Secretary of the Senate.

(Pub. L. 95-391, title III, § 310, Sept. 30, 1978, 92 Stat. 790; Pub. L. 104-186, title II, § 204(8), Aug. 20, 1996, 110 Stat. 1731.)

INAPPLICABILITY OF SECTION TO CERTAIN EMPLOYEES ON AND AFTER OCTOBER 1, 1983

Section 60j of this title, referred to in text, not to apply, on or after Oct. 1, 1983, to any individual whose pay is disbursed by the Secretary of the Senate except for individuals entitled to longevity compensation prior to Oct. 1, 1983, on the basis of service performed prior to such date, see section 60j-4 of this title.

AMENDMENTS

1996—Pub. L. 104-186 struck out "(a)" before "The provisions" and substituted "Chief Administrative Officer" for "Clerk" in two places.

§ 60j-3. Repealed. Pub. L. 97-276, § 101(e), Oct. 2, 1982, 96 Stat. 1189

Section, Pub. L. 95-391, title I, § 109, Sept. 30, 1978, 92 Stat. 773; Pub. L. 96-304, title I, § 107(c), July 8, 1980, 94 Stat. 890, provided for merit compensation for employees rated as outstanding and exceptional by Secretary of Senate and Sergeant at Arms and Doorkeeper, respectively.

EFFECTIVE DATE OF REPEAL

Section 101 of S. 2939, 97th Congress, 2d Session, as reported Sept. 22, 1982, and incorporated by reference in section 101(e) of Pub. L. 97-276, to be effective as if enacted into law, provided that the repeal is effective Oct. 1, 1982.

REPORTS COVERING FISCAL YEAR ENDING SEPTEMBER 30, 1982

Section 101 of S. 2939, 97th Congress, 2d Session, as reported Sept. 22, 1982, and incorporated by reference in section 101(e) of Pub. L. 97-276, to be effective as if enacted into law, provided in part that the reports required by subsec. (e) of this section with respect to the fiscal year ending Sept. 30, 1982, be filed notwithstanding the repeal. Subsec. (e) of this section had required that within thirty days following the end of each fiscal year, the Secretary of the Senate and the Sergeant at Arms and Doorkeeper file reports with the Senate Committee on Appropriations detailing the use and implementation of the authority contained in this section and that such reports include the names of all employees receiving merit compensation under authority of this section at the end of the fiscal year, the positions occupied by them and the date when each such employee first began to receive merit compensation.

§ 60j-4. Longevity compensation not applicable to individuals paid by Secretary of Senate; savings provision

Section 60j of this title on or after October 1, 1983 shall not apply to any individual whose pay is disbursed by the Secretary of the Senate; except that, any individual who prior to such date was entitled to longevity compensation under such section on the basis of service performed

[1] See References in Text note below.

prior to such date shall continue to be entitled to such compensation, but no individual shall accrue any longevity compensation on the basis of service performed on or after such date.

(Pub. L. 98–51, title I, §107, July 14, 1983, 97 Stat. 267.)

CODIFICATION

Section is from the Congressional Operations Appropriation Act, 1984, which is title I of the Legislative Branch Appropriation Act, 1984.

§ 60k. Application of rights and protections of Fair Labor Standards Act of 1938 to Congressional and Architect of Capitol employees

(a) House employees

(1) In general

Not later than 180 days after the date the minimum wage rate prescribed by section 6(a)(1) of the Fair Labor Standards Act of 1938 (29 U.S.C. 206(a)(1)) is increased pursuant to the amendment made by section 2, the rights and protections under the Fair Labor Standards Act of 1938 (29 U.S.C. 201 et seq.) shall apply with respect to any employee in an employment position in the House of Representatives and to any employing authority of the House of Representatives.

(2) Administration

In the administration of this subsection, the remedies and procedures under the Fair Employment Practices Resolution shall be applied. As used in this paragraph, the term "Fair Employment Practices Resolution" means House Resolution 558, One Hundredth Congress, agreed to October 4, 1988, as continued in effect by House Resolution 15, One Hundred First Congress, agreed to January 3, 1989.

(b) Architect of Capitol employees

Not later than 180 days after the date the minimum wage rate prescribed by section 6(a)(1) of the Fair Labor Standards Act of 1938 (29 U.S.C. 206(a)(1)) is increased pursuant to the amendment made by section 2, the rights and protections under the Fair Labor Standards Act of 1938 (29 U.S.C. 201 et seq.) shall apply with respect to individuals employed under the Office of the Architect of the Capitol.

(Pub. L. 101–157, §8, Nov. 17, 1989, 103 Stat. 944.)

REFERENCES IN TEXT

Section 2, referred to in text, is section 2 of Pub. L. 101–157, Nov. 17, 1989, 103 Stat. 938, which amended section 206(a)(1) of Title 29, Labor, to increase the minimum wage.

The Fair Labor Standards Act of 1938, referred to in text, is act June 25, 1938, ch. 676, 52 Stat. 1060, as amended, which is classified generally to chapter 8 (§201 et seq.) of Title 29. For complete classification of this Act to the Code, see section 201 of Title 29 and Tables.

House Resolution 558, referred to in subsec. (a)(2), was made applicable during the One Hundred Second Congress by Rule LI of the Rules of the House of Representatives of the One Hundred Second Congress. For the One Hundred Third Congress and One Hundred Fourth Congress, Rule LI was amended generally and, as so amended, contained provisions relating to fair employment practices. Rule LI was repealed by H. Res. No. 5,

§23(a), One Hundred Fifth Congress, Jan. 7, 1997. See section 1301 et seq. of this title.

§ 60l. Coverage of House and agencies of legislative branch

(a) Coverage of House

(1) In general

Notwithstanding any provision of title VII of the Civil Rights Act of 1964 (42 U.S.C. 2000e et seq.) or of other law, the purposes of such title shall, subject to paragraph (2), apply in their entirety to the House of Representatives.

(2) Employment in House

(A) Application

The rights and protections under title VII of the Civil Rights Act of 1964 (42 U.S.C. 2000e et seq.) shall, subject to subparagraph (B), apply with respect to any employee in an employment position in the House of Representatives and any employing authority of the House of Representatives.

(B) Administration

(i) In general

In the administration of this paragraph, the remedies and procedures made applicable pursuant to the resolution described in clause (ii) shall apply exclusively.

(ii) Resolution

The resolution referred to in clause (i) is the Fair Employment Practices Resolution (House Resolution 558 of the One Hundredth Congress, as agreed to October 4, 1988), as incorporated into the Rules of the House of Representatives of the One Hundred Second Congress as Rule LI,[1] or any other provision that continues in effect the provisions of such resolution.

(C) Exercise of rulemaking power

The provisions of subparagraph (B) are enacted by the House of Representatives as an exercise of the rulemaking power of the House of Representatives, with full recognition of the right of the House to change its rules, in the same manner, and to the same extent as in the case of any other rule of the House.

(b) Instrumentalities of Congress

(1) In general

The rights and protections under this title[1] and title VII of the Civil Rights Act of 1964 (42 U.S.C. 2000e et seq.) shall, subject to paragraph (2), apply with respect to the conduct of each instrumentality of the Congress.

(2) Establishment of remedies and procedures by instrumentalities

The chief official of each instrumentality of the Congress shall establish remedies and procedures to be utilized with respect to the rights and protections provided pursuant to paragraph (1). Such remedies and procedures shall apply exclusively, except for the employees who are defined as Senate employees, in section 2000e–16a(c)(1)[1] of title 42.

---

[1] See References in Text note below.

(3) Report to Congress

The chief official of each instrumentality of the Congress shall, after establishing remedies and procedures for purposes of paragraph (2), submit to the Congress a report describing the remedies and procedures.

(4) Definition of instrumentalities

For purposes of this section, instrumentalities of the Congress include the following: the Architect of the Capitol, the Congressional Budget Office, the General Accounting Office, the Government Printing Office, the Office of Technology Assessment, and the United States Botanic Garden.

(5) Construction

Nothing in this section shall alter the enforcement procedures for individuals protected under section 717 of title VII for the Civil Rights Act of 1964 (42 U.S.C. 2000e–16).

(Pub. L. 102–166, title I, §117, Nov. 21, 1991, 105 Stat. 1080.)

REFERENCES IN TEXT

The Civil Rights Act of 1964, referred to in subsecs. (a)(1), (2)(A) and (b)(1), is Pub. L. 88–352, July 2, 1964, 78 Stat. 252, as amended. Title VII of the Act is classified generally to subchapter VI (§2000e et seq.) of chapter 21 of Title 42, The Public Health and Welfare. For complete classification of this Act to the Code, see Short Title note set out under section 2000a of Title 42 and Tables.

Rule LI of the Rules of the House of Representatives, referred to in subsec. (a)(2)(B)(ii), was amended generally for the One Hundred Third Congress and, as so amended, contained provisions relating to fair employment practices. Rule LI was continued without change for the One Hundred Fourth Congress. Rule LI was repealed by H. Res. No. 5, §23(a), One Hundred Fifth Congress, Jan. 7, 1997. See section 1301 et seq. of this title.

This title, referred to in subsec. (b)(1), is title I of Pub. L. 102–166, Nov. 21, 1991, 105 Stat. 1071, which enacted this section and section 1981a of Title 42, The Public Health and Welfare, amended section 626 of Title 29, Labor, and sections 1981, 1988, 2000e, 2000e–1, 2000e–2, 2000e–4, 2000e–5, 2000e–16, 12111, and 12112 of Title 42, and enacted provisions set out as notes under sections 1981, 2000e, and 2000e–4 of Title 42. For complete classification of title I to the Code, see Tables.

Section 2000e–16a of title 42, referred to in subsec. (b)(2), was amended generally by Pub. L. 104–1, title V, §504(a)(1), Jan. 23, 1995, 109 Stat. 40, and as so amended, subsec. (c) of section 2000e–16a of title 42 no longer contains paragraphs and no longer defines the term "Senate employee". See section 1301(8) of this title.

EFFECTIVE DATE

Section effective Nov. 21, 1991, except as otherwise provided, see section 402(a) of Pub. L. 102–166, set out as an Effective Date of 1991 Amendment note under section 1981 of Title 42, The Public Health and Welfare.

§§ 60m, 60n. Repealed. Pub. L. 104–1, title V, § 504(b), Jan. 23, 1995, 109 Stat. 41

Section 60m, Pub. L. 103–3, title V, §501, Feb. 5, 1993, 107 Stat. 27; Pub. L. 103–283, title III, §312(f)(4), July 22, 1994, 108 Stat. 1447, related to family and medical leave for certain Senate employees. See section 1301 et seq. of this title.

Section 60n, Pub. L. 103–3, title V, §502, Feb. 5, 1993, 107 Stat. 28, related to family and medical leave for certain employees of House of Representatives. See section 1301 et seq. of this title.

SAVINGS PROVISION

Section 504(b) of Pub. L. 104–1 provided in part that sections 60m and 60n of this title are repealed, except as provided in section 1435 of this title.

§ 60*o*. Lump sum payment for accrued annual leave of House employees

(a) Approval; amount; source of payments

Upon the approval of the appropriate employing authority, an employee of the House of Representatives may be paid a lump sum for the accrued annual leave of the employee or for any other purpose. The lump sum—

(1) shall be paid in an amount not more than the lesser of—

(A) the amount of the monthly pay of the employee, as determined by the Chief Administrative Officer of the House of Representatives; or

(B) in the case of a lump sum payment for the accrued annual leave of the employee, the amount equal to the monthly pay of the employee, as determined by the Chief Administrative Officer of the House of Representatives, divided by 30, and multiplied by the number of days of the accrued annual leave of the employee;

(2) shall be paid—

(A) for clerk hire employees, from the clerk hire allowance of the Member;

(B) for committee employees, from amounts appropriated for committees; and

(C) for other employees, from amounts appropriated to the employing authority; and

(3) shall be based on the rate of pay in effect with respect to the employee on the last day of employment of the employee.

(b) Regulations

The Committee on House Oversight shall have authority to prescribe regulations to carry out this section.

(c) "Employee of the House of Representatives" defined

As used in this section, the term "employee of the House of Representatives" means an employee whose pay is disbursed by the Clerk of the House of Representatives or the Chief Administrative Officer of the House of Representatives, as applicable, except that such term does not include a uniformed or civilian support employee under the Capitol Police Board.

(d) Separations after June 30, 1995

Payments under this section may be made with respect to separations from employment taking place after June 30, 1995.

(Pub. L. 104–53, title I, §109, Nov. 19, 1995, 109 Stat. 522; Pub. L. 105–55, title I, §103(a), Oct. 7, 1997, 111 Stat. 1183.)

CODIFICATION

Section is from the Congressional Operations Appropriations Act, 1996, which is title I of the Legislative Branch Appropriations Act, 1996.

AMENDMENTS

1997—Subsec. (a). Pub. L. 105–55, §103(a)(1), (2), in introductory provisions, struck out "who is separated from employment," after "House of Representatives" and substituted "of the employee or for any other purpose" for "of the employee".

Subsec. (a)(1)(B). Pub. L. 105–55, § 103(a)(3), substituted "in the case of a lump sum payment for the accrued annual leave of the employee, the amount" for "the amount".

CHANGE OF NAME

Committee on House Oversight of House of Representatives changed to Committee on House Administration of House of Representatives by House Resolution No. 5, One Hundred Sixth Congress, Jan. 6, 1999.

EFFECTIVE DATE OF 1997 AMENDMENT

Section 103(b) of Pub. L. 105–55 provided that: "The amendments made by subsection (a) [amending this section] shall apply to fiscal years beginning on or after October 1, 1997."

LUMP SUM PAYMENT FOR ACCRUED ANNUAL LEAVE OF
SENATE EMPLOYEES

Pub. L. 106–554, § 1(a)(2) [title I, § 6], Dec. 21, 2000, 114 Stat. 2763, 2763A–97, provided that:

"(a) The head of the employing office of an employee of the Senate may, upon termination of employment of the employee, authorize payment of a lump sum for the accrued annual leave of that employee if—

"(1) the head of the employing office—

"(A) has approved a written leave policy authorizing employees to accrue leave and establishing the conditions upon which accrued leave may be paid; and

"(B) submits written certification to the Financial Clerk of the Senate of the number of days of annual leave accrued by the employee for which payment is to be made under the written leave policy of the employing office; and

"(2) there are sufficient funds to cover the lump sum payment.

"(b)(1) A lump sum payment under this section shall not exceed the lesser of—

"(A) twice the monthly rate of pay of the employee; or

"(B) the product of the daily rate of pay of the employee and the number of days of accrued annual leave of the employee.

"(2) The Secretary of the Senate shall determine the rates of pay of an employee under paragraph (1)(A) and (B) on the basis of the annual rate of pay of the employee in effect on the date of termination of employment.

"(c) Any payment under this section shall be paid from the appropriation account or fund used to pay the employee.

"(d) If an individual who received a lump sum payment under this section is reemployed as an employee of the Senate before the end of the period covered by the lump sum payment, the individual shall refund an amount equal to the applicable pay covering the period between the date of reemployment and the expiration of the lump sum period. Such amount shall be deposited to the appropriation account or fund used to pay the lump sum payment.

"(e) The Committee on Rules and Administration of the Senate may prescribe regulations to carry out this section.

"(f) In this section, the term—

"(1) 'employee of the Senate' means any employee whose pay is disbursed by the Secretary of the Senate, except that the term does not include a member of the Capitol Police or a civilian employee of the Capitol Police; and

"(2) 'head of the employing office' means any person with the final authority to appoint, hire, discharge, and set the terms, conditions, or privileges of the employment of an individual whose pay is disbursed by the Secretary of the Senate."

§ 60p. Payment for unaccrued leave

(a) In general

The Financial Clerk of the Senate is authorized to accept from an individual whose pay is disbursed by the Secretary of[1] Senate a payment representing pay for any period of unaccrued annual leave used by that individual, as certified by the head of the employing office of the individual making the payment.

(b) Withholding

The Financial Clerk of the Senate is authorized to withhold the amount referred to in subsection (a) of this section from any amount which is disbursed by the Secretary of the Senate and which is due to or on behalf of the individual described in subsection (a) of this section.

(c) Deposit

Any payment accepted under this section shall be deposited in the general fund of the Treasury as miscellaneous receipts.

(d) "Head of the employing office" defined

As used in this section, the term "head of the employing office" means any person with the final authority to appoint, hire, discharge, and set the terms, conditions, or privileges of the employment of an individual whose pay is disbursed by the Secretary of the Senate.

(e) Applicability

This section shall apply to fiscal year 1996 and each fiscal year thereafter.

(Pub. L. 104–197, title I, § 9, Sept. 16, 1996, 110 Stat. 2398.)

CODIFICATION

Section is from the Congressional Operations Appropriations Act, 1997, which is title I of the Legislative Branch Appropriations Act, 1997.

§ 61. Limit on rate of compensation of Senate officers and employees

No officer or employee of the Senate shall receive pay for any services performed by him at any rate higher than that provided for the office or employment to which he has been regularly appointed.

(Aug. 5, 1882, ch. 390, § 1, 22 Stat. 270.)

§ 61–1. Gross rate of compensation of employees paid by Secretary of Senate

(a) Annual rate; certification

(1) Whenever the rate of compensation of any employee whose compensation is disbursed by the Secretary of the Senate is fixed or adjusted on or after October 1, 1980, such rate as so fixed or adjusted shall be at a single whole dollar per annum gross rate and may not include a fractional part of a dollar.

(2) New or changed rates of compensation (other than changes in rates which are made by law) of any such employee (other than an employee who is an elected officer of the Senate) shall be certified in writing to the Disbursing Office of the Senate (and, for purposes of this paragraph, a new rate of compensation refers to

---

[1] So in original. Probably should be followed by "the".

compensation in the case of an appointment, transfer from one Senate appointing authority to another, or promotion by an appointing authority to a position the compensation for which is fixed by law). In the case of an appointment or other new rate of compensation, the certification must be received by such office on or before the day the rate of new compensation is to become effective. In any other case, the changed rate of compensation shall take effect on the first day of the month in which such certification is received (if such certification is received within the first ten days of such month), on the first day of the month after the month in which such certification is received (if the day on which such certification is received is after the twenty-fifth day of the month in which it is received), and on the sixteenth day of the month in which such certification is received (if such certification is received after the tenth day and before the twenty-sixth day of such month). Notwithstanding the preceding sentence, if the certification for a changed rate of compensation for an employee specifies an effective date of such change, such change shall become effective on the date so specified, but only if the date so specified is the first or sixteenth day of a month and is after the effective date prescribed in the preceding sentence; and, notwithstanding such sentence and the preceding provisions of this sentence, any changed rate of compensation for a new employee or an employee transferred from one appointing authority to another shall take effect on the date of such employee's appointment or transfer (as the case may be) if such date is later than the effective date for such changed rate of compensation as prescribed by such sentence.

(b) Conversion; increase in compensation

The rate of compensation of each employee whose compensation is disbursed by the Secretary of the Senate which was fixed before August 1, 1967, at a basic rate with respect to which additional compensation is payable by law shall be converted as of such date to the lowest per annum gross rate which is a multiple of $180 and which is not less than the aggregate rate of compensation (basic compensation plus additional compensation provided by law) which such employee was receiving immediately prior to such date. Any increments of longevity compensation to which an employee became entitled prior to August 1, 1967, under section 60j(b) of this title shall be excluded in converting such employee's rate of compensation under this subsection, but such employee's rate of gross compensation shall be increased by $540 (which shall be considered to be an increase under section 60j(b) of this title) for each such increment.

(c) Reference in other provisions to basic rates and additional compensation as reference to per annum gross rate

In any case in which the rate of compensation of any employee or position, or class of employees or positions, the compensation for which is disbursed by the Secretary of the Senate, or any maximum or minimum rate with respect to any such employee, position, or class, is referred to in or provided by statute or Senate resolution, and the rate so referred to or provided is a basic rate with respect to which additional compensation is provided by law, such statutory provision or resolution shall be deemed to refer, in lieu of such basic rate, to the per annum gross rate which an employee receiving such basic rate immediately prior to August 1, 1967, would receive (without regard to such statutory provision or resolution) under subsection (b) of this section on and after such date.

(d) Compensation of employees in office of Senator; limitation; titles of positions

(1)(A) Except as is otherwise provided in subparagraphs (B) and (C), the aggregate of gross compensation paid employees in the office of a Senator shall not exceed during each fiscal year the following:

$1,399,205 if the population of the State is less than 5,000,000;

$1,451,667 if such population is 5,000,000 but less than 6,000,000;

$1,504,132 if such population is 6,000,000 but less than 7,000,000;

$1,556,595 if such population is 7,000,000 but less than 8,000,000;

$1,609,059 if such population is 8,000,000 but less than 9,000,000;

$1,661,521 if such population is 9,000,000 but less than 10,000,000;

$1,713,987 if such population is 10,000,000 but less than 11,000,000;

$1,766,451 if such population is 11,000,000 but less than 12,000,000;

$1,818,913 if such population is 12,000,000 but less than 13,000,000;

$1,871,377 if such population is 13,000,000 but less than 14,000,000;

$1,923,841 if such population is 14,000,000 but less than 15,000,000;

$1,976,305 if such population is 15,000,000 but less than 16,000,000;

$2,028,770 if such population is 16,000,000 but less than 17,000,000;

$2,081,234 if such population is 17,000,000 but less than 18,000,000;

$2,114,796 if such population is 18,000,000 but less than 19,000,000;

$2,148,362 if such population is 19,000,000 but less than 20,000,000;

$2,181,928 if such population is 20,000,000 but less than 21,000,000;

$2,215,493 if such population is 21,000,000 but less than 22,000,000;

$2,249,059 if such population is 22,000,000 but less than 23,000,000;

$2,282,624 if such population is 23,000,000 but less than 24,000,000;

$2,316,186 if such population is 24,000,000 but less than 25,000,000;

$2,349,749 if such population is 25,000,000 but less than 26,000,000;

$2,383,317 if such population is 26,000,000 but less than 27,000,000;

$2,416,881 if such population is 27,000,000 but less than 28,000,000; and

$2,450,448 if such population is 28,000,000 or more.

For any fiscal year, the population of a State shall be deemed to be whichever of the following is the higher:

(I) the population of such State (as determined for purposes of this paragraph) for the preceding fiscal year; or

(II) the population of such State as of the first day of such fiscal year, as determined by the latest census (provisional or otherwise) conducted prior to such first day by the Bureau of the Census within the Department of Commerce.

If the population of any State, as determined under the preceding sentence, is not evenly divisible by 1,000,000, the population of such State shall be deemed to be increased to the next higher multiple of 1,000,000.

If, for any period after a fiscal year has begun, the census figures of the most recent census conducted prior to the first day of such year have not been officially released, then, for such period, in the administration of this paragraph, it shall be assumed that the population of each State is the same as such State's population (as determined for purposes of this paragraph) for the preceding fiscal year.

In the event that the term of office of a Senator begins after the first month of a fiscal year or ends (except by reason of death, resignation, or expulsion) before the last month of a fiscal year, the aggregate amount available for gross compensation of employees in the office of such Senator for such year shall be the applicable amount contained in the preceding table, divided by 12, and multiplied by the number of months in such year which are included in the Senator's term of office, counting any fraction of a month as a full month.

(B) In the case of gross compensation paid to employees in the office of a Senator for the period commencing January 1, 1988, and ending September 30, 1988, the total of—

(i) the aggregate amount of gross compensation which is paid to employees in the office of such Senator for such period, plus

(ii) the expenses paid to or on behalf of such Senator under authority of section 58 of this title (as determined after application of subsection (b) of such section, but without regard to paragraph (2)(A)(iv) thereof),

shall not exceed the aggregate of—

(iii) subject to the next sentence, the amount by which (I) the aggregate of the gross compensation which may be paid to employees in the office of such Senator for the fiscal year ending September 30, 1988, as determined under this subsection (but without regard to this subparagraph), exceeds (II) the aggregate amount of gross compensation which is paid to employees in the office of such Senator for that part of such fiscal year which precedes January 1, 1988, plus

(iv) the amount described in section 58(b)(2)(A)(iii) of this title.

In the event that the term of office of a Senator begins after the first month of the period which commences January 1, 1988, and ends September 30, 1988, or ends (except by reason of death, resignation, or expulsion) before the last month of such period, the amount computed pursuant to clause (iii) of this subparagraph (but before application of this sentence) shall be recalculated as follows: such amount, as so computed, shall be divided by 9, and multiplied by the number of months in such period which are included in the Senator's term of office, counting any fraction of a month as a full month.

(C) In the case of gross compensation paid to employees in the office of a Senator for the fiscal year beginning October 1, 1988, or any fiscal year thereafter, the total of—

(i) the aggregate amount of gross compensation which is paid to employees in the office of such Senator for such year, plus

(ii) the expenses paid to or on behalf of such Senator under authority of section 58 of this title (as determined after application of subsection (b) of such section, but without regard to paragraph (3)(A)(ii) and (iv) thereof),

shall not exceed the aggregate of—

(iii) the amount determined under subparagraph (A) for such year, plus

(iv) the amount described in section 58(b)(3) of this title (as determined without regard to subparagraph (A)(ii) and (iv) thereof).

(2) Within the limits prescribed by paragraph (1) of this subsection, Senators may fix the number and the rates of compensation of employees in their respective offices. The salary of an employee in a Senator's office shall not be fixed under this paragraph at a rate less than $1,966 or in excess of $140,559 per annum. A Senator may establish such titles for positions in his office as he may desire to designate, by written notification to the disbursing office of the Senate.

(e) Gross rate of compensation of employee of committee of Senate employed by joint committee, select committee, or standing committee

(1), (2) Repealed. Pub. L. 96–304, title I, § 112(b)(1), July 8, 1980, 94 Stat. 892.

(3) No employee of a committee of the Senate shall be paid at a gross rate in excess of $140,064, in case of an employee of a joint committee the expenses of which are paid from the contingent fund of the Senate, $140,559, in case of an employee of a select committee (including the conference majority and conference minority of the Senate), or $142,415, in case of an employee of any standing committee (including the majority and minority policy committees) of the Senate. For the purpose of this paragraph, an employee of a subcommittee shall be considered to be an employee of the full committee.

(f) General limitation

No officer or employee whose compensation is disbursed by the Secretary of the Senate shall be paid gross compensation at a rate less than $1,966 or in excess of $140,559 unless expressly authorized by law. The limitation on the minimum rate of gross compensation under this subsection shall not apply to any member or civilian employee of the Capitol Police whose compensation is disbursed by the Secretary of the Senate.

(Pub. L. 90–57, § 105(a)–(f), (j), July 28, 1967, 81 Stat. 141–144; Pub. L. 90–206, title II, § 214 (j)–(l), Dec. 16, 1967, 81 Stat. 637; Pub. L. 91–145, Dec. 12, 1969, 83 Stat. 340; Pub. L. 91–510, title III, § 305, Oct. 26, 1970, 84 Stat. 1181; Pub. L. 91–656, § 4, Jan. 8, 1971, 84 Stat. 1952; Pub. L. 92–184, ch. IV, Dec. 15, 1971, 85 Stat. 633; Pub. L. 92–607, ch. V, § 505, Oct. 31, 1972, 86 Stat. 1505; Pub. L. 93–145, Nov. 1, 1973, 87 Stat. 532; Pub. L. 93–245, ch. VI, Jan. 3, 1974, 87 Stat. 1078; Pub. L. 93–255, § 1, Mar. 27,

1974, 88 Stat. 52; Pub. L. 93–371, § 6, Aug. 13, 1974, 88 Stat. 430; Pub. L. 94–59, title I, § 102, July 25, 1975, 89 Stat. 274; Pub. L. 94–440, title I, § 101(a), Oct. 1, 1976, 90 Stat. 1443; Pub. L. 95–94, title I, § 111(d), Aug. 5, 1977, 91 Stat. 663; Pub. L. 95–391, title I, § 104(b), Sept. 30, 1978, 92 Stat. 772; Pub. L. 95–482, § 112, Oct. 18, 1978, 92 Stat. 1605; Pub. L. 96–304, title I, §§ 107(a), 112(b)(1), July 8, 1980, 94 Stat. 890, 892; Pub. L. 98–181, title I, § 1203(a), Nov. 30, 1983, 97 Stat. 1289; Pub. L. 98–367, title I, §§ 3(a), 12(a), (b), July 17, 1984, 98 Stat. 475, 476; Pub. L. 100–71, title I, § 3(a), July 11, 1987, 101 Stat. 423; Pub. L. 100–137, § 1(c)(1), Oct. 21, 1987, 101 Stat. 818; Pub. L. 100–202, § 101(i) [title I, § 1(a)], Dec. 22, 1987, 101 Stat. 1329–290, 1329–293; Pub. L. 104–186, title II, § 204(9), Aug. 20, 1996, 110 Stat. 1731; Pub. L. 105–18, title II, § 7001, June 12, 1997, 111 Stat. 192; Pub. L. 105–55, title I, § 5, Oct. 7, 1997, 111 Stat. 1181; Pub. L. 105–275, title I, § 8, Oct. 21, 1998, 112 Stat. 2434; Pub. L. 106–57, title I, § 2, Sept. 29, 1999, 113 Stat. 411.)

CODIFICATION

Section is comprised of subsecs. (a) to (f) and (j) of section 105 of Pub. L. 90–57, the Legislative Branch Appropriation Act, 1968. Subsec. (j), which was redesignated subsec. (g) of this section for purposes of codification, was repealed by Pub. L. 104–186. Other subsections of such section 105 provided as follows: subsecs. (g) and (h) amended section 60j(b) of this title and section 5533(c) of title 5, respectively; subsec. (i) repealed sections 60f, 72a–1, 72a–1a, and 72a–4 of this title and amended provisions set out as a note under section 60a–1 of this title; subsec. (k) is set out as an Effective Date note below.

AMENDMENTS

2000—Subsec. (d)(1)(A). The table was revised upward, effective Jan. 1, 2001, by section 6(b) of Salary Directive of President pro tempore of the Senate, Dec. 20, 2000, set out as a note under section 60a–1 of this title. Prior to such upward revision, the table, as revised by Salary Directive of President pro tempore of the Senate, Dec. 12, 1999, was set out as follows:

"$1,347,851 if the population of the State is less than 5,000,000;

"$1,398,388 if such population is 5,000,000 but less than 6,000,000;

"$1,448,927 if such population is 6,000,000 but less than 7,000,000;

"$1,499,465 if such population is 7,000,000 but less than 8,000,000;

"$1,550,003 if such population is 8,000,000 but less than 9,000,000;

"$1,600,540 if such population is 9,000,000 but less than 10,000,000;

"$1,651,080 if such population is 10,000,000 but less than 11,000,000;

"$1,701,619 if such population is 11,000,000 but less than 12,000,000;

"$1,752,155 if such population is 12,000,000 but less than 13,000,000;

"$1,802,694 if such population is 13,000,000 but less than 14,000,000;

"$1,853,232 if such population is 14,000,000 but less than 15,000,000;

"$1,903,771 if such population is 15,000,000 but less than 16,000,000;

"$1,954,310 if such population is 16,000,000 but less than 17,000,000;

"$2,004,849 if such population is 17,000,000 but less than 18,000,000;

"$2,037,179 if such population is 18,000,000 but less than 19,000,000;

"$2,069,513 if such population is 19,000,000 but less than 20,000,000;

"$2,101,847 if such population is 20,000,000 but less than 21,000,000;

"$2,134,180 if such population is 21,000,000 but less than 22,000,000;

"$2,166,514 if such population is 22,000,000 but less than 23,000,000;

"$2,198,847 if such population is 23,000,000 but less than 24,000,000;

"$2,231,178 if such population is 24,000,000 but less than 25,000,000;

"$2,263,509 if such population is 25,000,000 but less than 26,000,000;

"$2,295,845 if such population is 26,000,000 but less than 27,000,000;

"$2,328,177 if such population is 27,000,000 but less than 28,000,000; and

"$2,360,512 if such population is 28,000,000 or more."

Subsec. (d)(2). Figures "$1,893" and "$136,759" to be deemed to refer, effective Jan. 1, 2001, to the figures "$1,966" and "$140,559", respectively, see section 6(c) of Salary Directive of President pro tempore of the Senate, Dec. 20, 2000, set out as a note under section 60a–1 of this title.

Subsec. (e)(3). Figures "$136,264", "$136,759", and "$138,615" to be deemed to refer, effective Jan. 1, 2001, to the figures "$140,064", "$140,559", and "$142,415", respectively, see section 5(b) of Salary Directive of President pro tempore of the Senate, Dec. 20, 2000, set out as a note under section 60a–1 of this title.

Subsec. (f). Figures "$1,893" and "$136,759" to be deemed to refer, effective Jan. 1, 2001, to the figures "$1,966" and "$140,559", respectively, see section 7 of Salary Directive of President pro tempore of the Senate, Dec. 20, 2000, set out as a note under section 60a–1 of this title.

1999—Subsec. (d)(1)(A). The table was revised upward, effective Jan. 1, 2000, by section 6(b) of Salary Directive of President pro tempore of the Senate, Dec. 12, 1999, formerly set out as a note under section 60a–1 of this title.

Pub. L. 106–57 revised table upward, deeming dollar amounts in table to be increased by an additional $50,000 each.

Subsec. (d)(2). Figures "$1,823" and "$132,159" to be deemed to refer, effective Jan. 1, 2000, to the figures "$1,893" and "$136,759", respectively, see section 6(c) of Salary Directive of President pro tempore of the Senate, Dec. 12, 1999, formerly set out under section 60a–1 of this title.

Subsec. (e)(3). Figures "$131,664", "$132,159", and "$134,015" to be deemed to refer, effective Jan. 1, 2000, to the figures "$136,264", "$136,759", and "$138,615", respectively, see section 5(b) of Salary Directive of President pro tempore of the Senate, Dec. 12, 1999, formerly set out as a note under section 60a–1 of this title.

Subsec. (f). Figures "$1,823" and "$132,159" to be deemed to refer, effective Jan. 1, 2000, to the figures "$1,893" and "$136,759", respectively, see section 7 of Salary Directive of President pro tempore of the Senate, Dec. 12, 1999, formerly set out as a note under section 60a–1 of this title.

1998—Subsec. (d)(1)(A). The table was revised upward, effective Jan. 1, 1999, by section 6(b) of Salary Directive of President pro tempore of the Senate, Dec. 16, 1998, formerly set out as a note under section 60a–1 of this title.

Pub. L. 105–275 revised table upward, deeming dollar amounts in table to be increased by an additional $50,000 each.

Subsec. (d)(2). Figure "$1,768" to be deemed to refer, effective Jan. 1, 1999, to the figure "$1,823", see section 6(c) of Salary Directive of President pro tempore of the Senate, Dec. 16, 1998, formerly set out under section 60a–1 of this title.

Subsec. (f). Figure "$1,768" to be deemed to refer, effective Jan. 1, 1999, to the figure "$1,823", see section 7(a) of Salary Directive of President pro tempore of the Senate, Dec. 16, 1998, formerly set out as a note under section 60a–1 of this title.

1997—Subsec. (d)(1)(A). The table was revised upward, effective Jan. 1, 1998, by section 6(b) of Salary Directive of President pro tempore of the Senate, Dec. 19, 1997, formerly set out as a note under section 60a–1 of this title.

Pub. L. 105–55 revised table upward, effective Oct. 1, 1997, by deeming dollar amounts in table to be dollar amounts in that table as of Dec. 31, 1995, increased by 2 percent on Jan. 1, 1996, and by 2.3 percent on Jan. 1, 1997.

Subsec. (d)(2). Figures "$1,728" and "$129,059" to be deemed to refer, effective Jan. 1, 1998, to the figures "$1,768" and "$132,159", respectively, see section 6(c) of Salary Directive of President pro tempore of the Senate, Dec. 19, 1997, formerly set out as a note under section 60a–1 of this title.

Subsec. (e)(3). Figures "$128,564", "$129,059", and "$130,915" to be deemed to refer, effective Jan. 1, 1998, to the figures "$131,664", "$132,159", and "$134,015", respectively, see section 5(b) of Salary Directive of President pro tempore of the Senate, Dec. 19, 1997, formerly set out as a note under section 60a–1 of this title.

Subsec. (f). Pub. L. 105–18, § 7001, inserted at end "The limitation on the minimum rate of gross compensation under this subsection shall not apply to any member or civilian employee of the Capitol Police whose compensation is disbursed by the Secretary of the Senate."

Figures "$1,728" and "$129,059" to be deemed to refer, effective Jan. 1, 1998, to the figures '$1,768" and "$132,159", respectively, see section 7 of Salary Directive of President pro tempore of the Senate, Dec. 19, 1997, formerly set out as a note under section 60a–1 of this title.

1996—Subsec. (d)(1)(A). The table was revised upward, effective Jan. 1, 1997, by section 6(b) of Salary Directive of President pro tempore of the Senate, Dec. 18, 1996, formerly set out as a note under section 60a–1 of this title.

Subsec. (d)(2). Figure "$1,689" to be deemed to refer, effective Jan. 1, 1997, to the figure "$1,728", see section 6(c) of Salary Directive of President pro tempore of the Senate, Dec. 18, 1996, formerly set out as a note under section 60a–1 of this title.

Subsec. (f). Figure "$1,689" to be deemed to refer, effective Jan. 1, 1997, to the figure "$1,728", see section 7(a) of Salary Directive of President pro tempore of the Senate, Dec. 18, 1996, formerly set out as a note under section 60a–1 of this title.

Subsec. (g). Pub. L. 104–186 struck out subsec. (g) which read as follows: "The rate of compensation of each telephone operator on the United States Capitol telephone exchange and each member of the Capitol Police, whose compensation is disbursed by the Clerk of the House of Representatives shall be converted to a gross rate in accordance with the provisions of this section."

1995—Subsec. (d)(1)(A). The table was revised downward, effective Jan. 1, 1995, by section 6(b) of Salary Directive of President pro tempore of the Senate, Dec. 28, 1994, formerly set out as a note under section 60a–1 of this title.

Subsec. (d)(2). Figure "$1,655" increased, effective Jan. 1, 1995, to "$1,689", see section 6(c) of Salary Directive of President pro tempore of the Senate, Dec. 28, 1994, formerly set out as a note under section 60a–1 of this title.

Subsec. (f). Figure "$1,655" to be deemed to refer, effective Jan. 1, 1995, to the figure "$1,689", see section 7(a) of Salary Directive of President pro tempore of the Senate, Dec. 28, 1994, formerly set out as a note under section 60a–1 of this title.

1993—Subsec. (d)(1)(A). The table was revised upward, effective Jan. 1, 1993, by section 6(b) of Salary Directive of President pro tempore of the Senate, Dec. 17, 1992, formerly set out as a note under section 60a–1 of this title.

Subsec. (d)(2). Figures "$1,595" and "$124,959" increased, effective Jan. 1, 1993, to "$1,655" and "$129,059", respectively, see section 6(c) of Salary Directive of President pro tempore of the Senate, Dec. 17, 1992, formerly set out as a note under section 60a–1 of this title.

Subsec. (e)(3). Figures "$124,464", "$124,959", and "$126,815" to be deemed to refer, effective Jan. 1, 1993, to the figures "$128,564", "$129,059", and "$130,915", respectively, see section 5(b) of Salary Directive of President pro tempore of the Senate, Dec. 17, 1992, formerly set out as a note under section 60a–1 of this title.

Subsec. (f). Figures "$1,595" and "$124,959" to be deemed to refer, effective Jan. 1, 1993, to the figures "$1,655" and "$129,059", respectively, see section 7(a), (b) of Salary Directive of President pro tempore of the Senate, Dec. 17, 1992, formerly set out as a note under section 60a–1 of this title.

1992—Subsec. (d)(1)(A). The table was revised upward, effective Jan. 1, 1992, by section 6(b) of Salary Directive of President pro tempore of the Senate, Dec. 18, 1991, formerly set out as a note under section 60a–1 of this title.

Subsec. (d)(2). Figures "$1,530" and "$97,359" increased, effective Jan. 1, 1992, to "$1,595" and "$124,959", respectively, see section 6(c) of Salary Directive of President pro tempore of the Senate, Dec. 18, 1991, formerly set out as a note under section 60a–1 of this title.

Subsec. (e)(3). Figures "$96,864", "$97,359", and "$99,215" to be deemed to refer, effective Jan. 1, 1992, to the figures "$124,464", "$124,959", and "$126,815", respectively, see section 5(b) of Salary Directive of President pro tempore of the Senate, Dec. 18, 1991, formerly set out as a note under section 60a–1 of this title.

Subsec. (f). Figures "$1,530" and "$97,359" to be deemed to refer, effective Jan. 1, 1992, to the figures "$1,595" and "$124,959", respectively, see section 7(a), (b) of Salary Directive of President pro tempore of the Senate, Dec. 18, 1991, formerly set out as a note under section 60a–1 of this title.

1991—Subsec. (d)(1)(A). The table was revised upward, effective Jan. 1, 1991, by section 6(b) of Salary Directive of President pro tempore of the Senate, Dec. 20, 1990, formerly set out as a note under section 60a–1 of this title.

Subsec. (d)(2). Figures "$1,469" and "$84,959" increased, effective Jan. 1, 1991, to "$1,530" and "$97,359", respectively, see section 6(c) of Salary Directive of President pro tempore of the Senate, Dec. 20, 1990, formerly set out as a note under section 60a–1 of this title.

Subsec. (e)(3). Figures "$84,464", "$84,959", and "$86,815" (as increased to "$93,364", "$93,859", and "$95,715", respectively) to be deemed to refer, effective Jan. 1, 1991, to the figures "$96,864", "$97,359", and "$99,215", respectively, see section 5(b) of Salary Directive of President pro tempore of the Senate, Dec. 20, 1990, formerly set out as a note under section 60a–1 of this title.

Subsec. (f). Figures "$1,469" and "$84,959" (as increased to $93,859) to be deemed to refer, effective Jan. 1, 1991, to the figures "$1,530" and "$97,359", respectively, see section 7(a), (b) of Salary Directive of President pro tempore of the Senate, Dec. 20, 1990, formerly set out as a note under section 60a–1 of this title.

1990—Subsec. (d)(1)(A). The table was revised upward, effective Jan. 1, 1990, by section 6(b) of Salary Directive of President pro tempore of the Senate, Dec. 21, 1989, formerly set out as a note under section 60a–1 of this title.

Subsec. (d)(2). Figure "$1,417" increased, effective Jan. 1, 1990, to "$1,469", see section 6(c) of Salary Directive of President pro tempore of the Senate, Dec. 21, 1989, formerly set out as a note under section 60a–1 of this title.

Subsec. (f). Figure "$1,417" to be deemed to refer, effective Jan. 1, 1990, to figure "$1,469", see section 7(a) of Salary Directive of President pro tempore of the Senate, Dec. 21, 1989, formerly set out as a note under section 60a–1 of this title.

1989—Subsec. (d)(1)(A). The table was revised upward, effective Jan. 1, 1989, by section 6(b) of Salary Directive of President pro tempore of the Senate, Dec. 9, 1988, formerly set out as a note under section 60a–1 of this title.

Subsec. (d)(2). Figure "$1,361" increased, effective Jan. 1, 1989, to "$1,417", see section 6(c) of Salary Directive of President pro tempore of the Senate, Dec. 9, 1988, formerly set out as a note under section 60a–1 of this title.

Subsec. (f). Figure "$1,361" to be deemed to refer, effective Jan. 1, 1989, to figure "$1,417", see section 7(a) of Salary Directive of President pro tempore of the Senate, Dec. 9, 1988, formerly set out as a note under section 60a–1 of this title.

1988—Subsec. (d)(1)(A). The table was revised upward, effective Jan. 1, 1988, by section 6(b) of Salary Directive of President pro tempore of the Senate, Jan. 4, 1988, formerly set out as a note under section 60a–1 of this title.

Subsec. (d)(2). Figures "$1,334" and "$72,676" increased, effective Jan. 1, 1988, to "$1,361" and "$84,959", respectively, see section 6(c) of Salary Directive of President pro tempore of the Senate, Jan. 4, 1988, formerly set out as a note under section 60a–1 of this title.

Subsec. (e)(3). Figures "$72,166", "$72,676", and "$74,588" (as increased to "$78,545", "$79,100", and "$81,181", respectively) to be deemed to refer, effective Jan. 1, 1988, to the figures "$84,464", "$84,959", and "$86,815", respectively, see section 5(b) of Salary Directive of President pro tempore of the Senate, Jan. 4, 1988, formerly set out as a note under section 60a–1 of this title.

Subsec. (f). Figures "$1,334" and "$72,676" to be deemed to refer, effective Jan. 1, 1988, to the figures "$1,361" and "$84,959", respectively, see section 7(a), (b) of Salary Directive of President pro tempore of the Senate, Jan. 4, 1988, formerly set out as a note under section 60a–1 of this title.

1987—Subsec. (d)(1). Pub. L. 100–202 amended table and sentence immediately following table generally.

Pub. L. 100–137, §1(c)(1), designated existing provisions of par. (1) as subpar. (A), substituted "Except as otherwise provided in subparagraphs (B) and (C), the" for "The" in provision preceding table, and added subpars. (B) and (C).

Pub. L. 100–71 substituted "less than 6,000,000" for "less than 7,000,000" and inserted "$931,810 if such population is 6,000,000 but less than 7,000,000;".

The table was revised upward, effective Jan. 1, 1987, by section 6(b) of Salary Directive of President pro tempore of the Senate, Dec. 19, 1986, formerly set out as a note under section 60a–1 of this title.

Subsec. (d)(2). Figures "$1,295" and "$70,559" increased, effective Jan. 1, 1987, to "$1,334" and "$72,676", respectively, see section 6(c)(1) of Salary Directive of President pro tempore of the Senate, Dec. 19, 1986, formerly set out as a note under section 60a–1 of this title.

Subsec. (e)(3). Figures "$70,064", "$70,559", and "$72,415" to be deemed to refer, effective Jan. 1, 1987, to the figures "$72,166", "$72,676", and "$74,588", respectively, see section 5(b)(1) of Salary Directive of President pro tempore of the Senate, Dec. 19, 1986, formerly set out as a note under section 60a–1 of this title.

Subsec. (f). Figures "$1,295" and "$70,559" to be deemed to refer, effective Jan. 1, 1987, to the figures "$1,334" and "$72,676", respectively, see section 7(a), (b)(1) of Salary Directive of President pro tempore of the Senate, Dec. 19, 1986, formerly set out as a note under section 60a–1 of this title.

1985—Subsec. (d)(1). The table was revised upward, effective Jan. 1, 1985, by section 6(b) of Salary Directive of President pro tempore of the Senate, Jan. 4, 1985, formerly set out as a note under section 60a–1 of this title.

Subsec. (d)(2). Figures "$1,251" and "$68,172" increased, effective Jan. 1, 1985, to "$1,295" and "$70,559", respectively, see section 6(c)(1) of Salary Directive of President pro tempore of the Senate, Jan. 4, 1985, formerly set out as a note under section 60a–1 of this title.

Subsec. (e)(3). Figures "$67,694", "$68,172", and "$69,966" to be deemed to refer, effective Jan. 1, 1985, to the figures "$70,064", "$70,559", and "$72,415", respectively, see section 5(b)(1) of Salary Directive of President pro tempore of the Senate, Jan. 4, 1985, formerly set out as a note under section 60a–1 of this title.

Subsec. (f). Figures "$1,251" and "$68,172" to be deemed to refer, effective Jan. 1, 1985, to the figures "$1,295" and "$70,559", respectively, see section 7(a), (b)(1) of Salary Directive of President pro tempore of the Senate, Jan. 4, 1985, formerly set out as a note under section 60a–1 of this title.

1984—Subsec. (d)(1). Pub. L. 98–367, §3(a), struck out subpar. (A) designation, substituted "In the event that the term of office of a Senator begins after the first month of a fiscal year or ends (except by reason of death, resignation, or expulsion) before the last month of a fiscal year, the aggregate amount available for gross compensation of employees in the office of such Senator for such year shall be the applicable amount contained in the table included in the preceding sentence, divided by 12, and multiplied by the number of months in such year which are included in the Senator's term of office, counting any fraction of a month as a full month" for "In any fiscal year in which a Senator does not hold the office of Senator at least part of each month of that year, the aggregate amount available for gross compensation of employees in the office of that Senator shall be the applicable amount contained in the table included in this subparagraph, divided by 12, and multiplied by the number of months the Senator holds such office during that fiscal year, counting any fraction of a month as a full month", and struck out subpar. (B), which provided that the aggregate of payments of gross compensation made to employees in the office of a Senator during each fiscal year would not exceed at any time during such fiscal year one-twelfth of the applicable amount contained in the table included in former subpar. (A) multiplied by the number of months (counting a fraction of a month as a month) elapsing from the first month in that fiscal year in which the Senator held the office of Senator through the end of the current month for which the payment of gross compensation was to be made.

Subsec. (d)(1)(A). The table was revised upward, effective Jan. 1, 1984, by section 6(b) of Salary Directive of President pro tempore of the Senate, Dec. 20, 1983, formerly set out as a note under section 60a–1 of this title.

Subsec. (d)(2). Pub. L. 98–367, §12(a), substituted "The salary of an employee in a Senator's office shall not be fixed under this paragraph at a rate less than $1,251 or in excess of $68,172 per annum" for "The salary of an employee in a Senator's office shall not be fixed under this paragraph at a rate less than $1,251 per annum or in excess of $40,721 per annum except that (i) the salaries of three employees may be fixed at rates of not more than $64,106 per annum, (ii) the salaries of five employees may be fixed at rates of not more than $64,704 per annum, and (iii) the salary of one employee may be fixed at a rate of not more than $68,172 per annum".

Figures "$1,202", "$39,154", "$71,101", "$68,938", and "$72,061" increased, effective Jan. 1, 1984, to "$1,251", "$40,721", "$64,106", "$64,704", and "$68,172", respectively, see section 6(c)(1) of Salary Directive of President pro tempore of the Senate, Dec. 20, 1983, formerly set out as a note under section 60a–1 of this title.

Subsec. (e)(3). Pub. L. 98–367, §12(b), substituted "No employee of a committee of the Senate shall be paid at a gross rate in excess of $67,694, in case of an employee of a joint committee the expenses of which are paid from the contingent fund of the Senate, $68,172, in case of an employee of a select committee (including the conference majority and conference minority of the Senate), or $69,966, in case of an employee of any standing committee (including the majority and minority policy committees) of the Senate" for "No employee of any standing or select committee of the Senate (including the majority and minority policy committees and the conference majority and conference minority of the Senate), or of any joint committee the expenses of which are paid from the contingent fund of the Senate, shall be paid at a gross rate in excess of $64,106 per annum, except that (A) two employees of any such committee (other than the Committee on Appropriations), who are otherwise authorized to be paid at such rate, may be paid at gross rates not in excess of $65,661 per annum, and four such employees may be paid at gross rates not in excess of $69,966 per annum; and (B) sixteen employees of the Committee on Appropriations who are otherwise authorized to be paid at such rate, may be paid at gross rates not in excess of $65,661 per annum, and five such employees may be paid at gross rates not in excess of $69,966 per annum''.

Figures "$71,101", "$73,983", and "$78,066" (as reduced to "$61,640", "$63,135", and "$67,275", respectively, by section 304 of Pub. L. 98–51, 5 U.S.C. 5318 note) to be deemed to refer, effective Jan. 1, 1984, to the figures "$64,106", "$65,661", and "$69,966", respectively, see section 5(b)(1) of Salary Directive of President pro tempore of the Senate, Dec. 20, 1983, formerly set out as a note under section 60a–1 of this title.

Subsec. (f). Figure "$1,202" to be deemed to refer, effective Jan. 1, 1984, to the figure "$1,251", see section 7(a) of Salary Directive of President pro tempore of the Senate, Dec. 20, 1983, formerly set out as a note under section 60a–1 of this title.

Figure "$78,066" (as reduced to "$65,550" by section 304 of Pub. L. 98–51, 5 U.S.C. 5318 note) to be deemed to refer, effective Jan. 1, 1984, to the figure "$68,172", see section 7(b)(1) of Salary Directive of President pro tempore of the Senate, Dec. 20, 1983, formerly set out as a note under section 60a–1 of this title.

1983—Subsec. (a)(2). Pub. L. 98–181 amended par. (2) generally. Prior to amendment par. (2) read: "New or changed rates of compensation of any such employees shall be certified in writing to the disbursing office of the Senate on or before the day on which they are to become effective, except that in the case of any change, other than an appointment, to become effective on or after the first day and prior to the tenth day of any month, such certification may be made at any time not later than the tenth day of such month."

1982—Subsec. (d)(1)(A). The table was revised upward, effective Oct. 1, 1982, by section 6(b) of the Salary Directive of the President pro tempore of the Senate, Oct. 1, 1982, formerly set out as a note under section 60a–1 of this title.

Subsec. (d)(2). Figures "$1,155", "$37,648", "$68,366", "$66,286", and "$69,289" increased, effective Oct. 1, 1982, to "$1,202", "$39,154", "$71,101", "$68,938", and "$72,061", respectively, see section 6(c)(1) of Salary Directive of President pro tempore of the Senate, Oct. 1, 1982, formerly set out as a note under section 60a–1 of this title.

Subsec. (e)(3). Figures "$68,366", "$71,137", and "$75,063" to be deemed to refer, effective Oct. 1, 1982, to the figures "$71,101", "$73,983", and "$78,066", respectively, see section 5(b)(1) of Salary Directive of President pro tempore of the Senate, Oct. 1, 1982, formerly set out as a note under section 60a–1 of this title.

Subsec. (f). Figures "$1,155" and "$75,063" to be deemed to refer, effective Oct. 1, 1982, to the figures "$1,202" and "$78,066", respectively, see section 7(a), (b)(1) of Salary Directive of President pro tempore of the Senate, Oct. 1, 1982, formerly set out as a note under section 60a–1 of this title.

1981—Subsec. (d)(1)(A). The table was revised upward, effective Oct. 1, 1981, by section 6(b) of Salary Directive of President pro tempore of the Senate, Oct. 5, 1981, formerly set out as a note under section 60a–1 of this title.

Subsec. (d)(2). Figures "$1,102", "$35,923", "$63,250", and "$66,115" increased, effective Oct. 1, 1981, to the figures "$1,155", "$37,648", "$66,286", and "$69,289", respectively, and "$68,366 per annum" substituted for "the rate referred to in that portion of subsection (e)(3) of this section preceding subparagraph (A)", see section 6(c)(1) of Salary Directive of President pro tempore of the Senate, Oct. 5, 1981, formerly set out as a note under section 60a–1 of this title.

Subsec. (e)(3). Figures "$65,234", "$67,878", and "$71,625" to be deemed to refer, effective Oct. 1, 1981, to the figures "$68,366", "$71,137", and "$75,063", respectively, see section 5(b)(1) of Salary Directive of President pro tempore of the Senate, Oct. 5, 1981, formerly set out as a note under section 60a–1 of this title.

Subsec. (f). Figures "$1,102" and "$71,625" to be deemed to refer, effective Oct. 1, 1981, to the figures "$1,155" and "$75,063", respectively, see section 7(a), (b)(1) of Salary Directive of President pro tempore of the Senate, Oct. 5, 1981, formerly set out as a note under section 60a–1 of this title.

1980—Subsec. (a)(1). Pub. L. 96–304, § 107(a), substituted "October 1, 1980, such rate as so fixed or ad-justed shall be at a single whole dollar per annum gross rate and may not include a fractional part of a dollar" for "August 1, 1967, such rate as so fixed or adjusted shall be a single per annum gross rate which is a multiple of $202".

Subsec. (d)(1)(A). The table was revised upward, effective Oct. 1, 1980, by section 6(b) of Salary Directive of President pro tempore of the Senate, Oct. 1, 1980, formerly set out as a note under section 60a–1 of this title.

Subsec. (d)(2). Pub. L. 96–304, § 112(b)(1), substituted "that portion of subsection (e)(3) of this section preceding subparagraph (A)" for "subsection (e)(1) of this section".

Figures "$1,010", "$32,926", "$57,974", and "$60,600" increased, effective Oct. 1, 1980, to the figures "$1,102", "$35,923", "$63,250", and "$66,115", respectively, see section 6(c)(1) of Salary Directive of President pro tempore of the Senate, Oct. 1, 1980, formerly set out as a note under section 60a–1 of this title.

Subsec. (e). Pub. L. 96–304, § 112(b)(1), struck out par. (1) which provided that the professional staff members of standing committees of the Senate receive gross annual compensation to be fixed by the chairman at not to exceed $65,234, and par. (2) which provided that the rates of gross compensation of the clerical staff of each standing committee of the Senate, as fixed by the chairman, be for each committee, other than the Committee on Appropriations, one chief clerk and one assistant chief clerk at not to exceed $65,234, and not to exceed four other clerical assistants at not to exceed $26,006, and for the Committee on Appropriations, one chief clerk and one assistant chief clerk and two assistant clerks at not to exceed $65,234, such assistant clerks as may be necessary at not to exceed $39,228, and such other clerical assistants as may be necessary at not to exceed $26,006.

Figures "$23,836", "$35,956", "$59,792", "$62,216", and "$65,650" to be deemed to refer, effective Oct. 1, 1980, to the figures "$26,006", "$39,228", "$65,234", "$67,878" and "$71,625", respectively, see section 5(b)(1), (2) of Salary Directive of President pro tempore of the Senate, Oct. 1, 1980, formerly set out as a note under section 60a–1 of this title.

Subsec. (f). Figures "$1,010" and "$65,650" to be deemed to refer, effective Oct. 1, 1980, to the figures "$1,102" and "$71,625", respectively, see section 7(a), (b)(1) of Salary Directive of President pro tempore of the Senate, Oct. 1, 1980, formerly set out as a note under section 60a–1 of this title.

1979—Subsec. (a)(1). Figure "202" was substituted for figure "189" to reflect the use of the figure "202" as the multiple used for determining the general upward revision of salaries by Salary Directive of President pro tempore of the Senate, Oct. 13, 1979, formerly set out as a note under section 60a–1 of this title.

Subsec. (d)(1)(A). The table was revised upward, effective Oct. 1, 1979, by section 6(b) of Salary Directive of President pro tempore of the Senate, Oct. 13, 1979, formerly set out as a note under section 60a–1 of this title.

Subsec. (d)(2). Figures "$1,134", "$30,807", "$54,243", and "$56,700" increased, effective Oct. 1, 1979, to the figures "$1,010", "$32,926", "$57,974", and "$60,600", respectively, see section 6(c)(1) of Salary Directive of President pro tempore of the Senate, Oct. 13, 1979, formerly set out as a note under section 60a–1 of this title.

Subsec. (e). Figures "$22,302", "$33,642", "$55,944", "$58,212", and "$61,425" to be deemed to refer, effective Oct. 1, 1979, to the figures "$23,836", "$35,956", "$59,792", "$62,216", and "$65,650", respectively, see section 5(b)(1), (2), of Salary Directive of President pro tempore of the Senate, Oct. 13, 1979, formerly set out as a note under section 60a–1 of this title.

Subsec. (f). Figures "$1,134" and "$61,425" to be deemed to refer, effective Oct. 1, 1979, to the figures "$1,010" and "$65,650", respectively, see section 7(a), (b)(1) of Salary Directive of President pro tempore of the Senate, Oct. 13, 1979, formerly set out as a note under section 60a–1 of this title.

1978—Subsec. (a)(1). Figure "189" was substituted for figure "179" to reflect the use of the figure "189" as the multiple used for determining the general upward revision of salaries by Salary Directive of President pro tempore of the Senate, Oct. 9, 1978, formerly set out as a note under section 60a–1 of this title.

Subsec. (d)(1)(A). The table was revised upward, effective Oct. 1, 1978, by section 6(b) of Salary Directive of President pro tempore of the Senate, Oct. 9, 1978, formerly set out as a note under section 60a–1 of this title.

Pub. L. 95–391 inserted item in the table added by section 6(b) of Salary Directive of President pro tempore of the Senate dated Sept. 29, 1977, providing that the aggregate of gross compensation paid employees in the office of a Senator not exceed $664,627 if the population of that Senator's State is 8,000,000 but less than 9,000,000.

Subsec. (d)(2). Figures "$1,074", "$29,177", "$51,373", and "$53,700" increased, effective Oct. 1, 1978, to the figures "$1,134", "$30,807", "$54,243", and "$56,700", respectively, see section 6(c)(1) of Salary Directive of President pro tempore of the Senate, Oct. 9, 1978, formerly set out as a note under section 60a–1 of this title.

Subsec. (e). Figures "$21,122", "$31,862", "$52,984", "$55,132", and "$58,175" to be deemed to refer, effective Oct. 1, 1978, to the figures "$22,302", "$33,642", "$55,944", "$58,212", and "$61,425", respectively, see section 5(b)(1), (2) of Salary Directive of President pro tempore of the Senate, Oct. 9, 1978, formerly set out as a note under section 60a–1 of this title.

Subsec. (e)(3)(A). Pub. L. 95–482, § 112(1), (2), substituted "two employees" for "four employees" and "four such employees" for "two such employees".

Subsec. (e)(3)(B). Pub. L. 95–482, § 112(3), substituted "five such employees" for "three such employees".

Subsec. (f). Figures "$1,074" and "$58,175" to be deemed to refer, effective Oct. 1, 1978, to the figures "$1,134" and "$61,425", respectively, see section 7(a), (b)(1) of Salary Directive of President pro tempore of the Senate, Oct. 9, 1978, formerly set out as a note under section 60a–1 of this title.

1977—Subsec. (a)(1). Figure "179" was substituted for figure "167" to reflect the use of the figure "179" as the multiple used for determining the general upward revision of salaries by Salary Directive of President pro tempore of the Senate, Sept. 29, 1977, formerly set out as a note under section 60a–1 of this title.

Subsec. (d)(1)(A). The table was revised upward, effective Oct. 1, 1977, by section 6(b) of Salary Directive of President pro tempore of the Senate, Sept. 29, 1977, formerly set out as a note under section 60a–1 of this title.

Subsec. (d)(2). Figures "$1,169", "$27,221", "$47,929", and "$50,100" increased, effective Oct. 1, 1977, to the figures "$1,074", "$29,177", "$51,373", and "$53,700", respectively, see section 6(c)(1) of Salary Directive of President pro tempore of the Senate, Sept. 29, 1977, formerly set out as a note under section 60a–1 of this title.

Pub. L. 95–94 added cl. (i). Former cls. (i) and (ii) were redesignated (ii) and (iii), respectively.

Subsec. (e). Figures "$19,706", "$29,726", "$49,432", "$51,436", and "$54,275" to be deemed to refer, effective Oct. 1, 1977, to the figures "$21,122", "$31,862", "$52,984", "$55,132", and "$58,175", respectively, see section 5(b)(1), (2) of Salary Directive of President pro tempore of the Senate, Sept. 29, 1977, formerly set out as a note under section 60a–1 of this title.

Subsec. (f). Figures "$1,169" and "$54,275" to be deemed to refer, effective Oct. 1, 1977, to the figures "$1,074" and "$58,175", respectively, see section 7(a), (b)(1) of Salary Directive of President pro tempore of the Senate, Sept. 29, 1977, formerly set out as a note under section 60a–1 of this title.

1976—Subsec. (a)(1). Figure "167" was substituted for figure "159" to reflect the use of the figure "167" as the multiple used for determining the general upward revision of salaries by Salary Directive of President pro tempore of the Senate, Oct. 8, 1976, formerly set out as a note under section 60a–1 of this title.

Subsec. (d)(1). Pub. L. 94–440 substituted "fiscal year" for "calendar year" wherever appearing.

Subsec. (d)(1)(A). The table was revised upward, effective Oct. 1, 1976, by section 6(b) of Salary Directive of President pro tempore of the Senate, Oct. 8, 1976, formerly set out as a note under section 60a–1 of this title.

Subsec. (d)(2). Figures "$1,113", "$25,440", "$43,407", and "$45,315" increased, effective Oct. 1, 1976, to the figures "$1,169", "$27,221", "$47,929", and "$50,100", respectively, see section 6(c)(1) of Salary Directive of President pro tempore of the Senate, Oct. 8, 1976, formerly set out as a note under section 60a–1 of this title.

Subsec. (e). Figures "$18,762", "$27,666", "$44,679", "$46,587", and "$48,653" to be deemed to refer, effective Oct. 1, 1976, to the figures "$19,706", "$29,726", "$49,432", "$51,436", and "$54,275", respectively, see section 5(b)(1), (2), of Salary Directive of President pro tempore of the Senate, Oct. 8, 1976, formerly set out as a note under section 60a–1 of this title.

Subsec. (f). Figures "$1,113" and "$48,654" to be deemed to refer, effective Oct. 1, 1976, to the figures "$1,169" and "$54,275", respectively, see section 7(a), (b)(1), of Salary Directive of President pro tempore of the Senate, Oct. 8, 1976, formerly set out as a note under section 60a–1 of this title.

1975—Subsec. (a)(1). Figure "$159" was substituted for figure "$151" to reflect the use of the figure "$159" as the multiple used for determining the general upward revision of salaries by Salary Directive of President pro tempore of the Senate, Oct. 2, 1975, formerly set out as a note under section 60a–1 of this title.

Subsec. (d)(1)(A). The table was revised upward, effective Oct. 1, 1975, by section 6(b) of Salary Directive of President pro tempore of the Senate, Oct. 2, 1975, formerly set out as a note under section 60a–1 of this title.

Pub. L. 94–59 revised upward, effective July 1, 1975, the table covering the aggregate gross compensation paid employees in the office of a Senator.

Subsec. (d)(2). Figures "$1,057", "$24,160", "$41,223", and "$43,035" increased, effective Oct. 1, 1975, to the figures "$1,113", "$25,440", "$43,407", and "$45,315", respectively, see section 6(c)(1) of Salary Directive of President pro tempore of the Senate, Oct. 2, 1975, formerly set out as a note under section 60a–1 of this title.

Subsec. (e). Figures "$17,818", "$26,274", "$42,431", "$44,243", and "$46,206" to be deemed to refer, effective Oct. 1, 1975, to the figures "$18,762", "$27,666", "$44,679", "$46,587", and "$48,653", respectively, see section 5(b)(1), (2), of Salary Directive of President pro tempore of the Senate, Oct. 2, 1975, formerly set out as a note under section 60a–1 of this title.

Subsec. (f). Figures "$1,057" and "$46,206" to be deemed to refer, effective Oct. 1, 1975, to the figures "$1,113" and "$48,654", respectively, see section 7(a), (b)(1), of Salary Directive of President pro tempore of the Senate, Oct. 2, 1975, formerly set out as a note under section 60a–1 of this title.

1974—Subsec. (a)(1). Figure "$151" was substituted for figure "$285" to reflect the use of the figure "$151" as the multiple for determining the general upward revision of salaries by Salary Directive of President pro tempore of the Senate, Oct. 7, 1974, formerly set out as a note under section 60a–1 of this title.

Subsec. (d)(1)(A). The table was revised upward, effective Oct. 1, 1974, by section 6(b) of Salary Directive of President pro tempore of the Senate, Oct. 7, 1974, formerly set out as a note under section 60a–1 of this title.

Pub. L. 93–371 revised upward, effective July 1, 1974, the table covering the aggregate per annum gross rates of compensation of employees in the office of a Senator.

Subsec. (d)(2). Figures "$1,140," "$22,800," "$39,045," and "$40,755" increased, effective Oct. 1, 1974, to the figures "$1,057," "$24,160," "$41,223," and "$43,035," respectively, see section 6(c)(1) of Salary Directive of President pro tempore of the Senate, Oct. 7, 1974, formerly set out as a note under section 60a–1 of this title.

Subsec. (e). Figures "$16,815," "$24,795," "$40,185," "$41,895," and "$43,890" to be deemed to refer, effective Oct. 1, 1974, to the figures "$17,818," "$26,274," "$42,431," "$44,243," and "$46,206," respectively, see section 5(b)(1), (2), of Salary Directive of President pro tempore of the Senate, Oct. 7, 1974, formerly set out as a note under section 60a–1 of this title.

Subsec. (e)(1). Pub. L. 93–245 and Pub. L. 93–255 substituted "at not to exceed" for "ranging from $18,525 to".

Subsec. (e)(2)(A). Pub. L. 93–245 substituted "not to exceed" for "$8,265 to".

Subsec. (e)(2)(B). Pub. L. 93–245 substituted "not to exceed" for "$18,240 to", "$14,250 to", and "$8,265 to".

Subsec. (f). Figures "$1,140" and "$43,890" to be deemed to refer, effective Oct. 1, 1974, to the figures "$1,057" and "$46,206," respectively, see section 7(a), (b)(1), of Salary Directive of President pro tempore of the Senate, Oct. 7, 1974, formerly set out as a note under section 60a–1 of this title.

1973—Subsec. (a)(1). Figure "$285" was substituted for figure "$272" to reflect the use of the figure "$285" as the multiple for determining the general upward revision of salaries by Salary Directive of President pro tempore of the Senate, Oct. 4, 1973, formerly set out as a note under section 60a–1 of this title.

Subsec. (d)(1). The table was revised upward, effective Oct. 1, 1973, pursuant to Pub. L. 91–656, see section 6(b) of Salary Directive of President pro tempore of the Senate, Oct. 4, 1973, formerly set out under section 60a–1 of this title.

Pub. L. 93–145 revised upward, retroactive to July 1, 1973, the table covering the aggregate per annum gross rates of compensation of employees in the office of a Senator and, effective Jan. 1, 1974, designated such revised table as subpar. (A), added subpar. (B), and in subpar. (A) as so designated added following the table provisions covering calendar years in which a Senator does not hold the office of Senator at least part of each month for that year.

Subsec. (d)(2). Salary dollar limits were modified upward, effective Oct. 1, 1973, so as to substitute "$1,140" for "$1,128", "$22,800" for "$15,040", "$39,045" for "$24,400", and "$40,755" for "$25,568" pursuant to Pub. L. 91–656, see section 6(c)(1) of Salary Directive of President pro tempore of the Senate, Oct. 4, 1973, formerly set out under section 60a–1 of this title.

Pub. L. 93–145 raised from $23,652 to $24,400 in the case of two employees and from $23,312 to $24,400 in the case of one employee the maximum figure at which the salaries of such employees in a Senator's office may be set, raising thereby from two to five the number of employees in a Senator's office whose gross rates salary may be fixed at $24,400 per annum.

Subsec. (e). Figures "$18,525", "$40,185", "$8,265", "$14,250", "$24,795", "$16,815", "$18,240", "$41,895", and "$43,890" were substituted for figures "$18,496", "$38,352", "$8,160", "$14,144", "$23,664", "$16,048", "$18,224", "$39,984", and "$41,616", respectively, pursuant to Pub. L. 91–656, see section 5(b) of Salary Directive of President pro tempore of the Senate, Oct. 4, 1973, formerly set out under section 60a–1 of this title, which directed that the latter set of figures enumerated herein as appearing in subsec. (e) be deemed to refer to the former set of enumerated figures, effective Oct. 1, 1973.

Subsec. (e)(2)(B). Pub. L. 93–145 substituted "$18,224" for "$20,400".

Subsec. (f). Figures "$1,140" and "$43,890" were substituted for "$1,088" and "$41,616", respectively, pursuant to Pub. L. 91–656, see section 7 of Salary Directive of President pro tempore of the Senate, Oct. 4, 1973, formerly set out as a note under section 60a–1 of this title, under which the latter enumerated figures were to be deemed to refer to the former enumerated figures, effective Oct. 1, 1973.

1972—Subsec. (a)(1). Figure "$272" was substituted for figure "$259" to reflect the use of the figure "$272" as the multiple for determining the general upward revision of salaries by Salary Directive of President pro tempore of the Senate, Dec. 16, 1972, formerly set out as a note under section 60a–1 of this title.

Subsec. (d)(1). The table was revised upward, effective Jan. 1, 1973, by Salary Directive of President pro tempore of the Senate, Dec. 16, 1972, formerly set out as a note under section 60a–1 of this title.

Subsec. (d)(2). Figures "$1,295," "$20,720," "$27,972," "$33,929," "$35,483," and "$37,037" to be deemed to refer, effective Jan. 1, 1973, to the figures "$1,088," "$21,760," "$29,376," "$35,632," "$37,264," and "$38,896," respectively, see section 6(c)(1) of Salary Directive of President pro tempore of the Senate, Dec. 16, 1972, formerly set out as a note under section 60a–1 of this title.

Subsec. (e). Figures "$8,288," "$15,281," "$14,245," "$18,648," "$22,533," "$20,461," "$36,519," "$38,073," and "$39,627" to be deemed to refer, effective Jan. 1, 1973, to the figures "$8,160," "$16,048," "$14,144," "$18,496," "$23,664," "$20,400," "$38,352," "$39,984," and "$41,616," respectively, see section 5(b) of Salary Directive of President pro tempore of the Senate, Dec. 16, 1972, formerly set out under section 60a–1 of this title.

Pub. L. 92–607 substituted "three such employees" for "two such employees" in par. (3)(B).

Subsec. (f). Figures "$1,088" and "$41,616" were substituted for "$1,295" and "$39,627", respectively, pursuant to Pub. L. 91–656, see section 7 of Salary Directive of President pro tempore of the Senate, Dec. 16, 1972, formerly set out as a note under section 60a–1 of this title, under which the latter enumerated figures were to be deemed to refer to the former enumerated figures.

1971—Subsec. (a)(1). Figure "$259" was substituted for figure "$246" to reflect the use of the figure "$259" as the multiple for determining the general upward revision of salaries by Salary Directive of President pro tempore of the Senate, Dec. 23, 1971, formerly set out as a note under section 60a–1 of this title.

Figure "$246" was substituted for figure "$188" to reflect the use of the figure "$246" as the multiple for determining the general upward revision of salaries by Salary Directive of President pro tempore of the Senate, Jan. 15, 1971, formerly set out as a note under section 60a–1 of this title.

Subsec. (d)(1). The table was revised upward, effective Jan. 1, 1972, by Salary Directive of President pro tempore of the Senate, Dec. 23, 1971, formerly set out as a note under section 60a–1 of this title.

Pub. L. 92–184 revised upward, effective Jan. 1, 1972, the table covering the aggregate per annum gross rates of compensation of employees in the office of a Senator.

The table was revised upward, effective Feb. 1, 1971, by Salary Directive of President pro tempore of the Senate, Jan. 15, 1971, formerly set out as a note under section 60a–1 of this title.

Subsec. (d)(2). Figures "$1,230", "$19,680", "$26,568", "$32,226", "$33,702", "$35,178" to be deemed to refer, effective Jan. 1, 1972, to the figures "$1,295", "$20,720", "$27,972", "$33,929", "$35,483", and "$37,037", respectfully, see section 6(c) of Salary Directive of President pro tempore of the Senate, Dec. 23, 1971, formerly set out as a note under section 60a–1 of this title.

Figures "$1,095", "$17,520", "$23,652", "$28,689", "$30,003", and "$31,317" to be deemed to refer, effective Feb. 1, 1971, to the figures "$1,230", "$19,680", "$26,568", "$32,226", "$33,702", and "$35,178", respectively, see section 6(c) of Salary Directive of President pro tempore of the Senate, Jan. 15, 1971, formerly set out as a note under section 60a–1 of this title.

Subsec. (e). Figures "$8,118", "$14,514", "$14,022", "$18,450", "$21,402", "$20,418", "$32,712", "$34,104", and "$35,496" to be deemed to refer, effective Jan. 1, 1972, to the figures "$8,288", "$15,281", "$14,245", "$18,648", "$22,533", "$20,461", "$36,519", "$38,073", and "$39,627", respectively, see section 5(b) of Salary Directive of President pro tempore of the Senate, Dec. 23, 1971, formerly set out as a note under section 60a–1 of this title.

Figures "$7,888", "$13,688", "$13,920", "$18,328", "$20,184", "$20,416", "$32,712", "$34,014", and "$35,496" to be deemed to refer, effective Feb. 1, 1971, to the figures "$8,118", "$14,514", "$14,022", "$18,450", "$21,402", "$30,418", "$32,712", "$34,014", and "$35,496", respectively, see section 5(b) of Salary Directive of President pro tempore of the Senate, Jan. 15, 1971, formerly set out as a note under section 60a–1 of this title.

Subsec. (f). Figures "$1,230" and "$35,670" to be deemed to refer, effective Jan. 1, 1972, to the figures "$1,295" and "$39,627", respectively, see section 7 of Salary Directive of President pro tempore of the Senate,

Dec. 23, 1971, formerly set out as a note under section 60a–1 of this title.

Figures "$1,160" and "$35,496" to be deemed to refer, effective Feb. 1, 1971, to the figures "$1,230" and "$35,670", respectively, see section 7 of Salary Directive of President pro tempore of the Senate, Jan. 15, 1971, formerly set out as a note under section 60a–1 of this title.

1970—Subsec. (a)(1). Figure "$219" deemed on and after May 1, 1970, to refer to figure "$232", see section 3(a) of Salary Directive of President pro tempore of the Senate, Apr. 15, 1970, formerly set out as a note under section 60a–1 of this title.

Subsec. (d)(1). The table was revised upward, effective May 1, 1970, see section 2 of Salary Directive of President pro tempore of the Senate, Apr. 15, 1970, formerly set out as a note under section 60a–1 of this title.

Subsecs. (d)(2) to (f). Figures were increased, effective May 1, 1970, see section 3(b) of Salary Directive of President pro tempore of the Senate, Apr. 15, 1970, formerly set out as a note under section 60a–1 of this title.

Subsec. (e)(1). Pub. L. 91–510 increased range of gross annual compensation of professional staff members from "$14,852 to $23,312" to "$18,328 to $32,712".

Subsec. (e)(2). Pub. L. 91–510 increased range of gross compensation of clerical staff in subpar. (A) for chief clerk and assistant chief clerk from "$6,392 to $23,312" to "$7,888 to $32,712" and for other clerical assistants from "$6,392 to $11,092" to "$7,888 to $13,688" and in subpar. (B) for chief clerk, assistant chief clerk, and assistant clerks from "$16,544 to $23,312" to "$20,416 to $32,712", for necessary assistant clerks from "$11,280 to $16,356" to "$13,920 to $20,184", and for other necessary clerical assistants from "$6,392 to $11,092" to "$7,888 to $13,688".

Subsec. (e)(3). Pub. L. 91–510 increased gross rate of compensation from "$23,312" to "$32,712" per annum for certain employees of any standing or select committee of the Senate or joint committee expenses of which are paid from contingent fund of the Senate, in subpar. (A) for employees of any such committee from "$24,400" for two employees to "$34,104" for four employees and from "$25,568" for one employee to "$35,496" for two employees, and in subpar. (B) for employees of Committee on Appropriation from "$24,400" for seventeen employees to "$34,104" for sixteen employees and from "$25,568" for one employee to "$35,496" for two employees.

Subsec. (f). Pub. L. 91–510 increased minimum and maximum gross compensation limitation from "$1,128" and "$25,568" to "$1,160" and "$35,496", respectively, and deleted sentence providing that in any case in which the fixing of any salary rate in multiples as required by this section would result in a rate in excess of the maximum rate specified in this subsection, the rate so fixed shall be reduced to such maximum rate.

1969—Subsec. (a)(1). Figure "$199" deemed on and after July 1, 1969, to refer to figure "$219", see section 4(a) of Salary Directive of President pro tempore of the Senate, June 17, 1969, formerly set out as a note under section 60a–1 of this title.

Subsec. (d)(1). Pub. L. 91–145 increased the amounts in the table providing for Senators' clerk hire allowances by $23,652.

The table was revised upward, effective July 1, 1969, see section 2 of Salary Directive of President pro tempore of the Senate, June 17, 1969, formerly set out as a note under section 60a–1 of this title.

Subsec. (d)(2)(i). Pub. L. 91–145 substituted authorization for fixing the salary of two employees at gross rates of not more than $23,652 per annum for prior authorization for fixing the salary of one employee at a gross rate of not more than $18,988 per annum.

Subsecs. (d)(2) to (f). Figures were increased, effective July 1, 1969, see section 4(b) of Salary Directive of President pro tempore of the Senate, June 12, 1969, formerly set out as a note under section 60a–1 of this title.

1968—Subsec. (a)(1). Figure "$188" deemed on and after July 1, 1968, to refer to figure "$199", see section 1(g) of Salary Directive of President pro tempore of the Senate, June 12, 1968, formerly set out as a note under section 60a–1 of this title.

Subsec. (d)(1). The table was revised upward, effective July 1, 1968, see section 1(d)(1) of Salary Directive of President pro tempore of the Senate, June 12, 1968, formerly set out as a note under section 60a–1 of this title.

Subsecs. (d)(2) to (f). Figures were increased, effective July 1, 1968, see sections 1(g) and 2(b) of Salary Directive of President pro tempore of the Senate, June 12, 1968, formerly set out as a note under section 60a–1 of this title.

1967—Subsec. (a)(1). Pub. L. 90–206, § 214(j), substituted "$188" for "$180".

Subsec. (d)(1). Pub. L. 90–206, § 214(k), increased the aggregate amount of the per annum gross rates of compensation of employees in the office of a Senator.

Subsecs. (d)(2) to (f). Pub. L. 90–206, § 214(l), substituted "$1,128", "$6,392", "$11,092", "$11,280", "$14,852", "$15,040", "$16,356", "$16,544", "$18,988", "$23,312", "$24,440", and "$25,568" for "$1,080", "$6,120", "$10,620", "$10,800", "$14,220", "$14,400", "$15,660", "$15,840", "$18,180", "$22,320", "$23,400", and "$24,480", respectively, wherever appearing.

EFFECTIVE DATE OF 1999 AMENDMENT

Pub. L. 106–57, title I, § 2, Sept. 29, 1999, 113 Stat. 411, provided that the amendment made by section 2 is effective on and after Oct. 1, 1999.

EFFECTIVE DATE OF 1998 AMENDMENT

Pub. L. 105–275, title I, § 8, Oct. 21, 1998, 112 Stat. 2434, provided that the amendment made by section 8 is effective on and after Oct. 1, 1998.

EFFECTIVE DATE OF 1997 AMENDMENT

Section 5 of Pub. L. 105–55 provided that the amendment made by that section is effective on and after Oct. 1, 1997.

EFFECTIVE DATE OF 1987 AMENDMENTS

Section 101(i) [title I, § 1(b)] of Pub. L. 100–202 provided that: "The amendment made by this section [amending this section] shall be effective in the case of fiscal years beginning after September 30, 1987."

Section 1(c)(1) of Pub. L. 100–137 provided that the amendment made by that section is effective Jan. 1, 1988.

Section 3(a) of Pub. L. 100–71 provided that the amendment made by that section is effective July 1, 1987.

EFFECTIVE DATE OF 1984 AMENDMENT

Section 3(b) of Pub. L. 98–367 provided that: "The amendments made by subsection (a) of this section [amending this section] shall be effective with respect to fiscal years beginning after September 30, 1984."

Section 12(c) of Pub. L. 98–367 provided that: "The amendments made by subsection (a) of this section [amending this section] shall take effect on October 1, 1984."

EFFECTIVE DATE OF 1983 AMENDMENT

Section 1203(b) of Pub. L. 98–181 provided that: "The amendment made by subsection (a) [amending this section] shall be applicable in the case of new or changed rates of compensation which are certified to the Disbursing Office of the Senate on or after January 1, 1984."

EFFECTIVE DATE OF 1980 AMENDMENT

Amendment by section 107(a) of Pub. L. 96–304 effective Oct. 1, 1980, see section 107(d) of Pub. L. 96–304, set out as an Effective Date of 1980 Amendment note under section 60j of this title.

Section 112(b) of Pub. L. 96–304 provided that the amendment made by that section is effective as of the close of Feb. 28, 1981.

EFFECTIVE DATE OF 1977 AMENDMENT

Amendment by Pub. L. 95–94 effective Oct. 1, 1977, see section 111(f) of Pub. L. 95–94, set out as an Effective Date note under section 72a–1e of this title.

EFFECTIVE DATE OF 1976 AMENDMENT

Section 101(a) of Pub. L. 94–440 provided that the amendment made by that section is effective Oct. 1, 1976.

EFFECTIVE DATE OF 1974 AMENDMENT

Section 6 of Pub. L. 93–371 provided that the amendment made by that section is effective July 1, 1974.

EFFECTIVE DATE OF 1973 AMENDMENT

Section 101 of Pub. L. 93–145 provided that the upward revision of the table in subsec. (d)(1) and the amendment of subsec. (d)(2) of this section are effective July 1, 1973, but that the remaining amendments of subsec. (d)(1) by Pub. L. 93–145 [designating the revised table as subpar. (A), adding provisions following the table in such redesignated subpar. (A), and adding subpar. (B)] are effective Jan. 1, 1974.

EFFECTIVE DATE OF 1971 AMENDMENT

Section 401 of Pub. L. 92–184 provided that the amendment made by that section is effective Jan. 1, 1972.

EFFECTIVE DATE OF 1970 AMENDMENT

Amendment by Pub. L. 91–510 effective Jan. 1, 1971, see section 601(6) of Pub. L. 91–510, set out as a note under section 72a of this title.

EFFECTIVE DATE OF 1969 AMENDMENT

Section 101 of Pub. L. 91–145 provided that the amendment made by that section is effective Nov. 1, 1969.

EFFECTIVE DATE OF 1967 AMENDMENT

Amendment by Pub. L. 90–206 effective at beginning of first pay period which begins on or after Dec. 16, 1967, see section 220(a)(3) of Pub. L. 90–206, set out as a note under section 603 of Title 28, Judiciary and Judicial Procedure.

EFFECTIVE DATE

Section 105(k) of Pub. L. 90–57 provided that: "This section [enacting this section, amending section 60j of this title and section 5533 of Title 5, Government Organization and Employees, repealing sections 60f, 72a–1, 72a–1a, and 72a–4 of this title, and amending provisions set out as notes under section 60a–1 of this title] shall be effective from and after August 1, 1967."

1975 ADJUSTMENTS IN COMPENSATION IN MAXIMUM ANNUAL RATES TO EMPLOYEES IN OFFICES OF SENATORS, EMPLOYEES OF SENATORS, EMPLOYEES OF STANDING AND SELECT COMMITTEES AND JOINT COMMITTEES THE EXPENSES OF WHICH ARE PAID FROM SENATE CONTINGENT FUND, AND OFFICERS OR EMPLOYEES PAID BY SECRETARY OF SENATE

Pub. L. 94–59, title I, §105, July 25, 1975, 89 Stat. 275, as amended by Pub. L. 94–157, title I, §111(a), Dec. 18, 1975, 89 Stat. 832, provided in part that, effective July 1, 1975: "The two committee employees referred to in clause (A), and the three committee employees referred to in clause (B), of section 105(e)(3) of the Legislative Branch Appropriations Act, 1968, as amended and modified [subsec. (e)(3) of this section], whose salaries are appropriated under the heading 'Salaries, Officers and Employees' for 'Committee Employees' for the Senate during any fiscal year, and the two employees referred to in such clause (A) who are employees of any joint committee having legislative authority, may each be paid at a maximum annual rate of compensation not to exceed $38,000, except that the Committee on Commerce is authorized to pay two employees, in addition to the two employees referred to in clause (A) of such section, at such maximum annual rate of compensation during the fiscal year ending June 30, 1976, and the transition period ending September 30, 1976. The two committee employees, other than joint committee employees, referred to in clause (A) of section 105(e)(3) of

such Act [subsec. (e)(3) of this section] whose salaries are not appropriated under such heading may each be paid at a maximum annual rate of compensation not to exceed $37,500, except, that the two employees of the majority policy committee and the two employees of the minority policy committee referred to in clause (A) of section 105(e)(3) of such Act [subsec. (e)(3) of this section] may each be paid at a maximum annual rate of compensation not to exceed $38,000. The one employee in a Senator's office referred to in section 105(d)(2)(ii) of such Act [subsec. (d)(2)(ii) of this section] may be paid at a maximum annual rate of compensation not to exceed $38,000. Any officer or employee whose pay is subject to the maximum limitation referred to in section 105(f) of such Act [subsec. (f) of this section] may be paid at a maximum annual rate of compensation not to exceed $38,000. This section does not supersede (1) any provision of an order of the President pro tempore of the Senate authorizing a higher rate of compensation, and (2) any authority of the President pro tempore to adjust rates of compensation or limitations referred to in this paragraph under section 4 of the Federal Pay Comparability Act of 1970 [section 60a–1 of this title]."

Section 111(c) of Pub. L. 94–157 provided in part that amendment by section 111(a) of Pub. L. 94–157 inserting after "fiscal year" the words ", and the two employees referred to in such clause (A) who are employees of any joint committee having legislative authority," shall become effective Jan. 1, 1976, and no increase in salary shall be payable for any period prior to such date by reason of the amendment.

1974 ADJUSTMENTS IN COMPENSATION IN MAXIMUM ANNUAL RATES TO EMPLOYEES IN OFFICES OF SENATORS, PROFESSIONAL STAFF AND CLERICAL STAFF MEMBERS OF STANDING COMMITTEES, EMPLOYEES OF STANDING AND SELECT COMMITTEES AND JOINT COMMITTEES THE EXPENSES OF WHICH ARE PAID FROM SENATE CONTINGENT FUND, AND OFFICERS OR EMPLOYEES PAID BY SECRETARY OF SENATE

Pub. L. 93–371, §4, Aug. 13, 1974, 88 Stat. 429, as amended by Pub. L. 94–157, title I, §111(b), Dec. 18, 1975, 89 Stat. 832, provided in part that: "The two committee employees other than joint committee employees referred to in clause (A), and the three committee employees referred to in clause (B), of section 105(e)(3) of the Legislative Branch Appropriation Act, 1968, as amended and modified [subsec. (e)(3) of this section], may each be paid at a maximum annual rate of compensation not to exceed $37,050. The four committee employees other than joint committee employees, who are not employees of a joint committee having legislative authority, referred to in such clause (A) and the sixteen committee employees referred to in such clause (B) may each be paid at a maximum annual rate of compensation not to exceed $35,625. The one employee in a Senator's office referred to in section 105(d)(2)(ii) of such Act [subsec. (d)(2)(ii) of this section] may be paid at a maximum annual rate of compensation not to exceed $37,050. Any officer or employee whose pay is subject to the maximum limitation referred to in section 105(f) of such Act [subsec. (f) of this section] may be paid at a maximum annual rate of compensation not to exceed $37,050."

For provisions that section 101(4) of Pub. L. 93–371 [this note] do not supersede (1) any provision of an order of the President pro tempore of the Senate authorizing a higher rate of compensation, and (2) any authority of the President pro tempore to adjust rates and compensation or limitations referred to in this note under section 4 of the Federal Pay Comparability Act of 1970 [section 60a–1 of this title] and that the provisions of this note are effective July 1, 1974, see note under section 61a of this title.

Section 111(c) of Pub. L. 94–157 provided in part that amendment by section 111(b) of Pub. L. 94–157 inserting after "joint committee employees" the words ", who are not employees of a joint committee having legislative authority," shall become effective Jan. 1, 1976, and no increase in salary shall be payable for any period prior to such date by reason of the amendment.

AGGREGATE OF GROSS COMPENSATION FOR EMPLOYEES IN OFFICE OF SENATOR FOR EACH FISCAL YEAR; INCREASE IN AMOUNT; REDUCTION IN AMOUNTS FOR COMMITTEE CHAIRMEN, RANKING MINORITY MEMBERS, ETC.

Section 111(a), (b) of Pub. L. 95–94, as amended by Pub. L. 95–240, title II, §206, Mar. 7, 1978, 92 Stat. 117, eff. Oct. 1, 1977; Pub. L. 100–137, §3, Oct. 21, 1987, 101 Stat. 819; Pub. L. 102–392, title I, §1, Oct. 6, 1992, 106 Stat. 1706, eff. Oct. 1, 1992, provided that:

"(a) Except as provided in subsection (b), the aggregate of the gross compensation which may be paid to employees in the office of a Senator during each fiscal year under section 105(d) of the Legislative Branch Appropriation Act, 1968, as amended and modified (2 U.S.C. 61–1(d)), is increased by an amount equal to 3 times the maximum annual gross rate of compensation that may be paid to an employee of the office of a Senator.

"(b) [Repealed. Pub. L. 100–137, §3, Oct. 21, 1987, 101 Stat. 819]."

[The amount of the increase referred to in section 111(a) of Pub. L. 95–94, set out above, was set at $421,677 by §6(d) of the Salary Directive of President pro tempore of the Senate, Dec. 20, 2000, set out as a note under section 60a–1 of this title.]

[Prior increases in the amount of increase authorized by section 111(a) of Pub. L. 95–94, set out above, were contained in the following Salary Directives of President pro tempore of the Senate, formerly set out as notes under section 60a–1 of this title: Oct. 9, 1978, §6(d); Oct. 13, 1979, §6(d); Oct. 1, 1980, §6(d); Oct. 5, 1981, as amended Dec. 15, 1981, §6(d); Oct. 1, 1982, §6(d); Dec. 20, 1983, as amended May 2, 1984, §6(d); Jan. 4, 1985, §6(d); Dec. 19, 1986, §6(d); Jan. 4, 1988, §6(d); Dec. 9, 1988, §6(d); Dec. 21, 1989, §6(d); Dec. 20, 1990, §6(d); Dec. 18, 1991, §6(d); Dec. 17, 1992, §6(d); Dec. 28, 1994, §6(d); Dec. 18, 1996, §6(d); Dec. 19, 1997, §6(d); Dec. 16, 1998, §6(d); Dec. 12, 1999, §6(d).]

[Section 3 of Pub. L. 100–137 provided that the repeal of section 111(b) of Pub. L. 95–94 is effective as of the first day of the 100th Congress [Jan. 6, 1987]].

[S.Res. 34, Jan. 6, 1987, provided: "That subsection (b) of section 111 of the Legislative Branch Appropriation Act, 1978 (P.L. 95–94) [set out as a note above] shall not be effective during the 100th Congress." Similar provisions covering the 99th Congress were contained in S.Res. 85, §23, Feb. 28, 1985.]

LIMITATION ON 1987 INCREASES IN MAXIMUM ANNUAL RATES TO STAFF MEMBERS OF STANDING, SPECIAL, AND SELECT COMMITTEES OF SENATE AND JOINT COMMITTEES OF CONGRESS WHOSE FUNDS ARE DISBURSED BY SECRETARY OF SENATE

Section 5(b)(2)–(4) of Salary Directive of President pro tempore of the Senate, Dec. 19, 1986, formerly set out as a note under section 60a–1 of this title, provided that, notwithstanding the provisions of section 5(b)(1) of that Order, any individual occupying a position on the staff of a standing committee of the Senate or the majority or minority policy committee of the Senate to which such rate applied should not be paid at any time at an annual rate in excess of $1,000 less than the annual rate of compensation which was then or might thereafter, be in effect for those positions referred to in section 2(a) of that Order, that notwithstanding the provisions of section 5(b)(1) of that Order, any individual occupying a position on the staff of any special or select committee of the Senate or the conference majority or conference minority of the Senate to which any such rate applied should not be paid at any time at an annual rate in excess of $2,500 less than the annual rate of compensation which was then or might thereafter be in effect for those positions referred to in section 2(a) of that Order, and that notwithstanding the provisions of section 5(b)(1) of that Order, any individual occupying a position on the staff of any joint committee of the Congress whose funds are disbursed by the Secretary of the Senate to which any such rate ap-

plied should not be paid at any time at an annual rate in excess of $2,900 less than the annual rate of compensation which was then or might thereafter be in effect for those positions referred to in section 2(a) of that Order.

Similar provisions covering prior increases were contained in the following prior Salary Directives:

Section 5(b)(2)–(4) of Salary Directive of President pro tempore of the Senate, Jan. 4, 1985.

Section 5(b)(2)–(4) of Salary Directive of President pro tempore of the Senate, Dec. 20, 1983.

Section 5(b)(2)–(4) of Salary Directive of President pro tempore of the Senate, Oct. 1, 1982.

Section 5(b)(2)–(4) of Salary Directive of President pro tempore of the Senate, Oct. 5, 1981.

Section 5(b)(3)–(5) of Salary Directive of President pro tempore of the Senate, Oct. 1, 1980.

Section 5(b)(3)–(5) of Salary Directive of President pro tempore of the Senate, Oct. 13, 1979.

Section 5(b)(3)–(5) of Salary Directive of President pro tempore of the Senate, Oct. 9, 1978.

Section 5(b)(3)–(5) of Salary Directive of President pro tempore of the Senate, Sept. 29, 1977.

Section 5(b)(3)–(6) of Salary Directive of President pro tempore of the Senate, Oct. 8, 1976.

Section 5(b)(3)–(5) of Salary Directive of President pro tempore of the Senate, Oct. 2, 1975.

Section 5(b)(3)–(5) of Salary Directive of President pro tempore of the Senate, Oct. 7, 1974.

Section 5(b)(2) of Salary Directive of President pro tempore of the Senate, Oct. 4, 1973.

LIMITATION ON 1987 INCREASES IN MAXIMUM ANNUAL RATES TO EMPLOYEES IN OFFICES OF SENATORS

Section 6(c)(2) of Salary Directive of President pro tempore of the Senate, Dec. 19, 1986, formerly set out as a note under section 60a–1 of this title, provided that, notwithstanding the modification made by section 6(c)(1) of that Order, any individual occupying a position in a Senator's office should not be paid at any time at an annual rate in excess of $2,500 less than the annual rate of compensation which was then or might thereafter be in effect for those positions referred to in section 2(a) of that Order.

Similar provisions covering prior increases were contained in the following prior Salary Directives:

Section 6(c)(2) of Salary Directive of President pro tempore of the Senate, Jan. 4, 1985.

Section 6(c)(2) of Salary Directive of President pro tempore of the Senate, Dec. 20, 1983.

Section 6(c)(2) of Salary Directive of President pro tempore of the Senate, Oct. 1, 1982.

Section 6(c)(2) of Salary Directive of President pro tempore of the Senate, Oct. 5, 1981.

Section 6(c)(2) of Salary Directive of President pro tempore of the Senate, Oct. 1, 1980.

Section 6(c)(2) of Salary Directive of President pro tempore of the Senate, Oct. 13, 1979.

Section 6(c)(2) of Salary Directive of President pro tempore of the Senate, Oct. 9, 1978.

Section 6(c)(2) of Salary Directive of President pro tempore of the Senate, Sept. 29, 1977.

Section 6(c)(2), (3) of Salary Directive of President pro tempore of the Senate, Oct. 8, 1976.

Section 6(c)(2), (3) of Salary Directive of President pro tempore of the Senate, Oct. 2, 1975.

Section 6(c)(2)–(4) of Salary Directive of President pro tempore of the Senate, Oct. 7, 1974.

Section 6(c)(2) of Salary Directive of President pro tempore of the Senate, Oct. 4, 1973.

LIMITATION ON 1987 INCREASE IN MAXIMUM ANNUAL RATE TO OFFICERS OR EMPLOYEES PAID BY SECRETARY OF SENATE

Section 7(b)(2) of Salary Directive of President pro tempore of the Senate, Dec. 19, 1986, formerly set out as a note under section 60a–1 of this title, provided that, notwithstanding the provisions of section 7(b)(1) of that Order, any individual occupying a position to which such rate applied should not be paid at any time at an annual rate in excess of $2,500 less than the annual rate of compensation which was then or might thereafter be in effect for those positions referred to in section 2(a) of that Order.

Similar provisions covering prior increases were contained in the following prior Salary Directives:

Section 7(b)(2) of Salary Directive of President pro tempore of the Senate, Jan. 4, 1985.

Section 7(b)(2) of Salary Directive of President pro tempore of the Senate, Dec. 20, 1983.

Section 7(b)(2) of Salary Directive of President pro tempore of the Senate, Oct. 1, 1982.

Section 7(b)(2) of Salary Directive of President pro tempore of the Senate, Oct. 5, 1981.

Section 7(b)(2) of Salary Directive of President pro tempore of the Senate, Oct. 1, 1980.

Section 7(b)(2) of Salary Directive of President pro tempore of the Senate, Oct. 13, 1979.

Section 7(b)(2) of Salary Directive of President pro tempore of the Senate, Oct. 9, 1978.

Section 7(b)(2) of Salary Directive of President pro tempore of the Senate, Sept. 27, 1977.

Section 7(b)(2), (3) of Salary Directive of President pro tempore of the Senate, Oct. 8, 1976.

Section 7(b)(2), (3) of Salary Directive of President pro tempore of the Senate, Oct. 2, 1975.

Section 7(b)(2) of Salary Directive of President pro tempore of the Senate, Oct. 7, 1974.

Section 7(b) of Salary Directive of President pro tempore of the Senate, Oct. 4, 1973.

1977 ADDITION OF EMPLOYEES IN OFFICE OF SENATOR NOT TO EFFECT SECTION 6(c) OF ORDER OF PRESIDENT PRO TEMPORE ISSUED ON OCTOBER 8, 1976

Section 111(d) of Pub. L. 95–94 provided in part that: "The amendments made by this subsection [amending subsec. (d)(2) of this section] shall have no effect on section 6(c) of the Order of the President pro tempore issued on October 8, 1976, under section 4 of the Federal Pay Comparability Act of 1970 [set out as a note under section 60a–1 of this title]."

INCREASE IN ALLOWANCES FOR ADMINISTRATIVE AND CLERICAL ASSISTANCE TO SENATORS—1987

Pub. L. 100–17, title I, § 3(b), (c), July 11, 1987, 101 Stat. 423, provided that:

"(b) Effective July 1, 1987, the administrative and clerical allowance of each Senator from the State of Georgia and the State of North Carolina is increased to that allowed Senators from States having a population of six million but less than seven million, the population of said State having exceeded six million inhabitants.

"(c) Effective July 1, 1987, the administrative and clerical allowance of each Senator from the State of Indiana, the State of Massachusetts, the State of Missouri, and the State of Virginia, is that allowed Senators from States having a population of five million but less than six million."

INCREASE IN ALLOWANCES FOR ADMINISTRATIVE AND CLERICAL ASSISTANCE TO SENATORS—1986

Pub. L. 99–349, title I, § 1, July 2, 1986, 100 Stat. 741, provided that:

"(a) Effective October 1, 1985, the allowance for administrative and clerical assistance of each Senator from the State of Alabama is increased to that allowed Senators from States having a population of four million but less than five million, the population of said State having exceeded four million inhabitants.

"(b) Effective October 1, 1985, the allowance for administrative and clerical assistance of each Senator from the State of Florida is increased to that allowed Senators from States having a population of eleven million but less than twelve million, the population of said State having exceeded eleven million inhabitants."

INCREASE IN ALLOWANCES FOR ADMINISTRATIVE AND CLERICAL ASSISTANCE TO SENATORS—1985

Pub. L. 99–88, title I, § 191, Aug. 15, 1985, 99 Stat. 348, provided that: "Effective October 1, 1984, the allowance for administrative and clerical assistance of each Senator from the State of Missouri is increased to that allowed Senators from States having a population of five million but less than seven million, the population of said State having exceeded five million inhabitants."

INCREASE IN ALLOWANCES FOR ADMINISTRATIVE AND CLERICAL ASSISTANCE TO SENATORS—1983

Section 9 of Pub. L. 98–367 provided that: "Effective October 1, 1983, the allowance for administration and clerical assistance of each Senator from the State of Arizona is increased to that allowed to Senators from States having population of three million but less than four million, the population of such State having exceeded three million inhabitants."

INCREASE IN ALLOWANCES FOR ADMINISTRATIVE AND CLERICAL ASSISTANCE TO SENATORS—1982

Pub. L. 98–63, title I, § 901, July 30, 1983, 97 Stat. 335, provided that:

"(a) Effective October 1, 1982, the allowance for administrative and clerical assistance of each Senator from the State of Texas is increased to that allowed to Senators from States having a population of fifteen million but less than seventeen million, the population of said State having exceeded fifteen million inhabitants.

"(b) Effective October 1, 1982, the allowance for administrative and clerical assistance of each Senator from the State of Colorado is increased to that allowed to Senators from States having a population of three million but less than four million, the population of said State having exceeded three million inhabitants."

INCREASES IN ALLOWANCES FOR ADMINISTRATIVE AND CLERICAL ASSISTANCE TO SENATORS—1981

Pub. L. 97–257, title I, Sept. 10, 1982, 96 Stat. 849, provided that: "Effective October 1, 1981, the allowance for administrative and clerical assistance of each Senator from the State of Florida is increased to that allowed Senators from States having a population of ten million but less than eleven million, the population of said State having exceeded ten million inhabitants."

Pub. L. 97–12, title I, § 106, June 5, 1981, 95 Stat. 62, provided that:

"(a) Effective January 1, 1981, the allowance for administrative and clerical assistance of each Senator from the State of Florida is increased to that allowed Senators from States having a population of nine million but less than ten million, the population of said State having exceeded nine million inhabitants.

"(b) Effective January 1, 1981, the allowance for administrative and clerical assistance of each Senator from the State of Washington is increased to that allowed Senators from States having a population of four million but less than five million, the population of said State having exceeded four million inhabitants.

"(c) Effective January 1, 1981, the allowance for administrative and clerical assistance of each Senator from the States of Oklahoma and South Carolina is increased to that allowed Senators from States having a population of three million but less than four million, the population of said State having exceeded three million inhabitants."

INCREASE IN ALLOWANCES FOR ADMINISTRATIVE AND CLERICAL ASSISTANCE TO SENATORS—1979

Section 105 of Pub. L. 96–304 provided that: "Effective October 1, 1979, the allowance for administrative and clerical assistance of each Senator from the State of Louisiana is increased to that allowed Senators from States having a population of four million but less than five million, the population of said State having exceeded four million inhabitants."

Pub. L. 96–86, §111(a), (b), Oct. 12, 1979, 93 Stat. 660, 661, provided:

"(a) effective October 1, 1979, the allowance for administrative and clerical assistance of each Senator from the State of Minnesota is increased to that allowed Senators from States having a population of four million but less than five million, the population of said State having exceeded four million inhabitants;

"(b) effective October 1, 1979, the allowance for administrative and clerical assistance of each Senator from the State of Texas is increased to that allowed Senators from States having a population of thirteen million but less than fifteen million, the population of said State having exceeded thirteen million inhabitants;".

INCREASE IN ALLOWANCES FOR ADMINISTRATIVE AND CLERICAL ASSISTANCE TO SENATORS—1978

Section 104(a) of Pub. L. 95–391 provided that: "Effective April 1, 1978, the clerk-hire allowance of each Senator from the State of Georgia is increased to that allowed Senators from States having a population of five million but less than seven million, the population of said State having exceeded five million inhabitants."

INCREASE IN ALLOWANCES FOR ADMINISTRATIVE AND CLERICAL ASSISTANTS TO SENATORS—1977

Pub. L. 95–26, title I, May 4, 1977, 91 Stat. 81, provided in part: "That, effective April 1, 1977, the clerk hire allowance of each Senator from the State of Virginia shall be increased to that allowed Senators from States having a population of five million but less than seven million, the population of said State having exceeded five million inhabitants."

INCREASE IN ALLOWANCES FOR ADMINISTRATIVE AND CLERICAL ASSISTANCE TO SENATORS—1976

Pub. L. 94–157, title I, ch. IV, Dec. 18, 1975, 89 Stat. 830, provided: "That effective January 1, 1976, the clerk hire allowance of each Senator from the State of California shall be increased to that allowed Senators from States having a population of more than twenty-one million, the population of said State having exceeded twenty-one million inhabitants."

INCREASE IN ALLOWANCES FOR ADMINISTRATIVE AND CLERICAL ASSISTANCE TO SENATORS—1975

Pub. L. 94–32, title I, June 12, 1975, 89 Stat. 182, provided in part: "That effective January 1, 1975, the clerk hire allowance of each Senator from the State of Texas shall be increased to that allowed Senators from States having a population of more than twelve million, the population of said State having exceeded twelve million inhabitants."

INCREASE IN ALLOWANCES FOR ADMINISTRATIVE AND CLERICAL ASSISTANCE TO SENATORS—1974

Pub. L. 93–371, Aug. 13, 1974, 88 Stat. 425, provided in part: "That effective January 1, 1974, the clerk hire allowance of each Senator from the States of Arkansas and Arizona shall be increased to that allowed Senators from States having a population of two million, the population of each said State having exceeded two million inhabitants."

INCREASE IN ALLOWANCES FOR ADMINISTRATIVE AND CLERICAL ASSISTANCE TO SENATORS—1969

Pub. L. 91–145, Dec. 12, 1969, 83 Stat. 340, provided in part: "That the clerk hire allowance of each Senator from the State of Connecticut shall be increased to that allowed Senators from States having a population of three million, the population of said State having exceeded three million inhabitants."

INCREASE IN ALLOWANCES FOR ADMINISTRATIVE AND CLERICAL ASSISTANCE TO SENATORS—1968

Pub. L. 90–239, ch. IV, Jan. 2, 1968, 81 Stat. 774, provided in part that: "Effective January 1, 1968, the clerk

hire allowance of each Senator from the State of Indiana shall be increased to that allowed Senators from States having a population of five million, the population of said State having exceeded five million inhabitants; and that the clerk hire allowance of each Senator from the State of New Jersey shall be increased to that allowed Senators from States having a population of seven million, the population of said State having exceeded seven million inhabitants."

INCREASE IN ALLOWANCES FOR ADMINISTRATIVE AND CLERICAL ASSISTANCE TO SENATORS—1966

Pub. L. 89–697, ch. VI, Oct. 27, 1966, 80 Stat. 1063, provided: "That the clerk hire allowance of each Senator from the State of North Carolina shall be increased to that allowed Senators from States having a population of five million, the population of said State having exceeded five million inhabitants."

INCREASE IN ALLOWANCES FOR ADMINISTRATIVE AND CLERICAL ASSISTANCE TO SENATORS—1963

Pub. L. 88–25, title I, May 17, 1963, 77 Stat. 31, provided in part: "That the clerk hire allowance of each Senator from the State of California shall be increased to that allowed Senators from States having a population of over seventeen million, the population of said State having exceeded seventeen million inhabitants, that the clerk hire allowance of each Senator from the State of Georgia shall be increased to that allowed Senators from States having a population of four million, the population of said State having exceeded four million inhabitants, and that the clerk hire allowance of each Senator from the State of Washington shall be increased to that allowed Senators from States having a population of three million, the population of said State having exceeded three million inhabitants."

INCREASE IN ALLOWANCES FOR ADMINISTRATIVE AND CLERICAL ASSISTANCE TO SENATORS—1962

Pub. L. 87–545, title I, July 25, 1962, 76 Stat. 215, provided in part that:

"The basic clerk hire allowance of each Senator is hereby increased by $3,000.

"The clerk hire allowances of the Senators from the States of New York and Virginia are hereby increased so that the allowances of the Senators from the State of New York will be equal to that allowed Senators from States having a population of over seventeen million, the population of said State having exceeded seventeen million inhabitants, and so that allowances of Senators from the State of Virginia will be equal to that allowed Senators from States having a population of four million, the population of said State having exceeded four million inhabitants."

INCREASE IN ALLOWANCE FOR ADMINISTRATIVE AND CLERICAL ASSISTANCE TO SENATORS—1955

Act June 28, 1955, ch. 189, §4(d), (f), 69 Stat. 176, 177, as amended Aug. 21, 1959, Pub. L. 86–176, 73 Stat. 401; Aug. 20, 1964, Pub. L. 88–454, 78 Stat. 538; Aug. 27, 1966, Pub. L. 89–545, 80 Stat. 357; July 28, 1967, Pub. L. 90–57, §105(i)(6), 81 Stat. 144, provided that:

"(d)(1) The aggregate amount of the basic compensation authorized to be paid for administrative and clerical assistance and messenger service in the offices of Senators is hereby increased by—

"(A) $10,020 in the case of Senators from States the population of which is less than three million;

"(B) $10,920 in the case of Senators from States the population of which is three million or more but less than five million;

"(C) $11,760 in the case of Senators from States the population of which is five million or more but less than ten million; and

"(D) $11,880 in the case of Senators from States the population of which is ten million or more.

"(2) Notwithstanding the second proviso in the paragraph relating to the authority of Senators to rearrange the basic salaries of employees in their respective offices, which appears in the Legislative Branch Appropriation Act, 1947, as amended (2 U. S. C. 60f) [repealed], but subject to the limitations contained in paragraph (3) of this subsection, during the period beginning on the effective date of this subsection and ending on the last day of the first pay period which begins after the date of enactment of this Act [June 28, 1955] (A) the compensation of the administrative assistant in the office of each Senator may be fixed at a basic rate which together with additional compensation authorized by law will not exceed the maximum rate authorized by section 2 (b) of the Act of October 24, 1951 (Public Law 201, Eighty-second Congress), as amended [section 60e-6(b) of this title], (B) the compensation of one employee other than the administrative assistant in the office of each Senator may be fixed at a basic rate not to exceed $10,260 per annum, and (C) the compensation of any other employee in the office of a Senator may be fixed at a basic rate not to exceed $6,420 per annum.

"(3) Notwithstanding the third proviso in such paragraph [this section], any increase in the compensation of an employee in a Senator's office shall take effect on the effective date of this subsection or on the date such employee became employed, whichever is later, if (A) the certification filed by such Senator under such proviso so provides, (B) such certification is filed in the disbursing office of the Senate not later than fifteen days following the date of enactment of this Act [June 28, 1955], and (C) the amount of such increase does not exceed the amount of the increase which would be payable in the case of such employee if he were subject to the provisions of subsection (a) of this section [section 60e-7 of this title] plus any additional amount which may result from fixing the rate of basic compensation at the lowest multiple of $60 which will result in an increase not less than the amount of such increase which would be payable under subsection (a) [section 60e-7(a) of this title].

"(f) [Repealed. Pub. L. 90-57, § 105(i)(6), July 28, 1967, 81 Stat. 144, eff. Aug. 1, 1967.]"

INCREASE IN ALLOWANCE FOR ADMINISTRATIVE AND CLERICAL ASSISTANCE TO SENATORS—1951

Act Oct. 24, 1951, ch. 554, § 2(c)(1), 65 Stat. 614, provided that: "The aggregate amount of the basic compensation authorized to be paid for administrative and clerical assistance and messenger service in the offices of Senators is hereby increased by—

"(A) $4,140 in the case of Senators from States the population of which is less than three million;

"(B) $4,860 in the case of Senators from States the population of which is three million or more but less than five million;

"(C) $5,220 in the case of Senators from States the population of which is five million or more but less than ten million; and

"(D) $5,760 in the case of Senators from States the population of which is ten million or more."

1966 ADJUSTMENT OF BASIC COMPENSATION OF EMPLOYEES IN OFFICE OF SENATOR

Pub. L. 89-504, title III, § 302(f), July 18, 1966, 80 Stat. 295, provided that: "The basic compensation of each employee in the office of a Senator is hereby adjusted, effective on the first day of the month following the date of enactment of this Act [July 18, 1966], to the lowest multiple of $60 which will provide a gross rate of compensation not less than the gross rate such employee was receiving immediately prior thereto, except that the foregoing provisions of this subsection shall not apply in the case of any employee if on or before the fifteenth day following the date of enactment of this Act [July 18, 1966], the Senator by whom such employee is employed notifies the disbursing office of the Senate in writing that he does not wish such provisions to apply to such employee. No employee whose basic compensation is adjusted under this subsection shall receive any additional compensation under subsection

(a) [section 60e-13(a) of this title] for any period prior to the effective date of such adjustment during which such employee was employed in the office of the Senator by whom he is employed on the first day of the month following the enactment of this Act [July 18, 1966]. No additional compensation shall be paid to any person under subsection (a) [section 60e-13(a) of this title] for any period prior to the first day of the month following the date of enactment of this Act [July 18, 1966] during which such person was employed in the office of a Senator (other than a Senator by whom he is employed on such day) unless on or before the fifteenth day following the date of enactment of this Act [July 18, 1966] such Senator notifies the disbursing office of the Senate in writing that he wishes such employee to receive such additional compensation for such period. In any case in which, at the expiration of the time within which a Senator may give notice under this subsection, such Senator is deceased, such notice shall be deemed to have been given."

1965 ADJUSTMENT OF BASIC COMPENSATION OF EMPLOYEES IN OFFICE OF SENATOR

Pub. L. 89-301, § 11(f), Oct. 29, 1965, 79 Stat. 1121, provided that: "The basic compensation of each employee in the office of a Senator is hereby adjusted, effective on the first day of the month following the date of enactment of this Act [Oct. 29, 1965], to the lowest multiple of $60 which will provide a gross rate of compensation not less than the gross rate such employee was receiving immediately prior thereto, except that the foregoing provisions of this subsection shall not apply in the case of any employee if on or before the fifteenth day following the date of enactment of this Act [Oct. 29, 1965], the Senator by whom such employee is employed notifies the disbursing office of the Senate in writing that he does not wish such provisions to apply to such employee. No employee whose basic compensation is adjusted under this subsection shall receive any additional compensation under subsection (a) [section 60e-12(a) of this title] for any period prior to the effective date of such adjustment during which such employee was employed in the office of the Senator by whom he is employed on the first day of the month following the enactment of this Act [Oct. 29, 1965]. No additional compensation shall be paid to any person under subsection (a) [section 60e-12(a) of this title] for any period prior to the first day of the month following the date of enactment of this Act [Oct. 29, 1965] during which such person was employed in the office of a Senator (other than a Senator by whom he is employed on such day) unless on or before the fifteenth day following the date of enactment of this Act [Oct. 29, 1965] such Senator notifies the disbursing office of the Senate in writing that he wishes such employee to receive such additional compensation for such period. In any case in which, at the expiration of the time within which a Senator may give notice under this subsection, such Senator is deceased, such notice shall be deemed to have been given."

1964 ADJUSTMENT OF BASIC COMPENSATION OF EMPLOYEES IN OFFICE OF SENATOR

Pub. L. 88-426, title II, § 202(e), Aug. 14, 1964, 78 Stat. 413, provided that: "The basic compensation of each employee in the office of a Senator is hereby adjusted effective on the first day of the month following the date of enactment of this Act [Aug. 14, 1964], to the lowest multiple of $60 which will provide a gross rate of compensation not less than the gross rate such employee was receiving immediately prior thereto except that the foregoing provisions of this subsection shall not apply in the case of any employee if on or before the fifteenth day following the date of enactment of this Act [Aug. 14, 1964], the Senator by whom such employee is employed notifies the disbursing office of the Senate in writing that he does not wish such provisions to apply to such employee. No employee whose basic compensation is adjusted under this subsection shall receive any additional compensation under subsection (a) [section 60e–11(a) of this title] for any period prior to the effective date of such adjustment during which such employee was employed in the office of the Senator by whom he is employed on the first day of the month following the enactment of this Act [Aug. 14, 1964]. No additional compensation shall be paid to any person under subsection (a) [section 60e–11(a) of this title] for any period prior to the first day of the month following the date of enactment of this Act [Aug. 14, 1964] during which such person was employed in the office of a Senator (other than a Senator by whom he is employed on such day) unless on or before the fifteenth day following the date of enactment of this Act [Aug. 14, 1964] such Senator notifies the disbursing office of the Senate in writing that he wishes such employee to receive such additional compensation for such period. In any case in which, at the expiration of the time within which a Senator may give notice under this subsection, such Senator is deceased such notice shall be deemed to have been given."

1962 ADJUSTMENT OF BASIC COMPENSATION OF EMPLOYEES IN OFFICE OF SENATOR

Pub. L. 87–793, title VI, §1005(b), Oct. 11, 1962, 76 Stat. 867, provided that: "The basic compensation of each employee in the office of a Senator is hereby adjusted, effective on October 16, 1962, to the lowest multiple of $60 which will provide a gross rate of compensation not less than the gross rate such employee was receiving immediately prior thereto, except that the foregoing provisions of this subsection shall not apply in the case of any employee if on or before the fifteenth day following the date of enactment of this Act [Oct. 11, 1962] the Senator by whom such employee is employed notifies the disbursing office of the Senate in writing that he does not wish such provisions to apply to such employee. In any case in which, at the expiration of the time within which a Senator may give notice under this subsection, such Senator is deceased such notice shall be deemed to have been given."

1960 ADJUSTMENT OF BASIC COMPENSATION OF EMPLOYEES IN OFFICE OF SENATOR

Pub. L. 86–568, title I, §117(b), July 1, 1960, 74 Stat. 303, provided that: "The basic compensation of each employee in the office of a Senator is hereby adjusted, effective on July 1, 1960, to the lowest multiple of $60 which will provide a gross rate of compensation not less than the gross rate such employee was receiving immediately prior thereto, except that the foregoing provisions of this subsection shall not apply in the case of any employee if on or before the fifteenth day following the date of enactment of this Act [July 1, 1960] the Senator by whom such employee is employed notifies the disbursing office of the Senate in writing that he does not wish such provisions to apply to such employee. In any case in which, at the expiration of the time within which a Senator may give notice under this subsection, such Senator is deceased such notice shall be deemed to have been given."

1958 ADJUSTMENT OF BASIC COMPENSATION OF EMPLOYEES IN OFFICE OF SENATOR

Pub. L. 85–462, §4(b), June 20, 1958, 72 Stat. 207, provided that: "The basic compensation of each employee in the office of a Senator is hereby adjusted, effective on the first day of the month following the date of enactment of this Act [June 20, 1958], to the lowest multiple of $60 which will provide a gross rate of compensation not less than the gross rate such employee was receiving immediately prior thereto, except that the foregoing provisions of this subsection shall not apply in the case of any employee if on or before the fifteenth day following the date of enactment of this Act [June 20, 1958] the Senator by whom such employee is employed notifies the disbursing office of the Senate in writing that he does not wish such provisions to apply to such employee. No employee whose basic compensa-

tion is adjusted under this subsection shall receive any additional compensation under subsection (a) [section 60e–8(a) of this title] for any period prior to the effective date of such adjustment during which such employee was employed in the office of the Senator by whom he is employed on the first day of the month following the enactment of this Act [June 20, 1958]. No additional compensation shall be paid to any person under subsection (a) [section 60e–8(a) of this title] for any period prior to the first day of the month following the date of enactment of this Act [June 20, 1958] during which such person was employed in the office of a Senator (other than a Senator by whom he is employed on such day) unless on or before the fifteenth day following the date of enactment of this Act [June 20, 1958] such Senator notifies the disbursing office of the Senate in writing that he wishes such employee to receive such additional compensation for such period. In any case in which, at the expiration of the time within which a Senator may give notice under this subsection, such Senator is deceased such notice shall be deemed to have been given."

1955 ADJUSTMENT OF BASIC COMPENSATION OF EMPLOYEES IN OFFICE OF SENATOR

Act June 28, 1955, ch. 189, §4(e)(2), 69 Stat. 177, provided that: "The basic compensation of each employee in the office of a Senator on the effective date of this subsection is hereby adjusted to the lowest multiple of $60 which will provide basic compensation, plus additional compensation payable under subsection (a) [section 60e–7(a) of this title] and the provisions of law referred to in subsection (a) [section 60e–7(a) of this title], not less than the amount of basic compensation, plus additional compensation under the provisions of sections 501 and 502 of the Federal Employees' Pay Act of 1945, as amended [sections 60e–3 and 60e–4 of this title], and section 301 of the Postal Rate Revision and Federal Employees' Salary Act of 1948 [section 60e–4a of this title], which he is receiving on the effective date of this subsection."

COMPENSATION OF ADMINISTRATIVE ASSISTANT CHARGED TO SENATOR

Act Oct. 28, 1949, ch. 783, title I, §101(c)(1), 63 Stat. 974, provided that: "The basic compensation of the administrative assistant to a Senator shall be charged against the aggregate amount authorized to be paid for clerical assistance and messenger service in the office of such Senator."

ADDITIONAL INCREASE IN CLERK HIRE

Act Oct. 28, 1949, ch. 783, title I, §101(c)(2), 63 Stat. 974, provided that: "The aggregate amount of the basic compensation authorized to be paid for clerical assistance and messenger service in the office of each Senator is increased by $11,520."

INCREASE OF CLERK HIRE FOR SENATORS

Act Dec. 20, 1944, ch. 617, §2(b), 58 Stat. 832, effective Jan. 1, 1945, provided: "The aggregate amount of the basic compensation authorized to be paid to employees in the offices of Senators (including employees of standing committees of which Senators are chairmen) is hereby increased by (1) $4,020 in the case of each Senator from a State which has a population of less than four million inhabitants and (2) by $5,040 in the case of each Senator from a State which has a population of four million or more inhabitants."

RATE OF PAY FOR SENATE COMMITTEE STAFF MEMBERS FOR 1977 COMMITTEE SYSTEM REORGANIZATION

Pub. L. 95–4, Feb. 16, 1977, 91 Stat. 12, provided: "That (a) notwithstanding the limitations contained in section 105(e) of the Legislative Branch Appropriation Act, 1968, as amended and modified [subsec. (e) of this section], each eligible staff member of a new committee to whom section 703(d) of the Committee System Reorganization Amendments of 1977 [S. Res. 4, Feb. 4, 1977] applies may, during the transition period of such new committee, be paid gross annual compensation at the rate which that eligible staff member was receiving on January 4, 1977.

"(b) For purposes of subsection (a), the terms 'eligible staff member', 'new committee', and 'transition period' have the meanings given to them by section 701 of the Committee System Reorganization Amendments of 1977 [S. Res. 4, Feb. 4, 1977]."

1970 Increase in Pay Rates of Certain Employees of Legislative Branch

Adjustment by President pro tempore of Senate with respect to the Senate, by Finance Clerk of House with respect to the House of Representatives, and by Architect of the Capitol with respect to the Office of the Architect of the Capitol, effective on the first day of the first pay period which begins on or after Dec. 27, 1969, of the rates of pay of employees of the legislative branch subject to section 214 of Pub. L. 90–206, with certain exceptions, by the amounts of the adjustment for corresponding rates for employees subject to the General Schedule, set out in section 5332 of Title 5, which had been made by section 2 of Pub. L. 91–231 raising such rates by 6 percent, see Pub. L. 91–231, set out as a note under section 5332 of Title 5, Government Organization and Employees.

1968 and 1969 Increases in Compensation of Employees

This section deemed amended on and after July 1, 1969, see Salary Directives of President pro tempore of the Senate, June 12, 1968, and June 17, 1969, formerly set out as notes under section 60a–1 of this title.

Rates of Pay for Employees of Senate Select Committee To Study Governmental Operations With Respect to Intelligence Activities

Pub. L. 94–32, title I, §5, June 12, 1975, 89 Stat. 183, provided in part that: "Notwithstanding paragraph (3) of section 105(e) of the Legislative Branch Appropriations Act, 1968, as amended [subsec. (e)(3) of this section], two employees of the Senate Select Committee to Study Governmental Operations With Respect to Intelligence Activities may be paid at the highest gross rate provided in subparagraph (A) of such paragraph, and eleven employees of such committee may be paid at the next highest gross rate provided in such subparagraph."

Secretary of Senate To Fix Compensation of Legislative Clerk and Journal Clerk

Pub. L. 86–213, Sept. 1, 1959, 73 Stat. 443, authorized Secretary of Senate to fix compensation of legislative clerk and journal clerk, on and after Sept. 1, 1959, at not to exceed $7,620 basic per annum each.

Section Referred to in Other Sections

This section is referred to in sections 43d, 58, 61–1a, 61–1c of this title.

§ 61–1a. Availability of appropriated funds for payment to an individual of pay from more than one position; conditions

Notwithstanding any other provision of law, appropriated funds are available for payment to an individual of pay from more than one position, each of which is either in the office of a Senator and the pay of which is disbursed by the Secretary of the Senate or is in another office and the pay of which is disbursed by the Secretary of the Senate out of an appropriation under the heading "Salaries, Officers, and Employees", if the aggregate gross pay from those positions does not exceed the maximum rate specified in section 61–1(d)(2) of this title.

(Pub. L. 95–94, title I, §114, Aug. 5, 1977, 91 Stat. 665; Pub. L. 95–240, title II, §207, Mar. 7, 1978, 92 Stat. 117; Pub. L. 100–202, §101(i) [title I, §9], Dec. 22, 1987, 101 Stat. 1329–290, 1329–295.)

Codification

Section is from the Congressional Operations Appropriation Act, 1978, which is title I of the Legislative Branch Appropriation Act, 1978.

Amendments

1987—Pub. L. 100–202 amended section generally. Prior to amendment, section read as follows: "Notwithstanding any other provision of law, appropriated funds are available for payment to an individual of pay from more than one position, the pay for each of which is disbursed by the Secretary of the Senate out of an appropriation under the heading 'Salaries, Officers and Employees', if the aggregate gross pay from those positions does not exceed the amount specified in section 61–1(d)(2)(ii) of this title."

1978—Pub. L. 95–240 substituted provisions relating to pay disbursed by Secretary of Senate from appropriation with the heading for salaries, etc., for provisions requiring positions to be in office of a Senator and the pay for each disbursed by Secretary of Senate.

§ 61–1b. Availability of appropriations during first three months of any fiscal year for aggregate of payments of gross compensation made to employees from Senate appropriation account for "Salaries, Officers and Employees"

At no time during the first three months of any fiscal year (commencing with the fiscal year which begins October 1, 1984) shall the aggregate of payments of gross compensation made to employees out of any line item appropriation within the Senate appropriation account for "Salaries, Officers and Employees" (other than the line item appropriations, within such account for "Administrative, clerical, and legislative assistance to Senators" and for "Agency contributions") exceed twenty-five per centum of the total amount available for such line item appropriations for such fiscal year.

(Pub. L. 98–367, title I, §4, July 17, 1984, 98 Stat. 475.)

Codification

Section is from the Congressional Operations Appropriation Act, 1985, which is title I of the Legislative Branch Appropriations Act, 1985.

§ 61–1c. Aggregate gross compensation of employee of Senator of State with population under 5,000,000

(a) Notwithstanding the provisions of section 61–1(d)(1) of this title, and except as otherwise provided in subparagraph (C) of such subsection (d)(1), the aggregate of gross compensation paid employees in the office of a Senator shall not exceed during each fiscal year $1,012,083 if the population of his State is less than 5,000,000.

(b) Subsection (a) of this section shall take effect October 1, 1991.

(Pub. L. 102–90, title I, §5, Aug. 14, 1991, 105 Stat. 450.)

Codification

Section is from the Congressional Operations Appropriations Act, 1992, which is title I of the Legislative Branch Appropriations Act, 1992.

§ 61–2. Omitted

CODIFICATION

Section, Pub. L. 90–206, title II, §214(g)–(i), Dec. 16, 1967, 81 Stat. 636, provided for an increase in annual rate of gross compensation for pay periods after Dec. 16, 1967, for certain employees whose compensation is disbursed by Secretary of Senate and Clerk of House of Representatives.

§ 61a. Compensation of Secretary of Senate

The Secretary of the Senate shall be paid at an annual rate of compensation of $40,000.

(Pub. L. 88–426, title II, §203(g), Aug. 14, 1964, 78 Stat. 415; Pub. L. 93–371, §4, Aug. 13, 1974, 88 Stat. 429; Pub. L. 94–59, title I, §105, July 25, 1975, 89 Stat. 275.)

PRIOR PROVISIONS

A prior section 61a, act Aug. 5, 1955, ch. 568, §1, 69 Stat. 499, prescribed gross annual compensation of Secretary of Senate.

AMENDMENTS

1975—Pub. L. 94–59 substituted "an annual rate of compensation of $40,000" for "a rate of $38,760 per annum".

1974—Pub. L. 93–371 increased the annual rate of compensation from $27,500 to $38,760.

EFFECTIVE DATE OF 1975 AMENDMENT

Section 105 of Pub. L. 94–59 provided that the increase in the Secretary's rate of compensation to $40,000 is effective July 1, 1975.

EFFECTIVE DATE OF 1974 AMENDMENT

Section 4 of Pub. L. 93–371 provided in part that: "This paragraph [enacting sections 61h, 61h–1, 63a, and 64a–1 of this title, amending this section and sections 61a–3, 61b, 61e, 61g, 61j, and 273 of this title, and enacting provisions set out as notes under this section and sections 61–1 and 274 of this title] is effective July 1, 1974."

EFFECTIVE DATE

Section effective first day of first pay period which begins on or after July 1, 1964, to the extent provided in section 501(c) of Pub. L. 88–426, see section 501 of Pub. L. 88–426.

1974 ADJUSTMENT IN COMPENSATION NOT TO SUPERSEDE ADJUSTMENTS IN COMPENSATION OR LIMITATIONS BY PRESIDENT PRO TEMPORE OF THE SENATE

Section 4 of Pub. L. 93–371, eff. July 1, 1974, provided in part that: "This paragraph does not supersede (1) any provision of an order of the President pro tempore of the Senate authorizing a higher rate of compensation, and (2) any authority of the President pro tempore to adjust rates of compensation or limitations referred to in this paragraph under section 4 of the Federal Pay Comparability Act of 1970 [section 60a–1 of this title]."

INCREASES IN COMPENSATION

Increases in compensation of Secretary of Senate under authority of Federal Salary Act of 1967 (Pub. L. 90–206) and Federal Pay Comparability Act of 1970 (Pub. L. 91–656), see section 60a–1 of this title, and Salary Directives of President pro tempore of the Senate, set out as notes under that section.

§§ 61a–1, 61a–2. Omitted

CODIFICATION

Section 61a–1, acts June 27, 1956, ch. 453, §101, 70 Stat. 356; July 9, 1971, Pub. L. 92–51, §101, 85 Stat. 125, provided for rate of compensation of Chief Clerk of Senate which office was superseded by Assistant Secretary of Senate.

Section 61a–2, Pub. L. 88–426, title II, §202(i), Aug. 14, 1964, 78 Stat. 414; Pub. L. 95–94, title I, §108(a), Aug. 5, 1977, 91 Stat. 661, provided for rate of compensation for Postmaster and Assistant Postmaster of Senate. See section 61f–7 of this title which abolished all statutory positions in Office of Sergeant at Arms and Doorkeeper of Senate, with specified exceptions, effective Oct. 1, 1981, and authorized Sergeant at Arms and Doorkeeper of Senate to appoint and fix compensation of such employees as appropriate.

§ 61a–3. Compensation of Assistant Secretary of Senate

The Assistant Secretary of the Senate may be paid at a maximum annual rate of compensation not to exceed $39,000.

(Pub. L. 91–145, Dec. 12, 1969, 83 Stat. 340; Pub. L. 93–371, §4, Aug. 13, 1974, 88 Stat. 429; Pub. L. 94–59, title I, §105, July 25, 1975, 89 Stat. 275.)

AMENDMENTS

1975—Pub. L. 94–59 substituted "$39,000" for "$37,620", effective July 1, 1975.

1974—Pub. L. 93–371 substituted provision setting maximum annual rate of compensation of Assistant Secretary at not to exceed $37,620, for provisions authorizing Secretary of Senate to fix the compensation of Assistant Secretary at not to exceed $11,826 per annum, effective July 1, 1974.

CHANGE OF NAME

Assistant Secretary of the Senate deemed successor in references to Chief Clerk of Senate in all laws, rules, resolutions, and orders, effective July 1, 1971, under provisions of Pub. L. 92–51, July 9, 1971, 85 Stat. 125.

1974 ADJUSTMENT IN COMPENSATION NOT TO SUPERSEDE ADJUSTMENTS IN COMPENSATION OR LIMITATIONS BY PRESIDENT PRO TEMPORE OF THE SENATE

Adjustment in compensation by Pub. L. 93–371 not to supersede order of President pro tempore of the Senate authorizing higher rate of compensation or any authority of the President pro tempore to adjust rates of compensation or limitations under section 4 of the Federal Pay Comparability Act of 1970, see section 4 of Pub. L. 93–371, set out in part as a note under section 61a of this title.

INCREASES IN COMPENSATION

Increases in compensation of Assistant Secretary of the Senate under authority of Federal Salary Act of 1967 (Pub. L. 90–206) and Federal Pay Comparability Act of 1970 (Pub. L. 91–656), see section 60a–1 of this title, and Salary Directives of President pro tempore of the Senate, set out as notes under that section.

§ 61a–4. Repealed. Pub. L. 93–145, Nov. 1, 1973, 87 Stat. 531

Section, Pub. L. 91–145, Dec. 12, 1969, 83 Stat. 340; Pub. L. 91–382, Aug. 18, 1970, 84 Stat. 807, provided for appointment and salary of a Comptroller of the Senate and a secretary to the Comptroller.

EFFECTIVE DATE OF REPEAL

Pub. L. 93–145 provided that the repeal is effective July 1, 1973.

§ 61a–4a. Omitted

CODIFICATION

Section, Pub. L. 92–342, §101, July 10, 1972, 86 Stat. 433, authorized Comptroller of Senate to appoint and fix compensation of an auditor in lieu of a secretary. Section was omitted in view of repeal of section 61a–4 of this title which authorized appointment of a Comptroller of Senate by President pro tempore of the Senate and the appointment by Comptroller of Senate of a secretary, and repeal of section 61a–5 of this title which set out duties of Comptroller of Senate, one of which was to appoint a secretary.

§ 61a–5. Repealed. Pub. L. 93–145, Nov. 1, 1973, 87 Stat. 531

Section, Pub. L. 91–382, Aug. 18, 1970, 84 Stat. 807, set out the duties to be performed by the Comptroller of the Senate.

EFFECTIVE DATE OF REPEAL

Pub. L. 93–145 provided that the repeal is effective July 1, 1973.

§§ 61a–6 to 61a–8. Omitted

CODIFICATION

Sections were omitted for lack of general applicability. Sections were taken from the Legislative Branch Appropriation Act, 1971, the Legislative Branch Appropriation Act, 1972, and the Supplemental Appropriation Act, 1973, respectively, and provided for the appointment and compensation of specified employees of the Senate by the Secretary of the Senate.

Section 61a–6, Pub. L. 91–382, Aug. 18, 1970, 84 Stat. 808, was effective Aug. 1, 1970.

Section 61a–7, Pub. L. 92–51, July 9, 1971, 85 Stat. 125, was effective July 1, 1971.

Section 61a–8, Pub. L. 92–607, ch. V, Oct. 31, 1972, 86 Stat. 1504, was effective Nov. 1, 1972.

§ 61a–9. Advancement by Secretary of Senate of travel funds to employees under his jurisdiction for Federal Election Campaign Act travel expenses

The Secretary of the Senate is hereafter authorized to advance, in his discretion, to any designated employee under his jurisdiction, such sums as may be necessary, not exceeding $1,500, to defray official travel expenses in assisting the Secretary in carrying out his duties under the Federal Election Campaign Act of 1971 [2 U.S.C. 431 et seq.]. Any such employee shall, as soon as practicable, furnish to the Secretary a detailed voucher for such expenses incurred and make settlement with respect to any amount so advanced.

(Pub. L. 92–607, ch. V, § 504, Oct. 31, 1972, 86 Stat. 1505.)

REFERENCES IN TEXT

The Federal Election Campaign Act of 1971, referred to in text, is Pub. L. 92–225, Feb. 7, 1972, 86 Stat. 3, as amended, which is classified principally to chapter 14 (§ 431 et seq.) of this title. For complete classification of this Act to the Code, see Short Title note set out under section 431 of this title and Tables.

§ 61a–9a. Travel expenses of Secretary of Senate; advancement of travel funds to designated employees

For the purpose of carrying out his duties, the Secretary of the Senate is authorized to incur official travel expenses. The Secretary of the Senate is authorized to advance, in his discretion, to any designated employee under his jurisdiction, such sums as may be necessary, not exceeding $1,000, to defray official travel ex-

penses in assisting the Secretary in carrying out his duties. Any such employee shall, as soon as practicable, furnish to the Secretary a detailed voucher for such expenses incurred and make settlement with respect to any amount so advanced. Payments to carry out the provisions of this section shall be made from funds included in the appropriation "Miscellaneous Items" under the heading "Contingent Expenses of the Senate" upon vouchers approved by the Secretary of the Senate.

(Pub. L. 94–59, title I, § 101, July 25, 1975, 89 Stat. 273; Pub. L. 95–94, title I, § 106, Aug. 5, 1977, 91 Stat. 661; Pub. L. 95–355, title I, § 101, Sept. 8, 1978, 92 Stat. 533; Pub. L. 97–12, title I, § 102, June 5, 1981, 95 Stat. 61; Pub. L. 98–367, title I, § 1, July 17, 1984, 98 Stat. 474.)

AMENDMENTS

1984—Pub. L. 98–367 struck out provision that travel expenses could not exceed $10,000 during any fiscal year.

1981—Pub. L. 97–12 substituted "$10,000" for "$7,500".

1978—Pub. L. 95–355 substituted "$7,500" for "$5,500".

1977—Pub. L. 95–94 substituted "$5,500" for "$5,000".

EFFECTIVE DATE OF 1984 AMENDMENT

Section 1 of Pub. L. 98–367 provided that the amendment made by that section is effective with respect to fiscal years beginning on or after Oct. 1, 1983.

EFFECTIVE DATE OF 1981 AMENDMENT

Section 102 of Pub. L. 97–12 provided that the amendment made by that section is effective with respect to fiscal years beginning on or after Oct. 1, 1980.

EFFECTIVE DATE OF 1978 AMENDMENT

Section 101 of Pub. L. 95–355 provided that the amendment made by that section is effective with the fiscal year ending Sept. 30, 1978.

EFFECTIVE DATE OF 1977 AMENDMENT

Section 106 of Pub. L. 95–94 provided that the amendment made by that section is effective Oct. 1, 1977.

§ 61a–10. Omitted

CODIFICATION

Section, Pub. L. 93–145, Nov. 1, 1973, 87 Stat. 528, which was from the Legislative Branch Appropriation Act, 1974, and provided for appointment and compensation of specified Senate employees by Secretary of Senate, effective July 1, 1973, was omitted for lack of general applicability.

§ 61a–11. Abolition of statutory positions in Office of Secretary of Senate; Secretary's authority to establish and fix compensation for positions

Effective October 1, 1981, all statutory positions in the Office of the Secretary (other than the positions of the Secretary of the Senate, Assistant Secretary of the Senate, Parliamentarian, Financial Clerk, and Director of the Office of Classified National Security Information) are abolished, and in lieu of the positions hereby abolished the Secretary of the Senate is authorized to establish such number of positions as he deems appropriate and appoint and fix the compensation of employees to fill the positions so established; except that the annual rate of compensation payable to any employee appointed to fill any position established by the Secretary of the Senate shall not, for any period of time, be in excess of $1,000 less than the annual rate of compensation of the Secretary of the Senate for that period of time; and except that nothing in this section shall be construed to affect any position authorized by statute, if the compensation for such position is to be paid from the contingent fund of the Senate.

(Pub. L. 97–51, §114, Oct. 1, 1981, 95 Stat. 963.)

INCREASES IN COMPENSATION

Increases in compensation for Senate officers and employees under authority of Federal Pay Comparability Act of 1970 (Pub. L. 91–656), see Salary Directives of President pro tempore of the Senate, set out as notes under section 60a–1 of this title.

§ 61b. Compensation of Parliamentarian of Senate

The Parliamentarian of the Senate may be paid at a maximum annual rate of compensation not to exceed $39,000.

(Aug. 5, 1955, ch. 568, 69 Stat. 499; June 27, 1956, ch. 453, 70 Stat. 356; Pub. L. 93–371, §4, Aug. 13, 1974, 88 Stat. 429; Pub. L. 94–59, title I, §105, July 25, 1975, 89 Stat. 275.)

AMENDMENTS

1975—Pub. L. 94–59 substituted "$39,000" for "$37,620", effective July 1, 1975.

1974—Pub. L. 93–371 substituted provisions authorizing a maximum annual rate of compensation not to exceed $37,620 for Parliamentarian, for provisions authorizing a gross annual compensation of $15,500 for Parliamentarian and $7,620 for Assistant Parliamentarian, effective July 1, 1974.

1956—Act June 27, 1956, increased compensation of Parliamentarian of Senate from $8,820 basic annual compensation to $15,500 gross annual compensation, and basic annual compensation of Assistant Parliamentarian of Senate from $7,260 to $7,620, effective July 1, 1956.

1974 ADJUSTMENT IN COMPENSATION NOT TO SUPERSEDE ADJUSTMENTS IN COMPENSATION OR LIMITATIONS BY PRESIDENT PRO TEMPORE OF THE SENATE

Adjustment in compensation by Pub. L. 93–371 not to supersede order of President pro tempore of the Senate authorizing higher rate of compensation or any authority of the President pro tempore to adjust rates of compensation or limitations under section 4 of the Federal Pay Comparability Act of 1970, see section 4 of Pub. L. 93–371, set out in part as a note under section 61a of this title.

INCREASES IN COMPENSATION

Increases in compensation for Senate officers and employees under authority of Federal Salary Act of 1967 (Pub. L. 90–206) and Federal Pay Comparability Act of 1970 (Pub. L. 91– 656), see section 60a–1 of this title, and Salary Directives of President pro tempore of the Senate set out as notes under that section.

SECRETARY OF SENATE TO FIX COMPENSATION OF ASSISTANT PARLIAMENTARIAN

Pub. L. 86–213, Sept. 1, 1959, 73 Stat. 443, authorized Secretary of Senate to fix compensation of Assistant Parliamentarian, on and after Sept. 1, 1959, at not to exceed $7,620 basic per annum. See section 61a–11 of this title.

§§ 61b–1 to 61b–2. Omitted

CODIFICATION

Sections were omitted in view of section 61a–11 of this title which abolished all statutory positions in Of-

fice of Secretary of Senate, with specified exceptions, effective Oct. 1, 1981, and authorized Secretary of Senate to appoint and fix the compensation of such employees as appropriate.

Section 61b–1, Pub. L. 87–730, Oct. 2, 1962, 76 Stat. 680, provided for the appointment and compensation of a second assistant parliamentarian.

Section 61b–1a, Pub. L. 92–342, July 10, 1972, 86 Stat. 433; Pub. L. 95–94, title I, Aug. 5, 1977, 91 Stat. 654, provided for the appointment and compensation of a third assistant parliamentarian.

Section 61b–2, Pub. L. 90–608, ch. VII, §701, Oct. 21, 1968, 82 Stat. 1195, provided for the appointment and compensation of a Curator of Art and Antiquities.

§ 61b–3. Professional archivist; Secretary's authority to obtain services from General Services Administration

For each fiscal year (beginning with the fiscal year which ends September 30, 1982), the Secretary of the Senate is authorized to expend from the contingent fund of the Senate such amount as may be necessary to enable the Secretary to obtain from the General Services Administration the services of a professional archivist. Such services shall be obtained on a reimbursable basis and shall not be obtained except with the consent of the General Services Administration and the Committee on Rules and Administration.

(Pub. L. 97–92, title I, §125, Dec. 15, 1981, 95 Stat. 1198.)

REIMBURSEMENT OF ARCHIVIST OF THE UNITED STATES FOR EXPENDITURES FOR PROJECT TO PROVIDE FOR PRESERVATION OF RECORDS OF CONTINUING VALUE OF SENATE; PAYMENT, ETC., OF AMOUNTS

Pub. L. 97–257, title I, §107, Sept. 10, 1982, 96 Stat. 850, provided that: "For the fiscal year ending September 30, 1982, and for each of the next three succeeding fiscal years, the Secretary of the Senate is authorized to pay to the General Services Administration such amounts as may be necessary to reimburse the Archivist of the United States for expenditures made to conduct a project to provide for the proper preservation of the Senate's records of continuing value, which expenditures cannot be defrayed from funds otherwise available for such purpose. The aggregate of the sums paid to the General Services Administration under this section shall not exceed $300,000. Amounts paid under this section shall be paid from the contingent fund of the Senate on vouchers approved by the Secretary of the Senate."

§ 61c. Omitted

CODIFICATION

Section, Pub. L. 94–59, title I, July 25, 1975, 89 Stat. 270, which set the compensation for certain positions in office of Secretary of Senate, was omitted for lack of general applicability.

PRIOR PROVISIONS

A prior section 61c, acts Aug. 5, 1955, ch. 568, §1, 69 Stat. 499; June 27, 1956, ch. 453, 70 Stat. 356; Aug. 21, 1959, Pub. L. 86–176, 73 Stat. 398; Aug. 10, 1961, Pub. L. 87–130, 75 Stat. 320, set basic annual compensation of certain positions in office of Secretary of Senate.

§ 61c–1. Adjustment of rate of compensation by Secretary of Senate

Any specific rate of compensation established by law, as such rate has been increased or may hereafter be increased by or pursuant to law, for any position under the jurisdiction of the Secretary shall be considered as the maximum rate of compensation for that position, and the Secretary is authorized to adjust the rate of compensation of an individual occupying any such position to a rate not exceeding such maximum rate.

(Pub. L. 91–382, Aug. 18, 1970, 84 Stat. 808.)

INCREASES IN COMPENSATION

Increases in compensation for Senate officers and employees under authority of Federal Pay Comparability Act of 1970 (Pub. L. 91–656), see section 60a–1 of this title, and Salary Directives of President pro tempore of the Senate, set out as notes under that section.

§ 61c–2. Compensation of Assistants to Majority and Minority in Office of Secretary of Senate

The Assistant to the Majority of the Senate and the Assistant to the Minority of the Senate in the Office of the Secretary of the Senate may each be paid a maximum annual rate of compensation not to exceed $36,500.

(Pub. L. 94–59, title I, § 105, July 25, 1975, 89 Stat. 275.)

PRIOR PROVISIONS

Pub. L. 89–90, July 27, 1965, 79 Stat. 266, prescribed basic compensation of assistants to Majority and Minority at not more than $8,160 per annum each effective July 1, 1965.

Act May 19, 1956, ch. 313, Ch. XII, 70 Stat. 175, provided that basic compensation of assistant to majority and assistant to minority may be fixed by majority and minority leaders, respectively, at a rate not to exceed $8,820 per annum.

EFFECTIVE DATE

Section 105 of Pub. L. 94–59 provided that this section is effective July 1, 1975.

INCREASES IN COMPENSATION

Increases in compensation for Senate officers and employees under authority of Federal Pay Comparability Act of 1970 (Pub. L. 91–656), see Salary Directives of the President pro tempore of the Senate, set out as notes under section 60a–1 of this title.

§ 61d. Compensation of Chaplain of Senate

Effective with respect to pay periods beginning on or after December 22, 1987, the Chaplain of the Senate shall be compensated at a rate equal to the annual rate of basic pay for level IV of the Executive Schedule under section 5315 of title 5.

(Pub. L. 100–202, § 101(i) [title I, § 2(a)], Dec. 22, 1987, 101 Stat. 1329–290, 1329–294.)

CODIFICATION

Section is from the Congressional Operations Appropriations Act, 1988, which is title I of the Legislative Branch Appropriations Act, 1988.

PRIOR PROVISIONS

A prior section 61d, Pub. L. 93–145, Nov. 1, 1973, 87 Stat. 528; Pub. L. 95–26, title I, May 4, 1977, 91 Stat. 80; Pub. L. 96–38, title I, § 103, July 25, 1979, 93 Stat. 112; Pub. L. 97–51, § 121, Oct. 1, 1981, 95 Stat. 965, provided that effective October 1, 1981, the compensation of Chaplain of Senate would be $52,750.

Another prior section 61d, acts Aug. 5, 1955, ch. 568, § 1, 69 Stat. 499; July 12, 1960, Pub. L. 86–628, 74 Stat. 446; Aug. 14, 1964, Pub. L. 88–426, title II, § 203(h), 78 Stat. 415; Dec. 12, 1969, Pub. L. 91–145, 83 Stat. 340; Aug. 18, 1970,

Pub. L. 91–382, 84 Stat. 808, made provision for the appointment of a Secretary to Chaplain of Senate and prescribed compensation of Chaplain of Senate and Secretary to Chaplain.

INCREASES IN COMPENSATION

Increases in compensation for Senate officers and employees under authority of Federal Pay Comparability Act of 1970 (Pub. L. 91–656), see Salary Directives of President pro tempore of the Senate, set out as notes under section 60a–1 of this title.

§ 61d–1. Compensation of employees of Chaplain of Senate

The Chaplain of the Senate may appoint and fix the compensation of such employees as he deems appropriate, except that the amount which may be paid for any fiscal year as gross compensation for personnel in such Office for any fiscal year shall not exceed $147,000.

(Pub. L. 91–145, Dec. 12, 1969, 83 Stat. 340; Pub. L. 100–202, § 101(i) [title I, § 2(b)], Dec. 22, 1987, 101 Stat. 1329–290, 1329–294; Pub. L. 101–163, title I, § 10, Nov. 21, 1989, 103 Stat. 1046.)

PRIOR PROVISIONS

A prior section 61d–1, Pub. L. 93–371, Aug. 13, 1974, 88 Stat. 424; Pub. L. 96–38, title I, § 103, July 25, 1979, 93 Stat. 112, authorized Chaplain of Senate to appoint and fix compensation of a secretary at not to exceed $20,034 per annum.

AMENDMENTS

1989—Pub. L. 101–163 substituted "such employees as he deems appropriate, except that the amount which may be paid for any fiscal year as gross compensation for personnel in such Office for any fiscal year shall not exceed $147,000" for "a secretary".

1987—Pub. L. 100–202 amended section generally. Prior to amendment, section read as follows: "The Chaplain may appoint and fix the compensation of a secretary at not to exceed $8,541 per annum."

INCREASES IN COMPENSATION

Increases in compensation for Senate officers and employees under authority of Federal Pay Comparability Act of 1970 (Pub. L. 91–655), see Salary Directives of President pro tempore of the Senate, set out as notes under section 60a–1 of this title.

§ 61d–2. Postage allowance for Chaplain of Senate

The Secretary of the Senate is authorized and directed to procure and furnish each fiscal year (commencing with the fiscal year ending September 30, 1982) to the Chaplain of the Senate, upon the request of the Chaplain of the Senate, United States postage stamps in such amounts as may be necessary for the mailing of postal matters arising in connection with his official business.

(Pub. L. 97–51, § 127(b)(1), Oct. 1, 1981, 95 Stat. 966.)

PRIOR PROVISIONS

A prior section 61d–2, Pub. L. 94–303, title I, § 114, June 1, 1976, 90 Stat. 614, authorized a postage allowance for Chaplain of Senate, prior to repeal by section 127(b)(2) of Pub. L. 97–51.

§ 61d–3. Office of the Chaplain Expense Revolving Fund

(a) Establishment

There is established in the Treasury of the United States within the contingent fund of the

Senate a revolving fund, to be known as the "Office of the Chaplain Expense Revolving Fund" (hereafter referred to as the "fund"). The fund shall consist of all moneys collected or received with respect to the Office of the Chaplain of the Senate.

(b) Disbursements

The fund shall be available without fiscal year limitation for disbursement by the Secretary of the Senate, not to exceed $35,000 in any fiscal year, for the payment of official expenses incurred by the Chaplain of the Senate. In addition, moneys in the fund may be used to purchase food or food related items. The fund shall not be available for the payment of salaries.

(c) Deposits

All moneys (including donated moneys) received or collected with respect to the Office of the Chaplain of the Senate shall be deposited in the fund and shall be available for purposes of this section.

(d) Vouchers

Disbursements from the fund shall be made on vouchers approved by the Chaplain of the Senate.

(Pub. L. 104–53, title I, §2, Nov. 19, 1995, 109 Stat. 517; Pub. L. 105–275, title I, §2(a), Oct. 21, 1998, 112 Stat. 2433.)

CODIFICATION

Section is from the Congressional Operations Appropriations Act, 1996, which is title I of the Legislative Branch Appropriations Act, 1996.

AMENDMENTS

1998—Subsec. (b). Pub. L. 105–275 substituted "$35,000" for "$10,000".

EFFECTIVE DATE OF 1998 AMENDMENT

Pub. L. 105–275, title I, §2(b), Oct. 21, 1998, 112 Stat. 2433, provided that: "The amendment made by subsection (a) [amending this section] is effective on and after October 1, 1998."

§61e. Compensation of Sergeant at Arms and Doorkeeper of Senate

The Sergeant at Arms and Doorkeeper of the Senate shall be paid at an annual rate of compensation of $40,000.

(Pub. L. 88–426, title II, §203(g), Aug. 14, 1964, 78 Stat. 415; Pub. L. 93–371, §4, Aug. 13, 1974, 88 Stat. 429; Pub. L. 94–59, title I, §105, July 25, 1975, 89 Stat. 275.)

PRIOR PROVISIONS

A prior section 61e, act Aug. 5, 1955, ch. 568, §1, 69 Stat. 501, prescribed gross annual compensation of Sergeant at Arms of Senate.

AMENDMENTS

1975—Pub. L. 94–59 substituted "an annual rate of compensation of $40,000" for "a rate of $38,760 per annum", effective July 1, 1975.

1974—Pub. L. 93–371 substituted provisions authorizing Sergeant at Arms and Doorkeeper to be paid at an annual rate of compensation of $38,760, for provisions setting forth compensation of Sergeant at Arms at rate of $27,500 per annum, effective July 1, 1974.

EFFECTIVE DATE

Section effective on first day of first pay period which begins on or after July 1, 1964, except to the ex-

tent provided in section 501(c) of Pub. L. 88–426, see section 501 of Pub. L. 88–426.

1974 ADJUSTMENT IN COMPENSATION NOT TO SUPERSEDE ADJUSTMENTS IN COMPENSATION OR LIMITATIONS BY PRESIDENT PRO TEMPORE OF THE SENATE

Adjustment in compensation by Pub. L. 93–371 not to supersede order of President pro tempore of the Senate authorizing higher rate of compensation or any authority of President pro tempore to adjust rates of compensation or limitations under section 4 of the Federal Pay Comparability Act of 1970, see section 4 of Pub. L. 93–371, set out in part as a note under section 61a of this title.

INCREASES IN COMPENSATION

Increases in compensation for Senate officers and employees under authority of Federal Salary Act of 1967 (Pub. L. 90–206) and Federal Pay Comparability Act of 1970 (Pub. L. 91–656), see section 60a–1 of this title, and Salary Directives of President pro tempore of the Senate, set out as notes under that section.

§61e–1. Compensation of Deputy Sergeant at Arms and Doorkeeper of Senate

Effective August 1, 1979, the Sergeant at Arms and Doorkeeper may fix the compensation of the Deputy Sergeant at Arms and Doorkeeper at an annual rate not to exceed the maximum annual rate of compensation of the Assistant Secretary of the Senate.

(Pub. L. 94–226, §1(a), Mar. 9, 1976, 90 Stat. 203; Pub. L. 96–38, title I, §106(1), July 25, 1979, 93 Stat. 112.)

AMENDMENTS

1979—Pub. L. 96–38 raised the maximum annual rate of compensation of Deputy Sergeant at Arms and Doorkeeper of Senate to a rate the same as the maximum annual rate of compensation of Assistant Secretary of Senate.

EFFECTIVE DATE

Section 1(b) of Pub. L. 94–226 provided that: "Subsection (a) [enacting this section] shall take effect on January 1, 1976, and, notwithstanding any other provision of law, any increase in compensation made under authority of such subsection may take effect on that date or any date thereafter as prescribed by the Sergeant at Arms and Doorkeeper at the time of making such increase."

CHANGE OF NAME

Section 1(c) of Pub. L. 94–226 provided that: "Effective on the date of enactment of this resolution [Mar. 9, 1976] the title of the Procurement Officer, Auditor, and Deputy Sergeant at Arms is changed to Deputy Sergeant at Arms and Doorkeeper."

AUTHORITY OF PRESIDENT PRO TEMPORE OF THE SENATE TO RAISE OR ADJUST RATE OF COMPENSATION

Section 1(a) of Pub. L. 94–226 provided in part that: "This subsection [this section] does not supersede (1) any provision of an order of the President pro tempore of the Senate authorizing a higher rate of compensation, and (2) any authority of the President pro tempore to adjust the rate of compensation referred to in this subsection [this section] under section 4 of the Federal Pay Comparability Act of 1970 [section 60a–1 of this title]."

§61e–2. Compensation of Administrative Assistant to Sergeant at Arms and Doorkeeper of Senate

Effective August 1, 1979—

(1) the maximum annual rate of compensation of the Administrative Assistant to the Sergeant at Arms and Doorkeeper of the Senate shall be the same as the highest maximum annual rate of compensation that may be paid to an employee in the office of a Senator; and

(2) Omitted

(Pub. L. 96–38, title I, § 106(2), (3), July 25, 1979, 93 Stat. 112.)

CODIFICATION

Section consists of pars. (2) and (3) of section 106 of Pub. L. 96–38, Supplemental Appropriations Act, 1979. The paragraph numbers (2) and (3) in the original have been changed to (1) and (2) for purposes of codification.

Par. (2), relating to maximum annual rate of compensation of Executive Assistant to Sergeant at Arms and Doorkeeper of Senate, was omitted from the Code in view of section 61f–7 of this title which abolished all statutory positions in the Office of Sergeant at Arms and Doorkeeper of Senate, with specified exceptions, effective Oct. 1, 1981, and authorized Sergeant at Arms and Doorkeeper of Senate to appoint and fix compensation of such employees as appropriate.

§ 61e–3. Deputy Sergeant at Arms and Doorkeeper to act on death, resignation, disability, or absence of Sergeant at Arms and Doorkeeper of Senate

In the event of the death, resignation, or disability of the Sergeant at Arms and Doorkeeper of the Senate, the Deputy Sergeant at Arms and Doorkeeper shall act as Sergeant at Arms and Doorkeeper of the Senate in carrying out the duties and responsibilities of that office in all matters until such time as a new Sergeant at Arms and Doorkeeper of the Senate shall have been elected and qualified or such disability shall have been ended. For purposes of this section, the Sergeant at Arms and Doorkeeper of the Senate shall be considered as disabled only during such period of time as the Majority and Minority Leaders and the President Pro Tempore of the Senate certify jointly to the Senate that the Sergeant at Arms and Doorkeeper of the Senate is unable to perform his duties. In the event that the Sergeant at Arms and Doorkeeper of the Senate is absent, the Deputy Sergeant at Arms and Doorkeeper shall act during such absence as the Sergeant at Arms and Doorkeeper of the Senate in carrying out the duties and responsibilities of the office in all matters.

(Pub. L. 97–51, § 128, Oct. 1, 1981, 95 Stat. 966.)

§ 61e–4. Designation by Sergeant at Arms and Doorkeeper of Senate of persons to approve vouchers for payment of moneys

The Sergeant at Arms and Doorkeeper of the Senate (hereinafter in this section referred to as the "Sergeant at Arms") may designate one or more employees in the Office of the Sergeant at Arms and Doorkeeper of the Senate to approve, on his behalf, all vouchers, for payment of moneys, which the Sergeant at Arms is authorized to approve. Whenever the Sergeant at Arms makes a designation under the authority of the preceding sentence, he shall immediately notify the Committee on Rules and Administration in writing of the designation, and thereafter any approval of any voucher, for payment of moneys, by an employee so designated shall (until

such designation is revoked and the Sergeant at Arms notifies the Committee on Rules and Administration in writing of the revocation) be deemed and held to be approved by the Sergeant at Arms for all intents and purposes.

(Pub. L. 98–181, title I, § 1201, Nov. 30, 1983, 97 Stat. 1289.)

CODIFICATION

Section is from the Supplemental Appropriations Act, 1984.

§§ 61f, 61f–1. Omitted

Section 61f, acts Aug. 5, 1955, ch. 568, 69 Stat. 501; June 27, 1956, ch. 453, 70 Stat. 357; July 1, 1957, Pub. L. 85–75, 71 Stat. 245; July 31, 1958, Pub. L. 85–570, 72 Stat. 440; Aug. 21, 1959, Pub. L. 86–176, 73 Stat. 399; July 12, 1960, Pub. L. 86–628, 74 Stat. 447; Aug. 10, 1961, Pub. L. 87–130, 75 Stat. 321; Oct. 2, 1962, Pub. L. 87–730, 76 Stat. 681; Dec. 30, 1963, Pub. L. 88–248, 77 Stat. 804, prescribed the basic annual compensation of certain clerical, skilled, and unskilled employees in the office of Sergeant at Arms and Doorkeeper of Senate, and was omitted for lack of general applicability.

Section 61f–1, Pub. L. 91–382, Aug. 18, 1970, 84 Stat. 808, authorized Sergeant at Arms to employ certain additional personnel and prescribed their compensation, and was omitted for lack of general applicability.

§ 61f–1a. Travel expenses of Sergeant at Arms and Doorkeeper of Senate

For the purpose of carrying out his duties, the Sergeant at Arms and Doorkeeper of the Senate is authorized to incur official travel expenses during each fiscal year not to exceed the sums made available for such purpose under appropriations Acts. With the approval of the Sergeant at Arms and Doorkeeper of the Senate and in accordance with such regulations as may be promulgated by the Senate Committee on Rules and Administration, the Secretary of the Senate is authorized to advance to the Sergeant at Arms or to any designated employee under the jurisdiction of the Sergeant at Arms and Doorkeeper, such sums as may be necessary to defray official travel expenses incurred in carrying out the duties of the Sergeant at Arms and Doorkeeper. The receipt of any such sum so advanced to the Sergeant at Arms and Doorkeeper or to any designated employee shall be taken and passed by the accounting officers of the Government as a full and sufficient voucher; but it shall be the duty of the traveler, as soon as practicable, to furnish to the Secretary of the Senate a detailed voucher of the expenses incurred for the travel with respect to which the sum was so advanced, and make settlement with respect to such sum. Payments under this section shall be made from funds included in the appropriations account, within the contingent fund of the Senate, for the Sergeant at Arms and Doorkeeper of the Senate, upon vouchers approved by the Sergeant at Arms and Doorkeeper.

(Pub. L. 94–303, title I, § 117, June 1, 1976, 90 Stat. 615; Pub. L. 95–391, title I, § 106, Sept. 30, 1978, 92 Stat. 772; Pub. L. 96–86, § 111(c), Oct. 12, 1979, 93 Stat. 661; Pub. L. 97–12, title I, § 108, June 5, 1981, 95 Stat. 62; Pub. L. 100–458, title I, § 6, Oct. 1, 1988, 102 Stat. 2161; Pub. L. 101–520, title I, § 6, Nov. 5, 1990, 104 Stat. 2258.)

1990—Pub. L. 101–520 amended section generally. Prior to amendment, section read as follows: "For the purpose of carrying out his duties, the Sergeant at Arms and Doorkeeper of the Senate is authorized to incur official travel expenses not to exceed $250,000 during any fiscal year. With the approval of the Sergeant at Arms and Doorkeeper, the Secretary of the Senate is authorized to advance to any designated employee under the jurisdiction of the Sergeant at Arms and Doorkeeper such sums as may be necessary, not exceeding $1,000, to defray official travel expenses in assisting the Sergeant at Arms and Doorkeeper in carrying out his duties. Any such employee shall, as soon as practicable, furnish to the Sergeant at Arms and Doorkeeper a detailed voucher for such expenses incurred and make settlement with respect to any amount so advanced. For purposes of this section, official travel expenses includes travel expenses incurred in connection with training of employees only if the training has been approved by the Committee on Rules and Administration of the Senate. Payments under this section shall be made from funds included in the appropriation 'Miscellaneous Items' under the heading 'Contingent Expenses of the Senate' upon vouchers approved by the Sergeant at Arms and Doorkeeper."

1988—Pub. L. 100–458, which directed the substitution of "not to exceed $250,000 during any fiscal year" for "not to exceed $167,000 during any fiscal year" was executed by making the substitution for "not exceeding $167,000 during any fiscal year" as the probable intent of Congress because of absence of "not to exceed" in text.

1981—Pub. L. 97–12 substituted "$167,000" for "$92,000".

1979—Pub. L. 96–86 substituted "$92,000" for "$25,000".

1978—Pub. L. 95–391 substituted "$25,000" for "$10,000".

EFFECTIVE DATE OF 1990 AMENDMENT

Section 6 of Pub. L. 101–520 provided that the amendment made by that section is effective in the case of fiscal years which begin after Sept. 30, 1990.

EFFECTIVE DATE OF 1988 AMENDMENT

Section 6 of Pub. L. 100–458 provided that the amendment made by that section is effective with fiscal year ending Sept. 30, 1988.

EFFECTIVE DATE OF 1981 AMENDMENT

Section 108 of Pub. L. 97–12 provided that the amendment made by that section is effective with the fiscal year ending Sept. 30, 1981.

EFFECTIVE DATE OF 1979 AMENDMENT

Section 111(c) of Pub. L. 96–86 provided that the amendment made by that section is effective with the fiscal year ending Sept. 30, 1980.

§§ 61f–2 to 61f–6. Omitted

Sections were omitted for lack of general applicability. Sections were from the Legislative Branch Appropriation Act, 1972, the Supplemental Appropriation Act, 1972, the Supplemental Appropriation Act, 1973, the Legislative Branch Appropriation Act, 1974, and the Supplemental Appropriation Act, 1974, respectively, and provided for the appointment and compensation of specified Senate employees by the Sergeant at Arms.

Section 61f–2, Pub. L. 92–51, July 9, 1971, 85 Stat. 127, was effective July 1, 1971.

Section 61f–3, Pub. L. 92–184, ch. IV, Dec. 15, 1971, 85 Stat. 634, was effective Jan. 1, 1972.

Section 61f–4, Pub. L. 92–607, ch. V, Oct. 31, 1972, 86 Stat. 1504, was effective Nov. 1, 1972.

Section 61f–5, Pub. L. 93–145, Nov. 1, 1973, 87 Stat. 529, was effective July 1, 1973.

Section 61f–6, Pub. L. 93–245, ch. VI, Jan. 3, 1974, 87 Stat. 1078, was effective Dec. 1, 1973.

§ 61f–7. Abolition of statutory positions in Office of Sergeant at Arms and Doorkeeper of Senate; authority to establish and fix compensation for positions

Effective October 1, 1981, all statutory positions in the Office of the Sergeant at Arms and Doorkeeper of the Senate (other than the positions of the Sergeant at Arms and Doorkeeper of the Senate, Deputy Sergeant at Arms and Doorkeeper, and Administrative Assistant) are abolished, and in lieu of the positions hereby abolished the Sergeant at Arms and Doorkeeper of the Senate is authorized to establish such number of positions as he deems appropriate and appoint and fix the compensation of employees to fill the positions so established; except that the annual rate of compensation payable to any employee appointed to fill any position established by the Sergeant at Arms and Doorkeeper of the Senate shall not, for any period of time, be in excess of $1,000 less than the annual rate of compensation of the Sergeant at Arms and Doorkeeper of the Senate for that period of time; and except that nothing in this section shall be construed to affect any position authorized by statute, if the compensation for such position is to be paid from the contingent fund of the Senate.

(Pub. L. 97–51, § 116, Oct. 1, 1981, 95 Stat. 963.)

TRANSFER OF JURISDICTION OF SENATE CHAMBER PUBLIC ADDRESS SYSTEM FROM ARCHITECT OF CAPITOL TO SERGEANT AT ARMS AND DOORKEEPER OF SENATE

Pub. L. 102–90, title I, § 8, Aug. 14, 1991, 105 Stat. 451, provided that:

"(a) Effective October 1, 1991, the jurisdiction and control of the Senate chamber public address system is transferred from the Architect of the Capitol to the Sergeant at Arms and Doorkeeper of the Senate. In the case of any employee of the Architect of the Capitol transferred during fiscal year 1992 to the Sergeant at Arms and Doorkeeper of the Senate as an audio operator—

"(1) in the case of days of annual leave to the credit of any such employee as of the date such employee is transferred, the Architect of the Capitol is authorized to make payment to each such employee for that annual leave, and no such payment shall be considered a payment or compensation within the meaning of any law relating to dual compensation; and

"(2) for purposes of section 8339(m) of title 5, United States Code, the days of unused sick leave to the credit of any such employee as of the date such employee is transferred shall be included in the total service of such employee in connection with the computation of any annuity under subsections (a) through (e), (n), and (q) of such section.

"(b) The Architect of the Capitol shall provide the maintenance of the Senate chamber public address system until such system is replaced by a combined public address and audio broadcast system."

TRANSFER OF JURISDICTION OF ELEVATORS IN CAPITOL BUILDING UNDER CONTROL OF SENATE FROM ARCHITECT OF CAPITOL TO SERGEANT AT ARMS AND DOORKEEPER OF SENATE

Pub. L. 102–90, title I, § 9, Aug. 14, 1991, 105 Stat. 452, provided that:

"(a) Subject to subsection (b), those employees of the Architect of the Capitol engaged in operating elevators in that part of the United States Capitol Building under the control and jurisdiction of the United States Senate, together with the elevator operating functions performed by such employees, effective October 1, 1991, shall be transferred to the jurisdiction of the Sergeant at Arms and Doorkeeper of the Senate.

"(b) The Sergeant at Arms and Doorkeeper of the Senate is authorized to enter into an agreement or other arrangement with the Architect of the Capitol regarding the supervision of such employees."

INCREASES IN COMPENSATION

Increases in compensation for Senate officers and employees under authority of the Federal Pay Comparability Act of 1970 (Pub. L. 91–656), see Salary Directives of President pro tempore of the Senate, set out as notes under section 60a–1 of this title.

§ 61f–8. Use by Sergeant at Arms and Doorkeeper of Senate of individual consultants or organizations, and department and agency personnel

For each fiscal year (beginning with the fiscal year which ends September 30, 1982), the Sergeant at Arms and Doorkeeper of the Senate is hereby authorized to expend from the account for the Sergeant at Arms and Doorkeeper of the Senate, within the contingent fund of the Senate, an amount not to exceed $300,000:

(1) the procurement of the services, on a temporary basis, of individual consultants, or organizations thereof, with the prior consent of the Committee on Rules and Administration; such services may be procured by contract with the providers acting as independent contractors, or in the case of individuals, by employment at daily rates of compensation not in excess of the per diem equivalent of the highest gross rate of annual compensation which may be paid to employees of a standing committee of the Senate; and any such contract shall not be subject to the provisions of section 5 of title 41 or any other provision of law requiring advertising; and

(2) with the prior consent of the Government department or agency concerned and the Committee on Rules and Administration, use on a reimbursable basis (with reimbursement payable at the end of each calendar quarter for services rendered during such quarter) of the services of personnel of any such department or agency.

Payments made under this section shall be made upon vouchers approved by the Sergeant at Arms and Doorkeeper of the Senate.

(Pub. L. 97–51, § 117, Oct. 1, 1981, 95 Stat. 964; Pub. L. 97–257, title I, § 103, Sept. 10, 1982, 96 Stat. 849; Pub. L. 98–367, title I, § 7, July 17, 1984, 98 Stat. 475; Pub. L. 100–458, title I, § 7, Oct. 1, 1988, 102 Stat. 2162.)

AMENDMENTS

1988—Pub. L. 100–458 substituted "from the account for the Sergeant at Arms and Doorkeeper of the Senate, within the contingent fund of the Senate, an amount not to exceed $300,000:" for "from the contingent fund of the Senate an amount not to exceed $210,000 for:".

1984—Pub. L. 98–367 substituted "$210,000" for "$60,000".

1982—Par. (1). Pub. L. 97–257 substituted "the procurement of the services, on a temporary basis, of individual consultants, or organizations thereof, with the prior consent of the Committee on Rules and Administration; such services may be procured by contract with the providers acting as independent contractors, or in the case of individuals, by employment at daily rates of compensation not in excess of the per diem equivalent of the highest gross rate of annual com-

pensation which may be paid to employees of a standing committee of the Senate; and any such contract shall not be subject to the provisions of section 5 of title 41 or any other provision of law requiring advertising; and" for "the procurement of individual consultants, on a temporary or intermittent basis, at a daily rate of compensation not in excess of the per diem equivalent of the highest gross rate of annual compensation which may be paid to employees of a standing committee of the Senate with the prior consent of the Committee on Rules and Administration; and".

§ 61f–9. Employment of personnel by Sergeant at Arms and Doorkeeper of Senate at daily rates of compensation; authorization; limitation on amount of compensation

The Sergeant at Arms and Doorkeeper of the Senate, in carrying out the duties of his office, is authorized to employ personnel at daily rates of compensation; no individual so employed shall be paid at a daily rate of compensation which is in excess of the per diem equivalent of the highest gross rate of annual compensation which may be paid to employees of a standing committee of the Senate; and payments under authority of this section shall be made from the account, within the contingent fund of the Senate, for the "Sergeant at Arms and Doorkeeper of the Senate", upon vouchers approved by the Sergeant at Arms and Doorkeeper of the Senate.

(Pub. L. 98–367, title I, § 6, July 17, 1984, 98 Stat. 475.)

CODIFICATION

Section is from the Congressional Operations Appropriation Act, 1985, which is title I of the Legislative Branch Appropriations Act, 1985.

§ 61g. Compensation of Secretaries for Senate Majority and Minority

The Secretary for the Majority of the Senate (other than the incumbent holding office on April 1, 1977) and the Secretary for the Minority of the Senate shall each be paid at an annual rate of compensation of $39,500.

(Pub. L. 93–371, § 4, Aug. 13, 1974, 88 Stat. 429; Pub. L. 94–59, title I, § 105, July 25, 1975, 89 Stat. 275; Pub. L. 95–26, title I, § 102(a), May 4, 1977, 91 Stat. 82.)

PRIOR PROVISIONS

A prior section 61g, acts Aug. 5, 1955, ch. 568, 69 Stat. 502; June 27, 1956, ch. 453, § 101, 70 Stat. 357, prescribed the gross annual compensation of Secretaries of Senate Majority and Minority.

AMENDMENTS

1977—Pub. L. 95–26 substituted "April 1, 1977" for "July 1, 1975". Provisions covering the compensation of the incumbent holding the office of Secretary for the Majority of the Senate on July 1, 1975, were dropped as executed. See successor provisions set out as a note below.

1975—Pub. L. 94–59 increased annual rate of compensation of both Secretary for Majority of Senate and Secretary for Minority of Senate from $38,190 to $39,500 and substituted provisions excepting incumbent Secretary for Majority holding office on July 1, 1975, from mandatory payment of $39,500 rate but authorizing payment to him as long as he occupies that position at a maximum annual rate of compensation not to exceed $39,500 for provisions excepting Secretary for Majority holding office on June 15, 1974, from mandatory payment of the $38,190 rate but authorizing payment to him as long as he occupied that position at a maximum annual rate of compensation not to exceed $38,190.

EFFECTIVE DATE OF 1975 AMENDMENT

Section 105 of Pub. L. 94–59 provided that the increase in the rate of compensation to $39,500 is effective July 1, 1975.

EFFECTIVE DATE

Section effective July 1, 1974, see section 4 of Pub. L. 93–371, set out in part as an Effective Date of 1974 Amendment note under section 61a of this title.

COMPENSATION OF INCUMBENT HOLDING POSITION OF SECRETARY FOR THE MAJORITY ON APRIL 1, 1977

Section 102(b) of Pub. L. 95–26 provided that: "The Majority Leader of the Senate is authorized to fix the compensation of the Secretary for the Majority so long as the position is held by the incumbent holding such position on April 1, 1977."

1974 ADJUSTMENT IN COMPENSATION NOT TO SUPERSEDE ADJUSTMENTS IN COMPENSATION OR LIMITATIONS BY PRESIDENT PRO TEMPORE OF THE SENATE

Adjustment in compensation by Pub. L. 93–371 not to supersede order of President pro tempore of the Senate authorizing higher rate of compensation or any authority of President pro tempore to adjust rates of compensation or limitations under section 4 of the Federal Pay Comparability Act of 1970, see section 4 of Pub. L. 93–371, set out in part as a note under section 61a of this title.

INCREASES IN COMPENSATION

Increases in compensation for Senate officers and employees under authority of Federal Pay Comparability Act of 1970 (Pub. L. 91–656), see Salary Directives of President pro tempore of the Senate, set out as notes under section 60a–1 of this title.

1964 INCREASE IN GROSS ANNUAL COMPENSATION

Rates of gross compensation of Secretaries for Senate Majority and Minority, see section 202(f), (g) of Pub. L. 88–426, title II, Aug. 14, 1964, 78 Stat. 414, set out as a note under section 60a–1 of this title.

§§ 61g–1 to 61g–3. Omitted

CODIFICATION

Section 61g–1, Pub. L. 89–691, title IV, § 404, Oct. 15, 1966, 80 Stat. 1024, authorized, effective Oct. 1, 1966, Senate Majority Leader to fix the gross compensation of Secretary for Majority at not to exceed $25,611.05 per annum so long as position is held by present incumbent. See section 61g of this title.

Sections 61g–2 and 61g–3, Pub. L. 94–59, title I, July 25, 1975, 89 Stat. 272, originally classified to section 61g–3 and later reclassified to section 61g–2, authorized, effective July 1, 1975, and each fiscal year thereafter, Secretaries for Senate Majority and Minority to each appoint and fix compensation of an assistant during emergencies at specified rates of compensation for not more than six months in each fiscal year. Pub. L. 95–94, title I, Aug. 5, 1977, 91 Stat. 658, abolished such positions, effective Oct. 1, 1977, and authorized Secretaries concerned to appoint such employees as they deem appropriate. See section 61g–5 of this title.

§ 61g–4. Appointment and compensation of employees by Secretary of Conference of Majority of Senate and Secretary of Conference of Minority of Senate

Effective October 1, 1979, the Secretary of the Conference of the Majority and the Secretary of the Conference of the Minority are each authorized to appoint and fix the compensation of such employees as they deem appropriate: *Provided*, That the gross compensation paid to such employees shall not exceed $70,000 each fiscal year for each Secretary.

(Pub. L. 96–38, title I, § 102, July 25, 1979, 93 Stat. 111.)

CODIFICATION

Section is from the Supplemental Appropriations Act, 1979.

PRIOR PROVISIONS

A prior section 61g–4, Pub. L. 95–26, title I, § 100, May 4, 1977, 91 Stat. 80, authorized Secretary of Conference of Majority and Secretary of Conference of Minority each to appoint and fix compensation of an Executive Assistant and a Secretary. These positions were abolished by section 102 of Pub. L. 96–38, effective Oct. 1, 1979.

INCREASES IN COMPENSATION

Increases in compensation for Senate officers and employees under authority of Federal Pay Comparability Act of 1970 (Pub. L. 91–656), see Salary Directives of President pro tempore of the Senate, set out as notes under section 60a–1 of this title.

§ 61g–5. Appointment and compensation of employees by Secretaries for Senate Majority and Minority; gross compensation

Effective October 1, 1977, the Secretary for the Majority and the Secretary for the Minority are each authorized to appoint and fix the compensation of such employees as they deem appropriate: *Provided*, That the gross compensation paid to such employees shall not exceed $143,200 each fiscal year for each Secretary.

(Pub. L. 95–94, title I, Aug. 5, 1977, 91 Stat. 658, 659.)

CODIFICATION

Section is from the Congressional Operations Appropriation Act, 1978, which is title I of the Legislative Branch Appropriation Act, 1978.

INCREASES IN COMPENSATION

Increases in compensation for Senate officers and employees under authority of Federal Pay Comparability Act of 1970 (Pub. L. 91–656), see Salary Directives of President pro tempore of the Senate, set out as notes under section 60a–1 of this title.

§ 61g–6. Payment of expenses of Conference of Majority and Conference of Minority from Senate contingent fund

For each fiscal year (beginning with the fiscal year which ends September 30, 1982) there is authorized to be expended from the contingent fund of the Senate an amount, not in excess of $75,000, for the Conference of the Majority and an equal amount for the Conference of the Minority. Payments under this section shall be made only for expenses actually incurred by such a Conference in carrying out its functions, and shall be made upon certification and documentation of the expenses involved, by the Chairman of the Conference claiming payment hereunder and upon vouchers approved by such Chairman and by the Committee on Rules and Administration, except that vouchers shall not be required for payment of long-distance telephone calls.

(Pub. L. 97–51, § 120, Oct. 1, 1981, 95 Stat. 965; Pub. L. 97–276, Oct. 2, 1982, § 101(e), 96 Stat. 1189; Pub. L. 99–151, title I, § 1, Nov. 13, 1985, 99 Stat. 794; Pub. L. 101–163, title I, Nov. 21, 1989, 103 Stat. 1043; Pub. L. 101–520, title I, Nov. 5, 1990, 104 Stat. 2256.)

CODIFICATION

The 1982 amendment by Pub. L. 97–276 is based on section 105 of S. 2939, Ninety-seventh Congress, 2d Session, as reported Sept. 22, 1982, and incorporated by reference in section 101(e) of Pub. L. 97–276, to be effective as if enacted into law.

AMENDMENTS

1990—Pub. L. 101–520 substituted "$75,000" for "$50,000".

1989—Pub. L. 101–163 substituted "$50,000" for "$40,000".

1985—Pub. L. 99–151 inserted ", except that vouchers shall not be required for payment of long-distance telephone calls".

1982—Pub. L. 97–276 substituted "$40,000" for "$30,000". See Codification note above.

EFFECTIVE DATE OF 1990 AMENDMENT

Title I of Pub. L. 101–520 provided that the amendment made by Pub. L. 101–520 is effective in the case of fiscal years beginning after Sept. 30, 1990.

EFFECTIVE DATE OF 1989 AMENDMENT

Title I of Pub. L. 101–163 provided that the amendment made by Pub. L. 101–163 is effective in the case of fiscal years beginning after Sept. 30, 1989.

EFFECTIVE DATE OF 1982 AMENDMENT

Section 105 of S. 2939, Ninety-seventh Congress, 2d Session, as reported Sept. 22, 1982, and incorporated by reference in section 101(e) of Pub. L. 97–276, to be effective as if enacted into law, provided that the amendment made by that section is effective for fiscal years beginning after Sept. 30, 1981.

SECTION REFERRED TO IN OTHER SECTIONS

This section is referred to in section 61g–7 of this title.

§ 61g–6a. Salaries and expenses for Senate Majority and Minority Policy Committees and Senate Majority and Minority Conference Committees

(a) Transfer of funds for Policy Committees

(1) The Chairman of the Majority or Minority Policy Committee of the Senate may, during any fiscal year, at his or her election transfer funds from the appropriation account for salaries for the Majority and Minority Policy Committees of the Senate, to the account, within the contingent fund of the Senate, from which expenses are payable for such committees.

(2) The Chairman of the Majority or Minority Policy Committee of the Senate may, during any fiscal year, at his or her election transfer funds from the appropriation account for expenses, within the contingent fund of the Senate, for the Majority and Minority Policy Committees of the Senate, to the account from which salaries are payable for such committees.

(b) Transfer of funds for Conference Committees

(1) The Chairman of the Majority or Minority Conference Committee of the Senate may, during any fiscal year, at his or her election transfer funds from the appropriation account for salaries for the Majority and Minority Conference Committees of the Senate, to the account, within the contingent fund of the Senate, from which expenses are payable for such committees.

(2) The Chairman of the Majority or Minority Conference Committee of the Senate may, during any fiscal year, at his or her election transfer funds from the appropriation account for expenses, within the contingent fund of the Senate, for the Majority and Minority Conference Committees of the Senate, to the account from which salaries are payable for such committees.

(c) Availability of transferred funds

Any funds transferred under this section shall be—

(1) available for expenditure by such committee in like manner and for the same purposes as are other moneys which are available for expenditure by such committee from the account to which the funds were transferred; and

(2) made at such time or times as the Chairman shall specify in writing to the Senate Disbursing Office.

(d) Notification to Committee on Appropriations

The Chairman of a committee transferring funds under this section shall notify the Committee on Appropriations of the Senate of the transfer.

(Pub. L. 101–520, title I, § 1, Nov. 5, 1990, 104 Stat. 2257; Pub. L. 102–90, title I, § 1(a), Aug. 14, 1991, 105 Stat. 450; Pub. L. 104–53, title I, § 7[(a)], Nov. 19, 1995, 109 Stat. 518.)

CODIFICATION

Section is from the Congressional Operations Appropriations Act, 1991, which is title I of the Legislative Branch Appropriations Act, 1991.

AMENDMENTS

1995—Pub. L. 104–53 amended section generally. Prior to amendment, section read as follows: "The Chairman of the Majority or Minority Conference Committee of the Senate may, during any fiscal year (commencing with the fiscal year ending September 30, 1991), at his election transfer not more than $275,000 from the appropriation account for salaries for the Conference of the Majority and the Conference of the Minority of the Senate, to the account, within the contingent fund of the Senate, from which expenses are payable under section 61g–6 of this title. Any transfer of funds under authority of the preceding sentence shall be made at such time or times as such chairman shall specify in writing to the Senate Disbursing Office. Any funds so transferred by the Chairman of the Majority or Minority Conference Committee shall be available for expenditure by such committee in like manner and for the same purposes as are other moneys which are available for expenditure by such committee from the account, within the contingent fund of the Senate, from which expenses are payable under section 61g–6 of this title."

1991—Pub. L. 102–90 substituted "$275,000" for "$75,000".

EFFECTIVE DATE OF 1995 AMENDMENT

Section 7(b) of Pub. L. 104–53 provided that: "The amendment made by this section [amending this section] shall take effect on October 1, 1995, and shall be effective with respect to fiscal years beginning on or after that date."

EFFECTIVE DATE OF 1991 AMENDMENT

Section 1(b) of Pub. L. 102–90 provided that: "Subsection (a) [amending this section] shall take effect on October 1, 1991."

PRIOR PROVISIONS

Provisions similar to those in this section were contained in the following prior appropriation acts:

Pub. L. 101–163, title I, §1, Nov. 21, 1989, 103 Stat. 1044.
Pub. L. 100–458, title I, §1, Oct. 1, 1988, 102 Stat. 2161.
Pub. L. 100–202, §101(i) [title I, §7], Dec. 22, 1987, 101 Stat. 1329–290, 1329–294.

§ 61g–7. Services of consultants to Majority and Minority Conference Committee of Senate

(a) Authorization of expenditure with approval of Committee on Rules and Administration

Funds authorized to be expended under section 61g–6 of this title may be used by the Majority or Minority Conference Committee of the Senate, with the approval of the Committee on Rules and Administration, to procure the temporary services (not in excess of one year) or intermittent services of individual consultants, or organizations thereof, to make studies or advise the committee with respect to any matter within its jurisdiction or with respect to the administration of the affairs of the committee.

(b) Procurement by contract or employment

Such services in the case of individuals or organizations may be procured by contract as independent contractors, or in the case of individuals, by employment at daily rates of compensation not in excess of the per diem equivalent of the highest gross rate of compensation which may be paid to a regular employee of such committee. Such contracts shall not be subject to the provisions of section 5 of title 41 or any other provision of law requiring advertising.

(c) Selection of consultant or organization by Conference Committee chairman

Any such consultant or organization shall be selected for the Majority or Minority Conference Committee of the Senate by the chairman thereof.

(Pub. L. 99–88, title I, §195, Aug. 15, 1985, 99 Stat. 349; Pub. L. 104–197, title I, §1, Sept. 16, 1996, 110 Stat. 2396.)

CODIFICATION

Section is from the Supplemental Appropriations Act, 1985.

AMENDMENTS

1996—Subsec. (a). Pub. L. 104–197 inserted "or with respect to the administration of the affairs of the committee" before period at end.

§ 61g–8. Utilization of funds for specialized training of professional staff for Majority and Minority Conference Committee of Senate

Funds appropriated to the Conference of the Majority and funds appropriated to the Conference of the Minority for any fiscal year (commencing with the fiscal year ending September 30, 1991), may be utilized in such amounts as the Chairman of each Conference deems appropriate for the specialized training of professional staff, subject to such limitations, insofar as they are applicable, as are imposed by the Committee on Rules and Administration with respect to such training when provided to professional staff of standing committees of the Senate.

(Pub. L. 101–520, title I, §2, Nov. 5, 1990, 104 Stat. 2257.)

CODIFICATION

Section is from the Congressional Operations Appropriations Act, 1991, which is title I of the Legislative Branch Appropriations Act, 1991.

PRIOR PROVISIONS

Provisions relating to utilization of funds for specific fiscal year for specialized training of professional staff for Majority and Minority Conference Committee of Senate were contained in the following prior appropriation acts:

Pub. L. 101–163, title I, §2, Nov. 21, 1989, 103 Stat. 1044.
Pub. L. 100–458, title I, §2, Oct. 1, 1988, 102 Stat. 2161.
Pub. L. 100–202, §101(i) [title I], Dec. 22, 1987, 101 Stat. 1329–290, 1329–292.

§§ 61h, 61h–1. Omitted

CODIFICATION

Section 61h, Pub. L. 93–371, §4, Aug. 13, 1974, 88 Stat. 429; Pub. L. 94–59, title I, §105, July 25, 1975, 89 Stat. 275, set forth maximum annual rate of compensation for Assistant Secretaries for Senate Majority and Minority. Pub. L. 95–94, title I, Aug. 5, 1977, 91 Stat. 658, abolished such positions, effective Oct. 1, 1977, and authorized Secretaries concerned to appoint and fix compensation of such employees as they deem appropriate. See section 61g–5 of this title.

A prior section 61h, acts Aug. 5, 1955, ch. 568, 69 Stat. 502; June 27, 1956, ch. 453, 70 Stat. 357; Aug. 21, 1959, Pub. L. 86–176, 73 Stat. 399; Aug. 10, 1961, Pub. L. 87–130, 75 Stat. 321; July 27, 1965, Pub. L. 89–90, 79 Stat. 266, authorized basic per annum compensation of Assistant Secretaries for Senate Majority and Minority to be fixed by the respective Secretaries.

Section 61h–1, Pub. L. 93–371, §4, Aug. 13, 1974, 88 Stat. 429; Pub. L. 94–59, title I, §105, July 25, 1975, 89 Stat. 275, set a maximum annual rate of compensation of $38,000 for administrative assistants in Offices of Senate Majority and Minority Leaders. Positions established by Legislative Branch Appropriation Act, 1970, for Offices of Senate Majority and Minority Leaders, which Act, Pub. L. 91–145, Dec. 12, 1969, 83 Stat. 339, formerly classified to this section, authorized respective leaders to appoint an administrative assistant, were abolished, see title I of Pub. L. 95–26, 91 Stat. 80, set out below. See, also, section 61h–4 of this title.

A prior section 61h–1, Pub. L. 91–145, Dec. 12, 1969, 83 Stat. 339, authorized Senate Majority and Minority Leaders to each appoint and fix compensation of an administrative assistant, a legislative assistant, an executive secretary, and a clerical assistant in lieu of positions heretofore authorized by Senate Resolution 158, agreed to December 9, 1941, Pub. L. 86–30, approved May 20, 1959, and Senate Resolution 240, agreed to January 24, 1952.

ABOLITION OF POSITIONS IN OFFICES OF SENATE MAJORITY AND MINORITY LEADERS

Pub. L. 95–26, title I, May 4, 1977, 91 Stat. 80, provided in part: "That the positions established by the Legislative Branch Appropriation Act, 1970 [Pub. L. 91–145, Dec. 12, 1969, 83 Stat. 338], for the Offices of the Majority and Minority Leaders [of the Senate] are abolished effective April 1, 1977." The positions referred to were enumerated in Pub. L. 91–145, Dec. 12, 1969, 83 Stat. 339, classified to former section 61h–1 of this title, which authorized the respective leaders to appoint an administrative assistant, a legislative assistant, an executive secretary, and a clerical assistant in lieu of the positions authorized prior thereto by Senate Resolution

158, agreed to Dec. 9, 1941, Pub. L. 86–30, approved May 20, 1959, and Senate Resolution 240, agreed to Jan. 24, 1952. See section 61h–4 of this title.

§§ 61h–2, 61h–3. Omitted

CODIFICATION

Section 61h–2, Pub. L. 94–59, title I, § 105, July 25, 1975, 89 Stat. 275, set a maximum annual rate of compensation of $36,500 for legislative assistants in Offices of Senate Majority and Minority Leaders. Positions established by Legislative Branch Appropriation Act, 1970, for Offices of Senate Majority and Minority Leaders, which Act, Pub. L. 91–145, Dec. 12, 1969, 83 Stat. 339, classified to former section 61h–1 of this title, authorized the respective leaders to appoint a legislative assistant, were abolished, see Pub. L. 95–26, title I, May 4, 1977, 91 Stat. 80, set out as a note under section 61h–1 of this title. See, also, section 61h–4 of this title.

Section 61h–3, Pub. L. 94–59, title I, July 25, 1975, 89 Stat. 269, authorized Senate Majority and Minority Leaders to appoint and fix compensation of an executive secretary and a clerical assistant effective July 1, 1975. Positions established by Legislative Branch Appropriation Act, 1970, for Offices of Senate Majority and Minority Leaders, which Act, Pub. L. 91–145, Dec. 12, 1969, 83 Stat. 339, classified to former section 61h–1 of this title, authorized the respective leaders to appoint an executive secretary, and a clerical assistant, were abolished, see Pub. L. 95–26, title I, May 4, 1977, 91 Stat. 80, set out as a note under section 61h–1 of this title. See, also, section 61h–4 of this title.

§ 61h–4. Appointment of employees by Senate Majority and Minority Leaders; compensation

Effective April 1, 1977, the Majority Leader and the Minority Leader are each authorized to appoint and fix the compensation of such employees as they deem appropriate: *Provided*, That the gross compensation paid to such employees shall not exceed $191,700 each fiscal year for each Leader.

(Pub. L. 95–26, title I, May 4, 1977, 91 Stat. 80.)

CODIFICATION

Section is from the Supplemental Appropriations Act, 1977.

INCREASES IN COMPENSATION

Increases in compensation for Senate officers and employees under authority of Federal Pay Comparability Act of 1970 (Pub. L. 91–656), see Salary Directives of President pro tempore of the Senate, set out as notes under section 60a–1 of this title.

§ 61h–5. Assistants to Senate Majority and Minority Leaders for Floor Operations; establishment of positions; appointment; compensation

Effective October 1, 1983, there is established within the Offices of the Majority and Minority Leaders the positions of Assistant to the Majority Leader for Floor Operations and Assistant to the Minority Leader for Floor Operations, respectively. Individuals appointed to such positions by the Majority Leader and Minority Leader, respectively, shall receive compensation at a rate fixed by the appropriate Leader not to exceed the maximum annual rate of gross compensation of the Assistant Secretary of the Senate.

(Pub. L. 98–51, title I, § 101(a), July 14, 1983, 97 Stat. 265.)

CODIFICATION

Section is from the Congressional Operations Appropriation Act, 1984, which is title I of the Legislative Branch Appropriation Act, 1984.

PRIOR PROVISIONS

A prior section 61h–5, Pub. L. 95–26, title I, May 4, 1977, 91 Stat. 80, authorizing the Majority Leader and the Minority Leader to appoint, respectively, an Assistant to the Majority Leader for Floor Operations and an Assistant to the Minority Leader for Floor Operations, was omitted in view of section 101(b) of Pub. L. 98–51, which provided that: "Effective October 1, 1983, the positions of Assistant to the Majority Leader for Floor Operations and Assistant to the Minority Leader for Floor Operations established by the Supplemental Appropriations Act, 1977 (2 U.S.C. 61h–5), are abolished."

INCREASES IN COMPENSATION

Increases in compensation for Senate officers and employees under authority of Federal Pay Comparability Act of 1970 (Pub. L. 91–656), see Salary Directives of President pro tempore of the Senate, set out as notes under section 60a–1 of this title.

§ 61h–6. Appointment of consultants by Majority Leader, Minority Leader, Secretary of Senate, and Legislative Counsel of Senate; compensation

(a) The Majority Leader and the Minority Leader, are each authorized to appoint and fix the compensation of not more than four individual consultants, on a temporary or intermittent basis, at a daily rate of compensation not in excess of the per diem equivalent of the highest gross rate of annual compensation which may be paid to employees of a standing committee of the Senate. The President pro tempore of the Senate is authorized to appoint and fix the compensation of one consultant, on a temporary or intermittent basis, at a daily rate of compensation not in excess of that specified in the first sentence of this subsection. The Secretary of the Senate is authorized to appoint and fix the compensation of not more than two individual consultants, on a temporary or intermittent basis, at a daily rate of compensation not in excess of the per diem equivalent of the highest gross rate of annual compensation which may be paid to employees of a standing committee of the Senate. The Legislative Counsel of the Senate (subject to the approval of the President pro tempore) is authorized to appoint and fix the compensation of not more than two consultants, on a temporary or intermittent basis, at a daily rate of compensation not in excess of that specified in the first sentence of this section. The provisions of sections 8344 and 8468 of title 5 shall not apply to any individual serving in a position under this authority. Expenditures under this authority shall be paid from the contingent fund of the Senate upon vouchers approved by the President pro tempore, Majority Leader, Minority Leader, Secretary of the Senate, or Legislative Counsel of the Senate, as the case may be.

(b) Any or all appointments under this section may be at an annual rate of compensation rather than at a daily rate of compensation, but such annual rate shall not be in excess of the highest gross rate of annual compensation which may be paid to employees of a standing committee of the Senate.

(Pub. L. 95–26, title I, §101, May 4, 1977, 91 Stat. 82; Pub. L. 95–94, title I, §110(a), Aug. 5, 1977, 91 Stat. 662; Pub. L. 100–458, title I, §§4, 9, Oct. 1, 1988, 102 Stat. 2161, 2162; Pub. L. 101–302, title III, §314(a), May 25, 1990, 104 Stat. 245; Pub. L. 102–90, title I, §3, Aug. 14, 1991, 105 Stat. 450; Pub. L. 104–2, Feb. 9, 1995, 109 Stat. 45; Pub. L. 105–275, title I, §4(a), (b), Oct. 21, 1998, 112 Stat. 2433.)

CODIFICATION

Section is from the Supplemental Appropriations Act, 1977.

AMENDMENTS

1998—Subsec. (a). Pub. L. 105–275, §4(a), inserted after first sentence "The President pro tempore of the Senate is authorized to appoint and fix the compensation of one consultant, on a temporary or intermittent basis, at a daily rate of compensation not in excess of that specified in the first sentence of this subsection." and in penultimate sentence substituted "sections 8344 and 8468" for "section 8344".

Subsec. (b). Pub. L. 105–275, §4(b), substituted "Any or all appointments under this section may be" for "The Majority Leader, and the Minority Leader, in appointing individuals to consultant positions under authority of this section, may appoint one such individual to such position".

1995—Pub. L. 104–2, which directed the general amendment of section 61h–6 of title 2, was executed by amending section 101 of Pub. L. 95–26, which is classified to section 61h–6 of title 2, to reflect the probable intent of Congress, in subsec. (a) striking out provisions regarding appointment of two consultants at daily rate of compensation by President pro tempore of Senate and increasing number of appointments by Majority Leader of Senate from two to four consultants at daily rate of compensation, and in subsec. (b) striking out provisions regarding appointment of one consultant at an annual rate of compensation by President pro tempore of Senate.

1991—Subsec. (a). Pub. L. 102–90 which directed the insertion of "The Legislative Counsel of the Senate (subject to the approval of the President pro tempore) is authorized to appoint and fix the compensation of not more than 2 consultants, on a temporary or intermittent basis, at a daily rate of compensation not in excess of that specified in the first sentence of this section." immediately after the second sentence of this section and which directed the substitution of ", Secretary of the Senate, or Legislative Counsel of the Senate, as the case may be" for "and the Secretary of the Senate, respectively" in the last sentence of this section, was executed by making the insertion and the substitution for "and Secretary of the Senate, respectively", to reflect the probable intent of Congress.

1990—Pub. L. 101–302 designated existing provisions as subsec. (a) and added subsec. (b).

1988—Pub. L. 100–458 provided for appointment, compensation, and voucher approval of two consultants by President pro tempore of Senate and increased the number of appointments by Minority Leader of Senate from two to four individuals.

1977—Pub. L. 95–94 inserted two references to Secretary of Senate.

EFFECTIVE DATE OF 1998 AMENDMENT

Pub. L. 105–275, title I, §4(c), Oct. 21, 1998, 112 Stat. 2433, provided that: "This section [amending this section] is effective on and after the date of enactment of this Act [Oct. 21, 1998]."

EFFECTIVE DATE OF 1990 AMENDMENT

Section 314(b) of Pub. L. 101–302 provided that: "The amendments made by this section [amending this section] shall be effective in the case of appointments made after the date of enactment of this Act [May 25, 1990]."

EFFECTIVE DATE OF 1977 AMENDMENT

Section 110(b) of Pub. L. 95–94 provided that: "The amendments made by subsection (a) [amending this section] shall take effect on August 1, 1977."

§ 61h–7. Chiefs of Staff for Senate Majority and Minority Leaders; appointment; compensation

(a) There is established within the Offices of the Majority and Minority Leaders the positions of Chief of Staff for the Majority Leader and Chief of Staff for the Minority Leader, respectively. Individuals appointed to such positions by the Majority Leader and Minority Leader, respectively, shall receive compensation at a rate fixed by the appropriate Leader not to exceed the maximum annual rate of gross compensation of the Assistant Secretary of the Senate.

(b) Gross compensation for employees filling positions established by subsection (a) of this section for the fiscal year ending September 30, 1987, shall be paid out of any funds available in the Senate appropriation for such year under the item "Salaries, Officers and Employees".

(Pub. L. 101–163, title I, §9, Nov. 21, 1989, 103 Stat. 1046.)

CODIFICATION

Section is based on Senate Resolution No. 89, One Hundredth Congress, Jan. 28, 1987, which was enacted into permanent law by Pub. L. 101–163.

EFFECTIVE DATE

Section 9 of Pub. L. 101–163 provided that this section is effective on Jan. 28, 1987, the date on which Senate Resolution No. 89, One Hundredth Congress, was agreed to.

§§ 61i to 61j–1. Omitted

CODIFICATION

Section 61i, Pub. L. 86–30, title I, May 20, 1959, 73 Stat. 48, which was from the Second Supplemental Appropriation Act, 1959, authorized Senate Majority and Minority Leaders to fix, effective May 1, 1959, basic salaries of research assistants authorized by S. Res. 158, agreed to Dec. 9, 1941, at not to exceed $8,820 per annum. See section 61h–4 of this title.

Section 61j, Pub. L. 93–371, §4, Aug. 13, 1974, 88 Stat. 429; Pub. L. 94–59, title I, §105, July 25, 1975, 89 Stat. 275, set a maximum annual rate of compensation of $37,000 for administrative assistants in offices of Senate Majority and Minority Whips. Positions established by Legislative Branch Appropriation Act, 1970, for Offices of Senate Majority and Minority Whips, which Act, Pub. L. 91–145, Dec. 12, 1969, 83 Stat. 339, classified to former section 61j of this title, authorized the respective whips to appoint an administrative assistant, were abolished, see title I of Pub. L. 95–26, set out in part as a note under section 61h–1 of this title. See, also, section 61j–2 of this title.

A prior section 61j, Pub. L. 91–145, Dec. 12, 1969, 83 Stat. 339, authorized Senate Majority and Minority Whips to each appoint and fix compensation of an administrative assistant and an executive secretary.

Section 61j–1, Pub. L. 94–59, title I, July 25, 1975, 89 Stat. 270, authorized Senate Majority and Minority Whips, effective July 1, 1975, each to appoint and fix compensation of a legislative assistant. The positions established by Pub. L. 94–59 for the Offices of Majority and Minority Whips were abolished effective Apr. 1, 1977, by Pub. L. 95–26, title I, May 4, 1977, 91 Stat. 80, set out as a note under section 61h–1 of this title. See, also, section 61j–2 of this title.

§ 61j-2. Compensation and appointment of employees by Senate Majority and Minority Whips

Effective April 1, 1977, the Majority Whip and the Minority Whip are each authorized to appoint and fix the compensation of such employees as they deem appropriate: *Provided*, That the gross compensation paid to such employees shall not exceed $111,100 each fiscal year for each Whip.

(Pub. L. 95–26, title I, May 4, 1977, 91 Stat. 80.)

CODIFICATION

Section is from the Supplemental Appropriations Act, 1977.

INCREASES IN COMPENSATION

Increases in compensation for Senate officers and employees under authority of Federal Pay Comparability Act of 1970 (Pub. L. 91–656), see Salary Directives of President pro tempore of the Senate, set out as notes under section 60a–1 of this title.

§ 61k. Appointment and compensation of employees by President pro tempore of Senate

Effective October 1, 1979, the President pro tempore is authorized to appoint and fix the compensation of such employees as he deems appropriate: *Provided*, That the gross compensation paid to such employees shall not exceed $123,000 each fiscal year.

(Pub. L. 96–38, title I, § 101, July 25, 1979, 93 Stat. 111.)

CODIFICATION

Section is from the Supplemental Appropriations Act, 1979.

PRIOR PROVISIONS

A prior section 61k, Pub. L. 95–26, title I, May 4, 1977, 91 Stat. 79, authorized President pro tempore of Senate to appoint and fix compensation of an Administrative Assistant, a Legislative Assistant, and an Executive Secretary. These positions were abolished effective Oct. 1, 1979, by section 101 of Pub. L. 96–38.

INCREASES IN COMPENSATION

Increases in compensation for Senate officers and employees under authority of Federal Pay Comparability Act of 1970 (Pub. L. 91–656), see Salary Directives of President pro tempore of the Senate, set out as notes under section 60a–1 of this title.

§ 61l. Appointment and compensation of Administrative Assistant, Legislative Assistant, and Executive Secretary for Deputy President pro tempore of Senate

Effective April 1, 1977, the Deputy President pro tempore is authorized to appoint and fix the compensation of an Administrative Assistant at not to exceed $47,595 per annum; a Legislative Assistant at not to exceed $40,080 per annum, and an Executive Secretary at not to exceed $23,380 per annum.

(Pub. L. 95–26, title I, May 4, 1977, 91 Stat. 80.)

CODIFICATION

Section is from the Supplemental Appropriations Act, 1977.

INCREASES IN COMPENSATION

Increases in compensation for officers and employees of the Senate under authority of the Federal Pay Com-

parability Act of 1970 (Pub. L. 91–656), see Salary Directives of the President pro tempore of the Senate, set out as notes under section 60a–1 of this title.

§ 62. Limitation on compensation of Sergeant at Arms and Doorkeeper of Senate

The Sergeant at Arms and Doorkeeper of the Senate shall receive, directly or indirectly, no fees or other compensation or emolument whatever for performing the duties of the office, or in connection therewith, other than the salary prescribed by law.

(June 20, 1874, ch. 328, 18 Stat. 85; Mar. 3, 1875, ch. 129, 18 Stat. 344.)

§ 62a. Omitted

CODIFICATION

Section, act May 1, 1947, ch. 49, title I, 61 Stat. 58, accorded Sergeant at Arms of Senate the same priority as executive agencies under the Surplus Property Act of 1944 (50 App. U.S.C. 1611–1648). The Surplus Property Act of 1944 was repealed by act June 30, 1949, ch. 288, title V, § 503, 63 Stat. 399, and the priorities thereunder expired Dec. 31, 1949.

§ 62b. Transferred

CODIFICATION

Section, act July 26, 1949, ch. 366, 63 Stat. 482, which related to audits and reports by Comptroller General of fiscal records of House Sergeant at Arms, was transferred to section 81a of this title, and was subsequently repealed by Pub. L. 104–186.

§ 63. Repealed. Pub. L. 104–186, title II, § 204(21), Aug. 20, 1996, 110 Stat. 1733

Section, R.S. § 73, related to duties of Doorkeeper of Senate. Provisions of R.S. § 73 which related to duties of Doorkeeper of House of Representatives were classified to section 76 of this title prior to repeal by Pub. L. 104–186.

§ 64. Omitted

CODIFICATION

Section, R.S. § 56, authorizing payment on requisitions drawn by Secretary of Senate of moneys appropriated for compensation of Senate members and officers and for contingent Senate expenses, was omitted in view of the abolition of appropriation for the fund provided for in this section on and after July 1, 1935, and the authorization of annual definite appropriations by act June 26, 1934, ch. 756, § 14, 48 Stat. 1230.

§ 64–1. Employees of Senate Disbursing Office; designation by Secretary of Senate to administer oaths and affirmations

The Secretary of the Senate is on and after November 1, 1973, authorized to designate, in writing, employees of the Disbursing Office of the Senate to administer oaths and affirmations, with respect to matters relating to that Office, authorized or required by law or rules or orders of the Senate (including the oath of office required by section 3331 of title 5). During any period in which he is so designated, any such employee may administer such oaths and affirmations.

(Pub. L. 93–145, Nov. 1, 1973, 87 Stat. 532.)

§ 64–2. Transfers of funds by Secretary of Senate; approval of Committee on Appropriations

During any fiscal year (commencing with the fiscal year beginning October 1, 1982) the Secretary of the Senate is authorized to make such transfers between appropriations of funds available for disbursement by him during such year, subject to the approval of the Committee on Appropriations of the Senate.

(Pub. L. 97–276, §101(e), Oct. 2, 1982, 96 Stat. 1189.)

CODIFICATION

Section is based on section 104 of S. 2939, Ninety-seventh Congress, 2d Session, as reported Sept. 22, 1982, and incorporated by reference in section 101(e) of Pub. L. 97–276, to be effective as if enacted into law.

PRIOR PROVISIONS

A prior section 64–2, Pub. L. 95–26, title I, §108, May 4, 1977, 91 Stat. 85, provided that, on and after May 4, 1977, Secretary of Senate was authorized to transfer funds between appropriations with approval of a resolution of Senate.

TRANSFER OF FUNDS BY SECRETARY OF SENATE

Provisions authorizing Secretary of Senate, as Disbursing Officer of Senate, to make such transfers between appropriations of funds available for disbursement by him for specific fiscal years, as he deems appropriate, subject to customary reprograming procedures of Senate Committee on Appropriations were contained in the following appropriation acts:

Pub. L. 97–51, §113, Oct. 1, 1981, 95 Stat. 963.

Pub. L. 97–12, title I, §107, June 5, 1981, 95 Stat. 62.

§64–3. Reimbursement for Capitol Police salaries paid by Senate for service at Federal Law Enforcement Training Center

Notwithstanding any other provision of law, the Secretary of the Senate is authorized to receive moneys from the Department of the Treasury as reimbursements for salaries paid by the United States Senate in connection with certain officers and members of the United States Capitol Police serving as instructors at the Federal Law Enforcement Training Center. Moneys so received shall be deposited in the Treasury of the United States as miscellaneous receipts.

(Pub. L. 95–26, title I, §111, May 4, 1977, 91 Stat. 87.)

CODIFICATION

Section is from the Supplemental Appropriations Act, 1977.

§64a. Death, resignation, or disability of Secretary and Assistant Secretary of Senate; Financial Clerk deemed successor as disbursing officer

For any period during which both the Secretary and the Assistant Secretary of the Senate are unable (because of death, resignation, or disability) to discharge such Secretary's duties as disbursing officer of the Senate, the Financial Clerk of the Senate shall be deemed to be the successor of such Secretary as disbursing officer.

(Mar. 3, 1926, ch. 44, §1, 44 Stat. 162; Pub. L. 91–105, §2, Oct. 31, 1969, 83 Stat. 169; Pub. L. 91–382, Aug. 18, 1970, 84 Stat. 810; Pub. L. 92–310, title II, §220(g), June 6, 1972, 86 Stat. 204; Pub. L. 98–367, title I, §2(a), July 17, 1984, 98 Stat. 474.)

AMENDMENTS

1984—Pub. L. 98–367 substituted "For any period during which both the Secretary and the Assistant Sec-

retary of the Senate are unable (because of death, resignation, or disability) to discharge such Secretary's duties as disbursing officer of the Senate, the Financial Clerk of the Senate shall be deemed to be the successor of such Secretary as disbursing officer" for "In the event of the death, resignation, or disability of the Secretary of the Senate, the Financial Clerk of the Senate shall be deemed his successor as a disbursing officer and he shall serve as such disbursing officer until the end of the quarterly period during which a new Secretary shall have been elected and qualified, or such disability shall have been ended".

1972—Pub. L. 92–310 struck out provisions which related to the bond of the Financial Clerk.

1970—Pub. L. 91–382 substituted "Financial Clerk" for "Comptroller".

1969—Pub. L. 91–105 substituted the Comptroller of the Senate for the Financial Clerk of the Senate as the successor of the Secretary of the Senate in the event of the death, resignation, or disability of the Secretary.

EFFECTIVE DATE OF 1970 AMENDMENT

Pub. L. 91–382 provided that the amendment made by Pub. L. 91–382 is effective Aug. 1, 1970.

CERTIFICATION OF DISABILITY

Secretary of the Senate to be considered as disabled for purposes of this section only during such period of time as the Majority and Minority Leaders and the President pro tempore of the Senate certify jointly to the Senate that he is unable to perform his duties, see section 64b of this title.

SECTION REFERRED TO IN OTHER SECTIONS

This section is referred to in section 64b of this title.

§64a–1. Compensation of Financial Clerk of Senate

The Financial Clerk of the Senate may be paid at a maximum annual rate of compensation not to exceed $39,000.

(Pub. L. 93–371, §4, Aug. 13, 1974, 88 Stat. 429; Pub. L. 94–59, title I, §105, July 25, 1975, 89 Stat. 275.)

AMENDMENTS

1975—Pub. L. 94–59 substituted "$39,000" for "$37,620", effective July 1, 1975.

EFFECTIVE DATE

Section effective July 1, 1974, see section 4 of Pub. L. 93–371, set out in part as an Effective Date of 1974 Amendment note under section 61a of this title.

1974 ADJUSTMENT IN COMPENSATION NOT TO SUPERSEDE ADJUSTMENTS IN COMPENSATION OR LIMITATIONS BY PRESIDENT PRO TEMPORE OF THE SENATE

Adjustment in compensation by Pub. L. 93–371 not to supersede order of President pro tempore of the Senate authorizing higher rate of compensation or any authority of the President pro tempore to adjust rates of compensation or limitations under section 4 of the Federal Pay Comparability Act of 1970, see section 4 of Pub. L. 93–371, set out in part as a note under section 61a of this title.

INCREASES IN COMPENSATION

Increases in compensation for Senate officers and employees under authority of Federal Pay Comparability Act of 1970 (Pub. L. 91–656), see Salary Directives of President pro tempore of the Senate, set out as notes under section 60a–1 of this title.

§ 64b. Death, resignation, or disability of Secretary of Senate; Assistant Secretary of Senate to act as Secretary; written designation of absent status

In the event of the death, resignation, or disability of the Secretary of the Senate, the Assistant Secretary of the Senate shall act as Secretary in carrying out the duties and responsibilities of that office in all matters until such time as a new Secretary shall have been elected and qualified or such disability shall have been ended. For purposes of this section and section 64a of this title, the Secretary of the Senate shall be considered as disabled only during such period of time as the Majority and Minority Leaders and the President pro tempore of the Senate certify jointly to the Senate that the Secretary is unable to perform his duties. In the event that the Secretary of the Senate is absent or is to be absent for reasons other than disability (as provided in this paragraph), and makes a written designation that he is or will be so absent, the Assistant Secretary shall act during such absence as the Secretary in carrying out the duties and responsibilities of the office in all matters. The designation may be revoked in writing at any time by the Secretary, and is revoked whenever the Secretary making the designation dies, resigns, or is considered disabled in accordance with this paragraph.

(Pub. L. 92–184, ch. IV, Dec. 15, 1971, 85 Stat. 635; Pub. L. 93–371, § 1, Aug. 13, 1974, 88 Stat. 427; Pub. L. 98–367, title I, § 2(b), July 17, 1984, 98 Stat. 474.)

AMENDMENTS

1984—Pub. L. 98–367 struck out provisions relating to exception for duties of the Secretary as disbursing officer of the Senate.

1974—Pub. L. 93–371 inserted provisions relating to the absence of Secretary of Senate for reasons other than disability and the written designation of such absent status.

§ 65. Repealed. Pub. L. 92–310, title II, § 220(a), (c), June 6, 1972, 86 Stat. 204

Section, R.S. §§ 57, 59; acts Mar. 2, 1895, ch. 177, § 5, 28 Stat. 807; Oct. 31, 1951, ch. 655, § 13, 65 Stat. 715, required Secretary of Senate to give a bond in the sum of $20,000.

§ 65a. Insurance of office funds of Secretary of Senate and Sergeant at Arms; payment of premiums

The Secretary of the Senate and the Sergeant at Arms on and after June 27, 1956, are authorized and directed to protect the funds of their respective offices by purchasing insurance in an amount necessary to protect said funds against loss. Premiums on such insurance shall be paid out of the contingent fund of the Senate, upon vouchers approved by the chairman of the Committee on Rules and Administration.

(June 27, 1956, ch. 453, 70 Stat. 360.)

CODIFICATION

Section is from the Legislative Branch Appropriation Act, 1957, act June 27, 1956.

PRIOR PROVISIONS

Provisions similar to those in this section were contained in the following prior appropriation acts:

Aug. 5, 1955, ch. 568, 69 Stat. 504.
July 2, 1954, ch. 455, title I, 68 Stat. 400.
Aug. 1, 1953, ch. 304, title I, 67 Stat. 321.
July 9, 1952, ch. 598, 66 Stat. 467.
Oct. 11, 1951, ch. 485, 65 Stat. 392.
Sept. 6, 1950, ch. 896, Ch. II, 64 Stat. 597.
June 22, 1949, ch. 235, 63 Stat. 219.
June 14, 1948, ch. 467, 62 Stat. 425.

§ 65b. Advances to Sergeant at Arms of Senate for extraordinary expenses

The Secretary of the Senate on and after July 31, 1958, is authorized, in his discretion, to advance to the Sergeant at Arms of the Senate such sums as may be necessary, not exceeding $4,000, to meet any extraordinary expenses of the Senate.

(Pub. L. 85–570, July 31, 1958, 72 Stat. 442; Pub. L. 94–440, title I, § 108, Oct. 1, 1976, 90 Stat. 1445; Pub. L. 95–26, title I, § 104, May 4, 1977, 91 Stat. 82.)

AMENDMENTS

1977—Pub. L. 95–26 struck out "during any fiscal year" after "$4,000".

1976—Pub. L. 94–440 substituted "$4,000 during any fiscal year" for "$2,000".

§ 65c. Expense allowance for Secretary of Senate, Sergeant at Arms and Doorkeeper of Senate, and Secretaries for Senate Majority and Minority

(a) Notwithstanding any other provision of law, there is hereby established an account, within the Senate, to be known as the "Expense Allowance for the Secretary of the Senate, Sergeant at Arms and Doorkeeper of the Senate and Secretaries for the Majority and for the Minority, of the Senate" (hereinafter in this section referred to as the "Expense Allowance"). For each fiscal year (commencing with the fiscal year ending September 30, 1981) there shall be available from the Expense Allowance an expense allotment not to exceed $3,000 for each of the above specified officers. Amounts paid from the expense allotment of any such officer shall be paid to him only as reimbursement for actual expenses incurred by him and upon certification and documentation by him of such expenses. Amounts paid to any such officer pursuant to this section shall not be reported as income and shall not be allowed as a deduction under title 26.

(b) For the fiscal year ending September 30, 1981, and the succeeding fiscal year, the Secretary of the Senate shall transfer, for each such year, $8,000 to the Expense Allowance from "Miscellaneous Items" in the contingent fund of the Senate. For the fiscal year ending September 30, 1983, and for each fiscal year thereafter, there are authorized to be appropriated to the Expense Allowance such funds as may be necessary to carry out the provisions of subsection (a) of this section.

(Pub. L. 97–51, § 119, Oct. 1, 1981, 95 Stat. 964; Pub. L. 98–63, title I, July 30, 1983, 97 Stat. 334; Pub. L. 99–514, § 2, Oct. 22, 1986, 100 Stat. 2095.)

AMENDMENTS

1986—Subsec. (a). Pub. L. 99–514 substituted "Internal Revenue Code of 1986" for "Internal Revenue Code of

1954", which for purposes of codification was translated as "title 26" thus requiring no change in text.

1983—Subsec. (a). Pub. L. 98–63, which directed that "$3,000" be substituted for "$2,000" in first sentence of subsec. (a), was executed by making the substitution in second sentence as the probable intent of Congress.

EFFECTIVE DATE OF 1983 AMENDMENT

Title I of Pub. L. 98–63 provided that the amendment made by Pub. L. 98–63 is effective for fiscal years beginning on or after Oct. 1, 1982.

§ 65d. Funds advanced by Secretary of Senate to Sergeant at Arms and Doorkeeper of Senate to defray office expenses; accountability; maximum amount; vouchers

From funds available for any fiscal year (commencing with the fiscal year ending September 30, 1984), the Secretary of the Senate shall advance to the Sergeant at Arms and Doorkeeper of the Senate for the purpose of defraying office expenses such sums (for which the Sergeant at Arms and Doorkeeper shall be accountable) not in excess of $1,000 at any one time, as such Sergeant at Arms shall from time to time request; except that the aggregate of the sums so advanced during the fiscal year shall not exceed $10,000.

In accordance with the provisions of this section, a detailed voucher shall be submitted to the Secretary of the Senate by such Sergeant at Arms whenever necessary, in order to replenish funds expended.

(Pub. L. 98–51, title I, §104, July 14, 1983, 97 Stat. 266.)

CODIFICATION

Section is from the Congressional Operations Appropriation Act, 1984, which is title I of the Legislative Branch Appropriation Act, 1984.

§ 65e. Transferred

CODIFICATION

Section, Pub. L. 98–63, title I, July 30, 1983, 97 Stat. 333, which provided that effective with fiscal year 1983 and each fiscal year thereafter, the expense allowance of Majority and Minority Whips of Senate could not exceed $5,000 each fiscal year for each Whip, was transferred and executed to section 31a–1 of this title.

§ 65f. Funds for Secretary of Senate to assist in proper discharge within United States of responsibilities to foreign parliamentary groups or other foreign officials

(a) In general

On and after July 11, 1987, the Secretary of the Senate is authorized to use any available funds (but not in excess of $50,000 for any fiscal year), out of the appropriation account (within the Contingent Fund of the Senate) for the Secretary of the Senate, to assist him in the proper discharge, within the United States, of his appropriate responsibilities to members of foreign parliamentary groups or other foreign officials.

(b) Effective date

The provisions of subsection (a) of this section shall be effective in the case of expenditures for fiscal years ending after September 30, 1986.

(c) Transfer of funds

Upon the written request of the Secretary of the Senate, with the approval of the Committee on Appropriations of the Senate, there shall be transferred any amount of funds available under subsection (a) of this section specified in the request, but not to exceed $10,000 in any fiscal year, from the appropriation account (within the contingent fund of the Senate) for expenses of the Office of the Secretary of the Senate to the appropriation account for the expense allowance of the Secretary of the Senate. Any funds so transferred shall be available in like manner and for the same purposes as are other funds in the account to which the funds are transferred.

(Pub. L. 100–71, title I, §2, July 11, 1987, 101 Stat. 423; Pub. L. 102–90, title I, §4, Aug. 14, 1991, 105 Stat. 450; Pub. L. 105–18, title II, §7003(a), June 12, 1997, 111 Stat. 192.)

CODIFICATION

Section is from the Supplemental Appropriations Act, 1987.

AMENDMENTS

1997—Subsec. (c). Pub. L. 105–18 added subsec. (c).
1991—Subsec. (a). Pub. L. 102–90 substituted "On and after July 11, 1987, the Secretary of the Senate is authorized" for "The Secretary of the Senate is authorized" and "$50,000" for "$25,000".

EFFECTIVE DATE OF 1997 AMENDMENT

Section 7003(b) of Pub. L. 105–18 provided that: "The amendment made by subsection (a) [amending this section] shall be effective with respect to appropriations for fiscal years beginning on or after October 1, 1996."

§ 66. Repealed. Pub. L. 93–344, title V, § 505(1), July 12, 1974, 88 Stat. 322

Section, act June 19, 1934, ch. 648, title I, §1, 48 Stat. 1022, directed that the fiscal year for adjustment of accounts of Secretary of Senate for compensation and mileage of Senators extend from July 1 to June 30.

§ 66a. Restriction on payment of dual compensation by Secretary of Senate

Unless otherwise specifically authorized by law, no part of any appropriation disbursed by the Secretary of the Senate shall be available for payment of compensation to any person holding any position, for any period for which such person received compensation for holding any other position, the compensation for which is disbursed by the Secretary of the Senate.

(June 27, 1956, ch. 453, 70 Stat. 360.)

§ 67. Clerks to Senators-elect

A Senator entitled to receive his own salary may appoint the usual clerical assistants allowed Senators.

(Mar. 2, 1895, ch. 177, §1, 28 Stat. 766; Feb. 20, 1923, ch. 98, 42 Stat. 1266; June 19, 1934, ch. 648, title I, §1, 48 Stat. 1022.)

AMENDMENTS

1934—Act June 19, 1934, struck out provisions as to maximum of four clerical assistants and as to their compensation.

§ 67a. Employment of civilian employees of executive branch of Government by Senate Committee on Appropriations; restoration to former position

Whenever any person has left or leaves any civilian position in any department or agency in the executive branch of the Government in order to accept employment by the Senate Committee on Appropriations, he shall be carried on the rolls of such committee and shall be solely employed by such committee, and responsible only to it; but he shall be entitled upon making application to the Director of the Office of Personnel Management within thirty days after the termination of his employment by such committee (unless such employment is terminated for cause) to be restored to a position in the same or any other department or agency where an opening exists, comparable to the position which, according to the records of the department or agency which he left to accept employment by the Senate Committee on Appropriations or in the judgment of the Director of the Office of Personnel Management, such person would be occupying if he had remained in the employ of such department or agency during the time he was employed by such committee; and such person shall be restored to such position with the same seniority, status, and pay as if he had remained in the employ of the department or agency which he left, during such time. This section shall not be construed to require any person to be restored to a position in any department or agency after the expiration of the time for which he was appointed to the position which he left to accept employment by such committee.

(June 13, 1945, ch. 189, §1, 59 Stat. 243; July 1, 1946, ch. 530, 60 Stat. 392; 1978 Reorg. Plan No. 2, §102, eff. Jan. 1, 1979, 43 F.R. 36037, 92 Stat. 3783.)

AMENDMENTS

1946—Act July 1, 1946, reenacted section without change.

TRANSFER OF FUNCTIONS

"Director of the Office of Personnel Management" substituted in text for "Civil Service Commission" pursuant to Reorg. Plan No. 2 of 1978, §102, 43 F.R. 36037, 92 Stat. 3783, set out under section 1101 of Title 5, Government Organization and Employees, which transferred functions vested by statute in United States Civil Service Commission and Chairman thereof to Director of Office of Personnel Management (except as otherwise specified), effective Jan. 1, 1979, as provided by section 1–102 of Ex. Ord. No. 12107, Dec. 28, 1978, 44 F.R. 1055, set out under section 1101 of Title 5.

§ 68. Payments from Senate contingent fund

No payment shall be made from the contingent fund of the Senate unless sanctioned by the Committee on Rules and Administration of the Senate. Payments made upon vouchers or abstracts of disbursements of salaries approved by said Committee shall be deemed, held, and taken, and are declared to be conclusive upon all the departments and officers of the Government: *Provided*, That no payment shall be made from said contingent fund as additional salary or compensation to any officer or employee of the Senate.

(Oct. 2, 1888, ch. 1069, 25 Stat. 546; Aug. 2, 1946, ch. 753, §102, 60 Stat. 814; Pub. L. 93–554, title I, Dec. 27, 1974, 88 Stat. 1776; Pub. L. 104–186, title I, §105(c), Aug. 20, 1996, 110 Stat. 1722.)

CODIFICATION

Section is based on provisions of last par. on 25 Stat. 546, act of Oct. 2, 1888, ch. 1069, relating to payments

from contingent fund of Senate. Provisions of that par. relating to payments from contingent fund of House of Representatives were classified to section 95 of this title prior to being struck out by Pub. L. 104–186.

AMENDMENTS

1974—Pub. L. 93–554 inserted provision relating to applicability to payments made upon abstracts of disbursements of salaries.

1946—Act Aug. 2, 1946, substituted "Committee on Rules and Administration" for "Committee to Audit and Control Contingent Expenses".

EFFECTIVE DATE OF 1974 AMENDMENT

Title I of Pub. L. 93–554 provided that the amendment made by Pub. L. 93–554 is effective Jan. 1, 1975.

EFFECTIVE DATE OF 1946 AMENDMENT

Section 142 of act Aug. 2, 1946, provided that the amendment made by that act is effective Jan. 2, 1947.

SECTION REFERRED TO IN OTHER SECTIONS

This section is referred to in sections 288m, 601 of this title.

§ 68–1. Committee on Rules and Administration; designation of employees to approve vouchers for payments from Senate contingent fund

The Committee on Rules and Administration may authorize its chairman to designate any employee or employees of such Committee to approve in his behalf, all vouchers making payments from the contingent fund of the Senate, such approval to be deemed and held to be approval by the Committee on Rules and Administration for all intents and purposes.

(Pub. L. 93–145, Nov. 1, 1973, 87 Stat. 529; Pub. L. 97–51, §126, Oct. 1, 1981, 95 Stat. 965; Pub. L. 98–473, title I, §123A(c), Oct. 12, 1984, 98 Stat. 1970.)

AMENDMENTS

1984—Pub. L. 98–473 substituted "any employee or employees of such Committee" for "the committee Auditor and the committee Assistant Auditor".

1981—Pub. L. 97–51 substituted "the committee Auditor and the committee Assistant Auditor" for "one committee employee".

§ 68–2. Appropriations for contingent expenses of Senate; restrictions

Appropriations made for contingent expenses of the Senate shall not be used for the payment of personal services except upon the express and specific authorization of the Senate in whose behalf such services are rendered. Nor shall such appropriations be used for any expenses not intimately and directly connected with the routine legislative business of the Senate, and the General Accounting Office shall apply the provisions of this section in the settlement of the accounts of expenditures from said appropriations incurred for services or materials.

(Feb. 14, 1902, ch. 17, 32 Stat. 26; June 10, 1921, ch. 18, title III, §304, 42 Stat. 24; Pub. L. 104–186, title II, §204(45), Aug. 20, 1996, 110 Stat. 1737.)

CODIFICATION

Section is based on provisions of proviso on 32 Stat. 26, act of Feb. 14, 1902, ch. 17, the Urgent Deficiency Appropriation Act for the fiscal year 1902, as those provisions relate to appropriations for contingent expenses of Senate. Provisions of that proviso relating to appropriations for expenses of House of Representatives are classified to section 95a of this title.

Section was formerly classified to section 671 of Title 31 prior to the general revision and enactment of Title 31, Money and Finance, by Pub. L. 97–258, §1, Sept. 13, 1982, 96 Stat. 877.

AMENDMENTS

1996—Pub. L. 104–186 amended provisions relating to appropriations for expenses of House. See Codification note above.

TRANSFER OF FUNCTIONS

"General Accounting Office" substituted in text for "accounting officers of the Treasury" pursuant to act June 10, 1921, which transferred powers and duties of Comptroller, six auditors, and certain other employees of the Treasury to General Accounting Office. See section 701 et seq. of Title 31, Money and Finance.

§ 68–3. Separate accounts for "Secretary of the Senate" and for "Sergeant at Arms and Doorkeeper of the Senate"; establishment within Senate contingent fund; inclusion of funds in existing accounts

(a) Effective October 1, 1983—

(1) there shall be, within the contingent fund of the Senate, a separate account for the "Secretary of the Senate", and a separate account for the "Sergeant at Arms and Doorkeeper of the Senate";

(2) the account for "Automobiles and Maintenance", within the contingent fund of the Senate, is abolished, and funds for the purchase, lease, exchange, maintenance, and operation of vehicles for the Senate shall be included in the separate account, established by paragraph (1), for the "Sergeant at Arms and Doorkeeper of the Senate"; and

(3) the account for "Postage Stamps", within the contingent fund of the Senate, is abolished; and funds for special delivery postage of the Office of the Secretary of the Senate shall be included in the separate account, established by paragraph (1), for the "Secretary of the Senate"; funds for special delivery postage of the Sergeant at Arms and Doorkeeper of the Senate shall be included in the separate account, established by paragraph (1), for the "Sergeant at Arms and Doorkeeper of the Senate"; and postage stamps for the Secretaries for the Majority and the Minority and other offices and officers of the Senate, as authorized by law, shall be included in the account for "Miscellaneous Items", within the contingent fund of the Senate.

(b) Any provision of law which was enacted, or any Senate resolution which was agreed to, prior to October 1, 1983, and which authorizes moneys in the contingent fund of the Senate to be expended by or for the use of the Secretary of the Senate, or his office (whether generally or from a specified account within such fund) may on and after October 1, 1983, be construed to authorize such moneys to be expended from the separate account, within such fund, established by subsection (a)(1) of this section for the "Secretary of the Senate"; and any provision of law which was enacted prior to October 1, 1983, and which authorizes moneys in the contingent fund

of the Senate to be expended by or for the use of the Sergeant at Arms and Doorkeeper of the Senate, or his office (whether generally or from a specified account within such fund) may on and after October 1, 1983, be construed to authorize such moneys to be expended from the separate account, within such fund, established by subsection (a)(1) of this section for the "Sergeant at Arms and Doorkeeper of the Senate".

(Pub. L. 98–51, title I, §103, July 14, 1983, 97 Stat. 266.)

CODIFICATION

Section is from the Congressional Operations Appropriation Act, 1984, which is title I of the Legislative Branch Appropriation, 1984.

§ 68–4. Deposit of moneys for credit to account within Senate contingent fund for "Sergeant at Arms and Doorkeeper of the Senate"

Any provision of law which is enacted prior to October 1, 1983, and which directs the Sergeant at Arms and Doorkeeper of the Senate to deposit any moneys in the United States Treasury for credit to the account, within the contingent fund of the Senate, for "Miscellaneous Items", or for "Automobiles and Maintenance" shall, on and after October 1, 1983, be deemed to direct him to deposit such moneys in the United States Treasury for credit to the account, within the contingent fund of the Senate, for the "Sergeant at Arms and Doorkeeper of the Senate".

(Pub. L. 98–181, title I, §1202, Nov. 30, 1983, 97 Stat. 1289.)

CODIFICATION

Section is from the Supplemental Appropriations Act, 1984.

§ 68–5. Purchase, lease, exchange, maintenance, and operation of vehicles out of account for Sergeant at Arms and Doorkeeper of Senate within Senate contingent fund; authorization of appropriations

For each fiscal year (commencing with the fiscal year ending September 30, 1985) there is authorized to be appropriated to the account, within the contingent fund of the Senate, for the Sergeant at Arms and Doorkeeper of the Senate, such funds (which shall be in addition to funds authorized to be so appropriated for other purposes) as may be necessary for the purchase, lease, exchange, maintenance, and operation of vehicles as follows: one for the Vice President, one for the President pro tempore of the Senate, one for the Majority Leader of the Senate, one for the Minority Leader of the Senate, one for the Majority Whip of the Senate, one for the Minority Whip of the Senate, one for the attending physician, one as authorized by Senate Resolution 90 of the 100th Congress[1] such number as is needed for carrying mails, and for official use of the offices of the Secretary of the Senate, the Sergeant at Arms and Doorkeeper of the Senate, the Secretary for the Majority, and the Secretary for the Minority, and such additional

_____
[1] So in original. Probably should be followed by a comma.

number as is otherwise specifically authorized by law.

(Pub. L. 99–88, title I, § 192, Aug. 15, 1985, 99 Stat. 349; Pub. L. 100–202, § 101(i) [title I, § 3(a)], Dec. 22, 1987, 101 Stat. 1329–290, 1329–294.)

REFERENCES IN TEXT

Senate Resolution 90 of the 100th Congress, referred to in text, which was agreed to Jan. 28, 1987, provided in part for the Sergeant at Arms and Doorkeeper of the Senate to provide, by lease or purchase, and maintain an automobile for the former President pro tempore of the Senate.

CODIFICATION

Section is from the Supplemental Appropriations Act, 1985.

AMENDMENTS

1987—Pub. L. 100–202 substituted "one for the attending physician, one as authorized by Senate Resolution 90 of the 100th Congress" for "and" and inserted ", and such additional number as is otherwise specifically authorized by law".

EFFECTIVE DATE OF 1987 AMENDMENT

Section 101(i) [title I, § 3(b)] of Pub. L. 100–202 provided that: "The amendments made by subsection (a) [amending this section] shall be effective in the case of fiscal years ending after September 30, 1986."

§ 68–6. Transfers from appropriations account for expenses of Office of Secretary of Senate and Office of Sergeant at Arms and Doorkeeper of Senate

(a) The Secretary of the Senate is authorized, with the approval of the Senate Committee on Appropriations, to transfer, during any fiscal year (1) from the appropriations account, within the contingent fund of the Senate, for expenses of the Office of the Secretary of the Senate, such sums as he shall specify to the Senate appropriations account, appropriated under the headings "Salaries, Officers and Employees" and "Office of the Secretary", and (2) from the Senate appropriations account, appropriated under the headings "Salaries, Officers and Employees" and "Office of the Secretary" to the appropriations account, within the contingent fund of the Senate, for expenses of the Office of the Secretary of the Senate, such sums as he shall specify; and any funds so transferred shall be available in like manner and for the same purposes as are other funds in the account to which the funds are transferred.

(b) The Sergeant at Arms and Doorkeeper of the Senate is authorized, with the approval of the Senate Committee on Appropriations, to transfer, during any fiscal year, from the appropriations account, within the contingent fund of the Senate, for expenses of the Office of the Sergeant at Arms and Doorkeeper of the Senate, such sums as he shall specify to the appropriations account, appropriated under the headings "Salaries, Officers and Employees" and "Office of the Sergeant at Arms and Doorkeeper"; and any funds so transferred shall be available in like manner and for the same purposes as are other funds in the account to which the funds are transferred.

(Pub. L. 100–458, title I, § 3, Oct. 1, 1988, 102 Stat. 2161; Pub. L. 101–302, title III, § 317, May 25, 1990, 104 Stat. 247.)

CODIFICATION

Section is from the Congressional Operations Appropriations Act, 1989, which is title I of the Legislative Branch Appropriations Act, 1989.

AMENDMENTS

1990—Subsec. (a). Pub. L. 101–302 designated existing provisions as cl. (1) and added cl. (2).

PRIOR PROVISIONS

Provisions similar to those in this section were contained in the following prior appropriation act:
Pub. L. 100–202, § 101(i) [title I, § 8], Dec. 22, 1987, 101 Stat. 1329–290, 1329–295.

§ 68–6a. Transfers from appropriations account for expenses of Office of Sergeant at Arms and Doorkeeper of Senate

The Sergeant at Arms and Doorkeeper of the Senate is authorized, with the approval of the Senate Committee on Appropriations, to transfer, during any fiscal year, from the appropriations account, appropriated under the headings "Salaries, Officers and Employees" and "Office of the Sergeant at Arms and Doorkeeper", such sums as he shall specify to the appropriations account, within the contingent fund of the Senate, for expenses of the Office of the Sergeant at Arms and Doorkeeper of the Senate; and any funds so transferred shall be available in like manner and for the same purposes as are other funds in the account to which the funds are transferred.

(Pub. L. 101–520, title I, § 5, Nov. 5, 1990, 104 Stat. 2258.)

CODIFICATION

Section is from the Congressional Operations Appropriations Act, 1991, which is title I of the Legislative Branch Appropriations Act, 1991.

§ 68–7. Senate Office of Public Records Revolving Fund

(a) Establishment

There is established in the Treasury of the United States a revolving fund within the contingent fund of the Senate to be known as the "Senate Office of Public Records Revolving Fund" (hereafter in this section referred to as the "revolving fund").

(b) Source of moneys for deposit in Fund; availability of moneys in Fund

All moneys received on and after October 1, 1989, by the Senate Office of Public Records from fees and other charges for services shall be deposited to the credit of the revolving fund. Moneys in the revolving fund shall be available without fiscal year limitation for disbursement by the Secretary of the Senate for use in connection with the operation of the Senate Office of Public Records, including supplies, equipment, and other expenses.

(c) Vouchers

Disbursements from the revolving fund shall be made upon vouchers approved by the Secretary of the Senate.

(d) Regulations

The Secretary of the Senate is authorized to prescribe such regulations as may be necessary to carry out the provisions of this section.

(e) Transfer of moneys into Fund

To provide capital for the revolving fund, the Secretary of the Senate is authorized to transfer, from moneys appropriated for fiscal year 1990 to the account "Miscellaneous Items" in the contingent fund of the Senate, to the revolving fund such sum as he may determine necessary, not to exceed $30,000.

(Pub. L. 101–163, title I, §13, Nov. 21, 1989, 103 Stat. 1047.)

Section is from the Congressional Operations Appropriations Act, 1990, which is title I of the Legislative Branch Appropriations Act, 1990.

§ 68–8. Vouchering Senate office charges

(a) Senate support office charges

Charges for expenses of any office, the funds of which are disbursed by the Secretary of the Senate, may be vouchered by a Senate support office paying such expenses or to which such charges are owed for goods or services provided, if—

(1) such charges are paid on behalf of the office incurring such expenses by such Senate support office; or

(2) such charges are payable to such Senate support office for goods or services provided by such office to the office incurring such expenses.

(b) Payment charged to official funds

Payments under this section shall be charged to the official funds of the office on whose behalf the expenses were paid, or which received the goods or services for which payment is required.

(c) Certification

Any voucher submitted by a Senate support office pursuant to this section shall be accompanied by a certification from such office of the amount and that such purchases were of the nature that they could be charged to the official funds of the office on whose behalf charges were paid, or to which goods or services were provided.

(d) Regulations

Vouchers under this section shall be submitted and paid subject to such regulations as may be promulgated by the Committee on Rules and Administration.

(Pub. L. 103–69, title I, §1, Aug. 11, 1993, 107 Stat. 695.)

CODIFICATION

Section is from the Congressional Operations Appropriations Act, 1994, which is title I of the Legislative Branch Appropriations Act, 1994.

§ 68a. Materials, supplies, and fuel payments from Senate contingent fund

Payments from the contingent fund of the Senate for materials and supplies (including fuel) purchased on and after July 8, 1935, through the Administrator of General Services shall be made by check upon vouchers approved by the Committee on Rules and Administration of the Senate.

(July 8, 1935, ch. 374, 49 Stat. 463; Aug. 2, 1946, ch. 753, title I, §102, 60 Stat. 814; June 30, 1949, ch. 288, title I, §102(a), 63 Stat. 380.)

AMENDMENTS

1946—Act Aug. 2, 1946, substituted "Committee on Rules and Administration" for "Committee to Audit and Control Contingent Expenses".

CHANGE OF NAME

Effective Jan. 1, 1947, Procurement Division of Treasury Department changed to Bureau of Federal Supply by former regulation §5.7 of subpart A of Part 5 of Title 41, Public Contracts, 11 F.R. 13638, issued by Secretary of the Treasury.

Bureau of Federal Supply and its functions and duties transferred to Administrator of General Services by act June 30, 1949.

EFFECTIVE DATE OF 1946 AMENDMENT

Section 142 of act Aug. 2, 1946, provided that the amendment made by that act is effective Jan. 2, 1947.

§ 68b. Per diem and subsistence expenses from Senate contingent fund

No part of the appropriations made under the heading "Contingent Expenses of the Senate" on and after June 27, 1956 may be expended for per diem and subsistence expenses (as defined in section 5701 of title 5) at rates in excess of the rates prescribed by the Committee on Rules and Administration; except that (1) higher rates may be established by the Committee on Rules and Administration for travel beyond the limits of the continental United States, and (2) in accordance with regulations prescribed by the Committee on Rules and Administration of the Senate, reimbursement for such expenses may be made on an actual expense basis of not to exceed the daily rate prescribed by the Committee on Rules and Administration in the case of travel within the continental limits of the United States. This section shall not apply with respect to per diem or actual travel expenses incurred by Senators and employees in the office of a Senator which are reimbursed under section 58 of this title.

(June 27, 1956, ch. 453, 70 Stat. 360; Pub. L. 87–139, §7, Aug. 14, 1961, 75 Stat. 340; Pub. L. 91–114, §3, Nov. 10, 1969, 83 Stat. 190; Pub. L. 94–22, §8, May 19, 1975, 89 Stat. 86; Pub. L. 95–94, title I, §112(e), Aug. 5, 1977, 91 Stat. 664; Pub. L. 95–355, title I, §103, Sept. 8, 1978, 92 Stat. 533; Pub. L. 96–304, title I, §102(b), July 8, 1980, 94 Stat. 889.)

AMENDMENTS

1980—Pub. L. 96–304 substituted "prescribed by the Committee on Rules and Administration" for "in effect under section 5702 of title 5, for employees of agencies" in two places.

1978—Pub. L. 95–355 substituted provisions relating to applicability of rates under section 5702 of title 5, for employees of agencies, for provisions setting forth specific rates of $35 and $50 per day, respectively, for travel expenses.

1977—Pub. L. 95–94 inserted provisions relating to applicability to per diem or actual travel expenses incurred by a Senator or his employee reimbursed under section 58 of this title.

1975—Pub. L. 94–22 substituted "$35" and "$50" for "$25" and "$40", respectively.

1969—Pub. L. 91–114 increased maximum per diem rate from $16 to $25 and actual expense rate from $30 to $40.

1961—Pub. L. 87–139 increased maximum per diem rate from $12 to $16 and actual expense rate from $25 to $30.

Amendment by Pub. L. 95–94 effective Aug. 5, 1977, see section 112(f) of Pub. L. 95–94, set out as an Effective Date of 1977 Amendment note under section 58 of this title.

§ 68c. Computation of compensation for stenographic assistance of committees payable from Senate contingent fund

Compensation for stenographic assistance of committees paid out of the items under "Contingent Expenses of the Senate" on and after June 27, 1956 shall be computed at such rates and in accordance with such regulations as may be prescribed by the Committee on Rules and Administration, notwithstanding, and without regard to any other provision of law.

(June 27, 1956, ch. 453, 70 Stat. 360.)

§ 68d. Liquidation from appropriations of any unpaid obligations chargeable to rescinded unexpended balances of funds

If at the close of any fiscal year there is an unexpended balance of funds which were appropriated for such year (or for prior fiscal years) and which are subject to disbursement by the Secretary of the Senate for any purpose, then, if such unexpended balance is by law rescinded, any unpaid obligations chargeable to the balance so rescinded (or to appropriations for such purpose for prior years) shall be liquidated from any appropriations for the same general purpose, which, at the time of payment, are available for disbursement.

(Pub. L. 97–257, title I, § 106, Sept. 10, 1982, 96 Stat. 849.)

CODIFICATION

Section is from the Supplemental Appropriations Act, 1982.

§ 68e. Advance payments by Secretary of Senate

(a) Authorization

For fiscal year 1998, and each fiscal year thereafter, the Secretary of the Senate is authorized to make advance payments under a contract or other agreement to provide a service or deliver an article for the United States Government without regard to the provisions of section 3324 of title 31.

(b) Regulations

An advance payment authorized by subsection (a) of this section shall be made in accordance with regulations issued by the Committee on Rules and Administration of the Senate.

(c) Effective date

The authority granted by subsection (a) of this section shall not take effect until regulations are issued pursuant to subsection (b) of this section.

(Pub. L. 105–55, title I, § 1, Oct. 7, 1997, 111 Stat. 1179.)

CODIFICATION

Section is from the Congressional Operations Appropriations Act, 1998, which is title I of the Legislative Branch Appropriations Act, 1998.

§ 69. Expenses of committees payable from Senate contingent fund

When any duty is imposed upon a committee involving expenses that are ordered to be paid out of the contingent fund of the Senate, upon vouchers to be approved by the chairman of the committee charged with such duty, the receipt of such chairman for any sum advanced to him or his order out of said contingent fund by the Secretary of the Senate for committee expenses not involving personal services shall be taken and passed by the accounting officers of the Government as a full and sufficient voucher; but it shall be the duty of such chairman, as soon as practicable, to furnish to the Secretary of the Senate vouchers in detail for the expenses so incurred.

(Mar. 3, 1879, ch. 183, 20 Stat. 419; June 10, 1921, ch. 18, title III, § 304, 42 Stat. 24; June 22, 1949, ch. 235, § 101, 63 Stat. 218.)

AMENDMENTS

1949—Act June 22, 1949, inserted "for committee expenses not involving personal services" after "Secretary of the Senate", and omitted the requirement that the Secretary of the Senate file the vouchers with the General Accounting Office.

TRANSFER OF FUNCTIONS

Act June 10, 1921, transferred powers and duties of Comptroller, six auditors, and certain other officers of the Treasury to General Accounting Office.

§ 69–1. Availability of funds for franked mail expenses

Funds in the account, within the contingent fund of the Senate, available for the expenses of inquiries and investigations shall be available for franked mail expenses incurred by committees of the Senate the other expenses of which are paid from that account.

(Pub. L. 105–55, title I, § 6(b), Oct. 7, 1997, 111 Stat. 1181.)

CODIFICATION

Section is from the Congressional Operations Appropriations Act, 1998, which is title I of the Legislative Branch Appropriations Act, 1998.

EFFECTIVE DATE

Section 6(c) of Pub. L. 105–55 provided that: "This section [enacting this section] is effective for fiscal years beginning on and after October 1, 1997."

§ 69a. Orientation seminars, etc., for new Senators, Senate officials, or members of staffs of Senators or Senate officials; payment of expenses

Effective July 1, 1979, there is authorized an expense allowance for the Office of the Secretary of the Senate and the Office of Sergeant at Arms and Doorkeeper of the Senate which shall not exceed $10,000 each fiscal year for each such office. Payments made under this section shall be reimbursements only for actual expenses (including meals and food-related expenses) incurred in the course of conducting orientation seminars for Senators, Senate officials, or members of the staffs of Senators or Senate officials and other similar meetings, in the Capitol Building or the Senate Office Buildings. Such payments shall be made upon certification and documentation of such expenses by the Secretary and Sergeant at Arms, respectively, and shall be made out of the contingent fund of the Senate upon vouchers signed by the Secretary and the Sergeant at Arms, respectively. Amounts received as reimbursement of such expenses shall not be reported as income, and the expenses so reimbursed shall not be allowed as a deduction, under title 26.

(Pub. L. 96–38, title I, § 107(a), July 25, 1979, 93 Stat. 112; Pub. L. 99–88, title I, § 193, Aug. 15, 1985, 99 Stat. 349; Pub. L. 99–514, § 2, Oct. 22, 1986, 100 Stat. 2095; Pub. L. 100–202, § 101(i) [title I, § 6], Dec. 22, 1987, 101 Stat. 1329–290, 1329–294; Pub. L. 102–392, title I, § 3, Oct. 6, 1992, 106 Stat. 1706.)

CODIFICATION

Section is from the Supplemental Appropriations Act, 1979.

PRIOR PROVISIONS

A prior section 69a, Pub. L. 95–94, title I, § 105, Aug. 5, 1977, 91 Stat. 661, provided for expenditure of $1,000 during any fiscal year to conduct orientation seminars for new Senators and their staffs, prior to repeal effective July 1, 1979, by section 107(b) of Pub. L. 96–38.

AMENDMENTS

1992—Pub. L. 102–392 substituted "$10,000" for "$4,000".
1987—Pub. L. 100–202 substituted "$4,000" for "$2,000".
1986—Pub. L. 99–514 substituted "Internal Revenue Code of 1986" for "Internal Revenue Code of 1954", which for purposes of codification was translated as "title 26" thus requiring no change in text.
1985—Pub. L. 99–88 substituted "Senators, Senate officials, or members of the staffs of Senators or Senate officials" for "Senators and members of their staffs,".

EFFECTIVE DATE OF 1987 AMENDMENT

Section 101(i) [title I, § 6] of Pub. L. 100–202 provided that the amendment made by Pub. L. 100–202 is effective in the case of fiscal years beginning after Sept. 30, 1986.

§ 69b. Senate Leader's Lecture Series

(a) Establishment

There is established the Senate Leader's Lecture Series (hereinafter referred to as the "lecture series"). Expenses incurred in connection with the lecture series shall be paid from the appropriations account "Secretary of the Senate" within the contingent fund of the Senate and shall not exceed $30,000 in any fiscal year.

(b) Expenses covered

Payments for expenses in connection with the lecture series may cover expenses incurred by speakers, including travel, subsistence, and per diem, and the cost of receptions, including food, food related items, and hospitality.

(c) Payments for expenses

Payments for expenses of the lecture series shall be made on vouchers approved by the Secretary of the Senate.

(d) Effective date

This section is effective on and after October 1, 1997.

(Pub. L. 105–275, title I, § 5, Oct. 21, 1998, 112 Stat. 2433.)

CODIFICATION

Section is from the Congressional Operations Appropriations Act, 1999, which is title I of the Legislative Branch Appropriations Act, 1999.

§§ 70 to 72. Omitted

CODIFICATION

Section 70, act July 16, 1914, ch. 141, § 1, 38 Stat. 456, repealed resolutions passed prior to July 1, 1914, authorizing payment for clerical and messenger service.

Section 71, act July 11, 1919, ch. 6, § 1, 41 Stat. 57, was a provision in the Third Deficiency Act of 1919 authorizing Secretary of the Army to transfer to Sergeant at Arms of Senate motor equipment no longer required by the War Department. It is the opinion of the Department of the Army the section was intended to cover only surplus Army material on hand following World War I.

Section 72, acts Mar. 4, 1925, ch. 549, § 1, 43 Stat. 1291; May 13, 1926, ch. 294, § 1, 44 Stat. 542; Feb. 23, 1927, ch. 168, § 1, 44 Stat. 1152; May 14, 1928, ch. 551, § 1, 45 Stat. 522; Feb. 28, 1929, ch. 367, § 1, 45 Stat. 1392; June 6, 1930, ch. 407, § 1, 46 Stat. 509; Feb. 20, 1931, ch. 234, § 1, 46 Stat. 1179; June 30, 1932, ch. 314, § 1, 47 Stat. 387; Feb. 28, 1933, ch. 134, § 1, 47 Stat. 1356, related to Committee employees after termination of Congress, and was limited to the Legislative Branch Appropriation Acts of which it was a part.

§ 72a. Committee staffs

(a) Appointment of professional members; number; qualifications; termination of employment

Each standing committee of the Senate (other than the Committee on Appropriations) is authorized to appoint, by majority vote of the committee, not more than six professional staff members in addition to the clerical staffs. Such professional staff members shall be assigned to the chairman and the ranking minority member of such committee as the committee may deem advisable, except that whenever a majority of the minority members of such committee so request, two of such professional staff members may be selected for appointment by majority vote of the minority members and the committee shall appoint any staff members so selected. A staff member or members appointed pursuant to a request by the minority members of the committee shall be assigned to such committee business as such minority members deem advisable. Services of professional staff members appointed by majority vote of the committee may be terminated by a majority vote of the committee and services of professional staff members appointed pursuant to a request by the minority members of the committee shall be terminated by the committee when a majority of such minority members so request. Professional staff members authorized by this subsection shall be appointed on a permanent basis, without regard to political affiliation, and solely on the basis of fitness to perform the duties of their respective positions. Such professional staff members shall not engage in any work other than committee business and no other duties may be assigned to them.

(b) Professional members for Committee on Appropriations; examinations of executive agencies' operation

Subject to appropriations which it shall be in order to include in appropriation bills, the Committee on Appropriations of each House is authorized to appoint such staff, in addition to the clerk thereof and assistants for the minority, as each such committee, by a majority vote, shall determine to be necessary, such personnel, other than the minority assistants, to possess such qualifications as the committees respectively may prescribe, and the Committee on Appropriations of the House also is authorized to conduct studies and examinations of the organization and operation of any executive agency (including any agency the majority of the stock of which is owned by the Government of the United States) as it may deem necessary to assist it in connection with the determination of matters within its jurisdiction and in accordance with procedures authorized by the committee by a majority vote, including the rights and powers conferred by House Resolution Numbered 50, adopted January 9, 1945.

(c) Clerical employees; appointment; number; duties; termination of employment

The clerical staff of each standing committee of the Senate (other than the Committee on Appropriations), which shall be appointed by a majority vote of the committee, shall consist of not more than six clerks to be attached to the office of the chairman, to the ranking minority member, and to the professional staff, as the committee may deem advisable, except that whenever a majority of the minority members of such committee so requests, one of the members of the clerical staff may be selected for appointment by majority vote of such minority members and the committee shall appoint any staff member so selected. The clerical staff shall handle committee correspondence and stenographic work, both for the committee staff and for the chairman and ranking minority member on matters related to committee work, except that if a member of the clerical staff is appointed pursuant to a request by the minority members of the committee, such clerical staff member shall handle committee correspondence and stenographic work for the minority members of the committee and for any members of the committee staff appointed under subsection (a) of this section pursuant to request by such minority members, on matters related to committee work. Services of clerical staff members appointed by majority vote of the committee may be terminated by majority vote of the committee and services of clerical staff members appointed pursuant to a request by the minority members of the committee shall be terminated by the committee when a majority of such minority members so request.

(d) Recordation of committee hearings, data, etc.; access to records

All committee hearings, records, data, charts, and files shall be kept separate and distinct from the congressional office records of the Member serving as chairman of the committee; and such records shall be the property of the Congress and all members of the committee and the respective Houses shall have access to such records. Each committee is authorized to have printed and bound such testimony and other data presented at hearings held by the committee.

(e) Repealed. Pub. L. 91–510, title IV, § 477(a)(3), Oct. 26, 1970, 84 Stat. 1195

(f) Limitations on appointment of professional members

No committee shall appoint to its staff any experts or other personnel detailed or assigned from any department or agency of the Government, except with the written permission of the Committee on Rules and Administration of the Senate or the Committee on House Oversight of the House of Representatives, as the case may be.

(g) Appointments when no vacancy exists; payment from Senate contingent fund

In any case in which a request for the appointment of a minority staff member under subsection (a) or subsection (c) of this section is made at any time when no vacancy exists to which the appointment requested may be made—

(1) the person appointed pursuant to such a request under subsection (a) of this section may serve in addition to any other professional staff members authorized by such subsection and may be paid from the contingent fund of the Senate until such time as such a vacancy occurs, at which time such person shall be considered to have been appointed to such vacancy; and

(2) the person appointed pursuant to such a request under subsection (c) of this section may serve in addition to any other clerical staff members authorized by such subsection and may be paid, until otherwise provided, from the contingent fund of the Senate.

(h) Salary rates, assignment of facilities, and accessibility of committee records for minority staff appointees

Staff members appointed pursuant to a request by minority members of a committee under subsection (a) or subsection (c) of this section, and staff members appointed to assist minority members of subcommittees pursuant to authority of Senate resolution, shall be accorded equitable treatment with respect to the fixing of salary rates, the assignment of facilities, and the accessibility of committee records.

(i) Consultants for Senate and House standing committees; procurement of temporary or intermittent services; contracts; advertisement requirements inapplicable; selection method; qualifications report to Congressional committees

(1) Each standing committee of the Senate or House of Representatives is authorized, with the approval of the Committee on Rules and Administration in the case of standing committees of the Senate, or the Committee on House Oversight in the case of standing committees of the House of Representatives, within the limits of funds made available from the contingent fund of the Senate or the applicable accounts of the House of Representatives pursuant to resolutions which, in the case of the Senate, shall specify the maximum amounts which may be used for such purpose, approved by the appropriate House, to procure the temporary services (not in excess of one year) or intermittent serv-

ices of individual consultants, or organizations thereof, to make studies or advise the committee with respect to any matter within its jurisdiction or with respect to the administration of the affairs of the committee.

(2) Such services in the case of individuals or organizations may be procured by contract as independent contractors, or in the case of individuals by employment at daily rates of compensation not in excess of the per diem equivalent of the highest gross rate of compensation which may be paid to a regular employee of the committee. Such contracts shall not be subject to the provisions of section 5 of title 41 or any other provision of law requiring advertising.

(3) With respect to the standing committees of the Senate, any such consultant or organization shall be selected by the chairman and ranking minority member of the committee, acting jointly. With respect to the standing committees of the House of Representatives, the standing committee concerned shall select any such consultant or organization. The committee shall submit to the Committee on Rules and Administration in the case of standing committees of the Senate, and the Committee on House Oversight in the case of standing committees of the House of Representatives, information bearing on the qualifications of each consultant whose services are procured pursuant to this subsection, including organizations, and such information shall be retained by that committee and shall be made available for public inspection upon request.

(j) **Specialized training for professional staffs of Senate and House standing committees, Senate Appropriations Committee, Senate Majority and Minority Policy Committees, and joint committees whose funding is disbursed by Secretary of Senate or Chief Administrative Officer of House; assistance: pay, tuition, etc. while training; continued employment agreement; service credit: retirement, life insurance and health insurance**

(1) Each standing committee of the Senate or House of Representatives is authorized, with the approval of the Committee on Rules and Administration in the case of standing committees of the Senate, and the committee involved in the case of standing committees of the House of Representatives, and within the limits of funds made available from the contingent fund of the Senate or the applicable accounts of the House of Representatives pursuant to resolutions, which, in the case of the Senate, shall specify the maximum amounts which may be used for such purpose, approved by the appropriate House, to provide assistance for members of its professional staff in obtaining specialized training, whenever that committee determines that such training will aid the committee in the discharge of its responsibilities. Any joint committee of the Congress whose expenses are paid out of funds disbursed by the Secretary of the Senate or by the Chief Administrative Officer of the House of Representatives, the Committee on Appropriations of the Senate, and the Majority Policy Committee and Minority Policy Committee of the Senate are each authorized to expend, for the purpose of providing assistance in ac-

cordance with paragraphs (2), (3), and (4) of this subsection for members of its staff in obtaining such training, any part of amounts appropriated to that committee.

(2) Such assistance may be in the form of continuance of pay during periods of training or grants of funds to pay tuition, fees, or such other expenses of training, or both, as may be approved by the Committee on Rules and Administration or the Committee on House Administration, as the case may be.

(3) A committee providing assistance under this subsection shall obtain from any employee receiving such assistance such agreement with respect to continued employment with the committee as the committee may deem necessary to assure that it will receive the benefits of such employee's services upon completion of his training.

(4) During any period for which an employee is separated from employment with a committee for the purpose of undergoing training under this subsection, such employee shall be considered to have performed service (in nonpay status) as an employee of the committee at the rate of compensation received immediately prior to commencing such training (including any increases in compensation provided by law during the period of training) for the purposes of—

(A) subchapter III (relating to civil service retirement) of chapter 83 of title 5,

(B) chapter 87 (relating to Federal employees group life insurance) of title 5, and

(C) chapter 89 (relating to Federal employees group health insurance) of title 5.

(Aug. 2, 1946, ch. 753, title II, §202, 60 Stat. 834; July 30, 1947, ch. 361, title I, §101, 61 Stat. 611; Feb. 24, 1949, ch. 8, 63 Stat. 6; Aug. 5, 1955, ch. 568, §12, 69 Stat. 509; Pub. L. 85–462, §4(o), June 20, 1958, 72 Stat. 209; Pub. L. 88–426, title II, §202(j), Aug. 14, 1964, 78 Stat. 414; Pub. L. 91–510, title III, §§301(a)–(c), 303, 304, title IV, §477(a)(3), Oct. 26, 1970, 84 Stat. 1175, 1176, 1179, 1180, 1195; Pub. L. 92–136, §5, Oct. 11, 1971, 85 Stat. 378; Pub. L. 100–458, title III, §312, Oct. 1, 1988, 102 Stat. 2184; Pub. L. 104–186, title II, §204(10), (11), Aug. 20, 1996, 110 Stat. 1731; Pub. L. 105–55, title I, §105(a), Oct. 7, 1997, 111 Stat. 1184.)

PARTIAL REPEAL

Section 2(a) of S. Res. 274, Ninety-sixth Congress, Nov. 14, 1979, provided in part that, until otherwise provided by law or resolution of the Senate, the provisions of subsections (a) through (h) of this section shall not apply to committees of the Senate.

ABOLITION OF ADDITIONAL CLERICAL STAFF POSITIONS

Section 2(d) of Senate Resolution 281, Ninety-sixth Congress, approved March 11, 1980, provided that effective February 28, 1981, the additional clerical staff positions established by subsection (g) of this section (as in effect for committees of the Senate prior to November 14, 1979) are abolished.

CODIFICATION

A former subsec. (k) authorized additional professional staff members and clerical employees for specific

House committees. Committee staffs are now covered by the Rules of the House of Representatives. Former subsec. (k) was based on the following House resolutions which were enacted into permanent law:

Subsec. (k)(1) was based on House Resolution No. 172 of the Eighty-first Congress, which was enacted into permanent law by act June 22, 1949, ch. 235, § 105, 63 Stat. 230, and House Resolution No. 464 of the Eighty-first Congress, which was enacted into permanent law by act Oct. 11, 1951, ch. 485, § 105, 65 Stat. 403.

Subsec. (k)(2) was based on House Resolution No. 37 of the Eighty-second Congress, which was enacted into permanent law by act Oct. 11, 1951, ch. 485, § 105, 65 Stat. 403, House Resolution No. 393 of the Eighty-eighth Congress, which was enacted into permanent law by Pub. L. 88-454, § 103, Aug. 20, 1964, 78 Stat. 550, House Resolution No. 248 of the Eighty-ninth Congress, which was enacted into permanent law by Pub. L. 89-90, § 103, July 27, 1965, 79 Stat. 281, and House Resolution No. 640 of the Eighty-ninth Congress, which was enacted into permanent law by Pub. L. 89-545, § 103, Aug. 27, 1966, 80 Stat. 369.

Subsec. (k)(3) was based on House Resolution No. 554 of the Eighty-third Congress, which was enacted into permanent law by act July 2, 1954, ch. 455, § 103, 68 Stat. 409, House Resolution No. 468 of the Eighty-fourth Congress, which was enacted into permanent law by act June 27, 1956, ch. 453, § 103, 70 Stat. 370, House Resolution No. 126 of the Eighty-fifth Congress, which was enacted into permanent law by Pub. L. 85-75, § 103, July 1, 1957, 71 Stat. 256, House Resolution No. 525 of the Eighty-fifth Congress, which was enacted into permanent law by Pub. L. 85-570, § 103, July 31, 1958, 72 Stat. 453, and House Resolution No. 509 of the Eighty-seventh Congress, which was enacted into permanent law by Pub. L. 87-730, § 103, Oct. 2, 1962, 76 Stat. 693.

Subsec. (k)(4) was based on House Resolution No. 28 of the Eighty-fifth Congress, which was enacted into permanent law by Pub. L. 85-75, § 103, July 1, 1957, 71 Stat. 256, and section 2 of House Resolution No. 348 of the Eighty-seventh Congress, which was enacted into permanent law by Pub. L. 87-730, § 103, Oct. 2, 1962, 76 Stat. 693.

Subsec. (k)(5) was based on House Resolution No. 239 of the Eighty-fifth Congress, which was enacted into permanent law by Pub. L. 85-570, § 103, July 31, 1958, 72 Stat. 453, and House Resolution No. 225 of the Eighty-eighth Congress, which was enacted into permanent law by Pub. L. 88-248, § 103, Dec. 30, 1963, 77 Stat. 817.

AMENDMENTS

1997—Subsec. (j)(1). Pub. L. 105-55 amended directory language of Pub. L. 104-186, § 204(11). See 1996 Amendment note below.

1996—Subsec. (f). Pub. L. 104-186, § 204(10)(A), substituted "House Oversight" for "House Administration".

Subsec. (i)(1). Pub. L. 104-186, § 204(10), substituted "House Oversight" for "House Administration", "contingent fund of the Senate or the applicable accounts of the House of Representatives pursuant to resolutions which, in the case of the Senate," for "contingent funds of the respective Houses pursuant to resolutions, which", and "the appropriate House" for "such respective Houses".

Subsec. (i)(3). Pub. L. 104-186, § 204(10)(A), substituted "House Oversight" for "House Administration".

Subsec. (j)(1). Pub. L. 104-186, § 204(11), as amended by Pub. L. 105-55, § 105(a), substituted "committee involved in the case of standing committees of the House of Representatives, and within the limits of funds made available from the contingent fund of the Senate or the applicable accounts of the House of Representatives pursuant to resolutions, which, in the case of the Senate, shall specify the maximum amounts which may be used for such purpose, approved by the appropriate House" for "Committee on House Administration in the case of standing committees of the House of Representatives, and within the limits of funds made available from the contingent funds of the respective Houses pursuant to

resolutions, which shall specify the maximum amounts which may be used for such purpose, approved by such respective Houses" and "Chief Administrative Officer of the House of Representatives" for "Clerk of the House".

1988—Subsec. (i)(1). Pub. L. 100-458 inserted "or with respect to the administration of the affairs of the committee" before period at end.

1971—Subsec. (g). Pub. L. 92-136, § 5(a), permitted a clerical staff member, appointed at the request of the minority when no vacancy exists on the permanent staff, to continue to serve, in addition to any other clerical staff members authorized, and until otherwise provided, to continue to be paid from the contingent fund of the Senate, thereby eliminating the requirement, in the case of a clerical staff member, that this status continue until such time as a vacancy occurs, at which time such person is considered to be appointed to such vacancy.

Subsec. (j)(1). Pub. L. 92-136, § 5(b), authorized the same training opportunities for professional staff members of the Senate Appropriations Committee, the Senate Majority and Minority Policy Committees and joint committees whose expenses are paid out of funds disbursed by the Secretary of the Senate or the Clerk of the House, as are afforded to professional staff members of standing committees.

1970—Subsec. (a). Pub. L. 91-510, § 301(a), restricted the provisions to standing committees of the Senate, deleting "and the House of Representatives" after "Senate", increased numerical limitation of professional staff members from four to six, provided for appointment of two staff members by majority vote of minority members of a committee whenever majority of minority members so request and assignment of such appointees to such committee business as the minority members deem advisable, and substituted provision for termination of services of staff members appointed by majority vote of the committee and services of members appointed pursuant to request of minority members of the committee by the committee when majority of such minority members so request for prior termination provision by majority vote of the committee.

Subsec. (c). Pub. L. 91-510, § 301(b), inserted "of the Senate (other than the Committee on Appropriations)" after "each standing committee", provided for appointment of one clerical staff member by majority vote of minority members of a committee whenever majority of minority members so request and handling by such appointee of committee correspondence and stenographic work for minority members of the committee and for any members of the committee staff appointed under subsec. (a) of this section pursuant to request by the minority members, on matters related to committee work, and for termination of services of clerical staff members appointed by majority vote of the committee and services of members appointed pursuant to request of minority members of the committee by the committee when majority of such minority members so request.

Subsec. (e). Pub. L. 91-510, § 477(a)(3), repealed provisions prescribing basic annual compensation of professional staff members and clerical staff members of standing committees and limiting such compensation, together with additional compensation authorized by law, to maximum amount authorized by Classification Act of 1949.

Subsec. (g). Pub. L. 91-510, § 301(c), added subsec. (g). Former provisions, declaring any individual employed as a professional staff member of any committee as provided in this section ineligible for appointment to any office or position in executive branch of Government for period of one year after he shall have ceased to be such a member, were repealed by act Feb. 24, 1949, ch. 8, 63 Stat. 6.

Subsec. (h). Pub. L. 91-510, § 301(c), added subsec. (h) and struck out former provisions which related to employees of House and Senate Appropriation Committees through fiscal year 1947, all other committee employees through Jan. 31, 1947, and appropriations for compensation of committee employees as contained in Legislative Branch Appropriation Act, 1947, act July 1, 1946, ch. 530, 60 Stat. 386.

Subsec. (i). Pub. L. 91–510, § 303, added subsec. (i).

Subsec. (j). Pub. L. 91–510, § 304, added subsec. (j).

1964—Subsec. (e). Pub. L. 88–426 increased maximum basic annual compensation to professional staff members and clerical staff from $8,880 to highest amount which, together with additional compensation authorized by law, will not exceed maximum rate authorized by Classification Act of 1949, as amended.

1958—Subsec. (e). Pub. L. 85–462 substituted "$8,880" for "$8,820" in two places.

1955—Subsec. (e). Act Aug. 5, 1955, increased maximum basic annual compensation of professional staff and clerical staff from $8,000 to $8,820.

1949—Subsec. (g). Act Feb. 24, 1949, repealed subsec. (g).

1947—Subsec. (e). Act July 30, 1947, omitted figure $2,000 as lowest salary to be paid clerks.

CHANGE OF NAME

Committee on House Oversight of House of Representatives changed to Committee on House Administration of House of Representatives by House Resolution No. 5, One Hundred Sixth Congress, Jan. 6, 1999.

EFFECTIVE DATE OF 1997 AMENDMENT

Section 105(b) of Pub. L. 105–55 provided that: "The amendment made by subsection (a) [amending this section] shall take effect as of August 20, 1996."

EFFECTIVE DATE OF 1971 AMENDMENT

Amendment by Pub. L. 92–136 effective as of noon on Jan. 3, 1971, see section 9(a) of Pub. L. 92–136, set out as a note under section 190d of this title.

EFFECTIVE DATE OF 1970 AMENDMENT

Section 601 of Pub. L. 91–510 provided that:

"The foregoing provisions of this Act [see Short Title note below] shall take effect as follows:

"(1) Title I [enacting sections 190a–1 and 190a–2 and amending sections 190a, 190a–1, 190b to 190d, and 190f of this title], title II (except part 2 thereof) [enacting sections 190h to 190k of this title and chapter 22 of former Title 31, Money and Finance, and repealing section 190e of this title], title III (except section 203(d)(2), (d)(3), and (i) of the Legislative Reorganization Act of 1946, as amended by section 321 of this Act, and section 105(e) and (f) of the Legislative Branch Appropriation Act, 1968, as amended by section 305 of this Act) [enacting sections 28 and 29 of this title, amending sections 72a(a), (c), (g) to (j), and 166 of this title, enacting provisions set out as notes under this section and repealing provisions set out as a note under section 60a of this title], and title IV, of this Act [enacting chapters 10A and 13 and sections 60–1 and 88b–1 of this title and sections 166b–1a to 166b–1f, 184a, 193m–1, and 851 of Title 40, Public Buildings, Property, and Works, amending section 198 of this title and sections 2107, 5533, and 8332 of Title 5, Government Organization and Employees, repealing sections 60g, 60g–1, 72a(e), and 88c of this title and section 1106 of Title 8, Aliens and Nationality, and enacting provisions set out as notes under sections 88b–1 and 331 of this title, section 1106 of Title 8, and 166 and 851 of Title 40] shall become effective immediately prior to noon on January 3, 1971.

"(2) Part 2 of title II [amending section 11 of former Title 31] shall be effective with respect to fiscal years beginning on or after July 1, 1972.

"(3) Section 203(d)(2) and (3) of the Legislative Reorganization Act of 1946, as amended by section 321 of this Act [section 166(d)(2) and (3) of this title], shall become effective at the close of the first session of the Ninety-second Congress.

"(4) Section 203(i) of the Legislative Reorganization Act of 1946, as amended by section 321 of this Act [section 166(i) of this title], shall be effective with respect to fiscal years beginning on or after July 1, 1970.

"(5) Title V of this Act [sections 281 to 281b and 282 to 282e of this title] shall become effective on the date of enactment of this Act [Oct. 26, 1970].

"(6) Section 105(e) and (f) of the Legislative Branch Appropriation Act, 1968, as amended by section 305 of this Act [section 61–1(e) and (f) of this title] shall become effective on January 1, 1971."

EFFECTIVE DATE OF 1964 AMENDMENT

Amendment by Pub. L. 88–426 effective first day of first pay period which begins on or after July 1, 1964, except to the extent provided in section 501(c) of Pub. L. 88–426, see section 501 of Pub. L. 88–426.

EFFECTIVE DATE OF 1958 AMENDMENT

Amendment by Pub. L. 85–462 effective first day of first pay period which began on or after January 1, 1958, see section 17(a) of Pub. L. 85–462.

EFFECTIVE DATE OF 1955 AMENDMENT

Amendment by act Aug. 5, 1955, effective Aug. 1, 1955, see section 14 of that act.

EFFECTIVE DATE

Section 245 of title II of act Aug. 2, 1946, provided that: "This title [see Tables for classification] shall take effect on the date of its enactment [Aug. 2, 1946]; except that sections 202(a), (b), (c), (e), (f), and (h), 222, 223, 224, and 243 shall take effect on the day on which the Eightieth Congress convenes [Jan. 3, 1947]."

SHORT TITLE

Section 1 of Pub. L. 91–510 provided that Pub. L. 91–510 [enacting sections 28, 29, 60–1, 88b–1, 190a–1, 190a–2, 190h to 190k, 281 to 281b, 282 to 282e, 331 to 336, and 411 to 417 of this title, sections 1151 to 1157 and 1171 to 1176 of former Title 31, Money and Finance, and sections 166b–1a to 166b–1f, 184a, 193m–1, and 851 of Title 40, Public Buildings, Property, and Works, amending sections 61–1, 72a, 166, 190a, 190a–1, 190b to 190d, 190f, and 198 of this title, sections 2107, 5533, and 8332 of Title 5, Government Organization and Employees, and section 11 of former Title 31, repealing sections 60g, 60g–1, 88c, and 190e of this title and section 1106 of Title 8, Aliens and Nationality, enacting provisions set out as notes under sections 72a, 88b–1, 281, and 331 of this title and section 166 of Title 40, repealing provisions set out as a note under section 60a of this title, and abolishing Joint Committee on Immigration and Nationality established by former section 1106(a) of Title 8] may be cited as the "Legislative Reorganization Act of 1970."

Section 1(a) of act Aug. 2, 1946, provided that act Aug. 2, 1946 [enacting sections 72a, 72b–1, 74b, 75a–1, 88a, 132a, 132b, 145a, 166, 190 to 190a–2, 190b to 190f, 190g, 198, and 261 to 270 of this title, and sections 191a and 275 of former Title 5, Executive Departments and Government Officers and Employees, sections 1022(a) and 1024(b)(3) of Title 15, Commerce and Trade, sections 59 and 60 of former Title 31, Money and Finance, sections 525, 526, 527 to 533 of Title 33, Navigation and Navigable Waters, section 174d–1 of Title 40, Public Buildings, Property, and Works, and sections 1, 182c, and 402 of former Title 44, Public Printing and Documents], may be cited as the "Legislative Reorganization Act of 1946."

TRAVEL FOR STUDIES AND EXAMINATIONS OF EXECUTIVE AGENCIES

Pub. L. 104–53, title I, § 105, Nov. 19, 1995, 109 Stat. 521, provided that:

"(a) Notwithstanding any other provision of law, or any rule, regulation, or other authority, travel for studies and examinations under section 202(b) of the Legislative Reorganization Act of 1946 (2 U.S.C. 72a(b)) shall be governed by applicable laws or regulations of the House of Representatives or as promulgated from time to time by the Chairman of the Committee on Appropriations of the House of Representatives.

"(b) Subsection (a) shall take effect on the date of the enactment of this Act [Nov. 19, 1995] and shall apply to travel performed on or after that date."

OVERTIME PAY FOR FBI EMPLOYEES DETAILED TO HOUSE COMMITTEE ON APPROPRIATIONS

Pub. L. 103–283, title I, July 22, 1994, 108 Stat. 1430, provided in part: "That the Federal Bureau of Investigation, notwithstanding any other provision of law, may in any fiscal year pay all administrative uncontrollable overtime accrued by its employees while on detail to the Committee on Appropriations."

STAFF MEMBERS; REDUCTION IN NUMBER; SELECTION FOR MINORITY MEMBERS

Section 301(d) of Pub. L. 91–510 provided that: "Nothing in the amendments made by subsections (a) and (b) of this section [amending this section] shall be construed—

"(1) to require a reduction in—

"(A) the number of staff members authorized, prior to January 1, 1971, to be employed by any committee of the Senate, by statute or by annual or permanent resolution, or

"(B) the number of such staff members on such date assigned to, or authorized to be selected for appointment by or with the approval of, the minority members of any such committee; or

"(2) to authorize the selection for appointment of staff members by the minority members of a committee in any case in which two or more professional staff members or one or more clerical staff members, as the case may be, who are satisfactory to a majority of such minority members, are otherwise assigned to assist such minority members."

PROFESSIONAL STAFFS; INCREASE IN NUMBER

Section 301(e) of Pub. L. 91–510 provided that: "The additional professional staff members authorized to be employed by a committee by the amendment made by subsection (a) of this section [amending this section] shall be in addition to any other additional staff members authorized, prior to January 1, 1971, to be employed by any such committee."

INCREASES IN COMPENSATION

Increases in compensation for Senate and House officers and employees under authority of Federal Salary Act of 1967 (Pub. L. 90–206), Federal Pay Comparability Act of 1970 (Pub. L. 91–656), and Legislative Branch Appropriations Act, 1988 (Pub. L. 100–202), see sections 60a–1, 60a–2, and 60a–2a of this title, Salary Directives of President pro tempore of the Senate set out as notes under section 60a–1 of this title, and Salary Directives of Speaker of the House set out as notes under sections 60a–2 and 60a–2a of this title.

REORGANIZATION OF COMMITTEES AND PERSONNEL

Sections 102 and 121 of act Aug. 2, 1946, in amending Rule XXV of the Standing Rules of the Senate, and Rules X and XI of the Rules of the House of Representatives, reorganized the standing committees in the two Houses, and re-defined the jurisdiction of each such committee. The number of standing committees of the Senate was reduced from 33 to 13, and the number of such committees in the House of Representatives was reduced from 48 to 19. Section 142 of act Aug. 2, 1946, provided that sections 102 and 121 thereof should take effect on Jan. 2, 1947. For provisions of act Aug. 2, 1946, relating to appointment and compensation of clerical staffs of the revised committees and other personnel thereof, and retention of employees of existing committees, see this section and section 74a of this title.

OFFICE OF SENATE SECURITY

S. Res. 243, One Hundredth Congress, July 1, 1987, provided: "That (a) there is established, within the Office of the Secretary of the Senate (hereinafter referred to as the 'Secretary'), the Office of Senate Security (hereinafter referred to as the 'Office'), which shall be headed by a Director of Senate Security (hereinafter referred to as the 'Director'). The Office shall be under the policy direction of the Majority and Minority Leaders of the Senate, and shall be under the administrative direction and supervision of the Secretary.

"(b)(1) The Director shall be appointed by the Secretary after consultation with the Majority and Minority Leaders. The Secretary shall fix the compensation of the Director. Any appointment under this subsection shall be made solely on the basis of fitness to perform the duties of the position and without regard to political affiliation.

"(2) The Director, with the approval of the Secretary, and after consultation with the Chairman and Ranking Member of the Committee on Rules and Administration of the Senate, may establish such policies and procedures as may be necessary to carry out the provisions of this resolution. Commencing one year from the effective date of this resolution, the Director shall submit an annual report to the Majority and Minority Leaders and the Chairman and Ranking Member of the Committee on Rules and Administration on the status of security matters and the handling of classified information in the Senate, and the progress of the Office in achieving the mandates of this resolution.

"SEC. 2. (a) The Secretary shall appoint and fix the compensation of such personnel as may be necessary to carry out the provisions of this resolution. The Director, with the approval of the Secretary, shall prescribe the duties and responsibilities of such personnel. If a Director is not appointed, the Office shall be headed by an Acting Director. The Secretary shall appoint and fix the compensation of the Acting Director.

"(b) The Majority and Minority Leaders of the Senate may each designate a Majority staff assistant and a Minority staff assistant to serve as their liaisons to the Office. Upon such designation, the Secretary shall appoint and fix the compensation of the Majority and Minority liaison assistants.

"SEC. 3. (a) The Office is authorized, and shall have the responsibility, to develop, establish, and carry out policies and procedures with respect to such matters as:

"(1) the receipt, control, transmission, storage, destruction or other handling of classified information addressed to the United States Senate, the President of the Senate, or Members and employees of the Senate;

"(2) the processing of security clearance requests and renewals for officers and employees of the Senate;

"(3) establishing and maintaining a current and centralized record of security clearances held by officers and employees of the Senate, and developing recommendations for reducing the number of clearances held by such employees;

"(4) consulting and presenting briefings on security matters and the handling of classified information for the benefit of Members and employees of the Senate;

"(5) maintaining an active liaison on behalf of the Senate, or any committee thereof, with all departments and agencies of the United States on security matters; and

"(6) conducting periodic review of the practices and procedures employed by all offices of the Senate for the handling of classified information.

"(b) Within 180 days after the Director takes office, he shall develop, after consultation with the Secretary, a Senate Security Manual, to be printed and distributed to all Senate offices. The Senate Security Manual will prescribe the policies and procedures of the Office, and set forth regulations for all other Senate offices for the handling of classified information.

"(c) Within 90 days after taking office, the Director shall conduct a survey to determine the number of officers and employees of the Senate that have security clearances and report the findings of the survey to the

Majority and Minority Leaders and Secretary of the Senate together with recommendations regarding the feasibility of reducing the number of employees with such clearances.

"(d) The Office shall have authority—

"(1) to provide appropriate facilities in the United States Capitol for hearings of committees of the Senate at which restricted data or other classified information is to be presented or discussed;

"(2) to establish and operate a central repository in the United States Capitol for the safeguarding of classified information for which the Office is responsible; which shall include the classified records, transcripts, and materials of all closed sessions of the Senate; and

"(3) to administer and maintain oaths of secrecy under paragraph (2) of rule XXIX of the Standing Rules of the Senate and to establish such procedures as may be necessary to implement the provisions of such paragraph.

"Sec. 4. Funds appropriated for the fiscal year 1987 which would be available to carry out the purposes of the Interim Office of Senate Security but for the termination of such Office shall be available for the Office of Senate Security.

"Sec. 5. (a) All records, documents, data, materials, rooms, and facilities in the custody of the Interim Office of Senate Security at the time of its termination on July 10, 1987, are transferred to the Office established by subsection (a) of the first section of this resolution.

"(b) This resolution shall take effect on July 11, 1987."

S. Res. 229, One Hundredth Congress, June 5, 1987, established within the Office of the Secretary of the Senate an Interim Office of Senate Security with the same duties, functions, personnel, rooms, and facilities as the former Office of Classified National Security Information.

OFFICE OF CLASSIFIED NATIONAL SECURITY INFORMATION

Pub. L. 95–391, title I, § 105, Sept. 30, 1978, 92 Stat. 772, as amended by Pub. L. 97–51, § 115, Oct. 1, 1981, 95 Stat. 963, eff. Oct. 1, 1981; Pub. L. 99–492, § 2(a), Oct. 16, 1986, 100 Stat. 1240; Pub. L. 100–18, § 1(a), Apr. 3, 1987, 101 Stat. 262, established for the period beginning on Oct. 1, 1981, and ending on June 5, 1987, within the Office of the Secretary of the Senate, the Office of Classified National Security Information under the policy direction of the Majority Leader, the Minority Leader, and the chairman of the committee on Rules and Administration of the Senate, and under the administrative direction and supervision of the Secretary of the Senate with the responsibility for safeguarding such restricted data and such other classified information as any committee of the Senate may from time to time assign to it.

AUTHORIZATION OF APPROPRIATIONS

Section 244 of act Aug. 2, 1946, provided in part: "All necessary funds required to carry out the provisions of this Act [see Short Title note above for classification], by the Secretary of the Senate and the Clerk of the House, are hereby authorized to be appropriated."

SECTION REFERRED TO IN OTHER SECTIONS

This section is referred to in sections 72d, 288, 442 of this title.

§§ 72a–1, 72a–1a. Repealed. Pub. L. 90–57, § 105(i)(4), (5), July 28, 1967, 81 Stat. 144

Section 72a–1, acts Feb. 19, 1947, ch. 4, 61 Stat. 5; June 14, 1948, ch. 467, 62 Stat. 423, provided for compensation of clerical employees of Senate standing committees. See section 61–1(e) of this title.

Section 72a–1a, acts Aug. 5, 1955, ch. 568, § 1, 69 Stat. 505; June 20, 1958, Pub. L. 85–462, § 4(h), 72 Stat. 208; Aug. 27, 1966, Pub. L. 89–545, 80 Stat. 357, limited compensa-

tion of committee staff employees. See section 61–1(e) of this title.

EFFECTIVE DATE OF REPEAL

Repeal effective Aug. 1, 1967, see section 105(k) of Pub. L. 90–57, set out as an Effective Date note under section 61–1 of this title.

§ 72a–1b. Approval of employment and compensation of committee employees by House standing committees

Standing committees of the House shall have authority to approve the employment and compensation of committee employees (other than special and select committee employees) from the effective date of the beginning of each Congress, or such subsequent date as their service commenced.

(Pub. L. 87–130, § 103, Aug. 10, 1961, 75 Stat. 334.)

CODIFICATION

Section is based on House Resolution No. 16, Eighty-seventh Congress, Jan. 3, 1961, which was enacted into permanent law by Pub. L. 87–130.

INCREASES IN COMPENSATION

Increases in compensation for House officers and employees under authority of Federal Salary Act of 1967 (Pub. L. 90–206), Federal Pay Comparability Act of 1970 (Pub. L. 91–656), and Legislative Branch Appropriations Act, 1988 (Pub. L. 100–202), see sections 60a–2 and 60a–2a of this title, and Salary Directives of Speaker of the House, set out as notes under those sections.

§ 72a–1c. Repealed. Pub. L. 95–26, title I, § 106(f), May 4, 1977, 91 Stat. 84

Section, Pub. L. 94–59, title I, § 108, July 25, 1975, 89 Stat. 276; Pub. L. 94–440, title I, § 102, Oct. 1, 1976, 90 Stat. 1443, authorized Senators to hire staff assistance in connection with their committee memberships. See section 72a–1e of this title.

EFFECTIVE DATE OF REPEAL

Section 106(g)(1) of Pub. L. 95–26, title I, May 4, 1977, 91 Stat. 84, which provided that the repeal is effective Mar. 1, 1977, was repealed by Pub. L. 95–94, title I, § 111(e)(1), Aug. 5, 1977, 91 Stat. 663.

§ 72a–1d. Repealed. Pub. L. 95–94, title I, § 111(e)(1), Aug. 5, 1977, 91 Stat. 663

Section, Pub. L. 95–26, title I, § 106(a)–(e), May 4, 1977, 91 Stat. 83, 84, authorized Senators to employ individuals to assist with committee memberships of Senators and set forth compensation limitations and procedures applicable for employment of such individuals. See section 72a–1e of this title and section 111(a), (b) of Pub. L. 95–94, set out as a note under section 61–1 of this title for related provisions.

EFFECTIVE DATE OF REPEAL

Repeal effective Oct. 1, 1977, see section 111(f) of Pub. L. 95–94, set out as an Effective Date note under section 72a–1e of this title.

EFFECTIVE DATE AND SAVINGS PROVISIONS

Section 106(g) of Pub. L. 95–26, title I, May 4, 1977, 91 Stat. 84, provided that this section is effective Mar. 1, 1977, and set forth savings provisions relating to designations and availability of amounts for employees covered by section 72a–1d of this title, and was repealed by section 111(e)(1) of Pub. L. 95–94, title I, Aug. 5, 1977, 91 Stat. 663.

§ 72a–1e. Assistance to Senators with committee memberships by employees in office of Senator

(1) Designation

A Senator may designate employees in his office to assist him in connection with his membership on committees of the Senate. An employee may be designated with respect to only one committee.

(2) Certification; professional staff privileges

An employee designated by a Senator under this section shall be certified by him to the chairman and ranking minority member of the committee with respect to which such designation is made. Such employee shall be accorded all privileges of a professional staff member (whether permanent or investigatory) of such committee including access to all committee sessions and files, except that any such committee may restrict access to its sessions to one staff member per Senator at a time and require, if classified material is being handled or discussed, that any staff member possess the appropriate security clearance before being allowed access to such material or to discussion of it. Nothing contained in this paragraph shall be construed to prohibit a committee from adopting policies and practices with respect to the application of this section which are similar to the policies and practices adopted with respect to the application of section 705(c)(1)[1] of Senate Resolution 4, 95th Congress, and section 72a–1d(c)(1)[1] of this title.

(3) Termination

A Senator shall notify the chairman and ranking minority member of a committee whenever a designation of an employee under this section with respect to such committee is terminated.

(Pub. L. 95–94, title I, §111(c), Aug. 5, 1977, 91 Stat. 662.)

REFERENCES IN TEXT

Section 705(c)(1) of Senate Resolution 4, 95th Congress, referred to in par. (2), which was not classified to the Code, was repealed by Pub. L. 95–94, title I, §111(e)(2), Aug. 5, 1977, 91 Stat. 663.

Section 72a–1d(c)(1) of this title, referred to in par. (2), was repealed by Pub. L. 95–94, title I, §111(e)(1), Aug. 5, 1977, 91 Stat. 663.

CODIFICATION

Section is from the Congressional Operations Appropriation Act, 1978, which is title I of the Legislative Branch Appropriation Act, 1978.

EFFECTIVE DATE

Section 111(f) of Pub. L. 95–94 provided that: "This section, and the amendments made by subsection (d) and the repeals made by subsection (e) [enacting this section, amending section 61–1 of this title, enacting notes set out under section 61–1 of this title, and repealing notes set out under section 72a–1d of this title], shall take effect on October 1, 1977."

---

[1] See References in Text note below.

§ 72a–1f. Designation by Senator who is Chairman or Vice Chairman of Senate Select Committee on Ethics of employee in office of that Senator to perform part-time service for Committee; amount reimbursable; procedure applicable

Notwithstanding any other provisions of law, a Senator who is the Chairman or Vice Chairman of the Senate Select Committee on Ethics may designate one employee employed in his Senate office to perform part-time service for such Committee, and such Committee shall reimburse such Senator for such employee's services for the Committee by transferring from the contingent fund of the Senate, upon vouchers approved by the Chairman of such Committee, to such Senator's Administrative, Clerical, and Legislative Assistance Allowance, with respect to each pay period of such employee, an amount which bears the same ratio to such employee's salary (but not more than one-half of such salary) for such period, as the portion of the time spent (or to be spent) by such employee in performing services for such Committee during such period bears to the total time for which such employee worked (or will work) during such period (as determined by the Chairman of such Committee) for such Committee and in such Senator's office. Any funds transferred under authority of the preceding sentence to a Senator's Administrative, Clerical, and Legislative Assistance[1] shall be available for the same purposes and in like manner as funds therein which were not transferred thereto under such authority. For purposes of any law of the United States, a State, a territory, or a political subdivision thereof, an employee designated by a Senator pursuant to this section shall be considered to be an employee of such Senator's Senate office and not an employee of the Senate Select Committee on Ethics.

(Pub. L. 98–367, title I, §10, July 17, 1984, 98 Stat. 476.)

CODIFICATION

Section is from the Congressional Operations Appropriation Act, 1985, which is title I of the Legislative Branch Appropriations Act, 1985.

§ 72a–1g. Referral of ethics violations by Senate Ethics Committee to General Accounting Office for investigation

If the Committee on Ethics of the Senate determines that there is a reasonable basis to believe that a Member, officer, or employee of the Senate may have committed an ethics violation, the committee may request the Office of Special Investigations of the General Accounting Office to conduct factfinding and an investigation into the matter. The Office of Special Investigations shall promptly investigate the matter as directed by the committee.

(Pub. L. 101–194, title V, §501, Nov. 30, 1989, 103 Stat. 1753.)

---

[1] So in original. Probably should be "Assistance Allowance".

§§ 72a–2, 72a–3. Omitted

Section 72a–2, acts July 20, 1951, ch. 237, §§ 1–3, 65 Stat. 123; Aug. 5, 1955, ch. 568, §§ 1, 8, 69 Stat. 501, 509; Feb. 14, 1956, ch. 34, Ch. IV, 70 Stat. 13; June 27, 1956, ch. 453, 70 Stat. 357; July 28, 1967, Pub. L. 90–57, § 103, 81 Stat. 141; Aug. 18, 1970, Pub. L. 91–382, § 103, 84 Stat. 825, prescribed basic compensation of employees of House and Senate press, periodical, and radio galleries, and was omitted for lack of general applicability.

Section 72a–3, Pub. L. 91–382, Aug. 18, 1970, 84 Stat. 814, which related to computation of salaries and wages paid out of House appropriation items, was from the Legislative Branch Appropriation Act, 1971, and was not repeated in subsequent appropriation acts. See section 331 et seq. of this title. Similar provisions were contained in the following prior appropriation acts:

Pub. L. 91–145, Dec. 12, 1969, 83 Stat. 347.
Pub. L. 90–417, July 23, 1968, 82 Stat. 404.
Pub. L. 90–57, July 28, 1967, 81 Stat. 133.
Pub. L. 89–545, Aug. 27, 1966, 80 Stat. 361.
Pub. L. 89–90, July 27, 1965, 79 Stat. 273.
Pub. L. 88–454, Aug. 20, 1964, 78 Stat. 542.
Pub. L. 88–248, Dec. 30, 1963, 77 Stat. 809.
Pub. L. 87–730, Oct. 2, 1962, 76 Stat. 686.
Pub. L. 87–130, Aug. 10, 1961, 75 Stat. 327.
Pub. L. 86–628, July 12, 1960, 74 Stat. 453.
Pub. L. 86–176, Aug. 21, 1959, 73 Stat. 405.
Pub. L. 85–570, July 31, 1958, 72 Stat. 446.
Pub. L. 85–75, July 1, 1957, 71 Stat. 249.
June 27, 1956, ch. 453, 70 Stat. 363.
Aug. 5, 1955, ch. 568, 69 Stat. 513.
July 2, 1954, ch. 455, title I, 68 Stat. 403.

§ 72a–4. Repealed. Pub. L. 90–57, § 105(i)(1), July 28, 1967, 81 Stat. 144

Section, Pub. L. 85–75, July 1, 1957, 71 Stat. 246, provided for computation of salaries and wages paid out of Senate contingent-expense items. See section 61–1(b), (c) of this title.

Repeal effective Aug. 1, 1967, see section 105(k) of Pub. L. 90–57, set out as an Effective Date note under section 61–1 of this title.

§ 72b. Regulations governing availability of appropriations for House committee employees

Appropriations for committee employees shall be available in such amounts and under such regulations as may be approved by the Committee on House Oversight for compensation of employees of the standing committees of the House of Representatives, except the Committee on Appropriations.

(July 17, 1947, ch. 262, 61 Stat. 367; Pub. L. 104–186, title II, § 204(12), Aug. 20, 1996, 110 Stat. 1731.)

1996—Pub. L. 104–186 substituted "House Oversight" for "House Administration".

Committee on House Oversight of House of Representatives changed to Committee on House Administration of House of Representatives by House Resolution No. 5, One Hundred Sixth Congress, Jan. 6, 1999.

§ 72b–1. Omitted

Section, act Aug. 2, 1946, ch. 753, title I, § 134(b), 60 Stat. 832, related to reports of committees and subcommittees of the Senate and House of Representatives on employed personnel. See section 72c of this title and the Standing Rules of the Senate. Section 2(a) of Senate Resolution No. 274, Ninety-sixth Congress, Nov. 14, 1979, provided in part that this section, insofar as it relates to the Senate, is repealed.

§ 72c. Repealed. Pub. L. 104–186, title II, § 204(13), Aug. 20, 1996, 110 Stat. 1732

Section, act July 17, 1947, ch. 262, 61 Stat. 367, related to House committee reports on employed personnel.

§ 72d. Discretionary authority of Senate Committee on Appropriations

(a) In general

The Committee on Appropriations is authorized in its discretion—

(1) to hold hearings, report such hearings, and make investigations as authorized by paragraph 1 of rule XXVI of the Standing Rules of the Senate;

(2) to make expenditures from the contingent fund of the Senate;

(3) to employ personnel;

(4) with the prior consent of the Government department or agency concerned and the Committee on Rules and Administration to use, on a reimbursable or nonreimbursable basis, the services of personnel of any such department or agency;

(5) to procure the services of individual consultants, or organizations thereof (as authorized by section 72a(i) of this title and Senate Resolution 140, agreed to May 14, 1975); and

(6) to provide for the training of the professional staff of such committee (under procedures specified by section 72a(j) of this title).

(b) Omitted

(c) Effective date

This section shall be effective on and after October 1, 1998, or the date of enactment of this Act [October 21, 1998], whichever is later.

(Pub. L. 105–275, title I, § 10, Oct. 21, 1998, 112 Stat. 2435.)

Senate Resolution 140, agreed to May 14, 1975, referred to in subsec. (a)(5), is Senate Resolution 140, 94th Congress, which is not classified to the Code.

Section is comprised of section 10 of Pub. L. 105–275. Subsec. (b) of section 10 of Pub. L. 105–275 amended section 4 of Senate Resolution 54, 105th Congress, which is not classified to the Code.

Section is from the Congressional Operations Appropriations Act, 1999, which is title I of the Legislative Branch Appropriations Act, 1999.

§ 72d–1. Transfer of funds by Chairman of Senate Committee on Appropriations

(a) In general

(1) The Chairman of the Appropriations Committee of the Senate may, during any fiscal year, at his or her election transfer funds from the appropriation account for salaries for the Appropriations Committee of the Senate, to the account, within the contingent fund of the Senate, from which expenses are payable for such committee.

(2) The Chairman of the Appropriations Committee of the Senate may, during any fiscal year, at his or her election transfer funds from the appropriation account for expenses, within the contingent fund of the Senate, for the Appropriations Committee of the Senate, to the account from which salaries are payable for such committee.

(b) Availability of funds; times of transfer

Any funds transferred under this section shall be—

(1) available for expenditure by such committee in like manner and for the same purposes as are other moneys which are available for expenditure by such committee from the account to which the funds were transferred; and

(2) made at such time or times as the Chairman shall specify in writing to the Senate Disbursing Office.

(c) Effective date

This section shall take effect on October 1, 1998, and shall be effective with respect to fiscal years beginning on or after that date.

(Pub. L. 105–275, title I, § 11, Oct. 21, 1998, 112 Stat. 2435.)

CODIFICATION

Section is from the Congressional Operations Appropriations Act, 1999, which is title I of the Legislative Branch Appropriations Act, 1999.

§§ 73, 74. Omitted

CODIFICATION

Section 73, act Mar. 4, 1925, ch. 549, § 1, 43 Stat. 1292, related to clerk hire for Ways and Means Committee. See section 72a(c) of this title and Rules of House of Representatives.

Section 74, acts Mar. 3, 1893, No. 21, 27 Stat. 757; July 16, 1914, ch. 141, §§ 1, 6, 38 Stat. 454, 509; Mar. 4, 1915, ch. 141, §§ 1, 6, 38 Stat. 997, 1049; June 7, 1924, ch. 303, § 1, 43 Stat. 581, and Mar. 4, 1925, ch. 549, § 1, 43 Stat. 1286, related to clerk hire. See section 72a of this title.

REPEALS

R.S. § 53 and act May 24, 1924, ch. 183, § 1, 43 Stat. 149, formerly cited as a credit to section 74, were repealed by act Mar. 3, 1933, ch. 202, § 1, 47 Stat. 1428, and act June 20, 1929, ch. 33, § 6, 46 Stat. 39, respectively.

§ 74–1. Personal services in office of Speaker; payments

There shall be paid from the applicable accounts of the House of Representatives until otherwise provided by law, for personal services in the office of the Speaker of the House, an additional basic sum of $10,000 per annum.

(Pub. L. 87–730, § 103, Oct. 2, 1962, 76 Stat. 693; Pub. L. 104–186, title II, § 204(14), Aug. 20, 1996, 110 Stat. 1732.)

CODIFICATION

Section is based on House Resolution No. 487, Eighty-seventh Congress, Jan. 10, 1962, which was enacted into permanent law by Pub. L. 87–730.

AMENDMENTS

1996—Pub. L. 104–186 substituted "applicable accounts of the House of Representatives" for "contingent fund of the House".

§ 74–2. Omitted

Section, Pub. L. 88–248, § 103, Dec. 30, 1963, 77 Stat. 817; Pub. L. 89–90, § 103, July 27, 1965, 79 Stat. 81; Pub. L. 90–417, § 103, July 23, 1968, 82 Stat. 413, was based on House Resolutions No. 603, Apr. 16, 1962, and No. 685, Apr. 14, 1964, related to messengers in Office of Speaker, and was omitted for lack of general applicability.

§ 74a. Employment of administrative assistants for Speaker and House Majority and Minority Leaders; compensation; appropriations

The Speaker, the majority leader, and the minority leader of the House of Representatives are each authorized to employ an administrative assistant, who shall receive basic compensation at a rate not to exceed $8,000 a year. There is authorized to be appropriated such sums as may be necessary for the payment of such compensation.

(Aug. 2, 1946, ch. 753, title II, § 201(c), 60 Stat. 834.)

EFFECTIVE DATE

Section effective Aug. 2, 1946, see section 245 of act Aug. 2, 1946, set out as a note under section 72a of this title.

BASIC COMPENSATION OF ADMINISTRATIVE ASSISTANTS

Pub. L. 85–462, § 4(n), June 20, 1958, 72 Stat. 209, provided that: "The basic compensation of the Administrative Assistants to the Speaker, Majority Leader, Minority Leader, Majority Whip, and Minority Whip, shall be at the rate of $8,880 per annum."

House Resolution No. 127, Eighty-ninth Congress, Jan. 19, 1965, which was enacted into permanent law by Pub. L. 89–90, § 103, July 27, 1965, 79 Stat. 281, provided: "That effective January 3, 1965, there shall be payable from the contingent fund of the House, until otherwise provided by law, for any Member of the House who has served as majority leader and as minority leader of the House, an additional $8,880 basic per annum for an administrative assistant."

House Resolution No. 258, Eighty-ninth Congress, Mar. 9, 1965, which was enacted into permanent law by Pub. L. 89–90, § 103, July 27, 1965, 79 Stat. 281, provided: "That, effective March 1, 1965, there shall be payable from the contingent fund of the House of Representatives, until otherwise provided by law, an amount which will permit the payment of basic compensation per annum, at a rate not in excess of the highest amount which, together with additional compensation authorized by law, will not exceed the maximum rate authorized by the Classification Act of 1949, as amended, to the administrative assistant of each of the following:

"(1) the Speaker of the House;

"(2) the majority leader of the House;

"(3) the minority leader of the House;

"(4) the majority whip of the House;

"(5) the minority whip of the House;

"(6) each Member of the House who has served as Speaker of the House; and

"(7) each Member of the House who has served as majority leader, and as minority leader, of the House."

Section 207(c) of House Resolution 988, Ninety-third Congress, Oct. 8, 1974, provided for the compensation of the administrative assistants referred to in House Resolution 1015, Ninetieth Congress, Jan. 15, 1968, at a rate not in excess of the minimum rate of pay in effect for one pay level above that of employees (referred to in clause 6(a)(1) of Rule XI) to whom clause 6(c) of Rule XI of the Rules of the House of Representatives applied.

INCREASES IN COMPENSATION

Increases in compensation for House officers and employees under authority of Federal Salary Act of 1967

(Pub. L. 90–206), Federal Pay Comparability Act of 1970 (Pub. L. 91–656), and Legislative Branch Appropriations Act, 1988 (Pub. L. 100–202), see sections 60a–2 and 60a–2a of this title, and Salary Directives of Speaker of the House, set out as notes under those sections.

§ 74a–1. Omitted

CODIFICATION

Section, Pub. L. 87–367, title III, § 302(c), Oct. 4, 1961, 75 Stat. 793, provided that rate of gross annual compensation of Chief of Staff of Joint Committee on Internal Revenue Taxation was to be an amount equal to $17,500 as increased in the manner provided by sections 60e–8(d) and 60e–9(d) of this title. See section 74a–2 of this title.

A prior section 74a–1, act Aug. 5, 1955, ch. 568, § 9, 69 Stat. 509, prescribed compensation of Chief of Staff of Joint Committee on Internal Revenue Taxation.

§ 74a–2. Per annum rate of compensation of Chief of Staff of Joint Committee on Taxation

The per annum rate of compensation of the Chief of Staff of the Joint Committee on Taxation shall be the same as the per annum rate of compensation of the Legislative Counsel of the House of Representatives.

(Pub. L. 90–206, title II, § 214(e), Dec. 16, 1967, 81 Stat. 636; Pub. L. 103–437, § 2(a), Nov. 2, 1994, 108 Stat. 4581.)

AMENDMENTS

1994—Pub. L. 103–437 substituted "Joint Committee on Taxation" for "Joint Committee on Internal Revenue Taxation".

EFFECTIVE DATE

Section effective as of beginning of first pay period which begins on or after Oct. 1, 1967, see section 220(a)(2) of Pub. L. 90–206, set out as an Effective Date of 1967 Amendment note under section 5332 of Title 5, Government Organization and Employees.

CROSS REFERENCES

Compensation of Legislative Counsel of House of Representatives, see section 282b of this title.

§ 74a–3. Additional employees in offices of House Minority Leader, Majority Whip, and Chief Deputy Majority Whip; authorization; compensation

(a) Subject to the provisions of subsection (b) of this section, effective March 1, 1977, there shall be two additional employees in the office of the minority leader, and one additional employee each in the offices of the majority whip and the chief deputy majority whip.

(b) The annual rate of compensation for any individual employed under subsection (a) of this section shall not exceed the annual rate of basic pay of level V of the Executive Schedule of section 5316 of title 5, and until otherwise provided by law such compensation as may be necessary shall be paid from the applicable accounts of the House of Representatives.

(Pub. L. 95–94, title I, § 115, Aug. 5, 1977, 91 Stat. 668; Pub. L. 104–53, title I, § 103, Nov. 19, 1995, 109 Stat. 520; Pub. L. 104–186, title II, § 204(15)(A), Aug. 20, 1996, 110 Stat. 1732.)

CODIFICATION

Section is based on section 1 of House Resolution No. 393, Ninety-fifth Congress, Mar. 31, 1977, which was enacted into permanent law by Pub. L. 95–94.

Amendment by Pub. L. 104–53 is based on section 3(b) of House Resolution No. 113, One Hundred Fourth Congress, Mar. 10, 1995, which was enacted into permanent law by Pub. L. 104–53.

AMENDMENTS

1996—Subsec. (b). Pub. L. 104–186 substituted "applicable accounts of the House of Representatives" for "contingent fund of the House".

1995—Subsec. (a). Pub. L. 104–53 substituted "chief deputy majority whip" for "chief majority whip".

EFFECTIVE DATE OF 1995 AMENDMENT

Section 3(a) of House Resolution No. 113, One Hundred Fourth Congress, Mar. 10, 1995, as enacted into permanent law by Pub. L. 104–53, provided that: "Upon the enactment of this section into permanent law, the amendment made by subsection (b) [amending this section] shall take effect."

INCREASES IN COMPENSATION

Increases in compensation for House officers and employees under authority of Federal Salary Act of 1967 (Pub. L. 90–206), Federal Pay Comparability Act of 1970 (Pub. L. 91–656), and Legislative Branch Appropriations Act, 1988 (Pub. L. 100–202), see sections 60a–2 and 60a–2a of this title, and Salary Directives of Speaker of the House, set out as notes under those sections.

§ 74a–4. Additional amounts for personnel and equipment for House Majority and Minority Leaders and Majority and Minority Whips

Effective March 1, 1977, and until otherwise provided by law, there shall be paid out of the applicable accounts of the House of Representatives such additional amounts as may be necessary for office personnel, and rental or lease of necessary equipment, of each of the following officials of the House the following per annum amounts:

(1) The majority leader, $30,000.
(2) The minority leader, $30,000.
(3) The majority whip, $15,000.
(4) The minority whip, $15,000.

(Pub. L. 95–94, title I, § 115, Aug. 5, 1977, 91 Stat. 668; Pub. L. 104–186, title II, § 204(15)(B), Aug. 20, 1996, 110 Stat. 1732.)

CODIFICATION

Section is based on section 2 of House Resolution No. 393, Ninety-fifth Congress, Mar. 31, 1977, which was enacted into permanent law by Pub. L. 95–94.

AMENDMENTS

1996—Pub. L. 104–186 substituted "applicable accounts of the House of Representatives" for "contingent fund of the House".

SECTION REFERRED TO IN OTHER SECTIONS

This section is referred to in section 74a–5 of this title.

§ 74a–5. Limits on uses of funds provided under section 74a–4

The funds provided under the provisions of section 74a–4 of this title shall be limited to use for the compensation of additional personnel and other necessary official expenses.

(Pub. L. 98–51, title I, § 112, July 14, 1983, 97 Stat. 270; Pub. L. 104–186, title II, § 204(16), Aug. 20, 1996, 110 Stat. 1732.)

CODIFICATION

Section is from the Congressional Operations Appropriation Act, 1984, which is title I of the Legislative Branch Appropriation Act, 1984.

Section, as it applies to funds provided under section 333 of this title, is classified to section 333a of this title.

AMENDMENTS

1996—Pub. L. 104–186 made technical amendment to reference in original act which appears in text as reference to section 74a–4 of this title.

§ 74a–6. Repealed. Pub. L. 104–186, title II, § 204(17), Aug. 20, 1996, 110 Stat. 1732

Section, Pub. L. 103–283, title I, § 101, July 22, 1994, 108 Stat. 1430, provided for transfer of authority over Majority and Minority Printers of House to Director of Non-legislative and Financial Services of House.

§ 74a–7. Speaker's Office for Legislative Floor Activities

There is established in the House of Representatives an office to be known as the Speaker's Office for Legislative Floor Activities. The Speaker shall appoint and set the annual rate of pay for employees of the Office. The Office shall have the responsibility of assisting the Speaker in the management of legislative floor activity.

(Pub. L. 104–53, title I, § 103, Nov. 19, 1995, 109 Stat. 520.)

CODIFICATION

Section is based on section 223(b) of House Resolution No. 6, One Hundred Fourth Congress, Jan. 4, 1995, which was enacted into permanent law by Pub. L. 104–53.

§ 74a–8. Training and program development activities of Republican Conference and Democratic Steering and Policy Committee

(a) In general

There is hereby established an account in the House of Representatives for purposes of carrying out training and program development activities of the Republican Conference and the Democratic Steering and Policy Committee.

(b) Amounts, times, terms, and conditions of payment

Subject to the allocation described in subsection (c) of this section, funds in the account established under subsection (a) of this section shall be paid—

(1) for activities of the Republican Conference in such amounts, at such times, and under such terms and conditions as the Speaker of the House of Representatives may direct; and

(2) for activities of the Democratic Steering and Policy Committee in such amounts, at such times, and under such terms and conditions as the Minority Leader of the House of Representatives may direct.

(c) Allocation

Of the total amount in the account established under subsection (a) of this section—

(1) 50 percent shall be allocated to the Speaker for payments for activities of the Republican Conference; and

(2) 50 percent shall be allocated to the Minority Leader for payments for activities of the Democratic Steering and Policy Committee.

(d) Authorization of appropriations

There are authorized to be appropriated to the account under this section for fiscal year 1999 and each succeeding fiscal year such sums as may be necessary for training and program development activities of the Republican Conference and the Democratic Steering and Policy Committee during the fiscal year.

(Pub. L. 105–275, title I, § 103, Oct. 21, 1998, 112 Stat. 2438.)

CODIFICATION

Section is from the Congressional Operations Appropriations Act, 1999, which is title I of the Legislative Branch Appropriations Act, 1999.

§ 74a–9. Appointment of consultants by Speaker, Majority Leader, and Minority Leader of House; compensation

(a) The Speaker, Majority Leader, and Minority Leader of the House of Representatives are each authorized to appoint and fix the compensation of one consultant, on a temporary or intermittent basis, at a daily rate of compensation not in excess of the per diem equivalent of the highest gross rate of annual compensation which may be paid to employees of a standing committee of the House.

(b) This section shall apply with respect to fiscal year 1999 and each succeeding fiscal year.

(Pub. L. 105–275, title I, § 107, Oct. 21, 1998, 112 Stat. 2439.)

CODIFICATION

Section is from the Congressional Operations Appropriations Act, 1999, which is title I of the Legislative Branch Appropriations Act, 1999.

§ 74a–10. Lump sum allowances for House Minority Leader and Majority Whip

(a) The aggregate amount otherwise authorized to be appropriated for a fiscal year for the lump-sum allowance for the Office of the Minority Leader of the House of Representatives and the aggregate amount otherwise authorized to be appropriated for a fiscal year for the lump-sum allowance for the Office of the Majority Whip of the House of Representatives shall each be increased by $333,000.

(b) This section shall apply with respect to fiscal year 2000 and each succeeding fiscal year.

(Pub. L. 106–31, title III, § 3008, May 21, 1999, 113 Stat. 93.)

CODIFICATION

Section is from the 1999 Emergency Supplemental Appropriations Act.

§ 74a–11. Transfer of appropriations by House Leadership Offices

(a) In general

Each office described under the heading "HOUSE LEADERSHIP OFFICES" in the Act making appropriations for the legislative branch for a fiscal year may transfer any amounts appropriated for the office under such heading among the various categories of allowances and expenses for the office under such heading.

(b) Official expenses

Subsection (a) of this section shall not apply with respect to any amounts appropriated for official expenses.

(c) Applicability

This section shall apply with respect to fiscal year 1999 and each succeeding fiscal year.

(Pub. L. 106–31, title III, §3009, May 21, 1999, 113 Stat. 93.)

CODIFICATION

Section is from the 1999 Emergency Supplemental Appropriations Act.

§ 74b. Employment of additional administrative assistants

The Secretary of the Senate is authorized to employ such administrative assistants as may be necessary in order to carry out the provisions of this Act under the jurisdiction of the Secretary.

(Aug. 2, 1946, ch. 753, title II, §244, 60 Stat. 839; Pub. L. 104–186, title II, §204(18), Aug. 20, 1996, 110 Stat. 1732.)

REFERENCES IN TEXT

This Act, referred to in text, means act Aug. 2, 1946, ch. 753, 60 Stat. 812, as amended, known as the Legislative Reorganization Act of 1946. For complete classification of this Act to the Code, see Short Title note set out under section 72a of this title and Tables.

AMENDMENTS

1996—Pub. L. 104–186 substituted "is" for "and the Clerk of the House are" and "the jurisdiction of the Secretary" for "their respective jurisdictions".

EFFECTIVE DATE

Section effective Aug. 2, 1946, see section 245 of act Aug. 2, 1946, set out as a note under section 72a of this title.

SECTION REFERRED TO IN OTHER SECTIONS

This section is referred to in section 60j of this title.

§ 74c. Compensation of certain House minority employees

Effective January 3, 1977, and until otherwise provided by law, the rate of pay for each of the six positions of minority employee authorized by the Legislative Pay Act of 1929 and referred to in House Resolution 441 of the Ninety-first Congress shall be a per annum gross rate equal to the annual rate of basic pay of level IV of the Executive Schedule of section 5315 of title 5, unless a lower rate is established by the Minority Leader.

(Pub. L. 95–94, title I, §115, Aug. 5, 1977, 91 Stat. 668.)

REFERENCES IN TEXT

The Legislative Pay Act of 1929, referred to in text, is act June 20, 1929, ch. 33, 46 Stat. 32. For complete classification of this Act to the Code, see Tables.

House Resolution 441, referred to in text, is set out as a Prior Provisions note below.

CODIFICATION

Section is based on section 1 of House Resolution 119, Ninety-fifth Congress, Jan. 19, 1977, which was enacted into permanent law by Pub. L. 95–94.

PRIOR PROVISIONS

Provisions similar to those in this section were contained in House Resolution 441, Ninety-first Congress,

June 17, 1969, as enacted into permanent law by Pub. L. 91–145, §103, Dec. 12, 1969, 83 Stat. 359, which provided: "That, until otherwise provided by law—

"(1) The six positions of minority employee listed in House Resolution 8, Ninety-first Congress, as supplemented by House Resolution 238, Ninety-first Congress, and House Resolution 265, Ninety-first Congress, are hereby given position titles in the descending order in which those six positions are listed in House Resolution 8, as follows:

"(A) the position title of the position listed first is 'Floor Assistant to the Minority';

"(B) the position title of the position listed second is 'Floor Assistant to the Minority';

"(C) the position title of the position listed third is 'Floor Assistant to the Minority';

"(D) the position title of the position listed fourth is 'Floor Assistant to the Minority';

"(E) the position title of the position listed fifth is 'Pair Clerk to the Minority'; and

"(F) the position title of the position listed sixth is 'Staff Director to the Minority'.

"(2) Appointments to each position for which a position title is provided by subparagraph (1) of this section shall be made by action of the House of Representatives.

"(3) The rate of pay of each position for which a position title is provided by subparagraph (1) of this section shall be a per annum gross rate equal to the annual rate of basic pay of Level V of the Executive Schedule in section 5316 of title 5, United States Code, unless a different rate is provided for such position by action of the House of Representatives.

"SEC. 2. (a) The first section of this resolution shall not affect or change the appointments or continuity of employment of those employees who hold such positions on the date of adoption of this resolution [June 17, 1969].

"(b) In accordance with the authority of the House of Representatives under subparagraph (3) of the first section of this resolution, the respective per annum gross rates of pay of those positions for which position titles are provided by clauses (C), (D), (E), and (F) of subparagraph (1) of the first section of this resolution are as follows:

"(1) for the position subject to clause (C)—$29,160;

"(2) for the position subject to clause (D)—$25,200;

"(3) for the position subject to clause (E)—$28,440; and

"(4) for the position subject to subparagraph (F)—$28,080.

"SEC. 3. This resolution shall become effective as of the beginning of the calendar month in which this resolution is adopted [June 1969]."

DESIGNATION AND COMPENSATION OF THREE FURTHER MINORITY EMPLOYEES

House Resolution No. 7, One Hundred Fourth Congress, Jan. 4, 1995, which was enacted into permanent law by Pub. L. 104–53, title I, §103, Nov. 19, 1995, 109 Stat. 520, provided that: "In addition, the minority leader may appoint and set the annual rate of pay for up to three further minority employees."

§ 74d. Corrections Calendar Office

There is established in the House of Representatives an office to be known as the Corrections Calendar Office, which shall have the responsibility of assisting the Speaker in the management of the Corrections Calendar under the Rules of the House of Representatives. The Office shall have not more than five employees—

(1) who shall be appointed by the Speaker, in consultation with the minority leader; and

(2) whose annual rate of pay shall be established by the Speaker, but may not exceed 75 percent of the maximum annual rate under

the general limitation specified by the order of the Speaker in effect under section 60a–2a of this title.

(Pub. L. 105–55, title I, § 101, Oct. 7, 1997, 111 Stat. 1183.)

CODIFICATION

Section is based on House Resolution No. 7, One Hundred Fifth Congress, Jan. 7, 1997, which was enacted into permanent law by Pub. L. 105–55.

SECTION REFERRED TO IN OTHER SECTIONS

This section is referred to in section 74d–1 of this title.

§ 74d–1. Lump sum allowance for Corrections Calendar Office

There shall be a lump sum allowance of $300,000 per fiscal year for the salaries and expenses of the Corrections Calendar Office, established by section 74d of this title. Such amount shall be allocated between the majority party and the minority party as determined by the Speaker, in consultation with the minority leader.

(Pub. L. 105–55, title I, § 101, Oct. 7, 1997, 111 Stat. 1183.)

CODIFICATION

Section is based on section 1 of House Resolution No. 130, One Hundred Fifth Congress, Apr. 24, 1997, which was enacted into permanent law by Pub. L. 105–55.

SECTION REFERRED TO IN OTHER SECTIONS

This section is referred to in section 74d–2 of this title.

§ 74d–2. Effective date

The allowance under section 74d–1 of this title—

(1) shall be available beginning with the month of May 1997;

(2) through the end of September 1997, shall be paid from the applicable accounts of the House of Representatives on a pro rata basis; and

(3) beginning with fiscal year 1998, shall be paid as provided in appropriations Acts.

(Pub. L. 105–55, title I, § 101, Oct. 7, 1997, 111 Stat. 1183.)

CODIFICATION

Section is based on section 2 of House Resolution No. 130, One Hundred Fifth Congress, Apr. 24, 1997, which was enacted into permanent law by Pub. L. 105–55.

§ 75. Repealed. Pub. L. 92–310, title II, § 220(b), (c), June 6, 1972, 86 Stat. 204

Section, R.S. §§ 58, 59; act Mar. 2, 1895, ch. 177, § 5, 28 Stat. 807, required Clerk of House of Representatives to give a bond in the sum of $20,000.

§ 75–1. Repealed. Pub. L. 104–186, title II, § 204(22)(A)(iii), Aug. 20, 1996, 110 Stat. 1733

Section, based on H. Res. No. 8, par. (3), Ninety-fifth Congress, Jan. 4, 1977, enacted into permanent law by Pub. L. 95–94, title I, § 115, Aug. 5, 1977, 91 Stat. 668, related to compensation of Clerk of House.

A prior section 75–1, based on H. Res. No. 890, Ninety-second Congress, Oct. 4, 1972, enacted into permanent law by Pub. L. 92–607, ch. V, § 508, Oct. 31, 1972, 86 Stat.

1509, set forth the compensation of the Clerk at equal to the annual rate of basic pay fixed for level IV of the Executive Schedule under section 5315 of Title 5, Government Organization and Employees.

§ 75a. Death, resignation, etc., of Chief Administrative Officer of House; accounts and payments; liability of Chief Administrative Officer for acts and defaults of disbursing clerk

On and after June 8, 1942, in case of the death, resignation, separation from office, or disability of the Chief Administrative Officer of the House of Representatives, the accounts of the Chief Administrative Officer may be continued and payments made in his name by the disbursing clerk of the House of Representatives for a period extending not beyond the quarterly period during which a new Chief Administrative Officer shall have been appointed. Such accounts and payments shall be allowed and settled in the General Accounting Office, and the checks signed in the name of the former Chief Administrative Officer shall be honored by the Treasurer of the United States, in the same manner as if the former Chief Administrative Officer had continued in office. The former Chief Administrative Officer or his estate shall not be subject to any legal liability or penalty for the official acts and defaults of such disbursing clerk acting in the name or in the place of the former Chief Administrative Officer under this section, but such disbursing clerk shall be responsible therefor. The accounts and payments referred to in the second sentence shall be audited by the Inspector General of the House of Representatives.

(June 8, 1942, ch. 396, § 7, 56 Stat. 350; Pub. L. 92–310, title II, § 220(i), June 6, 1972, 86 Stat. 205; Pub. L. 104–186, title II, § 204(19), Aug. 20, 1996, 110 Stat. 1732.)

AMENDMENTS

1996—Pub. L. 104–186, § 204(19)(A), in first sentence, substituted "Chief Administrative Officer of the House of Representatives, the accounts of the Chief Administrative Officer" for "Clerk of the House of Representatives, the accounts of such Clerk" and "new Chief Administrative Officer shall have been appointed" for "new Clerk of the House of Representatives shall have been elected and qualified".

Pub. L. 104–186, § 204(19)(B), in second sentence, struck out ", audited," after "shall be allowed" and substituted "name of the former Chief Administrative Officer" for "name of the former Clerk of the House of Representatives" and "the former Chief Administrative Officer" for "such former Clerk".

Pub. L. 104–186, § 204(19)(C), in third sentence, substituted "The former Chief Administrative Officer" for "The former Clerk" and "the former Chief Administrative Officer" for "such former Clerk".

Pub. L. 104–186, § 204(19)(D), inserted at end "The accounts and payments referred to in the second sentence shall be audited by the Inspector General of the House of Representatives."

1972—Pub. L. 92–310 struck out provisions which related to the sureties on the bond of the former clerk, and which required the disbursing clerk to give a bond.

SECTION REFERRED TO IN OTHER SECTIONS

This section is referred to in section 75a–1 of this title.

§ 75a–1. Temporary appointments in case of vacancies or incapacity of House officers; compensation

(a) Temporary appointments in case of vacancy or incapacity in office of Clerk, Sergeant at Arms, Chief Administrative Officer, or Chaplain of House

In case of a vacancy, from whatever cause, in the office of Clerk, Sergeant at Arms, Chief Administrative Officer or Chaplain, of the House of Representatives, or in case of the incapacity or inability of the incumbent of any such office to perform the duties thereof, the Speaker of the House of Representatives may appoint a person to act as, and to exercise temporarily the duties of, Clerk, Sergeant at Arms, Chief Administrative Officer or Chaplain, as the case may be, until a person is chosen by the House of Representatives and duly qualifies as Clerk, Sergeant at Arms, Chief Administrative Officer or Chaplain, as the case may be, or until the termination of the incapacity or inability of the incumbent.

(b) Duties of temporary appointees

Any person appointed pursuant to this section shall exercise all the duties, shall have all the powers, and shall be subject to all the requirements and limitations applicable with respect to one chosen by the House of Representatives to fill the office involved; but nothing in this section shall be held to amend, repeal, or otherwise affect section 75a of this title.

(c) Compensation of temporary appointee

Any person appointed pursuant to this section shall be paid the compensation which he would receive if he were chosen by the House of Representatives to fill the office involved, unless such person is concurrently serving in any office or position the compensation for which is paid from the funds of the United States, in which case he shall receive no compensation for services rendered pursuant to his appointment under this section, and his compensation for performing the duties of such office other than the one to which he is appointed pursuant to this section shall be in full discharge for all services he performs for the United States while serving in such dual capacity.

(Aug. 2, 1946, ch. 753, § 208, as added Aug. 5, 1953, ch. 330, 67 Stat. 387; amended Pub. L. 104–186, title II, § 204(20), Aug. 20, 1996, 110 Stat. 1733.)

AMENDMENTS

1996—Subsec. (a). Pub. L. 104–186 substituted "Chief Administrative Officer" for "Doorkeeper, Postmaster," wherever appearing.

§§ 75b to 75e. Omitted

CODIFICATION

Section 75b, act May 1, 1947, ch. 49, title I, 61 Stat. 58, accorded Clerk of House the same priority as executive agencies under the Surplus Property Act of 1944 (50 App. U.S.C. 1611–1648). The Surplus Property Act of 1944 was repealed by act June 30, 1949, ch. 288, title V, § 503, 63 Stat. 399, and the priorities thereunder expired Dec. 31, 1949.

Sections 75c to 75e were omitted from the Code for lack of general applicability.

Section 75c, based on H. Res. No. 449, Sept. 21, 1961, enacted into permanent law by Pub. L. 87–730, § 103, Oct.

2, 1962, 76 Stat. 693, related to basic compensation of Assistant Tally Clerks in Office of Clerk of House.

Section 75d, based on H. Res. No. 331, June 7, 1961, enacted into permanent law by Pub. L. 87–730, § 103, Oct. 2, 1962, 76 Stat. 693, related to basic compensation of stationery and assistant stationery clerks.

Section 75e, based on H. Res. Nos. 225, 341, 402 and 773 of the 87th Congress, enacted into permanent law by Pub. L. 87–130, § 103, Aug. 10, 1961, 75 Stat. 334; Pub. L. 87–730, § 103, Oct. 2, 1962, 76 Stat. 693; Pub. L. 88–248, § 103, Dec. 30, 1963, 77 Stat. 817, related to compensation of certain laborers and clerks in offices of Clerk, Doorkeeper and Postmaster of House.

§§ 76 to 76a. Repealed. Pub. L. 104–186, title II, § 204(21), (22)(A)(iii), (23), Aug. 20, 1996, 110 Stat. 1733

Section 76, R.S. § 73, related to duties of Doorkeeper of House. Provisions of R.S. § 73 which related to duties of Doorkeeper of Senate were classified to section 63 of this title prior to repeal by Pub. L. 104–186.

Section 76–1, based on H. Res. No. 8, par. (3), Ninety-fifth Congress, Jan. 4, 1977, enacted into permanent law by Pub. L. 95–94, title I, § 115, Aug. 5, 1977, 91 Stat. 668, related to compensation of Doorkeeper of House.

A prior section 76–1 was based on provisions of H. Res. No. 890, Ninety-second Congress, Oct. 4, 1972, enacted into permanent law by Pub. L. 92–607, ch. V, § 508, Oct. 31, 1972, 86 Stat. 1509, relating to compensation of the Doorkeeper being equal to the annual rate of basic pay fixed for level IV of the Executive Schedule under section 5315 of Title 5, Government Organization and Employees, prior to those provisions being struck out by Pub. L. 104–186, title II, § 204(22)(B), Aug. 20, 1996, 110 Stat. 1733.

Another prior section 76–1, based on H. Res. No. 909, Eighty-ninth Congress, Sept. 8, 1966, enacted into permanent law by Pub. L. 89–697, ch. VI, § 601, Oct. 27, 1966, 80 Stat. 1064, set forth the compensation of the Doorkeeper at equal to the gross per annum rate of compensation of the Clerk of House and Sergeant at Arms of House, prior to being repealed by Pub. L. 104–186, title II, § 204(22)(B), Aug. 20, 1996, 110 Stat. 1733.

Section 76a, based on H. Res. No. 560, Eighty-seventh Congress, Mar. 27, 1962, enacted into permanent law by Pub. L. 87–730, § 103, Oct. 2, 1962, 76 Stat. 693, related to position of a special assistant in Office of Doorkeeper.

§ 76b. Omitted

CODIFICATION

Section 76b, based on H. Res. No. 603, §§ 2, 3, Eighty-seventh Congress, Apr. 16, 1962, enacted into permanent law by Pub. L. 88–248, § 103, Dec. 30, 1963, 77 Stat. 817, related to compensation of telephone clerks in Office of Doorkeeper, was omitted from Code in view of repeal of section 2 of H. Res. No. 603 by Pub. L. 104–186, title II, § 204(24) Aug. 20, 1996, 110 Stat. 1733.

§ 77. Sergeant at Arms of House; additional compensation

The Sergeant at Arms of the House of Representatives shall receive, directly or indirectly, no fees or other compensation or emolument whatever for performing the duties of the office, or in connection therewith, otherwise than the salary prescribed by law.

(June 20, 1874, ch. 328, 18 Stat. 87; Mar. 3, 1875, ch. 129, 18 Stat. 346.)

§ 77a. Repealed. Pub. L. 104–186, title II, § 204(22)(A)(iii), Aug. 20, 1996, 110 Stat. 1733

Section, based on H. Res. No. 8, par. (3), Ninety-fifth Congress, Jan. 4, 1977, enacted into permanent law by Pub. L. 95–94, title I, § 115, Aug. 5, 1977, 91 Stat. 668, related to compensation of Sergeant at Arms of House.

A prior section 77a, based on H. Res. No. 890, Ninety-second Congress, Oct. 4, 1972, enacted into permanent law by Pub. L. 92–607, ch. V, § 508, Oct. 31, 1972, 86 Stat. 1509, set forth the compensation of the Sergeant at Arms at equal to the annual rate of basic pay fixed for level IV of the Executive Schedule under section 5315 of Title 5, Government Organization and Employees.

§ 78. Duties of Sergeant at Arms

It shall be the duty of the Sergeant at Arms of the House of Representatives to attend the House during its sittings, to maintain order under the direction of the Speaker, and, pending the election of a Speaker or Speaker pro tempore, under the direction of the Clerk, execute the commands of the House and all processes issued by authority thereof, directed to him by the Speaker.

(Oct. 1, 1890, ch. 1256, § 1, 26 Stat. 645; Pub. L. 104–186, title II, § 204(25)(A), Aug. 20, 1996, 110 Stat. 1733.)

AMENDMENTS

1996—Pub. L. 104–186 struck out ", keep the accounts for the pay and mileage of Members and Delegates, and pay them as provided by law" after "directed to him by the Speaker".

LAW ENFORCEMENT AUTHORITY OF SERGEANT AT ARMS

Pub. L. 104–53, title III, § 313, Nov. 19, 1995, 109 Stat. 538, provided that:

"(a) The Sergeant at Arms of the House of Representatives shall have the same law enforcement authority, including the authority to carry firearms, as a member of the Capitol Police. The law enforcement authority under the preceding sentence shall be subject to the requirement that the Sergeant at Arms have the qualifications specified in subsection (b).

"(b) The qualifications referred to in subsection (a) are the following:

"(1) A minimum of five years of experience as a law enforcement officer before beginning service as the Sergeant at Arms.

"(2) Current certification in the use of firearms by the appropriate Federal law enforcement entity or an equivalent non-Federal entity.

"(3) Any other firearms qualification required for members of the Capitol Police.

"(c) The Committee on House Oversight [now Committee on House Administration] of the House of Representatives shall have authority to prescribe regulations to carry out this section."

§ 79. Symbol of office of Sergeant at Arms

The symbol of his office shall be the mace, which shall be borne by him while enforcing order on the floor.

(Oct. 1, 1890, ch. 1256, § 2, 26 Stat. 645.)

§ 80. Disbursement of compensation of House Members by Chief Administrative Officer

The moneys which have been, or may be, appropriated for the compensation and mileage of Members and Delegates shall be paid at the Treasury on requisitions drawn by the Chief Administrative Officer of the House of Representatives, and shall be kept, disbursed, and accounted for by him according to law, and he shall be a disbursing officer, but he shall not be entitled to any compensation additional to the salary fixed by law.

(Oct. 1, 1890, ch. 1256, § 3, 26 Stat. 645; Pub. L. 104–186, title II, § 204(25)(B), Aug. 20, 1996, 110 Stat. 1734.)

AMENDMENTS

1996—Pub. L. 104–186 substituted "Chief Administrative Officer" for "Sergeant-at-Arms".

§ 80a. Deductions by Chief Administrative Officer in disbursement of gratuity appropriations

The Chief Administrative Officer of the House of Representatives is authorized, in the disbursement of gratuity appropriations, to make deductions of such amounts as may be due to or through his office or as may be due the House of Representatives.

(May 29, 1928, ch. 853, § 1, 45 Stat. 885; Pub. L. 104–186, title II, § 204(26), Aug. 20, 1996, 110 Stat. 1734.)

AMENDMENTS

1996—Pub. L. 104–186 substituted "Chief Administrative Officer of the House of Representatives" for "Sergeant-at-Arms of the House".

§ 81. Repealed. Pub. L. 93–344, title V, § 505(2), July 12, 1974, 88 Stat. 322

Section, act July 2, 1954, ch. 455, title I, 68 Stat. 400, directed that the fiscal year for the adjustment of the accounts of Sergeant at Arms of House for compensation and mileage of Members, Delegates, and Resident Commissioner extend from July 1 to June 30.

§§ 81a to 81c. Repealed. Pub. L. 104–186, title II, § 204(27)–(29), Aug. 20, 1996, 110 Stat. 1734

Section 81a, act July 26, 1949, ch. 366, 63 Stat. 482, related to audits and reports of fiscal records of Sergeant at Arms of House.

Section 81b, based on H. Res. No. 465, Eighty-fourth Congress, Apr. 11, 1956, enacted into permanent law by act June 27, 1956, ch. 453, title I, § 103, 70 Stat. 370, related to payment from House contingent fund for restoration or adjustment of trust fund account of Sergeant at Arms.

Section 81c, based on H. Res. No. 144, Eighty-fifth Congress, Feb. 7, 1957, enacted into permanent law by Pub. L. 85–75, title I, § 103, July 1, 1957, 71 Stat. 256, related to purchase of and payment for insurance of office funds of Sergeant at Arms of House.

§ 82. Repealed. Pub. L. 92–310, title II, § 220(d), (e), June 6, 1972, 86 Stat. 204

Section, acts Oct. 1, 1890, ch. 1256, §§ 4, 5, 26 Stat. 645, 646; Mar. 2, 1895, ch. 177, § 5, 28 Stat. 807, required Sergeant at Arms of House of Representatives to give a bond in sum of $50,000.

§ 83. Tenure of office of Sergeant at Arms

Any person duly elected and qualified as Sergeant at Arms of the House of Representatives shall continue in said office until his successor is chosen and qualified subject, however, to removal by the House of Representatives.

(Oct. 1, 1890, ch. 1256, § 6, 26 Stat. 646.)

§§ 84, 84–1. Repealed. Pub. L. 104–186, title II, § 204(30), (31), Aug. 20, 1996, 110 Stat. 1734

Section 84, act Oct. 1, 1890, ch. 1256, § 7, 26 Stat. 646, related to statement of disbursements by Sergeant at Arms.

Section 84–1, based on H. Res. No. 6, Ninety-eighth Congress, Jan. 3, 1983, enacted into permanent law by Pub. L. 98–51, title I, § 110, July 14, 1983, 97 Stat. 269, fixed compensation of Postmaster of House of Representatives.

A prior section 84–1, based on H. Res. No. 393, §3, Ninety-fifth Congress, Mar. 31, 1977, enacted into permanent law by Pub. L. 95–94, title I, §115, Aug. 5, 1977, 91 Stat. 668, provided that per annum gross rate of compensation of Postmaster was to equal amount for level 13, step 5, of House Employees Schedule.

Another prior section 84–1, acts Aug. 5, 1955, ch. 568, §5, 69 Stat. 508; Dec. 16, 1967, Pub. L. 90–206, title II, §214(b), 81 Stat. 635, set forth compensation of Postmaster.

§ 84–2. Compensation of Chaplain of House

Effective May 1, 1977, and until otherwise provided by law, the per annum gross rate of compensation of the Chaplain of the House of Representatives shall be equal to the rate in effect from time to time for HS level 8, step 4, of the House Employees Schedule.

(Pub. L. 95–391, title I, §111, Sept. 30, 1978, 92 Stat. 777.)

REFERENCES IN TEXT

The House Employees Schedule, referred to in text, is provided for by section 293 of this title.

CODIFICATION

Section is based on section 3 of House Resolution No. 661, Ninety-fifth Congress, July 29, 1977, which was enacted into permanent law by Pub. L. 95–391.

PRIOR PROVISIONS

A prior section 84–2, Pub. L. 88–426, title II, §203(f), Aug. 14, 1964, 78 Stat. 415; H. Res. 313, 89th Cong., Mar. 31, 1965, as enacted by Pub. L. 89–90, §103, July 27, 1965, 79 Stat. 281; Pub. L. 90–206, title II, §214(b), Dec. 16, 1967, 81 Stat. 635, provided that the compensation of Chaplain of House shall be at a gross per annum rate which is equal to the gross per annum rate of compensation of Chaplain of Senate, subject to further increases.

COMPENSATION OF INDIVIDUAL HOLDING POSITION OF CHAPLAIN OF HOUSE OF REPRESENTATIVES ON JULY 14, 1983

House Resolution No. 7, Ninety-sixth Congress, Jan. 15, 1979, which was enacted into permanent law by Pub. L. 98–51, title I, §111(1), July 14, 1983, 97 Stat. 269, to be effective during the period in which the position of Chaplain of the House of Representatives is held by the individual holding the position on July 14, 1983, provided that: "The compensation of the Chaplain of the House of Representatives shall be equivalent to the highest rate of basic pay as in effect from time to time of level IV of the Executive Schedule in Section 5315 of Title V [5], United States Code."

INCREASES IN COMPENSATION

Increases in compensation for House officers and employees under authority of Federal Salary Act of 1967 (Pub. L. 90–206), Federal Pay Comparability Act of 1970 (Pub. L. 91–656), and Legislative Branch Appropriations Act, 1988 (Pub. L. 100–202), see sections 60a–2 and 60a–2a of this title, and Salary Directives of Speaker of the House, set out as notes under those sections.

§§ 84–3, 84–4. Omitted

CODIFICATION

Section 84–3, which related to compensation of Deputy Sergeant at Arms (charge of pairs), was based on House Resolution No. 138, Feb. 2, 1961, which was enacted into permanent law by Pub. L. 87–130, §103, Aug. 10, 1961, 75 Stat. 334. See section 291 et seq. of this title.

Section 84–4, which related to compensation of a clerk-messenger in office of Parliamentarian, was based on House Resolution No. 603, Apr. 16, 1962, which was enacted into permanent law by Pub. L. 88–248, §103,

Dec. 30, 1963, 77 Stat. 817, and was omitted because a lump-sum appropriation is now made for the Office of Parliamentarian.

§ 84a. Reporters for House of Representatives

No person shall be employed as a reporter for the House of Representatives without the approval of the Speaker.

(R.S. §54.)

CODIFICATION

R.S. §54 derived from act Apr. 2, 1872, ch. 79, §3, 17 Stat. 47.

§ 84a–1. Repealed. Pub. L. 104–186, title II, § 204(32), Aug. 20, 1996, 110 Stat. 1734

Section, based on H. Res. No. 1495, Ninety-fourth Congress, Sept. 30, 1976, enacted into permanent law by Pub. L. 95–94, title I, §115, Aug. 5, 1977, 91 Stat. 668; amended Pub. L. 101–509, title V, §529 [title I, §101(b)(4)(G)], Nov. 5, 1990, 104 Stat. 1427, 1440, related to adjustment of compensation of Official Reporter of Debates and Official Reporter to Committees.

§ 84b. Omitted

CODIFICATION

Section, acts July 17, 1947, ch. 262, 61 Stat. 365; Oct. 18, 1986, Pub. L. 99–500, §101(j), 100 Stat. 1783–287, and Oct. 30, 1986, Pub. L. 99–591, §101(j), 100 Stat. 3341–287; July 11, 1987, Pub. L. 100–71, title I, 101 Stat. 425, provided that on and after July 17, 1947, sums received from the sales of copies of transcripts of hearings of committees reported by such reporters be covered into the Treasury. See section 117e of this title.

Amendment of section by Pub. L. 99–500 and 99–591, as amended by Pub. L. 100–71, is based on section 104(b) of title I of H.R. 5203 (see House Report 99–805 as filed in the House on Aug. 15, 1986), and incorporated by reference in section 101(j) of Pub. L. 99–500 and 99–591, to be effective as if enacted into law. Pub. L. 99–591 is a corrected version of Pub. L. 99–500.

Provisions similar to those in this section were contained in appropriation acts which were classified to section 117a of this title.

§§ 85 to 88a. Repealed. Pub. L. 104–186, title II, § 204(33), (34)(A), Aug. 20, 1996, 110 Stat. 1734

Section 85, act Mar. 3, 1901, ch. 830, §1, 31 Stat. 968, related to performance of duties by employees of House.

Section 86, act Mar. 3, 1901, ch. 830, §1, 31 Stat. 968, related to division of salaries of employees of House.

Section 87, act Mar. 3, 1901, ch. 830, §1, 31 Stat. 968, related to requiring or permitting employees of House to sublet duties.

Section 88, act Mar. 3, 1901, ch. 830, §1, 31 Stat. 968, prescribed age limits of twelve and eighteen for service as pages in House of Representatives but made the restriction inapplicable to chief pages, riding pages, and telephone pages. See section 88b–1(b) of this title.

Section 88a, act Aug. 2, 1946, ch. 753, title II, §243, 60 Stat. 839, related to education of Congressional and Supreme Court pages, authorized appropriations, and allowed pages to elect to attend private or parochial schools.

§ 88b. Education of other minors who are Senate employees

The facilities provided for the education of Congressional and Supreme Court pages shall be available from and after January 2, 1947, also for the education of such other minors who are Senate employees as may be certified by the Secretary of the Senate to receive such education.

(Mar. 22, 1947, ch. 20, title I, 61 Stat. 16; Pub. L. 98–367, title I, § 103, July 17, 1984, 98 Stat. 479; Pub. L. 104–186, title II, § 204(35), Aug. 20, 1996, 110 Stat. 1735.)

CODIFICATION

The first paragraph of this section is based on act Mar. 22, 1947.

The second paragraph was based on H. Res. No. 279, Ninety-eighth Congress, July 21, 1983, enacted into permanent law by Pub. L. 98–367. See 1996 Amendment note below.

AMENDMENTS

1996—Pub. L. 104–186, in first par., substituted "Senate employees" for "congressional employees" and struck out "and the Clerk of the House of Representatives" after "Secretary of the Senate", and struck out second par. which read as follows: "This section shall not apply to any minor who is an employee of the House of Representatives or to any educational facility under the House of Representatives Page Board."

SECTION REFERRED TO IN OTHER SECTIONS

This section is referred to in title 40 section 184a.

§ 88b–1. Congressional pages

(a) Appointment conditions

A person shall not be appointed as a page of the Senate or House of Representatives—

(1) unless he agrees that, in the absence of unforeseen circumstances preventing his service as a page after his appointment, he will continue to serve as a page for the period specified in writing at the time of the appointment; and

(2) until complete information in writing is transmitted to his parent or parents, his legal guardian, or other appropriate person or persons acting as his parent or parents, with respect to the nature of the work of pages, their pay, their working conditions (including hours and scheduling of work), and the housing accommodations available to pages.

(b) Qualifications

A person shall not serve as a page—

(1) of the Senate before he has attained the age of fourteen years; or

(2) of the House of Representatives before he has attained the age of sixteen years.

(Pub. L. 91–510, title IV, § 491(a)–(d), Oct. 26, 1970, 84 Stat. 1198; Pub. L. 97–51, §§ 101(c), 123, Oct. 1, 1981, 95 Stat. 959, 965; Pub. L. 104–186, title II, § 204(36), Aug. 20, 1996, 110 Stat. 1735.)

CODIFICATION

Repeal of subsecs. (c) and (d) of this section is based on section 304(a) of H.R. 4120, as reported July 9, 1981, which was enacted into permanent law by section 101(c) of Pub. L. 97–51 and amended by section 123 of Pub. L. 97–51.

AMENDMENTS

1996—Subsec. (a)(1). Pub. L. 104–186, § 204(36)(A), substituted "the period specified in writing at the time of the appointment" for "a period of not less than two months".

Subsec. (b). Pub. L. 104–186, § 204(36)(B), substituted a period for "; or" at end of par. (2) and struck out concluding provisions which read as follows: "(except in the case of a chief page, telephone page, or riding page) during any session of the Congress which begins after he has attained the age of eighteen years."

1981—Subsecs. (c), (d). Pub. L. 97–51 struck out subsecs. (c) and (d) which had provided, respectively, that pay of pages of the Senate began not more than five days before the convening or reconvening of a session of the Congress or of the Senate and continued until the end of the month during which the Congress or the Senate adjourned or recessed or until the fourteenth day after such adjournment or recess, whichever was the later date, except that, in any case in which the Congress or the Senate adjourned or recessed on or before the last day of July for a period of at least thirty days but not more than forty-five days, such pay would continue until the end of such period of adjournment or recess, and that the pay of pages of the House of Representatives began not more than five days before the convening of a session of the Congress and continued until the end of the month during which the Congress adjourned sine die or recessed or until the fourteenth day after such adjournment or recess, whichever was the later date, except that, in any case in which the House adjourned or recessed on or before the last day of July in any year for a period of at least thirty days but not more than forty-five days, such pay would continue until the end of such period of adjournment or recess.

EFFECTIVE DATE

Subsecs. (a), (c), and (d) of this section effective immediately prior to noon on Jan. 3, 1971, see section 601(1) of Pub. L. 91–510, set out as an Effective Date of 1970 Amendment note under section 72a of this title.

Section 491(f) of Pub. L. 91–510 provided that: "Subsection (b) of this section shall become effective on January 3, 1971, but the provisions of such subsection limiting service as a page to persons who have attained the age of sixteen years shall not be construed to prohibit the continued service of any page appointed prior to the date of enactment of this Act [Oct. 26, 1970]."

PAY OF PAGES BETWEEN RECESS OR ADJOURNMENT

Prior to the repeal of subsecs. (c) and (d) of section 88b–1 of this title by Pub. L. 97–51, provisions for continuing the pay of pages of the Senate and House of Representatives during specific periods of recess or adjournment of Congress by making such subsecs. (b) and (c) inapplicable to the pay of pages during such periods, were contained in the following appropriation acts:

Pub. L. 97–12, title I, June 5, 1981, 95 Stat. 65.

Pub. L. 96–536, § 101(c), Dec. 16, 1980, 94 Stat. 3167.

Pub. L. 96–38, title III, § 303, July 25, 1979, 93 Stat. 142. Subsequently repealed by Pub. L. 97–51, §§ 101(c), 123, Oct. 1, 1981, 95 Stat. 965.

Pub. L. 95–391, title III, § 305, Sept. 30, 1978, 92 Stat. 789.

SECTION REFERRED TO IN OTHER SECTIONS

This section is referred to in title 40 section 184a.

§ 88b–2. House of Representatives Page Board; establishment and purpose

Until otherwise provided by law, there is hereby established a board to be known as the House of Representatives Page Board to ensure that the page program is conducted in a manner that is consistent with the efficient functioning of the House and the welfare of the pages.

(Pub. L. 97–377, title I, § 127, Dec. 21, 1982, 96 Stat. 1914.)

CODIFICATION

Section is based on section 1 of House Resolution No. 611, Ninety-seventh Congress, Nov. 30, 1982, which was enacted into permanent law by Pub. L. 97–377.

SECTION REFERRED TO IN OTHER SECTIONS

This section is referred to in sections 88b–3, 88b–4 of this title.

§ 88b–3. Membership of Page Board

(a) Appointed and designated members

The Page Board shall consist of—

(1) two Members of the House appointed by the Speaker and one Member of the House appointed by the minority leader; and

(2) the Clerk and the Sergeant at Arms of the House.

(b) "Member of the House" defined

As used in sections 88b–2 to 88b–4 of this title, the term "Member of the House" means a Representative in, and a Delegate or Resident Commissioner to, the Congress.

(Pub. L. 97–377, title I, §127, Dec. 21, 1982, 96 Stat. 1914; Pub. L. 104–186, title II, §204(37), Aug. 20, 1996, 110 Stat. 1735; Pub. L. 105–275, title I, §101(a), Oct. 21, 1998, 112 Stat. 2438.)

CODIFICATION

Section is based on section 2 of House Resolution No. 611, Ninety-seventh Congress, Nov. 30, 1982, which was enacted into permanent law by Pub. L. 97–377.

AMENDMENTS

1998—Subsec. (a)(3). Pub. L. 105–275 inserted "and" at end of par. (1), substituted a period for "; and" at end of par. (2), and struck out par. (3) which read as follows: "the Architect of the Capitol."

1996—Subsec. (a)(2). Pub. L. 104–186 substituted "Clerk and the Sergeant" for "Clerk, Doorkeeper, and Sergeant".

EFFECTIVE DATE OF 1998 AMENDMENT

Pub. L. 105–275, title I, §101(b), Oct. 21, 1998, 112 Stat. 2438, provided that: "The amendment made by subsection (a) [amending this section] shall apply with respect to the One Hundred Sixth Congress and each succeeding Congress."

SECTION REFERRED TO IN OTHER SECTIONS

This section is referred to in section 88b–4 of this title.

§ 88b–4. Regulations of Page Board

The Page Board shall have authority to prescribe such regulations as may be necessary to carry out sections 88b–2 to 88b–4 of this title.

(Pub. L. 97–377, title I, §127, Dec. 21, 1982, 96 Stat. 1914.)

CODIFICATION

Section is based on section 3 of House Resolution No. 611, Ninety-seventh Congress, Nov. 30, 1982, which was enacted into permanent law by Pub. L. 97–377.

SECTION REFERRED TO IN OTHER SECTIONS

This section is referred to in section 88b–3 of this title.

§ 88b–5. Page residence hall and page meal plan

(a) Revolving fund; establishment within House contingent fund

Effective at the beginning of the Ninety-eighth Congress and until otherwise provided by law, there is established a revolving fund within the contingent fund of the House of Representatives for the page residence hall and the page meal plan.

(b) Deposits in revolving fund; disbursements by Chief Administrative Officer of House

There shall be deposited in the revolving fund such amounts as may be received by the Chief Administrative Officer of the House of Representatives with respect to lodging, meals, and related services furnished for congressional pages. Amounts so deposited shall be available for disbursement by the Chief Administrative Officer of the House of Representatives, as determined by the Clerk of the House of Representatives, for expenses relating to the page residence hall and the page meal plan.

(c) Regulations

The House of Representatives Page Board shall prescribe such regulations as may be necessary to carry out this section.

(Pub. L. 98–51, title I, §110, July 14, 1983, 97 Stat. 269; Pub. L. 104–186, title II, §204(38), Aug. 20, 1996, 110 Stat. 1735.)

REFERENCES IN TEXT

The Ninety-eighth Congress, referred to in subsec. (a), convened on Jan. 3, 1983.

CODIFICATION

Section is based on House Resolution No. 64, Ninety-eighth Congress, Feb. 8, 1983, which was enacted into permanent law by Pub. L. 98–51.

Sections 1 to 4 of House Resolution No. 64 have been redesignated subsecs. (a) to (d) of this section, respectively, for purposes of codification.

AMENDMENTS

1996—Subsec. (b). Pub. L. 104–186, §204(38)(A), (B), substituted "Chief Administrative Officer of the House of Representatives" for "Clerk" in first sentence and "Chief Administrative Officer of the House of Representatives, as determined by the Clerk of the House of Representatives," for "Clerk" in second sentence.

Subsecs. (c), (d). Pub. L. 104–186, §204(38)(C), (D), redesignated subsec. (d) as (c) and struck out former subsec. (c) which read as follows: "As used in this section, the term 'Clerk' means the Clerk of the House of Representatives."

§ 88b–6. Repealed. Pub. L. 104–186, title II, § 204(39), Aug. 20, 1996, 110 Stat. 1735

Section, Pub. L. 98–63, title I, §902, July 30, 1983, 97 Stat. 336; Pub. L. 104–53, title I, §4, Nov. 19, 1995, 109 Stat. 517, related to withholding from salary charges for lodging, meals, and related services furnished Senate pages in page residence hall.

§ 88b–7. Daniel Webster Senate Page Residence Revolving Fund

(a) Establishment

There is established in the Treasury of the United States a revolving fund within the contingent fund of the Senate to be known as the Daniel Webster Senate Page Residence Revolving Fund (hereafter referred to in this section as the "fund"). The fund shall consist of all rental payments and other moneys collected or received by the Sergeant at Arms with regard to the Daniel Webster Senate Page Residence. All moneys in the fund shall be available without fiscal year limitation for disbursement by the Secretary of the Senate in connection with operation and maintenance of the Daniel Webster Senate Page Residence not normally performed by the Architect of the Capitol. In addition, such moneys may be used by the Sergeant at Arms to purchase food and food related items and fund activities for the pages.

(b) Deposit of moneys

All moneys received from rental payments and other moneys (including donated moneys) collected or received by the Sergeant at Arms with regard to the Daniel Webster Senate Page Residence shall be deposited in the fund and shall be available for purposes of this section.

(c) Vouchers

Disbursements from the fund shall be made upon vouchers approved by the Sergeant at Arms, or the designee of the Sergeant at Arms.

(d) Regulations

The Sergeant at Arms is authorized to prescribe such regulations as may be necessary to carry out the provisions of this section and to provide for the operations of the Daniel Webster Senate Page Residence.

(Pub. L. 103–283, title I, §4, July 22, 1994, 108 Stat. 1427; Pub. L. 104–53, title I, §6, Nov. 19, 1995, 109 Stat. 518.)

Codification

Section is from the Congressional Operations Appropriations Act, 1995, which is title I of the Legislative Branch Appropriations Act, 1995.

Amendments

1995—Subsec. (b). Pub. L. 104–53 inserted "(including donated moneys)" after "other moneys".

§ 88c. Repealed. Pub. L. 91–510, title IV, § 491(e), Oct. 26, 1970, 84 Stat. 1198

Section, acts June 14, 1948, ch. 467, 62 Stat. 426; Oct. 11, 1951, ch. 485, 65 Stat. 390; Oct. 13, 1964, Pub. L. 88–652, §16(b), 78 Stat. 1084, provided for compensation of pages of Senate and House.

Effective Date of Repeal

Repeal effective immediately prior to noon on Jan. 3, 1971, see section 601(1) of Pub. L. 91–510, set out as an Effective Date of 1970 Amendment note under section 72a of this title.

§ 88c–1. Repealed. Pub. L. 104–186, title II, § 204(40)(A), Aug. 20, 1996, 110 Stat. 1735

Section, based on H. Res. No. 234, §1, Ninety-eighth Congress, June 29, 1983, enacted into permanent law by Pub. L. 98–367, title I, §103, July 17, 1984, 98 Stat. 479, related to payment for educational services and related items for pages.

§ 88c–2. Academic year and summer term for page program

The page program shall consist of the two semesters of the academic year, plus a non-academic summer term.

(Pub. L. 98–367, title I, §103, July 17, 1984, 98 Stat. 479; Pub. L. 104–186, title II, § 204(40)(B), Aug. 20, 1996, 110 Stat. 1736.)

Codification

Section is based on section 2 of House Resolution No. 234, Ninety-eighth Congress, June 29, 1983, which was enacted into permanent law by Pub. L. 98–367.

Amendments

1996—Pub. L. 104–186 substituted "semesters of the academic year, plus a non-academic" for "terms of the academic year plus a".

Effective Date

Section 5 of House Resolution No. 234, Ninety-eighth Congress, June 29, 1983, as enacted into permanent law

by Pub. L. 98–367, provided that: "This resolution [enacting sections 88c–1 to 88c–4 of this title] shall take effect on the date on which this resolution is agreed to [June 29, 1983], except that section 3(a)(1)(A) and section 3(b)(2) [section 88c–3(a)(1)(A), (b)(2) of this title] shall apply to terms beginning after November 30, 1983."

Section Referred to in Other Sections

This section is referred to in section 88c–4 of this title.

§ 88c–3. Service of page during academic year and summer term; filling of vacancies; eligibility

(a)(1) Except as provided in subsection (b) of this section, a page serving during an academic year—

(A) shall be in the eleventh grade; and
(B) shall serve for one full semester or two full semesters.

(2) Except as provided in subsection (b) of this section, a page serving during the summer term—

(A) shall have completed the tenth grade; and
(B) shall not have begun the twelfth grade.

(b)(1) An unforeseen vacancy occurring in a page position during an academic year may be filled, except that no appointment may be made under this paragraph for service to begin on or after October 1 with respect to the first semester or on or after March 1 with respect to the second semester.

(2) An individual who has served as a congressional page at any time during each of any three semesters or terms, as the case may be, shall not be eligible to serve as a page.

(Pub. L. 98–367, title I, §103, July 17, 1984, 98 Stat. 479; Pub. L. 104–186, title II, § 204(40)(C)–(E), Aug. 20, 1996, 110 Stat. 1736.)

Codification

Section is based on section 3 of House Resolution No. 234, Ninety-eighth Congress, June 29, 1983, which was enacted into permanent law by Pub. L. 98–367.

Amendments

1996—Subsec. (a)(1)(B). Pub. L. 104–186, § 204(40)(C), substituted "semester or two full semesters" for "term or two full terms".

Subsec. (b)(1). Pub. L. 104–186, § 204(40)(D), substituted "except that no appointment may be made under this paragraph for service to begin on or after October 1 with respect to the first semester or on or after March 1 with respect to the second semester" for "but no appointment to fill that vacancy shall be for a period of less than two months".

Subsec. (b)(2). Pub. L. 104–186, § 204(40)(E), substituted "semesters or terms, as the case may be," for "terms".

Effective Date

Section effective June 29, 1983, except that subsecs. (a)(1)(A) and (b)(2) applicable to terms beginning after Nov. 30, 1983, see note set out under section 88c–2 of this title.

Section Referred to in Other Sections

This section is referred to in section 88c–4 of this title.

§ 88c–4. Definitions

As used in sections 88c–2 to 88c–4 of this title, the term—

(1) "academic year" means a regular school year, consisting of two semesters;

(2) "page" means a page of the House of Representatives, but such term does not include a full time, permanent employee of the House of Representatives with supervisory responsibility for pages; and

(3) "congressional page" means a page of the House of Representatives or the Senate.

(Pub. L. 98–367, title I, §103, July 17, 1984, 98 Stat. 479; Pub. L. 104–186, title II, §204(40)(F), Aug. 20, 1996, 110 Stat. 1736.)

CODIFICATION

Section is based on section 4 of House Resolution No. 234, Ninety-eighth Congress, June 29, 1983, which was enacted into permanent law by Pub. L. 98–367.

AMENDMENTS

1996—Par. (1). Pub. L. 104–186 substituted "semesters" for "terms".

EFFECTIVE DATE

Section effective June 29, 1983, see note set out under section 88c–2 of this title.

§89. Certificates to pay rolls of employees of House

The Clerk, Sergeant at Arms, and Chief Administrative Officer of the House of Representatives shall make certificate each month to their respective pay rolls, stating whether the persons named in such pay rolls and employed in their respective departments have been actually present at their respective places of duty and have actually performed the services for which compensation is provided in said pay rolls, and in each case where a person carried on such pay roll has been absent and has not performed the services in whole or in part for which payment is proposed, the reason for such absence and for such nonperformance of services shall be stated.

(Mar. 3, 1901, ch. 830, §1, 31 Stat. 968; Pub. L. 104–186, title II, §204(41), Aug. 20, 1996, 110 Stat. 1736.)

AMENDMENTS

1996—Pub. L. 104–186 substituted "and Chief Administrative Officer" for "Doorkeeper, and Postmaster".

§89a. Certification of indebtedness of employees of House; withholding of amount

Whenever an employee of the House of Representatives becomes indebted to the House of Representatives and fails to pay the indebtedness, the chairman of the committee or the elected officer of the House of Representatives that has jurisdiction over the activity under which the indebtedness arises may certify to the Chief Administrative Officer of the House of Representatives the amount of the indebtedness. The Chief Administrative Officer of the House of Representatives is authorized to withhold the amount so certified from any amount which is disbursed by him and which is due to, or on behalf of, such employee. Whenever an amount is withheld under this section, the appropriate account shall be credited in an amount equal to the amount so withheld. As used in this section, the term "employee of the House of Representa-

tives" means any person in the legislative branch of the Government whose salary, wages, or other compensation is disbursed by the Chief Administrative Officer of the House of Representatives.

(Pub. L. 85–492, July 2, 1958, 72 Stat. 293; Pub. L. 104–186, title II, §204(42), Aug. 20, 1996, 110 Stat. 1736.)

AMENDMENTS

1996—Pub. L. 104–186 substituted "and fails to pay the indebtedness, the chairman of the committee or the elected officer of the House of Representatives that has jurisdiction over the activity under which the indebtedness arises may certify to the Chief Administrative Officer of the House of Representatives the amount of the indebtedness" for ", or to the trust fund account in the office of the Sergeant at Arms of the House of Representatives, and such employee fails to pay such indebtedness, the chairman of the committee, or the elected officer, of the House of Representatives having jurisdiction of the activity under which such indebtedness arose, is authorized to certify to the Clerk of the House of Representatives the amount of such indebtedness" in first sentence and "Chief Administrative Officer" for "Clerk" in second and last sentences.

§§90, 91. Repealed. Pub. L. 104–186, title II, §204(33), Aug. 20, 1996, 110 Stat. 1734

Section 90, act Mar. 3, 1901, ch. 830, §1, 31 Stat. 968, related to removal from office of employees of House for violation of sections 85 to 87 and 89 of this title.

Section 91, acts Mar. 3, 1901, ch. 830, §1, 31 Stat. 968; Aug. 2, 1946, ch. 753, §121, 60 Stat. 822, related to investigations of violations of sections 85 to 87, 89, and 90 of this title.

§92. Employees of Members of House of Representatives

(a) In general

Under the Members' Representational Allowance, each Member of the House of Representatives may employ not more than 18 permanent employees and a total of not more than 4 additional employees in the following categories:

(1) Interns.

(2) Part-time employees.

(3) Shared employees.

(4) Temporary employees.

(5) Employees on leave without pay.

(b) Benefit exclusion

For purposes of this section, interns and temporary employees shall be excluded from the operation of the following provisions of title 5:

(1) Chapter 84 (relating to the Federal Employees' Retirement System).

(2) Chapter 87 (relating to life insurance).

(3) Chapter 89 (relating to health insurance).

(c) Definitions

As used in this section—

(1) the term "Member of the House of Representatives" means a Representative in, or a Delegate or Resident Commissioner to, the Congress;

(2) the term "intern" means, with respect to a Member of the House of Representatives, an individual who serves in the office of the Member for not more than 120 days in a 12-month period and whose service is primarily for the educational experience of the individual;

(3) the term "part-time employee" means, with respect to a Member of the House of Rep-

resentatives, an individual who is employed by the Member and whose normally assigned work schedule is not more than the equivalent of 15 full working days per month;

(4) the term "temporary employee" means, with respect to a Member of the House of Representatives, an individual who is employed for a specific purpose or task and who is employed for not more than 90 days in a 12-month period, except that the term of such employment may be extended with the written approval of the Committee on House Oversight; and

(5) the term "shared employee" means an employee who is paid by more than one employing authority of the House of Representatives.

(d) Regulations

The Committee on House Oversight shall have authority to prescribe regulations to carry out this section.

(Pub. L. 104–186, title I, §104, Aug. 20, 1996, 110 Stat. 1720; Pub. L. 105–55, title I, §104(a), Oct. 7, 1997, 111 Stat. 1183; Pub. L. 106–57, title I, §103(b), Sept. 29, 1999, 113 Stat. 416.)

CODIFICATION

Section is comprised of section 104 of Pub. L. 104–186. Subsec. (e)(1) of section 104 of Pub. L. 104–186 repealed former section 92 of this title. Subsec. (e)(2) and (3) of section 104 of Pub. L. 104–186 repealed provisions formerly set out as notes below.

PRIOR PROVISIONS

A prior section 92, acts Jan. 25, 1923, ch. 43, 42 Stat. 1217; July 25, 1939, ch. 352, §1, 53 Stat. 1080; Aug. 5, 1955, ch. 568, §11(b), 69 Stat. 509; Aug. 3, 1956, ch. 938, §1(b), 70 Stat. 990, related to payment of appropriations for clerk hire for Members of House of Representatives, Delegates, and Resident Commissioners, prior to repeal by Pub. L. 104–186, title I, §104(e)(1), Aug. 20, 1996, 110 Stat. 1721.

AMENDMENTS

1999—Pub. L. 106–57, §103(b)(2), struck out "Clerk hire" before "Employees" in section catchline.

Subsec. (a). Pub. L. 106–57, §103(b)(1), struck out "clerk hire" before "employees" in two places in introductory provisions.

1997—Subsec. (c)(2). Pub. L. 105–55 struck out "in the District of Columbia" after "office of the Member".

CHANGE OF NAME

Committee on House Oversight of House of Representatives changed to Committee on House Administration of House of Representatives by House Resolution No. 5, One Hundred Sixth Congress, Jan. 6, 1999.

EFFECTIVE DATE OF 1999 AMENDMENT

Amendment by Pub. L. 106–57 applicable with respect to the first session of the One Hundred Sixth Congress and each succeeding session of Congress, see section 103(c) of Pub. L. 106–57, set out as a note under section 57 of this title.

EFFECTIVE DATE OF 1997 AMENDMENT

Section 104(b) of Pub. L. 105–55 provided that: "The amendment made by subsection (a) [amending this section] shall apply with respect to fiscal years beginning on or after October 1, 1997."

EMPLOYMENT OF PERMANENT CLERKS

House Resolution No. 359, Ninety-sixth Congress, July 20, 1979, as enacted into permanent law by H.R. 7593, as passed the House of Representatives on July 21, 1980, and enacted into permanent law by Pub. L. 96–536, §101(c), Dec. 16, 1980, 94 Stat. 3167, which related to the employment of employees by Members of House of Representatives, Delegates, and Resident Commissioners, was repealed by Pub. L. 104–186, title I, §104(e)(2), Aug. 20, 1996, 110 Stat. 1721.

House Resolution No. 357, Ninety-first Congress, June 25, 1969, as enacted into permanent law by Pub. L. 91–145, §103, Dec. 12, 1969, 83 Stat. 359, which increased base Clerk Hire allowance of Members of House of Representatives and Resident Commissioner from Puerto Rico and authorized them to employ one additional clerk each, was repealed by Pub. L. 104–186, title I, §104(e)(3), Aug. 20, 1996, 110 Stat. 1721.

§ 92–1. Repealed. Pub. L. 104–186, title II, § 204(43), Aug. 20, 1996, 110 Stat. 1736

Section, based on H. Res. No. 294, §2, Eighty-eighth Congress, Aug. 14, 1964, as continued by H. Res. No. 7, Eighty-ninth Congress, Jan. 4, 1965, which was enacted into permanent law by Pub. L. 89–90, §103, July 27, 1965, 79 Stat. 281, related to place of performance of services for which clerk hire allowances were paid.

§ 92a. Pay of clerical assistants as affected by death of Senator or Representative

When a Senator or Member of the House of Representatives or Delegate or Resident Commissioner dies during his term of office the clerical assistants appointed by him, and then borne upon the pay rolls of the Senate or House of Representatives, shall be continued on such pay rolls in their respective positions and be paid for a period not longer than one month: *Provided,* That this shall not apply to clerical assistants of standing committees of the Senate or House of Representatives, when their service otherwise would continue beyond such period.

(Feb. 23, 1927, ch. 168, §1, 44 Stat. 1148.)

EMPLOYEES OF SENATE

Pub. L. 98–473, title I, §123A(a), Oct. 12, 1984, 98 Stat. 1969, provided that this section shall not apply to any employee of Senate.

SECTION REFERRED TO IN OTHER SECTIONS

This section is referred to in section 92b of this title.

§ 92b. Pay of clerical assistants as affected by death or resignation of Member of House

Notwithstanding the provisions of section 92a of this title, in case of the death or resignation of a Member of the House during his term of office, the clerical assistants designated by him and borne upon the clerk hire pay rolls of the House of Representatives on the date of such death or resignation shall be continued upon such pay rolls at their respective salaries until the successor to such Member of the House is elected to fill the vacancy.

(Aug. 21, 1935, ch. 600, §1, 49 Stat. 679; Apr. 24, 1950, ch. 96, 64 Stat. 82; July 15, 1952, ch. 759, §1, 66 Stat. 662; Pub. L. 89–554, §8(a), Sept. 6, 1966, 80 Stat. 657.)

AMENDMENTS

1966—Pub. L. 89–554 struck out sentence which related to retirement service credit.

1952—Joint Res. July 15, 1952, provided retirement credit to employees for time they were separated from employment following death or resignation of a Member and before election of his successor.

1950—Joint Res. Apr. 24, 1950, struck out second sentence which limited continuance of clerical assistants of deceased or resigned House Members on pay roll to six months.

EFFECTIVE DATE

Section 4 of act Aug. 21, 1935, provided that: "This joint resolution [enacting sections 92b to 92d of this title] shall be effective as of the beginning of the Seventy-fourth Congress, January 3, 1935."

SECTION REFERRED TO IN OTHER SECTIONS

This section is referred to in sections 92b–1, 92c, 92d of this title.

§ 92b–1. Termination of service of Members of House

(a) Until otherwise provided by law, for purposes of sections 92b, 92c, and 92d of this title, any termination of service during a term of office of a Member of the House that is not described in section 92b of this title shall be treated as if such termination were described in such section.

(b) The Clerk of the House shall take such action as may be necessary to apply the principles of section 92c of this title in the carrying out of sections 92b–1 to 92b–3 of this title.

(Pub. L. 97–51, § 101(c), Oct. 1, 1981, 95 Stat. 959.)

CODIFICATION

Section is based on section 1 of House Resolution 804, Ninety-sixth Congress, Oct. 2, 1980, as enacted into permanent law by H.R. 4120, as reported July 9, 1981, which was enacted into permanent law by section 101(c) of Pub. L. 97–51.

SECTION REFERRED TO IN OTHER SECTIONS

This section is referred to in sections 92b–2, 92b–3 of this title.

§ 92b–2. Authority to prescribe regulations

The Committee on House Oversight of the House of Representatives shall have authority to prescribe regulations for the carrying out of sections 92b–1 to 92b–3 of this title.

(Pub. L. 97–51, § 101(c), Oct. 1, 1981, 95 Stat. 959; Pub. L. 104–186, title II, § 204(44), Aug. 20, 1996, 110 Stat. 1736.)

CODIFICATION

Section is based on section 2 of House Resolution 804, Ninety-sixth Congress, Oct. 2, 1980, as enacted into permanent law by H.R. 4120, as reported July 9, 1981, which was enacted into permanent law by section 101(c) of Pub. L. 97–51.

AMENDMENTS

1996—Pub. L. 104–186 substituted "House Oversight of the House of Representatives" for "House Administration".

CHANGE OF NAME

Committee on House Oversight of House of Representatives changed to Committee on House Administration of House of Representatives by House Resolution No. 5, One Hundred Sixth Congress, Jan. 6, 1999.

SECTION REFERRED TO IN OTHER SECTIONS

This section is referred to in sections 92b–1, 92b–3 of this title.

§ 92b–3. Vouchers

Payments under sections 92b–1 to 92b–3 of this title shall be made on vouchers approved by the Committee on House Oversight of the House of Representatives and signed by the chairman of such committee.

(Pub. L. 97–51, § 101(c), Oct. 1, 1981, 95 Stat. 959; Pub. L. 104–186, title II, § 204(44), Aug. 20, 1996, 110 Stat. 1736.)

CODIFICATION

Section is based on section 3 of House Resolution 804, Ninety-sixth Congress, Oct. 2, 1980, as enacted into permanent law by H.R. 4120, as reported July 9, 1981, which was enacted into permanent law by section 101(c) of Pub. L. 97–51.

AMENDMENTS

1996—Pub. L. 104–186 substituted "House Oversight of the House of Representatives" for "House Administration".

CHANGE OF NAME

Committee on House Oversight of House of Representatives changed to Committee on House Administration of House of Representatives by House Resolution No. 5, One Hundred Sixth Congress, Jan. 6, 1999.

SECTION REFERRED TO IN OTHER SECTIONS

This section is referred to in sections 92b–1, 92b–2 of this title.

§ 92c. Performance of duties by clerical assistants of dead or resigned Member of House

Any clerical assistants who continue on the House pay rolls under the provisions of section 92b of this title shall, while so continued, perform their duties under the direction of the Clerk of the House, and he is authorized and directed to remove from such pay rolls any such clerks who are not attending to the duties for which their services are continued.

(Aug. 21, 1935, ch. 600, § 2, 49 Stat. 680.)

EFFECTIVE DATE

Section effective Jan. 3, 1935, see section 4 of act Aug. 21, 1935, set out as a note under section 92b of this title.

SECTION REFERRED TO IN OTHER SECTIONS

This section is referred to in section 92b–1 of this title.

§ 92d. "Member of the House" defined

As used in section 92b of this title the phrase "Member of the House" shall mean a Representative, Representative-elect, Delegate, Delegate-elect, Resident Commissioner, or Resident Commissioner-elect.

(Aug. 21, 1935, ch. 600, § 3, 49 Stat. 680.)

EFFECTIVE DATE

Section effective Jan. 3, 1935, see section 4 of act Aug. 21, 1935, set out as a note under section 92b of this title.

SECTION REFERRED TO IN OTHER SECTIONS

This section is referred to in section 92b–1 of this title.

§ 92e. Repealed. Pub. L. 98–473, title I, § 123A(b), Oct. 12, 1984, 98 Stat. 1969

Section, acts June 28, 1943, ch. 173, title I, 57 Stat. 223; June 26, 1944, ch. 277, title I, 58 Stat. 337; June 13, 1945, ch. 189, 59 Stat. 241; July 1, 1946, ch. 530, 60 Stat. 390, provided for continuation of salaries of clerical assistants to Senators upon death of that Senator in office.

§§ 93, 94. Omitted

Section 93, act June 28, 1886, No. 15, 24 Stat. 342, related to time of beginning of compensation of committee clerks. See section 72a of this title and Rules of House of Representatives.

Section 94, acts Mar. 4, 1925, ch. 549, § 1, 43 Stat. 1291; May 13, 1926, ch. 294, § 1, 44 Stat. 542; Feb. 23, 1927, ch. 168, § 1, 44 Stat. 1152; May 14, 1928, ch. 551, § 1, 45 Stat. 522; Feb. 28, 1929, ch. 367, § 1, 45 Stat. 1392; June 6, 1930, ch. 407, § 1, 46 Stat. 509; Feb. 20, 1931, ch. 234, § 1, 46 Stat. 1180; June 30, 1932, ch. 314, § 1, 47 Stat. 388; Feb. 28, 1933, ch. 134, § 1, 47 Stat. 1356, related to appointment and removal of janitors, and was limited to the appropriation acts of which it was a part.

§ 95. Omitted

Section was based on provisions of acts Oct. 2, 1888, ch. 1069, 25 Stat. 546; Mar. 4, 1911, ch. 240, 36 Stat. 1318; Aug. 2, 1946, ch. 753, § 121, 60 Stat. 822; Dec. 27, 1974, Pub. L. 93–554, title I, 88 Stat. 1776; Aug. 20, 1996, Pub. L. 104–186, title I, § 105(c), 110 Stat. 1722, relating to payments from contingent fund of House of Representatives prior to being struck out by Pub. L. 104–186. See section 95–1 of this title. Provisions of act Oct. 2, 1888, relating to payments from contingent fund of the Senate are classified to section 68 of this title.

§ 95–1. Payments from applicable accounts of House of Representatives

(a) In general

No payment may be made from the applicable accounts of the House of Representatives (as determined by the Committee on House Oversight of the House of Representatives), unless sanctioned by that Committee. Payments on vouchers approved in the manner directed by that Committee shall be deemed, held, and taken, and are declared to be conclusive upon all the departments and officers of the Government.

(b) Definitions

As used in this section—

(1) the term "applicable accounts of the House of Representatives" means accounts for salaries and expenses of committees (other than the Committee on Appropriations), the computer support organization of the House of Representatives, and allowances and expenses of Members of the House of Representatives, officers of the House of Representatives, and administrative and support offices of the House of Representatives; and

(2) the term "Member of the House of Representatives" means a Representative in, or a Delegate or Resident Commissioner to, the Congress.

(Pub. L. 104–186, title I, § 105, Aug. 20, 1996, 110 Stat. 1721.)

Section is comprised of section 105 of Pub. L. 104–186. Subsec. (c) of section 105 of Pub. L. 104–186 amended section 95 of this title.

Provisions similar to those in this section were contained in section 95 of this title prior to amendment by Pub. L. 104–186, § 105(c).

Committee on House Oversight of House of Representatives changed to Committee on House Adminis-

tration of House of Representatives by House Resolution No. 5, One Hundred Sixth Congress, Jan. 6, 1999.

§ 95a. Appropriations for expenses of House; restrictions

Appropriations made for expenses of the House of Representatives shall not be used for the payment of personal services except upon the express and specific authorization of the House in whose behalf such services are rendered. Nor shall such appropriations be used for any expenses not intimately and directly connected with the routine legislative business of the House of Representatives, and the General Accounting Office shall apply the provisions of this section in the settlement of the accounts of expenditures from said appropriations incurred for services or materials.

(Feb. 14, 1902, ch. 17, § 1, 32 Stat. 26; June 10, 1921, ch. 18, title III, § 304, 42 Stat. 24; Pub. L. 104–186, title II, § 204(45), Aug. 20, 1996, 110 Stat. 1737.)

Section is based on provisions of proviso on 32 Stat. 26, act of Feb. 14, 1902, ch. 17, the Urgent Deficiency Appropriation Act for the fiscal year 1902, relating to appropriations for contingent expenses of House of Representatives. Provisions of proviso relating to appropriations for expenses of Senate are classified to section 68–2 of this title.

Section was formerly classified to section 671 of Title 31 prior to the general revision and enactment of Title 31, Money and Finance, by Pub. L. 97–258, § 1, Sept. 13, 1982, 96 Stat. 877.

1996—Pub. L. 104–186 substituted "expenses of the House" for "contingent expenses of the House".

"General Accounting Office" substituted in text for "accounting officers of the Treasury" pursuant to act June 10, 1921, which transferred all powers and duties of the Comptroller, six auditors, and certain other employees of the Treasury to the General Accounting Office. See section 701 et seq. of Title 31, Money and Finance.

§ 95b. Transfers of amounts appropriated for House

(a) Transfers among categories of allowances and expenses

Amounts appropriated for any fiscal year for the House of Representatives under the heading "ALLOWANCES AND EXPENSES" may be transferred among the various categories of allowances and expenses under such heading, upon approval of the Committee on Appropriations of the House of Representatives.

(b) Transfers among offices and activities

Amounts appropriated for any fiscal year for the House of Representatives under the heading "SALARIES, OFFICERS AND EMPLOYEES" may be transferred among the various offices and activities under such heading, upon approval of the Committee on Appropriations of the House of Representatives.

(c) Transfers among various appropriations headings

(1) Amounts appropriated for any fiscal year for the House of Representatives under the head-

ings specified in paragraph (2) may be transferred among such headings, upon approval of the Committee on Appropriations of the House of Representatives.

(2) The headings referred to in paragraph (1) are "HOUSE LEADERSHIP OFFICES", "MEMBERS' CLERK HIRE", "COMMITTEE EMPLOYEES", "STANDING COMMITTEES, SPECIAL AND SELECT", "HOUSE INFORMATION SYSTEMS", "ALLOWANCES AND EXPENSES", "OFFICIAL MAIL COSTS", and "SALARIES, OFFICERS AND EMPLOYEES".

(Pub. L. 102-392, title I, §101, Oct. 6, 1992, 106 Stat. 1709.)

CODIFICATION

Section is from the Congressional Operations Appropriations Act, 1993, which is title I of the Legislative Branch Appropriations Act, 1993.

CATEGORIES OF ALLOWANCES AND EXPENSES

Pub. L. 105-55, title I, §102, Oct. 7, 1997, 111 Stat. 1183, provided that: "The funds and accounts specified in section 107(b) of the Legislative Branch Appropriations Act, 1996 (2 U.S.C. 123b note) shall be treated as categories of allowances and expenses for purposes of section 101(a) of the Legislative Branch Appropriations Act, 1993 (2 U.S.C. 95b(a))."

SECTION REFERRED TO IN OTHER SECTIONS

This section is referred to in section 95d of this title.

§ 95c. Advance payments

(a) Authorization

For fiscal year 1998 and each succeeding fiscal year, the Chief Administrative Officer of the House of Representatives is authorized to make advance payments under a contract or other agreement to provide a service or deliver an article for the United States Government without regard to the provisions of section 3324 of title 31.

(b) Regulations

An advance payment authorized by subsection (a) of this section shall be made in accordance with regulations issued by the Committee on House Oversight of the House of Representatives.

(c) Effective date

The authority granted by subsection (a) of this section shall not take effect until regulations are issued pursuant to subsection (b) of this section.

(Pub. L. 105-55, title I, §108, Oct. 7, 1997, 111 Stat. 1184.)

CODIFICATION

Section is from the Congressional Operations Appropriations Act, 1998, which is title I of the Legislative Branch Appropriations Act, 1998.

CHANGE OF NAME

Committee on House Oversight of House of Representatives changed to Committee on House Administration of House of Representatives by House Resolution No. 5, One Hundred Sixth Congress, Jan. 6, 1999.

§ 95d. Account in House of Representatives for Employees' Compensation Fund

(a) Establishment

There is hereby established an account in the House of Representatives for purposes of making payments of the House of Representatives to the Employees' Compensation Fund under section 8147 of title 5.

(b) Payments made from account

Notwithstanding any other provision of law, payments may be made from the account established under subsection (a) of this section at any time after October 7, 1997, without regard to the fiscal year for which the obligation to make such payments is incurred.

(c) Category of allowances and expenses

The account established under subsection (a) of this section shall be treated as a category of allowances and expenses for purposes of section 95b(a) of this title.

(Pub. L. 105-55, title I, §109, Oct. 7, 1997, 111 Stat. 1184.)

CODIFICATION

Section is from the Congressional Operations Appropriations Act, 1998, which is title I of the Legislative Branch Appropriations Act, 1998.

§§ 96 to 100. Repealed. Pub. L. 104-186, title II, § 204(46)-(51), Aug. 20, 1996, 110 Stat. 1737

Section 96, acts July 16, 1914, ch. 141, §1, 38 Stat. 462; Mar. 3, 1926, ch. 44, §1, 44 Stat. 163, related to payment of certain bills from moneys of House.

Section 96a, Pub. L. 103-69, title III, §311, Aug. 11, 1993, 107 Stat. 712, related to transfer of responsibility for legislative service organization financial activity to Clerk of House.

Section 97, act Mar. 2, 1895, ch. 177, §1, 28 Stat. 768, related to temporary committee on accounts of House.

Section 98, act Mar. 3, 1885, ch. 360, 23 Stat. 512, related to contracts for horses for service of House of Representatives.

Section 99, act Mar. 3, 1891, ch. 541, §1, 26 Stat. 914, related to contracts for horses and mail wagons for House of Representatives.

Section 100, act Mar. 3, 1901, ch. 830, §1, 31 Stat. 967, related to contracts for packing boxes for House.

§ 101. Subletting duties of employees of Senate or House

No employee of Congress, either in the Senate or House, shall sublet to, or hire, another to do or perform any part of the duties or work attached to the position to which he was appointed.

(Mar. 2, 1895, ch. 177, §1, 28 Stat. 771.)

§ 102. Repealed. Pub. L. 104-186, title II, § 204(52), Aug. 20, 1996, 110 Stat. 1737

Section, R.S. §§60, 61; Pub. L. 86-628, §105(c), July 12, 1960, 74 Stat. 461, required submission by Secretary of Senate and Clerk of House to two Houses of statements as to persons employed and as to expenditures and balances on hand and providing for printing of such reports as Senate and House documents. See sections 104a and 104b of this title.

§ 102a. Withdrawal of unexpended balances of appropriations

Notwithstanding the provisions of any other law, the unexpended balances of appropriations for the fiscal year 1955 and succeeding fiscal years which are subject to disbursement by the Secretary of the Senate or the Chief Administrative Officer of the House of Representatives shall be withdrawn as of June 30 of the second fiscal year following the year for which provided, except that the unexpended balances of such appropriations for the period commencing on July 1, 1976, and ending on September 30, 1976, and for each fiscal year beginning on or after October 1, 1976, shall be withdrawn as of September 30 of the second fiscal year following the period or year for which provided. Unpaid obligations chargeable to any of the balances so withdrawn or appropriations for prior years shall be liquidated from any appropriations for the same general purpose, which, at the time of payment, are available for disbursement.

(Pub. L. 85–58, ch. XI, June 21, 1957, 71 Stat. 190; Pub. L. 94–303, title I, § 118(a), June 1, 1976, 90 Stat. 615; Pub. L. 104–186, title II, § 204(53), Aug. 20, 1996, 110 Stat. 1737.)

AMENDMENTS

1996—Pub. L. 104–186 substituted "Chief Administrative Officer" for "Clerk".

1976—Pub. L. 94–303 provided that unexpended balances for period commencing July 1, 1976, and ending Sept. 30, 1976, and for each fiscal year beginning on or after Oct. 1, 1976, be withdrawn as of Sept. 30 of second fiscal year following period or year for which provided.

SECTION REFERRED TO IN OTHER SECTIONS

This section is referred to in title 40 section 188b–6.

§§ 103, 104. Omitted

CODIFICATION

Section 103, R.S. § 62, authorized Secretary of Senate and Clerk of House to require disbursing officers subject to their authority to return analytical statements and receipts for expenditures and to communicate such returns annually to Congress. See sections 104a and 104b of this title.

Section 104, R.S. § 63, required that all expenditures of Senate and House be made up to end of each fiscal year and reported to Congress at beginning of each regular session. See sections 104a and 104b of this title.

§ 104a. Semiannual statements of expenditures by Secretary of Senate and Chief Administrative Officer of House

(1) Commencing with the semiannual period beginning on July 1, 1964, and ending on December 31, 1964, and for each semiannual period thereafter, the Secretary of the Senate and the Chief Administrative Officer of the House of Representatives shall compile, and, not later than sixty days following the close of the semiannual period, submit to the Senate and House of Representatives, respectively, and make available to the public, in lieu of the reports and information required by sections 102, 103, and 104[1] of this title, and S. Res. 139, Eighty-sixth Congress, a report containing a detailed statement, by items, of the manner in which appropriations and other funds available for disbursement by the Secretary of the Senate and the Chief Administrative Officer of the House of Representatives, as the case may be, have been expended during the semiannual period covered by the report, including (1) the name of every person to whom any part of such appropriation has been paid, (2) if for anything furnished, the

quantity and price thereof, (3) if for services rendered, the nature of the services, the time employed, and the name, title, and specific amount paid to each person, and (4) a complete statement of all amounts appropriated, received, or expended, and any unexpended balances. Such reports shall include the information contained in statements of accountability and supporting vouchers submitted to the General Accounting Office pursuant to the provisions of section 3523(a) of title 31. Notwithstanding the foregoing provisions of this section, in any case in which the voucher or vouchers covering payment to any person for attendance as a witness before any committee of the Senate or House of Representatives, or any subcommittee thereof, during any semiannual period, indicate that all appearances of such person covered by such voucher or vouchers were as a witness in executive session of the committee or subcommittee, information regarding such payment, except for date of payment, voucher number, and amount paid, shall not be included in the report compiled pursuant to this subsection for such semiannual period. Any information excluded from a report for any semiannual period by reason of the foregoing sentence shall be included in the report compiled pursuant to this section for the succeeding semiannual period. Reports required to be submitted to the Senate and the House of Representatives under this section shall be printed as Senate and House documents, respectively.

(2) The report by the Secretary of the Senate under paragraph (1) for the semiannual period beginning on January 1, 1976, shall include the period beginning on July 1, 1976, and ending on September 30, 1976, and such semiannual period shall be treated as closing on September 30, 1976. Thereafter, the report by the Secretary of the Senate under paragraph (1) shall be for the semiannual periods beginning on October 1 and ending on March 31 and beginning on April 1 and ending on September 30 of each year.

(3) The report requirement relating to quantity, as contained in subparagraph (2) of paragraph (1), does not apply with respect to the Senate.

(4) Each report by the Secretary of the Senate required by paragraph (1) shall contain a separate summary of Senate accounts statement for each office of the Senate authorized to obligate appropriated funds, including each Senator's office, each officer of the Senate, and each committee of the Senate. The summary of Senate accounts statement shall include—

(A) the total amount of appropriations made available or allocated to the office;

(B) any supplemental appropriation, transfer of funds, or rescission and the effect of such action on the appropriation or allocation to the office;

(C) total expenses incurred for salary and office expenses; and

(D) the unexpended balance.

(5)(A) Notwithstanding the requirements of paragraph (1) relating to the level of detail of statement and itemization, each report by the Secretary of the Senate required under such paragraph shall be compiled at a summary level for each office of the Senate authorized to obligate appropriated funds.

---

[1] See References in Text note below.

(B) Subparagraph (A) shall not apply to the reporting of expenditures relating to personnel compensation, travel and transportation of persons, other contractual services, and acquisition of assets.

(C) In carrying out this paragraph the Secretary of the Senate shall apply the Standard Federal Object Classification of Expenses as the Secretary determines appropriate.

(Pub. L. 88–454, §105(a), Aug. 20, 1964, 78 Stat. 550; Pub. L. 88–656, Oct. 13, 1964, 78 Stat. 1088; Pub. L. 94–303, title I, §118(b)(1), June 1, 1976, 90 Stat. 615; Pub. L. 102–392, title I, §6, Oct. 6, 1992, 106 Stat. 1707; Pub. L. 103–283, title I, §3(a), July 22, 1994, 108 Stat. 1426; Pub. L. 104–186, title II, §204(54), Aug. 20, 1996, 110 Stat. 1738; Pub. L. 106–554, §1(a)(2) [title I, §1(a)], Dec. 21, 2000, 114 Stat. 2763, 2763A–95.)

INAPPLICABILITY OF SECTION TO HOUSE OF REPRESENTATIVES

Provisions of this section requiring submission and printing of statements and reports not applicable to the House of Representatives, see section 104b(e) of this title.

REFERENCES IN TEXT

Section 102 of this title, referred to in par. (1), was repealed by Pub. L. 104–186, title II, §204(52), Aug. 20, 1996, 110 Stat. 1737.

Sections 103 and 104 of this title, referred to in par. (1), were omitted from the Code.

CODIFICATION

In par. (1), "section 3523(a) of title 31" substituted for "section 117(a) of the Budget and Accounting Procedures Act of 1950 (31 U.S.C. 67(a))" on authority of Pub. L. 97–258, §4(b), Sept. 13, 1982, 96 Stat. 1067, the first section of which enacted Title 31, Money and Finance.

Section is based on the first paragraph of section 105 (a) of Pub. L. 88–454. Remainder of section 105(a) was classified to section 67 of former Title 31, which was repealed by Pub. L. 97–258, §5(b), Sept. 13, 1982, 96 Stat. 1068, and reenacted as section 3523 of Title 31, Money and Finance.

AMENDMENTS

2000—Par. (5). Pub. L. 106–554 added par. (5).

1996—Par. (1). Pub. L. 104–186 substituted "Chief Administrative Officer" for "Clerk" in two places.

1994—Pub. L. 103–283 added par. (4).

1992—Pub. L. 102–392 added par. (3).

1976—Pub. L. 94–303 designated existing provisions as par. (1) and added par. (2).

1964—Pub. L. 88–656 provided that information regarding persons paid by voucher for appearances as a witness before any committee of Congress in executive session shall not be included in semiannual report except for date of payment, voucher number, and amount paid, however, any information so excluded shall be included in next succeeding semiannual period.

EFFECTIVE DATE OF 2000 AMENDMENT

Pub. L. 106–554, §1(a)(2) [title I, §1(b)], Dec. 21, 2000, 114 Stat. 2763, 2763A–96, provided that:

"(1) IN GENERAL.—Subject to paragraph (2), the amendment made by this section [amending this section] shall take effect on the date of enactment of this Act [Dec. 21, 2000].

"(2) FIRST REPORT AFTER ENACTMENT.—The Secretary of the Senate may elect to compile and submit the report for the semiannual period during which the date of enactment of this section occurs, as if the amendment made by this section had not been enacted."

EFFECTIVE DATE OF 1994 AMENDMENT

Amendment by Pub. L. 103–283 effective with respect to reports and statements covering periods beginning on and after Oct. 1, 1994, and appropriations made and obligations incurred on and after such date, see section 3(c) of Pub. L. 103–283, set out as a note under section 59f of this title.

TERMINATION OF REPORTING REQUIREMENTS

For termination, effective May 15, 2000, of provisions of law requiring submittal to Congress of any annual, semiannual, or other regular periodic report listed in House Document No. 103–7 (in which the report required by this section is listed on page 1), see section 3003 of Pub. L. 104–66, as amended, set out as a note under section 1113 of Title 31, Money and Finance.

SECTION REFERRED TO IN OTHER SECTIONS

This section is referred to in section 104b of this title.

§ 104b. Report of disbursements for House of Representatives

(a) In general

Not later than 60 days after the last day of each semiannual period, the Chief Administrative Officer of the House of Representatives shall submit to the House of Representatives, with respect to that period, a detailed, itemized report of the disbursements for the operations of the House of Representatives.

(b) Contents

The report required by subsection (a) of this section shall include—

(1) the name of each person who receives a payment from the House of Representatives;

(2) the quantity and price of any item furnished to the House of Representatives;

(3) a description of any service rendered to the House of Representatives, together with a statement of the time required for the service, and the name, title, and amount paid to each person who renders the service;

(4) a statement of all amounts appropriated to, or received, or expended by the House of Representatives, and any unexpended balances of such amounts;

(5) the information submitted to the Comptroller General under section 3523(a) of title 31; and

(6) such additional information as may be required by regulation of the Committee on House Oversight of the House of Representatives.

(c) Exclusion

Notwithstanding subsection (b) of this section, if a voucher is for payment to an individual for attendance as a witness before a committee of the Congress in executive session, the report for the semiannual period in which the appearance occurs shall show only the date of payment, voucher number, and amount paid. Any information excluded from a report under the preceding sentence shall be included in the report for the next period.

(d) House document

Each report under this section shall be printed as a House document.

(e) Conforming provision

The provisions of—

(1) sections 102, 103, and 104[1] of this title; and

---

[1] See References in Text note below.

(2) section 104a of this title;

that require submission and printing of statements and reports are not applicable to the House of Representatives.

(f) Effective date

This section shall apply to the semiannual periods of January 1 through June 30 and July 1 through December 31 of each year, beginning with the semiannual period in which this section is enacted.

(Pub. L. 104–186, title I, § 106, Aug. 20, 1996, 110 Stat. 1722.)

REFERENCES IN TEXT

Section 102 of this title, referred to in subsec. (e)(1), was repealed by Pub. L. 104–186, title II, § 204(52), Aug. 20, 1996, 110 Stat. 1737.

Sections 103 and 104 of this title, referred to in subsec. (e)(1), were omitted from the Code.

CHANGE OF NAME

Committee on House Oversight of House of Representatives changed to Committee on House Administration of House of Representatives by House Resolution No. 5, One Hundred Sixth Congress, Jan. 6, 1999.

SIMILAR PROVISIONS

Provisions similar to those in this section are contained in section 104a of this title, but were made inapplicable to the House of Representatives by subsec. (e) of this section.

REPORTING PAYMENTS MADE TO WITNESSES BEFORE COMMITTEE ON STANDARDS OF OFFICIAL CONDUCT

Pub. L. 105–275, title I, § 105, Oct. 21, 1998, 112 Stat. 2439, provided that: "Notwithstanding any other provision of law or any other rule or regulation, any information on payments made by the Committee on Standards of Official Conduct of the House of Representatives to an individual for attendance as a witness before the Committee in executive session during a Congress shall be reported not later than the second semiannual report filed under section 106 of the House of Representatives Administrative Reform Technical Corrections Act (2 U.S.C. 104b) in the following Congress."

§ 105. Preparation and contents of statement of appropriations

The statement of all appropriations made during each session of Congress shall be prepared under the direction of the Committees on Appropriations of the Senate and House of Representatives, and said statement shall contain a chronological history of the regular appropriation bills passed during the session for which it is prepared. The statement shall indicate the amount of contracts authorized by appropriation Acts in addition to appropriations made therein, and shall also contain specific reference to all indefinite appropriations made each session and shall contain such additional information concerning estimates and appropriations as the committees may deem necessary.

(Oct. 19, 1888, ch. 1210, § 1, 25 Stat. 587; July 19, 1897, ch. 9, 30 Stat. 136; June 7, 1924, ch. 303, § 1, 43 Stat. 586.)

SECTION REFERRED TO IN OTHER SECTIONS

This section is referred to in title 44 section 725.

§ 106. Stationery for Senate; advertisements for

The Secretary of the Senate shall annually advertise, once a week for at least four weeks, in one or more of the principal papers published in the District of Columbia, for sealed proposals for supplying the Senate during the next session of Congress with the necessary stationery. The advertisement must describe the kind of stationery required, and must require the proposals to be accompanied with sufficient security for their performance.

(R.S. §§ 65, 66; Feb. 18, 1875, ch. 80, § 1, 18 Stat. 316; Pub. L. 104–186, title II, § 204(55), Aug. 20, 1996, 110 Stat. 1738.)

CODIFICATION

R.S. §§ 65, 66 derived from Res. Mar. 3, 1815, No. 11, 3 Stat. 249.

First sentence of section is based on R.S. § 65; second sentence of section is based on R.S. § 66.

AMENDMENTS

1996—Pub. L. 104–186 struck out "and Clerk of the House of Representatives" after "Secretary of the Senate" and "and House of Representatives, respectively," after "supplying the Senate".

SECTION REFERRED TO IN OTHER SECTIONS

This section is referred to in sections 108, 112 of this title.

§ 107. Opening bids for Senate and House stationery; awarding contracts

All such proposals shall be kept sealed until the day specified in such advertisement for opening the same, when the same shall be opened in the presence of at least two persons, and the contract shall be given to the lowest bidder, provided he shall give satisfactory security to perform the same, under a forfeiture not exceeding double the contract price in case of failure; and in case the lowest bidder shall fail to enter into such contract and give such security, within a time to be fixed in such advertisement, then the contract shall be given to the next lowest bidder, who shall enter into such contract, and give such security. And in case of failure by the person entering into such contract to perform the same, he and his sureties shall be liable for the forfeiture specified in such contract, as liquidated damages, to be sued for in the name of the United States.

(R.S. § 67; Feb. 18, 1875, ch. 80, § 1, 18 Stat. 316.)

CODIFICATION

R.S. § 67 derived from Res. Mar. 3, 1815, No. 11, 3 Stat. 249.

SECTION REFERRED TO IN OTHER SECTIONS

This section is referred to in sections 108, 112 of this title.

§ 108. Contracts for separate parts of Senate stationery

Sections 106 and 107 of this title shall not prevent the Secretary from contracting for separate parts of the supplies of stationery required to be furnished.

(R.S. § 68; Pub. L. 104–186, title II, § 204(56), Aug. 20, 1996, 110 Stat. 1738.)

CODIFICATION

R.S. § 68 derived from Res. Mar. 3, 1815, No. 11, 3 Stat. 249.

AMENDMENTS

1996—Pub. L. 104–186 substituted "the Secretary" for "either the Secretary or the Clerk".

SECTION REFERRED TO IN OTHER SECTIONS

This section is referred to in section 112 of this title.

§ 109. American goods to be preferred in purchases for Senate and House

The Secretary of the Senate and the Chief Administrative Officer of the House of Representatives shall, in disbursing the public moneys for the use of the two Houses, respectively, purchase only articles the growth and manufacture of the United States, provided the articles required can be procured of such growth and manufacture upon as good terms as to quality and price as are demanded for like articles of foreign growth and manufacture.

(R.S. § 69; Pub. L. 104–186, title II, § 204(57), Aug. 20, 1996, 110 Stat. 1738.)

CODIFICATION

R.S. § 69 derived from act June 17, 1844, ch. 105, § 1, 5 Stat. 681.

AMENDMENTS

1996—Pub. L. 104–186 substituted "Chief Administrative Officer" for "Clerk".

SECTION REFERRED TO IN OTHER SECTIONS

This section is referred to in section 112 of this title.

§ 110. Purchase of paper, envelopes, etc., for stationery rooms of Senate and House

Paper, envelopes, and blank books required by the stationery rooms of the Senate and House of Representatives for sale to Senators and Members for official use may be purchased from the Public Printer at actual cost thereof and payment therefor shall be made before delivery.

(June 5, 1920, ch. 253, § 1, 41 Stat. 1036.)

CHANGE OF NAME

Stationery room of House of Representatives redesignated Office Supply Service.

§ 111. Purchase of supplies for Senate and House

Supplies for use of the Senate and the House of Representatives may be purchased in accordance with the schedule of contract articles and prices of the Administrator of General Services.

(June 5, 1920, ch. 253, § 1, 41 Stat. 1036; Ex. Ord. No. 6166, June 10, 1933, § 1; June 30, 1949, ch. 288, title I, § 102, 63 Stat. 380.)

TRANSFER OF FUNCTIONS

Bureau of Federal Supply and its functions and duties transferred to Administrator of General Services by act June 30, 1949.

Effective Jan. 1, 1947, Procurement Division of Treasury Department changed to Bureau of Federal Supply by former regulation § 5.7 of subpart A of Part 5 of Title 41, Public Contracts, 11 F.R. 13638, issued by the Secretary of the Treasury.

Ex. Ord. No. 6166, abolished General Supply Committee of Treasury Department and vested it in Procurement Division. Public Buildings Branch of Procurement Division was in turn changed to Public Buildings Administration to be within Federal Works Agency by Reorg. Plan No. I, §§ 301, 303, eff. July 1, 1939, 4 F.R. 2729, 53 Stat. 1426, 1427.

§ 111a. Receipts from sales of items by Sergeant at Arms and Doorkeeper of Senate, to Senators, etc., to be credited to appropriation from which purchased

In any case in which appropriated funds are used by a Senator or a committee or office of the Senate to purchase from the Sergeant at Arms and Doorkeeper of the Senate items which were purchased by him from the appropriation for "miscellaneous items" under "Contingent Expenses of the Senate" in any appropriation Act, the amounts received by the Sergeant at Arms and Doorkeeper shall be deposited in the Treasury of the United States for credit to such appropriation. This section does not apply to amounts received from the sale of used or surplus furniture and equipment.

(Pub. L. 96–214, Mar. 24, 1980, 94 Stat. 122.)

§ 111b. Contracts to furnish property, supplies, or services to Congress; terms varying from those offered other entities of Federal Government

Notwithstanding any provision to the contrary in any contract which is entered into by any person and either the Administrator of General Services or a contracting officer of any executive agency and under which such person agrees to sell or lease to the Federal Government (or any one or more entities thereof) any unit of property, supplies, or services at a specified price or under specified terms and conditions (or both), such person may sell or lease to the Congress the same type of such property, supplies, or services at a unit price or under terms and conditions (or both) which are different from those specified in such contract; and any such sale or lease of any unit or units of such property, supplies, or services to the Congress shall not be taken into account for the purpose of determining the price at which, or the terms and conditions under which, such person is obligated under such contract to sell or lease any unit of such property, supplies, or services to any entity of the Federal Government other than the Congress. For purposes of the preceding sentence, any sale or lease of property, supplies, or services to the Senate (or any office or instrumentality thereof) or to the House of Representatives (or any office or instrumentality thereof) shall be deemed to be a sale or lease of such property, supplies, or services to the Congress.

(Pub. L. 98–63, title I, § 903(a), July 30, 1983, 97 Stat. 336.)

CODIFICATION

Section is from the Supplemental Appropriations Act, 1983.

EFFECTIVE DATE

Section 903(b) of Pub. L. 98–63 provided that: "The provisions of this section [enacting this section] shall take effect with respect to sales or leases of property, supplies, or services to the Congress after the date of enactment of this section [July 30, 1983]."

SALE OR LEASE OF PROPERTY, SUPPLIES, OR SERVICES TO CONGRESSIONAL BUDGET OFFICE DEEMED SALE OR LEASE TO CONGRESS

Sale or lease of property, supplies, or services to the Congressional Budget Office deemed a sale or lease of such property, supplies, or services to the Congress, see section 605 of this title.

SECTION REFERRED TO IN OTHER SECTIONS

This section is referred to in section 605 of this title.

§ 112. Purchases of stationery and materials for folding

Purchases of stationery and materials for folding shall be made in accordance with sections 106 to 109 of this title.

All contracts and bonds for purchases made under the authority of this section shall be filed with the Committee on Rules and Administration of the Senate.

(Mar. 3, 1887, ch. 392, § 1, 24 Stat. 596; Aug. 2, 1946 ch. 753, § 102, 60 Stat. 814; Pub. L. 104–186, title II, § 204(58), Aug. 20, 1996, 110 Stat. 1738.)

AMENDMENTS

1996—Pub. L. 104–186 struck out "or the Committee on Accounts of the House of Representatives respectively" before period at end.

1946—Act Aug. 2, 1946, substituted "Committee on Rules and Administration" for the "Committee to Audit and Control the Contingent Expenses".

EFFECTIVE DATE OF 1946 AMENDMENT

Section 142 of act Aug. 2, 1946, provided that the amendment made by that act is effective Jan. 2, 1947.

§§ 112a to 112d. Repealed. Pub. L. 91–139, § 2(a), Dec. 5, 1969, 83 Stat. 291

For subject matter of former sections 112a to 112d of this title, see section 112e of this title.

Section 112a, acts Mar. 25, 1953, ch. 10, § 1, 67 Stat. 7; Mar. 25, 1955, ch. 15, §§ 1, 2, 69 Stat. 13; Feb. 25, 1956, ch. 72, § 1, 70 Stat. 30; July 26, 1961, Pub. L. 87–107, § 1, 75 Stat. 221; Aug. 13, 1965, Pub. L. 89–122, 79 Stat. 517; Nov. 8, 1965, Pub. L. 89–342, 79 Stat. 1302, authorized electrical and mechanical office equipment for House Members, officers, and committees.

Section 112a–1, act Mar. 25, 1953, ch. 10, § 2, as added Feb. 25, 1956, ch. 72, § 2, 70 Stat. 31; amended July 26, 1961, Pub. L. 87–107, § 2, 75 Stat. 221; Oct. 9, 1965, Pub. L. 89–248, 79 Stat. 968; Oct. 24, 1967, Pub. L. 90–116, 81 Stat. 337, related to supply of additional typewriters.

Section 112a–2, act Mar. 25, 1953, ch. 10, § 3, as added Feb. 25, 1956, ch. 72, § 2, 70 Stat. 31, provided for payment for equipment supplied.

Section 112b, act Mar. 25, 1953, ch. 10, § 4, formerly § 2, 67 Stat. 8, renumbered § 4, Feb. 25, 1956, ch. 72, § 2, 70 Stat. 31, provided for registration and ownership of equipment supplied.

Section 112c, act Mar. 25, 1953, ch. 10, § 6, formerly § 4, 67 Stat. 8, renumbered § 6, Feb. 25, 1956, ch. 72, § 2, 70 Stat. 31, defined "Member".

Section 112d, act Mar. 25, 1953, ch. 10, § 7, formerly § 5, 67 Stat. 8, renumbered § 7, Feb. 25, 1956, ch. 72, § 2, 70 Stat. 31, related to the issuance of rules and regulations.

EFFECTIVE DATE OF REPEAL

Repeal effective at beginning of first calendar month which commenced on or after Dec. 5, 1969, see section 3 of Pub. L. 91–139, set out as an Effective Date note under section 112e of this title.

SAVINGS PROVISION

Section 2(b) of Pub. L. 91–139 provided that: "The repeal by subsection (a) of this section of the joint resolution of March 25, 1953 [sections 112a to 112d of this title], does not deprive any Member, officer, or committee of the House of Representatives, or the Resident Commissioner from Puerto Rico, of entitlement to the continued possession and use of office equipment furnished, under any provision of that joint resolution, to that Member, officer, committee, or the Resident Commissioner from Puerto Rico, and in use on the effective date of this Act [see Effective Date note set out under section 112e of this title]. However, the total value (less allowance for depreciation) of that equipment furnished to a Member or the Resident Commissioner under the first section and section 2 of the joint resolution of March 25, 1953, while in use by that Member or the Resident Commissioner on and after the effective date of this Act shall be taken into account for the purpose of determining the total value of equipment in use at any one time in the office of the Member or the Resident Commissioner under the regulations prescribed by the Committee on House Administration under the first section of this Act [section 112e of this title]."

§ 112e. Office equipment for House Members, officers, and committees

(a) Authority of Chief Administrative Officer

At the request of any Member, officer, or committee of the House of Representatives, or the Resident Commissioner from Puerto Rico, and with the approval of the Committee on House Oversight, but subject to the limitations prescribed by this Act, the Chief Administrative Officer of the House of Representatives shall furnish office equipment for use in the office of that Member, Resident Commissioner, officer, or committee. Office equipment so furnished is limited to equipment of those types and categories which the Committee on House Oversight shall prescribe.

(b) Registration and ownership

Office equipment furnished under this section shall be registered in the office of the Chief Administrative Officer of the House of Representatives and shall remain the property of the House of Representatives.

(c) Payment

The cost of office equipment furnished under this section shall be paid from the applicable accounts of the House of Representatives.

(d) Rules and regulations

The Committee on House Oversight shall prescribe such regulations as it considers necessary to carry out the purposes of this section.

(Pub. L. 91–139, § 1, Dec. 5, 1969, 83 Stat. 291; Pub. L. 104–186, title II, § 204(59), Aug. 20, 1996, 110 Stat. 1738.)

REFERENCES IN TEXT

This Act, referred to in subsec. (a), is Pub. L. 91–139, Dec. 5, 1969, 83 Stat. 291, which is classified generally to this section. For complete classification of this Act to the Code, see Tables.

AMENDMENTS

1996—Subsec. (a). Pub. L. 104–186, § 204(59)(A)(i), (B)(i), substituted "House Oversight" for "House Administration" in two places and "Chief Administrative Officer of the House of Representatives shall furnish" for "Clerk of the House shall furnish electrical and mechanical".

Subsec. (b). Pub. L. 104–186, § 204(59)(A)(ii), substituted "Chief Administrative Officer" for "Clerk".

Subsec. (c). Pub. L. 104–186, § 204(59)(B)(ii), substituted "applicable accounts" for "contingent fund".

Subsec. (d). Pub. L. 104–186, § 204(59)(B)(i), (iii), substituted "House Oversight" for "House Administration" and struck out at end "The regulations shall limit, on such basis as the committee considers appropriate, the total value of office equipment, with allowance for equipment depreciation, which may be in use at any one time in the office of a Member or the Resident Commissioner.''

CHANGE OF NAME

Committee on House Oversight of House of Representatives changed to Committee on House Administration of House of Representatives by House Resolution No. 5, One Hundred Sixth Congress, Jan. 6, 1999.

EFFECTIVE DATE

Section 3 of Pub. L. 91–139 provided that: "This Act [enacting this section and provisions set out as notes under this section and sections 112a to 112d of this title, and repealing sections 112a to 112d of this title] shall become effective at the beginning of the first calendar month which commences on or after the date of enactment of this Act [Dec. 5, 1969].''

§ 112f. Incidental use of equipment and supplies

(a) Notwithstanding any other provision of law, the Committee on House Oversight may prescribe by regulation appropriate conditions for the incidental use, for other than official business, of equipment and supplies owned or leased by, or the cost of which is reimbursed by, the House of Representatives.

(b) The authority of the Committee on House Oversight to prescribe regulations pursuant to subsection (a) of this section shall apply with respect to fiscal year 1999 and each succeeding fiscal year.

(Pub. L. 105–275, title I, § 106, Oct. 21, 1998, 112 Stat. 2439.)

CODIFICATION

Section is from the Congressional Operations Appropriations Act, 1999, which is title I of the Legislative Branch Appropriations Act, 1999.

CHANGE OF NAME

Committee on House Oversight of House of Representatives changed to Committee on House Administration of House of Representatives by House Resolution No. 5, One Hundred Sixth Congress, Jan. 6, 1999.

§ 113. Detailed reports of receipts and expenditures by Secretary of Senate and Chief Administrative Officer of House

The Secretary of the Senate and the Chief Administrative Officer of the House of Representatives, respectively, shall report to Congress on the first day of each regular session, and at the expiration of their terms of service, a full and complete statement of all their receipts and expenditures as such officers, showing in detail the items of expense, classifying them under the proper appropriations, and also showing the aggregate thereof, and exhibiting in a clear and concise manner the exact condition of all public moneys by them received, paid out, and remaining in their possession as such officers.

(R.S. § 70; Pub. L. 104–186, title II, § 204(60), Aug. 20, 1996, 110 Stat. 1738.)

CODIFICATION

R.S. § 70 derived from act July 15, 1870, ch. 302, § 1, 16 Stat. 365.

AMENDMENTS

1996—Pub. L. 104–186 substituted "Chief Administrative Officer" for "Clerk".

§ 114. Fees for copies from Senate journals

The Secretary of the Senate is entitled, for transcribing and certifying extracts from the journal of the Senate or the executive Journal of the Senate when the injunction of secrecy has been removed, except when such transcripts are required by an officer of the United States in a matter relating to the duties of his office, to receive from the persons for whom such transcripts are prepared the sum of 10 cents for each sheet containing one hundred words.

(R.S. § 71; Pub. L. 104–186, title II, § 204(61), Aug. 20, 1996, 110 Stat. 1738.)

CODIFICATION

R.S. § 71 derived from acts Sept. 15, 1789, ch. 14, § 6, 1 Stat. 69; Aug. 8, 1846, ch. 107, § 2, 9 Stat. 80; and Apr. 23, 1856, ch. 20, 11 Stat. 5.

AMENDMENTS

1996—Pub. L. 104–186 substituted "Secretary of the Senate is" for "Secretary of the Senate and the Clerk of the House of Representatives, respectively, are" and struck out "or from the journal of the House of Representatives," after "has been removed,".

§ 115. Index to House daily calendar

The index to the daily calendar of business of the House of Representatives shall be printed only on Monday of each week.

(Mar. 1, 1921, ch. 89, § 1, 41 Stat. 1181.)

§ 116. Repealed. May 29, 1928, ch. 901, § 1, 45 Stat. 995

Section, R.S. § 72, related to accounting by the Secretaries, Clerks, Sergeant at Arms, Postmasters, and Doorkeepers of Senate and House for property of the Government in their possession.

§ 117. Sale of waste paper and condemned furniture

It shall be the duty of the Secretary and Sergeant at Arms of the Senate to cause to be sold all waste paper and useless documents and condemned furniture that may accumulate, in their respective departments or offices, under the direction of the Committee on Rules and Administration of the Senate and cover the proceeds thereof into the Treasury.

(Aug. 7, 1882, ch. 433, § 1, 22 Stat. 337; May 29, 1928, ch. 901, § 1(122), 45 Stat. 995; Pub. L. 104–186, title II, § 204(62), Aug. 20, 1996, 110 Stat. 1739.)

AMENDMENTS

1996—Pub. L. 104–186 struck out "Clerk and Doorkeeper of the House of Representatives and the" before "Secretary and" and substituted "direction of the Committee on Rules and Administration of the Senate and cover" for "direction of the Committee on Accounts of their respective houses and cover".

REPORT ON SALES DISCONTINUED

Par. 122 of act May 29, 1928, provided for the discontinuance of reports on waste paper, etc., as follows: "122. Reports by the Clerk and Doorkeeper of the House and the Secretary and Sergeant at Arms of the Senate of the sales of waste paper and useless documents and condemned furniture, and so forth."

§ 117a. Omitted

CODIFICATION

Section, acts July 1, 1941, ch. 268, 55 Stat. 454; June 8, 1942, ch. 396, 56 Stat. 338; June 28, 1943, ch. 173, title I,

57 Stat. 228; June 26, 1944, ch. 277, title I, 58 Stat. 343; June 13, 1945, ch. 189, 59 Stat. 248; July 1, 1946, ch. 530, 60 Stat. 397, related to depositing in Treasury sums received from sale of transcripts of House committee hearings, and applied only to fiscal years covered by such acts. Permanent provisions were enacted by act July 17, 1947, ch. 262, 61 Stat. 365, and classified to section 84b of this title.

§ 117b. Disposal of used or surplus furniture and equipment by Sergeant at Arms and Doorkeeper of Senate; procedure; deposit of receipts

Effective October 1, 1981, the Sergeant at Arms and Doorkeeper of the Senate is authorized to dispose of used or surplus furniture and equipment by trade-in or by sale directly or through the General Services Administration. Receipts from the sale of such furniture and equipment shall be deposited in the United States Treasury for credit to the appropriation for "Miscellaneous Items" under the heading "Contingent Expenses of the Senate".

(Pub. L. 95–94, title I, §103, Aug. 5, 1977, 91 Stat. 660; Pub. L. 97–51, §118, Oct. 1, 1981, 95 Stat. 964.)

CODIFICATION

Section was formerly classified to section 59c of this title.

Section is from the Congressional Operations Appropriation Act, 1978, which is title I of the Legislative Branch Appropriation Act, 1978.

AMENDMENTS

1981—Pub. L. 97–51 substituted "Effective October 1, 1981" for "Effective October 1, 1977" and struck out provisions requiring that all receipts from the sale of furniture and equipment, other than such furniture and equipment as was replaced in kind, be deposited in the United States Treasury as miscellaneous receipts.

§ 117b–1. Receipts from sale of used or surplus furniture and furnishings of Senate

On and after October 1, 1982, receipts from the sale of used or surplus furniture and furnishings shall be deposited in the United States Treasury for credit to the appropriation for "Senate Office Buildings" under the heading "Architect of the Capitol."

(Pub. L. 97–276, §101(e), Oct. 2, 1982, 96 Stat. 1189.)

CODIFICATION

Section is based on title I (2d proviso under "Senate Office Buildings") of S. 2939, as reported Sept. 22, 1982, which was enacted into law by Pub. L. 97–276.

Section was formerly classified to section 170a of Title 40, Public Buildings, Property, and Works.

§ 117b–2. Transfer of excess or surplus educationally useful equipment to public schools

(a) Authorization

The Sergeant at Arms and Doorkeeper of the Senate may directly, or through the General Services Administration, transfer title to excess or surplus educationally useful equipment to a public school. Any such transfer shall be completed at the lowest possible cost to the public school and the Senate.

(b) Regulations

The Committee on Rules and Administration of the Senate shall prescribe regulations to carry out the provisions of this section.

(c) Deposit of receipts

Receipts from reimbursements for the costs of transfer of excess or surplus educationally useful equipment under this section,[1] shall be deposited in the United States Treasury for credit to the account for the "Sergeant at Arms and Doorkeeper of the Senate" within the contingent fund of the Senate.

(d) Definitions

For the purposes of this section:

(1) The term "public school" means a public elementary or secondary school as such terms are defined in section 8801 of title 20.

(2) The term "educationally useful equipment" means computers and related peripheral tools, including printers, modems, routers, servers, computer keyboards, scanners, and other telecommunications and research equipment, that are appropriate for use in public school education.

(e) Effective date

This section shall take effect beginning with fiscal year 1997 and shall be effective each fiscal year thereafter.

(Pub. L. 104–197, title I, §5, Sept. 16, 1996, 110 Stat. 2397.)

CODIFICATION

Section is from the Congressional Operations Appropriations Act, 1997, which is title I of the Legislative Branch Appropriations Act, 1997.

§ 117c. Disposal of used or surplus automobiles and trucks by Sergeant at Arms and Doorkeeper of Senate; procedure; deposit of receipts

On and after October 1, 1982, the Sergeant at Arms and Doorkeeper of the Senate is authorized to dispose of used or surplus automobiles and trucks by trade-in or by sale through the General Services Administration. Receipts from the sale of such automobiles and trucks shall be deposited in the United States Treasury for credit to the appropriation for "Automobiles and Maintenance" under the heading "Contingent Expenses of the Senate".

(Pub. L. 97–276, §101(e), Oct. 2, 1982, 96 Stat. 1189.)

CODIFICATION

Section is based on section 102 of S. 2939, Ninety-seventh Congress, 2d Session, as reported Sept. 22, 1982, and incorporated by reference in section 101(e) of Pub. L. 97–276, to be effective as if enacted into law.

§ 117d. Reimbursements to Sergeant at Arms and Doorkeeper of Senate for equipment provided to Senators, etc., which has been lost, stolen, damaged, or otherwise unaccounted for; deposit of receipts

The Sergeant at Arms and Doorkeeper of the Senate shall deposit in the United States Treasury for credit to the appropriation account, within the contingent fund of the Senate, for the "Sergeant at Arms and Doorkeeper of the Senate", all moneys received by him as reimbursement for equipment provided to Senators, com-

---

[1] So in original. Comma probably should not appear.

mittee chairmen, and other officers and employees of the Senate, which has been lost, stolen, damaged, or otherwise unaccounted for.

(Pub. L. 98–367, title I, § 5, July 17, 1984, 98 Stat. 475.)

CODIFICATION

Section is from the Congressional Operations Appropriation Act, 1985, which is title I of the Legislative Branch Appropriations Act, 1985.

§ 117e. Disposal of used or surplus furniture and equipment by Chief Administrative Officer of House; procedure; deposit of receipts

(1) The Chief Administrative Officer of the House of Representatives may dispose of used equipment of the House of Representatives, by trade-in or sale, directly or through the General Services Administration. Any direct disposal under the preceding sentence shall be in accordance with normal business practice and shall be at fair market value. Receipts from disposals under the first sentence of this section (together with receipts from sale of transcripts, waste paper and other items provided by law, and receipts for missing or damaged equipment) shall be deposited in the Treasury for credit to the appropriate account under the appropriation for "ALLOWANCES AND EXPENSES" under the heading "CONTINGENT EXPENSES OF THE HOUSE", and shall be available for expenditure in accordance with applicable law.

(2) If disposal in accordance with paragraph (1) is not feasible because of age, location, condition, or any other relevant factor, the Chief Administrative Officer may donate the equipment to the government of a State, to a local government, or to an organization that is described in section 501(c)(3) of title 26 and exempt from tax under section 501(a) of title 26. Except as provided in paragraph (3), a donation under this paragraph—

(A) shall be at no cost to the Government; and

(B) may be made only if the used equipment has no recoverable value because disposal in accordance with paragraph (1), under the most favorable terms available to the Government, would result in a loss to the Government.

(3)(A) In the case of computer-related equipment, during fiscal year 1998 the Chief Administrative Officer may donate directly the equipment to a public elementary or secondary school of the District of Columbia without regard to whether the donation meets the requirements of the second sentence of paragraph (2), except that the total number of workstations donated as a result of this paragraph may not exceed 1,000.

(B) In this paragraph—

(i) the term "computer-related equipment" includes desktops, laptops, printers, file servers, and peripherals which are appropriate for use in public school education;

(ii) the terms "public elementary school" and "public secondary school" have the meaning given such terms in section 8801 of title 20; and

(iii) the term "workstation" includes desktops and peripherals, file servers and peripherals, laptops and peripherals, printers and peripherals, and workstations and peripherals.

(C) The Committee on House Oversight shall have authority to issue regulations to carry out this paragraph.

(4) The Committee on House Oversight of the House of Representatives shall have authority to prescribe regulations to carry out this subsection.

(5) As used in this section—

(A) the term "State" means a State of the United States, the District of Columbia, the Commonwealth of Puerto Rico, and a territory or possession of the United States; and

(B) the term "used equipment" means such used or surplus equipment (including furniture and motor vehicles) as the Committee on House Oversight of the House of Representatives may prescribe by regulation.

(Pub. L. 99–500, § 101(j), Oct. 18, 1986, 100 Stat. 1783–287, and Pub. L. 99–591, § 101(j), Oct. 30, 1986, 100 Stat. 3341–287; Pub. L. 100–71, title I, July 11, 1987, 101 Stat. 425; Pub. L. 101–163, title I, § 103(a), Nov. 21, 1989, 103 Stat. 1049; Pub. L. 104–186, title II, § 204(63), Aug. 20, 1996, 110 Stat. 1739; Pub. L. 105–55, title I, § 106, Oct. 7, 1997, 111 Stat. 1184.)

CODIFICATION

Section is based on section 104(a) of title I of H.R. 5203 (see House Report 99–805 as filed in the House on Aug. 15, 1986), as incorporated by reference in section 101(j) of Pub. L. 99–500 and 99–591, as amended by Pub. L. 100–71, to be effective as if enacted into law.

Pub. L. 99–591 is a corrected version of Pub. L. 99–500.

AMENDMENTS

1997—Par. (2). Pub. L. 105–55, § 106(1), substituted "Except as provided in paragraph (3), a donation" for "A donation" in second sentence of introductory provisions.

Pars. (3) to (5). Pub. L. 105–55, § 106(2), (3), added par. (3) and redesignated former pars. (3) and (4) as (4) and (5), respectively.

1996—Pars. (1), (2). Pub. L. 104–186, § 204(63)(A), substituted "Chief Administrative Officer" for "Clerk".

Pars. (3), (4)(B). Pub. L. 104–186, § 204(63)(B), substituted "House Oversight" for "House Administration".

1989—Par. (1). Pub. L. 101–163, § 103(a)(1), (2), designated existing provisions as par. (1) and struck out at end "As used in this section, the term 'used equipment' means such used or surplus equipment (including furniture and motor vehicles) as the Committee on House Administration of the House of Representatives may prescribe by regulation."

Pars. (2) to (4). Pub. L. 101–163, § 103(a)(3), added pars. (2) to (4).

CHANGE OF NAME

Committee on House Oversight of House of Representatives changed to Committee on House Administration of House of Representatives by House Resolution No. 5, One Hundred Sixth Congress, Jan. 6, 1999.

EFFECTIVE DATE OF 1989 AMENDMENT

Section 103(c) of Pub. L. 101–163 provided that: "The amendments made by subsection (a) [amending this section] and the repeal made by subsection (b) [repealing section 59a of this title] shall take effect on October 1, 1989."

EFFECTIVE DATE OF 1987 AMENDMENT

Pub. L. 100–71 provided that the amendment made by Pub. L. 100–71 is effective Oct. 18, 1986.

EFFECTIVE DATE

Section 104(c) of title I of H.R. 5203 (see House Report 99–805 as filed in the House on Aug. 15, 1986), as incorporated by reference in section 101(j) of Pub. L. 99–500 and 99–591, as amended by Pub. L. 100–71, to be effective as if enacted into law, provided that: "This section and the amendment made by this section [enacting section 117e of this title and amending section 84b of this title] shall take effect on October 1, 1986."

SIMILAR PROVISIONS

Provisions similar to those in par. (1) of this section relating to disposition of receipts from sales of copies of transcripts were contained in former section 84b of this title.

§ 117f. Commissions and charges for public telephone or telecommunications services; deposit of receipts

(a) Authority of Chief Administrative Officer to receive commissions for providing public telephone service in House occupied areas

Effective October 1, 1988, the Chief Administrative Officer of the House of Representatives is authorized to receive commissions for providing public telephone service in space occupied by the United States House of Representatives.

(b) Authority of Chief Administrative Officer to receive legislative branch charges for provision of telephone or telecommunications services; exception

The Chief Administrative Officer is authorized to receive for deposit, amounts charged to any legislative branch entity, including the Congressional Budget Office and the Architect of the Capitol, for the provision of telephone or telecommunications services, except that no amount charged to the Members' Representational Allowance shall be deposited in accordance with this section.

(c) Deposit of receipts; availability for expenditure

Receipts from the commissions and charges set forth in subsections (a) and (b) of this section shall be deposited in the United States Treasury for credit to the appropriation for "Salaries and Expenses of the United States House of Representatives", and shall be available for expenditure upon the approval of the Committee on Appropriations of the House of Representatives.

(Pub. L. 100–458, title III, § 306, Oct. 1, 1988, 102 Stat. 2182; Pub. L. 104–186, title II, § 204(64), Aug. 20, 1996, 110 Stat. 1739.)

CODIFICATION

Section is from the Legislative Branch Appropriations Act, 1989.

AMENDMENTS

1996—Subsec. (a). Pub. L. 104–186, § 204(64)(A), substituted "Chief Administrative Officer" for "Clerk".

Subsec. (b). Pub. L. 104–186, § 204(64)(B), substituted "Chief Administrative Officer" for "Clerk", struck out "but not limited to Legislative Service Organizations," after "entity, including", and substituted ", except that no amount charged to the Members' Representational Allowance" for ": *Provided*, That no amounts charged to the official expense allowances of Members of the House".

§ 117g. Monies received by Attending Physician from sale of prescription drugs or other sources; deposit of receipts

On November 21, 1989, the Office of the Attending Physician Revolving Fund established by

the first undesignated paragraph under the center heading "OFFICE OF THE ATTENDING PHYSICIAN REVOLVING FUND" in title III of the Legislative Branch Appropriation Act, 1976 (89 Stat. 283) is abolished and all monies in the Fund on such date or subsequently received by the Attending Physician from the sale of prescription drugs or from any other source shall be deposited in the Treasury as miscellaneous receipts.

(Pub. L. 101–163, title I, Nov. 21, 1989, 103 Stat. 1051.)

REFERENCES IN TEXT

The first undesignated paragraph under the center heading "OFFICE OF THE ATTENDING PHYSICIAN REVOLVING FUND" in title III of the Legislative Branch Appropriation Act, 1976 [Pub. L. 94–59], referred to in text, is not classified to the Code.

CODIFICATION

Section is from the Congressional Operations Appropriations Act, 1990, which is title I of the Legislative Branch Appropriations Act, 1990.

§ 117h. Deposit of fees for services by Office of Attending Physician; availability of amounts deposited

(a) There is established a subaccount in the appropriation account for salaries and expenses of the House of Representatives for the deposit of fees received from Members and officers of the House of Representatives for services provided to such Members and officers by the Office of the Attending Physician. The amounts so deposited shall be available, subject to appropriation, for the operations of the Office of the Attending Physician.

(b) This section shall take effect at the beginning of the first month after October 1992.

(Pub. L. 102–392, title I, § 104, Oct. 6, 1992, 106 Stat. 1710.)

CODIFICATION

Section is from the Congressional Operations Appropriations Act, 1993, which is title I of the Legislative Branch Appropriations Act, 1993.

§ 117i. Revolving fund for House gymnasium; deposit of receipts; availability for expenditure

There is established in the Treasury a revolving fund for the House of Representatives gymnasium. The Architect of the Capitol shall deposit in the fund such amounts as the Architect may receive as gymnasium dues or assessments from Members of the House of Representatives and other authorized users of the gymnasium. The amounts so deposited shall be available for obligation by the Architect for expenses of the gymnasium.

(Pub. L. 102–392, title I, § 106, Oct. 6, 1992, 106 Stat. 1715.)

CODIFICATION

Section is from the Congressional Operations Appropriations Act, 1993, which is title I of the Legislative Branch Appropriations Act, 1993.

§ 117j. Fees for internal delivery in House of Representatives of nonpostage mail from outside sources

Effective with respect to fiscal years beginning with fiscal year 1995, in the case of mail from outside sources presented to the Chief Administrative Officer of the House of Representatives (other than mail through the Postal Service and mail with postage otherwise paid) for internal delivery in the House of Representatives, the Chief Administrative Officer is authorized to collect fees equal to the applicable postage. Amounts received by the Chief Administrative Officer as fees under the preceding sentence shall be deposited in the Treasury as miscellaneous receipts.

(Pub. L. 104–53, title I, §101, Nov. 19, 1995, 109 Stat. 520.)

CODIFICATION

Section is from the Congressional Operations Appropriations Act, 1996, which is title I of the Legislative Branch Appropriations Act, 1996.

§117k. Rebates under Government Travel Charge Card Program

Effective with respect to fiscal years beginning with fiscal year 1995, amounts received by the Chief Administrative Officer of the House of Representatives from the Administrator of General Services for rebates under the Government Travel Charge Card Program shall be deposited in the Treasury as miscellaneous receipts.

(Pub. L. 104–53, title I, §102, Nov. 19, 1995, 109 Stat. 520.)

CODIFICATION

Section is from the Congressional Operations Appropriations Act, 1996, which is title I of the Legislative Branch Appropriations Act, 1996.

§118. Actions against officers for official acts

In any action brought against any person for or on account of anything done by him while an officer of either House of Congress in the discharge of his official duty, in executing any order of such House, the United States attorney for the district within which the action is brought, on being thereto requested by the officer sued, shall enter an appearance in behalf of such officer; and all provisions of the eighth section of the Act of July 28, 1866, entitled "An Act to protect the revenue, and for other purposes", and also all provisions of the sections of former Acts therein referred to, so far as the same relate to the removal of suits, the withholding of executions, and the paying of judgments against revenue or other officers of the United States, shall become applicable to such action and to all proceedings and matters whatsoever connected therewith, and the defense of such action shall thenceforth be conducted under the supervision and direction of the Attorney General.

(Mar. 3, 1875, ch. 130, §8, 18 Stat. 401; June 25, 1948, ch. 646, §1, 62 Stat. 909.)

REFERENCES IN TEXT

The provisions of section 8 of act July 28, 1866, ch. 298, 14 Stat. 329, referred to in text, were contained generally in R.S. §643, which was incorporated in the former Judicial Code, §33, and was repealed by act June 25, 1948, ch. 646, §39, 62 Stat. 992. See sections 1442, 1446, and 1447 of Title 28, Judiciary and Judicial Procedure. Other provisions referred to were contained in R.S. §§771, 989, which were also repealed by act June 25, 1948. See sections 509, 547, and 2006, respectively, of Title 28.

CHANGE OF NAME

Act June 25, 1948, eff. Sept. 1, 1948, substituted "United States attorney" for "district attorney". See section 541 of Title 28, Judiciary and Judicial Procedure.

SECTION REFERRED TO IN OTHER SECTIONS

This section is referred to in section 118a of this title.

§118a. Officers of Senate

Section 118 of this title shall not apply to officers of the Senate.

(Pub. L. 95–521, title VII, §714(d), Oct. 26, 1978, 92 Stat. 1884.)

EFFECTIVE DATE

Section effective Jan. 3, 1979, see section 717 of Pub. L. 95–521, set out as a note under section 288 of this title.

§119. Stationery rooms of House and Senate; specification of classes of articles purchasable

The Committee on House Oversight of the House of Representatives and the Committee on Rules and Administration of the Senate, respectively, shall make and issue regulations specifying the classes of articles which may be purchased by or through the stationery rooms of the House and Senate.

(May 13, 1926, ch. 294, §2, 44 Stat. 552; Aug. 2, 1946, ch. 753, title I, §102, 60 Stat. 814; Pub. L. 104–186, title II, §204(65), Aug. 20, 1996, 110 Stat. 1739.)

AMENDMENTS

1996—Pub. L. 104–186 substituted "Committee on House Oversight" for "Committee on Accounts".

1946—Act Aug. 2, 1946, substituted "Committee on Rules and Administration" for "Committee to Audit and Control the Contingent Expenses".

CHANGE OF NAME

Committee on House Oversight of House of Representatives changed to Committee on House Administration of House of Representatives by House Resolution No. 5, One Hundred Sixth Congress, Jan. 6, 1999.

Stationery room of House of Representatives redesignated Office Supply Service.

EFFECTIVE DATE OF 1946 AMENDMENT

Section 142 of act Aug. 2, 1946, provided that the amendment made by that act is effective Jan. 2, 1947.

§119a. Repealed. Pub. L. 90–620, §3, Oct. 22, 1968, 82 Stat. 1309

Section, act July 2, 1954, ch. 455, 68 Stat. 397, provided that on and after July 2, 1954, the Senate Folding Room shall be known as the Senate Service Department. See section 740 of Title 44, Public Printing and Documents.

§120. Omitted

CODIFICATION

Section, act Feb. 23, 1927, ch. 168, §1, 44 Stat. 1150, changed the name of "clerk to Speaker's table" to "parliamentarian" and was omitted as executed.

§121. Senate restaurant deficit fund; deposit of proceeds from surcharge on orders

The Committee on Rules and Administration of the United States Senate is authorized and directed hereafter to add a minimum of 10 per centum to each order in excess of 10 cents served in the Senate restaurants and 20 per centum to all orders served outside of said restaurants, and the proceeds accruing therefrom shall be placed in a fund to be used in the payment of any deficit incurred in the management of such kitchens and restaurants.

(May 18, 1937, ch. 223, §1, 50 Stat. 173; Aug. 2, 1946, ch. 753, title I, §102, 60 Stat. 814.)

AMENDMENTS

1946—Act Aug. 2, 1946, substituted "Committee on Rules and Administration" for "Committee on Rules".

EFFECTIVE DATE OF 1946 AMENDMENT

Section 142 of act Aug. 2, 1946, provided that the amendment made by that act is effective Jan. 2, 1947.

SECTION REFERRED TO IN OTHER SECTIONS

This section is referred to in title 5 section 5363.

§ 121a. Repealed. Pub. L. 105–275, title I, § 6(h)(1), Oct. 21, 1998, 112 Stat. 2434

Section, Pub. L. 94–440, title I, §106, Oct. 1, 1976, 90 Stat. 1444; Pub. L. 95–26, title I, §107(a), May 4, 1977, 91 Stat. 85; Pub. L. 100–458, title I, §10(b), Oct. 1, 1988, 102 Stat. 2162, related to Senate Barber and Beauty Shops Revolving Fund.

EFFECTIVE DATE OF REPEAL

Repeal effective 30 days after Oct. 21, 1998, see section 121b–1(i) of this title.

§ 121b. Senate Beauty Shop

(a) Repealed. Pub. L. 105–275, title I, § 6(h)(2), Oct. 21, 1998, 112 Stat. 2434

(b) Omitted

(c) Creditable civilian service in Senate Building Beauty Shop for basic annuity

Any individual who, on October 1, 1988, is an employee of the Senate Building Beauty Shop and who, after having been employed by the Sergeant at Arms and Doorkeeper pursuant to subsection (a) of this section, attains 5 years of civilian service creditable under section 8411 of title 5, other than service credited pursuant to subsection (d) of this section, may be credited under such section for any service as an employee of the Senate Building Beauty Shop prior to October 1, 1988, if such employee makes a payment of the amount, determined by the Office of Personnel Management, that would have been deducted and withheld from the basic pay of such employee under section 8422 of title 5 for such period so credited, together with interest thereon.

(d) Creditable civilian service in Senate Building Beauty Shop for survivor annuities and disability benefits

Notwithstanding any other provision of this section, any service performed by an individual in the Senate Building Beauty Shop prior to October 1, 1988, is deemed to be civilian service creditable under section 8411 of title 5 for purposes of qualifying for survivor annuities and disability benefits under subchapters IV and V of chapter 84 of title 5, if such individual—

(1) on October 1, 1988, is an employee of the Senate Building Beauty Shop;

(2) on or after October 1, 1988, is employed by the Sergeant at Arms and Doorkeeper pursuant to subsection (a) of this section; and

(3) payment is made of an amount, determined by the Office of Personnel Management, which would have been deducted and withheld from the basic pay of such employee under section 8422 of title 5 for such period so credited, together with interest thereon.

(e) Certification concerning creditable service; acceptance by Office of Personnel Management

The Office of Personnel Management shall accept the certification of the Secretary of the Senate concerning creditable service for the purpose of this section.

(f) Effective date

The foregoing provisions of this section shall take effect on October 1, 1988.

(Pub. L. 100–458, title I, §10, Oct. 1, 1988, 102 Stat. 2162; Pub. L. 105–275, title I, §6(h)(2), Oct. 21, 1998, 112 Stat. 2434.)

CODIFICATION

Section is comprised of section 10 of Pub. L. 100–458. Subsec. (b) of section 10 amended former section 121a of this title.

Section is from the Congressional Operations Appropriations Act, 1989, which is title I of the Legislative Branch Appropriations Act, 1989.

AMENDMENTS

1998—Subsec. (a). Pub. L. 105–275 struck out subsec. (a) which read as follows: "The Sergeant at Arms and Doorkeeper of the Senate is authorized to employ, and fix the compensation of such employees as he determines necessary to operate the Senate Beauty Shop."

EFFECTIVE DATE OF 1998 AMENDMENT

Amendment by Pub. L. 105–275 effective 30 days after Oct. 21, 1998, see section 121b–1(i) of this title.

§ 121b–1. Senate Hair Care Services

(a) Appointment and compensation of personnel

The Sergeant at Arms and Doorkeeper of the Senate is authorized to appoint and fix the compensation of such employees as may be necessary to operate Senate Hair Care Services.

(b) Establishment of revolving fund

There is established in the Treasury of the United States within the contingent fund of the Senate a revolving fund to be known as the Senate Hair Care Services Revolving Fund (hereafter in this section referred to as the "revolving fund").

(c) Deposit and availability of moneys

(1) All moneys received by Senate Hair Care Services from fees for services or from any other source shall be deposited in the revolving fund.

(2) Moneys in the revolving fund shall be available without fiscal year limitation for disbursement by the Secretary of the Senate—

(A) for the payment of salaries of employees of Senate Hair Care Services; and

(B) for necessary supplies, equipment, and other expenses of Senate Hair Care Services.

(3) The provisions of section 193d of title 40, except for the provisions relating to solicita-

tion, shall not apply to any activity carried out pursuant to this section, subject to approval of such activities by the Committee on Rules and Administration.

(3)[1] Agency contributions for employees of Senate Hair Care Services shall be paid from the appropriations account for "SALARIES, OFFICERS AND EMPLOYEES".

(d) Disbursements upon vouchers

Disbursements from the revolving fund shall be made upon vouchers signed by the Sergeant at Arms and Doorkeeper of the Senate, except that vouchers shall not be required for the disbursement of salaries paid at an annual rate.

(e) Excess moneys

At the direction of the Committee on Rules and Administration, the Secretary of the Senate shall withdraw from the revolving fund and deposit in the Treasury of the United States as miscellaneous receipts all moneys in the revolving fund that the Committee may determine are in excess of the current and reasonably foreseeable needs of Senate Hair Care Services.

(f) Regulations

The Sergeant at Arms and Doorkeeper of the Senate are authorized to prescribe such regulations as may be necessary to carry out the provisions of this section, subject to the approval of the Committee on Rules and Administration.

(g) Transfer of unobligated balances

There is transferred to the revolving fund established by this section any unobligated balance in the fund established by section 121a of this title on the effective date of this section.

(h) Omitted

(i) Effective date

This section shall be effective on and after October 1, 1998, or 30 days after the date of enactment of this Act [October 21, 1998], whichever is later.

(Pub. L. 105–275, title I, §6, Oct. 21, 1998, 112 Stat. 2434; Pub. L. 106–57, title I, §4, Sept. 29, 1999, 113 Stat. 412; Pub. L. 106–554, §1(a)(2) [title I, §3(a)], Dec. 21, 2000, 114 Stat. 2763, 2763A–96.)

REFERENCES IN TEXT

Section 121a of this title, referred to in subsec. (g), was repealed by Pub. L. 105–275, title I, §6(h)(1), Oct. 21, 1998, 112 Stat. 2434.

CODIFICATION

Section is comprised of section 6 of Pub. L. 105–275. Subsec. (h) of section 6 of Pub. L. 105–275 amended section 121b of this title and repealed section 121a of this title.

Section is from the Congressional Operations Appropriations Act, 1999, which is title I of the Legislative Branch Appropriations Act, 1999.

AMENDMENTS

2000—Subsec. (c)(2)(A). Pub. L. 106–554, §1(a)(2) [title I, §3(a)(1)], struck out "and agency contributions" after "salaries".

Subsec. (c)(3). Pub. L. 106–554, §1(a)(2) [title I, §3(a)(2)], added par. (3) relating to agency contributions.

---

[1] So in original. Probably should be "(4)".

1999—Subsec. (c)(3). Pub. L. 106–57 added par. (3).

EFFECTIVE DATE OF 2000 AMENDMENT

Pub. L. 106–554, §1(a)(2) [title I, §3(b)], Dec. 21, 2000, 114 Stat. 2763, 2763A–96, provided that: "This section [amending this section] shall apply to pay periods beginning on or after October 1, 2000."

§ 121c. Office of Senate Health Promotion

(a) Establishment

The Sergeant at Arms and Doorkeeper of the Senate is authorized to establish an Office of Senate Health Promotion.

(b) Fees, assessments, and charges

(1) In carrying out this section, the Sergeant at Arms and Doorkeeper of the Senate is authorized to establish, or provide for the establishment of, exercise classes and other health services and activities on a continuing and regular basis. In providing for such classes, services, and activities, the Sergeant at Arms and Doorkeeper of the Senate is authorized to impose and collect fees, assessments, and other charges to defray the costs involved in promoting the health of Members, officers, and employees of the Senate. For purposes of this section, the term "employees of the Senate" shall have such meaning as the Sergeant at Arms, by regulation, may prescribe.

(2) All fees, assessments, and charges imposed and collected by the Sergeant at Arms pursuant to paragraph (1) shall be deposited in the revolving fund established pursuant to subsection (c) of this section and shall be available for purposes of this section.

(c) Senate Health Promotion Revolving Fund

There is established in the Treasury of the United States a revolving fund within the contingent fund of the Senate to be known as the Senate Health Promotion Revolving Fund (hereinafter referred to in this section as the "fund"). The fund shall consist of all amounts collected or received by the Sergeant at Arms and Doorkeeper of the Senate as fees, assessments, and other charges for activities and services to carry out the provisions of this section. All moneys in the fund shall be available without fiscal year limitation for disbursement by the Secretary of the Senate for promoting the health of Members, officers, and employees of the Senate. On or before December 31 of each year, the Secretary of the Senate shall withdraw from the fund and deposit in the Treasury of the United States as miscellaneous receipts all moneys in excess of $5,000 in the fund at the close of the preceding fiscal year.

(d) Vouchers

Disbursements from the revolving fund shall be made upon vouchers signed by the Sergeant at Arms and Doorkeeper of the Senate.

(e) Inapplicability of provisions prohibiting sales, advertisements, or solicitations in Capitol grounds

The provisions of section 193d of title 40 shall not be applicable to any class, service, or other activity carried out pursuant to the provisions of this section.

(f) Regulations

The provisions of this section shall be carried out in accordance with regulations which shall be promulgated by the Sergeant at Arms and Doorkeeper of the Senate and subject to approval at the beginning of each Congress by the Committee on Rules and Administration of the Senate.

(Pub. L. 101–163, title I, § 4, Nov. 21, 1989, 103 Stat. 1044; Pub. L. 102–90, title I, § 2, Aug. 14, 1991, 105 Stat. 450.)

CODIFICATION

Section is from the Congressional Operations Appropriations Act, 1990, which is title I of the Legislative Branch Appropriations Act, 1990.

AMENDMENTS

1991—Subsec. (c). Pub. L. 102–90 inserted at end "On or before December 31 of each year, the Secretary of the Senate shall withdraw from the fund and deposit in the Treasury of the United States as miscellaneous receipts all moneys in excess of $5,000 in the fund at the close of the preceding fiscal year."

§ 121d. Senate Gift Shop

(a) Establishment

The Secretary of the Senate is authorized to establish a Senate Gift Shop for the purpose of providing for the sale of gift items to Members of the Senate, staff, and the general public.

(b) Deposit of receipts

All moneys received from sales and other services by the Senate Gift Shop shall be deposited in the revolving fund established by subsection (c) of this section and shall be available for purposes of this section.

(c) Revolving fund

There is established in the Treasury of the United States a revolving fund within the contingent fund of the Senate to be known as the Senate Gift Shop Revolving Fund (hereafter referred to in this section as the "fund"). The fund shall consist of all amounts collected or received by the Secretary of the Senate from sales and services by the Senate Gift Shop. All moneys in the fund shall be available without fiscal year limitation for disbursement by the Secretary of the Senate in connection with the operation of the Senate Gift Shop, including supplies, equipment, and other expenses. In addition, such moneys may be used by the Secretary of the Senate to reimburse the Senate appropriations account, appropriated under the heading "SALARIES, OFFICERS AND EMPLOYEES" and "OFFICE OF THE SECRETARY", for amounts used from such account to pay the salaries of employees of the Senate Gift Shop.

(d) Exception to prohibition of sale or solicitation on Capitol Grounds

The provisions of section 193d of title 40 shall not be applicable to any activity carried out pursuant to this section.

(e) Transfer of moneys from Stationery Revolving Fund

To provide capital for the fund, the Secretary of the Senate is authorized to transfer, from moneys in the Stationery Revolving Fund in the contingent fund of the Senate, to the fund such sum as he may determine necessary, not to exceed $300,000.

(f) Authorization to expend from appropriations account for initial expenses

For the purpose of acquiring supplies, equipment, and meeting other initial expenses in implementing subsection (a) of this section, the Secretary of the Senate is authorized, upon October 6, 1992, to expend, from moneys appropriated to the appropriations account, within the contingent fund of the Senate, for expenses of the Secretary of the Senate, by the Legislative Branch Appropriations Act, 1991, such amounts as may be necessary to carry out this section.

(g) Disbursement on approved voucher

Disbursements from the fund shall be made upon vouchers approved by the Secretary of the Senate, or his designee.

(h) Regulations

The Secretary of the Senate is authorized to prescribe such regulations as may be necessary to carry out the provisions of this section.

(Pub. L. 102–392, title I, § 2, Oct. 6, 1992, 106 Stat. 1706.)

REFERENCES IN TEXT

The Legislative Branch Appropriations Act, 1991, referred to in subsec. (f), is Pub. L. 101–520, Nov. 5, 1990, 104 Stat. 2254. For complete classification of this Act to the Code, see Tables.

CODIFICATION

Section is from the Congressional Operations Appropriations Act, 1993, which is title I of the Legislative Branch Appropriations Act, 1993.

ADDITIONAL CAPITALIZATION

Pub. L. 103–283, title I, § 1, July 22, 1994, 108 Stat. 1426, provided that: "Effective on and after the date of enactment of this Act [July 22, 1994], the Secretary of the Senate, subject to the approval of the Committee on Appropriations of the Senate, is authorized to transfer up to $300,000 from any Senate appropriations account with respect to which the Secretary has disbursing authority to the revolving fund established under section 2(c) under the subheading 'ADMINISTRATIVE PROVISIONS' under the heading 'SENATE' in Public Law 102–392 (2 U.S.C. 121d(c)) to provide additional capitalization for such revolving fund. Any moneys so transferred shall be available for use in the same manner and to the same extent as the moneys otherwise in such revolving fund."

§ 121e. Payment of fees for services of Attending Physician and for use of Senate health and fitness facilities

(a) Regulations

The Senate Committee on Rules and Administration shall promulgate regulations—

(1) pertaining to the services provided by the Attending Physician and the operation and use of the Senate health and fitness facilities; and

(2) requiring the payment of fees for services received from the Attending Physician and for the use of the Senate health and fitness facilities pursuant to such regulations.

(b) Withholding of fees from salary

The Secretary of the Senate is authorized to withhold fees from the salary of an individual authorized by such regulations to receive such services from the Attending Physician and to use the Senate health and fitness facilities.

(c) Deposit in General Fund

The Secretary of the Senate shall remit all fees required by subsection (a)(2) of this section that are collected pursuant to subsection (b) of this section or by direct payment to the General Fund of the Treasury as miscellaneous receipts unless otherwise provided by law.

(d) Effective date

The provision[1] of this section shall take effect on April 9, 1992.

(Pub. L. 102–392, title III, § 314, Oct. 6, 1992, 106 Stat. 1723.)

CODIFICATION

Section is from the Legislative Branch Appropriations Act, 1993.

§ 121f. Senate Health and Fitness Facility Revolving Fund

(a) Establishment

There is established in the Treasury of the United States a revolving fund to be known as the Senate Health and Fitness Facility Revolving Fund ("the revolving fund").

(b) Deposit of receipts

The Architect of the Capitol shall deposit in the revolving fund—

(1) any amounts received as dues or other assessments for use of the Senate Health and Fitness Facility, and

(2) any amounts received from the operation of the Senate waste recycling program.

(c) Availability of funds

Subject to the approval of the Committee on Appropriations of the Senate, amounts in the revolving fund shall be available to the Architect of the Capitol, without fiscal year limitation, for payment of costs of the Senate Health and Fitness Facility.

(d) Withdrawal of excess amounts

The Architect of the Capitol shall withdraw from the revolving fund and deposit in the Treasury of the United States as miscellaneous receipts all moneys in the revolving fund that the Architect determines are in excess of the current and reasonably foreseeable needs of the Senate Health and Fitness Facility.

(e) Regulations

Subject to the approval of the Committee on Rules and Administration of the Senate, the Architect of the Capitol may issue such regulations as may be necessary to carry out the provisions of this section.

(Pub. L. 106–554, § 1(a)(2) [title I, § 4], Dec. 21, 2000, 114 Stat. 2763, 2763A–96.)

CODIFICATION

Section is from the Congressional Operations Appropriations Act, 2001, which is title I of the Legislative Branch Appropriations Act, 2001.

§ 122. Repealed. Pub. L. 95–391, title I, § 111, Sept. 30, 1978, 92 Stat. 777

Section, acts July 2, 1954, ch. 455, title I, 68 Stat. 403; Sept. 7, 1957, Pub. L. 85–301, § 1, 71 Stat. 622; Sept. 29,

1965, Pub. L. 89–211, § 1(a), 79 Stat. 857, provided for office space in the home districts of House Members and the Resident Commissioner from Puerto Rico.

The repeal of this section is based on section 6(b) of House Resolution No. 687, Ninety-fifth Congress, Sept. 20, 1977, which was enacted into permanent law by Pub. L. 95–391.

Similar provisions were contained in the following prior appropriation acts:

Aug. 1, 1953, ch. 304, title I, 67 Stat. 325.
July 9, 1952, ch. 598, 66 Stat. 470.

EFFECTIVE DATE OF REPEAL

Section 6(b) of House Resolution No. 687, Ninety-fifth Congress, Sept. 20, 1977, provided that the repeal of this section is applicable beginning on Jan. 3, 1978, upon the enactment of House Resolution No. 687 as permanent law, which was effected by Pub. L. 95–391, § 111.

§ 122a. Repealed. Pub. L. 104–186, title II, § 204(66), Aug. 20, 1996, 110 Stat. 1740

Section, acts July 2, 1954, ch. 455, title I, 68 Stat. 403; June 13, 1957, Pub. L. 85–54, 71 Stat. 82; H. Res. No. 831, Eighty-eighth Congress, Aug. 14, 1964, enacted into permanent law by act July 27, 1965, Pub. L. 89–90, § 103, 79 Stat. 281, related to reimbursement of House Members for office expenses outside District of Columbia.

REIMBURSEMENT OF EXPENSES OF HOUSE MEMBERS; MEMBER OF HOUSE OF REPRESENTATIVES AND MEMBER DEFINED

Section 302(a), (b), and (d) of H. Res. No. 287, Ninety-fifth Congress, Mar. 2, 1977, enacted into permanent law by Pub. L. 95–94, title I, § 115, Aug. 5, 1977, 91 Stat. 668, which related to reimbursement to Members of House of Representatives for official expenses incurred in United States, was repealed by Pub. L. 104–186, title II, § 203(20)(B), Aug. 20, 1996, 110 Stat. 1728.

§§ 122b to 122g. Repealed. Pub. L. 104–186, title II, § 204(67), Aug. 20, 1996, 110 Stat. 1740

Section 122b, based on H. Res. No. 687, § 1, Ninety-fifth Congress, Sept. 20, 1977, enacted into permanent law by Pub. L. 95–391, title I, § 111, Sept. 30, 1978, 92 Stat. 777, related to leasing of office space in home districts of House Members.

Section 122c, based on H. Res. No. 687, § 2, Ninety-fifth Congress, Sept. 20, 1977, enacted into permanent law by Pub. L. 95–391, title I, § 111, Sept. 30, 1978, 92 Stat. 777, related to determination of annual amount which could be disbursed on behalf of each Member under former sections 122b to 122g of this title.

Section 122d, based on H. Res. No. 687, § 3, Ninety-fifth Congress, Sept. 20, 1977, enacted into permanent law by Pub. L. 95–391, title I, § 111, Sept. 30, 1978, 92 Stat. 777, related to authorization by Committee on House Administration of disbursements under former sections 122b to 122g of this title.

Section 122e, based on H. Res. No. 687, § 4, Ninety-fifth Congress, Sept. 20, 1977, enacted into permanent law by Pub. L. 95–391, title I, § 111, Sept. 30, 1978, 92 Stat. 777, related to furnishing office equipment, carpeting, and draperies.

Section 122f, based on H. Res. No. 687, § 5, Ninety-fifth Congress, Sept. 20, 1977, enacted into permanent law by Pub. L. 95–391, title I, § 111, Sept. 30, 1978, 92 Stat. 777, authorized Committee on House Administration to prescribe rules and regulations to carry out former sections 122b to 122g of this title.

Section 122g, based on H. Res. No. 687, § 7, Ninety-fifth Congress, Sept. 20, 1977, enacted into permanent law by Pub. L. 95–391, title I, § 111, Sept. 30, 1978, 92 Stat. 777, defined terms for purposes of former sections 122b to 122g of this title.

§ 123. Repealed. June 27, 1956, ch. 453, § 105(m), 70 Stat. 372

Section, act Aug. 7, 1953, ch. 341, 67 Stat. 439, established a joint Senate and House Recording Facility re-

---

[1] So in original. Probably should be "provisions".

volving fund, provided for the disposition of monies, and required the coordinator of the Facility to give a penal bond. See section 123b(m) of this title.

§ 123a. Omitted

CODIFICATION

Section, act Aug. 5, 1955, ch. 568, § 1, 69 Stat. 500, which established the basic annual compensation of the coordinator, Joint Recording Facility, has been omitted because of section 123b(l) of this title which abolished the Joint Recording Facility positions and salaries established pursuant to the Legislative Branch Appropriation Act, 1948, and all subsequent acts.

§ 123b. House Recording Studio; Senate Recording Studio and Senate Photographic Studio

(a) Establishment

There is established the House Recording Studio, the Senate Recording Studio, and the Senate Photographic Studio.

(b) Assistance in making disk, film, and tape recordings; exclusiveness of use

The House Recording Studio shall assist Members of the House of Representatives in making disk, film, and tape recordings, and in performing such other functions and duties in connection with the making of such recordings as may be necessary. The Senate Recording Studio and the Senate Photographic Studio shall assist Members of the Senate and committees of the Senate in making disk, film, and tape recordings, and in performing such other functions and duties in connection with the making of such recordings as may be necessary. The House Recording Studio shall be for the exclusive use of Members of the House of Representatives (including the Delegates and the Resident Commissioner from Puerto Rico); the Senate Recording Studio and the Senate Photographic Studio shall be for the exclusive use of Members of the Senate, the Vice President, committees of the Senate, the Secretary of the Senate, and the Sergeant at Arms of the Senate.

(c) Operation of studios

The House Recording Studio shall be operated by the Chief Administrative Officer of the House of Representatives under the direction and control of a committee which is created (hereinafter referred to as the committee) composed of three Members of the House. Two members of the committee shall be from the majority party and one member shall be from the minority party, to be appointed by the Speaker. The committee is authorized to issue such rules and regulations relating to operation of the House Recording Studio as it may deem necessary.

The Senate Recording Studio and the Senate Photographic Studio shall be operated by the Sergeant at Arms of the Senate under the direction and control of the Committee on Rules and Administration of the Senate. The Committee on Rules and Administration is authorized to issue such rules and regulations relating to operation of the Senate Recording Studio and the Senate Photographic Studio as it may deem necessary.

(d) Prices of disk, film, and tape recordings; collection of moneys

The Chief Administrative Officer of the House of Representatives shall, subject to the approval of the committee, set the price of making disk, film, and tape recordings, and collect all moneys owed the House Recording Studio. The Committee on Rules and Administration of the Senate shall set the price of making disk, film, and tape recordings and all moneys owed the Senate Recording Studio and the Senate Photographic Studio shall be collected by the Sergeant at Arms of the Senate.

(e) Restrictions on expenditures

No moneys shall be expended or obligated for the House Recording Studio except as shall be pursuant to such regulations as the committee may approve. No moneys shall be expended or obligated by the Director of the Senate Recording Studio or the Director of the Senate Photographic Studio until approval therefor has been obtained from the Sergeant at Arms of the Senate.

(f) Appointment of Director and other employees of House Recording Studio

The Chief Administrative Officer of the House of Representatives is authorized, subject to the approval of the committee, to appoint a Director of the House Recording Studio and such other employees as are deemed necessary to the operation of the House Recording Studio.

(g) Revolving funds

There is established in the Treasury of the United States, a revolving fund for the House Recording Studio for the purposes of administering the duties of that studio. There is also established in the Treasury of the United States a revolving fund, within the contingent fund of the Senate, which shall be known as the "Senate Photographic Studio Revolving Fund", for the purpose of administering the duties of the Senate Photographic Studio; and there is established in the Treasury of the United States, a revolving fund, within the contingent fund of the Senate, which shall be known as the "Senate Recording Studio Revolving Fund", for the purpose of administering the duties of the Senate Recording Studio.

(h) Deposits in funds; availability of funds

All moneys received by the House Recording Studio from Members of the House of Representatives for disk, film, or tape recordings, or from any other source, shall be deposited by the Chief Administrative Officer of the House of Representatives in the revolving fund established for the House Recording Studio by subsection (g) of this section; moneys in such fund shall be available for disbursement therefrom by the Chief Administrative Officer of the House of Representatives for the care, maintenance, operation, and other expenses of the studio upon vouchers signed and approved in such manner as the committee shall prescribe. All moneys received by the Senate Recording Studio shall be deposited in the Senate Recording Studio Revolving Fund established by subsection (g) of this section and all funds received by the Senate Photographic Studio shall be deposited in the Senate Photographic Studio Revolving Fund established by such subsection; moneys in the Senate Recording Studio Revolving Fund shall be available for disbursement therefrom upon vouchers signed by the Sergeant at Arms and Doorkeeper of the Senate for the care, maintenance, operation, and other expenses of the Senate Recording Studio, and moneys in the Senate Photographic Studio Revolving Fund shall be available for disbursement therefrom upon vouchers signed by the Sergeant at Arms and Doorkeeper of the Senate for the care, maintenance, operation, and other expenses of the Senate Photographic Studio.

(i) Distribution of equity of Joint Senate and House Recording Facility Revolving Fund; assignment of existing studio facilities, equipment, materials and supplies; transfer of accounts; reserve fund; distribution of balance

(1) As soon as practicable after June 27, 1956, but no later than September 30, 1956, the equity of the Joint Senate and House Recording Facility Revolving Fund shall be distributed equally to the Senate and House of Representatives on the basis of an audit to be made by the General Accounting Office.

(2) The Sergeant at Arms of the Senate and the Clerk of the House of Representatives shall, subject to the approval of the committees mentioned in subsection (c) of this section, determine the assignment of existing studio facilities to the Senate and the House of Representatives, and also the existing equipment, materials and supplies to be transferred to the respective studios. The evaluation of equipment, materials and supplies transferred to each studio shall be on the basis of market value. Any other equipment, materials and supplies determined to be obsolete or not needed for the operation of the respective studio shall be disposed of to the best interest of the Government and the proceeds thereof deposited in the Joint Senate and House Recording Facility Revolving Fund.

(3) Accounts receivable, which on the effective date of liquidation, are due from Members and committees of the Senate shall be transferred to the Senate Studio, and those due from Members and committees of the House of Representatives shall be transferred to the House Studio.

(4) A sufficient reserve shall be set aside from the Joint Senate and House Recording Facility Revolving Fund to liquidate any outstanding accounts payable.

(5) After appropriate adjustments for the value of assets assigned or transferred to the Senate and House of Representatives, respectively, the balance in the Joint Senate and House Recording Facility Revolving Fund shall be distributed equally to the Senate and House of Representatives for deposit to the respective revolving funds authorized by this section.

(j) Availability of existing services and facilities

Pending acquisition of the stock, supplies, materials, and equipment necessary to properly equip both studios, the present services and facilities shall be made available to both studios in order that each studio may carry out its duty.

(k) Restrictions on employment

No person shall be an officer or employee of the House Recording Studio, Senate Recording Studio, or Senate Photographic Studio while he is engaged in any other business, profession, occupation, or employment which involves the performance of duties which are similar to those which would be performed by him as such an officer or employee of such studio unless approved in writing by the committee in the case of the House Recording Studio and the Senate Committee on Rules and Administration in the case of the Senate Recording Studio and the Senate Photographic Studio.

(l) Abolition of Joint Recording Facility positions and salaries

The Joint Recording Facility positions and salaries established pursuant to the Legislative Branch Appropriation Act, 1948, and all subsequent Acts are abolished.

(m) Repeals

Effective with the completion of the transfer provided for by subsection (i) of this section the joint resolution entitled "Joint resolution establishing in the Treasury of the United States a revolving fund within the contingent fund of the House of Representatives", approved August 7, 1953, is repealed.

(n) Repealed. Pub. L. 92–310, title II, § 220(j), June 6, 1972, 86 Stat. 205

(o) Authorization of appropriations

Such sums as may be necessary to carry out the provisions of this section are authorized to be appropriated.

(June 27, 1956, ch. 453, § 105, 70 Stat. 370; Pub. L. 88–652, § 16(a), Oct. 13, 1964, 78 Stat. 1084; Pub. L. 92–310, title II, § 220(j), June 6, 1972, 86 Stat. 205; Pub. L. 96–304, title I, § 108(a), July 8, 1980, 94 Stat. 890; Pub. L. 97–257, title I, § 102, Sept. 10, 1982, 96 Stat. 849; Pub. L. 101–520, title I, § 7(a), (c), (d), Nov. 5, 1990, 104 Stat. 2258, 2259; Pub. L. 104–186, title II, § 204(68), Aug. 20, 1996, 110 Stat. 1740.)

AMENDMENTS

1996—Subsecs. (c), (d), (f). Pub. L. 104–186, § 204(68)(A), substituted "Chief Administrative Officer" for "Clerk".

Subsec. (g). Pub. L. 104–186, § 204(68)(B), struck out "within the contingent fund of the House of Representatives" before "for the House Recording Studio".

Subsec. (h). Pub. L. 104–186, § 204(68)(A), substituted "Chief Administrative Officer" for "Clerk" in two places.

1990—Subsec. (g). Pub. L. 101–520, § 7(a), amended second sentence generally. Prior to amendment, second sentence read as follows: "There is also established in the Treasury of the United States, a revolving fund within the contingent fund of the Senate for the Senate Recording and Photographic Studios for the purposes of administering the duties of that studio."

Subsec. (h). Pub. L. 101–520, § 7(c), amended second sentence generally. Prior to amendment, second sentence read as follows: "All moneys received by the Senate Recording and Photographic Studios for disk, film, or tape recordings or from any other source, shall be deposited in the revolving fund established for the Senate Recording and Photographic Studios by subsection (g) of this section; moneys in such fund shall be available for disbursement therefrom upon vouchers signed and approved by the Sergeant at Arms for the care, maintenance, operation, and other expenses of the Senate Recording and Photographic Studios."

1982—Subsec. (b). Pub. L. 97–257 inserted reference to Secretary of Senate and Sergeant at Arms of Senate.

1972—Subsec. (n). Pub. L. 92–310 repealed subsec. (n) which required Directors of House and Senate Recording Studios to give bonds in sum of $20,000 each.

1964—Subsec. (f). Pub. L. 88–652 struck out "and fix the compensation of" after "to appoint".

EFFECTIVE DATE OF 1990 AMENDMENT

Section 7(b) of Pub. L. 101–520 provided that: "The amendment made by subsection (a) [amending this section] shall take effect on April 1, 1991, and, of the monies in the revolving fund within the contingent fund of the Senate for the Recording and Photographic Studios, as such fund was in existence immediately prior to the amendment made by subsection (a), $100,000 shall be deposited in the Senate Photographic Studio Revolving Fund (as established by the amendment made by subsection (a)) and the remainder shall be deposited into the Senate Recording Studio Revolving Fund (as so established)."

Section 7(c) of Pub. L. 101–520 provided that the amendment made by that section is effective Apr. 1, 1991.

EFFECTIVE DATE OF 1964 AMENDMENT

Amendment by Pub. L. 88–652 effective Jan. 1, 1965, see section 17 of Pub. L. 88–652, set out as an Effective Date note under section 291 of this title.

TRANSFER OF FUNCTIONS

References to Senate Recording Studio and Senate Photographic Studio substituted for "Senate Recording and Photographic Studios" wherever appearing in text pursuant to section 108(a) of Pub. L. 96–304, as amended by section 7(d) of Pub. L. 101–520, which is classified to section 123b–1(a) of this title, and which abolished entity known as Senate Recording and Photographic Studios, established instead Senate Recording Studio and Senate Photographic Studio, and made corresponding transfer of functions. Previously, "Senate Recording and Photographic Studios" had been substituted in text for "Senate Recording Studio" pursuant to section 108(a) of Pub. L. 96–304.

APPROPRIATIONS ACTS AS DETERMINING EXTENT OF AVAILABILITY OF FUNDS AND ACCOUNTS

Pub. L. 104–53, title I, §107, Nov. 19, 1995, 109 Stat. 522, provided that:

"(a) Each fund and account specified in subsection (b) shall be available only to the extent provided in appropriations Acts.

"(b) The funds and accounts referred to in subsection (a) are—

"(1) the revolving fund for the House Barber Shops, established by the paragraph under the heading 'HOUSE BARBER SHOPS REVOLVING FUND' in the matter relating to the House of Representatives in chapter III of title I of the Supplemental Appropriations Act, 1975 (Public Law 93–554; 88 Stat. 1776);

"(2) the revolving fund for the House Beauty Shop, established by the matter under the heading 'HOUSE BEAUTY SHOP' in the matter relating to administrative provisions for the House of Representatives in the Legislative Branch Appropriation Act, 1970 (Public Law 91–145; 83 Stat. 347);

"(3) the special deposit account established for the House of Representatives Restaurant by section 208 of the First Supplemental Civil Functions Appropriation Act, 1941 ([former] 40 U.S.C. 174k note); and

"(4) the revolving fund established for the House Recording Studio by section 105(g) of the Legislative Branch Appropriation Act, 1957 (2 U.S.C. 123b(g)).

"(c) This section shall take effect on October 1, 1995, and shall apply with respect to fiscal years beginning on or after that date."

§ 123b–1. Senate Recording Studio and Senate Photographic Studio as successors to Senate Recording and Photographic Studios; rules, regulations, and fees for photographs and photographic services

(a) The entity, in the Senate, known (prior to April 1, 1991) as the "Senate Recording and Pho-

tographic Studios" is abolished, and there is established in its stead the following two entities: the "Senate Recording Studio", and the "Senate Photographic Studio"; and there are transferred, from the entity known (prior to April 1, 1991) as the "Senate Recording and Photographic Studios" to the Senate Recording Studio all personnel, equipment, supplies, and funds which are available for, relate to, or are utilized in connection with, recording, and to the Senate Photographic Studio all personnel, equipment, supplies, and funds which are available for, relate to, or are utilized in connection with, photography.

(b)(1) The Sergeant at Arms and Doorkeeper of the Senate shall, subject to the approval of the majority and minority leaders, promulgate rules and regulations, and establish fees, for the provision of photographs and photographic services to be furnished by the Photographic Studio.

(2) Omitted.

(Pub. L. 96–304, title I, §108, July 8, 1980, 94 Stat. 890; Pub. L. 101–520, title I, §7(d), Nov. 5, 1990, 104 Stat. 2259.)

CODIFICATION

Words "prior to April 1, 1991", referred to in subsec. (a), were in the original "prior to this amendment" which was translated as meaning prior to the effective date of section 7(d) of Pub. L. 101–520, which amended subsec. (a) generally, to reflect the probable intent of Congress.

Subsec. (b)(2), which authorized the Sergeant at Arms and Doorkeeper of the Senate to appoint and fix the compensation of not more than 15 employees to carry out the functions of the Photographic Studio and provided that the Secretary of the Senate make payments of compensation, etc., of such personnel from certain funds appropriated for the Senate, was omitted in view of section 61f–7 of this title which abolished all statutory positions in the Office of the Sergeant at Arms and Doorkeeper of the Senate, with specified exceptions, effective Oct. 1, 1981, and authorized the Sergeant at Arms and Doorkeeper of the Senate to appoint and fix the compensation of such employees as appropriate.

AMENDMENTS

1990—Subsec. (a). Pub. L. 101–520 amended subsec. (a) generally. Prior to amendment, subsec. (a) read as follows: "The Senate Recording Studio hereafter shall be known as the Senate Recording and Photographic Studios. Subject to subsection (b) of this section, all references to the Senate Recording Studio (including the revolving fund) in any law, resolution, or regulation shall be considered as referring to the Senate Recording and Photographic Studios, and any provision of any law, resolution, or regulation which is applicable to the Senate Recording Studio shall be deemed to apply to the Senate Recording and Photographic Studios."

EFFECTIVE DATE OF 1990 AMENDMENT

Section 7(d) of Pub. L. 101–520 provided that the amendment made by that section is effective Apr. 1, 1991.

§ 123c. Data processing equipment, software, and services

Notwithstanding any other provision of law, the Sergeant at Arms, subject to the approval of the Committee on Rules and Administration, is hereafter authorized to enter into multi-year contracts for data processing equipment, software, and services.

(Pub. L. 94–32, title I, June 12, 1975, 89 Stat. 182; Pub. L. 95–26, title I, § 103, May 4, 1977, 91 Stat. 82.)

CODIFICATION

Section is from the Second Supplemental Appropriations Act, 1975.

AMENDMENTS

1977—Pub. L. 95–26 substituted "multi-year contracts for data processing equipment, software, and services" for "multi-year leases for automatic data processing equipment".

EFFECTIVE DATE

Title I of Pub. L. 94–32 provided that this section is effective June 12, 1975.

§ 123c–1. Advance payments for computer programing services

Notwithstanding any other provision of law, the Sergeant at Arms and Doorkeeper of the Senate, subject to the approval of the Committee on Rules and Administration, is on and after July 6, 1981, authorized to enter into contracts which provide for the making of advance payments for computer programing services.

(Pub. L. 97–20, July 6, 1981, 95 Stat. 104.)

§ 123d. Senate Computer Center

(a) Senate Computer Center Revolving Fund

(1) There is hereby established in the Treasury of the United States a revolving fund within the contingent fund of the Senate to be known as the Senate Computer Center Revolving Fund (hereafter in this section referred to as the "revolving fund").

(2) The revolving fund shall be available only for paying the salaries of personnel employed under subsection (c) of this section, and agency contributions attributable thereto, and for paying refunds under contracts entered into under subsection (b) of this section.

(3) Within 90 days after the end of each fiscal year, the Secretary of the Senate shall withdraw all amounts in the revolving fund in excess of $100,000, other than amounts required to make refunds under subsection (b)(2)(B) of this section, and shall deposit the amounts withdrawn in the Treasury of the United States as miscellaneous receipts.

(b) Contracts for use of Senate computer; approval; terms

(1) Subject to the provisions of paragraph (2), the Sergeant at Arms and Doorkeeper of the Senate is authorized to enter into contracts with any agency or instrumentality of the legislative branch for the use of any available time on the Senate computer.

(2) No contract may be entered into under paragraph (1) unless it has been approved by the Committee on Rules and Administration of the Senate, and no such contract may extend beyond the end of the fiscal year in which it is entered into. Each contract entered into under paragraph (1) shall contain—

(A) a provision requiring full advance payment for the amount of time contracted for, and

(B) a provision requiring refund of a proportionate amount of such advance payment if the total amount of time contracted for is not used.

Notwithstanding any other provision of law, any agency or instrumentality of the legislative branch is authorized to make advance payments under a contract entered into under paragraph (1).

(c) Additional personnel

To the extent that the personnel of the Senate Computer Center are unable to carry out the contracts entered into under subsection (b) of this section according to their terms and conditions, the Sergeant at Arms and Doorkeeper of the Senate is authorized to employ such additional personnel for the Senate Computer Center as may be necessary to carry out such contracts, and to pay the salaries of such additional personnel, and agency contributions attributable thereto, from the revolving fund. Such additional personnel may temporarily be assigned to perform the regular functions of the Senate Computer Center when their services are not needed to carry out such contracts.

(d) Disbursements

Disbursements from the revolving fund under subsections (b) and (c) of this section shall be made upon vouchers signed by the Sergeant at Arms and Doorkeeper of the Senate, except that vouchers shall not be required for the disbursement of salaries of employees paid at an annual rate.

(Pub. L. 94–303, title I, § 116, June 1, 1976, 90 Stat. 614.)

§ 123e. Senate legislative information system

(a) Development and implementation by Secretary of Senate

The Secretary of the Senate, with the oversight and approval of the Committee on Rules and Administration of the Senate, shall oversee the development and implementation of a comprehensive Senate legislative information system.

(b) Cooperative effort

In carrying out this section, the Secretary of the Senate shall consult and work with officers and employees of the House of Representatives. Legislative branch agencies and departments and agencies of the executive branch shall provide cooperation, consultation, and assistance as requested by the Secretary of the Senate to carry out this section.

(c) Funding

Any funds that were appropriated under the heading "Secretary of the Senate" for expenses of the Office of the Secretary of the Senate by the Legislative Branch Appropriations Act, 1995, to remain available until September 30, 1998, and that the Secretary determines are not needed for development of a financial management system for the Senate may, with the approval of the Committee on Appropriations of the Senate, be used to carry out the provisions of this section, and such funds shall be available through September 30, 2000.

(d) Regulations

The Committee on Rules and Administration of the Senate may prescribe such regulations as may be necessary to carry out the provisions of this section.

(e) Effective date

This section shall be effective for fiscal years beginning on or after October 1, 1996.

(Pub. L. 104–197, title I, §8, Sept. 16, 1996, 110 Stat. 2398.)

REFERENCES IN TEXT

The Legislative Branch Appropriations Act, 1995, referred to in subsec. (c), is Pub. L. 103–283, July 22, 1994, 108 Stat. 1423, as amended. Provisions under the heading "Secretary of the Senate" in Pub. L. 103–283 appear at 108 Stat. 1425, and are not classified to the Code.

CODIFICATION

Section is from the Congressional Operations Appropriations Act, 1997, which is title I of the Legislative Branch Appropriations Act, 1997.

§ 124. Arrangements for attendance at funeral of deceased House Members; payment of funeral expenses and expenses of attending funeral rites

Notwithstanding any other provision of law, the Sergeant at Arms of the House is authorized and directed on and after October 2, 1962, to make such arrangements as may be necessary for any committee of Members of the Senate and House of Representatives duly appointed to attend the funeral of a deceased Member of the House. Notwithstanding any other provision of law, there shall be paid out of the applicable accounts of the House of Representatives, under such rules and regulations as the Committee on House Oversight may prescribe, such sums as may be necessary to defray the funeral expenses of the deceased Member and to defray the expenses of such committee, the Sergeant at Arms of the House or a representative of his office, and the widow (or widower) or minor children, or both, of the deceased Member incurred in attending the funeral rites and burial of such Member.

(Pub. L. 87–730, §101, Oct. 2, 1962, 76 Stat. 686; Pub. L. 104–186, title II, §204(69), Aug. 20, 1996, 110 Stat. 1740.)

CODIFICATION

Section is from the Legislative Branch Appropriation Act, 1963.

PRIOR PROVISIONS

Provisions similar to those in this section were contained in the following prior appropriation acts:

Aug. 5, 1955, ch. 568, 69 Stat. 513.
July 2, 1954, ch. 455, title I, 68 Stat. 403.
Aug. 1, 1953, ch. 304, title I, 67 Stat. 325.

AMENDMENTS

1996—Pub. L. 104–186 substituted "applicable accounts of the House of Representatives" for "contingent fund of the House" and "House Oversight" for "House Administration".

CHANGE OF NAME

Committee on House Oversight of House of Representatives changed to Committee on House Administration of House of Representatives by House Resolution No. 5, One Hundred Sixth Congress, Jan. 6, 1999.

§ 125. Gratuities for survivors of deceased House employees; computation

The Chief Administrative Officer of the House of Representatives is on and after July 2, 1954, authorized to pay, from the applicable accounts of the House of Representatives, a gratuity to the widow, widower, or heirs-at-law, of each deceased employee of the House an amount equal to one month's salary for each year or part of year of the first six years service of such employee plus one-half of one month's salary for each year or part of year of such service in excess of six years to and including the eighteenth year of such service. Service computed hereunder shall include all Federal civilian employment, and military service where such service interrupted Federal civilian employment.

(July 2, 1954, ch. 455, title I, 68 Stat. 403; Pub. L. 104–186, title II, §204(70), Aug. 20, 1996, 110 Stat. 1740.)

AMENDMENTS

1996—Pub. L. 104–186 substituted "Chief Administrative Officer of the House of Representatives" for "Clerk of the House" and "applicable accounts of the House of Representatives" for "contingent fund of the House".

§ 125a. Death gratuity payments as gifts

Any death gratuity payment at any time specifically appropriated by any Act of Congress or at any time made out of the applicable accounts of the House of Representatives or the contingent fund of the Senate shall be held to have been a gift.

(June 5, 1952, ch. 369, Ch. I, 66 Stat. 101; Pub. L. 104–186, title II, §203(6), Aug. 20, 1996, 110 Stat. 1725.)

CODIFICATION

Section is also set out as section 38b of this title.

AMENDMENTS

1996—Pub. L. 104–186 substituted "applicable accounts of the House of Representatives or the contingent fund" for "contingent fund of the House of Representatives or".

§ 126. Repealed. Pub. L. 89–554, § 8, Sept. 6, 1966, 80 Stat. 658

Section, act Sept. 1, 1954, ch. 1208, title VI, §603, 68 Stat. 1116, provided that official reporters of Senate proceedings and their employees be considered officers or employees of the legislative branch within section 2091(a) of former Title 5. See section 8701(a)(3) of Title 5, Government Organization and Employees.

§ 126–1. Omitted

CODIFICATION

Section, Pub. L. 89–90, July 27, 1965, 79 Stat. 265; Pub. L. 90–239, ch. IV, Jan. 2, 1968, 81 Stat. 774; Pub. L. 94–59, title I, July 25, 1975, 89 Stat. 270; Pub. L. 96–38, title I, §105(1), July 25, 1979, 93 Stat. 112, which authorized Secretary of Senate to employ one chief reporter of debates, seven reporters of debates, one assistant reporter of debates, two clerks, and six expert transcribers, was omitted because of section 61a–11 of this title which abolished all statutory positions in the Office of the Secretary of the Senate, with specified exceptions, effective Oct. 1, 1981, and authorized Secretary of Senate to appoint and fix compensation of such employees as appropriate.

§ 126–2. Designation of reporters

The reporters of debates in the office of the Secretary of the Senate are hereby designated the official reporters of debates of the Senate.

(Pub. L. 89–545, Aug. 27, 1966, 80 Stat. 354.)

§ 126a. Omitted

CODIFICATION

Section, Pub. L. 86–628, July 12, 1960, 74 Stat. 447, related to appointment of reporters, transcribers and other employees by Official Reporter of Debates of Senate. See section 61a–11 of this title.

§ 126b. Substitute reporters of debates and expert transcribers; temporary reporters of debates and expert transcribers; payments from Senate contingent fund

The Secretary of the Senate is on and after June 5, 1981, authorized to employ, by contract or otherwise, substitute reporters of debates and expert transcribers at daily rates of compensation, or temporary reporters of debates and expert transcribers at annual rates of compensation; no temporary reporters of debates or expert transcribers may be employed under authority of this provision for more than ninety days in any fiscal year; and payments made under authority of this section shall be made from the contingent fund of the Senate upon vouchers approved by the Secretary of the Senate.

(Pub. L. 89–90, July 27, 1965, 79 Stat. 266; Pub. L. 97–12, title I, § 105, June 5, 1981, 95 Stat. 61.)

CODIFICATION

"On and after June 5, 1981" substituted in text for "hereafter", which probably meant after the date of enactment of Pub. L. 97–12 rather than the date of enactment of Pub. L. 89–90.

AMENDMENTS

1981—Pub. L. 97–12 amended section generally, substituting "authorized to employ, by contract or otherwise, substitute reporters of debates and expert transcribers at daily rates of compensation, or temporary reporters of debates and expert transcribers at annual rates of compensation; no temporary reporters of debates or expert transcribers may be employed under authority of this provision for more than ninety days in any fiscal year; and payments made under authority of this section shall be made from the contingent fund of the Senate upon vouchers approved by the Secretary of the Senate" for "authorized to obtain by contract or otherwise, emergency reporters and transcribers as may be necessary, payments therefor to be made form the contingent fund of the Senate".

§ 127. Repealed. Pub. L. 92–51, July 9, 1971, 85 Stat. 129

Section, Pub. L. 87–130, Aug. 10, 1961, 75 Stat. 323; Pub. L. 89–90, July 27, 1965, 79 Stat. 269; Pub. L. 91–145, Dec. 12, 1969, 83 Stat. 343, provided for reimbursement of transportation expenses of employees in Senator's office, authorizing eight round trips in any fiscal year and two additional mileage payments when office of Senator is from a State having a population of ten million or more inhabitants and requiring voucher certification of travel as being in line of official duty.

Similar provisions were contained in the following prior appropriation acts:

Act June 27, 1956, ch. 453, 70 Stat. 360, as amended by acts July 12, 1960, Pub. L. 86–628, 74 Stat. 449; Mar. 31, 1961, Pub. L. 87–14, title I, 75 Stat. 29.

Act Aug. 5, 1955, ch. 568, 69 Stat. 504.

EFFECTIVE DATE OF REPEAL

Pub. L. 92–51 provided that the repeal is effective July 1, 1971.

§ 127a. Reimbursement of transportation expenses for employees in office of House Member

The applicable accounts of the House of Representatives is [1] made available after August 28, 1965, for reimbursement of transportation expenses incurred by not to exceed two employees in the office of a Member of the House of Representatives (including the Resident Commissioner from Puerto Rico) for one round trip each, or incurred by not to exceed one employee for two round trips, in any calendar year between Washington, District of Columbia, and the place of residence of the Member representing the congressional district involved. Such payment shall be made only upon vouchers approved by the Member containing a certification by him that such travel was performed in line of official duty, but the mileage allowed for any such trip shall not exceed the round trip mileage by the nearest usual route between Washington, District of Columbia, and the Member's place of residence in the congressional district involved. The Committee on House Oversight of the House of Representatives shall make such rules and regulations as may be necessary to carry out this section.

(Pub. L. 89–147, § 3, Aug. 28, 1965, 79 Stat. 583; Pub. L. 104–186, title II, § 204(71), Aug. 20, 1996, 110 Stat. 1740.)

AMENDMENTS

1996—Pub. L. 104–186 substituted "applicable accounts" for "contingent fund" and "House Oversight" for "House Administration".

CHANGE OF NAME

Committee on House Oversight of House of Representatives changed to Committee on House Administration of House of Representatives by House Resolution No. 5, One Hundred Sixth Congress, Jan. 6, 1999.

§ 127b. Reimbursement of residential telecommunications expenses for House Members, officers, and employees

(a) Notwithstanding any other provision of law, official resources may be used during a fiscal year (beginning with fiscal year 1999), in accordance with regulations of the Committee on House Oversight, to reimburse a Member, officer, or employee of the House of Representatives for the ordinary and necessary expenses related to the official use of telecommunications lines in the residence of the Member, officer, or employee.

(b) The Committee on House Oversight shall promulgate such regulations as are necessary to implement this section.

(Pub. L. 105–275, title I, § 109, Oct. 21, 1998, 112 Stat. 2439.)

---

[1] So in original. Probably should be "are".

Section is from the Congressional Operations Appropriations Act, 1999, which is title I of the Legislative Branch Appropriations Act, 1999.

CHANGE OF NAME

Committee on House Oversight of House of Representatives changed to Committee on House Administration of House of Representatives by House Resolution No. 5, One Hundred Sixth Congress, Jan. 6, 1999.

§§ 128, 129. Repealed. Pub. L. 89–554, § 8(a), Sept. 6, 1966, 80 Stat. 658, 659

Section 128, act Aug. 5, 1955, ch. 568, 69 Stat. 513, authorized contributions for group life insurance of House employees from House contingent fund. See section 8708 of Title 5, Government Organization and Employees.

Section 129, Pub. L. 85–75, July 1, 1957, 71 Stat. 248, authorized contributions to retirement and disability fund from House contingent fund. See section 8334 of Title 5.

§ 130. Repealed. Pub. L. 95–391, title I, § 111, Sept. 30, 1978, 92 Stat. 777

Section, Pub. L. 87–730, § 103, Oct. 2, 1962, 76 Stat. 693; H. Res. 163, Mar. 19, 1975; Pub. L. 95–94, title I, § 115, Aug. 5, 1977, 91 Stat. 668, authorized payment of expenses of participation by House in interparliamentary institutions. See section 130–1 of this title.

The repeal of this section is based on a part of section 2 of House Resolution No. 1047, Ninety-fifth Congress, Apr. 4, 1978, which was enacted into permanent law by Pub. L. 95–391.

EFFECTIVE DATE OF REPEAL

Section 2 of House Resolution No. 1047, Ninety-fifth Congress, which was enacted into permanent law by Pub. L. 95–391, provided that the repeal is effective upon the enactment of House Resolution No. 1047 as permanent law, which was effected by Pub. L. 95–391, § 111, effective Sept. 30, 1978.

NINETY-FIFTH CONGRESS

Section 2 of House Resolution No. 1047, Ninety-fifth Congress, Apr. 4, 1978, enacted into permanent law by Pub. L. 95–391, provided that this section would not be effective in the Ninety-fifth Congress upon the adoption of H. Res. 1047.

AUTHORIZATION FOR PAYMENT OF EXPENSES FROM CONTINGENT FUND OF HOUSE OF REPRESENTATIVES FOR PARTICIPATORY ACTIVITIES

Section 1 of House Resolution No. 434, Ninety-fifth Congress, Mar. 31, 1977, enacted into permanent law by Pub. L. 95–94, title I, § 115, Aug. 5, 1977, 91 Stat. 668, which provided that, until otherwise provided by law, there was to have been paid out of the contingent fund of the House of Representatives such sums as may have been necessary, but not to exceed $15,000 in any calendar year, for the payment of expenses incurred in carrying out this section, was repealed by section 2 of H. Res. 1047, Ninety-fifth Congress, Apr. 4, 1978, which was enacted into permanent law by section 111 of Pub. L. 95–391, effective Sept. 30, 1978.

§ 130–1. Participation by House in interparliamentary institutions; reception of members of foreign legislative bodies and foreign officials; meetings with Government officials

(a) It is the purpose of this section to enable the House of Representatives more properly to discharge and coordinate its activities and responsibilities in connection with participation in various interparliamentary institutions, to facilitate the interchange and reception in the United States of members of foreign legislative bodies and permanent officials of foreign governments, and to enable the House of Representatives to host meetings with senior United States Government officials and other dignitaries in order to discuss matters relevant to United States relations with other countries.

(b) For payment of expenses incurred in carrying out subsection (a) of this section, there shall be paid out of the applicable accounts of the House of Representatives, until otherwise provided by law, such sums as may be necessary but not to exceed $80,000 in any calendar year. Such payments shall be made on vouchers signed by the chairman of the Committee on Foreign Affairs and approved by the Committee on House Oversight.

(Pub. L. 95–391, title I, § 111, Sept. 30, 1978, 92 Stat. 777; Pub. L. 103–437, § 2(b), Nov. 2, 1994, 108 Stat. 4581; Pub. L. 104–186, title II, § 204(72), Aug. 20, 1996, 110 Stat. 1741; Pub. L. 105–275, title I, § 102, Oct. 21, 1998, 112 Stat. 2438.)

CODIFICATION

Section is based on section 1 of House Resolution No. 1047, Ninety-fifth Congress, Apr. 4, 1978, which was enacted into permanent law by Pub. L. 95–391.

AMENDMENTS

1998—Subsec. (b). Pub. L. 105–275 substituted "$80,000" for "$55,000".

1996—Subsec. (b). Pub. L. 104–186 substituted "applicable accounts of the House of Representatives" for "contingent fund of the House" and "House Oversight" for "House Administration".

1994—Subsec. (b). Pub. L. 103–437 substituted "Committee on Foreign Affairs" for "Committee on International Relations".

CHANGE OF NAME

Committee on Foreign Affairs of House of Representatives treated as referring to Committee on International Relations of House of Representatives by section 1(a) of Pub. L. 104–14, set out as a note preceding section 21 of this title.

Committee on House Oversight of House of Representatives changed to Committee on House Administration of House of Representatives by House Resolution No. 5, One Hundred Sixth Congress, Jan. 6, 1999.

§ 130a. Nonpay status for Congressional employees studying under Congressional staff fellowships

(a) With respect to each employee of the Senate or House of Representatives—

(1) whose compensation is disbursed by the Secretary of the Senate or the Chief Administrative Officer of the House of Representatives, and

(2) who, on or after January 1, 1963 shall have been separated from employment with the Senate or House of Representatives in order to pursue certain studies under a congressional staff fellowship awarded by the American Political Science Association,

the period of time covered by such fellowship shall be held and considered to be service (in a nonpay status) in employment with the Senate or House of Representatives, as the case may be, at the rate of compensation received immediately prior to separation (including any increases in compensation provided by law during the period covered by such fellowship) for the purposes of the provisions of law specified in subsection (b) of this section, if the award of such fellowship to such employee is certified to the Secretary of the Senate or the Chief Administrative Officer of the House of Representatives, as appropriate, by the appointing authority concerned or, in the event of the death or disability of such appointing authority, is established to the satisfaction of the Secretary of the Senate or the Chief Administrative Officer of the House of Representatives by records or other evidence.

(b) The provisions of law referred to in subsection (a) of this section are—

(1) subchapter III (relating to civil service retirement) of chapter 83 of title 5;

(2) chapter 87 (relating to Federal employees group life insurance) of title 5; and

(3) chapter 89 (relating to Federal employees group health insurance) of title 5.

(Pub. L. 89–379, Mar. 30, 1966, 80 Stat. 94; Pub. L. 104–186, title II, §204(73), Aug. 20, 1996, 110 Stat. 1741.)

Amendments

1996—Pub. L. 104–186 designated existing provisions as subsec. (a), in par. (1) substituted "Chief Administrative Officer" for "Clerk", in provisions following par. (2) substituted "the purposes of the provisions of law specified in subsection (b) of this section, if the award" for "the purposes of—

"(A) subchapter III (relating to civil service retirement) of chapter 83 of title 5,

"(B) chapter 87 (relating to Federal employees group life insurance) of title 5, and

"(C) chapter 89 (relating to Federal employees group health insurance) of title 5,

if the award", "Chief Administrative Officer of the House of Representatives, as appropriate" for "Clerk of the House of Representatives, as appropriate", and "Chief Administrative Officer of the House of Representatives by records" for "Clerk of the House by records", and added subsec. (b).

§ 130b. Jury and witness service by Senate and House employees

(a) Definitions

For purposes of this section—

(1) "employee" means any individual whose pay is disbursed by the Secretary of the Senate or the Chief Administrative Officer of the House of Representatives; and

(2) "court of the United States" has the meaning given it by section 451 of title 28 and includes the United States District Court for the District of the Canal Zone, the District Court of Guam, and the District Court of the Virgin Islands.

(b) Service as juror or witness in connection with a judicial proceeding; prohibition against reduction of pay

The pay of an employee shall not be reduced during a period of absence with respect to which the employee is summoned (and permitted to respond to such summons by the appropriate authority of the House of the Congress disbursing his pay), in connection with a judicial proceeding by a court or authority responsible for the conduct of that proceeding, to serve—

(1) as a juror; or

(2) other than as provided in subsection (c) of this section, as a witness on behalf of any party in connection with any judicial proceeding to which the United States, the District of Columbia, or a State or local government is a party;

in the District of Columbia, a State, territory, or possession of the United States including the Commonwealth of Puerto Rico, the Canal Zone, or the Trust Territory of the Pacific Islands. For purposes of this subsection, "judicial proceeding" means any action, suit, or other judicial proceeding, including any condemnation, preliminary, informational, or other proceeding of a judicial nature, but does not include an administrative proceeding.

(c) Official duty

An employee is performing official duty during the period with respect to which he is summoned (and is authorized to respond to such summons by the House of the Congress disbursing his pay), or is assigned by such House, to—

(1) testify or produce official records on behalf of the United States or the District of Columbia; or

(2) testify in his official capacity or produce official records on behalf of a party other than the United States or the District of Columbia.

(d) Prohibition on receipt of jury or witness fees

(1) An employee may not receive fees for service—

(A) as juror in a court of the United States or the District of Columbia; or

(B) as a witness on behalf of the United States or the District of Columbia.

(2) If an employee receives an amount (other than travel expenses) for service as a juror or witness during a period in which his pay may not be reduced under subsection (b) of this section, or for which he is performing official duty under subsection (c) of this section, the employee shall remit such amount to the officer who disburses the pay of the employee, which amount shall be covered into the general fund of the Treasury as miscellaneous receipts.

(e) Travel expenses

(1) An employee summoned (and authorized to respond to such summons by the House of the Congress disbursing his pay), or assigned by such House, to testify or produce official records on behalf of the United States is entitled to travel expenses. If the case involves an activity in connection with which he is employed, the travel expenses shall be paid from funds otherwise available for the payment of travel expenses of such House in accordance with travel regulations of that House. If the case does not involve such an activity, the department, agency, or independent establishment of the United States on whose behalf he is so testifying or producing records shall pay to the employee his travel expenses out of appropriations otherwise available, and in accordance with regulation applicable, to that department, agency, or independent establishment for the payment of travel expenses.

(2) An employee summoned (and permitted to respond to such summons by the House of the

Congress disbursing his pay), or assigned by such House, to testify in his official capacity or produce official records on behalf of a party other than the United States, is entitled to travel expenses, unless any travel expenses are paid to the employee for his appearance by the court, authority, or party which caused him to be summoned.

(f) Rules and regulations

The Committee on Rules and Administration of the Senate and the Committee on House Oversight of the House of Representatives are authorized to prescribe, for employees of their respective Houses, such rules and regulations as may be necessary to carry out the provisions of this section.

(g) Congressional consent not conferred for production of official records or to testimony concerning activities related to employment

No provision of this section shall be construed to confer the consent of either House of the Congress to the production of official records of that House or to testimony by an employee of that House concerning activities related to his employment.

(Pub. L. 91–563, § 6, Dec. 19, 1970, 84 Stat. 1478; Pub. L. 94–310, § 2, June 15, 1976, 90 Stat. 687; Pub. L. 104–186, title II, § 204(74), (75), Aug. 20, 1996, 110 Stat. 1741.)

REFERENCES IN TEXT

For definition of Canal Zone, referred to in subsec. (b), see section 3602(b) of Title 22, Foreign Relations and Intercourse.

AMENDMENTS

1996—Subsec. (a)(1). Pub. L. 104–186, § 204(74), substituted "Chief Administrative Officer" for "Clerk".

Subsec. (f). Pub. L. 104–186, § 204(75), substituted "House Oversight" for "House Administration".

1976—Subsec. (b)(2). Pub. L. 94–310 substituted "other than as provided in subsection (c) of this section, as a witness on behalf of any party in connection with any judicial proceeding to which the United States, the District of Columbia, or a State or local government is a party" for "as a witness on behalf of a party other than the United States, the District of Columbia, or a private party".

CHANGE OF NAME

Committee on House Oversight of House of Representatives changed to Committee on House Administration of House of Representatives by House Resolution No. 5, One Hundred Sixth Congress, Jan. 6, 1999.

EFFECTIVE DATE OF 1976 AMENDMENT

Section 4 of Pub. L. 94–310 provided that: "The amendments made by this Act [amending this section and sections 6322 and 8906 of Title 5, Government Organization and Employees] shall take effect on October 1, 1976, or on the date of the enactment of this Act [June 15, 1976], whichever date is later."

TERMINATION OF TRUST TERRITORY OF THE PACIFIC ISLANDS

For termination of Trust Territory of the Pacific Islands, see note set out preceding section 1681 of Title 48, Territories and Insular Possessions.

TERMINATION OF UNITED STATES DISTRICT COURT FOR THE DISTRICT OF THE CANAL ZONE

For termination of the United States District Court for the District of the Canal Zone at end of the "transition period", being the 30 month period beginning Oct. 1, 1979, and ending midnight Mar. 31, 1982, see Paragraph 5 of Article XI of the Panama Canal Treaty of 1977 and sections 2101 and 2201 to 2203(a) of Pub. L. 96–70, title II, Sept. 27, 1979, 93 Stat. 493, formerly classified to sections 3831 and 3841 to 3843, respectively, of Title 22, Foreign Relations and Intercourse.

§ 130c. Waiver by Secretary of Senate of claims of United States arising out of erroneous payments to Vice President, Senator, or Senate employee paid by Secretary of Senate

(a) Waiver of claim for erroneous payment of pay or allowances

A claim of the United States against a person arising out of an erroneous payment of any pay or allowances, other than travel and transportation expenses and allowances, on or after July 25, 1974, to the Vice President, a Senator, or to an officer or employee whose pay is disbursed by the Secretary of the Senate, the collection of which would be against equity and good conscience and not in the best interests of the United States, may be waived in whole or in part by the Secretary of the Senate. An application for waiver shall be investigated by the Financial Clerk of the Senate who shall submit a written report of his investigation to the Secretary of the Senate. An application for waiver of a claim in an amount aggregating more than $1,500 may also be investigated by the Comptroller General of the United States who shall submit a written report of his investigation to the Secretary of the Senate.

(b) Prohibition of waiver

The Secretary of the Senate may not exercise his authority under this section to waive any claim—

(1) if, in his opinion, there exists, in connection with the claim, an indication of fraud, misrepresentation, fault, or lack of good faith on the part of the Vice President, the Senator, the officer or employee, or any other person having an interest in obtaining a waiver of the claim; or

(2) if the application for waiver is received in his office after the expiration of 3 years immediately following the date on which the erroneous payment of pay or allowances was discovered.

(c) Credit for waiver

In the audit and settlement of accounts of any accountable officer or official, full credit shall be given for any amounts with respect to which collection by the United States is waived under this section.

(d) Effect of waiver

An erroneous payment, the collection of which is waived under this section, is deemed a valid payment for all purposes.

(e) Construction with other laws

This section does not affect any authority under any other law to litigate, settle, compromise, or waive any claim of the United States.

(f) Rules and regulations

The Secretary of the Senate shall promulgate rules and regulations to carry out the provisions of this section.

(Pub. L. 93–359, § 2, July 25, 1974, 88 Stat. 394; Pub. L. 103–69, title III, § 315, Aug. 11, 1993, 107 Stat. 713; Pub. L. 104–316, title I, § 102(b), Oct. 19, 1996, 110 Stat. 3828.)

AMENDMENTS

1996—Subsec. (a). Pub. L. 104–316 in first sentence struck out ", if the claim is not the subject of an exception made by the Comptroller General in the account of any accountable officer or official" after "in part by the Secretary of the Senate", and in third sentence substituted "$1,500 may also" for "$1,500 shall also".

1993—Subsec. (a). Pub. L. 103–69 substituted "$1,500" for "$500".

EFFECTIVE DATE OF 1996 AMENDMENT

Section 101(e) of title I of Pub. L. 104–316 provided that:

"(1) IN GENERAL.—Except as provided in paragraph (2), this title [see Tables for classification] shall take effect on the date of enactment of this Act [Oct. 19, 1996].

"(2) EXCEPTIONS.—Sections 103(d), 105(b), and 116 [amending section 5584 of Title 5, Government Organization and Employees, section 2774 of Title 10, Armed Forces, and section 716 of Title 32, National Guard] shall take effect 60 days after the date of enactment of this Act."

§ 130d. Waiver by Speaker of House of claims of United States arising out of erroneous payments to officers or employees paid by Chief Administrative Officer of House

(a) Waiver of claim for erroneous payment of pay or allowances

A claim of the United States against a person arising out of an erroneous payment of any pay or allowances, other than travel and transportation expenses and allowances, on or after July 25, 1974, to an officer or employee whose pay is disbursed by the Chief Administrative Officer of the House of Representatives, the collection of which would be against equity and good conscience and not in the best interests of the United States, may be waived in whole or in part by the Speaker of the House.

(b) Investigation and report

An application for waiver of a claim shall be investigated by the Chief Administrative Officer of the House of Representatives who shall submit a written report of his investigation to the Speaker of the House.

(c) Prohibition of waiver

The Speaker of the House may not exercise his authority under this section to waive any claim—

(1) if, in his opinion, there exists, in connection with the claim, an indication of fraud, misrepresentation, fault, or lack of good faith on the part of the officer or employee or any other person having an interest in obtaining a waiver of the claim; or

(2) if the application for waiver is received in his office after the expiration of 3 years immediately following the date on which the erroneous payment of pay or allowances was discovered.

(d) Credit for waiver

In the audit and settlement of the accounts of any accountable officer or official, full credit shall be given for any amounts with respect to which collection by the United States is waived under this section.

(e) Effect of waiver

An erroneous payment, the collection of which is waived under this section, is deemed a valid payment for all purposes.

(f) Construction with other laws

This section does not affect any authority under any other law to litigate, settle, compromise, or waive any claim of the United States.

(g) Rules and regulations

The Speaker of the House shall prescribe rules and regulations to carry out the provisions of this section.

(Pub. L. 93–359, § 3, July 25, 1974, 88 Stat. 395; Pub. L. 104–186, title II, § 204(76), Aug. 20, 1996, 110 Stat. 1742; Pub. L. 104–316, title I, § 102(c), Oct. 19, 1996, 110 Stat. 3828.)

AMENDMENTS

1996—Subsec. (a). Pub. L. 104–316 struck out ", if the claim is not the subject of an exception made by the Comptroller General in the account of any accountable officer or official" before period at end.

Pub. L. 104–186 substituted "Chief Administrative Officer" for "Clerk".

Subsec. (b). Pub. L. 104–186 substituted "Chief Administrative Officer" for "Clerk".

§ 130e. Special Services Office

There is established, as a joint office of Congress, the Special Services Office, which (under the supervision and control of a board, to be known as the Special Services Board, comprised of the Sergeant at Arms of the House of Representatives, the Sergeant at Arms and Doorkeeper of the Senate, and the Architect of the Capitol) shall provide special services to Members of Congress, and to officers, employees, and guests of Congress.

(Pub. L. 101–163, title III, § 310, Nov. 21, 1989, 103 Stat. 1065; Pub. L. 104–53, title I, § 112, Nov. 19, 1995, 109 Stat. 525.)

CODIFICATION

Section is from the Legislative Branch Appropriations Act, 1990.

AMENDMENTS

1995—Pub. L. 104–53 substituted "Sergeant at Arms" for "Clerk" after "comprised of the" and "Architect of the Capitol" for "Librarian of Congress".

§ 130f. Office of General Counsel of House; administrative provisions

(a) Compliance with admission requirements

The General Counsel of the House of Representatives and any other counsel in the Office of the General Counsel of the House of Representatives, including any counsel specially retained by the Office of General Counsel, shall be entitled, for the purpose of performing the counsel's functions, to enter an appearance in any proceeding before any court of the United States or of any State or political subdivision thereof without compliance with any requirements for admission to practice before such court, except that the authorization conferred by this subsection shall not apply with respect to the admission of any such person to practice before the United States Supreme Court.

(b) Notification by Attorney General

The Attorney General shall notify the General Counsel of the House of Representatives with respect to any proceeding in which the United States is a party of any determination by the Attorney General or Solicitor General not to appeal any court decision affecting the constitutionality of an Act or joint resolution of Congress within such time as will enable the House to direct the General Counsel to intervene as a party in such proceeding pursuant to applicable rules of the House of Representatives.

(c) General Counsel definition

In this section, the term "General Counsel of the House of Representatives" means—

(1) the head of the Office of General Counsel established and operating under clause 8 of rule II of the Rules of the House of Representatives;

(2) the head of any successor office to the Office of General Counsel which is established after September 29, 1999; and

(3) any other person authorized and directed in accordance with the Rules of the House of Representatives to provide legal assistance and representation to the House in connection with the matters described in this section.

(d) Effective date

The provisions of this section shall become effective beginning with September 29, 1999.

(Pub. L. 106–57, title I, § 101, Sept. 29, 1999, 113 Stat. 414.)

CODIFICATION

Section is from the Congressional Operations Appropriations Act, 2000, which is title I of the Legislative Branch Appropriations Act, 2000.

CHAPTER 5—LIBRARY OF CONGRESS

§ 131. Collections composing Library; location

The Library of Congress, composed of the books, maps, and other publications which on December 1, 1873, remained in existence, from the collections theretofore united under authority of law and those added from time to time by purchase, exchange, donation, reservation from publications ordered by Congress, acquisition of material under the copyright law, and otherwise, shall be preserved in the Library Building.

(R.S. § 80; Feb. 19, 1897, ch. 265, § 1, 29 Stat. 545, 546; Pub. L. 94–553, title I, § 105(g), Oct. 19, 1976, 90 Stat. 2599; Pub. L. 100–202, § 101(i) [title III, § 310], Dec. 22, 1987, 101 Stat. 1329–290, 1329–310.)

CODIFICATION

R.S. § 80 derived from act Jan. 26, 1802, ch. 2, 2 Stat. 128; Res. Oct. 21, 1814, No. 3, 3 Stat. 246; act Jan. 30, 1815, ch. 27, 3 Stat. 195; act June 25, 1864, ch. 147, § 1, 13 Stat. 148; Res. July 25, 1866, No. 77, 14 Stat. 365; and act Mar. 2, 1867, ch. 167, § 1, 14 Stat. 464.

AMENDMENTS

1987—Pub. L. 100–202 struck out after first sentence "The law library shall be preserved in the Capitol in the rooms which were on July 4, 1872, appropriated to its use, and in such others as may hereafter be assigned thereto."

1976—Pub. L. 94–553 substituted "acquisition of material under the copyright law" for "deposit to secure copyright".

EFFECTIVE DATE OF 1976 AMENDMENT

Amendment by Pub. L. 94–553 effective Jan. 1, 1978, see section 102 of Pub. L. 94–553 set out as an Effective Date note preceding section 101 of Title 17, Copyrights.

TRANSFER TO LIBRARY BUILDING

Provisions for the removal of the Library to the Library Building, erected pursuant to act Apr. 15, 1886, ch. 50, 24 Stat. 12, and for the custody, care, and maintenance of that building, were made by act Feb. 19, 1897.

ORGANIZING AND MICROFILMING OF PRESIDENTIAL PAPERS; APPROPRIATION

Pub. L. 85–147, Aug. 16, 1957, 71 Stat. 368, as amended by Pub. L. 87–263, Sept. 21, 1961, 75 Stat. 544; Pub. L. 88–299, Apr. 27, 1964, 78 Stat. 183, provided: "That the Librarian of Congress is authorized and directed to arrange, index and microfilm the papers of the Presidents of the United States in the collections of the Library of Congress, in order to preserve their contents against destruction by war or other calamity and for the purpose of making them more readily available for study and research to the fullest possible extent consistent with any existing limitations that may have been imposed on the use of or the access to such papers by their donors or by those placing them on deposit with the Library of Congress. Neither the United States nor any officer or employee of the United States shall be liable for damages for infringement of literary property rights by reason of any activity authorized by this Act.

"SEC. 2. There are authorized to be appropriated such amounts as may be necessary to carry out the provisions of this Act."

§ 132. Departments of Library

The Library of Congress shall be arranged in two departments, a general library and a law library.

(R.S. § 81.)

R.S. § 81 derived from act July 14, 1832, ch. 221, § 1, 4 Stat. 579.

§ 132a. Appropriations for increase of general library

The unexpended balance of any sums appropriated by Congress for the increase of the general library, together with such sums as may hereafter be appropriated to the same purpose, shall be laid out under the direction of the Joint Committee of Congress on the Library.

(R.S. § 82; Feb. 7, 1902, No. 5, 32 Stat. 735; Aug. 2, 1946, ch. 753, title II, § 223, 60 Stat. 838.)

CODIFICATION

R.S. § 82 derived from acts Apr. 24, 1800, ch. 37, § 5, 2 Stat. 56, and Jan. 26, 1802, ch. 2, § 6, 2 Stat. 129.

AMENDMENTS

1946—Act Aug. 2, 1946, changed composition of Joint Committee. See section 132b of this title.

EFFECTIVE DATE OF 1946 AMENDMENT

Amendment by act Aug. 2, 1946, effective Jan. 3, 1947, see section 245 of that act, set out as a note under section 72a of this title.

§ 132a–1. Obligations for reimbursable and revolving fund activities; limitation

Effective for fiscal years beginning with fiscal year 1995, obligations for any reimbursable and revolving fund activities performed by the Library of Congress are limited to the total amounts provided (1) in the annual regular appropriations Act making appropriations for the legislative branch, or (2) in a supplemental appropriations Act that makes appropriations for the legislative branch.

(Pub. L. 103–69, title II, § 206, Aug. 11, 1993, 107 Stat. 706.)

§ 132a–2. Furniture, furnishings, and office and library equipment; transfer of funds

(a) Transfer of funds

In addition to any other transfer authority provided by law, during fiscal year 2001 and fiscal years thereafter, the Librarian of Congress may transfer to and among available accounts of the Library of Congress amounts appropriated to the Librarian from funds for the purchase, installation, maintenance, and repair of furniture, furnishings, and office and library equipment.

(b) Availability of funds

Any amounts transferred pursuant to subsection (a) of this section shall be merged with and be available for the same purpose and for the same period as the appropriation or account to which such amounts are transferred.

(c) Approval of Congress

The Librarian may transfer amounts pursuant to subsection (a) of this section only with the approval of the Committees on Appropriations of the House of Representatives and Senate.

(Pub. L. 106–554, § 1(a)(2) [title II, § 209], Dec. 21, 2000, 114 Stat. 2763, 2763A–114.)

CODIFICATION

Section is from the Legislative Branch Appropriations Act, 2001.

§ 132b. Joint Committee on the Library

The Joint Committee of Congress on the Library shall, on and after January 3, 1947, consist of the chairman and four members of the Committee on Rules and Administration of the Senate and the chairman and four members of the Committee on House Oversight of the House of Representatives.

(Aug. 2, 1946, ch. 753, title II, § 223, 60 Stat. 838; Pub. L. 104–186, title II, § 205, Aug. 20, 1996, 110 Stat. 1742.)

AMENDMENTS

1996—Pub. L. 104–186 substituted "House Oversight" for "House Administration".

CHANGE OF NAME

Committee on House Oversight of House of Representatives changed to Committee on House Administration of House of Representatives by House Resolution No. 5, One Hundred Sixth Congress, Jan. 6, 1999.

EFFECTIVE DATE

Section effective Jan. 3, 1947, see section 245 of act Aug. 2, 1946, set out as a note under section 72a of this title.

MEMBER OF COMMITTEE WITH RESPECT TO FINANCIAL MANAGEMENT AND BUDGET AND PROGRAM DEVELOPMENT

Pub. L. 106–554, § 1(a)(4) [div. A], Dec. 21, 2000, 114 Stat. 2763, 2763A–195, provided: "That notwithstanding any other provision of law, effective with the One Hundred Seventh Congress and each succeeding Congress the chair of the Subcommittee on the Legislative Branch of the Committee on Appropriations of the House of Representatives shall serve as a member of the Joint Committee on the Library with respect to the Library's financial management, organization, budget development and implementation, and program development and administration, as well as any other element of the mission of the Library of Congress which is subject to the requirements of Federal law."

§ 133. Joint Committee during recess of Congress

The portion of the Joint Committee of Congress on the Library on the part of the Senate remaining in office as Senators shall during the recess of Congress exercise the powers and discharge the duties conferred by law upon the Joint Committee of Congress on the Library.

(Mar. 3, 1883, ch. 141, § 2, 22 Stat. 592; Aug. 2, 1946, ch. 753, title II, § 223, 60 Stat. 838.)

AMENDMENTS

1946—Act Aug. 2, 1946, changed composition of Joint Committee. See section 132b of this title.

EFFECTIVE DATE OF 1946 AMENDMENT

Amendment by act Aug. 2, 1946, effective Jan. 3, 1947, see section 245 of that act, set out as a note under section 72a of this title.

§ 134. Incidental expenses of law library

The incidental expenses of the law library shall be paid out of the appropriations for the Library of Congress.

(R.S. § 83.)

R.S. § 83 derived from act July 14, 1832, ch. 221, § 3, 4 Stat. 579.

§ 135. Purchase of books for law library

The Librarian shall make the purchases of books for the law library, under the direction of and pursuant to the catalogue furnished him by the Chief Justice of the Supreme Court.

(R.S. § 84.)

R.S. § 84 derived from act July 14, 1832, ch. 221, § 4, 4 Stat. 579.

§ 135a. Books and sound-reproduction records for blind and other physically handicapped residents; annual appropriations; purchases

There is authorized to be appropriated annually to the Library of Congress, in addition to appropriations otherwise made to said Library, such sums for expenditure under the direction of the Librarian of Congress as may be necessary to provide books published either in raised characters, on sound-reproduction recordings or in any other form, and for purchase, maintenance, and replacement of reproducers for such sound-reproduction recordings, for the use of the blind and for other physically handicapped residents of the United States, including the several States, Territories, insular possessions, and the District of Columbia, all of which books, recordings, and reproducers will remain the property of the Library of Congress but will be loaned to blind and to other physically handicapped readers certified by competent authority as unable to read normal printed material as a result of physical limitations, under regulations prescribed by the Librarian of Congress for this service. In the purchase of books in either raised characters or in sound-reproduction recordings the Librarian of Congress, without reference to the provisions of section 5 of title 41, shall give preference to nonprofit-making institutions or agencies whose activities are primarily concerned with the blind and with other physically handicapped persons, in all cases where the prices or bids submitted by such institutions or agencies are, by said Librarian, under all the circumstances and needs involved, determined to be fair and reasonable.

(Mar. 3, 1931, ch. 400, § 1, 46 Stat. 1487; Mar. 4, 1933, ch. 279, 47 Stat. 1570; June 14, 1935, ch. 242, § 1, 49 Stat. 374; Apr. 23, 1937, ch. 125, § 1, 50 Stat. 72; June 7, 1939, ch. 191, 53 Stat. 812; June 6, 1940, ch. 255, 54 Stat. 245; Oct. 1, 1942, ch. 575, § 1, 56 Stat. 764; June 13, 1944, ch. 246, § 1, 58 Stat. 276; Aug. 8, 1946, ch. 868, § 1, 60 Stat. 908; July 3, 1952, ch. 566, 66 Stat. 326; Pub. L. 85–308, § 1, Sept. 7, 1957, 71 Stat. 630; Pub. L. 89–522, § 1, July 30, 1966, 80 Stat. 330.)

AMENDMENTS

1966—Pub. L. 89–522 amended section generally, extending availability of books and materials under this section by authorizing their loan to other physically handicapped residents, in addition to blind persons, certified by competent authority as unable to read normal printed material as a result of physical limitations.

1957—Pub. L. 85–308 authorized annual appropriation of necessary sums in lieu of provisions which limited annual appropriation to $1,125,000, and struck out limitation of $200,000 on amount of appropriated funds to be expended annually for books in raised characters.

1952—Act July 3, 1952, included children within its provisions as well as adults.

1946—Act Aug. 8, 1946, increased annual appropriation from $500,000 to $1,125,000.

1944—Act June 13, 1944, increased annual appropriation from $370,000 to $500,000, the amount allocated to sound-reproduction records from $250,000 to $400,000, and struck out provision allocating $20,000 to maintenance and replacement of Government-owned reproducers.

1942—Act Oct. 1, 1942, substituted "$370,000" for "$350,000", and inserted clause at end of first sentence relating to expenditure of not exceeding $20,000 for maintenance and replacement of reproducers for sound-reproduction records.

1940—Act June 6, 1940, substituted "$350,000" for "$275,000" and "$250,000" for "$175,000".

1939—Act June 7, 1939, inserted last sentence.

1937—Act Apr. 23, 1937, substituted "$275,000" for "$175,000" in two places and "$175,000" for "$75,000".

1935—Act June 14, 1935, substituted "$175,000" for "$100,000" and inserted provision that $100,000 of the $175,000 annual appropriation be expended for books in raised characters and the balance for sound-reproduction records.

1933—Act Mar. 4, 1933, inserted "published either in raised characters, on sound-reproduction records, or in any other form".

EFFECTIVE DATE OF 1957 AMENDMENT

Section 2 of Pub. L. 85–308 provided that: "This Act [amending this section] shall be applicable with respect to the fiscal year ending June 30, 1958, and for each fiscal year thereafter."

EFFECTIVE DATE OF 1946 AMENDMENT

Section 2 of act Aug. 8, 1946, provided: "This Act [amending this section] shall be applicable with respect to the fiscal year ending June 30, 1947, and for each fiscal year thereafter."

EFFECTIVE DATE OF 1944 AMENDMENT

Section 2 of act June 13, 1944, provided: "This Act [amending this section] shall be applicable with respect to the fiscal year ending June 30, 1945, and for each fiscal year thereafter."

EFFECTIVE DATE OF 1942 AMENDMENT

Section 2 of act Oct. 1, 1942, provided: "This Act [amending this section] shall be applicable with respect to the fiscal year ending June 30, 1943, and for each fiscal year thereafter."

EFFECTIVE DATE OF 1937 AMENDMENT

Section 2 of act Apr. 23, 1937, provided that: "This Act [amending this section] shall be applicable with respect to the fiscal year ending June 30, 1938, and for each fiscal year thereafter."

SECTION REFERRED TO IN OTHER SECTIONS

This section is referred to in section 135b of this title; title 17 section 121; title 39 section 3403.

§ 135a–1. Library of musical scores, instructional texts, and other specialized materials for use of blind persons or other physically handicapped residents; authorization of appropriations

(a) The Librarian of Congress shall establish and maintain a library of musical scores, instructional texts, and other specialized materials for the use of the blind and for other physically handicapped residents of the United States and its possessions in furthering their educational, vocational, and cultural opportunities in the field of music. Such scores, texts, and materials shall be made available on a loan basis under regulations developed by the Librarian or his designee in consultation with persons, organizations, and agencies engaged in work for the blind and for other physically handicapped persons.

(b) There are authorized to be appropriated such amounts as may be necessary to carry out the provisions of this section.

(Pub. L. 87–765, Oct. 9, 1962, 76 Stat. 763; Pub. L. 89–522, §2, July 30, 1966, 80 Stat. 331.)

AMENDMENTS

1966—Pub. L. 89–522 made the library of musical scores and materials available to other physically handicapped residents of the United States and added persons, organizations, and agencies engaged in work for physically handicapped persons to the groups with which the Librarian shall consult in making the materials available on a loan basis.

SECTION REFERRED TO IN OTHER SECTIONS

This section is referred to in section 135b of this title.

§135b. Local and regional centers; preference to blind and other physically handicapped veterans; rules and regulations; authorization of appropriations

(a) The Librarian of Congress may contract or otherwise arrange with such public or other nonprofit libraries, agencies, or organizations as he may deem appropriate to serve as local or regional centers for the circulation of (1) books, recordings, and reproducers referred to in section 135a of this title, and (2) musical scores, instructional texts, and other specialized materials referred to in section 135a–1 of this title, under such conditions and regulations as he may prescribe. In the lending of such books, recordings, reproducers, musical scores, instructional texts, and other specialized materials, preference shall at all times be given to the needs of the blind and of the other physically handicapped persons who have been honorably discharged from the Armed Forces of the United States.

(b) There are authorized to be appropriated such sums as may be necessary to carry out the purposes of this section.

(Mar. 3, 1931, ch. 400, §2, 46 Stat. 1487; Pub. L. 89–522, §1, July 30, 1966, 80 Stat. 330.)

AMENDMENTS

1966—Pub. L. 89–522 extended Librarian's authority to arrange for local and regional centers by authorizing him to contract with public or other nonprofit libraries, agencies, or organizations, extended field to include recordings, reproducers, musical scores, instructional texts, and other materials, substituted "Armed Forces of the United States" for "United States military or naval service", and extended veteran preference to include other physically handicapped individuals in addition to blind persons.

SECTION REFERRED TO IN OTHER SECTIONS

This section is referred to in title 39 section 3403.

§136. Librarian of Congress; appointment; rules and regulations

The Librarian of Congress shall be appointed by the President, by and with the advice and consent of the Senate. He shall make rules and regulations for the government of the Library.

(Feb. 19, 1897, ch. 265, §1, 29 Stat. 544, 546; Pub. L. 92–310, title II, §220(f), June 6, 1972, 86 Stat. 204.)

PRIOR PROVISIONS

R.S. §§88, 89, 4950, which were repealed by acts Feb. 28, 1933, ch. 131, §1, 47 Stat. 1349; Mar. 3, 1933, ch. 202, §1, 47 Stat. 1428, 1431.

AMENDMENTS

1972—Pub. L. 92–310 struck out provisions which required the Librarian of Congress to give a bond in the sum of $20,000.

§§136a, 136a–1. Omitted

CODIFICATION

Sections were superseded by section 136a–2 of this title.

Section 136a, Pub. L. 88–426, title II, §203(c), Aug. 14, 1964, 78 Stat. 415; Pub. L. 90–206, title II, §§219(2), 225(h), Dec. 16, 1967, 81 Stat. 639, 644; Pub. L. 94–82, title II, §204(b), Aug. 9, 1975, 89 Stat. 421, set compensation of Librarian of Congress at an annual rate equal to rate for positions at level IV of Executive Schedule.

A prior section 136a, acts Mar. 6, 1928, ch. 134, 45 Stat. 197; Oct. 15, 1949, ch. 695, §5(a), 63 Stat. 890, which contained similar provisions, was repealed by Pub. L. 89–554, §8(a), Sept. 6, 1966, 80 Stat. 647, 655.

Section 136a–1, Pub. L. 88–426, title II, §203(d), Aug. 14, 1964, 78 Stat. 415; Pub. L. 90–206, title II §§219(3), 225(h), Dec. 16, 1967, 81 Stat. 639, 644; Pub. L. 94–82, title II, §204(b), Aug. 9, 1975, 89 Stat. 421, set compensation of Deputy Librarian of Congress at an annual rate equal to rate for positions at level V of Executive Schedule.

§136a–2. Librarian of Congress and Deputy Librarian of Congress; compensation

Notwithstanding any other provision of law—

(1) the Librarian of Congress shall be compensated at an annual rate of pay which is equal to the annual rate of basic pay payable for positions at level II of the Executive Schedule under section 5313 of title 5; and

(2) the Deputy Librarian of Congress shall be compensated at an annual rate of pay which is equal to the annual rate of basic pay payable for positions at level III of the Executive Schedule under section 5314 of title 5.

(Pub. L. 98–63, title I, §904, July 30, 1983, 97 Stat. 336; Pub. L. 106–57, title II, §209(a), Sept. 29, 1999, 113 Stat. 424.)

AMENDMENTS

1999—Pub. L. 106–57 amended section generally. Prior to amendment, section read as follows:

"(a) Subject to subsection (b) of this section and notwithstanding any other provision of law—

"(1) the compensation of the Librarian of Congress shall be at an annual rate which is equal to the annual rate of basic pay payable for positions at level III of the Executive Schedule under section 5314 of title 5, and

"(2) the compensation of the Deputy Librarian of Congress shall be at an annual rate which is equal to the annual rate of basic pay payable for positions at level IV of the Executive Schedule under section 5315 of title 5.

"(b) The limitations contained in section 306 of S. 2939, Ninety-seventh Congress, as made applicable by section 101(e) of Public Law 97–276 (as amended by section 128(a) of Public Law 97–377) shall, after application of section 128(b) of Public law 97–377, be applicable to the compensation of the Librarian of Congress and the Deputy Librarian of Congress, as fixed by subsection (a) of this section."

EFFECTIVE DATE OF 1999 AMENDMENT

Pub. L. 106–57, title II, § 209(c), Sept. 29, 1999, 113 Stat. 424, provided that: "The amendments made by this section [amending this section and section 166 of this title] shall apply with respect to the first pay period which begins on or after the date of the enactment of this Act [Sept. 29, 1999] and each subsequent pay period."

EFFECTIVE DATE

Pub. L. 98–63, title I, § 904(c), July 30, 1983, 97 Stat. 337, provided that subsec. (a) of this section was to take effect on the first day of the first applicable pay period commencing on or after July 30, 1983, prior to being omitted in the general amendment of section 904 of Pub. L. 98–63 by section 209(a) of Pub. L. 106–57.

SALARY INCREASES

1987—Salaries of Librarian and Deputy Librarian increased respectively to $89,500 and $82,500 per annum, on recommendation of the President of the United States, see note set out under section 358 of this title.

1977—Salaries of Librarian and Deputy Librarian increased respectively to $50,000 and $47,500 per annum, on recommendation of the President of the United States, see note set out under section 358 of this title.

1969—Salaries of Librarian and Deputy Librarian increased respectively to $38,000 and $36,000 per annum, on recommendation of the President of the United States, see note set out under section 358 of this title.

§ 136b. Omitted

CODIFICATION

Section, act July 17, 1947, ch. 262, 61 Stat. 372, related to maximum salary for any position in the Library. See section 162a of this title.

§ 136c. Authorized additional expenses and services for which Library of Congress salary appropriations are available

From and after October 1, 1983, appropriations in this Act available to the Library of Congress for salaries shall be available for expenses of personnel security and suitability investigations of Library employees; special and temporary services (including employees engaged by day or hour or in piecework); and services as authorized by section 3109 of title 5.

(Pub. L. 98–51, title II, § 201, July 14, 1983, 97 Stat. 276.)

REFERENCES IN TEXT

This Act, referred to in text, is Pub. L. 98–51, July 14, 1983, 97 Stat. 263, known as the Legislative Branch Appropriations Act, 1984. For complete classification of this Act to the Code, see Tables.

§ 137. Use and regulation of law library

The justices of the Supreme Court shall have free access to the law library; and they are authorized to make regulations, not inconsistent with law, for the use of the same during the sittings of the court. But such regulations shall not restrict any person authorized to take books from the Library from having access to the law library, or using the books therein in the same manner as he may be entitled to use the books of the general Library.

(R.S. § 95.)

CODIFICATION

R.S. § 95 derived from act July 14, 1832, ch. 221, § 2, 4 Stat. 579.

§§ 137a, 137b. Omitted

CODIFICATION

Section 137a, R.S. § 94, related to persons specially privileged to use library. See last sentence of section 136 of this title, which gives Librarian of Congress power to make rules and regulations for government of library.

Section 137b, act Aug. 28, 1890, No. 41, 26 Stat. 678, which related to Interstate Commerce Commission and Chief of Army Engineering Corps, was omitted from the Code as superseded by the last sentence of section 136 of this title.

JOINT COMMITTEE REPORT

With reference to former section 137a of this title, the Joint Committee on the Library, in an official report March 3, 1897 (54th Cong., 2d Sess., Senate Report 1573) declared:

"Heretofore the Joint Committee on the Library has had authority to approve such rules and regulations as have been made by the Librarian of Congress, but the provision of law under which the Joint Committee has hitherto passed upon said rules and regulations would appear to be repealed by the more recent act (section 136 of this title) which places this power in the hands of the Librarian of Congress."

§ 137c. Withdrawal of books from Library of Congress

The chief judge and associate judges of the United States Court of Appeals for the District of Columbia and the chief judge and associate judges of the United States District Court for the District of Columbia are authorized to use and take books from the Library of Congress in the same manner and subject to the same regulations as justices of the Supreme Court of the United States.

(Joint Res. No. 9, Jan. 27, 1894, 28 Stat. 577; June 7, 1934, ch. 426, 48 Stat. 926; June 25, 1936, ch. 804, 49 Stat. 1921; June 25, 1948, ch. 646, § 32(a), (b), 62 Stat. 991; May 24, 1949, ch. 139, § 127, 63 Stat. 107.)

CHANGE OF NAME

Act June 25, 1948, eff. Sept. 1, 1948, as amended by act May 24, 1949, substituted "United States District Court for the District of Columbia" for "District Court of the United States for the District of Columbia", "chief judge" for "chief justice" and "associate judges" for "associate justices" wherever appearing.

Act June 25, 1936, substituted "District Court of the United States for the said District" for "Supreme Court for the said District".

Act June 7, 1934, substituted "United States Court of Appeals for the District of Columbia" for "Court of Appeals of the District of Columbia".

§ 138. Law library; hours kept open

The law library shall be kept open every day so long as either House of Congress is in session.

(July 11, 1888, ch. 615, § 1, 25 Stat. 262.)

§ 139. Omitted

CODIFICATION

Section, acts Feb. 19, 1897, ch. 265, § 1, 29 Stat. 546; Pub. L. 94–273, § 30, Apr. 21, 1976, 90 Stat. 380, which required the Librarian of Congress to make an annual report to Congress on the affairs of the Library, including copyright business and a detailed statement of receipts and expenditures, terminated, effective May 15, 2000, pursuant to section 3003 of Pub. L. 104–66, as amended, set out as a note under section 1113 of Title 31, Money and Finance. See, also, page 10 of House Document No. 103–7.

§ 140. Employees; fitness

All persons employed in and about said Library of Congress under the Librarian shall be appointed solely with reference to their fitness for their particular duties.

(Feb. 19, 1897, ch. 265, § 1, 29 Stat. 545; June 29, 1922, ch. 251, § 1, 42 Stat. 715.)

§ 141. Duties of Architect of the Capitol and Librarian of Congress

The Architect of the Capitol shall have charge of all structural work at the Library of Congress buildings and grounds (as defined in section 167j of this title), including all necessary repairs, the operation, maintenance, and repair of the mechanical plant and elevators, the care and maintenance of the grounds, and the purchasing of all equipment other than office equipment. The employees required for the performance of the foregoing duties shall be appointed by the Architect of the Capitol. All other duties on June 29, 1922, required to be performed by the Superintendent of the Library Building and Grounds shall be performed under the direction of the Librarian of Congress, who shall appoint the employees necessary therefor. The Librarian of Congress shall provide for the purchase and supply of office equipment and furniture for library purposes.

(June 29, 1922, ch. 251, § 1, 42 Stat. 715; Pub. L. 91–280, June 12, 1970, 84 Stat. 309; Pub. L. 101–520, title II, § 205(b), Nov. 5, 1990, 104 Stat. 2272; Pub. L. 101–562, § 2(a), Nov. 15, 1990, 104 Stat. 2780.)

AMENDMENTS

1990—Pub. L. 101–520 and Pub. L. 101–562 made substantively identical amendments, substituting reference to the Library of Congress buildings and grounds (as defined in section 167j of this title) for reference to the Library Building and on the grounds.

1970—Pub. L. 91–280 substituted "purchasing of all equipment other than office equipment" for "purchasing and supplying of all furniture and equipment for the building" in second sentence and inserted sentence at end.

EFFECTIVE DATE OF 1990 AMENDMENTS

Amendment by Pub. L. 101–520 and 101–562 effective on date [Nov. 6, 1991] Architect of the Capitol acquires the property and improvements described in Pub. L. 101–520, § 205(a), and Pub. L. 101–562, § 1, see section 205(e) of Pub. L. 101–520 and former section 2(d) of Pub. L. 101–562, set out as a Special Facilities Center; Acquisition note below.

ACQUISITION OF REAL PROPERTY FOR LIBRARY OF CONGRESS

Pub. L. 105–144, Dec. 15, 1997, 111 Stat. 2667, as amended by Pub. L. 106–554, § 1(a)(2) [title II, § 207], Dec. 21, 2000, 114 Stat. 2763, 2763A–114, provided that:

"SECTION 1. ACQUISITION OF FACILITY IN CULPEPER, VIRGINIA.

"(a) ACQUISITION.—The Architect of the Capitol may acquire on behalf of the United States Government by transfer of title, without reimbursement or transfer of funds, the following property:

"(1) Three parcels totaling approximately 41 acres, more or less, located in Culpeper County, Virginia, and identified as Culpeper County Tax Parcel Numbers 51–80B, 51–80C, and 51–80D, further described as real estate (consisting of 15.949 acres) conveyed to Federal Reserve Bank of Richmond by deed from Russell H. Inskeep and Jean H. Inskeep, his wife, dated October 1, 1964, and recorded October 7, 1964, in the Clerk's Office, Circuit Court of Culpeper County, Virginia, in Deed Book 177, page 431, and real estate (consisting of 20.498 acres and consisting of 4.502 acres) conveyed to Federal Reserve Bank of Richmond by deed from Russell H. Inskeep and Jean H. Inskeep, his wife, dated November 11, 1974, and recorded November 12, 1974, in the Clerk's Office, Circuit Court of Culpeper County, Virginia, in Deed Book 247, page 246.

"(2) Improvements to such real property.

"(b) USES.—Effective on the date on which the Architect of the Capitol acquires the property under subsection (a), such property shall be available to the Librarian of Congress for use as a national audiovisual conservation center.

"(c) TRANSFER PAYMENT BY ARCHITECT.—Notwithstanding the limitation on reimbursement or transfer of funds under subsection (a) of this section, the Architect of the Capitol may, not later than 90 days after acquisition of the property under this section, transfer funds to the entity from which the property was acquired by the Architect of the Capitol. Such transfers may not exceed a total of $16,500,000.

"SEC. 2. LIBRARY BUILDINGS AND GROUNDS.

"[Amended section 167j of this title.]

"SEC. 3. ACCEPTANCE OF TRANSFERRED GIFTS OR TRUST FUNDS.

"Gifts or trust funds given to the Library or the Library of Congress Trust Fund Board for the structural and mechanical work and refurbishment of Library buildings and grounds specified in section 1 shall be transferred to the Architect of the Capitol to be spent in accordance with the provisions of the first section of the Act of June 29, 1922 (2 U.S.C. 141).

"SEC. 4. FUND FOR TRANSFERRED FUNDS.

"There is established in the Treasury of the United States a fund consisting of those gifts or trust funds transferred to the Architect of the Capitol under section 3. Upon prior approval of the Committee on House Oversight [now Committee on House Administration] of the House of Representatives and Committee on Rules and Administration of the Senate, amounts in the fund shall be available to the Architect of the Capitol, subject to appropriation, to remain available until expended, for the structural and mechanical work and refurbishment of Library buildings and grounds. Such funds shall be available for expenditure in fiscal year 1998, subject to the prior approval of the Committee on House Oversight of the House of Representatives and the Committee on Rules and Administration of the Senate.

"SEC. 5. EFFECTIVE DATE.

"(a) IN GENERAL.—Except as provided in subsection (b), the provisions of this Act shall take effect on the date of the enactment of this Act [Dec. 15, 1997].

"(b) SPECIAL RULE FOR INCLUSION OF PROPERTY WITHIN LIBRARY BUILDINGS AND GROUNDS.—The amendment made by section 2 shall take effect upon the acquisition by the Architect of the Capitol of the property described in section 1."

TRANSFER OF PROPERTY BY SECRETARY OF ARMY TO PROVIDE FACILITIES TO ACCOMMODATE LONG-TERM STORAGE AND SERVICE NEEDS

Pub. L. 103–110, § 122, Oct. 21, 1993, 107 Stat. 1043, provided that:

"(a) Notwithstanding any other provision of law, the Secretary of the Army shall transfer, no later than

September 30, 1994, without reimbursement or transfer of funds, to the Architect of the Capitol, a portion of the real property, including improvements thereon, consisting of not more than 100 acres located at Fort George G. Meade in Anne Arundel County, Maryland, as determined under subsection (c).

"(b) The Architect of the Capitol shall, upon completion of the survey performed pursuant to subsection (c) and the transfer effected pursuant to subsection (a), utilize the transferred property to provide facilities to accommodate the varied long-term storage and service needs of the Library of Congress and other Legislative Branch agencies.

"(c) The exact acreage and legal description of the property to be transferred under this section shall be determined by a survey satisfactory to the Architect of the Capitol and the Secretary of the Army, and in consultation with officials of Anne Arundel County, Maryland.

"(d) Any real property and improvements thereon transferred pursuant to this section shall be under the jurisdiction of the Architect of the Capitol, subject to the rules and regulations providing for the use of such property as may be approved by the House Office Building Commission and the Senate Committee on Rules and Administration: *Provided,* That any existing improvements made available by the Architect to the Librarian of Congress, under the direction of the Joint Committee on the Library, or hereafter erected upon such real property pursuant to law for the purposes of providing for the long-term storage and service needs of the Library of Congress shall be subject to the provisions of sections 136, 141 and 167 to 167j of title 2, United States Code.

"(e) Portions of the real property and any improvements thereon transferred pursuant to this section that are not determined to be immediately required for storage or service needs by the Architect are authorized to be leased temporarily to the Secretary of the Army: *Provided,* That nominal lease payments made by the Secretary of the Army shall be credited to the appropriation 'Architect of the Capitol, Library Buildings and Grounds, Structural and Mechanical Care, No Year'.

"(f) There are authorized to be appropriated to the Architect of the Capitol such sums as may be necessary to carry out the provisions of this section."

SPECIAL FACILITIES CENTER; TEMPORARY RESTRICTION ON EVENING USE

Pub. L. 102–451, § 4, Oct. 23, 1992, 106 Stat. 2253, provided that: "No evening meetings may be held at the Library of Congress Special Facilities Center until an on-site parking plan for the property is approved by the Joint Committee on the Library."

SPECIAL FACILITIES CENTER; ACQUISITION

Section 205 of Pub. L. 101–520, as amended by Pub. L. 102–451, §§ 1–3, Oct. 23, 1992, 106 Stat. 2253, provided that:

"(a) The Architect of the Capitol may acquire on behalf of the United States Government by purchase, condemnation, transfer, or otherwise (1) all publicly or privately owned real property in lot 51 in square 869 in the District of Columbia, as that lot appears on the records in the office of the Surveyor of the District of Columbia on August 1, 1990, extending to the outer face of the curbs of the square in which it is located and including all alleys or parts of alleys and streets within the lot lines and curb lines surrounding such real property, and (2) improvements to such real property. The property acquired under this section shall be known as the 'Library of Congress Special Facilities Center' (hereinafter in this section referred to as the 'Center').

"(b) [Amended section 141 of this title.]

"(c) The property and improvements acquired under subsection (a) shall be repaired and altered, to the maximum extent feasible as determined by the Architect of the Capitol, in compliance with one of the nationally recognized model building codes and with other applicable nationally recognized codes (including electrical codes, fire and life safety codes, plumbing codes, as determined appropriate by the Architect), using the latest edition of the nationally recognized codes referred to in this paragraph.

"(d) [Amended section 167j of this title.]

"(e) Subsections (b) and (c) and the amendment made by subsection (d) shall take effect on the date [Nov. 6, 1991] the Architect of the Capitol acquires the property and improvements described in subsection (a).

"(f) There is authorized to be appropriated to the Architect of the Capitol $5,000,000 for carrying out the purposes of this section, to remain available until expended.

"(g) Effective on the date [Nov. 6, 1991] on which the Architect of the Capitol acquires the property known as St. Cecilia's School (Lot 51 in square 869) in the District of Columbia, as provided by law, such property shall be available to the Librarian of Congress for use—

"(1) as a day care center for children of employees of the Library of Congress and children of other employees of the legislative branch of the Government;

"(2) for staff training and development for employees of the Library of Congress;

"(3) for external training;

"(4) for general assembly and education programs of the Library;

"(5) for temporary living quarters and common areas for visiting scholars using the collections of the Library or participating in the programs of the Library; and

"(6) for other purposes relating to the operations of the Library of Congress.

Any use of such property shall be subject to approval by the Joint Committee on the Library, the Committee on House Administration of the House of Representatives, and the Committee on Rules and Administration of the Senate.

"(h)(1) The Librarian of Congress—

"(A) may charge fees for use of the Center under paragraphs (3), (4), and (5) of subsection (g); and

"(B) shall deposit the fees in the fund under paragraph (2).

"(2) There is established in the Treasury a fund which shall consist of amounts deposited under paragraph (1) and such other amounts as may be appropriated to the fund. The fund shall be—

"(A) available to the Librarian of Congress, in amounts specified in appropriations Acts, for the expenses of the Center; and

"(B) subject to audit by the Comptroller General at the discretion of the Comptroller General."

Similar provisions were contained in Pub. L. 101–562, §§ 1, 2, 4, Nov. 15, 1990, 104 Stat. 2780, 2781, which was repealed by Pub. L. 102–451, § 5, Oct. 23, 1992, 106 Stat. 2254, eff. Nov. 15, 1990.

ADDITIONAL BUILDING FOR LIBRARY OF CONGRESS

Pub. L. 86–469, May 14, 1960, 74 Stat. 132, authorized Architect of the Capitol, under direction and supervision of Joint Committee on the Library, to prepare preliminary plans and estimates of cost for an additional building for Library of Congress.

LIBRARY OF CONGRESS THOMAS JEFFERSON BUILDING

Pub. L. 104–208, div. A, title V, § 5402, Sept. 30, 1996, 110 Stat. 3009–511, provided that: "The Founders Hall instructional area in the House of Representatives Page School, located in the Thomas Jefferson Building of the Library of Congress, shall be known and designated as 'Bill Emerson Hall'."

Pub. L. 96–269, § 1, June 13, 1980, 94 Stat. 486, provided: "That the building in the block bounded by East Capitol Street, Second Street Southeast, Independence Avenue Southeast, and First Street Southeast, in the District of Columbia (commonly known as the Library of Congress Building or the Library of Congress Main Building), shall hereafter be known and designated as the 'Library of Congress Thomas Jefferson Building'.

Any reference in any law, map, regulation, document, record, or other paper of the United States to such building shall be held to be a reference to the Library of Congress Thomas Jefferson Building."

Pub. L. 94–264, Apr. 13, 1976, 90 Stat. 329, which had designated the Library of Congress Annex as the Library of Congress Thomas Jefferson Building, was repealed by Pub. L. 96–269, §3, June 13, 1980, 94 Stat. 486, as part of the redesignation of that building as the Library of Congress John Adams Building and the designation of the main building of the Library of Congress as the Library of Congress Thomas Jefferson Building.

LIBRARY OF CONGRESS JOHN ADAMS BUILDING

Pub. L. 96–269, §2, June 13, 1980, 94 Stat. 486, provided that: "The building in the block bounded by East Capitol Street, Second Street Southeast, Third Street Southeast, and Pennsylvania Avenue Southeast, in the District of Columbia (commonly known as the Library of Congress Thomas Jefferson Building or the Library of Congress Annex Building), shall hereafter be known and designated as the 'Library of Congress John Adams Building'. Any reference in any law, map, regulation, document, record, or other paper of the United States to such building shall be held to be a reference to the Library of Congress John Adams Building."

LIBRARY OF CONGRESS JAMES MADISON MEMORIAL BUILDING

Pub. L. 91–214, §2, Mar. 16, 1970, 84 Stat. 69, provided that: "Nothing contained in the Act of October 19, 1965 (79 Stat. 986) [set out as a note under this section], shall be construed to authorize the use of the third Library of Congress building authorized by such Act for general office building purposes."

Pub. L. 89–260, Oct. 19, 1965, 79 Stat. 987, as amended by Pub. L. 91–214, §1, Mar. 16, 1970, 84 Stat. 69; Pub. L. 94–219, Feb. 27, 1976, 90 Stat. 194; Pub. L. 95–548, Oct. 30, 1978, 92 Stat. 2064, provided: "That (a) the Architect of the Capitol under the direction jointly of the House Office Building Commission, the Senate Office Building Commission, and the Joint Committee on the Library, after consultation with a committee designated by the American Institute of Architects, is authorized and directed to construct (including, but not limited to, the preparation of all necessary designs, plans, and specifications) in square 732 in the District of Columbia a third Library of Congress fireproof building, which shall be known as the Library of Congress James Madison Memorial Building. The design of such building shall include a Madison Memorial Hall and shall be in keeping with the prevailing architecture of the Federal buildings on Capitol Hill. The Madison Memorial Hall shall be developed in consultation with the James Madison Memorial Commission.

"(b) In carrying out his authority under this joint resolution, the Architect of the Capitol, under the direction jointly of the House Office Building Commission, the Senate Office Building Commission, and the Joint Committee on the Library, is authorized (1) to provide for such equipment, such connections with the Capitol Power Plant and other utilities, such access facilities over or under public streets, such changes in the present Library of Congress buildings, such changes in or additions to the present tunnels, and such other appurtenant facilities, as may be necessary, and (2) to do such landscaping as may be necessary by reason of the construction authorized by this joint resolution.

"SEC. 2. The structural and mechanical care of the building authorized by this joint resolution and the care of the surrounding grounds shall be under the Architect of the Capitol.

"SEC. 3. There is hereby authorized to be appropriated not to exceed $130,675,000 to construct the building authorized by this joint resolution (including the preparation of all necessary designs, plans, and specifications).

"There is also authorized to be appropriated not exceeding $10,000 to pay the expenses of the James Madison Memorial Commission."

§ 141a. Design, installation, and maintenance of security systems; transfer of responsibility

The responsibility for design, installation, and maintenance of security systems to protect the physical security of the buildings and grounds of the Library of Congress is transferred from the Architect of the Capitol to the Capitol Police Board. Such design, installation, and maintenance shall be carried out under the direction of the Committee on House Oversight of the House of Representatives and the Committee on Rules and Administration of the Senate, and without regard to section 5 of title 41. Any alteration to a structural, mechanical, or architectural feature of the buildings and grounds of the Library of Congress that is required for a security system under the preceding sentence may be carried out only with the approval of the Architect of the Capitol.

(Pub. L. 105–277, div. B, title II, Oct. 21, 1998, 112 Stat. 2681–570.)

CHANGE OF NAME

Committee on House Oversight of House of Representatives changed to Committee on House Administration of House of Representatives by House Resolution No. 5, One Hundred Sixth Congress, Jan. 6, 1999.

§ 142. Omitted

CODIFICATION

Section, acts June 29, 1922, ch. 251, §1, 42 Stat. 715; Nov. 5, 1990, Pub. L. 101–520, title III, §307, 104 Stat. 2277, established office of administrative assistant and disbursing officer of Library of Congress which was abolished by section 142a of this title.

§ 142a. Office of administrative assistant and disbursing officer in Library of Congress abolished; transfer of duties to appointee of Librarian

From and after June 10, 1928, the office of administrative assistant and disbursing officer of the Library of Congress, created by section 142 of this title, is abolished and thereafter the duties required to be performed by the administrative assistant and disbursing officer shall be performed, under the direction of the Librarian of Congress, by such persons as the Librarian may appoint for those purposes.

(May 11, 1928, ch. 521, 45 Stat. 497; Pub. L. 92–310, title II, §220(h), June 6, 1972, 86 Stat. 205.)

REFERENCES IN TEXT

Section 142 of this title, referred to in text, was omitted from the Code.

AMENDMENTS

1972—Pub. L. 92–310 struck out provisions which required the person disbursing appropriations for Library of Congress and Botanic Garden to give a bond in sum of $30,000.

TRANSFER OF FUNCTIONS

Disbursement functions of all Government agencies, except Departments of the Army, Navy, and Air Force and Panama Canal transferred to Division of Disbursements, Treasury Department, by Ex. Ord. No. 6166, §4, June 10, 1933, and Ex. Ord. No. 6728, May 29, 1934.

Division subsequently consolidated with other agencies into Fiscal Service in Treasury Department by Reorg. Plan No. III of 1940, §1(a)(1), eff. June 30, 1940, 5

F.R. 2107, 54 Stat. 1231. See section 306 of Title 31, Money and Finance.

§ 142b. Certifying officers of the Library of Congress; accountability; relief by Comptroller General

On and after June 13, 1957, each officer and employee of the Library of Congress, including the Copyright Office, who has been duly authorized in writing by the Librarian of Congress to certify vouchers for payment from appropriations and funds, shall (1) be held responsible for the existence and correctness of the facts recited in the certificate or otherwise stated on the voucher or its supporting papers and for the legality of the proposed payment under the appropriation or fund involved; (2) [Repealed]; (3) be held responsible and accountable for the correctness of the computations of certified vouchers; and (4) be held accountable for and required to make good to the United States the amount of any illegal, improper, or incorrect payment resulting from any false, inaccurate, or misleading certificate made by him, as well as for any payment prohibited by law or which did not represent a legal obligation under the appropriation or fund involved: *Provided*, That the Comptroller General of the United States may, at his discretion, relieve such certifying officer or employee of liability for any payment otherwise proper whenever he finds (1) that the certification was based on official records and that such certifying officer or employee did not know, and by reasonable diligence and inquiry could not have ascertained, the actual facts, or (2) that the obligation was incurred in good faith, that the payment was not contrary to any statutory provision specifically prohibiting payments of the character involved, and the United States has received value for such payment: *Provided further*, That the Comptroller General shall relieve such certifying officer or employee of liability for an overpayment for transportation services made to any common carrier covered by section 3726 of title 31, whenever he finds that the overpayment occurred solely because the administrative examination made prior to payment of the transportation bill did not include a verification of transportation rates, freight classifications, or land grant deductions.

(Pub. L. 85–53, § 1, June 13, 1957, 71 Stat. 81; Pub. L. 92–310, title II, § 220(k), June 6, 1972, 86 Stat. 205.)

CODIFICATION

"Section 3726 of title 31" substituted in text for "title III, part II, section 322, of the Transportation Act of 1940, approved September 18, 1940 [31 U.S.C. 244]" on authority of Pub. L. 97–258, § 4(b), Sept. 13, 1982, 96 Stat. 1067, the first section of which enacted Title 31, Money and Finance.

AMENDMENTS

1972—Pub. L. 92–310 struck out provisions which required officers and employees of Library who are authorized to certify vouchers for payment to give a bond.

SECTION REFERRED TO IN OTHER SECTIONS

This section is referred to in section 142d of this title.

§ 142c. Enforcement of liability of certifying officers of Library of Congress

The liability of these certifying officers or employees shall be enforced in the same manner and to the same extent as now provided by law with respect to enforcement of the liability of disbursing and other accountable officers; and they shall have the right to apply for and obtain a decision by the Comptroller General on any question of law involved in a payment on any vouchers presented to them for certification.

(Pub. L. 85–53, § 2, June 13, 1957, 71 Stat. 81.)

§ 142d. Disbursing officer of the Library of Congress; disbursements in accordance with voucher; examination of vouchers; liability

The disbursing officer of the Library of Congress shall (1) disburse moneys of the Library of Congress only upon, and in strict accordance with, vouchers duly certified by the Librarian of Congress or by an officer or employee of the Library of Congress duly authorized in writing by the Librarian to certify such vouchers; (2) make such examination of vouchers as may be necessary to ascertain whether they are in proper form, and duly certified and approved; and (3) be held accountable accordingly: *Provided*, That the disbursing officer shall not be held accountable or responsible for any illegal, improper, or incorrect payment resulting from any false, inaccurate, or misleading certificate, the responsibility for which, under section 142b of this title, is imposed upon a certifying officer or employee of the Library of Congress.

(Pub. L. 85–53, § 3, June 13, 1957, 71 Stat. 81.)

§ 142e. Disbursing Officer of the Library of Congress; disbursements for Congressional Budget Office, accountability; financial management support to Congressional Budget Office under agreement of Librarian of Congress and Director of Congressional Budget Office; Congressional Budget Office certifying officers: voucher certifications, accountability, relief by Comptroller General

From and after January 1, 1976, the Disbursing Officer of the Library of Congress is authorized to disburse funds appropriated for the Congressional Budget Office, and the Library of Congress shall provide financial management support to the Congressional Budget Office as may be required and mutually agreed to by the Librarian of Congress and the Director of the Congressional Budget Office. The Library of Congress is further authorized to compute and disburse the basic pay of all personnel of the Congressional Budget Office pursuant to the provisions of section 5504 of title 5, except the Director, who as head of an agency, shall have pay computed and disbursed pursuant to the provisions of section 5505 of title 5.

All vouchers certified for payment by duly authorized certifying officers of the Library of Congress shall be supported with a certification by an officer or employee of the Congressional Budget Office duly authorized in writing by the Director of the Congressional Budget Office to certify payments from appropriations of the Congressional Budget Office. The Congressional

Budget Office certifying officers shall (1) be held responsible for the existence and correctness of the facts recited in the certificate or otherwise stated on the voucher or its supporting paper and the legality of the proposed payment under the appropriation or fund involved, (2) be held responsible and accountable for the correctness of the computations of certifications made, and (3) be held accountable for and required to make good to the United States the amount of any illegal, improper, or incorrect payment resulting from any false, inaccurate, or misleading certificate made by him, as well as for any payment prohibited by law which did not represent a legal obligation under the appropriation or fund involved: *Provided*, That the Comptroller General of the United States may, at his discretion, relieve such certifying officer or employee of liability for any payment otherwise proper whenever he finds (1) that the certification was based on official records and that such certifying officer or employee did not know, and by reasonable diligence and inquiry could not have ascertained the actual facts, or (2) that the obligation was incurred in good faith, that the payment was not contrary to any statutory provision specifically prohibiting payments of the character involved, and the United States has received value for such payment: *Provided further*, That the Comptroller General shall relieve such certifying officer or employee of liability for an overpayment for transportation services made to any common carrier covered by section 3726 of title 31, whenever he finds that the overpayment occurred solely because the administrative examination made prior to payment of the transportation bill did not include a verification of transportation rates, freight classifications, or land grant deductions.

The Disbursing Officer of the Library of Congress shall not be held accountable or responsible for any illegal, improper, or incorrect payment resulting from any false, inaccurate, or misleading certificate, the responsibility for which is imposed upon a certifying officer or employee of the Congressional Budget Office.

(Pub. L. 96–536, § 101(c), Dec. 16, 1980, 94 Stat. 3167.)

CODIFICATION

In the second par., "section 3726 of title 31" substituted for "section 244 of title 31" on authority of Pub. L. 97–258, § 4(b), Sept. 13, 1982, 96 Stat. 1067, the first section of which enacted Title 31, Money and Finance.

Section is based on section 207 of title II of H.R. 7593, as passed the House of Representatives on July 21, 1980, and incorporated by reference in section 101(c) of Pub. L. 96–536, to be effective as if enacted into law.

PRIOR PROVISIONS

Provisions similar to those in this section were contained in the following prior appropriation acts:

　Pub. L. 96–86, § 101(c) [H.R. 4390, title II, § 207], Oct. 12, 1979, 93 Stat. 657.

　Pub. L. 95–391, title II, § 207, Sept. 30, 1978, 92 Stat. 786.

　Pub. L. 95–94, title II, § 207, Aug. 5, 1977, 91 Stat. 678.

　Pub. L. 94–440, title VIII, § 808, Oct. 1, 1976, 90 Stat. 1458.

　Pub. L. 94–157, title I, ch. IV, Dec. 18, 1975, 89 Stat. 835.

§ 142f. Office of Technology Assessment; disbursement of funds, computation and disbursement of basic pay, and provision of financial management support by Library of Congress

From and after October 1, 1981, the Disbursing Officer of the Library of Congress is authorized to disburse funds appropriated for the Office of Technology Assessment, and the Library of Congress shall provide financial management support to the Office of Technology Assessment as may be required and mutually agreed to by the Librarian of Congress and the Director of the Office of Technology Assessment. The Library of Congress is further authorized to compute and disburse the basic pay of all personnel of the Office of Technology Assessment pursuant to the provisions of section 5504 of title 5.

All vouchers certified for payment by duly authorized certifying officers of the Library of Congress shall be supported with a certification by an officer or employee of the Office of Technology Assessment duly authorized in writing by the Director of the Office of Technology Assessment to certify payments from appropriations of the Office of Technology Assessment. The Office of Technology Assessment certifying officers shall (1) be held responsible for the existence and correctness of the facts recited in the certificate or otherwise stated on the voucher or its supporting paper and the legality of the proposed payment under the appropriation or fund involved, (2) be held responsible and accountable for the correctness of the computations of certifications made, and (3) be held accountable for and required to make good to the United States the amount of any illegal, improper, or incorrect payment resulting from any false, inaccurate, or misleading certificate made by him, as well as for any payment prohibited by law which did not represent a legal obligation under the appropriation or fund involved: *Provided*, That the Comptroller General of the United States may, at his discretion, relieve such certifying officer or employee of liability for any payment otherwise proper whenever he finds (1) that the certification was based on official records and that such certifying officer or employee did not know, and by reasonable diligence and inquiry could not have ascertained the actual facts, or (2) that the obligation was incurred in good faith, that the payment was not contrary to any statutory provision specifically prohibiting payments of the character involved, and the United States has received value for such payment: *Provided further*, That the Comptroller General shall relieve such certifying officer or employee of liability for an overpayment for transportation services made to any common carrier covered by section 3726 of title 31, whenever he finds that the overpayment occurred solely because of[1] the administrative examination made prior to payment of the transportation bill did not include a verification of transportation rates, freight classifications, or land grant deductions.

The Disbursing Officer of the Library of Congress shall not be held accountable or respon-

---

[1] So in original. The word "of" probably should not appear.

sible for any illegal, improper, or incorrect payment resulting from any false, inaccurate, or misleading certificate, the responsibility for which is imposed upon a certifying officer or employee of the Office of Technology Assessment.

(Pub. L. 97–51, §101(c), Oct. 1, 1981, 95 Stat. 959.)

CODIFICATION

In the second par., "section 3726 of title 31" substituted for "section 244 of title 31" on authority of Pub. L. 97–258, §4(b), Sept. 13, 1982, 96 Stat. 1067, the first section of which enacted Title 31, Money and Finance.

Section is based on section 205 of title II of H.R. 4120, as reported July 9, 1981, and incorporated by reference in section 101(c) of Pub. L. 97–51, to be effective as if enacted into law.

SECTION REFERRED TO IN OTHER SECTIONS

This section is referred to in sections 142h, 142j of this title.

§ 142g. Copyright Royalty Tribunal; computation and disbursement of pay of Tribunal personnel by Library of Congress

From and after October 1, 1983, the Library of Congress is authorized to compute and disburse basic pay of all personnel of the Copyright Royalty Tribunal pursuant to the provisions of section 5504 of title 5.

(Pub. L. 98–51, title II, §204, July 14, 1983, 97 Stat. 277.)

PRIOR PROVISIONS

Provisions similar to those in this section were contained in the following prior appropriation acts:

Pub. L. 97–276, §101(e) [S. 2939, title II, §204], Oct. 2, 1982, 96 Stat. 1189.
Pub. L. 97–51, §101(c) [H.R. 4120, title II, §204], Oct. 1, 1981, 95 Stat. 959.
Pub. L. 96–536, §101(c) [H.R. 7593, title II, §208], Dec. 16, 1980, 94 Stat. 3167.
Pub. L. 96–86, §101(c) [H.R. 4390, title II, §208], Oct. 12, 1979, 93 Stat. 657.
Pub. L. 95–391, title II, §208, Sept. 30, 1978, 92 Stat. 786.
Pub. L. 95–94, title II, §208, Aug. 5, 1977, 91 Stat. 678.

§ 142h. Biomedical Ethics Board; disbursement of funds, computation and disbursement of basic pay, and provision of financial management services and support by Library of Congress

Effective October 1, 1988, and to continue thereafter, the Disbursing Officer of the Library of Congress is authorized to—

(1) disburse funds appropriated for the Biomedical Ethics Board;

(2) compute and disburse the basic pay for all personnel of the Biomedical Ethics Board; and

(3) provide financial management services and support to the Biomedical Ethics Board,

in the same manner as provided with respect to the Office of Technology Assessment under section 142f of this title.

(Pub. L. 101–163, title I, Nov. 21, 1989, 103 Stat. 1054.)

PRIOR PROVISIONS

Provisions similar to those in this section were contained in the following prior appropriation act:
Pub. L. 100–458, title I, Oct. 1, 1988, 102 Stat. 2168.

§ 142i. United States Capitol Preservation Commission; provision of financial management services and support by Library of Congress

Effective June 15, 1989, the Library of Congress shall provide financial management services and support to the United States Capitol Preservation Commission as may be required and mutually agreed to by the Librarian of Congress and the Cochairmen of the United States Capitol Preservation Commission.

(Pub. L. 101–45, title I, June 30, 1989, 103 Stat. 107.)

§ 142j. John C. Stennis Center for Public Service Training and Development; disbursement of funds, computation and disbursement of basic pay, and provision of financial management services and support by Library of Congress; payment for services

From and after October 1, 1988, the Library of Congress is authorized to—

(1) disburse funds appropriated for the John C. Stennis Center for Public Service Training and Development;

(2) compute and disburse the basic pay for all personnel of the John C. Stennis Center for Public Service Training and Development;

(3) provide financial management services and support to the John C. Stennis Center for Public Service Training and Development, in the same manner as provided with respect to the Office of Technology Assessment under section 142f of this title; and

(4) collect from the funds appropriated for the John C. Stennis Center for Public Service Training and Development the full costs of providing the services specified in (1), (2), and (3) above, as provided under an agreement for services ordered under 31 U.S.C. 1535 and 1536.

(Pub. L. 101–163, title II, §205, Nov. 21, 1989, 103 Stat. 1060.)

§ 142k. Library of Congress disbursing office; payroll processing functions

From and after October 1, 1989, the Librarian of Congress shall take appropriate action to assure that no legislative branch employee whose salary is disbursed by the Library of Congress disbursing office is adversely affected by alternative ways of performing the personnel/payroll processing function.

(Pub. L. 101–163, title II, §206, Nov. 21, 1989, 103 Stat. 1060.)

§ 142l. Disbursing Officer of Library of Congress; disbursements for Office of Compliance; voucher certifications, accountability and relief by Comptroller General

From and after October 1, 1996, the Disbursing Officer of the Library of Congress is authorized to disburse funds appropriated for the Office of Compliance, and the Library of Congress shall provide financial management support to the Office of Compliance as may be required and mutually agreed to by the Librarian of Congress and the Executive Director of the Office of Compliance. The Library of Congress is further authorized to compute and disburse the basic pay of all personnel of the Office of Compliance pursuant to the provisions of section 5504 of title 5.

All vouchers certified for payment by duly authorized certifying officers of the Library of Congress shall be supported with a certification by an officer or employee of the Office of Compliance duly authorized in writing by the Executive Director of the Office of Compliance to certify payments from appropriations of the Office of Compliance. The Office of Compliance certifying officers shall (1) be held responsible for the existence and correctness of the facts recited in the certificate or otherwise stated on the voucher or its supporting paper and the legality of the proposed payment under the appropriation or fund involved, (2) be held responsible and accountable for the correctness of the computations of certifications made, and (3) be held accountable for and required to make good to the United States the amount of any illegal, improper, or incorrect payment resulting from any false, inaccurate, or misleading certificate made by them, as well as for any payment prohibited by law which did not represent a legal obligation under the appropriation or fund involved: *Provided,* That the Comptroller General of the United States may, at his discretion, relieve such certifying officer or employee of liability for any payment otherwise proper whenever he finds (1) that the certification was based on official records and that such certifying officer or employee did not know, and by reasonable diligence and inquiry could not have ascertained the actual facts, or (2) that the obligation was incurred in good faith, that the payment was not contrary to any statutory provision specifically prohibiting payments of the character involved, and the United States has received value for such payment: *Provided further,* That the Comptroller General shall relieve such certifying officer or employee of liability for an overpayment for transportation services made to any common carrier covered by section 3726 of title 31, whenever he finds that the overpayment occurred solely because the administrative examination made prior to payment of the transportation bill did not include a verification of transportation rates, freight classifications, or land grant deductions.

The Disbursing Officer of the Library of Congress shall not be held accountable or responsible for any illegal, improper, or incorrect payment resulting from any false, inaccurate, or misleading certificate, the responsibility for which is imposed upon a certifying officer or employee of the Office of Compliance.

(Pub. L. 104–197, title II, §208, Sept. 16, 1996, 110 Stat. 2409.)

§ 143. Appropriations for Library Building and Grounds

All appropriations made to the Architect of the Capitol on account of the Library Building and Grounds shall be disbursed for that purpose in the same manner as other appropriations under his control.

(June 29, 1922, ch. 251, §3, 42 Stat. 715.)

TRANSFER OF FUNCTIONS

Disbursement functions of all Government agencies except Departments of the Army, Navy, and Air Force and Panama Canal transferred to Division of Disbursements, Treasury Department, by Ex. Ord. No. 6166, §4, June 10, 1933, and Ex. Ord. No. 6728, May 29, 1934.

Division subsequently consolidated with other agencies into Fiscal Service in Treasury Department by Reorg. Plan No. III of 1940, §1(a)(1), eff. June 30, 1940, 5 F.R. 2107, 54 Stat. 1231. See section 306 of Title 31, Money and Finance.

§ 143a. Disbursement of funds

From and after October 1, 1978, funds available to the Library of Congress may be expended to reimburse the Department of State for medical services rendered to employees of the Library of Congress stationed abroad and for contracting on behalf of and hiring alien employees for the Library of Congress under compensation plans comparable to those authorized by section 444 of the Foreign Service Act of 1946, as amended (22 U.S.C. 889(a)), for purchase or hire of passenger motor vehicles; for payment of travel, storage and transportation of household goods, and transportation and per diem expenses for families enroute (not to exceed twenty-four); for benefits comparable to those payable under sections 911(9), 911(11), and 941 of the Foreign Service Act of 1946, as amended (22 U.S.C. 1136(9), 1136(11), and 1156, respectively); and travel benefits comparable with those which are now or hereafter may be granted single employees of the Agency for International Development, including single Foreign Service personnel assigned to A.I.D. projects, by the Administrator of the Agency for International Development—or his designee—under the authority of section 2396(b) of title 22; subject to such rules and regulations as may be issued by the Librarian of Congress.

(Pub. L. 96–536, §101(c), Dec. 16, 1980, 94 Stat. 3167.)

REFERENCES IN TEXT

Sections 444, 911(9), 911(11), and 941 of the Foreign Service Act of 1946, referred to in text, were repealed by section 2205(1) of the Foreign Service Act of 1980, Pub. L. 96–465, title II, Oct. 17, 1980, 94 Stat. 2159. The Foreign Service Act of 1980 is classified principally to chapter 52 (§3901 et seq.) of Title 22, Foreign Relations and Intercourse. Section 2401(c) of the 1980 Act (22 U.S.C. 4172(c)) provides in part that references in law to provisions of the Foreign Service Act of 1946 shall be deemed to include reference to the corresponding provisions of the 1980 Act. For provisions corresponding to the above cited sections of the 1946 Act, see sections 408, 901(6), 901(8), and 904 of the 1980 Act (22 U.S.C. 3968, 4081(6), 4081(8), 4084).

CODIFICATION

Section is based on section 203 of title II of H.R. 7593, as passed the House of Representatives on July 21, 1980, and incorporated by reference in section 101(c) of Pub. L. 96–536, to be effective as if enacted into law.

PRIOR PROVISIONS

Provisions similar to those in this section were contained in the following prior appropriation acts:

Pub. L. 96–86, §101(c) [H.R. 4390, title II, §203], Oct. 12, 1979, 93 Stat. 657.

Pub. L. 95–391, title II, §203, Sept. 30, 1978, 92 Stat. 785.

Pub. L. 95–94, title II, §203, Aug. 5, 1977, 91 Stat. 677.

Pub. L. 94–440, title VIII, §803, Oct. 1, 1976, 90 Stat. 1457.

Pub. L. 94–59, title VII, §703, July 25, 1975, 89 Stat. 295.
Pub. L. 93–371, Aug. 13, 1974, 88 Stat. 441.
Pub. L. 93–145, Nov. 1, 1973, 87 Stat. 545.
Pub. L. 92–342, July 10, 1972, 86 Stat. 446.
Pub. L. 92–51, July 9, 1971, 85 Stat. 141.
Pub. L. 91–382, Aug. 18, 1970, 84 Stat. 823.
Pub. L. 91–145, Dec. 12, 1969, 83 Stat. 357.
Pub. L. 90–417, July 28, 1968, 82 Stat. 411.
Pub. L. 90–57, July 28, 1967, 81 Stat. 140.
Pub. L. 89–545, Aug. 27, 1966, 80 Stat. 368.

§ 143b. Payments in advance for subscriptions or other charges

From and after October 1, 1980, payments in advance for subscriptions or other charges for bibliographical data, publications, materials in any other form, and services may be made by the Librarian of Congress whenever he determines it to be more prompt, efficient, or economical to do so in the interest of carrying out required Library programs.

(Pub. L. 96–536, §101(c), Dec. 16, 1980, 94 Stat. 3167.)

CODIFICATION

Section is based on section 204 of title II of H.R. 7593, as passed the House of Representatives on July 21, 1980, and incorporated by reference in section 101(c) of Pub. L. 96–536, to be effective as if enacted into law.

PRIOR PROVISIONS

Provisions similar to those in this section were contained in the following prior appropriation acts:
Pub. L. 96–86, §101(c) [H.R. 4390, title II, §204], Oct. 12, 1979, 93 Stat. 657.
Pub. L. 95–391, title II, §204, Sept. 30, 1978, 92 Stat. 786.
Pub. L. 95–94, title II, §204, Aug. 5, 1977, 91 Stat. 677.
Pub. L. 94–440, title VIII, §804, Oct. 1, 1976, 90 Stat. 1457.
Pub. L. 94–59, title VII, §704, July 25, 1975, 89 Stat. 295.
Pub. L. 93–371, Aug. 13, 1974, 88 Stat. 441.
Pub. L. 93–145, Nov. 1, 1973, 87 Stat. 545.
Pub. L. 92–342, July 10, 1972, 86 Stat. 447.
Pub. L. 92–51, July 9, 1971, 85 Stat. 142.
Pub. L. 91–382, Aug. 18, 1970, 84 Stat. 823.
Pub. L. 91–145, Dec. 12, 1969, 83 Stat. 357.
Pub. L. 90–417, July 23, 1968, 82 Stat. 411.
Pub. L. 90–57, July 28, 1967, 81 Stat. 140.

§ 144. Copies of Statutes at Large

Ten of the copies of the Statutes at Large, published by Little, Brown & Co., which were deposited in the Library prior to February 5, 1859, shall be retained by the Librarian for the use of the justices of the Supreme Court, during the terms of court.

(R.S. §96.)

CODIFICATION

R.S. §96 derived from act Feb. 5, 1859, ch. 22, §11, 11 Stat. 381.

§ 145. Copies of journals and documents

Two copies of the journals and documents, and of each book printed by either House of Congress, well bound in calf, shall be deposited in the Library, and must not be taken therefrom.

(R.S. §97.)

CODIFICATION

R.S. §97 derived from Res. Jan. 2, 1857, No. 5, §5, 11 Stat. 253.

§ 145a. Periodical binding of printed hearings of committee testimony

The Librarian of the Library of Congress is authorized and directed to have bound at the end of each session of Congress the printed hearings of testimony taken by each committee of the Congress at the preceding session.

(Aug. 2, 1946, ch. 753, title I, §141, 60 Stat. 834.)

EFFECTIVE DATE

Section effective Aug. 2, 1946, see section 142 of act Aug. 2, 1946.

§ 146. Deposit of Journals of Senate and House

Twenty-five copies of the public Journals of the Senate, and of the House of Representatives, shall be deposited in the Library of the United States, at the seat of government, to be delivered to Members of Congress during any session, and to all other persons authorized by law to use the books in the Library, upon their application to the Librarian, and giving their responsible receipts for the same, in like manner as for other books.

(R.S. §98.)

CODIFICATION

R.S. §98 derived from Res. Dec. 27, 1813, No. 1, 3 Stat. 140; Res. July 20, 1840, No. 5, 5 Stat. 409.

§ 147. Repealed. Oct. 25, 1951, ch. 562, §1(*l*), 65 Stat. 638

Section, act June 6, 1900, ch. 791, §1, 31 Stat. 642, related to bound volumes from files of House of Representatives. See sections 2103 and 2114 of Title 44, Public Printing and Documents.

§ 148. Repealed. Oct. 31, 1951, ch. 654, §1(*l*), 65 Stat. 701

Section, act Feb. 25, 1903, ch. 755, §1, 32 Stat. 865, related to transfer of books from executive departments to Library. See sections 471(c) and 472 of Title 40, Public Buildings, Property, and Works.

§ 149. Transfer of books to other libraries

The Librarian of Congress may from time to time transfer to other governmental libraries within the District of Columbia, including the Public Library, books and material in the possession of the Library of Congress in his judgment no longer necessary to its uses, but in the judgment of the custodians of such other collections likely to be useful to them, and may dispose of or destroy such material as has become useless: *Provided,* That no records of the Federal Government shall be transferred, disposed of, or destroyed under the authority granted in this section.

(Mar. 4, 1909, ch. 297, §1, 35 Stat. 858; Oct. 25, 1951, ch. 562, §4(1), 65 Stat. 640.)

AMENDMENTS

1951—Act Oct. 25, 1951, inserted proviso.

§ 150. Sale of copies of card indexes and other publications

The Librarian of Congress is authorized to furnish to such institutions or individuals as may desire to buy them, such copies of the card indexes and other publications of the Library as may not be required for its ordinary transactions, and charge for the same a price which will cover their cost and ten per centum added, and all moneys received by him shall be deposited in the Treasury and shall be credited to the appropriation for necessary expenses for the preparation and distribution of catalog cards and other publications of the Library.

(June 28, 1902, ch. 1301, § 1, 32 Stat. 480; Pub. L. 95–94, title IV, § 405(a), Aug. 5, 1977, 91 Stat. 682.)

AMENDMENTS

1977—Pub. L. 95–94 inserted provisions relating to crediting of the moneys deposited in the Treasury.

EFFECTIVE DATE OF 1977 AMENDMENT

Section 405(b) of Pub. L. 95–94 provided that: "The amendment made by subsection (a) [amending this section] shall take effect on October 1, 1977."

§ 151. Smithsonian Library

The library collected by the Smithsonian Institution under the provisions of the Act of August 10, 1846, chapter 25, and removed from the building of that institution, with the consent of the Regents thereof, to the Library of Congress, shall, while there deposited, be subject to the same regulations as the Library of Congress, except as hereinafter provided.

(R.S. § 99.)

REFERENCES IN TEXT

Act of August 10, 1846, chapter 25, referred to in text, probably should be act Aug. 10, 1846, ch. 178, 9 Stat. 102, which was entitled "An Act to establish the 'Smithsonian Institution', for the increase and diffusion of knowledge among men".

CODIFICATION

R.S. § 99 derived from act Apr. 5, 1866, ch. 25, § 1, 14 Stat. 13.

SECTION REFERRED TO IN OTHER SECTIONS

This section is referred to in section 152 of this title.

§ 152. Care and use of Smithsonian Library

The Smithsonian Institution shall have the use of the library referred to in section 151 of this title in like manner as before its removal. All the books, maps, and charts of the Smithsonian Library shall be properly cared for and preserved in like manner as are those of the Congressional Library; from which the Smithsonian Library shall not be removed except on reimbursement by the Smithsonian Institution to the Treasury of the United States of expenses incurred in binding and in taking care of the same, or upon such terms and conditions as shall be mutually agreed upon by Congress and the Regents of the Institution.

(R.S. § 100.)

CODIFICATION

R.S. § 100 derived from act Apr. 5, 1866, ch. 25, § 2, 14 Stat. 13.

§ 153. Control of library of House of Representatives

The library of the House of Representatives shall be under the control and direction of the Librarian of Congress, who shall provide all needful books of reference therefor. The librarian, two assistant librarians, and assistant in the library, shall be appointed by the Clerk of the House, with the approval of the Speaker of the House of Representatives. No removals shall be made from the said positions except for cause reported to and approved by the Committee on Rules.

(Mar. 3, 1901, ch. 830, § 1, 31 Stat. 964.)

§ 154. Library of Congress Trust Fund Board; members; quorum; seal; rules and regulations

A board is created and established, to be known as the "Library of Congress Trust Fund Board" (hereinafter referred to as the board), which shall consist of the Secretary of the Treasury (or an Assistant Secretary designated in writing by the Secretary of the Treasury), the chairman and the vice chair of the Joint Committee on the Library, the Librarian of Congress, two persons appointed by the President for a term of five years each (the first appointments being for three and five years, respectively), four persons appointed by the Speaker of the House of Representatives (in consultation with the minority leader of the House of Representatives) for a term of five years each (the first appointments being for two, three, four, and five years, respectively), and four persons appointed by the majority leader of the Senate (in consultation with the minority leader of the Senate) for a term of five years each (the first appointments being for two, three, four, and five years, respectively). Upon request of the chair of the Board, any member whose term has expired may continue to serve on the Trust Fund Board until the earlier of the date on which such member's successor is appointed or the expiration of the 1-year period which begins on the date such member's term expires. Seven members of the board shall constitute a quorum for the transaction of business, and the board shall have an official seal, which shall be judicially noticed. The board may adopt rules and regulations in regard to its procedure and the conduct of its business.

(Mar. 3, 1925, ch. 423, § 1, 43 Stat. 1107; Pub. L. 95–277, May 12, 1978, 92 Stat. 236; Pub. L. 102–246, §§ 1, 2, Feb. 18, 1992, 106 Stat. 31; Pub. L. 106–481, title II, § 201, Nov. 9, 2000, 114 Stat. 2190.)

CODIFICATION

Section is comprised of first par. of section 1 of act Mar. 3, 1925. Second par. of section 1 is classified to section 155 of this title.

AMENDMENTS

2000—Pub. L. 106–481 inserted "and the vice chair" after "the chairman" and "Upon request of the chair of the Board, any member whose term has expired may continue to serve on the Trust Fund Board until the earlier of the date on which such member's successor is appointed or the expiration of the 1-year period which begins on the date such member's term expires." after first sentence and substituted "Seven members of the board" for "Nine members of the board".

1992—Pub. L. 102–246 struck out "and" after "Librarian of Congress," inserted ", four persons appointed by the Speaker of the House of Representatives (in consultation with the minority leader of the House of Representatives) for a term of five years each (the first appointments being for two, three, four, and five years, respectively), and four persons appointed by the majority leader of the Senate (in consultation with the minority leader of the Senate) for a term of five years each (the first appointments being for two, three, four, and five years, respectively)" after "respectively)", and substituted "Nine" for "Three".

1978—Pub. L. 95–277 inserted "(or an Assistant Secretary designated in writing by the Secretary of the Treasury)".

EFFECTIVE DATE OF 2000 AMENDMENT

Pub. L. 106–481, title II, § 202, Nov. 9, 2000, 114 Stat. 2191, provided that: "The amendments made by this title [amending this section] shall take effect on the date of the enactment of this Act [Nov. 9, 2000]."

SHORT TITLE

Act Mar. 3, 1925, enacting sections 154 to 162 and 163 of this title, is popularly known as the "Library of Congress Trust Fund Board Act".

SECTION REFERRED TO IN OTHER SECTIONS

This section is referred to in section 160 of this title.

§ 155. Compensation and expenses of Library of Congress Trust Fund Board

No compensation shall be paid to the members of the board for their services as such members, but they shall be reimbursed for the expenses necessarily incurred by them, out of the income from the fund or funds in connection with which such expenses are incurred. The voucher of the chairman of the board shall be sufficient evidence that the expenses are properly allowable. Any expenses of the board, including the cost of its seal, not properly chargeable to the income of any trust fund held by it, shall be estimated for in the annual estimates of the librarian for the maintenance of the Library of Congress.

(Mar. 3, 1925, ch. 423, § 1, 43 Stat. 1107.)

CODIFICATION

Section is comprised of second par. of section 1 of act Mar. 3, 1925. First par. of section 1 is classified to section 154 of this title.

SECTION REFERRED TO IN OTHER SECTIONS

This section is referred to in section 160 of this title.

§ 156. Gifts, etc., to Library of Congress Trust Fund Board

The Board is authorized to accept, receive, hold, and administer such gifts, bequests, or devises of property for the benefit of, or in connection with, the Library, its collections, or its service, as may be approved by the Board and by the Joint Committee on the Library.

(Mar. 3, 1925, ch. 423, § 2, formerly § 1, 43 Stat. 1107, renumbered Apr. 13, 1936, ch. 213, 49 Stat. 1205.)

CODIFICATION

Section is comprised of first par. of section 2 of act Mar. 3, 1925. Second, third, and fourth pars. of section 2 are classified to sections 157, 158, and 158a of this title, respectively.

SECTION REFERRED TO IN OTHER SECTIONS

This section is referred to in sections 158a, 160 of this title.

§ 157. Funds of Library of Congress Trust Fund Board; management of

The moneys or securities composing the trust funds given or bequeathed to the board shall be receipted for by the Secretary of the Treasury, who shall invest, reinvest, or retain investments as the board may from time to time determine. The income as and when collected shall be deposited with the Treasurer of the United States, who shall enter it in a special account to the credit of the Library of Congress and subject to disbursement by the librarian for the purposes in each case specified; and the Treasurer of the United States is authorized to honor the requisitions of the librarian made in such manner and in accordance with such regulations as the Treasurer may from time to time prescribe: *Provided, however*, That the board is not authorized to engage in any business nor to exercise any voting privilege which may be incidental to securities in its hands, nor shall the board make any investments that could not lawfully be made by a trust company in the District of Columbia, except that it may make any investments directly authorized by the instrument of gift, and may retain any investments accepted by it.

(Mar. 3, 1925, ch. 423, § 2, formerly § 1, 43 Stat. 1107, renumbered Apr. 13, 1936, ch. 213, 49 Stat. 1205.)

CODIFICATION

Section is comprised of second par. of section 2 of act Mar. 3, 1925. First, third, and fourth pars. of section 2 are classified to sections 156, 158, and 158a of this title, respectively.

SECTION REFERRED TO IN OTHER SECTIONS

This section is referred to in sections 158a, 160 of this title.

§ 158. Deposits by Library of Congress Trust Fund Board with Treasurer of United States

In the absence of any specification to the contrary, the board may deposit the principal sum, in cash, with the Treasurer of the United States as a permanent loan to the United States Treasury, and the Treasurer shall thereafter credit such deposit with interest at a rate which is the higher of the rate of 4 per centum per annum or a rate which is 0.25 percentage points less than a rate determined by the Secretary of the Treasury, taking into consideration the current average market yield on outstanding long-term marketable obligations of the United States, adjusted to the nearest one-eighth of 1 per centum, payable semi-annually, such interest, as income, being subject to disbursement by the Librarian of Congress for the purposes specified: *Provided, however*, That the total of such principal sums at any time so held by the Treasurer under this authorization shall not exceed the sum of $10,000,000.

(Mar. 3, 1925, ch. 423, § 2, formerly § 1, 43 Stat. 1107; renumbered § 2, Apr. 13, 1936, ch. 213, 49 Stat. 1205; amended June 23, 1936, ch. 734, 49 Stat. 1894; Pub. L. 87–522, July 3, 1962, 76 Stat. 135; Pub. L. 94–289, May 22, 1976, 90 Stat. 521.)

CODIFICATION

Section is comprised of third par. of section 2 of act Mar. 3, 1925. First, second, and fourth pars. of section 2 are classified to sections 156, 157, and 158a of this title, respectively.

AMENDMENTS

1976—Pub. L. 94–289 substituted "a rate which is the higher of the rate of 4 per centum per annum or a rate which is 0.25 percentage points less than a rate determined by the Secretary of the Treasury, taking into consideration the current average market yield on outstanding long-term marketable obligations of the United States, adjusted to the nearest one-eighth of 1 per centum" for "the rate of 4 per centum per annum".

1962—Pub. L. 87–522 increased the total amount of deposits which can be held by the Treasurer from $5,000,000 to $10,000,000.

1936—Act June 23, 1936, substituted "in the absence of any specification to the contrary" for "Should any gift or bequest so provide".

SECTION REFERRED TO IN OTHER SECTIONS

This section is referred to in section 160 of this title.

§ 158a. Temporary possession of gifts of money or securities to Library of Congress; investment

In the case of a gift of money or securities offered to the Library of Congress, if, because of conditions attached by the donor or similar considerations, expedited action is necessary, the Librarian of Congress may take temporary possession of the gift, subject to approval under section 156 of this title. The gift shall be receipted for and invested, reinvested, or retained as provided in section 157 of this title, except that—

(1) a gift of securities may not be invested or reinvested; and

(2) any investment or reinvestment of a gift of money shall be made in an interest bearing obligation of the United States or an obligation guaranteed as to principal and interest by the United States.

If the gift is not so approved within the 12-month period after the Librarian so takes possession, the principal of the gift shall be returned to the donor and any income earned during that period shall be available for use with respect to the Library of Congress as provided by law.

(Mar. 3, 1925, ch. 423, § 2(par.), as added Pub. L. 102–246, § 3, Feb. 18, 1992, 106 Stat. 31.)

CODIFICATION

Section is comprised of fourth par. of section 2 of act Mar. 3, 1925, as added by Pub. L. 102–246. First, second, and third pars. of section 2 are classified to sections 156, 157, and 158 of this title, respectively.

§ 159. Perpetual succession and suits by or against Library of Congress Trust Fund Board

The board shall have perpetual succession, with all the usual powers and obligations of a trustee, including the power to sell, except as herein limited, in respect of all property, moneys, or securities which shall be conveyed, transferred, assigned, bequeathed, delivered, or paid over to it for the purposes above specified. The board may be sued in the United States District Court for the District of Columbia, which is given jurisdiction of such suits, for the purpose of enforcing the provisions of any trust accepted by it.

(Mar. 3, 1925, ch. 423, § 3, 43 Stat. 1108; Jan. 27, 1926, ch. 6, § 1, 44 Stat. 2; June 25, 1936, ch. 804, 49 Stat. 1921; June 25, 1948, ch. 646, § 32(a), 62 Stat. 991; May 24, 1949, ch. 139, § 127, 63 Stat. 107.)

AMENDMENTS

1926—Act Jan. 27, 1926, inserted "including the power to sell" in first sentence.

CHANGE OF NAME

Act June 25, 1948, eff. Sept. 1, 1948, as amended by act May 24, 1949, substituted "United States District Court for the District of Columbia" for "district court of the United States for the District of Columbia".

Act June 25, 1936, provided that the Supreme Court of the District of Columbia is to be known as the District Court of the United States for the District of Columbia.

SECTION REFERRED TO IN OTHER SECTIONS

This section is referred to in section 160 of this title.

§ 160. Disbursement of gifts, etc., to Library

Nothing in sections 154 to 162 and 163[1] of this title shall be construed as prohibiting or restricting the Librarian of Congress from accepting in the name of the United States gifts or bequests of money for immediate disbursement in the interest of the Library, its collections, or its service. Such gifts or bequests, after acceptance by the librarian, shall be paid by the donor or his representative to the Treasurer of the United States, whose receipts shall be their acquittance. The Treasurer of the United States shall enter them in a special account to the credit of the Library of Congress and subject to disbursement by the librarian for the purposes in each case specified.

Upon agreement by the Librarian of Congress and the Board, a gift or bequest accepted by the Librarian under the first paragraph of this section may be invested or reinvested in the same manner as provided for trust funds under section 157 of this title.

(Mar. 3, 1925, ch. 423, § 4, 43 Stat. 1108; Pub. L. 105–55, title II, § 208, Oct. 7, 1997, 111 Stat. 1194.)

REFERENCES IN TEXT

Section 163 of this title, referred to in text, was omitted from the Code.

AMENDMENTS

1997—Pub. L. 105–55 added second par.

§ 161. Tax exemption of gifts, etc., to Library of Congress

Gifts or bequests or devises to or for the benefit of the Library of Congress, including those to the board, and the income therefrom, shall be exempt from all Federal taxes, including all taxes levied by the District of Columbia.

(Mar. 3, 1925, ch. 423, § 5, 43 Stat. 1108; Oct. 2, 1942, ch. 576, 56 Stat. 765.)

AMENDMENTS

1942—Act Oct. 2, 1942, included devises in the exemptions, and exempted gifts, bequests and devises, and the income therefrom, from taxes levied by the District of Columbia.

SECTION REFERRED TO IN OTHER SECTIONS

This section is referred to in section 160 of this title; title 26 section 2055.

---

[1] See References in Text note below.

§ 162. Compensation of Library of Congress employees

Employees of the Library of Congress who perform special functions for the performance of which funds have been entrusted to the board or the librarian, or in connection with cooperative undertakings in which the Library of Congress is engaged, shall not be subject to section 209 of title 18; and section 5533 of title 5 shall not apply to any additional compensation so paid to such employees.

(Mar. 3, 1925, ch. 423, §6, 43 Stat. 1108; Jan. 27, 1926, ch. 6, §2, 44 Stat. 2; Pub. L. 88–448, title IV, §401(j), Aug. 19, 1964, 78 Stat. 491.)

CODIFICATION

"Section 209 of title 18" substituted in text for reference to the Act of March 3, 1917, 39 Stat. 1106 (5 U.S.C. 66), on authority of (1) act June 25, 1948, ch. 645, 62 Stat. 683, section 1 of which enacted Title 18, Crimes and Criminal Procedure, and which enacted in section 1914 of Title 18 the provisions formerly classified to section 66 of Title 5; and (2) section 2 of Pub. L. 87–849, Oct. 23, 1962, 76 Stat. 1126, which repealed section 1914 of Title 18 and supplanted it with section 209, and which provided that exemptions from section 1914 shall be deemed exemptions from section 209. For further details, see Exemptions note set out under section 203 of Title 18.

"Section 5533 of title 5" substituted in text for "section 301 of the Dual Compensation Act [5 U.S.C. 3105]" on authority of sec. 7(b) of Pub. L. 89–554, Sept. 6, 1966, 80 Stat. 631, the first section of which enacted Title 5, Government Organization and Employees.

Section was formerly classified to sections 60 and 65 of Title 5 prior to the general revision and enactment of Title 5, Government Organization and Employees, by Pub. L. 89–554, Sept. 6, 1966, 80 Stat. 378.

AMENDMENTS

1964—Pub. L. 88–448 substituted "and section 301 of the Dual Compensation Act [5 U.S.C. 3105] shall not apply to any additional compensation so paid to such employees" for "nor shall any additional compensation so paid to such employees be construed as a double salary under the provisions of section 6 of the Act making appropriations for the legislative, executive, and judicial expenses of the Government for the fiscal year ending June 30, 1917, as amended (Thirty-ninth Statutes at Large, page 582) [5 U.S.C. 58]".

1926—Act Jan. 27, 1926, struck out the comma after "undertakings".

EFFECTIVE DATE OF 1964 AMENDMENT

Amendment by Pub. L. 88–448 effective on first day of first month which begins later than the ninetieth day following Aug. 19, 1964, see section 403 of Pub. L. 88–448.

SECTION REFERRED TO IN OTHER SECTIONS

This section is referred to in sections 160, 162a of this title; title 5 section 5533.

§ 162a. Gross salary of Library of Congress employees

Hereafter the gross salary of any position in the Library which is augmented by payment of an honorarium from other than appropriated funds under terms of section 162 of this title shall not exceed an amount, which when combined with such honorarium, will exceed the maximum salary provided in chapter 51 and subchapter III of chapter 53 of title 5.

(June 22, 1949, ch. 235, §101, 63 Stat. 226; Oct. 28, 1949, ch. 782, title XI, §1106(a), 63 Stat. 972.)

CODIFICATION

"Chapter 51 and subchapter III of chapter 53 of title 5" substituted in text for "the Classification Act of 1949" on authority of section 7(b) of Pub. L. 89–554, Sept. 6, 1966, 80 Stat. 631, section 1 of which enacted Title 5, Government Organization and Employees.

AMENDMENTS

1949—Act Oct. 28, 1949, substituted "Classification Act of 1949" for "Classification Act of 1923".

REPEALS

Act Oct. 28, 1949, ch. 782, cited as a credit to this section, was repealed (subject to a savings clause) by Pub. L. 89–554, Sept. 6, 1966, §8, 80 Stat. 632, 655.

§ 162b. Little Scholars Child Development Center; employee compensation and personnel matters

(a) Election of coverage; creditable service; qualification for survivor annuities and disability benefits; contributions to thrift savings plan; certification concerning creditable service

(1) This subsection shall apply to any individual who—

(A) is employed by the Library of Congress Child Development Center (known as the "Little Scholars Child Development Center", in this section referred to as the "Center") established under section 205(g)(1) of the Legislative Branch Appropriations Act, 1991; and

(B) makes an election to be covered by this subsection with the Librarian of Congress, not later than the later of—

(i) 60 days after December 21, 2000; or

(ii) 60 days after the date the individual begins such employment.

(2)(A) Any individual described under paragraph (1) may be credited, under section 8411 of title 5 for service as an employee of the Center before December 21, 2000, if such employee makes a payment of the deposit under section 8411(f)(2) of such title without application of section 8411(b)(3) of such title.

(B) An individual described under paragraph (1) shall be credited under section 8411 of title 5 for any service as an employee of the Center on or after December 21, 2000, if such employee has such amounts deducted and withheld from his pay as determined by the Office of Personnel Management which would be deducted and withheld from the basic pay of an employee under section 8422 of title 5.

(3) Notwithstanding any other provision of this subsection, any service performed by an individual described under paragraph (1) as an employee of the Center is deemed to be civilian service creditable under section 8411 of title 5 for purposes of qualifying for survivor annuities and disability benefits under subchapters IV and V of chapter 84 of such title, if such individual makes payment of an amount, determined by the Office of Personnel Management, which would have been deducted and withheld from the basic pay of such individual if such individual had been an employee subject to section 8422 of title 5 for such period so credited, together with interest thereon.

(4) An individual described under paragraph (1) shall be deemed an employee for purposes of chapter 84 of title 5, including subchapter III of

such title,[1] and may make contributions under section 8432 of such title effective for the first applicable pay period beginning on or after the date such individual elects coverage under this section.

(5) The Office of Personnel Management shall accept the certification of the Librarian of Congress concerning creditable service for purposes of this subsection.

(b) Health insurance coverage

Any individual who is employed by the Center on or after the date of enactment of this Act [December 21, 2000], shall be deemed an employee under section 8901(1) of title 5 for purposes of health insurance coverage under chapter 89 of such title. An individual who is an employee of the Center on the date of enactment of this Act may elect coverage under this subsection before the 60th day after the date of enactment of this Act, and during such periods as determined by the Office of Personnel Management for employees of the Center employed after such date.

(c) Life insurance coverage

An individual who is employed by the Center shall be deemed an employee under section 8701(a) of title 5 for purposes of life insurance coverage under chapter 87 of such title.

(d) Government contributions by Librarian from available appropriations

Government contributions for individuals receiving benefits under this section, as computed under sections 8423, 8432, 8708, and 8906[2] shall be made by the Librarian of Congress from any appropriations available to the Library of Congress.

(e) Payroll and personnel functions of Library of Congress

The Library of Congress, directly or by agreement with its designated representative, shall—

(1) process payroll for Center employees, including making deductions and withholdings from the pay of employees in the amounts determined under sections 8422, 8432, 8707, and 8905 of title 5;

(2) maintain appropriate personnel and payroll records for Center employees, and transmit appropriate information and records to the Office of Personnel Management; and

(3) transmit funds for Government and employee contributions under this section to the Office of Personnel Management.

(f) Responsibilities of Center

The Center shall—

(1) pay to the Library of Congress funds sufficient to cover the gross salary and the employer's share of taxes under section 3111 of title 26 for Center employees, in amounts computed by the Library of Congress;

(2) as required by the Library of Congress, reimburse the Library of Congress for reasonable administrative costs incurred under subsection (e)(1) of this section;

(3) comply with regulations and procedures prescribed by the Librarian of Congress for administration of this section;

(4) maintain appropriate records on all Center employees, as required by the Librarian of Congress; and

(5) consult with the Librarian of Congress on the administration and implementation of this section.

(g) Regulations

The Librarian of Congress may prescribe regulations to carry out this section.

(Pub. L. 106–554, § 1(a)(2) [title II, § 210], Dec. 21, 2000, 114 Stat. 2763, 2763A–114.)

REFERENCES IN TEXT

Section 205(g)(1) of the Legislative Branch Appropriations Act, 1991, referred to in subsec. (a)(1)(A), is section 205(g)(1) of Pub. L. 101–520, which is set out as a note under section 141 of this title.

§ 163. Omitted

CODIFICATION

Section, act Mar. 3, 1925, ch. 423, § 7, 43 Stat. 1108, which required the Library of Congress Trust Fund Board to submit an annual report to Congress on moneys or securities received and held and operations, terminated, effective May 15, 2000, pursuant to section 3003 of Pub. L. 104–66, as amended, set out as a note under section 1113 of Title 31, Money and Finance. See, also, page 10 of House Document No. 103–7.

§ 164. Index and digest of State legislation; preparation

The Librarian of Congress is authorized and directed to prepare biennially an index to the legislation of the States of the United States enacted during the biennium, together with a supplemental digest of the more important legislation of the period.

(Feb. 10, 1927, ch. 99, § 1, 44 Stat. 1066; Feb. 28, 1929, ch. 367, § 1, 45 Stat. 1398.)

AMENDMENTS

1929—Act Feb. 28, 1929, repealed provision that the Librarian of Congress report biennially to Congress an index and digest of State legislation.

SECTION REFERRED TO IN OTHER SECTIONS

This section is referred to in sections 164a, 165 of this title.

§ 164a. Official distribution of State legislation index and digest

The Librarian of Congress is directed to have the indexes and digests authorized by section 164 of this title printed and bound for official distribution only.

(Feb. 28, 1929, ch. 367, § 1, 45 Stat. 1398.)

§ 165. Authorization for appropriation for biennial index

There is authorized to be appropriated annually for carrying out the provisions of section 164 of this title the sum of $30,000, to remain available until expended.

(Feb. 10, 1927, ch. 99, § 2, 44 Stat. 1066.)

§ 166. Congressional Research Service

(a) Redesignation of Legislative Reference Service

The Legislative Reference Service in the Library of Congress is hereby continued as a sepa-

---

[1] So in original. Probably should be "chapter".
[2] So in original. Probably should be followed by "of title 5".

rate department in the Library of Congress and is redesignated the "Congressional Research Service".

(b) Functions and objectives

It is the policy of Congress that—

(1) the Librarian of Congress shall, in every possible way, encourage, assist, and promote the Congressional Research Service in—

(A) rendering to Congress the most effective and efficient service,

(B) responding most expeditiously, effectively, and efficiently to the special needs of Congress, and

(C) discharging its responsibilities to Congress;

and

(2) the Librarian of Congress shall grant and accord to the Congressional Research Service complete research independence and the maximum practicable administrative independence consistent with these objectives.

(c) Appointment and compensation of Director, Deputy Director, and other necessary personnel; minimum grade for Senior Specialists; placement in grades GS–16, 17, and 18 of Specialists and Senior Specialists; appointment without regard to civil service laws and political affiliation and on basis of fitness to perform duties

(1) After consultation with the Joint Committee on the Library, the Librarian of Congress shall appoint the Director of the Congressional Research Service. The basic pay of the Director shall be at a per annum rate equal to the rate of basic pay provided for level III of the Executive Schedule under section 5314 of title 5.

(2) The Librarian of Congress, upon the recommendation of the Director, shall appoint a Deputy Director of the Congressional Research Service and all other necessary personnel thereof. The basic pay of the Deputy Director shall be fixed in accordance with chapter 51 (relating to classification) and subchapter III (relating to General Schedule pay rates) of chapter 53 of title 5, but without regard to section 5108(a) of such title. The basic pay of all other necessary personnel of the Congressional Research Service shall be fixed in accordance with chapter 51 (relating to classification) and subchapter III (relating to General Schedule pay rates) of chapter 53 of title 5, except that—

(A) the grade of Senior Specialist in each field within the purview of subsection (e) of this section shall not be less than the highest grade in the executive branch of the Government to which research analysts and consultants, without supervisory responsibility, are currently assigned; and

(B) the positions of Specialist and Senior Specialist in the Congressional Research Service may be placed in GS–16, 17, and 18 of the General Schedule of section 5332 of title 5, without regard to section 5108(a) of such title, subject to the prior approval of the Joint Committee on the Library, of the placement of each such position in any of such grades.

(3) Each appointment made under paragraphs (1) and (2) of this subsection and subsection (e) of this section shall be without regard to the civil service laws, without regard to political affiliation, and solely on the basis of fitness to perform the duties of the position.

(d) Duties of Service; assistance to Congressional committees; list of terminating programs and subjects for analysis; legislative data, studies, etc.; information research; digest of bills, preparation; legislation, purpose and effect, and preparation of memoranda; information and research capability, development

It shall be the duty of the Congressional Research Service, without partisan bias—

(1) upon request, to advise and assist any committee of the Senate or House of Representatives and any joint committee of Congress in the analysis, appraisal, and evaluation of legislative proposals within that committee's jurisdiction, or of recommendations submitted to Congress, by the President or any executive agency, so as to assist the committee in—

(A) determining the advisability of enacting such proposals;

(B) estimating the probable results of such proposals and alternatives thereto; and

(C) evaluating alternative methods for accomplishing those results;

and, by providing such other research and analytical services as the committee considers appropriate for these purposes, otherwise to assist in furnishing a basis for the proper evaluation and determination of legislative proposals and recommendations generally; and in the performance of this duty the Service shall have authority, when so authorized by a committee and acting as the agent of that committee, to request of any department or agency of the United States the production of such books, records, correspondence, memoranda, papers, and documents as the Service considers necessary, and such department or agency of the United States shall comply with such request; and further, in the performance of this and any other relevant duty, the Service shall maintain continuous liaison with all committees;

(2) to make available to each committee of the Senate and House of Representatives and each joint committee of the two Houses, at the opening of a new Congress, a list of programs and activities being carried out under existing law scheduled to terminate during the current Congress, which are within the jurisdiction of the committee;

(3) to make available to each committee of the Senate and House of Representatives and each joint committee of the two Houses, at the opening of a new Congress, a list of subjects and policy areas which the committee might profitably analyze in depth;

(4) upon request, or upon its own initiative in anticipation of requests, to collect, classify, and analyze in the form of studies, reports, compilations, digests, bulletins, indexes, translations, and otherwise, data having a bearing on legislation, and to make such data available and serviceable to committees and Members of the Senate and House of Representatives and joint committees of Congress;

(5) upon request, or upon its own initiative in anticipation of requests, to prepare and pro-

vide information, research, and reference materials and services to committees and Members of the Senate and House of Representatives and joint committees of Congress to assist them in their legislative and representative functions;

(6) to prepare summaries and digests of bills and resolutions of a public general nature introduced in the Senate or House of Representatives;

(7) upon request made by any committee or Member of the Congress, to prepare and transmit to such committee or Member a concise memorandum with respect to one or more legislative measures upon which hearings by any committee of the Congress have been announced, which memorandum shall contain a statement of the purpose and effect of each such measure, a description of other relevant measures of similar purpose or effect previously introduced in the Congress, and a recitation of all action taken theretofore by or within the Congress with respect to each such other measure; and

(8) to develop and maintain an information and research capability, to include Senior Specialists, Specialists, other employees, and consultants, as necessary, to perform the functions provided for in this subsection.

(e) Specialists and Senior Specialists; appointment; fields of appointment

The Librarian of Congress is authorized to appoint in the Congressional Research Service, upon the recommendation of the Director, Specialists and Senior Specialists in the following broad fields:

(1) agriculture;

(2) American government and public administration;

(3) American public law;

(4) conservation;

(5) education;

(6) engineering and public works;

(7) housing;

(8) industrial organization and corporation finance;

(9) international affairs;

(10) international trade and economic geography;

(11) labor and employment;

(12) mineral economics;

(13) money and banking;

(14) national defense;

(15) price economics;

(16) science;

(17) social welfare;

(18) taxation and fiscal policy;

(19) technology;

(20) transportation and communications;

(21) urban affairs;

(22) veterans' affairs; and

(23) such other broad fields as the Director may consider appropriate.

Such Specialists and Senior Specialists, together with such other employees of the Congressional Research Service as may be necessary, shall be available for special work with the committees and Members of the Senate and House of Representatives and the joint committees of Congress for any of the purposes of subsection (d) of this section.

(f) Duties of Director; establishment and change of research and reference divisions or other organizational units, or both

The Director is authorized—

(1) to classify, organize, arrange, group, and divide, from time to time, as he considers advisable, the requests for advice, assistance, and other services submitted to the Congressional Research Service by committees and Members of the Senate and House of Representatives and joint committees of Congress, into such classes and categories as he considers necessary to—

(A) expedite and facilitate the handling of the individual requests submitted by Members of the Senate and House of Representatives,

(B) promote efficiency in the performance of services for committees of the Senate and House of Representatives and joint committees of Congress, and

(C) provide a basis for the efficient performance by the Congressional Research Service of its legislative research and related functions generally,

and

(2) to establish and change, from time to time, as he considers advisable, within the Congressional Research Service, such research and reference divisions or other organizational units, or both, as he considers necessary to accomplish the purposes of this section.

(g) Budget estimates

The Director of the Congressional Research Service will submit to the Librarian of Congress for review, consideration, evaluation, and approval, the budget estimates of the Congressional Research Service for inclusion in the Budget of the United States Government.

(h) Experts or consultants, individual or organizational, and persons and organizations with specialized knowledge; procurement of temporary or intermittent assistance; contracts, nonpersonal and personal service; advertisement requirements inapplicable; end product; pay; travel time

(1) The Director of the Congressional Research Service may procure the temporary or intermittent assistance of individual experts or consultants (including stenographic reporters) and of persons learned in particular or specialized fields of knowledge—

(A) by nonpersonal service contract, without regard to any provision of law requiring advertising for contract bids, with the individual expert, consultant, or other person concerned, as an independent contractor, for the furnishing by him to the Congressional Research Service of a written study, treatise, theme, discourse, dissertation, thesis, summary, advisory opinion, or other end product; or

(B) by employment (for a period of not more than one year) in the Congressional Research Service of the individual expert, consultant, or other person concerned, by personal service contract or otherwise, without regard to the position classification laws, at a rate of pay not in excess of the per diem equivalent of the highest rate of basic pay then currently in effect for the General Schedule of section 5332 of title 5, including payment of such rate for necessary travel time.

(2) The Director of the Congressional Research Service may procure by contract, without regard to any provision of law requiring advertising for contract bids, the temporary (for respective periods not in excess of one year) or intermittent assistance of educational, research, or other organizations of experts and consultants (including stenographic reporters) and of educational, research, and other organizations of persons learned in particular or specialized fields of knowledge.

(i) Special report to Joint Committee on the Library

The Director of the Congressional Research Service shall prepare and file with the Joint Committee on the Library at the beginning of each regular session of Congress a separate and special report covering, in summary and in detail, all phases of activity of the Congressional Research Service for the immediately preceding fiscal year.

(j) Authorization of appropriations

There are hereby authorized to be appropriated to the Congressional Research Service each fiscal year such sums as may be necessary to carry on the work of the Service.

(Aug. 2, 1946, ch. 753, title II, § 203, 60 Stat. 836; Oct. 28, 1949, ch. 782, title XI, § 1106(a), 63 Stat. 972; Pub. L. 91–510, title III, § 321(a), Oct. 26, 1970, 84 Stat. 1181; Pub. L. 99–190, § 133, Dec. 19, 1985, 99 Stat. 1322; Pub. L. 106–57, title II, § 209(b), Sept. 29, 1999, 113 Stat. 424.)

REFERENCES IN TEXT

The civil service laws, referred to in subsec. (c)(3), are set forth in Title 5, Government Organization and Employees. See, particularly, section 3301 et seq. of that title.

AMENDMENTS

1999—Subsec. (c)(1). Pub. L. 106–57 substituted second sentence for former second sentence which read as follows: "The basic pay of the Director shall be at a per annum rate equal to the rate of basic pay provided for level V of the Executive Schedule contained in section 5316 of title 5."

1985—Subsec. (g). Pub. L. 99–190 amended subsec. (g) generally. Prior to amendment subsec. (g) read as follows: "In order to facilitate the study, consideration, evaluation, and determination by the Congress of the budget requirements of the Congressional Research Service for each fiscal year, the Librarian of Congress shall receive from the Director and submit, for inclusion in the Budget of the United States Government, the budget estimates of the Congressional Research Service which shall be prepared separately by the Director in detail for each fiscal year as a separate item of the budget estimates of the Library of Congress for such fiscal year."

1970—Subsec. (a). Pub. L. 91–510 substituted provision for continuation of Legislative Reference Service, redesignated "Congressional Research Service", for prior authorization for establishment of Legislative Reference Service and deleted second sentence, cls. (1) to (3), prescribing as duties of such Service for the Congress and its committees, the giving of advice and assistance, making data available, and preparing summaries and digests of public hearings before committees and of bills and resolutions of public nature, which

was incorporated in subsec. (d)(1), (d)(4), and (d)(6), respectively, of this section.

Subsec. (b). Pub. L. 91–510 added subsec. (b). Former subsec. (b)(1) provided for appointment of director, assistant director, and other necessary personnel of Legislative Reference Service, without regard to civil-service laws, without reference to political affiliations, on ground of fitness to perform duties of the office, for compensation in accordance with Classification Act of 1949, with a prescribed minimum for senior specialists in the various fields, and made all employees of the Service subject to civil-service retirement laws, now incorporated in subsec. (c)(1), (2)(A), and (3) of this section and sections 8331(1)(viii) and 8347(j) of Title 5, Government Organization and Employees. Former subsec. (b)(2) provided for appointment of senior specialists in certain enumerated fields and was covered in subsec. (e) of this section.

Subsec. (c). Pub. L. 91–510 incorporated in provisions added as subsec. (c) provisions of former subsec. (b) (1), and in revising them, provided in par. (1) for consultation with Joint Committee on the Library before appointment of Director and for basic pay rate of Director equal to level V of Executive Schedule, provided in par. (2) for appointment, upon recommendation of the Director, of a Deputy Director and made references to classification and General Schedule pay rate provisions of revised Title 5, reenacted as subpar. (A) proviso of second sentence of former subsec. (b)(1), and added subpar. (B), and in par. (3) reenacted part of first sentence of former subsec. (b)(1).

Subsec. (d). Pub. L. 91–510 incorporated in provisions added as subsec. (d) second sentence, cls. (1) to (3), of former subsec. (a), and in revising the provision, added pars. (2), (3), (5), (7), and (8), substituted "Congressional Research Service" for "Legislative Reference Service", reenacted introductory "without partisan bias" provision of former cl. (2), incorporated in par. (1) former cl. (1), substituting "proposals within that committee's jurisdiction" for "proposals pending before it" and "otherwise to assist in furnishing a basis for the proper evaluation and determination of legislative proposals and recommendations generally" for "otherwise to assist in furnishing a basis for the proper determination of measures before the committee", added subpars. (A) to (C), provision for assistance by providing other research and analytical services, authorization for production of books, records, etc., compliance with request for such production, and maintenance of liaison with all committees, incorporated in par. (4) former cl. (2), substituting "collect" for "gather" and including analysis in form of studies and reports, and making data available to joint committees, and incorporated in par. (6) former cl. (3), omitting provision respecting summaries and digests of public hearings before committees of Congress.

Subsec. (e). Pub. L. 91–510 incorporated in provisions added as subsec. (e) provisions of former subsec. (b)(2), and in revising them, in introductory text, substituted "Congressional Research Service" for "Legislative Reference Service" and authorized appointments "upon the recommendation of the Director", including Specialists; provided numerical item designations for broad fields listed in prior paragraph in run-on form, added fields of national defense, science, technology, urban affairs, and other broad fields as deemed appropriate by the Director in items (14), (16), (19), (21), and (23), and combined separate fields of "full employment" and "labor" in "labor and employment" in item (11); and in last sentence, included Senior Specialists and substituted "such other employees of the Congressional Research Service" for "such other members of the staff" and "special work with the committees and Members of the Senate and House of Representatives and the joint committees of Congress for any of the purposes of subsection (d) of this section" for "special work with the appropriate committees of Congress for any of the purposes set out in subsection (a)(1) of this section".

Subsecs. (f) to (i). Pub. L. 91–510 added subsecs. (f) to (i).

Subsec. (j). Pub. L. 91–510 incorporated in provisions added as subsec. (j) appropriations authorization of section 203(c) of Act Aug. 2, 1946, which had also provided $550,000, $650,000, and $750,000, for fiscal years ending June 30, 1947, 1948, and 1949, respectively.

1949—Subsec. (b)(1). Act Oct. 28, 1949, substituted "Classification Act of 1949" for "Classification Act of 1923".

EFFECTIVE DATE OF 1999 AMENDMENT

Amendment by Pub. L. 106–57 applicable with respect to the first pay period which begins on or after Sept. 29, 1999 and each subsequent pay period, see section 209(c) of Pub. L. 106–57, set out as a note under section 136a–2 of this title.

EFFECTIVE DATE OF 1970 AMENDMENT

Amendment of provisions, other than enactment of subsecs. (d)(2), (3) and (i) of this section, and enactment of subsecs. (d)(2), (3) and (i) by Pub. L. 91–510 effective immediately prior to noon on Jan. 3, 1971, at the close of the first session of the Ninety-second Congress, and with respect to fiscal years beginning on or after July 1, 1970, respectively, see section 601(1), (3), and (4) of Pub. L. 91–510, set out as a note under section 72a of this title.

EFFECTIVE DATE

Section effective Aug. 2, 1946, see section 245 of that act, set out as a note under section 72a of this title.

REPEALS

Act Oct. 28, 1949, ch. 782, cited as a credit to this section, was repealed (subject to a savings clause) by Pub. L. 89–554, Sept. 6, 1966, §8, 80 Stat. 632, 655.

REFERENCES IN OTHER LAWS TO GS–16, 17, OR 18 PAY RATES

References in laws to the rates of pay for GS–16, 17, or 18, or to maximum rates of pay under the General Schedule, to be considered references to rates payable under specified sections of Title 5, Government Organization and Employees, see section 529 [title I, §101(c)(1)] of Pub. L. 101–509, set out in a note under section 5376 of Title 5.

COMPENSATION OF DIRECTOR OF CONGRESSIONAL RESEARCH SERVICE

Pub. L. 105–275, title I, Oct. 21, 1998, 112 Stat. 2444, which provided that the compensation of the Director of the Congressional Research Service, Library of Congress, was to be at an annual rate equal to the annual rate of basic pay for positions at level IV of the Executive Schedule under section 5315 of title 5, was from the Legislative Branch Appropriations Act, 1999, and was not repeated in subsequent appropriations acts. Similar provisions were contained in the following prior appropriation acts:

Pub. L. 105–55, title I, Oct. 7, 1997, 111 Stat. 1190.
Pub. L. 104–197, title I, Sept. 16, 1996, 110 Stat. 2406.
Pub. L. 104–53, title I, Nov. 19, 1995, 109 Stat. 529.
Pub. L. 103–283, title I, July 22, 1994, 108 Stat. 1435.
Pub. L. 103–69, title I, Aug. 11, 1993, 107 Stat. 703.
Pub. L. 102–392, title I, Oct. 6, 1992, 106 Stat. 1715.
Pub. L. 102–90, title I, Aug. 14, 1991, 105 Stat. 460.
Pub. L. 101–520, title I, Nov. 5, 1990, 104 Stat. 2269.
Pub. L. 101–163, title I, Nov. 21, 1989, 103 Stat. 1057.
Pub. L. 100–458, title I, Oct. 1, 1988, 102 Stat. 2171.
Pub. L. 100–202, §101(i) [title I], Dec. 22, 1987, 101 Stat. 1329–290, 1329–303.
Pub. L. 99–500, §101(j) [H.R. 5203, title I], Oct. 18, 1986, 100 Stat. 1783–287, and Pub. L. 99–591, §101(j), Oct. 30, 1986, 100 Stat. 3341–287.
Pub. L. 99–151, title I, Nov. 13, 1985, 99 Stat. 802.
Pub. L. 98–367, title I, July 17, 1984, 98 Stat. 484.

§ 167. Buildings and grounds; designation of employees as police

The Librarian of Congress may designate employees of the Library of Congress as police for duty with respect to the Library of Congress buildings and adjacent streets. The rank structure and pay for employees so designated shall be the same as the rank structure and pay for the Capitol Police.

(Aug. 4, 1950, ch. 561, §1, 64 Stat. 411; Pub. L. 90–610, §1, Oct. 21, 1968, 82 Stat. 1201; Pub. L. 93–175, §1, Dec. 5, 1973, 87 Stat. 693; Pub. L. 100–135, §1(a), Oct. 16, 1987, 101 Stat. 811.)

AMENDMENTS

1987—Pub. L. 100–135 amended section generally. Prior to amendment, section read as follows:

"(a) The Librarian of Congress may designate employees of the Library of Congress as special policemen for duty in connection with policing of the Library of Congress buildings and grounds and adjacent streets and shall fix their rates of basic pay as follows:

"(1) Private GS–7—step one through five;
"(2) Sergeant GS–8—step one through five;
"(3) Lieutenant GS–9—step one through five;
"(4) Senior Lieutenant GS–10—step one through five; and
"(5) Captain GS–11—step one through seven.

"(b) The Librarian of Congress may apply the provisions of subchapter V of chapter 55 of title 5 to members of the special police force of the Library of Congress."

1973—Subsec. (a)(1). Pub. L. 93–175 substituted "Private GS–7—step one through five" for "Private—not to exceed the rate for GS–5, Step 5".

Subsec. (a)(2). Pub. L. 93–175 substituted "Sergeant GS–8—step one through five" for "Sergeant—not to exceed the rate for GS–6, Step 5".

Subsec. (a)(3). Pub. L. 93–175 substituted "Lieutenant GS–9—step one through five" for "Lieutenant—not to exceed the rate for GS–7, Step 5".

Subsec. (a)(4). Pub. L. 93–175 substituted "Senior Lieutenant GS–10—step one through five" for "Senior Lieutenant—not to exceed the rate for GS–9, Step 5".

Subsec. (a)(5). Pub. L. 93–175 substituted "Captain GS–11—step one through seven" for "Captain—not to exceed the rate for GS–10, Step 5".

1968—Pub. L. 90–610 struck out provisions which permitted the Librarian to designate employees as special policemen without additional compensation, and inserted provisions permitting designation of employees as special employees, prescribing their rates of basic pay, and empowering the Librarian to apply the provisions of subchapter V of chapter 55 of title 5 to members of the special police force.

EFFECTIVE DATE OF 1987 AMENDMENT

Section 3 of Pub. L. 100–135 provided that: "The amendments made by section 1 [amending sections 167 and 167h of this title and section 5102 of Title 5, Government Organization and Employees] shall apply with respect to pay periods beginning after September 30, 1987, except that any pay increase for employees of the Library of Congress, pursuant to the amendments made by such section, shall be subject to appropriation and shall be implemented in four approximately equal annual increments, so that pay parity with the Capitol Police occurs beginning with the first pay period beginning after September 30, 1990."

EFFECTIVE DATE OF 1973 AMENDMENT

Section 2 of Pub. L. 93–175 provided that: "The amendment made by this Act [amending this section] shall take effect on the first day of the first pay period which begins on or after the date of enactment of this Act [Dec. 5, 1973]."

EFFECTIVE DATE OF 1968 AMENDMENT

Section 3 of Pub. L. 90–610 provided that: "The amendments made by this Act [amending this section and section 5102 of Title 5, Government Organization and Employees] shall take effect on the first day of the first pay period which begins on or after the date of enactment of this Act [Oct. 21, 1968]. Notwithstanding any provisions of this Act, no rate of basic pay shall be reduced by reason of the enactment of this Act."

TRANSITION RULE FOR CERTAIN EMPLOYEES

Section 2 of Pub. L. 100–135 provided that:

"(a) IN GENERAL.—Notwithstanding the amendments made by section 1 [amending this section, section 167h of this title, and section 5102 of Title 5, Government Organization and Employees], each identified employee shall be paid in accordance with prior law until the earliest of—

"(1) the first pay period during which the employee does not perform Sunday work or night work;

"(2) the first pay period for which the pay of the employee, computed in accordance with the amendments made by section 1 and without regard to this section, exceeds the pay computed under prior law; or

"(3) the first pay period beginning after September 30, 1989.

"(b) DEFINITIONS.—As used in this section—

"(1) the term 'identified employee' means an employee identified by the Librarian of Congress as an employee who (with respect to each of the thirteen pay periods immediately before the first pay period to which the amendments made by section 1 apply) is designated by the Librarian for police duty, at the rank of private, and receives additional pay for Sunday work or night work under section 5544 or section 5545 of title 5, United States Code; and

"(2) the term 'prior law' means the first section of the Act entitled 'An Act relating to the policing of the buildings and grounds of the Library of Congress', approved August 4, 1950 (2 U.S.C. 167), as in effect immediately before the first pay period to which the amendments made by section 1 apply."

SECTION REFERRED TO IN OTHER SECTIONS

This section is referred to in sections 167h, 167j of this title; title 5 section 5102.

§ 167a. Public use of Library of Congress grounds

Public travel in and occupancy of the Library of Congress grounds is restricted to the sidewalks and other paved surfaces.

(Aug. 4, 1950, ch. 561, § 2, 64 Stat. 411.)

SECTION REFERRED TO IN OTHER SECTIONS

This section is referred to in sections 167f, 167g, 167h, 167i, 167j of this title.

§ 167b. Sales, advertisements, and solicitations in Library buildings and grounds

It shall be unlawful to offer or expose any article for sale in the Library of Congress buildings or grounds; to display any sign, placard, or other form of advertisement therein; or to solicit fares, alms, subscriptions, or contributions therein.

(Aug. 4, 1950, ch. 561, § 3, 64 Stat. 411.)

SECTION REFERRED TO IN OTHER SECTIONS

This section is referred to in sections 167f, 167g, 167h, 167i, 167j of this title.

§ 167c. Injuries to Library property

It shall be unlawful to step or climb upon, remove, or in any way injure any statue, seat, wall fountain, or other erection or achitectural[1] feature, or any tree, shrub, plant, or turf in the Library of Congress buildings or grounds.

(Aug. 4, 1950, ch. 561, § 4, 64 Stat. 411.)

---

[1] So in original. Probably should be "architectural".

SECTION REFERRED TO IN OTHER SECTIONS

This section is referred to in sections 167f, 167g, 167h, 167i, 167j of this title.

§ 167d. Firearms or fireworks; speeches; objectionable language in Library buildings and grounds

It shall be unlawful to discharge any firearm, firework or explosive, set fire to any combustible, make any harangue or oration, or utter loud, threatening, or abusive language in the Library of Congress buildings or grounds.

(Aug. 4, 1950, ch. 561, § 5, 64 Stat. 411.)

SECTION REFERRED TO IN OTHER SECTIONS

This section is referred to in sections 167f, 167g, 167h, 167i, 167j of this title.

§ 167e. Parades, assemblages or display of flags in Library buildings and grounds

It shall be unlawful to parade, stand, or move in processions or assemblages in the Library of Congress buildings or grounds, or to display therein any flag, banner, or device designed or adapted to bring into public notice any party, organization, or movement.

(Aug. 4, 1950, ch. 561, § 6, 64 Stat. 411.)

SECTION REFERRED TO IN OTHER SECTIONS

This section is referred to in sections 167f, 167g, 167h, 167i, 167j of this title.

§ 167f. Regulations for Library buildings and grounds; publication; effective date

(a) In addition to the restrictions and requirements specified in sections 167a to 167e of this title, the Librarian of Congress may prescribe such regulations as may be deemed necessary for the adequate protection of the Library of Congress buildings and grounds and of persons and property therein, and for the maintenance of suitable order and decorum within the Library of Congress buildings and grounds.

(b) All regulations promulgated under the authority of this section shall be printed in one or more of the daily newspapers published in the District of Columbia, and shall not become effective until the expiration of ten days after the date of such publication.

(Aug. 4, 1950, ch. 561, § 7, 64 Stat. 411.)

SECTION REFERRED TO IN OTHER SECTIONS

This section is referred to in sections 167g, 167h, 167j of this title.

§ 167g. Prosecution and punishment of offenses in Library buildings and grounds

Whoever violates any provision of sections 167a to 167e of this title, or of any regulation prescribed under section 167f of this title, commits a Class B misdemeanor, prosecution for such offenses to be had in the Superior Court of the District of Columbia upon information by the United States attorney or any of his assistants: *Provided,* That in any case where, in the commission of any such offense, public property is damaged in an amount exceeding $100, the person commits a Class D felony.

(Aug. 4, 1950, ch. 561, § 8, 64 Stat. 412; Pub. L. 88–60, § 1, July 8, 1963, 77 Stat. 77; Pub. L. 91–358,

§ 111, July 29, 1970, 84 Stat. 473; Pub. L. 101–562, § 3, Nov. 15, 1990, 104 Stat. 2781.)

AMENDMENTS

1990—Pub. L. 101–562 substituted "commits a Class B misdemeanor" for "shall be fined not more than $100 or imprisoned not more than sixty days, or both" and "the person commits a Class D felony" for "the period of imprisonment for the offense may not be more than five years".

CHANGE OF NAME

"District of Columbia Court of General Sessions" substituted in text for "Municipal Court for the District of Columbia" pursuant to act Apr. 1, 1942, ch. 207, §§ 1, 4, 56 Stat. 190, 192, which consolidated into a single court powers and functions of Police Court of District of Columbia and Municipal Court of District of Columbia, and Pub. L. 87–873, § 1, Oct. 23, 1962, 76 Stat. 1171 and Pub. L. 88–60, § 1, July 8, 1963, 77 Stat. 77, which both redesignated the "Municipal Court for the District of Columbia" as the "District of Columbia Court of General Sessions".

"District of Columbia Court of General Sessions" changed to "Superior Court of the District of Columbia" pursuant to Pub. L. 91–358, which provided that such change is effective the first day of the seventh calendar month which begins after July 29, 1970.

SECTION REFERRED TO IN OTHER SECTIONS

This section is referred to in section 167j of this title.

§ 167h. Jurisdiction of police within Library buildings, grounds, and adjacent streets

The police provided for in section 167 of this title shall have the power, within the Library of Congress buildings and grounds and adjacent streets, to enforce and make arrests for violations of any provision of sections 167a to 167e of this title, of any regulation prescribed under section 167f of this title, or of any law of the United States, any law of the District of Columbia, or of any State, or any regulation promulgated pursuant thereto: *Provided*, That the Metropolitan Police force of the District of Columbia are authorized to make arrests within the Library of Congress buildings and grounds for any violations of any such laws or regulations, but such authority shall not be construed as authorizing the Metropolitan Police force, except with the consent or upon the request of the Librarian of Congress or his assistants, to enter the Library of Congress buildings to make arrests in response to complaints or to serve warrants or to patrol the Library of Congress buildings or grounds.

(Aug. 4, 1950, ch. 561, § 9, 64 Stat. 412; Pub. L. 93–198, title VII, § 739(g)(9), Dec. 24, 1973, 87 Stat. 829; Pub. L. 100–135, § 1(b)(1), Oct. 16, 1987, 101 Stat. 811.)

AMENDMENTS

1987—Pub. L. 100–135 substituted "The police" for "The special police".

1973—Pub. L. 93–198 inserted reference to violations of any law of the District of Columbia.

EFFECTIVE DATE OF 1987 AMENDMENT

Amendment by Pub. L. 100–135 applicable with respect to pay periods beginning after Sept. 30, 1987, except that any pay increase for employees of Library of Congress, pursuant to such amendment, to be subject to appropriation and to be implemented in four approximately equal annual increments, so that pay par-

ity with Capitol Police occurs beginning with first pay period beginning after Sept. 30, 1990, see section 3 of Pub. L. 100–135, set out as a note under section 167 of this title.

EFFECTIVE DATE OF 1973 AMENDMENT

Section 771(e) of Pub. L. 93–198 provided that the amendment made by Pub. L. 93–198 is effective Jan. 2, 1975, if a majority of the registered qualified electors in the District of Columbia voting on the charter issue in the charter referendum accept the charter set out in Title IV of Pub. L. 93–198, Dec. 24, 1973, 87 Stat. 785. The charter was approved by the voters on May 7, 1974.

SECTION REFERRED TO IN OTHER SECTIONS

This section is referred to in section 167j of this title.

§ 167i. Suspension of prohibitions against use of Library buildings and grounds

In order to permit the observance of authorized ceremonies within the Library of Congress buildings and grounds, the Librarian of Congress may suspend for such occasions so much of the prohibitions contained in sections 167a to 167e of this title as may be necessary for the occasion, but only if responsible officers shall have been appointed, and arrangements determined which are adequate, in the judgment of the Librarian, for the maintenance of suitable order and decorum in the proceedings, and for the protection of the Library buildings and grounds and of persons and property therein.

(Aug. 4, 1950, ch. 561, § 10, 64 Stat. 412.)

SECTION REFERRED TO IN OTHER SECTIONS

This section is referred to in section 167j of this title.

§ 167j. Area comprising Library of Congress grounds; "buildings and grounds" defined

(a) For the purposes of sections 167 to 167j of this title the Library of Congress grounds shall be held to extend to the line of the face of the east curb of First Street Southeast, between B Street Southeast and East Capitol Street; to the line of the face of the south curb of East Capitol Street, between First Street Southeast and Second Street Southeast; to the line of the face of the west curb of Second Street Southeast, between East Capitol Street and B Street Southeast; to the line of the face of the north curb of B Street Southeast, between First Street Southeast and Second Street Southeast; and to the line of the face of the east curb of Second Street Southeast, between Pennsylvania Avenue Southeast and the north side of the alley separating the Library Annex Building and the Folger Shakespeare Library; to the line of the north side of the same alley, between Second Street Southeast and Third Street Southeast; to the line of the face of the west curb of Third Street Southeast, between the north side of the same alley and B Street Southeast; to the line of the face of the north curb of B Street Southeast, between Third Street Southeast and Pennsylvania Avenue Southeast; to the line of the face of the northeast curb of Pennsylvania Avenue Southeast, between B Street Southeast and Second Street Southeast.

(b) For the purposes of sections 167 to 167j of this title, the term "Library of Congress buildings and grounds" shall include (1) the whole or any part of any building or structure which is occupied under lease or otherwise by the Library of Congress and is subject to supervision and control by the Librarian of Congress, (2) the land upon which there is situated any building or structure which is occupied wholly by the Library of Congress, and (3) any subway or enclosed passageway connecting two or more buildings or structures occupied in whole or in part by the Library of Congress.

(c) For the purpose of sections 167 to 167j of this title, the term "Library of Congress buildings and grounds" shall include (1) all real property in lot 51 in square 869 in the District of Columbia, as that lot appears on the records in the office of the Surveyor of the District of Columbia on August 1, 1990, extending to the outer face of the curbs of the square in which it is located and including all alleys or parts of alleys and streets within the lot lines and curb lines surrounding such real property, and (2) improvements to such real property.

(d) For the purposes of sections 167 to 167j of this title, the term "Library of Congress buildings and grounds" shall include the following property:

(1) Three parcels totaling approximately 41 acres, more or less, located in Culpeper County, Virginia, and identified as Culpeper County Tax Parcel Numbers 51–80B, 51–80C, and 51–80D, further described as real estate (consisting of 15.949 acres) conveyed to Federal Reserve Bank of Richmond by deed from Russell H. Inskeep and Jean H. Inskeep, his wife, dated October 1, 1964, and recorded October 7, 1964, in the Clerk's Office, Circuit Court of Culpeper County, Virginia, in Deed Book 177, page 431; and real estate (consisting of 20.498 acres and consisting of 4.502 acres) conveyed to Federal Reserve Bank of Richmond by deed from Russell H. Inskeep and Jean H. Inskeep, his wife, dated November 11, 1974, and recorded November 12, 1974, in the Clerk's Office, Circuit Court of Culpeper County, Virginia, in Deed Book 247, page 246.

(2) Improvements to such real property.

(Aug. 4, 1950, ch. 561, § 11, 64 Stat. 412; Pub. L. 91–281, June 17, 1970, 84 Stat. 309; Pub. L. 101–520, title II, § 205(d), Nov. 5, 1990, 104 Stat. 2272; Pub. L. 101–562, § 2(c), Nov. 15, 1990, 104 Stat. 2780; Pub. L. 105–144, § 2, Dec. 15, 1997, 111 Stat. 2667.)

Amendments

1997—Subsec. (d). Pub. L. 105–144 added subsec. (d).
1990—Subsec. (c). Pub. L. 101–520 and Pub. L. 101–562 made substantively identical amendments, adding subsec. (c).
1970—Pub. L. 91–281 designated existing provisions as subsec. (a) and added subsec. (b).

Effective Date of 1997 Amendment

Amendment by Pub. L. 105–144 effective upon acquisition by Architect of the Capitol of property described in section 1 of Pub. L. 105–144, see section 5 of Pub. L. 105–144, set out as an Acquisition of Real Property for Library of Congress note under section 141 of this title.

Effective Date of 1990 Amendments

Amendment by Pub. L. 101–520 and Pub. L. 101–562 effective on date [Nov. 6, 1991] Architect of the Capitol acquires the property and improvements described in Pub. L. 101–520, § 205(a), and Pub. L. 101–562, § 1, see sec-

tion 205(e) of Pub. L. 101–520 and former section 2(d) of Pub. L. 101–562, set out as a Special Facilities Center; Acquisition note under section 141 of this title.

Section Referred to in Other Sections

This section is referred to in section 141 of this title; title 40 section 136.

§ 168. Constitution of the United States; preparation and publication of revised edition; annotations; supplements; decennial editions and supplements

The Librarian of Congress shall have prepared—

(1) a hardbound revised edition of the Constitution of the United States of America—Analysis and Interpretation, published as Senate Document Numbered 39, Eighty-eighth Congress (referred to hereinafter as the "Constitution Annotated"), which shall contain annotations of decisions of the Supreme Court of the United States through the end of the October 1971 term of the Supreme Court, construing provisions of the Constitution;

(2) upon the completion of each of the October 1973, October 1975, October 1977, and October 1979 terms of the Supreme Court, a cumulative pocket-part supplement to the hardbound revised edition of the Constitution Annotated prepared pursuant to clause (1), which shall contain cumulative annotations of all such decisions rendered by the Supreme Court after the end of the October 1971 term;

(3) upon the completion of the October 1981 term of the Supreme Court, and upon the completion of each tenth October term of the Supreme Court thereafter, a hardbound decennial revised edition of the Constitution Annotated, which shall contain annotations of all decisions theretofore rendered by the Supreme Court construing provisions of the Constitution; and

(4) upon the completion of the October 1983 term of the Supreme Court, and upon the completion of each subsequent October term of the Supreme Court beginning in an odd-numbered year (the final digit of which is not a 1), a cumulative pocket-part supplement to the most recent hardbound decennial revised edition of the Constitution Annotated, which shall contain cumulative annotations of all such decisions rendered by the Supreme Court which were not included in that hardbound decennial revised edition of the Constitution Annotated.

(Pub. L. 91–589, § 1, Dec. 24, 1970, 84 Stat. 1586.)

Section Referred to in Other Sections

This section is referred to in sections 168b, 168d of this title.

§ 168a. Printing of Constitution Annotated as Senate documents

All hardbound revised editions and all cumulative pocket-part supplements shall be printed as Senate documents.

(Pub. L. 91–589, § 2, Dec. 24, 1970, 84 Stat. 1586.)

Section Referred to in Other Sections

This section is referred to in section 168d of this title.

§ 168b. Printing and distribution of additional copies of Constitution Annotated

There shall be printed four thousand eight hundred and seventy additional copies of the hardbound revised editions prepared pursuant to clause (1) of section 168 of this title and of all cumulative pocket-part supplements thereto, of which two thousand six hundred and thirty-four copies shall be for the use of the House of Representatives, one thousand two hundred and thirty-six copies shall be for the use of the Senate, and one thousand copies shall be for the use of the Joint Committee on Printing. All Members of the Congress, Vice Presidents of the United States, and Delegates and Resident Commissioners, newly elected subsequent to the issuance of the hardbound revised edition prepared pursuant to such clause and prior to the first hardbound decennial revised edition, who did not receive a copy of the edition prepared pursuant to such clause, shall, upon timely request, receive one copy of such edition and the then current cumulative pocket-part supplement and any further supplements thereto. All Members of the Congress, Vice Presidents of the United States, and Delegates and Resident Commissioners, no longer serving after the issuance of the hardbound revised edition prepared pursuant to such clause and who received such edition, may receive one copy of each cumulative pocket-part supplement thereto upon timely request.

(Pub. L. 91–589, § 3, Dec. 24, 1970, 84 Stat. 1586.)

SECTION REFERRED TO IN OTHER SECTIONS

This section is referred to in section 168d of this title.

§ 168c. Printing and distribution of decennial editions and supplements to Constitution Annotated

Additional copies of each hardbound decennial revised edition and of the cumulative pocket-part supplements thereto shall be printed and distributed in accordance with the provisions of any concurrent resolution hereafter adopted with respect thereto.

(Pub. L. 91–589, § 4, Dec. 24, 1970, 84 Stat. 1587.)

SECTION REFERRED TO IN OTHER SECTIONS

This section is referred to in section 168d of this title.

§ 168d. Authorization of appropriations for Constitution Annotated

There are authorized to be appropriated such sums, to remain available until expended, as may be necessary to carry out the provisions of sections 168 to 168d of this title.

(Pub. L. 91–589, § 5, Dec. 24, 1970, 84 Stat. 1587.)

§ 169. Positions in Library of Congress exempt from citizenship requirement

From and after October 1, 1983, not to exceed fifteen positions in the Library of Congress may be exempt from the provisions of appropriation Acts concerning the employment of aliens during the current fiscal year, but the Librarian shall not make any appointment to any such position until he has ascertained that he cannot secure for such appointments a person in any of the categories specified in such provisions who possesses the special qualifications for the particular position and also otherwise meets the general requirements for employment in the Library of Congress.

(Pub. L. 98–51, title II, § 202, July 14, 1983, 97 Stat. 276.)

PRIOR PROVISIONS

Provisions similar to those in this section were contained in the following prior appropriation acts:

Oct. 2, 1982, Pub. L. 97–276, § 101(e) [S. 2939, title II, § 202], 96 Stat. 1189.

Oct. 1, 1981, Pub. L. 97–51, § 101(c) [H.R. 4120, title II, § 202], 95 Stat. 959.

Dec. 16, 1980, Pub. L. 96–536, § 101(c) [H.R. 7593, title II, § 202], 94 Stat. 3167.

Oct. 12, 1979, Pub. L. 96–86, § 101(c) [H.R. 4390, title II, § 202], 93 Stat. 657.

Sept. 30, 1978, Pub. L. 95–391, title II, § 202, 92 Stat. 785.

Aug. 5, 1977, Pub. L. 95–94, title II, § 202, 91 Stat. 677.

Oct. 1, 1976, Pub. L. 94–440, title VIII, § 802, 90 Stat. 1457.

July 25, 1975, Pub. L. 94–59, title VII, § 702, 89 Stat. 294.

Aug. 13, 1974, Pub. L. 93–371, 88 Stat. 441.

Nov. 1, 1973, Pub. L. 93–145, 87 Stat. 547.

July 10, 1972, Pub. L. 92–342, 86 Stat. 446.

July 9, 1971, Pub. L. 92–51, 85 Stat. 141.

Aug. 18, 1970, Pub. L. 91–382, 84 Stat. 823.

Dec. 12, 1969, Pub. L. 91–145, 83 Stat. 357.

July 23, 1968, Pub. L. 90–417, 82 Stat. 411.

July 28, 1967, Pub. L. 90–57, 81 Stat. 140.

Aug. 27, 1966, Pub. L. 89–545, 80 Stat. 368.

July 27, 1965, Pub. L. 89–90, 79 Stat. 280.

Aug. 20, 1964, Pub. L. 88–454, 78 Stat. 548.

Dec. 30, 1963, Pub. L. 88–248, 77 Stat. 816.

Oct. 2, 1962, Pub. L. 87–730, 76 Stat. 692.

Aug. 10, 1961, Pub. L. 87–130, 75 Stat. 333.

July 12, 1960, Pub. L. 86–628, 74 Stat. 459.

Aug. 21, 1959, Pub. L. 86–176, 73 Stat. 411.

July 31, 1958, Pub. L. 85–570, 72 Stat. 452.

July 1, 1957, Pub. L. 85–75, 71 Stat. 255.

June 27, 1956, ch. 453, 70 Stat. 368.

Aug. 5, 1955, ch. 568, 69 Stat. 518.

July 2, 1954, ch. 455, 68 Stat. 408.

Aug. 1, 1953, ch. 304, 67 Stat. 330.

July 9, 1952, ch. 598, 66 Stat. 476.

Oct. 11, 1951, ch. 485, 65 Stat. 400.

Sept. 6, 1950, ch. 896, Ch. II, 64 Stat. 606.

June 22, 1949, ch. 235, 63 Stat. 228.

June 14, 1948, ch. 467, 62 Stat. 434.

July 17, 1947, ch. 262, 61 Stat. 374.

July 1, 1946, ch. 530, 60 Stat. 405.

June 13, 1945, ch. 189, 59 Stat. 256.

June 26, 1944, ch. 277, 58 Stat. 351.

June 28, 1943, ch. 173, 57 Stat. 236.

§ 170. American Television and Radio Archives

(a) Establishment and maintenance in Library of Congress; purpose; determination of composition, cataloging, indexing and availability by Librarian

The Librarian of Congress (hereinafter referred to as the "Librarian") shall establish and maintain in the Library of Congress a library to be known as the American Television and Radio Archives (hereinafter referred to as the "Archives"). The purpose of the Archives shall be to preserve a permanent record of the television and radio programs which are the heritage of the people of the United States and to provide access to such programs to historians and scholars without encouraging or causing copyright infringement.

(1) The Librarian, after consultation with interested organizations and individuals, shall determine and place in the Archives such copies and phonorecords of television and radio programs transmitted to the public in the United States and in other countries which are of present or potential public or cultural interest, historical significance, cognitive value, or otherwise worthy of preservation, including copies and phonorecords of published and unpublished transmission programs—

  (A) acquired in accordance with sections 407 and 408 of title 17; and

  (B) transferred from the existing collections of the Library of Congress; and

  (C) given to or exchanged with the Archives by other libraries, archives, organizations, and individuals; and

  (D) purchased from the owner thereof.

(2) The Librarian shall maintain and publish appropriate catalogs and indexes of the collections of the Archives, and shall make such collections available for study and research under the conditions prescribed under this section.

(b) Reproduction, compilation, and distribution for research of regularly scheduled newscasts or on-the-spot coverage of news events by Librarian; promulgation of regulations

Notwithstanding the provisions of section 106 of title 17, the Librarian is authorized with respect to a transmission program which consists of a regularly scheduled newscast or on-the-spot coverage of news events and, under standards and conditions that the Librarian shall prescribe by regulation—

(1) to reproduce a fixation of such a program, in the same or another tangible form, for the purposes of preservation or security or for distribution under the conditions of clause (3) of this subsection;

(2) to compile, without abridgment or any other editing, portions of such fixations according to subject matter, and to reproduce such compilations for the purpose of clause (1) of this subsection; and

(3) to distribute a reproduction made under clause (1) or (2) of this subsection—

  (A) by loan to a person engaged in research; and

  (B) for deposit in a library or archives which meets the requirements of section 108(a) of title 17,

in either case for use only in research and not for further reproduction or performance.

(c) Liability for copyright infringement by Librarian or any employee of Librarian

The Librarian or any employee of the Library who is acting under the authority of this section shall not be liable in any action for copyright infringement committed by any other person unless the Librarian or such employee knowingly participated in the act of infringement committed by such person. Nothing in this section shall be construed to excuse or limit liability under title 17 for any act not authorized by that title or this section, or for any act performed by a person not authorized to act under that title or this section.

(d) Short title

This section may be cited as the "American Television and Radio Archives Act".

(Pub. L. 94–553, title I, §113, Oct. 19, 1976, 90 Stat. 2601.)

EFFECTIVE DATE

Section effective Jan. 1, 1978, see section 102 of Pub. L. 94–553, set out as a note preceding section 101 of Title 17, Copyrights.

§ 171. Congressional declaration of findings and purpose as to Center for the Book

The Congress hereby finds and declares—

(1) that the Congress of the United States on April 24, 1800, established for itself a library of the Congress;

(2) that in 1815, the Congress purchased the personal library of the third President of the United States which contained materials on every science known to man and described such a collection as a "substratum of a great national library";

(3) that the Congress of the United States in recognition of the importance of printing and its impact on America purchased the Gutenberg Bible in 1930 for the Nation for placement in the Library of Congress;

(4) that the Congress of the United States has through statute and appropriations made this library accessible to any member of the public;

(5) that this collection of books and other library materials has now become one of the greatest libraries in civilization;

(6) that the book and the printed word have had the most profound influence on American civilization and learning and have been the very foundation on which our democratic principles have survived through our two hundred-year history;

(7) that in the year 1977, the Congress of the United States assembled hereby declares its reaffirmation of the importance of the printed word and the book and recognizes the importance of a Center for the Book to the continued study and development of written record as central to our understanding of ourselves and our world.

It is therefore the purpose of sections 171 to 175 of this title to establish a Center for the Book in the Library of Congress to provide a program for the investigation of the transmission of human knowledge and to heighten public interest in the role of books and printing in the diffusion of this knowledge.

(Pub. L. 95–129, §1, Oct. 13, 1977, 91 Stat. 1151.)

SECTION REFERRED TO IN OTHER SECTIONS

This section is referred to in section 172 of this title.

§ 172. Definitions

As used in sections 171 to 175 of this title—

(1) the term Center means the Center for the Book;

(2) the term Librarian means the Librarian of Congress.

(Pub. L. 95–129, §2, Oct. 13, 1977, 91 Stat. 1151.)

SECTION REFERRED TO IN OTHER SECTIONS

This section is referred to in section 171 of this title.

§ 173. Establishment of Center for the Book

There is hereby established in the Library of Congress a Center for the Book.

The Center shall be under the direction of the Librarian of Congress.

(Pub. L. 95–129, § 3, Oct. 13, 1977, 91 Stat. 1151.)

SECTION REFERRED TO IN OTHER SECTIONS

This section is referred to in sections 171, 172 of this title.

§ 174. Function of Center for the Book

The Librarian through the Center shall stimulate public interest and research in the role of the book in the diffusion of knowledge through such activities as a visiting scholar program accompanied by lectures, exhibits, publications, and any other related activities.

(Pub. L. 95–129, § 4, Oct. 13, 1977, 91 Stat. 1152.)

SECTION REFERRED TO IN OTHER SECTIONS

This section is referred to in sections 171, 172 of this title.

§ 175. Administrative provisions

The Librarian of Congress, in carrying out the Center's functions, is authorized to—

(1) prescribe such regulations as he deems necessary;

(2) receive money and other property donated, bequeathed, or devised for the purposes of the Center, and to use, sell, or otherwise dispose of such property for the purposes of carrying out the Center's functions, without reference to Federal disposal statutes; and

(3) accept and utilize the services of voluntary and noncompensated personnel and reimburse them for travel expenses, including per diem, as authorized by section 5703 of title 5.

(Pub. L. 95–129, § 5, Oct. 13, 1977, 91 Stat. 1152.)

SECTION REFERRED TO IN OTHER SECTIONS

This section is referred to in sections 171, 172 of this title.

§ 176. Mass Book Deacidification Facility; operation by Librarian of Congress

Notwithstanding any other provision of law, the Librarian of Congress shall equip, furnish, operate, and maintain the Library of Congress Mass Book Deacidification Facility.

(Pub. L. 98–427, § 2, Sept. 28, 1984, 98 Stat. 1656.)

AUTHORIZATION TO CONSTRUCT FACILITY

Section 1 of Pub. L. 98–427 provided: "That the Librarian of Congress is authorized and directed, subject to the supervision and construction authority of a Federal civilian or military agency, to construct the Library of Congress Mass Book Deacidification Facility in accordance with the general design developed by the Library of Congress and reviewed by the Architect of the Capitol, as set forth in the document entitled 'Library of Congress Mass Book Deacidification Facility, Engineering, Design, and Cost Estimate and Drawings', dated December 1983. Such facility shall be constructed on Federal property within seventy-five miles of the United States Capitol Building."

AUTHORIZATION OF APPROPRIATION

Section 3 of Pub. L. 98–427 provided that: "There are authorized to be appropriated for fiscal years beginning after September 30, 1983, sums not to exceed $11,500,000 to carry out the provisions of this Act [enacting this section and a provision set out as a note under this section]."

§ 177. Poet Laureate Consultant in Poetry

(a) Recognition

The Congress recognizes that the Consultant in Poetry to the Library of Congress has for some time occupied a position of prominence in the life of the Nation, has spoken effectively for literary causes, and has occasionally performed duties and functions sometimes associated with the position of poet laureate in other nations and societies. Individuals are appointed to the position of Consultant in Poetry by the Librarian of Congress for one- or two-year terms solely on the basis of literary merit, and are compensated from endowment funds administered by the Library of Congress Trust Fund Board. The Congress further recognizes this position is equivalent to that of Poet Laureate of the United States.

(b) Position established

(1) There is established in the Library of Congress the position of Poet Laureate Consultant in Poetry. The Poet Laureate Consultant in Poetry shall be appointed by the Librarian of Congress pursuant to the same procedures of appointment as established on December 20, 1985, for the Consultant in Poetry to the Library of Congress.

(2) Each department and office of the Federal Government is encouraged to make use of the services of the Poet Laureate Consultant in Poetry for ceremonial and other occasions of celebration under such procedures as the Librarian of Congress shall approve designed to assure that participation under this paragraph does not impair the continuation of the work of the individual chosen to fill the position of Poet Laureate Consultant in Poetry.

(c) Poetry program

(1) The Chairperson of the National Endowment for the Arts, with the advice of the National Council on the Arts, shall annually sponsor a program at which the Poet Laureate Consultant in Poetry will present a major work or the work of other distinguished poets.

(2) There are authorized to be appropriated to the National Endowment for the Arts $10,000 for the fiscal year 1987 and for each succeeding fiscal year ending prior to October 1, 1990, for the purpose of carrying out this subsection.

(Pub. L. 99–194, title VI, § 601, Dec. 20, 1985, 99 Stat. 1347.)

§§ 178 to 178*l*. Repealed. Pub. L. 102–307, title II, § 214, June 26, 1992, 106 Stat. 272

Section 178, Pub. L. 100–446, title I, § 1, Sept. 27, 1988, 102 Stat. 1782, related to Congressional findings on national film preservation.

Section 178a, Pub. L. 100–446, title I, § 2, Sept. 27, 1988, 102 Stat. 1782, related to establishment of a National Film Registry.

Section 178b, Pub. L. 100–446, title I, § 3, Sept. 27, 1988, 102 Stat. 1782, related to the duties of Librarian of Congress with respect to the National Film Registry.

Section 178c, Pub. L. 100–446, title I, § 4, Sept. 27, 1988, 102 Stat. 1784, related to film labeling requirements.

Section 178d, Pub. L. 100–446, title I, §5, Sept. 27, 1988, 102 Stat. 1785, related to misuse of National Film Registry seal.

Section 178e, Pub. L. 100–446, title I, §6, Sept. 27, 1988, 102 Stat. 1785, related to remedies for film labeling violations or for misusing the National Film Registry seal.

Section 178f, Pub. L. 100–446, title I, §7, Sept. 27, 1988, 102 Stat. 1785, related to exclusivity of remedies provided in former section 178e of this title.

Section 178g, Pub. L. 100–446, title I, §8, Sept. 27, 1988, 102 Stat. 1785; Pub. L. 102–378, §5(c), Oct. 2, 1992, 106 Stat. 1358, related to establishment of National Film Preservation Board.

Section 178h, Pub. L. 100–446, title I, §9, Sept. 27, 1988, 102 Stat. 1787, related to staff of National Film Registry Board and authority of Board to procure services of experts and consultants.

Section 178i, Pub. L. 100–446, title I, §10, Sept. 27, 1988, 102 Stat. 1787, related to powers of National Film Registry Board.

Section 178j, Pub. L. 100–446, title I, §11, Sept. 27, 1988, 102 Stat. 1787, contained definitions.

Section 178k, Pub. L. 100–446, title I, §12, Sept. 27, 1988, 102 Stat. 1788, authorized appropriations.

Section 178l, Pub. L. 100–446, title I, §13, Sept. 27, 1988, 102 Stat. 1788, provided effective date, sunset, and savings provisions for former sections 178 to 178l of this title.

For similar provisions, see section 179l et seq. of this title.

SHORT TITLE

Pub. L. 100–446, title I, §1, Sept. 27, 1988, 102 Stat. 1782, which provided that sections 178 to 178l of this title were to be cited as the "National Film Preservation Act of 1988" was repealed by Pub. L. 102–307, title III, §214, June 26, 1992, 106 Stat. 272.

§§ 179 to 179k. Repealed. Pub. L. 104–285, title I, § 114, Oct. 11, 1996, 110 Stat. 3382

Section 179, Pub. L. 102–307, title II, §202, June 26, 1992, 106 Stat. 267, required Librarian of Congress to establish National Film Registry for purpose of maintaining and preserving culturally, historically, or aesthetically significant films.

Section 179a, Pub. L. 102–307, title II, §203, June 26, 1992, 106 Stat. 267, required Librarian of Congress to conduct study of film preservation, to establish film preservation program and guidelines and procedures for inclusion of films in National Film Registry, and to report to Congress on films selected and activities undertaken.

Section 179b, Pub. L. 102–307, title II, §204, June 26, 1992, 106 Stat. 268, related to establishment of National Film Preservation Board and provided for number and appointment of members, chairperson, term of office, quorum, basic pay, meetings, and conflict of interest.

Section 179c, Pub. L. 102–307, title II, §205, June 26, 1992, 106 Stat. 270, related to responsibilities and powers of Board, including consultation with Librarian with respect to inclusion of films in Registry, consideration of films nominated for inclusion in Registry, and general powers.

Section 179d, Pub. L. 102–307, title II, §206, June 26, 1992, 106 Stat. 270, related to National Film Registry Collection of Library of Congress, including provisions relating to acquisition of archival quality copies and additional materials, ownership of copies and additional materials by United States, and maintenance of and access to Collection.

Section 179e, Pub. L. 102–307, title II, §207, June 26, 1992, 106 Stat. 271, related to seal of National Film Registry.

Section 179f, Pub. L. 102–307, title II, §208, June 26, 1992, 106 Stat. 271, provided that district courts of United States were to have jurisdiction to prevent and restrain unlawful use of seal.

Section 179g, Pub. L. 102–307, title II, §209, June 26, 1992, 106 Stat. 271, provided that remedies provided in section 179f were to be exclusive.

Section 179h, Pub. L. 102–307, title II, §210, June 26, 1992, 106 Stat. 271, authorized Librarian to appoint and fix pay of staff and to procure services of experts and consultants.

Section 179i, Pub. L. 102–307, title II, §211, June 26, 1992, 106 Stat. 271, defined terms for purpose of sections 179 to 179k of this title.

Section 179j, Pub. L. 102–307, title II, §212, June 26, 1992, 106 Stat. 272, authorized to be appropriated to Librarian necessary sums to carry out sections 179 to 179k of this title.

Section 179k, Pub. L. 102–307, title II, §213, June 26, 1992, 106 Stat. 272, provided that sections 179 to 179k of this title were effective for 4 years beginning June 26, 1992, and applicable to any copy of any film, including copies of films selected for inclusion in National Film Registry under National Film Preservation Act of 1988.

For similar provisions, see section 179l et seq. of this title.

SHORT TITLE

Pub. L. 102–307, title II, §201, June 26, 1992, 106 Stat. 267, which provided that title II of Pub. L. 102–307, which enacted sections 179 to 179k of this title and repealed sections 178 to 178l of this title and provisions set out as a note under section 178 of this title, was to be cited as the "National Film Preservation Act of 1992", was repealed by Pub. L. 104–285, title I, §114, Oct. 11, 1996, 110 Stat. 3382.

§ 179l. National Film Registry of Library of Congress

The Librarian of Congress (hereafter in sections 179l to 179w of this title referred to as the "Librarian") shall continue the National Film Registry established and maintained under the National Film Preservation Act of 1988 (Public Law 100–446), and the National Film Preservation Act of 1992 (Public Law 102–307) pursuant to the provisions of sections 179l to 179w of this title, for the purpose of maintaining and preserving films that are culturally, historically, or aesthetically significant.

(Pub. L. 104–285, title I, §102, Oct. 11, 1996, 110 Stat. 3377.)

TERMINATION OF SECTION

For termination of section, see section 179w of this title.

REFERENCES IN TEXT

Sections 179l to 179w of the title, referred to in text, was in the original "this Act" the first place appearing and "this title" the second place appearing, both of which were translated as meaning title I of Pub. L. 104–285, Oct. 11, 1996, 110 Stat. 3377, which is classified principally to sections 179l to 179w of this title. For complete classification of title I to the Code, see Short Title note below and Tables.

The National Film Preservation Act of 1988, referred to in text, is Pub. L. 100–446, title I, §§1–13, Sept. 27, 1988, 102 Stat. 1782–1788, which was classified to sections 178 to 178l of this title and was repealed by Pub. L. 102–307, title II, §214, June 26, 1992, 106 Stat. 272.

The National Film Preservation Act of 1992, referred to in text, is title II of Pub. L. 102–307, June 26, 1992, 106 Stat. 267, which was classified principally to sections 179 to 179k of this title and was repealed by Pub. L. 104–285, title I, §114, Oct. 11, 1996, 110 Stat. 3382.

PRIOR PROVISIONS

Prior provisions similar to sections 179l to 179w of this title were contained in former section 179 et seq. of this title.

SHORT TITLE

Section 101 of title I of Pub. L. 104–285 provided that: "This title [enacting this section and sections 179m to

179w of this title and repealing sections 179 to 179k of this title and provisions set out as a note under section 179 of this title] may be cited as the 'National Film Preservation Act of 1996'.''

ACT REFERRED TO IN OTHER SECTIONS

The National Film Preservation Act of 1996 is referred to in title 36 section 151702.

SECTION REFERRED TO IN OTHER SECTIONS

This section is referred to in sections 179s, 179t, 179u, 179v, 179w of this title.

§ 179m. Duties of Librarian of Congress

(a) Powers

(1) In general

The Librarian shall, after consultation with the Board established pursuant to section 179n of this title—

(A) continue the implementation of the comprehensive national film preservation program for motion pictures established under the National Film Preservation Act of 1992, in conjunction with other film archivists, educators and historians, copyright owners, film industry representatives, and others involved in activities related to film preservation, taking into account the objectives of the national film preservation study and the comprehensive national plan conducted under the National Film Preservation Act of 1992. This program shall—

(i) coordinate activities to assure that efforts of archivists and copyright owners, and others in the public and private sector, are effective and complementary;

(ii) generate public awareness of and support for these activities;

(iii) increase accessibility of films for educational purposes; and

(iv) undertake studies and investigations of film preservation activities as needed, including the efficacy of new technologies, and recommend solutions to improve these practices;

(B) establish criteria and procedures under which films may be included in the National Film Registry, except that no film shall be eligible for inclusion in the National Film Registry until 10 years after such film's first publication;

(C) establish procedures under which the general public may make recommendations to the Board regarding the inclusion of films in the National Film Registry; and

(D) determine which films satisfy the criteria established under subparagraph (B) and qualify for inclusion in the National Film Registry, except that the Librarian shall not select more than 25 films each year for inclusion in the Registry.

(2) Publication of films in Registry

The Librarian shall publish in the Federal Register the name of each film that is selected for inclusion in the National Film Registry.

(3) Seal

The Librarian shall provide a seal to indicate that a film has been included in the National Film Registry and is the Registry ver-

sion of that film. The Librarian shall establish guidelines for approval of the use of the seal in accordance with subsection (b) of this section.

(b) Use of seal

The seal provided under subsection (a)(3) of this section may only be used on film copies of the Registry version of a film. Such seal may be used only after the Librarian has given approval to those persons seeking to apply the seal in accordance with the guidelines under subsection (a)(3) of this section. In the case of copyrighted works, only the copyright owner or an authorized licensee of the copyright owner may place or authorize the placement of the seal on any film copy of a Registry version of a film selected for inclusion in the National Film Registry, and the Librarian may place the seal on any film copy of the Registry version of any film that is maintained in the National Film Registry Collection in the Library of Congress. Anyone authorized to place the seal on any film copy of any Registry version of a film may accompany such seal with the following language: ''This film was selected for inclusion in the National Film Registry by the National Film Preservation Board of the Library of Congress because of its cultural, historical, or aesthetic significance.''.

(Pub. L. 104–285, title I, § 103, Oct. 11, 1996, 110 Stat. 3377.)

TERMINATION OF SECTION

For termination of section, see section 179w of this title.

REFERENCES IN TEXT

The National Film Preservation Act of 1992, referred to in subsec. (a)(1)(A), is title II of Pub. L. 102–307, June 26, 1992, 106 Stat. 267, which was classified principally to sections 179 to 179k of this title and was repealed by Pub. L. 104–285, title I, § 114, Oct. 11, 1996, 110 Stat. 3382.

SECTION REFERRED TO IN OTHER SECTIONS

This section is referred to in sections 179l, 179o, 179q, 179s, 179t, 179u, 179v, 179w of this title.

§ 179n. National Film Preservation Board

(a) Number and appointment

(1) Members

The Librarian shall establish in the Library of Congress a National Film Preservation Board to be comprised of 20 members, who shall be selected by the Librarian in accordance with this section. Subject to subparagraphs (C) and (N), the Librarian shall request each organization listed in subparagraphs (A) through (Q) to submit a list of three candidates qualified to serve as a member of the Board. Except for the members-at-large appointed under subparagraph[1] (2), the Librarian shall appoint one member from each such list submitted by such organizations, and shall designate from that list an alternate who may attend at Board expense those meetings to which the individual appointed to the Board cannot attend. The organizations are the following:

(A) The Academy of Motion Picture Arts and Sciences.

---

[1] So in original. Probably should be "paragraph".

(B) The Directors Guild of America.

(C) The Writers Guild of America. The Writers Guild of America East and the Writers Guild of America West shall each nominate three candidates, and a representative from one organization shall be selected as the member and a representative from the other organization as the alternate.

(D) The National Society of Film Critics.

(E) The Society for Cinema Studies.

(F) The American Film Institute.

(G) The Department of Film and Television of the School of Theater, Film and Television at the University of California, Los Angeles.

(H) The Department of Film and Television of the Tisch School of the Arts at New York University.

(I) The University Film and Video Association.

(J) The Motion Picture Association of America.

(K) The Alliance of Motion Picture and Television Producers.

(L) The Screen Actors Guild of America.

(M) The National Association of Theater Owners.

(N) The American Society of Cinematographers and the International Photographers Guild, which shall jointly submit one list of three candidates from which a member and alternate will be selected.

(O) The United States Members of the International Federation of Film Archives.

(P) The Association of Moving Image Archivists.

(Q) The Society of Composers and Lyricists.

(2) Members-at-large

In addition to the members appointed under paragraph (1), the Librarian shall appoint up to three members-at-large. The Librarian shall also select an alternate for each member[2] at-large, who may attend at Board expense those meetings which the member[2] at-large cannot attend.

(b) Chair

The Librarian shall appoint one member of the Board to serve as Chair.

(c) Term of office

(1) Terms

The term of each member of the Board shall be 4 years, except that there shall be no limit to the number of terms that any individual member may serve.

(2) Removal of member or organization

The Librarian shall have the authority to remove any member of the Board, or the organization listed in subsection (a) of this section such member represents, if the member, or organization, over any consecutive 2-year period, fails to attend at least one regularly scheduled Board meeting.

(3) Vacancies

A vacancy in the Board shall be filled in the manner in which the original appointment was

made under subsection (a) of this section, except that the Librarian may fill the vacancy from a list of candidates previously submitted by the organization or organizations involved. Any member appointed to fill a vacancy before the expiration of the term for which his or her predecessor was appointed shall be appointed for the remainder of such term.

(d) Quorum

11 members of the Board shall constitute a quorum but a lesser number may hold hearings.

(e) Reimbursement of expenses

Members of the Board shall serve without pay, but may be reimbursed for the actual and necessary traveling and subsistence expenses incurred by them in the performance of the duties of the Board.

(f) Meetings

The Board shall meet at least once each fiscal year. Meetings shall be at the call of the Librarian.

(g) Conflict of interest

The Librarian shall establish rules and procedures to address any potential conflict of interest between a member of the Board and responsibilities of the Board.

(Pub. L. 104–285, title I, § 104, Oct. 11, 1996, 110 Stat. 3378.)

TERMINATION OF SECTION

For termination of section, see section 179w of this title.

SECTION REFERRED TO IN OTHER SECTIONS

This section is referred to in sections 179*l*, 179m, 179s, 179t, 179u, 179v, 179w of this title.

§ 179o. Responsibilities and powers of Board

(a) In general

The Board shall review nominations of films submitted to it for inclusion in the National Film Registry and consult with the Librarian, as provided in section 179m of this title, with respect to the inclusion of such films in the Registry and the preservation of these and other films that are culturally, historically, or aesthetically significant.

(b) Nomination of films

The Board shall consider, for inclusion in the National Film Registry, nominations submitted by the general public as well as representatives of the film industry, such as the guilds and societies representing actors, directors, screenwriters, cinematographers, and other creative artists, producers, and film critics, archives and other film preservation organizations, and representatives of academic institutions with film study programs. The Board shall nominate not more than 25 films each year for inclusion in the Registry.

(c) Powers

(1) In general

The Board may, for the purpose of carrying out its duties, hold such hearings, sit and act at such times and places, take such testimony, and receive such evidence, as the Librarian and the Board consider appropriate.

---

[2] So in original. Probably should be followed by a hyphen.

(2) Service on Foundation

Two sitting members of the Board shall be appointed by the Librarian, and shall serve, as Board members of the National Film Preservation Foundation, in accordance with section 151703 of title 36.

(Pub. L. 104–285, title I, § 105, Oct. 11, 1996, 110 Stat. 3380.)

TERMINATION OF SECTION

For termination of section, see section 179w of this title.

CODIFICATION

"Section 151703 of title 36" substituted in subsec. (c)(2) for "section 203", meaning section 203 of the National Film Preservation Act of 1996, on authority of Pub. L. 105–225, § 5(b), Aug. 12, 1998, 112 Stat. 1499, the first section of which enacted Title 36, Patriotic and National Observances, Ceremonies, and Organizations.

SECTION REFERRED TO IN OTHER SECTIONS

This section is referred to in sections 179*l*, 179s, 179t, 179u, 179v, 179w of this title.

§ 179p. National Film Registry Collection of Library of Congress

(a) Acquisition of archival quality copies

The Librarian shall endeavor to obtain, by gift from the owner, an archival quality copy of the Registry version of each film included in the National Film Registry. Whenever possible, the Librarian shall endeavor to obtain the best surviving materials, including preprint materials. Copyright owners and others possessing copies of such materials are strongly encouraged, to further the preservation purposes of this Act, to provide preprint and other archival elements to the Library of Congress.

(b) Additional materials

The Librarian shall endeavor to obtain, for educational and research purposes, additional materials related to each film included in the National Film Registry, such as background materials, production reports, shooting scripts (including continuity scripts) and other similar materials.

(c) Property of United States

All copies of films on the National Film Registry that are received as gifts or bequests by the Librarian and other materials received by the Librarian under subsection (b) of this section, shall become the property of the United States Government, subject to the provisions of title 17.

(d) National Film Registry Collection

All copies of films on the National Film Registry that are received by the Librarian under subsection (a) of this section, and other materials received by the Librarian under subsection (b) of this section, shall be maintained in the Library of Congress and be known as the "National Film Registry Collection of the Library of Congress". The Librarian shall, by regulation, and in accordance with title 17, provide for reasonable access to the films and other materials in such collection for scholarly and research purposes.

(Pub. L. 104–285, title I, § 106, Oct. 11, 1996, 110 Stat. 3380.)

TERMINATION OF SECTION

For termination of section, see section 179w of this title.

REFERENCES IN TEXT

This Act, referred to in subsec. (a), is Pub. L. 104–285, Oct. 11, 1996, 110 Stat. 3377, which enacted this section and sections 179*l* to 179*o* and 179q to 179w of this title and sections 5701 to 5708 of former Title 36, Patriotic Societies and Observances, repealed sections 179 to 179k of this title, enacted provisions set out as a note under section 179*l* of this title, and repealed provisions set out as a note under section 179 of this title. Sections 5701 to 5708 of former Title 36 were repealed and reenacted as chapter 1517 (§ 151701 et seq.) of Title 36, Patriotic and National Observances, Ceremonies, and Organizations, by Pub. L. 105–225, § 5(b), Aug. 12, 1998, 112 Stat. 1499, the first section of which enacted Title 36. For complete classification of this Act to the Code, see Tables.

SECTION REFERRED TO IN OTHER SECTIONS

This section is referred to in sections 179*l*, 179s, 179t, 179u, 179v, 179w of this title.

§ 179q. Seal of National Film Registry

(a) Use of seal

(1) Prohibition on distribution and exhibition

No person shall knowingly distribute or exhibit to the public a version of a film or any copy of a film which bears the seal described in section 179m(a)(3) of this title if such film—

  (A) is not included in the National Film Registry; or

  (B) is included in the National Film Registry, but such film or film copy has not been approved for use of the seal by the Librarian pursuant to section 179m(a)(1)(D) of this title.

(2) Prohibition on promotion

No person shall knowingly use the seal described in section 179m(a)(3) of this title to promote any version of a film or film copy other than a Registry version.

(b) Effective date of seal

The use of the seal described in section 179m(a)(3) of this title shall be effective for each film after the Librarian publishes in the Federal Register, in accordance with section 179m(a)(2) of this title, the name of that film as selected for inclusion in the National Film Registry.

(Pub. L. 104–285, title I, § 107, Oct. 11, 1996, 110 Stat. 3381.)

TERMINATION OF SECTION

For termination of section, see section 179w of this title.

SECTION REFERRED TO IN OTHER SECTIONS

This section is referred to in sections 179*l*, 179r, 179s, 179t, 179u, 179v, 179w of this title.

§ 179r. Remedies

(a) Jurisdiction

The several district courts of the United States shall have jurisdiction, for cause shown, to prevent and restrain violations of section 179q(a) of this title.

(b) Relief

(1) Removal of seal

Except as provided in paragraph (2), relief for violation of section 179q(a) of this title

shall be limited to the removal of the seal of
the National Film Registry from the film involved in the violation.

(2) Fine and injunctive relief

In the case of a pattern or practice of the
willful violation of section 179q(a) of this title,
the United States district courts may order a
civil fine of not more than $10,000 and appro-
priate injunctive relief.

(Pub. L. 104–285, title I, §108, Oct. 11, 1996, 110
Stat. 3381.)

TERMINATION OF SECTION

*For termination of section, see section 179w of
this title.*

SECTION REFERRED TO IN OTHER SECTIONS

This section is referred to in sections 179*l*, 179s, 179t,
179u, 179v, 179w of this title.

§ 179s. Limitations of remedies

The remedies provided in section 179r of this
title shall be the exclusive remedies under sections 179*l* to 179w of this title, or any other Federal or State law, regarding the use of the seal
described in section 179m(a)(3) of this title.

(Pub. L. 104–285, title I, §109, Oct. 11, 1996, 110
Stat. 3381.)

TERMINATION OF SECTION

*For termination of section, see section 179w of
this title.*

SECTION REFERRED TO IN OTHER SECTIONS

This section is referred to in sections 179*l*, 179t, 179u,
179v, 179w of this title.

§ 179t. Staff of Board; experts and consultants

(a) Staff

The Librarian may appoint and fix the pay of
such personnel as the Librarian considers appropriate to carry out sections 179*l* to 179w of this
title.

(b) Experts and consultants

The Librarian may, in carrying out sections
179*l* to 179w of this title, procure temporary and
intermittent services under section 3109(b) of
title 5, but at rates for individuals not to exceed
the daily equivalent of the maximum rate of
basic pay payable for GS–15 of the General
Schedule. In no case may a member of the Board
or an alternate be paid as an expert or consultant under this section.

(Pub. L. 104–285, title I, §110, Oct. 11, 1996, 110
Stat. 3381.)

TERMINATION OF SECTION

*For termination of section, see section 179w of
this title.*

REFERENCES IN TEXT

The General Schedule, referred to in subsec. (b), is set
out under section 5332 of Title 5, Government Organization and Employees.

SECTION REFERRED TO IN OTHER SECTIONS

This section is referred to in sections 179*l*, 179s, 179u,
179v, 179w of this title.

§ 179u. Definitions

As used in sections 179*l* to 179w of this title—

(1) the term "Librarian" means the Librarian of Congress;

(2) the term "Board" means the National
Film Preservation Board;

(3) the term "film" means a "motion picture" as defined in section 101 of title 17, except that such term does not include any work
not originally fixed on film stock, such as a
work fixed on videotape or laser disk;

(4) the term "publication" means "publication" as defined in section 101 of title 17; and

(5) the term "Registry version" means, with
respect to a film, the version of a film first
published, or as complete a version as bona
fide preservation and restoration activities by
the Librarian, an archivist other than the Librarian, or the copyright owner can compile in
those cases where the original material has
been irretrievably lost.

(Pub. L. 104–285, title I, §111, Oct. 11, 1996, 110
Stat. 3382.)

TERMINATION OF SECTION

*For termination of section, see section 179w of
this title.*

SECTION REFERRED TO IN OTHER SECTIONS

This section is referred to in sections 179*l*, 179s, 179t,
179v, 179w of this title.

§ 179v. Authorization of appropriations

There are authorized to be appropriated to the
Librarian such sums as may be necessary to
carry out the purposes of sections 179*l* to 179w of
this title, but in no fiscal year shall such sum
exceed $250,000.

(Pub. L. 104–285, title I, §112, Oct. 11, 1996, 110
Stat. 3382.)

TERMINATION OF SECTION

*For termination of section, see section 179w of
this title.*

SECTION REFERRED TO IN OTHER SECTIONS

This section is referred to in sections 179*l*, 179s, 179t,
179u, 179w of this title.

§ 179w. Effective date

The provisions of sections 179*l* to 179w of this
title shall be effective for 7 years beginning on
October 11, 1996. The provisions of sections 179*l*
to 179w of this title shall apply to any copy of
any film, including those copies of films selected
for inclusion in the National Film Registry
under the National Film Preservation Act of
1988 and the National Film Preservation Act of
1992, except that any film so selected under either Act shall be deemed to have been selected
for the National Film Registry under sections
179*l* to 179w of this title.

(Pub. L. 104–285, title I, §113, Oct. 11, 1996, 110
Stat. 3382.)

REFERENCES IN TEXT

The National Film Preservation Act of 1988, referred
to in text, is Pub. L. 100–446, title I, §§1–13, Sept. 27,
1988, 102 Stat. 1782–1788, which was classified to sections
178 to 178*l* of this title and was repealed by Pub. L.
102–307, title II, §214, June 26, 1992, 106 Stat. 272.

The National Film Preservation Act of 1992, referred
to in text, is title II of Pub. L. 102–307, June 26, 1992, 106

Stat. 267, which was classified principally to sections 179 to 179k of this title and was repealed by Pub. L. 104–285, title I, § 114, Oct. 11, 1996, 110 Stat. 3382.

SECTION REFERRED TO IN OTHER SECTIONS

This section is referred to in sections 179l, 179s, 179t, 179u, 179v of this title.

§ 180. Legislative information retrieval system

(a) Purpose

The purpose of this section is to reduce the cost of information support for the Congress by eliminating duplication among systems which provide electronic access by Congress to legislative information.

(b) "Legislative information" defined

As used in this section, the term "legislative information" means information, prepared within the legislative branch, consisting of the text of publicly available bills, amendments, committee hearings, and committee reports, the text of the Congressional Record, data relating to bill status, data relating to legislative activity, and other similar public information that is directly related to the legislative process.

(c) Development of single system to serve entire Congress

Pursuant to the plan approved under subsection (d) of this section and consistent with the provisions of any other law, the Library of Congress or the entity designated by that plan shall develop and maintain, in coordination with other appropriate entities of the legislative branch, a single legislative information retrieval system to serve the entire Congress.

(d) Development and approval of plan

The Library shall develop a plan for creation of this system, taking into consideration the findings and recommendations of the study directed by House Report No. 103–517 to identify and eliminate redundancies in congressional information systems. This plan must be approved by the Committee on Rules and Administration of the Senate, the Committee on House Oversight of the House of Representatives, and the Committees on Appropriations of the Senate and the House of Representatives. The Library shall provide these committees with regular status reports on the development of the plan.

(e) Availability of information to public

In formulating its plan, the Library shall examine issues regarding efficient ways to make this information available to the public. This analysis shall be submitted to the Committees on Appropriations of the Senate and the House of Representatives as well as the Committee on Rules and Administration of the Senate, and the Committee on House Oversight of the House of Representatives for their consideration and possible action.

(Pub. L. 104–53, title II, § 209, Nov. 19, 1995, 109 Stat. 532.)

CHANGE OF NAME

Committee on House Oversight of House of Representatives changed to Committee on House Administration of House of Representatives by House Resolution No. 5, One Hundred Sixth Congress, Jan. 6, 1999.

§ 181. Program for exchange of information among legislative branch agencies

(a) On September 16, 1996, there shall be established a program for providing the widest possible exchange of information among legislative branch agencies with the long-range goal of improving information technology planning and evaluation. The Committee on House Oversight of the House of Representatives and the Committee on Rules and Administration of the Senate are requested to determine the structure and operation of this program and to provide appropriate oversight. All of the appropriate offices and agencies of the legislative branch as defined below shall participate in this program for information exchange, and shall report annually on the extent and nature of their participation in their budget submissions to the Committee on Appropriations of the House of Representatives and the Committee on Appropriations of the Senate.

(b) As used in this section—

(1) the term "offices and agencies of the legislative branch" means, the office of the Clerk of the House, the office of the Secretary of the Senate, the office of the Architect of the Capitol, the General Accounting Office, the Government Printing Office, the Library of Congress, the Congressional Research Service, the Congressional Budget Office, the Chief Administrative Officer of the House of Representatives, and the Sergeant at Arms of the Senate; and

(2) the term "technology" refers to any form of computer hardware and software; computer-based systems, services, and support for the creation, processing, exchange, and delivery of information; and telecommunications systems, and the associated hardware and software, that provide for voice, data, or image communication.

(Pub. L. 104–197, title III, § 314, Sept. 16, 1996, 110 Stat. 2415.)

CHANGE OF NAME

Committee on House Oversight of House of Representatives changed to Committee on House Administration of House of Representatives by House Resolution No. 5, One Hundred Sixth Congress, Jan. 6, 1999.

§ 182. Cooperative Acquisitions Program Revolving Fund

(a) Establishment

Effective October 1, 1997, there is established in the Treasury of the United States a revolving fund to be known as the Cooperative Acquisitions Program Revolving Fund (in this section referred to as the "revolving fund"). Moneys in the revolving fund shall be available to the Librarian of Congress, without fiscal year limitation, for financing the cooperative acquisitions program (in this section referred to as the "program") under which the Library acquires foreign publications and research materials on behalf of participating institutions on a cost-recovery basis. Obligations under the revolving fund are limited to amounts specified in the appropriations Act for that purpose for any fiscal year.

(b) Amounts deposited

The revolving fund shall consist of—

(1) any amounts appropriated by law for the purposes of the revolving fund;

(2) any amounts held by the Librarian as of October 1, 1997 or October 7, 1997, whichever is later, that were collected as payment for the Library's indirect costs of the program; and

(3) the difference between (A) the total value of the supplies, equipment, gift fund balances, and other assets of the program, and (B) the total value of the liabilities (including unfunded liabilities such as the value of accrued annual leave of employees) of the program.

(c) Credits to revolving fund

The revolving fund shall be credited with all advances and amounts received as payment for purchases under the program and services and supplies furnished to program participants, at rates estimated by the Librarian to be adequate to recover the full direct and indirect costs of the program to the Library over a reasonable period of time.

(d) Unobligated balances

Any unobligated and unexpended balances in the revolving fund that the Librarian determines to be in excess of amounts needed for activities financed by the revolving fund, shall be deposited in the Treasury of the United States as miscellaneous receipts. Amounts needed for activities financed by the revolving fund means the direct and indirect costs of the program, including the costs of purchasing, shipping, binding of books and other library materials; supplies, materials, equipment and services needed in support of the program; salaries and benefits; general overhead; and travel.

(e) Annual report

Not later than March 31 of each year, the Librarian of Congress shall prepare and submit to Congress an audited financial statement for the revolving fund for the preceding fiscal year. The audit shall be conducted in accordance with Government Auditing Standards for financial audits issued by the Comptroller General of the United States.

(Pub. L. 105–55, title II, § 207, Oct. 7, 1997, 111 Stat. 1193.)

§ 182a. Revolving fund for audio and video duplication services associated with audiovisual conservation center

(a) Establishment

There is hereby established in the Treasury a revolving fund for audio and video duplication and delivery services provided by the Librarian of Congress (hereafter in sections 182a to 182d of this title referred to as the "Librarian") which are associated with the national audiovisual conservation center established under the Act entitled "An Act to authorize acquisition of certain real property for the Library of Congress, and for other purposes", approved December 15, 1997 (Public Law 105–144; 2 U.S.C. 141 note).

(b) Fees for services

The Librarian may charge a fee for providing services described in subsection (a) of this section, and shall deposit any such fees charged into the revolving fund under this section.

(c) Contents of fund

(1) In general

The revolving fund under this section shall consist of the following amounts:

(A) Amounts deposited by the Librarian under subsection (b) of this section.

(B) Any other amounts received by the Librarian which are attributable to the services described in subsection (a) of this section.

(C) Amounts deposited by the Librarian under paragraph (2).

(D) Such other amounts as may be appropriated under law.

(2) Deposit of funds during transition

The Librarian shall transfer to the revolving fund under this section the following:

(A) Any obligated, unexpended balances existing as of the date of the transfer which are attributable to the services described in subsection (a) of this section.

(B) An amount equal to the difference as of such date between—

(i) the total value of the supplies, inventories, equipment, gift fund balances, and other assets attributable to such services; and

(ii) the total value of the liabilities attributable to such services.

(d) Use of amounts in fund

Amounts in the revolving fund under this section shall be available to the Librarian, in amounts specified in appropriations Acts and without fiscal year limitation, to carry out the services described in subsection (a) of this section.

(Pub. L. 106–481, title I, § 101, Nov. 9, 2000, 114 Stat. 2187.)

REFERENCES IN TEXT

Sections 182a to 182d of this title, referred to in subsec. (a), was in the original "this Act", meaning Pub. L. 106–481, Nov. 9, 2000, 114 Stat. 2187, known as the Library of Congress Fiscal Operations Improvement Act of 2000, which enacted this section and sections 182b to 182d of this title, amended section 154 of this title, and enacted provisions set out as notes under this section and section 154 of this title. For complete classification of this Act to the Code, see Short Title note below and Tables.

EFFECTIVE DATE

Pub. L. 106–481, title I, § 105, Nov. 9, 2000, 114 Stat. 2190, provided that: "The provisions of this title [enacting this section and sections 182b to 182d of this title and provisions set out as a note under this section] shall apply with respect to fiscal year 2002 and each succeeding fiscal year."

SHORT TITLE

Pub. L. 106–481, § 1, Nov. 9, 2000, 114 Stat. 2187, provided that: "This Act [enacting this section and sections 182b to 182d of this title, amending section 154 of this title, and enacting provisions set out as notes under this section and section 154 of this title] may be cited as the 'Library of Congress Fiscal Operations Improvement Act of 2000'."

§ 182b. Revolving fund for gift shop, decimal classification, photo duplication, and related services

(a) Establishment

There is hereby established in the Treasury a revolving fund for the following programs and activities of the Librarian:

(1) Decimal classification development.

(2) The operation of a gift shop or other sales of items associated with collections, exhibits, performances, and special events of the Library of Congress.

(3) Document reproduction and microfilming services.

(b) Individual accounting requirement

A separate account shall be maintained in the revolving fund under this section with respect to the programs and activities described in each of the paragraphs of subsection (a) of this section.

(c) Fees for services

The Librarian may charge a fee for services under any of the programs and activities described in subsection (a) of this section, and shall deposit any such fees charged into the account of the revolving fund under this section for such program or activity.

(d) Contents of accounts in fund

(1) In general

Each account of the revolving fund under this section shall consist of the following amounts:

(A) Amounts deposited by the Librarian under subsection (c) of this section.

(B) Any other amounts received by the Librarian which are attributable to the programs and activities covered by such account.

(C) Amounts deposited by the Librarian under paragraph (2).

(D) Such other amounts as may be appropriated under law.

(2) Deposit of funds during transition

The Librarian shall transfer to each account of the revolving fund under this section the following:

(A) Any obligated, unexpended balances existing as of the date of the transfer which are attributable to the programs and activities covered by such account.

(B) An amount equal to the difference as of such date between—

(i) the total value of the supplies, inventories, equipment, gift fund balances, and other assets attributable to such programs and activities; and

(ii) the total value of the liabilities attributable to such programs and activities.

(e) Use of amounts

Amounts in the accounts of the revolving fund under this section shall be available to the Librarian, in amounts specified in appropriations Acts and without fiscal year limitation, to carry out the programs and activities covered by such accounts.

(Pub. L. 106–481, title I, § 102, Nov. 9, 2000, 114 Stat. 2188.)

EFFECTIVE DATE

Section applicable with respect to fiscal year 2002 and each succeeding fiscal year, see section 105 of Pub. L. 106–481, set out as a note under section 182a of this title.

§ 182c. Revolving fund for FEDLINK program and Federal Research program

(a) Establishment

There is hereby established in the Treasury a revolving fund for the Federal Library and Information Network program (hereafter in sections 182a to 182d of this title referred to as the "FEDLINK program") of the Library of Congress (as described in subsection (f)(1) of this section) and the Federal Research program of the Library of Congress (as described in subsection (f)(2) of this section).

(b) Individual accounting requirement

A separate account shall be maintained in the revolving fund under this section with respect to the programs described in subsection (a) of this section.

(c) Fees for services

(1) In general

The Librarian may charge a fee for services under the FEDLINK program and the Federal Research program, and shall deposit any such fees charged into the account of the revolving fund under this section for such program.

(2) Advances of funds

Participants in the FEDLINK program and the Federal Research program shall pay for products and services of the program by advance of funds—

(A) if the Librarian determines that amounts in the Revolving Fund[1] are otherwise insufficient to cover the costs of providing such products and services; or

(B) upon agreement between participants and the Librarian.

(d) Contents of fund

(1) In general

Each account of the revolving fund under this section shall consist of the following amounts:

(A) Amounts deposited by the Librarian under subsection (c) of this section.

(B) Any other amounts received by the Librarian which are attributable to the program covered by such account.

(C) Amounts deposited by the Librarian under paragraph (2).

(D) Such other amounts as may be appropriated under law.

(2) Deposit of funds during transition

Notwithstanding section 1535(d) of title 31, the Librarian shall transfer to the appropriate account of the revolving fund under this section the following:

(A) Any obligated, unexpended balances existing as of the date of the transfer which are attributable to the FEDLINK program or the Federal Research program.

(B) An amount equal to the difference as of such date between—

---

[1] So in original. Probably should not be capitalized.

(i) the total value of the supplies, inventories, equipment, gift fund balances, and other assets attributable to such program; and

(ii) the total value of the liabilities attributable to such program.

(e) Use of amounts in fund

Amounts in the accounts of the revolving fund under this section shall be available to the Librarian, in amounts specified in appropriations Acts and without fiscal year limitation, to carry out the program covered by each such account.

(f) Programs described

(1) FEDLINK

In this section, the "FEDLINK program" is the program of the Library of Congress under which the Librarian provides the following services on behalf of participating Federal libraries, Federal information centers, other entities of the Federal Government, and the District of Columbia:

(A) The procurement of commercial information services, publications in any format, and library support services.

(B) Related accounting services.

(C) Related education, information, and support services.

(2) Federal Research program

In this section, the "Federal Research program" is the program of the Library of Congress under which the Librarian provides research reports, translations, and analytical studies for entities of the Federal Government and the District of Columbia (other than any program of the Congressional Research Service).

(Pub. L. 106–481, title I, § 103, Nov. 9, 2000, 114 Stat. 2189.)

References in Text

Sections 182a to 182d of this title, referred to in subsec. (a), was in the original "this Act", meaning Pub. L. 106–481, Nov. 9, 2000, 114 Stat. 2187, known as the Library of Congress Fiscal Operations Improvement Act of 2000, which enacted this section and sections 182b to 182d of this title, amended section 154 of this title, and enacted provisions set out as notes under this section and section 154 of this title. For complete classification of this Act to the Code, see Short Title note set out under section 182a of this title and Tables.

Effective Date

Section applicable with respect to fiscal year 2002 and each succeeding fiscal year, see section 105 of Pub. L. 106–481, set out as a note under section 182a of this title.

§ 182d. Audits by Comptroller General

Each of the revolving funds established under sections 182a to 182d of this title shall be subject to audit by the Comptroller General at the Comptroller General's discretion.

(Pub. L. 106–481, title I, § 104, Nov. 9, 2000, 114 Stat. 2190.)

Effective Date

Section applicable with respect to fiscal year 2002 and each succeeding fiscal year, see section 105 of Pub. L. 106–481, set out as a note under section 182a of this title.

§ 183. Written history of the House of Representatives

(a) In general

Subject to available funding and in accordance with the requirements of this section and section 183a of this title, the Librarian of Congress shall prepare, print, distribute, and arrange for the funding of, a new and complete written history of the House of Representatives, in consultation with the Committee on House Administration. In preparing this written history, the Librarian of Congress shall consult, commission, or engage the services or participation of, eminent historians, Members, and former Members of the House of Representatives.

(b) Guidelines

In carrying out subsection (a) of this section, the Librarian of Congress shall take into account the following:

(1) The history should be an illustrated, narrative history of the House of Representatives, organized chronologically.

(2) The history's intended audience is the general reader, as well as Members of Congress and their staffs.

(3) The history should include a discussion of the First and Second Continental Congresses and the Constitutional Convention, especially with regard to their roles in creating the House of Representatives.

(c) Printing

(1) In general

The Librarian of Congress shall arrange for the printing of the history.

(2) Printing arrangements

The printing may be performed—

(A) by the Public Printer pursuant to the provisions of chapter 5 of title 44;

(B) under a cooperative arrangement among the Librarian of Congress, a private funding source obtained pursuant to subsection (e) of this section, and a publisher in the private sector; or

(C) under subparagraphs (A) and (B).

(3) Internet dissemination

Any arrangement under paragraph (2) shall include terms for dissemination of the history over the Internet via facilities maintained by the United States Government.

(4) Member copies

To the extent that the history is printed by the Public Printer, copies of the history provided to the Congress under subsection (d) of this section shall be charged to the Government Printing Office's congressional allotment for printing and binding.

(d) Distribution

The Librarian of Congress shall make the history available for sale to the public, and shall make available, free of charge, 5 copies to each Member of the House of Representatives and 250 copies to the Senate.

(e) Private funding

The Librarian of Congress shall solicit and accept funding for the preparation, publication, marketing, and public distribution of the history from private individuals, organizations, or entities.

(Pub. L. 106–99, § 2, Nov. 12, 1999, 113 Stat. 1330.)

REFERENCES IN TEXT

This section and section 183a of this title, referred to in subsec. (a), was in the original "this Act", meaning Pub. L. 106–99, which enacted this section and section 183a of this title and provisions set out as a note under this section. For complete classification of this Act to the Code, see Short Title note set out under this section and Tables.

SHORT TITLE

Pub. L. 106–99, § 1, Nov. 12, 1999, 113 Stat. 1330, provided that: "This Act [enacting this section and section 183a of this title] may be cited as the 'History of the House Awareness and Preservation Act'."

§ 183a. Oral history of the House of Representatives

(a) In general

The Librarian of Congress shall accept for deposit, preserve, maintain, and make accessible an oral history of the House of Representatives, as told by its Members and former Members, compiled and updated (on a voluntary or contract basis) by the United States Association of Former Members of Congress or other private organization. In carrying out this section, the Librarian of Congress may enlist the voluntary aid or assistance of such organization, or may contract with it for such services as may be necessary.

(b) Definition of oral history

In this section, the term "oral history" means a story or history consisting of personal recollection as recorded by any one or more of the following means:

(1) Interviews.
(2) Transcripts.
(3) Audio recordings.
(4) Video recordings.
(5) Such other form or means as may be suitable for the recording and preservation of such information.

(Pub. L. 106–99, § 3, Nov. 12, 1999, 113 Stat. 1331.)

SECTION REFERRED TO IN OTHER SECTIONS

This section is referred to in section 183 of this title.

CHAPTER 6—CONGRESSIONAL AND COMMITTEE PROCEDURE; INVESTIGATIONS

§ 190. Repealed. S. Res. 4, § 301(b), Feb. 4, 1977

Section, act Aug. 2, 1946, ch. 753, title I, § 137, 60 Stat. 832, directed that controversies arising as to the jurisdiction of any standing committee of the Senate with respect to any proposed legislation be decided by the presiding officer of the Senate in favor of the committee having jurisdiction over the subject matter which predominated in the proposed legislation.

§§ 190a to 190a–2. Repealed. S. Res. 274, § 2(a), Nov. 14, 1979

Section 190a, acts Aug. 2, 1946, ch. 753, title 1, § 133, 60 Stat. 381; Oct. 26, 1970, Pub. L. 91–510, title I, §§ 102(a), 103(a), 104(a), 105(a), 106(a), 107(a), 108(a), 110(a), 84 Stat. 1143–1149; Dec. 16, 1970, Pub. L. 91–552, § 1(2), 84 Stat. 1440; Oct. 11, 1971, Pub. L. 92–136, § 3(a), (b), 85 Stat. 377; S. Res. 9, § 2, Nov. 5, 1975, related to meetings of the standing committees of the Senate. See the Standing Rules of the Senate.

Section 190a–1, act Aug. 2, 1946, ch. 753, title I, § 133A, as added Oct. 26, 1970, Pub. L. 91–510, title I, §§ 111(a)(1), 112(a), 113(a), 114(a), 115(a), 116(a), 84 Stat. 1151–1153; S. Res. 9, § 2, Nov. 5, 1975, related to Senate committee hearing procedures. See Standing Rules of the Senate.

Section 190a–2, act Aug. 2, 1946, ch. 753, title I, § 133B, as added Oct. 26, 1970, Pub. L. 91–510, title I, § 130(a), 84 Stat. 1163, related to Senate committee rules. See Standing Rules of the Senate.

§ 190a–3. Repealed. S. Res. 9, § 2, Nov. 5, 1975

Section, Pub. L. 93–344, title I, § 102(d), July 12, 1974, 88 Stat. 301, provided that meetings of Senate Committee on the Budget or any subcommittee thereof be open to public except in certain specified instances.

§§ 190b, 190c. Repealed. S. Res. 274, § 2(a), Nov. 14, 1979

Section 190b, acts Aug. 2, 1946, ch. 753, title I, § 134(a), (c), 60 Stat. 831, 832; Oct. 26, 1970, Pub. L. 91–510, title I, § 117(a), 84 Stat. 1155; Dec. 16, 1970, Pub. L. 91–552, § 1(6), 84 Stat. 1440; July 12, 1974, Pub. L. 93–344, title IX, § 903(a), 88 Stat. 331; S. Res. 4, § 402(c), Feb. 4, 1977, related to authority of Senate standing committees and subcommittees. See Standing Rules of the Senate.

Section 190c, acts Aug. 2, 1946, ch. 753, title I, § 135, 60 Stat. 832; Oct. 26, 1970, Pub. L. 91–510, title I, § 125(a)(2), 84 Stat. 1159, related to Senate conference reports. See Standing Rules of the Senate.

§ 190d. Legislative review by standing committees of the Senate and the House of Representatives

(a) Scope of assistance

In order to assist the Congress in—

(1) its analysis, appraisal, and evaluation of the application, administration, and execution of the laws enacted by the Congress, and

(2) its formulation, consideration, and enactment of such modifications of or changes in those laws, and of such additional legislation, as may be necessary or appropriate,

each standing committee of the Senate and the House of Representatives shall review and study, on a continuing basis, the application, administration, and execution of those laws, or parts of laws, the subject matter of which is within the jurisdiction of that committee. Such committees may carry out the required analysis, appraisal, and evaluation themselves, or by contract, or may require a Government agency to do so and furnish a report thereon to the Congress. Such committees may rely on such techniques as pilot testing, analysis of costs in comparison with benefits, or provision for evaluation after a defined period of time.

(b) Reports to the Senate and the House of Representatives

In each odd-numbered year beginning on or after January 1, 1973, each standing committee of the Senate shall submit, not later than March 31, to the Senate, and each standing committee of the House shall submit, not later than January 2, to the House, a report on the activities of that committee under this section during the Congress ending at noon on January 3 of such year.

(c) Exceptions

The preceding provisions of this section do not apply to the Committees on Appropriations and the Budget of the Senate and the Committees on Appropriations, the Budget, House Oversight, Rules, and Standards of Official Conduct of the House.

(Aug. 2, 1946, ch. 753, title I, § 136, 60 Stat. 832; Pub. L. 91–510, title I, § 118(a)(1), Oct. 26, 1970, 84 Stat. 1156; Pub. L. 92–136, § 1, Oct. 11, 1971, 85 Stat. 376; Pub. L. 93–344, title VII, § 701, title IX, § 903(b), July 12, 1974, 88 Stat. 325, 331; Pub. L. 104–186, title II, § 206(1), Aug. 20, 1996, 110 Stat. 1742.)

PARTIAL REPEAL

Section 2(a), S. Res. 274, Ninety-sixth Congress, Nov. 14, 1979, provided in part that this section, insofar as it relates to the Senate, is repealed. See Standing Rules of the Senate.

AMENDMENTS

1996—Subsec. (c). Pub. L. 104–186 substituted "House Oversight" for "House Administration".

1974—Subsec. (a). Pub. L. 93–344, § 701, authorized the committees to carry out the required analysis, appraisal, and evaluation themselves, or by contract, or

to require a Government agency to do so and furnish a report thereon to the Congress, and authorized the committees to rely on such techniques as pilot testing, analysis of costs in comparison with benefits, or provision for evaluation after a defined period of time.

Subsec. (c). Pub. L. 93–344, § 903(b), substituted "Committees on Appropriations and the Budget of the Senate and the Committees on Appropriations, the Budget," for "Committee on Appropriations of the Senate and the Committee on Appropriations,".

1971—Subsec. (a). Pub. L. 92–136 substituted "Congress" for "Senate" in provisions preceding cl. (1) and inserted reference to the House of Representatives in provisions following cl. (2).

Subsec. (b). Pub. L. 92–136 substituted "In each odd-numbered year beginning on or after January 1, 1973, each" for "Each" and "March 31, to the Senate, and each standing committee of the House shall submit, not later than January 2, to the House," for "March 31 of each odd-numbered year beginning on and after January 1, 1973, to the Senate".

Subsec. (c). Pub. L. 92–136 inserted reference to Committees on Appropriations, House Administration, Rules, and Standards of Official Conduct of the House.

1970—Subsec. (a). Pub. L. 91–510 incorporated existing subject matter in provisions designated as subsec. (a), restricted the text to standing committees of Senate, revised phraseology to require standing committees to review and study, on a continuing basis, application, administration, and execution of laws and parts of laws for prior provision for exercise of continuous watchfulness of execution of laws by administrative agencies concerned, and in providing for assistance to the Senate, rather than the Congress, included analysis and evaluation of laws enacted by Congress and substituted provision for formulation, consideration, and enactment of modifications or changes in the laws and of additional legislation as necessary or appropriate for prior provisions for assistance in developing amendments or related legislation as may be necessary.

Subsecs. (b), (c). Pub. L. 91–510 added subsecs. (b) and (c).

CHANGE OF NAME

Committee on House Oversight of House of Representatives changed to Committee on House Administration of House of Representatives by House Resolution No. 5, One Hundred Sixth Congress, Jan. 6, 1999.

EFFECTIVE DATE OF 1971 AMENDMENT

Section 9(a) of Pub. L. 92–136 provided that: "The amendments made by the first section [amending this section] section 2, and section 5 of this Act [amending section 72a of this title] shall become effective as of noon on January 3, 1971."

EFFECTIVE DATE OF 1970 AMENDMENT

Amendment by Pub. L. 91–510 effective immediately prior to noon on Jan. 3, 1971, see section 601(1) of Pub. L. 91–510, set out as a note under section 72a of this title.

EFFECTIVE DATE

Section effective Jan. 2, 1947, see section 142 of act Aug. 2, 1946.

§ 190e. Repealed. Pub. L. 91–510, title II, § 242(b)(1), Oct. 26, 1970, 84 Stat. 1172

Section, act Aug. 2, 1946, ch. 753, title I, § 138, 60 Stat. 832, related to report of legislative budget by Committee on Ways and Means and Committee on Appropriations of House and Committee on Finance and Committee on Appropriations of Senate, its contents, and concurrent resolution adopting the budget. See Rules of the House of Representatives and Standing Rules of the Senate.

EFFECTIVE DATE OF REPEAL

Repeal effective immediately prior to noon on Jan. 3, 1971, see section 601(1) of Pub. L. 91–510, set out as an

Effective Date of 1970 Amendment note under section 72a of this title.

§ 190f. General appropriation bills

(a) Repealed. Pub. L. 91–510, title I, § 108(d), Oct. 26, 1970, 84 Stat. 1149

(b) Standard appropriation classification schedule

The Committees on Appropriations of the two Houses are authorized and directed, acting jointly, to develop a standard appropriation classification schedule which will clearly define in concise and uniform accounts the subtotals of appropriations asked for by agencies in the executive branch of the Government. That part of the printed hearings containing each such agency's request for appropriations shall be preceded by such a schedule.

(c) Nonconsideration if a provision reappropriates unexpended balances

No general appropriation bill or amendment thereto shall be received or considered in either House if it contains a provision reappropriating unexpended balances of appropriations; except that this provision shall not apply to appropriations in continuation of appropriations for public works on which work has commenced.

(Aug. 2, 1946, ch. 753, title I, §139(a), (b), (c), 60 Stat. 833; Pub. L. 91–510, title I, §108(d), Oct. 26, 1970, 84 Stat. 1149.)

PARTIAL REPEAL

Section 2(a), S. Res. 274, Ninety-sixth Congress, Nov. 14, 1979, provided in part that this section, insofar as it relates to the Senate, is repealed. See Standing Rules of the Senate.

CODIFICATION

Section constitutes subsections (a) to (c) of section 139 of act Aug. 2, 1946. Subsection (d) of section 139, which required the two Houses of Congress to make a study of existing permanent appropriations with a view to limiting the number thereof and to recommending what permanent appropriations should be discontinued, and of the disposition of funds resulting from the sale of Government property or services by all departments and agencies in the executive branch of the Government with a view to recommending a uniform system of control with respect to those funds, was omitted from the Code as being of a temporary character.

AMENDMENTS

1970—Subsec. (a). Pub. L. 91–510 repealed prohibition against consideration of any general appropriation bill in either House unless prior to such consideration printed committee hearings and reports on the bill have been available for at least three calendar days for the Members of the House considering the bill, which was incorporated in section 190a(f) of this title.

EFFECTIVE DATE OF 1970 AMENDMENT

Amendment by Pub. L. 91–510 effective immediately prior to noon on Jan. 3, 1971, see section 601(1) of Pub. L. 91–510, set out as a note under section 72a of this title.

EFFECTIVE DATE

Section effective Jan. 2, 1947, see section 142 of act Aug. 2, 1946.

§ 190g. Nonconsideration of certain private bills and resolutions

No private bill or resolution (including so-called omnibus claims or pension bills), and no amendment to any bill or resolution, authorizing or directing (1) the payment of money for property damages, for personal injuries or death for which suit may be instituted under the Federal Tort Claims Act, or for a pension (other than to carry out a provision of law or treaty stipulation); (2) the construction of a bridge across a navigable stream; or (3) the correction of a military or naval record, shall be received or considered in either the Senate or the House of Representatives.

(Aug. 2, 1946, ch. 753, title I, §131, 60 Stat. 831.)

PARTIAL REPEAL

Section 2(a), S. Res. 274, Ninety-sixth Congress, Nov. 14, 1979, provided in part that this section, insofar as it relates to the Senate, is repealed. See Standing Rules of the Senate.

REFERENCES IN TEXT

The Federal Tort Claims Act, referred to in text, is classified generally to section 1346(b) and chapter 171 (§2671 et seq.) of Title 28, Judiciary and Judicial Procedure.

EFFECTIVE DATE

Section effective Jan. 2, 1947, see section 142 of act Aug. 2, 1946.

§ 190h. Repealed. S. Res. 9, § 2, Nov. 5, 1975

Section, Pub. L. 91–510, title II, §242(a), Oct. 26, 1970, 84 Stat. 1171, provided that each meeting conducted by Senate Committee on Appropriations be open to the public except when testimony to be taken might relate to a matter of national security, tend to reflect adversely on character or reputation of witness or other individual, or divulge matters deemed confidential under other provisions of law or regulations.

§§ 190i to 190k. Repealed. S. Res. 274, § 2(b), Nov. 14, 1979

Section 190i, Pub. L. 91–510, title II, § 243, Oct. 26, 1970, 84 Stat. 1173, related to actions and procedures of the Committee on Appropriations of Senate. See Standing Rules of the Senate.

Section 190j, Pub. L. 91–510, title II, § 252(a), Oct. 26, 1970, 84 Stat. 1173; Aug. 1, 1946, ch. 724, § 302(d), as added Aug. 30, 1954, ch. 1073, § 1, as added Sept. 20, 1977, Pub. L. 95–110, § 1, 91 Stat. 884, related to cost estimates in reports of Senate committees accompanying certain legislative measures and to other Senate committee operations. See Standing Rules of the Senate.

Section 190k, Pub. L. 91–510, title II, § 253(a), (b), Oct. 26, 1970, 84 Stat. 1174, related to appropriations on an annual basis for continuing programs and activities and review by Senate and joint committees. See Standing Rules of the Senate.

§ 190*l*. Private claims pending before Congress; taking of testimony

Any committee of either House of Congress before which any private claim against the United States may at any time be pending, being first thereto authorized by the House appointing them, may order testimony to be taken, and books and papers to be examined, and copies thereof proved, before any standing master in chancery within the judicial district where such testimony or evidence is to be taken. Such master in chancery, upon receiving a copy of the order of such committee, signed by its chairman, setting forth the time and place when and where such examination is to be had, the questions to be investigated, and, so far as may be known to the committee, the names of the witnesses to be examined on the part of the United States, and the general nature of the books, papers, and documents to be proved, if known, shall proceed to give to such private parties reasonable notice of the time and place of such examination, unless such notice shall have been or shall be given by such committee or its chairman, or by the attorney or agent of the United States, or waived by such private party. And such master shall issue subpoenas for such witnesses as may have been named in the order of such committee, and such others as the agent or other representative of the United States hereinafter mentioned shall request. And he shall also issue subpoenas at the request of such private party, or parties, for such witnesses within such judicial district as they may desire: *Provided*, That the United States shall not be liable for the fees of any officer for serving any subpoena for any private party, nor for the fees of any witness on behalf of such party. Said committee may inform the United States attorney for the district where the testimony is to be taken of the time, place, and object of such examination, and request his attendance in behalf of the Government in conducting such examination, in which case it shall be his duty to attend in person, or by an assistant employed by him, to conduct such examination on the part of the United States, or such committee may, at its option, appoint an agent or attorney, or one of its own members, for that purpose, as they may deem best; and in that event, if the committee shall not be unanimous, the minority of the committee may also appoint such agent or attorney or member of such committee to attend and take part in such examination.

(Feb. 3, 1879, ch. 40, § 1, 20 Stat. 278; Mar. 3, 1911, ch. 231, § 291, 36 Stat. 1167; June 25, 1948, ch. 646, § 1, 62 Stat. 909.)

CODIFICATION

This section and section 190m of this title were an act entitled "An act to provide for taking testimony, to be used before Congress, in cases of private claims against the United States."

The original text referred to "any standing master in chancery of the circuit of the United States within the judicial district where such testimony or evidence is to be taken." The words "of the circuit of the United States" were omitted as inappropriate since the abolition of circuit courts by act Mar. 3, 1911.

Section was formerly classified to section 229 of Title 31 prior to the general revision and enactment of Title 31, Money and Finance, by Pub. L. 97–258, § 1, Sept. 13, 1982, 96 Stat. 877.

CHANGE OF NAME

Act June 25, 1948, eff. Sept. 1, 1948, substituted "United States attorney" for "district attorney of the United States". See section 541 of Title 28, Judiciary and Judicial Procedure, and Historical and Revision Notes thereunder.

SECTION REFERRED TO IN OTHER SECTIONS

This section is referred to in section 190m of this title.

§ 190m. Subpoena for taking testimony; compensation of officers and witnesses; return of depositions

It shall be the duty of the marshal of the United States for the district in which the testimony is to be taken to serve, or cause to be served, all subpoenas issued in behalf of the United States under this section and section 190*l* of this title, in the same manner as if issued by the district court for his district; and he shall, upon being first paid his fees therefor, serve any subpoenas that may be issued at the instance of such private party or parties. And the said master may, in his discretion, appoint any other person to serve any subpoena. Such master shall have full power to administer oaths to witnesses, and the same power to issue attachments to compel the attendance of witnesses and the production of books, papers, and documents, as the district court of his district would have in a case pending before it; and it shall be his duty to report the conduct of contumacious witnesses before him to the House of Congress appointing such committee. The compensation of such master in chancery, and the fees of marshals and deputy marshals, and of any person appointed to serve papers, shall be the same as for like services in equity cases in the district court of the United States; and the compensation of witnesses shall be the same as for like attendance and travel of witnesses before such district courts; and all such fees and compensation of officers and witnesses on behalf of the United States, and other expenses of all investigations which may be had under the provisions of this section and section 190*l* of this title on the part of the United States, shall be paid out of the contingent fund of the Senate, in the case of a committee of the Senate, or the applicable accounts of the House of Representatives, in the case of a committee of the House of Representatives. Said master, when the examination is concluded, shall attach together all the depositions and exhibits, and attach thereto his certificate setting forth or referring to the authority by which they were taken, any notices he may have given, the names of the witnesses for whom subpoenas or attachments were issued, the names of witnesses who attended, with the time of attendance and mileage and fees of each witness on behalf of the United States, which he may require to be shown by affidavit, his own fees, the fees of the marshal, his deputies or other persons serving papers, giving the items, and such other facts in relation to the circumstances connected with the taking of the depositions as he may deem material. He shall then seal up such depositions and papers securely, direct them to the chairman of such committee at Washington, stating briefly on the outside the nature of the contents, and place the same in the post office, paying the postage thereon; and said package shall be opened only in the presence of such committee. The chairman of any committee ordering testimony to be taken under this section and section 190*l* of this title shall, at least ten days before the time fixed for such examination, and within two days after the adoption of such order, cause a copy thereof to be directed and delivered to the Attorney General of the United

States, or sent to him by mail at the Department of Justice, to enable him to give such instructions as he may deem best to the United States attorney of the district where such testimony is to be taken, who may, and, if required by the Attorney General, shall, though not requested by the committee, appear for the United States in person or by assistant, and take such part in such examination as the Attorney General shall direct.

(Feb. 3, 1879, ch. 40, §2, 20 Stat. 279; Mar. 3, 1911, ch. 231, §291, 36 Stat. 1167; June 25, 1948, ch. 646, §1, 62 Stat. 909; Pub. L. 104–186, title II, §206(2), Aug. 20, 1996, 110 Stat. 1742.)

CODIFICATION

Upon its incorporation into the Code, references in this section to the circuit courts were omitted or changed to refer to the district courts to conform to act Mar. 3, 1911, which abolished the circuit courts.

Section was formerly classified to section 230 of Title 31 prior to the general revision and enactment of Title 31, Money and Finance, by Pub. L. 97–258, §1, Sept. 13, 1982, 96 Stat. 877.

AMENDMENTS

1996—Pub. L. 104–186 substituted "contingent fund of the Senate, in the case of a committee of the Senate, or the applicable accounts of the House of Representatives, in the case of a committee of the House of Representatives." for "contingent fund of the branch of Congress appointing such committee."

CHANGE OF NAME

Act June 25, 1948, eff. Sept. 1, 1948, substituted "United States attorney" for "district attorney of the United States". See section 541 of Title 28, Judiciary and Judicial Procedure, and Historical and Revision Notes thereunder.

§ 191. Oaths to witnesses

The President of the Senate, the Speaker of the House of Representatives, or a chairman of any joint committee established by a joint or concurrent resolution of the two Houses of Congress, or of a committee of the whole, or of any committee of either House of Congress, is empowered to administer oaths to witnesses in any case under their examination.

Any member of either House of Congress may administer oaths to witnesses in any matter depending in either House of Congress of which he is a Member, or any committee thereof.

(R.S. §101; June 26, 1884, ch. 123, 23 Stat. 60; June 22, 1938, ch. 594, 52 Stat. 942, 943.)

CODIFICATION

R.S. §101 derived from acts May 3, 1798, ch. 36, §1, 1 Stat. 554, and Feb. 8, 1817, ch. 10, 3 Stat. 345.

R.S. §101 constitutes first sentence, and act June 26, 1884, constitutes second sentence.

AMENDMENTS

1938—Act June 22, 1938, reenacted section without change.

§ 192. Refusal of witness to testify or produce papers

Every person who having been summoned as a witness by the authority of either House of Congress to give testimony or to produce papers upon any matter under inquiry before either House, or any joint committee established by a joint or concurrent resolution of the two Houses of Congress, or any committee of either House of Congress, willfully makes default, or who, having appeared, refuses to answer any question pertinent to the question under inquiry, shall be deemed guilty of a misdemeanor, punishable by a fine of not more than $1,000 nor less than $100 and imprisonment in a common jail for not less than one month nor more than twelve months.

(R.S. §102; June 22, 1938, ch. 594, 52 Stat. 942.)

CODIFICATION

R.S. §102 derived from act Jan. 24, 1857, ch. 19, §1, 11 Stat. 155.

AMENDMENTS

1938—Act June 22, 1938, reenacted section without change.

SECTION REFERRED TO IN OTHER SECTIONS

This section is referred to in section 194 of this title.

§ 193. Privilege of witnesses

No witness is privileged to refuse to testify to any fact, or to produce any paper, respecting which he shall be examined by either House of Congress, or by any joint committee established by a joint or concurrent resolution of the two Houses of Congress, or by any committee of either House, upon the ground that his testimony to such fact or his production of such paper may tend to disgrace him or otherwise render him infamous.

(R.S. §103; June 22, 1938, ch. 594, 52 Stat. 942.)

CODIFICATION

R.S. §103 derived from act Jan. 24, 1862, ch. 11, 12 Stat. 333.

AMENDMENTS

1938—Act June 22, 1938, reenacted section without change.

§ 194. Certification of failure to testify or produce; grand jury action

Whenever a witness summoned as mentioned in section 192 of this title fails to appear to testify or fails to produce any books, papers, records, or documents, as required, or whenever any witness so summoned refuses to answer any question pertinent to the subject under inquiry before either House, or any joint committee established by a joint or concurrent resolution of the two Houses of Congress, or any committee or subcommittee of either House of Congress, and the fact of such failure or failures is reported to either House while Congress is in session or when Congress is not in session, a statement of fact constituting such failure is reported to and filed with the President of the Senate or the Speaker of the House, it shall be the duty of the said President of the Senate or Speaker of the House, as the case may be, to certify, and he shall so certify, the statement of facts aforesaid under the seal of the Senate or House, as the case may be, to the appropriate United States attorney, whose duty it shall be to bring the matter before the grand jury for its action.

(R.S. § 104; July 13, 1936, ch. 884, 49 Stat. 2041; June 22, 1938, ch. 594, 52 Stat. 942.)

CODIFICATION

R.S. § 104 derived from act Jan. 24, 1857, ch. 19, § 3, 11 Stat. 156.

AMENDMENTS

1938—Act June 22, 1938, substituted "section 102" for "section 102 of the Revised Statutes" and inserted "or any joint committee established by a joint or concurrent resolution of the two Houses of Congress".

1936—Act July 13, 1936, substituted "section 102 of the Revised Statutes" for "section 102", inserted provisions as to failure to produce and refusal to answer, required a statement of facts constituting the failure to be reported to and filed with the President of the Senate or the Speaker of the House, and directed that said President or Speaker certify the facts to the appropriate United States attorney in lieu of prior certification to the district attorney for the District of Columbia.

SECTION REFERRED TO IN OTHER SECTIONS

This section is referred to in sections 288d, 288g of this title.

§ 194a. Request by Congressional committees to officers or employees of Federal departments, agencies, etc., concerned with foreign countries or multilateral organizations for expression of views and opinions

Upon the request of a committee of either House of Congress, a joint committee of Congress, or a member of such committee, any officer or employee of the Department of State, the Agency for International Development, or any other department, agency, or independent establishment of the United States Government primarily concerned with matters relating to foreign countries or multilateral organizations may express his views and opinions, and make recommendations he considers appropriate, if the request of the committee or member of the committee relates to a subject which is within the jurisdiction of that committee.

(Pub. L. 92–352, title V, § 502, July 13, 1972, 86 Stat. 496; Pub. L. 93–126, § 17, Oct. 18, 1973, 87 Stat. 455; Pub. L. 105–277, div. G, subdiv. A, title XII, § 1225(g), title XIII, § 1335(n), Oct. 21, 1998, 112 Stat. 2681–775, 2681–789.)

AMENDMENTS

1998—Pub. L. 105–277, § 1335(n), struck out "the United States Information Agency," after "Department of State,".

Pub. L. 105–277, § 1225(g), struck out "the United States Arms Control and Disarmament Agency," after "International Development,".

1973—Pub. L. 93–126 substituted "or employee of" for "appointed by the President, by and with the advice and consent of the Senate, to a position in".

EFFECTIVE DATE OF 1998 AMENDMENT

Amendment by section 1225(g) of Pub. L. 105–277 effective Apr. 1, 1999, see section 1201 of Pub. L. 105–277, set out as an Effective Date note under section 6511 of Title 22, Foreign Relations and Intercourse.

Amendment by section 1335(n) of Pub. L. 105–277 effective Oct. 1, 1999, see section 1301 of Pub. L. 105–277, set out as an Effective Date note under section 6531 of Title 22, Foreign Relations and Intercourse.

§ 194b. Omitted

CODIFICATION

Section, Pub. L. 100–418, title V, § 5421, Aug. 23, 1988, 102 Stat. 1468, which directed President or head of ap-

propriate department or agency to include in every recommendation or report made to Congress on legislation which might affect ability of United States firms to compete in domestic and international commerce a statement of impact of such legislation on international trade and public interest and ability of United States firms engaged in the manufacture, sale, distribution, or provision of goods or services to compete in foreign or domestic markets, ceased to be effective six years from Aug. 23, 1988, pursuant to subsec. (c) of section.

§ 195. Fees of witnesses in District of Columbia

Witnesses residing in the District of Columbia and not in the service of the government of said District or of the United States, who shall be summoned to give testimony before any committee of the House of Representatives, shall not be allowed exceeding $2 for each day's attendance before said committee.

(May 1, 1876, ch. 88, 19 Stat. 41.)

HOUSE RULE ON PAY OF WITNESSES

Rule XI, clause 5, Rules of the House of Representatives, provides that: "Witnesses appearing before the House or any of its committees shall be paid the same per diem rate as established, authorized, and regulated by the Committee on House Administration for Members, Delegates, the Resident Commissioner, and employees of the House, plus actual expenses of travel to or from the place of examination. Such per diem may not be paid when a witness has been summoned at the place of examination."

§ 195a. Restriction on payment of witness fees or travel and subsistence expenses to persons subpenaed by Congressional committees

No part of any appropriation disbursed by the Secretary of the Senate shall be available on and after July 12, 1960, for the payment to any person, at the time of the service upon him of a subpena requiring his attendance at any inquiry or hearing conducted by any committee of the Congress or of the Senate or any subcommittee of any such committee, of any witness fee or any sum of money as an advance payment of any travel or subsistence expense which may be incurred by such person in responding to that subpena.

(Pub. L. 86–628, July 12, 1960, 74 Stat. 449.)

§ 195b. Fees for witnesses requested to appear before Majority Policy Committee or Minority Policy Committee

Any witness requested to appear before the Majority Policy Committee or the Minority Policy Committee shall be entitled to a witness fee for each full day spent in traveling to and from the place at which he is to appear, and reimbursement of actual and necessary transportation expenses incurred in traveling to and from that place, at rates not to exceed those rates paid witnesses appearing before committees of the Senate.

(Pub. L. 93–371, § 7, Aug. 13, 1974, 88 Stat. 431.)

§ 196. Senate resolutions for investigations; limit of cost

Senate resolutions providing for inquiries and investigations shall contain a limit of cost of such investigation, which limit shall not be exceeded except by vote of the Senate authorizing additional amounts.

(Mar. 3, 1926, ch. 44, § 1, 44 Stat. 162.)

§ 197. Compensation of employees

The rate of compensation for any position under the appropriations now available for, or hereafter made for, expenses of inquiries and investigations of the Senate or expenses of special and select committees of the House of Representatives shall not exceed the rates fixed under chapter 51 and subchapter III of chapter 53 of title 5, for positions with comparable duties; and the salary limitations of $3,600 attached to appropriations heretofore made for expenses of inquiries and investigations of the Senate or for expenses of special and select committees of the House of Representatives are repealed.

(Feb. 9, 1937, ch. 9, title I, § 1, 50 Stat. 9; Oct. 28, 1949, ch. 782, title XI, § 1106(a), 63 Stat. 972.)

CODIFICATION

"Chapter 51 and subchapter III of chapter 53 of title 5" substituted in text for "the Classification Act of 1949" on authority of section 7(b) of Pub. L. 89–554, Sept. 6, 1966, 80 Stat. 631, section 1 of which enacted Title 5, Government Organization and Employees.

AMENDMENTS

1949—Act Oct. 28, 1949, substituted "Classification Act of 1949" for "Classification Act of 1923".

REPEALS

Act Oct. 28, 1949, ch. 782, cited as a credit to this section, was repealed (subject to a savings clause) by Pub. L. 89–554, Sept. 6, 1966, § 8, 80 Stat. 632, 655.

§ 198. Adjournment

(a) Unless otherwise provided by the Congress, the two Houses shall—

(1) adjourn sine die not later than July 31 of each year; or

(2) in the case of an odd-numbered year, provide, not later than July 31 of such year, by concurrent resolution adopted in each House by roll-call vote, for the adjournment of the two Houses from that Friday in August which occurs at least thirty days before the first Monday in September (Labor Day) of such year to the second day after Labor Day.

(b) This section shall not be applicable in any year if on July 31 of such year a state of war exists pursuant to a declaration of war by the Congress.

(Aug. 2, 1946, ch. 753, title I, § 132, 60 Stat. 831; Pub. L. 91–510, title IV, § 461(b), Oct. 26, 1970, 84 Stat. 1193.)

AMENDMENTS

1970—Pub. L. 95–110, in amending section generally, incorporated existing subject matter in subsec. (a)(1), substituted therein an adjournment date not later than July 31 of each year for prior provision for a date not later than last day (Sundays excepted) in month of July in each year, added subsec. (a)(2), added subsec. (b) which incorporated former exception to adjournment in time of war, and deleted another exception to adjournment during national emergency proclaimed by the President.

EFFECTIVE DATE OF 1970 AMENDMENT

Amendment by Pub. L. 91–510 effective immediately prior to noon on Jan. 3, 1971, see section 601(1) of Pub.

L. 91–510, set out as a note under section 72a of this title.

EFFECTIVE DATE

Section effective Jan. 2, 1947, see section 142 of act Aug. 2, 1946.

§ 199. Member of commission, board, etc., appointed by President pro tempore of Senate; recommendation process; applicability

(a) Any provision of law which provides that any member of a commission, board, committee, advisory group, or similar body is to be appointed by the President pro tempore of the Senate shall be construed to require that the appointment be made—

(1) upon recommendation of the Majority Leader of the Senate, if such provision of law specifies that the appointment is to be made on the basis of the appointee's affiliation with the majority political party,

(2) upon the recommendation of the Minority Leader of the Senate, if such provision of law specifies that the appointment is to be made on the basis of the appointee's affiliation with the minority party, and

(3) upon the joint recommendation of the Majority Leader of the Senate and the Minority Leader of the Senate, if such provision of law does not specify that the appointment is to be made on the appointee's affiliation with the majority or minority political party.

(b) The provisions of subsection (a) of this section shall be applicable in the case of appointments made after December 22, 1980, pursuant to provisions of law enacted on, before, and after December 22, 1980.

(Pub. L. 96–576, § 3, Dec. 22, 1980, 94 Stat. 3355.)

CHAPTER 7—CONTESTED ELECTIONS

§§ 201 to 226. Repealed. Pub. L. 91–138, § 18, Dec. 5, 1969, 83 Stat. 290

The subject matter of former sections 201 to 226 of this title is covered generally by chapter 12 of this title.

Section 201, R.S. § 105, provided that whenever any person intended to contest an election of any member of House of Representatives he had to give notice in writing to that member within thirty days of result of such election.

Section 202, R.S. § 106, provided that a member of House of Representatives whose election was contested serve an answer within thirty days after service of notice upon him.

Section 203, R.S. § 107; Mar. 2, 1875, ch. 119, § 2, 18 Stat. 338, provided time and order for taking testimony.

Section 204, R.S. § 108, provided for taking of depositions upon notice to other party.

Section 205, R.S. § 109, provided that testimony in contested election cases could be taken at two or more places at same time.

Section 206, R.S. § 110; June 7, 1878, ch. 160, 20 Stat. 99; July 1, 1898, ch. 541, § 38, 30 Stat. 555, made provision for issuance of subpoenas by specified officers.

Section 207, R.S. § 111, set forth requisite contents of subpoenas.

Section 208, R.S. § 112, authorized issuance of subpoenas by justices of the peace.

Section 209, R.S. § 113, made provision for taking of depositions by written consent.

Section 210, R.S. § 114, required that each witness be served with a subpoena at least five days prior to date he was required to attend.

Section 211, R.S. § 115, exempted witness from attendance at examinations out of county in which they resided or were served with a subpoena.

Section 212, R.S. § 116, mandated a $20 penalty to be recovered by party issuing subpoena, and a possible indictment for a misdemeanor, for failure of party summoned to attend or testify, unless prevented by sickness or unavoidable necessity.

Section 213, R.S. § 117, provided that depositions of witnesses residing outside district be taken before any officer authorized to take testimony in contested election cases in district in which witness resided.

Section 214, R.S. § 118, required selection of qualified officers to officiate jointly with officer named in notice.

Section 215, R.S. § 119, provided that at taking of any deposition under this chapter, either party could appear and act in person, or by agent or attorney.

Section 216, R.S. § 120, made provision for examination of witnesses through device of taking their depositions before a qualified officer.

Section 217, R.S. § 121, provided that testimony to be taken by either party be confined to proof or disproof of facts alleged or denied in notice and answer.

Section 218, R.S. § 122, required officer to reduce to writing testimony of witnesses, together with questions proposed by parties, and have this writing duly attested by witnesses.

Section 219, R.S. § 123, empowered officer to require production of papers.

Section 220, R.S. § 124, provided that taking of testimony might, if so stated in notice, be adjourned from day to day.

Section 221, R.S. § 125, provided that notice to take depositions, with proof of service thereof, and a copy of the subpoena, where one has been served, be attached to depositions when completed.

Section 222, R.S. § 126, provided that a copy of notice of contest and of answer of returned member, be prefixed to depositions taken and transmitted with them to Clerk of House of Representatives.

Section 223, R.S. § 127; Mar. 2, 1875, ch. 119, § 1, 18 Stat. 338; Mar. 2, 1887, ch. 318, 24 Stat. 445, covered procedure followed by Clerk of House of Representatives once the sealed testimony was forwarded to him by officer who took testimony.

Section 224, R.S. § 128, fixed witness fees to be paid by party at whose instance witness was summoned.

Section 225, R.S. § 129, provided that each officer employed pursuant to this chapter be entitled to receive from party who employed him, such fees as were allowed for similar services in State wherein such service was rendered.

Section 226, R.S. § 130; Mar. 3, 1879, ch. 182, § 1, 20 Stat. 400, limited payments of expenses to contestee or contestant to $2,000, and then, only upon filing of a detailed account of expenses with Clerk of Committee on Elections.

EFFECTIVE DATE OF REPEAL

Repeal applicable with respect to any general or special election for Representative in, or Resident Commissioner to, the Congress of the United States occurring after December 5, 1969, see section 19 of Pub. L. 91–138, set out as an Effective Date note under section 381 of this title.

CHAPTER 8—FEDERAL CORRUPT PRACTICES

§§ 241 to 248. Repealed. Pub. L. 92–225, title IV, § 405, Feb. 7, 1972, 86 Stat. 20

Sections, act Feb. 28, 1925, ch. 368, title III, §§ 302–309, 43 Stat. 1070–1073, provided for:

Section 241, amended Dec. 23, 1971, Pub. L. 92–220, § 2, 85 Stat. 795, definitions;

Section 242, chairman and treasurer of political committees, duties as to contributions, and accounts and receipts;

Section 243, accounts of contributions received;

Section 244, statements by treasurer filed with Clerk of House of Representatives;

Section 245, statements by others than political committee filed with Clerk of House of Representatives;

Section 246, statements by candidates for Senator, Representative, Delegate, or Resident Commissioner filed with Secretary of Senate and Clerk of House of Representatives;

Section 247, statements: verification, preservation, and inspection; and

Section 248, limitation upon amount of expenditures by candidate.

Such former provisions are covered generally by chapter 14 (§ 431 et seq.) of this title.

EFFECTIVE DATE OF REPEAL

Repeal effective 60 days after Feb. 7, 1972, see section 408 of Pub. L. 92–225, set out as an Effective Date note under section 431 of this title.

§§ 249 to 251. Repealed. June 25, 1948, ch. 645, § 21, 62 Stat. 862, eff. Sept. 1, 1948

Section 249, act Feb. 28, 1925, ch. 368, title III, § 310, 43 Stat. 1073, related to promises or pledges by candidates. See section 599 of Title 18, Crimes and Criminal Procedure.

Section 250, act Feb. 28, 1925, ch. 368, title III, § 311, 43 Stat. 1073, related to expenditures to influence voting. See section 597 of Title 18.

Section 251, acts Feb. 28, 1925, ch. 368, title III, § 313, 43 Stat. 1074; June 25, 1943, ch. 144, § 9, 57 Stat. 167; June 23, 1947, ch. 120, title III, § 304, 61 Stat. 159, related to political contributions by national banks, corporations, or labor unions. See section 441b of this title.

§§ 252 to 256. Repealed. Pub. L. 92–225, title IV, § 405, Feb. 7, 1972, 86 Stat. 20

Sections 252 to 255, act Feb. 28, 1925, ch. 368, title III, §§ 314–317, 43 Stat. 1074, provided for general penalties for violations, expenses of election contests, no effect on State laws, and partial invalidity.

Section 256, act Feb. 28, 1925, ch. 368, title III, § 301, 43 Stat. 1070, provided for citation of act Feb. 28, 1925, as the "Federal Corrupt Practices Act".

Such former provisions are covered generally by chapter 14 (§ 431 et seq.) of this title.

EFFECTIVE DATE OF REPEAL

Repeal effective 60 days after Feb. 7, 1972, see section 408 of Pub. L. 92–225, set out as an Effective Date note under section 431 of this title.

CHAPTER 8A—REGULATION OF LOBBYING

§§ 261 to 270. Repealed. Pub. L. 104–65, § 11(a), Dec. 19, 1995, 109 Stat. 701

Section 261, act Aug. 2, 1946, ch. 753, title III, § 302, 60 Stat. 839, defined terms used in this chapter.

Section 262, act Aug. 2, 1946, ch. 753, title III, § 303, 60 Stat. 840, related to detailed accounts of contributions and retention of receipted bills of expenditures.

Section 263, act Aug. 2, 1946, ch. 753, title III, § 304, 60 Stat. 840, required receipts for contributions.

Section 264, act Aug. 2, 1946, ch. 753, title III, § 305, 60 Stat. 840, required filing of statements of accounts with Clerk of House.

Section 265, act Aug. 2, 1946, ch. 753, title III, § 306, 60 Stat. 841, related to proper filing and preservation of statements filed with Clerk of House.

Section 266, act Aug. 2, 1946, ch. 753, title III, § 307, 60 Stat. 841, related to persons to whom chapter was applicable.

Section 267, act Aug. 2, 1946, ch. 753, title III, § 308, 60 Stat. 841, related to registration of lobbyists with Secretary of Senate and Clerk of House and required compilation of information required.

Section 268, act Aug. 2, 1946, ch. 753, title III, § 309, 60 Stat. 842, required that reports and statements be made under oath.

Section 269, act Aug. 2, 1946, ch. 753, title III, § 310, 60 Stat. 842, related to penalties and prohibitions for violations of this chapter.

Section 270, act Aug. 2, 1946, ch. 753, title III, § 311, 60 Stat. 842, related to exemptions from this chapter.

For provisions relating to disclosure of lobbying activities to influence the Federal Government, see section 1601 et seq. of this title.

EFFECTIVE DATE OF REPEAL

Repeal effective Jan. 1, 1996, except as otherwise provided, see section 24 of Pub. L. 104–65, set out as an Effective Date note under section 1601 of this title.

SHORT TITLE

Act Aug. 2, 1946, title III, § 301, 60 Stat. 839, provided that title III of act Aug. 2, 1946 (enacting this chapter), could be cited as the "Federal Regulation of Lobbying Act", prior to repeal by Pub. L. 104–65, § 11(a), Dec. 19, 1995, 109 Stat. 701.

CHAPTER 9—OFFICE OF LEGISLATIVE COUNSEL

SUBCHAPTER I—SENATE

CHANGE OF NAME

Act June 2, 1924, ch. 234, § 1101, 43 Stat. 353, classified to sections 271 to 277 of this title, changed legislative drafting service to office of the legislative counsel, and draftsman to legislative counsel.

SUBCHAPTER I—SENATE

§ 271. Establishment

There shall be in the Senate an office to be known as the Office of the Legislative Counsel, and to be under the direction of the Legislative Counsel of the Senate.

(Feb. 24, 1919, ch. 18, § 1303(a), (d), 40 Stat. 1141; June 2, 1924, ch. 234, title XI, § 1101, 43 Stat. 353.)

CODIFICATION

As originally enacted, section provided for creation of an office of the legislative counsel to be under the direction of two legislative counsels. In view of nonapplicability of section to Speaker, employee, etc., of the House of Representatives pursuant to section 531 of

Pub. L. 91–510, set out as a note under section 281 of this title, section has been revised to limit applicability to Senate and creation therein of Office of Legislative Counsel. See section 281 of this title for provisions establishing Office of the Legislative Counsel for the House of Representatives and section 282 of this title for provisions vesting management, etc., in the Legislative Counsel.

APPROPRIATIONS

Section 204 of act Aug. 2, 1946, ch. 753, 60 Stat. 837, provided: "There is hereby authorized to be appropriated for the work of the Office of the Legislative Counsel the following sums:

"(1) For the fiscal year ending June 30, 1947, $150,000;
"(2) For the fiscal year ending June 30, 1948, $200,000;
"(3) For the fiscal year ending June 30, 1949, $250,000;
"(4) For the fiscal year ending June 30, 1950, $250,000; and
"(5) For each fiscal year thereafter such sums as may be necessary to carry on the work of the Office."

[Section 204 was made effective Aug. 2, 1946, by section 245 of act Aug. 2, 1946, set out as a note under section 72a of this title.]

§ 272. Legislative Counsel

The Legislative Counsel shall be appointed by the President pro tempore of the Senate, without reference to political affiliations and solely on the ground of fitness to perform the duties of the office.

(Feb. 24, 1919, ch. 18, § 1303(a), (d), 40 Stat. 1141; June 2, 1924, ch. 234, title XI, § 1101, 43 Stat. 353; Sept. 20, 1941, ch. 412, title VI, § 602, 55 Stat. 726.)

CODIFICATION

Provisions authorizing appointment of a legislative counsel for the House of Representatives by the Speaker were omitted in view of nonapplicability of section to Speaker, employee, etc., of the House of Representatives pursuant to section 531 of Pub. L. 91–510, set out as a note under section 281 of this title. See section 282 of this title for provisions authorizing appointment, etc., of Legislative Counsel of the House of Representatives.

AMENDMENTS

1941—Act Sept. 20, 1941, substituted "President pro tempore of the Senate" for "President of the Senate."

§ 273. Compensation

The Legislative Counsel of the Senate shall be paid at an annual rate of compensation of $40,000.

(Feb. 24, 1919, ch. 18, § 1303(d), as added June 2, 1924, ch. 234, title XI, § 1101, 43 Stat. 353; amended June 18, 1940, ch. 396, § 1, 54 Stat. 472; Sept. 20, 1941, ch. 412, title VI, § 602, 55 Stat. 726; Oct. 15, 1949, ch. 695, § 6(c), 63 Stat. 881; Aug. 5, 1955, ch. 568, §§ 9, 101, 69 Stat. 509, 514; Pub. L. 85–75, July 1, 1957, 71 Stat. 250; Pub. L. 88–426, title II, § 203(g), Aug. 14, 1964, 78 Stat. 415; Pub. L. 93–371, § 4, Aug. 13, 1974, 88 Stat. 429; Pub. L. 94–59, title I, § 105, July 25, 1975, 89 Stat. 275.)

CODIFICATION

Provisions setting forth authority for the allocation of the positions of legislative counsel to the appropriate grade in the compensation schedules of section 1112 of former Title 5 and the setting of rates of compensation thereunder by the President pro tempore of the Senate and the Speaker of the House of Representatives and prescribing the annual rate of compensation of the Legislative Counsel of the House of Representatives as an amount equal to $15,000, increased by an amount which is the same percentage of $15,000 as the percentage set forth in section 4(c) of the Federal Employees Salary Increase Act of 1955 were omitted in view of nonapplicability of section to Speaker, employee, etc., of the House of Representatives pursuant to section 531 of Pub. L. 91–510, set out as a note under section 281 of this title. See section 282b of this title for provisions setting forth compensation of Legislative Counsel of House of Representatives.

AMENDMENTS

1975—Pub. L. 94–59 substituted "an annual rate of compensation of $40,000" for "a gross annual compensation of $38,760 per annum" as the rate of compensation of the Legislative Counsel of the Senate, effective July 1, 1975.

1974—Pub. L. 93–371 substituted provisions authorizing the Legislative Counsel of the Senate to be paid at an annual rate of compensation of $38,760, for provisions setting forth the gross annual compensation of the Legislative Counsel as $27,500 per annum, effective July 1, 1974.

1964—Pub. L. 88–426 provided that the compensation of the Legislative Counsel of the Senate shall be at the rate of $27,500 per annum.

1957—Pub. L. 85–75 increased the gross compensation of the Legislative Counsel of the Senate from $15,500 to $17,500 per annum, effective July 1, 1957.

1955—Act Aug. 5, 1955, increased the compensation of the Legislative Counsel of the Senate from a basic compensation of $12,000, to a gross annual compensation of $15,500, and the compensation of the Legislative Counsel of the House was increased from a basic compensation of $12,000 to an annual rate of compensation of $15,000 increased by the percentage set forth in section 4(c) of the Federal Employees Salary Increase Act of 1955.

1949—Act Oct. 15, 1949, increased the compensation of the Legislative Counsel of both House and the Senate from $10,000 to $12,000 per annum.

1941—Act Sept. 20, 1941, substituted "President pro tempore of the Senate" for "President of the Senate".

1940—Act June 18, 1940, provided that thereafter the compensation of the Legislative Counsel of the Senate shall be at the rate of $10,000 per annum so long as the present incumbent held the position.

EFFECTIVE DATE OF 1949 AMENDMENT

Section 9 of act Oct. 15, 1949, provided that: "This Act shall take effect on the first day of the first pay period which begins after the date of enactment of this Act [Oct. 15, 1949]."

REPEALS

Act Mar. 10, 1928, ch. 167, § 23(a), 45 Stat. 279, formerly cited as a credit to this section, was repealed by Pub. L. 89–554, § 8(a), Sept. 6, 1966, 80 Stat. 647.

1974 ADJUSTMENT IN COMPENSATION NOT TO SUPERSEDE ADJUSTMENTS IN COMPENSATION OR LIMITATIONS BY PRESIDENT PRO TEMPORE OF THE SENATE

Adjustment in compensation by Pub. L. 93–371 not to supersede order of President pro tempore of the Senate authorizing higher rate of compensation or any authority of the President pro tempore to adjust rates of compensation or limitations under section 4 of the Federal Pay Comparability Act of 1970, see section 4 of Pub. L. 93–371, set out in part as a note under section 61a of this title.

INCREASES IN COMPENSATION

Increases in compensation for officers and employees of the Senate under authority of the Federal Pay Comparability Act of 1970 (Pub. L. 91–656), see Salary Directives of the President pro tempore of the Senate, set out as notes under section 60a–1 of this title.

§ 274. Staff; office equipment and supplies

The Legislative Counsel shall, subject to the approval of the President pro tempore of the Senate, employ and fix the compensation of such Assistant Counsel, clerks, and other employees, and purchase such furniture, office equipment, books, stationery, and other supplies, as may be necessary for the proper performance of the duties of the Office and as may be appropriated for by Congress.

(Feb. 24, 1919, ch. 18, § 1303(a), (d), 40 Stat. 1141; June 2, 1924, ch. 234, title XI, § 1101, 43 Stat. 353; Sept. 20, 1941, ch. 412, title VI, § 602, 55 Stat. 726.)

CODIFICATION

As originally enacted, section also provided for legislative counsel of House of Representatives, subject to approval of Speaker, to employ and fix the compensation of assistant counsel, clerks, etc. In view of nonapplicability of section to Speaker, employee, etc., of the House of Representatives pursuant to section 531 of Pub. L. 91–510, set out as a note under section 281 of this title, section has been revised to limit applicability to authority of Legislative Counsel of the Senate. See section 282a et seq. of this title for provisions relating to appointment of staff, etc., for Office of Legislative Counsel of the House of Representatives.

AMENDMENTS

1941—Act Sept. 20, 1941, substituted "President pro tempore of the Senate" for "President of the Senate".

DESIGNATION OF DEPUTY LEGISLATIVE COUNSEL

Pub. L. 106–57, title I, § 6, Sept. 29, 1999, 113 Stat. 412, provided that: "The Legislative Counsel may, subject to the approval of the President pro tempore of the Senate, designate one of the Senior Counsels appointed under section 102 of the Legislative Branch Appropriation Act, 1979 (2 U.S.C. 274 note; Public Law 95–391; 92 Stat. 771) as Deputy Legislative Counsel. The Deputy Legislative Counsel shall perform the functions of the Legislative Counsel during the absence or disability of the Legislative Counsel, or when the office is vacant."

SENIOR COUNSEL

Pub. L. 85–75, July 1, 1957, 71 Stat. 251, provided in part that: "No more than three employees in the Office of the Legislative Counsel of the Senate may be designated as Senior Counsel, whose compensation shall be $15,500 gross per annum each."

ADDITIONAL SENIOR COUNSEL

Pub. L. 95–391, title I, § 102, Sept. 30, 1978, 92 Stat. 771, provided that: "Effective October 1, 1978, the number of employees in the Office of the Legislative Counsel of the Senate who may be designated as, and receive the compensation of, a Senior Counsel is increased to five."

Pub. L. 88–248, Dec. 30, 1963, 77 Stat. 804, provided in part: "That effective July 1, 1963, one additional employee in the Office of the Legislative Counsel of the Senate may be designated as Senior Counsel, and the compensation of the additional employee so designated shall be equal to the gross per annum rate presently authorized for other employees so designated."

INCREASES IN COMPENSATION OF FOUR SENIOR COUNSELS

Pub. L. 94–59, title I, § 105, July 25, 1975, 89 Stat. 275, eff. July 1, 1975, provided in part that the four Senior Counsels in the Office of the Legislative Counsel of the Senate shall each be paid at an annual rate of compensation of $39,000.

Pub. L. 93–371, § 4, Aug. 13, 1974, 88 Stat. 429, eff. July 1, 1974, provided in part that the four Senior Counsels in the Office of the Legislative Counsel of the Senate shall each be paid at an annual rate of compensation of $37,620.

1974 ADJUSTMENT IN COMPENSATION NOT TO SUPERSEDE ADJUSTMENTS IN COMPENSATION OR LIMITATIONS BY PRESIDENT PRO TEMPORE OF THE SENATE

Adjustment in compensation by Pub. L. 93–371 not to supersede order of President pro tempore of the Senate authorizing higher rate of compensation or any authority of the President pro tempore to adjust rates of compensation or limitations under section 4 of the Federal Pay Comparability Act of 1970, see section 4 of Pub. L. 93–371, set out in part as a note under section 61a of this title.

INCREASES IN COMPENSATION

Increases in compensation for officers and employees of the Senate under authority of the Federal Pay Comparability Act of 1970 (Pub. L. 91–656), see Salary Directives of the President pro tempore of the Senate, set out as notes under section 60a–1 of this title.

§ 275. Functions

The Office of the Legislative Counsel shall aid in drafting public bills and resolutions or amendments thereto on the request of any committee of the Senate but the Committee on Rules and Administration of the Senate may determine the preference, if any, to be given to such requests of the committees. The Legislative Counsel shall, from time to time, prescribe rules and regulations for the conduct of the work of the Office for the committees, subject to the approval of such Committee on Rules and Administration.

(Feb. 24, 1919, ch. 18, § 1303(b), (d), 40 Stat. 1141; June 2, 1924, ch. 234, title XI, § 1101, 43 Stat. 353; Aug. 2, 1946, ch. 753, title I, §§ 102, 121, 60 Stat. 814, 822.)

CODIFICATION

Provisions setting forth functions of office of legislative counsel with respect to the House of Representatives and the committees thereof were omitted in view of nonapplicability of section to Speaker, employee, etc., of the House of Representatives pursuant to section 531 of Pub. L. 91–510, set out as a note under section 281 of this title. See section 281b of this title for functions of Office of Legislative Counsel of House of Representatives.

AMENDMENTS

1946—Act Aug. 2, 1946, substituted "Committee on Rules and Administration" for "Library Committee of the Senate" and "Committee on House Administration" for "Library Committee of the House of Representatives".

EFFECTIVE DATE OF 1946 AMENDMENT

Section 142 of act Aug. 2, 1946, provided that the amendment made by that act is effective Jan. 2, 1947.

§ 276. Disbursement of appropriations

All appropriations for the Office of the Legislative Counsel shall be disbursed by the Secretary of the Senate.

(Feb. 24, 1919, ch. 18, § 1303(c), (d), 40 Stat. 1142; June 2, 1924, ch. 234, title XI, § 1101, 43 Stat. 353.)

CODIFICATION

As originally enacted, section provided for disbursement of one-half of appropriations for office of legislative counsel by Secretary of Senate and one-half by Clerk of House of Representatives. In view of nonapplicability of section to Speaker, employee, etc., of the House of Representatives pursuant to section 531 of

Pub. L. 91–510, set out as a note under section 281 of this title, section has been revised to limit application to Office of the Legislative Counsel of the Senate. See section 282c of this title for provisions relating to expenditures by Legislative Counsel of the House of Representatives.

§ 276a. Expenditures

With the approval of the President Pro Tempore of the Senate, the Legislative Counsel of the Senate may make such expenditures as may be necessary or appropriate for the functioning of the Office of the Legislative Counsel of the Senate.

(Pub. L. 98–51, title I, § 105, July 14, 1983, 97 Stat. 267.)

CODIFICATION

Section was enacted as part of the Congressional Operations Appropriation Act, 1984, which is title I of the Legislative Branch Appropriation Act, 1984, and not as part of section 1303 of act Feb. 24, 1919 which comprises this subchapter.

§ 276b. Travel and related expenses

Funds expended by the Legislative Counsel of the Senate for travel and related expenses shall be subject to the same regulations and limitations (insofar as they are applicable) as those which the Senate Committee on Rules and Administration prescribes for application to travel and related expenses for which payment is authorized to be made from the contingent fund of the Senate.

(Pub. L. 98–51, title I, § 106, July 14, 1983, 97 Stat. 267.)

CODIFICATION

Section was enacted as part of the Congressional Operations Appropriation Act, 1984, which is title I of the Legislative Branch Appropriation Act, 1984, and not as part of section 1303 of act Feb. 24, 1919 which comprises this subchapter.

Section, as it relates to funds expended by the Senate Legal Counsel, is classified to section 288n of this title.

§ 277. Repealed. Pub. L. 93–191, § 13, Dec. 18, 1973, 87 Stat. 746

Section, act Feb. 24, 1919, ch. 18, § 1303(d), as added June 2, 1924, ch. 234, title XI, § 1101, 43 Stat. 353, provided for free transmission of official mail matter of legislative counsel. Official mail matter of Legislative Counsel of House of Representatives is covered by section 282d of this title.

EFFECTIVE DATE OF REPEAL

Repeal effective Dec. 18, 1973, see section 14 of Pub. L. 93–191, set out as an Effective Date of 1973 Amendment note under section 3210 of Title 39, Postal Service.

SUBCHAPTER II—HOUSE OF REPRESENTATIVES

PART I—PURPOSE, POLICY, AND FUNCTION

§ 281. Establishment

There is established in the House of Representatives an office to be known as the Office of the Legislative Counsel, referred to hereinafter in this subchapter as the "Office".

(Pub. L. 91–510, title V, § 501, Oct. 26, 1970, 84 Stat. 1201.)

EFFECTIVE DATE

Subchapter effective Oct. 26, 1970, see section 601(5) of Pub. L. 91–510, set out as an Effective Date of 1970 Amendment note under section 72a of this title.

TRANSFER OF FUNCTIONS; NONAPPLICABILITY OF SECTIONS 271 TO 277 TO THE HOUSE

Section 531 of Pub. L. 91–510 provided that: "Any individual who on the date of the enactment of this Act [Oct. 26, 1970] is serving under an appointment by the Speaker as Legislative Counsel of the House of Representatives shall continue as Legislative Counsel of the House of Representatives in accordance with this subtitle [this subchapter]. All personnel, positions, property, records, and unexpended balances of appropriations of or for that part of the Office of the Legislative Counsel established under section 1303 of the Revenue Act of 1918 (2 U.S.C., ch. 9) [sections 271 to 277 of this title] employed or held in or for the House of Representatives shall be transferred to the Office established under this subtitle; and, effective upon the date of enactment of this Act, the provisions of section 1303 of the Revenue Act of 1918 shall have no further applicability of any kind to the Speaker or to any committee, officer, employee, or property of the House of Representatives."

§ 281a. Purpose and policy

The purpose of the Office shall be to advise and assist the House of Representatives, and its committees and Members, in the achievement of a clear, faithful, and coherent expression of legislative policies. The Office shall maintain impartiality as to issues of legislative policy to be determined by the House of Representatives, and shall not advocate the adoption or rejection of any legislation except when duly requested by the Speaker or a committee to comment on a proposal directly affecting the functions of the Office. The Office shall maintain the attorney-client relationship with respect to all communications between it and any Member or committee of the House.

(Pub. L. 91–510, title V, § 502, Oct. 26, 1970, 84 Stat. 1202.)

SECTION REFERRED TO IN OTHER SECTIONS

This section is referred to in section 281b of this title.

§ 281b. Functions

The functions of the Office shall be as follows:

(1) Upon request of the managers on the part of the House at any conference on the disagreeing votes of the two Houses, to advise and assist the managers on the part of the House in the course of the conference, and to assist the committee of conference in the preparation of the conference report and any accompanying explanatory statement.

(2) Upon request of any committee of the House, or any joint committee having authority to report legislation to the House, to advise and assist the committee in the consideration of any legislation before it, and to assist the committee in the preparation of drafts of any such legislation, amendments thereto, and reports thereon.

(3) Upon request of any Member having control of time during the consideration of any legislation by the House, to have in attendance on the floor of the House not more than two members of the staff of the Office (and, in

his discretion, the Legislative Counsel) to advise and assist such Member and, to the extent feasible, any other Member, in the course of such consideration.

(4) Upon request of any Member, subject to such reasonable restrictions as the Legislative Counsel may impose with the approval of the Speaker on the proportion of the resources of the Office which may be devoted to the requests of any one Member, to prepare drafts of legislation and to furnish drafting advice with respect to drafts of legislation prepared by others.

(5) At the direction of the Speaker, to perform on behalf of the House of Representatives any legal services which are within the capabilities of the Office and the performance of which would not be inconsistent with the provisions of section 281a of this title or the preceding provisions of this section.

(Pub. L. 91–510, title V, § 503, Oct. 26, 1970, 84 Stat. 1202.)

PART II—ADMINISTRATION

§ 282. Legislative Counsel

The management, supervision, and administration of the Office are vested in the Legislative Counsel, who shall be appointed by the Speaker of the House of Representatives without regard to political affiliation and solely on the basis of fitness to perform the duties of the position. Any person so appointed shall serve at the pleasure of the Speaker.

(Pub. L. 91–510, title V, § 521, Oct. 26, 1970, 84 Stat. 1202.)

§ 282a. Staff; Deputy Legislative Counsel; delegation of functions

(a) With the approval of the Speaker, or in accordance with policies and procedures approved by the Speaker, the Legislative Counsel shall appoint such attorneys and other employees as may be necessary for the prompt and efficient performance of the functions of the Office. Any such appointment shall be made without regard to political affiliation and solely on the basis of fitness to perform the duties of the position. Any person so appointed may be removed by the Legislative Counsel with the approval of the Speaker, or in accordance with policies and procedures approved by the Speaker.

(b)(1) One of the attorneys appointed under subsection (a) of this section shall be designated by the Legislative Counsel as Deputy Legislative Counsel. During the absence or disability of the Legislative Counsel, or when the office is vacant, the Deputy Legislative Counsel shall perform the functions of the Legislative Counsel.

(2) The Legislative Counsel may delegate to the Deputy Legislative Counsel and to other employees appointed under subsection (a) of this section such of his functions as he considers necessary or appropriate.

(Pub. L. 91–510, title V, § 522, Oct. 26, 1970, 84 Stat. 1203; Pub. L. 92–51, § 101, July 9, 1971, 85 Stat. 132.)

AMENDMENTS

1971—Subsec. (b). Pub. L. 92–51 substituted provisions for designation of one attorney as Deputy Legislative

Counsel to perform functions of Legislative Counsel during his absence or disability or when office is vacant and for delegation of functions to Deputy Legislative Counsel and other employees for former provisions for appointment of full-time Office Administrator to exercise management, supervisory, and administrative functions of the Office as delegated to him by the Legislative Counsel.

§ 282b. Compensation

(a) The Legislative Counsel shall be paid at a per annum gross rate equal to the rate of basic pay, as in effect from time to time, for level III of the Executive Schedule of section 5314 of title 5.

(b) Members of the staff of the Office other than the Legislative Counsel shall be paid at per annum gross rates fixed by the Legislative Counsel with the approval of the Speaker or in accordance with policies approved by the Speaker, but not in excess of the rate of basic pay for one pay level above the maximum pay level for employees of the House of Representatives provided under clause 6(c) of Rule XI of the Rules of the House of Representatives.

(Pub. L. 91–510, title V, § 523, Oct. 26, 1970, 84 Stat. 1203; Pub. L. 95–94, title I, § 115, Aug. 5, 1977, 91 Stat. 668.)

REFERENCES IN TEXT

Clause 6(c) of Rule XI of the Rules of the House of Representatives, referred to in text, was amended generally for the One Hundred First Congress, and, as so amended, does not refer to specific pay levels. The Rules were amended generally by House Resolution No. 5, One Hundred Sixth Congress, Jan. 6, 1999, and, as so amended, provisions formerly appearing in clause 6(c) of Rule XI, as amended for the One Hundred First Congress, are now contained in clause 9(c) of Rule X.

CODIFICATION

Amendment by Pub. L. 95–94 is based on par. (2) of House Resolution No. 8, Ninety-fifth Congress, Jan. 4, 1977, which was enacted into permanent law by Pub. L. 95–94.

PRIOR PROVISIONS

House Resolution 312, 89th Congress, Mar. 31, 1965, which was enacted into permanent law by section 103 of Pub. L. 89–90, July 27, 1965, 79 Stat. 281, provided that effective Apr. 1, 1965, the compensation of the Legislative Counsel of the House of Representatives shall be at a gross per annum rate which is equal to the gross per annum rate of compensation of the Legislative Counsel of the Senate, and that the additional sums necessary to carry out this resolution shall be paid out of the contingent fund of the House until otherwise provided by law.

AMENDMENTS

1977—Subsec. (b). Pub. L. 95–94 substituted provisions authorizing compensation at a rate not in excess of the rate of basic pay for one pay level above the maximum pay level for House employees provided under cl. 6(c) of Rule XI of the Rules of the House of Representatives, for provisions authorizing compensation at per annum gross rates not in excess of a per annum gross rate equal to the rate of basic pay for level V of the Executive Schedule of section 5316 of title 5.

INCREASES IN COMPENSATION

Increases in compensation for House officers and employees under authority of Federal Salary Act of 1967 (Pub. L. 90–206), Federal Pay Comparability Act of 1970 (Pub. L. 91–656), and Legislative Branch Appropriations Act, 1988 (Pub. L. 100–202), see sections 60a–2 and 60a–2a of this title, and Salary Directives of Speaker of the House, set out as notes under those sections.

§ 282c. Expenditures

In accordance with policies and procedures approved by the Speaker, the Legislative Counsel may make such expenditures as may be necessary or appropriate for the functioning of the Office.

(Pub. L. 91–510, title V, § 524, Oct. 26, 1970, 84 Stat. 1203.)

§ 282d. Official mail matter

The Legislative Counsel may send the official mail matter of the Office as franked mail under section 3210 of title 39.

(Pub. L. 91–510, title V, § 525, Oct. 26, 1970, 84 Stat. 1203; Pub. L. 92–51, § 101, July 9, 1971, 85 Stat. 132.)

AMENDMENTS

1971—Pub. L. 92–51 substituted provision for Legislative Counsel to send official mail matter of the Office as franked mail under section 3210 of title 39, for former provision granting the Office the same privilege of free transmission of official mail matter as other offices of the United States Government.

§ 282e. Authorization of appropriations

There are authorized to be appropriated, for the fiscal year ending June 30, 1971, and for each fiscal year thereafter, such sums as may be necessary to carry out this subchapter and to increase the efficiency of the Office and the quality of the services which it provides.

(Pub. L. 91–510, title V, § 526, Oct. 26, 1970, 84 Stat. 1203.)

CHAPTER 9A—OFFICE OF LAW REVISION COUNSEL

§ 285. Establishment

There is established in the House of Representatives an office to be known as the Office of the Law Revision Counsel, referred to hereinafter in this chapter as the "Office".

(Pub. L. 93–554, title I, ch. III, § 101, Dec. 27, 1974, 88 Stat. 1777.)

CODIFICATION

Section is based on section 205(a) of House Resolution No. 988, Ninety-third Congress, Oct. 8, 1974, which was enacted into permanent law by Pub. L. 93–554.

EFFECTIVE DATE

Section 101 of Pub. L. 93–554 provided that the enactment of House Resolution No. 988, Ninety-third Congress, Oct. 8, 1974, into permanent law is effective on Jan. 2, 1975. This chapter is derived from enactment into permanent law of section 205 of House Resolution No. 988.

§ 285a. Purpose and policy

The principal purpose of the Office shall be to develop and keep current an official and positive codification of the laws of the United States. The Office shall maintain impartiality as to issues of legislative policy to be determined by the House.

(Pub. L. 93–554, title I, ch. III, § 101, Dec. 27, 1974, 88 Stat. 1777.)

CODIFICATION

Section is based on section 205(b) of House Resolution No. 988, Ninety-third Congress, Oct. 8, 1974, which was enacted into permanent law by Pub. L. 93–554.

§ 285b. Functions

The functions of the Office shall be as follows:

(1) To prepare, and submit to the Committee on the Judiciary one title at a time, a complete compilation, restatement, and revision of the general and permanent laws of the United States which conforms to the understood policy, intent, and purpose of the Congress in the original enactments, with such amendments and corrections as will remove ambiguities, contradictions, and other imperfections both of substance and of form, separately stated, with a view to the enactment of each title as positive law.

(2) To examine periodically all of the public laws enacted by the Congress and submit to the Committee on the Judiciary recommendations for the repeal of obsolete, superfluous, and superseded provisions contained therein.

(3) To prepare and publish periodically a new edition of the United States Code (including those titles which are not yet enacted into positive law as well as those titles which have been so enacted), with annual cumulative supplements reflecting newly enacted laws.

(4) To classify newly enacted provisions of law to their proper positions in the Code where the titles involved have not yet been enacted into positive law.

(5) To prepare and submit periodically such revisions in the titles of the Code which have been enacted into positive law as may be necessary to keep such titles current.

(6) To prepare and publish periodically new editions of the District of Columbia Code, with annual cumulative supplements reflecting newly enacted laws, through publication of the fifth annual cumulative supplement to the 1973 edition of such Code.

(7) To provide the Committee on the Judiciary with such advice and assistance as the committee may request in carrying out its functions with respect to the revision and codification of the Federal statutes.

(Pub. L. 93–554, title I, ch. III, § 101, Dec. 27, 1974, 88 Stat. 1777; Pub. L. 94–386, § 1, Aug. 14, 1976, 90 Stat. 1170.)

CODIFICATION

Section is based on section 205(c) of House Resolution No. 988, Ninety-third Congress, Oct. 8, 1974, which was enacted into permanent law by Pub. L. 93–554.

AMENDMENTS

1976—Par. (6). Pub. L. 94–386 substituted "through publication of the fifth annual cumulative supplement to the 1973 edition of such Code" for "until such time as the District of Columbia Self–Government and Governmental Reorganization Act becomes effective".

PREPARATION AND PUBLICATION OF NEW EDITION OF THE DISTRICT OF COLUMBIA CODE UNDER DIRECTION OF COUNCIL OF THE DISTRICT OF COLUMBIA

Section 2 of Pub. L. 94–386 provided that:

"(a) After publication by the Law Revision Counsel of the fifth annual cumulative supplement to the 1973 edition of the District of Columbia Code, new editions of the District of Columbia Code (and annual cumulative supplements thereto) shall be prepared and published under the direction of the Council of the District of Columbia and shall set forth the general and permanent laws relating to or in force in the District of Columbia, whether enacted by the Congress or by the Council of the District of Columbia, except such laws as are of application in the District of Columbia by reason of being laws of the United States general and permanent in nature.

"(b) After completion of the printing of the fifth annual cumulative supplement to the 1973 edition of the District of Columbia Code, the Public Printer shall, as the Council of the District of Columbia may request, either—

"(1) furnish to the Council of the District of Columbia, on such terms as the Public Printer (in consultation with the Joint Committee on Printing) deems appropriate, the type used in preparing the 1973 edition of the District of Columbia Code and the fifth annual cumulative supplement to such edition; or

"(2) make such arrangements with the Council of the District of Columbia as the Public Printer (in consultation with the Joint Committee on Printing) deems appropriate for the printing by the Government Printing Office of future editions of the District of Columbia Code, and annual cumulative supplements thereto, prepared under the direction of the Council of the District of Columbia."

§ 285c. Law Revision Counsel

The management, supervision, and administration of the Office are vested in the Law Revision Counsel, who shall be appointed by the Speaker without regard to political affiliation and solely on the basis of fitness to perform the duties of the position. Any person so appointed shall serve at the pleasure of the Speaker.

(Pub. L. 93–554, title I, ch. III, § 101, Dec. 27, 1974, 88 Stat. 1777.)

CODIFICATION

Section is based on section 205(d) of House Resolution No. 988, Ninety-third Congress, Oct. 8, 1974, which was enacted into permanent law by Pub. L. 93–554.

§ 285d. Staff; Deputy Law Revision Counsel; delegation of functions

(1) With the approval of the Speaker, or in accordance with policies and procedures approved by the Speaker, the Law Revision Counsel shall appoint such employees as may be necessary for the prompt and efficient performance of the functions of the Office. Any such appointment shall be made without regard to political affiliation and solely on the basis of fitness to perform the duties of the position. Any person so appointed may be removed by the Law Revision Counsel with the approval of the Speaker, or in accordance with policies and procedures approved by the Speaker.

(2)(A) One of the employees appointed under paragraph (1) shall be designated by the Law Revision Counsel as Deputy Law Revision Counsel. During the absence or disability of the Law Revision Counsel, or when the office is vacant, the Deputy Law Revision Counsel shall perform the functions of the Law Revision Counsel.

(B) The Law Revision Counsel may delegate to the Deputy Law Revision Counsel and to other employees appointed under paragraph (1) such of his or her functions as he or she considers necessary or appropriate.

(Pub. L. 93–554, title I, ch. III, § 101, Dec. 27, 1974, 88 Stat. 1777.)

CODIFICATION

Section is based on section 205(e) of House Resolution No. 988, Ninety-third Congress, Oct. 8, 1974, which was enacted into permanent law by Pub. L. 93–554.

§ 285e. Compensation

The Law Revision Counsel shall be paid at a per annum gross rate not to exceed level IV of the Executive Schedule of section 5315 of title 5; and members of the staff of the Office other than the Law Revision Counsel shall be paid at per annum gross rates fixed by the Law Revision Counsel with the approval of the Speaker or in accordance with policies approved by the Speaker, but not in excess of a per annum gross rate equal to level V of such schedule.

(Pub. L. 93–554, title I, ch. III, § 101, Dec. 27, 1974, 88 Stat. 1777.)

CODIFICATION

Section is based on section 205(f) of House Resolution No. 988, Ninety-third Congress, Oct. 8, 1974, which was enacted into permanent law by Pub. L. 93–554.

INCREASES IN COMPENSATION

Increases in compensation for House officers and employees under authority of Federal Salary Act of 1967 (Pub. L. 90–206), Federal Pay Comparability Act of 1970 (Pub. L. 91–656), and Legislative Branch Appropriations Act, 1988 (Pub. L. 100–202), see sections 60a–2 and 60a–2a of this title, and Salary Directives of Speaker of the House, set out as notes under those sections.

§ 285f. Expenditures

In accordance with policies and procedures approved by the Speaker, the Law Revision Counsel is authorized to make such expenditures as may be necessary or appropriate for the functioning of the Office.

(Pub. L. 93–554, title I, ch. III, § 101, Dec. 27, 1974, 88 Stat. 1777.)

CODIFICATION

Section is based on section 205(g) of House Resolution No. 988, Ninety-third Congress, Oct. 8, 1974, which was enacted into permanent law by Pub. L. 93–554.

§ 285g. Availability of applicable accounts of House

Until such time as funds are appropriated by law to carry out the purpose of this chapter, the applicable accounts of the House of Representatives shall be available for such purpose.

(Pub. L. 93–554, title I, ch. III, § 101, Dec. 27, 1974, 88 Stat. 1777; Pub. L. 104–186, title II, § 207, Aug. 20, 1996, 110 Stat. 1742.)

CODIFICATION

Section is based on section 205(h) of House Resolution No. 988, Ninety-third Congress, Oct. 8, 1974, which was enacted into permanent law by Pub. L. 93–554.

AMENDMENTS

1996—Pub. L. 104–186 substituted "applicable accounts of the House of Representatives" for "contingent fund of the House".

CHAPTER 9B—LEGISLATIVE CLASSIFICATION OFFICE

§§ 286 to 286g. Repealed. Pub. L. 104–186, title II, § 208, Aug. 20, 1996, 110 Stat. 1742

Section 286, based on H. Res. No. 988, § 203(a), Ninety-third Congress, Oct. 8, 1974, enacted into permanent law by Pub. L. 93–554, title I, ch. III, § 101, Dec. 27, 1974, 88 Stat. 1777, established Legislative Classification Office in House of Representatives.

Section 286a, based on H. Res. No. 988, § 203(b), Ninety-third Congress, Oct. 8, 1974, enacted into permanent law by Pub. L. 93–554, title I, ch. III, § 101, Dec. 27, 1974, 88 Stat. 1777, related to purpose and policy of Legislative Classification Office.

Section 286b, based on H. Res. No. 988, § 203(c), Ninety-third Congress, Oct. 8, 1974, enacted into permanent law by Pub. L. 93–554, title I, ch. III, § 101, Dec. 27, 1974, 88 Stat. 1777, related to functions of Legislative Classification Office.

Section 286c, based on H. Res. No. 988, § 203(d), Ninety-third Congress, Oct. 8, 1974, enacted into permanent law by Pub. L. 93–554, title I, ch. III, § 101, Dec. 27, 1974, 88 Stat. 1777, related to functions and appointment of Staff Director of Legislative Classification Office.

Section 286d, based on H. Res. No. 988, § 203(e), Ninety-third Congress, Oct. 8, 1974, enacted into permanent law by Pub. L. 93–554, title I, ch. III, § 101, Dec. 27, 1974, 88 Stat. 1777, related to appointment of staff, Deputy Staff Director, and delegation of functions of Legislative Classification Office.

Section 286e, based on H. Res. No. 988, § 203(f), Ninety-third Congress, Oct. 8, 1974, enacted into permanent law by Pub. L. 93–554, title I, ch. III, § 101, Dec. 27, 1974, 88 Stat. 1777, related to compensation of Staff Director and staff of Legislative Classification Office.

Section 286f, based on H. Res. No. 988, § 203(g), Ninety-third Congress, Oct. 8, 1974, enacted into permanent law by Pub. L. 93–554, title I, ch. III, § 101, Dec. 27, 1974, 88 Stat. 1777, related to expenditures of Legislative Classification Office.

Section 286g, based on H. Res. No. 988, § 203(h), Ninety-third Congress, Oct. 8, 1974, enacted into permanent law by Pub. L. 93–554, title I, ch. III, § 101, Dec. 27, 1974, 88 Stat. 1777, provided that contingent fund of House was available to carry out this chapter.

CHAPTER 9C—OFFICE OF PARLIAMENTARIAN OF HOUSE OF REPRESENTATIVES

§ 287. Establishment

There is hereby established in the House of Representatives an office to be known as the Office of the Parliamentarian, hereinafter in this chapter referred to as the "Office".

(Pub. L. 95–94, title I, § 115, Aug. 5, 1977, 91 Stat. 668.)

Section is based on section 1 of House Resolution No. 502, Ninety-fifth Congress, Apr. 20, 1977, which was enacted into permanent law by Pub. L. 95–94.

EFFECTIVE DATE

Section 6 of House Resolution No. 502, Apr. 20, 1977, as enacted into permanent law by section 115 of Pub. L. 95–94, provided that: "This resolution [this chapter] shall take effect as of March 1, 1977, and shall continue in effect until otherwise provided by law."

§ 287a. Parliamentarian

The management, supervision, and administration of the Office shall be vested in the Parliamentarian, who shall be appointed by the Speaker of the House of Representatives without regard to political affiliation and solely on the basis of fitness to perform the duties of the position. Any person so appointed shall serve at the pleasure of the Speaker.

(Pub. L. 95–94, title I, § 115, Aug. 5, 1977, 91 Stat. 668.)

CODIFICATION

Section is based on section 2 of House Resolution No. 502, Ninety-fifth Congress, Apr. 20, 1977, which was enacted into permanent law by Pub. L. 95–94.

§ 287b. Staff; Deputy Parliamentarian; delegation of functions

(a) With the approval of the Speaker, or in accordance with policies and procedures approved by the Speaker, the Parliamentarian shall appoint such attorneys and other employees as may be necessary for the prompt and efficient performance of the functions of the Office. Any such appointment shall be made without regard to political affiliation and solely on the basis of fitness to perform the duties of the position. Any person so appointed may be removed by the Parliamentarian with the approval of the Speaker, or in accordance with policies and procedures approved by the Speaker.

(b)(1) One of the attorneys appointed under subsection (a) of this section shall be designated by the Parliamentarian as Deputy Parliamentarian. During the absence or disability of the Parliamentarian, or when the office is vacant, the Deputy Parliamentarian shall perform the functions of the Parliamentarian.

(2) The Parliamentarian may delegate to the Deputy Parliamentarian and to other employees appointed under subsection (a) of this section such of the functions of the Parliamentarian as the Parliamentarian considers necessary or appropriate.

(Pub. L. 95–94, title I, § 115, Aug. 5, 1977, 91 Stat. 668.)

CODIFICATION

Section is based on section 3 of House Resolution No. 502, Ninety-fifth Congress, Apr. 20, 1977, which was enacted into permanent law by Pub. L. 95–94.

§ 287c. Compensation

(a) The Parliamentarian shall be paid at a per annum gross rate established by the Speaker but not in excess of the rate of basic pay determined from time to time under subsection (b) of section 3 of the Speaker's salary directive of June 11, 1968.

(b) Members of the staff of the Office other than the Parliamentarian shall be paid at per annum gross rates fixed by the Parliamentarian with the approval of the Speaker or in accordance with policies approved by the Speaker, but not in excess of the rate of basic pay set forth in subsection (a) of this section.

(Pub. L. 95–94, title I, § 115, Aug. 5, 1977, 91 Stat. 668.)

REFERENCES IN TEXT

Subsection (b) of section 3 of the Speaker's salary directive of June 11, 1968, referred to in subsec. (a), is set out as a note under section 60a–2 of this title.

CODIFICATION

Section is based on section 4 of House Resolution No. 502, Ninety-fifth Congress, Apr. 20, 1977, which was enacted into permanent law by Pub. L. 95–94.

PRIOR PROVISIONS

House Resolution No. 904, Eighty-eighth Congress, Oct. 3, 1964, provided: "That effective January 1, 1965, the salary of the Parliamentarian of the House of Representatives shall be at the gross rate of $28,500. The additional sums necessary to carry out this resolution shall be paid out of the contingent fund of the House until otherwise provided by law."

INCREASES IN COMPENSATION

Increases in compensation for House officers and employees under authority of Federal Salary Act of 1967 (Pub. L. 90–206), Federal Pay Comparability Act of 1970 (Pub. L. 91–656), and Legislative Branch Appropriations Act, 1988 (Pub. L. 100–202), see sections 60a–2 and 60a–2a of this title, and Salary Directives of Speaker of the House, set out as notes under those sections.

§ 287d. Expenditures

In accordance with policies and procedures approved by the Speaker, the Parliamentarian may make such expenditures as may be necessary or appropriate for the functioning of the Office.

(Pub. L. 95–94, title I, § 115, Aug. 5, 1977, 91 Stat. 668.)

CODIFICATION

Section is based on section 5 of House Resolution No. 502, Ninety-fifth Congress, Apr. 20, 1977, which was enacted into permanent law by Pub. L. 95–94.

CHAPTER 9D—OFFICE OF SENATE LEGAL COUNSEL

§ 288. Office of Senate Legal Counsel

(a) Establishment; appointment of Counsel and Deputy Counsel; Senate approval; reappointment; compensation

(1) There is established, as an office of the Senate, the Office of Senate Legal Counsel (hereinafter referred to as the "Office"), which shall be headed by a Senate Legal Counsel (hereinafter referred to as the "Counsel"); and there shall be a Deputy Senate Legal Counsel (hereinafter referred to as the "Deputy Counsel") who shall perform such duties as may be assigned to him by the Counsel and who, during any absence, disability, or vacancy in the position of the Counsel, shall serve as Acting Senate Legal Counsel.

(2) The Counsel and the Deputy Counsel each shall be appointed by the President pro tempore of the Senate from among recommendations submitted by the majority and minority leaders of the Senate. Any appointment made under this paragraph shall be made without regard to political affiliation and solely on the basis of fitness to perform the duties of the position. Any person appointed as Counsel or Deputy Counsel shall be learned in the law, a member of the bar of a State or the District of Columbia, and shall not engage in any other business, vocation, or employment during the term of such appointment.

(3)(A) Any appointment made under paragraph (2) shall become effective upon approval by resolution of the Senate. The Counsel and the Deputy Counsel shall each be appointed for a term of service which shall expire at the end of the Congress following the Congress during which the Counsel or Deputy Counsel, respectively, is appointed except that the Senate may, by resolution, remove either the Counsel or the Deputy Counsel prior to the termination of any term of service. The Counsel and the Deputy Counsel may be reappointed at the termination of any term of service.

(B) The first Counsel and the first Deputy Counsel shall be appointed, approved, and begin service within ninety days after January 3, 1979, and thereafter the Counsel and Deputy Counsel shall be appointed, approved, and begin service within thirty days after the beginning of the session of the Congress immediately following the termination of a Counsel's or Deputy Counsel's term of service or within sixty days after a vacancy occurs in either position.

(4) The Counsel shall receive compensation at a rate equal to the annual rate of basic pay for level III of the Executive Schedule under section 5314 of title 5. The Deputy Counsel shall receive compensation at a rate equal to the annual rate of basic pay for level IV of the Executive Schedule under section 5315 of title 5.

(b) Assistant counsels and other personnel; compensation; appointment; removal

(1) The Counsel shall select and fix the compensation of such Assistant Senate Legal Counsels (hereinafter referred to as "Assistant Counsels") and of such other personnel, within the limits of available funds, as may be necessary to carry out the provisions of this chapter and may prescribe the duties and responsibilities of such personnel. The compensation fixed for each Assistant Counsel shall not be in excess of a rate equal to the annual rate of basic pay for level V of the Executive Schedule under section 5316 of title 5. Any selection made under this paragraph shall be made without regard to political affiliation and solely on the basis of fitness to perform the duties of the position. Any individual selected as an Assistant Counsel shall be learned in the law, a member of the bar of a State or the District of Columbia, and shall not engage in any other business, vocation, or employment during his term of service. The Counsel may remove any individual appointed under this paragraph.

(2) For purposes of pay (other than the rate of pay of the Counsel and Deputy Counsel) and employment benefits, right, and privileges, all personnel of the Office shall be treated as employees of the Senate.

(c) Consultants

In carrying out the functions of the Office, the Counsel may procure the temporary (not to exceed one year) or intermittent services of individual consultants (including outside counsel), or organizations thereof, in the same manner and under the same conditions as a standing committee of the Senate may procure such services under section 72a(i) of this title.

(d) Policies and procedures

The Counsel may establish such policies and procedures as may be necessary to carry out the provisions of this chapter.

(e) Delegation of duties

The counsel[1] may delegate authority for the performance of any function imposed by this chapter except any function imposed upon the Counsel under section 288e(b) of this title.

(f) Attorney-client relationship

The Counsel and other employees of the Office shall maintain the attorney-client relationship with respect to all communications between them and any Member, officer, or employee of the Senate.

(Pub. L. 95–521, title VII, § 701, Oct. 26, 1978, 92 Stat. 1875.)

REFERENCES IN TEXT

This chapter, referred to in subsecs. (b)(1), (d), and (e), was in the original "this title", meaning title VII of Pub. L. 95–521, which enacted this chapter, section 118a of this title, and section 1364 of Title 28, Judiciary and Judicial Procedure, and amended sections 3210, 3216, and 3219 of Title 39, Postal Service. For complete classification of title VII to the Code, see Tables.

EFFECTIVE DATE

Section 717 of title VII of Pub. L. 95–521 provided that: "This title [enacting this chapter, section 118a of this title, section 1364 of Title 28, Judiciary and Judicial Procedure, amending sections 3210, 3216, and 3219 of Title 39, Postal Service, and enacting provisions set out as notes under this section] shall take effect on January 3, 1979."

SEPARABILITY

Section 715 of title VII of Pub. L. 95–521 provided that: "If any part of this title or any amendment made by this title [enacting this chapter, section 118a of this title, section 1364 of Title 28, Judiciary and Judicial Procedure, amending sections 3210, 3216, and 3219 of Title 39, Postal Service, and enacting provisions set out as notes under this section] is held invalid, the remainder of the title and any amendment made by this title shall not be affected thereby. If any provision of any part of this title or of any amendment made by this title, or the application thereof to any person or circumstance is held invalid, the provisions of other parts and of any amendment made by this title and their application to other persons or circumstances shall not be affected thereby."

INCREASES IN COMPENSATION

Increases in compensation for Senate officers and employees under authority of Federal Pay Comparability Act of 1970 (Pub. L. 91–656), see Salary Directives of President pro tempore of the Senate, set out as notes under section 60a–1 of this title.

§ 288a. Senate Joint Leadership Group

(a) Accountability of Office

The Office shall be directly accountable to the Joint Leadership Group in the performance of the duties of the Office.

(b) Membership

For purposes of this chapter, the Joint Leadership Group shall consist of the following Members:

(1) The President pro tempore (or if he so designates, the Deputy President pro tempore) of the Senate.

(2) The majority and minority leaders of the Senate.

(3) The Chairman and ranking minority Member of the Committee on the Judiciary of the Senate.

(4) The Chairman and ranking minority Member of the committee of the Senate which has jurisdiction over the contingent fund of the Senate.

(c) Assistance of Secretary of Senate

The Joint Leadership Group shall be assisted in the performance of its duties by the Secretary of the Senate.

(Pub. L. 95–521, title VII, § 702, Oct. 26, 1978, 92 Stat. 1877.)

§ 288b. Requirements for authorizing representation activity

(a) Direction of Joint Leadership Group or Senate resolution

The Counsel shall defend the Senate or a committee, subcommittee, Member, officer, or employee of the Senate under section 288c of this title only when directed to do so by two-thirds of the Members of the Joint Leadership Group or by the adoption of a resolution by the Senate.

(b) Civil action to enforce subpena

The Counsel shall bring a civil action to enforce a subpena of the Senate or a committee or subcommittee of the Senate under section 288d of this title only when directed to do so by the adoption of a resolution by the Senate.

(c) Intervention or appearance

The Counsel shall intervene or appear as amicus curiae under section 288e of this title only when directed to do so by a resolution adopted by the Senate when such intervention or appearance is to be made in the name of the Senate or in the name of an officer, committee, subcommittee, or chairman of a committee or subcommittee of the Senate.

(d) Immunity proceedings

The Counsel shall serve as the duly authorized representative in obtaining an order granting immunity under section 288f of this title of—

(1) the Senate when directed to do so by an affirmative vote of a majority of the Members present of the Senate; or

(2) a committee or subcommittee of the Senate when directed to do so by an affirmative vote of two-thirds of the members of the full committee.

(e) Resolution recommendations

The Office shall make no recommendation with respect to the consideration of a resolution under this section.

(Pub. L. 95–521, title VII, § 703, Oct. 26, 1978, 92 Stat. 1877.)

SECTION REFERRED TO IN OTHER SECTIONS

This section is referred to in sections 288c, 288d, 288e, 288f, 288j of this title.

---

[1] So in original. Probably should be capitalized.

§ 288c. Defending the Senate, committee, subcommittee, member, officer, or employee of Senate

(a) Except as otherwise provided in subsection (b) of this section, when directed to do so pursuant to section 288b(a) of this title, the Counsel shall—

(1) defend the Senate, a committee, subcommittee, Member, officer, or employee of the Senate in any civil action pending in any court of the United States or of a State or political subdivision thereof, in which the Senate, such committee, subcommittee, Member, officer, or employee is made a party defendant and in which there is placed in issue the validity of any proceeding of, or action, including issuance of any subpena or order, taken by the Senate, or such committee, subcommittee, Member, officer, or employee in its or his official or representative capacity; or

(2) defend the Senate or a committee, subcommittee, Member, officer, or employee of the Senate in any proceeding with respect to any subpena or order directed to the Senate or such committee, subcommittee, Member, officer, or employee in its or his official or representative capacity.

(b) Representation of a Member, officer, or employee under subsection (a) of this section shall be undertaken by the Counsel only upon the consent of such Member, officer, or employee.

(Pub. L. 95–521, title VII, § 704, Oct. 26, 1978, 92 Stat. 1877.)

<small>SECTION REFERRED TO IN OTHER SECTIONS</small>

This section is referred to in sections 288b, 288g, 288k of this title.

§ 288d. Enforcement of Senate subpena or order

(a) Institution of civil actions

When directed to do so pursuant to section 288b(b) of this title, the Counsel shall bring a civil action under any statute conferring jurisdiction on any court of the United States (including section 1365 of title 28), to enforce, to secure a declaratory judgment concerning the validity of, or to prevent a threatened failure or refusal to comply with, any subpena or order issued by the Senate or a committee or a subcommittee of the Senate authorized to issue a subpena or order.

(b) Actions in name of committees and subcommittees

Any directive to the Counsel to bring a civil action pursuant to subsection (a) of this section in the name of a committee or subcommittee of the Senate shall, for such committee or subcommittee, constitute authorization to bring such action within the meaning of any statute conferring jurisdiction on any court of the United States.

(c) Consideration of resolutions authorizing actions

It shall not be in order in the Senate to consider a resolution to direct the Counsel to bring a civil action pursuant to subsection (a) of this section in the name of a committee or subcommittee unless—

(1) such resolution is reported by a majority of the members voting, a majority being present, of such committee or committee of which such subcommittee is a subcommittee, and

(2) the report filed by such committee or committee of which such subcommittee is a subcommittee contains a statement of—

(A) the procedure followed in issuing such subpena;

(B) the extent to which the party subpenaed has complied with such subpena;

(C) any objections or privileges raised by the subpenaed party; and

(D) the comparative effectiveness of bringing a civil action under this section, certification of a criminal action for contempt of Congress, and initiating a contempt proceeding before the Senate.

(d) Rules of Senate

The provisions of subsection (c) of this section are enacted—

(1) as an exercise of the rulemaking power of the Senate, and, as such, they shall be considered as part of the rules of the Senate, and such rules shall supersede any other rule of the Senate only to the extent that rule is inconsistent therewith; and

(2) with full recognition of the constitutional right of the Senate to change such rules (so far as relating to the procedure in the Senate) at any time, in the same manner, and to the same extent as in the case of any other rule of the Senate.

(e) Committee reports

A report filed pursuant to subsection (c)(2) of this section shall not be receivable in any court of law to the extent such report is in compliance with such subsection.

(f) Omitted

(g) Certification of failure to testify; contempt

Nothing in this section shall limit the discretion of—

(1) the President pro tempore of the Senate in certifying to the United States Attorney for the District of Columbia any matter pursuant to section 194 of this title; or

(2) the Senate to hold any individual or entity in contempt of the Senate.

(Pub. L. 95–521, title VII, § 705, Oct. 26, 1978, 92 Stat. 1878; Pub. L. 99–336, § 6(a)(2), June 19, 1986, 100 Stat. 639.)

<small>CODIFICATION</small>

Subsec. (f) of this section amended title 28 by adding section 1364 and by adding item 1364 to the chapter analysis.

<small>AMENDMENTS</small>

1986—Subsec. (a). Pub. L. 99–336 substituted "section 1365 of title 28" for "section 1364 of title 28".

<small>SECTION REFERRED TO IN OTHER SECTIONS</small>

This section is referred to in sections 288b, 288j of this title.

§ 288e. Intervention or appearance

(a) Actions or proceedings

When directed to do so pursuant to section 288b(c) of this title, the Counsel shall intervene or appear as amicus curiae in the name of the Senate, or in the name of an officer, committee, subcommittee, or chairman of a committee or subcommittee of the Senate in any legal action or proceeding pending in any court of the United States or of a State or political subdivision thereof in which the powers and responsibilities of Congress under the Constitution of the United States are placed in issue. The Counsel shall be authorized to intervene only if standing to intervene exists under section 2 of article III of the Constitution of the United States.

(b) Notification; publication

The Counsel shall notify the Joint Leadership Group of any legal action or proceeding in which the Counsel is of the opinion that intervention or appearance as amicus curiae under subsection (a) of this section is in the interest of the Senate. Such notification shall contain a description of the legal action or proceeding together with the reasons that the Counsel is of the opinion that intervention or appearance as amicus curiae is in the interest of the Senate. The Joint Leadership Group shall cause said notification to be published in the Congressional Record for the Senate.

(c) Powers and responsibilities of Congress

The Counsel shall limit any intervention or appearance as amicus curiae in an action or proceeding to issues relating to the powers and responsibilities of Congress.

(Pub. L. 95–521, title VII, § 706, Oct. 26, 1978, 92 Stat. 1880.)

SECTION REFERRED TO IN OTHER SECTIONS

This section is referred to in sections 288, 288b, 288k, 288l of this title.

§ 288f. Immunity proceedings

When directed to do so pursuant to section 288b(d) of this title, the Counsel shall serve as the duly authorized representative of the Senate or a committee or subcommittee of the Senate in requesting a United States district court to issue an order granting immunity pursuant to section 6005 of title 18.

(Pub. L. 95–521, title VII, § 707, Oct. 26, 1978, 92 Stat. 1880.)

SECTION REFERRED TO IN OTHER SECTIONS

This section is referred to in section 288b of this title.

§ 288g. Advisory and other functions

(a) Cooperation with persons, committees, subcommittees, and offices

The Counsel shall advise, consult, and cooperate with—

(1) the United States Attorney for the District of Columbia with respect to any criminal proceeding for contempt of Congress certified by the President pro tempore of the Senate pursuant to section 194 of this title;

(2) the committee of the Senate with the responsibility to identify any court proceeding or action which is of vital interest to the Senate;

(3) the Comptroller General, the General Accounting Office, the Office of Legislative

Counsel of the Senate, and the Congressional Research Service, except that none of the responsibilities and authority assigned by this chapter to the Counsel shall be construed to affect or infringe upon any functions, powers, or duties of the aforementioned;

(4) any Member, officer, or employee of the Senate not represented under section 288c of this title with regard to obtaining private legal counsel for such Member, officer, or employee;

(5) the President pro tempore of the Senate, the Secretary of[1] Senate, the Sergeant-at-Arms of the Senate, and the Parliamentarian of the Senate, regarding any subpena, order, or request for withdrawal of papers presented to the Senate which raises a question of the privileges of the Senate; and

(6) any committee or subcommittee of the Senate in promulgating and revising their rules and procedures for the use of congressional investigative powers and with respect to questions which may arise in the course of any investigation.

(b) Legal research files

The Counsel shall compile and maintain legal research files of materials from court proceedings which have involved Congress, a House of Congress, an office or agency of Congress, or any committee, subcommittee, Member, officer, or employee of Congress. Public court papers and other research memoranda which do not contain information of a confidential or privileged nature shall be made available to the public consistent with any applicable procedures set forth in such rules of the Senate as may apply and the interests of the Senate.

(c) Miscellaneous duties

The Counsel shall perform such other duties consistent with the purposes and limitations of this chapter as the Senate may direct.

(Pub. L. 95–521, title VII, § 708, Oct. 26, 1978, 92 Stat. 1880.)

§ 288h. Defense of certain constitutional powers

In performing any function under this chapter, the Counsel shall defend vigorously when placed in issue—

(1) the constitutional privilege from arrest or from being questioned in any other place for any speech or debate under section 6 of article I of the Constitution of the United States;

(2) the constitutional power of the Senate to be judge of the elections, returns, and qualifications of its own Members and to punish or expel a Member under section 5 of article I of the Constitution of the United States;

(3) the constitutional power of the Senate to except from publication such parts of its journal as in its judgment may require secrecy;

(4) the constitutional power of the Senate to determine the rules of its proceedings;

(5) the constitutional power of Congress to make all laws as shall be necessary and proper for carrying into execution the constitutional powers of Congress and all other powers vested

---

[1] So in original. Probably should be "of the".

by the Constitution in the Government of the United States, or in any department or office thereof;

(6) all other constitutional powers and responsibilities of the Senate or of Congress; and

(7) the constitutionality of Acts and joint resolutions of the Congress.

(Pub. L. 95–521, title VII, § 709, Oct. 26, 1978, 92 Stat. 1881.)

§ 288i. Representation conflict or inconsistency

(a) Notification

In the carrying out of the provisions of this chapter, the Counsel shall notify the Joint Leadership Group, and any party represented or person affected, of the existence and nature of any conflict or inconsistency between the representation of such party or person and the carrying out of any other provision of this chapter or compliance with professional standards and responsibilities.

(b) Solution; publication in Congressional Record; review

Upon receipt of such notification, the members of the Joint Leadership Group shall recommend the action to be taken to avoid or resolve the conflict or inconsistency. If such recommendation is made by a two-thirds vote, the Counsel shall take such steps as may be necessary to resolve the conflict or inconsistency as recommended. If not, the members of the Joint Leadership Group shall cause the notification of conflict or inconsistency and recommendation with respect to resolution thereof to be published in the Congressional Record of the Senate. If the Senate does not direct the Counsel within fifteen days from the date of publication in the Record to resolve the conflict in another manner, the Counsel shall take such action as may be necessary to resolve the conflict or inconsistency as recommended. Any instruction or determination made pursuant to this subsection shall not be reviewable in any court of law.

(c) Computation of period following publication

For purposes of the computation of the fifteen day period in subsection (b) of this section—

(1) continuity of session is broken only by an adjournment of Congress sine die; and

(2) the days on which the Senate is not in session because of an adjournment of more than three days to a date certain are excluded.

(d) Reimbursement

The Senate may by resolution authorize the reimbursement of any Member, officer, or employee of the Senate who is not represented by the Counsel for fees and costs, including attorneys' fees, reasonably incurred in obtaining representation. Such reimbursement shall be from funds appropriated to the contingent fund of the Senate.

(Pub. L. 95–521, title VII, § 710, Oct. 26, 1978, 92 Stat. 1882.)

§ 288j. Consideration of resolutions to direct counsel

(a) Procedure; rules

(1) A resolution introduced pursuant to section 288b of this title shall not be referred to a committee, except as otherwise required under section 288d(c) of this title. Upon introduction, or upon being reported if required under section 288d(c) of this title, whichever is later, it shall at any time thereafter be in order (even though a previous motion to the same effect has been disagreed to) to move to proceed to the consideration of such resolution. A motion to proceed to the consideration of a resolution shall be highly privileged and not debatable. An amendment to such motion shall not be in order, and it shall not be in order to move to reconsider the vote by which such motion is agreed to.

(2) With respect to a resolution pursuant to section 288b(a) of this title, the following rules apply:

(A) If the motion to proceed to the consideration of the resolution is agreed to, debate thereon shall be limited to not more than ten hours, which shall be divided equally between, and controlled by, those favoring and those opposing the resolution. A motion further to limit debate shall not be debatable. No amendment to the resolution shall be in order. No motion to recommit the resolution shall be in order, and it shall not be in order to reconsider the vote by which the resolution is agreed to.

(B) Motions to postpone, made with respect to the consideration of the resolution, and motions to proceed to the consideration of other business, shall be decided without debate.

(C) All appeals from the decisions of the Chair relating to the application of the rules of the Senate to the procedure relating to the resolution shall be decided without debate.

(b) "Committee" defined

For purposes of this chapter, other than section 288b of this title, the term "committee" includes standing, select, and special committees of the Senate established by law or resolution.

(c) Rules of the Senate

The provisions of this section are enacted—

(1) as an exercise of the rulemaking power of the Senate, and, as such, they shall be considered as part of the rules of the Senate, and such rules shall supersede any other rule of the Senate only to the extent that rule is inconsistent therewith; and

(2) with full recognition of the constitutional right of the Senate to change such rules at any time, in the same manner, and to the same extent as in the case of any other rule of the Senate.

(Pub. L. 95–521, title VII, § 711, Oct. 26, 1978, 92 Stat. 1882.)

§ 288k. Attorney General relieved of responsibility

(a) Upon receipt of written notice that the Counsel has undertaken, pursuant to section 288c(a) of this title, to perform any representational service with respect to any designated party in any action or proceeding pending or to be instituted, the Attorney General shall—

(1) be relieved of any responsibility with respect to such representational service;

(2) have no authority to perform such service in such action or proceeding except at the request or with the approval of the Senate; and

(3) transfer all materials relevant to the representation authorized under section 288c(a) of this title to the Counsel, except that nothing in this subsection shall limit any right of the Attorney General under existing law to intervene or appear as amicus curiae in such action or proceeding.

(b) The Attorney General shall notify the Counsel with respect to any proceeding in which the United States is a party of any determination by the Attorney General or Solicitor General not to appeal any court decision affecting the constitutionality of an Act or joint resolution of Congress within such time as will enable the Senate to direct the Counsel to intervene as a party in such proceeding pursuant to section 288e of this title.

(Pub. L. 95–521, title VII, § 712, Oct. 26, 1978, 92 Stat. 1883.)

§ 288*l*. Procedural provisions

(a) Intervention or appearance

Permission to intervene as a party or to appear as amicus curiae under section 288e of this title shall be of right and may be denied by a court only upon an express finding that such intervention or appearance is untimely and would significantly delay the pending action or that standing to intervene has not been established under section 2 of article III of the Constitution of the United States.

(b) Compliance with admission requirements

The Counsel, the Deputy Counsel, or any designated Assistant Counsel or counsel specially retained by the Office shall be entitled, for the purpose of performing his functions under this chapter, to enter an appearance in any proceeding before any court of the United States or of a State or political subdivision thereof without compliance with any requirement for admission to practice before such court, except that the authorization conferred by this subsection shall not apply with respect to the admission of any such person to practice before the United States Supreme Court.

(c) Standing to sue; jurisdiction

Nothing in this chapter shall be construed to confer standing on any party seeking to bring, or jurisdiction on any court with respect to, any civil or criminal action against Congress, either House of Congress, a Member of Congress, a committee or subcommittee of a House of Congress, any office or agency of Congress, or any officer or employee of a House of Congress or any office or agency of Congress.

(Pub. L. 95–521, title VII, § 713, Oct. 26, 1978, 92 Stat. 1883.)

§ 288m. Contingent fund

The expenses of the Office shall be paid from the contingent fund of the Senate in accordance with section 68 of this title, and upon vouchers approved by the Counsel.

(Pub. L. 95–521, title VII, § 716, Oct. 26, 1978, 92 Stat. 1885.)

§ 288n. Travel and related expenses

Funds expended by the Senate Legal Counsel for travel and related expenses shall be subject to the same regulations and limitations (insofar as they are applicable) as those which the Senate Committee on Rules and Administration prescribes for application to travel and related expenses for which payment is authorized to be made from the contingent fund of the Senate.

(Pub. L. 98–51, title I, § 106, July 14, 1983, 97 Stat. 267.)

CODIFICATION

Section was enacted as part of the Congressional Operations Appropriation Act, 1984, which is title I of the Legislative Branch Appropriation Act, 1984, and not as part of title VII of Pub. L. 95–521 which in part comprises this chapter.

Section, as it relates to funds expended by the Legislative Counsel of the Senate, is classified to section 276b of this title.

CHAPTER 10—CLASSIFICATION OF EMPLOYEES OF HOUSE OF REPRESENTATIVES

§ 291. Congressional declaration of purpose

It is the purpose of this chapter to provide a classification system for the equitable establishment and adjustment of rates of compensation for, and for the efficient utilization of personnel in, certain positions under the House of Representatives to which this chapter applies, through—

(1) the creation and maintenance of orderly and equitable compensation relationships for such positions—

(A) in accordance with the principle of equal pay for substantially equal work, and

(B) with due regard to (i) differences in the levels of difficulty, responsibility, and qualification requirements of the work, (ii) the kind of work performed, (iii) satisfactory performance, and (iv) length of service;

(2) the application of appropriate position standards and position descriptions for such positions; and

(3) the adoption of organization and position titles in the House which accurately reflect the respective functions, duties, and responsibilities of those organizations and positions in the House to which this chapter applies.

(Pub. L. 88–652, § 2, Oct. 13, 1964, 78 Stat. 1079.)

REFERENCES IN TEXT

This chapter, referred to in text, was in the original "this Act", meaning Pub. L. 88–652, Oct. 13, 1964, 78

Stat. 1079, known as the House Employees Position Classification Act, which enacted this chapter and amended sections 88c and 123b of this title. For complete classification of this Act to the Code, see Short Title note set out below and Tables.

EFFECTIVE DATE

Section 17 of Pub. L. 88–652 provided that: "This Act [enacting this chapter and amending sections 88c and 123b of this title] shall become effective on January 1, 1965."

SHORT TITLE

Section 1 of Pub. L. 88–652 provided that: "This Act [enacting this chapter and amending sections 88c and 123b of this title] may be cited as the 'House Employees Position Classification Act'."

SAVINGS PROVISION

Section 15 of Pub. L. 88–652 provided that:

"(a) Notwithstanding any provision of this Act [this chapter], the aggregate (gross) rate of compensation of any employee immediately prior to the effective date of this Act [Jan. 1, 1965] shall not be reduced by reason of the enactment of this Act.

"(b) For the purposes of applicable law relating to the payment to any individual of compensation from more than one civilian office or position, each employee of the House to whom this Act applies who, immediately prior to the effective date of this Act—

"(1) is receiving basic compensation from more than one civilian office or position and

"(2) is in compliance with such law

shall be held and considered to be in compliance with such law on and after such effective date, notwithstanding the enactment of this Act, so long as such employee continues to receive, without break in service of more than thirty days, the same or lower rate of basic compensation in a position to which this Act does not apply."

§ 292. Positions affected

This chapter shall apply to—

(1) all positions under the Clerk, the Sergeant at Arms, the Chief Administrative Officer, and the Inspector General of the House of Representatives, except the positions of telephone operator and positions on the United States Capitol Police force;

(2) the position of minority pair clerk in the House;

(3) all positions under the House Recording Studio; and

(4) all positions under the House Radio and Television Correspondents' Gallery and the House Periodical Press Gallery.

(Pub. L. 88–652, §3, Oct. 13, 1964, 78 Stat. 1079; Pub. L. 104–53, title I, §108(1), Nov. 19, 1995, 109 Stat. 522.)

AMENDMENTS

1995—Par. (1). Pub. L. 104–53 substituted "Chief Administrative Officer, and the Inspector General" for "Doorkeeper, and the Postmaster,".

§ 293. Compensation schedules

(a)(1) The Committee on House Oversight of the House of Representatives (hereinafter referred to as the "committee") shall establish and maintain, and, from time to time, may revise, for positions, to which this chapter applies (other than positions within the purview of subsection (b) of this section the compensation for which is fixed and adjusted from time to time in accordance with prevailing rates), a compensation schedule of per annum rates, which shall be known as the "House Employees Schedule" and for which the symbol shall be "HS", subject to the following provisions:

(A) Such schedule shall be composed of such number of compensation levels as the committee deems appropriate.

(B) Each compensation level shall consist of twelve compensation steps.

(C) The per annum rate of compensation for each compensation step of each compensation level shall be in such amount as the committee deems appropriate, except that the per annum rate of compensation for the maximum compensation step of the highest compensation level shall not exceed the maximum rate of compensation authorized by chapter 51 and subchapter III of chapter 53 of title 5.

(2) The rates of compensation for such positions shall be in accordance with such schedule.

(b) The committee shall establish and maintain, and, from time to time, may revise, for positions under the Clerk, the Sergeant at Arms, the Chief Administrative Officer, and the Inspector General of the House of Representatives, the compensation for which, in the judgment of the committee, should be fixed and adjusted from time to time in accordance with prevailing rates, a compensation schedule providing for per annum or per hour rates, or both, established in accordance with prevailing rates and consisting of such number of compensation levels and steps as the committee deems appropriate, which shall be known as the "House Wage Schedule" and for which the symbol shall be "HWS". The rates of compensation for such positions shall be in accordance with such schedule.

(Pub. L. 88–652, §4, Oct. 13, 1964, 78 Stat. 1079; Pub. L. 104–53, title I, §108(2), Nov. 19, 1995, 109 Stat. 522; Pub. L. 104–186, title II, §209(1), Aug. 20, 1996, 110 Stat. 1743.)

AMENDMENTS

1996—Subsec. (a)(1). Pub. L. 104–186 substituted "House Oversight" for "House Administration".

1995—Subsec. (b). Pub. L. 104–53 substituted "Chief Administrative Officer, and the Inspector General" for "Doorkeeper, and the Postmaster,".

CHANGE OF NAME

Committee on House Oversight of House of Representatives changed to Committee on House Administration of House of Representatives by House Resolution No. 5, One Hundred Sixth Congress, Jan. 6, 1999.

INCREASES IN COMPENSATION

Increases in compensation for House officers and employees under authority of Federal Salary Act of 1967 (Pub. L. 90–206), Federal Pay Comparability Act of 1970 (Pub. L. 91–656), and Legislative Branch Appropriations Act, 1988 (Pub. L. 100–202), see sections 60a–2 and 60a–2a of this title, and Salary Directives of Speaker of the House, set out as notes under those sections.

§§ 293a to 293c. Omitted

Section 293a, Pub. L. 89–301, §11(c), Oct. 29, 1965, 79 Stat. 1120, required compensation of employees of House of Representatives whose compensation is fixed under this chapter to be increased by amounts equal to increases provided by section 60e–12(a) of this title.

Section 293b, Pub. L. 89–504, title III, §302(c), July 18, 1966, 80 Stat. 295, required compensation of employees of House of Representatives whose compensation is fixed under this chapter to be increased by amounts equal to increases provided by section 60e–13(a) of this title.

Section 293c, Pub. L. 90–206, title II, § 214(c), Dec. 16, 1967, 81 Stat. 636, required compensation of employees of House of Representatives whose compensation is fixed under this chapter to be increased by amounts equal to increases provided by section 60e–14(a) of this title.

§ 294. Position standards and descriptions

(a)(1) It shall be the duty of the committee to prescribe, revise, and (on a current basis) maintain position standards which shall apply to positions (in existence on, or established after, January 1, 1965) under the House of Representatives to which this chapter applies.

(2) The position standards shall—

(A) provide for the separation of such positions into appropriate classes for pay and personnel purposes on the basis of reasonable similarity with respect to types of positions, qualification requirements of positions, and levels of difficulty and responsibility of work, and

(B) govern the placement of such positions in their respective appropriate compensation levels of the appropriate compensation schedule.

(b)(1) Subject to review and approval by the committee, the Clerk, the Sergeant at Arms, the Chief Administrative Officer, and the Inspector General of the House of Representatives, shall prepare, revise, and (on a current basis) maintain, at such times and in such form as the committee deems appropriate, position descriptions of the respective positions (in existence on, or established after, January 1, 1965) under the House of Representatives to which this chapter applies which are under their respective jurisdictions, including—

(A) with respect to the Clerk, positions under the House Recording Studio,

(B) with respect to the Sergeant at Arms, the position of minority pair clerk in the House, and

(C) with respect to the Chief Administrative Officer, positions under the House Radio and Television Correspondents' Gallery and the House Periodical Press Gallery.

(2) The position descriptions shall—

(A) describe in detail the actual duties, responsibilities, and qualification requirements of the work of each of such positions,

(B) provide a position title for such position which accurately reflects such duties and responsibilities, and

(C) govern the placement of such position in its appropriate class.

(c) The Clerk, the Sergeant at Arms, the Chief Administrative Officer, and the Inspector General of the House of Representatives, shall transmit to the committee, at such times and in such form as the committee deems appropriate, all position descriptions required by subsection (b) of this section to be prepared, provided, and currently maintained by them, together with such other pertinent information as the committee may require, in order that the committee

shall have, at all times, current information with respect to such position descriptions, the positions to which such descriptions apply, and related personnel matters within the purview of this chapter. Such information so transmitted shall be kept on file in the committee.

(d) Notwithstanding any other provision of this chapter, the committee shall have authority, which may be exercised at any time in its discretion, to—

(1) conduct surveys and studies of all organization units, and the positions therein, to which this chapter applies;

(2) ascertain on a current basis the facts with respect to the duties, responsibilities, and qualification requirements of any position to which this chapter applies;

(3) prepare and revise the position description of any such position;

(4) place any such position in its appropriate class and compensation level;

(5) decide whether any such position is in its appropriate class and compensation level;

(6) change any such position from one class or compensation level to any other class or compensation level whenever the facts warrant; and

(7) prescribe such organization and position titles as may be appropriate to carry out the purposes of this chapter.

All such actions of the committee shall be binding on the House officer and organization unit concerned and shall be the basis for payment of compensation and for other personnel benefits and transactions until otherwise changed by the committee.

(Pub. L. 88–652, § 5, Oct. 13, 1964, 78 Stat. 1080; Pub. L. 104–53, title I, § 108(3), (4), Nov. 19, 1995, 109 Stat. 522; Pub. L. 104–186, title II, § 209(2), Aug. 20, 1996, 110 Stat. 1743.)

Amendments

1996—Subsec. (b)(1)(C). Pub. L. 104–186 substituted "Chief Administrative Officer" for "Doorkeeper".

1995—Subsec. (b)(1). Pub. L. 104–53 substituted "Chief Administrative Officer, and the Inspector General" for "Doorkeeper, and the Postmaster".

Subsec. (c). Pub. L. 104–53 substituted "Chief Administrative Officer, and the Inspector General" for "Doorkeeper, and the Postmaster,".

Transfer of Functions

Certain functions of Recording Studio and Officers of House of Representatives transferred to Director of Non-legislative and Financial Services by section 7 of House Resolution No. 423, One Hundred Second Congress, Apr. 9, 1992. Director of Non-legislative and Financial Services replaced by Chief Administrative Officer of House of Representatives by House Resolution No. 6, One Hundred Fourth Congress, Jan. 4, 1995.

Section Referred to in Other Sections

This section is referred to in section 295 of this title.

§ 295. Placement of positions in compensation schedules

The committee shall place each position (in existence on, or established after, January 1, 1965) under the House of Representatives to which this chapter applies in its appropriate class, and in its appropriate compensation level of the appropriate compensation schedule, in accordance with the position standards and position descriptions provided for in section 294 of this title. The committee is authorized, when circumstances so warrant, to change any such position from one class or compensation level to another class or compensation level. All actions of the committee under this section shall be binding on the House officer and organization unit concerned and shall be the basis for payment of compensation and for other personnel benefits and transactions until otherwise changed by the committee.

(Pub. L. 88–652, § 6, Oct. 13, 1964, 78 Stat. 1081.)

§ 296. Step increases; waiting periods; service in Armed Forces; automatic advancement

(a) Each employee in a compensation level of the House Employees Schedule (HS), who has not attained the highest schedule rate of compensation for the compensation level (HS level) in which his position is placed, shall be advanced successively to the next higher step of such HS level, as follows:

(1) to steps 2, 3, and 4, respectively—at the beginning of the first pay period following the completion, without break in service of more than thirty months, of one year of satisfactory service in the next lower step;

(2) to steps 5, 6, and 7, respectively—at the beginning of the first pay period following the completion, without break in service of more than thirty months, of two years of satisfactory service in the next lower step;

(3) to steps 8, 9, and 10, respectively—at the beginning of the first pay period following the completion, without break in service of more than thirty months, of three years of satisfactory service in the next lower step; and

(4) to steps 11 and 12, respectively—at the beginning of the first pay period following the completion, without break in service of more than thirty months, of five years of satisfactory service in the next lower step.

(b) The receipt of an increase in compensation during any of the waiting periods of service specified in subsection (a) of this section shall cause a new full waiting period of service to commence for further step increases under such subsection.

(c) Any increase in compensation granted by law, or granted by reason of an increase made by the committee in the rates of compensation of the House Employees Schedule, to employees within the purview of subsection (a) of this section shall not be held or considered to be an increase in compensation for the purposes of subsection (b) of this section.

(d) The benefit of successive step increases under subsection (a) of this section shall be preserved, under regulations prescribed by the committee, for employees whose continuous service is interrupted by service in the Armed Forces of the United States.

(e) The committee shall establish and maintain, and, from time to time, may revise, a system of automatic advancement, by successive step increases in compensation, on the basis of satisfactory service performed, without break in service of more than thirty months, for employees subject to the House Wage Schedule (HWS).

In the operation of such system of step increases the committee may prescribe regulations to the effect that—

(1) the receipt of an increase in compensation during any of the waiting periods of service required for advancement by step increases under such system shall cause a new full waiting period of service to commence for further step increases under such system;

(2) any increase in compensation granted by law, or granted by reason of an increase made by the committee in the rates of compensation of the House Wage Schedule, to employees within the purview of such system of step increases shall not be held or considered to be an increase in compensation for the purposes of subparagraph (1) of this subsection; and

(3) the benefit of successive step increases under such system of step increases shall be preserved, under regulations prescribed by the committee, for employees whose continuous service is interrupted by service in the Armed Forces of the United States.

(Pub. L. 88–652, § 7, Oct. 13, 1964, 78 Stat. 1081.)

§ 297. Appointments and reclassifications to higher compensation levels

(a) Each employee in a compensation level of the House Employees Schedule (HS), who is appointed to a position in a higher compensation level of such schedule, or whose position is placed in a higher compensation level of such schedule pursuant to a reclassification of such position, shall be paid compensation in such higher compensation level, in accordance with the following provisions, whichever is first applicable in the following numerical order of precedence:

(1) at the rate of the lowest step for which the rate of compensation equals the rate of compensation for that step, in the compensation level from which he is appointed, which is two steps above the step in such level which he had attained immediately prior to such appointment;

(2) at the rate of the lowest step for which the rate of compensation exceeds, by not less than two steps of the compensation level from which he is appointed, his rate of compensation immediately prior to such appointment; or

(3) at the rate of the highest step of such higher compensation level, or at his rate of compensation immediately prior to such appointment, whichever rate is the higher.

(b) The committee may provide by regulations for the payment of compensation, at an appropriate compensation step determined in accordance with such regulations, to each employee subject to the House Wage Schedule (HWS) who is appointed to a position in a higher compensation level of such schedule or whose position is placed in a higher compensation level of such schedule pursuant to a reclassification of such position.

(Pub. L. 88–652, § 8, Oct. 13, 1964, 78 Stat. 1082.)

§ 298. Reductions in compensation level

Each employee in a position of a compensation level of the House Employees Schedule (HS) or the House Wage Schedule (HWS), whose employment in such position and level is terminated and who is reemployed, with or without break in service, in a position in a lower compensation level (HS level or HWS level) of such schedule, or whose position is placed in a lower compensation level of such schedule pursuant to a reclassification of such position, shall be placed by the committee in such step of such lower compensation level as the committee deems appropriate.

(Pub. L. 88–652, § 9, Oct. 13, 1964, 78 Stat. 1083.)

§ 299. Repealed. Pub. L. 106–554, § 1(a)(2) [title I, § 102(a)], Dec. 21, 2000, 114 Stat. 2763, 2763A–100

Section, Pub. L. 88–652, § 10, Oct. 13, 1964, 78 Stat. 1083, related to compensation level of individual appointed to position subject to House Employees Schedule or House Wage Schedule.

EFFECTIVE DATE OF REPEAL

Pub. L. 106–554, § 1(a)(2) [title I, § 102(b)], Dec. 21, 2000, 114 Stat. 2763, 2763A–100, provided that: "The amendment made by subsection (a) [repealing this section] shall apply with respect to employees appointed on or after October 1, 2000."

§ 300. Establishment of positions; payment from applicable accounts

The committee may authorize the establishment of additional positions of the kind to which this chapter applies, on a permanent basis or on a temporary basis of not to exceed six months' duration, whenever, in the judgment of the committee, such action is warranted in the interests of the orderly and efficient operation of the House of Representatives. The compensation of each such position may be paid out of the applicable accounts of the House of Representatives until otherwise provided by law. An additional position of the kind to which this chapter applies shall not be established without authorization of the committee.

(Pub. L. 88–652, § 11, Oct. 13, 1964, 78 Stat. 1083; Pub. L. 104–186, title II, § 209(3), Aug. 20, 1996, 110 Stat. 1743.)

AMENDMENTS

1996—Pub. L. 104–186 substituted "applicable accounts" for "contingent fund".

§ 301. Preservation of existing appointing authorities

This chapter shall not be held or considered to change or otherwise affect—

(1) any authority to establish positions under the House of Representatives which are not within the purview of this chapter, or

(2) any authority to make appointments to positions under the House of Representatives, irrespective of whether such positions are within the purview of this chapter.

(Pub. L. 88–652, § 12, Oct. 13, 1964, 78 Stat. 1083.)

§ 302. Regulations

The committee is authorized to prescribe such regulations as may be necessary to carry out the purposes of this chapter.

(Pub. L. 88–652, § 13, Oct. 13, 1964, 78 Stat. 1084.)

§ 303. Dual compensation

For the purposes of applicable law relating to the payment to any employee subject to the House Employees Schedule or the House Wage Schedule of compensation from more than one civilian office or position, the rate of basic compensation of each employee subject to any such schedule shall be held and considered to be that rate which, when increased by additional compensation then currently authorized by law for House employees generally, equals or most nearly equals the per annum rate of compensation of such employee under such schedule.

(Pub. L. 88–652, § 14, Oct. 13, 1964, 78 Stat. 1084.)

SECTION REFERRED TO IN OTHER SECTIONS

This section is referred to in section 60e–13 of this title.

CHAPTER 10A—PAYROLL ADMINISTRATION IN HOUSE OF REPRESENTATIVES

§ 331. Single per annum gross rates of pay for employees

Whenever the rate of pay of an employee whose pay is disbursed by the Chief Administrative Officer of the House of Representatives is fixed or adjusted on or after the effective date of this section, that rate, as so fixed or adjusted, shall be a single per annum gross rate.

(Pub. L. 91–510, title IV, § 471, Oct. 26, 1970, 84 Stat. 1193; Pub. L. 104–186, title II, § 210(1), Aug. 20, 1996, 110 Stat. 1743.)

AMENDMENTS

1996—Pub. L. 104–186 substituted "Chief Administrative Officer" for "Clerk".

EFFECTIVE DATE

Chapter effective immediately prior to noon on Jan. 3, 1971, see section 601(1) of Pub. L. 91–510, set out as an Effective Date of 1970 Amendment note under section 72a of this title.

INCONSISTENT PROVISIONS

Section 477(b) of Pub. L. 91–510 provided that: "All provisions of law inconsistent with any provision of this Part [enacting this chapter, amending section 5533(c) of Title 5, Government Organization and Employees, and repealing sections 60g, 60g–1 and 72a(e) of this title] are hereby superseded to the extent of the inconsistency."

§ 332. Repealed. Pub. L. 104–186, title II, § 210(2)(A), Aug. 20, 1996, 110 Stat. 1743

Section, Pub. L. 91–510, title IV, § 472, Oct. 26, 1970, 84 Stat. 1194, directed single per annum gross rates of clerk hire allowances of Members determined on basis of population.

§ 333. Single per annum gross rates of allowances for personal services in offices of Speaker, Leaders, and Whips

The allowance for additional office personnel in the office of each of the following officials of the House of Representatives shall be at a single per annum gross rate, as follows:

(1) the Speaker, $110,000.
(2) the Majority Leader, $90,000.
(3) the Minority Leader, $55,000.
(4) the Majority Whip, $55,000.
(5) the Minority Whip, $55,000.

(Pub. L. 91–510, title IV, § 473, Oct. 26, 1970, 84 Stat. 1194.)

SECTION REFERRED TO IN OTHER SECTIONS

This section is referred to in section 333a of this title.

§ 333a. Limits on uses of funds provided under section 333

The funds provided under the provisions of section 333 of this title shall be limited to use for the compensation of additional personnel and other necessary official expenses.

(Pub. L. 98–51, title I, § 112, July 14, 1983, 97 Stat. 270; Pub. L. 104–186, title II, § 204(16), Aug. 20, 1996, 110 Stat. 1732.)

CODIFICATION

Section was enacted as part of the Congressional Operations Appropriation Act, 1984, which is title I of the Legislative Branch Appropriation Act, 1984, and not as part of part 6 (§§ 471–477) of title IV of Pub. L. 91–510 which in part comprises this chapter.

Section, as it applies to funds provided under section 74a–4 of this title, is classified to section 74a–5 of this title.

AMENDMENTS

1996—Pub. L. 104–186 made technical amendment to reference in original act which appears in text as reference to section 333 of this title.

§ 334. Repealed. Pub. L. 104–186, title II, § 210(3)(A), Aug. 20, 1996, 110 Stat. 1743

Section, Pub. L. 91–510, title IV, § 474, Oct. 26, 1970, 84 Stat. 1194, directed Clerk of House to convert existing basic pay rates to per annum gross pay rates.

§ 335. Obsolete references in existing law to basic pay rates

In any case in which—

(1) the rate of pay of any employee or position, or class of employees or positions, the pay for whom or for which is disbursed by the Chief Administrative Officer of the House of Representatives, or any maximum or minimum rate with respect to any such employee, position, or class, is referred to in or provided by statute or House resolution; and

(2) the rate so referred to or provided is a basic rate with respect to which additional pay is provided by law;

such statutory provision or resolution shall be deemed to refer, in lieu of such basic rate, to the per annum gross rate which an employee receiving such basic rate immediately prior to the effective date of this section would receive, without regard to such statutory provision or resolu-

tion, under section 334[1] of this title on and after such date.

(Pub. L. 91–510, title IV, § 475, Oct. 26, 1970, 84 Stat. 1195; Pub. L. 104–186, title II, § 210(4), Aug. 20, 1996, 110 Stat. 1743.)

REFERENCES IN TEXT

Section 334 of this title, referred to in text, was repealed by Pub. L. 104–186, title II, § 210(3)(A), Aug. 20, 1996, 110 Stat. 1743.

AMENDMENTS

1996—Par. (1). Pub. L. 104–186 substituted "Chief Administrative Officer" for "Clerk".

§ 336. Saving provision

The provisions of this chapter shall not be construed to—

(1) limit or otherwise affect any authority for the making of any appointment to, or for fixing or adjusting the pay for, any position for which the pay is disbursed by the Chief Administrative Officer of the House of Representatives; or

(2) affect the continuity of employment of, or reduce the pay of, any employee whose pay is disbursed by the Chief Administrative Officer of the House.

(Pub. L. 91–510, title IV, § 476, Oct. 26, 1970, 84 Stat. 1195; Pub. L. 104–186, title II, § 210(5), Aug. 20, 1996, 110 Stat. 1743.)

REFERENCES IN TEXT

This chapter, referred to in text, was in the original "this Part", meaning part 6 (§§ 471–477) of title IV of Pub. L. 91–510, Oct. 26, 1970, 84 Stat. 1193, which enacted this chapter, amended section 5533 of Title 5, Government Organization and Employees, repealed sections 60g, 60g–1, and 72a of this title, and enacted provisions set out as a note under section 331 of this title. For complete classification of part 6 to the Code, see Tables.

AMENDMENTS

1996—Pars. (1), (2). Pub. L. 104–186 substituted "Chief Administrative Officer" for "Clerk".

CHAPTER 11—CITIZENS' COMMISSION ON PUBLIC SERVICE AND COMPENSATION

_____
[1] See References in Text note below.

CHAPTER REFERRED TO IN OTHER SECTIONS

This chapter is referred to in section 31 of this title; title 3 section 104; title 5 sections 5312 to 5316; title 26 section 7456; title 28 sections 5, 44, 135, 252.

§ 351. Establishment

There is hereby established a commission to be known as the Citizens' Commission on Public Service and Compensation (hereinafter referred to as the "Commission").

(Pub. L. 90–206, title II, § 225(a), Dec. 16, 1967, 81 Stat. 642; Pub. L. 101–194, title VII, § 701(a), Nov. 30, 1989, 103 Stat. 1763.)

AMENDMENTS

1989—Pub. L. 101–194 substituted "Citizens' Commission on Public Service and Compensation" for "Commission on Executive, Legislative, and Judicial Salaries".

EFFECTIVE DATE

Chapter effective Dec. 16, 1967, see section 220(a)(1) of Pub. L. 90–206, set out as a note under section 3110 of Title 5, Government Organization and Employees.

§ 352. Membership

(1) The Commission shall be composed of 11 members, who shall be appointed from private life as follows:

(A) 2 appointed by the President of the United States;

(B) 1 appointed by the President pro tempore of the Senate, upon the recommendation of the majority and minority leaders of the Senate;

(C) 1 appointed by the Speaker of the House of Representatives;

(D) 2 appointed by the Chief Justice of the United States; and

(E) 5 appointed by the Administrator of General Services in accordance with paragraph (4).

(2) No person shall serve as a member of the Commission who is—

(A) an officer or employee of the Federal Government;

(B) registered (or required to register) under the Federal Regulation of Lobbying Act;[1] or

(C) a parent, sibling, spouse, child, or dependent relative, of anyone under subparagraph (A) or (B).

(3) The persons appointed under subparagraphs (A) through (D) of paragraph (1) shall be selected without regard to political affiliation, and should be selected from among persons who have experience or expertise in such areas as government, personnel management, or public administration.

(4) The Administrator of General Services shall by regulation establish procedures under which persons shall be selected for appointment under paragraph (1)(E). Such procedures—

(A) shall be designed in such a way so as to provide for the maximum degree of geographic diversity practicable among members under paragraph (1)(E);

(B) shall include provisions under which those members shall be chosen by lot from among names randomly selected from voter registration lists; and

---

[1] See References in Text note below.

(C) shall otherwise comply with applicable provisions of this section.

(5) The chairperson shall be designated by the President.

(6) A vacancy in the membership of the Commission shall be filled in the manner in which the original appointment was made.

(7) Each member of the Commission shall be paid at the rate of $100 for each day such member is engaged upon the work of the Commission and shall be allowed travel expenses, including a per diem allowance, in accordance with section 5703 of title 5, when engaged in the performance of services for the Commission.

(8)(A) The terms of office of persons first appointed as members of the Commission shall be for the period of the 1993 fiscal year of the Federal Government, and shall begin not later than February 14, 1993.

(B) After the close of the 1993 fiscal year of the Federal Government, persons shall be appointed as members of the Commission with respect to every fourth fiscal year following the 1993 fiscal year. The terms of office of persons so appointed shall be for the period of the fiscal year with respect to which the appointment is made, except that, if any appointment is made after the beginning and before the close of any such fiscal year, the term of office based on such appointment shall be for the remainder of such fiscal year.

(C)(i) Notwithstanding any provision of subparagraph (A) or (B), members of the Commission may continue to serve after the close of a fiscal year, if the date designated by the President under section 357 of this title (relating to the date by which the Commission is to submit its report to the President) is subsequent to the close of such fiscal year, and only if or to the extent necessary to allow the Commission to submit such report.

(ii) Notwithstanding any provision of section 353 of this title, authority under such section shall remain available, after the close of a fiscal year, so long as members of the Commission continue to serve.

(Pub. L. 90–206, title II, § 225(b), Dec. 16, 1967, 81 Stat. 642; Pub. L. 99–190, § 135(a), Dec. 19, 1985, 99 Stat. 1322; Pub. L. 101–194, title VII, § 701(b), Nov. 30, 1989, 103 Stat. 1763.)

REFERENCES IN TEXT

The Federal Regulation of Lobbying Act, referred to in par. (2)(B), is title III of act Aug. 2, 1946, ch. 753, 60 Stat. 839, which was classified generally to chapter 8A (§ 261 et seq.) of this title, prior to repeal by Pub. L. 104–65, § 11(a), Dec. 19, 1995, 109 Stat. 701. For complete classification of this Act to the Code, see Tables.

AMENDMENTS

1989—Pub. L. 101–194 amended section generally, substituting pars. (1) to (8) for former pars. (1) to (5).
1985—Par. (3). Pub. L. 99–190 inserted "and with respect to fiscal year 1987" at end of first sentence.

SECTION REFERRED TO IN OTHER SECTIONS

This section is referred to in sections 353, 356 of this title.

§ 353. Executive Director; additional personnel; detail of personnel of other agencies

(1) Without regard to the provisions of title 5 governing appointments in the competitive serv-

ice, and the provisions of chapter 51 and subchapter III of chapter 53 of such title, relating to classification and General Schedule pay rates, and on a temporary basis for periods covering all or part of any fiscal year referred to in subparagraphs (A) and (B) of section 352(8) of this title—

(A) the Commission is authorized to appoint an Executive Director and fix his basic pay at the rate provided for level V of the Executive Schedule by section 5316 of title 5; and

(B) with the approval of the Commission, the Executive Director is authorized to appoint and fix the basic pay (at respective rates not in excess of the maximum rate of the General Schedule in section 5332 of title 5) of such additional personnel as may be necessary to carry out the function of the Commission.

(2) Upon the request of the Commission, the head of any department, agency, or establishment of any branch of the Federal Government is authorized to detail, on a reimbursable basis, for periods covering all or part of any fiscal year referred to in subparagraphs (A) and (B) of section 352(8) of this title, any of the personnel of such department, agency, or establishment to assist the Commission in carrying out its function.

(Pub. L. 90–206, title II, § 225(c), Dec. 16, 1967, 81 Stat. 643; Pub. L. 101–194, title VII, § 701(c), Nov. 30, 1989, 103 Stat. 1764.)

REFERENCES IN TEXT

The provisions of title 5 governing appointments in the competitive service, referred to in par. (1), are classified generally to section 3301 et seq. of Title 5, Government Organization and Employees.

AMENDMENTS

1989—Pub. L. 101–194 substituted "subparagraphs (A) and (B) of section 352(8) of this title" for "section 352(2) and (3) of this title" in pars. (1) and (2).

REFERENCES IN OTHER LAWS TO GS–16, 17, OR 18 PAY RATES

References in laws to the rates of pay for GS–16, 17, or 18, or to maximum rates of pay under the General Schedule, to be considered references to rates payable under specified sections of Title 5, Government Organization and Employees, see section 529 [title I, § 101(c)(1)] of Pub. L. 101–509, set out in a note under section 5376 of Title 5.

SECTION REFERRED TO IN OTHER SECTIONS

This section is referred to in section 352 of this title.

§ 354. Use of United States mails

The Commission may use the United States mails in the same manner and upon the same conditions as other departments and agencies of the United States.

(Pub. L. 90–206, title II, § 225(d), Dec. 16, 1967, 81 Stat. 643.)

§ 355. Administrative support services

The Administrator of General Services shall provide administrative support services for the Commission on a reimbursable basis.

(Pub. L. 90–206, title II, § 225(e), Dec. 16, 1967, 81 Stat. 643.)

§ 356. Functions

The Commission shall conduct, in each of the respective fiscal years referred to in subparagraphs (A) and (B) of section 352(8) of this title, a review of the rates of pay of—

(A) the Vice President of the United States, Senators, Members of the House of Representatives, the Resident Commissioner from Puerto Rico, the Speaker of the House of Representatives, the President pro tempore of the Senate, and the majority and minority leaders of the Senate and the House of Representatives;

(B) offices and positions in the legislative branch referred to in subsections (a), (b), (c), and (d) of section 203 of the Federal Legislative Salary Act of 1964 (78 Stat. 415; Public Law 88–426);

(C) justices, judges, and other personnel in the judicial branch referred to in section 403 of the Federal Judicial Salary Act of 1964 (78 Stat. 434; Public Law 88–426) except bankruptcy judges, but including the judges of the United States Court of Federal Claims;

(D) offices and positions under the Executive Schedule in subchapter II of chapter 53 of title 5; and

(E) the Governors of the Board of Governors of the United States Postal Service appointed under section 202 of title 39.

Such review by the Commission shall be made for the purpose of determining and providing—

(i) the appropriate pay levels and relationships between and among the respective offices and positions covered by such review, and

(ii) the appropriate pay relationships between such offices and positions and the offices and positions subject to the provisions of chapter 51 and subchapter III of chapter 53 of title 5, relating to classification and General Schedule pay rates.

In reviewing the rates of pay of the offices or positions referred to in subparagraph (D) of this section, the Commission shall determine and consider the appropriateness of the executive levels of such offices and positions.

(Pub. L. 90–206, title II, § 225(f), Dec. 16, 1967, 81 Stat. 643; Pub. L. 91–375, § 6(a), Aug. 12, 1970, 84 Stat. 775; Pub. L. 94–82, title II, § 206(a), Aug. 9, 1975, 89 Stat. 423; Pub. L. 95–598, title III, § 301, Nov. 6, 1978, 92 Stat. 2673; Pub. L. 97–164, title I, § 143, Apr. 2, 1982, 96 Stat. 45; Pub. L. 99–190, § 135(b), Dec. 19, 1985, 99 Stat. 1322; Pub. L. 100–202, § 101(a) [title IV, § 408(c)], Dec. 22, 1987, 101 Stat. 1329, 1329–27; Pub. L. 101–194, title VII, § 701(d), Nov. 30, 1989, 103 Stat. 1764; Pub. L. 102–572, title IX, § 902(b)(1), Oct. 29, 1992, 106 Stat. 4516.)

REFERENCES IN TEXT

The rates of pay of the offices and positions in the legislative branch, referred to in par. (B), are set out in section 136a–2 of this title; sections 703(f) and 731(c) of Title 31, Money and Finance; sections 162a and 166b–3a of Title 40, Public Buildings, Property, and Works; and section 303 of Title 44, Public Printing and Documents.

The rates of pay of justices, judges, and other personnel in the judicial branch, referred to in par. (C), are set out in section 867 of Title 10, Armed Forces; section 7443 of Title 26, Internal Revenue Code; and sections 5,

44, 135, 173, 213, 252, 603, and 792 of Title 28, Judiciary and Judicial Procedure.

AMENDMENTS

1992—Par. (C). Pub. L. 102–572 substituted "United States Court of Federal Claims" for "United States Claims Court".

1989—Pub. L. 101–194 substituted "subparagraphs (A) and (B) of section 352(8) of this title" for "section 352(2) and (3) of this title".

1987—Par. (C). Pub. L. 100–202 substituted "except bankruptcy judges, but including" for "and magistrates and".

1985—Pub. L. 99–190 inserted last sentence relating to review of rates of pay of offices or positions.

1982—Par. (C). Pub. L. 97–164 inserted reference to judges of the United States Claims Court.

1978—Par. (C). Pub. L. 95–598 struck out reference to section 402(d) and inserted reference to magistrates.

1975—Par. (A). Pub. L. 94–82 inserted "the Vice President of the United States" before "Senators", and "the Speaker of the House of Representatives, the President pro tempore of the Senate, and the majority and minority leaders of the Senate and the House of Representatives" after "Puerto Rico".

1970—Par. (E). Pub. L. 91–375 added par. (E).

EFFECTIVE DATE OF 1992 AMENDMENT

Amendment by Pub. L. 102–572 effective Oct. 29, 1992, see section 911 of Pub. L. 102–572, set out as a note under section 171 of Title 28, Judiciary and Judicial Procedure.

EFFECTIVE DATE OF 1987 AMENDMENT

Amendment by Pub. L. 100–202 effective Oct. 1, 1988, and any salary affected by the amendment to be adjusted at beginning of first applicable pay period commencing on or after such date, see section 101(a) [title IV, § 408(d)] of Pub. L. 100–202, set out as a note under section 153 of Title 28, Judiciary and Judicial Procedure.

EFFECTIVE DATE OF 1982 AMENDMENT

Amendment by Pub. L. 97–164 effective Oct. 1, 1982, see section 402 of Pub. L. 97–164, set out as a note under section 171 of Title 28, Judiciary and Judicial Procedure.

EFFECTIVE DATE OF 1978 AMENDMENT

Amendment by Pub. L. 95–598 effective Oct. 1, 1979, see section 402(a) of Pub. L. 95–598, set out as an Effective Date note preceding section 101 of Title 11, Bankruptcy.

EFFECTIVE DATE OF 1970 AMENDMENT

Amendment by Pub. L. 91–375 effective within 1 year after Aug. 12, 1970, on date established therefor by the Board of Governors of the United States Postal Service and published by it in the Federal Register, see section 15(a) of Pub. L. 91–375, set out as an Effective Date note preceding section 101 of Title 39, Postal Service.

EFFECTIVE RATES OF PAY PENDING CHANGES IN RATES PURSUANT TO FEDERAL SALARY ACT OF 1967

Section 206(b) of Pub. L. 94–82 provided that: "Until such time as a change in the rate of pay of the offices referred to in the amendment made by subsection (a) of this section [amending par. (A) of this section] occurs under the provisions of the Federal Salary Act of 1967 (2 U.S.C. 351–361), as amended by subsection (a) of this section, such rates of pay shall be the rates of pay in effect immediately prior to the date of enactment of this Act [Aug. 9, 1975], as adjusted under sections 203 and 204 of this title [amending sections 31, 60a note, 136a and 136a–1 of this title, section 104 of Title 3, The President, sections 42a and 51a of former Title 31, Money and Finance, sections 162a and 166b of Title 40, Public Buildings, Property, and Works, and section 303 of Title 44, Public Printing and Documents]."

SECTION REFERRED TO IN OTHER SECTIONS

This section is referred to in sections 60a–2a, 357, 358, 362, 363, 364 of this title.

§ 356a. Omitted

CODIFICATION

Section, Pub. L. 94–440, title II, § 100, Oct. 1, 1976, 90 Stat. 1446, the Legislative Branch Appropriation Act, 1977, which provided salary rate limitations for positions or offices referred to in section 356 of this title, applied to fiscal year 1977 and was not repealed in subsequent appropriation acts. See decision B–145492 of the Comptroller General of the United States, dated Sept. 21, 1976. Pub. L. 94–440, title II, § 100, is set out as a note under section 5318 of Title 5, Government Organization and Employees.

§ 357. Report by Commission to President with respect to pay

The Commission shall submit to the President a report of the results of each review conducted by the Commission with respect to rates of pay for the offices and positions within the purview of subparagraphs (A), (B), (C), and (D) of section 356 of this title, together with its recommendations. Each such report shall be submitted on such date as the President may designate but not later than December 15 next following the close of the fiscal year in which the review is conducted by the Commission.

(Pub. L. 90–206, title II, § 225(g), Dec. 16, 1967, 81 Stat. 644; Pub. L. 99–190, § 135(c), Dec. 19, 1985, 99 Stat. 1322; Pub. L. 101–194, title VII, § 701(e), Nov. 30, 1989, 103 Stat. 1764.)

AMENDMENTS

1989—Pub. L. 101–194 amended section catchline generally and in text substituted "Commission with respect to rates of pay for" for "Commission of" and "December 15 next following the close of the fiscal year in which the review is conducted by the Commission." for "December 15 of the fiscal year in which the review is conducted by the Commission."

1985—Pub. L. 99–190 substituted "December 15" for "January 1 next following the close".

1985 FISCAL YEAR RECOMMENDATIONS ON PAY RATES OF OFFICES AND POSITIONS

Section 135(g) of Pub. L. 99–190 provided that: "Notwithstanding section 225(g) of such Act (2 U.S.C. 357), the Commission on Executive, Legislative, and Judicial Salaries shall not make recommendations on the rates of pay of offices and positions within the purview of subparagraphs (A), (B), (C), and (D) of section 225(f) of such Act (2 U.S.C. 356) in connection with the review of rates of pay of such offices and positions conducted by the Commission in fiscal year 1985."

SECTION REFERRED TO IN OTHER SECTIONS

This section is referred to in sections 352, 358, 362, 363 of this title.

§ 358. Recommendations of President with respect to pay

(1) After considering the report and recommendations of the Commission submitted under section 357 of this title, the President shall transmit to Congress his recommendations with respect to the exact rates of pay, for offices and positions within the purview of subparagraphs (A), (B), (C), and (D) of section 356 of this title, which the President considers to be fair and rea-

sonable in light of the Commission's report and recommendations, the prevailing market value of the services rendered in the offices and positions involved, the overall economic condition of the country, and the fiscal condition of the Federal Government.

(2) The President shall transmit his recommendations under this section to Congress on the first Monday after January 3 of the first calendar year beginning after the date on which the Commission submits its report and recommendations to the President under section 357 of this title.

(Pub. L. 90–206, title II, § 225(h), Dec. 16, 1967, 81 Stat. 644; Pub. L. 99–190, § 135(d), Dec. 19, 1985, 99 Stat. 1322; Pub. L. 101–194, title VII, § 701(f), Nov. 30, 1989, 103 Stat. 1765.)

AMENDMENTS

1989—Pub. L. 101–194 amended section generally. Prior to amendment, section read as follows: "The President shall include, in the budget next transmitted under section 1105(a) of title 31 by him to the Congress after the date of the submission of the report and recommendations of the Commission under section 357 of this title, his recommendations with respect to the exact rates of pay which he deems advisable, for those offices and positions within the purview of subparagraphs (A), (B), (C), and (D) of section 356 of this title."

1985—Pub. L. 99–190 inserted reference to section 1105(a) of title 31, and struck out last sentence defining "budget".

COMMISSION'S FIRST REPORT AFTER JULY 30, 1983, TO INCLUDE RECOMMENDATION FOR APPROPRIATE SALARY FOR MEMBERS OF CONGRESS; PROHIBITION ON RECEIPT OF HONORARIA

Pub. L. 98–63, title I, § 908(e), July 30, 1983, 97 Stat. 338, which directed Commission on Executive, Legislative, and Judicial Salaries to include in first report required to be submitted by it after July 30, 1983, a recommendation for an appropriate salary for Members, which recommendation was to assume a prohibition on receipt of honoraria by Members, was repealed by Pub. L. 102–90, title I, § 6(c), Aug. 14, 1991, 105 Stat. 451.

COMPENSATION AND EMOLUMENTS OF ATTORNEY GENERAL

Pub. L. 94–2, Feb. 18, 1975, 89 Stat. 4, provided in part that the compensation and other emoluments attached to the Office of the Attorney General on and after Feb. 4, 1975, shall be those that on or after Feb. 18, 1975, attach to offices and positions at level I of the Executive Schedule (section 5312 of Title 5).

RECOMMENDATIONS FOR INCREASES IN EXECUTIVE, LEGISLATIVE, AND JUDICIAL SALARIES

Transmitted to Congress Jan. 9, 1989

H.Doc. No. 101–21, Cong. Rec., vol. 135, pt. 1, p. 251, Jan. 19, 1989

Dear Mr. Speaker: (Dear Mr. President:)[1]
As required by section 225 of the Federal Salary Act of 1967, Public Law 90–206 (2 U.S.C. 351 et seq.), the latest Quadrennial Commission on Executive, Legislative, and Judicial Salaries ("Commission") has submitted to me recommendations on salaries for Senators, Representatives, Federal judges, Cabinet officers, and other agency heads, and certain other officials in the executive, legislative, and judicial branches.

The statute requires that, in the budget next submitted after receipt of the report of the Commission, I set forth recommendations for adjustment of these salaries. Pursuant to section 225(i), as amended by section 135 of Public Law 99–190 [2 U.S.C. 359], these recommendations will be effective unless Congress dis-

approves the recommendation by a joint resolution within 30 days following the transmittal of my budget.

The Commission's report, submitted to me on December 14, 1988, documented both the substantial erosion in the real level of Federal executive pay that has occurred since 1969 and the recruitment and retention problems that have resulted, especially for the Federal judiciary. The Commission is to be commended for its diligent and conscientious effort to address the complicated and complex problems associated with Federal pay levels.

The Commission found that Federal executives and legislators have experienced a decline of approximately 35 percent in real salaries since 1969. In contrast, the salaries of General Schedule employees have declined by only 8 percent over the same period. The Commission's recommendations go a long way towards compensating for this salary erosion, but they do not make up the full gap. For example, for an official at Executive Level II, which is also the Congressional salary rate, the salary level adjusted for inflation since 1969 would be $140,340, while the Commission's recommendation is $135,000.

Every one of the Commissions that has met over the past 20 years concluded that a pay increase for key Federal officials was necessary. Each Commission found that pay for senior Government officials fell far behind that of their counterparts in the private sector. They also surmised that we cannot afford a Government composed primarily of those wealthy enough to serve.

In accepting the Commission's salary recommendations, I recognize that we are under a mandate to reduce the Federal deficit and hold the costs of Government to an absolute minimum. Thus, while I have decided to propose a pay increase that accepts in full the salary recommendations made by the Commissioners in their report to me last month, this proposal will not increase the deficit; the funding for the pay increase will be fully absorbed within proposed budget levels.

This increase fulfills my promise made in January 1987, that, assuming continued progress toward eliminating the deficit and favorable economic conditions, I would recommend another step toward overcoming the erosion of real income.

While this represents a substantial increase in salaries, it is coupled with the salutary recommendation of a ban on receipt of all honoraria in all branches of Government. Although my recommendation concerning honoraria has no legal effect, I urge the swiftest possible consideration of this important reform. The Commission further recommended that Congress enact legislation to bar officials in the three branches from receiving honoraria. I endorse these recommendations of the Commission as an appropriate step toward better government. A salary increase and a prohibition on receipt of honoraria together will help ensure that the Government is able to attract and keep talented senior officials and that the questions that arise from outside payments of honoraria are put to rest.

Accordingly, pursuant to subparagraphs (A), (B), (C), and (D) of section 225(f) and section 225(h) of Public Law 90–206 (81 Stat. 643 and 644), as amended [2 U.S.C. 356(A)–(D), 358] [this section]:

For the Vice President of the United States	$175,000
For offices and positions under the Executive Schedule in subchapter II of chapter 53 of title 5, United States Code, as follows:	
Positions at level I	155,000
Positions at level II	135,000
Positions at level III	125,000
Positions at level IV	120,000
Positions at level V	115,000
For the Speaker of the House of Representatives	175,000

For the President Pro Tempore of the Senate, majority leader and minority leader of the Senate, and majority leader and minority leader of the House of Representatives 155,000

For Senators, Members of the House of Representatives, Delegates to the House of Representatives, and the Resident Commissioner from Puerto Rico 135,000

For other officers and positions in the legislative branch as follows:

> Comptroller General of the United States 135,000
> Deputy Comptroller General of the United States, Librarian of Congress, and Architect of the Capitol 125,000
> General Counsel of the General Accounting Office, Deputy Librarian of Congress, and Assistant Architect of the Capitol 120,000

For Justices, judges, and other personnel in the judicial branch as follows:

> Chief Justice of the United States 175,000
> Associate Justices of the Supreme Court 165,000
> Judges:
>> U.S. Courts of Appeals 140,000
>> Court of Military Appeals 140,000
>> U.S. District Courts 135,000
>> Court of International Trade 135,000
>> Tax Court of the United States 135,000
>> U.S. Claims Court 135,000

Sincerely,

RONALD REAGAN.

¹ **Editorial note.** This is the text of identical letters addressed to the Speaker of the House of Representatives and the President of the Senate, which were transmitted on January 9, 1989.

DISAPPROVAL OF SALARY RECOMMENDATIONS FOR 1989 INCREASES

Pub. L. 101–1, Feb. 7, 1989, 102 Stat. 3, provided: "That the Congress disapproves in their entirety the recommendations transmitted to the Congress by the President on January 9, 1989, under section 225(h) of the Federal Salary Act of 1967."

PRIOR SALARY RECOMMENDATIONS

A prior recommendation of the President for increases in executive, legislative, and judicial salaries, which was transmitted to Congress on Jan. 5, 1987 (52 F.R. 4125; 101 Stat. 1967), was disapproved by Pub. L. 100–6, § 3, Feb. 12, 1987, 101 Stat. 94. However, such recommendation became effective pursuant to section 359 of this title.

A prior recommendation of the President for increases in executive, legislative, and judicial salaries, which was transmitted to Congress on Jan. 7, 1981 (H.Doc. No. 97–6, Cong. Rec., vol. 127, pt. 1, p. 241, Jan. 9, 1981), was disapproved by House Resolution No. 109, Ninety-sixth Congress, Mar. 12, 1981, Senate Resolution No. 89, Ninety-sixth Congress, Mar. 12, 1981, Senate Resolution No. 90, Ninety-sixth Congress, Mar. 12, 1981, Senate Resolution No. 91, Ninety-sixth Congress, Mar. 12, 1981, and Senate Resolution No. 92, Ninety-sixth Congress, Mar. 12, 1981.

A prior recommendation of the President for increases in executive, legislative, and judicial salaries was transmitted to Congress on Jan. 17, 1977 (42 F.R. 10297; 91 Stat. 1643).

A prior recommendation of the President for increases in executive, legislative, and judicial salaries was transmitted to Congress on Jan. 15, 1969 (34 F.R. 2241; 83 Stat. 863).

SECTION REFERRED TO IN OTHER SECTIONS

This section is referred to in sections 359, 360, 362 of this title.

§ 359. Effective date of recommendations of President

(1) None of the President's recommendations under section 358 of this title shall take effect unless approved under paragraph (2).

(2)(A) The recommendations of the President under section 358 of this title shall be considered approved under this paragraph if there is enacted into law a bill or joint resolution approving such recommendations in their entirety. This bill or joint resolution shall be passed by recorded vote to reflect the vote of each Member of Congress thereon.

(B)(i) The provisions of this subparagraph are enacted by the Congress—

(I) as an exercise of the rulemaking power of the Senate and the House of Representatives and as such shall be considered as part of the rules of each House, and shall supersede other rules only to the extent that they are inconsistent therewith; and

(II) with full recognition of the constitutional right of either House to change the rules (so far as they relate to the procedures of that House) at any time, in the same manner, and to the same extent as in the case of any other rule of that House.

(ii) During the 60-calendar-day period beginning on the date that the President transmits his recommendations to the Congress under section 358 of this title, it shall be in order as a matter of highest privilege in each House of Congress to consider a bill or joint resolution, if offered by the majority leader of such House (or a designee), approving such recommendations in their entirety.

(3) Except as provided in paragraph (4), any recommended pay adjustment approved under paragraph (2) shall take effect as of the date proposed by the President under section 358 of this title with respect to such adjustment.

(4)(A) Notwithstanding the approval of the President's pay recommendations in accordance with paragraph (2), none of those recommendations shall take effect unless, between the date on which the bill or resolution approving those recommendations is signed by the President (or otherwise becomes law) and the earliest date as of which the President proposes (under section 358 of this title) that any of those recommendations take effect, an election of Representatives shall have intervened.

(B) For purposes of this paragraph, the term "election of Representatives" means an election held on the Tuesday following the first Monday of November in any even-numbered calendar year.

(Pub. L. 90–206, title II, § 225(i), Dec. 16, 1967, 81 Stat. 644; Pub. L. 95–19, title IV, § 401(a), Apr. 12, 1977, 91 Stat. 45; Pub. L. 99–190, § 135(e), Dec. 19, 1985, 99 Stat. 1322; Pub. L. 101–194, title VII, § 701(g), Nov. 30, 1989, 103 Stat. 1765.)

AMENDMENTS

1989—Pub. L. 101–194 amended section generally. Prior to amendment, section read as follows:

"(1) The recommendations of the President which are transmitted to the Congress pursuant to section 358 of this title shall be effective as provided in paragraph (2) of this section unless any such recommendation is disapproved by a joint resolution agreed to by the Congress not later than the last day of the 30-day period which begins on the date of which such recommendations are transmitted to the Congress.

"(2) The effective date of the rate or rates of pay which take effect for an office or position under paragraph (1) of this section shall be the first day of the first pay period which begins for such office or position after the end of the 30-day period described in such paragraph."

1985—Par. (1). Pub. L. 99–190 amended par. (1) generally, substituting provisions relating to the effective date of Presidential recommendations transmitted to Congress pursuant to section 358 of this title, for provisions relating to voting requirements and procedures for Presidential recommendations to Congress.

Par. (2). Pub. L. 99–190 amended par. (2) generally, substituting provisions relating to effective date of rates of pay for offices or positions under par. (1), for provisions relating to later operative dates of Presidential recommendations.

1977—Par. (1). Pub. L. 95–19 substituted provisions directing each house of the Congress to conduct a separate vote within sixty days on each Presidential recommendation with respect to the offices and positions described in section 356(A), (B), (C), and (D) of this title, with the votes to be recorded so as to reflect the votes of each individual member and with each recommendation, if approved, to become effective for the offices and positions covered at the beginning of the first pay period which begins after the thirtieth day following the approval of the recommendation by the second house of the Congress to approve the recommendation, for provisions directing that all or part of the recommendations of the President transmitted to the Congress in the budget under section 358 of this title be effective at the beginning of the first pay period beginning after the thirtieth day following the transmittal of the recommendations to the budget, but only to the extent that, between the date of transmittal of the recommendations in the budget and the beginning of the pay period, there has not been enacted into law a statute establishing rates of pay other than the rates set in the recommendation, neither house of the Congress specifically disapproves all or part of the recommendations, or both.

Par. (2). Pub. L. 95–19 reenacted par. (2) without change.

SECTION REFERRED TO IN OTHER SECTIONS

This section is referred to in section 360 of this title.

§ 360. Effect of recommendations on existing law and prior recommendations

The recommendations of the President taking effect as provided in section 359 of this title shall be held and considered to modify, supersede, or render inapplicable, as the case may be, to the extent inconsistent therewith—

(A) all provisions of law enacted prior to the effective date or dates of all or part (as the case may be) of such recommendations (other than any provision of law enacted with respect to such recommendations in the period beginning on the date the President transmits his recommendations to the Congress under section 358 of this title and ending on the date of their approval under section 359(2) of this title), and

(B) any prior recommendations of the President which take effect under this chapter.

(Pub. L. 90–206, title II, § 225(j), Dec. 16, 1967, 81 Stat. 644; Pub. L. 95–19, title IV, § 401(b), Apr. 12, 1977, 91 Stat. 46; Pub. L. 99–190, § 135(f), Dec. 19, 1985, 99 Stat. 1322; Pub. L. 101–194, title VII, § 701(h), Nov. 30, 1989, 103 Stat. 1766.)

AMENDMENTS

1989—Cl. (A). Pub. L. 101–194 substituted "(other than any provision of law enacted with respect to such recommendations in the period beginning on the date the President transmits his recommendations to the Congress under section 358 of this title and ending on the date of their approval under section 359(2) of this title), and" for "(other than any provision of law enacted in the period specified section 359 of this title with respect to such recommendations), and".

1985—Pub. L. 99–190 substituted "taking effect as provided in section 359 of this title shall" for "transmitted to the Congress immediately following a review conducted by the Commission in one of the fiscal years referred to in section 352(2) and (3) of this title shall, if approved by the Congress as provided in section 359 of this title,", and in cl. (A) struck out "in paragraph (1) of" before "section 359 of this title".

1977—Pub. L. 95–19 inserted ", if approved by the Congress as provided in section 359 of this title,".

§ 361. Publication of recommendations

The recommendations of the President which take effect shall be printed in the Statutes at Large in the same volume as public laws and shall be printed in the Federal Register and included in the Code of Federal Regulations.

(Pub. L. 90–206, title II, § 225(k), Dec. 16, 1967, 81 Stat. 644.)

§ 362. Requirements applicable to recommendations

Notwithstanding any other provision of this chapter, the recommendations submitted by the Commission to the President under section 357 of this title, and the recommendations transmitted by the President to the Congress under section 358 of this title, shall be in conformance with the following:

(1) Any recommended pay adjustment shall specify the date as of which it is proposed that such adjustment take effect.

(2) The proposed effective date of a pay adjustment may occur no earlier than January 1 of the second fiscal year, and no later than December 31 next following the close of the fifth fiscal year, beginning after the fiscal year in which the Commission conducts its review under section 356 of this title.

(3)(A)(i) The rates of pay recommended for the Speaker of the House of Representatives, the Vice President of the United States, and the Chief Justice of the United States, respectively, shall be equal.

(ii) The rates of pay recommended for the majority and minority leaders of the Senate and the House of Representatives, the President pro tempore of the Senate, and each office or position under section 5312 of title 5 (relating to level I of the Executive Schedule), respectively, shall be equal.

(iii) The rates of pay recommended for a Senator, a Member of the House of Representatives, the Resident Commissioner from Puerto Rico, a Delegate to the House of Representatives, a judge of a district court of the United States, a judge of the United States Court of International Trade, and each office or position under section 5313 of title 5 (relating to level II of the Executive Schedule), respectively, shall be equal.

(B) Nothing in this section shall be considered to require that the rate recommended for any office or position by the President under section 358 of this title be the same as the rate recommended for such office or position by the Commission under section 357 of this title.

(Pub. L. 90–206, title II, § 225(*l*), as added Pub. L. 101–194, title VII, § 701(i), Nov. 30, 1989, 103 Stat. 1766.)

§ 363. Additional function

The Commission shall, whenever it conducts a review under section 356 of this title, also conduct a review under this section relating to any recruitment or retention problems, and any public policy issues involved in maintaining appropriate ethical standards, with respect to any offices or positions within the Federal public service. Any findings or recommendations under this section shall be included by the Commission as part of its report to the President under section 357 of this title.

(Pub. L. 90–206, title II, § 225(m), as added Pub. L. 101–194, title VII, § 701(j), Nov. 30, 1989, 103 Stat. 1767.)

§ 364. Provision relating to certain other pay adjustments

(1) A provision of law increasing the rate of pay payable for an office or position within the purview of subparagraph (A), (B), (C), or (D) of section 356 of this title shall not take effect before the beginning of the Congress following the Congress during which such provision is enacted.

(2) For purposes of this section, a provision of law enacted during the period beginning on the Tuesday following the first Monday of November of an even-numbered year of any Congress and ending at noon on the following January 3 shall be considered to have been enacted during the first session of the following Congress.

(3) Nothing in this section shall be considered to apply with respect to any pay increase—

(A) which takes effect under the preceding sections of this chapter;

(B) which is based on a change in the Employment Cost Index (as determined under section 704(a)(1) of the Ethics Reform Act of 1989) or which is in lieu of any pay adjustment which might otherwise be made in a year based on a change in such index (as so determined); or

(C) which takes effect under section 702 or 703 of the Ethics Reform Act of 1989.

(Pub. L. 90–206, title II, § 225(n), as added Pub. L. 101–194, title VII, § 701(k), Nov. 30, 1989, 103 Stat. 1767.)

REFERENCES IN TEXT

Sections 702, 703, and 704(a)(1) of the Ethics Reform Act of 1989, referred to in par. (3)(B), (C), are sections 702, 703, and 704(a)(1) of Pub. L. 101–194 which are set out as notes under sections 5303 and 5318 of Title 5, Government Organization and Employees.

CHAPTER 12—CONTESTED ELECTIONS

§ 381. Definitions

For purposes of this chapter:

(1) The term "election" means an official general or special election to choose a Representative in, or Delegate or Resident Commissioner to, the Congress, but that term does not include a primary election, or a caucus or convention of a political party.

(2) The term "candidate" means an individual (A) whose name is printed on the official ballot for election to the office of Representative in, or Delegate or Resident Commissioner to, the Congress, or (B) notwithstanding his name is not printed on such ballot, who seeks election to the office of Representative in, or Delegate or Resident Commissioner to, the Congress by write-in votes, provided that he is qualified for such office and that, under the law of the State in which the congressional district is located, write-in voting for such office is permitted and he is eligible to receive write-in votes in such election.

(3) The term "contestant" means an individual who contests the election of a Member of the House of Representatives under this chapter.

(4) The term "contestee" means a Member of the House of Representatives whose election is contested under this chapter.

(5) The term "Member of the House of Representatives" means an incumbent Representative in, or Delegate or Resident Commissioner to, the Congress, or an individual who has been elected to such office but has not taken the oath of office.

(6) The term "Clerk" means the Clerk of the House of Representatives.

(7) The term "committee" means the Committee on House Oversight of the House of Representatives.

(8) The term "State" means a State of the United States and any territory or possession of the United States.

(9) The term "write-in vote" means a vote cast for a person whose name does not appear on the official ballot by writing in the name of such person on such ballot or by any other method prescribed by the law of the State in which the election is held.

(Pub. L. 91–138, § 2, Dec. 5, 1969, 83 Stat. 284; Pub. L. 104–186, title II, § 211(1), (2), Aug. 20, 1996, 110 Stat. 1743, 1744.)

AMENDMENTS

1996—Pub. L. 104–186, § 211(1)(A)–(C), substituted "chapter:" for "chapter—" in introductory provisions, redesignated subdivs. (a) to (i) as pars. (1) to (9), respectively, and realigned margins of pars. (1) to (9).

Par. (1). Pub. L. 104–186, § 211(2)(A), substituted ", or Delegate or Resident Commissioner to, the Congress, but that term" for "or Resident Commissioner to the Congress of the United States, but".

Par. (2). Pub. L. 104–186, § 211(2)(B), substituted "office of Representative in, or Delegate or Resident Commissioner to, the Congress" for "House of Representatives of the United States" in subpar. (A) and "House of Representatives" in subpar. (B).

Pub. L. 104–186, § 211(1)(D), redesignated pars. (1) and (2) as subpars. (A) and (B), respectively.

Pars. (3), (4). Pub. L. 104–186, § 211(2)(C), (D), struck out "of the United States" after "House of Representatives".

Par. (5). Pub. L. 104–186, § 211(2)(E), substituted "term 'Member of the House of Representatives' means an incumbent Representative in, or Delegate or Resident Commissioner to, the Congress, or an individual who has been elected to such office" for "term 'Member' means an incumbent Representative in or Resident Commissioner to the Congress of the United States, or an individual who has been elected to either of such offices".

Par. (6). Pub. L. 104–186, § 211(2)(F), struck out "of the United States" after "House of Representatives".

Par. (7). Pub. L. 104–186, § 211(2)(G), substituted "House Oversight of the House of Representatives" for "House Administration of the House of Representatives of the United States".

Par. (8). Pub. L. 104–186, § 211(2)(H), substituted "means a State of the United States and any territory or" for "includes territory and".

Par. (9). Pub. L. 104–186, § 211(1)(A), (C), redesignated former subsec. (i) as par. (9).

CHANGE OF NAME

Committee on House Oversight of House of Representatives changed to Committee on House Administration of House of Representatives by House Resolution No. 5, One Hundred Sixth Congress, Jan. 6, 1999.

EFFECTIVE DATE

Section 19 of Pub. L. 91–138 provided that: "The provisions of, and the repeals made by, this Act [enacting this chapter and repealing sections 201 to 226 of this title] shall apply with respect to any general or special election for Representative in, or Resident Commissioner to, the Congress of the United States occurring after the date of enactment of this Act [Dec. 5, 1969]."

SHORT TITLE

Section 1 of Pub. L. 91–138 provided that: "This Act [enacting this chapter and repealing sections 201 to 226 of this title] may be cited as the 'Federal Contested Elections Act'."

§ 382. Notice of contest

(a) Filing of notice

Whoever, having been a candidate for election in the last preceding election and claiming a right to such office, intends to contest the election of a Member of the House of Representatives, shall, within thirty days after the result of such election shall have been declared by the officer of Board of Canvassers authorized by law to declare such result, file with the Clerk and serve upon the contestee written notice of his intention to contest such election.

(b) Contents and form of notice

Such notice shall state with particularity the grounds upon which contestant contests the election and shall state that an answer thereto must be served upon contestant under section 383 of this title within thirty days after service of such notice. Such notice shall be signed by contestant and verified by his oath or affirmation.

(c) Service of notice; proof of service

Service of the notice of contest upon contestee shall be made as follows:

(1) by delivering a copy to him personally;

(2) by leaving a copy at his dwelling house or usual place of abode with a person of discretion not less than sixteen years of age then residing therein;

(3) by leaving a copy at his principal office or place of business with some person then in charge thereof;

(4) by delivering a copy to an agent authorized by appointment to receive service of such notice;

(5) by mailing a copy by registered or certified mail addressed to contestee at his residence or principal office or place of business. Service by mail is complete upon mailing; or

(6) the verified return by the person so serving such notice, setting forth the time and

manner of such service shall be proof of same, and the return post office receipt shall be proof of the service of said notice mailed by registered or certified mail as aforesaid. Proof of service shall be made to the Clerk promptly and in any event within the time during which the contestee must answer the notice of contest. Failure to make proof of service does not affect the validity of the service.

(Pub. L. 91–138, § 3, Dec. 5, 1969, 83 Stat. 284; Pub. L. 104–186, title II, § 211(3), Aug. 20, 1996, 110 Stat. 1744.)

AMENDMENTS

1996—Subsec. (a). Pub. L. 104–186, § 211(3)(A), struck out "to the House of Representatives" after "for election".

Subsec. (c)(4), (5). Pub. L. 104–186, § 211(3)(B), struck out "or" at end of par. (4) and inserted "or" at end of par. (5).

SECTION REFERRED TO IN OTHER SECTIONS

This section is referred to in sections 383, 394 of this title.

§ 383. Response of contestee

(a) Answer

Any contestee upon whom a notice of contest as described in section 382 of this title shall be served, shall, within thirty days after the service thereof, serve upon contestant a written answer to such notice, admitting or denying the averments upon which contestant relies. If contestee is without knowledge or information sufficient to form a belief as to the truth of an averment, he shall so state and this shall have the effect of a denial. Such answer shall set forth affirmatively any other defenses, in law or fact, on which contestee relies. Contestee shall sign and verify such answer by oath or affirmation.

(b) Defenses by motion prior to answer

At the option of contestee, the following defenses may be made by motion served upon contestant prior to contestee's answer:

(1) Insufficiency of service of notice of contest.
(2) Lack of standing of contestant.
(3) Failure of notice of contest to state grounds sufficient to change result of election.
(4) Failure of contestant to claim right to contestee's seat.

(c) Motion for more definite statement

If a notice of contest to which an answer is required is so vague or ambiguous that the contestee cannot reasonably be required to frame a responsive answer, he may move for a more definite statement before interposing his answer. The motion shall point out the defects complained of and the details desired. If the motion is granted and the order of the committee is not obeyed within ten days after notice of the order or within such other time as the committee may fix, the committee may dismiss the action, or make such order as it deems just.

(d) Time for serving answer after service of motion

Service of a motion permitted under this section alters the time for serving the answer as follows, unless a different time is fixed by order

of the committee: If the committee denies the motion or postpones its disposition until the hearing on the merits, the answer shall be served within ten days after notice of such action. If the committee grants a motion for a more definite statement the answer shall be served within ten days after service of the more definite statement.

(Pub. L. 91–138, § 4, Dec. 5, 1969, 83 Stat. 285.)

SECTION REFERRED TO IN OTHER SECTIONS

This section is referred to in sections 382, 386 of this title.

§ 384. Service and filing of papers other than notice of contest

(a) Modes of service

Except for the notice of contest, every paper required to be served shall be served upon the attorney representing the party, or, if he is not represented by an attorney, upon the party himself. Service upon the attorney or upon a party shall be made:

(1) by delivering a copy to him personally;
(2) by leaving it at his principal office with some person then in charge thereof; or if the office is closed or the person to be served has no office, leaving it at his dwelling house or usual place of abode with a person of discretion not less than sixteen years of age then residing therein; or
(3) by mailing it addressed to the person to be served at his residence or principal office. Service by mail is complete upon mailing.

(b) Filing of papers with clerk

All papers subsequent to the notice of contest required to be served upon the opposing party shall be filed with the Clerk either before service or within a reasonable time thereafter.

(c) Proof of service

Papers filed subsequent to the notice of contest shall be accompanied by proof of service showing the time and manner of service, made by affidavit of the person making service or by certificate of an attorney representing the party in whose behalf service is made. Failure to make proof of service does not affect the validity of such service.

(Pub. L. 91–138, § 5, Dec. 5, 1969, 83 Stat. 286.)

§ 385. Default of contestee

The failure of contestee to answer the notice of contest or to otherwise defend as provided by this chapter shall not be deemed an admission of the truth of the averments in the notice of contest. Notwithstanding such failure, the burden is upon contestant to prove that the election results entitle him to contestee's seat.

(Pub. L. 91–138, § 6, Dec. 5, 1969, 83 Stat. 286.)

§ 386. Deposition

(a) Oral examination

Either party may take the testimony of any person, including the opposing party, by deposition upon oral examination for the purpose of discovery or for use as evidence in the contested election case, or for both purposes. Depositions shall be taken only within the time for the taking of testimony prescribed in this section.

(b) Scope of examination

Witnesses may be examined regarding any matter, not privileged, which is relevant to the subject matter involved in the pending contested election case, whether it relates to the claim or defense of the examining party or the claim or defense of the opposing party, including the existence, description, nature, custody, condition and location of any books, papers, documents, or other tangible things and the identity and location of persons having knowledge of relevant facts. After the examining party has examined the witness the opposing party may cross examine.

(c) Order and time of taking testimony

The order in which the parties may take testimony shall be as follows:

(1) Contestant may take testimony within thirty days after service of the answer, or, if no answer is served within the time provided in section 383 of this title, within thirty days after the time for answer has expired.

(2) Contestee may take testimony within thirty days after contestant's time for taking testimony has expired.

(3) If contestee has taken any testimony or has filed testimonial affidavits or stipulations under section 387(c) of this title, contestant may take rebuttal testimony within ten days after contestee's time for taking testimony has expired.

(d) Officer before whom testimony may be taken

Testimony shall be taken before an officer authorized to administer oaths by the laws of the United States or of the place where the examination is held.

(e) Subpena

Attendance of witnesses may be compelled by subpena as provided in section 388 of this title.

(f) Taking of testimony by party or his agent

At the taking of testimony, a party may appear and act in person, or by his agent or attorney.

(g) Conduct of examination; recordation of testimony; notation of objections; interrogatories

The officer before whom testimony is to be taken shall put the witness under oath and shall personally, or by someone acting under his direction and in his presence, record the testimony of the witness. The testimony shall be taken stenographically and transcribed. All objections made at the time of examination to the qualifications of the officer taking the deposition, or to the manner of taking it, or to the evidence presented, or the conduct of any party, and any other objection to the proceedings, shall be noted by the officer upon the deposition. Evidence objected to shall be taken subject to the objections. In lieu of participating in the oral examination, a party served with a notice of deposition may transmit written interrogatories to the officer, who shall propound them to the witness and record the answers verbatim.

(h) Examination of deposition by witness; signature of witness or officer; use of deposition

When the testimony is fully transcribed, the deposition shall be submitted to the witness for examination and shall be read to or by him, unless such examination and reading are waived by the witness and the parties. Any changes in the form or substance which the witness desires to make shall be entered upon the deposition by the officer with a statement of the reasons given by the witness for making them. The deposition shall be signed by the witness, unless the parties by stipulation waive the signing or the witness is ill or cannot be found or refuses to sign. If the deposition is not signed by the witness, the officer shall sign it and note on the deposition the fact of the waiver or of the illness or the absence of the witness or the fact of refusal to sign together with the reason, if any, given therefor; and the deposition may then be used as fully as though signed, unless on a motion to suppress, the committee rules that the reasons given for the refusal to sign require rejection of the deposition in whole or in part.

(Pub. L. 91–138, § 7, Dec. 5, 1969, 83 Stat. 286.)

SECTION REFERRED TO IN OTHER SECTIONS

This section is referred to in section 387 of this title.

§ 387. Notice of depositions

(a) Time for service; form

A party desiring to take the deposition of any person upon oral examination shall serve written notice on the opposing party not later than two days before the date of the examination. The notice shall state the time and place for taking the deposition and the name and address of each person to be examined. A copy of such notice, together with proof of such service thereof, shall be attached to the deposition when it is filed with the Clerk.

(b) Testimony by stipulation

By written stipulation of the parties, the deposition of a witness may be taken without notice. A copy of such stipulation shall be attached to the deposition when it is filed with the Clerk.

(c) Testimony by affidavit; time for filing

By written stipulation of the parties, the testimony of any witness of either party may be filed in the form of an affidavit by such witness or the parties may agree what a particular witness would testify to if his deposition were taken. Such testimonial affidavits or stipulations shall be filed within the time limits prescribed for the taking of testimony in section 386 of this title.

(Pub. L. 91–138, § 8, Dec. 5, 1969, 83 Stat. 287.)

SECTION REFERRED TO IN OTHER SECTIONS

This section is referred to in section 386 of this title.

§ 388. Subpena for attendance at deposition

(a) Issuance

Upon application of any party, a subpena for attendance at a deposition shall be issued by:

(1) a judge or clerk of the United States district court for the district in which the place of examination is located;

(2) a judge or clerk of any court of record of the State in which the place of examination is located; or

(3) a judge or clerk of any court of record of the county in which the place of examination is located.

(b) Time, method, and proof of service

Service of the subpena shall be made upon the witness no later than three days before the day on which his attendance is directed. A subpena may be served by any person who is not a party to the contested election case and is not less than eighteen years of age. Service of a subpena upon a person named therein shall be made by delivering a copy thereof to such person and by tendering to him the fee for one day's attendance and the mileage allowed by section 389 of this title. Written proof of service shall be made under oath by the person making same and shall be filed with the Clerk.

(c) Place of examination

A witness may be required to attend an examination only in the county wherein he resides or is employed, or transacts his business in person, or is served with a subpena, or within forty miles of the place of service.

(d) Form

Every subpena shall state the name and title of the officer issuing same and the title of the contested election case, and shall command each person to whom it is directed to attend and give testimony at a time and place and before an officer specified therein.

(e) Production of documents

A subpena may also command the person to whom it is directed to produce the books, papers, documents, or other tangible things designated therein, but the committee, upon motion promptly made and in any event at or before the time specified in the subpena for compliance therewith, may (1) quash or modify the subpena if it is unreasonable or oppressive, or (2) condition denial of the motion upon the advancement by the party in whose behalf the subpena is issued of the reasonable cost of producing the books, papers, documents, or tangible things. In the case of public records or documents, copies thereof, certified by the person having official custody thereof, may be produced in lieu of the originals.

(Pub. L. 91–138, § 9, Dec. 5, 1969, 83 Stat. 288.)

SECTION REFERRED TO IN OTHER SECTIONS

This section is referred to in section 386 of this title.

§ 389. Officer and witness fees

(a) Each judge, clerk of court, or other officer who issues any subpena or takes a deposition and each person who serves any subpena or other paper herein authorized to be entitled to receive from the party at whose instance the service shall have been performed such fees as are allowed for similar services in the district courts of the United States.

(b) Witnesses whose depositions are taken shall be entitled to receive from the party at whose instance the witness appeared the same fees and travel allowance paid to witnesses subpenaed to appear before the House of Representatives or its committees.

(Pub. L. 91–138, § 10, Dec. 5, 1969, 83 Stat. 288.)

SECTION REFERRED TO IN OTHER SECTIONS

This section is referred to in section 388 of this title.

§ 390. Penalty for failure to appear, testify, or produce documents

Every person who, having been subpenaed as a witness under this chapter to give testimony or to produce documents, willfully makes default, or who, having appeared, refuses to answer any question pertinent to the contested election case, shall be deemed guilty of a misdemeanor punishable by fine of not more than $1,000 nor less than $100 or imprisonment for not less than one month nor more than twelve months, or both.

(Pub. L. 91–138, § 11, Dec. 5, 1969, 83 Stat. 288.)

§ 391. Certification and filing of depositions

(a) Sealing of papers; deposit with clerk

The officer before whom any deposition is taken shall certify thereon that the witness was duly sworn by him and that the deposition is a true record of the testimony given by the witness. He shall then securely seal the deposition, together with any papers produced by the witness and the notice of deposition or stipulation, if the deposition was taken without notice, in an envelope endorsed with the title of the contested election case and marked "Deposition of (here insert name of witness)" and shall within thirty days after completion of the witness' testimony, file it with the Clerk.

(b) Notification of filing

After filing the deposition, the officer shall promptly notify the parties of its filing.

(c) Copy of deposition to parties or deponents

Upon payment of reasonable charges therefor, not to exceed the charges allowed in the district court of the United States for the district wherein the place of examination is located, the officer shall furnish a copy of deposition to any party or the deponent.

(Pub. L. 91–138, § 12, Dec. 5, 1969, 83 Stat. 289.)

§ 392. Record

(a) Hearing on papers, depositions, and exhibits

Contested election cases shall be heard by the committee on the papers, depositions, and exhibits filed with the Clerk. Such papers, depositions, and exhibits shall constitute the record of the case.

(b) Appendix to contestant's brief

Contestant shall print as an appendix to his brief those portions of the record which he desires the committee to consider in order to decide the case and such other portions of the record as may be prescribed by the rules of the committee.

(c) Appendix to contestee's brief

Contestee shall print as an appendix to his brief those portions of the record not printed by contestant which contestee desires the committee to consider in order to decide the case.

(d) Contestant's brief; service on contestee

Within forty-five days after the time for both parties to take testimony has expired, contestant shall serve on contestee his printed brief of the facts and authorities relied on to establish his case together with his appendix.

(e) Contestee's brief; service on contestant

Within thirty days of service of contestant's brief and appendix, contestee shall serve on contestant his printed brief of the facts and authorities relied on to establish his case together with his appendix.

(f) Reply brief of contestant

Within ten days after service of contestee's brief and appendix, contestant may serve on contestee a printed reply brief.

(g) Form of briefs; number of copies served and filed

The form and length of the briefs, the form of the appendixes, and the number of copies to be served and filed shall be in accordance with such rules as the committee may prescribe.

(Pub. L. 91–138, § 13, Dec. 5, 1969, 83 Stat. 289.)

§ 393. Filing of pleadings, motions, depositions, appendixes, briefs, and other papers

(a) Filings of pleadings, motions, depositions, appendixes, briefs, and other papers shall be accomplished by:

　(1) delivering a copy thereof to the Clerk of the House of Representatives at his office in Washington, District of Columbia, or to a member of his staff at such office; or

　(2) mailing a copy thereof, by registered or certified mail, addressed to the Clerk at the House of Representatives, Washington, District of Columbia: *Provided*, That if such copy is not actually received, another copy shall be filed within a reasonable time; and

　(3) delivering or mailing, simultaneously with the delivery or mailing of a copy thereof under paragraphs (1) and (2) of this subsection, such additional copies as the committee may by rule prescribe.

(b) All papers filed with the Clerk pursuant to this chapter shall be promptly transmitted by him to the committee.

(Pub. L. 91–138, § 14, Dec. 5, 1969, 83 Stat. 289.)

§ 394. Computation of time

(a) Method of computing time

In computing any period of time prescribed or allowed by this chapter or by the rules or any order of the committee, the day of the act, event, or default after which the designated period of time begins to run shall not be included. The last day of the period so computed shall be included, unless it is a Saturday, a Sunday, or a legal holiday, in which event the period shall run until the end of the next day which is neither a Saturday, a Sunday, nor a legal holiday. When the period of time prescribed or allowed is less than seven days, intermediate Saturdays, Sundays, and legal holidays shall be excluded in the computation. For the purposes of this chapter, "legal holiday" shall mean New Year's Day, Washington's Birthday, Memorial Day, Independence Day, Labor Day, Veterans Day, Thanksgiving Day, Christmas Day, and any other day appointed as a holiday by the President or the Congress of the United States.

(b) Service by mail

Whenever a party has the right or is required to do some act or take some proceeding within a prescribed period after the service of a pleading, motion, notice, brief, or other paper upon him, which is served upon him by mail, three days shall be added to the prescribed period.

(c) Enlargement of time

When by this chapter or by the rules or any order of the committee an act is required or allowed to be done at or within a specified time, the committee, for good cause shown, may at any time in its discretion (1) with or without motion or notice, order the period enlarged if request therefor is made before the expiration of the period originally prescribed or as extended by a previous order, or (2) upon motion made after the expiration of the specified period, permit the act to be done where the failure to act was the result of excusable neglect, but it shall not extend the time for serving and filing the notice of contest under section 382 of this title.

(Pub. L. 91–138, § 15, Dec. 5, 1969, 83 Stat. 290.)

§ 395. Death of contestant

In the event of the death of the contestant, the contested election case shall abate.

(Pub. L. 91–138, § 16, Dec. 5, 1969, 83 Stat. 290.)

§ 396. Allowance of party's expenses

The committee may allow any party reimbursement from the applicable accounts of the House of Representatives of his reasonable expenses of the contested election case, including reasonable attorneys fees, upon the verified application of such party accompanied by a complete and detailed account of his expenses and supporting vouchers and receipts.

(Pub. L. 91–138, § 17, Dec. 5, 1969, 83 Stat. 290; Pub. L. 104–186, title II, § 211(4), Aug. 20, 1996, 110 Stat. 1744.)

AMENDMENTS

1996—Pub. L. 104–186 substituted "applicable accounts" for "contingent fund".

CHAPTER 13—JOINT COMMITTEE ON CONGRESSIONAL OPERATIONS

§§ 411 to 417. Repealed. Pub. L. 104–186, title II, § 212(1)(A), (2), Aug. 20, 1996, 110 Stat. 1745

Section 411, Pub. L. 91–510, title IV, § 401, Oct. 26, 1970, 84 Stat. 1187, created a 10-member Joint Committee on Congressional Operations.

Section 412, Pub. L. 91–510, title IV, § 402, Oct. 26, 1970, 84 Stat. 1187, enumerated duties of Joint Committee.

Section 412a, based on H. Res. No. 988, § 206, Ninety-third Congress, Oct. 8, 1974, enacted into permanent law by Pub. L. 93–554, title I, ch. III, § 101, Dec. 27, 1974, 88 Stat. 1777, related to continuing study of jurisdiction of House standing committees by House members of Joint Committee, periodic report to House Committee on Rules, and contents and purposes of such report.

Section 413, Pub. L. 91–510, title IV, § 403, Oct. 26, 1970, 84 Stat. 1188, related to powers of Joint Committee, including rulemaking, issuing subpenas, and administering oaths.

Section 414, Pub. L. 91–510, title IV, § 404, Oct. 26, 1970, 84 Stat. 1188, authorized Joint Committee to appoint and manage professional staff members and to utilize Government services, personnel, consultants, and experts.

Section 415, Pub. L. 91–510, title IV, § 405, Oct. 26, 1970, 84 Stat. 1188, related to records of Joint Committee.

Section 416, Pub. L. 91–510, title IV, § 406, Oct. 26, 1970, 84 Stat. 1189, established Office of Placement and Office Management which was subject to supervision and control of Joint Committee.

Section 417, Pub. L. 91–510, title IV, § 407, Oct. 26, 1970, 84 Stat. 1189, directed that expenses of Joint Committee be paid from contingent fund of House of Representatives.

CHAPTER 14—FEDERAL ELECTION CAMPAIGNS

SUBCHAPTER I—DISCLOSURE OF FEDERAL CAMPAIGN FUNDS

CHAPTER REFERRED TO IN OTHER SECTIONS

This chapter is referred to in section 61a–9 of this title.

SUBCHAPTER I—DISCLOSURE OF FEDERAL CAMPAIGN FUNDS

SUBCHAPTER REFERRED TO IN OTHER SECTIONS

This subchapter is referred to in section 455 of this title.

§ 431. Definitions

When used in this Act:

(1) The term "election" means—

(A) a general, special, primary, or runoff election;

(B) a convention or caucus of a political party which has authority to nominate a candidate;

(C) a primary election held for the selection of delegates to a national nominating convention of a political party; and

(D) a primary election held for the expression of a preference for the nomination of individuals for election to the office of President.

(2) The term "candidate" means an individual who seeks nomination for election, or election, to Federal office, and for purposes of this paragraph, an individual shall be deemed to seek nomination for election, or election—

(A) if such individual has received contributions aggregating in excess of $5,000 or has made expenditures aggregating in excess of $5,000; or

(B) if such individual has given his or her consent to another person to receive contributions or make expenditures on behalf of such individual and if such person has received such contributions aggregating in excess of $5,000 or has made such expenditures aggregating in excess of $5,000.

(3) The term "Federal office" means the office of President or Vice President, or of Senator or Representative in, or Delegate or Resident Commissioner to, the Congress.

(4) The term "political committee" means—

(A) any committee, club, association, or other group of persons which receives contributions aggregating in excess of $1,000 during a calendar year or which makes expenditures aggregating in excess of $1,000 during a calendar year; or

(B) any separate segregated fund established under the provisions of section 441b(b) of this title; or

(C) any local committee of a political party which receives contributions aggregating in excess of $5,000 during a calendar year, or makes payments exempted from the definition of contribution or expenditure as defined in paragraphs (8) and (9) aggregating in excess of $5,000 during a calendar year, or makes contributions aggregating in excess of $1,000 during a calendar year or makes expenditures aggregating in excess of $1,000 during a calendar year.

(5) The term "principal campaign committee" means a political committee designated and authorized by a candidate under section 432(e)(1) of this title.

(6) The term "authorized committee" means the principal campaign committee or any other political committee authorized by a candidate under section 432(e)(1) of this title to receive contributions or make expenditures on behalf of such candidate.

(7) The term "connected organization" means any organization which is not a political committee but which directly or indirectly establishes, administers or financially supports a political committee.

(8)(A) The term "contribution" includes—

(i) any gift, subscription, loan, advance, or deposit of money or anything of value made by any person for the purpose of influencing any election for Federal office; or

(ii) the payment by any person of compensation for the personal services of another person which are rendered to a political committee without charge for any purpose.

(B) The term "contribution" does not include—

(i) the value of services provided without compensation by any individual who volunteers on behalf of a candidate or political committee;

(ii) the use of real or personal property, including a church or community room used on a regular basis by members of a community for noncommercial purposes, and the cost of invitations, food, and beverages, voluntarily provided by an individual to any candidate or any political committee of a political party in rendering voluntary personal services on the individual's residential premises or in the church or community room for candidate-related or political party-related activities, to the extent that the cumulative value of such invitations, food, and beverages provided by such individual on behalf of any single candidate does not exceed $1,000 with respect to any single election, and on behalf of all political committees of a political party does not exceed $2,000 in any calendar year;

(iii) the sale of any food or beverage by a vendor for use in any candidate's campaign or for use by or on behalf of any political committee of a political party at a charge less than the normal comparable charge, if such charge is at least equal to the cost of such food or beverage to the vendor, to the extent that the cumulative value of such activity by such vendor on behalf of any single candidate does not exceed $1,000 with respect to any single election, and on behalf of all political committees of a political party does not exceed $2,000 in any calendar year;

(iv) any unreimbursed payment for travel expenses made by any individual on behalf of any candidate or any political committee of a political party, to the extent that the cumulative value of such activity by such individual on behalf of any single candidate does not exceed $1,000 with respect to any single election, and on behalf of all political committees of a political party does not exceed $2,000 in any calendar year;

(v) the payment by a State or local committee of a political party of the costs of preparation, display, or mailing or other distribution incurred by such committee with respect to a printed slate card or sample ballot, or other printed listing, of 3 or more candidates for any public office for which an election is held in the State in which such committee is organized, except that this clause shall not apply to any cost incurred by such committee with respect to a display of any such listing made on broadcasting stations, or in newspapers, magazines, or similar types of general public political advertising;

(vi) any payment made or obligation incurred by a corporation or a labor organization which, under section 441b(b) of this title, would not constitute an expenditure by such corporation or labor organization;

(vii) any loan of money by a State bank, a federally chartered depository institution, or a depository institution the deposits or accounts of which are insured by the Federal Deposit Insurance Corporation, Federal Savings and Loan Insurance Corporation, or the National Credit Union Administration, other than any overdraft made with respect to a checking or savings account, made in accordance with applicable law and in the ordinary course of business, but such loan—

(I) shall be considered a loan by each endorser or guarantor, in that proportion of the unpaid balance that each endorser or guarantor bears to the total number of endorsers or guarantors;

(II) shall be made on a basis which assures repayment, evidenced by a written instrument, and subject to a due date or amortization schedule; and

(III) shall bear the usual and customary interest rate of the lending institution;

(viii) any gift, subscription, loan, advance, or deposit of money or anything of value to a national or a State committee of a political party specifically designated to defray any cost for construction or purchase of any office facility not acquired for the purpose of influencing the election of any candidate in any particular election for Federal office;

(ix) any legal or accounting services rendered to or on behalf of—

(I) any political committee of a political party if the person paying for such services is the regular employer of the person rendering such services and if such services are not attributable to activities which directly further the election of any designated candidate to Federal office; or

(II) an authorized committee of a candidate or any other political committee, if the person paying for such services is the regular employer of the individual rendering such services and if such services are solely for the purpose of ensuring compliance with this Act or chapter 95 or chapter 96 of title 26,

but amounts paid or incurred by the regular employer for such legal or accounting services shall be reported in accordance with section 434(b) of this title by the committee receiving such services;

(x) the payment by a State or local committee of a political party of the costs of campaign materials (such as pins, bumper stickers, handbills, brochures, posters, party tabloids, and yard signs) used by such committee in connection with volunteer activities on behalf of nominees of such party: *Provided*, That—

(1) such payments are not for the costs of campaign materials or activities used in connection with any broadcasting, newspaper, magazine, billboard, direct mail, or similar type of general public communication or political advertising;

(2) such payments are made from contributions subject to the limitations and prohibitions of this Act; and

(3) such payments are not made from contributions designated to be spent on behalf of a particular candidate or particular candidates;

(xi) the payment by a candidate, for nomination or election to any public office (including State or local office), or authorized committee of a candidate, of the costs of campaign materials which include information on or referenced to any other candidate and which are used in connection with volunteer activities (including pins, bumper stickers, handbills, brochures, posters, and yard signs, but not including the use of broadcasting, newspapers, magazines, billboards, direct mail, or similar types of general public communication or political advertising): *Provided,* That such payments are made from contributions subject to the limitations and prohibitions of this Act;

(xii) the payment by a State or local committee of a political party of the costs of voter registration and get-out-the-vote activities conducted by such committee on behalf of nominees of such party for President and Vice President: *Provided,* That—

(1) such payments are not for the costs of campaign materials or activities used in connection with any broadcasting, newspaper, magazine, billboard, direct mail, or similar type of general public communication or political advertising;

(2) such payments are made from contributions subject to the limitations and prohibitions of this Act; and

(3) such payments are not made from contributions designated to be spent on behalf of a particular candidate or candidates;

(xiii) payments made by a candidate or the authorized committee of a candidate as a condition of ballot access and payments received by any political party committee as a condition of ballot access;

(xiv) any honorarium (within the meaning of section 441i of this title); and

(xv) any loan of money derived from an advance on a candidate's brokerage account, credit card, home equity line of credit, or other line of credit available to the candidate, if such loan is made in accordance with applicable law and under commercially reasonable terms and if the person making such loan makes loans derived from an advance on the candidate's brokerage account, credit card, home equity line of credit, or other line of credit in the normal course of the person's business.

(9)(A) The term "expenditure" includes—

(i) any purchase, payment, distribution, loan, advance, deposit, or gift of money or anything of value, made by any person for the purpose of influencing any election for Federal office; and

(ii) a written contract, promise, or agreement to make an expenditure.

(B) The term "expenditure" does not include—

(i) any news story, commentary, or editorial distributed through the facilities of any broadcasting station, newspaper, magazine, or other periodical publication, unless such facilities are owned or controlled by any political party, political committee, or candidate;

(ii) nonpartisan activity designed to encourage individuals to vote or to register to vote;

(iii) any communication by any membership organization or corporation to its members, stockholders, or executive or administrative personnel, if such membership organization or corporation is not organized primarily for the purpose of influencing the nomination for election, or election, of any individual to Federal office, except that the costs incurred by a membership organization (including a labor organization) or by a corporation directly attributable to a communication expressly advocating the election or defeat of a clearly identified candidate (other than a communication primarily devoted to subjects other than the express advocacy of the election or defeat of a clearly identified candidate), shall, if such costs exceed $2,000 for any election, be reported to the Commission in accordance with section 434(a)(4)(A)(i) of this title, and in accordance with section 434(a)(4)(A)(ii) of this title with respect to any general election;

(iv) the payment by a State or local committee of a political party of the costs of preparation, display, or mailing or other distribution incurred by such committee with respect to a printed slate card or sample ballot, or other printed listing, of 3 or more candidates for any public office for which an election is held in the State in which such committee is organized, except that this clause shall not apply to costs incurred by such committee with respect to a display of any such listing made on broadcasting stations, or in newspapers, magazines, or similar types of general public political advertising;

(v) any payment made or obligation incurred by a corporation or a labor organization which, under section 441b(b) of this title, would not constitute an expenditure by such corporation or labor organization;

(vi) any costs incurred by an authorized committee or candidate in connection with the solicitation of contributions on behalf of such candidate, except that this clause shall not apply with respect to costs incurred by an authorized committee of a candidate in excess of an amount equal to 20 percent of the expenditure limitation applicable to such candidate under section 441a(b) of this title, but all such costs shall be reported in accordance with section 434(b) of this title;

(vii) the payment of compensation for legal or accounting services—

(I) rendered to or on behalf of any political committee of a political party if the person paying for such services is the regular employer of the individual rendering such services, and if such services are not attributable to activities which directly further the election of any designated candidate to Federal office; or

(II) rendered to or on behalf of a candidate or political committee if the person paying for such services is the regular employer of the individual rendering such services, and if such services are solely for the purpose of ensuring compliance with this Act or chapter 95 or chapter 96 of title 26,

but amounts paid or incurred by the regular employer for such legal or accounting services shall be reported in accordance with section 434(b) of this title by the committee receiving such services;

(viii) the payment by a State or local committee of a political party of the costs of campaign materials (such as pins, bumper stickers, handbills, brochures, posters, party tabloids, and yard signs) used by such committee in connection with volunteer activities on behalf of nominees of such party: *Provided,* That—

(1) such payments are not for the costs of campaign materials or activities used in connection with any broadcasting, newspaper, magazine, billboard, direct mail, or similar type of general public communication or political advertising;

(2) such payments are made from contributions subject to the limitations and prohibitions of this Act; and

(3) such payments are not made from contributions designated to be spent on behalf of a particular candidate or particular candidates;

(ix) the payment by a State or local committee of a political party of the costs of voter registration and get-out-the-vote activities conducted by such committee on behalf of nominees of such party for President and Vice President: *Provided*, That—

(1) such payments are not for the costs of campaign materials or activities used in connection with any broadcasting, newspaper, magazine, billboard, direct mail, or similar type of general public communication or political advertising;

(2) such payments are made from contributions subject to the limitations and prohibitions of this Act; and

(3) such payments are not made from contributions designated to be spent on behalf of a particular candidate or candidates; and

(x) payments received by a political party committee as a condition of ballot access which are transferred to another political party committee or the appropriate State official.

(10) The term "Commission" means the Federal Election Commission.

(11) The term "person" includes an individual, partnership, committee, association, corporation, labor organization, or any other organization or group of persons, but such term does not include the Federal Government or any authority of the Federal Government.

(12) The term "State" means a State of the United States, the District of Columbia, the Commonwealth of Puerto Rico, or a territory or possession of the United States.

(13) The term "identification" means—

(A) in the case of any individual, the name, the mailing address, and the occupation of such individual, as well as the name of his or her employer; and

(B) in the case of any other person, the full name and address of such person.

(14) The term "national committee" means the organization which, by virtue of the bylaws of a political party, is responsible for the day-to-day operation of such political party at the national level, as determined by the Commission.

(15) The term "State committee" means the organization which, by virtue of the bylaws of a political party, is responsible for the day-to-day operation of such political party at the State level, as determined by the Commission.

(16) The term "political party" means an association, committee, or organization which nominates a candidate for election to any Federal office whose name appears on the election ballot as the candidate of such association, committee, or organization.

(17) The term "independent expenditure" means an expenditure by a person expressly advocating the election or defeat of a clearly identified candidate which is made without cooperation or consultation with any candidate, or any authorized committee or agent of such candidate, and which is not made in concert with, or at the request or suggestion of, any candidate, or any authorized committee or agent of such candidate.

(18) The term "clearly identified" means that—

(A) the name of the candidate involved appears;

(B) a photograph or drawing of the candidate appears; or

(C) the identity of the candidate is apparent by unambiguous reference.

(19) The term "Act" means the Federal Election Campaign Act of 1971 as amended.

(Pub. L. 92–225, title III, § 301, Feb. 7, 1972, 86 Stat. 11; Pub. L. 93–443, title II, §§ 201(a), 208(c)(1), Oct. 15, 1974, 88 Stat. 1272, 1286; Pub. L. 94–283, title I, §§ 102, 115(d), (h), May 11, 1976, 90 Stat. 478, 495, 496; Pub. L. 96–187, title I, § 101, Jan. 8, 1980, 93 Stat. 1339; Pub. L. 99–514, § 2, Oct. 22, 1986, 100 Stat. 2095; Pub. L. 106–346, § 101(a) [title V, § 502(b)], Oct. 23, 2000, 114 Stat. 1356, 1356A–49.)

REFERENCES IN TEXT

The Federal Election Campaign Act of 1971, as amended, referred to in par. (19), is Pub. L. 92–225, Feb. 7, 1972, 86 Stat. 3, as amended, which is classified principally to this chapter. For complete classification of this Act to the Code, see Short Title notes set out below and Tables.

AMENDMENTS

2000—Par. (8)(B)(xv). Pub. L. 106–346 added cl. (xv).

1986—Pars. (8)(B)(ix)(II), (9)(A)(vii)(II). Pub. L. 99–514 substituted "Internal Revenue Code of 1986" for "Internal Revenue Code of 1954", which for purposes of codification was translated as "title 26" thus requiring no change in text.

1980—Pub. L. 96–187 changed the section designations from letters to numbers, and as so redesignated, substantially redefined the terms applicable to the provisions of this Act.

1976—Subsec. (a)(2). Pub. L. 94–283, § 102(a), substituted "party which has authority to nominate" for "party held to nominate".

Subsec. (e)(2). Pub. L. 94–283, § 102(b), substituted "written contract, promise, or agreement," for "contract, promise, or agreement, expressed or implied,".

Subsec. (e)(4). Pub. L. 94–283, § 102(c), inserted provisions establishing an exception for legal or accounting services.

Subsec. (e)(5). Pub. L. 94–283, §§ 102(d), (e), 115(d) (1), substituted "section 441b(b) of this title" for "the last paragraph of section 610 of title 18, United States Code" in cl. (F), added cls. (G), (H), and (I), and, in the provisions following cl. (I), substituted "person" for "individual".

Subsec. (f)(4). Pub. L. 94–283, §§ 102(f), 115(d)(2), inserted provisions in cl. (C) requiring the reporting to the Commission of costs directly attributable to a communication expressly advocating the election or defeat of a clearly identifiable candidate if those costs should exceed $2,000 per election, substituted "section 441b(b) of this title" for "the last paragraph of section 610 of title 18, United States Code" in cl. (H), and added cls. (I), (J), and (K).

Subsec. (n). Pub. L. 94–283, § 115(h), substituted "section 432(e) (1) of this title" for "section 432(f)(1) of this title".

Subsec. (*o*) to (q). Pub. L. 94–283, § 102(g)(3), added subsecs. (*o*) to (q).

1974—Pub. L. 93–443, § 201(a)(1), inserted introductory reference to title IV of this Act, which for purposes of codification is translated as subchapter II of this chapter.

Subsec. (a)(5). Pub. L. 93–443, § 201(a)(2), struck out from definition of "election" the election of delegates to a constitutional convention for proposing amendments to the Constitution of the United States.

Subsec. (d). Pub. L. 93–443, § 201(a)(3), inserted reference to "club," before "association" and substituted "other group of persons" and "receives" for "organization" and "accepts".

Subsec. (e). Pub. L. 93–443, § 201(a)(4), transferred the word "means" after introductory word "contribution" to become the initial word in pars. (1) to (4); in par. (1), incorporated existing provisions in provisions designated subpars. (A) and (B), and deleted former provisions respecting contributions for the purpose of influencing the nomination for election, or election, of any person as a presidential election or for the purpose of influencing the election of delegates to a constitutional convention for proposing amendments to the Constitution of the United States; in par. (2), provided for express or implied transactions; in par. (3), substitution of "funds received by a political committee which are transferred to such committee from another political committee or other source" for "a transfer of funds between political committees"; inserted at end of par. (4) the word "but"; and added par. (5).

Subsec. (f). Pub. L. 93–443, § 201(a)(5), transferred the word "means" following introductory word "expenditure" to become the initial word in pars. (1) to (3); in par. (1), incorporated existing provisions in provisions designated subpars. (A) to (C) and deleted end text reading ", or for the purpose of influencing the election of delegates to a constitutional convention for proposing amendments to the Constitution of the United States"; in par. (2), provided for express or implied transactions; in par. (3), substituted "the transfer of funds by a political committee to another political committee; but" for "a transfer of funds between political committees"; and added par. (4).

Subsec. (g). Pub. L. 93–443, § 208(c)(1), substituted definition of "Commission" for "supervisory officer".

Subsecs. (j) to (n). Pub. L. 93–443, § 201(a)(6)–(8), added subsecs. (j) to (n).

EFFECTIVE DATE OF 2000 AMENDMENT

Pub. L. 106–346, § 101(a) [title V, § 502(d)], Oct. 23, 2000, 114 Stat. 1356, 1356A–50, provided that: "The amendments made by this section [amending this section and section 434 of this title] shall apply with respect to elections occurring after January 2001."

EFFECTIVE DATE OF 1980 AMENDMENT

Section 301 of Pub. L. 96–187 provided that:

"(a) Except as provided in subsection (b), the amendments made by this Act [see Short Title of 1980 Amendment note set out below] are effective upon enactment [Jan. 8, 1980].

"(b) For authorized committees of candidates for President and Vice President, section 304(b) of the Federal Election Campaign Act of 1971 [section 434(b) of this title] shall be effective for elections occurring after January 1, 1981."

EFFECTIVE DATE OF 1974 AMENDMENT

Section 410 of Pub. L. 93–443 provided that:

"(a) Except as provided by subsection (b) and subsection (c), the foregoing provisions of this Act [enacting sections 437a to 437h, 439a to 439c, 455 and 456 of this title sections 614 to 617 of Title 18, Crimes and Criminal Procedure, and sections 9031 to 9042 of Title 26, Internal Revenue Code, amending sections 431 to 437, 438, 439, 451 to 453 of this title, sections 1501 to 1503 of Title 5, Government Organization and Employees, sections 591, 608, 610, 611, and 613 of Title 18, sections 276, 6012, and 9002

to 9012 of Title 26, and section 315 of Title 47, Telegraphs, Telephones, and Radiotelegraphs, repealing section 440 of this title, section 9021 of Title 26, and sections 801 to 805 of Title 47, and enacting provisions set out as notes under this section and sections 432, 434, 437c, and 438 of this title, sections 591 and 608 of Title 18, and section 9006 of Title 26] shall become effective January 1, 1975.

"(b) Section 104 [set out as a note under section 591 of Title 18] and the amendment made by section 301 [amending section 453 of this title] shall become effective on the date of the enactment of this Act [Oct. 15, 1974].

"(c)(1) The amendments made by sections 403(a), 404, 405, 406, 408, and 409 [enacting sections 9031 to 9042, amending sections 276, 9002, 9003, 9004, 9005, 9006, 9007, 9008, 9009, 9010, 9011, and 9012, and repealing section 9021 of Title 26] shall apply with respect to taxable years beginning after December 31, 1974.

"(2) The amendment made by section 407 [amending section 6012 of Title 26] shall apply with respect to taxable years beginning after December 31, 1971."

EFFECTIVE DATE

Section 408, formerly § 406, of Pub. L. 92–225 as renumbered Pub. L. 93–443, title III, § 302, Oct. 15, 1974, 88 Stat. 1289, provided that: "Except as provided in section 401 of this Act [section 451 of this title], the provisions of this Act [see Short Title note set out below] shall become effective on December 31, 1971, or sixty days after the date of enactment of this Act [Feb. 7, 1972], whichever is later."

SHORT TITLE OF 1980 AMENDMENT

Section 1 of Pub. L. 96–187 provided: "That this Act [amending this section and sections 432 to 434, 437, 437c, 437d, 437f to 439a, 439c, 441a to 441i of this title, section 3132 of Title 5, Government Organization and Employees, sections 602, 603, and 607 of Title 18, Crimes and Criminal Procedure, section 901a of Title 22, Foreign Relations and Intercourse, section 9008 of Title 26, Internal Revenue Code, and section 5043 of Title 42, The Public Health and Welfare; repealing sections 435, 436, 437b, 437e, 439b, and 441j of this title and section 591 of Title 18; and enacting provisions set out as notes under this section] may be cited as the 'Federal Election Campaign Act Amendments of 1979'."

SHORT TITLE OF 1976 AMENDMENT

Section 1 of Pub. L. 94–283 provided that: "This Act [enacting sections 441a to 441j of this title, amending this section and sections 432, 434, 436, 437b to 439c, and 455 of this title, section 591 of Title 18, Crimes and Criminal Procedure, and sections 9002, 9003, 9004, 9006, 9007, 9008, 9009, 9012, 9032, 9033, 9034, 9035, and 9039 of Title 26, Internal Revenue Code, repealing sections 437a, 441, and 456 of this title and sections 608, 610, 611, 612, 613, 614, 615, 616, and 617 of Title 18, and enacting provisions set out as notes under sections 437c, 437f, and 441 of this title and sections 9002, 9004, and 9035 of Title 26] may be cited as the 'Federal Election Campaign Act Amendments of 1976'."

SHORT TITLE OF 1974 AMENDMENT

Section 1 of Pub. L. 93–443 provided: "That this Act [enacting sections 437a to 437h, 439a to 439c, 455, and 456 of this title, sections 614 to 617 of Title 18, Crimes and Criminal Procedure, and sections 9031 to 9042 of Title 26, Internal Revenue Code; amending this section and sections 432 to 437, 438, 439 and 451 to 453 of this title, sections 1501 to 1503 of Title 5, Government Organization and Employees, sections 591, 608, 610, 611, and 613 of Title 18, sections 276, 6012, 9002 to 9012 of Title 26, and section 315 of Title 47, Telegraphs, Telephones, and Radiotelegraphs; repealing section 440 of this title, section 9021 of Title 26, and sections 801 to 805 of Title 47; and enacting provisions set out as notes under this section and sections 434, 437c, and 438 of this title, sections 591 and 608 of Title 18, and section 9006 of Title 26] may be cited as the 'Federal Election Campaign Act Amendments of 1974'.''

SHORT TITLE

Section 1 of Pub. L. 92–225 provided: ''That this Act [enacting this chapter and chapter 7 of Title 47, Telegraphs, Telephones, and Radiotelegraphs, amending sections 591, 600, 608, 610, and 611 of Title 18, Crimes and Criminal Procedure, and sections 312 and 315 of Title 47, repealing sections 241 to 256 of this title and section 609 of Title 18, and enacting provisions set out as notes under this section and section 801 of Title 47] may be cited as the 'Federal Election Campaign Act of 1971'.''

TRANSFER OF FUNCTIONS

Federal Savings and Loan Insurance Corporation abolished and functions transferred, see Pub. L. 101–73, title IV, §§ 401–406, Aug. 9, 1989, 103 Stat. 354–363, set out as a note under section 1437 of Title 12, Banks and Banking.

TRANSITION PROVISIONS

Section 303 of Pub. L. 96–187 provided that:
''(a) The Federal Election Commission shall transmit to the Congress proposed rules and regulations necessary for the purpose of implementing the provisions of this Act, and the amendments made by this Act [see Short Title of 1980 Amendment note set out above], prior to February 29, 1980.

''(b) The provisions of section 311(d) of the Federal Election Campaign Act of 1971 [section 438(d) of this title] allowing disapproval of rules and regulations by either House of Congress within 30 legislative days after receipt shall, with respect to rules and regulations required to be proposed under subsection (a) of this section, be deemed to allow such disapproval within 15 legislative days after receipt.''

VOTING SYSTEM STUDY; REPORT TO CONGRESS; COST OF STUDY

Section 302 of Pub. L. 96–187, as amended by Pub. L. 100–418, title V, § 5115(c), Aug. 23, 1988, 102 Stat. 1433, provided that: ''The Federal Election Commission with the cooperation and assistance of the National Institute of Standards and Technology, shall conduct a preliminary study with respect to the future development of voluntary engineering and procedural performance standards for voting systems used in the United States. The Commission shall report to the Congress the results of the study, and such report shall include recommendations, if any, for the implementation of a program of such standards (including estimates of the costs and time requirements of implementing such a program). The cost of the study shall be paid out of any funds otherwise available to defray the expenses of the Commission.''

SECTION REFERRED TO IN OTHER SECTIONS

This section is referred to in sections 58, 59e, 433, 437a of this title; title 18 sections 602, 603, 607; title 20 section 1094; title 22 section 3944; title 42 sections 1973gg–1, 5043.

§ 432. Organization of political committees

(a) Treasurer; vacancy; official authorizations

Every political committee shall have a treasurer. No contribution or expenditure shall be accepted or made by or on behalf of a political committee during any period in which the office of treasurer is vacant. No expenditure shall be made for or on behalf of a political committee without the authorization of the treasurer or his or her designated agent.

(b) Account of contributions; segregated funds

(1) Every person who receives a contribution for an authorized political committee shall, no later than 10 days after receiving such contribution, forward to the treasurer such contribution, and if the amount of the contribution is in excess of $50 the name and address of the person making the contribution and the date of receipt.

(2) Every person who receives a contribution for a political committee which is not an authorized committee shall—

(A) if the amount of the contribution is $50 or less, forward to the treasurer such contribution no later than 30 days after receiving the contribution; and

(B) if the amount of the contribution is in excess of $50, forward to the treasurer such contribution, the name and address of the person making the contribution, and the date of receipt of the contribution, no later than 10 days after receiving the contribution.

(3) All funds of a political committee shall be segregated from, and may not be commingled with, the personal funds of any individual.

(c) Recordkeeping

The treasurer of a political committee shall keep an account of—

(1) all contributions received by or on behalf of such political committee;

(2) the name and address of any person who makes any contribution in excess of $50, together with the date and amount of such contribution by any person;

(3) the identification of any person who makes a contribution or contributions aggregating more than $200 during a calendar year, together with the date and amount of any such contribution;

(4) the identification of any political committee which makes a contribution, together with the date and amount of any such contribution; and

(5) the name and address of every person to whom any disbursement is made, the date, amount, and purpose of the disbursement, and the name of the candidate and the office sought by the candidate, if any, for whom the disbursement was made, including a receipt, invoice, or canceled check for each disbursement in excess of $200.

(d) Preservation of records and copies of reports

The treasurer shall preserve all records required to be kept by this section and copies of all reports required to be filed by this subchapter for 3 years after the report is filed. For any report filed in electronic format under section 434(a)(11) of this title, the treasurer shall retain a machine-readable copy of the report as the copy preserved under the preceding sentence.

(e) Principal and additional campaign committees; designations, status of candidate, authorized committees, etc.

(1) Each candidate for Federal office (other than the nominee for the office of Vice President) shall designate in writing a political committee in accordance with paragraph (3) to serve as the principal campaign committee of such candidate. Such designation shall be made no later than 15 days after becoming a candidate. A candidate may designate additional political committees in accordance with paragraph (3) to

serve as authorized committees of such candidate. Such designation shall be in writing and filed with the principal campaign committee of such candidate in accordance with subsection (f)(1) of this section.

(2) Any candidate described in paragraph (1) who receives a contribution, or any loan for use in connection with the campaign of such candidate for election, or makes a disbursement in connection with such campaign, shall be considered, for purposes of this Act, as having received the contribution or loan, or as having made the disbursement, as the case may be, as an agent of the authorized committee or committees of such candidate.

(3)(A) No political committee which supports or has supported more than one candidate may be designated as an authorized committee, except that—

(i) the candidate for the office of President nominated by a political party may designate the national committee of such political party as a principal campaign committee, but only if that national committee maintains separate books of account with respect to its function as a principal campaign committee; and

(ii) candidates may designate a political committee established solely for the purpose of joint fundraising by such candidates as an authorized committee.

(B) As used in this section, the term "support" does not include a contribution by any authorized committee in amounts of $1,000 or less to an authorized committee of any other candidate.

(4) The name of each authorized committee shall include the name of the candidate who authorized such committee under paragraph (1). In the case of any political committee which is not an authorized committee, such political committee shall not include the name of any candidate in its name.

(5) The name of any separate segregated fund established pursuant to section 441b(b) of this title shall include the name of its connected organization.

(f) Filing with and receipt of designations, statements, and reports by principal campaign committee

(1) Notwithstanding any other provision of this Act, each designation, statement, or report of receipts or disbursements made by an authorized committee of a candidate shall be filed with the candidate's principal campaign committee.

(2) Each principal campaign committee shall receive all designations, statements, and reports required to be filed with it under paragraph (1) and shall compile and file such designations, statements, and reports in accordance with this Act.

(g) Filing with and receipt of designations, statements, and reports by Secretary of Senate; forwarding to Commission; filing requirements with Commission; public inspection and preservation of designations, etc.

(1) Designations, statements, and reports required to be filed under this Act by a candidate for the office of Senator, by the principal campaign committee of such candidate, and by the Republican and Democratic Senatorial Campaign Committees shall be filed with the Secretary of the Senate, who shall receive such designations, statements, and reports, as custodian for the Commission.

(2) The Secretary of the Senate shall forward a copy of any designation, statement, or report filed with the Secretary under this subsection to the Commission as soon as possible (but no later than 2 working days) after receiving such designation, statement, or report.

(3) All designations, statements, and reports required to be filed under this Act, except designations, statements, and reports filed in accordance with paragraph (1), shall be filed with the Commission.

(4) The Secretary of the Senate shall make the designations, statements, and reports received under this subsection available for public inspection and copying in the same manner as the Commission under section 438(a)(4) of this title, and shall preserve such designations, statements, and reports in the same manner as the Commission under section 438(a)(5) of this title.

(h) Campaign depositories; designations, maintenance of accounts, etc.; petty cash fund for disbursements; record of disbursements

(1) Each political committee shall designate one or more State banks, federally chartered depository institutions, or depository institutions the deposits or accounts of which are insured by the Federal Deposit Insurance Corporation, the Federal Savings and Loan Insurance Corporation, or the National Credit Union Administration, as its campaign depository or depositories. Each political committee shall maintain at least one checking account and such other accounts as the committee determines at a depository designated by such committee. All receipts received by such committee shall be deposited in such accounts. No disbursements may be made (other than petty cash disbursements under paragraph (2)) by such committee except by check drawn on such accounts in accordance with this section.

(2) A political committee may maintain a petty cash fund for disbursements not in excess of $100 to any person in connection with a single purchase or transaction. A record of all petty cash disbursements shall be maintained in accordance with subsection (c)(5) of this section.

(i) Reports and records, compliance with requirements based on best efforts

When the treasurer of a political committee shows that best efforts have been used to obtain, maintain, and submit the information required by this Act for the political committee, any report or any records of such committee shall be considered in compliance with this Act or chapter 95 or chapter 96 of title 26.

(Pub. L. 92–225, title III, § 302, Feb. 7, 1972, 86 Stat. 12; Pub. L. 93–443, title II, §§ 202, 208(c)(2), Oct. 15, 1974, 88 Stat. 1275, 1286; Pub. L. 94–283, title I, § 103, May 11, 1976, 90 Stat. 480; Pub. L. 96–187, title I, § 102, Jan. 8, 1980, 93 Stat. 1345; Pub. L. 99–514, § 2, Oct. 22, 1986, 100 Stat. 2095; Pub. L. 104–79, §§ 1(b), 3(a), Dec. 28, 1995, 109 Stat. 791, 792; Pub. L. 105–61, title VI, § 637, Oct. 10, 1997, 111 Stat. 1316.)

This Act, referred to in text, means the Federal Election Campaign Act of 1971, as amended, as defined by section 431 of this title.

AMENDMENTS

1997—Subsec. (g)(1). Pub. L. 105–55 struck out "and" after "Senator," and inserted "and by the Republican and Democratic Senatorial Campaign Committees" after "candidate,".

1995—Subsec. (d). Pub. L. 104–79, §1(b), inserted at end "For any report filed in electronic format under section 434(a)(11) of this title, the treasurer shall retain a machine-readable copy of the report as the copy preserved under the preceding sentence."

Subsec. (g)(1). Pub. L. 104–79, §3(a)(1), (2), redesignated par. (2) as (1) and struck out former par. (1) which read as follows: "Designations, statements, and reports required to be filed under this Act by a candidate or by an authorized committee of a candidate for the office of Representative in, or Delegate or Resident Commissioner to, the Congress, and by the principal campaign committee of such a candidate, shall be filed with the Clerk of the House of Representatives, who shall receive such designations, statements, and reports as custodian for the Commission."

Subsec. (g)(2). Pub. L. 104–79, §3(a)(2), (3), redesignated par. (3) as (2), struck out "Clerk of the House of Representatives and the" before "Secretary of the Senate", and substituted "filed with the Secretary" for "filed with them". Former par. (2) redesignated (1).

Subsec. (g)(3). Pub. L. 104–79, §3(a)(2), (4), redesignated par. (4) as (3) and substituted "paragraph (1)" for "paragraphs (1) and (2)". Former par. (3) redesignated (2).

Subsec. (g)(4). Pub. L. 104–79, §3(a)(2), (5), redesignated par. (5) as (4) and struck out "Clerk of the House of Representatives and the" before "Secretary of the Senate". Former par. (4) redesignated (3).

Subsec. (g)(5). Pub. L. 104–79, §3(a)(2), redesignated par. (5) as (4).

1986—Subsec. (i). Pub. L. 99–514 substituted "Internal Revenue Code of 1986" for "Internal Revenue Code of 1954", which for purposes of codification was translated as "title 26" thus requiring no change in text.

1980—Subsec. (a). Pub. L. 96–187 struck out reference to the chairman as a person authorized to accept or make a contribution on behalf of a political committee.

Subsec. (b). Pub. L. 96–187 redesignated subsec. (b) as par. (1) of subsec. (b), substituted "for an authorized political committee shall, no later than 10 days after receiving such contribution, forward to the treasurer such contribution, and if the amount of the contribution is in excess of $50 the name and address of the person making the contribution and the date of the receipt." for "in excess of $50 for a political committee shall, on demand of the treasurer, and in any event within five days after receipt of such contribution, render to the treasurer a detailed account thereof, including the amount of the contribution and the identification of the person making such contribution, and the date on which received. All funds of a political committee shall be segregated from, and may not be commingled with, any personal funds of officers, members, or associates of such committee.", and added pars. (2) and (3).

Subsec. (c). Pub. L. 96–187 substituted "The treasurer of a political committee shall keep an account of" for "It shall be the duty of the treasurer of a political committee to keep a detailed and exact account of" in introductory clause; substituted in par. (1) "all contributions received by or on behalf of such political committee" for "all contributions made to or for such committee"; substituted in par. (2) "the name and address of any person who makes any contribution in excess of $50, together with the date and amount of such contribution by any person" for "the identification of every person making a contribution in excess of $50, and the date and amount thereof and, if a person's con-

tributions aggregating more than $100, the account shall include occupation, and the principal place of business (if any)"; substituted in par. (3) "the identification of any person who makes a contribution or contributions aggregating more than $200 during a calendar year, together with the date and amount of any such contribution" for "all expenditures made by or on behalf of such committee; and"; substituted in par. (4) "the identification of any political committee which makes a contribution, together with the date and amount of any such contribution, and" for "the identification of every person to whom any expenditure is made, the date and amount thereof and the name and address of, and office sought by, each candidate on whose behalf such expenditure was made", and added par. (5).

Subsec. (d). Pub. L. 96–187 substituted provisions requiring the treasurer to preserve all records required by this section and copies of all reports to be filed by this subchapter for 3 years after the filing of the report for provisions requiring the treasurer to keep receipted bills for expenditures in excess of $100, and for expenditures of lesser amounts if the aggregate amount to the same person during a calendar year exceeds $100, such receipts to be kept for a period to be determined by the Secretary.

Subsec. (e). Pub. L. 96–187 in par. (1) substituted provisions requiring a written designation of a political committee no later than 15 days after becoming a candidate, with the designation of additional committees to be filed with the principal committee, for provisions prohibiting the designation of a committee as the principal campaign committee of more than one candidate except that the presidential candidate may nominate the national committee of a political party as his principal campaign committee; in par. (2) substituted provisions considering any candidate receiving a contribution or loan or making a disbursement as an agent of the authorized committees for provisions requiring the filing of any report or statement of contributions required to be filed with the Commission to be filed instead with the principal campaign committee; in par. (3) redesignated existing provisions as introductory clause of par. (3)(A), and in such clause as so redesignated, substituted provision that no political committee which supports or has supported more than one candidate may be designated as an authorized committee for provisions requiring principal committee to receive reports and statements and to compile and file such reports and statements together with its own reports and statements with the Commission, and added pars. (3)(A)(i), (ii), (4) and (5).

Subsecs. (f) to (i). Pub. L. 96–187 added subsecs. (f) to (i).

1976—Subsec. (b). Pub. L. 94–283, §103(a), substituted "$50" for "$10".

Subsec. (c)(2). Pub. L. 94–283, §103(b), substituted "$50" for "$10".

Subsecs. (e), (f). Pub. L. 94–283, §103(c), (d), redesignated subsec. (f) as (e) and in par. (1) of subsec. (e) as so redesignated inserted provision that occasional, isolated, or incidental support of a candidate not be construed as support for such a candidate for purposes of determining whether a political committee supports more than one candidate. Former subsec. (e) providing for the giving of notice by a candidate that a political committee soliciting funds on his behalf is not authorized to do so and that he is not responsible for the activities of that committee was eliminated.

1974—Subsec. (b). Pub. L. 93–443, §202(a)(1), substituted "of the contribution and the identification" for ", the name and address (occupation and principal place of business, if any)".

Subsec. (c)(2). Pub. L. 93–443, §202(a)(2), (3), substituted "identification" for "full name and mailing address (occupation and the principal place of business, if any)" before "of every person" and inserted end text reading "and, if a person's contributions aggregate more than $100, the account shall include occupation, and the principal place of business (if any)".

Subsec. (c)(4). Pub. L. 93–443, § 202(a)(2), substituted "identification" for "full name and mailing address (occupation and the principal place of business, if any)" before "of every person".

Subsec. (d). Pub. L. 93–443, § 208(c)(2), substituted "Commission" for "supervisory officers".

Subsec. (f). Pub. L. 93–443, § 202(b), substituted provisions respecting principal campaign committees for prior provisions respecting notice of funds solicitation by political committees and availability for purchase of annual reports of the political committees from the Superintendent of Documents made available through the Public Printer, now covered in section 435(b) of this title.

EFFECTIVE DATE OF 1995 AMENDMENT

Section 1(c) of Pub. L. 104–79 provided that: "The amendments made by subsection (a) and subsection (b) [amending this section and section 434 of this title] shall apply with respect to reports for periods beginning after December 31, 1996."

Section 3(d) of Pub. L. 104–79 provided that: "The amendments made by this section [amending this section and sections 434 and 438 of this title] shall apply with respect to reports, designations, and statements required to be filed after December 31, 1995."

EFFECTIVE DATE OF 1980 AMENDMENT

Amendment by Pub. L. 96–187 effective Jan. 8, 1980, see section 301(a) of Pub. L. 96–187, set out as a note under section 431 of this title.

EFFECTIVE DATE OF 1974 AMENDMENT

Amendment by Pub. L. 93–443 effective Jan. 1, 1975, see section 410(a) of Pub. L. 93–443, set out as a note under section 431 of this title.

TRANSFER OF FUNCTIONS

Federal Savings and Loan Insurance Corporation abolished and functions transferred, see Pub. L. 101–73, title IV, §§ 401–406, Aug. 9, 1989, 103 Stat. 354–363, set out as a note under section 1437 of Title 12, Banks and Banking.

SECTION REFERRED TO IN OTHER SECTIONS

This section is referred to in sections 431, 433 of this title; title 18 sections 603, 607; title 26 section 527.

§ 433. Registration of political committees

(a) Statements of organizations

Each authorized campaign committee shall file a statement of organization no later than 10 days after designation pursuant to section 432(e)(1) of this title. Each separate segregated fund established under the provisions of section 441b(b) of this title shall file a statement of organization no later than 10 days after establishment. All other committees shall file a statement of organization within 10 days after becoming a political committee within the meaning of section 431(4) of this title.

(b) Contents of statements

The statement of organization of a political committee shall include—

(1) the name, address, and type of committee;

(2) the name, address, relationship, and type of any connected organization or affiliated committee;

(3) the name, address, and position of the custodian of books and accounts of the committee;

(4) the name and address of the treasurer of the committee;

(5) if the committee is authorized by a candidate, the name, address, office sought, and party affiliation of the candidate; and

(6) a listing of all banks, safety deposit boxes, or other depositories used by the committee.

(c) Change of information in statements

Any change in information previously submitted in a statement of organization shall be reported in accordance with section 432(g) of this title no later than 10 days after the date of the change.

(d) Termination, etc., requirements and authorities

(1) A political committee may terminate only when such a committee files a written statement, in accordance with section 432(g) of this title, that it will no longer receive any contributions or make any disbursements and that such committee has no outstanding debts or obligations.

(2) Nothing contained in this subsection may be construed to eliminate or limit the authority of the Commission to establish procedures for—

(A) the determination of insolvency with respect to any political committee;

(B) the orderly liquidation of an insolvent political committee, and the orderly application of its assets for the reduction of outstanding debts; and

(C) the termination of an insolvent political committee after such liquidation and application of assets.

(Pub. L. 92–225, title III, § 303, Feb. 7, 1972, 86 Stat. 14; Pub. L. 93–443, title II, §§ 203, 208(c)(3), Oct. 15, 1974, 88 Stat. 1276, 1286; Pub. L. 96–187, title I, § 103, Jan. 8, 1980, 93 Stat. 1347.)

AMENDMENTS

1980—Subsec. (a). Pub. L. 96–187 substituted provisions requiring each authorized campaign committee, each segregated fund established under section 441b(b) of this title, and all other committees to file a statement of organization 10 days after establishment for provisions requiring each political committee anticipating the receipt or expenditure during the calendar year of an amount exceeding $1,000 to file with the Commission a statement of organization within 10 days after organization or 10 days after receipt of information causing the anticipation of receipt or expenditure in excess of $1,000 and requiring each committee in existence on the date of enactment of this Act to file a statement of organization at such time as the Commission prescribes.

Subsec. (b). Pub. L. 96–187 inserted "of a political committee" in introductory clause; in par. (1) inserted reference to type of committee; in par. (2) inserted reference to type of organization or affiliated committee; in par. (3) substituted provisions relating to the name, address and position of custodian of books and accounts for provisions relating to area, scope or jurisdiction of the committee; in par. (4) substituted provisions relating to the name and address of the treasurer for provisions relating to the name, address and position of the custodian of books and accounts; in par. (5) substituted provisions relating to the name, address, office sought and party affiliation of the candidate for provisions relating to the name, address and position of principal officers including officers of the finance committee; in par. (6) substituted provisions relating to listings of banks, safety deposit boxes, etc. for provisions relating to name and address, office sought and political affiliation of supported candidates, and struck out pars. (7) to (11) relating to other information.

Subsec. (c). Pub. L. 96–187 substituted "in accordance with section 432(g) of this title no later than 10 days after the date of the change" for "to the Commission within a ten-day period following the change".

Subsec. (d). Pub. L. 96–187 redesignated existing provisions as par. (1), substituted provisions relating to termination of a political committee by written statement in accordance with section 432(g) of this title for provisions relating to notification to the Commission in the event of disbandment or determination no longer to receive contributions during the calendar year of an amount exceeding $1,000, and added par. (2).

Subsec. (e). Pub. L. 96–187 struck out subsec. (e) relating to filing of required reports and notifications with the appropriate principal campaign committee instead of the Commission in the case of a political committee which is not a principal campaign committee.

1974—Pub. L. 93–443, § 208(c)(3)(A), substituted "Commission" for "supervisory officer" wherever appearing.

Subsec. (a). Pub. L. 93–443, § 208(c)(3)(B), substituted "it prescribes" for "he prescribes".

Subsec. (e). Pub. L. 93–443, § 203, added subsec. (e).

Effective Date of 1980 Amendment

Amendment by Pub. L. 96–187 effective Jan. 8, 1980, see section 301(a) of Pub. L. 96–187, set out as a note under section 431 of this title.

Effective Date of 1974 Amendment

Amendment by Pub. L. 93–443 effective Jan. 1, 1975, see section 410(a) of Pub. L. 93–443, set out as a note under section 431 of this title.

Section Referred to in Other Sections

This section is referred to in section 441a of this title; title 18 section 608; title 26 section 9008.

§ 434. Reporting requirements

(a) Receipts and disbursements by treasurers of political committees; filing requirements

(1) Each treasurer of a political committee shall file reports of receipts and disbursements in accordance with the provisions of this subsection. The treasurer shall sign each such report.

(2) If the political committee is the principal campaign committee of a candidate for the House of Representatives or for the Senate—

(A) in any calendar year during which there is regularly scheduled election for which such candidate is seeking election, or nomination for election, the treasurer shall file the following reports:

(i) a pre-election report, which shall be filed no later than the 12th day before (or posted by registered or certified mail no later than the 15th day before) any election in which such candidate is seeking election, or nomination for election, and which shall be complete as of the 20th day before such election;

(ii) a post-general election report, which shall be filed no later than the 30th day after any general election in which such candidate has sought election, and which shall be complete as of the 20th day after such general election; and

(iii) additional quarterly reports, which shall be filed no later than the 15th day after the last day of each calendar quarter, and which shall be complete as of the last day of each calendar quarter: except that the report for the quarter ending December 31 shall be filed no later than January 31 of the following calendar year; and

(B) in any other calendar year the following reports shall be filed:

(i) a report covering the period beginning January 1 and ending June 30, which shall be filed no later than July 31; and

(ii) a report covering the period beginning July 1 and ending December 31, which shall be filed no later than January 31 of the following calendar year.

(3) If the committee is the principal campaign committee of a candidate for the office of President—

(A) in any calendar year during which a general election is held to fill such office—

(i) the treasurer shall file monthly reports if such committee has on January 1 of such year, received contributions aggregating $100,000 or made expenditures aggregating $100,000 or anticipates receiving contributions aggregating $100,000 or more or making expenditures aggregating $100,000 or more during such year: such monthly reports shall be filed no later than the 20th day after the last day of each month and shall be complete as of the last day of the month, except that, in lieu of filing the report otherwise due in November and December, a pre-general election report shall be filed in accordance with paragraph (2)(A)(i), a post-general election report shall be filed in accordance with paragraph (2)(A)(ii), and a year end report shall be filed no later than January 31 of the following calendar year;

(ii) the treasurer of the other principal campaign committees of a candidate for the office of President shall file a pre-election report or reports in accordance with paragraph (2)(A)(i), a post-general election report in accordance with paragraph (2)(A)(ii), and quarterly reports in accordance with paragraph (2)(A)(iii); and

(iii) if at any time during the election year a committee filing under paragraph (3)(A)(ii) receives contributions in excess of $100,000 or makes expenditures in excess of $100,000, the treasurer shall begin filing monthly reports under paragraph (3)(A)(i) at the next reporting period; and

(B) in any other calendar year, the treasurer shall file either—

(i) monthly reports, which shall be filed no later than the 20th day after the last day of each month and shall be complete as of the last day of the month; or

(ii) quarterly reports, which shall be filed no later than the 15th day after the last day of each calendar quarter and which shall be complete as of the last day of each calendar quarter.

(4) All political committees other than authorized committees of a candidate shall file either—

(A)(i) quarterly reports, in a calendar year in which a regularly scheduled general election is held, which shall be filed no later than the 15th day after the last day of each calendar quarter: except that the report for the quarter ending on December 31 of such calendar year shall be filed no later than January 31 of the following calendar year;

(ii) a pre-election report, which shall be filed no later than the 12th day before (or posted by registered or certified mail no later than the 15th day before) any election in which the committee makes a contribution to or expenditure on behalf of a candidate in such election, and which shall be complete as of the 20th day before the election;

(iii) a post-general election report, which shall be filed no later than the 30th day after the general election and which shall be complete as of the 20th day after such general election; and

(iv) in any other calendar year, a report covering the period beginning January 1 and ending June 30, which shall be filed no later than July 31 and a report covering the period beginning July 1 and ending December 31, which shall be filed no later than January 31 of the following calendar year; or

(B) monthly reports in all calendar years which shall be filed no later than the 20th day after the last day of the month and shall be complete as of the last day of the month, except that, in lieu of filing the reports otherwise due in November and December of any year in which a regularly scheduled general election is held, a pre-general election report shall be filed in accordance with paragraph (2)(A)(i), a post-general election report shall be filed in accordance with paragraph (2)(A)(ii), and a year end report shall be filed no later than January 31 of the following calendar year.

(5) If a designation, report, or statement filed pursuant to this Act (other than under paragraph (2)(A)(i) or (4)(A)(ii), or the second sentence of subsection (c)(2) of this section) is sent by registered or certified mail, the United States postmark shall be considered the date of filing of the designation, report, or statement.

(6)(A) The principal campaign committee of a candidate shall notify the Secretary or the Commission, and the Secretary of State, as appropriate, in writing, of any contribution of $1,000 or more received by any authorized committee of such candidate after the 20th day, but more than 48 hours before, any election. This notification shall be made within 48 hours after the receipt of such contribution and shall include the name of the candidate and the office sought by the candidate, the identification of the contributor, and the date of receipt and amount of the contribution.

(B) The notification required under this paragraph shall be in addition to all other reporting requirements under this Act.

(7) The reports required to be filed by this subsection shall be cumulative during the calendar year to which they relate, but where there has been no change in an item reported in a previous report during such year, only the amount need be carried forward.

(8) The requirement for a political committee to file a quarterly report under paragraph (2)(A)(iii) or paragraph (4)(A)(i) shall be waived if such committee is required to file a pre-election report under paragraph (2)(A)(i), or paragraph (4)(A)(ii) during the period beginning on the 5th day after the close of the calendar quarter and ending on the 15th day after the close of the calendar quarter.

(9) The Commission shall set filing dates for reports to be filed by principal campaign committees of candidates seeking election, or nomination for election, in special elections and political committees filing under paragraph (4)(A) which make contributions to or expenditures on behalf of a candidate or candidates in special elections. The Commission shall require no more than one pre-election report for each election and one post-election report for the election which fills the vacancy. The Commission may waive any reporting obligation of committees required to file for special elections if any report required by paragraph (2) or (4) is required to be filed within 10 days of a report required under this subsection. The Commission shall establish the reporting dates within 5 days of the setting of such election and shall publish such dates and notify the principal campaign committees of all candidates in such election of the reporting dates.

(10) The treasurer of a committee supporting a candidate for the office of Vice President (other than the nominee of a political party) shall file reports in accordance with paragraph (3).

(11)(A) The Commission shall promulgate a regulation under which a person required to file a designation, statement, or report under this Act—

(i) is required to maintain and file a designation, statement, or report for any calendar year in electronic form accessible by computers if the person has, or has reason to expect to have, aggregate contributions or expenditures in excess of a threshold amount determined by the Commission; and

(ii) may maintain and file a designation, statement, or report in electronic form or an alternative form if not required to do so under the regulation promulgated under clause (i).

(B) The Commission shall make a designation, statement, report, or notification that is filed electronically with the Commission accessible to the public on the Internet not later than 24 hours after the designation, statement, report, or notification is received by the Commission.

(C) In promulgating a regulation under this paragraph, the Commission shall provide methods (other than requiring a signature on the document being filed) for verifying designations, statements, and reports covered by the regulation. Any document verified under any of the methods shall be treated for all purposes (including penalties for perjury) in the same manner as a document verified by signature.

(D) As used in this paragraph, the term "report" means, with respect to the Commission, a report, designation, or statement required by this Act to be filed with the Commission.

(b) Contents of reports

Each report under this section shall disclose—

(1) the amount of cash on hand at the beginning of the reporting period;

(2) for the reporting period and the calendar year (or election cycle, in the case of an authorized committee of a candidate for Federal office), the total amount of all receipts, and the total amount of all receipts in the following categories:

(A) contributions from persons other than political committees;

(B) for an authorized committee, contributions from the candidate;

(C) contributions from political party committees;

(D) contributions from other political committees;

(E) for an authorized committee, transfers from other authorized committees of the same candidate;

(F) transfers from affiliated committees and, where the reporting committee is a political party committee, transfers from other political party committees, regardless of whether such committees are affiliated;

(G) for an authorized committee, loans made by or guaranteed by the candidate;

(H) all other loans;

(I) rebates, refunds, and other offsets to operating expenditures;

(J) dividends, interest, and other forms of receipts; and

(K) for an authorized committee of a candidate for the office of President, Federal funds received under chapter 95 and chapter 96 of title 26;

(3) the identification of each—

(A) person (other than a political committee) who makes a contribution to the reporting committee during the reporting period, whose contribution or contributions have an aggregate amount or value in excess of $200 within the calendar year (or election cycle, in the case of an authorized committee of a candidate for Federal office), or in any lesser amount if the reporting committee should so elect, together with the date and amount of any such contribution;

(B) political committee which makes a contribution to the reporting committee during the reporting period, together with the date and amount of any such contribution;

(C) authorized committee which makes a transfer to the reporting committee;

(D) affiliated committee which makes a transfer to the reporting committee during the reporting period and, where the reporting committee is a political party committee, each transfer of funds to the reporting committee from another political party committee, regardless of whether such committees are affiliated, together with the date and amount of such transfer;

(E) person who makes a loan to the reporting committee during the reporting period, together with the identification of any endorser or guarantor of such loan, and the date and amount or value of such loan;

(F) person who provides a rebate, refund, or other offset to operating expenditures to the reporting committee in an aggregate amount or value in excess of $200 within the calendar year (or election cycle, in the case of an authorized committee of a candidate for Federal office), together with the date and amount of such receipt; and

(G) person who provides any dividend, interest, or other receipt to the reporting committee in an aggregate value or amount in excess of $200 within the calendar year (or election cycle, in the case of an authorized

committee of a candidate for Federal office), together with the date and amount of any such receipt;

(4) for the reporting period and the calendar year (or election cycle, in the case of an authorized committee of a candidate for Federal office), the total amount of all disbursements, and all disbursements in the following categories:

(A) expenditures made to meet candidate or committee operating expenses;

(B) for authorized committees, transfers to other committees authorized by the same candidate;

(C) transfers to affiliated committees and, where the reporting committee is a political party committee, transfers to other political party committees, regardless of whether they are affiliated;

(D) for an authorized committee, repayment of loans made by or guaranteed by the candidate;

(E) repayment of all other loans;

(F) contribution refunds and other offsets to contributions;

(G) for an authorized committee, any other disbursements;

(H) for any political committee other than an authorized committee—

(i) contributions made to other political committees;

(ii) loans made by the reporting committees;

(iii) independent expenditures;

(iv) expenditures made under section 441a(d) of this title; and

(v) any other disbursements; and

(I) for an authorized committee of a candidate for the office of President, disbursements not subject to the limitation of section 441a(b) of this title;

(5) the name and address of each—

(A) person to whom an expenditure in an aggregate amount or value in excess of $200 within the calendar year is made by the reporting committee to meet a candidate or committee operating expense, together with the date, amount, and purpose of such operating expenditure;

(B) authorized committee to which a transfer is made by the reporting committee;

(C) affiliated committee to which a transfer is made by the reporting committee during the reporting period and, where the reporting committee is a political party committee, each transfer of funds by the reporting committee to another political party committee, regardless of whether such committees are affiliated, together with the date and amount of such transfers;

(D) person who receives a loan repayment from the reporting committee during the reporting period, together with the date and amount of such loan repayment; and

(E) person who receives a contribution refund or other offset to contributions from the reporting committee where such contribution was reported under paragraph (3)(A) of this subsection, together with the date and amount of such disbursement;

(6)(A) for an authorized committee, the name and address of each person who has received any disbursement not disclosed under paragraph (5) in an aggregate amount or value in excess of $200 within the calendar year (or election cycle, in the case of an authorized committee of a candidate for Federal office), together with the date and amount of any such disbursement;

(B) for any other political committee, the name and address of each—

(i) political committee which has received a contribution from the reporting committee during the reporting period, together with the date and amount of any such contribution;

(ii) person who has received a loan from the reporting committee during the reporting period, together with the date and amount of such loan;

(iii) person who receives any disbursement during the reporting period in an aggregate amount or value in excess of $200 within the calendar year (or election cycle, in the case of an authorized committee of a candidate for Federal office), in connection with an independent expenditure by the reporting committee, together with the date, amount, and purpose of any such independent expenditure and a statement which indicates whether such independent expenditure is in support of, or in opposition to, a candidate, as well as the name and office sought by such candidate, and a certification, under penalty of perjury, whether such independent expenditure is made in cooperation, consultation, or concert, with, or at the request or suggestion of, any candidate or any authorized committee or agent of such committee;

(iv) person who receives any expenditure from the reporting committee during the reporting period in connection with an expenditure under section 441a(d) of this title, together with the date, amount, and purpose of any such expenditure as well as the name of, and office sought by, the candidate on whose behalf the expenditure is made; and

(v) person who has received any disbursement not otherwise disclosed in this paragraph or paragraph (5) in an aggregate amount or value in excess of $200 within the calendar year (or election cycle, in the case of an authorized committee of a candidate for Federal office), from the reporting committee within the reporting period, together with the date, amount, and purpose of any such disbursement;

(7) the total sum of all contributions to such political committee, together with the total contributions less offsets to contributions and the total sum of all operating expenditures made by such political committee, together with total operating expenditures less offsets to operating expenditures, for both the reporting period and the calendar year (or election cycle, in the case of an authorized committee of a candidate for Federal office); and

(8) the amount and nature of outstanding debts and obligations owed by or to such political committee; and where such debts and obli-gations are settled for less than their reported amount or value, a statement as to the circumstances and conditions under which such debts or obligations were extinguished and the consideration therefor.

(c) Statements by other than political committees; filing; contents; indices of expenditures

(1) Every person (other than a political committee) who makes independent expenditures in an aggregate amount or value in excess of $250 during a calendar year shall file a statement containing the information required under subsection (b)(3)(A) of this section for all contributions received by such person.

(2) Statements required to be filed by this subsection shall be filed in accordance with subsection (a)(2) of this section, and shall include—

(A) the information required by subsection (b)(6)(B)(iii) of this section, indicating whether the independent expenditure is in support of, or in opposition to, the candidate involved;

(B) under penalty of perjury, a certification whether or not such independent expenditure is made in cooperation, consultation, or concert, with, or at the request or suggestion of, any candidate or any authorized committee or agent of such candidate; and

(C) the identification of each person who made a contribution in excess of $200 to the person filing such statement which was made for the purpose of furthering an independent expenditure.

Any independent expenditure (including those described in subsection (b)(6)(B)(iii) of this section) aggregating $1,000 or more made after the 20th day, but more than 24 hours, before any election shall be filed within 24 hours after such independent expenditure is made. Such statement shall be filed with the Secretary or the Commission and the Secretary of State and shall contain the information required by subsection (b)(6)(B)(iii) of this section indicating whether the independent expenditure is in support of, or in opposition to, the candidate involved. Notwithstanding subsection (a)(5) of this section, the time at which the statement under this subsection is received by the Secretary, the Commission, or any other recipient to whom the notification is required to be sent shall be considered the time of filing of the statement with the recipient.

(3) The Commission shall be responsible for expeditiously preparing indices which set forth, on a candidate-by-candidate basis, all independent expenditures separately, including those reported under subsection (b)(6)(B)(iii) of this section, made by or for each candidate, as reported under this subsection, and for periodically publishing such indices on a timely pre-election basis.

(d) Filing by facsimile device or electronic mail

(1) Any person who is required to file a statement under subsection (c) of this section, except statements required to be filed electronically pursuant to subsection (a)(11)(A)(i) of this section may file the statement by facsimile device or electronic mail, in accordance with such regulations as the Commission may promulgate.

(2) The Commission shall make a document which is filed electronically with the Commis-

sion pursuant to this paragraph accessible to the public on the Internet not later than 24 hours after the document is received by the Commission.

(3) In promulgating a regulation under this paragraph, the Commission shall provide methods (other than requiring a signature on the document being filed) for verifying the documents covered by the regulation. Any document verified under any of the methods shall be treated for all purposes (including penalties for perjury) in the same manner as a document verified by signature.

(Pub. L. 92–225, title III, § 304, Feb. 7, 1972, 86 Stat. 14; Pub. L. 93–443, title II, §§ 204(a)–(d), 208(c)(4), Oct. 15, 1974, 88 Stat. 1276–1278, 1286; Pub. L. 94–283, title I, § 104, May 11, 1976, 90 Stat. 480; Pub. L. 96–187, title I, § 104, Jan. 8, 1980, 93 Stat. 1348; Pub. L. 99–514, § 2, Oct. 22, 1986, 100 Stat. 2095; Pub. L. 104–79, §§ 1(a), 3(b), Dec. 28, 1995, 109 Stat. 791, 792; Pub. L. 106–58, title VI, §§ 639(a), 641(a), Sept. 29, 1999, 113 Stat. 476, 477; Pub. L. 106–346, § 101(a) [title V, § 502(a), (c)], Oct. 23, 2000, 114 Stat. 1356, 1356A–49.)

References in Text

This Act, referred to in subsec. (a)(5), (6)(B), (11)(A), (D), means the Federal Election Campaign Act of 1971, as amended, as defined by section 431 of this title.

Prior Provisions

Provisions similar to those comprising subsec. (c) of this section were contained in section 305 of Pub. L. 92–225, title III, Feb. 7, 1972, 86 Stat. 16 (section 435 of this title) prior to amendment of section 305 of Pub. L. 92–225 by Pub. L. 93–433.

Amendments

2000—Subsec. (a)(5). Pub. L. 106–346, § 101(a) [title V, § 502(c)(2)], substituted "or (4)(A)(ii), or the second sentence of subsection (c)(2) of this section" for "or (4)(A)(ii)".

Subsec. (c)(2). Pub. L. 106–346, § 101(a) [title V, § 502(c)(1)], in concluding provisions, substituted "shall be filed within" for "shall be reported within" and inserted at end "Notwithstanding subsection (a)(5) of this section, the time at which the statement under this subsection is received by the Secretary, the Commission, or any other recipient to whom the notification is required to be sent shall be considered the time of filing of the statement with the recipient."

Subsec. (d). Pub. L. 106–346, § 101(a) [title V, § 502(a)], added subsec. (d).

1999—Subsec. (a)(11). Pub. L. 106–58, § 639(a), added par. (11) and struck out former par. (11) which read as follows:

"(11)(A) The Commission shall permit reports required by this Act to be filed and preserved by means of computer disk or any other appropriate electronic format or method, as determined by the Commission.

"(B) In carrying out subparagraph (A) with respect to filing of reports, the Commission shall provide for one or more methods (other than requiring a signature on the report being filed) for verifying reports filed by means of computer disk or other electronic format or method. Any verification under the preceding sentence shall be treated for all purposes (including penalties for perjury) in the same manner as a verification by signature.

"(C) As used in this paragraph, the term 'report' means, with respect to the Commission, a report, designation, or statement required by this Act to be filed with the Commission."

Subsec. (b)(2) to (4), (6), (7). Pub. L. 106–58, § 641(a), which directed insertion of "(or election cycle, in the case of an authorized committee of a candidate for Fed-

eral office)" after "calendar year" wherever appearing in pars. (2)–(4), (6), (7) of section 304(b) of the Federal Election Campaign Act, was executed by making the insertions in this section, which is section 304(b) of the Federal Election Campaign Act of 1971, to reflect the probable intent of Congress.

1995—Subsec. (a)(6)(A). Pub. L. 104–79, § 3(b)(1), substituted "notify the Secretary" for "notify the Clerk, the Secretary," in first sentence.

Subsec. (a)(11). Pub. L. 104–79, § 1(a), added par. (11).

Subsec. (c)(2). Pub. L. 104–79, § 3(b)(2), substituted "filed with the Secretary" for "filed with the Clerk, the Secretary," in last sentence.

1986—Subsec. (b)(2)(K). Pub. L. 99–514 substituted "Internal Revenue Code of 1986" for "Internal Revenue Code of 1954", which for purposes of codification was translated as "title 26" thus requiring no change in text.

1980—Pub. L. 96–187 completely revised this section by changing the reporting requirements of candidates and committees so as to substantially reduce the maximum number of reports to be filed while maintaining full and adequate disclosure of campaign activities.

1976—Subsec. (a)(1)(C). Pub. L. 94–283, § 104(a), inserted provisions covering reports which must be filed in any year in which a candidate is not on the ballot for election to Federal office.

Subsec. (a)(2). Pub. L. 94–283, § 104(b), substituted "committee authorized by a candidate to raise contributions or make expenditures on his behalf, other than the candidate's principal campaign committee, shall file the reports required under this section with the candidate's principal campaign committee" for "committee which is not a principal campaign committee shall file the reports required under this section with the appropriate principal campaign committee".

Subsec. (b). Pub. L. 94–283, § 104(c), added par. (13), redesignated former par. (13) as (14), and provided that committee treasurers and candidates be deemed to be in compliance with this subsection when they show that best efforts have been used to obtain and submit the information required by this subsection.

Subsec. (e). Pub. L. 94–283, § 104(d), designated existing provisions as par. (1), substituted "independent expenditures expressly advocating the election or defeat of a clearly identifiable candidate" for "expenditures" "$100 during a calendar year" for "$100 within a calendar year", and ", on a form prepared by the Commission, a statement containing the information required of a person who makes a contribution in excess of $100 to a candidate or political committee and the information required of a candidate or political committee receiving such a contribution" for "a statement containing the information required by this section. Statements required by this subsection shall be filed on the dates on which reports by political committees are filed but need not be cumulative", and added pars. (2) and (3).

1974—Subsec. (a)(1). Pub. L. 93–443, §§ 204(a)(1), (2), 208(c)(4)(A), substituted provisions of cls. (A) to (D) respecting filing of reports and that "Any contribution of $1,000 or more received after the fifteenth day, but more than 48 hours, before any election shall be reported within 48 hours after its receipt." for prior requirement that "Such reports shall be filed on the tenth day of March, June, and September, in each year, and on the fifteenth and fifth days next preceding the date on which an election is held, and also by the thirty-first day of January. Such reports shall be complete as of such date as the supervisory officer may prescribe, which shall not be less than five days before the date of filing, except that any contribution of $5,000 or more received after the last report is filed prior to the election shall be reported within forty-eight hours after its receipt."; designated existing provisions as par. (1), inserting introductory text "Except as provided by paragraph (2),"; and substituted "Commission" and "it" for "appropriate supervisory officer" and "him" in first sentence, respectively.

Subsec. (a)(2), (3). Pub. L. 93–443, § 204(a)(2), added pars. (2) and (3).

Subsec. (b)(5). Pub. L. 93–443, § 204(b)(1), required information respecting guarantors.

Subsec. (b)(8). Pub. L. 93–443, § 204(b)(2), required the report to disclose the total receipts less transfers between political committees which support the same candidate and which do not support more than one candidate.

Subsec. (b)(9), (10). Pub. L. 93–443, § 204(b)(3), substituted "identification" for "full name and mailing address (occupation and the principal place of business, if any)" in pars. (9) and (10).

Subsec. (b)(11). Pub. L. 93–443, § 204(b)(4), required the report to disclose the total expenditures less transfers between political committees which support the same candidate and which do not support more than one candidate.

Subsec. (b)(12). Pub. L. 93–443, §§ 204(b)(5), 208(c)(4)(B), required the report to include a statement as to the circumstances and conditions under which any debt or obligation is extinguished and the consideration therefor and substituted "Commission" for "supervisory officer".

Subsec. (b)(13). Pub. L. 93–443, § 208(c)(4)(B), substituted "Commission" for "supervisory officer".

Subsecs. (d), (e). Pub. L. 93–443, § 204(c), added subsec. (d) and incorporated provisions of former section 435 of this title in provisions designated as subsec. (e), substituting "Commission" for "supervisory officer" therein.

Effective Date of 2000 Amendment

Amendment by Pub. L. 106–346 applicable with respect to elections occurring after January 2001, see section 101(a) [title V, § 502(d)] of Pub. L. 106–346, set out as a note under section 431 of this title.

Effective Date of 1999 Amendment

Pub. L. 106–58, title VI, § 639(b), Sept. 29, 1999, 113 Stat. 476, provided that: "The amendments made by this section [amending this section] shall be effective for reporting periods beginning after December 31, 2000."

Pub. L. 106–58, title VI, § 641(b), Sept. 29, 1999, 113 Stat. 477, provided that: "The amendment made by this section [amending this section] shall become effective with respect to reporting periods beginning after December 31, 2000."

Effective Date of 1995 Amendment

Amendment by section 1(a) of Pub. L. 104–79 applicable with respect to reports for periods beginning after Dec. 31, 1996, see section 1(c) of Pub. L. 104–79, set out as a note under section 432 of this title.

Amendment by section 3(b) of Pub. L. 104–79 applicable with respect to reports, designations, and statements required to be filed after Dec. 31, 1995, see section 3(d) of Pub. L. 104–79, set out as a note under section 432 of this title.

Effective Date of 1980 Amendment

Amendment by Pub. L. 96–187 effective Jan. 8, 1980, with subsec. (b) of this section applicable to authorized committees for President and Vice President in elections occurring after Jan. 1, 1981, see section 301 of Pub. L. 96–187, set out as a note under section 431 of this title.

Effective Date of 1974 Amendment

Amendment by Pub. L. 93–443 effective Jan. 1, 1975, see section 410(a) of Pub. L. 93–443, set out as a note under section 431 of this title.

Report Required To Be Filed By January 31, 1975

Section 204(e) of Pub. L. 93–443 provided that notwithstanding the amendment to this section as to the time to file reports, nothing in Pub. L. 93–443 [see Short Title note set out under section 431 of this title] is to be construed as waiving the report required to be filed by Jan. 31, 1975 under the provisions of this section as in effect on Oct. 15, 1974, the date of enactment of Pub. L. 93–443.

Section Referred to in Other Sections

This section is referred to in sections 431, 432, 437g, 438 of this title.

§§ 435, 436. Repealed. Pub. L. 96–187, title I, § 105(1), Jan. 8, 1980, 93 Stat. 1354

Section 435, Pub. L. 92–225, title III, § 305, Feb. 7, 1972, 86 Stat. 16; Pub. L. 93–443, title II, § 205(a), Oct. 15, 1974, 88 Stat. 1278, related to requirements for campaign advertising.

Section 436, Pub. L. 92–225, title III, § 306, Feb. 7, 1972, 86 Stat. 16; Pub. L. 93–443, title II, §§ 206, 207, 208(c)(5), Oct. 15, 1974, 88 Stat. 1278, 1279, 1286; Pub. L. 94–283, title I, § 115(a), May 11, 1976, 90 Stat. 495, set forth formal requirements respecting reports and statements.

Effective Date of Repeal

Repeal effective Jan. 8, 1980, see section 301(a) of Pub. L. 96–187, set out as an Effective Date of 1980 Amendment note under section 431 of this title.

§ 437. Reports on convention financing

Each committee or other organization which—

(1) represents a State, or a political subdivision thereof, or any group of persons, in dealing with officials of a national political party with respect to matters involving a convention held in such State or political subdivision to nominate a candidate for the office of President or Vice President, or

(2) represents a national political party in making arrangements for the convention of such party held to nominate a candidate for the office of President or Vice President,

shall, within 60 days following the end of the convention (but not later than 20 days prior to the date on which presidential and vice-presidential electors are chosen), file with the Commission a full and complete financial statement, in such form and detail as it may prescribe, of the sources from which it derived its funds, and the purpose for which such funds were expended.

(Pub. L. 92–225, title III, § 305, formerly § 307, Feb. 7, 1972, 86 Stat. 16; Pub. L. 93–443, title II, § 208(c)(6), Oct. 15, 1974, 88 Stat. 1286; renumbered § 305 and amended Pub. L. 96–187, title I, §§ 105(2), 112(a), Jan. 8, 1980, 93 Stat. 1354, 1366.)

Amendments

1980—Pub. L. 96–187 substituted "60" and "20" for "sixty" and "twenty", respectively, and struck out "Federal Election" before "Commission".

1974—Pub. L. 93–443 substituted "Federal Election Commission" and "it" for "Comptroller General of the United States" and "he", respectively.

Effective Date of 1980 Amendment

Amendment by Pub. L. 96–187 effective Jan. 8, 1980, see section 301(a) of Pub. L. 96–187, set out as a note under section 431 of this title.

Effective Date of 1974 Amendment

Amendment by Pub. L. 93–443 effective Jan. 1, 1975, see section 410(a) of Pub. L. 93–443, set out as a note under section 431 of this title.

Section Referred to in Other Sections

This section is referred to in section 437d of this title; title 18 section 591.

§437a. Repealed. Pub. L. 94–283, title I, §105, May 11, 1976, 90 Stat. 481

Section, Pub. L. 92–225, title III, §308, as added Pub. L. 93–443, title II, §208(a), Oct. 15, 1974, 88 Stat. 1279, required the filing of reports with the Commission by certain named persons other than individuals who act to influence others to vote for or against political candidates. See section 441d et seq. of this title.

SAVINGS PROVISION

Repeal by Pub. L. 94–283 not to release or extinguish any penalty, forfeiture, or liability incurred under this section, with this section or penalty to be treated as remaining in force for the purpose of sustaining any proper action or prosecution for the enforcement of any penalty, forfeiture, or liability, see section 114 of Pub. L. 94–283, set out as a note under section 441 of this title.

§437b. Repealed. Pub. L. 96–187, title I, §105(1), Jan. 8, 1980, 93 Stat. 1354

Section, Pub. L. 92–225, title III, §308, formerly §309, as added Pub. L. 93–443, title II, §208(a), Oct. 15, 1974, 88 Stat. 1280; renumbered §308 and amended Pub. L. 94–283, title I, §§105, 106, 115(i), May 11, 1976, 90 Stat. 481, 496, set forth provisions respecting designation, etc., of campaign depositories.

EFFECTIVE DATE OF REPEAL

Repeal effective Jan. 8, 1980, see section 301(a) of Pub. L. 96–187, set out as an Effective Date of 1980 Amendment note under section 431 of this title.

§437c. Federal Election Commission

(a) Establishment; membership; term of office; vacancies; qualifications; compensation; chairman and vice chairman

(1) There is established a commission to be known as the Federal Election Commission. The Commission is composed of the Secretary of the Senate and the Clerk of the House of Representatives or their designees, ex officio and without the right to vote, and 6 members appointed by the President, by and with the advice and consent of the Senate. No more than 3 members of the Commission appointed under this paragraph may be affiliated with the same political party.

(2)(A) Members of the Commission shall serve for a single term of 6 years, except that of the members first appointed—

(i) two of the members, not affiliated with the same political party, shall be appointed for terms ending on April 30, 1977;

(ii) two of the members, not affiliated with the same political party, shall be appointed for terms ending on April 30, 1979; and

(iii) two of the members, not affiliated with the same political party, shall be appointed for terms ending on April 30, 1981.

(B) A member of the Commission may serve on the Commission after the expiration of his or her term until his or her successor has taken office as a member of the Commission.

(C) An individual appointed to fill a vacancy occurring other than by the expiration of a term of office shall be appointed only for the unexpired term of the member he or she succeeds.

(D) Any vacancy occurring in the membership of the Commission shall be filled in the same manner as in the case of the original appointment.

(3) Members shall be chosen on the basis of their experience, integrity, impartiality, and good judgment and members (other than the Secretary of the Senate and the Clerk of the House of Representatives) shall be individuals who, at the time appointed to the Commission, are not elected or appointed officers or employees in the executive, legislative, or judicial branch of the Federal Government. Such members of the Commission shall not engage in any other business, vocation, or employment. Any individual who is engaging in any other business, vocation, or employment at the time of his or her appointment to the Commission shall terminate or liquidate such activity no later than 90 days after such appointment.

(4) Members of the Commission (other than the Secretary of the Senate and the Clerk of the House of Representatives) shall receive compensation equivalent to the compensation paid at level IV of the Executive Schedule (5 U.S.C. 5315).

(5) The Commission shall elect a chairman and a vice chairman from among its members (other than the Secretary of the Senate and the Clerk of the House of Representatives) for a term of one year. A member may serve as chairman only once during any term of office to which such member is appointed. The chairman and the vice chairman shall not be affiliated with the same political party. The vice chairman shall act as chairman in the absence or disability of the chairman or in the event of a vacancy in such office.

(b) Administration, enforcement, and formulation of policy; exclusive jurisdiction of civil enforcement; Congressional authorities or functions with respect to elections for Federal office

(1) The Commission shall administer, seek to obtain compliance with, and formulate policy with respect to, this Act and chapter 95 and chapter 96 of title 26. The Commission shall have exclusive jurisdiction with respect to the civil enforcement of such provisions.

(2) Nothing in this Act shall be construed to limit, restrict, or diminish any investigatory, informational, oversight, supervisory, or disciplinary authority or function of the Congress or any committee of the Congress with respect to elections for Federal office.

(c) Voting requirements; delegation of authorities

All decisions of the Commission with respect to the exercise of its duties and powers under the provisions of this Act shall be made by a majority vote of the members of the Commission. A member of the Commission may not delegate to any person his or her vote or any decisionmaking authority or duty vested in the Commission by the provisions of this Act, except that the affirmative vote of 4 members of the Commission shall be required in order for the Commission to take any action in accordance with paragraph (6), (7), (8), or (9) of section 437d(a) of this title or with chapter 95 or chapter 96 of title 26.

(d) Meetings

The Commission shall meet at least once each month and also at the call of any member.

(e) Rules for conduct of activities; judicial notice of seal; principal office

The Commission shall prepare written rules for the conduct of its activities, shall have an official seal which shall be judicially noticed, and shall have its principal office in or near the District of Columbia (but it may meet or exercise any of its powers anywhere in the United States).

(f) Staff director and general counsel; appointment and compensation; appointment and compensation of personnel and procurement of intermittent services by staff director; use of assistance, personnel, and facilities of Federal agencies and departments; counsel for defense of actions

(1) The Commission shall have a staff director and a general counsel who shall be appointed by the Commission. The staff director shall be paid at a rate not to exceed the rate of basic pay in effect for level IV of the Executive Schedule (5 U.S.C. 5315). The general counsel shall be paid at a rate not to exceed the rate of basic pay in effect for level V of the Executive Schedule (5 U.S.C. 5316). With the approval of the Commission, the staff director may appoint and fix the pay of such additional personnel as he or she considers desirable without regard to the provisions of title 5 governing appointments in the competitive service.

(2) With the approval of the Commission, the staff director may procure temporary and intermittent services to the same extent as is authorized by section 3109(b) of title 5, but at rates for individuals not to exceed the daily equivalent of the annual rate of basic pay in effect for grade GS–15 of the General Schedule (5 U.S.C. 5332).

(3) In carrying out its responsibilities under this Act, the Commission shall, to the fullest extent practicable, avail itself of the assistance, including personnel and facilities of other agencies and departments of the United States. The heads of such agencies and departments may make available to the Commission such personnel, facilities, and other assistance, with or without reimbursement, as the Commission may request.

(4) Notwithstanding the provisions of paragraph (2), the Commission is authorized to appear in and defend against any action instituted under this Act, either (A) by attorneys employed in its office, or (B) by counsel whom it may appoint, on a temporary basis as may be necessary for such purpose, without regard to the provisions of title 5 governing appointments in the competitive service, and whose compensation it may fix without regard to the provisions of chapter 51 and subchapter III of chapter 53 of such title. The compensation of counsel so appointed on a temporary basis shall be paid out of any funds otherwise available to pay the compensation of employees of the Commission.

(Pub. L. 92–225, title III, § 306, formerly § 310, as added Pub. L. 93–443, title II, § 208(a), Oct. 15, 1974, 88 Stat. 1280; renumbered § 309 and amended Pub. L. 94–283, title I, §§ 101(a)–(d), 105, May 11, 1976, 90 Stat. 475, 476, 481; renumbered § 306 and amended Pub. L. 96–187, title I, §§ 105(3), (6), 112(b), Jan. 8, 1980, 93 Stat. 1354, 1366; Pub. L. 99–514, § 2, Oct. 22, 1986, 100 Stat. 2095; Pub. L. 105–61, title V, § 512(a), Oct. 10, 1997, 111 Stat. 1305.)

REFERENCES IN TEXT

This Act, referred to in subsecs. (b), (c), and (f)(3), (4), means the Federal Election Campaign Act of 1971, as amended, as defined by section 431 of this title.

The provisions of title 5 governing appointments in the competitive service, referred to in subsec. (f)(1), (4), are classified generally to section 3301 et seq. of Title 5, Government Organization and Employees.

AMENDMENTS

1997—Subsec. (a)(2)(A). Pub. L. 105–61 substituted "for a single term of 6 years" for "for terms of 6 years" in introductory provisions.

1986—Subsec. (c). Pub. L. 99–514 substituted "Internal Revenue Code of 1986" for "Internal Revenue Code of 1954", which for purposes of codification was translated as "title 26" thus requiring no change in text.

1980—Subsec. (a). Pub. L. 96–187, § 105(6), in par. (1) inserted "or their designees," before "ex officio", and struck out "of the United States" after "President"; in par. (2)(B) inserted "or her" after "his" in two places; in par. (2)(C) inserted "or she" after "he"; in par. (3) struck out "maturity" before "experience", substituted "and members (other than the Secretary of the Senate and the Clerk of the House of Representatives) shall be individuals who, at the time appointed to the Commission" for "and shall be chosen from among individuals who, at the time of their appointment", substituted "Such members of the Commission" for "Members of the Commission" and substituted "of his or her appointment to the Commission" for "such individual begins to serve as a member of the Commission"; and in par. (5) substituted "A member may serve as Chairman only once" for "No member may serve as Chairman more often than once".

Subsec. (b)(1). Pub. L. 96–187, § 105(6), substituted "exclusive jurisdiction" for "exclusive primary jurisdiction".

Subsec. (c). Pub. L. 96–187, § 105(6), substituted "provisions of this Act" for "provisions of this subchapter" in first sentence, and substituted "A member of the Commission may not delegate to any person his or her vote or any decisionmaking authority or duty vested in the Commission by the provisions of this Act, except that the affirmative vote of 4 members of the Commission shall be required in order for the Commission to take any action in accordance with paragraph (6), (7), (8), or (9) of section 437d(a) of this title or with chapter 95 or chapter 96 of title 26." for "except that the affirmative vote of 4 members of the Commission shall be required in order for the Commission to establish guidelines for compliance with the provisions of this Act or with chapter 95 or chapter 96 of title 26, or for the Commission to take any action in accordance with paragraph (6), (7), (8), or (10) of section 437d(a) of this title. A member of the Commission may not delegate to any person his vote or any decisionmaking authority or duty vested in the Commission by the provisions of this subchapter".

Pub. L. 96–187, § 112(b), purported to substitute "section 307(a)" for "section 310(a)", referred to in text as "section 437d(a) of this title". However, that substitution had been made in the general amendment of the subsection by section 105(6) of Pub. L. 96–187. See preceding paragraph.

Subsec. (f). Pub. L. 96–187, § 105(6), in par. (1) inserted "or she" after "as he"; in par. (3) struck out "Government" after "United States"; and added par. (4).

1976—Subsec. (a)(1). Pub. L. 94–283, § 101(a), changed provisions covering the appointment and confirmation of the six members of the Commission other than the Secretary of the Senate and the Clerk of the House of Representatives by substituting a requirement that they be appointed by the President of the United States, by and with the advice and consent of the Senate, for a requirement that appointment be made by the President, the President pro tempore of the Senate, and the Speaker of the House, with confirmation by a majority of both Houses of the Congress, and made technical changes in the provisions covering the political affiliation of the six appointees so as to accommodate the changed appointment and confirmation procedures.

Subsec. (a)(2). Pub. L. 94–283, § 101(b), provided that members of the Commission serve for terms of 6 years, except that members first appointed serve for staggered terms as designated by the President, and inserted provision that a member may serve on the Commission after the expiration of his term until his successor has taken office as a member of the Commission.

Subsec. (a)(3). Pub. L. 94–283, § 101(c)(1), inserted provisions that Commission members may not engage in other businesses, vocations, or employment, but allowed appointees one year after beginning service as members of the Commission to terminate or liquidate other businesses, vocations, or employment which they may be engaged in when they begin their service as Commission members.

Subsec. (b). Pub. L. 94–283, § 101(c)(2), designated existing provisions as par. (1), substituted "chapter 95 and chapter 96 of title 26" for "sections 608, 610, 611, 613, 614, 615, 616, and 617 of Title 18" and "shall have exclusive primary jurisdiction" for "has primary jurisdiction", and added par. (2).

Subsec. (c). Pub. L. 94–283, § 101(c)(3), provided that the affirmative vote of 4 members of the Commission shall be required in order for the Commission to establish guidelines for compliance with the provisions of this Act or with chapter 95 or chapter 96 of title 26, or for the Commission to take any action in accordance with paragraph (6), (7), (8), or (10) of section 437d(a) of this title.

Subsec. (f)(1). Pub. L. 94–283, § 101(d), provided that the appointment and the fixing of pay of additional personnel by the staff director may be done without regard to the provisions of title 5 governing appointments in the competitive service.

EFFECTIVE DATE OF 1997 AMENDMENT

Section 512(b) of Pub. L. 105–61, as amended by Pub. L. 105–119, title VI, § 631, Nov. 26, 1997, 111 Stat. 2523, provided that: "The amendment made by subsection (a) [amending this section] shall apply with respect to individuals nominated by the President to be members of the Federal Election Commission after December 31, 1997 unless the President announced his intent to nominate the individual prior to November 30, 1997."

EFFECTIVE DATE OF 1980 AMENDMENT

Amendment by Pub. L. 96–187 effective Jan. 8, 1980, see section 301(a) of Pub. L. 96–187, set out as a note under section 431 of this title.

EFFECTIVE DATE

Section effective Jan. 1, 1975, see section 410(a) of Pub. L. 93–443, set out as an Effective Date of 1974 Amendment note under section 431 of this title.

OPERATION OF FEDERAL ELECTION COMMISSION AFTER 1976 AMENDMENT OF FEDERAL ELECTION CAMPAIGN ACT; APPOINTMENT OF COMMISSION MEMBERS; TRANSFER OF PERSONNEL, LIABILITIES, CONTRACTS, PROPERTY, AND RECORDS, OF COMMISSION; REFERENCES TO COMMISSION PRIOR TO AMENDMENT DEEMED REFERENCES TO COMMISSION AS CONSTITUTED AFTER 1976 AMENDMENT OF FEDERAL ELECTION CAMPAIGN ACT

Section 101(e)–(g) of Pub. L. 94–283 provided for the transition of the Federal Election Commission as it was reconstituted under the Federal Election Campaign Act of 1971 as amended by Pub. L. 94–283 by providing for appointment of members, transfer of personnel, liabilities, contracts, property, and records, and savings provisions for orders, determinations, rules opinions, and proceedings issued, pending, or commenced before such amendments.

TRANSITIONAL PROVISION PENDING APPOINTMENT AND QUALIFICATION OF MEMBERS AND GENERAL COUNSEL OF FEDERAL ELECTION COMMISSION AND TRANSFER OF RECORDS, DOCUMENTS, MEMORANDUMS, AND OTHER PAPERS

Section 208(b) of Pub. L. 93–443 provided transitional authority for the Comptroller General, the Secretary of the Senate, and the Clerk of the House of Representatives pending the appointment and qualification of the members and general counsel of the Federal Election Commission and authority for transfer of records, documents, memorandums, and other papers to the Commission.

SECTION REFERRED TO IN OTHER SECTIONS

This section is referred to in title 26 sections 9002, 9032.

§ 437d. Powers of Commission

(a) Specific authorities

The Commission has the power—

(1) to require by special or general orders, any person to submit, under oath, such written reports and answers to questions as the Commission may prescribe;

(2) to administer oaths or affirmations;

(3) to require by subpena, signed by the chairman or the vice chairman, the attendance and testimony of witnesses and the production of all documentary evidence relating to the execution of its duties;

(4) in any proceeding or investigation, to order testimony to be taken by deposition before any person who is designated by the Commission and has the power to administer oaths and, in such instances, to compel testimony and the production of evidence in the same manner as authorized under paragraph (3);

(5) to pay witnesses the same fees and mileage as are paid in like circumstances in the courts of the United States;

(6) to initiate (through civil actions for injunctive, declaratory, or other appropriate relief), defend (in the case of any civil action brought under section 437g(a)(8) of this title) or appeal any civil action in the name of the Commission to enforce the provisions of this Act and chapter 95 and chapter 96 of title 26, through its general counsel;

(7) to render advisory opinions under section 437f of this title;

(8) to develop such prescribed forms and to make, amend, and repeal such rules, pursuant to the provisions of chapter 5 of title 5, as are necessary to carry out the provisions of this Act and chapter 95 and chapter 96 of title 26; and

(9) to conduct investigations and hearings expeditiously, to encourage voluntary compliance, and to report apparent violations to the appropriate law enforcement authorities.

(b) Judicial orders for compliance with subpenas and orders of Commission; contempt of court

Upon petition by the Commission, any United States district court within the jurisdiction of which any inquiry is being carried on may, in case of refusal to obey a subpena or order of the Commission issued under subsection (a) of this section, issue an order requiring compliance. Any failure to obey the order of the court may be punished by the court as a contempt thereof.

(c) Civil liability for disclosure of information

No person shall be subject to civil liability to any person (other than the Commission or the United States) for disclosing information at the request of the Commission.

(d) Concurrent transmissions to Congress or Member of budget estimates, etc.; prior submission of legislative recommendations, testimony, or comments on legislation

(1) Whenever the Commission submits any budget estimate or request to the President or the Office of Management and Budget, it shall concurrently transmit a copy of such estimate or request to the Congress.

(2) Whenever the Commission submits any legislative recommendation, or testimony, or comments on legislation, requested by the Congress or by any Member of the Congress, to the President or the Office of Management and Budget, it shall concurrently transmit a copy thereof to the Congress or to the Member requesting the same. No officer or agency of the United States shall have any authority to require the Commission to submit its legislative recommendations, testimony, or comments on legislation, to any office or agency of the United States for approval, comments, or review, prior to the submission of such recommendations, testimony, or comments to the Congress.

(e) Exclusive civil remedy for enforcement

Except as provided in section 437g(a)(8) of this title, the power of the Commission to initiate civil actions under subsection (a)(6) of this section shall be the exclusive civil remedy for the enforcement of the provisions of this Act.

(Pub. L. 92–225, title III, §307, formerly §311, as added Pub. L. 93–443, title II, §208(a), Oct. 15, 1974, 88 Stat. 1282; renumbered §310 and amended Pub. L. 94–283, title I, §§105, 107, 115(b), May 11, 1976, 90 Stat. 481, 495; renumbered §307 and amended Pub. L. 96–187, title I, §§105(3), 106, Jan. 8, 1980, 93 Stat. 1354, 1356; Pub. L. 99–514, §2, Oct. 22, 1986, 100 Stat. 2095.)

REFERENCES IN TEXT

This Act, referred to in subsecs. (a)(6), (8), and (e), means the Federal Election Campaign Act of 1971, as amended, as defined by section 431 of this title.

AMENDMENTS

1986—Subsec. (a)(6), (8). Pub. L. 99–514 substituted "Internal Revenue Code of 1986" for "Internal Revenue Code of 1954", which for purposes of codification was translated as "title 26" thus requiring no change in text.

1980—Subsec. (a). Pub. L. 96–187, §106, in par. (1) substituted "under oath, such written reports and answers to questions as the Commission may prescribe" for "in writing such reports and answers to questions as the Commission may prescribe" and struck out provision that such submission be made within such reasonable time and under oath as determined by the Commission; in par. (4) struck out "of this subsection" after "paragraph (3)"; in par. (6) substituted "section 437g(a)(8)" for "section 437g(a)(9)", and substituted "to enforce the provisions of this Act" for "for the purpose of enforcing the provisions of this Act"; struck out par. (9) relating to formulation of general policy respecting administration of this Act and chapters 95 and 96 of title 26; and redesignated former par. (10) as (9).

Subsec. (b). Pub. L. 96–187, §106, reworded subsec. (b) without substantive changes.

Subsec. (c). Pub. L. 96–187, §106, reenacted subsec. (c) without change.

Subsec. (d). Pub. L. 96–187, §106, struck out "of the United States" after "President" in pars. (1) and (2).

Subsec. (e). Pub. L. 96–187, §106, substituted "section 437g(a)(8)" for "section 437g(a)(9)".

1976—Subsec. (a)(6). Pub. L. 94–283, §107(b)(1), substituted "civil actions" for "civil proceedings" and inserted "(in the case of any civil action brought under section 437g(a) (9) of this title)" after "defend" and "and chapter 95 and chapter 96 of title 26" after "this Act".

Subsec. (a)(7). Pub. L. 94–283, §115(b), substituted "section 312" for "section 313" in the original to accommodate the renumbering of section 313 of Pub. L. 92–225 as section 312 of Pub. L. 92–225 by section 105 of Pub. L. 94–283. Since both the original and substituted references translate as "section 437f of this title" no change in text was required.

Subsec. (a)(8). Pub. L. 94–283, §107(a)(1), inserted "to develop such prescribed forms and to" before "to make, amend, and repeal" and inserted "and chapter 95 and chapter 96 of title 26" after "provisions of this Act".

Subsec. (a)(9). Pub. L. 94–283, §107(a)(2), substituted "and chapter 95 and chapter 96 of title 26; and" for "and sections 608, 610, 611, 613, 614, 615, 616, and 617 of title 18;".

Subsecs. (a)(10), (11). Pub. L. 94–283, §107(a)(3), redesignated par. (11) as par. (10). Former par. (10), which covered the development of prescribed forms under subsection (a)(1) of this section, was struck out.

Subsec. (e). Pub. L. 94–283, §107(b)(2), added subsec. (e).

EFFECTIVE DATE OF 1980 AMENDMENT

Amendment by Pub. L. 96–187 effective Jan. 8, 1980, see section 301(a) of Pub. L. 96–187, set out as a note under section 431 of this title.

EFFECTIVE DATE

Section effective Jan. 1, 1975, see section 410(a) of Pub. L. 93–443, set out as an Effective Date of 1974 Amendment note under section 431 of this title.

SECTION REFERRED TO IN OTHER SECTIONS

This section is referred to in section 437c of this title.

§ 437e. Repealed. Pub. L. 96–187, title I, § 105(1), Jan. 8, 1980, 93 Stat. 1354

Section, Pub. L. 92–225, title III, §311, formerly §312, as added Pub. L. 93–443, title II, §208(a), Oct. 15, 1974, 88 Stat. 1283; renumbered §311, Pub. L. 94–283, title I, §105, May 11, 1976, 90 Stat. 481, related to reports to the President and Congress.

EFFECTIVE DATE OF REPEAL

Repeal effective Jan. 8, 1980, see section 301(a) of Pub. L. 96–187, set out as an Effective Date of 1980 Amendment note under section 431 of this title.

§ 437f. Advisory opinions

(a) Requests by persons, candidates, or authorized committees; subject matter; time for response

(1) Not later than 60 days after the Commission receives from a person a complete written request concerning the application of this Act, chapter 95 or chapter 96 of title 26, or a rule or regulation prescribed by the Commission, with respect to a specific transaction or activity by the person, the Commission shall render a written advisory opinion relating to such transaction or activity to the person.

(2) If an advisory opinion is requested by a candidate, or any authorized committee of such

candidate, during the 60-day period before any election for Federal office involving the requesting party, the Commission shall render a written advisory opinion relating to such request no later than 20 days after the Commission receives a complete written request.

(b) Procedures applicable to initial proposal of rules or regulations, and advisory opinions

Any rule of law which is not stated in this Act or in chapter 95 or chapter 96 of title 26 may be initially proposed by the Commission only as a rule or regulation pursuant to procedures established in section 438(d) of this title. No opinion of an advisory nature may be issued by the Commission or any of its employees except in accordance with the provisions of this section.

(c) Persons entitled to rely upon opinions; scope of protection for good faith reliance

(1) Any advisory opinion rendered by the Commission under subsection (a) of this section may be relied upon by—

(A) any person involved in the specific transaction or activity with respect to which such advisory opinion is rendered; and

(B) any person involved in any specific transaction or activity which is indistinguishable in all its material aspects from the transaction or activity with respect to which such advisory opinion is rendered.

(2) Notwithstanding any other provisions of law, any person who relies upon any provision or finding of an advisory opinion in accordance with the provisions of paragraph (1) and who acts in good faith in accordance with the provisions and findings of such advisory opinion shall not, as a result of any such act, be subject to any sanction provided by this Act or by chapter 95 or chapter 96 of title 26.

(d) Requests made public; submission of written comments by interested public

The Commission shall make public any request made under subsection (a) of this section for an advisory opinion. Before rendering an advisory opinion, the Commission shall accept written comments submitted by any interested party within the 10-day period following the date the request is made public.

(Pub. L. 92–225, title III, § 308, formerly § 313, as added Pub. L. 93–443, title II, § 208(a), Oct. 15, 1974, 88 Stat. 1283; renumbered § 312 and amended Pub. L. 94–283, title I, §§ 105, 108(a), May 11, 1976, 90 Stat. 481, 482; renumbered § 308 and amended Pub. L. 96–187, title I, §§ 105(4), 107(a), Jan. 8, 1980, 93 Stat. 1354, 1357; Pub. L. 99–514, § 2, Oct. 22, 1986, 100 Stat. 2095.)

REFERENCES IN TEXT

This Act, referred to in subsecs. (a)(1), (b), and (c)(2), means the Federal Election Campaign Act of 1971, as amended, as defined by section 431 of this title.

AMENDMENTS

1986—Subsecs. (a)(1), (b), (c)(2). Pub. L. 99–514 substituted "Internal Revenue Code of 1986" for "Internal Revenue Code of 1954", which for purposes of codification was translated as "title 26" thus requiring no change in text.
1980—Subsec. (a). Pub. L. 96–187, § 107, redesignated existing provisions as par. (1), substituted provisions

requiring the Commission to render a written advisory opinion no later than 60 days after receiving a written request concerning the application of this Act, chapters 95 or 96 of title 26, or a rule or regulation for provisions requiring a written advisory opinion within a reasonable time in response to a written request by any individual holding Federal office, candidate for Federal office, any political committee or the national committee of a political party, provisions requiring promulgation of a rule or regulation pursuant to procedures established by section 438(c) of this title, and prohibiting issuance of advisory opinions except in accordance with the provisions of this section, and added par. (2).

Subsec. (b). Pub. L. 96–187, § 107, struck out the par. (1) and (2) designations and substituted provisions requiring any rule of law not stated in this Act or chapter 95 or 96 of title 26 be initially proposed as a rule or regulation pursuant to the procedures of section 438(d) of this title, and provisions prohibiting issuance of an advisory opinion except in accordance with the provisions of this section for provisions holding any person relying upon an advisory opinion free from any sanction provided by this Act or chapter 95 or 96 of title 26, and provisions allowing reliance on an advisory opinion by any person in the specific transaction and any person involved in a transaction indistinguishable from the transaction with respect to which such opinion was rendered.

Subsec. (c). Pub. L. 96–187, § 107, redesignated existing provisions as par. (1), substituted provisions allowing reliance on any advisory opinion by any person involved in the specific transaction or activity to which such opinion was rendered and any person involved in a transaction or activity indistinguishable from the transaction with respect to which such opinion was rendered for provisions mandating that any request for an advisory opinion be made public and allowing any interested party to transmit written comments to the Commission prior to the rendering of its opinion, and added par. (2).

Subsec. (d). Pub. L. 96–187, § 107, added subsec. (d).
1976—Subsec. (a). Pub. L. 94–283, § 108(a), added national committees of political parties to the enumeration of persons and political bodies authorized to request advisory opinions, substituted the application of general rules of law as stated in the Act or in chapter 95 or 96 of title 26 or as prescribed by rules or regulations of the Commission to specific factual situations for the resolution of the question of whether or not any specific transaction or activity by an individual, candidate, or political committee would constitute a violation of the Act as the subject matter of advisory opinions, and inserted requirement that rules or regulations forming the basis for rules of law be rules or regulations proposed pursuant to section 438(c) of this title and that advisory opinions be issued only in accordance with the provisions of this section.

Subsec. (b). Pub. L. 94–283, § 108(a), designated existing provisions as par. (1), substituted provisions that any person who relies upon any finding or provision of an advisory opinion in accordance with the provisions of paragraph (2) and who acts in good faith in accordance with the provisions and findings of the advisory opinion shall not, as a result of that act, be subject to any sanctions provided by the Act or by chapter 95 or 96 of title 26 for provisions that any person with respect to whom an advisory opinion was rendered under subsection (a) who acted in good faith in accordance with the provisions and findings of an advisory opinion would be presumed to be in compliance with the Act, and added par. (2).

EFFECTIVE DATE OF 1980 AMENDMENT

Amendment by Pub. L. 96–187 effective Jan. 8, 1980, see section 301(a) of Pub. L. 96–187, set out as a note under section 431 of this title.

EFFECTIVE DATE

Section effective Jan. 1, 1975, see section 410(a) of Pub. L. 93–443, set out as an Effective Date of 1974 Amendment note under section 431 of this title.

CONFORMANCE OF ADVISORY OPINIONS ISSUED PRIOR TO MAY 11, 1976, TO REQUIREMENTS IMPOSED UNDER 1976 AMENDMENTS

Section 108(b) of Pub. L. 94–283 provided that: "The Commission shall, no later than 90 days after the date of the enactment of this Act [May 11, 1976], conform the advisory opinions issued before such date of enactment to the requirements established by section 312 (a) of the Act [subsec. (a) of this section], as amended by subsection (a) of this section. The provisions of section 312(b) of the Act [subsec. (b) of this section], as amended by subsection (a) of this section, shall apply with respect to all advisory opinions issued before the date of the enactment of this Act as conformed to meet the requirements of section 312(a) of the Act, as amended by subsection (a) of this section."

SECTION REFERRED TO IN OTHER SECTIONS

This section is referred to in section 437d of this title.

§ 437g. Enforcement

(a) Administrative and judicial practice and procedure

(1) Any person who believes a violation of this Act or of chapter 95 or chapter 96 of title 26 has occurred, may file a complaint with the Commission. Such complaint shall be in writing, signed and sworn to by the person filing such complaint, shall be notarized, and shall be made under penalty of perjury and subject to the provisions of section 1001 of title 18. Within 5 days after receipt of a complaint, the Commission shall notify, in writing, any person alleged in the complaint to have committed such a violation. Before the Commission conducts any vote on the complaint, other than a vote to dismiss, any person so notified shall have the opportunity to demonstrate, in writing, to the Commission within 15 days after notification that no action should be taken against such person on the basis of the complaint. The Commission may not conduct any investigation or take any other action under this section solely on the basis of a complaint of a person whose identity is not disclosed to the Commission.

(2) If the Commission, upon receiving a complaint under paragraph (1) or on the basis of information ascertained in the normal course of carrying out its supervisory responsibilities, determines, by an affirmative vote of 4 of its members, that it has reason to believe that a person has committed, or is about to commit, a violation of this Act or chapter 95 or chapter 96 of title 26, the Commission shall, through its chairman or vice chairman, notify the person of the alleged violation. Such notification shall set forth the factual basis for such alleged violation. The Commission shall make an investigation of such alleged violation, which may include a field investigation or audit, in accordance with the provisions of this section.

(3) The general counsel of the Commission shall notify the respondent of any recommendation to the Commission by the general counsel to proceed to a vote on probable cause pursuant to paragraph (4)(A)(i). With such notification, the general counsel shall include a brief stating the position of the general counsel on the legal and factual issues of the case. Within 15 days of receipt of such brief, respondent may submit a brief stating the position of such respondent on the legal and factual issues of the case, and re-plying to the brief of general counsel. Such briefs shall be filed with the Secretary of the Commission and shall be considered by the Commission before proceeding under paragraph (4).

(4)(A)(i) Except as provided in clauses[1] (ii) and subparagraph (C), if the Commission determines, by an affirmative vote of 4 of its members, that there is probable cause to believe that any person has committed, or is about to commit, a violation of this Act or of chapter 95 or chapter 96 of title 26, the Commission shall attempt, for a period of at least 30 days, to correct or prevent such violation by informal methods of conference, conciliation, and persuasion, and to enter into a conciliation agreement with any person involved. Such attempt by the Commission to correct or prevent such violation may continue for a period of not more than 90 days. The Commission may not enter into a conciliation agreement under this clause except pursuant to an affirmative vote of 4 of its members. A conciliation agreement, unless violated, is a complete bar to any further action by the Commission, including the bringing of a civil proceeding under paragraph (6)(A).

(ii) If any determination of the Commission under clause (i) occurs during the 45-day period immediately preceding any election, then the Commission shall attempt, for a period of at least 15 days, to correct or prevent the violation involved by the methods specified in clause (i).

(B)(i) No action by the Commission or any person, and no information derived, in connection with any conciliation attempt by the Commission under subparagraph (A) may be made public by the Commission without the written consent of the respondent and the Commission.

(ii) If a conciliation agreement is agreed upon by the Commission and the respondent, the Commission shall make public any conciliation agreement signed by both the Commission and the respondent. If the Commission makes a determination that a person has not violated this Act or chapter 95 or chapter 96 of title 26, the Commission shall make public such determination.

(C)(i) Notwithstanding subparagraph (A), in the case of a violation of any requirement of section 434(a) of this title, the Commission may—

(I) find that a person committed such a violation on the basis of information obtained pursuant to the procedures described in paragraphs (1) and (2); and

(II) based on such finding, require the person to pay a civil money penalty in an amount determined under a schedule of penalties which is established and published by the Commission and which takes into account the amount of the violation involved, the existence of previous violations by the person, and such other factors as the Commission considers appropriate.

(ii) The Commission may not make any determination adverse to a person under clause (i) until the person has been given written notice and an opportunity to be heard before the Commission.

---

[1] So in original. Probably should be "clause".

(iii) Any person against whom an adverse determination is made under this subparagraph may obtain a review of such determination in the district court of the United States for the district in which the person resides, or transacts business, by filing in such court (prior to the expiration of the 30-day period which begins on the date the person receives notification of the determination) a written petition requesting that the determination be modified or set aside.

(5)(A) If the Commission believes that a violation of this Act or of chapter 95 or chapter 96 of title 26 has been committed, a conciliation agreement entered into by the Commission under paragraph (4)(A) may include a requirement that the person involved in such conciliation agreement shall pay a civil penalty which does not exceed the greater of $5,000 or an amount equal to any contribution or expenditure involved in such violation.

(B) If the Commission believes that a knowing and willful violation of this Act or of chapter 95 or chapter 96 of title 26 has been committed, a conciliation agreement entered into by the Commission under paragraph (4)(A) may require that the person involved in such conciliation agreement shall pay a civil penalty which does not exceed the greater of $10,000 or an amount equal to 200 percent of any contribution or expenditure involved in such violation.

(C) If the Commission by an affirmative vote of 4 of its members, determines that there is probable cause to believe that a knowing and willful violation of this Act which is subject to subsection (d) of this section, or a knowing and willful violation of chapter 95 or chapter 96 of title 26, has occurred or is about to occur, it may refer such apparent violation to the Attorney General of the United States without regard to any limitations set forth in paragraph (4)(A).

(D) In any case in which a person has entered into a conciliation agreement with the Commission under paragraph (4)(A), the Commission may institute a civil action for relief under paragraph (6)(A) if it believes that the person has violated any provision of such conciliation agreement. For the Commission to obtain relief in any civil action, the Commission need only establish that the person has violated, in whole or in part, any requirement of such conciliation agreement.

(6)(A) If the Commission is unable to correct or prevent any violation of this Act or of chapter 95 or chapter 96 of title 26, by the methods specified in paragraph (4), the Commission may, upon an affirmative vote of 4 of its members, institute a civil action for relief, including a permanent or temporary injunction, restraining order, or any other appropriate order (including an order for a civil penalty which does not exceed the greater of $5,000 or an amount equal to any contribution or expenditure involved in such violation) in the district court of the United States for the district in which the person against whom such action is brought is found, resides, or transacts business.

(B) In any civil action instituted by the Commission under subparagraph (A), the court may grant a permanent or temporary injunction, restraining order, or other order, including a civil penalty which does not exceed the greater of $5,000 or an amount equal to any contribution or expenditure involved in such violation, upon a proper showing that the person involved has committed, or is about to commit (if the relief sought is a permanent or temporary injunction or a restraining order), a violation of this Act or chapter 95 or chapter 96 of title 26.

(C) In any civil action for relief instituted by the Commission under subparagraph (A), if the court determines that the Commission has established that the person involved in such civil action has committed a knowing and willful violation of this Act or of chapter 95 or chapter 96 of title 26, the court may impose a civil penalty which does not exceed the greater of $10,000 or an amount equal to 200 percent of any contribution or expenditure involved in such violation.

(7) In any action brought under paragraph (5) or (6), subpenas for witnesses who are required to attend a United States district court may run into any other district.

(8)(A) Any party aggrieved by an order of the Commission dismissing a complaint filed by such party under paragraph (1), or by a failure of the Commission to act on such complaint during the 120-day period beginning on the date the complaint is filed, may file a petition with the United States District Court for the District of Columbia.

(B) Any petition under subparagraph (A) shall be filed, in the case of a dismissal of a complaint by the Commission, within 60 days after the date of the dismissal.

(C) In any proceeding under this paragraph the court may declare that the dismissal of the complaint or the failure to act is contrary to law, and may direct the Commission to conform with such declaration within 30 days, failing which the complainant may bring, in the name of such complainant, a civil action to remedy the violation involved in the original complaint.

(9) Any judgment of a district court under this subsection may be appealed to the court of appeals, and the judgment of the court of appeals affirming or setting aside, in whole or in part, any such order of the district court shall be final, subject to review by the Supreme Court of the United States upon certiorari or certification as provided in section 1254 of title 28.

(10) Repealed. Pub. L. 98–620, title IV, § 402(1)(A), Nov. 8, 1984, 98 Stat. 3357.

(11) If the Commission determines after an investigation that any person has violated an order of the court entered in a proceeding brought under paragraph (6), it may petition the court for an order to hold such person in civil contempt, but if it believes the violation to be knowing and willful it may petition the court for an order to hold such person in criminal contempt.

(12)(A) Any notification or investigation made under this section shall not be made public by the Commission or by any person without the written consent of the person receiving such notification or the person with respect to whom such investigation is made.

(B) Any member or employee of the Commission, or any other person, who violates the provisions of subparagraph (A) shall be fined not more than $2,000. Any such member, employee, or other person who knowingly and willfully violates the provisions of subparagraph (A) shall be fined not more than $5,000.

(b) Notice to persons not filing required reports prior to institution of enforcement action; publication of identity of persons and unfiled reports

Before taking any action under subsection (a) of this section against any person who has failed to file a report required under section 434(a)(2)(A)(iii) of this title for the calendar quarter immediately preceding the election involved, or in accordance with section 434(a)(2)(A)(i) of this title, the Commission shall notify the person of such failure to file the required reports. If a satisfactory response is not received within 4 business days after the date of notification, the Commission shall, pursuant to section 438(a)(7) of this title, publish before the election the name of the person and the report or reports such person has failed to file.

(c) Reports by Attorney General of apparent violations

Whenever the Commission refers an apparent violation to the Attorney General, the Attorney General shall report to the Commission any action taken by the Attorney General regarding the apparent violation. Each report shall be transmitted within 60 days after the date the Commission refers an apparent violation, and every 30 days thereafter until the final disposition of the apparent violation.

(d) Penalties; defenses; mitigation of offenses

(1)(A) Any person who knowingly and willfully commits a violation of any provision of this Act which involves the making, receiving, or reporting of any contribution or expenditure aggregating $2,000 or more during a calendar year shall be fined, or imprisoned for not more than one year, or both. The amount of this fine shall not exceed the greater of $25,000 or 300 percent of any contribution or expenditure involved in such violation.

(B) In the case of a knowing and willful violation of section 441b(b)(3) of this title, the penalties set forth in this subsection shall apply to a violation involving an amount aggregating $250 or more during a calendar year. Such violation of section 441b(b)(3) of this title may incorporate a violation of section 441c(b), 441f, and 441g of this title.

(C) In the case of a knowing and willful violation of section 441h of this title, the penalties set forth in this subsection shall apply without regard to whether the making, receiving, or reporting of a contribution or expenditure of $1,000 or more is involved.

(2) In any criminal action brought for a violation of any provision of this Act or of chapter 95 or chapter 96 of title 26, any defendant may evidence their lack of knowledge or intent to commit the alleged violation by introducing as evidence a conciliation agreement entered into between the defendant and the Commission under subsection (a)(4)(A) of this section which specifically deals with the act or failure to act constituting such violation and which is still in effect.

(3) In any criminal action brought for a violation of any provision of this Act or of chapter 95 or chapter 96 of title 26, the court before which such action is brought shall take into account, in weighing the seriousness of the violation and in considering the appropriateness of the penalty to be imposed if the defendant is found guilty, whether—

(A) the specific act or failure to act which constitutes the violation for which the action was brought is the subject of a conciliation agreement entered into between the defendant and the Commission under subparagraph (a)(4)(A);

(B) the conciliation agreement is in effect; and

(C) the defendant is, with respect to the violation involved, in compliance with the conciliation agreement.

(Pub. L. 92–225, title III, § 309, formerly § 314, as added Pub. L. 93–443, title II, § 208(a), Oct. 15, 1974, 88 Stat. 1284; renumbered § 313 and amended Pub. L. 94–283, title I, §§ 105, 109, May 11, 1976, 90 Stat. 481, 483; renumbered § 309 and amended Pub. L. 96–187, title I, §§ 105(4), 108, Jan. 8, 1980, 93 Stat. 1354, 1358; Pub. L. 98–620, title IV, § 402(1)(A), Nov. 8, 1984, 98 Stat. 3357; Pub. L. 99–514, § 2, Oct. 22, 1986, 100 Stat. 2095; Pub. L. 106–58, title VI, § 640(a), (b), Sept. 29, 1999, 113 Stat. 476, 477.)

REFERENCES IN TEXT

This Act, referred to in subsecs. (a) and (d), means the Federal Election Campaign Act of 1971, as amended, as defined by section 431 of this title.

PRIOR PROVISIONS

Provisions similar to those comprising subsec. (a) of this section were contained in section 308(d) of Pub. L. 92–225, title III, Feb. 7, 1972, 86 Stat. 18 (section 438(d) of this title), prior to amendment of section 308 of Pub. L. 92–225 by Pub. L. 93–443.

AMENDMENTS

1999—Subsec. (a)(4)(A)(i). Pub. L. 106–58, § 640(a)(1), substituted "clauses (ii) and subparagraph (C)" for "clause (ii)".

Subsec. (a)(4)(C). Pub. L. 106–58, § 640(a)(2), added subpar. (C).

Subsec. (a)(6)(A). Pub. L. 106–58, § 640(b), substituted "paragraph (4)" for "paragraph (4)(A)".

1986—Subsecs. (a)(1), (2), (4)(A)(i), (B)(ii), (5)(A) to (C), (6), (d)(2), (3). Pub. L. 99–514 substituted "Internal Revenue Code of 1986" for "Internal Revenue Code of 1954", which for purposes of codification was translated as "title 26" thus requiring no change in text.

1984—Subsec. (a)(10). Pub. L. 98–620 struck out par. (10) which provided that any action brought under subsec. (a) be advanced on the docket of the court in which filed and put ahead of all other actions (other than other actions brought under this subsec. or under section 437h of this title).

1980—Pub. L. 96–187, § 108, substantially revised provisions of this section in order to facilitate the Commission's more expeditious handling of complaints, and implementation of enforcement proceedings.

1976—Subsec. (a). Pub. L. 94–283, § 109, generally revised provisions of subsec. (a) to reflect enactment of sections 441a to 441j of this title and repeal of sections 608 and 610 to 617 of title 18 and to update the operations of the Commission.

Subsecs. (b), (c). Pub. L. 94–283, § 109, reenacted subsec. (b) without change and added subsec. (c).

EFFECTIVE DATE OF 1999 AMENDMENT

Pub. L. 106–58, title VI, § 640(c), Sept. 29, 1999, 113 Stat. 477, provided that: "The amendments made by this section [amending this section] shall apply with respect to violations occurring between January 1, 2000 and December 31, 2001.''

EFFECTIVE DATE OF 1984 AMENDMENT

Amendment by Pub. L. 98–620 not applicable to cases pending on Nov. 8, 1984, see section 403 of Pub. L. 98–620, set out as an Effective Date note under section 1657 of Title 28, Judiciary and Judicial Procedure.

EFFECTIVE DATE OF 1980 AMENDMENT

Amendment by Pub. L. 96–187 effective Jan. 8, 1980, see section 301(a) of Pub. L. 96–187, set out as a note under section 431 of this title.

EFFECTIVE DATE

Section effective Jan. 1, 1975, see section 410(a) of Pub. L. 93–443, set out as an Effective Date of 1974 Amendment note under section 431 of this title.

SECTION REFERRED TO IN OTHER SECTIONS

This section is referred to in section 437d of this title.

§ 437h. Judicial review

The Commission, the national committee of any political party, or any individual eligible to vote in any election for the office of President may institute such actions in the appropriate district court of the United States, including actions for declaratory judgment, as may be appropriate to construe the constitutionality of any provision of this Act. The district court immediately shall certify all questions of constitutionality of this Act to the United States court of appeals for the circuit involved, which shall hear the matter sitting en banc.

(Pub. L. 92–225, title III, § 310, formerly § 315, as added Pub. L. 93–443, title II, § 208(a), Oct. 15, 1974, 88 Stat. 1285; renumbered § 314 and amended Pub. L. 94–283, title I, §§ 105, 115(e), May 11, 1976, 90 Stat. 481, 496; renumbered § 310 and amended Pub. L. 96–187, title I, §§ 105(4), 112(c), Jan. 8, 1980, 93 Stat. 1354, 1366; Pub. L. 98–620, title IV, § 402(1)(B), Nov. 8, 1984, 98 Stat. 3357; Pub. L. 100–352, § 6(a), June 27, 1988, 102 Stat. 663.)

REFERENCES IN TEXT

This Act, referred to in text, means the Federal Election Campaign Act of 1971, as amended, as defined by section 431 of this title.

AMENDMENTS

1988—Pub. L. 100–352 struck out ''(a)'' before ''The Commission'' and struck out subsec. (b) which read as follows: ''Notwithstanding any other provision of law, any decision on a matter certified under subsection (a) of this section shall be reviewable by appeal directly to the Supreme Court of the United States. Such appeal shall be brought no later than 20 days after the decision of the court of appeals.''

1984—Subsec. (c). Pub. L. 98–620 struck out subsec. (c) which provided for advancement on appellate docket and expedited disposition of any matter certified under subsec. (a) of this section.

1980—Subsec. (a). Pub. L. 96–187, § 112(c), struck out ''of the United States'' after ''office of President''.

1976—Subsec. (a). Pub. L. 94–283, § 115(e), struck out references to sections 608, 610, 611, 613, 614, 615, 616, and 617 of title 18.

EFFECTIVE DATE OF 1988 AMENDMENT

Amendment by Pub. L. 100–352 effective ninety days after June 27, 1988, except that such amendment not to apply to cases pending in Supreme Court on such effec-

tive date or affect right to review or manner of reviewing judgment or decree of court which was entered before such effective date, see section 7 of Pub. L. 100–352, set out as a note under section 1254 of Title 28, Judiciary and Judicial Procedure.

EFFECTIVE DATE OF 1984 AMENDMENT

Amendment by Pub. L. 98–620 not applicable to cases pending on Nov. 8, 1984, see section 403 of Pub. L. 98–620, set out as an Effective Date note under section 1657 of Title 28, Judiciary and Judicial Procedure.

EFFECTIVE DATE OF 1980 AMENDMENT

Amendment by Pub. L. 96–187 effective Jan. 8, 1980, see section 301(a) of Pub. L. 96–187, set out as a note under section 431 of this title.

EFFECTIVE DATE

Section effective Jan. 1, 1975, see section 410(a) of Pub. L. 93–443, set out as an Effective Date of 1974 Amendment note under section 431 of this title.

§ 438. Administrative provisions

(a) Duties of Commission

The Commission shall—

(1) prescribe forms necessary to implement this Act;

(2) prepare, publish, and furnish to all persons required to file reports and statements under this Act a manual recommending uniform methods of bookkeeping and reporting;

(3) develop a filing, coding, and cross-indexing system consistent with the purposes of this Act;

(4) within 48 hours after the time of the receipt by the Commission of reports and statements filed with it, make them available for public inspection, and copying, at the expense of the person requesting such copying, except that any information copied from such reports or statements may not be sold or used by any person for the purpose of soliciting contributions or for commercial purposes, other than using the name and address of any political committee to solicit contributions from such committee. A political committee may submit 10 pseudonyms on each report filed in order to protect against the illegal use of names and addresses of contributors, provided such committee attaches a list of such pseudonyms to the appropriate report. The Secretary or the Commission shall exclude these lists from the public record;

(5) keep such designations, reports, and statements for a period of 10 years from the date of receipt, except that designations, reports, and statements that relate solely to candidates for the House of Representatives shall be kept for 5 years from the date of their receipt;

(6)(A) compile and maintain a cumulative index of designations, reports, and statements filed under this Act, which index shall be published at regular intervals and made available for purchase directly or by mail;

(B) compile, maintain, and revise a separate cumulative index of reports and statements filed by multi-candidate committees, including in such index a list of multi-candidate committees; and

(C) compile and maintain a list of multi-candidate committees, which shall be revised and made available monthly;

(7) prepare and publish periodically lists of authorized committees which fail to file reports as required by this Act;

(8) prescribe rules, regulations, and forms to carry out the provisions of this Act, in accordance with the provisions of subsection (d) of this section;

(9) transmit to the President and to each House of the Congress no later than June 1 of each year, a report which states in detail the activities of the Commission in carrying out its duties under this Act, and any recommendations for any legislative or other action the Commission considers appropriate; and

(10) serve as a national clearinghouse for the compilation of information and review of procedures with respect to the administration of Federal elections. The Commission may enter into contracts for the purpose of conducting studies under this paragraph. Reports or studies made under this paragraph shall be available to the public upon the payment of the cost thereof, except that copies shall be made available without cost, upon request, to agencies and branches of the Federal Government.

(b) Audits and field investigations

The Commission may conduct audits and field investigations of any political committee required to file a report under section 434 of this title. All audits and field investigations concerning the verification for, and receipt and use of, any payments received by a candidate or committee under chapter 95 or chapter 96 of title 26 shall be given priority. Prior to conducting any audit under this subsection, the Commission shall perform an internal review of reports filed by selected committees to determine if the reports filed by a particular committee meet the threshold requirements for substantial compliance with the Act. Such thresholds for compliance shall be established by the Commission. The Commission may, upon an affirmative vote of 4 of its members, conduct an audit and field investigation of any committee which does meet the threshold requirements established by the Commission. Such audit shall be commenced within 30 days of such vote, except that any audit of an authorized committee of a candidate, under the provisions of this subsection, shall be commenced within 6 months of the election for which such committee is authorized.

(c) Statutory provisions applicable to forms and information-gathering activities

Any forms prescribed by the Commission under subsection (a)(1) of this section, and any information-gathering activities of the Commission under this Act, shall not be subject to the provisions of section 3512[1] of title 44.

(d) Rules, regulations, or forms; issuance, procedures applicable, etc.

(1) Before prescribing any rule, regulation, or form under this section or any other provision of this Act, the Commission shall transmit a statement with respect to such rule, regulation, or form to the Senate and the House of Representatives, in accordance with this subsection. Such statement shall set forth the proposed rule, regulation, or form, and shall contain a detailed explanation and justification of it.

(2) If either House of the Congress does not disapprove by resolution any proposed rule or regulation submitted by the Commission under this section within 30 legislative days after the date of the receipt of such proposed rule or regulation or within 10 legislative days after the date of receipt of such proposed form, the Commission may prescribe such rule, regulation, or form.

(3) For purposes of this subsection, the term "legislative day" means, with respect to statements transmitted to the Senate, any calendar day on which the Senate is in session, and with respect to statements transmitted to the House of Representatives, any calendar day on which the House of Representatives is in session.

(4) For purposes of this subsection, the terms "rule" and "regulation" mean a provision or series of interrelated provisions stating a single, separable rule of law.

(5)(A) A motion to discharge a committee of the Senate from the consideration of a resolution relating to any such rule, regulation, or form or a motion to proceed to the consideration of such a resolution, is highly privileged and shall be decided without debate.

(B) Whenever a committee of the House of Representatives reports any resolution relating to any such form, rule or regulation, it is at any time thereafter in order (even though a previous motion to the same effect has been disagreed to) to move to proceed to the consideration of the resolution. The motion is highly privileged and is not debatable. An amendment to the motion is not in order, and is not in order to move to reconsider the vote by which the motion is agreed to or disagreed with.

(e) Scope of protection for good faith reliance upon rules or regulations

Notwithstanding any other provision of law, any person who relies upon any rule or regulation prescribed by the Commission in accordance with the provisions of this section and who acts in good faith in accordance with such rule or regulation shall not, as a result of such act, be subject to any sanction provided by this Act or by chapter 95 or chapter 96 of title 26.

(f) Promulgation of rules, regulations, and forms by Commission and Internal Revenue Service; report to Congress on cooperative efforts

In prescribing such rules, regulations, and forms under this section, the Commission and the Internal Revenue Service shall consult and work together to promulgate rules, regulations, and forms which are mutually consistent. The Commission shall report to the Congress annually on the steps it has taken to comply with this subsection.

(Pub. L. 92–225, title III, § 311, formerly § 308, Feb. 7, 1972, 86 Stat. 16; renumbered § 316 and amended Pub. L. 93–443, title II, §§ 208(a), (c)(7)–(10), 209(a)(1), (b), Oct. 15, 1974, 88 Stat. 1279, 1286, 1287; renumbered § 315 and amended Pub. L. 94–283, title I, §§ 105, 110, May 11, 1976, 90 Stat. 481, 486; renumbered § 311 and amended Pub. L. 96–187, title I, §§ 105(4), 109, Jan. 8, 1980, 93 Stat. 1354, 1362; Pub. L. 99–514, § 2, Oct. 22, 1986, 100 Stat.

---

[1] See References in Text note below.

2095; Pub. L. 104–79, § 3(c), Dec. 28, 1995, 109 Stat. 792.)

REFERENCES IN TEXT

This Act, referred to in text, means the Federal Election Campaign Act of 1971, as amended, as defined by section 431 of this title.

Section 3512 of title 44, referred to in subsec. (c), which related to requirements for the collection of information by independent Federal regulatory agencies, was a part of chapter 35 of Title 44, Public Printing and Documents. Chapter 35 was amended generally by the Paperwork Reduction Act of 1980 (Pub. L. 96–511) and subsequently by the Paperwork Reduction Act of 1995 (Pub. L. 104–13).

AMENDMENTS

1995—Subsec. (a)(4). Pub. L. 104–79 substituted "Secretary" for "Clerk, Secretary,".

1986—Subsecs. (b), (e). Pub. L. 99–514 substituted "Internal Revenue Code of 1986" for "Internal Revenue Code of 1954", which for purposes of codification was translated as "title 26" thus requiring no change in text.

1980—Subsec. (a). Pub. L. 96–187, § 109, substituted in introductory clause "The Commission shall" for "It shall be the duty of the Commission".

Subsec. (a)(1). Pub. L. 96–187, § 109, substituted "prescribe forms necessary to implement this Act" for "to develop and furnish to the person required by the provisions of this Act prescribed forms for the making of the reports and statements required to be filed with it under this subchapter".

Subsec. (a)(2). Pub. L. 96–187, § 109, substituted "prepare, publish, and furnish to all persons required to file reports and statements under this Act" for "to prepare, publish, and furnish to the person required to file such reports and statements".

Subsec. (a)(3). Pub. L. 96–187, § 109, struck out "to" before "develop" and substituted "consistent with the purposes of this Act" for "consonant with the purposes of this subchapter".

Subsec. (a)(4). Pub. L. 96–187, § 109, substituted provisions making available for inspection and copying reports and statements within 48 hours after receipt and prohibiting the sale or use of any information for soliciting contributions or for commercial purposes other than using names and addresses of any political committee and allowing a political committee to submit 10 pseudonyms on each report to protect against illegal use of names and addresses of contributors, such lists to be excluded from the public record, for provisions making available for public inspection and copying reports and statements as soon as practicable but no later than the end of the second day following the day during which it was received, and to permit copying by hand or duplicating machine at the person's own expense, provided that no information so copied be sold or utilized for purposes of soliciting contributions or for commercial purposes.

Subsec. (a)(5). Pub. L. 96–187, § 109, substituted "keep such designations, reports" for "to preserve such reports", "except that designations, reports, and statements that relate" for "except that reports and statements relating" and "shall be kept" for "shall be preserved".

Subsec. (a)(6). Pub. L. 96–187, § 109, redesignated existing provisions as subpar. (A), added subpars. (B) and (C), and in subpar. (A) as so designated substituted provisions for the compilation and maintenance of a cumulative index of designations, reports, and statements filed under this Act, to be published at regular intervals and made available for direct or mail purchase for provisions for compilation and maintenance of such index to be published in the Federal Register at regular intervals to be made available for direct or mail purchase at reasonable prices, and for compilation and maintenance of a separate cumulative index of reports and statements of political committees supporting more than one candidate including a listing of the date of registration of such committee and the date of qualification to make expenditures under section 441a(a)(2), to be revised on the same basis as the other cumulative indices.

Subsec. (a)(7). Pub. L. 96–187, § 109, substituted provisions requiring preparation and publication periodically lists of committees failing to file reports as required by this Act for provisions requiring preparation and publication from time to time of special reports listing candidates for whom reports were filed as required and candidates for whom reports were not filed.

Subsec. (a)(8). Pub. L. 96–187, § 109, substituted provisions for rules, regulations and forms to carry out the provisions of this Act in accordance with subsec. (d) for provisions mandating audits and field investigations with respect to reports and statements and failure to file such and giving priority to auditing and field investigation verification and receipt and use of payments received by a candidate.

Subsec. (a)(9). Pub. L. 96–187, § 109, substituted provisions for transmittal to the President and Congress no later than June 1 of each year a report of Commission activities and recommendations for legislation for provisions for reporting apparent violations of law to appropriate law enforcement authorities.

Subsec. (a)(10). Pub. L. 96–187, § 109, substituted provisions authorizing the Commission to serve as a national clearinghouse for compilation of information and review procedures with respect to administration of Federal elections, and to enter into contracts to conduct studies, to be made available to the public upon payment of costs except that copies be made available without cost to agencies and branches of the Federal Government for provisions for prescription of rules and regulations to carry out the provisions of this subchapter in accordance with the provisions of subsec. (c) of this section.

Subsec. (b). Pub. L. 96–187, § 109, substituted provisions for the conduct of audits and field investigations with priority to verification for, and receipt and use of payments received by a candidate or committee under chapter 95 or 96 of title 26, and performance of internal review of reports of selected committees to determine compliance with threshold requirements of this Act, such requirements to be established by the Commission, audits and investigations to be undertaken upon affirmative vote of 4 members within 30 days of such vote except audits of an authorized committee of a candidate to be commenced within 6 months of the election for which such committee was authorized, for provisions declaring it the duty of the Commission to act as a national clearinghouse for information in respect to administration of elections, to enter into contracts to conduct independent studies of administration of elections, such studies to be published by the Commission and copies made available to the general public.

Subsec. (c). Pub. L. 96–187, § 109, substituted provisions exempting from the provisions of section 3512 of title 44 any forms prescribed by the Commission and any information-gathering activities of the Commission for provisions of pars. (1) to (5) relating to prescribing of rules and regulations and approval thereof by either the Senate or the House of Representatives, and definition of "legislative days" and "rule or regulation".

Subsec. (d)(1). Pub. L. 96–187, § 109, substituted provisions for transmittal to Congress of a statement with respect to any rule, regulation or form prior to its prescription, such statement setting forth such rule, etc., and a detailed explanation and justification, for provisions of subpars. (A) to (C) prescribing rules and regulations to carry out the provisions of this subchapter including rules and regulations relating to reports and statements to be filed by a candidate or delegate or Resident Commissioner to Congress, candidate for office of Senator, such reports to be made available to the public by the Clerk and Secretary of the House of Representatives and Senate, respectively.

Subsec. (d)(2). Pub. L. 96–187, § 109, substituted provisions permitting the Commission to prescribe a rule or regulation in the absence of disapproval by resolution of either House of Congress within 30 legislative days after the date of receipt of such proposed rule or regulation or within 10 legislative days after receipt of such proposed form for provisions that it is the duty of the Clerk and Secretary of the House of Representatives and Senate, respectively, to cooperate with the Commission in carrying out its duties under this Act and to furnish such services and facilities as may be required.

Subsec. (d)(3), (4). Pub. L. 96–187, § 109, added pars. (3) and (4).

Subsecs. (e), (f). Pub. L. 96–187, § 109, added subsecs. (e) and (f).

1976—Subsec. (a)(6). Pub. L. 94–283, § 110(a)(1), inserted provisions covering and index of reports and statements filed by committees supporting more than one candidate.

Subsec. (a)(8). Pub. L. 94–283, § 110(a)(2), inserted provisions giving priority to auditing and field investigating of the verification for, and the receipt and use of, any payments received by a candidate under chapter 95 or 96 of title 26.

Subsec. (c)(2). Pub. L. 94–283, § 110(b)(1), inserted provision for priority consideration by the House of Representatives of a motion to consider resolutions relating to a rule or regulation reported by a committee of the House.

Subsec. (c)(5). Pub. L. 94–283, § 110(b)(2), added par. (5).

1974—Subsec. (a). Pub. L. 93–443, § 208(c)(8), substituted "Commission" for "supervisory officer" in introductory provision.

Subsec. (a)(1), (4). Pub. L. 93–443, § 208(c)(9)(A), (B), substituted "him" for "it" in pars. (1) and (4).

Subsec. (a)(6). Pub. L. 93–443, § 209(a)(1), substituted provisions respecting index of reports and statements and publication thereof in Federal Register for provisions respecting compilation and maintenance of current list of candidate statements.

Subsec. (a)(7). Pub. L. 93–443, § 209(a)(1), substituted provision for preparation and publication of special reports listing candidates for whom reports were filed as required by this subchapter and those candidates for whom such reports were not filed as so required for provisions respecting publication of annual reports and compilations of data.

Subsec. (a)(8). Pub. L. 93–443, § 209(a)(1), redesignated par. (11) as (8) and struck out former par. (8) provision for preparation and publication of special reports comparing the various totals and categories of contributions and expenditures made with respect to preceding elections.

Subsec. (a)(9). Pub. L. 93–443, § 209(a)(1), redesignated par. (12) as (9) and struck out former par. (9) provision for preparation and publication of other reports.

Subsec. (a)(10). Pub. L. 93–443, § 209(a)(1), (b)(1), redesignated par. (13) as (10), inserted end text reading ", in accordance with the provisions of subsection (c) of this section", and struck out former par. (10) provision for dissemination of information.

Subsec. (a)(11) to (13). Pub. L. 93–443, § 209(a)(1), redesignated pars. (11) to (13) as (8) to (10), respectively.

Subsec. (b). Pub. L. 93–443, §§ 208(c)(10)(A), (B), 209(b)(2)(A), substituted "Commission" for "Comptroller General" wherever appearing and "its" for "his" in second sentence and struck out provision that "Nothing in this subsection shall be construed to authorize the Comptroller General to require the inclusion of any comment or recommendation of the Comptroller General in any such study.", redesignated subsec. (c) as (b) and struck out former subsec. (b) provisions respecting Federal and State filing of reports, including procedures for Federal copies in satisfaction of State requirements to eliminate multiple filings.

Subsec. (c). Pub. L. 93–443, § 209(b)(2)(A), (B), added subsec. (c) and redesignated former subsec. (c) as (b).

Subsec. (d). Pub. L. 93–443, § 209(b)(2)(A), (B), added subsec. (d) and struck out former subsec. (d) provisions respecting violations, the paragraphs relating to: (1) complaints, investigations, notice and hearing, Federal civil actions for injunction, restraining orders, or other appropriate orders, venue, and bond; (2) subpenas; (3) review by court of appeals and time for petition of review; (4) finality of appellate judgment and review by Supreme Court; and (5) docket advancement and priorities, provisions now covered by section 437g(a) of this title.

EFFECTIVE DATE OF 1995 AMENDMENT

Amendment by Pub. L. 104–79 applicable with respect to reports, designations, and statements required to be filed after Dec. 31, 1995, see section 3(d) of Pub. L. 104–79, set out as a note under section 432 of this title.

EFFECTIVE DATE OF 1980 AMENDMENT

Amendment by Pub. L. 96–187 effective Jan. 8, 1980, see section 301(a) of Pub. L. 96–187, set out as a note under section 431 of this title.

TERMINATION OF REPORTING REQUIREMENTS

For termination, effective May 15, 2000, of provisions in subsecs. (a)(9) and (f) of this section relating to submittal of annual reports to Congress, see section 3003 of Pub. L. 104–66, as amended, set out as a note under section 1113 of Title 31, Money and Finance, and page 168 of House Document No. 103–7.

TRANSITION PROVISIONS

Disapproval of rules and regulations by either House of Congress under subsec. (d) of this section within 30 legislative days after receipt to be deemed to allow such disapproval within 15 days with respect to rules and regulations implementing Pub. L. 96–187 proposed under section 303(a) of Pub. L. 96–187, see section 303(b) of Pub. L. 96–187, set out as a note under section 431 of this title.

ANNUAL REPORTS FOR CALENDAR YEARS BEGINNING AFTER DEC. 31, 1972

Section 209(a)(2) of Pub. L. 93–443 provided that: "Notwithstanding section 308(a)(7) of the Federal Election Campaign Act of 1971 [subsec. (a)(7) of this section] (relating to an annual report by the supervisory officer), as in effect on the day before the effective date of the amendments made by paragraph (1) of this subsection, no such annual report shall be required with respect to any calendar year beginning after December 31, 1972."

SECTION REFERRED TO IN OTHER SECTIONS

This section is referred to in sections 432, 437f, 437g, 439c of this title.

§ 439. Statements filed with State officers; "appropriate State" defined; duties of State officers; waiver of duplicate filing requirement for States with electronic access

(a) Statements filed; "appropriate State" defined

(1) A copy of each report and statement required to be filed by any person under this Act shall be filed by such person with the Secretary of State (or equivalent State officer) of the appropriate State, or, if different, the officer of such State who is charged by State law with maintaining State election campaign reports. The chief executive officer of such State shall designate any such officer and notify the Commission of any such designation.

(2) For purposes of this subsection, the term "appropriate State" means—

(A) for statements and reports in connection with the campaign for nomination for election of a candidate to the office of President or Vice President, each State in which an expenditure is made on behalf of the candidate; and

(B) for statements and reports in connection with the campaign for nomination for election, or election, of a candidate to the office of Senator or Representative in, or Delegate or Resident Commissioner to, the Congress, the State in which the candidate seeks election; except that political committees other than authorized committees are only required to file, and Secretaries of State required to keep, that portion of the report applicable to candidates seeking election in that State.

(b) Duties of State officers

The Secretary of State (or equivalent State officer), or the officer designated under subsection (a)(1) of this section, shall—

(1) receive and maintain in an orderly manner all reports and statements required by this Act to be filed therewith;

(2) keep such reports and statements (either in original filed form or in facsimile copy by microfilm or otherwise) for 2 years after their date of receipt;

(3) make each report and statement filed therewith available as soon as practicable (but within 48 hours of receipt) for public inspection and copying during regular business hours, and permit copying of any such report or statement by hand or by duplicating machine at the request of any person, except that such copying shall be at the expense of the person making the request; and

(4) compile and maintain a current list of all reports and statements pertaining to each candidate.

(c) Waiver; electronic access

Subsections (a) and (b) of this section shall not apply with respect to any State that, as determined by the Commission, has a system that permits electronic access to, and duplication of, reports and statements that are filed with the Commission.

(Pub. L. 92–225, title III, § 312, formerly § 309, Feb. 7, 1972, 86 Stat. 18; renumbered § 317 and amended Pub. L. 93–443, title II, § 208(a), (c)(11), Oct. 15, 1974, 88 Stat. 1279, 1287; renumbered § 316, Pub. L. 94–283, title I, § 105, May 11, 1976, 90 Stat. 481; renumbered § 312 and amended Pub. L. 96–187, title I, §§ 105(4), 110, Jan. 8, 1980, 93 Stat. 1354, 1364; Pub. L. 104–79, § 2, Dec. 28, 1995, 109 Stat. 791.)

REFERENCES IN TEXT

This Act, referred to in subsecs. (a)(1) and (b)(1), means the Federal Election Campaign Act of 1971, as amended, as defined by section 431 of this title.

AMENDMENTS

1995—Subsec. (c). Pub. L. 104–79 added subsec. (c).

1980—Subsec. (a). Pub. L. 96–187, § 110, in revising text, added par. (1), incorporating part of first sentence reading "A copy of each statement required to be filed with the Commissioner by this subchapter shall be filed with the Secretary of State (or, if there is no office of Secretary of State, the equivalent State officer) of the appropriate State."; and reenacted as par. (2) definition provision of second sentence, redesignating as cl. (A) prior cl. (1) provisions, inserting reference to statements respecting the campaign, striking out reference to campaign for election and provision for expenditure by the candidate, and redesignating as cl. (B) prior cl. (2), inserting reference to statements respecting the campaign and requirement only for political committees other than authorized committees to file and Secretaries of State to keep that portion of report applicable to candidates seeking election in that State.

Subsec. (b). Pub. L. 96–187, § 110, in revising text, provided for performance of the prescribed duties by the officer designated under subsec. (a)(1); substituted in cl. (1) "reports and statements required by this Act to be filed therewith" for "reports and statements required by this subchapter to be filed with him"; substituted in cl. (2) requirement of a 2 year retention period for reports and statements after receipt in original form or in facsimile copy by microfilm for ten year retention period after such receipt and five year period when relating to House of Representatives candidates; required in cl. (3) that filed reports and statements be available within 48 hours of receipt rather than no later than end of day of receipt; and provided in cl. (4) for inclusion of reports in current list and exclusion of parts of statements.

1974—Subsec. (a). Pub. L. 93–443, § 208(c)(11), substituted "the Commission" for "a supervisory officer".

EFFECTIVE DATE OF 1980 AMENDMENT

Amendment by Pub. L. 96–187 effective Jan. 8, 1980, see section 301(a) of Pub. L. 96–187, set out as a note under section 431 of this title.

EFFECTIVE DATE OF 1974 AMENDMENT

Amendment by Pub. L. 93–443 effective Jan. 1, 1975, see section 410(a) of Pub. L. 93–443, set out as a note under section 431 of this title.

§ 439a. Use of contributed amounts for certain purposes

Amounts received by a candidate as contributions that are in excess of any amount necessary to defray his expenditures, and any other amounts contributed to an individual for the purpose of supporting his or her activities as a holder of Federal office, may be used by such candidate or individual, as the case may be, to defray any ordinary and necessary expenses incurred in connection with his or her duties as a holder of Federal office, may be contributed to any organization described in section 170(c) of title 26, or may be used for any other lawful purpose, including transfers without limitation to any national, State, or local committee of any political party; except that no such amounts may be converted by any person to any personal use, other than to defray any ordinary and necessary expenses incurred in connection with his or her duties as a holder of Federal office.

(Pub. L. 92–225, title III, § 313, formerly § 318, as added Pub. L. 93–443, title II, § 210, Oct. 15, 1974, 88 Stat. 1288; renumbered § 317, Pub. L. 94–283, title I, § 105, May 11, 1976, 90 Stat. 481; renumbered § 313 and amended Pub. L. 96–187, title I, §§ 105(4), 113, Jan. 8, 1980, 93 Stat. 1354, 1366; Pub. L. 99–514, § 2, Oct. 22, 1986, 100 Stat. 2095; Pub. L. 101–194, title V, § 504(a), Nov. 30, 1989, 103 Stat. 1755.)

AMENDMENTS

1989—Pub. L. 101–194 struck out ", with respect to any individual who is not a Senator or Representative in, or Delegate or Resident Commissioner to, the Congress on January 8, 1980," after "except that".

1986—Pub. L. 99–514 substituted "Internal Revenue Code of 1986" for "Internal Revenue Code of 1954", which for purposes of codification was translated as "title 26" thus requiring no change in text.

1980—Pub. L. 96–187, § 113, substituted "his or her activities", "incurred in connection with his or her duties," and "may be contributed to any organization" for "his activities", "incurred by him in connection with his duties", and "may be contributed by him to any organization", respectively; authorized use of contributions for transfers without limitation to any national, State, or local committee of any political party but prohibited with respect to any individual who is not a Senator or Representative in, or Delegate or Resident Commissioner to the Congress on Jan. 8, 1980, conversion to any personal use, other than to defray any ordinary and necessary expenses incurred in connection with his or her duties as a holder of Federal office; and struck out requirement for disclosure of contributions and expenditures under Commission rules when such disclosure is not otherwise required under this subchapter and authorization for Commission to prescribe rules to carry out this section.

EFFECTIVE DATE OF 1989 AMENDMENT

Section 504(b) of Pub. L. 101–194 provided that: "The amendment made by subsection (a) [amending this section]—

"(1) in the case of an individual who serves as a Senator or Representative in, or Delegate or Resident Commissioner to, the Congress in the 102nd Congress or an earlier Congress, shall apply, except as provided in paragraph (2), to the use of excess amounts totaling more than the amount equal to the unobligated balance on hand on the date of the enactment of this Act [Nov. 30, 1989]; and

"(2) in the case of an individual who serves as a Senator or Representative in, or Delegate or Resident Commissioner to, the Congress after the 102nd Congress (including an individual referred to in paragraph (1) who so serves), shall apply to the use of any excess amount on or after the first day of such service."

EFFECTIVE DATE OF 1980 AMENDMENT

Amendment by Pub. L. 96–187 effective Jan. 8, 1980, see section 301(a) of Pub. L. 96–187, set out as a note under section 431 of this title.

EFFECTIVE DATE

Section effective Jan. 1, 1975, see section 410(a) of Pub. L. 93–443, set out as an Effective Date of 1974 Amendment note under section 431 of this title.

§ 439b. Repealed. Pub. L. 96–187, title I, § 105(1), Jan. 8, 1980, 93 Stat. 1354

Section, Pub. L. 92–225, title III, § 318, formerly § 319, as added Pub. L. 93–443, title II, § 210, Oct. 15, 1974, 88 Stat. 1289; renumbered § 318, Pub. L. 94–283, title I, § 105, May 11, 1976, 90 Stat. 481, set forth prohibitions respecting franked solicitations.

EFFECTIVE DATE OF REPEAL

Repeal effective Jan. 8, 1980, see section 301(a) of Pub. L. 96–187, set out as an Effective Date of 1980 Amendment note under section 431 of this title.

§ 439c. Authorization of appropriations

There are authorized to be appropriated to the Commission for the purpose of carrying out its functions under this Act, and under chapters 95 and 96 of title 26, not to exceed $5,000,000 for the fiscal year ending June 30, 1975. There are authorized to be appropriated to the Commission $6,000,000 for the fiscal year ending June 30, 1976, $1,500,000 for the period beginning July 1, 1976, and ending September 30, 1976, $6,000,000 for the fiscal year ending September 30, 1977, $7,811,500 for the fiscal year ending September 30, 1978, and $9,400,000 (of which not more than $400,000 are authorized to be appropriated for the national clearinghouse function described in section 438(a)(10) of this title) for the fiscal year ending September 30, 1981.

(Pub. L. 92–225, title III, § 314, formerly § 320, as added Pub. L. 93–443, title II, § 210, Oct. 15, 1974, 88 Stat. 1289; renumbered § 319 and amended Pub. L. 94–283, title I, §§ 105, 113, May 11, 1976, 90 Stat. 481, 495; Pub. L. 95–127, Oct. 12, 1977, 91 Stat. 1110; renumbered § 314, Pub. L. 96–187, title I, § 105(5), Jan. 8, 1980, 93 Stat. 1354; Pub. L. 96–253, May 29, 1980, 94 Stat. 398; Pub. L. 99–514, § 2, Oct. 22, 1986, 100 Stat. 2095.)

REFERENCES IN TEXT

This Act, referred to in text, means the Federal Election Campaign Act of 1971, as amended, as defined by section 431 of this title.

AMENDMENTS

1986—Pub. L. 99–514 substituted "Internal Revenue Code of 1986" for "Internal Revenue Code of 1954", which for purposes of codification was translated as "title 26" thus requiring no change in text.

1980—Pub. L. 96–253 inserted provisions authorizing appropriations of $9,400,000 for fiscal year ending Sept. 30, 1981.

1977—Pub. L. 95–127 inserted provisions authorizing appropriations of $7,811,500 for fiscal year ending Sept. 30, 1978.

1976—Pub. L. 94–283, § 113, inserted provisions authorizing appropriations through fiscal year ending Sept. 30, 1977.

EFFECTIVE DATE

Section effective Jan. 1, 1975, see section 410(a) of Pub. L. 93–443, set out as an Effective Date of 1974 Amendment note under section 431 of this title.

§ 440. Repealed. Pub. L. 93–443, title I, § 101(f)(4), Oct. 15, 1974, 88 Stat. 1268

Section, Pub. L. 92–225, title III, § 310, Feb. 7, 1972, 86 Stat. 19, related to prohibition of contributions in the name of another. See section 441f of this title.

EFFECTIVE DATE OF REPEAL

Repeal effective Jan. 1, 1975, see section 410(a) of Pub. L. 93–443, set out as an Effective Date of 1974 Amendment note under section 431 of this title.

§ 441. Repealed. Pub. L. 94–283, title I, § 112(1), May 11, 1976, 90 Stat. 486

Section, Pub. L. 92–225, title III, § 320, formerly § 311, Feb. 7, 1972, 86 Stat. 19; renumbered § 321, Pub. L. 93–443, title II, § 208(a), Oct. 15, 1974, 88 Stat. 1279; renumbered § 320, Pub. L. 94–283, title I, § 105, May 11, 1976, 90 Stat. 481, provided penalties of not more than $1,000 fine or not more than 1 year imprisonment, or both for violations of this subchapter. See section 441j of this title.

SAVINGS PROVISION

Section 114 of Pub. L. 94–283 provided that: "Except as otherwise provided by this Act [see Short Title of 1976 Amendment note set out under section 431 of this title], the repeal by this Act of any section or penalty shall not have the effect of releasing or extinguishing any penalty, forfeiture, or liability incurred under such section or penalty, and such section or penalty shall be treated as remaining in force for the purpose of sustaining any proper action or prosecution for the enforcement of any penalty, forfeiture, or liability."

§ 441a. Limitations on contributions and expenditures

(a) Dollar limits on contributions

(1) No person shall make contributions—

(A) to any candidate and his authorized political committees with respect to any election for Federal office which, in the aggregate, exceed $1,000;

(B) to the political committees established and maintained by a national political party, which are not the authorized political committees of any candidate, in any calendar year which, in the aggregate, exceed $20,000; or

(C) to any other political committee in any calendar year which, in the aggregate, exceed $5,000.

(2) No multicandidate political committee shall make contributions—

(A) to any candidate and his authorized political committees with respect to any election for Federal office which, in the aggregate, exceed $5,000;

(B) to the political committees established and maintained by a national political party, which are not the authorized political committees of any candidate, in any calendar year, which, in the aggregate, exceed $15,000; or

(C) to any other political committee in any calendar year which, in the aggregate, exceed $5,000.

(3) No individual shall make contributions aggregating more than $25,000 in any calendar year. For purposes of this paragraph, any contribution made to a candidate in a year other than the calendar year in which the election is held with respect to which such contribution is made, is considered to be made during the calendar year in which such election is held.

(4) The limitations on contributions contained in paragraphs (1) and (2) do not apply to transfers between and among political committees which are national, State, district, or local committees (including any subordinate committee thereof) of the same political party. For purposes of paragraph (2), the term "multicandidate political committee" means a political committee which has been registered under section 433 of this title for a period of not less than 6 months, which has received contributions from more than 50 persons, and, except for any State political party organization, has made contributions to 5 or more candidates for Federal office.

(5) For purposes of the limitations provided by paragraph (1) and paragraph (2), all contributions made by political committees established or financed or maintained or controlled by any corporation, labor organization, or any other person, including any parent, subsidiary, branch, division, department, or local unit of such corporation, labor organization, or any other person, or by any group of such persons, shall be considered to have been made by a single political committee, except that (A) nothing in this sentence shall limit transfers between political committees of funds raised through joint fund raising efforts; (B) for purposes of the limitations provided by paragraph (1) and paragraph (2) all contributions made by a single political committee established or financed or maintained or controlled by a national committee of a political party and by a single political committee established or financed or maintained or controlled by the State committee of a political party shall not be considered to have been made by a single political committee; and

(C) nothing in this section shall limit the transfer of funds between the principal campaign committee of a candidate seeking nomination or election to a Federal office and the principal campaign committee of that candidate for nomination or election to another Federal office if (i) such transfer is not made when the candidate is actively seeking nomination or election to both such offices; (ii) the limitations contained in this Act on contributions by persons are not exceeded by such transfer; and (iii) the candidate has not elected to receive any funds under chapter 95 or chapter 96 of title 26. In any case in which a corporation and any of its subsidiaries, branches, divisions, departments, or local units, or a labor organization and any of its subsidiaries, branches, divisions, departments, or local units establish or finance or maintain or control more than one separate segregated fund, all such separate segregated funds shall be treated as a single separate segregated fund for purposes of the limitations provided by paragraph (1) and paragraph (2).

(6) The limitations on contributions to a candidate imposed by paragraphs (1) and (2) of this subsection shall apply separately with respect to each election, except that all elections held in any calendar year for the office of President of the United States (except a general election for such office) shall be considered to be one election.

(7) For purposes of this subsection—

(A) contributions to a named candidate made to any political committee authorized by such candidate to accept contributions on his behalf shall be considered to be contributions made to such candidate;

(B)(i) expenditures made by any person in cooperation, consultation, or concert, with, or at the request or suggestion of, a candidate, his authorized political committees, or their agents, shall be considered to be a contribution to such candidate;

(ii) the financing by any person of the dissemination, distribution, or republication, in whole or in part, of any broadcast or any written, graphic, or other form of campaign materials prepared by the candidate, his campaign committees, or their authorized agents shall be considered to be an expenditure for purposes of this paragraph; and

(C) contributions made to or for the benefit of any candidate nominated by a political party for election to the office of Vice President of the United States shall be considered to be contributions made to or for the benefit of the candidate of such party for election to the office of President of the United States.

(8) For purposes of the limitations imposed by this section, all contributions made by a person, either directly or indirectly, on behalf of a particular candidate, including contributions which are in any way earmarked or otherwise directed through an intermediary or conduit to such candidate, shall be treated as contributions from such person to such candidate. The intermediary or conduit shall report the original source and the intended recipient of such contribution to the Commission and to the intended recipient.

(b) Dollar limits on expenditures by candidates for office of President of United States

(1) No candidate for the office of President of the United States who is eligible under section 9003 of title 26 (relating to condition for eligibility for payments) or under section 9033 of title 26 (relating to eligibility for payments) to receive payments from the Secretary of the Treasury may make expenditures in excess of—

(A) $10,000,000, in the case of a campaign for nomination for election to such office, except the aggregate of expenditures under this subparagraph in any one State shall not exceed the greater of 16 cents multiplied by the voting age population of the State (as certified under subsection (e) of this section), or $200,000; or

(B) $20,000,000 in the case of a campaign for election to such office.

(2) For purposes of this subsection—

(A) expenditures made by or on behalf of any candidate nominated by a political party for election to the office of Vice President of the United States shall be considered to be expenditures made by or on behalf of the candidate of such party for election to the office of President of the United States; and

(B) an expenditure is made on behalf of a candidate, including a vice presidential candidate, if it is made by—

(i) an authorized committee or any other agent of the candidate for purposes of making any expenditure; or

(ii) any person authorized or requested by the candidate, an authorized committee of the candidate, or an agent of the candidate, to make the expenditure.

(c) Increases on limits based on increases in price index

(1) At the beginning of each calendar year (commencing in 1976), as there become available necessary data from the Bureau of Labor Statistics of the Department of Labor, the Secretary of Labor shall certify to the Commission and publish in the Federal Register the percent difference between the price index for the 12 months preceding the beginning of such calendar year and the price index for the base period. Each limitation established by subsection (b) of this section and subsection (d) of this section shall be increased by such percent difference. Each amount so increased shall be the amount in effect for such calendar year.

(2) For purposes of paragraph (1)—

(A) the term "price index" means the average over a calendar year of the Consumer Price Index (all items—United States city average) published monthly by the Bureau of Labor Statistics; and

(B) the term "base period" means the calendar year 1974.

(d) Expenditures by national committee, State committee, or subordinate committee of State committee in connection with general election campaign of candidates for Federal office

(1) Notwithstanding any other provision of law with respect to limitations on expenditures or limitations on contributions, the national committee of a political party and a State committee of a political party, including any subordinate committee of a State committee, may make expenditures in connection with the general election campaign of candidates for Federal office, subject to the limitations contained in paragraphs (2) and (3) of this subsection.

(2) The national committee of a political party may not make any expenditure in connection with the general election campaign of any candidate for President of the United States who is affiliated with such party which exceeds an amount equal to 2 cents multiplied by the voting age population of the United States (as certified under subsection (e) of this section). Any expenditure under this paragraph shall be in addition to any expenditure by a national committee of a political party serving as the principal campaign committee of a candidate for the office of President of the United States.

(3) The national committee of a political party, or a State committee of a political party, including any subordinate committee of a State committee, may not make any expenditure in connection with the general election campaign of a candidate for Federal office in a State who is affiliated with such party which exceeds—

(A) in the case of a candidate for election to the office of Senator, or of Representative from a State which is entitled to only one Representative, the greater of—

(i) 2 cents multiplied by the voting age population of the State (as certified under subsection (e) of this section); or

(ii) $20,000; and

(B) in the case of a candidate for election to the office of Representative, Delegate, or Resident Commissioner in any other State, $10,000.

(e) Certification and publication of estimated voting age population

During the first week of January 1975, and every subsequent year, the Secretary of Commerce shall certify to the Commission and publish in the Federal Register an estimate of the voting age population of the United States, of each State, and of each congressional district as of the first day of July next preceding the date of certification. The term "voting age population" means resident population, 18 years of age or older.

(f) Prohibited contributions and expenditures

No candidate or political committee shall knowingly accept any contribution or make any expenditure in violation of the provisions of this section. No officer or employee of a political committee shall knowingly accept a contribution made for the benefit or use of a candidate, or knowingly make any expenditure on behalf of a candidate, in violation of any limitation imposed on contributions and expenditures under this section.

(g) Attribution of multi-State expenditures to candidate's expenditure limitation in each State

The Commission shall prescribe rules under which any expenditure by a candidate for presidential nominations for use in 2 or more States shall be attributed to such candidate's expenditure limitation in each such State, based on the voting age population in such State which can reasonably be expected to be influenced by such expenditure.

(h) Senatorial candidates

Notwithstanding any other provision of this Act, amounts totaling not more than $17,500 may be contributed to a candidate for nomination for election, or for election, to the United States Senate during the year in which an election is held in which he is such a candidate, by the Republican or Democratic Senatorial Campaign Committee, or the national committee of a political party, or any combination of such committees.

(Pub. L. 92–225, title III, § 315, formerly § 320, as added Pub. L. 94–283, title I, § 112(2), May 11, 1976, 90 Stat. 486; renumbered § 315, Pub. L. 96–187, title I, § 105(5), Jan. 8, 1980, 93 Stat. 1354; amended Pub. L. 99–514, § 2, Oct. 22, 1986, 100 Stat. 2095.)

REFERENCES IN TEXT

This Act, referred to in subsecs. (a)(5) and (h), means the Federal Election Campaign Act of 1971, as amended, as defined by section 431 of this title.

CODIFICATION

Another section 320 of Pub. L. 92–225, which was classified to section 441 of this title, was repealed by Pub. L. 94–283, title I, § 112(1), May 11, 1976, 90 Stat. 486.

AMENDMENTS

1986—Subsecs. (a)(5), (b)(1). Pub. L. 99–514 substituted "Internal Revenue Code of 1986" for "Internal Revenue Code of 1954", which for purposes of codification was translated as "title 26" thus requiring no change in text.

SECTION REFERRED TO IN OTHER SECTIONS

This section is referred to in section 434 of this title; title 5 section 7323; title 26 sections 9004, 9008, 9034, 9035.

§ 441b. Contributions or expenditures by national banks, corporations, or labor organizations

(a) It is unlawful for any national bank, or any corporation organized by authority of any law of Congress, to make a contribution or expenditure in connection with any election to any political office, or in connection with any primary election or political convention or caucus held to select candidates for any political office, or for any corporation whatever, or any labor organization, to make a contribution or expenditure in connection with any election at which presidential and vice presidential electors or a Senator or Representative in, or a Delegate or Resident Commissioner to, Congress are to be voted for, or in connection with any primary election or political convention or caucus held to select candidates for any of the foregoing offices, or for any candidate, political committee, or other person knowingly to accept or receive any contribution prohibited by this section, or any officer or any director of any corporation or any national bank or any officer of any labor organization to consent to any contribution or expenditure by the corporation, national bank, or labor organization, as the case may be, prohibited by this section.

(b)(1) For the purposes of this section the term "labor organization" means any organization of any kind, or any agency or employee representation committee or plan, in which employees participate and which exists for the purpose, in whole or in part, of dealing with employers concerning grievances, labor disputes, wages, rates of pay, hours of employment, or conditions of work.

(2) For purposes of this section and section 79l(h) of title 15, the term "contribution or expenditure" shall include any direct or indirect payment, distribution, loan, advance, deposit, or gift of money, or any services, or anything of value (except a loan of money by a national or State bank made in accordance with the applicable banking laws and regulations and in the ordinary course of business) to any candidate, campaign committee, or political party or organization, in connection with any election to any of the offices referred to in this section, but shall not include (A) communications by a corporation to its stockholders and executive or administrative personnel and their families or by a labor organization to its members and their families on any subject; (B) nonpartisan registration and get-out-the-vote campaigns by a corporation aimed at its stockholders and executive or administrative personnel and their families, or by a labor organization aimed at its members and their families; and (C) the establishment, administration, and solicitation of contributions to a separate segregated fund to be utilized for political purposes by a corporation, labor organization, membership organization, cooperative, or corporation without capital stock.

(3) It shall be unlawful—

(A) for such a fund to make a contribution or expenditure by utilizing money or anything of value secured by physical force, job discrimination, financial reprisals, or the threat of force, job discrimination, or financial reprisal; or by dues, fees, or other moneys required as a condition of membership in a labor organization or as a condition of employment, or by moneys obtained in any commercial transaction;

(B) for any person soliciting an employee for a contribution to such a fund to fail to inform such employee of the political purposes of such fund at the time of such solicitation; and

(C) for any person soliciting an employee for a contribution to such a fund to fail to inform such employee, at the time of such solicitation, of his right to refuse to so contribute without any reprisal.

(4)(A) Except as provided in subparagraphs (B), (C), and (D), it shall be unlawful—

(i) for a corporation, or a separate segregated fund established by a corporation, to solicit contributions to such a fund from any person other than its stockholders and their families and its executive or administrative personnel and their families, and

(ii) for a labor organization, or a separate segregated fund established by a labor organization, to solicit contributions to such a fund from any person other than its members and their families.

(B) It shall not be unlawful under this section for a corporation, a labor organization, or a separate segregated fund established by such corporation or such labor organization, to make 2 written solicitations for contributions during the calendar year from any stockholder, executive or administrative personnel, or employee of a corporation or the families of such persons. A solicitation under this subparagraph may be made only by mail addressed to stockholders, executive or administrative personnel, or employees at their residence and shall be so designed that the corporation, labor organization, or separate segregated fund conducting such solicitation cannot determine who makes a contribution of $50 or less as a result of such solicitation and who does not make such a contribution.

(C) This paragraph shall not prevent a membership organization, cooperative, or corporation without capital stock, or a separate segregated fund established by a membership organization, cooperative, or corporation without capital stock, from soliciting contributions to such a fund from members of such organization, cooperative, or corporation without capital stock.

(D) This paragraph shall not prevent a trade association or a separate segregated fund established by a trade association from soliciting contributions from the stockholders and executive or administrative personnel of the member corporations of such trade association and the families of such stockholders or personnel to the extent that such solicitation of such stockholders and personnel, and their families, has been separately and specifically approved by the member corporation involved, and such member corporation does not approve any such solicitation by more than one such trade association in any calendar year.

(5) Notwithstanding any other law, any method of soliciting voluntary contributions or of facilitating the making of voluntary contributions to a separate segregated fund established by a corporation, permitted by law to corporations with regard to stockholders and executive or administrative personnel, shall also be permitted to labor organizations with regard to their members.

(6) Any corporation, including its subsidiaries, branches, divisions, and affiliates, that utilizes a method of soliciting voluntary contributions or facilitating the making of voluntary contributions, shall make available such method, on written request and at a cost sufficient only to reimburse the corporation for the expenses incurred thereby, to a labor organization representing any members working for such corporation, its subsidiaries, branches, divisions, and affiliates.

(7) For purposes of this section, the term "executive or administrative personnel" means individuals employed by a corporation who are paid on a salary, rather than hourly, basis and who have policymaking, managerial, professional, or supervisory responsibilities.

(Pub. L. 92–225, title III, §316, formerly §321, as added Pub. L. 94–283, title I, §112(2), May 11, 1976, 90 Stat. 490; renumbered §316 and amended Pub. L. 96–187, title I, §§105(5), 112(d), Jan. 8, 1980, 93 Stat. 1354, 1366.)

AMENDMENTS

1980—Subsec. (b)(4)(B). Pub. L. 96–187, §112(d), substituted "It" for "it".

EFFECTIVE DATE OF 1980 AMENDMENT

Amendment by Pub. L. 96–187 effective Jan. 8, 1980, see section 301(a) of Pub. L. 96–187, set out as a note under section 431 of this title.

SECTION REFERRED TO IN OTHER SECTIONS

This section is referred to in sections 432, 433, 437g, 441c of this title.

§441c. Contributions by government contractors

(a) Prohibition

It shall be unlawful for any person—

(1) who enters into any contract with the United States or any department or agency thereof either for the rendition of personal services or furnishing any material, supplies, or equipment to the United States or any department or agency thereof or for selling any land or building to the United States or any department or agency thereof, if payment for the performance of such contract or payment for such material, supplies, equipment, land, or building is to be made in whole or in part from funds appropriated by the Congress, at any time between the commencement of negotiations for and the later of (A) the completion of performance under; or (B) the termination of negotiations for, such contract or furnishing of material, supplies, equipment, land, or buildings, directly or indirectly to make any contribution of money or other things of value, or to promise expressly or impliedly to make any such contribution to any political party, committee, or candidate for public office or to any person for any political purpose or use; or

(2) knowingly to solicit any such contribution from any such person for any such purpose during any such period.

(b) Separate segregated funds

This section does not prohibit or make unlawful the establishment or administration of, or the solicitation of contributions to, any separate segregated fund by any corporation, labor organization, membership organization, cooperative, or corporation without capital stock for the purpose of influencing the nomination for election, or election, of any person to Federal office, unless the provisions of section 441b of this title prohibit or make unlawful the establishment or administration of, or the solicitation of contributions to, such fund. Each specific prohibition, allowance, and duty applicable to a corporation, labor organization, or separate segregated fund under section 441b of this title applies to a corporation, labor organization, or separate segregated fund to which this subsection applies.

(c) "Labor organization" defined

For purposes of this section, the term "labor organization" has the meaning given it by section 441b(b)(1) of this title.

(Pub. L. 92–225, title III, §317, formerly §322, as added Pub. L. 94–283, title I, §112(2), May 11, 1976, 90 Stat. 492; renumbered §317, Pub. L. 96–187, title I, §105(5), Jan. 8, 1980, 93 Stat. 1354.)

REFERENCES IN TEXT

Section 441b of this title, referred to in subsecs. (b) and (c), was in the original "section 321" meaning section 321 of Pub. L. 92–225 which is classified to section 441g of this title. In view of the renumbering of section 321 as section 316 by section 105(5) of Pub. L. 96–187, the reference has been translated as reading "section 316" to reflect the probable intent of Congress.

SECTION REFERRED TO IN OTHER SECTIONS

This section is referred to in section 437g of this title.

§ 441d. Publication and distribution of statements and solicitations; charge for newspaper or magazine space

(a) Whenever any person makes an expenditure for the purpose of financing communications expressly advocating the election or defeat of a clearly identified candidate, or solicits any contribution through any broadcasting station, newspaper, magazine, outdoor advertising facility, direct mailing, or any other type of general public political advertising, such communication—

(1) if paid for and authorized by a candidate, an authorized political committee of a candidate, or its agents, shall clearly state that the communication has been paid for by such authorized political committee, or[1]

(2) if paid for by other persons but authorized by a candidate, an authorized political committee of a candidate, or its agents, shall clearly state that the communication is paid for by such other persons and authorized by such authorized political committee;[1]

(3) if not authorized by a candidate, an authorized political committee of a candidate, or its agents, shall clearly state the name of the person who paid for the communication and state that the communication is not authorized by any candidate or candidate's committee.

(b) No person who sells space in a newspaper or magazine to a candidate or to the agent of a candidate, for use in connection with such candidate's campaign, may charge any amount for such space which exceeds the amount charged for comparable use of such space for other purposes.

(Pub. L. 92–225, title III, § 318, formerly § 323, as added Pub. L. 94–283, title I, § 112(2), May 11, 1976, 90 Stat. 493; renumbered § 318 and amended Pub. L. 96–187, title I, §§ 105(5), 111, Jan. 8, 1980, 93 Stat. 1354, 1365.)

AMENDMENTS

1980—Subsec. (a). Pub. L. 96–187, § 111, designated existing provisions as subsec. (a), and in revising text, provided for solicitation of contributions; prescribed three categories of communications: (1) paid for and authorized by the candidate, (2) paid for by others but authorized by the candidate, and (3) not authorized by the candidate for prior two categories where (1) authorized and (2) not authorized by the candidate; struck out requirement for statement in accordance with regulations of Commission and in a conspicuous manner; and struck out from the communication not authorized by the candidate statement of name of affiliated or connected organization required to be disclosed under section 433 (b)(2) of this title.

---

[1] So in original. The word "or" probably should appear at the end of par. (2).

Subsec. (b). Pub. L. 96–187, § 111, added subsec. (b).

EFFECTIVE DATE OF 1980 AMENDMENT

Amendment by Pub. L. 96–187 effective Jan. 8, 1980, see section 301(a) of Pub. L. 96–187, set out as a note under section 431 of this title.

§ 441e. Contributions by foreign nationals

(a) It shall be unlawful for a foreign national directly or through any other person to make any contribution of money or other thing of value, or to promise expressly or impliedly to make any such contribution, in connection with an election to any political office or in connection with any primary election, convention, or caucus held to select candidates for any political office; or for any person to solicit, accept, or receive any such contribution from a foreign national.

(b) As used in this section, the term "foreign national" means—

(1) a foreign principal, as such term is defined by section 611(b) of title 22, except that the term "foreign national" shall not include any individual who is a citizen of the United States; or

(2) an individual who is not a citizen of the United States and who is not lawfully admitted for permanent residence, as defined by section 1101(a)(20) of title 8.

(Pub. L. 92–225, title III, § 319, formerly § 324, as added Pub. L. 94–283, title I, § 112(2), May 11, 1976, 90 Stat. 493; renumbered § 319, Pub. L. 96–187, title I, § 105(5), Jan. 8, 1980, 93 Stat. 1354.)

§ 441f. Contributions in name of another prohibited

No person shall make a contribution in the name of another person or knowingly permit his name to be used to effect such a contribution, and no person shall knowingly accept a contribution made by one person in the name of another person.

(Pub. L. 92–225, title III, § 320, formerly § 325, as added Pub. L. 94–283, title I, § 112(2), May 11, 1976, 90 Stat. 494; renumbered § 320, Pub. L. 96–187, title I, § 105(5), Jan. 8, 1980, 93 Stat. 1354.)

SECTION REFERRED TO IN OTHER SECTIONS

This section is referred to in section 437g of this title.

§ 441g. Limitation on contribution of currency

No person shall make contributions of currency of the United States or currency of any foreign country to or for the benefit of any candidate which, in the aggregate, exceed $100, with respect to any campaign of such candidate for nomination for election, or for election, to Federal office.

(Pub. L. 92–225, title III, § 321, formerly § 326, as added Pub. L. 94–283, title I, § 112(2), May 11, 1976, 90 Stat. 494; renumbered § 321, Pub. L. 96–187, title I, § 105(5), Jan. 8, 1980, 93 Stat. 1354.)

SECTION REFERRED TO IN OTHER SECTIONS

This section is referred to in section 437g of this title.

§ 441h. Fraudulent misrepresentation of campaign authority

No person who is a candidate for Federal office or an employee or agent of such a candidate shall—

(1) fraudulently misrepresent himself or any committee or organization under his control as speaking or writing or otherwise acting for or on behalf of any other candidate or political party or employee or agent thereof on a matter which is damaging to such other candidate or political party or employee or agent thereof; or

(2) willfully and knowingly participate in or conspire to participate in any plan, scheme, or design to violate paragraph (1).

(Pub. L. 92–225, title III, § 322, formerly § 327, as added Pub. L. 94–283, title I, § 112(2), May 11, 1976, 90 Stat. 494; renumbered § 322, Pub. L. 96–187, title I, § 105(5), Jan. 8, 1980, 93 Stat. 1354.)

SECTION REFERRED TO IN OTHER SECTIONS

This section is referred to in section 437g of this title.

§ 441i. Repealed. Pub. L. 102–90, title I, § 6(d), Aug. 14, 1991, 105 Stat. 451

Section, Pub. L. 92–225, title III, § 323, formerly § 328, as added Pub. L. 94–283, title I, § 112(2), May 11, 1976, 90 Stat. 494; amended Pub. L. 95–216, title V, § 502(a), Dec. 20, 1977, 91 Stat. 1565; renumbered § 323, Pub. L. 96–187, title I, § 105(5), Jan. 8, 1980, 93 Stat. 1354; amended Pub. L. 97–51, § 130(a), Oct. 1, 1981, 95 Stat. 966; Pub. L. 98–63, title I, § 908(g), July 30, 1983, 97 Stat. 338; Pub. L. 101–194, title VI, § 601(b)(1), Nov. 30, 1989, 103 Stat. 1762; Pub. L. 101–280, § 7(b)(1) [(d)(1)], May 4, 1990, 104 Stat. 161, related to acceptance of excessive honorariums.

§ 441j. Repealed. Pub. L. 96–187, title I, § 105(1), Jan. 8, 1980, 93 Stat. 1354

Section, Pub. L. 92–225, title III, § 329, as added Pub. L. 94–283, title I, § 112(2), May 11, 1976, 90 Stat. 494, set forth provisions respecting penalties for violations of the Federal Election Campaign Act of 1971.

EFFECTIVE DATE OF REPEAL

Repeal effective Jan. 8, 1980, see section 301(a) of Pub. L. 96–187, set out as an Effective Date of 1980 Amendment note under section 431 of this title.

§ 442. Authority to procure technical support and other services and incur travel expenses; payment of such expenses

For the purpose of carrying out his duties under the Federal Election Campaign Act of 1971, the Secretary of the Senate is authorized, from and after July 1, 1972, (1) to procure technical support services, (2) to procure the temporary or intermittent services of individual technicians, experts, or consultants, or organizations thereof, in the same manner and under the same conditions, to the extent applicable, as a standing committee of the Senate may procure such services under section 72a(i) of this title, (3) with the prior consent of the Government department or agency concerned and the Committee on Rules and Administration, to use on a reimbursable basis the services of personnel of any such department or agency, and (4) to incur official travel expenses. Payments to carry out the provisions of this paragraph shall be made from funds included in the appropria-

tion "Miscellaneous Items" under the heading "Contingent Expenses of the Senate" upon vouchers approved by the Secretary of the Senate. All sums received by the Secretary under authority of the Federal Election Campaign Act of 1971 shall be covered into the Treasury as miscellaneous receipts.

(Pub. L. 92–342, § 101, July 10, 1972, 86 Stat. 435.)

REFERENCES IN TEXT

The Federal Election Campaign Act of 1971, referred to in text, is Pub. L. 92–225, Feb. 7, 1972, 86 Stat. 3, as amended, which is classified principally to this chapter. For complete classification of this Act to the Code, see Short Title note set out under section 431 of this title and Tables.

CODIFICATION

Section was enacted as part of Legislative Branch Appropriation Act, 1973 and not as a part of Federal Election Campaign Act of 1971 which comprises this chapter.

SUBCHAPTER II—GENERAL PROVISIONS

§ 451. Extension of credit by regulated industries; regulations

The Secretary of Transportation, the Federal Communications Commission, and the Surface Transportation Board shall each maintain,[1] its own regulations with respect to the extension of credit, without security, by any person regulated by the Secretary under subpart II of part A of subtitle VII of title 49, or such Commission or Board, to any candidate for Federal office, or to any person on behalf of such a candidate, for goods furnished or services rendered in connection with the campaign of such candidate for nomination for election, or election, to such office.

(Pub. L. 92–225, title IV, § 401, Feb. 7, 1972, 86 Stat. 19; Pub. L. 93–443, title II, § 201(b)(1), Oct. 15, 1974, 88 Stat. 1275; Pub. L. 103–272, § 4(a), July 5, 1994, 108 Stat. 1360; Pub. L. 104–88, title III, § 313, Dec. 29, 1995, 109 Stat. 948; Pub. L. 104–287, § 6(g), Oct. 11, 1996, 110 Stat. 3399.)

REFERENCES IN TEXT

Subpart II of part A of subtitle VII of title 49, referred to in text, is set out in section 41101 et seq. of Title 49, Transportation.

AMENDMENTS

1996—Pub. L. 104–287 substituted "the Secretary" for "such Secretary".

1995—Pub. L. 104–88 inserted "or Board" after "or such Commission" and substituted "Surface Transportation Board shall each maintain" for "Interstate Commerce Commission shall each promulgate, within ninety days after February 7, 1972".

1994—Pub. L. 103–272 substituted "Secretary of Transportation" for "Civil Aeronautics Board" and "Secretary under subpart II of part A of subtitle VII of title 49, or such Commission," for "Board or Commission".

1974—Pub. L. 93–443 struck out "(as such term is defined in section 431(c) of this title)" after "Federal office".

EFFECTIVE DATE OF 1995 AMENDMENT

Amendment by Pub. L. 104–88 effective Jan. 1, 1996, see section 2 of Pub. L. 104–88, set out as an Effective Date note under section 701 of Title 49, Transportation.

---

[1] So in original. The comma probably should not appear.

EFFECTIVE DATE OF 1974 AMENDMENT

Amendment by Pub. L. 93–443 effective Jan. 1, 1975, see section 410(a) of Pub. L. 93–443, set out as a note under section 431 of this title.

§ 452. Prohibition against use of certain Federal funds for election activities

No part of any funds appropriated to carry out the Economic Opportunity Act of 1964 [42 U.S.C. 2701 et seq.] shall be used to finance, directly or indirectly, any activity designed to influence the outcome of any election to Federal office, or any voter registration activity, or to pay the salary of any officer or employee of the Office of Economic Opportunity who, in his official capacity as such an officer or employee, engages in any such activity.

(Pub. L. 92–225, title IV, § 402, Feb. 7, 1972, 86 Stat. 19; Pub. L. 93–443, title II, § 201(b)(2), Oct. 15, 1974, 88 Stat. 1275.)

REFERENCES IN TEXT

The Economic Opportunity Act of 1964, referred to in text, is Pub. L. 88–452, Aug. 20, 1964, 78 Stat. 508, as amended, which was classified generally to chapter 34 (§ 2701 et seq.) of Title 42, The Public Health and Welfare, prior to repeal, except for titles VIII and X, by Pub. L. 97–35, title VI, § 683(a), Aug. 13, 1981, 95 Stat. 519. Titles VIII and X of the Act are classified generally to subchapters VIII (§ 2991 et seq.) and X (§ 2996 et seq.) of chapter 34 of Title 42. For complete classification of this Act to the Code, see Tables.

AMENDMENTS

1974—Pub. L. 93–443 struck out reference to section 431(a) and (c) of this title for definition of "election" and "Federal office".

EFFECTIVE DATE OF 1974 AMENDMENT

Amendment by Pub. L. 93–443 effective Jan. 1, 1975, see section 410(a) of Pub. L. 93–443, set out as a note under section 431 of this title.

OFFICE OF ECONOMIC OPPORTUNITY

Pub. L. 93–644, § 9(a), Jan. 4, 1975, 88 Stat. 2310 [42 U.S.C. 2941], amended the Economic Opportunity Act of 1964 [42 U.S.C. 2701 et seq.] to create the Community Services Administration, an independent agency in the executive branch, as the successor authority to the Office of Economic Opportunity, and provided that references to the Office of Economic Opportunity or to its Director were deemed to refer to the Community Services Administration or to its Director. The Community Services Administration was terminated when the Economic Opportunity Act of 1964, except for titles VIII and X, was repealed, effective Oct. 1, 1981, by section 683(a) of Pub. L. 97–35, title VI, Aug. 13, 1981, 95 Stat. 519, which is classified to 42 U.S.C. 9912(a). An Office of Community Services, headed by a Director, was established in the Department of Health and Human Services by section 676 of Pub. L. 97–35, which is classified to 42 U.S.C. 9905.

§ 453. State laws affected

The provisions of this Act, and of rules prescribed under this Act, supersede and preempt any provision of State law with respect to election to Federal office.

(Pub. L. 92–225, title IV, § 403, Feb. 7, 1972, 86 Stat. 20; Pub. L. 93–443, title III, § 301, Oct. 15, 1974, 88 Stat. 1289.)

REFERENCES IN TEXT

This Act, referred to in text, means the Federal Election Campaign Act of 1971, as amended, as defined by section 431 of this title.

AMENDMENTS

1974—Pub. L. 93–443 substituted provision for Pub. L. 92–225 and rules thereunder to supersede and preempt any provision of State law with respect to election to Federal office for prior provisions which in former subsec. (a) stated that nothing in Pub. L. 92–225 shall be deemed to invalidate or make inapplicable any provision of State law, except where compliance with such provision would result in a violation of Pub. L. 92–225 and in former subsec. (b) stated that no provision of State law shall be construed to prohibit any person from taking any action authorized by Pub. L. 92–225 or from making any expenditure which he could lawfully make under Pub. L. 92–225.

EFFECTIVE DATE OF 1974 AMENDMENT

Amendment by Pub. L. 93–443 effective Oct. 15, 1974, see section 410(b) of Pub. L. 93–443, set out as a note under section 431 of this title.

§ 454. Partial invalidity

If any provision of this Act, or the application thereof to any person or circumstance, is held invalid, the validity of the remainder of the Act and the application of such provision to other persons and circumstances shall not be affected thereby.

(Pub. L. 92–225, title IV, § 404, Feb. 7, 1972, 86 Stat. 20.)

REFERENCES IN TEXT

This Act, referred to in text, means the Federal Election Campaign Act of 1971, as amended, as defined by, section 431 of this title.

§ 455. Period of limitations

(a) No person shall be prosecuted, tried, or punished for any violation of subchapter I of this chapter, unless the indictment is found or the information is instituted within 3 years after the date of the violation.

(b) Notwithstanding any other provision of law—

(1) the period of limitations referred to in subsection (a) of this section shall apply with respect to violations referred to in such subsection committed before, on, or after the effective date of this section; and

(2) no criminal proceeding shall be instituted against any person for any act or omission which was a violation of any provision of subchapter I of this chapter, as in effect on December 31, 1974, if such act or omission does not constitute a violation of any such provision, as amended by the Federal Election Campaign Act Amendments of 1974.

Nothing in this subsection shall affect any proceeding pending in any court of the United States on January 1, 1975.

(Pub. L. 92–225, title IV, § 406, as added Pub. L. 93–443, title III, § 302, Oct. 15, 1974, 88 Stat. 1289; amended Pub. L. 94–283, title I, § 115(f), May 11, 1976, 90 Stat. 496.)

REFERENCES IN TEXT

The Federal Election Campaign Act Amendments of 1974, referred to in subsec. (b)(2), is Pub. L. 93–433, Oct. 15, 1974, 88 Stat. 1263, as amended. For complete classification of this Act to the Code, see Short Title of 1974 Amendment note set out under section 431 of this title and Tables.

1976—Subsec. (a). Pub. L. 94–283, §115(f)(1), struck out references to sections 608, 610, 611, 613, 614, 615, 616, and 617 of title 18.

Subsec. (b)(2). Pub. L. 94–283, §115(f)(2), struck out references to sections 608, 610, 611, and 613 of title 18.

EFFECTIVE DATE

Section effective Jan. 1, 1975, see section 410(a) of Pub. L. 93–443, set out as an Effective Date of 1974 Amendment note under section 431 of this title.

§ 456. Repealed. Pub. L. 94–283, title I, § 111, May 11, 1976, 90 Stat. 486

Section, Pub. L. 92–225, title IV, §407, as added Pub. L. 93–443, title III, §302, Oct. 15, 1974, 88 Stat. 1290, gave Commission additional enforcement authority by providing for disqualification of candidates for Federal office from elections for Federal office for a period of time following a finding by Commission that candidate failed to file a required report.

SAVINGS PROVISION

Repeal by Pub. L. 94–283 not to release or extinguish any penalty, forfeiture, or liability incurred under this section or penalty, with this section or penalty to be treated as remaining in force for the purpose of sustaining any proper action or prosecution for the enforcement of any penalty, forfeiture, or liability, see section 114 of Pub. L. 94–283, set out as a note under section 441 of this title.

CHAPTER 15—OFFICE OF TECHNOLOGY ASSESSMENT

§ 471. Congressional findings and declaration of purpose

The Congress hereby finds and declares that:

(a) As technology continues to change and expand rapidly, its applications are—

(1) large and growing in scale; and

(2) increasingly extensive, pervasive, and critical in their impact, beneficial and adverse, on the natural and social environment.

(b) Therefore, it is essential that, to the fullest extent possible, the consequences of technological applications be anticipated, understood, and considered in determination of public policy on existing and emerging national problems.

(c) The Congress further finds that:

(1) the Federal agencies presently responsible directly to the Congress are not designed

to provide the legislative branch with adequate and timely information, independently developed, relating to the potential impact of technological applications, and

(2) the present mechanisms of the Congress do not and are not designed to provide the legislative branch with such information.

(d) Accordingly, it is necessary for the Congress to—

(1) equip itself with new and effective means for securing competent, unbiased information concerning the physical, biological, economic, social, and political effects of such applications; and

(2) utilize this information, whenever appropriate, as one factor in the legislative assessment of matters pending before the Congress, particularly in those instances where the Federal Government may be called upon to consider support for, or management or regulation of, technological applications.

(Pub. L. 92–484, § 2, Oct. 13, 1972, 86 Stat. 797.)

SHORT TITLE

Section 1 of Pub. L. 92–484 provided: "That this Act [enacting this chapter and amending section 1862 of Title 42, The Public Health and Welfare] may be cited as the 'Technology Assessment Act of 1972'."

TERMINATION OF OFFICE OF TECHNOLOGY ASSESSMENT

Pub. L. 104–53, title I, §§ 113, 114, Nov. 19, 1995, 109 Stat. 526, provided that:

"SEC. 113. Upon enactment of this Act [Nov. 19, 1995] all employees of the Office of Technology Assessment for 183 days preceding termination of employment who are terminated as a result of the elimination of the Office and who are not otherwise gainfully employed may continue to be paid by the Office of Technology Assessment at their respective salaries for a period not to exceed 60 calendar days following the employee's date of termination or until the employee becomes otherwise gainfully employed whichever is earlier. Any day for which a former employee receives a payment under this section shall be counted as Federal service for purposes of determining entitlement to benefits, including retirement, annual and sick leave earnings, and health and life insurance. A statement in writing to the Director of the Office of Technology Assessment or his designee by any such employee that he was not gainfully employed during such period or the portion thereof for which payment is claimed shall be accepted as prima facie evidence that he was not so employed.

"SEC. 114. Notwithstanding the provisions of the Federal Property and Administrative Services Act of 1949, as amended [40 U.S.C. 471 et seq.], or any other provision of law, upon the abolition of the Office of Technology Assessment, all records and property of the Office (including the Unix system, all computer hardware and software, all library collections and research materials, and all photocopying equipment), shall be under the administrative control of the Architect of the Capitol. Not later than December 31, 1995, the Architect shall submit a proposal to transfer such records and property to appropriate support agencies of the Legislative Branch which request such transfer, and shall carry out such transfer subject to the approval of the Committees on Appropriations of the House of Representatives and the Senate."

SECTION REFERRED TO IN OTHER SECTIONS

This section is referred to in section 472 of this title.

§ 472. Office of Technology Assessment

(a) Creation

In accordance with the findings and declaration of purpose in section 471 of this title, there is hereby created the Office of Technology Assessment (hereinafter referred to as the "Office") which shall be within and responsible to the legislative branch of the Government.

(b) Composition

The Office shall consist of a Technology Assessment Board (hereinafter referred to as the "Board") which shall formulate and promulgate the policies of the Office, and a Director who shall carry out such policies and administer the operations of the Office.

(c) Functions and duties

The basic function of the Office shall be to provide early indications of the probable beneficial and adverse impacts of the applications of technology and to develop other coordinate information which may assist the Congress. In carrying out such function, the Office shall:

(1) identify existing or probable impacts of technology or technological programs;

(2) where possible, ascertain cause-and-effect relationships;

(3) identify alternative technological methods of implementing specific programs;

(4) identify alternative programs for achieving requisite goals;

(5) make estimates and comparisons of the impacts of alternative methods and programs;

(6) present findings of completed analyses to the appropriate legislative authorities;

(7) identify areas where additional research or data collection is required to provide adequate support for the assessments and estimates described in paragraph (1) through (5) of this subsection; and

(8) undertake such additional associated activities as the appropriate authorities specified under subsection (d) of this section may direct.

(d) Initiation of assessment activities

Assessment activities undertaken by the Office may be initiated upon the request of:

(1) the chairman of any standing, special, or select committee of either House of the Congress, or of any joint committee of the Congress, acting for himself or at the request of the ranking minority member or a majority of the committee members;

(2) the Board; or

(3) the Director, in consultation with the Board.

(e) Availability of information

Assessments made by the Office, including information, surveys, studies, reports, and findings related thereto, shall be made available to the initiating committee or other appropriate committees of the Congress. In addition, any such information, surveys, studies, reports, and findings produced by the Office may be made available to the public except where—

(1) to do so would violate security statutes; or

(2) the Board considers it necessary or advisable to withhold such information in accordance with one or more of the numbered paragraphs in section 552(b) of title 5.

(Pub. L. 92–484, § 3, Oct. 13, 1972, 86 Stat. 797.)

SECTION REFERRED TO IN OTHER SECTIONS

This section is referred to in section 476 of this title.

§ 473. Technology Assessment Board

(a) Membership

The Board shall consist of thirteen members as follows:

(1) six Members of the Senate, appointed by the President pro tempore of the Senate, three from the majority party and three from the minority party;

(2) six Members of the House of Representatives appointed by the Speaker of the House of Representatives, three from the majority party and three from the minority party; and

(3) the Director, who shall not be a voting member.

(b) Execution of functions during vacancies; filling of vacancies

Vacancies in the membership of the Board shall not affect the power of the remaining members to execute the functions of the Board and shall be filled in the same manner as in the case of the original appointment.

(c) Chairman and vice chairman, selection procedure

The Board shall select a chairman and a vice chairman from among its members at the beginning of each Congress. The vice chairman shall act in the place and stead of the chairman in the absence of the chairman. The chairmanship and the vice chairmanship shall alternate between the Senate and the House of Representatives with each Congress. The chairman during each even-numbered Congress shall be selected by the Members of the House of Representatives on the Board from among their number. The vice chairman during each Congress shall be chosen in the same manner from that House of Congress other than the House of Congress of which the chairman is a Member.

(d) Meetings; powers of Board

The Board is authorized to sit and act at such places and times during the sessions, recesses, and adjourned periods of Congress, and upon a vote of a majority of its members, to require by subpena or otherwise the attendance of such witnesses and the production of such books, papers, and documents, to administer such oaths and affirmations, to take such testimony, to procure such printing and binding, and to make such expenditures, as it deems advisable. The Board may make such rules respecting its organization and procedures as it deems necessary, except that no recommendation shall be reported from the Board unless a majority of the Board assent. Subpenas may be issued over the signature of the chairman of the Board or of any voting member designated by him or by the Board, and may be served by such person or persons as may be designated by such chairman or member. The chairman of the Board or any voting member thereof may administer oaths or affirmations to witnesses.

(Pub. L. 92–484, § 4, Oct. 13, 1972, 86 Stat. 798.)

§ 474. Director of Office of Technology Assessment

(a) Appointment; term; compensation

The Director of the Office of Technology Assessment shall be appointed by the Board and shall serve for a term of six years unless sooner removed by the Board. He shall receive basic pay at the rate provided for level III of the Executive Schedule under section 5314 of title 5.

(b) Powers and duties

In addition to the powers and duties vested in him by this chapter, the Director shall exercise such powers and duties as may be delegated to him by the Board.

(c) Deputy Director; appointment; functions; compensation

The Director may appoint with the approval of the Board, a Deputy Director who shall perform such functions as the Director may prescribe and who shall be Acting Director during the absence or incapacity of the Director or in the event of a vacancy in the office of Director. The Deputy Director shall receive basic pay at the rate provided for level IV of the Executive Schedule under section 5315 of title 5.

(d) Restrictions on outside employment activities of Director and Deputy Director

Neither the Director nor the Deputy Director shall engage in any other business, vocation, or employment than that of serving as such Director or Deputy Director, as the case may be; nor shall the Director or Deputy Director, except with the approval of the Board, hold any office in, or act in any capacity for, any organization, agency, or institution with which the Office makes any contract or other arrangement under this chapter.

(Pub. L. 92–484, § 5, Oct. 13, 1972, 86 Stat. 799.)

§ 475. Powers of Office of Technology Assessment

(a) Use of public and private personnel and organizations; formation of special ad hoc task forces; contracts with governmental, etc., agencies and instrumentalities; advance, progress, and other payments; utilization of services of voluntary and uncompensated personnel; acquisition, holding, and disposal of real and personal property; promulgation of rules and regulations

The Office shall have the authority, within the limits of available appropriations, to do all things necessary to carry out the provisions of this chapter, including, but without being limited to, the authority to—

(1) make full use of competent personnel and organizations outside the Office, public or private, and form special ad hoc task forces or make other arrangements when appropriate;

(2) enter into contracts or other arrangements as may be necessary for the conduct of the work of the Office with any agency or instrumentality of the United States, with any State, territory, or possession or any political subdivision thereof, or with any person, firm, association, corporation, or educational institution, with or without reimbursement, without performance or other bonds, and without regard to section 5 of title 41;

(3) make advance, progress, and other payments which relate to technology assessment without regard to the provisions of section 3324(a) and (b) of title 31;

(4) accept and utilize the services of voluntary and uncompensated personnel nec-

essary for the conduct of the work of the Office and provide transportation and subsistence as authorized by section 5703 of title 5, for persons serving without compensation;

(5) acquire by purchase, lease, loan, or gift, and hold and dispose of by sale, lease, or loan, real and personal property of all kinds necessary for or resulting from the exercise of authority granted by this chapter; and

(6) prescribe such rules and regulations as it deems necessary governing the operation and organization of the Office.

(b) Recordkeeping by contractors and other parties entering into contracts and other arrangements with Office; availability of books and records to Office and Comptroller General for audit and examination

Contractors and other parties entering into contracts and other arrangements under this section which involve costs to the Government shall maintain such books and related records as will facilitate an effective audit in such detail and in such manner as shall be prescribed by the Office, and such books and records (and related documents and papers) shall be available to the Office and the Comptroller General of the United States, or any of their duly authorized representatives, for the purpose of audit and examination.

(c) Operation of laboratories, pilot plants, or test facilities

The Office, in carrying out the provisions of this chapter, shall not, itself, operate any laboratories, pilot plants, or test facilities.

(d) Requests to executive departments or agencies for information, suggestions, estimates, statistics, and technical assistance; duty of executive departments and agencies to furnish information, etc.

The Office is authorized to secure directly from any executive department or agency information, suggestions, estimates, statistics, and technical assistance for the purpose of carrying out its functions under this chapter. Each such executive department or agency shall furnish the information, suggestions, estimates, statistics, and technical assistance directly to the Office upon its request.

(e) Requests to heads of executive departments or agencies for detail of personnel; reimbursement

On request of the Office, the head of any executive department or agency may detail, with or without reimbursement, any of its personnel to assist the Office in carrying out its functions under this chapter.

(f) Appointment and compensation of personnel

The Director shall, in accordance with such policies as the Board shall prescribe, appoint and fix the compensation of such personnel as may be necessary to carry out the provisions of this chapter.

(Pub. L. 92–484, §6, Oct. 13, 1972, 86 Stat. 799.)

CODIFICATION

In subsec. (a)(3), "section 3324(a) and (b) of title 31" substituted for "section 3648 of the Revised Statutes (31

U.S.C. 529)" on authority of Pub. L. 97–258, §4(b), Sept. 13, 1982, 96 Stat. 1067, the first section of which enacted Title 31, Money and Finance.

§ 476. Technology Assessment Advisory Council

(a) Establishment; composition

The Office shall establish a Technology Assessment Advisory Council (hereinafter referred to as the "Council"). The Council shall be composed of the following twelve members:

(1) ten members from the public, to be appointed by the Board, who shall be persons eminent in one or more fields of the physical, biological, or social sciences or engineering or experienced in the administration of technological activities, or who may be judged qualified on the basis of contributions made to educational or public activities;

(2) the Comptroller General; and

(3) the Director of the Congressional Research Service of the Library of Congress.

(b) Duties

The Council, upon request by the Board, shall—

(1) review and make recommendations to the Board on activities undertaken by the Office or on the initiation thereof in accordance with section 472(d) of this title;

(2) review and make recommendations to the Board on the findings of any assessment made by or for the Office; and

(3) undertake such additional related tasks as the Board may direct.

(c) Chairman and Vice Chairman; election by Council from members appointed from public; terms and conditions of service

The Council by majority vote, shall elect from its members appointed under subsection (a)(1) of this section a Chairman and a Vice Chairman, who shall serve for such time and under such conditions as the Council may prescribe. In the absence of the Chairman, or in the event of his incapacity, the Vice Chairman shall act as Chairman.

(d) Terms of office of members appointed from public; reappointment

The term of office of each member of the Council appointed under subsection (a)(1) of this section shall be four years except that any such member appointed to fill a vacancy occurring prior to the expiration of the term for which his predecessor was appointed shall be appointed for the remainder of such term. No person shall be appointed a member of the Council under subsection (a)(1) of this section more than twice. Terms of the members appointed under subsection (a)(1) of this section shall be staggered so as to establish a rotating membership according to such method as the Board may devise.

(e) Payment to Comptroller General and Director of Congressional Research Service of travel and other necessary expenses; payment to members appointed from public of compensation and reimbursement for travel, subsistence, and other necessary expenses

(1) The members of the Council other than those appointed under subsection (a)(1) of this section shall receive no pay for their services as

members of the Council, but shall be allowed necessary travel expenses (or, in the alternative, mileage for use of privately owned vehicles and payments when traveling on official business at not to exceed the payment prescribed in regulations implementing section 5702 and in[1] 5704 of title 5), and other necessary expenses incurred by them in the performance of duties vested in the Council, without regard to the provisions of subchapter 1 of chapter 57 and section 5731 of title 5, and regulations promulgated thereunder.

(2) The members of the Council appointed under subsection (a)(1) of this section shall receive compensation for each day engaged in the actual performance of duties vested in the Council at rates of pay not in excess of the daily equivalent of the highest rate of basic pay set forth in the General Schedule of section 5332(a) of title 5, and in addition shall be reimbursed for travel, subsistence, and other necessary expenses in the manner provided for other members of the Council under paragraph (1) of this subsection.

(Pub. L. 92–484, §7, Oct. 13, 1972, 86 Stat. 800; Pub. L. 99–234, title I, §107(a), Jan. 2, 1986, 99 Stat. 1759.)

AMENDMENTS

1986—Subsec. (e)(1). Pub. L. 99–234 substituted "payments when traveling on official business at not to exceed the payment prescribed in regulations implementing section 5702 and in" for "a per diem in lieu of subsistence at not to exceed the rate prescribed in sections 5702 and".

EFFECTIVE DATE OF 1986 AMENDMENT

Amendment by Pub. L. 99–234 effective on effective date of regulations to be promulgated not later than 150 days after Jan. 2, 1986, or 180 days after Jan. 2, 1986, whichever occurs first, see section 301(a) of Pub. L. 99–234, set out as a note under section 5701 of Title 5, Government Organization and Employees.

TERMINATION OF ADVISORY COUNCILS

Advisory councils in existence on Jan. 5, 1973, to terminate not later than the expiration of the 2-year period following Jan. 5, 1973, unless, in the case of a council established by the President or an officer of the Federal Government, such council is renewed by appropriate action prior to the expiration of such 2-year period, or in the case of a council established by the Congress, its duration is otherwise provided by law. See sections 3(2) and 14 of Pub. L. 92–463, Oct. 6, 1972, 86 Stat. 770, 776, set out in the Appendix to Title 5, Government Organization and Employees.

REFERENCES IN OTHER LAWS TO GS–16, 17, OR 18 PAY RATES

References in laws to the rates of pay for GS–16, 17, or 18, or to maximum rates of pay under the General Schedule, to be considered references to rates payable under specified sections of Title 5, Government Organization and Employees, see section 529 [title I, §101(c)(1)] of Pub. L. 101–509, set out in a note under section 5376 of Title 5.

§477. Utilization of services of Library of Congress

(a) Authority of Librarian to make available services and assistance of Congressional Research Service

To carry out the objectives of this chapter, the Librarian of Congress is authorized to make available to the Office such services and assistance of the Congressional Research Service as may be appropriate and feasible.

(b) Scope of services and assistance

Such services and assistance made available to the Office shall include, but not be limited to, all of the services and assistance which the Congressional Research Service is otherwise authorized to provide to the Congress.

(c) Services or responsibilities performed by Congressional Research Service for Congress not altered or modified; authority of Librarian to establish within Congressional Research Service additional divisions, etc.

Nothing in this section shall alter or modify any services or responsibilities, other than those performed for the Office, which the Congressional Research Service under law performs for or on behalf of the Congress. The Librarian is, however, authorized to establish within the Congressional Research Service such additional divisions, groups, or other organizational entities as may be necessary to carry out the purpose of this chapter.

(d) Reimbursement for services and assistance

Services and assistance made available to the Office by the Congressional Research Service in accordance with this section may be provided with or without reimbursement from funds of the Office, as agreed upon by the Board and the Librarian of Congress.

(Pub. L. 92–484, §8, Oct. 13, 1972, 86 Stat. 801.)

§478. Utilization of services of General Accounting Office

(a) Authority of General Accounting Office to furnish financial and administrative services

Financial and administrative services (including those related to budgeting, accounting, financial reporting, personnel, and procurement) and such other services as may be appropriate shall be provided the Office by the General Accounting Office.

(b) Scope of services and assistance

Such services and assistance to the Office shall include, but not be limited to, all of the services and assistance which the General Accounting Office is otherwise authorized to provide to the Congress.

(c) Services or responsibilities performed by General Accounting Office for Congress not altered or modified

Nothing in this section shall alter or modify any services or responsibilities, other than those performed for the Office, which the General Accounting Office under law performs for or on behalf of the Congress.

(d) Reimbursement for services and assistance

Services and assistance made available to the Office by the General Accounting Office in accordance with this section may be provided with or without reimbursement from funds of the Office, as agreed upon by the Board and the Comptroller General.

(Pub. L. 92–484, §9, Oct. 13, 1972, 86 Stat. 802.)

§ 479. Coordination of activities with National Science Foundation

The Office shall maintain a continuing liaison with the National Science Foundation with respect to—

(1) grants and contracts formulated or activated by the Foundation which are for purposes of technology assessment; and

(2) the promotion of coordination in areas of technology assessment, and the avoidance of unnecessary duplication or overlapping of research activities in the development of technology assessment techniques and programs.

(Pub. L. 92–484, § 10(a), Oct. 13, 1972, 86 Stat. 802.)

§ 480. Omitted

CODIFICATION

Section, Pub. L. 92–484, § 11, Oct. 13, 1972, 86 Stat. 802, which required the Office of Technology Assessment to submit an annual report to Congress on technology assessment and technological areas and programs requiring future analysis, terminated, effective May 15, 2000, pursuant to section 3003 of Pub. L. 104–66, as amended, set out as a note under section 1113 of Title 31, Money and Finance. See, also, page 10 of House Document No. 103–7.

§ 481. Authorization of appropriations; availability of appropriations

(a) To enable the Office to carry out its powers and duties, there is hereby authorized to be appropriated to the Office, out of any money in the Treasury not otherwise appropriated, not to exceed $5,000,000 in the aggregate for the two fiscal years ending June 30, 1973, and June 30, 1974, and thereafter such sums as may be necessary.

(b) Appropriations made pursuant to the authority provided in subsection (a) of this section shall remain available for obligation, for expenditure, or for obligation and expenditure for such period or periods as may be specified in the Act making such appropriations.

(Pub. L. 92–484, § 12, Oct. 13, 1972, 86 Stat. 803.)

CHAPTER 16—CONGRESSIONAL MAILING STANDARDS

§ 501. House Commission on Congressional Mailing Standards

(a) Establishment; designation

There is established a special commission of the House of Representatives, designated the "House Commission on Congressional Mailing Standards" (herein referred to as the "Commission").

(b) Membership; political party representation; Chairman; vacancies; quorum

The Commission shall be composed of six Members appointed by the Speaker of the House, three from the majority political party, and three from the minority political party, in the House. The Speaker shall designate as Chairman of the Commission, from among the members of the Committee on Post Office and Civil Service of the House, one of the Members appointed to the Commission. A vacancy in the membership of the Commission shall be filled in the same manner as the original appointment. Four members of the Commission shall constitute a quorum to do business.

(c) Assistance and use of personnel, including chief counsel, of Committee on Post Office and Civil Service of the House

In performing its duties and functions, the Commission may use such personnel, office space, equipment, and facilities of, and obtain such other assistance from, the Committee on Post Office and Civil Service of the House, as such committee shall make available to the Commission. Such personnel and assistance shall include, in all cases, the services and assistance of the chief counsel or other head of the professional staff (by whatever title designated) of such committee. All assistance so furnished to the Commission by the Committee on Post Office and Civil Service shall be sufficient to enable the Commission to perform its duties and functions efficiently and effectively.

(d) Advisory opinions or consultations respecting franked mail for persons entitled to franking privilege; franking privilege regulations

The Commission shall provide guidance, assistance, advice, and counsel, through advisory opinions or consultations, in connection with the mailing or contemplated mailing of franked mail under section 3210, 3211, 3212, 3213(2), 3218, or 3219, in connection with the operation of section 3215, of title 39, and in connection with any other Federal law (other than any law which imposes any criminal penalty) or any rule of the House of Representatives relating to franked mail, upon the request of any Member of the House or Member-elect, Resident Commissioner or Resident Commissioner-elect, Delegate or Delegate-elect, any former Member of the House or former Member-elect, Resident Commissioner or Resident Commissioner-elect, Delegate or Delegate-elect, any surviving spouse of any of the foregoing (or any individual designated by the Clerk of the House under section 3218 of title 39), or any other House official or former House official, entitled to send mail as franked mail under any of those sections. The Commission shall prescribe regulations governing the proper use of the franking privilege under those sections by such persons.

(e) Complaint of franked mail violations; investigation; notice and hearing; conclusiveness of findings; decision of Commission; judicial review; reference of certain violations to Committee on Standards of Official Conduct of the House for appropriate action and enforcement; administrative procedure regulations

Any complaint by any person that a violation of any section of title 39 referred to in subsection (d) of this section (or any other Federal law which does not include any criminal penalty or any rule of the House of Representatives relating to franked mail) is about to occur, or has occurred within the immediately preceding period of one year, by any person referred to in such subsection (d), shall contain pertinent factual material and shall conform to regulations prescribed by the Commission. The Commission, if it determines there is reasonable justification for the complaint, shall conduct an investigation of the matter, including an investigation of reports and statements filed by the complainant with respect to the matter which is the subject of the complaint. The Commission shall afford to the person who is the subject of the complaint due notice and, if it determines that there is substantial reason to believe that such violation has occurred or is about to occur, opportunity for all parties to participate in a hearing before the Commission. The Commission shall issue a written decision on each complaint under this subsection not later than thirty days after such a complaint has been filed or, if a hearing is held, not later than thirty days after the conclusion of such hearing. Such decision shall be based on written findings of fact in the case by the Commission. Such findings of fact by the Commission on which its decision is based are binding and conclusive for all judicial and administrative purposes, including purposes of any judicial challenge or review. Any judicial review of such decision, if ordered on any ground, shall be limited to matters of law. If the Commission finds in its written decision, that a serious and willful violation has occurred or is about to occur, it may refer such decision to the Committee on Standards of Official Conduct of the House of Representatives for appropriate action and enforcement by the committee concerned in accordance with applicable rules and precedents of the House and such other standards as may be prescribed by such committee. In the case of a former Member of the House or a former Member-elect, a former Resident Commissioner or Delegate or Resident Commissioner-elect or Delegate-elect, any surviving spouse of any of the foregoing (or any individual designated by the Clerk of the House under section 3218 of title 39), or any other former House official, if the Commission finds in its written decision that any serious and willful violation has occurred or is about to occur, then the Commission may refer the matter to any appropriate law enforcement agency or official for appropriate remedial action. Notwithstanding any other provision of law, no court or administrative body in the United States or in any territory thereof shall have jurisdiction to entertain any civil action of any character concerning or related to a violation of the franking laws or an abuse of the franking privilege by any person listed under subsection (d) of this section as entitled to send mail as franked mail, except judicial review of the decisions of the Commission under this subsection. The Commission shall prescribe regulations for the holding of investigations and hearings, the conduct of proceedings, and the rendering of decisions under this subsection providing for equitable procedures and the protection of individual, public, and Government interests. The regulations shall, insofar as practicable, contain the substance of the administrative procedure provisions of sections 551–559, and 701–706, of title 5. These regulations shall govern matters under this subsection subject to judicial review thereof.

(f) Procedural considerations; sessions, place and time; subpenas, issuance and service; oaths and affirmations; testimony; printing and binding; expenditures; organizational and procedural regulations; majority assent

The Commission may sit and act at such places and times during the sessions, recesses, and adjourned periods of Congress, require by subpena or otherwise the attendance of such witnesses and the production of such books, papers, and documents, administer such oaths and affirmations, take such testimony, procure such printing and binding, and make such expenditures, as the Commission considers advisable. The Commission may make such rules respecting its organization and procedures as it considers necessary, except that no action shall be taken by the Commission unless a majority of the Commission assent. Subpenas may be issued over the signature of the Chairman of the Commission or of any member designated by him or by the Commission, and may be served by such person or persons as may be designated by such

Chairman or member. The Chairman of the Commission or any member thereof may administer oaths or affirmations to witnesses.

(g) Property of Commission; records; voting record; location of records, data, and files

The Commission shall keep a complete record of all its actions, including a record of the votes on any question on which a record vote is demanded. All records, data, and files of the Commission shall be the property of the Commission and shall be kept in the offices of the Commission or such other places as the Commission may direct.

(Pub. L. 93–191, § 5, Dec. 18, 1973, 87 Stat. 742; Pub. L. 93–255, § 3(a), Mar. 27, 1974, 88 Stat. 52; Pub. L. 97–69, § 7, Oct. 26, 1981, 95 Stat. 1043.)

AMENDMENTS

1981—Subsec. (d). Pub. L. 97–69, § 7(a)(1), (b), inserted references to Federal laws (other than laws which impose criminal penalties), to rules of the House of Representatives relating to franked mail, to former Members of the House of Representatives or Members-elect, Resident Commissioners or Resident Commissioners-elect, Delegates or Delegates-elect, and former House officials, and to individuals designated by the Clerk of the House under section 3218 of title 39.

Subsec. (e). Pub. L. 97–69, § 7(a)(2), (c), inserted reference to Federal laws that do not include criminal penalties or rules of the House of Representatives relating to franked mail and inserted provision that, in the case of a former Member of the House or a former Member-elect, a former Resident Commissioner or Delegate or Resident Commissioner-elect or Delegate-elect, any surviving spouse of any of the foregoing (or any individual designated by the Clerk of the House under section 3218 of title 39), or any other former House official, if the Commission finds in its written decision that any serious and willful violation has occurred or is about to occur, then the Commission may refer the matter to any appropriate law enforcement agency or official for appropriate remedial action.

1974—Subsec. (d). Pub. L. 93–255 inserted reference to section 3219 of title 39.

EFFECTIVE DATE

Section effective Dec. 18, 1973, see section 14 of Pub. L. 93–191, set out as an Effective Date of 1973 Amendment note under section 3210 of Title 39, Postal Service.

ABOLITION OF HOUSE COMMITTEE ON POST OFFICE AND CIVIL SERVICE

Committee on Post Office and Civil Service of House of Representatives abolished by House Resolution No. 6, One Hundred Fourth Congress, Jan. 4, 1995. References to Committee on Post Office and Civil Service with respect to House Commission on Congressional Mailing Standards treated as referring to Committee on House Oversight, see section 1(b) of Pub. L. 104–14, set out as a note preceding section 21 of this title. Committee on House Oversight of House of Representatives changed to Committee on House Administration of House of Representatives by House Resolution No. 5, One Hundred Sixth Congress, Jan. 6, 1999.

§ 502. Select Committee on Standards and Conduct of the Senate

(a) Advisory opinions or consultations respecting franked mail for persons entitled to franking privilege; franking privilege regulations

The Select Committee on Standards and Conduct of the Senate shall provide guidance, assistance, advice and counsel, through advisory opinions or consultations, in connection with the mailing or contemplated mailing of franked mail under section 3210, 3211, 3212, 3213(2), 3218, or 3219, and in connection with the operation of section 3215, of title 39, upon the request of any Member of the Senate or Member-elect, surviving spouse of any of the foregoing, or other Senate official, entitled to send mail as franked mail under any of those sections. The select committee shall prescribe regulations governing the proper use of the franking privilege under those sections by such persons.

(b) Complaint of franked mail violations; investigation; notice and hearing; decision of select committee; enforcement

Any complaint filed by any person with the select committee that a violation of any section of title 39 referred to in subsection (a) of this section is about to occur or has occurred within the immediately preceding period of one year, by any person referred to in such subsection (a), shall contain pertinent factual material and shall conform to regulations prescribed by the select committee. The select committee, if it determines there is reasonable justification for the complaint, shall conduct an investigation of the matter, including an investigation of reports and statements filed by the complainant with respect to the matter which is the subject of the complaint. The committee shall afford to the person who is the subject of the complaint due notice and, if it determines that there is substantial reason to believe that such violation has occurred or is about to occur, opportunity for all parties to participate in a hearing before the select committee. The select committee shall issue a written decision on each complaint under this subsection not later than thirty days after such a complaint has been filed or, if a hearing is held, not later than thirty days after the conclusion of such hearing. Such decision shall be based on written findings of fact in the case by the select committee. If the select committee finds, in its written decision, that a violation has occurred or is about to occur, the committee may take such action and enforcement as it considers appropriate in accordance with applicable rules, precedents, and standing orders of the Senate, and such other standards as may be prescribed by such committee.

(c) Administrative or judicial jurisdiction of civil actions respecting franking law violations or abuses of franking privilege dependent on filing of complaint with select committee and rendition of decision by such committee

Notwithstanding any other provision of law, no court or administrative body in the United States or in any territory thereof shall have jurisdiction to entertain any civil action of any character concerning or related to a violation of the franking laws or an abuse of the franking privilege by any person listed under subsection (a) of this section as entitled to send mail as franked mail, until a complaint has been filed with the select committee and the committee has rendered a decision under subsection (b) of this section.

(d) Administrative procedure regulations

The select committee shall prescribe regulations for the holding of investigations and hearings, the conduct of proceedings, and the rendering of decisions under this subsection providing for equitable procedures and the protection of individual, public, and Government interests. The regulations shall, insofar as practicable, contain the substance of the administrative procedure provisions of sections 551 to 559 and 701 to 706, of title 5. These regulations shall govern matters under this subsection subject to judicial review thereof.

(e) Property of Senate; records of select committee; voting record; location of records, data, and files

The select committee shall keep a complete record of all its actions, including a record of the votes on any question on which a record vote is demanded. All records, data, and files of the select committee shall be the property of the Senate and shall be kept in the offices of the select committee or such other places as the committee may direct.

(Pub. L. 93–191, § 6, Dec. 18, 1973, 87 Stat. 744; Pub. L. 93–255, § 3(b), Mar. 27, 1974, 88 Stat. 52.)

AMENDMENTS

1974—Subsec. (a). Pub. L. 93–255 inserted reference to section 3219 of title 39.

EFFECTIVE DATE

Section effective Dec. 18, 1973, see section 14 of Pub. L. 93–191, set out as an Effective Date of 1973 Amendment note under section 3210 of Title 39, Postal Service.

CHAPTER 17—CONGRESSIONAL BUDGET OFFICE

CHAPTER REFERRED TO IN OTHER SECTIONS

This chapter is referred to in section 622 of this title.

§ 601. Establishment

(a) In general

(1) There is established an office of the Congress to be known as the Congressional Budget Office (hereinafter in this chapter referred to as the "Office"). The Office shall be headed by a Director; and there shall be a Deputy Director who shall perform such duties as may be assigned to him by the Director and, during the absence or incapacity of the Director or during a vacancy in that office, shall act as Director.

(2) The Director shall be appointed by the Speaker of the House of Representatives and the President pro tempore of the Senate after considering recommendations received from the Committees on the Budget of the House and the Senate, without regard to political affiliation and solely on the basis of his fitness to perform his duties. The Deputy Director shall be appointed by the Director.

(3) The term of office of the Director shall be 4 years and shall expire on January 3 of the year preceding each Presidential election. Any individual appointed as Director to fill a vacancy prior to the expiration of a term shall serve only for the unexpired portion of that term. An individual serving as Director at the expiration of a term may continue to serve until his successor is appointed. Any Deputy Director shall serve until the expiration of the term of office of the Director who appointed him (and until his successor is appointed), unless sooner removed by the Director.

(4) The Director may be removed by either House by resolution.

(5)(A) The Director shall receive compensation at an annual rate of pay that is equal to the lower of—

     (i) the highest annual rate of compensation of any officer of the Senate; or

     (ii) the highest annual rate of compensation of any officer of the House of Representatives.

(B) The Deputy Director shall receive compensation at an annual rate of pay that is $1,000 less than the annual rate of pay received by the Director, as determined under subparagraph (A).

(b) Personnel

The Director shall appoint and fix the compensation of such personnel as may be necessary to carry out the duties and functions of the Office. All personnel of the Office shall be appointed without regard to political affiliation and solely on the basis of their fitness to perform their duties. The Director may prescribe the duties and responsibilities of the personnel of the Office, and delegate to them authority to perform any of the duties, powers, and functions imposed on the Office or on the Director. For purposes of pay (other than pay of the Director and Deputy Director) and employment benefits, rights, and privileges, all personnel of the Office shall be treated as if they were employees of the House of Representatives.

(c) Experts and consultants

In carrying out the duties and functions of the Office, the Director may procure the temporary (not to exceed one year) or intermittent services of experts or consultants or organizations thereof by contract as independent contractors, or, in the case of individual experts or consultants, by employment at rates of pay not in excess of the daily equivalent of the highest rate of basic pay payable under the General Schedule of section 5332 of title 5.

(d) Relationship to executive branch

The Director is authorized to secure information, data, estimates, and statistics directly from the various departments, agencies, and establishments of the executive branch of Government and the regulatory agencies and commissions of the Government. All such departments, agencies, establishments, and regulatory agencies and commissions shall furnish the Director any available material which he determines to be necessary in the performance of his duties and functions (other than material the disclosure of which would be a violation of law). The Director is also authorized, upon agreement with the head of any such department, agency, establishment, or regulatory agency or commission, to utilize its services, facilities, and personnel with or without reimbursement; and the head of each such department, agency, establishment, or regulatory agency or commission is authorized to provide the Office such services, facilities, and personnel.

(e) Relationship to other agencies of Congress

In carrying out the duties and functions of the Office, and for the purpose of coordinating the operations of the Office with those of other congressional agencies with a view to utilizing most effectively the information, services, and capabilities of all such agencies in carrying out the various responsibilities assigned to each, the Director is authorized to obtain information, data, estimates, and statistics developed by the General Accounting Office,[1] and the Library of Congress, and (upon agreement with them) to utilize their services, facilities, and personnel with or without reimbursement. The Comptroller General,[1] and the Librarian of Congress,[1] are authorized to provide the Office with the information, data, estimates, and statistics, and the services, facilities, and personnel, referred to in the preceding sentence.

(f) Revenue estimates

For the purposes of revenue legislation which is income, estate and gift, excise, and payroll taxes (i.e., Social Security), considered or enacted in any session of Congress, the Congressional Budget Office shall use exclusively during that session of Congress revenue estimates provided to it by the Joint Committee on Taxation. During that session of Congress such revenue estimates shall be transmitted by the Congressional Budget Office to any committee of the House of Representatives or the Senate requesting such estimates, and shall be used by such Committees in determining such estimates. The Budget Committees of the Senate and House shall determine all estimates with respect to scoring points of order and with respect to the execution of the purposes of this Act.

(g) Authorization of appropriations

There are authorized to be appropriated to the Office for each fiscal year such sums as may be necessary to enable it to carry out its duties and functions. Until sums are first appropriated pursuant to the preceding sentence, but for a period not exceeding 12 months following the effective date of this subsection, the expenses of the Office shall be paid from the contingent fund of the Senate, in accordance with section 68 of this title, and upon vouchers approved by the Director.

(Pub. L. 93–344, title II, § 201, July 12, 1974, 88 Stat. 302; Pub. L. 99–177, title II, § 273, Dec. 12, 1985, 99 Stat. 1098, renumbered § 201(g) of Pub. L. 93–344, Pub. L. 101–508, title XIII, § 13202(b), Nov. 5, 1990, 104 Stat. 1388–615; Pub. L. 101–508, title XIII, § 13202(a), (c), Nov. 5, 1990, 104 Stat. 1388–615; Pub. L. 105–33, title X, § 10102, Aug. 5, 1997, 111 Stat. 678; Pub. L. 106–113, div. B, § 1000(a)(5) [title II, § 224], Nov. 29, 1999, 113 Stat. 1536, 1501A–299.)

REFERENCES IN TEXT

This Act, referred to in subsec. (f), means Pub. L. 93–344, July 12, 1974, 88 Stat. 297, as amended, known as the Congressional Budget and Impoundment Control Act of 1974, which enacted chapters 17, 17A and 17B, and section 190a–3 of this title and sections 11a, 11c, 11d, 1020a of former Title 31, Money and Finance, amended sections 11, 665, 701, 1020, 1151, 1152, 1153, and 1154 of former Title 31, section 105 of Title 1, General Provisions, sections 190b and 190d of this title, repealed sections 571 and 581c–1 of former Title 31, and sections 66 and 81 of this title, and enacted provisions set out as notes under sections 190a–1, 621, 632, and 682 of this title, section 105 of Title 1, and section 1020 of former Title 31. For complete classification of this Act to the Code, see Short Title note set out under section 621 of this title and Tables.

CODIFICATION

Pub. L. 101–508, § 12302(b), transferred section 273 of Pub. L. 99–177, which was classified to section 921 of this title, to subsec. (g) (now (f)) of this section, relating to revenue estimates.

AMENDMENTS

1999—Subsec. (a)(5). Pub. L. 106–113 amended par. (5) generally. Prior to amendment, par. (5) read as follows: "The Director shall receive compensation at a per annum gross rate equal to the rate of basic pay, as in effect from time to time, for level III of the Executive Schedule in section 5314 of title 5. The Deputy Director shall receive compensation at a per annum gross rate equal to the rate of basic pay, as so in effect, for level IV of the Executive Schedule in section 5315 of such title."

1997—Subsec. (a)(3). Pub. L. 105–33, § 10102(a), substituted "The term of office of the Director shall be 4 years and shall expire on January 3 of the year preceding each Presidential election." for "The term of office of the Director first appointed shall expire at noon on January 3, 1979, and the terms of office of Directors subsequently appointed shall expire at noon on January 3 of each fourth year thereafter."

Subsec. (e). Pub. L. 105–33, § 10102(b), inserted "and" before "the Library", struck out "and the Office of Technology Assessment," after "Library of Congress,", inserted "and" before "the Librarian", and struck out ", and the Technology Assessment Board" after "Librarian of Congress".

Subsecs. (f), (g). Pub. L. 105–33, § 10102(c), redesignated subsec. (g), relating to revenue estimates, as (f).

1990—Subsec. (f). Pub. L. 101–508, § 13202(a), redesignated subsec. (f), relating to authorization of appropriations, as (g).

---

[1] So in original. Comma probably should not appear.

Subsec. (g). Pub. L. 101–508, § 13202(a), redesignated subsec. (f), relating to authorization of appropriations, as (g).

Pub. L. 101–508, § 12302(b), (c), redesignated section 921 of this title as subsec. (g) of this section, inserted heading "Revenue estimates" and substituted "this Act" for "this title and the Congressional Budget and Impoundment Control Act of 1974".

Effective Date

Subsec. (a) effective July 12, 1974, see section 905(a) of Pub. L. 93–344, and subsecs. (b) to (f) effective on day on which first Director of Congressional Budget Office is appointed under subsec. (a), see section 905(a), (b) of Pub. L. 93–344, formerly set out as a note under section 621 of this title.

Short Title

Pub. L. 93–344, which enacted this chapter, to be cited in its entirety as the "Congressional Budget and Impoundment Control Act of 1974", with titles I through IX thereof to be cited as the "Congressional Budget Act of 1974", see section 1(a) of Pub. L. 93–344, set out as a note under section 621 of this title.

References in Other Laws to GS–16, 17, or 18 Pay Rates

References in laws to the rates of pay for GS–16, 17, or 18, or to maximum rates of pay under the General Schedule, to be considered references to rates payable under specified sections of Title 5, Government Organization and Employees, see section 529 [title I, § 101(c)(1)] of Pub. L. 101–509, set out in a note under section 5376 of Title 5.

Section Referred to in Other Sections

This section is referred to in section 603 of this title.

§ 602. Duties and functions

(a) Assistance to budget committees

It shall be the primary duty and function of the Office to provide to the Committees on the Budget of both Houses information which will assist such committees in the discharge of all matters within their jurisdictions, including (1) information with respect to the budget, appropriation bills, and other bills authorizing or providing new budget authority or tax expenditures, (2) information with respect to revenues, receipts, estimated future revenues and receipts, and changing revenue conditions, and (3) such related information as such Committee may request.

(b) Assistance to Committees on Appropriations, Ways and Means, and Finance

At the request of the Committee on Appropriations of either House, the Committee on Ways and Means of the House of Representatives, or the Committee on Finance of the Senate, the Office shall provide to such Committee any information which will assist it in the discharge of matters within its jurisdiction, including information described in clauses (1) and (2) of subsection (a) of this section and such related information as the Committee may request.

(c) Assistance to other committees and Members

(1) At the request of any other committee of the House of Representatives or the Senate or any joint committee of the Congress, the Office shall provide to such committee or joint committee any information compiled in carrying out clauses (1) and (2) of subsection (a) of this section, and, to the extent practicable, such additional information related to the foregoing as may be requested.

(2) At the request of any committee of the Senate or the House of Representatives, the Office shall, to the extent practicable, consult with and assist such committee in analyzing the budgetary or financial impact of any proposed legislation that may have—

(A) a significant budgetary impact on State, local, or tribal governments;

(B) a significant financial impact on the private sector; or

(C) a significant employment impact on the private sector.

(3) At the request of any Member of the House or Senate, the Office shall provide to such Member any information compiled in carrying out clauses (1) and (2) of subsection (a) of this section, and, to the extent available, such additional information related to the foregoing as may be requested.

(d) Assignment of office personnel to committees and joint committees

At the request of the Committee on the Budget of either House, personnel of the Office shall be assigned, on a temporary basis, to assist such committee. At the request of any other committee of either House or any joint committee of the Congress, personnel of the Office may be assigned, on a temporary basis, to assist such committee or joint committee with respect to matters directly related to the applicable provisions of subsection (b) or (c) of this section.

(e) Reports to budget committees

(1) On or before February 15 of each year, the Director shall submit to the Committees on the Budget of the House of Representatives and the Senate a report, for the fiscal year commencing on October 1 of that year, with respect to fiscal policy, including (A) alternative levels of total revenues, total new budget authority, and total outlays (including related surpluses and deficits), (B) the levels of tax expenditures under existing law, taking into account projected economic factors and any changes in such levels based on proposals in the budget submitted by the President for such fiscal year, and (C) a statement of the levels of budget authority and outlays for each program assumed to be extended in the baseline, as provided in section 907(b)(2)(A) of this title and for excise taxes assumed to be extended under section 907(b)(2)(C) of this title. Such report shall also include a discussion of national budget priorities, including alternative ways of allocating new budget authority and budget outlays for such fiscal year among major programs or functional categories, taking into account how such alternative allocations will meet major national needs and affect balanced growth and development of the United States.

(2) The Director shall from time to time submit to the Committees on the Budget of the House of Representatives and the Senate such further reports (including reports revising the report required by paragraph (1)) as may be necessary or appropriate to provide such Committees with information, data, and analyses for the performance of their duties and functions.

(3) On or before January 15 of each year, the Director, after consultation with the appropriate committees of the House of Representatives and Senate, shall submit to the Congress a report listing (A) all programs and activities funded during the fiscal year ending September 30 of that calendar year for which authorizations for appropriations have not been enacted for that fiscal year, and (B) all programs and activities for which authorizations for appropriations have been enacted for the fiscal year ending September 30 of that calendar year, but for which no authorizations for appropriations have been enacted for the fiscal year beginning October 1 of that calendar year.

(f) Use of computers and other techniques

The Director may equip the Office with up-to-date computer capability (upon approval of the Committee on House Oversight of the House of Representatives and the Committee on Rules and Administration of the Senate), obtain the services of experts and consultants in computer technology, and develop techniques for the evaluation of budgetary requirements.

(g) Studies

(1) Continuing studies

The Director of the Congressional Budget Office shall conduct continuing studies to enhance comparisons of budget outlays, credit authority, and tax expenditures.

(2) Federal mandate studies

(A) At the request of any Chairman or ranking member of the minority of a Committee of the Senate or the House of Representatives, the Director shall, to the extent practicable, conduct a study of a legislative proposal containing a Federal mandate.

(B) In conducting a study on intergovernmental mandates under subparagraph (A), the Director shall—

(i) solicit and consider information or comments from elected officials (including their designated representatives) of State, local, or tribal governments as may provide helpful information or comments;

(ii) consider establishing advisory panels of elected officials or their designated representatives, of State, local, or tribal governments if the Director determines that such advisory panels would be helpful in performing responsibilities of the Director under this section; and

(iii) if, and to the extent that the Director determines that accurate estimates are reasonably feasible, include estimates of—

(I) the future direct cost of the Federal mandate to the extent that such costs significantly differ from or extend beyond the 5-year period after the mandate is first effective; and

(II) any disproportionate budgetary effects of Federal mandates upon particular industries or sectors of the economy, States, regions, and urban or rural or other types of communities, as appropriate.

(C) In conducting a study on private sector mandates under subparagraph (A), the Direc-

tor shall provide estimates, if and to the extent that the Director determines that such estimates are reasonably feasible, of—

(i) future costs of Federal private sector mandates to the extent that such mandates differ significantly from or extend beyond the 5-year time period referred to in subparagraph (B)(iii)(I);

(ii) any disproportionate financial effects of Federal private sector mandates and of any Federal financial assistance in the bill or joint resolution upon any particular industries or sectors of the economy, States, regions, and urban or rural or other types of communities; and

(iii) the effect of Federal private sector mandates in the bill or joint resolution on the national economy, including the effect on productivity, economic growth, full employment, creation of productive jobs, and international competitiveness of United States goods and services.

(Pub. L. 93–344, title II, § 202, July 12, 1974, 88 Stat. 304; Pub. L. 99–177, title II, § 221, Dec. 12, 1985, 99 Stat. 1060; Pub. L. 101–508, title XIII, § 13112(a)(3), Nov. 5, 1990, 104 Stat. 1388–608; Pub. L. 104–4, title I, § 102(1), Mar. 22, 1995, 109 Stat. 60; Pub. L. 104–186, title II, § 213, Aug. 20, 1996, 110 Stat. 1745; Pub. L. 105–33, title X, § 10103, Aug. 5, 1997, 111 Stat. 678.)

AMENDMENTS

1997—Subsec. (a). Pub. L. 105–33, § 10103(a), inserted "primary" before "duty" in first sentence.

Subsec. (e). Pub. L. 105–33, § 10103(b), redesignated subsec. (f) as (e) and struck out heading and text of former subsec. (e). Text of par. (1) of subsec. (e) read as follows: "The duties, functions, and personnel of the Joint Committee on Reduction of Federal Expenditures are transferred to the Office, and the Joint Committee is abolished." Par. (2) of subsec. (e) repealed section 571 of former Title 31, Money and Finance.

Subsec. (e)(1)(C). Pub. L. 105–33, § 10103(c), added subpar. (C).

Subsecs. (f) to (h). Pub. L. 105–33, § 10103(b), redesignated subsecs. (g) and (h) as (f) and (g), respectively.

1996—Subsec. (g). Pub. L. 104–186 substituted "House Oversight" for "House Administration".

1995—Subsec. (c)(2), (3). Pub. L. 104–4, § 102(1)(A), added par. (2) and redesignated former par. (2) as (3).

Subsec. (h). Pub. L. 104–4, § 102(1)(B), amended heading and text of subsec. (h) generally. Prior to amendment, text read as follows: "The Director shall conduct continuing studies to enhance comparisons of budget outlays, credit authority, and tax expenditures."

1990—Subsecs. (a)(1), (f)(1). Pub. L. 101–508 substituted "new budget authority" for "budget authority" in subsec. (a)(1) and second sentence of subsec. (f)(1).

1985—Subsec. (f)(1). Pub. L. 99–177, § 221(a), substituted "February 15" for "April 1".

Subsec. (f)(3). Pub. L. 99–177, § 221(b), added par. (3).

Subsec. (h). Pub. L. 99–177, § 221(c), added subsec. (h).

CHANGE OF NAME

Committee on House Oversight of House of Representatives changed to Committee on House Administration of House of Representatives by House Resolution No. 5, One Hundred Sixth Congress, Jan. 6, 1999.

EFFECTIVE DATE OF 1995 AMENDMENT

Amendment by Pub. L. 104–4 effective Jan. 1, 1996, or on the date 90 days after appropriations are made available as authorized under section 1516 of this title, whichever is earlier, and applicable to legislation considered on and after such date, see section 110 of Pub.

L. 104–4, set out as an Effective Date note under section 1511 of this title.

EFFECTIVE DATE OF 1985 AMENDMENT

Amendment by Pub. L. 99–177 effective Dec. 12, 1985, and applicable with respect to fiscal years beginning after Sept. 30, 1985, see section 275(a)(1) of Pub. L. 99–177, set out as an Effective and Termination Dates note under section 900 of this title.

EFFECTIVE DATE

Section effective on day on which first Director of Congressional Budget Office is appointed under section 601(a) of this title, see section 905(b) of Pub. L. 93–344, formerly set out as a note under section 621 of this title.

CREDIT REFORM

Pub. L. 100–119, title II, § 212, Sept. 29, 1987, 101 Stat. 787, provided that: "The Congressional Budget Office, in consultation with the General Accounting Office, shall study and report to Congress on Federal direct loan and loan guarantee programs for fiscal year 1987 and fiscal year 1988. The report shall be submitted as soon as practicable to all congressional committees of appropriate jurisdiction. The report shall provide information and recommendations on: (1) more accurately measuring the costs to the Federal Government of such credit programs, (2) comparing the cost of credit programs to other forms of Federal assistance, and (3) improving the allocation of resources between credit and other programs. The report shall also discuss the considerations involved in establishing a system for using the information on the costs of credit programs as part of the budget process."

§ 603. Public access to budget data

(a) Right to copy

Except as provided in subsections (c), (d), and (e) of this section, the Director shall make all information, data, estimates, and statistics obtained under section 601(d) and (e) of this title available for public copying during normal business hours, subject to reasonable rules and regulations, and shall to the extent practicable, at the request of any person, furnish a copy of any such information, data, estimates, or statistics upon payment by such person of the cost of making and furnishing such copy.

(b) Index

The Director shall develop and maintain filing, coding, and indexing systems that identify the information, data, estimates, and statistics to which subsection (a) of this section applies and shall make such systems available for public use during normal business hours.

(c) Exceptions

Subsection (a) of this section shall not apply to information, data, estimates, and statistics—

(1) which are specifically exempted from disclosure by law; or

(2) which the Director determines will disclose—

(A) matters necessary to be kept secret in the interests of national defense or the confidential conduct of the foreign relations of the United States;

(B) information relating to trade secrets or financial or commercial information pertaining specifically to a given person if the information has been obtained by the Government on a confidential basis, other than

through an application by such person for a specific financial or other benefit, and is required to be kept secret in order to prevent undue injury to the competitive position of such person; or

(C) personnel or medical data or similar data the disclosure of which would constitute a clearly unwarranted invasion of personal privacy;

unless the portions containing such matters, information, or data have been excised.

(d) Information obtained for committees and Members

Subsection (a) of this section shall apply to any information, data, estimates, and statistics obtained at the request of any committee, joint committee, or Member unless such committee, joint committee, or Member has instructed the Director not to make such information, data, estimates, or statistics available for public copying.

(e) Level of confidentiality

With respect to information, data, estimates, and statistics obtained under sections 601(d) and 601(e) of this title, the Director shall maintain the same level of confidentiality as is required by law of the department, agency, establishment, or regulatory agency or commission from which it is obtained. Officers and employees of the Congressional Budget Office shall be subject to the same statutory penalties for unauthorized disclosure or use as officers or employees of the department, agency, establishment, or regulatory agency or commission from which it is obtained.

(Pub. L. 93–344, title II, § 203, July 12, 1974, 88 Stat. 305; Pub. L. 106–554, § 1(a)(7) [title III, § 310(b)], Dec. 21, 2000, 114 Stat. 2763, 2763A–639.)

AMENDMENTS

2000—Subsec. (a). Pub. L. 106–554, § 1(a)(7) [title III, § 310(b)(2)], substituted "subsections (c), (d), and (e)" for "subsections (c) and (d)".
Subsec. (e). Pub. L. 106–554, § 1(a)(7) [title III, § 310(b)(1)], added subsec. (e).

EFFECTIVE DATE

Section effective on day on which first Director of Congressional Budget Office is appointed under section 601(a) of this title, see section 905(b) of Pub. L. 93–344, formerly set out as a note under section 621 of this title.

§ 604. Omitted

CODIFICATION

Section, Pub. L. 94–440, title V, § 500, Oct. 1, 1976, 90 Stat. 1452, the Legislative Appropriation Act, 1977, which authorized the Congressional Budget Office to contract without regard to section 5 of Title 41, Public Contracts, applied to fiscal year 1977 and was not repeated in subsequent appropriation acts. Similar provisions were contained in the following prior appropriation act:

Pub. L. 94–157, title I, Dec. 18, 1975, 89 Stat. 834.

§ 605. Sale or lease of property, supplies, or services

(a) Any sale or lease of property, supplies, or services to the Congressional Budget Office shall be deemed to be a sale or lease to the Congress subject to section 111b of this title.

(b) Subsection (a) of this section shall apply with respect to fiscal years beginning after September 30, 1996.

(Pub. L. 104–197, title I, § 104, Sept. 16, 1996, 110 Stat. 2404.)

REFERENCES IN TEXT

Section 111b of this title, referred to in subsec. (a), was in the original a reference to section 903 of the Supplemental Appropriations Act, 1983, Pub. L. 98–63, title I, July 30, 1983, 97 Stat. 336, which is classified to section 111b of this title and in part as a note set out under section 111b of this title.

CODIFICATION

Section was enacted as part of the appropriation act cited as the credit to this section, and not as part of title II of the Congressional Budget and Impoundment Control Act of 1974 which comprises this chapter.

PRIOR PROVISIONS

Provisions similar to those in this section were contained in the following prior appropriation acts:

Pub. L. 104–53, title I, Nov. 19, 1995, 109 Stat. 527.
Pub. L. 103–283, title I, July 22, 1994, 108 Stat. 1433.
Pub. L. 103–69, title I, Aug. 11, 1993, 107 Stat. 701.
Pub. L. 102–392, title I, Oct. 6, 1992, 106 Stat. 1713.
Pub. L. 102–90, title I, Aug. 14, 1991, 105 Stat. 458.
Pub. L. 101–520, title I, Nov. 5, 1990, 104 Stat. 2266.
Pub. L. 101–163, title I, Nov. 21, 1989, 103 Stat. 1054.
Pub. L. 100–458, title I, Oct. 1, 1988, 102 Stat. 2169.
Pub. L. 100–202, § 101(i) [title I], Dec. 22, 1987, 101 Stat. 1329–290, 1329–300.
Pub. L. 99–500, § 101(j) [H.R. 5203, title I], Oct. 18, 1986, 100 Stat. 1783–287, and Pub. L. 99–591, § 101(j), Oct. 30, 1986, 100 Stat. 3341–287.
Pub. L. 99–151, title I, Nov. 13, 1985, 99 Stat. 800.
Pub. L. 98–367, title I, July 17, 1984, 98 Stat. 482.

§ 606. Disposition of surplus or obsolete property

(a) The Director of the Congressional Budget Office shall have the authority, within the limits of available appropriations, to dispose of surplus or obsolete personal property by inter-agency transfer, donation, or discarding.

(b) Subsection (a) of this section shall apply with respect to fiscal years beginning after September 30, 1996.

(Pub. L. 104–197, title I, § 105, Sept. 16, 1996, 110 Stat. 2404.)

CODIFICATION

Section was enacted as part of the appropriation act cited as the credit to this section, and not as part of title II of the Congressional Budget and Impoundment Control Act of 1974 which comprises this chapter.

PRIOR PROVISIONS

Provisions similar to those in this section were contained in the following prior appropriation acts:

Pub. L. 104–53, title I, Nov. 19, 1995, 109 Stat. 527.
Pub. L. 103–283, title I, July 22, 1994, 108 Stat. 1433.
Pub. L. 103–69, title I, Aug. 11, 1993, 107 Stat. 701.

§ 607. Lump-sum payments for annual leave to separated employees

(a) The Director of the Congressional Budget Office shall have the authority to make lump-sum payments to separated employees of the Congressional Budget Office for unused annual leave.

(b) Subsection (a) of this section shall apply with respect to fiscal years beginning after September 30, 1996.

(Pub. L. 104–197, title I, § 106, Sept. 16, 1996, 110 Stat. 2404.)

CODIFICATION

Section was enacted as part of the Congressional Operations Appropriations Act, 1997, which is title I of the Legislative Branch Appropriations Act, 1997, and not as part of title II of the Congressional Budget and Impoundment Control Act of 1974 which comprises this chapter.

§ 608. Lump-sum payments to enhance staff recruitment and to reward exceptional performance

(a) The Director of the Congressional Budget Office shall have the authority to make lump-sum payments to enhance staff recruitment and to reward exceptional performance by an employee or a group of employees.

(b) Subsection (a) of this section shall apply with respect to fiscal years beginning after September 30, 1999.

(Pub. L. 106–57, title I, § 106, Sept. 29, 1999, 113 Stat. 418.)

CODIFICATION

Section was enacted as part of the Congressional Operations Appropriations Act, 2000, which is title I of the Legislative Branch Appropriations Act, 2000, and not as part of title II of the Congressional Budget and Impoundment Control Act of 1974 which comprises this chapter.

CHAPTER 17A—CONGRESSIONAL BUDGET AND FISCAL OPERATIONS

§ 621. Congressional declaration of purpose

The Congress declares that it is essential—

(1) to assure effective congressional control over the budgetary process;

(2) to provide for the congressional determination each year of the appropriate level of Federal revenues and expenditures;

(3) to provide a system of impoundment control;

(4) to establish national budget priorities; and

(5) to provide for the furnishing of information by the executive branch in a manner that will assist the Congress in discharging its duties.

(Pub. L. 93–344, § 2, July 12, 1974, 88 Stat. 298.)

CODIFICATION

Section was formerly classified to section 1301 of Title 31 prior to the general revision and enactment of Title 31, Money and Finance, by Pub. L. 97–258, § 1, Sept. 13, 1982, 96 Stat. 877.

EFFECTIVE DATE

Section 905 of Pub. L. 93–344 provided effective dates for Pub. L. 93–344 prior to repeal by Pub. L. 105–33, title X, § 10120(a), Aug. 5, 1997, 111 Stat. 696.

SHORT TITLE OF 1999 AMENDMENT

Pub. L. 106–141, § 1, Dec. 7, 1999, 113 Stat. 1699, provided that: "This Act [amending sections 658b and 658c of this title] may be cited as the 'State Flexibility Clarification Act'."

SHORT TITLE OF 1981 AMENDMENT

Pub. L. 97–108, § 1, Dec. 23, 1981, 95 Stat. 1510, provided: "That this Act [amending section 653 of this title and enacting provisions set out as notes under section 653 of this title] may be cited as the 'State and Local Government Cost Estimate Act of 1981'."

SHORT TITLE

Section 1(a) of Pub. L. 93–344, as amended by Pub. L. 104–130, § 4(a), Apr. 9, 1996, 110 Stat. 1211, provided that: "This Act [enacting chapters 17, 17A and 17B, and section 190a–3 of this title, and sections 11a, 11c, 11d, and 1020a of former Title 31, amending section 105 of Title 1, General Provisions, sections 190b and 190d of this title, and sections 11, 665, 701, 1020, and 1151, 1152, 1153, and 1154 of former Title 31, repealing sections 66 and 81 of this title, and sections 571 and 581c–1 of former Title 31, and enacting provisions set out as notes under sections 190a–1, 621, 632, and 682 of this title, section 105 of Title 1, General Provisions, and 1020 of former Title 31] may be cited as the 'Congressional Budget and Impoundment Control Act of 1974'. Titles I through IX may be cited as the 'Congressional Budget Act of 1974'. Parts A and B of title X [enacting subchapters I and II of chapter 17B of this title] may be cited as the 'Impoundment Control Act of 1974'. Part C of title X [enacting subchapter III of chapter 17B of this title] may be cited as the 'Line Item Veto Act of 1996'."

Pub. L. 93–344, title V, § 500, as added Pub. L. 101–508, title XIII, § 13201(a), Nov. 5, 1990, 104 Stat. 1388–609, provided that: "This title [enacting subchapter III of this chapter] may be cited as the 'Federal Credit Reform Act of 1990'."

FINANCIAL SAFETY AND SOUNDNESS OF GOVERNMENT-SPONSORED ENTERPRISES

Pub. L. 101–508, title XIII, § 13501, Nov. 5, 1990, 104 Stat. 1388–628, provided that:

"(a) DEFINITION.—For purposes of this section, the terms 'Government-sponsored enterprise' and 'GSE' mean the Farm Credit System (including the Farm Credit Banks, Banks for Cooperatives, and Federal Agricultural Mortgage Corporation), the Federal Home Loan Bank System, the Federal Home Loan Mortgage Corporation, the Federal National Mortgage Association, and the Student Loan Marketing Association.

"(b) TREASURY DEPARTMENT STUDY AND PROPOSED LEGISLATION.—

"(1) The Department of the Treasury shall prepare and submit to Congress no later than April 30, 1991, a study of GSEs and recommended legislation.

"(2) The study shall include an objective assessment of the financial soundness of GSEs, the adequacy of the existing regulatory structure for GSEs, the financial exposure of the Federal Government posed by GSEs, and the effects of GSE activities on Treasury borrowing.

"(c) CONGRESSIONAL BUDGET OFFICE STUDY.—

"(1) The Congressional Budget Office shall prepare and submit to Congress no later than April 30, 1991, a study of GSEs.

"(2) The study shall include an analysis of the financial risks each GSE assumes, how Congress may improve its understanding of those risks, the supervision and regulation of GSEs' risk management, the financial exposure of the Federal Government posed by GSEs, and the effects of GSE activities on Treasury borrowing. The study shall also include an analysis of alternative models for oversight of GSEs and of the costs and benefits of each alternative model to the Government and to the markets and beneficiaries served by GSEs.

"(d) ACCESS TO RELEVANT INFORMATION.—

"(1) For the studies required by this section, each GSE shall provide full and prompt access to the Secretary of the Treasury and the Director of the Congressional Budget Office to its books and records and other information requested by the Secretary of the Treasury or the Director of the Congressional Budget Office.

"(2) In preparing the studies required by this section, the Secretary of the Treasury and the Director of the Congressional Budget Office may request information from, or the assistance of, any Federal department or agency authorized by law to supervise the activities of a GSE.

"(e) CONFIDENTIALITY OF RELEVANT INFORMATION.—

"(1) The Secretary of the Treasury and the Director of the Congressional Budget Office shall determine and maintain the confidentiality of any book, record, or information made available by a GSE under this section in a manner consistent with the level of confidentiality established for the material by the GSE involved.

"(2) The Department of the Treasury shall be exempt from section 552 of title 5, United States Code, for any book, record, or information made available under subsection (d) and determined by the Secretary of the Treasury to be confidential under this subsection.

"(3) Any officer or employee of the Department of the Treasury shall be subject to the penalties set forth in section 1906 of title 18, United States Code, if—

"(A) by virtue of his or her employment or official position, he or she has possession of or access to any book, record, or information made available under and determined to be confidential under this section; and

"(B) he or she discloses the material in any manner other than—

"(i) to an officer or employee of the Department of the Treasury; or

"(ii) pursuant to the exception set forth in such section 1906.

"(4) The Congressional Budget Office shall be exempt from section 203 of the Congressional Budget Act of 1974 [2 U.S.C. 603] with respect to any book, record, or information made available under this subsection and determined by the Director to be confidential under paragraph (1).

"(f) REQUIREMENT TO REPORT LEGISLATION.—(1) The committees of jurisdiction in the House shall prepare and report to the House no later than September 15, 1991, legislation to ensure the financial soundness of GSEs and to minimize the possibility that a GSE might require future assistance from the Government.

"(2) It is the sense of the Senate that the committees of jurisdiction in the Senate shall prepare and report to the Senate no later than September 15, 1991, legislation to ensure the financial safety and soundness of GSEs and to minimize the possibility that a GSE might require future assistance from the Government.

"(f) [sic] PRESIDENT'S BUDGET.—The President's annual budget submission shall include an analysis of the financial condition of the GSEs and the financial exposure of the Government, if any, posed by GSEs.''

MULTIYEAR AUTHORIZATIONS AND 2-YEAR APPROPRIATIONS FOR SELECTED AGENCIES AND ACCOUNTS

Pub. L. 100–119, title II, § 201, Sept. 29, 1987, 101 Stat. 784, provided that: "It is the sense of the Congress that the Congress should undertake an experiment with multiyear authorizations and 2-year appropriations for selected agencies and accounts. An evaluation of the efficacy and desirability of such experiment should be conducted at the end of the 2-year period. The appropriate committees are directed to develop a plan in consultation with the leadership of the House and Senate to implement this experiment."

FINANCIAL MANAGEMENT REFORM

Pub. L. 100–119, title II, § 203, Sept. 29, 1987, 101 Stat. 784, provided that: "It is the sense of the Congress that the Congress should undertake a coordinated effort to identify problems and develop specific recommendations to reform the financial management systems of the United States Government, including consideration of the use of generally accepted accounting principles."

EXERCISE OF CONGRESSIONAL RULEMAKING POWER

Section 904 of Pub. L. 93–344, as amended by Pub. L. 99–177, title II, § 271(a), Dec. 12, 1985, 99 Stat. 1094; Pub. L. 101–508, title XIII, §§ 13112(a)(11), 13208(a), Nov. 5, 1990, 104 Stat. 1388–608, 1388–619; Pub. L. 104–130, § 4(c), Apr. 9, 1996, 110 Stat. 1212; Pub. L. 105–33, title X, § 10119, Aug. 5, 1997, 111 Stat. 695, provided that:

"(a) The provisions of this title and of titles I, III, IV, and V and the provisions of sections 701, 703,, [sic] 1017, 1025, and 1027 [enacting this chapter (except subchapter IV) and sections 190a–3, 688, 691d, and 691f of this title, amending the Rules of the House of Representatives and the Standing Rules of the Senate, and sections 190b and 190d of this title, and enacting provisions set out as notes under this section and sections 190a–1 and 632 of this title] are enacted by the Congress—

"(1) as an exercise of the rulemaking power of the House of Representatives and the Senate, respectively, and as such they shall be considered as part of the rules of each House, respectively, or of that House to which they specifically apply, and such rules shall supersede other rules only to the extent that they are inconsistent therewith; and

"(2) with full recognition of the constitutional right of either House to change such rules (so far as relating to such House) at any time, in the same manner, and to the same extent as in the case of any other rule of such House.

"(b) Any provision of title III or IV [enacting subchapters I and II of this chapter] may be waived or suspended in the Senate by a majority vote of the Members voting, a quorum being present, or by the unanimous consent of the Senate.

"(c) WAIVERS.—

"(1) PERMANENT.—Sections 305(b)(2), 305(c)(4), 306, 310(d)(2), 313, 904(c), and 904(d) of this Act [sections 636(b)(2), (c)(4), 637, 641(d)(2), and 644 of this title and subsecs. (c) and (d) of this note] may be waived or suspended in the Senate only by the affirmative vote of three-fifths of the Members, duly chosen and sworn.

"(2) TEMPORARY.—Sections 301(i), 302(c), 302(f), 310(g), 311(a), 312(b), and 312(c) of this Act [sections 632(i), 633(c), (f), 641(g), 642(a), and 643(b), (c) of this title] and sections 258(a)(4)(C), 258A(b)(3)(C)(I) [(i)], 258B(f)(1), 258B(h)(1), 258(h)(3) [258B(h)(3)], 258C(a)(5), and 258C(b)(1) of the Balanced Budget and Emergency Deficit Control Act of 1985 [sections 907a(a)(4)(C), 907b(b)(3)(C)(i), 907c(f)(1), (h)(1), (3), and 907d(a)(5), (b)(1) of this title] may be waived or suspended in the Senate only by the affirmative vote of three-fifths of the Members, duly chosen and sworn.

"(d) APPEALS.—

"(1) PROCEDURE.—Appeals in the Senate from the decisions of the Chair relating to any provision of title III or IV [enacting subchapters I and II of this chapter] or section 1017 [section 688 of this title] shall, except as otherwise provided therein, be limited to 1 hour, to be equally divided between, and controlled by, the mover and the manager of the resolution, concurrent resolution, reconciliation bill, or rescission bill, as the case may be.

"(2) PERMANENT.—An affirmative vote of three-fifths of the Members, duly chosen and sworn, shall be required in the Senate to sustain an appeal of the ruling of the Chair on a point of order raised under sections 305(b)(2), 305(c)(4), 306, 310(d)(2), 313, 904(c), and 904(d) of this Act [sections 636(b)(2), (c)(4), 637, 641(d)(2), 644 of this title and subsecs. (c) and (d) of this note].

"(3) TEMPORARY.—An affirmative vote of three-fifths of the Members, duly chosen and sworn, shall be required in the Senate to sustain an appeal of the ruling of the Chair on a point of order raised under sections 301(i), 302(c), 302(f), 310(g), 311(a), 312(b), and 312(c) of this Act and sections 258(a)(4)(C), 258A(b)(3)(C)(I) [(i)], 258B(f)(1), 258B(h)(1), 258(h)(3) [258B(h)(3)], 258C(a)(5), and 258C(b)(1) of the Balanced Budget and Emergency Deficit Control Act of 1985.

"(e) EXPIRATION OF CERTAIN SUPERMAJORITY VOTING REQUIREMENTS.—Subsections (c)(2) and (d)(3) shall expire on September 30, 2002.''

ACT REFERRED TO IN OTHER SECTIONS

The Congressional Budget Act of 1974 is referred to in sections 907a, 907b, 907c, of this title; title 7 section 1446c–1; title 22 sections 2718, 4715; title 33 section 2326a; title 50 App. sections 1989b–8, 1989c–7.

The Congressional Budget and Impoundment Control Act of 1974 is referred to in section 907a of this title; title 16 sections 544l, 1606; title 22 sections 2295b, 5857; title 42 section 11303.

§ 622. Definitions

For purposes of this Act—

(1) The terms "budget outlays" and "outlays" mean, with respect to any fiscal year, expenditures and net lending of funds under budget authority during such year.

(2) BUDGET AUTHORITY AND NEW BUDGET AUTHORITY.—

(A) IN GENERAL.—The term "budget authority" means the authority provided by Federal law to incur financial obligations, as follows:

(i) provisions of law that make funds available for obligation and expenditure (other than borrowing authority), including the authority to obligate and expend the proceeds of offsetting receipts and collections;

(ii) borrowing authority, which means authority granted to a Federal entity to borrow and obligate and expend the borrowed funds, including through the issuance of promissory notes or other monetary credits;

(iii) contract authority, which means the making of funds available for obligation but not for expenditure; and

(iv) offsetting receipts and collections as negative budget authority, and the reduction thereof as positive budget authority.

(B) LIMITATIONS ON BUDGET AUTHORITY.— With respect to the Federal Hospital Insurance Trust Fund, the Supplementary Medical Insurance Trust Fund, the Unemployment Trust Fund, and the railroad retirement account, any amount that is precluded from obligation in a fiscal year by a provision of law (such as a limitation or a benefit formula) shall not be budget authority in that year.

(C) NEW BUDGET AUTHORITY.—The term "new budget authority" means, with respect to a fiscal year—

(i) budget authority that first becomes available for obligation in that year, including budget authority that becomes available in that year s[1] a result of a reappropriation; or

(ii) a change in any account in the availability of unobligated balances of budget authority carried over from a prior year, resulting from a provision of law first effective in that year;

and includes a change in the estimated level of new budget authority provided in indefinite amounts by existing law.

(3) The term "tax expenditures" means those revenue losses attributable to provisions of the Federal tax laws which allow a special exclusion, exemption, or deduction from gross income or which provide a special credit, a preferential rate of tax, or a deferral of tax liability; and the term "tax expenditures budget" means an enumeration of such tax expenditures.

(4) The term "concurrent resolution on the budget" means—

(A) a concurrent resolution setting forth the congressional budget for the United States Government for a fiscal year as provided in section 632 of this title; and

(B) any other concurrent resolution revising the congressional budget for the United States Government for a fiscal year as described in section 635 of this title.

(5) The term "appropriation Act" means an Act referred to in section 105 of title 1.

(6) The term "deficit" means, with respect to a fiscal year, the amount by which outlays exceeds[2] receipts during that year.

(7) The term "surplus" means, with respect to a fiscal year, the amount by which receipts exceeds[2] outlays during that year.

(8) The term "government-sponsored enterprise" means a corporate entity created by a law of the United States that—

(A)(i) has a Federal charter authorized by law;

(ii) is privately owned, as evidenced by capital stock owned by private entities or individuals;

(iii) is under the direction of a board of directors, a majority of which is elected by private owners;

(iv) is a financial institution with power to—

(I) make loans or loan guarantees for limited purposes such as to provide credit for specific borrowers or one sector; and

(II) raise funds by borrowing (which does not carry the full faith and credit of the Federal Government) or to guarantee the debt of others in unlimited amounts; and

(B)(i) does not exercise powers that are reserved to the Government as sovereign (such as the power to tax or to regulate interstate commerce);

(ii) does not have the power to commit the Government financially (but it may be a recipient of a loan guarantee commitment made by the Government); and

(iii) has employees whose salaries and expenses are paid by the enterprise and are not Federal employees subject to title 5.

(9) The term "entitlement authority" means—

(A) the authority to make payments (including loans and grants), the budget authority for which is not provided for in advance by appropriation Acts, to any person or government if, under the provisions of the law containing that authority, the United States is obligated to make such payments to persons or governments who meet the requirements established by that law; and

(B) the food stamp program.

(10) The term "credit authority" means authority to incur direct loan obligations or to incur primary loan guarantee commitments.

(Pub. L. 93–344, §3, July 12, 1974, 88 Stat. 299; Aug. 1, 1946, ch. 724, title I, §302(c), as added Aug. 30, 1954, ch. 1073, §1, as added Pub. L. 95–110, §1, Sept. 20, 1977, 91 Stat. 884, renumbered title I, Pub. L. 102–486, title IX, §902(a)(8), Oct. 24, 1992, 106 Stat. 2944; Pub. L. 99–177, title II, §§201(a), 232(b), Dec. 12, 1985, 99 Stat. 1039, 1062; Pub. L. 99–514, §2, Oct. 22, 1986, 100 Stat. 2095; Pub. L. 100–119, title I, §106(a), Sept. 29, 1987, 101 Stat. 780; Pub. L. 100–203, title VIII, §8003(c), Dec. 22, 1987, 101 Stat. 1330–282; Pub. L. 101–508, title XIII, §§13112(a)(2), 13201(b)(1), 13211(a), Nov. 5, 1990, 104 Stat. 1388–607, 1388–614, 1388–620; Pub. L. 105–33, title X, §10101, Aug. 5, 1997, 111 Stat. 678.)

---

[1] So in original. Probably should be "as".

[2] So in original. Probably should be "exceed".

REFERENCES IN TEXT

This Act, referred to in text, means Pub. L. 93–344, July 12, 1974, 88 Stat. 297, as amended, known as the Congressional Budget and Impoundment Control Act of 1974, which enacted chapters 17, 17A and 17B, and section 190a–3 of this title and sections 11a, 11c, 11d, 1020a of former Title 31, Money and Finance, amended sections 11, 665, 701, 1020, 1151, 1152, 1153, and 1154 of former Title 31, section 105 of Title 1, General Provisions, sections 190b and 190d of this title, repealed sections 571 and 581c–1 of former Title 31, and sections 66 and 81 of this title, and enacted provisions set out as notes under sections 190a–1, 621, 632, and 682 of this title, section 105 of Title 1, and section 1020 of former Title 31. For complete classification of this Act to the Code, see Short Title note set out under section 621 of this title and Tables.

CODIFICATION

Section was formerly classified to section 1302 of Title 31 prior to the general revision and enactment of Title 31, Money and Finance, by Pub. L. 97–258, § 1, Sept. 13, 1982, 96 Stat. 877.

AMENDMENTS

1997—Par. (9). Pub. L. 105–33 amended par. (9) generally. Prior to amendment, par. (9) read as follows: "The term 'entitlement authority' means spending authority described by section 651(c)(2)(C) of this title."

1990—Par. (2). Pub. L. 101–508, § 13211(a), amended par. (2) generally. Prior to amendment, par. (2) read as follows: "The term 'budget authority' means authority provided by law to enter into obligations which will result in immediate or future outlays involving Government funds or to collect offsetting receipts., except that such term does not include authority to insure or guarantee the repayment of indebtedness incurred by another person or government. The term includes the cost for direct loan and loan guarantee programs, as those terms are defined by subchapter III of this chapter".

Pub. L. 101–508, § 13201(b)(1), inserted at end: "The term includes the cost for direct loan and loan guarantee programs, as those terms are defined by subchapter III of this chapter".

Pars. (6) to (8). Pub. L. 101–508, § 13112(a)(2), added pars. (6) to (8) and struck out former par. (6) which defined "deficit" and contained provisions relating to calculation of the deficit, former par. (7) which defined "maximum deficit amount", and former par. (8) which defined "off-budget Federal entity".

1987—Par. (7)(C). Pub. L. 100–203, § 8003(c)(1), (2), redesignated subpar. (D) as (C). Former subpar. (C), which provided for maximum deficit amount of $108,000,000,000 for fiscal year beginning Oct. 1, 1987, was struck out.

Par. (7)(D) to (I). Pub. L. 100–203, § 8003(c)(2)–(7), redesignated subpars. (E) to (I) as (D) to (H), respectively. Former subpar. (D) redesignated (C).

Pub. L. 100–119 inserted subpars. (D) to (I) and struck out former subpars. (D) to (F) which read as follows:

"(D) with respect to the fiscal year beginning October 1, 1988, $72,000,000,000;

"(E) with respect to the fiscal year beginning October 1, 1989, $36,000,000,000; and

"(F) with respect to the fiscal year beginning October 1, 1990, zero."

1986—Par. (6). Pub. L. 99–514 substituted "Internal Revenue Code of 1986" for "Internal Revenue Code of 1954", which for purposes of codification was translated as "title 26" thus requiring no change in text.

1985—Par. (2). Pub. L. 99–177, § 201(a)(2), inserted reference to the collection of offsetting receipts, effective Apr. 15, 1986.

Par. (4). Pub. L. 99–177, § 232(b), struck out subpar. (B) relating to concurrent resolutions as provided in section 641 of this title, and redesignated subpar. (C) as (B).

Pars. (6) to (10). Pub. L. 99–177, § 201(a)(1), added pars. (6) to (10).

1977—Pub. L. 95–110 struck out designation "(a)" before "For the purpose of this chapter" and struck out subsec. (b) which provided that Members of the respective Houses of Congress who were members of the Joint Committee on Atomic Energy were to be treated as standing committees of their respective Houses of Congress.

EFFECTIVE DATE OF 1990 AMENDMENT

Section 13211(b) of Pub. L. 101–508 provided that: "The amendment made by subsection (a) [amending this section] shall be effective for fiscal year 1992 and subsequent fiscal years."

EFFECTIVE DATE OF 1985 AMENDMENT

Amendment by sections 201(a)(1) and 232(b) of Pub. L. 99–177 effective Dec. 12, 1985, and applicable with respect to fiscal years beginning after Sept. 30, 1985, and amendment by section 201(a)(2) of Pub. L. 99–177 effective Apr. 15, 1986, see section 275(a)(1), (2)(A) of Pub. L. 99–177, as amended, set out as an Effective and Termination Dates note under section 900 of this title.

SECTION REFERRED TO IN OTHER SECTIONS

This section is referred to in sections 900, 1602 of this title; title 39 section 2009a; title 50 section 403f.

§ 623. Continuing study of additional budget reform proposals

(a) The Committees on the Budget of the House of Representatives and the Senate shall study on a continuing basis proposals designed to improve and facilitate methods of congressional budgetmaking. The proposals to be studied shall include, but are not limited to, proposals for—

(1) improving the information base required for determining the effectiveness of new programs by such means as pilot testing survey research, and other experimental and analytical techniques;

(2) improving analytical and systematic evaluation of the effectiveness of existing programs;

(3) establishing maximum and minimum time limitations for program authorization; and

(4) developing techniques of human resource accounting and other means of providing noneconomic as well as economic evaluation measures.

(b) The Committee on the Budget of each House shall, from time to time, report to its House the results of the study carried on by it under subsection (a) of this section, together with its recommendations.

(c) Nothing in this section shall preclude studies to improve the budgetary process by any other committee of the House of Representatives or the Senate or any joint committee of the Congress.

(Pub. L. 93–344, title VII, § 703, July 12, 1974, 88 Stat. 326.)

CODIFICATION

Section was formerly classified to section 1303 of Title 31 prior to the general revision and enactment of Title 31, Money and Finance, by Pub. L. 97–258, § 1, Sept. 13, 1982, 96 Stat. 877.

SUBCHAPTER I—CONGRESSIONAL BUDGET PROCESS

SUBCHAPTER REFERRED TO IN OTHER SECTIONS

This subchapter is referred to in sections 632, 907a, 907b, 907c of this title; title 42 section 6247.

§ 631. Timetable

The timetable with respect to the congressional budget process for any fiscal year is as follows:

On or before:	Action to be completed:
First Monday in February.	President submits his budget.
February 15	Congressional Budget Office submits report to Budget Committees.
Not later than 6 weeks after President submits budget.	Committees submit views and estimates to Budget Committees.
April 1	Senate Budget Committee reports concurrent resolution on the budget.
April 15	Congress completes action on concurrent resolution on the budget.
May 15	Annual appropriation bills may be considered in the House.
June 10	House Appropriations Committee reports last annual appropriation bill.
June 15	Congress completes action on reconciliation legislation.
June 30	House completes action on annual appropriation bills.
October 1	Fiscal year begins.

(Pub. L. 93–344, title III, § 300, July 12, 1974, 88 Stat. 306; Pub. L. 99–177, title II, § 201(b), Dec. 12, 1985, 99 Stat. 1040; Pub. L. 101–508, title XIII, § 13112(a)(4), Nov. 5, 1990, 104 Stat. 1388–608; Pub. L. 105–33, title X, § 10104(a), Aug. 5, 1997, 111 Stat. 679.)

CODIFICATION

Section was formerly classified to section 1321 of Title 31 prior to the general revision and enactment of Title 31, Money and Finance, by Pub. L. 97–258, § 1, Sept. 13, 1982, 96 Stat. 877.

AMENDMENTS

1997—Pub. L. 105–33 substituted "Not later than 6 weeks after President submits budget" for "February 25".

1990—Pub. L. 101–508 substituted "First Monday in February" for "First Monday after January 3".

1985—Pub. L. 99–177 amended section generally. Prior to the amendment the timetable was on or before: November 10—President submits current services budget; 15th day after Congress meets—President submits his budget; March 15—Committees and joint committees submit reports to Budget Committees; April 1—Congressional Budget Office submits reports to Budget Committees; April 15—Budget Committees report first concurrent resolution on the budget to their Houses; May 15—Committees report bills and resolutions authorizing new budget authority; May 15—Congress completes action on first concurrent resolution on the budget; 7th day after Labor Day—Congress completes action on bills and resolutions providing new budget authority and new spending authority; September 15—Congress completes action on second required concurrent resolution on the budget; September 25—Congress completes action on reconciliation bill or resolution, or

both, implementing second required concurrent resolution; October 1—Fiscal year begins.

EFFECTIVE DATE OF 1985 AMENDMENT

Amendment by Pub. L. 99–177 effective Dec. 12, 1985, and applicable with respect to fiscal years beginning after Sept. 30, 1985, see section 275(a)(1) of Pub. L. 99–177, set out as an Effective and Termination Dates note under section 900 of this title.

EFFECTIVE DATE

Subchapter applicable with respect to the fiscal year beginning Oct. 1, 1976, and succeeding fiscal years, except as section 906 of Pub. L. 93–344, formerly set out as a note under section 632 of this title, makes provision for possible application of this section to the fiscal year beginning July 1, 1975, see section 905(c) of Pub. L. 93–344, formerly set out as an Effective Date note under section 621 of this title.

§ 632. Annual adoption of concurrent resolution on the budget

(a) Content of concurrent resolution on the budget

On or before April 15 of each year, the Congress shall complete action on a concurrent resolution on the budget for the fiscal year beginning on October 1 of such year. The concurrent resolution shall set forth appropriate levels for the fiscal year beginning on October 1 of such year and for at least each of the 4 ensuing fiscal years for the following—

(1) totals of new budget authority and outlays;

(2) total Federal revenues and the amount, if any, by which the aggregate level of Federal revenues should be increased or decreased by bills and resolutions to be reported by the appropriate committees;

(3) the surplus or deficit in the budget;

(4) new budget authority and outlays for each major functional category, based on allocations of the total levels set forth pursuant to paragraph (1);

(5) the public debt;

(6) For[1] purposes of Senate enforcement under this subchapter, outlays of the old-age, survivors, and disability insurance program established under title II of the Social Security Act [42 U.S.C. 401 et seq.] for the fiscal year of the resolution and for each of the 4 succeeding fiscal years; and

(7) For[1] purposes of Senate enforcement under this subchapter, revenues of the old-age, survivors, and disability insurance program established under title II of the Social Security Act (and the related provisions of the Internal Revenue Code of 1986 [26 U.S.C. 1 et seq.]) for the fiscal year of the resolution and for each of the 4 succeeding fiscal years.

The concurrent resolution shall not include the outlays and revenue totals of the old age,[2] survivors, and disability insurance program established under title II of the Social Security Act or the related provisions of the Internal Revenue Code of 1986 in the surplus or deficit totals required by this subsection or in any other sur-

---

[1] So in original. Probably should not be capitalized.
[2] So in original. Probably should be "old-age,".

plus or deficit totals required by this subchapter.

(b) Additional matters in concurrent resolution

The concurrent resolution on the budget may—

(1) set forth, if required by subsection (f) of this section, the calendar year in which, in the opinion of the Congress, the goals for reducing unemployment set forth in section 4(b) of the Employment Act of 1946 [15 U.S.C. 1022a(b)] should be achieved;

(2) include reconciliation directives described in section 641 of this title;

(3) require a procedure under which all or certain bills or resolutions providing new budget authority or new entitlement authority for such fiscal year shall not be enrolled until the Congress has completed action on any reconciliation bill or reconciliation resolution or both required by such concurrent resolution to be reported in accordance with section 641(b) of this title;

(4) set forth such other matters, and require such other procedures, relating to the budget, as may be appropriate to carry out the purposes of this Act;

(5) include a heading entitled "Debt Increase as Measure of Deficit" in which the concurrent resolution shall set forth the amounts by which the debt subject to limit (in section 3101 of title 31) has increased or would increase in each of the relevant fiscal years;

(6) include a heading entitled "Display of Federal Retirement Trust Fund Balances" in which the concurrent resolution shall set forth the balances of the Federal retirement trust funds;

(7) set forth procedures in the Senate whereby committee allocations, aggregates, and other levels can be revised for legislation if that legislation would not increase the deficit, or would not increase the deficit when taken with other legislation enacted after the adoption of the resolution, for the first fiscal year or the total period of fiscal years covered by the resolution;

(8) set forth procedures to effectuate pay-as-you-go in the House of Representatives; and

(9) set forth direct loan obligation and primary loan guarantee commitment levels.

(c) Consideration of procedures or matters which have effect of changing any rule of House

If the Committee on the Budget of the House of Representatives reports any concurrent resolution on the budget which includes any procedure or matter which has the effect of changing any rule of the House of Representatives, such concurrent resolution shall then be referred to the Committee on Rules with instructions to report it within five calendar days (not counting any day on which the House is not in session). The Committee on Rules shall have jurisdiction to report any concurrent resolution referred to it under this paragraph with an amendment or amendments changing or striking out any such procedure or matter.

(d) Views and estimates of other committees

Within 6 weeks after the President submits a budget under section 1105(a) of title 31, or at such time as may be requested by the Committee on the Budget, each committee of the House of Representatives having legislative jurisdiction shall submit to the Committee on the Budget of the House and each committee of the Senate having legislative jurisdiction shall submit to the Committee on the Budget of the Senate its views and estimates (as determined by the committee making such submission) with respect to all matters set forth in subsections (a) and (b) of this section which relate to matters within the jurisdiction or functions of such committee. The Joint Economic Committee shall submit to the Committees on the Budget of both Houses its recommendations as to the fiscal policy appropriate to the goals of the Employment Act of 1946 [15 U.S.C. 1021 et seq.]. Any other committee of the House of Representatives or the Senate may submit to the Committee on the Budget of its House, and any joint committee of the Congress may submit to the Committees on the Budget of both Houses, its views and estimates with respect to all matters set forth in subsections (a) and (b) of this section which relate to matters within its jurisdiction or functions. Any Committee[3] of the House of Representatives or the Senate that anticipates that the committee will consider any proposed legislation establishing, amending, or reauthorizing any Federal program likely to have a significant budgetary impact on any State, local, or tribal government, or likely to have a significant financial impact on the private sector, including any legislative proposal submitted by the executive branch likely to have such a budgetary or financial impact, shall include its views and estimates on that proposal to the Committee on the Budget of the applicable House.

(e) Hearings and report

(1) In general

In developing the concurrent resolution on the budget referred to in subsection (a) of this section for each fiscal year, the Committee on the Budget of each House shall hold hearings and shall receive testimony from Members of Congress and such appropriate representatives of Federal departments and agencies, the general public, and national organizations as the committee deems desirable. Each of the recommendations as to short-term and medium-term goals set forth in the report submitted by the members of the Joint Economic Committee under subsection (d) of this section may be considered by the Committee on the Budget of each House as part of its consideration of such concurrent resolution, and its report may reflect its views thereon, including its views on how the estimates of revenues and levels of budget authority and outlays set forth in such concurrent resolution are designed to achieve any goals it is recommending.

(2) Required contents of report

The report accompanying the resolution shall include—

(A) a comparison of the levels of total new budget authority, total outlays, total reve-

---

[3] So in original. Probably should not be capitalized.

nues, and the surplus or deficit for each fiscal year set forth in the resolution with those requested in the budget submitted by the President;

(B) with respect to each major functional category, an estimate of total new budget authority and total outlays, with the estimates divided between discretionary and mandatory amounts;

(C) the economic assumptions that underlie each of the matters set forth in the resolution and any alternative economic assumptions and objectives the committee considered;

(D) information, data, and comparisons indicating the manner in which, and the basis on which, the committee determined each of the matters set forth in the resolution;

(E) the estimated levels of tax expenditures (the tax expenditures budget) by major items and functional categories for the President's budget and in the resolution; and

(F) allocations described in section 633(a) of this title.

(3) Additional contents of report

The report accompanying the resolution may include—

(A) a statement of any significant changes in the proposed levels of Federal assistance to State and local governments;

(B) an allocation of the level of Federal revenues recommended in the resolution among the major sources of such revenues;

(C) information, data, and comparisons on the share of total Federal budget outlays and of gross domestic product devoted to investment in the budget submitted by the President and in the resolution;

(D) the assumed levels of budget authority and outlays for public buildings, with a division between amounts for construction and repair and for rental payments; and

(E) other matters, relating to the budget and to fiscal policy, that the committee deems appropriate.

(f) Achievement of goals for reducing unemployment

(1) If, pursuant to section 4(c) of the Employment Act of 1946 [15 U.S.C. 1022a(c)], the President recommends in the Economic Report that the goals for reducing unemployment set forth in section 4(b) of such Act [15 U.S.C. 1022a(b)] be achieved in a year after the close of the five-year period prescribed by such subsection, the concurrent resolution on the budget for the fiscal year beginning after the date on which such Economic Report is received by the Congress may set forth the year in which, in the opinion of the Congress, such goals can be achieved.

(2) After the Congress has expressed its opinion pursuant to paragraph (1) as to the year in which the goals for reducing unemployment set forth in section 4(b) of the Employment Act of 1946 [15 U.S.C. 1022a(b)] can be achieved, if, pursuant to section 4(e) of such Act [15 U.S.C. 1022a(e)], the President recommends in the Economic Report that such goals be achieved in a year which is different from the year in which the Congress has expressed its opinion that such goals should be achieved, either in its action

pursuant to paragraph (1) or in its most recent action pursuant to this paragraph, the concurrent resolution on the budget for the fiscal year beginning after the date on which such Economic Report is received by the Congress may set forth the year in which, in the opinion of the Congress, such goals can be achieved.

(3) It shall be in order to amend the provision of such resolution setting forth such year only if the amendment thereto also proposes to alter the estimates, amounts, and levels (as described in subsection (a) of this section) set forth in such resolution in germane fashion in order to be consistent with the economic goals (as described in sections 3(a)(2) and 4(b) of the Employment Act of 1946 [15 U.S.C. 1022(a)(2), 1022(a)(b)]) which such amendment proposes can be achieved by the year specified in such amendment.

(g) Economic assumptions

(1) It shall not be in order in the Senate to consider any concurrent resolution on the budget for a fiscal year, or any amendment thereto, or any conference report thereon, that sets forth amounts and levels that are determined on the basis of more than one set of economic and technical assumptions.

(2) The joint explanatory statement accompanying a conference report on a concurrent resolution on the budget shall set forth the common economic assumptions upon which such joint statement and conference report are based, or upon which any amendment contained in the joint explanatory statement to be proposed by the conferees in the case of technical disagreement, is based.

(3) Subject to periodic reestimation based on changed economic conditions or technical estimates, determinations under titles III and IV of the Congressional Budget Act of 1974 [2 U.S.C. 631 et seq., 651 et seq.] shall be based upon such common economic and technical assumptions.

(h) Budget Committee's consultation with committees

The Committee on the Budget of the House of Representatives shall consult with the committees of its House having legislative jurisdiction during the preparation, consideration, and enforcement of the concurrent resolution on the budget with respect to all matters which relate to the jurisdiction or functions of such committees.

(i) Social security point of order

It shall not be in order in the Senate to consider any concurrent resolution on the budget (or amendment, motion, or conference report on the resolution) that would decrease the excess of social security revenues over social security outlays in any of the fiscal years covered by the concurrent resolution. No change in chapter 1 of the Internal Revenue Code of 1986 [26 U.S.C. 1 et seq.] shall be treated as affecting the amount of social security revenues unless such provision changes the income tax treatment of social security benefits.

(Pub. L. 93–344, title III, § 301, July 12, 1974, 88 Stat. 306; Pub. L. 95–523, title III, §§ 303(a), 304, Oct. 27, 1978, 92 Stat. 1905, 1906; Pub. L. 99–177, title II, § 201(b), Dec. 12, 1985, 99 Stat. 1040; Pub.

L. 100–119, title I, § 106(d), title II, § 208(a), Sept. 29, 1987, 101 Stat. 781, 786; Pub. L. 100–418, title V, § 5302, Aug. 23, 1988, 102 Stat. 1462; Pub. L. 101–508, title XIII, §§ 13112(a)(5), 13203, 13204, 13301(b), 13303(a), (b), Nov. 5, 1990, 104 Stat. 1388–608, 1388–615, 1388–616, 1388–623, 1388–625; Pub. L. 104–4, title I, § 102(2), Mar. 22, 1995, 109 Stat. 62; Pub. L. 105–33, title X, § 10105(a)–(f)(1), Aug. 5, 1997, 111 Stat. 679, 680.)

References in Text

The Social Security Act, referred to in subsec. (a), is act Aug. 14, 1935, ch. 531, 49 Stat. 620, as amended. Title II of the Social Security Act is classified generally to subchapter II (§ 401 et seq.) of chapter 7 of Title 42, The Public Health and Welfare. For complete classification of this Act to the Code, see section 1305 of Title 42 and Tables.

The Internal Revenue Code of 1986, referred to in subsecs. (a) and (i), is classified generally to Title 26, Internal Revenue Code.

This Act, referred to in subsec. (b)(4), means Pub. L. 93–344, July 12, 1974, 88 Stat. 297, as amended, known as the Congressional Budget and Impoundment Control Act of 1974, which enacted chapters 17, 17A and 17B, and section 190a–3 of this title and sections 11a, 11c, 11d, 1020a of former Title 31, Money and Finance, amended sections 11, 665, 701, 1020, 1151, 1152, 1153 and 1154 of former Title 31, section 105 of Title 1, General Provisions, sections 190b and 190d of this title, repealed sections 571 and 581c–1 of former Title 31 and sections 66 and 81 of this title, and enacted provisions set out as notes under sections 190a–1, 621, 632, and 682 of this title, section 105 of Title 1, and section 1020 of former Title 31. For complete classification of this Act to the Code, see Short Title note set out under section 621 of this title and Tables.

The Employment Act of 1946, referred to in subsec. (d), is act Feb. 20, 1946, ch. 33, 60 Stat. 23, as amended, which is classified generally to chapter 21 (§ 1021 et seq.) of Title 15, Commerce and Trade. For complete classification of this Act to the Code, see Short Title note set out under section 1021 of Title 15 and Tables.

The Congressional Budget Act of 1974, referred to in subsec. (g)(3), is titles I through IX of Pub. L. 93–344, July 12, 1974, 88 Stat. 297, as amended. Titles III and IV of the Act are classified generally to this subchapter (§ 631 et seq.) and subchapter II (§ 651 et seq.) of this chapter. For complete classification of this Act to the Code, see Short Title note set out under section 621 of this title and Tables.

Codification

Section was formerly classified to section 1322 of Title 31 prior to the general revision and enactment of Title 31, Money and Finance, by Pub. L. 97–258, § 1, Sept. 13, 1982, 96 Stat. 877.

Amendments

1997—Subsec. (a). Pub. L. 105–33, § 10105(a), in introductory provisions, substituted "and for at least each of the 4 ensuing fiscal years" for ", and planning levels for each of the two ensuing fiscal years,".

Subsec. (a)(1), (4). Pub. L. 105–33, § 10105(b), substituted "and outlays" for ", budget outlays, direct loan obligations, and primary loan guarantee commitments".

Subsec. (b)(7). Pub. L. 105–33, § 10105(c)(1), added par. (7) and struck out former par. (7) which related to setting forth pay-as-you-go procedures for the Senate.

Subsec. (b)(9). Pub. L. 105–33, § 10105(c)(2), (3), added par. (9).

Subsec. (d). Pub. L. 105–33, § 10105(d), in first sentence, inserted "or at such time as may be requested by the Committee on the Budget," after "title 31,".

Subsec. (e). Pub. L. 105–33, § 10105(e), designated existing provisions as par. (1), inserted par. heading, added pars. (2) and (3), and struck out former last sentence

consisting of pars. (1) to (9) which contained requirements for contents of report to accompany the concurrent resolution on the budget.

Subsec. (i). Pub. L. 105–33, § 10105(f)(1), inserted heading and substituted "(or amendment, motion, or conference report on the resolution)" for "as reported to the Senate".

1995—Subsec. (d). Pub. L. 104–4 inserted at end "Any Committee of the House of Representatives or the Senate that anticipates that the committee will consider any proposed legislation establishing, amending, or reauthorizing any Federal program likely to have a significant budgetary impact on any State, local, or tribal government, or likely to have a significant financial impact on the private sector, including any legislative proposal submitted by the executive branch likely to have such a budgetary or financial impact, shall include its views and estimates on that proposal to the Committee on the Budget of the applicable House."

1990—Subsec. (a). Pub. L. 101–508, § 13301(b), inserted at end: "The concurrent resolution shall not include the outlays and revenue totals of the old age, survivors, and disability insurance program established under title II of the Social Security Act or the related provisions of the Internal Revenue Code of 1986 in the surplus or deficit totals required by this subsection or in any other surplus or deficit totals required by this subchapter."

Subsec. (a)(6), (7). Pub. L. 101–508, § 13303(a), added pars. (6) and (7).

Subsec. (b)(5), (6). Pub. L. 101–508, § 13203, added pars. (5) and (6).

Subsec. (b)(7), (8). Pub. L. 101–508, § 13204, added pars. (7) and (8).

Subsec. (d). Pub. L. 101–508, § 13112(a)(5), substituted "Within 6 weeks after the President submits a budget under section 1105(a) of title 31" for "On or before February 25 of each year".

Subsec. (i). Pub. L. 101–508, § 13303(b), amended subsec. (i) generally, substituting present provisions for former provisions relating to maximum deficit amounts.

1988—Subsec. (e)(10). Pub. L. 100–418 temporarily added par. (10). See Effective and Termination Dates of 1988 Amendment note below.

1987—Subsec. (g). Pub. L. 100–119, § 208(a), amended subsec. (g) generally. Prior to amendment, subsec. (g) read as follows: "The joint explanatory statement accompanying a conference report on a concurrent resolution on the budget shall set forth the common economic assumptions upon which such joint statement and conference report are based, or upon which any amendment contained in the joint explanatory statement to be proposed by the conferees in the case of technical disagreement is based."

Subsec. (i)(2). Pub. L. 100–119, § 106(d), designated existing provisions as subpar. (A) and added subpars. (B) and (C).

1985—Pub. L. 99–177 substituted "Adoption of concurrent resolution on the budget" for "Adoption of first concurrent resolution" in section catchline.

Subsec. (a). Pub. L. 99–177 amended subsec. (a) generally, substituting provisions relating to content of concurrent resolution on the budget, for provisions relating to action required to be completed by May 15 of each year.

Subsec. (b). Pub. L. 99–177 amended subsec. (b) generally, inserting provisions relating to achievement of goals for reducing unemployment and provisions relating to reconciliation directives described in section 641 of this title.

Subsec. (c). Pub. L. 99–177 amended subsec. (c) generally, substituting provisions relating to consideration of procedures or matters which have the effect of changing any rule of the House of Representatives, for provisions relating to submission on or before March 15 of each year of the views and estimates of other committees.

Subsec. (d). Pub. L. 99–177 amended subsec. (d) generally, substituting provisions relating to views and estimates of other committees, for provisions relating to hearings and report in developing the first concurrent resolution on the budget.

Subsec. (e). Pub. L. 99–177 amended subsec. (e) generally, substituting provisions relating to hearings and report in developing the concurrent resolution on the budget, for provisions relating to achievement of goals for reducing unemployment.

Subsecs. (f) to (i). Pub. L. 99–177, §§ 201(b), 275(b)(2)(B), in amending section generally, added subsecs. (f) to (i).

1978—Subsec. (a)(6), (7). Pub. L. 95–523, § 304(a), added par. (6) and redesignated former par. (6) as (7).

Subsec. (d). Pub. L. 95–523, § 303(a), which directed insertion in subsec. (c) provisions relating to consideration by the Committee on the Budget of each House respecting short-term and medium-term goals set forth in the Joint Economic Committee report and the reflection of its views in its report and insertion of "also" after "concurrent resolution shall" was executed to subsec. (d) to reflect the probable intent of Congress.

Subsec. (e). Pub. L. 95–523, § 304(b), added subsec. (e).

EFFECTIVE DATE OF 1995 AMENDMENT

Amendment by Pub. L. 104–4 effective Jan. 1, 1996, or on the date 90 days after appropriations are made available as authorized under section 1516 of this title, whichever is earlier, and applicable to legislation considered on and after such date, see section 110 of Pub. L. 104–4, set out as an Effective Date note under section 1511 of this title.

EFFECTIVE DATE OF 1990 AMENDMENT

Section 13306 of Pub. L. 101–508 provided that: "Sections 13301, 13302, and 13303 and any amendments made by such sections [amending this section and sections 633 and 642 of this title and enacting provisions set out as notes under this section] shall apply with respect to fiscal years beginning on or after October 1, 1990. Section 13304 [amending section 401 of Title 42, The Public Health and Welfare] shall be effective for annual reports of the Board of Trustees issued in or after calendar year 1991."

EFFECTIVE AND TERMINATION DATES OF 1988 AMENDMENT

Amendment by Pub. L. 100–418 effective for fiscal years 1989, 1990, 1991, and 1992, see section 5303 of Pub. L. 100–418, set out as a note under section 1105 of Title 31, Money and Finance.

EFFECTIVE DATE OF 1985 AMENDMENT

Amendment by Pub. L. 99–177 effective Dec. 12, 1985, and applicable with respect to fiscal years beginning after Sept. 30, 1985, see section 275(a)(1) of Pub. L. 99–177, set out as an Effective and Termination Dates note under section 900 of this title.

EXCLUSION OF SOCIAL SECURITY FROM ALL BUDGETS

Section 13301(a) of Pub. L. 101–508 provided that: "Notwithstanding any other provision of law, the receipts and disbursements of the Federal Old-Age and Survivors Insurance Trust Fund and the Federal Disability Insurance Trust Fund shall not be counted as new budget authority, outlays, receipts, or deficit or surplus for purposes of—

"(1) the budget of the United States Government as submitted by the President,

"(2) the congressional budget, or

"(3) the Balanced Budget and Emergency Deficit Control Act of 1985 [see Short Title note set out under section 900 of this title]."

PROTECTION OF OASDI TRUST FUNDS IN HOUSE OF REPRESENTATIVES

Section 13302 of Pub. L. 101–508 provided that:

"(a) IN GENERAL.—It shall not be in order in the House of Representatives to consider any bill or joint resolution, as reported, or any amendment thereto or conference report thereon, if, upon enactment—

"(1)(A) such legislation under consideration would provide for a net increase in OASDI benefits of at least 0.02 percent of the present value of future taxable payroll for the 75-year period utilized in the most recent annual report of the Board of Trustees provided pursuant to section 201(c)(2) of the Social Security Act [42 U.S.C. 401(c)(2)], and (B) such legislation under consideration does not provide at least a net increase, for such 75-year period, in OASDI taxes of the amount by which the net increase in such benefits exceeds 0.02 percent of the present value of future taxable payroll for such 75-year period,

"(2)(A) such legislation under consideration would provide for a net increase in OASDI benefits (for the 5-year estimating period for such legislation under consideration), (B) such net increase, together with the net increases in OASDI benefits resulting from previous legislation enacted during that fiscal year or any of the previous 4 fiscal years (as estimated at the time of enactment) which are attributable to those portions of the 5-year estimating periods for such previous legislation that fall within the 5-year estimating period for such legislation under consideration, exceeds $250,000,000, and (C) such legislation under consideration does not provide at least a net increase, for the 5-year estimating period for such legislation under consideration, in OASDI taxes which, together with net increases in OASDI taxes resulting from such previous legislation which are attributable to those portions of the 5-year estimating periods for such previous legislation that fall within the 5-year estimating period for such legislation under consideration, equals the amount by which the net increase derived under subparagraph (B) exceeds $250,000,000;

"(3)(A) such legislation under consideration would provide for a net decrease in OASDI taxes of at least 0.02 percent of the present value of future taxable payroll for the 75-year period utilized in the most recent annual report of the Board of Trustees provided pursuant to section 201(c)(2) of the Social Security Act, and (B) such legislation under consideration does not provide at least a net decrease, for such 75-year period, in OASDI benefits of the amount by which the net decrease in such taxes exceeds 0.02 percent of the present value of future taxable payroll for such 75-year period, or

"(4)(A) such legislation under consideration would provide for a net decrease in OASDI taxes (for the 5-year estimating period for such legislation under consideration), (B) such net decrease, together with the net decreases in OASDI taxes resulting from previous legislation enacted during that fiscal year or any of the previous 4 fiscal years (as estimated at the time of enactment) which are attributable to those portions of the 5-year estimating periods for such previous legislation that fall within the 5-year estimating period for such legislation under consideration, exceeds $250,000,000, and (C) such legislation under consideration does not provide at least a net decrease, for the 5-year estimating period for such legislation under consideration, in OASDI benefits which, together with net decreases in OASDI benefits resulting from such previous legislation which are attributable to those portions of the 5-year estimating periods for such previous legislation that fall within the 5-year estimating period for such legislation under consideration, equals the amount by which the net decrease derived under subparagraph (B) exceeds $250,000,000.

"(b) APPLICATION.—In applying paragraph (3) or (4) of subsection (a), any provision of any bill or joint resolution, as reported, or any amendment thereto, or conference report thereon, the effect of which is to provide for a net decrease for any period in taxes described in subsection (c)(2)(A) shall be disregarded if such bill, joint resolution, amendment, or conference report also includes a provision the effect of which is to provide for a net increase of at least an equivalent amount for such period in medicare taxes.

"(c) DEFINITIONS.—For purposes of this subsection:

"(1) The term 'OASDI benefits' means the benefits under the old-age, survivors, and disability insurance programs under title II of the Social Security Act [42 U.S.C. 401 et seq.].

"(2) The term 'OASDI taxes' means—

"(A) the taxes imposed under sections 1401(a), 3101(a), and 3111(a) of the Internal Revenue Code of 1986 [26 U.S.C. 1401(a), 3101(a), 3111(a)], and

"(B) the taxes imposed under chapter 1 of such Code [26 U.S.C. 1 et seq.] (to the extent attributable to section 86 of such Code [26 U.S.C. 86]).

"(3) The term 'medicare taxes' means the taxes imposed under sections 1401(b), 3101(b), and 3111(b) of the Internal Revenue Code of 1986.

"(4) The term 'previous legislation' shall not include legislation enacted before fiscal year 1991.

"(5) The term '5-year estimating period' means, with respect to any legislation, the fiscal year in which such legislation becomes or would become effective and the next 4 fiscal years.

"(6) No provision of any bill or resolution, or any amendment thereto or conference report thereon, involving a change in chapter 1 of the Internal Revenue Code of 1986 shall be treated as affecting the amount of OASDI taxes referred to in paragraph (2)(B) unless such provision changes the income tax treatment of OASDI benefits."

BALANCED FEDERAL BUDGETS; CONGRESSIONAL BUDGET COMMITTEE REPORTS BY APRIL 15, 1979, 1980, AND 1981, OF BALANCED FISCAL YEAR BUDGETS FOR 1981 AND 1982

Pub. L. 96–5, § 5, Apr. 2, 1979, 93 Stat. 8, which provided that Congress shall balance the Federal budget, that the Budget Committees were to report, by April 15, 1979, a fiscal year budget for 1981 that would be in balance, and also a fiscal year budget for 1982 that would be in balance, and by April 15, 1980, a fiscal year budget for 1981 that would be in balance, and by April 15, 1981, a fiscal year budget for 1982 that would be in balance, and that the Budget Committees were to show the consequences of each budget on each budget function and on the economy, setting forth the effects on revenues, spending, employment, inflation, and national security, was repealed by Pub. L. 97–258, § 5(b), Sept. 13, 1982, 96 Stat. 1068.

APPLICATION OF CONGRESSIONAL BUDGET PROCESS TO FISCAL YEAR BEGINNING JULY 1, 1975

Section 906 of Pub. L. 93–344 provided for application of provisions of this subchapter and sections 602(f), 651, and 652 of this title with respect to the fiscal year beginning July 1, 1975, to the extent agreed to by the Committees on the Budget of the House of Representatives and the Senate, prior to repeal by Pub. L. 105–33, title X, § 10120(a), Aug. 5, 1997, 111 Stat. 696.

SECTION REFERRED TO IN OTHER SECTIONS

This section is referred to in sections 622, 633, 635, 636, 641, 655, 907d of this title; title 31 section 1105.

§ 633. Committee allocations

(a) Committee spending allocations

(1) Allocation among committees

The joint explanatory statement accompanying a conference report on a concurrent resolution on the budget shall include an allocation, consistent with the resolution recommended in the conference report, of the levels for the first fiscal year of the resolution, for at least each of the ensuing 4 fiscal years, and a total for that period of fiscal years (except in the case of the Committee on Appropriations only for the fiscal year of that resolution) of—

(A) total new budget authority; and

(B) total outlays;

among each committee of the House of Representatives or the Senate that has jurisdiction over legislation providing or creating such amounts.

(2) No double counting

In the House of Representatives, any item allocated to one committee may not be allocated to another committee.

(3) Further division of amounts

(A) In the Senate

In the Senate, the amount allocated to the Committee on Appropriations shall be further divided among the categories specified in section 900(c)(4) of this title and shall not exceed the limits for each category set forth in section 901(c) of this title.

(B) In the House

In the House of Representatives, the amounts allocated to each committee for each fiscal year, other than the Committee on Appropriations, shall be further divided between amounts provided or required by law on the date of filing of that conference report and amounts not so provided or required. The amounts allocated to the Committee on Appropriations shall be further divided—

(i) between discretionary and mandatory amounts or programs, as appropriate; and

(ii) consistent with the categories specified in section 900(c)(4) of this title.

(4) Amounts not allocated

In the House of Representatives or the Senate, if a committee receives no allocation of new budget authority or outlays, that committee shall be deemed to have received an allocation equal to zero for new budget authority or outlays.

(5) Adjusting allocation of discretionary spending in the House of Representatives

(A) If a concurrent resolution on the budget is not adopted by April 15, the chairman of the Committee on the Budget of the House of Representatives shall submit to the House, as soon as practicable, an allocation under paragraph (1) to the Committee on Appropriations consistent with the discretionary spending levels in the most recently agreed to concurrent resolution on the budget for the appropriate fiscal year covered by that resolution.

(B) As soon as practicable after an allocation under paragraph (1) is submitted under this section, the Committee on Appropriations shall make suballocations and report those suballocations to the House of Representatives.

(b) Suballocations by Appropriations Committees

As soon as practicable after a concurrent resolution on the budget is agreed to, the Committee on Appropriations of each House (after consulting with the Committee on Appropriations of the other House) shall suballocate each amount allocated to it for the budget year under subsection (a) of this section among its subcommittees. Each Committee on Appropriations shall promptly report to its House suballocations made or revised under this subsection. The Committee on Appropriations of the House of Representatives shall further divide among its subcommittees the divisions made under subsection (a)(3)(B) of this section and promptly report those divisions to the House.

(c) Point of order

After the Committee on Appropriations has received an allocation pursuant to subsection (a) of this section for a fiscal year, it shall not be in order in the House of Representatives or the Senate to consider any bill, joint resolution, amendment, motion, or conference report within the jurisdiction of that committee providing new budget authority for that fiscal year, until that committee makes the suballocations required by subsection (b) of this section.

(d) Subsequent concurrent resolutions

In the case of a concurrent resolution on the budget referred to in section 635 of this title, the allocations under subsection (a) of this section and the subdivisions under subsection (b) of this section shall be required only to the extent necessary to take into account revisions made in the most recently agreed to concurrent resolution on the budget.

(e) Alteration of allocations

At any time after a committee reports the allocations required to be made under subsection (b) of this section, such committee may report to its House an alteration of such allocations. Any alteration of such allocations must be consistent with any actions already taken by its House on legislation within the committee's jurisdiction.

(f) Legislation subject to point of order

(1) In the House of Representatives

After the Congress has completed action on a concurrent resolution on the budget for a fiscal year, it shall not be in order in the House of Representatives to consider any bill, joint resolution, or amendment providing new budget authority for any fiscal year, or any conference report on any such bill or joint resolution, if—

(A) the enactment of such bill or resolution as reported;

(B) the adoption and enactment of such amendment; or

(C) the enactment of such bill or resolution in the form recommended in such conference report,

would cause the applicable allocation of new budget authority made under subsection (a) or (b) of this section for the first fiscal year or the total of fiscal years to be exceeded.

(2) In the Senate

After a concurrent resolution on the budget is agreed to, it shall not be in order in the Senate to consider any bill, joint resolution, amendment, motion, or conference report that would cause—

(A) in the case of any committee except the Committee on Appropriations, the appli-

cable allocation of new budget authority or outlays under subsection (a) of this section for the first fiscal year or the total of fiscal years to be exceeded; or

(B) in the case of the Committee on Appropriations, the applicable suballocation of new budget authority or outlays under subsection (b) of this section to be exceeded.

(g) Pay-as-you-go exception in the House

(1) In general

(A) Subsection (f)(1) of this section and, after April 15, section 634(a) of this title shall not apply to any bill or joint resolution, as reported, amendment thereto, or conference report thereon if, for each fiscal year covered by the most recently agreed to concurrent resolution on the budget—

(i) the enactment of that bill or resolution as reported;

(ii) the adoption and enactment of that amendment; or

(iii) the enactment of that bill or resolution in the form recommended in that conference report,

would not increase the deficit, and, if the sum of any revenue increases provided in legislation already enacted during the current session (when added to revenue increases, if any, in excess of any outlay increase provided by the legislation proposed for consideration) is at least as great as the sum of the amount, if any, by which the aggregate level of Federal revenues should be increased as set forth in that concurrent resolution and the amount, if any, by which revenues are to be increased pursuant to pay-as-you-go procedures under section 632(b)(8) of this title, if included in that concurrent resolution.

(B) Section 642(a) of this title, as that section applies to revenues, shall not apply to any bill, joint resolution, amendment thereto, or conference report thereon if, for each fiscal year covered by the most recently agreed to concurrent resolution on the budget—

(i) the enactment of that bill or resolution as reported;

(ii) the adoption and enactment of that amendment; or

(iii) the enactment of that bill or resolution in the form recommended in that conference report,

would not increase the deficit, and, if the sum of any outlay reductions provided in legislation already enacted during the current session (when added to outlay reductions, if any, in excess of any revenue reduction provided by the legislation proposed for consideration) is at least as great as the sum of the amount, if any, by which the aggregate level of Federal outlays should be reduced as required by that concurrent resolution and the amount, if any, by which outlays are to be reduced pursuant to pay-as-you-go procedures under section 632(b)(8) of this title, if included in that concurrent resolution.

(2) Revised allocations

(A) As soon as practicable after Congress agrees to a bill or joint resolution that would have been subject to a point of order under subsection (f)(1) of this section but for the exception provided in paragraph (1)(A) or would have been subject to a point of order under section 642(a) of this title but for the exception provided in paragraph (1)(B), the chairman of the committee[1] on the Budget of the House of Representatives shall file with the House appropriately revised allocations under subsection (a) of this section and revised functional levels and budget aggregates to reflect that bill.

(B) Such revised allocations, functional levels, and budget aggregates shall be considered for the purposes of this Act as allocations, functional levels, and budget aggregates contained in the most recently agreed to concurrent resolution on the budget.

(Pub. L. 93–344, title III, § 302, July 12, 1974, 88 Stat. 308; Pub. L. 99–177, title II, § 201(b), Dec. 12, 1985, 99 Stat. 1044; Pub. L. 101–508, title XIII, §§ 13112(a)(6), (7), 13201(b)(2), (3), 13207(a)(1)(A), (B), (2), 13303(c), Nov. 5, 1990, 104 Stat. 1388–608, 1388–614, 1388–617, 1388–618, 1388–625; Pub. L. 105–33, title X, § 10106, Aug. 5, 1997, 111 Stat. 680.)

REFERENCES IN TEXT

This Act, referred to in subsec. (g)(2)(B), means Pub. L. 93–344, July 12, 1974, 88 Stat. 297, as amended, known as the Congressional Budget and Impoundment Control Act of 1974, which enacted chapters 17, 17A, and 17B and section 190a–3 of this title and sections 11a, 11c, 11d, 1020a of former Title 31, Money and Finance, amended sections 11, 665, 701, 1020, 1151, 1152, 1153, and 1154 of former Title 31, section 105 of Title 1, General Provisions, and sections 190b and 190d of this title, repealed sections 571 and 581c–1 of former Title 31, and sections 66 and 81 of this title, and enacted provisions set out as notes under sections 190a–1, 621, 632, and 682 of this title, section 105 of Title 1, and section 1020 of former Title 31. For complete classification of this Act to the Code, see Short Title note set out under section 621 of this title and Tables.

CODIFICATION

Section was formerly classified to section 1323 of Title 31 prior to the general revision and enactment of Title 31, Money and Finance, by Pub. L. 97–258, § 1, Sept. 13, 1982, 96 Stat. 877.

AMENDMENTS

1997—Subsec. (a). Pub. L. 105–33, § 10106(a), added subsec. (a) and struck out former subsec. (a) which required inclusion of certain allocations to committees of the House of Representatives and of the Senate in the joint explanatory statement accompanying a conference report on a concurrent resolution on the budget.

Subsec. (b). Pub. L. 105–33, § 10106(a), added subsec. (b) and struck out former subsec. (b) which required committees of each House to subdivide among their subcommittees the allocations of budget outlays and new budget authority allocated to them in joint explanatory statement accompanying conference report on concurrent resolution on budget and required further subdivisions of such allocations by subcommittees.

Subsec. (c). Pub. L. 105–33, § 10106(b), reenacted heading without change and amended text generally. Prior to amendment, text read as follows: "It shall not be in order in the House of Representatives or the Senate to consider any bill, joint resolution, amendment, motion, or conference report, providing—

"(1) new budget authority for a fiscal year; or

"(2) new spending authority as described in section 651(c)(2) of this title for a fiscal year;

within the jurisdiction of any committee which has received an appropriate allocation of such authority pursuant to subsection (a) of this section for such fiscal year, unless and until such committee makes the allocation or subdivisions required by subsection (b) of this section, in connection with the most recently agreed to concurrent resolution on the budget for such fiscal year."

Subsec. (f)(1). Pub. L. 105–33, § 10106(c)(1), substituted "providing new budget authority for any fiscal year" for "providing new budget authority for such fiscal year or new entitlement authority effective during such fiscal year" in introductory provisions and "applicable allocation of new budget authority made under subsection (a) or (b) of this section for the first fiscal year or the total of fiscal years to be exceeded." for "appropriate allocation made pursuant to subsection (b) of this section for such fiscal year of new discretionary budget authority or new entitlement authority to be exceeded." in concluding provisions.

Subsec. (f)(2). Pub. L. 105–33, § 10106(c)(2), reenacted heading without change and amended text generally. Prior to amendment, text provided that consideration in the Senate was not in order for certain bills, joint resolutions, amendments, motions, or conference reports that provided for budget outlays, new budget authority, or new spending authority in excess of certain allocations.

Subsec. (g). Pub. L. 105–33, § 10106(d), amended heading and text of subsec. (g) generally. Prior to amendment, text read as follows: "For purposes of this section, the levels of new budget authority, spending authority as described in section 651(c)(2) of this title, outlays, and new credit authority for a fiscal year shall be determined on the basis of estimates made by the Committee on the Budget of the House of Representatives or the Senate, as the case may be."

1990—Subsec. (a)(1). Pub. L. 101–508, § 13201(b)(3)(A), substituted "and total entitlement authority" for "total entitlement authority, and total credit authority", "or such entitlement authority" for "such entitlement authority, or such credit authority", and "and entitlement authority" for "entitlement authority, and credit authority".

Subsec. (a)(2). Pub. L. 101–508, § 13303(c)(1), inserted "social security outlays for the fiscal year of the resolution and for each of the 4 succeeding fiscal years," after "appropriate levels of".

Pub. L. 101–508, § 13201(b)(3)(B), substituted "total budget outlays and total new budget authority" for "total budget outlays, total new budget authority and new credit authority".

Pub. L. 101–508, § 13112(a)(6), struck out "the House of Representatives and" after "among each committee of".

Subsec. (b)(1)(A). Pub. L. 101–508, § 13201(b)(3)(C), substituted "budget outlays and new budget authority" for "budget outlays, new budget authority, and new credit authority".

Subsec. (c). Pub. L. 101–508, § 13207(a)(1)(A), substituted "bill, joint resolution, amendment, motion, or conference report" for "bill or resolution, or amendment thereto".

Subsec. (c)(3). Pub. L. 101–508, § 13201(b)(3)(D), struck out par. (3) which read as follows: "new credit authority for a fiscal year;".

Subsec. (f)(1). Pub. L. 101–508, § 13207(a)(1)(B), inserted "joint" before "resolution" the second and third places appearing in introductory provisions.

Pub. L. 101–508, § 13201(b)(3)(E), substituted "year or new entitlement authority effective during such fiscal year," for "year, new entitlement authority effective during such fiscal year, or new credit authority for such fiscal year," in introductory provisions and "authority or new entitlement authority" for "authority, new entitlement authority, or new credit authority" in closing provisions.

Subsec. (f)(2). Pub. L. 101–508, § 13303(c)(3), inserted three sentences at end beginning with "In applying this paragraph—".

---

[1] So in original. Probably should be capitalized.

Pub. L. 101–508, § 13303(c)(2), which directed the insertion of "or provides for social security outlays in excess of the appropriate allocation of social security outlays under subsection (a) of this section for the fiscal year of the resolution or for the total of that year and the 4 succeeding fiscal years" before the period, was executed by making the insertion before the period at end of first sentence, as the probable intent of Congress, in view of the applicability of the amendment. See Effective and Termination Dates of 1990 Amendment note below.

Pub. L. 101–508, § 13207(a)(2), substituted "outlays, new budget authority, or new spending authority (as defined in section 651(c)(2) of this title)" for "outlays or new budget authority".

Pub. L. 101–508, § 13207(a)(1)(B), substituted "bill, joint resolution, amendment, motion, or conference report" for "bill or resolution (including a conference report thereon), or any amendment to a bill or resolution".

Pub. L. 101–508, § 13201(b)(2), temporarily inserted "or new credit authority" after "new budget authority". See Effective and Termination Dates of 1990 Amendment note below.

Pub. L. 101–508, § 13112(a)(7), inserted "(A)" after "in excess of", substituted "under subsection (a) of this section, or (B) the appropriate allocation (if any) of such outlays or authority reported under subsection (b) of this section" for "under subsection (b) of this section", and inserted after first sentence "Subparagraph (A) shall not apply to any bill, resolution, amendment, motion, or conference report that is within the jurisdiction of the Committee on Appropriations."

1985—Pub. L. 99–177 substituted "Committee allocations" for "Matters to be included in joint statement of managers; reports by committees" in section catchline.

Subsec. (a). Pub. L. 99–177 amended subsec. (a) generally, providing for separate provisions relating to allocations of totals for the House of Representatives and for the Senate, with respect to the joint explanatory statement accompanying the conference report on a concurrent resolution on the budget.

Subsec. (b). Pub. L. 99–177 amended subsec. (b) generally, inserting applicability to new credit authority.

Subsec. (c). Pub. L. 99–177 amended subsec. (c) generally, substituting provisions relating to point of order for provisions relating to subsequent concurrent resolutions.

Subsecs. (d) to (g). Pub. L. 99–177, in amending section generally, added subsecs. (d) to (g).

EFFECTIVE AND TERMINATION DATES OF 1990 AMENDMENT

Section 13201(b)(2) of Pub. L. 101–508 provided that the amendment made by that section is effective Jan. 1, 1991, for fiscal year 1991 only.

Section 13201(b)(3) of Pub. L. 101–508 provided that the amendment made by that section is effective for fiscal years beginning after Sept. 30, 1991.

Amendment by section 13303(c) of Pub. L. 101–508 applicable with respect to fiscal years beginning on or after Oct. 1, 1990, see section 13306 of Pub. L. 101–508, set out as an Effective Date of 1990 Amendment note under section 632 of this title.

EFFECTIVE DATE OF 1985 AMENDMENT

Amendment by Pub. L. 99–177 effective Dec. 12, 1985, and applicable with respect to fiscal years beginning after Sept. 30, 1985, except that such amendment, insofar as it relates to subsecs. (c), (f), and (g) of this section, to become effective Apr. 15, 1986, see section 275(a)(1), (2)(A) of Pub. L. 99–177, set out as an Effective and Termination Dates note under section 900 of this title.

SECTION REFERRED TO IN OTHER SECTIONS

This section is referred to in sections 632, 634, 639, 641, 642, 645, 651, 907a, 907c of this title.

§ 634. Concurrent resolution on the budget must be adopted before budget-related legislation is considered

(a) In general

Until the concurrent resolution on the budget for a fiscal year has been agreed to, it shall not be in order in the House of Representatives, with respect to the first fiscal year covered by that resolution, or the Senate, with respect to any fiscal year covered by that resolution, to consider any bill or joint resolution, amendment or motion thereto, or conference report thereon that—

(1) first provides new budget authority for that fiscal year;

(2) first provides an increase or decrease in revenues during that fiscal year;

(3) provides an increase or decrease in the public debt limit to become effective during that fiscal year;

(4) in the Senate only, first provides new entitlement authority for that fiscal year; or

(5) in the Senate only, first provides for an increase or decrease in outlays for that fiscal year.

(b) Exceptions in House

In the House of Representatives, subsection (a) of this section does not apply—

(1)(A) to any bill or joint resolution, as reported, providing advance discretionary new budget authority that first becomes available for the first or second fiscal year after the budget year; or

(B) to any bill or joint resolution, as reported, first increasing or decreasing revenues in a fiscal year following the fiscal year to which the concurrent resolution applies;

(2) after May 15, to any general appropriation bill or amendment thereto; or

(3) to any bill or joint resolution unless it is reported by a committee.

(c) Application to appropriation measures in Senate

(1) In general

Until the concurrent resolution on the budget for a fiscal year has been agreed to and an allocation has been made to the Committee on Appropriations of the Senate under section 633(a) of this title for that year, it shall not be in order in the Senate to consider any appropriation bill or joint resolution, amendment or motion thereto, or conference report thereon for that year or any subsequent year.

(2) Exception

Paragraph (1) does not apply to appropriations legislation making advance appropriations for the first or second fiscal year after the year the allocation referred to in that paragraph is made.

(Pub. L. 93–344, title III, § 303, July 12, 1974, 88 Stat. 309; Pub. L. 99–177, title II, § 201(b), Dec. 12, 1985, 99 Stat. 1046; Pub. L. 101–508, title XIII, §§ 13205, 13207(a)(1)(C), Nov. 5, 1990, 104 Stat. 1388–616, 1388–617; Pub. L. 105–33, title X, § 10107(a), Aug. 5, 1997, 111 Stat. 683.)

CODIFICATION

Section was formerly classified to section 1324 of Title 31 prior to the general revision and enactment of

Title 31, Money and Finance, by Pub. L. 97–258, §1, Sept. 13, 1982, 96 Stat. 877.

AMENDMENTS

1997—Pub. L. 105–33 amended section catchline and text generally. Prior to amendment, text provided that concurrent resolution on the budget must be adopted before legislation providing new budget authority, new spending authority, new credit authority, or changes in revenues or public debt limit could be considered.

1990—Subsec. (a). Pub. L. 101–508, §13207(a)(1)(C), substituted "bill, joint resolution, amendment, motion, or conference report" for "bill or resolution (or amendment thereto)".

Pub. L. 101–508, §13205(a)(4), inserted "(or, in the Senate, a concurrent resolution on the budget covering such fiscal year)" after "fiscal year" in closing provisions.

Subsec. (a)(5), (6). Pub. L. 101–508, §13205(a)(1)–(3), added pars. (5) and (6) and struck out former par. (5) which read as follows: "new credit authority for a fiscal year,".

Subsec. (b). Pub. L. 101–508, §13205(b), designated existing provisions as par. (1) and substituted "In the House of Representatives, subsection (a)" for "Subsection (a)", redesignated former pars. (1) and (2) as subpars. (A) and (B), respectively, and added par. (2).

1985—Pub. L. 99–177 inserted reference to new credit authority in section catchline.

Subsec. (a). Pub. L. 99–177 amended subsec. (a) generally, substituting provisions respecting new entitlement authority or new credit authority, for provisions respecting new spending authority.

Subsec. (b). Pub. L. 99–177 amended subsec. (b) generally, inserting provisions relating to applicability of subsec. (a) after May 15 of any calendar year.

Subsec. (c). Pub. L. 99–177 amended subsec. (c) generally, inserting references to amendments of bills or resolutions wherever appearing.

EFFECTIVE DATE OF 1985 AMENDMENT

Amendment by Pub. L. 99–177 effective Dec. 12, 1985, and applicable with respect to fiscal years beginning after Sept. 30, 1985, see section 275(a)(1) of Pub. L. 99–177, set out as an Effective and Termination Dates note under section 900 of this title.

SECTION REFERRED TO IN OTHER SECTIONS

This section is referred to in sections 633, 907c of this title.

§ 635. Permissible revisions of concurrent resolutions on the budget

At any time after the concurrent resolution on the budget for a fiscal year has been agreed to pursuant to section 632 of this title, and before the end of such fiscal year, the two Houses may adopt a concurrent resolution on the budget which revises or reaffirms the concurrent resolution on the budget for such fiscal year most recently agreed to.

(Pub. L. 93–344, title III, §304, July 12, 1974, 88 Stat. 310; Pub. L. 99–177, title II, §201(b), Dec. 12, 1985, 99 Stat. 1047; Pub. L. 100–119, title II, §208(b), Sept. 29, 1987, 101 Stat. 786; Pub. L. 101–508, title XIII, §13112(a)(8), Nov. 5, 1990, 104 Stat. 1388–608; Pub. L. 105–33, title X, §10108, Aug. 5, 1997, 111 Stat. 684.)

CODIFICATION

Section was formerly classified to section 1325 of Title 31 prior to the general revision and enactment of Title 31, Money and Finance, by Pub. L. 97–258, §1, Sept. 13, 1982, 96 Stat. 877.

AMENDMENTS

1997—Pub. L. 105–33 designated subsec. (a) as entire section and struck out subsec. (a) heading "In general"

and subsec. (b) heading and text. Prior to amendment, text of subsec. (b) read as follows: "The provisions of section 632(g) of this title shall apply with respect to concurrent resolutions on the budget under this section (and amendments thereto and conference reports thereon) in the same way they apply to concurrent resolutions on the budget under such section 632(g) of this title (and amendments thereto and conference reports thereon)."

1990—Subsecs. (b), (c). Pub. L. 101–508 redesignated subsec. (c) as (b) and struck out former subsec. (b) which read as follows: "The provisions of section 632(i) of this title shall apply with respect to concurrent resolutions on the budget under this section (and amendments thereto and conference reports thereon) in the same way they apply to concurrent resolutions on the budget under such section 632(i) of this title (and amendments thereto and conference reports thereon)."

1987—Subsec. (c). Pub. L. 100–119 added subsec. (c).

1985—Pub. L. 99–177, in amending section generally, inserted "Permissible" before "revisions" in section catchline, designated existing provisions as subsec. (a), struck out "first" after "after the", and added subsec. (b).

EFFECTIVE DATE OF 1985 AMENDMENT

Amendment by Pub. L. 99–177 effective Dec. 12, 1985, and applicable with respect to fiscal years beginning after Sept. 30, 1985, see section 275(a)(1) of Pub. L. 99–177, set out as an Effective and Termination Dates note under section 900 of this title.

SECTION REFERRED TO IN OTHER SECTIONS

This section is referred to in sections 622, 633, 636, 641, 655 of this title.

§ 636. Provisions relating to consideration of concurrent resolutions on the budget

(a) Procedure in House after report of Committee; debate

(1) When a concurrent resolution on the budget has been reported by the Committee on the Budget of the House of Representatives and has been referred to the appropriate calendar of the House, it shall be in order on any day thereafter, subject to clause 2(*l*)(6) of rule XI[1] of the Rules of the House of Representatives, to move to proceed to the consideration of the concurrent resolution. The motion is highly privileged and is not debatable. An amendment to the motion is not in order and it is not in order to move to reconsider the vote by which the motion is agreed to or disagreed to.

(2) General debate on any concurrent resolution on the budget in the House of Representatives shall be limited to not more than 10 hours, which shall be divided equally between the majority and minority parties, plus such additional hours of debate as are consumed pursuant to paragraph (3). A motion further to limit debate is not debatable. A motion to recommit the concurrent resolution is not in order, and it is not in order to move to reconsider the vote by which the concurrent resolution is agreed to or disagreed to.

(3) Following the presentation of opening statements on the concurrent resolution on the budget for a fiscal year by the chairman and ranking minority member of the Committee on the Budget of the House, there shall be a period of up to four hours for debate on economic goals and policies.

---

[1] See References in Text note below.

(4) Only if a concurrent resolution on the budget reported by the Committee on the Budget of the House sets forth the economic goals (as described in sections 1022(a)(2) and 1022a(b) of title 15) which the estimates, amounts, and levels (as described in section 632(a) of this title) set forth in such resolution are designed to achieve, shall it be in order to offer to such resolution an amendment relating to such goals, and such amendment shall be in order only if it also proposes to alter such estimates, amounts, and levels in germane fashion in order to be consistent with the goals proposed in such amendment.

(5) Consideration of any concurrent resolution on the budget by the House of Representatives shall be in the Committee of the Whole, and the resolution shall be considered for amendment under the five-minute rule in accordance with the applicable provisions of rule XXIII[2] of the Rules of the House of Representatives. After the Committee rises and reports the resolution back to the House, the previous question shall be considered as ordered on the resolution and any amendments thereto to final passage without intervening motion; except that it shall be in order at any time prior to final passage (notwithstanding any other rule or provision of law) to adopt an amendment (or a series of amendments) changing any figure or figures in the resolution as so reported to the extent necessary to achieve mathematical consistency.

(6) Debate in the House of Representatives on the conference report on any concurrent resolution on the budget shall be limited to not more than 5 hours, which shall be divided equally between the majority and minority parties. A motion further to limit debate is not debatable. A motion to recommit the conference report is not in order, and it is not in order to move to reconsider the vote by which the conference report is agreed to or disagreed to.

(7) Appeals from decisions of the Chair relating to the application of the Rules of the House of Representatives to the procedure relating to any concurrent resolution on the budget shall be decided without debate.

(b) Procedure in Senate after report of Committee; debate; amendments

(1) Debate in the Senate on any concurrent resolution on the budget, and all amendments thereto and debatable motions and appeals in connection therewith, shall be limited to not more than 50 hours, except that with respect to any concurrent resolution referred to in section 635(a)[2] of this title all such debate shall be limited to not more than 15 hours. The time shall be equally divided between, and controlled by, the majority leader and the minority leader or their designees.

(2) Debate in the Senate on any amendment to a concurrent resolution on the budget shall be limited to 2 hours, to be equally divided between, and controlled by, the mover and the manager of the concurrent resolution, and debate on any amendment to an amendment, debatable motion, or appeal shall be limited to 1 hour, to be equally divided between, and controlled by, the mover and the manager of the concurrent resolution, except that in the event the manager of the concurrent resolution is in favor of any such amendment, motion, or appeal, the time in opposition thereto shall be controlled by the minority leader or his designee. No amendment that is not germane to the provisions of such concurrent resolution shall be received. Such leaders, or either of them, may, from the time under their control on the passage of the concurrent resolution, allot additional time to any Senator during the consideration of any amendment, debatable motion, or appeal.

(3) Following the presentation of opening statements on the concurrent resolution on the budget for a fiscal year by the chairman and ranking minority member of the Committee on the Budget of the Senate, there shall be a period of up to four hours for debate on economic goals and policies.

(4) Subject to the other limitations of this Act, only if a concurrent resolution on the budget reported by the Committee on the Budget of the Senate sets forth the economic goals (as described in sections 1022(a)(2) and 1022a(b) of title 15) which the estimates, amounts, and levels (as described in section 632(a) of this title) set forth in such resolution are designed to achieve, shall it be in order to offer to such resolution an amendment relating to such goals, and such amendment shall be in order only if it also proposes to alter such estimates, amounts, and levels in germane fashion in order to be consistent with the goals proposed in such amendment.

(5) A motion to further limit debate is not debatable. A motion to recommit (except a motion to recommit with instructions to report back within a specified number of days, not to exceed 3, not counting any day on which the Senate is not in session) is not in order. Debate on any such motion to recommit shall be limited to 1 hour, to be equally divided between, and controlled by, the mover and the manager of the concurrent resolution.

(6) Notwithstanding any other rule, an amendment or series of amendments to a concurrent resolution on the budget proposed in the Senate shall always be in order if such amendment or series of amendments proposes to change any figure or figures then contained in such concurrent resolution so as to make such concurrent resolution mathematically consistent or so as to maintain such consistency.

(c) Action on conference reports in Senate

(1) A motion to proceed to the consideration of the conference report on any concurrent resolution on the budget (or a reconciliation bill or resolution) may be made even though a previous motion to the same effect has been disagreed to.

(2) During the consideration in the Senate of the conference report (or a message between Houses) on any concurrent resolution on the budget, and all amendments in disagreement, and all amendments thereto, and debatable motions and appeals in connection therewith, debate shall be limited to 10 hours, to be equally divided between, and controlled by, the majority leader and minority leader or their designees. Debate on any debatable motion or appeal related to the conference report (or a message be-

----

[2] See References in Text note below.

tween Houses) shall be limited to 1 hour, to be equally divided between, and controlled by, the mover and the manager of the conference report (or a message between Houses).

(3) Should the conference report be defeated, debate on any request for a new conference and the appointment of conferees shall be limited to 1 hour, to be equally divided between, and controlled by, the manager of the conference report and the minority leader or his designee, and should any motion be made to instruct the conferees before the conferees are named, debate on such motion shall be limited to one-half hour, to be equally divided between, and controlled by, the mover and the manager of the conference report. Debate on any amendment to any such instructions shall be limited to 20 minutes, to be equally divided between and controlled by the mover and the manager of the conference report. In all cases when the manager of the conference report is in favor of any motion, appeal, or amendment, the time in opposition shall be under the control of the minority leader or his designee.

(4) In any case in which there are amendments in disagreement, time on each amendment shall be limited to 30 minutes, to be equally divided between, and controlled by, the manager of the conference report and the minority leader or his designee. No amendment that is not germane to the provisions of such amendments shall be received.

(d) Concurrent resolution must be consistent in Senate

It shall not be in order in the Senate to vote on the question of agreeing to—

(1) a concurrent resolution on the budget unless the figures then contained in such resolution are mathematically consistent; or

(2) a conference report on a concurrent resolution on the budget unless the figures contained in such resolution, as recommended in such conference report, are mathematically consistent.

(Pub. L. 93–344, title III, §305, July 12, 1974, 88 Stat. 310; Pub. L. 95–523, title III, §303(b), (c), Oct. 27, 1978, 92 Stat. 1905, 1906; Pub. L. 99–177, title II, §201(b), Dec. 12, 1985, 99 Stat. 1047; Pub. L. 100–119, title II, §209, Sept. 29, 1987, 101 Stat. 787; Pub. L. 100–203, title VIII, §8003(d), Dec. 22, 1987, 101 Stat. 1330–282; Pub. L. 101–508, title XIII, §§13209, 13210(1), Nov. 5, 1990, 104 Stat. 1388–619, 1388–620; Pub. L. 105–33, title X, §10109(a), Aug. 5, 1997, 111 Stat. 684.)

REFERENCES IN TEXT

The Rules of the House of Representatives for the One Hundred Sixth Congress were adopted and amended generally by House Resolution No. 5, One Hundred Sixth Congress, Jan. 6, 1999. Provisions formerly appearing in clause 2(*l*)(6) of rule XI, referred to in subsec. (a)(1), are now contained in clause 4 of rule XIII. Provisions formerly appearing in rule XXIII, referred to in subsec. (a)(5), are now contained in rule XVIII.

Section 635(a) of this title, referred to in subsec. (b)(1), was redesignated section 635 of this title by Pub. L. 105–33, title X, §10108(1), Aug. 5, 1997, 111 Stat. 684.

This Act, referred to in subsec. (b)(4), means Pub. L. 93–344, July 12, 1974, 88 Stat. 297, as amended, known as the Congressional Budget and Impoundment Control Act of 1974, which enacted chapters 17, 17A and 17B, and section 190a–3 of this title and sections 11a, 11c, 11d,

1020a of former Title 31, Money and Finance, amended sections 11, 665, 701, 1020, 1151, 1152, 1153, and 1154 of former Title 31, section 105 of Title 1, General Provisions, sections 190b and 190d of this title, repealed sections 571 and 581c–1 of former Title 31 and sections 66 and 81 of this title, and enacted provisions set out as notes under sections 190a–1, 621, 632, and 682 of this title, section 105 of Title 1, and section 1020 of former Title 31. For complete classification of this Act to the Code, see Short Title note set out under section 621 of this title and Tables.

CODIFICATION

Section was formerly classified to section 1326 of Title 31 prior to the general revision and enactment of Title 31, Money and Finance, by Pub. L. 97–258, §1, Sept. 13, 1982, 96 Stat. 877.

AMENDMENTS

1997—Subsec. (a)(1). Pub. L. 105–33 amended par. (1) generally. Prior to amendment, par. (1) read as follows: "When the Committee on the Budget of the House of Representatives has reported any concurrent resolution on the budget, it is in order at any time after the fifth day (excluding Saturdays, Sundays, and legal holidays) following the day on which the report upon such resolution by the Committee on the Budget has been available to Members of the House and, if applicable, after the first day (excluding Saturdays, Sundays, and legal holidays) following the day on which a report upon such resolution by the Committee on Rules pursuant to section 632(c) of this title has been available to Members of the House (even though a previous motion to the same effect has been disagreed to) to move to proceed to the consideration of the concurrent resolution. The motion is highly privileged and is not debatable. An amendment to the motion is not in order, and it is not in order to move to reconsider the vote by which the motion is agreed to or disagreed to."

1990—Subsec. (c)(1). Pub. L. 101–508, §13209(1), struck out at beginning "The conference report on any concurrent resolution on the budget shall be in order in the Senate at any time after the third day (excluding Saturdays, Sundays, and legal holidays) following the day on which such conference report is reported and is available to Members of the Senate." and inserted "on any concurrent resolution on the budget (or a reconciliation bill or resolution)" after "consideration of the conference report".

Subsec. (c)(2). Pub. L. 101–508, §13209(2), inserted "(or a message between Houses)" after "conference report" wherever appearing.

Subsecs. (d), (e). Pub. L. 101–508, §13210(1), redesignated subsec. (e) as (d) and struck out former subsec. (d) which read as follows: "If at the end of 7 days (excluding Saturdays, Sundays, and legal holidays) after the conferees of both Houses have been appointed to a committee of conference on a concurrent resolution on the budget, the conferees are unable to reach agreement with respect to all matters in disagreement between the two Houses, then the conferees shall submit to their respective Houses, on the first day thereafter on which their House is in session—

"(1) a conference report recommending those matters on which they have agreed and reporting in disagreement those matters on which they have not agreed; or

"(2) a conference report in disagreement, if the matter in disagreement is an amendment which strikes out the entire text of the concurrent resolution and inserts a substitute text."

1987—Subsec. (c)(2). Pub. L. 100–203, §8003(d), inserted a comma after "therewith".

Pub. L. 100–119 inserted "and all amendments in disagreement, and all amendments thereto, and debatable motions and appeals in connection therewith" after "budget,".

1985—Subsec. (a). Pub. L. 99–177, in amending subsec. (a) generally, in par. (1) inserted provisions relating to applicability of report after first day and substituted "fifth day" for "tenth day", in par. (3) struck out "first" before "concurrent", in par. (5) substituted "considered for" for "read for", struck out par. (7) relating to motions to postpone, and redesignated par. (8) as (7).

Subsec. (b). Pub. L. 99–177, in amending subsec. (b) generally, in par. (1) substituted "any concurrent" for "the second required concurrent" and "635(a)" for "641(a)", in par. (3) struck out "first" before "concurrent", and in par. (4) inserted provisions relating to applicability of other limitations of this Act.

Subsecs. (c) to (e). Pub. L. 99–177, in amending section generally, reenacted subsecs. (c) to (e) without change.

1978—Subsec. (a). Pub. L. 95–523, § 303(b), inserted in par. (2) ", plus such additional hours of debate as are consumed pursuant to paragraph (3)" after "and minority parties", added pars. (3) and (4) and redesignated existing pars. (3) to (6) as (6) to (9), respectively. Existing pars. (3) to (6) were renumbered (5) to (8), respectively, as the probable intent of Congress, notwithstanding the language of section 303(b)(2) of Pub. L. 95–523 directing that existing pars. (3) to (6) be redesignated (6) to (9), respectively.

Subsec. (b). Pub. L. 95–523, § 303(c), added pars. (3) and (4) and redesignated existing pars. (3) and (4) as (6) and (7), respectively. Existing pars. (3) and (4) were renumbered (5) and (6), respectively, as the probable intent of Congress, notwithstanding the language of section 303(c)(1) of Pub. L. 95–523 directing that existing pars. (3) and (4) be redesignated (6) and (7), respectively.

EFFECTIVE DATE OF 1985 AMENDMENT

Amendment by Pub. L. 99–177 effective Dec. 12, 1985, and applicable with respect to fiscal years beginning after Sept. 30, 1985, see section 275(a)(1) of Pub. L. 99–177, set out as an Effective and Termination Dates note under section 900 of this title.

SECTION REFERRED TO IN OTHER SECTIONS

This section is referred to in sections 641, 907d of this title.

§ 637. Legislation dealing with Congressional budget must be handled by Budget Committees

No bill, resolution, amendment, motion, or conference report, dealing with any matter which is within the jurisdiction of the Committee on the Budget of either House shall be considered in that House unless it is a bill or resolution which has been reported by the Committee on the Budget of that House (or from the consideration of which such committee has been discharged) or unless it is an amendment to such a bill or resolution.

(Pub. L. 93–344, title III, § 306, July 12, 1974, 88 Stat. 313; Pub. L. 99–177, title II, § 201(b), Dec. 12, 1985, 99 Stat. 1050; Pub. L. 101–508, title XIII, § 13207(a)(1)(D), Nov. 5, 1990, 104 Stat. 1388–617.)

CODIFICATION

Section was formerly classified to section 1327 of Title 31 prior to the general revision and enactment of Title 31, Money and Finance, by Pub. L. 97–258, § 1, Sept. 13, 1982, 96 Stat. 877.

AMENDMENTS

1990—Pub. L. 101–508 substituted "bill, resolution, amendment, motion, or conference report" for "bill or resolution, and no amendment to any bill or resolution".

1985—Pub. L. 99–177 reenacted section without change.

EFFECTIVE DATE OF 1985 AMENDMENT

Amendment by Pub. L. 99–177 effective Dec. 12, 1985, and applicable with respect to fiscal years beginning

after Sept. 30, 1985, see section 275(a)(1) of Pub. L. 99–177, set out as an Effective and Termination Dates note under section 900 of this title.

SECTION REFERRED TO IN OTHER SECTIONS

This section is referred to in section 907c of this title.

§ 638. House committee action on all appropriation bills to be completed by June 10

On or before June 10 of each year, the Committee on Appropriations of the House of Representatives shall report annual appropriation bills providing new budget authority under the jurisdiction of all of its subcommittees for the fiscal year which begins on October 1 of that year.

(Pub. L. 93–344, title III, § 307, July 12, 1974, 88 Stat. 313; Pub. L. 99–177, title II, § 201(b), Dec. 12, 1985, 99 Stat. 1051.)

CODIFICATION

Section was formerly classified to section 1328 of Title 31 prior to the general revision and enactment of Title 31, Money and Finance, by Pub. L. 97–258, § 1, Sept. 13, 1982, 96 Stat. 877.

AMENDMENTS

1985—Pub. L. 99–177 substituted "by June 10" for "before first appropriation bill is reported" in section catchline, and amended section generally. Prior to amendment, section read as follows: "Prior to reporting the first regular appropriation bill for each fiscal year, the Committee on Appropriations of the House of Representatives shall, to the extent practicable, complete subcommittee markup and full committee action on all regular appropriation bills for that year and submit to the House a summary report comparing the committee's recommendations with the appropriate levels of budget outlays and new budget authority as set forth in the most recently agreed to concurrent resolution on the budget for that year."

EFFECTIVE DATE OF 1985 AMENDMENT

Amendment by Pub. L. 99–177 effective Dec. 12, 1985, and applicable with respect to fiscal years beginning after Sept. 30, 1985, see section 275(a)(1) of Pub. L. 99–177, set out as an Effective and Termination Dates note under section 900 of this title.

§ 639. Reports, summaries, and projections of Congressional budget actions

(a) Reports on legislation providing new budget authority or providing increase or decrease in revenues or tax expenditures

(1) Whenever a committee of either House reports to its House a bill or joint resolution, or committee amendment thereto, providing new budget authority (other than continuing appropriations) or providing an increase or decrease in revenues or tax expenditures for a fiscal year (or fiscal years), the report accompanying that bill or joint resolution shall contain a statement, or the committee shall make available such a statement in the case of an approved committee amendment which is not reported to its House, prepared after consultation with the Director of the Congressional Budget Office—

(A) comparing the levels in such measure to the appropriate allocations in the reports submitted under section 633(b) of this title for the most recently agreed to concurrent resolution on the budget for such fiscal year (or fiscal years);

(B) containing a projection by the Congressional Budget Office of how such measure will affect the levels of such budget authority, budget outlays, revenues, or tax expenditures under existing law for such fiscal year (or fiscal years) and each of the four ensuing fiscal years, if timely submitted before such report is filed; and

(C) containing an estimate by the Congressional Budget Office of the level of new budget authority for assistance to State and local governments provided by such measure, if timely submitted before such report is filed.

(2) Whenever a conference report is filed in either House and such conference report or any amendment reported in disagreement or any amendment contained in the joint statement of managers to be proposed by the conferees in the case of technical disagreement on such bill or joint resolution provides new budget authority (other than continuing appropriations) or provides an increase or decrease in revenues for a fiscal year (or fiscal years), the statement of managers accompanying such conference report shall contain the information described in paragraph (1), if available on a timely basis. If such information is not available when the conference report is filed, the committee shall make such information available to Members as soon as practicable prior to the consideration of such conference report.

(b) Up-to-date tabulations of Congressional budget action

(1) The Director of the Congressional Budget Office shall issue to the committees of the House of Representatives and the Senate reports on at least a monthly basis detailing and tabulating the progress of congressional action on bills and joint resolutions providing new budget authority or providing an increase or decrease in revenues or tax expenditures for each fiscal year covered by a concurrent resolution on the budget. Such reports shall include but are not limited to an up-to-date tabulation comparing the appropriate aggregate and functional levels (including outlays) included in the most recently adopted concurrent resolution on the budget with the levels provided in bills and joint resolutions reported by committees or adopted by either House or by the Congress, and with the levels provided by law for the fiscal year preceding the first fiscal year covered by the appropriate concurrent resolution.

(2) The Committee on the Budget of each House shall make available to Members of its House summary budget scorekeeping reports. Such reports—

(A) shall be made available on at least a monthly basis, but in any case frequently enough to provide Members of each House an accurate representation of the current status of congressional consideration of the budget;

(B) shall include, but are not limited to, summaries of tabulations provided under subsection (b)(1) of this section; and

(C) shall be based on information provided under subsection (b)(1) of this section without substantive revision.

The chairman of the Committee on the Budget of the House of Representatives shall submit such reports to the Speaker.

(c) Five-year projection of Congressional budget action

As soon as practicable after the beginning of each fiscal year, the Director of the Congressional Budget Office shall issue a report projecting for the period of 5 fiscal years beginning with such fiscal year—

(1) total new budget authority and total budget outlays for each fiscal year in such period;

(2) revenues to be received and the major sources thereof, and the surplus or deficit, if any, for each fiscal year in such period;

(3) tax expenditures for each fiscal year in such period; and

(4) entitlement authority for each fiscal year in such period.

(Pub. L. 93–344, title III, §308, July 12, 1974, 88 Stat. 313; Pub. L. 99–177, title II, §201(b), Dec. 12, 1985, 99 Stat. 1051; Pub. L. 101–508, title XIII, §13206, Nov. 5, 1990, 104 Stat. 1388–617; Pub. L. 105–33, title X, §10110, Aug. 5, 1997, 111 Stat. 685.)

CODIFICATION

Section was formerly classified to section 1329 of Title 31 prior to the general revision and enactment of Title 31, Money and Finance, by Pub. L. 97–258, §1, Sept. 13, 1982, 96 Stat. 877.

AMENDMENTS

1997—Subsec. (a). Pub. L. 105–33, §10110(1)(A), struck out ", new spending authority, or new credit authority," after "new budget authority" in heading.

Subsec. (a)(1). Pub. L. 105–33, §10110(4), in introductory provisions, substituted "bill or joint resolution" for "bill or resolution" in two places.

Pub. L. 105–33, §10110(1)(D), in introductory provisions, struck out ", new spending authority described in section 651(c)(2) of this title, or new credit authority," after "continuing appropriations)".

Subsec. (a)(1)(B). Pub. L. 105–33, §10110(1)(C), substituted "revenues, or tax expenditures" for "spending authority, revenues, tax expenditures, direct loan obligations, or primary loan guarantee commitments".

Pub. L. 105–33, §10110(1)(B), redesignated subpar. (C) as (B) and struck out former subpar. (B) which read as follows: "including an identification of any new spending authority described in section 651(c)(2) of this title which is contained in such measure and a justification for the use of such financing method instead of annual appropriations;".

Subsec. (a)(1)(C), (D). Pub. L. 105–33, §10110(1)(B), redesignated subpars. (C) and (D) as (B) and (C), respectively.

Subsec. (a)(2). Pub. L. 105–33, §10110(4), substituted "bill or joint resolution" for "bill or resolution".

Pub. L. 105–33, §10110(1)(D), struck out ", new spending authority described in section 651(c)(2) of this title, or new credit authority," after "continuing appropriations)".

Subsec. (b)(1). Pub. L. 105–33, §10110(4), substituted "bills and joint resolutions" for "bills and resolutions" in two places.

Pub. L. 105–33, §10110(2), struck out ", new spending authority described in section 651(c)(2) of this title, or new credit authority," after "new budget authority".

Subsec. (c)(3) to (5). Pub. L. 105–33, §10110(3), inserted "and" at end of par. (3), substituted a period for "; and" at end of par. (4), and struck out par. (5) which read as follows: "credit authority for each fiscal year in such period."

1990—Subsec. (a)(1). Pub. L. 101–508, §13206(a)(1), inserted "(or fiscal years)" after "fiscal year" in introductory provisions and in subpars. (A) and (C).

Subsec. (a)(2). Pub. L. 101–508, §13206(b), inserted "(or fiscal years)" after "fiscal year".

Subsec. (b)(1). Pub. L. 101–508, § 13206(c), substituted "for each fiscal year covered by a concurrent resolution on the budget" for "for a fiscal year" in first sentence, and "the first fiscal year covered by the appropriate concurrent resolution" for "such fiscal year" in second sentence.

1985—Subsec. (a). Pub. L. 99–177, in amending subsec. (a) generally, designated existing provisions as par. (1), substituted provisions relating to reports on legislation providing new budget authority, new spending authority, or new credit authority, or providing an increase or decrease in revenues or tax expenditures, for provisions relating to reports on legislation providing new budget authority or tax expenditures, and added par. (2).

Subsec. (b). Pub. L. 99–177, in amending subsec. (b) generally, designated existing provisions as par. (1), substituted provisions relating to issuance of reports on a monthly basis and contents of such reports, for provisions relating to issuance of reports on a periodic basis and contents of such reports, and added par. (2).

Subsec. (c). Pub. L. 99–177 amended subsec. (c) generally, adding pars. (4) and (5).

Amendment by Pub. L. 99–177 effective Dec. 12, 1985, and applicable with respect to fiscal years beginning after Sept. 30, 1985, see section 275(a)(1) of Pub. L. 99–177, set out as an Effective and Termination Dates note under section 900 of this title.

§ 640. House approval of regular appropriation bills

It shall not be in order in the House of Representatives to consider any resolution providing for an adjournment period of more than three calendar days during the month of July until the House of Representatives has approved annual appropriation bills providing new budget authority under the jurisdiction of all the subcommittees of the Committee on Appropriations for the fiscal year beginning on October 1 of such year. For purposes of this section, the chairman of the Committee on Appropriations of the House of Representatives shall periodically advise the Speaker as to changes in jurisdiction among its various subcommittees.

(Pub. L. 93–344, title III, § 309, July 12, 1974, 88 Stat. 314; Pub. L. 99–177, title II, § 201(b), Dec. 12, 1985, 99 Stat. 1052.)

CODIFICATION

Section was formerly classified to section 1330 of Title 31 prior to the general revision and enactment of Title 31, Money and Finance, by Pub. L. 97–258, § 1, Sept. 13, 1982, 96 Stat. 877.

AMENDMENTS

1985—Pub. L. 99–177 substituted "House approval of regular appropriation bills" for "Completion of action on bills providing new budget authority and certain new spending authority" in section catchline, and amended section generally. Prior to amendment, section read as follows: "Except as otherwise provided pursuant to this subchapter, not later than the seventh day after Labor Day of each year, the Congress shall complete action on all bills and resolutions—

"(1) providing new budget authority for the fiscal year beginning on October 1 of such year, other than supplemental, deficiency, and continuing appropriation bills and resolutions, and other than the reconciliation bill for such year, if required to be reported under section 641(c) of this title; and

"(2) providing new spending authority described in section 651(c)(2)(C) of this title which is to become effective during such fiscal year.

Paragraph (1) shall not apply to any bill or resolution if legislation authorizing the enactment of new budget authority to be provided in such bill or resolution has not been timely enacted."

Amendment by Pub. L. 99–177 effective Dec. 12, 1985, and applicable with respect to fiscal years beginning after Sept. 30, 1985, see section 275(a)(1) of Pub. L. 99–177, set out as an Effective and Termination Dates note under section 900 of this title.

§ 641. Reconciliation

(a) Inclusion of reconciliation directives in concurrent resolutions on the budget

A concurrent resolution on the budget for any fiscal year, to the extent necessary to effectuate the provisions and requirements of such resolution, shall—

(1) specify the total amount by which—

(A) new budget authority for such fiscal year;

(B) budget authority initially provided for prior fiscal years;

(C) new entitlement authority which is to become effective during such fiscal year; and

(D) credit authority for such fiscal year,

contained in laws, bills, and resolutions within the jurisdiction of a committee, is to be changed and direct that committee to determine and recommend changes to accomplish a change of such total amount;

(2) specify the total amount by which revenues are to be changed and direct that the committees having jurisdiction to determine and recommend changes in the revenue laws, bills, and resolutions to accomplish a change of such total amount;

(3) specify the amounts by which the statutory limit on the public debt is to be changed and direct the committee having jurisdiction to recommend such change; or

(4) specify and direct any combination of the matters described in paragraphs (1), (2), and (3) (including a direction to achieve deficit reduction).

(b) Legislative procedure

If a concurrent resolution containing directives to one or more committees to determine and recommend changes in laws, bills, or resolutions is agreed to in accordance with subsection (a) of this section, and—

(1) only one committee of the House or the Senate is directed to determine and recommend changes, that committee shall promptly make such determination and recommendations and report to its House reconciliation legislation containing such recommendations; or

(2) more than one committee of the House or the Senate is directed to determine and recommend changes, each such committee so directed shall promptly make such determination and recommendations and submit such recommendations to the Committee on the Budget of its House, which, upon receiving all such recommendations, shall report to its House reconciliation legislation carrying out all such recommendations without any substantive revision.

For purposes of this subsection, a reconciliation resolution is a concurrent resolution directing the Clerk of the House of Representatives or the Secretary of the Senate, as the case may be, to make specified changes in bills and resolutions which have not been enrolled.

(c) Compliance with reconciliation directions

(1) Any committee of the House of Representatives or the Senate that is directed, pursuant to a concurrent resolution on the budget, to determine and recommend changes of the type described in paragraphs (1) and (2) of subsection (a) of this section with respect to laws within its jurisdiction, shall be deemed to have complied with such directions—

(A) if—

(i) the amount of the changes of the type described in paragraph (1) of such subsection recommended by such committee do not exceed or fall below the amount of the changes such committee was directed by such concurrent resolution to recommend under such paragraph by more than[1]

(I) in the Senate, 20 percent of the total of the amounts of the changes such committee was directed to make under paragraphs (1) and (2) of such subsection; or

(II) in the House of Representatives, 20 percent of the sum of the absolute value of the changes the committee was directed to make under paragraph (1) and the absolute value of the changes the committee was directed to make under paragraph (2); and

(ii) the amount of the changes of the type described in paragraph (2) of such subsection recommended by such committee do not exceed or fall below the amount of the changes such committee was directed by such concurrent resolution to recommend under that paragraph by more than[1]

(I) in the Senate, 20 percent of the total of the amounts of the changes such committee was directed to make under paragraphs (1) and (2) of such subsection; or

(II) in the House of Representatives, 20 percent of the sum of the absolute value of the changes the committee was directed to make under paragraph (1) and the absolute value of the changes the committee was directed to make under paragraph (2); and

(B) if the total amount of the changes recommended by such committee is not less than the total of the amounts of the changes such committee was directed to make under paragraphs (1) and (2) of such subsection.

(2)(A) Upon the reporting to the Committee on the Budget of the Senate of a recommendation that shall be deemed to have complied with such directions solely by virtue of this subsection, the chairman of that committee may file with the Senate appropriately revised allocations under section 633(a) of this title and revised functional levels and aggregates to carry out this subsection.

(B) Upon the submission to the Senate of a conference report recommending a reconciliation bill or resolution in which a committee shall be deemed to have complied with such directions solely by virtue of this subsection, the chairman of the Committee on the Budget of the Senate may file with the Senate appropriately revised allocations under section 633(a) of this title and revised functional levels and aggregates to carry out this subsection.

(C) Allocations, functional levels, and aggregates revised pursuant to this paragraph shall be considered to be allocations, functional levels, and aggregates contained in the concurrent resolution on the budget pursuant to section 632 of this title.

(D) Upon the filing of revised allocations pursuant to this paragraph, the reporting committee shall report revised allocations pursuant to section 633(b) of this title to carry out this subsection.

(d) Limitation on amendments to reconciliation bills and resolutions

(1) It shall not be in order in the House of Representatives to consider any amendment to a reconciliation bill or reconciliation resolution if such amendment would have the effect of increasing any specific budget outlays above the level of such outlays provided in the bill or resolution (for the fiscal years covered by the reconciliation instructions set forth in the most recently agreed to concurrent resolution on the budget), or would have the effect of reducing any specific Federal revenues below the level of such revenues provided in the bill or resolution (for such fiscal years), unless such amendment makes at least an equivalent reduction in other specific budget outlays, an equivalent increase in other specific Federal revenues, or an equivalent combination thereof (for such fiscal years), except that a motion to strike a provision providing new budget authority or new entitlement authority may be in order.

(2) It shall not be in order in the Senate to consider any amendment to a reconciliation bill or reconciliation resolution if such amendment would have the effect of decreasing any specific budget outlay reductions below the level of such outlay reductions provided (for the fiscal years covered) in the reconciliation instructions which relate to such bill or resolution set forth in a resolution providing for reconciliation, or would have the effect of reducing Federal revenue increases below the level of such revenue increases provided (for such fiscal years) in such instructions relating to such bill or resolution, unless such amendment makes a reduction in other specific budget outlays, an increase in other specific Federal revenues, or a combination thereof (for such fiscal years) at least equivalent to any increase in outlays or decrease in revenues provided by such amendment, except that a motion to strike a provision shall always be in order.

(3) Paragraphs (1) and (2) shall not apply if a declaration of war by the Congress is in effect.

(4) For purposes of this section, the levels of budget outlays and Federal revenues for a fiscal year shall be determined on the basis of estimates made by the Committee on the Budget of the House of Representatives or of the Senate, as the case may be.

(5) The Committee on Rules of the House of Representatives may make in order amendments to achieve changes specified by reconcili-

ation directives contained in a concurrent resolution on the budget if a committee or committees of the House fail to submit recommended changes to its Committee on the Budget pursuant to its instruction.

(e) Procedure in Senate

(1) Except as provided in paragraph (2), the provisions of section 636 of this title for the consideration in the Senate of concurrent resolutions on the budget and conference reports thereon shall also apply to the consideration in the Senate of reconciliation bills reported under subsection (b) of this section and conference reports thereon.

(2) Debate in the Senate on any reconciliation bill reported under subsection (b) of this section, and all amendments thereto and debatable motions and appeals in connection therewith, shall be limited to not more than 20 hours.

(f) Completion of reconciliation process

It shall not be in order in the House of Representatives to consider any resolution providing for an adjournment period of more than three calendar days during the month of July until the House of Representatives has completed action on the reconciliation legislation for the fiscal year beginning on October 1 of the calendar year to which the adjournment resolution pertains, if reconciliation legislation is required to be reported by the concurrent resolution on the budget for such fiscal year.

(g) Limitation on changes to Social Security Act

Notwithstanding any other provision of law, it shall not be in order in the Senate or the House of Representatives to consider any reconciliation bill or reconciliation resolution reported pursuant to a concurrent resolution on the budget agreed to under section 632 or 635 of this title, or a joint resolution pursuant to section 907d of this title, or any amendment thereto or conference report thereon, that contains recommendations with respect to the old-age, survivors, and disability insurance program established under title II of the Social Security Act [42 U.S.C. 401 et seq.].

(Pub. L. 93–344, title III, § 310, July 12, 1974, 88 Stat. 315; Pub. L. 99–177, title II, § 201(b), Dec. 12, 1985, 99 Stat. 1053; Pub. L. 101–508, title XIII, §§ 13112(a)(9), 13207(c), (d), 13210(2), Nov. 5, 1990, 104 Stat. 1388–608, 1388–618 to 1388–620; Pub. L. 105–33, title X, § 10111, Aug. 5, 1997, 111 Stat. 685.)

REFERENCES IN TEXT

The Social Security Act, referred to in subsec. (g), is act Aug. 14, 1935, ch. 531, 49 Stat. 620, as amended. Title II of the Social Security Act is classified generally to subchapter II (§ 401 et seq.) of chapter 7 of Title 42, The Public Health and Welfare. For complete classification of this Act to the Code, see section 1305 of Title 42 and Tables.

CODIFICATION

Section was formerly classified to section 1331 of Title 31 prior to the general revision and enactment of Title 31, Money and Finance, by Pub. L. 97–258, § 1, Sept. 13, 1982, 96 Stat. 877.

AMENDMENTS

1997—Subsec. (c)(1)(A)(i). Pub. L. 105–33, § 10111(1), substituted subcls. (I) and (II) for "20 percent of the total

of the amounts of the changes such committee was directed to make under paragraphs (1) and (2) of such subsection, and''.

Subsec. (c)(1)(A)(ii). Pub. L. 105–33, § 10111(2), substituted subcls. (I) and (II) for "20 percent of the total of the amounts of the changes such committee was directed to make under paragraphs (1) and (2) of such subsection; and''.

1990—Subsec. (a)(4). Pub. L. 101–508, § 13207(d), inserted before period at end "(including a direction to achieve deficit reduction)''.

Subsec. (c). Pub. L. 101–508, § 13207(c), designated existing provisions as par. (1), redesignated former par. (1) and subpars. (A) and (B) thereof as subpar. (A) and cls. (i) and (ii), respectively, redesignated former par. (2) as subpar. (B) of par. (1), and added par. (2).

Subsec. (f). Pub. L. 101–508, § 13210(2), struck out par. (1) heading "In general" and text which directed Congress to complete action on any reconciliation bill or reconciliation resolution reported under subsec. (b) of this section not later than June 15 of each year, and struck out the par. (2) designation and heading "Point of order in the House of Representatives''.

Subsec. (g). Pub. L. 101–508, § 13112(a)(9), substituted "joint resolution pursuant" for "resolution pursuant" and "section 907d of this title" for "section 904(b) of this title''.

1985—Pub. L. 99–177 substituted "Reconciliation" for "Second required concurrent resolution and reconciliation process" in section catchline.

Subsec. (a). Pub. L. 99–177 amended subsec. (a) generally, inserting provisions relating to new entitlement authority and credit authority, and deleting provision that any such concurrent resolution could be reported, and the report accompanying it could be filed, in either House notwithstanding that that House was not in session on the day on which such concurrent resolution is reported.

Subsec. (b). Pub. L. 99–177 amended subsec. (b) generally, substituting provisions relating to legislative procedure respecting concurrent resolutions with directives to committees to determine and recommend changes in laws, etc., for provisions relating to completion of action on concurrent resolutions.

Subsec. (c). Pub. L. 99–177 amended subsec. (c) generally, substituting provisions relating to compliance with reconciliation directives, for provisions relating to the reconciliation process.

Subsec. (d). Pub. L. 99–177 amended subsec. (d) generally, substituting provisions relating to limitations on amendments to reconciliation bills and resolutions, for provisions relating to completion of the reconciliation process.

Subsec. (e). Pub. L. 99–177 amended subsec. (e) generally, substituting references to subsec. (b) for references to subsec. (c) wherever appearing, and deleting references to reconciliation resolutions.

Subsec. (f). Pub. L. 99–177 amended subsec. (f) generally, inserting provision that Congress complete action on reconciliation bills or resolutions reported under subsec. (b) not later than June 15 of each year and revising provisions relating to adjournment periods of the House of Representatives with respect to completion of action on fiscal year reconciliation legislation.

Subsec. (g). Pub. L. 99–177, in amending section generally, added subsec. (g).

EFFECTIVE DATE OF 1985 AMENDMENT

Amendment by Pub. L. 99–177 effective Dec. 12, 1985, and applicable with respect to fiscal years beginning after Sept. 30, 1985, except that such amendment, insofar as it relates to subsecs. (c), (d), and (g) of this section, to become effective Apr. 15, 1986, see section 275(a)(1), (2)(A) of Pub. L. 99–177, set out as an Effective and Termination Dates note under section 900 of this title.

SECTION REFERRED TO IN OTHER SECTIONS

This section is referred to in sections 632, 644, 907a, 907d of this title.

§ 642. Budget-related legislation must be within appropriate levels

(a) Enforcement of budget aggregates

(1) In House of Representatives

Except as provided by subsection (c) of this section, after the Congress has completed action on a concurrent resolution on the budget for a fiscal year, it shall not be in order in the House of Representatives to consider any bill, joint resolution, amendment, motion, or conference report providing new budget authority or reducing revenues, if—

(A) the enactment of that bill or resolution as reported;

(B) the adoption and enactment of that amendment; or

(C) the enactment of that bill or resolution in the form recommended in that conference report;

would cause the level of total new budget authority or total outlays set forth in the applicable concurrent resolution on the budget for the first fiscal year to be exceeded, or would cause revenues to be less than the level of total revenues set forth in that concurrent resolution for the first fiscal year or for the total of that first fiscal year and the ensuing fiscal years for which allocations are provided under section 633(a) of this title, except when a declaration of war by the Congress is in effect.

(2) In Senate

After a concurrent resolution on the budget is agreed to, it shall not be in order in the Senate to consider any bill, joint resolution, amendment, motion, or conference report that—

(A) would cause the level of total new budget authority or total outlays set forth for the first fiscal year in the applicable resolution to be exceeded; or

(B) would cause revenues to be less than the level of total revenues set forth for that first fiscal year or for the total of that first fiscal year and the ensuing fiscal years in the applicable resolution for which allocations are provided under section 633(a) of this title.

(3) Enforcement of social security levels in Senate

After a concurrent resolution on the budget is agreed to, it shall not be in order in the Senate to consider any bill, joint resolution, amendment, motion, or conference report that would cause a decrease in social security surpluses or an increase in social security deficits relative to the levels set forth in the applicable resolution for the first fiscal year or for the total of that fiscal year and the ensuing fiscal years for which allocations are provided under section 633(a) of this title.

(b) Social security levels

(1) In general

For purposes of subsection (a)(3) of this section, social security surpluses equal the excess of social security revenues over social security outlays in a fiscal year or years with such an excess and social security deficits equal the excess of social security outlays over social security revenues in a fiscal year or years with such an excess.

(2) Tax treatment

For purposes of subsection (a)(3) of this section, no provision of any legislation involving a change in chapter 1 of the Internal Revenue Code of 1986 [26 U.S.C. 1 et seq.] shall be treated as affecting the amount of social security revenues or outlays unless that provision changes the income tax treatment of social security benefits.

(c) Exception in House of Representatives

Subsection (a)(1) of this section shall not apply in the House of Representatives to any bill, joint resolution, or amendment that provides new budget authority for a fiscal year or to any conference report on any such bill or resolution, if—

(1) the enactment of that bill or resolution as reported;

(2) the adoption and enactment of that amendment; or

(3) the enactment of that bill or resolution in the form recommended in that conference report;

would not cause the appropriate allocation of new budget authority made pursuant to section 633(a) of this title for that fiscal year to be exceeded.

(Pub. L. 93–344, title III, § 311, July 12, 1974, 88 Stat. 316; Pub. L. 99–177, title II, § 201(b), Dec. 12, 1985, 99 Stat. 1055; Pub. L. 100–119, title I, § 106(e)(1), Sept. 29, 1987, 101 Stat. 781; Pub. L. 101–508, title XIII, §§ 13112(a)(10), 13207(a)(1)(E), 13303(d), Nov. 5, 1990, 104 Stat. 1388–608, 1388–617, 1388–626; Pub. L. 105–33, title X, § 10112(a), Aug. 5, 1997, 111 Stat. 686.)

REFERENCES IN TEXT

The Internal Revenue Code of 1986, referred to in subsec. (b)(2), is classified generally to Title 26, Internal Revenue Code.

CODIFICATION

Section was formerly classified to section 1332 of Title 31 prior to the general revision and enactment of Title 31, Money and Finance, by Pub. L. 97–258, § 1, Sept. 13, 1982, 96 Stat. 877.

AMENDMENTS

1997—Pub. L. 105–33 amended section catchline and text generally. Prior to amendment, section provided that new budget authority, new spending authority, and revenue legislation had to be within appropriate levels.

1990—Subsec. (a). Pub. L. 101–508, § 13303(d), designated existing provisions as par. (1), redesignated former pars. (1) to (3) thereof as subpars. (A) to (C), respectively, and added par. (2).

Pub. L. 101–508, § 13207(a)(1)(E), substituted "bill, joint resolution, amendment, motion, or conference report" for "bill, resolution, or amendment" and struck out "or any conference report on any such bill or resolution" after "reducing revenues for such fiscal year,".

Pub. L. 101–508, § 13112(a)(10), in closing provisions, substituted "except in the case that a declaration of war by the Congress is in effect" for "or, in the Senate, would otherwise result in a deficit for such fiscal year that—

"(A) for fiscal year 1989 or any subsequent fiscal year, exceeds the maximum deficit amount specified for such fiscal year in section 622(7) of this title; and

"(B) for fiscal year 1988 or 1989, exceeds the amount of the estimated deficit for such fiscal year based on laws and regulations in effect on January 1 of the calendar year in which such fiscal year begins as measured using the budget baseline specified in section 901(a)(6) of this title minus $23,000,000,000 for fiscal year 1988 or $36,000,000,000 for fiscal year 1989;

except to the extent that paragraph (1) of section 632(i) of this title or section 635(b) of this title, as the case may be, does not apply by reason of paragraph (2) of such subsection.''

1987—Subsec. (a). Pub. L. 100–119 substituted "would otherwise result in a deficit for such fiscal year that—

"(A) for fiscal year 1989 or any subsequent fiscal year, exceeds the maximum deficit amount specified for such fiscal year in section 622(7) of this title; and

"(B) for fiscal year 1988 or 1989, exceeds the amount of the estimated deficit for such fiscal year based on laws and regulations in effect on January 1 of the calendar year in which such fiscal year begins as measured using the budget baseline specified in section 901(a)(6) of this title minus $23,000,000,000 for fiscal year 1988 or $36,000,000,000 for fiscal year 1989;

except to the extent that paragraph (1) of section 632(i) of this title or section 635(b) of this title, as the case may be, does not apply by reason of paragraph (2) of such subsection" for "would otherwise result in a deficit for such fiscal year that exceeds the maximum deficit amount specified for such fiscal year in section 622(7) of this title (except to the extent that paragraph (1) of section 632(i) of this title or section 635(b) of this title, as the case may be, does not apply by reason of paragraph (2) of such subsection)".

1985—Subsec. (a). Pub. L. 99–177 amended subsec. (a) generally, striking out references to sections 641 and 651 of this title, and inserting provisions relating to nonconsideration in Senate of any bill, resolution, etc., resulting in a fiscal year deficit exceeding maximum deficit amount specified in section 622(7) of this title, with certain exceptions.

Subsec. (b). Pub. L. 99–177 amended subsec. (b) generally, substituting provisions setting forth exceptions in the House of Representatives for certain bills, etc., under subsec. (a) of this section, for provisions relating to determination of outlays and revenues.

Subsec. (c). Pub. L. 99–177, in amending section generally, added subsec. (c).

EFFECTIVE DATE OF 1990 AMENDMENT

Amendment by section 13303(d) of Pub. L. 101–508 applicable with respect to fiscal years beginning on or after Oct. 1, 1990, see section 13306 of Pub. L. 101–508, set out as a note under section 632 of this title.

EFFECTIVE DATE OF 1985 AMENDMENT

Amendment by Pub. L. 99–177 effective Dec. 12, 1985, and applicable with respect to fiscal years beginning after Sept. 30, 1985, see section 275(a)(1) of Pub. L. 99–177, set out as an Effective and Termination Dates note under section 900 of this title.

SECTION REFERRED TO IN OTHER SECTIONS

This section is referred to in sections 633, 907a of this title.

§ 643. Determinations and points of order

(a) Budget Committee determinations

For purposes of this subchapter and subchapter II of this chapter, the levels of new budget authority, outlays, direct spending, new entitlement authority, and revenues for a fiscal year shall be determined on the basis of estimates made by the Committee on the Budget of the House of Representatives or the Senate, as applicable.

(b) Discretionary spending point of order in Senate

(1) In general

Except as otherwise provided in this subsection, it shall not be in order in the Senate to consider any bill or resolution (or amendment, motion, or conference report on that bill or resolution) that would exceed any of the discretionary spending limits in section 251(c) of the Balanced Budget and Emergency Deficit Control Act of 1985 [2 U.S.C. 901(c)].

(2) Exceptions

This subsection shall not apply if a declaration of war by the Congress is in effect or if a joint resolution pursuant to section 258 of the Balanced Budget and Emergency Deficit Control Act of 1985 [2 U.S.C. 907a] has been enacted.

(c) Maximum deficit amount point of order in Senate

It shall not be in order in the Senate to consider any concurrent resolution on the budget for a fiscal year, or to consider any amendment to that concurrent resolution, or to consider a conference report on that concurrent resolution, if—

(1) the level of total outlays for the first fiscal year set forth in that concurrent resolution or conference report exceeds; or

(2) the adoption of that amendment would result in a level of total outlays for that fiscal year that exceeds;

the recommended level of Federal revenues for that fiscal year, by an amount that is greater than the maximum deficit amount, if any, specified in the Balanced Budget and Emergency Deficit Control Act of 1985 for that fiscal year.

(d) Timing of points of order in Senate

A point of order under this Act may not be raised against a bill, resolution, amendment, motion, or conference report while an amendment or motion, the adoption of which would remedy the violation of this Act, is pending before the Senate.

(e) Points of order in Senate against amendments between Houses

Each provision of this Act that establishes a point of order against an amendment also establishes a point of order in the Senate against an amendment between the Houses. If a point of order under this Act is raised in the Senate against an amendment between the Houses and the point of order is sustained, the effect shall be the same as if the Senate had disagreed to the amendment.

(f) Effect of point of order in Senate

In the Senate, if a point of order under this Act against a bill or resolution is sustained, the Presiding Officer shall then recommit the bill or resolution to the committee of appropriate jurisdiction for further consideration.

(Pub. L. 93–344, title III, § 312, as added Pub. L. 101–508, title XIII, § 13207(b)(1), Nov. 5, 1990, 104 Stat. 1388–618; amended Pub. L. 105–33, title X, § 10113(a), Aug. 5, 1997, 111 Stat. 687.)

REFERENCES IN TEXT

The Balanced Budget and Emergency Deficit Control Act of 1985, referred to in subsec. (c), is title II of Pub.

L. 99–177, Dec. 12, 1985, 99 Stat. 1038, as amended, which enacted chapter 20 (§ 900 et seq.) and sections 654 to 656 of this title, amended sections 602, 622, 631 to 642, and 651 to 653 of this title, sections 1104 to 1106 and 1109 of Title 31, Money and Finance, and section 911 of Title 42, The Public Health and Welfare, repealed section 661 of this title, enacted provisions set out as notes under section 900 of this title and section 911 of Title 42, and amended provisions set out as a note under section 621 of this title. For complete classification of this Act to the Code, see Short Title note set out under section 900 of this title and Tables.

This Act, referred to in subsecs. (d) to (f), means Pub. L. 93–344, July 12, 1974, 88 Stat. 297, as amended, known as the Congressional Budget and Impoundment Control Act of 1974, which enacted chapters 17, 17A, and 17B and section 190a–3 of this title and sections 11a, 11c, 11d, 1020a of former Title 31, Money and Finance, amended sections 11, 665, 701, 1020, 1151, 1152, 1153, and 1154 of former Title 31, section 105 of Title 1, General Provisions, and sections 190b and 190d of this title, repealed sections 571 and 581c–1 of former Title 31 and sections 66 and 81 of this title, and enacted provisions set out as notes under sections 190a–1, 621, 632, and 682 of this title, section 105 of Title 1, and section 1020 of former Title 31. For complete classification of this Act to the Code, see Short Title note set out under section 621 of this title and Tables.

AMENDMENTS

1997—Pub. L. 105–33 amended section catchline and text generally. Prior to amendment, section consisted of subsecs. (a) and (b) and provided that each provision of this Act that established point of order against an amendment also established point of order in Senate against an amendment between Houses and prescribed effect of sustaining point of order against an amendment or bill under this Act.

§ 644. Extraneous matter in reconciliation legislation

(a) In general

When the Senate is considering a reconciliation bill or a reconciliation resolution pursuant to section 641 of this title (whether that bill or resolution originated in the Senate or the House) or section 907d of this title, upon a point of order being made by any Senator against material extraneous to the instructions to a committee which is contained in any title or provision of the bill or resolution or offered as an amendment to the bill or resolution, and the point of order is sustained by the Chair, any part of said title or provision that contains material extraneous to the instructions to said Committee as defined in subsection (b) of this section shall be deemed stricken from the bill and may not be offered as an amendment from the floor.

(b) Extraneous provisions

(1)(A) Except as provided in paragraph (2), a provision of a reconciliation bill or reconciliation resolution considered pursuant to section 641 of this title shall be considered extraneous if such provision does not produce a change in outlays or revenues, including changes in outlays and revenues brought about by changes in the terms and conditions under which outlays are made or revenues are required to be collected (but a provision in which outlay decreases or revenue increases exactly offset outlay increases or revenue decreases shall not be considered extraneous by virtue of this subparagraph); (B) any provision producing an increase in outlays or decrease in revenues shall be considered extraneous if the net effect of provisions reported by the committee reporting the title containing the provision is that the committee fails to achieve its reconciliation instructions; (C) a provision that is not in the jurisdiction of the committee with jurisdiction over said title or provision shall be considered extraneous; (D) a provision shall be considered extraneous if it produces changes in outlays or revenues which are merely incidental to the non-budgetary components of the provision; (E) a provision shall be considered to be extraneous if it increases, or would increase, net outlays, or if it decreases, or would decrease, revenues during a fiscal year after the fiscal years covered by such reconciliation bill or reconciliation resolution, and such increases or decreases are greater than outlay reductions or revenue increases resulting from other provisions in such title in such year; and (F) a provision shall be considered extraneous if it violates section 641(g) of this title.

(2) A Senate-originated provision shall not be considered extraneous under paragraph (1)(A) if the Chairman and Ranking Minority Member of the Committee on the Budget and the Chairman and Ranking Minority Member of the Committee which reported the provision certify that: (A) the provision mitigates direct effects clearly attributable to a provision changing outlays or revenues and both provisions together produce a net reduction in the deficit; (B) the provision will result in a substantial reduction in outlays or a substantial increase in revenues during fiscal years after the fiscal years covered by the reconciliation bill or reconciliation resolution; (C) a reduction of outlays or an increase in revenues is likely to occur as a result of the provision, in the event of new regulations authorized by the provision or likely to be proposed, court rulings on pending litigation, or relationships between economic indices and stipulated statutory triggers pertaining to the provision, other than the regulations, court rulings or relationships currently projected by the Congressional Budget Office for scorekeeping purposes; or (D) such provision will be likely to produce a significant reduction in outlays or increase in revenues but, due to insufficient data, such reduction or increase cannot be reliably estimated.

(3) A provision reported by a committee shall not be considered extraneous under paragraph (1)(C) if (A) the provision is an integral part of a provision or title, which if introduced as a bill or resolution would be referred to such committee, and the provision sets forth the procedure to carry out or implement the substantive provisions that were reported and which fall within the jurisdiction of such committee; or (B) the provision states an exception to, or a special application of, the general provision or title of which it is a part and such general provision or title if introduced as a bill or resolution would be referred to such committee.

(c) Extraneous materials

Upon the reporting or discharge of a reconciliation bill or resolution pursuant to section 641 of this title in the Senate, and again upon the submission of a conference report on such a reconciliation bill or resolution, the Committee on the Budget of the Senate shall submit for the record a list of material considered to be extraneous under subsections (b)(1)(A), (b)(1)(B), and (b)(1)(E) of this section to the instructions of a committee as provided in this section. The inclusion or exclusion of a provision shall not constitute a determination of extraneousness by the Presiding Officer of the Senate.

(d) Conference reports

When the Senate is considering a conference report on, or an amendment between the Houses in relation to, a reconciliation bill or reconciliation resolution pursuant to section 641 of this title, upon—

(1) a point of order being made by any Senator against extraneous material meeting the definition of subsections (b)(1)(A), (b)(1)(B), (b)(1)(D), (b)(1)(E), or (b)(1)(F) of this section, and

(2) such point of order being sustained,

such material contained in such conference report or amendment shall be deemed stricken, and the Senate shall proceed, without intervening action or motion, to consider the question of whether the Senate shall recede from its amendment and concur with a further amendment, or concur in the House amendment with a further amendment, as the case may be, which further amendment shall consist of only that portion of the conference report or House amendment, as the case may be, not so stricken. Any such motion in the Senate shall be debatable for two hours. In any case in which such point of order is sustained against a conference report (or Senate amendment derived from such conference report by operation of this subsection), no further amendment shall be in order.

(e) General point of order

Notwithstanding any other law or rule of the Senate, it shall be in order for a Senator to raise a single point of order that several provisions of a bill, resolution, amendment, motion, or conference report violate this section. The Presiding Officer may sustain the point of order as to some or all of the provisions against which the Senator raised the point of order. If the Presiding Officer so sustains the point of order as to some of the provisions (including provisions of an amendment, motion, or conference report) against which the Senator raised the point of order, then only those provisions (including provisions of an amendment, motion, or conference report) against which the Presiding Officer sustains the point of order shall be deemed stricken pursuant to this section. Before the Presiding Officer rules on such a point of order, any Senator may move to waive such a point of order as it applies to some or all of the provisions against which the point of order was raised. Such a motion to waive is amendable in accordance with the rules and precedents of the Senate. After the Presiding Officer rules on such a point of order, any Senator may appeal the ruling of the Presiding Officer on such a point of order as it applies to some or all of the provisions on which the Presiding Officer ruled.

(Pub. L. 93–344, title III, § 313, formerly Pub. L. 99–272, title XX, § 20001, Apr. 7, 1986, 100 Stat. 390, as amended Pub. L. 99–509, title VII, § 7006, Oct.

21, 1986, 100 Stat. 1949; Pub. L. 100–119, title II, § 205(a), (b), Sept. 29, 1987, 101 Stat. 784; renumbered § 313 of Pub. L. 93–344 and amended Pub. L. 101–508, title XIII, § 13214(a)–(b)(4), Nov. 5, 1990, 104 Stat. 1388–621, 1388–622; Pub. L. 105–33, title X, § 10113(b)(1), Aug. 5, 1997, 111 Stat. 688.)

CODIFICATION

Prior to redesignation by Pub. L. 101–508, this section was section 20001 of Pub. L. 99–272, which was not classified to the Code, and subsec. (c) (now (d)) of this section (relating to point of order) was subsec. (a) of the first section of Senate Resolution No. 286, Ninety-ninth Congress, Dec. 19, 1985.

AMENDMENTS

1997—Subsec. (c). Pub. L. 105–33, § 10113(b)(1)(A), redesignated subsec. (c), relating to point of order, as (d).

Subsec. (d). Pub. L. 105–33, § 10113(b)(1)(A), redesignated subsec. (c), relating to point of order, as (d) and inserted heading. Former subsec. (d) redesignated (e).

Subsec. (e). Pub. L. 105–33, § 10113(b)(1)(B), redesignated subsec. (d) as (e) and struck out heading and text of former subsec. (e). Text read as follows: "For purposes of this section, the levels of new budget authority, budget outlays, new entitlement authority, and revenues for a fiscal year shall be determined on the basis of estimates made by the Committee on the Budget of the Senate."

1990—Pub. L. 101–508, § 13214(b)(2)(A), inserted "Extraneous matter in reconciliation legislation" as section catchline.

Pub. L. 101–508, § 13214(b)(1), redesignated section 20001 of Pub. L. 99–272 as this section.

Subsec. (a). Pub. L. 101–508, § 13214(a)(1)(A), inserted heading "In general".

Pub. L. 101–508, § 13214(b)(4)(B), substituted "subsection (b) of this section" for "subsection (d) of this section".

Pub. L. 101–508, § 13214(b)(4)(A), made technical amendment to reference to section 641 of this title to reflect change in reference to corresponding section of original act.

Pub. L. 101–508, § 13214(b)(2)(B), struck out at end "An affirmative vote of three-fifths of the Members, duly chosen and sworn, shall be required to sustain an appeal of the ruling of the Chair on a point of order raised under this section, as well as to waive or suspend the provisions of this subsection."

Pub. L. 101–508, § 13214(a)(1)(B), inserted "(whether that bill or resolution originated in the Senate or the House) or section 907d of this title" after "section 641 of this title".

Subsec. (b). Pub. L. 101–508, § 13214(b)(2)(B), (C), redesignated subsec. (d) as (b) and struck out former subsec. (b) which provided that no motion to waive or suspend the requirement of section 636(b)(2) of this title, as it related to germaneness with respect to a reconciliation bill or resolution, could be agreed to unless supported by an affirmative vote of three-fifths of the Members, duly chosen and sworn, which super-majority was to be required to successfully appeal the ruling of the Chair on a point of order raised under that section, as well as to waive or suspend the provisions of this subsection.

Pub. L. 101–508, § 13214(a)(2), inserted heading "Extraneous provisions".

Subsec. (b)(1)(A). Pub. L. 101–508, § 13214(b)(4)(A), made technical amendment to reference to section 641 of this title to reflect change in reference to corresponding section of original act.

Pub. L. 101–508, § 13214(a)(3), inserted before semicolon "(but a provision in which outlay decreases or revenue increases exactly offset outlay increases or revenue decreases shall not be considered extraneous by virtue of this subparagraph)".

Subsec. (b)(1)(F). Pub. L. 101–508, § 13214(a)(4)–(6), added subpar. (F).

Subsec. (b)(2). Pub. L. 101–508, § 13214(a)(7), substituted "A Senate-originated provision" for "A provision".

Subsec. (b)(2)(C). Pub. L. 101–508, §13214(b)(4)(C), inserted "or" after "scorekeeping purposes;".

Subsec. (c). Pub. L. 101–508, §13214(b)(4)(F), which directed the substitution of "this subsection" for "this resolution" in par. (2), was executed to last sentence of subsec. (c) as the probable intent of Congress.

Pub. L. 101–508, §13214(b)(4)(E), substituted "(b)(1)(A), (b)(1)(B), (b)(1)(D), (b)(1)(E), or (b)(1)(F) of this section" for "(d)(1)(A) or (d)(1)(D) of section 20001 of the Consolidated Omnibus Budget Reconciliation Act of 1985".

Pub. L. 101–508, §13214(b)(4)(D), substituted "When" for "when".

Pub. L. 101–508, §13214(b)(4)(A), made technical amendment to reference to section 641 of this title to reflect change in reference to corresponding section of original act.

Pub. L. 101–508, §13214(b)(3), redesignated as subsec. (c), relating to point of order, subsec. (a) of the first section of Senate Resolution No. 286, Ninety-ninth Congress, Dec. 19, 1985, as amended by Senate Resolution No. 509, Ninety-ninth Congress, Oct. 16, 1986.

Pub. L. 101–508, §13214(b)(2)(C), redesignated subsec. (e), relating to extraneous materials, as (c).

Pub. L. 101–508, §13214(b)(2)(B), struck out subsec. (c) which provided for effective and termination dates of this section.

Subsec. (d). Pub. L. 101–508, §13214(b)(2)(C), redesignated subsec. (f) as (d). Former subsec. (d) redesignated (b).

Subsecs. (e) to (g). Pub. L. 101–508, §13214(a)(8), (b)(2)(C), added subsecs. (e) to (g) and redesignated them as subsecs. (c) to (e), respectively.

1987—Subsec. (c). Pub. L. 100–119, §205(a), substituted "September 30, 1992" for "January 2, 1988".

Subsec. (d)(1)(E). Pub. L. 100–119, §205(b), which directed that cl. (E) be added to subsec. (d)(1)(A), was executed to subsec. (d)(1), as the probable intent of Congress.

1986—Subsec. (c). Pub. L. 99–509, §7006(b), substituted "January 2, 1988" for "January 2, 1987".

Pub. L. 99–509, §7006(c), substituted "section 20001" for "section 1201" in Senate Resolution No. 286, Ninety-ninth Congress, Dec. 19, 1985. See 1990 Amendment note above.

Subsec. (d)(2). Pub. L. 99–509, §7006(a)(1), substituted "paragraph (1)(A) if the Chairman and Ranking Minority Member of the Committee on the Budget and the Chairman and Ranking Minority Member of the Committee which reported the provision certify that" for "(1)(A) above if" in introductory provisions.

Subsec. (d)(2)(A). Pub. L. 99–509, §7006(a)(2), substituted "the provision mitigates" for "it is designed to mitigate the".

Subsec. (d)(2)(B). Pub. L. 99–509, §7006(a)(3), substituted "the provision" for "it".

Subsec. (d)(3). Pub. L. 99–509, §7006(a)(4), added par. (3).

§ 645. Adjustments

(a) Adjustments

(1) In general

After the reporting of a bill or joint resolution, the offering of an amendment thereto, or the submission of a conference report thereon, the chairman of the Committee on the Budget of the House of Representatives or the Senate shall make the adjustments set forth in paragraph (2) for the amount of new budget authority in that measure (if that measure meets the requirements set forth in subsection (b) of this section) and the outlays flowing from that budget authority.

(2) Matters to be adjusted

The adjustments referred to in paragraph (1) are to be made to—

(A) the discretionary spending limits, if any, set forth in the appropriate concurrent resolution on the budget;

(B) the allocations made pursuant to the appropriate concurrent resolution on the budget pursuant to section 633(a) of this title; and

(C) the budgetary aggregates as set forth in the appropriate concurrent resolution on the budget.

(b) Amounts of adjustments

The adjustment referred to in subsection (a) of this section shall be—

(1) an amount provided and designated as an emergency requirement pursuant to section 901(b)(2)(A) or 902(e) of this title;

(2) an amount provided for continuing disability reviews subject to the limitations in section 901(b)(2)(C) of this title;

(3) for any fiscal year through 2002, an amount provided that is the dollar equivalent of the Special Drawing Rights with respect to—

(A) an increase in the United States quota as part of the International Monetary Fund Eleventh General Review of Quotas (United States Quota); or

(B) any increase in the maximum amount available to the Secretary of the Treasury pursuant to section 286e–2 of title 22, as amended from time to time (New Arrangements to Borrow);

(4) an amount provided not to exceed $1,884,000,000 for the period of fiscal years 1998 through 2000 for arrearages for international organizations, international peacekeeping, and multilateral development banks;

(5) an amount provided for an earned income tax credit compliance initiative but not to exceed—

(A) with respect to fiscal year 1998, $138,000,000 in new budget authority;

(B) with respect to fiscal year 1999, $143,000,000 in new budget authority;

(C) with respect to fiscal year 2000, $144,000,000 in new budget authority;

(D) with respect to fiscal year 2001, $145,000,000 in new budget authority; and

(E) with respect to fiscal year 2002, $146,000,000 in new budget authority; or

(6) in the case of an amount for adoption incentive payments (as defined in section 901(b)(2)(G) of this title) for fiscal year 1999, 2000, 2001, 2002, or 2003 for the Department of Health and Human Services, an amount not to exceed $20,000,000.

(c) Application of adjustments

The adjustments made pursuant to subsection (a) of this section for legislation shall—

(1) apply while that legislation is under consideration;

(2) take effect upon the enactment of that legislation; and

(3) be published in the Congressional Record as soon as practicable.

(d) Reporting revised suballocations

Following any adjustment made under subsection (a) of this section, the Committees on Appropriations of the Senate and the House of Representatives may report appropriately revised suballocations under section 633(b) of this title to carry out this section.

(e) Definitions for CDRs

As used in subsection (b)(2) of this section—

(1) the term "continuing disability reviews" shall have the same meaning as provided in section 901(b)(2)(C)(ii) of this title; and

(2) the term "new budget authority" shall have the same meaning as the term "additional new budget authority" and the term "outlays" shall have the same meaning as "additional outlays" in that section.

(Pub. L. 93–344, title III, § 314, as added Pub. L. 105–33, title X, § 10114(a), Aug. 5, 1997, 111 Stat. 688; amended Pub. L. 105–89, title II, § 201(b)(2), Nov. 19, 1997, 111 Stat. 2125.)

AMENDMENTS

1997—Subsec. (b)(6). Pub. L. 105–89 added par. (6).

EFFECTIVE DATE OF 1997 AMENDMENT

Amendment by Pub. L. 105–89 effective Nov. 19, 1997, except as otherwise provided, with delay permitted if State legislation is required, see section 501 of Pub. L. 105–89, set out as a note under section 622 of Title 42, The Public Health and Welfare.

§ 645a. Effect of adoption of special order of business in House of Representatives

For purposes of a reported bill or joint resolution considered in the House of Representatives pursuant to a special order of business, the term "as reported" in this subchapter or subchapter II of this chapter shall be considered to refer to the text made in order as an original bill or joint resolution for the purpose of amendment or to the text on which the previous question is ordered directly to passage, as the case may be.

(Pub. L. 93–344, title III, § 315, as added Pub. L. 105–33, title X, § 10115(a), Aug. 5, 1997, 111 Stat. 690.)

SUBCHAPTER II—FISCAL PROCEDURES

SUBCHAPTER REFERRED TO IN OTHER SECTIONS

This subchapter is referred to in sections 632, 643, 645a, 907b, 907c of this title.

PART A—GENERAL PROVISIONS

§ 651. Budget-related legislation not subject to appropriations

(a) Controls on certain budget-related legislation not subject to appropriations

It shall not be in order in either the House of Representatives or the Senate to consider any bill or joint resolution (in the House of Representatives only, as reported), amendment, motion, or conference report that provides—

(1) new authority to enter into contracts under which the United States is obligated to make outlays;

(2) new authority to incur indebtedness (other than indebtedness incurred under chapter 31 of title 31) for the repayment of which the United States is liable; or

(3) new credit authority;

unless that bill, joint resolution, amendment, motion, or conference report also provides that the new authority is to be effective for any fiscal year only to the extent or in the amounts provided in advance in appropriation Acts.

(b) Legislation providing new entitlement authority

(1) POINT OF ORDER.—It shall not be in order in either the House of Representatives or the Senate to consider any bill or joint resolution (in the House of Representatives only, as reported), amendment, motion, or conference report that provides new entitlement authority that is to become effective during the current fiscal year.

(2) If any committee of the House of Representatives or the Senate reports any bill or resolution which provides new entitlement authority which is to become effective during a fiscal year and the amount of new budget authority which will be required for such fiscal year if such bill or resolution is enacted as so reported exceeds the appropriate allocation of new budget authority reported under section 633(b) of this title in connection with the most recently agreed to concurrent resolution on the budget for such fiscal year, such bill or resolution shall then be referred to the Committee on Appropriations of the Senate or may then be referred to the Committee on Appropriations of the House, as the case may be, with instructions to report it, with the committee's recommendations, within 15 calendar days (not counting any day on which that House is not in session) beginning with the day following the day on which it is so referred. If the Committee on Appropriations of either House fails to report a bill or resolution referred to it under this paragraph within such 15-day period, the committee shall automatically be discharged from further consideration of such bill or resolution and such bill or resolution shall be placed on the appropriate calendar.

(3) The Committee on Appropriations of each House shall have jurisdiction to report any bill or resolution referred to it under paragraph (2) with an amendment which limits the total amount of new spending authority provided in such bill or resolution.

(c) Exceptions

(1) Subsections (a) and (b) of this section shall not apply to new authority described in those subsections if outlays from that new authority will flow—

(A) from a trust fund established by the Social Security Act (as in effect on July 12, 1974) [42 U.S.C. 301 et seq.]; or

(B) from any other trust fund, 90 percent or more of the receipts of which consist or will consist of amounts (transferred from the general fund of the Treasury) equivalent to amounts of taxes (related to the purposes for which such outlays are or will be made) received in the Treasury under specified provisions of the Internal Revenue Code of 1986 [26 U.S.C. 1 et seq.].

(2) Subsections (a) and (b) of this section shall not apply to new authority described in those subsections to the extent that—

(A) the outlays resulting therefrom are made by an organization which is (i) a mixed-ownership Government corporation (as defined in section 9101(2) of title 31), or (ii) a wholly owned Government corporation (as defined in section 9101(3) of title 31) which is specifically exempted by law from compliance with any or all of the provisions of chapter 91 of title 31, as of December 12, 1985; or

(B) the outlays resulting therefrom consist exclusively of the proceeds of gifts or bequests made to the United States for a specific purpose.

(Pub. L. 93–344, title IV, § 401, July 12, 1974, 88 Stat. 317; Pub. L. 99–177, title II, § 211, Dec. 12, 1985, 99 Stat. 1056; Pub. L. 99–514, § 2, Oct. 22, 1986, 100 Stat. 2095; Pub. L. 101–508, title XIII, § 13207(a)(1)(F), (G), Nov. 5, 1990, 104 Stat. 1388–617, 1388–618; Pub. L. 105–33, title X, § 10116(a)(1)–(5), Aug. 5, 1997, 111 Stat. 690, 691.)

REFERENCES IN TEXT

The Social Security Act, referred to in subsec. (c)(1)(A), is act Aug. 14, 1935, ch. 531, 49 Stat. 620, as amended, which is classified generally to chapter 7 (§ 301 et seq.) of Title 42, The Public Health and Welfare. For complete classification of this Act to the Code, see section 1305 of Title 42 and Tables.

The Internal Revenue Code of 1986, referred to in subsec. (c)(1)(B), is classified generally to Title 26, Internal Revenue Code.

CODIFICATION

In subsec. (c)(2)(A), "section 9101(2) of title 31", "section 9101(3) of title 31", and "chapter 91 of title 31" were substituted for "section 201 of the Government Corporation Control Act [31 U.S.C. 856]", "section 101 of such Act [31 U.S.C. 846]", and "that Act", respectively, on authority of Pub. L. 97–258, § 4(b), Sept. 13, 1982, 96 Stat. 1067, the first section of which enacted Title 31, Money and Finance.

Section was formerly classified to section 1351 of Title 31 prior to the general revision and enactment of Title 31, Money and Finance, by Pub. L. 97–258, § 1, Sept. 13, 1982, 96 Stat. 877.

AMENDMENTS

1997—Pub. L. 105–33, § 10116(a)(1)(A), substituted "Budget-related legislation not subject to appropriations" for "Bills providing new spending authority" as section catchline.

Subsec. (a). Pub. L. 105–33, § 10116(a)(1)(B), added subsec. (a) and struck out heading and text of former subsec. (a). Text read as follows: "It shall not be in order in either the House of Representatives or the Senate to consider any bill, joint resolution, amendment, motion, or conference report, as reported to its House which provides new spending authority described in subsection (c)(2)(A) or (B) of this section, unless that bill, resolution, conference report, or amendment also provides that such new spending authority as described in subsection (c)(2)(A) or (B) of this section is to be effective for any fiscal year only to such extent or in such amounts as are provided in appropriation Acts."

Subsec. (b). Pub. L. 105–33, § 10116(a)(2)(A), inserted "new" before "entitlement" in heading.

Subsec. (b)(1). Pub. L. 105–33, § 10116(a)(2)(B), added par. (1) and struck out former par. (1) which read as follows: "It shall not be in order in either the House of Representatives or the Senate to consider any bill, joint resolution, amendment, motion, or conference report, as reported to its House, which provides new spending authority described in subsection (c)(2)(C) of this section which is to become effective before the first day of the fiscal year which begins during the calendar year in which such bill or resolution is reported."

Subsec. (b)(2). Pub. L. 105–33, § 10116(a)(2)(C), substituted "new entitlement authority" for "new spending authority described in subsection (c)(2)(C) of this section" and "of the Senate or may then be referred to the Committee on Appropriations of the House, as the case may be," for "of that House".

Subsec. (c). Pub. L. 105–33, § 10116(a)(5), redesignated subsec. (d) as (c).

Pub. L. 105–33, § 10116(a)(3), struck out subsec. (c) which defined terms "new spending authority" and "spending authority".

Subsec. (d). Pub. L. 105–33, § 10116(a)(5), redesignated subsec. (d) as (c).

Subsec. (d)(1). Pub. L. 105–33, § 10116(a)(4)(A), which directed substitution of "new authority described in those subsections if outlays from that new authority will flow" for "new spending authority if the budget authority for outlays which result from such new spending authority is derived", was executed by making the substitution for "new spending authority if the budget authority for outlays which will result from such new spending authority is derived" in introductory provisions to reflect the probable intent of Congress.

Subsec. (d)(2), (3). Pub. L. 105–33, § 10116(a)(4)(B), (C), redesignated par. (3) as (2), substituted "new authority described in those subsections" for "new spending authority" in introductory provisions, and struck out former par. (2) which read as follows: "Subsections (a) and (b) of this section shall not apply to new spending authority which is an amendment to or extension of chapter 67 of title 31, or a continuation of the program of fiscal assistance to State and local governments provided by that chapter, to the extent so provided in the bill or resolution providing such authority."

1990—Subsec. (a). Pub. L. 101–508, § 13207(a)(1)(F), substituted "bill, joint resolution, amendment, motion, or conference report" for "bill, resolution, or conference report" and struck out "(or any amendment which provides such new spending authority)" after "subsection (c)(2)(A) or (B) of this section".

Subsec. (b)(1). Pub. L. 101–508, § 13207(a)(1)(G), substituted "bill, joint resolution, amendment, motion, or conference report, as reported to its House" for "bill or resolution" and struck out "(or any amendment which provides such new spending authority)" after "subsection (c)(2)(C) of this section".

1986—Subsec. (d)(1)(B). Pub. L. 99–514 substituted "Internal Revenue Code of 1986" for "Internal Revenue Code of 1954".

1985—Subsec. (a). Pub. L. 99–177 amended subsec. (a) generally, inserting provisions relating to applicability to conference reports.

Subsec. (b). Pub. L. 99–177, in amending section generally, reenacted subsec. (b) without change.

Subsec. (c). Pub. L. 99–177, in amending subsec. (c) generally, added pars. (2)(D) and (E).

Subsec. (d). Pub. L. 99–177, in amending subsec. (d) generally, reenacted pars. (1) and (2) without change, and inserted reference to December 12, 1985, in par. (3).

EFFECTIVE DATE OF 1985 AMENDMENT

Amendment by Pub. L. 99–177 effective Dec. 12, 1985, and applicable with respect to fiscal years beginning after Sept. 30, 1985, see section 275(a)(1) of Pub. L. 99–177, set out as an Effective and Termination Dates note under section 900 of this title.

EFFECTIVE DATE

Section 905(c) of Pub. L. 93–344 (formerly set out as a note under section 621 of this title) provided that except as provided in section 906 of Pub. L. 93–344 (formerly set out as a note under section 632 of this title) this section shall take effect on the first day of the second regular session of the Ninety-fourth Congress.

SECTION REFERRED TO IN OTHER SECTIONS

This section is referred to in section 907c of this title; title 7 section 6617; title 15 section 4110; title 16 section 543h; title 25 sections 1300h–8, 1771d; title 33 section 2326a; title 42 sections 1962d–19, 10309, 11713; title 43 section 390g–7; title 50 App. section 1989b–9.

§ 652. Repealed. Pub. L. 105–33, title X, § 10116(b), Aug. 5, 1997, 111 Stat. 692

Section, Pub. L. 93–344, title IV, § 402, July 12, 1974, 88 Stat. 318; Pub. L. 99–177, title II, § 212, Dec. 12, 1985, 99 Stat. 1058; Pub. L. 101–508, title XIII, § 13207(a)(1)(H), Nov. 5, 1990, 104 Stat. 1388–618, related to legislation providing new credit authority.

§ 653. Analysis by Congressional Budget Office

The Director of the Congressional Budget Office shall, to the extent practicable, prepare for each bill or resolution of a public character reported by any committee of the House of Representatives or the Senate (except the Committee on Appropriations of each House), and submit to such committee—

(1) an estimate of the costs which would be incurred in carrying out such bill or resolution in the fiscal year in which it is to become effective and in each of the 4 fiscal years following such fiscal year, together with the basis for each such estimate;

(2) a comparison of the estimates of costs described in paragraph (1) with any available estimates of costs made by such committee or by any Federal agency; and

(3) a description of each method for establishing a Federal financial commitment contained in such bill or resolution.

The estimates, comparison, and description so submitted shall be included in the report accompanying such bill or resolution if timely submitted to such committee before such report is filed.

(Pub. L. 93–344, title IV, § 402, formerly § 403, July 12, 1974, 88 Stat. 320; Pub. L. 97–108, § 2(a), Dec. 23, 1981, 95 Stat. 1510; Pub. L. 99–177, title II, § 213, Dec. 12, 1985, 99 Stat. 1059; Pub. L. 104–4, title I, § 104, Mar. 22, 1995, 109 Stat. 62; renumbered § 402, Pub. L. 105–33, title X, § 10116(c)(1), Aug. 5, 1997, 111 Stat. 692.)

CODIFICATION

Section was formerly classified to section 1353 of Title 31 prior to the general revision and enactment of Title 31, Money and Finance, by Pub. L. 97–258, § 1, Sept. 13, 1982, 96 Stat. 877.

PRIOR PROVISIONS

A prior section 402 of Pub. L. 93–344 was classified to section 652 of this title prior to repeal by Pub. L. 105–33.

AMENDMENTS

1995—Subsec. (a). Pub. L. 104–4, § 104(2), struck out subsection designation.

Subsec. (a)(2). Pub. L. 104–4, § 104(1)(A), (C), redesignated par. (3) as (2) and struck out former par. (2), which read as follows: "an estimate of the cost which would be incurred by State and local governments in carrying out or complying with any significant bill or resolution in the fiscal year in which it is to become effective and in each of the four fiscal years following such fiscal year, together with the basis for each such estimate;".

Subsec. (a)(3). Pub. L. 104–4, § 104(1)(C), redesignated par. (4) as (3). Former par. (3) redesignated (2).

Pub. L. 104–4, § 104(1)(B), which directed the substitution of "paragraph (1)" for "paragraphs (1) and (2)", was executed by making the substitution for "paragraph (1) and (2)" to reflect the probable intent of Congress.

Subsec. (a)(4). Pub. L. 104–4, § 104(1)(C), redesignated par. (4) as (3).

Subsecs. (b), (c). Pub. L. 104–4, § 104(3), struck out subsecs. (b) and (c) which read as follows:

"(b) For purposes of subsection (a)(2) of this section, the term 'local government' has the same meaning as in section 6501 of title 31.

"(c) For purposes of subsection (a)(2) of this section, the term 'significant bill or resolution' is defined as any bill or resolution which in the judgment of the Di-

rector of the Congressional Budget Office is likely to result in an annual cost to State and local governments of $200,000,000 or more, or is likely to have exceptional fiscal consequences for a geographic region or a particular level of government."

1985—Subsec. (a). Pub. L. 99–177 added par. (4) and substituted "estimates, comparison, and description" for "estimates and comparison" in last sentence.

1981—Subsec. (a). Pub. L. 97–108, § 2(a)(1)–(6), designated existing provisions as subsec. (a), added par. (2), redesignated former par. (2) as (3), in par. (3) as so redesignated, substituted "estimates" for "estimate" in two places, and substituted reference to pars. (1) and (2) for reference to par. (1), and in provision following par. (3) substituted "estimates" for "estimate".

Subsecs. (b) and (c). Pub. L. 97–108, § 2(a)(7), added subsecs. (b) and (c).

EFFECTIVE DATE OF 1995 AMENDMENT

Amendment by Pub. L. 104–4 effective Jan. 1, 1996, or on the date 90 days after appropriations are made available as authorized under section 1516 of this title, whichever is earlier, and applicable to legislation considered on and after such date, see section 110 of Pub. L. 104–4, set out as an Effective Date note under section 1511 of this title.

EFFECTIVE DATE OF 1985 AMENDMENT

Amendment by Pub. L. 99–177 effective Dec. 12, 1985, and applicable with respect to fiscal years beginning after Sept. 30, 1985, see section 275(a)(1) of Pub. L. 99–177, set out as an Effective and Termination Dates note under section 900 of this title.

EFFECTIVE DATE OF 1981 AMENDMENT

Section 2(b) of Pub. L. 97–108 provided that: "The amendments made by subsection (a) [amending this section] shall apply with respect to bills or resolutions reported by committees of the House of Representatives and the Senate after September 30, 1982."

EFFECTIVE DATE

Amendment by Pub. L. 93–344 effective on day on which first Director of Congressional Budget Office is appointed under section 601(a) of this title, see section 905(b) of Pub. L. 93–344, formerly set out as an Effective Date note under section 621 of this title.

AUTHORIZATION OF APPROPRIATIONS

Section 3 of Pub. L. 97–108 provided that: "There are authorized to be appropriated such sums as may be necessary to carry out this Act [amending this section and enacting provisions set out as notes under this section and section 621 of this title]."

EXPIRATION OF AUTHORIZATION

Section 4 of Pub. L. 97–108, which provided for expiration on Sept. 30, 1987, of authorization granted under Pub. L. 97–108, which amended this section and enacted provisions set out as notes under sections 621 and 653 of this title, was repealed by Pub. L. 100–119, title II, § 204, Sept. 29, 1987, 101 Stat. 784.

§ 654. Study by General Accounting Office of forms of Federal financial commitment not reviewed annually by Congress

The General Accounting Office shall study those provisions of law which provide mandatory spending and report to the Congress its recommendations for the appropriate form of financing for activities or programs financed by such provisions not later than eighteen months after December 12, 1985. Such report shall be revised from time to time.

(Pub. L. 93–344, title IV, § 404, formerly § 405, as added Pub. L. 99–177, title II, § 214, Dec. 12, 1985,

99 Stat. 1059; renumbered § 404 and amended Pub. L. 105–33, title X, § 10116(c)(1), (2), Aug. 5, 1997, 111 Stat. 692.)

PRIOR PROVISIONS

A prior section 404 of Pub. L. 93–344, which is not classified to the Code, was renumbered section 403 by Pub. L. 105–33, title X, § 10116(c)(1), Aug. 5, 1997, 111 Stat. 692.

AMENDMENTS

1997—Pub. L. 105–33, § 10116(c)(2), substituted "mandatory spending" for "spending authority as described by section 651(c)(2) of this title and which provide permanent appropriations,".

EFFECTIVE DATE

Section effective Dec. 12, 1985, and applicable with respect to fiscal years beginning after Sept. 30, 1985, see section 275(a)(1) of Pub. L. 99–177, set out as an Effective and Termination Dates note under section 900 of this title.

§ 655. Off-budget agencies, programs, and activities

(a) Notwithstanding any other provision of law, budget authority, credit authority, and estimates of outlays and receipts for activities of the Federal budget which are off-budget immediately prior to December 12, 1985, not including activities of the Federal Old-Age and Survivors Insurance and Federal Disability Insurance Trust Funds, shall be included in a budget submitted pursuant to section 1105 of title 31 and in a concurrent resolution on the budget reported pursuant to section 632 or section 635 of this title and shall be considered, for purposes of this Act, budget authority, outlays, and spending authority in accordance with definitions set forth in this Act.

(b) All receipts and disbursements of the Federal Financing Bank with respect to any obligations which are issued, sold, or guaranteed by a Federal agency shall be treated as a means of financing such agency for purposes of section 1105 of title 31 and for purposes of this Act.

(Pub. L. 93–344, title IV, § 405, formerly § 406, as added Pub. L. 99–177, title II, § 214, Dec. 12, 1985, 99 Stat. 1059; renumbered § 405, Pub. L. 105–33, title X, § 10116(c)(1), Aug. 5, 1997, 111 Stat. 692.)

REFERENCES IN TEXT

This Act, referred to in text, means Pub. L. 93–344, July 12, 1974, 88 Stat. 297, as amended, known as the Congressional Budget and Impoundment Control Act of 1974, which enacted chapters 17, 17A, and 17B, and section 190a–3 of this title and sections 11a, 11c, 11d, 1020a of former Title 31, Money and Finance, amended sections 11, 665, 701, 1020, 1151, 1152, 1153, and 1154 of former Title 31, section 105 of Title 1, General Provisions, sections 190b and 190d of this title, repealed sections 571 and 581c–1 of former Title 31, and sections 66 and 81 of this title, and enacted provisions set out as notes under sections 190a–1, 621, 632, and 682 of this title, section 105 of Title 1, and section 1020 of former Title 31. For complete classification of this Act to the Code, see Short Title note set out under section 621 of this title and Tables.

PRIOR PROVISIONS

A prior section 405 of Pub. L. 93–344 was renumbered section 404 and is classified to section 654 of this title.

EFFECTIVE DATE

Section effective Dec. 12, 1985, and applicable with respect to fiscal years beginning after Sept. 30, 1985, see

section 275(a)(1) of Pub. L. 99–177, set out as an Effective and Termination Dates note under section 900 of this title.

SECTION REFERRED TO IN OTHER SECTIONS

This section is referred to in section 661d of this title.

§ 656. Member User Group

The Speaker of the House of Representatives, after consulting with the Minority Leader of the House, may appoint a Member User Group for the purpose of reviewing budgetary scorekeeping rules and practices of the House and advising the Speaker from time to time on the effect and impact of such rules and practices.

(Pub. L. 93–344, title IV, § 406, formerly § 407, as added Pub. L. 99–177, title II, § 214, Dec. 12, 1985, 99 Stat. 1060; renumbered § 406, Pub. L. 105–33, title X, § 10116(c)(1), Aug. 5, 1997, 111 Stat. 692.)

PRIOR PROVISIONS

A prior section 406 of Pub. L. 93–344 was renumbered section 405 and is classified to section 655 of this title.

EFFECTIVE DATE

Section effective Dec. 12, 1985, and applicable with respect to fiscal years beginning after Sept. 30, 1985, see section 275(a)(1) of Pub. L. 99–177, set out as an Effective and Termination Dates note under section 900 of this title.

PART B—FEDERAL MANDATES

PART REFERRED TO IN OTHER SECTIONS

This part is referred to in section 1511 of this title.

§ 658. Definitions

For purposes of this part:

(1) Agency

The term "agency" has the same meaning as defined in section 551(1) of title 5, but does not include independent regulatory agencies.

(2) Amount

The term "amount", with respect to an authorization of appropriations for Federal financial assistance, means the amount of budget authority for any Federal grant assistance program or any Federal program providing loan guarantees or direct loans.

(3) Direct costs

The term "direct costs"—

(A)(i) in the case of a Federal intergovernmental mandate, means the aggregate estimated amounts that all State, local, and tribal governments would be required to spend or would be prohibited from raising in revenues in order to comply with the Federal intergovernmental mandate; or

(ii) in the case of a provision referred to in paragraph (5)(A)(ii), means the amount of Federal financial assistance eliminated or reduced;

(B) in the case of a Federal private sector mandate, means the aggregate estimated amounts that the private sector will be required to spend in order to comply with the Federal private sector mandate;

(C) shall be determined on the assumption that—

(i) State, local, and tribal governments, and the private sector will take all reasonable steps necessary to mitigate the costs resulting from the Federal mandate, and will comply with applicable standards of practice and conduct established by recognized professional or trade associations; and

(ii) reasonable steps to mitigate the costs shall not include increases in State, local, or tribal taxes or fees; and

(D) shall not include—

(i) estimated amounts that the State, local, and tribal governments (in the case of a Federal intergovernmental mandate) or the private sector (in the case of a Federal private sector mandate) would spend—

(I) to comply with or carry out all applicable Federal, State, local, and tribal laws and regulations in effect at the time of the adoption of the Federal mandate for the same activity as is affected by that Federal mandate; or

(II) to comply with or carry out State, local, and tribal governmental programs, or private-sector business or other activities in effect at the time of the adoption of the Federal mandate for the same activity as is affected by that mandate; or

(ii) expenditures to the extent that such expenditures will be offset by any direct savings to the State, local, and tribal governments, or by the private sector, as a result of—

(I) compliance with the Federal mandate; or

(II) other changes in Federal law or regulation that are enacted or adopted in the same bill or joint resolution or proposed or final Federal regulation and that govern the same activity as is affected by the Federal mandate.

(4) Direct savings

The term "direct savings", when used with respect to the result of compliance with the Federal mandate—

(A) in the case of a Federal intergovernmental mandate, means the aggregate estimated reduction in costs to any State, local, or tribal government as a result of compliance with the Federal intergovernmental mandate; and

(B) in the case of a Federal private sector mandate, means the aggregate estimated reduction in costs to the private sector as a result of compliance with the Federal private sector mandate.

(5) Federal intergovernmental mandate

The term "Federal intergovernmental mandate" means—

(A) any provision in legislation, statute, or regulation that—

(i) would impose an enforceable duty upon State, local, or tribal governments, except—

(I) a condition of Federal assistance; or

(II) a duty arising from participation in a voluntary Federal program, except as provided in subparagraph (B));[1] or

(ii) would reduce or eliminate the amount of authorization of appropriations for—

(I) Federal financial assistance that would be provided to State, local, or tribal governments for the purpose of complying with any such previously imposed duty unless such duty is reduced or eliminated by a corresponding amount; or

(II) the control of borders by the Federal Government; or reimbursement to State, local, or tribal governments for the net cost associated with illegal, deportable, and excludable aliens, including court-mandated expenses related to emergency health care, education or criminal justice; when such a reduction or elimination would result in increased net costs to State, local, or tribal governments in providing education or emergency health care to, or incarceration of, illegal aliens; except that this subclause shall not be in effect with respect to a State, local, or tribal government, to the extent that such government has not fully cooperated in the efforts of the Federal Government to locate, apprehend, and deport illegal aliens;

(B) any provision in legislation, statute, or regulation that relates to a then-existing Federal program under which $500,000,000 or more is provided annually to State, local, and tribal governments under entitlement authority, if the provision—

(i)(I) would increase the stringency of conditions of assistance to State, local, or tribal governments under the program; or

(II) would place caps upon, or otherwise decrease, the Federal Government's responsibility to provide funding to State, local, or tribal governments under the program; and

(ii) the State, local, or tribal governments that participate in the Federal program lack authority under that program to amend their financial or programmatic responsibilities to continue providing required services that are affected by the legislation, statute, or regulation.

(6) Federal mandate

The term "Federal mandate" means a Federal intergovernmental mandate or a Federal private sector mandate, as defined in paragraphs (5) and (7).

(7) Federal private sector mandate

The term "Federal private sector mandate" means any provision in legislation, statute, or regulation that—

(A) would impose an enforceable duty upon the private sector except—

(i) a condition of Federal assistance; or

---

[1] So in original. Second closing parenthesis probably should not appear.

(ii) a duty arising from participation in a voluntary Federal program; or

(B) would reduce or eliminate the amount of authorization of appropriations for Federal financial assistance that will be provided to the private sector for the purposes of ensuring compliance with such duty.

(8) Local government

The term "local government" has the same meaning as defined in section 6501(6) of title 31.

(9) Private sector

The term "private sector" means all persons or entities in the United States, including individuals, partnerships, associations, corporations, and educational and nonprofit institutions, but shall not include State, local, or tribal governments.

(10) Regulation; rule

The term "regulation" or "rule" (except with respect to a rule of either House of the Congress) has the meaning of "rule" as defined in section 601(2) of title 5.

(11) Small government

The term "small government" means any small governmental jurisdictions defined in section 601(5) of title 5 and any tribal government.

(12) State

The term "State" has the same meaning as defined in section 6501(9) of title 31.

(13) Tribal government

The term "tribal government" means any Indian tribe, band, nation, or other organized group or community, including any Alaska Native village or regional or village corporation as defined in or established pursuant to the Alaska Native Claims Settlement Act (85 Stat. 688; 43 U.S.C. 1601 et seq.) which is recognized as eligible for the special programs and services provided by the United States to Indians because of their special status as Indians.

(Pub. L. 93–344, title IV, § 421, as added Pub. L. 104–4, title I, § 101(a)(2), Mar. 22, 1995, 109 Stat. 50.)

REFERENCES IN TEXT

The Alaska Native Claims Settlement Act, referred to in par. (13), is Pub. L. 92–203, Dec. 18, 1971, 85 Stat. 688, as amended, which is classified generally to chapter 33 (§ 1601 et seq.) of Title 43, Public Lands. For complete classification of this Act to the Code, see Short Title note set out under section 1601 of Title 43 and Tables.

EFFECTIVE DATE

Part effective Jan. 1, 1996, or on the date 90 days after appropriations are made available as authorized under section 1516 of this title, whichever is earlier, and applicable to legislation considered on and after such date, see section 110 of Pub. L. 104–4, set out as a note under section 1511 of this title.

SECTION REFERRED TO IN OTHER SECTIONS

This section is referred to in sections 658b, 658c, 1502, 1515 of this title.

§ 658a. Exclusions

This part shall not apply to any provision in a bill, joint resolution, amendment, motion, or conference report before Congress that—

(1) enforces constitutional rights of individuals;

(2) establishes or enforces any statutory rights that prohibit discrimination on the basis of race, color, religion, sex, national origin, age, handicap, or disability;

(3) requires compliance with accounting and auditing procedures with respect to grants or other money or property provided by the Federal Government;

(4) provides for emergency assistance or relief at the request of any State, local, or tribal government or any official of a State, local, or tribal government;

(5) is necessary for the national security or the ratification or implementation of international treaty obligations;

(6) the President designates as emergency legislation and that the Congress so designates in statute; or

(7) relates to the old-age, survivors, and disability insurance program under title II of the Social Security Act [42 U.S.C. 401 et seq.] (including taxes imposed by sections 3101(a) and 3111(a) of title 26 (relating to old-age, survivors, and disability insurance)).

(Pub. L. 93–344, title IV, § 422, as added Pub. L. 104–4, title I, § 101(a)(2), Mar. 22, 1995, 109 Stat. 53.)

REFERENCES IN TEXT

The Social Security Act, referred to in par. (7), is act Aug. 14, 1935, ch. 531, 49 Stat. 620, as amended. Title II of the Act is classified generally to subchapter II (§ 401 et seq.) of chapter 7 of Title 42, The Public Health and Welfare. For complete classification of this Act to the Code, see section 1305 of Title 42 and Tables.

SECTION REFERRED TO IN OTHER SECTIONS

This section is referred to in section 1515 of this title.

§ 658b. Duties of Congressional committees

(a) In general

When a committee of authorization of the Senate or the House of Representatives reports a bill or joint resolution of public character that includes any Federal mandate, the report of the committee accompanying the bill or joint resolution shall contain the information required by subsections (c) and (d) of this section.

(b) Submission of bills to Director

When a committee of authorization of the Senate or the House of Representatives orders reported a bill or joint resolution of a public character, the committee shall promptly provide the bill or joint resolution to the Director of the Congressional Budget Office and shall identify to the Director any Federal mandates contained in the bill or resolution.

(c) Reports on Federal mandates

Each report described under subsection (a) of this section shall contain—

(1) an identification and description of any Federal mandates in the bill or joint resolution, including the direct costs to State, local,

and tribal governments, and to the private sector, required to comply with the Federal mandates;

(2) a qualitative, and if practicable, a quantitative assessment of costs and benefits anticipated from the Federal mandates (including the effects on health and safety and the protection of the natural environment); and

(3) a statement of the degree to which a Federal mandate affects both the public and private sectors and the extent to which Federal payment of public sector costs or the modification or termination of the Federal mandate as provided under section 658d(a)(2) of this title would affect the competitive balance between State, local, or tribal governments and the private sector including a description of the actions, if any, taken by the committee to avoid any adverse impact on the private sector or the competitive balance between the public sector and the private sector.

(d) Intergovernmental mandates

If any of the Federal mandates in the bill or joint resolution are Federal intergovernmental mandates, the report required under subsection (a) of this section shall also contain—

(1)(A) a statement of the amount, if any, of increase or decrease in authorization of appropriations under existing Federal financial assistance programs, or of authorization of appropriations for new Federal financial assistance, provided by the bill or joint resolution and usable for activities of State, local, or tribal governments subject to the Federal intergovernmental mandates;

(B) a statement of whether the committee intends that the Federal intergovernmental mandates be partly or entirely unfunded, and if so, the reasons for that intention; and

(C) if funded in whole or in part, a statement of whether and how the committee has created a mechanism to allocate the funding in a manner that is reasonably consistent with the expected direct costs among and between the respective levels of State, local, and tribal government;

(2) any existing sources of Federal assistance in addition to those identified in paragraph (1) that may assist State, local, and tribal governments in meeting the direct costs of the Federal intergovernmental mandates; and

(3) if the bill or joint resolution would make the reduction specified in section 658(5)(B)(i)(II) of this title, a statement of how the committee specifically intends the States to implement the reduction and to what extent the legislation provides additional flexibility, if any, to offset the reduction.

(e) Preemption clarification and information

When a committee of authorization of the Senate or the House of Representatives reports a bill or joint resolution of public character, the committee report accompanying the bill or joint resolution shall contain, if relevant to the bill or joint resolution, an explicit statement on the extent to which the bill or joint resolution is intended to preempt any State, local, or tribal law, and, if so, an explanation of the effect of such preemption.

(f) Publication of statement from Director
(1) In general

Upon receiving a statement from the Director under section 658c of this title, a committee of the Senate or the House of Representatives shall publish the statement in the committee report accompanying the bill or joint resolution to which the statement relates if the statement is available at the time the report is printed.

(2) Other publication of statement of Director

If the statement is not published in the report, or if the bill or joint resolution to which the statement relates is expected to be considered by the Senate or the House of Representatives before the report is published, the committee shall cause the statement, or a summary thereof, to be published in the Congressional Record in advance of floor consideration of the bill or joint resolution.

(Pub. L. 93–344, title IV, §423, as added Pub. L. 104–4, title I, §101(a)(2), Mar. 22, 1995, 109 Stat. 53; amended Pub. L. 106–141, §2(a), Dec. 7, 1999, 113 Stat. 1699.)

AMENDMENTS

1999—Subsec. (d)(3). Pub. L. 106–141 added par. (3).

SECTION REFERRED TO IN OTHER SECTIONS

This section is referred to in sections 658d, 1515 of this title.

§ 658c. Duties of Director; statements on bills and joint resolutions other than appropriations bills and joint resolutions

(a) Federal intergovernmental mandates in reported bills and resolutions

For each bill or joint resolution of a public character reported by any committee of authorization of the Senate or the House of Representatives, the Director of the Congressional Budget Office shall prepare and submit to the committee a statement as follows:

(1) Contents

If the Director estimates that the direct cost of all Federal intergovernmental mandates in the bill or joint resolution will equal or exceed $50,000,000 (adjusted annually for inflation) in the fiscal year in which any Federal intergovernmental mandate in the bill or joint resolution (or in any necessary implementing regulation) would first be effective or in any of the 4 fiscal years following such fiscal year, the Director shall so state, specify the estimate, and briefly explain the basis of the estimate.

(2) Estimates

Estimates required under paragraph (1) shall include estimates (and brief explanations of the basis of the estimates) of—

(A) the total amount of direct cost of complying with the Federal intergovernmental mandates in the bill or joint resolution;

(B) if the bill or resolution contains an authorization of appropriations under section 658d(a)(2)(B) of this title, the amount of new budget authority for each fiscal year for a period not to exceed 10 years beyond the effective date necessary for the direct cost of the intergovernmental mandate; and

(C) the amount, if any, of increase in authorization of appropriations under existing Federal financial assistance programs, or of authorization of appropriations for new Federal financial assistance, provided by the bill or joint resolution and usable by State, local, or tribal governments for activities subject to the Federal intergovernmental mandates.

(3) Additional flexibility information

The Director shall include in the statement submitted under this subsection, in the case of legislation that makes changes as described in section 658(5)(B)(i)(II) of this title—

(A) if no additional flexibility is provided in the legislation, a description of whether and how the States can offset the reduction under existing law; or

(B) if additional flexibility is provided in the legislation, whether the resulting savings would offset the reductions in that program assuming the States fully implement that additional flexibility.

(4) Estimate not feasible

If the Director determines that it is not feasible to make a reasonable estimate that would be required under paragraphs (1) and (2), the Director shall not make the estimate, but shall report in the statement that the reasonable estimate cannot be made and shall include the reasons for that determination in the statement. If such determination is made by the Director, a point of order under this part shall lie only under section 658d(a)(1) of this title and as if the requirement of section 658d(a)(1) of this title had not been met.

(b) Federal private sector mandates in reported bills and joint resolutions

For each bill or joint resolution of a public character reported by any committee of authorization of the Senate or the House of Representatives, the Director of the Congressional Budget Office shall prepare and submit to the committee a statement as follows:

(1) Contents

If the Director estimates that the direct cost of all Federal private sector mandates in the bill or joint resolution will equal or exceed $100,000,000 (adjusted annually for inflation) in the fiscal year in which any Federal private sector mandate in the bill or joint resolution (or in any necessary implementing regulation) would first be effective or in any of the 4 fiscal years following such fiscal year, the Director shall so state, specify the estimate, and briefly explain the basis of the estimate.

(2) Estimates

Estimates required under paragraph (1) shall include estimates (and a brief explanation of the basis of the estimates) of—

(A) the total amount of direct costs of complying with the Federal private sector mandates in the bill or joint resolution; and

(B) the amount, if any, of increase in authorization of appropriations under existing Federal financial assistance programs, or of authorization of appropriations for new Federal financial assistance, provided by the bill

or joint resolution usable by the private sector for the activities subject to the Federal private sector mandates.

(3) Estimate not feasible

If the Director determines that it is not feasible to make a reasonable estimate that would be required under paragraphs (1) and (2), the Director shall not make the estimate, but shall report in the statement that the reasonable estimate cannot be made and shall include the reasons for that determination in the statement.

(c) Legislation falling below direct costs thresholds

If the Director estimates that the direct costs of a Federal mandate will not equal or exceed the thresholds specified in subsections (a) and (b) of this section, the Director shall so state and shall briefly explain the basis of the estimate.

(d) Amended bills and joint resolutions; conference reports

If a bill or joint resolution is passed in an amended form (including if passed by one House as an amendment in the nature of a substitute for the text of a bill or joint resolution from the other House) or is reported by a committee of conference in amended form, and the amended form contains a Federal mandate not previously considered by either House or which contains an increase in the direct cost of a previously considered Federal mandate, then the committee of conference shall ensure, to the greatest extent practicable, that the Director shall prepare a statement as provided in this subsection or a supplemental statement for the bill or joint resolution in that amended form.

(Pub. L. 93–344, title IV, § 424, as added Pub. L. 104–4, title I, § 101(a)(2), Mar. 22, 1995, 109 Stat. 55; amended Pub. L. 106–141, § 2(b), Dec. 7, 1999, 113 Stat. 1699.)

AMENDMENTS

1999—Subsec. (a)(3), (4). Pub. L. 106–141 added par. (3) and redesignated former par. (3) as (4).

SECTION REFERRED TO IN OTHER SECTIONS

This section is referred to in sections 658b, 658d, 1515 of this title.

§ 658d. Legislation subject to point of order

(a) In general

It shall not be in order in the Senate or the House of Representatives to consider—

(1) any bill or joint resolution that is reported by a committee unless the committee has published a statement of the Director on the direct costs of Federal mandates in accordance with section 658b(f) of this title before such consideration, except this paragraph shall not apply to any supplemental statement prepared by the Director under section 658c(d) of this title; and

(2) any bill, joint resolution, amendment, motion, or conference report that would increase the direct costs of Federal intergovernmental mandates by an amount that causes the thresholds specified in section 658c(a)(1) of this title to be exceeded, unless—

(A) the bill, joint resolution, amendment, motion, or conference report provides new budget authority or new entitlement authority in the House of Representatives or direct spending authority in the Senate for each fiscal year for such mandates included in the bill, joint resolution, amendment, motion, or conference report in an amount equal to or exceeding the direct costs of such mandate; or

(B) the bill, joint resolution, amendment, motion, or conference report includes an authorization for appropriations in an amount equal to or exceeding the direct costs of such mandate, and—

(i) identifies a specific dollar amount of the direct costs of such mandate for each year up to 10 years during which such mandate shall be in effect under the bill, joint resolution, amendment, motion or conference report, and such estimate is consistent with the estimate determined under subsection (e) of this section for each fiscal year;

(ii) identifies any appropriation bill that is expected to provide for Federal funding of the direct cost referred to under clause (i); and

(iii)(I) provides that for any fiscal year the responsible Federal agency shall determine whether there are insufficient appropriations for that fiscal year to provide for the direct costs under clause (i) of such mandate, and shall (no later than 30 days after the beginning of the fiscal year) notify the appropriate authorizing committees of Congress of the determination and submit either—

(aa) a statement that the agency has determined, based on a re-estimate of the direct costs of such mandate, after consultation with State, local, and tribal governments, that the amount appropriated is sufficient to pay for the direct costs of such mandate; or

(bb) legislative recommendations for either implementing a less costly mandate or making such mandate ineffective for the fiscal year;

(II) provides for expedited procedures for the consideration of the statement or legislative recommendations referred to in subclause (I) by Congress no later than 30 days after the statement or recommendations are submitted to Congress; and

(III) provides that such mandate shall—

(aa) in the case of a statement referred to in subclause (I)(aa), cease to be effective 60 days after the statement is submitted unless Congress has approved the agency's determination by joint resolution during the 60-day period;

(bb) cease to be effective 60 days after the date the legislative recommendations of the responsible Federal agency are submitted to Congress under subclause (I)(bb) unless Congress provides otherwise by law; or

(cc) in the case that such mandate that has not yet taken effect, continue not to be effective unless Congress provides otherwise by law.

(b) Rule of construction

The provisions of subsection (a)(2)(B)(iii) of this section shall not be construed to prohibit or otherwise restrict a State, local, or tribal government from voluntarily electing to remain subject to the original Federal intergovernmental mandate, complying with the programmatic or financial responsibilities of the original Federal intergovernmental mandate and providing the funding necessary consistent with the costs of Federal agency assistance, monitoring, and enforcement.

(c) Committee on Appropriations

(1) Application

The provisions of subsection (a) of this section—

(A) shall not apply to any bill or resolution reported by the Committee on Appropriations of the Senate or the House of Representatives; except

(B) shall apply to—

(i) any legislative provision increasing direct costs of a Federal intergovernmental mandate contained in any bill or resolution reported by the Committee on Appropriations of the Senate or House of Representatives;

(ii) any legislative provision increasing direct costs of a Federal intergovernmental mandate contained in any amendment offered to a bill or resolution reported by the Committee on Appropriations of the Senate or House of Representatives;

(iii) any legislative provision increasing direct costs of a Federal intergovernmental mandate in a conference report accompanying a bill or resolution reported by the Committee on Appropriations of the Senate or House of Representatives; and

(iv) any legislative provision increasing direct costs of a Federal intergovernmental mandate contained in any amendments in disagreement between the two Houses to any bill or resolution reported by the Committee on Appropriations of the Senate or House of Representatives.

(2) Certain provisions stricken in Senate

Upon a point of order being made by any Senator against any provision listed in paragraph (1)(B), and the point of order being sustained by the Chair, such specific provision shall be deemed stricken from the bill, resolution, amendment, amendment in disagreement, or conference report and may not be offered as an amendment from the floor.

(d) Determinations of applicability to pending legislation

For purposes of this section, in the Senate, the presiding officer of the Senate shall consult with the Committee on Governmental Affairs, to the extent practicable, on questions concerning the applicability of this part to a pending bill, joint resolution, amendment, motion, or conference report.

(e) Determinations of Federal mandate levels

For purposes of this section, in the Senate, the levels of Federal mandates for a fiscal year shall be determined based on the estimates made by the Committee on the Budget.

(Pub. L. 93–344, title IV, §425, as added Pub. L. 104–4, title I, §101(a)(2), Mar. 22, 1995, 109 Stat. 56.)

SECTION REFERRED TO IN OTHER SECTIONS

This section is referred to in sections 658b, 658c, 658e, 1512, 1515 of this title.

§ 658e. Provisions relating to House of Representatives

(a) Enforcement in House of Representatives

It shall not be in order in the House of Representatives to consider a rule or order that waives the application of section 658d of this title.

(b) Disposition of points of order

(1) Application to House of Representatives

This subsection shall apply only to the House of Representatives.

(2) Threshold burden

In order to be cognizable by the Chair, a point of order under section 658d of this title or subsection (a) of this section must specify the precise language on which it is premised.

(3) Question of consideration

As disposition of points of order under section 658d of this title or subsection (a) of this section, the Chair shall put the question of consideration with respect to the proposition that is the subject of the points of order.

(4) Debate and intervening motions

A question of consideration under this section shall be debatable for 10 minutes by each Member initiating a point of order and for 10 minutes by an opponent on each point of order, but shall otherwise be decided without intervening motion except one that the House adjourn or that the Committee of the Whole rise, as the case may be.

(5) Effect on amendment in order as original text

The disposition of the question of consideration under this subsection with respect to a bill or joint resolution shall be considered also to determine the question of consideration under this subsection with respect to an amendment made in order as original text.

(Pub. L. 93–344, title IV, §426, as added Pub. L. 104–4, title I, §101(a)(2), Mar. 22, 1995, 109 Stat. 59.)

SECTION REFERRED TO IN OTHER SECTIONS

This section is referred to in section 1515 of this title.

§ 658f. Requests to Congressional Budget Office from Senators

At the written request of a Senator, the Director shall, to the extent practicable, prepare an estimate of the direct costs of a Federal intergovernmental mandate contained in an amendment of such Senator.

(Pub. L. 93–344, title IV, §427, as added Pub. L. 104–4, title I, §101(a)(2), Mar. 22, 1995, 109 Stat. 59.)

SECTION REFERRED TO IN OTHER SECTIONS

This section is referred to in section 1515 of this title.

§ 658g. Clarification of application

(a) In general

This part applies to any bill, joint resolution, amendment, motion, or conference report that reauthorizes appropriations, or that amends existing authorizations of appropriations, to carry out any statute, or that otherwise amends any statute, only if enactment of the bill, joint resolution, amendment, motion, or conference report—

(1) would result in a net reduction in or elimination of authorization of appropriations for Federal financial assistance that would be provided to State, local, or tribal governments for use for the purpose of complying with any Federal intergovernmental mandate, or to the private sector for use to comply with any Federal private sector mandate, and would not eliminate or reduce duties established by the Federal mandate by a corresponding amount; or

(2) would result in a net increase in the aggregate amount of direct costs of Federal intergovernmental mandates or Federal private sector mandates other than as described in paragraph (1).

(b) Direct costs

(1) In general

For purposes of this part, the direct cost of the Federal mandates in a bill, joint resolution, amendment, motion, or conference report that reauthorizes appropriations, or that amends existing authorizations of appropriations, to carry out a statute, or that otherwise amends any statute, means the net increase, resulting from enactment of the bill, joint resolution, amendment, motion, or conference report, in the amount described under paragraph (2)(A) over the amount described under paragraph (2)(B).

(2) Amounts

The amounts referred to under paragraph (1) are—

(A) the aggregate amount of direct costs of Federal mandates that would result under the statute if the bill, joint resolution, amendment, motion, or conference report is enacted; and

(B) the aggregate amount of direct costs of Federal mandates that would result under the statute if the bill, joint resolution, amendment, motion, or conference report were not enacted.

(3) Extension of authorization of appropriations

For purposes of this section, in the case of legislation to extend authorization of appropriations, the authorization level that would be provided by the extension shall be compared to the authorization level for the last year in which authorization of appropriations is already provided.

(Pub. L. 93–344, title IV, §428, as added Pub. L. 104–4, title I, §101(a)(2), Mar. 22, 1995, 109 Stat. 59.)

SECTION REFERRED TO IN OTHER SECTIONS

This section is referred to in section 1515 of this title.

SUBCHAPTER III—CREDIT REFORM

SUBCHAPTER REFERRED TO IN OTHER SECTIONS

This subchapter is referred to in section 900 of this title; title 12 sections 635, 635i–6; title 22 sections 2124, 2186, 2197; title 23 section 181; title 31 section 3720C; title 38 section 3722; title 42 sections 254b, 292i; title 47 section 614.

§ 661. Purposes

The purposes of this subchapter are to—

(1) measure more accurately the costs of Federal credit programs;

(2) place the cost of credit programs on a budgetary basis equivalent to other Federal spending;

(3) encourage the delivery of benefits in the form most appropriate to the needs of beneficiaries; and

(4) improve the allocation of resources among credit programs and between credit and other spending programs.

(Pub. L. 93–344, title V, § 501, as added Pub. L. 101–508, title XIII, § 13201(a), Nov. 5, 1990, 104 Stat. 1388–610.)

PRIOR PROVISIONS

A prior section 661, Pub. L. 93–344, title VI, § 606, July 12, 1974, 88 Stat. 325, directed that Budget Committees of House and Senate study, on a continuing basis, any provisions of law which exempt agencies or programs from inclusion in the budget and make recommendations from time to time with regard to terminating or modifying such provisions, prior to repeal by Pub. L. 99–177, title II, §§ 223, 275(a)(1), Dec. 12, 1985, 99 Stat. 1060, 1100, effective Dec. 12, 1985, and applicable with respect to fiscal years beginning after Sept. 30, 1985.

A prior section 501 of Pub. L. 93–344, title V, July 12, 1974, 88 Stat. 321, was classified to section 1020 of former Title 31, prior to repeal and reenactment as section 1102 of Title 31, Money and Finance, by Pub. L. 97–258, § 5(b), Sept. 13, 1982, 96 Stat. 1068, the first section of which enacted Title 31.

SHORT TITLE

For short title of title V of Pub. L. 93–344, which enacted this subchapter, as the "Federal Credit Reform Act of 1990", see section 500 of Pub. L. 93–344, set out as a note under section 621 of this title.

§ 661a. Definitions

For purposes of this subchapter—

(1) The term "direct loan" means a disbursement of funds by the Government to a non-Federal borrower under a contract that requires the repayment of such funds with or without interest. The term includes the purchase of, or participation in, a loan made by another lender and financing arrangements that defer payment for more than 90 days, including the sale of a government[1] asset on credit terms. The term does not include the acquisition of a federally guaranteed loan in satisfaction of default claims or the price support loans of the Commodity Credit Corporation.

(2) The term "direct loan obligation" means a binding agreement by a Federal agency to

---

[1] So in original. Probably should be capitalized.

make a direct loan when specified conditions are fulfilled by the borrower.

(3) The term "loan guarantee" means any guarantee, insurance, or other pledge with respect to the payment of all or a part of the principal or interest on any debt obligation of a non-Federal borrower to a non-Federal lender, but does not include the insurance of deposits, shares, or other withdrawable accounts in financial institutions.

(4) The term "loan guarantee commitment" means a binding agreement by a Federal agency to make a loan guarantee when specified conditions are fulfilled by the borrower, the lender, or any other party to the guarantee agreement.

(5)(A) The term "cost" means the estimated long-term cost to the Government of a direct loan or loan guarantee or modification thereof, calculated on a net present value basis, excluding administrative costs and any incidental effects on governmental receipts or outlays.

(B) The cost of a direct loan shall be the net present value, at the time when the direct loan is disbursed, of the following estimated cash flows:

(i) loan disbursements;

(ii) repayments of principal; and

(iii) payments of interest and other payments by or to the Government over the life of the loan after adjusting for estimated defaults, prepayments, fees, penalties, and other recoveries;

including the effects of changes in loan terms resulting from the exercise by the borrower of an option included in the loan contract.

(C) The cost of a loan guarantee shall be the net present value, at the time when the guaranteed loan is disbursed, of the following estimated cash flows:

(i) payments by the Government to cover defaults and delinquencies, interest subsidies, or other payments; and

(ii) payments to the Government including origination and other fees, penalties and recoveries;

including the effects of changes in loan terms resulting from the exercise by the guaranteed lender of an option included in the loan guarantee contract, or by the borrower of an option included in the guaranteed loan contract.

(D) The cost of a modification is the difference between the current estimate of the net present value of the remaining cash flows under the terms of a direct loan or loan guarantee contract, and the current estimate of the net present value of the remaining cash flows under the terms of the contract, as modified.

(E) In estimating net present values, the discount rate shall be the average interest rate on marketable Treasury securities of similar maturity to the cash flows of the direct loan or loan guarantee for which the estimate is being made.

(F) When funds are obligated for a direct loan or loan guarantee, the estimated cost shall be based on the current assumptions, adjusted to incorporate the terms of the loan contract, for the fiscal year in which the funds are obligated.

(6) The term "credit program account" means the budget account into which an appropriation to cover the cost of a direct loan or loan guarantee program is made and from which such cost is disbursed to the financing account.

(7) The term "financing account" means the non-budget account or accounts associated with each credit program account which holds balances, receives the cost payment from the credit program account, and also includes all other cash flows to and from the Government resulting from direct loan obligations or loan guarantee commitments made on or after October 1, 1991.

(8) The term "liquidating account" means the budget account that includes all cash flows to and from the Government resulting from direct loan obligations or loan guarantee commitments made prior to October 1, 1991.

These accounts shall be shown in the budget on a cash basis.

(9) The term "modification" means any Government action that alters the estimated cost of an outstanding direct loan (or direct loan obligation) or an outstanding loan guarantee (or loan guarantee commitment) from the current estimate of cash flows. This includes the sale of loan assets, with or without recourse, and the purchase of guaranteed loans. This also includes any action resulting from new legislation, or from the exercise of administrative discretion under existing law, that directly or indirectly alters the estimated cost of outstanding direct loans (or direct loan obligations) or loan guarantees (or loan guarantee commitments) such as a change in collection procedures.

(10) The term "current" has the same meaning as in section 900(c)(9) of this title.

(11) The term "Director" means the Director of the Office of Management and Budget.

(Pub. L. 93–344, title V, §502, as added Pub. L. 101–508, title XIII, §13201(a), Nov. 5, 1990, 104 Stat. 1388–610; amended Pub. L. 105–33, title X, §10117(a), Aug. 5, 1997, 111 Stat. 692.)

PRIOR PROVISIONS

A prior section 502 of Pub. L. 93–344, title V, July 12, 1974, 88 Stat. 321, was set out as a note under section 1020 of former Title 31, prior to repeal by Pub. L. 97–258, §5(b), Sept. 13, 1982, 96 Stat. 1068.

AMENDMENTS

1997—Par. (1). Pub. L. 105–33, §10117(a)(1), inserted "and financing arrangements that defer payment for more than 90 days, including the sale of a government asset on credit terms" after "another lender".

Par. (5)(A). Pub. L. 105–33, §10117(a)(2), inserted "or modification thereof" after "or loan guarantee".

Par. (5)(B), (C). Pub. L. 105–33, §10117(a)(3), added subpars. (B) and (C) and struck out former subpars. (B) and (C) which read as follows:

"(B) The cost of a direct loan shall be the net present value, at the time when the direct loan is disbursed, of the following cash flows:

"(i) loan disbursements;

"(ii) repayments of principal; and

"(iii) payments of interest and other payments by or to the Government over the life of the loan after

adjusting for estimated defaults, prepayments, fees, penalties and other recoveries.

"(C) The cost of a loan guarantee shall be the net present value when a guaranteed loan is disbursed of the cash flow from—

"(i) estimated payments by the Government to cover defaults and delinquencies, interest subsidies, or other payments, and

"(ii) the estimated payments to the Government including origination and other fees, penalties and recoveries."

Par. (5)(D). Pub. L. 105–33, §10117(a)(4), amended subpar. (D) generally. Prior to amendment, subpar. (D) read as follows: "Any Government action that alters the estimated net present value of an outstanding direct loan or loan guarantee (except modifications within the terms of existing contracts or through other existing authorities) shall be counted as a change in the cost of that direct loan or loan guarantee. The calculation of such changes shall be based on the estimated present value of the direct loan or loan guarantee at the time of modification."

Par. (5)(E). Pub. L. 105–33, §10117(a)(5), inserted "the cash flows of" after "similar maturity to".

Par. (5)(F). Pub. L. 105–33, §10117(a)(6), added subpar. (F).

Pars. (9) to (11). Pub. L. 105–33, §10117(a)(7), added pars. (9) and (10) and redesignated former par. (9) as (11).

SECTION REFERRED TO IN OTHER SECTIONS

This section is referred to in section 661d of this title; title 10 sections 2540d, 2873; title 12 sections 635i–5, 1701z–11, 1715*l*, 1715z–1, 1715z–13a, 1721, 1735f–20, 4707; title 14 section 682; title 15 sections 636, 683, 697; title 22 sections 290m–2, 2151f, 2152b, 2431d, 2431e, 2431f; title 25 section 4195; title 31 section 3711; title 42 section 1490p–2; title 46 App. sections 1273, 1279e.

§ 661b. OMB and CBO analysis, coordination, and review

(a) In general

For the executive branch, the Director shall be responsible for coordinating the estimates required by this subchapter. The Director shall consult with the agencies that administer direct loan or loan guarantee programs.

(b) Delegation

The Director may delegate to agencies authority to make estimates of costs. The delegation of authority shall be based upon written guidelines, regulations, or criteria consistent with the definitions in this subchapter.

(c) Coordination with Congressional Budget Office

In developing estimation guidelines, regulations, or criteria to be used by Federal agencies, the Director shall consult with the Director of the Congressional Budget Office.

(d) Improving cost estimates

The Director and the Director of the Congressional Budget Office shall coordinate the development of more accurate data on historical performance of direct loan and loan guarantee programs. They shall annually review the performance of outstanding direct loans and loan guarantees to improve estimates of costs. The Office of Management and Budget and the Congressional Budget Office shall have access to all agency data that may facilitate the development and improvement of estimates of costs.

(e) Historical credit program costs

The Director shall review, to the extent possible, historical data and develop the best possible estimates of adjustments that would convert aggregate historical budget data to credit reform accounting.

(f) Administrative costs

The Director and the Director of the Congressional Budget Office shall each analyze and report to Congress on differences in long-term administrative costs for credit programs versus grant programs by January 31, 1992. Their reports shall recommend to Congress any changes, if necessary, in the treatment of administrative costs under credit reform accounting.

(Pub. L. 93–344, title V, § 503, as added Pub. L. 101–508, title XIII, § 13201(a), Nov. 5, 1990, 104 Stat. 1388–611.)

PRIOR PROVISIONS

A prior section 503 of Pub. L. 93–344, title V, July 12, 1974, 88 Stat. 321, was classified to section 701 of former Title 31, prior to repeal and reenactment in section 1552(a) of Title 31, Money and Finance, by Pub. L. 97–258, § 5(b), Sept. 13, 1982, 96 Stat. 1068, the first section of which enacted Title 31.

§ 661c. Budgetary treatment

(a) President's budget

Beginning with fiscal year 1992, the President's budget shall reflect the costs of direct loan and loan guarantee programs. The budget shall also include the planned level of new direct loan obligations or loan guarantee commitments associated with each appropriations request.

(b) Appropriations required

Notwithstanding any other provision of law, new direct loan obligations may be incurred and new loan guarantee commitments may be made for fiscal year 1992 and thereafter only to the extent that—

(1) new budget authority to cover their costs is provided in advance in an appropriations Act;

(2) a limitation on the use of funds otherwise available for the cost of a direct loan or loan guarantee program has been provided in advance in an appropriations Act; or

(3) authority is otherwise provided in appropriation Acts.

(c) Exemption for mandatory programs

Subsections (b) and (e) of this section shall not apply to a direct loan or loan guarantee program that—

(1) constitutes an entitlement (such as the guaranteed student loan program or the veterans' home loan guaranty program); or

(2) all existing credit programs of the Commodity Credit Corporation on November 5, 1990.

(d) Budget accounting

(1) The authority to incur new direct loan obligations, make new loan guarantee commitments, or modify outstanding direct loans (or direct loan obligations) or loan guarantees (or loan guarantee commitments) shall constitute new budget authority in an amount equal to the cost of the direct loan or loan guarantee in the fiscal year in which definite authority becomes available or indefinite authority is used. Such

budget authority shall constitute an obligation of the credit program account to pay to the financing account.

(2) The outlays resulting from new budget authority for the cost of direct loans or loan guarantees described in paragraph (1) shall be paid from the credit program account into the financing account and recorded in the fiscal year in which the direct loan or the guaranteed loan is disbursed or its costs altered.

(3) All collections and payments of the financing accounts shall be a means of financing.

(e) Modifications

An outstanding direct loan (or direct loan obligation) or loan guarantee (or loan guarantee commitment) shall not be modified in a manner that increases its costs unless budget authority for the additional cost has been provided in advance in an appropriations Act.

(f) Reestimates

When the estimated cost for a group of direct loans or loan guarantees for a given credit program made in a single fiscal year is reestimated in a subsequent year, the difference between the reestimated cost and the previous cost estimate shall be displayed as a distinct and separately identified subaccount in the credit program account as a change in program costs and a change in net interest. There is hereby provided permanent indefinite authority for these reestimates.

(g) Administrative expenses

All funding for an agency's administration of a direct loan or loan guarantee program shall be displayed as distinct and separately identified subaccounts within the same budget account as the program's cost.

(Pub. L. 93–344, title V, § 504, as added Pub. L. 101–508, title XIII, § 13201(a), Nov. 5, 1990, 104 Stat. 1388–612; amended Pub. L. 105–33, title X, § 10117(b), Aug. 5, 1997, 111 Stat. 693.)

PRIOR PROVISIONS

A prior section 504 of Pub. L. 93–344, title V, July 12, 1974, 88 Stat. 322, was classified to section 1020a of former Title 31, prior to repeal by Pub. L. 97–258, § 5(b), Sept. 13, 1982, 96 Stat. 1068.

AMENDMENTS

1997—Subsec. (b)(1). Pub. L. 105–33, § 10117(b)(1), amended par. (1) generally. Prior to amendment, par. (1) read as follows: "appropriations of budget authority to cover their costs are made in advance;".

Subsec. (b)(2). Pub. L. 105–33, § 10117(b)(2), substituted "has been provided in advance in an appropriations Act" for "is enacted".

Subsec. (c). Pub. L. 105–33, § 10117(b)(3), substituted "Subsections (b) and (e)" for "Subsection (b)".

Subsec. (d)(1). Pub. L. 105–33, § 10117(b)(4), substituted "modify outstanding direct loans (or direct loan obligations) or loan guarantees (or loan guarantee commitments)" for "directly or indirectly alter the costs of outstanding direct loans and loan guarantees".

Subsec. (e). Pub. L. 105–33, § 10117(b)(5), amended heading and text of subsec. (e) generally. Prior to amendment, text read as follows: "A direct loan obligation or loan guarantee commitment shall not be modified in a manner that increases its cost unless budget authority for the additional cost is appropriated, or is available out of existing appropriations or from other budgetary resources."

SECTION REFERRED TO IN OTHER SECTIONS

This section is referred to in section 661d of this title; title 16 section 1854; title 22 sections 2195, 2197; title 31 section 3711; title 42 sections 254b, 4822; title 45 section 822.

§ 661d. Authorizations

(a) Authorization of appropriations for costs

There are authorized to be appropriated to each Federal agency authorized to make direct loan obligations or loan guarantee commitments, such sums as may be necessary to pay the cost associated with such direct loan obligations or loan guarantee commitments.

(b) Authorization for financing accounts

In order to implement the accounting required by this subchapter, the President is authorized to establish such non-budgetary accounts as may be appropriate.

(c) Treasury transactions with financing accounts

The Secretary of the Treasury shall borrow from, receive from, lend to, or pay to the financing accounts such amounts as may be appropriate. The Secretary of the Treasury may prescribe forms and denominations, maturities, and terms and conditions for the transactions described above, except that the rate of interest charged by the Secretary on lending to financing accounts (including amounts treated as lending to financing accounts by the Federal Financing Bank (hereinafter in this subsection referred to as the "Bank")) pursuant to section 655(b)[1] of this title) and the rate of interest paid to financing accounts on uninvested balances in financing accounts shall be the same as the rate determined pursuant to section 661a(5)(E) of this title. For guaranteed loans financed by the Bank and treated as direct loans by a Federal agency pursuant to section 655(b)[1] of this title, any fee or interest surcharge (the amount by which the interest rate charged exceeds the rate determined pursuant to section 661a(5)(E) of this title) that the Bank charges to a private borrower pursuant to section 2285(c) of title 12 shall be considered a cash flow to the Government for the purposes of determining the cost of the direct loan pursuant to section 661a(5) of this title. All such amounts shall be credited to the appropriate financing account. The Bank is authorized to require reimbursement from a Federal agency to cover the administrative expenses of the Bank that are attributable to the direct loans financed for that agency. All such payments by an agency shall be considered administrative expenses subject to section 661c(g) of this title. This subsection shall apply to transactions related to direct loan obligations or loan guarantee commitments made on or after October 1, 1991. The authorities described above shall not be construed to supersede or override the authority of the head of a Federal agency to administer and operate a direct loan or loan guarantee program. All of the transactions provided in this subsection shall be subject to the provisions of subchapter II of chapter 15 of title 31. Cash balances of the financing accounts in excess of current requirements shall be maintained in a form of uninvested funds and the Secretary of the Treasury shall pay interest on these funds.

(d) Authorization for liquidating accounts

(1) Amounts in liquidating accounts shall be available only for payments resulting from direct loan obligations or loan guarantee commitments made prior to October 1, 1991, for—

(A) interest payments and principal repayments to the Treasury or the Federal Financing Bank for amounts borrowed;

(B) disbursements of loans;

(C) default and other guarantee claim payments;

(D) interest supplement payments;

(E) payments for the costs of foreclosing, managing, and selling collateral that are capitalized or routinely deducted from the proceeds of sales;

(F) payments to financing accounts when required for modifications;

(G) administrative expenses, if—

(i) amounts credited to the liquidating account would have been available for administrative expenses under a provision of law in effect prior to October 1, 1991; and

(ii) no direct loan obligation or loan guarantee commitment has been made, or any modification of a direct loan or loan guarantee has been made, since September 30, 1991; or

(H) such other payments as are necessary for the liquidation of such direct loan obligations and loan guarantee commitments.

(2) Amounts credited to liquidating accounts in any year shall be available only for payments required in that year. Any unobligated balances in liquidating accounts at the end of a fiscal year shall be transferred to miscellaneous receipts as soon as practicable after the end of the fiscal year.

(3) If funds in liquidating accounts are insufficient to satisfy obligations and commitments of such accounts, there is hereby provided permanent, indefinite authority to make any payments required to be made on such obligations and commitments.

(e) Authorization of appropriations for implementation expenses

There are authorized to be appropriated to existing accounts such sums as may be necessary for salaries and expenses to carry out the responsibilities under this subchapter.

(f) Reinsurance

Nothing in this subchapter shall be construed as authorizing or requiring the purchase of insurance or reinsurance on a direct loan or loan guarantee from private insurers. If any such reinsurance for a direct loan or loan guarantee is authorized, the cost of such insurance and any recoveries to the Government shall be included in the calculation of the cost.

(g) Eligibility and assistance

Nothing in this subchapter shall be construed to change the authority or the responsibility of a Federal agency to determine the terms and conditions of eligibility for, or the amount of assistance provided by a direct loan or a loan guarantee.

---

[1] See References in Text note below.

(Pub. L. 93–344, title V, § 505, as added Pub. L. 101–508, title XIII, § 13201(a), Nov. 5, 1990, 104 Stat. 1388–613; amended Pub. L. 105–33, title X, § 10117(c), Aug. 5, 1997, 111 Stat. 694.)

REFERENCES IN TEXT

Section 655(b) of this title, referred to in subsec. (c), was in the original "section 406(b)" and was translated as reading "section 405(b)", meaning section 405(b) of Pub. L. 93–344, to reflect the probable intent of Congress because of context and because section 406 does not contain a subsec. (b).

PRIOR PROVISIONS

A prior section 505 of Pub. L. 93–344, title V, July 12, 1974, 88 Stat. 322, repealed sections 66 and 81 of this title.

AMENDMENTS

1997—Subsec. (c). Pub. L. 105–33, § 10117(c)(2), substituted "supersede" for "supercede".

Pub. L. 105–33, § 10117(c)(1), inserted before period at end of second sentence ", except that the rate of interest charged by the Secretary on lending to financing accounts (including amounts treated as lending to financing accounts by the Federal Financing Bank (hereinafter in this subsection referred to as the 'Bank') pursuant to section 655(b) of this title) and the rate of interest paid to financing accounts on uninvested balances in financing accounts shall be the same as the rate determined pursuant to section 661a(5)(E) of this title. For guaranteed loans financed by the Bank and treated as direct loans by a Federal agency pursuant to section 655(b) of this title, any fee or interest surcharge (the amount by which the interest rate charged exceeds the rate determined pursuant to section 661a(5)(E) of this title) that the Bank charges to a private borrower pursuant to section 2285(c) of title 12 shall be considered a cash flow to the Government for the purposes of determining the cost of the direct loan pursuant to section 661a(5) of this title. All such amounts shall be credited to the appropriate financing account. The Bank is authorized to require reimbursement from a Federal agency to cover the administrative expenses of the Bank that are attributable to the direct loans financed for that agency. All such payments by an agency shall be considered administrative expenses subject to section 661c(g) of this title. This subsection shall apply to transactions related to direct loan obligations or loan guarantee commitments made on or after October 1, 1991".

Subsec. (d). Pub. L. 105–33, § 10117(c)(3), amended heading and text of subsec. (d) generally. Prior to amendment, text read as follows: "If funds in liquidating accounts are insufficient to satisfy the obligations and commitments of said accounts, there is hereby provided permanent, indefinite authority to make any payments required to be made on such obligations and commitments."

SECTION REFERRED TO IN OTHER SECTIONS

This section is referred to in title 22 section 2197.

§ 661e. Treatment of deposit insurance and agencies and other insurance programs

(a) In general

This subchapter shall not apply to the credit or insurance activities of the Federal Deposit Insurance Corporation, National Credit Union Administration, Resolution Trust Corporation, Pension Benefit Guaranty Corporation, National Flood Insurance, National Insurance Development Fund, Crop Insurance, or Tennessee Valley Authority.

(b) Study

The Director and the Director of the Congressional Budget Office shall each study whether the accounting for Federal deposit insurance programs should be on a cash basis on the same basis as loan guarantees, or on a different basis. Each Director shall report findings and recommendations to the President and the Congress on or before May 31, 1991.

(c) Access to data

For the purposes of subsection (b) of this section, the Office of Management and Budget and the Congressional Budget Office shall have access to all agency data that may facilitate these studies.

(Pub. L. 93–344, title V, § 506, as added Pub. L. 101–508, title XIII, § 13201(a), Nov. 5, 1990, 104 Stat. 1388–614; amended Pub. L. 105–33, title X, § 10117(d), Aug. 5, 1997, 111 Stat. 695.)

PRIOR PROVISIONS

A prior section 506 of Pub. L. 93–344, title V, July 12, 1974, 88 Stat. 322, amended section 105 of Title 1, General Provisions, and enacted provisions set out as a note under section 105 of Title 1, prior to the general revision of title V of Pub. L. 93–344 by Pub. L. 101–508.

AMENDMENTS

1997—Pub. L. 105–33 struck out subsec. (a) designation and heading, redesignated pars. (1) to (3) of former subsec. (a) as subsecs. (a) to (c), respectively, inserted subsec. headings, and substituted "subsection (b) of this section" for "paragraph (2)" in subsec. (c).

§ 661f. Effect on other laws

(a) Effect on other laws

This subchapter shall supersede, modify, or repeal any provision of law enacted prior to November 5, 1990, to the extent such provision is inconsistent with this subchapter. Nothing in this subchapter shall be construed to establish a credit limitation on any Federal loan or loan guarantee program.

(b) Crediting of collections

Collections resulting from direct loans obligated or loan guarantees committed prior to October 1, 1991, shall be credited to the liquidating accounts of Federal agencies. Amounts so credited shall be available, to the same extent that they were available prior to November 5, 1990, to liquidate obligations arising from such direct loans obligated or loan guarantees committed prior to October 1, 1991, including repayment of any obligations held by the Secretary of the Treasury or the Federal Financing Bank. The unobligated balances of such accounts that are in excess of current needs shall be transferred to the general fund of the Treasury. Such transfers shall be made from time to time but, at least once each year.

(Pub. L. 93–344, title V, § 507, as added Pub. L. 101–508, title XIII, § 13201(a), Nov. 5, 1990, 104 Stat. 1388–614.)

SUBCHAPTER IV—BUDGET AGREEMENT ENFORCEMENT PROVISIONS

§§ 665 to 665e. Repealed. Pub. L. 105–33, title X, § 10118(a), Aug. 5, 1997, 111 Stat. 695

Section 665, Pub. L. 93–344, title VI, § 601, as added Pub. L. 101–508, title XIII, § 13111, Nov. 5, 1990, 104 Stat. 1388–602; amended Pub. L. 103–66, title XIV, § 14002(a), (b), Aug. 10, 1993, 107 Stat. 683, defined terms and provided for points of order in cases where measures would exceed discretionary spending limits.

A prior section 601 of Pub. L. 93–344, title VI, July 12, 1974, 88 Stat. 323, was classified to section 11 of former Title 31, prior to repeal and reenactment as sections 1105(a)(15), 1106(b), and 1108(d) of Title 31, Money and Finance, by Pub. L. 97–258, §5(b), Sept. 13, 1982, 96 Stat. 1068, the first section of which enacted Title 31.

Section 665a, Pub. L. 93–344, title VI, §602, as added Pub. L. 101–508, title XIII, §13111, Nov. 5, 1990, 104 Stat. 1388–603; amended Pub. L. 103–322, title XXXI, §310001(f)(1), Sept. 13, 1994, 108 Stat. 2103, related to committee allocations and enforcement.

A prior section 602 of Pub. L. 93–344, title VI, July 12, 1974, 88 Stat. 324, was classified to section 11 of former Title 31, prior to repeal and reenactment as section 1106(a) of Title 31, Money and Finance, by Pub. L. 97–258, §5(b), Sept. 13, 1982, 96 Stat. 1068, the first section of which enacted Title 31.

Section 665b, Pub. L. 93–344, title VI, §603, as added Pub. L. 101–508, title XIII, §13111, Nov. 5, 1990, 104 Stat. 1388–605, related to consideration of legislation before adoption of budget resolution for that fiscal year.

A prior section 603 of Pub. L. 93–344, title VI, July 12, 1974, 88 Stat. 324, was classified to section 11 of former Title 31, prior to repeal and reenactment in section 1105(a)(1)–(14) of Title 31, Money and Finance, by Pub. L. 97–258, §5(b), Sept. 13, 1982, 96 Stat. 1068, the first section of which enacted Title 31.

Section 665c, Pub. L. 93–344, title VI, §604, as added Pub. L. 101–508, title XIII, §13111, Nov. 5, 1990, 104 Stat. 1388–605, related to reconciliation directives regarding pay-as-you-go requirements.

A prior section 604 of Pub. L. 93–344, title VI, July 12, 1974, 88 Stat. 324, was classified to section 11 of former Title 31, prior to repeal and reenactment in section 1105(a)(1)–(14) of Title 31, Money and Finance, by Pub. L. 97–258, §5(b), Sept. 13, 1982, 96 Stat. 1068, the first section of which enacted Title 31.

Section 665d, Pub. L. 93–344, title VI, §605, as added Pub. L. 101–508, title XIII, §13111, Nov. 5, 1990, 104 Stat. 1388–606, related to application of section 642 of this title and points of order in Senate for measures exceeding specified maximum deficit amount.

A prior section 605 of Pub. L. 93–344, title VI, July 12, 1974, 88 Stat. 325, was classified to section 11a of former Title 31, prior to repeal and reenactment in section 1109 of Title 31, Money and Finance, by Pub. L. 97–258, §5(b), Sept. 13, 1982, 96 Stat. 1068, the first section of which enacted Title 31.

Section 665e, Pub. L. 93–344, title VI, §606, as added Pub. L. 101–508, title XIII, §13111, Nov. 5, 1990, 104 Stat. 1388–606; amended Pub. L. 104–121, title I, §103(c), Mar. 29, 1996, 110 Stat. 849; Pub. L. 104–193, title II, §211(d)(5)(C), Aug. 22, 1996, 110 Stat. 2192, related to 5-year budget resolutions and requirement that budget resolutions conform to Balanced Budget and Emergency Deficit Control Act of 1985.

EFFECTIVE DATE

Section 607 of title VI of Pub. L. 93–344, as added by Pub. L. 101–508, title XIII, §13111, Nov. 5, 1990, 104 Stat. 1388–607, and amended by Pub. L. 103–66, title XIV, §14002(c)(3)(B), Aug. 10, 1993, 107 Stat. 684, provided that title VI of Pub. L. 93–344, enacting this subchapter, was effective Nov. 5, 1990, and was applicable to fiscal years 1991 to 1998, prior to repeal by Pub. L. 105–33, title X, §10118(a), Aug. 5, 1997, 111 Stat. 695.

A prior section 606 of Pub. L. 93–344, title VI, July 12, 1974, 88 Stat. 325, was classified to section 661 of this title, prior to repeal by Pub. L. 99–177, title II, §223, Dec. 12, 1985, 99 Stat. 1060.

CHAPTER 17B—IMPOUNDMENT CONTROL AND LINE ITEM VETO

SUBCHAPTER I—GENERAL PROVISIONS

CHAPTER REFERRED TO IN OTHER SECTIONS

This chapter is referred to in title 22 section 3224a; title 31 section 1512; title 42 section 6240.

SUBCHAPTER I—GENERAL PROVISIONS

SUBCHAPTER REFERRED TO IN OTHER SECTIONS

This subchapter is referred to in section 691 of this title.

§ 681. Disclaimer

Nothing contained in this Act, or in any amendments made by this Act, shall be construed as—

(1) asserting or conceding the constitutional powers or limitations of either the Congress or the President;

(2) ratifying or approving any impoundment heretofore or hereafter executed or approved by the President or any other Federal officer or employee, except insofar as pursuant to statutory authorization then in effect;

(3) affecting in any way the claims or defenses of any party to litigation concerning any impoundment; or

(4) superseding any provision of law which requires the obligation of budget authority or the making of outlays thereunder.

(Pub. L. 93–344, title X, § 1001, July 12, 1974, 88 Stat. 332.)

REFERENCES IN TEXT

This Act, referred to in provision preceding par. (1), means Pub. L. 93–344, July 12, 1974, 88 Stat. 297, as amended, known as the Congressional Budget and Impoundment Control Act of 1974, which enacted chapters 17, 17A, and 17B, and section 190a–3 of this title and sections 11a, 11c, 11d, 1020a of former Title 31, amended sections 11, 665, 701, 1020, 1151, 1152, 1153, and 1154 of former Title 31, section 105 of Title 1, General Provisions, sections 190b and 190d of this title, repealed sections 571 and 581c–1 of former Title 31 and sections 66 and 81 of this title, and enacted provisions set out as notes under sections 190a–1, 621, 632, and 682 of this title, section 105 of Title 1, and section 1020 of former Title 31. For complete classification of this Act to the Code, see Short Title note set out under section 621 of this title and Tables.

CODIFICATION

Section was formerly classified to section 1400 of Title 31 prior to the general revision and enactment of Title 31, Money and Finance, by Pub. L. 97–258, § 1, Sept. 13, 1982, 96 Stat. 877.

EFFECTIVE DATE

Chapter effective July 12, 1974, see section 905(a) of Pub. L. 93–344, formerly set out as a note under section 621 of this title.

SHORT TITLE OF 1996 AMENDMENT

Pub. L. 104–130, § 1, Apr. 9, 1996, 110 Stat. 1200, provided that: "This Act [enacting subchapter III (§ 691 et seq.) of this chapter and provisions set out as a note under section 691 of this title and amending provisions set out as notes under section 621 of this title] may be cited as the 'Line Item Veto Act'."

SHORT TITLE

Section 1(a) of Pub. L. 93–344 (set out as a note under section 621 of this title) provided, in part, that: "Parts A and B of title X [subchapters I and II of this chapter] may be cited as the 'Impoundment Control Act of 1974'. Part C of title X [subchapter III of this chapter] may be cited as the 'Line Item Veto Act of 1996'."

SUBCHAPTER II—CONGRESSIONAL CONSIDERATION OF PROPOSED RESCISSIONS, RESERVATIONS, AND DEFERRALS OF BUDGET AUTHORITY

SUBCHAPTER REFERRED TO IN OTHER SECTIONS

This subchapter is referred to in section 691 of this title.

§ 682. Definitions

For purposes of sections 682 to 688 of this title—

(1) "deferral of budget authority" includes—

(A) withholding or delaying the obligation or expenditure of budget authority (whether by establishing reserves or otherwise) provided for projects or activities; or

(B) any other type of Executive action or inaction which effectively precludes the obligation or expenditure of budget authority, including authority to obligate by contract in advance of appropriations as specifically authorized by law;

(2) "Comptroller General" means the Comptroller General of the United States;

(3) "rescission bill" means a bill or joint resolution which only rescinds, in whole or in part, budget authority proposed to be rescinded in a special message transmitted by the President under section 683 of this title, and upon which the Congress completes action before the end of the first period of 45 calendar days of continuous session of the Congress after the date on which the President's message is received by the Congress;

(4) "impoundment resolution" means a resolution of the House of Representatives or the Senate which only expresses its disapproval of a proposed deferral of budget authority set forth in a special message transmitted by the President under section 684 of this title; and

(5) continuity of a session of the Congress shall be considered as broken only by an adjournment of the Congress sine die, and the days on which either House is not in session because of an adjournment of more than 3 days to a day certain shall be excluded in the computation of the 45-day period referred to in paragraph (3) of this section and in section 683 of this title, and the 25-day periods referred to in sections 687 and 688(b)(1) of this title. If a special message is transmitted under section 683 of this title during any Congress and the last session of such Congress adjourns sine die before the expiration of 45 calendar days of continuous session (or a special message is so transmitted after the last session of the Congress adjourns sine die), the message shall be deemed to have been retransmitted on the first day of the succeeding Congress and the 45-day period referred to in paragraph (3) of this section and in section 683 of this title (with respect to such message) shall commence on the day after such first day.

(Pub. L. 93–344, title X, § 1011, July 12, 1974, 88 Stat. 333.)

CODIFICATION

Section was formerly classified to section 1401 of Title 31 prior to the general revision and enactment of

Title 31, Money and Finance, by Pub. L. 97–258, § 1, Sept. 13, 1982, 96 Stat. 877.

SECTION REFERRED TO IN OTHER SECTIONS

This section is referred to in title 45 sections 721, 726.

§ 683. Rescission of budget authority

(a) Transmittal of special message

Whenever the President determines that all or part of any budget authority will not be required to carry out the full objectives or scope of programs for which it is provided or that such budget authority should be rescinded for fiscal policy or other reasons (including the termination of authorized projects or activities for which budget authority has been provided), or whenever all or part of budget authority provided for only one fiscal year is to be reserved from obligation for such fiscal year, the President shall transmit to both Houses of Congress a special message specifying—

(1) the amount of budget authority which he proposes to be rescinded or which is to be so reserved;

(2) any account, department, or establishment of the Government to which such budget authority is available for obligation, and the specific project or governmental functions involved;

(3) the reasons why the budget authority should be rescinded or is to be so reserved;

(4) to the maximum extent practicable, the estimated fiscal, economic, and budgetary effect of the proposed rescission or of the reservation; and

(5) all facts, circumstances, and considerations relating to or bearing upon the proposed rescission or the reservation and the decision to effect the proposed rescission or the reservation, and to the maximum extent practicable, the estimated effect of the proposed rescission or the reservation upon the objects, purposes, and programs for which the budget authority is provided.

(b) Requirement to make available for obligation

Any amount of budget authority proposed to be rescinded or that is to be reserved as set forth in such special message shall be made available for obligation unless, within the prescribed 45-day period, the Congress has completed action on a rescission bill rescinding all or part of the amount proposed to be rescinded or that is to be reserved. Funds made available for obligation under this procedure may not be proposed for rescission again.

(Pub. L. 93–344, title X, § 1012, July 12, 1974, 88 Stat. 333; Pub. L. 100–119, title II, § 207, Sept. 29, 1987, 101 Stat. 786.)

CODIFICATION

Section was formerly classified to section 1402 of Title 31 prior to the general revision and enactment of Title 31, Money and Finance, by Pub. L. 97–258, § 1, Sept. 13, 1982, 96 Stat. 877.

AMENDMENTS

1987—Subsec. (b). Pub. L. 100–119 inserted at end "Funds made available for obligation under this procedure may not be proposed for rescission again."

SECTION REFERRED TO IN OTHER SECTIONS

This section is referred to in sections 682, 684, 685, 686 of this title.

§ 684. Proposed deferrals of budget authority

(a) Transmittal of special message

Whenever the President, the Director of the Office of Management and Budget, the head of any department or agency of the United States, or any officer or employee of the United States proposes to defer any budget authority provided for a specific purpose or project, the President shall transmit to the House of Representatives and the Senate a special message specifying—

(1) the amount of the budget authority proposed to be deferred;

(2) any account, department, or establishment of the Government to which such budget authority is available for obligation, and the specific projects or governmental functions involved;

(3) the period of time during which the budget authority is proposed to be deferred;

(4) the reasons for the proposed deferral, including any legal authority invoked to justify the proposed deferral;

(5) to the maximum extent practicable, the estimated fiscal, economic, and budgetary effect of the proposed deferral; and

(6) all facts, circumstances, and considerations relating to or bearing upon the proposed deferral and the decision to effect the proposed deferral, including an analysis of such facts, circumstances, and considerations in terms of their application to any legal authority, including specific elements of legal authority, invoked to justify such proposed deferral, and to the maximum extent practicable, the estimated effect of the proposed deferral upon the objects, purposes, and programs for which the budget authority is provided.

A special message may include one or more proposed deferrals of budget authority. A deferral may not be proposed for any period of time extending beyond the end of the fiscal year in which the special message proposing the deferral is transmitted to the House and the Senate.

(b) Consistency with legislative policy

Deferrals shall be permissible only—

(1) to provide for contingencies;

(2) to achieve savings made possible by or through changes in requirements or greater efficiency of operations; or

(3) as specifically provided by law.

No officer or employee of the United States may defer any budget authority for any other purpose.

(c) Exception

The provisions of this section do not apply to any budget authority proposed to be rescinded or that is to be reserved as set forth in a special message required to be transmitted under section 683 of this title.

(Pub. L. 93–344, title X, § 1013, July 12, 1974, 88 Stat. 334; Pub. L. 100–119, title II, § 206(a), Sept. 29, 1987, 101 Stat. 785.)

CODIFICATION

Section was formerly classified to section 1403 of Title 31 prior to the general revision and enactment of Title 31, Money and Finance, by Pub. L. 97–258, § 1, Sept. 13, 1982, 96 Stat. 877.

1987—Pub. L. 100–119 amended section generally, substituting substantially similar provisions in subsecs. (a) and (c) and substituting subsec. (b) for former subsec. (b) which read as follows: "Any amount of budget authority proposed to be deferred, as set forth in a special message transmitted under subsection (a) of this section, shall be made available for obligation if either House of Congress passes an impoundment resolution disapproving such proposed deferral."

SECTION REFERRED TO IN OTHER SECTIONS

This section is referred to in sections 682, 685, 686 of this title.

§ 685. Transmission of messages; publication

(a) Delivery to House and Senate

Each special message transmitted under section 683 or 684 of this title shall be transmitted to the House of Representatives and the Senate on the same day, and shall be delivered to the Clerk of the House of Representatives if the House is not in session, and to the Secretary of the Senate if the Senate is not in session. Each special message so transmitted shall be referred to the appropriate committee of the House of Representatives and the Senate. Each such message shall be printed as a document of each House.

(b) Delivery to Comptroller General

A copy of each special message transmitted under section 683 or 684 of this title, shall be transmitted to the Comptroller General on the same day it is transmitted to the House of Representatives and the Senate. In order to assist the Congress in the exercise of its functions under section 683 or 684 of this title, the Comptroller General shall review each such message and inform the House of Representatives and the Senate as promptly as practicable with respect to—

(1) in the case of a special message transmitted under section 683 of this title, the facts surrounding the proposed rescission or the reservation of budget authority (including the probable effects thereof); and

(2) in the case of a special message transmitted under section 684 of this title, (A) the facts surrounding each proposed deferral of budget authority (including the probable effects thereof) and (B) whether or not (or to what extent), in his judgment, such proposed deferral is in accordance with existing statutory authority.

(c) Transmission of supplementary messages

If any information contained in a special message transmitted under section 683 or 684 of this title is subsequently revised, the President shall transmit to both Houses of Congress and the Comptroller General a supplementary message stating and explaining such revision. Any such supplementary message shall be delivered, referred, and printed as provided in subsection (a) of this section. The Comptroller General shall promptly notify the House of Representatives and the Senate of any changes in the information submitted by him under subsection (b) of this section which may be necessitated by such revision.

(d) Printing in Federal Register

Any special message transmitted under section 683 or 684 of this title, and any supplementary message transmitted under subsection (c) of this section, shall be printed in the first issue of the Federal Register published after such transmittal.

(e) Cumulative reports of proposed rescissions, reservations, and deferrals of budget authority

(1) The President shall submit a report to the House of Representatives and the Senate, not later than the 10th day of each month during a fiscal year, listing all budget authority for that fiscal year with respect to which, as of the first day of such month—

(A) he has transmitted a special message under section 683 of this title with respect to a proposed rescission or a reservation; and

(B) he has transmitted a special message under section 684 of this title proposing a deferral.

Such report shall also contain, with respect to each such proposed rescission or deferral, or each such reservation, the information required to be submitted in the special message with respect thereto under section 683 or 684 of this title.

(2) Each report submitted under paragraph (1) shall be printed in the first issue of the Federal Register published after its submission.

(Pub. L. 93–344, title X, § 1014, July 12, 1974, 88 Stat. 335.)

CODIFICATION

Section was formerly classified to section 1404 of Title 31 prior to the general revision and enactment of Title 31, Money and Finance, by Pub. L. 97–258, § 1, Sept. 13, 1982, 96 Stat. 877.

EX. ORD. NO. 11845. DELEGATION OF CERTAIN REPORTING FUNCTIONS TO DIRECTOR OF OFFICE OF MANAGEMENT AND BUDGET

Ex. Ord. No. 11845, Mar. 24, 1975, 40 F.R. 13299, as amended by Ex. Ord. No. 12608, Sept. 9, 1987, 52 F.R. 34617, provided:

By virtue of the authority vested in me by the Impoundment Control Act of 1974 (Public Law 93–344; 88 Stat. 332, (2 U.S.C. 681 et seq.), hereinafter referred to as the Act) [subchapters I and II of this chapter], and section 301 of title 3 of the United States Code, the Director of the Office of Management and Budget is hereby designated and empowered to exercise, as of October 1, 1974 without ratification or other action of the President (1) the functions required by sections 1014(b) and 1014(d) of the Act [subsecs. (b) and (d) of this section] of transmitting to the Comptroller General of the United States and to the Office of the Federal Register copies of special messages transmitted pursuant to section 1012 or 1013 (2 U.S.C. 683 and 684) of the Act; and (2) the function conferred upon the President by section 1014(e) of the Act (2 U.S.C. 685(e)) of submitting to the Congress cumulative reports of proposed rescissions, reservations, and deferrals of budget authority.

§ 686. Reports by Comptroller General

(a) Failure to transmit special message

If the Comptroller General finds that the President, the Director of the Office of Management and Budget, the head of any department or agency of the United States, or any other officer or employee of the United States—

(1) is to establish a reserve or proposes to defer budget authority with respect to which the President is required to transmit a special message under section 683 or 684 of this title; or

(2) has ordered, permitted, or approved the establishment of such a reserve or a deferral of budget authority;

and that the President has failed to transmit a special message with respect to such reserve or deferral, the Comptroller General shall make a report on such reserve or deferral and any available information concerning it to both Houses of Congress. The provisions of sections 682 to 688 of this title shall apply with respect to such reserve or deferral in the same manner and with the same effect as if such report of the Comptroller General were a special message transmitted by the President under section 683 or 684 of this title, and, for purposes of sections 682 to 688 of this title, such report shall be considered a special message transmitted under section 683 or 684 of this title.

(b) Incorrect classification of special message

If the President has transmitted a special message to both Houses of Congress in accordance with section 683 or 684 of this title, and the Comptroller General believes that the President so transmitted the special message in accordance with one of those sections when the special message should have been transmitted in accordance with the other of those sections, the Comptroller General shall make a report to both Houses of the Congress setting forth his reasons.

(Pub. L. 93–344, title X, § 1015, July 12, 1974, 88 Stat. 336.)

CODIFICATION

Section was formerly classified to section 1405 of Title 31 prior to the general revision and enactment of Title 31, Money and Finance, by Pub. L. 97–258, § 1, Sept. 13, 1982, 96 Stat. 877.

REAFFIRMATION

Pub. L. 100–119, title II, § 206(c), Sept. 29, 1987, 101 Stat. 786, provided that: "Sections 1015 and 1016 of the Impoundment Control Act of 1974 [2 U.S.C. 686, 687] are reaffirmed."

§ 687. Suits by Comptroller General

If, under this chapter, budget authority is required to be made available for obligation and such budget authority is not made available for obligation, the Comptroller General is hereby expressly empowered, through attorneys of his own selection, to bring a civil action in the United States District Court for the District of Columbia to require such budget authority to be made available for obligation, and such court is hereby expressly empowered to enter in such civil action, against any department, agency, officer, or employee of the United States, any decree, judgment, or order which may be necessary or appropriate to make such budget authority available for obligation. No civil action shall be brought by the Comptroller General under this section until the expiration of 25 calendar days of continuous session of the Congress following the date on which an explanatory statement by the Comptroller General of the circumstances

giving rise to the action contemplated has been filed with the Speaker of the House of Representatives and the President of the Senate.

(Pub. L. 93–344, title X, § 1016, July 12, 1974, 88 Stat. 336; Pub. L. 98–620, title IV, § 402(35), Nov. 8, 1984, 98 Stat. 3360; Pub. L. 100–119, title II, § 206(b), Sept. 29, 1987, 101 Stat. 786.)

CODIFICATION

Section was formerly classified to section 1406 of Title 31 prior to the general revision and enactment of Title 31, Money and Finance, by Pub. L. 97–258, § 1, Sept. 13, 1982, 96 Stat. 877.

AMENDMENTS

1987—Pub. L. 100–119 substituted "If, under this chapter" for "If, under section 683(b) or 684(b) of this title".
1984—Pub. L. 98–620 struck out provision requiring that the courts give precedence to civil actions brought under this section, and to appeals and writs from decisions in such actions, over all other civil actions, appeals, and writs.

EFFECTIVE DATE OF 1984 AMENDMENT

Amendment by Pub. L. 98–620 not applicable to cases pending on Nov. 8, 1984, see section 403 of Pub. L. 98–620, set out as an Effective Date note under section 1657 of Title 28, Judiciary and Judicial Procedure.

REAFFIRMATION

For provision reaffirming this section, see section 206(c) of Pub. L. 100–119, set out as a note under section 686 of this title.

SECTION REFERRED TO IN OTHER SECTIONS

This section is referred to in section 682 of this title.

§ 688. Procedure in House of Representatives and Senate

(a) Referral

Any rescission bill introduced with respect to a special message or impoundment resolution introduced with respect to a proposed deferral of budget authority shall be referred to the appropriate committee of the House of Representatives or the Senate, as the case may be.

(b) Discharge of committee

(1) If the committee to which a rescission bill or impoundment resolution has been referred has not reported it at the end of 25 calendar days of continuous session of the Congress after its introduction, it is in order to move either to discharge the committee from further consideration of the bill or resolution or to discharge the committee from further consideration of any other rescission bill with respect to the same special message or impoundment resolution with respect to the same proposed deferral, as the case may be, which has been referred to the committee.

(2) A motion to discharge may be made only by an individual favoring the bill or resolution, may be made only if supported by one-fifth of the Members of the House involved (a quorum being present), and is highly privileged in the House and privileged in the Senate (except that it may not be made after the committee has reported a bill or resolution with respect to the same special message or the same proposed deferral, as the case may be); and debate thereon shall be limited to not more than 1 hour, the

time to be divided in the House equally between those favoring and those opposing the bill or resolution, and to be divided in the Senate equally between, and controlled by, the majority leader and the minority leader or their designees. An amendment to the motion is not in order, and it is not in order to move to reconsider the vote by which the motion is agreed to or disagreed to.

(c) Floor consideration in House

(1) When the committee of the House of Representatives has reported, or has been discharged from further consideration of, a rescission bill or impoundment resolution, it shall at any time thereafter be in order (even though a previous motion to the same effect has been disagreed to) to move to proceed to the consideration of the bill or resolution. The motion shall be highly privileged and not debatable. An amendment to the motion shall not be in order, nor shall it be in order to move to reconsider the vote by which the motion is agreed to or disagreed to.

(2) Debate on a rescission bill or impoundment resolution shall be limited to not more than 2 hours, which shall be divided equally between those favoring and those opposing the bill or resolution. A motion further to limit debate shall not be debatable. In the case of an impoundment resolution, no amendment to, or motion to recommit, the resolution shall be in order. It shall not be in order to move to reconsider the vote by which a rescission bill or impoundment resolution is agreed to or disagreed to.

(3) Motions to postpone, made with respect to the consideration of a rescission bill or impoundment resolution, and motions to proceed to the consideration of other business, shall be decided without debate.

(4) All appeals from the decisions of the Chair relating to the application of the Rules of the House of Representatives to the procedure relating to any rescission bill or impoundment resolution shall be decided without debate.

(5) Except to the extent specifically provided in the preceding provisions of this subsection, consideration of any rescission bill or impoundment resolution and amendments thereto (or any conference report thereon) shall be governed by the Rules of the House of Representatives applicable to other bills and resolutions, amendments, and conference reports in similar circumstances.

(d) Floor consideration in Senate

(1) Debate in the Senate on any rescission bill or impoundment resolution, and all amendments thereto (in the case of a rescission bill) and debatable motions and appeals in connection therewith, shall be limited to not more than 10 hours. The time shall be equally divided between, and controlled by, the majority leader and the minority leader or their designees.

(2) Debate in the Senate on any amendment to a rescission bill shall be limited to 2 hours, to be equally divided between, and controlled by, the mover and the manager of the bill. Debate on any amendment to an amendment, to such a bill, and debate on any debatable motion or appeal in connection with such a bill or an im-

poundment resolution shall be limited to 1 hour, to be equally divided between, and controlled by, the mover and the manager of the bill or resolution, except that in the event the manager of the bill or resolution is in favor of any such amendment, motion, or appeal, the time in opposition thereto, shall be controlled by the minority leader or his designee. No amendment that is not germane to the provisions of a rescission bill shall be received. Such leaders, or either of them, may, from the time under their control on the passage of a rescission bill or impoundment resolution, allot additional time to any Senator during the consideration of any amendment, debatable motion, or appeal.

(3) A motion to further limit debate is not debatable. In the case of a rescission bill, a motion to recommit (except a motion to recommit with instructions to report back within a specified number of days, not to exceed 3, not counting any day on which the Senate is not in session) is not in order. Debate on any such motion to recommit shall be limited to one hour, to be equally divided between, and controlled by, the mover and the manager of the concurrent resolution. In the case of an impoundment resolution, no amendment or motion to recommit is in order.

(4) The conference report on any rescission bill shall be in order in the Senate at any time after the third day (excluding Saturdays, Sundays, and legal holidays) following the day on which such a conference report is reported and is available to Members of the Senate. A motion to proceed to the consideration of the conference report may be made even though a previous motion to the same effect has been disagreed to.

(5) During the consideration in the Senate of the conference report on any rescission bill, debate shall be limited to 2 hours to be equally divided between, and controlled by, the majority leader and minority leader or their designees. Debate on any debatable motion or appeal related to the conference report shall be limited to 30 minutes, to be equally divided between, and controlled by, the mover and the manager of the conference report.

(6) Should the conference report be defeated, debate on any request for a new conference and the appointment of conferees shall be limited to one hour, to be equally divided between, and controlled by, the manager of the conference report and the minority leader or his designee, and should any motion be made to instruct the conferees before the conferees are named, debate on such motion shall be limited to 30 minutes, to be equally divided between, and controlled by, the mover and the manager of the conference report. Debate on any amendment to any such instructions shall be limited to 20 minutes, to be equally divided between, and controlled by, the mover and the manager of the conference report. In all cases when the manager of the conference report is in favor of any motion, appeal, or amendment, the time in opposition shall be under the control of the minority leader or his designee.

(7) In any case in which there are amendments in disagreement, time on each amendment shall be limited to 30 minutes, to be equally divided between, and controlled by, the manager of the

conference report and the minority leader or his designee. No amendment that is not germane to the provisions of such amendments shall be received.

(Pub. L. 93–344, title X, § 1017, July 12, 1974, 88 Stat. 337.)

CODIFICATION

Section was formerly classified to section 1407 of Title 31 prior to the general revision and enactment of Title 31, Money and Finance, by Pub. L. 97–258, § 1, Sept. 13, 1982, 96 Stat. 877.

SECTION REFERRED TO IN OTHER SECTIONS

This section is referred to in section 682 of this title; title 22 section 3224a; title 45 sections 721, 726.

SUBCHAPTER III—LINE ITEM VETO

TERMINATION OF SUBCHAPTER

For termination of subchapter, see Effective and Termination Dates note set out under section 691 of this title.

CONSTITUTIONALITY OF LINE ITEM VETO

For decision holding line item veto unconstitutional, see *Clinton v. City of New York*, 524 U.S. 417, 118 S.Ct. 2091, 141 L.Ed. 2d 393 (1998).

SUBCHAPTER REFERRED TO IN OTHER SECTIONS

This subchapter is referred to in section 692 of this title.

§ 691. Line item veto authority

(a) In general

Notwithstanding the provisions of subchapters I and II of this chapter, and subject to the provisions of this subchapter, the President may, with respect to any bill or joint resolution that has been signed into law pursuant to Article I, section 7, of the Constitution of the United States, cancel in whole—

(1) any dollar amount of discretionary budget authority;

(2) any item of new direct spending; or

(3) any limited tax benefit;

if the President—

(A) determines that such cancellation will—

(i) reduce the Federal budget deficit;

(ii) not impair any essential Government functions; and

(iii) not harm the national interest; and

(B) notifies the Congress of such cancellation by transmitting a special message, in accordance with section 691a of this title, within five calendar days (excluding Sundays) after the enactment of the law providing the dollar amount of discretionary budget authority, item of new direct spending, or limited tax benefit that was canceled.

(b) Identification of cancellations

In identifying dollar amounts of discretionary budget authority, items of new direct spending, and limited tax benefits for cancellation, the President shall—

(1) consider the legislative history, construction, and purposes of the law which contains such dollar amounts, items, or benefits;

(2) consider any specific sources of information referenced in such law or, in the absence of specific sources of information, the best available information; and

(3) use the definitions contained in section 691e of this title in applying this subchapter to the specific provisions of such law.

(c) Exception for disapproval bills

The authority granted by subsection (a) of this section shall not apply to any dollar amount of discretionary budget authority, item of new direct spending, or limited tax benefit contained in any law that is a disapproval bill as defined in section 691e of this title.

(Pub. L. 93–344, title X, § 1021, as added Pub. L. 104–130, § 2(a), Apr. 9, 1996, 110 Stat. 1200.)

TERMINATION OF SECTION

For termination of section by section 5 of Pub. L. 104–130, see Effective and Termination Dates note below.

EFFECTIVE AND TERMINATION DATES

Section 5 of Pub. L. 104–130 provided that: "This Act [enacting this subchapter and provisions set out as a note under section 681 of this title and amending provisions set out as notes under section 621 of this title] and the amendments made by it shall take effect and apply to measures enacted on the earlier of—

"(1) the day after the enactment into law, pursuant to Article I, section 7, of the Constitution of the United States, of an Act entitled 'An Act to provide for a seven-year plan for deficit reduction and achieve a balanced Federal budget.'; or

"(2) January 1, 1997;

and shall have no force or effect on or after January 1, 2005."

SECTION REFERRED TO IN OTHER SECTIONS

This section is referred to in sections 691a, 691c, 691f of this title.

§ 691a. Special messages

(a) In general

For each law from which a cancellation has been made under this subchapter, the President shall transmit a single special message to the Congress.

(b) Contents

(1) The special message shall specify—

(A) the dollar amount of discretionary budget authority, item of new direct spending, or limited tax benefit which has been canceled, and provide a corresponding reference number for each cancellation;

(B) the determinations required under section 691(a) of this title, together with any supporting material;

(C) the reasons for the cancellation;

(D) to the maximum extent practicable, the estimated fiscal, economic, and budgetary effect of the cancellation;

(E) all facts, circumstances and considerations relating to or bearing upon the cancellation, and to the maximum extent practicable, the estimated effect of the cancellation upon the objects, purposes and programs for which the canceled authority was provided; and

(F) include the adjustments that will be made pursuant to section 691c of this title to the discretionary spending limits under section 901(c) of this title and an evaluation of the effects of those adjustments upon the sequestration procedures of section 901 of this title.

(2) In the case of a cancellation of any dollar amount of discretionary budget authority or item of new direct spending, the special message shall also include, if applicable—

(A) any account, department, or establishment of the Government for which such budget authority was to have been available for obligation and the specific project or governmental functions involved;

(B) the specific States and congressional districts, if any, affected by the cancellation; and

(C) the total number of cancellations imposed during the current session of Congress on States and congressional districts identified in subparagraph (B).

(c) Transmission of special messages to House and Senate

(1) The President shall transmit to the Congress each special message under this subchapter within five calendar days (excluding Sundays) after enactment of the law to which the cancellation applies. Each special message shall be transmitted to the House of Representatives and the Senate on the same calendar day. Such special message shall be delivered to the Clerk of the House of Representatives if the House is not in session, and to the Secretary of the Senate if the Senate is not in session.

(2) Any special message transmitted under this subchapter shall be printed in the first issue of the Federal Register published after such transmittal.

(Pub. L. 93–344, title X, § 1022, as added Pub. L. 104–130, § 2(a), Apr. 9, 1996, 110 Stat. 1201; amended Pub. L. 105–33, title X, § 10121(a), Aug. 5, 1997, 111 Stat. 696.)

TERMINATION OF SECTION

For termination of section by section 5 of Pub. L. 104–130, see Effective and Termination Dates note set out under section 691 of this title.

AMENDMENTS

1997—Subsec. (b)(1)(F). Pub. L. 105–33 substituted "section 901(c) of this title" for "section 665 of this title".

SECTION REFERRED TO IN OTHER SECTIONS

This section is referred to in section 691 of this title.

§ 691b. Cancellation effective unless disapproved

(a) In general

The cancellation of any dollar amount of discretionary budget authority, item of new direct spending, or limited tax benefit shall take effect upon receipt in the House of Representatives and the Senate of the special message notifying the Congress of the cancellation. If a disapproval bill for such special message is enacted into law, then all cancellations disapproved in that law shall be null and void and any such dollar amount of discretionary budget authority, item of new direct spending, or limited tax benefit shall be effective as of the original date provided in the law to which the cancellation applied.

(b) Commensurate reductions in discretionary budget authority

Upon the cancellation of a dollar amount of discretionary budget authority under subsection (a) of this section, the total appropriation for each relevant account of which that dollar amount is a part shall be simultaneously reduced by the dollar amount of that cancellation.

(Pub. L. 93–344, title X, § 1023, as added Pub. L. 104–130, § 2(a), Apr. 9, 1996, 110 Stat. 1202.)

TERMINATION OF SECTION

For termination of section by section 5 of Pub. L. 104–130, see Effective and Termination Dates note set out under section 691 of this title.

§ 691c. Deficit reduction

(a) In general

(1) Discretionary budget authority

OMB shall, for each dollar amount of discretionary budget authority and for each item of new direct spending canceled from an appropriation law under section 691(a) of this title—

(A) reflect the reduction that results from such cancellation in the estimates required by section 251(a)(7) of the Balanced Budget and Emergency Deficit Control Act of 1985 [2 U.S.C. 901(a)(7)] in accordance with that Act [2 U.S.C. 900 et seq.], including an estimate of the reduction of the budget authority and the reduction in outlays flowing from such reduction of budget authority for each outyear; and

(B) include a reduction to the discretionary spending limits for budget authority and outlays in accordance with the Balanced Budget and Emergency Deficit Control Act of 1985 [2 U.S.C. 900 et seq.] for each applicable fiscal year set forth in section 251(c) of the Balanced Budget and Emergency Deficit Control Act of 1985 [2 U.S.C. 901(c)] by amounts equal to the amounts for each fiscal year estimated pursuant to subparagraph (A).

(2) Direct spending and limited tax benefits

(A) OMB shall, for each item of new direct spending or limited tax benefit canceled from a law under section 691(a) of this title, estimate the deficit decrease caused by the cancellation of such item or benefit in that law and include such estimate as a separate entry in the report prepared pursuant to section 252(d) of the Balanced Budget and Emergency Deficit Control Act of 1985 [2 U.S.C. 902(d)].

(B) OMB shall not include any change in the deficit resulting from a cancellation of any item of new direct spending or limited tax benefit, or the enactment of a disapproval bill for any such cancellation, under this subchapter in the estimates and reports required by sections 252(b) and 254 of the Balanced Budget and Emergency Deficit Control Act of 1985 [2 U.S.C. 902(b), 904].

(b) Adjustments to spending limits

After ten calendar days (excluding Sundays) after the expiration of the time period in section 691d(b)(1) of this title for expedited congressional consideration of a disapproval bill for a special message containing a cancellation of discretionary budget authority, OMB shall make the reduction included in subsection (a)(1)(B) of this section as part of the next sequester report required by section 254 of the Balanced Budget and Emergency Deficit Control Act of 1985 [2 U.S.C. 904].

(c) Exception

Subsection (b) of this section shall not apply to a cancellation if a disapproval bill or other law that disapproves that cancellation is enacted into law prior to 10 calendar days (excluding Sundays) after the expiration of the time period set forth in section 691d(b)(1) of this title.

(d) Congressional Budget Office estimates

As soon as practicable after the President makes a cancellation from a law under section 691(a) of this title, the Director of the Congressional Budget Office shall provide the Committees on the Budget of the House of Representatives and the Senate with an estimate of the reduction of the budget authority and the reduction in outlays flowing from such reduction of budget authority for each outyear.

(Pub. L. 93–344, title X, §1024, as added Pub. L. 104–130, §2(a), Apr. 9, 1996, 110 Stat. 1202; amended Pub. L. 105–33, title X, §10121(b), Aug. 5, 1997, 111 Stat. 696.)

TERMINATION OF SECTION

For termination of section by section 5 of Pub. L. 104–130, see Effective and Termination Dates note set out under section 691 of this title.

REFERENCES IN TEXT

The Balanced Budget and Emergency Deficit Control Act of 1985, referred to in subsec. (a)(1), is title II of Pub. L. 99–177, Dec. 12, 1985, 99 Stat. 1038, as amended, which enacted chapter 20 (§900 et seq.) and sections 654 to 656 of this title, amended sections 602, 622, 631 to 642, and 651 to 653 of this title, sections 1104 to 1106, and 1109 of Title 31, Money and Finance, and section 911 of Title 42, The Public Health and Welfare, repealed section 661 of this title, enacted provisions set out as notes under section 900 of this title and section 911 of Title 42, and amended provisions set out as a note under section 621 of this title. For complete classification of this Act to the Code, see Short Title note set out under section 900 of this title and Tables.

AMENDMENTS

1997—Subsec. (a)(1). Pub. L. 105–33 substituted "section 251(c) of the Balanced Budget and Emergency Deficit Control Act of 1985" for "section 665(a)(2) of this title".

SECTION REFERRED TO IN OTHER SECTIONS

This section is referred to in section 691a of this title.

§691d. Expedited congressional consideration of disapproval bills

(a) Receipt and referral of special message

Each special message transmitted under this subchapter shall be referred to the Committee on the Budget and the appropriate committee or committees of the Senate and the Committee on the Budget and the appropriate committee or committees of the House of Representatives. Each such message shall be printed as a document of the House of Representatives.

(b) Time period for expedited procedures

(1) There shall be a congressional review period of 30 calendar days of session, beginning on the first calendar day of session after the date on which the special message is received in the House of Representatives and the Senate, during which the procedures contained in this section shall apply to both Houses of Congress.

(2) In the House of Representatives the procedures set forth in this section shall not apply after the end of the period described in paragraph (1).

(3) If Congress adjourns at the end of a Congress prior to the expiration of the period described in paragraph (1) and a disapproval bill was then pending in either House of Congress or a committee thereof (including a conference committee of the two Houses of Congress), or was pending before the President, a disapproval bill for the same special message may be introduced within the first five calendar days of session of the next Congress and shall be treated as a disapproval bill under this subchapter, and the time period described in paragraph (1) shall commence on the day of introduction of that disapproval bill.

(c) Introduction of disapproval bills

(1) In order for a disapproval bill to be considered under the procedures set forth in this section, the bill must meet the definition of a disapproval bill and must be introduced no later than the fifth calendar day of session following the beginning of the period described in subsection (b)(1) of this section.

(2) In the case of a disapproval bill introduced in the House of Representatives, such bill shall include in the first blank space referred to in section 691e(6)(C) of this title a list of the reference numbers for all cancellations made by the President in the special message to which such disapproval bill relates.

(d) Consideration in House of Representatives

(1) Any committee of the House of Representatives to which a disapproval bill is referred shall report it without amendment, and with or without recommendation, not later than the seventh calendar day of session after the date of its introduction. If any committee fails to report the bill within that period, it is in order to move that the House discharge the committee from further consideration of the bill, except that such a motion may not be made after the committee has reported a disapproval bill with respect to the same special message. A motion to discharge may be made only by a Member favoring the bill (but only at a time or place designated by the Speaker in the legislative schedule of the day after the calendar day on which the Member offering the motion announces to the House his intention to do so and the form of the motion). The motion is highly privileged. Debate thereon shall be limited to not more than one hour, the time to be divided in the House equally between a proponent and an opponent. The previous question shall be considered as ordered on the motion to its adoption without intervening motion. A motion to reconsider the vote by which the motion is agreed to or disagreed to shall not be in order.

(2) After a disapproval bill is reported or a committee has been discharged from further consideration, it is in order to move that the House resolve into the Committee of the Whole

House on the State of the Union for consideration of the bill. If reported and the report has been available for at least one calendar day, all points of order against the bill and against consideration of the bill are waived. If discharged, all points of order against the bill and against consideration of the bill are waived. The motion is highly privileged. A motion to reconsider the vote by which the motion is agreed to or disagreed to shall not be in order. During consideration of the bill in the Committee of the Whole, the first reading of the bill shall be dispensed with. General debate shall proceed, shall be confined to the bill, and shall not exceed one hour equally divided and controlled by a proponent and an opponent of the bill. The bill shall be considered as read for amendment under the five-minute rule. Only one motion to rise shall be in order, except if offered by the manager. No amendment to the bill is in order, except any Member if supported by 49 other Members (a quorum being present) may offer an amendment striking the reference number or numbers of a cancellation or cancellations from the bill. Consideration of the bill for amendment shall not exceed one hour excluding time for recorded votes and quorum calls. No amendment shall be subject to further amendment, except pro forma amendments for the purposes of debate only. At the conclusion of the consideration of the bill for amendment, the Committee shall rise and report the bill to the House with such amendments as may have been adopted. The previous question shall be considered as ordered on the bill and amendments thereto to final passage without intervening motion. A motion to reconsider the vote on passage of the bill shall not be in order.

(3) Appeals from decisions of the Chair regarding application of the rules of the House of Representatives to the procedure relating to a disapproval bill shall be decided without debate.

(4) It shall not be in order to consider under this subsection more than one disapproval bill for the same special message except for consideration of a similar Senate bill (unless the House has already rejected a disapproval bill for the same special message) or more than one motion to discharge described in paragraph (1) with respect to a disapproval bill for that special message.

(e) Consideration in Senate

(1) Referral and reporting

Any disapproval bill introduced in the Senate shall be referred to the appropriate committee or committees. A committee to which a disapproval bill has been referred shall report the bill not later than the seventh day of session following the date of introduction of that bill. If any committee fails to report the bill within that period, that committee shall be automatically discharged from further consideration of the bill and the bill shall be placed on the Calendar.

(2) Disapproval bill from House

When the Senate receives from the House of Representatives a disapproval bill, such bill shall not be referred to committee and shall be placed on the Calendar.

(3) Consideration of single disapproval bill

After the Senate has proceeded to the consideration of a disapproval bill for a special message, then no other disapproval bill originating in that same House relating to that same message shall be subject to the procedures set forth in this subsection.

(4) Amendments

(A) Amendments in order

The only amendments in order to a disapproval bill are—

(i) an amendment that strikes the reference number of a cancellation from the disapproval bill; and

(ii) an amendment that only inserts the reference number of a cancellation included in the special message to which the disapproval bill relates that is not already contained in such bill.

(B) Waiver or appeal

An affirmative vote of three-fifths of the Senators, duly chosen and sworn, shall be required in the Senate—

(i) to waive or suspend this paragraph; or

(ii) to sustain an appeal of the ruling of the Chair on a point of order raised under this paragraph.

(5) Motion nondebatable

A motion to proceed to consideration of a disapproval bill under this subsection shall not be debatable. It shall not be in order to move to reconsider the vote by which the motion to proceed was adopted or rejected, although subsequent motions to proceed may be made under this paragraph.

(6) Limit on consideration

(A) After no more than 10 hours of consideration of a disapproval bill, the Senate shall proceed, without intervening action or debate (except as permitted under paragraph (9)), to vote on the final disposition thereof to the exclusion of all amendments not then pending and to the exclusion of all motions, except a motion to reconsider or to table.

(B) A single motion to extend the time for consideration under subparagraph (A) for no more than an additional five hours is in order prior to the expiration of such time and shall be decided without debate.

(C) The time for debate on the disapproval bill shall be equally divided between the Majority Leader and the Minority Leader or their designees.

(7) Debate on amendments

Debate on any amendment to a disapproval bill shall be limited to one hour, equally divided and controlled by the Senator proposing the amendment and the majority manager, unless the majority manager is in favor of the amendment, in which case the minority manager shall be in control of the time in opposition.

(8) No motion to recommit

A motion to recommit a disapproval bill shall not be in order.

(9) Disposition of Senate disapproval bill

If the Senate has read for the third time a disapproval bill that originated in the Senate, then it shall be in order at any time thereafter to move to proceed to the consideration of a disapproval bill for the same special message received from the House of Representatives and placed on the Calendar pursuant to paragraph (2), strike all after the enacting clause, substitute the text of the Senate disapproval bill, agree to the Senate amendment, and vote on final disposition of the House disapproval bill, all without any intervening action or debate.

(10) Consideration of House message

Consideration in the Senate of all motions, amendments, or appeals necessary to dispose of a message from the House of Representatives on a disapproval bill shall be limited to not more than four hours. Debate on each motion or amendment shall be limited to 30 minutes. Debate on any appeal or point of order that is submitted in connection with the disposition of the House message shall be limited to 20 minutes. Any time for debate shall be equally divided and controlled by the proponent and the majority manager, unless the majority manager is a proponent of the motion, amendment, appeal, or point of order, in which case the minority manager shall be in control of the time in opposition.

(f) Consideration in conference

(1) Convening of conference

In the case of disagreement between the two Houses of Congress with respect to a disapproval bill passed by both Houses, conferees should be promptly appointed and a conference promptly convened, if necessary.

(2) House consideration

(A) Notwithstanding any other rule of the House of Representatives, it shall be in order to consider the report of a committee of conference relating to a disapproval bill provided such report has been available for one calendar day (excluding Saturdays, Sundays, or legal holidays, unless the House is in session on such a day) and the accompanying statement shall have been filed in the House.

(B) Debate in the House of Representatives on the conference report and any amendments in disagreement on any disapproval bill shall each be limited to not more than one hour equally divided and controlled by a proponent and an opponent. A motion to further limit debate is not debatable. A motion to recommit the conference report is not in order, and it is not in order to move to reconsider the vote by which the conference report is agreed to or disagreed to.

(3) Senate consideration

Consideration in the Senate of the conference report and any amendments in disagreement on a disapproval bill shall be limited to not more than four hours equally divided and controlled by the Majority Leader and the Minority Leader or their designees. A motion to recommit the conference report is not in order.

(4) Limits on scope

(A) When a disagreement to an amendment in the nature of a substitute has been referred to a conference, the conferees shall report those cancellations that were included in both the bill and the amendment, and may report a cancellation included in either the bill or the amendment, but shall not include any other matter.

(B) When a disagreement on an amendment or amendments of one House to the disapproval bill of the other House has been referred to a committee of conference, the conferees shall report those cancellations upon which both Houses agree and may report any or all of those cancellations upon which there is disagreement, but shall not include any other matter.

(Pub. L. 93–344, title X, § 1025, as added Pub. L. 104–130, § 2(a), Apr. 9, 1996, 110 Stat. 1203.)

TERMINATION OF SECTION

For termination of section by section 5 of Pub. L. 104–130, see Effective and Termination Dates note set out under section 691 of this title.

SECTION REFERRED TO IN OTHER SECTIONS

This section is referred to in section 691c of this title.

§ 691e. Definitions

As used in this subchapter:

(1) Appropriation law

The term "appropriation law" means an Act referred to in section 105 of title 1, including any general or special appropriation Act, or any Act making supplemental, deficiency, or continuing appropriations, that has been signed into law pursuant to Article I, section 7, of the Constitution of the United States.

(2) Calendar day

The term "calendar day" means a standard 24-hour period beginning at midnight.

(3) Calendar days of session

The term "calendar days of session" shall mean only those days on which both Houses of Congress are in session.

(4) Cancel

The term "cancel" or "cancellation" means—

(A) with respect to any dollar amount of discretionary budget authority, to rescind;

(B) with respect to any item of new direct spending—

(i) that is budget authority provided by law (other than an appropriation law), to prevent such budget authority from having legal force or effect;

(ii) that is entitlement authority, to prevent the specific legal obligation of the United States from having legal force or effect; or

(iii) through the food stamp program, to prevent the specific provision of law that results in an increase in budget authority or outlays for that program from having legal force or effect; and

(C) with respect to a limited tax benefit, to prevent the specific provision of law that provides such benefit from having legal force or effect.

(5) Direct spending

The term "direct spending" means—

(A) budget authority provided by law (other than an appropriation law);

(B) entitlement authority; and

(C) the food stamp program.

(6) Disapproval bill

The term "disapproval bill" means a bill or joint resolution which only disapproves one or more cancellations of dollar amounts of discretionary budget authority, items of new direct spending, or limited tax benefits in a special message transmitted by the President under this subchapter and—

(A) the title of which is as follows: "A bill disapproving the cancellations transmitted by the President on _____", the blank space being filled in with the date of transmission of the relevant special message and the public law number to which the message relates;

(B) which does not have a preamble; and

(C) which provides only the following after the enacting clause: "That Congress disapproves of cancellations _____", the blank space being filled in with a list by reference number of one or more cancellations contained in the President's special message, "as transmitted by the President in a special message on _____", the blank space being filled in with the appropriate date, "regarding _____.", the blank space being filled in with the public law number to which the special message relates.

(7) Dollar amount of discretionary budget authority

(A) Except as provided in subparagraph (B), the term "dollar amount of discretionary budget authority" means the entire dollar amount of budget authority—

(i) specified in an appropriation law, or the entire dollar amount of budget authority required to be allocated by a specific proviso in an appropriation law for which a specific dollar figure was not included;

(ii) represented separately in any table, chart, or explanatory text included in the statement of managers or the governing committee report accompanying such law;

(iii) required to be allocated for a specific program, project, or activity in a law (other than an appropriation law) that mandates the expenditure of budget authority from accounts, programs, projects, or activities for which budget authority is provided in an appropriation law;

(iv) represented by the product of the estimated procurement cost and the total quantity of items specified in an appropriation law or included in the statement of managers or the governing committee report accompanying such law; or

(v) represented by the product of the estimated procurement cost and the total quantity of items required to be provided in a law (other than an appropriation law) that mandates the expenditure of budget authority from accounts, programs, projects, or activities for which budget authority is provided in an appropriation law.

(B) The term "dollar amount of discretionary budget authority" does not include—

(i) direct spending;

(ii) budget authority in an appropriation law which funds direct spending provided for in other law;

(iii) any existing budget authority rescinded or canceled in an appropriation law; or

(iv) any restriction, condition, or limitation in an appropriation law or the accompanying statement of managers or committee reports on the expenditure of budget authority for an account, program, project, or activity, or on activities involving such expenditure.

(8) Item of new direct spending

The term "item of new direct spending" means any specific provision of law that is estimated to result in an increase in budget authority or outlays for direct spending relative to the most recent levels calculated pursuant to section 907 of this title.

(9) Limited tax benefit

(A) The term "limited tax benefit" means—

(i) any revenue-losing provision which provides a Federal tax deduction, credit, exclusion, or preference to 100 or fewer beneficiaries under title 26 in any fiscal year for which the provision is in effect; and

(ii) any Federal tax provision which provides temporary or permanent transitional relief for 10 or fewer beneficiaries in any fiscal year from a change to title 26.

(B) A provision shall not be treated as described in subparagraph (A)(i) if the effect of that provision is that—

(i) all persons in the same industry or engaged in the same type of activity receive the same treatment;

(ii) all persons owning the same type of property, or issuing the same type of investment, receive the same treatment; or

(iii) any difference in the treatment of persons is based solely on—

(I) in the case of businesses and associations, the size or form of the business or association involved;

(II) in the case of individuals, general demographic conditions, such as income, marital status, number of dependents, or tax return filing status;

(III) the amount involved; or

(IV) a generally-available election under title 26.

(C) A provision shall not be treated as described in subparagraph (A)(ii) if—

(i) it provides for the retention of prior law with respect to all binding contracts or other legally enforceable obligations in existence on a date contemporaneous with congressional action specifying such date; or

(ii) it is a technical correction to previously enacted legislation that is estimated to have no revenue effect.

(D) For purposes of subparagraph (A)—

(i) all businesses and associations which are related within the meaning of sections

707(b) and 1563(a) of title 26 shall be treated as a single beneficiary;

(ii) all qualified plans of an employer shall be treated as a single beneficiary;

(iii) all holders of the same bond issue shall be treated as a single beneficiary; and

(iv) if a corporation, partnership, association, trust or estate is the beneficiary of a provision, the shareholders of the corporation, the partners of the partnership, the members of the association, or the beneficiaries of the trust or estate shall not also be treated as beneficiaries of such provision.

(E) For purposes of this paragraph, the term "revenue-losing provision" means any provision which results in a reduction in Federal tax revenues for any one of the two following periods—

(i) the first fiscal year for which the provision is effective; or

(ii) the period of the 5 fiscal years beginning with the first fiscal year for which the provision is effective.

(F) The terms used in this paragraph shall have the same meaning as those terms have generally in title 26, unless otherwise expressly provided.

(10) OMB

The term "OMB" means the Director of the Office of Management and Budget.

(Pub. L. 93–344, title X, § 1026, as added Pub. L. 104–130, § 2(a), Apr. 9, 1996, 110 Stat. 1207; amended Pub. L. 105–33, title X, § 10122, Aug. 5, 1997, 111 Stat. 697.)

TERMINATION OF SECTION

For termination of section by section 5 of Pub. L. 104–130, see Effective and Termination Dates note set out under section 691 of this title.

AMENDMENTS

1997—Par. (7)(A)(iv). Pub. L. 105–33 substituted "; or" for "; and".

SECTION REFERRED TO IN OTHER SECTIONS

This section is referred to in sections 691, 691d, 691f of this title.

§ 691f. Identification of limited tax benefits

(a) Statement by Joint Tax Committee

The Joint Committee on Taxation shall review any revenue or reconciliation bill or joint resolution which includes any amendment to title 26 that is being prepared for filing by a committee of conference of the two Houses, and shall identify whether such bill or joint resolution contains any limited tax benefits. The Joint Committee on Taxation shall provide to the committee of conference a statement identifying any such limited tax benefits or declaring that the bill or joint resolution does not contain any limited tax benefits. Any such statement shall be made available to any Member of Congress by the Joint Committee on Taxation immediately upon request.

(b) Statement included in legislation

(1) Notwithstanding any other rule of the House of Representatives or any rule or prece-

dent of the Senate, any revenue or reconciliation bill or joint resolution which includes any amendment to title 26 reported by a committee of conference of the two Houses may include, as a separate section of such bill or joint resolution, the information contained in the statement of the Joint Committee on Taxation, but only in the manner set forth in paragraph (2).

(2) The separate section permitted under paragraph (1) shall read as follows: "Section 1021(a)(3) of the Congressional Budget and Impoundment Control Act of 1974 shall _____ apply to _____.", with the blank spaces being filled in with—

(A) in any case in which the Joint Committee on Taxation identifies limited tax benefits in the statement required under subsection (a), the word "only" in the first blank space and a list of all of the specific provisions of the bill or joint resolution identified by the Joint Committee on Taxation in such statement in the second blank space; or

(B) in any case in which the Joint Committee on Taxation declares that there are no limited tax benefits in the statement required under subsection (a), the word "not" in the first blank space and the phrase "any provision of this Act" in the second blank space.

(c) President's authority

If any revenue or reconciliation bill or joint resolution is signed into law pursuant to Article I, section 7, of the Constitution of the United States—

(1) with a separate section described in subsection (b)(2) of this section, then the President may use the authority granted in section 691(a)(3) of this title only to cancel any limited tax benefit in that law, if any, identified in such separate section; or

(2) without a separate section described in subsection (b)(2) of this section, then the President may use the authority granted in section 691(a)(3) of this title to cancel any limited tax benefit in that law that meets the definition in section 691e of this title.

(d) Congressional identifications of limited tax benefits

There shall be no judicial review of the congressional identification under subsections (a) and (b) of this section of a limited tax benefit in a conference report.

(Pub. L. 93–344, title X, § 1027, as added Pub. L. 104–130, § 2(a), Apr. 9, 1996, 110 Stat. 1210.)

TERMINATION OF SECTION

For termination of section by section 5 of Pub. L. 104–130, see Effective and Termination Dates note set out under section 691 of this title.

REFERENCES IN TEXT

Section 1021(a)(3) of the Congressional Budget and Impoundment Control Act of 1974, referred to in subsec. (b)(2), is classified to section 691(a)(3) of this title.

§ 692. Judicial review

(a) Expedited review

(1) Any Member of Congress or any individual adversely affected by part C of title X of the Congressional Budget and Impoundment Control

Act of 1974 [2 U.S.C. 691 et seq.] may bring an action, in the United States District Court for the District of Columbia, for declaratory judgment and injunctive relief on the ground that any provision of this part violates the Constitution.

(2) A copy of any complaint in an action brought under paragraph (1) shall be promptly delivered to the Secretary of the Senate and the Clerk of the House of Representatives, and each House of Congress shall have the right to intervene in such action.

(3) Nothing in this section or in any other law shall infringe upon the right of the House of Representatives to intervene in an action brought under paragraph (1) without the necessity of adopting a resolution to authorize such intervention.

(b) Appeal to Supreme Court

Notwithstanding any other provision of law, any order of the United States District Court for the District of Columbia which is issued pursuant to an action brought under paragraph (1) of subsection (a) of this section shall be reviewable by appeal directly to the Supreme Court of the United States. Any such appeal shall be taken by a notice of appeal filed within 10 calendar days after such order is entered; and the jurisdictional statement shall be filed within 30 calendar days after such order is entered. No stay of an order issued pursuant to an action brought under paragraph (1) of subsection (a) of this section shall be issued by a single Justice of the Supreme Court.

(c) Expedited consideration

It shall be the duty of the District Court for the District of Columbia and the Supreme Court of the United States to advance on the docket and to expedite to the greatest possible extent the disposition of any matter brought under subsection (a) of this section.

(Pub. L. 104–130, §3, Apr. 9, 1996, 110 Stat. 1211.)

TERMINATION OF SECTION

For termination of section by section 5 of Pub. L. 104–130, see Effective and Termination Dates note set out under section 691 of this title.

REFERENCES IN TEXT

The Congressional Budget and Impoundment Control Act of 1974, referred to in subsec. (a)(1), is Pub. L. 93–344, July 12, 1974, 88 Stat. 297, as amended. Part C of title X of the Act is classified generally to subchapter III (§691 et seq.) of this chapter. For complete classification of this Act to the Code, see Short Title note set out under section 621 of this title and Tables.

CODIFICATION

Section was enacted as part of the Line Item Veto Act, and not as part of the Line Item Veto Act of 1996 which comprises this subchapter.

CHAPTER 18—LEGISLATIVE PERSONNEL FINANCIAL DISCLOSURE REQUIREMENTS

§§ 701 to 709. Transferred

CODIFICATION

Sections 701 to 709, comprising title I of the Ethics in Government Act of 1978, Pub. L. 95–521, was amended generally by Pub. L. 101–194, title II, §202, Nov. 30, 1989, 103 Stat. 1724, effective Jan. 1, 1991, and was transferred

to section 101 et seq. of the Appendix to Title 5, Government Organization and Employees.

Section 701, Pub. L. 95–521, title I, §101, Oct. 26, 1978, 92 Stat. 1824; Pub. L. 96–19, §§2(a)(1), (b), (c)(1), 4(b)(1), (d)–(f), 5, June 13, 1979, 93 Stat. 37, 38, 40, related to legislative personnel financial disclosure.

Section 702, Pub. L. 95–521, title I, §102, Oct. 26, 1978, 92 Stat. 1825; Pub. L. 96–19, §§3(a)(1), (b), 6(a), 7(a)–(d)(1), (f), 9(b), (c)(1), (j), June 13, 1979, 93 Stat. 39–43; Pub. L. 97–51, §130(b), Oct. 1, 1981, 95 Stat. 966; Pub. L. 98–150, §10, Nov. 11, 1983, 97 Stat. 962, related to contents of reports.

Section 703, Pub. L. 95–521, title I, §103, Oct. 26, 1978, 92 Stat. 1831; Pub. L. 96–19, §§4(b)(2), 9(a), June 13, 1979, 93 Stat. 40, 42, related to filing of reports.

Section 704, Pub. L. 95–521, title I, §104, Oct. 26, 1978, 92 Stat. 1832; Pub. L. 96–19, §8(a), June 13, 1979, 93 Stat. 41, related to accessibility of reports.

Section 705, Pub. L. 95–521, title I, §105, Oct. 26, 1978, 92 Stat. 1833, related to review and compliance procedures.

Section 706, Pub. L. 95–521, title I, §106, Oct. 26, 1978, 92 Stat. 1833, related to failure to file or filing false reports.

Section 707, Pub. L. 95–521, title I, §107, Oct. 26, 1978, 92 Stat. 1834; Pub. L. 96–19, §9(d), (g), June 13, 1979, 93 Stat. 42, 43; Pub. L. 99–514, §2, Oct. 22, 1986, 100 Stat. 2095, related to definitions.

Section 708, Pub. L. 95–521, title I, §108, Oct. 26, 1978, 92 Stat. 1835; Pub. L. 96–19, §9(t), June 13, 1979, 93 Stat. 44, related to State laws affected.

Section 709, Pub. L. 95–521, title I, §109, Oct. 26, 1978, 92 Stat. 1836, related to study by Comptroller General.

CHAPTER 19—CONGRESSIONAL AWARD PROGRAM

SUBCHAPTER I—CONGRESSIONAL AWARD PROGRAM

SUBCHAPTER I—CONGRESSIONAL AWARD PROGRAM

§ 801. Establishment, etc., of Congressional Award Board

There is established a board to be known as the Congressional Award Board (hereinafter in this subchapter referred to as the "Board"), which shall be responsible for administering the Congressional Award Program described under section 802 of this title. The Board shall not be an agency or instrumentality of the United States, and the United States is not liable for any obligation or liability incurred by the Board.

(Pub. L. 96–114, title I, §101, formerly §2, Nov. 16, 1979, 93 Stat. 851; renumbered title I, §101, and amended Pub. L. 106–533, §1(b)(1)–(3), Nov. 22, 2000, 114 Stat. 2553.)

AMENDMENTS

2000—Pub. L. 106–533, §1(b)(3)(A), substituted "subchapter" for "chapter".

Pub. L. 106–533, §1(b)(3)(B), made technical amendment to reference in original act which appears in text as reference to section 802 of this title.

SHORT TITLE OF 1992 AMENDMENT

Pub. L. 102–457, §1, Oct. 23, 1992, 106 Stat. 2265, provided that: "This Act [amending sections 804 and 808 of this title] may be cited as the 'Congressional Award Act Amendments of 1992'."

SHORT TITLE OF 1990 AMENDMENT

Pub. L. 101–525, §1, Nov. 6, 1990, 104 Stat. 2305, provided that: "This Act [amending sections 802, 803, and 806 to 808 of this title and enacting provisions set out as a note under section 808 of this title] may be cited as the 'Congressional Award Amendments of 1990'."

SHORT TITLE OF 1988 AMENDMENT

Pub. L. 100–674, §1, Nov. 17, 1988, 102 Stat. 3996, provided that: "This Act [amending sections 802, 803, and 806 to 808 of this title and enacting provisions set out as a note under section 803 of this title] may be cited as the 'Congressional Award Act Amendments of 1988'."

SHORT TITLE OF 1985 AMENDMENT

Pub. L. 99–161, §1, Nov. 25, 1985, 99 Stat. 934, provided that: "This Act [amending sections 802, 803, and 806 to 808 of this title and repealing provisions set out as a note under section 803 of this title] may be cited as the 'Congressional Award Amendments of 1985'."

SHORT TITLE

Pub. L. 96–114, title II, §201, as added by Pub. L. 106–533, §1(a), Nov. 22, 2000, 114 Stat. 2545, provided that: "This title [enacting subchapter II of this chapter] may be cited as the 'Congressional Recognition for Excellence in Arts Education Act'."

Section 1 of Pub. L. 96–114 provided that: "This Act [enacting this chapter] may be cited as the 'Congressional Award Act'."

§ 802. Program

(a) Establishment, functions, and purposes; nature of awards

The Board shall establish and administer a program to be known as the Congressional Award Program, which shall be designed to promote initiative, achievement, and excellence among youths in the areas of public service, personal development, and physical and expedition fitness. Under the program medals shall be awarded to young people within the United States, aged fourteen through twenty-three (subject to such exceptions as the Board may prescribe), who have satisfied the standards of achievement established by the Board under subsection (b) of this section. Each medal shall consist of gold-plate over bronze, rhodium over bronze, or bronze and shall be struck in accordance with subsection (f) of this section.

(b) Implementation requirements for Board

In carrying out the Congressional Award Program, the Board shall—

(1) establish the standards of achievement required for young people to qualify as recipients of the medals and establish such procedures as may be required to verify that individuals satisfy such qualifications;

(2) designate the recipients of the medals in accordance with the standards established under paragraph (1) of this subsection;

(3) delineate such roles as the Board considers to be appropriate for the Director and Regional Directors in administering the Congressional Award, and set forth in the bylaws of the Board the duties, salaries, and benefits of the Director and Regional Directors;

(4) raise funds for the operation of the program; and

(5) take such other actions as may be appropriate for the administration of the Congressional Award Program.

No salary established by the Board under paragraph (3) shall exceed $75,000 per annum, except that for calendar years after 1986, such limit shall be increased in proportion to increases in the Consumer Price Index.

(c) Presentation of awards

The Board shall arrange for the presentation of the awards to the recipients and shall provide for participation by Members of Congress in such presentation, when appropriate. To the extent possible, recipients shall be provided with opportunities to exchange information and views with Members of Congress during the presentation of the awards.

(d) Scholarships for recipients of Congressional Award Gold, Silver, and Bronze Medals

The Board may award scholarships in such amounts as the Board determines to be appropriate to any recipient of the Congressional Award Gold, Silver, and Bronze Medals.

(e) Omitted

(f) Congressional Award Program medals

(1) Design and striking

The Secretary of the Treasury shall strike the medals described in subsection (a) of this section and awarded by the Board under this chapter. Subject to subsection (a) of this section, the medals shall be of such quantity, design, and specifications as the Secretary of the Treasury may determine, after consultation with the Board.

(2) National medals

The medals struck pursuant to this chapter are National medals for purposes of chapter 51 of title 31.

(3) Authorization of appropriations

There are authorized to be charged against the Numismatic Public Enterprise Fund such amounts as may be necessary to pay for the cost of the medals struck pursuant to this chapter.

(Pub. L. 96–114, title I, §102, formerly §3, Nov. 16, 1979, 93 Stat. 851; Pub. L. 99–161, §4(a)–(c), Nov. 25, 1985, 99 Stat. 934; Pub. L. 100–674, §2(a), Nov. 17, 1988, 102 Stat. 3996; Pub. L. 101–525, §3, Nov. 6, 1990, 104 Stat. 2305; Pub. L. 103–329, title VI, §637, Sept. 30, 1994, 108 Stat. 2431; Pub. L. 106–63, §1(a), Oct. 1, 1999, 113 Stat. 510; renumbered title I, §102, and amended Pub. L. 106–533, §1(b)(1), (2), (4), Nov. 22, 2000, 114 Stat. 2553.)

§ 803. Board organization

(a) Membership; composition; appointment criteria; derivation of appointment

(1) The Board shall consist of 25 members, as follows:

(A) Six members appointed by the majority leader of the Senate, 1 of whom shall be a recipient of the Congressional Award.

(B) Six members appointed by the minority leader of the Senate, 1 of whom shall be a a[1] local Congressional Award program volunteer.

(C) Six members appointed by the Speaker of the House of Representatives, 1 of whom shall be a a[1] local Congressional Award program volunteer.

(D) Six members appointed by the minority leader of the House of Representatives, 1 of

---

[1] So in original.

whom shall be a recipient of the Congressional Award.

(E) The Director of the Board, who shall serve as a nonvoting member.

(2) In making appointments to the Board, the congressional leadership shall consider recommendations submitted by any interested party, including any member of the Board. One of the members appointed under each of subparagraphs (A) through (D) of paragraph (1) shall be a member of the Congress.

(3) Individuals appointed to the Board shall have an interest in one or more of the fields of concern of the Congressional Award Program.

(4) For the purpose of determining the derivation of the appointment of any person appointed to the Board under this section, if there is a change in the status of majority and minority between the parties of the House or the Senate, each person appointed under this section shall be deemed to have been appointed by the leadership position set out in subsection (a)(1) of this section of the party of the individual who made the initial appointment of such person.

(b) Terms of appointed members; reappointment

(1) Appointed members of the Board shall continue to serve at the pleasure of the officer by whom they are appointed, and (unless reappointed under paragraph (3)) shall serve for a term of 4 years.

(2) For the purpose of adjusting the terms of Board members to allow for staggered appointments, the following distribution of Board terms shall take effect at the first meeting of the Board occurring after November 6, 1990:

(A) Those members who have served 10 years or more, as of the date of such meeting, shall have an appointment expiring on a date 2 years from October 1, 1990.

(B) Those members who have served for 6 months or less, as of the date of such meeting, shall have an appointment expiring on a date 6 years from October 11, 1990.

(C) All other members shall apportion the remaining Board positions between equal numbers of 2 and 4 year terms (providing that if there are an unequal number of remaining members, there shall be a predominance of 4 year terms), such apportionment to be made by lot.

(3)(A) Subject to the limitations in subparagraphs (B) and (C) of this paragraph, members of the Board may be reappointed, provided that no member may serve more than 2 consecutive terms.

(B) Members of the Board covered under paragraph (2)(A) of this section[2] shall not be eligible for reappointment to the Board. Members of the Board covered under subparagraphs (B) and (C) of paragraph (2) of this section[2] may be reappointed for 1 additional consecutive 4 year term.

(C) Members of the Board who serve as chairman of the Board shall not have the time during which they serve as chairman used in the computation of their period of service for purposes of this paragraph and paragraph (2).

_____
[2] So in original. Probably should be "subsection".

(c) Vacancies in membership

(1) Any vacancy in the Board shall be filled in the same manner in which the original appointment was made.

(2) Any appointed member of the Board may continue to serve after the expiration of his term until his successor has taken office.

(3) Vacancies in the membership of the Board shall not affect its power to function if there remain sufficient members to constitute a quorum under subsection (d) of this section.

(d) Notice; quorum

(1) A meeting of the Board may be convened only if—

(A) notice of the meeting was provided to each member in accordance with the bylaws; and

(B) not less than 11 members are present for the meeting at the time given in the notice.

(2) A majority of the members present when a meeting is convened shall constitute a quorum for the remainder of the meeting.

(e) Compensation for travel expenses of members

Members of the Board shall serve without pay but may be compensated for reasonable travel expenses incurred by them in the performance of their duties as members of the Board.

(f) Meetings

The Board shall meet at least twice a year at the call of the Chairman (with at least one meeting in the District of Columbia) and at such other times as the Chairman may determine to be appropriate. The Chairman shall call a meeting of the Board whenever one-third of the members of the Board submit written requests for such a meeting.

(g) Chairman and Vice Chairman

The Chairman and the Vice Chairman of the Board shall be elected from among the members of the Board by a majority vote of the Board for such terms as the Board determines. The Vice Chairman shall perform the duties of the Chairman in his absence.

(h) Appointment, functions, etc., of committees; membership

(1) The Board may appoint such committees, and assign to the committees such functions, as may be appropriate to assist the Board in carrying out its duties under this chapter. Members of such committees may include the members of the Board or such other qualified individuals as the Board may select.

(2) Any employee or officer of the Federal Government may serve as a member of a committee created by the Board, but may not receive compensation for services performed for such a committee.

(i) Bylaws and regulations; contents; transmittal to Congress

The Board shall establish such bylaws and other regulations as may be appropriate to enable the Board to carry out its functions under this chapter. Such bylaws and other regulations shall include provisions to prevent any conflict of interest, or the appearance of any conflict of interest, in the procurement and employment actions taken by the Board or by any officer or employee of the Board. Such bylaws shall include appropriate fiscal control, funds accountability, and operating principles to ensure compliance with the provisions of section 806 of this title. A copy of such bylaws shall be transmitted to each House of Congress not later than 90 days after November 25, 1985, and not later than 10 days after any subsequent amendment or revision of such bylaws.

(j) Removal from Board

Any member of the Board who fails to attend 4 consecutive Board meetings scheduled pursuant to the bylaws of the Board and for which proper notice has been given under such bylaws, or to send a designee of such member (approved in advance by the Board under provisions of its bylaws), is, by operation of this subsection, removed, for cause, from the Board as of the date of the last meeting from which they are absent. The Chairman of the Board shall take such steps as are necessary to inform members who have 3 absences of this subsection. The Chairman shall notify the House and the Senate, including the appropriate committees of each body, whenever there is a vacancy created by the operation of this subsection.

(Pub. L. 96–114, title I, § 103, formerly § 4, Nov. 16, 1979, 93 Stat. 852; Pub. L. 98–33, § 1, May 25, 1983, 97 Stat. 194; Pub. L. 99–161, §§ 2, 4(d), (e), Nov. 25, 1985, 99 Stat. 934, 935; Pub. L. 100–674, § 2(b), Nov. 17, 1988, 102 Stat. 3996; Pub. L. 101–525, §§ 4–6, Nov. 6, 1990, 104 Stat. 2305, 2306; Pub. L. 106–63, § 1(b), Oct. 1, 1999, 113 Stat. 510; renumbered title I, § 103, and amended Pub. L. 106–533, § 1(b)(1), (2), (5), Nov. 22, 2000, 114 Stat. 2553, 2554.)

AMENDMENTS

2000—Subsec. (i). Pub. L. 106–533, § 1(b)(5), made technical amendment to reference in original act which appears in text as reference to section 806 of this title.

1999—Subsec. (a)(1)(A). Pub. L. 106–63, § 1(b)(1), substituted "recipient of the Congressional Award" for "member of the Congressional Award Association".

Subsec. (a)(1)(B), (C). Pub. L. 106–63, § 1(b)(2), substituted "a local Congressional Award program volunteer" for "representative of a local Congressional Award Council".

Subsec. (a)(1)(D). Pub. L. 106–63, § 1(b)(1), substituted "recipient of the Congressional Award" for "member of the Congressional Award Association".

1990—Subsec. (a)(4). Pub. L. 101–525, § 4, added par. (4).

Subsec. (b). Pub. L. 101–525, § 5, designated existing provision as par. (1) and substituted "and (unless reappointed under paragraph (3)) shall serve for a term of 4 years" for "but (unless reappointed) shall not serve for more than four years", and added pars. (2) and (3).

Subsec. (j). Pub. L. 101–525, § 6, added subsec. (j).

1988—Subsec. (a)(1). Pub. L. 100–674, § 2(b)(1), in introductory provisions, substituted "25" for "thirty-three", in subpars. (A) to (D), substituted "Six members" for "Eight members", in subpars. (A) and (D), inserted ", 1 of whom shall be a member of the Congressional Award Association", and in subpars. (B) and (C), inserted ", 1 of whom shall be a representative of a local Congressional Award Council".

Subsec. (d). Pub. L. 100–674, § 2(b)(2), amended subsec. (d) generally. Prior to amendment, subsec. (d) read as follows: "A majority of the members of the Board shall constitute a quorum."

1985—Subsec. (a)(2). Pub. L. 99–161, § 2(1), inserted "One of the members appointed under each of subparagraphs (A) through (D) of paragraph (1) shall be a member of the Congress."

Subsec. (b). Pub. L. 99–161, § 2(2), amended subsec. (b) generally, substituting provisions for continuance of service of appointed members at pleasure of appointing officer, but unless reappointed, for not more than four years, for provisions limiting term of service to six years with exceptions for first appointed members and individuals appointed to Board after March 31, 1983, whose terms were limited.

Subsec. (c)(2) to (4). Pub. L. 99–161, § 2(3), struck out par. (2) limiting term of service of any member appointed to fill out an unexpired term to remainder of that term and redesignated pars. (3) and (4) as (2) and (3), respectively.

Subsec. (f). Pub. L. 99–161, § 4(d), substituted "meet at least twice a year at the call of the Chairman (with at least one meeting in the District of Columbia)" for "meet annually at the call of the Chairman".

Subsec. (i). Pub. L. 99–161, § 4(e), inserted requirement that bylaws and other regulations include provisions preventing conflict of interest, and include appropriate fiscal control, funds accountability, etc., to comply with section 806 of this title, and inserted provisions requiring transmittal of a copy of such bylaws to each House of Congress within specified periods of time.

1983—Subsec. (a)(1). Pub. L. 98–33, § 1(a)(1), (2), substituted "thirty-three" for "seventeen" in the matter preceding subpar. (A), and substituted "Eight" for "Four" in each of subpars. (A) through (D).

Subsec. (a)(2). Pub. L. 98–33, § 1(a)(3), struck out "or the Committee for the Establishment and Promotion of the Congressional Award" after "member of the Board".

Subsec. (b). Pub. L. 98–33, § 1(b), designated existing provisions as par. (1); in par. (1), as so designated, redesignated pars. (1) to (3) as subpars. (A) to (C), respectively, and substituted "Except as provided in paragraph (2), appointed" for "Appointed"; and added par. (2).

TRANSITION PROVISIONS

Section 3 of Pub. L. 100–674 provided that: "Not later than 120 days after the date of the enactment of this Act [Nov. 17, 1988], the congressional leadership shall appoint members to fill vacancies on the Congressional Award Board in accordance with section 4(a) of the Congressional Award Act [2 U.S.C. 803(a)] (as amended by section 2(b)). In filling such vacancies, the congressional leadership shall first appoint members from the Congressional Award Association and local Congressional Award Councils in accordance with section 4(a) of the Congressional Award Act (as amended by section 2(b))."

EXCEPTIONAL TERMS FOR CERTAIN BOARD MEMBERS

Section 2 of Pub. L. 98–33, relating to exceptional terms for certain individuals appointed to the Congressional Award Board, Nov. 25, 1985, 99 Stat. 936, was repealed by Pub. L. 99–161, § 5, Nov. 25, 1985, 99 Stat. 936.

§ 804. Administration

(a) Director; status; appointment and term; removal

In the administration of the Congressional Award Program, the Board shall be assisted by a Director, who shall be the principal executive of the program and who shall supervise the affairs of the Board. The Director shall be appointed by a majority vote of the Board, and shall serve for such term as the Board may determine. The Director may be removed by a majority vote of the Board.

(b) Functions of Director

The Director shall, in consultation with the Board—

(1) formulate programs to carry out the policies of the Congressional Award Program;

(2) establish such divisions within the Congressional Award Program as may be appropriate; and

(3) employ and provide for the compensation of such personnel as may be necessary to carry out the Congressional Award Program, subject to such policies as the Board shall prescribe under its bylaws.

(c) Requirements regarding financial operations; noncompliance with requirements

(1) The Director shall, in consultation with the Board, ensure that appropriate procedures for fiscal control and fund accounting are established for the financial operations of the Congressional Award Program, and that such operations are administered by personnel with expertise in accounting and financial management. Such personnel may be retained under contract. In carrying out this paragraph, the Director shall ensure that the liabilities of the Board do not, for any calendar year, exceed the assets of the Board.

(2)(A) The Comptroller General of the United States shall determine, for calendar years 1993[1] 1994, 1995, 1996, 1997, 1998, 1999, 2000, 2001, 2002, 2003, and 2004, whether the Director has substantially complied with paragraph (1). The findings made by the Comptroller General under the preceding sentence shall be included in the first report submitted under section 807(b)[2] of this title after December 31, 1994.

(B) If the Director fails to substantially comply with paragraph (1), the Board shall take such actions as may be necessary to prepare, pursuant to section 808[2] of this title, for the orderly cessation of the activities of the Board.

(Pub. L. 96–114, title I, §104, formerly §5, Nov. 16, 1979, 93 Stat. 853; Pub. L. 102–457, §2, Oct. 23, 1992, 106 Stat. 2265; Pub. L. 104–208, div. A, title V, §5401(a), Sept. 30, 1996, 110 Stat. 3009–511; Pub. L. 106–63, §1(c), Oct. 1, 1999, 113 Stat. 510; renumbered title I, §104, Pub. L. 106–533, §1(b)(1), (2), Nov. 22, 2000, 114 Stat. 2553.)

REFERENCES IN TEXT

Sections 807(b) and 808 of this title, referred to in subsec. (c)(2), were in the original references to sections 8(b) and 9 which were renumbered sections 107(b) and 108 by Pub. L. 106–533, §1(b)(2), Nov. 22, 2000, 114 Stat. 2553.

AMENDMENTS

1999—Subsec. (c)(2)(A). Pub. L. 106–63 substituted "1998, 1999, 2000, 2001, 2002, 2003, and 2004" for "and 1998".

1996—Subsec. (c)(2)(A). Pub. L. 104–208 substituted "1994, 1995, 1996, 1997, and 1998" for "and 1994".

1992—Subsec. (c). Pub. L. 102–457 added subsec. (c).

§805. Regional award directors of program; appointment criteria

Regional award directors may be appointed by the Board, upon recommendation of the Director, for any State or other appropriate geographic area of the United States. The Director shall make such recommendations with respect to a State or geographic area only after soliciting recommendations regarding such appointments from public and private youth organizations within such State or geographic area.

---

[1] So in original. Probably should be followed by a comma.
[2] See References in Text note below.

(Pub. L. 96–114, title I, §105, formerly §6, Nov. 16, 1979, 93 Stat. 853; renumbered title I, §105, Pub. L. 106–533, §1(b)(1), (2), Nov. 22, 2000, 114 Stat. 2553.)

§806. Powers, functions, and limitations

(a) General operating and expenditure authority

Subject to such limitations as may be provided for under this section, the Board may take such actions and make such expenditures as may be necessary to carry out the Congressional Award Program, except that—

(1) the Board shall carry out its functions and make expenditures with only such resources as are available to the Board from sources other than the Federal Government; and

(2) the Board shall not take any actions which would disqualify the Board from treatment (for tax purposes) as an organization described in section 501(c)(3) of title 26.

(b) Mandatory functions

(1) The Board shall establish such functions and procedures as may be necessary to carry out the provisions of this chapter.

(2) The functions established by the Board under paragraph (1) shall include—

(A) communication with local Congressional Award Councils concerning the Congressional Award Program;

(B) provision, upon the request of any local Congressional Award Council, of such technical assistance as may be necessary to assist such council with its responsibilities, including the provision of medals, the preparation and provision of applications, guidance on disposition of applications, arrangements with respect to local award ceremonies, and other responsibilities of such council;

(C) conduct of outreach activities to establish new local Congressional Award Councils, particularly in inner-city areas and rural areas;

(D) in addition to those activities authorized under subparagraph (C), conduct of outreach activities to encourage, where appropriate, the establishment and development of Statewide Congressional Award Councils;

(E) fundraising;

(F) conduct of an annual Gold Medal Awards ceremony in the District of Columbia;

(G) consideration of implementation of the provisions of this chapter relating to scholarships; and

(H) carrying out of duties relating to management of the national office of the Congressional Award Program, including supervision of office personnel and of the office budget.

(c) Statewide Congressional Award Councils; establishment, purposes, duties, etc.

(1) In carrying out its functions with respect to Statewide Congressional Award Councils (hereinafter in this subsection referred to as Statewide Councils) under subsection (b) of this section, the Board shall develop guidelines, criteria, and standards for the formation of Statewide Councils. In order to create a Statewide Council, Members of Congress and Senators from each respective State are encouraged to work jointly with the Board.

(2) The establishment of Statewide Councils is intended to—

(A) facilitate expanded public participation and involvement in the program; and

(B) promote greater opportunities for involvement by members of the State congressional delegation.

(3) The duties and responsibilities of each Statewide Council established pursuant to this section shall include, but not be limited to, the following:

(A) promoting State and local awareness of the Congressional Award Program;

(B) review of participant records and activities;

(C) review and verification of information on, and recommendation of, candidates to the national board for approval;

(D) planning and organization of bronze and silver award ceremonies;

(E) assisting gold award recipients with travel to and from the national gold award ceremony; and

(F) designation of a Statewide coordinator to serve as a liaison between the State and local boards and the national board.

(4) Each Statewide Council established pursuant to this section is authorized to receive public monetary and in-kind contributions, which may be made available to local boards to supplement or defray operating expenses. The Board shall adopt appropriate financial management methods in order to ensure the proper accounting of these funds.

(5) Each Statewide Council established pursuant to this section shall comply with the standard charter requirements of the national board of directors.

(d) Contracting authority

The Board may enter into and perform such contracts as may be appropriate to carry out its business, but the Board may not enter into any contract which would obligate the Board to expend an amount greater than the amount available to the Board for the purpose of such contract during the fiscal year in which the expenditure is made.

(e) Obtaining and acceptance of non-Federal funds and resources; indirect resources

(1) Subject to the provisions of paragraph (2), the Board may seek and accept funds and other resources to carry out its activities. The Board may not accept any funds or other resources which are—

(A) donated with a restriction on their use unless such restriction merely provides that such funds or other resources be used in furtherance of the Congressional Award Program or a specific regional or local program; and

(B) donated subject to the condition that the identity of the donor of the funds or resources shall remain anonymous.

The Board may permit donors to use the name of the Board or the name "Congressional Award Program" in advertising.

(2) Except as otherwise provided in this chapter, the Board may not receive any Federal funds or resources. The Board may benefit from in-kind and indirect resources provided by Offices of Members of Congress or the Congress. Further, the Board is not prohibited from receiving indirect benefits from efforts or activities undertaken in collaboration with entities which receive Federal funds or resources.

(f) Acceptance and utilization of services of voluntary, uncompensated personnel

The Board may accept and utilize the services of voluntary, uncompensated personnel.

(g) Lease, etc., of real or personal property

The Board may lease (or otherwise hold), acquire, or dispose of real or personal property necessary for, or relating to, the duties of the Board.

(h) Fiscal authority

The Board shall have no power—

(1) to issue bonds, notes, debentures, or other similar obligations creating long-term indebtedness;

(2) to issue any share of stock or to declare or pay any dividends; or

(3) to provide for any part of the income or assets of the Board to inure to the benefit of any director, officer, or employee of the Board except as reasonable compensation for services or reimbursement for expenses.

(i) Establishment, functions, etc., of private nonprofit corporation; articles of incorporation of corporation; compensation, etc., for director, officer, or employee of corporation

(1) The Board shall provide for the establishment of a private nonprofit corporation for the sole purpose of assisting the Board to carry out the Congressional Award Program, and shall delegate to the corporation such duties as it considers appropriate.

(2) The articles of incorporation of the corporation established under this subsection shall provide that—

(A) the members of the Board of Directors of the corporation shall be the members of the Board, and the Director of the corporation shall be the Director of the Board; and

(B) the extent of the authority of the corporation shall be the same as that of the Board.

(3) No director, officer, or employee of any corporation established under this subsection may receive compensation, travel expenses, or benefits from both the corporation and the Board.

(Pub. L. 96–114, title I, §106, formerly §7, Nov. 16, 1979, 93 Stat. 854; Pub. L. 99–161, §4(f), Nov. 25, 1985, 99 Stat. 935; Pub. L. 99–514, §2, Oct. 22, 1986, 100 Stat. 2095; Pub. L. 100–674, §2(c), Nov. 17, 1988, 102 Stat. 3996; Pub. L. 101–525, §7, Nov. 6, 1990, 104 Stat. 2306; renumbered title I, §106, Pub. L. 106–533, §1(b)(1), (2), Nov. 22, 2000, 114 Stat. 2553.)

AMENDMENTS

1990—Subsec. (a). Pub. L. 101–525, §7(a), which directed the insertion of "(a)" after the section designation, was not executed in view of existing subsec. (a) designation.

Subsec. (b)(2)(C). Pub. L. 101–525, §7(b)(1)(A), substituted "conduct" for "conducting" and struck out "State and" after "new".

Subsec. (b)(2)(D), (E). Pub. L. 101–525, §7(b)(1)(B), added subpar. (D) and redesignated former subpar. (D) as (E). Former subpar. (E) redesignated (F).

Subsec. (b)(2)(F). Pub. L. 101–525, §7(b)(1)(B), (C), redesignated subpar. (E) as (F) and substituted "conduct" for "conducting". Former subpar. (F) redesignated (G).

Subsec. (b)(2)(G), (H). Pub. L. 101–525, §7(b)(1)(B), redesignated subpars. (F) and (G) as (G) and (H), respectively.

Subsecs. (c), (d). Pub. L. 101–525, §7(b)(2), added subsec. (c). Former subsecs. (c) and (d) redesignated (d) and (e), respectively.

Subsec. (e). Pub. L. 101–525, §7(b)(2), (c), redesignated subsec. (d) as (e) and amended it generally. Prior to amendment, subsec. (e) read as follows: "The Board may seek and accept, from sources other than the Federal Government, funds and other resources to carry out its activities. The Board may not accept any funds or other resources which are—

"(1) donated with a restriction on their use unless such restriction merely provides that such funds or other resources be used in furtherance of the Congressional Award Program; or

"(2) donated subject to the condition that the identity of the donor of the funds or resources shall remain anonymous.

The Board may permit donors to use the name of the Board or the name 'Congressional Award Program' in advertising." Former subsec. (e) redesignated (f).

Subsecs. (f) to (i). Pub. L. 101–525, §7(b)(2), redesignated subsecs. (e) to (h) as (f) to (i), respectively.

1988—Pub. L. 100–674, §2(c)(1), substituted "Powers, functions, and limitations" for "Powers and limitations of Board" in section catchline.

Subsecs. (b) to (h). Pub. L. 100–674, §2(c)(2), added subsec. (b) and redesignated former subsecs. (b) to (g) as (c) to (h), respectively.

1986—Subsec. (a)(2). Pub. L. 99–514 substituted "Internal Revenue Code of 1986" for "Internal Revenue Code of 1954", which for purposes of codification was translated as "title 26" thus requiring no change in text.

1985—Subsec. (c). Pub. L. 99–161 inserted at end "The Board may permit donors to use the name of the Board or the name 'Congressional Award Program' in advertising."

SECTION REFERRED TO IN OTHER SECTIONS

This section is referred to in sections 803, 807 of this title.

§ 807. Audits and evaluation

(a) Annual audits by Comptroller General; access to books, documents, papers, and records

The financial records of the Board and of any corporation established under section 806(i)[1] of this title shall be audited annually by the Comptroller General of the United States (hereinafter in this section referred to as the "Comptroller General"). The Comptroller General, or any duly authorized representative of the Comptroller General, shall have access for the purpose of audit to any books, documents, papers, and records of the Board or such corporation (or any agent of the Board or such corporation) which, in the opinion of the Comptroller General, may be pertinent to the Congressional Award Program.

(b) Annual report to Congress on audit results

The Comptroller General shall submit to appropriate officers, committees, and subcommittees of the Congress, by May 15th of each calendar year, a report on the results of the audit of the financial records and on any such additional areas as the Comptroller General determines deserve or require evaluation.

---

[1] See References in Text note below.

(Pub. L. 96–114, title I, §107, formerly §8, Nov. 16, 1979, 93 Stat. 855; Pub. L. 99–161, §4(g), Nov. 25, 1985, 99 Stat. 935; Pub. L. 100–674, §2(e), Nov. 17, 1988, 102 Stat. 3998; Pub. L. 101–525, §8, Nov. 6, 1990, 104 Stat. 2308; renumbered title I, §107, Pub. L. 106–533, §1(b)(1), (2), Nov. 22, 2000, 114 Stat. 2553.)

REFERENCES IN TEXT

Section 806(i) of this title, referred to in subsec. (a), was in the original a reference to section 7(i) which was renumbered section 106 by Pub. L. 106–533, §1(b)(2), Nov. 22, 2000, 114 Stat. 2553.

AMENDMENTS

1990—Subsec. (a). Pub. L. 101–525, §8(1), substituted "section 806(i) of this title" for "section 806(h) of this title" and "annually" for "at least biennially".

Subsec. (b). Pub. L. 101–525, §8(2), added subsec. (b) and struck out former subsec. (b) which required audit to assess adequacy of fiscal control and funds accountability procedures and propriety of expenses.

Subsecs. (c), (d). Pub. L. 101–525, §8(2), struck out subsec. (c) which required the Comptroller General to include in report on first audit performed after Nov. 25, 1985, an evaluation of programs and activities under this chapter and specified contents of such evaluation, and subsec. (d) which directed that report on first audit performed after Nov. 25, 1985, was to be submitted on or before May 15, 1988.

1988—Subsec. (a). Pub. L. 100–674 substituted "section 806(h)" for "section 806(g)".

1985—Pub. L. 99–161, §4(g)(1), inserted "and evaluation" after "Audits" in section catchline.

Subsec. (a). Pub. L. 99–161, §4(g)(2)–(4), designated existing provisions as subsec. (a), substituted "shall be audited at least biennially" for "may be audited", and struck out "at such times as the Comptroller General may determine to be appropriate" after "referred to as the 'Comptroller General')".

Subsecs. (b) to (d). Pub. L. 99–161, §4(g)(5), added subsecs. (b) to (d).

SECTION REFERRED TO IN OTHER SECTIONS

This section is referred to in section 804 of this title.

§ 808. Termination

The Board shall terminate October 1, 2004.

(Pub. L. 96–114, title I, §108, formerly §9, Nov. 16, 1979, 93 Stat. 855; Pub. L. 99–161, §3, Nov. 25, 1985, 99 Stat. 934; Pub. L. 100–674, §2(d), Nov. 17, 1988, 102 Stat. 3997; Pub. L. 101–525, §2(a), Nov. 6, 1990, 104 Stat. 2305; Pub. L. 102–457, §3, Oct. 23, 1992, 106 Stat. 2266; Pub. L. 104–208, div. A, title V, §5401(b), Sept. 30, 1996, 110 Stat. 3009–511; Pub. L. 106–63, §1(d), Oct. 1, 1999, 113 Stat. 510; renumbered title I, §108, Pub. L. 106–533, §1(b)(1), (2), Nov. 22, 2000, 114 Stat. 2553.)

AMENDMENTS

1999—Pub. L. 106–63 substituted "October 1, 2004" for "October 1, 1999".

1996—Pub. L. 104–208 substituted "1999" for "1995".

1992—Pub. L. 102–457 substituted "1995" for "1992".

1990—Pub. L. 101–525 amended section generally, substituting present provision for provisions which had: in subsec. (a) directed that the Board terminate on Nov. 15, 1989; in subsec. (b) provided for alternative termination dates; in subsec. (c) required reports to Congress; in subsecs. (d) and (e) required certification of compliance and verification of information, respectively; and in subsec. (f) mandated dissolution of corporations established by the Board prior to its termination.

1988—Pub. L. 100–674 amended section generally. Prior to amendment, section read as follows: "The Board shall terminate on November 16, 1988. Upon termination of the Board, the Board shall take such actions as may be required to provide for the dissolution of any corporation established by the Board under section 806(g) of this title. The Board shall set forth, in its by-laws, the procedures for dissolution to be followed by the Board.''

1985—Pub. L. 99–161 substituted ''on November 16, 1988'' for ''six years after November 16, 1979''.

SAVINGS PROVISION

Section 5401(c) of div. A of Pub. L. 104–208 provided that: ''During the period of October 1, 1995, through the date of the enactment of this section [Sept. 30, 1996], all actions and functions of the Congressional Award Board under the Congressional Award Act [2 U.S.C. 801 et seq.] shall have the same effect as though no lapse or termination of the Congressional Award Board ever occurred.''

Section 2(b) of Pub. L. 101–525 provided that: ''During the period of October 1, 1990, through the date of the enactment of this section [Nov. 6, 1990], all actions and functions of the Congressional Award Board under the Congressional Award Act (2 U.S.C. 801 et seq.) shall have the same effect as though no lapse or termination of the Board ever occurred.''

SECTION REFERRED TO IN OTHER SECTIONS

This section is referred to in section 804 of this title.

SUBCHAPTER II—CONGRESSIONAL RECOGNITION FOR EXCELLENCE IN ARTS EDUCATION

§ 811. Findings

Congress makes the following findings:

(1) Arts literacy is a fundamental purpose of schooling for all students.

(2) Arts education stimulates, develops, and refines many cognitive and creative skills, critical thinking and nimbleness in judgment, creativity and imagination, cooperative decisionmaking, leadership, high-level literacy and communication, and the capacity for problem-posing and problem-solving.

(3) Arts education contributes significantly to the creation of flexible, adaptable, and knowledgeable workers who will be needed in the 21st century economy.

(4) Arts education improves teaching and learning.

(5) Where parents and families, artists, arts organizations, businesses, local civic and cultural leaders, and institutions are actively engaged in instructional programs, arts education is more successful.

(6) Effective teachers of the arts should be encouraged to continue to learn and grow in mastery of their art form as well as in their teaching competence.

(7) The 1999 study, entitled ''Gaining the Arts Advantage: Lessons from School Districts that Value Arts Education'', found that the literacy, education, programs, learning and growth described in paragraphs (1) through (6) contribute to successful districtwide arts education.

(8) Despite all of the literacy, education, programs, learning and growth findings described in paragraphs (1) through (6), the 1997 National Assessment of Educational Progress reported that students lack sufficient opportunity for participatory learning in the arts.

(9) The Arts Education Partnership, a coalition of national and State education, arts,

business, and civic groups, is an excellent example of one organization that has demonstrated its effectiveness in addressing the purposes described in section 814(a) of this title and the capacity and credibility to administer arts education programs of national significance.

(Pub. L. 96–114, title II, § 202, as added Pub. L. 106–533, § 1(a), Nov. 22, 2000, 114 Stat. 2545.)

SECTION REFERRED TO IN OTHER SECTIONS

This section is referred to in section 814 of this title.

§ 812. Definitions

In this subchapter:

(1) Arts Education Partnership

The term ''Arts Education Partnership'' means a private, nonprofit coalition of education, arts, business, philanthropic, and government organizations that demonstrates and promotes the essential role of arts education in enabling all students to succeed in school, life, and work, and was formed in 1995.

(2) Board

The term ''Board'' means the Congressional Recognition for Excellence in Arts Education Awards Board established under section 813 of this title.

(3) Elementary school; secondary school

The terms ''elementary school'' and ''secondary school'' mean—

(A) a public or private elementary school or secondary school (as the case may be), as defined in section 8801 of title 20; or

(B) a bureau[1] funded school as defined in section 2026 of title 25.

(4) State

The term ''State'' means each of the several States of the United States, the District of Columbia, the Commonwealth of Puerto Rico, Guam, American Samoa, the United States Virgin Islands, the Commonwealth of the Northern Mariana Islands, the Republic of the Marshall Islands, the Federated States of Micronesia, and the Republic of Palau.

(Pub. L. 96–114, title II, § 203, as added Pub. L. 106–533, § 1(a), Nov. 22, 2000, 114 Stat. 2546.)

§ 813. Establishment of Board

There is established within the legislative branch of the Federal Government a Congressional Recognition for Excellence in Arts Education Awards Board. The Board shall be responsible for administering the awards program described in section 814 of this title.

(Pub. L. 96–114, title II, § 204, as added Pub. L. 106–533, § 1(a), Nov. 22, 2000, 114 Stat. 2546.)

SECTION REFERRED TO IN OTHER SECTIONS

This section is referred to in section 812 of this title.

§ 814. Board duties

(a) Awards program established

The Board shall establish and administer an awards program to be known as the ''Congres-

_____
[1] So in original. Probably should be ''Bureau''.

sional Recognition for Excellence in Arts Education Awards Program''. The purpose of the program shall be to—

(1) celebrate the positive impact and public benefits of the arts;

(2) encourage all elementary schools and secondary schools to integrate the arts into the school curriculum;

(3) spotlight the most compelling evidence of the relationship between the arts and student learning;

(4) demonstrate how community involvement in the creation and implementation of arts policies enriches the schools;

(5) recognize school administrators and faculty who provide quality arts education to students;

(6) acknowledge schools that provide professional development opportunities for their teachers;

(7) create opportunities for students to experience the relationship between early participation in the arts and developing the life skills necessary for future personal and professional success;

(8) increase, encourage, and ensure comprehensive, sequential arts learning for all students; and

(9) expand student access to arts education in schools in every community.

(b) Duties

(1) School awards

The Board shall—

(A) make annual awards to elementary schools and secondary schools in the States in accordance with criteria established under subparagraph (B), which awards—

(i) shall be of such design and materials as the Board may determine, including a well-designed certificate or a work of art, designed for the awards event by an appropriate artist; and

(ii) shall be reflective of the dignity of Congress;

(B) establish criteria required for a school to receive the award, and establish such procedures as may be necessary to verify that the school meets the criteria, which criteria shall include criteria requiring—

(i) that the school—

(I) provides comprehensive, sequential arts learning; and

(II) integrates the arts throughout the curriculum in subjects other than the arts; and

(ii) 3 of the following:

(I) that the community serving the school is actively involved in shaping and implementing the arts policies and programs of the school;

(II) that the school principal supports the policy of arts education for all students;

(III) that arts teachers in the school are encouraged to learn and grow in mastery of their art form as well as in their teaching competence;

(IV) that the school actively encourages the use of arts assessment techniques for improving student, teacher, and administrative performance; and

(V) that school leaders engage the total school community in arts activities that create a climate of support for arts education; and

(C) include, in the procedures necessary for verification that a school meets the criteria described in subparagraph (B), written evidence of the specific criteria, and supporting documentation, that includes—

(i) 3 letters of support for the school from community members, which may include a letter from—

(I) the school's Parent Teacher Association (PTA);

(II) community leaders, such as elected or appointed officials; and

(III) arts organizations or institutions in the community that partner with the school; and

(ii) the completed application for the award signed by the principal or other education leader such as a school district arts coordinator, school board member, or school superintendent;

(D) determine appropriate methods for disseminating information about the program and make application forms available to schools;

(E) delineate such roles as the Board considers to be appropriate for the Director in administering the program, and set forth in the bylaws of the Board the duties, salary, and benefits of the Director;

(F) raise funds for the operation of the program;

(G) determine, and inform Congress regarding, the national readiness for interdisciplinary individual student awards described in paragraph (2), on the basis of the framework established in the 1997 National Assessment of Educational Progress and such other criteria as the Board determines appropriate; and

(H) take such other actions as may be appropriate for the administration of the Congressional Recognition for Excellence in Arts Education Awards Program.

(2) Student awards

(A) In general

At such time as the Board determines appropriate, the Board—

(i) shall make annual awards to elementary school and secondary school students for individual interdisciplinary arts achievement; and

(ii) establish criteria for the making of the awards.

(B) Award model

The Board may use as a model for the awards the Congressional Award Program and the President's Physical Fitness Award Program.

(c) Presentation

The Board shall arrange for the presentation of awards under this section to the recipients and shall provide for participation by Members of Congress in such presentation, when appropriate.

(d) Date of announcement

The Board shall determine an appropriate date or dates for announcement of the awards under this section, which date shall coincide with a National Arts Education Month or a similarly designated day, week or month, if such designation exists.

(e) Report

(1) In general

The Board shall prepare and submit an annual report to Congress not later than March 1 of each year summarizing the activities of the Congressional Recognition for Excellence in Arts Education Awards Program during the previous year and making appropriate recommendations for the program. Any minority views and recommendations of members of the Board shall be included in such reports.

(2) Contents

The annual report shall contain the following:

(A) Specific information regarding the methods used to raise funds for the Congressional Recognition for Excellence in Arts Education Awards Program and a list of the sources of all money raised by the Board.

(B) Detailed information regarding the expenditures made by the Board, including the percentage of funds that are used for administrative expenses.

(C) A description of the programs formulated by the Director under section 816(b)(1) of this title, including an explanation of the operation of such programs and a list of the sponsors of the programs.

(D) A detailed list of the administrative expenditures made by the Board, including the amounts expended for salaries, travel expenses, and reimbursed expenses.

(E) A list of schools given awards under the program, and the city, town, or county, and State in which the school is located.

(F) An evaluation of the state of arts education in schools, which may include anecdotal evidence of the effect of the Congressional Recognition for Excellence in Arts Education Awards Program on individual school curriculum.

(G) On the basis of the findings described in section 811 of this title and the purposes of the Congressional Recognition for Excellence in Arts Education Awards Program described in subsection (a) of this section, a recommendation regarding the national readiness to make individual student awards under subsection (b)(2) of this section.

(Pub. L. 96–114, title II, § 205, as added Pub. L. 106–533, § 1(a), Nov. 22, 2000, 114 Stat. 2546.)

Section Referred to in Other Sections

This section is referred to in sections 811, 813, 815 of this title.

§ 815. Composition of Board; Advisory Board

(a) Composition

(1) In general

The Board shall consist of 9 members as follows:

(A) 2 Members of the Senate appointed by the Majority Leader of the Senate.

(B) 2 Members of the Senate appointed by the Minority Leader of the Senate.

(C) 2 Members of the House of Representatives appointed by the Speaker of the House of Representatives.

(D) 2 Members of the House of Representatives appointed by the Minority Leader of the House of Representatives.

(E) The Director of the Board, who shall serve as a nonvoting member.

(2) Advisory Board

There is established an Advisory Board to assist and advise the Board with respect to its duties under this subchapter, that shall consist of 15 members appointed—

(A) in the case of the initial such members of the Advisory Board, by the leaders of the Senate and House of Representatives making the appointments under paragraph (1), from recommendations received from organizations and entities involved in the arts such as businesses, civic and cultural organizations, and the Arts Education Partnership steering committee; and

(B) in the case of any other such members of the Advisory Board, by the Board.

(3) Special rule for Advisory Board

In making appointments to the Advisory Board, the individuals and entity making the appointments under paragraph (2) shall consider recommendations submitted by any interested party, including any member of the Board.

(4) Interest

(A) In general

Members of Congress appointed to the Board shall have an interest in 1 of the purposes described in section 814(a) of this title.

(B) Diversity

The membership of the Advisory Board shall represent a balance of artistic and education professionals, including at least 1 representative who teaches in each of the following disciplines:

(i) Music.

(ii) Theater.

(iii) Visual Arts.

(iv) Dance.

(b) Terms

(1) Board

Members of the Board shall serve for terms of 6 years, except that of the members first appointed—

(A) 1 Member of the House of Representatives and 1 Member of the Senate shall serve for terms of 2 years;

(B) 1 Member of the House of Representatives and 1 Member of the Senate shall serve for terms of 4 years; and

(C) 2 Members of the House of Representatives and 2 Members of the Senate shall serve for terms of 6 years,

as determined by lot when all such members have been appointed.

(2) Advisory Board

Members of the Advisory Board shall serve for terms of 6 years, except that of the members first appointed, 3 shall serve for terms of 2 years, 4 shall serve for terms of 4 years, and 8 shall serve for terms of 6 years, as determined by lot when all such members have been appointed.

(c) Vacancy

(1) In general

Any vacancy in the membership of the Board or Advisory Board shall be filled in the same manner in which the original appointment was made.

(2) Term

Any member appointed to fill a vacancy occurring before the expiration of the term for which the member's predecessor was appointed shall be appointed only for the remainder of such term.

(3) Extension

Any appointed member of the Board or Advisory Board may continue to serve after the expiration of the member's term until the member's successor has taken office.

(4) Special rule

Vacancies in the membership of the Board shall not affect the Board's power to function if there remain sufficient members of the Board to constitute a quorum under subsection (d) of this section.

(d) Quorum

A majority of the members of the Board shall constitute a quorum.

(e) Compensation

Members of the Board and Advisory Board shall serve without pay but may be compensated, from amounts in the trust fund, for reasonable travel expenses incurred by the members in the performance of their duties as members of the Board.

(f) Meetings

The Board shall meet annually at the call of the Chairperson and at such other times as the Chairperson may determine to be appropriate. The Chairperson shall call a meeting of the Board whenever ⅓ of the members of the Board submit written requests for such a meeting.

(g) Officers

The Chairperson and the Vice Chairperson of the Board shall be elected from among the members of the Board, by a majority vote of the members of the Board, for such terms as the Board determines. The Vice Chairperson shall perform the duties of the Chairperson in the absence of the Chairperson.

(h) Committees

(1) In general

The Board may appoint such committees, and assign to the committees such functions, as may be appropriate to assist the Board in carrying out its duties under this subchapter. Members of such committees may include the members of the Board or the Advisory Board.

(2) Special rule

Any employee or officer of the Federal Government may serve as a member of a committee created by the Board, but may not receive compensation for services performed for such a committee.

(i) Bylaws and other requirements

The Board shall establish such bylaws and other requirements as may be appropriate to enable the Board to carry out the Board's duties under this subchapter.

(Pub. L. 96–114, title II, §206, as added Pub. L. 106–533, §1(a), Nov. 22, 2000, 114 Stat. 2549.)

Termination of Advisory Boards

Advisory boards established after Jan. 5, 1973, to terminate not later than the expiration of the 2-year period beginning on the date of their establishment, unless, in the case of a board established by the President or an officer of the Federal Government, such board is renewed by appropriate action prior to the expiration of such 2-year period, or in the case of a board established by the Congress, its duration is otherwise provided for by law. See sections 3(2) and 14 of Pub. L. 92–463, Oct. 6, 1972, 86 Stat. 770, 776, set out in the Appendix to Title 5, Government Organization and Employees.

§ 816. Administration

(a) In general

In the administration of the Congressional Recognition for Excellence in Arts Education Awards Program, the Board shall be assisted by a Director, who shall be the principal executive of the program and who shall supervise the affairs of the Board. The Director shall be appointed by a majority vote of the Board.

(b) Director's responsibilities

The Director shall, in consultation with the Board—

(1) formulate programs to carry out the policies of the Congressional Recognition for Excellence in Arts Education Awards Program;

(2) establish such divisions within the Congressional Recognition for Excellence in Arts Education Awards Program as may be appropriate; and

(3) employ and provide for the compensation of such personnel as may be necessary to carry out the Congressional Recognition for Excellence in Arts Education Awards Program, subject to such policies as the Board shall prescribe under its bylaws.

(c) Application

Each school or student desiring an award under this subchapter shall submit an application to the Board at such time, in such manner and accompanied by such information as the Board may require.

(Pub. L. 96–114, title II, §207, as added Pub. L. 106–533, §1(a), Nov. 22, 2000, 114 Stat. 2551.)

Section Referred to in Other Sections

This section is referred to in section 814 of this title.

§ 817. Limitations

(a) In general

Subject to such limitations as may be provided for under this section, the Board may take such actions and make such expenditures as may be necessary to carry out the Congressional Recognition for Excellence in Arts Education Awards Program, except that the Board shall carry out its functions and make expenditures with only such resources as are available to the Board from the Congressional Recognition for Excellence in Arts Education Awards Trust Fund under section 817c of this title.

(b) Contracts

The Board may enter into such contracts as may be appropriate to carry out the business of the Board, but the Board may not enter into any contract which will obligate the Board to expend an amount greater than the amount available to the Board for the purpose of such contract during the fiscal year in which the expenditure is made.

(c) Gifts

The Board may seek and accept, from sources other than the Federal Government, funds and other resources to carry out the Board's activities. The Board may not accept any funds or other resources that are—

(1) donated with a restriction on their use unless such restriction merely provides that such funds or other resources be used in furtherance of the Congressional Recognition for Excellence in Arts Education Awards Program; or

(2) donated subject to the condition that the identity of the donor of the funds or resources shall remain anonymous.

(d) Volunteers

The Board may accept and utilize the services of voluntary, uncompensated personnel.

(e) Real or personal property

The Board may lease (or otherwise hold), acquire, or dispose of real or personal property necessary for, or relating to, the duties of the Board.

(f) Prohibitions

The Board shall have no power—

(1) to issue bonds, notes, debentures, or other similar obligations creating long-term indebtedness;

(2) to issue any share of stock or to declare or pay any dividends; or

(3) to provide for any part of the income or assets of the Board to inure to the benefit of any director, officer, or employee of the Board except as reasonable compensation for services or reimbursement for expenses.

(Pub. L. 96–114, title II, § 208, as added Pub. L. 106–533, § 1(a), Nov. 22, 2000, 114 Stat. 2551.)

SECTION REFERRED TO IN OTHER SECTIONS

This section is referred to in section 817c of this title.

§ 817a. Audits

The financial records of the Board may be audited by the Comptroller General of the United States at such times as the Comptroller General may determine to be appropriate. The Comptroller General, or any duly authorized representative of the Comptroller General, shall have access for the purpose of audit to any books, documents, papers, and records of the Board (or any agent of the Board) which, in the opinion of the Comptroller General, may be pertinent to the Congressional Recognition for Excellence in Arts Education Awards Program.

(Pub. L. 96–114, title II, § 209, as added Pub. L. 106–533, § 1(a), Nov. 22, 2000, 114 Stat. 2552.)

§ 817b. Termination

The Board shall terminate 6 years after November 22, 2000. The Board shall set forth, in its bylaws, the procedures for dissolution to be followed by the Board.

(Pub. L. 96–114, title II, § 210, as added Pub. L. 106–533, § 1(a), Nov. 22, 2000, 114 Stat. 2552.)

§ 817c. Trust fund

(a) Establishment of fund

There shall be established in the Treasury of the United States a trust fund which shall be known as the "Congressional Recognition for Excellence in Arts Education Awards Trust Fund". The fund shall be administered by the Board, and shall consist of amounts donated to the Board under section 817(c) of this title and amounts credited to the fund under subsection (d) of this section.

(b) Investment

(1) In general

It shall be the duty of the Secretary of the Treasury to invest, at the direction of the Director of the Board, such portion of the fund that is not, in the judgment of the Director of the Board, required to meet the current needs of the fund.

(2) Authorized investments

Such investments shall be in public debt obligations with maturities suitable to the needs of the fund, as determined by the Director of the Board. Investments in public debt obligations shall bear interest at rates determined by the Secretary of the Treasury taking into consideration the current market yield on outstanding marketable obligations of the United States of comparable maturity.

(c) Authority to sell obligations

Any obligation acquired by the fund may be sold by the Secretary of the Treasury at the market price.

(d) Proceeds from certain transactions credited to fund

The interest on, and the proceeds from the sale or redemption of, any obligations held in the fund shall be credited to and form a part of the fund.

(Pub. L. 96–114, title II, § 211, as added Pub. L. 106–533, § 1(a), Nov. 22, 2000, 114 Stat. 2552.)

SECTION REFERRED TO IN OTHER SECTIONS

This section is referred to in section 817 of this title.

CHAPTER 19A—JOHN HEINZ COMPETITIVE EXCELLENCE AWARD

§ 831. John Heinz Competitive Excellence Award

(a) Establishment

There is hereby established the John Heinz Competitive Excellence Award, which shall be evidenced by a national medal bearing the inscription "John Heinz Competitive Excellence Award". The medal, to be minted by the United States Mint and provided to the Congress, shall be of such design and bear such additional inscriptions as the Secretary of the Treasury may prescribe, in consultation with the Majority and Minority Leaders of the Senate, the Speaker and the Minority Leader of the House of Representatives, and the family of Senator John Heinz. The medal shall be—

(1) three inches in diameter; and

(2) made of bronze obtained from recycled sources.

(b) Award categories

(1) In general

Two separate awards may be given under this section in each year. One such award may be given to a qualifying individual (including employees of any State or local government, or the Federal Government), and 1 such award may be given to a qualifying organization, institution, or business.

(2) Limitation

No award shall be made under this section to an entity in either category described in paragraph (1) in any year if there is no qualified individual, organization, institution, or business recommended under subsection (c) of this section for an award in such category in that year.

(c) Qualification criteria for award

(1) Selection panel

A selection panel shall be established, comprised of a total of 8 persons, including—

(A) 2 persons appointed by the Majority Leader of the Senate;

(B) 2 persons appointed by the Minority Leader of the Senate;

(C) 2 persons appointed by the Speaker of the House of Representatives; and

(D) 2 persons appointed by the Minority Leader of the House of Representatives.

(2) Qualification

An individual, organization, institution, or business may qualify for an award under this section only if such individual, organization, institution, or business—

(A) is nominated to the Majority or Minority Leader of the Senate or to the Speaker or the Minority Leader of the House of Representatives by a member of the Senate or the House of Representatives;

(B) permits a rigorous evaluation by the Office of Technology Assessment of the way in which such individual, organization, institution, or business has demonstrated excellence in promoting United States industrial competitiveness; and

(C) meets such other requirements as the selection panel determines to be appropriate to achieve the objectives of this section.

(3) Evaluation

An evaluation of each nominee shall be conducted by the Office of Technology Assessment. The Office of Technology Assessment shall work with the selection panel to establish appropriate procedures for evaluating nominees.

(4) Panel review

The selection panel shall review the Office of Technology Assessment's evaluation of each nominee and may, based on those evaluations, recommend 1 award winner for each year for each category described in subsection (b)(1) of this section to the Majority and Minority Leaders of the Senate and the Speaker and the Minority Leader of the House of Representatives.

(d) Presentation of award

(1) In general

The Majority and Minority Leaders of the Senate and the Speaker and the Minority Leader of the House of Representatives shall make the award to an individual and an organization, institution, or business that has demonstrated excellence in promoting United States industrial competitiveness in the international marketplace through technological innovation, productivity improvement, or improved competitive strategies.

(2) Ceremonies

The presentation of an award under this section shall be made by the Majority and Minority Leaders of the Senate and the Speaker and the Minority Leader of the House of Representatives, with such ceremonies as they may deem proper.

(3) Publicity

An individual, organization, institution, or business to which an award is made under this section may publicize its receipt of such award and use the award in its advertising, but it shall be ineligible to receive another award in the same category for a period of 5 years.

(e) Publication of evaluations

(1) Summary of evaluations

The Office of Technology Assessment shall ensure that all nominees receive a detailed summary of any evaluation conducted of such nominee under subsection (c) of this section.

(2) Summary of competitiveness strategy

The Office of Technology Assessment shall also make available to all nominees and the public a summary of each award winner's competitiveness strategy. Proprietary information shall not be included in any such summary without the consent of the award winner.

(f) Reimbursement of costs

The Majority and Minority Leaders of the Senate and the Speaker and the Minority Lead-

er of the House of Representatives are authorized to seek and accept gifts from public and private sources to defray the cost of implementing
this section.

(Pub. L. 102–429, title III, § 301, Oct. 21, 1992, 106
Stat. 2205.)

CHAPTER 20—EMERGENCY POWERS TO ELIMINATE BUDGET DEFICITS

SUBCHAPTER I—ELIMINATION OF DEFICITS IN EXCESS OF MAXIMUM DEFICIT AMOUNT

TERMINATION OF SUBCHAPTER

*For termination of subchapter, see Effective
and Termination Dates note set out under section 900 of this title.*

SUBCHAPTER REFERRED TO IN OTHER SECTIONS

This subchapter is referred to in section 922 of this
title; title 22 section 5853; title 38 section 113; title 39
section 2009a; title 42 section 300aa–15.

§ 900. Statement of budget enforcement through sequestration; definitions

(a) Omitted

(b) General statement of budget enforcement through sequestration

This subchapter provides for budget enforcement as called for in House Concurrent Resolution 84 (105th Congress, 1st session).

(c) Definitions

As used in this subchapter:

(1) The terms "budget authority", "new budget authority", "outlays", and "deficit" have the meanings given to such terms in section 3 of the Congressional Budget and Impoundment Control Act of 1974 [2 U.S.C. 622] and "discretionary spending limit" shall mean the amounts specified in section 901 of this title.

(2) The terms "sequester" and "sequestration" refer to or mean the cancellation of budgetary resources provided by discretionary appropriations or direct spending law.

(3) The term "breach" means, for any fiscal year, the amount (if any) by which new budget authority or outlays for that year (within a category of discretionary appropriations) is above that category's discretionary spending limit for new budget authority or outlays for that year, as the case may be.

(4)(A) The term "category" means the subsets of discretionary appropriations in section 901(c) of this title. Discretionary appropriations in each of the categories shall be those designated in the joint explanatory statement accompanying the conference report on the Balanced Budget Act of 1997. New accounts or activities shall be categorized only after consultation with the committees[1] on Appropriations and the Budget of the House of Representatives and the Senate and that consultation shall, to the extent practicable, include written communication to such committees that affords such committees the opportunity to comment before official action is taken with respect to new accounts or activities.

(B) The term "highway category" refers to the following budget accounts or portions thereof that are subject to the obligation limitations on contract authority set forth in the Transportation Equity Act for the 21st Century:

(i) 69–8083–0–7–401 (Federal-Aid Highways).

(ii) 69–8020–0–7–401 (Highway Traffic Safety Grants).

(iii) 69–8048–0–7–401 (National Motor Carrier Safety Program).

(iv) 69–8016–0–7–401 (Operations and Research NHTSA).

(C) The term "mass transit category" refers to the following budget accounts or portions thereof that are subject to the obligation limitations on contract authority provided in the Transportation Equity Act for the 21st Century or for which appropriations are provided pursuant to authorizations contained in that Act (except that appropriations provided pursuant to section 5338(h) of title 49, as amended by the Transportation Equity Act for the 21st Century, shall not be included in this category):

(i) 69–8191–0–7–401 (Mass Transit Capital Fund).

(ii) 69–8350–0–7–401 (Trust Fund Share of Expenses).

(iii) 69–1129–0–1–401 (Formula Grants).

(iv) 69–1120–0–1–401 (Administrative Expenses).

(v) 69–1136–0–1–401 (University Transportation Centers).

(vi) 69–1137–0–1–401 (Transit Planning and Research).

Such term also refers to the Washington Metropolitan Transit Authority account (69–1128–0–1–401) only for fiscal year 1999 only for appropriations provided pursuant to authorizations contained in section 14 of Public Law 96–184 and Public Law 101–551.

(D) SPECIAL RULE.—(i) Any outlays in excess of the discretionary spending limit set forth in section 901(c) of this title for the highway or mass transit category, as adjusted, for the budget year shall be considered nondefense category outlays or discretionary category outlays.

(ii) If the obligation limitations for accounts in the highway or mass transit category provided in an appropriation Act for a fiscal year exceed the obligation limitations set forth in section 8103 of the Transportation Equity Act for the 21st Century for that year, as adjusted, the estimated outlays flowing for each outyear from such excess obligations calculated pursuant to clause (iii) shall be attributed to the discretionary category in that outyear.

(iii) For purposes of clause (ii), outlays from excess obligations shall be determined using the average of the spendout rates for that category in the baseline.

(E) The term "conservation spending category" means discretionary appropriations for conservation activities in the following budget accounts or portions thereof providing appropriations to preserve and protect lands, habitat, wildlife, and other natural resources, to provide recreational opportunities, and for related purposes:

(i) 14–5033 Bureau of Land Management Land Acquisition.

(ii) 14–5020 Fish and Wildlife Service Land Acquisition.

(iii) 14–5035 National Park Service Land Acquisition and State Assistance.

(iv) 12–9923 Forest Service Land Acquisition.

(v) 14–5143 Fish and Wildlife Service Cooperative Endangered Species Conservation Fund.

(vi) 14–5241 Fish and Wildlife Service North American Wetlands Conservation Fund.

(vii) 14–1694 Fish and Wildlife Service State Wildlife Grants.

(viii) 14–0804 United States Geological Survey Surveys, Investigations, and Research, the State Planning Partnership programs: Community/Federal Information Partnership, Urban Dynamics, and Decision Support for Resource Management.

---

[1] So in original. Probably should be capitalized.

(ix) 12–1105 Forest Service State and Private Forestry, the Forest Legacy Program, Urban and Community Forestry, and Smart Growth Partnerships.

(x) 14–1031 National Park Service Urban Park and Recreation Recovery program.

(xi) 14–5140 National Park Service Historic Preservation Fund.

(xii) Youth Conservation Corps.

(xiii) 14–1114 Bureau of Land Management Payments in Lieu of Taxes.

(xiv) Federal Infrastructure Improvement (as established in title VIII of the Department of the Interior and Related Agencies Appropriations Act, 2001).

(xv) 13–1460 NOAA Procurement Acquisition and Construction, the National Marine Sanctuaries and the National Estuarine Research Reserve Systems.

(xvi) 13–1450 NOAA Operations, Research, and Facilities, the Coastal Zone Management Act programs, the National Marine Sanctuaries, the National Estuarine Research Reserve Systems, and Coral Restoration programs.

(xvii) 13–1451 NOAA Pacific Coastal Salmon Recovery.

(F) The term "Federal and State Land and Water Conservation Fund sub-category" means discretionary appropriations for activities in the accounts described in (E)(i)–(E)(iv)[2] or portions thereof.

(G) The term "State and Other Conservation sub-category" means discretionary appropriations for activities in the accounts described in (E)(v)–(E)(ix),[2] with the exception of Urban and Community Forestry as described in (E)(ix),[2] or portions thereof.

(H) The term "Urban and Historic Preservation sub-category" means discretionary appropriations for activities in the accounts described in (E)(ix)–(E)(xii),[2] with the exception of Forest Legacy and Smart Growth Partnerships as described in (E)(ix),[2] or portions thereof.

(I) The term "Payments in Lieu of Taxes sub-category" means discretionary appropriations for activities in the account described in (E)(xiii)[2] or portions thereof.

(J) The term "Federal Deferred Maintenance sub-category" means discretionary appropriations for activities in the account described in (E)(xiv)[2] or portions thereof.

(K) The term "Coastal Assistance sub-category" means discretionary appropriations for activities in the accounts described in (E)(xv)–(E)(xvii)[2] or portions thereof.

(5) The term "baseline" means the projection (described in section 907 of this title) of current-year levels of new budget authority, outlays, receipts, and the surplus or deficit into the budget year and the outyears.

(6) The term "budgetary resources" means new budget authority, unobligated balances, direct spending authority, and obligation limitations.

(7) The term "discretionary appropriations" means budgetary resources (except to fund direct-spending programs) provided in appropriation Acts.

(8) The term "direct spending" means—

(A) budget authority provided by law other than appropriation Acts;

(B) entitlement authority; and

(C) the food stamp program.

(9) The term "current" means, with respect to OMB estimates included with a budget submission under section 1105(a) of title 31, the estimates consistent with the economic and technical assumptions underlying that budget and with respect to estimates made after that budget submission that are not included with it, estimates consistent with the economic and technical assumptions underlying the most recently submitted President's budget.

(10) The term "real economic growth", with respect to any fiscal year, means the growth in the gross national product during such fiscal year, adjusted for inflation, consistent with Department of Commerce definitions.

(11) The term "account" means an item for which appropriations are made in any appropriation Act and, for items not provided for in appropriation Acts, such term means an item for which there is a designated budget account identification code number in the President's budget.

(12) The term "budget year" means, with respect to a session of Congress, the fiscal year of the Government that starts on October 1 of the calendar year in which that session begins.

(13) The term "current year" means, with respect to a budget year, the fiscal year that immediately precedes that budget year.

(14) The term "outyear" means, with respect to a budget year, any of the first 4 fiscal years that follow the budget year.

(15) The term "OMB" means the Director of the Office of Management and Budget.

(16) The term "CBO" means the Director of the Congressional Budget Office.

(17) As used in this subchapter, all references to entitlement authority shall include the list of mandatory appropriations included in the joint explanatory statement of managers accompanying the conference report on the Balanced Budget Act of 1997.

(18) The term "deposit insurance" refers to the expenses[3] the Federal deposit insurance agencies, and other Federal agencies supervising insured depository institutions, resulting from full funding of, and continuation of, the deposit insurance guarantee commitment in effect under current estimates.

(19) The term "asset sale" means the sale to the public of any asset (except for those assets covered by title V of the Congressional Budget Act of 1974 [2 U.S.C. 661 et seq.]), whether physical or financial, owned in whole or in part by the United States.

(Pub. L. 99–177, title II, § 250, as added Pub. L. 101–508, title XIII, § 13101(a), Nov. 5, 1990, 104 Stat. 1388–574, and Pub. L. 99–177, title II, § 250(c)(21), formerly § 257(12), as added Pub. L. 100–119, title I, § 102(b)(7), Sept. 29, 1987, 101 Stat. 774, renumbered § 250(c)(21), Pub. L. 101–508, title

---

[2] So in original. Probably should be preceded by "subparagraph".

[3] So in original. Probably should be followed by "of".

XIII, §13101(b), Nov. 5, 1990, 104 Stat. 1388–589; amended Pub. L. 105–33, title X, §§10202, 10204(a)(2), 10208(a)(2), Aug. 5, 1997, 111 Stat. 697, 702, 708; Pub. L. 105–178, title VIII, §8101(c), (f), June 9, 1998, 112 Stat. 489; Pub. L. 105–206, title IX, §9013(b), July 22, 1998, 112 Stat. 865; Pub. L. 106–291, title VIII, §801(c), Oct. 11, 2000, 114 Stat. 1028.)

TERMINATION OF SECTION

For termination of section by section 275(b) of Pub. L. 99–177, as amended, see Effective and Termination Dates note set out below.

REFERENCES IN TEXT

House Concurrent Resolution 84, referred to in subsec. (b), is H. Con. Res. 84, June 5, 1997, 111 Stat. 2710, which is not classified to the Code.

The Balanced Budget Act of 1997, referred to in subsec. (c)(4)(A), (17), is Pub. L. 105–33, Aug. 5, 1997, 111 Stat. 251. For complete classification of this Act to the Code, see Tables.

The Transportation Equity Act for the 21st Century, referred to in subsec. (c)(4)(B), (C), (D)(ii), is Pub. L. 105–178, June 9, 1998, 112 Stat. 107, as amended. Section 8103 of the Act is set out as a note under section 901 of this title. For complete classification of this Act to the Code, see section 1(a) of Pub. L. 105–178, set out as a Short Title of 1998 Amendment note under section 101 of Title 23, Highways, and Tables.

Section 14 of Public Law 96–184, referred to in subsec. (c)(4)(C), probably means section 14 of Pub. L. 91–143, as added by Pub. L. 96–184, §2, Jan. 3, 1980, 93 Stat. 1320, which is not classified to the Code.

Public Law 101–551, referred to in subsec. (c)(4)(C), is Pub. L. 101–551, Nov. 15, 1990, 104 Stat. 2733, which is not classified to the Code.

The Department of the Interior and Related Agencies Appropriations Act, 2001, referred to in subsec. (c)(4)(E)(xiv), is Pub. L. 106–291, Oct. 11, 2000, 114 Stat. 922. Title VIII of the Act amended this section and section 901 of this title. For complete classification of this Act to the Code, see Tables.

The Congressional Budget Act of 1974, referred to in subsec. (c)(19), is titles I through IX of Pub. L. 93–344, July 12, 1974, 88 Stat. 297, as amended. Title V of the Act, known as the Federal Credit Reform Act of 1990, was added by Pub. L. 101–508, title XIII, §13201(a), Nov. 5, 1990, 104 Stat. 1388–609, and is classified generally to subchapter III (§661 et seq.) of chapter 17A of this title. For complete classification of this Act to the Code, see Short Title note set out under section 621 of this title and Tables.

CODIFICATION

Subsection (a) of this section, which provided a partial table of contents for this subchapter was omitted from the Code.

Pub. L. 101–508, §13101(b), transferred section 257(12) of Pub. L. 99–177, which was classified to section 907(12) of this title, to subsec. (c)(21) (now (c)(19)) of this section.

AMENDMENTS

2000—Subsec. (c)(4)(E) to (K). Pub. L. 106–291 added subpars. (E) to (K).

1998—Subsec. (c)(4). Pub. L. 105–178, §8101(c), designated existing provisions as subpar. (A) and added subpars. (B) to (D).

Subsec. (c)(4)(C). Pub. L. 105–178, §8101(f), as added by Pub. L. 105–206, §9013(b), in introductory provisions, substituted "Century or" for "Century and" and "as amended by the Transportation Equity Act for the 21st Century" for "as amended by this section", and inserted concluding provisions.

1997—Subsec. (a). Pub. L. 105–33, §§10204(a)(2), 10208(a)(2), amended table of contents. See Codification note above.

Subsec. (b). Pub. L. 105–33, §10202(a), substituted present text for former text which read as follows:

"This subchapter provides for the enforcement of the deficit reduction assumed in House Concurrent Resolution 310 (101st Congress, second session) and the applicable deficit targets for fiscal years 1991 through 1995. Enforcement, as necessary, is to be implemented through sequestration—

"(1) to enforce discretionary spending levels assumed in that resolution (with adjustments as provided hereinafter);

"(2) to enforce the requirement that any legislation increasing direct spending or decreasing revenues be on a pay-as-you-go basis; and

"(3) to enforce the deficit targets specifically set forth in the Congressional Budget and Impoundment Control Act of 1974 (with adjustments as provided hereinafter);

applied in the order set forth above."

Subsec. (c)(1). Pub. L. 105–33, §10202(b)(1), struck out "(but including the treatment specified in section 907(b)(3) of this title of the Hospital Insurance Trust Fund) and the terms 'maximum deficit amount'" before "and 'discretionary" and substituted "section 901" for "section 601 of that Act as adjusted under sections 901 and 903".

Subsec. (c)(4). Pub. L. 105–33, §10202(b)(2), added par. (4) and struck out former par. (4) which read as follows: "The term 'category' means:

"(A) For fiscal years 1991, 1992, and 1993, any of the following subsets of discretionary appropriations: defense, international, or domestic. Discretionary appropriations in each of the three categories shall be those so designated in the joint statement of managers accompanying the conference report on the Omnibus Budget Reconciliation Act of 1990. New accounts or activities shall be categorized in consultation with the Committees on Appropriations and the Budget of the House of Representatives and the Senate.

"(B) For fiscal years 1994 and 1995, all discretionary appropriations.

Contributions to the United States to offset the cost of Operation Desert Shield shall not be counted within any category."

Subsec. (c)(6). Pub. L. 105–33, §10202(b)(3), added par. (6) and struck out former par. (6) which read as follows: "The term 'budgetary resources' means—

"(A) with respect to budget year 1991, new budget authority; unobligated balances; new loan guarantee commitments or limitations; new direct loan obligations, commitments, or limitations; direct spending authority; and obligation limitations; or

"(B) with respect to budget year 1992, 1993, 1994, or 1995, new budget authority; unobligated balances; direct spending authority; and obligation limitations."

Subsec. (c)(9). Pub. L. 105–33, §10202(b)(4), substituted "that budget submission that are not included with it" for "submission of the fiscal year 1992 budget that are not included with a budget submission".

Subsec. (c)(14). Pub. L. 105–33, §10202(b)(5), inserted "first 4" before "fiscal years" and struck out "through fiscal year 1995" after "the budget year".

Subsec. (c)(17). Pub. L. 105–33, §10202(b)(6), (7), redesignated par. (18) as (17), substituted "Balanced Budget Act of 1997" for "Omnibus Budget Reconciliation Act of 1990", and struck out former par. (17) which read as follows: "For purposes of sections 902 and 903 of this title, legislation enacted during the second session of the One Hundred First Congress shall be deemed to have been enacted before November 5, 1990."

Subsec. (c)(18). Pub. L. 105–33, §10202(b)(6), (8), redesignated par. (19) as (18) and substituted "the Federal deposit insurance agencies, and other Federal agencies supervising insured depository institutions, resulting from full funding of, and continuation of, the deposit insurance guarantee commitment in effect under current estimates." for "of the Federal Deposit Insurance Corporation and the funds it incorporates, the Resolution Trust Corporation, the National Credit Union Administration and the funds it incorporates, the Office of Thrift Supervision, the Comptroller of the Currency

Assessment Fund, and the RTC Office of Inspector General." Former par. (18) redesignated (17).

Subsec. (c)(19). Pub. L. 105–33, §10202(b)(9), added par. (19) and struck out former par. (19) which read as follows: "The sale of an asset means the sale to the public of any asset, whether physical or financial, owned in whole or in part by the United States. The term 'prepayment of a loan' means payments to the United States made in advance of the schedules set by law or contract when the financial asset is first acquired, such as the prepayment to the Federal Financing Bank of loans guaranteed by the Rural Electrification Administration. If a law or contract allows a flexible payment schedule, the term 'in advance' shall mean in advance of the slowest payment schedule allowed under such law or contract."

Pub. L. 105–33, §10202(b)(6), redesignated par. (21) as (19). Former par. (19) redesignated (18).

Subsec. (c)(20). Pub. L. 105–33, §10202(b)(6), struck out par. (20) which read as follows: "The term 'composite outlay rate' means the percent of new budget authority that is converted to outlays in the fiscal year for which the budget authority is provided and subsequent fiscal years, as follows:

"(A) For the international category, 46 percent for the first year, 20 percent for the second year, 16 percent for the third year, and 8 percent for the fourth year.

"(B) For the domestic category, 53 percent for the first year, 31 percent for the second year, 12 percent for the third year, and 2 percent for the fourth year."

Subsec. (c)(21). Pub. L. 105–33, §10202(b)(6), redesignated par. (21) as (19).

1990—Subsec. (c)(21). Pub. L. 101–508, §13101(b), redesignated section 907(12) of this title as par. (21).

EFFECTIVE DATE OF 1998 AMENDMENT

Title IX of Pub. L. 105–206 effective simultaneously with enactment of Pub. L. 105–178 and to be treated as included in Pub. L. 105–178 at time of enactment, and provisions of Pub. L. 105–178, as in effect on day before July 22, 1998, that are amended by title IX of Pub. L. 105–206 to be treated as not enacted, see section 9016 of Pub. L. 105–206, set out as a note under section 101 of Title 23, Highways.

EFFECTIVE AND TERMINATION DATES

Pub. L. 103–66, title XIV, §14002(c)(3)(A), Aug. 10, 1993, 107 Stat. 684, which provided that, notwithstanding section 275(b) of Pub. L. 99–177, set out below, sections 900, 901, 902, and 904 to 908 of this title were to expire on Sept. 30, 1998, was repealed by Pub. L. 105–33, title X, §10212(b), Aug. 5, 1997, 111 Stat. 712.

Section 275 of title II of Pub. L. 99–177, as amended by Pub. L. 100–119, title I, §106(c), title II, §210(b), Sept. 29, 1987, 101 Stat. 780, 787; Pub. L. 101–508, title XIII, §§13112(b), 13208(b), Nov. 5, 1990, 104 Stat. 1388–608, 1388–619; Pub. L. 105–33, title X, §10212(a), Aug. 5, 1997, 111 Stat. 712, provided that:

"(a) IN GENERAL.—

"(1) Except as provided in paragraph (2) and in subsections (b) and (c), this title and the amendments made by this title [see Short Title note below] shall become effective on the date of the enactment of this title [Dec. 12, 1985] and shall apply with respect to fiscal years beginning after September 30, 1985.

"(2)(A) The amendment made by section 201(a)(2) [amending section 622(2) of this title], and the amendment made by section 201(b) [( ] insofar as it relates to subsections (c), (f), and (g) of section 302 of the Congressional Budget Act of 1974 [section 633(c), (f), and (g) of this title] and to subsections (c), (d), and (g) of section 310 of that Act [section 641(c), (d), and (g) of this title]), shall become effective April 15, 1986.

"(B) The amendment made by section 212 [amending section 652 of this title] shall become effective February 1, 1986.

"(b) EXPIRATION.—Sections 251, 253, 258B, and 271(b) of this Act [sections 901, 903, and 907c of this title and pro-

visions set out as a note below], and sections 1105(f) and 1106(c) of title 31, United States Code, shall expire September 30, 2002. The remaining sections of part C of this title [enacting this subchapter] shall expire September 30, 2006.

"(c) OASDI TRUST FUNDS.—The amendments made by part D [amending section 911 of Title 42, The Public Health and Welfare, and enacting provisions set out as a note under section 911 of Title 42] shall apply as provided in such part."

[Amendment of section 275(b)(2) of Pub. L. 99–177, set out above, by section 13208(b) of Pub. L. 101–508 could not be executed because of general amendment of section 275(b) by section 13112(b) of Pub. L. 101–508.]

SHORT TITLE OF 1997 AMENDMENT

Section 10001(a) of title X of Pub. L. 105–33 provided that: "This title [enacting sections 645 and 645a of this title, amending this section, sections 601, 602, 622, 631 to 636, 639, 641, 641 to 644, 651, 654, 661a, 661c to 661e, 691a, 691c, 691e, 901, 902, 904 to 907, and 922 of this title, section 1105 of Title 31, Money and Finance, and section 911 of Title 42, The Public Health and Welfare, repealing sections 652, 665 to 665e, 901a, and 908 of this title and section 14212 of Title 42, enacting provisions set out as notes under this section and section 902 of this title, amending provisions set out as notes under this section and section 621 of this title, and repealing provisions set out as notes under this section and sections 621, 631, and 665 of this title] may be cited as the 'Budget Enforcement Act of 1997'."

SHORT TITLE OF 1990 AMENDMENT

Section 13001(a) of title XIII of Pub. L. 101–508 provided that: "This title [enacting this section and sections 643, 661 to 661f, 665 to 665e, and 907a to 907d of this title, amending sections 601, 602, 622, 631 to 637, 639, 641, 642, 644, 651, 652, and 901 to 907 of this title, section 1022 of Title 15, Commerce and Trade, sections 1105, 1341, and 1342 of Title 31, Money and Finance, and section 401 of Title 42, The Public Health and Welfare, transferring section 921 of this title to section 601(g) of this title, repealing section 909 of this title, enacting provisions set out as notes under this section and sections 621, 622, 632, 633, 665, and 902 of this title, and amending provisions set out as notes under this section and sections 621 and 632 of this title] may be cited as the 'Budget Enforcement Act of 1990'."

SHORT TITLE OF 1987 AMENDMENT

Section 101(b) of title I of Pub. L. 100–119 provided that: "This title [enacting section 908 of this title, amending sections 622, 632, 642, 901 to 907, and 922 of this title and section 1105 of Title 31, Money and Finance, enacting provisions set out as notes under section 1395ww of Title 42, The Public Health and Welfare, and amending provisions set out as notes under section 901 of this title and sections 1320b–8 and 1395ww of Title 42] may be cited as the 'Balanced Budget and Emergency Deficit Control Reaffirmation Act of 1987'."

SHORT TITLE

Section 200(a) of title II of Pub. L. 99–177 provided that: "This title [enacting this chapter and sections 654 to 656 of this title, amending sections 602, 622, 631 to 642, and 651 to 653 of this title, sections 1104 to 1106 and 1109 of Title 31, Money and Finance, and section 911 of Title 42, The Public Health and Welfare, repealing section 661 of this title, enacting provisions set out as notes under this section and section 911 of Title 42, and amending provisions set out as a note under section 621 of this title] may be cited as the 'Balanced Budget and Emergency Deficit Control Act of 1985'."

PURPOSE OF SUBTITLE B OF TITLE X OF PUB. L. 105–33

Section 10201 of title X of Pub. L. 105–33 provided that: "The purpose of this subtitle [subtitle B (§§10201–10213) of title X of Pub. L. 105–33, amending this section, sections 901, 902, 904 to 907, and 922 of this title, section 1105 of Title 31, Money and Finance, and section 911 of Title 42, The Public Health and Welfare, repealing sections 901a and 908 of this title and section 14212 of Title 42, enacting provisions set out as a note under section 902 of this title, and amending and repealing provisions set out as notes under this section] is to extend discretionary spending limits and pay-as-you-go requirements."

RESTRICTION ON ELIMINATION OR REDUCTION OF PROGRAMS RELATING TO ENERGY AND WATER DEVELOPMENT

Pub. L. 102–377, title V, §503, Oct. 2, 1992, 106 Stat. 1342, provided that: "None of the programs, projects or activities as defined in the reports accompanying this Act or subsequent Energy and Water Development Appropriations Acts, may be eliminated or disproportionately reduced due to the application of 'Savings and Slippage', 'general reduction', or the provision of Public Law 99–177 [see Short Title note above] or Public Law 100–119 [see section 213 of Pub. L. 100–119 set out below] unless such reports expressly provide otherwise."

WAIVERS AND SUSPENSIONS IN THE SENATE

Section 271(b) of Pub. L. 99–177, as amended by Pub. L. 100–119, title II, §211, Sept. 29, 1987, 101 Stat. 787, provided that: "Sections 301(i), 302(c), 302(f), 304(b), 310(d), 310(g), and 311(a) of the Congressional Budget Act of 1974 [sections 632(i), 633(c), 633(f), former 635(b), 641(d), 641(g), and 642(a) of this title] may be waived or suspended in the Senate only by the affirmative vote of three-fifths of the Members, duly chosen and sworn. This subsection shall not apply to any joint resolution reported or discharged pursuant to section 254(a) of this joint resolution [section 904(a) of this title]."

[For effective and termination dates of section 271(b) of Pub. L. 99–177, see section 275(a)(1), (b) of Pub. L. 99–177, as amended, set out as a note above.]

APPEALS OF RULINGS

Section 271(c) of Pub. L. 99–177, as added by Pub. L. 100–119, title II, §210(a), Sept. 29, 1987, 101 Stat. 787, provided that: "An affirmative vote of three-fifths of the Members of the Senate, duly chosen and sworn, shall be required in the Senate to sustain an appeal of the ruling of the Chair on a point of order raised under section 301(i), 302(c), 302(f), 304(b), 306, 310(d), 310(g), or 311(a) of the Congressional Budget Act of 1974 [sections 632(i), 633(c), 633(f), 635(b), 637, 641(d), 641(g), or 642(a) of this title]."

[For effective date of section 271(c) of Pub. L. 99–177, see section 275(a)(1) of Pub. L. 99–177, as amended, set out as a note above.]

EXERCISE OF CONGRESSIONAL RULEMAKING POWER

Pub. L. 103–66, title XIV, §14004, Aug. 10, 1993, 107 Stat. 685, provided that: "The Congress enacts the provisions of this part [probably should be "this title", amending sections 665, 901, 902, and 904 of this title, enacting provisions set out as notes under this section and section 902 of this title, and amending provisions set out as notes under section 665 of this title]—

"(1) as an exercise of the rule-making power of the Senate and the House of Representatives, respectively, and as such these provisions shall be considered as part of the rules of each House, respectively, or of that House to which they specifically apply, and such rules shall supersede other rules only to the extent that they are inconsistent therewith; and

"(2) with full recognition of the constitutional right of either House to change such rules (so far as relating to such House) at any time, in the same manner, and to the same extent as in the case of any other rule of such House."

Section 13305 of title XIII of Pub. L. 101–508 provided that: "This title and the amendments made by it [see Short Title of 1990 Amendment note above] are enacted by the Congress—

"(1) as an exercise of the rulemaking power of the House of Representatives and the Senate, respectively, and as such they shall be considered as a part of the rules of each House, respectively, or of that House to which they specifically apply, and such rules shall supersede other rules only to the extent that they are inconsistent therewith; and

"(2) with full recognition of the constitutional right of either House to change such rules (so far as relating to such House) at any time, in the same manner, and to the same extent as in the case of any other rule of such House."

Section 213 of Pub. L. 100–119 provided that: "This Act and the amendments made by this Act [enacting sections 908 and 909 of this title, amending sections 622, 632, 635, 636, 642, 683, 684, 687, 901 to 907, and 922 of this title and sections 1105 and 3101 of Title 31, Money and Finance, enacting provisions set out as notes under sections 602, 621, 686, and 901 of this title and section 1395ww of Title 42, The Public Health and Welfare, amending provisions set out as notes under section 901 of this title and sections 1320b–8 and 1395ww of Title 42, and repealing provisions set out as a note under section 653 of this title], other than those relating to the activities of the executive and judicial branches of the Government, are enacted by Congress—

"(1) as an exercise of the rulemaking power of the House of Representatives and the Senate, respectively, and as such they shall be considered as part of the rules of each House, respectively, or of that House to which they specifically apply, and such rules shall supersede other rules only to the extent that they are inconsistent therewith; and

"(2) with full recognition of the constitutional right of either House to change such rules (so far as relating to such House) at any time, in the same manner and to the same extent as in the case of any other rule of such House."

Section 271(d), formerly section 271(c), of Pub. L. 99–177, as redesignated by Pub. L. 100–119, title II, §210(a), Sept. 29, 1987, 101 Stat. 787, provided that: "The provisions of this title [see Short Title note above], other than those relating to the activities of the executive and judicial branches of the Government, are enacted by the Congress—

"(1) as an exercise of the rulemaking power of the House of Representatives and the Senate, respectively, and as such they shall be considered as part of the rules of each House, respectively, or of that House to which they specifically apply, and such rules shall supersede other rules only to the extent that they are inconsistent therewith; and

"(2) with full recognition of the constitutional right of either House to change such rules (so far as relating to such House) at any time, in the same manner and to the same extent as in the case of any other rule of such House."

RESTORATION OF TRUST FUND INVESTMENTS; FUNDS BORROWED OR NOT INVESTED DURING DELAYS IN RAISING PUBLIC DEBT LIMIT

For provisions restoring various trust and retirement funds administered by the Secretary of the Treasury to the position in which they would have been if debt limit increases had been delayed, including transferring amounts to the funds to compensate those funds for current and prospective losses arising from premature redemption of some long term securities when the debt limit was reached, see notes set out under section 3101 of Title 31, Money and Finance.

EX. ORD. NO. 12857. BUDGET CONTROL

Ex. Ord. No. 12857, Aug. 4, 1993, 58 F.R. 42181, provided:

By the authority vested in me as President of the United States by the Constitution and the laws of the United States of America, including section 1105 of title 31, United States Code, it is hereby ordered as follows:

SECTION 1. *Purpose.* The purpose of this order is to create a mechanism to monitor total costs of direct spending programs, and, in the event that actual or projected costs exceed targeted levels, to require that the budget address adjustments in direct spending.

SEC. 2. *Establishment of Direct Spending Targets.*

(a) *In General.* The initial direct spending targets for each of fiscal years 1994 through 1997 shall equal total outlays for all direct spending except net interest and deposit insurance as determined by the Director of the Office of Management and Budget (Director) under subsection (b).

(b) *Initial Report by Director.* (1) Not later than 30 days after the date of enactment of the Omnibus Budget Reconciliation Act of 1993 (OBRA) [Aug. 10, 1993], the Director shall submit a report to the Congress setting forth projected direct spending targets for each of fiscal years 1994 through 1997.

(2) The Director's projections shall be based on legislation enacted as of 5 days before the report is submitted under paragraph (1). To the extent feasible, the Director shall use the same economic and technical assumptions used in preparing the concurrent resolution on the budget for fiscal year 1994 (H.Con.Res. 64).

(c) *Adjustments.* Direct spending targets shall be subsequently adjusted by the Director under Section 6.

SEC. 3. *Annual Review of Direct Spending and Receipts by President.* As part of each budget submitted under section 1105(a) of title 31, United States Code, the Director shall provide an annual review of direct spending and receipts, which include (1) information supporting the adjustment of direct spending targets pursuant to Section 6, (2) information on total outlays for programs covered by the direct spending targets, including actual outlays for the prior fiscal year and projected outlays for the current fiscal year and the 5 succeeding fiscal years, and (3) information on the major categories of Federal receipts, including a comparison between the levels of those receipts and the levels projected as of the date of enactment of OBRA [Aug. 10, 1993].

SEC. 4. *Special Direct Spending Message by President.* (a) *Trigger.* In the event that the information submitted under Section 3 indicates—

(1) that actual outlays for direct spending in the prior fiscal year exceeded the applicable direct spending target, or

(2) that outlays for direct spending for the current or budget year are projected to exceed the applicable direct spending targets, the Director shall include in the budget a special direct spending message meeting the requirements of subsection (b) of this Section.

(b) *Contents.* (1) The special direct spending message shall include:

(A) An explanation of any adjustments to the direct spending targets pursuant to Section 6.

(B) An analysis of the variance in direct spending over the adjusted direct spending targets.

(C) The President's recommendations for addressing the direct spending overages, if any, in the prior, current, or budget year.

(2) The recommendations may consist of any of the following:

(A) Proposed legislative changes to reduce outlays, increase revenues, or both, in order to recoup or eliminate the overage for the prior, current, and budget years in the current year, the budget year, and the 4 out-years.

(B) Proposed legislative changes to reduce outlays, increase revenues, or both, in order to recoup or eliminate part of the overage for the prior, current, and budget year in the current year, the budget year, and the 4 out-years, accompanied by a finding by the President that, because of economic conditions or for other specified reasons, only some of the overage should be recouped or eliminated by outlay reductions or revenue increases, or both.

(C) A proposal to make no legislative changes to recoup or eliminate any overage, accompanied by a finding by the President that, because of economic conditions or for other specified reasons, no legislative changes are warranted.

(3) Any proposed legislative change under paragraph (2) to reduce outlays may include reductions in direct spending or in the discretionary spending limits under section 601 of the Congressional Budget Act of 1974 [former 2 U.S.C. 665].

SEC. 5. *Proposed Special Direct Spending Resolution.* If the President recommends reductions consistent with subsection [Section] 4 (b)(2)(A) or (B), the special direct spending message shall include the text of a special direct spending resolution implementing the President's recommendations through reconciliation directives instructing the appropriate committees of the House of Representatives and Senate to determine and recommend changes in laws within their jurisdictions to reduce outlays or increase revenues by specified amounts. If the President recommends no reductions pursuant to Section 4 (b)(2)(C), the special direct spending message shall include the text of a special resolution concurring in the President's recommendation of no legislative action.

SEC. 6. *Adjustments to Direct Spending Targets.*

(a) *Required Annual Adjustments.* Prior to the submission of the President's budget for each of fiscal years 1995 through 1997, the Director shall adjust the direct spending targets in accordance with this Section. Any such adjustments shall be reflected in the targets used in the report under Section 3 and message (if any) under Section 4.

(b) *Adjustment for Increases in Beneficiaries.* (1) The Director shall adjust the direct spending targets for increases (if any) in actual or projected numbers of beneficiaries under direct spending programs for which the number of beneficiaries is a variable in determining costs.

(2) The adjustment shall be made by—

(A) computing, for each program under paragraph (1), the percentage change between (i) the annual average number of beneficiaries under that program (including actual numbers of beneficiaries for the prior fiscal year and projections for the budget and subsequent fiscal years) to be used in the President's budget with which the adjustments will be submitted, and (ii) the annual average number of beneficiaries used in the adjustments made by the Director in the previous year (or, in the case of adjustments made in 1994, the annual average number of beneficiaries used in the Director's initial report under Section 2(b));

(B) applying the percentages computed under subparagraph (A) to the projected levels of outlays for each program consistent with the direct spending targets in effect immediately prior to the adjustment; and

(C) adding the results of the calculations required by subparagraph (B) to the direct spending targets in effect immediately prior to the adjustment.

(3) No adjustment shall be made for any program for a fiscal year in which the percentage increase computed under paragraph (2)(A) is less than or equal to zero.

(c) *Adjustments for Revenue Legislation.* The Director shall adjust the targets as follows:

(1) they shall be increased by the amount of any increase in receipts; or

(2) they shall be decreased by the amount of any decrease in receipts, resulting from receipts legislation enacted after the date of enactment of OBRA [Aug. 10, 1993], except legislation enacted in response to the message transmitted under Section 4.

(d) *Adjustments To Reflect Congressional Decisions.* Upon enactment of a reconciliation bill enacted in response to a message submitted under Section 4, the Director shall adjust direct spending targets for the current year, the budget year, and each outyear through 1997 by—

(1) increasing the target for the current year and the budget year by the amount stated for that year in that reconciliation bill (but if a separate vote was required by Congressional rules, only if that vote has occurred); and

(2) decreasing the target for the current, budget, and outyears through 1997 by the amount of reductions in direct spending enacted in that reconciliation bill.

(e) *Designated Emergencies.* The Director shall adjust the targets to reflect the costs of legislation that is designated as an emergency by Congress and the President under section 252(e) of the Balanced Budget and Emergency Deficit Control Act of 1985 [2 U.S.C. 902(e)].

SEC. 7. *Relationship to Balanced Budget and Emergency Deficit Control Act.* Recommendations pursuant to Section 4 shall include a provision specifying that reductions in outlays or increases in receipts resulting from that legislation shall not be taken into account for purposes of any budget enforcement procedures under the Balanced Budget and Emergency Deficit Control Act of 1985 [2 U.S.C. 900 et seq.].

SEC. 8. *Estimating Margin.* For any fiscal year for which the overage is less than one-half of 1 percent of the direct spending target for that year, the procedures set forth in Section 4 shall not apply.

SEC. 9. *Means-Tested Programs.* In making recommendations under Section 4, the Director shall seriously consider all other alternatives before proposing reductions in means-tested programs.

SEC. 10. *Effective Date.* This order shall take effect upon enactment of OBRA [Aug. 10, 1993]. This order shall apply to direct spending targets for fiscal years 1994 through 1997 and shall expire at the end of fiscal year 1997.

WILLIAM J. CLINTON.

EX. ORD. NO. 12858. DEFICIT REDUCTION FUND

Ex. Ord. No. 12858, Aug. 4, 1993, 58 F.R. 42185, provided:

By the authority vested in me as President of the United States by the Constitution and the laws of the United States of America, including sections 1104 and 1105 of title 31, United States Code, it is hereby ordered as follows:

SECTION 1. *Purpose.* It is essential to guarantee that the net deficit reduction achieved by the Omnibus Budget Reconciliation Act of 1993 [Pub. L. 103–66, see Tables for classification] is dedicated exclusively to reducing the deficit.

SEC. 2. *Deficit Reduction Fund.*

(a) *Establishment of the Fund.* There is established a separate account in the Treasury, known as the Deficit Reduction Fund, which shall receive the net deficit reduction achieved by the Omnibus Budget Reconciliation Act of 1993 [Pub. L. 103–66, see Tables for classification] as called for in subsection (b) of this order.

(b) *Amounts in Fund.* Beginning upon enactment of the Omnibus Budget Reconciliation Act of 1993 [Aug. 10, 1993], the Deficit Reduction Fund shall receive any increases in total revenues resulting from enactment of such Act on a daily basis. In addition, on a daily basis, the Secretary of the Treasury shall enter into such account an amount equivalent to the net deficit reduction achieved as a result of all spending reductions resulting from such Act. The cumulative fiscal year amounts for the combination of all such revenue increases and spending reductions shall be equal to:

(1) for fiscal year 1994, $60,292,000,000;
(2) for fiscal year 1995, $70,437,000,000;
(3) for fiscal year 1996, $92,061,000,000;
(4) for fiscal year 1997, $125,881,000,000;
(5) for fiscal year 1998, $146,939,000,000.

Within 30 days of enactment of the Omnibus Budget Reconciliation Act of 1993, the foregoing amounts may be adjusted by the Director of the Office of Management and Budget to reflect the final scoring of such Act.

(c) *Status of Amounts in Fund.* (i) The amounts in the Deficit Reduction Fund shall be used exclusively to redeem maturing debt obligations of the Treasury of the United States held by foreign governments in the amounts specified in subsection (b).

(ii) The amounts in the Deficit Reduction Fund as set forth in subsection (b) that result from increases in total revenues and spending reductions shall not be available for new spending or to finance measures that increase the deficit for purposes of budget enforcement procedures under the Balanced Budget and Emergency Deficit Control Act of 1985 (2 U.S.C. 901–922 [900–922]).

(d) *Effect on Other Funds.* Establishment of and transfers to the Deficit Reduction Fund shall not affect trust fund transfers that may be authorized or required by provisions of the Omnibus Reconciliation Act of 1993 or any other provision of law.

SEC. 3. *Requirement for the President To Report Annually on the Status of the Fund.* The Director of the Office of Management and Budget shall include in the President's Budget transmitted under section 1105 of title 31, United States Code, information about the Deficit Reduction Fund, including a separate statement of amounts in and Federal debt redeemed by that Fund.

SEC. 4. *Implementation.* The Secretary of the Treasury and the Director of the Office of Management and Budget shall each take such actions as may be necessary, within their respective authorities, promptly to carry out this order.

SEC. 5. *Effective Date.* This order shall take effect upon enactment of the Omnibus Budget Reconciliation Act of 1993 [Aug. 10, 1993].

WILLIAM J. CLINTON.

ACT REFERRED TO IN OTHER SECTIONS

The Balanced Budget and Emergency Deficit Control Act of 1985 (see Short Title note above) is referred to in sections 643, 691c of this title; title 7 section 1446; title 10 section 2814; title 12 section 2250; title 21 section 379g; title 22 sections 2295b, 3751, 5857; title 25 section 2010; title 38 section 113; title 39 section 2009a; title 42 sections 1382, 8621, 11303, 14211; title 48 section 1469a–1.

SECTION REFERRED TO IN OTHER SECTIONS

This section is referred to in sections 633, 661a of this title; title 45 section 821; title 50 App. section 1989b–9.

§ 901. Enforcing discretionary spending limits

(a) Enforcement

(1) Sequestration

Within 15 calendar days after Congress adjourns to end a session and on the same day as a sequestration (if any) under section 902 of this title and section 903 of this title, there shall be a sequestration to eliminate a budget-year breach, if any, within any category.

(2) Eliminating a breach

Each non-exempt account within a category shall be reduced by a dollar amount calculated by multiplying the baseline level of sequestrable budgetary resources in that account at that time by the uniform percentage necessary to eliminate a breach within that category; except that the health programs set forth in section 906(e) of this title shall not be reduced by more than 2 percent and the uniform percent applicable to all other programs under this paragraph shall be increased (if necessary) to a level sufficient to eliminate that breach. If, within a category, the discretionary spending limits for both new budget authority and outlays are breached, the uniform percentage shall be calculated by—

(A) first, calculating the uniform percentage necessary to eliminate the breach in new budget authority, and

(B) second, if any breach in outlays remains, increasing the uniform percentage to a level sufficient to eliminate that breach.

(3) Military personnel

If the President uses the authority to exempt any military personnel from sequestration under section 905(f) of this title, each account within subfunctional category 051 (other than those military personnel accounts for which the authority provided under section 905(f) of this title has been exercised) shall be further reduced by a dollar amount calculated by multiplying the enacted level of non-exempt budgetary resources in that account at that time by the uniform percentage necessary to offset the total dollar amount by which outlays are not reduced in military personnel accounts by reason of the use of such authority.

(4) Part-year appropriations

If, on the date specified in paragraph (1), there is in effect an Act making or continuing appropriations for part of a fiscal year for any budget account, then the dollar sequestration calculated for that account under paragraphs (2) and (3) shall be subtracted from—

(A) the annualized amount otherwise available by law in that account under that or a subsequent part-year appropriation; and

(B) when a full-year appropriation for that account is enacted, from the amount otherwise provided by the full-year appropriation.

(5) Look-back

If, after June 30, an appropriation for the fiscal year in progress is enacted that causes a breach within a category for that year (after taking into account any sequestration of amounts within that category), the discretionary spending limits for that category for the next fiscal year shall be reduced by the amount or amounts of that breach.

(6) Within-session sequestration

If an appropriation for a fiscal year in progress is enacted (after Congress adjourns to end the session for that budget year and before July 1 of that fiscal year) that causes a breach within a category for that year (after taking into account any prior sequestration of amounts within that category), 15 days later there shall be a sequestration to eliminate that breach within that category following the procedures set forth in paragraphs (2) through (4).

(7) Estimates

(A) CBO estimates

As soon as practicable after Congress completes action on any discretionary appropriation, CBO, after consultation with the Committees on the Budget of the House of Representatives and the Senate, shall provide OMB with an estimate of the amount of discretionary new budget authority and outlays for the current year (if any) and the budget year provided by that legislation.

(B) OMB estimates and explanation of differences

Not later than 7 calendar days (excluding Saturdays, Sundays, and legal holidays) after the date of enactment of any discretionary appropriation, OMB shall transmit a report to the House of Representatives and to the Senate containing the CBO estimate of that legislation, an OMB estimate of the amount of discretionary new budget authority and outlays for the current year (if any)

and the budget year provided by that legislation, and an explanation of any difference between the 2 estimates. If during the preparation of the report OMB determines that there is a significant difference between OMB and CBO, OMB shall consult with the Committees on the Budget of the House of Representatives and the Senate regarding that difference and that consultation shall include, to extent practicable, written communication to those committees that affords such committees the opportunity to comment before the issuance of the report.

(C) Assumptions and guidelines

OMB estimates under this paragraph shall be made using current economic and technical assumptions. OMB shall use the OMB estimates transmitted to the Congress under this paragraph. OMB and CBO shall prepare estimates under this paragraph in conformance with scorekeeping guidelines determined after consultation among the House and Senate Committees on the Budget, CBO, and OMB.

(D) Annual appropriations

For purposes of this paragraph, amounts provided by annual appropriations shall include any new budget authority and outlays for the current year (if any) and the budget year in accounts for which funding is provided in that legislation that result from previously enacted legislation.

(b) Adjustments to discretionary spending limits

(1) Preview report

(A) CONCEPTS AND DEFINITIONS.—When the President submits the budget under section 1105 of title 31, OMB shall calculate and the budget shall include adjustments to discretionary spending limits (and those limits as cumulatively adjusted) for the budget year and each outyear to reflect changes in concepts and definitions. Such changes shall equal the baseline levels of new budget authority and outlays using up-to-date concepts and definitions minus those levels using the concepts and definitions in effect before such changes. Such changes may only be made after consultation with the committees[1] on Appropriations and the Budget of the House of Representatives and the Senate and that consultation shall include written communication to such committees that affords such committees the opportunity to comment before official action is taken with respect to such changes.

(B) ADJUSTMENT TO ALIGN HIGHWAY SPENDING WITH REVENUES.—(i) When the President submits the budget under section 1105 of title 31, OMB shall calculate and the budget shall include adjustments to the highway category for the budget year and each outyear as provided in clause (ii)(I)(cc).

(ii)(I)(aa) OMB shall take the actual level of highway receipts for the year before the current year and subtract the sum of the estimated level of highway receipts in subclause (II) plus any amount previously calculated under item (bb) for that year.

---

[1] So in original. Probably should be capitalized.

(bb) OMB shall take the current estimate of highway receipts for the budget year and subtract the estimated level of receipts for that year.

(cc) OMB shall take the sum of the amounts calculated under items (aa) and (bb), add that sum to the amount of obligations set forth in section 8103 of the Transportation Equity Act for the 21st Century for the highway category for the budget year, and calculate the outlay change resulting from that change in obligations relative to that amount for the budget year and each outyear using current estimates. After making the calculation under the preceding sentence, OMB shall adjust the amount of obligations set forth in that section for the budget year by adding the sum of the amounts calculated under items (aa) and (bb).

(II) The estimated level of highway receipts for the purposes of this clause are—

    (aa) for fiscal year 1998, $22,164,000,000;
    (bb) for fiscal year 1999, $32,619,000,000;
    (cc) for fiscal year 2000, $28,066,000,000;
    (dd) for fiscal year 2001, $28,506,000,000;
    (ee) for fiscal year 2002, $28,972,000,000; and
    (ff) for fiscal year 2003, $29,471,000,000.

(III) In this clause, the term "highway receipts" means the governmental receipts credited to the highway account of the Highway Trust Fund.

(C)(i) In addition to the adjustment required by subparagraph (B), when the President submits the budget under section 1105 of title 31 for fiscal years[2] 2000, 2001, 2002, or 2003, OMB shall calculate and the budget shall include for the budget year and each outyear an adjustment to the limits on outlays for the highway category and the mass transit category equal to—

(I) the outlays for the applicable category calculated assuming obligation levels consistent with the estimates prepared pursuant to subparagraph (D), as adjusted, using current technical assumptions; minus

(II) the outlays for the applicable category set forth in the subparagraph (D) estimates, as adjusted.

(ii) The adjustment made pursuant to clause (i) in the fiscal years 2002 and 2003 budget submissions of the President under section 1105(a) of title 31 shall not exceed 4 percent plus cumulative carryovers. In this clause, the term "cumulative carryovers" means the total of each amount by which outlays for the highway and mass transit category for any fiscal year are less than the outlay limit for that category, as adjusted, for that year less any amount of carryover used in the previous year.

(D)(i) When OMB and CBO submit their final sequester report for fiscal year 1999, that report shall include an estimate of the outlays for each of the categories that would result in fiscal years 2000 through 2003 from obligations at the levels specified in section 8103 of the Transportation Equity Act for the 21st Century using current assumptions.

(ii) When the President submits the budget under section 1105 of title 31 for fiscal years[2]

2000, 2001, 2002, or 2003, OMB shall adjust the estimates made in clause (i) by the adjustments by subparagraphs (B) and (C).

(E) OMB shall consult with the Committees on the Budget and include a report on adjustments under subparagraphs (B) and (C) in the preview report.

(2) Sequestration reports

When OMB submits a sequestration report under section 904(e), (f), or (g) of this title for a fiscal year, OMB shall calculate, and the sequestration report and subsequent budgets submitted by the President under section 1105(a) of title 31 shall include adjustments to discretionary spending limits (and those limits as adjusted) for the fiscal year and each succeeding year through 2002, as follows:

(A) Emergency appropriations

If, for any fiscal year, appropriations for discretionary accounts are enacted that the President designates as emergency requirements and that the Congress so designates in statute, the adjustment shall be the total of such appropriations in discretionary accounts designated as emergency requirements and the outlays flowing in all fiscal years from such appropriations. This subparagraph shall not apply to appropriations to cover agricultural crop disaster assistance.

(B) Special outlay allowance

If, in any fiscal year, outlays for a category exceed the discretionary spending limit for that category but new budget authority does not exceed its limit for that category (after application of the first step of a sequestration described in subsection (a)(2) of this section, if necessary), the adjustment in outlays for a fiscal year is the amount of the excess but not to exceed 0.5 percent of the sum of the adjusted discretionary spending limits on outlays for that fiscal year.

(C) Continuing disability reviews

(i) If a bill or joint resolution making appropriations for a fiscal year is enacted that specifies an amount for continuing disability reviews under the heading "Limitation on Administrative Expenses" for the Social Security Administration, the adjustments for that fiscal year shall be the additional new budget authority provided in that Act for such reviews for that fiscal year and the additional outlays flowing from such amounts, but shall not exceed—

(I) for fiscal year 1998, $290,000,000 in additional new budget authority and $338,000,000 in additional outlays;

(II) for fiscal year 1999, $520,000,000 in additional new budget authority and $520,000,000 in additional outlays;

(III) for fiscal year 2000, $520,000,000 in additional new budget authority and $520,000,000 in additional outlays;

(IV) for fiscal year 2001, $520,000,000 in additional new budget authority and $520,000,000 in additional outlays; and

(V) for fiscal year 2002, $520,000,000 in additional new budget authority and $520,000,000 in additional outlays.

---

[2] So in original. Probably should be "year".

(ii) As used in this subparagraph—

(I) the term "continuing disability reviews" means reviews or redeterminations as defined under section 401(g)(1)(A) of title 42 and reviews and redeterminations authorized under section 211 of the Personal Responsibility and Work Opportunity Reconciliation Act of 1996;

(II) the term "additional new budget authority" means the amount provided for a fiscal year, in excess of $200,000,000, in an appropriations Act and specified to pay for the costs of continuing disability reviews under the heading "Limitation on Administrative Expenses" for the Social Security Administration; and

(III) the term "additional outlays" means outlays, in excess of $200,000,000 in a fiscal year, flowing from the amounts specified for continuing disability reviews under the heading "Limitation on Administrative Expenses" for the Social Security Administration, including outlays in that fiscal year flowing from amounts specified in Acts enacted for prior fiscal years (but not before 1996).

(D) Allowance for IMF

If an appropriation bill or joint resolution is enacted for a fiscal year through 2002 that includes an appropriation with respect to clause (i) or (ii), the adjustment shall be the amount of budget authority in the measure that is the dollar equivalent of the Special Drawing Rights with respect to—

(i) an increase in the United States quota as part of the International Monetary Fund Eleventh General Review of Quotas (United States Quota); or

(ii) any increase in the maximum amount available to the Secretary of the Treasury pursuant to section 286e-2 of title 22, as amended from time to time (New Arrangements to Borrow).

(E) Allowance for international arrearages

(i) Adjustments

If an appropriation bill or joint resolution is enacted for fiscal year 1998, 1999, or 2000 that includes an appropriation for arrearages for international organizations, international peacekeeping, and multilateral development banks for that fiscal year, the adjustment shall be the amount of budget authority in that measure and the outlays flowing in all fiscal years from that budget authority.

(ii) Limitations

The total amount of adjustments made pursuant to this subparagraph for the period of fiscal years 1998 through 2000 shall not exceed $1,884,000,000 in budget authority.

(F) EITC compliance initiative

If an appropriation bill or joint resolution is enacted for a fiscal year that includes an appropriation for an earned income tax credit compliance initiative, the adjustment shall be the amount of budget authority in that measure for that initiative and the out-

lays flowing in all fiscal years from that budget authority, but not to exceed—

(i) with respect to fiscal year 1998, $138,000,000 in new budget authority and $131,000,000 in outlays;

(ii) with respect to fiscal year 1999, $143,000,000 in new budget authority and $143,000,000 in outlays;

(iii) with respect to fiscal year 2000, $144,000,000 in new budget authority and $144,000,000 in outlays;

(iv) with respect to fiscal year 2001, $145,000,000 in new budget authority and $145,000,000 in outlays; and

(v) with respect to fiscal year 2002, $146,000,000 in new budget authority and $146,000,000 in outlays.

(G) Adoption incentive payments

Whenever a bill or joint resolution making appropriations for fiscal year 1999, 2000, 2001, 2002, or 2003 is enacted that specifies an amount for adoption incentive payments pursuant to this subchapter for the Department of Health and Human Services—

(i) the adjustments for new budget authority shall be the amounts of new budget authority provided in that measure for adoption incentive payments, but not to exceed $20,000,000; and

(ii) the adjustment for outlays shall be the additional outlays flowing from such amount.

(H) Conservation spending

(i) If a bill or resolution making appropriations for any fiscal year appropriates an amount for the conservation spending category that is less than the limit for the conservation spending category as specified in subsection (c) of this section, then the adjustment for new budget authority and outlays for the following fiscal year for that category shall be the amount of new budget authority and outlays that equals the difference between the amount appropriated and the amount of that category specified in subsection (c) of this section.

(ii) If a bill or resolution making appropriations for any fiscal year appropriates an amount for any conservation spending sub-category that is less than the limit for that conservation spending sub-category as specified in subsections (c)(11)–(c)(16) of this section, then the adjustment for new budget authority for the following fiscal year for that sub-category shall be the amount of new budget authority that equals the difference between the amount appropriated and the amount of that sub-category specified in subsection (c)(11)–(c)(16) of this section.

(iii) The total amount provided for any conservation activity within the conservation spending category may not exceed any authorized ceiling for that activity.

(c) Discretionary spending limit

As used in this subchapter, the term "discretionary spending limit" means—

(1) with respect to fiscal year 1997, for the discretionary category, the current adjusted limits of new budget authority and outlays;

(2) with respect to fiscal year 1998—

(A) for the defense category: $269,000,000,000 in new budget authority and $266,823,000,000 in outlays;

(B) for the nondefense category: $252,357,000,000 in new budget authority and $282,853,000,000 in outlays; and

(C) for the violent crime reduction category: $5,500,000,000 in new budget authority and $3,592,000,000 in outlays;

(3) with respect to fiscal year 1999—

(A) for the defense category: $271,500,000,000 in new budget authority and $266,518,000,000 in outlays;

(B) for the nondefense category: $255,699,000,000 in new budget authority and $287,850,000,000 in outlays;

(C) for the violent crime reduction category: $5,800,000,000 in new budget authority and $4,953,000,000 in outlays;

(D) for the highway category: $21,885,000,000 in outlays; and

(E) for the mass transit category: $4,401,000,000 in outlays;

(4) with respect to fiscal year 2000—

(A) for the discretionary category: $532,693,000,000 in new budget authority and $558,711,000,000 in outlays;

(B) for the violent crime reduction category: $4,500,000,000 in new budget authority and $5,554,000,000 in outlays;

(C) for the highway category: $24,436,000,000 in outlays; and

(D) for the mass transit category: $4,761,000,000 in outlays;

(5) with respect to fiscal year 2001—

(A) for the discretionary category: $637,000,000,000 in new budget authority and $612,695,000,000 in outlays;

(B) for the highway category: $26,204,000,000 in outlays; and

(C) for the mass transit category: $5,190,000,000 in outlays;

(6) with respect to fiscal year 2002—

(A) for the discretionary category: $551,074,000,000 in new budget authority and $560,799,000,000 in outlays;

(B) for the highway category: $26,977,000,000 in outlays;

(C) for the mass transit category: $5,709,000,000 in outlays; and and[3]

(D) for the conservation spending category: $1,760,000,000, in new budget authority and $1,232,000,000 in outlays;

(7) with respect to fiscal year 2003—

(A) for the highway category: $27,728,000,000 in outlays;

(B) for the mass transit category: $6,256,000,000 in outlays; and

(C) for the conservation spending category: $1,920,000,000, in new budget authority and $1,872,000,000 in outlays;

(8) with respect to fiscal year 2004 for the conservation spending category: $2,080,000,000, in new budget authority and $2,032,000,000 in outlays;

(9) with respect to fiscal year 2005 for the conservation spending category: $2,240,000,000, in new budget authority and $2,192,000,000 in outlays;

(10) with respect to fiscal year 2006 for the conservation spending category: $2,400,000,000, in new budget authority and $2,352,000,000 in outlays;

(11) with respect to each fiscal year 2002 through 2006 for the Federal and State Land and Water Conservation Fund sub-category of the conservation spending category: $540,000,000 in new budget authority and the outlays flowing therefrom;

(12) with respect to each fiscal year 2002 through 2006 for the State and Other Conservation sub-category of the conservation spending category: $300,000,000 in new budget authority and the outlays flowing therefrom;

(13) with respect to each fiscal year 2002 through 2006 for the Urban and Historic Preservation sub-category of the conservation spending category: $160,000,000 in new budget authority and the outlays flowing therefrom;

(14) with respect to each fiscal year 2002 through 2006 for the Payments in Lieu of Taxes sub-category of the conservation spending category: $50,000,000 in new budget authority and the outlays flowing therefrom;

(15) with respect to each fiscal year 2002 through 2006 for the Federal Deferred Maintenance sub-category of the conservation spending category: $150,000,000 in new budget authority and the outlays flowing therefrom;

(16) with respect to fiscal year 2002 for the Coastal Assistance sub-category of the conservation spending category: $440,000,000 in new budget authority and the outlays flowing therefrom; with respect to fiscal year 2003 for the Coastal Assistance sub-category of the conservation spending category: $480,000,000 in new budget authority and the outlays flowing therefrom; with respect to fiscal year 2004 for the Coastal Assistance sub-category of the conservation spending category: $520,000,000 in new budget authority and the outlays flowing therefrom; with respect to fiscal year 2005 for the Coastal Assistance sub-category of the conservation spending category: $560,000,000 in new budget authority and the outlays flowing therefrom; and with respect to fiscal year 2006 for the Coastal Assistance sub-category of the conservation spending category: $600,000,000 in new budget authority and the outlays flowing therefrom;

as adjusted in strict conformance with subsection (b) of this section.

(Pub. L. 99–177, title II, §251, Dec. 12, 1985, 99 Stat. 1063; Pub. L. 100–119, title I, §102(a), Sept. 29, 1987, 101 Stat. 754; Pub. L. 100–203, title VIII, §8003(f), Dec. 22, 1987, 101 Stat. 1330–282; Pub. L. 101–508, title XIII, §13101(a), (e)(2), Nov. 5, 1990, 104 Stat. 1388–577, 1388–593; Pub. L. 103–66, title XIV, §14002(c)(1), Aug. 10, 1993, 107 Stat. 683; Pub. L. 103–87, title V, §571, Sept. 30, 1993, 107 Stat. 971; Pub. L. 103–306, title V, §562, Aug. 23, 1994, 108 Stat. 1649; Pub. L. 103–354, title I, §119(d)(1), Oct. 13, 1994, 108 Stat. 3208; Pub. L. 104–121, title I, §103(b), Mar. 29, 1996, 110 Stat. 848; Pub. L. 104–193, title II, §211(d)(5)(B), Aug. 22, 1996, 110

[3] So in original.

Stat. 2191; Pub. L. 104–208, div. A, title I, § 101(c) [title V, § 577], Sept. 30, 1996, 110 Stat. 3009–121, 3009–169; Pub. L. 105–33, title X, § 10203(a), (b), Aug. 5, 1997, 111 Stat. 698, 701; Pub. L. 105–89, title II, § 201(b)(1), Nov. 19, 1997, 111 Stat. 2125; Pub. L. 105–178, title VIII, § 8101(a), (d), June 9, 1998, 112 Stat. 488, 490; Pub. L. 106–291, title VIII, § 801(a), (b), Oct. 11, 2000, 114 Stat. 1026, 1027; Pub. L. 106–429, § 101(a) [title VII, § 701(a)], Nov. 6, 2000, 114 Stat. 1900, 1900A–64.)

TERMINATION OF SECTION

For termination of section by section 275(b) of Pub. L. 99–177, as amended, see Effective and Termination Dates note set out under section 900 of this title.

REFERENCES IN TEXT

Section 8103 of the Transportation Equity Act for the 21st Century, referred to in subsec. (b)(1)(B)(ii)(I)(cc), (D)(i), is section 8103 of Pub. L. 105–178, which is set out as a note below.

Section 211 of the Personal Responsibility and Work Opportunity Reconciliation Act of 1996, referred to in subsec. (b)(2)(C)(ii)(I), is section 211 of Pub. L. 104–193, which amended this section, section 665e of this title, and section 1382c of Title 42, The Public Health and Welfare, enacted provisions set out as a note under section 1382c of Title 42, and amended provisions set out as a note under section 401 of Title 42.

CODIFICATION

Pub. L. 101–508, § 13101(e)(2), redesignated former subsec. (a)(6)(I) of this section as section 257(e) of Pub. L. 99–177, which is classified to section 907(e) of this title.

AMENDMENTS

2000—Subsec. (b)(2)(H). Pub. L. 106–291, § 801(b), added subpar. (H).

Subsec. (c)(5)(A). Pub. L. 106–429 added subpar. (A) and struck out former subpar. (A) which read as follows: "for the discretionary category: $542,032,000,000 in new budget authority and $564,396,000,000 in outlays;".

Subsec. (c)(6)(D). Pub. L. 106–291, § 801(a)(1), added subpar. (D).

Subsec. (c)(7)(C). Pub. L. 106–291, § 801(a)(2), added subpar. (C).

Subsec. (c)(8) to (16). Pub. L. 106–291, § 801(a)(3), added pars. (8) to (16).

1998—Subsec. (b)(1). Pub. L. 105–178, § 8101(d), designated existing provisions as subpar. (A), inserted heading, and added subpars. (B) to (E).

Subsec. (c)(3)(D), (E). Pub. L. 105–178, § 8101(a)(1), added subpars. (D) and (E).

Subsec. (c)(4)(C), (D). Pub. L. 105–178, § 8101(a)(2), added subpars. (C) and (D).

Subsec. (c)(5). Pub. L. 105–178, § 8101(a)(3), substituted a dash for comma after "2001", designated remaining provisions as subpar. (A), realigned margins, struck out "and" at end, and added subpars. (B) and (C).

Subsec. (c)(6). Pub. L. 105–178, § 8101(a)(4), substituted a dash for comma after "2002", designated remaining provisions as subpar. (A), realigned margins, and added subpars. (B) and (C).

Subsec. (c)(7). Pub. L. 105–178, § 8101(a)(5), added par. (7).

1997—Subsec. (a). Pub. L. 105–33, § 10203(a)(1), struck out "Fiscal Years 1991–1998" before "Enforcement" in heading.

Subsec. (a)(3). Pub. L. 105–33, § 10203(a)(2), substituted "section 905(f)" for "section 905(h)" in two places.

Subsec. (a)(7). Pub. L. 105–33, § 10203(a)(3), added par. (7) and struck out heading and text of former par. (7). Text read as follows: "As soon as practicable after Congress completes action on any discretionary appropriation, CBO, after consultation with the Committees on the Budget of the House of Representatives and the

Senate, shall provide OMB with an estimate of the amount of discretionary new budget authority and outlays for the current year (if any) and the budget year provided by that legislation. Within 5 calendar days after the enactment of any discretionary appropriation, OMB shall transmit a report to the House of Representatives and to the Senate containing the CBO estimate of that legislation, an OMB estimate of the amount of discretionary new budget authority and outlays for the current year (if any) and the budget year provided by that legislation, and an explanation of any difference between the two estimates. For purposes of this paragraph, amounts provided by annual appropriations shall include any new budget authority and outlays for those years in accounts for which funding is provided in that legislation that result from previously enacted legislation. Those OMB estimates shall be made using current economic and technical assumptions. OMB shall use the OMB estimates transmitted to the Congress under this paragraph for the purposes of this subsection. OMB and CBO shall prepare estimates under this paragraph in conformance with scorekeeping guidelines determined after consultation among the House and Senate Committees on the Budget, CBO, and OMB."

Subsec. (b). Pub. L. 105–33, § 10203(a)(4), added subsec. (b) and struck out heading and text of former subsec. (b) which provided that when the President submitted the budget for a budget year from 1992 to 1998, OMB was to calculate, and the budget was to include, adjustments to discretionary spending limits reflecting certain enumerated factors and provided that when OMB submitted a sequestration report for a fiscal year from 1991 to 1998, OMB was to calculate, and the sequestration report and subsequent budgets were to include, adjustments to discretionary spending limits reflecting certain enumerated factors.

Subsec. (b)(2)(G). Pub. L. 105–89 added subpar. (G).

Subsec. (c). Pub. L. 105–33, § 10203(b), added subsec. (c).

1996—Subsec. (b)(2)(G). Pub. L. 104–208 substituted "fiscal years 1994, 1995, and 1997" for "fiscal year 1994 and 1995" in two places.

Subsec. (b)(2)(H). Pub. L. 104–121 added subpar. (H).

Subsec. (b)(2)(H)(i). Pub. L. 104–193, § 211(d)(5)(B)(i), substituted "$175,000,000" for "$25,000,000" and "$310,000,000" for "$160,000,000" in subcl. (II), and "$245,000,000" for "$145,000,000" and "$470,000,000" for "$370,000,000" in subcl. (III).

Subsec. (b)(2)(H)(ii)(I). Pub. L. 104–193, § 211(d)(5)(B)(ii), amended subcl. (I) generally. Prior to amendment, subcl. (I) read as follows: "the term 'continuing disability reviews' has the meaning given such term by section 401(g)(1)(A) of title 42;".

1994—Subsec. (b)(2)(D)(i). Pub. L. 103–354 inserted at end "This subparagraph shall not apply to appropriations to cover agricultural crop disaster assistance."

Subsec. (b)(2)(G). Pub. L. 103–306 substituted "1994 and 1995" for "1994" in two places.

1993—Subsec. (a). Pub. L. 103–66, § 14002(c)(1)(A), substituted "1998" for "1995" in heading.

Subsec. (b)(1). Pub. L. 103–66, § 14002(c)(1)(B)(i), in introductory provisions, substituted "1995, 1996, 1997, or 1998" for "or 1995" and "outyear through 1998" for "outyear through 1995".

Subsec. (b)(1)(B)(iii). Pub. L. 103–66, § 14002(c)(1)(B)(ii), added cl. (iii).

Subsec. (b)(2). Pub. L. 103–66, § 14002(c)(1)(B)(iii), in introductory provisions, substituted "1995, 1996, 1997, or 1998" for "or 1995" and "year through 1998" for "year through 1995".

Subsec. (b)(2)(D)(i). Pub. L. 103–66, § 14002(c)(1)(B)(iv), substituted "for any fiscal year," for "for fiscal year 1991, 1992, 1993, 1994, or 1995,".

Subsec. (b)(2)(E)(iv). Pub. L. 103–66, § 14002(c)(1)(B)(v), added cl. (iv).

Subsec. (b)(2)(F). Pub. L. 103–66, § 14002(c)(1)(B)(vi), inserted before period at end ", and not to exceed 0.5 percent of the adjusted descretionary [sic] spending limit on outlays for the fiscal year in fiscal year 1996, 1997, or 1998".

Subsec. (b)(2)(G). Pub. L. 103–87 added subpar. (G).

1990—Pub. L. 101–508, §13101(a), amended section generally, substituting subsecs. (a) and (b) relating to enforcement of discretionary spending limits for former subsecs. (a) to (e) relating to reporting of excess deficits.

Subsec. (a)(6)(I). Pub. L. 101–508, §13101(e)(2), redesignated subsec. (a)(6)(I) of this section as section 907(e) of this title.

1987—Pub. L. 100–119 amended section generally, substituting provisions consisting of subsecs. (a) to (e) relating to reports by Director of CBO to Director of OMB and to Congress and by Director of OMB to President and Congress for provisions consisting of subsecs. (a) to (g) relating to joint reports by Directors of CBO and OMB to Comptroller General and report by Comptroller General to President and Congress.

Subsec. (a)(6)(B). Pub. L. 100–203, §8003(f), struck out "and" before "contract authority" and inserted provision whereby the authority to provide insurance through the Federal Housing Administration Fund be continued.

EFFECTIVE DATE OF 1997 AMENDMENT

Amendment by Pub. L. 105–89 effective Nov. 19, 1997, except as otherwise provided, with delay permitted if State legislation is required, see section 501 of Pub. L. 105–89, set out as a note under section 622 of Title 42, The Public Health and Welfare.

EFFECTIVE DATE OF 1994 AMENDMENT

Section 119(d)(1) of Pub. L. 103–354 provided that the amendment made by that section is effective Jan. 1, 1995.

ADJUSTMENT FOR ROUNDING

Pub. L. 106–429, §101(a) [title VII, §701(c)], Nov. 6, 2000, 114 Stat. 1900, 1900A–64, provided that: "Under the terms of section 251(b)(2) of the Balanced Budget and Emergency Deficit Control Act of 1985 [2 U.S.C. 901(b)(2)] adjustments for rounding shall be provided for the first amount referred to in section 251(c)(5)(A) of such Act [2 U.S.C. 901(c)(5)(A)], as amended by this section, equal to 0.5 percent of such amount."

Pub. L. 106–113, div. B, §1000(a)(5) [title III, §307], Nov. 29, 1999, 113 Stat. 1536, 1501A–306, provided that: "Under the terms of section 251(b)(2) of Public Law 99–177 [2 U.S.C. 901(b)(2)], an adjustment for rounding shall be provided for the first amount referred to in section 251(c)(4)(A) of such Act [2 U.S.C. 901(c)(4)(A)] equal to 0.2 percent of such amount."

OFFSETTING ADJUSTMENT IN DISCRETIONARY SPENDING LIMITS

Pub. L. 105–178, title VIII, §8101(b), June 9, 1998, 112 Stat. 489, as amended by Pub. L. 105–206, title IX, §9013(a), July 22, 1998, 112 Stat. 865, provided that:

"(1) ADJUSTMENT OF NONDEFENSE CATEGORY FOR FY1999.—The discretionary spending limit set forth in section 251(c)(3)(B) of the Balanced Budget and Emergency Deficit Control Act of 1985 [2 U.S.C. 901(c)(3)(B)], as adjusted in conformance with section 251(b) of that Act, is reduced by $859,000,000 in new budget authority and $25,144,000,000 in outlays.

"(2) ADJUSTMENT OF DISCRETIONARY CATEGORY FOR FY2000.—The discretionary spending limit set forth in section 251(c)(4)(A) of the Balanced Budget and Emergency Deficit Control Act of 1985 [2 U.S.C. 901(c)(4)(A)], as adjusted in conformance with section 251(b) of that Act, is reduced by $859,000,000 in new budget authority and $26,009,000,000 in outlays.

"(3) ADJUSTMENT OF DISCRETIONARY SPENDING LIMIT FOR FY2001.—The discretionary spending limit set forth in section 251(c)(5)(A) of the Balanced Budget and Emergency Deficit Control Act of 1985 [2 U.S.C. 901(c)(5)(A)], as adjusted in conformance with section 251(b) of that Act, is reduced by $859,000,000 in new budget authority and $26,329,000,000 in outlays.

"(4) ADJUSTMENT OF DISCRETIONARY SPENDING LIMIT FOR FY2002.—The discretionary spending limit set forth

in section 251(c)(6)(A) of the Balanced Budget and Emergency Deficit Control Act of 1985 [2 U.S.C. 901(c)(6)(A)], as adjusted in conformance with section 251(b) of that Act, is reduced by $859,000,000 in new budget authority and $26,675,000,000 in outlays."

LEVEL OF OBLIGATION LIMITATIONS

Pub. L. 105–178, title VIII, §8103, June 9, 1998, 112 Stat. 492, provided that:

"(a) HIGHWAY CATEGORY.—For the purposes of section 251(b) of the Balanced Budget and Emergency Deficit Control Act of 1985 [2 U.S.C. 901(b)], the level of obligation limitations for the highway category is—

"(1) for fiscal year 1999, $25,883,000,000;

"(2) for fiscal year 2000, $26,629,000,000;

"(3) for fiscal year 2001, $27,158,000,000;

"(4) for fiscal year 2002, $27,767,000,000; and

"(5) for fiscal year 2003, $28,233,000,000.

"(b) MASS TRANSIT CATEGORY.—For the purposes of section 251(b) of the Balanced Budget and Emergency Deficit Control Act of 1985, the level of obligation limitations for the mass transit category is—

"(1) for fiscal year 1999, $5,365,000,000;

"(2) for fiscal year 2000, $5,797,000,000;

"(3) for fiscal year 2001, $6,271,000,000;

"(4) for fiscal year 2002, $6,747,000,000; and

"(5) for fiscal year 2003, $7,226,000,000.

For purposes of this subsection, the term 'obligation limitations' means the sum of budget authority and obligation limitations."

SECTION REFERRED TO IN OTHER SECTIONS

This section is referred to in sections 633, 643, 645, 691a, 691c, 900, 902, 903, 904, 907 of this title; title 16 section 556c; title 23 section 110; title 38 sections 113, 1729A; title 39 section 2009a; title 42 sections 5203, 8621; title 43 section 1474a.

§ 901a. Repealed. Pub. L. 105–33, title X, § 10204(a)(1), Aug. 5, 1997, 111 Stat. 702

Section, Pub. L. 99–177, title II, §251A, as added Pub. L. 103–322, title XXXI, §310001(g)(1), Sept. 13, 1994, 108 Stat. 2104, related to sequestration with respect to Violent Crime Reduction Trust Fund.

§ 902. Enforcing pay-as-you-go

(a) Purpose

The purpose of this section is to assure that any legislation enacted before October 1, 2002, affecting direct spending or receipts that increases the deficit will trigger an offsetting sequestration.

(b) Sequestration

(1) Timing

Not later than 15 calendar days after the date Congress adjourns to end a session and on the same day as a sequestration (if any) under section 901 or 903 of this title, there shall be a sequestration to offset the amount of any net deficit increase caused by all direct spending and receipts legislation enacted before October 1, 2002, as calculated under paragraph (2).

(2) Calculation of deficit increase

OMB shall calculate the amount of deficit increase or decrease by adding—

(A) all OMB estimates for the budget year of direct spending and receipts legislation transmitted under subsection (d) of this section;

(B) the estimated amount of savings in direct spending programs applicable to budget year resulting from the prior year's sequestration under this section or section 903 of this title, if any, as published in OMB's final sequestration report for that prior year; and

(C) any net deficit increase or decrease in the current year resulting from all OMB estimates for the current year of direct spending and receipts legislation transmitted under subsection (d) of this section that were not reflected in the final OMB sequestration report for the current year.

(c) Eliminating a deficit increase

(1) The amount required to be sequestered in a fiscal year under subsection (b) of this section shall be obtained from non-exempt direct spending accounts from actions taken in the following order:

(A) First

All reductions in automatic spending increases specified in section 906(a) of this title shall be made.

(B) Second

If additional reductions in direct spending accounts are required to be made, the maximum reductions permissible under sections 906(b) of this title (guaranteed and direct student loans) and 906(c) of this title (foster care and adoption assistance) shall be made.

(C) Third

(i) If additional reductions in direct spending accounts are required to be made, each remaining non-exempt direct spending account shall be reduced by the uniform percentage necessary to make the reductions in direct spending required by paragraph (1); except that the medicare programs specified in section 906(d) of this title shall not be reduced by more than 4 percent and the uniform percentage applicable to all other direct spending programs under this paragraph shall be increased (if necessary) to a level sufficient to achieve the required reduction in direct spending.

(ii) For purposes of determining reductions under clause (i), outlay reductions (as a result of sequestration of Commodity Credit Corporation commodity price support contracts in the fiscal year of a sequestration) that would occur in the following fiscal year shall be credited as outlay reductions in the fiscal year of the sequestration.

(2) For purposes of this subsection, accounts shall be assumed to be at the level in the baseline.

(d) Estimates

(1) CBO estimates

As soon as practicable after Congress completes action on any direct spending or receipts legislation, CBO shall provide an estimate to OMB of that legislation.

(2) OMB estimates

Not later than 7 calendar days (excluding Saturdays, Sundays, and legal holidays) after the date of enactment of any direct spending or receipts legislation, OMB shall transmit a report to the House of Representatives and to the Senate containing—

(A) the CBO estimate of that legislation;

(B) an OMB estimate of that legislation using current economic and technical assumptions; and

(C) an explanation of any difference between the 2 estimates.

(3) Significant differences

If during the preparation of the report under paragraph (2) OMB determines that there is a significant difference between the OMB and CBO estimates, OMB shall consult with the Committees on the Budget of the House of Representatives and the Senate regarding that difference and that consultation, to the extent practicable, shall include written communication to such committees that affords such committees the opportunity to comment before the issuance of that report.

(4) Scope of estimates

The estimates under this section shall include the amount of change in outlays or receipts for the current year (if applicable), the budget year, and each outyear excluding any amounts resulting from—

(A) full funding of, and continuation of, the deposit insurance guarantee commitment in effect under current estimates; and

(B) emergency provisions as designated under subsection (e) of this section.

(5) Scorekeeping guidelines

OMB and CBO, after consultation with each other and the Committees on the Budget of the House of Representatives and the Senate, shall—

(A) determine common scorekeeping guidelines; and

(B) in conformance with such guidelines, prepare estimates under this section.

(e) Emergency legislation

If a provision of direct spending or receipts legislation is enacted that the President designates as an emergency requirement and that the Congress so designates in statute, the amounts of new budget authority, outlays, and receipts in all fiscal years resulting from that provision shall be designated as an emergency requirement in the reports required under subsection (d) of this section. This subsection shall not apply to direct spending provisions to cover agricultural crop disaster assistance.

(Pub. L. 99–177, title II, § 252, Dec. 12, 1985, 99 Stat. 1072; Pub. L. 100–119, title I, § 102(a), Sept. 29, 1987, 101 Stat. 764; Pub. L. 100–203, title VIII, § 8003(e), Dec. 22, 1987, 101 Stat. 1330–282; Pub. L. 101–508, title XIII, § 13101(a), Nov. 5, 1990, 104 Stat. 1388–581; Pub. L. 103–66, title XIV, § 14003(a), Aug. 10, 1993, 107 Stat. 684; Pub. L. 103–354, title I, § 119(d)(2), Oct. 13, 1994, 108 Stat. 3208; Pub. L. 105–33, title X, § 10205, Aug. 5, 1997, 111 Stat. 702.)

TERMINATION OF SECTION

For termination of section by section 275(b) of Pub. L. 99–177, as amended, see Effective and Termination Dates note set out under section 900 of this title.

AMENDMENTS

1997—Subsec. (a). Pub. L. 105–33, § 10205(1), added subsec. (a) and struck out heading and text of former subsec. (a). Text read as follows: "The purpose of this section is to assure that any legislation (enacted after November 5, 1990) affecting direct spending or receipts that increases the deficit in any fiscal year covered by this Act will trigger an offsetting sequestration."

Subsec. (b). Pub. L. 105–33, § 10205(1), added subsec. (b) and struck out heading and text of former subsec. (b) which required sequestrations at the end of a session of Congress to offset amount of any net deficit increase in that fiscal year and prior fiscal year caused by all direct spending and receipts legislation enacted after Nov. 5, 1990.

Subsec. (c)(1)(B). Pub. L. 105–33, § 10205(2), inserted "and direct" after "guaranteed".

Subsec. (d). Pub. L. 105–33, § 10205(3), amended heading and text of subsec. (d) generally. Prior to amendment, text read as follows: "As soon as practicable after Congress completes action on any direct spending or receipts legislation enacted after November 5, 1990, after consultation with the Committees on the Budget of the House of Representatives and the Senate, CBO shall provide OMB with an estimate of the amount of change in outlays or receipts, as the case may be, in each fiscal year through fiscal year 1998 resulting from that legislation. Within 5 calendar days after the enactment of any direct spending or receipts legislation enacted after November 5, 1990, OMB shall transmit a report to the House of Representatives and to the Senate containing such CBO estimate of that legislation, an OMB estimate of the amount of change in outlays or receipts, as the case may be, in each fiscal year through fiscal year 1998 resulting from that legislation, and an explanation of any difference between the two estimates. Those OMB estimates shall be made using current economic and technical assumptions. OMB and CBO shall prepare estimates under this paragraph in conformance with scorekeeping guidelines determined after consultation among the House and Senate Committees on the Budget, CBO, and OMB."

Subsec. (e). Pub. L. 105–33, § 10205(4), struck out ", for any fiscal year from 1991 through 1998," after "If" and "through 1995" after "receipts in all fiscal years".

1994—Subsec. (e). Pub. L. 103–354 inserted at end "This subsection shall not apply to direct spending provisions to cover agricultural crop disaster assistance."

1993—Subsec. (a). Pub. L. 103–66, § 14003(a)(1), which directed the substitution of "Fiscal year 1992–1998 enforcement" for "Fiscal year 1992–1995 enforcement" in heading, was executed by substituting "Fiscal years 1992–1998 enforcement" for "Fiscal years 1992–1995 enforcement", to reflect the probable intent of Congress.

Subsec. (d). Pub. L. 103–66, § 14003(a)(2), substituted "through fiscal year 1998" for "through fiscal year 1995" in two places.

Subsec. (e). Pub. L. 103–66, § 14003(a)(3), substituted "for any fiscal year 1991 through 1998" for "for fiscal year 1991, 1992, 1993, 1994, or 1995".

1990—Pub. L. 101–508 amended section generally, substituting subsecs. (a) to (e) relating to enforcement of pay-as-you-go for former subsecs. (a) to (g) relating to Presidential order.

1987—Pub. L. 100–119 amended section generally to reflect substitution of Director of OMB for Comptroller General as official submitting reports under section 901 of this title and to revise provisions relating to content of Presidential orders issued in accordance with those reports.

Subsec. (c)(2)(F)(ii). Pub. L. 100–203, § 8003(e), substituted "proposed" for "made".

Effective Date of 1994 Amendment

Section 119(d)(2) of Pub. L. 103–354 provided that the amendment made by that section is effective Jan. 1, 1995.

Conforming Paygo Scorecard With Transportation Equity Act For 21st Century

Pub. L. 105–178, title VIII, § 8102, June 9, 1998, 112 Stat. 492, as amended by Pub. L. 105–206, title IX, § 9013(c),

July 22, 1998, 112 Stat. 865, provided that: "Upon the enactment of this Act [June 9, 1998], the Director of the Office of Management and Budget shall not make any estimates under section 252(d) of the Balanced Budget and Emergency Deficit Control Act of 1985 [2 U.S.C. 902(d)] of changes in direct spending outlays and receipts for any fiscal year resulting from this title [see Tables for classification] or from section 1102 of this Act [23 U.S.C. 104 note]."

Reduction of Preexisting Balances and Exclusion of Effects of Pub. L. 105–33 From Paygo Scorecard

Section 10213 of Pub. L. 105–33 provided that: "Upon the enactment of this Act [Aug. 5, 1997], the Director of the Office of Management and Budget shall—

"(1) reduce any balances of direct spending and receipts legislation for any fiscal year under section 252 of the Balanced Budget and Emergency Deficit Control Act of 1985 [2 U.S.C. 902] to zero; and

"(2) not make any estimates of changes in direct spending outlays and receipts under subsection (d) of that section for any fiscal year resulting from the enactment of this Act [see Tables for classification] or of the Taxpayer Relief Act of 1997 [Pub. L. 105–34, see Tables for classification]."

Reduction of Direct Spending and Receipts Legislation Balances

Section 14003(c) of Pub. L. 103–66 provided that: "Upon enactment of this Act [Aug. 10, 1993], the director of the Office of Management and Budget shall reduce the balances of direct spending and receipts legislation applicable to each fiscal year under section 252 of the Balanced Budget and Emergency Deficit Control Act of 1985 [2 U.S.C. 902] by an amount equal to the net deficit reduction achieved through the enactment in this Act [see Tables for classification] of direct spending and receipts legislation for that year."

Section Referred to in Other Sections

This section is referred to in sections 645, 691c, 901, 903, 904, 906, 907, 907d of this title; title 7 section 1446; title 16 sections 3834, 3837d, 3839c; title 19 section 3624; title 31 section 1341; title 38 section 1729A; title 39 section 2009a.

§ 903. Enforcing deficit targets

(a) Sequestration

Within 15 calendar days after Congress adjourns to end a session (other than of the One Hundred First Congress) and on the same day as a sequestration (if any) under section 901 of this title and section 902 of this title, but after any sequestration required by section 901 of this title (enforcing discretionary spending limits) or section 902 of this title (enforcing pay-as-you-go), there shall be a sequestration to eliminate the excess deficit (if any remains) if it exceeds the margin.

(b) Excess deficit; margin

The excess deficit is, if greater than zero, the estimated deficit for the budget year, minus—

(1) the maximum deficit amount for that year;

(2) the amounts for that year designated as emergency direct spending or receipts legislation under section 902(e) of this title; and

(3) for any fiscal year in which there is not a full adjustment for technical and economic reestimates, the deposit insurance reestimate for that year, if any, calculated under subsection (h) of this section.

The "margin" for fiscal year 1992 or 1993 is zero and for fiscal year 1994 or 1995 is $15,000,000,000.

(c) Dividing sequestration

To eliminate the excess deficit in a budget year, half of the required outlay reductions shall be obtained from non-exempt defense accounts (accounts designated as function 050 in the President's fiscal year 1991 budget submission) and half from non-exempt, non-defense accounts (all other non-exempt accounts).

(d) Defense

Each non-exempt defense account shall be reduced by a dollar amount calculated by multiplying the level of sequestrable budgetary resources in that account at that time by the uniform percentage necessary to carry out subsection (c) of this section, except that, if any military personnel are exempt, adjustments shall be made under the procedure set forth in section 901(a)(3) of this title.

(e) Non-defense

Actions to reduce non-defense accounts shall be taken in the following order:

(1) First

All reductions in automatic spending increases under section 906(a) of this title shall be made.

(2) Second

If additional reductions in non-defense accounts are required to be made, the maximum reduction permissible under sections 906(b) of this title (guaranteed student loans) and 906(c) of this title (foster care and adoption assistance) shall be made.

(3) Third

(A) If additional reductions in non-defense accounts are required to be made, each remaining non-exempt, non-defense account shall be reduced by the uniform percentage necessary to make the reductions in non-defense outlays required by subsection (c) of this section, except that—

(i) the medicare program specified in section 906(d) of this title shall not be reduced by more than 2 percent in total including any reduction of less than 2 percent made under section 902 of this title or, if it has been reduced by 2 percent or more under section 902 of this title, it may not be further reduced under this section; and

(ii) the health programs set forth in section 906(e) of this title shall not be reduced by more than 2 percent in total (including any reduction made under section 901 of this title),

and the uniform percent applicable to all other programs under this subsection shall be increased (if necessary) to a level sufficient to achieve the required reduction in non-defense outlays.

(B) For purposes of determining reductions under subparagraph (A), outlay reduction (as a result of sequestration of Commodity Credit Corporation commodity price support contracts in the fiscal year of a sequestration) that would occur in the following fiscal year shall be credited as outlay reductions in the fiscal year of the sequestration.

(f) Baseline assumptions; part-year appropriations

(1) Budget assumptions

For purposes of subsections (b), (c), (d), and (e) of this section, accounts shall be assumed to be at the level in the baseline minus any reductions required to be made under sections 901 and 902 of this title.

(2) Part-year appropriations

If, on the date specified in subsection (a) of this section, there is in effect an Act making or continuing appropriations for part of a fiscal year for any non-exempt budget account, then the dollar sequestration calculated for that account under subsection (d) or (e) of this section, as applicable, shall be subtracted from—

(A) the annualized amount otherwise available by law in that account under that or a subsequent part-year appropriation; and

(B) when a full-year appropriation for that account is enacted, from the amount otherwise provided by the full-year appropriation; except that the amount to be sequestered from that account shall be reduced (but not below zero) by the savings achieved by that appropriation when the enacted amount is less than the baseline for that account.

(g) Adjustments to maximum deficit amounts

(1) Adjustments

(A) When the President submits the budget for fiscal year 1992, the maximum deficit amounts for fiscal years 1992, 1993, 1994, and 1995 shall be adjusted to reflect up-to-date reestimates of economic and technical assumptions and any changes in concepts or definitions. When the President submits the budget for fiscal year 1993, the maximum deficit amounts for fiscal years 1993, 1994, and 1995 shall be further adjusted to reflect up-to-date reestimates of economic and technical assumptions and any changes in concepts or definitions.

(B) When submitting the budget for fiscal year 1994, the President may choose to adjust the maximum deficit amounts for fiscal years 1994 and 1995 to reflect up-to-date reestimates of economic and technical assumptions. If the President chooses to adjust the maximum deficit amount when submitting the fiscal year 1994 budget, the President may choose to invoke the same adjustment procedure when submitting the budget for fiscal year 1995. In each case, the President must choose between making no adjustment or the full adjustment described in paragraph (2). If the President chooses to make that full adjustment, then those procedures for adjusting discretionary spending limits described in sections 901(b)(1)(C)[1] and 901(b)(2)(E)[1] of this title, otherwise applicable through fiscal year 1993 or 1994 (as the case may be), shall be deemed to apply for fiscal year 1994 (and 1995 if applicable).

(C) When the budget for fiscal year 1994 or 1995 is submitted and the sequestration reports for those years under section 904 of

---

[1] See References in Text note below.

this title are made (as applicable), if the President does not choose to make the adjustments set forth in subparagraph (B), the maximum deficit amount for that fiscal year shall be adjusted by the amount of the adjustment to discretionary spending limits first applicable for that year (if any) under section 901(b) of this title.

(D) For each fiscal year the adjustments required to be made with the submission of the President's budget for that year shall also be made when OMB submits the sequestration update report and the final sequestration report for that year, but OMB shall continue to use the economic and technical assumptions in the President's budget for that year.

Each adjustment shall be made by increasing or decreasing the maximum deficit amounts set forth in section 665[1] of this title.

(2) Calculations of adjustments

The required increase or decrease shall be calculated as follows:

(A) The baseline deficit or surplus shall be calculated using up-to-date economic and technical assumptions, using up-to-date concepts and definitions, and, in lieu of the baseline levels of discretionary appropriations, using the discretionary spending limits set forth in section 665[1] of this title as adjusted under section 901 of this title.

(B) The net deficit increase or decrease caused by all direct spending and receipts legislation enacted after November 5, 1990 (after adjusting for any sequestration of direct spending accounts) shall be calculated for each fiscal year by adding—

(i) the estimates of direct spending and receipts legislation transmitted under section 902(d) of this title applicable to each such fiscal year; and

(ii) the estimated amount of savings in direct spending programs applicable to each such fiscal year resulting from the prior year's sequestration under this section or section 902 of this title of direct spending, if any, as contained in OMB's final sequestration report for that year.

(C) The amount calculated under subparagraph (B) shall be subtracted from the amount calculated under subparagraph (A).

(D) The maximum deficit amount set forth in section 665[1] of this title shall be subtracted from the amount calculated under subparagraph (C).

(E) The amount calculated under subparagraph (D) shall be the amount of the adjustment required by paragraph (1).

(h) Treatment of deposit insurance

(1) Initial estimates

The initial estimates of the net costs of federal deposit insurance for fiscal year 1994 and fiscal year 1995 (assuming full funding of, and continuation of, the deposit insurance guarantee commitment in effect on the date of the submission of the budget for fiscal year 1993) shall be set forth in that budget.

(2) Reestimates

For fiscal year 1994 and fiscal year 1995, the amount of the reestimate of deposit insurance costs shall be calculated by subtracting the amount set forth under paragraph (1) for that year from the current estimate of deposit insurance costs (but assuming full funding of, and continuation of, the deposit insurance guarantee commitment in effect on the date of submission of the budget for fiscal year 1993).

(Pub. L. 99–177, title II, § 253, Dec. 12, 1985, 99 Stat. 1078; Pub. L. 100–119, title I, § 103, Sept. 29, 1987, 101 Stat. 775; Pub. L. 101–508, title XIII, § 13101(a), Nov. 5, 1990, 104 Stat. 1388–583.)

TERMINATION OF SECTION

For termination of section by section 275(b) of Pub. L. 99–177, as amended, see Effective and Termination Dates note set out under section 900 of this title.

REFERENCES IN TEXT

Section 901 of this title, referred to in subsec. (g)(1)(B), was amended by Pub. L. 105–33, title X, § 10203(a)(4), Aug. 5, 1997, 111 Stat. 699, by striking out subsec. (b) and adding a new subsec. (b). In the new subsec. (b), par. (1) does not contain a subpar. (C) and par. (2)(E) relates to allowance for international arrearages. Prior to amendment, section 901(b)(2)(E) related to special allowance for discretionary new budget authority.

Section 665 of this title, referred to in subsec. (g)(1), (2)(A), (D), was repealed by Pub. L. 105–33, title X, § 10118(a), Aug. 5, 1997, 111 Stat. 695.

CODIFICATION

November 5, 1990, referred to in subsec. (g)(2)(B), was in the original "the date of enactment of this section", which was translated as meaning the date of enactment of Pub. L. 101–508, which amended this section generally, to reflect the probable intent of Congress.

AMENDMENTS

1990—Pub. L. 101–508 amended section generally, substituting provisions relating to enforcement of deficit targets for provisions relating to compliance report by Comptroller General.

1987—Pub. L. 100–119 amended section generally, designating existing provisions as par. (1), substituting "(or December 15, 1987, in the case of the fiscal year 1988)" for "(or on or before April 1, 1986, in the case of the fiscal year 1986)", and adding pars. (2) and (3).

SECTION REFERRED TO IN OTHER SECTIONS

This section is referred to in sections 901, 902, 904, 906, 907, 907d of this title.

§ 904. Reports and orders

(a) Timetable

The timetable with respect to this subchapter for any budget year is as follows:

Date:	Action to be completed:
January 21	Notification regarding optional adjustment of maximum deficit amount.
5 days before the President's budget submission.	CBO sequestration preview report.
The President's budget submission.	OMB sequestration preview report.
August 10	Notification regarding military personnel.
August 15	CBO sequestration update report.
August 20	OMB sequestration update report.
10 days after end of session.	CBO final sequestration report.

Date:	Action to be completed:
15 days after end of session.	OMB final sequestration report; Presidential order.

(b) Submission and availability of reports

Each report required by this section shall be submitted, in the case of CBO, to the House of Representatives, the Senate and OMB and, in the case of OMB, to the House of Representatives, the Senate, and the President on the day it is issued. On the following day a notice of the report shall be printed in the Federal Register.

(c) Sequestration preview reports

(1) Reporting requirement

On the dates specified in subsection (a) of this section, OMB and CBO shall issue a preview report regarding discretionary, pay-as-you-go, and deficit sequestration based on laws enacted through those dates.

(2) Discretionary sequestration report

The preview reports shall set forth estimates for the current year and each subsequent year through 2002 of the applicable discretionary spending limits for each category and an explanation of any adjustments in such limits under section 901 of this title.

(3) Pay-as-you-go sequestration reports

The preview reports shall set forth, for the current year and the budget year, estimates for each of the following:

(A) The amount of net deficit increase or decrease, if any, calculated under subsection 902(b) of this title.

(B) A list identifying each law enacted and sequestration implemented after November 5, 1990, included in the calculation of the amount of deficit increase or decrease and specifying the budgetary effect of each such law.

(C) The sequestration percentage or (if the required sequestration percentage is greater than the maximum allowable percentage for medicare) percentages necessary to eliminate a deficit increase under section 902(c) of this title.

(4) Deficit sequestration reports

The preview reports shall set forth for the budget year estimates for each of the following:

(A) The maximum deficit amount, the estimated deficit calculated under section 903(b) of this title, the excess deficit, and the margin.

(B) The amount of reductions required under section 902 of this title, the excess deficit remaining after those reductions have been made, and the amount of reductions required from defense accounts and the reductions required from non-defense accounts.

(C) The sequestration percentage necessary to achieve the required reduction in defense accounts under section 903(d) of this title.

(D) The reductions required under sections 903(e)(1) and 903(e)(2) of this title.

(E) The sequestration percentage necessary to achieve the required reduction in non-defense accounts under section 903(e)(3) of this title.

The CBO report need not set forth the items other than the maximum deficit amount for fiscal year 1992, 1993, or any fiscal year for which the President notifies the House of Representatives and the Senate that he will adjust the maximum deficit amount under the option under section 903(g)(1)(B) of this title.

(5) Explanation of differences

The OMB reports shall explain the differences between OMB and CBO estimates for each item set forth in this subsection.

(d) Notification regarding military personnel

On or before the date specified in subsection (a) of this section, the President shall notify the Congress of the manner in which he intends to exercise flexibility with respect to military personnel accounts under section 905(f) of this title.

(e) Sequestration update reports

On the dates specified in subsection (a) of this section, OMB and CBO shall issue a sequestration update report, reflecting laws enacted through those dates, containing all of the information required in the sequestration preview reports.

(f) Final sequestration reports

(1) Reporting requirement

On the dates specified in subsection (a) of this section, OMB and CBO shall issue a final sequestration report, updated to reflect laws enacted through those dates.

(2) Discretionary sequestration reports

The final reports shall set forth estimates for each of the following:

(A) For the current year and each subsequent year through 2002 the applicable discretionary spending limits for each category and an explanation of any adjustments in such limits under section 901 of this title.

(B) For the current year and the budget year the estimated new budget authority and outlays for each category and the breach, if any, in each category.

(C) For each category for which a sequestration is required, the sequestration percentages necessary to achieve the required reduction.

(D) For the budget year, for each account to be sequestered, estimates of the baseline level of sequestrable budgetary resources and resulting outlays and the amount of budgetary resources to be sequestered and resulting outlay reductions.

(3) Pay-as-you-go and deficit sequestration reports

The final reports shall contain all the information required in the pay-as-you-go and deficit sequestration preview reports. In addition, these reports shall contain, for the budget year, for each account to be sequestered, estimates of the baseline level of sequestrable budgetary resources and resulting outlays and the amount of budgetary resources to be sequestered and resulting outlay reductions. The reports shall also contain estimates of the effects on outlays of the sequestration in each outyear for direct spending programs.

(4) Explanation of differences

The OMB report shall explain any differences between OMB and CBO estimates of the amount of any net deficit change calculated under subsection[1] 902(b) of this title, any excess deficit, any breach, and any required sequestration percentage. The OMB report shall also explain differences in the amount of sequesterable[2] resources for any budget account to be reduced if such difference is greater than $5,000,000.

(5) Presidential order

On the date specified in subsection (a) of this section, if in its final sequestration report OMB estimates that any sequestration is required, the President shall issue an order fully implementing without change all sequestrations required by the OMB calculations set forth in that report. This order shall be effective on issuance.

(g) Within-session sequestration reports and order

If an appropriation for a fiscal year in progress is enacted (after Congress adjourns to end the session for that budget year and before July 1 of that fiscal year) that causes a breach, 10 days later CBO shall issue a report containing the information required in paragraph (f)(2). Fifteen days after enactment, OMB shall issue a report containing the information required in paragraphs (f)(2) and (f)(4). On the same day as the OMB report, the President shall issue an order fully implementing without change all sequestrations required by the OMB calculations set forth in that report. This order shall be effective on issuance.

(h) GAO compliance report

Upon request of the Committee on the Budget of the House of Representatives or the Senate, the Comptroller General shall submit to the Congress and the President a report on—

(1) the extent to which each order issued by the President under this section complies with all of the requirements contained in this subchapter, either certifying that the order fully and accurately complies with such requirements or indicating the respects in which it does not; and

(2) the extent to which each report issued by OMB or CBO under this section complies with all of the requirements contained in this subchapter, either certifying that the report fully and accurately complies with such requirements or indicating the respects in which it does not.

(i) Low-growth report

At any time, CBO shall notify the Congress if—

(1) during the period consisting of the quarter during which such notification is given, the quarter preceding such notification, and the 4 quarters following such notification, CBO or OMB has determined that real eco-

nomic growth is projected or estimated to be less than zero with respect to each of any 2 consecutive quarters within such period; or

(2) the most recent of the Department of Commerce's advance preliminary or final reports of actual real economic growth indicate that the rate of real economic growth for each of the most recently reported quarter and the immediately preceding quarter is less than one percent.

(j) Economic and technical assumptions

In all reports required by this section, OMB shall use the same economic and technical assumptions as used in the most recent budget submitted by the President under section 1105(a) of title 31.

(Pub. L. 99–177, title II, § 254, Dec. 12, 1985, 99 Stat. 1078; Pub. L. 100–119, title I, §§ 102(b)(1), 106(e)(2), Sept. 29, 1987, 101 Stat. 773, 781; Pub. L. 101–508, title XIII, § 13101(a), Nov. 5, 1990, 104 Stat. 1388–586; Pub. L. 103–66, title XIV, §§ 14002(c)(2), 14003(b), Aug. 10, 1993, 107 Stat. 684, 685; Pub. L. 103–322, title XXXI, § 310001(g)(2), Sept. 13, 1994, 108 Stat. 2105; Pub. L. 104–316, title I, § 102(d), Oct. 19, 1996, 110 Stat. 3828; Pub. L. 105–33, title X, § 10206, Aug. 5, 1997, 111 Stat. 704.)

TERMINATION OF SECTION

For termination of section by section 275(b) of Pub. L. 99–177, as amended, see Effective and Termination Dates note set out under section 900 of this title.

CODIFICATION

November 5, 1990, referred to in subsec. (c)(3)(B), was in the original "the date of enactment of this section", which was translated as meaning the date of enactment of Pub. L. 101–508, which amended this section generally, to reflect the probable intent of Congress.

AMENDMENTS

1997—Subsec. (c). Pub. L. 105–33, § 10206(1), (2), redesignated subsec. (d) as (c), substituted "2002" for "1998" in par. (2), and struck out heading and text of former subsec. (c). Text read as follows: "With respect to budget year 1994 or 1995, on the date specified in subsection (a) of this section the President shall notify the House of Representatives and the Senate of his decision regarding the optional adjustment of the maximum deficit amount (as allowed under section 903(g)(1)(B) of this title)."

Subsec. (d). Pub. L. 105–33, § 10206(1), (3), redesignated subsec. (e) as (d) and substituted "section 905(f)" for "section 905(h)". Former subsec. (d) redesignated (c).

Subsec. (e). Pub. L. 105–33, § 10206(1), redesignated subsec. (f) as (e). Former subsec. (e) redesignated (d).

Subsec. (f). Pub. L. 105–33, § 10206(1), redesignated subsec. (g) as (f). Former subsec. (f) redesignated (e).

Subsec. (f)(2)(A). Pub. L. 105–33, § 10206(4)(A), substituted "2002" for "1998".

Subsec. (f)(3). Pub. L. 105–33, § 10206(4)(B), struck out "through 1998" after "each outyear".

Subsec. (f)(4) to (6). Pub. L. 105–33, § 10206(4)(C), redesignated pars. (5) and (6) as (4) and (5), respectively, and struck out heading and text of former par. (4). Text read as follows: "The final reports shall set forth for the budget year estimates for each of the following:

"(A) The amount of budget authority appropriated from the Violent Crime Reduction Trust Fund and outlays resulting from those appropriations.

"(B) The sequestration percentage and reductions, if any, required under section 901a of this title."

Subsec. (g). Pub. L. 105–33, § 10206(1), (5), redesignated subsec. (h) as (g) and substituted "paragraph (f)(2)" for

---

[1] So in original. Probably should be "section".

[2] So in original. Probably should be "sequestrable".

"paragraph (g)(2)" and "paragraphs (f)(2) and (f)(4)" for "paragraphs (g)(2) and (g)(4)". Former subsec. (g) redesignated (f).

Subsecs. (h) to (k). Pub. L. 105–33, § 10206(1), redesignated subsecs. (i) to (k) as (h) to (j), respectively. Former subsec. (h) redesignated (g).

1996—Subsec. (a). Pub. L. 104–316, § 102(d)(1), struck out item at end of timetable relating to GAO compliance report.

Subsec. (i). Pub. L. 104–316, § 102(d)(2), in introductory provisions substituted "Upon request of the Committee on the Budget of the House of Representatives or the Senate" for "On the date specified in subsection (a) of this section".

1994—Subsec. (g)(4) to (6). Pub. L. 103–322 added par. (4) and redesignated former pars. (4) and (5) as (5) and (6), respectively.

1993—Subsecs. (d)(2), (g)(2)(A), (3). Pub. L. 103–66 substituted "1998" for "1995".

1990—Pub. L. 101–508 amended section generally, substituting provisions setting out timetable and requisite content of reports and orders developed as part of sequestration process for former provisions relating to special Congressional procedures in the event of recession, Congressional responses to Presidential orders, and treatment of certain resolutions as reconciliation bills.

1987—Subsec. (b)(1)(A). Pub. L. 100–119, § 102(b)(1), substituted "the Director of OMB" for "the Comptroller General".

Subsec. (b)(1)(E). Pub. L. 100–119, § 106(e)(2), inserted provisions relating to maximum deficit amount for fiscal year 1988 or 1989.

FISCAL YEAR DEFICIT CONTROL MEASURES

1991—Pub. L. 102–27, title IV, § 401(b), Apr. 10, 1991, 105 Stat. 154, provided that: "Upon the enactment of this Act [Apr. 10, 1991], the order issued by the President on November 9, 1990 [set out below], pursuant to sections 251 and 254 of the Balanced Budget and Emergency Deficit Control Act of 1985, as amended, [2 U.S.C. 901, 904] is hereby rescinded. Any action taken to implement this order shall be reversed, and any sequestrable resource that has been reduced or sequestered by such order is hereby restored, revived, or released and shall be available to the same extent and for the same purpose as if the order had not been issued."

Section 13401 of Pub. L. 101–508 provided that:

"(a) ORDER RESCINDED.—Upon the enactment of this Act [Nov. 5, 1990], the orders issued by the President on August 25, 1990, and October 15, 1990 [set out below], pursuant to section 252 of the Balanced Budget and Emergency Deficit Control Act of 1985 [2 U.S.C. 902] are hereby rescinded.

"(b) AMOUNTS RESTORED.—Any action taken to implement the orders referred to in subsection (a) shall be reversed, and any sequestrable resource that has been reduced or sequestered by such orders is hereby restored, revived, or released and shall be available to the same extent and for the same purpose as if the orders had not been issued.

"(c) FURLOUGHED EMPLOYEES.—(1) Federal employees furloughed as a result of the lapse in appropriations from midnight October 5, 1990, until the enactment of House Joint Resolution 666 [Pub. L. 101–412, which was approved Oct. 9, 1990] shall be compensated at their standard rate of compensation for the period during which there was a lapse in appropriations.

"(2) All obligations incurred in anticipation of the appropriations made and authority granted by House Joint Resolution 666 for the purposes of maintaining the essential level of activity to protect life and property and bringing about orderly termination of government functions are hereby ratified and approved if otherwise in accord with the provisions of that Act [Pub. L. 101–412, Oct. 9, 1990, 104 Stat. 894]."

Pub. L. 101–467, § 105, Oct. 28, 1990, 104 Stat. 1087, provided that:

"(a) Any order on sequestration for fiscal year 1991 issued before, on, or after the date of enactment of this joint resolution [Oct. 28, 1990] pursuant to section 252 of the Balanced Budget and Emergency Deficit Control Act of 1985 [2 U.S.C. 902] is suspended and no action shall be taken to implement any such order.

"(b) Subsection (a) shall cease to be effective on the date set forth in section 101(b)(B) [Nov. 5, 1990]."

Pub. L. 101–461, § 113, Oct. 25, 1990, 104 Stat. 1078, provided that:

"(a) Any order on sequestration for fiscal year 1991 issued before, on, or after the date of enactment of this joint resolution [Oct. 25, 1990] pursuant to section 252 of the Balanced Budget and Emergency Deficit Control Act of 1985 [2 U.S.C. 902] is suspended and no action shall be taken to implement any such order.

"(b) Subsection (a) shall cease to be effective on the date set forth in section 108(c) [Oct. 27, 1990]."

Pub. L. 101–444, § 113, Oct. 19, 1990, 104 Stat. 1033, provided that:

"(a) Any order on sequestration for fiscal year 1991 issued before, on, or after the date of enactment of this joint resolution [Oct. 19, 1990] pursuant to section 252 of the Balanced Budget and Emergency Deficit Control Act of 1985 [2 U.S.C. 902] is suspended and no action shall be taken to implement any such order.

"(b) Subsection (a) shall cease to be effective on the date set forth in section 108(c) [Oct. 24, 1990]."

Pub. L. 101–412, § 113, Oct. 9, 1990, 104 Stat. 897, provided that:

"(a) Any order on sequestration for fiscal year 1991 issued before, on, or after the date of enactment of this joint resolution [Oct. 9, 1990] pursuant to section 252 of the Balanced Budget and Emergency Deficit Control Act of 1985 [2 U.S.C. 902] is suspended and no action shall be taken to implement any such order.

"(b) Subsection (a) shall cease to be effective on the date set forth in section 108(c) [Oct. 19, 1990]."

Pub. L. 101–403, title I, § 113, Oct. 1, 1990, 104 Stat. 870, provided that:

"(a) Any order on sequestration for fiscal year 1991 issued before, on, or after the date of enactment of this joint resolution [Oct. 1, 1990] pursuant to section 252 of the Balanced Budget and Emergency Deficit Control Act of 1985 [2 U.S.C. 902] is suspended and no action shall be taken to implement any such order.

"(b) Subsection (a) shall cease to be effective on the date set forth in section 108(c) [Oct. 5, 1990]."

Final Order of the President of the United States, Nov. 9, 1990, 26 Weekly Compilation of Presidential Documents 1797, Nov. 12, 1990, provided:

By the authority vested in me as President by the statutes of the United States of America, including section 254 of the Balanced Budget and Emergency Deficit Control Act of 1985 (Public Law 99–177) [2 U.S.C. 904], as amended by the Balanced Budget and Emergency Deficit Control Reaffirmation Act of 1987 (Public Law 100–119) and Title XIII of the Omnibus Reconciliation Act of 1990 (Public Law 101–508) (hereafter referred to as "the Act"), I hereby order that the following actions be taken immediately to implement the sequestrations and reductions determined by the Director of the Office of Management and Budget as set forth in his report dated November 9, 1990, under sections 251 and 254 of the Act [2 U.S.C. 901, 904]:

(1) Budgetary resources for each non-exempt account within the international category of discretionary spending shall be reduced as specified by the Director of the Office of Management and Budget in his report of November 9, 1990.

(2) Pursuant to sections 250(c)(6) and 251 [2 U.S.C. 900(c)(6), 901], budgetary resources subject to sequestration shall be new budget authority; new loan guarantee commitments or limitations; new direct loan obligations, commitments, or limitations; and obligation limitations.

(3) For accounts making commitments for guaranteed loans as authorized by substantive law, the head of each Department or agency is directed to reduce the level of such commitments or obligations to the extent necessary to conform to the limitations established by the Act [Pub. L. 99–177, title II, see Short Title note set

out under 2 U.S.C. 900] and specified by the Director of the Office of Management and Budget in his report of November 9, 1990.

All sequestrations shall be made in strict accordance with the specifications of the November 9th report of the Director of the Office of Management and Budget and the requirements of sections 251 and 254.

GEORGE BUSH.

Final Order of the President of the United States, Oct. 15, 1990, 55 F.R. 41977, provided:

By the authority vested in me as President by the statutes of the United States of America, including section 252 of the Balanced Budget and Emergency Deficit Control Act of 1985 (Public Law 99–177) [2 U.S.C. 902], as amended by the Balanced Budget and Emergency Deficit Control Reaffirmation Act of 1987 (Public Law 100–119) (hereafter referred to as "the Act"), I hereby order that the following actions shall be taken to implement the sequestrations and reductions determined by the Director of the Office of Management and Budget as set forth in his report dated October 15, 1990, under section 251 of the Act [2 U.S.C. 901]:

(1) Each automatic spending increase that would, but for the provisions of the Act, take effect during fiscal year 1991 is permanently sequestered or reduced as provided in section 252.

(2) The following are sequestered as provided in section 252: new budget authority; unobligated balances; new loan guarantee commitments or limitations; new direct loan obligations, commitments, or limitations; spending authority as defined in section 401(c)(2) of the Congressional Budget Act of 1974, as amended [2 U.S.C. 651(c)(2)]; and obligation limitations.

(3) For accounts making payments otherwise required by substantive law, the head of each Department or agency is directed to modify the calculation of each such payment to the extent necessary to reduce the estimate of total required payments for the fiscal year by the amount specified by the Director of the Office of Management and Budget in his report of October 15, 1990.

(4) For accounts making commitments for guaranteed loans as authorized by substantive law, the head of each Department or agency is directed to reduce the level of such commitments or obligations to the extent necessary to conform to the limitations established by the Act and specified by the Director of the Office of Management and Budget in his report of October 15, 1990.

All reductions and sequestrations shall be made in strict accordance with the specifications of the October 15th report of the Director of the Office of Management and Budget and the requirements of section 252(b).

This order supersedes the Initial Order issued on August 25, 1990 [see above].

This order shall be published in the Federal Register.

GEORGE BUSH.

Initial Order of the President of the United States, Aug. 25, 1990, 55 F.R. 35133, which provided emergency deficit control measures for fiscal year 1991, was superseded by Final Order of the President, Oct. 15, 1990, 55 F.R. 41977, set out above.

1990—Pub. L. 101–239, title VI, §6001, Dec. 19, 1989, 103 Stat. 2139, provided that: "Notwithstanding any other provision of law (including section 11002 [set out below] or any other provision of this Act, other than section 6201 [set out below]), the reductions in the amount of payments required under title XVIII of the Social Security Act [42 U.S.C. 1395 et seq.] made by the final sequester order issued by the President on October 16, 1989 [set out below], pursuant to section 252(b) of the Balanced Budget and Emergency Deficit Control Act of 1985 [2 U.S.C. 902(b)] shall continue to be effective (as provided by sections 252(a)(4)(B) and 256(d)(2) of such Act [2 U.S.C. 902(a)(4)(B), 906(d)(2)]) through December 31, 1989, with respect to payments for items and services under part A of such title [42 U.S.C. 1395c et seq.] (including payments under section 1886 of such title [42

U.S.C. 1395ww] attributable or allocated to such part). Each such payment made for items and services provided during fiscal year 1990 after such date shall be increased by 1.42 percent above what it would otherwise be under this Act."

Pub. L. 101–239, title VI, §6101, Dec. 19, 1989, 103 Stat. 2168, provided that: "Notwithstanding any other provision of law (including any other provision of this Act, other than section 6201 [set out below]), the reductions in the amount of payments required under title XVIII of the Social Security Act [42 U.S.C. 1395 et seq.] made by the final sequester order issued by the President on October 16, 1989, pursuant to section 252(b) of the Balanced Budget and Emergency Deficit Control Act of 1985 [2 U.S.C. 902(b)] shall continue to be effective (as provided by sections 252(a)(4)(B) and 256(d)(2) of such Act [2 U.S.C. 902(a)(4)(B), 906(d)(2)]) through March 31, 1990, with respect to payments for items and services under part B of such title [42 U.S.C. 1395j et seq.]."

Pub. L. 101–239, title VI, §6201, Dec. 19, 1989, 103 Stat. 2225, provided that: "Notwithstanding any other provision of law (including section 11002 [set out below] or any other provision of this Act), the reductions in the amount of payments required under title XVIII of the Social Security Act [42 U.S.C. 1395 et seq.] made by the final sequester order issued by the President on October 16, 1989 [set out below], pursuant to section 252(b) of the Balanced Budget and Emergency Deficit Control Act of 1985 [2 U.S.C. 902(b)] shall continue to be effective (as provided by sections 252(a)(4)(B) and 256(d)(2) of such Act [2 U.S.C. 902(a)(4)(B), 906(d)(2)]) through December 31, 1989, with respect to payments under section 1833(a)(1)(A) or 1876 of the Social Security Act [42 U.S.C. 1395l(a)(1)(A), 1395mm], section 402 of the Social Security Amendments of 1967 [section 402 of Pub. L. 90–248, enacting 42 U.S.C. 1395b–1, and amending 42 U.S.C. 1395ll], or section 222 of the Social Security Amendments of 1972 [section 222 of Pub. L. 92–603, amending 42 U.S.C. 1395b–1 and enacting provisions set out as a note under 42 U.S.C. 1395b–1]. Each such payment made during fiscal year 1990 after such date shall be increased by 1.42 percent above what it would otherwise be under this Act."

Pub. L. 101–239, title XI, §11002, Dec. 19, 1989, 103 Stat. 2490, provided that:

"(a) ORDER RESCINDED.—(1) Upon the issuance of a new final order by the President under subsection (b)(4) [set out below], the order issued by the President on October 16, 1989 [set out below], pursuant to section 252 of the Balanced Budget and Emergency Deficit Control Act of 1985 [2 U.S.C. 902] is rescinded.

"(2) Except as otherwise provided in sections 6001, 6101, and 6201 [set out above], and subject to subsection (b), any action taken to implement the order issued by the President on October 16, 1989, shall be reversed, and any sequesterable budgetary resource that has been reduced or sequestered by such order is restored, revived, or released and shall be available to the same extent and for the same purposes as if an order had not been issued.

"(3) For purposes of section[s] 702(d) and 1101(c) of the Ethics Reform Act of 1989 [Pub. L. 101–194, 5 U.S.C. 5305 note, 2 U.S.C. 31–1 note], the order issued by the President on October 16, 1989, pursuant to section 252 of the Balanced Budget and Emergency Deficit Control Act of 1985 [2 U.S.C. 902] is deemed to be rescinded on January 31, 1990.

"(b) ADJUSTED REDUCTION.—

"(1) Before the close of the fifteenth calendar day beginning after the date of enactment of this Act [Dec. 19, 1989], the Director of OMB shall issue a revised report using the exact budget baseline set forth in the report of October 16, 1989 [set out below], and following the requirements, specifications, definitions, and calculations required by the Balanced Budget and Emergency Deficit Control Act of 1985 [Pub. L. 99–177, title II, see Short Title note set out under 2 U.S.C. 901] for the final report issued under section 251(c)(2) [2 U.S.C. 901(c)(2)] for fiscal year 1990, except that the aggregate outlay reduction to be achieved shall be an amount equal to $16.1 billion multiplied by 130 divided by 365. Calculations made to carry out the preceding sentence shall take into account the reductions and cancellations achieved by paragraphs (2) and (3) and shall not be affected by subsection (d).

"(2) Notwithstanding any provision of law other than this paragraph, the reductions and cancellations in the student loan programs described in section 256(c) of the Balanced Budget and Emergency Deficit Control Act of 1985 [2 U.S.C. 906(c)] achieved by the order issued by the President on October 16, 1989, shall remain in effect through December 31, 1989, and no reductions or cancellations in such programs shall be made by the order issued under paragraph (4).

"(3) Notwithstanding any provision of law other than this paragraph, any automatic spending increase suspended or cancelled by the order issued by the President on October 16, 1989, shall be paid at a rate that is 130/365ths less than the rate that would have been paid under the laws providing for such automatic spending increase.

"(4) On the date that the Director submits a revised report to the President under paragraph (1) for fiscal year 1990, the President shall issue a new final order to make all of the reductions and cancellations specified in such report in conformity with section 252(a)(2) of the Balanced Budget and Emergency Deficit Control Act of 1985 [2 U.S.C. 902(a)(2)]. Such order shall be deemed to have become effective on October 16, 1989.

"(c) COMPLIANCE REPORT BY COMPTROLLER GENERAL.— Before the close of the thirtieth day beginning after the date the President issues a new final order under subsection (b)(4), the Comptroller General shall submit to the Congress and the President a compliance report setting forth the information required under section 253 of the Balanced Budget and Emergency Deficit Control Act of 1985 [2 U.S.C. 903] with respect to such order.

"(d) NO DOUBLE REDUCTION IN MEDICARE.—With respect to items and services described in section 6001, 6101, or 6201 [set out above] for periods for which reductions are made pursuant to the respective sections, no reduction shall be made under subsection (b)."

New Final Order of the President of the United States, Dec. 27, 1989, 54 F.R. 53469, provided:

By the authority vested in me as President by the statutes of the United States of America, including section 252 of the Balanced Budget and Emergency Deficit Control Act of 1985 (Public Law 99–177) [2 U.S.C. 902], as amended by the Balanced Budget and Emergency Deficit Control Reaffirmation Act of 1987 (Public Law 100–119) (hereafter referred to as "the Act"), and section 11002 of the Omnibus [Budget] Reconciliation Act of 1989 (Public Law 101–239) ("OBRA") [set out above], I hereby order that the following actions be taken to implement the sequestrations and reductions determined by the Director of the Office of Management and Budget as set forth in his report dated December 27, 1989, under section 251 of the Act [2 U.S.C. 901] and section 11002 of the OBRA:

(1) Each automatic spending increase that would, but for the provisions of the Act, take effect during fiscal year 1990 is permanently sequestered or reduced as provided in section 252 of the Act and section 11002 of OBRA.

(2) The following are sequestered as provided in section 252 of the Act and section 11002 of OBRA: new budget authority; unobligated balances; new loan guarantee commitments or limitations; new direct loan obligations, commitments, or limitations; spending authority as defined in section 401(c)(2) of the Congressional Budget Act of 1974, as amended [2 U.S.C. 651(c)(2)]; and obligation limitations.

(3) For accounts making payments otherwise required by substantive law, the head of each department or agency is directed to modify the calculation of each such payment to the extent necessary to reduce the estimate of total required payments for the fiscal year by the amount specified by the Director of the Office of

Management and Budget in his report of December 27, 1989.

(4) For accounts making commitments for guaranteed loans or obligations for direct loans as authorized by substantive law, the head of each department or agency is directed to reduce the level of such commitments or obligations to the extent necessary to conform to the limitations established by the Act and by OBRA and specified by the Director of the Office of Management and Budget in his report of December 27, 1989.

All reductions and sequestrations shall be made in strict accordance with the specifications of the December 27th report of the Director of the Office of Management and Budget and the requirements of section 252(b) of the Act and section 11002 of OBRA.

This order shall be deemed to have become effective on October 16, 1989, as provided in section 11002 of OBRA.

This order shall be published [in the] Federal Register.

GEORGE BUSH.

Final Order of the President of the United States, Oct. 16, 1989, 54 F.R. 42795, which provided emergency deficit control measures for fiscal year 1990, was rescinded by section 11002(a) of Pub. L. 101–239, set out above, upon issuance of New Final Order of the President of the United States, Dec. 27, 1989, 54 F.R. 53469, set out above.

Initial Order of the President of the United States, Aug. 25, 1989, 54 F.R. 35627, which provided emergency deficit control measures for fiscal year 1990, was superseded by Final Order of the President, Oct. 16, 1989, 54 F.R. 42795.

1989—Final Order of the President of the United States, Oct. 15, 1988, 53 F.R. 40696.

Initial Order of the President of the United States, Aug. 25, 1988, 53 F.R. 32881.

1988—Pub. L. 100–203, title IV, §§ 4001, 4041(b), 4061, title VIII, § 8002, Dec. 22, 1987, 101 Stat. 1330–42, 1330–84, 1330–100, 1330–281.

Pub. L. 100–202, § 1, Dec. 22, 1987, 101 Stat. 1329.

Order of the President of the United States, Nov. 20, 1987, 52 F.R. 44960.

Order of the President of the United States, Oct. 20, 1987, 52 F.R. 39205.

1986—Pub. L. 99–366, July 31, 1986, 100 Stat. 773.

Pub. L. 99–349, title II, § 202, July 2, 1986, 100 Stat. 748.

Pub. L. 99–255, Mar. 7, 1986, 100 Stat. 39, as amended by Pub. L. 99–322, § 1, May 23, 1986, 100 Stat. 494.

Order of the President of the United States, Feb. 1, 1986, 51 F.R. 4291.

SECTION REFERRED TO IN OTHER SECTIONS

This section is referred to in sections 691c, 901, 903, 905, 906, 907a, 907b, 907c, 907d, 922 of this title; title 21 section 379g.

§ 905. Exempt programs and activities

(a) Social security benefits and tier I railroad retirement benefits

Benefits payable under the old-age, survivors, and disability insurance program established under title II of the Social Security Act [42 U.S.C. 401 et seq.], and benefits payable under section 231b(a), 231b(f)(3), 231c(a), or 231c(f) of title 45, shall be exempt from reduction under any order issued under this subchapter.

(b) Veterans programs

The following programs shall be exempt from reduction under any order issued under this subchapter:

National Service Life Insurance Fund (36-8132-0-7-701);

Service-Disabled Veterans Insurance Fund (36-4012-0-3-701);

Veterans Special Life Insurance Fund (36-8455-0-8-701);

Veterans Reopened Insurance Fund (36-4010-0-3-701);

United States Government Life Insurance Fund (36-8150-0-7-701);

Veterans Insurance and Indemnities (36-0120-0-1-701);

Special Therapeutic and Rehabilitation Activities Fund (36-4048-0-3-703);

Canteen Service Revolving Fund (36-4014-0-3-705);

Benefits under chapter 21 of title 38 relating to specially adapted housing and mortgage-protection life insurance for certain veterans with service-connected disabilities (36-0120-0-1-701);

Benefits under section 2307 of title 38 relating to burial benefits for veterans who die as a result of service-connected disability (36-0155-0-1-701);

Benefits under chapter 39 of title 38 relating to automobiles and adaptive equipment for certain disabled veterans and members of the Armed Forces (36-0137-0-1-702);

Compensation (36-0153-0-1-701); and

Pensions (36-0154-0-1-701).

Benefits under chapter 35 of title 38 related to educational assistance for survivors and dependents of certain veterans with service-connected disabilities (36-0137-0-1-702);

Assistance and services under chapter 31 of title 38 relating to training and rehabilitation for certain veterans with service-connected disabilities (36-0137-0-1-702);

Benefits under subchapters I, II, and III of chapter 37 of title 38 relating to housing loans for certain veterans and for the spouses and surviving spouses of certain veterans Guaranty and Indemnity Program Account (36-1119-0-1-704);

Loan Guaranty Program Account (36-1025-0-1-704); and

Direct Loan Program Account (36-1024-0-1-704).

(c) Net interest

No reduction of payments for net interest (all of major functional category 900) shall be made under any order issued under this subchapter.

(d) Earned income tax credit

Payments to individuals made pursuant to section 32 of title 26 shall be exempt from reduction under any order issued under this subchapter.

(e) Non-defense unobligated balances

Unobligated balances of budget authority carried over from prior fiscal years, except balances in the defense category, shall be exempt from reduction under any order issued under this subchapter.

(f) Optional exemption of military personnel

(1) In general

The President may, with respect to any military personnel account, exempt that account from sequestration or provide for a lower uniform percentage reduction than would otherwise apply.

(2) Limitation

The President may not use the authority provided by paragraph (1) unless the President notifies the Congress of the manner in which such authority will be exercised on or before the date specified in section 904(a) of this title for the budget year.

(g) Other programs and activities

(1)(A) The following budget accounts and activities shall be exempt from reduction under any order issued under this subchapter:

Activities resulting from private donations, bequests, or voluntary contributions to the Government;

Activities financed by voluntary payments to the Government for goods or services to be provided for such payments;

Administration of Territories, Northern Mariana Islands Covenant grants (14-0412-0-1-806);

Alaska Power Administration, Operations and maintenance (89-0304-0-1-271);

Appropriations for the District of Columbia (to the extent they are appropriations of locally raised funds);

Bonneville Power Administration fund and borrowing authority established pursuant to section 13 of Public Law 93–454 (1974), as amended [16 U.S.C. 838k] (89-4045-0-3-271);

Bureau of Indian Affairs, Indian land and water claims settlements and miscellaneous payments to Indians (14-2303-0-1-452);

Bureau of Indian Affairs Miscellaneous trust funds (14-9973-0-7-999);

Claims, judgments, and relief acts (20-1895-0-1-808);

Compact of Free Association (14-0415-0-1-808);

Compensation of the President (11-0001-0-1-802);

Conservation Reserve Program (12-2319-0-1-302);

Customs Service, miscellaneous permanent appropriations (20-9922-0-2-806);

Comptroller of the Currency, Assessment funds (20-8413-0-8-373);

Dual benefits payments account (60-0111-0-1-601);

Exchange stabilization fund (20-4444-0-3-155);

Farm Credit Administration, Limitation on Administrative Expenses (78-4131-0-3-351);

Farm Credit System Financial Assistance Corporation, interest payment (20-1850-0-1-908);

Farm Credit System Financial Assistance Corporation, interest payments (20-1850-0-1-351);

Federal Deposit Insurance Corporation, Bank Insurance Fund (51-4064-0-3-373);

Federal Deposit Insurance Corporation, FSLIC Resolution Fund (51-4065-0-3-373);

Federal Deposit Insurance Corporation, Savings Association Insurance Fund (51-4066-0-3-373);

Federal Housing Finance Board (95-4039-0-3-371);

Federal payment to the railroad retirement accounts (60-0113-0-1-601);

Foreign military sales trust fund (11-8242-0-7-155);

Health professions graduate student loan insurance fund program account (75-0340-0-1-552);

Higher education facilities loans (91-0240-01-502);

Internal Revenue Collections for Puerto Rico (20-5737-0-2-806);

Intragovernmental funds, including those from which the outlays are derived primarily from resources paid in from other government accounts, except to the extent such funds are augmented by direct appropriations for the fiscal year during which an order is in effect;

Panama Canal Commission, Panama Canal Revolving Fund (95-4061-0-3-403);

Medical facilities guarantee and loan fund, Federal interest subsidies for medical facilities (75-9931-0-3-550);

National Credit Union Administration operating fund (25-4056-0-3-373);

National Credit Union Administration, Central liquidity facility (25-4470-0-3-373);

National Credit Union Administration, Credit union share insurance fund (25-4468-0-3-373);

Office of Thrift Supervision (20-4108-0-3-373);

Payment of Vietnam and USS Pueblo prisoner-of-war claims (15-0104-0-1-153);

Payment to civil service retirement and disability fund (24-0200-0-1-805);

Payment to Judiciary Trust Funds (10-0941-0-1-752);

Payments to copyright owners (03-5175-0-2-376);

Payments to health care trust funds (75-0580-0-1-571);

Payments to military retirement fund (97-0040-0-1-054);

Payments to social security trust funds (75-0404-0-1-651);

Payments to the foreign service retirement and disability fund (11-1036-0-1-153 and 19-0540-0-1-153);

Payments to trust funds from excise taxes or other receipts properly creditable to such trust funds;

Payments to the United States territories, fiscal assistance (14-0418-0-1-806);

Payments to widows and heirs of deceased Members of Congress (00-0215-0-1-801);

Postal service fund (18-4020-0-3-372);

Resolution Trust Corporation Revolving Fund (22-4055-0-3-373);

Salaries of Article III judges;

Soldiers and Airmen's Home, payment of claims (84-8930-0-7-705);

Southeastern Power Administration, Operations and maintenance (89-0302-0-1-271);

Southwestern Power Administration, Operations and maintenance (89-0303-0-1-271);

Tennessee Valley Authority fund, except non-power programs and activities (64-4110-0-3-999);

Thrift Savings Fund;

United States Enrichment Corporation (95-4054-0-3-271);

Vaccine Injury Compensation (75-0320-0-1-551);

Vaccine Injury Compensation Program Trust Fund (20-8175-0-7-551);

United States Enrichment Corporation;

Washington Metropolitan Area Transit Authority, interest payments (46-0300-0-1-401);

Western Area Power Administration, Construction, rehabilitation, operations, and maintenance (89-5068-0-2-271); and

Western Area Power Administration, Colorado River basins power marketing fund (89-4452-0-3-271).

(B) The following Federal retirement and disability accounts and activities shall be exempt from reduction under any order issued under this subchapter:

Black Lung Disability Trust Fund (20-8144-0-7-601);

Central Intelligence Agency retirement and disability system fund (56-3400-0-1-054);

Civil service retirement and disability fund (24-8135-0-7-602);

Comptrollers general retirement system (05-0107-0-1-801);

Foreign service retirement and disability fund (19-8186-0-7-602);

Judicial survivors' annuities fund (10-8110-0-7-602);

Judicial Officers' Retirement Fund (10-8122-0-7-602);

Claims Judges' Retirement Fund (10-8124-0-7-602);

Special workers compensation expenses, Longshoremen's and harborworkers' compensation benefits (16-9971-0-7-601);

Military retirement fund (97-8097-0-7-602);

National Oceanic and Atmospheric Administration retirement (13-1450-0-1-306);

Pensions for former Presidents (47-0105-0-1-802);

Railroad Industry Pension Fund (60-8011-0-7-601);

Railroad supplemental annuity pension fund (60-8012-0-7-602);

Retired pay, Coast Guard (69-0241-0-1-403);

Retirement pay and medical benefits for commissioned officers, Public Health Service (75-0379-0-1-551);

Special benefits, Federal Employees' Compensation Act (16-1521-0-1-600);

Special benefits for disabled coal miners (75-0409-0-1-601); and

Tax Court judges survivors annuity fund (23-8115-0-7-602).

(2) Prior legal obligations of the Government in the following budget accounts and activities shall be exempt from any order issued under this subchapter:

Biomass energy development (20-0114-0-1-271);

United States Treasury check forgery insurance fund (20-4109-0-3-803);

Credit liquidating accounts;

Employees life insurance fund (24-8424-0-8-602);

Energy security reserve (Synthetic Fuels Corporation) (20-0112-0-1-271);

Federal Aviation Administration, Aviation insurance revolving fund (69-4120-0-3-402);

Federal Crop Insurance Corporation fund (12-4085-0-3-351);

Federal Emergency Management Agency, National flood insurance fund (58-4236-0-3-453);

Federal Emergency Management Agency, National insurance development fund (58-4235-0-3-451);

Geothermal resources development fund (89-0206-0-1-271);

Homeowners assistance fund, Defense (97-4090-0-3-051);

International Trade Administration, Operations and administration (13-1250-0-1-376);

Low-rent public housing, Loans and other expenses (86-4098-0-3-604);

Maritime Administration, War-risk insurance revolving fund (69-4302-0-3-403);

Overseas Private Investment Corporation (71-4030-0-3-151);

Pension Benefit Guaranty Corporation fund (16-4204-0-3-601);

Rail service assistance (69-0122-0-1-401); and

Department of Veterans Affairs, Servicemen's group life insurance fund (36-4009-0-3-701).

(h) Low-income programs

The following programs shall be exempt from reduction under any order issued under this subchapter:

Block grants to States for temporary assistance for needy families;

Child nutrition programs (with the exception of special milk programs) (12-3539-0-1-605);

Temporary assistance for needy families (75-1552-0-1-609);

Contingency fund (75-1522-0-1-609);

Child care entitlement to States (75-1550-0-1-609);

Commodity supplemental food program (12-3512-0-1-605);

Food stamp programs (12-3505-0-1-605 and 12-3550-0-1-605);

Grants to States for Medicaid (75-0512-0-1-551);

Supplemental Security Income Program (75-0406-0-1-609); and [1]

Special supplemental nutrition program for women, infants, and children (WIC) (12-3510-0-1-605); [1]

Family support payments to States (75-1501-0-1-609); [2]

(i) Identification of programs

For purposes of subsections (b), (g), and (h) of this section, each account is identified by the designated budget account identification code number set forth in the Budget of the United States Government 1998–Appendix, and an activity within an account is designated by the name of the activity and the identification code number of the account.

(Pub. L. 99–177, title II, §255, Dec. 12, 1985, 99 Stat. 1082; Pub. L. 99–509, title VII, §7002(a), Oct. 21, 1986, 100 Stat. 1949; Pub. L. 99–514, §2, Oct. 22, 1986, 100 Stat. 2095; Pub. L. 100–86, title V, §506(a), Aug. 10, 1987, 101 Stat. 634; Pub. L. 100–119, title I, §104(a)(1), (2), (b), (c)(1), Sept. 29, 1987, 101 Stat. 775–777; Pub. L. 101–73, title VII, §743(a), (c), Aug. 9, 1989, 103 Stat. 437; Pub. L. 101–220, §8, Dec. 12, 1989, 103 Stat. 1881; Pub. L. 101–508, title XIII, §13101(c), Nov. 5, 1990, 104 Stat. 1388–589; Pub. L. 102–54, §13(a), June 13, 1991, 105 Stat. 274; Pub. L. 102–83, §5(c)(2), Aug. 6, 1991, 105 Stat. 406; Pub. L. 102–486, title IX, §902(d), Oct. 24, 1992, 106 Stat. 2944; Pub. L. 102–572, title VI, §601, Oct. 29, 1992, 106 Stat. 4514; Pub. L. 104–193, title I, §110(r)(1), Aug. 22, 1996, 110 Stat. 2175; Pub. L. 104–208, div. A, title II, §2704(d)(10), Sept. 30, 1996, 110 Stat. 3009–489; Pub. L. 105–33, title X, §10207, Aug. 5, 1997, 111 Stat. 704.)

TERMINATION OF SECTION

For termination of section by section 275(b) of Pub. L. 99–177, as amended, see Effective and

[1] So in original. The word "and" probably should follow "(12-3510-0-1-605);".

[2] So in original. The semicolon probably should be a period.

Termination Dates note set out under section 900 of this title.

REFERENCES IN TEXT

The Social Security Act, referred to in subsec. (a), is act Aug. 14, 1935, ch. 531, 49 Stat. 620, as amended. Title II of the Social Security Act is classified generally to subchapter II (§401 et seq.) of Title 42, The Public Health and Welfare. For complete classification of this Act to the Code, see section 1305 of Title 42 and Tables.

The Federal Employees' Compensation Act, referred to in subsec. (g)(1)(B), which is act Sept. 7, 1916, ch. 458, 39 Stat. 742, was repealed and the provisions thereof reenacted as subchapter I of chapter 81 of Title 5, Government Organization and Employees, by Pub. L. 89–554, Sept. 6, 1966, 80 Stat. 378.

AMENDMENTS

1997—Subsec. (b). Pub. L. 105–33, §10207(a), substituted "Veterans Insurance and Indemnities" for "Veterans Insurance and Indemnity", "Canteen Service Revolving Fund" for "Veterans' Canteen Service Revolving Fund", "(36-0120-0-1-701)" for "(36-0137-0-1-702)" in item relating to benefits under chapter 21 of title 38, "Compensation" for "Veterans' compensation", and "Pensions" for "Veterans' pensions" and inserted at end items relating to benefits under chapter 35 of title 38, assistance and services under chapter 31 of title 38, benefits under subchapters I, II, and III of chapter 37 of title 38, Loan Guaranty Program Account, and Direct Loan Program Account.

Subsec. (f). Pub. L. 105–33, §10207(b), amended heading and text of subsec. (f) generally. Prior to amendment, text read as follows: "Outlays for programs specified in paragraph (1) of section 907 of this title shall be subject to reduction only in accordance with the procedures established in section 901(a)(3)(C) and 906(b) of this title."

Subsec. (g)(1)(A). Pub. L. 105–33, §10207(c)(1)(KK), inserted items relating to Thrift Savings Fund, United States Enrichment Corporation (95-4054-0-3-271), Vaccine Injury Compensation, and Vaccine Injury Compensation Program Trust Fund.

Pub. L. 105–33, §10207(c)(1)(JJ), inserted "Revolving Fund (22-4055-0-3-373)" before semicolon in item relating to the Resolution Trust Corporation.

Pub. L. 105–33, §10207(c)(1)(II), struck out "Resolution Funding Corporation;" after item relating to postal service fund.

Pub. L. 105–33, §10207(c)(1)(HH), substituted "806" for "852" in item relating to payments to the United States territories.

Pub. L. 105–33, §10207(c)(1)(GG), struck out "Payments to state and local government fiscal assistance trust fund (20-2111-0-1-851);" after item relating to payments to social security trust funds.

Pub. L. 105–33, §10207(c)(1)(FF), substituted "651" for "571" in item relating to payments to social security trust funds.

Pub. L. 105–33, §10207(c)(1)(EE), struck out "Compact of Free Association, economic assistance pursuant to Public Law 99–658 (14-0415-0-1-806);" after item relating to payments to military retirement fund.

Pub. L. 105–33, §10207(c)(1)(DD), substituted "571" for "572" in item relating to payments to health care trust funds.

Pub. L. 105–33, §10207(c)(1)(CC), inserted item relating to Office of Thrift Supervision.

Pub. L. 105–33, §10207(c)(1)(BB), substituted "Credit union share" for "credit union share" and inserted before semicolon "(25-4468-0-3-373)" in third item relating to National Credit Union Administration.

Pub. L. 105–33, §10207(c)(1)(AA), substituted "Central" for "central" and inserted before semicolon "(25-4470-0-3-373)" in second item relating to National Credit Union Administration.

Pub. L. 105–33, §10207(c)(1)(Z), inserted "operating fund (25-4056-0-3-373)" before semicolon in first item relating to National Credit Union Administration.

Pub. L. 105–33, §10207(c)(1)(Y), substituted "(75-9931-0-3-550)" for "(75-4430-0-3-551)" in item relating to medical facilities guarantee and loan fund.

Pub. L. 105–33, § 10207(c)(1)(X), substituted "Panama Canal Commission, Panama Canal Revolving Fund (95-4061-0-3-403);" for "Panama Canal Commission, operating expenses (95-5190-0-2-403), and Panama Canal Commission, capital outlay (95-5190-0-2-403);".

Pub. L. 105–33, § 10207(c)(1)(W), substituted "806" for "852" in item relating to internal revenue collections for Puerto Rico.

Pub. L. 105–33, § 10207(c)(1)(V), struck out "and insurance" after "Higher education facilities loans".

Pub. L. 105–33, § 10207(c)(1)(U), inserted "program account" after "fund" and substituted "(75-0340-0-1-552)" for "(Health Education Assistance Loan Program) (75-4305-0-3-553)" in item relating to health professions graduate student loan insurance fund.

Pub. L. 105–33, § 10207(c)(1)(T), substituted "accounts" for "account" after "Federal payment to the railroad retirement".

Pub. L. 105–33, § 10207(c)(1)(S), inserted "(95-4039-0-3-371)" before semicolon in item relating to Federal Housing Finance Board.

Pub. L. 105–33, § 10207(c)(1)(R), inserted "(51-4066-0-3-373)" before semicolon in third item relating to Federal Deposit Insurance Corporation.

Pub. L. 105–33, § 10207(c)(1)(Q), inserted "(51-4065-0-3-373)" before semicolon in second item relating to Federal Deposit Insurance Corporation.

Pub. L. 105–33, § 10207(c)(1)(P), inserted "(51-4064-0-3-373)" before semicolon in first item relating to Federal Deposit Insurance Corporation.

Pub. L. 105–33, § 10207(c)(1)(O), struck out "Federal Deposit Insurance Corporation;" after item relating to Farm Credit System Financial Assistance Corporation, interest payments (20-1850-0-1-351).

Pub. L. 105–33, § 10207(c)(1)(N), inserted items relating to Farm Credit Administration and Farm Credit System Financial Assistance Corporation, interest payment (20-1850-0-1-908).

Pub. L. 105–33, § 10207(c)(1)(M), struck out "Eastern Indian land claims settlement fund (14-2202-0-1-806);" after item relating to dual benefits payments account.

Pub. L. 105–33, § 10207(c)(1)(L), struck out "Director of the Office of Thrift Supervision;" after item relating to Comptroller of the Currency.

Pub. L. 105–33, § 10207(c)(1)(K), inserted ", Assessment funds (20-8413-0-8-373)" before semicolon in item relating to the Comptroller of the Currency.

Pub. L. 105–33, § 10207(c)(1)(J), substituted "806" for "852" in item relating to the Customs Service.

Pub. L. 105–33, § 10207(c)(1)(I), inserted item relating to Conservation Reserve Program.

Pub. L. 105–33, § 10207(c)(1)(H), inserted item relating to Compact of Free Association.

Pub. L. 105–33, § 10207(c)(1)(G), struck out "Coinage profit fund (20-5811-0-2-803);" after item relating to claims, judgments, and relief acts.

Pub. L. 105–33, § 10207(c)(1)(F), substituted "808" for "806" in item relating to claims, judgments, and relief acts.

Pub. L. 105–33, § 10207(c)(1)(E), struck out "Claims, defense (97-0102-0-1-051);" after second item relating to Bureau of Indian Affairs.

Pub. L. 105–33, § 10207(c)(1)(D), substituted "Miscellaneous trust funds" for "miscellaneous trust funds, tribal trust funds" in second item relating to Bureau of Indian Affairs.

Pub. L. 105–33, § 10207(c)(1)(C), inserted "Indian land and water claims settlements and" after comma in first item relating to Bureau of Indian Affairs.

Pub. L. 105–33, § 10207(c)(1)(B), struck out "Thrift Savings Fund (26-8141-0-7-602);" after item relating to administration of Territories, Northern Mariana Islands Covenant grants.

Pub. L. 105–33, § 10207(c)(1)(A), inserted item relating to activities financed by voluntary payments to Government.

Subsec. (g)(1)(B). Pub. L. 105–33, § 10207(c)(2)(E), substituted "Railroad Industry Pension Fund" for "Railroad retirement tier II".

Pub. L. 105–33, § 10207(c)(2)(D), inserted "Special workers compensation expenses," before "Longshoremen's and harborworkers' compensation benefits".

Pub. L. 105–33, § 10207(c)(2)(C), substituted "Claims Judges' Retirement Fund" for "Court of Federal Claims Judges' Retirement Fund".

Pub. L. 105–33, § 10207(c)(2)(B), substituted "Black Lung Disability Trust Fund" for "Black lung benefits".

Pub. L. 105–33, § 10207(c)(2)(A), substituted "The following Federal retirement and disability accounts" for "The following budget accounts" in introductory provisions.

Subsec. (g)(2). Pub. L. 105–33, § 10207(c)(3)(E), struck out items "Credit union share insurance fund (25-4468-0-3-371);" and "Economic development revolving fund (13-4406-0-3-452);" after item relating to credit liquidating accounts, item "Export-Import Bank of the United States, Limitation of program activity (83-4027-0-3-155);" after item relating to energy security reserve (Synthetic Fuels Corporation), item "Federal Deposit Insurance Corporation (51-8419-0-8-371);" after item relating to Federal Crop Insurance Corporation fund, items "Federal Housing Administration fund (86-4070-0-3-371);", "Federal ship financing fund (69-4301-0-3-403);", and "Federal ship financing fund, fishing vessels (13-4417-0-3-376);" after item relating to Federal Emergency Management Agency National insurance development fund, items "Government National Mortgage Association, Guarantees of mortgage-backed securities (86-4238-0-3-371);" and "Health education loans (75-4307-0-3-553);" after item relating to geothermal resources development fund, item "Indian loan guarantee and insurance fund (14-4410-0-3-452);" after item relating to homeowners assistance fund, defense, and items "Railroad rehabilitation and improvement financing fund (69-4411-0-3-401);", "Rural development insurance fund (12-4155-0-3-452);", "Rural electric and telephone revolving fund (12-4230-8-3-271);", "Rural housing insurance fund (12-4141-0-3-371);", "Small Business Administration, Business loan and investment fund (73-4154-0-3-376);", "Small Business Administration, Lease guarantees revolving fund (73-4157-0-3-376);", "Small Business Administration, Pollution control equipment contract guarantee revolving fund (73-4147-0-3-376);", "Small Business Administration, Surety bond guarantees revolving fund (73-4156-0-3-376);", and "Department of Veterans Affairs, Loan guaranty revolving fund (36-4025-0-3-704);" after item relating to rail service assistance.

Pub. L. 105–33, § 10207(c)(3)(D), inserted item relating to credit liquidating accounts.

Pub. L. 105–33, § 10207(c)(3)(C), struck out "Community development grant loan guarantees (86-0162-0-1-451);" after item relating to United States Treasury check forgery insurance fund.

Pub. L. 105–33, § 10207(c)(3)(B), substituted "United States Treasury check forgery insurance fund" for "Check forgery insurance fund".

Pub. L. 105–33, § 10207(c)(3)(A), struck out items "Agency for International Development, Housing, and other credit guarantee programs (72-4340-0-3-151);" and "Agricultural credit insurance fund (12-4140-0-3-351);" after "order issued under this subchapter:".

Subsec. (h). Pub. L. 105–33, § 10207(f), struck out heading and text of subsec. (h) relating to optional exemption of military personnel. Text read as follows:

"(1) The President may, with respect to any military personnel account, exempt that account from sequestration or provide for a lower uniform percentage reduction than would otherwise apply.

"(2) The President may not use the authority provided by paragraph (1) unless he notifies the Congress of the manner in which such authority will be exercised on or before the initial snapshot date for the budget year."

Pub. L. 105–33, § 10207(d)(4), inserted item relating to family support payments to States.

Pub. L. 105–33, § 10207(d)(3), substituted item relating to special supplemental nutrition program for women, infants, and children (WIC) for "Women, infants, and children program (12-3510-0-1-605).".

Pub. L. 105–33, § 10207(d)(2), inserted items relating to temporary assistance for needy families, contingency fund, and child care entitlement to States.

Pub. L. 105–33, § 10207(d)(1), substituted item relating to child nutrition programs for "Child nutrition (12-3539-0-1-605);".

Subsec. (i). Pub. L. 105–33, § 10207(e), amended heading and text of subsec. (i) generally. Prior to amendment, text read as follows: "For purposes of subsections (g) and (h) of this section, programs are identified by the designated budget account identification code numbers set forth in the Budget of the United States Government, 1986—Appendix."

1996—Subsec. (g)(1)(A). Pub. L. 104–208, which directed the amendment of subpar. (A) by substituting "Deposit Insurance Fund" for "Bank Insurance Fund" and by striking "Federal Deposit Insurance Corporation, Savings Association Insurance fund;", was not executed. See Effective Date of 1996 Amendments note below.

Subsec. (h). Pub. L. 104–193 substituted "Block grants to States for temporary assistance for needy families;" for "Aid to families with dependent children (75-0412-0-1-609);".

1992—Subsec. (g)(1)(A). Pub. L. 102–572, § 601(b), inserted item relating to payment to Judiciary Trust Funds.

Pub. L. 102–486 inserted item relating to United States Enrichment Corporation.

Subsec. (g)(1)(B). Pub. L. 102–572, § 601(a), inserted items relating to Judicial Officers' Retirement Fund and Court of Federal Claims Judges' Retirement Fund.

1991—Subsec. (b). Pub. L. 102–83 substituted "section 2307 of title 38" for "section 907 of title 38" in item relating to burial benefits for veterans.

Subsec. (g)(2). Pub. L. 102–54 substituted last two items relating to Department of Veterans Affairs for items relating to Veterans Administration, Loan guaranty revolving fund, and Veterans Administration, Servicemen's group life insurance fund.

1990—Subsec. (a). Pub. L. 101–508, § 13101(c)(1), amended subsec. (a) generally. Prior to amendment, subsec. (a) read as follows: "Increases in benefits payable under the old-age, survivors, and disability insurance program established under title II of the Social Security Act, or in benefits payable under section 231b(a), 231b(f)(3), 231c(a), or 231c(f) of title 45, shall not be considered "automatic spending increases" for purposes of this title; and no reduction in any such increase or in any of the benefits involved shall be made under any order issued under this subchapter."

Subsec. (e). Pub. L. 101–508, § 13101(c)(2), amended subsec. (e) generally. Prior to amendment, subsec. (e) read as follows: "Offsetting receipts and collections shall not be reduced under any order issued under this subchapter."

Subsec. (g)(1)(B). Pub. L. 101–508, § 13101(c)(3), inserted item relating to railroad supplemental annuity pension fund.

Subsec. (h). Pub. L. 101–508, § 13101(c)(4), added subsec. (h) relating to optional exemption of military personnel.

1989—Subsec. (g)(1)(A). Pub. L. 101–220 inserted item relating to Farm Credit System Financial Assistance Corporation, interest payments, after item relating to Exchange stabilization fund.

Pub. L. 101–73, § 743(a)(1), inserted item relating to Director of the Office of Thrift Supervision after item relating to Comptroller of the Currency.

Pub. L. 101–73, § 743(a)(2), substituted items relating to Federal Deposit Insurance Corporation, Bank Insurance Fund; Federal Deposit Insurance Corporation, FSLIC Resolution Fund; and Federal Deposit Insurance Corporation, Savings Association Insurance Fund; for item relating to Federal Home Loan Bank Board.

Pub. L. 101–73, § 743(a)(3), substituted item relating to Federal Housing Finance Board for item relating to Federal Home Loan Bank Board, Federal Savings and Loan Insurance Corporation.

Pub. L. 101–73, § 743(a)(4), inserted items relating to Resolution Funding Corporation and Resolution Trust Corporation after item relating to Postal service fund.

Subsec. (g)(2). Pub. L. 101–73, § 743(c), struck out item relating to Federal Savings and Loan Insurance Corporation fund (82-4037-0-3-371).

1987—Subsec. (b). Pub. L. 100–119, § 104(b)(1), inserted items relating to National Service Life Insurance Fund, Service-Disabled Veterans Insurance Fund, Veterans Special Life Insurance Fund, Veterans Reopened Insurance Fund, United States Government Life Insurance Fund, Veterans Insurance and Indemnity, Special Therapeutic and Rehabilitation Activities Fund, Veterans' Canteen Service Revolving Fund, benefits under chapter 21 of title 38 relating to specially adapted and mortgage-protection life insurance for certain veterans and service-connected disabilities, benefits under section 907 of title 38 relating to burial benefits for veterans who die as a result of service-connected disability, and benefits under chapter 39 of title 38 relating to automobiles and adaptive equipment for certain disabled veterans and members of the Armed Forces.

Subsec. (g)(1). Pub. L. 100–119, § 104(a)(2), (b)(2), (3), designated existing provisions of par. (1) as subpar. (A); inserted items relating to Administration of Territories, Northern Mariana Islands Covenant grants, Thrift Savings Fund, Bureau of Indian Affairs, miscellaneous payments to Indians, Customs Service, miscellaneous permanent appropriations, higher education facilities loans and insurance, Internal Revenue Collections for Puerto Rico, Panama Canal Commission operating expenses and Panama Canal Commission capital outlay, to medical facilities guarantee and loan fund, Federal interest subsidies for medical facilities, Compact of Free Association, economic assistance pursuant to Public Law 99–658, payments to United States territories, fiscal assistance, payments to widows and heirs of deceased Members of Congress, and Washington Metropolitan Area Transit Authority, interest payments; and added subpar. (B).

Pub. L. 100–86 inserted items relating to Comptroller of the Currency; Federal Deposit Insurance Corporation; Federal Home Loan Bank Board; Federal Home Loan Bank Board, Federal Savings and Loan Insurance Corporation; National Credit Union Administration; National Credit Union Administration, central liquidity facility; and National Credit Union Administration, credit union share insurance fund.

Subsec. (g)(2). Pub. L. 100–119, § 104(c)(1), struck out following items relating to Veterans Administration: national service life insurance fund, service-disabled veterans insurance fund, United States Government life insurance fund, veterans insurance and indemnities, veterans reopened insurance fund, and veterans special life insurance fund.

Subsec. (h). Pub. L. 100–119, § 104(a)(1), inserted item relating to commodity supplemental food program.

1986—Subsec. (d). Pub. L. 99–514 substituted "Internal Revenue Code of 1986" for "Internal Revenue Code of 1954", which for purposes of codification was translated as "title 26" thus requiring no change in text.

Subsec. (g)(1). Pub. L. 99–509 inserted item relating to dual benefits payments account.

EFFECTIVE DATE OF 1996 AMENDMENTS

Amendment by Pub. L. 104–208 effective Jan. 1, 1999, if no insured depository institution is a savings association on that date, see section 2704(c) of Pub. L. 104–208, set out as a note under section 1821 of Title 12, Banks and Banking.

Amendment by Pub. L. 104–193 effective July 1, 1997, with transition rules relating to State options to accelerate such date, rules relating to claims, actions, and proceedings commenced before such date, rules relating to closing out of accounts for terminated or substantially modified programs and continuance in office of Assistant Secretary for Family Support, and provisions relating to termination of entitlement under AFDC program, see section 116 of Pub. L. 104–193, as amended, set out as an Effective Date note under section 601 of Title 42, The Public Health and Welfare.

EFFECTIVE DATE OF 1992 AMENDMENT

Section 1101(a) of Pub. L. 102–572 provided that: "Except as otherwise provided in this Act, the provisions of this Act and the amendments made by this Act [see Tables for classification] shall take effect on January 1, 1993.''

EFFECTIVE DATE OF 1986 AMENDMENT

Section 7002(b) of Pub. L. 99–509 provided that: "The amendment made by subsection (a) [amending this section] shall apply to fiscal years beginning after September 30, 1986."

SOLDIERS' AND AIRMEN'S HOME

The Soldiers' and Airmen's Home, referred to in subsec. (g)(1)(A), was incorporated into the Armed Forces Retirement Home by section 411 of Title 24, Hospitals and Asylums.

TERMINATION OF UNITED STATES SYNTHETIC FUELS CORPORATION

The United States Synthetic Fuels Corporation was terminated by Pub. L. 99–272, title VII, § 7403(b), Apr. 7, 1986, 100 Stat. 144, set out as a note under section 8791 of Title 42, The Public Health and Welfare.

SECTION REFERRED TO IN OTHER SECTIONS

This section is referred to in sections 901, 904 of this title; title 16 section 839d–1; title 38 section 7298.

§ 906. General and special sequestration rules

(a) Automatic spending increases

Automatic spending increases are increases in outlays due to changes in indexes in the following programs:

    (1) Special milk program; and

    (2) Vocational rehabilitation basic State grants.

In those programs all amounts other than the automatic spending increases shall be exempt from reduction under any order issued under this subchapter.

(b) Student loans

For all student loans under part B or D of title IV of the Higher Education Act of 1965 [20 U.S.C. 1071 et seq., 1087a et seq.] made during the period when a sequestration order under section 904 of this title is in effect as required by section 902 or 903 of this title, origination fees under sections 438(c)(2) and 455(c) of that Act [20 U.S.C. 1087–1(c)(2), 1087e(c)] shall each be increased by 0.50 percentage point.

(c) Treatment of foster care and adoption assistance programs

Any order issued by the President under section 904 of this title shall make the reduction which is otherwise required under the foster care and adoption assistance programs (established by part E of title IV of the Social Security Act [42 U.S.C. 670 et seq.]) only with respect to payments and expenditures made by States in which increases in foster care maintenance payment rates or adoption assistance payment rates (or both) are to take effect during the fiscal year involved, and only to the extent that the required reduction can be accomplished by applying a uniform percentage reduction to the Federal matching payments that each such State would otherwise receive under section 474 of that Act [42 U.S.C. 674] (for such fiscal year) for that portion of the State's payments which is attributable to the increases taking effect during that year. No State's matching payments from the Federal Government for foster care

maintenance payments or for adoption assistance maintenance payments may be reduced by a percentage exceeding the applicable domestic sequestration percentage. No State may, after December 12, 1985, make any change in the timetable for making payments under a State plan approved under part E of title IV of the Social Security Act which has the effect of changing the fiscal year in which expenditures under such part are made.

(d) Special rules for Medicare program

(1) Calculation of reduction in individual payment amounts

To achieve the total percentage reduction in those programs required by sections 902 and 903 of this title, and notwithstanding section 710 of the Social Security Act [42 U.S.C. 911], OMB shall determine, and the applicable Presidential order under section 904 of this title shall implement, the percentage reduction that shall apply to payments under the health insurance programs under title XVIII of the Social Security Act [42 U.S.C. 1395 et seq.] for services furnished after the order is issued, such that the reduction made in payments under that order shall achieve the required total percentage reduction in those payments for that fiscal year as determined on a 12-month basis.

(2) Timing of application of reductions

(A) In general

Except as provided in subparagraph (B), if a reduction is made under paragraph (1) in payment amounts pursuant to a sequestration order, the reduction shall be applied to payment for services furnished during the effective period of the order. For purposes of the previous sentence, in the case of inpatient services furnished for an individual, the services shall be considered to be furnished on the date of the individual's discharge from the inpatient facility.

(B) Payment on the basis of cost reporting periods

In the case in which payment for services of a provider of services is made under title XVIII of the Social Security Act [42 U.S.C. 1395 et seq.] on a basis relating to the reasonable cost incurred for the services during a cost reporting period of the provider, if a reduction is made under paragraph (1) in payment amounts pursuant to a sequestration order, the reduction shall be applied to payment for costs for such services incurred at any time during each cost reporting period of the provider any part of which occurs during the effective period of the order, but only (for each such cost reporting period) in the same proportion as the fraction of the cost reporting period that occurs during the effective period of the order.

(3) No increase in beneficiary charges in assignment-related cases

If a reduction in payment amounts is made under paragraph (1) for services for which payment under part B of title XVIII of the Social Security Act [42 U.S.C. 1395j et seq.] is made on the basis of an assignment described in section 1842(b)(3)(B)(ii) [42 U.S.C. 1395u(b)(3)(B)(ii)], in accordance with section 1842(b)(6)(B) [42 U.S.C. 1395u(b)(6)(B)], or under the procedure described in section 1870(f)(1) [42 U.S.C. 1395gg(f)(1)], of such Act, the person furnishing the services shall be considered to have accepted payment of the reasonable charge for the services, less any reduction in payment amount made pursuant to a sequestration order, as payment in full.

(4) No effect on computation of AAPCC

In computing the adjusted average per capita cost for purposes of section 1876(a)(4) of the Social Security Act [42 U.S.C. 1395mm(a)(4)], the Secretary of Health and Human Services shall not take into account any reductions in payment amounts which have been or may be effected under this subchapter.

(e) Community and migrant health centers, Indian health services and facilities, and veterans' medical care

(1) The maximum permissible reduction in budget authority for any account listed in paragraph (2) for any fiscal year, pursuant to an order issued under section 904 of this title, shall be 2 percent.

(2) The accounts referred to in paragraph (1) are as follows:

(A) Community health centers (75-0350-0-1-550).

(B) Migrant health centers (75-0350-0-1-550).

(C) Indian health facilities (75-0391-0-1-551).

(D) Indian health services (75-0390-0-1-551).

(E) Veterans' medical care (36-0160-0-1-703).

For purposes of the preceding provisions of this paragraph, programs are identified by the designated budget account identification code numbers set forth in the Budget of the United States Government—Appendix.

(f) Treatment of child support enforcement program

Notwithstanding any change in the display of budget accounts, any order issued by the President under section 904 of this title shall accomplish the full amount of any required reduction in expenditures under sections 455 and 458 of the Social Security Act [42 U.S.C. 655, 658] by reducing the Federal matching rate for State administrative costs under such program, as specified (for the fiscal year involved) in section 455(a) of such Act, to the extent necessary to reduce such expenditures by that amount.

(g) Federal pay

(1) In general

For purposes of any order issued under section 904 of this title—

(A) Federal pay under a statutory pay system, and

(B) elements of military pay,

shall be subject to reduction under an order in the same manner as other administrative expense components of the Federal budget; except that no such order may reduce or have the effect of reducing the rate of pay to which any individual is entitled under any such statutory pay system (as increased by any amount payable under section 5304 of title 5 or section

302 of the Federal Employees Pay Comparability Act of 1990) or the rate of any element of military pay to which any individual is entitled under title 37, or any increase in rates of pay which is scheduled to take effect under section 5303 of title 5, section 1009 of title 37, or any other provision of law.

(2) Definitions

For purposes of this subsection:

(A) The term "statutory pay system" shall have the meaning given that term in section 5302(1) of title 5.

(B) The term "elements of military pay" means—

(i) the elements of compensation of members of the uniformed services specified in section 1009 of title 37,

(ii) allowances provided members of the uniformed services under sections 403a and 405 of such title, and

(iii) cadet pay and midshipman pay under section 203(c) of such title.

(C) The term "uniformed services" shall have the meaning given that term in section 101(3) of title 37.

(h) Treatment of Federal administrative expenses

(1) Notwithstanding any other provision of this title,[1] administrative expenses incurred by the departments and agencies, including independent agencies, of the Federal Government in connection with any program, project, activity, or account shall be subject to reduction pursuant to an order issued under section 904 of this title, without regard to any exemption, exception, limitation, or special rule which is otherwise applicable with respect to such program, project, activity, or account under this subchapter.

(2) Notwithstanding any other provision of law, administrative expenses of any program, project, activity, or account which is self-supporting and does not receive appropriations shall be subject to reduction under a sequester order, unless specifically exempted in this subchapter.

(3) Payments made by the Federal Government to reimburse or match administrative costs incurred by a State or political subdivision under or in connection with any program, project, activity, or account shall not be considered administrative expenses of the Federal Government for purposes of this section, and shall be subject to reduction or sequestration under this subchapter to the extent (and only to the extent) that other payments made by the Federal Government under or in connection with that program, project, activity, or account are subject to such reduction or sequestration; except that Federal payments made to a State as reimbursement of administrative costs incurred by such State under or in connection with the unemployment compensation programs specified in subsection (h)(1)[1] of this section shall be subject to reduction or sequestration under this subchapter notwithstanding the exemption otherwise granted to such programs under that subsection.

---

[1] See References in Text note below.

(4) Notwithstanding any other provision of law, this subsection shall not apply with respect to the following:

  (A) Comptroller of the Currency.
  (B) Federal Deposit Insurance Corporation.
  (C) Office of Thrift Supervision.
  (D) National Credit Union Administration.
  (E) National Credit Union Administration, central liquidity facility.
  (F) Federal Retirement Thrift Investment Board.
  (G) Resolution Trust Corporation.
  (H) Farm Credit Administration.

(i) Treatment of payments and advances made with respect to unemployment compensation programs

(1) For purposes of section 904 of this title—

  (A) any amount paid as regular unemployment compensation by a State from its account in the Unemployment Trust Fund (established by section 904(a) of the Social Security Act [42 U.S.C. 1104(a)]),

  (B) any advance made to a State from the Federal unemployment account (established by section 904(g) of such Act [42 U.S.C. 1104(g)]) under title XII of such Act [42 U.S.C. 1321 et seq.] and any advance appropriated to the Federal unemployment account pursuant to section 1203 of such Act [42 U.S.C. 1323], and

  (C) any payment made from the Federal Employees Compensation Account (as established under section 909 of such Act [42 U.S.C. 1109]) for the purpose of carrying out chapter 85 of title 5 and funds appropriated or transferred to or otherwise deposited in such Account,

shall not be subject to reduction.

(2)(A) A State may reduce each weekly benefit payment made under the Federal-State Extended Unemployment Compensation Act of 1970 for any week of unemployment occurring during any period with respect to which payments are reduced under an order issued under section 904 of this title by a percentage not to exceed the percentage by which the Federal payment to the State under section 204 of such Act is to be reduced for such week as a result of such order.

(B) A reduction by a State in accordance with subparagraph (A) shall not be considered as a failure to fulfill the requirements of section 3304(a)(11) of title 26.

(j) Commodity Credit Corporation

(1) Powers and authorities of the Commodity Credit Corporation

This title [2] shall not restrict the Commodity Credit Corporation in the discharge of its authority and responsibility as a corporation to buy and sell commodities in world trade, to use the proceeds as a revolving fund to meet other obligations and otherwise operate as a corporation, the purpose for which it was created.

(2) Reduction in payments made under contracts

(A) Loan eligibility under any contract entered into with a person by the Commodity Credit Corporation prior to the time an order

has been issued under section 904 of this title shall not be reduced by an order subsequently issued. Subject to subparagraph (B), after an order is issued under such section for a fiscal year, any cash payments for loans or loan deficiencies made by the Commodity Credit Corporation shall be subject to reduction under the order.

(B) Each loan contract entered into with producers or producer cooperatives with respect to a particular crop of a commodity and subject to reduction under subparagraph (A) shall be reduced in accordance with the same terms and conditions. If some, but not all, contracts applicable to a crop of a commodity have been entered into prior to the issuance of an order under section 904 of this title, the order shall provide that the necessary reduction in payments under contracts applicable to the commodity be uniformly applied to all contracts for the next succeeding crop of the commodity, under the authority provided in paragraph (3).

(3) Delayed reduction in outlays permissible

Notwithstanding any other provision of this title,[2] if an order under section 904 of this title is issued with respect to a fiscal year, any reduction under the order applicable to contracts described in paragraph (1) may provide for reductions in outlays for the account involved to occur in the fiscal year following the fiscal year to which the order applies.

(4) Uniform percentage rate of reduction and other limitations

All reductions described in paragraph (2) which are required to be made in connection with an order issued under section 904 of this title with respect to a fiscal year shall be made so as to ensure that outlays for each program, project, activity, or account involved are reduced by a percentage rate that is uniform for all such programs, projects, activities, and accounts, and may not be made so as to achieve a percentage rate of reduction in any such item exceeding the rate specified in the order.

(5) Dairy program

Notwithstanding any other provision of this subsection, as the sole means of achieving any reduction in outlays under the milk price support program, the Secretary of Agriculture shall provide for a reduction to be made in the price received by producers for all milk produced in the United States and marketed by producers for commercial use. That price reduction (measured in cents per hundred weight of milk marketed) shall occur under section 1446(d)(2)(A) of title 7, shall begin on the day any sequestration order is issued under section 904 of this title, and shall not exceed the aggregate amount of the reduction in outlays under the milk price support program that otherwise would have been achieved by reducing payments for the purchase of milk or the products of milk under this subsection during the applicable fiscal year.

(6) Certain authority not to be limited

Nothing in this joint resolution shall limit or reduce, in any way, any appropriation that

[2] See References in Text note below.

provides the Commodity Credit Corporation with budget authority to cover the Corporation's net realized losses.

(k) Effects of sequestration

The effects of sequestration shall be as follows:

(1) Budgetary resources sequestered from any account shall be permanently cancelled, except as provided in paragraph (5).

(2) Except as otherwise provided, the same percentage sequestration shall apply to all programs, projects, and activities within a budget account (with programs, projects, and activities as delineated in the appropriation Act or accompanying report for the relevant fiscal year covering that account, or for accounts not included in appropriation Acts, as delineated in the most recently submitted President's budget).

(3) Administrative regulations or similar actions implementing a sequestration shall be made within 120 days of the sequestration order. To the extent that formula allocations differ at different levels of budgetary resources within an account, program, project, or activity, the sequestration shall be interpreted as producing a lower total appropriation, with the remaining amount of the appropriation being obligated in a manner consistent with program allocation formulas in substantive law.

(4) Except as otherwise provided, obligations in sequestered accounts shall be reduced only in the fiscal year in which a sequester occurs.

(5) If an automatic spending increase is sequestered, the increase (in the applicable index) that was disregarded as a result of that sequestration shall not be taken into account in any subsequent fiscal year.

(6) Budgetary resources sequestered in revolving, trust, and special fund accounts and offsetting collections sequestered in appropriation accounts shall not be available for obligation during the fiscal year in which the sequestration occurs, but shall be available in subsequent years to the extent otherwise provided in law.

(Pub. L. 99–177, title II, § 256, Dec. 12, 1985, 99 Stat. 1086; Pub. L. 99–514, § 2, Oct. 22, 1986, 100 Stat. 2095; Pub. L. 100–86, title V, § 506(b), Aug. 10, 1987, 101 Stat. 634; Pub. L. 100–119, title I, §§ 102(b)(2), (3), (11), 104(a)(3), (4), Sept. 29, 1987, 101 Stat. 773, 775, 776; Pub. L. 101–73, title VII, § 743(b), Aug. 9, 1989, 103 Stat. 437; Pub. L. 101–508, title XIII, § 13101(d), Nov. 5, 1990, 104 Stat. 1388–589; Pub. L. 101–509, title V, § 529 [title I, § 101(b)(2)(A), (4)(H)], Nov. 5, 1990, 104 Stat. 1427, 1439, 1440; Pub. L. 104–193, title I, § 110(r)(2), Aug. 22, 1996, 110 Stat. 2175; Pub. L. 105–33, title X, § 10208(a)(1), (b)–(g), Aug. 5, 1997, 111 Stat. 708–710.)

TERMINATION OF SECTION

For termination of section by section 275(b) of Pub. L. 99–177, as amended, see Effective and Termination Dates note set out under section 900 of this title.

REFERENCES IN TEXT

The Higher Education Act of 1965, referred to in subsec. (b), is Pub. L. 89–329, Nov. 8, 1965, 79 Stat. 1219, as amended. Parts B and D of title IV of the Act are classified generally to parts B (§ 1071 et seq.) and C (§ 1087a et seq.) of subchapter IV of chapter 28 of Title 20, Education. For complete classification of this Act to the Code, see Short Title note set out under section 1001 of Title 20 and Tables.

The Social Security Act, referred to in subsecs. (c), (d)(1), (2)(B), (3), and (i)(1)(B), is act Aug. 14, 1935, ch. 531, 49 Stat. 620, as amended. Part E of title IV of the Social Security Act is classified generally to part E (§ 670 et seq.) of subchapter IV of chapter 7 of Title 42, The Public Health and Welfare. Titles XII and XVIII of the Social Security Act are classified generally to subchapters XII (§ 1321 et seq.) and XVIII (§ 1395 et seq.), respectively, of chapter 7 of Title 42. Part B of title XVIII of the Social Security Act is classified generally to part B (§ 1395j et seq.) of subchapter XVIII of chapter 7 of Title 42. For complete classification of this Act to the Code, see section 1305 of Title 42 and Tables.

Section 302 of the Federal Employees Pay Comparability Act of 1990, referred to in subsec. (g)(1), is section 529 [title III, § 302] of Pub. L. 101–509, which is set out as a note under section 5304 of Title 5, Government Organization and Employees.

This title, referred to in subsecs. (h)(1) and (j)(1), (3), means title II (§ 200 et seq.) of Pub. L. 99–177, Dec. 12, 1985, 99 Stat. 1038, known as the Balanced Budget and Emergency Deficit Control Act of 1985. For complete classification of this Act to the Code, see Short Title note set out under section 900 of this title and Tables.

This joint resolution, referred to in subsec. (j)(6), means Pub. L. 99–177, Dec. 12, 1985, 99 Stat. 1037, as amended, which enacted this chapter and sections 654 to 656 of this title, amended sections 602, 622, 631 to 642, and 651 to 653 of this title, sections 1104 to 1106, 1109, and 3101 of Title 31, Money and Finance, and section 911 of Title 42, The Public Health and Welfare, repealed section 661 of this title, enacted provisions set out as notes under section 900 of this title and section 911 of Title 42, and amended provisions set out as a note under section 621 of this title. For complete classification of this Act to the Code, see Tables.

Subsec. (h)(1) of this section, referred to in subsec. (h)(3), was redesignated subsec. (i)(1) of this section by Pub. L. 101–508, title XIII, § 13101(d)(2), Nov. 5, 1990, 104 Stat. 1388–589.

The Federal-State Extended Unemployment Compensation Act of 1970, referred to in subsec. (i)(2)(A), is title II of Pub. L. 91–373, Aug. 10, 1970, 84 Stat. 708, as amended, which is classified generally as a note under section 3304 of Title 26, Internal Revenue Code. Section 204 of such Act is set out in the note under section 3304 of Title 26. For complete classification of this Act to the Code, see Tables.

AMENDMENTS

1997—Pub. L. 105–33, § 10208(a)(1), substituted "General and special sequestration rules" for "Exceptions, limitations, and special rules" as section catchline.

Subsec. (a). Pub. L. 105–33, § 10208(b), redesignated pars. (2) and (3) as (1) and (2), respectively, and struck out former par. (1) which read as follows: "National Wool Act;".

Subsec. (b). Pub. L. 105–33, § 10208[(c)], amended subsec. (b) generally, substituting new heading and text for former text consisting of pars. (1) to (3) relating to reductions required to be achieved from student loan programs operated under part B of title IV of the Higher Education Act of 1965 as a consequence of a sequestration order. Amendment was executed to reflect the probable intent of Congress based on language directing the general amendment of subsec. (b), appearing in the conference report for H.R. 2015, H. Rept. No. 105–217, 105th Congress, as adopted by the House of Representatives and Senate.

Subsec. (e)(1). Pub. L. 105–33, § 10208(d), substituted "shall be 2 percent." for "shall be—" and struck out subpars. (A) and (B) which read as follows:

"(A) 1 percent in the case of the fiscal year 1986, and

"(B) 2 percent in the case of any subsequent fiscal year."

Subsec. (h)(2). Pub. L. 105–33, § 10208(e)(1), substituted "this subchapter" for "this joint resolution".

Subsec. (h)(4)(D). Pub. L. 105–33, § 10208(e)(2), redesignated subpar. (E) as (D) and struck out former subpar. (D) which read as follows: "Office of Thrift Supervision."

Subsec. (h)(4)(E) to (G). Pub. L. 105–33, § 10208(e)(2), redesignated subpars. (F), (G), and (I) as (E), (F), and (G), respectively. Former subpar. (E) redesignated (D).

Subsec. (h)(4)(H). Pub. L. 105–33, § 10208(e)(2), added subpar. (H) and struck out former subpar. (H) which read as follows: "Resolution Funding Corporation."

Subsec. (h)(4)(I). Pub. L. 105–33, § 10208(e)(2), redesignated subpar. (I) as (G).

Subsec. (j)(2) to (5). Pub. L. 105–33, § 10208(f), added pars. (2) to (5) and struck out former pars. (2) to (5) which related to reduction in payments made under contracts, delayed reduction in outlays permissible, uniform percentage rate of reduction and other limitations, and no double reduction for agricultural price support and income protection programs.

Subsec. (k)(1). Pub. L. 105–33, § 10208(g)(1), struck out "other than a trust or special fund account" after "from any account" and inserted ", except as provided in paragraph (5)" before period.

Subsec. (k)(6). Pub. L. 105–33, § 10208(g)(2), amended par. (6) generally. Prior to amendment, par. (6) read as follows: "Except as otherwise provided, sequestration in trust and special fund accounts for which obligations are indefinite shall be taken in a manner to ensure that obligations in the fiscal year of a sequestration are reduced, from the level that would actually have occurred, by the applicable sequestration percentage."

1996—Subsecs. (k), (l). Pub. L. 104–193 redesignated subsec. (l) as (k) and struck out former subsec. (k) which related to special rules for JOBS portion of AFDC, providing that any order under section 904 accomplish full amount of any required sequestration of job opportunities and basic skills training program, and setting forth new allotment formula.

1990—Subsec. (a). Pub. L. 101–508, § 13101(d)(1), amended subsec. (a) generally, substituting provisions relating to automatic spending increases for provisions relating to effect of reductions and sequestrations.

Subsec. (b). Pub. L. 101–508, § 13101(d)(3), substituted "section 904 of this title" for "section 902 of this title" in pars. (1) to (3).

Pub. L. 101–508, § 13101(d)(2), redesignated subsec. (c) as (b). Former subsec. (b) redesignated (h).

Subsec. (c). Pub. L. 101–508, § 13101(d)(4), inserted after first sentence "No State's matching payments from the Federal Government for foster care maintenance payments or for adoption assistance maintenance payments may be reduced by a percentage exceeding the applicable domestic sequestration percentage."

Pub. L. 101–508, § 13101(d)(3), substituted "section 904 of this title" for "section 902 of this title".

Pub. L. 101–508, § 13101(d)(2), redesignated subsec. (f) as (c). Former subsec. (c) redesignated (b).

Subsec. (d)(1). Pub. L. 101–508, § 13101(d)(5), amended par. (1) generally. Prior to amendment, par. (1) read as follows: "The maximum permissible reduction for the health insurance programs under title XVIII of the Social Security Act for any fiscal year, pursuant to an order issued under section 902 of this title, consists only of a reduction of—

"(A) 1 percent in the case of fiscal year 1986, and

"(B) 2 percent (or such higher percentage as may apply as determined in accordance with section 902(a)(4)(B)(ii) of this title) in the case of any subsequent fiscal year,

in each separate payment amount otherwise made for a covered service under those programs without regard to this subchapter."

Subsec. (d)(2)(C). Pub. L. 101–508, § 13101(d)(6), struck out subpar. (C) which read as follows: "For purposes of this paragraph, the effective period of a sequestration order for fiscal year 1986 is the period beginning on March 1, 1986, and ending on September 30, 1986."

Subsec. (e). Pub. L. 101–508, § 13101(d)(2), redesignated subsec. (k) as (e). Former subsec. (e) redesignated (f).

Subsec. (e)(1). Pub. L. 101–508, § 13101(d)(3), substituted "section 904 of this title" for "section 902 of this title".

Subsec. (f). Pub. L. 101–508, § 13101(d)(3), substituted "section 904 of this title" for "section 902 of this title".

Pub. L. 101–508, § 13101(d)(2), redesignated subsec. (e) as (f). Former subsec. (f) redesignated (c).

Subsec. (g)(1). Pub. L. 101–509, § 529 [title I, § 101(b)(4)(H)], in closing provisions, inserted "(as increased by any amount payable under section 5304 of title 5 or section 302 of the Federal Employees Pay Comparability Act of 1990)" after "pay system" and substituted "5303" for "5305".

Pub. L. 101–508, § 13101(d)(3), substituted "section 904 of this title" for "section 902 of this title".

Subsec. (g)(2)(A). Pub. L. 101–509, § 529 [title I, § 101(b)(2)(A)], substituted "5302(1)" for "5301(c)".

Subsec. (h). Pub. L. 101–508, § 13101(d)(2), redesignated subsec. (b) as (h). Former subsec. (h) redesignated (i).

Subsec. (h)(1). Pub. L. 101–508, § 13101(d)(3), substituted "section 904 of this title" for "section 902 of this title".

Subsec. (i). Pub. L. 101–508, § 13101(d)(2), redesignated subsec. (h) as (i) and struck out former subsec. (i) which related to treatment of mine worker disability compensation increases as automatic spending increases.

Subsec. (i)(1), (2)(A). Pub. L. 101–508, § 13101(d)(3), substituted "section 904 of this title" for "section 902 of this title".

Subsec. (j). Pub. L. 101–508, § 13101(d)(3), substituted "section 904 of this title" for "section 902 of this title" wherever appearing in pars. (2) to (5).

Subsec. (k). Pub. L. 101–508, § 13101(d)(2), added subsec. (k). Former subsec. (k) redesignated (e).

Subsec. (l). Pub. L. 101–508, § 13101(d)(2), added subsec. (l) and struck out former subsec. (l) which related to treatment of obligated balances.

1989—Subsec. (b)(4)(C). Pub. L. 101–73, § 743(b)(1), substituted "Office of Thrift Supervision" for "Federal Home Loan Bank Board".

Subsec. (b)(4)(D). Pub. L. 101–73, § 743(b)(2), substituted "Office of Thrift Supervision" for "Federal Savings and Loan Insurance Corporation".

Subsec. (b)(4)(H), (I). Pub. L. 101–73, § 743(b)(3), added subpars. (H) and (I).

1987—Subsec. (a)(2). Pub. L. 100–119, § 102(b)(2), amended par. (2) generally. Prior to amendment, par. (2) read as follows: "Any amount of new budget authority, unobligated balances, obligated balances, new loan guarantee commitments, new direct loan obligations, spending authority (as defined in section 651(c)(2) of this title), or obligation limitations which is sequestered or reduced pursuant to an order issued under section 902 of this title is permanently cancelled, with the exception of amounts sequestered in special or trust funds, which shall remain in such funds and be available in accordance with and to the extent permitted by law, including the provisions of this Act."

Subsec. (b)(4). Pub. L. 100–86 added par. (4).

Subsec. (b)(4)(G). Pub. L. 100–119, § 104(a)(3), added subpar. (G).

Subsec. (d)(1)(B). Pub. L. 100–119, § 102(b)(11), inserted "(or such higher percentage as may apply as determined in accordance with section 902(a)(4)(B)(ii) of this title)".

Subsec. (e). Pub. L. 100–119, § 104(a)(4), substituted "Notwithstanding any change in the display of budget accounts, any order" for "Any order".

Subsec. (l). Pub. L. 100–119, § 102(b)(3), amended subsec. (l) generally, striking out provisions which had created an "existing contract" exception to the rule of obligated balances not being subject to reduction under an order issued under section 902 of this title, under which existing contracts in major functional category 050 (other than (A) those contracts which included a specified penalty for cancellation or modification by the Government and which if so cancelled or modified would have resulted (due to such penalty) in a net loss to the Government for the fiscal year, and (B) those contracts the reduction of which would have violated the legal obligations of the Government) were subject to reduction, in accordance with section 901(d)(3) of this title, under an order issued under section 902 of this title.

1986—Subsec. (h)(2)(B). Pub. L. 99–514 substituted "Internal Revenue Code of 1986" for "Internal Revenue Code of 1954", which for purposes of codification was translated as "title 26" thus requiring no change in text.

EFFECTIVE DATE OF 1996 AMENDMENT

Amendment by Pub. L. 104–193 effective July 1, 1997, with transition rules relating to State options to accelerate such date, rules relating to claims, actions, and proceedings commenced before such date, rules relating to closing out of accounts for terminated or substantially modified programs and continuance in office of Assistant Secretary for Family Support, and provisions relating to termination of entitlement under AFDC program, see section 116 of Pub. L. 104–193, set out as a note under section 601 of Title 42, The Public Health and Welfare.

EFFECTIVE DATE OF 1990 AMENDMENT

Amendment by Pub. L. 101–509 effective on such date as the President shall determine, but not earlier than 90 days, and not later than 180 days, after Nov. 5, 1990, see section 529 [title III, § 305] of Pub. L. 101–509, set out as a note under section 5301 of Title 5, Government Organization and Employees.

SECTION REFERRED TO IN OTHER SECTIONS

This section is referred to in sections 901, 902, 903, 922 of this title; title 12 section 1772c.

§ 907. The baseline

(a) In general

For any budget year, the baseline refers to a projection of current-year levels of new budget authority, outlays, revenues, and the surplus or deficit into the budget year and the outyears based on laws enacted through the applicable date.

(b) Direct spending and receipts

For the budget year and each outyear, the baseline shall be calculated using the following assumptions:

(1) In general

Laws providing or creating direct spending and receipts are assumed to operate in the manner specified in those laws for each such year and funding for entitlement authority is assumed to be adequate to make all payments required by those laws.

(2) Exceptions

(A)(i) No program established by a law enacted on or before August 5, 1997, with estimated current year outlays greater than $50,000,000 shall be assumed to expire in the budget year or the outyears. The scoring of new programs with estimated outlays greater than $50,000,000 a year shall be based on scoring by the Committees on Budget or OMB, as applicable. OMB, CBO, and the Budget Committees shall consult on the scoring of such programs where there are differenes[1] between CBO and OMB.

(ii) On the expiration of the suspension of a provision of law that is suspended under section 7301 of title 7 and that authorizes a program with estimated fiscal year outlays that are greater than $50,000,000, for purposes of clause (i), the program shall be assumed to continue to operate in the same manner as the program operated immediately before the expiration of the suspension.

(B) The increase for veterans' compensation for a fiscal year is assumed to be the same as that required by law for veterans' pensions unless otherwise provided by law enacted in that session.

(C) Excise taxes dedicated to a trust fund, if expiring, are assumed to be extended at current rates.

(D) If any law expires before the budget year or any outyear, then any program with estimated current year outlays greater than $50,000,000 that operates under that law shall be assumed to continue to operate under that law as in effect immediately before its expiration.

(3) Hospital Insurance Trust Fund

Notwithstanding any other provision of law, the receipts and disbursements of the Hospital Insurance Trust Fund shall be included in all calculations required by this Act.

(c) Discretionary appropriations

For the budget year and each outyear, the baseline shall be calculated using the following assumptions regarding all amounts other than those covered by subsection (b) of this section:

(1) Inflation of current-year appropriations

Budgetary resources other than unobligated balances shall be at the level provided for the budget year in full-year appropriation Acts. If for any account a full-year appropriation has not yet been enacted, budgetary resources other than unobligated balances shall be at the level available in the current year, adjusted sequentially and cumulatively for expiring housing contracts as specified in paragraph (2), for social insurance administrative expenses as specified in paragraph (3), to offset pay absorption and for pay annualization as specified in paragraph (4), for inflation as specified in paragraph (5), and to account for changes required by law in the level of agency payments for personnel benefits other than pay.

(2) Expiring housing contracts

New budget authority to renew expiring multiyear subsidized housing contracts shall be adjusted to reflect the difference in the number of such contracts that are scheduled to expire in that fiscal year and the number expiring in the current year, with the per-contract renewal cost equal to the average current-year cost of renewal contracts.

(3) Social insurance administrative expenses

Budgetary resources for the administrative expenses of the following trust funds shall be adjusted by the percentage change in the beneficiary population from the current year to that fiscal year: the Federal Hospital Insurance Trust Fund, the Supplementary Medical Insurance Trust Fund, the Unemployment Trust Fund, and the railroad retirement account.

[1] So in original. Probably should be "differences".

(4) Pay annualization; offset to pay absorption

Current-year new budget authority for Federal employees shall be adjusted to reflect the full 12-month costs (without absorption) of any pay adjustment that occurred in that fiscal year.

(5) Inflators

The inflator used in paragraph (1) to adjust budgetary resources relating to personnel shall be the percent by which the average of the Bureau of Labor Statistics Employment Cost Index (wages and salaries, private industry workers) for that fiscal year differs from such index for the current year. The inflator used in paragraph (1) to adjust all other budgetary resources shall be the percent by which the average of the estimated gross domestic product chain-type price index for that fiscal year differs from the average of such estimated index for the current year.

(6) Current-year appropriations

If, for any account, a continuing appropriation is in effect for less than the entire current year, then the current-year amount shall be assumed to equal the amount that would be available if that continuing appropriation covered the entire fiscal year. If law permits the transfer of budget authority among budget accounts in the current year, the current-year level for an account shall reflect transfers accomplished by the submission of, or assumed for the current year in, the President's original budget for the budget year.

(d) Up-to-date concepts

In deriving the baseline for any budget year or outyear, current-year amounts shall be calculated using the concepts and definitions that are required for that budget year.

(e) Asset sales

Amounts realized from the sale of an asset shall not be included in estimates under section 901, 902, or 903 of this title if that sale would result in a financial cost to the Federal Government as determined pursuant to scorekeeping guidelines.

(Pub. L. 99–177, title II, § 257, formerly §§ 251(a)(6)(I), 257, Dec. 12, 1985, 99 Stat. 1092; Pub. L. 100–119, title I, §§ 102(a), (b)(4)–(8), 104(c)(2), 106(b), Sept. 29, 1987, 101 Stat. 754, 773, 774, 777, 780; renumbered § 257 and amended Pub. L. 101–508, title XIII, § 13101(b), (e)(1), (2), Nov. 5, 1990, 104 Stat. 1388–589, 1388–591, 1388–593; Pub. L. 105–33, title X, § 10209(a), Aug. 5, 1997, 111 Stat. 710.)

Termination of Section

For termination of section by section 275(b) of Pub. L. 99–177, as amended, see Effective and Termination Dates note set out under section 900 of this title.

References in Text

This Act, referred to in subsec. (b)(3), means Pub. L. 99–177, Dec. 12, 1985, 99 Stat. 1037, as amended, which enacted this chapter and sections 654 to 656 of this title, amended sections 602, 622, 631 to 642, and 651 to 653 of this title, sections 1104 to 1106, 1109, and 3101 of Title 31, Money and Finance, and section 911 of Title 42, The Public Health and Welfare, repealed section 661 of this title, enacted provisions set out as notes under section 900 of this title and section 911 of Title 42, and amended provisions set out as a note under section 621 of this title. For complete classification of this Act to the Code, see Tables.

Codification

Pub. L. 101–508, § 13101(b), redesignated former par. (12) of this section as section 250(c)(21) (now 250(c)(19)) of Pub. L. 99–177, which is classified to section 900(c)(19) of this title.

Pub. L. 101–508, § 13101(e)(2), transferred section 251(a)(6)(I) of Pub. L. 99–177, which was classified to section 901(a)(6)(I) of this title, to subsec. (e) of this section.

Amendments

1997—Subsec. (b)(2)(A). Pub. L. 105–33, § 10209(a)(1), amended subpar. (A) generally. Prior to amendment, subpar. (A) read as follows: "No program with estimated current-year outlays greater than $50 million shall be assumed to expire in the budget year or outyears."

Subsec. (b)(2)(D). Pub. L. 105–33, § 10209(a)(2), added subpar. (D).

Subsec. (c)(5). Pub. L. 105–33, § 10209(a)(3), substituted "domestic product chain-type price index" for "national product fixed-weight price index".

Subsec. (e). Pub. L. 105–33, § 10209(a)(4), added subsec. (e) and struck out former subsec. (e) which read as follows: "The sale of an asset or prepayment of a loan shall not alter the deficit or produce any net deficit reduction in the budget baseline, except that the budget baseline estimate shall include asset sales mandated by law before September 18, 1987, and routine, ongoing asset sales and loan prepayments at levels consistent with agency operations in fiscal year 1986;".

1990—Pub. L. 101–508, § 13101(e)(1), amended section generally, substituting provisions relating to baseline for provisions relating to definitions.

Subsec. (e). Pub. L. 101–508, § 13101(e)(2), redesignated section 901(a)(6)(I) of this title as subsec. (e) of this section, and substituted "The" for "assuming, for purposes of this paragraph and subparagraph (A)(i) of paragraph (3), that the".

1987—Pub. L. 100–119, § 102(a), amended section 901 of this title generally, adding subsec. (a)(6)(I). See 1990 Amendment note above.

Par. (1). Pub. L. 100–119, § 104(c)(2), struck out provisions of former subpar. (A) that "automatic spending increase" meant increases in budget outlays due to changes in indexes in the following Federal programs:

"Black lung benefits (20–8144–0–7–601);
"Central Intelligence Agency retirement and disability system fund (56–3400–0–1–054);
"Civil service retirement and disability fund (24–8135–0–7–602);
"Comptrollers general retirement system (05–0107–0–1–801);
"Foreign service retirement and disability fund (19–8186–0–7–602);
"Judicial survivors' annuities fund (10–8110–0–7–602);
"Longshoremen's and harborworkers' compensation benefits (16–9971–0–7–601);
"Military retirement fund (97–8097–0–7–602);
"National Oceanic and Atmospheric Administration retirement (13–1450–0–1–306);
"Pensions for former Presidents (47–0105–0–1–802);
"Railroad retirement tier II (60–8011–0–7–601);
"Retired pay, Coast Guard (69–0241–0–1–403);
"Retirement pay and medical benefits for commissioned officers, Public Health Service (75–0379–0–1–551);
"Special benefits, Federal Employees' Compensation Act (16–1521–0–1–600);
"Special benefits for disabled coal miners (75–0409–0–1–601); and
"Tax Court judges survivors annuity fund (23–8115–0–7–602)."

Par. (7). Pub. L. 100–119, §102(b)(4), amended par. (7) generally. Prior to amendment, par. (7) read as follows: "The terms 'sequester' and 'sequestration' (subject to section 902(a)(4) of this title) refer to or mean the cancellation of new budget authority, unobligated balances, obligated balances, new loan guarantee commitments, new direct loan obligations, and spending authority as defined in section 651(c)(2) of this title, and the reduction of obligation limitations."

Par. (9). Pub. L. 100–119, §102(b)(5), added par. (9).

Par. (10). Pub. L. 100–119, §106(b), added par. (10).

Par. (11). Pub. L. 100–119, §102(b)(6), added par. (11).

Par. (12). Pub. L. 100–119, §102(b)(7), added par. (12).

Pars. (13), (14). Pub. L. 100–119, §102(b)(8), added pars. (13) and (14).

DEFINITION OF TERMS USED IN BALANCED BUDGET AND EMERGENCY DEFICIT CONTROL ACT OF 1985

Pub. L. 101–163, title III, §315, Nov. 21, 1989, 103 Stat. 1066, provided that: "Effective in the case of this Act and any subsequent Act making appropriations for the Legislative Branch, for purposes of the Balanced Budget and Emergency Deficit Control Act of 1985 (Public Law 99–177), as amended [see Short Title note set out under section 900 of this title], or any other Act which requires a uniform percentage reduction in accounts in this Act and any subsequent Act making appropriations for the Legislative Branch, the accounts under the general heading 'Senate', and the accounts under the general heading 'House of Representatives', shall each be considered to be one appropriation account and one 'program, project, and activity'."

Pub. L. 100–202, §101(i) [title III, §306], Dec. 22, 1987, 101 Stat. 1329–290, 1329–309, provided that: "Hereafter, for purposes of the Balanced Budget and Emergency Deficit Control Act of 1985 (Public Law 99–177), as amended [see Short Title note set out under section 900 of this title], the term 'program, project, and activity' shall be synonymous with each appropriation account in this Act [see Tables for classification], except that the accounts under the general heading 'House of Representatives' shall be considered one appropriation account and one 'program, project, and activity', and the accounts under the general heading 'Senate' shall be considered one appropriation account and one 'program, project, and activity'."

COST-OF-LIVING ADJUSTMENTS IN CERTAIN FEDERAL BENEFITS

Pub. L. 99–509, title VII, §7001, Oct. 21, 1986, 100 Stat. 1948, provided that:

"(a) IN GENERAL.—Benefits which are payable in calendar year 1987, 1988, 1989, 1990, or 1991, under programs listed in section 257(1)(A) of the Balanced Budget and Emergency Deficit Control Act of 1985 (Public Law 99–177), [2 U.S.C. 907(1)(A)], including any cost-of-living adjustment in such benefits, shall not be subject to modification, suspension, or reduction in such calendar year pursuant to a Presidential order issued under such Act [see Short Title note set out under 2 U.S.C. 900].

"(b) DEFINITION.—For purposes of this section, the term 'cost-of-living adjustment' means any increase or change in the amount of a benefit or in standards relating to such benefit under any provision of Federal law which requires such increase or change as a result of any change in the Consumer Price Index (or any component thereof) or any other index which measures costs, prices, or wages."

SECTION REFERRED TO IN OTHER SECTIONS

This section is referred to in sections 602, 691e, 900 of this title; title 7 section 7251; title 31 section 1105; title 38 section 1729A; title 42 section 603.

§ 907a. Suspension in event of war or low growth

(a) Procedures in event of low-growth report

(1) Trigger

Whenever CBO issues a low-growth report under section 254(j),[1] the Majority Leader of the House of Representatives may, and the Majority Leader of the Senate shall, introduce a joint resolution (in the form set forth in paragraph (2)) declaring that the conditions specified in section 254(j)[1] are met and suspending the relevant provisions of this title,[1] titles III and VI[1] of the Congressional Budget Act of 1974 [2 U.S.C. 631 et seq.], and section 1103 of title 31.

(2) Form of joint resolution

(A) The matter after the resolving clause in any joint resolution introduced pursuant to paragraph (1) shall be as follows: "That the Congress declares that the conditions specified in section 254(j)[1] of the Balanced Budget and Emergency Deficit Control Act of 1985 are met, and the implementation of the Congressional Budget and Impoundment Control Act of 1974, chapter 11 of title 31, United States Code, and part C of the Balanced Budget and Emergency Deficit Control Act of 1985 are modified as described in section 258(b) of the Balanced Budget and Emergency Deficit Control Act of 1985."

(B) The title of the joint resolution shall be "Joint resolution suspending certain provisions of law pursuant to section 258(a)(2) of the Balanced Budget and Emergency Deficit Control Act of 1985."; and the joint resolution shall not contain any preamble.

(3) Committee action

Each joint resolution introduced pursuant to paragraph (1) shall be referred to the appropriate committees of the House of Representatives or the Committee on the Budget of the Senate, as the case may be; and such Committee shall report the joint resolution to its House without amendment on or before the fifth day on which such House is in session after the date on which the joint resolution is introduced. If the Committee fails to report the joint resolution within the five-day period referred to in the preceding sentence, it shall be automatically discharged from further consideration of the joint resolution, and the joint resolution shall be placed on the appropriate calendar.

(4) Consideration of joint resolution

(A) A vote on final passage of a joint resolution reported to the Senate or discharged pursuant to paragraph (3) shall be taken on or before the close of the fifth calendar day of session after the date on which the joint resolution is reported or after the Committee has been discharged from further consideration of the joint resolution. If prior to the passage by one House of a joint resolution of that House, that House receives the same joint resolution from the other House, then—

(i) the procedure in that House shall be the same as if no such joint resolution had been received from the other House, but

_____
[1] See References in Text note below.

(ii) the vote on final passage shall be on the joint resolution of the other House.

When the joint resolution is agreed to, the Clerk of the House of Representatives (in the case of a House joint resolution agreed to in the House of Representatives) or the Secretary of the Senate (in the case of a Senate joint resolution agreed to in the Senate) shall cause the joint resolution to be engrossed, certified, and transmitted to the other House of the Congress as soon as practicable.

(B)(i) In the Senate, a joint resolution under this paragraph shall be privileged. It shall not be in order to move to reconsider the vote by which the motion is agreed to or disagreed to.

(ii) Debate in the Senate on a joint resolution under this paragraph, and all debatable motions and appeals in connection therewith, shall be limited to not more than five hours. The time shall be equally divided between, and controlled by, the majority leader and the minority leader or their designees.

(iii) Debate in the Senate on any debatable motion or appeal in connection with a joint resolution under this paragraph shall be limited to not more than one hour, to be equally divided between, and controlled by, the mover and the manager of the joint resolution, except that in the event the manager of the joint resolution is in favor of any such motion or appeal, the time in opposition thereto shall be controlled by the minority leader or his designee.

(iv) A motion in the Senate to further limit debate on a joint resolution under this paragraph is not debatable. A motion to table or to recommit a joint resolution under this paragraph is not in order.

(C) No amendment to a joint resolution considered under this paragraph shall be in order in the Senate.

(b) Suspension of sequestration procedures

Upon the enactment of a declaration of war or a joint resolution described in subsection (a) of this section—

(1) the subsequent issuance of any sequestration report or any sequestration order is precluded;

(2) sections 302(f), 310(d), 311(a), and title VI[2] of the Congressional Budget Act of 1974 [2 U.S.C. 633(f), 641(d), 642(a)] are suspended; and

(3) section 1103 of title 31 is suspended.

(c) Restoration of sequestration procedures

(1) In the event of a suspension of sequestration procedures due to a declaration of war, then, effective with the first fiscal year that begins in the session after the state of war is concluded by Senate ratification of the necessary treaties, the provisions of subsection (b) of this section triggered by that declaration of war are no longer effective.

(2) In the event of a suspension of sequestration procedures due to the enactment of a joint resolution described in subsection (a) of this section, then, effective with regard to the first fiscal year beginning at least 12 months after the enactment of that resolution, the provisions of

subsection (b) of this section triggered by that resolution are no longer effective.

(Pub. L. 99–177, title II, § 258, as added Pub. L. 101–508, title XIII, § 13101(f), Nov. 5, 1990, 104 Stat. 1388–593.)

TERMINATION OF SECTION

For termination of section by section 275(b) of Pub. L. 99–177, as amended, see Effective and Termination Dates note set out under section 900 of this title.

REFERENCES IN TEXT

Section 254 and section 254 of the Balanced Budget and Emergency Deficit Control Act of 1985, referred to in subsec. (a)(1), (2)(A), mean section 254 of Pub. L. 99–177, which is classified to section 904 of this title, and was amended by Pub. L. 105–33, title X, § 10206(1), Aug. 5, 1997, 111 Stat. 704, by redesignating subsecs. (j) and (k) as (i) and (j), respectively.

This title, referred to in subsec. (a)(1), means title II (§ 200 et seq.) of Pub. L. 99–177, Dec. 12, 1985, 99 Stat. 1038, as amended, known as the Balanced Budget and Emergency Deficit Control Act of 1985. For complete classification of this Act to the Code, see Short Title note set out under section 900 of this title and Tables.

The Congressional Budget Act of 1974, referred to in subsecs. (a)(1) and (b)(2), is titles I to IX of Pub. L. 93–344, July 12, 1974, 88 Stat. 297, as amended. Title III of the Act is classified generally to subchapter I (§ 631 et seq.) of chapter 17A of this title. Title VI of the Act was classified generally to subchapter IV (§ 665 et seq.) of chapter 17A of this title prior to repeal by Pub. L. 105–33, title X, § 10118(a), Aug. 5, 1997, 111 Stat. 695. For complete classification of this Act to the Code, see Short Title note set out under section 621 of this title and Tables.

The Congressional Budget and Impoundment Control Act of 1974, referred to in subsec. (a)(2)(A), is Pub. L. 93–344, July 12, 1974, 88 Stat. 297, as amended. For complete classification of this Act to the Code, see Short Title note set out under section 621 of this title and Tables.

Part C of the Balanced Budget and Emergency Deficit Control Act of 1985, referred to in subsec. (a)(2)(A), is classified generally to this subchapter. Section 258 of the Act is classified to this section.

PRIOR PROVISIONS

A prior section 258 of Pub. L. 99–177 was classified to section 908 of this title prior to repeal by Pub. L. 105–33, title X, § 10210, Aug. 5, 1997, 111 Stat. 711.

SECTION REFERRED TO IN OTHER SECTIONS

This section is referred to in section 643 of this title.

§ 907b. Modification of Presidential order

(a) Introduction of joint resolution

At any time after the Director of OMB issues a final sequestration report under section 904 of this title for a fiscal year, but before the close of the twentieth calendar day of the session of Congress beginning after the date of issuance of such report, the majority leader of either House of Congress may introduce a joint resolution which contains provisions directing the President to modify the most recent order issued under section 904 of this title or provide an alternative to reduce the deficit for such fiscal year. After the introduction of the first such joint resolution in either House of Congress in any calendar year, then no other joint resolution introduced in such House in such calendar year shall be subject to the procedures set forth in this section.

---

[2] See References in Text note below.

(b) Procedures for consideration of joint resolutions

(1) Referral to committee

A joint resolution introduced in the Senate under subsection (a) of this section shall not be referred to a committee of the Senate and shall be placed on the calendar pending disposition of such joint resolution in accordance with this subsection.

(2) Consideration in Senate

On or after the third calendar day (excluding Saturdays, Sundays, and legal holidays) beginning after a joint resolution is introduced under subsection (a) of this section, notwithstanding any rule or precedent of the Senate, including Rule XXII of the Standing Rules of the Senate, it is in order (even though a previous motion to the same effect has been disagreed to) for any Member of the Senate to move to proceed to the consideration of the joint resolution. The motion is not in order after the eighth calendar day (excluding Saturdays, Sundays, and legal holidays) beginning after a joint resolution (to which the motion applies) is introduced. The joint resolution is privileged in the Senate. A motion to reconsider the vote by which the motion is agreed to or disagreed to shall not be in order. If a motion to proceed to the consideration of the joint resolution is agreed to, the Senate shall immediately proceed to consideration of the joint resolution without intervening motion, order, or other business, and the joint resolution shall remain the unfinished business of the Senate until disposed of.

(3) Debate in Senate

(A) In the Senate, debate on a joint resolution introduced under subsection (a) of this section, amendments thereto, and all debatable motions and appeals in connection therewith shall be limited to not more than 10 hours, which shall be divided equally between the majority leader and the minority leader (or their designees).

(B) A motion to postpone, or a motion to proceed to the consideration of other business is not in order. A motion to reconsider the vote by which the joint resolution is agreed to or disagreed to is not in order, and a motion to recommit the joint resolution is not in order.

(C)(i) No amendment that is not germane to the provisions of the joint resolution or to the order issued under section 904 of this title shall be in order in the Senate. In the Senate, an amendment, any amendment to an amendment, or any debatable motion or appeal is debatable for not to exceed 30 minutes to be equally divided between, and controlled by, the mover and the majority leader (or their designees), except that in the event that the majority leader favors the amendment, motion, or appeal, the minority leader (or the minority leader's designee) shall control the time in opposition to the amendment, motion, or appeal.

(ii) In the Senate, an amendment that is otherwise in order shall be in order notwithstanding the fact that it amends the joint resolution in more than one place or amends language previously amended. It shall not be in order in the Senate to vote on the question of agreeing to such a joint resolution or any amendment thereto unless the figures then contained in such joint resolution or amendment are mathematically consistent.

(4) Vote on final passage

Immediately following the conclusion of the debate on a joint resolution introduced under subsection (a) of this section, a single quorum call at the conclusion of the debate if requested in accordance with the rules of the Senate, and the disposition of any pending amendments under paragraph (3), the vote on final passage of the joint resolution shall occur.

(5) Appeals

Appeals from the decisions of the Chair shall be decided without debate.

(6) Conference reports

In the Senate, points of order under titles III, IV, and VI[1] of the Congressional Budget Act of 1974 [2 U.S.C. 631 et seq., 651 et seq.] are applicable to a conference report on the joint resolution or any amendments in disagreement thereto.

(7) Resolution from other House

If, before the passage by the Senate of a joint resolution of the Senate introduced under subsection (a) of this section, the Senate receives from the House of Representatives a joint resolution introduced under subsection (a) of this section, then the following procedures shall apply:

(A) The joint resolution of the House of Representatives shall not be referred to a committee and shall be placed on the calendar.

(B) With respect to a joint resolution introduced under subsection (a) of this section in the Senate—

(i) the procedure in the Senate shall be the same as if no joint resolution had been received from the House; but

(ii)(I) the vote on final passage shall be on the joint resolution of the House if it is identical to the joint resolution then pending for passage in the Senate; or

(II) if the joint resolution from the House is not identical to the joint resolution then pending for passage in the Senate and the Senate then passes the Senate joint resolution, the Senate shall be considered to have passed the House joint resolution as amended by the text of the Senate joint resolution.

(C) Upon disposition of the joint resolution received from the House, it shall no longer be in order to consider the resolution originated in the Senate.

(8) Senate action on House resolution

If the Senate receives from the House of Representatives a joint resolution introduced under subsection (a) of this section after the Senate has disposed of a Senate originated res-

---

[1] See References in Text note below.

olution which is identical to the House passed joint resolution, the action of the Senate with regard to the disposition of the Senate originated joint resolution shall be deemed to be the action of the Senate with regard to the House originated joint resolution. If it is not identical to the House passed joint resolution, then the Senate shall be considered to have passed the joint resolution of the House as amended by the text of the Senate joint resolution.

(Pub. L. 99–177, title II, §258A, as added Pub. L. 101–508, title XIII, §13101(f), Nov. 5, 1990, 104 Stat. 1388–595.)

TERMINATION OF SECTION

For termination of section by section 275(b) of Pub. L. 99–177, as amended, see Effective and Termination Dates note set out under section 900 of this title.

REFERENCES IN TEXT

The Congressional Budget Act of 1974, referred to in subsec. (b)(6), is titles I to IX of Pub. L. 93–344, July 12, 1974, 88 Stat. 297, as amended. Titles III and IV of the Act are classified generally to subchapters I (§631 et seq.) and II (§651 et seq.), respectively, of chapter 17A of this title. Title VI of the Act was classified generally to subchapter IV (§665 et seq.) of chapter 17A of this title prior to repeal by Pub. L. 105–33, title X, §10118(a), Aug. 5, 1997, 111 Stat. 695. For complete classification of this Act to the Code, see Short Title note set out under section 621 of this title and Tables.

§ 907c. Flexibility among defense programs, projects, and activities

(a) Reductions beyond amount specified in Presidential order

Subject to subsections (b), (c), and (d) of this section, new budget authority and unobligated balances for any programs, projects, or activities within major functional category 050 (other than a military personnel account) may be further reduced beyond the amount specified in an order issued by the President under section 904 of this title for such fiscal year. To the extent such additional reductions are made and result in additional outlay reductions, the President may provide for lesser reductions in new budget authority and unobligated balances for other programs, projects, or activities within major functional category 050 for such fiscal year, but only to the extent that the resulting outlay increases do not exceed the additional outlay reductions, and no such program, project, or activity may be increased above the level actually made available by law in appropriation Acts (before taking sequestration into account). In making calculations under this subsection, the President shall use account outlay rates that are identical to those used in the report by the Director of OMB under section 904 of this title.

(b) Base closures prohibited

No actions taken by the President under subsection (a) of this section for a fiscal year may result in a domestic base closure or realignment that would otherwise be subject to section 2687 of title 10.

(c) Report and joint resolution required

The President may not exercise the authority provided by this paragraph[1] for a fiscal year unless—

(1) the President submits a single report to Congress specifying, for each account, the detailed changes proposed to be made for such fiscal year pursuant to this section;

(2) that report is submitted within 5 calendar days of the start of the next session of Congress; and

(3) a joint resolution affirming or modifying the changes proposed by the President pursuant to this paragraph[1] becomes law.

(d) Introduction of joint resolution

Within 5 calendar days of session after the President submits a report to Congress under subsection (c)(1) of this section for a fiscal year, the majority leader of each House of Congress shall (by request) introduce a joint resolution which contains provisions affirming the changes proposed by the President pursuant to this paragraph.[1]

(e) Form and title of joint resolution

(1) The matter after the resolving clause in any joint resolution introduced pursuant to subsection (d) of this section shall be as follows: "That the report of the President as submitted on [Insert Date] under section 258B is hereby approved."

(2) The title of the joint resolution shall be "Joint resolution approving the report of the President submitted under section 258B of the Balanced Budget and Emergency Deficit Control Act of 1985."

(3) Such joint resolution shall not contain any preamble.

(f) Calendaring and consideration of joint resolution in Senate

(1) A joint resolution introduced in the Senate under subsection (d) of this section shall be referred to the Committee on Appropriations, and if not reported within 5 calendar days (excluding Saturdays, Sundays, and legal holidays) from the date of introduction shall be considered as having been discharged therefrom and shall be placed on the appropriate calendar pending disposition of such joint resolution in accordance with this subsection. In the Senate, no amendment proposed in the Committee on Appropriations shall be in order other than an amendment (in the nature of a substitute) that is germane or relevant to the provisions of the joint resolution or to the order issued under section 904 of this title. For purposes of this paragraph, an amendment shall be considered to be relevant if it relates to function 050 (national defense).

(2) On or after the third calendar day (excluding Saturdays, Sundays, and legal holidays) beginning after a joint resolution is placed on the Senate calendar, notwithstanding any rule or precedent of the Senate, including Rule XXII of the Standing Rules of the Senate, it is in order (even though a previous motion to the same effect has been disagreed to) for any Member of the Senate to move to proceed to the consideration of the joint resolution. The motion is not

---

[1] So in original. Probably should be "section".

in order after the eighth calendar day (excluding
Saturdays, Sundays, and legal holidays) beginning after such joint resolution is placed on the
appropriate calendar. The motion is not debatable. The joint resolution is privileged in the
Senate. A motion to reconsider the vote by
which the motion is agreed to or disagreed to
shall not be in order. If a motion to proceed to
the consideration of the joint resolution is
agreed to, the Senate shall immediately proceed
to consideration of the joint resolution without
intervening motion, order, or other business,
and the joint resolution shall remain the unfinished business of the Senate until disposed of.

(g) Debate of joint resolution; motions

(1) In the Senate, debate on a joint resolution
introduced under subsection (d) of this section,
amendments thereto, and all debatable motions
and appeals in connection therewith shall be
limited to not more than 10 hours, which shall
be divided equally between the majority leader
and the minority leader (or their designees).

(2) A motion to postpone, or a motion to proceed to the consideration of other business is
not in order. A motion to reconsider the vote by
which the joint resolution is agreed to or disagreed to is not in order. In the Senate, a motion to recommit the joint resolution is not in
order.

(h) Amendment of joint resolution

(1) No amendment that is not germane or relevant to the provisions of the joint resolution or
to the order issued under section 904 of this title
shall be in order in the Senate. For purposes of
this paragraph, an amendment shall be considered to be relevant if it relates to function 050
(national defense). In the Senate, an amendment, any amendment to an amendment, or any
debatable motion or appeal is debatable for not
to exceed 30 minutes to be equally divided between, and controlled by, the mover and the majority leader (or their designees), except that in
the event that the majority leader favors the
amendment, motion, or appeal, the minority
leader (or the minority leader's designee) shall
control the time in opposition to the amendment, motion, or appeal.

(2) In the Senate, an amendment that is otherwise in order shall be in order notwithstanding
the fact that it amends the joint resolution in
more than one place or amends language previously amended, so long as the amendment
makes or maintains mathematical consistency.
It shall not be in order in the Senate to vote on
the question of agreeing to such a joint resolution or any amendment thereto unless the figures then contained in such joint resolution or
amendment are mathematically consistent.

(3) It shall not be in order in the Senate to
consider any amendment to any joint resolution
introduced under subsection (d) of this section
or any conference report thereon if such amendment or conference report would have the effect
of decreasing any specific budget outlay reductions below the level of such outlay reductions
provided in such joint resolution unless such
amendment or conference report makes a reduction in other specific budget outlays at least
equivalent to any increase in outlays provided
by such amendment or conference report.

(4) For purposes of the application of paragraph (3), the level of outlays and specific budget outlay reductions provided in an amendment
shall be determined on the basis of estimates
made by the Committee on the Budget of the
Senate.

(i) Vote on final passage of joint resolution

Immediately following the conclusion of the
debate on a joint resolution introduced under
subsection (d) of this section, a single quorum
call at the conclusion of the debate if requested
in accordance with the rules of the Senate, and
the disposition of any pending amendments
under subsection (h) of this section, the vote on
final passage of the joint resolution shall occur.

(j) Appeal from decision of Chair

Appeals from the decisions of the Chair relating to the application of the rules of the Senate
to the procedure relating to a joint resolution
described in subsection (d) of this section shall
be decided without debate.

(k) Conference reports

In the Senate, points of order under titles III
and IV of the Congressional Budget Act of 1974
[2 U.S.C. 631 et seq., 651 et seq.] (including points
of order under sections 302(c), 303(a), 306, and
401(b)(1) [2 U.S.C. 633(c), 634(a), 637, 651(b)(1)]) are
applicable to a conference report on the joint
resolution or any amendments in disagreement
thereto.

(*l*) Resolution from other House

If, before the passage by the Senate of a joint
resolution of the Senate introduced under subsection (d) of this section, the Senate receives
from the House of Representatives a joint resolution introduced under subsection (d) of this
section, then the following procedures shall
apply:

(1) The joint resolution of the House of Representatives shall not be referred to a committee.

(2) With respect to a joint resolution introduced under subsection (d) of this section in
the Senate—

(A) the procedure in the Senate shall be
the same as if no joint resolution had been
received from the House; but

(B)(i) the vote on final passage shall be on
the joint resolution of the House if it is identical to the joint resolution then pending for
passage in the Senate; or

(ii) if the joint resolution from the House
is not identical to the joint resolution then
pending for passage in the Senate and the
Senate then passes the Senate joint resolution, the Senate shall be considered to have
passed the House joint resolution as amended by the text of the Senate joint resolution.

(3) Upon disposition of the joint resolution
received from the House, it shall no longer be
in order to consider the joint resolution originated in the Senate.

(m) Senate action on House resolution

If the Senate receives from the House of Representatives a joint resolution introduced under
subsection (d) of this section after the Senate
has disposed of a Senate originated joint resolu-

tion which is identical to the House passed joint resolution, the action of the Senate with regard to the disposition of the Senate originated joint resolution shall be deemed to be the action of the Senate with regard to the House originated joint resolution. If it is not identical to the House passed joint resolution, then the Senate shall be considered to have passed the joint resolution of the House as amended by the text of the Senate joint resolution.

(Pub. L. 99–177, title II, § 258B, as added Pub. L. 101–508, title XIII, § 13101(g), Nov. 5, 1990, 104 Stat. 1388–597.)

TERMINATION OF SECTION

For termination of section by section 275(b) of Pub. L. 99–177, as amended, see Effective and Termination Dates note set out under section 900 of this title.

REFERENCES IN TEXT

Section 258B, referred to in subsec. (e)(1), (2), means section 258B of Pub. L. 99–177, which is classified to this section.

The Congressional Budget Act of 1974, referred to in subsec. (k), is titles I to IX of Pub. L. 93–344, July 12, 1974, 88 Stat. 297, as amended. Titles III and IV of the Act are classified generally to subchapters I (§ 631 et seq.) and II (§ 651 et seq.) of chapter 17A of this title. For complete classification of this Act to the Code, see Short Title note set out under section 621 of this title and Tables.

§ 907d. Special reconciliation process

(a) Reporting of resolutions and reconciliation bills and resolutions, in Senate

(1) Committee alternatives to Presidential order

After the submission of an OMB sequestration update report under section 904 of this title that envisions a sequestration under section 902 or 903 of this title, each standing committee of the Senate may, not later than October 10, submit to the Committee on the Budget of the Senate information of the type described in section 632(d) of this title with respect to alternatives to the order envisioned by such report insofar as such order affects laws within the jurisdiction of the committee.

(2) Initial Budget Committee action

After the submission of such a report, the Committee on the Budget of the Senate may, not later than October 15, report to the Senate a resolution. The resolution may affirm the impact of the order envisioned by such report, in whole or in part. To the extent that any part is not affirmed, the resolution shall state which parts are not affirmed and shall contain instructions to committees of the Senate of the type referred to in section 641(a) of this title, sufficient to achieve at least the total level of deficit reduction contained in those sections which are not affirmed.

(3) Response of committees

Committees instructed pursuant to paragraph (2), or affected thereby, shall submit their responses to the Budget Committee no later than 10 days after the resolution referred to in paragraph (2) is agreed to, except that if only one such Committee is so instructed such Committee shall, by the same date, report to the Senate a reconciliation bill or reconciliation resolution containing its recommendations in response to such instructions. A committee shall be considered to have complied with all instructions to it pursuant to a resolution adopted under paragraph (2) if it has made recommendations with respect to matters within its jurisdiction which would result in a reduction in the deficit at least equal to the total reduction directed by such instructions.

(4) Budget Committee action

Upon receipt of the recommendations received in response to a resolution referred to in paragraph (2), the Budget Committee shall report to the Senate a reconciliation bill or reconciliation resolution, or both, carrying out all such recommendations without any substantive revisions. In the event that a committee instructed in a resolution referred to in paragraph (2) fails to submit any recommendation (or, when only one committee is instructed, fails to report a reconciliation bill or resolution) in response to such instructions, the Budget Committee shall include in the reconciliation bill or reconciliation resolution reported pursuant to this subparagraph legislative language within the jurisdiction of the noncomplying committee to achieve the amount of deficit reduction directed in such instructions.

(5) Point of order

It shall not be in order in the Senate to consider any reconciliation bill or reconciliation resolution reported under paragraph (4) with respect to a fiscal year, any amendment thereto, or any conference report thereon if—

(A) the enactment of such bill or resolution as reported;

(B) the adoption and enactment of such amendment; or

(C) the enactment of such bill or resolution in the form recommended in such conference report,

would cause the amount of the deficit for such fiscal year to exceed the maximum deficit amount for such fiscal year, unless the low-growth report submitted under section 904 of this title projects negative real economic growth for such fiscal year, or for each of any two consecutive quarters during such fiscal year.

(6) Treatment of certain amendments

In the Senate, an amendment which adds to a resolution reported under paragraph (2) an instruction of the type referred to in such paragraph shall be in order during the consideration of such resolution if such amendment would be in order but for the fact that it would be held to be non-germane on the basis that the instruction constitutes new matter.

(7) "Day" defined

For purposes of paragraphs (1), (2), and (3), the term "day" shall mean any calendar day on which the Senate is in session.

(b) Procedures

(1) In general

Except as provided in paragraph (2), in the Senate the provisions of sections 636 and 641 of this title for the consideration of concurrent resolutions on the budget and conference reports thereon shall also apply to the consideration of resolutions, and reconciliation bills and reconciliation resolutions reported under this paragraph and conference reports thereon.

(2) Limit on debate

Debate in the Senate on any resolution reported pursuant to subsection (a)(2) of this section, and all amendments thereto and debatable motions and appeals in connection therewith, shall be limited to 10 hours.

(3) Limitation on amendments

Section 641(d)(2) of this title shall apply to reconciliation bills and reconciliation resolutions reported under this subsection.

(4) Bills and resolutions received from the House

Any bill or resolution received in the Senate from the House, which is a companion to a reconciliation bill or reconciliation resolution of the Senate for the purposes of this subsection, shall be considered in the Senate pursuant to the provisions of this subsection.

(5) "Resolution" defined

For purposes of this subsection, the term "resolution" means a simple, joint, or concurrent resolution.

(Pub. L. 99–177, title II, § 258C, as added Pub. L. 101–508, title XIII, § 13101(g), Nov. 5, 1990, 104 Stat. 1388–600.)

TERMINATION OF SECTION

For termination of section by section 275(b) of Pub. L. 99–177, as amended, see Effective and Termination Dates note set out under section 900 of this title.

SECTION REFERRED TO IN OTHER SECTIONS

This section is referred to in sections 641, 644 of this title.

§ 908. Repealed. Pub. L. 105–33, title X, § 10210, Aug. 5, 1997, 111 Stat. 711

Section, Pub. L. 99–177, title II, § 258, as added Pub. L. 100–119, title I, § 105(a), Sept. 29, 1987, 101 Stat. 778, related to modification of Presidential order.

§ 909. Repealed. Pub. L. 101–508, title XIII, § 13212, Nov. 5, 1990, 104 Stat. 1388–621

Section, Pub. L. 100–119, title II, § 202, Sept. 29, 1987, 101 Stat. 784, prohibited counting as savings transfer of Government actions from one year to another.

SUBCHAPTER II—OPERATION AND REVIEW

§ 921. Transferred

CODIFICATION

Section, Pub. L. 99–177, title II, § 273, Dec. 12, 1985, 99 Stat. 1098, which related to revenue estimates, was redesignated as section 201(g) of Pub. L. 93–344 by section 13202(b) of Pub. L. 101–508 and is classified to section 601(f) of this title.

§ 922. Judicial review

(a) Expedited review

(1) Any Member of Congress may bring an action, in the United States District Court for the District of Columbia, for declaratory judgment and injunctive relief on the ground that any order that might be issued pursuant to section 904 of this title violates the Constitution.

(2) Any Member of Congress, or any other person adversely affected by any action taken under this title,[1] may bring an action, in the United States District Court for the District of Columbia, for declaratory judgment and injunctive relief concerning the constitutionality of this title.[1]

(3) Any Member of Congress may bring an action, in the United States District Court for the District of Columbia, for declaratory and injunctive relief on the ground that the terms of an order issued under section 904 of this title do not comply with the requirements of this title.[1]

(4) A copy of any complaint in an action brought under paragraph (1), (2), or (3) shall be promptly delivered to the Secretary of the Senate and the Clerk of the House of Representatives, and each House of Congress shall have the right to intervene in such action.

(5) Any action brought under paragraph (1), (2), or (3) shall be heard and determined by a three-judge court in accordance with section 2284 of title 28.

Nothing in this section or in any other law shall infringe upon the right of the House of Representatives to intervene in an action brought under paragraph (1), (2), or (3) without the necessity of adopting a resolution to authorize such intervention.

(b) Appeal to Supreme Court

Notwithstanding any other provision of law, any order of the United States District Court for the District of Columbia which is issued pursuant to an action brought under paragraph (1), (2), or (3) of subsection (a) of this section shall be reviewable by appeal directly to the Supreme Court of the United States. Any such appeal shall be taken by a notice of appeal filed within 10 days after such order is entered; and the jurisdictional statement shall be filed within 30 days after such order is entered. No stay of an order issued pursuant to an action brought under paragraph (1), (2), or (3) of subsection (a) of this section shall be issued by a single Justice of the Supreme Court.

(c) Expedited consideration

It shall be the duty of the District Court for the District of Columbia and the Supreme Court of the United States to advance on the docket and to expedite to the greatest possible extent the disposition of any matter brought under subsection (a) of this section.

(d) Noncompliance with sequestration procedures

(1) If it is finally determined by a court of competent jurisdiction that an order issued by

---

[1] See References in Text note below.

the President under section 904 of this title for any fiscal year—

(A) does not reduce automatic spending increases under any program specified in section 906(a) of this title if such increases are required to be reduced by subchapter I of this chapter (or reduces such increases by a greater extent than is so required), or

(B) does not sequester the amount of budgetary resources which is required to be sequestered by subchapter I of this chapter (or sequesters more than that amount) with respect to any program, project, activity, or account,

the President shall, within 20 days after such determination is made, revise the order in accordance with such determination.

(2) If the order issued by the President under section 904 of this title for any fiscal year—

(A) does not reduce any automatic spending increase to the extent that such increase is required to be reduced by subchapter I of this chapter,

(B) does not sequester any amount of new budget authority, new loan guarantee commitments, new direct loan obligations, or spending authority which is required to be sequestered by subchapter I of this chapter, or

(C) does not reduce any obligation limitation by the amount by which such limitation is required to be reduced under subchapter I of this chapter,

on the claim or defense that the constitutional powers of the President prevent such sequestration or reduction or permit the avoidance of such sequestration or reduction, and such claim or defense is finally determined by the Supreme Court of the United States to be valid, then the entire order issued pursuant to section 904 of this title for such fiscal year shall be null and void.

(e) Timing of relief

No order of any court granting declaratory or injunctive relief from the order of the President issued under section 904 of this title, including but not limited to relief permitting or requiring the expenditure of funds sequestered by such order, shall take effect during the pendency of the action before such court, during the time appeal may be taken, or, if appeal is taken, during the period before the court to which such appeal is taken has entered its final order disposing of such action.

(f) Preservation of other rights

The rights created by this section are in addition to the rights of any person under law, subject to subsection (e) of this section.

(g) Economic data and assumptions

The economic data and economic assumptions used by the Director of OMB in computing the figures specified in any report issued by the Director of OMB under section 904 of this title, shall not be subject to review in any judicial or administrative proceeding.

(Pub. L. 99–177, title II, § 274, Dec. 12, 1985, 99 Stat. 1098; Pub. L. 100–119, title I, § 102(b)(9), (10), Sept. 29, 1987, 101 Stat. 774, 775; Pub. L. 105–33, title X, § 10211, Aug. 5, 1997, 111 Stat. 711.)

REFERENCES IN TEXT

This title, referred to in subsec. (a)(2), (3), means title II (§ 200 et seq.) of Pub. L. 99–177, Dec. 12, 1985, 99 Stat. 1038, known as the Balanced Budget and Emergency Deficit Control Act of 1985. For complete classification of this Act to the code, see Short Title note set out under section 901 of this title and Tables.

AMENDMENTS

1997—Subsec. (a)(1), (3). Pub. L. 105–33, § 10211(1), substituted "section 904" for "section 902".

Subsec. (d)(1). Pub. L. 105–33, § 10211(1), substituted "section 904" for "section 902(b)" in introductory provisions.

Subsec. (d)(1)(A). Pub. L. 105–33, § 10211(2), substituted "906(a) of this title if" for "907(1) of this title to the extent that" and inserted "or" at end.

Subsec. (d)(1)(B). Pub. L. 105–33, § 10211(3), substituted "budgetary resources" for "new budget authority, new loan guarantee commitments, new direct loan obligations, or spending authority". Directory language directing the striking of "or" after the comma was executed by striking "or" after "account," and not after "activity," to reflect the probable intent of Congress.

Subsec. (d)(1)(C). Pub. L. 105–33, § 10211(4), struck out subpar. (C) which read as follows: "does not reduce obligation limitations by the amount by which such limitations are required to be reduced under subchapter I of this chapter (or reduces such limitations by more than that amount) with respect to any program, project, activity, or account,".

Subsec. (d)(2). Pub. L. 105–33, § 10211(1), substituted "section 904" for "section 902(b)" in introductory and concluding provisions.

Subsec. (e). Pub. L. 105–33, § 10211(1), substituted "section 904" for "section 902".

Subsec. (f). Pub. L. 105–33, § 10211(5), redesignated subsec. (g) as (f) and struck out heading and text of former subsec. (f) consisting of pars. (1) to (5) relating to alternative procedures for joint reports of directors.

Subsec. (g). Pub. L. 105–33, § 10211(6), substituted "figures" for "base levels of total revenues and total budget outlays, as" and "section 904 of this title" for "section 901(a)(2)(B) or (c)(2) of this title,".

Pub. L. 105–33, § 10211(5), redesignated subsec. (h) as (g). Former subsec. (g) redesignated (f).

Subsec. (h). Pub. L. 105–33, § 10211(5), redesignated subsec. (h) as (g).

1987—Subsec. (f)(1). Pub. L. 100–119, § 102(b)(9)(A), added par. (1) and struck out former par. (1) which read as follows: "In the event that any of the reporting procedures described in section 901 of this title are invalidated, then any report of the Directors referred to in section 901(a) or (c)(1) of this title shall be transmitted to the joint committee established under this subsection."

Subsec. (f)(2), (3). Pub. L. 100–119, § 102(b)(9)(B), substituted "Director of CBO" for "Directors" wherever appearing.

Subsec. (f)(5). Pub. L. 100–119, § 102(b)(9)(C), substituted "section 901(a)(2)(B) or (c)(2)" for "section 901(b) or (c)(2)".

Subsec. (h). Pub. L. 100–119, § 102(b)(10), substituted "and economic assumptions" for ", assumptions, and methodologies", "Director of OMB" for "Comptroller General" in two places, and "section 901(a)(2)(B)" for "section 901(b)".

CHAPTER 21—CIVIC ACHIEVEMENT AWARD PROGRAM IN HONOR OF OFFICE OF SPEAKER OF HOUSE OF REPRESENTATIVES

§§ 1001 to 1004. Repealed. Pub. L. 101–483, Oct. 31, 1990, 104 Stat. 1166

Section 1001, Pub. L. 100–158, § 1, Nov. 9, 1987, 101 Stat. 896, related to support for Civic Achievement Award Program in Honor of Office of Speaker of House of Representatives.

Section 1002, Pub. L. 100–158, § 2, Nov. 9, 1987, 101 Stat. 897; Pub. L. 101–118, §§ 2, 3, Oct. 17, 1989, 103 Stat. 698, related to a description of Civic Achievement Award Program conducted by Close Up Foundation, categories of awards, a national committee to advise Close Up Foundation, and participation by libraries.

Section 1003, Pub. L. 100–158, § 3, Nov. 9, 1987, 101 Stat. 897, related to audit and reporting requirements of Comptroller General and Close Up Foundation with regard to Civic Achievement Award Program.

Section 1004, Pub. L. 100–158, § 4, Nov. 9, 1987, 101 Stat. 898; Pub. L. 101–118, § 1, Oct. 17, 1989, 103 Stat. 698, related to authorization of appropriations to carry out Civic Achievement Award Program.

PREAMBLE

Preamble to Pub. L. 100–158 was repealed by Pub. L. 101–483, Oct. 31, 1990, 104 Stat. 1166.

CHAPTER 22—JOHN C. STENNIS CENTER FOR PUBLIC SERVICE TRAINING AND DEVELOPMENT

§ 1101. Congressional findings

The Congress makes the following findings:

(1) Senator John C. Stennis of the State of Mississippi has served his State and country with distinction for more than 60 years as a public servant, including service in the United States Senate for a period of 41 years.

(2) Senator Stennis has a distinguished record as a United States Senator, including service as the first Chairman of the Select Committee on Ethics, Chairman of the Committee on Armed Services, Chairman of the Committee on Appropriations, and President pro tempore of the Senate.

(3) Senator Stennis has long maintained a special interest in and devotion to the development of leadership and excellence in public service.

(4) There is a compelling need to encourage outstanding young people to pursue public service on a career basis and to provide public service leadership training opportunities for individuals serving in State and local governments and for individuals serving as employees of Members of Congress.

(5) It would be a fitting tribute to Senator Stennis and to his leadership, integrity, and years of devoted public service to establish in his name a center for the training and development of leadership and excellence in public service.

(Pub. L. 100–458, title I, § 112, Oct. 1, 1988, 102 Stat. 2172.)

SHORT TITLE

Section 111 of Pub. L. 100–458 provided that: "This subtitle [subtitle B (§§ 111–121) of title I of Pub. L. 100–458, enacting this chapter] may be cited as the 'John C. Stennis Center for Public Service Training and Development Act'."

§ 1102. Definitions

In this chapter:

(1) The term "Center" means the John C. Stennis Center for Public Service Training and Development established under section 1103(a) of this title.

(2) The term "Board" means the Board of Trustees of the John C. Stennis Center for Public Service Training and Development established under section 1103(b) of this title.

(3) The term "fund" means the John C. Stennis Center for Public Service Training and Development Trust Fund provided for under section 1105 of this title.

(Pub. L. 100–458, title I, § 113, Oct. 1, 1988, 102 Stat. 2172.)

§ 1103. Establishment of John C. Stennis Center for Public Service Training and Development

(a) Establishment

There is established in the legislative branch of the Government a center to be known as the "John C. Stennis Center for Public Service Training and Development".

(b) Board of Trustees

The Center shall be subject to the supervision and direction of a Board of Trustees. The Board shall be composed of seven members, as follows:

(1) Two members to be appointed by the majority leader of the Senate.

(2) One member to be appointed by the minority leader of the Senate.

(3) Two members to be appointed by the Speaker of the House of Representatives.

(4) One member to be appointed by the minority leader of the House of Representatives.

(5) The Executive Director of the Center, who shall serve as an ex officio member of the Board.

(c) Term of office

The term of office of each member of the Board appointed under paragraphs (1), (2), (3), and (4) of subsection (b) of this section shall be six years, except that—

(1) the members first appointed under paragraphs (1) and (2) shall serve, as designated by the majority leader of the Senate, one for a term of two years, one for a term of four years, and one for a term of six years;

(2) the members first appointed under paragraphs (3) and (4) shall serve, as designated by the Speaker of the House of Representatives, one for a term of two years, one for a term of four years, and one for a term of six years; and

(3) a member appointed to fill a vacancy shall serve for the remainder of the term for which his predecessor was appointed and shall be appointed in the same manner as the original appointment for that vacancy was made.

(d) Travel and subsistence pay

Members of the Board (other than the Executive Director) shall serve without pay, but shall be entitled to reimbursement for travel, subsistence, and other necessary expenses incurred in the performance of their duties.

(e) Location of Center

The Center shall be located at or near Starkville, Mississippi, the location of Mississippi State University.

(Pub. L. 100–458, title I, § 114, Oct. 1, 1988, 102 Stat. 2173.)

SECTION REFERRED TO IN OTHER SECTIONS

This section is referred to in section 1102 of this title.

§ 1104. Purposes and authority of Center

(a) Purposes of Center

The purposes of the Center shall be—

(1) to increase awareness of the importance of public service, to foster among the youth of the United States greater recognition and understanding of the role of public service in the development of the United States, and to promote public service as a career choice;

(2) to provide training and development opportunities for State and local elected government officials and employees of State and local governments in order to assist such officials and employees to become more effective and more efficient in performing their public duties and develop their potential for accepting increased public service opportunities; and

(3) to provide training and development opportunities for those employees of Members of the Congress who perform key roles in helping Members of Congress serve the people of the United States.

(b) Authority of Center

The Center is authorized, consistent with this chapter, to develop such programs, activities, and services as it considers appropriate to carry out the purpose of this chapter. Such authority shall include the following:

(1) The development and implementation of educational programs for secondary and postsecondary schools and colleges designed—

(A) to improve the attitude of students toward public service;

(B) to encourage students to consider public service as a career goal;

(C) to create a better understanding of the important role that people in public service have played in the growth and development of the United States; and

(D) to foster a sense of civic responsibility among the youth of the United States.

(2) The development and implementation of programs designed—

(A) to enhance skills and abilities of public service employees and elected officials at the State and local levels of government;

(B) to make such officials more productive and effective in the performance of their duties; and

(C) to help prepare such employees and officials to assume greater responsibilities in the field of public service.

(3) The development and implementation of congressional staff training programs designed to equip congressional staff personnel to perform their duties more effectively and efficiently.

(4) The development and implementation of media and telecommunications production capabilities to assist the Center in expanding the reach of its programs throughout the United States.

(5) The establishment of library and research facilities for the collection and compilation of research materials for use in carrying out the programs of the Center.

(c) Program priorities

The Board of Trustees shall determine the priority of the programs to be carried out under this chapter and the amount of funds to be allocated for such programs.

(Pub. L. 100–458, title I, § 115, Oct. 1, 1988, 102 Stat. 2173.)

SECTION REFERRED TO IN OTHER SECTIONS

This section is referred to in section 1108, 1151 of this title.

§ 1105. John C. Stennis Center for Public Service Development Trust Fund

(a) Establishment of fund

There is established in the Treasury of the United States a trust fund to be known as the "John C. Stennis Center for Public Service Development Trust Fund". The fund shall consist of amounts appropriated to it pursuant to section 1110 of this title and amounts credited to it under subsection (d) of this section.

(b) Investment of fund assets

(1) It shall be the duty of the Secretary of the Treasury to invest in full the amounts appropriated to the fund. Such investments may be made only in interest bearing obligations of the United States or in obligations guaranteed as to both principal and interest by the United States. For such purpose, such obligations may be acquired on original issue at the issue price or by purchase of outstanding obligations at the marketplace.

(2) The purposes for which obligations of the United States may be issued under chapter 31 of title 31 are hereby extended to authorize the issuance at par of special obligations exclusively to the fund. Such special obligations shall bear interest at a rate equal to the average rate of interest, computed as to the end of the calendar month next preceding the date of such issue, borne by all marketable interest bearing obligations of the United States then forming a part of the public debt, except that when such average rate is not a multiple of one-eighth of one per-

cent, the rate of interest of such special obligations shall be the multiple of one-eighth of one percent next lower than such average rate. Such special obligations shall be issued only if the Secretary determines that the purchase of other interest bearing obligations of the United States, or of obligations guaranteed as to both principal and interest by the United States or original issue or at the market price, is not in the public interest.

(c) Authority to sell obligations

Any obligation acquired by the fund (except special obligations issued exclusively to the fund) may be sold by the Secretary of the Treasury at the market price, and such special obligations may be redeemed at par plus accrued interest.

(d) Proceeds from certain transactions credited to fund

In addition to the appropriations received pursuant to section 1110 of this title, the interest on, and the proceeds from the sale or redemption of, any obligations held in the fund pursuant to section 1108(a) of this title, shall be credited to and form a part of the fund.

(Pub. L. 100–458, title I, § 116, Oct. 1, 1988, 102 Stat. 2174; Pub. L. 101–520, title III, § 313(a), Nov. 5, 1990, 104 Stat. 2282.)

CODIFICATION

In subsec. (b)(2), "chapter 31 of title 31" substituted for "the Second Liberty Bond Act" on authority of Pub. L. 97–258, § 4(b), Sept. 13, 1982, 96 Stat. 1067, the first section of which enacted Title 31, Money and Finance.

AMENDMENTS

1990—Subsec. (d). Pub. L. 101–520 amended subsec. (d) generally. Prior to amendment, subsec. (d) read as follows: "The interest on, and the proceeds from the sale or redemption of, any obligations held in the fund shall be credited to and form a part of the fund."

SECTION REFERRED TO IN OTHER SECTIONS

This section is referred to in sections 1102, 1108, 1151 of this title.

§ 1106. Expenditures and audit of trust fund

(a) In general

The Secretary of the Treasury is authorized to pay to the Center from the interest and earnings of the fund, and moneys credited to the fund pursuant to section 1108(a) of this title, such sums as the Board determines are necessary and appropriate to enable the Center to carry out the provisions of this chapter.

(b) Audit by GAO

The activities of the Center under this chapter may be audited by the General Accounting Office under such rules and regulations as may be prescribed by the Comptroller General of the United States. Representatives of the General Accounting Office shall have access to all books, accounts, records, reports, and files and all other papers, things, or property belonging to or in use by the Center, pertaining to such activities and necessary to facilitate the audit.

(Pub. L. 100–458, title I, § 117, Oct. 1, 1988, 102 Stat. 2175; Pub. L. 101–520, title III, § 313(b), Nov. 5, 1990, 104 Stat. 2282.)

AMENDMENTS

1990—Subsec. (a). Pub. L. 101–520 amended subsec. (a) generally. Prior to amendment, subsec. (a) read as follows: "The Secretary of the Treasury is authorized to pay to the Center from the interest and earnings of the fund such sums as the Board determines are necessary and appropriate to enable the Center to carry out the provisions of this chapter."

SECTION REFERRED TO IN OTHER SECTIONS

This section is referred to in section 1151 of this title.

§ 1107. Executive Director of Center

(a) Appointment by Board

(1) There shall be an Executive Director of the Center who shall be appointed by the Board. The Executive Director shall be the chief executive officer of the Center and shall carry out the functions of the Center subject to the supervision and direction of the Board. The Executive Director shall carry out such other functions consistent with the provisions of this chapter as the Board shall prescribe.

(2) The Executive Director shall not be eligible to serve as Chairman of the Board.

(b) Compensation

The Executive Director of the Center shall be compensated at the rate specified for employees in grade GS–18 of the General Schedule under section 5332 of title 5.

(Pub. L. 100–458, title I, § 118, Oct. 1, 1988, 102 Stat. 2175.)

REFERENCES IN OTHER LAWS TO GS–16, 17, OR 18 PAY RATES

References in laws to the rates of pay for GS–16, 17, or 18, or to maximum rates of pay under the General Schedule, to be considered references to rates payable under specified sections of Title 5, Government Organization and Employees, see section 529 [title I, § 101(c)(1)] of Pub. L. 101–509, set out in a note under section 5376 of Title 5.

§ 1108. Administrative provisions

(a) In general

In order to carry out the provisions of this chapter, the Center may—

(1) appoint and fix the compensation of such personnel as may be necessary to carry out the provisions of this chapter, except that in no case shall employees other than the Executive Director be compensated at a rate to exceed the maximum rate for employees in grade GS–15 of the General Schedule under section 5332 of title 5;

(2) procure temporary and intermittent services of experts and consultants as are necessary to the extent authorized by section 3109 of title 5, but at rates not to exceed the rate specified at the time of such service for grade GS–18 under section 5332 of such title;

(3) prescribe such regulations as it considers necessary governing the manner in which its functions shall be carried out;

(4) solicit and receive money and other property donated, bequeathed, or devised, without condition or restriction other than it be used for the purposes of the Center, and to use, sell, or otherwise dispose of such property for the purpose of carrying out its functions;

(5) accept and utilize the services of voluntary and noncompensated personnel and reimburse them for travel expenses, including per diem, as authorized by section 5703 of title 5;

(6) enter into contracts, grants, or other arrangements, or modifications thereof, to carry out the provisions of this chapter, and such contracts or modifications thereof may, with the concurrence of two-thirds of the members of the Board, be entered into without performance or other bonds, and without regard to section 5 of title 41;

(7) make expenditures for official reception and representation expenses as well as expenditures for meals, entertainment and refreshments in connection with official training sessions or other authorized programs or activities;

(8) apply for, receive and use for the purposes of the Center grants or other assistance from Federal sources;

(9) establish, receive and use for the purposes of the Center fees or other charges for goods or services provided in fulfilling the Center's purposes to persons not enumerated in section 1104(b) of this title;

(10) invest, as specified in section 1105(b) of this title, moneys authorized to be received under this section; and

(11) make other necessary expenditures.

(b) Omitted

(Pub. L. 100–458, title I, § 119, Oct. 1, 1988, 102 Stat. 2176; Pub. L. 101–163, title III, § 320, Nov. 21, 1989, 103 Stat. 1068; Pub. L. 101–520, title III, § 313(c), Nov. 5, 1990, 104 Stat. 2282.)

CODIFICATION

Subsection (b), which required the Center to submit an annual report to Congress on its operations under this chapter, terminated, effective May 15, 2000, pursuant to section 3003 of Pub. L. 104–66, as amended, set out as a note under section 1113 of Title 31, Money and Finance. See, also, page 143 of House Document No. 103–7.

AMENDMENTS

1990—Subsec. (a)(6) to (11). Pub. L. 101–520 struck out "and" at end of par. (6), added pars. (7) to (11), and struck out former par. (7) which read as follows: "To make other necessary expenditures including official reception and representation expenses."

1989—Subsec. (a)(7). Pub. L. 101–163 substituted "To make other necessary expenditures including official reception and representation expenses" for "make other necessary expenditures".

REFERENCES IN OTHER LAWS TO GS–16, 17, OR 18 PAY RATES

References in laws to the rates of pay for GS–16, 17, or 18, or to maximum rates of pay under the General Schedule, to be considered references to rates payable under specified sections of Title 5, Government Organization and Employees, see section 529 [title I, § 101(c)(1)] of Pub. L. 101–509, set out in a note under section 5376 of Title 5.

SECTION REFERRED TO IN OTHER SECTIONS

This section is referred to in sections 1105, 1106, 1151 of this title.

§ 1109. Authorization for appropriations

There are authorized to be appropriated such sums as may be necessary to carry out this chapter.

(Pub. L. 100–458, title I, § 120, Oct. 1, 1988, 102 Stat. 2176.)

§ 1110. Appropriations

There is appropriated to the fund the sum of $7,500,000 to carry out this chapter.

(Pub. L. 100–458, title I, § 121, Oct. 1, 1988, 102 Stat. 2176.)

SECTION REFERRED TO IN OTHER SECTIONS

This section is referred to in section 1105 of this title.

CHAPTER 22A—CENTER FOR RUSSIAN LEADERSHIP DEVELOPMENT

§ 1151. Center for Russian Leadership Development

(a) Establishment

(1) In general

There is established in the legislative branch of the Government a center to be known as the "Center for Russian Leadership Development" (the "Center").

(2) Board of Trustees

The Center shall be subject to the supervision and direction of a Board of Trustees which shall be composed of nine members as follows:

(A) Two members appointed by the Speaker of the House of Representatives, one of whom shall be designated by the Majority Leader of the House of Representatives and one of whom shall be designated by the Minority Leader of the House of Representatives.

(B) Two members appointed by the President pro tempore of the Senate, one of whom shall be designated by the Majority Leader of the Senate and one of whom shall be designated by the Minority Leader of the Senate.

(C) The Librarian of Congress.

(D) Four private individuals with interests in improving United States and Russian relations, designated by the Librarian of Congress.

Each member appointed under this paragraph shall serve for a term of 3 years. Any vacancy shall be filled in the same manner as the original appointment and the individual so appointed shall serve for the remainder of the term. Members of the Board shall serve without pay, but shall be entitled to reimbursement for travel, subsistence, and other necessary expenses incurred in the performance of their duties.

(b) Purpose and authority of the Center

(1) Purpose

The purpose of the Center is to establish, in accordance with the provisions of paragraph

(2), a program to enable emerging political leaders of Russia at all levels of government to gain significant, firsthand exposure to the American free market economic system and the operation of American democratic institutions through visits to governments and communities at comparable levels in the United States.

(2) Grant program

Subject to the provisions of paragraphs (3) and (4), the Center shall establish a program under which the Center annually awards grants to government or community organizations in the United States that seek to establish programs under which those organizations will host Russian nationals who are emerging political leaders at any level of government.

(3) Restrictions

(A) Duration

The period of stay in the United States for any individual supported with grant funds under the program shall not exceed 30 days.

(B) Limitation

The number of individuals supported with grant funds under the program shall not exceed 3,000 in any fiscal year.

(C) Use of funds

Grant funds under the program shall be used to pay—

(i) the costs and expenses incurred by each program participant in traveling between Russia and the United States and in traveling within the United States;

(ii) the costs of providing lodging in the United States to each program participant, whether in public accommodations or in private homes; and

(iii) such additional administrative expenses incurred by organizations in carrying out the program as the Center may prescribe.

(4) Application

(A) In general

Each organization in the United States desiring a grant under this section shall submit an application to the Center at such time, in such manner, and accompanied by such information as the Center may reasonably require.

(B) Contents

Each application submitted pursuant to subparagraph (A) shall—

(i) describe the activities for which assistance under this section is sought;

(ii) include the number of program participants to be supported;

(iii) describe the qualifications of the individuals who will be participating in the program; and

(iv) provide such additional assurances as the Center determines to be essential to ensure compliance with the requirements of this section.

(c) Establishment of Fund

(1) In general

There is established in the Treasury of the United States a trust fund to be known as the "Russian Leadership Development Center Trust Fund" (the "Fund") which shall consist of amounts which may be appropriated, credited, or transferred to it under this section.

(2) Donations

Any money or other property donated, bequeathed, or devised to the Center under the authority of this section shall be credited to the Fund.

(3) Fund management

(A) In general

The provisions of subsections (b), (c), and (d) of section 1105 of this title, and the provisions of section 1106(b) of this title, shall apply to the Fund.

(B) Expenditures

The Secretary of the Treasury is authorized to pay to the Center from amounts in the Fund such sums as the Board of Trustees of the Center determines are necessary and appropriate to enable the Center to carry out the provisions of this section.

(d) Executive Director

The Board shall appoint an Executive Director who shall be the chief executive officer of the Center and who shall carry out the functions of the Center subject to the supervision and direction of the Board of Trustees. The Executive Director of the Center shall be compensated at the annual rate specified by the Board, but in no event shall such rate exceed level III of the Executive Schedule under section 5314 of title 5.

(e) Administrative provisions

(1) In general

The provisions of section 1108 of this title shall apply to the Center.

(2) Support provided by Library of Congress

The Library of Congress may disburse funds appropriated to the Center, compute and disburse the basic pay for all personnel of the Center, provide administrative, legal, financial management, and other appropriate services to the Center, and collect from the Fund the full costs of providing services under this paragraph, as provided under an agreement for services ordered under sections 1535 and 1536 of title 31.

(f) Authorization of appropriations

There are authorized to be appropriated such sums as may be necessary to carry out this section.

(g) Transfer of funds

Any amounts appropriated for use in the program established under section 3011 of the 1999 Emergency Supplemental Appropriations Act (Public Law 106–31; 113 Stat. 93) shall be transferred to the Fund and shall remain available without fiscal year limitation.

(h) Effective dates

(1) In general

This section shall take effect on December 21, 2000.

(2) Transfer

Subsection (g) of this section shall only apply to amounts which remain unexpended on and after the date the Board of Trustees of the Center certifies to the Librarian of Congress that grants are ready to be made under the program established under this section.

(Pub. L. 106–554, § 1(a)(2) [title III, § 313], Dec. 21, 2000, 114 Stat. 2763, 2763A–120.)

REFERENCES IN TEXT

Section 3011 of the 1999 Emergency Supplemental Appropriations Act, referred to in subsec. (g), is section 3011 of Pub. L. 106–31, which is set out as a note below.

RUSSIAN LEADERSHIP PROGRAM

Pub. L. 106–31, title III, § 3011, May 21, 1999, 113 Stat. 93, as amended by Pub. L. 106–113, div. B, § 1000(a)(2) [title V, § 585], Nov. 29, 1999, 113 Stat. 1535, 1501A–117, provided that:

"(a) PURPOSE.—It is the purpose of this section to establish, in accordance with the provisions of this section—

"(1) a pilot program within the Library of Congress for fiscal years 1999 and 2000; and

"(2) a permanent program within the Executive agency designated by the President of the United States for fiscal years 2001 and thereafter,

to enable emerging political leaders of Russia at all levels of government to gain significant, firsthand exposure to the American free market economic system and the operation of American democratic institutions through visits to governments and communities at comparable levels in the United States.

"(b) GRANTS.—

"(1) IN GENERAL.—The head of the administering agency shall annually award grants to government or community organizations in the United States that seek to establish programs under which those organizations will host eligible Russians for the purpose described in subsection (a).

"(2) DURATION.—The period of stay in the United States for any eligible Russian supported with grant funds under this section shall not exceed 30 days.

"(3) LIMITATION.—The number of eligible Russians supported with grant funds under this section shall not exceed 3,000 in any fiscal year.

"(4) ADMINISTRATION.—

"(A) IN GENERAL.—Subject to the availability of appropriations, the head of the administering agency—

"(i) may contract with nongovernmental organizations having expertise in carrying out the activities described in subsection (a) for the purpose of carrying out the administrative functions of the program (other than the awarding of grants); and

"(ii) may, without regard to the civil service laws and regulations (or, in the case of the Librarian of Congress, any requirement for competition in hiring), appoint and terminate an executive director and such other additional personnel as may be necessary to enable the administering agency to perform its duties under this section.

"(B) WAIVER OF COMPETITIVE BIDDING.—The Librarian of Congress, after consultation with the Joint Committee on the Library of Congress, may enter into contracts under subparagraph (A)(i) to carry out the pilot program during fiscal years 1999 and 2000 without regard to section 3709 of the Revised Statutes [41 U.S.C. 5] or any other requirement for competitive contracting or the providing of notice of contracting opportunities.

"(c) USE OF FUNDS.—Grants awarded under subsection (b) shall be used to pay—

"(1) the costs and expenses incurred by each program participant in traveling between Russia and the United States and in traveling within the United States;

"(2) the costs of providing lodging in the United States to each program participant, whether in public accommodations or in private homes; and

"(3) such additional administrative expenses incurred by organizations in carrying out the program as the head of the administering agency may prescribe.

"(d) APPLICATION.—

"(1) IN GENERAL.—Each organization in the United States desiring a grant under this section shall submit an application to the head of the administering agency at such time, in such manner, and accompanied by such information as such head may reasonably require.

"(2) CONTENTS.—Each application submitted pursuant to paragraph (1) shall—

"(A) describe the activities for which assistance under this section is sought;

"(B) include the number of program participants to be supported;

"(C) describe the qualifications of the individuals who will be participating in the program; and

"(D) provide such additional assurances as the head of the administering agency determines to be essential to ensure compliance with the requirements of this section.

"(3) WAIVER.—The Librarian of Congress may waive the requirement of this subsection in carrying out the pilot program during fiscal years 1999 and 2000.

"(e) ADVISORY BOARD.—

"(1) IN GENERAL.—There is established a Russian Leadership Program Advisory Board which shall advise the head of the administering agency as to the carrying out of the permanent program during fiscal years 2001 and thereafter.

"(2) MEMBERSHIP.—The Advisory Board under paragraph (1) shall consist of—

"(A) two members appointed by the Speaker of the House of Representatives, of whom one shall be designated by the Majority Leader of the House of Representatives and one shall be designated by the Minority Leader of the House of Representatives;

"(B) two members appointed by the President pro tempore of the Senate, of whom one shall be designated by the Majority Leader of the Senate and one shall be designated by the Minority Leader of the Senate;

"(C) the Librarian of Congress;

"(D) a private individual with expertise in international exchange programs, designated by the Librarian of Congress; and

"(E) an officer or employee of the administering agency, designated by the head of the administering agency.

"(3) TERMS.—Each member appointed under paragraph (2) shall serve for a term of 3 years. Any vacancy shall be filled in the same manner as the original appointment and the individual so appointed shall serve for the remainder of the term.

"(f) REPORTING.—The head of the administering agency shall, not later than 3 months following the close of each fiscal year for which such agency administered the program, report to Congress with respect to the conduct of such program during such fiscal year. Such report shall include information with respect to the number of participants in the program and the cost of the program, and any recommendations on improvements necessary to enable the program to carry out the purposes of this section.

"(g) FUNDING.—

"(1) FISCAL YEAR 1999.—

"(A) IN GENERAL.—Of funds made available under the heading 'SENATE' under title I of the Legislative [Branch] Appropriations Act, 1999 (Public Law 105–275; 112 Stat. 2430 et seq.) [see Tables for classification], $10,000,000 shall be made available, subject to the approval of the Committee on Appropriations of the Senate, to the administering agency to carry out the program.

"(B) USE OF FUNDS AT CLOSE OF FISCAL YEAR.—Funds made available under this paragraph which are unexpended and unobligated as of the close of fiscal year 1999 shall no longer be available for such purpose and shall be available for the purpose originally appropriated.

"(2) FISCAL YEAR 2000 AND SUBSEQUENT FISCAL YEARS.—

"(A) AUTHORIZATION OF APPROPRIATIONS.—There are authorized to be appropriated to the administering agency for fiscal years 2000 and thereafter such sums as may be necessary to carry out the program.

"(B) AVAILABILITY OF FUNDS.—Amounts appropriated pursuant to subparagraph (A) are authorized to remain available until expended.

"(h) DEFINITIONS.—In this section:

"(1) ADMINISTERING AGENCY.—The term 'administering agency' means—

"(A) for fiscal years 1999 and 2000, the Library of Congress; and

"(B) for fiscal year 2001, and subsequent fiscal years, the Executive agency designated by the President of the United States under subsection (a)(2).

"(2) ELIGIBLE RUSSIAN.—The term 'eligible Russian' means a Russian national who is an emerging political leader at any level of government.

"(3) PROGRAM.—The term 'program' means the grant program established under this section.

"(4) PROGRAM PARTICIPANT.—The term 'program participant' means an eligible Russian selected for participation in the program."

CHAPTER 23—GOVERNMENT EMPLOYEE RIGHTS

§§ 1201, 1202. Transferred

CODIFICATION

Section 1201, Pub. L. 102–166, title III, § 301, Nov. 21, 1991, 105 Stat. 1088; Pub. L. 103–283, title III, § 312(f)(1), July 22, 1994, 108 Stat. 1446; Pub. L. 104–1, title V, § 504(a)(1), Jan. 23, 1995, 109 Stat. 40, which provided for short title of chapter as the "Government Employee Rights Act of 1991", provided purpose of chapter as establishing procedures to protect the rights of certain government employees with respect to their public employment, and defined "violation" for purposes of chapter, was transferred to section 2000e–16a of Title 42, The Public Health and Welfare.

Section 1202, Pub. L. 102–166, title III, § 302, Nov. 21, 1991, 105 Stat. 1088; Pub. L. 104–1, title V, § 504(a)(1), Jan. 23, 1995, 109 Stat. 40, which prohibited certain discriminatory practices affecting State employees, and provided for remedies, was transferred to section 2000e–16b of Title 42, The Public Health and Welfare.

§§ 1203 to 1218. Repealed. Pub. L. 104–1, title V, § 504(a)(2), (5), Jan. 23, 1995, 109 Stat. 41

Section 1203, Pub. L. 102–166, title III, § 303, Nov. 21, 1991, 105 Stat. 1088, related to establishment of Office of Senate Fair Employment Practices.

Section 1204, Pub. L. 102–166, title III, § 304, Nov. 21, 1991, 105 Stat. 1090, related to Senate procedure for consideration of alleged violations of employee rights.

Section 1205, Pub. L. 102–166, title III, § 305, Nov. 21, 1991, 105 Stat. 1090; Pub. L. 103–283, title III, § 312(f)(2), July 22, 1994, 108 Stat. 1446, related to counseling of Senate employees alleging violations of rights.

Section 1206, Pub. L. 102–166, title III, § 306, Nov. 21, 1991, 105 Stat. 1091, related to mediation of disputes between Senate employees and employing offices.

Section 1207, Pub. L. 102–166, title III, § 307, Nov. 21, 1991, 105 Stat. 1091, related to formal complaints by Senate employees and hearings.

Section 1207a, Pub. L. 103–50, ch. XII, § 1205, July 2, 1993, 107 Stat. 269; Pub. L. 103–211, title II, § 2001(a)–(c), Feb. 12, 1994, 108 Stat. 22, related to Settlements and Awards Reserve appropriation account.

Section 1208, Pub. L. 102–166, title III, § 308, Nov. 21, 1991, 105 Stat. 1092, related to review by Select Committee on Ethics of decisions on violations of rights of Senate employees.

Section 1209, Pub. L. 102–166, title III, § 309, Nov. 21, 1991, 105 Stat. 1093; Pub. L. 102–392, title III, § 316(a), Oct. 6, 1992, 106 Stat. 1724; Pub. L. 103–50, ch. XII, § 1204(a), July 2, 1993, 107 Stat. 268, related to judicial review of decisions regarding violations of rights of Senate employees.

Section 1210, Pub. L. 102–166, title III, § 310, Nov. 21, 1991, 105 Stat. 1094, related to resolution of complaints for violations of rights of Senate employees.

Section 1211, Pub. L. 102–166, title III, § 311, Nov. 21, 1991, 105 Stat. 1094, related to costs of attending hearings on violations of Senate employee rights.

Section 1212, Pub. L. 102–166, title III, § 312, Nov. 21, 1991, 105 Stat. 1094; Pub. L. 103–283, title III, § 312(f)(3), July 22, 1994, 108 Stat. 1446, prohibited intimidation or reprisal against Senate employees for exercising rights under this chapter.

Section 1213, Pub. L. 102–166, title III, § 313, Nov. 21, 1991, 105 Stat. 1095, related to confidentiality of proceedings under this chapter.

Section 1214, Pub. L. 102–166, title III, § 314, Nov. 21, 1991, 105 Stat. 1095, provided that this chapter was enacted as an exercise of rulemaking power of Senate.

Section 1215, Pub. L. 102–166, title III, § 316, Nov. 21, 1991, 105 Stat. 1095, related to consideration of political affiliation and place of residence in Senate employment decisions.

Section 1216, Pub. L. 102–166, title III, § 317, Nov. 21, 1991, 105 Stat. 1096, related to exclusiveness of this chapter as remedy for discriminatory practices relative to Senate employment.

Section 1217, Pub. L. 102–166, title III, § 318, Nov. 21, 1991, 105 Stat. 1096, expressed sense of Senate that legislation be enacted giving employees of other instrumentalities of Congress rights comparable to those granted in this chapter.

Section 1218, Pub. L. 102–166, title III, § 319, Nov. 21, 1991, 105 Stat. 1096, reaffirmed Senate's commitment to Rule XLII of Standing Rules of the Senate, relating to employment discrimination on basis of race, color, religion, sex, national origin, age, or state of physical handicap.

SAVINGS PROVISION

Section 504(a)(2), (5) of Pub. L. 104–1 provided in part that sections 1203 to 1218 of this title are repealed, except as provided in section 1435 of this title.

§ 1219. Repealed. Pub. L. 104–331, § 5(a), Oct. 26, 1996, 110 Stat. 4072

Section, Pub. L. 102–166, title III, § 303, formerly § 320, Nov. 21, 1991, 105 Stat. 1096; renumbered § 303 and amended Pub. L. 104–1, title V, § 504(a)(3), (4), Jan. 23, 1995, 109 Stat. 41, provided protection from discriminatory practices with respect to employment of Presidential appointees.

A prior section 303 of Pub. L. 102–166 was classified to section 1203 of this title prior to repeal by Pub. L. 104–1.

EFFECTIVE DATE OF REPEAL

Section 5(b) of Pub. L. 104–331 provided that: "This section [repealing this section and enacting provisions set out as a note below] shall take effect on October 1, 1997."

SAVINGS PROVISION

Section 5(c) of Pub. L. 104–331 provided that: "The repeal under this section [repealing this section] shall not affect proceedings under such section 303 in which a complaint was filed before the effective date of this section [Oct. 1, 1997], and orders shall be issued in such proceedings and appeals shall be taken therefrom as if this section had not been enacted."

§ 1220. Transferred

CODIFICATION

Section, Pub. L. 102–166, title III, § 304, formerly § 321, Nov. 21, 1991, 105 Stat. 1097; renumbered § 304 and amended Pub. L. 104–1, title V, § 504(a)(3), (4), Jan. 23, 1995, 109 Stat. 41, which provided for application of provisions of section 1202 to previously exempt State employees, enforcement by administrative action, judicial review, and attorney fees, was transferred to section 2000e–16c of Title 42, The Public Health and Welfare.

§ 1221. Repealed. Pub. L. 104–1, title V, § 504(a)(2), Jan. 23, 1995, 109 Stat. 41

Section, Pub. L. 102–166, title III, § 322, Nov. 21, 1991, 105 Stat. 1098, related to severability.

SAVINGS PROVISION

Section 504(a)(2) of Pub. L. 104–1 provided in part that section 1221 of this title is repealed, except as provided in section 1435 of this title.

§ 1222. Repealed. Pub. L. 102–392, title III, § 316(b), Oct. 6, 1992, 106 Stat. 1724

Section, Pub. L. 102–166, title III, § 323, Nov. 21, 1991, 105 Stat. 1098, required President or Member of Senate to reimburse appropriate Federal account for payment made on his or her behalf for violation of this chapter.

§§ 1223, 1224. Repealed. Pub. L. 104–1, title V, § 504(a)(2), Jan. 23, 1995, 109 Stat. 41

Section 1223, Pub. L. 102–166, title III, § 324, Nov. 21, 1991, 105 Stat. 1099, related to reports of Senate committees.

Section 1224, Pub. L. 102–166, title III, § 325, Nov. 21, 1991, 105 Stat. 1099, related to intervention and expedited reviews of certain appeals based on constitutionality of sections 1209 and 1219 of this title.

SAVINGS PROVISION

Section 504(a)(2) of Pub. L. 104–1 provided in part that sections 1223 and 1224 of this title are repealed, except as provided in section 1435 of this title.

CHAPTER 24—CONGRESSIONAL ACCOUNTABILITY

SUBCHAPTER I—GENERAL

SUBCHAPTER I—GENERAL

SUBCHAPTER REFERRED TO IN OTHER SECTIONS

This subchapter is referred to in section 1434 of this title.

§ 1301. Definitions

Except as otherwise specifically provided in this chapter, as used in this chapter:

(1) Board

The term "Board" means the Board of Directors of the Office of Compliance.

(2) Chair

The term "Chair" means the Chair of the Board of Directors of the Office of Compliance.

(3) Covered employee

The term "covered employee" means any employee of—

  (A) the House of Representatives;
  (B) the Senate;
  (C) the Capitol Guide Service;
  (D) the Capitol Police;
  (E) the Congressional Budget Office;
  (F) the Office of the Architect of the Capitol;
  (G) the Office of the Attending Physician;
  (H) the Office of Compliance; or
  (I) the Office of Technology Assessment.

(4) Employee

The term "employee" includes an applicant for employment and a former employee.

(5) Employee of the Office of the Architect of the Capitol

The term "employee of the Office of the Architect of the Capitol" includes any employee of the Office of the Architect of the Capitol, the Botanic Garden, or the Senate Restaurants.

(6) Employee of the Capitol Police

The term "employee of the Capitol Police" includes any member or officer of the Capitol Police.

(7) Employee of the House of Representatives

The term "employee of the House of Representatives" includes an individual occupying a position the pay for which is disbursed by the Clerk of the House of Representatives, or another official designated by the House of Representatives, or any employment position in an entity that is paid with funds derived from the clerk-hire allowance of the House of Representatives but not any such individual employed by any entity listed in subparagraphs (C) through (I) of paragraph (3).

(8) Employee of the Senate

The term "employee of the Senate" includes any employee whose pay is disbursed by the Secretary of the Senate, but not any such individual employed by any entity listed in subparagraphs (C) through (I) of paragraph (3).

(9) Employing office

The term "employing office" means—

  (A) the personal office of a Member of the House of Representatives or of a Senator;
  (B) a committee of the House of Representatives or the Senate or a joint committee;
  (C) any other office headed by a person with the final authority to appoint, hire, discharge, and set the terms, conditions, or privileges of the employment of an employee of the House of Representatives or the Senate; or
  (D) the Capitol Guide Board, the Capitol Police Board, the Congressional Budget Office, the Office of the Architect of the Capitol, the Office of the Attending Physician, the Office of Compliance, and the Office of Technology Assessment.

(10) Executive Director

The term "Executive Director" means the Executive Director of the Office of Compliance.

(11) General Counsel

The term "General Counsel" means the General Counsel of the Office of Compliance.

(12) Office

The term "Office" means the Office of Compliance.

(Pub. L. 104–1, title I, § 101, Jan. 23, 1995, 109 Stat. 4.)

REFERENCES IN TEXT

This chapter, referred to in text, was in the original "this Act", meaning Pub. L. 104–1, Jan. 23, 1995, 109 Stat. 3, as amended, which is classified principally to this chapter. For complete classification of this Act to the Code, see Short Title note below and Tables.

SHORT TITLE

Section 1(a) of Pub. L. 104–1 provided that: "This Act [enacting this chapter, amending sections 1201, 1202, 1219, and 1220 of this title, section 6381 of Title 5, Government Organization and Employees, sections 203, 633a, 2611, and 2617 of Title 29, Labor, section 166b–7 of Title 40, Public Buildings, Property, and Works, and sections 2000e–16 and 12209 of Title 42, The Public Health and Welfare, repealing sections 60m, 60n, 1203 to 1218, 1221, 1223, and 1224 of this title, and enacting provisions set out as a note under section 751 of Title 31, Money and Finance] may be cited as the 'Congressional Accountability Act of 1995'."

SECTION REFERRED TO IN OTHER SECTIONS

This section is referred to in section 1316a of this title.

§ 1302. Application of laws

(a) Laws made applicable

The following laws shall apply, as prescribed by this chapter, to the legislative branch of the Federal Government:

  (1) The Fair Labor Standards Act of 1938 (29 U.S.C. 201 et seq.).
  (2) Title VII of the Civil Rights Act of 1964 (42 U.S.C. 2000e et seq.).
  (3) The Americans with Disabilities Act of 1990 (42 U.S.C. 12101 et seq.).
  (4) The Age Discrimination in Employment Act of 1967 (29 U.S.C. 621 et seq.).
  (5) The Family and Medical Leave Act of 1993 (29 U.S.C. 2611 et seq.).
  (6) The Occupational Safety and Health Act of 1970 (29 U.S.C. 651 et seq.).
  (7) Chapter 71 (relating to Federal service labor-management relations) of title 5.
  (8) The Employee Polygraph Protection Act of 1988 (29 U.S.C. 2001 et seq.).
  (9) The Worker Adjustment and Retraining Notification Act (29 U.S.C. 2101 et seq.).
  (10) The Rehabilitation Act of 1973 (29 U.S.C. 701 et seq.).
  (11) Chapter 43 (relating to veterans' employment and reemployment) of title 38.

(b) Laws which may be made applicable

(1) In general

The Board shall review provisions of Federal law (including regulations) relating to (A) the terms and conditions of employment (including hiring, promotion, demotion, termination, salary, wages, overtime compensation, benefits, work assignments or reassignments, grievance and disciplinary procedures, protection from discrimination in personnel actions, occupational health and safety, and family and medical and other leave) of employees, and (B) access to public services and accommodations.

(2) Board report

Beginning on December 31, 1996, and every 2 years thereafter, the Board shall report on (A) whether or to what degree the provisions described in paragraph (1) are applicable or inapplicable to the legislative branch, and (B) with respect to provisions inapplicable to the legislative branch, whether such provisions should be made applicable to the legislative branch. The presiding officers of the House of Representatives and the Senate shall cause each such report to be printed in the Congressional Record and each such report shall be referred to the committees of the House of Representatives and the Senate with jurisdiction.

(3) Reports of congressional committees

Each report accompanying any bill or joint resolution relating to terms and conditions of employment or access to public services or accommodations reported by a committee of the House of Representatives or the Senate shall—

(A) describe the manner in which the provisions of the bill or joint resolution apply to the legislative branch; or

(B) in the case of a provision not applicable to the legislative branch, include a statement of the reasons the provision does not apply.

On the objection of any Member, it shall not be in order for the Senate or the House of Representatives to consider any such bill or joint resolution if the report of the committee on such bill or joint resolution does not comply with the provisions of this paragraph. This paragraph may be waived in either House by majority vote of that House.

(Pub. L. 104–1, title I, §102, Jan. 23, 1995, 109 Stat. 5.)

REFERENCES IN TEXT

The Fair Labor Standards Act of 1938, referred to in subsec. (a)(1), is act June 25, 1938, ch. 676, 52 Stat. 1060, as amended, which is classified generally to chapter 8 (§201 et seq.) of Title 29, Labor. For complete classification of this Act to the Code, see section 201 of Title 29 and Tables.

The Civil Rights Act of 1964, referred to in subsec. (a)(2), is Pub. L. 88–352, July 2, 1964, 78 Stat. 252, as amended. Title VII of the Act is classified generally to subchapter VI (§2000e et seq.) of chapter 21 of Title 42, The Public Health and Welfare. For complete classification of this Act to the Code, see Short Title note set out under section 2000a of Title 42 and Tables.

The Americans with Disabilities Act of 1990, referred to in subsec. (a)(3), is Pub. L. 101–336, July 26, 1990, 104 Stat. 327, as amended, which is classified principally to chapter 126 (§12101 et seq.) of Title 42. For complete classification of this Act to the Code, see Short Title note set out under section 12101 of Title 42 and Tables.

The Age Discrimination in Employment Act of 1967, referred to in subsec. (a)(4), is Pub. L. 90–202, Dec. 15, 1967, 81 Stat. 602, as amended, which is classified generally to chapter 14 (§621 et seq.) of Title 29, Labor. For complete classification of this Act to the Code, see Short Title note set out under section 621 of Title 29 and Tables.

The Family and Medical Leave Act of 1993, referred to in subsec. (a)(5), is Pub. L. 103–3, Feb. 5, 1993, 107 Stat.

6, as amended, which enacted sections 60m and 60n of this title, sections 6381 to 6387 of Title 5, Government Organization and Employees, and chapter 28 (§2601 et seq.) of Title 29, Labor, amended section 2105 of Title 5, and enacted provisions set out as notes under section 2601 of Title 29. For complete classification of this Act to the Code, see Short Title note set out under section 2601 of Title 29 and Tables.

The Occupational Safety and Health Act of 1970, referred to in subsec. (a)(6), is Pub. L. 91–596, Dec. 29, 1970, 84 Stat. 1590, as amended, which is classified principally to chapter 15 (§651 et seq.) of Title 29. For complete classification of this Act to the Code, see Short Title note set out under section 651 of Title 29 and Tables.

The Employee Polygraph Protection Act of 1988, referred to in subsec. (a)(8), is Pub. L. 100–347, June 27, 1988, 102 Stat. 646, as amended, which is classified generally to chapter 22 (§2001 et seq.) of Title 29. For complete classification of this Act to the Code, see Short Title note set out under section 2001 of Title 29 and Tables.

The Worker Adjustment and Retraining Notification Act, referred to in subsec. (a)(9), is Pub. L. 100–379, Aug. 4, 1988, 102 Stat. 890, which is classified generally to chapter 23 (§2101 et seq.) of Title 29. For complete classification of this Act to the Code, see Short Title note set out under section 2101 of Title 29 and Tables.

The Rehabilitation Act of 1973, referred to in subsec. (a)(10), is Pub. L. 93–112, Sept. 26, 1973, 87 Stat. 355, as amended, which is classified generally to chapter 16 (§701 et seq.) of Title 29. For complete classification of this Act to the Code, see Short Title note set out under section 701 of Title 29 and Tables.

SECTION REFERRED TO IN OTHER SECTIONS

This section is referred to in sections 1381, 1382, 1405, 1431 of this title.

SUBCHAPTER II—EXTENSION OF RIGHTS AND PROTECTIONS

SUBCHAPTER REFERRED TO IN OTHER SECTIONS

This subchapter is referred to in sections 1384, 1405, 1434 of this title.

PART A—EMPLOYMENT DISCRIMINATION, FAMILY AND MEDICAL LEAVE, FAIR LABOR STANDARDS, EMPLOYEE POLYGRAPH PROTECTION, WORKER ADJUSTMENT AND RETRAINING, EMPLOYMENT AND REEMPLOYMENT OF VETERANS, AND INTIMIDATION

PART REFERRED TO IN OTHER SECTIONS

This part is referred to in sections 1316a, 1361, 1401, 1402, 1407 of this title.

§1311. Rights and protections under title VII of Civil Rights Act of 1964, Age Discrimination in Employment Act of 1967, Rehabilitation Act of 1973, and title I of Americans with Disabilities Act of 1990

(a) Discriminatory practices prohibited

All personnel actions affecting covered employees shall be made free from any discrimination based on—

(1) race, color, religion, sex, or national origin, within the meaning of section 703 of the Civil Rights Act of 1964 (42 U.S.C. 2000e–2);

(2) age, within the meaning of section 15 of the Age Discrimination in Employment Act of 1967 (29 U.S.C. 633a); or

(3) disability, within the meaning of section 501 of the Rehabilitation Act of 1973 (29 U.S.C. 791) and sections 102 through 104 of the Americans with Disabilities Act of 1990 (42 U.S.C. 12112–12114).

(b) Remedy

(1) Civil rights

The remedy for a violation of subsection (a)(1) of this section shall be—

(A) such remedy as would be appropriate if awarded under section 706(g) of the Civil Rights Act of 1964 (42 U.S.C. 2000e–5(g)); and

(B) such compensatory damages as would be appropriate if awarded under section 1981 of title 42, or as would be appropriate if awarded under sections 1981a(a)(1), 1981a(b)(2), and, irrespective of the size of the employing office, 1981a(b)(3)(D) of title 42.

(2) Age discrimination

The remedy for a violation of subsection (a)(2) of this section shall be—

(A) such remedy as would be appropriate if awarded under section 15(c) of the Age Discrimination in Employment Act of 1967 (29 U.S.C. 633a(c)); and

(B) such liquidated damages as would be appropriate if awarded under section 7(b) of such Act (29 U.S.C. 626(b)).

In addition, the waiver provisions of section 7(f) of such Act (29 U.S.C. 626(f)) shall apply to covered employees.

(3) Disabilities discrimination

The remedy for a violation of subsection (a)(3) of this section shall be—

(A) such remedy as would be appropriate if awarded under section 505(a)(1) of the Rehabilitation Act of 1973 (29 U.S.C. 794a(a)(1)) or section 107(a) of the Americans with Disabilities Act of 1990 (42 U.S.C. 12117(a)); and

(B) such compensatory damages as would be appropriate if awarded under sections 1981a(a)(2), 1981a(a)(3), 1981a(b)(2), and, irrespective of the size of the employing office, 1981a(b)(3)(D) of title 42.

(c) Omitted

(d) Effective date

This section shall take effect 1 year after January 23, 1995.

(Pub. L. 104–1, title II, § 201, Jan. 23, 1995, 109 Stat. 7.)

CODIFICATION

Section is comprised of section 201 of Pub. L. 104–1. Subsec. (c) of section 201 of Pub. L. 104–1 amended section 633a of Title 29, Labor, and sections 2000e–16 and 12209 of Title 42, The Public Health and Welfare.

SECTION REFERRED TO IN OTHER SECTIONS

This section is referred to in sections 1331, 1408, 1415, 1432, 1435 of this title.

§ 1312. Rights and protections under Family and Medical Leave Act of 1993

(a) Family and medical leave rights and protections provided

(1) In general

The rights and protections established by sections 101 through 105 of the Family and Medical Leave Act of 1993 (29 U.S.C. 2611 through 2615) shall apply to covered employees.

(2) Definitions

For purposes of the application described in paragraph (1)—

(A) the term "employer" as used in the Family and Medical Leave Act of 1993 means any employing office, and

(B) the term "eligible employee" as used in the Family and Medical Leave Act of 1993 means a covered employee who has been employed in any employing office for 12 months and for at least 1,250 hours of employment during the previous 12 months.

(b) Remedy

The remedy for a violation of subsection (a) of this section shall be such remedy, including liquidated damages, as would be appropriate if awarded under paragraph (1) of section 107(a) of the Family and Medical Leave Act of 1993 (29 U.S.C. 2617(a)(1)).

(c) Omitted

(d) Regulations

(1) In general

The Board shall, pursuant to section 1384 of this title, issue regulations to implement the rights and protections under this section.

(2) Agency regulations

The regulations issued under paragraph (1) shall be the same as substantive regulations promulgated by the Secretary of Labor to implement the statutory provisions referred to in subsection (a) of this section except insofar as the Board may determine, for good cause shown and stated together with the regulation, that a modification of such regulations would be more effective for the implementation of the rights and protections under this section.

(e) Effective date

(1) In general

Subsections (a) and (b) of this section shall be effective 1 year after January 23, 1995.

(2) General Accounting Office and Library of Congress

Subsection (c) of this section shall be effective 1 year after transmission to the Congress of the study under section 1371 of this title.

(Pub. L. 104–1, title II, § 202, Jan. 23, 1995, 109 Stat. 9.)

REFERENCES IN TEXT

The Family and Medical Leave Act of 1993, referred to in subsec. (a)(2), is Pub. L. 103–3, Feb. 5, 1993, 107 Stat. 6, as amended, which enacted sections 60m and 60n of this title, sections 6381 to 6387 of Title 5, Government Organization and Employees, and chapter 28 (§ 2601 et seq.) of Title 29, Labor, amended section 2105 of Title 5, and enacted provisions set out as notes under section 2601 of Title 29. For complete classification of this Act to the Code, see Short Title note set out under section 2601 of Title 29 and Tables.

Subsection (c) of this section, referred to in subsec. (e)(2), amended section 6381 of Title 5, Government Organization and Employees, and sections 2611 and 2617 of Title 29, Labor.

CODIFICATION

Section is comprised of section 202 of Pub. L. 104–1. Subsec. (c) of section 202 of Pub. L. 104–1 amended section 6381 of Title 5, Government Organization and Employees, and sections 2611 and 2617 of Title 29, Labor.

SECTION REFERRED TO IN OTHER SECTIONS

This section is referred to in section 1435 of this title.

§1313. Rights and protections under Fair Labor Standards Act of 1938

(a) Fair labor standards

(1) In general

The rights and protections established by subsections (a)(1) and (d) of section 6, section 7, and section 12(c) of the Fair Labor Standards Act of 1938 (29 U.S.C. 206 (a)(1) and (d), 207, 212(c)) shall apply to covered employees.

(2) Interns

For the purposes of this section, the term "covered employee" does not include an intern as defined in regulations under subsection (c) of this section.

(3) Compensatory time

Except as provided in regulations under subsection (c)(3) of this section and in subsection (c)(4) of this section, covered employees may not receive compensatory time in lieu of overtime compensation.

(b) Remedy

The remedy for a violation of subsection (a) of this section shall be such remedy, including liquidated damages, as would be appropriate if awarded under section 16(b) of the Fair Labor Standards Act of 1938 (29 U.S.C. 216(b)).

(c) Regulations to implement section

(1) In general

The Board shall, pursuant to section 1384 of this title, issue regulations to implement this section.

(2) Agency regulations

Except as provided in paragraph (3), the regulations issued under paragraph (1) shall be the same as substantive regulations promulgated by the Secretary of Labor to implement the statutory provisions referred to in subsection (a) of this section except insofar as the Board may determine, for good cause shown and stated together with the regulation, that a modification of such regulations would be more effective for the implementation of the rights and protections under this section.

(3) Irregular work schedules

The Board shall issue regulations for covered employees whose work schedules directly depend on the schedule of the House of Representatives or the Senate that shall be comparable to the provisions in the Fair Labor Standards Act of 1938 [29 U.S.C. 201 et seq.] that apply to employees who have irregular work schedules.

(4) Law enforcement

Law enforcement personnel of the Capitol Police who are subject to the exemption under section 7(k) of the Fair Labor Standards Act of 1938 (29 U.S.C. 207(k)) may elect to receive compensatory time off in lieu of overtime compensation for hours worked in excess of the maximum for their work period.

(d) Omitted

(e) Effective date

Subsections (a) and (b) of this section shall be effective 1 year after January 23, 1995.

(Pub. L. 104–1, title II, §203, Jan. 23, 1995, 109 Stat. 10; Pub. L. 104–197, title III, §312, Sept. 16, 1996, 110 Stat. 2415.)

REFERENCES IN TEXT

The Fair Labor Standards Act of 1938, referred to in subsec. (c)(3), is act June 25, 1938, ch. 676, 52 Stat. 1060, as amended, which is classified generally to chapter 8 (§201 et seq.) of Title 29, Labor. For complete classification of this Act to the Code, see section 201 of Title 29 and Tables.

CODIFICATION

Section is comprised of section 203 of Pub. L. 104–1. Subsec. (d) of section 203 of Pub. L. 104–1 amended section 203 of Title 29, Labor.

AMENDMENTS

1996—Subsec. (a)(3). Pub. L. 104–197, §312(a), inserted "and in subsection (c)(4) of this section" after "subsection (c)(3) of this section".

Subsec. (c)(4). Pub. L. 104–197, §312(b), added par. (4).

§1314. Rights and protections under Employee Polygraph Protection Act of 1988

(a) Polygraph practices prohibited

(1) In general

No employing office, irrespective of whether a covered employee works in that employing office, may require a covered employee to take a lie detector test where such a test would be prohibited if required by an employer under paragraph (1), (2), or (3) of section 3 of the Employee Polygraph Protection Act of 1988 (29 U.S.C. 2002(1), (2), or (3)). In addition, the waiver provisions of section 6(d) of such Act (29 U.S.C. 2005(d)) shall apply to covered employees.

(2) Definitions

For purposes of this section, the term "covered employee" shall include employees of the General Accounting Office and the Library of Congress and the term "employing office" shall include the General Accounting Office and the Library of Congress.

(3) Capitol Police

Nothing in this section shall preclude the Capitol Police from using lie detector tests in accordance with regulations under subsection (c) of this section.

(b) Remedy

The remedy for a violation of subsection (a) of this section shall be such remedy as would be appropriate if awarded under section 6(c)(1) of the Employee Polygraph Protection Act of 1988 (29 U.S.C. 2005(c)(1)).

(c) Regulations to implement section

(1) In general

The Board shall, pursuant to section 1384 of this title, issue regulations to implement this section.

(2) Agency regulations

The regulations issued under paragraph (1) shall be the same as substantive regulations promulgated by the Secretary of Labor to implement the statutory provisions referred to in subsections (a) and (b) of this section except insofar as the Board may determine, for good cause shown and stated together with the regulation, that a modification of such regulations would be more effective for the implementation of the rights and protections under this section.

(d) Effective date

(1) In general

Except as provided in paragraph (2), subsections (a) and (b) of this section shall be effective 1 year after January 23, 1995.

(2) General Accounting Office and Library of Congress

This section shall be effective with respect to the General Accounting Office and the Library of Congress 1 year after transmission to the Congress of the study under section 1371 of this title.

(Pub. L. 104–1, title II, § 204, Jan. 23, 1995, 109 Stat. 10.)

§ 1315. Rights and protections under Worker Adjustment and Retraining Notification Act

(a) Worker adjustment and retraining notification rights

(1) In general

No employing office shall be closed or a mass layoff ordered within the meaning of section 3 of the Worker Adjustment and Retraining Notification Act (29 U.S.C. 2102) until the end of a 60-day period after the employing office serves written notice of such prospective closing or layoff to representatives of covered employees or, if there are no representatives, to covered employees.

(2) Definitions

For purposes of this section, the term "covered employee" shall include employees of the General Accounting Office and the Library of Congress and the term "employing office" shall include the General Accounting Office and the Library of Congress.

(b) Remedy

The remedy for a violation of subsection (a) of this section shall be such remedy as would be appropriate if awarded under paragraphs (1), (2), and (4) of section 5(a) of the Worker Adjustment and Retraining Notification Act (29 U.S.C. 2104(a)(1), (2), and (4)).

(c) Regulations to implement section

(1) In general

The Board shall, pursuant to section 1384 of this title, issue regulations to implement this section.

(2) Agency regulations

The regulations issued under paragraph (1) shall be the same as substantive regulations promulgated by the Secretary of Labor to implement the statutory provisions referred to in subsection (a) of this section except insofar as the Board may determine, for good cause shown and stated together with the regula-

tion, that a modification of such regulations would be more effective for the implementation of the rights and protections under this section.

(d) Effective date

(1) In general

Except as provided in paragraph (2), subsections (a) and (b) of this section shall be effective 1 year after January 23, 1995.

(2) General Accounting Office and Library of Congress

This section shall be effective with respect to the General Accounting Office and the Library of Congress 1 year after transmission to the Congress of the study under section 1371 of this title.

(Pub. L. 104–1, title II, § 205, Jan. 23, 1995, 109 Stat. 11.)

§ 1316. Rights and protections relating to veterans' employment and reemployment

(a) Employment and reemployment rights of members of uniformed services

(1) In general

It shall be unlawful for an employing office to—

(A) discriminate, within the meaning of subsections (a) and (b) of section 4311 of title 38, against an eligible employee;

(B) deny to an eligible employee reemployment rights within the meaning of sections 4312 and 4313 of title 38; or

(C) deny to an eligible employee benefits within the meaning of sections 4316, 4317, and 4318 of title 38.

(2) Definitions

For purposes of this section—

(A) the term "eligible employee" means a covered employee performing service in the uniformed services, within the meaning of section 4303(13) of title 38, whose service has not been terminated upon occurrence of any of the events enumerated in section 4304 of title 38,

(B) the term "covered employee" includes employees of the General Accounting Office and the Library of Congress, and

(C) the term "employing office" includes the General Accounting Office and the Library of Congress.

(b) Remedy

The remedy for a violation of subsection (a) of this section shall be such remedy as would be appropriate if awarded under paragraphs (1), (2)(A), and (3) of section 4323(c) of title 38.

(c) Regulations to implement section

(1) In general

The Board shall, pursuant to section 1384 of this title, issue regulations to implement this section.

(2) Agency regulations

The regulations issued under paragraph (1) shall be the same as substantive regulations promulgated by the Secretary of Labor to implement the statutory provisions referred to in subsection (a) of this section except to the extent that the Board may determine, for good cause shown and stated together with the regulation, that a modification of such regulations would be more effective for the implementation of the rights and protections under this section.

(d) Effective date

(1) In general

Except as provided in paragraph (2), subsections (a) and (b) of this section shall be effective 1 year after January 23, 1995.

(2) General Accounting Office and Library of Congress

This section shall be effective with respect to the General Accounting Office and the Library of Congress 1 year after transmission to the Congress of the study under section 1371 of this title.

(Pub. L. 104–1, title II, § 206, Jan. 23, 1995, 109 Stat. 12.)

SECTION REFERRED TO IN OTHER SECTIONS

This section is referred to in section 1361 of this title.

§ 1316a. Legislative branch appointments

(1) Definitions

For the purposes of this section, the terms "covered employee" and "Board" shall each have the meaning given such term by section 101 of the Congressional Accountability Act of 1995 (2 U.S.C. 1301).

(2) Rights and protections

The rights and protections established under section 2108, sections 3309 through 3312, and subchapter I of chapter 35, of title 5, shall apply to covered employees.

(3) Remedies

(A) In general

The remedy for a violation of paragraph (2) shall be such remedy as would be appropriate if awarded under applicable provisions of title 5 in the case of a violation of the relevant corresponding provision (referred to in paragraph (2)) of such title.

(B) Procedure

The procedure for consideration of alleged violations of paragraph (2) shall be the same as apply under section 401 of the Congressional Accountability Act of 1995 [2 U.S.C. 1401] (and the provisions of law referred to therein) in the case of an alleged violation of part A of title II of such Act [2 U.S.C. 1311 et seq.].

(4) Regulations to implement section

(A) In general

The Board shall, pursuant to section 304 of the Congressional Accountability Act of 1995 (2 U.S.C. 1384), issue regulations to implement this section.

(B) Agency regulations

The regulations issued under subparagraph (A) shall be the same as the most relevant substantive regulations (applicable with respect to the executive branch) promulgated to implement the statutory provisions referred to in paragraph (2) except insofar as the Board may determine, for good cause shown and stated together with the regulation, that a modification of such regulations would be more effective for the implementation of the rights and protections under this section.

(C) Coordination

The regulations issued under subparagraph (A) shall be consistent with section 225 of the Congressional Accountability Act of 1995 (2 U.S.C. 1361).

(5) Applicability

Notwithstanding any other provision of this section, the term "covered employee" shall not, for purposes of this section, include an employee—

(A) whose appointment is made by the President with the advice and consent of the Senate;

(B) whose appointment is made by a Member of Congress or by a committee or subcommittee of either House of Congress; or

(C) who is appointed to a position, the duties of which are equivalent to those of a Senior Executive Service position (within the meaning of section 3132(a)(2) of title 5).

(6) Effective date

Paragraphs (2) and (3) shall be effective as of the effective date of the regulations under paragraph (4).

(Pub. L. 105–339, § 4(c), Oct. 31, 1998, 112 Stat. 3185.)

REFERENCES IN TEXT

The Congressional Accountability Act of 1995, referred to in par. (3)(B), is Pub. L. 104–1, Jan. 23, 1995, 109 Stat. 3, as amended. Part A of title II of the Act enacted this part and amended section 6381 of Title 5, Government Organization and Employees, sections 203, 633a, 2611, and 2617 of Title 29, Labor, and sections 2000e–16 and 12209 of Title 42, The Public Health and Welfare. For complete classification of part A to the Code, see Tables.

CODIFICATION

Section was enacted as part of the Veterans Employment Opportunities Act of 1998, and not as part of the Congressional Accountability Act of 1995 which comprises this chapter.

§ 1317. Prohibition of intimidation or reprisal

(a) In general

It shall be unlawful for an employing office to intimidate, take reprisal against, or otherwise discriminate against, any covered employee because the covered employee has opposed any practice made unlawful by this chapter, or because the covered employee has initiated proceedings, made a charge, or testified, assisted, or participated in any manner in a hearing or other proceeding under this chapter.

(b) Remedy

The remedy available for a violation of subsection (a) of this section shall be such legal or equitable remedy as may be appropriate to redress a violation of subsection (a) of this section.

(Pub. L. 104–1, title II, § 207, Jan. 23, 1995, 109 Stat. 13.)

This chapter, referred to in subsec. (a), was in the original "this Act", meaning Pub. L. 104–1, Jan. 23, 1995, 109 Stat. 3, as amended, which is classified principally to this chapter. For complete classification of this Act to the Code, see Short Title note set out under section 1301 of this title and Tables.

PART B—PUBLIC SERVICES AND ACCOMMODATIONS UNDER AMERICANS WITH DISABILITIES ACT OF 1990

PART REFERRED TO IN OTHER SECTIONS

This part is referred to in section 1407 of this title.

§ 1331. Rights and protections under Americans with Disabilities Act of 1990 relating to public services and accommodations; procedures for remedy of violations

(a) Entities subject to this section

The requirements of this section shall apply to—

(1) each office of the Senate, including each office of a Senator and each committee;

(2) each office of the House of Representatives, including each office of a Member of the House of Representatives and each committee;

(3) each joint committee of the Congress;

(4) the Capitol Guide Service;

(5) the Capitol Police;

(6) the Congressional Budget Office;

(7) the Office of the Architect of the Capitol (including the Senate Restaurants and the Botanic Garden);

(8) the Office of the Attending Physician;

(9) the Office of Compliance; and

(10) the Office of Technology Assessment.

(b) Discrimination in public services and accommodations

(1) Rights and protections

The rights and protections against discrimination in the provision of public services and accommodations established by sections 201 through 230, 302, 303, and 309 of the Americans with Disabilities Act of 1990 (42 U.S.C. 12131–12150, 12182, 12183, and 12189) shall apply to the entities listed in subsection (a) of this section.

(2) Definitions

For purposes of the application of title II of the Americans with Disabilities Act of 1990 (42 U.S.C. 12131 et seq.) under this section, the term "public entity" means any entity listed in subsection (a) of this section that provides public services, programs, or activities.

(c) Remedy

The remedy for a violation of subsection (b) of this section shall be such remedy as would be appropriate if awarded under section 203 or 308(a) of the Americans with Disabilities Act of 1990 (42 U.S.C. 12133, 12188(a)), except that, with respect to any claim of employment discrimination asserted by any covered employee, the exclusive remedy shall be under section 1311 of this title.

(d) Available procedures

(1) Charge filed with General Counsel

A qualified individual with a disability, as defined in section 201(2) of the Americans with Disabilities Act of 1990 (42 U.S.C. 12131(2)), who alleges a violation of subsection (b) of this section by an entity listed in subsection (a) of this section, may file a charge against any entity responsible for correcting the violation with the General Counsel within 180 days of the occurrence of the alleged violation. The General Counsel shall investigate the charge.

(2) Mediation

If, upon investigation under paragraph (1), the General Counsel believes that a violation of subsection (b) of this section may have occurred and that mediation may be helpful in resolving the dispute, the General Counsel may request, but not participate in, mediation under subsections (b) through (d) of section 1403 of this title between the charging individual and any entity responsible for correcting the alleged violation.

(3) Complaint, hearing, Board review

If mediation under paragraph (2) has not succeeded in resolving the dispute, and if the General Counsel believes that a violation of subsection (b) of this section may have occurred, the General Counsel may file with the Office a complaint against any entity responsible for correcting the violation. The complaint shall be submitted to a hearing officer for decision pursuant to subsections (b) through (h) of section 1405 of this title and any person who has filed a charge under paragraph (1) may intervene as of right, with the full rights of a party. The decision of the hearing officer shall be subject to review by the Board pursuant to section 1406 of this title.

(4) Judicial review

A charging individual who has intervened under paragraph (3) or any respondent to the complaint, if aggrieved by a final decision of the Board under paragraph (3), may file a petition for review in the United States Court of Appeals for the Federal Circuit, pursuant to section 1407 of this title.

(5) Compliance date

If new appropriated funds are necessary to comply with an order requiring correction of a violation of subsection (b) of this section, compliance shall take place as soon as possible, but no later than the fiscal year following the end of the fiscal year in which the order requiring correction becomes final and not subject to further review.

(e) Regulations to implement section

(1) In general

The Board shall, pursuant to section 1384 of this title, issue regulations to implement this section.

(2) Agency regulations

The regulations issued under paragraph (1) shall be the same as substantive regulations promulgated by the Attorney General and the Secretary of Transportation to implement the statutory provisions referred to in subsection (b) of this section except to the extent that the Board may determine, for good cause shown and stated together with the regulation, that a modification of such regulations would be more effective for the implementation of the rights and protections under this section.

(3) Entity responsible for correction

The regulations issued under paragraph (1) shall include a method of identifying, for purposes of this section and for categories of violations of subsection (b) of this section, the entity responsible for correction of a particular violation.

(f) Periodic inspections; report to Congress; initial study

(1) Periodic inspections

On a regular basis, and at least once each Congress, the General Counsel shall inspect the facilities of the entities listed in subsection (a) of this section to ensure compliance with subsection (b) of this section.

(2) Report

On the basis of each periodic inspection, the General Counsel shall, at least once every Congress, prepare and submit a report—

(A) to the Speaker of the House of Representatives, the President pro tempore of the Senate, and the Office of the Architect of the Capitol, or other entity responsible, for correcting the violation of this section uncovered by such inspection, and

(B) containing the results of the periodic inspection, describing any steps necessary to correct any violation of this section, assessing any limitations in accessibility to and usability by individuals with disabilities associated with each violation, and the estimated cost and time needed for abatement.

(3) Initial period for study and corrective action

The period from January 23, 1995, until December 31, 1996, shall be available to the Office of the Architect of the Capitol and other entities subject to this section to identify any violations of subsection (b) of this section, to determine the costs of compliance, and to take any necessary corrective action to abate any violations. The Office shall assist the Office of the Architect of the Capitol and other entities listed in subsection (a) of this section by arranging for inspections and other technical assistance at their request. Prior to July 1, 1996, the General Counsel shall conduct a thorough inspection under paragraph (1) and shall submit the report under paragraph (2) for the One Hundred Fourth Congress.

(4) Detailed personnel

The Attorney General, the Secretary of Transportation, and the Architectural and Transportation Barriers Compliance Board may, on request of the Executive Director, detail to the Office such personnel as may be necessary to advise and assist the Office in carrying out its duties under this section.

(g) Omitted

(h) Effective date

(1) In general

Subsections (b), (c), and (d) of this section shall be effective on January 1, 1997.

(2) General Accounting Office, Government Printing Office, and Library of Congress

Subsection (g) of this section shall be effective 1 year after transmission to the Congress of the study under section 1371 of this title.

(Pub. L. 104–1, title II, §210, Jan. 23, 1995, 109 Stat. 13.)

REFERENCES IN TEXT

The Americans with Disabilities Act of 1990, referred to in subsec. (b)(2), is Pub. L. 101–336, July 26, 1990, 104 Stat. 327, as amended. Title II of the Act is classified generally to subchapter II (§12131 et seq.) of chapter 126 of Title 42, The Public Health and Welfare. For complete classification of this Act to the Code, see Short Title note set out under section 12101 of Title 42 and Tables.

Subsection (g) of this section, referred to in subsec. (h)(2), amended section 12209 of Title 42.

CODIFICATION

Section is comprised of section 210 of Pub. L. 104–1. Subsec. (g) of section 210 of Pub. L. 104–1 amended section 12209 of Title 42, The Public Health and Welfare.

SECTION REFERRED TO IN OTHER SECTIONS

This section is referred to in sections 1341, 1361, 1407, 1414, 1415, 1416, 1435 of this title.

PART C—OCCUPATIONAL SAFETY AND HEALTH ACT OF 1970

PART REFERRED TO IN OTHER SECTIONS

This part is referred to in section 1407 of this title.

§ 1341. Rights and protections under Occupational Safety and Health Act of 1970; procedures for remedy of violations

(a) Occupational safety and health protections

(1) In general

Each employing office and each covered employee shall comply with the provisions of section 5 of the Occupational Safety and Health Act of 1970 (29 U.S.C. 654).

(2) Definitions

For purposes of the application under this section of the Occupational Safety and Health Act of 1970 [29 U.S.C. 651 et seq.]—

(A) the term "employer" as used in such Act means an employing office;

(B) the term "employee" as used in such Act means a covered employee;

(C) the term "employing office" includes the General Accounting Office, the Library of Congress, and any entity listed in subsection (a) of section 1331 of this title that is responsible for correcting a violation of this section, irrespective of whether the entity has an employment relationship with any covered employee in any employing office in which such a violation occurs; and

(D) the term "employee" includes employees of the General Accounting Office and the Library of Congress.

(b) Remedy

The remedy for a violation of subsection (a) of this section shall be an order to correct the violation, including such order as would be appropriate if issued under section 13(a) of the Occupational Safety and Health Act of 1970 (29 U.S.C. 662(a)).

(c) Procedures

(1) Requests for inspections

Upon written request of any employing office or covered employee, the General Counsel shall exercise the authorities granted to the Secretary of Labor by subsections (a), (d), (e), and (f) of section 8 of the Occupational Safety and Health Act of 1970 (29 U.S.C. 657(a), (d), (e), and (f)) to inspect and investigate places of employment under the jurisdiction of employing offices.

(2) Citations, notices, and notifications

For purposes of this section, the General Counsel shall exercise the authorities granted to the Secretary of Labor in sections 9 and 10 of the Occupational Safety and Health Act of 1970 (29 U.S.C. 658 and 659), to issue—

(A) a citation or notice to any employing office responsible for correcting a violation of subsection (a) of this section; or

(B) a notification to any employing office that the General Counsel believes has failed to correct a violation for which a citation has been issued within the period permitted for its correction.

(3) Hearings and review

If after issuing a citation or notification, the General Counsel determines that a violation has not been corrected, the General Counsel may file a complaint with the Office against the employing office named in the citation or notification. The complaint shall be submitted to a hearing officer for decision pursuant to subsections (b) through (h) of section 1405 of this title, subject to review by the Board pursuant to section 1406 of this title.

(4) Variance procedures

An employing office may request from the Board an order granting a variance from a standard made applicable by this section. For the purposes of this section, the Board shall exercise the authorities granted to the Secretary of Labor in sections 6(b)(6) and 6(d) of the Occupational Safety and Health Act of 1970 (29 U.S.C. 655(b)(6) and 655(d)) to act on any employing office's request for a variance. The Board shall refer the matter to a hearing officer pursuant to subsections (b) through (h) of section 1405 of this title, subject to review by the Board pursuant to section 1406 of this title.

(5) Judicial review

The General Counsel or employing office aggrieved by a final decision of the Board under paragraph (3) or (4), may file a petition for review with the United States Court of Appeals for the Federal Circuit pursuant to section 1407 of this title.

(6) Compliance date

If new appropriated funds are necessary to correct a violation of subsection (a) of this section for which a citation is issued, or to comply with an order requiring correction of such a violation, correction or compliance shall take place as soon as possible, but not later than the end of the fiscal year following the fiscal year in which the citation is issued or the order requiring correction becomes final and not subject to further review.

(d) Regulations to implement section

(1) In general

The Board shall, pursuant to section 1384 of this title, issue regulations to implement this section.

(2) Agency regulations

The regulations issued under paragraph (1) shall be the same as substantive regulations promulgated by the Secretary of Labor to implement the statutory provisions referred to in subsection (a) of this section except to the extent that the Board may determine, for good cause shown and stated together with the regulation, that a modification of such regulations would be more effective for the implementation of the rights and protections under this section.

(3) Employing office responsible for correction

The regulations issued under paragraph (1) shall include a method of identifying, for purposes of this section and for different categories of violations of subsection (a) of this section, the employing office responsible for correction of a particular violation.

(e) Periodic inspections; report to Congress

(1) Periodic inspections

On a regular basis, and at least once each Congress, the General Counsel, exercising the same authorities of the Secretary of Labor as under subsection (c)(1) of this section, shall conduct periodic inspections of all facilities of the House of Representatives, the Senate, the Capitol Guide Service, the Capitol Police, the Congressional Budget Office, the Office of the Architect of the Capitol, the Office of the Attending Physician, the Office of Compliance, the Office of Technology Assessment, the Library of Congress, and the General Accounting Office to report on compliance with subsection (a) of this section.

(2) Report

On the basis of each periodic inspection, the General Counsel shall prepare and submit a report—

(A) to the Speaker of the House of Representatives, the President pro tempore of the Senate, and the Office of the Architect of the Capitol or other employing office responsible for correcting the violation of this section uncovered by such inspection, and

(B) containing the results of the periodic inspection, identifying the employing office responsible for correcting the violation of this section uncovered by such inspection, describing any steps necessary to correct any violation of this section, and assessing any risks to employee health and safety associated with any violation.

(3) Action after report

If a report identifies any violation of this section, the General Counsel shall issue a citation or notice in accordance with subsection (c)(2)(A) of this section.

(4) Detailed personnel

The Secretary of Labor may, on request of the Executive Director, detail to the Office such personnel as may be necessary to advise and assist the Office in carrying out its duties under this section.

(f) Initial period for study and corrective action

The period from January 23, 1995, until December 31, 1996, shall be available to the Office of the Architect of the Capitol and other employing offices to identify any violations of subsection (a) of this section, to determine the costs of compliance, and to take any necessary corrective action to abate any violations. The Office shall assist the Office of the Architect of the Capitol and other employing offices by arranging for inspections and other technical assistance at their request. Prior to July 1, 1996, the General Counsel shall conduct a thorough inspection under subsection (e)(1) of this section and shall submit the report under subsection (e)(2) of this section for the One Hundred Fourth Congress.

(g) Effective date

(1) In general

Except as provided in paragraph (2), subsections (a), (b), (c), and (e)(3) of this section shall be effective on January 1, 1997.

(2) General Accounting Office and Library of Congress

This section shall be effective with respect to the General Accounting Office and the Library of Congress 1 year after transmission to the Congress of the study under section 1371 of this title.

(Pub. L. 104–1, title II, §215, Jan. 23, 1995, 109 Stat. 16.)

REFERENCES IN TEXT

The Occupational Safety and Health Act of 1970, referred to in subsec. (a)(2), is Pub. L. 91–596, Dec. 29, 1970, 84 Stat. 1590, as amended, which is classified principally to chapter 15 (§651 et seq.) of Title 29, Labor. For complete classification of this Act to the Code, see Short Title note set out under section 651 of Title 29 and Tables.

SECTION REFERRED TO IN OTHER SECTIONS

This section is referred to in sections 1407, 1414, 1415, 1416 of this title.

PART D—LABOR-MANAGEMENT RELATIONS

PART REFERRED TO IN OTHER SECTIONS

This part is referred to in section 1407 of this title.

§1351. Application of chapter 71 of title 5 relating to Federal service labor-management relations; procedures for remedy of violations

(a) Labor-management rights

(1) In general

The rights, protections, and responsibilities established under sections 7102, 7106, 7111 through 7117, 7119 through 7122, and 7131 of title 5 shall apply to employing offices and to covered employees and representatives of those employees.

(2) "Agency" defined

For purposes of the application under this section of the sections referred to in paragraph (1), the term "agency" shall be deemed to include an employing office.

(b) Remedy

The remedy for a violation of subsection (a) of this section shall be such remedy, including a remedy under section 7118(a)(7) of title 5, as would be appropriate if awarded by the Federal Labor Relations Authority to remedy a violation of any provision made applicable by subsection (a) of this section.

(c) Authorities and procedures for implementation and enforcement

(1) General authorities of Board; petitions

For purposes of this section and except as otherwise provided in this section, the Board shall exercise the authorities of the Federal Labor Relations Authority under sections 7105, 7111, 7112, 7113, 7115, 7117, 7118, and 7122 of title 5 and of the President under section 7103(b) of title 5. For purposes of this section, any petition or other submission that, under chapter 71 of title 5, would be submitted to the Federal Labor Relations Authority shall, if brought under this section, be submitted to the Board. The Board shall refer any matter under this paragraph to a hearing officer for decision pursuant to subsections (b) through (h) of section 1405 of this title, subject to review by the Board pursuant to section 1406 of this title. The Board may direct that the General Counsel carry out the Board's investigative authorities under this paragraph.

(2) General authorities of the General Counsel; charges of unfair labor practice

For purposes of this section and except as otherwise provided in this section, the General Counsel shall exercise the authorities of the General Counsel of the Federal Labor Relations Authority under sections 7104 and 7118 of title 5. For purposes of this section, any charge or other submission that, under chapter 71 of title 5, would be submitted to the General Counsel of the Federal Labor Relations Authority shall, if brought under this section, be submitted to the General Counsel. If any person charges an employing office or a labor organization with having engaged in or engaging in an unfair labor practice and makes such charge within 180 days of the occurrence of the alleged unfair labor practice, the General Counsel shall investigate the charge and may file a complaint with the Office. The complaint shall be submitted to a hearing officer for decision pursuant to subsections (b) through (h) of section 1405 of this title, subject to review by the Board pursuant to section 1406 of this title.

(3) Judicial review

Except for matters referred to in paragraphs (1) and (2) of section 7123(a) of title 5, the General Counsel or the respondent to the complaint, if aggrieved by a final decision of the Board under paragraph (1) or (2) of this subsection, may file a petition for judicial review in the United States Court of Appeals for the Federal Circuit pursuant to section 1407 of this title.

(4) Exercise of impasses panel authority; requests

For purposes of this section and except as otherwise provided in this section, the Board shall exercise the authorities of the Federal Service Impasses Panel under section 7119 of title 5. For purposes of this section, any request that, under chapter 71 of title 5, would be presented to the Federal Service Impasses Panel shall, if made under this section, be presented to the Board. At the request of the Board, the Executive Director shall appoint a mediator or mediators to perform the functions of the Federal Service Impasses Panel under section 7119 of title 5.

(d) Regulations to implement section

(1) In general

The Board shall, pursuant to section 1384 of this title, issue regulations to implement this section.

(2) Agency regulations

Except as provided in subsection (c) of this section, the regulations issued under paragraph (1) shall be the same as substantive regulations promulgated by the Federal Labor Relations Authority to implement the statutory provisions referred to in subsection (a) of this section except—

(A) to the extent that the Board may determine, for good cause shown and stated together with the regulation, that a modification of such regulations would be more effective for the implementation of the rights and protections under this section; or

(B) as the Board deems necessary to avoid a conflict of interest or appearance of a conflict of interest.

(e) Specific regulations regarding application to certain offices of Congress

(1) Regulations required

The Board shall issue regulations pursuant to section 1384 of this title on the manner and extent to which the requirements and exemptions of chapter 71 of title 5 should apply to covered employees who are employed in the offices listed in paragraph (2). The regulations shall, to the greatest extent practicable, be consistent with the provisions and purposes of chapter 71 of title 5 and of this chapter, and shall be the same as substantive regulations issued by the Federal Labor Relations Authority under chapter 71 of title 5, except—

(A) to the extent that the Board may determine, for good cause shown and stated together with the regulation, that a modification of such regulations would be more effective for the implementation of the rights and protections under this section; and

(B) that the Board shall exclude from coverage under this section any covered employees who are employed in offices listed in paragraph (2) if the Board determines that such exclusion is required because of—

(i) a conflict of interest or appearance of a conflict of interest; or

(ii) Congress' constitutional responsibilities.

(2) Offices referred to

The offices referred to in paragraph (1) include—

(A) the personal office of any Member of the House of Representatives or of any Senator;

(B) a standing, select, special, permanent, temporary, or other committee of the Senate or House of Representatives, or a joint committee of Congress;

(C) the Office of the Vice President (as President of the Senate), the Office of the President pro tempore of the Senate, the Office of the Majority Leader of the Senate, the Office of the Minority Leader of the Senate, the Office of the Majority Whip of the Senate, the Office of the Minority Whip of the Senate, the Conference of the Majority of the Senate, the Conference of the Minority of the Senate, the Office of the Secretary of the Conference of the Majority of the Senate, the Office of the Secretary of the Conference of the Minority of the Senate, the Office of the Secretary for the Majority of the Senate, the Office of the Secretary for the Minority of the Senate, the Majority Policy Committee of the Senate, the Minority Policy Committee of the Senate, and the following offices within the Office of the Secretary of the Senate: Offices of the Parliamentarian, Bill Clerk, Legislative Clerk, Journal Clerk, Executive Clerk, Enrolling Clerk, Official Reporters of Debate, Daily Digest, Printing Services, Captioning Services, and Senate Chief Counsel for Employment;

(D) the Office of the Speaker of the House of Representatives, the Office of the Majority Leader of the House of Representatives, the Office of the Minority Leader of the House of Representatives, the Offices of the Chief Deputy Majority Whips, the Offices of the Chief Deputy Minority Whips and the following offices within the Office of the Clerk of the House of Representatives: Offices of Legislative Operations, Official Reporters of Debate, Official Reporters to Committees, Printing Services, and Legislative Information;

(E) the Office of the Legislative Counsel of the Senate, the Office of the Senate Legal Counsel, the Office of the Legislative Counsel of the House of Representatives, the Office of the General Counsel of the House of Representatives, the Office of the Parliamentarian of the House of Representatives, and the Office of the Law Revision Counsel;

(F) the offices of any caucus or party organization;

(G) the Congressional Budget Office, the Office of Technology Assessment, and the Office of Compliance; and

(H) such other offices that perform comparable functions which are identified under regulations of the Board.

(f) Effective date

(1) In general

Except as provided in paragraph (2), subsections (a) and (b) of this section shall be effective on October 1, 1996.

(2) Certain offices

With respect to the offices listed in subsection (e)(2) of this section, to the covered employees of such offices, and to representatives of such employees, subsections (a) and

(b) of this section shall be effective on the effective date of regulations under subsection (e) of this section.

(Pub. L. 104–1, title II, § 220, Jan. 23, 1995, 109 Stat. 19.)

REFERENCES IN TEXT

This chapter, referred to in subsec. (e)(1), was in the original "this Act", meaning Pub. L. 104–1, Jan. 23, 1995, 109 Stat. 3, as amended, which is classified principally to this chapter. For complete classification of this Act to the Code, see Short Title note set out under section 1301 of this title and Tables.

SECTION REFERRED TO IN OTHER SECTIONS

This section is referred to in sections 1407, 1411, 1414 of this title.

PART E—GENERAL

§ 1361. Generally applicable remedies and limitations

(a) Attorney's fees

If a covered employee, with respect to any claim under this chapter, or a qualified person with a disability, with respect to any claim under section 1331 of this title, is a prevailing party in any proceeding under section 1405, 1406, 1407, or 1408 of this title, the hearing officer, Board, or court, as the case may be, may award attorney's fees, expert fees, and any other costs as would be appropriate if awarded under section 2000e–5(k) of title 42.

(b) Interest

In any proceeding under section 1405, 1406, 1407, or 1408 of this title, the same interest to compensate for delay in payment shall be made available as would be appropriate if awarded under section 2000e–16(d) of title 42.

(c) Civil penalties and punitive damages

No civil penalty or punitive damages may be awarded with respect to any claim under this chapter.

(d) Exclusive procedure

(1) In general

Except as provided in paragraph (2), no person may commence an administrative or judicial proceeding to seek a remedy for the rights and protections afforded by this chapter except as provided in this chapter.

(2) Veterans

A covered employee under section 1316 of this title may also utilize any provisions of chapter 43 of title 38 that are applicable to that employee.

(e) Scope of remedy

Only a covered employee who has undertaken and completed the procedures described in sections 1402 and 1403 of this title may be granted a remedy under part A of this subchapter.

(f) Construction

(1) Definitions and exemptions

Except where inconsistent with definitions and exemptions provided in this chapter, the definitions and exemptions in the laws made applicable by this chapter shall apply under this chapter.

(2) Size limitations

Notwithstanding paragraph (1), provisions in the laws made applicable under this chapter (other than the Worker Adjustment and Retraining Notification Act [29 U.S.C. 2101 et seq.]) determining coverage based on size, whether expressed in terms of numbers of employees, amount of business transacted, or other measure, shall not apply in determining coverage under this chapter.

(3) Executive branch enforcement

This chapter shall not be construed to authorize enforcement by the executive branch of this chapter.

(Pub. L. 104–1, title II, § 225, Jan. 23, 1995, 109 Stat. 22.)

REFERENCES IN TEXT

This chapter, referred to in subsecs. (a), (c), (d)(1), and (f), was in the original "this Act", meaning Pub. L. 104–1, Jan. 23, 1995, 109 Stat. 3, as amended, which is classified principally to this chapter. For complete classification of this Act to the Code, see Short Title note set out under section 1301 of this title and Tables.

Part A of this subchapter, referred to in subsec. (e), was in the original "part A of this title", meaning part A (§§ 201–207) of title II of Pub. L. 104–1, Jan. 23, 1995, 109 Stat. 7, which enacted part A of this subchapter and amended section 6381 of Title 5, Government Organization and Employees, sections 203, 633a, 2611, and 2617 of Title 29, Labor, and sections 2000e–16 and 12209 of Title 42, The Public Health and Welfare. For complete classification of part A to the Code, see Tables.

The Worker Adjustment and Retraining Notification Act, referred to in subsec. (f)(2), is Pub. L. 100–379, Aug. 4, 1988, 102 Stat. 890, which is classified generally to chapter 23 (§ 2101 et seq.) of Title 29, Labor. For complete classification of this Act to the Code, see Short Title note set out under section 2101 of Title 29 and Tables.

SECTION REFERRED TO IN OTHER SECTIONS

This section is referred to in section 1316a of this title.

PART F—STUDY

§ 1371. Study and recommendations regarding General Accounting Office, Government Printing Office, and Library of Congress

(a) In general

The Board shall undertake a study of—

(1) the application of the laws listed in subsection (b) of this section to—

(A) the General Accounting Office;

(B) the Government Printing Office; and

(C) the Library of Congress; and

(2) the regulations and procedures used by the entities referred to in paragraph (1) to apply and enforce such laws to themselves and their employees.

(b) Applicable statutes

The study under this section shall consider the application of the following laws:

(1) Title VII of the Civil Rights Act of 1964 (42 U.S.C. 2000e et seq.), and related provisions of section 2302 of title 5.

(2) The Age Discrimination in Employment Act of 1967 (29 U.S.C. 621 et seq.), and related provisions of section 2302 of title 5.

(3) The Americans with Disabilities Act of 1990 (42 U.S.C. 12101 et seq.), and related provisions of section 2302 of title 5.

(4) The Family and Medical Leave Act of 1993 (29 U.S.C. 2611 et seq.), and related provisions of sections 6381 through 6387 of title 5.

(5) The Fair Labor Standards Act of 1938 (29 U.S.C. 201 et seq.), and related provisions of sections 5541 through 5550a of title 5.

(6) The Occupational Safety and Health Act of 1970 (29 U.S.C. 651 et seq.), and related provisions of section 7902 of title 5.

(7) The Rehabilitation Act of 1973 (29 U.S.C. 701 et seq.).

(8) Chapter 71 (relating to Federal service labor-management relations) of title 5.

(9) The General Accounting Office Personnel Act of 1980 (31 U.S.C. 731 et seq.).

(10) The Employee Polygraph Protection Act of 1988 (29 U.S.C. 2001 et seq.).

(11) The Worker Adjustment and Retraining Notification Act (29 U.S.C. 2101 et seq.).

(12) Chapter 43 (relating to veterans' employment and reemployment) of title 38.

(c) Contents of study and recommendations

The study under this section shall evaluate whether the rights, protections, and procedures, including administrative and judicial relief, applicable to the entities listed in paragraph (1) of subsection (a) of this section and their employees are comprehensive and effective and shall include recommendations for any improvements in regulations or legislation, including proposed regulatory or legislative language.

(d) Deadline and delivery of study

Not later than December 31, 1996—

(1) the Board shall prepare and complete the study and recommendations required under this section; and

(2) the Board shall transmit such study and recommendations (with the Board's comments) to the head of each entity considered in the study, and to the Congress by delivery to the Speaker of the House of Representatives and President pro tempore of the Senate for referral to the appropriate committees of the House of Representatives and of the Senate.

(Pub. L. 104–1, title II, § 230, Jan. 23, 1995, 109 Stat. 23; Pub. L. 104–53, title III, § 309(a), (b), Nov. 19, 1995, 109 Stat. 538.)

REFERENCES IN TEXT

The Civil Rights Act of 1964, referred to in subsec. (b)(1), is Pub. L. 88–352, July 2, 1964, 78 Stat. 252, as amended. Title VII of the Act is classified generally to subchapter VI (§ 2000e et seq.) of chapter 21 of Title 42, The Public Health and Welfare. For complete classification of this Act to the Code, see Short Title note set out under section 2000a of Title 42 and Tables.

The Age Discrimination in Employment Act of 1967, referred to in subsec. (b)(2), is Pub. L. 90–202, Dec. 15, 1967, 81 Stat. 602, as amended, which is classified generally to chapter 14 (§ 621 et seq.) of Title 29, Labor. For complete classification of this Act to the Code, see Short Title note set out under section 621 of Title 29 and Tables.

The Americans with Disabilities Act of 1990, referred to in subsec. (b)(3), is Pub. L. 101–336, July 26, 1990, 104 Stat. 327, as amended, which is classified principally to chapter 126 (§ 12101 et seq.) of Title 42, The Public Health and Welfare. For complete classification of this Act to the Code, see Short Title note set out under section 12101 of Title 42 and Tables.

The Family and Medical Leave Act of 1993, referred to in subsec. (b)(4), is Pub. L. 103–3, Feb. 5, 1993, 107 Stat. 6, as amended, which enacted sections 60m and 60n of this title, sections 6381 to 6387 of Title 5, Government Organization and Employees, and chapter 28 (§ 2601 et seq.) of Title 29, Labor, amended section 2105 of Title 5, and enacted provisions set out as notes under section 2601 of Title 29. For complete classification of this Act to the Code, see Short Title note set out under section 2601 of Title 29 and Tables.

The Fair Labor Standards Act of 1938, referred to in subsec. (b)(5), is act June 25, 1938, ch. 676, 52 Stat. 1060, as amended, which is classified generally to chapter 8 (§ 201 et seq.) of Title 29. For complete classification of this Act to the Code, see section 201 of Title 29 and Tables.

The Occupational Safety and Health Act of 1970, referred to in subsec. (b)(6), is Pub. L. 91–596, Dec. 29, 1970, 84 Stat. 1590, as amended, which is classified principally to chapter 15 (§ 651 et seq.) of Title 29. For complete classification of this Act to the Code, see Short Title note set out under section 651 of Title 29 and Tables.

The Rehabilitation Act of 1973, referred to in subsec. (b)(7), is Pub. L. 93–112, Sept. 26, 1973, 87 Stat. 355, as amended, which is classified generally to chapter 16 (§ 701 et seq.) of Title 29. For complete classification of this Act to the Code, see Short Title note set out under section 701 of Title 29 and Tables.

The General Accounting Office Personnel Act of 1980, referred to in subsec. (b)(9), is Pub. L. 96–191, Feb. 15, 1980, 94 Stat. 27, which is classified principally to section 52–1 et seq. of former Title 31, Money and Finance, and which was substantially repealed by Pub. L. 97–258, § 5(b), Sept. 13, 1982, 96 Stat. 1068, and reenacted by the first section thereof principally in subchapters III (§ 731 et seq.) and IV (§ 751 et seq.) of chapter 7 of Title 31, Money and Finance.

The Employee Polygraph Protection Act of 1988, referred to in subsec. (b)(10), is Pub. L. 100–347, June 27, 1988, 102 Stat. 646, as amended, which is classified generally to chapter 22 (§ 2001 et seq.) of Title 29, Labor. For complete classification of this Act to the Code, see Short Title note set out under section 2001 of Title 29 and Tables.

The Worker Adjustment and Retraining Notification Act, referred to in subsec. (b)(11), is Pub. L. 100–379, Aug. 4, 1988, 102 Stat. 890, which is classified generally to chapter 23 (§ 2101 et seq.) of Title 29. For complete classification of this Act to the Code, see Short Title note set out under section 2101 of Title 29 and Tables.

AMENDMENTS

1995—Subsec. (a). Pub. L. 104–53, § 309(a), substituted "Board" for "Administrative Conference of the United States" in introductory provisions.

Subsec. (d)(1). Pub. L. 104–53, § 309(b), substituted "Board" for "Administrative Conference of the United States" and struck out "and shall submit the study and recommendations to the Board" before semicolon.

EFFECTIVE DATE OF 1995 AMENDMENT

Section 309(c) of Pub. L. 104–53 provided that: "The amendments made by this section [amending this section] shall take effect only if the Administrative Conference of the United States ceases to exist prior to the completion and submission of the study to the Board as required by section 230 of the Congressional Accountability Act of 1995 (2 U.S.C. 1371). [See provision of title II of Pub. L. 104–52, set out as a note preceding section 591 of Title 5, Government Organization and Employees.]"

SECTION REFERRED TO IN OTHER SECTIONS

This section is referred to in sections 1312, 1314, 1315, 1316, 1331, 1341 of this title.

SUBCHAPTER III—OFFICE OF COMPLIANCE

SUBCHAPTER REFERRED TO IN OTHER SECTIONS

This subchapter is referred to in section 1434 of this title.

§ 1381. Establishment of Office of Compliance

(a) Establishment

There is established, as an independent office within the legislative branch of the Federal Government, the Office of Compliance.

(b) Board of Directors

The Office shall have a Board of Directors. The Board shall consist of 5 individuals appointed jointly by the Speaker of the House of Representatives, the Majority Leader of the Senate, and the Minority Leaders of the House of Representatives and the Senate. Appointments of the first 5 members of the Board shall be completed not later than 90 days after January 23, 1995.

(c) Chair

The Chair shall be appointed from members of the Board jointly by the Speaker of the House of Representatives, the Majority Leader of the Senate, and the Minority Leaders of the House of Representatives and the Senate.

(d) Board of Directors qualifications

(1) Specific qualifications

Selection and appointment of members of the Board shall be without regard to political affiliation and solely on the basis of fitness to perform the duties of the Office. Members of the Board shall have training or experience in the application of the rights, protections, and remedies under one or more of the laws made applicable under section 1302 of this title.

(2) Disqualifications for appointments

(A) Lobbying

No individual who engages in, or is otherwise employed in, lobbying of the Congress and who is required under the Federal Regulation of Lobbying Act[1] to register with the Clerk of the House of Representatives or the Secretary of the Senate shall be eligible for appointment to, or service on, the Board.

(B) Incompatible office

No member of the Board appointed under subsection (b) of this section may hold or may have held the position of Member of the House of Representatives or Senator, may hold the position of officer or employee of the House of Representatives, Senate, or instrumentality or other entity of the legislative branch, or may have held such a position (other than the position of an officer or employee of the General Accounting Office Personnel Appeals Board, an officer or employee of the Office of Fair Employment Practices of the House of Representatives, or officer or employee of the Office of Senate Fair Employment Practices) within 4 years of the date of appointment.

(3) Vacancies

A vacancy on the Board shall be filled in the manner in which the original appointment was made.

(e) Term of office

(1) In general

Except as provided in paragraph (2), membership on the Board shall be for 5 years. A member of the Board who is appointed to a term of office of more than 3 years shall only be eligible for appointment for a single term of office.

(2) First appointments

Of the members first appointed to the Board—

(A) 1 shall have a term of office of 3 years,

(B) 2 shall have a term of office of 4 years, and

(C) 2 shall have a term of office of 5 years, 1 of whom shall be the Chair,

as designated at the time of appointment by the persons specified in subsection (b) of this section.

(f) Removal

(1) Authority

Any member of the Board may be removed from office by a majority decision of the appointing authorities described in subsection (b) of this section, but only for—

(A) disability that substantially prevents the member from carrying out the duties of the member,

(B) incompetence,

(C) neglect of duty,

(D) malfeasance, including a felony or conduct involving moral turpitude, or

(E) holding an office or employment or engaging in an activity that disqualifies the individual from service as a member of the Board under subsection (d)(2) of this section.

(2) Statement of reasons for removal

In removing a member of the Board, the Speaker of the House of Representatives and the President pro tempore of the Senate shall state in writing to the member of the Board being removed the specific reasons for the removal.

(g) Compensation

(1) Per diem

Each member of the Board shall be compensated at a rate equal to the daily equivalent of the annual rate of basic pay prescribed for level V of the Executive Schedule under section 5316 of title 5 for each day (including travel time) during which such member is engaged in the performance of the duties of the Board. The rate of pay of a member may be prorated based on the portion of the day during which the member is engaged in the performance of Board duties.

(2) Travel expenses

Each member of the Board shall receive travel expenses, including per diem in lieu of subsistence, at rates authorized for employees of agencies under subchapter I of chapter 57 of title 5, for each day the member is engaged in the performance of duties away from the home or regular place of business of the member.

(h) Duties

The Office shall—

(1) carry out a program of education for Members of Congress and other employing authorities of the legislative branch of the Federal Government respecting the laws made ap-

---

[1] See References in Text note below.

plicable to them and a program to inform individuals of their rights under laws applicable to the legislative branch of the Federal Government;

(2) in carrying out the program under paragraph (1), distribute the telephone number and address of the Office, procedures for action under subchapter IV of this chapter, and any other information appropriate for distribution, distribute such information to employing offices in a manner suitable for posting, provide such information to new employees of employing offices, distribute such information to the residences of covered employees, and conduct seminars and other activities designed to educate employing offices and covered employees; and

(3) compile and publish statistics on the use of the Office by covered employees, including the number and type of contacts made with the Office, on the reason for such contacts, on the number of covered employees who initiated proceedings with the Office under this chapter and the result of such proceedings, and on the number of covered employees who filed a complaint, the basis for the complaint, and the action taken on the complaint.

(i) Congressional oversight

The Board and the Office shall be subject to oversight (except with respect to the disposition of individual cases) by the Committee on Rules and Administration and the Committee on Governmental Affairs of the Senate and the Committee on House Oversight of the House of Representatives.

(j) Opening of Office

The Office shall be open for business, including receipt of requests for counseling under section 1402 of this title, not later than 1 year after January 23, 1995.

(k) Financial disclosure reports

Members of the Board and officers and employees of the Office shall file the financial disclosure reports required under title I of the Ethics in Government Act of 1978 with the Clerk of the House of Representatives.

(Pub. L. 104–1, title III, § 301, Jan. 23, 1995, 109 Stat. 24.)

REFERENCES IN TEXT

The Federal Regulation of Lobbying Act, referred to in subsec. (d)(2)(A), is title III of act Aug. 2, 1946, ch. 753, 60 Stat. 839, which was classified generally to chapter 8A (§ 261 et seq.) of this title prior to repeal by Pub. L. 104–65, § 11(a), Dec. 19, 1995, 109 Stat. 701. See section 1601 et seq. of this title.

This chapter, referred to in subsec. (h)(3), was in the original "this Act", meaning Pub. L. 104–1, Jan. 23, 1995, 109 Stat. 3, as amended, which is classified principally to this chapter. For complete classification of this Act to the Code, see Short Title note set out under section 1301 of this title and Tables.

The Ethics in Government Act of 1978, referred to in subsec. (k), is Pub. L. 95–521, Oct. 26, 1978, 92 Stat. 1824, as amended. Title I of the Act is set out in the Appendix to Title 5, Government Organization and Employees. For complete classification of this Act to the Code, see Short Title note set out under section 101 of Pub. L. 95–521 in the Appendix to Title 5 and Tables.

CHANGE OF NAME

Committee on House Oversight of House of Representatives changed to Committee on House Adminis-

tration of House of Representatives by House Resolution No. 5, One Hundred Sixth Congress, Jan. 6, 1999.

SECTION REFERRED TO IN OTHER SECTIONS

This section is referred to in section 1382 of this title.

§ 1382. Officers, staff, and other personnel

(a) Executive Director

(1) Appointment and removal

(A) In general

The Chair, subject to the approval of the Board, shall appoint and may remove an Executive Director. Selection and appointment of the Executive Director shall be without regard to political affiliation and solely on the basis of fitness to perform the duties of the Office. The first Executive Director shall be appointed no later than 90 days after the initial appointment of the Board of Directors.

(B) Qualifications

The Executive Director shall be an individual with training or expertise in the application of laws referred to in section 1302(a) of this title.

(C) Disqualifications

The disqualifications in section 1381(d)(2) of this title shall apply to the appointment of the Executive Director.

(2) Compensation

The Chair may fix the compensation of the Executive Director. The rate of pay for the Executive Director may not exceed the annual rate of basic pay prescribed for level V of the Executive Schedule under section 5316 of title 5.

(3) Term

The term of office of the Executive Director shall be a single term of 5 years, except that the first Executive Director shall have a single term of 7 years.

(4) Duties

The Executive Director shall serve as the chief operating officer of the Office. Except as otherwise specified in this chapter, the Executive Director shall carry out all of the responsibilities of the Office under this chapter.

(b) Deputy Executive Directors

(1) In general

The Chair, subject to the approval of the Board, shall appoint and may remove a Deputy Executive Director for the Senate and a Deputy Executive Director for the House of Representatives. Selection and appointment of a Deputy Executive Director shall be without regard to political affiliation and solely on the basis of fitness to perform the duties of the office. The disqualifications in section 1381(d)(2) of this title shall apply to the appointment of a Deputy Executive Director.

(2) Term

The term of office of a Deputy Executive Director shall be a single term of 5 years, except that the first Deputy Executive Directors shall have a single term of 6 years.

(3) Compensation

The Chair may fix the compensation of the Deputy Executive Directors. The rate of pay for a Deputy Executive Director may not exceed 96 percent of the annual rate of basic pay prescribed for level V of the Executive Schedule under section 5316 of title 5.

(4) Duties

The Deputy Executive Director for the Senate shall recommend to the Board regulations under section 1384(a)(2)(B)(i) of this title, maintain the regulations and all records pertaining to the regulations, and shall assume such other responsibilities as may be delegated by the Executive Director. The Deputy Executive Director for the House of Representatives shall recommend to the Board the regulations under section 1384(a)(2)(B)(ii) of this title, maintain the regulations and all records pertaining to the regulations, and shall assume such other responsibilities as may be delegated by the Executive Director.

(c) General Counsel

(1) In general

The Chair, subject to the approval of the Board, shall appoint a General Counsel. Selection and appointment of the General Counsel shall be without regard to political affiliation and solely on the basis of fitness to perform the duties of the Office. The disqualifications in section 1381(d)(2) of this title shall apply to the appointment of a General Counsel.

(2) Compensation

The Chair may fix the compensation of the General Counsel. The rate of pay for the General Counsel may not exceed the annual rate of basic pay prescribed for level V of the Executive Schedule under section 5316 of title 5.

(3) Duties

The General Counsel shall—

(A) exercise the authorities and perform the duties of the General Counsel as specified in this chapter; and

(B) otherwise assist the Board and the Executive Director in carrying out their duties and powers, including representing the Office in any judicial proceeding under this chapter.

(4) Attorneys in the office of the General Counsel

The General Counsel shall appoint, and fix the compensation of, and may remove, such additional attorneys as may be necessary to enable the General Counsel to perform the General Counsel's duties.

(5) Term

The term of office of the General Counsel shall be a single term of 5 years.

(6) Removal

(A) Authority

The General Counsel may be removed from office by the Chair but only for—

(i) disability that substantially prevents the General Counsel from carrying out the duties of the General Counsel,

(ii) incompetence,

(iii) neglect of duty,

(iv) malfeasance, including a felony or conduct involving moral turpitude, or

(v) holding an office or employment or engaging in an activity that disqualifies the individual from service as the General Counsel under paragraph (1).

(B) Statement of reasons for removal

In removing the General Counsel, the Speaker of the House of Representatives and the President pro tempore of the Senate shall state in writing to the General Counsel the specific reasons for the removal.

(d) Other staff

The Executive Director shall appoint, and fix the compensation of, and may remove, such other additional staff, including hearing officers, but not including attorneys employed in the office of the General Counsel, as may be necessary to enable the Office to perform its duties.

(e) Detailed personnel

The Executive Director may, with the prior consent of the department or agency of the Federal Government concerned, use on a reimbursable or nonreimbursable basis the services of personnel of any such department or agency, including the services of members or personnel of the General Accounting Office Personnel Appeals Board.

(f) Consultants

In carrying out the functions of the Office, the Executive Director may procure the temporary (not to exceed 1 year) or intermittent services of consultants.

(Pub. L. 104–1, title III, § 302, Jan. 23, 1995, 109 Stat. 26.)

§ 1383. Procedural rules

(a) In general

The Executive Director shall, subject to the approval of the Board, adopt rules governing the procedures of the Office, including the procedures of hearing officers, which shall be submitted for publication in the Congressional Record. The rules may be amended in the same manner.

(b) Procedure

The Executive Director shall adopt rules referred to in subsection (a) of this section in accordance with the principles and procedures set forth in section 553 of title 5. The Executive Director shall publish a general notice of proposed rulemaking under section 553(b) of title 5, but, instead of publication of a general notice of proposed rulemaking in the Federal Register, the Executive Director shall transmit such notice to the Speaker of the House of Representatives and the President pro tempore of the Senate for publication in the Congressional Record on the first day on which both Houses are in session following such transmittal. Before adopting rules, the Executive Director shall provide a comment period of at least 30 days after publication of a general notice of proposed rulemaking. Upon adopting rules, the Executive Director shall transmit notice of such action together with a copy of such rules to the Speaker of the House of Representatives and the President pro tempore of the Senate for publication in the Congressional Record on the first day on which both Houses are in session following such transmittal. Rules shall be considered issued by the Executive Director as of the date on which they are published in the Congressional Record.

(Pub. L. 104–1, title III, § 303, Jan. 23, 1995, 109 Stat. 28.)

§ 1384. Substantive regulations

(a) Regulations

(1) In general

The procedures applicable to the regulations of the Board issued for the implementation of this chapter, which shall include regulations the Board is required to issue under subchapter II of this chapter (including regulations on the appropriate application of exemptions under the laws made applicable in subchapter II of this chapter) are as prescribed in this section.

(2) Rulemaking procedure

Such regulations of the Board—
(A) shall be adopted, approved, and issued in accordance with subsection (b) of this section; and
(B) shall consist of 3 separate bodies of regulations, which shall apply, respectively, to—
(i) the Senate and employees of the Senate;
(ii) the House of Representatives and employees of the House of Representatives; and
(iii) all other covered employees and employing offices.

(b) Adoption by Board

The Board shall adopt the regulations referred to in subsection (a)(1) of this section in accordance with the principles and procedures set forth in section 553 of title 5 and as provided in the following provisions of this subsection:

(1) Proposal

The Board shall publish a general notice of proposed rulemaking under section 553(b) of title 5, but, instead of publication of a general notice of proposed rulemaking in the Federal Register, the Board shall transmit such notice to the Speaker of the House of Representatives and the President pro tempore of the Senate for publication in the Congressional Record on the first day on which both Houses are in session following such transmittal. Such notice shall set forth the recommendations of the Deputy Director for the Senate in regard to regulations under subsection (a)(2)(B)(i) of this section, the recommendations of the Deputy Director for the House of Representatives in regard to regulations under subsection (a)(2)(B)(ii) of this section, and the recommendations of the Executive Director for regulations under subsection (a)(2)(B)(iii) of this section.

(2) Comment

Before adopting regulations, the Board shall provide a comment period of at least 30 days after publication of a general notice of proposed rulemaking.

(3) Adoption

After considering comments, the Board shall adopt regulations and shall transmit notice of such action together with a copy of such regulations to the Speaker of the House of Representatives and the President pro tempore of the Senate for publication in the Congressional Record on the first day on which both Houses are in session following such transmittal.

(4) Recommendation as to method of approval

The Board shall include a recommendation in the general notice of proposed rulemaking and in the regulations as to whether the regulations should be approved by resolution of the Senate, by resolution of the House of Representatives, by concurrent resolution, or by joint resolution.

(c) Approval of regulations

(1) In general

Regulations referred to in paragraph (2)(B)(i) of subsection (a) of this section may be approved by the Senate by resolution or by the Congress by concurrent resolution or by joint resolution. Regulations referred to in paragraph (2)(B)(ii) of subsection (a) of this section may be approved by the House of Representatives by resolution or by the Congress by concurrent resolution or by joint resolution. Regulations referred to in paragraph (2)(B)(iii) may be approved by Congress by concurrent resolution or by joint resolution.

(2) Referral

Upon receipt of a notice of adoption of regulations under subsection (b)(3) of this section, the presiding officers of the House of Representatives and the Senate shall refer such notice, together with a copy of such regulations, to the appropriate committee or committees of the House of Representatives and of the Senate. The purpose of the referral shall be to consider whether such regulations should be approved, and, if so, whether such approval should be by resolution of the House of Representatives or of the Senate, by concurrent resolution or by joint resolution.

(3) Joint referral and discharge in the Senate

The presiding officer of the Senate may refer the notice of issuance of regulations, or any resolution of approval of regulations, to one committee or jointly to more than one committee. If a committee of the Senate acts to report a jointly referred measure, any other committee of the Senate must act within 30 calendar days of continuous session, or be automatically discharged.

(4) One-House resolution or concurrent resolution

In the case of a resolution of the House of Representatives or the Senate or a concurrent resolution referred to in paragraph (1), the matter after the resolving clause shall be the following: "The following regulations issued by the Office of Compliance on _____ are hereby approved:" (the blank space being appropriately filled in, and the text of the regulations being set forth).

(5) Joint resolution

In the case of a joint resolution referred to in paragraph (1), the matter after the resolving clause shall be the following: "The following regulations issued by the Office of Compliance on _____ are hereby approved and shall have the force and effect of law:" (the blank space being appropriately filled in, and the text of the regulations being set forth).

(d) Issuance and effective date

(1) Publication

After approval of regulations under subsection (c) of this section, the Board shall submit the regulations to the Speaker of the House of Representatives and the President pro tempore of the Senate for publication in the Congressional Record on the first day on which both Houses are in session following such transmittal.

(2) Date of issuance

The date of issuance of regulations shall be the date on which they are published in the Congressional Record under paragraph (1).

(3) Effective date

Regulations shall become effective not less than 60 days after the regulations are issued, except that the Board may provide for an earlier effective date for good cause found (within the meaning of section 553(d)(3) of title 5) and published with the regulation.

(e) Amendment of regulations

Regulations may be amended in the same manner as is described in this section for the adoption, approval, and issuance of regulations, except that the Board may, in its discretion, dispense with publication of a general notice of proposed rulemaking of minor, technical, or urgent amendments that satisfy the criteria for dispensing with publication of such notice pursuant to section 553(b)(B) of title 5.

(f) Right to petition for rulemaking

Any interested party may petition to the Board for the issuance, amendment, or repeal of a regulation.

(g) Consultation

The Executive Director, the Deputy Directors, and the Board—

(1) shall consult, with regard to the development of regulations, with—

(A) the Chair of the Administrative Conference of the United States;

(B) the Secretary of Labor;

(C) the Federal Labor Relations Authority; and

(D) the Director of the Office of Personnel Management; and

(2) may consult with any other persons with whom consultation, in the opinion of the Board, the Executive Director, or Deputy Directors, may be helpful.

(Pub. L. 104–1, title III, §304, Jan. 23, 1995, 109 Stat. 29.)

REFERENCES IN TEXT

Subchapter II of this chapter, referred to in subsec. (a)(1), was in the original "title II", meaning title II of Pub. L. 104–1, Jan. 23, 1995, 109 Stat. 7, as amended, which enacted subchapter II of this chapter and amended section 6381 of Title 5, Government Organization and Employees, sections 203, 633a, 2611, and 2617 of Title 29, Labor, and sections 2000e–16 and 12209 of Title 42, The Public Health and Welfare. For complete classification of title II to the Code, see Tables.

SECTION REFERRED TO IN OTHER SECTIONS

This section is referred to in sections 1312, 1313, 1314, 1315, 1316, 1316a, 1331, 1341, 1351, 1382, 1409, 1431 of this title.

§ 1385. Expenses

(a) Authorization of appropriations

Beginning in fiscal year 1995, and for each fiscal year thereafter, there are authorized to be appropriated for the expenses of the Office such sums as may be necessary to carry out the functions of the Office. Until sums are first appropriated pursuant to the preceding sentence, but for a period not exceeding 12 months following January 23, 1995—

(1) one-half of the expenses of the Office shall be paid from funds appropriated for allowances and expenses of the House of Representatives, and

(2) one-half of the expenses of the Office shall be paid from funds appropriated for allowances and expenses of the Senate,

upon vouchers approved by the Executive Director, except that a voucher shall not be required for the disbursement of salaries of employees who are paid at an annual rate. The Clerk of the House of Representatives and the Secretary of the Senate are authorized to make arrangements for the division of expenses under this subsection, including arrangements for one House of Congress to reimburse the other House of Congress.

(b) Financial and administrative services

The Executive Director may place orders and enter into agreements for goods and services with the head of any agency, or major organizational unit within an agency, in the legislative or executive branch of the United States in the same manner and to the same extent as agencies are authorized under sections 1535 and 1536 of title 31 to place orders and enter into agreements.

(c) Witness fees and allowances

Except for covered employees, witnesses before a hearing officer or the Board in any proceeding under this chapter other than rulemaking shall be paid the same fee and mileage allowances as are paid subpoenaed witnesses in the courts of the United States. Covered employees who are summoned, or are assigned by their employer, to testify in their official capacity or to produce official records in any proceeding under this chapter shall be entitled to travel expenses under subchapter I and section 5751 of chapter 57 of title 5.

(Pub. L. 104–1, title III, §305, Jan. 23, 1995, 109 Stat. 31.)

SUBCHAPTER IV—ADMINISTRATIVE AND JUDICIAL DISPUTE-RESOLUTION PROCEDURES

SUBCHAPTER REFERRED TO IN OTHER SECTIONS

This subchapter is referred to in sections 1381, 1434 of this title.

§ 1401. Procedure for consideration of alleged violations

Except as otherwise provided, the procedure for consideration of alleged violations of part A of subchapter II of this chapter consists of—

(1) counseling as provided in section 1402 of this title;

(2) mediation as provided in section 1403 of this title; and

(3) election, as provided in section 1404 of this title, of either—

(A) a formal complaint and hearing as provided in section 1405 of this title, subject to Board review as provided in section 1406 of this title, and judicial review in the United States Court of Appeals for the Federal Circuit as provided in section 1407 of this title, or

(B) a civil action in a district court of the United States as provided in section 1408 of this title.

In the case of an employee of the Office of the Architect of the Capitol or of the Capitol Police, the Executive Director, after receiving a request for counseling under section 1402 of this title, may recommend that the employee use the grievance procedures of the Architect of the Capitol or the Capitol Police for resolution of the employee's grievance for a specific period of time, which shall not count against the time available for counseling or mediation.

(Pub. L. 104–1, title IV, § 401, Jan. 23, 1995, 109 Stat. 32.)

REFERENCES IN TEXT

Part A of subchapter II of this chapter, referred to in text, was in the original "part A of title II", meaning part A (§§ 201–207) of title II of Pub. L. 104–1, Jan. 23, 1995, 109 Stat. 7, as amended, which enacted part A of subchapter II of this chapter and amended section 6381 of Title 5, Government Organization and Employees, sections 203, 633a, 2611, and 2617 of Title 29, Labor, and sections 2000e–16 and 12209 of Title 42, The Public Health and Welfare. For complete classification of part A to the Code, see Tables.

SECTION REFERRED TO IN OTHER SECTIONS

This section is referred to in sections 1316a, 1414 of this title.

§ 1402. Counseling

(a) In general

To commence a proceeding, a covered employee alleging a violation of a law made applicable under part A of subchapter II of this chapter shall request counseling by the Office. The Office shall provide the employee with all relevant information with respect to the rights of the employee. A request for counseling shall be made not later than 180 days after the date of the alleged violation.

(b) Period of counseling

The period for counseling shall be 30 days unless the employee and the Office agree to reduce the period. The period shall begin on the date the request for counseling is received.

(c) Notification of end of counseling period

The Office shall notify the employee in writing when the counseling period has ended.

(Pub. L. 104–1, title IV, § 402, Jan. 23, 1995, 109 Stat. 32.)

SECTION REFERRED TO IN OTHER SECTIONS

This section is referred to in sections 452, 1361, 1381, 1401, 1403, 1408, 1435 of this title.

§ 1403. Mediation

(a) Initiation

Not later than 15 days after receipt by the employee of notice of the end of the counseling period under section 1402 of this title, but prior to and as a condition of making an election under section 1404 of this title, the covered employee who alleged a violation of a law shall file a request for mediation with the Office.

(b) Process

Mediation under this section—

(1) may include the Office, the covered employee, the employing office, and one or more individuals appointed by the Executive Director after considering recommendations by organizations composed primarily of individuals experienced in adjudicating or arbitrating personnel matters, and

(2) shall involve meetings with the parties separately or jointly for the purpose of resolving the dispute between the covered employee and the employing office.

(c) Mediation period

The mediation period shall be 30 days beginning on the date the request for mediation is received. The mediation period may be extended for additional periods at the joint request of the covered employee and the employing office. The Office shall notify in writing the covered employee and the employing office when the mediation period has ended.

(d) Independence of mediation process

No individual, who is appointed by the Executive Director to mediate, may conduct or aid in a hearing conducted under section 1405 of this title with respect to the same matter or shall be subject to subpoena or any other compulsory process with respect to the same matter.

(Pub. L. 104–1, title IV, § 403, Jan. 23, 1995, 109 Stat. 32.)

SECTION REFERRED TO IN OTHER SECTIONS

This section is referred to in sections 452, 1331, 1361, 1401, 1405, 1408, 1435 of this title.

§ 1404. Election of proceeding

Not later than 90 days after a covered employee receives notice of the end of the period of mediation, but no sooner than 30 days after receipt of such notification, such covered employee may either—

(1) file a complaint with the Office in accordance with section 1405 of this title, or

(2) file a civil action in accordance with section 1408 of this title in the United States dis-

trict court for the district in which the employee is employed or for the District of Columbia.

(Pub. L. 104–1, title IV, § 404, Jan. 23, 1995, 109 Stat. 33.)

Section Referred to in Other Sections

This section is referred to in sections 1401, 1403, 1408 of this title.

§ 1405. Complaint and hearing

(a) In general

A covered employee may, upon the completion of mediation under section 1403 of this title, file a complaint with the Office. The respondent to the complaint shall be the employing office—

(1) involved in the violation, or

(2) in which the violation is alleged to have occurred,

and about which mediation was conducted.

(b) Dismissal

A hearing officer may dismiss any claim that the hearing officer finds to be frivolous or that fails to state a claim upon which relief may be granted.

(c) Hearing officer

(1) Appointment

Upon the filing of a complaint, the Executive Director shall appoint an independent hearing officer to consider the complaint and render a decision. No Member of the House of Representatives, Senator, officer of either the House of Representatives or the Senate, head of an employing office, member of the Board, or covered employee may be appointed to be a hearing officer. The Executive Director shall select hearing officers on a rotational or random basis from the lists developed under paragraph (2). Nothing in this section shall prevent the appointment of hearing officers as full-time employees of the Office or the selection of hearing officers on the basis of specialized expertise needed for particular matters.

(2) Lists

The Executive Director shall develop master lists, composed of—

(A) members of the bar of a State or the District of Columbia and retired judges of the United States courts who are experienced in adjudicating or arbitrating the kinds of personnel and other matters for which hearings may be held under this chapter, and

(B) individuals expert in technical matters relating to accessibility and usability by persons with disabilities or technical matters relating to occupational safety and health.

In developing lists, the Executive Director shall consider candidates recommended by the Federal Mediation and Conciliation Service or the Administrative Conference of the United States.

(d) Hearing

Unless a complaint is dismissed before a hearing, a hearing shall be—

(1) conducted in closed session on the record by the hearing officer;

(2) commenced no later than 60 days after filing of the complaint under subsection (a) of this section, except that the Office may, for good cause, extend up to an additional 30 days the time for commencing a hearing; and

(3) conducted, except as specifically provided in this chapter and to the greatest extent practicable, in accordance with the principles and procedures set forth in sections 554 through 557 of title 5.

(e) Discovery

Reasonable prehearing discovery may be permitted at the discretion of the hearing officer.

(f) Subpoenas

(1) In general

At the request of a party, a hearing officer may issue subpoenas for the attendance of witnesses and for the production of correspondence, books, papers, documents, and other records. The attendance of witnesses and the production of records may be required from any place within the United States. Subpoenas shall be served in the manner provided under rule 45(b) of the Federal Rules of Civil Procedure.

(2) Objections

If a person refuses, on the basis of relevance, privilege, or other objection, to testify in response to a question or to produce records in connection with a proceeding before a hearing officer, the hearing officer shall rule on the objection. At the request of the witness or any party, the hearing officer shall (or on the hearing officer's own initiative, the hearing officer may) refer the ruling to the Board for review.

(3) Enforcement

(A) In general

If a person fails to comply with a subpoena, the Board may authorize the General Counsel to apply, in the name of the Office, to an appropriate United States district court for an order requiring that person to appear before the hearing officer to give testimony or produce records. The application may be made within the judicial district where the hearing is conducted or where that person is found, resides, or transacts business. Any failure to obey a lawful order of the district court issued pursuant to this section may be held by such court to be a civil contempt thereof.

(B) Service of process

Process in an action or contempt proceeding pursuant to subparagraph (A) may be served in any judicial district in which the person refusing or failing to comply, or threatening to refuse or not to comply, resides, transacts business, or may be found, and subpoenas for witnesses who are required to attend such proceedings may run into any other district.

(g) Decision

The hearing officer shall issue a written decision as expeditiously as possible, but in no case more than 90 days after the conclusion of the hearing. The written decision shall be transmitted by the Office to the parties. The decision shall state the issues raised in the complaint, describe the evidence in the record, contain findings of fact and conclusions of law, contain a determination of whether a violation has occurred, and order such remedies as are appropriate pursuant to subchapter II of this chapter. The decision shall be entered in the records of the Office. If a decision is not appealed under section 1406 of this title to the Board, the decision shall be considered the final decision of the Office.

(h) Precedents

A hearing officer who conducts a hearing under this section shall be guided by judicial decisions under the laws made applicable by section 1302 of this title and by Board decisions under this chapter.

(Pub. L. 104–1, title IV, §405, Jan. 23, 1995, 109 Stat. 33.)

REFERENCES IN TEXT

This chapter, referred to in subsecs. (c)(2)(A), (d)(3), and (h), was in the original "this Act", meaning Pub. L. 104–1, Jan. 23, 1995, 109 Stat. 3, as amended, which is classified principally to this chapter. For complete classification of this Act to the Code, see Short Title note set out under section 1301 of this title and Tables.

Rule 45(b) of the Federal Rules of Civil Procedure, referred to in subsec. (f)(1), is set out in the Appendix to Title 28, Judiciary and Judicial Procedure.

Subchapter II of this chapter, referred to in subsec. (g), was in the original "title II", meaning title II of Pub. L. 104–1, Jan. 23, 1995, 109 Stat. 7, as amended, which enacted subchapter II of this chapter and amended section 6381 of Title 5, Government Organization and Employees, sections 203, 633a, 2611, and 2617 of Title 29, Labor, and sections 2000e–16 and 12209 of Title 42, The Public Health and Welfare. For complete classification of title II to the Code, see Tables.

SECTION REFERRED TO IN OTHER SECTIONS

This section is referred to in sections 1331, 1341, 1351, 1361, 1401, 1403, 1404, 1406, 1407, 1411, 1413, 1416, 1435 of this title.

§ 1406. Appeal to Board

(a) In general

Any party aggrieved by the decision of a hearing officer under section 1405(g) of this title may file a petition for review by the Board not later than 30 days after entry of the decision in the records of the Office.

(b) Parties' opportunity to submit argument

The parties to the hearing upon which the decision of the hearing officer was made shall have a reasonable opportunity to be heard, through written submission and, in the discretion of the Board, through oral argument.

(c) Standard of review

The Board shall set aside a decision of a hearing officer if the Board determines that the decision was—

(1) arbitrary, capricious, an abuse of discretion, or otherwise not consistent with law;
(2) not made consistent with required procedures; or
(3) unsupported by substantial evidence.

(d) Record

In making determinations under subsection (c) of this section, the Board shall review the whole record, or those parts of it cited by a party, and due account shall be taken of the rule of prejudicial error.

(e) Decision

The Board shall issue a written decision setting forth the reasons for its decision. The decision may affirm, reverse, or remand to the hearing officer for further proceedings. A decision that does not require further proceedings before a hearing officer shall be entered in the records of the Office as a final decision.

(Pub. L. 104–1, title IV, §406, Jan. 23, 1995, 109 Stat. 35.)

SECTION REFERRED TO IN OTHER SECTIONS

This section is referred to in sections 1331, 1341, 1351, 1361, 1401, 1405, 1407, 1411, 1416 of this title.

§ 1407. Judicial review of Board decisions and enforcement

(a) Jurisdiction

(1) Judicial review

The United States Court of Appeals for the Federal Circuit shall have jurisdiction over any proceeding commenced by a petition of—

(A) a party aggrieved by a final decision of the Board under section 1406(e) of this title in cases arising under part A of subchapter II of this chapter,
(B) a charging individual or a respondent before the Board who files a petition under section 1331(d)(4) of this title,
(C) the General Counsel or a respondent before the Board who files a petition under section 1341(c)(5) of this title, or
(D) the General Counsel or a respondent before the Board who files a petition under section 1351(c)(3) of this title.

The court of appeals shall have exclusive jurisdiction to set aside, suspend (in whole or in part), to determine the validity of, or otherwise review the decision of the Board.

(2) Enforcement

The United States Court of Appeals for the Federal Circuit shall have jurisdiction over any petition of the General Counsel, filed in the name of the Office and at the direction of the Board, to enforce a final decision under section 1405(g) or 1406(e) of this title with respect to a violation of part A, B, C, or D of subchapter II of this chapter.

(b) Procedures

(1) Respondents

(A) In any proceeding commenced by a petition filed under subsection (a)(1)(A) or (B) of this section, or filed by a party other than the General Counsel under subsection (a)(1)(C) or (D) of this section, the Office shall be named respondent and any party before the Board may be named respondent by filing a notice of election with the court within 30 days after service of the petition.

(B) In any proceeding commenced by a petition filed by the General Counsel under subsection (a)(1)(C) or (D) of this section, the prevailing party in the final decision entered under section 1406(e) of this title shall be named respondent, and any other party before the Board may be named respondent by filing a notice of election with the court within 30 days after service of the petition.

(C) In any proceeding commenced by a petition filed under subsection (a)(2) of this section, the party under section 1405 or 1406 of this title that the General Counsel determines has failed to comply with a final decision under section 1405(g) or 1406(e) of this title shall be named respondent.

(2) Intervention

Any party that participated in the proceedings before the Board under section 1406 of this title and that was not made respondent under paragraph (1) may intervene as of right.

(c) Law applicable

Chapter 158 of title 28 shall apply to judicial review under paragraph (1) of subsection (a) of this section, except that—

(1) with respect to section 2344 of title 28, service of a petition in any proceeding in which the Office is a respondent shall be on the General Counsel rather than on the Attorney General;

(2) the provisions of section 2348 of title 28, on the authority of the Attorney General, shall not apply;

(3) the petition for review shall be filed not later than 90 days after the entry in the Office of a final decision under section 1406(e) of this title; and

(4) the Office shall be an "agency" as that term is used in chapter 158 of title 28.

(d) Standard of review

To the extent necessary for decision in a proceeding commenced under subsection (a)(1) of this section and when presented, the court shall decide all relevant questions of law and interpret constitutional and statutory provisions. The court shall set aside a final decision of the Board if it is determined that the decision was—

(1) arbitrary, capricious, an abuse of discretion, or otherwise not consistent with law;

(2) not made consistent with required procedures; or

(3) unsupported by substantial evidence.

(e) Record

In making determinations under subsection (d) of this section, the court shall review the whole record, or those parts of it cited by a party, and due account shall be taken of the rule of prejudicial error.

(Pub. L. 104–1, title IV, § 407, Jan. 23, 1995, 109 Stat. 35.)

Section Referred to in Other Sections

This section is referred to in sections 1331, 1341, 1351, 1361, 1401, 1409, 1410, 1411, 1413, 1416 of this title.

§ 1408. Civil action

(a) Jurisdiction

The district courts of the United States shall have jurisdiction over any civil action commenced under section 1404 of this title and this section by a covered employee who has completed counseling under section 1402 of this title and mediation under section 1403 of this title. A civil action may be commenced by a covered employee only to seek redress for a violation for which the employee has completed counseling and mediation.

(b) Parties

The defendant shall be the employing office alleged to have committed the violation, or in which the violation is alleged to have occurred.

(c) Jury trial

Any party may demand a jury trial where a jury trial would be available in an action against a private defendant under the relevant law made applicable by this chapter. In any case in which a violation of section 1311 of this title is alleged, the court shall not inform the jury of the maximum amount of compensatory damages available under section 1311(b)(1) or 1311(b)(3) of this title.

(Pub. L. 104–1, title IV, § 408, Jan. 23, 1995, 109 Stat. 37.)

Section Referred to in Other Sections

This section is referred to in sections 1361, 1401, 1404, 1409, 1410, 1411, 1413, 1435 of this title.

§ 1409. Judicial review of regulations

In any proceeding brought under section 1407 or 1408 of this title in which the application of a regulation issued under this chapter is at issue, the court may review the validity of the regulation in accordance with the provisions of subparagraphs (A) through (D) of section 706(2) of title 5, except that with respect to regulations approved by a joint resolution under section 1384(c) of this title, only the provisions of section 706(2)(B) of title 5 shall apply. If the court determines that the regulation is invalid, the court shall apply, to the extent necessary and appropriate, the most relevant substantive executive agency regulation promulgated to implement the statutory provisions with respect to which the invalid regulation was issued. Except as provided in this section, the validity of regulations issued under this chapter is not subject to judicial review.

(Pub. L. 104–1, title IV, § 409, Jan. 23, 1995, 109 Stat. 37.)

Section Referred to in Other Sections

This section is referred to in section 1410 of this title.

§ 1410. Other judicial review prohibited

Except as expressly authorized by sections 1407, 1408, and 1409 of this title, the compliance or noncompliance with the provisions of this chapter and any action taken pursuant to this chapter shall not be subject to judicial review.

(Pub. L. 104–1, title IV, § 410, Jan. 23, 1995, 109 Stat. 37.)

§ 1411. Effect of failure to issue regulations

In any proceeding under section 1405, 1406, 1407, or 1408 of this title, except a proceeding to enforce section 1351 of this title with respect to offices listed under section 1351(e)(2) of this title, if the Board has not issued a regulation on a matter for which this chapter requires a regulation to be issued, the hearing officer, Board, or court, as the case may be, shall apply, to the extent necessary and appropriate, the most relevant substantive executive agency regulation promulgated to implement the statutory provision at issue in the proceeding.

(Pub. L. 104–1, title IV, §411, Jan. 23, 1995, 109 Stat. 37.)

§ 1412. Expedited review of certain appeals

(a) In general

An appeal may be taken directly to the Supreme Court of the United States from any interlocutory or final judgment, decree, or order of a court upon the constitutionality of any provision of this chapter.

(b) Jurisdiction

The Supreme Court shall, if it has not previously ruled on the question, accept jurisdiction over the appeal referred to in subsection (a) of this section, advance the appeal on the docket, and expedite the appeal to the greatest extent possible.

(Pub. L. 104–1, title IV, §412, Jan. 23, 1995, 109 Stat. 38.)

§ 1413. Privileges and immunities

The authorization to bring judicial proceedings under sections 1405(f)(3), 1407, and 1408 of this title shall not constitute a waiver of sovereign immunity for any other purpose, or of the privileges of any Senator or Member of the House of Representatives under article I, section 6, clause 1, of the Constitution, or a waiver of any power of either the Senate or the House of Representatives under the Constitution, including under article I, section 5, clause 3, or under the rules of either House relating to records and information within its jurisdiction.

(Pub. L. 104–1, title IV, §413, Jan. 23, 1995, 109 Stat. 38.)

§ 1414. Settlement of complaints

Any settlement entered into by the parties to a process described in section 1331, 1341, 1351, or 1401 of this title shall be in writing and not become effective unless it is approved by the Executive Director. Nothing in this chapter shall affect the power of the Senate and the House of Representatives, respectively, to establish rules governing the process by which a settlement may be entered into by such House or by any employing office of such House.

(Pub. L. 104–1, title IV, §414, Jan. 23, 1995, 109 Stat. 38.)

§ 1415. Payments

(a) Awards and settlements

Except as provided in subsection (c) of this section, only funds which are appropriated to an account of the Office in the Treasury of the United States for the payment of awards and settlements may be used for the payment of awards and settlements under this chapter. There are authorized to be appropriated for such account such sums as may be necessary to pay such awards and settlements. Funds in the ac-

count are not available for awards and settlements involving the General Accounting Office, the Government Printing Office, or the Library of Congress.

(b) Compliance

Except as provided in subsection (c) of this section, there are authorized to be appropriated such sums as may be necessary for administrative, personnel, and similar expenses of employing offices which are needed to comply with this chapter.

(c) OSHA, accommodation, and access requirements

Funds to correct violations of section 1311(a)(3), 1331, or 1341 of this title may be paid only from funds appropriated to the employing office or entity responsible for correcting such violations. There are authorized to be appropriated such sums as may be necessary for such funds.

(Pub. L. 104–1, title IV, §415, Jan. 23, 1995, 109 Stat. 38.)

§ 1416. Confidentiality

(a) Counseling

All counseling shall be strictly confidential, except that the Office and a covered employee may agree to notify the employing office of the allegations.

(b) Mediation

All mediation shall be strictly confidential.

(c) Hearings and deliberations

Except as provided in subsections (d), (e), and (f) of this section, all proceedings and deliberations of hearing officers and the Board, including any related records, shall be confidential. This subsection shall not apply to proceedings under section 1341 of this title, but shall apply to the deliberations of hearing officers and the Board under that section.

(d) Release of records for judicial action

The records of hearing officers and the Board may be made public if required for the purpose of judicial review under section 1407 of this title.

(e) Access by committees of Congress

At the discretion of the Executive Director, the Executive Director may provide to the Committee on Standards of Official Conduct of the House of Representatives and the Select Committee on Ethics of the Senate access to the records of the hearings and decisions of the hearing officers and the Board, including all written and oral testimony in the possession of the Office. The Executive Director shall not provide such access until the Executive Director has consulted with the individual filing the complaint at issue, and until a final decision has been entered under section 1405(g) or 1406(e) of this title.

(f) Final decisions

A final decision entered under section 1405(g) or 1406(e) of this title shall be made public if it is in favor of the complaining covered employee, or in favor of the charging party under section 1331 of this title, or if the decision reverses a decision of a hearing officer which had been in favor of the covered employee or charging party. The Board may make public any other decision at its discretion.

(Pub. L. 104–1, title IV, § 416, Jan. 23, 1995, 109 Stat. 38.)

SUBCHAPTER V—MISCELLANEOUS PROVISIONS

§ 1431. Exercise of rulemaking powers

The provisions of sections 1302(b)(3) and 1384(c) of this title are enacted—

(1) as an exercise of the rulemaking power of the House of Representatives and the Senate, respectively, and as such they shall be considered as part of the rules of such House, respectively, and such rules shall supersede other rules only to the extent that they are inconsistent therewith; and

(2) with full recognition of the constitutional right of either House to change such rules (so far as relating to such House) at any time, in the same manner, and to the same extent as in the case of any other rule of each House.

(Pub. L. 104–1, title V, § 501, Jan. 23, 1995, 109 Stat. 39.)

§ 1432. Political affiliation and place of residence

(a) In general

It shall not be a violation of any provision of section 1311 of this title to consider the—

(1) party affiliation;

(2) domicile; or

(3) political compatibility with the employing office;

of an employee referred to in subsection (b) of this section with respect to employment decisions.

(b) "Employee" defined

For purposes of subsection (a) of this section, the term "employee" means—

(1) an employee on the staff of the leadership of the House of Representatives or the leadership of the Senate;

(2) an employee on the staff of a committee or subcommittee of—

(A) the House of Representatives;

(B) the Senate; or

(C) a joint committee of the Congress;

(3) an employee on the staff of a Member of the House of Representatives or on the staff of a Senator;

(4) an officer of the House of Representatives or the Senate or a congressional employee who is elected by the House of Representatives or Senate or is appointed by a Member of the House of Representatives or by a Senator (in addition an employee described in paragraph (1), (2), or (3)); or

(5) an applicant for a position that is to be occupied by an individual described in any of paragraphs (1) through (4).

(Pub. L. 104–1, title V, § 502, Jan. 23, 1995, 109 Stat. 39.)

§ 1433. Nondiscrimination rules of House and Senate

The Select Committee on Ethics of the Senate and the Committee on Standards of Official Conduct of the House of Representatives retain full power, in accordance with the authority provided to them by the Senate and the House, with respect to the discipline of Members, officers, and employees for violating rules of the Senate and the House on nondiscrimination in employment.

(Pub. L. 104–1, title V, § 503, Jan. 23, 1995, 109 Stat. 40.)

§ 1434. Judicial branch coverage study

The Judicial Conference of the United States shall prepare a report for submission by the Chief Justice of the United States to the Congress on the application to the judicial branch of the Federal Government of—

(1) the Fair Labor Standards Act of 1938 (29 U.S.C. 201 et seq.);

(2) title VII of the Civil Rights Act of 1964 (42 U.S.C. 2000e et seq.);

(3) the Americans with Disabilities Act of 1990 (42 U.S.C. 12101 et seq.);

(4) the Age Discrimination in Employment Act of 1967 (29 U.S.C. 621 et seq.);

(5) the Family and Medical Leave Act of 1993 (29 U.S.C. 2611 et seq.);

(6) the Occupational Safety and Health Act of 1970 (29 U.S.C. 651 et seq.);

(7) chapter 71 (relating to Federal service labor-management relations) of title 5;

(8) the Employee Polygraph Protection Act of 1988 (29 U.S.C. 2001 et seq.);

(9) the Worker Adjustment and Retraining Notification Act (29 U.S.C. 2101 et seq.);

(10) the Rehabilitation Act of 1973 (29 U.S.C. 701 et seq.); and

(11) chapter 43 (relating to veterans' employment and reemployment) of title 38.

The report shall be submitted to Congress not later than December 31, 1996, and shall include any recommendations the Judicial Conference may have for legislation to provide to employees of the judicial branch the rights, protections, and procedures under the listed laws, including administrative and judicial relief, that are comparable to those available to employees of the legislative branch under subchapters I through IV of this chapter.

(Pub. L. 104–1, title V, § 505, Jan. 23, 1995, 109 Stat. 41.)

REFERENCES IN TEXT

The Fair Labor Standards Act of 1938, referred to in par. (1), is act June 25, 1938, ch. 676, 52 Stat. 1060, as amended, which is classified generally to chapter 8 (§ 201 et seq.) of Title 29, Labor. For complete classification of this Act to the Code, see section 201 of Title 29 and Tables.

The Civil Rights Act of 1964, referred to in par. (2), is Pub. L. 88–352, July 2, 1964, 78 Stat. 252, as amended. Title VII of the Act is classified generally to subchapter VI (§ 2000e et seq.) of chapter 21 of Title 42, The Public Health and Welfare. For complete classification of this Act to the Code, see Short Title note set out under section 2000a of Title 42 and Tables.

The Americans with Disabilities Act of 1990, referred to in par. (3), is Pub. L. 101–336, July 26, 1990, 104 Stat.

parameter.

327, as amended, which is classified principally to chapter 126 (§ 12101 et seq.) of Title 42. For complete classification of this Act to the Code, see Short Title note set out under section 12101 of Title 42 and Tables.

The Age Discrimination in Employment Act of 1967, referred to in par. (4), is Pub. L. 90–202, Dec. 15, 1967, 81 Stat. 602, as amended, which is classified generally to chapter 14 (§ 621 et seq.) of Title 29, Labor. For complete classification of this Act to the Code, see Short Title note set out under section 621 of Title 29 and Tables.

The Family and Medical Leave Act of 1993, referred to in par. (5), is Pub. L. 103–3, Feb. 5, 1993, 107 Stat. 6, as amended, which enacted sections 60m and 60n of this title, sections 6381 to 6387 of Title 5, Government Organization and Employees, and chapter 28 (§ 2601 et seq.) of Title 29, Labor, amended section 2105 of Title 5, and enacted provisions set out as notes under section 2601 of Title 29. For complete classification of this Act to the Code, see Short Title note set out under section 2601 of Title 29 and Tables.

The Occupational Safety and Health Act of 1970, referred to in par. (6), is Pub. L. 91–596, Dec. 29, 1970, 84 Stat. 1590, as amended, which is classified principally to chapter 15 (§ 651 et seq.) of Title 29. For complete classification of this Act to the Code, see Short Title note set out under section 651 of Title 29 and Tables.

The Employee Polygraph Protection Act of 1988, referred to in par. (8), is Pub. L. 100–347, June 27, 1988, 102 Stat. 646, as amended, which is classified generally to chapter 22 (§ 2001 et seq.) of Title 29. For complete classification of this Act to the Code, see Short Title note set out under section 2001 of Title 29 and Tables.

The Worker Adjustment and Retraining Notification Act, referred to in par. (9), is Pub. L. 100–379, Aug. 4, 1988, 102 Stat. 890, which is classified generally to chapter 23 (§ 2101 et seq.) of Title 29. For complete classification of this Act to the Code, see Short Title note set out under section 2101 of Title 29 and Tables.

The Rehabilitation Act of 1973, referred to in par. (10), is Pub. L. 93–112, Sept. 26, 1973, 87 Stat. 355, as amended, which is classified generally to chapter 16 (§ 701 et seq.) of Title 29. For complete classification of this Act to the Code, see Short Title note set out under section 701 of Title 29 and Tables.

Subchapter II of this chapter, referred to in text, was in the original a reference to title II of this Act, meaning title II of Pub. L. 104–1, Jan. 23, 1995, 109 Stat. 7, as amended, which enacted subchapter II of this chapter and amended section 6381 of Title 5, Government Organization and Employees, sections 203, 633a, 2611, and 2617 of Title 29, Labor, and sections 2000e–16 and 12209 of Title 42, The Public Health and Welfare. For complete classification of title II to the Code, see Tables.

§ 1435. Savings provisions

(a) Transition provisions for employees of House of Representatives and of Senate

(1) Claims arising before effective date

If, as of the date on which section 1311 of this title takes effect, an employee of the Senate or the House of Representatives has or could have requested counseling under section 305[1] of the Government Employees Rights Act of 1991 or Rule LI of the House of Representatives, including counseling for alleged violations of family and medical leave rights under title V of the Family and Medical Leave Act of 1993, the employee may complete, or initiate and complete, all procedures under the Government Employees Rights Act of 1991 and Rule LI, and the provisions of that Act and Rule shall remain in effect with respect to, and provide the exclusive procedures for, those

[1] See References in Text note below.

claims until the completion of all such procedures.

(2) Claims arising between effective date and opening of Office

If a claim by an employee of the Senate or House of Representatives arises under section 1311 or 1312 of this title after the effective date of such sections, but before the opening of the Office for receipt of requests for counseling or mediation under sections 1402 and 1403 of this title, the provisions of the Government Employees Rights Act of 1991 and Rule LI of the House of Representatives relating to counseling and mediation shall remain in effect, and the employee may complete under that Act or Rule the requirements for counseling and mediation under sections 1402 and 1403 of this title. If, after counseling and mediation is completed, the Office has not yet opened for the filing of a timely complaint under section 1405 of this title, the employee may elect—

(A) to file a complaint under section 307 of the Government Employees Rights Act of 1991[1] or Rule LI of the House of Representatives, and thereafter proceed exclusively under that Act or Rule, the provisions of which shall remain in effect until the completion of all proceedings in relation to the complaint, or

(B) to commence a civil action under section 1408 of this title.

(3) Section 1207a of this title

With respect to payments of awards and settlements relating to Senate employees under paragraph (1) of this subsection, section 1207a[1] of this title remains in effect.

(b) Transition provisions for employees of Architect of Capitol

(1) Claims arising before effective date

If, as of the date on which section 1311 of this title takes effect, an employee of the Architect of the Capitol has or could have filed a charge or complaint regarding an alleged violation of section 166b–7(e)(2)[1] of title 40, the employee may complete, or initiate and complete, all procedures under section 166b–7(e)[1] of title 40, the provisions of which shall remain in effect with respect to, and provide the exclusive procedures for, that claim until the completion of all such procedures.

(2) Claims arising between effective date and opening of Office

If a claim by an employee of the Architect of the Capitol arises under section 1311 or 1312 of this title after the effective date of those provisions, but before the opening of the Office for receipt of requests for counseling or mediation under sections 1402 and 1403 of this title, the employee may satisfy the requirements for counseling and mediation by exhausting the requirements prescribed by the Architect of the Capitol in accordance with section 166b–7(e)(3)[1] of title 40. If, after exhaustion of those requirements the Office has not yet opened for the filing of a timely complaint under section 1405 of this title, the employee may elect—

(A) to file a charge with the General Accounting Office Personnel Appeals Board pursuant to section 166b–7(e)(3)[1] of title 40, and thereafter proceed exclusively under section 166b–7(e)[1] of title 40, the provisions of which shall remain in effect until the completion of all proceedings in relation to the charge, or

(B) to commence a civil action under section 1408 of this title.

(c) Transition provision relating to matters other than employment under section 12209 of title 42

With respect to matters other than employment under section 12209 of title 42, the rights, protections, remedies, and procedures of section 12209 of title 42 shall remain in effect until section 1331 of this title takes effect with respect to each of the entities covered by section 12209 of title 42.

(Pub. L. 104–1, title V, § 506, Jan. 23, 1995, 109 Stat. 42.)

REFERENCES IN TEXT

For the effective dates of sections 1311, 1312, and 1331 of this title, referred to in text, see sections 1311(d), 1312(e), and 1331(h), respectively, of this title.

Rule LI of the Rules of the House of Representatives, referred to in subsec. (a)(1), (2), was repealed by H. Res. No. 5, § 23(a), One Hundred Fifth Congress, Jan. 7, 1997.

The Family and Medical Leave Act of 1993, referred to in subsec. (a)(1), is Pub. L. 103–3, Feb. 5, 1993, 107 Stat. 6. Title V of the Act was classified generally to sections 60m and 60n of this title prior to repeal, except as provided by this section, by Pub. L. 104–1, title V, § 504(b), Jan. 23, 1995, 109 Stat. 41. For complete classification of this Act to the Code, see Short Title note set out under section 2601 of Title 29, Labor, and Tables.

The Government Employees Rights Act of 1991, referred to in subsec. (a)(1), (2), probably means the Government Employee Rights Act of 1991, which is title III of Pub. L. 102–166, Nov. 21, 1991, 105 Stat. 1088, as amended, and is classified generally to sections 2000e–16a to 2000e–16c of Title 42, The Public Health and Welfare. Sections 305 and 307 of the Act were classified to sections 1205 and 1207, respectively, of this title prior to repeal, except as provided in this section, by Pub. L. 104–1, title V, § 504(a)(2), Jan. 23, 1995, 109 Stat. 41. For complete classification of this Act to the Code, see section 2000e–16a(a) of Title 42 and Tables.

Section 1207a of this title, referred to in subsec. (a)(3), was repealed, except as provided in this section, by Pub. L. 104–1, title V, § 504(a)(5), Jan. 23, 1995, 109 Stat. 41.

Section 166b–7(e) of title 40, referred to in subsec. (b), was repealed, except as provided in this section, by Pub. L. 104–1, title V, § 504(c)(1), Jan. 23, 1995, 109 Stat. 41.

§ 1436. Repealed. Pub. L. 106–57, title III, § 313, Sept. 29, 1999, 113 Stat. 428

Section, Pub. L. 104–1, title V, § 507, Jan. 23, 1995, 109 Stat. 43; Pub. L. 105–275, title I, § 12, Oct. 21, 1998, 112 Stat. 2436, related to use of frequent flyer miles.

§ 1437. Sense of Senate regarding adoption of simplified and streamlined acquisition procedures for Senate acquisitions

It is the sense of the Senate that the Committee on Rules and Administration of the Senate should review the rules applicable to purchases by Senate offices to determine whether they are consistent with the acquisition simplification and streamlining laws enacted in the Federal Acquisition Streamlining Act of 1994 (Public Law 103–355).

(Pub. L. 104–1, title V, § 508, Jan. 23, 1995, 109 Stat. 44.)

REFERENCES IN TEXT

The Federal Acquisition Streamlining Act of 1994, referred to in text, is Pub. L. 103–355, Oct. 13, 1994, 108 Stat. 3243. For complete classification of this Act to the Code, see Short Title of 1994 Amendment note set out under section 251 of Title 41, Public Contracts, and Tables.

§ 1438. Severability

If any provision of this chapter or the application of such provision to any person or circumstance is held to be invalid, the remainder of this chapter and the application of the provisions of the remainder to any person or circumstance shall not be affected thereby.

(Pub. L. 104–1, title V, § 509, Jan. 23, 1995, 109 Stat. 44.)

REFERENCES IN TEXT

This chapter, referred to in text, was in the original "this Act", meaning Pub. L. 104–1, Jan. 23, 1995, 109 Stat. 3, as amended, which is classified principally to this chapter. For complete classification of this Act to the Code, see Short Title note set out under section 1301 of this title and Tables.

CHAPTER 25—UNFUNDED MANDATES REFORM

§ 1501. Purposes

The purposes of this chapter are—

(1) to strengthen the partnership between the Federal Government and State, local, and tribal governments;

(2) to end the imposition, in the absence of full consideration by Congress, of Federal mandates on State, local, and tribal governments without adequate Federal funding, in a manner that may displace other essential State, local, and tribal governmental priorities;

(3) to assist Congress in its consideration of proposed legislation establishing or revising Federal programs containing Federal mandates affecting State, local, and tribal governments, and the private sector by—

(A) providing for the development of information about the nature and size of mandates in proposed legislation; and

(B) establishing a mechanism to bring such information to the attention of the Senate and the House of Representatives before the Senate and the House of Representatives vote on proposed legislation;

(4) to promote informed and deliberate decisions by Congress on the appropriateness of Federal mandates in any particular instance;

(5) to require that Congress consider whether to provide funding to assist State, local, and tribal governments in complying with Federal mandates, to require analyses of the impact of private sector mandates, and through the dissemination of that information provide informed and deliberate decisions by Congress

and Federal agencies and retain competitive balance between the public and private sectors;

(6) to establish a point-of-order vote on the consideration in the Senate and House of Representatives of legislation containing significant Federal intergovernmental mandates without providing adequate funding to comply with such mandates;

(7) to assist Federal agencies in their consideration of proposed regulations affecting State, local, and tribal governments, by—

(A) requiring that Federal agencies develop a process to enable the elected and other officials of State, local, and tribal governments to provide input when Federal agencies are developing regulations; and

(B) requiring that Federal agencies prepare and consider estimates of the budgetary impact of regulations containing Federal mandates upon State, local, and tribal governments and the private sector before adopting such regulations, and ensuring that small governments are given special consideration in that process; and

(8) to begin consideration of the effect of previously imposed Federal mandates, including the impact on State, local, and tribal governments of Federal court interpretations of Federal statutes and regulations that impose Federal intergovernmental mandates.

(Pub. L. 104–4, § 2, Mar. 22, 1995, 109 Stat. 48.)

REFERENCES IN TEXT

This chapter, referred to in text, was in the original "this Act", meaning Pub. L. 104–4, Mar. 22, 1995, 109 Stat. 48, known as the Unfunded Mandates Reform Act of 1995. For complete classification of this Act to the Code, see Short Title note below and Tables.

SHORT TITLE

Section 1 of Pub. L. 104–4 provided that: "This Act [enacting this chapter and sections 658 to 658g of this title, amending sections 602, 632, and 653 of this title, and enacting provisions set out as notes under sections 1511 and 1531 of this title] may be cited as the 'Unfunded Mandates Reform Act of 1995'."

§ 1502. Definitions

For purposes of this chapter—

(1) except as provided in section 1555 of this title, the terms defined under section 658 of this title shall have the meanings as so defined; and

(2) the term "Director" means the Director of the Congressional Budget Office.

(Pub. L. 104–4, § 3, Mar. 22, 1995, 109 Stat. 49.)

SECTION REFERRED TO IN OTHER SECTIONS

This section is referred to in section 1555 of this title.

§ 1503. Exclusions

This chapter shall not apply to any provision in a bill, joint resolution, amendment, motion, or conference report before Congress and any provision in a proposed or final Federal regulation that—

(1) enforces constitutional rights of individuals;

(2) establishes or enforces any statutory rights that prohibit discrimination on the

basis of race, color, religion, sex, national origin, age, handicap, or disability;

(3) requires compliance with accounting and auditing procedures with respect to grants or other money or property provided by the Federal Government;

(4) provides for emergency assistance or relief at the request of any State, local, or tribal government or any official of a State, local, or tribal government;

(5) is necessary for the national security or the ratification or implementation of international treaty obligations;

(6) the President designates as emergency legislation and that the Congress so designates in statute; or

(7) relates to the old-age, survivors, and disability insurance program under title II of the Social Security Act [42 U.S.C. 401 et seq.] (including taxes imposed by sections 3101(a) and 3111(a) of title 26 (relating to old-age, survivors, and disability insurance)).

(Pub. L. 104–4, § 4, Mar. 22, 1995, 109 Stat. 49.)

REFERENCES IN TEXT

The Social Security Act, referred to in par. (7), is act Aug. 14, 1935, ch. 531, 49 Stat. 620, as amended. Title II of the Act is classified generally to subchapter II (§ 401 et seq.) of chapter 7 of Title 42, The Public Health and Welfare. For complete classification of this Act to the Code, see section 1305 of Title 42 and Tables.

§ 1504. Agency assistance

Each agency shall provide to the Director such information and assistance as the Director may reasonably request to assist the Director in carrying out this chapter.

(Pub. L. 104–4, § 5, Mar. 22, 1995, 109 Stat. 50.)

SUBCHAPTER I—LEGISLATIVE ACCOUNTABILITY AND REFORM

§ 1511. Cost of regulations

(a) Sense of Congress

It is the sense of the Congress that Federal agencies should review and evaluate planned regulations to ensure that the cost estimates provided by the Congressional Budget Office will be carefully considered as regulations are promulgated.

(b) Statement of cost

At the request of a committee chairman or ranking minority member, the Director shall, to the extent practicable, prepare a comparison between—

(1) an estimate by the relevant agency, prepared under section 1532 of this title, of the costs of regulations implementing an Act containing a Federal mandate; and

(2) the cost estimate prepared by the Congressional Budget Office for such Act when it was enacted by the Congress.

(c) Cooperation of Office of Management and Budget

At the request of the Director of the Congressional Budget Office, the Director of the Office of Management and Budget shall provide data and cost estimates for regulations implementing an Act containing a Federal mandate covered by part B of title IV of the Congressional Budget and Impoundment Control Act of 1974 [2 U.S.C. 658 et seq.].

(Pub. L. 104–4, title I, § 103, Mar. 22, 1995, 109 Stat. 62.)

REFERENCES IN TEXT

The Congressional Budget and Impoundment Control Act of 1974, referred to in subsec. (c), is Pub. L. 93–344, July 12, 1974, 88 Stat. 297, as amended. Part B of title IV of the Act is classified generally to part B (§ 658 et seq.) of subchapter II of chapter 17A of this title. For complete classification of this Act to the Code, see Short Title note set out under section 621 of this title and Tables.

EFFECTIVE DATE

Section 110 of title I of Pub. L. 104–4 provided that: "This title [enacting this subchapter and sections 658 to 658g of this title and amending sections 602, 632, and 653 of this title] shall take effect on January 1, 1996 or on the date 90 days after appropriations are made available as authorized under section 109 [section 1516 of this title], whichever is earlier and shall apply to legislation considered on and after such date."

§ 1512. Consideration for Federal funding

Nothing in this chapter shall preclude a State, local, or tribal government that already complies with all or part of the Federal intergovernmental mandates included in the bill, joint resolution, amendment, motion, or conference report from consideration for Federal funding under section 658d(a)(2) of this title for the cost of the mandate, including the costs the State, local, or tribal government is currently paying and any additional costs necessary to meet the mandate.

(Pub. L. 104–4, title I, § 105, Mar. 22, 1995, 109 Stat. 62.)

REFERENCES IN TEXT

This chapter, referred to in text, was in the original "this Act", meaning Pub. L. 104–4, Mar. 22, 1995, 109 Stat. 48, known as the Unfunded Mandates Reform Act of 1995. For complete classification of this Act to the Code, see Short Title note set out under section 1501 of this title and Tables.

§ 1513. Impact on local governments

(a) Findings

The Senate finds that—

(1) the Congress should be concerned about shifting costs from Federal to State and local authorities and should be equally concerned about the growing tendency of States to shift costs to local governments;

(2) cost shifting from States to local governments has, in many instances, forced local governments to raise property taxes or curtail sometimes essential services; and

(3) increases in local property taxes and cuts in essential services threaten the ability of many citizens to attain and maintain the American dream of owning a home in a safe, secure community.

(b) Sense of Senate

It is the sense of the Senate that—

(1) the Federal Government should not shift certain costs to the State, and States should end the practice of shifting costs to local gov-

ernments, which forces many local governments to increase property taxes;

(2) States should end the imposition, in the absence of full consideration by their legislatures, of State issued mandates on local governments without adequate State funding, in a manner that may displace other essential government priorities; and

(3) one primary objective of this chapter and other efforts to change the relationship among Federal, State, and local governments should be to reduce taxes and spending at all levels and to end the practice of shifting costs from one level of government to another with little or no benefit to taxpayers.

(Pub. L. 104–4, title I, § 106, Mar. 22, 1995, 109 Stat. 63.)

§ 1514. Enforcement in House of Representatives

(a) Omitted

(b) Committee on Rules reports on waived points of order

The Committee on Rules shall include in the report required by clause 1(d) of rule XI (relating to its activities during the Congress) of the Rules of the House of Representatives a separate item identifying all waivers of points of order relating to Federal mandates, listed by bill or joint resolution number and the subject matter of that measure.

(Pub. L. 104–4, title I, § 107, Mar. 22, 1995, 109 Stat. 63.)

CODIFICATION

Section is comprised of section 107 of Pub. L. 104–4. Subsec. (a) of section 107 of Pub. L. 104–4 amended the Rules of the House of Representatives, which are not classified to the Code.

SECTION REFERRED TO IN OTHER SECTIONS

This section is referred to in section 1515 of this title.

§ 1515. Exercise of rulemaking powers

The provisions of sections 658 to 658g and 1514 of this title are enacted by Congress—

(1) as an exercise of the rulemaking power of the Senate and the House of Representatives, respectively, and as such they shall be considered as part of the rules of such House, respectively, and such rules shall supersede other rules only to the extent that they are inconsistent therewith; and

(2) with full recognition of the constitutional right of either House to change such rules (so far as relating to such House) at any time, in the same manner, and to the same extent as in the case of any other rule of each House.

(Pub. L. 104–4, title I, § 108, Mar. 22, 1995, 109 Stat. 63.)

§ 1516. Authorization of appropriations

There are authorized to be appropriated to the Congressional Budget Office $4,500,000 for each of the fiscal years 1996, 1997, 1998, 1999, 2000, 2001, and 2002 to carry out the provisions of this subchapter.

(Pub. L. 104–4, title I, § 109, Mar. 22, 1995, 109 Stat. 64.)

REFERENCES IN TEXT

This subchapter, referred to in text, was in the original "this title", meaning title I of Pub. L. 104–4, Mar. 22, 1995, 109 Stat. 50, which enacted this subchapter and sections 658 to 658g of this title, amended sections 602, 632, and 653 of this title, and enacted provisions set out as a note under section 1511 of this title.

SUBCHAPTER II—REGULATORY ACCOUNTABILITY AND REFORM

§ 1531. Regulatory process

Each agency shall, unless otherwise prohibited by law, assess the effects of Federal regulatory actions on State, local, and tribal governments, and the private sector (other than to the extent that such regulations incorporate requirements specifically set forth in law).

(Pub. L. 104–4, title II, § 201, Mar. 22, 1995, 109 Stat. 64.)

EFFECTIVE DATE

Section 209 of title II of Pub. L. 104–4 provided that: "This title [enacting this subchapter] and the amendments made by this title shall take effect on the date of the enactment of this Act [Mar. 22, 1995]."

REGULATORY PLANNING AND REVIEW

For provisions stating regulatory philosophy and principles and setting forth regulatory organization, procedures, and guidelines for centralized review of new and existing regulations to make the regulatory process more efficient, see Ex. Ord. No. 12866, Sept. 30, 1993, 58 F.R. 51735, set out as a note under section 601 of Title 5, Government Organization and Employees.

§ 1532. Statements to accompany significant regulatory actions

(a) In general

Unless otherwise prohibited by law, before promulgating any general notice of proposed rulemaking that is likely to result in promulgation of any rule that includes any Federal mandate that may result in the expenditure by State, local, and tribal governments, in the aggregate, or by the private sector, of $100,000,000 or more (adjusted annually for inflation) in any 1 year, and before promulgating any final rule for which a general notice of proposed rulemaking was published, the agency shall prepare a written statement containing—

(1) an identification of the provision of Federal law under which the rule is being promulgated;

(2) a qualitative and quantitative assessment of the anticipated costs and benefits of the Federal mandate, including the costs and benefits to State, local, and tribal governments or the private sector, as well as the effect of the Federal mandate on health, safety, and the natural environment and such an assessment shall include—

(A) an analysis of the extent to which such costs to State, local, and tribal governments may be paid with Federal financial assistance (or otherwise paid for by the Federal Government); and

(B) the extent to which there are available Federal resources to carry out the intergovernmental mandate;

(3) estimates by the agency, if and to the extent that the agency determines that accurate estimates are reasonably feasible, of—

(A) the future compliance costs of the Federal mandate; and

(B) any disproportionate budgetary effects of the Federal mandate upon any particular regions of the nation or particular State, local, or tribal governments, urban or rural or other types of communities, or particular segments of the private sector;

(4) estimates by the agency of the effect on the national economy, such as the effect on productivity, economic growth, full employment, creation of productive jobs, and international competitiveness of United States goods and services, if and to the extent that the agency in its sole discretion determines that accurate estimates are reasonably feasible and that such effect is relevant and material; and

(5)(A) a description of the extent of the agency's prior consultation with elected representatives (under section 1534 of this title) of the affected State, local, and tribal governments;

(B) a summary of the comments and concerns that were presented by State, local, or tribal governments either orally or in writing to the agency; and

(C) a summary of the agency's evaluation of those comments and concerns.

(b) Promulgation

In promulgating a general notice of proposed rulemaking or a final rule for which a statement under subsection (a) of this section is required, the agency shall include in the promulgation a summary of the information contained in the statement.

(c) Preparation in conjunction with other statement

Any agency may prepare any statement required under subsection (a) of this section in conjunction with or as a part of any other statement or analysis, provided that the statement or analysis satisfies the provisions of subsection (a) of this section.

(Pub. L. 104–4, title II, § 202, Mar. 22, 1995, 109 Stat. 64.)

SECTION REFERRED TO IN OTHER SECTIONS

This section is referred to in sections 1511, 1535, 1536, 1571 of this title; title 5 section 801.

§ 1533. Small government agency plan

(a) Effects on small governments

Before establishing any regulatory requirements that might significantly or uniquely affect small governments, agencies shall have developed a plan under which the agency shall—

(1) provide notice of the requirements to potentially affected small governments, if any;

(2) enable officials of affected small governments to provide meaningful and timely input in the development of regulatory proposals containing significant Federal intergovernmental mandates; and

(3) inform, educate, and advise small governments on compliance with the requirements.

(b) Authorization of appropriations

There are authorized to be appropriated to each agency to carry out the provisions of this section and for no other purpose, such sums as are necessary.

(Pub. L. 104–4, title II, § 203, Mar. 22, 1995, 109 Stat. 65.)

SECTION REFERRED TO IN OTHER SECTIONS

This section is referred to in section 1571 of this title; title 5 section 801.

§ 1534. State, local, and tribal government input

(a) In general

Each agency shall, to the extent permitted in law, develop an effective process to permit elected officers of State, local, and tribal governments (or their designated employees with authority to act on their behalf) to provide meaningful and timely input in the development of regulatory proposals containing significant Federal intergovernmental mandates.

(b) Meetings between State, local, tribal and Federal officers

The Federal Advisory Committee Act (5 U.S.C. App.) shall not apply to actions in support of intergovernmental communications where—

(1) meetings are held exclusively between Federal officials and elected officers of State, local, and tribal governments (or their designated employees with authority to act on their behalf) acting in their official capacities; and

(2) such meetings are solely for the purposes of exchanging views, information, or advice relating to the management or implementation of Federal programs established pursuant to public law that explicitly or inherently share intergovernmental responsibilities or administration.

(c) Implementing guidelines

No later than 6 months after March 22, 1995, the President shall issue guidelines and instructions to Federal agencies for appropriate implementation of subsections (a) and (b) of this section consistent with applicable laws and regulations.

(Pub. L. 104–4, title II, § 204, Mar. 22, 1995, 109 Stat. 65.)

REFERENCES IN TEXT

The Federal Advisory Committee Act, referred to in subsec. (b), is Pub. L. 92–463, Oct. 6, 1972, 86 Stat. 770, as amended, which is set out in the Appendix to Title 5, Government Organization and Employees.

DELEGATION OF AUTHORITY TO ISSUE GUIDELINES AND INSTRUCTIONS

Memorandum of President of the United States, Aug. 25, 1995, 60 F.R. 45039, provided:

Memorandum for the Director of the Office of Management and Budget

By the authority vested in me as President by the Constitution and laws of the United States, including section 204(c) of the Unfunded Mandates Reform Act of 1995 (Public Law 104–4) [2 U.S.C. 1534(c)] and section 301 of title 3 of the United States Code, I hereby delegate to the Director of the Office of Management and Budget the authority vested in the President to issue the guidelines and instructions to Federal agencies required by section 204(c) of that Act.

You are authorized and directed to publish this memorandum in the Federal Register.

WILLIAM J. CLINTON.

SECTION REFERRED TO IN OTHER SECTIONS

This section is referred to in section 1532 of this title;
title 5 section 801.

§ 1535. Least burdensome option or explanation required

(a) In general

Except as provided in subsection (b) of this
section, before promulgating any rule for which
a written statement is required under section
1532 of this title, the agency shall identify and
consider a reasonable number of regulatory alternatives and from those alternatives select
the least costly, most cost-effective or least burdensome alternative that achieves the objectives of the rule, for—

(1) State, local, and tribal governments, in
the case of a rule containing a Federal intergovernmental mandate; and

(2) the private sector, in the case of a rule
containing a Federal private sector mandate.

(b) Exception

The provisions of subsection (a) of this section
shall apply unless—

(1) the head of the affected agency publishes
with the final rule an explanation of why the
least costly, most cost-effective or least burdensome method of achieving the objectives of
the rule was not adopted; or

(2) the provisions are inconsistent with law.

(c) OMB certification

No later than 1 year after March 22, 1995, the
Director of the Office of Management and Budget shall certify to Congress, with a written explanation, agency compliance with this section
and include in that certification agencies and
rulemakings that fail to adequately comply
with this section.

(Pub. L. 104–4, title II, § 205, Mar. 22, 1995, 109
Stat. 66.)

SECTION REFERRED TO IN OTHER SECTIONS

This section is referred to in title 5 section 801.

§ 1536. Assistance to Congressional Budget Office

The Director of the Office of Management and
Budget shall—

(1) collect from agencies the statements prepared under section 1532 of this title; and

(2) periodically forward copies of such statements to the Director of the Congressional
Budget Office on a reasonably timely basis
after promulgation of the general notice of
proposed rulemaking or of the final rule for
which the statement was prepared.

(Pub. L. 104–4, title II, § 206, Mar. 22, 1995, 109
Stat. 66.)

§ 1537. Pilot program on small government flexibility

(a) In general

The Director of the Office of Management and
Budget, in consultation with Federal agencies,
shall establish pilot programs in at least 2 agencies to test innovative, and more flexible regulatory approaches that—

(1) reduce reporting and compliance burdens
on small governments; and

(2) meet overall statutory goals and objectives.

(b) Program focus

The pilot programs shall focus on rules in effect or proposed rules, or a combination thereof.

(Pub. L. 104–4, title II, § 207, Mar. 22, 1995, 109
Stat. 67.)

§ 1538. Annual statements to Congress on agency compliance

No later than 1 year after March 22, 1995, and
annually thereafter, the Director of the Office of
Management and Budget shall submit to the
Congress, including the Committee on Governmental Affairs of the Senate and the Committee
on Government Reform and Oversight of the
House of Representatives, a written report detailing compliance by each agency during the
preceding reporting period with the requirements of this subchapter.

(Pub. L. 104–4, title II, § 208, Mar. 22, 1995, 109
Stat. 67.)

CHANGE OF NAME

Committee on Government Reform and Oversight of
House of Representatives changed to Committee on
Government Reform of House of Representatives by
House Resolution No. 5, One Hundred Sixth Congress,
Jan. 6, 1999.

SUBCHAPTER III—REVIEW OF FEDERAL MANDATES

§ 1551. Baseline study of costs and benefits

(a) In general

No later than 18 months after March 22, 1995,
the Advisory Commission on Intergovernmental
Relations (hereafter in this subchapter referred
to as the "Advisory Commission"), in consultation with the Director, shall complete a study to
examine the measurement and definition issues
involved in calculating the total costs and benefits to State, local, and tribal governments of
compliance with Federal law.

(b) Considerations

The study required by this section shall consider—

(1) the feasibility of measuring indirect costs
and benefits as well as direct costs and benefits of the Federal, State, local, and tribal relationship; and

(2) how to measure both the direct and indirect benefits of Federal financial assistance
and tax benefits to State, local, and tribal
governments.

(Pub. L. 104–4, title III, § 301, Mar. 22, 1995, 109
Stat. 67.)

SECTION REFERRED TO IN OTHER SECTIONS

This section is referred to in section 1556 of this title.

§ 1552. Report on Federal mandates by Advisory Commission on Intergovernmental Relations

(a) In general

The Advisory Commission on Intergovernmental Relations shall in accordance with this
section—

(1) investigate and review the role of Federal
mandates in intergovernmental relations and

their impact on State, local, tribal, and Federal government objectives and responsibilities, and their impact on the competitive balance between State, local, and tribal governments, and the private sector and consider views of and the impact on working men and women on those same matters;

(2) investigate and review the role of unfunded State mandates imposed on local governments;

(3) make recommendations to the President and the Congress regarding—

(A) allowing flexibility for State, local, and tribal governments in complying with specific Federal mandates for which terms of compliance are unnecessarily rigid or complex;

(B) reconciling any 2 or more Federal mandates which impose contradictory or inconsistent requirements;

(C) terminating Federal mandates which are duplicative, obsolete, or lacking in practical utility;

(D) suspending, on a temporary basis, Federal mandates which are not vital to public health and safety and which compound the fiscal difficulties of State, local, and tribal governments, including recommendations for triggering such suspension;

(E) consolidating or simplifying Federal mandates, or the planning or reporting requirements of such mandates, in order to reduce duplication and facilitate compliance by State, local, and tribal governments with those mandates;

(F) establishing common Federal definitions or standards to be used by State, local, and tribal governments in complying with Federal mandates that use different definitions or standards for the same terms or principles; and

(G)(i) the mitigation of negative impacts on the private sector that may result from relieving State, local, and tribal governments from Federal mandates (if and to the extent that such negative impacts exist on the private sector); and

(ii) the feasibility of applying relief from Federal mandates in the same manner and to the same extent to private sector entities as such relief is applied to State, local, and tribal governments; and

(4) identify and consider in each recommendation made under paragraph (3), to the extent practicable—

(A) the specific Federal mandates to which the recommendation applies, including requirements of the departments, agencies, and other entities of the Federal Government that State, local, and tribal governments utilize metric systems of measurement; and

(B) any negative impact on the private sector that may result from implementation of the recommendation.

(b) Criteria

(1) In general

The Commission shall establish criteria for making recommendations under subsection (a) of this section.

(2) Issuance of proposed criteria

The Commission shall issue proposed criteria under this subsection no later than 60 days after March 22, 1995, and thereafter provide a period of 30 days for submission by the public of comments on the proposed criteria.

(3) Final criteria

No later than 45 days after the date of issuance of proposed criteria, the Commission shall—

(A) consider comments on the proposed criteria received under paragraph (2);

(B) adopt and incorporate in final criteria any recommendations submitted in those comments that the Commission determines will aid the Commission in carrying out its duties under this section; and

(C) issue final criteria under this subsection.

(c) Preliminary report

(1) In general

No later than 9 months after March 22, 1995, the Commission shall—

(A) prepare and publish a preliminary report on its activities under this subchapter, including preliminary recommendations pursuant to subsection (a) of this section;

(B) publish in the Federal Register a notice of availability of the preliminary report; and

(C) provide copies of the preliminary report to the public upon request.

(2) Public hearings

The Commission shall hold public hearings on the preliminary recommendations contained in the preliminary report of the Commission under this subsection.

(d) Final report

No later than 3 months after the date of the publication of the preliminary report under subsection (c) of this section, the Commission shall submit to the Congress, including the Committee on Government Reform and Oversight of the House of Representatives, the Committee on Governmental Affairs of the Senate, the Committee on the Budget of the Senate, and the Committee on the Budget of the House of Representatives, and to the President a final report on the findings, conclusions, and recommendations of the Commission under this section.

(e) Priority to mandates that are subject of judicial proceedings

In carrying out this section, the Advisory Commission shall give the highest priority to immediately investigating, reviewing, and making recommendations regarding Federal mandates that are the subject of judicial proceedings between the United States and a State, local, or tribal government.

(f) "State mandate" defined

For purposes of this section the term "State mandate" means any provision in a State statute or regulation that imposes an enforceable duty on local governments, the private sector, or individuals, including a condition of State assistance or a duty arising from participation in a voluntary State program.

(Pub. L. 104–4, title III, § 302, Mar. 22, 1995, 109 Stat. 67.)

CHANGE OF NAME

Committee on Government Reform and Oversight of House of Representatives changed to Committee on Government Reform of House of Representatives by House Resolution No. 5, One Hundred Sixth Congress, Jan. 6, 1999.

SECTION REFERRED TO IN OTHER SECTIONS

This section is referred to in section 1556 of this title.

§ 1553. Special authorities of Advisory Commission

(a) Experts and consultants

For purposes of carrying out this subchapter, the Advisory Commission may procure temporary and intermittent services of experts or consultants under section 3109(b) of title 5.

(b) Detail of staff of Federal agencies

Upon request of the Executive Director of the Advisory Commission, the head of any Federal department or agency may detail, on a reimbursable basis, any of the personnel of that department or agency to the Advisory Commission to assist it in carrying out this subchapter.

(c) Administrative support services

Upon the request of the Advisory Commission, the Administrator of General Services shall provide to the Advisory Commission, on a reimbursable basis, the administrative support services necessary for the Advisory Commission to carry out its duties under this subchapter.

(d) Contract authority

The Advisory Commission may, subject to appropriations, contract with and compensate government and private persons (including agencies) for property and services used to carry out its duties under this subchapter.

(Pub. L. 104–4, title III, § 303, Mar. 22, 1995, 109 Stat. 69.)

§ 1554. Annual report to Congress regarding Federal court rulings

No later than 4 months after March 22, 1995, and no later than March 15 of each year thereafter, the Advisory Commission on Intergovernmental Relations shall submit to the Congress, including the Committee on Government Reform and Oversight of the House of Representatives and the Committee on Governmental Affairs of the Senate, and to the President a report describing any Federal court case to which a State, local, or tribal government was a party in the preceding calendar year that required such State, local, or tribal government to undertake responsibilities or activities, beyond those such government would otherwise have undertaken, to comply with Federal statutes and regulations.

(Pub. L. 104–4, title III, § 304, Mar. 22, 1995, 109 Stat. 70.)

CHANGE OF NAME

Committee on Government Reform and Oversight of House of Representatives changed to Committee on Government Reform of House of Representatives by House Resolution No. 5, One Hundred Sixth Congress, Jan. 6, 1999.

§ 1555. "Federal mandate" defined

Notwithstanding section 1502 of this title, for purposes of this subchapter the term "Federal mandate" means any provision in statute or regulation or any Federal court ruling that imposes an enforceable duty upon State, local, or tribal governments including a condition of Federal assistance or a duty arising from participation in a voluntary Federal program.

(Pub. L. 104–4, title III, § 305, Mar. 22, 1995, 109 Stat. 70.)

SECTION REFERRED TO IN OTHER SECTIONS

This section is referred to in section 1502 of this title.

§ 1556. Authorization of appropriations

There are authorized to be appropriated to the Advisory Commission to carry out section 1551 of this title and section 1552 of this title, $500,000 for each of fiscal years 1995 and 1996.

(Pub. L. 104–4, title III, § 306, Mar. 22, 1995, 109 Stat. 70.)

SUBCHAPTER IV—JUDICIAL REVIEW

§ 1571. Judicial review

(a) Agency statements on significant regulatory actions

(1) In general

Compliance or noncompliance by any agency with the provisions of sections 1532 and 1533(a)(1) and (2) of this title shall be subject to judicial review only in accordance with this section.

(2) Limited review of agency compliance or noncompliance

(A) Agency compliance or noncompliance with the provisions of sections 1532 and 1533(a)(1) and (2) of this title shall be subject to judicial review only under section 706(1) of title 5, and only as provided under subparagraph (B).

(B) If an agency fails to prepare the written statement (including the preparation of the estimates, analyses, statements, or descriptions) under section 1532 of this title or the written plan under section 1533(a)(1) and (2) of this title, a court may compel the agency to prepare such written statement.

(3) Review of agency rules

In any judicial review under any other Federal law of an agency rule for which a written statement or plan is required under sections 1532 and 1533(a)(1) and (2) of this title, the inadequacy or failure to prepare such statement (including the inadequacy or failure to prepare any estimate, analysis, statement or description) or written plan shall not be used as a basis for staying, enjoining, invalidating or otherwise affecting such agency rule.

(4) Certain information as part of record

Any information generated under sections 1532 and 1533(a)(1) and (2) of this title that is part of the rulemaking record for judicial review under the provisions of any other Federal law may be considered as part of the record for judicial review conducted under such other provisions of Federal law.

(5) Application of other Federal law

For any petition under paragraph (2) the provisions of such other Federal law shall control all other matters, such as exhaustion of administrative remedies, the time for and manner of seeking review and venue, except that if such other Federal law does not provide a limitation on the time for filing a petition for judicial review that is less than 180 days, such limitation shall be 180 days after a final rule is promulgated by the appropriate agency.

(6) Effective date

This subsection shall take effect on October 1, 1995, and shall apply only to any agency rule for which a general notice of proposed rulemaking is promulgated on or after such date.

(b) Judicial review and rule of construction

Except as provided in subsection (a) of this section—

(1) any estimate, analysis, statement, description or report prepared under this chapter, and any compliance or noncompliance with the provisions of this chapter, and any determination concerning the applicability of the provisions of this chapter shall not be subject to judicial review; and

(2) no provision of this chapter shall be construed to create any right or benefit, substantive or procedural, enforceable by any person in any administrative or judicial action.

(Pub. L. 104–4, title IV, § 401, Mar. 22, 1995, 109 Stat. 70.)

REFERENCES IN TEXT

This chapter, referred to in subsec. (b), was in the original "this Act", meaning Pub. L. 104–4, Mar. 22, 1995, 109 Stat. 48, known as the Unfunded Mandates Reform Act of 1995. For complete classification of this Act to the Code, see Short Title note set out under section 1501 of this title and Tables.

CHAPTER 26—DISCLOSURE OF LOBBYING ACTIVITIES

CHAPTER REFERRED TO IN OTHER SECTIONS

This chapter is referred to in title 18 section 219; title 22 section 613; title 31 section 1352.

§ 1601. Findings

The Congress finds that—

(1) responsible representative Government requires public awareness of the efforts of paid lobbyists to influence the public decision-making process in both the legislative and executive branches of the Federal Government;

(2) existing lobbying disclosure statutes have been ineffective because of unclear statutory language, weak administrative and enforcement provisions, and an absence of clear guidance as to who is required to register and what they are required to disclose; and

(3) the effective public disclosure of the identity and extent of the efforts of paid lobbyists to influence Federal officials in the conduct of Government actions will increase public confidence in the integrity of Government.

(Pub. L. 104–65, § 2, Dec. 19, 1995, 109 Stat. 691.)

EFFECTIVE DATE

Section 24 of Pub. L. 104–65 provided that:

"(a) Except as otherwise provided in this section, this Act [see Short Title note below] and the amendments made by this Act shall take effect on January 1, 1996.

"(b) The repeals and amendments made under sections 9, 10, 11, and 12 [amending section 4804 of Title 15, Commerce and Trade, section 219 of Title 18, Crimes and Criminal Procedure, sections 611, 613, 614, 616, 618, and 4002 of Title 22, Foreign Relations and Intercourse, section 1352 of Title 31, Money and Finance, and section 1490p of Title 42, The Public Health and Welfare, repealing sections 261 to 270 of this title and section 3537b of Title 42, and repealing provisions set out as a note under section 261 of this title] shall take effect as provided under subsection (a), except that such repeals and amendments—

"(1) shall not affect any proceeding or suit commenced before the effective date under subsection (a), and in all such proceedings or suits, proceedings shall be had, appeals taken, and judgments rendered in the same manner and with the same effect as if this Act had not been enacted; and

"(2) shall not affect the requirements of Federal agencies to compile, publish, and retain information filed or received before the effective date of such repeals and amendments."

SHORT TITLE OF 1998 AMENDMENT

Pub. L. 105–166, § 1(a), Apr. 6, 1998, 112 Stat. 38, provided that: "This Act [amending sections 1602, 1604, and 1610 of this title and section 613 of Title 22, Foreign Relations and Intercourse] may be cited as the 'Lobbying Disclosure Technical Amendments Act of 1998'."

SHORT TITLE

Section 1 of Pub. L. 104–65 provided that: "This Act [enacting this chapter, amending sections 3304 of Title

5, Government Organization and Employees, section 102 of Pub. L. 95–521, set out in the Appendix to Title 5, section 4804 of Title 15, Commerce and Trade, sections 207 and 219 of Title 18, Crimes and Criminal Procedure, section 2171 of Title 19, Customs Duties, sections 611, 613, 614, 616, 618, 621, and 4002 of Title 22, Foreign Relations and Intercourse, section 1352 of Title 31, Money and Finance, and section 1490p of Title 42, The Public Health and Welfare, repealing sections 261 to 270 of this title and section 3537b of Title 42, enacting provisions set out as notes under this section, section 3304 of Title 5, section 102 of Pub. L. 95–521, set out in the Appendix to Title 5, and section 207 of Title 18, and repealing provisions set out as a note under section 261 of this title] may be cited as the 'Lobbying Disclosure Act of 1995'.''

§ 1602. Definitions

As used in this chapter:

(1) Agency

The term "agency" has the meaning given that term in section 551(1) of title 5.

(2) Client

The term "client" means any person or entity that employs or retains another person for financial or other compensation to conduct lobbying activities on behalf of that person or entity. A person or entity whose employees act as lobbyists on its own behalf is both a client and an employer of such employees. In the case of a coalition or association that employs or retains other persons to conduct lobbying activities, the client is the coalition or association and not its individual members.

(3) Covered executive branch official

The term "covered executive branch official" means—

(A) the President;

(B) the Vice President;

(C) any officer or employee, or any other individual functioning in the capacity of such an officer or employee, in the Executive Office of the President;

(D) any officer or employee serving in a position in level I, II, III, IV, or V of the Executive Schedule, as designated by statute or Executive order;

(E) any member of the uniformed services whose pay grade is at or above O–7 under section 201 of title 37; and

(F) any officer or employee serving in a position of a confidential, policy-determining, policy-making, or policy-advocating character described in section 7511(b)(2)(B) of title 5.

(4) Covered legislative branch official

The term "covered legislative branch official" means—

(A) a Member of Congress;

(B) an elected officer of either House of Congress;

(C) any employee of, or any other individual functioning in the capacity of an employee of—

(i) a Member of Congress;

(ii) a committee of either House of Congress;

(iii) the leadership staff of the House of Representatives or the leadership staff of the Senate;

(iv) a joint committee of Congress; and

(v) a working group or caucus organized to provide legislative services or other assistance to Members of Congress; and

(D) any other legislative branch employee serving in a position described under section 109(13) of the Ethics in Government Act of 1978 (5 U.S.C. App.).

(5) Employee

The term "employee" means any individual who is an officer, employee, partner, director, or proprietor of a person or entity, but does not include—

(A) independent contractors; or

(B) volunteers who receive no financial or other compensation from the person or entity for their services.

(6) Foreign entity

The term "foreign entity" means a foreign principal (as defined in section 1(b) of the Foreign Agents Registration Act of 1938 (22 U.S.C. 611(b)).

(7) Lobbying activities

The term "lobbying activities" means lobbying contacts and efforts in support of such contacts, including preparation and planning activities, research and other background work that is intended, at the time it is performed, for use in contacts, and coordination with the lobbying activities of others.

(8) Lobbying contact

(A) Definition

The term "lobbying contact" means any oral or written communication (including an electronic communication) to a covered executive branch official or a covered legislative branch official that is made on behalf of a client with regard to—

(i) the formulation, modification, or adoption of Federal legislation (including legislative proposals);

(ii) the formulation, modification, or adoption of a Federal rule, regulation, Executive order, or any other program, policy, or position of the United States Government;

(iii) the administration or execution of a Federal program or policy (including the negotiation, award, or administration of a Federal contract, grant, loan, permit, or license); or

(iv) the nomination or confirmation of a person for a position subject to confirmation by the Senate.

(B) Exceptions

The term "lobbying contact" does not include a communication that is—

(i) made by a public official acting in the public official's official capacity;

(ii) made by a representative of a media organization if the purpose of the communication is gathering and disseminating news and information to the public;

(iii) made in a speech, article, publication or other material that is distributed and made available to the public, or through radio, television, cable television, or other medium of mass communication;

(iv) made on behalf of a government of a foreign country or a foreign political party and disclosed under the Foreign Agents Registration Act of 1938 (22 U.S.C. 611 et seq.);

(v) a request for a meeting, a request for the status of an action, or any other similar administrative request, if the request does not include an attempt to influence a covered executive branch official or a covered legislative branch official;

(vi) made in the course of participation in an advisory committee subject to the Federal Advisory Committee Act;

(vii) testimony given before a committee, subcommittee, or task force of the Congress, or submitted for inclusion in the public record of a hearing conducted by such committee, subcommittee, or task force;

(viii) information provided in writing in response to an oral or written request by a covered executive branch official or a covered legislative branch official for specific information;

(ix) required by subpoena, civil investigative demand, or otherwise compelled by statute, regulation, or other action of the Congress or an agency, including any communication compelled by a Federal contract, grant, loan, permit, or license;

(x) made in response to a notice in the Federal Register, Commerce Business Daily, or other similar publication soliciting communications from the public and directed to the agency official specifically designated in the notice to receive such communications;

(xi) not possible to report without disclosing information, the unauthorized disclosure of which is prohibited by law;

(xii) made to an official in an agency with regard to—

(I) a judicial proceeding or a criminal or civil law enforcement inquiry, investigation, or proceeding; or

(II) a filing or proceeding that the Government is specifically required by statute or regulation to maintain or conduct on a confidential basis,

if that agency is charged with responsibility for such proceeding, inquiry, investigation, or filing;

(xiii) made in compliance with written agency procedures regarding an adjudication conducted by the agency under section 554 of title 5 or substantially similar provisions;

(xiv) a written comment filed in the course of a public proceeding or any other communication that is made on the record in a public proceeding;

(xv) a petition for agency action made in writing and required to be a matter of public record pursuant to established agency procedures;

(xvi) made on behalf of an individual with regard to that individual's benefits, employment, or other personal matters involving only that individual, except that this clause does not apply to any communication with—

(I) a covered executive branch official, or

(II) a covered legislative branch official (other than the individual's elected Members of Congress or employees who work under such Members' direct supervision),

with respect to the formulation, modification, or adoption of private legislation for the relief of that individual;

(xvii) a disclosure by an individual that is protected under the amendments made by the Whistleblower Protection Act of 1989, under the Inspector General Act of 1978, or under another provision of law;

(xviii) made by—

(I) a church, its integrated auxiliary, or a convention or association of churches that is exempt from filing a Federal income tax return under paragraph 2(A)(i) of section 6033(a) of title 26, or

(II) a religious order that is exempt from filing a Federal income tax return under paragraph (2)(A)(iii) of such section 6033(a); and

(xix) between—

(I) officials of a self-regulatory organization (as defined in section 3(a)(26) of the Securities Exchange Act [15 U.S.C. 78c(a)(26)]) that is registered with or established by the Securities and Exchange Commission as required by that Act [15 U.S.C. 78a et seq.] or a similar organization that is designated by or registered with the Commodities Future Trading Commission as provided under the Commodity Exchange Act [7 U.S.C. 1 et seq.]; and

(II) the Securities and Exchange Commission or the Commodities Future Trading Commission, respectively;

relating to the regulatory responsibilities of such organization under that Act.

(9) Lobbying firm

The term "lobbying firm" means a person or entity that has 1 or more employees who are lobbyists on behalf of a client other than that person or entity. The term also includes a self-employed individual who is a lobbyist.

(10) Lobbyist

The term "lobbyist" means any individual who is employed or retained by a client for financial or other compensation for services that include more than one lobbying contact, other than an individual whose lobbying activities constitute less than 20 percent of the time engaged in the services provided by such individual to that client over a six month period.

(11) Media organization

The term "media organization" means a person or entity engaged in disseminating information to the general public through a newspaper, magazine, other publication, radio, television, cable television, or other medium of mass communication.

(12) Member of Congress

The term "Member of Congress" means a Senator or a Representative in, or Delegate or Resident Commissioner to, the Congress.

(13) Organization

The term "organization" means a person or entity other than an individual.

(14) Person or entity

The term "person or entity" means any individual, corporation, company, foundation, association, labor organization, firm, partnership, society, joint stock company, group of organizations, or State or local government.

(15) Public official

The term "public official" means any elected official, appointed official, or employee of—

(A) a Federal, State, or local unit of government in the United States other than—

(i) a college or university;

(ii) a government-sponsored enterprise (as defined in section 622(8) of this title);

(iii) a public utility that provides gas, electricity, water, or communications;

(iv) a guaranty agency (as defined in section 1085(j) of title 20), including any affiliate of such an agency; or

(v) an agency of any State functioning as a student loan secondary market pursuant to section 1085(d)(1)(F) of title 20;

(B) a Government corporation (as defined in section 9101 of title 31);

(C) an organization of State or local elected or appointed officials other than officials of an entity described in clause (i), (ii), (iii), (iv), or (v) of subparagraph (A);

(D) an Indian tribe (as defined in section 450b(e) of title 25;[1]

(E) a national or State political party or any organizational unit thereof; or

(F) a national, regional, or local unit of any foreign government, or a group of governments acting together as an international organization.

(16) State

The term "State" means each of the several States, the District of Columbia, and any commonwealth, territory, or possession of the United States.

(Pub. L. 104–65, § 3, Dec. 19, 1995, 109 Stat. 691; Pub. L. 105–166, §§ 2, 3, Apr. 6, 1998, 112 Stat. 38.)

REFERENCES IN TEXT

This chapter, referred to in text, was in the original "this Act" meaning Pub. L. 104–65, Dec. 19, 1995, 109 Stat. 691, known as the Lobbying Disclosure Act of 1995. For complete classification of this Act to the Code, see Short Title note set out under section 1601 of this title and Tables.

Levels I, II, III, IV, and V of the Executive Schedule, referred to in par. (3)(D), are set out in sections 5312, 5313, 5314, 5315, and 5316, respectively, of Title 5, Government Organization and Employees.

Section 109(13) of the Ethics in Government Act of 1978, referred to in par. (4)(D), is section 109(13) of Pub. L. 95–521, which is set out in the Appendix to Title 5.

The Foreign Agents Registration Act of 1938, referred to in par. (8)(B)(iv), is act June 8, 1938, ch. 327, 52 Stat.

[1] So in original. A closing parenthesis probably should precede the semicolon.

631, as amended, which is classified generally to subchapter II (§ 611 et seq.) of chapter 11 of Title 22, Foreign Relations and Intercourse. For complete classification of this Act to the Code, see Short Title note set out under section 611 of Title 22 and Tables.

The Federal Advisory Committee Act, referred to in par. (8)(B)(vi), is Pub. L. 92–463, Oct. 6, 1972, 86 Stat. 770, as amended, which is set out in the Appendix to Title 5, Government Organization and Employees.

The Whistleblower Protection Act of 1989, referred to in par. (8)(B)(xvii), is Pub. L. 101–12, Apr. 10, 1989, 103 Stat. 16, as amended, which enacted subchapters II [5 U.S.C. 1211 et seq.] and III [5 U.S.C. 1221 et seq.] of chapter 12 and section 3352 of Title 5, Government Organization and Employees, amended sections 1201 to 1206, 1209, 1211, 2302, 2303, 3393, 7502, 7512, 7521, 7542, 7701, and 7703 of Title 5 and section 4139 of Title 22, Foreign Relations and Intercourse, repealed sections 1207 and 1208 of Title 5, and enacted provisions set out as notes under sections 1201, 1211, and 5509 of Title 5. For complete classification of this Act to the Code, see Short Title of 1989 Amendment note set out under section 1201 of Title 5 and Tables.

The Inspector General Act of 1978, referred to in par. (8)(B)(xvii), is Pub. L. 95–452, Oct. 12, 1978, 92 Stat. 1101, as amended, which is set out in the Appendix to Title 5.

The Securities Exchange Act, referred to in par. (8)(B)(xix), probably means the Securities Exchange Act of 1934, act June 6, 1934, ch. 404, 48 Stat. 881, as amended, which is classified generally to chapter 2B (§ 78a et seq.) of Title 15, Commerce and Trade. For complete classification of this Act to the Code, see section 78a of Title 15 and Tables.

The Commodity Exchange Act, referred to in par. (8)(B)(xix), is act Sept. 21, 1922, ch. 369, 42 Stat. 998, as amended, which is classified generally to chapter 1 (§ 1 et seq.) of Title 7, Agriculture. For complete classification of this Act to the Code, see section 1 of Title 7 and Tables.

AMENDMENTS

1998—Par. (3)(F). Pub. L. 105–166, § 2, substituted "7511(b)(2)(B)" for "7511(b)(2)".

Par. (8)(B)(ix). Pub. L. 105–166, § 3(a), inserted before semicolon at end ", including any communication compelled by a Federal contract, grant, loan, permit, or license".

Par. (15)(F). Pub. L. 105–166, § 3(b), inserted before period at end ", or a group of governments acting together as an international organization".

SECTION REFERRED TO IN OTHER SECTIONS

This section is referred to in section 1610 of this title; title 15 section 4804; title 18 section 219; title 22 section 4002.

§ 1603. Registration of lobbyists

(a) Registration

(1) General rule

No later than 45 days after a lobbyist first makes a lobbying contact or is employed or retained to make a lobbying contact, whichever is earlier, such lobbyist (or, as provided under paragraph (2), the organization employing such lobbyist), shall register with the Secretary of the Senate and the Clerk of the House of Representatives.

(2) Employer filing

Any organization that has 1 or more employees who are lobbyists shall file a single registration under this section on behalf of such employees for each client on whose behalf the employees act as lobbyists.

(3) Exemption

(A) General rule

Notwithstanding paragraphs (1) and (2), a person or entity whose—

(i) total income for matters related to lobbying activities on behalf of a particular client (in the case of a lobbying firm) does not exceed and is not expected to exceed $5,000; or

(ii) total expenses in connection with lobbying activities (in the case of an organization whose employees engage in lobbying activities on its own behalf) do not exceed or are not expected to exceed $20,000,

(as estimated under section 1604 of this title) in the semiannual period described in section 1604(a) of this title during which the registration would be made is not required to register under this subsection with respect to such client.

(B) Adjustment

The dollar amounts in subparagraph (A) shall be adjusted—

(i) on January 1, 1997, to reflect changes in the Consumer Price Index (as determined by the Secretary of Labor) since December 19, 1995; and

(ii) on January 1 of each fourth year occurring after January 1, 1997, to reflect changes in the Consumer Price Index (as determined by the Secretary of Labor) during the preceding 4-year period,

rounded to the nearest $500.

(b) Contents of registration

Each registration under this section shall contain—

(1) the name, address, business telephone number, and principal place of business of the registrant, and a general description of its business or activities;

(2) the name, address, and principal place of business of the registrant's client, and a general description of its business or activities (if different from paragraph (1));

(3) the name, address, and principal place of business of any organization, other than the client, that—

(A) contributes more than $10,000 toward the lobbying activities of the registrant in a semiannual period described in section 1604(a) of this title; and

(B) in whole or in major part plans, supervises, or controls such lobbying activities.

(4) the name, address, principal place of business, amount of any contribution of more than $10,000 to the lobbying activities of the registrant, and approximate percentage of equitable ownership in the client (if any) of any foreign entity that—

(A) holds at least 20 percent equitable ownership in the client or any organization identified under paragraph (3);

(B) directly or indirectly, in whole or in major part, plans, supervises, controls, directs, finances, or subsidizes the activities of the client or any organization identified under paragraph (3); or

(C) is an affiliate of the client or any organization identified under paragraph (3) and

has a direct interest in the outcome of the lobbying activity;

(5) a statement of—

(A) the general issue areas in which the registrant expects to engage in lobbying activities on behalf of the client; and

(B) to the extent practicable, specific issues that have (as of the date of the registration) already been addressed or are likely to be addressed in lobbying activities; and

(6) the name of each employee of the registrant who has acted or whom the registrant expects to act as a lobbyist on behalf of the client and, if any such employee has served as a covered executive branch official or a covered legislative branch official in the 2 years before the date on which such employee first acted (after December 19, 1995) as a lobbyist on behalf of the client, the position in which such employee served.

(c) Guidelines for registration

(1) Multiple clients

In the case of a registrant making lobbying contacts on behalf of more than 1 client, a separate registration under this section shall be filed for each such client.

(2) Multiple contacts

A registrant who makes more than 1 lobbying contact for the same client shall file a single registration covering all such lobbying contacts.

(d) Termination of registration

A registrant who after registration—

(1) is no longer employed or retained by a client to conduct lobbying activities, and

(2) does not anticipate any additional lobbying activities for such client,

may so notify the Secretary of the Senate and the Clerk of the House of Representatives and terminate its registration.

(Pub. L. 104–65, §4, Dec. 19, 1995, 109 Stat. 696.)

Section Referred to in Other Sections

This section is referred to in sections 1604, 1609, 1610 of this title.

§1604. Reports by registered lobbyists

(a) Semiannual report

No later than 45 days after the end of the semiannual period beginning on the first day of each January and the first day of July of each year in which a registrant is registered under section 1603 of this title, each registrant shall file a report with the Secretary of the Senate and the Clerk of the House of Representatives on its lobbying activities during such semiannual period. A separate report shall be filed for each client of the registrant.

(b) Contents of report

Each semiannual report filed under subsection (a) of this section shall contain—

(1) the name of the registrant, the name of the client, and any changes or updates to the information provided in the initial registration;

(2) for each general issue area in which the registrant engaged in lobbying activities on

behalf of the client during the semiannual filing period—

    (A) a list of the specific issues upon which a lobbyist employed by the registrant engaged in lobbying activities, including, to the maximum extent practicable, a list of bill numbers and references to specific executive branch actions;

    (B) a statement of the Houses of Congress and the Federal agencies contacted by lobbyists employed by the registrant on behalf of the client;

    (C) a list of the employees of the registrant who acted as lobbyists on behalf of the client; and

    (D) a description of the interest, if any, of any foreign entity identified under section 1603(b)(4) of this title in the specific issues listed under subparagraph (A);

    (3) in the case of a lobbying firm, a good faith estimate of the total amount of all income from the client (including any payments to the registrant by any other person for lobbying activities on behalf of the client) during the semiannual period, other than income for matters that are unrelated to lobbying activities; and

    (4) in the case of a registrant engaged in lobbying activities on its own behalf, a good faith estimate of the total expenses that the registrant and its employees incurred in connection with lobbying activities during the semiannual filing period.

(c) Estimates of income or expenses

For purposes of this section, estimates of income or expenses shall be made as follows:

    (1) Estimates of amounts in excess of $10,000 shall be rounded to the nearest $20,000.

    (2) In the event income or expenses do not exceed $10,000, the registrant shall include a statement that income or expenses totaled less than $10,000 for the reporting period.

(Pub. L. 104–65, §5, Dec. 19, 1995, 109 Stat. 697; Pub. L. 105–166, §4(c), Apr. 6, 1998, 112 Stat. 39.)

AMENDMENTS

1998—Subsec. (c)(3). Pub. L. 105–166 struck out par. (3) which read as follows: "A registrant that reports lobbying expenditures pursuant to section 6033(b)(8) of title 26 may satisfy the requirement to report income or expenses by filing with the Secretary of the Senate and the Clerk of the House of Representatives a copy of the form filed in accordance with section 6033(b)(8)."

SECTION REFERRED TO IN OTHER SECTIONS

This section is referred to in sections 1602, 1603, 1610 of this title.

§ 1605. Disclosure and enforcement

The Secretary of the Senate and the Clerk of the House of Representatives shall—

    (1) provide guidance and assistance on the registration and reporting requirements of this chapter and develop common standards, rules, and procedures for compliance with this chapter;

    (2) review, and, where necessary, verify and inquire to ensure the accuracy, completeness, and timeliness of registration and reports;

    (3) develop filing, coding, and cross-indexing systems to carry out the purpose of this chapter, including—

    (A) a publicly available list of all registered lobbyists, lobbying firms, and their clients; and

    (B) computerized systems designed to minimize the burden of filing and maximize public access to materials filed under this chapter;

    (4) make available for public inspection and copying at reasonable times the registrations and reports filed under this chapter;

    (5) retain registrations for a period of at least 6 years after they are terminated and reports for a period of at least 6 years after they are filed;

    (6) compile and summarize, with respect to each semiannual period, the information contained in registrations and reports filed with respect to such period in a clear and complete manner;

    (7) notify any lobbyist or lobbying firm in writing that may be in noncompliance with this chapter; and

    (8) notify the United States Attorney for the District of Columbia that a lobbyist or lobbying firm may be in noncompliance with this chapter, if the registrant has been notified in writing and has failed to provide an appropriate response within 60 days after notice was given under paragraph (7).

(Pub. L. 104–65, §6, Dec. 19, 1995, 109 Stat. 698.)

REFERENCES IN TEXT

This chapter, referred to in pars. (1), (3), (4), (7), and (8), was in the original "this Act" meaning Pub. L. 104–65, Dec. 19, 1995, 109 Stat. 691, known as the Lobbying Disclosure Act of 1995. For complete classification of this Act to the Code, see Short Title note set out under section 1601 of this title and Tables.

§ 1606. Penalties

Whoever knowingly fails to—

    (1) remedy a defective filing within 60 days after notice of such a defect by the Secretary of the Senate or the Clerk of the House of Representatives; or

    (2) comply with any other provision of this chapter;

shall, upon proof of such knowing violation by a preponderance of the evidence, be subject to a civil fine of not more than $50,000, depending on the extent and gravity of the violation.

(Pub. L. 104–65, §7, Dec. 19, 1995, 109 Stat. 699.)

REFERENCES IN TEXT

This chapter, referred to in par. (2), was in the original "this Act" meaning Pub. L. 104–65, Dec. 19, 1995, 109 Stat. 691, known as the Lobbying Disclosure Act of 1995. For complete classification of this Act to the Code, see Short Title note set out under section 1601 of this title and Tables.

§ 1607. Rules of construction

(a) Constitutional rights

Nothing in this chapter shall be construed to prohibit or interfere with—

    (1) the right to petition the Government for the redress of grievances;

    (2) the right to express a personal opinion; or

    (3) the right of association,

protected by the first amendment to the Constitution.

(b) Prohibition of activities

Nothing in this chapter shall be construed to prohibit, or to authorize any court to prohibit, lobbying activities or lobbying contacts by any person or entity, regardless of whether such person or entity is in compliance with the requirements of this chapter.

(c) Audit and investigations

Nothing in this chapter shall be construed to grant general audit or investigative authority to the Secretary of the Senate or the Clerk of the House of Representatives.

(Pub. L. 104–65, § 8, Dec. 19, 1995, 109 Stat. 699.)

REFERENCES IN TEXT

This chapter, referred to in text, was in the original "this Act" meaning Pub. L. 104–65, Dec. 19, 1995, 109 Stat. 691, known as the Lobbying Disclosure Act of 1995. For complete classification of this Act to the Code, see Short Title note set out under section 1601 of this title and Tables.

§ 1608. Severability

If any provision of this chapter, or the application thereof, is held invalid, the validity of the remainder of this chapter and the application of such provision to other persons and circumstances shall not be affected thereby.

(Pub. L. 104–65, § 13, Dec. 19, 1995, 109 Stat. 701.)

REFERENCES IN TEXT

This chapter, referred to in text, was in the original "this Act" meaning Pub. L. 104–65, Dec. 19, 1995, 109 Stat. 691, known as the Lobbying Disclosure Act of 1995. For complete classification of this Act to the Code, see Short Title note set out under section 1601 of this title and Tables.

§ 1609. Identification of clients and covered officials

(a) Oral lobbying contacts

Any person or entity that makes an oral lobbying contact with a covered legislative branch official or a covered executive branch official shall, on the request of the official at the time of the lobbying contact—

(1) state whether the person or entity is registered under this chapter and identify the client on whose behalf the lobbying contact is made; and

(2) state whether such client is a foreign entity and identify any foreign entity required to be disclosed under section 1603(b)(4) of this title that has a direct interest in the outcome of the lobbying activity.

(b) Written lobbying contacts

Any person or entity registered under this chapter that makes a written lobbying contact (including an electronic communication) with a covered legislative branch official or a covered executive branch official shall—

(1) if the client on whose behalf the lobbying contact was made is a foreign entity, identify such client, state that the client is considered a foreign entity under this chapter, and state whether the person making the lobbying contact is registered on behalf of that client under section 1603 of this title; and

(2) identify any other foreign entity identified pursuant to section 1603(b)(4) of this title that has a direct interest in the outcome of the lobbying activity.

(c) Identification as covered official

Upon request by a person or entity making a lobbying contact, the individual who is contacted or the office employing that individual shall indicate whether or not the individual is a covered legislative branch official or a covered executive branch official.

(Pub. L. 104–65, § 14, Dec. 19, 1995, 109 Stat. 702.)

REFERENCES IN TEXT

This chapter, referred to in subsecs. (a)(1) and (b), was in the original "this Act" meaning Pub. L. 104–65, Dec. 19, 1995, 109 Stat. 691, known as the Lobbying Disclosure Act of 1995. For complete classification of this Act to the Code, see Short Title note set out under section 1601 of this title and Tables.

§ 1610. Estimates based on tax reporting system

(a) Entities covered by section 6033(b) of title 26

A person, other than a lobbying firm, that is required to report and does report lobbying expenditures pursuant to section 6033(b)(8) of title 26 may—

(1) make a good faith estimate (by category of dollar value) of applicable amounts that would be required to be disclosed under such section for the appropriate semiannual period to meet the requirements of sections 1603(a)(3) and 1604(b)(4) of this title; and

(2) for all other purposes consider as lobbying contacts and lobbying activities only—

(A) lobbying contacts with covered legislative branch officials (as defined in section 1602(4) of this title) and lobbying activities in support of such contacts; and

(B) lobbying of Federal executive branch officials to the extent that such activities are influencing legislation as defined in section 4911(d) of title 26.

(b) Entities covered by section 162(e) of title 26

A person, other than a lobbying firm, who is required to account and does account for lobbying expenditures pursuant to section 162(e) of title 26 may—

(1) make a good faith estimate (by category of dollar value) of applicable amounts that would not be deductible pursuant to such section for the appropriate semiannual period to meet the requirements of sections 1603(a)(3) and 1604(b)(4) of this title; and

(2) for all other purposes consider as lobbying contacts and lobbying activities only—

(A) lobbying contacts with covered legislative branch officials (as defined in section 1602(4) of this title) and lobbying activities in support of such contacts; and

(B) lobbying of Federal executive branch officials to the extent that amounts paid or costs incurred in connection with such activities are not deductible pursuant to section 162(e) of title 26.

(c) Disclosure of estimate

Any registrant that elects to make estimates required by this chapter under the procedures authorized by subsection (a) or (b) of this section for reporting or threshold purposes shall—

(1) inform the Secretary of the Senate and the Clerk of the House of Representatives that

the registrant has elected to make its estimates under such procedures; and

(2) make all such estimates, in a given calendar year, under such procedures.

(d) Study

Not later than March 31, 1997, the Comptroller General of the United States shall review reporting by registrants under subsections (a) and (b) of this section and report to the Congress—

(1) the differences between the definition of "lobbying activities" in section 1602(7) of this title and the definitions of "lobbying expenditures", "influencing legislation", and related terms in sections 162(e) and 4911 of title 26, as each are implemented by regulations;

(2) the impact that any such differences may have on filing and reporting under this chapter pursuant to this subsection; and

(3) any changes to this chapter or to the appropriate sections of title 26 that the Comptroller General may recommend to harmonize the definitions.

(Pub. L. 104–65, §15, Dec. 19, 1995, 109 Stat. 702; Pub. L. 105–166, §4(a), (b), Apr. 6, 1998, 112 Stat. 38.)

REFERENCES IN TEXT

This chapter, referred to in subsecs. (c) and (d)(2), (3), was in the original "this Act" meaning Pub. L. 104–65, Dec. 19, 1995, 109 Stat. 691, known as the Lobbying Disclosure Act of 1995. For complete classification of this Act to the Code, see Short Title note set out under section 1601 of this title and Tables.

AMENDMENTS

1998—Subsec. (a). Pub. L. 105–166, §4(a)(1), in introductory provisions, substituted "A person, other than a lobbying firm," for "A registrant".

Subsec. (a)(2). Pub. L. 105–166, §4(a)(2), amended par. (2) generally. Prior to amendment, par. (2) read as follows: "in lieu of using the definition of 'lobbying activities' in section 1602(7) of this title, consider as lobbying activities only those activities that are influencing legislation as defined in section 4911(d) of title 26."

Subsec. (b). Pub. L. 105–166, §4(b)(1), in introductory provisions, substituted "A person, other than a lobbying firm, who is required to account and does account for lobbying expenditures pursuant to" for "A registrant that is subject to".

Subsec. (b)(2). Pub. L. 105–166, §4(b)(2), amended par. (2) generally. Prior to amendment, par. (2) read as follows: "in lieu of using the definition of 'lobbying activities' in section 1602(7) of this title, consider as lobbying activities only those activities, the costs of which are not deductible pursuant to section 162(e) of title 26."

§ 1611. Exempt organizations

An organization described in section 501(c)(4) of title 26 which engages in lobbying activities shall not be eligible for the receipt of Federal funds constituting an award, grant, or loan.

(Pub. L. 104–65, §18, Dec. 19, 1995, 109 Stat. 703; Pub. L. 104–99, title I, §129(a), Jan. 26, 1996, 110 Stat. 34.)

AMENDMENTS

1996—Pub. L. 104–99 substituted "award, grant, or loan" for "award, grant, contract, loan, or any other form".

EFFECTIVE DATE OF 1996 AMENDMENT

Section 129(b) of Pub. L. 104–99 provided that: "The amendment made by subsection (a) [amending this sec-

tion] shall take effect as if included in the Lobbying Disclosure Act of 1995 [Pub. L. 104–65] on the date of the enactment of such Act [Dec. 19, 1995]."

[For provision that notwithstanding section 106 of Pub. L. 104–99 [110 Stat. 27], section 129 of Pub. L. 104–99 [see above] to remain in effect as if enacted as part of Pub. L. 104–134, see section 21103 of Pub. L. 104–134, set out as a note following note captioned 501 First Street SE., District of Columbia; Disposal of Real Property, under section 175 of Title 40, Public Buildings, Property, and Works].

§ 1612. Sense of Senate that lobbying expenses should remain nondeductible

(a) Findings

The Senate finds that ordinary Americans generally are not allowed to deduct the costs of communicating with their elected representatives.

(b) Sense of Senate

It is the sense of the Senate that lobbying expenses should not be tax deductible.

(Pub. L. 104–65, §23, Dec. 19, 1995, 109 Stat. 705.)

CHAPTER 27—SOUND RECORDING PRESERVATION BY THE LIBRARY OF CONGRESS

SUBCHAPTER I—NATIONAL RECORDING REGISTRY

CHAPTER REFERRED TO IN OTHER SECTIONS

This chapter is referred to in title 36 section 152402.

SUBCHAPTER I—NATIONAL RECORDING REGISTRY

SUBCHAPTER REFERRED TO IN OTHER SECTIONS

This subchapter is referred to in section 1724 of this title.

§ 1701. National Recording Registry of the Library of Congress

The Librarian of Congress shall establish the National Recording Registry for the purpose of maintaining and preserving sound recordings that are culturally, historically, or aesthetically significant.

(Pub. L. 106–474, title I, § 101, Nov. 9, 2000, 114 Stat. 2085.)

SHORT TITLE

Pub. L. 106–474, § 1, Nov. 9, 2000, 114 Stat. 2085, provided that: "This Act [enacting this chapter and chapter 1524 of Title 36, Patriotic and National Observances, Ceremonies, and Organizations] may be cited as the 'National Recording Preservation Act of 2000'."

§ 1702. Duties of Librarian of Congress

(a) Establishment of criteria and procedures

For purposes of carrying out this subchapter, the Librarian shall—

(1) establish criteria and procedures under which sound recordings may be included in the National Recording Registry, except that no sound recording shall be eligible for inclusion in the National Recording Registry until 10 years after the recording's creation;

(2) establish procedures under which the general public may make recommendations to the National Recording Preservation Board established under subchapter III of this chapter regarding the inclusion of sound recordings in the National Recording Registry; and

(3) determine which sound recordings satisfy the criteria established under paragraph (1) and select such recordings for inclusion in the National Recording Registry.

(b) Publication of sound recordings in the Registry

The Librarian shall publish in the Federal Register the name of each sound recording that is selected for inclusion in the National Recording Registry.

(Pub. L. 106–474, title I, § 102, Nov. 9, 2000, 114 Stat. 2085.)

SECTION REFERRED TO IN OTHER SECTIONS

This section is referred to in section 1703 of this title.

§ 1703. Seal of the National Recording Registry

(a) In general

The Librarian shall provide a seal to indicate that a sound recording has been included in the National Recording Registry and is the Registry version of that recording.

(b) Use of seal

The Librarian shall establish guidelines for approval of the use of the seal provided under subsection (a) of this section, and shall include in the guidelines the following:

(1) The seal may only be used on recording copies of the Registry version of a sound recording.

(2) The seal may be used only after the Librarian has given approval to those persons seeking to apply the seal in accordance with the guidelines.

(3) In the case of copyrighted mass distributed, broadcast, or published works, only the copyright legal owner or an authorized licensee of that copyright owner may place or authorize the placement of the seal on any recording copy of the Registry version of any sound recording that is maintained in the National Recording Registry Collection in the Library of Congress.

(4) Anyone authorized to place the seal on any recording copy of any Registry version of a sound recording may accompany such seal with the following language: "This sound recording is selected for inclusion in the National Recording Registry by the Librarian of Congress in consultation with the National Recording Preservation Board of the Library of Congress because of its cultural, historical, or aesthetic significance."

(c) Effective date of the seal

The use of the seal provided under subsection (a) of this section with respect to a sound recording shall be effective beginning on the date the Librarian publishes in the Federal Register (in accordance with section 1702(b) of this title) the name of the recording, as selected for inclusion in the National Recording Registry.

(d) Prohibited uses of the seal

(1) Prohibition on distribution and exhibition

No person may knowingly distribute or exhibit to the public a version of a sound recording or any copy of a sound recording which bears the seal described in subsection (a) of this section if such recording—

(A) is not included in the National Recording Registry; or

(B) is included in the National Recording Registry but has not been approved for use of the seal by the Librarian pursuant to the guidelines established under subsection (b) of this section.

(2) Prohibition on promotion

No person may knowingly use the seal described in subsection (a) of this section to promote any version of a sound recording or recording copy other than a Registry version.

(e) Remedies for violations

(1) Jurisdiction

The several district courts of the United States shall have jurisdiction, for cause shown, to prevent and restrain violations of subsection (d) of this section.

(2) Relief

(A) Removal of seal

Except as provided in subparagraph (B), relief for violation of subsection (d) of this section shall be limited to the removal of the seal from the sound recording involved in the violation.

(B) Fine and injunctive relief

In the case of a pattern or practice of the willful violation of subsection (d) of this section, the court may order a civil fine of not more than $10,000 and appropriate injunctive relief.

(3) Limitation of remedies

The remedies provided in this subsection shall be the exclusive remedies under this chapter, or any other Federal or State law, regarding the use of the seal described in subsection (a) of this section.

(Pub. L. 106–474, title I, §103, Nov. 9, 2000, 114 Stat. 2086.)

§ 1704. National Recording Registry Collection of the Library of Congress

(a) In general

All copies of sound recordings on the National Recording Registry that are received by the Librarian under subsection (b) of this section shall be maintained in the Library of Congress and be known as the "National Recording Registry Collection of the Library of Congress". The Librarian shall by regulation and in accordance with title 17 provide for reasonable access to the sound recordings and other materials in such collection for scholarly and research purposes.

(b) Acquisition of quality copies

(1) In general

The Librarian shall seek to obtain, by gift from the owner, a quality copy of the Registry version of each sound recording included in the National Recording Registry.

(2) Limit on number of copies

Not more than one copy of the same version or take of any sound recording may be preserved in the National Recording Registry. Nothing in the preceding sentence may be construed to prohibit the Librarian from making or distributing copies of sound recordings included in the Registry for purposes of carrying out this Act.

(c) Property of United States

All copies of sound recordings on the National Recording Registry that are received by the Librarian under subsection (b) of this section shall become the property of the United States Government, subject to the provisions of title 17.

(Pub. L. 106–474, title I, §104, Nov. 9, 2000, 114 Stat. 2087.)

REFERENCES IN TEXT

This Act, referred to in subsec. (b)(2), is Pub. L. 106–474, Nov. 9, 2000, 114 Stat. 2085, known as the National Recording Preservation Act of 2000, which en-

acted this chapter and chapter 1524 (§152401 et seq.) of Title 36, Patriotic and National Observances, Ceremonies, and Organizations. For complete classification of this Act to the Code, see Short Title note set out under section 1701 of this title and Tables.

SUBCHAPTER II—NATIONAL SOUND RECORDING PRESERVATION PROGRAM

§ 1711. Establishment of program by Librarian of Congress

(a) In general

The Librarian shall, after consultation with the National Recording Preservation Board established under subchapter III of this chapter, implement a comprehensive national sound recording preservation program, in conjunction with other sound recording archivists, educators and historians, copyright owners, recording industry representatives, and others involved in activities related to sound recording preservation, and taking into account studies conducted by the Board.

(b) Contents of program specified

The program established under subsection (a) of this section shall—

(1) coordinate activities to assure that efforts of archivists and copyright owners, and others in the public and private sector, are effective and complementary;

(2) generate public awareness of and support for these activities;

(3) increase accessibility of sound recordings for educational purposes;

(4) undertake studies and investigations of sound recording preservation activities as needed, including the efficacy of new technologies, and recommend solutions to improve these practices; and

(5) utilize the audiovisual conservation center of the Library of Congress at Culpeper, Virginia, to ensure that preserved sound recordings included in the National Recording Registry are stored in a proper manner and disseminated to researchers, scholars, and the public as may be appropriate in accordance with title 17 and the terms of any agreements between the Librarian and persons who hold copyrights to such recordings.

(Pub. L. 106–474, title I, §111, Nov. 9, 2000, 114 Stat. 2087.)

§ 1712. Promoting accessibility and public awareness of sound recordings

The Librarian shall carry out activities to make sound recordings included in the National Recording Registry more broadly accessible for research and educational purposes and to generate public awareness and support of the Registry and the comprehensive national sound recording preservation program established under this subchapter.

(Pub. L. 106–474, title I, §112, Nov. 9, 2000, 114 Stat. 2088.)

SUBCHAPTER III—NATIONAL RECORDING PRESERVATION BOARD

SUBCHAPTER REFERRED TO IN OTHER SECTIONS

This subchapter is referred to in sections 1702, 1711 of this title.

§ 1721. Establishment

The Librarian shall establish in the Library of Congress a National Recording Preservation Board whose members shall be selected in accordance with the procedures described in section 1722 of this title.

(Pub. L. 106–474, title I, § 121, Nov. 9, 2000, 114 Stat. 2088.)

§ 1722. Appointment of members

(a) Selections from lists submitted by organizations

(1) In general

The Librarian shall request each organization described in paragraph (2) to submit a list of three candidates qualified to serve as a member of the Board. The Librarian shall appoint one member from each such list, and shall designate from that list an alternate who may attend at Board expense those meetings which the individual appointed to the Board cannot attend.

(2) Organizations described

The organizations described in this paragraph are as follows:

(A) National Academy of Recording Arts and Sciences (NARAS).

(B) Recording Industry Association of America (RIAA).

(C) Association for Recorded Sound Collections (ARSC).

(D) American Society of Composers, Authors and Publishers (ASCAP).

(E) Broadcast Music, Inc. (BMI).

(F) Songwriters Association (SESAC).

(G) American Federation of Musicians (AF of M).

(H) Music Library Association.

(I) American Musicological Society.

(J) National Archives and Record Administration.

(K) National Association of Recording Merchandisers (NARM).

(L) Society for Ethnomusicology.

(M) American Folklore Society.

(N) Country Music Foundation.

(O) Audio Engineering Society (AES).

(P) National Academy of Popular Music.

(Q) Digital Media Association (DiMA).

(b) Other members

In addition to the members appointed under subsection (a) of this section, the Librarian may appoint not more than five members-at-large. The Librarian shall select an alternate for each member-at-large, who may attend at Board expense those meetings that the member-at-large cannot attend.

(c) Chair

The Librarian shall appoint one member of the Board to serve as Chair.

(d) Term of office

(1) Terms

The term of each member of the Board shall be 4 years, except that there shall be no limit to the number of terms that any individual member may serve.

(2) Removal of member of organization

The Librarian shall have the authority to remove any member of the Board (or, in the case of a member appointed under subsection (a)(1) of this section, the organization that such member represents) if the member or organization over any consecutive 2-year period fails to attend at least one regularly scheduled Board meeting.

(3) Vacancies

A vacancy in the Board shall be filled in the manner in which the original appointment was made under subsection (a) of this section, except that the Librarian may fill the vacancy from a list of candidates previously submitted by the organization or organizations involved. Any member appointed to fill a vacancy shall be appointed for the remainder of the term of the member's predecessor.

(Pub. L. 106–474, title I, § 122, Nov. 9, 2000, 114 Stat. 2088.)

SECTION REFERRED TO IN OTHER SECTIONS

This section is referred to in section 1721 of this title.

§ 1723. Service of members; meetings

(a) Reimbursement of expenses

Members of the Board shall serve without pay, but may receive travel expenses, including per diem in lieu of subsistence, in accordance with sections 5702 and 5703 of title 5.

(b) Conflict of interest

The Librarian shall establish rules and procedures to address any potential conflict of interest between a member of the Board and responsibilities of the Board.

(c) Meetings

The Board shall meet at least once each fiscal year. Meetings shall be at the call of the Librarian.

(d) Quorum

Eleven members of the Board shall constitute a quorum for the transaction of business.

(Pub. L. 106–474, title I, § 123, Nov. 9, 2000, 114 Stat. 2089.)

§ 1724. Responsibilities of Board

(a) Review and recommendation of nominations for National Recording Registry

(1) In general

The Board shall review nominations of sound recordings submitted to it for inclusion in the National Recording Registry and advise the Librarian, as provided in subchapter I of this chapter, with respect to the inclusion of such recordings in the Registry and the preservation of these and other sound recordings that are culturally, historically, or aesthetically significant.

(2) Source of nominations

The Board shall consider for inclusion in the National Recording Registry nominations submitted by the general public as well as representatives of sound recording archives and the sound recording industry (such as the guilds and societies representing sound recording artists) and other creative artists.

(b) Study and report on sound recording preservation and restoration

The Board shall conduct a study and issue a report on the following issues:

(1) The current state of sound recording archiving, preservation and restoration activities.

(2) Taking into account the research and other activities carried out by or on behalf of the National Audio-Visual Conservation Center at Culpeper, Virginia—

(A) the methodology and standards needed to make the transition from analog "open reel" preservation of sound recordings to digital preservation of sound recordings; and

(B) standards for access to preserved sound recordings by researchers, educators, and other interested parties.

(3) The establishment of clear standards for copying old sound recordings (including equipment specifications and equalization guidelines).

(4) Current laws and restrictions regarding the use of archives of sound recordings, including recommendations for changes in such laws and restrictions to enable the Library of Congress and other nonprofit institutions in the field of sound recording preservation to make their collections available to researchers in a digital format.

(5) Copyright and other laws applicable to the preservation of sound recordings.

(Pub. L. 106–474, title I, § 124, Nov. 9, 2000, 114 Stat. 2089.)

§ 1725. General powers of Board

(a) In general

The Board may, for the purpose of carrying out its duties, hold such hearings, sit and act at such times and places, take such testimony, and receive such evidence, as the Librarian and the Board consider appropriate.

(b) Service on Foundation

Two sitting members of the Board shall be appointed by the Librarian and shall serve as members of the board of directors of the National Recording Preservation Foundation, in accordance with section 152403 of title 36.

(Pub. L. 106–474, title I, § 125, Nov. 9, 2000, 114 Stat. 2090.)

SUBCHAPTER IV—GENERAL PROVISIONS

§ 1741. Definitions

As used in this chapter:

(1) The term "Librarian" means the Librarian of Congress.

(2) The term "Board" means the National Recording Preservation Board.

(3) The term "sound recording" has the meaning given such term in section 101 of title 17.

(4) The term "publication" has the meaning given such term in section 101 of title 17.

(5) The term "Registry version" means, with respect to a sound recording, the version of a recording first published or offered for mass distribution whether as a publication or a broadcast, or as complete a version as bona fide preservation and restoration activities by the Librarian, an archivist other than the Librarian, or the copyright legal owner can compile in those cases where the original material has been irretrievably lost or the recording is unpublished.

(Pub. L. 106–474, title I, § 131, Nov. 9, 2000, 114 Stat. 2090.)

§ 1742. Staff; experts and consultants

(a) Staff

The Librarian may appoint and fix the pay of such personnel as the Librarian considers appropriate to carry out this chapter.

(b) Experts and consultants

The Librarian may, in carrying out this chapter, procure temporary and intermittent services under section 3109(b) of title 5, but at rates for individuals not to exceed the daily equivalent of the maximum rate of basic pay payable for level 15 of the General Schedule. In no case may a member of the Board (including an alternate member) be paid as an expert or consultant under this section.

(Pub. L. 106–474, title I, § 132, Nov. 9, 2000, 114 Stat. 2091.)

REFERENCES IN TEXT

The General Schedule, referred to in subsec. (b), is set out under section 5332 of Title 5, Government Organization and Employees.

§ 1743. Authorization of appropriations

There are authorized to be appropriated to the Librarian for each of the first 7 fiscal years beginning on or after November 9, 2000, such sums as may be necessary to carry out this chapter, except that the amount authorized for any fiscal year may not exceed $250,000.

(Pub. L. 106–474, title I, § 133, Nov. 9, 2000, 114 Stat. 2091.)

TITLE 3—THE PRESIDENT

This title was enacted by act June 25, 1948, ch. 644, § 1, 62 Stat. 672

AMENDMENTS

1996—Pub. L. 104–331, § 2(c), Oct. 26, 1996, 110 Stat. 4068, added item for chapter 5.

1951—Act Oct. 31, 1951, ch. 655, § 4, 65 Stat. 711, added item for chapter 4.

POSITIVE LAW; CITATION

This title has been made positive law by section 1 of act June 25, 1948, ch. 644, 62 Stat. 672, which provided in part that: "Title 3 of the United States Code, entitled 'The President', is codified and enacted into positive law and may be cited as '3 U. S. C., §—.'"

SAVINGS CLAUSE

Section 2 of act June 25, 1948, provided that: "The provisions of title 3, 'The President', set out in section 1 of this Act, shall be construed as a continuation of existing law and no loss of rights, interruption of jurisdiction, nor prejudice to matters pending on the effective date of this Act shall result from its enactment."

REPEALS

Section 3 of act June 25, 1948, provided that the sections or parts thereof of the Statutes at Large or the Revised Statutes covering provisions codified in this Act are repealed insofar as the provisions appeared in former Title 3, and provided that any rights or liabilities now existing under the repealed sections or parts thereof shall not be affected by the repeal.

PRIOR REPEALS

Former sections 21 and 22 relating to performance of presidential duties in absence of both the President and Vice President were repealed by act July 18, 1947, ch. 264, § 1(g), 61 Stat. 381.

TABLE SHOWING DISPOSITION OF ALL SECTIONS OF FORMER TITLE 3

Title 3 Former Sections	Revised Statutes Statutes at Large	Title 3 New Sections
1	R.S. § 131	1
2	R.S. § 132	3
3	R.S. § 133	4
4	R.S. § 134	2
5	Feb. 3, 1887, ch. 90, § 1, 24 Stat. 373	7
5a	May 29, 1928, ch. 859, § 1, 45 Stat. 945 June 5, 1934, ch. 390, § 6(a), 48 Stat. 879.	7

TABLE SHOWING DISPOSITION OF ALL SECTIONS OF FORMER TITLE 3—Continued

Title 3 Former Sections	Revised Statutes Statutes at Large	Title 3 New Sections
6	Feb. 3, 1887, ch. 90, § 2, 24 Stat. 373	5
7	Feb. 3, 1887, ch. 90, § 3, 24 Stat. 373	6
7a	May 29, 1928, ch. 859, § 2, 45 Stat. 946	6
8	R.S. § 137	8
9	R.S. § 138	9
9a	May 29, 1928, ch. 859, § 3, 45 Stat. 946	9
10	R.S. § 139	10
11	R.S. § 140 Oct. 19, 1888, ch. 1216, § 1, 25 Stat. 613.	11
11a	May 29, 1928, ch. 859, § 4, 45 Stat. 946	11
11b	May 29, 1928, ch. 859, § 5, 45 Stat. 946 June 5, 1934, ch. 390, § 6(b), 48 Stat. 879..	12
11c	May 29, 1928, ch. 859, § 6, 45 Stat. 946 June 5, 1934, ch. 390, § 6(c), 48 Stat. 879.	13
12	Oct. 19, 1888, ch. 1216, § 1, 25 Stat. 613	11, 12
13	R.S. § 141 Oct. 19, 1888, ch. 1216, § 2, 25 Stat. 613.	13
14	R.S. § 143	11
15	R.S. § 144	11
16	R.S. § 145	14
17	Feb. 3, 1887, ch. 90, § 4, 24 Stat. 373. June 5, 1934, ch. 390, § 7, 48 Stat. 879.	15
18	Feb. 3, 1887, ch. 90, § 5, 24 Stat. 374	18
19	Feb. 3, 1887, ch. 90, § 6, 24 Stat. 375	17
20	Feb. 3, 1887, ch. 90, § 7, 24 Stat. 375	16
21	Jan. 19, 1886, ch. 4, § 1, 24 Stat. 1	19
22	Jan. 19, 1886, ch. 4, § 2, 24 Stat. 1	19
23	R.S. § 151	20
24	July 18, 1947, ch. 264, § 1(a–f), 61 Stat. 380, 381. July 26, 1947, ch. 343, § 311, 61 Stat. 509..	19
41	R.S. § 152 June 5, 1934, ch. 390, § 1, 48 Stat. 879.	101
42	R.S. § 153 Mar. 4, 1909, ch. 297, § 1, 35 Stat. 859.	102
43	June 23, 1906, ch. 3523, 34 Stat. 454 Aug. 2, 1946, ch. 744, § 17(c), 60 Stat. 811.	103
44	R.S. § 154 Feb. 26, 1907, ch. 1635, § 4, 34 Stat. 993. Mar. 4, 1925, ch. 549, § 4, 43 Stat. 1301. Aug. 2, 1946, ch. 753, § 601(a), 60 Stat. 850.	104
45	Apr. 22, 1926, ch. 171, § 1, 44 Stat. 305	105
45a	Apr. 3, 1939, ch. 36, § 301, 53 Stat. 565	106
46	June 12, 1922, ch. 218, 42 Stat. 636 Feb. 13, 1923, ch. 72, 42 Stat. 1227. June 7, 1924, ch. 292, § 1, 43 Stat. 521. Mar. 3, 1925, ch. 468, § 1, 43 Stat. 1198, 1199. Apr. 22, 1926, ch. 171, § 1, 44 Stat. 305. Feb. 11, 1927, ch. 104, § 1, 44 Stat. 1069. May 16, 1928, ch. 580, § 1, 45 Stat. 573. Feb. 20, 1929, ch. 270, § 1, 45 Stat. 1230. Apr. 19, 1930, ch. 201, § 1, 46 Stat. 229. Feb. 23, 1931, ch. 281, § 1, 46 Stat. 1355. June 30, 1932, ch. 330, § 1, 47 Stat. 452. June 16, 1933, ch. 101, § 1, 48 Stat. 284. Mar. 28, 1934, ch. 102, § 1, 48 Stat. 509. Feb. 2, 1935, ch. 3, § 1, 49 Stat. 6. Mar. 19, 1936, ch. 156, § 1, 49 Stat. 1148. June 28, 1937, ch. 396, § 1, 50 Stat. 350. May 23, 1938, ch. 259, § 1, 52 Stat. 411. Mar. 16, 1939, ch. 11, § 1, 53 Stat 524. Apr. 8, 1940, ch. 107, § 1, 54 Stat. 112. Apr. 5, 1941, ch. 40, § 1, 55 Stat. 93. June 27, 1942, ch. 450, § 1, 56 Stat. 392. June 26, 1943, ch. 145, § 101, 57 Stat. 169. June 27, 1944, ch. 286, § 101, 58 Stat. 361. May 3, 1945, ch. 106, § 101, 59 Stat. 106. Mar. 28, 1946, ch. 113, § 101, 60 Stat. 61.	107
47	Mar. 4, 1911, ch. 285, § 1, 36 Stat. 1404	108
48	June 25, 1910, ch. 384, § 9, 36 Stat. 773	109
49	R.S. § 1829 Feb. 26, 1925, ch. 377, §§ 1, 2, 43 Stat. 1091.	110
50	R.S. § 1832	109
51	R.S. § 1833	109
52	R.S. § 1834	109
53	June 23, 1913, ch. 3, § 1, 38 Stat. 23	201
54	June 9, 1941, ch. 189, 55 Stat. 247	Elim.
61	Sept. 14, 1922, ch. 308, § 1, 42 Stat. 841	202

[1] Chapter heading amended by Pub. L. 95–179 without a corresponding amendment of chapter analysis.

CHAPTER 1—PRESIDENTIAL ELECTIONS AND VACANCIES

AMENDMENTS

1984—Pub. L. 98–497, title I, § 107(e)(3), Oct. 19, 1984, 98 Stat. 2292, substituted "Archivist of the United States" for "Administrator of General Services" in items 6 and 12.

1961—Pub. L. 87–389, § 2(b), Oct. 4, 1961, 75 Stat. 820, added item 21.

1951—Act Oct. 31, 1951, ch. 655, § 5, 65 Stat. 711, substituted "Administrator of General Services" for "Secretary of State" in items 6 and 12.

§ 1. Time of appointing electors

The electors of President and Vice President shall be appointed, in each State, on the Tuesday next after the first Monday in November, in every fourth year succeeding every election of a President and Vice President.

(June 25, 1948, ch. 644, 62 Stat. 672.)

SHORT TITLE OF 1996 AMENDMENT

Pub. L. 104–331, § 1(a), Oct. 26, 1996, 110 Stat. 4053, provided that: "This Act [enacting sections 401, 402, 411 to 417, 421, 425, 431, 435, 451 to 456, and 471 of this title and sections 1296, 1413, and 3901 to 3908 of Title 28, Judiciary and Judicial Procedure, amending sections 1346 and 2402 of Title 28, repealing section 1219 of Title 2, The Congress, and enacting provisions set out as notes under section 401 of this title, section 1219 of Title 2, and section 1296 of Title 28] may be cited as the 'Presidential and Executive Office Accountability Act'."

SHORT TITLE OF 1988 AMENDMENT

Pub. L. 100–398, § 1, Aug. 17, 1988, 102 Stat. 985, provided that: "This Act [amending sections 3345, 3348, and 5723 of Title 5, Government Organization and Employees, and enacting and amending provisions set out as notes under section 102 of this title] may be cited as the 'Presidential Transitions Effectiveness Act'."

CONSTITUTIONAL PROVISIONS

Time of choosing electors, see Const. Art. 2, § 1, cl. 3.

SECTION REFERRED TO IN OTHER SECTIONS

This section is referred to in title 18 sections 871, 1751.

§ 2. Failure to make choice on prescribed day

Whenever any State has held an election for the purpose of choosing electors, and has failed to make a choice on the day prescribed by law, the electors may be appointed on a subsequent day in such a manner as the legislature of such State may direct.

(June 25, 1948, ch. 644, 62 Stat. 672.)

SECTION REFERRED TO IN OTHER SECTIONS

This section is referred to in title 18 sections 871, 1751.

§ 3. Number of electors

The number of electors shall be equal to the number of Senators and Representatives to which the several States are by law entitled at the time when the President and Vice President to be chosen come into office; except, that where no apportionment of Representatives has been made after any enumeration, at the time of choosing electors, the number of electors shall be according to the then existing apportionment of Senators and Representatives.

(June 25, 1948, ch. 644, 62 Stat. 672.)

§ 4. Vacancies in electoral college

Each State may, by law, provide for the filling of any vacancies which may occur in its college of electors when such college meets to give its electoral vote.

(June 25, 1948, ch. 644, 62 Stat. 673.)

§ 5. Determination of controversy as to appointment of electors

If any State shall have provided, by laws enacted prior to the day fixed for the appointment of the electors, for its final determination of any controversy or contest concerning the appointment of all or any of the electors of such State, by judicial or other methods or procedures, and such determination shall have been made at least six days before the time fixed for the meeting of the electors, such determination made pursuant to such law so existing on said day, and made at least six days prior to said time of meeting of the electors, shall be conclusive, and shall govern in the counting of the electoral

---
[1] So in original. Does not conform to section catchline.

votes as provided in the Constitution, and as hereinafter regulated, so far as the ascertainment of the electors appointed by such State is concerned.

(June 25, 1948, ch. 644, 62 Stat. 673.)

SECTION REFERRED TO IN OTHER SECTIONS

This section is referred to in section 15 of this title.

§ 6. Credentials of electors; transmission to Archivist of the United States and to Congress; public inspection

It shall be the duty of the executive of each State, as soon as practicable after the conclusion of the appointment of the electors in such State by the final ascertainment, under and in pursuance of the laws of such State providing for such ascertainment, to communicate by registered mail under the seal of the State to the Archivist of the United States a certificate of such ascertainment of the electors appointed, setting forth the names of such electors and the canvass or other ascertainment under the laws of such State of the number of votes given or cast for each person for whose appointment any and all votes have been given or cast; and it shall also thereupon be the duty of the executive of each State to deliver to the electors of such State, on or before the day on which they are required by section 7 of this title to meet, six duplicate-originals of the same certificate under the seal of the State; and if there shall have been any final determination in a State in the manner provided for by law of a controversy or contest concerning the appointment of all or any of the electors of such State, it shall be the duty of the executive of such State, as soon as practicable after such determination, to communicate under the seal of the State to the Archivist of the United States a certificate of such determination in form and manner as the same shall have been made; and the certificate or certificates so received by the Archivist of the United States shall be preserved by him for one year and shall be a part of the public records of his office and shall be open to public inspection; and the Archivist of the United States at the first meeting of Congress thereafter shall transmit to the two Houses of Congress copies in full of each and every such certificate so received at the National Archives and Records Administration.

(June 25, 1948, ch. 644, 62 Stat. 673; Oct. 31, 1951, ch. 655, § 6, 65 Stat. 711; Pub. L. 98–497, title I, § 107(e)(1), (2)(A), Oct. 19, 1984, 98 Stat. 2291.)

AMENDMENTS

1984—Pub. L. 98–497 substituted "Archivist of the United States" for "Administrator of General Services" in section catchline and wherever appearing in text and "National Archives and Records Administration" for "General Services Administration".

1951—Act Oct. 31, 1951, substituted "Administrator of General Services" for "Secretary of State" in section catchline and several places in text, and for "Secretary of State of the United States" in one place, and "General Services Administration" for "State Department".

EFFECTIVE DATE OF 1984 AMENDMENT

Amendment by Pub. L. 98–497 effective Apr. 1, 1985, see section 301 of Pub. L. 98–497, set out as a note under section 2102 of Title 44, Public Printing and Documents.

TERMINATION OF REPORTING REQUIREMENTS

For termination, effective May 15, 2000, of provisions of law requiring submittal to Congress of any annual, semiannual, or other regular periodic report listed in House Document No. 103–7 (in which the requirement under this section that the Archivist transmit to Congress copies of certificates of ascertainment is listed as a report on page 179), see section 3003 of Pub. L. 104–66, as amended, set out as a note under section 1113 of Title 31, Money and Finance.

SECTION REFERRED TO IN OTHER SECTIONS

This section is referred to in section 15 of this title.

§ 7. Meeting and vote of electors

The electors of President and Vice President of each State shall meet and give their votes on the first Monday after the second Wednesday in December next following their appointment at such place in each State as the legislature of such State shall direct.

(June 25, 1948, ch. 644, 62 Stat. 673.)

CONSTITUTIONAL PROVISIONS

Day of voting by electors, see Const. Art. II, § 1, cl. 3. Voting by electors, see Const. Amend. XII.

SECTION REFERRED TO IN OTHER SECTIONS

This section is referred to in section 6 of this title.

§ 8. Manner of voting

The electors shall vote for President and Vice President, respectively, in the manner directed by the Constitution.

(June 25, 1948, ch. 644, 62 Stat. 674.)

§ 9. Certificates of votes for President and Vice President

The electors shall make and sign six certificates of all the votes given by them, each of which certificates shall contain two distinct lists, one of the votes for President and the other of the votes for Vice President, and shall annex to each of the certificates one of the lists of the electors which shall have been furnished to them by direction of the executive of the State.

(June 25, 1948, ch. 644, 62 Stat. 674.)

SECTION REFERRED TO IN OTHER SECTIONS

This section is referred to in section 12 of this title.

§ 10. Sealing and endorsing certificates

The electors shall seal up the certificates so made by them, and certify upon each that the lists of all the votes of such State given for President, and of all the votes given for Vice President, are contained therein.

(June 25, 1948, ch. 644, 62 Stat. 674.)

§ 11. Disposition of certificates

The electors shall dispose of the certificates so made by them and the lists attached thereto in the following manner:

First. They shall forthwith forward by registered mail one of the same to the President of the Senate at the seat of government.

Second. Two of the same shall be delivered to the secretary of state of the State, one of which shall be held subject to the order of the President of the Senate, the other to be preserved by him for one year and shall be a part of the public records of his office and shall be open to public inspection.

Third. On the day thereafter they shall forward by registered mail two of such certificates and lists to the Archivist of the United States at the seat of government, one of which shall be held subject to the order of the President of the Senate. The other shall be preserved by the Archivist of the United States for one year and shall be a part of the public records of his office and shall be open to public inspection.

Fourth. They shall forthwith cause the other of the certificates and lists to be delivered to the judge of the district in which the electors shall have assembled.

(June 25, 1948, ch. 644, 62 Stat. 674; Oct. 31, 1951, ch. 655, § 7, 65 Stat. 712; Pub. L. 98–497, title I, § 107(e)(1), Oct. 19, 1984, 98 Stat. 2291.)

AMENDMENTS

1984—Pub. L. 98–497 substituted "Archivist of the United States" for "Administrator of General Services" two places in par. "Third".

1951—Act Oct. 31, 1951, substituted "Administrator of General Services" for "Secretary of State" two places in par. "Third".

EFFECTIVE DATE OF 1984 AMENDMENT

Amendment by Pub. L. 98–497 effective Apr. 1, 1985, see section 301 of Pub. L. 98–497, set out as a note under section 2102 of Title 44, Public Printing and Documents.

SECTION REFERRED TO IN OTHER SECTIONS

This section is referred to in section 12 of this title.

§ 12. Failure of certificates of electors to reach President of the Senate or Archivist of the United States; demand on State for certificate

When no certificate of vote and list mentioned in sections 9 and 11 of this title from any State shall have been received by the President of the Senate or by the Archivist of the United States by the fourth Wednesday in December, after the meeting of the electors shall have been held, the President of the Senate or, if he be absent from the seat of government, the Archivist of the United States shall request, by the most expeditious method available, the secretary of state of the State to send up the certificate and list lodged with him by the electors of such State; and it shall be his duty upon receipt of such request immediately to transmit same by registered mail to the President of the Senate at the seat of government.

(June 25, 1948, ch. 644, 62 Stat. 674; Oct. 31, 1951, ch. 655, § 8, 65 Stat. 712; Pub. L. 98–497, title I, § 107(e)(1), (2)(B), Oct. 19, 1984, 98 Stat. 2291.)

AMENDMENTS

1984—Pub. L. 98–497 substituted "Archivist of the United States" for "Administrator of General Services" in section catchline and two places in text.

1951—Act Oct. 31, 1951, substituted "Administrator of General Services" for "Secretary of State" in section catchline and two places in text.

EFFECTIVE DATE OF 1984 AMENDMENT

Amendment by Pub. L. 98–497 effective Apr. 1, 1985, see section 301 of Pub. L. 98–497, set out as a note under section 2102 of Title 44, Public Printing and Documents.

§ 13. Same; demand on district judge for certificate

When no certificates of votes from any State shall have been received at the seat of government on the fourth Wednesday in December, after the meeting of the electors shall have been held, the President of the Senate or, if he be absent from the seat of government, the Archivist of the United States shall send a special messenger to the district judge in whose custody one certificate of votes from that State has been lodged, and such judge shall forthwith transmit that list by the hand of such messenger to the seat of government.

(June 25, 1948, ch. 644, 62 Stat. 674; Oct. 31, 1951, ch. 655, § 9, 65 Stat. 712; Pub. L. 98–497, title I, § 107(e)(1), Oct. 19, 1984, 98 Stat. 2291.)

AMENDMENTS

1984—Pub. L. 98–497 substituted "Archivist of the United States" for "Administrator of General Services".

1951—Act Oct. 31, 1951, substituted "Administrator of General Services" for "Secretary of State".

EFFECTIVE DATE OF 1984 AMENDMENT

Amendment by Pub. L. 98–497 effective Apr. 1, 1985, see section 301 of Pub. L. 98–497, set out as a note under section 2102 of Title 44, Public Printing and Documents.

SECTION REFERRED TO IN OTHER SECTIONS

This section is referred to in section 14 of this title.

§ 14. Forfeiture for messenger's neglect of duty

Every person who, having been appointed, pursuant to section 13 of this title, to deliver the certificates of the votes of the electors to the President of the Senate, and having accepted such appointment, shall neglect to perform the services required from him, shall forfeit the sum of $1,000.

(June 25, 1948, ch. 644, 62 Stat. 675.)

§ 15. Counting electoral votes in Congress

Congress shall be in session on the sixth day of January succeeding every meeting of the electors. The Senate and House of Representatives shall meet in the Hall of the House of Representatives at the hour of 1 o'clock in the afternoon on that day, and the President of the Senate shall be their presiding officer. Two tellers shall be previously appointed on the part of the Senate and two on the part of the House of Representatives, to whom shall be handed, as they are opened by the President of the Senate, all the certificates and papers purporting to be certificates of the electoral votes, which certificates and papers shall be opened, presented, and acted upon in the alphabetical order of the States, beginning with the letter A; and said tellers, having then read the same in the presence and hearing of the two Houses, shall make a list of the votes as they shall appear from the said certificates; and the votes having been ascertained and counted according to the rules in this subchapter provided, the result of the same shall be delivered to the President of the Senate, who shall thereupon announce the state of the vote, which announcement shall be deemed a sufficient declaration of the persons, if any, elected President and Vice President of the United States, and, together with a list of the votes, be entered on the Journals of the two Houses. Upon such reading of any such certificate or paper, the President of the Senate shall call for objections, if any. Every objection shall be made in writing, and shall state clearly and concisely, and without argument, the ground thereof, and shall be signed by at least one Senator and one Member of the House of Representatives before the same shall be received. When all objections so made to any vote or paper from a State shall have been received and read, the Senate shall thereupon withdraw, and such objections shall be submitted to the Senate for its decision; and the Speaker of the House of Representatives shall, in like manner, submit such objections to the House of Representatives for its decision; and no electoral vote or votes from any State which shall have been regularly given by electors whose appointment has been lawfully certified to according to section 6 of this title from which but one return has been received shall be rejected, but the two Houses concurrently may reject the vote or votes when they agree that such vote or votes have not been so regularly given by electors whose appointment has been so certified. If more than one return or paper purporting to be a return from a State shall have been received by the President of the Senate, those votes, and those only, shall be counted which shall have been regularly given by the electors who are shown by the determination mentioned in section 5 of this title to have been appointed, if the determination in said section provided for shall have been made, or by such successors or substitutes, in case of a vacancy in the board of electors so ascertained, as have been appointed to fill such vacancy in the mode provided by the laws of the State; but in case there shall arise the question which of two or more of such State authorities determining what electors have been appointed, as mentioned in section 5 of this title, is the lawful tribunal of such State, the votes regularly given of those electors, and those only, of such State shall be counted whose title as electors the two Houses, acting separately, shall concurrently decide is supported by the decision of such State so authorized by its law; and in such case of more than one return or paper purporting to be a return from a State, if there shall have been no such determination of the question in the State aforesaid, then those votes, and those only, shall be counted which the two Houses shall concurrently decide were cast by lawful electors appointed in accordance with the laws of the State, unless the two Houses, acting separately, shall concurrently decide such votes not to be the lawful votes of the legally appointed electors of such State. But if the two Houses shall disagree in respect of the counting of such votes, then, and in that case, the votes of the electors whose appointment shall have been certified by the executive of the State, under the seal thereof, shall be counted. When the two Houses have voted, they shall immediately again meet, and the presiding officer shall then announce the decision of the questions submitted. No votes or papers from any other State shall be acted upon until the objec-

tions previously made to the votes or papers from any State shall have been finally disposed of.

(June 25, 1948, ch. 644, 62 Stat. 675.)

COUNTING OF ELECTORAL VOTES

1996—Pub. L. 104–296, §2, Oct. 11, 1996, 110 Stat. 3558, provided that: "The meeting of the Senate and House of Representatives to be held in January 1997 pursuant to section 15 of title 3, United States Code, to count the electoral votes for President and Vice President cast by the electors in December 1996 shall be held on January 9, 1997 (rather than on the date specified in the first sentence of that section)."
1989—Pub. L. 100–646, Nov. 9, 1988, 102 Stat. 3341, provided: "That in carrying out the procedure set forth in section 15 of title, 3, United States Code, for 1989, 'the fourth day of January' shall be substituted for 'the sixth day of January' in the first sentence of such section."
1985—Pub. L. 98–456, Oct. 9, 1984, 98 Stat. 1748, provided: "That, in carrying out the procedure set forth in section 15 of title 3, United States Code, for 1985, 'the seventh day of January' shall be substituted for 'the sixth day of January' in the first sentence of such section."

§ 16. Same; seats for officers and Members of two Houses in joint meeting

At such joint meeting of the two Houses seats shall be provided as follows: For the President of the Senate, the Speaker's chair; for the Speaker, immediately upon his left; the Senators, in the body of the Hall upon the right of the presiding officer; for the Representatives, in the body of the Hall not provided for the Senators; for the tellers, Secretary of the Senate, and Clerk of the House of Representatives, at the Clerk's desk; for the other officers of the two Houses, in front of the Clerk's desk and upon each side of the Speaker's platform. Such joint meeting shall not be dissolved until the count of electoral votes shall be completed and the result declared; and no recess shall be taken unless a question shall have arisen in regard to counting any such votes, or otherwise under this subchapter, in which case it shall be competent for either House, acting separately, in the manner hereinbefore provided, to direct a recess of such House not beyond the next calendar day, Sunday excepted, at the hour of 10 o'clock in the forenoon. But if the counting of the electoral votes and the declaration of the result shall not have been completed before the fifth calendar day next after such first meeting of the two Houses, no further or other recess shall be taken by either House.

(June 25, 1948, ch. 644, 62 Stat. 676.)

§ 17. Same; limit of debate in each House

When the two Houses separate to decide upon an objection that may have been made to the counting of any electoral vote or votes from any State, or other question arising in the matter, each Senator and Representative may speak to such objection or question five minutes, and not more than once; but after such debate shall have lasted two hours it shall be the duty of the presiding officer of each House to put the main question without further debate.

(June 25, 1948, ch. 644, 62 Stat. 676.)

§ 18. Same; parliamentary procedure at joint meeting

While the two Houses shall be in meeting as provided in this chapter, the President of the Senate shall have power to preserve order; and no debate shall be allowed and no question shall be put by the presiding officer except to either House on a motion to withdraw.

(June 25, 1948, ch. 644, 62 Stat. 676; Sept. 3, 1954, ch. 1263, § 3, 68 Stat. 1227.)

AMENDMENTS

1954—Act Sept. 3, 1954, substituted "chapter" for "subchapter".

§ 19. Vacancy in offices of both President and Vice President; officers eligible to act

(a)(1) If, by reason of death, resignation, removal from office, inability, or failure to qualify, there is neither a President nor Vice President to discharge the powers and duties of the office of President, then the Speaker of the House of Representatives shall, upon his resignation as Speaker and as Representative in Congress, act as President.

(2) The same rule shall apply in the case of the death, resignation, removal from office, or inability of an individual acting as President under this subsection.

(b) If, at the time when under subsection (a) of this section a Speaker is to begin the discharge of the powers and duties of the office of President, there is no Speaker, or the Speaker fails to qualify as Acting President, then the President pro tempore of the Senate shall, upon his resignation as President pro tempore and as Senator, act as President.

(c) An individual acting as President under subsection (a) or subsection (b) of this section shall continue to act until the expiration of the then current Presidential term, except that—

(1) if his discharge of the powers and duties of the office is founded in whole or in part on the failure of both the President-elect and the Vice-President-elect to qualify, then he shall act only until a President or Vice President qualifies; and

(2) if his discharge of the powers and duties of the office is founded in whole or in part on the inability of the President or Vice President, then he shall act only until the removal of the disability of one of such individuals.

(d)(1) If, by reason of death, resignation, removal from office, inability, or failure to qualify, there is no President pro tempore to act as President under subsection (b) of this section, then the officer of the United States who is highest on the following list, and who is not under disability to discharge the powers and duties of the office of President shall act as President: Secretary of State, Secretary of the Treasury, Secretary of Defense, Attorney General, Secretary of the Interior, Secretary of Agriculture, Secretary of Commerce, Secretary of Labor, Secretary of Health and Human Services, Secretary of Housing and Urban Development, Secretary of Transportation, Secretary of Energy, Secretary of Education, Secretary of Veterans Affairs.

(2) An individual acting as President under this subsection shall continue so to do until the expiration of the then current Presidential term, but not after a qualified and prior-entitled individual is able to act, except that the removal of the disability of an individual higher on the list contained in paragraph (1) of this subsection or the ability to qualify on the part of an individual higher on such list shall not terminate his service.

(3) The taking of the oath of office by an individual specified in the list in paragraph (1) of this subsection shall be held to constitute his resignation from the office by virtue of the holding of which he qualifies to act as President.

(e) Subsections (a), (b), and (d) of this section shall apply only to such officers as are eligible to the office of President under the Constitution. Subsection (d) of this section shall apply only to officers appointed, by and with the advice and consent of the Senate, prior to the time of the death, resignation, removal from office, inability, or failure to qualify, of the President pro tempore, and only to officers not under impeachment by the House of Representatives at the time the powers and duties of the office of President devolve upon them.

(f) During the period that any individual acts as President under this section, his compensation shall be at the rate then provided by law in the case of the President.

(June 25, 1948, ch. 644, 62 Stat. 677; Pub. L. 89–174, § 6(a), Sept. 9, 1965, 79 Stat. 669; Pub. L. 89–670, § 10(a), Oct. 15, 1966, 80 Stat. 948; Pub. L. 91–375, § 6(b), Aug. 12, 1970, 84 Stat. 775; Pub. L. 95–91, title VII, § 709(g), Aug. 4, 1977, 91 Stat. 609; Pub. L. 96–88, title V, § 508(a), Oct. 17, 1979, 93 Stat. 692; Pub. L. 100–527, § 13(a), Oct. 25, 1988, 102 Stat. 2643.)

AMENDMENTS

1988—Subsec. (d)(1). Pub. L. 100–527 inserted reference to Secretary of Veterans Affairs.

1979—Subsec. (d)(1). Pub. L. 96–88 substituted "Secretary of Health and Human Services" for "Secretary of Health, Education, and Welfare" and inserted reference to Secretary of Education.

1977—Subsec. (d)(1). Pub. L. 95–91 inserted reference to Secretary of Energy.

1970—Subsec. (d)(1). Pub. L. 91–375 struck out "Postmaster General," after "Attorney General,".

1966—Subsec. (d)(1). Pub. L. 89–670 inserted reference to Secretary of Transportation.

1965—Subsec. (d)(1). Pub. L. 89–174 inserted reference to Secretary of Health, Education, and Welfare and Secretary of Housing and Urban Development.

EFFECTIVE DATE OF 1988 AMENDMENT

Amendment by Pub. L. 100–527 effective Mar. 15, 1989, see section 18(a) of Pub. L. 100–527, set out as a Department of Veterans Affairs Act note under section 301 of Title 38, Veterans' Benefits.

EFFECTIVE DATE OF 1979 AMENDMENT

Amendment by Pub. L. 96–88 effective May 4, 1980, with specified exceptions, see section 601 of Pub. L. 96–88, set out as an Effective Date note under section 3401 of Title 20, Education.

EFFECTIVE DATE OF 1970 AMENDMENT

Amendment by Pub. L. 91–375 effective within 1 year after Aug. 12, 1970, on date established therefor by Board of Governors of United States Postal Service and published by it in Federal Register, see section 16(a), formerly section 15(a) of Pub. L. 91–375, set out as an Effective Date note preceding section 101 of Title 39, Postal Service.

EFFECTIVE DATE OF 1966 AMENDMENT

Amendment by Pub. L. 89–670 effective Apr. 1, 1967, as prescribed by President and published in Federal Register, see section 16(a), formerly §15(a), of Pub. L. 89–670, and Ex. Ord. No. 11340, Mar. 30, 1967, 32 F.R. 5453.

EFFECTIVE DATE OF 1965 AMENDMENT

Amendment by Pub. L. 89–174 effective upon expiration of first period of sixty calendar days following Sept. 9, 1965 or on earlier date specified by Executive order, see section 11(a) of Pub. L. 89–174 set out as an Effective Date note under section 3531 of Title 42, The Public Health and Welfare.

SECTION REFERRED TO IN OTHER SECTIONS

This section is referred to in title 18 section 871.

§ 20. Resignation or refusal of office

The only evidence of a refusal to accept, or of a resignation of the office of President or Vice President, shall be an instrument in writing, declaring the same, and subscribed by the person refusing to accept or resigning, as the case may be, and delivered into the office of the Secretary of State.

(June 25, 1948, ch. 644, 62 Stat. 678.)

PRESIDENTIAL RECORDINGS AND MATERIALS PRESERVATION ACT

For protection and preservation of tape recordings of conversations involving former President Richard M. Nixon, see sections 101 to 106 of Pub. L. 93–526, set out as a note under section 2107 of Title 44, Public Printing and Documents.

SECTION REFERRED TO IN OTHER SECTIONS

This section is referred to in title 18 section 871.

§ 21. Definitions

As used in this chapter the term—
(a) "State" includes the District of Columbia.
(b) "executives of each State" includes the Board of Commissioners of the District of Columbia.

(Added Pub. L. 87–389, §2(a), Oct. 4, 1961, 75 Stat. 820.)

TRANSFER OF FUNCTIONS

Except as otherwise provided in Reorg. Plan No. 3 of 1967, eff. Aug. 11, 1967 (in part), 32 F.R. 11669, 81 Stat. 948, functions of Board of Commissioners of District of Columbia transferred to Commissioner of District of Columbia by section 401 of Reorg. Plan No. 3 of 1967. Office of Commissioner of District of Columbia, as established by Reorg. Plan No. 3 of 1967, abolished as of noon Jan. 2, 1975, by Pub. L. 93–198, title VII, §711, Dec. 24, 1973, 87 Stat. 818, and replaced by office of Mayor of District of Columbia by section 421 of Pub. L. 93–198.

CHAPTER 2—OFFICE AND COMPENSATION OF PRESIDENT

AMENDMENTS

1998—Pub. L. 105–339, §4(b)(2), Oct. 31, 1998, 112 Stat. 3185, added item 115.

1978—Pub. L. 95–570, §§1(b), 2(b), 3(b), 5(b)(2), (c)(2), Nov. 2, 1978, 92 Stat. 2447, 2449, 2450, 2451, substituted in item 105 "Assistance and services for the President" for "Compensation of secretaries and executive, administrative, and staff assistants to President"; in item 106 "Assistance and services for the Vice President" for "Administrative assistants"; in item 107 "Domestic Policy Staff and Office of Administration; personnel" for "Detail of employees of executive departments to office of President"; in item 108 "Assistance to the President for unanticipated needs" for "Accommodations for vehicles"; and in item 109 "the Executive Residence at the White House" for "Executive Mansion"; inserted in item 110 "the Executive Residence at the" before "White House"; and added items 112, 113 and 114.

EXECUTIVE OFFICE PERSONNEL BACKGROUND INVESTIGATIONS; LEAVES OF ABSENCE

Pub. L. 103–329, title VI, §632, Sept. 30, 1994, 108 Stat. 2425, provided that:

"(a) IN GENERAL.—Hereafter, the employment of any individual within the Executive Office of the President shall be placed on leave without pay status if the individual—

"(1) has not, within 30 days of commencing such employment or by October 31, 1994 (whichever occurs later), submitted a completed questionnaire for sensitive positions (SF–86) or equivalent form; or

"(2) has not, within 6 months of commencing such employment or by October 31, 1994 (whichever occurs later), had his or her background investigation, if completed, forwarded by the counsel to the President to the United States Secret Service for issuance of the appropriate access pass.

"(b) EXEMPTION.—Subsection (a) shall not apply to any individual specifically exempted from such subsection by the President or his designee."

REORGANIZATION PLAN NO. 1 OF 1977

42 F.R. 56101, 91 Stat. 1633, as amended by Pub. L. 97–195, §1(c)(5), June 16, 1982, 96 Stat. 115

Prepared by the President and transmitted to the Senate and the House of Representatives in Congress assembled, July 15, 1977,[1] pursuant to the provisions of Chapter 9 of Title 5 of the United States Code.

EXECUTIVE OFFICE OF THE PRESIDENT

SECTION 1. REDESIGNATION OF DOMESTIC COUNCIL STAFF

The Domestic Council staff is hereby designated the Domestic Policy Staff and shall consist of such staff personnel as are determined by the President to be necessary to assure that the needs of the President for prompt and comprehensive advice are met with respect to matters of economic and domestic policy. The staff

---

[1] As amended Sept. 15, 1977.

shall continue to be headed by an Executive Director who shall be an Assistant to the President, designated by the President, as provided in Section 203 of Reorganization Plan No. 2 of 1970 [set out in Title 5, Appendix]. The Executive Director shall perform such functions as the President may from time to time direct.

SEC. 2. ESTABLISHMENT OF AN OFFICE OF ADMINISTRATION

There is hereby established in the Executive Office of the President the Office of Administration which shall be headed by the President. There shall be a Director of the Office of Administration. The Director shall be appointed by the President and shall serve as chief administrative officer of the Office of Administration. The President is authorized to fix the compensation and duties of the Director.

The Office of Administration shall provide components of the Executive Office of the President with such administrative services as the President shall from time to time direct.

SEC. 3. ABOLITION OF COMPONENTS

The following components of the Executive Office of the President are hereby abolished:
A. The Domestic Council;
B. The Office of Drug Abuse Policy;
C. The Office of Telecommunications Policy; and
D. The Economic Opportunity Council.

SEC. 4. APPOINTMENT OF THE ASSISTANT SECRETARY OF COMMERCE FOR COMMUNICATIONS AND INFORMATION

There shall be in the Department of Commerce an Assistant Secretary for Communications and Information who shall be appointed by the President, by and with the advice and consent of the Senate. [As amended Pub. L. 97–195, § 1(c)(5), June 16, 1982, 96 Stat. 115.]

SEC. 5. TRANSFERS OF FUNCTIONS

The following functions shall be transferred:
A. All functions vested in the Director of the Office of Science and Technology Policy and in the Office of Science and Technology Policy pursuant to sections 205(a)(2), 206 and 209 of the National Science and Technology Policy, Organization, and Priorities Act of 1976 (Public Law 94–282; 90 Stat. 459) [42 U.S.C. 6614(a)(2), 6615 and 6618], are hereby transferred to the Director of the National Science Foundation. The Intergovernmental Science, Engineering, and Technology Advisory Panel, the President's Committee on Science and Technology, and the Federal Coordinating Council for Science, Engineering and Technology, established in accordance with the provisions of Titles II, III, IV of the National Science and Technology Policy, Organization, and Priorities Act of 1976 [42 U.S.C. 6611 et seq., 6631 et seq., and 6651 et seq.], are hereby abolished, and their functions transferred to the President.
B. Those functions of the Office of Telecommunications Policy and of its Director relating to:
(1) the preparation of Presidential telecommunications policy options including, but not limited to those related to the procurement and management of Federal telecommunications systems, national security, and emergency matters; and
(2) disposition of appeals from assignments of radio frequencies to stations of the United States Government;
are hereby transferred to the President who may delegate such functions within the Executive Office of the President as the President may from time to time deem desirable. All other functions of the Office of Telecommunications Policy and of its Director are hereby transferred to the Secretary of Commerce who shall provide for the performance of such functions.
C. The functions of the Office of Drug Abuse Policy and its Director are hereby transferred to the President, who may delegate such functions within the Executive Office of the President as the President may from time to time deem desirable.

D. The functions of the Domestic Council are hereby transferred to the President, who may delegate such functions within the Executive Office of the President as the President may from time to time deem desirable.
E. Those functions of the Council on Environmental Quality and the Office of Environmental Quality relating to the evaluation provided for by Section 11 of the Federal Nonnuclear Energy Research and Development Act of 1974 (Public Law 93–577, 88 Stat. 1878) [42 U.S.C. 5910], are hereby transferred to the Administrator of the Environmental Protection Agency.
F. Those functions of the Office of Management and Budget and its Director relating to the Committee Management Secretariat (Public Law 92–463, 86 Stat. 770, as amended by Public Law 94–409, 90 Stat. 1247) [see section 7 of the Federal Advisory Committee Act, Pub. L. 92–463, Oct. 6, 1972, 86 Stat. 774, as amended, set out in Title 5, Appendix] are hereby transferred to the Administrator of General Services.
G. The functions of the Economic Opportunity Council are hereby transferred to the President, who may delegate such functions within the Executive Office of the President as the President may from time to time deem desirable.

SEC. 6. INCIDENTAL TRANSFERS

So much of the personnel, property, records, and unexpended balances of appropriations, allocations and other funds employed, used, held, available, or to be made available in connection with the functions transferred under this Plan, as the Director of the Office of Management and Budget shall determine, shall be transferred to the appropriate department, agency, or component at such time or times as the Director of the Office of Management and Budget shall provide, except that no such unexpended balances transferred shall be used for purposes other than those for which the appropriation was originally made. The Director of the Office of Management and Budget shall provide for terminating the affairs of all agencies abolished herein and for such further measures and dispositions as such Director deems necessary to effectuate the purposes of this Reorganization Plan.

SEC. 7. EFFECTIVE DATE

This Reorganization Plan shall become effective at such time or times on or before April 1, 1978, as the President shall specify, but not sooner than the earliest time allowable under Section 906 of Title 5 of the United States Code.

MESSAGE OF THE PRESIDENT

To the Congress of the United States:
I herewith transmit my plan for the Reorganization of the Executive Office of the President (EOP), Reorganization Plan No. 1 of 1977. This plan is the first of a series I intend to submit under the reorganization authority vested in me by the Reorganization Act of 1977 (Public Law 95–17) [5 U.S.C. 901–912]. It adheres to the purposes set forth in Section 901(a) of the Act [5 U.S.C. 901(a)].
This plan in conjunction with the other steps I am taking will:
Eliminate seven of the seventeen units now within the EOP and modify the rest. There were 19 units when I took office; the President's Foreign Intelligence Advisory Board and the Economic Policy Board have already been abolished. Thus with this plan I will have eliminated nine of 19 EOP units.
Reduce EOP staffing by about 250 which includes the White House staff reduction of 134 or 28 percent which I have already ordered.
Improve efficiency by centralizing administrative functions; and
Improve the process by which information is provided for Presidential decisionmaking.
These recommendations arise from a careful, systematic study of the EOP. They are based on the premise

that the EOP exists to serve the President and should be structured to meet his needs. They will reduce waste and cost while improving the service the President, and the nation, receive from the EOP.

The EOP now consists of the immediate White House Office, the Vice President's Office, the Office of Management and Budget, and fourteen other agencies. The EOP has a budget authority of about $80,000,000 and 1,712 full time employees.

The White House Office concentrates on close personal support including policy and political advice and administrative and operational services. The Office of the Vice President provides similar support to him. OMB's primary mission is to develop and implement the budget; it also carries out a number of management and reorganization activities.

Three EOP units have responsibility for policy development:

    National Security Council.
    Domestic Council.
    Council on International Economic Policy.

The other 11 are more specialized offices that offer analysis and advice, help develop policy in certain areas, or carry out special projects. These are:

    Council of Economic Advisers.
    Council on Wage and Price Stability.
    Office of the Special Representative for Trade Negotiations.
    Council on Environmental Quality.
    Office of Science and Technology Policy.
    Office of Drug Abuse Policy.
    Office of Telecommunications Policy.
    Intelligence Oversight Board.
    Federal Property Council.
    Energy Resources Council.
    Economic Opportunity Council.

To make the EOP more effective, four steps are necessary:

    I. Strengthen management of policy issues.
    II. Limit the EOP, wherever possible, to functions directly related to the President's work.
    III. Centralize administrative services.
    IV. Reduce size of White House and EOP staffs.

I. STRENGTHEN PROCESS MANAGEMENT OF POLICY ISSUES

Perhaps the most important function of the President's staff is to make sure he has the wide variety of views and facts he needs to make decisions. By building a more orderly system for collecting information and advice, the President can make sure that he will hear all the views he should—and hear them in time. To better insure that this happens, I am taking the following actions to:

    Institute for domestic and economic issues, a system similar to the Presidential Review Memorandum process currently used for National Security issues.

    Create a committee of Presidential advisers, chaired by the Vice President, to set priorities among issues and oversee their staffing.

    Assure that Presidential decision memoranda on policy issues are coordinated with Cabinet and EOP advisers most involved with the issue.

    Consolidate under the Staff Secretary the two current White House paper circulation systems.

    Appoint a group of advisers to review the decision-making process periodically.

    Give the Assistant to the President for Domestic Affairs and Policy clear responsibility for managing the way in which domestic and most economic policy issues are prepared for Presidential decision.

    Assign follow-up responsibility for Presidential decisions as follows: immediate follow-up will be handled by the NSC or Domestic Policy Staff most directly involved in the issue; long term follow-up on selected issues will be handled by the Assistant to the President for Intergovernmental Relations.

These actions recognize that the White House and Executive Office staff must use their proximity to the President to insure that the full resources of the government and the public are brought to bear on Presidential decisions in a timely fashion. It is my purpose in instituting these changes to strengthen Cabinet participation in Presidential decisions.

II. RATIONALIZE EOP STRUCTURE BY LIMITING EOP, WHEREVER POSSIBLE, TO FUNCTIONS WHICH BEAR A CLOSE RELATIONSHIP TO THE WORK OF THE PRESIDENT

As the President's principal staff institution, there are several major things the EOP must do:

    Provide day-to-day operational support (e.g., scheduling, appointments) and help the President communicate with the public, the Congress, and the press.

    Manage the budget and coordinate Administration positions on matters before the Congress.

    Manage the Presidential decisionmaking processes efficiently and fairly, and bring the President the widest possible range of opinions.

    Help the President: plan and set priorities; monitor and evaluate progress toward achieving the President's objectives; understand and resolve major conflicts among line subordinates; manage crises, especially in national security matters.

In order to restructure the EOP around these basic functions, the functions of seven units should be discontinued or transferred, and ten units, including the White House Office, should be retained but modified.

Seven units should be discontinued or their functions transferred. These are:

    1. Office of Drug Abuse Policy.
    2. Office of Telecommunications Policy.
    3. Council on International Economic Policy.
    4. Federal Property Council.
    5. Energy Resources Council.
    6. Economic Opportunity Council.
    7. Domestic Council.

The functions of the Office of Drug Abuse Policy (ODAP) can be performed by a smaller staff reporting to a Presidential adviser in the EOP. The Office itself will be discontinued.

Much of the work done by the Office of Telecommunications Policy (OTP) can be more effectively performed outside the EOP. It is important that the EOP have the capacity to resolve differences and that the President have immediate advice on telecommunications and information policy, especially on national security, emergency preparedness and privacy issues. This only requires a small staff within EOP. The Office of Management and Budget would take responsibility for Federal telecommunications procurement and management policy and arbitration of interagency disputes about frequency allocation. All other functions except developing Presidential policy options would be transferred to a new office within the Department of Commerce, headed by a new Assistant Secretary for Communications and Information, who will perform many of the functions previously performed by the head of the OTP.

I propose that the Economic Opportunity Council be discontinued; it is dormant and its only active function (preparation of the Catalogue of Federal Domestic Assistance) is being performed by OMB. Three other units are also inactive and should be discontinued: Council on International Economic Policy, the Federal Property Council, and the Energy Resources Council.

The Domestic Council should be abolished. It has rarely functioned as a Council, because it is too large and its membership too diverse to make decisions efficiently. Its functions have been performed entirely by its staff. This Domestic Policy Staff should report to the Assistant to the President for Domestic Affairs and Policy. Under the policy process system described earlier, they should manage the process which coordinates the making of domestic and most economic policy. They should work closely with the Cabinet departments and agencies to insure that the views of the Cabinet and agency heads are brought to the President before decisions are made.

The ten EOP units which will continue with some modification are:

    1. White House Office.

2. Office of the Vice President.
3. Office of Management and Budget.
4. Council on Environmental Quality.
5. Council of Economic Advisers.
6. Office of Science and Technology Policy.
7. Office of the Special Representative for Trade Negotiations.
8. National Security Council.
9. Intelligence Oversight Board.
10. Council on Wage and Price Stability.

The operations of the Office of the Vice President reflect the combination of constitutional, statutory, and Presidentially assigned duties that make it unique among EOP units. Because his interests and assignments cover the same range as the President's, the Vice President requires a staff with expertise in diverse areas. Its basic functions should not be changed. However, I propose that certain support functions—involving accounting, personnel services, and supply—be transferred to a centralized EOP Administrative Unit.

The Office of Management and Budget would remain as a separate entity in the EOP, but some functional changes should be made. Four functions should be transferred from OMB to other parts of the government:

Administration to the new EOP Central Administrative Unit;

Executive Department/Labor Relations (except for Pay Agent, Executive Level Pools, and Legislative Analysis) to the Civil Service Commission;

Advisory Committee Management Secretariat to the General Services Administration;

Statistical Policy (except Forms Clearance) to the Department of Commerce.

I have asked the OMB to reorganize its management arm to emphasize major Presidential initiatives, such as reorganization, program evaluation, paperwork reduction, and regulatory reform.

The Council on Environmental Quality (CEQ) should remain in the EOP as an environmental adviser to the President. The CEQ's major purpose is to provide an independent assessment of our policies for improving the environment. Toward this end, it will analyze long term trends and conditions in the environment. It will advise OMB on the reorganization of natural resources functions within the Federal government. The Council will retain the functions it now has under NEPA and Executive Order No. 11514 with the exception of routine review of the adequacy of impact statements and the administrative aspects of their receipt and handling. The EPA will take over CEQ's evaluation responsibility under the Federal Nonnuclear Energy Research Development Act of 1974 [section 5901 et seq. of Title 42, The Public Health and Welfare]. The CEQ will continue to review and publish the Annual Report on Environmental Quality.

The strength of the Council of Economic Advisers (CEA) lies in its economic analysis of current policy choices. It also presents objective economic data, makes macroeconomic forecasts, and analyzes economic trends and their impact on the national economy. It will continue with a small reduction in staff.

The Office of Science and Technology Policy (OSTP) should retain those science, engineering, and technology functions which can be so useful in helping the President and his advisers make decisions about policy and budget issues. Instead of the Intergovernmental Science, Engineering, and Technology Advisory Panels, the President should rely on an intergovernmental relations working group, chaired by the Science Adviser. The Federal Coordinating Council on Science and Technology should operate as a sub-Cabinet working group chaired by the Science Adviser. The reorganization work of the President's Committee on Science and Technology would be part of the overall reorganization effort. The responsibility for preparing certain reports should be transferred to the National Science Foundation.

The proposal places manageable limits on OSTP's broad mandate while emphasizing functions that support the President.

The Office of the Special Representative for Trade Negotiations (STR) is now operating effectively and will be retained essentially as is. With the difficult negotiations now underway in Geneva, the benefits of transferring the STR to another agency are outweighed by the potential reduction in its effectiveness as an international negotiator.

The National Security Council (NSC) will be retained in its present form and its staff slightly reduced.

Intelligence Oversight Board (IOB) should be retained to insure that abuses of the past are not repeated and to emphasize Presidential concerns regarding intelligence issues.

The Council of Wage and Price Stability (COWPS) is a necessary weapon in the continuing fight against inflation and will be retained. To be sure that its work is closely coordinated with the economic analyses performed by the Council of Economic Advisers (CEA), COWPS should be directed by the Chairman of CEA.

III. CENTRALIZE ADMINISTRATIVE FUNCTIONS

About 380 (22 percent) of the full-time, permanent EOP personnel perform administrative support services in EOP units. Most EOP units besides the White House and OMB are too small to provide a full complement of administrative services. They depend on the White House, OMB, GSA, other federal departments, or several of these sources for many of these services. This approach is inefficient; the quality is uneven and the coordination poor. Some services are duplicated, others inconsistently distributed (excess capacity in some units and deficiencies in others), and most too costly.

I propose to combine administrative support operations into a Central Administrative Unit in EOP to provide support in administrative services common to all EOP entities. It should be a separate EOP entity because of the need to assure equal access by all other units.

This consolidation will result in:

Saving of roughly 40 positions and about $1.1 million, improved and more innovative services.

A focus for monitoring the efficiency and responsibility of administrative services.

A base for an effective EOP budget/planning system through which the President can manage an integrated EOP rather than a collection of disparate units.

The EOP has never before been organized as a single, unified entity serving the President. It is only by viewing it as a whole that we can improve efficiency through steps like the Central Administrative Unit.

IV. REDUCE THE SIZE OF WHITE HOUSE AND EOP STAFFS

I am reducing the White House staff by 28 percent, from the 485 I inherited from my predecessor to 351. This involves cuts in my policy and administrative staffs as well as transfers to the Central Administrative Unit.

I estimate that this plan and the other steps I am taking will reduce staff levels in the EOP by about 250, from 1,712 full-time permanent positions to about 1,460 and will save the taxpayers at least $6 million.

As in the rest of the government, I will be reluctant to add staff unless necessary to help me do my job better.

I ask that you support me in improving the operations of the Executive Office of the President by approving the attached reorganization plan.

In summary this plan would:

Abolish the Domestic Council and establish a Domestic Policy Staff.

Establish within the EOP a Central Administrative Unit.

Transfer certain functions of the Council on Environmental Quality to the President for redelegation.

Abolish the Office of Drug Abuse Policy and vest functions in the President for redelegation.

Abolish the Office of Telecommunications Policy and transfer functions to the Department of Commerce and to the President for redelegation.

Create an Assistant Secretary of Commerce for Communications and Information.

Vest some Office of Science and Technology Policy functions in the President for redelegation.

Abolish the Economic Opportunity Council and vest those functions in the President for redelegation.

Transfer the Committee Management Secretariat function of the Office of Management and Budget to the President for redelegation.

Make other incidental transfers attendant to those mentioned above.

Each of the changes set forth in the plan accompanying this message is necessary to accomplish one or more of the purposes set forth in Section 901(a) of Title 5 of the United States Code. I have taken care to determine that all functions abolished by the plan are done so only under statutory authority provided by Section 903(b) of Title 5 of the United States Code. The provisions in the plan for the appointment and pay of any head or officer of any agency have been found by me to be necessary.

As we continue our studies of other parts of the Executive Branch, we will find more ways to improve services in the EOP and elsewhere. This plan is only a beginning, but I am confident that it represents a major step toward a more efficient government that will serve the needs of the people and the President well.

JIMMY CARTER.

THE WHITE HOUSE, July 15, 1977.

ABOLITION OF OFFICE OF TELECOMMUNICATIONS POLICY

For effective date of the abolition of the Office of Telecommunications Policy and its transfer of functions, implementing Reorg. Plan No. 1 of 1977, set out above, see Ex. Ord. No. 12046, Mar. 27, 1978, 43 F.R. 13349, set out as a note under section 305 of Title 47, Telegraphs, Telephones, and Radiotelegraphs.

EX. ORD. NO. 12028. OFFICE OF ADMINISTRATION IN EXECUTIVE OFFICE OF PRESIDENT

Ex. Ord. No. 12028, Dec. 12, 1977, 42 F.R. 62895, as amended by Ex. Ord. No. 12122, Feb. 26, 1979, 44 F.R. 11197, provided:

By virtue of the authority vested in me by the Constitution and statutes of the United States of America, including the National Security Act of 1947, as amended [act July 26, 1947, ch. 343, 61 Stat. 495], Reorganization Plan No. 2 of 1970 (5 U.S.C. App.), Section 202 of the Budget and Accounting Procedures Act of 1950 (31 U.S.C. 581c) [31 U.S.C. 1531], and Reorganization Plan No. 1 of 1977 (42 FR 56101 (October 21, 1977)) [set out above], and as President of the United States of America, in order to effectuate the establishment of the Office of Administration in the Executive Office of the President, it is hereby ordered as follows:

SECTION 1. The establishment, provided by Section 2 of Reorganization Plan No. 1 of 1977 (42 F.R. 56101), of the Office of Administration in the Executive Office of the President shall be effective, as authorized by Section 7 of that Plan, on December 4, 1977.

SEC. 2. The Director of the Office of Administration, hereinafter referred to as the Director, shall report to the President. As the chief administrative officer of the Office of Administration, the Director shall be responsible for ensuring that the Office of Administration provides units within the Executive Office of the President common administrative support and services.

SEC. 3. (a) The Office of Administration shall provide common administrative support and services to all units within the Executive Office of the President, except for such services provided primarily in direct support of the President. The Office of Administration shall, upon request, assist the White House Office in performing its role of providing those administrative services which are primarily in direct support of the President.

(b) The common administrative support and services provided by the Office of Administration shall encompass all types of administrative support and services

that may be used by, or useful to, units within the Executive Office of the President. Such services and support shall include, but not be limited to, providing support services in the following administrative areas:

(1) personnel management services, including equal employment opportunity programs;

(2) financial management services;

(3) data processing, including support and services;

(4) library, records, and information services;

(5) office services and operations, including: mail, messenger, printing and duplication, graphics, word processing, procurement, and supply services; and

(6) any other administrative support or service which will achieve financial savings and increase efficiency through centralization of the supporting service.

(c) Administrative support and services shall be provided to all units within the Executive Office of the President in a manner consistent with available funds and other resources, or in accord with Section 7 of the Act of May 21, 1920 (41 Stat. 613), as amended (31 U.S.C. 686, referred to as the Economy Act) [31 U.S.C. 1535, 1536].

SEC. 4. (a) Subject to such direction or approval as the President may provide or require, the Director shall organize the Office of Administration, contract for supplies and services, and do all other things that the President, as head of the Office of Administration, might do.

(b) The Director is designated to perform the functions of the President under Section 107(b) of Title 3 of the United States Code.

(c) The Director may appoint and fix the pay of employees pursuant to the provisions of Section 107(b)(1)(A) of Title 3 of the United States Code without regard to any other provision of law regulating the employment or compensation of persons in the Government service. Under that section the Director may also fix the pay of an employee serving in a competitive position or in the career service in order to avoid the pay limitation imposed by Section 114 of Title 3 of the United States Code. The provisions of other laws regulating the employment or compensation of persons in the Government service shall continue to apply to such employee.

(d) The Director shall not be accountable for the program and management responsibilities of units within the Executive Office of the President; the head of each unit shall remain responsible for those functions.

SEC. 5. The primary responsibility for performing all administrative support and service functions of units within the Executive Office of the President shall be transferred and reassigned to the Office of Administration; except to the extent those functions are vested by law in the head of such a unit, other than the President; and except to the extent those functions are performed by the White House Office primarily in direct support of the President.

SEC. 6. The records, property, personnel, and unexpended balances of appropriations, available or to be made available, which relate to the functions transferred or reassigned by this Order from units within the Executive Office of the President to the Office of Administration, shall be transferred to the Office of Administration.

SEC. 7. (a) The Director of the Office of Management and Budget shall make such determinations, issue such orders, and take all actions necessary or appropriate to effectuate the transfers or reassignments provided by this Order, including the transfer of funds, records, property, and personnel.

(b) Such transfers shall become effective on April 1, 1978, or at such earlier time or times as the Director of the Office of Management and Budget determines, after consultation with the Director of the Office of Administration and other appropriate units within the Executive Office of the President.

JIMMY CARTER.

Ex. Ord. No. 12045. Implementation of Reorganization Plan Relating to Domestic Council, Domestic Policy Staff, Office of Drug Abuse Policy, and Economic Opportunity Council

Ex. Ord. No. 12045, Mar. 27, 1978, 43 F.R. 13347, provided:

By virtue of the authority vested in me by the Constitution and laws of the United States of America, including Section 7 of Reorganization Plan No. 1 of 1977 (42 F.R. 56101 (October 21, 1977)) [set out above], Section 202 of the Budget and Accounting Procedures Act of 1950 (31 U.S.C. 581c) [31 U.S.C. 1531], and Section 301 of Title 3 of the United States Code, and as President of the United States of America, in order to provide for transfers of the functions of the Office of Drug Abuse Policy, the Domestic Council, and the Economic Opportunity Council, and the abolition of the Office of Drug Abuse Policy, and Domestic Council, and the Economic Opportunity Council, and for other purposes, it is hereby ordered as follows:

SECTION 1. (a) The transfer of all functions of the Domestic Council, as provided by Section 5D of Reorganization Plan No. 1 of 1977 (42 F.R. 56101), is hereby effective.

(b) The redesignation of the Domestic Council Staff as the Domestic Policy Staff and the other provisions of Section 1 of Reorganization Plan No. 1 of 1977 (42 F.R. 56101), are hereby effective.

(c) The abolition of the Domestic Council, as provided by Section 3A of Reorganization Plan No. 1 of 1977 (42 F.R. 56101), is hereby effective.

(d) The Domestic Policy Staff shall perform such functions as the President may from time to time direct.

SEC. 2. (a) The transfer of all functions of the Office of Drug Abuse Policy and its Director, as provided by Section 5C of Reorganization Plan No. 1 of 1977 (42 F.R. 56101), is hereby effective.

(b) The abolition of the Office of Drug Abuse Policy, as provided by Section 3B of Reorganization Plan No. 1 of 1977 (42 F.R. 56101), is hereby effective.

(c) The Domestic Policy Staff shall assist the President in the performance of the functions transferred by Section 5C of Reorganization Plan No. 1 of 1977 (42 F.R. 56101).

SEC. 3. (a) The transfer of all functions of the Economic Opportunity Council, as provided by Section 5G of Reorganization Plan No. 1 of 1977 (42 F.R. 56101), is hereby effective.

(b) The abolition of the Economic Opportunity Council, as provided by Section 3D Reorganization Plan No. 1 of 1977 (42 F.R. 56101), is hereby effective.

SEC. 4. All provisions of Reorganization Plan No. 1 of 1977 (42 F.R. 56101) not made effective on or prior to the effective date of this Order are hereby effective.

SEC. 5. The records, property, personnel, and unexpended balances of appropriations, available or to be made available, which relate to the functions transferred, assigned, or delegated as provided in this Order are hereby transferred as appropriate.

SEC. 6. The Director of the Office of Management and Budget shall make such determinations, issue such orders, and take all actions necessary or appropriate to effectuate the transfers or reassignments provided in this Order, including the transfer of funds, records, property, and personnel.

SEC. 7. This Order shall be effective March 26, 1978.

JIMMY CARTER.

EXECUTIVE ORDER NO. 12133

Ex. Ord. No. 12133, May 9, 1979, 44 F.R. 27635, which related to the drug policy functions of the Domestic Policy Staff, was revoked by Ex. Ord. No. 12368, June 24, 1982, 47 F.R. 27843, set out as a note under section 1112 of Title 21, Food and Drugs.

Ex. Ord. No. 12134. Transfer of Printing and Duplicating Service Activity of Office of Administration to Department of Navy

Ex. Ord. No. 12134, May 9, 1979, 44 F.R. 27637, provided:

By the authority vested in me as President by the Constitution and laws of the United States of America, including Reorganization Plan No. 2 of 1970 (5 U.S.C. App.), Section 202 of the Budget and Accounting Procedures Act of 1950 (31 U.S.C. 581c) [31 U.S.C. 1531], and Reorganization Plan No. 1 of 1977 (42 F.R. 56101; 5 U.S.C. App.) [also set out above], and in order to provide for the transfer of the printing and duplicating service activity from the Office of Administration in the Executive Office of the President to the Department of the Navy, it is hereby ordered as follows:

1–101. (a) The primary responsibility for performing the common and usual administrative support and services that are related to printing and duplication and that are assigned to the Office of Administration in the Executive Office of the President by Section 3(b)(5) of Executive Order No. 12028, as amended [set out above], is transferred and reassigned to the Department of the Navy.

(b) The Department of the Navy shall be primarily responsible for providing to the Office of Administration, both onsite and offsite, that common and usual administrative support and service related to printing and duplication. It shall be provided in a manner consistent with available funds and other resources, or in accord with Section 7 of the Act of May 21, 1920 (41 Stat. 613), as amended (31 U.S.C. 686, referred to as the Economy Act) [31 U.S.C. 1535, 1536].

1–102. The records, property, personnel, and unexpended balances of appropriations, available or to be made available, which relate to the functions transferred or reassigned by this Order, shall be transferred to the Department of the Navy.

1–103. The Director of the Office of Management and Budget shall make such determinations, issue such orders, and take all actions necessary or appropriate to effectuate the transfers or reassignments provided by this Order, including the transfer of funds, records, property, and personnel.

1–104. Such transfers shall be effective on May 6, 1979.

JIMMY CARTER.

Ex. Ord. No. 12859. Establishment of Domestic Policy Council

Ex. Ord. No. 12859, Aug. 16, 1993, 58 F.R. 44101, provided:

By the authority vested in me as President by the Constitution and the laws of the United States of America, including sections 105, 107, and 301 of title 3, United States Code, it is hereby ordered as follows:

SECTION 1. *Establishment*. There is established the Domestic Policy Council ("the Council").

SEC. 2. *Membership*. The Council shall comprise the:

(a) President, who shall serve as a Chairman of the Council;

(b) Vice President;

(c) Secretary of Health and Human Services;

(d) Attorney General;

(e) Secretary of Labor;

(f) Secretary of Veterans Affairs;

(g) Secretary of the Interior;

(h) Secretary of Education;

(i) Secretary of Housing and Urban Development;

(j) Secretary of Agriculture;

(k) Secretary of Transportation;

(l) Secretary of Commerce;

(m) Secretary of Energy;

(n) Secretary of the Treasury;

(o) Administrator of the Environmental Protection Agency;

(p) Chair of the Council of Economic Advisers;

(q) Director of the Office of Management and Budget;

(r) Assistant to the President for Economic Policy;

(s) Assistant to the President for Domestic Policy;

(t) Assistant to the President and Director of the Office of National Service;

(u) Senior Advisor to the President for Policy Development;

(v) Director, Office of National Drug Control Policy;

(w) AIDS Policy Coordinator; and

(x) Such other officials of Executive departments and agencies as the President may, from time to time, designate.

SEC. 3. *Meeting of the Council.* The President, or upon his direction, the Assistant to the President for Domestic Policy ("the Assistant"), may convene meetings of the Council. The President shall preside over the meetings of the Council, provided that in his absence the Vice President, and in his absence the Assistant, will preside.

SEC. 4. *Functions.* (a) The principal functions of the Council are: (1) to coordinate the domestic policy-making process; (2) to coordinate domestic policy advice to the President; (3) to ensure that domestic policy decisions and programs are consistent with the President's stated goals, and to ensure that those goals are being effectively pursued; and (4) to monitor implementation of the President's domestic policy agenda. The Assistant may take such actions, including drafting a Charter, as may be necessary or appropriate to implement such functions.

(b) All executive departments and agencies, whether or not represented on the Council, shall coordinate domestic policy through the Council.

(c) In performing the foregoing functions, the Assistant will, when appropriate, work with the Assistant to the President for National Security Affairs and the Assistant to the President for Economic Policy.

SEC. 5. *Administration.* (a) The Council may function through established or ad hoc committees, task forces or interagency groups.

(b) The Council shall have a staff to be headed by the Assistant to the President for Domestic Policy. The Council shall have such staff and other assistance as may be necessary to carry out the provisions of this order.

(c) All executive departments and agencies shall cooperate with the Council and provide such assistance, information, and advice to the Council as the Council may request, to the extent permitted by law.

WILLIAM J. CLINTON.

§ 101. Commencement of term of office

The term of four years for which a President and Vice President shall be elected, shall, in all cases, commence on the 20th day of January next succeeding the day on which the votes of the electors have been given.

(June 25, 1948, ch. 644, 62 Stat. 678.)

SHORT TITLE OF 2000 AMENDMENT

Pub. L. 106–293, § 1, Oct. 12, 2000, 114 Stat. 1035, provided that: "This Act [amending provisions set out as a note under section 102 of this title] may be cited as the 'Presidential Transition Act of 2000'."

DWIGHT D. EISENHOWER EXECUTIVE OFFICE BUILDING

Pub. L. 106–92, Nov. 9, 1999, 113 Stat. 1309, provided that:

"SECTION 1. DESIGNATION OF DWIGHT D. EISENHOWER EXECUTIVE OFFICE BUILDING.

"The Old Executive Office Building located at 17th Street and Pennsylvania Avenue, NW, in Washington, District of Columbia, shall be known and designated as the 'Dwight D. Eisenhower Executive Office Building'.

"SEC. 2. REFERENCES.

"Any reference in a law, map, regulation, document, paper, or other record of the United States to the building referred to in section 1 shall be deemed to be a reference to the 'Dwight D. Eisenhower Executive Office Building'."

Pub. L. 100–461, title V, § 590, Oct. 1, 1988, 102 Stat. 2268–52, as amended by Pub. L. 106–92, § 2, Nov. 9, 1999, 113 Stat. 1309, provided that:

"(a) ACCEPTANCE OF GIFTS OF MONEY AND PROPERTY.— The Director of the Office of Administration is authorized to—

"(1) accept, hold, administer, utilize and sell gifts and bequests of property, both real and personal, and loans of personal property other than money; and

"(2) accept and utilize voluntary and uncompensated services;

for the purpose of aiding, benefiting, or facilitating the work of preservation, restoration, renovation, rehabilitation, or historic furnishing of the Dwight D. Eisenhower Executive Office Building and the grounds thereof.

"(b) ESTABLISHMENT OF FUND.—There is established in the Treasury a fund for use in accordance with the provisions of this section. Amounts of money and proceeds from the sale of property accepted under subsection (a) shall be deposited in the fund, which shall be available to the Director of the Office of Administration. Such funds shall be held in trust by the Secretary of the Treasury.

"(c) USE OF FUND.—Property accepted pursuant to this section or the proceeds from the sale thereof, shall be used as nearly as possible in accordance with the terms of the gift or bequest. Any use or sale of property accepted pursuant to this section, and any use of proceeds from such sale, shall be subject to the disapproval of the Administrator of General Services within 30 days after the Administrator receives notice of such use or sale. The Director of the Office of Administration shall not accept any gift under this section that is expressly conditioned on any expenditure not to be met from the gift itself unless such expenditure has been approved by an Act of Congress.

"(d) TAXES.—For the purpose of the Federal income, estate, and gift tax laws, property accepted under this section shall be considered as a gift, bequest, or devise to the United States."

PRESIDENT'S ADVISORY COMMISSION ON PRESIDENTIAL OFFICE SPACE

Act Aug. 3, 1956, ch. 925, 70 Stat. 979, as amended by Pub. L. 85–3, Jan. 25, 1957, 71 Stat. 4, created a President's Advisory Commission on Presidential Office Space to study the problem of providing more adequate office space for the White House Office and the other agencies of the Executive Office of the President. Pursuant to section 1(b) of act Aug. 3, 1956, the Commission was required to report to the President its findings and recommendations within 10 months after Aug. 3, 1956, and section 2(g) of act Aug. 3, 1956, provided that the Commission should cease to exist 30 days after the submission of its final report.

§ 102. Compensation of the President

The President shall receive in full for his services during the term for which he shall have been elected compensation in the aggregate amount of $400,000 a year, to be paid monthly, and in addition an expense allowance of $50,000 to assist in defraying expenses relating to or resulting from the discharge of his official duties, for which expense allowance no accounting, other than for income tax purposes, shall be made by him. He shall be entitled also to the use of the furniture and other effects belonging to the United States and kept in the Executive Residence at the White House.

(June 25, 1948, ch. 644, 62 Stat. 678; Jan. 19, 1949, ch. 2, § 1(a), 63 Stat. 4; Oct. 20, 1951, ch. 521, title VI, § 619(a), 65 Stat. 569; Pub. L. 91–1, § 1, Jan. 17, 1969, 83 Stat. 3; Pub. L. 95–570, § 5(a), Nov. 2, 1978, 92 Stat. 2450; Pub. L. 106–58, title VI, § 644(a), Sept. 29, 1999, 113 Stat. 478.)

AMENDMENTS

1999—Pub. L. 106–58 substituted "$400,000" for "$200,000".

1978—Pub. L. 95–570 substituted "Executive Residence at the White House" for "Executive Mansion".

1969—Pub. L. 91–1 substituted "$200,000" for "$100,000".

1951—Act Oct. 20, 1951, made President's expense allowance taxable.

1949—Act Jan. 19, 1949, increased salary from $75,000 to $100,000 per year, and gave President a yearly expense account of $50,000 for which he was to make no accounting and which was tax free.

EFFECTIVE DATE OF 1999 AMENDMENT

Pub. L. 106–58, title VI, § 644(b), Sept. 29, 1999, 113 Stat. 478, provided that: "The amendment made by this section [amending this section] shall take effect at noon on January 20, 2001."

EFFECTIVE DATE OF 1978 AMENDMENT

Section 6(a) of Pub. L. 95–570 provided that: "The amendments made by this Act [enacting sections 107, 108, 112, 113, and 114 of this title, amending sections 102, 103, 105, 106, 109, 110, and 202 of this title, repealing section 107 of this title, and enacting provisions set out as a note under section 107 of this title] shall apply to any fiscal year which begins on or after October 1, 1978."

EFFECTIVE DATE OF 1969 AMENDMENT

Section 2 of Pub. L. 91–1 provided that: "The amendment made by this Act [amending this section] shall take effect at noon on January 20, 1969."

EFFECTIVE DATE OF 1951 AMENDMENT

Section 619(e) of act Oct. 20, 1951, provided that: "The amendments made by subsections (a) and (b) of this section [amending this section and section 111 of this title] shall become effective at noon on January 20, 1953, and the amendments made by subsections (c) and (d) [amending sections 31a and 31b of Title 2, The Congress] shall become effective at noon on January 3, 1953."

EFFECTIVE DATE OF 1949 AMENDMENT

Amendment by act Jan. 19, 1949, effective noon, Jan. 19, 1949, see section 3 of that act.

DISCLOSURE OF IN-KIND CONTRIBUTIONS TO 1988–1989 TRANSITION

Pub. L. 100–398, § 5, Aug. 17, 1988, 102 Stat. 987, provided that:

"(a) DISCLOSURE AS CONDITION OF RECEIPT OF FUNDS.—The President-elect and Vice-President-elect (as a condition for receiving services under section 3 and for funds provided under section 6(a)(1) of the Presidential Transition Act of 1963 [Pub. L. 88–277] (3 U.S.C. 102 note) shall provide an estimate to the Administrator of General Services of the aggregate value of in-kind contributions made during the period beginning on November 9, 1988, through January 20, 1989, received for transition activities for—

"(1) transportation;

"(2) hotel and other accommodations;

"(3) suitable office space; and

"(4) furniture, furnishings, office machines and equipment, and office supplies.

"(b) FORM AND AVAILABILITY OF ESTIMATES.—The estimates made under subsection (a) shall be—

"(1) in the form of a report to the Administrator of General Services within 90 days after January 20, 1989; and

"(2) made available to the public by the Administrator upon receipt by the Administrator."

PRESIDENTIAL TRANSITION ACT OF 1963

Pub. L. 88–277, Mar. 7, 1964, 78 Stat. 153, as amended by Pub. L. 94–499, §§ 1, 2, Oct. 14, 1976, 90 Stat. 2380; Pub. L. 100–398, §§ 2(a), 3, 4, Aug. 17, 1988, 102 Stat. 985, 986; Pub. L. 106–293, § 2, Oct. 12, 2000, 114 Stat. 1035, provided: "That this Act may be cited as the 'Presidential Transition Act of 1963.'

"PURPOSE OF THIS ACT

"SEC. 2. The Congress declares it to be the purpose of this Act to promote the orderly transfer of the executive power in connection with the expiration of the term of office of a President and the inauguration of a new President. The national interest requires that such transitions in the office of President be accomplished so as to assure continuity in the faithful execution of the laws and in the conduct of the affairs of the Federal Government, both domestic and foreign. Any disruption occasioned by the transfer of the executive power could produce results detrimental to the safety and well-being of the United States and its people. Accordingly, it is the intent of the Congress that appropriate actions be authorized and taken to avoid or minimize any disruption. In addition to the specific provisions contained in this Act directed toward that purpose, it is the intent of the Congress that all officers of the Government so conduct the affairs of the Government for which they exercise responsibility and authority as (1) to be mindful of problems occasioned by transitions in the office of President, (2) to take appropriate lawful steps to avoid or minimize disruptions that might be occasioned by the transfer of the executive power, and (3) otherwise to promote orderly transitions in the office of President.

"SERVICES AND FACILITIES AUTHORIZED TO BE PROVIDED TO PRESIDENTS-ELECT AND VICE-PRESIDENTS-ELECT

"SEC. 3. (a) The Administrator of General Services, referred to hereafter in this Act as 'the Administrator,' is authorized to provide, upon request, to each President-elect and each Vice-President-elect, for use in connection with his preparations for the assumption of official duties as President or Vice President necessary services and facilities, including the following:

"(1) Suitable office space appropriately equipped with furniture, furnishings, office machines and equipment, and office supplies, as determined by the Administrator, after consultation with the President-elect, the Vice-President-elect, or their designee provided for in subsection (e) of this section, at such place or places within the United States as the President-elect or Vice-President-elect shall designate.

"(2) Payment of the compensation of members of office staffs designated by the President-elect or Vice-President-elect at rates determined by them not to exceed the rate provided by the Classification Act of 1949, as amended [chapter 51 and subchapter III of chapter 53 of title 5], for grade GS–18: Provided, That any employee of any agency of any branch of the Government may be detailed to such staffs on a reimbursable basis with the consent of the head of the agency; and while so detailed such employee shall be responsible only to the President-elect or Vice-President-elect for the performance of his duties: Provided further, That any employee so detailed shall continue to receive the compensation provided pursuant to law for his regular employment, and shall retain the rights and privileges of such employment without interruption. Notwithstanding any other law, persons receiving compensation as members of office staffs under this subsection, other than those detailed from agencies, shall not be held or considered to be employees of the Federal Government except for purposes of the Civil Service Retirement Act [section 8301 et seq. of title 5], the Federal Employees' Compensation Act [section 8501 et seq. of title 5], the Federal Employees' Group Life Insurance Act of 1954 [section 8701 et seq. of title 5], and the Federal Employees Health Benefits Act of 1959 [section 8901 et seq. of title 5].

"(3) Payment of expenses for the procurement of services of experts or consultants or organizations thereof for the President-elect or Vice-President-elect, as authorized for the head of any department by section 15 of the Administrative Expenses Act of 1946, as amended (5 U.S.C. 55a) [section 3109 of title 5].

"(4)(A) Payment of travel expenses and subsistence allowances, including rental of Government or hired motor vehicles, found necessary by the President-elect or Vice-President-elect, as authorized for persons employed intermittently or for persons serving without compensation by section 5 of the Administrative Expenses Act of 1946, as amended (5 U.S.C. 73b–2) [section 5703 of title 5], as may be appropriate;

"(B) When requested by the President-elect or Vice-President-elect or their designee, and approved by the President, Government aircraft may be provided for transition purposes on a reimbursable basis; when requested by the President-elect, the Vice-President-elect, or the designee of the President-elect or Vice-President-elect, aircraft may be chartered for transition purposes; and any collections from the Secret Service, press, or others occupying space on chartered aircraft shall be deposited to the credit of the appropriations made under section 6 of this Act.

"(5) Communications services found necessary by the President-elect or Vice-President-elect.

"(6) Payment of expenses for necessary printing and binding, notwithstanding the Act of January 12, 1895, and the Act of March 1, 1919, as amended (44 U.S.C. 111) [section 501 of title 44].

"(7) Reimbursement to the postal revenues in amounts equivalent to the postage that would otherwise be payable on mail matter referred to in subsection (d) of this section.

"(8)(A)(i) Not withstanding subsection (b), payment of expenses during the transition for briefings, workshops, or other activities to acquaint key prospective Presidential appointees with the types of problems and challenges that most typically confront new political appointees when they make the transition from campaign and other prior activities to assuming the responsibility for governance after inauguration.

"(ii) Activities under this paragraph may include interchange between such appointees and individuals who—

"(I) held similar leadership roles in prior administrations;

"(II) are department or agency experts from the Office of Management and Budget or an Office of Inspector General of a department or agency; or

"(III) are relevant staff from the General Accounting Office.

"(iii) Activities under this paragraph may include training or orientation in records management to comply with section 2203 of title 44, United States Code, including training on the separation of Presidential records and personal records to comply with subsection (b) of that section.

"(iv) Activities under this paragraph may include training or orientation in human resources management and performance-based management.

"(B) Activities under this paragraph shall be conducted primarily for individuals the President-elect intends to nominate as department heads or appoint to key positions in the Executive Office of the President.

"(9)(A) Notwithstanding subsection (b), development of a transition directory by the Administrator of General Services Administration, in consultation with the Archivist of the United States (head of the National Archives and Records Administration) for activities conducted under paragraph (8).

"(B) The transition directory shall be a compilation of Federal publications and materials with supplementary materials developed by the Administrator that provides information on the officers, organization, and statutory and administrative authorities, functions, duties, responsibilities, and mission of each department and agency.

"(10)(A) Notwithstanding subsection (b), consultation by the Administrator with any candidate for President or Vice President to develop a systems architecture plan for the computer and communications systems of the candidate to coordinate a transition to Federal systems, if the candidate is elected.

"(B) Consultations under this paragraph shall be conducted at the discretion of the Administrator.

"(b) The Administrator may not expend funds for the provision of services and facilities under section 3 of this Act in connection with any obligations incurred by the President-elect or Vice-President-elect—

"(1) before the day following the date of the general elections held to determine the electors of President and Vice President under section 1 or 2 of title 3, United States Code; or

"(2) after 30 days after the date of the inauguration of the President-elect as President and the inauguration of the Vice-President-elect as Vice President.

"(c) The terms 'President-elect' and 'Vice-President-elect' as used in this Act shall mean such persons as are the apparent successful candidates for the office of President and Vice President, respectively, as ascertained by the Administrator following the general elections held to determine the electors of President and Vice President in accordance with title 3, United States Code, sections 1 and 2.

"(d) Each President-elect shall be entitled to conveyance within the United States and its territories and possessions of all mail matter, including airmail, sent by him in connection with his preparations for the assumption of official duties as President, and such mail matter shall be transmitted as penalty mail as provided in title 39, United States Code, section 4152 [now section 3202 of title 39]. Each Vice-President-elect shall be entitled to conveyance within the United States and its territories and possessions of all mail matter, including airmail, sent by him under his written autograph signature in connection with his preparations for the assumption of official duties as Vice President.

"(e) Each President-elect and Vice-President-elect may designate to the Administrator an assistant authorized to make on his behalf such designations or findings of necessity as may be required in connection with the services and facilities to be provided under this Act. Not more than 10 per centum of the total expenditures under this Act for any President-elect or Vice-President-elect may be made upon the basis of a certificate by him or the assistant designated by him pursuant to this section that such expenditures are classified and are essential to the national security, and that they accord with the provisions of subsections (a), (b), and (d) of this section.

"(f) In the case where the President-elect is the incumbent President or in the case where the Vice-President-elect is the incumbent Vice President, there shall be no expenditures of funds for the provision of services and facilities to such incumbent under this Act, and any funds appropriated for such purposes shall be returned to the general funds of the Treasury.

"SERVICES AND FACILITIES AUTHORIZED TO BE PROVIDED TO FORMER PRESIDENTS AND FORMER VICE PRESIDENTS

"SEC. 4. The Administrator is authorized to provide, upon request, to each former President and each former Vice President, for a period not to exceed seven months from 30 days before the date of the expiration of his term of office as President or Vice President, for use in connection with winding up the affairs of his office, necessary services and facilities of the same general character as authorized by this Act to be provided to Presidents-elect and Vice-Presidents-elect. Any person appointed or detailed to serve a former President or former Vice President under authority of this section shall be appointed or detailed in accordance with, and shall be subject to, all of the provisions of section 3 of this Act applicable to persons appointed or detailed under authority of that section. The provisions of the Act of August 25, 1958 (72 Stat. 838; 3 U.S.C. 102, note), other than subsections (a) and (e) shall not become effective with respect to a former President until six months after the expiration of his term of office as President.

"DISCLOSURES OF FINANCING AND PERSONNEL; LIMITATION ON ACCEPTANCE OF DONATIONS

"SEC. 5. (a)(1) The President-elect and Vice-President-elect (as a condition for receiving services under section 3 and for funds provided under section 6(a)(1)) shall disclose to the Administrator the date of contribution, source, amount, and expenditure thereof of all money, other than funds from the Federal Government, and including currency of the United States and of any foreign nation, checks, money orders, or any other negotiable instruments payable on demand, received either before or after the date of the general elections for use in the preparation of the President-elect or Vice-President-elect for the assumption of official duties as President or Vice President.

"(2) The President-elect and Vice-President-elect (as a condition for receiving such services and funds) shall make available to the Administrator and the Comptroller General all information concerning such contributions as the Administrator or Comptroller General may require for purposes of auditing both the public and private funding used in the activities authorized by this Act.

"(3) Disclosures made under paragraph (1) shall be—

"(A) in the form of a report to the Administrator within 30 days after the inauguration of the President-elect as President and the Vice-President-elect as Vice President; and

"(B) made available to the public by the Administrator upon receipt by the Administrator.

"(b)(1) The President-elect and Vice-President-elect (as a condition for receiving services provided under section 3 and funds provided under section 6(a)(1)) shall make available to the public—

"(A) the names and most recent employment of all transition personnel (full-time or part-time, public or private, or volunteer) who are members of the President-elect or Vice-President-elect's Federal department or agency transition teams; and

"(B) information regarding the sources of funding which support the transition activities of each transition team member.

"(2) Disclosures under paragraph (1) shall be made public before the initial transition team contact with a Federal department or agency and shall be updated as necessary.

"(c) The President-elect and Vice-President-elect (as a condition for receiving services under section 3 and for funds provided under section 6(a)(1)) shall not accept more than $5,000 from any person, organization, or other entity for purposes of carrying out activities authorized by this Act.

"AUTHORIZATION OF APPROPRIATIONS"

"SEC. 6. (a) There are hereby authorized to be appropriated to the Administrator such funds as may be necessary for carrying out the purposes of this Act, except that with respect to any one Presidential transition—

"(1) not more than $3,500,000 may be appropriated for the purposes of providing services and facilities to the President-elect and Vice President-elect under section 3, and

"(2) not more than $1,500,000 may be appropriated for the purposes of providing services and facilities to the former President and former Vice President under section 4, except that any amount appropriated pursuant to this paragraph in excess of $1,250,000 shall be returned to the general fund of the Treasury in the case where the former Vice President is the incumbent President.

The President shall include in the budget transmitted to Congress, for each fiscal year in which his regular term of office will expire, a proposed appropriation for carrying out the purposes of this Act.

"(b) The amounts authorized to be appropriated under subsection (a) shall be increased by an inflation adjusted amount, based on increases in the cost of transition services and expenses which have occurred in the years following the most recent Presidential transition, and shall be included in the proposed appropriation transmitted by the President under the last sentence of subsection (a)."

[Pub. L. 100–398, §2(b), Aug. 17, 1988, 102 Stat. 985, provided that: "The amendments made by subsection (a) of this section [renumbering and amending section 6 of Pub. L. 88–277, set out above] shall be effective upon enactment [Aug. 17, 1988], except that the amendment

made by paragraph (7) of such subsection [enacting subsec. (b) of section 6 of Pub. L. 88–277, set out above] shall take effect on October 1, 1989."]

[Pub. L. 94–499, §3, Oct. 14, 1976, 90 Stat. 2380, provided that amendment of section 5 of Pub. L. 88–277 [set out above] by section 1 of Pub. L. 94–499, respecting revision of appropriation authorization, shall be effective Oct. 14, 1976.]

[References in laws to the rates of pay for GS–16, 17, or 18, or to maximum rates of pay under the General Schedule, to be considered references to rates payable under specified sections of Title 5, Government Organization and Employees, see section 529 [title I, §101(c)(1)] of Pub. L. 101–509, set out in a note under section 5376 of Title 5.]

EXPENSE ALLOWANCE: USE; REVERSION OF UNEXPENDED PORTION; NONTAXABLE

Provisions prohibiting expenditure of funds made available for official expenses for any other purpose, requiring reversion of any unused amount to the Treasury pursuant to 31 U.S.C. 1552, and providing that none of the funds made available for official expenses shall be considered as taxable to the President were contained in the following appropriation acts:

Pub. L. 106–554, §1(a)(3) [title III], Dec. 21, 2000, 114 Stat. 2763, 2763A–136.
Pub. L. 106–58, title III, Sept. 29, 1999, 113 Stat. 444.
Pub. L. 105–277, div. A, §101(h) [title III], Oct. 21, 1998, 112 Stat. 2681–480, 2681–492.
Pub. L. 105–61, title III, Oct. 10, 1997, 111 Stat. 1290.
Pub. L. 104–208, div. A, title I, §101(f) [title III], Sept. 30, 1996, 110 Stat. 3009–314, 3009–326.
Pub. L. 104–52, title III, Nov. 19, 1995, 109 Stat. 477.
Pub. L. 103–329, title III, Sept. 30, 1994, 108 Stat. 2392.
Pub. L. 103–123, title III, Oct. 28, 1993, 107 Stat. 1235.
Pub. L. 102–393, title III, Oct. 6, 1992, 106 Stat. 1738.
Pub. L. 102–141, title III, Oct. 28, 1991, 105 Stat. 844.
Pub. L. 101–509, title III, Nov. 5, 1990, 104 Stat. 1399.
Pub. L. 101–136, title III, Nov. 3, 1989, 103 Stat. 790.
Pub. L. 100–440, title III, Sept. 22, 1988, 102 Stat. 1728.
Pub. L. 100–202, §101(m) [title III], Dec. 22, 1987, 101 Stat. 1329–390, 1329–398.
Pub. L. 99–500, §101(m) [title III], Oct. 18, 1986, 100 Stat. 1783–308, 1783–315, and Pub. L. 99–591, §101(m) [title III, §301], Oct. 30, 1986, 100 Stat. 3341–308, 3341–315.
Pub. L. 99–190, §101(h) [H.R. 3036, title III], Dec. 19, 1985, 99 Stat. 1291.
Pub. L. 98–473, §101(j) [H.R. 5798, title III], Oct. 12, 1984, 98 Stat. 1963.
Pub. L. 98–151, §101(f) [H.R. 4139, title III], Nov. 14, 1983, 97 Stat. 973.
Pub. L. 97–377, title I, §101(a) [incorporating H.R. 4121, title III, for FY 1982], Dec. 21, 1982, 96 Stat. 1830.
Pub. L. 97–92, §101(a) [H.R. 4121, title III], Dec. 15, 1981, 95 Stat. 1183.
Pub. L. 96–536, §101(a) [incorporating Pub. L. 96–74, title III], Dec. 16, 1980, 94 Stat. 3166.
Pub. L. 96–74, title III, Sept. 29, 1979, 93 Stat. 563.

FORMER PRESIDENTS; ALLOWANCE; SELECTION, COMPENSATION, AND STATUS OF OFFICE STAFF; OFFICE SPACE; WIDOW'S ALLOWANCE, TERMINATION; "FORMER PRESIDENT" DEFINED

Pub. L. 85–745, Aug. 25, 1958, 72 Stat. 838, as amended by Pub. L. 86–682, §12(c), Sept. 2, 1960, 74 Stat. 730; Pub. L. 88–426, title I, §124, Aug. 14, 1964, 78 Stat. 412; Pub. L. 89–554, §8(a), Sept. 6, 1966, 80 Stat. 660; Pub. L. 90–206, title II, §224(c), Dec. 16, 1967, 81 Stat. 642; Pub. L. 91–231, §7, Apr. 15, 1970, 84 Stat. 198; Pub. L. 91–658, §6, Jan. 8, 1971, 84 Stat. 1963; Pub. L. 95–138, §1, Oct. 18, 1977, 91 Stat. 1170; Pub. L. 103–123, title IV, §6(a), Oct. 28, 1993, 107 Stat. 1246; Pub. L. 103–329, title V, §531, Sept. 30, 1994, 108 Stat. 2413; Pub. L. 104–52, title V, §523, Nov. 19, 1995, 109 Stat. 495; Pub. L. 105–61, title IV, §409(a), Oct. 10, 1997, 111 Stat. 1299, provided that:

"(a) Each former President shall be entitled for the remainder of his life to receive from the United States a monetary allowance at a rate per annum, payable monthly by the Secretary of the Treasury, which is equal to the annual rate of basic pay, as in effect from time to time, of the head of an executive department, as defined in section 101 of title 5, United States Code. However, such allowance shall not be paid for any period during which such former President holds an appointive or elective office or position in or under the Federal Government or the government of the District of Columbia to which is attached a rate of pay other than a nominal rate.

"(b) The Administrator of General Services shall, without regard to the civil-service and classification laws, provide for each former President an office staff. Persons employed under this subsection shall be selected by the former President and shall be responsible only to him for the performance of their duties. Each former President shall fix basic rates of compensation for persons employed for him under this paragraph which in the aggregate shall not exceed $96,000 per annum except that for the first 30-month period during which a former President is entitled to staff assistance under this subsection, such rates of compensation in the aggregate shall not exceed $150,000 per annum. The annual rate of compensation payable to any such person shall not exceed the highest annual rate of basic pay now or hereafter provided by law for positions at level II of the Executive Schedule under section 5313 of title 5, United States Code.

"(c) The Administrator of General Services shall furnish for each former President suitable office space appropriately furnished and equipped, as determined by the Administrator, at such place within the United States as the former President shall specify.

"(d) [Repealed. Pub. L. 86–682, §12(c), Sept. 2, 1960, 74 Stat. 730. See sections 3214 and 3216 of title 39.]

"(e) The widow of each former President shall be entitled to receive from the United States a monetary allowance at a rate of $20,000 per annum, payable monthly by the Secretary of the Treasury, if such widow shall waive the right to each other annuity or pension to which she is entitled under any other Act of Congress. The monetary allowance of such widow—

"(1) commences on the day after the former President dies;

"(2) terminates on the last day of the month before such widow—

"(A) dies; or

"(B) remarries before becoming 60 years of age; and

"(3) is not payable for any period during which such widow holds an appointive or elective office or position in or under the Federal Government or the government of the District of Columbia to which is attached a rate of pay other than a nominal rate.

"(f) As used in this section, the term 'former President' means a person—

"(1) who shall have held the office of President of the United States of America;

"(2) whose service in such office shall have terminated other than by removal pursuant to section 4 of article II of the Constitution of the United States of America; and

"(3) who does not then currently hold such office.

"(g) There are authorized to be appropriated to the Administrator of General Services up to $1,000,000 for each former President and up to $500,000 for the spouse of each former President each fiscal year for security and travel related expenses: *Provided*, That under the provisions set forth in section 3056, paragraph (a), subparagraph (3) of title 18, United States Code, the former President and/or spouse was not receiving protection for a lifetime provided by the United States Secret Service under section 3056 paragraph (a) subparagraph (3) of title 18, United States Code; the protection provided by the United States Secret Service expired at its designated time; or the protection provided by the United States Secret Service was declined prior to authorized expiration in lieu of these funds."

[Pub. L. 95–138, §2, Oct. 18, 1977, 91 Stat. 1170, provided that: "The amendment made by the first section of this Act [amending Pub. L. 87–745, set out above] shall take effect October 1, 1977."]

FORMER PRESIDENT EISENHOWER; ALLOWANCE; COMPENSATION OF OFFICE STAFF; WIDOW'S PENSION

Allowance to former President Eisenhower as precluding entitlement to pay of General of the Army, compensation of office staff to former President to be reduced by pay of military assistants to the General of the Army, and benefits of widow of former President unaffected by restoration of military status, see Appointment of General of the Army note under former sections 1691 to 1697 of Title 50, Appendix, War and National Defense.

SECTION REFERRED TO IN OTHER SECTIONS

This section is referred to in title 10 section 1091; title 20 section 1018; title 31 section 3524; title 38 section 7437.

§ 103. Traveling expenses

There may be expended for or on account of the traveling expenses of the President of the United States such sum as Congress may from time to time appropriate, not exceeding $100,000 per annum, such sum when appropriated to be expended in the discretion of the President and accounted for on his certificate solely.

(June 25, 1948, ch. 644, 62 Stat. 678; Pub. L. 95–570, §4, Nov. 2, 1978, 92 Stat. 2450.)

AMENDMENTS

1978—Pub. L. 95–570 substituted "$100,000" for "$40,000".

EFFECTIVE DATE OF 1978 AMENDMENT

Amendment by Pub. L. 95–570 applicable to any fiscal year beginning on or after Oct. 1, 1978, see section 6(a) of Pub. L. 95–570, set out as a note under section 102 of this title.

SECTION REFERRED TO IN OTHER SECTIONS

This section is referred to in title 31 section 3524.

§ 104. Salary of the Vice President

(a) The per annum rate of salary of the Vice President of the United States shall be the rate determined for such position under chapter 11 of title 2, as adjusted under this section. Subject to subsection (b), effective at the beginning of the first month in which an adjustment takes effect under section 5303 of title 5 in the rates of pay under the General Schedule, the salary of the Vice President shall be adjusted by an amount, rounded to the nearest multiple of $100 (or if midway between multiples of $100, to the nearest higher multiple of $100), equal to the percentage of such per annum rate which corresponds to the most recent percentage change in the ECI (relative to the date described in the next sentence), as determined under section 704(a)(1) of the Ethics Reform Act of 1989. The appropriate date under this sentence is the first day of the fiscal year in which such adjustment in the rates of pay under the General Schedule takes effect.

(b) In no event shall the percentage adjustment taking effect under the second and third sentences of subsection (a) in any calendar year (before rounding) exceed the percentage adjustment taking effect in such calendar year under section 5303 of title 5 in the rates of pay under the General Schedule.

(June 25, 1948, ch. 644, 62 Stat. 678; Jan. 19, 1949, ch. 2, §1(b), 63 Stat. 4; Mar. 2, 1955, ch. 9, §4(c), 69 Stat. 11; Pub. L. 88–426, title III, §304(a), Aug. 14, 1964, 78 Stat. 422; Pub. L. 91–67, §1, Sept. 15, 1969, 83 Stat. 106; Pub. L. 94–82, title II, §203, Aug. 9, 1975, 89 Stat. 420; Pub. L. 97–257, title I, §105(b), Sept. 10, 1982, 96 Stat. 849; Pub. L. 101–194, title VII, §704(a)(2)(A), Nov. 30, 1989, 103 Stat. 1769; Pub. L. 101–509, title V, §529 [title I, §101(b)(4)(I)], Nov. 5, 1990, 104 Stat. 1427, 1440; Pub. L. 103–356, title I, §101(2), Oct. 13, 1994, 108 Stat. 3410.)

References in Text

The General Schedule, referred to in text, is set out under section 5332 of Title 5, Government Organization and Employees.

Section 704(a)(1) of the Ethics Reform Act of 1989, referred to in subsec. (a), is section 704(a)(1) of Pub. L. 101–194, which is set out as a note under section 5318 of Title 5.

Amendments

1994—Pub. L. 103–356 designated existing provisions as subsec. (a), substituted "Subject to subsection (b), effective" for "Effective" in second sentence, and added subsec. (b).

1990—Pub. L. 101–509 substituted "5303" for "5305".

1989—Pub. L. 101–194 substituted "corresponds to the most recent percentage change in the ECI (relative to the date described in the next sentence), as determined under section 704(a)(1) of the Ethics Reform Act of 1989. The appropriate date under this sentence is the first day of the fiscal year in which such adjustment in the rates of pay under the General Schedule takes effect" for "corresponds to the overall average percentage (as set forth in the report transmitted to the Congress under section 5305 of title 5) of the adjustment in such rates of pay".

1982—Pub. L. 97–257 struck out requirement for payment of salary on a monthly basis.

1975—Pub. L. 94–82 substituted provisions for a rate of salary to be determined under chapter 11 of title 2, as adjusted under this section, with adjustments equal to the percentage of such per annum rate which corresponds to the overall average percentage of the adjustment in such rates of pay for provisions for a per annum rate of salary of $62,500.

1969—Pub. L. 91–67 increased salary from $43,000 to $62,500.

1964—Pub. L. 88–426 increased salary from $35,000 to $43,000.

1955—Act Mar. 2, 1955, increased salary from $30,000 to $35,000.

1949—Act Jan. 19, 1949, increased salary from $20,000 to $30,000.

Effective Date of 1994 Amendment

Section 101 of Pub. L. 101–356 provided that the amendment made by that section is effective Dec. 31, 1994.

Effective Date of 1990 Amendment

Amendment by Pub. L. 101–509 effective on such date as the President shall determine, but not earlier than 90 days, and not later than 180 days, after Nov. 5, 1990, see section 529 [title III, §305] of Pub. L. 101–509, set out as a note under section 5301 of Title 5, Government Organization and Employees.

Effective Date of 1989 Amendment

Amendment by Pub. L. 101–194 effective Jan. 1, 1991, see section 704(b) of Pub. L. 101–194, set out as a note under section 5318 of Title 5, Government Organization and Employees.

Effective Date of 1982 Amendment

Amendment by Pub. L. 97–257 effective in the case of compensation payable for months after December 1981,

see section 105(c) of Pub. L. 97–257, set out as a note under section 60c–1 of Title 2, The Congress.

Effective Date of 1969 Amendment

Section 3 of Pub. L. 91–67 provided that: "The amendments made by this Act [amending this section and section 31 of Title 2, The Congress] shall become effective on March 1, 1969."

Effective Date of 1964 Amendment

Amendment by Pub. L. 88–426 effective on first day of first pay period which begins on or after July 1, 1964, except to the extent provided in section 501(c) of Pub. L. 88–426, see section 504 of Pub. L. 88–426.

Effective Date of 1955 Amendment

Amendment by act Mar. 2, 1955, effective Mar. 1, 1955, see section 5 of that act, set out as a note under section 31 of Title 2, The Congress.

Effective Date of 1949 Amendment

Amendment by act Jan. 19, 1949, effective noon, Jan. 20, 1949, see section 3 of that act.

Salary Increases

2001—Ex. Ord. No. 13182, Dec. 23, 2000, 65 F.R. 82879, 66 F.R. 10057, set out as a note under section 5332 of Title 5, Government Organization and Employees, provided for the adjustment of pay rates effective Jan. 1, 2001.

2000—Ex. Ord. No. 13144, Dec. 21, 1999, 64 F.R. 72237, which provided for the adjustment of pay rates effective Jan. 1, 2000, was superseded by Ex. Ord. No. 13182, Dec. 23, 2000, 65 F.R. 82879, set out as a note under section 5332 of Title 5.

1999—Ex. Ord. No. 13106, Dec. 7, 1998, 63 F.R. 68151, which provided for the adjustment of pay rates effective Jan. 1, 1999, was substantially superseded by Ex. Ord. No. 13144, Dec. 21, 1999, 64 F.R. 72237, formerly set out as a note under section 5332 of Title 5.

1998—Ex. Ord. No. 13071, Dec. 29, 1997, 62 F.R. 68521, which provided for the adjustment of pay rates effective Jan. 1, 1998, was superseded by Ex. Ord. No. 13106, Dec. 7, 1998, 63 F.R. 68151, formerly set out as a note under section 5332 of Title 5.

1997—Ex. Ord. No. 13033, Dec. 27, 1996, 61 F.R. 68987, which provided for the adjustment of pay rates effective Jan. 1, 1997, was superseded by Ex. Ord. No. 13071, Dec. 29, 1997, 62 F.R. 68521, formerly set out as a note under section 5332 of Title 5.

1996—Ex. Ord. No. 12984, Dec. 28, 1995, 61 F.R. 237, which provided for the adjustment of pay rates effective Jan. 1, 1996, was superseded by Ex. Ord. No. 13033, Dec. 27, 1996, 61 F.R. 68987, formerly set out as a note under section 5332 of Title 5.

1995—Ex. Ord. No. 12944, Dec. 28, 1994, 60 F.R. 309, which provided for the adjustment of pay rates effective Jan. 1, 1995, was superseded by Ex. Ord. No. 12984, Dec. 28, 1995, 61 F.R. 237, formerly set out as a note under section 5332 of Title 5.

1993—Ex. Ord. No. 12826, Dec. 30, 1992, 57 F.R. 62909, which provided for the adjustment of pay rates effective Jan. 1, 1993, was superseded by Ex. Ord. No. 12944, Dec. 28, 1994, 60 F.R. 309, formerly set out as a note under section 5332 of Title 5.

1992—Ex. Ord. No. 12786, Dec. 26, 1991, 56 F.R. 67453, which provided for the adjustment of pay rates effective Jan. 1, 1992, was superseded by Ex. Ord. No. 12826, Dec. 30, 1992, 57 F.R. 62909, formerly set out as a note under section 5332 of Title 5.

1991—Ex. Ord. No. 12736, Dec. 12, 1990, 55 F.R. 51385, which provided for the adjustment of pay rates effective Jan. 1, 1991, was superseded by Ex. Ord. No. 12786, Dec. 26, 1991, 56 F.R. 67453, formerly set out as a note under section 5332 of Title 5.

1990—Ex. Ord. No. 12698, Dec. 23, 1989, 54 F.R. 53473, which provided for adjustments of pay rates effective Jan. 1, 1990, and Jan. 31, 1990, was superseded by Ex. Ord. No. 12736, Dec. 12, 1990, 55 F.R. 51385, formerly set out as a note under section 5332 of Title 5.

1989—Pub. L. 101–194, title VII, § 703(a)(2), Nov. 30, 1989, 103 Stat. 1768, set out as a note under section 5318 of Title 5, provided that effective Jan. 1, 1991, the rate of basic pay for the Vice President shall be increased in the amount of 25 percent of the rate (as last in effect before the increase).

Ex. Ord. No. 12663, Jan. 6, 1989, 54 F.R. 791, which provided for the adjustment of pay rates effective Jan. 1, 1989, was superseded by Ex. Ord. No. 12698, Dec. 23, 1989, 54 F.R. 53473, formerly set out as a note under section 5332 of Title 5.

1988—Ex. Ord. No. 12622, Dec. 31, 1987, 53 F.R. 222, which provided for the adjustment of pay rates effective Jan. 1, 1988, was superseded by Ex. Ord. No. 12663, Jan. 6, 1989, 54 F.R. 791, formerly set out as a note under section 5332 of Title 5.

1987—Salary of the Vice President increased to $115,000 per annum, on recommendation of the President of the United States, see note set out under section 358 of Title 2, The Congress.

Ex. Ord. No. 12578, Dec. 31, 1986, 52 F.R. 505, which provided for the adjustment of pay rates effective Jan. 1, 1987, was superseded by Ex. Ord. No. 12622, Dec. 31, 1987, 53 F.R. 222, formerly set out as a note under section 5332 of Title 5.

1985—Ex. Ord. No. 12496, Dec. 28, 1984, 50 F.R. 211, as amended by Ex. Ord. No. 12540, Dec. 30, 1985, 51 F.R. 577, which provided for the adjustment of pay rates effective Jan. 1, 1985, was superseded by Ex. Ord. No. 12578, Dec. 31, 1986, 52 F.R. 505, formerly set out as a note under section 5332 of Title 5.

1984—Ex. Ord. No. 12456, Dec. 30, 1983, 49 F.R. 347, as amended Ex. Ord. No. 12477, May 23, 1984, 49 F.R. 22041; Ex. Ord. No. 12487, Sept. 14, 1984, 49 F.R. 36493, which provided for the adjustment of pay rates effective Jan. 1, 1984, was superseded by Ex. Ord. No. 12496, Dec. 28, 1984, 50 F.R. 211, as amended by Ex. Ord. No. 12540, Dec. 30, 1985, 51 F.R. 577, formerly set out as a note under section 5332 of Title 5.

1982—Ex. Ord. No. 12387, Oct. 8, 1982, 47 F.R. 44981, which provided for the adjustment of pay rates effective Oct. 1, 1982, was superseded by Ex. Ord. No. 12456, Dec. 30, 1983, 49 F.R. 347, as amended Ex. Ord. No. 12477, May 23, 1984, 49 F.R. 22041; Ex. Ord. No. 12487, Sept. 14, 1983, 49 F.R. 36493, formerly set out as a note under section 5332 of Title 5.

Maximum rate payable after Dec. 17, 1982, increased from $79,125 to $91,000, see Pub. L. 97–377, title I, § 129(b)–(d), Dec. 21, 1982, 96 Stat. 1914, set out as a note under section 5318 of Title 5.

Limitations on use of funds for fiscal year ending Sept. 30, 1983, appropriated by any Act to pay the salary or pay of any individual in legislative, executive, or judicial branch in position equal to or above level V of the Executive Schedule, see section 101(e) of Pub. L. 97–276, as amended, set out as a note under section 5318 of Title 5.

1981—Ex. Ord. No. 12330, Oct. 15, 1981, 46 F.R. 50921, which provided for the adjustment of pay rates effective Oct. 1, 1981, was superseded by Ex. Ord. No. 12387, Oct. 8, 1982, 47 F.R. 44981, formerly set out as a note under section 5332 of Title 5.

Limitations on use of funds for fiscal year ending Sept. 30, 1982, appropriated by any Act to pay the salary or pay of any individual in legislative, executive, or judicial branch in position equal to or above level V of the Executive Schedule, see sections 101(g) and 141 of Pub. L. 97–92, set out as a note under section 5318 of Title 5.

1980—Ex. Ord. No. 12248, Oct. 16, 1981, 45 F.R. 69199, which provided for the adjustment of pay rates effective Oct. 1, 1980, was superseded by Ex. Ord. No. 12330, Oct. 15, 1981, 46 F.R. 50921, formerly set out as a note under section 5332 of Title 5.

Limitations on use of funds for fiscal year ending Sept. 30, 1981, appropriated by any Act to pay the salary or pay of any individual in legislative, executive, or judicial branch in position equal to or above Level V of the Executive Schedule, see section 101(c) of Pub. L. 96–536, as amended, set out as a note under section 5318 of Title 5.

1979—Ex. Ord. No. 12165, Oct. 9, 1979, 44 F.R. 58671, as amended by Ex. Ord. No. 12200, Mar. 12, 1980, 45 F.R. 16443, which provided for the adjustment of pay rates effective Oct. 1, 1979, was superseded by Ex. Ord. No. 12248, Oct. 16, 1980, 45 F.R. 69199, formerly set out as a note under section 5332 of Title 5.

Applicability to funds appropriated by any Act for fiscal year ending Sept. 30, 1980, of limitation of section 304 of Pub. L. 95–391 on use of funds to pay the salary or pay of any individual in legislative, executive, or judicial branch in position equal to or above Level V of the Executive Schedule, see section 101 of Pub. L. 96–86, set out as a note under section 5318 of Title 5.

1978—Ex. Ord. No. 12087, Oct. 7, 1978, 43 F.R. 46823, which provided for the adjustment of pay rates effective Oct. 1, 1978, was superseded by Ex. Ord. No. 12165, Oct. 9, 1979, 44 F.R. 58671, formerly set out as a note under section 5332 of Title 5.

Limitations on use of funds for fiscal year ending Sept. 30, 1979, appropriated by any Act to pay the salary or pay of any individual in legislative, executive, or judicial branch in position equal to or above Level V of the Executive Schedule, see section 304 of Pub. L. 95–391 and section 613 of Pub. L. 95–429, set out as a note under section 5318 of Title 5.

1977—Salary of the Vice President of the United States increased to $75,000 per annum on recommendation of the President of the United States, see note set out under section 358 of Title 2, The Congress.

Pub. L. 95–66, § 1(1), July 11, 1977, 91 Stat. 270, set out as a note under section 5318 of Title 5, Government Organization and Employees, provided that the first adjustment which, but for the enactment of Pub. L. 95–66, would have been made in the annual rate of pay for the Vice President under the second sentence of this section after July 11, 1977, would not take effect.

1976—Ex. Ord. No. 11941, Oct. 1, 1976, 41 F.R. 43899, as amended by Ex. Ord. No. 11943, Oct. 25, 1976, 41 F.R. 47213, which provided for the adjustment of pay rates effective Oct. 1, 1976, was superseded by Ex. Ord. No. 12010, Sept. 28, 1977, 42 F.R. 52365, formerly set out as a note under section 5332 of Title 5.

1975—Ex. Ord. No. 11883, Oct. 6, 1975, 40 F.R. 47091, which provided for the adjustment of pay rates effective Oct. 1, 1975, was superseded by Ex. Ord. No. 11941, Oct. 1, 1976, 41 F.R. 43899, as amended by Ex. Ord. No. 11943, Oct. 25, 1976, 41 F.R. 47213, formerly set out as a note under section 5332 of Title 5.

SECTION REFERRED TO IN OTHER SECTIONS

This section is referred to in title 5 sections 9502, 9503, 9505; title 35 section 3.

§ 105. Assistance and services for the President

(a)(1) Subject to the provisons[1] of paragraph (2) of this subsection, the President is authorized to appoint and fix the pay of employees in the White House Office without regard to any other provision of law regulating the employment or compensation of persons in the Government service. Employees so appointed shall perform such official duties as the President may prescribe.

(2) The President may, under paragraph (1) of this subsection, appoint and fix the pay of not more than—

　(A) 25 employees at rates not to exceed the rate of basic pay then currently paid for level II of the Executive Schedule of section 5313 of title 5; and in addition

　(B) 25 employees at rates not to exceed the rate of basic pay then currently paid for level III of the Executive Schedule of section 5314 of title 5; and in addition

---

[1] So in original. Probably should be "provisions".

(C) 50 employees at rates not to exceed the maximum rate of basic pay then currently paid for GS–18 of the General Schedule of section 5332 of title 5; and in addition

(D) such number of other employees as he may determine to be appropriate at rates not to exceed the minimum rate of basic pay then currently paid for GS–16 of the General Schedule of section 5332 of title 5.

(b)(1) Subject to the provisions of paragraph (2) of this subsection, the President is authorized to appoint and fix the pay of employees in the Executive Residence at the White House without regard to any other provision of law regulating the employment or compensation of persons in the Government service. Employees so appointed shall perform such official duties as the President may prescribe.

(2) The President may, under paragraph (1) of this subsection, appoint and fix the pay of not more than—

(A) 3 employees at rates not to exceed the maximum rate of basic pay then currently paid for GS–18 of the General Schedule of section 5332 of title 5; and in addition

(B) such number of other employees as he may determine to be appropriate at rates not to exceed the minimum rate of basic pay then currently paid for GS–16 of the General Schedule of section 5332 of title 5.

(c) The President is authorized to procure for the White House Office and the Executive Residence at the White House, as provided in appropriation Acts, temporary or intermittent services of experts and consultants, as described in and in accordance with the first two sentences of section 3109(b) of title 5—

(1) in the case of the White House Office, at respective daily rates of pay for individuals which are not more than the daily equivalent of the rate of basic pay then currently paid for level II of the Executive Schedule of section 5313 of title 5; and

(2) in the case of the Executive Residence, at respective daily rates of pay for individuals which are not more than the daily equivalent of the maximum rate of basic pay then currently paid for GS–18 of the General Schedule of section 5332 of title 5.

Notwithstanding such section 3109(b), temporary services of any expert or consultant described in such section 3109(b) may be procured for a period in excess of one year if the President determines such procurement is necessary.

(d) There are authorized to be appropriated each fiscal year to the President such sums as may be necessary for—

(1) the care, maintenance, repair, alteration, refurnishing, improvement, air-conditioning, heating, and lighting (including electric power and fixtures) of the Executive Residence at the White House;

(2) the official expenses of the White House Office;

(3) the official entertainment expenses of the President;

(4) the official entertainment expenses for allocation within the Executive Office of the President; and

(5) the subsistence expenses of persons in the Government service while traveling on official business in connection with the travel of the President.

Sums appropriated under this subsection for expenses described in paragraphs (1), (3), and (5) may be expended as the President may determine, notwithstanding the provisions of any other law. Such sums shall be accounted for solely on the certificate of the President, except that, with respect to such expenses, the Comptroller General may inspect all necessary books, documents, papers, and records relating to any such expenditures solely for the purpose of verifying that all such expenditures related to expenses in paragraph (1), (3), or (5). The Comptroller General shall certify to Congress the fact of such verification, and shall report any such expenses not expended for such purpose.

(e) Assistance and services authorized pursuant to this section to the President are authorized to be provided to the spouse of the President in connection with assistance provided by such spouse to the President in the discharge of the President's duties and responsibilities. If the President does not have a spouse, such assistance and services may be provided for such purposes to a member of the President's family whom the President designates.

(June 25, 1948, ch. 644, 62 Stat. 678; Oct. 15, 1949, ch. 695, §2(a), 63 Stat. 880; July 31, 1956, ch. 804, title I, §109, 70 Stat. 740; Pub. L. 87–367, title III, §303(h), Oct. 4, 1961, 75 Stat. 794; Pub. L. 88–426, title III, §304(b), Aug. 14, 1964, 78 Stat. 422; Pub. L. 90–222, title I, §111(c), Dec. 23, 1967, 81 Stat. 726; Pub. L. 95–570, §1(a), Nov. 2, 1978, 92 Stat. 2445.)

Amendments

1978—Pub. L. 95–570 inserted provisions relating to appointment and determination of pay by President of employees in the White House Office and the Executive Residence at the White House; procurement by President of temporary or intermittent services of experts and consultants and pay of such experts and consultants; appropriation of sums for the care, maintenance, etc., of the Executive Residence at the White House, the official expenses of the White House Office, the official entertainment expenses of the President, the official entertainment expenses for allocation within the Executive Office, and the subsistence expenses of Government personnel while traveling on official business in connection with the travel of the President; accounting of sums by President; inspection, certification and report to Congress by the Comptroller General concerning expenditures; and allotment of assistance and services to spouse of President or to a member of President's family; struck out provisions which authorized President to fix compensation of six administrative assistants, Executive Secretaries of the National Security Council, the National Aeronautics and Space Council, and the Economic Opportunity Council, and eight other secretaries or other immediate staff assistants in the White House Office, at rates of basic pay not to exceed the rate of Executive level II.

1967—Pub. L. 90–222 inserted position of Executive Secretary of the Economic Opportunity Council.

1964—Pub. L. 88–426 included Executive Secretary of the National Aeronautics and Space Council, and substituted provisions permitting President to fix compensation of enumerated personnel at rates of basic compensation not more than that of level II of the Federal Executive Salary Schedule for provisions which limited compensation of such personnel to two at rates not more than $22,500, three at not more than $21,000, seven at not more than $20,000 and three at not more than $18,500 per annum.

1961—Pub. L. 87–367 authorized President to increase compensation of three assistants to the President from $17,500 to $18,500 per annum.

1956—Act July 31, 1956, authorized President to fix compensation of an additional three secretaries or other immediate staff assistants, substituted "$22,500" for "$20,000", "$21,000" for "$18,000", and "$20,000" for "$15,000", and provided for payment of three at rates not exceeding $17,500 per annum.

1949—Act Oct. 15, 1949, increased compensation of secretaries, and executive, administrative, and staff assistants.

EFFECTIVE DATE OF 1978 AMENDMENT

Amendment by Pub. L. 95–570 applicable to any fiscal year beginning on or after Oct. 1, 1978, see section 6(a) of Pub. L. 95–570, set out as a note under section 102 of this title.

EFFECTIVE DATE OF 1967 AMENDMENT

Amendment by Pub. L. 90–222 effective immediately on enactment of Pub. L. 90–222, which was approved on Dec. 23, 1967, see section 401 of Pub. L. 90–222, set out as a note under section 2702 of Title 42, The Public Health and Welfare.

EFFECTIVE DATE OF 1964 AMENDMENT

Amendment by Pub. L. 88–426 effective on first day of first pay period which begins on or after July 1, 1964, except to the extent provided in section 501(c) of Pub. L. 88–426, see section 501 of Pub. L. 88–426.

EFFECTIVE DATE OF 1961 AMENDMENT

Amendment by Pub. L. 87–367 effective at beginning of first pay period which begins on or after sixtieth day following Oct. 4, 1961, see section 305 of Pub. L. 87–367.

EFFECTIVE DATE OF 1956 AMENDMENT

Amendment by act July 31, 1956, effective at beginning of first pay period commencing after June 30, 1956, see section 120 of act July 31, 1956.

EFFECTIVE DATE OF 1949 AMENDMENT

Amendment by act Oct. 15, 1949, effective on first day of first pay period after Oct. 15, 1949, see section 9 of that act, set out as a note under section 273 of Title 2, The Congress.

REPEALS

Act July 31, 1956, ch. 804, title I, § 109, 70 Stat. 740, cited as a credit to this section, was repealed by Pub. L. 88–426, title III, § 305(1), Aug. 14, 1964, 78 Stat. 422.

ABOLITION OF NATIONAL AERONAUTICS AND SPACE COUNCIL

National Aeronautics and Space Council, including office of Executive Secretary of Council, together with functions of Council, abolished by section 3(a)(4) of 1973 Reorg. Plan No. 1, effective July 1, 1973, set out in the Appendix to Title 5, Government Organization and Employees.

REFERENCES IN OTHER LAWS TO GS–16, 17, OR 18 PAY RATES

References in laws to the rates of pay for GS–16, 17, or 18, or to maximum rates of pay under the General Schedule, to be considered references to rates payable under specified sections of Title 5, Government Organization and Employees, see section 529 [title I, § 101(c)(1)] of Pub. L. 101–509, set out in a note under section 5376 of Title 5.

SECTION REFERRED TO IN OTHER SECTIONS

This section is referred to in section 115 of this title; title 18 sections 207, 1751; title 26 section 3121; title 31 section 3524; title 42 section 410.

§ 106. Assistance and services for the Vice President

(a) In order to enable the Vice President to provide assistance to the President in connection with the performance of functions specially assigned to the Vice President by the President in the discharge of executive duties and responsibilities, the Vice President is authorized—

(1) without regard to any other provision of law regulating the employment or compensation of persons in the Government service, to appoint and fix the pay of not more than—

(A) 5 employees at rates not to exceed the rate of basic pay then currently paid for level II of the Executive Schedule of section 5313 of title 5; and in addition

(B) 3 employees at rates not to exceed the rate of basic pay then currently paid for level III of the Executive Schedule of section 5314 of title 5; and in addition

(C) 3 employees at rates not to exceed the maximum rate of basic pay then currently paid for GS–18 of the General Schedule of section 5332 of title 5; and in addition

(D) such number of other employees as he may determine to be appropriate at rates not to exceed the minimum rate of basic pay then currently paid for GS–16 of the General Schedule of section 5332 of title 5; and

(2) to procure, as provided in appropriation Acts, temporary or intermittent services of experts and consultants, as described in and in accordance with the first two sentences of section 3109(b) of title 5, at respective daily rates of pay for individuals which are not more than the daily equivalent of the rate of basic pay then currently paid for level II of the Executive Schedule of section 5313 of title 5.

Notwithstanding such section 3109(b), temporary services of any expert or consultant described in such section 3109(b) may be procured under paragraph (2) of this subsection for a period in excess of one year if the Vice President determines such procurement is necessary.

(b) In order to carry out the executive duties and responsibilities referred to in subsection (a), there are authorized to be appropriated each fiscal year to the Vice President such sums as may be necessary for—

(1) the official expenses of the Office of the Vice President;

(2) the official entertainment expenses of the Vice President; and

(3) the subsistence expenses of persons in the Government service while traveling on official business in connection with the travel of the Vice President.

Sums appropriated under this subsection for expenses described in paragraphs (2) and (3) may be expended as the Vice President may determine, notwithstanding the provisions of any other law. Such sums shall be accounted for solely on the certificate of the Vice President, except that, with respect to such expenses, the Comptroller General may inspect all necessary books, documents, papers, and records relating to any such expenditures solely for the purpose of verifying that all such expenditures related to expenses in paragraph (2) or (3). The Comptroller General shall certify to Congress the fact of such verification, and shall report any such expenses not expended for such purpose.

(c) Assistance and services authorized pursuant to this section to the Vice President are authorized to be provided to the spouse of the Vice President in connection with assistance provided by such spouse to the Vice President in the discharge of the Vice President's executive duties and responsibilities. If the Vice President does not have a spouse, such assistance and services may be provided for such purposes to a member of the Vice President's family whom the Vice President designates.

(June 25, 1948, ch. 644, 62 Stat. 678; Oct. 15, 1949, ch. 695, § 2(b), 63 Stat. 880; Pub. L. 95–570, § 1(a), Nov. 2, 1978, 92 Stat. 2446.)

AMENDMENTS

1978—Pub. L. 95–570 inserted provisions relating to appointment and determination of pay by the Vice President of employees and procurement by the Vice President of temporary or intermittent services of experts and consultants to enable the Vice President to provide assistance to the President; appropriation of sums for the official expenses of the Office of the Vice President, the official entertainment expenses of the Vice President, and subsistence expenses of Government personnel while traveling on official business in connection with the travel of the Vice President; accounting of sums by the Vice President; inspection, certification and report to Congress by the Comptroller General concerning expenditures; and allotment of assistance and services to the spouse of the Vice President or to a member of the Vice President's family; struck out provisions which authorized the President to appoint and fix compensation of not to exceed six administrative assistants and directed that each assistant perform such duties as the President prescribed.

1949—Act Oct. 15, 1949, struck out salary provisions. See section 105 of this title.

EFFECTIVE DATE OF 1978 AMENDMENT

Amendment by Pub. L. 95–570 applicable to any fiscal year beginning on or after Oct. 1, 1978, see section 6(a) of Pub. L. 95–570, set out as a note under section 102 of this title.

EFFECTIVE DATE OF 1949 AMENDMENT

Amendment by act Oct. 15, 1949, effective on first day of first pay period after Oct. 15, 1949, see section 9 of that act, set out as a note under section 273 of Title 2, The Congress.

REFERENCES IN OTHER LAWS TO GS–16, 17, OR 18 PAY RATES

References in laws to the rates of pay for GS–16, 17, or 18, or to maximum rates of pay under the General Schedule, to be considered references to rates payable under specified sections of Title 5, Government Organization and Employees, see section 529 [title I, § 101(c)(1)] of Pub. L. 101–509, set out in a note under section 5376 of Title 5.

FORMER PRESIDENT'S OFFICE STAFF

See note under section 102 of this title.

EX. ORD. NO. 11456. SPECIAL ASSISTANT TO THE PRESIDENT FOR LIAISON WITH FORMER PRESIDENTS

Ex. Ord. No. 11456, Feb. 14, 1969, 34 F.R. 2301, provided: By virtue of the authority vested in me as President of the United States, it is hereby ordered as follows:

SECTION 1. There shall be in the White House Office a Special Assistant to the President for Liaison with Former Presidents (referred to hereinafter as the Special Assistant).

SEC. 2. (a) On behalf of the President, the Special Assistant shall maintain channels of communication between the President and each former living President of the United States, to the end that (1) each such former President shall be kept abreast of such developments as the President may desire; and (2) the President may avail himself of the counsel and advice of any or all of such former Presidents with respect to major matters, particularly of a national security nature, currently confronting the President.

(b) The Special Assistant shall also—

(1) Keep each former President currently informed of the major aspects of such principal international and domestic problems as the President directs;

(2) Arrange to secure from such former Presidents, or any of them, and convey to the President, their views on such issues as the President may designate; and

(3) Arrange to secure and convey to the President such views as any of the former Presidents may wish to communicate to the President on any issue of current interest or concern.

SEC. 3. (a) The Secretary of State, the Secretary of Defense, the Director of the Central Intelligence Agency, and the Executive Secretary of the National Security Council shall each designate a member of his staff as a point of contact for the Special Assistant. The Special Assistant may call upon such designated staff members to supply information and render such other appropriate assistance as he may require in carrying out his duties under section 2 of this Order.

(b) Upon request of the Special Assistant, the head of any department or agency of the Federal Government shall designate a member of his staff as a point of contact to supply information and assistance for the Special Assistant in the performance of his duties in the same manner as provided in subsection (a) for staff members designated pursuant to that subsection.

SEC. 4. The Special Assistant shall be appointed by the President and shall serve at the pleasure of the President. He shall receive compensation at such rate as the President, consonant with law, may prescribe.

SEC. 5. (a) The Special Assistant shall have such staff and other assistance as may be necessary to carry out his duties under this Order.

(b) The Special Assistant shall be provided with such office space as may be necessary to carry out his duties under this Order, and shall also be provided with such office space, and maintenance thereof, as may be necessary for the use of former Presidents at the seat of Government when they are engaged in any effort of interest or concern to the President.

SEC. 6. (a) The compensation and expenses of the Special Assistant and members of his staff shall be paid from the appropriation under the heading "Special" in the Executive Office Appropriation Act, 1969, or any corresponding appropriation which may be made for subsequent fiscal years, or from such other appropriated funds as may be available under law.

(b) The General Services Administration shall provide, on a reimbursable basis, such administrative services and facilities for the Special Assistant as the White House Office may request.

RICHARD NIXON.

SECTION REFERRED TO IN OTHER SECTIONS

This section is referred to in sections 114, 115 of this title; title 18 sections 207, 1751; title 26 section 3121; title 31 section 3524; title 42 section 410.

§ 107. Domestic Policy Staff and Office of Administration; personnel

(a) In order to enable the Domestic Policy Staff to perform its functions, the President (or his designee) is authorized—

(1) without regard to any other provision of law regulating the employment or compensation of persons in the Government service, to appoint and fix the pay of not more than—

(A) 6 employees at rates not to exceed the rate of basic pay then currently paid for level III of the Executive Schedule of section 5314 of title 5; and in addition

(B) 18 employees at rates not to exceed the maximum rate of basic pay then currently paid for GS–18 of the General Schedule of section 5332 of title 5; and in addition

(C) such number of other employees as he may determine to be appropriate at rates not to exceed the minimum rate of basic pay then currently paid for GS–16 of the General Schedule of section 5332 of title 5; and

(2) to procure, as provided in appropriation Acts, temporary or intermittent services of experts and consultants, as described in and in accordance with the first two sentences of section 3109(b) of title 5, at respective daily rates of pay for individuals which are not more than the daily equivalent of the rate of basic pay then currently paid for level III of the Executive Schedule of section 5314 of title 5.

(b)(1) In order to enable the Office of Administration to perform its functions, the President (or his designee) is authorized—

(A) without regard to such other provisions of law as the President may specify which regulate the employment and compensation of persons in the Government service, to appoint and fix the pay of not more than—

(i) 5 employees at rates not to exceed the rate of basic pay then currently paid for level III of the Executive Schedule of section 5314 of title 5; and in addition

(ii) 5 employees at rates not to exceed the maximum rate of basic pay then currently paid for GS–18 of the General Schedule of section 5332 of title 5; and

(B) to procure, as provided in appropriation Acts, temporary or intermittent services of experts and consultants, as described in and in accordance with the first two sentences of section 3109(b) of title 5, at respective daily rates of pay for individuals which are not more than the daily equivalent of the maximum rate of basic pay then currently paid for GS–18 of the General Schedule of section 5332 of title 5.

(2) In addition to any authority granted under paragraph (1) of this subsection, the President (or his designee) is authorized to employ individuals in the Office of Administration in accordance with section 3101 of title 5 and provisions relating thereto. Any individual so employed under the authority granted under such section 3101 shall be subject to the limitation specified in section 114 of this title.

(c) There are authorized to be appropriated each fiscal year such sums as may be necessary for the official expenses of the Domestic Policy Staff and the Office of Administration.

(Added Pub. L. 95–570, § 2(a), Nov. 2, 1978, 92 Stat. 2448.)

PRIOR PROVISIONS

A prior section 107, act June 25, 1948, ch. 644, 62 Stat. 679, providing that employees of the executive departments and independent establishments of the executive branch of the Government might be detailed from time to time to the White House Office for temporary assistance, was repealed by section 2(a) of Pub. L. 95–570. See section 112 of this title.

EFFECTIVE DATE

Section applicable to any fiscal year beginning on or after Oct. 1, 1978, see section 6(a) of Pub. L. 95–570, set out as an Effective Date of 1978 Amendment note under section 102 of this title.

REFERENCES IN OTHER LAWS TO GS–16, 17, OR 18 PAY RATES

References in laws to the rates of pay for GS–16, 17, or 18, or to maximum rates of pay under the General Schedule, to be considered references to rates payable under specified sections of Title 5, Government Organization and Employees, see section 529 [title I, § 101(c)(1)] of Pub. L. 101–509, set out in a note under section 5376 of Title 5.

APPLICABILITY OF SUBSEC. (b) TO CURRENT EMPLOYEES OF OFFICE OF ADMINISTRATION

Section 6(b) of Pub. L. 95–570 provided that: "In the case of an individual—

"(1) who is an employee of the Office of Administration as of the date of the enactment of this Act [Nov. 2, 1978], and

"(2) whose position would be terminated or whose rate of basic pay would be reduced (but for this subsection) by reason of section 107(b) of title 3, United States Code (as amended by this Act) [subsec. (b) of this section],

such employee may be allowed to continue to hold such position and receive basic pay at the rate in effect on the effective date of this Act [see Effective Date of 1978 Amendment note set out under section 102 of this title] during the period which begins on such date and ends 2 years after such date so long as such employee continues as an employee of the Office of Administration."

SECTION REFERRED TO IN OTHER SECTIONS

This section is referred to in section 115 of this title; title 26 section 3121; title 42 section 410.

§ 108. Assistance to the President for unanticipated needs

(a) There is authorized to be appropriated to the President an amount not to exceed $1,000,000 each fiscal year to enable the President, in his discretion, to meet unanticipated needs for the furtherance of the national interest, security, or defense, including personnel needs and needs for services described in section 3109(b) of title 5, and administrative expenses related thereto, without regard to any provision of law regulating the employment or compensation of persons in the Government service or regulating expenditures of Government funds.

(b) The President shall transmit a report to each House of the Congress for each fiscal year beginning on or after the effective date of this subsection which sets forth the purposes for which expenditures were made under this section for such fiscal year and the amount expended for each such purpose. Each such report shall be transmitted no later than 60 days after the close of the fiscal year covered by such report.

(c) An individual may not be paid under the authority of this section at a rate of pay in excess of the rate of basic pay then currently paid for level II of the Executive Schedule of section 5313 of title 5.

(Added Pub. L. 95–570, § 2(a), Nov. 2, 1978, 92 Stat. 2449.)

REFERENCES IN TEXT

For the effective date of this subsection, referred to in subsec. (b), see section 6(a) of Pub. L. 95–570, set out as an Effective Date of 1978 Amendment note under section 102 of this title.

PRIOR PROVISIONS

A prior section 108, act June 25, 1948, ch. 644, 62 Stat. 679, directing the Quartermaster General of the Army to provide suitable accommodations for the horses, carriages, and other vehicles of the President and of the Executive Office, was repealed by act June 28, 1950, ch. 383, title IV, § 401(j), 64 Stat. 271.

Insofar as prior section 108, by virtue of a former proviso in section 401 of act June 28, 1950, continued to remain in effect to the extent that it was applicable to the Department of the Air Force, and the United States Air Force, it was additionally repealed by act Sept. 19, 1951, ch. 407, title IV, § 401(a)(1), 65 Stat. 333.

Act Oct. 31, 1951, ch. 654, § 1(2), 65 Stat. 701, repealed that part of act Mar. 4, 1911, ch. 285, § 1, 36 Stat. 1404, from which prior section 108, as enacted by act June 25, 1948, ch. 644, § 1, 62 Stat. 672, had been derived. That part of the 1911 act had previously been repealed by section 3 of the 1948 act.

EFFECTIVE DATE

Section applicable to any fiscal year beginning on or after Oct. 1, 1978, see section 6(a) of Pub. L. 95–570, set out as an Effective Date of 1978 Amendment note under section 102 of this title.

§ 109. Public property in and belonging to the Executive Residence at the White House

The steward, housekeeper, or such other employee of the Executive Residence at the White House as the President may designate, shall under the direction of the President, have the charge and custody of and be responsible for the plate, furniture, and public property therein. A complete inventory, in proper books, shall be made annually in the month of June, under the direction of the Director of the National Park Service, of all the public property in and belonging to the Executive Residence at the White House, showing when purchased, its cost, condition, and final disposition. This inventory shall be submitted to the President for his approval, and shall then be kept for reference in the office of the Director of the National Park Service, which shall furnish a copy thereof to the steward, housekeeper, or other employee responsible for the property.

(June 25, 1948, ch. 644, 62 Stat. 679; Pub. L. 92–310, title II, § 201, June 6, 1972, 86 Stat. 202; Pub. L. 95–570, § 5(b)(1), Nov. 2, 1978, 92 Stat. 2450.)

AMENDMENTS

1978—Pub. L. 95–570 substituted in section catchline "the Executive Residence at the White House" for "Executive Mansion" and in text "Executive Residence at the White House" for "Executive Mansion" in two places.

1972—Pub. L. 92–310 struck out provisions which required a bond in the sum of $10,000 from the person having charge and custody of the plate, furniture, and public property.

EFFECTIVE DATE OF 1978 AMENDMENT

Amendment by Pub. L. 95–570 applicable to any fiscal year beginning on or after Oct. 1, 1978, see section 6(a) of Pub. L. 95–570, set out as a note under section 102 of this title.

TRANSFER OF FUNCTIONS

Functions of all other officers of Department of the Interior and functions of all agencies and employees of

such Department, with two exceptions, transferred to Secretary of the Interior, with power vested in him to authorize their performance or performance of any of his functions by any of such officers, agencies, and employees, by 1950 Reorg. Plan No. 3, §§ 1, 2, eff. May 24, 1950, 15 F.R. 3174, 64 Stat. 1262, set out in the Appendix to Title 5, Government Organization and Employees.

§ 110. Furniture for the Executive Residence at the White House

All furniture purchased for the use of the Executive Residence at the White House shall be, as far as practicable, of domestic manufacture. With a view to conserving in the Executive Residence at the White House the best specimens of the early American furniture and furnishings, and for the purpose of maintaining the interior of the Executive Residence at the White House in keeping with its original design, the Director of the National Park Service is authorized and directed, with the approval of the President, to accept donations of furniture and furnishings for use in the Executive Residence at the White House, all such articles thus donated to become the property of the United States and to be accounted for as such. The said Director of the National Park Service is further authorized and directed, with the approval of the President, to appoint a temporary committee composed of one representative of the American Federation of Arts, one representative of the National Commission of Fine Arts, one representative of the National Academy of Design, one member of the American Institute of Architects, and five members representing the public at large; the said committee to have full power to select and pass on the articles in question and to recommend the same for acceptance.

(June 25, 1948, ch. 644, 62 Stat. 679; Pub. L. 95–570, § 5(c)(1), Nov. 2, 1978, 92 Stat. 2451.)

AMENDMENTS

1978—Pub. L. 95–570 inserted in section catchline "the Executive Residence at the" before "White House" and substituted in text "Executive Residence at the White House" for "President's House" and "Executive Residence at the White House" for "White House" wherever appearing.

EFFECTIVE DATE OF 1978 AMENDMENT

Amendment by Pub. L. 95–570 applicable to any fiscal year beginning on or after Oct. 1, 1978, see section 6(a) of Pub. L. 95–570, set out as a note under section 102 of this title.

TRANSFER OF FUNCTIONS

Functions of officers of Department of the Interior and functions of all agencies and employees of such Department, with two exceptions, transferred to Secretary of the Interior, see Transfer of Functions note set out under section 109 of this title.

COMMISSION ON RENOVATION OF THE EXECUTIVE MANSION

Act Apr. 14, 1949, ch. 51, 63 Stat. 45, authorized appointment of a commission of six to supervise and approve all construction plans and work necessary to remedy the present unsafe conditions in the Executive Mansion and to modernize same.

WHITE HOUSE; ADMINISTRATION; PRESERVATION OF MUSEUM CHARACTER; ARTICLES OF HISTORIC OR ARTISTIC INTEREST

Pub. L. 87–286, Sept. 22, 1961, 75 Stat. 586, provided: "That all of that portion of reservation numbered 1 in the city of Washington, District of Columbia, which is within the President's park enclosure, comprising eighteen and seven one-hundredths acres, shall continue to be known as the White House and shall be administered pursuant to the Act of August 25, 1916 (39 Stat. 535; 16 U.S.C. 1-3), and Acts supplementary thereto and amendatory thereof. In carrying out this Act primary attention shall be given to the preservation and interpretation of the museum character of the principal corridor on the ground floor and the principal public rooms on the first floor of the White House, but nothing done under this Act shall conflict with the administration of the Executive offices of the President or with the use and occupancy of the buildings and grounds as the home of the President and his family and for his official purposes.

"SEC. 2. Articles of furniture, fixtures, and decorative objects of the White House, when declared by the President to be of historic or artistic interest, together with such similar articles, fixtures, and objects as are acquired by the White House in the future when similarly so declared, shall thereafter be considered to be inalienable and the property of the White House. Any such article, fixture, or object when not in use or on display in the White House shall be transferred by direction of the President as a loan to the Smithsonian Institution for its care, study, and storage or exhibition and such articles, fixtures, and objects shall be returned to the White House from the Smithsonian Institution on notice by the President.

"SEC. 3. Nothing in this Act shall alter any privileges, powers, or duties vested in the White House Police and the United States Secret Service, Treasury Department, by section 202 of title 3, United States Code, and section 3056 of title 18, United States Code."

EX. ORD. NO. 11145. CURATOR OF WHITE HOUSE; COMMITTEE FOR PRESERVATION OF WHITE HOUSE

Ex. Ord. No. 11145, Mar. 7, 1964, 29 F.R. 3189, as amended by Ex. Ord. No. 11565, Oct. 13, 1970, 35 F.R. 16155, provided:

WHEREAS the White House, as the home of the highest elective officer of the United States

—symbolizes the American ideal of responsible self-government

—is emblematic of our democracy and our national purpose

—has been intimately associated with the personal and social life of the Presidents of the United States and many of their official acts

—occupies a particular place in the heart of every American citizen, and

WHEREAS certain historic rooms and entranceways in the White House

—possess great human interest and historic significance

—traditionally have been open to visitors

—have provided pleasure and patriotic inspiration to millions of our citizens

—have come to be regarded as a public museum and the proud possession of all Americans, and

WHEREAS the Congress by law (Act of September 22, 1961), (75 Stat. 586) [set out as a note under this section] has authorized the care and preservation of the historic and artistic contents of the White House and has given the President certain responsibilities with regard thereto:

NOW, THEREFORE, by virtue of the authority vested in me as President of the United States, it is ordered as follows:

SECTION 1. (a) There shall be in the White House a Curator of the White House. The Curator shall assist in the preservation and protection of the articles of furniture, fixtures, and decorative objects used or displayed in the principal corridor on the ground floor and the principal public rooms on the first floor of the White House, and in such other areas in the White House as the President may designate.

(b) The Curator shall report to the President and shall make recommendations with respect to the articles, fixtures, and objects to be declared by the President, under section 2 of the Act of September 22, 1961, to be of historic or artistic interest.

SEC. 2. There is hereby established the Committee for the Preservation of the White House, hereinafter referred to as the "Committee". The Committee shall be composed of the Director of the National Park Service, the Curator of the White House, the Secretary of the Smithsonian Institution, the Chairman of the Commission of Fine Arts, the Director of the National Gallery of Art, the Chief Usher of the White House, and so many other members as the President may from time to time appoint. The Director of the National Park Service shall serve as Chairman of the Committee and shall designate an employee of that Service to act as Executive Secretary of the Committee. Members of the Committee shall serve without compensation.

SEC. 3. (a) The Committee shall report to the President and shall advise the Director of the National Park Service with respect to the discharge of his responsibility under the Act of September 22, 1961, for the preservation and the interpretation of the museum character of the principal corridor on the ground floor and the principal public rooms on the first floor of the White House. Among other things, the Committee shall make recommendations as to the articles of furniture, fixtures, and decorative objects which shall be used or displayed in the aforesaid areas of the White House and as to the decor and arrangements therein best suited to enhance the historic and artistic values of the White House and of such articles, fixtures, and objects.

(b) The Committee shall cooperate with the White House Historical Association, a nonprofit organization heretofore formed under the laws of the District of Columbia.

(c) The Committee is authorized to invite individuals who are distinguished or interested in the fine arts to attend its meetings or otherwise to assist in carrying out its functions.

SEC. 4. Consonant with law, each Federal department and agency represented on the Committee shall furnish necessary assistance to the Committee in accordance with section 214 of the Act of May 3, 1945, 59 Stat. 134 (31 U.S.C. 691) [31 U.S.C. 1346(b)]. The Department of the Interior shall furnish necessary administrative services for the Committee.

EXTENSION OF TERM OF COMMITTEE FOR THE PRESERVATION OF THE WHITE HOUSE

Term of the Committee for the Preservation of the White House extended until Dec. 31, 1978, by Ex. Ord. No. 11948, Dec. 20, 1976, 41 F.R. 55705, formerly set out as a note under section 14 of the Federal Advisory Committee Act in the Appendix to Title 5, Government Organization and Employees.

Term of the Committee for the Preservation of the White House extended until Dec. 31, 1980, by Ex. Ord. No. 12110, Dec. 28, 1978, 44 F.R. 1069, formerly set out as a note under section 14 of the Federal Advisory Committee Act in the Appendix to Title 5.

Term of the Committee for the Preservation of the White House extended until Dec. 31, 1982, by Ex. Ord. No. 12258, Dec. 31, 1980, 46 F.R. 1251, formerly set out as a note under section 14 of the Federal Advisory Committee Act in the Appendix to Title 5.

Term of the Committee for the Preservation of the White House extended until Sept. 30, 1984, by Ex. Ord. No. 12399, Dec. 31, 1982, 48 F.R. 379, formerly set out as a note under section 14 of the Federal Advisory Committee Act in the Appendix to Title 5.

Term of the Committee for the Preservation of the White House extended until Sept. 30, 1985, by Ex. Ord. No. 12489, Sept. 28, 1984, 49 F.R. 38927, formerly set out as a note under section 14 of the Federal Advisory Committee Act in the Appendix to Title 5.

Term of the Committee for the Preservation of the White House extended until Sept. 30, 1987, by Ex. Ord. No. 12534, Sept. 30, 1985, 50 F.R. 40319, formerly set out as a note under section 14 of the Federal Advisory Committee Act in the Appendix to Title 5.

Term of the Committee for the Preservation of the White House extended until Sept. 30, 1989, by Ex. Ord. No. 12610, Sept. 30, 1987, 52 F.R. 36901, formerly set out as a note under section 14 of the Federal Advisory Committee Act in the Appendix to Title 5.

Term of the Committee for the Preservation of the White House extended until Sept. 30, 1991, by Ex. Ord. No. 12692, Sept. 29, 1989, 54 F.R. 40627, formerly set out as a note under section 14 of the Federal Advisory Committee Act in the Appendix to Title 5.

Term of the Committee for the Preservation of the White House extended until Sept. 30, 1993, by Ex. Ord. No. 12774, Sept. 27, 1991, 56 F.R. 49835, formerly set out as a note under section 14 of the Federal Advisory Committee Act in the Appendix to Title 5.

Term of the Committee for the Preservation of the White House extended until Sept. 30, 1995, by Ex. Ord. No. 12869, Sept. 30, 1993, 58 F.R. 51751, formerly set out as a note under section 14 of the Federal Advisory Committee Act in the Appendix to Title 5.

Term of the Committee for the Preservation of the White House extended until Sept. 30, 1997, by Ex. Ord. No. 12974, Sept. 29, 1995, 60 F.R. 51875, formerly set out as a note under section 14 of the Federal Advisory Committee Act in the Appendix to Title 5.

Term of the Committee for the Preservation of the White House extended until Sept. 30, 1999, by Ex. Ord. No. 13062, Sept. 29, 1997, 62 F.R. 51755, formerly set out as a note under section 14 of the Federal Advisory Committee Act in the Appendix to Title 5.

Term of the Committee for the Preservation of the White House extended until Sept. 30, 2001, by Ex. Ord. No. 13138, Sept. 30, 1999, 64 F.R. 53879, set out as a note under section 14 of the Federal Advisory Committee Act in the Appendix to Title 5.

§ 111. Expense allowance of Vice President

There shall be paid to the Vice President in equal monthly installments an expense allowance of $10,000 per annum to assist in defraying expenses relating to or resulting from the discharge of his official duties, for which no accounting, other than for income tax purposes, shall be made by him.

(Added Jan. 19, 1949, ch. 2, § 1(c), 63 Stat. 4; amended Oct. 20, 1951, ch. 521, title VI, § 619(b), 65 Stat. 570.)

AMENDMENTS

1951—Act Oct. 20, 1951, made Vice President's expense allowance taxable.

EFFECTIVE DATE OF 1951 AMENDMENT

Amendment by act Oct. 20, 1951, effective at noon on Jan. 20, 1953, see section 619(e) of that act, set out as a note under section 102 of this title.

EFFECTIVE DATE

Section effective noon, Jan. 20, 1949, see section 3 of act Jan. 19, 1949.

OFFICIAL TEMPORARY RESIDENCE OF THE VICE PRESIDENT

Pub. L. 93–346, July 12, 1974, 88 Stat. 340, as amended by Pub. L. 93–552, title VI, § 609(a), Dec. 27, 1974, 88 Stat. 1764, provided: "That effective July 1, 1974, the Government-owned house together with furnishings, associated grounds (consisting of twelve acres, more or less), and related facilities which have heretofore been used as the residence of the Chief of Naval Operations, Department of the Navy, shall, on and after such date be available for, and are hereby designated as, the temporary official residence of the Vice President of the United States.

"SEC. 2. The temporary official residence of the Vice President shall be adequately staffed and provided with such appropriate equipment, furnishings, dining facilities, services, and other provisions as may be required, under the supervision and direction of the Vice President, to enable him to perform and discharge appropriately the duties, functions, and obligations associated with his high office.

"SEC. 3. The Secretary of the Navy shall, subject to the supervision and control of the Vice President, provide for the military staffing and the care and maintenance of the grounds of the temporary official residence of the Vice President and, subject to reimbursement therefor out of funds appropriated for such purposes, provide for the civilian staffing, care, maintenance, repair, improvement, alteration, and furnishing of such residence.

"SEC. 4. There is hereby authorized to be appropriated such sums as may be necessary from time to time to carry out the foregoing provisions of this joint resolution. During any interim period until and before any such funds are so appropriated, the Secretary of the Navy shall make provision for staffing and other appropriate services in connection with the temporary official residence of the Vice President from funds available to the Department of the Navy, subject to reimbursement therefor from funds subsequently appropriated to carry out the purposes of this joint resolution.

"SEC. 5. After the date on which the Vice President moves into the temporary official residence provided for in this joint resolution no funds may be expended for the maintenance, care, repair, furnishing, or security of any residence for the Vice President other than the temporary official residence provided for in this joint resolution unless the expenditure of such funds is specifically authorized by law enacted after such date.

"SEC. 6. The Secretary of the Navy is authorized and directed, with the approval of the Vice President, to accept donations of money or property for the furnishing of or making improvements in or about the temporary official residence of the Vice President, all such donations to become the property of the United States and to be accounted for as such.

"SEC. 7. [Amended section 202 of this title].

"SEC. 8. [Amended section 3056(a) of title 18].

"SEC. 9. It is the sense of Congress that living accommodations, generally equivalent to those available to the highest ranking officer on active duty in each of the other military services, should be provided for the Chief of Naval Operations."

OFFICIAL RESIDENCE FOR THE VICE PRESIDENT; DESIGN AND CONSTRUCTION; AUTHORIZATION OF APPROPRIATION

Pub. L. 89–386, Apr. 9, 1966, 80 Stat. 106, provided: "That the Administrator of General Services is hereby authorized to plan, design, and construct an official residence for the Vice President of the United States in the District of Columbia.

"SEC. 2. The Administrator is further authorized to use as a site for such residence Federal land and property comprising approximately ten acres at the United States Naval Observatory, the specific area and boundaries thereof to be determined jointly by the General Services Administration and the Department of the Navy: Provided, That any roads and improvements thereon for which there is a continued need may be relocated and reconstructed.

"SEC. 3. The Administrator is further authorized to provide for the care, maintenance, repair, improvement, alteration, and furnishing of the official residence and grounds, including heating, lighting, and air conditioning, which services shall be provided at the expense of the United States.

"SEC. 4. The Administrator of General Services is further authorized to accept cash gifts, furniture, and furnishings and other types of gifts on behalf of the United States for use in constructing and furnishing the official residence but without further conditions on use, all such articles thus given to become the property of the United States.

"SEC. 5. There is authorized to be appropriated to the General Services Administration, the sum of $750,000 for planning, design, construction, and costs incidental thereto, including the cost of initial furnishings.

"SEC. 6. There is further authorized to be appropriated to the General Services Administration, annually, such amounts as may be necessary to carry out the purposes of section 3."

§ 112. Detail of employees of executive departments

The head of any department, agency, or independent establishment of the executive branch of the Government may detail, from time to time, employees of such department, agency, or establishment to the White House Office, the Executive Residence at the White House, the Office of the Vice President, the Domestic Policy Staff, and the Office of Administration. Any such office to which an employee has been detailed for service to such office shall reimburse the detailing department, agency, or establishment for the pay of each employee thereof—

(1) who is so detailed, and

(2) who is performing services which have been or would otherwise be performed by an employee of such office,

for any period occurring during any fiscal year after 180 calendar days after the employee is detailed in such year.

(Added Pub. L. 95–570, § 3(a), Nov. 2, 1978, 92 Stat. 2449.)

EFFECTIVE DATE

Section applicable to any fiscal year beginning on or after Oct. 1, 1978, see section 6(a) of Pub. L. 95–570, set out as an Effective Date of 1978 Amendment note under section 102 of this title.

SECTION REFERRED TO IN OTHER SECTIONS

This section is referred to in section 113 of this title.

§ 113. Personnel report

(a) The President shall transmit to each House of the Congress, and make available to the public, reports containing information described in subsection (b) for each fiscal year beginning on or after the effective date of this section. Each such report shall be transmitted no later than 60 days after the close of the fiscal year covered by such report and shall contain a statement of such information for such year.

(b) Each report required under subsection (a) shall contain—

(1) the number of employees who are paid at a rate of basic pay equal to or greater than the rate of basic pay then currently paid for level V of the Executive Schedule of section 5316 of title 5 and who are employed in the White House Office, the Executive Residence at the White House, the Office of the Vice President, the Domestic Policy Staff, or the Office of Administration, and the aggregate amount paid to such employees;

(2) the number of employees employed in such offices who are paid at a rate of basic pay which is equal to or greater than the minimum rate of basic pay then currently paid for GS–16 of the General Schedule of section 5332 of title 5 but which is less than the rate then currently paid for level V of the Executive Schedule of section 5316 of title V[1] and the aggregate amount paid to such employees;

(3) the number of employees employed in such offices who are paid at a rate of basic pay which is less than the minimum rate then currently paid for GS–16 of the General Schedule of section 5332 of title V[1], and the aggregate amount paid to such employees;

(4) the number of individuals detailed under section 112 of this title for more than 30 days to each such office, the number of days in excess of 30 each individual was detailed, and the aggregate amount of reimbursement made as provided by the provisions of section 112 of this title; and

(5) the number of individuals whose services as experts or consultants are procured under this chapter for service in any such office, the total number of days employed, and the aggregate amount paid to procure such services.

The information required under this subsection to be in any report shall be shown both in the aggregate and by office involved.

(Added Pub. L. 95–570, § 3(a), Nov. 2, 1978, 92 Stat. 2449.)

REFERENCES IN TEXT

For the effective date of this section, referred to in subsec. (a), see section 6(a) of Pub. L. 95–570, set out as an Effective Date of 1978 Amendment note under section 102 of this title.

EFFECTIVE DATE

Section applicable to any fiscal year beginning on or after Oct. 1, 1978, see section 6(a) of Pub. L. 95–570, set out as an Effective Date of 1978 Amendment note under section 102 of this title.

TERMINATION OF REPORTING REQUIREMENTS

For termination, effective May 15, 2000, of provisions of law requiring submittal to Congress of any annual, semiannual, or other regular periodic report listed in House Document No. 103–7 (in which the report required by subsec. (a) of this section is listed on page 21), see section 3003 of Pub. L. 104–66, as amended, set out as a note under section 1113 of Title 31, Money and Finance.

REFERENCES IN OTHER LAWS TO GS–16, 17, OR 18 PAY RATES

References in laws to the rates of pay for GS–16, 17, or 18, or to maximum rates of pay under the General Schedule, to be considered references to rates payable under specified sections of Title 5, Government Organization and Employees, see section 529 [title I, § 101(c)(1)] of Pub. L. 101–509, set out in a note under section 5376 of Title 5.

REPORT ON WHITE HOUSE OFFICE PERSONNEL

Pub. L. 103–270, § 6, June 30, 1994, 108 Stat. 737, provided that:

"(a) SUBMISSION OF REPORT.—On July 1 of each year, the President shall submit a report described in subsection (b) to the Committee on Governmental Affairs of the Senate and the Committee on Government Operations of the House of Representatives.

"(b) CONTENTS.—A report under subsection (a) shall, except as provided in subsection (c), include—

"(1) a list of each individual—

"(A) employed by the White House Office; or

"(B) detailed to the White House Office; and

"(2) with regard to each individual described in paragraph (1), the individual's—

"(A) name;

"(B) position and title; and

"(C) annual rate of pay.

"(c) EXCLUSION FROM REPORT.—If the President determines that disclosure of any item of information de-

---

[1] So in original. Probably should be title "5".

scribed in subsection (b) with respect to any particular individual would not be in the interest of the national defense or foreign policy of the United States—

"(1) a report under subsection (a) shall—

"(A) exclude such information with respect to that individual; and

"(B) include a statement of the number of individuals with respect to whom such information has been excluded; and

"(2) at the request of the Committee on Governmental Affairs of the Senate or the Committee on Government Operations of the House of Representatives, the information that was excluded from the report shall be made available for inspection by such committee."

[Committee on Government Operations of House of Representatives treated as referring to Committee on Government Reform and Oversight of House of Representatives by section 1(a) of Pub. L. 104–14, set out as a note under section 21 of Title 2, The Congress. Committee on Government Reform and Oversight of House of Representatives changed to Committee on Government Reform of House of Representatives by House Resolution No. 5, One Hundred Sixth Congress, Jan. 6, 1999.]

[Section 6 of Pub. L. 103–270, set out above, effective Jan. 1, 1995, see section 7(i) of Pub. L. 103–270, set out as an Effective Date of 1994 Amendment; Transition Provisions note under section 591 of Title 28, Judiciary and Judicial Procedure.]

§ 114. General pay limitation

Notwithstanding any provision of law, other than the provisions of this chapter, no employee of the White House Office, the Executive Residence at the White House, the Domestic Policy Staff, or the Office of Administration, nor any employee under the Vice President appointed under section 106 of this title, may be paid at a rate of basic pay in excess of the minimum rate of basic pay then currently paid for GS–16 of the General Schedule of section 5332 of title 5.

(Added Pub. L. 95–570, § 3(a), Nov. 2, 1978, 92 Stat. 2450.)

EFFECTIVE DATE

Section applicable to any fiscal year beginning on or after Oct. 1, 1978, see section 6(a) of Pub. L. 95–570, set out as an Effective Date of 1978 Amendment note under section 102 of this title.

REFERENCES IN OTHER LAWS TO GS–16, 17, OR 18 PAY RATES

References in laws to the rates of pay for GS–16, 17, or 18, or to maximum rates of pay under the General Schedule, to be considered references to rates payable under specified sections of Title 5, Government Organization and Employees, see section 529 [title I, § 101(c)(1)] of Pub. L. 101–509, set out in a note under section 5376 of Title 5.

SECTION REFERRED TO IN OTHER SECTIONS

This section is referred to in section 107 of this title.

§ 115. Veterans' preference

(a) Subject to subsection (b), appointments under sections 105, 106, and 107 shall be made in accordance with section 2108, and sections 3309 through 3312, of title 5.

(b) Subsection (a) shall not apply to any appointment to a position the rate of basic pay for which is at least equal to the minimum rate established for positions in the Senior Executive Service under section 5382 of title 5 and the duties of which are comparable to those described

in section 3132(a)(2) of such title or to any other position if, with respect to such position, the President makes certification—

(1) that such position is—

(A) a confidential or policy-making position; or

(B) a position for which political affiliation or political philosophy is otherwise an important qualification; and

(2) that any individual selected for such position is expected to vacate the position at or before the end of the President's term (or terms) of office.

Each individual appointed to a position described in the preceding sentence as to which the expectation described in paragraph (2) applies shall be notified as to such expectation, in writing, at the time of appointment to such position.

(Added Pub. L. 105–339, § 4(b)(1), Oct. 31, 1998, 112 Stat. 3185.)

CHAPTER 3—PROTECTION OF THE PRESIDENT; UNITED STATES SECRET SERVICE UNIFORMED DIVISION

AMENDMENTS

1977—Pub. L. 95–179, Nov. 15, 1977, 91 Stat. 1371, substituted "United States Secret Service Uniformed Division" for "Executive Protective Service" in chapter heading and in item 202.

1975—Pub. L. 94–196, § 1(d)(2), Dec. 31, 1975, 89 Stat. 1110, added item 208 and renumbered former item 208 as 209.

1970—Pub. L. 91–217, § 1(2), Mar. 19, 1970, 84 Stat. 74, substituted "Executive Protective Service" for "White House Police" in chapter heading and in item 202.

1951—Act July 16, 1951, ch. 226, § 5(b), 65 Stat. 122, struck out item 201 "Protection of President and family authorized".

[§ 201. Repealed. July 16, 1951, ch. 226, § 5(a), 65 Stat. 122]

Section, act June 25, 1948, ch. 644, 62 Stat. 680, related to protection of President and family. See section 3056 of Title 18, Crimes and Criminal Procedure.

§ 202. United States Secret Service Uniformed Division; establishment, control, and supervision; privileges, powers, and duties

There is hereby created and established a permanent police force, to be known as the "United States Secret Service Uniformed Division". Subject to the supervision of the Secretary of the Treasury, the United States Secret Service Uni-

---

[1] Section repealed without amending analysis.

formed Division shall perform such duties as the Director, United States Secret Service, may prescribe in connection with the protection of the following: (1) the White House in the District of Columbia; (2) any building in which Presidential offices are located; (3) the Treasury Building and grounds; (4) the President and members of his immediate family; (5) foreign diplomatic missions located in the metropolitan area of the District of Columbia; (6) the temporary official residence of the Vice President and grounds in the District of Columbia; (7) the Vice President and members of his immediate family; (8) foreign diplomatic missions located in metropolitan areas (other than the District of Columbia) in the United States where there are located twenty or more such missions headed by full-time officers, except that such protection shall be provided only (A) on the basis of extraordinary protective need, (B) upon request of the affected metropolitan area, and (C) when the extraordinary protective need arises at or in association with a visit to (i) a permanent mission to, or an observer mission invited to participate in the work of, an international organization of which the United States is a member; or (ii) an international organization of which the United States is a member, except that such protection may also be provided for motorcades and at other places associated with any such visit and may be extended at places of temporary domicile in connection with any such visit;

(9) foreign consular and diplomatic missions located in such areas in the United States, its territories and possessions, as the President, on a case-by-case basis, may direct; and

(10) visits of foreign government officials to metropolitan areas (other than the District of Columbia) where there are located 20 or more consular or diplomatic missions staffed by accredited personnel, including protection for motorcades and at other places associated with such visits when such officials are in the United States to conduct official business with the United States Government.

The members of such force shall possess privileges and powers similar to those of the members of the Metropolitan Police of the District of Columbia.

(June 25, 1948, ch. 644, 62 Stat. 680; Pub. L. 87–481, §1, June 8, 1962, 76 Stat. 95; Pub. L. 91–217, §1(2), (3), Mar. 19, 1970, 84 Stat. 74; Pub. L. 93–346, §7, July 12, 1974, as added Pub. L. 93–552, title VI, §609(a), Dec. 27, 1974, 88 Stat. 1765; Pub. L. 94–196, §1(a), (b), Dec. 31, 1975, 89 Stat. 1109; Pub. L. 95–179, Nov. 15, 1977, 91 Stat. 1371; Pub. L. 95–570, §5(d), Nov. 2, 1978, 92 Stat. 2451; Pub. L. 97–418, §1(a), Jan. 4, 1983, 96 Stat. 2089; Pub. L. 99–500, §101(m) [title VI, §622], Oct. 18, 1986, 100 Stat. 1783–308, 1783–333; Pub. L. 99–591, §101(m) [title VI, §622], Oct. 30, 1986, 100 Stat. 3341–308, 3341–333; Pub. L. 102–138, title I, §135(b)(1)–(3), Oct. 28, 1991, 105 Stat. 666, 667; Pub. L. 102–499, §3(a), Oct. 24, 1992, 106 Stat. 3264.)

AMENDMENTS

1992—Cl. (10). Pub. L. 102–499 substituted "when such officials are in the United States to conduct official business with the United States Government" for ", pursuant to invitations of the United States Government".

1991—Cl. (8)(C). Pub. L. 102–138, §135(b)(1), amended subcl. (C) generally. Prior to amendment, subcl. (C) read as follows: "when the extraordinary protective need arises in association with a visit to or occurs at a permanent mission to an international organization of which the United States is a member or an observer mission invited to participate in the work of such organization, provided that such protection may be provided for motorcades and at other places associated with such a visit and may be extended at places of temporary domicile in connection with such a visit; and".

Cl. (9). Pub. L. 102–138, §135(b)(2), amended cl. (9) generally. Prior to amendment, cl. (9) read as follows: "foreign diplomatic missions located in such areas in the United States, its territories and possessions, as the President, on a case-by-case basis, may direct."

Cl. (10). Pub. L. 102–138, §135(b)(3), added cl. (10).

1986—Cls. (3) to (9). Pub. L. 99–500 and Pub. L. 99–591 added cl. (3), redesignated cls. (3) to (8) as (4) to (9), respectively, and in cl. (7), as so redesignated, substituted "immediate" for "immediately".

1983—Cl. (7). Pub. L. 97–418 inserted "may be provided for motorcades and at other places associated with such a visit" after "protection".

1978—Pub. L. 95–570 substituted "White House" for "Executive Mansion and grounds".

1977—Pub. L. 95–179 substituted "United States Secret Service Uniformed Division" for "Executive Protective Service" in section catchline and wherever appearing in text.

1975—Pub. L. 94–196 added cl. (7), redesignated former cl. (7) as (8) and substituted "in such areas" for "in such other areas".

1974—Cls. (5) to (7). Pub. L. 93–552 added cls. (5) and (6) and redesignated former cl. (5) as (7).

1970—Pub. L. 91–217 substituted "Executive Protective Service" for "White House Police", substituted the Director, United States Secret Service, for the Secretary of the Treasury as the immediate director of Service operations, and added foreign diplomatic missions located in the metropolitan area of the District of Columbia and foreign diplomatic missions located in other areas as the President may direct to the enumerated list of areas under protection.

1962—Pub. L. 87–481 transferred control and supervision of White House Police from Chief of Secret Service Division to Secretary of the Treasury and required such force to perform duties in connection with protection of any building in which White House offices are located and the President and members of his immediate family.

CHANGE OF NAME

Pub. L. 95–179, Nov. 15, 1977, 91 Stat. 1371, provided in part that: "Any reference in any other law or in any regulation, document, record, or other paper of the United States to the Executive Protective Service shall be held to be a reference to the United States Secret Service Uniformed Division."

Pub. L. 91–297, title II, §202, June 30, 1970, 84 Stat. 358, provided that: "All laws of the United States in force on the date of enactment of this title [June 30, 1970] in which reference is made to the White House Police force are amended by substituting 'Executive Protective Service' for each such reference."

EFFECTIVE DATE OF 1992 AMENDMENT

Section 3(b) of Pub. L. 102–499 provided that: "The amendment made by subsection (a) [amending this section] shall be deemed to have become effective as of October 1, 1991."

EFFECTIVE DATE OF 1991 AMENDMENT

Section 135(b)(4) of Pub. L. 102–138 provided that:

"(A) Except as provided in subparagraph (B), the amendments made by this subsection [amending this section] shall take effect October 1, 1991.

"(B) The amendments made by paragraph (1) [amending this section] shall be deemed to have become effective as of January 1, 1989."

EFFECTIVE DATE OF 1983 AMENDMENT

Section 2 of Pub. L. 97–418 provided that: "The amendments made by the first section of this Act [amending sections 202 and 208 of this title] shall take effect on the date of enactment of this Act [Jan. 4, 1983], except that no amount authorized to be appropriated by the amendment made by subsection (b) of the first section of this Act [amending section 208(b) of this title] may be made available for use or obligation prior to October 1, 1982."

EFFECTIVE DATE OF 1978 AMENDMENT

Amendment by Pub. L. 95–570 applicable to any fiscal year beginning on or after Oct. 1, 1978, see section 6(a) of Pub. L. 95–570, set out as a note under section 102 of this title.

EFFECTIVE DATE OF 1975 AMENDMENT

Section 1(e) of Pub. L. 94–196 provided that: "The amendments made by subsections (a), (b), and (d) of this section [enacting section 208 of this title and amending this section] shall take effect as of July 1, 1974."

EFFECTIVE DATE OF 1974 AMENDMENT

Section 609(b) of Pub. L. 93–552 provided that: "Except as otherwise provided therein, the amendment made by subsection (a) of this section [amending this section, provisions set out as a note under section 111 of this title, and section 3056 of Title 18, Crimes and Criminal Procedure] shall become effective July 12, 1974."

TRANSFER OF FUNCTIONS

Functions of all officers of Department of the Treasury, and functions of all agencies and employees of such Department, transferred, with certain exceptions, to Secretary of the Treasury, with power vested in him to authorize their performance or performance of any of his functions, by any of such officers, agencies, and employees, by 1950 Reorg. Plan No. 26, §§1, 2, eff. July 31, 1950, 15 F.R. 4935, 64 Stat. 1280, set out in the Appendix to Title 5, Government Organization and Employees. Secret Service, referred to in this section, is an agency in Department of the Treasury.

REIMBURSEMENT TO STATE AND LOCAL GOVERNMENTS FOR PROTECTIVE SERVICES FOR FOREIGN MISSIONS

Section 135(b)(5) of Pub. L. 102–138 provided that: "Protective services provided by a State or local government at any time during the period beginning on January 1, 1989, and ending on September 30, 1991, which were performed in connection with visits described in section 202(8) of title 3, United States Code, as amended by this subsection, shall be deemed to be reimbursement obligations entered into pursuant to section 208(a) of that title as if the amendment made by paragraph (1) of this subsection [amending this section] was in effect during that period and the services had been requested by the Secretary of State."

SECTION REFERRED TO IN OTHER SECTIONS

This section is referred to in sections 208, 209 of this title; title 12 section 3414; title 22 sections 2709, 4304, 4314.

§ 203. Personnel, appointment, and vacancies

(a) The United States Secret Service Uniformed Division shall consist of such number of officers, with grades corresponding to similar officers of the Metropolitan Police force, and of such number of privates, with grade corresponding to that of private of the highest grade in the Metropolitan Police force, as may be necessary.

(b) Members of the United States Secret Service Uniformed Division shall be recruited under the civil service laws and regulations on a nationwide basis. Members of such Service may also be appointed from the members of the Metropolitan Police force and the United States Park Police force from lists furnished by the officers in charge of such forces. Whenever any vacancy is created in the Metropolitan Police force or the United States Park Police force as the result of an appointment to the United States Secret Service Uniformed Division, such vacancy shall be filled in the manner provided by law. In the period of time which follows the date of enactment of this sentence and precedes January 1, 1975, not more than thirty members of the Metropolitan Police force may be appointed annually to the United States Secret Service Uniformed Division.

(June 25, 1948, ch. 644, 62 Stat. 680; Aug. 15, 1950, ch. 715, §2, 64 Stat. 448; June 28, 1952, ch. 481, 66 Stat. 283; Pub. L. 87–481, §2, June 8, 1962, 76 Stat. 95; Pub. L. 91–217, §1(1), (4)–(6), Mar. 19, 1970, 84 Stat. 74, 75; Pub. L. 94–196, §1(c), Dec. 31, 1975, 89 Stat. 1109; Pub. L. 95–179, Nov. 15, 1977, 91 Stat. 1371; Pub. L. 104–208, div. A, title I, §101(f) [title I], Sept. 30, 1996, 110 Stat. 3009–314, 3009–324.)

REFERENCES IN TEXT

The civil service laws, referred to in subsec. (b), are set forth in Title 5, Government Organization and Employees. See, particularly, section 3301 et seq. of Title 5.

The date of enactment of this sentence, referred to in subsec. (b), is Mar. 19, 1970, the date of enactment of Pub. L. 91–217.

AMENDMENTS

1996—Subsec. (a). Pub. L. 104–208 struck out "but not exceeding twelve hundred in number" before period at end.

1977—Pub. L. 95–179 substituted "United States Secret Service Uniformed Division" for "Executive Protective Service" wherever appearing in subsecs. (a) and (b).

1975—Subsec. (a). Pub. L. 94–196 increased maximum number of Executive Protective Service from eight hundred and fifty to twelve hundred.

1970—Subsec. (a). Pub. L. 91–217, §1(1), (4), (5), substituted "Executive Protective Service" for "White House Police force", "eight hundred and fifty" for "two hundred and fifty", and struck out provisions limiting the appointment of White House Police to appointment from lists provided by the Metropolitan Police force and in the United States Park Police force and covering the filling of vacancies.

Subsec. (b). Pub. L. 91–217, §1(6), substituted "Executive Protective Service" for "White House Police force" and inserted provisions for the recruiting of personnel on a nationwide basis and from lists provided by the Metropolitan Police force and the United States Park Police force and placed a limit of 30 on the number to be appointed from the Metropolitan Police force annually until Jan. 1, 1975.

1962—Subsec. (a). Pub. L. 87–481 increased force from 170 to 250 members.

1952—Subsec. (a). Act June 28, 1952, increased force from 133 to 170 members.

1950—Subsec. (a). Act Aug. 15, 1950, increased force from 110 to 133 members.

TEMPORARY EXCEPTIONS TO LIMITATION

Acts Aug. 11, 1951, ch. 301, title I, 65 Stat. 185; June 30, 1952, ch. 523, title I, 66 Stat. 290, made appropriations for salaries and expenses of the White House Police force for fiscal years 1952 and 1953, and provided that the appropriations should be available for additional personnel without regard for the limitation contained in this section. The provisions were not repeated in the Treasury Department Appropriation Act, 1954, act June 18, 1953, ch. 132, title I, 67 Stat. 67.

SECTION REFERRED TO IN OTHER SECTIONS

This section is referred to in section 209 of this title.

§204. Grades, salaries, and transfers of appointees

(a) No person shall be appointed a member of the United States Secret Service Uniformed Division at a grade lower than the grade held by him as a member of the Metropolitan Police force or of the United States Park Police force at the time of his appointment.

(b) A member of the United States Secret Service Uniformed Division shall receive a salary at the rate provided for the corresponding grade in the Metropolitan Police force (including longevity increases provided by section 401 of the District of Columbia Police and Firemen's Salary Act of 1958), and he shall be furnished with uniforms and other necessary equipment similar to the uniforms and equipment furnished the United States Park Police, and he shall be entitled to the same leave allowances as a member of the United States Park Police force.

(c) Any member of the United States Secret Service Uniformed Division appointed thereto from the Metropolitan Police force or the United States Park Police force may be transferred to the organization of which he was a member at the time of such appointment.

(June 25, 1948, ch. 644, 62 Stat. 680; June 20, 1953, ch. 146, title IV, §402, 67 Stat. 76; Pub. L. 85–584, title V, §502(a), Aug. 1, 1958, 72 Stat. 485; Pub. L. 91–217, §1(1), Mar. 19, 1970, 84 Stat. 74; Pub. L. 95–179, Nov. 15, 1977, 91 Stat. 1371.)

REFERENCES IN TEXT

Section 401 of the District of Columbia Police and Firemen's Salary Act of 1958, referred to in subsec. (b), is section 401 of Pub. L. 85–584, title IV, Aug. 1, 1958, 72 Stat. 484.

AMENDMENTS

1977—Pub. L. 95–179 substituted "United States Secret Service Uniformed Division" for "Executive Protective Service" wherever appearing.

1970—Pub. L. 91–217 substituted "Executive Protective Service" for "White House Police force" wherever appearing in subsecs. (a), (b), and (c).

1958—Subsec. (b). Pub. L. 85–584 substituted "section 401 of the District of Columbia Police and Firemen's Salary Act of 1958" for "section 102 of the District of Columbia Police and Firemen's Salary Act of 1953".

1953—Subsec. (b). Act June 20, 1953, inserted references to longevity pay.

EFFECTIVE DATE OF 1953 AMENDMENT

Section 407 of act June 20, 1953, provided that: "This Act [amending this section] shall take effect on July 1, 1953."

CONVERSION TO NEW SALARY SCHEDULE

Pub. L. 106–554, §1(a)(4) [div. B, title IX, §905], Dec. 21, 2000, 114 Stat. 2763, 2763A–306, provided that:

"(a) IN GENERAL.—

"(1) DETERMINATION OF RATES OF BASIC PAY.—Effective on the first day of the 1st pay period beginning 6 months after the date of enactment of this Act [Dec. 21, 2000], the Secretary of the Treasury shall fix the rates of basic pay for officers and members of the United States Secret Service Uniformed Division, and the Secretary of the Interior shall fix the rates of basic pay for officers and members of the United States Park Police, in accordance with this subsection.

"(2) PLACEMENT ON REVISED SALARY SCHEDULE.—

"(A) IN GENERAL.—Each officer and member shall be placed in and receive basic compensation at the corresponding scheduled service step of the salary schedule under section 501(c) of the District of Columbia Police and Firemen's Salary Act of 1958 [Pub. L. 85–584, title V, Aug. 1, 1958, 72 Stat. 485] (as amended by section 902(a)) in accordance with the member's total years of creditable service, receiving credit for all service step adjustments. If the scheduled rate of pay for the step to which the officer or member would be assigned in accordance with this paragraph is lower than the officer's or member's salary immediately prior to the enactment of this paragraph, the officer or member will be placed in and receive compensation at the next higher service step.

"(B) CREDIT FOR INCREASES DURING TRANSITION.—Each member whose position is to be converted to the salary schedule under section 501(b) of the District of Columbia Police and Firemen's Salary Act of 1958 (as amended by subsection (a)) and who, prior to the effective date of this section [set out below] has earned, but has not been credited with, an increase in his or her rate of pay shall be afforded that increase before such member is placed in the corresponding service step in the salary schedule under section 501(b).

"(C) CREDITABLE SERVICE DESCRIBED.—For purposes of this paragraph, an officer's or member's creditable service is any police service in pay status with the United States Secret Service Uniformed Division, United States Park Police, or Metropolitan Police Department.

"(b) HOLD HARMLESS FOR CURRENT TOTAL COMPENSATION.—Notwithstanding any other provision of law, if the total rate of compensation for an officer or employee for any pay period occurring after conversion to the salary schedule pursuant to subsection (a) (determined by taking into account any locality-based comparability adjustments, longevity pay, and other adjustments paid in addition to the rate of basic compensation) is less than the officer's or employee's total rate of compensation (as so determined) on the date of enactment [Dec. 21, 2000], the rate of compensation for the officer or employee for the pay period shall be equal to—

"(1) the rate of compensation on the date of enactment (as so determined); increased by

"(2) a percentage equal to 50 percent of sum of the percentage adjustments made in the rate of basic compensation under section 501(c) of the District of Columbia Police and Firemen's Salary Act of 1958 (as amended by subsection (a)) for pay periods occurring after the date of enactment and prior to the pay period involved.

"(c) CONVERSION NOT TREATED AS TRANSFER OR PROMOTION.—The conversion of positions and individuals to appropriate classes of the salary schedule under section 501(c) of the District of Columbia Police and Firemen's Salary Act of 1958 (as amended by section 902(a)) and the initial adjustments of rates of basic pay of those positions and individuals in accordance with subsection (a) shall not be considered to be transfers or promotions within the meaning of section 304 of the District of Columbia Police and Firemen's Salary Act of 1958 [Pub. L. 85–584, title III, Aug. 1, 1958, 72 Stat. 484] (sec. 4–413, D.C. Code).

"(d) TRANSFER OF CREDIT FOR SATISFACTORY SERVICE.—Each individual whose position is converted to the salary schedule under section 501(c) of the District of Columbia Police and Firemen's Salary Act of 1958 (as amended by section 902(a)) in accordance with subsection (a) shall be granted credit for purposes of such individual's first service step adjustment under the salary schedule in such section 501(c) for all satisfactory service performed by the individual since the individual's last increase in basic pay prior to the adjustment under that section.

"(e) ADJUSTMENT TO TAKE INTO ACCOUNT GENERAL SCHEDULE ADJUSTMENTS DURING TRANSITION.—The rates provided under the salary schedule under section 501(c) of the District of Columbia Police and Firemen's Salary Act of 1958 (as amended by section 902(a)) shall be increased by the percentage of any annual adjustment applicable to the General Schedule authorized under section 5303 of title 5, United States Code, which takes effect during the period which begins on the date of the enactment of this Act [Dec. 21, 2000] and ends on the first day of the first pay period beginning 6 months after the date of enactment of this Act.

"(f) CONVERSION NOT TREATED AS SALARY INCREASE FOR PURPOSES OF CERTAIN PENSIONS AND ALLOWANCES.— The conversion of positions and individuals to appropriate classes of the salary schedule under section 501(c) of the District of Columbia Police and Firemen's Salary Act of 1958 (as amended by section 2[902](a)) and the initial adjustments of rates of basic pay of those positions and individuals in accordance with subsection (a) shall not be treated as an increase in salary for purposes of section 3 of the Act entitled 'An Act to provide increased pensions for widows and children of deceased members of the Police Department and the Fire Department of the District of Columbia', approved August 4, 1949 [ch. 394, 63 Stat. 566] (sec. 4–604, D.C. Code), or section 301 of the District of Columbia Police and Firemen's Salary Act of 1953 [June 20, 1953, ch. 146, title III, 67 Stat. 75] (sec. 4–605, D.C. Code)."

[Pub. L. 106–554, §1(a)(4) [div. B, title IX, §909], Dec. 21, 2000, 114 Stat. 2763, 2763A–310, provided that: "Except as provided in section 908(c) [114 Stat. 2763A–310], this title [enacting provisions set out as notes above and under sections 5301, 5304, and 5305 of Title 5, Government Organization and Employees, and amending provisions set out as a note under section 5305 of Title 5] and the amendments made by this title shall become effective on the first day of the first pay period beginning 6 months after the date of enactment [Dec. 21, 2000]."]

SECRET SERVICE UNIFORMED DIVISION COMPENSATION

Pub. L. 105–61, title I, §118, Oct. 10, 1997, 111 Stat. 1285, provided that:

"(a) NEW RATES OF BASIC PAY.—[Amended Pub. L. 85–584, title V, §501, Aug. 1, 1958, 72 Stat. 485.]

"(b) CONVERSION TO NEW SALARY SCHEDULE.—

"(1)(A) Effective on the first day of the first pay period beginning after the date of enactment of this section [Oct. 10, 1997], the Secretary of the Treasury shall fix the rates of basic pay for members of the United States Secret Service Uniformed Division in accordance with this paragraph.

"(B) Subject to subparagraph (C), each officer and member receiving basic compensation, immediately prior to the effective date of this section, at one of the scheduled rates in the salary schedule in section 101 of the District of Columbia Police and Firemen's Salary Act of 1958 [Pub. L. 85–584, title I, Aug. 1, 1958, 72 Stat. 481], as adjusted by law and as in effect prior to the effective date of this section, shall be placed in and receive basic compensation at the corresponding scheduled service step of the salary schedule under subsection (a)(4).

"(C)(i) The Assistant Chief and the Chief of the United States Secret Service Uniformed Division shall be placed in and receive basic compensation in salary class 10 and salary class 11, respectively, in the appropriate service step in the new salary class in accordance with section 304 of the District of Columbia Police and Firemen's Salary Act of 1958 [Pub. L. 85–584, title III, Aug. 1, 1958, 72 Stat. 484] (District of Columbia Code, section 4–413).

"(ii) Each member whose position is to be converted to the salary schedule under section 501(c) of the District of Columbia Police and Firemen's Salary Act of 1958 [Pub. L. 85–584, title V, Aug. 1, 1958, 72 Stat. 485] (District of Columbia Code, section 4–416(c)) as amended by this section, in accordance with subsection (a) of this section, and who, prior to the effective date of this section has earned, but has not been credited with, an increase in his or her rate of pay

shall be afforded that increase before such member is placed in the corresponding service step in the salary schedule under section 501(c).

"(2) Except in the cases of the Assistant Chief and the Chief of the United States Secret Service Uniformed Division, the conversion of positions and individuals to appropriate classes of the salary schedule under section 501(c) of the District of Columbia Police and Firemen's Salary Act of 1958 (District of Columbia Code, section 4–416(c)) as amended by this section, and the initial adjustments of rates of basic pay of those positions and individuals, in accordance with paragraph (1) of this subsection, shall not be considered to be transfers or promotions within the meaning of section 304 of the District of Columbia Police and Firemen's Salary Act of 1958 (District of Columbia Code, section 4–413).

"(3) Each member whose position is converted to the salary schedule under section 501(c) of the District of Columbia Police and Firemen's Salary Act of 1958 (District of Columbia Code, section 4–416(c)) as amended by this section, in accordance with subsection (a) of this section, shall be granted credit for purposes of such member's first service step adjustment under the salary schedule in such section 510(c) for all satisfactory service performed by the member since the member's last increase in basic pay prior to the adjustment under that section.

"(c) LIMITATION ON PAY PERIOD EARNINGS.—[Amended act Aug. 15, 1950, ch. 715, 64 Stat. 477.]

"(d) SAVINGS PROVISION.—On the effective date of this section, any existing special salary rates authorized for members of the United States Secret Service Uniformed Division under section 5305 of title 5, United States Code (or any previous similar provision of law) and any special rates of pay or special pay adjustments under section 403, 404, or 405 of the Federal Law Enforcement Pay Reform Act of 1990 [Pub. L. 101–509, §529 [title IV, §§403–405], 5 U.S.C. 5305 note] applicable to members of the United States Secret Service Uniformed Division shall be rendered inapplicable.

"(e) CONFORMING AMENDMENT.—[Amended Pub. L. 101–509, §529 [title IV, §405], set out as a note under section 5305 of Title 5, Government Organization and Employees.]

"(f) EFFECTIVE DATE.—The provisions of this section shall become effective on the first day of the first pay period beginning after the date of enactment of this Act [Oct. 10, 1997]."

SECTION REFERRED TO IN OTHER SECTIONS

This section is referred to in section 209 of this title.

[§ 205. Repealed. Pub. L. 91–217, § 1(7), Mar. 19, 1970, 84 Stat. 75]

Section, act June 25, 1948, ch. 644, 62 Stat. 680, provided for appointment of members of White House Police force in accordance with civil service laws. See section 203(b) of this title.

§ 206. Privileges of civil-service appointees

Members of the United States Secret Service Uniformed Division not appointed from the Metropolitan Police force or the United States Park Police force shall be entitled to the same privileges as to salary, grade, uniforms, equipment, transfer, leave, relief funds, retirement, and refunds as members appointed from the Metropolitan Police force and the United States Park Police force.

(June 25, 1948, ch. 644, 62 Stat. 681; Pub. L. 91–217, §1(8), Mar. 19, 1970, 84 Stat. 75; Pub. L. 95–179, Nov. 15, 1977, 91 Stat. 1371.)

AMENDMENTS

1977—Pub. L. 95–179 substituted "United States Secret Service Uniformed Division" for "Executive Protective Service".

1970—Pub. L. 91–217 substituted "Members of the Executive Protective Service not appointed from the Metropolitan Police force or the United States Park Police force" for "Members appointed pursuant to section 205 of this title".

§ 207. Participation in police and firemen's relief fund

(a) For the purposes of retirement under section 12 of the Act entitled "An Act making appropriations to provide for the expenses of the government of the District of Columbia for the fiscal year ending June 30, 1917, and for other purposes,[1] approved September 1, 1916, as amended, service with the United States Park Police force shall be deemed service with the United States Secret Service Uniformed Division.

(b) Any member of the Metropolitan Police force appointed to the United States Secret Service Uniformed Division shall continue to be subject to the provisions of section 12 of such Act, and appointment of such member to the United States Secret Service Uniformed Division or transfer of such member to his former organization shall not affect any right, privilege, or duty of such member under the provisions of such section of such Act.

(June 25, 1948, ch. 644, 62 Stat. 681; Pub. L. 91–217, §1(1), Mar. 19, 1970, 84 Stat. 74; Pub. L. 95–179, Nov. 15, 1977, 91 Stat. 1371.)

REFERENCES IN TEXT

Section 12 of the Act entitled "An Act making appropriations to provide for the expenses of the government of the District of Columbia for the fiscal year ending June 30, 1917, and for other purposes," approved September 1, 1916, as amended, referred to in text, is act Sept. 1, 1916, ch. 433, §12, 39 Stat. 718, as amended.

AMENDMENTS

1977—Pub. L. 95–179 substituted "United States Secret Service Uniformed Division" for "Executive Protective Service" wherever appearing.

1970—Pub. L. 91–217 substituted "Executive Protective Service" for "White House Police force" wherever appearing.

SECTION REFERRED TO IN OTHER SECTIONS

This section is referred to in section 209 of this title.

§ 208. Reimbursement of State and local governments

(a) In carrying out the functions pursuant to sections 202(8) and 202(10), the Secretary of Treasury may utilize, with their consent, on a reimbursable basis, the services, personnel, equipment, and facilities of State and local governments, and is authorized to reimburse such State and local governments for the utilization of such services, personnel, equipment, and facilities. The Secretary of Treasury may carry out the functions pursuant to sections 202(8) and 202(10) by contract. The authority of this subsection may be transferred by the President to the Secretary of State. In carrying out any duty under sections 202(8) and 202(10), the Secretary of State is authorized to utilize any authority available to the Secretary under title II of the State Department Basic Authorities Act of 1956.

(b) There is authorized to be appropriated, in addition to such sums as have been heretofore appropriated under this section—

(1) $10,000,000 for each fiscal year beginning after September 30, 1991, for the payment of reimbursement obligations entered into under subsection (a) without regard to the fiscal year such obligations were entered into, including obligations entered into before such date; and

(2) $8,000,000 for the payment of reimbursement obligations entered into under subsection (a) before October 1, 1991, except that not more than $4,000,000 of this amount shall be obligated or expended during fiscal year 1992.

Amounts appropriated under this subsection shall remain available until expended.

(Added Pub. L. 94–196, §1(d)(1), Dec. 31, 1975, 89 Stat. 1109; amended Pub. L. 97–418, §1(b), Jan. 4, 1983, 96 Stat. 2089; Pub. L. 99–93, title I, §126(c), Aug. 16, 1985, 99 Stat. 418; Pub. L. 99–399, title IV, §410, Aug. 27, 1986, 100 Stat. 866; Pub. L. 102–138, title I, §135(a)(1), (2), (c), Oct. 28, 1991, 105 Stat. 666, 667.)

REFERENCES IN TEXT

Title II of the State Department Basic Authorities Act of 1956, referred to in subsec. (a), is title II of act Aug. 1, 1956, ch. 841, as added Aug. 24, 1982, Pub. L. 97–241, title II, §202(b), 96 Stat. 283, known as the Foreign Missions Act, which is classified principally to chapter 53 (§4301 et seq.) of Title 22, Foreign Relations and Intercourse. For complete classification of title II to the Code, see Short Title note set out under section 4301 of Title 22 and Tables.

PRIOR PROVISIONS

A prior section 208 was renumbered 209 by Pub. L. 94–196.

AMENDMENTS

1991—Subsec. (a). Pub. L. 102–138, §135(c), substituted "sections 202(8) and 202(10)" for "section 202(7)" wherever appearing.

Subsec. (b)(1). Pub. L. 102–138, §135(a)(1), substituted "$10,000,000" for "$7,000,000", "1991" for "1982", and "without regard to the fiscal year such obligations were entered into, including obligations entered into before such date" for "after such date".

Subsec. (b)(2). Pub. L. 102–138, §135(a)(2), substituted "$8,000,000" for "$17,700,000" and "1991, except that not more than $4,000,000 of this amount shall be obligated or expended during fiscal year 1992" for "1982".

1986—Subsec. (a). Pub. L. 99–399 authorized the Secretary of State, in carrying out any duty under section 202(7), to utilize the authority under title II of the State Department Basic Authorities Act of 1956.

1985—Subsec. (a). Pub. L. 99–93 inserted sentence authorizing the Secretary of Treasury to carry out the functions pursuant to section 202(7) by contract.

1983—Subsec. (b). Pub. L. 97–418 substituted provisions authorizing appropriation of $7,000,000 for each fiscal year beginning after Sept. 30, 1982, and $17,700,000 for obligations entered into before that date, for provisions authorizing to be appropriated not more than $3,500,000 for any fiscal year.

EFFECTIVE DATE OF 1991 AMENDMENT

Section 135(a)(3) of Pub. L. 102–138 provided that: "The amendments made by this subsection [amending this section] shall take effect on October 1, 1991."

EFFECTIVE DATE OF 1985 AMENDMENT

Amendment by Pub. L. 99–93 effective Oct. 1, 1985, see section 126(e) of Pub. L. 99–93, set out as an Effective

---

[1] So in original. Probably should be followed by close quotation.

Date note under section 4314 of Title 22, Foreign Relations and Intercourse.

Amendment by Pub. L. 97–418 effective Jan. 4, 1983, except that no amount authorized to be appropriated by such amendment may be made available for use or obligation prior to Oct. 1, 1982, see section 2 of Pub. L. 97–418, set out as a note under section 202 of this title.

Section effective July 1, 1974, see section 1(e) of Pub. L. 94–196, set out as an Effective Date of 1975 Amendment note under section 202 of this title.

Ex. Ord. No. 12478, May 23, 1984, 49 F.R. 22053, provided:

By authority vested in me as President by the Constitution and statutes of the United States of America, and in accordance with the provisions of the Act of December 31, 1975, Public Law 94–196 (89 Stat. 1109), codified as sections 202(7) and 208(a) of Title 3, United States Code, as amended, it is hereby ordered as follows:

SECTION 1. There is transferred to the Secretary of State authority to determine the need for and to approve terms and conditions of the provision of reimbursable extraordinary protective activities for foreign diplomatic missions pursuant to section 202(7), and the authority to make reimbursements to State and local governments for services, personnel, equipment, and facilities pursuant to section 208(a) of Title 3, United States Code;

SEC. 2. There are transferred to the Secretary of State such unexpended moneys as may have been appropriated to the Department of the Treasury for the purpose of permitting reimbursements to be made under the provisions of section 208(a) of Title 3, United States Code;

SEC. 3. The authority transferred pursuant to this Order shall be exercised in coordination with protective security programs administered by the Secretary of State under the Foreign Missions Act of 1982 [22 U.S.C. 4301 et seq.]; authority available under that Act may also be applied to any foreign mission to which section 202(7) applies; and

SEC. 4. This Order shall be effective on October 1, 1984.

RONALD REAGAN.

This section is referred to in section 209 of this title; title 22 section 4314.

§ 209. Appropriation to carry out provisions

There is authorized to be appropriated, out of any money in the Treasury not otherwise appropriated, such sums as may be necessary to carry out the provisions of sections 202–204, 207, and 208 of this title.

(June 25, 1948, ch. 644, 62 Stat. 681, § 208; renumbered § 209, Pub. L. 94–196, § 1(d)(1), Dec. 31, 1975, 89 Stat. 1109.)

CHAPTER 4—DELEGATION OF FUNCTIONS

Similar provisions were contained in former chapter 4, comprising former sections 301 to 303 of this title, which was set out here but which was not a part of this title. Former sections 301 to 303 were derived from act Aug. 8, 1950, ch. 646, §§ 1–3, 64 Stat. 419, and were repealed by section 56(j) of act Oct. 31, 1951. Subsec. (l) of section 56 provided that the repeal should not affect any rights or liabilities existing under the repealed sections on the effective date of the repeal (Oct. 31, 1951).

§ 301. General authorization to delegate functions; publication of delegations

The President of the United States is authorized to designate and empower the head of any department or agency in the executive branch, or any official thereof who is required to be appointed by and with the advice and consent of the Senate, to perform without approval, ratification, or other action by the President (1) any function which is vested in the President by law, or (2) any function which such officer is required or authorized by law to perform only with or subject to the approval, ratification, or other action of the President: *Provided,* That nothing contained herein shall relieve the President of his responsibility in office for the acts of any such head or other official designated by him to perform such functions. Such designation and authorization shall be in writing, shall be published in the Federal Register, shall be subject to such terms, conditions, and limitations as the President may deem advisable, and shall be revocable at any time by the President in whole or in part.

(Added Oct. 31, 1951, ch. 655, § 10, 65 Stat. 712.)

Functions vested by law (including reorganization plan) in Bureau of the Budget or Director of Bureau of the Budget transferred to President by section 101 of 1970 Reorg. Plan No. 2, eff. July 1, 1970, 35 F.R. 7959, 84 Stat. 2085. Section 102 of 1970 Reorg. Plan No. 2, redesignated Bureau of the Budget as Office of Management and Budget and Director of Bureau of the Budget as Director of Office of Management and Budget. See Reorganization Plan No. 2 of 1970, set out in the Appendix to Title 5, Government Organization and Employees.

For similar provisions contained in prior law, and saving clause in connection therewith, see note preceding this section.

Ex. Ord. No. 10250, June 5, 1951, 16 F.R. 5385, as amended by Ex. Ord. No. 10732, Oct. 10, 1957, 22 F.R. 8135; Ex. Ord. No. 10752, Feb. 12, 1958, 23 F.R. 973; Pub. L. 101–509, title V, § 529 [title I, § 112(c)], Nov. 5, 1990, 104 Stat. 1427, 1454, provided:

1. The Secretary of the Interior is hereby designated and empowered to perform the following-described functions of the President without the approval, ratification, or other action of the President:

(a) The authority vested in the President by section 1 of the act of July 10, 1935, ch. 375, 49 Stat. 477 [see 16 U.S.C. 19e to 19n], to appoint members of the National Park Trust Fund Board.

(b) The authority vested in the President by section 2059 of the Revised Statutes [25 U.S.C. 62] to discontinue any Indian agency, or transfer the same, from the place or tribe designated by law to such other place or tribe as the public service may require.

(c) The authority vested in the President by section 6 of the act of May 17, 1882, ch. 168, 22 Stat. 88, as amended [25 U.S.C. 63], to consolidate two or more Indian agencies into one, to consolidate one or more Indian tribes, and to abolish such agencies as are thereby rendered unnecessary.

(d) The authority vested in the President by the act of March 1, 1907, ch. 2285, 34 Stat. 1016 [25 U.S.C. 140], to divert appropriations made for certain purposes to other uses for the benefit of the several Indian tribes: *Provided*, That the Secretary of the Interior shall make to the Congress reports required in connection with action taken by him under this provision.

(e) The authority vested in the President by section 5 of the act of February 8, 1887, ch. 119, 24 Stat. 389, as amended [25 U.S.C. 348], by the act of December 24, 1942, ch. 814, 56 Stat. 1081 [25 U.S.C. 348a], by the act of June 21, 1906, ch. 3504, 34 Stat. 326 [25 U.S.C. 391], and by section 3 of the act of January 12, 1891, 26 Stat. 712, as amended by section 3 of the act of March 2, 1917, ch. 146, 39 Stat. 976, to extend trust periods on land patents issued to Indians and to continue restrictions on alienation.

(f) The authority vested in the President by section 4705(b) of the Internal Revenue Code of 1954 [former 26 U.S.C. 4705(b)] to authorize certain persons in the Virgin Islands to obtain certain drugs for legitimate medical purposes without regard to order forms, and by section 4762(b) of such Code [former 26 U.S.C. 4762(b)] to provide for the registration of and the imposition of special and transfer taxes upon persons in the Virgin Islands who import, manufacture, produce, compound, sell, deal in, dispense, prescribe, administer, or give away marihuana: *Provided*, That the Secretary of the Interior shall perform the functions referred to in this subsection in consultation with the Department of the Treasury.

(g) The authority vested in the President by section 2343 of the Revised Statutes [30 U.S.C. 46] to establish additional land districts and to appoint necessary officers under existing laws when deemed necessary for the public convenience in executing certain provisions of law with respect to mineral lands and mining.

(h) The authority vested in the President by section 2252 of the Revised Statutes as affected by section 403 of Reorganization Plan No. 3 of 1946, 60 Stat. 1100 [43 U.S.C. 121], to order the discontinuance of any land office and the transfer of any of its business and archives to any other land office within the same State or Territory.

(i) The authority vested in the President by section 2250 of the Revised Statutes [43 U.S.C. 125] to discontinue a land office in a land district under certain circumstances and to annex the same to some other adjoining land district.

(j) The authority vested in the President by section 2251 of the Revised Statutes [43 U.S.C. 126] to change the location of the land offices in the several land districts established by law and to relocate the same from time to time at such point in the district as may be deemed expedient.

(k) The authority vested in the President by section 2253 of the Revised Statutes [43 U.S.C. 127], to change and reestablish the boundaries of land districts.

(*l*) The authority vested in the President by section 2 of the act of March 2, 1917, ch. 145, 39 Stat. 951, as amended [48 U.S.C. 737], to approve the payment out of the Treasury for other purposes of money derived from any tax levied or assessed for a special purpose in Puerto Rico.

(m) The authority vested in the President by section 7 of the act of March 2, 1917, ch. 145, 39 Stat. 954, as amended [48 U.S.C. 748], to convey to the people of Puerto Rico lands, buildings, or interests in lands, or other property owned by the United States, and to accept lands, buildings, or other interests or property by legislative grant from Puerto Rico.

(n) The authority vested in the President by section 3(b) of the act of March 3, 1925, ch. 426, 43 Stat. 1111, as amended [see 50 U.S.C. 167d], to approve regulations governing the production and sale of helium for medical, scientific, and commercial use.

(*o*) The authority vested in the President by section 6 of the act of April 26, 1906, ch. 1876, 34 Stat. 139, to remove from office the principal chief of the Choctaw, Cherokee, Creek, or Seminole tribe or the governor of the Chickasaw tribe, to declare any such office vacant, and to fill any vacancy in any such office arising from removal, disability, or death of the incumbent.

(p) The authority vested in the President by section 28 of the act of April 26, 1906, ch. 1876, 34 Stat. 148, to approve acts, ordinances, or resolutions of the tribal council or legislature of the Choctaw, Chickasaw, Cherokee, Creek, and Seminole tribes or nations, and to approve contracts, involving the payment or expenditure of money or affecting property belonging to any of the said tribes or nations, made by them or any of them or by any officer thereof.

(q) [Superseded by section 3 of Ex. Ord. No. 10752, Feb. 12, 1958, 23 F.R. 973, set out as a note under 15 U.S.C. 715j].

(r) The authority vested in the President by section 55 of the act of April 30, 1900, 31 Stat. 150, as amended [48 U.S.C. 562], and by section 4 of the act of August 24, 1954, 68 Stat. 785, as amended [48 U.S.C. 562*o*], to approve the issuance of bonds or other instruments of indebtedness by the Territory of Hawaii.

2. The Secretary of the Interior is hereby designated and empowered to perform, without the approval, ratification, or other action of the President, the following functions which have heretofore, under the respective provisions of law cited, required the approval, ratification, or other action of the President in connection with their performance by the Secretary of the Interior:

(a) The authority vested in the Secretary of the Interior by section 1 of the act of June 6, 1942, ch. 380, 56 Stat. 326 [16 U.S.C. 459r], to convey or lease to the States or to the political subdivisions thereof any or all of certain recreational demonstration projects and lands and equipment comprised within such projects or any parts of such projects; and to transfer to other Federal agencies any of the said recreational demonstration areas that may be of use to such agencies.

(b) The authority vested in the Secretary of the Interior by section 3 of the act of July 3, 1918, ch. 128, 40 Stat. 755, as amended, and as affected by section 4(f) of Reorganization Plan No. II, effective July 1, 1939, 53 Stat. 1433 [16 U.S.C. 704], to promulgate regulations permitting and governing the hunting, taking, capture, killing, possession, sale, purchase, shipment, transportation, carriage, or export of any migratory bird included in the terms of certain conventions, or any part, nest, or egg thereof.

3. As used in this order, the term "functions" embraces duties, powers, responsibilities, authority, or discretion, and the term "perform" may be construed to mean "exercise".

4. All actions heretofore taken by the President in respect of the matters affected by this order and in force at the time of the issuance of this order, including regulations prescribed by the President in respect of such matters, shall, except as they may be inconsistent with the provisions of this order, remain in effect until modified or revoked pursuant to the authority conferred by this order.

5. The Secretary of the Interior is hereby authorized to redelegate to the Deputy Secretary of the Interior any of the authority delegated to the Secretary of the Interior by section 1 of this order.

EX. ORD. NO. 10289. DELEGATION OF FUNCTIONS TO
SECRETARY OF THE TREASURY

Ex. Ord. No. 10289, Sept. 17, 1951, 16 F.R. 9499, as amended by Ex. Ord. No. 10583, Dec. 18, 1954, 19 F.R. 8725; Ex. Ord. No. 10882, July 18, 1960, 25 F.R. 6869; Ex. Ord. No. 11110, June 4, 1963, 28 F.R. 5605; Ex. Ord. No. 11825, Dec. 31, 1974, 40 F.R. 1003; Ex. Ord. No. 12608, Sept. 9, 1987, 52 F.R. 34617, provided:

1. The Secretary of the Treasury is hereby designated and empowered to perform the following-described functions of the President without the approval, ratification, or other action of the President:

(a) The authority vested in the President by section 1 of the act of August 1, 1914, ch. 223, 38 Stat. 609, 623, as amended [19 U.S.C. 2], (1) to rearrange, by consolidation or otherwise, the several customs-collection districts, (2) to discontinue ports of entry by abolishing the same and establishing others in their stead, and (3) to change from time to time the location of the headquarters in any customs-collection district as the needs of the service may require.

(b) The authority vested in the President by section 1 of the Anti-Smuggling Act of August 5, 1935, c. 438, 49 Stat. 517 [19 U.S.C. 1701], (1) to find and declare that at any place or within any area on the high seas adjacent to but outside customs waters any vessel or vessels hover or are being kept off the coast of the United States and that, by virtue of the presence of any such vessel or vessels at such place or within such area, the unlawful introduction or removal into or from the United States of any merchandise or person is being, or may be, occasioned, promoted, or threatened, (2) to find and declare that certain waters on the high seas are in such proximity to such vessel or vessels that such unlawful introduction or removal of merchandise or persons may be carried on by or to or from such vessel or vessels, and (3) to find and declare that, within any customs-enforcement area, the circumstances no longer exist which gave rise to the declaration of such area as a customs-enforcement area.

(c) The authority vested in the President by section 1 of the Act of August 26, 1985, Public Law 98–89, 97 Stat. 510 (46 U.S.C. 3101); to suspend the provisions of law requiring the inspection of foreign-built vessels admitted to American registry.

(d) The authority vested in the President by section 5 of the act of May 28, 1908, ch. 212, 35 Stat. 425, as amended (46 U.S.C. Appendix 104), to determine (as a prerequisite to the extension of reciprocal privileges by the Commissioner of Customs) that yachts used and employed exclusively as pleasure vessels and belonging to any resident of the United States are allowed to arrive at and depart from any foreign port and to cruise in the waters of such port without entering or clearing at the custom-house thereof and without the payment of any charges for entering or clearing, dues, duty per ton, tonnage taxes, or charges for cruising licenses.

(e) The authority vested in the President by section 2 of the act of March 24, 1908, ch. 96, 35 Stat. 46 (46 U.S.C. Appendix 134), to name the hospital ships to which section 1 of the said act [46 U.S.C. Appendix 133], shall apply and to indicate the time when the exemptions thereby provided for shall begin and end.

(f) The authority vested in the President by section 4228 of the Revised Statutes, as amended (46 U.S.C. Appendix 141), (1) to declare that—upon satisfactory proof being given by the government of any foreign nation that no discriminating duties of tonnage or imports are imposed or levied in the ports of such nation upon vessels wholly belonging to citizens of the United States, or upon the produce, manufactures or merchandise imported in the same from the United States or from any foreign country—the foreign discriminating duties of tonnage and impost within the United States are suspended and discontinued, so far as respect the vessels of such foreign nation, and the produce, manufactures, or merchandise imported into the United States from such foreign nation, or from any other foreign country, and (2) to suspend in part the operation of section 4219 of the Revised Statutes, as amended (46 U.S.C. Appendix 121), and section IV, J, subsection 1 of the act of October 3, 1913, c. 16 38 Stat. 195, as amended (46 U.S.C. Appendix 146), so that foreign vessels from a country imposing partial discriminating tonnage duties upon American vessels, or partial discriminating import duties upon American merchandise, may enjoy in our ports the identical privileges which the same class of American vessels and merchandise may enjoy in such country: *Provided*, That prior to the issuance of an order of the Secretary of the Treasury suspending and discontinuing (wholly or in part) discriminating tonnage duties, imposts, and import duties within the United States, the Department of State shall obtain and furnish to the Secretary of the Treasury the proof required by the said sections 4228, as amended, as the basis for that order.

(g) The authority vested in the President by section 3650 of the Internal Revenue Code [section 3650 of the Internal Revenue Code of 1939] [see 26 U.S.C. 7621], to establish convenient collection districts (for the purpose of assessing, levying, and collecting the taxes provided by the internal revenue laws), and from time to time to alter such districts.

(h) The authority which is now vested in the President by section 2564(b) of the Internal Revenue Code [section 2564(b) of the Internal Revenue Code of 1939], and which on and after January 1, 1955, will be vested in the President by section 4735(b) of the Internal Revenue Code of 1954 [former 26 U.S.C. 4735(b)], to issue, in accordance with the provisions of the said section 2564(b) or 4735(b), as the case may be, orders providing for the registration and the imposition of a special tax upon all persons in the Canal Zone who produce, import, compound, deal in, dispense, sell, distribute, or give away narcotic drugs.

(i) The authority vested in the President by Section 5318 of the Revised Statutes, as amended (19 U.S.C. 540), to employ suitable vessels other than Coast Guard cutters in the execution of laws providing for the collection of duties on imports and tonnage;[.]

2. The Secretary of the Treasury is hereby designated and empowered to perform without the approval, ratification, or other action of the President the following functions which have heretofore, under the respective provisions of law cited, required the approval of the President in connection with their performance by the Secretary of the Treasury:

(a) The authority vested in the Secretary of the Treasury by section 6 of the act of July 8, 1937, ch. 444, 50 Stat. 480 [40 U.S.C. 728], to make rules and regulations necessary for the execution of the functions vested in the Secretary of the Treasury by the said act, as amended.

(b), (c) [Revoked by Ex. Ord. No. 11110, June 4, 1963, 28 F.R. 5605.]

(d) [Revoked by Ex. Ord. No. 11825, Dec. 31, 1974, 40 F.R. 1003.]

(e) The authority vested in the Secretary of the Treasury by section 1 of Title II of the act of June 15, 1917, ch. 30, 40 Stat. 220 [50 U.S.C. 191], to make rules and regulations governing the anchorage and movement of any vessel, foreign or domestic, in the territorial waters of the United States.

3. (a) The Secretary of the Treasury and the Postmaster General [now United States Postal Service] are hereby designated and empowered jointly to prescribe without the approval of the President regulations, under section 1 of the act of July 8, 1937, ch. 444, 50 Stat. 479 [40 U.S.C. 721], governing the shipment of valuables by the executive departments, independent establishments, agencies, wholly-owned corporations, officers, and employees of the United States.

(b) The Postmaster General [now United States Postal Service] is hereby designated and empowered to exercise without the approval, ratification, or other action of the President the authority vested in the President by section 504(b) of Title 18 of the United States Code to approve regulations issued by the Secretary of the Treasury under the authority of the said section 504(b) (relating to the printing, publishing, or importation, or the making or importation of the necessary plates for such printing or publishing, of postage stamps for philatelic purposes) [see section 504(2) of title 18], and to approve any amendment or repeal of any of such regulations by the Secretary of the Treasury.

4. As used in this order, the term "functions" embraces duties, powers, responsibilities, authority, or discretion, and the term "perform" may be construed to mean "exercise".

5. All actions heretofore taken by the President in respect of the matters affected by this order and in force at the time of the issuance of this order, including regulations prescribed by the President in respect of such

matters, shall, except as they may be inconsistent with the provisions of this order, remain in effect until amended, modified, or revoked pursuant to the authority conferred by this order.

Ex. Ord. No. 10530. Delegation of Miscellaneous Functions

Ex. Ord. No. 10530, May 10, 1954, 19 F.R. 2709, as amended by Ex. Ord. No. 10573, Oct. 26, 1954, 19 F.R. 6899; Ex. Ord. No. 10682, Oct. 22, 1956, 21 F.R. 8129; Ex. Ord. No. 10759, Mar. 17, 1958, 23 F.R. 1803; Ex. Ord. No. 10790, Nov. 20, 1958, 23 F.R. 9051; Ex. Ord. No. 10836, Sept. 8, 1959, 24 F.R. 7269; Ex. Ord. No. 10852, Nov. 27, 1959, 24 F.R. 9565; Ex. Ord. No. 10889, Oct. 5, 1960, 25 F.R. 9633; Ex. Ord. No. 10903, Jan. 9, 1961, 26 F.R. 217; Ex. Ord. No. 10960, Aug. 21, 1961, 26 F.R. 7823; Ex. Ord. No. 10970, Oct. 27, 1961, 26 F.R. 10149; Ex. Ord. No. 11012, Mar. 27, 1962, 27 F.R. 2983; Ex. Ord. No. 11116, Aug. 5, 1963, 28 F.R. 8075; Ex. Ord. No. 11164, Aug. 1, 1964, 29 F.R. 11257; Ex. Ord. No. 11184, Oct. 13, 1964, 29 F.R. 14155; Ex. Ord. No. 11196, Feb. 2, 1965, 30 F.R. 1171; Ex. Ord. No. 11222, May 8, 1965, 30 F.R. 6469; Ex. Ord. No. 11228, June 14, 1965, 30 F.R. 7739; Ex. Ord. No. 11230, § 2(1), (3), (5) to (14), June 28, 1965, 30 F.R. 8447; Ex. Ord. No. 12107, Dec. 28, 1978, 44 F.R. 1055; Pub. L. 98–497, title I, § 103(b)(1), Oct. 19, 1984, 98 Stat. 2283; Ex. Ord. No. 12608, Sept. 9, 1987, 52 F.R. 34617, provided:

Part I—Director of the Bureau of the Budget

[Superseded by Ex. Ord. No. 11230, § 2(1), (3), (5)–(14), June 28, 1965, 30 F.R. 8447]

Part II—The Office of Personnel Management

[Superseded by Ex. Ord. No. 11228, § 3(1), (2), (5), June 14, 1965, 30 F.R. 7739]

Part III—The Housing and Home Finance Administrator

[Superseded by Ex. Ord. No. 11196, Feb. 2, 1965, 30 F.R. 1171]

Part IV

The Federal Communications Commission

Sec. 5. (a) The Federal Communications Commission is hereby designated and empowered to exercise, without the approval, ratification, or other action of the President, all authority vested in the President by the act of May 27, 1921, ch. 12, 42 Stat. 8 [47 U.S.C. 34 to 39], including the authority to issue, withhold, or revoke licenses to land or operate submarine cables in the United States: *Provided,* That no such license shall be granted or revoked by the Commission except after obtaining approval of the Secretary of State and such advice from any executive department or establishment of the Government as the Commission may deem necessary. The Commission is authorized and directed to receive all applications for the said licenses.

(b) Executive Order No. 3513 of July 9, 1921, as amended by Executive Order No. 6779 of June 30, 1934, is hereby revoked.

Part V

The Attorney General and the Archivist of the United States

Sec. 6. The Attorney General and the Archivist of the United States are hereby designated and empowered jointly to perform the following-described functions without the approval, ratification, or other action of the President:

(a) The authority vested in the President by section 5(a) of the act of July 26, 1935, ch. 417, 49 Stat. 501, as amended (44 U.S.C. 1505(a)), to determine from time to time the documents or classes of documents having general applicability and legal effect.

(b) The authority vested in the President by sections 6, 11(a), and 11(f) of said act, as amended (44 U.S.C. 1506; 1510(a) and 1510(f)), to approve (or disapprove), respectively, (1) regulations, prescribed by the Administrative Committee of the Federal Register, for carrying out the provisions of that act (including the regulations referred to in section 5(b) of the act (44 U.S.C. 1505(b)), authorizing publication in the Federal Register of certain documents or classes of documents), (2) actions of the Administrative Committee of the Federal Register requiring, from time to time, the preparation and publication in special or supplemental editions of the Federal Register of complete codifications of the documents, described in the said section 11(a) (44 U.S.C. 1510(a)), of each agency of the Government, and (3) regulations, prescribed by the Administrative Committee of the Federal Register, for carrying out the provisions of section 11 (44 U.S.C. 1510) of the said act, as amended.

Part VI

General Provisions

Sec. 7. All actions heretofore taken by the President in respect of the matters affected by this order and in force at the time of the issuance of this order, including any regulations prescribed or approved by the President in respect of such matters, shall, except as they may be inconsistent with the provisions of this order, remain in effect until amended, modified, or revoked pursuant to the authority conferred by this order.

Sec. 8. As used in this order, the term "functions" embraces duties, powers, responsibilities, authority, or discretion, and the term "perform" may be construed to mean "exercise."

Ex. Ord. No. 10621. Delegation of Functions to Secretary of Defense

Ex. Ord. No. 10621, July 1, 1955, 20 F.R. 4759, as amended by Ex. Ord. No. 11294, Aug. 4, 1966, 31 F.R. 10601; Ex. Ord. No. 12396, Dec. 9, 1982, 47 F.R. 55897; Ex. Ord. No. 12561, July 1, 1986, 51 F.R. 24299, provided:

Section 1. The Secretary of Defense, and, as designated by the said Secretary for this purpose, any of the Secretaries, Under Secretaries, and Assistant Secretaries of the military departments, are hereby designated and empowered to perform the following-described functions of the President without the approval, ratification, or other action of the President:

(a) The authority vested in the President by the act of March 3, 1901, ch. 852, 31 Stat. 1107, 1133 [10 U.S.C. 5941, 7291], to establish and modify, as the needs of the service may require, a classification of vessels of the Navy, and to formulate appropriate rules governing assignments to command of vessels and squadrons.

(b) The authority vested in the President by the act of August 22, 1912, ch. 335, 37 Stat. 382, 331 [see 10 U.S.C. 509, 1171], to approve regulations of the Secretary of the Navy under which any enlisted man may be discharged within three months before the expiration of the term of his enlistment, and under which an enlisted man may voluntarily extend the term of his enlistment.

(c) The authority vested in the President by the act of May 22, 1928, ch. 688, 45 Stat. 712 [10 U.S.C. 6152], to approve regulations governing the advancement of public funds to naval personnel when required to meet expenses of officers and men detailed on emergency shore duty.

(d) The authority vested in the President by the act of June 22, 1938, ch. 567, 52 Stat. 839, as amended [10 U.S.C. 5083, 5133, 5148, 5201], section 201(a) of the act of August 25, 1941, ch. 409, 55 Stat. 680 [10 U.S.C. 5063, 5064], section 3 of the act of December 28, 1945, ch. 604, 59 Stat. 666, as amended [10 U.S.C. 5138], section 2 of the act of August 1, 1946, ch. 727, 60 Stat. 779 [10 U.S.C. 5150], and section 7(a) of the act of March 5, 1948, ch. 98, 62 Stat. 68 [see Department of Defense Reorganization Order set out as a note under 10 U.S.C. 5111], to authorize, in his discretion, for any officer of the Regular Navy or Marine Corps who retires while serving as Chief of Naval Operations, as Chief of a Bureau of the Navy Department, as Judge Advocate General of the

Navy, as Commandant of the Marine Corps, as Director of Budgets and Reports, as Chief of the Dental Division, as Chief of Naval Research, or as Chief of Naval Material, or while serving in a lower rank if he has previously served in any of such offices two and one-half years or more, retirement in the highest grade or rank in which he so served and with retired pay based on that rank.

(e) The authority vested in the President by the act of June 15, 1940, ch. 374, 54 Stat. 400, to prescribe from time to time the number of warrant and commissioned warrant officers for the Marine Corps.

(f) The authority vested in the President by the act of June 24, 1941, ch. 231, 55 Stat. 260 [10 U.S.C. 7306], to approve the use for experimental purposes of vessels of the United States Navy stricken from the Navy Register pursuant to the act of August 5, 1882, 22 Stat. 296, as amended [10 U.S.C. 7304].

(g) The authority vested in the President by section 302 of the act of June 22, 1944, ch. 268, 58 Stat. 287 [see 10 U.S.C. 1554], to approve or disapprove the proceedings and decisions of boards of review established under that section by the Secretary of the Army, the Secretary of the Air Force, or the Secretary of the Navy, and to issue orders in such cases.

(h) The authority vested in the President by Section 102(a) of the Federal Civilian Employee and Contractor Travel Expenses Act of 1985, 5 U.S.C. 5702(a), to establish maximum rates of per diem allowances and reimbursements for the actual and necessary expenses of official travel for employees of the Government to the extent that such authority pertains to travel status in localities in Alaska, Hawaii, the Commonwealth of Puerto Rico, and possessions of the United States.

SEC. 2. The Secretary of Defense, and, as designated by the said Secretary for this purpose, the Deputy Secretary of Defense and any of the Assistant Secretaries of Defense, are hereby designated and empowered to perform the following-described functions of the President without the approval, ratification, or other action of the President:

(a) The authority vested in the President by section 1547 of the Revised Statutes of the United States [10 U.S.C. 6011], to approve alterations made by the Secretary of the Navy in Navy Regulations.

(b) The authority vested in the President by section 1 of the act of April 9, 1906, ch. 1370, 34 Stat. 104 [10 U.S.C. 6961], to approve the dismissal by the Secretary of the Navy of a midshipman from the United States Naval Academy.

SEC. 3. All actions heretofore taken by the President with respect to the matters affected by this order and in force and effect at the time of the issuance of this order, including any regulations prescribed or approved by the President with respect to such matters, shall, except as they may be inconsistent with the provisions of this order, remain in force and effect until amended, modified, or revoked pursuant to the authority conferred by this order.

SEC. 4. As used in this order, the term "functions" includes duties, powers, responsibilities, authority, and discretion, and the term "perform" may be construed to mean "exercise".

EX. ORD. NO. 10637. DELEGATION OF FUNCTIONS TO
SECRETARY OF THE TREASURY

Ex. Ord. No. 10637, Sept. 16, 1955, 20 F.R. 7025, provided:

SECTION 1. The Secretary of the Treasury is hereby designated and empowered to perform the following-described functions without the approval, ratification, or other action of the President:

(a) The authority vested in the President by section 149 of title 14 of the United States Code, in his discretion, to detail officers and enlisted men of the Coast Guard to assist foreign governments in matters concerning which the Coast Guard may be of assistance.

(b) The authority vested in the President by section 229 of title 14 of the United States Code [see 14 U.S.C. 281 et seq.], to revoke the commission of any officer on the active list of the Coast Guard who, at the date of such revocation, has had less than three years of continuous service as a commissioned officer in the Coast Guard, and to prescribe regulations relating to such revocations.

(c) The authority vested in the President by section 232 of title 14 of the United States Code [see 14 U.S.C. 291], in his discretion, to retire from active service any commissioned officer of the Coast Guard, upon his own application, who has completed twenty years of active service in the Coast Guard, Navy, Army, Air Force, or Marine Corps, or the Reserve Components thereof.

(d) The authority vested in the President by section 235 of title 14 of the United States Code [see 14 U.S.C. 251 et seq.], to retire, to approve the retirement of, to place out of line of promotion, and to approve the placing out of line of promotion of, officers of the Coast Guard.

(e) The authority vested in the President by section 492 of title 14 of the United States Code to present a distinguished service medal (including incidental items) to any person who, while serving in any capacity with the Coast Guard, distinguishes himself by exceptionally meritorious service to the Government in a duty of great responsibility.

(f) The authority vested in the President by section 493 of title 14 of the United States Code to present the Coast Guard medal (including incidental items) to any person who, while serving in any capacity with the Coast Guard, distinguishes himself by heroism not involving actual conflict with an enemy.

(g) The authority vested in the President by section 494 of title 14 of the United States Code to award emblems, insignia, rosettes, and other devices, to the extent that such authority relates to the awarding of such items to be worn with the distinguished service medal or the Coast Guard medal.

(h) The authority vested in the President by section 498 of title 14 of the United States Code to make posthumous awards of decorations and to designate representatives to receive such awards, to the extent that such authority relates to the awarding of the distinguished service medal or the Coast Guard medal, or ribbons, emblems, insignia, rosettes, or other devices corresponding thereto.

(i) The authority vested in the President by section 499 of title 14 of the United States Code to make rules, regulations, and orders to the extent that they shall relate to the authority described in sections 1(f), 1(g), and 1(h) above.

(j) The authority vested in the President by the first paragraph of section 806 of the act of September 8, 1916, ch. 463, 39 Stat. 799 [15 U.S.C. 77], to direct the detention of any vessel, American or foreign, by withholding clearance or by formal notice forbidding departure; but such authority shall be exercised by the Secretary of the Treasury only upon a finding by the President that there is reasonable ground to believe that the vessel concerned is making or giving undue or unreasonable preference or advantage to any party, or is subjecting any party to undue or unreasonable prejudice, disadvantage, injury, or discrimination, as described in the said paragraph; and the authority so vested to revoke, modify, or renew any such direction.

(k) The authority vested in the President by the second paragraph of the said section 806 of the act of September 8, 1916 [15 U.S.C. 77], to withhold clearance from one or more vessels of a belligerent country or government until such belligerent shall restore to American vessels and American citizens reciprocal liberty of commerce and equal facilities for trade, and the authority to direct that similar privileges and facilities, if any, enjoyed by vessels and citizens of such belligerent in the United States or its possessions be refused to vessels or citizens of such belligerent; but such authority shall not, in either instance, be exercised by the Secretary of the Treasury with respect to any vessel or citizen of such belligerent unless and until the President proclaims that the belligerent nation concerned is denying privileges and facilities to American vessels as described in the said paragraph.

(*l*) The authority vested in the President by section 963(a) of title 18 of the United States Code to detain, in accordance with the provisions of such section, any armed vessel, or any vessel, domestic or foreign (other than one which has entered the ports of the United States as a public vessel), which is manifestly built for warlike purposes or has been converted or adapted from a private vessel to one suitable for warlike use, and to determine, in each case, whether the proof required by such section is satisfactory.

(m) The authority vested in the President by section 967(a) of title 18 of the United States Code, during a war in which the United States is a neutral nation, to withhold clearance from or to any vessel, domestic or foreign, or, by service of formal notice upon the owner, master, or person in command or in charge of any domestic vessel not required to secure clearances, and to forbid its departure from port or from the United States, whenever there is reasonable cause to believe that such vessel is about to carry fuel, arms, ammunition, men, supplies, dispatches, or information to any warship, tender, or supply ship of a foreign belligerent nation in violation of the laws, treaties, or obligations of the United States under the law of nations.

(n) The authority vested in the President by section 10(a) of the act of November 4, 1939, ch. 2, 54 Stat. 9 [22 U.S.C. 450(a)], to require the owner, master, or person in command of a vessel to give a bond to the United States, as prescribed by the said section 10(a).

(*o*) The authority vested in the President by section 10(b) of the act of November 4, 1939, ch. 2, 54 Stat. 9 [22 U.S.C. 450(b)], to prohibit the departure of a vessel from a port of the United States, in accordance with the provisions of the said section 10(b).

(p) The authority vested in the President by section 2 of the act of August 18, 1914, ch. 256, 38 Stat. 699 [46 U.S.C. 8103(h)(2)], to suspend, in his discretion, by order, so far and for such length of time as he may deem desirable, the provisions of law prescribing that all watch officers of vessels of the United States registered for foreign trade shall be citizens of the United States.

(q) The authority vested in the President by section 2 of the act of October 17, 1940, ch. 896, 54 Stat. 1201 [former 46 U.S.C. 643b], to extend, whenever in his judgment the national interest requires, the provisions of subsection (b) of section 4551, Revised Statutes, as amended [46 U.S.C. 7304], to such additional class or classes of vessels and to such waters as he may designate.

(r) The authority vested in the Secretary of the Treasury by the first paragraph of section 1 of Title II of the act of June 15, 1917, ch. 30, 40 Stat. 220, as amended [50 U.S.C. 191], during a national emergency proclaimed as provided in the said paragraph, (1) to make rules and regulations governing the anchorage and movement of any vessel, foreign or domestic, in the territorial waters of the United States, and (2) to take full possession and control of such vessel for the purposes set forth in the said paragraph.

(s) The authority vested in the President by section 6 of the act of July 24, 1941, ch. 320, 55 Stat. 604, as amended (34 U.S.C. 350e) [see Historical and Revision Notes set out under 10 U.S.C. 5501], to make appointments of officers below flag rank without the advice and consent of the Senate, to the extent that such authority relates, pursuant to section 11(b) of the said act, as amended (34 U.S.C. 350j) [see 14 U.S.C. 214, 275], to officers of the United States Coast Guard.

SEC. 2. The Secretary of the Treasury is hereby designated and empowered to perform without the approval, ratification, or other action of the President the following described functions to the extent that they relate to the United States Coast Guard:

(a) The authority vested in the President by Article 4(a) of the Uniform Code of Military Justice (section 1 of the act of May 5, 1950, ch. 169, 64 Stat. 110) [10 U.S.C. 804], to convene a general court-martial to try any dismissed officer, upon application by the officer concerned for trial by court-martial.

(b) The authority vested in the President by Articles 4(c) and 75 of the Uniform Code of Military Justice (64 Stat. 110, 132) [10 U.S.C. 804, 875], to reappoint a discharged officer to such commissioned rank and precedence as the former officer would have attained had he not been dismissed, and to direct the extent to which any such reappointment shall affect the promotion status of other officers.

(c) The authority vested in the President by section 10 of the act of May 5, 1950, ch. 169, 64 Stat. 146 [10 U.S.C. 1161, 6408], to drop from the rolls any officer who has been absent without authority from his place of duty for a period of three months or more, or who, having been found guilty by the civil authorities of any offense, is finally sentenced to confinement in a Federal or State penitentiary or correctional institution.

(d) The authority vested in the President by section 219 of the Armed Forces Reserve Act, approved July 9, 1952 (66 Stat. 487) [10 U.S.C. 12203], to make appointments of Reserves in commissioned grades below flag officer grades.

(e) The authority vested in the President by section 221 of the said Armed Forces Reserve Act [10 U.S.C. 12203], to determine the tenure in office of commissioned officers of the reserve.

(f) The authority vested in the President by section 248 of the said Armed Forces Reserve Act [see 10 U.S.C. 12681, 12682], to effect the discharge of commissioned officers of the reserve.

(g) The authority vested in the President by section 6 of the act of February 21, 1946, ch. 34, 60 Stat. 27 [10 U.S.C. 6323], as made applicable to the Coast Guard Reserve by section 755(a) of Title 14 of the United States Code, in his discretion, to place upon the retired list any officer of the Coast Guard Reserve, upon his own application, who has completed more than twenty years of active service as described in the said section 6.

SEC. 3. All actions heretofore taken by the President with respect to the matters affected by this order and in force at the time of issuance of this order, including any regulations prescribed or approved by the President with respect to such matters, shall, except as they may be inconsistent with the provisions of this order, remain in effect until amended, modified, or revoked pursuant to the authority conferred by this order.

SEC. 4. As used in this order, the term "functions" embraces duties, powers, responsibilities, authority, or discretion, and the term "perform" may be construed to mean "exercise".

SEC. 5. Whenever the entire Coast Guard operates as a service in the Navy, the references to the Secretary of the Treasury in the introductory portions of sections 1 and 2 of this order shall be deemed to be references to the Secretary of the Navy.

DWIGHT D. EISENHOWER.

EX. ORD. NO. 10661. DELEGATION OF FUNCTIONS TO SECRETARY OF DEFENSE AND SECRETARY OF COMMERCE

Ex. Ord. No. 10661, Feb. 27, 1956, 21 F.R. 1315, provided:

SECTION 1. The Secretary of Defense, and, when designated by the Secretary of Defense for such purpose, the Secretary of the Army are hereby designated and empowered to exercise, without the approval, ratification, or other action of the President, the authority vested in the President by the first section of the act of June 26, 1946, ch. 493, 60 Stat. 311, as amended [10 U.S.C. 4344, 9344], to designate persons from the American Republics (other than the United States) and Canada who may be permitted to receive instruction at the United States Military Academy at West Point, New York.

SEC. 2. The Secretary of Defense, and, when designated by the Secretary of Defense for such purpose, the Secretary of the Navy are hereby designated and empowered to exercise, without the approval, ratification, or other action of the President, the following-described authority to designate persons who may be permitted to receive instruction at the United States Naval Academy at Annapolis, Maryland:

(a) The authority vested in the President by the act of July 14, 1941, ch. 292, 55 Stat. 589, as amended [10 U.S.C. 6957], with respect to persons from the American Republics (other than the United States) and Canada.

(b) The authority vested in the President by the act of June 24, 1948, ch. 616, 62 Stat. 583 [10 U.S.C. 6957], with respect to Filipinos.

SEC. 3. The Secretary of Defense, and, when designated by the Secretary of Defense for such purpose, the Secretary of the Air Force are hereby designated and empowered to exercise, without the approval, ratification, or other action of the President, the authority vested in the President by the first section of the said act of June 26, 1946, as made applicable to the United States Air Force Academy by section 5 of the act of April 1, 1954, ch. 127, 68 Stat. 48 [10 U.S.C. 9344], to designate persons from the American Republics (other than the United States) and Canada who may be permitted to receive instruction at the United States Air Force Academy.

SEC. 4. The Secretary of Commerce is hereby designated and empowered to exercise, without the approval, ratification, or other action of the President, the authority vested in the President by the act of August 9, 1946, ch. 928, 60 Stat. 961 [former 46 U.S.C. 1126b], to designate persons from the American Republics (other than the United States) who may be permitted to receive instruction in the United States Merchant Marine Cadet Corps and at the United States Merchant Marine Academy at Kings Point, New York.

SEC. 5. No person shall be designated under the authority of this order to receive instruction except after consultation by the designating officer with the Secretary of State.

DWIGHT D. EISENHOWER.

EX. ORD. NO. 10950. DELEGATION OF FUNCTIONS TO SECRETARY OF THE INTERIOR

EX. ORD. NO. 10950, June 27, 1961, 26 F.R. 5787, as amended by Pub. L. 101–509, title V, § 529 [title I, § 112(c)], Nov. 5, 1990, 104 Stat. 1427, 1454, provided:

By virtue of the authority vested in me by section 6(b) of the Alaska Statehood Act of July 7, 1958 (72 Stat. 339) [set out as a note preceding 48 U.S.C. 21], and as President of the United States, I hereby designate the Secretary of the Interior as my representative to exercise the authority vested in me by section 6(b) of the act to approve selections of land made by the State of Alaska under the provisions of section 6(b) in instances in which those selections include land lying north and west of the line described in section 10(b) of the act: *Provided*, That no selection by the State shall be approved pursuant to this order, in whole or in part, without the concurrence of the Secretary of Defense or his designated representative.

As the Secretary of the Interior may direct, the Deputy Secretary of the Interior, an Assistant Secretary of the Interior, the Director of the Bureau of Land Management, or the Operations Supervisors of the Bureau of Land Management in Alaska are severally authorized to exercise the authority vested in the Secretary by this order.

EX. ORD. NO. 11012. DELEGATION OF FUNCTIONS TO ADMINISTRATOR OF GENERAL SERVICES

EX. ORD. NO. 11012, Mar. 27, 1962, 27 F.R. 2983, as amended by Ex. Ord. No. 11230, § 2(11), June 28, 1965, 30 F.R. 8447; Ex. Ord. No. 12608, Sept. 9, 1987, 52 F.R. 34617, provided:

By virtue of the authority vested in me by Section 301 of Title 3 of the United States Code, and as President of the United States, it is hereby ordered as follows:

SECTION 1. [Superseded by Ex. Ord. No. 11230, § 2(11), June 28, 1965, 30 F.R. 8447.]

SEC. 2. The Administrator of General Services is hereby designated and empowered to exercise, without the approval, ratification, or other action of the President, so much of the authority vested in the President by

Section 1(b) of the Act of August 2, 1946, ch. 744, 60 Stat. 807 (5 U.S.C. 73b–1(b)) [5 U.S.C. 5724], as pertains to the establishment of the rates to be used in reimbursing civilian officers or employees of the Government on a commuted basis in lieu of the payment of actual expenses of transportation, packing, crating, temporary storage, drayage, and unpacking of their household goods and personal effects in the case of transfers from one official station to another within the continental United States for permanent duty.

SEC. 3. The initial regulations to be issued by the Director of the Office of Management and Budget and by the Administrator of General Services under the authority delegated to each of them by this order shall be effective on the same date and effective as of that date the following-described Executive orders are revoked:

(a) Executive Order No. 9778 of September 10, 1946.
(b) Executive Order No. 9805 of November 25, 1946.
(c) Executive Order No. 9933 of February 27, 1948.
(d) Executive Order No. 9997 of September 8, 1948.
(e) Executive Order No. 10069 of July 14, 1949.
(f) Executive Order No. 10177 of October 27, 1950.
(g) Executive Order No. 10196 of December 20, 1950.
(h) Executive Order No. 10274 of July 18, 1951.
(i) Executive Order No. 10381 of August 6, 1952.
(j) Executive Order No. 10507 of December 10, 1953.

SEC. 4. Existing regulations prescribed by the Director of the Office of Management and Budget under the authority of Section 1(b) of Executive Order No. 10530, as amended and in effect immediately prior to the issuance of this order, shall remain in effect until they are superseded in pursuance of the provisions of this order.

EX. ORD. NO. 11023. DELEGATION OF FUNCTIONS TO SECRETARY OF COMMERCE

EX. ORD. NO. 11023, May 28, 1962, 27 F.R. 5131, as amended by Ex. Ord. No. 12608, Sept. 9, 1987, 52 F.R. 34617, provided:

By virtue of the authority vested in me by section 301 of title 3, of the United States Code, and as President of the United States, it is ordered as follows:

SECTION 1. The Secretary of Commerce is hereby designated and empowered to perform the following-described functions without the approval, ratification, or other action of the President:

(a) The authority contained in section 6(b) of the Coast and Geodetic Survey Commissioned Officers Act of 1948 (62 Stat. 298; 33 U.S.C. 853e(b)) to revoke the commissions of ensigns of the National Oceanic and Atmospheric Administration who are found not fully qualified and to separate such ensigns from the commissioned service.

(b) The authority vested in the President by section 12(a) of the Coast and Geodetic Survey Commissioned Officers Act of 1948, as amended (75 Stat. 506; 33 U.S.C. 853j–1(a)), to make temporary appointments in the grade of ensign in the National Oceanic and Atmospheric Administration.

(c) The authority vested in the President by section 12(b) of the Coast and Geodetic Survey Commissioned Officers Act of 1948, as amended (75 Stat. 506; 33 U.S.C. 853j–1(b)), to temporarily promote officers in the permanent grade of ensign in the National Oceanic and Atmospheric Administration, and to appoint such officers to the grade of lieutenant junior grade whenever vacancies exist in higher grades.

(d) The authority vested in the President by section 12 (c) of the Coast and Geodetic Survey Commissioned Officers Act of 1948, as amended (75 Stat. 506; 33 U.S.C. 853j–1(c)), to temporarily promote any officer one grade.

(e) The authority vested in the President by section 13(b) of the Coast and Geodetic Survey Commissioned Officers Act of 1948, as amended (75 Stat. 506; 33 U.S.C. 853k(b)), to defer the retirement of an officer of the National Oceanic and Atmospheric Administration serving in a rank above that of captain who has attained the age of sixty-two years.

(f) The authority vested in the President by section 14 of the Coast and Geodetic Survey Commissioned Officers Act of 1948, as amended (75 Stat. 506; 33 U.S.C. 853*l*), to retire from the active service any commissioned officer of the National Oceanic and Atmospheric Administration, upon his own application, who has completed twenty years of active service in the National Oceanic and Atmospheric Administration.

(g) The authority vested in the President by section 23(a) of the Coast and Geodetic Survey Commissioned Officers Act of 1948, as amended (75 Stat. 506; 33 U.S.C. 853t(a)), (1) to find that any officer appointed under section 23 is not qualified for service, (2) to revoke the commissions of officers in respect of whom such findings are made, and (3) to prescribe the regulations referred to in that section.

(h) The authority contained in section 1(1) of the Act of December 3, 1942 (56 Stat. 1038; 33 U.S.C. 854a–1(1)) to temporarily promote to higher ranks or grades, upon recommendation of the Secretary of the military department concerned, commissioned officers of the National Oceanic and Atmospheric Administration transferred to the military departments.

(i) The authority contained in section 1(2) of the Act of December 3, 1942 (56 Stat. 1038; 33 U.S.C. 854a–1(2)) to temporarily promote commissioned officers of the National Oceanic and Atmospheric Administration to fill vacancies in ranks and grades caused by transfer of commissioned officers to the service and jurisdiction of the military departments.

(j) The authority contained in section 1(3) of the Act of December 3, 1942 (56 Stat. 1038; 33 U.S.C. 854a–1(3)) to temporarily appoint deck officers and junior engineers to the grade of ensign to fill vacancies caused by transfer of officers to the military departments.

(k) The authority vested in the President by section 16 of the Act of May 22, 1917 (40 Stat. 87; 33 U.S.C. 855), to transfer to service and jurisdiction of the Department of Defense, as he may deem to be to the best interest of the country, vessels, equipment, stations, and personnel of the National Oceanic and Atmospheric Administration; but the Secretary of Commerce may effect such transfers only during the existence of a state of national emergency proclaimed by President. Commissioned officers so transferred shall serve under their commissions in the National Oceanic and Atmospheric Administration and while so serving shall constitute a part of the active armed forces of the United States and shall be under the direct orders of, and shall be subject to the applicable laws, regulations, and orders for the government of, the armed forces to which they are transferred, respectively. The Secretary of Commerce may return such vessels, equipment, stations, and personnel to the jurisdiction of the Department of Commerce, but in time of national emergency such return shall be effected only with the concurrence of the Secretary of Defense.

(*l*) The authority vested in the President by section 8 of the Act of August 6, 1947 (61 Stat. 788; 33 U.S.C. 883h) to employ public vessels, and to give instructions for regulating their conduct, to carry out the provisions of the Act of August 6, 1947; but the employment by the Secretary of Commerce of vessels, except those of the Department of Commerce or of any subordinate entity thereof, shall require the concurrence of the head of the department or other executive agency having custody or control of the vessel.

SEC. 2. Upon receipt by the Secretary of Commerce from the President or from the President's representative of information showing that the Senate has confirmed nominees of the President for appointment as commissioned officers of the National Oceanic and Atmospheric Administration, and without any further action on the part of the President, (1) the Secretary of Commerce or an officer of the Department of Commerce designated by the Secretary may, upon completion of statutory requirements for such appointments, tender offers of appointment to the nominees and upon acceptance such persons shall be deemed to be appointed accordingly, (2) the Secretary of Commerce, in the name of the President, shall issue to each such person a commission evidencing the appointment of such

persons accordingly, and (3) the commissions of such persons shall be deemed to have been signed by the President. The effective date specified in any commission so issued shall be deemed, for all purposes, to be the date of the appointment evidenced by such commission.

SEC. 3. In connection with making appointments or promotions under authority delegated to him by subsections (b), (c), (d), (h), (i), and (j) of section 1 of this order, the Secretary of Commerce shall issue to each person appointed or promoted by him thereunder a certificate evidencing the appointment or promotion of such person. Such certificate may be issued in the name of the President.

SEC. 4. Any requirement of any provision of law that commissions of officers under the direction and control of the Secretary of Commerce be signed by the President before the seal of the Department of Commerce may be affixed thereto shall, in the case of officers appointed under the procedure set forth in section 2 of this order and in the case of officers appointed or promoted under authority delegated by subsections (b), (c), (d), (h), (i), and (j) of section 1 of this order, be deemed to be satisfied by signature of the commission or certificate by the Secretary of Commerce, before the departmental seal is affixed thereto.

SEC. 5. The Secretary of Commerce is hereby authorized to accept, in the name of the President, the resignation of a commissioned officer, either permanent or temporary, of the National Oceanic and Atmospheric Administration.

SEC. 6. The authority delegated by the provisions of subsections (b), (c), (d), (h), (i), and (j) of section 1 of this order shall be deemed to include the authority to terminate any appointment or promotion made under the provisions of law referred to in those subsections.

SEC. 7. All actions heretofore taken by the President with respect to the matters affected by this order and in force at the time of issuance of this order, including any regulations prescribed or approved by the President with respect to such matters shall, except as they may be inconsistent with the provisions of this order, remain in effect until amended, modified or revoked pursuant to the authority conferred by this order. The following are hereby superseded: (1) Letter of the President to the Secretary of Commerce, dated April 23, 1929, and relating to the general subject of section 2 of this order, and (2) letter of the Secretary to the President, dated July 1, 1919, and directed to the Secretary of Commerce, relating to the general subject of section 5 of this order.

SEC. 8. As used in this order the term "functions" embraces duties, powers, responsibilities, authority or discretion, and the term "perform" may be construed to mean "exercise".

EX. ORD. NO. 11110. AMENDMENT OF EXECUTIVE ORDER NO. 10289, RELATING TO PERFORMANCE OF CERTAIN FUNCTIONS OF DEPARTMENT OF THE TREASURY

Ex. Ord. No. 11110, June 4, 1963, 28 F.R. 5605, provided:

By virtue of the authority vested in me by section 301 of Title 3 of the United States Code, it is ordered as follows:

SECTION 1. Executive Order No. 10289 of September 19, 1951, as amended [set out as a note under this section], is hereby further amended—

(a) By adding at the end of paragraph 1 thereof the following subparagraph (j):

"(j) The authority vested in the President by paragraph (b) of section 43 of the Act of May 12, 1933, as amended (31 U.S.C. 821(b)) [31 U.S.C. 5301(a), (b)] to issue silver certificates against any silver bullion, silver, or standard silver dollars in the Treasury not then held for redemption of any outstanding silver certificates, to prescribe the denominations of such silver certificates, and to coin standard silver dollars and subsidiary silver currency for their redemption," and

(b) By revoking subparagraphs (b) and (c) of paragraph 2 thereof.

SEC. 2. The amendments made by this order shall not affect any act done, or any right accruing or accrued or any suit or proceeding had or commenced in any civil or criminal cause prior to the date of this order but all such liabilities shall continue and may be enforced as if said amendments had not been made.

JOHN F. KENNEDY.

Ex. Ord. No. 11228. Delegation of Functions to Office of Personnel Management

Ex. Ord. No. 11228, June 14, 1965, 30 F.R. 7739, as amended by Ex. Ord. No. 11257, Nov. 13, 1965, 30 F.R. 14353; Ex. Ord. No. 12107, Dec. 28, 1978, 44 F.R. 1055, provided:

By virtue of the authority vested in me by Section 301 of Title 3 of the United States Code, and as President of the United States, it is hereby ordered as follows—

SECTION 1. The Office of Personnel Management is hereby designated and empowered to exercise, without the approval, ratification, or other action of the President, the following:

(1) The authority vested in the Office of Personnel Management by Section 605 of the Federal Employees Pay Act of 1945, 59 Stat. 304 (5 U.S.C. 945) [5 U.S.C. 5504(c), 5548, 6101(c)], to issue, subject to the approval of the President, regulations necessary for the administration of certain provisions of that Act insofar as the Act affects officers and employees in or under the executive branch of the Government.

(2) The authority vested in the President by Section 203(f) of the Annual and Sick Leave Act of 1951, 65 Stat. 680 (5 U.S.C. 2062(f)) [5 U.S.C. 6305(a)], to prescribe regulations governing the granting of leave of absence as described in that Section.

(3) Except as to Presidential appointees, the authority vested in the President (A) by Section 204 of the Act of June 30, 1932, 47 Stat. 404 (5 U.S.C. 3323(a)], to exempt from automatic separation from the service under that Section any person when, in his judgment, the public interest so requires and (B) by Section 5(c) of the Civil Service Retirement Act, 70 Stat. 748 (5 U.S.C. 2255(c)) [5 U.S.C. 8335(c)], to exempt from automatic separation from the service under Section 5 of that Act [5 U.S.C. 8335] any employee when, in his judgment, the public interest so requires.

(4) The authority vested in the President by Section 9(b) (8) of the Federal Employees Salary Act of 1965 (approved October 29, 1965) [5 U.S.C. 5595(a)(2)] to prescribe rules and regulations excluding officers or employees from the application of Section 9 of that Act [5 U.S.C. 5595].

(5) The authority vested in the President by Section 9(c) of the Federal Employees Salary Act of 1965 [5 U.S.C. 5595(b)(2)] to prescribe rules and regulations governing severance pay.

SEC. 2. The Director of the Office of Personnel Management is hereby designated and empowered to exercise, without the approval, ratification, or other action of the President, the authority vested in the President by Section 304(e) of the Government Employees' Incentive Awards Act, 68 Stat. 1113 (5 U.S.C. 2123(e)) [5 U.S.C. 4502(d)], to determine the activity primarily benefiting, or the various activities benefiting, from any suggestion, invention, superior accomplishment, or other personal effort of any civilian officer or employee of the Government which constitutes the basis of any Presidential award or honorary recognition made or granted under Section 304(b) of that Act (5 U.S.C. 2123(b)) [5 U.S.C. 4501(2)(A), 4504].

SEC 3. The following are hereby superseded:

(1) Part II of Executive Order No. 10530 of May 10, 1954.

(2) Executive Order No. 10682 of October 22, 1956.

(3) Section 5 of Executive Order No. 10800 of January 15, 1959.

(4) Executive Order No. 10835 of August 21, 1959.

(5) So much of Section 2 of Executive Order No. 10903 of January 9, 1961, as added paragraph (e) of Section 2 of Executive Order No. 10530 of May 10, 1954.

SEC. 4. (a) Unless inappropriate, references in this Order to any statute or to any provision of any statute shall be deemed to include references thereto as amended from time to time.

(b) Unless inappropriate, any reference in any Executive order to any Executive order which is superseded by this Order, or to any Executive order provision so superseded, shall hereafter be deemed to refer to this Order or to the provision of Section 1 or Section 2 of this Order, if any, which corresponds to the superseded provision.

SEC. 5. All actions heretofore taken by the President or by his delegates in respect of the matters affected by Sections 1 and 2 of this Order and in force at the time of the issuance of this Order, including any regulations prescribed or approved by the President or by his delegates in respect of such matters, shall, except as they may be inconsistent with the provisions, of this Order, remain in effect until amended, modified, or revoked pursuant to the authority conferred by this Order unless sooner terminated by operation of law.

EXECUTIVE ORDER NO. 11230

Ex. Ord. No. 11230, June 28, 1965, 30 F.R. 8847, as amended by Ex. Ord. No. 11275, Mar. 31, 1966, 31 F.R. 5283; Ex. Ord. No. 11290, July 21, 1966, 31 F.R. 10067; Ex. Ord. No. 11294, Aug. 4, 1966, 31 F.R. 10601, delegating certain functions of the President to the Director of the Bureau of the Budget, was superseded by Ex. Ord. No. 11609, July 22, 1971, 36 F.R. 13747, set out as a note under this section.

EXECUTIVE ORDER NO. 11294

Ex. Ord. No. 11294, Aug. 4, 1966, 31 F.R. 10601, as amended by Ex. Ord. No. 11609, July 22, 1971, 36 F.R. 13747, which delegated functions of the President to establish maximum rates of per diem allowances for certain travel, was revoked by Ex. Ord. No. 12561, July 1, 1986, 51 F.R. 24299, set out as a note under section 5702 of Title 5, Government Organization and Employees.

Ex. Ord. No. 11390. Delegation of Functions to Secretary of Defense

Ex. Ord. No. 11390, Jan. 22, 1968, 33 F.R. 841, as amended by Ex. Ord. No. 11601, June 29, 1971, 36 F.R. 12473; Ex. Ord. No. 12396, Dec. 9, 1982, 47 F.R. 55897; Ex. Ord. No. 12608, Sept. 9, 1987, 52 F.R. 34617, provided:

By virtue of the authority vested in me by section 301 of title 3 of the United States Code, and as President of the United States, it is ordered as follows:

SECTION 1. The Secretary of Defense, and, as designated by the said Secretary for this purpose, any of the Secretaries, Under Secretaries, and Assistant Secretaries of the military departments, are hereby designated and empowered to perform the following-described functions of the President without the approval, ratification, or other action of the President:

(1) [Revoked by Ex. Ord. No. 12608, Sept. 9, 1987, 52 F.R. 34617.]

(2), (3) [Revoked by Ex. Ord. No. 12396, Dec. 9, 1982, 47 F.R. 55897.]

(4) The authority vested in the President by sections 565 and 599 [now 12243] of title 10, United States Code, to suspend, in time of war or emergency, any provision of law relative to promotion and mandatory retirement or separation of warrant officers of the armed forces.

(5) The authority vested in the President by sections 4337 and 9337 of title 10, United States Code, to appoint the chaplains at the United States Military and Air Force Academies.

(6) The authority vested in the President by sections 4302(a) and 9302(a) of title 10, United States Code, to approve regulations concerning instruction of enlisted members of the Army and Air Force.

(7) [Revoked by Ex. Ord. No. 12608, Sept. 9, 1987, 52 F.R. 34617.]

(8) The authority vested in the President by sections 5139 and 5149 of title 10, United States Code, relating to the retirement of the Chief of the Medical Service Corps, the Deputy Judge Advocate General, and the Assistant Judge Advocate General, of the Navy.

(9) [Revoked by Ex. Ord. No. 12396, Dec. 9, 1982, 47 F.R. 55897.]

(10) The authority vested in the President by section 2102(a) of title 10, United States Code, to prescribe regulations governing the establishment and maintenance of senior reserve officers' Training Corps units at civilian educational institutions.

(11) The authority vested in the President by section 123 of title 10, and section 111 of title 32, United States Code, to suspend in time of war or national emergency those provisions cited therein relating to promotion of reserve officers.

(12) [Revoked by Ex. Ord. No. 12396, Dec. 9, 1982, 47 F.R. 55897.]

(13) The authority vested in the President by section 6223(b) of title 10, United States Code, relating to members of the Marine Corps Band.

(14) The authority vested in the President by section 425 of title 37, United States Code, to approve concert tours of the Navy Band and the Marine Corps Band.

(15) [Revoked by Ex. Ord. No. 12396, Dec. 9, 1982, 47 F.R. 55897.]

SEC. 2. All actions heretofore taken by or for the President with respect to the matters affected by this order and in force and effect at the time of the issuance of this order, including any regulations prescribed or approved by the President with respect to such matters, shall, except as they may be inconsistent with the provisions of this order, remain in force and effect until amended, modified, or revoked pursuant to the authority conferred by this order.

EX. ORD. NO. 11423. DELEGATION OF FUNCTIONS TO SECRETARY OF STATE RESPECTING CERTAIN FACILITIES CONSTRUCTED AND MAINTAINED ON UNITED STATES BORDERS

Ex. Ord. No. 11423, Aug. 16, 1968, 33 F.R. 11741, as amended by Ex. Ord. No. 12847, May 17, 1993, 58 F.R. 29511, provided:

WHEREAS the proper conduct of the foreign relations of the United States requires that executive permission be obtained for the construction and maintenance at the borders of the United States of facilities connecting the United States with a foreign country; and

WHEREAS such executive permission has from time to time been sought and granted in the form of Presidential permits for the construction, connection, operation, and maintenance at the borders of the United States of such border crossing facilities as water supply and oil pipelines, aerial tramways and cable cars, submarine cables, and lines for the transmission of electric energy; and

WHEREAS Executive Order No. 10485 of September 3, 1953 [set out as a note under section 717b of title 15], empowers the Federal Power Commission [Secretary of Energy] to issue permits for the construction, operation, maintenance, or connection, at the borders of the United States, of facilities for the transmission of electric energy between the United States and a foreign country and for the importation or exportation of natural gas to or from a foreign country; and

WHEREAS Executive Order No. 10530 of May 10, 1954 [set out as a note under this section], empowers the Federal Communications Commission to issue and revoke licenses to land submarine cables in the United States; and

WHEREAS it is desirable to provide a systematic method in connection with the issuance of permits for the construction and maintenance of other such facilities connecting the United States with a foreign country:

NOW, THEREFORE, by virtue of the authority vested in me as President of the United States and Commander in Chief of the Armed Forces of the United States and in conformity with the provisions of section 301 of title 3, United States Code, it is ordered as follows:

SECTION 1. (a) Except with respect to facilities covered by Executive Order Nos. 10485 [15 U.S.C. 717b note] and 10530 [set out above], the Secretary of State is hereby designated and empowered to receive all applications for permits for the construction, connection, operation, or maintenance, at the borders of the United States, of: (i) pipelines, conveyor belts, and similar facilities for the exportation or importation of petroleum, petroleum products, coal, minerals, or other products to or from a foreign country; (ii) facilities for the exportation or importation of water or sewage to or from a foreign country; (iii) facilities for the transportation of persons or things, or both, to or from a foreign country; (iv) bridges, to the extent that congressional authorization is not required; and (v) similar facilities above or below ground.

(b) With respect to applications received pursuant to subsection (a)(i) above, the Secretary of State shall request the views of the Secretary of the Treasury, the Secretary of Defense, the Attorney General, the Secretary of the Interior, the Secretary of Commerce, the Secretary of Transportation, the Interstate Commerce Commission, and the Director of the Office of Emergency Planning. With respect to applications received pursuant to subsection (a)(ii) above, the Secretary of State shall request the views of the Secretary of Defense and the Secretary of the Interior. With respect to applications received pursuant to subsection (a)(iii), (iv) or (v) above, the Secretary of State shall request the views of the Secretary of the Treasury, the Secretary of Defense, the Attorney General, and the Secretary of Transportation.

(c) The Secretary of State may also consult with such other department and agency heads and with such state and local government officials as he deems appropriate with respect to each application. All federal government officials consulted by the Secretary of State pursuant to this section shall provide such information and render such assistance as he may request, consistent with their competence and authority.

(d) If the Secretary of State finds, after consideration of the views obtained pursuant to subsections (b) and (c), that issuance of a permit to the applicant would serve the national interest, he shall prepare a permit, in such form and with such terms and conditions as the national interest may in his judgment require, and shall notify the officials required to be consulted under subsection (b) above of his proposed determination that the permit be issued.

(e) If the Secretary of State finds, after consideration of the views obtained pursuant to subsections (b) and (c), that issuance of a permit to the applicant would not serve the national interest, he shall notify the officials required to be consulted under subsection (b) above of his proposed determination that the application be denied.

(f) The Secretary of State shall issue or deny the permit in accordance with his proposed determination unless, within fifteen days after notification pursuant to subsection (d) or (e) above, an official required to be consulted under subsection (b) above shall notify the Secretary of State that he disagrees with the Secretary's proposed determination and requests the Secretary to refer the application to the President. In the event of such a request, the Secretary of State shall refer the application, together with statements of the views of the several officials involved, to the President for his consideration and final decision.

SEC. 2. (a) The Secretary of State may provide for the publication in the Federal Register of notice of receipt of applications, for the receipt of public comments on applications, and for publication in the Federal Register of notice of issuance or denial of applications.

(b) The Secretary of State is authorized to issue such further rules and regulations, and to prescribe such further procedures, as he may from time to time deem necessary or desirable for the exercise of the authority conferred upon him by this order.

SEC. 3. The authority of the Secretary of State hereunder is supplemental to, and does not supersede, existing authorities or delegations relating to importation, exportation, transmission, or transportation to or from a foreign country. All permits heretofore issued with respect to matters described in section 1 of this order, and in force at the time of issuance of this order, and all permits issued hereunder, shall remain in effect in accordance with their terms unless and until modified, amended, suspended, or revoked by the President or, upon compliance with the procedures provided for in this order, by the Secretary of State.

[Interstate Commerce Commission abolished and functions of Commission transferred, except as otherwise provided in Pub. L. 104–88, to Surface Transportation Board effective Jan. 1, 1996, by section 702 of Title 49, Transportation, and section 101 of Pub. L. 104–88, set out as a note under section 701 of Title 49. References to Interstate Commerce Commission deemed to refer to Surface Transportation Board, a member or employee of the Board, or Secretary of Transportation, as appropriate, see section 205 of Pub. L. 104–88, set out as a note under section 701 of Title 49.]

EX. ORD. NO. 11592. DELEGATION OF FUNCTIONS TO DIRECTOR OF OFFICE OF MANAGEMENT AND BUDGET

Ex. Ord. No. 11592, May 6, 1971, 36 F.R. 8555, provided:

By virtue of the authority vested in me by section 301 of title 3 of the United States Code, and as President of the United States, the Director of the Office of Management and Budget is hereby designated and empowered to exercise, without the approval, ratification, or other action of the President, the function of granting the approvals authorized or required to be granted by the President by any of the provisions of the River and Harbor Act of 1970 and the Flood Control Act of 1970, Public Law 91–611, approved December 31, 1970.

RICHARD NIXON.

EX. ORD. NO. 11609. DELEGATION OF CERTAIN FUNCTIONS VESTED IN THE PRESIDENT TO OTHER OFFICERS OF THE GOVERNMENT

Ex. Ord. No. 11609, July 22, 1971, 36 F.R. 13747, as amended by Ex. Ord. No. 11713, Apr. 21, 1973, 38 F.R. 10069; Ex. Ord. No. 11779, Apr. 19, 1974, 39 F.R. 14185; Ex. Ord. No. 12107, Dec. 28, 1978, 44 F.R. 1055; Ex. Ord. No. 12215, May 27, 1980, 45 F.R. 36043; Ex. Ord. No. 12466, Feb. 27, 1984, 49 F.R. 7349, eff. Nov. 14, 1983; Ex. Ord. No. 12522, June 24, 1985, 50 F.R. 26337, eff. Oct. 12, 1984; Ex. Ord. No. 12608, Sept. 9, 1987, 52 F.R. 34617; Ex. Ord. No. 12822, Nov. 16, 1992, 57 F.R. 54289, eff. Jan. 1, 1992, provided:

By virtue of the authority vested in me by section 301 of title 3 of the United States Code, and as President of the United States, it is hereby ordered as follows:

SECTION 1. *General Services Administration.* The Administrator of General Services is hereby designated and empowered to exercise, without the approval, ratification, or other action of the President, the following:

(1) The authority of the President under 5 U.S.C. 4111(b) to prescribe regulations with respect to reductions to be made from payments by the Government to employees for travel, subsistence, or other expenses incident to training in a non-Government facility or to attendance at a meeting.

(2) The authority of the President under the last sentence of 5 U.S.C. 5702(a) to establish maximum rates of per diem allowances to the extent that such authority pertains to travel status of employees (as defined in 5 U.S.C. 5701) while enroute to, from, or between localities situated outside the 48 contiguous States of the United States and the District of Columbia.

(3) The authority of the President under 5 U.S.C. 5707 to prescribe regulations necessary for the administration of subchapter I of chapter 57 of title 5 of the United States Code [section 5701 et seq. of title 5] (relating to travel and subsistence expenses and mileage allowances).

(4) The authority of the President under 5 U.S.C. 5722(a) to prescribe regulations with respect to the payment of travel expenses and transportation expenses of household goods and personal effects.

(5) The authority of the President under 5 U.S.C. 5723(a) to prescribe regulations with respect to the payment of travel expenses and transportation expenses.

(6) The authority of the President under 5 U.S.C. 5724 to prescribe the regulations provided for therein (relating to travel and transportation expenses and other matters).

(7)(a) The authority of the President under 5 U.S.C. 5724(a) to prescribe the regulations provided for therein, relating to (i) the availability of appropriations or other funds of agencies for the reimbursement of described expenses of employees for whom the Government pays expenses of travel and transportation under 5 U.S.C. 5724(a), (ii) the entitlement of employees to amounts related to their basic pay, and (iii) the allowance, payment, and receipt of expenses and benefits to former employees who are reemployed by nontemporary appointments.

(b) In consultation with the Secretary of the Treasury, the authority of the President under 5 U.S.C. 5724b to prescribe the regulations provided for therein relating to reimbursement of Federal, State, and city income taxes for travel, transportation, and relocation expenses of employees, transferred at Government expense, furnished in kind or for which reimbursement or an allowance is provided.

(c) The authority of the President under 5 U.S.C. 5724c to prescribe the regulations provided for therein pursuant to which each agency shall carry out its responsibilities under 5 U.S.C. 5724c; *provided,* that the Director of Central Intelligence, after consultation with the Administrator of General Services, shall prescribe such regulations for the Central Intelligence Agency.

(8) The authority of the President under 5 U.S.C. 5726 to prescribe the regulations provided for therein, relating to (i) the definition of "household goods and personal effects", (ii) allowable storage expenses and related transportation, and (iii) the allowance of nontemporary storage expenses or storage at Government expense in Government-owned facilities (including related transportation and other expenses).

(9) The authority of the President under 5 U.S.C. 5727 to prescribe the regulations provided for therein, relating to the transportation at Government expense of privately owned motor vehicles.

(10) The authority of the President under 5 U.S.C. 5728 (a) and (b) to prescribe the regulations provided for therein, relating to the payment by an agency from its appropriations of the expenses of round trip travel of an employee, and the transportation of his immediate family, in described circumstances.

(11) The authority of the President under 5 U.S.C. 5729(a) and (b) to prescribe the regulations provided for therein, relating to (i) the payment by an agency from its appropriations of the expenses of transporting the immediate family of an employee and of shipping his household goods and personal effects, and (ii) the reimbursement from its appropriations by an agency of an employee for the proper transportation expense of returning his immediate family and household goods and personal effects, both in described circumstances.

(12) The authority of the President under 5 U.S.C. 5731(a) to prescribe the regulations provided for therein, relating to certifications respecting transportation accommodations.

(13) The authority of the President under 5 U.S.C. 5742(b) to prescribe regulations with respect to the payment of expenses when an employee dies.

(14) The authority of the President under the last sentence of paragraph (c) of section 32 of title III of the Act of July 22, 1937, c. 517, 50 Stat. 525 (7 U.S.C. 1011(c)), to transfer to Federal, State, or Territorial agencies lands acquired by the Secretary of Agriculture under section 32(a) of that Act.

(15) The authority of the President under section 340 of the Consolidated Farmers Home Administration Act of 1961, 75 Stat. 318 (7 U.S.C. 1990), in his discretion to transfer to the Secretary of Agriculture any right, interest or title held by the United States in any lands acquired in the program of national defense and no longer needed for that program, and to determine the suitability of the lands to be transferred, for the pur-

poses referred to in that section: *Provided*, That the exercise by the Administrator of the authority delegated to him by this paragraph (15) shall require the concurrence of the Secretary of Defense as to the absence of further need of the lands for the national defense program.

(16) The authority of the President under section 4(k) of the Tennessee Valley Authority Act, 55 Stat. 599 (16 U.S.C. 831c(k)), to approve transfers under paragraphs (a) and (c) of that section, other than leases for terms of less than 20 years and conveyances of property having a value not in excess of $500.

(17) The authority of the President under section 7(b) of the Tennessee Valley Authority Act of May 18, 1933, 48 Stat. 63 (16 U.S.C. 831f(b)), to provide for the transfer to the Tennessee Valley Authority of the use, possession, and control of real or personal property of the United States deemed by the Administrator of General Services to be necessary and proper for the purposes of that Authority as stated in that Act.

(18) The authority of the President under section 1 of the Act of March 4, 1927, c. 505, 44 Stat. 1422 (20 U.S.C. 191), to transfer to the jurisdiction of the Secretary of Agriculture for the purposes of that Act any land belonging to the United States within or adjacent to the District of Columbia located along the Anacostia River North of Benning Bridge.

(19) That part of the authority of the President under section 7(a) of the Act of July 17, 1959, P.L. 86–91, 73 Stat. 216, as amended (20 U.S.C. 905(a)), which consists of authority to prescribe regulations relating to storage (including packing, drayage, unpacking, and transportation to and from storage) of household effects and personal possessions.

(20) The authority of the Administrator of General Services under section 210(i) of the Federal Property and Administrative Services Act of 1949, as amended (40 U.S.C. 490(i)) to prescribe regulations relating to the installation, repair, and replacement of sidewalks.

(21) The authority of the President under section 108 of the Housing Act of July 15, 1949, c. 338, 63 Stat. 419, as amended (42 U.S.C. 1458), to transfer, or cause to be transferred, to the Secretary of Housing and Urban Development any right, title or interest held by the Federal Government or any department or agency thereof in any land (including buildings thereon) which is surplus to the needs of the Government and which a local public agency certifies will be within the area of a project being planned by it.

(22), (23) [Revoked by Ex. Ord. No. 12215, May 27, 1980, 45 F.R. 36043.]

SEC. 2. *Department of the Treasury.* The Secretary of the Treasury is hereby designated and empowered to exercise, without the approval, ratification, or other action of the President, the following:

(1) The authority under 5 U.S.C. 5943(a) to make recommendations to the President concerning the meeting of losses sustained by employees and members of the uniformed services while serving in a foreign country due to appreciation of foreign currency in its relation to the American dollar.

(2) The authority under 5 U.S.C. 5943(d) to report annually to the Congress on expenditures made under 5 U.S.C. 5943(d).

SEC. 3. *Department of Health and Human Services.* The Secretary of Health and Human Services is hereby designated and empowered to exercise, without the approval, ratification, or other action of the President, the following:

(1) The authority of the President under the first section of the Act entitled "An Act to authorize the operation of stands in Federal buildings by blind persons, to enlarge the economic opportunities of the blind, and for other purposes," approved June 20, 1936, 49 Stat. 1559, as amended (20 U.S.C. 107), to approve regulations prescribed by the heads of the respective departments and agencies thereunder.

(2) The authority of the Secretary of Health and Human Services under section 2 of the Act of August 4, 1947, c. 478, 61 Stat. 751, as amended (24 U.S.C. 168a) to fix per diem rates for care of patients in Saint Elizabeths Hospital.

SEC. 4. (a) *Department of State.* The Secretary of State is hereby designated and empowered to exercise his authority under section 12 of the Act of August 1, 1956, 70 Stat. 892 (22 U.S.C. 2679) (being authority to prescribe certain maximum rates of per diem in lieu of subsistence (or of similar allowances therefor)), without the approval, ratification, or other action of the President.

(b) The Secretary of State is hereby designated and empowered to exercise the authority of the President under section 9 of the United Nations Participation Act of 1945 (59 Stat. 619), as amended by section 15 of Public Law 93–126 (87 Stat. 454–455) [22 U.S.C. 287e–1].

SEC. 5. *Department of Defense.* The Secretary of Defense is hereby designated and empowered to exercise the authority of the President under the last sentence of section 4 of the Act of May 10, 1943, c. 95, 57 Stat. 81 (24 U.S.C. 34) to prescribe from time to time uniform rates of charges for hospitalization and dispensary services: *Provided*, That the authority hereby delegated may not be redelegated to any officer in the Department of the Navy, Department of the Air Force, or Department of the Army.

SEC. 6. *Department of Health and Human Services; Department of Defense.* The following are hereby designated and empowered to exercise, without the approval, ratification, or other action of the President, the authority of the President under 10 U.S.C. 1085 to establish uniform rates of reimbursement for inpatient medical or dental care:

(1) The Secretary of Health and Human Services in respect of such care in a facility under his jurisdiction.

(2) The Secretary of Defense in respect of such care in a facility of an armed force under the jurisdiction of a military department.

SEC. 7. *Veterans Administration.* (a) The Administrator of Veterans Affairs is hereby designated and empowered to exercise the authority of the President under 10 U.S.C. 1074(b) to approve uniform rates of reimbursement for care provided in facilities operated by the Administrator.

(b) Section 2 of Executive Order No. 11302 of September 6, 1966, as amended by Executive Order No. 11429 of September 9, 1968 [set out as a note under section 111 of Title 38, Veterans' Benefits], is hereby further amended by substituting for the words "allowance of not more than six cents a mile" the following: "allowance, in such amount per mile as the Administrator shall from time to time fix pursuant to 38 U.S.C. 111 as affected by this order,".

SEC. 8. *Office of Personnel Management.* The Office of Personnel Management is hereby designated and empowered to exercise, without the approval, ratification, or other action of the President, the following:

(1) The authority of the President under 5 U.S.C. 5514(b) to approve regulations prescribed by the head of each agency to carry out 5 U.S.C. 5514 and section 3(a) of the Act of July 15, 1954, c. 509, 68 Stat. 483, 31 U.S.C. 581d [31 U.S.C. 3530(d)] (relating to installment deductions from pay for indebtedness because of erroneous payment).

(2) The authority of the President under 5 U.S.C. 5903 to prescribe regulations necessary for the uniform administration of subchapter I of chapter 59 of title 5 of the United States Code [5 U.S.C. 5901 et seq.] (relating to uniform allowances).

(3) The authority of the President under 5 U.S.C. 5942 to prescribe regulations establishing rates at which an allowance based on duty (except temporary duty) at remote work sites will be paid and defining and designating the sites, areas and groups of positions to which the rates apply.

(4) The authority of the President under 5 U.S.C. 5942a to prescribe regulations governing the payment of allowances to employees assigned to duty at Johnston Island for the purposes of maintaining the employees' spouses or dependents, or both, at a location other than Johnston Island.

SEC. 9. *Office of Management and Budget.* The Director of the Office of Management and Budget is hereby designated and empowered to exercise, without the approval, ratification, or other action of the President, the following:

(1) The authority of the President under 5 U.S.C. 5911(f) to issue the regulations provided for therein (relating to the provision, occupancy, and availability of quarters and facilities, the determination of rates and charges therefor, and other related matters, as are necessary and appropriate to carry out the provision of section 5911).

(2) The authority of the President under 10 U.S.C. 126(a) to approve the transfers of balances of appropriations provided for therein.

(3) The authority of the President under section 202 of the Budget and Accounting Procedures Act of September 12, 1950, 64 Stat. 833 (31 U.S.C. 581c) [31 U.S.C. 1531] to approve the transfers of balances of appropriations provided for in subsections (a) and (b) of that section.

(4) The authority of the President under the last sentence of section 11 of the Act of June 6, 1924, c. 270, 43 Stat. 463 (40 U.S.C. 72), to approve (i) the designation of lands to be acquired by condemnation, (ii) contracts for purchase of lands, and (iii) agreements between the National Capital Planning Commission and officials of the States of Maryland and Virginia.

(5) The authority of the President under section 1 of the Act of December 22, 1928, c. 48, 45 Stat. 1070 (40 U.S.C. 72a), to approve contracts for acquisition of land subject to limited rights reserved to the grantor and for the acquisition of limited permanent rights in land adjoining park property.

(6) The authority of the President under section 407(b) of the Act of August 30, 1957, 71 Stat. 556 (42 U.S.C. 1594j(b)) [see 10 U.S.C. 2830], to approve regulations (relating to the rental of substandard housing for members of the uniformed services) prescribed pursuant to that section. The Secretaries referred to in section 407(c) of that Act shall furnish the Director of the Office of Management and Budget such reports with respect to matters within the scope of the regulations so approved as he may require and at such times as he may specify.

(7) The authority of the President under 44 U.S.C. 1108 to approve the use, from the appropriations available for printing and binding, of such sums as are necessary for the printing of journals, magazines, periodicals, and similar publications.

(8) The authority of the President under the paragraph appearing under the heading "Expenses of Management Improvement" in title III of the Treasury, Post Office, and Executive Office Appropriation Act, 1971, P.L. 91–422, 84 Stat. 877, or by any reenactment of the provisions of that paragraph in the same or in a different amount of funds, to allocate to any agency or office of the executive branch (including the Office of Management and Budget) funds appropriated by that paragraph or by any such reenactment of it. The Director of the Office of Management and Budget shall from time to time report to the President concerning activities carried on by executive agencies and offices with funds allocated under this paragraph and shall, consonant with law, exercise such direction and control with respect to those activities as he shall deem appropriate.

SEC. 10. *General Provisions.* (a) Unless inappropriate, any reference in this order to any provision of law shall be deemed to include reference thereto as amended from time to time and as affected by Reorganization Plan No. 2 of 1970 (35 F.R. 7959).

(b) Unless inappropriate, any reference in any Executive order to any Executive order which is superseded by this order, or to any Executive order provision so superseded, shall hereafter be deemed to refer to this order or to the provision of the preceding section of this order, if any, which corresponds to the superseded provision.

(c) All actions heretofore taken by the President, the Director of the Bureau of the Budget, or the Director of the Office of Management and Budget in respect of the matters affected by the provisions of the preceding sec-

tions of this order and in force at the time of the issuance of this order, including any regulations prescribed or approved by any of them in respect of such matters, shall, except as may be inconsistent with the provisions of this order, remain in effect until amended, modified, or revoked pursuant to the authority conferred by this order unless sooner terminated by operation of law.

SEC. 11. *Orders superseded.* The following are hereby superseded:

(1) Executive Order No. 10604 of April 22, 1955.

(2) Executive Order No. 11230 of June 28, 1965.

(3) Executive Order No. 11275 of March 31, 1966.

(4) Executive Order No. 11290 of July 21, 1966.

(5) Section 3 of Executive Order No. 11294 of August 4, 1966.

(6) To the extent that it is inconsistent with this order, Executive Order No. 11541 of July 1, 1970.

SEC. 12. *Taking effect.* This order shall be effective immediately except that paragraphs (1) to (13), inclusive, and paragraph (19), of section 1 hereof shall become effective ninety days after the date of this order.

CHANGE OF NAME

References to Administrator of Veterans' Affairs and to Veterans' Administration deemed to refer to Secretary of Veterans Affairs and to Department of Veterans Affairs, respectively, pursuant to section 10 of Pub. L. 100–527, set out as a Department of Veterans Affairs Act note under section 301 of Title 38, Veterans' Benefits.

EX. ORD. NO. 11690. DELEGATION OF FUNCTIONS TO EXECUTIVE DIRECTOR OF DOMESTIC COUNCIL

Ex. Ord. No. 11690, Dec. 14, 1972, 37 F.R. 26815, provided:

By virtue of the authority vested in me by the Constitution and statutes of the United States, Part II of Reorganization Plan No. 2 of 1970 [set out in 5 App. U.S.C.], and as President of the United States, it is ordered as follows:

SECTION 1. *Functions of the Executive Director of the Domestic Council.* In addition to the functions heretofore assigned, the Executive Director of the Domestic Council shall assist the President with respect to intergovernmental relations generally. In addition, he shall:

(1) serve as the coordinator for the prompt handling and solution of Federal-State-local problems brought to the attention of the President or Vice President by executive and legislative officers of State and local governments;

(2) identify and report to the President on recurring intergovernmental problems of a Federal interdepartmental and interprogram nature;

(3) explore and report to the President on ways and means of strengthening the headquarters and interagency relationships of Federal field offices as they relate to intergovernmental activities;

(4) maintain continuing liaison with intergovernmental units in Federal departments and agencies; and

(5) review procedures utilized by Federal executive agencies for affording State and local officials an opportunity to confer and comment on Federal assistance programs and other intergovernmental issues, and propose methods of strengthening such procedures.

SEC. 2. *Administrative Arrangements.* (a) All Federal departments, agencies, and interagency councils and committees having an impact on intergovernmental relations, and all Federal Executive Boards, shall extend full cooperation and assistance to the Director in carrying out his responsibilities under this order. The Director shall, upon request, assist all Federal departments and agencies with problems that may arise between them and the executive agencies or elected officials of State and local governments.

(b) The head of each Federal department and agency shall designate an appropriate official with broad general experience in his department or agency to serve, upon request of the Director, as a point of contact in carrying out Federal-State-local liaison activities under this order.

SEC. 3. *Construction.* Nothing in this order shall be construed as subjecting any department, establishment, or other instrumentality of the executive branch of the Federal Government or the head thereof, or any function vested by law in or assigned pursuant to law, to any such agency or head, to the authority of any other such agency or head or as abrogating, modifying, or restricting any such function in any manner.

SEC. 4. *Revocation.* Executive Order No. 11455 of February 14, 1969, entitled "Establishing an Office of Intergovernmental Relations", is hereby revoked.

SEC. 5. *Records, Property, Personnel, and Funds.* The records, property, personnel, and unexpended balances, available or to be made available, of appropriations, allocations, and other funds of the Office of Intergovernmental Relations are hereby transferred to the Domestic Council.

SEC. 6. *Effective Date.* This Order shall be effective thirty days after this date.

RICHARD NIXON.

ABOLITION OF DOMESTIC COUNCIL

The Domestic Council, referred to in section 5 of Ex. Ord. No. 11690, Dec. 14, 1972, 31 F.R. 26815, was abolished and its functions transferred to the President with power to delegate such functions within the Executive Office of the President pursuant to Reorg. Plan No. 1 of 1977, §§1, 3, 5D, 42 F.R. 56101, 91 Stat. 1633, set out preceding section 101 of this title, effective on or before Apr. 1, 1978, at such time as specified by the President. Ex. Ord. No. 12045, Mar. 27, 1978, 43 F.R. 13347, set out preceding section 101 of this title, provided that the abolition and transfer of functions of the Domestic Council be effective Mar. 26, 1978.

EXECUTIVE ORDER NO. 11713

Ex. Ord. No. 11713, Apr. 21, 1973, 38 F.R. 10069, which related to the delegation of functions to the Administrator of General Services, was revoked by section 1–404 of Ex. Ord. No. 12215, May 27, 1980, 45 F.R. 36045, set out as a note under section 3601 of Title 22, Foreign Relations and Intercourse.

EX. ORD. NO. 11732. DELEGATION OF FUNCTIONS TO SECRETARY OF HOUSING AND URBAN DEVELOPMENT

Ex. Ord. No. 11732, July 30, 1973, 38 F.R. 20429, provided:

By virtue of the authority vested in me by section 301 of title 3 of the United States Code, the Secretary of Housing and Urban Development is hereby designated and empowered to exercise, without approval, ratification, or other action by the President, the functions vested in the President by sections 305 and 301 of the National Housing Act, as amended (12 U.S.C. 1720 and 1716, respectively), relating to the authorization of the purchase of mortgages by the Government National Mortgage Association in connection with its special assistance functions and the determination that such action is in the public interest.

RICHARD NIXON.

EXECUTIVE ORDER NO. 11784

Ex. Ord. No. 11784, May 30, 1974, 39 F.R. 19443, which related to the delegation of certain authority to the Administrator of General Services to issue regulations relating to joint funding, was superseded by Ex. Ord. No. 11867, June 19, 1975, 40 F.R. 26253, formerly set out as a note under section 7103 of Title 31, Money and Finance.

EX. ORD. NO. 12001. TRANSFERRING CERTAIN BICENTENNIAL FUNCTIONS TO SECRETARY OF THE INTERIOR

Ex. Ord. No. 12001, June 29, 1977, 42 F.R. 33709, provided:

By virtue of the authority vested in me by Section 7(b) of the Act of December 11, 1973 (87 Stat. 701) [Pub.

L. 93–179], hereinafter referred to as the Act, Section 202(b) of the Budget and Accounting Procedures Act of 1950 (64 Stat. 838, 31 U.S.C. 581c(b)) [31 U.S.C. 1531], and Section 301 of Title 3 of the United States Code, and as President of the United States of America it is hereby ordered as follows:

SECTION 1. The Secretary of the Interior, hereinafter referred to as the Secretary, shall, through existing National Park Service programs, provide for the continuation of appropriate commemoration of events relating to the American Revolution until December 31, 1983.

SEC. 2. The Secretary shall administer existing contracts and grants of the American Revolution Bicentennial Administration, hereinafter referred to as ARBA.

SEC. 3. In performing the functions described in Sections 1 and 2 of this Order, the Secretary may, in addition to any other available authority, exercise the following powers under the Act which are hereby transferred to him for such purposes until December 31, 1983, except as otherwise provided in subsection (b) of this Section:

(a) All powers described in Section 2(f) of the Act with respect to the expenditure of funds donated to ARBA prior to the effective date of this Order, and the expenditure of revenues received or which may be received pursuant to contracts described in Section 2 of this Order.

(b) Until December 31, 1977, all powers exercised by ARBA prior to the effective date of this Order which relate to enforcement of Section 2(i) of the Act.

(c) All powers described in Section 5(a) of the Act.

SEC. 4. All personnel, records, property and appropriations, including all funds and revenues described in Section 3(a) of this Order, as relate to the powers and functions assigned or transferred by this Order are hereby transferred to the Secretary.

SEC. 5. The Director of the Office of Management and Budget shall make such determinations and issue such orders as may be necessary or appropriate to carry out the transfers provided by this Order.

SEC. 6. Executive Order No. 11840 of February 18, 1975, is hereby revoked.

SEC. 7. This Order shall be effective June 30, 1977.

JIMMY CARTER.

EX. ORD. NO. 12152. DELEGATION OF FUNCTIONS TO DIRECTOR OF OFFICE OF MANAGEMENT AND BUDGET

Ex. Ord. No. 12152, Aug. 14, 1979, 44 F.R. 48143, provided:

By the authority vested in me as President by the Constitution and statutes of the United States of America, including Section 301 of Title 3 of the United States Code, and in order to ensure the continued delegation of certain functions which had been previously assigned but which are now vested directly in the President by virtue of H.R. 4616 [Pub. L. 96–54, Aug. 14, 1979, 93 Stat. 381] that I have signed into law today, it is hereby ordered that the functions vested in the President by Sections 305(b), 4111(b), and 4112(a) of Title 5 of the United States Code are hereby delegated to the Director of the Office of Management and Budget.

JIMMY CARTER.

EX. ORD. NO. 12396. DELEGATION OF FUNCTIONS TO SECRETARY OF DEFENSE

Ex. Ord. No. 12396, Dec. 9, 1982, 47 F.R. 55897, provided:

By the authority vested in me as President of the United States of America by Section 301 of Title 3 of the United States Code, and in order to delegate certain functions concerning the appointment, promotion, and retirement of commissioned officers of the Armed Forces, it is hereby ordered as follows:

SECTION 1. The Secretary of Defense is designated to perform, without approval, ratification, or other action by the President, the following functions vested in the President:

(a) The authority vested in the President by Sections 618(b)(1) and 628(d)(1) of Title 10 of the United States

Code, to approve, modify, or disapprove the report of a selection board.

(b) The authority vested in the President by Section 629(a) of Title 10 of the United States Code, to remove the name of any officer from a promotion list to any grade below commodore or brigadier general.

(c) The authority vested in the President by Section 624(c) of Title 10 of the United States Code, to appoint officers in the grades of first lieutenant and captain in the Army, Air Force, and Marine Corps or in the grades of lieutenant (junior grade) and lieutenant in the Navy.

(d) The authority vested in the President by Section 5721(c) of Title 10 of the United States Code, to make certain temporary appointments to the grade of lieutenant commander.

(e) The authority vested in the President by Section 6323(a) of Title 10 of the United States Code, to approve the application of an officer of the Navy or the Marine Corps for retirement after the completion of more than 20 years of active service and to designate the month in which such retirements shall become effective.

(f) The authority vested in the President by Sections 3918 and 8918 of Title 10 of the United States Code, to approve the request of a regular commissioned officer of the Army or the Air Force to retire after at least 30 years of service.

(g) Nothing in this Section shall be deemed to delegate the authority vested in the President by Section 618(c) of Title 10 to remove a name from a selection board report.

SEC. 2. (a) The Secretary of Defense is designated to perform during a time of war or national emergency the following functions vested in the President, without the approval, ratification, or other action by the President.

(1) The authority vested in the President by Section 526 of Title 10 of the United States Code, to suspend the operation of any provision of Sections 523, 524 [now 12011], or 525 of Title 10 of the United States Code, relating to the authorized strength of commissioned officers.

(2) The authority vested in the President by subsections (a) and (b) of Section 603 of Title 10 of the United States Code, to make or vacate certain temporary commissioned appointments.

(3) The authority vested in the President by Section 644 [see 123] of Title 10 of the United States Code, to suspend the operation of any law relating to the promotion, involuntary retirement, or separation of commissioned officers of the Army, Navy, Air Force, or Marine Corps.

(b) The authority delegated to the Secretary of Defense by this Section may not be exercised during the time of a national emergency declared by the President, unless the exercise of any such authority is specifically directed by the President in accordance with Section 301 of the National Emergencies Act (50 U.S.C. 1631).

(c) The Secretary of Defense shall ensure that actions taken pursuant to the authority delegated by this Section are accounted for as required by Section 401 of the National Emergencies Act (50 U.S.C. 1641).

SEC. 3. The authority delegated to the Secretary of Defense by this Order may be redelegated to the Deputy Secretary of Defense, any of the Assistant Secretaries of Defense, and to any of the Secretaries of the military departments who may further subdelegate such authority to subordinates who are appointed to their office by the President with the advice and consent of the Senate.

SEC. 4. All actions taken by, for, or on behalf of the President with respect to the functions delegated by this Order, which actions would be valid if taken pursuant to this Order, are ratified.

SEC. 5. (a) Executive Order No. 10621, as amended [set out above], is further amended by revoking subsections (g), (h), (j), (k), (l), (m), and (n) of Section 1 thereof.

(b) Executive Order No. 11390, as amended [set out above], is further amended by revoking subsections 2, 3, 9, 12, and 15 of Section 1 thereof.

(c) Executive Order No. 12239 is revoked.

RONALD REAGAN.

EX. ORD. NO. 12781. DELEGATION OF FUNCTIONS AND AUTHORITIES, DEVELOPMENT OF REQUIREMENTS AND REGULATIONS, AND CORRECTION OF TITLE

Ex. Ord. No. 12781, Nov. 20, 1991, 56 F.R. 59203, provided:

By the authority vested in me as President by the Constitution and the laws of the United States of America, including section 3603 of the Financial Reports Act of 1988 (22 U.S.C. 5351 et seq.) [22 U.S.C. 5353], section 274A(d)(2) and (4) of the Immigration and Nationality Act ("Act"), as amended (8 U.S.C. 1324a(d)(2) and (4)), sections 4561, 6082, and 9561 of title 10 of the United States Code, the Act of June 14, 1987 [1897], ch. 2, 30 Stat. 11, 36 (16 U.S.C. 473), section 301 of title 3 of the United States Code, and in order to: (1) delegate functions concerning discussions with foreign governments to improve access by U.S. banking and financial organizations; (2) delegate authority concerning a national employment verification system; (3) delegate authority concerning the development of requirements and regulations for a uniform military ration; and (4) correct the title of the Nez Perce National Forest, it is hereby ordered as follows:

SECTION 1. Functions Concerning Discussions with Foreign Governments to Improve Access by U.S. Banking and Financial Organizations. The functions vested in the President by section 3603 of the Financial Reports Act of 1988 (22 U.S.C. 5353) are hereby delegated to the Secretary of the Treasury. This delegation is not in derogation of, and shall not affect, the existing authorities of the United States Trade Representative.

SEC. 2. Authority Concerning the Employment Verification System. The authority conferred upon the President by section 274A(d)(4) of the Act [8 U.S.C. 1324a(d)(4)], to undertake demonstration projects of different changes in the requirements of the employment verification system, is delegated to the Attorney General. Demonstration projects shall be conducted consistent with the restrictions in section 274A(d)(2) of the Act and shall not extend for a period longer than 3 years. This authority may be redelegated.

SEC. 3. Authority, Requirements, and Regulations Concerning a Uniform Military Ration.

(a) Authority. The Secretary of Defense is hereby designated and empowered to exercise, without the approval, ratification, or other action by the President, the authority conferred upon the President by section 4561(a), sections 6082(a) and (d), and section 9561(a) of title 10 of the United States Code. Under this authority the Secretary may prescribe a uniform military ration applicable to the Army, Navy, and Air Force.

(b) Requirements. (1) Components and Quantities. The components and the quantities of the uniform military ration shall reflect military member preferences and satisfy nutritional requirements. (2) Monetary Value. The monetary value of the uniform military ration shall be equal to the monetary value of the ration in effect on the day before the effective date of this order. (3) Index. The Secretary of Defense shall establish, as of the effective date of this order, an index composed of a representative market basket of items equal in value to the ration value. Subsequent to the effective date of this order, and based upon the changing prices of food components in the index, the Secretaries of the military departments shall periodically redetermine the monetary value of the ration. The Secretary of Defense shall review the index periodically, but not less than once a year, to ensure that it reflects changes in food service technology, scientific advances in nutrition, the requirements of the Armed Forces of the United States, and the food preferences of the enlisted members. Increases or decreases in the monetary value of the ration that result from changes in the composition of the food items making up the index shall not exceed 2 percent of the ration value annually.

(c) Regulations. Under regulations of the Secretary of Defense, the Secretary of the Army, the Secretary of the Navy, and the Secretary of the Air Force are authorized, for their respective military departments, to prescribe the issue of special allowances and such special or supplemental rations, defined by component, quantity, or monetary value, as they may consider appropriate. Executive Order No. 11339 of March 28, 1967, is hereby revoked.

SEC. 4. *Correction of Title of the Nez Perce National Forest.* Executive Order No. 854 of June 26, 1908, is hereby amended by retitling the "Nezperce National Forest" the "Nez Perce National Forest."

SEC. 5. This order shall take effect immediately.

GEORGE BUSH.

§ 302. Scope of delegation of functions

The authority conferred by this chapter shall apply to any function vested in the President by law if such law does not affirmatively prohibit delegation of the performance of such function as herein provided for, or specifically designate the officer or officers to whom it may be delegated. This chapter shall not be deemed to limit or derogate from any existing or inherent right of the President to delegate the performance of functions vested in him by law, and nothing herein shall be deemed to require express authorization in any case in which such an official would be presumed in law to have acted by authority or direction of the President.

(Added Oct. 31, 1951, ch. 655, § 10, 65 Stat. 712.)

SIMILAR PROVISIONS; REPEAL; SAVING CLAUSE

For similar provisions contained in prior law, and saving clause in connection therewith, see note preceding section 301 of this title.

SECTION REFERRED TO IN OTHER SECTIONS

This section is referred to in title 31 section 1537.

§ 303. Definitions

As used in this chapter, the term "function" embraces any duty, power, responsibility, authority, or discretion vested in the President or other officer concerned, and the terms "perform" and "performance" may be construed to mean "exercise".

(Added Oct. 31, 1951, ch. 655, § 10, 65 Stat. 712.)

SIMILAR PROVISIONS; REPEAL; SAVING CLAUSE

For similar provisions contained in prior law, and saving clause in connection therewith, see note preceding section 301 of this title.

CHAPTER 5—EXTENSION OF CERTAIN RIGHTS AND PROTECTIONS TO PRESIDENTIAL OFFICES

SUBCHAPTER I—GENERAL PROVISIONS

CHAPTER REFERRED TO IN OTHER SECTIONS

This chapter is referred to in title 28 sections 1296, 1346, 1413, 3901, 3902, 3903, 3904, 3905, 3906, 3907.

SUBCHAPTER I—GENERAL PROVISIONS

§ 401. Definitions

(a) IN GENERAL.—Except as otherwise specifically provided in this chapter, as used in this chapter:

(1) BOARD.—The term "Board" means the Merit Systems Protection Board under chapter 12 of title 5.

(2) COVERED EMPLOYEE.—The term "covered employee" means any employee of an employing office.

(3) EMPLOYEE.—The term "employee" includes an applicant for employment and a former employee.

(4) EMPLOYING OFFICE.—The term "employing office" means—

(A) each office, agency, or other component of the Executive Office of the President;

(B) the Executive Residence at the White House; and

(C) the official residence (temporary or otherwise) of the Vice President.

---

[1] So in original. Does not conform to section catchline.

(b) DEFINITIONS RELATING TO CERTAIN MAT-
TERS.—For purposes of applying this chapter
with respect to any practice or other matter—

(1) to which section 411 relates, the terms
"employing office" and "covered employee"
shall each be considered to have the meaning
given to the term by such section;

(2) to which section 412 relates, the term
"covered employee" means a covered employee described in section 412(a)(2)(B);

(3) to which section 413 relates, the term
"covered employee" excludes interns and volunteers, as described in section 413(a)(2); and

(4) to which section 416 relates, the term
"covered employee" means a covered employee described in section 416(a)(2).

(Added Pub. L. 104–331, §2(a), Oct. 26, 1996, 110
Stat. 4054.)

REGULATIONS

Section 2(b) of Pub. L. 104–331 provided that: "Appropriate measures shall be taken to ensure that—

"(1) any regulations required to implement section
411 of title 3, United States Code, shall be in effect by
October 1, 1997; and

"(2) any other regulations needed to implement
chapter 5 of title 3, United States Code, shall be in effect as soon as practicable, but not later than October 1, 1998."

APPLICABILITY OF FUTURE EMPLOYMENT LAWS

Section 4 of Pub. L. 104–331 provided that:

"(a) IN GENERAL.—Each provision of Federal law that
is made applicable to the legislative branch under section 102 of the Congressional Accountability Act of 1995
(2 U.S.C. 1302), and that is enacted later than 12 months
after the date of the enactment of this Act [Oct. 26,
1996], shall be deemed to apply with respect to 'employing offices' and 'covered employees' (within the meaning of section 401 of title 3, United States Code, as
added by this Act), unless such law specifically provides otherwise and expressly cites this section.

"(b) REGULATIONS.—

"(1) IN GENERAL.—The President, or the designee of
the President, shall issue regulations to implement
such provision.

"(2) AGENCY REGULATIONS.—The regulations issued
under paragraph (1) to implement a provision shall be
the same as substantive regulations promulgated by
the head of the appropriate executive agency to implement the provision, except to the extent that the
President or designee may determine, for good cause
shown and stated together with the regulation, that
a modification of such regulations would be more effective for the implementation of the rights and protections under the section."

SECTION REFERRED TO IN OTHER SECTIONS

This section is referred to in title 28 section 3908.

§ 402. Application of laws

The following laws shall apply, as prescribed
by this chapter, to all employing offices (including employing offices within the meaning of section 411, to the extent prescribed therein):

(1) The Fair Labor Standards Act of 1938.

(2) Title VII of the Civil Rights Act of 1964.

(3) The Americans with Disabilities Act of
1990.

(4) The Age Discrimination in Employment
Act of 1967.

(5) The Family and Medical Leave Act of
1993.

(6) The Occupational Safety and Health Act
of 1970.

(7) Chapter 71 (relating to Federal service
labor-management relations) of title 5.

(8) The Employee Polygraph Protection Act
of 1988.

(9) The Worker Adjustment and Retraining
Notification Act.

(10) The Rehabilitation Act of 1973.

(11) Chapter 43 (relating to veterans' employment and reemployment) of title 38.

(Added Pub. L. 104–331, §2(a), Oct. 26, 1996, 110
Stat. 4054.)

REFERENCES IN TEXT

The Fair Labor Standards Act of 1938, referred to in
par. (1), is act June 25, 1938, ch. 676, 52 Stat. 1060, as
amended, which is classified generally to chapter 8
(§201 et seq.) of Title 29, Labor. For complete classification of this Act to the Code, see section 201 of Title 29
and Tables.

The Civil Rights Act of 1964, referred to in par. (2), is
Pub. L. 88–352, July 2, 1964, 78 Stat. 252, as amended.
Title VII of the Act is classified generally to subchapter VI (§2000e et seq.) of chapter 21 of Title 42, The
Public Health and Welfare. For complete classification
of this Act to the Code, see Short Title note set out
under section 2000a of Title 42 and Tables.

The Americans with Disabilities Act of 1990, referred
to in par. (3), is Pub. L. 101–336, July 26, 1990, 104 Stat.
327, as amended, which is classified principally to chapter 126 (§12101 et seq.) of Title 42. For complete classification of this Act to the Code, see Short Title note
set out under section 12101 of Title 42 and Tables.

The Age Discrimination in Employment Act of 1967,
referred to in par. (4), is Pub. L. 90–202, Dec. 15, 1967, 81
Stat. 602, as amended, which is classified generally to
chapter 14 (§621 et seq.) of Title 29, Labor. For complete
classification of this Act to the Code, see Short Title
note set out under section 621 of Title 29 and Tables.

The Family and Medical Leave Act of 1993, referred to
in par. (5), is Pub. L. 103–3, Feb. 5, 1993, 107 Stat. 6, as
amended, which enacted sections 60m and 60n of Title
2, The Congress, sections 6381 to 6387 of Title 5, Government Organization and Employees, and chapter 28
(§2601 et seq.) of Title 29, amended section 2105 of Title
5, and enacted provisions set out as notes under section
2601 of Title 29. For complete classification of this Act
to the Code, see Short Title note set out under section
2601 of Title 29 and Tables.

The Occupational Safety and Health Act of 1970, referred to in par. (6), is Pub. L. 91–596, Dec. 29, 1970, 84
Stat. 1590, as amended, which is classified principally
to chapter 15 (§651 et seq.) of Title 29. For complete
classification of this Act to the Code, see Short Title
note set out under section 651 of Title 29 and Tables.

The Employee Polygraph Protection Act of 1988, referred to in par. (8), is Pub. L. 100–347, June 27, 1988, 102
Stat. 646, as amended, which is classified generally to
chapter 22 (§2001 et seq.) of Title 29. For complete classification of this Act to the Code, see Short Title note
set out under section 2001 of Title 29 and Tables.

The Worker Adjustment and Retraining Notification
Act, referred to in par. (9), is Pub. L. 100–379, Aug. 4,
1988, 102 Stat. 890, which is classified generally to chapter 23 (§2101 et seq.) of Title 29. For complete classification of this Act to the Code, see Short Title note set
out under section 2101 of Title 29 and Tables.

The Rehabilitation Act of 1973, referred to in par. (10),
is Pub. L. 93–112, Sept. 26, 1973, 87 Stat. 355, as amended,
which is classified generally to chapter 16 (§701 et seq.)
of Title 29. For complete classification of this Act to
the Code, see Short Title note set out under section 701
of Title 29 and Tables.

SUBCHAPTER II—EXTENSION OF RIGHTS AND PROTECTIONS

PART A—EMPLOYMENT DISCRIMINATION, FAMILY AND MEDICAL LEAVE, FAIR LABOR STANDARDS, EMPLOYEE POLYGRAPH PROTECTION, WORKER ADJUSTMENT AND RETRAINING, EMPLOYMENT AND REEMPLOYMENT OF VETERANS, AND INTIMIDATION

PART REFERRED TO IN OTHER SECTIONS

This part is referred to in sections 435, 451, 452, 454 of this title.

§ 411. Rights and protections under title VII of the Civil Rights Act of 1964, the Age Discrimination in Employment Act of 1967, the Rehabilitation Act of 1973, and title I of the Americans with Disabilities Act of 1990

(a) DISCRIMINATORY PRACTICES PROHIBITED.—All personnel actions affecting covered employees shall be made free from any discrimination based on—

(1) race, color, religion, sex, or national origin, within the meaning of section 703 of the Civil Rights Act of 1964;

(2) age, within the meaning of section 15 of the Age Discrimination in Employment Act of 1967; or

(3) disability, within the meaning of section 501 of the Rehabilitation Act of 1973 and sections 102 through 104 of the Americans with Disabilities Act of 1990.

(b) REMEDY.—

(1) CIVIL RIGHTS.—The remedy for a violation of subsection (a)(1) shall be—

(A) such damages as would be appropriate if awarded under section 706(g) of the Civil Rights Act of 1964; and

(B) such compensatory damages as would be appropriate if awarded under section 1977 of the Revised Statutes, or as would be appropriate if awarded under sections 1977A(a)(1), 1977A(b)(2), and, irrespective of the size of the employing office, 1977A(b)(3)(D) of the Revised Statutes.

(2) AGE DISCRIMINATION.—The remedy for a violation of subsection (a)(2) shall be—

(A) such damages as would be appropriate if awarded under section 15(c) of the Age Discrimination in Employment Act of 1967; and

(B) such liquidated damages as would be appropriate if awarded under section 7(b) of such Act.

In addition, the waiver provisions of section 7(f) of such Act shall apply to covered employees.

(3) DISABILITIES DISCRIMINATION.—The remedy for a violation of subsection (a)(3) shall be—

(A) such damages as would be appropriate if awarded under section 505(a)(1) of the Rehabilitation Act of 1973 or section 107(a) of the Americans with Disabilities Act of 1990; and

(B) such compensatory damages as would be appropriate if awarded under sections 1977A(a)(2), 1977A(a)(3), 1977A(b)(2), and, irrespective of the size of the employing office, 1977A(b)(3)(D) of the Revised Statutes.

(c) DEFINITIONS.—Except as otherwise specifically provided in this section, as used in this section:

(1) COVERED EMPLOYEE.—The term "covered employee" means any employee of a unit of the executive branch, including the Executive Office of the President, whether appointed by the President or by any other appointing authority in the executive branch, who is not otherwise entitled to bring an action under any of the statutes referred to in subsection (a), but does not include any individual—

(A) whose appointment is made by and with the advice and consent of the Senate;

(B) who is appointed to an advisory committee, as defined in section 3(2) of the Federal Advisory Committee Act; or

(C) who is a member of the uniformed services.

(2) EMPLOYING OFFICE.—The term "employing office", with respect to a covered employee, means the office, agency, or other entity in which the covered employee is employed (or sought employment or was employed in the case of an applicant or former employee, respectively).

(d) REGULATIONS TO IMPLEMENT SECTION.—

(1) IN GENERAL.—The President, or the designee of the President, shall issue regulations to implement paragraphs (1) and (3) of subsection (a) and paragraphs (1) and (3) of subsection (b).

(2) AGENCY REGULATIONS.—The regulations issued under paragraph (1) shall be the same as substantive regulations promulgated by the appropriate officer of an executive agency to implement the statutory provisions referred to in paragraphs (1) and (3) of subsection (a) and paragraphs (1) and (3) of subsection (b)—

(A) except to the extent that the President or designee may determine, for good cause shown and stated together with the regulation, that a modification of such regulations would be more effective for the implementation of the rights and protections under this section; and

(B) except that the President or designee may, at the discretion of the President or designee, issue regulations to implement a provision of section 717 of the Civil Rights Act of 1964 or section 501 of the Rehabilitation Act of 1973 that applies to employees in the executive branch of the Federal Government in lieu of an analogous statutory provision referred to in paragraph (1) or (3) of subsection (a) or paragraph (1) or (3) of subsection (b), if the issuance of such regulations—

(i) would be equally effective for the implementation of the rights and protections under this section; and

(ii) would promote uniformity in the application of Federal law to employees in the executive branch of the Federal Government.

(e) APPLICABILITY.—Subsections (a) through (c), and section 417 (to the extent that it relates to any matter under this section), shall apply with respect to violations occurring on or after the effective date of this chapter.

(f) EFFECTIVE DATE.—This section shall take effect on October 1, 1997.

(Added Pub. L. 104–331, §2(a), Oct. 26, 1996, 110 Stat. 4055.)

REFERENCES IN TEXT

Sections 703, 706, and 717 of the Civil Rights Act of 1964, referred to in subsecs. (a)(1), (b)(1)(A), and (d)(2)(B), are classified to sections 2000e–2, 2000e–5, and 2000e–16, respectively, of Title 42, The Public Health and Welfare.

Sections 7 and 15 of the Age Discrimination in Employment Act of 1967, referred to in subsecs. (a)(1) and (b)(2), are classified to sections 626 and 633a, respectively, of Title 29, Labor.

Sections 501 and 505 of the Rehabilitation Act of 1973, referred to in subsecs. (a)(3), (b)(3)(A), and (d)(2)(B), are classified to sections 791 and 794a, respectively, of Title 29.

Sections 102 to 104 and 107 of the Americans with Disabilities Act of 1990, referred to in subsecs. (a)(3) and (b)(3)(A), are classified to sections 12112 to 12114 and 12117, respectively, of Title 42, The Public Health and Welfare.

Sections 1977 and 1977A of the Revised Statutes, referred to in subsec. (b)(1)(B), (3)(B), are classified to sections 1981 and 1981a, respectively, of Title 42.

Section 3(2) of the Federal Advisory Committee Act, referred to in subsec. (c)(1)(B), is section 3(2) of Pub. L. 92–463, which is set out in the Appendix to Title 5, Government Organization and Employees.

The effective date of this chapter, referred to in subsec. (e), is Oct. 1, 1997, unless otherwise provided, see section 471 of this title.

EFFECTIVE DATE

Subsec. (d) of this section effective Oct. 26, 1996, see section 471(b) of this title.

REGULATIONS

For provisions requiring that appropriate measures be taken to ensure that any regulations required to implement this section be in effect by Oct. 1, 1997, see section 2(b)(1) of Pub. L. 104–331, set out as a note under section 401 of this title.

SECTION REFERRED TO IN OTHER SECTIONS

This section is referred to in sections 401, 402, 421, 454, 471 of this title; title 28 section 3901.

§ 412. Rights and protections under the Family and Medical Leave Act of 1993

(a) FAMILY AND MEDICAL LEAVE RIGHTS AND PROTECTIONS PROVIDED.—

(1) IN GENERAL.—The rights and protections established by sections 101 through 105 of the Family and Medical Leave Act of 1993 shall apply to covered employees.

(2) DEFINITIONS.—For purposes of the application described in paragraph (1)—

(A) the term "employer" as used in the Family and Medical Leave Act of 1993 means any employing office; and

(B) the term "eligible employee" as used in the Family and Medical Leave Act of 1993 means a covered employee who has been employed in any employing office for 12 months and for at least 1,250 hours of employment during the previous 12 months.

(b) REMEDY.—The remedy for a violation of subsection (a) shall be such remedy, including liquidated damages, as would be appropriate if awarded under paragraph (1) of section 107(a) of the Family and Medical Leave Act of 1993.

(c) REGULATIONS TO IMPLEMENT SECTION.—

(1) IN GENERAL.—The President, or the designee of the President, shall issue regulations to implement this section.

(2) AGENCY REGULATIONS.—The regulations issued under paragraph (1) shall be the same as substantive regulations promulgated by the Secretary of Labor to implement the statutory provisions referred to in subsections (a) and (b)—

(A) except to the extent that the President or designee may determine, for good cause shown and stated together with the regulation, that a modification of such regulations would be more effective for the implementation of the rights and protections under this section; and

(B) except that the President or designee may, at the discretion of the President or designee, issue regulations to implement a provision of subchapter V of chapter 63 of title 5, United States Code, that applies to employees in the executive branch of the Federal Government in lieu of an analogous statutory provision referred to in subsection (a) or (b), if the issuance of such regulations—

(i) would be equally effective for the implementation of the rights and protections under this section; and

(ii) would promote uniformity in the application of Federal law to employees in the executive branch of the Federal Government.

(d) EFFECTIVE DATE.—Subsections (a) and (b) shall take effect on the earlier of—

(1) the effective date of regulations issued under subsection (c); or

(2) October 1, 1998.

(Added Pub. L. 104–331, §2(a), Oct. 26, 1996, 110 Stat. 4057.)

REFERENCES IN TEXT

The Family and Medical Leave Act of 1993, referred to in subsecs. (a) and (b), is Pub. L. 103–3, Feb. 5, 1993, 107 Stat. 6, as amended, which enacted sections 60m and 60n of Title 2, The Congress, sections 6381 to 6387 of Title 5, Government Organization and Employees, and chapter 28 (§2601 et seq.) of Title 29, Labor, amended section 2105 of Title 5, and enacted provisions set out as notes under section 2601 of Title 29. Sections 101 to 105 and 107 of the Act are classified to sections 2611 to 2615 and 2617, respectively, of Title 29. For complete classification of this Act to the Code, see Short Title note set out under section 2601 of Title 29 and Tables.

EFFECTIVE DATE

Subsec. (c) of this section effective Oct. 26, 1996, see section 471(b) of this title.

SECTION REFERRED TO IN OTHER SECTIONS

This section is referred to in sections 401, 471 of this title.

§ 413. Rights and protections under the Fair Labor Standards Act of 1938

(a) FAIR LABOR STANDARDS.—

(1) IN GENERAL.—The rights and protections established by subsections (a)(1) and (d) of section 6, section 7, and section 12(c) of the Fair Labor Standards Act of 1938 shall apply to covered employees.

(2) INTERNS AND VOLUNTEERS.—For the purposes of this section, the term "covered employee" does not include an intern or a volunteer as defined in regulations under subsection (c).

(3) COMPENSATORY TIME.—Except as provided in regulations under subsection (c)(3), covered employees may not receive compensatory time in lieu of overtime compensation.

(b) REMEDY.—The remedy for a violation of subsection (a) shall be such damages, including liquidated damages, as would be appropriate if awarded under section 16(b) of the Fair Labor Standards Act of 1938.

(c) REGULATIONS TO IMPLEMENT SECTION.—

(1) IN GENERAL.—The President, or the designee of the President, shall issue regulations to implement this section.

(2) AGENCY REGULATIONS.—Except as provided in paragraph (3), the regulations issued under paragraph (1) shall be the same as substantive regulations promulgated by the Secretary of Labor to implement the statutory provisions referred to in subsections (a) and (b) except to the extent that the President or designee may determine, for good cause shown and stated together with the regulation, that a modification of such regulations would be more effective for the implementation of the rights and protections under this section.

(3) IRREGULAR WORK SCHEDULES.—The President or designee shall issue regulations for covered employees whose work schedules directly depend on the schedule of the President or the Vice President that shall be comparable to the provisions in the Fair Labor Standards Act of 1938 that apply to employees who have irregular work schedules.

(d) EFFECTIVE DATE.—Subsections (a) and (b) shall take effect on the earlier of—

(1) the effective date of regulations issued under subsection (c); or

(2) October 1, 1998.

(Added Pub. L. 104–331, § 2(a), Oct. 26, 1996, 110 Stat. 4058.)

REFERENCES IN TEXT

The Fair Labor Standards Act of 1938, referred to in subsecs. (a)(1), (b), and (c)(3), is act June 25, 1938, ch. 676, 52 Stat. 1060, as amended, which is classified generally to chapter 8 (§ 201 et seq.) of Title 29, Labor. Sections 6, 7, 12, and 16 of the Act are classified to sections 206, 207, 212, and 216, respectively, of Title 29. For complete classification of this Act to the Code, see section 201 of Title 29 and Tables.

EFFECTIVE DATE

Subsec. (c) of this section effective Oct. 26, 1996, see section 471(b) of this title.

SECTION REFERRED TO IN OTHER SECTIONS

This section is referred to in sections 401, 471 of this title.

§ 414. Rights and protections under the Employee Polygraph Protection Act of 1988

(a) POLYGRAPH PRACTICES PROHIBITED.—No employing office may require a covered employee to take a lie detector test where such a test would be prohibited if required by an employer under paragraph (1), (2), or (3) of section 3 of the Employee Polygraph Protection Act of 1988. In addition, the waiver provisions of section 6(d) of such Act shall apply to covered employees.

(b) REMEDY.—The remedy for a violation of subsection (a) shall be such damages as would be appropriate if awarded under section 6(c)(1) of the Employee Polygraph Protection Act of 1988.

(c) REGULATIONS TO IMPLEMENT SECTION.—

(1) IN GENERAL.—The President, or the designee of the President, shall issue regulations to implement this section.

(2) AGENCY REGULATIONS.—The regulations issued under paragraph (1) shall be the same as substantive regulations promulgated by the Secretary of Labor to implement the statutory provisions referred to in subsections (a) and (b) except to the extent that the President or designee may determine, for good cause shown and stated together with the regulation, that a modification of such regulations would be more effective for the implementation of the rights and protections under this section.

(d) EFFECTIVE DATE.—Subsections (a) and (b) shall take effect on the earlier of—

(1) the effective date of regulations issued under subsection (c); or

(2) October 1, 1998.

(Added Pub. L. 104–331, § 2(a), Oct. 26, 1996, 110 Stat. 4058.)

REFERENCES IN TEXT

Sections 3 and 6 of the Employee Polygraph Protection Act of 1988, referred to in subsecs. (a) and (b), are classified to sections 2002 and 2005, respectively, of Title 29, Labor.

EFFECTIVE DATE

Subsec. (c) of this section effective Oct. 26, 1996, see section 471(b) of this title.

SECTION REFERRED TO IN OTHER SECTIONS

This section is referred to in section 471 of this title.

§ 415. Rights and protections under the Worker Adjustment and Retraining Notification Act

(a) WORKER ADJUSTMENT AND RETRAINING NOTIFICATION RIGHTS.—

(1) IN GENERAL.—Except as provided in paragraph (2), no employing office shall be closed or mass layoff ordered within the meaning of section 3 of the Worker Adjustment and Retraining Notification Act until the end of a 60-day period after the employing office serves written notice of such prospective closing or layoff to representatives of covered employees or, if there are no representatives, to covered employees.

(2) EXCEPTION.—

(A) IN GENERAL.—In the event that a President (hereinafter in this paragraph referred to as the "previous President") is not elected to a successive term in office as a result of the election of a new President—

(i) no notice or waiting period shall be required under paragraph (1) with respect to the separation of any individual described in subparagraph (B), if such separation occurs pursuant to a closure or mass layoff ordered after the term of the new President commences; and

(ii) if any individual is separated from service, or begins a period of leave under the Family and Medical Leave Act of 1993, before such term commences, nothing in this chapter shall require reinstatement or restoration to employment of the individual after such term commences.

(B) DESCRIPTION OF INDIVIDUALS.—An individual described in this subparagraph is any covered employee serving pursuant to an appointment made during—

(i) the term of office of the previous President; or

(ii) any term, earlier than the term referred to in clause (i), during which such previous President served as President or Vice President.

(b) REMEDY.—The remedy for a violation of subsection (a) shall be such damages as would be appropriate if awarded under paragraphs (1), (2), and (4) of section 5(a) of the Worker Adjustment and Retraining Notification Act.

(c) REGULATIONS TO IMPLEMENT SECTION.—

(1) IN GENERAL.—The President, or the designee of the President, shall issue regulations to implement this section.

(2) AGENCY REGULATIONS.—The regulations issued under paragraph (1) shall be the same as substantive regulations promulgated by the Secretary of Labor to implement the statutory provisions referred to in subsections (a) and (b) except to the extent that the President or designee may determine, for good cause shown and stated together with the regulation, that a modification of such regulations would be more effective for the implementation of the rights and protections under this section.

(d) EFFECTIVE DATE.—Subsections (a) and (b) shall take effect on the earlier of—

(1) the effective date of regulations issued under subsection (c); or

(2) October 1, 1998.

(Added Pub. L. 104–331, § 2(a), Oct. 26, 1996, 110 Stat. 4059.)

REFERENCES IN TEXT

Sections 3 and 5 of the Worker Adjustment and Retraining Notification Act, referred to in subsecs. (a)(1) and (b), are classified to sections 2102 and 2104, respectively, of Title 29, Labor.

The Family and Medical Leave Act of 1993, referred to in subsec. (a)(2)(A)(ii), is Pub. L. 103–3, Feb. 5, 1993, 107 Stat. 6, as amended, which enacted sections 60m and 60n of Title 2, The Congress, sections 6381 to 6387 of Title 5, Government Organization and Employees, and chapter 28 (§ 2601 et seq.) of Title 29, amended section 2105 of Title 5, and enacted provisions set out as notes under section 2601 of Title 29. For complete classification of this Act to the Code, see Short Title note set out under section 2601 of Title 29 and Tables.

EFFECTIVE DATE

Subsec. (c) of this section effective Oct. 26, 1996, see section 471(b) of this title.

SECTION REFERRED TO IN OTHER SECTIONS

This section is referred to in section 471 of this title.

§ 416. Rights and protections relating to veterans' employment and reemployment

(a) EMPLOYMENT AND REEMPLOYMENT RIGHTS OF MEMBERS OF THE UNIFORMED SERVICES.—

(1) IN GENERAL.—It shall be unlawful for an employing office to—

(A) discriminate, within the meaning of subsections (a) and (b) of section 4311 of title 38, against an eligible employee;

(B) deny to an eligible employee reemployment rights within the meaning of sections 4312 and 4313 of title 38; or

(C) deny to an eligible employee benefits within the meaning of sections 4316, 4317, and 4318 of title 38.

(2) DEFINITION.—For purposes of this section, the term "eligible employee" means a covered employee performing service in the uniformed services, within the meaning of section 4303(13) of title 38, whose service has not been terminated upon the occurrence of any of the events enumerated in section 4304 of such title.

(b) REMEDY.—The remedy for a violation of subsection (a) shall be such damages as would be appropriate if awarded under paragraphs (1) and (2)(A) of section 4323(c) of title 38.

(c) REGULATIONS TO IMPLEMENT SECTION.—

(1) IN GENERAL.—The President, or the designee of the President, shall issue regulations to implement this section.

(2) AGENCY REGULATIONS.—The regulations issued under paragraph (1) shall be the same as substantive regulations promulgated by the Secretary of Labor to implement the statutory provisions referred to in subsections (a) and (b)—

(A) except to the extent that the President or designee may determine, for good cause shown and stated together with the regulation, that a modification of such regulations would be more effective for the implementation of the rights and protections under this section; and

(B) except that the President or designee may, at the discretion of the President or designee, issue regulations to implement a provision of section 4314 or 4324 of title 38, United States Code, that applies to employees in the executive branch of the Federal Government in lieu of an analogous statutory provision referred to in subsection (a) or (b), if the issuance of such regulations—

(i) would be equally effective for the implementation of the rights and protections under this section; and

(ii) would promote uniformity in the application of Federal law to employees in the executive branch of the Federal Government.

(d) EFFECTIVE DATE.—Subsections (a) and (b) shall take effect on the earlier of—

(1) the effective date of regulations issued under subsection (c); or

(2) October 1, 1998.

(Added Pub. L. 104–331, § 2(a), Oct. 26, 1996, 110 Stat. 4060.)

EFFECTIVE DATE

Subsec. (c) of this section effective Oct. 26, 1996, see section 471(b) of this title.

SECTION REFERRED TO IN OTHER SECTIONS

This section is referred to in sections 401, 435, 471 of this title.

§ 417. Prohibition of intimidation or reprisal

(a) IN GENERAL.—It shall be unlawful for an employing office to intimidate, take reprisal against, or otherwise discriminate against, any covered employee because the covered employee has opposed any practice made unlawful by this chapter, or because the covered employee has initiated proceedings, made a charge, or testified, assisted, or participated in any manner in a hearing or other proceeding under this chapter.

(b) REMEDY.—A violation of subsection (a) may be remedied by any legal remedy available to redress the practice opposed by the covered employee or other violation of law as to which the covered employee initiated proceedings, made a charge, or engaged in other conduct protected under subsection (a).

(Added Pub. L. 104–331, §2(a), Oct. 26, 1996, 110 Stat. 4061.)

SECTION REFERRED TO IN OTHER SECTIONS

This section is referred to in sections 411, 454 of this title.

PART B—PUBLIC ACCESS PROVISIONS UNDER THE AMERICANS WITH DISABILITIES ACT OF 1990

§ 421. Rights and protections under the Americans with Disabilities Act of 1990

(a) RIGHTS AND PROTECTIONS.—The rights and protections against discrimination in the provision of public services and accommodations established by sections 201, 202, and 204, and sections 302, 303, and 309, of the Americans with Disabilities Act of 1990 shall apply, to the extent that public services, programs, or activities are provided, with respect to the White House and its appurtenant grounds and gardens, the Dwight D. Eisenhower Executive Office Building, the New Executive Office Buildings, and any other facility to the extent that offices are provided for employees of the Executive Office of the President.

(b) REMEDY.—The remedy for a violation of subsection (a) shall be such remedy as would be appropriate if awarded under section 203 or 308 of the Americans with Disabilities Act of 1990, as the case may be, except that, with respect to any claim of employment discrimination, the exclusive remedy shall be under section 411 of this title. A remedy under the preceding sentence shall be enforced in accordance with applicable provisions of such section 203 or 308, as the case may be.

(c) DEFINITION.—For purposes of the application under this section of the Americans with Disabilities Act of 1990, the term "public entity" as used in such Act, means, to the extent that public services, programs, or activities are provided, the White House and its appurtenant grounds and gardens, the Dwight D. Eisenhower Executive Office Building, the New Executive Office Buildings, and any other facility to the extent that offices are provided for employees of the Executive Office of the President.

(d) REGULATIONS TO IMPLEMENT SECTION.—

(1) IN GENERAL.—The President, or the designee of the President, shall issue regulations to implement this section.

(2) AGENCY REGULATIONS.—The regulations issued under paragraph (1) shall be the same as substantive regulations promulgated by the appropriate officer of an executive agency to implement the statutory provisions referred to in subsections (a) and (b)—

(A) except to the extent that the President or designee may determine, for good cause shown and stated together with the regulation, that a modification of such regulations would be more effective for the implementation of the rights and protections under this section; and

(B) except that the President or designee may, at the discretion of the President or designee, issue regulations to implement a provision of section 1, 2, 3, or 6 of the Act entitled "An Act to insure that certain buildings financed with Federal funds are so designed and constructed as to be accessible to the physically handicapped", approved August 12, 1968 (commonly known as the "Architectural Barriers Act of 1968") or section 501 of the Rehabilitation Act of 1973 that applies to agencies of the executive branch of the Federal Government in lieu of an analogous statutory provision referred to in subsection (a) or (b), if the issuance of such regulations—

(i) would be equally effective for the implementation of the rights and protections under this section; and

(ii) would promote uniformity in the application of Federal law to agencies of the executive branch of the Federal Government.

(e) EFFECTIVE DATE.—Subsections (a), (b), and (c) shall take effect on the earlier of—

(1) the effective date of regulations issued under subsection (d); or

(2) October 1, 1998.

(Added Pub. L. 104–331, §2(a), Oct. 26, 1996, 110 Stat. 4061; amended Pub. L. 106–92, §2, Nov. 9, 1999, 113 Stat. 1309.)

REFERENCES IN TEXT

The Americans with Disabilities Act of 1990, referred to in subsecs. (a) to (c), is Pub. L. 101–336, July 26, 1990, 104 Stat. 327, as amended, which is classified principally to chapter 126 (§12101 et seq.) of Title 42, The Public Health and Welfare. Sections 201 to 204, 302, 303, 308, and 309 of the Act are classified to sections 12131 to 12134, 12182, 12183, 12188, and 12189, respectively, of Title 42. For complete classification of this Act to the Code, see Short Title note set out under section 12101 of Title 42 and Tables.

Sections 1, 2, 3, and 6 of the Act of August 12, 1968, commonly known as the Architectural Barriers Act of 1968, referred to in subsec. (d)(2)(B), are classified to sections 4151 to 4153 and 4156, respectively, of Title 42.

Section 501 of the Rehabilitation Act of 1973, referred to in subsec. (d)(2)(B), is classified to section 791 of Title 29, Labor.

AMENDMENTS

1999—Subsecs. (a), (c). Pub. L. 106–92 substituted "Dwight D. Eisenhower Executive Office Building" for "Old Executive Office Building".

EFFECTIVE DATE

Subsec. (d) of this section effective Oct. 26, 1996, see section 471(b) of this title.

SECTION REFERRED TO IN OTHER SECTIONS

This section is referred to in sections 435, 471 of this title; title 28 section 3905.

PART C—OCCUPATIONAL SAFETY AND HEALTH ACT OF 1970

PART REFERRED TO IN OTHER SECTIONS

This part is referred to in title 28 section 1296.

§ 425. Rights and protections under the Occupational Safety and Health Act of 1970; procedures for remedy of violations

(a) OCCUPATIONAL SAFETY AND HEALTH PROTECTIONS.—

(1) IN GENERAL.—Each employing office and each covered employee shall comply with the provisions of section 5 of the Occupational Safety and Health Act of 1970.

(2) DEFINITIONS.—For purposes of the application under this section of the Occupational Safety and Health Act of 1970—

(A) the term "employer" as used in such Act means an employing office; and

(B) the term "employee" as used in such Act means a covered employee.

(b) REMEDY.—The remedy for a violation of subsection (a) shall be an order to correct the violation, including such order as would be appropriate if issued under section 13(a) of the Occupational Safety and Health Act of 1970.

(c) PROCEDURES.—

(1) REQUESTS FOR INSPECTIONS.—Upon written request of any employing office or covered employee, the Secretary of Labor shall have the authority to inspect and investigate places of employment under the jurisdiction of employing offices in accordance with subsections (a), (d), (e), and (f) of section 8 of the Occupational Safety and Health Act of 1970.

(2) CITATIONS, NOTICES, AND NOTIFICATIONS.—The Secretary of Labor shall have the authority, in accordance with sections 9 and 10 of the Occupational Safety and Health Act of 1970, to issue—

(A) a citation or notice to any employing office responsible for correcting a violation of subsection (a); or

(B) a notification to any employing office that the Secretary of Labor believes has failed to correct a violation for which a citation has been issued within the period permitted for its correction.

(3) HEARINGS AND REVIEW.—If after issuing a citation or notification, the Secretary of Labor determines that a violation has not been corrected—

(A) the citation and notification shall be deemed a final order (within the meaning of section 10(b) of the Occupational Safety and Health Act of 1970) if the employer fails to notify the Secretary of Labor within 15 days (excluding Saturdays, Sundays, and Federal holidays) after receipt of the notice that the employer intends to contest the citation or notification; or

(B) opportunity for a hearing before the Occupational Safety and Health Review Commission shall be afforded in accordance with section 10(c) of the Occupational Safety

and Health Act of 1970, if the employer gives timely notice to the Secretary that he intends to contest the citation or notification.

(4) VARIANCE PROCEDURES.—An employing office may request from the Secretary of Labor an order granting a variance from a standard made applicable by this section, in accordance with sections 6(b)(6) and 6(d) of the Occupational Safety and Health Act of 1970.

(5) JUDICIAL REVIEW.—Any person or employing office aggrieved by a final decision of the Occupational Safety and Health Review Commission under paragraph (3) or the Secretary of Labor under paragraph (4) may file a petition for review with the United States Court of Appeals for the Federal Circuit under section 1296 of title 28.

(6) COMPLIANCE DATE.—If new appropriated funds are necessary to correct a violation of subsection (a) for which a citation is issued, or to comply with an order requiring correction of such a violation, correction or compliance shall take place as soon as possible, but not later than the end of the fiscal year following the fiscal year in which the citation is issued or the order requiring correction becomes final and not subject to further review.

(d) REGULATIONS TO IMPLEMENT SECTION.—

(1) IN GENERAL.—The President, or the designee of the President, shall issue regulations to implement this section.

(2) AGENCY REGULATIONS.—The regulations issued under paragraph (1) shall be the same as substantive regulations promulgated by the Secretary of Labor to implement the statutory provisions referred to in subsections (a) and (b)—

(A) except to the extent that the President or designee may determine, for good cause shown and stated together with the regulation, that a modification of such regulations would be more effective for the implementation of the rights and protections under this section; and

(B) except that the President or designee may, at the discretion of the President or designee, issue regulations to implement a provision of section 19 of the Occupational Safety and Health Act of 1970 that applies to agencies or employees of the executive branch of the Federal Government in lieu of an analogous statutory provision referred to in subsection (a) or (b), if the issuance of such regulations—

(i) would be equally effective for the implementation of the rights and protections under this section; and

(ii) would promote uniformity in the application of Federal law to employees in the executive branch of the Federal Government.

(3) EMPLOYING OFFICE RESPONSIBLE FOR CORRECTION.—The regulations issued under paragraph (1) shall include a method of identifying, for purposes of this section and for different categories of violations of subsection (a), the employing office responsible for correction of a particular violation.

(e) EFFECTIVE DATE.—Subsections (a) through (c) shall take effect on the earlier of—

(1) the effective date of regulations issued under subsection (d); or

(2) October 1, 1998.

(Added Pub. L. 104–331, § 2(a), Oct. 26, 1996, 110 Stat. 4062.)

REFERENCES IN TEXT

The Occupational Safety and Health Act of 1970, referred to in subsecs. (a) to (c)(4) and (d)(2)(B), is Pub. L. 91–596, Dec. 29, 1970, 84 Stat. 1590, as amended, which is classified principally to chapter 15 (§ 651 et seq.) of Title 29, Labor. Sections 5, 6, 8 to 10, 13, and 19 of the Act are classified to sections 654, 655, 657 to 659, 662, and 668, respectively, of Title 29. For complete classification of this Act to the Code, see Short Title note set out under section 651 of Title 29 and Tables.

EFFECTIVE DATE

Subsec. (d) of this section effective Oct. 26, 1996, see section 471(b) of this title.

SECTION REFERRED TO IN OTHER SECTIONS

This section is referred to in section 471 of this title.

PART D—LABOR-MANAGEMENT RELATIONS

PART REFERRED TO IN OTHER SECTIONS

This part is referred to in title 28 section 1296.

§ 431. Application of chapter 71 of title 5, relating to Federal service labor-management relations; procedures for remedy of violations

(a) LABOR-MANAGEMENT RIGHTS.—Subject to subsection (d), chapter 71 of title 5 shall apply to employing offices and to covered employees and representatives of those employees, except that covered employees shall not have a right to reinstatement pursuant to section 7118(a)(7)(C) or 7123 of title 5.

(b) DEFINITION.—For purposes of the application under this section of chapter 71 of title 5, the term "agency" as used in such chapter means an employing office.

(c) REGULATIONS TO IMPLEMENT SECTION.—

(1) IN GENERAL.—The Federal Labor Relations Authority shall issue regulations to implement this section.

(2) AGENCY REGULATIONS.—Except as provided in subsection (d), the regulations issued under paragraph (1) shall be the same as substantive regulations promulgated by the Authority to implement the statutory provisions referred to in subsection (a), except—

(A) to the extent the Authority may determine, for good cause shown and stated together with the regulation, that a modification of such regulations would be more effective for the implementation of the rights and protections under this section; or

(B) as the Authority may determine that a modification of such regulations is necessary to avoid a conflict of interest or appearance of a conflict of interest.

(d) SPECIFIC REGULATIONS REGARDING APPLICATIONS TO CERTAIN EMPLOYING OFFICES.—

(1) REGULATIONS REQUIRED.—The Authority shall issue regulations on the manner and the extent to which the requirements and exemptions of chapter 71 of title 5 should apply to covered employees who are employed in the offices listed in paragraph (2). The regulations shall, to the greatest extent practicable, be consistent with the provisions and purposes of chapter 71 of title 5 and of this chapter, and shall be the same as the substantive regulations issued by the Authority under such chapter, except—

(A) to the extent the Authority may determine, for good cause shown and stated together with the regulation, that a modification of such regulations would be more effective for the implementation of the rights and protections under this section; and

(B) that the Authority shall exclude from coverage under this section any covered employees who are employed in offices listed in paragraph (2) if the Authority determines that such exclusion is required because of—

(i) a conflict of interest or appearance of a conflict of interest; or

(ii) the President's or Vice President's constitutional responsibilities.

(2) OFFICES REFERRED TO.—The offices referred to in paragraph (1) include—

(A) the White House Office;

(B) the Executive Residence at the White House;

(C) the Office of the Vice President;

(D) the Office of Policy Development;

(E) the Council of Economic Advisers;

(F) the National Security Council;

(G) the Office of Management and Budget; and

(H) the Office of National Drug Control Policy.

(e) EFFECTIVE DATE.—

(1) IN GENERAL.—Except as provided in paragraph (2), subsections (a) and (b) shall take effect on the earlier of—

(A) the effective date of regulations issued under subsection (c); or

(B) October 1, 1998.

(2) CERTAIN EMPLOYING OFFICES.—Subsections (a) and (b) shall take effect, with respect to employing offices, and employees of employing offices, referred to in subsection (d)(2), on the earlier of—

(A) the effective date of regulations issued under subsection (d); or

(B) October 1, 1998.

(Added Pub. L. 104–331, § 2(a), Oct. 26, 1996, 110 Stat. 4064.)

EFFECTIVE DATE

Subsecs. (c) and (d) of this section effective Oct. 26, 1996, see section 471(b) of this title.

SECTION REFERRED TO IN OTHER SECTIONS

This section is referred to in section 471 of this title.

PART E—GENERAL

§ 435. Generally applicable remedies and limitations

(a) ATTORNEY'S FEES.—If a covered employee, with respect to any claim under this chapter, or a qualified person with a disability, with respect to any claim under section 421, is a prevailing party in any proceeding under section 453(1), the administrative agency may award attorney's fees, expert fees, and any other costs as would be appropriate if awarded under section 706(k) of the Civil Rights Act of 1964.

(b) INTEREST.—In any proceeding under section 453(1), the same interest to compensate for delay in payment shall be made available as would be appropriate if awarded under section 717(d) of the Civil Rights Act of 1964.

(c) CIVIL PENALTIES AND PUNITIVE DAMAGES.—Except as otherwise provided in this chapter, no civil penalty or punitive damages may be awarded with respect to any claim under this chapter.

(d) EXCLUSIVE PROCEDURE.—

(1) IN GENERAL.—Except as provided in paragraph (2), no person may commence an administrative or judicial proceeding to seek a remedy for the rights and protections afforded by this chapter except as provided in this chapter and in sections 1296 and 1346(g) and chapter 179 of title 28.

(2) VETERANS.—A covered employee under section 416 may also utilize any provisions of chapter 43 of title 38 that are applicable to that employee.

(e) SCOPE OF REMEDY.—Only a covered employee who has undertaken and completed the procedures described in section 452 may be granted a remedy under part A of this subchapter.

(f) CONSTRUCTION.—

(1) DEFINITIONS AND EXEMPTIONS.—Except where inconsistent with definitions and exemptions provided in this chapter, the definitions and exemptions in the laws made applicable by this chapter shall apply under this chapter.

(2) SIZE LIMITATIONS.—Notwithstanding paragraph (1), provisions in the laws made applicable under this chapter (other than paragraphs (2) and (3) of section 2(a) of the Worker Adjustment and Retraining Notification Act) determining coverage based on size, whether expressed in terms of numbers of employees, amount of business transacted, or other measure, shall not apply in determining coverage under this chapter.

(g) POLITICAL AFFILIATION.—It shall not be a violation of any provision of this chapter to consider, or make any employment decision based on, the party affiliation, or political compatibility with the employing office, of an employee who is a covered employee.

(Added Pub. L. 104–331, § 2(a), Oct. 26, 1996, 110 Stat. 4066.)

REFERENCES IN TEXT

Sections 706 and 717 of the Civil Rights Act of 1964, referred to in subsecs. (a) and (b), are classified to sections 2000e–5 and 2000e–16, respectively, of Title 42, The Public Health and Welfare.

Section 2 of the Worker Adjustment and Retraining Notification Act, referred to in subsec. (f)(2), is classified to section 2101 of Title 29, Labor.

SUBCHAPTER III—ADMINISTRATIVE AND JUDICIAL DISPUTE RESOLUTION PROCEDURES

§ 451. Procedure for consideration of alleged violations

The procedure for consideration of alleged violations of part A of subchapter II consists of—

(1) counseling and mediation as provided in section 452; and

(2) election, as provided in section 453, of either—

(A) an administrative proceeding as provided in section 453(1) and judicial review as provided in section 1296 of title 28; or

(B) a civil action in a district court of the United States as provided in section 1346(g) of title 28.

(Added Pub. L. 104–331, § 2(a), Oct. 26, 1996, 110 Stat. 4067.)

§ 452. Counseling and mediation

(a) IN GENERAL.—The President, or the designee of the President, shall by regulation establish procedures substantially similar to those under sections 402 and 403 of the Congressional Accountability Act of 1995 for the counseling and mediation of alleged violations of a law made applicable under part A of subchapter II.

(b) EXHAUSTION REQUIREMENT.—A covered employee who has not exhausted counseling and mediation under subsection (a) shall be ineligible to make any election under section 453 or otherwise pursue any further form of relief under this subchapter.

(Added Pub. L. 104–331, § 2(a), Oct. 26, 1996, 110 Stat. 4067.)

REFERENCES IN TEXT

Sections 402 and 403 of the Congressional Accountability Act of 1995, referred to in subsec. (a), are classified to sections 1402 and 1403, respectively, of Title 2, The Congress.

EFFECTIVE DATE

Section effective Oct. 1, 1997, except that subsec. (a) of this section effective Oct. 26, 1996, see section 471 of this title.

SECTION REFERRED TO IN OTHER SECTIONS

This section is referred to in sections 435, 451, 456, 471 of this title.

§ 453. Election of proceeding

Not later than 90 days after a covered employee receives notice of the end of the period of mediation, but no sooner than 30 days after receipt of such notification, such covered employee may either—

(1) file a complaint with the appropriate agency, as determined under section 454; or

(2) file a civil action under section 1346(g) of title 28.

(Added Pub. L. 104–331, § 2(a), Oct. 26, 1996, 110 Stat. 4067.)

SECTION REFERRED TO IN OTHER SECTIONS

This section is referred to in sections 435, 451, 452, 455 of this title; title 28 section 1346.

§ 454. Appropriate agencies

(a) IN GENERAL.—Except as provided in subsection (b), the appropriate agency under this section with respect to an alleged violation of part A of subchapter II shall be the Board. The complaint in an action involving such an alleged violation shall be processed under the procedures specified by the President, or the designee of the President, in such regulations as the President or designee may issue.

(b) EXCEPTIONS.—

(1) DISCRIMINATION.—For purposes of any action arising under section 411 (or any action alleging intimidation, reprisal, or discrimination under section 417 relating to any practice made unlawful under section 411), the appropriate agency shall be the Equal Employment Opportunity Commission, and the complaint in any such action shall be processed under the same administrative procedures as any such complaint filed by any employee in the executive branch of the Federal Government (other than a covered employee).

(2) MIXED CASES.—In the case of any covered employee (within the meaning of section 411) who has been affected by an action which an employee of an executive agency may appeal to the Board and who alleges that a basis for the action was discrimination prohibited by section 411 (or any action alleging intimidation, reprisal, or discrimination under section 417 relating to any practice made unlawful under section 411), the initial appropriate agency shall be the Board, and such matter shall thereafter be processed in accordance with section 7702(a)–(d) (disregarding paragraph (2) of such subsection (a)) and (f) of title 5.

(3) JUDICIAL REVIEW.—Notwithstanding any other provision of law (including any provision of law referenced in paragraph (1) or (2)), judicial review of any administrative decision under this subsection shall be by appeal to the United States Court of Appeals for the Federal Circuit under section 1296 of title 28.

(Added Pub. L. 104–331, § 2(a), Oct. 26, 1996, 110 Stat. 4067.)

EFFECTIVE DATE

Section effective Oct. 1, 1997, except that subsec. (a) of this section effective Oct. 26, 1996, see section 471 of this title.

SECTION REFERRED TO IN OTHER SECTIONS

This section is referred to in sections 453, 471 of this title; title 28 section 1296.

§ 455. Effect of failure to issue regulations

In any proceeding under section 453(1), if the President, or the designee of the President, has not issued a regulation on a matter for which this chapter requires a regulation to be issued, the administrative agency shall apply, to the extent necessary and appropriate, the most relevant substantive executive agency regulation promulgated to implement the statutory provision at issue in the proceeding.

(Added Pub. L. 104–331, § 2(a), Oct. 26, 1996, 110 Stat. 4068.)

§ 456. Confidentiality

(a) COUNSELING.—All counseling under section 452 shall be strictly confidential, except that, with the consent of the covered employee, the employing office may be notified.

(b) MEDIATION.—All mediation under section 452 shall be strictly confidential.

(Added Pub. L. 104–331, § 2(a), Oct. 26, 1996, 110 Stat. 4068.)

SUBCHAPTER IV—EFFECTIVE DATE

§ 471. Effective date

(a) IN GENERAL.—Except as otherwise provided in this chapter, this chapter shall take effect on October 1, 1997.

(b) REGULATIONS.—Sections 411(d), 412(c), 413(c), 414(c), 415(c), 416(c), 421(d), 425(d), 431(c), 431(d), 452(a), and 454(a) shall take effect on the date of enactment of this Act.[1]

(Added Pub. L. 104–331, § 2(a), Oct. 26, 1996, 110 Stat. 4068.)

REFERENCES IN TEXT

The date of enactment of this Act, referred to in subsec. (b), probably means the date of enactment of Pub. L. 104–331, which enacted this chapter and was approved Oct. 26, 1996.

---

[1] See References in Text note below.

TITLE 4—FLAG AND SEAL, SEAT OF GOVERNMENT, AND THE STATES

This title was enacted by act July 30, 1947, ch. 389, § 1, 61 Stat. 641

AMENDMENTS

1951—Act Oct. 31, 1951, ch. 655, §11, 65 Stat. 713, added item for chapter 5.

POSITIVE LAW; CITATION

This title has been made positive law by section 1 of act July 30, 1947, ch. 389, 61 Stat. 641, which provided in part that: "title 4 of the United States Code, entitled 'Flag and seal, Seat of Government, and the States', is codified and enacted into positive law and may be cited as '4 U. S. C., §—'".

REPEALS

Section 2 of act July 30, 1947, provided that the sections or parts thereof of the Statutes at Large or the Revised Statutes covering provisions codified in this Act are repealed insofar as the provisions appeared in former Title 4, and provided that any rights or liabilities now existing under the repealed sections or parts thereof shall not be affected by the repeal.

TABLE SHOWING DISPOSITION OF ALL SECTIONS OF FORMER TITLE 4

Title 4 Former Sections	Revised Statutes Statutes at Large	Title 4 New Sections
1	R.S. §§1791, 1792	1
2	R.S. §1792	2
3	Feb. 8, 1917, ch. 34, 39 Stat. 900	3
4	R.S. §1793	41
5	R.S. §§203 (first clause), 1794	42
6	R.S. §1795	71
7	R.S. §1796	72
8	R.S. §4798	73
9	R.S. §1836	101
10	R.S. §1837	102
11	R.S. §1838	103
12	June 16, 1936, ch. 582, §10, 49 Stat. 1521 ...... Oct. 9, 1940, ch. 787, 54 Stat. 1060.	104
13	Oct. 9, 1940, ch. 787, §1, 54 Stat. 1059	105
14	Oct. 9, 1940, ch. 787, §2, 54 Stat. 1060	106
15	Oct. 9, 1940, ch. 787, §3, 54 Stat. 1060	107
16	Oct. 9, 1940, ch. 787, §4, 54 Stat. 1060	108
17	Oct. 9, 1940, ch. 787, §5, 54 Stat. 1060	109
18	Oct. 9, 1940, ch. 787, §6, 54 Stat. 1060	110

CHAPTER 1—THE FLAG

AMENDMENTS

1998—Pub. L. 105–225, §2(b), Aug. 12, 1998, 112 Stat. 1498, added items 4 to 10.

§ 1. Flag; stripes and stars on

The flag of the United States shall be thirteen horizontal stripes, alternate red and white; and the union of the flag shall be forty-eight stars, white in a blue field.

(July 30, 1947, ch. 389, 61 Stat. 642.)

SHORT TITLE OF 2000 AMENDMENT

Pub. L. 106–252, §1, July 28, 2000, 114 Stat. 626, provided that: "This Act [enacting sections 116 to 126 of this title and provisions set out as a note under section 116 of this title] may be cited as the 'Mobile Telecommunications Sourcing Act'."

EXECUTIVE ORDER NO. 10798

Ex. Ord. No. 10798, Jan. 3, 1959, 24 F.R. 79, which prescribed proportions and sizes of flags until July 4, 1960, was revoked by section 33 of Ex. Ord. No. 10834, set out as a note under this section.

EX. ORD. NO. 10834. PROPORTIONS AND SIZES OF FLAGS AND POSITION OF STARS

Ex. Ord. No. 10834, Aug. 21, 1959, 24 F.R. 6865, provided:

WHEREAS the State of Hawaii has this day been admitted into the Union; and

WHEREAS section 2 of title 4 of the United States Code provides as follows: "On the admission of a new State into the Union one star shall be added to the union of the flag; and such addition shall take effect on the fourth day of July then next succeeding such admission."; and

WHEREAS the Federal Property and Administrative Services Act of 1949 (63 Stat. 377), as amended [see Short Title note under section 471 of Title 40, Public Buildings, Property, and Works] authorizes the President to prescribe policies and directives governing the procurement and utilization of property by executive agencies; and

WHEREAS the interests of the Government require that orderly and reasonable provision be made for various matters pertaining to the flag and that appropriate regulations governing the procurement and utilization of national flags and union jacks by executive agencies be prescribed:

NOW, THEREFORE, by virtue of the authority vested in me as President of the United States and as Commander in Chief of the armed forces of the United States, and the Federal Property and Administrative Services Act of 1949, as amended [see Short Title note under section 471 of Title 40, Public Buildings, Property, and Works], it is hereby ordered as follows:

PART I—DESIGN OF THE FLAG

SECTION 1. The flag of the United States shall have thirteen horizontal stripes, alternate red and white, and a union consisting of white stars on a field of blue.

SEC. 2. The positions of the stars in the union of the flag and in the union jack shall be as indicated on the attachment to this order, which is hereby made a part of this order.

SEC. 3. The dimensions of the constituent parts of the flag shall conform to the proportions set forth in the attachment referred to in section 2 of this order.

PART II—REGULATIONS GOVERNING EXECUTIVE AGENCIES

SEC. 21. The following sizes of flags are authorized for executive agencies:

Size	Dimensions of Flag	
	Hoist (width)	Fly (length)
	Feet	Feet
(1)	20.00	38.00
(2)	10.00	19.00
(3)	8.95	17.00
(4)	7.00	11.00
(5)	5.00	9.50
(6)	4.33	5.50
(7)	3.50	6.65
(8)	3.00	4.00
(9)	3.00	5.70
(10)	2.37	4.50
(11)	1.32	2.50

SEC. 22. Flags manufactured or purchased for the use of executive agencies:

(a) Shall conform to the provisions of Part I of this order, except as may be otherwise authorized pursuant to the provisions of section 24, or except as otherwise authorized by the provisions of section 21, of this order.

(b) Shall conform to the provisions of section 21 of this order, except as may be otherwise authorized pursuant to the provisions of section 24 of this order.

SEC. 23. The exterior dimensions of each union jack manufactured or purchased for executive agencies shall equal the respective exterior dimensions of the union of a flag of a size authorized by or pursuant to this order. The size of the union jack flown with the national flag shall be the same as the size of the union of that national flag.

SEC. 24. (a) The Secretary of Defense in respect of procurement for the Department of Defense (including military colors) and the Administrator of General Services in respect of procurement for executive agencies other than the Department of Defense may, for cause which the Secretary or the Administrator, as the case may be, deems sufficient, make necessary minor adjustments in one or more of the dimensions or proportionate dimensions prescribed by this order, or authorize proportions or sizes other than those prescribed by section 3 or section 21 of this order.

(b) So far as practicable, (1) the actions of the Secretary of Defense under the provisions of section 24(a) of this order, as they relate to the various organizational elements of the Department of Defense, shall be coordinated, and (2) the Secretary and the Administrator shall mutually coordinate their actions under that section.

SEC. 25. Subject to such limited exceptions as the Secretary of Defense in respect of the Department of Defense, and the Administrator of General Services in respect of executive agencies other than the Department of Defense, may approve, all national flags and union jacks now in the possession of executive agencies, or hereafter acquired by executive agencies under contracts awarded prior to the date of this order, including those so possessed or so acquired by the General Services Administration, for distribution to other agencies, shall be utilized until unserviceable.

PART III—GENERAL PROVISIONS

SEC. 31. The flag prescribed by Executive Order No. 10798 of January 3, 1959, shall be the official flag of the United States until July 4, 1960, and on that date the flag prescribed by Part I of this order shall become the official flag of the United States; but this section shall neither derogate from section 24 or section 25 of this order nor preclude the procurement, for executive agencies, of flags provided for by or pursuant to this order at any time after the date of this order.

SEC. 32. As used in this order, the term "executive agencies" means the executive departments and independent establishments in the executive branch of the Government, including wholly-owned Government corporations.

SEC. 33. Executive Order No. 10798 of January 3, 1959, is hereby revoked.

DWIGHT D. EISENHOWER.

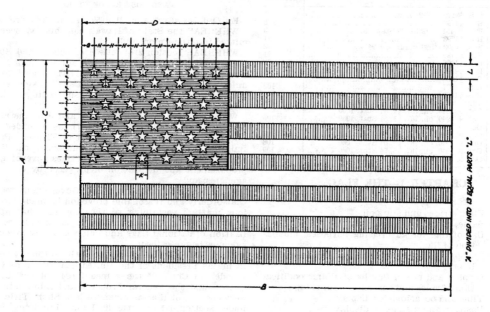

Standard proportions

Hoist (width) of flag 1.0	Fly (length) of flag 1.9	Hoist (width) of Union 0.5385 (⁷⁄₁₃)	Fly (length) of Union 0.76	0.054	0.054	0.063	0.063	Diameter of star 0.0616	Width of stripe 0.0769 (¹⁄₁₃)
A	B	C	D	E	F	G	H	K	L

SECTION REFERRED TO IN OTHER SECTIONS

This section is referred to in section 5 of this title.

§ 2. Same; additional stars

On the admission of a new State into the Union one star shall be added to the union of the flag; and such addition shall take effect on the fourth day of July then next succeeding such admission.

(July 30, 1947, ch. 389, 61 Stat. 642.)

SECTION REFERRED TO IN OTHER SECTIONS

This section is referred to in section 5 of this title.

§ 3. Use of flag for advertising purposes; mutilation of flag

Any person who, within the District of Columbia, in any manner, for exhibition or display, shall place or cause to be placed any word, figure, mark, picture, design, drawing, or any advertisement of any nature upon any flag, standard, colors, or ensign of the United States of America; or shall expose or cause to be exposed to public view any such flag, standard, colors, or ensign upon which shall have been printed, painted, or otherwise placed, or to which shall be attached, appended, affixed, or annexed any word, figure, mark, picture, design, or drawing, or any advertisement of any nature; or who, within the District of Columbia, shall manufacture, sell, expose for sale, or to public view, or give away or have in possession for sale, or to be given away or for use for any purpose, any article or substance being an article of merchandise, or a receptacle for merchandise or article or thing for carrying or transporting merchandise, upon which shall have been printed, painted, attached, or otherwise placed a representation of any such flag, standard, colors, or ensign, to advertise, call attention to, decorate, mark, or distinguish the article or substance on which so placed shall be deemed guilty of a misdemeanor and shall be punished by a fine not exceeding $100 or by imprisonment for not more than thirty days, or both, in the discretion of the court. The words "flag, standard, colors, or ensign", as used herein, shall include any flag, standard, colors, ensign, or any picture or representation of either, or of any part or parts of either, made of any substance or represented on any substance, of any size evidently purporting to be either of said flag, standard, colors, or ensign of the United States of America or a picture or a representation of either, upon which shall be shown the colors, the stars and the stripes, in any number of either thereof, or of any part or parts of either, by which the average person seeing the same without deliberation may believe the same to represent the flag, colors, standard, or ensign of the United States of America.

(July 30, 1947, ch. 389, 61 Stat. 642; Pub. L. 90–381, §3, July 5, 1968, 82 Stat. 291.)

AMENDMENTS

1968—Pub. L. 90–381 struck out "; or who, within the District of Columbia, shall publicly mutilate, deface, defile or defy, trample upon, or cast contempt, either by word or act, upon any such flag, standard, colors, or ensign," after "substance on which so placed".

§ 4. Pledge of allegiance to the flag; manner of delivery

The Pledge of Allegiance to the Flag, "I pledge allegiance to the Flag of the United States of America, and to the Republic for which it stands, one Nation under God, indivisible, with liberty and justice for all.", should be rendered by standing at attention facing the flag with the right hand over the heart. When not in uniform men should remove their headdress with their right hand and hold it at the left shoulder, the hand being over the heart. Persons in uniform should remain silent, face the flag, and render the military salute.

(Added Pub. L. 105–225, §2(a), Aug. 12, 1998, 112 Stat. 1494.)

HISTORICAL AND REVISION NOTES

Revised Section	Source (U.S. Code)	Source (Statutes at Large)
4	36:172.	June 22, 1942, ch. 435, §7, 56 Stat. 380; Dec. 22, 1942, ch. 806, §7, 56 Stat. 1077; Dec. 28, 1945, ch. 607, 59 Stat. 668; June 14, 1954, ch. 297, 68 Stat. 249; July 7, 1976, Pub. L. 94–344, (19), 90 Stat. 813.

§ 5. Display and use of flag by civilians; codification of rules and customs; definition

The following codification of existing rules and customs pertaining to the display and use of the flag of the United States of America is established for the use of such civilians or civilian groups or organizations as may not be required to conform with regulations promulgated by one or more executive departments of the Government of the United States. The flag of the United States for the purpose of this chapter shall be defined according to sections 1 and 2 of this title and Executive Order 10834 issued pursuant thereto.

(Added Pub. L. 105–225, §2(a), Aug. 12, 1998, 112 Stat. 1494.)

HISTORICAL AND REVISION NOTES

Revised Section	Source (U.S. Code)	Source (Statutes at Large)
5	36:173.	June 22, 1942, ch. 435, §1, 56 Stat. 377; Dec. 22, 1942, ch. 806, §1, 56 Stat. 1074; July 7, 1976, Pub. L. 94–344, (1), 90 Stat. 810.

REFERENCES IN TEXT

Executive Order 10834, referred to in text, is set out as a note under section 1 of this title.

§ 6. Time and occasions for display

(a) It is the universal custom to display the flag only from sunrise to sunset on buildings and on stationary flagstaffs in the open. However, when a patriotic effect is desired, the flag may be displayed 24 hours a day if properly illuminated during the hours of darkness.

(b) The flag should be hoisted briskly and lowered ceremoniously.

(c) The flag should not be displayed on days when the weather is inclement, except when an all weather flag is displayed.

(d) The flag should be displayed on all days, especially on New Year's Day, January 1; Inauguration Day, January 20; Martin Luther King Jr.'s birthday, third Monday in January; Lincoln's Birthday, February 12; Washington's Birthday, third Monday in February; Easter Sunday (variable); Mother's Day, second Sunday in May; Armed Forces Day, third Saturday in May; Memorial Day (half-staff until noon), the last Monday in May; Flag Day, June 14; Independence Day, July 4; Labor Day, first Monday in September; Constitution Day, September 17; Columbus Day, second Monday in October; Navy Day, October 27; Veterans Day, November 11; Thanksgiving Day, fourth Thursday in November; Christmas Day, December 25; and such other days as may be proclaimed by the President of the United States; the birthdays of States (date of admission); and on State holidays.

(e) The flag should be displayed daily on or near the main administration building of every public institution.

(f) The flag should be displayed in or near every polling place on election days.

(g) The flag should be displayed during school days in or near every schoolhouse.

(Added Pub. L. 105–225, § 2(a), Aug. 12, 1998, 112 Stat. 1494; amended Pub. L. 106–80, § 1, Oct. 25, 1999, 113 Stat. 1285.)

HISTORICAL AND REVISION NOTES

Revised Section	Source (U.S. Code)	Source (Statutes at Large)
6	36:174.	June 22, 1942, ch. 435, § 2, 56 Stat. 378; Dec. 22, 1942, ch. 806, § 2, 56 Stat. 1074; July 7, 1976, Pub. L. 94–344, (2)–(5), 90 Stat. 810.

In subsection (d), the words "Veterans Day" are substituted for "Armistice Day" because of the Act of June 1, 1954 (ch. 250, 68 Stat. 168).

AMENDMENTS

1999—Subsec. (d). Pub. L. 106–80 inserted "Martin Luther King Jr.'s birthday, third Monday in January;" after "January 20;".

§ 7. Position and manner of display

The flag, when carried in a procession with another flag or flags, should be either on the marching right; that is, the flag's own right, or, if there is a line of other flags, in front of the center of that line.

(a) The flag should not be displayed on a float in a parade except from a staff, or as provided in subsection (i) of this section.

(b) The flag should not be draped over the hood, top, sides, or back of a vehicle or of a railroad train or a boat. When the flag is displayed on a motorcar, the staff shall be fixed firmly to the chassis or clamped to the right fender.

(c) No other flag or pennant should be placed above or, if on the same level, to the right of the flag of the United States of America, except during church services conducted by naval chaplains at sea, when the church pennant may be flown above the flag during church services for the personnel of the Navy. No person shall display the flag of the United Nations or any other national or international flag equal, above, or in a position of superior prominence or honor to, or in place of, the flag of the United States at any place within the United States or any Territory or possession thereof: *Provided*, That nothing in this section shall make unlawful the continuance of the practice heretofore followed of displaying the flag of the United Nations in a position of superior prominence or honor, and other national flags in positions of equal prominence or honor, with that of the flag of the United States at the headquarters of the United Nations.

(d) The flag of the United States of America, when it is displayed with another flag against a wall from crossed staffs, should be on the right, the flag's own right, and its staff should be in front of the staff of the other flag.

(e) The flag of the United States of America should be at the center and at the highest point of the group when a number of flags of States or localities or pennants of societies are grouped and displayed from staffs.

(f) When flags of States, cities, or localities, or pennants of societies are flown on the same halyard with the flag of the United States, the latter should always be at the peak. When the flags are flown from adjacent staffs, the flag of the United States should be hoisted first and lowered last. No such flag or pennant may be placed above the flag of the United States or to the United States flag's right.

(g) When flags of two or more nations are displayed, they are to be flown from separate staffs of the same height. The flags should be of approximately equal size. International usage forbids the display of the flag of one nation above that of another nation in time of peace.

(h) When the flag of the United States is displayed from a staff projecting horizontally or at an angle from the window sill, balcony, or front of a building, the union of the flag should be placed at the peak of the staff unless the flag is at half-staff. When the flag is suspended over a sidewalk from a rope extending from a house to a pole at the edge of the sidewalk, the flag should be hoisted out, union first, from the building.

(i) When displayed either horizontally or vertically against a wall, the union should be uppermost and to the flag's own right, that is, to the observer's left. When displayed in a window, the flag should be displayed in the same way, with the union or blue field to the left of the observer in the street.

(j) When the flag is displayed over the middle of the street, it should be suspended vertically with the union to the north in an east and west street or to the east in a north and south street.

(k) When used on a speaker's platform, the flag, if displayed flat, should be displayed above and behind the speaker. When displayed from a staff in a church or public auditorium, the flag of the United States of America should hold the position of superior prominence, in advance of the audience, and in the position of honor at the clergyman's or speaker's right as he faces the audience. Any other flag so displayed should be placed on the left of the clergyman or speaker or to the right of the audience.

(*l*) The flag should form a distinctive feature of the ceremony of unveiling a statue or monument, but it should never be used as the covering for the statue or monument.

(m) The flag, when flown at half-staff, should be first hoisted to the peak for an instant and then lowered to the half-staff position. The flag should be again raised to the peak before it is lowered for the day. On Memorial Day the flag should be displayed at half-staff until noon only, then raised to the top of the staff. By order of the President, the flag shall be flown at half-staff upon the death of principal figures of the United States Government and the Governor of a State, territory, or possession, as a mark of respect to their memory. In the event of the death of other officials or foreign dignitaries, the flag is to be displayed at half-staff according to Presidential instructions or orders, or in accordance with recognized customs or practices not inconsistent with law. In the event of the death of a present or former official of the government of any State, territory, or possession of the United States, the Governor of that State, territory, or possession may proclaim that the National flag shall be flown at half-staff. The flag shall be flown at half-staff 30 days from the death of the President or a former President; 10 days from the day of death of the Vice President, the Chief Justice or a retired Chief Justice of the United States, or the Speaker of the House of Representatives; from the day of death until interment of an Associate Justice of the Supreme Court, a Secretary of an executive or military department, a former Vice President, or the Governor of a State, territory, or possession; and on the day of death and the following day for a Member of Congress. The flag shall be flown at half-staff on Peace Officers Memorial Day, unless that day is also Armed Forces Day. As used in this subsection—

(1) the term "half-staff" means the position of the flag when it is one-half the distance between the top and bottom of the staff;

(2) the term "executive or military department" means any agency listed under sections 101 and 102 of title 5, United States Code; and

(3) the term "Member of Congress" means a Senator, a Representative, a Delegate, or the Resident Commissioner from Puerto Rico.

(n) When the flag is used to cover a casket, it should be so placed that the union is at the head and over the left shoulder. The flag should not be lowered into the grave or allowed to touch the ground.

(*o*) When the flag is suspended across a corridor or lobby in a building with only one main entrance, it should be suspended vertically with the union of the flag to the observer's left upon entering. If the building has more than one main entrance, the flag should be suspended vertically near the center of the corridor or lobby with the

union to the north, when entrances are to the east and west or to the east when entrances are to the north and south. If there are entrances in more than two directions, the union should be to the east.

(Added Pub. L. 105–225, § 2(a), Aug. 12, 1998, 112 Stat. 1495.)

HISTORICAL AND REVISION NOTES

Revised Section	Source (U.S. Code)	Source (Statutes at Large)
7	36:175.	June 22, 1942, ch. 435, § 3, 56 Stat. 378; Dec. 22, 1942, ch. 806, § 3, 56 Stat. 1075; July 9, 1953, ch. 183, 67 Stat. 142; July 7, 1976, Pub. L. 94–344, (6)–(11), 90 Stat. 811; Sept. 13, 1994, Pub. L. 103–322, title XXXII, § 320922(b), 108 Stat. 2131.

PROC. NO. 3044. DISPLAY OF FLAG AT HALF-STAFF UPON DEATH OF CERTAIN OFFICIALS AND FORMER OFFICIALS

Proc. No. 3044, Mar. 1, 1954, 19 F.R. 1235, as amended by Proc. No. 3948, Dec. 12, 1969, 34 F.R. 19699, provided:

WHEREAS it is appropriate that the flag of the United States of America be flown at half-staff on Federal buildings, grounds, and facilities upon the death of principal officials and former officials of the Government of the United States and the Governors of the States, Territories, and possessions of the United States as a mark of respect to their memory; and

WHEREAS it is desirable that rules be prescribed for the uniform observance of this mark of respect by all executive departments and agencies of the Government, and as a guide to the people of the Nation generally on such occasions:

NOW, THEREFORE, I, DWIGHT D. EISENHOWER, President of the United States of America and Commander in Chief of the armed forces of the United States, do hereby prescribe and proclaim the following rules with respect to the display of the flag of the United States of America at half-staff upon the death of the officials hereinafter designated:

1. The flag of the United States shall be flown at half-staff on all buildings, grounds, and naval vessels of the Federal Government in the District of Columbia and throughout the United States and its Territories and possessions for the period indicated upon the death of any of the following-designated officials or former officials of the United States:

(a) The President or a former President: for thirty days from the day of death.

The flag shall also be flown at half-staff for such period at all United States embassies, legations, and other facilities abroad, including all military facilities and naval vessels and stations.

(b) The Vice President, the Chief Justice or a retired Chief Justice of the United States, or the Speaker of the House of Representatives: for ten days from the day of death.

(c) An Associate Justice of the Supreme Court, a member of the Cabinet, a former Vice President, the President pro tempore of the Senate, the Majority Leader of the Senate, the Minority Leader of the Senate, the Majority Leader of the House of Representatives, or the Minority Leader of the House of Representatives: from the day of death until interment.

2. The flag of the United States shall be flown at half-staff on all buildings, grounds, and naval vessels of the Federal Government in the metropolitan area of the District of Columbia on the day of death and on the following day upon the death of a United States Senator, Representative, Territorial Delegate, or the Resident Commissioner from the Commonwealth of Puerto Rico, and it shall also be flown at half-staff on all buildings, grounds, and naval vessels of the Federal Government in the State, Congressional District, Territory, or Commonwealth of such Senator, Representative, Delegate,

or Commissioner, respectively, from the day of death until interment.

3. The flag of the United States shall be flown at half-staff on all buildings and grounds of the Federal Government in a State, Territory, or possession of the United States upon the death of the Governor of such State, Territory, or possession from the day of death until interment.

4. In the event of the death of other officials, former officials, or foreign dignitaries, the flag of the United States shall be displayed at half-staff in accordance with such orders or instructions as may be issued by or at the direction of the President, or in accordance with recognized customs or practices not inconsistent with law.

5. The heads of the several departments and agencies of the Government may direct that the flag of the United States be flown at half-staff on buildings, grounds, or naval vessels under their jurisdiction on occasions other than those specified herein which they consider proper, and that suitable military honors be rendered as appropriate.

IN WITNESS WHEREOF, I have hereunto set my hand and caused the Seal of the United States of America to be affixed.

DONE at the City of Washington this 1st day of March in the year of our Lord nineteen hundred and fifty-four, and of the Independence of the United States of America the one hundred and seventy-eighth.

[SEAL]

DWIGHT D. EISENHOWER.

SECTION REFERRED TO IN OTHER SECTIONS

This section is referred to in title 10 section 2249b; title 36 section 136.

§ 8. Respect for flag

No disrespect should be shown to the flag of the United States of America; the flag should not be dipped to any person or thing. Regimental colors, State flags, and organization or institutional flags are to be dipped as a mark of honor.

(a) The flag should never be displayed with the union down, except as a signal of dire distress in instances of extreme danger to life or property.

(b) The flag should never touch anything beneath it, such as the ground, the floor, water, or merchandise.

(c) The flag should never be carried flat or horizontally, but always aloft and free.

(d) The flag should never be used as wearing apparel, bedding, or drapery. It should never be festooned, drawn back, nor up, in folds, but always allowed to fall free. Bunting of blue, white, and red, always arranged with the blue above, the white in the middle, and the red below, should be used for covering a speaker's desk, draping the front of the platform, and for decoration in general.

(e) The flag should never be fastened, displayed, used, or stored in such a manner as to permit it to be easily torn, soiled, or damaged in any way.

(f) The flag should never be used as a covering for a ceiling.

(g) The flag should never have placed upon it, nor on any part of it, nor attached to it any mark, insignia, letter, word, figure, design, picture, or drawing of any nature.

(h) The flag should never be used as a receptacle for receiving, holding, carrying, or delivering anything.

(i) The flag should never be used for advertising purposes in any manner whatsoever. It should not be embroidered on such articles as cushions or handkerchiefs and the like, printed or otherwise impressed on paper napkins or boxes or anything that is designed for temporary use and discard. Advertising signs should not be fastened to a staff or halyard from which the flag is flown.

(j) No part of the flag should ever be used as a costume or athletic uniform. However, a flag patch may be affixed to the uniform of military personnel, firemen, policemen, and members of patriotic organizations. The flag represents a living country and is itself considered a living thing. Therefore, the lapel flag pin being a replica, should be worn on the left lapel near the heart.

(k) The flag, when it is in such condition that it is no longer a fitting emblem for display, should be destroyed in a dignified way, preferably by burning.

(Added Pub. L. 105–225, § 2(a), Aug. 12, 1998, 112 Stat. 1497.)

HISTORICAL AND REVISION NOTES

Revised Section	Source (U.S. Code)	Source (Statutes at Large)
8	36:176.	June 22, 1942, ch. 435, § 4, 56 Stat. 379; Dec. 22, 1942, ch. 806, § 4, 56 Stat. 1076; July 7, 1976, Pub. L. 94–344, (12)–(16), 90 Stat. 812.

§ 9. Conduct during hoisting, lowering or passing of flag

During the ceremony of hoisting or lowering the flag or when the flag is passing in a parade or in review, all persons present except those in uniform should face the flag and stand at attention with the right hand over the heart. Those present in uniform should render the military salute. When not in uniform, men should remove their headdress with their right hand and hold it at the left shoulder, the hand being over the heart. Aliens should stand at attention. The salute to the flag in a moving column should be rendered at the moment the flag passes.

(Added Pub. L. 105–225, § 2(a), Aug. 12, 1998, 112 Stat. 1498.)

HISTORICAL AND REVISION NOTES

Revised Section	Source (U.S. Code)	Source (Statutes at Large)
9	36:177.	June 22, 1942, ch. 435, § 5, 56 Stat. 380; Dec. 22, 1942, ch. 806, § 5, 56 Stat. 1077; July 7, 1976, Pub. L. 94–344, (17), 90 Stat. 812.

§ 10. Modification of rules and customs by President

Any rule or custom pertaining to the display of the flag of the United States of America, set forth herein, may be altered, modified, or repealed, or additional rules with respect thereto may be prescribed, by the Commander in Chief of the Armed Forces of the United States, whenever he deems it to be appropriate or desirable; and any such alteration or additional rule shall be set forth in a proclamation.

(Added Pub. L. 105–225, §2(a), Aug. 12, 1998, 112 Stat. 1498.)

HISTORICAL AND REVISION NOTES

Revised Section	Source (U.S. Code)	Source (Statutes at Large)
10	36:178.	June 22, 1942, ch. 435, §8, 56 Stat. 380; Dec. 22, 1942, ch. 806, §8, 56 Stat. 1077; July 7, 1976, Pub. L. 94–344, (20), 90 Stat. 813.

REFERENCES IN TEXT

Herein, referred to in text, means sections 4 to 10 of this title.

PROC. NO. 2605. THE FLAG OF THE UNITED STATES

Proc. No. 2605, Feb. 18, 1944, 9 F.R. 1957, 58 Stat. 1126, provided:

The flag of the United States of America is universally representative of the principles of the justice, liberty, and democracy enjoyed by the people of the United States; and

People all over the world recognize the flag of the United States as symbolic of the United States; and

The effective prosecution of the war requires a proper understanding by the people of other countries of the material assistance being given by the Government of the United States:

NOW, THEREFORE, by virtue of the power vested in me by the Constitution and laws of the United States, particularly by the Joint Resolution approved June 22, 1942, as amended by the Joint Resolution approved December 22, 1942 [now sections 4 to 10 of this title], as President and Commander in Chief, it is hereby proclaimed as follows:

1. The use of the flag of the United States or any representation thereof, if approved by the Foreign Economic Administration, on labels, packages, cartons, cases, or other containers for articles or products of the United States intended for export as lend-lease aid, as relief and rehabilitation aid, or as emergency supplies for the Territories and possessions of the United States, or similar purposes, shall be considered a proper use of the flag of the United States and consistent with the honor and respect due to the flag.

2. If any article or product so labelled, packaged or otherwise bearing the flag of the United States or any representation thereof, as provided for in section 1, should, by force of circumstances, be diverted to the ordinary channels of domestic trade, no person shall be considered as violating the rules and customs pertaining to the display of the flag of the United States, as set forth in the Joint Resolution approved June 22, 1942, as amended by the Joint Resolution approved December 22, 1942 (U.S.C., Supp. II, title 36, secs. 171–178) [now sections 4 to 10 of this title] for possessing, transporting, displaying, selling or otherwise transferring any such article or product solely because the label, package, carton, case, or other container bears the flag of the United States or any representation thereof.

SECTION REFERRED TO IN OTHER SECTIONS

This section is referred to in title 10 section 2249b.

CHAPTER 2—THE SEAL

Sec.
41. Seal of the United States.
42. Same; custody and use of.

§ 41. Seal of the United States

The seal heretofore used by the United States in Congress assembled is declared to be the seal of the United States.

(July 30, 1947, ch. 389, 61 Stat. 643.)

§ 42. Same; custody and use of

The Secretary of State shall have the custody and charge of such seal. Except as provided by section 2902(a) of title 5, the seal shall not be affixed to any instrument without the special warrant of the President therefor.

(July 30, 1947, ch. 389, 61 Stat. 643; Pub. L. 89–554, §2(a), Sept. 6, 1966, 80 Stat. 608.)

AMENDMENTS

1966—Pub. L. 89–554 struck out provisions which required the Secretary of State to make out and record, and to affix the seal to, all civil commissions for officers of the United States appointed by the President. See section 2902(a) of Title 5, Government Organization and Employees.

EX. ORD. NO. 10347. AFFIXING OF SEAL WITHOUT SPECIAL WARRANT

Ex. Ord. No. 10347, Apr. 18, 1952, 17 F.R. 3521, as amended by Ex. Ord. No. 11354, May 23, 1967, 32 F.R. 7695; Ex. Ord. No. 11517, Mar. 19, 1970, 35 F.R. 4937, provided:

By virtue of the authority vested in me by section 301 of title 3 of the United States Code (section 10, Public Law 248, approved October 31, 1951, 65 Stat. 713), and as President of the United States, I hereby authorize and direct the Secretary of State to affix the Seal of the United States, pursuant to section 42 of title 4 of the United States Code [this section], without any special warrant therefor, other than this order, to each document included within any of the following classes of documents when such document has been signed by the President and, in the case of any such document to which the counter-signature of the Secretary of State is required to be affixed, has been counter-signed by the said Secretary:

1. Proclamations by the President of treaties, conventions, protocols, or other international agreements.

2. Instruments of ratification of treaties.

3. Full powers to negotiate treaties and to exchange ratifications.

4. Letters of credence and recall and other communications from the President to heads of foreign governments.

5. Exequaturs issued to those foreign consular officers in the United States whose commissions bear the signature of the chief of state which they represent.

CHAPTER 3—SEAT OF THE GOVERNMENT

Sec.
71. Permanent seat of Government.
72. Public offices; at seat of Government.
73. Same; removal from seat of Government.

§ 71. Permanent seat of Government

All that part of the territory of the United States included within the present limits of the District of Columbia shall be the permanent seat of government of the United States.

(July 30, 1947, ch. 389, 61 Stat. 643.)

§ 72. Public offices; at seat of Government

All offices attached to the seat of government shall be exercised in the District of Columbia, and not elsewhere, except as otherwise expressly provided by law.

(July 30, 1947, ch. 389, 61 Stat. 643.)

§ 73. Same; removal from seat of Government

In case of the prevalence of a contagious or epidemic disease at the seat of government, the

President may permit and direct the removal of any or all the public offices to such other place or places as he shall deem most safe and convenient for conducting the public business.

(July 30, 1947, ch. 389, 61 Stat. 643.)

SECTION REFERRED TO IN OTHER SECTIONS

This section is referred to in title 42 section 97.

CHAPTER 4—THE STATES

AMENDMENTS

2000—Pub. L. 106–252, § 2(b), July 28, 2000, 114 Stat. 633, added items 116 to 126.

1998—Pub. L. 105–261, div. A, title X, § 1075(a)(2), Oct. 17, 1998, 112 Stat. 2138, added item 115.

1996—Pub. L. 104–95, § 1(b), Jan. 10, 1996, 109 Stat. 980, added item 114.

1977—Pub. L. 95–67, § 1(b), July 19, 1977, 91 Stat. 271, added item 113.

1966—Pub. L. 89–554, § 2(b), Sept. 6, 1966, 80 Stat. 608, added item 111 and redesignated former item 111 as 112.

1949—Act May 24, 1949, ch. 139, § 129(a), 63 Stat. 107, added item 111.

CIVIL AND CRIMINAL JURISDICTION OVER INDIANS

Amendment of State Constitutions to remove legal impediment to the assumption of civil and criminal jurisdiction in accordance with the provisions of section 1162 of Title 18 and section 1360 of Title 28, see act Aug. 15, 1953, ch. 505, § 6, 67 Stat. 590, set out as a note under

---

[1] So in original. Does not conform to section catchline.
[2] So in original. Probably should be followed by a period.

section 1360 of Title 28, Judiciary and Judicial Procedure.

Consent of United States to other States to assume jurisdiction with respect to criminal offenses or civil causes of action, or with respect to both, as provided for in section 1162 of Title 18 and section 1360 of Title 28, see act Aug. 15, 1953, ch. 505, § 7, 67 Stat. 590, set out as a note under section 1360 of Title 28.

§ 101. Oath by members of legislatures and officers

Every member of a State legislature, and every executive and judicial officer of a State, shall, before he proceeds to execute the duties of his office, take an oath in the following form, to wit: "I, A B, do solemnly swear that I will support the Constitution of the United States."

(July 30, 1947, ch. 389, 61 Stat. 643.)

§ 102. Same; by whom administered

Such oath may be administered by any person who, by the law of the State, is authorized to administer the oath of office; and the person so administering such oath shall cause a record or certificate thereof to be made in the same manner, as by the law of the State, he is directed to record or certify the oath of office.

(July 30, 1947, ch. 389, 61 Stat. 644.)

§ 103. Assent to purchase of lands for forts

The President of the United States is authorized to procure the assent of the legislature of any State, within which any purchase of land has been made for the erection of forts, magazines, arsenals, dockyards, and other needful buildings, without such consent having been obtained.

(July 30, 1947, ch. 389, 61 Stat. 644.)

§ 104. Tax on motor fuel sold on military or other reservation[1] reports to State taxing authority

(a) All taxes levied by any State, Territory, or the District of Columbia upon, with respect to, or measured by, sales, purchases, storage, or use of gasoline or other motor vehicle fuels may be levied, in the same manner and to the same extent, with respect to such fuels when sold by or through post exchanges, ship stores, ship service stores, commissaries, filling stations, licensed traders, and other similar agencies, located on United States military or other reservations, when such fuels are not for the exclusive use of the United States. Such taxes, so levied, shall be paid to the proper taxing authorities of the State, Territory, or the District of Columbia, within whose borders the reservation affected may be located.

(b) The officer in charge of such reservation shall, on or before the fifteenth day of each month, submit a written statement to the proper taxing authorities of the State, Territory, or the District of Columbia within whose borders the reservation is located, showing the amount of such motor fuel with respect to which taxes are payable under subsection (a) for the preceding month.

---

[1] So in original. Probably should be followed by a semicolon.

(c) As used in this section, the term "Territory" shall include Guam.

(July 30, 1947, ch. 389, 61 Stat. 644; Aug. 1, 1956, ch. 827, 70 Stat. 799.)

AMENDMENTS

1956—Subsec. (c) added by act Aug. 1, 1956.

CIVIL AIRPORTS OWNED BY UNITED STATES SUBJECT TO SECTIONS 104 TO 110; SALES OR USE TAXES: FUELS FOR AIRCRAFT OR OTHER SERVICING OF AIRCRAFT; LANDING OR TAKING OFF CHARGES; LEASES

Section 210 of Pub. L. 91–258, title II, May 21, 1970, 84 Stat. 253, provided that:

"(a) Nothing in this title or in any other law of the United States shall prevent the application of sections 104 through 110 of title 4 of the United States Code to civil airports owned by the United States.

"(b) Subsection (a) shall not apply to—

"(1) sales or use taxes in respect of fuels for aircraft or in respect of other servicing of aircraft, or

"(2) taxes, fees, head charges, or other charges in respect of the landing or taking off of aircraft or aircraft passengers or freight.

"(c) In the case of any lease in effect on September 28, 1969, subsection (a) shall not authorize the levy or collection of any tax in respect of any transaction occurring, or any service performed, pursuant to such lease before the expiration of such lease (determined without regard to any renewal or extension of such lease made after September 28, 1969). For purposes of the preceding sentence, the term 'lease' includes a contract."

SECTION REFERRED TO IN OTHER SECTIONS

This section is referred to in section 110 of this title.

§ 105. State, and so forth, taxation affecting Federal areas; sales or use tax

(a) No person shall be relieved from liability for payment of, collection of, or accounting for any sales or use tax levied by any State, or by any duly constituted taxing authority therein, having jurisdiction to levy such a tax, on the ground that the sale or use, with respect to which such tax is levied, occurred in whole or in part within a Federal area; and such State or taxing authority shall have full jurisdiction and power to levy and collect any such tax in any Federal area within such State to the same extent and with the same effect as though such area was not a Federal area.

(b) The provisions of subsection (a) shall be applicable only with respect to sales or purchases made, receipts from sales received, or storage or use occurring, after December 31, 1940.

(July 30, 1947, ch. 389, 61 Stat. 644.)

TAXATION WITH RESPECT TO ESSENTIAL SUPPORT ACTIVITIES OR FUNCTIONS OF NON-GOVERNMENTAL PERSONS IN CONGRESSIONALLY-CONTROLLED LOCATIONS IN DISTRICT OF COLUMBIA

Pub. L. 100–202, § 101(i) [title III, § 307], Dec. 22, 1987, 101 Stat. 1329–290, 1329–309, as amended by Pub. L. 104–186, title II, § 214, Aug. 20, 1996, 110 Stat. 1745, provided that:

"(a) Notwithstanding section 105 of title 4, United States Code, or any other provision of law, no person shall be required to pay, collect, or account for any sales, use, or similar excise tax, or any personal property tax, with respect to an essential support activity or function conducted by a nongovernmental person in the Capitol, the House Office Buildings, the Senate Office Buildings, the Capitol Grounds, or any other location under the control of the Congress in the District of Columbia.

"(b) As used in this section—

"(1) the term 'essential support activity or function' means a support activity or function so designated by the Committee on House Oversight [now Committee on House Administration] of the House of Representatives or the Committee on Rules and Administration of the Senate, acting jointly or separately, as appropriate;

"(2) the term 'personal property tax' means a tax of a State, a subdivision of a State, or any other authority of a State, that is levied on, levied with respect to, or measured by, the value of personal property;

"(3) the term 'sales, use, or similar excise tax' means a tax of a State, a subdivision of a State, or any other authority of a State, that is levied on, levied with respect to, or measured by, sales, receipts from sales, or purchases, or by storage, possession, or use of personal property; and

"(4) the term 'State' means a State of the United States, the District of Columbia, or a territory or possession of the United States.

"(c) This section shall apply to any sale, receipt, purchase, storage, possession, use, or valuation taking place after December 31, 1986."

SECTION REFERRED TO IN OTHER SECTIONS

This section is referred to in sections 107, 108, 109, 110 of this title; title 36 section 220307.

§ 106. Same; income tax

(a) No person shall be relieved from liability for any income tax levied by any State, or by any duly constituted taxing authority therein, having jurisdiction to levy such a tax, by reason of his residing within a Federal area or receiving income from transactions occurring or services performed in such area; and such State or taxing authority shall have full jurisdiction and power to levy and collect such tax in any Federal area within such State to the same extent and with the same effect as though such area was not a Federal area.

(b) The provisions of subsection (a) shall be applicable only with respect to income or receipts received after December 31, 1940.

(July 30, 1947, ch. 389, 61 Stat. 644.)

SECTION REFERRED TO IN OTHER SECTIONS

This section is referred to in sections 107, 108, 109, 110 of this title.

§ 107. Same; exception of United States, its instrumentalities, and authorized purchases[1] therefrom

(a) The provisions of sections 105 and 106 of this title shall not be deemed to authorize the levy or collection of any tax on or from the United States or any instrumentality thereof, or the levy or collection of any tax with respect to sale, purchase, storage, or use of tangible personal property sold by the United States or any instrumentality thereof to any authorized purchaser.

(b) A person shall be deemed to be an authorized purchaser under this section only with respect to purchases which he is permitted to make from commissaries, ship's stores, or voluntary unincorporated organizations of personnel of any branch of the Armed Forces of the

---

[1] So in original. Probably should be "purchasers".

United States, under regulations promulgated by the departmental Secretary having jurisdiction over such branch.

(July 30, 1947, ch. 389, 61 Stat. 645; Sept. 3, 1954, ch. 1263, § 4, 68 Stat. 1227.)

AMENDMENTS

1954—Subsec. (b). Act Sept. 3, 1954, substituted "personnel of any branch of the Armed Forces of the United States" for "Army or Navy personnel".

SECTION REFERRED TO IN OTHER SECTIONS

This section is referred to in sections 108, 110 of this title.

§ 108. Same; jurisdiction of United States over Federal areas unaffected

The provisions of sections 105–110 of this title shall not for the purposes of any other provision of law be deemed to deprive the United States of exclusive jurisdiction over any Federal area over which it would otherwise have exclusive jurisdiction or to limit the jurisdiction of the United States over any Federal area.

(July 30, 1947, ch. 389, 61 Stat. 645.)

SECTION REFERRED TO IN OTHER SECTIONS

This section is referred to in section 110 of this title.

§ 109. Same; exception of Indians

Nothing in sections 105 and 106 of this title shall be deemed to authorize the levy or collection of any tax on or from any Indian not otherwise taxed.

(July 30, 1947, ch. 389, 61 Stat. 645.)

SECTION REFERRED TO IN OTHER SECTIONS

This section is referred to in sections 108, 110 of this title.

§ 110. Same; definitions

As used in sections 105–109 of this title—

(a) The term "person" shall have the meaning assigned to it in section 3797 of title 26.

(b) The term "sales or use tax" means any tax levied on, with respect to, or measured by, sales, receipts from sales, purchases, storage, or use of tangible personal property, except a tax with respect to which the provisions of section 104 of this title are applicable.

(c) The term "income tax" means any tax levied on, with respect to, or measured by, net income, gross income, or gross receipts.

(d) The term "State" includes any Territory or possession of the United States.

(e) The term "Federal area" means any lands or premises held or acquired by or for the use of the United States or any department, establishment, or agency, of the United States; and any Federal area, or any part thereof, which is located within the exterior boundaries of any State, shall be deemed to be a Federal area located within such State.

(July 30, 1947, ch. 389, 61 Stat. 645.)

REFERENCES IN TEXT

Section 3797 of title 26, referred to in subsec. (a), is a reference to section 3797 of the Internal Revenue Code of 1939, which was repealed by section 7851 of the Inter-

nal Revenue Code of 1954, Title 26, and is covered by section 7701(a)(1) of Title 26. The Internal Revenue Code of 1954 was redesignated the Internal Revenue Code of 1986 by Pub. L. 99–514, § 2, Oct. 22, 1986, 100 Stat. 2095. For table of comparisons of the 1939 Code to the 1986 Code, see Table I preceding section 1 of Title 26, Internal Revenue Code. See also section 7852(b) of Title 26, Internal Revenue Code, for provision that references in any other law to a provision of the 1939 Code, unless expressly incompatible with the intent thereof, shall be deemed a reference to the corresponding provision of the 1986 Code.

SECTION REFERRED TO IN OTHER SECTIONS

This section is referred to in sections 108, 113, 114 of this title.

§ 111. Same; taxation affecting Federal employees; income tax

(a) GENERAL RULE.—The United States consents to the taxation of pay or compensation for personal service as an officer or employee of the United States, a territory or possession or political subdivision thereof, the government of the District of Columbia, or an agency or instrumentality of one or more of the foregoing, by a duly constituted taxing authority having jurisdiction, if the taxation does not discriminate against the officer or employee because of the source of the pay or compensation.

(b) TREATMENT OF CERTAIN FEDERAL EMPLOYEES EMPLOYED AT FEDERAL HYDROELECTRIC FACILITIES LOCATED ON THE COLUMBIA RIVER.—Pay or compensation paid by the United States for personal services as an employee of the United States at a hydroelectric facility—

(1) which is owned by the United States;

(2) which is located on the Columbia River; and

(3) portions of which are within the States of Oregon and Washington,

shall be subject to taxation by the State or any political subdivision thereof of which such employee is a resident.

(c) TREATMENT OF CERTAIN FEDERAL EMPLOYEES EMPLOYED AT FEDERAL HYDROELECTRIC FACILITIES LOCATED ON THE MISSOURI RIVER.—Pay or compensation paid by the United States for personal services as an employee of the United States at a hydroelectric facility—

(1) which is owned by the United States;

(2) which is located on the Missouri River; and

(3) portions of which are within the States of South Dakota and Nebraska,

shall be subject to taxation by the State or any political subdivision thereof of which such employee is a resident.

(Added Pub. L. 89–554, § 2(c), Sept. 6, 1966, 80 Stat. 608; amended Pub. L. 105–261, div. A, title X, § 1075(b)(1), Oct. 17, 1998, 112 Stat. 2138.)

HISTORICAL AND REVISION NOTES

Derivation	U.S. Code	Revised Statutes and Statutes at Large
....	5 U.S.C. 84a ...	Apr. 12, 1939, ch. 59, § 4, 53 Stat. 575.

The words "received after December 31, 1938," are omitted as obsolete. The words "pay or" are added before "compensation" for clarity as the word "pay" is used throughout title 5, United States Code, to refer to the remuneration, salary, wages, or compensation for the personal services of a Federal employee. The word "territory" is not capitalized as there are no longer any "Territories." The words "to tax such compensation" are omitted as unnecessary.

AMENDMENTS

1998—Pub. L. 105–261 designated existing provisions as subsec. (a), inserted heading, and added subsecs. (b) and (c).

EFFECTIVE DATE OF 1998 AMENDMENT

Pub. L. 105–261, div. A, title X, § 1075(b)(2), Oct. 17, 1998, 112 Stat. 2139, provided that: "The amendment made by this subsection [amending this section] shall apply to pay and compensation paid after the date of the enactment of this Act [Oct. 17, 1998]."

§ 112. Compacts between States for cooperation in prevention of crime; consent of Congress

(a) The consent of Congress is hereby given to any two or more States to enter into agreements or compacts for cooperative effort and mutual assistance in the prevention of crime and in the enforcement of their respective criminal laws and policies, and to establish such agencies, joint or otherwise, as they may deem desirable for making effective such agreements and compacts.

(b) For the purpose of this section, the term "States" means the several States and Alaska, Hawaii, the Commonwealth of Puerto Rico, the Virgin Islands, Guam, and the District of Columbia.

(Added May 24, 1949, ch. 139, § 129(b), 63 Stat. 107, § 112, formerly § 111; amended Aug. 3, 1956, ch. 941, 70 Stat. 1020; Pub. L. 87–406, Feb. 16, 1962, 76 Stat. 9; renumbered § 112, Pub. L. 89–554, § 2(c), Sept. 6, 1966, 80 Stat. 608.)

HISTORICAL AND REVISION NOTE

This section [section 129(b) of Act May 24, 1949] incorporates in title 4, U.S.C. (enacted into positive law by act of July 30, 1947 (ch. 389, § 1, 61 Stat. 641), the provisions of former section 420 of title 18, U.S.C. (act of June 6, 1934, ch. 406, 48 Stat. 909), which, in the course of the revision of such title 18, was omitted therefrom and recommended for transfer to such title 4. (See table 7—Transferred sections, p. A219, H. Rept. No. 304, April 24, 1947, to accompany H.R. 3190, 80th Cong.).

AMENDMENTS

1962—Subsec. (b). Pub. L. 87–406 inserted "Guam" after "the Virgin Islands,".

1956—Act Aug. 3, 1956, designated existing provisions as subsec. (a) and added subsec. (b).

ADMISSION OF ALASKA AND HAWAII TO STATEHOOD

Alaska was admitted into the Union on Jan. 3, 1959, on issuance of Proc. No. 3269, Jan. 3, 1959, 24 F.R. 81, 73 Stat. c16, and Hawaii was admitted into the Union on Aug. 21, 1959, on issuance of Proc. No. 3309, Aug. 21, 1959, 24 F.R. 6868, 73 Stat. c74. For Alaska Statehood Law, see Pub. L. 85–508, July 7, 1958, 72 Stat. 339, set out as a note preceding former section 21 of Title 48, Territories and Insular Possessions. For Hawaii Statehood Law, see Pub. L. 86–3, Mar. 18, 1959, 73 Stat. 4, set out as a note preceding former section 491 of Title 48.

§ 113. Residence of Members of Congress for State income tax laws

(a) No State, or political subdivision thereof, in which a Member of Congress maintains a place of abode for purposes of attending sessions of Congress may, for purposes of any income tax (as defined in section 110(c) of this title) levied by such State or political subdivision thereof—

(1) treat such Member as a resident or domiciliary of such State or political subdivision thereof; or

(2) treat any compensation paid by the United States to such Member as income for services performed within, or from sources within, such State or political subdivision thereof,

unless such Member represents such State or a district in such State.

(b) For purposes of subsection (a)—

(1) the term "Member of Congress" includes the delegates from the District of Columbia, Guam, and the Virgin Islands, and the Resident Commissioner from Puerto Rico; and

(2) the term "State" includes the District of Columbia.

(Added Pub. L. 95–67, § 1(a), July 19, 1977, 91 Stat. 271.)

EFFECTIVE DATE

Section 1(c) of Pub. L. 95–67 provided that: "The amendments made by subsections (a) and (b) [enacting this section and amending analysis preceding section 101 of this title] shall be effective with respect to all taxable years, whether beginning before, on, or after the date of the enactment of this Act [July 19, 1977]."

RESIDENCE OF MEMBERS OF CONGRESS FOR STATE PERSONAL PROPERTY TAX ON MOTOR VEHICLES

Pub. L. 99–190, § 101(c) [H.R. 3067, § 131], Dec. 19, 1985, 99 Stat. 1224; Pub. L. 100–202, § 106, Dec. 22, 1987, 101 Stat. 1329–433, provided that:

"(a) No State, or political subdivision thereof, in which a Member of Congress maintains a place of abode for purposes of attending sessions of Congress may impose a personal property tax with respect to any motor vehicle owned by such Member (or by the spouse of such Member) unless such Member represents such State or a district in such State.

"(b) For purposes of this section—

"(1) the term 'Member of Congress' includes the delegates from the District of Columbia, Guam, and the Virgin Islands, and the Resident Commissioner from Puerto Rico;

"(2) the term 'State' includes the District of Columbia; and

"(3) the term 'personal property tax' means any tax imposed on an annual basis and levied on, with respect to, or measured by, the market value or assessed value of an item of personal property.

"(c) This section shall apply to all taxable periods beginning on or after January 1, 1985."

§ 114. Limitation on State income taxation of certain pension income

(a) No State may impose an income tax on any retirement income of an individual who is not a resident or domiciliary of such State (as determined under the laws of such State).

(b) For purposes of this section—

(1) The term "retirement income" means any income from—

(A) a qualified trust under section 401(a) of the Internal Revenue Code of 1986 that is exempt under section 501(a) from taxation;

(B) a simplified employee pension as defined in section 408(k) of such Code;

(C) an annuity plan described in section 403(a) of such Code;

(D) an annuity contract described in section 403(b) of such Code;

(E) an individual retirement plan described in section 7701(a)(37) of such Code;

(F) an eligible deferred compensation plan (as defined in section 457 of such Code);

(G) a governmental plan (as defined in section 414(d) of such Code);

(H) a trust described in section 501(c)(18) of such Code; or

(I) any plan, program, or arrangement described in section 3121(v)(2)(C) of such Code, if such income—

(i) is part of a series of substantially equal periodic payments (not less frequently than annually) made for—

(I) the life or life expectancy of the recipient (or the joint lives or joint life expectancies of the recipient and the designated beneficiary of the recipient), or

(II) a period of not less than 10 years, or

(ii) is a payment received after termination of employment and under a plan, program, or arrangement (to which such employment relates) maintained solely for the purpose of providing retirement benefits for employees in excess of the limitations imposed by 1 or more of sections 401(a)(17), 401(k), 401(m), 402(g), 403(b), 408(k), or 415 of such Code or any other limitation on contributions or benefits in such Code on plans to which any of such sections apply.

Such term includes any retired or retainer pay of a member or former member of a uniform service computed under chapter 71 of title 10, United States Code.

(2) The term "income tax" has the meaning given such term by section 110(c).

(3) The term "State" includes any political subdivision of a State, the District of Columbia, and the possessions of the United States.

(e)[1] Nothing in this section shall be construed as having any effect on the application of section 514 of the Employee Retirement Income Security Act of 1974.

(Added Pub. L. 104–95, §1(a), Jan. 10, 1996, 109 Stat. 979.)

REFERENCES IN TEXT

The Internal Revenue Code of 1986, referred to in subsec. (b)(1), is classified generally to Title 26, Internal Revenue Code.

Section 514 of the Employee Retirement Income Security Act of 1974, referred to in subsec. (e), is classified to section 1144 of Title 29, Labor.

EFFECTIVE DATE

Section 1(c) of Pub. L. 104–95 provided that: "The amendments made by this section [enacting this section] shall apply to amounts received after December 31, 1995."

§ 115. Limitation on State authority to tax compensation paid to individuals performing services at Fort Campbell, Kentucky

Pay and compensation paid to an individual for personal services at Fort Campbell, Kentucky, shall be subject to taxation by the State or any political subdivision thereof of which such employee is a resident.

(Added Pub. L. 105–261, div. A, title X, § 1075(a)(1), Oct. 17, 1998, 112 Stat. 2138.)

EFFECTIVE DATE

Pub. L. 105–261, div. A, title X, § 1075(a)(3), Oct. 17, 1998, 112 Stat. 2138, provided that: "The amendments made by this subsection [enacting this section] shall apply to pay and compensation paid after the date of the enactment of this Act [Oct. 17, 1998]."

§ 116. Rules for determining State and local government treatment of charges related to mobile telecommunications services

(a) APPLICATION OF THIS SECTION THROUGH SECTION 126.—This section through[1] 126 of this title apply to any tax, charge, or fee levied by a taxing jurisdiction as a fixed charge for each customer or measured by gross amounts charged to customers for mobile telecommunications services, regardless of whether such tax, charge, or fee is imposed on the vendor or customer of the service and regardless of the terminology used to describe the tax, charge, or fee.

(b) GENERAL EXCEPTIONS.—This section through[1] 126 of this title do not apply to—

(1) any tax, charge, or fee levied upon or measured by the net income, capital stock, net worth, or property value of the provider of mobile telecommunications service;

(2) any tax, charge, or fee that is applied to an equitably apportioned amount that is not determined on a transactional basis;

(3) any tax, charge, or fee that represents compensation for a mobile telecommunications service provider's use of public rights of way or other public property, provided that such tax, charge, or fee is not levied by the taxing jurisdiction as a fixed charge for each customer or measured by gross amounts charged to customers for mobile telecommunication services;

(4) any generally applicable business and occupation tax that is imposed by a State, is applied to gross receipts or gross proceeds, is the legal liability of the home service provider, and that statutorily allows the home service provider to elect to use the sourcing method required in this section through[1] 126 of this title;

(5) any fee related to obligations under section 254 of the Communications Act of 1934; or

(6) any tax, charge, or fee imposed by the Federal Communications Commission.

(c) SPECIFIC EXCEPTIONS.—This section through[1] 126 of this title—

(1) do not apply to the determination of the taxing situs of prepaid telephone calling services;

(2) do not affect the taxability of either the initial sale of mobile telecommunications services or subsequent resale of such services, whether as sales of such services alone or as a part of a bundled product, if the Internet Tax Freedom Act would preclude a taxing jurisdiction from subjecting the charges of the sale of

---

[1] So in original. No subsecs. (c) and (d) have been enacted.

[1] So in original. Probably should be followed by "section".

such services to a tax, charge, or fee, but this section provides no evidence of the intent of Congress with respect to the applicability of the Internet Tax Freedom Act to such charges; and

(3) do not apply to the determination of the taxing situs of air-ground radiotelephone service as defined in section 22.99 of title 47 of the Code of Federal Regulations as in effect on June 1, 1999.

(Added Pub. L. 106–252, §2(a), July 28, 2000, 114 Stat. 626.)

REFERENCES IN TEXT

Section 254 of the Communications Act of 1934, referred to in subsec. (b)(5), is classified to section 254 of Title 47, Telegraphs, Telephones, and Radiotelegraphs.

The Internet Tax Freedom Act, referred to in subsec. (c)(2), is title XI of Pub. L. 105–277, div. C, Oct. 21, 1998, 112 Stat. 2681–719, which is set out as a note under section 151 of Title 47, Telegraphs, Telephones, and Radiotelegraphs.

EFFECTIVE DATE; APPLICATION OF AMENDMENT

Pub. L. 106–252, §3, July 28, 2000, 114 Stat. 633, provided that:

"(a) EFFECTIVE DATE.—Except as provided in subsection (b), this Act [enacting this section and sections 117 to 126 of this title and provisions set out as a note under section 1 of this title] and the amendment made by this Act shall take effect on the date of the enactment of this Act [July 28, 2000].

"(b) APPLICATION OF ACT.—The amendment made by this Act [enacting this section and sections 117 to 126 of this title] shall apply only to customer bills issued after the first day of the first month beginning more than 2 years after the date of the enactment of this Act [July 28, 2000]."

SECTION REFERRED TO IN OTHER SECTIONS

This section is referred to in sections 117, 118, 123, 124, 125, 126 of this title.

§ 117. Sourcing rules

(a) TREATMENT OF CHARGES FOR MOBILE TELECOMMUNICATIONS SERVICES.—Notwithstanding the law of any State or political subdivision of any State, mobile telecommunications services provided in a taxing jurisdiction to a customer, the charges for which are billed by or for the customer's home service provider, shall be deemed to be provided by the customer's home service provider.

(b) JURISDICTION.—All charges for mobile telecommunications services that are deemed to be provided by the customer's home service provider under sections 116 through 126 of this title are authorized to be subjected to tax, charge, or fee by the taxing jurisdictions whose territorial limits encompass the customer's place of primary use, regardless of where the mobile telecommunication services originate, terminate, or pass through, and no other taxing jurisdiction may impose taxes, charges, or fees on charges for such mobile telecommunications services.

(Added Pub. L. 106–252, §2(a), July 28, 2000, 114 Stat. 627.)

EFFECTIVE DATE; APPLICATION OF AMENDMENT

Section effective July 28, 2000, and applicable only to customer bills issued after the first day of the first month beginning more than 2 years after July 28, 2000, see section 3 of Pub. L. 106–252, set out as a note under section 116 of this title.

SECTION REFERRED TO IN OTHER SECTIONS

This section is referred to in sections 116, 118, 123, 124, 125, 126 of this title.

§ 118. Limitations

Sections 116 through 126 of this title do not—

(1) provide authority to a taxing jurisdiction to impose a tax, charge, or fee that the laws of such jurisdiction do not authorize such jurisdiction to impose; or

(2) modify, impair, supersede, or authorize the modification, impairment, or supersession of the law of any taxing jurisdiction pertaining to taxation except as expressly provided in sections 116 through 126 of this title.

(Added Pub. L. 106–252, §2(a), July 28, 2000, 114 Stat. 627.)

EFFECTIVE DATE; APPLICATION OF AMENDMENT

Section effective July 28, 2000, and applicable only to customer bills issued after the first day of the first month beginning more than 2 years after July 28, 2000, see section 3 of Pub. L. 106–252, set out as a note under section 116 of this title.

SECTION REFERRED TO IN OTHER SECTIONS

This section is referred to in sections 116, 117, 123, 124, 125, 126 of this title.

§ 119. Electronic databases for nationwide standard numeric jurisdictional codes

(a) ELECTRONIC DATABASE.—

(1) PROVISION OF DATABASE.—A State may provide an electronic database to a home service provider or, if a State does not provide such an electronic database to home service providers, then the designated database provider may provide an electronic database to a home service provider.

(2) FORMAT.—(A) Such electronic database, whether provided by the State or the designated database provider, shall be provided in a format approved by the American National Standards Institute's Accredited Standards Committee X12, that, allowing for de minimis deviations, designates for each street address in the State, including to the extent practicable, any multiple postal street addresses applicable to one street location, the appropriate taxing jurisdictions, and the appropriate code for each taxing jurisdiction, for each level of taxing jurisdiction, identified by one nationwide standard numeric code.

(B) Such electronic database shall also provide the appropriate code for each street address with respect to political subdivisions which are not taxing jurisdictions when reasonably needed to determine the proper taxing jurisdiction.

(C) The nationwide standard numeric codes shall contain the same number of numeric digits with each digit or combination of digits referring to the same level of taxing jurisdiction throughout the United States using a format similar to FIPS 55–3 or other appropriate standard approved by the Federation of Tax Administrators and the Multistate Tax Commission, or their successors. Each address shall be provided in standard postal format.

(b) NOTICE; UPDATES.—A State or designated database provider that provides or maintains an electronic database described in subsection (a) shall provide notice of the availability of the then current electronic database, and any subsequent revisions thereof, by publication in the manner normally employed for the publication of informational tax, charge, or fee notices to taxpayers in such State.

(c) USER HELD HARMLESS.—A home service provider using the data contained in an electronic database described in subsection (a) shall be held harmless from any tax, charge, or fee liability that otherwise would be due solely as a result of any error or omission in such database provided by a State or designated database provider. The home service provider shall reflect changes made to such database during a calendar quarter not later than 30 days after the end of such calendar quarter for each State that issues notice of the availability of an electronic database reflecting such changes under subsection (b).

(Added Pub. L. 106–252, § 2(a), July 28, 2000, 114 Stat. 627.)

EFFECTIVE DATE; APPLICATION OF AMENDMENT

Section effective July 28, 2000, and applicable only to customer bills issued after the first day of the first month beginning more than 2 years after July 28, 2000, see section 3 of Pub. L. 106–252, set out as a note under section 116 of this title.

SECTION REFERRED TO IN OTHER SECTIONS

This section is referred to in sections 116, 117, 118, 120, 123, 124, 125, 126 of this title.

§ 120. Procedure if no electronic database provided

(a) SAFE HARBOR.—If neither a State nor designated database provider provides an electronic database under section 119, a home service provider shall be held harmless from any tax, charge, or fee liability in such State that otherwise would be due solely as a result of an assignment of a street address to an incorrect taxing jurisdiction if, subject to section 121, the home service provider employs an enhanced zip code to assign each street address to a specific taxing jurisdiction for each level of taxing jurisdiction and exercises due diligence at each level of taxing jurisdiction to ensure that each such street address is assigned to the correct taxing jurisdiction. If an enhanced zip code overlaps boundaries of taxing jurisdictions of the same level, the home service provider must designate one specific jurisdiction within such enhanced zip code for use in taxing the activity for such enhanced zip code for each level of taxing jurisdiction. Any enhanced zip code assignment changed in accordance with section 121 is deemed to be in compliance with this section. For purposes of this section, there is a rebuttable presumption that a home service provider has exercised due diligence if such home service provider demonstrates that it has—

(1) expended reasonable resources to implement and maintain an appropriately detailed electronic database of street address assignments to taxing jurisdictions;

(2) implemented and maintained reasonable internal controls to promptly correct misassignments of street addresses to taxing jurisdictions; and

(3) used all reasonably obtainable and usable data pertaining to municipal annexations, incorporations, reorganizations and any other changes in jurisdictional boundaries that materially affect the accuracy of such database.

(b) TERMINATION OF SAFE HARBOR.—Subsection (a) applies to a home service provider that is in compliance with the requirements of subsection (a), with respect to a State for which an electronic database is not provided under section 119 until the later of—

(1) 18 months after the nationwide standard numeric code described in section 119(a) has been approved by the Federation of Tax Administrators and the Multistate Tax Commission; or

(2) 6 months after such State or a designated database provider in such State provides such database as prescribed in section 119(a).

(Added Pub. L. 106–252, § 2(a), July 28, 2000, 114 Stat. 628.)

EFFECTIVE DATE; APPLICATION OF AMENDMENT

Section effective July 28, 2000, and applicable only to customer bills issued after the first day of the first month beginning more than 2 years after July 28, 2000, see section 3 of Pub. L. 106–252, set out as a note under section 116 of this title.

SECTION REFERRED TO IN OTHER SECTIONS

This section is referred to in sections 116, 117, 118, 121, 123, 124, 125, 126 of this title.

§ 121. Correction of erroneous data for place of primary use

(a)[1] IN GENERAL.—A taxing jurisdiction, or a State on behalf of any taxing jurisdiction or taxing jurisdictions within such State, may—

(1) determine that the address used for purposes of determining the taxing jurisdictions to which taxes, charges, or fees for mobile telecommunications services are remitted does not meet the definition of place of primary use in section 124(8) and give binding notice to the home service provider to change the place of primary use on a prospective basis from the date of notice of determination if—

(A) if the taxing jurisdiction making such determination is not a State, such taxing jurisdiction obtains the consent of all affected taxing jurisdictions within the State before giving such notice of determination; and

(B) before the taxing jurisdiction gives such notice of determination, the customer is given an opportunity to demonstrate in accordance with applicable State or local tax, charge, or fee administrative procedures that the address is the customer's place of primary use;

(2) determine that the assignment of a taxing jurisdiction by a home service provider under section 120 does not reflect the correct taxing jurisdiction and give binding notice to the home service provider to change the assignment on a prospective basis from the date of notice of determination if—

(A) if the taxing jurisdiction making such determination is not a State, such taxing ju-

_____
[1] So in original. No subsec. (b) was enacted.

risdiction obtains the consent of all affected taxing jurisdictions within the State before giving such notice of determination; and

(B) the home service provider is given an opportunity to demonstrate in accordance with applicable State or local tax, charge, or fee administrative procedures that the assignment reflects the correct taxing jurisdiction.

(Added Pub. L. 106–252, § 2(a), July 28, 2000, 114 Stat. 629.)

EFFECTIVE DATE; APPLICATION OF AMENDMENT

Section effective July 28, 2000, and applicable only to customer bills issued after the first day of the first month beginning more than 2 years after July 28, 2000, see section 3 of Pub. L. 106–252, set out as a note under section 116 of this title.

SECTION REFERRED TO IN OTHER SECTIONS

This section is referred to in sections 116, 117, 118, 120, 122, 123, 124, 125, 126 of this title.

§ 122. Determination of place of primary use

(a) PLACE OF PRIMARY USE.—A home service provider shall be responsible for obtaining and maintaining the customer's place of primary use (as defined in section 124). Subject to section 121, and if the home service provider's reliance on information provided by its customer is in good faith, a taxing jurisdiction shall—

(1) allow a home service provider to rely on the applicable residential or business street address supplied by the home service provider's customer; and

(2) not hold a home service provider liable for any additional taxes, charges, or fees based on a different determination of the place of primary use for taxes, charges, or fees that are customarily passed on to the customer as a separate itemized charge.

(b) ADDRESS UNDER EXISTING AGREEMENTS.— Except as provided in section 121, a taxing jurisdiction shall allow a home service provider to treat the address used by the home service provider for tax purposes for any customer under a service contract or agreement in effect 2 years after the date of the enactment of the Mobile Telecommunications Sourcing Act as that customer's place of primary use for the remaining term of such service contract or agreement, excluding any extension or renewal of such service contract or agreement, for purposes of determining the taxing jurisdictions to which taxes, charges, or fees on charges for mobile telecommunications services are remitted.

(Added Pub. L. 106–252, § 2(a), July 28, 2000, 114 Stat. 630.)

REFERENCES IN TEXT

The date of the enactment of the Mobile Telecommunications Sourcing Act, referred to in subsec. (b), is the date of enactment of Pub. L. 106–252, which was approved July 28, 2000.

EFFECTIVE DATE; APPLICATION OF AMENDMENT

Section effective July 28, 2000, and applicable only to customer bills issued after the first day of the first month beginning more than 2 years after July 28, 2000, see section 3 of Pub. L. 106–252, set out as a note under section 116 of this title.

SECTION REFERRED TO IN OTHER SECTIONS

This section is referred to in sections 116, 117, 118, 123, 124, 125, 126 of this title.

§ 123. Scope; special rules

(a) ACT DOES NOT SUPERSEDE CUSTOMER'S LIABILITY TO TAXING JURISDICTION.—Nothing in sections 116 through 126 modifies, impairs, supersedes, or authorizes the modification, impairment, or supersession of, any law allowing a taxing jurisdiction to collect a tax, charge, or fee from a customer that has failed to provide its place of primary use.

(b) ADDITIONAL TAXABLE CHARGES.—If a taxing jurisdiction does not otherwise subject charges for mobile telecommunications services to taxation and if these charges are aggregated with and not separately stated from charges that are subject to taxation, then the charges for nontaxable mobile telecommunications services may be subject to taxation unless the home service provider can reasonably identify charges not subject to such tax, charge, or fee from its books and records that are kept in the regular course of business.

(c) NONTAXABLE CHARGES.—If a taxing jurisdiction does not subject charges for mobile telecommunications services to taxation, a customer may not rely upon the nontaxability of charges for mobile telecommunications services unless the customer's home service provider separately states the charges for nontaxable mobile telecommunications services from taxable charges or the home service provider elects, after receiving a written request from the customer in the form required by the provider, to provide verifiable data based upon the home service provider's books and records that are kept in the regular course of business that reasonably identifies the nontaxable charges.

(Added Pub. L. 106–252, § 2(a), July 28, 2000, 114 Stat. 630.)

REFERENCES IN TEXT

Act, referred to in subsec. (a), probably means the Mobile Telecommunications Sourcing Act, Pub. L. 106–252, July 28, 2000, 114 Stat. 626, which enacted sections 116 to 126 of this title and provisions set out as notes under sections 1 and 116 of this title. For complete classification of this Act to the Code, see Short Title of 2000 Amendment note set out under section 1 of this title and Tables.

EFFECTIVE DATE; APPLICATION OF AMENDMENT

Section effective July 28, 2000, and applicable only to customer bills issued after the first day of the first month beginning more than 2 years after July 28, 2000, see section 3 of Pub. L. 106–252, set out as a note under section 116 of this title.

SECTION REFERRED TO IN OTHER SECTIONS

This section is referred to in sections 116, 117, 118, 124, 125, 126 of this title.

§ 124. Definitions

In sections 116 through 126 of this title:

(1) CHARGES FOR MOBILE TELECOMMUNICATIONS SERVICES.—The term "charges for mobile telecommunications services" means any charge for, or associated with, the provision of commercial mobile radio service, as defined in

section 20.3 of title 47 of the Code of Federal Regulations as in effect on June 1, 1999, or any charge for, or associated with, a service provided as an adjunct to a commercial mobile radio service, that is billed to the customer by or for the customer's home service provider regardless of whether individual transmissions originate or terminate within the licensed service area of the home service provider.

(2) CUSTOMER.—

(A) IN GENERAL.—The term "customer" means—

(i) the person or entity that contracts with the home service provider for mobile telecommunications services; or

(ii) if the end user of mobile telecommunications services is not the contracting party, the end user of the mobile telecommunications service, but this clause applies only for the purpose of determining the place of primary use.

(B) The term "customer" does not include—

(i) a reseller of mobile telecommunications service; or

(ii) a serving carrier under an arrangement to serve the customer outside the home service provider's licensed service area.

(3) DESIGNATED DATABASE PROVIDER.—The term "designated database provider" means a corporation, association, or other entity representing all the political subdivisions of a State that is—

(A) responsible for providing an electronic database prescribed in section 119(a) if the State has not provided such electronic database; and

(B) approved by municipal and county associations or leagues of the State whose responsibility it would otherwise be to provide such database prescribed by sections 116 through 126 of this title.

(4) ENHANCED ZIP CODE.—The term "enhanced zip code" means a United States postal zip code of 9 or more digits.

(5) HOME SERVICE PROVIDER.—The term "home service provider" means the facilities-based carrier or reseller with which the customer contracts for the provision of mobile telecommunications services.

(6) LICENSED SERVICE AREA.—The term "licensed service area" means the geographic area in which the home service provider is authorized by law or contract to provide commercial mobile radio service to the customer.

(7) MOBILE TELECOMMUNICATIONS SERVICE.—The term "mobile telecommunications service" means commercial mobile radio service, as defined in section 20.3 of title 47 of the Code of Federal Regulations as in effect on June 1, 1999.

(8) PLACE OF PRIMARY USE.—The term "place of primary use" means the street address representative of where the customer's use of the mobile telecommunications service primarily occurs, which must be—

(A) the residential street address or the primary business street address of the customer; and

(B) within the licensed service area of the home service provider.

(9) PREPAID TELEPHONE CALLING SERVICES.—The term "prepaid telephone calling service" means the right to purchase exclusively telecommunications services that must be paid for in advance, that enables the origination of calls using an access number, authorization code, or both, whether manually or electronically dialed, if the remaining amount of units of service that have been prepaid is known by the provider of the prepaid service on a continuous basis.

(10) RESELLER.—The term "reseller"—

(A) means a provider who purchases telecommunications services from another telecommunications service provider and then resells, uses as a component part of, or integrates the purchased services into a mobile telecommunications service; and

(B) does not include a serving carrier with which a home service provider arranges for the services to its customers outside the home service provider's licensed service area.

(11) SERVING CARRIER.—The term "serving carrier" means a facilities-based carrier providing mobile telecommunications service to a customer outside a home service provider's or reseller's licensed service area.

(12) TAXING JURISDICTION.—The term "taxing jurisdiction" means any of the several States, the District of Columbia, or any territory or possession of the United States, any municipality, city, county, township, parish, transportation district, or assessment jurisdiction, or any other political subdivision within the territorial limits of the United States with the authority to impose a tax, charge, or fee.

(Added Pub. L. 106–252, §2(a), July 28, 2000, 114 Stat. 631.)

EFFECTIVE DATE; APPLICATION OF AMENDMENT

Section effective July 28, 2000, and applicable only to customer bills issued after the first day of the first month beginning more than 2 years after July 28, 2000, see section 3 of Pub. L. 106–252, set out as a note under section 116 of this title.

SECTION REFERRED TO IN OTHER SECTIONS

This section is referred to in sections 116, 117, 118, 121, 122, 123, 125, 126 of this title.

§ 125. Nonseverability

If a court of competent jurisdiction enters a final judgment on the merits that—

(1) is based on Federal law;

(2) is no longer subject to appeal; and

(3) substantially limits or impairs the essential elements of sections 116 through 126 of this title,

then sections 116 through 126 of this title are invalid and have no legal effect as of the date of entry of such judgment.

(Added Pub. L. 106–252, §2(a), July 28, 2000, 114 Stat. 632.)

EFFECTIVE DATE; APPLICATION OF AMENDMENT

Section effective July 28, 2000, and applicable only to customer bills issued after the first day of the first month beginning more than 2 years after July 28, 2000, see section 3 of Pub. L. 106–252, set out as a note under section 116 of this title.

SECTION REFERRED TO IN OTHER SECTIONS

This section is referred to in sections 116, 117, 118, 123, 124, 126 of this title.

§ 126. No inference

(a) INTERNET TAX FREEDOM ACT.—Nothing in sections 116 through this section of this title shall be construed as bearing on Congressional intent in enacting the Internet Tax Freedom Act or to modify or supersede the operation of such Act.

(b) TELECOMMUNICATIONS ACT OF 1996.—Nothing in sections 116 through this section of this title shall limit or otherwise affect the implementation of the Telecommunications Act of 1996 or the amendments made by such Act.

(Added Pub. L. 106–252, § 2(a), July 28, 2000, 114 Stat. 632.)

REFERENCES IN TEXT

The Internet Tax Freedom Act, referred to in subsec. (a), is title XI of Pub. L. 105–277, div. C, Oct. 21, 1998, 112 Stat. 2681–719, which is set out as a note under section 151 of Title 47, Telegraphs, Telephones, and Radiotelegraphs.

The Telecommunications Act of 1996, referred to in subsec. (b), is Pub. L. 104–104, Feb. 8, 1996, 110 Stat. 56. For complete classification of this Act to the Code, see Short Title of 1996 Amendment note set out under section 609 of Title 47, Telegraphs, Telephones, and Radiotelegraphs, and Tables.

EFFECTIVE DATE; APPLICATION OF AMENDMENT

Section effective July 28, 2000, and applicable only to customer bills issued after the first day of the first month beginning more than 2 years after July 28, 2000, see section 3 of Pub. L. 106–252, set out as a note under section 116 of this title.

SECTION REFERRED TO IN OTHER SECTIONS

This section is referred to in sections 116, 117, 118, 123, 124, 125 of this title.

CHAPTER 5—OFFICIAL TERRITORIAL PAPERS

AMENDMENTS

1951—Chapter added by act Oct. 31, 1951, ch. 655, § 12, 65 Stat. 713.

SIMILAR PROVISIONS; REPEAL; SAVING CLAUSE; DELEGATION OF FUNCTIONS; TRANSFER OF PROPERTY AND PERSONNEL

Similar provisions were contained in former chapter 5, comprising former sections 141 to 146, which was set out here but which was not a part of this title. Former sections 141 to 146 were derived from: acts Mar. 3, 1925, ch. 419, §§ 1, 2, 43 Stat. 1104; Mar. 3, 1925, ch. 419, §§ 3, 4, as added Feb. 28, 1929, ch. 385, 45 Stat. 1412, 1413; Feb. 28, 1929, ch. 385, 45 Stat. 1412 (in addition to the provisions added to said act Mar. 3, 1925); Mar. 22, 1935, ch. 39, § 1 (part), 49 Stat. 69; Feb. 14, 1936, ch. 70, 49 Stat. 1139; May 15, 1936, ch. 405, § 1 (part), 49 Stat. 1311; June 16, 1937, ch. 359, § 1 (part), 50 Stat. 262, 263; June 28, 1937, ch. 386, 50 Stat. 323, 324; Apr. 27, 1938, ch. 180, § 1 (part), 52 Stat. 249; June 29, 1939, ch. 248, title I (part), 53 Stat. 886; July 31, 1945, ch. 336, 59 Stat. 510, 511; 1946 Proc. No. 2714, Dec. 31, 1946, 12 F.R. 1; act Oct. 28, 1949, ch. 782, title XI, § 1106(a), 63 Stat. 972; 1950 Reorg. Plan No. 20, § 1, eff. May 24, 1950, 15 F.R. 3178, 64 Stat. 1272; act July 7, 1950, ch. 452, 64 Stat. 320. All of the foregoing provisions, with the exception of 1946 Proc. No. 2714, act Oct. 28, 1949, § 1106(a), and 1950 Reorg. Plan No. 20, were repealed by act Oct. 31, 1951, ch. 655, § 56(k)(1)–(11), 65 Stat. 730. Subsec. (l) of section 56 provided that the repeal should not affect any rights or liabilities existing under the repealed statutes on the effective date of the repeal (Oct. 31, 1951). For delegation of functions under the repealed statutes, and for transfer of records, property, personnel, and funds, see sections 3 and 4 of said 1950 Reorg. Plan No. 20, set out in the Appendix to Title 5, Government Organization and Employees.

§ 141. Collection, preparation and publication

The Archivist of the United States, hereinafter referred to in this chapter as the "Archivist", shall continue to completion the work of collecting, editing, copying, and suitably arranging for issuance as a Government publication, the official papers relating to the Territories from which States of the United States were formed, in the national archives, as listed in Parker's "Calendar of Papers in Washington" Archives Relating to the Territories of the United States (to 1873)", being publication numbered 148 of the Carnegie Institution of Washington, together with such additional papers of like character which may be found.

(Added Oct. 31, 1951, ch. 655, § 12, 65 Stat. 713; amended Pub. L. 98–497, title I, § 107(f), Oct. 19, 1984, 98 Stat. 2292.)

AMENDMENTS

1984—Pub. L. 98–497 substituted "Archivist of the United States" and "Archivist" for "Administrator of General Services" and "Administrator", respectively.

EFFECTIVE DATE OF 1984 AMENDMENT

Amendment by Pub. L. 98–497 effective Apr. 1, 1985, see section 301 of Pub. L. 98–497, set out as a note under section 2102 of Title 44, Public Printing and Documents.

SIMILAR PROVISIONS; REPEAL; SAVING CLAUSE; DELEGATION OF FUNCTIONS; TRANSFER OF PROPERTY AND PERSONNEL

See note preceding this section.

SECTION REFERRED TO IN OTHER SECTIONS

This section is referred to in sections 142, 143, 144 of this title.

§ 142. Appointment of experts

For the purpose of carrying on the work prescribed by section 141 of this title, the Archivist, without regard to the Classification Act of 1949 and the civil service laws and regulations thereunder, may engage the services, either in or outside of the District of Columbia, of not to exceed five historical experts who are especially informed on the various phases of the territorial history of the United States and are especially qualified for the editorial work necessary in arranging such territorial papers for publication.

(Added Oct. 31, 1951, ch. 655, § 12, 65 Stat. 714; amended Pub. L. 98–497, title I, § 107(f), Oct. 19, 1984, 98 Stat. 2292.)

REFERENCES IN TEXT

The Classification Act of 1949, referred to in text, is act Oct. 28, 1949, ch. 782, 63 Stat. 954, which was repealed by Pub. L. 89–554, § 8(a), Sept. 6, 1966, 80 Stat. 632, and reenacted by the first section thereof as chapter 51 and subchapter III of chapter 53 of Title 5, Government Organization and Employees.

The civil service laws, referred to in text, are set forth in Title 5. See, particularly, section 3301 et seq. of Title 5.

AMENDMENTS

1984—Pub. L. 98–497 substituted "Archivist" for "Administrator".

EFFECTIVE DATE OF 1984 AMENDMENT

Amendment by Pub. L. 98–497 effective Apr. 1, 1985, see section 301 of Pub. L. 98–497, set out as a note under section 2102 of Title 44, Public Printing and Documents.

SIMILAR PROVISIONS; REPEAL; SAVING CLAUSE; DELEGATION OF FUNCTIONS; TRANSFER OF PROPERTY AND PERSONNEL

See note preceding section 141 of this title.

§ 143. Employment and utilization of other personnel; cost of copy reading and indexing

(a) In carrying out his functions under this chapter, the Archivist may employ such clerical assistants as may be necessary.

(b) The work of copy reading and index making for the publication of the papers described in section 141 of this title shall be done by the regular editorial staff of the National Archives and Records Administration, and the cost of this particular phase of the work (prorated each month according to the number of hours spent and the annual salaries of the clerks employed) shall be charged against the annual appropriations made under section 146 of this title.

(Added Oct. 31, 1951, ch. 655, § 12, 65 Stat. 714; amended Pub. L. 98–497, title I, § 107(f), Oct. 19, 1984, 98 Stat. 2292.)

AMENDMENTS

1984—Subsec. (a). Pub. L. 98–497 substituted "Archivist" for "Administrator".

Subsec. (b). Pub. L. 98–497 substituted "National Archives and Records Administration" for "General Services Administration".

EFFECTIVE DATE OF 1984 AMENDMENT

Amendment by Pub. L. 98–497 effective Apr. 1, 1985, see section 301 of Pub. L. 98–497, set out as a note under section 2102 of Title 44, Public Printing and Documents.

SIMILAR PROVISIONS; REPEAL; SAVING CLAUSE; DELEGATION OF FUNCTIONS; TRANSFER OF PROPERTY AND PERSONNEL

See note preceding section 141 of this title.

§ 144. Cooperation of departments and agencies

The heads of the several executive departments and independent agencies and establishments shall cooperate with the Archivist in the work prescribed by section 141 of this title by permitting access to any records deemed by him to be necessary to the completion of such work.

(Added Oct. 31, 1951, ch. 655, § 12, 65 Stat. 714; amended Pub. L. 98–497, title I, § 107(f), Oct. 19, 1984, 98 Stat. 2292.)

AMENDMENTS

1984—Pub. L. 98–497 substituted "Archivist" for "Administrator".

EFFECTIVE DATE OF 1984 AMENDMENT

Amendment by Pub. L. 98–497 effective Apr. 1, 1985, see section 301 of Pub. L. 98–497, set out as a note under section 2102 of Title 44, Public Printing and Documents.

SIMILAR PROVISIONS; REPEAL; SAVING CLAUSE; DELEGATION OF FUNCTIONS; TRANSFER OF PROPERTY AND PERSONNEL

See note preceding section 141 of this title.

§ 145. Printing and distribution

(a) The Public Printer shall print and bind each volume of the official papers relating to the Territories of the United States as provided for in this chapter, of which—

(1) four hundred and twenty copies shall be delivered to the Superintendent of Documents, Government Printing Office, for distribution, on the basis of one copy each, and as directed by the Archivist, to those historical associations, commissions, museums, or libraries and other nondepository libraries, not to exceed eight in number within each State, Territory, or Possession, which have been or may be designated by the Governor thereof to receive such copies;

(2) one hundred copies shall be delivered to the National Archives and Records Administration for the use of that Administration; and

(3) one hundred copies shall be delivered to the Superintendent of Documents for distribution in such manner and number as may be authorized and directed by the Joint Committee on Printing.

(b) The historical associations, commissions, museums, or libraries and other nondepository libraries within each State, Territory, or Possession which have been or may be designated by the Governor thereof to receive the publications referred to in subsection (a) of this section, shall, during their existence, receive the succeeding volumes, the distribution of which shall be made by the Superintendent of Documents in accordance with lists of designations transmitted to him by the Archivist. A new designation may be made to the Archivist by the Governor only when a designated association, commission, museum, or library shall cease to exist, or when authorized by law.

(Added Oct. 31, 1951, ch. 655, § 12, 65 Stat. 714; amended Pub. L. 98–497, title I, § 107(f), Oct. 19, 1984, 98 Stat. 2292.)

AMENDMENTS

1984—Subsec. (a)(1). Pub. L. 98–497 substituted "Archivist" for "Administrator".

Subsec. (a)(2). Pub. L. 98–497 substituted "National Archives and Records Administration" for "General Services Administration".

Subsec. (b). Pub. L. 98–497 substituted "Archivist" for "Administrator" in two places.

EFFECTIVE DATE OF 1984 AMENDMENT

Amendment by Pub. L. 98–497 effective Apr. 1, 1985, see section 301 of Pub. L. 98–497, set out as a note under section 2102 of Title 44, Public Printing and Documents.

SIMILAR PROVISIONS; REPEAL; SAVING CLAUSE; DELEGATION OF FUNCTIONS; TRANSFER OF PROPERTY AND PERSONNEL

See note preceding section 141 of this title.

§ 146. Authorization of appropriations

For the purposes of this chapter, there are authorized to be appropriated, out of any money in the Treasury not otherwise appropriated, sums of not more than $50,000 for any one fiscal year.

(Added Oct. 31, 1951, ch. 655, § 12, 65 Stat. 715.)

SIMILAR PROVISIONS; REPEAL; SAVING CLAUSE; DELEGATION OF FUNCTIONS; TRANSFER OF PROPERTY AND PERSONNEL

See note preceding section 141 of this title.

SECTION REFERRED TO IN OTHER SECTIONS

This section is referred to in section 143 of this title.

TITLE 5—GOVERNMENT ORGANIZATION AND EMPLOYEES

Sections 101 to end appear in this volume

This title was enacted by Pub. L. 89–554, §1, Sept. 6, 1966, 80 Stat. 378

AMENDMENTS

1979—Pub. L. 96–54, §2(a)(1), Aug. 14, 1979, 93 Stat. 381, substituted "Civil Service Functions and Responsibilities" for "The United States Civil Service Commission" in item for part II.

TABLE SHOWING DISPOSITION OF ALL SECTIONS OF FORMER TITLE 5

Title 5 *Former Sections*	Title 5 *New Sections*
1, 2	101
3	Rep.
4	3345
5	3346
6	3347
7	3348
8	3349
9	5535
10	2901
11, 12	2902
13–14a, 15	Rep.
16	3331
16a	2903, 2904
17, 17a	Rep.
17b, 17c	2905
18	2903
19	Rep.
20	2904
21	2906
21a	3332
21b	5507
22	301
22–1 (less 3d–5th provisos)	7532
22–1 (3d proviso)	3571, 5594
22–1 (4th and 5th provisos)	7312
22–2	7533
22–3	7531
22a	302
23–26c	Rep.
27	6106
28	6105
29, 29a, 30 to 30b–1, 30c to 30e–1, 30f–30m.	Rep.
30n	6322
30n–1	T. 28 §1823
30o	5537
30p	5515
30q	6321
30r(a)	6323
30r(b)	3551
30r(c)	502, 5534
30r(d)	2105
31–31b, 32	Rep.
33	7154
34–35a, 36–37a	Rep.
38	3341
39, 40	3342
41	T. 14 §632
42, 42a	Rep.
43	3101
43a	3102
44	T. 31 §492–1 (See Rev. T. 31 Table)
45	Rep.

TABLE SHOWING DISPOSITION OF ALL SECTIONS OF FORMER TITLE 5—Continued

Title 5 *Former Sections*	Title 5 *New Sections*
46	3103
46a	5511
46b	5513
46c	T. 31 §699a (See Rev. T. 31 Table)
46d, 46e	5514
47	3103; T. 18 §1916
47a	8301; T. 10 §1221
48	T. 28 §514
49	3106
50	5501; T. 18 §1916
51	5536
52	5502
53	3108
54	3107
55	Rep.
55a	3109
56	5503
57–59c	Rep.
60	T. 2 §162
61	D.C. Code, §31–1009
61a	5552
61a–1(a), (f)	5534a
61a–1(b)–(e)	Rep.
61b (1st, 2d sentences)	5551
61b (3d–5th sentences)	6306
61b (6th sentence)	5551
61c–61e	Rep.
61f	5582
61g	5581
61h	5583
61i	5581
61j	5582
61k	5581
62–64a	Rep.
65	T. 2 §162
66	T. 18 §1914
67	T. 7 §2220
68	T. 8 §1353c
69	5535, 5536
70	5536
70a, 70b	5945
70c	5942
71	5536
72	5535
73, 73a	Rep.
73b	5731
73b–1(a), (b)	5724
73b–1(c)	5730
73b–1(d)	5725
73b–1(e)	5726
73b–1(f)	5727
73b–2	5703
73b–3(a) (less 3d–6th provisos)	5722
73b–3(a) (3d, 4th provisos)	5728
73b–3(a) (5th, 6th provisos)	5729
73b–3 (less (a))	5723
73b–4	T. 41 §5a
73b–4a, 73b–4b	5724a
73b–4c	5726
73b–4d	5724
73b–4e	5724a
73b–4f	5724
73b–5	5732
73c	5727
73c–1, 73c–2, 73d	Rep.
73e	5731
73f, 74–75a	Rep.

Title 5 Former Sections	Title 5 New Sections
75a–1	Elim.
75b–75d, 76	Rep.
76a	T. 20 § 244a
77, 77a	Rep.
78, 78a, 78a–1, 79, 80	T. 31 §§ 638a–638e (See Rev. T. 31 Table)
81, 81a	Rep.
82	5512
83	5946
84	5505
84a	T. 4 § 111
84b, 84c	5517
84d	5518
85	5502
86	Rep.
86a	6104
87–87c	6103
88	T. 31 § 554 (See Rev. T. 31 Table)
89	Rep.
90	T. 28 § 414
91	T. 28 § 520
92	Rep.
92a	2903
93	303
93a	Rep.
94	304
95, 95a	503
96	304
97, 98	Rep.
99, 100	Rep. See T. 18 § 207.
101	501
102	Rep.
103	5741
103a, 103b	5742
104	T. 31 § 492–2 (See Rev. T. 31 Table)
104a, 105	Rep.
105a	2954
106	2952
107	Rep.
108	T. 44 § 121 (See Rev. T. 44 Table)
109	Rep.
110	T. 40 § 484–1
111, 112	Rep.
113	7351
114	7341
114a	7342 note
115, 115a	7341
116	Elim.
116a, 117	Rep.
118	T. 31 § 686–2 (See Rev. T. 31 Table)
118a	5912
118b	T. 31 § 530a (See Rev. T. 31 Table)
118c	5943
118c–1 to 118e	Rep.
118f	5944
118g	7903
118h	5941
118i(a) (1st 4 sentences)	7324
118i(a) (5th sentence)	7327
118i(b) (less last proviso, and less last sentence).	7325
118i(b) (last proviso, last sentence).	Elim.
118i(c)	1308
118j, 118j–1	Rep.
118k(a)	1501, 1502
118k(b)	1504, 1505, 1506
118k(c)	1508
118k(d)	1302, 1507
118k(e), (f)	1501
118k–1	1501, 7324
118k–2	1501
118k–3	7324
118l	1501, 7324
118m	7327
118n	1503, 7326
118o	7323
118p	7311
118q	3333
118r	T. 18 § 1918
119–123	Elim.
124–131a, 132–133r	Rep.

Title 5 Former Sections	Title 5 New Sections
133s, 133t	Elim.
133u, 133v	Rep.
133w	Elim.
133x to 133y–16	Rep.
133z	901
133z–1	903
133z–2	904
133z–3	905
133z–4	906
133z–5, 133z–6	902
133z–7, 133z–8	907
133z–9	906
133z–10	908
133z–11 to 133z–15	909–913
134	T. 40 § 721
134a	T. 40 § 722
134b	T. 40 § 723
134b–1	T. 40 § 724
134b–2	T. 40 § 725
134c	T. 40 § 726
134d	T. 40 § 727
134e	T. 40 § 728
134f	T. 40 § 729
134g, 134h	T. 40 § 721 note
135–138j	Rep.
139–139f	T. 44 §§ 421–427 (See Rev. T. 44 Table)
140, 140a	T. 31 §§ 483a, 483b (See Rev. T. 31 Table)
141–149	Rep.
150	7901
150e–150i	T. 10 § 2575
150j	T. 10 §§ 4712, 9712
150j–1 to 150j–3	T. 10 §§ 4713, 9713
150k	2105
150k–1(a)	8171
150k–1(b)	8172
150k–1(c)	8173
150m–150o	T. 10 § 2541
150p	T. 10 § 2572
150q–150t	T. 10 § 2601
151	T. 22 § 2651
151a	T. 22 § 2652
151b	T. 22 § 2653
151c	T. 22 § 2658
151d to 152–1	Rep.
152a	T. 22 § 2654
152b	T. 22 § 2655
152c, 152d, 153	Rep.
153a	T. 22 § 2663
154	T. 22 § 2664
154a	Rep.
155	T. 22 § 2665
156	T. 22 § 2656
157	Rep.
158	T. 22 § 2657
159, 160	Rep.
161	T. 22 § 2659
162–164	Rep.
165	T. 22 § 2660
166–168d	Rep.
169	T. 22 § 2661
170	T. 22 § 2668
170a	T. 22 § 2681
170b	T. 22 § 2682
170c	T. 22 § 2683
170d	Rep.
170e	T. 22 § 2666
170e–1	T. 22 § 2667
170f	T. 22 § 2662
170g	T. 22 § 2669
170h	T. 22 § 2670
170i	T. 22 § 2671
170j	T. 22 § 2672
170k	T. 22 § 2673
170l	T. 22 § 2674
170m	T. 22 § 2675
170n	T. 22 § 2676
170o	T. 22 § 2677
170p	T. 22 § 2678
170q	T. 22 § 2679
170r, 170s	Rep.
170t	T. 22 § 2680
170u	T. 22 § 2684
171	T. 10 §§ 131, 133

Title 5 Former Sections	Title 5 New Sections
171–1	T. 50 § 408
171–2	T. 50 § 409
171a(a), (b)	T. 10 § 133
171a(c)	T. 10 §§ 125, 136, 141, 3010, 3012, 5011, 5031, 8010, 8012
171a(d)	T. 10 § 133
171a(e)	T. 10 § 132
171a(f)	T. 10 § 133
171a(g)–(i)	Elim.
171a(j)	T. 10 § 124
171a–1	T. 10 § 133
171b	Rep.
171c	T. 10 §§ 134–136, 718, 2358
171c–1, 171c–2, 171d to 171d–2	Rep.
171e	T. 10 § 171
171f	T. 10 §§ 141, 142
171g	T. 10 § 143
171h, 171i	Rep.
171j	T. 10 § 173
171j–1 to 171l	Rep.
171m	T. 50 § 411
171m–1	T. 10 § 2211
171n	T. 50 § 410
171o	Rep.
171p, 171q	T. 10 § 1581
171r	T. 10 § 1582
171s	T. 10 §§ 3230, 5416, 8230
171s–1	T. 31 § 700 (See Rev. T. 31 Table)
171t	T. 10 § 2571
171u	Rep.
171v	T. 10 § 1583
171w	T. 10 § 2385
171x, 171y	Rep.
171y–1	T. 10 §§ 3205, 5417, 8205
171z	T. 10 § 2661
171z–1	T. 10 § 2681
171z–2	T. 31 § 700a (See Rev. T. 31 Table)
171z–3 to 171z–5	T. 10 §§ 2673–2675
172	T. 10 § 136
172a	T. 10 §§ 3014, 5061, 8014
172b, 172c	T. 10 §§ 2203, 2204
172d	T. 10 § 2208
172d–1	T. 10 § 2210
172e	T. 10 § 2209
172f	T. 10 § 126
172g, 172h	T. 10 §§ 2205, 2206
172i	T. 10 § 2701
172j	T. 50 § 412
173	T. 10 § 2451
173a	Rep.
173b	T. 10 § 2451
173c–173e	T. 10 §§ 2452–2454
173f–173h	T. 10 § 2455
173i	T. 10 § 2456
174	T. 31 § 650a (See Rev. T. 31 Table)
174a	T. 37 § 412
174b	T. 10 § 2666
174c	Elim.
174d	T. 10 § 2207
174e	T. 10 § 2387
174f	Elim.
174g	T. 31 § 638f (See Rev. T. 31 Table)
174h	Elim.
174i	T. 31 § 700b (See Rev. T. 31 Table)
181	T. 10 § 3012
181–1(a)	T. 10 § 3012
181–1(b)	Elim.
181–1(c)	T. 10 § 101(5); T. 50 § 409(a)
181–1(d)	T. 10 § 3011
181–1(e)	T. 10 § 3062
181–2	T. 10 § 3012
181–3	T. 10 § 3001
181–4	T. 10 §§ 3012, 4532
181–5	T. 10 §§ 3013, 3017
181a, 182, 182a, 183, 184	Rep.
185–187	T. 10 § 3016
187a, 188, 189	Rep.
189a	T. 10 §§ 4025, 9025
189b	Rep.
189c	T. 10 § 2632
189d	Rep.
190	T. 10 § 3012

Title 5 Former Sections	Title 5 New Sections
191	T. 10 § 4831
191a	T. 10 § 1552
192, 192a, 193–194a, 195–197	Rep.
198	T. 10 § 4714
199	T. 10 §§ 3693, 8693
200	T. 10 § 1551
201	Rep.
202	T. 10 §§ 4565, 9565
203–207i, 208–213	Rep.
214	Elim.
215–216a, 217	Rep.
218	T. 10 § 2381
219–219b, 220	Rep.
221	T. 10 §§ 4540, 9540
222	T. 31 § 649a (See Rev. T. 31 Table)
223	Rep.
224	T. 22 § 276aa
225	T. 22 § 276bb
226	T. 22 § 276cc
227	T. 22 § 276dd
228	T. 22 § 276ee
229–232	Rep.
233–233c	(See former 150q–150t)
234–234f	Rep.
235	T. 10 § 4531
235a	T. 10 § 4503
235b	T. 10 § 174
235c	T. 10 § 1584
235d	T. 10 § 2352
235e	T. 10 §§ 2353, 2357
235f, 235g	T. 10 §§ 2354, 2355
235h	T. 10 §§ 174, 2356
241–245	T. 10 §§ 1001–1005 (See Rev. T. 31 Table)
245a	Rep. and Elim.
246	T. 31 § 1006 (See Rev. T. 31 Table)
246a	Rep.
247–248a	T. 31 §§ 1007–1009 (See Rev. T. 31 Table)
248b	Rep.
248c–248e	T. 31 §§ 1010, 1011, 1013 (See Rev. T. 31 Table)
249, 249a	Rep.
249b, 250	T. 31 §§ 1014, 1015 (See Rev. T. 31 Table)
251	Rep.
252–258a, 259–265	T. 31 §§ 1016–1030 (See Rev. T. 31 Table)
266–269	Rep.
270, 271	Elim.
272–274	Rep.
275	T. 10 § 1552
276	Rep.
277	T. 31 § 1031 (See Rev. T. 31 Table)
281	T. 19 § 2071
281a	T. 19 § 2072
281b	T. 19 § 2073
281c	T. 21 § 163
281d, 281e	Rep.
281f	T. 19 § 2072
281g	T. 19 § 2074
282	T. 21 § 161
282a	T. 21 § 162
282b	T. 21 § 164
282c	T. 21 § 165
291	T. 28 §§ 501, 503
292	T. 28 § 502
293	T. 28 § 505
293a	Rep.
294	T. 28 § 504
295, 295–1	T. 28 § 506
295a	Rep.
295b	Rep. and Elim.
296	Rep.
297	Rep. and Elim.
297a	Rep.
298	T. 28 § 543
298a	5108
299	T. 28 § 533
300	T. 28 §§ 533, 534
300a	T. 18 §§ 3052, 3107
300b	T. 31 § 224b (See Rev. T. 31 Table)

TABLE SHOWING DISPOSITION OF ALL SECTIONS OF
FORMER TITLE 5—Continued

TABLE SHOWING DISPOSITION OF ALL SECTIONS OF
FORMER TITLE 5—Continued

Title 5 Former Sections	Title 5 New Sections
300c, 300c–1	Rep.
300d	T. 28 § 536
300e–302	Rep.
303, 304	T. 28 §§ 511, 512
305	T. 28 § 521; T. 44 § 296a (See Rev. T. 44 Table)
306	T. 28 § 516
306a	Rep.
307	T. 28 § 513
308	Rep.
309	T. 28 § 518
310	T. 28 § 515
311	Rep.
311a	T. 28 § 535
312	T. 28 §§ 543, 547, 548
313	T. 28 § 514
314	3106
315	T. 28 § 515
316	T. 28 § 517
317	T. 28 §§ 547, 569
318	T. 28 §§ 549, 569
319	T. 28 § 523
320, 321	Rep.
322	T. 31 § 1010 (See Rev. T. 31 Table)
323, 324	T. 28 § 547
325	T. 31 § 1012 (See Rev. T. 31 Table)
326	T. 31 § 1011 (See Rev. T. 31 Table)
327	T. 28 § 547
328	T. 31 § 1013 (See Rev. T. 31 Table)
329	T. 28 §§ 547, 569
330, 331	T. 28 § 547
332	Rep. See Fed. Rules Civ. Proc. rule 2.
333	T. 28 § 522
334–339	Rep.
340	T. 28 § 534
341	T. 28 § 524
341a	T. 28 § 568
341b	T. 28 § 526
341c	T. 28 §§ 536, 537
341d	T. 8 § 1555
341e	T. 28 § 525
341f	T. 18 § 4010
341g	T. 18 § 4011
341h	T. 42 § 250a
342	T. 8 § 1551
342a	Elim.
342b	T. 8 § 1552
342b–1	T. 8 § 1553
342c	T. 8 § 1353a
342d	T. 8 § 1353b
342e	T. 8 § 1353d
342f	Rep.
342g	T. 8 § 1554
342h–342k	Elim.
342l	T. 8 § 1557
361	Rep. See T. 39 §§ 201, 203.
362	Rep. See T. 39 § 207.
363, 363a, 364	Rep. See T. 39 § 204.
364–1(a)	Rep. See T. 39 §§ 204, 401.
364–1(b), 364a, 364b	Rep.
365	Rep. See T. 39 § 1011.
366	Rep. See T. 39 § 401.
367	Rep. See T. 39 § 2201.
368	Rep.
369	Rep. See T. 39 §§ 202, 401, 403, 404.
370	Rep. See T. 39 §§ 1001, 1006.
371	Rep.
372, 373	Rep. See T. 39 § 407.
374	Rep. See T. 39 § 2202.
375	Rep. See T. 39 § 407.
376	Rep.
377	Rep. See T. 39 § 401.
378–382	Rep.
383, 384	Rep. See T. 39 § 2601.
385–388	Rep.
389	Rep. See T. 39 § 5213.
390, 391	Rep.
392	Rep. See T. 39 § 2603.
393	Rep. See T. 39 § 401.
411	T. 10 § 5031

Title 5 Former Sections	Title 5 New Sections
411a(a)	T. 10 § 101(5); T. 50 § 409(b)
411a(b)	T. 10 § 5012
411a(c)	T. 10 §§ 5013, 5402
411b, 412	T. 10 § 5031
412a	T. 10 §§ 6952, 7202–7211, 7214, 7215, 7218, 7301, 7472, 7478, 7571, 7572, 7576, 7578, 7579
412b	T. 10 § 2381
413	T. 10 § 5031
414, 415, 415a	Rep.
415b	T. 10 § 7473
415c	T. 10 § 7472
415d	T. 10 § 2632
415e, 416, 417	Rep.
418	T. 10 § 7216
419	T. 10 § 7221
419a	T. 10 § 7220
419b	T. 10 § 7222
419c	T. 10 § 7202
420, 420a, 421	T. 10 § 5034
421a	Rep.
421a–1	T. 10 §§ 5034, 5036
421b	T. 10 §§ 5033, 5036
421c	T. 10 § 7211
421d	T. 10 § 7204
421e	T. 10 §§ 7203, 7205
421f	T. 10 §§ 7207–7209
421g	T. 10 §§ 6081, 7204, 7205, 7211, 7214, 7218, 7571, 7572, 7576, 7579
422, 422a, 423	Rep.
423a	T. 10 §§ 5081, 5082, 5111
423b	T. 10 § 5081
423c–423f	T. 10 §§ 5085–5088
423g, 423h	T. 10 §§ 5111, 5112
423i	T. 10 § 5082
423j	T. 10 § 5036
423k	T. 10 §§ 5085, 5086, 5088, 5111
424	T. 10 § 5081
425	Rep.
425a	T. 10 §§ 5083, 5133, 5148, 5201
426, 426a	Rep.
427	T. 10 § 5081
427a	T. 10 § 5084
428	T. 10 § 5148
429	T. 10 §§ 5131, 5132
430	T. 10 § 5132
430a	T. 10 § 7303
430b	T. 10 § 5132
431	T. 10 § 5132
432	T. 10 §§ 5137, 5141, 5146, 5147
432a	T. 10 § 5135
433	T. 10 § 5147
434	T. 10 §§ 5141, 5144
435	T. 10 § 5145
436	Rep.
437	T. 10 § 5146
438	T. 10 § 5137
439	T. 10 §§ 5133, 5136
440	T. 10 §§ 5137, 5146
441	T. 10 §§ 5133, 5148
441a	T. 10 § 5133
442, 443	Rep.
444	T. 10 § 5149
445	T. 10 §§ 5135, 5147
446	T. 10 §§ 5135, 5141
447	T. 10 §§ 5135, 5144
448	T. 10 § 5145
448a	T. 10 § 5135
448b	T. 10 § 5145
449	T. 10 §§ 5135, 5146
450	Rep.
451	T. 10 § 5137
452	T. 10 §§ 5134–5136
453	T. 10 § 5149
454	Rep.
455	T. 10 § 5132
456	Rep.
456a	T. 10 § 1552
456b, 456c	T. 10 § 5138
456d	T. 10 § 6029
457	T. 10 § 7391
457a, 457b	Rep.
458	T. 10 §§ 7392, 7394
458a	T. 10 § 7393
459	T. 10 § 7394

Title 5 Former Sections	Title 5 New Sections
460, 460a	Rep.
461	T. 10 § 7395
462	Rep.
463	T. 10 § 7395
464	T. 10 § 7396
465	Rep.
466	T. 10 § 7217
467, 468, 468a, 469, 470	Rep.
471	T. 10 §§ 5063, 5064
475	T. 10 §§ 5150, 5151
475a, 475b	T. 10 § 5150
475c	T. 10 § 5153
475d	T. 10 §§ 5151, 5152
475e	T. 10 § 7522
475f	Rep.
475g	T. 10 § 174
475h	T. 10 § 1584
475i	T. 10 § 2352
475j	T. 10 §§ 2353, 2357
475k, 475l	T. 10 §§ 2354, 2355
475m	T. 10 §§ 174, 2356
476, 476a, 476b	T. 10 §§ 1581, 1582
477–477c	(See former 150q–150t)
481	T. 43 § 1451
481a	T. 43 § 1452
482	T. 43 § 1453
482a	Rep.
483	T. 43 § 1454
483–1	Rep. and Elim.
483–2	Rep.
483a	T. 43 § 1455
484	T. 43 § 1456
485	T. 43 § 1457
486	T. 43 § 1458
487	T. 43 § 1459
488	T. 43 § 1460
489	T. 43 § 1461
490	Rep. See T. 28 § 1733.
491	T. 43 § 1462
492	T. 43 § 1463
493	T. 43 § 1464
494	Rep.
495	T. 43 § 1465
496, 496a, 497	Rep.
498	T. 43 § 1466
499, 500	Rep.
501	Elim.
502	T. 43 § 1467
503	T. 43 § 1468
511	T. 7 § 2201
512	T. 7 § 2202
513	T. 7 § 2203
514	T. 7 § 2204
514a	T. 7 § 2210
514b	T. 7 § 2211
514c	Rep.
514d (1st, 3d pars.)	Rep.
514d (2d par.)	3101
515	T. 7 § 2205
516	T. 7 § 2206
516a	T. 7 § 450c
516b (less 3d sentence)	T. 7 § 450d
516b (3d sentence)	5109
516c	T. 7 § 450e
516d	T. 7 § 450f
516e	T. 7 § 450g
517	T. 7 § 2212
517a	Rep.
517b	T. 7 § 2213
517c	Rep.
518	Elim.
518a	T. 7 § 2214
519	T. 7 § 2215
520	T. 7 § 2216
520a	T. 7 § 2232
521	T. 7 § 2217
522	T. 7 § 2218
523–527	Rep.
528	T. 7 § 2219
529	Rep.
530	T. 7 § 2221
531	T. 7 § 2222
532	T. 7 § 2223
533	T. 7 § 2224
534–537	Rep.

Title 5 Former Sections	Title 5 New Sections
538	T. 7 § 2227
539–541b	Rep.
541c	T. 7 § 2233
541d	T. 7 § 2228
541e	T. 7 § 2229
542	T. 7 § 2234
542–1	T. 7 § 2235
542–2	T. 7 § 2236
542a	T. 7 § 2237
542b	T. 7 § 2238
542c	T. 7 § 2239
543	T. 7 § 2240
543a	T. 7 § 2230
543b	T. 7 § 2231
544–548	Rep.
549	T. 7 § 2241
550	Rep.
551	T. 7 § 2242
552	T. 7 § 2243
552a	T. 7 § 2244
553	T. 7 § 2245
554	T. 7 § 2246
555	T. 7 § 2247
556, 556a	Rep.
556b	T. 7 § 2248
557	T. 7 § 2207
557a	T. 7 § 2208
558	T. 7 § 2209
558a, 559–562	Rep.
563	T. 7 § 450b
564	T. 7 § 2220
564a	T. 7 § 2249
565	Rep.
565a	T. 7 § 2250
565b	T. 7 § 2250a
566	T. 7 § 2251
567	T. 7 § 2253
568	Rep.
568a	T. 7 § 2254
568b	Rep.
569	T. 7 § 2252
570	T. 7 § 2255
571	T. 7 § 2256
572	T. 7 § 2257
573	T. 7 § 2258
574	T. 7 § 2225
574a	T. 7 § 2226
575	T. 7 § 2259
576	T. 7 § 2260
577	T. 7 § 2261
578	T. 7 § 2262
579	T. 7 § 2263
591	T. 15 § 1501
591a	T. 15 § 1502
591b	T. 15 § 1503
592	T. 15 § 1504
592a	T. 15 § 1505
592a–1, 592a–2	Rep.
592a–3	T. 15 § 1506
592a–4	T. 15 § 1507
592b	T. 15 § 1508
592c, 592d, 593	Rep.
593a	T. 15 § 1509
594	T. 15 § 1510
595	Rep.
596	T. 15 § 1512
596a	T. 15 § 1514
597	T. 15 § 1511
597a, 597a–1, 597b–597d	Rep.
598	T. 15 § 1515
599	T. 15 § 1513
600–600b	Rep.
601	T. 15 § 1516
601a–601d	T. 15 §§ 189, 189a, 192, 192a
602	T. 15 § 1517
603	T. 15 § 1518
604	T. 15 § 1519
605	Rep.
606	T. 15 § 1520
606a	Rep.
607	T. 15 § 1521
608	Rep.
608a	T. 15 § 1522
608b	T. 15 § 1523
608c	T. 15 § 1524

TABLE SHOWING DISPOSITION OF ALL SECTIONS OF
FORMER TITLE 5—Continued

TABLE SHOWING DISPOSITION OF ALL SECTIONS OF
FORMER TITLE 5—Continued

Title 5 Former Sections	Title 5 New Sections	Title 5 Former Sections	Title 5 New Sections
611	T. 29 § 551	630e	T. 40 § 755
611a	T. 29 § 552	630f	Rep.
611b	T. 29 § 553	630g	T. 40 § 756
611c	Rep. and Elim.	630g–1	T. 40 § 757
612, 613	Rep.	630g–2	T. 40 § 759
613a	T. 29 § 554	630h	T. 40 § 758
613b	T. 29 § 555	630i	Elim.
614	Rep.	630j	Rep.
615	T. 29 § 556	631	3301, 7301
616	T. 29 § 557	631a, 631b(a)	Elim.
617	T. 29 § 558	631b(b), (c)	3304
618	T. 29 § 559	632 (1st par.)	1101
619	Rep.	632 (2d–4th pars.)	1102
620	T. 29 § 560	632 (5th par.)	1103
621	T. 29 § 561	633(1)	1301, 3302
622	T. 29 § 562	633(2)1	3304
622a	T. 29 § 563	633(2)2	3318
623	T. 42 § 3501	633(2)3	3306
623a	T. 42 § 3508	633(2)4	3321
623b	T. 42 § 3503	633(2)5	7321
623c	T. 42 § 3504	633(2)6	7152, 7322
623d	T. 42 § 3505	633(2)7	1302, 3304
623e	T. 42 § 3507	633(2)8	2951, 3302
623f	T. 42 § 3506	633(2)9	7153
623g	T. 42 § 3502	633(3)	1302, 1307
623h	T. 42 § 3501a	633(4)	1303
623i	Elim.	633(5)	1308
624	T. 42 § 3531	633a–633e	Rep.
624a	T. 42 § 3532	634	1306
624b	T. 42 § 3533	635 (1st 5 sentences)	1104, 1105
624c	T. 42 § 3534	635 (6th sentence)	1105, 3305
624d	T. 42 § 3535	635 (7th sentence)	3304
624e	T. 42 § 3536	636	Rep.
624f	T. 42 § 3537	637	T. 18 § 1917
626(a)	T. 10 § 8012	638	2102, 3304, 3361
626(b)	Rep.	638a	Rep.
626(c)	T. 10 § 101(5); T. 50 § 409(c)	638b	3307, 3322
626(d)	T. 10 § 8013	639	Rep.
626(e)	T. 10 § 8012	640	7352
626(f)	T. 10 § 8033	641	3319
626(g)	T. 10 § 8011	642	3303
626–1	T. 10 § 8013, 8017	642a	2953
626–2	T. 10 §§ 8012, 9532	643–645b	Rep.
626a	T. 10 § 8012	645c–645e	Elim.
626b	T. 10 § 8013	646–651b	Rep.
626c(a), (f)	T. 10 § 8062	652(a)	7501
626c(b)	T. 10 § 743	652(b)	5591–5593
626c(c)–(e), 626c–1 to 626c–3, 626d, 626e.	Rep.	652(c)	7101
		652(d)	7102
626f	(See former 150p)	652a–652c	5596
626g–626j	(See former 150q–150t)	653, 654	Rep.
626k	Rep.	655–657	1304
626l, 626m	T. 10 § 9441	658	Elim.
626n	T. 10 § 2632	659	3327
626o	Rep.	661–663b, 664–669a, 670–672c, 673–673b.	Rep.
626p	T. 10 § 9774		
626q, 626r	T. 10 § 9301	673c (1st par., less provisos)	Rep.
626s to 626s–2	T. 10 § 2481	673c (1st proviso)	6102
626s–3	T. 10 § 2667	673c (2d, 3d provisos)	5544
626s–4, 626s–5	Rep.	673c (2d par.), 674–678b	Rep.
626s–6	T. 10 § 2667	679	Elim.
626t, 626u	T. 10 § 1581	680–684, 691, 691a, 692–692d, 693 to 693–2, 693a–693d, 694, 649a, 695, 695a, 696, 696a, 697, 697a, 698–698b, 699, 699a, 700, 700a, 701, 701a, 702, 702a, 703, 703a, 704, 704a, 705, 705a, 706, 706a, 707, 707a, 708, 708a, 709–615.	Rep.
626v–626y, 627	Rep.		
627a	T. 10 §§ 8208, 8215		
627b	T. 10 §§ 8071, 8208, 8297, 8299, 8305, 8504, 8685, 8888, 8915, 8916, 8927, 8962, 8991		
627c	Rep.	715a	3323
627d	T. 10 § 8256	715b–715d, 716–718a, 719, 719–1, 719a, 719b, 720–729a, 730–736c, 737–739b, 740, 740a.	Rep.
627e	T. 10 § 8685		
627f	T. 10 §§ 8549, 8580, 8818		
627g–627l	Rep.	740b–740i	(See former 2281–2288)
628	T. 10 § 9531	745–745r	Rep.
628a	T. 10 § 9503	751	8102
628b	T. 10 § 174	752	8117
628c	T. 10 § 1584	753	8105
628d	T. 10 § 2352	754	8106
628e	T. 10 §§ 2353, 2357	755(a), (b)	8107
628f, 628g	T. 10 §§ 2354, 2355	755(c)	8108
628h	T. 10 §§ 174, 2356	755(d)	8109
630	T. 40 § 751	756(a)	8110
630a	T. 40 § 752	756(b)	8111
630b	T. 40 § 753	756(c)	8112
630c	Rep.	756(d)	8113
630d	T. 40 § 754		

Title 5 Former Sections	Title 5 New Sections
756a	Rep.
757	8116
758	8118
759(a)	8103
759(b)	8104
759(c)	3315a
760(A)	8133
760(B)	8101, 8133
760(C)–(G)	8133
760(H)	8101
760(I)–(K)	8133
760(L)	T. 18 § 1921
760(M)	8101
761	8134
762	8114
763	8115
764	8135
765–767	8119
768, 769	8121
770	8122
771, 772, 773(a)	8123
773(b)	8127; T. 18 § 292
773(c)	8125
774(a)	8120
774(b)	T. 18 § 1922
775	8130
776	8131
777	8132
778	8145
779	8120
780	8126
781	8145
782	Rep.
783	8145, 8149
784(a)	8148
784(b), (c)	7902
785	8147
786	8124
787	8128
788	8129
789	T. 18 § 1920
790	8101
791	8131
791–1 to 791–3, 791–4(a)	Rep.
791–4(b)	8150
791a	Rep.
791b	Elim.
792	Rep.
793 (1st par.)	8146
793 (2d par., 1st sentence)	8146
793 (2d par., 2d sentence)	8138
793 (2d par., 3d, 4th sentences)	8146
793 (3d par.)	8146
793 (4th par., 1st sentence)	8138
793 (4th par., 2d sentence)	8136
793 (5th par., 1st through 6th sentences).	8137
793 (5th par., 7th sentence)	8128
793 (5th par., 8th sentence)	8137
793a(a), (b)	8146a
793a(c)	8101
794	8101, 8139
795–797a, 798–801	Rep.
802	8140
803(a)–(c)	8141
803(d)	Rep.
803a	8150
821–823	Rep.
823a	(See former 73c)
824–834	Rep.
835	5701
836	5702
837	5704
838	5705
839	5706
840	5707
841, 842	5708
851	1302, 2108
852 (1st 2 sentences)	3309, 3310
852 (less 1st 2 sentences)	Elim.
853	3311
854	3308, 3312, 3351, 3363, 3504
855	3306, 3319
856	3313
857	3317, 3318, 3364

Title 5 Former Sections	Title 5 New Sections
858	3320
859	3305
860	1302
861	3501–3503
862	3316
863	3315, 7512, 7701
864	3315, 3318
865	3314
866, 867	Rep.
868	1302, 7701
869	3320
901(a)	5541
901(b)	Rep.
901(c)	T. 2 § 60e–2. Rep. in part.
901(d), (e)	5541
902	5541; T. 2 § 60e–2
911	5542
912	5543
912a, 912b	5542
913	5544
914	5506
921	5545
921a	5546
922	5546
926	5545
931	T. 2 § 60e–3
932	T. 2 § 60e–4
932a	T. 2 § 60e–5
932b	T. 2 § 60e–6
932c(a)–(c)	T. 2 § 60e–7
932c(d)	8331
932d(a)–(c)	T. 2 § 60e–8
932d(d)	8331
932d(e)	Rep.
932d(f)	T. 2 § 60e–8
932e(a)–(e)	T. 2 § 60e–9
932e(f)	8331
932f(a)–(d)	T. 2 § 60e–10
932f(e)	8331
932f(f)	T. 2 § 60e–10
932f(g)	Rep.
932g(a)–(c)	T. 2 § 60e–11
932g(d)	8331
932g(e)	T. 2 § 60e–11
932h(a), (b)	T. 2 § 60e–12
932h(c)	8331
932h(d)	T. 2 § 60e–12
932i(a), (b)	T. 2 § 60e–13
932i(c)	8331
932i(d), (e)	T. 2 § 60e–13
933	5544; T. 2 § 60e–2b
933a	T. 31 § 46a (See Rev. T. 31 Table)
934, 935	Rep.
941	5549
942–942b	Rep.
943	5547
943a	Rep.
944(a)	6101
944(b), (c)	5504
944(d)	5504, 6101
945	5504, 5548, 6101
946	5342
947–954	Rep.
955	T. 2 § 60e–4a
956–958	Rep.
1001	551
1002	552
1003	553
1004	554
1005	555
1006	556
1007	557
1008	558
1009	701–706
1010 (1st sentence)	3105
1010 (2d sentence)	7521
1010 (3d sentence)	4301, 5335, 5362
1010 (4th sentence)	3344
1010 (5th sentence)	1305
1011	559
1012–1014	500
1031–1040	T. 28 §§ 2341–2350
1041	T. 28 § 2352
1042	T. 28 § 2351
1045(a)–(d)	Elim.

Title 5 Former Sections	Title 5 New Sections
1045(e)	571
1045a	572
1045b	573
1045c	574
1045d	575
1045e	576
1051	5352, 5353
1052	5351
1053	8144
1054	8331, 8332
1055	5354
1056	Rep.
1057	5355
1058	5356
1071	5101
1072, 1072a	5115
1073	Rep.
1074	7154
1075	Rep.
1076	Elim.
1081	5102
1082	5102, 5341, 5342
1083	5103
1084(a)	T. 2 §60e–2a
1084(b), (c)	5102, 5103
1085	305
1091	5102
1092, 1093	5106
1094	5105
1101	5112
1102	5107, 5110
1103	5110
1104	5111
1105(a)–(l)	3324, 5108
1105(m)	Rep.
1105a	5114
1105b	Elim.
1106	5113
1107	5337
1111, 1112	5104
1113	5332
1114–1116	Rep.
1117	5595
1121	5335
1122	5336
1123	5335, 5336
1124, 1125	Rep.
1131	5333
1132	5334
1133	5333
1134	5545
1141, 1142	Rep.
1151	305
1152, 1153	Rep.
1161	3104, 3325, 5361
1162(a)	3325
1162(b)	5361
1162(c)	3104
1163	3104
1171	5301
1172	5302
1173	5303
1174	5304
1181	5343
1182(a)	5344, 5581
1182(b)	8331
1182(c)	5344
1183	8704
1184	Rep.
2001	4301
2002	4302
2003	4307
2004	4303
2005	4304
2006	4305
2007(a)	4308
2007(b)–(d)	4306
2061	5508, 6301, 6305
2061a	5551, 6302
2062(a), (b)	6303
2062(c), (d)	6304
2062(e)	6303
2062(f)	6305
2062(g)	6310
2062(h)	6302

Title 5 Former Sections	Title 5 New Sections
2062(i)	6303
2062a, 2062b	Rep.
2063	6307
2064(a)–(c)	6302
2064(d)	6309
2064(e)	6308
2065	6311
2066(a)	6304
2066(b)–(d)	Rep.
2067	6301
2068–2070	Rep.
2071	6324
2091(a)	8701, 8716
2091(b)	8701
2091(c)	8706
2091(d)	8701, 8716
2092(a)–(c)	8704
2092(d)	Rep.
2093	8705
2094(a) (1st par.)	8707
2094(a) (2d par.)	8702
2094(b)	8708
2094(c), (d)	8714. Elim. in part.
2095	8706
2096	8709, 8710
2097	8711, 8712
2098	8703
2099	Elim.
2100	8716. Elim. in part.
2101	8713. Elim. in part.
2102	1308. Elim. in part.
2103	8715. Elim. in part.
2121	1308, 4506
2122	4501
2123(a)	4503
2123(b)	4504
2123(c)	4505
2123(d), (e)	4502
2123(f)	3362
2123(g)	4502
2131	5901
2132	5901, 8331
2133	5901
2134	5902
2151	T. 10 §1481
2152, 2153	T. 10 §§1481, 1482
2154	T. 10 §1481
2155–2160	T. 10 §§1483–1488
2161, 2162	T. 10 §1482
2163	Rep.
2171	T. 42 §1973cc–1
2172	T. 42 §1973cc–2
2173	T. 42 §1973cc–3
2181	T. 42 §1973cc–11
2182	T. 42 §1973cc–12
2183	T. 42 §1973cc–13
2184	T. 42 §1973cc–14
2185	T. 42 §1973cc–15
2191	T. 42 §1973cc–21
2192	T. 42 §1973cc–22
2193	T. 42 §1973cc–23
2194	T. 42 §1973cc–24
2195	T. 42 §1973cc–25
2196	T. 42 §1973cc–26
2201–2209	Rep.
2210	5311
2211(a)	5312
2211(b)(1)–(14)	5313
2211(b)(15) (less proviso)	Elim.
2211(b)(15) (proviso)	5314
2211(b)(16)–(19)	5313
2211(c)(1)–(38)	5314
2211(c)(39) (less proviso)	Elim.
2211(c)(39) (proviso)	5315
2211(c)(40)–(45)	5314
2211(c)(46) (less proviso)	Elim.
2211(c)(46) (proviso)	5315
2211(c)(47)	5314
2211(d)	5315
2211(e)	5316
2211(f)	5317
2211(g)	5315, 5316
2212	5363
2213	5364
2251(a)–(g)	8331

TABLE SHOWING DISPOSITION OF ALL SECTIONS OF
FORMER TITLE 5—Continued

Title 5 Former Sections	Title 5 New Sections
2251(h)–(j)	8341
2251(k)–(t)	8331
2252(a)–(d)	8331
2252(e)	8347
2252(f)	8331, 8347
2252(g)	8331, 8332
2252(h)	8331, 8332, 8347
2253(a)–(e)	8332
2253(f), (g)	8333
2253(h)–(j)	8332
2254	8334
2255	8335
2256(a)–(e)	8336
2256(f)	8333, 8336
2257	8337
2258	8338
2259	8339
2260	8341
2261	8342
2262	8343
2263(a)	3323
2263(b), (c)	8344
2264	8345
2265	8346
2266(a)–(e)	8347
2266(f)	1308
2266(g)	8347
2267	8348
2268	8340
2281	8311
2282	8312
2283(a)	8314
2283(b), (c)	8315
2283a	8313
2284(a), (b)	8316
2284(c), (d)	8317
2284a(a)	8317
2284a(b)	8316
2285(a), (b)	8318
2285(c)	8320
2286	8321
2287	8319
2288	8322
2301(1)–(3)	Elim.
2301(4)	4117
2302	4101
2303	4102
2304	4113
2305	4118
2306	4103
2307	4104
2308	4105
2309	4109
2310	4108
2311	4106
2312, 2313	4107
2314	4114
2315	4115
2316	4116
2317(a)	4113
2317(b), (c)	1308
2318(a)	4111
2318(b)	4110
2318(c)	4111
2318(d)	4107
2318(e)	4117
2319	4112
2331	3343, 3581
2332	3343
2333	3582, 3583
2334	3584
2351–2356	T. 20 §§ 901–906
2357	5334
2358(a)	5541, 6301
2358(b)	T. 20 § 907
2358(c)	8331, 8701
2371–2379	T. 42 § 4271–4279
3001	8901
3002(a)–(f)	8901, 8905, 8913
3002(g)	Rep.
3003	8903
3004	8904
3005	8902
3006	8906
3007	8909

TABLE SHOWING DISPOSITION OF ALL SECTIONS OF
FORMER TITLE 5—Continued

Title 5 Former Sections	Title 5 New Sections
3008(a)	Rep.
3008(b)	8909
3009(a), (b)	8913
3009(c)	8908
3009(d)	8907
3010	8910
3011	1308
3012	8911
3013(a)	1104, 5109
3013(b)	Rep.
3014	8912
3031	Elim.
3032	5921
3033–3035	5922
3036	5923
3037	5924
3038	5925
3039	5913
3051–3060	Elim.
3071	5521
3072	5522
3073	5523
3074	5524
3075	5525
3076	5527
3077	Rep.
3078	5526
3101	3326, 3501, 5531, 6303. Elim. in part.
3102(a)–(e)	5532
3102(f)–(h)	Elim.
3103	3326
3104	Elim.
3105(a)–(d)	5533
3105(e)	Elim.
3105(f)	5533
3121–3127	5911

ENACTING CLAUSE

Section 1 of Pub. L. 89–554, Sept. 6, 1966, 80 Stat. 378, provided in part: "That the laws relating to the organization of the Government of the United States and to its civilian officers and employees, generally, are revised, codified, and enacted as title 5 of the United States Code, entitled 'Government Organization and Employees', and may be cited as '5 U.S.C., §   '."

LEGISLATIVE PURPOSE: INCONSISTENT PROVISIONS

Section 7(a) of Pub. L. 89–554, Sept. 6, 1966, 80 Stat. 631, provided that: "The legislative purpose in enacting sections 1–6 of this Act is to restate, without substantive change, the laws replaced by those sections on the effective date of this Act [Sept. 6, 1966]. Laws effective after June 30, 1965, that are inconsistent with this Act are considered as superseding it to the extent of the inconsistency."

REFERENCES TO OTHER LAWS

Section 7(b) of Pub. L. 89–554, Sept. 6, 1966, 80 Stat. 631, provided that: "A reference to a law replaced by sections 1–6 of this Act, including a reference in a regulation, order, or other law, is deemed to refer to the corresponding provision enacted by this Act."

OUTSTANDING ORDERS, RULES AND REGULATIONS

Section 7(c) of Pub. L. 89–554, Sept. 6, 1966, 80 Stat. 631, provided that: "An order, rule, or regulation in effect under a law replaced by sections 1–6 of this Act continues in effect under the corresponding provision enacted by this Act until repealed, amended, or superseded."

SAVINGS PROVISION

Section 7(d) of Pub. L. 89–554, Sept. 6, 1966, 80 Stat. 631, provided that: "An action taken or an offense committed under a law replaced by sections 1–6 of this Act is deemed to have been taken or committed under the corresponding provision enacted by this Act."

LEGISLATIVE CONSTRUCTION

Section 7(e) of Pub. L. 89–554, Sept. 6, 1966, 80 Stat. 631, provided that: "An inference of a legislative construction is not to be drawn by reason of the location in the United States Code of a provision enacted by this Act or by reason of the caption or catchline thereof."

PAY, ALLOWANCES, COMPENSATION, OR ANNUITY

Section 7(f) of Pub. L. 89–554, Sept. 6, 1966, 80 Stat. 631, provided that: "The enactment of this Act does not increase or decrease the pay, allowances, compensation, or annuity of any person."

SEPARABILITY

Section 7(g) of Pub. L. 89–554, Sept. 6, 1966, 80 Stat. 631, provided that: "If a provision enacted by this Act is held invalid, all valid provisions that are separable from the invalid provision remain in effect. If a provision of this Act is held invalid in one or more of its applications, the provision remains in effect in all valid applications that are severable from the invalid application or applications."

APPLICABILITY TO COMMISSIONED OFFICERS OF PUBLIC HEALTH SERVICE AND COAST AND GEODETIC SURVEY

Section 7(h) of Pub. L. 89–554, Sept. 6, 1966, 80 Stat. 632, provided that: "Sections 1–6 of this Act shall be construed to apply to commissioned officers of the Public Health Service and commissioned officers of the Coast and Geodetic Survey [now the National Oceanic and Atmospheric Administration] to the same extent that the laws replaced by those sections applied to these officers immediately before the date of enactment of this Act [Sept. 6, 1966]."

REPEALS

Section 8(a) of Pub. L. 89–554, Sept. 6, 1966, 80 Stat. 632, repealed the sections or parts thereof of the Revised Statutes or Statutes at Large codified in this title, except with respect to rights and duties that matured, penalties that were incurred, and proceedings that were begun, before Sept. 6, 1966, and except as provided by section 7 of Pub. L. 89–554.

Section 8(c) of Pub. L. 89–554, Sept. 6, 1966, 80 Stat. 632, provided that: "The repeal of a law by this Act may not be construed as a legislative inference that the provision was or was not in effect before its repeal."

CONTINUATION OF RIGHT TO DEFERRED ANNUITY

Section 8(b) of Pub. L. 89–554, Sept. 6, 1966, 80 Stat. 632, provided that: "The right to a deferred annuity on satisfaction of the conditions attached thereto is continued notwithstanding the repeal of the law conferring the right."

IMPROVEMENT OF UNITED STATES CODE BY PUB. L. 90–83; LEGISLATIVE PURPOSE; INCONSISTENT PROVISIONS; CORRESPONDING PROVISIONS; SAVINGS AND SEPARABILITY OF PROVISIONS

Section 9(a)–(g) of Pub. L. 90–83, Sept. 11, 1967, 81 Stat. 222, provided that:

"(a) The legislative purpose in enacting sections 1–8 of this Act is to restate, without substantive change, the laws replaced by those sections on the effective date of this Act. Laws effective after February 21, 1967, that are inconsistent with this Act are considered as superseding it to the extent of the inconsistency.

"(b) A reference to a law replaced by sections 1–8 of this Act, including a reference in a regulation, order, or other law, is deemed to refer to the corresponding provision enacted by this Act.

"(c) An order, rule, or regulation in effect under a law replaced by sections 1–8 of this Act continues in effect under the corresponding provision enacted by this Act until repealed, amended, or superseded.

"(d) An action taken or an offense committed under a law replaced by sections 1–8 of this Act is deemed to have been taken or committed under the corresponding provision enacted by this Act.

"(e) An inference of a legislative construction is not to be drawn by reason of the location in the United States Code of a provision enacted by this Act or by reason of the caption or catchline thereof.

"(f) The enactment of this Act does not increase or decrease the pay, allowances, compensation, or annuity of any person.

"(g) If a provision enacted by this Act is held invalid, all valid provisions that are severable from the invalid provision remain in effect. If a provision of this Act is held invalid in one or more of its applications, the provision remains in effect in all valid applications that are severable from the invalid application or applications."

TITLE REFERRED TO IN OTHER SECTIONS

This title is referred to in title 2 sections 353, 437c, 622, 1316a; title 7 sections 84, 1765a, 1988, 6981, 7317; title 10 sections 1408, 1552, 1603, 1606, 2164; title 12 sections 1422b, 1795f, 1821, 2278a–3, 2279aa–3, 2405, 3307; title 14 section 186; title 15 sections 634d, 648, 649a, 2206, 2451, 6804; title 16 sections 410cc–36, 410ww–24, 410ccc–22, 450ss–3, 469j, 583j–1, 712f, 1401, 3702, 4005, 4604, 5804; title 18 sections 202, 3006A; title 20 sections 76k, 80g, 80o, 80q–4, 971, 1004, 1018, 1067j, 1098, 1137, 1138b, 1213c, 1221e, 1417, 1505, 3413, 3425, 3461, 4416, 5509, 5826, 6011, 6021, 6031, 9011, 9105, 9252; title 21 sections 394, 1908; title 22 sections 1622d, 2124c, 2421, 2581, 2905, 3008, 3652, 3664, 4606, 4823, 5421, 6204, 6207; title 24 section 417; title 25 sections 640d–11, 1661, 2021, 2022, 2704, 2707, 3113, 3505, 3731; title 26 sections 7471, 7803, 9010, 9040; title 28 sections 375, 561, 601, 625, 1877; title 29 sections 762, 783, 1147, 1808; title 30 section 1724; title 31 sections 301, 732, 733; title 33 section 1123; title 35 section 3; title 36 sections 151304, 151704, 152404; title 37 section 7257; title 38 sections 106, 707, 4103, 4312, 4322, 5303A, 7281, 7403, 7406, 7425, 7453, 7802; title 40 sections 136, 873, 1106; title 41 section 422; title 42 sections 217a, 237, 282, 285a–2, 285a–4, 285b–3, 288–4, 290aa, 299c–1, 299c–5, 300v–2, 903, 904, 907a, 1314, 1320a–4, 1320b–9, 1320c–2, 1395b–6, 1395m, 1395oo, 1395ww, 1863, 1975b, 2000e–4, 2210, 3015, 3525, 3533, 3788, 4025, 4372, 4768, 5149, 5404, 5667g–2, 7231, 7412, 8104, 10704, 12314, 12373, 12619, 12651e, 12651f, 14196; title 43 section 1731; title 46 App. sections 41, 1295g; title 49 sections 325, 32306; title 50 section 2081; title 50 App. section 2153.

PART I—THE AGENCIES GENERALLY

AMENDMENTS

1996—Pub. L. 104–121, title II, §253, Mar. 29, 1996, 110 Stat. 874, added item for chapter 8.

CHAPTER 1—ORGANIZATION

CHAPTER REFERRED TO IN OTHER SECTIONS

This chapter is referred to in title 15 section 2225a; title 19 section 2571.

---

[1] Pub. L. 90–83 added section 500 to chapter 5 without making a corresponding change in Part analysis.

[2] Editorially supplied. Chapter 6 added by Pub. L. 96–354 without a corresponding amendment of Part analysis.

§ 101. Executive departments

The Executive departments are:
  The Department of State.
  The Department of the Treasury.
  The Department of Defense.
  The Department of Justice.
  The Department of the Interior.
  The Department of Agriculture.
  The Department of Commerce.
  The Department of Labor.
  The Department of Health and Human Services.
  The Department of Housing and Urban Development.
  The Department of Transportation.
  The Department of Energy.
  The Department of Education.
  The Department of Veterans Affairs.

(Pub. L. 89–554, Sept. 6, 1966, 80 Stat. 378; Pub. L. 89–670, §10(b), Oct. 15, 1966, 80 Stat. 948; Pub. L. 91–375, §6(c)(1), Aug. 12, 1970, 84 Stat. 775; Pub. L. 95–91, title VII, §710(a), Aug. 4, 1977, 91 Stat. 609; Pub. L. 96–88, title V, §508(b), Oct. 17, 1979, 93 Stat. 692; Pub. L. 100–527, §13(b), Oct. 25, 1988, 102 Stat. 2643.)

HISTORICAL AND REVISION NOTES

Derivation	U.S. Code	Revised Statutes and Statutes at Large
....	5 U.S.C. 1.	R.S. §158. Feb. 9, 1889, ch. 122, §1 (38th through 54th words), 25 Stat. 659. Feb. 14, 1903, ch. 552, §1 (83d through 99th words), 32 Stat. 825. Mar. 4, 1913, ch. 141, §1 (75th through 91st words), 37 Stat. 736. Aug. 10, 1949, ch. 412, §4 "Sec. 201(c)", 63 Stat. 579. July 31, 1956, ch. 802, §1(a), 70 Stat. 732.
....	5 U.S.C. 2.	R.S. §159.

The reference in former section 1 to the application of the provisions of this title, referring to title IV of the Revised Statutes, is omitted as unnecessary as the application of those provisions is stated in the text.

The statement in former section 2 that the use of the word "department" means one of the Executive departments named in former section 1 is omitted as unnecessary as the words "Executive department" are used in this title when Executive department is meant.

"The Department of Commerce" is substituted for "The Department of Commerce and Labor" on authority of the act of March 4, 1913, ch. 141, §1, 37 Stat. 736.

AMENDMENTS

1988—Pub. L. 100–527 inserted "The Department of Veterans Affairs."

1979—Pub. L. 96–88 substituted "Department of Health and Human Services" for "Department of Health, Education, and Welfare" and inserted "The Department of Education."

1977—Pub. L. 95–91 inserted "The Department of Energy."

1970—Pub. L. 91–375 struck out "The Post Office Department."

1966—Pub. L. 89–670 inserted "The Department of Housing and Urban Development." and "The Department of Transportation."

EFFECTIVE DATE OF 1988 AMENDMENT

Amendment by Pub. L. 100–527 effective Mar. 15, 1989, see section 18(a) of Pub. L. 100–527, set out as a Department of Veterans Affairs Act note under section 301 of Title 38, Veterans' Benefits.

EFFECTIVE DATE OF 1979 AMENDMENT

Amendment by Pub. L. 96–88 effective May 4, 1980, with specified exceptions, see section 601 of Pub. L. 96–88, set out as an Effective Date note under section 3401 of Title 20, Education.

EFFECTIVE DATE OF 1970 AMENDMENT

Amendment by Pub. L. 91–375 effective within 1 year after Aug. 12, 1970, on date established therefor by Board of Governors of United States Postal Service and published by it in Federal Register, see section 15(a) of Pub L. 91–375, set out as an Effective Date note preceding section 101 of Title 39, Postal Service.

EFFECTIVE DATE OF 1966 AMENDMENT

Amendment by Pub. L. 89–670 effective Apr. 1, 1967, as prescribed by the President and published in the Federal Register, see section 16(a), formerly §15(a), of Pub. L. 89–670 and Ex. Ord. No. 11340, Mar. 30, 1967, 32 F.R. 5453.

PROHIBITION AGAINST CONSTRUCTION THAT WOULD RENDER APPLICABLE TO THE DEPARTMENT OF TRANSPORTATION PROVISIONS OF LAW INCONSISTENT WITH PUB. L. 89–670 CREATING THE DEPARTMENT OF TRANSPORTATION

Section 10(c) of Pub. L. 89–670, which provided that the amendment made to this section by section 10(b) of Pub. L. 89–670 was not to be construed to make applicable to the Department any provision of law inconsistent with Pub. L. 89–670, was repealed by Pub. L. 104–287, §7(5), Oct. 11, 1996, 110 Stat. 3400.

SECTION REFERRED TO IN OTHER SECTIONS

This section is referred to in title 4 section 7; title 18 sections 115, 351, 1030, 6001; title 28 section 451; title 31 sections 1343, 1344; title 41 sections 403, 601; title 42 sections 8262c, 10156, 10222.

§ 102. Military departments

The military departments are:
  The Department of the Army.
  The Department of the Navy.
  The Department of the Air Force.

(Pub. L. 89–554, Sept. 6, 1966, 80 Stat. 378.)

HISTORICAL AND REVISION NOTES

The section is supplied to avoid the necessity for defining "military departments" each time it is used in this title. See section 101(7) of title 10.

SECTION REFERRED TO IN OTHER SECTIONS

This section is referred to in title 4 section 7; title 15 sections 638, 3703; title 18 section 6001; title 26 section 6050M; title 29 sections 203, 633a; title 31 section 1344; title 35 section 201; title 38 section 4303; title 41 sections 48b, 403, 601; title 42 sections 2000e–16, 10156, 10222.

§ 103. Government corporation

For the purpose of this title—

  (1) "Government corporation" means a corporation owned or controlled by the Government of the United States; and

  (2) "Government controlled corporation" does not include a corporation owned by the Government of the United States.

(Pub. L. 89–554, Sept. 6, 1966, 80 Stat. 378.)

HISTORICAL AND REVISION NOTES

The section is supplied to avoid the necessity for defining "Government corporation" and "Government controlled corporation" each time it is used in this title.

SECTION REFERRED TO IN OTHER SECTIONS

This section is referred to in title 20 section 1155; title 26 section 6402; title 31 sections 1344, 3332; title 42 section 12651.

§ 104. Independent establishment

For the purpose of this title, "independent establishment" means—

(1) an establishment in the executive branch (other than the United States Postal Service or the Postal Rate Commission) which is not an Executive department, military department, Government corporation, or part thereof, or part of an independent establishment; and

(2) the General Accounting Office.

(Pub. L. 89–554, Sept. 6, 1966, 80 Stat. 379; Pub. L. 91–375, § 6(c)(2), Aug. 12, 1970, 84 Stat. 775.)

HISTORICAL AND REVISION NOTES

The section is supplied to avoid the necessity for defining "independent establishment" each time it is used in this title.

Certain agencies are not independent establishments under the definition since they are constituent agencies or parts of an independent establishment. However, these agencies would continue to be subject to the provisions of this title applicable to the independent establishment of which they are a constituent or part. Also, the definition does not expand or abridge any rights or authority possessed by these agencies as no substantive changes are intended, see section 7(a) of the bill.

AMENDMENTS

1970—Par. (1). Pub. L. 91–375 inserted "(other than the United States Postal Service or the Postal Rate Commission)" after "executive branch".

EFFECTIVE DATE OF 1970 AMENDMENT

Amendment by Pub. L. 91–375 effective within 1 year after Aug. 12, 1970, on date established therefor by Board of Governors of United States Postal Service and published by it in Federal Register, see section 15(a) of Pub. L. 91–375, set out as an Effective Date note preceding section 101 of Title 39, Postal Service.

SECTION REFERRED TO IN OTHER SECTIONS

This section is referred to in title 22 sections 6203, 6563; title 41 sections 403, 601.

§ 105. Executive agency

For the purpose of this title, "Executive agency" means an Executive department, a Government corporation, and an independent establishment.

(Pub. L. 89–554, Sept. 6, 1966, 80 Stat. 379.)

HISTORICAL AND REVISION NOTES

The section is supplied to avoid the necessity for defining "Executive agency" each time it is used in this title.

SECTION REFERRED TO IN OTHER SECTIONS

This section is referred to in sections 306, 5372b, 5948 of this title; title 7 section 2132; title 10 section 2014; title 12 section 1749bbb–10b; title 15 sections 638, 3301, 3703, 4901, 5802, 6617; title 16 section 2602; title 22 sections 2685, 3641, 6502, 6765; title 29 sections 203, 633a; title 31 section 1353; title 35 section 201; title 38 sections 4211, 4303; title 39 section 416; title 40 section 913; title 41 sec-

tion 48b; title 42 sections 2000e–16, 4071, 4902, 6361, 6964, 7911, 8241, 8802, 10101; title 43 section 2003; title 50 section 1601.

CHAPTER 3—POWERS

Sec.
301. Departmental regulations.
302. Delegation of authority.
303. Oaths to witnesses.
304. Subpenas.
305. Systematic agency review of operations.
306. Strategic plans.

AMENDMENTS

1993—Pub. L. 103–62, § 11(a), Aug. 3, 1993, 107 Stat. 295, added item 306.

§ 301. Departmental regulations

The head of an Executive department or military department may prescribe regulations for the government of his department, the conduct of its employees, the distribution and performance of its business, and the custody, use, and preservation of its records, papers, and property. This section does not authorize withholding information from the public or limiting the availability of records to the public.

(Pub. L. 89–554, Sept. 6, 1966, 80 Stat. 379.)

HISTORICAL AND REVISION NOTES

Derivation	U.S. Code	Revised Statutes and Statutes at Large
....	5 U.S.C. 22.	R.S. § 161. Aug. 12, 1958, Pub. L. 85–619, 72 Stat. 547.

The words "Executive department" are substituted for "department" as the definition of "department" applicable to this section is coextensive with the definition of "Executive department" in section 101. The words "not inconsistent with law" are omitted as surplusage as a regulation which is inconsistent with law is invalid.

The words "or military department" are inserted to preserve the application of the source law. Before enactment of the National Security Act Amendments of 1949 (63 Stat. 578), the Department of the Army, the Department of the Navy, and the Department of the Air Force were Executive departments. The National Security Act Amendments of 1949 established the Department of Defense as an Executive Department including the Department of the Army, the Department of the Navy, and the Department of the Air Force as military departments, not as Executive departments. However, the source law for this section, which was in effect in 1949, remained applicable to the Secretaries of the military departments by virtue of section 12(g) of the National Security Act Amendments of 1949 (63 Stat. 591), which provided:

"All laws, orders, regulations, and other actions relating to the National Military Establishment, the Departments of the Army, the Navy, or the Air Force, or to any officer or activity of such establishment or such departments, shall, except to the extent inconsistent with the provisions of this Act, have the same effect as if this Act had not been enacted; but, after the effective date of this Act, any such law, order, regulation, or other action which vested functions in or otherwise related to any officer, department, or establishment, shall be deemed to have vested such function in or relate to the officer, or department, executive or military, succeeding the officer, department, or establishment in which such function was vested. For purposes of this subsection the Department of Defense shall be deemed the department succeeding the National Military Establishment, and the military departments of

Army, Navy, and Air Force shall be deemed the departments succeeding the Executive Departments of Army, Navy, and Air Force.''

This section was part of title IV of the Revised Statutes. The Act of July 26, 1947, ch. 343, § 201(d), as added Aug. 10, 1949, ch. 412, § 4, 63 Stat. 579 (former 5 U.S.C. 171–1), which provides ''Except to the extent inconsistent with the provisions of this Act [National Security Act of 1947], the provisions of title IV of the Revised Statutes as now or hereafter amended shall be applicable to the Department of Defense'' is omitted from this title but is not repealed.

Standard changes are made to conform with the definitions applicable and the style of this title as outlined in the preface to the report.

IMPROVEMENTS IN IDENTIFICATION-RELATED DOCUMENTS

Pub. L. 104–208, div. C, title VI, § 656, Sept. 30, 1996, 110 Stat. 3009–716, as amended by Pub. L. 106–69, title III, § 355, Oct. 9, 1999, 113 Stat. 1027, provided that:

''(a) BIRTH CERTIFICATES.—

''(1) STANDARDS FOR ACCEPTANCE BY FEDERAL AGENCIES.—

''(A) IN GENERAL.—

''(i) GENERAL RULE.—Subject to clause (ii), a Federal agency may not accept for any official purpose a certificate of birth, unless the certificate—

''(I) is a birth certificate (as defined in paragraph (3)); and

''(II) conforms to the standards set forth in the regulation promulgated under subparagraph (B).

''(ii) APPLICABILITY.—Clause (i) shall apply only to a certificate of birth issued after the day that is 3 years after the date of the promulgation of a final regulation under subparagraph (B). Clause (i) shall not be construed to prevent a Federal agency from accepting for official purposes any certificate of birth issued on or before such day.

''(B) REGULATION.—

''(i) CONSULTATION WITH GOVERNMENT AGENCIES.—The President shall select 1 or more Federal agencies to consult with State vital statistics offices, and with other appropriate Federal agencies designated by the President, for the purpose of developing appropriate standards for birth certificates that may be accepted for official purposes by Federal agencies, as provided in subparagraph (A).

''(ii) SELECTION OF LEAD AGENCY.—Of the Federal agencies selected under clause (i), the President shall select 1 agency to promulgate, upon the conclusion of the consultation conducted under such clause, a regulation establishing standards of the type described in such clause.

''(iii) DEADLINE.—The agency selected under clause (ii) shall promulgate a final regulation under such clause not later than the date that is 1 year after the date of the enactment of this Act [Sept. 30, 1996].

''(iv) MINIMUM REQUIREMENTS.—The standards established under this subparagraph—

''(I) at a minimum, shall require certification of the birth certificate by the State or local custodian of record that issued the certificate, and shall require the use of safety paper, the seal of the issuing custodian of record, and other features designed to limit tampering, counterfeiting, and photocopying, or otherwise duplicating, the birth certificate for fraudulent purposes;

''(II) may not require a single design to which birth certificates issued by all States must conform; and

''(III) shall accommodate the differences between the States in the manner and form in which birth records are stored and birth certificates are produced from such records.

''(2) GRANTS TO STATES.—

''(A) ASSISTANCE IN MEETING FEDERAL STANDARDS.—

''(i) IN GENERAL.—Beginning on the date a final regulation is promulgated under paragraph (1)(B), the Secretary of Health and Human Services, acting through the Director of the National Center for Health Statistics and after consulting with the head of any other agency designated by the President, shall make grants to States to assist them in issuing birth certificates that conform to the standards set forth in the regulation.

''(ii) ALLOCATION OF GRANTS.—The Secretary shall provide grants to States under this subparagraph in proportion to the populations of the States applying to receive a grant and in an amount needed to provide a substantial incentive for States to issue birth certificates that conform to the standards described in clause (i).

''(B) ASSISTANCE IN MATCHING BIRTH AND DEATH RECORDS.—

''(i) IN GENERAL.—The Secretary of Health and Human Services, acting through the Director of the National Center for Health Statistics and after consulting with the head of any other agency designated by the President, shall make grants to States to assist them in developing the capability to match birth and death records, within each State and among the States, and to note the fact of death on the birth certificates of deceased persons. In developing the capability described in the preceding sentence, a State that receives a grant under this subparagraph shall focus first on individuals born after 1950.

''(ii) ALLOCATION AND AMOUNT OF GRANTS.—The Secretary shall provide grants to States under this subparagraph in proportion to the populations of the States applying to receive a grant and in an amount needed to provide a substantial incentive for States to develop the capability described in clause (i).

''(C) DEMONSTRATION PROJECTS.—The Secretary of Health and Human Services, acting through the Director of the National Center for Health Statistics, shall make grants to States for a project in each of 5 States to demonstrate the feasibility of a system under which persons otherwise required to report the death of individuals to a State would be required to provide to the State's office of vital statistics sufficient information to establish the fact of death of every individual dying in the State within 24 hours of acquiring the information.

''(3) BIRTH CERTIFICATE.—As used in this subsection, the term 'birth certificate' means a certificate of birth—

''(A) of—

''(i) an individual born in the United States; or

''(ii) an individual born abroad—

''(I) who is a citizen or national of the United States at birth; and

''(II) whose birth is registered in the United States; and

''(B) that—

''(i) is a copy, issued by a State or local authorized custodian of record, of an original certificate of birth issued by such custodian of record; or

''(ii) was issued by a State or local authorized custodian of record and was produced from birth records maintained by such custodian of record.

''[(b) Repealed. Pub. L. 106–69, title III, § 355, Oct. 9, 1999, 113 Stat. 1027.]

''(c) REPORT.—Not later than 1 year after the date of the enactment of this Act [Sept. 30, 1996], the Secretary of Health and Human Services shall submit a report to the Congress on ways to reduce the fraudulent obtaining and the fraudulent use of birth certificates, including any such use to obtain a social security account number or a State or Federal document related to identification or immigration.

''(d) FEDERAL AGENCY DEFINED.—For purposes of this section, the term 'Federal agency' means any of the following:

"(1) An Executive agency (as defined in section 105 of title 5, United States Code).

"(2) A military department (as defined in section 102 of such title).

"(3) An agency in the legislative branch of the Government of the United States.

"(4) An agency in the judicial branch of the Government of the United States."

EQUAL OPPORTUNITY IN FEDERAL EMPLOYMENT

Establishment of equal employment opportunity programs by heads of Executive departments and agencies, see Ex. Ord. No. 11246, Sept. 24, 1965, 30 F.R. 12319 and Ex. Ord. No. 11478, Aug. 8, 1969, 34 F.R. 12985, set out as notes under section 2000e of Title 42, The Public Health and Welfare.

§ 302. Delegation of authority

(a) For the purpose of this section, "agency" has the meaning given it by section 5721 of this title.

(b) In addition to the authority to delegate conferred by other law, the head of an agency may delegate to subordinate officials the authority vested in him—

(1) by law to take final action on matters pertaining to the employment, direction, and general administration of personnel under his agency; and

(2) by section 3702 of title 44 to authorize the publication of advertisements, notices, or proposals.

(Pub. L. 89–554, Sept. 6, 1966, 80 Stat. 379; Pub. L. 94–183, § 2(1), Dec. 31, 1975, 89 Stat. 1057.)

HISTORICAL AND REVISION NOTES

Derivation	U.S. Code	Revised Statutes and Statutes at Large
....	5 U.S.C. 22a.	Aug. 2, 1946, ch. 744, § 12, 60 Stat. 809.

Clause (2) of former section 22a is omitted because of the repeal of R.S. § 3683 (31 U.S.C. 675) by the Act of Sept. 12, 1950, ch. 946, § 301(76), 64 Stat. 843.

The word "agency" is substituted for "department" and defined to conform to the definition of "department" in section 18 of the Act of Aug. 2, 1946, ch. 744, 60 Stat. 811.

In subsection (b), the words "In addition to the authority to delegate conferred by other law," are added for clarity and in recognition of the various reorganization plans which generally have transferred all functions of the departments and agencies to the heads thereof and have authorized them to delegate the functions to subordinates.

Standard changes are made to conform with the definitions applicable and the style of this title as outlined in the preface to the report.

AMENDMENTS

1975—Subsec. (b)(2). Pub. L. 94–183 substituted "3702" for "324".

§ 303. Oaths to witnesses

(a) An employee of an Executive department lawfully assigned to investigate frauds on or attempts to defraud the United States, or irregularity or misconduct of an employee or agent of the United States, may administer an oath to a witness attending to testify or depose in the course of the investigation.

(b) An employee of the Department of Defense lawfully assigned to investigative duties may administer oaths to witnesses in connection with an official investigation.

(Pub. L. 89–554, Sept. 6, 1966, 80 Stat. 379; Pub. L. 94–213, Feb. 13, 1976, 90 Stat. 179.)

HISTORICAL AND REVISION NOTES

Derivation	U.S. Code	Revised Statutes and Statutes at Large
....	5 U.S.C. 93.	R.S. § 183. Mar. 2, 1901, ch. 809, § 3, 31 Stat. 951. Feb. 13, 1911, ch. 43, 36 Stat. 898.

The word "employee" is substituted for "officer or clerk" in view of the definition in section 2105. The words "Executive department" are substituted for "departments" as the definition of "department" applicable to this section is coextensive with the definition of "Executive department" in section 101. So much as related to the Armed Forces is omitted as superseded by section 636 of title 14 and section 936(b) of title 10.

This section was part of title IV of the Revised Statutes. The Act of July 26, 1947, ch. 343, § 201(d), as added Aug. 10, 1949, ch. 412, § 4, 63 Stat. 579 (formerly 5 U.S.C. 171–1), which provides "Except to the extent inconsistent with the provisions of this Act [National Security Act of 1947], the provisions of title IV of the Revised Statutes as now or hereafter amended shall be applicable to the Department of Defense" is omitted from this title but is not repealed.

Standard changes are made to conform with the definitions applicable and the style of this title as outlined in the preface to the report.

AMENDMENTS

1976—Pub. L. 94–213 designated existing provisions as subsec. (a) and added subsec. (b).

§ 304. Subpenas

(a) The head of an Executive department or military department or bureau thereof in which a claim against the United States is pending may apply to a judge or clerk of a court of the United States to issue a subpena for a witness within the jurisdiction of the court to appear at a time and place stated in the subpena before an individual authorized to take depositions to be used in the courts of the United States, to give full and true answers to such written interrogatories and cross-interrogatories as may be submitted with the application, or to be orally examined and cross-examined on the subject of the claim.

(b) If a witness, after being served with a subpena, neglects or refuses to appear, or, appearing, refuses to testify, the judge of the district in which the subpena issued may proceed, on proper process, to enforce obedience to the subpena, or to punish for disobedience, in the same manner as a court of the United States may in case of process of subpena ad testificandum issued by the court.

(Pub. L. 89–554, Sept. 6, 1966, 80 Stat. 379.)

HISTORICAL AND REVISION NOTES

Derivation	U.S. Code	Revised Statutes and Statutes at Large
(a)	5 U.S.C. 94.	R.S. § 184.
(b)	5 U.S.C. 96.	R.S. § 186.

In subsection (a), the words "Executive department" are substituted for "department" as the definition of "department" applicable to this section is coextensive with the definition of "Executive department" in section 101. The word "thereof" is added to reflect the proper relationship between "department" and "bureau" as reflected in title IV of the Revised Statutes of 1878. The words "in any State, District, or Territory" are omitted as unnecessary. The word "individual" is substituted for "officer" as the definition of "officer" in section 2104 is narrower than the word "officer" in R.S. § 184 which word includes "officers" as defined in section 2104 as well as notaries public who are not "officers" under section 2104, but are "officers" as that word is used in R.S. § 184.

In subsection (a), the words "or military department" are inserted to preserve the application of the source law. Before enactment of the National Security Act Amendments of 1949 (63 Stat. 578), the Department of the Army, the Department of the Navy, and the Department of the Air Force were Executive departments. The National Security Act Amendments of 1949 established the Department of Defense as an Executive Department including the Department of the Army, the Department of the Navy, and the Department of the Air Force as military departments, not as Executive departments. However, the source law for this section, which was in effect in 1949, remained applicable to the Secretaries of the military departments by virtue of section 12(g) of the National Security Act Amendments of 1949 (63 Stat. 591), which is set out in the reviser's note for section 301.

This section was part of title IV of the Revised Statutes. The Act of July 26, 1947, ch. 343, § 201(d), as added Aug. 10, 1949, ch. 412, § 4, 63 Stat. 579 (former 5 U.S.C. 171–1), which provides "Except to the extent inconsistent with the provisions of this Act [National Security Act of 1947], the provisions of title IV of the Revised Statutes as now or hereafter amended shall be applicable to the Department of Defense" is omitted from this title but is not repealed.

Standard changes are made to conform with the definitions applicable and the style of this title as outlined in the preface to the report.

SECTION REFERRED TO IN OTHER SECTIONS

This section is referred to in section 503 of this title.

§ 305. Systematic agency review of operations

(a) For the purpose of this section, "agency" means an Executive agency, but does not include—

(1) a Government controlled corporation;
(2) the Tennessee Valley Authority;
(3) the Virgin Islands Corporation;
(4) the Atomic Energy Commission;
(5) the Central Intelligence Agency;
(6) the Panama Canal Commission; or
(7) the National Security Agency, Department of Defense.

(b) Under regulations prescribed and administered by the President, each agency shall review systematically the operations of each of its activities, functions, or organization units, on a continuing basis.

(c) The purpose of the reviews includes—

(1) determining the degree of efficiency and economy in the operation of the agency's activities, functions, or organization units;
(2) identifying the units that are outstanding in those respects; and
(3) identifying the employees whose personal efforts have caused their units to be outstanding in efficiency and economy of operations.

(Pub. L. 89–554, Sept. 6, 1966, 80 Stat. 380; Pub. L. 96–54, § 2(a)(2), Aug. 14, 1979, 93 Stat. 381; Pub. L. 96–70, title III, § 3302(e)(1), Sept. 27, 1979, 93 Stat. 498; Pub. L. 97–468, title VI, § 615(b)(1)(A), Jan. 14, 1983, 96 Stat. 2578.)

HISTORICAL AND REVISION NOTES

Derivation	U.S. Code	Revised Statutes and Statutes at Large
(a)	5 U.S.C. 1085.	Oct. 28, 1949, ch. 782, § 205, 63 Stat. 957.
(b), (c)	5 U.S.C. 1151.	Oct. 28, 1949, ch. 782, § 1001, 63 Stat. 971.

Subsection (a) is based in part on former sections 1081 and 1082, which are carried into section 5102.

In subsection (a)(1), the exception of "a Government controlled corporation" is added to preserve the application of this section to "corporations wholly owned by the United States". This is necessary as the defined term "Executive agency" includes the defined term "Government corporation" and the latter includes both Government owned and controlled corporations. Thus the exclusion of Government controlled corporations, which are distinct from wholly owned corporations, operates to preserve the application of this section to wholly owned corporations. The exception for the Inland Waterways Corporation in former section 1082(13) is omitted on authority of the Act of July 19, 1963, Pub. L. 88–67, 77 Stat. 81. The exceptions for Production Credit Corporations and Federal Intermediate Credit Banks in former section 1082(18) and (19) are omitted as they are no longer "corporations wholly owned by the United States". Under the Farm Credit Act of 1956, 70 Stat. 659, the Production Credit Corporations were merged in the Federal Intermediate Credit Banks, and pursuant to that Act the Federal Intermediate Credit Banks have ceased to be corporations wholly owned by the United States.

In subsection (a)(7), the words "Panama Canal Company" are substituted for "Panama Railroad Company" on authority of the Act of Sept. 26, 1950, ch. 1049, § 2(a)(2), 64 Stat. 1038.

Standard changes are made to conform with the definitions applicable and the style of this title as outlined in the preface to the report.

AMENDMENTS

1983—Subsec. (a)(3) to (8). Pub. L. 97–468 struck out par. (3), which excluded The Alaska Railroad, and redesignated pars. (4) to (8) as (3) to (7), respectively.

1979—Subsec. (a)(7). Pub. L. 96–70 substituted "Commission" for "Company".

Subsec. (b). Pub. L. 96–54 substituted "President" for "Director of the Bureau of the Budget".

EFFECTIVE DATE OF 1983 AMENDMENT

Amendment by Pub. L. 97–468 effective on date of transfer of Alaska Railroad to the State [Jan. 5, 1985], pursuant to section 1203 of Title 45, Railroads, see section 615(b) of Pub. L. 97–468.

EFFECTIVE DATE OF 1979 AMENDMENTS

Amendment by Pub. L. 96–70 effective Oct. 1, 1979, see section 3304 of Pub. L. 96–70, set out as an Effective Date note under section 3601 of Title 22, Foreign Relations and Intercourse.

Section 2(b) of Pub. L. 96–54 provided that: "Except as otherwise expressly provided in subsection (a), the amendments made by subsection (a) [amending sections 305, 1308, 2101, 2105, 2106, 2108, 3102, 3132, 3302, 3305, 3315, 3317, 3324, 3326, 3503, 4102, 4109, 4111, 4112, 4701, 5102, 5108, 5311 to 5316, 5333 to 5335, 5347, 5504, 5514, 5516, 5521, 5545, 5550a, 5562, 5581, 5584, 5596, 5702, 5903, 5943, 6104, 6304, 6305, 6323, 6325, 7325, 7327, 7701, 7702, 8331, 8332, 8339, 8347, 8701, 8901, and 8906 of this title], shall take effect July 12, 1979, or the date of the enactment of this Act [Aug. 14, 1979], whichever is earlier."

TRANSFER OF FUNCTIONS

Atomic Energy Commission abolished and functions transferred by sections 5814 and 5841 of Title 42, The Public Health and Welfare. See also Transfer of Functions notes set out under those sections.

DELEGATION OF FUNCTIONS

Functions of President under subsec. (b) of this section delegated to Director of Office of Management and Budget, see Ex. Ord. No. 12152, Aug. 14, 1979, 44 F.R. 48143, set out as a note under section 301 of Title 3, The President.

DISSOLUTION OF VIRGIN ISLANDS CORPORATION

Virgin Islands Corporation established to have succession until June 30, 1969, unless sooner dissolved by Act of Congress, by act June 30, 1949, ch. 285, 63 Stat. 350, as amended (48 U.S.C. 1407 et seq.). Corporation terminated its program June 30, 1965, and dissolved July 1, 1966. Act June 30, 1949, was repealed by Pub. L. 97–357, title III, § 308(e), Oct. 19, 1982, 96 Stat. 1710.

SECTION REFERRED TO IN OTHER SECTIONS

This section is referred to in section 7204 of this title; title 10 sections 4540, 7212, 9540.

§ 306. Strategic plans

(a) No later than September 30, 1997, the head of each agency shall submit to the Director of the Office of Management and Budget and to the Congress a strategic plan for program activities. Such plan shall contain—

(1) a comprehensive mission statement covering the major functions and operations of the agency;

(2) general goals and objectives, including outcome-related goals and objectives, for the major functions and operations of the agency;

(3) a description of how the goals and objectives are to be achieved, including a description of the operational processes, skills and technology, and the human, capital, information, and other resources required to meet those goals and objectives;

(4) a description of how the performance goals included in the plan required by section 1115(a) of title 31 shall be related to the general goals and objectives in the strategic plan;

(5) an identification of those key factors external to the agency and beyond its control that could significantly affect the achievement of the general goals and objectives; and

(6) a description of the program evaluations used in establishing or revising general goals and objectives, with a schedule for future program evaluations.

(b) The strategic plan shall cover a period of not less than five years forward from the fiscal year in which it is submitted. The strategic plan shall be updated and revised at least every three years, except that the strategic plan for the Department of Defense shall be updated and revised at least every four years.

(c) The performance plan required by section 1115 of title 31 shall be consistent with the agency's strategic plan. A performance plan may not be submitted for a fiscal year not covered by a current strategic plan under this section.

(d) When developing a strategic plan, the agency shall consult with the Congress, and shall solicit and consider the views and suggestions of those entities potentially affected by or interested in such a plan.

(e) The functions and activities of this section shall be considered to be inherently Governmental functions. The drafting of strategic plans under this section shall be performed only by Federal employees.

(f) For purposes of this section the term "agency" means an Executive agency defined under section 105, but does not include the Central Intelligence Agency, the General Accounting Office, the Panama Canal Commission, the United States Postal Service, and the Postal Rate Commission.

(Added Pub. L. 103–62, § 3, Aug. 3, 1993, 107 Stat. 286; amended Pub. L. 106–65, div. A, title IX, § 902, Oct. 5, 1999, 113 Stat. 717.)

AMENDMENTS

1999—Subsec. (b). Pub. L. 106–65 substituted ". The strategic plan shall be updated and revised at least every three years, except that the strategic plan for the Department of Defense shall be updated and revised at least every four years." for ", and shall be updated and revised at least every three years."

CONSTRUCTION

No provision or amendment made by Pub. L. 103–62 to be construed as creating any right, privilege, benefit, or entitlement for any person who is not an officer or employee of the United States acting in such capacity, and no person not an officer or employee of the United States acting in such capacity to have standing to file any civil action in any court of the United States to enforce any provision or amendment made by Pub. L. 103–62, or to be construed as superseding any statutory requirement, see section 10 of Pub. L. 103–62, set out as a note under section 1115 of Title 31, Money and Finance.

SECTION REFERRED TO IN OTHER SECTIONS

This section is referred to in title 7 section 3123; title 15 section 638; title 23 section 508; title 31 sections 1115, 1117, 1118, 1119; title 40 section 1425.

CHAPTER 5—ADMINISTRATIVE PROCEDURE

[1] So in original. Does not conform to section catchline.

AMENDMENTS

1996—Pub. L. 104–320, §§4(b)(2), 10(b), 11(b)(2), (d)(2), Oct. 19, 1996, 110 Stat. 3871, 3873, 3874, in item 569 substituted "Encouraging negotiated rulemaking" for "Role of the Administrative Conference of the United States and other entities", added items 570a and 584, and struck out item 582 "Compilation of information".

1992—Pub. L. 102–354, §4, Aug. 26, 1992, 106 Stat. 945, substituted headings of subchapters III, IV, and V and items 561 to 570, 571 to 583, and 591 to 596 for former heading of subchapter III and former items 571 to 576 relating to Administrative Conference of the United States, former heading of subchapter IV and former items 581 to 593 relating to alternative means of dispute resolution in the administrative process, and former heading of subchapter IV and former items 581 to 590 relating to negotiated rulemaking procedure.

1990—Pub. L. 101–648, §3(b), Nov. 29, 1990, 104 Stat. 4976, added heading of subchapter IV and items 581 to 590 relating to negotiated rulemaking procedure.

Pub. L. 101–552, §4(c), Nov. 15, 1990, 104 Stat. 2745, added heading of subchapter IV and items 581 to 593 [renumbered 571 to 583] relating to alternative means of dispute resolution.

1986—Pub. L. 99–470, §2(b), Oct. 14, 1986, 100 Stat. 1198, substituted "Authorization of appropriations" for "Appropriations" in item 576.

1985—Pub. L. 99–80, §6, Aug. 5, 1985, 99 Stat. 186, revived item 504 and repealed Pub. L. 96–481, title II, §203(c), Oct. 21, 1980, 94 Stat. 2327, which provided for the repeal, effective Oct. 1, 1984, of item 504.

1980—Pub. L. 96–481, title II, §203(a)(2), (c), Oct. 21, 1980, 94 Stat. 2327, added item 504 "Costs and fees of parties", and repealed that item effective Oct. 1, 1984.

1976—Pub. L. 94–409, §3(b), Sept. 13, 1976, 90 Stat. 1246, added item 552b.

1974—Pub. L. 93–579, §4, Dec. 31, 1974, 88 Stat. 1905, added item 552a.

1967—Pub. L. 90–83, §1(1)(B), Sept. 11, 1967, 81 Stat. 195, added item 500.

Pub. L. 90–23, §2, June 5, 1967, 81 Stat. 56, substituted "Public information; agency rules, opinions, orders, records and proceedings" for "Publication of information, rules, opinions, orders, and public records" in item 552.

CHAPTER REFERRED TO IN OTHER SECTIONS

This chapter is referred to in title 2 section 437d; title 12 sections 1467a, 1730a, 1786, 1818, 2266, 4582, 4633; title 15 sections 77s, 637, 648, 656, 687e, 1541, 1691b, 1715, 2703, 3803; title 16 section 460aa–3; title 20 sections 1068, 7711; title 21 section 342; title 25 sections 450j, 450l, 458aaa–5, 954; title 29 sections 1861, 2939; title 30 section 811; title 33 section 701n; title 39 sections 204, 410, 3001, 3603; title 42 sections 300j–6, 9613, 11504; title 43 section 1740; title 44 section 3507; title 45 sections 1116, 1212; title 46 App. section 1241p; title 49 section 106.

SUBCHAPTER I—GENERAL PROVISIONS

§ 500. Administrative practice; general provisions

(a) For the purpose of this section—

(1) "agency" has the meaning given it by section 551 of this title; and

(2) "State" means a State, a territory or possession of the United States including a Commonwealth, or the District of Columbia.

(b) An individual who is a member in good standing of the bar of the highest court of a State may represent a person before an agency on filing with the agency a written declaration that he is currently qualified as provided by this subsection and is authorized to represent the particular person in whose behalf he acts.

(c) An individual who is duly qualified to practice as a certified public accountant in a State may represent a person before the Internal Revenue Service of the Treasury Department on filing with that agency a written declaration that he is currently qualified as provided by this subsection and is authorized to represent the particular person in whose behalf he acts.

(d) This section does not—

(1) grant or deny to an individual who is not qualified as provided by subsection (b) or (c) of this section the right to appear for or represent a person before an agency or in an agency proceeding;

(2) authorize or limit the discipline, including disbarment, of individuals who appear in a representative capacity before an agency;

(3) authorize an individual who is a former employee of an agency to represent a person before an agency when the representation is prohibited by statute or regulation; or

(4) prevent an agency from requiring a power of attorney as a condition to the settlement of a controversy involving the payment of money.

(e) Subsections (b)–(d) of this section do not apply to practice before the United States Patent and Trademark Office with respect to patent matters that continue to be covered by chapter 3 (sections 31–33) of title 35.

(f) When a participant in a matter before an agency is represented by an individual qualified under subsection (b) or (c) of this section, a notice or other written communication required or permitted to be given the participant in the matter shall be given to the representative in addition to any other service specifically required by statute. When a participant is represented by more than one such qualified representative, service on any one of the representatives is sufficient.

(Added Pub. L. 90–83, §1(1)(A), Sept. 11, 1967, 81 Stat. 195; amended Pub. L. 106–113, div. B, §1000(a)(9) [title IV, §4732(b)(2)], Nov. 29, 1999, 113 Stat. 1536, 1501A–583.)

HISTORICAL AND REVISION NOTES

Section of title 5	Source (U.S. Code)	Source (Revised Statutes at Large)
500(a)	5 App.: 1014.	Nov. 8, 1965, Pub. L. 89–332, §3, 79 Stat. 1281.
500(b)–(e) ...	5 App.: 1012.	Nov. 8, 1965, Pub. L. 89–332, §1, 79 Stat. 1281.
500(f)	5 App.: 1013.	Nov. 8, 1965, Pub. L. 89–332, §2, 79 Stat. 1281.

The definition of "State" in subsection (a)(2) is supplied for convenience and is based on the words "State, possession, territory, Commonwealth, or District of Columbia" in subsections (a) and (b) of 5 App. U.S.C. 1012.

In subsection (d), the words "This section does not" are substituted for "nothing herein shall be construed".

In subsection (d)(3), the word "employee" is substituted for "officer or employee" to conform to the definition of "employee" in 5 U.S.C. 2105.

AMENDMENTS

1999—Subsec. (e). Pub. L. 106–113 substituted "United States Patent and Trademark Office" for "Patent Office".

EFFECTIVE DATE OF 1999 AMENDMENT

Amendment by Pub. L. 106–113 effective 4 months after Nov. 29, 1999, see section 1000(a)(9) [title IV, §4731] of Pub. L. 106–113, set out as a note under section 1 of Title 35, Patents.

SECTION REFERRED TO IN OTHER SECTIONS

This section is referred to in title 31 section 330; title 38 section 5901; title 49 section 703.

§ 501. Advertising practice; restrictions

An individual, firm, or corporation practicing before an agency of the United States may not use the name of a Member of either House of Congress or of an individual in the service of the United States in advertising the business.

(Pub. L. 89–554, Sept. 6, 1966, 80 Stat. 381.)

HISTORICAL AND REVISION NOTES

Derivation	U.S. Code	Revised Statutes and Statutes at Large
....	5 U.S.C. 101.	Apr. 27, 1916, ch. 89, §1, 39 Stat. 54.

The words "may not" are substituted for "It shall be unlawful for". The words "agency of the United States" are substituted for "any department or office of the Government". The words "an individual in the service of the United States" are substituted for "officer of the Government" in view of the definitions in sections 2104 and 2105.

Standard changes are made to conform with the definitions applicable and the style of this title as outlined in the preface to the report.

§ 502. Administrative practice; Reserves and National Guardsmen

Membership in a reserve component of the armed forces or in the National Guard does not prevent an individual from practicing his civilian profession or occupation before, or in connection with, an agency of the United States.

(Pub. L. 89–554, Sept. 6, 1966, 80 Stat. 381.)

HISTORICAL AND REVISION NOTES

Derivation	U.S. Code	Revised Statutes and Statutes at Large
....	5 U.S.C. 30r(c) (2d sentence).	Aug. 10, 1956, ch. 1041, §29(c) (2d sentence), 70A Stat. 632.

Standard changes are made to conform with the definitions applicable and the style as outlined in the preface to the report.

§ 503. Witness fees and allowances

(a) For the purpose of this section, "agency" has the meaning given it by section 5721 of this title.

(b) A witness is entitled to the fees and allowances allowed by statute for witnesses in the courts of the United States when—

(1) he is subpenaed under section 304(a) of this title; or

(2) he is subpenaed to and appears at a hearing before an agency authorized by law to hold hearings and subpena witnesses to attend the hearings.

(Pub. L. 89–554, Sept. 6, 1966, 80 Stat. 381.)

HISTORICAL AND REVISION NOTES

Derivation	U.S. Code	Revised Statutes and Statutes at Large
....	5 U.S.C. 95.	R.S. §185.
....	5 U.S.C. 95a.	Aug. 2, 1946, ch. 744, §10, 60 Stat. 809.

Former sections 95 and 95a are combined and restated for clarity and brevity. The words "or expenses in the case of Government officers and employees" are omitted as covered by section 1823 of title 28. The word "agency" is substituted for "department" and defined to conform to the definition of "department" in section 18 of the Act of Aug. 2, 1946, ch. 744, 60 Stat. 811.

This section was part of title IV of the Revised Statutes. The Act of July 26, 1947, ch. 343, §201(d), as added Aug. 10, 1949, ch. 412, §4, 63 Stat. 579 (former 5 U.S.C. 171–1), which provides "Except to the extent inconsistent with the provisions of this Act [National Security Act of 1947], the provisions of title IV of the Revised Statutes as now or hereafter amended shall be applicable to the Department of Defense" is omitted from this title but is not repealed.

Standard changes are made to conform with the definitions applicable and the style of this title as outlined in the preface to the report.

§ 504. Costs and fees of parties

(a)(1) An agency that conducts an adversary adjudication shall award, to a prevailing party other than the United States, fees and other expenses incurred by that party in connection with that proceeding, unless the adjudicative officer of the agency finds that the position of the agency was substantially justified or that special circumstances make an award unjust. Whether or not the position of the agency was substantially justified shall be determined on the basis of the administrative record, as a whole, which is made in the adversary adjudication for which fees and other expenses are sought.

(2) A party seeking an award of fees and other expenses shall, within thirty days of a final disposition in the adversary adjudication, submit to the agency an application which shows that the party is a prevailing party and is eligible to receive an award under this section, and the amount sought, including an itemized statement from any attorney, agent, or expert witness representing or appearing in behalf of the party stating the actual time expended and the rate at which fees and other expenses were computed. The party shall also allege that the position of the agency was not substantially justified. When the United States appeals the underlying merits of an adversary adjudication, no decision on an application for fees and other expenses in connection with that adversary adjudication shall be made under this section until a final and unreviewable decision is rendered by the court on the appeal or until the underlying merits of the case have been finally determined pursuant to the appeal.

(3) The adjudicative officer of the agency may reduce the amount to be awarded, or deny an award, to the extent that the party during the course of the proceedings engaged in conduct which unduly and unreasonably protracted the final resolution of the matter in controversy. The decision of the adjudicative officer of the agency under this section shall be made a part of the record containing the final decision of the agency and shall include written findings and conclusions and the reason or basis therefor. The decision of the agency on the application for fees and other expenses shall be the final administrative decision under this section.

(4) If, in an adversary adjudication arising from an agency action to enforce a party's compliance with a statutory or regulatory requirement, the demand by the agency is substantially in excess of the decision of the adjudicative officer and is unreasonable when compared with such decision, under the facts and circumstances of the case, the adjudicative officer shall award to the party the fees and other expenses related to defending against the excessive demand, unless the party has committed a willful violation of law or otherwise acted in bad faith, or special circumstances make an award unjust. Fees and expenses awarded under this paragraph shall be paid only as a consequence of appropriations provided in advance.

(b)(1) For the purposes of this section—
(A) "fees and other expenses" includes the reasonable expenses of expert witnesses, the reasonable cost of any study, analysis, engineering report, test, or project which is found by the agency to be necessary for the preparation of the party's case, and reasonable attorney or agent fees (The amount of fees awarded under this section shall be based upon prevailing market rates for the kind and quality of the services furnished, except that (i) no expert witness shall be compensated at a rate in excess of the highest rate of compensation for expert witnesses paid by the agency involved, and (ii) attorney or agent fees shall not be awarded in excess of $125 per hour unless the agency determines by regulation that an increase in the cost of living or a special factor, such as the limited availability of qualified attorneys or agents for the proceedings involved, justifies a higher fee.);

(B) "party" means a party, as defined in section 551(3) of this title, who is (i) an individual whose net worth did not exceed $2,000,000 at the time the adversary adjudication was initiated, or (ii) any owner of an unincorporated business, or any partnership, corporation, association, unit of local government, or organization, the net worth of which did not exceed $7,000,000 at the time the adversary adjudication was initiated, and which had not more than 500 employees at the time the adversary adjudication was initiated; except that an organization described in section 501(c)(3) of the Internal Revenue Code of 1986 (26 U.S.C. 501(c)(3)) exempt from taxation under section 501(a) of such Code, or a cooperative association as defined in section 15(a) of the Agricultural Marketing Act (12 U.S.C. 1141j(a)), may be a party regardless of the net worth of such organization or cooperative association or for purposes of subsection (a)(4), a small entity as defined in section 601;

(C) "adversary adjudication" means (i) an adjudication under section 554 of this title in which the position of the United States is represented by counsel or otherwise, but excludes an adjudication for the purpose of establishing or fixing a rate or for the purpose of granting or renewing a license, (ii) any appeal of a decision made pursuant to section 6 of the Contract Disputes Act of 1978 (41 U.S.C. 605) before an agency board of contract appeals as provided in section 8 of that Act (41 U.S.C. 607), (iii) any hearing conducted under chapter 38 of title 31, and (iv) the Religious Freedom Restoration Act of 1993;

(D) "adjudicative officer" means the deciding official, without regard to whether the official is designated as an administrative law judge, a hearing officer or examiner, or otherwise, who presided at the adversary adjudication;

(E) "position of the agency" means, in addition to the position taken by the agency in the adversary adjudication, the action or failure to act by the agency upon which the adversary adjudication is based; except that fees and other expenses may not be awarded to a party for any portion of the adversary adjudication in which the party has unreasonably protracted the proceedings; and

(F) "demand" means the express demand of the agency which led to the adversary adjudication, but does not include a recitation by the agency of the maximum statutory penalty (i) in the administrative complaint, or (ii) elsewhere when accompanied by an express demand for a lesser amount.

(2) Except as otherwise provided in paragraph (1), the definitions provided in section 551 of this title apply to this section.

(c)(1) After consultation with the Chairman of the Administrative Conference of the United States, each agency shall by rule establish uniform procedures for the submission and consideration of applications for an award of fees and other expenses. If a court reviews the underlying decision of the adversary adjudication, an award for fees and other expenses may be made only pursuant to section 2412(d)(3) of title 28, United States Code.

(2) If a party other than the United States is dissatisfied with a determination of fees and other expenses made under subsection (a), that party may, within 30 days after the determination is made, appeal the determination to the court of the United States having jurisdiction to review the merits of the underlying decision of the agency adversary adjudication. The court's determination on any appeal heard under this paragraph shall be based solely on the factual record made before the agency. The court may modify the determination of fees and other expenses only if the court finds that the failure to make an award of fees and other expenses, or the calculation of the amount of the award, was unsupported by substantial evidence.

(d) Fees and other expenses awarded under this subsection shall be paid by any agency over which the party prevails from any funds made available to the agency by appropriation or otherwise.

(e) The Chairman of the Administrative Conference of the United States, after consultation with the Chief Counsel for Advocacy of the Small Business Administration, shall report annually to the Congress on the amount of fees and other expenses awarded during the preceding fiscal year pursuant to this section. The report shall describe the number, nature, and amount of the awards, the claims involved in the controversy, and any other relevant information which may aid the Congress in evaluating the scope and impact of such awards. Each agency shall provide the Chairman with such information as is necessary for the Chairman to comply with the requirements of this subsection.

(f) No award may be made under this section for costs, fees, or other expenses which may be awarded under section 7430 of the Internal Revenue Code of 1986.

(Added Pub. L. 96–481, title II, § 203(a)(1), (c), Oct. 21, 1980, 94 Stat. 2325, 2327; revived and amended Pub. L. 99–80, §§ 1, 6, Aug. 5, 1985, 99 Stat. 183, 186; Pub. L. 99–509, title VI, § 6103(c), Oct. 21, 1986, 100 Stat. 1948; Pub. L. 99–514, § 2, Oct. 22, 1986, 100 Stat. 2095; Pub. L. 100–647, title VI, § 6239(b), Nov. 10, 1988, 102 Stat. 3746; Pub. L. 103–141, § 4(b), Nov. 16, 1993, 107 Stat. 1489; Pub. L. 104–121, title II, § 231, Mar. 29, 1996, 110 Stat. 862.)

REFERENCES IN TEXT

The Religious Freedom Restoration Act of 1993, referred to in subsec. (b)(1)(C)(iv), is Pub. L. 103–141, Nov. 16, 1993, 107 Stat. 1488, which is classified principally to chapter 21B (§ 2000bb et seq.) of Title 42, The Public Health and Welfare. For complete classification of this Act to the Code, see Short Title note set out under section 2000bb of Title 42 and Tables.

Section 7430 of the Internal Revenue Code of 1986, referred to in subsec. (f), is classified to section 7430 of Title 26, Internal Revenue Code.

AMENDMENTS

1996—Subsec. (a)(4). Pub. L. 104–121, § 231(a), added par. (4).

Subsec. (b)(1)(A)(ii). Pub. L. 104–121, § 231(b)(1), substituted "$125" for "$75".

Subsec. (b)(1)(B). Pub. L. 104–121, § 231(b)(2), inserted before semicolon at end "or for purposes of subsection (a)(4), a small entity as defined in section 601".

Subsec. (b)(1)(F). Pub. L. 104–121, § 231(b)(3)–(5), added subpar. (F).

1993—Subsec. (b)(1)(C). Pub. L. 103–141 added cl. (iv).

1988—Subsec. (f). Pub. L. 100–647 added subsec. (f).

1986—Subsec. (b)(1)(B). Pub. L. 99–514 substituted "Internal Revenue Code of 1986" for "Internal Revenue Code of 1954".

Subsec. (b)(1)(C)(iii). Pub. L. 99–509 added cl. (iii).

1985—Subsec. (a)(1). Pub. L. 99–80, § 1(a)(1), (2), struck out "as a party to the proceeding" after "the position of the agency", and inserted "Whether or not the position of the agency was substantially justified shall be determined on the basis of the administrative record, as a whole, which is made in the adversary adjudication for which fees and other expenses are sought."

Subsec. (a)(2). Pub. L. 99–80, § 1(b), inserted "When the United States appeals the underlying merits of an adversary adjudication, no decision on an application for fees and other expenses in connection with that adversary adjudication shall be made under this section until a final and unreviewable decision is rendered by the court on the appeal or until the underlying merits of the case have been finally determined pursuant to the appeal."

Subsec. (a)(3). Pub. L. 99–80, § 1(a)(3), inserted "The decision of the agency on the application for fees and other expenses shall be the final administrative decision under this section."

Subsec. (b)(1)(B). Pub. L. 99–80, § 1(c)(1), amended subpar. (B) generally. Prior to amendment, subpar. (B) read as follows: "'party' means a party, as defined in section 551(3) of this title, which is an individual, partnership, corporation, association, or public or private organization other than an agency, but excludes (i) any individual whose net worth exceeded $1,000,000 at the time the adversary adjudication was initiated, and any sole owner of an unincorporated business, or any partnership, corporation, association, or organization whose net worth exceeded $5,000,000 at the time the adversary adjudication was initiated, except that an organization described in section 501(c)(3) of the Internal Revenue Code of 1954 (26 U.S.C. 501(c)(3)) exempt from taxation under section 501(a) of the Code and a cooperative association as defined in section 15(a) of the Agricultural Marketing Act (12 U.S.C. 1141j(a)), may be a party regardless of the net worth of such organization or cooperative association, and (ii) any sole owner of an unincorporated business, or any partnership, corporation, association, or organization, having more than 500 employees at the time the adversary adjudication was initiated;".

Subsec. (b)(1)(C). Pub. L. 99–80, § 1(c)(2), designated existing provisions of subpar. (C) as cl. (i) thereof by inserting "(i)" before "an adjudication under", added cl. (ii), and struck out "and" after the semicolon at the end.

Subsec. (b)(1)(D), (E). Pub. L. 99–80, § 1(c)(3), substituted "; and" for the period at end of subpar. (D), and added subpar. (E).

Subsec. (c)(2). Pub. L. 99–80, § 1(d), amended par. (2) generally. Prior to amendment, par. (2) read as follows: "A party dissatisfied with the fee determination made under subsection (a) may petition for leave to appeal to the court of the United States having jurisdiction to review the merits of the underlying decision of the agency adversary adjudication. If the court denies the petition for leave to appeal, no appeal may be taken from the denial. If the court grants the petition, it may modify the determination only if it finds that the failure to make an award, or the calculation of the amount of the award, was an abuse of discretion."

Subsec. (d). Pub. L. 99–80, § 1(e), amended subsec. (d) generally. Prior to amendment, subsec. (d) read as follows:

"(1) Fees and other expenses awarded under this section may be paid by any agency over which the party prevails from any funds made available to the agency, by appropriation or otherwise, for such purpose. If not paid by any agency, the fees and other expenses shall be paid in the same manner as the payment of final judgments is made pursuant to section 2414 of title 28, United States Code.

"(2) There is authorized to be appropriated to each agency for each of the fiscal years 1982, 1983, and 1984, such sums as may be necessary to pay fees and other expenses awarded under this section in such fiscal years."

1980—Pub. L. 96–481, § 203(c), which provided for the repeal of this section effective Oct. 1, 1984, was itself repealed and this section was revived by section 6 of Pub. L. 99–80, set out as a note below.

EFFECTIVE DATE OF 1996 AMENDMENT

Section 233 of Pub. L. 104–121 provided that: "The amendments made by sections 331 and 332 [probably means sections 231 and 232, amending this section and section 2412 of Title 28, Judiciary and Judicial Procedure] shall apply to civil actions and adversary adjudications commenced on or after the date of the enactment of this subtitle [Mar. 29, 1996]."

EFFECTIVE DATE OF 1988 AMENDMENT

Amendment by Pub. L. 100–647 applicable to proceedings commencing after Nov. 10, 1988, see section 6239(d) of Pub. L. 100–647, set out as a note under section 7430 of Title 26, Internal Revenue Code.

EFFECTIVE DATE OF 1986 AMENDMENT

Amendment by Pub. L. 99–509 effective Oct. 21, 1986, and applicable to any claim or statement made, presented or submitted on or after such date, see section 6104 of Pub. L. 99–509, set out as an Effective Date note under section 3801 of Title 31, Money and Finance.

EFFECTIVE DATE OF 1985 AMENDMENT

Section 7 of Pub. L. 99–80 provided that:

"(a) IN GENERAL.—Except as otherwise provided in this section, the amendments made by this Act [reviving and amending this section and section 2412(d) of Title 28, Judiciary and Judicial Procedure, and amending and repealing provisions set out as notes under those sections] shall apply to cases pending on or commenced on or after the date of the enactment of this Act [Aug. 5, 1985].

"(b) APPLICABILITY OF AMENDMENTS TO CERTAIN PRIOR CASES.—The amendments made by this Act shall apply to any case commenced on or after October 1, 1984, and finally disposed of before the date of the enactment of this Act [Aug. 5, 1985], except that in any such case, the 30-day period referred to in section 504(a)(2) of title 5, United States Code, or section 2412(d)(1)(B) of title 28, United States Code, as the case may be, shall be deemed to commence on the date of the enactment of this Act.

"(c) APPLICABILITY OF AMENDMENTS TO PRIOR BOARD OF CONTRACTS APPEALS CASES.—Section 504(b)(1)(C)(ii) of title 5, United States Code, as added by section 1(c)(2) of this Act, and section 2412(d)(2)(E) of title 28, United States Code, as added by section 2(c)(2) of this Act, shall apply to any adversary adjudication pending on or commenced on or after October 1, 1981, in which applications for fees and other expenses were timely filed and were dismissed for lack of jurisdiction."

EFFECTIVE DATE

Section 208 of title II of Pub. L. 96–481, as amended by Pub. L. 99–80, § 5, Aug. 5, 1985, 99 Stat. 186, provided that: "This title and the amendments made by this title [see Short Title note below] shall take effect on [on] October 1, 1981, and shall apply to any adversary adjudication, as defined in section 504(b)(1)(C) of title 5, United States Code, and any civil action or adversary adjudication described in section 2412 of title 28, United States Code, which is pending on, or commenced on or after, such date. Awards may be made for fees and other expenses incurred before October 1, 1981, in any such adversary adjudication or civil action."

Section 203(c) of Pub. L. 96–481 which provided that effective Oct. 1, 1984, this section is repealed, except

that the provisions of this section shall continue to apply through final disposition of any adversary adjudication initiated before the date of repeal, was itself repealed by Pub. L. 99–80, § 6(b)(1), Aug. 5, 1985, 99 Stat. 186.

SHORT TITLE

Section 201 of title II of Pub. L. 96–481 provided that: "This title [enacting this section, amending section 634 of Title 15, Commerce and Trade, section 2412 of Title 28, Judiciary and Judicial Procedure, Rule 37 of the Federal Rules of Civil Procedure, set out in Title 28 Appendix, and section 1988 of Title 42, The Public Health and Welfare, and enacting provisions set out as notes under this section and section 2412 of Title 28] may be cited as the 'Equal Access to Justice Act'."

TERMINATION OF REPORTING REQUIREMENTS

For termination, effective May 15, 2000, of provisions in subsec. (e) of this section relating to annual report to Congress on the amount of fees and other expenses, see section 3003 of Pub. L. 104–66, as amended, set out as a note under section 1113 of Title 31, Money and Finance, and page 153 of House Document No. 103–7.

TERMINATION OF ADMINISTRATIVE CONFERENCE OF UNITED STATES

For termination of Administrative Conference of United States, see provision of title IV of Pub. L. 104–52, set out as a note preceding section 591 of this title.

PROHIBITION ON USE OF ENERGY AND WATER DEVELOPMENT APPROPRIATIONS TO PAY INTERVENING PARTIES IN REGULATORY OR ADJUDICATORY PROCEEDINGS

Pub. L. 102–377, title V, § 502, Oct. 2, 1992, 106 Stat. 1342, provided that: "None of the funds in this Act or subsequent Energy and Water Development Appropriations Acts shall be used to pay the expenses of, or otherwise compensate, parties intervening in regulatory or adjudicatory proceedings funded in such Acts."

REVIVAL OF PREVIOUSLY REPEALED PROVISIONS

Section 6 of Pub. L. 99–80 provided that:

"(a) REVIVAL OF CERTAIN EXPIRED PROVISIONS.—Section 504 of title 5, United States Code, and the item relating to that section in the table of sections of chapter 5 of title 5, United States Code, and subsection (d) of section 2412 of title 28, United States Code, shall be effective on or after the date of the enactment of this Act [Aug. 5, 1985] as if they had not been repealed by sections 203(c) and 204(c) of the Equal Access to Justice Act [Pub. L. 96–481].

"(b) REPEALS.—

"(1) Section 203(c) of the Equal Access to Justice Act [which repealed this section] is hereby repealed.

"(2) Section 204(c) of the Equal Access to Justice Act [which repealed section 2412(d) of title 28] is hereby repealed."

CONGRESSIONAL FINDINGS AND PURPOSES

Section 202 of title II of Pub. L. 96–481 provided that:

"(a) The Congress finds that certain individuals, partnerships, corporations, and labor and other organizations may be deterred from seeking review of, or defending against, unreasonable governmental action because of the expense involved in securing the vindication of their rights in civil actions and in administrative proceedings.

"(b) The Congress further finds that because of the greater resources and expertise of the United States the standard for an award of fees against the United States should be different from the standard governing an award against a private litigant, in certain situations.

"(c) It is the purpose of this title [see Short Title note above]—

"(1) to diminish the deterrent effect of seeking review of, or defending against, governmental action by providing in specified situations an award of attorney fees, expert witness fees, and other costs against the United States; and

"(2) to insure the applicability in actions by or against the United States of the common law and statutory exceptions to the 'American rule' respecting the award of attorney fees."

LIMITATION ON PAYMENTS

Section 207 of title II of Pub. L. 96–481, which provided that the payment of judgments, fees and other expenses in the same manner as the payment of final judgments as provided in this Act [probably should be "this title", see Short Title note above] would be effective only to the extent and in such amounts as are provided in advance in appropriation Acts, was repealed by Pub. L. 99–80, § 4, Aug. 5, 1985, 99 Stat. 186.

SECTION REFERRED TO IN OTHER SECTIONS

This section is referred to in title 15 section 634b; title 18 section 293; title 20 section 1234; title 25 section 450m–1; title 28 section 2412; title 42 section 3612.

SUBCHAPTER II—ADMINISTRATIVE PROCEDURE

SHORT TITLE

The provisions of this subchapter and chapter 7 of this title were originally enacted by act June 11, 1946, ch. 324, 60 Stat. 237, popularly known as the "Administrative Procedure Act". That Act was repealed as part of the general revision of this title by Pub. L. 89–554 and its provisions incorporated into this subchapter and chapter 7 hereof.

SUBCHAPTER REFERRED TO IN OTHER SECTIONS

This subchapter is referred to in sections 571, 592, 7118, 7134, 8902, 8902a of this title; title 2 sections 501, 502; title 7 sections 136d, 1642, 6911; title 12 sections 635a–2, 1437, 1441a, 1749bbb–17, 1959, 2278a–10, 3349, 4525, 4545; title 15 sections 78dd–1, 78dd–2, 78ggg, 266, 1715, 3412, 3710a, 5103, 5308; title 16 sections 460aa–3, 470q, 470hh; title 17 sections 701, 802; title 19 sections 1337, 1677c; title 20 section 107d–2; title 21 sections 360kk, 811, 824, 875, 958, 971; title 22 sections 277d–24, 1623, 1645n, 4116; title 23 sections 134, 135; title 25 section 954; title 28 section 509; title 29 sections 156, 164, 213, 481, 628, 792, 1137; title 30 sections 184, 956; title 31 sections 321, 3801, 3803; title 33 sections 524, 597, 2313; title 39 section 3008; title 41 section 43a; title 42 sections 1436c, 2000e–12, 2231, 2236, 2454, 3789d, 6212, 6241, 6393, 7191, 7276, 7420, 7607, 11346, 12116, 12206; title 43 section 1624; title 45 sections 1116, 1212; title 46 sections 7702, 9303; title 47 sections 303, 305, 310, 409; title 49 sections 721, 5303, 11123, 11324, 13905, 20143, 40103, 46102, 46105; title 50 sections 167h, 835; title 50 App. sections 463, 2159.

§ 551. Definitions

For the purpose of this subchapter—

(1) "agency" means each authority of the Government of the United States, whether or not it is within or subject to review by another agency, but does not include—

(A) the Congress;

(B) the courts of the United States;

(C) the governments of the territories or possessions of the United States;

(D) the government of the District of Columbia;

or except as to the requirements of section 552 of this title—

(E) agencies composed of representatives of the parties or of representatives of organizations of the parties to the disputes determined by them;

(F) courts martial and military commissions;

(G) military authority exercised in the field in time of war or in occupied territory; or

(H) functions conferred by sections 1738, 1739, 1743, and 1744 of title 12; chapter 2 of title 41; subchapter II of chapter 471 of title 49; or sections 1884, 1891–1902, and former section 1641(b)(2), of title 50, appendix;

(2) "person" includes an individual, partnership, corporation, association, or public or private organization other than an agency;

(3) "party" includes a person or agency named or admitted as a party, or properly seeking and entitled as of right to be admitted as a party, in an agency proceeding, and a person or agency admitted by an agency as a party for limited purposes;

(4) "rule" means the whole or a part of an agency statement of general or particular applicability and future effect designed to implement, interpret, or prescribe law or policy or describing the organization, procedure, or practice requirements of an agency and includes the approval or prescription for the future of rates, wages, corporate or financial structures or reorganizations thereof, prices, facilities, appliances, services or allowances therefor or of valuations, costs, or accounting, or practices bearing on any of the foregoing;

(5) "rule making" means agency process for formulating, amending, or repealing a rule;

(6) "order" means the whole or a part of a final disposition, whether affirmative, negative, injunctive, or declaratory in form, of an agency in a matter other than rule making but including licensing;

(7) "adjudication" means agency process for the formulation of an order;

(8) "license" includes the whole or a part of an agency permit, certificate, approval, registration, charter, membership, statutory exemption or other form of permission;

(9) "licensing" includes agency process respecting the grant, renewal, denial, revocation, suspension, annulment, withdrawal, limitation, amendment, modification, or conditioning of a license;

(10) "sanction" includes the whole or a part of an agency—

(A) prohibition, requirement, limitation, or other condition affecting the freedom of a person;

(B) withholding of relief;

(C) imposition of penalty or fine;

(D) destruction, taking, seizure, or withholding of property;

(E) assessment of damages, reimbursement, restitution, compensation, costs, charges, or fees;

(F) requirement, revocation, or suspension of a license; or

(G) taking other compulsory or restrictive action;

(11) "relief" includes the whole or a part of an agency—

(A) grant of money, assistance, license, authority, exemption, exception, privilege, or remedy;

(B) recognition of a claim, right, immunity, privilege, exemption, or exception; or

(C) taking of other action on the application or petition of, and beneficial to, a person;

(12) "agency proceeding" means an agency process as defined by paragraphs (5), (7), and (9) of this section;

(13) "agency action" includes the whole or a part of an agency rule, order, license, sanction, relief, or the equivalent or denial thereof, or failure to act; and

(14) "ex parte communication" means an oral or written communication not on the public record with respect to which reasonable prior notice to all parties is not given, but it shall not include requests for status reports on any matter or proceeding covered by this subchapter.

(Pub. L. 89–554, Sept. 6, 1966, 80 Stat. 381; Pub. L. 94–409, §4(b), Sept. 13, 1976, 90 Stat. 1247; Pub. L. 103–272, §5(a), July 5, 1994, 108 Stat. 1373.)

HISTORICAL AND REVISION NOTES

Derivation	U.S. Code	Revised Statutes and Statutes at Large
(1)	5 U.S.C. 1001(a).	June 11, 1946, ch. 324, §2(a), 60 Stat. 237. Aug. 8, 1946, ch. 870, §302, 60 Stat. 918. Aug. 10, 1946, ch. 951, §601, 60 Stat. 993. Mar. 31, 1947, ch. 30, §6(a), 61 Stat. 37. June 30, 1947, ch. 163, §210, 61 Stat. 201. Mar. 30, 1948, ch. 161, §301, 62 Stat. 99.
(2)–(13)	5 U.S.C. 1001 (less (a)).	June 11, 1946, ch. 324, §2 (less (a)), 60 Stat. 237.

In paragraph (1), the sentence "Nothing in this Act shall be construed to repeal delegations of authority as provided by law," is omitted as surplusage since there is nothing in the Act which could reasonably be so construed.

In paragraph (1)(G), the words "or naval" are omitted as included in "military".

In paragraph (1)(H), the words "functions which by law expire on the termination of present hostilities, within any fixed period thereafter, or before July 1, 1947" are omitted as executed. Reference to the "Selective Training and Service Act of 1940" is omitted as that Act expired Mar. 31, 1947. Reference to the "Sugar Control Extension Act of 1947" is omitted as that Act expired on Mar. 31, 1948. References to the "Housing and Rent Act of 1947, as amended" and the "Veterans' Emergency Housing Act of 1946" have been consolidated as they are related. The reference to former section 1641(b)(2) of title 50, appendix, is retained notwithstanding its repeal by §111(a)(1) of the Act of Sept. 21, 1961, Pub. L. 87–256, 75 Stat. 538, since §111(c) of the Act provides that a reference in other Acts to a provision of law repealed by §111(a) shall be considered to be a reference to the appropriate provisions of Pub. L. 87–256.

In paragraph (2), the words "of any character" are omitted as surplusage.

In paragraph (3), the words "and a person or agency admitted by an agency as a party for limited purposes" are substituted for "but nothing herein shall be construed to prevent an agency from admitting any person or agency as a party for limited purposes".

In paragraph (9), a comma is supplied between the words "limitation" and "amendment" to correct an editorial error of omission.

In paragraph (10)(C), the words "of any form" are omitted as surplusage.

Standard changes are made to conform with the definitions applicable and the style of this title as outlined in the preface to the report.

CODIFICATION

Section 551 of former Title 5, Executive Departments and Government Officers and Employees, was transferred to section 2242 of Title 7, Agriculture.

AMENDMENTS

1994—Par. (1)(H). Pub. L. 103–272 substituted "subchapter II of chapter 471 of title 49; or sections" for "or sections 1622,".

1976—Par. (14). Pub. L. 94–409 added par. (14).

EFFECTIVE DATE OF 1976 AMENDMENT

Amendment by Pub. L. 94–409 effective 180 days after Sept. 13, 1976, see section 6 of Pub. L. 94–409, set out as an Effective Date note under section 552b of this title.

STUDY AND REPORTS ON ADMINISTRATIVE SUBPOENAS

Pub. L. 106–544, §7, Dec. 19, 2000, 114 Stat. 2719, provided that:

"(a) STUDY ON USE OF ADMINISTRATIVE SUBPOENAS.— Not later than December 31, 2001, the Attorney General, in consultation with the Secretary of the Treasury, shall complete a study on the use of administrative subpoena power by executive branch agencies or entities and shall report the findings to the Committees on the Judiciary of the Senate and the House of Representatives. Such report shall include—

"(1) a description of the sources of administrative subpoena power and the scope of such subpoena power within executive branch agencies;

"(2) a description of applicable subpoena enforcement mechanisms;

"(3) a description of any notification provisions and any other provisions relating to safeguarding privacy interests;

"(4) a description of the standards governing the issuance of administrative subpoenas; and

"(5) recommendations from the Attorney General regarding necessary steps to ensure that administrative subpoena power is used and enforced consistently and fairly by executive branch agencies.

"(b) REPORT ON FREQUENCY OF USE OF ADMINISTRATIVE SUBPOENAS.—

"(1) IN GENERAL.—The Attorney General and the Secretary of the Treasury shall report in January of each year to the Committees on the Judiciary of the Senate and the House of Representatives on the number of administrative subpoenas issued by them under this section and the identity of the agency or component of the Department of Justice or the Department of the Treasury issuing the subpoena and imposing the charges.

"(2) EXPIRATION.—The reporting requirement of this subsection shall terminate in 3 years after the date of the enactment of this section [Dec. 19, 2000]."

SECTION REFERRED TO IN OTHER SECTIONS

This section is referred to in sections 500, 504, 552, 562, 571, 592, 595, 601, 701, 804, 3344, 3348 of this title; title 2 sections 501, 502, 658, 1602; title 7 section 6997; title 15 sections 78d–1, 78w, 632, 637c, 766, 2053, 3412, 3416, 6501; title 16 section 470w; title 22 sections 3731, 6033, 6741; title 26 sections 6103, 9041; title 30 sections 185, 956; title 31 sections 3901, 6101, 7501; title 41 section 422; title 42 sections 2231, 2992c, 6107, 6241, 6393, 7191, 8259, 8262, 11317, 11504; title 46 sections 7702, 9303; title 47 sections 155, 409; title 49 sections 106, 11324; title 50 App. sections 2159, 2412.

§ 552. Public information; agency rules, opinions, orders, records, and proceedings

(a) Each agency shall make available to the public information as follows:

(1) Each agency shall separately state and currently publish in the Federal Register for the guidance of the public—

(A) descriptions of its central and field organization and the established places at which, the employees (and in the case of a uniformed service, the members) from whom, and the methods whereby, the public may obtain information, make submittals or requests, or obtain decisions;

(B) statements of the general course and method by which its functions are channeled and determined, including the nature and requirements of all formal and informal procedures available;

(C) rules of procedure, descriptions of forms available or the places at which forms may be obtained, and instructions as to the scope and contents of all papers, reports, or examinations;

(D) substantive rules of general applicability adopted as authorized by law, and statements of general policy or interpretations of general applicability formulated and adopted by the agency; and

(E) each amendment, revision, or repeal of the foregoing.

Except to the extent that a person has actual and timely notice of the terms thereof, a person may not in any manner be required to resort to, or be adversely affected by, a matter required to be published in the Federal Register and not so published. For the purpose of this paragraph, matter reasonably available to the class of persons affected thereby is deemed published in the Federal Register when incorporated by reference therein with the approval of the Director of the Federal Register.

(2) Each agency, in accordance with published rules, shall make available for public inspection and copying—

(A) final opinions, including concurring and dissenting opinions, as well as orders, made in the adjudication of cases;

(B) those statements of policy and interpretations which have been adopted by the agency and are not published in the Federal Register;

(C) administrative staff manuals and instructions to staff that affect a member of the public;

(D) copies of all records, regardless of form or format, which have been released to any person under paragraph (3) and which, because of the nature of their subject matter, the agency determines have become or are likely to become the subject of subsequent requests for substantially the same records; and

(E) a general index of the records referred to under subparagraph (D);

unless the materials are promptly published and copies offered for sale. For records created on or after November 1, 1996, within one year after such date, each agency shall make such records available, including by computer telecommunications or, if computer telecommunications means have not been established by the agency, by other electronic means. To the extent required to prevent a clearly unwarranted invasion of personal privacy, an agency may delete identifying details when it makes available or publishes an opinion, statement of policy, interpretation, staff manual, instruction, or copies of

records referred to in subparagraph (D). However, in each case the justification for the deletion shall be explained fully in writing, and the extent of such deletion shall be indicated on the portion of the record which is made available or published, unless including that indication would harm an interest protected by the exemption in subsection (b) under which the deletion is made. If technically feasible, the extent of the deletion shall be indicated at the place in the record where the deletion was made. Each agency shall also maintain and make available for public inspection and copying current indexes providing identifying information for the public as to any matter issued, adopted, or promulgated after July 4, 1967, and required by this paragraph to be made available or published. Each agency shall promptly publish, quarterly or more frequently, and distribute (by sale or otherwise) copies of each index or supplements thereto unless it determines by order published in the Federal Register that the publication would be unnecessary and impracticable, in which case the agency shall nonetheless provide copies of such index on request at a cost not to exceed the direct cost of duplication. Each agency shall make the index referred to in subparagraph (E) available by computer telecommunications by December 31, 1999. A final order, opinion, statement of policy, interpretation, or staff manual or instruction that affects a member of the public may be relied on, used, or cited as precedent by an agency against a party other than an agency only if—

(i) it has been indexed and either made available or published as provided by this paragraph; or

(ii) the party has actual and timely notice of the terms thereof.

(3)(A) Except with respect to the records made available under paragraphs (1) and (2) of this subsection, each agency, upon any request for records which (i) reasonably describes such records and (ii) is made in accordance with published rules stating the time, place, fees (if any), and procedures to be followed, shall make the records promptly available to any person.

(B) In making any record available to a person under this paragraph, an agency shall provide the record in any form or format requested by the person if the record is readily reproducible by the agency in that form or format. Each agency shall make reasonable efforts to maintain its records in forms or formats that are reproducible for purposes of this section.

(C) In responding under this paragraph to a request for records, an agency shall make reasonable efforts to search for the records in electronic form or format, except when such efforts would significantly interfere with the operation of the agency's automated information system.

(D) For purposes of this paragraph, the term "search" means to review, manually or by automated means, agency records for the purpose of locating those records which are responsive to a request.

(4)(A)(i) In order to carry out the provisions of this section, each agency shall promulgate regulations, pursuant to notice and receipt of public comment, specifying the schedule of fees applicable to the processing of requests under this section and establishing procedures and guidelines for determining when such fees should be waived or reduced. Such schedule shall conform to the guidelines which shall be promulgated, pursuant to notice and receipt of public comment, by the Director of the Office of Management and Budget and which shall provide for a uniform schedule of fees for all agencies.

(ii) Such agency regulations shall provide that—

(I) fees shall be limited to reasonable standard charges for document search, duplication, and review, when records are requested for commercial use;

(II) fees shall be limited to reasonable standard charges for document duplication when records are not sought for commercial use and the request is made by an educational or noncommercial scientific institution, whose purpose is scholarly or scientific research; or a representative of the news media; and

(III) for any request not described in (I) or (II), fees shall be limited to reasonable standard charges for document search and duplication.

(iii) Documents shall be furnished without any charge or at a charge reduced below the fees established under clause (ii) if disclosure of the information is in the public interest because it is likely to contribute significantly to public understanding of the operations or activities of the government and is not primarily in the commercial interest of the requester.

(iv) Fee schedules shall provide for the recovery of only the direct costs of search, duplication, or review. Review costs shall include only the direct costs incurred during the initial examination of a document for the purposes of determining whether the documents must be disclosed under this section and for the purposes of withholding any portions exempt from disclosure under this section. Review costs may not include any costs incurred in resolving issues of law or policy that may be raised in the course of processing a request under this section. No fee may be charged by any agency under this section—

(I) if the costs of routine collection and processing of the fee are likely to equal or exceed the amount of the fee; or

(II) for any request described in clause (ii) (II) or (III) of this subparagraph for the first two hours of search time or for the first one hundred pages of duplication.

(v) No agency may require advance payment of any fee unless the requester has previously failed to pay fees in a timely fashion, or the agency has determined that the fee will exceed $250.

(vi) Nothing in this subparagraph shall supersede fees chargeable under a statute specifically providing for setting the level of fees for particular types of records.

(vii) In any action by a requester regarding the waiver of fees under this section, the court shall determine the matter de novo: *Provided,* That the court's review of the matter shall be limited to the record before the agency.

(B) On complaint, the district court of the United States in the district in which the complainant resides, or has his principal place of business, or in which the agency records are situated, or in the District of Columbia, has jurisdiction to enjoin the agency from withholding agency records and to order the production of any agency records improperly withheld from the complainant. In such a case the court shall determine the matter de novo, and may examine the contents of such agency records in camera to determine whether such records or any part thereof shall be withheld under any of the exemptions set forth in subsection (b) of this section, and the burden is on the agency to sustain its action. In addition to any other matters to which a court accords substantial weight, a court shall accord substantial weight to an affidavit of an agency concerning the agency's determination as to technical feasibility under paragraph (2)(C) and subsection (b) and reproducibility under paragraph (3)(B).

(C) Notwithstanding any other provision of law, the defendant shall serve an answer or otherwise plead to any complaint made under this subsection within thirty days after service upon the defendant of the pleading in which such complaint is made, unless the court otherwise directs for good cause shown.

[(D) Repealed. Pub. L. 98–620, title IV, § 402(2), Nov. 8, 1984, 98 Stat. 3357.]

(E) The court may assess against the United States reasonable attorney fees and other litigation costs reasonably incurred in any case under this section in which the complainant has substantially prevailed.

(F) Whenever the court orders the production of any agency records improperly withheld from the complainant and assesses against the United States reasonable attorney fees and other litigation costs, and the court additionally issues a written finding that the circumstances surrounding the withholding raise questions whether agency personnel acted arbitrarily or capriciously with respect to the withholding, the Special Counsel shall promptly initiate a proceeding to determine whether disciplinary action is warranted against the officer or employee who was primarily responsible for the withholding. The Special Counsel, after investigation and consideration of the evidence submitted, shall submit his findings and recommendations to the administrative authority of the agency concerned and shall send copies of the findings and recommendations to the officer or employee or his representative. The administrative authority shall take the corrective action that the Special Counsel recommends.

(G) In the event of noncompliance with the order of the court, the district court may punish for contempt the responsible employee, and in the case of a uniformed service, the responsible member.

(5) Each agency having more than one member shall maintain and make available for public inspection a record of the final votes of each member in every agency proceeding.

(6)(A) Each agency, upon any request for records made under paragraph (1), (2), or (3) of this subsection, shall—

(i) determine within 20 days (excepting Saturdays, Sundays, and legal public holidays) after the receipt of any such request whether to comply with such request and shall immediately notify the person making such request of such determination and the reasons therefor, and of the right of such person to appeal to the head of the agency any adverse determination; and

(ii) make a determination with respect to any appeal within twenty days (excepting Saturdays, Sundays, and legal public holidays) after the receipt of such appeal. If on appeal the denial of the request for records is in whole or in part upheld, the agency shall notify the person making such request of the provisions for judicial review of that determination under paragraph (4) of this subsection.

(B)(i) In unusual circumstances as specified in this subparagraph, the time limits prescribed in either clause (i) or clause (ii) of subparagraph (A) may be extended by written notice to the person making such request setting forth the unusual circumstances for such extension and the date on which a determination is expected to be dispatched. No such notice shall specify a date that would result in an extension for more than ten working days, except as provided in clause (ii) of this subparagraph.

(ii) With respect to a request for which a written notice under clause (i) extends the time limits prescribed under clause (i) of subparagraph (A), the agency shall notify the person making the request if the request cannot be processed within the time limit specified in that clause and shall provide the person an opportunity to limit the scope of the request so that it may be processed within that time limit or an opportunity to arrange with the agency an alternative time frame for processing the request or a modified request. Refusal by the person to reasonably modify the request or arrange such an alternative time frame shall be considered as a factor in determining whether exceptional circumstances exist for purposes of subparagraph (C).

(iii) As used in this subparagraph, "unusual circumstances" means, but only to the extent reasonably necessary to the proper processing of the particular requests—

(I) the need to search for and collect the requested records from field facilities or other establishments that are separate from the office processing the request;

(II) the need to search for, collect, and appropriately examine a voluminous amount of separate and distinct records which are demanded in a single request; or

(III) the need for consultation, which shall be conducted with all practicable speed, with another agency having a substantial interest in the determination of the request or among two or more components of the agency having substantial subject-matter interest therein.

(iv) Each agency may promulgate regulations, pursuant to notice and receipt of public comment, providing for the aggregation of certain requests by the same requestor, or by a group of requestors acting in concert, if the agency reasonably believes that such requests actually constitute a single request, which would otherwise satisfy the unusual circumstances specified in this subparagraph, and the requests involve clearly related matters. Multiple requests involving unrelated matters shall not be aggregated.

(C)(i) Any person making a request to any agency for records under paragraph (1), (2), or (3) of this subsection shall be deemed to have exhausted his administrative remedies with respect to such request if the agency fails to comply with the applicable time limit provisions of this paragraph. If the Government can show exceptional circumstances exist and that the agency is exercising due diligence in responding to the request, the court may retain jurisdiction and allow the agency additional time to complete its review of the records. Upon any determination by an agency to comply with a request for records, the records shall be made promptly available to such person making such request. Any notification of denial of any request for records under this subsection shall set forth the names and titles or positions of each person responsible for the denial of such request.

(ii) For purposes of this subparagraph, the term "exceptional circumstances" does not include a delay that results from a predictable agency workload of requests under this section, unless the agency demonstrates reasonable progress in reducing its backlog of pending requests.

(iii) Refusal by a person to reasonably modify the scope of a request or arrange an alternative time frame for processing a request (or a modified request) under clause (ii) after being given an opportunity to do so by the agency to whom the person made the request shall be considered as a factor in determining whether exceptional circumstances exist for purposes of this subparagraph.

(D)(i) Each agency may promulgate regulations, pursuant to notice and receipt of public comment, providing for multitrack processing of requests for records based on the amount of work or time (or both) involved in processing requests.

(ii) Regulations under this subparagraph may provide a person making a request that does not qualify for the fastest multitrack processing an opportunity to limit the scope of the request in order to qualify for faster processing.

(iii) This subparagraph shall not be considered to affect the requirement under subparagraph (C) to exercise due diligence.

(E)(i) Each agency shall promulgate regulations, pursuant to notice and receipt of public comment, providing for expedited processing of requests for records—

(I) in cases in which the person requesting the records demonstrates a compelling need; and

(II) in other cases determined by the agency.

(ii) Notwithstanding clause (i), regulations under this subparagraph must ensure—

(I) that a determination of whether to provide expedited processing shall be made, and notice of the determination shall be provided to the person making the request, within 10 days after the date of the request; and

(II) expeditious consideration of administrative appeals of such determinations of whether to provide expedited processing.

(iii) An agency shall process as soon as practicable any request for records to which the agency has granted expedited processing under this subparagraph. Agency action to deny or affirm denial of a request for expedited processing pursuant to this subparagraph, and failure by an agency to respond in a timely manner to such a request shall be subject to judicial review under paragraph (4), except that the judicial review shall be based on the record before the agency at the time of the determination.

(iv) A district court of the United States shall not have jurisdiction to review an agency denial of expedited processing of a request for records after the agency has provided a complete response to the request.

(v) For purposes of this subparagraph, the term "compelling need" means—

(I) that a failure to obtain requested records on an expedited basis under this paragraph could reasonably be expected to pose an imminent threat to the life or physical safety of an individual; or

(II) with respect to a request made by a person primarily engaged in disseminating information, urgency to inform the public concerning actual or alleged Federal Government activity.

(vi) A demonstration of a compelling need by a person making a request for expedited processing shall be made by a statement certified by such person to be true and correct to the best of such person's knowledge and belief.

(F) In denying a request for records, in whole or in part, an agency shall make a reasonable effort to estimate the volume of any requested matter the provision of which is denied, and shall provide any such estimate to the person making the request, unless providing such estimate would harm an interest protected by the exemption in subsection (b) pursuant to which the denial is made.

(b) This section does not apply to matters that are—

(1)(A) specifically authorized under criteria established by an Executive order to be kept secret in the interest of national defense or foreign policy and (B) are in fact properly classified pursuant to such Executive order;

(2) related solely to the internal personnel rules and practices of an agency;

(3) specifically exempted from disclosure by statute (other than section 552b of this title), provided that such statute (A) requires that the matters be withheld from the public in such a manner as to leave no discretion on the issue, or (B) establishes particular criteria for withholding or refers to particular types of matters to be withheld;

(4) trade secrets and commercial or financial information obtained from a person and privileged or confidential;

(5) inter-agency or intra-agency memorandums or letters which would not be available by law to a party other than an agency in litigation with the agency;

(6) personnel and medical files and similar files the disclosure of which would constitute a clearly unwarranted invasion of personal privacy;

(7) records or information compiled for law enforcement purposes, but only to the extent that the production of such law enforcement records or information (A) could reasonably be expected to interfere with enforcement proceedings, (B) would deprive a person of a right to a fair trial or an impartial adjudication, (C) could reasonably be expected to constitute an unwarranted invasion of personal privacy, (D) could reasonably be expected to disclose the identity of a confidential source, including a State, local, or foreign agency or authority or any private institution which furnished information on a confidential basis, and, in the case of a record or information compiled by criminal law enforcement authority in the course of a criminal investigation or by an agency conducting a lawful national security intelligence investigation, information furnished by a confidential source, (E) would disclose techniques and procedures for law enforcement investigations or prosecutions, or would disclose guidelines for law enforcement investigations or prosecutions if such disclosure could reasonably be expected to risk circumvention of the law, or (F) could reasonably be expected to endanger the life or physical safety of any individual;

(8) contained in or related to examination, operating, or condition reports prepared by, on behalf of, or for the use of an agency responsible for the regulation or supervision of financial institutions; or

(9) geological and geophysical information and data, including maps, concerning wells.

Any reasonably segregable portion of a record shall be provided to any person requesting such record after deletion of the portions which are exempt under this subsection. The amount of information deleted shall be indicated on the released portion of the record, unless including that indication would harm an interest protected by the exemption in this subsection under which the deletion is made. If technically feasible, the amount of the information deleted shall be indicated at the place in the record where such deletion is made.

(c)(1) Whenever a request is made which involves access to records described in subsection (b)(7)(A) and—

(A) the investigation or proceeding involves a possible violation of criminal law; and

(B) there is reason to believe that (i) the subject of the investigation or proceeding is not aware of its pendency, and (ii) disclosure of the existence of the records could reasonably be expected to interfere with enforcement proceedings,

the agency may, during only such time as that circumstance continues, treat the records as not subject to the requirements of this section.

(2) Whenever informant records maintained by a criminal law enforcement agency under an informant's name or personal identifier are requested by a third party according to the informant's name or personal identifier, the agency may treat the records as not subject to the requirements of this section unless the informant's status as an informant has been officially confirmed.

(3) Whenever a request is made which involves access to records maintained by the Federal Bu-

reau of Investigation pertaining to foreign intelligence or counterintelligence, or international terrorism, and the existence of the records is classified information as provided in subsection (b)(1), the Bureau may, as long as the existence of the records remains classified information, treat the records as not subject to the requirements of this section.

(d) This section does not authorize withholding of information or limit the availability of records to the public, except as specifically stated in this section. This section is not authority to withhold information from Congress.

(e)(1) On or before February 1 of each year, each agency shall submit to the Attorney General of the United States a report which shall cover the preceding fiscal year and which shall include—

(A) the number of determinations made by the agency not to comply with requests for records made to such agency under subsection (a) and the reasons for each such determination;

(B)(i) the number of appeals made by persons under subsection (a)(6), the result of such appeals, and the reason for the action upon each appeal that results in a denial of information; and

(ii) a complete list of all statutes that the agency relies upon to authorize the agency to withhold information under subsection (b)(3), a description of whether a court has upheld the decision of the agency to withhold information under each such statute, and a concise description of the scope of any information withheld;

(C) the number of requests for records pending before the agency as of September 30 of the preceding year, and the median number of days that such requests had been pending before the agency as of that date;

(D) the number of requests for records received by the agency and the number of requests which the agency processed;

(E) the median number of days taken by the agency to process different types of requests;

(F) the total amount of fees collected by the agency for processing requests; and

(G) the number of full-time staff of the agency devoted to processing requests for records under this section, and the total amount expended by the agency for processing such requests.

(2) Each agency shall make each such report available to the public including by computer telecommunications, or if computer telecommunications means have not been established by the agency, by other electronic means.

(3) The Attorney General of the United States shall make each report which has been made available by electronic means available at a single electronic access point. The Attorney General of the United States shall notify the Chairman and ranking minority member of the Committee on Government Reform and Oversight of the House of Representatives and the Chairman and ranking minority member of the Committees on Governmental Affairs and the Judiciary of the Senate, no later than April 1 of the year in which each such report is issued, that such reports are available by electronic means.

(4) The Attorney General of the United States, in consultation with the Director of the Office of Management and Budget, shall develop reporting and performance guidelines in connection with reports required by this subsection by October 1, 1997, and may establish additional requirements for such reports as the Attorney General determines may be useful.

(5) The Attorney General of the United States shall submit an annual report on or before April 1 of each calendar year which shall include for the prior calendar year a listing of the number of cases arising under this section, the exemption involved in each case, the disposition of such case, and the cost, fees, and penalties assessed under subparagraphs (E), (F), and (G) of subsection (a)(4). Such report shall also include a description of the efforts undertaken by the Department of Justice to encourage agency compliance with this section.

(f) For purposes of this section, the term—

(1) "agency" as defined in section 551(1) of this title includes any executive department, military department, Government corporation, Government controlled corporation, or other establishment in the executive branch of the Government (including the Executive Office of the President), or any independent regulatory agency; and

(2) "record" and any other term used in this section in reference to information includes any information that would be an agency record subject to the requirements of this section when maintained by an agency in any format, including an electronic format.

(g) The head of each agency shall prepare and make publicly available upon request, reference material or a guide for requesting records or information from the agency, subject to the exemptions in subsection (b), including—

(1) an index of all major information systems of the agency;

(2) a description of major information and record locator systems maintained by the agency; and

(3) a handbook for obtaining various types and categories of public information from the agency pursuant to chapter 35 of title 44, and under this section.

(Pub. L. 89–554, Sept. 6, 1966, 80 Stat. 383; Pub. L. 90–23, §1, June 5, 1967, 81 Stat. 54; Pub. L. 93–502, §§1–3, Nov. 21, 1974, 88 Stat. 1561–1564; Pub. L. 94–409, §5(b), Sept. 13, 1976, 90 Stat. 1247; Pub. L. 95–454, title IX, §906(a)(10), Oct. 13, 1978, 92 Stat. 1225; Pub. L. 98–620, title IV, §402(2), Nov. 8, 1984, 98 Stat. 3357; Pub. L. 99–570, title I, §§1802, 1803, Oct. 27, 1986, 100 Stat. 3207–48, 3207–49; Pub. L. 104–231, §§3–11, Oct. 2, 1996, 110 Stat. 3049–3054.)

HISTORICAL AND REVISION NOTES
1966 ACT

Derivation	U.S. Code	Revised Statutes and Statutes at Large
....	5 U.S.C. 1002.	June 11, 1946, ch. 324, §3, 60 Stat. 238.

In subsection (b)(3), the words "formulated and" are omitted as surplusage. In the last sentence of subsection (b), the words "in any manner" are omitted as surplusage since the prohibition is all inclusive.

Standard changes are made to conform with the definitions applicable and the style of this title as outlined in the preface to the report.

1967 ACT

Section 1 [of Pub. L. 90–23] amends section 552 of title 5, United States Code, to reflect Public Law 89–487.

In subsection (a)(1)(A), the words "employees (and in the case of a uniformed service, the member)" are substituted for "officer" to retain the coverage of Public Law 89–487 and to conform to the definitions in 5 U.S.C. 2101, 2104, and 2105.

In the last sentence of subsection (a)(2), the words "A final order * * * may be relied on * * * only if" are substituted for "No final order * * * may be relied upon * * * unless"; and the words "a party other than an agency" and "the party" are substituted for "a private party" and "the private party", respectively, on authority of the definition of "private party" in 5 App. U.S.C. 1002(g).

In subsection (a)(3), the words "the responsible employee, and in the case of a uniformed service, the responsible member" are substituted for "the responsible officers" to retain the coverage of Public Law 89–487 and to conform to the definitions in 5 U.S.C. 2101, 2104, and 2105.

In subsection (a)(4), the words "shall maintain and make available for public inspection a record" are substituted for "shall keep a record * * * and that record shall be available for public inspection".

In subsection (b)(5) and (7), the words "a party other than an agency" are substituted for "a private party" on authority of the definition of "private party" in 5 App. U.S.C. 1002(g).

In subsection (c), the words "This section does not authorize" and "This section is not authority" are substituted for "Nothing in this section authorizes" and "nor shall this section be authority", respectively.

5 App. U.S.C. 1002(g), defining "private party" to mean a party other than an agency, is omitted since the words "party other than an agency" are substituted for the words "private party" wherever they appear in revised 5 U.S.C. 552.

5 App. U.S.C. 1002(h), prescribing the effective date, is omitted as unnecessary. That effective date is prescribed by section 4 of this bill.

CODIFICATION

Section 552 of former Title 5, Executive Departments and Government Officers and Employees, was transferred to section 2243 of Title 7, Agriculture.

AMENDMENTS

1996—Subsec. (a)(2). Pub. L. 104–231, §4(4), (5), in first sentence struck out "and" at end of subpar. (B) and inserted subpars. (D) and (E).

Pub. L. 104–231, §4(7), inserted after first sentence "For records created on or after November 1, 1996, within one year after such date, each agency shall make such records available, including by computer telecommunications or, if computer telecommunications means have not been established by the agency, by other electronic means."

Pub. L. 104–231, §4(1), in second sentence substituted "staff manual, instruction, or copies of records referred to in subparagraph (D)" for "or staff manual or instruction".

Pub. L. 104–231, §4(2), inserted before period at end of third sentence ", and the extent of such deletion shall be indicated on the portion of the record which is made available or published, unless including that indication would harm an interest protected by the exemption in subsection (b) under which the deletion is made".

Pub. L. 104–231, §4(3), inserted after third sentence "If technically feasible, the extent of the deletion shall be indicated at the place in the record where the deletion was made."

Pub. L. 104–231, §4(6), which directed the insertion of the following new sentence after the fifth sentence "Each agency shall make the index referred to in subparagraph (E) available by computer telecommunications by December 31, 1999.", was executed by making the insertion after the sixth sentence, to reflect the probable intent of Congress and the addition of a new sentence by section 4(3) of Pub. L. 104–231.

Subsec. (a)(3). Pub. L. 104–231, §5, inserted subpar. (A) designation after "(3)", redesignated subpars. (A) and (B) as cls. (i) and (ii), respectively, and added subpars. (B) to (D).

Subsec. (a)(4)(B). Pub. L. 104–231, §6, inserted at end "In addition to any other matters to which a court accords substantial weight, a court shall accord substantial weight to an affidavit of an agency concerning the agency's determination as to technical feasibility under paragraph (2)(C) and subsection (b) and reproducibility under paragraph (3)(B)."

Subsec. (a)(6)(A)(i). Pub. L. 104–231, §8(b), substituted "20 days" for "ten days".

Subsec. (a)(6)(B). Pub. L. 104–231, §7(b), amended subpar. (B) generally. Prior to amendment, subpar. (B) read as follows: "In unusual circumstances as specified in this subparagraph, the time limits prescribed in either clause (i) or clause (ii) of subparagraph (A) may be extended by written notice to the person making such request setting forth the reasons for such extension and the date on which a determination is expected to be dispatched. No such notice shall specify a date that would result in an extension for more than ten working days. As used in this subparagraph, 'unusual circumstances' means, but only to the extent reasonably necessary to the proper processing of the particular request—

"(i) the need to search for and collect the requested records from field facilities or other establishments that are separate from the office processing the request;

"(ii) the need to search for, collect, and appropriately examine a voluminous amount of separate and distinct records which are demanded in a single request; or

"(iii) the need for consultation, which shall be conducted with all practicable speed, with another agency having a substantial interest in the determination of the request or among two or more components of the agency having substantial subject-matter interest therein."

Subsec. (a)(6)(C). Pub. L. 104–231, §7(c), designated existing provisions as cl. (i) and added cls. (ii) and (iii).

Subsec. (a)(6)(D). Pub. L. 104–231, §7(a), added subpar. (D).

Subsec. (a)(6)(E), (F). Pub. L. 104–231, §8(a), (c), added subpars. (E) and (F).

Subsec. (b). Pub. L. 104–231, §9, inserted at end of closing provisions "The amount of information deleted shall be indicated on the released portion of the record, unless including that indication would harm an interest protected by the exemption in this subsection under which the deletion is made. If technically feasible, the amount of the information deleted shall be indicated at the place in the record where such deletion is made."

Subsec. (e). Pub. L. 104–231, §10, amended subsec. (e) generally, revising and restating provisions relating to reports to Congress.

Subsec. (f). Pub. L. 104–231, §3, amended subsec. (f) generally. Prior to amendment, subsec. (f) read as follows: "For purposes of this section, the term 'agency' as defined in section 551(1) of this title includes any executive department, military department, Government corporation, Government controlled corporation, or other establishment in the executive branch of the Government (including the Executive Office of the President), or any independent regulatory agency."

Subsec. (g). Pub. L. 104–231, §11, added subsec. (g).

1986—Subsec. (a)(4)(A). Pub. L. 99–570, §1803, amended subpar. (A) generally. Prior to amendment, subpar. (A) read as follows: "In order to carry out the provisions of this section, each agency shall promulgate regulations, pursuant to notice and receipt of public comment, specifying a uniform schedule of fees applicable to all constituent units of such agency. Such fees shall be limited to reasonable standard charges for document search and duplication and provide for recovery of only the direct costs of such search and duplication. Documents shall be furnished without charge or at a reduced charge where the agency determines that waiver or reduction of the fee is in the public interest because furnishing the information can be considered as primarily benefiting the general public."

Subsec. (b)(7). Pub. L. 99–570, § 1802(a), amended par. (7) generally. Prior to amendment, par. (7) read as follows: "investigatory records compiled for law enforcement purposes, but only to the extent that the production of such records would (A) interfere with enforcement proceedings, (B) deprive a person of a right to a fair trial or an impartial adjudication, (C) constitute an unwarranted invasion of personal privacy, (D) disclose the identity of a confidential source, and, in the case of a record compiled by a criminal law enforcement authority in the course of a criminal investigation, or by an agency conducting a lawful national security intelligence investigation, confidential information furnished only by the confidential source, (E) disclose investigative techniques and procedures, or (F) endanger the life or physical safety of law enforcement personnel;".

Subsecs. (c) to (f). Pub. L. 99–570, § 1802(b), added subsec. (c) and redesignated former subsecs. (c) to (e) as (d) to (f), respectively.

1984—Subsec. (a)(4)(D). Pub. L. 98–620 repealed subpar. (D) which provided for precedence on the docket and expeditious disposition of district court proceedings authorized by subsec. (a).

1978—Subsec. (a)(4)(F). Pub. L. 95–454 substituted references to the Special Counsel for references to the Civil Service Commission wherever appearing and reference to his findings for reference to its findings.

1976—Subsec. (b)(3). Pub. L. 94–409 inserted provision excluding section 552b of this title from applicability of exemption from disclosure and provision setting forth conditions for statute specifically exempting disclosure.

1974—Subsec. (a)(2). Pub. L. 93–502, § 1(a), substituted provisions relating to maintenance and availability of current indexes, for provisions relating to maintenance and availability of a current index, and inserted provisions relating to publication and distribution of copies of indexes or supplements thereto.

Subsec. (a)(3). Pub. L. 93–502, § 1(b)(1), substituted provisions requiring requests to reasonably describe records for provisions requiring requests, for identifiable records, and struck out provisions setting forth procedures to enjoin agencies from withholding the requested records and ordering their production.

Subsec. (a)(4), (5). Pub. L. 93–502, § 1(b)(2), added par. (4) and redesignated former par. (4) as (5).

Subsec. (a)(6). Pub. L. 93–502, § 1(c), added par. (6).

Subsec. (b)(1). Pub. L. 93–502, § 2(a), designated existing provisions as cl. (A), substituted "authorized under criteria established by an" for "required by", and added cl. (B).

Subsec. (b)(7). Pub. L. 93–502, § 2(b), substituted provisions relating to exemption for investigatory records compiled for law enforcement purposes, for provisions relating to exemption for investigatory files compiled for law enforcement purposes.

Subsec. (b), foll. par. (9). Pub. L. 93–502, § 2(c), inserted provision relating to availability of segregable portion of records.

Subsecs. (d), (e). Pub. L. 93–502, § 3, added subsecs. (d) and (e).

1967—Subsec. (a). Pub. L. 90–23 substituted introductory statement requiring every agency to make available to the public certain information for former introductory provision excepting from disclosure (1) any function of the United States requiring secrecy in the public interest or (2) any matter relating to internal management of an agency, covered in subsec. (b)(1) and (2) of this section.

Subsec. (a)(1). Pub. L. 90–23 incorporated provisions of: former subsec. (b)(1) in (A), inserting requirement of

publication of names of officers as sources of information and provision for public to obtain decisions, and striking out publication requirement for delegations by the agency of final authority; former subsec. (b)(2), introductory part, in (B); former subsec. (b)(2), concluding part, in (C), inserting publication requirement for rules of procedure and descriptions of forms available or the places at which forms may be obtained; former subsec. (b)(3), introductory part, in (D), inserting requirement of general applicability of substantive rules and interpretations, added clause (E), substituted exemption of any person from failure to resort to any matter or from being adversely affected by any matter required to be published in the Federal Register but not so published for former subsec. (b)(3), concluding part, excepting from publication rules addressed to and served upon named persons in accordance with laws and final sentence reading "A person may not be required to resort to organization or procedure not so published" and inserted provision deeming matter, which is reasonably available, as published in the Federal Register when such matter is incorporated by reference in the Federal Register with the approval of its Director.

Subsec. (a)(2). Pub. L. 90–23 incorporated provisions of former subsec. (c), provided for public copying of records, struck out requirement of agency publication of final opinions or orders and authority for secrecy and withholding of opinions and orders required for good cause to be held confidential and not cited as precedents, latter provision now superseded by subsec. (b) of this section, designated existing subsec. (c) as clause (A), including provision for availability of concurring and dissenting opinions, inserted provisions for availability of policy statements and interpretations in clause (B) and staff manuals and instructions in clause (C), deletion of personal identifications from records to protect personal privacy with written justification therefor, and provision for indexing and prohibition of use of records not indexed against any private party without actual and timely notice of the terms thereof.

Subsec. (a)(3). Pub. L. 90–23 incorporated provisions of former subsec. (d) and substituted provisions requiring identifiable agency records to be made available to any person upon request and compliance with rules as to time, place, and procedure for inspection, and payment of fees and provisions for Federal district court proceedings de novo for enforcement by contempt of noncompliance with court's orders with the burden on the agency and docket precedence for such proceedings for former provisions requiring matters of official record to be made available to persons properly and directly concerned except information held confidential for good cause shown, the latter provision superseded by subsec. (b) of this section.

Subsec. (a)(4). Pub. L. 90–23 added par. (4).

Subsec. (b). Pub. L. 90–23 added subsec. (b) which superseded provisions excepting from disclosure any function of the United States requiring secrecy in the public interest or any matter relating to internal management of an agency, formerly contained in former subsec. (a), final opinions or orders required for good cause to be held confidential and not cited as precedents, formerly contained in subsec. (c), and information held confidential for good cause found, contained in former subsec. (d) of this section.

Subsec. (c). Pub. L. 90–23 added subsec. (c).

CHANGE OF NAME

Committee on Government Reform and Oversight of House of Representatives changed to Committee on Government Reform of House of Representatives by House Resolution No. 5, One Hundred Sixth Congress, Jan. 6, 1999.

EFFECTIVE DATE OF 1996 AMENDMENT

Section 12 of Pub. L. 104–231 provided that:
"(a) IN GENERAL.—Except as provided in subsection (b), this Act [amending this section and enacting provi-

sions set out as notes below] shall take effect 180 days after the date of the enactment of this Act [Oct. 2, 1996].

"(b) PROVISIONS EFFECTIVE ON ENACTMENT [sic].—Sections 7 and 8 [amending this section] shall take effect one year after the date of the enactment of this Act [Oct. 2, 1996]."

EFFECTIVE DATE OF 1986 AMENDMENT

Section 1804 of Pub. L. 99–570 provided that:

"(a) The amendments made by section 1802 [amending this section] shall be effective on the date of enactment of this Act [Oct. 27, 1986], and shall apply with respect to any requests for records, whether or not the request was made prior to such date, and shall apply to any civil action pending on such date.

"(b)(1) The amendments made by section 1803 [amending this section] shall be effective 180 days after the date of enactment of this Act [Oct. 27, 1986], except that regulations to implement such amendments shall be promulgated by such 180th day.

"(2) The amendments made by section 1803 [amending this section] shall apply with respect to any requests for records, whether or not the request was made prior to such date, and shall apply to any civil action pending on such date, except that review charges applicable to records requested for commercial use shall not be applied by an agency to requests made before the effective date specified in paragraph (1) of this subsection or before the agency has finally issued its regulations."

EFFECTIVE DATE OF 1984 AMENDMENT

Amendment by Pub. L. 98–620 not applicable to cases pending on Nov. 8, 1984, see section 403 of Pub. L. 98–620, set out as an Effective Date note under section 1657 of Title 28, Judiciary and Judicial Procedure.

EFFECTIVE DATE OF 1978 AMENDMENT

Amendment by Pub. L. 95–454 effective 90 days after Oct. 13, 1978, see section 907 of Pub. L. 95–454, set out as a note under section 1101 of this title.

EFFECTIVE DATE OF 1976 AMENDMENT

Amendment by Pub. L. 94–409 effective 180 days after Sept. 13, 1976, see section 6 of Pub. L. 94–409, set out as an Effective Date note under section 552b of this title.

EFFECTIVE DATE OF 1974 AMENDMENT

Section 4 of Pub. L. 93–502 provided that: "The amendments made by this Act [amending this section] shall take effect on the ninetieth day beginning after the date of enactment of this Act [Nov. 21, 1974]."

EFFECTIVE DATE OF 1967 AMENDMENT

Section 4 of Pub. L. 90–23 provided that: "This Act [amending this section] shall be effective July 4, 1967, or on the date of enactment [June 5, 1967], whichever is later."

SHORT TITLE OF 1996 AMENDMENT

Section 1 of Pub. L. 104–231 provided that: "This Act [amending this section and enacting provisions set out as notes under this section] may be cited as the 'Electronic Freedom of Information Act Amendments of 1996'."

SHORT TITLE OF 1986 AMENDMENT

Section 1801 of Pub. L. 99–570 provided that: "This subtitle [subtitle N (§§ 1801–1804) of title I of Pub. L. 99–570, amending this section and enacting provisions set out as a note under this section] may be cited as the 'Freedom of Information Reform Act of 1986'."

SHORT TITLE

This section is popularly known as the "Freedom of Information Act".

DISCLOSURE OF INFORMATION ON JAPANESE IMPERIAL GOVERNMENT

Pub. L. 106–567, title VIII, Dec. 27, 2000, 114 Stat. 2864, provided that:

"SEC. 801. SHORT TITLE.

"This title may be cited as the 'Japanese Imperial Government Disclosure Act of 2000'.

"SEC. 802. DESIGNATION.

"(a) DEFINITIONS.—In this section:

"(1) AGENCY.—The term 'agency' has the meaning given such term under section 551 of title 5, United States Code.

"(2) INTERAGENCY GROUP.—The term 'Interagency Group' means the Nazi War Crimes and Japanese Imperial Government Records Interagency Working Group established under subsection (b).

"(3) JAPANESE IMPERIAL GOVERNMENT RECORDS.—The term 'Japanese Imperial Government records' means classified records or portions of records that pertain to any person with respect to whom the United States Government, in its sole discretion, has grounds to believe ordered, incited, assisted, or otherwise participated in the experimentation on, and persecution of, any person because of race, religion, national origin, or political opinion, during the period beginning September 18, 1931, and ending on December 31, 1948, under the direction of, or in association with—

"(A) the Japanese Imperial Government;

"(B) any government in any area occupied by the military forces of the Japanese Imperial Government;

"(C) any government established with the assistance or cooperation of the Japanese Imperial Government; or

"(D) any government which was an ally of the Japanese Imperial Government.

"(4) RECORD.—The term 'record' means a Japanese Imperial Government record.

"(b) ESTABLISHMENT OF INTERAGENCY GROUP.—

"(1) IN GENERAL.—Not later than 60 days after the date of the enactment of this Act [Dec. 27, 2000], the President shall designate the Working Group established under the Nazi War Crimes Disclosure Act (Public Law 105–246; 5 U.S.C. 552 note) to also carry out the purposes of this title with respect to Japanese Imperial Government records, and that Working Group shall remain in existence for 3 years after the date on which this title takes effect. Such Working Group is redesignated as the 'Nazi War Crimes and Japanese Imperial Government Records Interagency Working Group'.

"(2) MEMBERSHIP.—[Amended Pub. L. 105–246, set out as a note below.]

"(c) FUNCTIONS.—Not later than 1 year after the date of the enactment of this Act [Dec. 27, 2000], the Interagency Group shall, to the greatest extent possible consistent with section 803—

"(1) locate, identify, inventory, recommend for declassification, and make available to the public at the National Archives and Records Administration, all classified Japanese Imperial Government records of the United States;

"(2) coordinate with agencies and take such actions as necessary to expedite the release of such records to the public; and

"(3) submit a report to Congress, including the Committee on Government Reform and the Permanent Select Committee on Intelligence of the House of Representatives, and the Committee on the Judiciary and the Select Committee on Intelligence of the Senate, describing all such records, the disposition of such records, and the activities of the Interagency Group and agencies under this section.

"(d) FUNDING.—There is authorized to be appropriated such sums as may be necessary to carry out the provisions of this title.

"SEC. 803. REQUIREMENT OF DISCLOSURE OF RECORDS.

"(a) RELEASE OF RECORDS.—Subject to subsections (b), (c), and (d), the Japanese Imperial Government Records Interagency Working Group shall release in their entirety Japanese Imperial Government records.

"(b) EXEMPTIONS.—An agency head may exempt from release under subsection (a) specific information, that would—

"(1) constitute an unwarranted invasion of personal privacy;

"(2) reveal the identity of a confidential human source, or reveal information about an intelligence source or method when the unauthorized disclosure of that source or method would damage the national security interests of the United States;

"(3) reveal information that would assist in the development or use of weapons of mass destruction;

"(4) reveal information that would impair United States cryptologic systems or activities;

"(5) reveal information that would impair the application of state-of-the-art technology within a United States weapon system;

"(6) reveal United States military war plans that remain in effect;

"(7) reveal information that would impair relations between the United States and a foreign government, or undermine ongoing diplomatic activities of the United States;

"(8) reveal information that would impair the current ability of United States Government officials to protect the President, Vice President, and other officials for whom protection services are authorized in the interest of national security;

"(9) reveal information that would impair current national security emergency preparedness plans; or

"(10) violate a treaty or other international agreement.

"(c) APPLICATIONS OF EXEMPTIONS.—

"(1) IN GENERAL.—In applying the exemptions provided in paragraphs (2) through (10) of subsection (b), there shall be a presumption that the public interest will be served by disclosure and release of the records of the Japanese Imperial Government. The exemption may be asserted only when the head of the agency that maintains the records determines that disclosure and release would be harmful to a specific interest identified in the exemption. An agency head who makes such a determination shall promptly report it to the committees of Congress with appropriate jurisdiction, including the Committee on the Judiciary and the Select Committee on Intelligence of the Senate and the Committee on Government Reform and the Permanent Select Committee on Intelligence of the House of Representatives.

"(2) APPLICATION OF TITLE 5.—A determination by an agency head to apply an exemption provided in paragraphs (2) through (9) of subsection (b) shall be subject to the same standard of review that applies in the case of records withheld under section 552(b)(1) of title 5, United States Code.

"(d) RECORDS RELATED TO INVESTIGATIONS OR PROSECUTIONS.—This section shall not apply to records—

"(1) related to or supporting any active or inactive investigation, inquiry, or prosecution by the Office of Special Investigations of the Department of Justice; or

"(2) solely in the possession, custody, or control of the Office of Special Investigations.

"SEC. 804. EXPEDITED PROCESSING OF REQUESTS FOR JAPANESE IMPERIAL GOVERNMENT RECORDS.

"For purposes of expedited processing under section 552(a)(6)(E) of title 5, United States Code, any person who was persecuted in the manner described in section 802(a)(3) and who requests a Japanese Imperial Government record shall be deemed to have a compelling need for such record.

"SEC. 805. EFFECTIVE DATE.

"The provisions of this title shall take effect on the date that is 90 days after the date of the enactment of this Act [Dec. 27, 2000]."

NAZI WAR CRIMES DISCLOSURE

Pub. L. 105–246, Oct. 8, 1998, 112 Stat. 1859, as amended by Pub. L. 106–567, § 802(b)(2), Dec. 27, 2000, 114 Stat. 2865, provided that:

"SECTION 1. SHORT TITLE.

"This Act may be cited as the 'Nazi War Crimes Disclosure Act'.

"SEC. 2. ESTABLISHMENT OF NAZI WAR CRIMINAL RECORDS INTERAGENCY WORKING GROUP.

"(a) DEFINITIONS.—In this section the term—

"(1) 'agency' has the meaning given such term under section 551 of title 5, United States Code;

"(2) 'Interagency Group' means the Nazi War Criminal Records Interagency Working Group [redesignated Nazi War Crimes and Japanese Imperial Government Records Interagency Working Group, see section 802(b)(1) of Pub. L. 106–567, set out above] established under subsection (b);

"(3) 'Nazi war criminal records' has the meaning given such term under section 3 of this Act; and

"(4) 'record' means a Nazi war criminal record.

"(b) ESTABLISHMENT OF INTERAGENCY GROUP.—

"(1) IN GENERAL.—Not later than 60 days after the date of enactment of this Act [Oct. 8, 1998], the President shall establish the Nazi War Criminal Records Interagency Working Group, which shall remain in existence for 3 years after the date the Interagency Group is established.

"(2) MEMBERSHIP.—The President shall appoint to the Interagency Group individuals whom the President determines will most completely and effectively carry out the functions of the Interagency Group within the time limitations provided in this section, including the Director of the Holocaust Museum, the Historian of the Department of State, the Archivist of the United States, the head of any other agency the President considers appropriate, and no more than 4 other persons who shall be members of the public, of whom 3 shall be persons appointed under the provisions of this Act in effect on October 8, 1998..[sic] The head of an agency appointed by the President may designate an appropriate officer to serve on the Interagency Group in lieu of the head of such agency.

"(3) INITIAL MEETING.—Not later than 90 days after the date of enactment of this Act, the Interagency Group shall hold an initial meeting and begin the functions required under this section.

"(c) FUNCTIONS.—Not later than 1 year after the date of enactment of this Act [Oct. 8, 1998], the Interagency Group shall, to the greatest extent possible consistent with section 3 of this Act—

"(1) locate, identify, inventory, recommend for declassification, and make available to the public at the National Archives and Records Administration, all classified Nazi war criminal records of the United States;

"(2) coordinate with agencies and take such actions as necessary to expedite the release of such records to the public; and

"(3) submit a report to Congress, including the Committee on the Judiciary of the Senate and the Committee on Government Reform and Oversight [now Committee on Government Reform] of the House of Representatives, describing all such records, the disposition of such records, and the activities of the Interagency Group and agencies under this section.

"(d) FUNDING.—There are authorized to be appropriated such sums as may be necessary to carry out the provisions of this Act.

"SEC. 3. REQUIREMENT OF DISCLOSURE OF RECORDS REGARDING PERSONS WHO COMMITTED NAZI WAR CRIMES.

"(a) NAZI WAR CRIMINAL RECORDS.—For purposes of this Act, the term 'Nazi war criminal records' means classified records or portions of records that—

"(1) pertain to any person with respect to whom the United States Government, in its sole discretion, has grounds to believe ordered, incited, assisted, or otherwise participated in the persecution of any person because of race, religion, national origin, or political opinion, during the period beginning on March 23, 1933, and ending on May 8, 1945, under the direction of, or in association with—

"(A) the Nazi government of Germany;

"(B) any government in any area occupied by the military forces of the Nazi government of Germany;

"(C) any government established with the assistance or cooperation of the Nazi government of Germany; or

"(D) any government which was an ally of the Nazi government of Germany; or

"(2) pertain to any transaction as to which the United States Government, in its sole discretion, has grounds to believe—

"(A) involved assets taken from persecuted persons during the period beginning on March 23, 1933, and ending on May 8, 1945, by, under the direction of, on behalf of, or under authority granted by the Nazi government of Germany or any nation then allied with that government; and

"(B) such transaction was completed without the assent of the owners of those assets or their heirs or assigns or other legitimate representatives.

"(b) RELEASE OF RECORDS.—

"(1) IN GENERAL.—Subject to paragraphs (2), (3), and (4), the Nazi War Criminal Records Interagency Working Group shall release in their entirety Nazi war criminal records that are described in subsection (a).

"(2) EXCEPTION FOR PRIVACY, ETC.—An agency head may exempt from release under paragraph (1) specific information, that would—

"(A) constitute a clearly unwarranted invasion of personal privacy;

"(B) reveal the identity of a confidential human source, or reveal information about the application of an intelligence source or method, or reveal the identity of a human intelligence source when the unauthorized disclosure of that source would clearly and demonstrably damage the national security interests of the United States;

"(C) reveal information that would assist in the development or use of weapons of mass destruction;

"(D) reveal information that would impair United States cryptologic systems or activities;

"(E) reveal information that would impair the application of state-of-the-art technology within a United States weapon system;

"(F) reveal actual United States military war plans that remain in effect;

"(G) reveal information that would seriously and demonstrably impair relations between the United States and a foreign government, or seriously and demonstrably undermine ongoing diplomatic activities of the United States;

"(H) reveal information that would clearly and demonstrably impair the current ability of United States Government officials to protect the President, Vice President, and other officials for whom protection services, in the interest of national security, are authorized;

"(I) reveal information that would seriously and demonstrably impair current national security emergency preparedness plans; or

"(J) violate a treaty or international agreement.

"(3) APPLICATION OF EXEMPTIONS.—

"(A) IN GENERAL.—In applying the exemptions listed in subparagraphs (B) through (J) of paragraph (2), there shall be a presumption that the public interest in the release of Nazi war criminal records will be served by disclosure and release of the records. Assertion of such exemption may only be made when the agency head determines that disclosure and release would be harmful to a specific interest identified in the exemption. An agency head who makes such a determination shall promptly report it to the committees of Congress with appropriate jurisdiction, including the Committee on the Judiciary of the Senate and the Committee on Government Reform and Oversight [now

Committee on Government Reform] of the House of Representatives. The exemptions set forth in paragraph (2) shall constitute the only authority pursuant to which an agency head may exempt records otherwise subject to release under paragraph (1).

"(B) APPLICATION OF TITLE 5.—A determination by an agency head to apply an exemption listed in subparagraphs (B) through (I) of paragraph (2) shall be subject to the same standard of review that applies in the case of records withheld under section 552(b)(1) of title 5, United States Code.

"(4) LIMITATION ON APPLICATION.—This subsection shall not apply to records—

"(A) related to or supporting any active or inactive investigation, inquiry, or prosecution by the Office of Special Investigations of the Department of Justice; or

"(B) solely in the possession, custody, or control of that office.

"(c) INAPPLICABILITY OF NATIONAL SECURITY ACT OF 1947 EXEMPTION.—Section 701(a) of the National Security Act of 1947 (50 U.S.C. 431[(a)]) shall not apply to any operational file, or any portion of any operational file, that constitutes a Nazi war criminal record under section 3 of this Act.

"SEC. 4. EXPEDITED PROCESSING OF FOIA REQUESTS FOR NAZI WAR CRIMINAL RECORDS.

"(a) EXPEDITED PROCESSING.—For purposes of expedited processing under section 552(a)(6)(E) of title 5, United States Code, any requester of a Nazi war criminal record shall be deemed to have a compelling need for such record.

"(b) REQUESTER.—For purposes of this section, the term 'requester' means any person who was persecuted in the manner described under section 3(a)(1) of this Act who requests a Nazi war criminal record.

"SEC. 5. EFFECTIVE DATE.

"This Act and the amendments made by this Act shall take effect on the date that is 90 days after the date of enactment of this Act [Oct. 8, 1998]."

CONGRESSIONAL STATEMENT OF FINDINGS AND PURPOSE; PUBLIC ACCESS TO INFORMATION IN ELECTRONIC FORMAT

Section 2 of Pub. L. 104–231 provided that:

"(a) FINDINGS.—The Congress finds that—

"(1) the purpose of section 552 of title 5, United States Code, popularly known as the Freedom of Information Act, is to require agencies of the Federal Government to make certain agency information available for public inspection and copying and to establish and enable enforcement of the right of any person to obtain access to the records of such agencies, subject to statutory exemptions, for any public or private purpose;

"(2) since the enactment of the Freedom of Information Act in 1966, and the amendments enacted in 1974 and 1986, the Freedom of Information Act has been a valuable means through which any person can learn how the Federal Government operates;

"(3) the Freedom of Information Act has led to the disclosure of waste, fraud, abuse, and wrongdoing in the Federal Government;

"(4) the Freedom of Information Act has led to the identification of unsafe consumer products, harmful drugs, and serious health hazards;

"(5) Government agencies increasingly use computers to conduct agency business and to store publicly valuable agency records and information; and

"(6) Government agencies should use new technology to enhance public access to agency records and information.

"(b) PURPOSES.—The purposes of this Act [see Short Title of 1996 Amendment note above] are to—

"(1) foster democracy by ensuring public access to agency records and information;

"(2) improve public access to agency records and information;

"(3) ensure agency compliance with statutory time limits; and

"(4) maximize the usefulness of agency records and information collected, maintained, used, retained, and disseminated by the Federal Government."

FREEDOM OF INFORMATION ACT EXEMPTION FOR CERTAIN OPEN SKIES TREATY DATA

Pub. L. 103–236, title V, § 533, Apr. 30, 1994, 108 Stat. 480, provided that:

"(a) IN GENERAL.—Data with respect to a foreign country collected by sensors during observation flights conducted in connection with the Treaty on Open Skies, including flights conducted prior to entry into force of the treaty, shall be exempt from disclosure under the Freedom of Information Act—

"(1) if the country has not disclosed the data to the public; and

"(2) if the country has not, acting through the Open Skies Consultative Commission or any other diplomatic channel, authorized the United States to disclose the data to the public.

"(b) STATUTORY CONSTRUCTION.—This section constitutes a specific exemption within the meaning of section 552(b)(3) of title 5, United States Code.

"(c) DEFINITIONS.—For the purposes of this section—

"(1) the term 'Freedom of Information Act' means the provisions of section 552 of title 5, United States Code;

"(2) the term 'Open Skies Consultative Commission' means the commission established pursuant to Article X of the Treaty on Open Skies; and

"(3) the term 'Treaty on Open Skies' means the Treaty on Open Skies, signed at Helsinki on March 24, 1992."

CLASSIFIED NATIONAL SECURITY INFORMATION

For provisions relating to a response to a request for information under this section when the fact of its existence or nonexistence is itself classified or when it was originally classified by another agency, see Ex. Ord. No. 12958, § 3.7, Apr. 17, 1995, 60 F.R. 19835, set out as a note under section 435 of Title 50, War and National Defense.

EXECUTIVE ORDER NO. 12174

Ex. Ord. No. 12174, Nov. 30, 1979, 44 F.R. 69609, which related to minimizing Federal paperwork, was revoked by Ex. Ord. No. 12291, Feb. 17, 1981, 46 F.R. 13193, formerly set out as a note under section 601 of this title.

EX. ORD. NO. 12600. PREDISCLOSURE NOTIFICATION PROCEDURES FOR CONFIDENTIAL COMMERCIAL INFORMATION

Ex. Ord. No. 12600, June 23, 1987, 52 F.R. 23781, provided:

By the authority vested in me as President by the Constitution and statutes of the United States of America, and in order to provide predisclosure notification procedures under the Freedom of Information Act [5 U.S.C. 552] concerning confidential commercial information, and to make existing agency notification provisions more uniform, it is hereby ordered as follows:

SECTION 1. The head of each Executive department and agency subject to the Freedom of Information Act [5 U.S.C. 552] shall, to the extent permitted by law, establish procedures to notify submitters of records containing confidential commercial information as described in section 3 of this Order, when those records are requested under the Freedom of Information Act [FOIA], 5 U.S.C. 552, as amended, if after reviewing the request, the responsive records, and any appeal by the requester, the department or agency determines that it may be required to disclose the records. Such notice requires that an agency use good-faith efforts to advise submitters of confidential commercial information of the procedures established under this Order. Further, where notification of a voluminous number of submitters is required, such notification may be accomplished by posting or publishing the notice in a place reasonably calculated to accomplish notification.

SEC. 2. For purposes of this Order, the following definitions apply:

(a) "Confidential commercial information" means records provided to the government by a submitter that arguably contain material exempt from release under Exemption 4 of the Freedom of Information Act, 5 U.S.C. 552(b)(4), because disclosure could reasonably be expected to cause substantial competitive harm.

(b) "Submitter" means any person or entity who provides confidential commercial information to the government. The term "submitter" includes, but is not limited to, corporations, state governments, and foreign governments.

SEC. 3. (a) For confidential commercial information submitted prior to January 1, 1988, the head of each Executive department or agency shall, to the extent permitted by law, provide a submitter with notice pursuant to section 1 whenever:

(i) the records are less than 10 years old and the information has been designated by the submitter as confidential commercial information; or

(ii) the department or agency has reason to believe that disclosure of the information could reasonably be expected to cause substantial competitive harm.

(b) For confidential commercial information submitted on or after January 1, 1988, the head of each Executive department or agency shall, to the extent permitted by law, establish procedures to permit submitters of confidential commercial information to designate, at the time the information is submitted to the Federal government or a reasonable time thereafter, any information the disclosure of which the submitter claims could reasonably be expected to cause substantial competitive harm. Such agency procedures may provide for the expiration, after a specified period of time or changes in circumstances, of designations of competitive harm made by submitters. Additionally, such procedures may permit the agency to designate specific classes of information that will be treated by the agency as if the information had been so designated by the submitter. The head of each Executive department or agency shall, to the extent permitted by law, provide the submitter notice in accordance with section 1 of this Order whenever the department or agency determines that it may be required to disclose records:

(i) designated pursuant to this subsection; or

(ii) the disclosure of which the department or agency has reason to believe could reasonably be expected to cause substantial competitive harm.

SEC. 4. When notification is made pursuant to section 1, each agency's procedures shall, to the extent permitted by law, afford the submitter a reasonable period of time in which the submitter or its designee may object to the disclosure of any specified portion of the information and to state all grounds upon which disclosure is opposed.

SEC. 5. Each agency shall give careful consideration to all such specified grounds for nondisclosure prior to making an administrative determination of the issue. In all instances when the agency determines to disclose the requested records, its procedures shall provide that the agency give the submitter a written statement briefly explaining why the submitter's objections are not sustained. Such statement shall, to the extent permitted by law, be provided a reasonable number of days prior to a specified disclosure date.

SEC. 6. Whenever a FOIA requester brings suit seeking to compel disclosure of confidential commercial information, each agency's procedures shall require that the submitter be promptly notified.

SEC. 7. The designation and notification procedures required by this Order shall be established by regulations, after notice and public comment. If similar procedures or regulations already exist, they should be reviewed for conformity and revised where necessary. Existing procedures or regulations need not be modified if they are in compliance with this Order.

SEC. 8. The notice requirements of this Order need not be followed if:

(a) The agency determines that the information should not be disclosed;

(b) The information has been published or has been officially made available to the public;

(c) Disclosure of the information is required by law (other than 5 U.S.C. 552);

(d) The disclosure is required by an agency rule that (1) was adopted pursuant to notice and public comment, (2) specifies narrow classes of records submitted to the agency that are to be released under the Freedom of Information Act [5 U.S.C. 552], and (3) provides in exceptional circumstances for notice when the submitter provides written justification, at the time the information is submitted or a reasonable time thereafter, that disclosure of the information could reasonably be expected to cause substantial competitive harm;

(e) The information requested is not designated by the submitter as exempt from disclosure in accordance with agency regulations promulgated pursuant to section 7, when the submitter had an opportunity to do so at the time of submission of the information or a reasonable time thereafter, unless the agency has substantial reason to believe that disclosure of the information would result in competitive harm; or

(f) The designation made by the submitter in accordance with agency regulations promulgated pursuant to section 7 appears obviously frivolous; except that, in such case, the agency must provide the submitter with written notice of any final administrative disclosure determination within a reasonable number of days prior to the specified disclosure date.

SEC. 9. Whenever an agency notifies a submitter that it may be required to disclose information pursuant to section 1 of this Order, the agency shall also notify the requester that notice and an opportunity to comment are being provided the submitter. Whenever an agency notifies a submitter of a final decision pursuant to section 5 of this Order, the agency shall also notify the requester.

SEC. 10. This Order is intended only to improve the internal management of the Federal government, and is not intended to create any right or benefit, substantive or procedural, enforceable at law by a party against the United States, its agencies, its officers, or any person.

RONALD REAGAN.

EX. ORD. NO. 13110. NAZI WAR CRIMES AND JAPANESE IMPERIAL GOVERNMENT RECORDS INTERAGENCY WORKING GROUP

Ex. Ord. No. 13110, Jan. 11, 1999, 64 F.R. 2419, provided:

By the authority vested in me as President by the Constitution and the laws of the United States of America, including the Nazi War Crimes Disclosure Act (Public Law 105–246) (the "Act") [5 U.S.C. 552 note], it is hereby ordered as follows:

SECTION 1. *Establishment of Working Group.* There is hereby established the Nazi War Criminal Records Interagency Working Group [now Nazi War Crimes and Japanese Imperial Government Records Interagency Working Group] (Working Group). The function of the Group shall be to locate, inventory, recommend for declassification, and make available to the public at the National Archives and Records Administration all classified Nazi war criminal records of the United States, subject to certain designated exceptions as provided in the Act. The Working Group shall coordinate with agencies and take such actions as necessary to expedite the release of such records to the public.

SEC. 2. *Schedule.* The Working Group should complete its work to the greatest extent possible and report to the Congress within 1 year.

SEC. 3. *Membership.* (a) The Working Group shall be composed of the following members:

(1) Archivist of the United States (who shall serve as Chair of the Working Group);

(2) Secretary of Defense;

(3) Attorney General;

(4) Director of Central Intelligence;

(5) Director of the Federal Bureau of Investigation;

(6) Director of the United States Holocaust Memorial Museum;

(7) Historian of the Department of State; and

(8) Three other persons appointed by the President.

(b) The Senior Director for Records and Access Management of the National Security Council will serve as the liaison to and attend the meetings of the Working Group. Members of the Working Group who are full-time Federal officials may serve on the Working Group through designees.

SEC. 4. *Administration.* (a) To the extent permitted by law and subject to the availability of appropriations, the National Archives and Records Administration shall provide the Working Group with funding, administrative services, facilities, staff, and other support services necessary for the performance of the functions of the Working Group.

(b) The Working Group shall terminate 3 years from the date of this Executive order.

WILLIAM J. CLINTON.

SECTION REFERRED TO IN OTHER SECTIONS

This section is referred to in sections 551, 552a, 552b, 566, 574, 1216, 7133 of this title; title 2 sections 472, 501, 502; title 7 sections 12, 450i, 499f, 608d, 948, 1314g, 1314i, 1508, 1636, 1637b, 1642, 2279b, 5651, 5662, 5906, 7035; title 8 section 1182; title 10 sections 128, 130b, 1034, 1102, 1506, 2304, 2305, 2306a, 2328, 2371; title 12 sections 1786, 1818, 1828, 1831o, 4611; title 14 section 645; title 15 sections 18a, 57b–2, 78m, 78o–5, 78q, 78w, 78x, 78dd–1, 78dd–2, 79z–5c, 80a–30, 80b–10a, 278n, 719d, 773, 796, 1314, 1335a, 2055, 2217, 2613, 3364, 3710a, 4019, 4104, 4107, 4305, 4403, 4606, 4912, 5104, 5308, 7006; title 16 sections 973j, 1402, 4304, 5937; title 18 sections 207, 208, 1838; title 19 sections 1333, 1431, 1509, 1625, 1677f, 2418, 3315; title 20 sections 1078, 1087–2, 6512; title 21 sections 360c, 360j, 379, 379f, 830, 1904, 1908; title 22 sections 2200a, 3902, 4355, 4415, 4604, 4607, 4833, 5841, 6713, 6744; title 25 sections 450c, 450k, 1951, 2716; title 26 sections 6103, 6110, 7611, 7803; title 28 sections 594, 1657; title 29 sections 1310, 1343, 2635; title 30 section 1604; title 31 sections 716, 1352, 3729, 3733, 5319; title 33 sections 524, 941, 1513; title 35 sections 202, 209; title 38 sections 501, 502, 7451; title 39 sections 410, 3016; title 41 sections 253, 253b, 254b, 423, 706; title 42 sections 263b, 300v–2, 300aa–25, 405, 1306, 1320c–9, 2167, 2168, 2454, 2996d, 3027, 4332, 5916, 5919, 6272–6274, 7135, 7412, 8103, 9122, 9208, 9660, 10704, 13385; title 44 sections 2201, 2204, 2206, 3501, 3504, 3506; title 46 sections 4309, 6305, 7702, 9303; title 46 App. section 1705; title 49 sections 106, 706, 10706, 10709, 11162, 14123; title 50 sections 403–5b, 431; title 50 App. sections 463, 2158, 2159, 2170, 2406, 2411.

§ 552a. Records maintained on individuals

(a) DEFINITIONS.—For purposes of this section—

(1) the term "agency" means agency as defined in section 552(e)[1] of this title;

(2) the term "individual" means a citizen of the United States or an alien lawfully admitted for permanent residence;

(3) the term "maintain" includes maintain, collect, use, or disseminate;

(4) the term "record" means any item, collection, or grouping of information about an individual that is maintained by an agency, including, but not limited to, his education, financial transactions, medical history, and criminal or employment history and that contains his name, or the identifying number, symbol, or other identifying particular assigned to the individual, such as a finger or voice print or a photograph;

(5) the term "system of records" means a group of any records under the control of any agency from which information is retrieved by the name of the individual or by some identi-

---

[1] See References in Text note below.

fying number, symbol, or other identifying particular assigned to the individual;

(6) the term "statistical record" means a record in a system of records maintained for statistical research or reporting purposes only and not used in whole or in part in making any determination about an identifiable individual, except as provided by section 8 of title 13;

(7) the term "routine use" means, with respect to the disclosure of a record, the use of such record for a purpose which is compatible with the purpose for which it was collected;

(8) the term "matching program"—

(A) means any computerized comparison of—

(i) two or more automated systems of records or a system of records with non-Federal records for the purpose of—

(I) establishing or verifying the eligibility of, or continuing compliance with statutory and regulatory requirements by, applicants for, recipients or beneficiaries of, participants in, or providers of services with respect to, cash or in-kind assistance or payments under Federal benefit programs, or

(II) recouping payments or delinquent debts under such Federal benefit programs, or

(ii) two or more automated Federal personnel or payroll systems of records or a system of Federal personnel or payroll records with non-Federal records,

(B) but does not include—

(i) matches performed to produce aggregate statistical data without any personal identifiers;

(ii) matches performed to support any research or statistical project, the specific data of which may not be used to make decisions concerning the rights, benefits, or privileges of specific individuals;

(iii) matches performed, by an agency (or component thereof) which performs as its principal function any activity pertaining to the enforcement of criminal laws, subsequent to the initiation of a specific criminal or civil law enforcement investigation of a named person or persons for the purpose of gathering evidence against such person or persons;

(iv) matches of tax information (I) pursuant to section 6103(d) of the Internal Revenue Code of 1986, (II) for purposes of tax administration as defined in section 6103(b)(4) of such Code, (III) for the purpose of intercepting a tax refund due an individual under authority granted by section 404(e), 464, or 1137 of the Social Security Act; or (IV) for the purpose of intercepting a tax refund due an individual under any other tax refund intercept program authorized by statute which has been determined by the Director of the Office of Management and Budget to contain verification, notice, and hearing requirements that are substantially similar to the procedures in section 1137 of the Social Security Act;

(v) matches—

(I) using records predominantly relating to Federal personnel, that are performed for routine administrative purposes (subject to guidance provided by the Director of the Office of Management and Budget pursuant to subsection (v)); or

(II) conducted by an agency using only records from systems of records maintained by that agency;

if the purpose of the match is not to take any adverse financial, personnel, disciplinary, or other adverse action against Federal personnel;

(vi) matches performed for foreign counterintelligence purposes or to produce background checks for security clearances of Federal personnel or Federal contractor personnel;

(vii) matches performed incident to a levy described in section 6103(k)(8) of the Internal Revenue Code of 1986; or

(viii) matches performed pursuant to section 202(x)(3) or 1611(e)(1) of the Social Security Act (42 U.S.C. 402(x)(3), 1382(e)(1));

(9) the term "recipient agency" means any agency, or contractor thereof, receiving records contained in a system of records from a source agency for use in a matching program;

(10) the term "non-Federal agency" means any State or local government, or agency thereof, which receives records contained in a system of records from a source agency for use in a matching program;

(11) the term "source agency" means any agency which discloses records contained in a system of records to be used in a matching program, or any State or local government, or agency thereof, which discloses records to be used in a matching program;

(12) the term "Federal benefit program" means any program administered or funded by the Federal Government, or by any agent or State on behalf of the Federal Government, providing cash or in-kind assistance in the form of payments, grants, loans, or loan guarantees to individuals; and

(13) the term "Federal personnel" means officers and employees of the Government of the United States, members of the uniformed services (including members of the Reserve Components), individuals entitled to receive immediate or deferred retirement benefits under any retirement program of the Government of the United States (including survivor benefits).

(b) CONDITIONS OF DISCLOSURE.—No agency shall disclose any record which is contained in a system of records by any means of communication to any person, or to another agency, except pursuant to a written request by, or with the prior written consent of, the individual to whom the record pertains, unless disclosure of the record would be—

(1) to those officers and employees of the agency which maintains the record who have a need for the record in the performance of their duties;

(2) required under section 552 of this title;

(3) for a routine use as defined in subsection (a)(7) of this section and described under subsection (e)(4)(D) of this section;

(4) to the Bureau of the Census for purposes of planning or carrying out a census or survey or related activity pursuant to the provisions of title 13;

(5) to a recipient who has provided the agency with advance adequate written assurance that the record will be used solely as a statistical research or reporting record, and the record is to be transferred in a form that is not individually identifiable;

(6) to the National Archives and Records Administration as a record which has sufficient historical or other value to warrant its continued preservation by the United States Government, or for evaluation by the Archivist of the United States or the designee of the Archivist to determine whether the record has such value;

(7) to another agency or to an instrumentality of any governmental jurisdiction within or under the control of the United States for a civil or criminal law enforcement activity if the activity is authorized by law, and if the head of the agency or instrumentality has made a written request to the agency which maintains the record specifying the particular portion desired and the law enforcement activity for which the record is sought;

(8) to a person pursuant to a showing of compelling circumstances affecting the health or safety of an individual if upon such disclosure notification is transmitted to the last known address of such individual;

(9) to either House of Congress, or, to the extent of matter within its jurisdiction, any committee or subcommittee thereof, any joint committee of Congress or subcommittee of any such joint committee;

(10) to the Comptroller General, or any of his authorized representatives, in the course of the performance of the duties of the General Accounting Office;

(11) pursuant to the order of a court of competent jurisdiction; or

(12) to a consumer reporting agency in accordance with section 3711(e) of title 31.

(c) ACCOUNTING OF CERTAIN DISCLOSURES.—Each agency, with respect to each system of records under its control, shall—

(1) except for disclosures made under subsections (b)(1) or (b)(2) of this section, keep an accurate accounting of—

(A) the date, nature, and purpose of each disclosure of a record to any person or to another agency made under subsection (b) of this section; and

(B) the name and address of the person or agency to whom the disclosure is made;

(2) retain the accounting made under paragraph (1) of this subsection for at least five years or the life of the record, whichever is longer, after the disclosure for which the accounting is made;

(3) except for disclosures made under subsection (b)(7) of this section, make the accounting made under paragraph (1) of this sub-

section available to the individual named in the record at his request; and

(4) inform any person or other agency about any correction or notation of dispute made by the agency in accordance with subsection (d) of this section of any record that has been disclosed to the person or agency if an accounting of the disclosure was made.

(d) ACCESS TO RECORDS.—Each agency that maintains a system of records shall—

(1) upon request by any individual to gain access to his record or to any information pertaining to him which is contained in the system, permit him and upon his request, a person of his own choosing to accompany him, to review the record and have a copy made of all or any portion thereof in a form comprehensible to him, except that the agency may require the individual to furnish a written statement authorizing discussion of that individual's record in the accompanying person's presence;

(2) permit the individual to request amendment of a record pertaining to him and—

(A) not later than 10 days (excluding Saturdays, Sundays, and legal public holidays) after the date of receipt of such request, acknowledge in writing such receipt; and

(B) promptly, either—

(i) make any correction of any portion thereof which the individual believes is not accurate, relevant, timely, or complete; or

(ii) inform the individual of its refusal to amend the record in accordance with his request, the reason for the refusal, the procedures established by the agency for the individual to request a review of that refusal by the head of the agency or an officer designated by the head of the agency, and the name and business address of that official;

(3) permit the individual who disagrees with the refusal of the agency to amend his record to request a review of such refusal, and not later than 30 days (excluding Saturdays, Sundays, and legal public holidays) from the date on which the individual requests such review, complete such review and make a final determination unless, for good cause shown, the head of the agency extends such 30-day period; and if, after his review, the reviewing official also refuses to amend the record in accordance with the request, permit the individual to file with the agency a concise statement setting forth the reasons for his disagreement with the refusal of the agency, and notify the individual of the provisions for judicial review of the reviewing official's determination under subsection (g)(1)(A) of this section;

(4) in any disclosure, containing information about which the individual has filed a statement of disagreement, occurring after the filing of the statement under paragraph (3) of this subsection, clearly note any portion of the record which is disputed and provide copies of the statement and, if the agency deems it appropriate, copies of a concise statement of the reasons of the agency for not making the amendments requested, to persons or other

agencies to whom the disputed record has been disclosed; and

(5) nothing in this section shall allow an individual access to any information compiled in reasonable anticipation of a civil action or proceeding.

(e) AGENCY REQUIREMENTS.—Each agency that maintains a system of records shall—

(1) maintain in its records only such information about an individual as is relevant and necessary to accomplish a purpose of the agency required to be accomplished by statute or by executive order of the President;

(2) collect information to the greatest extent practicable directly from the subject individual when the information may result in adverse determinations about an individual's rights, benefits, and privileges under Federal programs;

(3) inform each individual whom it asks to supply information, on the form which it uses to collect the information or on a separate form that can be retained by the individual—

(A) the authority (whether granted by statute, or by executive order of the President) which authorizes the solicitation of the information and whether disclosure of such information is mandatory or voluntary;

(B) the principal purpose or purposes for which the information is intended to be used;

(C) the routine uses which may be made of the information, as published pursuant to paragraph (4)(D) of this subsection; and

(D) the effects on him, if any, of not providing all or any part of the requested information;

(4) subject to the provisions of paragraph (11) of this subsection, publish in the Federal Register upon establishment or revision a notice of the existence and character of the system of records, which notice shall include—

(A) the name and location of the system;

(B) the categories of individuals on whom records are maintained in the system;

(C) the categories of records maintained in the system;

(D) each routine use of the records contained in the system, including the categories of users and the purpose of such use;

(E) the policies and practices of the agency regarding storage, retrievability, access controls, retention, and disposal of the records;

(F) the title and business address of the agency official who is responsible for the system of records;

(G) the agency procedures whereby an individual can be notified at his request if the system of records contains a record pertaining to him;

(H) the agency procedures whereby an individual can be notified at his request how he can gain access to any record pertaining to him contained in the system of records, and how he can contest its content; and

(I) the categories of sources of records in the system;

(5) maintain all records which are used by the agency in making any determination about any individual with such accuracy, rel-

evance, timeliness, and completeness as is reasonably necessary to assure fairness to the individual in the determination;

(6) prior to disseminating any record about an individual to any person other than an agency, unless the dissemination is made pursuant to subsection (b)(2) of this section, make reasonable efforts to assure that such records are accurate, complete, timely, and relevant for agency purposes;

(7) maintain no record describing how any individual exercises rights guaranteed by the First Amendment unless expressly authorized by statute or by the individual about whom the record is maintained or unless pertinent to and within the scope of an authorized law enforcement activity;

(8) make reasonable efforts to serve notice on an individual when any record on such individual is made available to any person under compulsory legal process when such process becomes a matter of public record;

(9) establish rules of conduct for persons involved in the design, development, operation, or maintenance of any system of records, or in maintaining any record, and instruct each such person with respect to such rules and the requirements of this section, including any other rules and procedures adopted pursuant to this section and the penalties for noncompliance;

(10) establish appropriate administrative, technical, and physical safeguards to insure the security and confidentiality of records and to protect against any anticipated threats or hazards to their security or integrity which could result in substantial harm, embarrassment, inconvenience, or unfairness to any individual on whom information is maintained;

(11) at least 30 days prior to publication of information under paragraph (4)(D) of this subsection, publish in the Federal Register notice of any new use or intended use of the information in the system, and provide an opportunity for interested persons to submit written data, views, or arguments to the agency; and

(12) if such agency is a recipient agency or a source agency in a matching program with a non-Federal agency, with respect to any establishment or revision of a matching program, at least 30 days prior to conducting such program, publish in the Federal Register notice of such establishment or revision.

(f) AGENCY RULES.—In order to carry out the provisions of this section, each agency that maintains a system of records shall promulgate rules, in accordance with the requirements (including general notice) of section 553 of this title, which shall—

(1) establish procedures whereby an individual can be notified in response to his request if any system of records named by the individual contains a record pertaining to him;

(2) define reasonable times, places, and requirements for identifying an individual who requests his record or information pertaining to him before the agency shall make the record or information available to the individual;

(3) establish procedures for the disclosure to an individual upon his request of his record or

information pertaining to him, including special procedure, if deemed necessary, for the disclosure to an individual of medical records, including psychological records, pertaining to him;

(4) establish procedures for reviewing a request from an individual concerning the amendment of any record or information pertaining to the individual, for making a determination on the request, for an appeal within the agency of an initial adverse agency determination, and for whatever additional means may be necessary for each individual to be able to exercise fully his rights under this section; and

(5) establish fees to be charged, if any, to any individual for making copies of his record, excluding the cost of any search for and review of the record.

The Office of the Federal Register shall biennially compile and publish the rules promulgated under this subsection and agency notices published under subsection (e)(4) of this section in a form available to the public at low cost.

(g)(1) CIVIL REMEDIES.—Whenever any agency

(A) makes a determination under subsection (d)(3) of this section not to amend an individual's record in accordance with his request, or fails to make such review in conformity with that subsection;

(B) refuses to comply with an individual request under subsection (d)(1) of this section;

(C) fails to maintain any record concerning any individual with such accuracy, relevance, timeliness, and completeness as is necessary to assure fairness in any determination relating to the qualifications, character, rights, or opportunities of, or benefits to the individual that may be made on the basis of such record, and consequently a determination is made which is adverse to the individual; or

(D) fails to comply with any other provision of this section, or any rule promulgated thereunder, in such a way as to have an adverse effect on an individual,

the individual may bring a civil action against the agency, and the district courts of the United States shall have jurisdiction in the matters under the provisions of this subsection.

(2)(A) In any suit brought under the provisions of subsection (g)(1)(A) of this section, the court may order the agency to amend the individual's record in accordance with his request or in such other way as the court may direct. In such a case the court shall determine the matter de novo.

(B) The court may assess against the United States reasonable attorney fees and other litigation costs reasonably incurred in any case under this paragraph in which the complainant has substantially prevailed.

(3)(A) In any suit brought under the provisions of subsection (g)(1)(B) of this section, the court may enjoin the agency from withholding the records and order the production to the complainant of any agency records improperly withheld from him. In such a case the court shall determine the matter de novo, and may examine the contents of any agency records in camera to determine whether the records or any portion

thereof may be withheld under any of the exemptions set forth in subsection (k) of this section, and the burden is on the agency to sustain its action.

(B) The court may assess against the United States reasonable attorney fees and other litigation costs reasonably incurred in any case under this paragraph in which the complainant has substantially prevailed.

(4) In any suit brought under the provisions of subsection (g)(1)(C) or (D) of this section in which the court determines that the agency acted in a manner which was intentional or willful, the United States shall be liable to the individual in an amount equal to the sum of—

(A) actual damages sustained by the individual as a result of the refusal or failure, but in no case shall a person entitled to recovery receive less than the sum of $1,000; and

(B) the costs of the action together with reasonable attorney fees as determined by the court.

(5) An action to enforce any liability created under this section may be brought in the district court of the United States in the district in which the complainant resides, or has his principal place of business, or in which the agency records are situated, or in the District of Columbia, without regard to the amount in controversy, within two years from the date on which the cause of action arises, except that where an agency has materially and willfully misrepresented any information required under this section to be disclosed to an individual and the information so misrepresented is material to establishment of the liability of the agency to the individual under this section, the action may be brought at any time within two years after discovery by the individual of the misrepresentation. Nothing in this section shall be construed to authorize any civil action by reason of any injury sustained as the result of a disclosure of a record prior to September 27, 1975.

(h) RIGHTS OF LEGAL GUARDIANS.—For the purposes of this section, the parent of any minor, or the legal guardian of any individual who has been declared to be incompetent due to physical or mental incapacity or age by a court of competent jurisdiction, may act on behalf of the individual.

(i)(1) CRIMINAL PENALTIES.—Any officer or employee of an agency, who by virtue of his employment or official position, has possession of, or access to, agency records which contain individually identifiable information the disclosure of which is prohibited by this section or by rules or regulations established thereunder, and who knowing that disclosure of the specific material is so prohibited, willfully discloses the material in any manner to any person or agency not entitled to receive it, shall be guilty of a misdemeanor and fined not more than $5,000.

(2) Any officer or employee of any agency who willfully maintains a system of records without meeting the notice requirements of subsection (e)(4) of this section shall be guilty of a misdemeanor and fined not more than $5,000.

(3) Any person who knowingly and willfully requests or obtains any record concerning an individual from an agency under false pretenses shall be guilty of a misdemeanor and fined not more than $5,000.

(j) GENERAL EXEMPTIONS.—The head of any agency may promulgate rules, in accordance with the requirements (including general notice) of sections 553(b)(1), (2), and (3), (c), and (e) of this title, to exempt any system of records within the agency from any part of this section except subsections (b), (c)(1) and (2), (e)(4)(A) through (F), (e)(6), (7), (9), (10), and (11), and (i) if the system of records is—

(1) maintained by the Central Intelligence Agency; or

(2) maintained by an agency or component thereof which performs as its principal function any activity pertaining to the enforcement of criminal laws, including police efforts to prevent, control, or reduce crime or to apprehend criminals, and the activities of prosecutors, courts, correctional, probation, pardon, or parole authorities, and which consists of (A) information compiled for the purpose of identifying individual criminal offenders and alleged offenders and consisting only of identifying data and notations of arrests, the nature and disposition of criminal charges, sentencing, confinement, release, and parole and probation status; (B) information compiled for the purpose of a criminal investigation, including reports of informants and investigators, and associated with an identifiable individual; or (C) reports identifiable to an individual compiled at any stage of the process of enforcement of the criminal laws from arrest or indictment through release from supervision.

At the time rules are adopted under this subsection, the agency shall include in the statement required under section 553(c) of this title, the reasons why the system of records is to be exempted from a provision of this section.

(k) SPECIFIC EXEMPTIONS.—The head of any agency may promulgate rules, in accordance with the requirements (including general notice) of sections 553(b)(1), (2), and (3), (c), and (e) of this title, to exempt any system of records within the agency from subsections (c)(3), (d), (e)(1), (e)(4)(G), (H), and (I) and (f) of this section if the system of records is—

(1) subject to the provisions of section 552(b)(1) of this title;

(2) investigatory material compiled for law enforcement purposes, other than material within the scope of subsection (j)(2) of this section: *Provided, however,* That if any individual is denied any right, privilege, or benefit that he would otherwise be entitled by Federal law, or for which he would otherwise be eligible, as a result of the maintenance of such material, such material shall be provided to such individual, except to the extent that the disclosure of such material would reveal the identity of a source who furnished information to the Government under an express promise that the identity of the source would be held in confidence, or, prior to the effective date of this section, under an implied promise that the identity of the source would be held in confidence;

(3) maintained in connection with providing protective services to the President of the United States or other individuals pursuant to section 3056 of title 18;

(4) required by statute to be maintained and used solely as statistical records;

(5) investigatory material compiled solely for the purpose of determining suitability, eligibility, or qualifications for Federal civilian employment, military service, Federal contracts, or access to classified information, but only to the extent that the disclosure of such material would reveal the identity of a source who furnished information to the Government under an express promise that the identity of the source would be held in confidence, or, prior to the effective date of this section, under an implied promise that the identity of the source would be held in confidence;

(6) testing or examination material used solely to determine individual qualifications for appointment or promotion in the Federal service the disclosure of which would compromise the objectivity or fairness of the testing or examination process; or

(7) evaluation material used to determine potential for promotion in the armed services, but only to the extent that the disclosure of such material would reveal the identity of a source who furnished information to the Government under an express promise that the identity of the source would be held in confidence, or, prior to the effective date of this section, under an implied promise that the identity of the source would be held in confidence.

At the time rules are adopted under this subsection, the agency shall include in the statement required under section 553(c) of this title, the reasons why the system of records is to be exempted from a provision of this section.

(*l*)(1) ARCHIVAL RECORDS.—Each agency record which is accepted by the Archivist of the United States for storage, processing, and servicing in accordance with section 3103 of title 44 shall, for the purposes of this section, be considered to be maintained by the agency which deposited the record and shall be subject to the provisions of this section. The Archivist of the United States shall not disclose the record except to the agency which maintains the record, or under rules established by that agency which are not inconsistent with the provisions of this section.

(2) Each agency record pertaining to an identifiable individual which was transferred to the National Archives of the United States as a record which has sufficient historical or other value to warrant its continued preservation by the United States Government, prior to the effective date of this section, shall, for the purposes of this section, be considered to be maintained by the National Archives and shall not be subject to the provisions of this section, except that a statement generally describing such records (modeled after the requirements relating to records subject to subsections (e)(4)(A) through (G) of this section) shall be published in the Federal Register.

(3) Each agency record pertaining to an identifiable individual which is transferred to the National Archives of the United States as a record which has sufficient historical or other value to warrant its continued preservation by the United States Government, on or after the effective date of this section, shall, for the purposes

of this section, be considered to be maintained by the National Archives and shall be exempt from the requirements of this section except subsections (e)(4)(A) through (G) and (e)(9) of this section.

(m)(1) GOVERNMENT CONTRACTORS.—When an agency provides by a contract for the operation by or on behalf of the agency of a system of records to accomplish an agency function, the agency shall, consistent with its authority, cause the requirements of this section to be applied to such system. For purposes of subsection (i) of this section any such contractor and any employee of such contractor, if such contract is agreed to on or after the effective date of this section, shall be considered to be an employee of an agency.

(2) A consumer reporting agency to which a record is disclosed under section 3711(e) of title 31 shall not be considered a contractor for the purposes of this section.

(n) MAILING LISTS.—An individual's name and address may not be sold or rented by an agency unless such action is specifically authorized by law. This provision shall not be construed to require the withholding of names and addresses otherwise permitted to be made public.

(o) MATCHING AGREEMENTS.—(1) No record which is contained in a system of records may be disclosed to a recipient agency or non-Federal agency for use in a computer matching program except pursuant to a written agreement between the source agency and the recipient agency or non-Federal agency specifying—

(A) the purpose and legal authority for conducting the program;

(B) the justification for the program and the anticipated results, including a specific estimate of any savings;

(C) a description of the records that will be matched, including each data element that will be used, the approximate number of records that will be matched, and the projected starting and completion dates of the matching program;

(D) procedures for providing individualized notice at the time of application, and notice periodically thereafter as directed by the Data Integrity Board of such agency (subject to guidance provided by the Director of the Office of Management and Budget pursuant to subsection (v)), to—

(i) applicants for and recipients of financial assistance or payments under Federal benefit programs, and

(ii) applicants for and holders of positions as Federal personnel,

that any information provided by such applicants, recipients, holders, and individuals may be subject to verification through matching programs;

(E) procedures for verifying information produced in such matching program as required by subsection (p);

(F) procedures for the retention and timely destruction of identifiable records created by a recipient agency or non-Federal agency in such matching program;

(G) procedures for ensuring the administrative, technical, and physical security of the records matched and the results of such programs;

(H) prohibitions on duplication and redisclosure of records provided by the source agency within or outside the recipient agency or the non-Federal agency, except where required by law or essential to the conduct of the matching program;

(I) procedures governing the use by a recipient agency or non-Federal agency of records provided in a matching program by a source agency, including procedures governing return of the records to the source agency or destruction of records used in such program;

(J) information on assessments that have been made on the accuracy of the records that will be used in such matching program; and

(K) that the Comptroller General may have access to all records of a recipient agency or a non-Federal agency that the Comptroller General deems necessary in order to monitor or verify compliance with the agreement.

(2)(A) A copy of each agreement entered into pursuant to paragraph (1) shall—

(i) be transmitted to the Committee on Governmental Affairs of the Senate and the Committee on Government Operations of the House of Representatives; and

(ii) be available upon request to the public.

(B) No such agreement shall be effective until 30 days after the date on which such a copy is transmitted pursuant to subparagraph (A)(i).

(C) Such an agreement shall remain in effect only for such period, not to exceed 18 months, as the Data Integrity Board of the agency determines is appropriate in light of the purposes, and length of time necessary for the conduct, of the matching program.

(D) Within 3 months prior to the expiration of such an agreement pursuant to subparagraph (C), the Data Integrity Board of the agency may, without additional review, renew the matching agreement for a current, ongoing matching program for not more than one additional year if—

(i) such program will be conducted without any change; and

(ii) each party to the agreement certifies to the Board in writing that the program has been conducted in compliance with the agreement.

(p) VERIFICATION AND OPPORTUNITY TO CONTEST FINDINGS.—(1) In order to protect any individual whose records are used in a matching program, no recipient agency, non-Federal agency, or source agency may suspend, terminate, reduce, or make a final denial of any financial assistance or payment under a Federal benefit program to such individual, or take other adverse action against such individual, as a result of information produced by such matching program, until—

(A)(i) the agency has independently verified the information; or

(ii) the Data Integrity Board of the agency, or in the case of a non-Federal agency the Data Integrity Board of the source agency, determines in accordance with guidance issued by the Director of the Office of Management and Budget that—

(I) the information is limited to identification and amount of benefits paid by the source agency under a Federal benefit program; and

(II) there is a high degree of confidence that the information provided to the recipient agency is accurate;

(B) the individual receives a notice from the agency containing a statement of its findings and informing the individual of the opportunity to contest such findings; and

(C)(i) the expiration of any time period established for the program by statute or regulation for the individual to respond to that notice; or

(ii) in the case of a program for which no such period is established, the end of the 30-day period beginning on the date on which notice under subparagraph (B) is mailed or otherwise provided to the individual.

(2) Independent verification referred to in paragraph (1) requires investigation and confirmation of specific information relating to an individual that is used as a basis for an adverse action against the individual, including where applicable investigation and confirmation of—

(A) the amount of any asset or income involved;

(B) whether such individual actually has or had access to such asset or income for such individual's own use; and

(C) the period or periods when the individual actually had such asset or income.

(3) Notwithstanding paragraph (1), an agency may take any appropriate action otherwise prohibited by such paragraph if the agency determines that the public health or public safety may be adversely affected or significantly threatened during any notice period required by such paragraph.

(q) SANCTIONS.—(1) Notwithstanding any other provision of law, no source agency may disclose any record which is contained in a system of records to a recipient agency or non-Federal agency for a matching program if such source agency has reason to believe that the requirements of subsection (p), or any matching agreement entered into pursuant to subsection (o), or both, are not being met by such recipient agency.

(2) No source agency may renew a matching agreement unless—

(A) the recipient agency or non-Federal agency has certified that it has complied with the provisions of that agreement; and

(B) the source agency has no reason to believe that the certification is inaccurate.

(r) REPORT ON NEW SYSTEMS AND MATCHING PROGRAMS.—Each agency that proposes to establish or make a significant change in a system of records or a matching program shall provide adequate advance notice of any such proposal (in duplicate) to the Committee on Government Operations of the House of Representatives, the Committee on Governmental Affairs of the Senate, and the Office of Management and Budget in order to permit an evaluation of the probable or potential effect of such proposal on the privacy or other rights of individuals.

(s) BIENNIAL REPORT.—The President shall biennially submit to the Speaker of the House of Representatives and the President pro tempore of the Senate a report—

(1) describing the actions of the Director of the Office of Management and Budget pursuant to section 6 of the Privacy Act of 1974 during the preceding 2 years;

(2) describing the exercise of individual rights of access and amendment under this section during such years;

(3) identifying changes in or additions to systems of records;

(4) containing such other information concerning administration of this section as may be necessary or useful to the Congress in reviewing the effectiveness of this section in carrying out the purposes of the Privacy Act of 1974.

(t)(1) EFFECT OF OTHER LAWS.—No agency shall rely on any exemption contained in section 552 of this title to withhold from an individual any record which is otherwise accessible to such individual under the provisions of this section.

(2) No agency shall rely on any exemption in this section to withhold from an individual any record which is otherwise accessible to such individual under the provisions of section 552 of this title.

(u) DATA INTEGRITY BOARDS.—(1) Every agency conducting or participating in a matching program shall establish a Data Integrity Board to oversee and coordinate among the various components of such agency the agency's implementation of this section.

(2) Each Data Integrity Board shall consist of senior officials designated by the head of the agency, and shall include any senior official designated by the head of the agency as responsible for implementation of this section, and the inspector general of the agency, if any. The inspector general shall not serve as chairman of the Data Integrity Board.

(3) Each Data Integrity Board—

(A) shall review, approve, and maintain all written agreements for receipt or disclosure of agency records for matching programs to ensure compliance with subsection (o), and all relevant statutes, regulations, and guidelines;

(B) shall review all matching programs in which the agency has participated during the year, either as a source agency or recipient agency, determine compliance with applicable laws, regulations, guidelines, and agency agreements, and assess the costs and benefits of such programs;

(C) shall review all recurring matching programs in which the agency has participated during the year, either as a source agency or recipient agency, for continued justification for such disclosures;

(D) shall compile an annual report, which shall be submitted to the head of the agency and the Office of Management and Budget and made available to the public on request, describing the matching activities of the agency, including—

(i) matching programs in which the agency has participated as a source agency or recipient agency;

(ii) matching agreements proposed under subsection (o) that were disapproved by the Board;

(iii) any changes in membership or structure of the Board in the preceding year;

(iv) the reasons for any waiver of the requirement in paragraph (4) of this section for completion and submission of a cost-benefit analysis prior to the approval of a matching program;

(v) any violations of matching agreements that have been alleged or identified and any corrective action taken; and

(vi) any other information required by the Director of the Office of Management and Budget to be included in such report;

(E) shall serve as a clearinghouse for receiving and providing information on the accuracy, completeness, and reliability of records used in matching programs;

(F) shall provide interpretation and guidance to agency components and personnel on the requirements of this section for matching programs;

(G) shall review agency recordkeeping and disposal policies and practices for matching programs to assure compliance with this section; and

(H) may review and report on any agency matching activities that are not matching programs.

(4)(A) Except as provided in subparagraphs (B) and (C), a Data Integrity Board shall not approve any written agreement for a matching program unless the agency has completed and submitted to such Board a cost-benefit analysis of the proposed program and such analysis demonstrates that the program is likely to be cost effective.[2]

(B) The Board may waive the requirements of subparagraph (A) of this paragraph if it determines in writing, in accordance with guidelines prescribed by the Director of the Office of Management and Budget, that a cost-benefit analysis is not required.

(C) A cost-benefit analysis shall not be required under subparagraph (A) prior to the initial approval of a written agreement for a matching program that is specifically required by statute. Any subsequent written agreement for such a program shall not be approved by the Data Integrity Board unless the agency has submitted a cost-benefit analysis of the program as conducted under the preceding approval of such agreement.

(5)(A) If a matching agreement is disapproved by a Data Integrity Board, any party to such agreement may appeal the disapproval to the Director of the Office of Management and Budget. Timely notice of the filing of such an appeal shall be provided by the Director of the Office of Management and Budget to the Committee on Governmental Affairs of the Senate and the Committee on Government Operations of the House of Representatives.

(B) The Director of the Office of Management and Budget may approve a matching agreement notwithstanding the disapproval of a Data Integrity Board if the Director determines that—

(i) the matching program will be consistent with all applicable legal, regulatory, and policy requirements;

(ii) there is adequate evidence that the matching agreement will be cost-effective; and

(iii) the matching program is in the public interest.

(C) The decision of the Director to approve a matching agreement shall not take effect until 30 days after it is reported to committees described in subparagraph (A).

(D) If the Data Integrity Board and the Director of the Office of Management and Budget disapprove a matching program proposed by the inspector general of an agency, the inspector general may report the disapproval to the head of the agency and to the Congress.

(6) In the reports required by paragraph (3)(D), agency matching activities that are not matching programs may be reported on an aggregate basis, if and to the extent necessary to protect ongoing law enforcement or counterintelligence investigations.

(v) OFFICE OF MANAGEMENT AND BUDGET RESPONSIBILITIES.—The Director of the Office of Management and Budget shall—

(1) develop and, after notice and opportunity for public comment, prescribe guidelines and regulations for the use of agencies in implementing the provisions of this section; and

(2) provide continuing assistance to and oversight of the implementation of this section by agencies.

(Added Pub. L. 93–579, §3, Dec. 31, 1974, 88 Stat. 1897; amended Pub. L. 94–183, §2(2), Dec. 31, 1975, 89 Stat. 1057; Pub. L. 97–365, §2, Oct. 25, 1982, 96 Stat. 1749; Pub. L. 97–375, title II, §201(a), (b), Dec. 21, 1982, 96 Stat. 1821; Pub. L. 97–452, §2(a)(1), Jan. 12, 1983, 96 Stat. 2478; Pub. L. 98–477, §2(c), Oct. 15, 1984, 98 Stat. 2211; Pub. L. 98–497, title I, §107(g), Oct. 19, 1984, 98 Stat. 2292; Pub. L. 100–503, §§2–6(a), 7, 8, Oct. 18, 1988, 102 Stat. 2507–2514; Pub. L. 101–508, title VII, §7201(b)(1), Nov. 5, 1990, 104 Stat. 1388–334; Pub. L. 103–66, title XIII, §13581(c), Aug. 10, 1993, 107 Stat. 611; Pub. L. 104–193, title I, §110(w), Aug. 22, 1996, 110 Stat. 2175; Pub. L. 104–226, §1(b)(3), Oct. 2, 1996, 110 Stat. 3033; Pub. L. 104–316, title I, §115(g)(2)(B), Oct. 19, 1996, 110 Stat. 3835; Pub. L. 105–34, title X, §1026(b)(2), Aug. 5, 1997, 111 Stat. 925; Pub. L. 105–362, title XIII, §1301(d), Nov. 10, 1998, 112 Stat. 3293; Pub. L. 106–170, title IV, §402(a)(2), Dec. 17, 1999, 113 Stat. 1908.)

REFERENCES IN TEXT

Section 552(e) of this title, referred to in subsec. (a)(1), was redesignated section 552(f) of this title by section 1802(b) of Pub. L. 99–570.

Section 6103 of the Internal Revenue Code of 1986, referred to in subsec. (a)(8)(B)(iv), (vii), is classified to section 6103 of Title 26, Internal Revenue Code.

Sections 404, 464, and 1137 of the Social Security Act, referred to in subsec. (a)(8)(B)(iv), are classified to sections 604, 664, and 1320b–7, respectively, of Title 42, The Public Health and Welfare.

For effective date of this section, referred to in subsecs. (k)(2), (5), (7), (l)(2), (3), and (m), see Effective Date note below.

Section 6 of the Privacy Act of 1974, referred to in subsec. (s)(1), is section 6 of Pub. L. 93–579, which was set out below and was repealed by section 6(c) of Pub. L. 100–503.

For classification of the Privacy Act of 1974, referred to in subsec. (s)(4), see Short Title note below.

CODIFICATION

Section 552a of former Title 5, Executive Departments and Government Officers and Employees, was transferred to section 2244 of Title 7, Agriculture.

[2] So in original. Probably should be "cost-effective."

AMENDMENTS

1999—Subsec. (a)(8)(B)(viii). Pub. L. 106–170 added cl. (viii).

1998—Subsec. (u)(6), (7). Pub. L. 105–362 redesignated par. (7) as (6), substituted "paragraph (3)(D)" for "paragraphs (3)(D) and (6)", and struck out former par. (6) which read as follows: "The Director of the Office of Management and Budget shall, annually during the first 3 years after the date of enactment of this subsection and biennially thereafter, consolidate in a report to the Congress the information contained in the reports from the various Data Integrity Boards under paragraph (3)(D). Such report shall include detailed information about costs and benefits of matching programs that are conducted during the period covered by such consolidated report, and shall identify each waiver granted by a Data Integrity Board of the requirement for completion and submission of a cost-benefit analysis and the reasons for granting the waiver."

1997—Subsec. (a)(8)(B)(vii). Pub. L. 105–34 added cl. (vii).

1996—Subsec. (a)(8)(B)(iv)(III). Pub. L. 104–193 substituted "section 404(e), 464," for "section 464".

Subsec. (a)(8)(B)(v) to (vii). Pub. L. 104–226 inserted "or" at end of cl. (v), struck out "or" at end of cl. (vi), and struck out cl. (vii) which read as follows: "matches performed pursuant to section 6103(l)(12) of the Internal Revenue Code of 1986 and section 1144 of the Social Security Act;".

Subsecs. (b)(12), (m)(2). Pub. L. 104–316 substituted "3711(e)" for "3711(f)".

1993—Subsec. (a)(8)(B)(vii). Pub. L. 103–66 added cl. (vii).

1990—Subsec. (p). Pub. L. 101–508 amended subsec. (p) generally, restating former pars. (1) and (3) as par. (1), adding provisions relating to Data Integrity Boards, and restating former pars. (2) and (4) as (2) and (3), respectively.

1988—Subsec. (a)(8) to (13). Pub. L. 100–503, §5, added pars. (8) to (13).

Subsec. (e)(12). Pub. L. 100–503, §3(a), added par. (12).

Subsec. (f). Pub. L. 100–503, §7, substituted "biennially" for "annually" in last sentence.

Subsecs. (o) to (q). Pub. L. 100–503, §2(2), added subsecs. (o) to (q). Former subsecs. (o) to (q) redesignated (r) to (t), respectively.

Subsec. (r). Pub. L. 100–503, §3(b), inserted "and matching programs" in heading and amended text generally. Prior to amendment, text read as follows: "Each agency shall provide adequate advance notice to Congress and the Office of Management and Budget of any proposal to establish or alter any system of records in order to permit an evaluation of the probable or potential effect of such proposal on the privacy and other personal or property rights of individuals or the disclosure of information relating to such individuals, and its effect on the preservation of the constitutional principles of federalism and separation of powers."

Pub. L. 100–503, §2(1), redesignated former subsec. (o) as (r).

Subsec. (s). Pub. L. 100–503, §8, substituted "Biennial" for "Annual" in heading, "biennially submit" for "annually submit" in introductory provisions, "preceding 2 years" for "preceding year" in par. (1), and "such years" for "such year" in par. (2).

Pub. L. 100–503, §2(1), redesignated former subsec. (p) as (s).

Subsec. (t). Pub. L. 100–503, §2(1), redesignated former subsec. (q) as (t).

Subsec. (u). Pub. L. 100–503, §4, added subsec. (u).

Subsec. (v). Pub. L. 100–503, §6(a), added subsec. (v).

1984—Subsec. (b)(6). Pub. L. 98–497, §107(g)(1), substituted "National Archives and Records Administration" for "National Archives of the United States", and "Archivist of the United States or the designee of the Archivist" for "Administrator of General Services or his designee".

Subsec. (l)(1). Pub. L. 98–497, §107(g)(2), substituted "Archivist of the United States" for "Administrator of General Services" in two places.

Subsec. (q). Pub. L. 98–477 designated existing provisions as par. (1) and added par. (2).

1983—Subsec. (b)(12). Pub. L. 97–452 substituted "section 3711(f) of title 31" for "section 3(d) of the Federal Claims Collection Act of 1966 (31 U.S.C. 952(d))".

Subsec. (m)(2). Pub. L. 97–452 substituted "section 3711(f) of title 31" for "section 3(d) of the Federal Claims Collection Act of 1966 (31 U.S.C. 952(d))".

1982—Subsec. (b)(12). Pub. L. 97–365, §2(a), added par. (12).

Subsec. (e)(4). Pub. L. 97–375, §201(a), substituted "upon establishment or revision" for "at least annually" after "Federal Register".

Subsec. (m). Pub. L. 97–365, §2(b), designated existing provisions as par. (1) and added par. (2).

Subsec. (p). Pub. L. 97–375, §201(b), substituted provisions requiring annual submission of a report by the President to the Speaker of the House and President pro tempore of the Senate relating to the Director of the Office of Management and Budget, individual rights of access, changes or additions to systems of records, and other necessary or useful information, for provisions which had directed the President to submit to the Speaker of the House and the President of the Senate, by June 30 of each calendar year, a consolidated report, separately listing for each Federal agency the number of records contained in any system of records which were exempted from the application of this section under the provisions of subsections (j) and (k) of this section during the preceding calendar year, and the reasons for the exemptions, and such other information as indicate efforts to administer fully this section.

1975—Subsec. (g)(5). Pub. L. 94–183 substituted "to September 27, 1975" for "to the effective date of this section".

CHANGE OF NAME

Committee on Government Operations of House of Representatives treated as referring to Committee on Government Reform and Oversight of House of Representatives by section 1(a) of Pub. L. 104–14, set out as a note under section 21 of Title 2, The Congress. Committee on Government Reform and Oversight of House of Representatives changed to Committee on Government Reform of House of Representatives by House Resolution No. 5, One Hundred Sixth Congress, Jan. 6, 1999.

EFFECTIVE DATE OF 1999 AMENDMENT

Amendment by Pub. L. 106–170 applicable to individuals whose period of confinement in an institution commences on or after the first day of the fourth month beginning after December 1999, see section 402(a)(4) of Pub. L. 106–170, set out as a note under section 402 of Title 42, The Public Health and Welfare.

EFFECTIVE DATE OF 1997 AMENDMENT

Amendment by Pub. L. 105–34 applicable to levies issued after Aug. 5, 1997, see section 1026(c) of Pub. L. 105–34, set out as a note under section 6103 of Title 26, Internal Revenue Code.

EFFECTIVE DATE OF 1996 AMENDMENT

Amendment by Pub. L. 104–193 effective July 1, 1997, with transition rules relating to State options to accelerate such date, rules relating to claims, actions, and proceedings commenced before such date, rules relating to closing out of accounts for terminated or substantially modified programs and continuance in office of Assistant Secretary for Family Support, and provisions relating to termination of entitlement under AFDC program, see section 116 of Pub. L. 104–193, as amended, set out as an Effective Date note under section 601 of Title 42, The Public Health and Welfare.

EFFECTIVE DATE OF 1993 AMENDMENT

Amendment by Pub. L. 103–66 effective Jan. 1, 1994, see section 13581(d) of Pub. L. 103–66, set out as a note under section 1395y of Title 42, The Public Health and Welfare.

EFFECTIVE DATE OF 1988 AMENDMENT

Section 10 of Pub. L. 100–503, as amended by Pub. L. 101–56, § 2, July 19, 1989, 103 Stat. 149, provided that:

"(a) IN GENERAL.—Except as provided in subsections (b) and (c), the amendments made by this Act [amending this section and repealing provisions set out as a note below] shall take effect 9 months after the date of enactment of this Act [Oct. 18, 1988].

"(b) EXCEPTIONS.—The amendment made by sections 3(b), 6, 7, and 8 of this Act [amending this section and repealing provisions set out as a note below] shall take effect upon enactment.

"(c) EFFECTIVE DATE DELAYED FOR EXISTING PROGRAMS.—In the case of any matching program (as defined in section 552a(a)(8) of title 5, United States Code, as added by section 5 of this Act) in operation before June 1, 1989, the amendments made by this Act (other than the amendments described in subsection (b)) shall take effect January 1, 1990, if—

"(1) such matching program is identified by an agency as being in operation before June 1, 1989; and

"(2) such identification is—

"(A) submitted by the agency to the Committee on Governmental Affairs of the Senate, the Committee on Government Operations of the House of Representatives, and the Office of Management and Budget before August 1, 1989, in a report which contains a schedule showing the dates on which the agency expects to have such matching program in compliance with the amendments made by this Act, and

"(B) published by the Office of Management and Budget in the Federal Register, before September 15, 1989."

EFFECTIVE DATE OF 1984 AMENDMENT

Amendment by Pub. L. 98–497 effective Apr. 1, 1985, see section 301 of Pub. L. 98–497, set out as a note under section 2102 of Title 44, Public Printing and Documents.

EFFECTIVE DATE

Section 8 of Pub. L. 93–579 provided that: "The provisions of this Act [enacting this section and provisions set out as notes under this section] shall be effective on and after the date of enactment [Dec. 31, 1974], except that the amendments made by sections 3 and 4 [enacting this section and amending analysis preceding section 500 of this title] shall become effective 270 days following the day on which this Act is enacted."

SHORT TITLE OF 1990 AMENDMENT

Section 7201(a) of Pub. L. 101–508 provided that: "This section [amending this section and enacting provisions set out as notes below] may be cited as the 'Computer Matching and Privacy Protection Amendments of 1990'."

SHORT TITLE OF 1989 AMENDMENT

Pub. L. 101–56, § 1, July 19, 1989, 103 Stat. 149, provided that: "This Act [amending section 10 of Pub. L. 100–503, set out as a note above] may be cited as the 'Computer Matching and Privacy Protection Act Amendments of 1989'."

SHORT TITLE OF 1988 AMENDMENT

Section 1 of Pub. L. 100–503 provided that: "This Act [amending this section, enacting provisions set out as notes above and below, and repealing provisions set out as a note below] may be cited as the 'Computer Matching and Privacy Protection Act of 1988'."

SHORT TITLE

Section 1 of Pub. L. 93–579 provided: "That this Act [enacting this section and provisions set out as notes under this section] may be cited as the 'Privacy Act of 1974'."

TERMINATION OF REPORTING REQUIREMENTS

For termination, effective May 15, 2000, of reporting provisions in subsec. (s) of this section, see section 3003

of Pub. L. 104–66, as amended, set out as a note under section 1113 of Title 31, Money and Finance, and page 31 of House Document No. 103–7.

DELEGATION OF FUNCTIONS

Functions of Director of Office of Management and Budget under this section delegated to Administrator for Office of Information and Regulatory Affairs by section 3 of Pub. L. 96–511, Dec. 11, 1980, 94 Stat. 2825, set out as a note under section 3503 of Title 44, Public Printing and Documents.

PUBLICATION OF GUIDANCE UNDER SUBSECTION (p)(1)(A)(ii)

Section 7201(b)(2) of Pub. L. 101–508 provided that: "Not later than 90 days after the date of the enactment of this Act [Nov. 5, 1990], the Director of the Office of Management and Budget shall publish guidance under subsection (p)(1)(A)(ii) of section 552a of title 5, United States Code, as amended by this Act."

LIMITATION ON APPLICATION OF VERIFICATION REQUIREMENT

Section 7201(c) of Pub. L. 101–508 provided that: "Section 552a(p)(1)(A)(ii)(II) of title 5, United States Code, as amended by section 2 [probably means section 7201(b)(1) of Pub. L. 101–508], shall not apply to a program referred to in paragraph (1), (2), or (4) of section 1137(b) of the Social Security Act (42 U.S.C. 1320b–7), until the earlier of—

"(1) the date on which the Data Integrity Board of the Federal agency which administers that program determines that there is not a high degree of confidence that information provided by that agency under Federal matching programs is accurate; or

"(2) 30 days after the date of publication of guidance under section 2(b) [probably means section 7201(b)(2) of Pub. L. 101–508, set out as a note above]."

EFFECTIVE DATE DELAYED FOR CERTAIN EDUCATION BENEFITS COMPUTER MATCHING PROGRAMS

Pub. L. 101–366, title II, § 206(d), Aug. 15, 1990, 104 Stat. 442, provided that:

"(1) In the case of computer matching programs between the Department of Veterans Affairs and the Department of Defense in the administration of education benefits programs under chapters 30 and 32 of title 38 and chapter 106 of title 10, United States Code, the amendments made to section 552a of title 5, United States Code, by the Computer Matching and Privacy Protection Act of 1988 [Pub. L. 100–503] (other than the amendments made by section 10(b) of that Act) [see Effective Date of 1988 Amendment note above] shall take effect on October 1, 1990.

"(2) For purposes of this subsection, the term 'matching program' has the same meaning provided in section 552a(a)(8) of title 5, United States Code."

IMPLEMENTATION GUIDANCE FOR 1988 AMENDMENTS

Section 6(b) of Pub. L. 100–503 provided that: "The Director shall, pursuant to section 552a(v) of title 5, United States Code, develop guidelines and regulations for the use of agencies in implementing the amendments made by this Act [amending this section and repealing provisions set out as a note below] not later than 8 months after the date of enactment of this Act [Oct. 18, 1988]."

CONSTRUCTION OF 1988 AMENDMENTS

Section 9 of Pub. L. 100–503 provided that: "Nothing in the amendments made by this Act [amending this section and repealing provisions set out as a note below] shall be construed to authorize—

"(1) the establishment or maintenance by any agency of a national data bank that combines, merges, or links information on individuals maintained in systems of records by other Federal agencies;

"(2) the direct linking of computerized systems of records maintained by Federal agencies;

"(3) the computer matching of records not otherwise authorized by law; or

"(4) the disclosure of records for computer matching except to a Federal, State, or local agency."

CONGRESSIONAL FINDINGS AND STATEMENT OF PURPOSE

Section 2 of Pub. L. 93–579 provided that:

"(a) The Congress finds that—

"(1) the privacy of an individual is directly affected by the collection, maintenance, use, and dissemination of personal information by Federal agencies;

"(2) the increasing use of computers and sophisticated information technology, while essential to the efficient operations of the Government, has greatly magnified the harm to individual privacy that can occur from any collection, maintenance, use, or dissemination of personal information;

"(3) the opportunities for an individual to secure employment, insurance, and credit, and his right to due process, and other legal protections are endangered by the misuse of certain information systems;

"(4) the right to privacy is a personal and fundamental right protected by the Constitution of the United States; and

"(5) in order to protect the privacy of individuals identified in information systems maintained by Federal agencies, it is necessary and proper for the Congress to regulate the collection, maintenance, use, and dissemination of information by such agencies.

"(b) The purpose of this Act [enacting this section and provisions set out as notes under this section] is to provide certain safeguards for an individual against an invasion of personal privacy by requiring Federal agencies, except as otherwise provided by law, to—

"(1) permit an individual to determine what records pertaining to him are collected, maintained, used, or disseminated by such agencies;

"(2) permit an individual to prevent records pertaining to him obtained by such agencies for a particular purpose from being used or made available for another purpose without his consent;

"(3) permit an individual to gain access to information pertaining to him in Federal agency records, to have a copy made of all or any portion thereof, and to correct or amend such records;

"(4) collect, maintain, use, or disseminate any record of identifiable personal information in a manner that assures that such action is for a necessary and lawful purpose, that the information is current and accurate for its intended use, and that adequate safeguards are provided to prevent misuse of such information;

"(5) permit exemptions from the requirements with respect to records provided in this Act only in those cases where there is an important public policy need for such exemption as has been determined by specific statutory authority; and

"(6) be subject to civil suit for any damages which occur as a result of willful or intentional action which violates any individual's rights under this Act."

PRIVACY PROTECTION STUDY COMMISSION

Section 5 of Pub. L. 93–579, as amended by Pub. L. 95–38, June 1, 1977, 91 Stat. 179, which established the Privacy Protection Study Commission and provided that the Commission study data banks, automated data processing programs and information systems of governmental, regional and private organizations to determine standards and procedures in force for protection of personal information, that the Commission report to the President and Congress the extent to which requirements and principles of section 552a of title 5 should be applied to the information practices of those organizations, and that it make other legislative recommendations to protect the privacy of individuals while meeting the legitimate informational needs of government and society, ceased to exist on September 30, 1977, pursuant to section 5(g) of Pub. L. 93–579.

GUIDELINES AND REGULATIONS FOR MAINTENANCE OF PRIVACY AND PROTECTION OF RECORDS OF INDIVIDUALS

Section 6 of Pub. L. 93–579, which provided that the Office of Management and Budget shall develop guidelines and regulations for use of agencies in implementing provisions of this section and provide continuing assistance to and oversight of the implementation of the provisions of such section by agencies, was repealed by Pub. L. 100–503, §6(c), Oct. 18, 1988, 102 Stat. 2513.

DISCLOSURE OF SOCIAL SECURITY NUMBER

Section 7 of Pub. L. 93–579 provided that:

"(a)(1) It shall be unlawful for any Federal, State or local government agency to deny to any individual any right, benefit, or privilege provided by law because of such individual's refusal to disclose his social security account number.

"(2) the [The] provisions of paragraph (1) of this subsection shall not apply with respect to—

"(A) any disclosure which is required by Federal statute, or

"(B) the disclosure of a social security number to any Federal, State, or local agency maintaining a system of records in existence and operating before January 1, 1975, if such disclosure was required under statute or regulation adopted prior to such date to verify the identity of an individual.

"(b) Any Federal, State, or local government agency which requests an individual to disclose his social security account number shall inform that individual whether that disclosure is mandatory or voluntary, by what statutory or other authority such number is solicited, and what uses will be made of it."

AUTHORIZATION OF APPROPRIATIONS TO PRIVACY PROTECTION STUDY COMMISSION

Section 9 of Pub. L. 93–579, as amended by Pub. L. 94–394, Sept. 3, 1976, 90 Stat. 1198, authorized appropriations for the period beginning July 1, 1975, and ending on September 30, 1977.

CLASSIFIED NATIONAL SECURITY INFORMATION

For provisions relating to a response to a request for information under this section when the fact of its existence or nonexistence is itself classified or when it was originally classified by another agency, see Ex. Ord. No. 12958, §3.7, Apr. 17, 1995, 60 F.R. 19835, set out as a note under section 435 of Title 50, War and National Defense.

SECTION REFERRED TO IN OTHER SECTIONS

This section is referred to in sections 552b, 1212, 3111, 7133, 8148 of this title; title 7 sections 2204b, 2279b, 7035; title 10 sections 1102, 1506, 1588; title 12 section 1715z; title 14 section 645; title 15 section 278g–3; title 16 sections 410cc–35, 1536; title 19 section 1631; title 20 sections 1080a, 1090, 9010; title 22 section 4355; title 25 section 3205; title 26 sections 6103, 7852; title 29 section 1908; title 31 sections 3701, 3711, 3716, 3718, 3729, 3733, 7701; title 38 sections 3684A, 5701; title 39 section 410; title 42 sections 247b–4, 300aa–25, 402, 405, 904, 1306, 3544, 9660, 14614, 14616; title 44 sections 2906, 3501, 3504, 3506; title 46 sections 7702, 9303; title 49 section 30305; title 50 section 403–5b; title 50 App. section 2159.

§ 552b. Open meetings

(a) For purposes of this section—

(1) the term "agency" means any agency, as defined in section 552(e)[1] of this title, headed by a collegial body composed of two or more individual members, a majority of whom are appointed to such position by the President with the advice and consent of the Senate, and any subdivision thereof authorized to act on behalf of the agency;

(2) the term "meeting" means the deliberations of at least the number of individual

[1] See References in Text note below.

agency members required to take action on behalf of the agency where such deliberations determine or result in the joint conduct or disposition of official agency business, but does not include deliberations required or permitted by subsection (d) or (e); and

(3) the term "member" means an individual who belongs to a collegial body heading an agency.

(b) Members shall not jointly conduct or dispose of agency business other than in accordance with this section. Except as provided in subsection (c), every portion of every meeting of an agency shall be open to public observation.

(c) Except in a case where the agency finds that the public interest requires otherwise, the second sentence of subsection (b) shall not apply to any portion of an agency meeting, and the requirements of subsections (d) and (e) shall not apply to any information pertaining to such meeting otherwise required by this section to be disclosed to the public, where the agency properly determines that such portion or portions of its meeting or the disclosure of such information is likely to—

(1) disclose matters that are (A) specifically authorized under criteria established by an Executive order to be kept secret in the interests of national defense or foreign policy and (B) in fact properly classified pursuant to such Executive order;

(2) relate solely to the internal personnel rules and practices of an agency;

(3) disclose matters specifically exempted from disclosure by statute (other than section 552 of this title), provided that such statute (A) requires that the matters be withheld from the public in such a manner as to leave no discretion on the issue, or (B) establishes particular criteria for withholding or refers to particular types of matters to be withheld;

(4) disclose trade secrets and commercial or financial information obtained from a person and privileged or confidential;

(5) involve accusing any person of a crime, or formally censuring any person;

(6) disclose information of a personal nature where disclosure would constitute a clearly unwarranted invasion of personal privacy;

(7) disclose investigatory records compiled for law enforcement purposes, or information which if written would be contained in such records, but only to the extent that the production of such records or information would (A) interfere with enforcement proceedings, (B) deprive a person of a right to a fair trial or an impartial adjudication, (C) constitute an unwarranted invasion of personal privacy, (D) disclose the identity of a confidential source and, in the case of a record compiled by a criminal law enforcement authority in the course of a criminal investigation, or by an agency conducting a lawful national security intelligence investigation, confidential information furnished only by the confidential source, (E) disclose investigative techniques and procedures, or (F) endanger the life or physical safety of law enforcement personnel;

(8) disclose information contained in or related to examination, operating, or condition reports prepared by, on behalf of, or for the use of an agency responsible for the regulation or supervision of financial institutions;

(9) disclose information the premature disclosure of which would—

(A) in the case of an agency which regulates currencies, securities, commodities, or financial institutions, be likely to (i) lead to significant financial speculation in currencies, securities, or commodities, or (ii) significantly endanger the stability of any financial institution; or

(B) in the case of any agency, be likely to significantly frustrate implementation of a proposed agency action,

except that subparagraph (B) shall not apply in any instance where the agency has already disclosed to the public the content or nature of its proposed action, or where the agency is required by law to make such disclosure on its own initiative prior to taking final agency action on such proposal; or

(10) specifically concern the agency's issuance of a subpena, or the agency's participation in a civil action or proceeding, an action in a foreign court or international tribunal, or an arbitration, or the initiation, conduct, or disposition by the agency of a particular case of formal agency adjudication pursuant to the procedures in section 554 of this title or otherwise involving a determination on the record after opportunity for a hearing.

(d)(1) Action under subsection (c) shall be taken only when a majority of the entire membership of the agency (as defined in subsection (a)(1)) votes to take such action. A separate vote of the agency members shall be taken with respect to each agency meeting a portion or portions of which are proposed to be closed to the public pursuant to subsection (c), or with respect to any information which is proposed to be withheld under subsection (c). A single vote may be taken with respect to a series of meetings, a portion or portions of which are proposed to be closed to the public, or with respect to any information concerning such series of meetings, so long as each meeting in such series involves the same particular matters and is scheduled to be held no more than thirty days after the initial meeting in such series. The vote of each agency member participating in such vote shall be recorded and no proxies shall be allowed.

(2) Whenever any person whose interests may be directly affected by a portion of a meeting requests that the agency close such portion to the public for any of the reasons referred to in paragraph (5), (6), or (7) of subsection (c), the agency, upon request of any one of its members, shall vote by recorded vote whether to close such meeting.

(3) Within one day of any vote taken pursuant to paragraph (1) or (2), the agency shall make publicly available a written copy of such vote reflecting the vote of each member on the question. If a portion of a meeting is to be closed to the public, the agency shall, within one day of the vote taken pursuant to paragraph (1) or (2) of this subsection, make publicly available a full written explanation of its action closing the portion together with a list of all persons expected to attend the meeting and their affiliation.

(4) Any agency, a majority of whose meetings may properly be closed to the public pursuant to paragraph (4), (8), (9)(A), or (10) of subsection (c), or any combination thereof, may provide by regulation for the closing of such meetings or portions thereof in the event that a majority of the members of the agency votes by recorded vote at the beginning of such meeting, or portion thereof, to close the exempt portion or portions of the meeting, and a copy of such vote, reflecting the vote of each member on the question, is made available to the public. The provisions of paragraphs (1), (2), and (3) of this subsection and subsection (e) shall not apply to any portion of a meeting to which such regulations apply: *Provided*, That the agency shall, except to the extent that such information is exempt from disclosure under the provisions of subsection (c), provide the public with public announcement of the time, place, and subject matter of the meeting and of each portion thereof at the earliest practicable time.

(e)(1) In the case of each meeting, the agency shall make public announcement, at least one week before the meeting, of the time, place, and subject matter of the meeting, whether it is to be open or closed to the public, and the name and phone number of the official designated by the agency to respond to requests for information about the meeting. Such announcement shall be made unless a majority of the members of the agency determines by a recorded vote that agency business requires that such meeting be called at an earlier date, in which case the agency shall make public announcement of the time, place, and subject matter of such meeting, and whether open or closed to the public, at the earliest practicable time.

(2) The time or place of a meeting may be changed following the public announcement required by paragraph (1) only if the agency publicly announces such change at the earliest practicable time. The subject matter of a meeting, or the determination of the agency to open or close a meeting, or portion of a meeting, to the public, may be changed following the public announcement required by this subsection only if (A) a majority of the entire membership of the agency determines by a recorded vote that agency business so requires and that no earlier announcement of the change was possible, and (B) the agency publicly announces such change and the vote of each member upon such change at the earliest practicable time.

(3) Immediately following each public announcement required by this subsection, notice of the time, place, and subject matter of a meeting, whether the meeting is open or closed, any change in one of the preceding, and the name and phone number of the official designated by the agency to respond to requests for information about the meeting, shall also be submitted for publication in the Federal Register.

(f)(1) For every meeting closed pursuant to paragraphs (1) through (10) of subsection (c), the General Counsel or chief legal officer of the agency shall publicly certify that, in his or her opinion, the meeting may be closed to the public and shall state each relevant exemptive provision. A copy of such certification, together with a statement from the presiding officer of the

meeting setting forth the time and place of the meeting, and the persons present, shall be retained by the agency. The agency shall maintain a complete transcript or electronic recording adequate to record fully the proceedings of each meeting, or portion of a meeting, closed to the public, except that in the case of a meeting, or portion of a meeting, closed to the public pursuant to paragraph (8), (9)(A), or (10) of subsection (c), the agency shall maintain either such a transcript or recording, or a set of minutes. Such minutes shall fully and clearly describe all matters discussed and shall provide a full and accurate summary of any actions taken, and the reasons therefor, including a description of each of the views expressed on any item and the record of any rollcall vote (reflecting the vote of each member on the question). All documents considered in connection with any action shall be identified in such minutes.

(2) The agency shall make promptly available to the public, in a place easily accessible to the public, the transcript, electronic recording, or minutes (as required by paragraph (1)) of the discussion of any item on the agenda, or of any item of the testimony of any witness received at the meeting, except for such item or items of such discussion or testimony as the agency determines to contain information which may be withheld under subsection (c). Copies of such transcript, or minutes, or a transcription of such recording disclosing the identity of each speaker, shall be furnished to any person at the actual cost of duplication or transcription. The agency shall maintain a complete verbatim copy of the transcript, a complete copy of the minutes, or a complete electronic recording of each meeting, or portion of a meeting, closed to the public, for a period of at least two years after such meeting, or until one year after the conclusion of any agency proceeding with respect to which the meeting or portion was held, whichever occurs later.

(g) Each agency subject to the requirements of this section shall, within 180 days after the date of enactment of this section, following consultation with the Office of the Chairman of the Administrative Conference of the United States and published notice in the Federal Register of at least thirty days and opportunity for written comment by any person, promulgate regulations to implement the requirements of subsections (b) through (f) of this section. Any person may bring a proceeding in the United States District Court for the District of Columbia to require an agency to promulgate such regulations if such agency has not promulgated such regulations within the time period specified herein. Subject to any limitations of time provided by law, any person may bring a proceeding in the United States Court of Appeals for the District of Columbia to set aside agency regulations issued pursuant to this subsection that are not in accord with the requirements of subsections (b) through (f) of this section and to require the promulgation of regulations that are in accord with such subsections.

(h)(1) The district courts of the United States shall have jurisdiction to enforce the requirements of subsections (b) through (f) of this section by declaratory judgment, injunctive relief, or other relief as may be appropriate. Such actions may be brought by any person against an agency prior to, or within sixty days after, the meeting out of which the violation of this section arises, except that if public announcement of such meeting is not initially provided by the agency in accordance with the requirements of this section, such action may be instituted pursuant to this section at any time prior to sixty days after any public announcement of such meeting. Such actions may be brought in the district court of the United States for the district in which the agency meeting is held or in which the agency in question has its headquarters, or in the District Court for the District of Columbia. In such actions a defendant shall serve his answer within thirty days after the service of the complaint. The burden is on the defendant to sustain his action. In deciding such cases the court may examine in camera any portion of the transcript, electronic recording, or minutes of a meeting closed to the public, and may take such additional evidence as it deems necessary. The court, having due regard for orderly administration and the public interest, as well as the interests of the parties, may grant such equitable relief as it deems appropriate, including granting an injunction against future violations of this section or ordering the agency to make available to the public such portion of the transcript, recording, or minutes of a meeting as is not authorized to be withheld under subsection (c) of this section.

(2) Any Federal court otherwise authorized by law to review agency action may, at the application of any person properly participating in the proceeding pursuant to other applicable law, inquire into violations by the agency of the requirements of this section and afford such relief as it deems appropriate. Nothing in this section authorizes any Federal court having jurisdiction solely on the basis of paragraph (1) to set aside, enjoin, or invalidate any agency action (other than an action to close a meeting or to withhold information under this section) taken or discussed at any agency meeting out of which the violation of this section arose.

(i) The court may assess against any party reasonable attorney fees and other litigation costs reasonably incurred by any other party who substantially prevails in any action brought in accordance with the provisions of subsection (g) or (h) of this section, except that costs may be assessed against the plaintiff only where the court finds that the suit was initiated by the plaintiff primarily for frivolous or dilatory purposes. In the case of assessment of costs against an agency, the costs may be assessed by the court against the United States.

(j) Each agency subject to the requirements of this section shall annually report to the Congress regarding the following:

(1) The changes in the policies and procedures of the agency under this section that have occurred during the preceding 1-year period.

(2) A tabulation of the number of meetings held, the exemptions applied to close meetings, and the days of public notice provided to close meetings.

(3) A brief description of litigation or formal complaints concerning the implementation of this section by the agency.

(4) A brief explanation of any changes in law that have affected the responsibilities of the agency under this section.

(k) Nothing herein expands or limits the present rights of any person under section 552 of this title, except that the exemptions set forth in subsection (c) of this section shall govern in the case of any request made pursuant to section 552 to copy or inspect the transcripts, recordings, or minutes described in subsection (f) of this section. The requirements of chapter 33 of title 44, United States Code, shall not apply to the transcripts, recordings, and minutes described in subsection (f) of this section.

(l) This section does not constitute authority to withhold any information from Congress, and does not authorize the closing of any agency meeting or portion thereof required by any other provision of law to be open.

(m) Nothing in this section authorizes any agency to withhold from any individual any record, including transcripts, recordings, or minutes required by this section, which is otherwise accessible to such individual under section 552a of this title.

(Added Pub. L. 94–409, §3(a), Sept. 13, 1976, 90 Stat. 1241; amended Pub. L. 104–66, title III, §3002, Dec. 21, 1995, 109 Stat. 734.)

REFERENCES IN TEXT

Section 552(e) of this title, referred to in subsec. (a)(1), was redesignated section 552(f) of this title by section 1802(b) of Pub. L. 99–570.

180 days after the date of enactment of this section, referred to in subsec. (g), means 180 days after the date of enactment of Pub. L. 94–409, which was approved Sept. 13, 1976.

AMENDMENTS

1995—Subsec. (j). Pub. L. 104–66 amended subsec. (j) generally. Prior to amendment, subsec. (j) read as follows: "Each agency subject to the requirements of this section shall annually report to Congress regarding its compliance with such requirements, including a tabulation of the total number of agency meetings open to the public, the total number of meetings closed to the public, the reasons for closing such meetings, and a description of any litigation brought against the agency under this section, including any costs assessed against the agency in such litigation (whether or not paid by the agency)."

EFFECTIVE DATE

Section 6 of Pub. L. 94–409 provided that:

"(a) Except as provided in subsection (b) of this section, the provisions of this Act [see Short Title note set out below] shall take effect 180 days after the date of its enactment [Sept. 13, 1976].

"(b) Subsection (g) of section 552b of title 5, United States Code, as added by section 3(a) of this Act, shall take effect upon enactment [Sept. 13, 1976]."

SHORT TITLE

Section 1 of Pub. L. 94–409 provided: "That this Act [enacting this section, amending sections 551, 552, 556, and 557 of this title, section 10 of Pub. L. 92–463, set out in the Appendix to this title, and section 410 of Title 39, and enacting provisions set out as notes under this section] may be cited as the 'Government in the Sunshine Act'."

TERMINATION OF REPORTING REQUIREMENTS

For termination, effective May 15, 2000, of provisions of law requiring submittal to Congress of any annual, semiannual, or other regular periodic report listed in House Document No. 103–7 (in which the report required by subsec. (j) of this section is listed on page 151), see section 3003 of Pub. L. 104–66, as amended, set out as a note under section 1113 of Title 31, Money and Finance.

TERMINATION OF ADMINISTRATIVE CONFERENCE OF UNITED STATES

For termination of Administrative Conference of United States, see provision of title IV of Pub. L. 104–52, set out as a note preceding section 591 of this title.

DECLARATION OF POLICY AND STATEMENT OF PURPOSE

Section 2 of Pub. L. 94–409 provided that: "It is hereby declared to be the policy of the United States that the public is entitled to the fullest practicable information regarding the decisionmaking processes of the Federal Government. It is the purpose of this Act [see Short Title note set out above] to provide the public with such information while protecting the rights of individuals and the ability of the Government to carry out its responsibilities."

SECTION REFERRED TO IN OTHER SECTIONS

This section is referred to in section 552 of this title; title 7 section 945; title 19 section 2347; title 20 section 6021; title 22 sections 4605, 4833; title 39 section 410; title 42 sections 2996c, 7171, 8103, 10703, 14195; title 44 section 2204; title 45 sections 1116, 1212; title 46 sections 7702, 9303; title 49 section 703; title 50 App. sections 2158, 2159.

§ 553. Rule making

(a) This section applies, according to the provisions thereof, except to the extent that there is involved—

(1) a military or foreign affairs function of the United States; or

(2) a matter relating to agency management or personnel or to public property, loans, grants, benefits, or contracts.

(b) General notice of proposed rule making shall be published in the Federal Register, unless persons subject thereto are named and either personally served or otherwise have actual notice thereof in accordance with law. The notice shall include—

(1) a statement of the time, place, and nature of public rule making proceedings;

(2) reference to the legal authority under which the rule is proposed; and

(3) either the terms or substance of the proposed rule or a description of the subjects and issues involved.

Except when notice or hearing is required by statute, this subsection does not apply—

(A) to interpretative rules, general statements of policy, or rules of agency organization, procedure, or practice; or

(B) when the agency for good cause finds (and incorporates the finding and a brief statement of reasons therefor in the rules issued) that notice and public procedure thereon are impracticable, unnecessary, or contrary to the public interest.

(c) After notice required by this section, the agency shall give interested persons an opportunity to participate in the rule making through submission of written data, views, or arguments with or without opportunity for oral presentation. After consideration of the relevant matter presented, the agency shall incorporate in the rules adopted a concise general statement of their basis and purpose. When rules are required by statute to be made on the record after opportunity for an agency hearing, sections 556 and 557 of this title apply instead of this subsection.

(d) The required publication or service of a substantive rule shall be made not less than 30 days before its effective date, except—

(1) a substantive rule which grants or recognizes an exemption or relieves a restriction;

(2) interpretative rules and statements of policy; or

(3) as otherwise provided by the agency for good cause found and published with the rule.

(e) Each agency shall give an interested person the right to petition for the issuance, amendment, or repeal of a rule.

(Pub. L. 89–554, Sept. 6, 1966, 80 Stat. 383.)

HISTORICAL AND REVISION NOTES

Derivation	U.S. Code	Revised Statutes and Statutes at Large
....	5 U.S.C. 1003.	June 11, 1946, ch. 324, § 4, 60 Stat. 238.

In subsection (a)(1), the words "or naval" are omitted as included in "military".

In subsection (b), the word "when" is substituted for "in any situation in which".

In subsection (c), the words "for oral presentation" are substituted for "to present the same orally in any manner". The words "sections 556 and 557 of this title apply instead of this subsection" are substituted for "the requirements of sections 1006 and 1007 of this title shall apply in place of the provisions of this subsection".

Standard changes are made to conform with the definitions applicable and the style of this title as outlined in the preface to the report.

CODIFICATION

Section 553 of former Title 5, Executive Departments and Government Officers and Employees, was transferred to section 2245 of Title 7, Agriculture.

EXECUTIVE ORDER NO. 12044

Ex. Ord. No. 12044, Mar. 23, 1978, 43 F.R. 12661, as amended by Ex. Ord. No. 12221, June 27, 1980, 45 F.R. 44249, which related to the improvement of Federal regulations, was revoked by Ex. Ord. No. 12291, Feb. 17, 1981, 46 F.R. 13193, formerly set out as a note under section 601 of this title.

SECTION REFERRED TO IN OTHER SECTIONS

This section is referred to in sections 552a, 556, 561, 566, 601, 603, 604, 611, 1103, 1105, 5304 of this title; title 2 sections 501, 502, 1383, 1384; title 7 sections 499c, 499f, 927, 944a, 2013, 2014, 2707, 4604, 4906, 6802, 6804, 7251, 7253, 7281, 7412, 7804; title 8 sections 1288, 1372; title 9 section 306; title 12 sections 635, 1441a, 1710, 1735f–17, 1828, 3336, 4004, 4008, 4112, 4308, 4526, 4589, 4611; title 15 sections 18a, 45a, 57a, 78l, 78s, 78ggg, 1193, 1203, 1262, 1277, 1474, 1476, 1604, 1693b, 2058, 2079, 2082, 2309, 2603, 2604, 2605, 2618, 2643, 2703, 2823, 3412, 3803, 4017, 4404, 5624, 5711, 5721, 5724, 6004, 6102, 6502, 6765; title 16 sections 620a, 839b, 971d, 1379, 1381, 1383b, 1463, 1533, 1535, 1604, 1821, 1822, 3341, 3604, 3636, 3801, 5504; title 19 section 2561; title 20 sections 1098a, 1221e–4, 1232, 1406, 1461, 6104; title 21 sections 358, 463; title 25 sections 450c, 450k; title 28 section 994; title 30 sections 185, 811, 936, 1211, 1468, 1751; title 33 sections 1231, 1322, 1504; title 35 sections 2, 3; title 38 sections 501, 502; title 40 section 333; title 41 sections 43a, 47, 422; title 42 sections 289d, 290aa–10, 300g–1, 300h, 421, 902, 1320a–7c, 1395ff, 1395hh, 1437d, 1437u, 1437z–3, 1796c, 2210a, 2992b–1, 4029, 4905, 5403, 5506, 5919, 6239, 6306, 7191, 7407, 7502, 7511a, 7607, 8275, 8411, 9112, 9127, 9204, 9605, 10155, 10193, 11023, 11376, 11387, 12725, 12879, 12898, 12898a, 13603, 13643; title 43 section 1740; title 44 section 2206; title 46 sections 7702, 9303, 14104; title 46 App. sections 1241f, 1716; title 49 sections 5103, 20103, 24308, 31136, 31317, 32502, 32902, 40103, 60102; title 50 App. sections 2158, 2159, 2412.

§ 554. Adjudications

(a) This section applies, according to the provisions thereof, in every case of adjudication required by statute to be determined on the record after opportunity for an agency hearing, except to the extent that there is involved—

(1) a matter subject to a subsequent trial of the law and the facts de novo in a court;

(2) the selection or tenure of an employee, except a[1] administrative law judge appointed under section 3105 of this title;

(3) proceedings in which decisions rest solely on inspections, tests, or elections;

(4) the conduct of military or foreign affairs functions;

(5) cases in which an agency is acting as an agent for a court; or

(6) the certification of worker representatives.

(b) Persons entitled to notice of an agency hearing shall be timely informed of—

(1) the time, place, and nature of the hearing;

(2) the legal authority and jurisdiction under which the hearing is to be held; and

(3) the matters of fact and law asserted.

When private persons are the moving parties, other parties to the proceeding shall give prompt notice of issues controverted in fact or law; and in other instances agencies may by rule require responsive pleading. In fixing the time and place for hearings, due regard shall be had for the convenience and necessity of the parties or their representatives.

(c) The agency shall give all interested parties opportunity for—

(1) the submission and consideration of facts, arguments, offers of settlement, or proposals of adjustment when time, the nature of the proceeding, and the public interest permit; and

(2) to the extent that the parties are unable so to determine a controversy by consent, hearing and decision on notice and in accordance with sections 556 and 557 of this title.

(d) The employee who presides at the reception of evidence pursuant to section 556 of this title shall make the recommended decision or initial decision required by section 557 of this title, unless he becomes unavailable to the agency. Except to the extent required for the disposition of ex parte matters as authorized by law, such an employee may not—

(1) consult a person or party on a fact in issue, unless on notice and opportunity for all parties to participate; or

(2) be responsible to or subject to the supervision or direction of an employee or agent engaged in the performance of investigative or prosecuting functions for an agency.

An employee or agent engaged in the performance of investigative or prosecuting functions for an agency in a case may not, in that or a factually related case, participate or advise in the decision, recommended decision, or agency review pursuant to section 557 of this title, except as witness or counsel in public proceedings. This subsection does not apply—

(A) in determining applications for initial licenses;

(B) to proceedings involving the validity or application of rates, facilities, or practices of public utilities or carriers; or

(C) to the agency or a member or members of the body comprising the agency.

(e) The agency, with like effect as in the case of other orders, and in its sound discretion, may issue a declaratory order to terminate a controversy or remove uncertainty.

(Pub. L. 89–554, Sept. 6, 1966, 80 Stat. 384; Pub. L. 95–251, § 2(a)(1), Mar. 27, 1978, 92 Stat. 183.)

HISTORICAL AND REVISION NOTES

Derivation	U.S. Code	Revised Statutes and Statutes at Large
....	5 U.S.C. 1004.	June 11, 1946, ch. 324, § 5, 60 Stat. 239.

In subsection (a)(2), the word "employee" is substituted for "officer or employee of the United States" in view of the definition of "employee" in section 2105.

In subsection (a)(4), the word "naval" is omitted as included in "military".

In subsection (a)(5), the word "or" is substituted for "and" since the exception is applicable if any one of the factors are involved.

In subsection (a)(6), the word "worker" is substituted for "employee", since the latter is defined in section 2105 as meaning Federal employees.

In subsection (b), the word "When" is substituted for "In instances in which".

In subsection (c)(2), the comma after the word "hearing" is omitted to correct an editorial error.

In subsection (d), the words "The employee" and "such an employee" are substituted in the first two sentences for "The same officers" and "such officers" in view of the definition of "employee" in section 2105. The word "officer" is omitted in the third and fourth sentences as included in "employee" as defined in section 2105. The prohibition in the third and fourth sentences is restated in positive form. In paragraph (C) of the last sentence, the words "in any manner" are omitted as surplusage.

Standard changes are made to conform with the definitions applicable and the style of this title as outlined in the preface to the report.

CODIFICATION

Section 554 of former Title 5, Executive Departments and Government Officers and Employees, was transferred to section 2246 of Title 7, Agriculture.

AMENDMENTS

1978—Subsec. (a)(2). Pub. L. 95–251 substituted "administrative law judge" for "hearing examiner".

SECTION REFERRED TO IN OTHER SECTIONS

This section is referred to in sections 504, 552b, 556, 557, 8124 of this title; title 2 sections 501, 502, 1405, 1602; title 7 sections 86, 87e, 87f–1, 1359ii, 3804, 3805; title 8 sections 1324a, 1324c, 1375; title 12 sections 1817, 1818, 2268, 3413; title 15 sections 78d–1, 1274, 2064, 2066, 2605, 2615,

---

[1] So in original.

3412, 6765; title 16 sections 429b–1, 470ff, 773f, 796, 823b, 839f, 973f, 1174, 1437, 1536, 1540, 1852, 1856, 1858, 2407, 2437, 2602, 3142, 3373, 3636, 5010, 5507; title 18 section 3625; title 20 sections 1234, 6083; title 21 sections 321, 333, 342, 346a, 360e, 844a, 1041; title 22 section 6761; title 29 sections 214, 216, 659, 1813, 1853; title 30 sections 185, 804, 811, 815, 817, 818, 821, 938, 1264, 1268, 1275, 1293, 1426, 1462; title 33 sections 919, 1319, 1321, 1367, 1504; title 38 section 7101A; title 41 section 422; title 42 sections 262, 300g–3, 300h–2, 300gg–22, 2000e–16c, 2000e–17, 2282a, 3783, 3789d, 4910, 6303, 6971, 7407, 7413, 7419, 7502, 7511a, 7524, 7607, 7920, 8433, 9112, 9152, 9609, 9610; title 43 sections 1656, 1766; title 45 section 905; title 46 sections 7702, 9303; title 46 App. section 1187e; title 47 sections 409, 503; title 49 sections 521, 13902, 20104; title 50 App. sections 16, 2159, 2410, 2412.

§ 555. Ancillary matters

(a) This section applies, according to the provisions thereof, except as otherwise provided by this subchapter.

(b) A person compelled to appear in person before an agency or representative thereof is entitled to be accompanied, represented, and advised by counsel or, if permitted by the agency, by other qualified representative. A party is entitled to appear in person or by or with counsel or other duly qualified representative in an agency proceeding. So far as the orderly conduct of public business permits, an interested person may appear before an agency or its responsible employees for the presentation, adjustment, or determination of an issue, request, or controversy in a proceeding, whether interlocutory, summary, or otherwise, or in connection with an agency function. With due regard for the convenience and necessity of the parties or their representatives and within a reasonable time, each agency shall proceed to conclude a matter presented to it. This subsection does not grant or deny a person who is not a lawyer the right to appear for or represent others before an agency or in an agency proceeding.

(c) Process, requirement of a report, inspection, or other investigative act or demand may not be issued, made, or enforced except as authorized by law. A person compelled to submit data or evidence is entitled to retain or, on payment of lawfully prescribed costs, procure a copy or transcript thereof, except that in a nonpublic investigatory proceeding the witness may for good cause be limited to inspection of the official transcript of his testimony.

(d) Agency subpenas authorized by law shall be issued to a party on request and, when required by rules of procedure, on a statement or showing of general relevance and reasonable scope of the evidence sought. On contest, the court shall sustain the subpena or similar process or demand to the extent that it is found to be in accordance with law. In a proceeding for enforcement, the court shall issue an order requiring the appearance of the witness or the production of the evidence or data within a reasonable time under penalty of punishment for contempt in case of contumacious failure to comply.

(e) Prompt notice shall be given of the denial in whole or in part of a written application, petition, or other request of an interested person made in connection with any agency proceeding. Except in affirming a prior denial or when the denial is self-explanatory, the notice shall be accompanied by a brief statement of the grounds for denial.

(Pub. L. 89–554, Sept. 6, 1966, 80 Stat. 385.)

HISTORICAL AND REVISION NOTES

Derivation	U.S. Code	Revised Statutes and Statutes at Large
....	5 U.S.C. 1005.	June 11, 1946, ch. 324, §6, 60 Stat. 240.

In subsection (b), the words "is entitled" are substituted for "shall be accorded the right". The word "officers" is omitted as included in "employees" in view of the definition of "employee" in section 2105. The words "With due regard for the convenience and necessity of the parties or their representatives and within a reasonable time" are substituted for "with reasonable dispatch" and "except that due regard shall be had for the convenience and necessity of the parties or their representatives". The prohibition in the last sentence is restated in positive form and the words "This subsection does not" are substituted for "Nothing herein shall be construed either to".

In subsection (c), the words "in any manner or for any purpose" are omitted as surplusage.

In subsection (e), the word "brief" is substituted for "simple". The words "of the grounds for denial" are substituted for "of procedural or other grounds" for clarity.

Standard changes are made to conform with the definitions applicable and the style of this title as outlined in the preface to the report.

CODIFICATION

Section 555 of former Title 5, Executive Departments and Government Officers and Employees, was transferred to section 2247 of Title 7, Agriculture.

SECTION REFERRED TO IN OTHER SECTIONS

This section is referred to in title 2 sections 501, 502, 1405; title 8 section 1375; title 16 sections 1536, 3636; title 18 section 3625; title 30 section 185; title 41 section 422; title 42 sections 2000e–16c, 7407, 7502, 7511a, 7607; title 46 sections 7702, 9303; title 50 App. sections 16, 2159, 2410, 2412.

§ 556. Hearings; presiding employees; powers and duties; burden of proof; evidence; record as basis of decision

(a) This section applies, according to the provisions thereof, to hearings required by section 553 or 554 of this title to be conducted in accordance with this section.

(b) There shall preside at the taking of evidence—

(1) the agency;

(2) one or more members of the body which comprises the agency; or

(3) one or more administrative law judges appointed under section 3105 of this title.

This subchapter does not supersede the conduct of specified classes of proceedings, in whole or in part, by or before boards or other employees specially provided for by or designated under statute. The functions of presiding employees and of employees participating in decisions in accordance with section 557 of this title shall be conducted in an impartial manner. A presiding or participating employee may at any time disqualify himself. On the filing in good faith of a timely and sufficient affidavit of personal bias or other disqualification of a presiding or participating employee, the agency shall determine the matter as a part of the record and decision in the case.

(c) Subject to published rules of the agency and within its powers, employees presiding at hearings may—

(1) administer oaths and affirmations;

(2) issue subpenas authorized by law;

(3) rule on offers of proof and receive relevant evidence;

(4) take depositions or have depositions taken when the ends of justice would be served;

(5) regulate the course of the hearing;

(6) hold conferences for the settlement or simplification of the issues by consent of the parties or by the use of alternative means of dispute resolution as provided in subchapter IV of this chapter;

(7) inform the parties as to the availability of one or more alternative means of dispute resolution, and encourage use of such methods;

(8) require the attendance at any conference held pursuant to paragraph (6) of at least one representative of each party who has authority to negotiate concerning resolution of issues in controversy;

(9) dispose of procedural requests or similar matters;

(10) make or recommend decisions in accordance with section 557 of this title; and

(11) take other action authorized by agency rule consistent with this subchapter.

(d) Except as otherwise provided by statute, the proponent of a rule or order has the burden of proof. Any oral or documentary evidence may be received, but the agency as a matter of policy shall provide for the exclusion of irrelevant, immaterial, or unduly repetitious evidence. A sanction may not be imposed or rule or order issued except on consideration of the whole record or those parts thereof cited by a party and supported by and in accordance with the reliable, probative, and substantial evidence. The agency may, to the extent consistent with the interests of justice and the policy of the underlying statutes administered by the agency, consider a violation of section 557(d) of this title sufficient grounds for a decision adverse to a party who has knowingly committed such violation or knowingly caused such violation to occur. A party is entitled to present his case or defense by oral or documentary evidence, to submit rebuttal evidence, and to conduct such cross-examination as may be required for a full and true disclosure of the facts. In rule making or determining claims for money or benefits or applications for initial licenses an agency may, when a party will not be prejudiced thereby, adopt procedures for the submission of all or part of the evidence in written form.

(e) The transcript of testimony and exhibits, together with all papers and requests filed in the proceeding, constitutes the exclusive record for decision in accordance with section 557 of this title and, on payment of lawfully prescribed costs, shall be made available to the parties. When an agency decision rests on official notice of a material fact not appearing in the evidence in the record, a party is entitled, on timely request, to an opportunity to show the contrary.

(Pub. L. 89–554, Sept. 6, 1966, 80 Stat. 386; Pub. L. 94–409, §4(c), Sept. 13, 1976, 90 Stat. 1247; Pub. L. 95–251, §2(a)(1), Mar. 27, 1978, 92 Stat. 183; Pub. L. 101–552, §4(a), Nov. 15, 1990, 104 Stat. 2737.)

HISTORICAL AND REVISION NOTES

Derivation	U.S. Code	Revised Statutes and Statutes at Large
....	5 U.S.C. 1006.	June 11, 1946, ch. 324, §7, 60 Stat. 241.

In subsection (b), the words "hearing examiners" are substituted for "examiners" in paragraph (3) for clarity. The prohibition in the second sentence is restated in positive form and the words "This subchapter does not" are substituted for "but nothing in this chapter shall be deemed to". The words "employee" and "employees" are substituted for "officer" and "officers" in view of the definition of "employee" in section 2105. The sentence "A presiding or participating employee may at any time disqualify himself." is substituted for the words "Any such officer may at any time withdraw if he deems himself disqualified."

Standard changes are made to conform with the definitions applicable and the style of this title as outlined in the preface to the report.

AMENDMENTS

1990—Subsec. (c)(6). Pub. L. 101–552, §4(a)(1), inserted before semicolon at end "or by the use of alternative means of dispute resolution as provided in subchapter IV of this chapter".

Subsec. (c)(7) to (11). Pub. L. 101–552, §4(a)(2), added pars. (7) and (8) and redesignated former pars. (7) and (8) and redesignated former pars. (7) to (9) as (9) to (11), respectively.

1978—Subsec. (b)(3). Pub. L. 95–251 substituted "administrative law judges" for "hearing examiners".

1976—Subsec. (d). Pub. L. 94–409 inserted provisions relating to consideration by agency of a violation under section 557(d) of this title.

EFFECTIVE DATE OF 1976 AMENDMENT

Amendment by Pub. L. 94–409 effective 180 days after Sept. 13, 1976, see section 6 of Pub. L. 94–409, set out as an Effective Date note under section 552b of this title.

HEARING EXAMINERS EMPLOYED BY DEPARTMENT OF AGRICULTURE

Functions vested by this subchapter in hearing examiners employed by Department of Agriculture not included in functions of officers, agencies, and employees of that Department transferred to Secretary of Agriculture by 1953 Reorg. Plan No. 2, §1, eff. June 4, 1953, 18 F.R. 3219, 67 Stat. 633, set out in the Appendix to this title.

HEARING EXAMINERS EMPLOYED BY DEPARTMENT OF COMMERCE

Functions vested by this subchapter in hearing examiners employed by Department of Commerce not included in functions of officers, agencies, and employees of that Department transferred to Secretary of Commerce by 1950 Reorg. Plan No. 5, §1, eff. May 24, 1950, 15 F.R. 3174, 64 Stat. 1263, set out in the Appendix to this title.

HEARING EXAMINERS EMPLOYED BY DEPARTMENT OF THE INTERIOR

Functions vested by this subchapter in hearing examiners employed by Department of the Interior not included in functions of officers, agencies, and employees of that Department transferred to Secretary of the Interior by 1950 Reorg. Plan No. 3, §1, eff. May 24, 1950, 15 F.R. 3174, 64 Stat. 1262, set out in the Appendix to this title.

HEARING EXAMINERS EMPLOYED BY DEPARTMENT OF JUSTICE

Functions vested by this subchapter in hearing examiners employed by Department of Justice not included in functions of officers, agencies, and employees of that

Department transferred to Attorney General by 1950 Reorg. Plan No. 2, §1, eff. May 24, 1950, 15 F.R. 3173, 64 Stat. 1261, set out in the Appendix to this title.

HEARING EXAMINERS EMPLOYED BY DEPARTMENT OF LABOR

Functions vested by this subchapter in hearing examiners employed by Department of Labor not included in functions of officers, agencies, and employees of that Department transferred to Secretary of Labor by 1950 Reorg. Plan No. 6, §1, eff. May 24, 1950, 15 F.R. 3174, 64 Stat. 1263, set out in the Appendix to this title.

HEARING EXAMINERS EMPLOYED BY DEPARTMENT OF THE TREASURY

Functions vested by this subchapter in hearing examiners employed by Department of the Treasury not included in functions of officers, agencies, and employees of that Department transferred to Secretary of the Treasury by 1950 Reorg. Plan. No. 26, §1, eff. July 31, 1950, 15 F.R. 4935, 64 Stat. 1280, set out in the Appendix to this title.

SECTION REFERRED TO IN OTHER SECTIONS

This section is referred to in sections 553, 554, 557, 558, 706, 3105 of this title; title 2 sections 501, 502, 1405; title 7 sections 86, 87e, 87f–1, 1359ii, 2023, 2707, 3804, 3805, 4604, 4906, 6802, 6804, 7804; title 8 sections 1182, 1375; title 15 sections 57a, 2605, 3412; title 16 sections 796, 839f, 1536, 2602, 3636; title 20 section 1234; title 21 sections 321, 342, 379e, 1041; title 22 sections 1037a, 4136; title 30 sections 185, 811, 1415; title 33 sections 907, 1319, 1321; title 39 sections 404, 3624, 3661; title 41 section 422; title 42 sections 300h–2, 1320a–7c, 2000e–16c, 2241, 7171, 7407, 7413, 7502, 7511a, 7524, 7607, 9612, 11504; title 46 sections 7702, 9303; title 47 section 155; title 49 sections 31136, 31317; title 50 App. sections 16, 2159, 2410, 2412.

§ 557. Initial decisions; conclusiveness; review by agency; submissions by parties; contents of decisions; record

(a) This section applies, according to the provisions thereof, when a hearing is required to be conducted in accordance with section 556 of this title.

(b) When the agency did not preside at the reception of the evidence, the presiding employee or, in cases not subject to section 554(d) of this title, an employee qualified to preside at hearings pursuant to section 556 of this title, shall initially decide the case unless the agency requires, either in specific cases or by general rule, the entire record to be certified to it for decision. When the presiding employee makes an initial decision, that decision then becomes the decision of the agency without further proceedings unless there is an appeal to, or review on motion of, the agency within time provided by rule. On appeal from or review of the initial decision, the agency has all the powers which it would have in making the initial decision except as it may limit the issues on notice or by rule. When the agency makes the decision without having presided at the reception of the evidence, the presiding employee or an employee qualified to preside at hearings pursuant to section 556 of this title shall first recommend a decision, except that in rule making or determining applications for initial licenses—

(1) instead thereof the agency may issue a tentative decision or one of its responsible employees may recommend a decision; or

(2) this procedure may be omitted in a case in which the agency finds on the record that due and timely execution of its functions imperatively and unavoidably so requires.

(c) Before a recommended, initial, or tentative decision, or a decision on agency review of the decision of subordinate employees, the parties are entitled to a reasonable opportunity to submit for the consideration of the employees participating in the decisions—

(1) proposed findings and conclusions; or

(2) exceptions to the decisions or recommended decisions of subordinate employees or to tentative agency decisions; and

(3) supporting reasons for the exceptions or proposed findings or conclusions.

The record shall show the ruling on each finding, conclusion, or exception presented. All decisions, including initial, recommended, and tentative decisions, are a part of the record and shall include a statement of—

(A) findings and conclusions, and the reasons or basis therefor, on all the material issues of fact, law, or discretion presented on the record; and

(B) the appropriate rule, order, sanction, relief, or denial thereof.

(d)(1) In any agency proceeding which is subject to subsection (a) of this section, except to the extent required for the disposition of ex parte matters as authorized by law—

(A) no interested person outside the agency shall make or knowingly cause to be made to any member of the body comprising the agency, administrative law judge, or other employee who is or may reasonably be expected to be involved in the decisional process of the proceeding, an ex parte communication relevant to the merits of the proceeding;

(B) no member of the body comprising the agency, administrative law judge, or other employee who is or may reasonably be expected to be involved in the decisional process of the proceeding, shall make or knowingly cause to be made to any interested person outside the agency an ex parte communication relevant to the merits of the proceeding;

(C) a member of the body comprising the agency, administrative law judge, or other employee who is or may reasonably be expected to be involved in the decisional process of such proceeding who receives, or who makes or knowingly causes to be made, a communication prohibited by this subsection shall place on the public record of the proceeding:

(i) all such written communications;

(ii) memoranda stating the substance of all such oral communications; and

(iii) all written responses, and memoranda stating the substance of all oral responses, to the materials described in clauses (i) and (ii) of this subparagraph;

(D) upon receipt of a communication knowingly made or knowingly caused to be made by a party in violation of this subsection, the agency, administrative law judge, or other employee presiding at the hearing may, to the extent consistent with the interests of justice and the policy of the underlying statutes, require the party to show cause why his claim or interest in the proceeding should not be dismissed, denied, disregarded, or otherwise adversely affected on account of such violation; and

(E) the prohibitions of this subsection shall apply beginning at such time as the agency may designate, but in no case shall they begin to apply later than the time at which a proceeding is noticed for hearing unless the person responsible for the communication has knowledge that it will be noticed, in which case the prohibitions shall apply beginning at the time of his acquisition of such knowledge.

(2) This subsection does not constitute authority to withhold information from Congress.

(Pub. L. 89–554, Sept. 6, 1966, 80 Stat. 387; Pub. L. 94–409, § 4(a), Sept. 13, 1976, 90 Stat. 1246.)

HISTORICAL AND REVISION NOTES

Derivation	U.S. Code	Revised Statutes and Statutes at Large
....	5 U.S.C. 1007.	June 11, 1946, ch. 324, § 8, 60 Stat. 242.

In subsection (b), the word "employee" is substituted for "officer" and "officers" in view of the definition of "employee" in section 2105. The word "either" is added after the word "requires" in the first sentence to eliminate the need for parentheses. The words "the presiding employee or an employee qualified to preside at hearings under section 556 of this title" are substituted for "such officers" in the last sentence. The word "initial" is omitted before "decision", the final word in the first sentence and the sixth word of the fourth sentence, to avoid confusion between the "initial decision" of the presiding employee and the "initial decision" of the agency.

In subsection (c), the word "employees" is substituted for "officers" in view of the definition of "employee" in section 2105.

Standard changes are made to conform with the definitions applicable and the style of this title as outlined in the preface to the report.

CODIFICATION

Section 557 of former Title 5, Executive Departments and Government Officers and Employees, was transferred to section 2207 of Title 7, Agriculture.

Section 557a of former Title 5, Executive Departments and Government Officers and Employees, was transferred to section 2208 of Title 7.

AMENDMENTS

1976—Subsec. (d). Pub. L. 94–409 added subsec. (d).

EFFECTIVE DATE OF 1976 AMENDMENT

Amendment by Pub. L. 94–409 effective 180 days after Sept. 13, 1976, see section 6 of Pub. L. 94–409, set out as an Effective Date note under section 552b of this title.

SECTION REFERRED TO IN OTHER SECTIONS

This section is referred to in sections 553, 554, 556, 558, 706, 3105 of this title; title 2 sections 501, 502, 1405; title 7 sections 86, 87e, 87f–1, 2023, 2707, 4604, 4906, 6802, 6804, 7804; title 8 section 1375; title 15 sections 57a, 2605, 3412; title 16 sections 796, 839f, 2602, 3636; title 20 section 1234; title 21 section 321; title 30 sections 185, 811, 823, 1415; title 39 sections 404, 3624, 3661; title 41 section 422; title 42 sections 1320a–7c, 1395ww, 1485, 2000e–16c, 2241, 7407, 7502, 7511a, 7607, 11504; title 46 sections 7702, 9303; title 49 sections 31136, 31317; title 50 App. sections 16, 2159, 2410, 2412.

§ 558. Imposition of sanctions; determination of applications for licenses; suspension, revocation, and expiration of licenses

(a) This section applies, according to the provisions thereof, to the exercise of a power or authority.

(b) A sanction may not be imposed or a substantive rule or order issued except within jurisdiction delegated to the agency and as authorized by law.

(c) When application is made for a license required by law, the agency, with due regard for the rights and privileges of all the interested parties or adversely affected persons and within a reasonable time, shall set and complete proceedings required to be conducted in accordance with sections 556 and 557 of this title or other proceedings required by law and shall make its decision. Except in cases of willfulness or those in which public health, interest, or safety requires otherwise, the withdrawal, suspension, revocation, or annulment of a license is lawful only if, before the institution of agency proceedings therefor, the licensee has been given—

(1) notice by the agency in writing of the facts or conduct which may warrant the action; and

(2) opportunity to demonstrate or achieve compliance with all lawful requirements.

When the licensee has made timely and sufficient application for a renewal or a new license in accordance with agency rules, a license with reference to an activity of a continuing nature does not expire until the application has been finally determined by the agency.

(Pub. L. 89–554, Sept. 6, 1966, 80 Stat. 388.)

HISTORICAL AND REVISION NOTES

Derivation	U.S. Code	Revised Statutes and Statutes at Large
....	5 U.S.C. 1008.	June 11, 1946, ch. 324, § 9, 60 Stat. 242.

In subsection (b), the prohibition is restated in positive form.

In subsection (c), the words "within a reasonable time" are substituted for "with reasonable dispatch". The last two sentences are restated for conciseness and clarity and to restate the prohibition in positive form.

Standard changes are made to conform with the definitions applicable and the style of this title as outlined in the preface to the report.

CODIFICATION

Section 558 of former Title 5, Executive Departments and Government Officers and Employees, was transferred to section 2209 of Title 7, Agriculture.

SECTION REFERRED TO IN OTHER SECTIONS

This section is referred to in title 2 sections 501, 502; title 16 section 1824; title 30 section 185; title 41 section 422; title 42 sections 2236, 7651g; title 45 section 312; title 46 sections 7702, 9303; title 50 App. sections 2159, 2412.

§ 559. Effect on other laws; effect of subsequent statute

This subchapter, chapter 7, and sections 1305, 3105, 3344, 4301(2)(E), 5372, and 7521 of this title, and the provisions of section 5335(a)(B) of this title that relate to administrative law judges, do not limit or repeal additional requirements imposed by statute or otherwise recognized by law. Except as otherwise required by law, requirements or privileges relating to evidence or procedure apply equally to agencies and persons. Each agency is granted the authority necessary to comply with the requirements of this subchapter through the issuance of rules or otherwise. Subsequent statute may not be held to supersede or modify this subchapter, chapter 7, sections 1305, 3105, 3344, 4301(2)(E), 5372, or 7521 of this title, or the provisions of section 5335(a)(B) of this title that relate to administrative law judges, except to the extent that it does so expressly.

(Pub. L. 89–554, Sept. 6, 1966, 80 Stat. 388; Pub. L. 90–623, §1(1), Oct. 22, 1968, 82 Stat. 1312; Pub. L. 95–251, §2(a)(1), Mar. 27, 1978, 92 Stat. 183; Pub. L. 95–454, title VIII, §801(a)(3)(B)(iii), Oct. 13, 1978, 92 Stat. 1221.)

HISTORICAL AND REVISION NOTES

Derivation	U.S. Code	Revised Statutes and Statutes at Large
....	5 U.S.C. 1011.	June 11, 1946, ch. 324, §12, 60 Stat. 244.

In the first and last sentences, the words "This subchapter, chapter 7, and sections 1305, 3105, 3344, 4301(2)(E), 5362, and 7521, and the provisions of section 5335(a)(B) of this title that relate to hearing examiners" are substituted for "this Act" to reflect the codification of the Act in this title. The words "to diminish the constitutional rights of any person or" are omitted as surplusage as there is nothing in the Act that can reasonably be construed to diminish those rights and because a statute may not operate in derogation of the Constitution.

The third sentence of former section 1011 is omitted as covered by technical section 7. The sixth sentence of former section 1011 is omitted as executed.

Standard changes are made to conform with the definitions applicable and the style of this title as outlined in the preface to the report.

AMENDMENTS

1978—Pub. L. 95–454 substituted "5372" for "5362" wherever appearing.

Pub. L. 95–251 substituted "administrative law judges" for "hearing examiners" wherever appearing.

1968—Pub. L. 90–623 inserted "of this title" after "7521" wherever appearing.

EFFECTIVE DATE OF 1978 AMENDMENT

Amendment by Pub. L. 95–454 effective on first day of first applicable pay period beginning on or after the 90th day after Oct. 13, 1978, see section 801(a)(4) of Pub. L. 95–454, set out as an Effective Date note under section 5361 of this title.

EFFECTIVE DATE OF 1968 AMENDMENT

Amendment by Pub. L. 90–623 intended to restate without substantive change the law in effect on Oct. 22, 1968, see section 6 of Pub. L. 90–623, set out as a note under section 5334 of this title.

SECTION REFERRED TO IN OTHER SECTIONS

This section is referred to in title 2 sections 501, 502; title 15 section 1541; title 30 sections 185, 823, 956; title 41 section 422; title 46 sections 7702, 9303; title 50 App. sections 2159, 2412.

SUBCHAPTER III—NEGOTIATED RULEMAKING PROCEDURE

PRIOR PROVISIONS

A prior subchapter III (§571 et seq.) was redesignated subchapter V (§591 et seq.) of this chapter.

AMENDMENTS

1992—Pub. L. 102–354, §3(a)(1), Aug. 26, 1992, 106 Stat. 944, redesignated subchapter IV of this chapter relating to negotiated rulemaking procedure as this subchapter.

SUBCHAPTER REFERRED TO IN OTHER SECTIONS

This subchapter is referred to in title 20 sections 2326, 6511; title 23 section 202; title 25 sections 450k, 458gg, 458aaa–16, 4116; title 42 sections 1320d–1, 1395w–26, 1437g, 1485.

§ 561. Purpose

The purpose of this subchapter is to establish a framework for the conduct of negotiated rulemaking, consistent with section 553 of this title, to encourage agencies to use the process when it enhances the informal rulemaking process. Nothing in this subchapter should be construed as an attempt to limit innovation and experimentation with the negotiated rulemaking process or with other innovative rulemaking procedures otherwise authorized by law.

(Added Pub. L. 101–648, §3(a), Nov. 29, 1990, 104 Stat. 4970, §581; renumbered §561, Pub. L. 102–354, §3(a)(2), Aug. 26, 1992, 106 Stat. 944.)

AMENDMENTS

1992—Pub. L. 102–354 renumbered section 581 of this title as this section.

EFFECTIVE DATE OF REPEAL; SAVINGS PROVISION

Section 5 of Pub. L. 101–648, as amended by Pub. L. 102–354, §5(a)(2), Aug. 26, 1992, 106 Stat. 945, which provided that subchapter III of chapter 5 of title 5 and the table of sections corresponding to such subchapter, were repealed, effective 6 years after Nov. 29, 1990, except for then pending proceedings, was repealed by Pub. L. 104–320, §11(a), Oct. 19, 1996, 110 Stat. 3873.

SHORT TITLE OF 1992 AMENDMENT

Section 1 of Pub. L. 102–354 provided that: "This Act [amending sections 565, 568, 569, 571, 577, 580, 581, and 593 of this title, section 10 of Title 9, Arbitration, and section 173 of Title 29, Labor, renumbering sections 571 to 576, 581 to 590, and 581 to 593 as 591 to 596, 561 to 570, and 571 to 583, respectively, of this title, and amending provisions set out as notes under this section and section 571 of this title] may be cited as the 'Administrative Procedure Technical Amendments Act of 1991'."

SHORT TITLE

Section 1 of Pub. L. 101–648 provided that: "This Act [enacting this subchapter] may be cited as the 'Negotiated Rulemaking Act of 1990'."

CONGRESSIONAL FINDINGS

Section 2 of Pub. L. 101–648 provided that: "The Congress makes the following findings:

"(1) Government regulation has increased substantially since the enactment of the Administrative Procedure Act [see Short Title note set out preceding section 551 of this title].

"(2) Agencies currently use rulemaking procedures that may discourage the affected parties from meeting and communicating with each other, and may cause parties with different interests to assume conflicting and antagonistic positions and to engage in expensive and time-consuming litigation over agency rules.

"(3) Adversarial rulemaking deprives the affected parties and the public of the benefits of face-to-face negotiations and cooperation in developing and reaching agreement on a rule. It also deprives them of the benefits of shared information, knowledge, expertise, and technical abilities possessed by the affected parties.

"(4) Negotiated rulemaking, in which the parties who will be significantly affected by a rule participate in the development of the rule, can provide significant advantages over adversarial rulemaking.

"(5) Negotiated rulemaking can increase the acceptability and improve the substance of rules, making it less likely that the affected parties will resist enforcement or challenge such rules in court. It may also shorten the amount of time needed to issue final rules.

"(6) Agencies have the authority to establish negotiated rulemaking committees under the laws establishing such agencies and their activities and under the Federal Advisory Committee Act (5 U.S.C. App.). Several agencies have successfully used negotiated rulemaking. The process has not been widely used by other agencies, however, in part because such agencies are unfamiliar with the process or uncertain as to the authority for such rulemaking."

AUTHORIZATION OF APPROPRIATIONS

Section 4 of Pub. L. 101–648, as amended by Pub. L. 102–354, §5(a)(1), Aug. 26, 1992, 106 Stat. 945, authorized additional appropriations to Administrative Conference of the United States to carry out Pub. L. 101–648 in fiscal years 1991, 1992, and 1993.

§ 562. Definitions

For the purposes of this subchapter, the term—

(1) "agency" has the same meaning as in section 551(1) of this title;

(2) "consensus" means unanimous concurrence among the interests represented on a negotiated rulemaking committee established under this subchapter, unless such committee—

(A) agrees to define such term to mean a general but not unanimous concurrence; or

(B) agrees upon another specified definition;

(3) "convener" means a person who impartially assists an agency in determining whether establishment of a negotiated rulemaking committee is feasible and appropriate in a particular rulemaking;

(4) "facilitator" means a person who impartially aids in the discussions and negotiations among the members of a negotiated rulemaking committee to develop a proposed rule;

(5) "interest" means, with respect to an issue or matter, multiple parties which have a similar point of view or which are likely to be affected in a similar manner;

(6) "negotiated rulemaking" means rulemaking through the use of a negotiated rulemaking committee;

(7) "negotiated rulemaking committee" or "committee" means an advisory committee established by an agency in accordance with this subchapter and the Federal Advisory Committee Act to consider and discuss issues for the purpose of reaching a consensus in the development of a proposed rule;

(8) "party" has the same meaning as in section 551(3) of this title;

(9) "person" has the same meaning as in section 551(2) of this title;

(10) "rule" has the same meaning as in section 551(4) of this title; and

(11) "rulemaking" means "rule making" as that term is defined in section 551(5) of this title.

(Added Pub. L. 101–648, §3(a), Nov. 29, 1990, 104 Stat. 4970, §582; renumbered §562, Pub. L. 102–354, §3(a)(2), Aug. 26, 1992, 106 Stat. 944.)

REFERENCES IN TEXT

The Federal Advisory Committee Act, referred to in par. (7), is Pub. L. 92–463, Oct. 6, 1972, 86 Stat. 770, as amended, which is set out in the Appendix to this title.

AMENDMENTS

1992—Pub. L. 102–354 renumbered section 582 of this title as this section.

§ 563. Determination of need for negotiated rulemaking committee

(a) DETERMINATION OF NEED BY THE AGENCY.— An agency may establish a negotiated rulemaking committee to negotiate and develop a proposed rule, if the head of the agency determines that the use of the negotiated rulemaking procedure is in the public interest. In making such a determination, the head of the agency shall consider whether—

(1) there is a need for a rule;

(2) there are a limited number of identifiable interests that will be significantly affected by the rule;

(3) there is a reasonable likelihood that a committee can be convened with a balanced representation of persons who—

(A) can adequately represent the interests identified under paragraph (2); and

(B) are willing to negotiate in good faith to reach a consensus on the proposed rule;

(4) there is a reasonable likelihood that a committee will reach a consensus on the proposed rule within a fixed period of time;

(5) the negotiated rulemaking procedure will not unreasonably delay the notice of proposed rulemaking and the issuance of the final rule;

(6) the agency has adequate resources and is willing to commit such resources, including technical assistance, to the committee; and

(7) the agency, to the maximum extent possible consistent with the legal obligations of the agency, will use the consensus of the committee with respect to the proposed rule as the basis for the rule proposed by the agency for notice and comment.

(b) USE OF CONVENERS.—

(1) PURPOSES OF CONVENERS.—An agency may use the services of a convener to assist the agency in—

(A) identifying persons who will be significantly affected by a proposed rule, including residents of rural areas; and

(B) conducting discussions with such persons, and to ascertain whether the establishment of a negotiated rulemaking committee is feasible and appropriate in the particular rulemaking.

(2) DUTIES OF CONVENERS.—The convener shall report findings and may make recommendations to the agency. Upon request of the agency, the convener shall ascertain the names of persons who are willing and qualified to represent interests that will be significantly affected by the proposed rule, including residents of rural areas. The report and any

recommendations of the convener shall be made available to the public upon request.

(Added Pub. L. 101–648, §3(a), Nov. 29, 1990, 104 Stat. 4970, §583; renumbered §563, Pub. L. 102–354, §3(a)(2), Aug. 26, 1992, 106 Stat. 944.)

AMENDMENTS

1992—Pub. L. 102–354 renumbered section 583 of this title as this section.

NEGOTIATED RULEMAKING COMMITTEES

Pub. L. 104–320, §11(e), Oct. 19, 1996, 110 Stat. 3874, provided that: "The Director of the Office of Management and Budget shall—

"(1) within 180 days of the date of the enactment of this Act [Oct. 19, 1996], take appropriate action to expedite the establishment of negotiated rulemaking committees and committees established to resolve disputes under the Administrative Dispute Resolution Act [Pub. L. 101–552, see Short Title note set out under section 571 of this title], including, with respect to negotiated rulemaking committees, eliminating any redundant administrative requirements related to filing a committee charter under section 9 of the Federal Advisory Committee Act (5 U.S.C. App.) and providing public notice of such committee under section 564 of title 5, United States Code; and

"(2) within one year of the date of the enactment of this Act, submit recommendations to Congress for any necessary legislative changes."

SECTION REFERRED TO IN OTHER SECTIONS

This section is referred to in title 23 section 202; title 25 section 4116.

§ 564. Publication of notice; applications for membership on committees

(a) PUBLICATION OF NOTICE.—If, after considering the report of a convener or conducting its own assessment, an agency decides to establish a negotiated rulemaking committee, the agency shall publish in the Federal Register and, as appropriate, in trade or other specialized publications, a notice which shall include—

(1) an announcement that the agency intends to establish a negotiated rulemaking committee to negotiate and develop a proposed rule;

(2) a description of the subject and scope of the rule to be developed, and the issues to be considered;

(3) a list of the interests which are likely to be significantly affected by the rule;

(4) a list of the persons proposed to represent such interests and the person or persons proposed to represent the agency;

(5) a proposed agenda and schedule for completing the work of the committee, including a target date for publication by the agency of a proposed rule for notice and comment;

(6) a description of administrative support for the committee to be provided by the agency, including technical assistance;

(7) a solicitation for comments on the proposal to establish the committee, and the proposed membership of the negotiated rulemaking committee; and

(8) an explanation of how a person may apply or nominate another person for membership on the committee, as provided under subsection (b).

(b) APPLICATIONS FOR MEMBERSHIP OR[1] COMMITTEE.—Persons who will be significantly affected by a proposed rule and who believe that their interests will not be adequately represented by any person specified in a notice under subsection (a)(4) may apply for, or nominate another person for, membership on the negotiated rulemaking committee to represent such interests with respect to the proposed rule. Each application or nomination shall include—

(1) the name of the applicant or nominee and a description of the interests such person shall represent;

(2) evidence that the applicant or nominee is authorized to represent parties related to the interests the person proposes to represent;

(3) a written commitment that the applicant or nominee shall actively participate in good faith in the development of the rule under consideration; and

(4) the reasons that the persons specified in the notice under subsection (a)(4) do not adequately represent the interests of the person submitting the application or nomination.

(c) PERIOD FOR SUBMISSION OF COMMENTS AND APPLICATIONS.—The agency shall provide for a period of at least 30 calendar days for the submission of comments and applications under this section.

(Added Pub. L. 101–648, §3(a), Nov. 29, 1990, 104 Stat. 4971, §584; renumbered §564, Pub. L. 102–354, §3(a)(2), Aug. 26, 1992, 106 Stat. 944.)

AMENDMENTS

1992—Pub. L. 102–354 renumbered section 584 of this title as this section.

SECTION REFERRED TO IN OTHER SECTIONS

This section is referred to in section 565 of this title; title 25 section 4116; title 42 section 1395w–26.

§ 565. Establishment of committee

(a) ESTABLISHMENT.—

(1) DETERMINATION TO ESTABLISH COMMITTEE.—If after considering comments and applications submitted under section 564, the agency determines that a negotiated rulemaking committee can adequately represent the interests that will be significantly affected by a proposed rule and that it is feasible and appropriate in the particular rulemaking, the agency may establish a negotiated rulemaking committee. In establishing and administering such a committee, the agency shall comply with the Federal Advisory Committee Act with respect to such committee, except as otherwise provided in this subchapter.

(2) DETERMINATION NOT TO ESTABLISH COMMITTEE.—If after considering such comments and applications, the agency decides not to establish a negotiated rulemaking committee, the agency shall promptly publish notice of such decision and the reasons therefor in the Federal Register and, as appropriate, in trade or other specialized publications, a copy of which shall be sent to any person who applied for, or nominated another person for membership on the negotiating[1] rulemaking committee to represent such interests with respect to the proposed rule.

(b) MEMBERSHIP.—The agency shall limit membership on a negotiated rulemaking com-

---

[1] So in original. Probably should be "on".

[1] So in original. Probably should be "negotiated".

mittee to 25 members, unless the agency head determines that a greater number of members is necessary for the functioning of the committee or to achieve balanced membership. Each committee shall include at least one person representing the agency.

(c) ADMINISTRATIVE SUPPORT.—The agency shall provide appropriate administrative support to the negotiated rulemaking committee, including technical assistance.

(Added Pub. L. 101–648, § 3(a), Nov. 29, 1990, 104 Stat. 4972, § 585; renumbered § 565 and amended Pub. L. 102–354, § 3(a)(2), (3), Aug. 26, 1992, 106 Stat. 944.)

REFERENCES IN TEXT

The Federal Advisory Committee Act, referred to in subsec. (a)(1), is Pub. L. 92–463, Oct. 6, 1972, 86 Stat. 770, as amended, which is set out in the Appendix to this title.

AMENDMENTS

1992—Pub. L. 102–354, § 3(a)(2), renumbered section 585 of this title as this section.

Subsec. (a)(1). Pub. L. 102–354, § 3(a)(3), substituted "section 564" for "section 584".

SECTION REFERRED TO IN OTHER SECTIONS

This section is referred to in title 23 section 202; title 25 sections 458gg, 458aaa–16, 4116; title 42 section 1395w–26.

§ 566. Conduct of committee activity

(a) DUTIES OF COMMITTEE.—Each negotiated rulemaking committee established under this subchapter shall consider the matter proposed by the agency for consideration and shall attempt to reach a consensus concerning a proposed rule with respect to such matter and any other matter the committee determines is relevant to the proposed rule.

(b) REPRESENTATIVES OF AGENCY ON COMMITTEE.—The person or persons representing the agency on a negotiated rulemaking committee shall participate in the deliberations and activities of the committee with the same rights and responsibilities as other members of the committee, and shall be authorized to fully represent the agency in the discussions and negotiations of the committee.

(c) SELECTING FACILITATOR.—Notwithstanding section 10(e) of the Federal Advisory Committee Act, an agency may nominate either a person from the Federal Government or a person from outside the Federal Government to serve as a facilitator for the negotiations of the committee, subject to the approval of the committee by consensus. If the committee does not approve the nominee of the agency for facilitator, the agency shall submit a substitute nomination. If a committee does not approve any nominee of the agency for facilitator, the committee shall select by consensus a person to serve as facilitator. A person designated to represent the agency in substantive issues may not serve as facilitator or otherwise chair the committee.

(d) DUTIES OF FACILITATOR.—A facilitator approved or selected by a negotiated rulemaking committee shall—

(1) chair the meetings of the committee in an impartial manner;

(2) impartially assist the members of the committee in conducting discussions and negotiations; and

(3) manage the keeping of minutes and records as required under section 10(b) and (c) of the Federal Advisory Committee Act, except that any personal notes and materials of the facilitator or of the members of a committee shall not be subject to section 552 of this title.

(e) COMMITTEE PROCEDURES.—A negotiated rulemaking committee established under this subchapter may adopt procedures for the operation of the committee. No provision of section 553 of this title shall apply to the procedures of a negotiated rulemaking committee.

(f) REPORT OF COMMITTEE.—If a committee reaches a consensus on a proposed rule, at the conclusion of negotiations the committee shall transmit to the agency that established the committee a report containing the proposed rule. If the committee does not reach a consensus on a proposed rule, the committee may transmit to the agency a report specifying any areas in which the committee reached a consensus. The committee may include in a report any other information, recommendations, or materials that the committee considers appropriate. Any committee member may include as an addendum to the report additional information, recommendations, or materials.

(g) RECORDS OF COMMITTEE.—In addition to the report required by subsection (f), a committee shall submit to the agency the records required under section 10(b) and (c) of the Federal Advisory Committee Act.

(Added Pub. L. 101–648, § 3(a), Nov. 29, 1990, 104 Stat. 4973, § 586; renumbered § 566, Pub. L. 102–354, § 3(a)(2), Aug. 26, 1992, 106 Stat. 944.)

REFERENCES IN TEXT

Section 10 of the Federal Advisory Committee Act, referred to in subsecs. (c), (d)(3), and (g), is section 10 of Pub. L. 92–463, which is set out in the Appendix to this title.

AMENDMENTS

1992—Pub. L. 102–354 renumbered section 586 of this title as this section.

SECTION REFERRED TO IN OTHER SECTIONS

This section is referred to in title 42 section 1395w–26.

§ 567. Termination of committee

A negotiated rulemaking committee shall terminate upon promulgation of the final rule under consideration, unless the committee's charter contains an earlier termination date or the agency, after consulting the committee, or the committee itself specifies an earlier termination date.

(Added Pub. L. 101–648, § 3(a), Nov. 29, 1990, 104 Stat. 4974, § 587; renumbered § 567, Pub. L. 102–354, § 3(a)(2), Aug. 26, 1992, 106 Stat. 944.)

AMENDMENTS

1992—Pub. L. 102–354 renumbered section 587 of this title as this section.

§ 568. Services, facilities, and payment of committee member expenses

(a) SERVICES OF CONVENERS AND FACILITATORS.—

(1) IN GENERAL.—An agency may employ or enter into contracts for the services of an individual or organization to serve as a convener or facilitator for a negotiated rulemaking committee under this subchapter, or may use the services of a Government employee to act as a convener or a facilitator for such a committee.

(2) DETERMINATION OF CONFLICTING INTERESTS.—An agency shall determine whether a person under consideration to serve as convener or facilitator of a committee under paragraph (1) has any financial or other interest that would preclude such person from serving in an impartial and independent manner.

(b) SERVICES AND FACILITIES OF OTHER ENTITIES.—For purposes of this subchapter, an agency may use the services and facilities of other Federal agencies and public and private agencies and instrumentalities with the consent of such agencies and instrumentalities, and with or without reimbursement to such agencies and instrumentalities, and may accept voluntary and uncompensated services without regard to the provisions of section 1342 of title 31. The Federal Mediation and Conciliation Service may provide services and facilities, with or without reimbursement, to assist agencies under this subchapter, including furnishing conveners, facilitators, and training in negotiated rulemaking.

(c) EXPENSES OF COMMITTEE MEMBERS.—Members of a negotiated rulemaking committee shall be responsible for their own expenses of participation in such committee, except that an agency may, in accordance with section 7(d) of the Federal Advisory Committee Act, pay for a member's reasonable travel and per diem expenses, expenses to obtain technical assistance, and a reasonable rate of compensation, if—

(1) such member certifies a lack of adequate financial resources to participate in the committee; and

(2) the agency determines that such member's participation in the committee is necessary to assure an adequate representation of the member's interest.

(d) STATUS OF MEMBER AS FEDERAL EMPLOYEE.—A member's receipt of funds under this section or section 569 shall not conclusively determine for purposes of sections 202 through 209 of title 18 whether that member is an employee of the United States Government.

(Added Pub. L. 101–648, § 3(a), Nov. 29, 1990, 104 Stat. 4974, § 588; renumbered § 568 and amended Pub. L. 102–354, § 3(a)(2), (4), Aug. 26, 1992, 106 Stat. 944.)

REFERENCES IN TEXT

Section 7(d) of the Federal Advisory Committee Act, referred to in subsec. (c), is section 7(d) of Pub. L. 92–463, which is set out in the Appendix to this title.

AMENDMENTS

1992—Pub. L. 102–354, § 3(a)(2), renumbered section 588 of this title as this section.

Subsec. (d). Pub. L. 102–354, § 3(a)(4), substituted "section 569" for "section 589".

§ 569. Encouraging negotiated rulemaking

(a) The President shall designate an agency or designate or establish an interagency committee to facilitate and encourage agency use of negotiated rulemaking. An agency that is considering, planning, or conducting a negotiated rulemaking may consult with such agency or committee for information and assistance.

(b) To carry out the purposes of this subchapter, an agency planning or conducting a negotiated rulemaking may accept, hold, administer, and utilize gifts, devises, and bequests of property, both real and personal if that agency's acceptance and use of such gifts, devises, or bequests do not create a conflict of interest. Gifts and bequests of money and proceeds from sales of other property received as gifts, devises, or bequests shall be deposited in the Treasury and shall be disbursed upon the order of the head of such agency. Property accepted pursuant to this section, and the proceeds thereof, shall be used as nearly as possible in accordance with the terms of the gifts, devises, or bequests.

(Added Pub. L. 101–648, § 3(a), Nov. 29, 1990, 104 Stat. 4975, § 589; renumbered § 569 and amended Pub. L. 102–354, § 3(a)(2), (5), Aug. 26, 1992, 106 Stat. 944; Pub. L. 104–320, § 11(b)(1), Oct. 19, 1996, 110 Stat. 3873.)

AMENDMENTS

1996—Pub. L. 104–320 in section catchline substituted "Encouraging negotiated rulemaking" for "Role of the Administrative Conference of the United States and other entities", and in text added subsecs. (a) and (b) and struck out former subsecs. (a) to (g) which related to: in subsec. (a), consultation by agencies; in subsec. (b), roster of potential conveners and facilitators; in subsec. (c), procedures to obtain conveners and facilitators; in subsec. (d), compilation of data on negotiated rulemaking and report to Congress; in subsec. (e), training in negotiated rulemaking; in subsec. (f), payment of expenses of agencies; and in subsec. (g), use of funds of the conference.

1992—Pub. L. 102–354, § 3(a)(2), renumbered section 589 of this title as this section.

Subsec. (d)(2). Pub. L. 102–354, § 3(a)(5)(A), substituted "section 566" for "section 586".

Subsec. (f)(2). Pub. L. 102–354, § 3(a)(5)(B), substituted "section 568(c)" for "section 588(c)".

Subsec. (g). Pub. L. 102–354, § 3(a)(5)(C), substituted "section 595(c)(12)" for "section 575(c)(12)".

SECTION REFERRED TO IN OTHER SECTIONS

This section is referred to in section 568 of this title.

§ 570. Judicial review

Any agency action relating to establishing, assisting, or terminating a negotiated rulemaking committee under this subchapter shall not be subject to judicial review. Nothing in this section shall bar judicial review of a rule if such judicial review is otherwise provided by law. A rule which is the product of negotiated rulemaking and is subject to judicial review shall not be accorded any greater deference by a court than a rule which is the product of other rulemaking procedures.

(Added Pub. L. 101–648, § 3(a), Nov. 29, 1990, 104 Stat. 4976, § 590; renumbered § 570, Pub. L. 102–354, § 3(a)(2), Aug. 26, 1992, 106 Stat. 944.)

AMENDMENTS

1992—Pub. L. 102–354 renumbered section 590 of this title as this section.

§ 570a. Authorization of appropriations

There are authorized to be appropriated such sums as may be necessary to carry out the purposes of this subchapter.

(Added Pub. L. 104–320, §11(d)(1), Oct. 19, 1996, 110 Stat. 3873.)

SUBCHAPTER IV—ALTERNATIVE MEANS OF DISPUTE RESOLUTION IN THE ADMINISTRATIVE PROCESS

CODIFICATION

Another subchapter IV (§ 581 et seq.) relating to negotiated rulemaking procedure was redesignated subchapter III (§ 561 et seq.) of this chapter.

AMENDMENTS

1992—Pub. L. 102–354, §3(b)(1), Aug. 26, 1992, 106 Stat. 944, transferred this subchapter so as to appear immediately after subchapter III of this chapter.

SUBCHAPTER REFERRED TO IN OTHER SECTIONS

This subchapter is referred to in section 556 of this title; title 12 section 4806; title 25 sections 450j, 450l; title 28 section 2672; title 29 section 173; title 41 section 605.

§ 571. Definitions

For the purposes of this subchapter, the term—

(1) "agency" has the same meaning as in section 551(1) of this title;

(2) "administrative program" includes a Federal function which involves protection of the public interest and the determination of rights, privileges, and obligations of private persons through rule making, adjudication, licensing, or investigation, as those terms are used in subchapter II of this chapter;

(3) "alternative means of dispute resolution" means any procedure that is used to resolve issues in controversy, including, but not limited to, conciliation, facilitation, mediation, fact-finding, minitrials, arbitration, and use of ombuds, or any combination thereof;

(4) "award" means any decision by an arbitrator resolving the issues in controversy;

(5) "dispute resolution communication" means any oral or written communication prepared for the purposes of a dispute resolution proceeding, including any memoranda, notes or work product of the neutral, parties or non-party participant; except that a written agreement to enter into a dispute resolution proceeding, or final written agreement or arbitral award reached as a result of a dispute resolution proceeding, is not a dispute resolution communication;

(6) "dispute resolution proceeding" means any process in which an alternative means of dispute resolution is used to resolve an issue in controversy in which a neutral is appointed and specified parties participate;

(7) "in confidence" means, with respect to information, that the information is provided—

(A) with the expressed intent of the source that it not be disclosed; or

(B) under circumstances that would create the reasonable expectation on behalf of the source that the information will not be disclosed;

(8) "issue in controversy" means an issue which is material to a decision concerning an administrative program of an agency, and with which there is disagreement—

(A) between an agency and persons who would be substantially affected by the decision; or

(B) between persons who would be substantially affected by the decision;

(9) "neutral" means an individual who, with respect to an issue in controversy, functions specifically to aid the parties in resolving the controversy;

(10) "party" means—

(A) for a proceeding with named parties, the same as in section 551(3) of this title; and

(B) for a proceeding without named parties, a person who will be significantly affected by the decision in the proceeding and who participates in the proceeding;

(11) "person" has the same meaning as in section 551(2) of this title; and

(12) "roster" means a list of persons qualified to provide services as neutrals.

(Added Pub. L. 101–552, §4(b), Nov. 15, 1990, 104 Stat. 2738, §581; renumbered §571 and amended Pub. L. 102–354, §§3(b)(2), 5(b)(1), (2), Aug. 26, 1992, 106 Stat. 944, 946; Pub. L. 104–320, §2, Oct. 19, 1996, 110 Stat. 3870.)

CODIFICATION

Section 571 of former Title 5, Executive Departments and Government Officers and Employees, was transferred to section 2256 of Title 7, Agriculture.

PRIOR PROVISIONS

A prior section 571 was renumbered section 591 of this title.

AMENDMENTS

1996—Par. (3). Pub. L. 104–320, §2(1), struck out ", in lieu of an adjudication as defined in section 551(7) of this title," after "any procedure that is used", struck out "settlement negotiations," after "but not limited to," and substituted "arbitration, and use of ombuds" for "and arbitration".

Par. (8). Pub. L. 104–320, §2(2), substituted "decision;" for "decision," at end of subpar. (B), and struck out closing provisions which read as follows: "except that such term shall not include any matter specified under section 2302 or 7121(c) of this title;".

1992—Pub. L. 102–354, §3(b)(2), renumbered section 581 of this title as this section.

Par. (3). Pub. L. 102–354, §5(b)(1), inserted comma after "including".

Par. (8). Pub. L. 102–354, §5(b)(2), amended par. (8) generally. Prior to amendment, par. (8) read as follows: "'issue in controversy' means an issue which is material to a decision concerning an administrative program of an agency, and with which there is disagreement between the agency and persons who would be substantially affected by the decision but shall not extend to matters specified under the provisions of sections 2302 and 7121(c) of title 5;".

TERMINATION DATE; SAVINGS PROVISION

Section 11 of Pub. L. 101–552, as amended by Pub. L. 104–106, div. D, title XLIII, §4321(i)(5), Feb. 10, 1996, 110 Stat. 676, which provided that the authority of agencies to use dispute resolution proceedings under this Act [see Short Title note below] was to terminate on Oct. 1, 1995, except with respect to pending proceedings, was repealed by Pub. L. 104–320, §9, Oct. 19, 1996, 110 Stat. 3872.

SHORT TITLE OF 1996 AMENDMENT

Section 1 of Pub. L. 104–320 provided that: "This Act [enacting sections 570a and 584 of this title, amending this section, sections 569, 573 to 575, 580, 581, and 583 of this title, section 2304 of Title 10, Armed Forces, section 1491 of Title 28, Crimes and Criminal Procedure, section 173 of Title 29, Labor, section 3556 of Title 31, Money and Finance, and sections 253 and 605 of Title 41, Public Contracts, repealing section 582 of this title, enacting provisions set out as notes under section 563 of this title, section 1491 of Title 28, and section 3556 of Title 31, amending provisions set out as notes under this section, and repealing provisions set out as notes under this section and section 561 of this title] may be cited as the 'Administrative Dispute Resolution Act of 1996'."

SHORT TITLE

Section 1 of Pub. L. 101–552 provided that: "This Act [enacting this subchapter, amending section 556 of this title, section 10 of Title 9, Arbitration, section 2672 of Title 28, Judiciary and Judicial Procedure, section 173 of Title 29, Labor, section 3711 of Title 31, Money and Finance, and sections 605 and 607 of Title 41, Public Contracts, and enacting provisions set out as notes under this section] may be cited as the 'Administrative Dispute Resolution Act'."

CONGRESSIONAL FINDINGS

Section 2 of Pub. L. 101–552 provided that: "The Congress finds that—

"(1) administrative procedure, as embodied in chapter 5 of title 5, United States Code, and other statutes, is intended to offer a prompt, expert, and inexpensive means of resolving disputes as an alternative to litigation in the Federal courts;

"(2) administrative proceedings have become increasingly formal, costly, and lengthy resulting in unnecessary expenditures of time and in a decreased likelihood of achieving consensual resolution of disputes;

"(3) alternative means of dispute resolution have been used in the private sector for many years and, in appropriate circumstances, have yielded decisions that are faster, less expensive, and less contentious;

"(4) such alternative means can lead to more creative, efficient, and sensible outcomes;

"(5) such alternative means may be used advantageously in a wide variety of administrative programs;

"(6) explicit authorization of the use of well-tested dispute resolution techniques will eliminate ambiguity of agency authority under existing law;

"(7) Federal agencies may not only receive the benefit of techniques that were developed in the private sector, but may also take the lead in the further development and refinement of such techniques; and

"(8) the availability of a wide range of dispute resolution procedures, and an increased understanding of the most effective use of such procedures, will enhance the operation of the Government and better serve the public."

PROMOTION OF ALTERNATIVE MEANS OF DISPUTE RESOLUTION

Section 3 of Pub. L. 101–552, as amended by Pub. L. 104–320, § 4(a), Oct. 19, 1996, 110 Stat. 3871, provided that:

"(a) PROMULGATION OF AGENCY POLICY.—Each agency shall adopt a policy that addresses the use of alternative means of dispute resolution and case management. In developing such a policy, each agency shall—

"(1) consult with the agency designated by, or the interagency committee designated or established by, the President under section 573 of title 5, United States Code, to facilitate and encourage agency use of alternative dispute resolution under subchapter IV of chapter 5 of such title; and

"(2) examine alternative means of resolving disputes in connection with—

"(A) formal and informal adjudications;

"(B) rulemakings;

"(C) enforcement actions;

"(D) issuing and revoking licenses or permits;

"(E) contract administration;

"(F) litigation brought by or against the agency; and

"(G) other agency actions.

"(b) DISPUTE RESOLUTION SPECIALISTS.—The head of each agency shall designate a senior official to be the dispute resolution specialist of the agency. Such official shall be responsible for the implementation of—

"(1) the provisions of this Act [see Short Title note above] and the amendments made by this Act; and

"(2) the agency policy developed under subsection (a).

"(c) TRAINING.—Each agency shall provide for training on a regular basis for the dispute resolution specialist of the agency and other employees involved in implementing the policy of the agency developed under subsection (a). Such training should encompass the theory and practice of negotiation, mediation, arbitration, or related techniques. The dispute resolution specialist shall periodically recommend to the agency head agency employees who would benefit from similar training.

"(d) PROCEDURES FOR GRANTS AND CONTRACTS.—

"(1) Each agency shall review each of its standard agreements for contracts, grants, and other assistance and shall determine whether to amend any such standard agreements to authorize and encourage the use of alternative means of dispute resolution.

"(2)(A) Within 1 year after the date of the enactment of this Act [Nov. 15, 1990], the Federal Acquisition Regulation shall be amended, as necessary, to carry out this Act [see Short Title note above] and the amendments made by this Act.

"(B) For purposes of this section, the term 'Federal Acquisition Regulation' means the single system of Government-wide procurement regulation referred to in section 6(a) of the Office of Federal Procurement Policy Act (41 U.S.C. 405(a))."

USE OF NONATTORNEYS

Section 9 of Pub. L. 101–552 provided that:

"(a) REPRESENTATION OF PARTIES.—Each agency, in developing a policy on the use of alternative means of dispute resolution under this Act [see Short Title note above], shall develop a policy with regard to the representation by persons other than attorneys of parties in alternative dispute resolution proceedings and shall identify any of its administrative programs with numerous claims or disputes before the agency and determine—

"(1) the extent to which individuals are represented or assisted by attorneys or by persons who are not attorneys; and

"(2) whether the subject areas of the applicable proceedings or the procedures are so complex or specialized that only attorneys may adequately provide such representation or assistance.

"(b) REPRESENTATION AND ASSISTANCE BY NONATTORNEYS.—A person who is not an attorney may provide representation or assistance to any individual in a claim or dispute with an agency, if—

"(1) such claim or dispute concerns an administrative program identified under subsection (a);

"(2) such agency determines that the proceeding or procedure does not necessitate representation or assistance by an attorney under subsection (a)(2); and

"(3) such person meets any requirement of the agency to provide representation or assistance in such a claim or dispute.

"(c) DISQUALIFICATION OF REPRESENTATION OR ASSISTANCE.—Any agency that adopts regulations under subchapter IV of chapter 5 of title 5, United States Code, to permit representation or assistance by persons who are not attorneys shall review the rules of practice before such agency to—

"(1) ensure that any rules pertaining to disqualification of attorneys from practicing before the agency shall also apply, as appropriate, to other persons who provide representation or assistance; and

"(2) establish effective agency procedures for enforcing such rules of practice and for receiving complaints from affected persons."

DEFINITIONS

Section 10 of Pub. L. 101–552, as amended by Pub. L. 102–354, § 5(b)(6), Aug. 26, 1992, 106 Stat. 946, provided that: "As used in this Act [see Short Title note above], the terms 'agency', 'administrative program', and 'alternative means of dispute resolution' have the meanings given such terms in section 571 of title 5, United States Code (enacted as section 581 of title 5, United States Code, by section 4(b) of this Act, and redesignated as section 571 of such title by section 3(b) of the Administrative Procedure Technical Amendments Act of 1991 [Pub. L. 102–354])."

SECTION REFERRED TO IN OTHER SECTIONS

This section is referred to in title 12 section 4806.

§ 572. General authority

(a) An agency may use a dispute resolution proceeding for the resolution of an issue in controversy that relates to an administrative program, if the parties agree to such proceeding.

(b) An agency shall consider not using a dispute resolution proceeding if—

(1) a definitive or authoritative resolution of the matter is required for precedential value, and such a proceeding is not likely to be accepted generally as an authoritative precedent;

(2) the matter involves or may bear upon significant questions of Government policy that require additional procedures before a final resolution may be made, and such a proceeding would not likely serve to develop a recommended policy for the agency;

(3) maintaining established policies is of special importance, so that variations among individual decisions are not increased and such a proceeding would not likely reach consistent results among individual decisions;

(4) the matter significantly affects persons or organizations who are not parties to the proceeding;

(5) a full public record of the proceeding is important, and a dispute resolution proceeding cannot provide such a record; and

(6) the agency must maintain continuing jurisdiction over the matter with authority to alter the disposition of the matter in the light of changed circumstances, and a dispute resolution proceeding would interfere with the agency's fulfilling that requirement.

(c) Alternative means of dispute resolution authorized under this subchapter are voluntary procedures which supplement rather than limit other available agency dispute resolution techniques.

(Added Pub. L. 101–552, § 4(b), Nov. 15, 1990, 104 Stat. 2739, § 582; renumbered § 572, Pub. L. 102–354, § 3(b)(2), Aug. 26, 1992, 106 Stat. 944.)

CODIFICATION

Section 572 of former Title 5, Executive Departments and Government Officers and Employees, was transferred to section 2257 of Title 7, Agriculture.

PRIOR PROVISIONS

A prior section 572 was renumbered section 592 of this title.

AMENDMENTS

1992—Pub. L. 102–354 renumbered section 582 of this title as this section.

SECTION REFERRED TO IN OTHER SECTIONS

This section is referred to in section 575 of this title; title 9 section 10; title 41 section 605.

§ 573. Neutrals

(a) A neutral may be a permanent or temporary officer or employee of the Federal Government or any other individual who is acceptable to the parties to a dispute resolution proceeding. A neutral shall have no official, financial, or personal conflict of interest with respect to the issues in controversy, unless such interest is fully disclosed in writing to all parties and all parties agree that the neutral may serve.

(b) A neutral who serves as a conciliator, facilitator, or mediator serves at the will of the parties.

(c) The President shall designate an agency or designate or establish an interagency committee to facilitate and encourage agency use of dispute resolution under this subchapter. Such agency or interagency committee, in consultation with other appropriate Federal agencies and professional organizations experienced in matters concerning dispute resolution, shall—

(1) encourage and facilitate agency use of alternative means of dispute resolution; and

(2) develop procedures that permit agencies to obtain the services of neutrals on an expedited basis.

(d) An agency may use the services of one or more employees of other agencies to serve as neutrals in dispute resolution proceedings. The agencies may enter into an interagency agreement that provides for the reimbursement by the user agency or the parties of the full or partial cost of the services of such an employee.

(e) Any agency may enter into a contract with any person for services as a neutral, or for training in connection with alternative means of dispute resolution. The parties in a dispute resolution proceeding shall agree on compensation for the neutral that is fair and reasonable to the Government.

(Added Pub. L. 101–552, § 4(b), Nov. 15, 1990, 104 Stat. 2739, § 583; renumbered § 573, Pub. L. 102–354, § 3(b)(2), Aug. 26, 1992, 106 Stat. 944; amended Pub. L. 104–320, § 7(b), Oct. 19, 1996, 110 Stat. 3872.)

CODIFICATION

Section 573 of former Title 5, Executive Departments and Government Officers and Employees, was transferred to section 2258 of Title 7, Agriculture.

PRIOR PROVISIONS

A prior section 573 was renumbered section 593 of this title.

AMENDMENTS

1996—Subsec. (c). Pub. L. 104–320, § 7(b)(1), added subsec. (c) and struck out former subsec. (c) which related to power of Administrative Conference of the United States to establish and utilize standards for neutrals and to enter into contracts for services of neutrals.

Subsec. (e). Pub. L. 104–320, § 7(b)(2), struck out "on a roster established under subsection (c)(2) or a roster maintained by other public or private organizations, or individual'' after ''contract with any person''.

1992—Pub. L. 102–354 renumbered section 583 of this title as this section.

SECTION REFERRED TO IN OTHER SECTIONS

This section is referred to in section 577 of this title; title 29 section 173.

§ 574. Confidentiality

(a) Except as provided in subsections (d) and (e), a neutral in a dispute resolution proceeding shall not voluntarily disclose or through discovery or compulsory process be required to disclose any dispute resolution communication or any communication provided in confidence to the neutral, unless—

(1) all parties to the dispute resolution proceeding and the neutral consent in writing, and, if the dispute resolution communication was provided by a nonparty participant, that participant also consents in writing;

(2) the dispute resolution communication has already been made public;

(3) the dispute resolution communication is required by statute to be made public, but a neutral should make such communication public only if no other person is reasonably available to disclose the communication; or

(4) a court determines that such testimony or disclosure is necessary to—

(A) prevent a manifest injustice;

(B) help establish a violation of law; or

(C) prevent harm to the public health or safety,

of sufficient magnitude in the particular case to outweigh the integrity of dispute resolution proceedings in general by reducing the confidence of parties in future cases that their communications will remain confidential.

(b) A party to a dispute resolution proceeding shall not voluntarily disclose or through discovery or compulsory process be required to disclose any dispute resolution communication, unless—

(1) the communication was prepared by the party seeking disclosure;

(2) all parties to the dispute resolution proceeding consent in writing;

(3) the dispute resolution communication has already been made public;

(4) the dispute resolution communication is required by statute to be made public;

(5) a court determines that such testimony or disclosure is necessary to—

(A) prevent a manifest injustice;

(B) help establish a violation of law; or

(C) prevent harm to the public health and safety,

of sufficient magnitude in the particular case to outweigh the integrity of dispute resolution proceedings in general by reducing the confidence of parties in future cases that their communications will remain confidential;

(6) the dispute resolution communication is relevant to determining the existence or meaning of an agreement or award that resulted from the dispute resolution proceeding or to the enforcement of such an agreement or award; or

(7) except for dispute resolution communications generated by the neutral, the dispute resolution communication was provided to or was available to all parties to the dispute resolution proceeding.

(c) Any dispute resolution communication that is disclosed in violation of subsection (a) or (b), shall not be admissible in any proceeding relating to the issues in controversy with respect to which the communication was made.

(d)(1) The parties may agree to alternative confidential procedures for disclosures by a neutral. Upon such agreement the parties shall inform the neutral before the commencement of the dispute resolution proceeding of any modifications to the provisions of subsection (a) that will govern the confidentiality of the dispute resolution proceeding. If the parties do not so inform the neutral, subsection (a) shall apply.

(2) To qualify for the exemption established under subsection (j), an alternative confidential procedure under this subsection may not provide for less disclosure than the confidential procedures otherwise provided under this section.

(e) If a demand for disclosure, by way of discovery request or other legal process, is made upon a neutral regarding a dispute resolution communication, the neutral shall make reasonable efforts to notify the parties and any affected nonparty participants of the demand. Any party or affected nonparty participant who receives such notice and within 15 calendar days does not offer to defend a refusal of the neutral to disclose the requested information shall have waived any objection to such disclosure.

(f) Nothing in this section shall prevent the discovery or admissibility of any evidence that is otherwise discoverable, merely because the evidence was presented in the course of a dispute resolution proceeding.

(g) Subsections (a) and (b) shall have no effect on the information and data that are necessary to document an agreement reached or order issued pursuant to a dispute resolution proceeding.

(h) Subsections (a) and (b) shall not prevent the gathering of information for research or educational purposes, in cooperation with other agencies, governmental entities, or dispute resolution programs, so long as the parties and the specific issues in controversy are not identifiable.

(i) Subsections (a) and (b) shall not prevent use of a dispute resolution communication to resolve a dispute between the neutral in a dispute resolution proceeding and a party to or participant in such proceeding, so long as such dispute resolution communication is disclosed only to the extent necessary to resolve such dispute.

(j) A dispute resolution communication which is between a neutral and a party and which may not be disclosed under this section shall also be exempt from disclosure under section 552(b)(3).

(Added Pub. L. 101–552, § 4(b), Nov. 15, 1990, 104 Stat. 2740, § 584; renumbered § 574, Pub. L. 102–354, § 3(b)(2), Aug. 26, 1992, 106 Stat. 944; amended Pub. L. 104–320, § 3, Oct. 19, 1996, 110 Stat. 3870.)

CODIFICATION

Section 574 of former Title 5, Executive Departments and Government Officers and Employees, was transferred to section 2255 of Title 7, Agriculture.

Section 574a of former Title 5, Executive Departments and Government Officers and Employees, was transferred to section 2226 of Title 7.

PRIOR PROVISIONS

A prior section 574 was renumbered section 594 of this title.

AMENDMENTS

1996—Subsecs. (a), (b). Pub. L. 104–320, § 3(a), in introductory provisions struck out "any information concerning" after "be required to disclose".

Subsec. (b)(7). Pub. L. 104–320, § 3(b), amended par. (7) generally. Prior to amendment, par. (7) read as follows: "the dispute resolution communication was provided to or was available to all parties to the dispute resolution proceeding".

Subsec. (d). Pub. L. 104–320, § 3(c), designated existing provisions as par. (1) and added par. (2).

Subsec. (j). Pub. L. 104–320, § 3(d), amended subsec. (j) generally. Prior to amendment, subsec. (j) read as follows: "This section shall not be considered a statute specifically exempting disclosure under section 552(b)(3) of this title."

1992—Pub. L. 102–354 renumbered section 584 of this title as this section.

§ 575. Authorization of arbitration

(a)(1) Arbitration may be used as an alternative means of dispute resolution whenever all parties consent. Consent may be obtained either before or after an issue in controversy has arisen. A party may agree to—

(A) submit only certain issues in controversy to arbitration; or

(B) arbitration on the condition that the award must be within a range of possible outcomes.

(2) The arbitration agreement that sets forth the subject matter submitted to the arbitrator shall be in writing. Each such arbitration agreement shall specify a maximum award that may be issued by the arbitrator and may specify other conditions limiting the range of possible outcomes.

(3) An agency may not require any person to consent to arbitration as a condition of entering into a contract or obtaining a benefit.

(b) An officer or employee of an agency shall not offer to use arbitration for the resolution of issues in controversy unless such officer or employee—

(1) would otherwise have authority to enter into a settlement concerning the matter; or

(2) is otherwise specifically authorized by the agency to consent to the use of arbitration.

(c) Prior to using binding arbitration under this subchapter, the head of an agency, in consultation with the Attorney General and after taking into account the factors in section 572(b), shall issue guidance on the appropriate use of binding arbitration and when an officer or employee of the agency has authority to settle an issue in controversy through binding arbitration.

(Added Pub. L. 101–552, § 4(b), Nov. 15, 1990, 104 Stat. 2742, § 585; renumbered § 575, Pub. L. 102–354, § 3(b)(2), Aug. 26, 1992, 106 Stat. 944; amended Pub. L. 104–320, § 8(c), Oct. 19, 1996, 110 Stat. 3872.)

CODIFICATION

Section 575 of former Title 5, Executive Departments and Government Officers and Employees, was transferred to section 2259 of Title 7, Agriculture.

PRIOR PROVISIONS

A prior section 575 was renumbered section 595 of this title.

AMENDMENTS

1996—Subsec. (a)(2). Pub. L. 104–320, § 8(c)(1), (2), substituted "The" for "Any" and inserted at end "Each such arbitration agreement shall specify a maximum award that may be issued by the arbitrator and may specify other conditions limiting the range of possible outcomes."

Subsec. (b). Pub. L. 104–320, § 8(c)(3), in introductory provisions substituted "shall not offer to use arbitration for the resolution of issues in controversy unless" for "may offer to use arbitration for the resolution of issues in controversy, if", and in par. (1) substituted "would otherwise have authority" for "has authority".

Subsec. (c). Pub. L. 104–320, § 8(c)(4), added subsec. (c).

1992—Pub. L. 102–354 renumbered section 585 of this title as this section.

§ 576. Enforcement of arbitration agreements

An agreement to arbitrate a matter to which this subchapter applies is enforceable pursuant to section 4 of title 9, and no action brought to enforce such an agreement shall be dismissed nor shall relief therein be denied on the grounds that it is against the United States or that the United States is an indispensable party.

(Added Pub. L. 101–552, § 4(b), Nov. 15, 1990, 104 Stat. 2742, § 586; renumbered § 576, Pub. L. 102–354, § 3(b)(2), Aug. 26, 1992, 106 Stat. 944.)

CODIFICATION

Section 576 of former Title 5, Executive Departments and Government Officers and Employees, was transferred to section 2260 of Title 7, Agriculture.

PRIOR PROVISIONS

A prior section 576 was renumbered section 596 of this title.

AMENDMENTS

1992—Pub. L. 102–354 renumbered section 586 of this title as this section.

§ 577. Arbitrators

(a) The parties to an arbitration proceeding shall be entitled to participate in the selection of the arbitrator.

(b) The arbitrator shall be a neutral who meets the criteria of section 573 of this title.

(Added Pub. L. 101–552, § 4(b), Nov. 15, 1990, 104 Stat. 2742, § 587; renumbered § 577 and amended Pub. L. 102–354, § 3(b)(2), (3), Aug. 26, 1992, 102 Stat. 944, 945.)

AMENDMENTS

1992—Pub. L. 102–354, § 3(b)(2), renumbered section 587 of this title as this section.

Subsec. (b). Pub. L. 102–354, § 3(b)(3), substituted "section 573" for "section 583".

§ 578. Authority of the arbitrator

An arbitrator to whom a dispute is referred under this subchapter may—

(1) regulate the course of and conduct arbitral hearings;

(2) administer oaths and affirmations;

(3) compel the attendance of witnesses and production of evidence at the hearing under the provisions of section 7 of title 9 only to the extent the agency involved is otherwise authorized by law to do so; and

(4) make awards.

(Added Pub. L. 101–552, § 4(b), Nov. 15, 1990, 104 Stat. 2742, § 588; renumbered § 578, Pub. L. 102–354, § 3(b)(2), Aug. 26, 1992, 106 Stat. 944.)

AMENDMENTS

1992—Pub. L. 102–354 renumbered section 588 of this title as this section.

§ 579. Arbitration proceedings

(a) The arbitrator shall set a time and place for the hearing on the dispute and shall notify the parties not less than 5 days before the hearing.

(b) Any party wishing a record of the hearing shall—

(1) be responsible for the preparation of such record;

(2) notify the other parties and the arbitrator of the preparation of such record;

(3) furnish copies to all identified parties and the arbitrator; and

(4) pay all costs for such record, unless the parties agree otherwise or the arbitrator determines that the costs should be apportioned.

(c)(1) The parties to the arbitration are entitled to be heard, to present evidence material to the controversy, and to cross-examine witnesses appearing at the hearing.

(2) The arbitrator may, with the consent of the parties, conduct all or part of the hearing by telephone, television, computer, or other electronic means, if each party has an opportunity to participate.

(3) The hearing shall be conducted expeditiously and in an informal manner.

(4) The arbitrator may receive any oral or documentary evidence, except that irrelevant, immaterial, unduly repetitious, or privileged evidence may be excluded by the arbitrator.

(5) The arbitrator shall interpret and apply relevant statutory and regulatory requirements, legal precedents, and policy directives.

(d) No interested person shall make or knowingly cause to be made to the arbitrator an unauthorized ex parte communication relevant to the merits of the proceeding, unless the parties agree otherwise. If a communication is made in violation of this subsection, the arbitrator shall ensure that a memorandum of the communication is prepared and made a part of the record, and that an opportunity for rebuttal is allowed. Upon receipt of a communication made in violation of this subsection, the arbitrator may, to the extent consistent with the interests of justice and the policies underlying this subchapter, require the offending party to show cause why the claim of such party should not be resolved against such party as a result of the improper conduct.

(e) The arbitrator shall make the award within 30 days after the close of the hearing, or the date of the filing of any briefs authorized by the arbitrator, whichever date is later, unless—

(1) the parties agree to some other time limit; or

(2) the agency provides by rule for some other time limit.

(Added Pub. L. 101–552, § 4(b), Nov. 15, 1990, 104 Stat. 2742, § 589; renumbered § 579, Pub. L. 102–354, § 3(b)(2), Aug. 26, 1992, 106 Stat. 944.)

AMENDMENTS

1992—Pub. L. 102–354 renumbered section 589 of this title as this section.

§ 580. Arbitration awards

(a)(1) Unless the agency provides otherwise by rule, the award in an arbitration proceeding under this subchapter shall include a brief, informal discussion of the factual and legal basis for the award, but formal findings of fact or conclusions of law shall not be required.

(2) The prevailing parties shall file the award with all relevant agencies, along with proof of service on all parties.

(b) The award in an arbitration proceeding shall become final 30 days after it is served on all parties. Any agency that is a party to the proceeding may extend this 30-day period for an additional 30-day period by serving a notice of such extension on all other parties before the end of the first 30-day period.

(c) A final award is binding on the parties to the arbitration proceeding, and may be enforced pursuant to sections 9 through 13 of title 9. No action brought to enforce such an award shall be dismissed nor shall relief therein be denied on the grounds that it is against the United States or that the United States is an indispensable party.

(d) An award entered under this subchapter in an arbitration proceeding may not serve as an estoppel in any other proceeding for any issue that was resolved in the proceeding. Such an award also may not be used as precedent or otherwise be considered in any factually unrelated proceeding, whether conducted under this subchapter, by an agency, or in a court, or in any other arbitration proceeding.

(Added Pub. L. 101–552, § 4(b), Nov. 15, 1990, 104 Stat. 2743, § 590; renumbered § 580 and amended Pub. L. 102–354, §§ 3(b)(2), 5(b)(3), Aug. 26, 1992, 106 Stat. 944, 946; Pub. L. 104–320, § 8(a), Oct. 19, 1996, 110 Stat. 3872.)

AMENDMENTS

1996—Subsec. (c). Pub. L. 104–320, § 8(a), redesignated subsec. (d) as (c) and struck out former subsec. (c) which read as follows: "The head of any agency that is a party to an arbitration proceeding conducted under this subchapter is authorized to terminate the arbitration proceeding or vacate any award issued pursuant to the proceeding before the award becomes final by serving on all other parties a written notice to that effect, in which case the award shall be null and void. Notice shall be provided to all parties to the arbitration proceeding of any request by a party, nonparty participant or other person that the agency head terminate the arbitration proceeding or vacate the award. An employee or agent engaged in the performance of investigative or prosecuting functions for an agency may not, in that or a factually related case, advise in a decision under this subsection to terminate an arbitration proceeding or to vacate an arbitral award, except as witness or counsel in public proceedings."

Subsecs. (d), (e). Pub. L. 104–320, § 8(a)(2), redesignated subsec. (e) as (d). Former subsec. (d) redesignated (c).

Subsecs. (f), (g). Pub. L. 104–320, § 8(a)(1), struck out subsecs. (f) and (g) which read as follows:

"(f) An arbitral award that is vacated under subsection (c) shall not be admissible in any proceeding relating to the issues in controversy with respect to which the award was made.

"(g) If an agency head vacates an award under subsection (c), a party to the arbitration (other than the United States) may within 30 days of such action petition the agency head for an award of fees and other expenses (as defined in section 504(b)(1)(A) of this title) incurred in connection with the arbitration proceeding. The agency head shall award the petitioning party those fees and expenses that would not have been incurred in the absence of such arbitration proceeding, unless the agency head or his or her designee finds that special circumstances make such an award unjust. The procedures for reviewing applications for awards shall, where appropriate, be consistent with those set forth in subsection (a)(2) and (3) of section 504 of this title. Such fees and expenses shall be paid from the funds of the agency that vacated the award."

1992—Pub. L. 102–354, § 3(b)(2), renumbered section 590 of this title as this section.

Subsec. (g). Pub. L. 102–354, § 5(b)(3), substituted "fees and other expenses" for "attorney fees and expenses".

SECTION REFERRED TO IN OTHER SECTIONS

This section is referred to in title 9 section 10.

§ 581. Judicial Review [1]

(a) Notwithstanding any other provision of law, any person adversely affected or aggrieved by an award made in an arbitration proceeding conducted under this subchapter may bring an action for review of such award only pursuant to the provisions of sections 9 through 13 of title 9.

(b) A decision by an agency to use or not to use a dispute resolution proceeding under this subchapter shall be committed to the discretion of the agency and shall not be subject to judicial review, except that arbitration shall be subject to judicial review under section 10(b) of title 9.

(Added Pub. L. 101–552, § 4(b), Nov. 15, 1990, 104 Stat. 2744, § 591; renumbered § 581 and amended Pub. L. 102–354, § 3(b)(2), (4), Aug. 26, 1992, 106 Stat. 944, 945; Pub. L. 104–320, § 8(b), Oct. 19, 1996, 110 Stat. 3872.)

PRIOR PROVISIONS

A prior section 581 was renumbered section 571 of this title.

Another prior section 581 was renumbered section 561 of this title.

AMENDMENTS

1996—Subsec. (b). Pub. L. 104–320, which directed that section 581(d) of this title be amended by striking "(1)" after "(b)" and by striking par. (2), was executed to subsec. (b) of this section to reflect the probable intent of Congress. Prior to amendment, par. (2) read as follows: "A decision by the head of an agency under section 580 to terminate an arbitration proceeding or vacate an arbitral award shall be committed to the discretion of the agency and shall not be subject to judicial review."

1992—Pub. L. 102–354, § 3(b)(2), renumbered section 591 of this title as this section.

Subsec. (b)(2). Pub. L. 102–354, § 3(b)(4), substituted "section 580" for "section 590".

---

[1] So in original. Probably should not be capitalized.

[§ 582. Repealed. Pub. L. 104–320, § 4(b)(1), Oct. 19, 1996, 110 Stat. 3871]

Section, added Pub. L. 101–552, § 4(b), Nov. 15, 1990, 104 Stat. 2744, § 592; renumbered § 582, Pub. L. 102–354, § 3(b)(2), Aug. 26, 1992, 106 Stat. 944, related to compilation of data on use of alternative means of dispute resolution in conducting agency proceedings.

§ 583. Support services

For the purposes of this subchapter, an agency may use (with or without reimbursement) the services and facilities of other Federal agencies, State, local, and tribal governments, public and private organizations and agencies, and individuals, with the consent of such agencies, organizations, and individuals. An agency may accept voluntary and uncompensated services for purposes of this subchapter without regard to the provisions of section 1342 of title 31.

(Added Pub. L. 101–552, § 4(b), Nov. 15, 1990, 104 Stat. 2745, § 593; renumbered § 583, Pub. L. 102–354, § 3(b)(2), Aug. 26, 1992, 106 Stat. 944; amended Pub. L. 104–320, § 5, Oct. 19, 1996, 110 Stat. 3871.)

PRIOR PROVISIONS

Prior sections 583 to 590 were renumbered sections 573 to 580 of this title, respectively.

Other prior sections 583 to 590 were renumbered sections 563 to 570 of this title, respectively.

AMENDMENTS

1996—Pub. L. 104–320 inserted "State, local, and tribal governments," after "other Federal agencies,".

1992—Pub. L. 102–354 renumbered section 593 of this title as this section.

§ 584. Authorization of appropriations

There are authorized to be appropriated such sums as may be necessary to carry out the purposes of this subchapter.

(Added Pub. L. 104–320, § 10(a), Oct. 19, 1996, 110 Stat. 3873.)

SUBCHAPTER V—ADMINISTRATIVE CONFERENCE OF THE UNITED STATES

AMENDMENTS

1992—Pub. L. 102–354, § 2(1), Aug. 26, 1992, 106 Stat. 944, redesignated subchapter III of this chapter as this subchapter.

TERMINATION OF ADMINISTRATIVE CONFERENCE OF UNITED STATES

Pub. L. 104–52, title IV, Nov. 19, 1995, 109 Stat. 480, provided: "For necessary expenses of the Administrative Conference of the United States, established under subchapter V of chapter 5 of title 5, United States Code, $600,000: Provided, That these funds shall only be available for the purposes of the prompt and orderly termination of the Administrative Conference of the United States by February 1, 1996."

§ 591. Purpose

It is the purpose of this subchapter to provide suitable arrangements through which Federal agencies, assisted by outside experts, may cooperatively study mutual problems, exchange information, and develop recommendations for action by proper authorities to the end that private rights may be fully protected and regulatory activities and other Federal responsibilities may be carried out expeditiously in the public interest.

(Pub. L. 89–554, Sept. 6, 1966, 80 Stat. 388, § 571; renumbered § 591, Pub. L. 102–354, § 2(2), Aug. 26, 1992, 106 Stat. 944.)

HISTORICAL AND REVISION NOTES

Derivation	U.S. Code	Revised Statutes and Statutes at Large
....	5 U.S.C. 1045(e).	Aug. 30, 1964, Pub. L. 88–499, § 2(e), 78 Stat. 615.

The words "this subchapter" are substituted for "this Act" to reflect the codification of the Administrative Conference Act in this subchapter.

Standard changes are made to conform with the definitions applicable and the style of this title as outlined in the preface to the report.

PRIOR PROVISIONS

A prior section 591 was renumbered section 581 of this title.

AMENDMENTS

1992—Pub. L. 102–354 renumbered section 571 of this title as this section.

§ 592. Definitions

For the purpose of this subchapter—

(1) "administrative program" includes a Federal function which involves protection of the public interest and the determination of rights, privileges, and obligations of private persons through rule making, adjudication, licensing, or investigation, as those terms are used in subchapter II of this chapter, except that it does not include a military or foreign affairs function of the United States;

(2) "administrative agency" means an authority as defined by section 551(1) of this title; and

(3) "administrative procedure" means procedure used in carrying out an administrative program and is to be broadly construed to include any aspect of agency organization, procedure, or management which may affect the equitable consideration of public and private interests, the fairness of agency decisions, the speed of agency action, and the relationship of operating methods to later judicial review, but does not include the scope of agency responsibility as established by law or matters of substantive policy committed by law to agency discretion.

(Pub. L. 89–554, Sept. 6, 1966, 80 Stat. 388, § 572; renumbered § 592, Pub. L. 102–354, § 2(2), Aug. 26, 1992, 106 Stat. 944.)

HISTORICAL AND REVISION NOTES

Derivation	U.S. Code	Revised Statutes and Statutes at Large
....	5 U.S.C. 1045a.	Aug. 30, 1964, Pub. L. 88–499, § 3, 78 Stat. 615.

In paragraph (1), the words "subchapter II of this chapter" are substituted for "the Administrative Procedure Act (5 U.S.C. 1001–1011)" to reflect the codification of the Act in this title. The word "naval" is omitted as included in "military".

In paragraph (2), the words "section 551(1) of this title" are substituted for "section 2(a) of the Administrative Procedure Act (5 U.S.C. 1001(a))".

Standard changes are made to conform with the definitions applicable and the style of this title as outlined in the preface to the report.

PRIOR PROVISIONS

A prior section 592 was renumbered section 582 of this title and was subsequently repealed.

AMENDMENTS

1992—Pub. L. 102–354 renumbered section 572 of this title as this section.

§ 593. Administrative Conference of the United States

(a) The Administrative Conference of the United States consists of not more than 101 nor less than 75 members appointed as set forth in subsection (b) of this section.

(b) The Conference is composed of—

(1) a full-time Chairman appointed for a 5-year term by the President, by and with the advice and consent of the Senate. The Chairman is entitled to pay at the highest rate established by statute for the chairman of an independent regulatory board or commission, and may continue to serve until his successor is appointed and has qualified;

(2) the chairman of each independent regulatory board or commission or an individual designated by the board or commission;

(3) the head of each Executive department or other administrative agency which is designated by the President, or an individual designated by the head of the department or agency;

(4) when authorized by the Council referred to in section 595(b) of this title, one or more appointees from a board, commission, department, or agency referred to in this subsection, designated by the head thereof with, in the case of a board or commission, the approval of the board or commission;

(5) individuals appointed by the President to membership on the Council who are not otherwise members of the Conference; and

(6) not more than 40 other members appointed by the Chairman, with the approval of the Council, for terms of 2 years, except that the number of members appointed by the Chairman may at no time be less than one-third nor more than two-fifths of the total number of members. The Chairman shall select the members in a manner which will provide broad representation of the views of private citizens and utilize diverse experience. The members shall be members of the practicing bar, scholars in the field of administrative law or government, or others specially informed by knowledge and experience with respect to Federal administrative procedure.

(c) Members of the Conference, except the Chairman, are not entitled to pay for service. Members appointed from outside the Federal Government are entitled to travel expenses, including per diem instead of subsistence, as authorized by section 5703 of this title for individuals serving without pay.

(Pub. L. 89–554, Sept. 6, 1966, 80 Stat. 389, § 573; Pub. L. 99–470, § 1, Oct. 14, 1986, 100 Stat. 1198; renumbered § 593 and amended Pub. L. 102–354, § 2(2), (3), Aug. 26, 1992, 106 Stat. 944.)

HISTORICAL AND REVISION NOTES

Derivation	U.S. Code	Revised Statutes and Statutes at Large
....	5 U.S.C. 1045b.	Aug. 30, 1964, Pub. L. 88–499, § 4, 78 Stat. 616.

In subsection (a), the words "There is hereby established" are omitted as executed. The words "hereinafter referred to as the 'Conference'" are omitted as unnecessary as the title "Administrative Conference of the United States" is fully set out the first time it is used in each section of this chapter.

In subsection (b)(4), the words "referred to in section 575(b) of this title" are inserted for clarity.

In subsection (c), the words "by section 5703 of this title" are substituted for "by law (5 U.S.C. 73b–2)" to reflect the codification of that section in title 5.

Standard changes are made to conform with the definitions applicable and the style of this title as outlined in the preface to the report.

PRIOR PROVISIONS

A prior section 593 was renumbered section 583 of this title.

AMENDMENTS

1992—Pub. L. 102–354, § 2(2), renumbered section 573 of this title as this section.

Subsec. (b)(4). Pub. L. 102–354, § 2(3), substituted "section 595(b)" for "section 575(b)".

1986—Subsec. (a). Pub. L. 99–470, § 1(a)(1), substituted "101" for "91".

Subsec. (b)(6). Pub. L. 99–470, § 1(a)(2), substituted "40" for "36".

TERMINATION OF ADMINISTRATIVE CONFERENCE OF UNITED STATES

For termination of Administrative Conference of United States, see note set out preceding section 591 of this title.

DEVELOPMENT OF ADMINISTRATIVE CONFERENCE

The Administrative Conference of the United States, established as a permanent body by the Administrative Conference Act, Pub. L. 88–499, Aug. 30, 1964, 78 Stat. 615, was preceded by two temporary Conferences. The first was called by President Eisenhower in 1953 and adopted a final report which was transmitted to the President who acknowledged receipt of it on March 3, 1955. The second was established by President Kennedy by Executive Order No. 10934, Apr. 14, 1961, 26 F.R. 3233, which, by its terms, called for a final report to the President by December 31, 1962. The final report recommended a continuing Conference consisting of both government personnel and outside experts.

§ 594. Powers and duties of the Conference

To carry out the purpose of this subchapter, the Administrative Conference of the United States may—

(1) study the efficiency, adequacy, and fairness of the administrative procedure used by administrative agencies in carrying out administrative programs, and make recommendations to administrative agencies, collectively or individually, and to the President, Congress, or the Judicial Conference of the United States, in connection therewith, as it considers appropriate;

(2) arrange for interchange among administrative agencies of information potentially useful in improving administrative procedure;

(3) collect information and statistics from administrative agencies and publish such reports as it considers useful for evaluating and improving administrative procedure;

(4) enter into arrangements with any administrative agency or major organizational unit within an administrative agency pursuant to which the Conference performs any of the functions described in this section; and

(5) provide assistance in response to requests relating to the improvement of administrative procedure in foreign countries, subject to the concurrence of the Secretary of State, the Administrator of the Agency for International Development, or the Director of the United States Information Agency, as appropriate, except that—

(A) such assistance shall be limited to the analysis of issues relating to administrative procedure, the provision of training of foreign officials in administrative procedure, and the design or improvement of administrative procedure, where the expertise of members of the Conference is indicated; and

(B) such assistance may only be undertaken on a fully reimbursable basis, including all direct and indirect administrative costs.

Payment for services provided by the Conference pursuant to paragraph (4) shall be credited to the operating account for the Conference and shall remain available until expended.

(Pub. L. 89–554, Sept. 6, 1966, 80 Stat. 390, § 574; Pub. L. 101–422, § 2, Oct. 12, 1990, 104 Stat. 910; renumbered § 594, Pub. L. 102–354, § 2(2), Aug. 26, 1992, 106 Stat. 944; Pub. L. 102–403, Oct. 9, 1992, 106 Stat. 1968.)

HISTORICAL AND REVISION NOTES

Derivation	U.S. Code	Revised Statutes and Statutes at Large
....	5 U.S.C. 1045c.	Aug. 30, 1964, Pub. L. 88–499, § 5, 78 Stat. 616.

Standard changes are made to conform with the definitions applicable and the style of this title as outlined in the preface to the report.

AMENDMENTS

1992—Pub. L. 102–354 renumbered section 574 of this title as this section.

Par. (4). Pub. L. 102–403 amended par. (4) generally. Prior to amendment, par. (4) read as follows: "enter into arrangements with any administrative agency or major organizational unit within an administrative agency pursuant to which the Conference performs any of the functions described in paragraphs (1), (2), and (3)."

Par. (5). Pub. L. 102–403 which directed addition of par. (5) at end of section, was executed by adding par. (5) after par. (4) and before concluding provisions, to reflect the probable intent of Congress.

1990—Pub. L. 101–422 added par. (4) and concluding provisions.

TERMINATION OF ADMINISTRATIVE CONFERENCE OF UNITED STATES

For termination of Administrative Conference of United States, see note set out preceding section 591 of this title.

TRANSFER OF FUNCTIONS

United States Information Agency (other than Broadcasting Board of Governors and International Broadcasting Bureau) abolished and functions transferred to Secretary of State, see sections 6531 and 6532 of Title 22, Foreign Relations and Intercourse.

§ 595. Organization of the Conference

(a) The membership of the Administrative Conference of the United States meeting in plenary session constitutes the Assembly of the Conference. The Assembly has ultimate authority over all activities of the Conference. Specifically, it has the power to—

(1) adopt such recommendations as it considers appropriate for improving administrative procedure. A member who disagrees with a recommendation adopted by the Assembly is entitled to enter a dissenting opinion and an alternate proposal in the record of the Conference proceedings, and the opinion and proposal so entered shall accompany the Conference recommendation in a publication or distribution thereof; and

(2) adopt bylaws and regulations not inconsistent with this subchapter for carrying out the functions of the Conference, including the creation of such committees as it considers necessary for the conduct of studies and the development of recommendations for consideration by the Assembly.

(b) The Conference includes a Council composed of the Chairman of the Conference, who is Chairman of the Council, and 10 other members appointed by the President, of whom not more than one-half shall be employees of Federal regulatory agencies or Executive departments. The President may designate a member of the Council as Vice Chairman. During the absence or incapacity of the Chairman, or when that office is vacant, the Vice Chairman shall serve as Chairman. The term of each member, except the Chairman, is 3 years. When the term of a member ends, he may continue to serve until a successor is appointed. However, the service of any member ends when a change in his employment status would make him ineligible for Council membership under the conditions of his original appointment. The Council has the power to—

(1) determine the time and place of plenary sessions of the Conference and the agenda for the sessions. The Council shall call at least one plenary session each year;

(2) propose bylaws and regulations, including rules of procedure and committee organization, for adoption by the Assembly;

(3) make recommendations to the Conference or its committees on a subject germane to the purpose of the Conference;

(4) receive and consider reports and recommendations of committees of the Conference and send them to members of the Conference with the views and recommendations of the Council;

(5) designate a member of the Council to preside at meetings of the Council in the absence or incapacity of the Chairman and Vice Chairman;

(6) designate such additional officers of the Conference as it considers desirable;

(7) approve or revise the budgetary proposals of the Chairman; and

(8) exercise such other powers as may be delegated to it by the Assembly.

(c) The Chairman is the chief executive of the Conference. In that capacity he has the power to—

(1) make inquiries into matters he considers important for Conference consideration, including matters proposed by individuals inside or outside the Federal Government;

(2) be the official spokesman for the Conference in relations with the several branches and agencies of the Federal Government and with interested organizations and individuals outside the Government, including responsibility for encouraging Federal agencies to carry out the recommendations of the Conference;

(3) request agency heads to provide information needed by the Conference, which information shall be supplied to the extent permitted by law;

(4) recommend to the Council appropriate subjects for action by the Conference;

(5) appoint, with the approval of the Council, members of committees authorized by the bylaws and regulations of the Conference;

(6) prepare, for approval of the Council, estimates of the budgetary requirements of the Conference;

(7) appoint and fix the pay of employees, define their duties and responsibilities, and direct and supervise their activities;

(8) rent office space in the District of Columbia;

(9) provide necessary services for the Assembly, the Council, and the committees of the Conference;

(10) organize and direct studies ordered by the Assembly or the Council, to contract for the performance of such studies with any public or private persons, firm, association, corporation, or institution under title III of the Federal Property and Administrative Services Act of 1949, as amended (41 U.S.C. 251–260), and to use from time to time, as appropriate, experts and consultants who may be employed in accordance with section 3109 of this title at rates not in excess of the maximum rate of pay for grade GS–15 as provided in section 5332 of this title;

(11) utilize, with their consent, the services and facilities of Federal agencies and of State and private agencies and instrumentalities with or without reimbursement;

(12) accept, hold, administer, and utilize gifts, devises, and bequests of property, both real and personal, for the purpose of aiding and facilitating the work of the Conference. Gifts and bequests of money and proceeds from sales of other property received as gifts, devises, or bequests shall be deposited in the Treasury and shall be disbursed upon the order of the Chairman. Property accepted pursuant to this section, and the proceeds thereof, shall be used as nearly as possible in accordance with the terms of the gifts, devises, or bequests. For purposes of Federal income, estate, or gift taxes, property accepted under this section shall be considered as a gift, devise, or bequest to the United States;

(13) accept voluntary and uncompensated services, notwithstanding the provisions of section 1342 of title 31;

(14) on request of the head of an agency, furnish assistance and advice on matters of administrative procedure;

(15) exercise such additional authority as the Council or Assembly delegates to him; and

(16) request any administrative agency to notify the Chairman of its intent to enter into any contract with any person outside the agency to study the efficiency, adequacy, or fairness of an agency proceeding (as defined in section 551(12) of this title).

The Chairman shall preside at meetings of the Council and at each plenary session of the Conference, to which he shall make a full report concerning the affairs of the Conference since the last preceding plenary session. The Chairman, on behalf of the Conference, shall transmit to the President and Congress an annual report and such interim reports as he considers desirable.

(Pub. L. 89–554, Sept. 6, 1966, 80 Stat. 390, §575; Pub. L. 92–526, §1, Oct. 21, 1972, 86 Stat. 1048; Pub. L. 97–258, §3(a)(1), Sept. 13, 1982, 96 Stat. 1062; Pub. L. 101–422, §3, Oct. 12, 1990, 104 Stat. 910; renumbered §595, Pub. L. 102–354, §2(2), Aug. 26, 1992, 106 Stat. 944.)

HISTORICAL AND REVISION NOTES

Derivation	U.S. Code	Revised Statutes and Statutes at Large
....	5 U.S.C. 1045d.	Aug. 30, 1964, Pub. L. 88–499, §6, 78 Stat. 617.

In subsection (b), the words "except that the Council members initially appointed shall serve for one, two, or three years, as designated by the President" are omitted as executed, existing rights being preserved by technical section 8.

In subsection (b)(1), the words "the sessions" are substituted for "such meetings" for clarity as elsewhere the word "sessions" refers to sessions of the Conference and "meetings" refers to meetings of the Council.

In subsection (c)(7), the words "subject to the civil service and classification laws" are omitted as unnecessary inasmuch as appointments in the executive branch are made subject to the civil service laws and pay is fixed under classification laws unless specifically excepted. The words "and fix the pay of" are added for clarity.

Standard changes are made to conform with the definitions applicable and the style of this title as outlined in the preface to the report.

REFERENCES IN TEXT

The Federal Property and Administrative Services Act of 1949, referred to in subsec. (c)(10), is act June 30, 1949, ch. 288, 63 Stat. 377, as amended. Title III of that Act is classified generally to subchapter IV (§251 et seq.) of chapter 4 of Title 41, Public Contracts. For complete classification of this Act to the Code, see Short Title note set out under section 471 of Title 40, Public Buildings, Property, and Works, and Tables.

AMENDMENTS

1992—Pub. L. 102–354 renumbered section 575 of this title as this section.

1990—Subsec. (c)(16). Pub. L. 101–422 added par. (16).

1982—Subsec. (c)(13). Pub. L. 97–258 substituted "section 1342 of title 31" for "section 3679(b) of the Revised Statutes (31 U.S.C. 665(b))".

1972—Subsec. (c)(10). Pub. L. 92–526, §1(a), inserted provisions authorizing contracts for the performance of such studies with any public or private persons, etc., under title III of the Federal Property and Administrative Services Act of 1949, as amended, and substituted provisions authorizing the payment of experts and consultants in accordance with rates not in excess of the maximum rate of pay for grade GS–15 as provided in section 5332 of this title, for provisions authorizing the payment of such individuals at rates not in excess of $100 a day.

Subsec. (c)(11) to (15). Pub. L. 92–526, §1(b), added pars. (11) to (13) and redesignated former pars. (11) and (12) as (14) and (15), respectively.

TERMINATION OF ADMINISTRATIVE CONFERENCE OF UNITED STATES

For termination of Administrative Conference of United States, see note set out preceding section 591 of this title.

SECTION REFERRED TO IN OTHER SECTIONS

This section is referred to in section 593 of this title.

§ 596. Authorization of appropriations

There are authorized to be appropriated to carry out the purposes of this subchapter not more than $2,000,000 for fiscal year 1990, $2,100,000 for fiscal year 1991, $2,200,000 for fiscal year 1992, $2,300,000 for fiscal year 1993, and $2,400,000 for fiscal year 1994. Of any amounts appropriated under this section, not more than $1,500 may be made available in each fiscal year for official representation and entertainment expenses for foreign dignitaries.

(Pub. L. 89–554, Sept. 6, 1966, 80 Stat. 391, §576; Pub. L. 91–164, Dec. 24, 1969, 83 Stat. 446; Pub. L. 92–526, §2, Oct. 21, 1972, 86 Stat. 1048; Pub. L. 95–293, §1(a), June 13, 1978, 92 Stat. 317; Pub. L. 97–330, Oct. 15, 1982, 96 Stat. 1618; Pub. L. 99–470, §2(a), Oct. 14, 1986, 100 Stat. 1198; Pub. L. 101–422, §1, Oct. 12, 1990, 104 Stat. 910; renumbered §596, Pub. L. 102–354, §2(2), Aug. 26, 1992, 106 Stat. 944.)

HISTORICAL AND REVISION NOTES

Derivation	U.S. Code	Revised Statutes and Statutes at Large
....	5 U.S.C. 1045e.	Aug. 30, 1964, Pub. L. 88–499, §7, 78 Stat. 618.

The word "hereby" is omitted as unnecessary.

Standard changes are made to conform with the definitions applicable and the style of this title as outlined in the preface to the report.

AMENDMENTS

1992—Pub. L. 102–354 renumbered section 576 of this title as this section.

1990—Pub. L. 101–422 amended section generally. Prior to amendment, section read as follows: "There are authorized to be appropriated to carry out the purposes of this subchapter not more than $1,600,000 for fiscal year 1986 and not more than $2,000,000 for each fiscal year thereafter up to and including fiscal year 1990. Of any amounts appropriated under this section, not more than $1,000 may be made available in each fiscal year for official reception and entertainment expenses for foreign dignitaries."

1986—Pub. L. 99–470 substituted "Authorization of appropriations" for "Appropriations" in section catchline and amended text generally. Prior to amendment, text read as follows: "There are authorized to be appropriated to carry out the purposes of this subchapter sums not to exceed $2,300,000 for the fiscal year ending September 30, 1982, and not to exceed $2,300,000 for each fiscal year thereafter up to and including the fiscal year ending September 30, 1986."

1982—Pub. L. 97–330 substituted provisions authorizing appropriations of not to exceed $2,300,000 for fiscal year ending Sept. 30, 1982, and not to exceed $2,300,000 for each fiscal year thereafter up to and including fiscal year ending Sept. 30, 1986, for provisions that had authorized appropriations of not to exceed $1,700,000 for fiscal year ending Sept. 30, 1979, $2,000,000 for fiscal year ending Sept. 30, 1980, $2,300,000 for fiscal year ending Sept. 30, 1981, and $2,300,000 for fiscal year ending Sept. 30, 1982.

1978—Pub. L. 95–293 substituted provisions authorizing appropriations for fiscal years ending Sept. 30, 1979, Sept. 30, 1980, Sept. 30, 1981, and Sept. 30, 1982, of $1,700,000, $2,000,000, $2,300,000, and $2,300,000, respectively, for provisions authorizing appropriations for fiscal years ending June 30, 1974, June 30, 1975, June 30, 1976, June 30, 1977, and June 30, 1978, of $760,000, $805,000, $850,000, $900,000, and $950,000, respectively, and provisions authorizing for each fiscal year thereafter such sums as may be necessary.

1972—Pub. L. 92–526 substituted provisions authorizing to be appropriated necessary sums not in excess of $760,000 for fiscal year ending June 30, 1974, $805,000 for fiscal year ending June 30, 1975, $850,000 for fiscal year ending June 30, 1976, $900,000 for fiscal year ending June 30, 1977, and $950,000 for fiscal year ending June 30, 1978, and each fiscal year thereafter, for provisions authorizing to be appropriated necessary sums, not in excess of $450,000 per annum.

1969—Pub. L. 91–164 substituted "$450,000 per annum" for "$250,000".

EFFECTIVE DATE OF 1978 AMENDMENT

Section 1(b) of Pub. L. 95–293 provided that: "The amendment made by subsection (a) [amending this section] shall take effect October 1, 1977."

CHAPTER 6—THE ANALYSIS OF REGULATORY FUNCTIONS

CHAPTER REFERRED TO IN OTHER SECTIONS

This chapter is referred to in title 16 sections 1379, 1855; title 42 sections 1302, 7661f.

§ 601. Definitions

For purposes of this chapter—

(1) the term "agency" means an agency as defined in section 551(1) of this title;

(2) the term "rule" means any rule for which the agency publishes a general notice of proposed rulemaking pursuant to section 553(b) of this title, or any other law, including any rule of general applicability governing Federal grants to State and local governments for which the agency provides an opportunity for notice and public comment, except that the term "rule" does not include a rule of particular applicability relating to rates, wages, corporate or financial structures or reorganizations thereof, prices, facilities, appliances, services, or allowances therefor or to valuations, costs or accounting, or practices relating to such rates, wages, structures, prices, appliances, services, or allowances;

(3) the term "small business" has the same meaning as the term "small business concern" under section 3 of the Small Business Act, un-

less an agency, after consultation with the Office of Advocacy of the Small Business Administration and after opportunity for public comment, establishes one or more definitions of such term which are appropriate to the activities of the agency and publishes such definition(s) in the Federal Register;

(4) the term "small organization" means any not-for-profit enterprise which is independently owned and operated and is not dominant in its field, unless an agency establishes, after opportunity for public comment, one or more definitions of such term which are appropriate to the activities of the agency and publishes such definition(s) in the Federal Register;

(5) the term "small governmental jurisdiction" means governments of cities, counties, towns, townships, villages, school districts, or special districts, with a population of less than fifty thousand, unless an agency establishes, after opportunity for public comment, one or more definitions of such term which are appropriate to the activities of the agency and which are based on such factors as location in rural or sparsely populated areas or limited revenues due to the population of such jurisdiction, and publishes such definition(s) in the Federal Register;

(6) the term "small entity" shall have the same meaning as the terms "small business", "small organization" and "small governmental jurisdiction" defined in paragraphs (3), (4) and (5) of this section; and

(7) the term "collection of information"—

(A) means the obtaining, causing to be obtained, soliciting, or requiring the disclosure to third parties or the public, of facts or opinions by or for an agency, regardless of form or format, calling for either—

(i) answers to identical questions posed to, or identical reporting or recordkeeping requirements imposed on, 10 or more persons, other than agencies, instrumentalities, or employees of the United States; or

(ii) answers to questions posed to agencies, instrumentalities, or employees of the United States which are to be used for general statistical purposes; and

(B) shall not include a collection of information described under section 3518(c)(1) of title 44, United States Code.

(8) RECORDKEEPING REQUIREMENT.—The term "recordkeeping requirement" means a requirement imposed by an agency on persons to maintain specified records.

(Added Pub. L. 96–354, § 3(a), Sept. 19, 1980, 94 Stat. 1165; amended Pub. L. 104–121, title II, § 241(a)(2), Mar. 29, 1996, 110 Stat. 864.)

REFERENCES IN TEXT

Section 3 of the Small Business Act, referred to in par. (3), is classified to section 632 of Title 15, Commerce and Trade.

AMENDMENTS

1996—Pars. (7), (8). Pub. L. 104–121 added pars. (7) and (8).

EFFECTIVE DATE OF 1996 AMENDMENT

Section 245 of title II of Pub. L. 104–121 provided that: "This subtitle [subtitle D (§§ 241–245) of title II of Pub.

L. 104–121, amending this section and sections 603 to 605, 609, 611, and 612 of this title and enacting provisions set out as a note under section 609 of this title] shall become effective on the expiration of 90 days after the date of enactment of this subtitle [Mar. 29, 1996], except that such amendments shall not apply to interpretative rules for which a notice of proposed rulemaking was published prior to the date of enactment.''

EFFECTIVE DATE

Section 4 of Pub. L. 96–354 provided that: "The provisions of this Act [enacting this chapter] shall take effect January 1, 1981, except that the requirements of sections 603 and 604 of title 5, United States Code (as added by section 3 of this Act) shall apply only to rules for which a notice of proposed rulemaking is issued on or after January 1, 1981.''

SHORT TITLE OF 1996 AMENDMENT

Section 1 of Pub. L. 104–121 provided that: "This Act [enacting sections 801 to 808 of this title, section 657 of Title 15, Commerce and Trade, and sections 1320b–15 and 1383e of Title 42, The Public Health and Welfare, amending this section and sections 504, 603 to 605, 609, 611, and 612 of this title, sections 665e and 901 of Title 2, The Congress, section 648 of Title 15, section 2412 of Title 28, Judiciary and Judicial Procedure, section 3101 of Title 31, Money and Finance, and sections 401, 402, 403, 405, 422, 423, 425, 902, 903, 1382, 1382c, 1383, and 1383c of Title 42, enacting provisions set out as notes under this section and sections 504, 609, and 801 of this title and sections 401, 402, 403, 405, 902, 1305, 1320b–15, and 1382 of Title 42, amending provisions set out as a note under section 631 of Title 15, and repealing provisions set out as a note under section 425 of Title 42] may be cited as the 'Contract with America Advancement Act of 1996'.''

SHORT TITLE

Section 1 of Pub. L. 96–354 provided: "That this Act [enacting this chapter] may be cited as the 'Regulatory Flexibility Act'.''

ASSESSMENT OF FEDERAL REGULATIONS AND POLICIES ON FAMILIES

Pub. L. 105–277, div. A, §101(h) [title VI, §654], Oct. 21, 1998, 112 Stat. 2681–480, 2681–528, provided that:

"(a) PURPOSES.—The purposes of this section are to—

"(1) require agencies to assess the impact of proposed agency actions on family well-being; and

"(2) improve the management of executive branch agencies.

"(b) DEFINITIONS.—In this section—

"(1) the term 'agency' has the meaning given the term 'Executive agency' by section 105 of title 5, United States Code, except such term does not include the General Accounting Office; and

"(2) the term 'family' means—

"(A) a group of individuals related by blood, marriage, adoption, or other legal custody who live together as a single household; and

"(B) any individual who is not a member of such group, but who is related by blood, marriage, or adoption to a member of such group, and over half of whose support in a calendar year is received from such group.

"(c) FAMILY POLICYMAKING ASSESSMENT.—Before implementing policies and regulations that may affect family well-being, each agency shall assess such actions with respect to whether—

"(1) the action strengthens or erodes the stability or safety of the family and, particularly, the marital commitment;

"(2) the action strengthens or erodes the authority and rights of parents in the education, nurture, and supervision of their children;

"(3) the action helps the family perform its functions, or substitutes governmental activity for the function;

"(4) the action increases or decreases disposable income or poverty of families and children;

"(5) the proposed benefits of the action justify the financial impact on the family;

"(6) the action may be carried out by State or local government or by the family; and

"(7) the action establishes an implicit or explicit policy concerning the relationship between the behavior and personal responsibility of youth, and the norms of society.

"(d) GOVERNMENTWIDE FAMILY POLICY COORDINATION AND REVIEW.—

"(1) CERTIFICATION AND RATIONALE.—With respect to each proposed policy or regulation that may affect family well-being, the head of each agency shall—

"(A) submit a written certification to the Director of the Office of Management and Budget and to Congress that such policy or regulation has been assessed in accordance with this section; and

"(B) provide an adequate rationale for implementation of each policy or regulation that may negatively affect family well-being.

"(2) OFFICE OF MANAGEMENT AND BUDGET.—The Director of the Office of Management and Budget shall—

"(A) ensure that policies and regulations proposed by agencies are implemented consistent with this section; and

"(B) compile, index, and submit annually to the Congress the written certifications received pursuant to paragraph (1)(A).

"(3) OFFICE OF POLICY DEVELOPMENT.—The Office of Policy Development shall—

"(A) assess proposed policies and regulations in accordance with this section;

"(B) provide evaluations of policies and regulations that may affect family well-being to the Director of the Office of Management and Budget; and

"(C) advise the President on policy and regulatory actions that may be taken to strengthen the institutions of marriage and family in the United States.

"(e) ASSESSMENTS UPON REQUEST BY MEMBERS OF CONGRESS.—Upon request by a Member of Congress relating to a proposed policy or regulation, an agency shall conduct an assessment in accordance with subsection (c), and shall provide a certification and rationale in accordance with subsection (d).

"(f) JUDICIAL REVIEW.—This section is not intended to create any right or benefit, substantive or procedural, enforceable at law by a party against the United States, its agencies, its officers, or any person.''

SMALL BUSINESS REGULATORY FAIRNESS

Sections 201 to 224 of title II of Pub. L. 104–121 provided that:

"SEC. 201. SHORT TITLE.

"This title [enacting sections 801 to 808 of this title and section 657 of Title 15, Commerce and Trade, amending this section, sections 504, 603 to 605, 609, 611, and 612 of this title, section 648 of Title 15, and section 2412 of Title 28, Judiciary and Judicial Procedure, enacting provisions set out as notes under this section and sections 504, 609, and 801 of this title, and amending provisions set out as a note under section 631 of Title 15] may be cited as the 'Small Business Regulatory Enforcement Fairness Act of 1996'.

"SEC. 202. FINDINGS.

"Congress finds that—

"(1) a vibrant and growing small business sector is critical to creating jobs in a dynamic economy;

"(2) small businesses bear a disproportionate share of regulatory costs and burdens;

"(3) fundamental changes that are needed in the regulatory and enforcement culture of Federal agencies to make agencies more responsive to small business can be made without compromising the statutory missions of the agencies;

"(4) three of the top recommendations of the 1995 White House Conference on Small Business involve reforms to the way government regulations are developed and enforced, and reductions in government paperwork requirements;

"(5) the requirements of chapter 6 of title 5, United States Code, have too often been ignored by government agencies, resulting in greater regulatory burdens on small entities than necessitated by statute; and

"(6) small entities should be given the opportunity to seek judicial review of agency actions required by chapter 6 of title 5, United States Code.

"SEC. 203. PURPOSES.

"The purposes of this title are—

"(1) to implement certain recommendations of the 1995 White House Conference on Small Business regarding the development and enforcement of Federal regulations;

"(2) to provide for judicial review of chapter 6 of title 5, United States Code;

"(3) to encourage the effective participation of small businesses in the Federal regulatory process;

"(4) to simplify the language of Federal regulations affecting small businesses;

"(5) to develop more accessible sources of information on regulatory and reporting requirements for small businesses;

"(6) to create a more cooperative regulatory environment among agencies and small businesses that is less punitive and more solution-oriented; and

"(7) to make Federal regulators more accountable for their enforcement actions by providing small entities with a meaningful opportunity for redress of excessive enforcement activities.

"SUBTITLE A—REGULATORY COMPLIANCE SIMPLIFICATION

"SEC. 211. DEFINITIONS.

"For purposes of this subtitle—

"(1) the terms 'rule' and 'small entity' have the same meanings as in section 601 of title 5, United States Code;

"(2) the term 'agency' has the same meaning as in section 551 of title 5, United States Code; and

"(3) the term 'small entity compliance guide' means a document designated as such by an agency.

"SEC. 212. COMPLIANCE GUIDES.

"(a) COMPLIANCE GUIDE.—For each rule or group of related rules for which an agency is required to prepare a final regulatory flexibility analysis under section 604 of title 5, United States Code, the agency shall publish one or more guides to assist small entities in complying with the rule, and shall designate such publications as 'small entity compliance guides'. The guides shall explain the actions a small entity is required to take to comply with a rule or group of rules. The agency shall, in its sole discretion, taking into account the subject matter of the rule and the language of relevant statutes, ensure that the guide is written using sufficiently plain language likely to be understood by affected small entities. Agencies may prepare separate guides covering groups or classes of similarly affected small entities, and may cooperate with associations of small entities to develop and distribute such guides.

"(b) COMPREHENSIVE SOURCE OF INFORMATION.—Agencies shall cooperate to make available to small entities through comprehensive sources of information, the small entity compliance guides and all other available information on statutory and regulatory requirements affecting small entities.

"(c) LIMITATION ON JUDICIAL REVIEW.—An agency's small entity compliance guide shall not be subject to judicial review, except that in any civil or administrative action against a small entity for a violation occurring after the effective date of this section, the content of the small entity compliance guide may be considered as evidence of the reasonableness or appropriateness of any proposed fines, penalties or damages.

"SEC. 213. INFORMAL SMALL ENTITY GUIDANCE.

"(a) GENERAL.—Whenever appropriate in the interest of administering statutes and regulations within the jurisdiction of an agency which regulates small entities, it shall be the practice of the agency to answer inquiries by small entities concerning information on, and advice about, compliance with such statutes and regulations, interpreting and applying the law to specific sets of facts supplied by the small entity. In any civil or administrative action against a small entity, guidance given by an agency applying the law to facts provided by the small entity may be considered as evidence of the reasonableness or appropriateness of any proposed fines, penalties or damages sought against such small entity.

"(b) PROGRAM.—Each agency regulating the activities of small entities shall establish a program for responding to such inquiries no later than 1 year after enactment of this section [Mar. 29, 1996], utilizing existing functions and personnel of the agency to the extent practicable.

"(c) REPORTING.—Each agency regulating the activities of small business shall report to the Committee on Small Business and Committee on Governmental Affairs of the Senate and the Committee on Small Business and Committee on the Judiciary of the House of Representatives no later than 2 years after the date of the enactment of this section on the scope of the agency's program, the number of small entities using the program, and the achievements of the program to assist small entity compliance with agency regulations.

"SEC. 214. SERVICES OF SMALL BUSINESS DEVELOPMENT CENTERS.

"(a) [Amended section 648 of Title 15, Commerce and Trade.]

"(b) Nothing in this Act [see Short Title of 1996 Amendment note, above] in any way affects or limits the ability of other technical assistance or extension programs to perform or continue to perform services related to compliance assistance.

"SEC. 215. COOPERATION ON GUIDANCE.

"Agencies may, to the extent resources are available and where appropriate, in cooperation with the States, develop guides that fully integrate requirements of both Federal and State regulations where regulations within an agency's area of interest at the Federal and State levels impact small entities. Where regulations vary among the States, separate guides may be created for separate States in cooperation with State agencies.

"SEC. 216. EFFECTIVE DATE.

"This subtitle and the amendments made by this subtitle shall take effect on the expiration of 90 days after the date of enactment of this subtitle [Mar. 29, 1996].

"SUBTITLE B—REGULATORY ENFORCEMENT REFORMS

"SEC. 221. DEFINITIONS.

"For purposes of this subtitle—

"(1) the terms 'rule' and 'small entity' have the same meanings as in section 601 of title 5, United States Code;

"(2) the term 'agency' has the same meaning as in section 551 of title 5, United States Code; and

"(3) the term 'small entity compliance guide' means a document designated as such by an agency.

"SEC. 222. SMALL BUSINESS AND AGRICULTURE ENFORCEMENT OMBUDSMAN.

"[Enacted section 657 of Title 15, Commerce and Trade.]

"SEC. 223. RIGHTS OF SMALL ENTITIES IN ENFORCEMENT ACTIONS.

"(a) IN GENERAL.—Each agency regulating the activities of small entities shall establish a policy or program within 1 year of enactment of this section [Mar. 29, 1996] to provide for the reduction, and under appropriate circumstances for the waiver, of civil penalties for violations of a statutory or regulatory requirement by a small entity. Under appropriate circumstances, an agency may consider ability to pay in determining penalty assessments on small entities.

"(b) CONDITIONS AND EXCLUSIONS.—Subject to the requirements or limitations of other statutes, policies or programs established under this section shall contain conditions or exclusions which may include, but shall not be limited to—

"(1) requiring the small entity to correct the violation within a reasonable correction period;

"(2) limiting the applicability to violations discovered through participation by the small entity in a compliance assistance or audit program operated or supported by the agency or a State;

"(3) excluding small entities that have been subject to multiple enforcement actions by the agency;

"(4) excluding violations involving willful or criminal conduct;

"(5) excluding violations that pose serious health, safety or environmental threats; and

"(6) requiring a good faith effort to comply with the law.

"(c) REPORTING.—Agencies shall report to the Committee on Small Business and Committee on Governmental Affairs of the Senate and the Committee on Small Business and Committee on Judiciary of the House of Representatives no later than 2 years after the date of enactment of this section [Mar. 29, 1996] on the scope of their program or policy, the number of enforcement actions against small entities that qualified or failed to qualify for the program or policy, and the total amount of penalty reductions and waivers.

"SEC. 224. EFFECTIVE DATE.

"This subtitle and the amendments made by this subtitle shall take effect on the expiration of 90 days after the date of enactment of this subtitle [Mar. 29, 1996]."

EFFECTS OF DEREGULATION ON RURAL AMERICA

Pub. L. 101–574, title III, § 309, Nov. 15, 1990, 104 Stat. 2831, provided that:

"(a) STUDY.—The Office of Technology Assessment shall conduct a study of the effects of deregulation on the economic vitality of rural areas. Such study shall include, but not be limited to, a thorough analysis of the impact of deregulation on—

"(1) the number of loans made by financial institutions to small businesses located in rural areas, a change in the level of security interests required for such loans, and the cost of such loans to rural small businesses for creation and expansion;

"(2) airline service in cities and towns with populations of 100,000 or less, including airline fare, the number of flights available, number of seats available, scheduling of flights, continuity of service, number of markets being served by large and small airlines, availability of nonstop service, availability of direct service, number of economic cancellations, number of flight delays, the types of airplanes used, and time delays;

"(3) the availability and costs of bus, rail and trucking transportation for businesses located in rural areas;

"(4) the availability and costs of state-of-the-art telecommunications services to small businesses located in rural areas, including voice telephone service, private (not multiparty) telephone service, reliable facsimile document and data transmission, competitive long distance carriers, cellular (mobile) telephone service, multifrequency tone signaling services such as touchtone services, custom-calling services (including three-way calling, call forwarding, and call waiting), voicemail services, and 911 emergency services with automatic number identification;

"(5) the availability and costs to rural schools, hospitals, and other public facilities, of sending and receiving audio and visual signals in cases where such ability will enhance the quality of services provided to rural residents and businesses; and

"(6) the availability and costs of services enumerated in paragraphs (1) through (5) in urban areas compared to rural areas.

"(b) REPORT.—Not later than 12 months after the date of enactment of this title [Nov. 15, 1990], the Office of Technology Assessment shall transmit to Congress a report on the results of the study conducted under subsection (a) together with its recommendations on how to address the problems facing small businesses in rural areas."

CONGRESSIONAL FINDINGS AND DECLARATION OF PURPOSE

Section 2 of Pub. L. 96–354 provided that:

"(a) The Congress finds and declares that—

"(1) when adopting regulations to protect the health, safety and economic welfare of the Nation, Federal agencies should seek to achieve statutory goals as effectively and efficiently as possible without imposing unnecessary burdens on the public;

"(2) laws and regulations designed for application to large scale entities have been applied uniformly to small businesses, small organizations, and small governmental jurisdictions even though the problems that gave rise to government action may not have been caused by those smaller entities;

"(3) uniform Federal regulatory and reporting requirements have in numerous instances imposed unnecessary and disproportionately burdensome demands including legal, accounting and consulting costs upon small businesses, small organizations, and small governmental jurisdictions with limited resources;

"(4) the failure to recognize differences in the scale and resources of regulated entities has in numerous instances adversely affected competition in the marketplace, discouraged innovation and restricted improvements in productivity;

"(5) unnecessary regulations create entry barriers in many industries and discourage potential entrepreneurs from introducing beneficial products and processes;

"(6) the practice of treating all regulated businesses, organizations, and governmental jurisdictions as equivalent may lead to inefficient use of regulatory agency resources, enforcement problems, and, in some cases, to actions inconsistent with the legislative intent of health, safety, environmental and economic welfare legislation;

"(7) alternative regulatory approaches which do not conflict with the stated objectives of applicable statutes may be available which minimize the significant economic impact of rules on small businesses, small organizations, and small governmental jurisdictions;

"(8) the process by which Federal regulations are developed and adopted should be reformed to require agencies to solicit the ideas and comments of small businesses, small organizations, and small governmental jurisdictions to examine the impact of proposed and existing rules on such entities, and to review the continued need for existing rules.

"(b) It is the purpose of this Act [enacting this chapter] to establish as a principle of regulatory issuance that agencies shall endeavor, consistent with the objectives of the rule and of applicable statutes, to fit regulatory and informational requirements to the scale of the businesses, organizations, and governmental jurisdictions subject to regulation. To achieve this principle, agencies are required to solicit and consider flexible regulatory proposals and to explain the rationale for their actions to assure that such proposals are given serious consideration."

EXECUTIVE ORDER NO. 12291

Ex. Ord. No. 12291, Feb. 17, 1981, 46 F.R. 13193, which established requirements for agencies to follow in promulgating regulations, reviewing existing regulations, and developing legislative proposals concerning regulation, was revoked by Ex. Ord. No. 12866, § 11, Sept. 30, 1993, 58 F.R. 51735, set out below.

EXECUTIVE ORDER NO. 12498

Ex. Ord. No. 12498, Jan. 4, 1985, 50 F.R. 1036, which established a regulatory planning process by which to develop and publish a regulatory program for each year, was revoked by Ex. Ord. No. 12866, § 11, Sept. 30, 1993, 58 F.R. 51735, set out below.

EXECUTIVE ORDER NO. 12606

Ex. Ord. No. 12606, Sept. 2, 1987, 52 F.R. 34188, which provided criteria for executive departments and agencies to follow in making policies and regulations to ensure consideration of effect of those policies and regulations on autonomy and rights of the family, was revoked by Ex. Ord. No. 13045, § 7, Apr. 21, 1997, 62 F.R. 19888, set out as a note under section 4321 of Title 42, The Public Health and Welfare.

EXECUTIVE ORDER NO. 12612

Ex. Ord. No. 12612, Oct. 26, 1987, 52 F.R. 41685, which set out fundamental federalism principles and policy-making criteria for executive departments and agencies to follow in formulating and implementing policies and limited the instances when executive departments and agencies could construe a Federal statute to preempt State law, was revoked by Ex. Ord. No. 13132, § 10(b), Aug. 4, 1999, 64 F.R. 43259, set out below.

EX. ORD. NO. 12630. GOVERNMENTAL ACTIONS AND INTERFERENCE WITH CONSTITUTIONALLY PROTECTED PROPERTY RIGHTS

Ex. Ord. No. 12630, Mar. 15, 1988, 53 F.R. 8859, provided:

By the authority vested in me as President by the Constitution and laws of the United States of America, and in order to ensure that government actions are undertaken on a well-reasoned basis with due regard for fiscal accountability, for the financial impact of the obligations imposed on the Federal government by the Just Compensation Clause of the Fifth Amendment, and for the Constitution, it is hereby ordered as follows:

SECTION 1. *Purpose.* (a) The Fifth Amendment of the United States Constitution provides that private property shall not be taken for public use without just compensation. Government historically has used the formal exercise of the power of eminent domain, which provides orderly processes for paying just compensation, to acquire private property for public use. Recent Supreme Court decisions, however, in reaffirming the fundamental protection of private property rights provided by the Fifth Amendment and in assessing the nature of governmental actions that have an impact on constitutionally protected property rights, have also reaffirmed that governmental actions that do not formally invoke the condemnation power, including regulations, may result in a taking for which just compensation is required.

(b) Responsible fiscal management and fundamental principles of good government require that government decision-makers evaluate carefully the effect of their administrative, regulatory, and legislative actions on constitutionally protected property rights. Executive departments and agencies should review their actions carefully to prevent unnecessary takings and should account in decision-making for those takings that are necessitated by statutory mandate.

(c) The purpose of this Order is to assist Federal departments and agencies in undertaking such reviews and in proposing, planning, and implementing actions with due regard for the constitutional protections provided by the Fifth Amendment and to reduce the risk of undue or inadvertent burdens on the public fisc resulting from lawful governmental action. In furtherance of the purpose of this Order, the Attorney General shall, consistent with the principles stated herein and in consultation with the Executive departments and agencies, promulgate Guidelines for the Evaluation of Risk and Avoidance of Unanticipated Takings to which each Executive department or agency shall refer in making the evaluations required by this Order or in otherwise taking any action that is the subject of this Order. The Guidelines shall be promulgated no later than May 1, 1988, and shall be disseminated to all units

of each Executive department and agency no later than July 1, 1988. The Attorney General shall, as necessary, update these guidelines to reflect fundamental changes in takings law occurring as a result of Supreme Court decisions.

SEC. 2. *Definitions.* For the purpose of this Order: (a) "Policies that have takings implications" refers to Federal regulations, proposed Federal regulations, proposed Federal legislation, comments on proposed Federal legislation, or other Federal policy statements that, if implemented or enacted, could effect a taking, such as rules and regulations that propose or implement licensing, permitting, or other condition requirements or limitations on private property use, or that require dedications or exactions from owners of private property. "Policies that have takings implications" does not include:

(1) Actions abolishing regulations, discontinuing governmental programs, or modifying regulations in a manner that lessens interference with the use of private property;

(2) Actions taken with respect to properties held in trust by the United States or in preparation for or during treaty negotiations with foreign nations;

(3) Law enforcement actions involving seizure, for violations of law, of property for forfeiture or as evidence in criminal proceedings;

(4) Studies or similar efforts or planning activities;

(5) Communications between Federal agencies or departments and State or local land-use planning agencies regarding planned or proposed State or local actions regulating private property regardless of whether such communications are initiated by a Federal agency or department or are undertaken in response to an invitation by the State or local authority;

(6) The placement of military facilities or military activities involving the use of Federal property alone; or

(7) Any military or foreign affairs functions (including procurement functions thereunder) but not including the U.S. Army Corps of Engineers civil works program.

(b) Private property refers to all property protected by the Just Compensation Clause of the Fifth Amendment.

(c) "Actions" refers to proposed Federal regulations, proposed Federal legislation, comments on proposed Federal legislation, applications of Federal regulations to specific property, or Federal governmental actions physically invading or occupying private property, or other policy statements or actions related to Federal regulation or direct physical invasion or occupancy, but does not include:

(1) Actions in which the power of eminent domain is formally exercised;

(2) Actions taken with respect to properties held in trust by the United States or in preparation for or during treaty negotiations with foreign nations;

(3) Law enforcement actions involving seizure, for violations of law, of property for forfeiture or as evidence in criminal proceedings;

(4) Studies or similar efforts or planning activities;

(5) Communications between Federal agencies or departments and State or local land-use planning agencies regarding planned or proposed State or local actions regulating private property regardless of whether such communications are initiated by a Federal agency or department or are undertaken in response to an invitation by the State or local authority;

(6) The placement of military facilities or military activities involving the use of Federal property alone; or

(7) Any military or foreign affairs functions (including procurement functions thereunder), but not including the U.S. Army Corps of Engineers civil works program.

SEC. 3. *General Principles.* In formulating or implementing policies that have takings implications, each Executive department and agency shall be guided by the following general principles:

(a) Governmental officials should be sensitive to, anticipate, and account for, the obligations imposed by the Just Compensation Clause of the Fifth Amendment in planning and carrying out governmental actions so that they do not result in the imposition of unanticipated or undue additional burdens on the public fisc.

(b) Actions undertaken by governmental officials that result in a physical invasion or occupancy of private property, and regulations imposed on private property that substantially affect its value or use, may constitute a taking of property. Further, governmental action may amount to a taking even though the action results in less than a complete deprivation of all use or value, or of all separate and distinct interests in the same private property and even if the action constituting a taking is temporary in nature.

(c) Government officials whose actions are taken specifically for purposes of protecting public health and safety are ordinarily given broader latitude by courts before their actions are considered to be takings. However, the mere assertion of a public health and safety purpose is insufficient to avoid a taking. Actions to which this Order applies asserted to be for the protection of public health and safety, therefore, should be undertaken only in response to real and substantial threats to public health and safety, be designed to advance significantly the health and safety purpose, and be no greater than is necessary to achieve the health and safety purpose.

(d) While normal governmental processes do not ordinarily effect takings, undue delays in decision-making during which private property use if interfered with carry a risk of being held to be takings. Additionally, a delay in processing may increase significantly the size of compensation due if a taking is later found to have occurred.

(e) The Just Compensation Clause is self-actuating, requiring that compensation be paid whenever governmental action results in a taking of private property regardless of whether the underlying authority for the action contemplated a taking or authorized the payment of compensation. Accordingly, governmental actions that may have a significant impact on the use or value of private property should be scrutinized to avoid undue or unplanned burdens on the public fisc.

SEC. 4. *Department and Agency Action.* In addition to the fundamental principles set forth in Section 3, Executive departments and agencies shall adhere, to the extent permitted by law, to the following criteria when implementing policies that have takings implications:

(a) When an Executive department or agency requires a private party to obtain a permit in order to undertake a specific use of, or action with respect to, private property, any conditions imposed on the granting of a permit shall:

(1) Serve the same purpose that would have been served by a prohibition of the use or action; and

(2) Substantially advance that purpose.

(b) When a proposed action would place a restriction on a use of private property, the restriction imposed on the use shall not be disproportionate to the extent to which the use contributes to the overall problem that the restriction is imposed to redress.

(c) When a proposed action involves a permitting process or any other decision-making process that will interfere with, or otherwise prohibit, the use of private property pending the completion of the process, the duration of the process shall be kept to the minimum necessary.

(d) Before undertaking any proposed action regulating private property use for the protection of public health or safety, the Executive department or agency involved shall, in internal deliberative documents and any submissions to the Director of the Office of Management and Budget that are required:

(1) Identify clearly, with as much specificity as possible, the public health or safety risk created by the private property use that is the subject of the proposed action;

(2) Establish that such proposed action substantially advances the purpose of protecting public health and safety against the specifically identified risk;

(3) Establish to the extent possible that the restrictions imposed on the private property are not disproportionate to the extent to which the use contributes to the overall risk; and

(4) Estimate, to the extent possible, the potential cost to the government in the event that a court later determines that the action constituted a taking.

In instances in which there is an immediate threat to health and safety that constitutes an emergency requiring immediate response, this analysis may be done upon completion of the emergency action.

SEC. 5. *Executive Department and Agency Implementation.* (a) The head of each Executive department and agency shall designate an official to be responsible for ensuring compliance with this Order with respect to the actions of the department or agency.

(b) Executive departments and agencies shall, to the extent permitted by law, identify the takings implications of proposed regulatory actions and address the merits of those actions in light of the identified takings implications, if any, in all required submissions made to the Office of Management and Budget. Significant takings implications should also be identified and discussed in notices of proposed rule-making and messages transmitting legislative proposals to the Congress stating the departments' and agencies' conclusions on the takings issues.

(c) Executive departments and agencies shall identify each existing Federal rule and regulation against which a takings award has been made or against which a takings claim is pending including the amount of each claim or award. A "takings" award has been made or a "takings" claim pending if the award was made, or the pending claim brought, pursuant to the Just Compensation Clause of the Fifth Amendment. An itemized compilation of all such awards made in Fiscal Years 1985, 1986, and 1987 and all such pending claims shall be submitted to the Director, Office of Management and Budget, on or before May 16, 1988.

(d) Each Executive department and agency shall submit annually to the Director, Office of Management and Budget, and to the Attorney General an itemized compilation of all awards of just compensation entered against the United States for takings, including awards of interest as well as monies paid pursuant to the provisions of the Uniform Relocation Assistance and Real Property Acquisition Policies Act of 1970, 42 U.S.C. 4601.

(e)(1) The Director, Office of Management and Budget, and the Attorney General shall each, to the extent permitted by law, take action to ensure that the policies of the Executive departments and agencies are consistent with the principles, criteria, and requirements stated in Sections 1 through 5 of this Order, and the Office of Management and Budget shall take action to ensure that all takings awards levied against agencies are properly accounted for in agency budget submissions.

(2) In addition to the guidelines required by Section 1 of this Order, the Attorney General shall, in consultation with each Executive department and agency to which this Order applies, promulgate such supplemental guidelines as may be appropriate to the specific obligations of that department or agency.

SEC. 6. *Judicial Review.* This Order is intended only to improve the internal management of the Executive branch and is not intended to create any right or benefit, substantive or procedural, enforceable at law by a party against the United States, its agencies, its officers, or any person.

RONALD REAGAN.

EX. ORD. NO. 12861. ELIMINATION OF ONE-HALF OF
EXECUTIVE BRANCH INTERNAL REGULATIONS

Ex. Ord. No. 12861, Sept. 11, 1993, 58 F.R. 48255, provided:

By the authority vested in me as President by the Constitution and the laws of the United States of America, including section 301 of title 3, United States

Code, and section 1111 of title 31, United States Code, and to cut 50 percent of the executive branch's internal regulations in order to streamline and improve customer service to the American people, it is hereby ordered as follows:

SECTION 1. *Regulatory Reductions.* Each executive department and agency shall undertake to eliminate not less than 50 percent of its civilian internal management regulations that are not required by law within 3 years of the effective date of this order. An agency internal management regulation, for the purposes of this order, means an agency directive or regulation that pertains to its organization, management, or personnel matters. Reductions in agency internal management regulations shall be concentrated in areas that will result in the greatest improvement in productivity, streamlining of operations, and improvement in customer service.

SEC. 2. *Coverage.* This order applies to all executive branch departments and agencies.

SEC. 3. *Implementation.* The Director of the Office of Management and Budget shall issue instructions regarding the implementation of this order, including exemptions necessary for the delivery of essential services and compliance with applicable law.

SEC. 4. *Independent Agencies.* All independent regulatory commissions and agencies are requested to comply with the provisions of this order.

WILLIAM J. CLINTON.

EX. ORD. NO. 12866. REGULATORY PLANNING AND REVIEW

Ex. Ord. No. 12866, Sept. 30, 1993, 58 F.R. 51735, provided:

The American people deserve a regulatory system that works for them, not against them: a regulatory system that protects and improves their health, safety, environment, and well-being and improves the performance of the economy without imposing unacceptable or unreasonable costs on society; regulatory policies that recognize that the private sector and private markets are the best engine for economic growth; regulatory approaches that respect the role of State, local, and tribal governments; and regulations that are effective, consistent, sensible, and understandable. We do not have such a regulatory system today.

With this Executive order, the Federal Government begins a program to reform and make more efficient the regulatory process. The objectives of this Executive order are to enhance planning and coordination with respect to both new and existing regulations; to reaffirm the primacy of Federal agencies in the regulatory decision-making process; to restore the integrity and legitimacy of regulatory review and oversight; and to make the process more accessible and open to the public. In pursuing these objectives, the regulatory process shall be conducted so as to meet applicable statutory requirements and with due regard to the discretion that has been entrusted to the Federal agencies.

Accordingly, by the authority vested in me as President by the Constitution and the laws of the United States of America, it is hereby ordered as follows:

SECTION 1. *Statement of Regulatory Philosophy and Principles.*

(a) *The Regulatory Philosophy.* Federal agencies should promulgate only such regulations as are required by law, are necessary to interpret the law, or are made necessary by compelling public need, such as material failures of private markets to protect or improve the health and safety of the public, the environment, or the well-being of the American people. In deciding whether and how to regulate, agencies should assess all costs and benefits of available regulatory alternatives, including the alternative of not regulating. Costs and benefits shall be understood to include both quantifiable measures (to the fullest extent that these can be usefully estimated) and qualitative measures of costs and benefits that are difficult to quantify, but nevertheless essential to consider. Further, in choosing among alternative regulatory approaches, agencies should select those approaches that maximize net benefits (including potential economic, environmental, public health and safety, and other advantages; distributive impacts; and equity), unless a statute requires another regulatory approach.

(b) *The Principles of Regulation.* To ensure that the agencies' regulatory programs are consistent with the philosophy set forth above, agencies should adhere to the following principles, to the extent permitted by law and where applicable:

(1) Each agency shall identify the problem that it intends to address (including, where applicable, the failures of private markets or public institutions that warrant new agency action) as well as assess the significance of that problem.

(2) Each agency shall examine whether existing regulations (or other law) have created, or contributed to, the problem that a new regulation is intended to correct and whether those regulations (or other law) should be modified to achieve the intended goal of regulation more effectively.

(3) Each agency shall identify and assess available alternatives to direct regulation, including providing economic incentives to encourage the desired behavior, such as user fees or marketable permits, or providing information upon which choices can be made by the public.

(4) In setting regulatory priorities, each agency shall consider, to the extent reasonable, the degree and nature of the risks posed by various substances or activities within its jurisdiction.

(5) When an agency determines that a regulation is the best available method of achieving the regulatory objective, it shall design its regulations in the most cost-effective manner to achieve the regulatory objective. In doing so, each agency shall consider incentives for innovation, consistency, predictability, the costs of enforcement and compliance (to the government, regulated entities, and the public), flexibility, distributive impacts, and equity.

(6) Each agency shall assess both the costs and the benefits of the intended regulation and, recognizing that some costs and benefits are difficult to quantify, propose or adopt a regulation only upon a reasoned determination that the benefits of the intended regulation justify its costs.

(7) Each agency shall base its decisions on the best reasonably obtainable scientific, technical, economic, and other information concerning the need for, and consequences of, the intended regulation.

(8) Each agency shall identify and assess alternative forms of regulation and shall, to the extent feasible, specify performance objectives, rather than specifying the behavior or manner of compliance that regulated entities must adopt.

(9) Wherever feasible, agencies shall seek views of appropriate State, local, and tribal officials before imposing regulatory requirements that might significantly or uniquely affect those governmental entities. Each agency shall assess the effects of Federal regulations on State, local, and tribal governments, including specifically the availability of resources to carry out those mandates, and seek to minimize those burdens that uniquely or significantly affect such governmental entities, consistent with achieving regulatory objectives. In addition, as appropriate, agencies shall seek to harmonize Federal regulatory actions with related State, local, and tribal regulatory and other governmental functions.

(10) Each agency shall avoid regulations that are inconsistent, incompatible, or duplicative with its other regulations or those of other Federal agencies.

(11) Each agency shall tailor its regulations to impose the least burden on society, including individuals, businesses of differing sizes, and other entities (including small communities and governmental entities), consistent with obtaining the regulatory objectives, taking into account, among other things, and to the extent practicable, the costs of cumulative regulations.

(12) Each agency shall draft its regulations to be simple and easy to understand, with the goal of minimizing

the potential for uncertainty and litigation arising from such uncertainty.

SEC. 2. *Organization.* An efficient regulatory planning and review process is vital to ensure that the Federal Government's regulatory system best serves the American people.

(a) *The Agencies.* Because Federal agencies are the repositories of significant substantive expertise and experience, they are responsible for developing regulations and assuring that the regulations are consistent with applicable law, the President's priorities, and the principles set forth in this Executive order.

(b) *The Office of Management and Budget.* Coordinated review of agency rulemaking is necessary to ensure that regulations are consistent with applicable law, the President's priorities, and the principles set forth in this Executive order, and that decisions made by one agency do not conflict with the policies or actions taken or planned by another agency. The Office of Management and Budget (OMB) shall carry out that review function. Within OMB, the Office of Information and Regulatory Affairs (OIRA) is the repository of expertise concerning regulatory issues, including methodologies and procedures that affect more than one agency, this Executive order, and the President's regulatory policies. To the extent permitted by law, OMB shall provide guidance to agencies and assist the President, the Vice President, and other regulatory policy advisors to the President in regulatory planning and shall be the entity that reviews individual regulations, as provided by this Executive order.

(c) *The Vice President.* The Vice President is the principal advisor to the President on, and shall coordinate the development and presentation of recommendations concerning, regulatory policy, planning, and review, as set forth in this Executive order. In fulfilling their responsibilities under this Executive order, the President and the Vice President shall be assisted by the regulatory policy advisors within the Executive Office of the President and by such agency officials and personnel as the President and the Vice President may, from time to time, consult.

SEC. 3. *Definitions.* For purposes of this Executive order:

(a) "Advisors" refers to such regulatory policy advisors to the President as the President and Vice President may from time to time consult, including, among others: (1) the Director of OMB; (2) the Chair (or another member) of the Council of Economic Advisers; (3) the Assistant to the President for Economic Policy; (4) the Assistant to the President for Domestic Policy; (5) the Assistant to the President for National Security Affairs; (6) the Assistant to the President for Science and Technology; (7) the Assistant to the President for Intergovernmental Affairs; (8) the Assistant to the President and Staff Secretary; (9) the Assistant to the President and Chief of Staff to the Vice President; (10) the Assistant to the President and Counsel to the President; (11) the Deputy Assistant to the President and Director of the White House Office on Environmental Policy; and (12) the Administrator of OIRA, who also shall coordinate communications relating to this Executive order among the agencies, OMB, the other Advisors, and the Office of the Vice President.

(b) "Agency," unless otherwise indicated, means any authority of the United States that is an "agency" under 44 U.S.C. 3502(1), other than those considered to be independent regulatory agencies, as defined in 44 U.S.C. 3502(10).

(c) "Director" means the Director of OMB.

(d) "Regulation" or "rule" means an agency statement of general applicability and future effect, which the agency intends to have the force and effect of law, that is designed to implement, interpret, or prescribe law or policy or to describe the procedure or practice requirements of an agency. It does not, however, include:

(1) Regulations or rules issued in accordance with the formal rulemaking provisions of 5 U.S.C. 556, 557;

(2) Regulations or rules that pertain to a military or foreign affairs function of the United States, other than procurement regulations and regulations involving the import or export of non-defense articles and services;

(3) Regulations or rules that are limited to agency organization, management, or personnel matters; or

(4) Any other category of regulations exempted by the Administrator of OIRA.

(e) "Regulatory action" means any substantive action by an agency (normally published in the Federal Register) that promulgates or is expected to lead to the promulgation of a final rule or regulation, including notices of inquiry, advance notices of proposed rulemaking, and notices of proposed rulemaking.

(f) "Significant regulatory action" means any regulatory action that is likely to result in a rule that may:

(1) Have an annual effect on the economy of $100 million or more or adversely affect in a material way the economy, a sector of the economy, productivity, competition, jobs, the environment, public health or safety, or State, local, or tribal governments or communities;

(2) Create a serious inconsistency or otherwise interfere with an action taken or planned by another agency;

(3) Materially alter the budgetary impact of entitlements, grants, user fees, or loan programs or the rights and obligations of recipients thereof; or

(4) Raise novel legal or policy issues arising out of legal mandates, the President's priorities, or the principles set forth in this Executive order.

SEC. 4. *Planning Mechanism.* In order to have an effective regulatory program, to provide for coordination of regulations, to maximize consultation and the resolution of potential conflicts at an early stage, to involve the public and its State, local, and tribal officials in regulatory planning, and to ensure that new or revised regulations promote the President's priorities and the principles set forth in this Executive order, these procedures shall be followed, to the extent permitted by law:

(a) *Agencies' Policy Meeting.* Early in each year's planning cycle, the Vice President shall convene a meeting of the Advisors and the heads of agencies to seek a common understanding of priorities and to coordinate regulatory efforts to be accomplished in the upcoming year.

(b) *Unified Regulatory Agenda.* For purposes of this subsection, the term "agency" or "agencies" shall also include those considered to be independent regulatory agencies, as defined in 44 U.S.C. 3502(10). Each agency shall prepare an agenda of all regulations under development or review, at a time and in a manner specified by the Administrator of OIRA. The description of each regulatory action shall contain, at a minimum, a regulation identifier number, a brief summary of the action, the legal authority for the action, any legal deadline for the action, and the name and telephone number of a knowledgeable agency official. Agencies may incorporate the information required under 5 U.S.C. 602 and [former] 41 U.S.C. 402 into these agendas.

(c) *The Regulatory Plan.* For purposes of this subsection, the term "agency" or "agencies" shall also include those considered to be independent regulatory agencies, as defined in 44 U.S.C. 3502(10). (1) As part of the Unified Regulatory Agenda, beginning in 1994, each agency shall prepare a Regulatory Plan (Plan) of the most important significant regulatory actions that the agency reasonably expects to issue in proposed or final form in that fiscal year or thereafter. The Plan shall be approved personally by the agency head and shall contain at a minimum:

(A) A statement of the agency's regulatory objectives and priorities and how they relate to the President's priorities;

(B) A summary of each planned significant regulatory action including, to the extent possible, alternatives to be considered and preliminary estimates of the anticipated costs and benefits;

(C) A summary of the legal basis for each such action, including whether any aspect of the action is required by statute or court order;

(D) A statement of the need for each such action and, if applicable, how the action will reduce risks to public health, safety, or the environment, as well as how the magnitude of the risk addressed by the action relates to other risks within the jurisdiction of the agency;

(E) The agency's schedule for action, including a statement of any applicable statutory or judicial deadlines; and

(F) The name, address, and telephone number of a person the public may contact for additional information about the planned regulatory action.

(2) Each agency shall forward its Plan to OIRA by June 1st of each year.

(3) Within 10 calendar days after OIRA has received an agency's Plan, OIRA shall circulate it to other affected agencies, the Advisors, and the Vice President.

(4) An agency head who believes that a planned regulatory action of another agency may conflict with its own policy or action taken or planned shall promptly notify, in writing, the Administrator of OIRA, who shall forward that communication to the issuing agency, the Advisors, and the Vice President.

(5) If the Administrator of OIRA believes that a planned regulatory action of an agency may be inconsistent with the President's priorities or the principles set forth in this Executive order or may be in conflict with any policy or action taken or planned by another agency, the Administrator of OIRA shall promptly notify, in writing, the affected agencies, the Advisors, and the Vice President.

(6) The Vice President, with the Advisors' assistance, may consult with the heads of agencies with respect to their Plans and, in appropriate instances, request further consideration or inter-agency coordination.

(7) The Plans developed by the issuing agency shall be published annually in the October publication of the Unified Regulatory Agenda. This publication shall be made available to the Congress; State, local, and tribal governments; and the public. Any views on any aspect of any agency Plan, including whether any planned regulatory action might conflict with any other planned or existing regulation, impose any unintended consequences on the public, or confer any unclaimed benefits on the public, should be directed to the issuing agency, with a copy to OIRA.

(d) *Regulatory Working Group.* Within 30 days of the date of this Executive order, the Administrator of OIRA shall convene a Regulatory Working Group ("Working Group"), which shall consist of representatives of the heads of each agency that the Administrator determines to have significant domestic regulatory responsibility, the Advisors, and the Vice President. The Administrator of OIRA shall chair the Working Group and shall periodically advise the Vice President on the activities of the Working Group. The Working Group shall serve as a forum to assist agencies in identifying and analyzing important regulatory issues (including, among others (1) the development of innovative regulatory techniques, (2) the methods, efficacy, and utility of comparative risk assessment in regulatory decision-making, and (3) the development of short forms and other streamlined regulatory approaches for small businesses and other entities). The Working Group shall meet at least quarterly and may meet as a whole or in subgroups of agencies with an interest in particular issues or subject areas. To inform its discussions, the Working Group may commission analytical studies and reports by OIRA, the Administrative Conference of the United States, or any other agency.

(e) *Conferences.* The Administrator of OIRA shall meet quarterly with representatives of State, local, and tribal governments to identify both existing and proposed regulations that may uniquely or significantly affect those governmental entities. The Administrator of OIRA shall also convene, from time to time, conferences with representatives of businesses, nongovernmental organizations, and the public to discuss regulatory issues of common concern.

SEC. 5. *Existing Regulations.* In order to reduce the regulatory burden on the American people, their fami-

lies, their communities, their State, local, and tribal governments, and their industries; to determine whether regulations promulgated by the executive branch of the Federal Government have become unjustified or unnecessary as a result of changed circumstances; to confirm that regulations are both compatible with each other and not duplicative or inappropriately burdensome in the aggregate; to ensure that all regulations are consistent with the President's priorities and the principles set forth in this Executive order, within applicable law; and to otherwise improve the effectiveness of existing regulations: (a) Within 90 days of the date of this Executive order, each agency shall submit to OIRA a program, consistent with its resources and regulatory priorities, under which the agency will periodically review its existing significant regulations to determine whether any such regulations should be modified or eliminated so as to make the agency's regulatory program more effective in achieving the regulatory objectives, less burdensome, or in greater alignment with the President's priorities and the principles set forth in this Executive order. Any significant regulations selected for review shall be included in the agency's annual Plan. The agency shall also identify any legislative mandates that require the agency to promulgate or continue to impose regulations that the agency believes are unnecessary or outdated by reason of changed circumstances.

(b) The Administrator of OIRA shall work with the Regulatory Working Group and other interested entities to pursue the objectives of this section. State, local, and tribal governments are specifically encouraged to assist in the identification of regulations that impose significant or unique burdens on those governmental entities and that appear to have outlived their justification or be otherwise inconsistent with the public interest.

(c) The Vice President, in consultation with the Advisors, may identify for review by the appropriate agency or agencies other existing regulations of an agency or groups of regulations of more than one agency that affect a particular group, industry, or sector of the economy, or may identify legislative mandates that may be appropriate for reconsideration by the Congress.

SEC. 6. *Centralized Review of Regulations.* The guidelines set forth below shall apply to all regulatory actions, for both new and existing regulations, by agencies other than those agencies specifically exempted by the Administrator of OIRA:

(a) *Agency Responsibilities.* (1) Each agency shall (consistent with its own rules, regulations, or procedures) provide the public with meaningful participation in the regulatory process. In particular, before issuing a notice of proposed rulemaking, each agency should, where appropriate, seek the involvement of those who are intended to benefit from and those expected to be burdened by any regulation (including, specifically, State, local, and tribal officials). In addition, each agency should afford the public a meaningful opportunity to comment on any proposed regulation, which in most cases should include a comment period of not less than 60 days. Each agency also is directed to explore and, where appropriate, use consensual mechanisms for developing regulations, including negotiated rulemaking.

(2) Within 60 days of the date of this Executive order, each agency head shall designate a Regulatory Policy Officer who shall report to the agency head. The Regulatory Policy Officer shall be involved at each stage of the regulatory process to foster the development of effective, innovative, and least burdensome regulations and to further the principles set forth in this Executive order.

(3) In addition to adhering to its own rules and procedures and to the requirements of the Administrative Procedure Act [5 U.S.C. 551 et seq., 701 et seq.], the Regulatory Flexibility Act [5 U.S.C. 601 et seq.], the Paperwork Reduction Act [44 U.S.C. 3501 et seq.], and other applicable law, each agency shall develop its regulatory actions in a timely fashion and adhere to the following procedures with respect to a regulatory action:

(A) Each agency shall provide OIRA, at such times and in the manner specified by the Administrator of OIRA, with a list of its planned regulatory actions, indicating those which the agency believes are significant regulatory actions within the meaning of this Executive order. Absent a material change in the development of the planned regulatory action, those not designated as significant will not be subject to review under this section unless, within 10 working days of receipt of the list, the Administrator of OIRA notifies the agency that OIRA has determined that a planned regulation is a significant regulatory action within the meaning of this Executive order. The Administrator of OIRA may waive review of any planned regulatory action designated by the agency as significant, in which case the agency need not further comply with subsection (a)(3)(B) or subsection (a)(3)(C) of this section.

(B) For each matter identified as, or determined by the Administrator of OIRA to be, a significant regulatory action, the issuing agency shall provide to OIRA:

(i) The text of the draft regulatory action, together with a reasonably detailed description of the need for the regulatory action and an explanation of how the regulatory action will meet that need; and

(ii) An assessment of the potential costs and benefits of the regulatory action, including an explanation of the manner in which the regulatory action is consistent with a statutory mandate and, to the extent permitted by law, promotes the President's priorities and avoids undue interference with State, local, and tribal governments in the exercise of their governmental functions.

(C) For those matters identified as, or determined by the Administrator of OIRA to be, a significant regulatory action within the scope of section 3(f)(1), the agency shall also provide to OIRA the following additional information developed as part of the agency's decision-making process (unless prohibited by law):

(i) An assessment, including the underlying analysis, of benefits anticipated from the regulatory action (such as, but not limited to, the promotion of the efficient functioning of the economy and private markets, the enhancement of health and safety, the protection of the natural environment, and the elimination or reduction of discrimination or bias) together with, to the extent feasible, a quantification of those benefits;

(ii) An assessment, including the underlying analysis, of costs anticipated from the regulatory action (such as, but not limited to, the direct cost both to the government in administering the regulation and to businesses and others in complying with the regulation, and any adverse effects on the efficient functioning of the economy, private markets (including productivity, employment, and competitiveness), health, safety, and the natural environment), together with, to the extent feasible, a quantification of those costs; and

(iii) An assessment, including the underlying analysis, of costs and benefits of potentially effective and reasonably feasible alternatives to the planned regulation, identified by the agencies or the public (including improving the current regulation and reasonably viable nonregulatory actions), and an explanation why the planned regulatory action is preferable to the identified potential alternatives.

(D) In emergency situations or when an agency is obligated by law to act more quickly than normal review procedures allow, the agency shall notify OIRA as soon as possible and, to the extent practicable, comply with subsections (a)(3)(B) and (C) of this section. For those regulatory actions that are governed by a statutory or court-imposed deadline, the agency shall, to the extent practicable, schedule rulemaking proceedings so as to permit sufficient time for OIRA to conduct its review, as set forth below in subsection (b)(2) through (4) of this section.

(E) After the regulatory action has been published in the Federal Register or otherwise issued to the public, the agency shall:

(i) Make available to the public the information set forth in subsections (a)(3)(B) and (C);

(ii) Identify for the public, in a complete, clear, and simple manner, the substantive changes between the draft submitted to OIRA for review and the action subsequently announced; and

(iii) Identify for the public those changes in the regulatory action that were made at the suggestion or recommendation of OIRA.

(F) All information provided to the public by the agency shall be in plain, understandable language.

(b) *OIRA Responsibilities.* The Administrator of OIRA shall provide meaningful guidance and oversight so that each agency's regulatory actions are consistent with applicable law, the President's priorities, and the principles set forth in this Executive order and do not conflict with the policies or actions of another agency. OIRA shall, to the extent permitted by law, adhere to the following guidelines:

(1) OIRA may review only actions identified by the agency or by OIRA as significant regulatory actions under subsection (a)(3)(A) of this section.

(2) OIRA shall waive review or notify the agency in writing of the results of its review within the following time periods:

(A) For any notices of inquiry, advance notices of proposed rulemaking, or other preliminary regulatory actions prior to a Notice of Proposed Rulemaking, within 10 working days after the date of submission of the draft action to OIRA;

(B) For all other regulatory actions, within 90 calendar days after the date of submission of the information set forth in subsections (a)(3)(B) and (C) of this section, unless OIRA has previously reviewed this information and, since that review, there has been no material change in the facts and circumstances upon which the regulatory action is based, in which case, OIRA shall complete its review within 45 days; and

(C) The review process may be extended (1) once by no more than 30 calendar days upon the written approval of the Director and (2) at the request of the agency head.

(3) For each regulatory action that the Administrator of OIRA returns to an agency for further consideration of some or all of its provisions, the Administrator of OIRA shall provide the issuing agency a written explanation for such return, setting forth the pertinent provision of this Executive order on which OIRA is relying. If the agency head disagrees with some or all of the bases for the return, the agency head shall so inform the Administrator of OIRA in writing.

(4) Except as otherwise provided by law or required by a Court, in order to ensure greater openness, accessibility, and accountability in the regulatory review process, OIRA shall be governed by the following disclosure requirements:

(A) Only the Administrator of OIRA (or a particular designee) shall receive oral communications initiated by persons not employed by the executive branch of the Federal Government regarding the substance of a regulatory action under OIRA review;

(B) All substantive communications between OIRA personnel and persons not employed by the executive branch of the Federal Government regarding a regulatory action under review shall be governed by the following guidelines: (i) A representative from the issuing agency shall be invited to any meeting between OIRA personnel and such person(s);

(ii) OIRA shall forward to the issuing agency, within 10 working days of receipt of the communication(s), all written communications, regardless of format, between OIRA personnel and any person who is not employed by the executive branch of the Federal Government, and the dates and names of individuals involved in all substantive oral communications (including meetings to which an agency representative was invited, but did not attend, and telephone conversations between OIRA personnel and any such persons); and

(iii) OIRA shall publicly disclose relevant information about such communication(s), as set forth below in subsection (b)(4)(C) of this section.

(C) OIRA shall maintain a publicly available log that shall contain, at a minimum, the following information pertinent to regulatory actions under review:

(i) The status of all regulatory actions, including if (and if so, when and by whom) Vice Presidential and Presidential consideration was requested;

(ii) A notation of all written communications forwarded to an issuing agency under subsection (b)(4)(B)(ii) of this section; and

(iii) The dates and names of individuals involved in all substantive oral communications, including meetings and telephone conversations, between OIRA personnel and any person not employed by the executive branch of the Federal Government, and the subject matter discussed during such communications.

(D) After the regulatory action has been published in the Federal Register or otherwise issued to the public, or after the agency has announced its decision not to publish or issue the regulatory action, OIRA shall make available to the public all documents exchanged between OIRA and the agency during the review by OIRA under this section.

(5) All information provided to the public by OIRA shall be in plain, understandable language.

SEC. 7. *Resolution of Conflicts.* To the extent permitted by law, disagreements or conflicts between or among agency heads or between OMB and any agency that cannot be resolved by the Administrator of OIRA shall be resolved by the President, or by the Vice President acting at the request of the President, with the relevant agency head (and, as appropriate, other interested government officials). Vice Presidential and Presidential consideration of such disagreements may be initiated only by the Director, by the head of the issuing agency, or by the head of an agency that has a significant interest in the regulatory action at issue. Such review will not be undertaken at the request of other persons, entities, or their agents.

Resolution of such conflicts shall be informed by recommendations developed by the Vice President, after consultation with the Advisors (and other executive branch officials or personnel whose responsibilities to the President include the subject matter at issue). The development of these recommendations shall be concluded within 60 days after review has been requested.

During the Vice Presidential and Presidential review period, communications with any person not employed by the Federal Government relating to the substance of the regulatory action under review and directed to the Advisors or their staffs or to the staff of the Vice President shall be in writing and shall be forwarded by the recipient to the affected agency(ies) for inclusion in the public docket(s). When the communication is not in writing, such Advisors or staff members shall inform the outside party that the matter is under review and that any comments should be submitted in writing.

At the end of this review process, the President, or the Vice President acting at the request of the President, shall notify the affected agency and the Administrator of OIRA of the President's decision with respect to the matter.

SEC. 8. *Publication.* Except to the extent required by law, an agency shall not publish in the Federal Register or otherwise issue to the public any regulatory action that is subject to review under section 6 of this Executive order until (1) the Administrator of OIRA notifies the agency that OIRA has waived its review of the action or has completed its review without any requests for further consideration, or (2) the applicable time period in section 6(b)(2) expires without OIRA having notified the agency that it is returning the regulatory action for further consideration under section 6(b)(3), whichever occurs first. If the terms of the preceding sentence have not been satisfied and an agency wants to publish or otherwise issue a regulatory action, the head of that agency may request Presidential consideration through the Vice President, as provided under section 7 of this order. Upon receipt of this request, the Vice President shall notify OIRA and the Advisors. The guidelines and time period set forth in section 7 shall apply to the publication of regulatory actions for which Presidential consideration has been sought.

SEC. 9. *Agency Authority.* Nothing in this order shall be construed as displacing the agencies' authority or responsibilities, as authorized by law.

SEC. 10. *Judicial Review.* Nothing in this Executive order shall affect any otherwise available judicial review of agency action. This Executive order is intended only to improve the internal management of the Federal Government and does not create any right or benefit, substantive or procedural, enforceable at law or equity by a party against the United States, its agencies or instrumentalities, its officers or employees, or any other person.

SEC. 11. *Revocations.* Executive Orders Nos. 12291 and 12498; all amendments to those Executive orders; all guidelines issued under those orders; and any exemptions from those orders heretofore granted for any category of rule are revoked.

WILLIAM J. CLINTON.

EXECUTIVE ORDER NO. 12875

Ex. Ord. No. 12875, Oct. 26, 1993, 58 F.R. 58093, which provided for the reduction of unfunded mandates on State, local, or tribal governments and increased flexibility for State and local waivers of statutory or regulatory requirements, was revoked by Ex. Ord. No. 13132, § 10(b), Aug. 4, 1999, 64 F.R. 43259, set out below.

EXECUTIVE ORDER NO. 13083

Ex. Ord. No. 13083, May 14, 1998, 63 F.R. 27651, which listed fundamental federalism principles and federalism policymaking criteria to guide agencies in formulating and implementing policies and required agencies to have a process to permit State and local governments to provide input into the development of regulatory policies that have federalism implications and to streamline the State and local government waiver process, was revoked by Ex. Ord. No. 13132, § 10(b), Aug. 4, 1999, 64 F.R. 43259, set out below.

EXECUTIVE ORDER NO. 13095

Ex. Ord. No. 13095, Aug. 5, 1998, 63 F.R. 42565, which suspended Ex. Ord. No. 13083, was revoked by Ex. Ord. No. 13132, § 10(b), Aug. 4, 1999, 64 F.R. 43259, set out below.

EX. ORD. NO. 13107. IMPLEMENTATION OF HUMAN RIGHTS TREATIES

Ex. Ord. No. 13107, Dec. 10, 1998, 63 F.R. 68991, provided:

By the authority vested in me as President by the Constitution and the laws of the United States of America, and bearing in mind the obligations of the United States pursuant to the International Covenant on Civil and Political Rights (ICCPR), the Convention Against Torture and Other Cruel, Inhuman or Degrading Treatment or Punishment (CAT), the Convention on the Elimination of All Forms of Racial Discrimination (CERD), and other relevant treaties concerned with the protection and promotion of human rights to which the United States is now or may become a party in the future, it is hereby ordered as follows:

SECTION 1. *Implementation of Human Rights Obligations.* (a) It shall be the policy and practice of the Government of the United States, being committed to the protection and promotion of human rights and fundamental freedoms, fully to respect and implement its obligations under the international human rights treaties to which it is a party, including the ICCPR, the CAT, and the CERD.

(b) It shall also be the policy and practice of the Government of the United States to promote respect for international human rights, both in our relationships with all other countries and by working with and strengthening the various international mechanisms for the promotion of human rights, including, *inter alia,* those of the United Nations, the International Labor Organization, and the Organization of American States.

SEC. 2. *Responsibility of Executive Departments and Agencies.* (a) All executive departments and agencies (as defined in 5 U.S.C. 101–105, including boards and commissions, and hereinafter referred to collectively as "agency" or "agencies") shall maintain a current awareness of United States international human rights obligations that are relevant to their functions and shall perform such functions so as to respect and implement those obligations fully. The head of each agency shall designate a single contact officer who will be responsible for overall coordination of the implementation of this order. Under this order, all such agencies shall retain their established institutional roles in the implementation, interpretation, and enforcement of Federal law and policy.

(b) The heads of agencies shall have lead responsibility, in coordination with other appropriate agencies, for questions concerning implementation of human rights obligations that fall within their respective operating and program responsibilities and authorities or, to the extent that matters do not fall within the operating and program responsibilities and authorities of any agency, that most closely relate to their general areas of concern.

SEC. 3. *Human Rights Inquiries and Complaints.* Each agency shall take lead responsibility, in coordination with other appropriate agencies, for responding to inquiries, requests for information, and complaints about violations of human rights obligations that fall within its areas of responsibility or, if the matter does not fall within its areas of responsibility, referring it to the appropriate agency for response.

SEC. 4. *Interagency Working Group on Human Rights Treaties.* (a) There is hereby established an Interagency Working Group on Human Rights Treaties for the purpose of providing guidance, oversight, and coordination with respect to questions concerning the adherence to and implementation of human rights obligations and related matters.

(b) The designee of the Assistant to the President for National Security Affairs shall chair the Interagency Working Group, which shall consist of appropriate policy and legal representatives at the Assistant Secretary level from the Department of State, the Department of Justice, the Department of Labor, the Department of Defense, the Joint Chiefs of Staff, and other agencies as the chair deems appropriate. The principal members may designate alternates to attend meetings in their stead.

(c) The principal functions of the Interagency Working Group shall include:

(i) coordinating the interagency review of any significant issues concerning the implementation of this order and analysis and recommendations in connection with pursuing the ratification of human rights treaties, as such questions may from time to time arise;

(ii) coordinating the preparation of reports that are to be submitted by the United States in fulfillment of treaty obligations;

(iii) coordinating the responses of the United States Government to complaints against it concerning alleged human rights violations submitted to the United Nations, the Organization of American States, and other international organizations;

(iv) developing effective mechanisms to ensure that legislation proposed by the Administration is reviewed for conformity with international human rights obligations and that these obligations are taken into account in reviewing legislation under consideration by the Congress as well;

(v) developing recommended proposals and mechanisms for improving the monitoring of the actions by the various States, Commonwealths, and territories of the United States and, where appropriate, of Native Americans and Federally recognized Indian tribes, including the review of State, Commonwealth, and territorial laws for their conformity with relevant treaties, the provision of relevant information for reports and other monitoring purposes, and the promotion of effective remedial mechanisms;

(vi) developing plans for public outreach and education concerning the provisions of the ICCPR, CAT, CERD, and other relevant treaties, and human rights-related provisions of domestic law;

(vii) coordinating and directing an annual review of United States reservations, declarations, and understandings to human rights treaties, and matters as to which there have been nontrivial complaints or allegations of inconsistency with or breach of international human rights obligations, in order to determine whether there should be consideration of any modification of relevant reservations, declarations, and understandings to human rights treaties, or United States practices or laws. The results and recommendations of this review shall be reviewed by the head of each participating agency;

(viii) making such other recommendations as it shall deem appropriate to the President, through the Assistant to the President for National Security Affairs, concerning United States adherence to or implementation of human rights treaties and related matters; and

(ix) coordinating such other significant tasks in connection with human rights treaties or international human rights institutions, including the Inter-American Commission on Human Rights and the Special Rapporteurs and complaints procedures established by the United Nations Human Rights Commission.

(d) The work of the Interagency Working Group shall not supplant the work of other interagency entities, including the President's Committee on the International Labor Organization, that address international human rights issues.

SEC. 5. *Cooperation Among Executive Departments and Agencies.* All agencies shall cooperate in carrying out the provisions of this order. The Interagency Working Group shall facilitate such cooperative measures.

SEC. 6. *Judicial Review, Scope, and Administration.* (a) Nothing in this order shall create any right or benefit, substantive or procedural, enforceable by any party against the United States, its agencies or instrumentalities, its officers or employees, or any other person.

(b) This order does not supersede Federal statutes and does not impose any justiciable obligations on the executive branch.

(c) The term "treaty obligations" shall mean treaty obligations as approved by the Senate pursuant to Article II, section 2, clause 2 of the United States Constitution.

(d) To the maximum extent practicable and subject to the availability of appropriations, agencies shall carry out the provisions of this order.

WILLIAM J. CLINTON.

REGULATORY REFORM—WAIVER OF PENALTIES AND REDUCTION OF REPORTS

Memorandum of President of the United States, Apr. 21, 1995, 60 F.R. 20621, provided:

Memorandum for
The Secretary of State
The Secretary of the Treasury
The Secretary of Defense
The Attorney General
The Secretary of the Interior
The Secretary of Agriculture
The Secretary of Commerce
The Secretary of Labor
The Secretary of Health and Human Services
The Secretary of Housing and Urban Development
The Secretary of Transportation
The Secretary of Energy
The Secretary of Education
The Secretary of Veterans Affairs
The Administrator, Environmental Protection Agency
The Administrator, Small Business Administration
The Secretary of the Army
The Secretary of the Navy
The Secretary of the Air Force
The Director, Federal Emergency Management Agency
The Administrator, National Aeronautics and Space Administration

The Director, National Science Foundation

The Acting Archivist of the United States

The Administrator of General Services

The Chair, Railroad Retirement Board

The Chairperson, Architectural and Transportation Barriers Compliance Board

The Executive Director, Pension Benefit Guaranty Corporation

On March 16, I announced that the Administration would implement new policies to give compliance officials more flexibility in dealing with small business and to cut back on paperwork. These Governmentwide policies, as well as the specific agency actions I announced, are part of this Administration's continuing commitment to sensible regulatory reform. With your help and cooperation, we hope to move the Government toward a more flexible, effective, and user friendly approach to regulation.

A. *Actions*: This memorandum directs the designated department and agency heads to implement the policies set forth below.

1. *Authority to Waive Penalties.* (a) To the extent permitted by law, each agency shall use its discretion to modify the penalties for small businesses in the following situations. Agencies shall exercise their enforcement discretion to waive the imposition of all or a portion of a penalty when the violation is corrected within a time period appropriate to the violation in question. For those violations that may take longer to correct than the period set by the agency, the agency shall use its enforcement discretion to waive up to 100 percent of the financial penalties if the amounts waived are used to bring the entity into compliance. The provisions in paragraph 1(a) of this memorandum shall apply only where there has been a good faith effort to comply with applicable regulations and the violation does not involve criminal wrongdoing or significant threat to health, safety, or the environment.

(b) Each agency shall, by June 15, 1995, submit a plan to the Director of the Office of Management and Budget ("Director") describing the actions it will take to implement the policies in paragraph 1(a) of this memorandum. The plan shall provide that the agency will implement the policies described in paragraph 1(a) of this memorandum on or before July 14, 1995. Plans should include information on how notification will be given to frontline workers and small businesses.

2. *Cutting Frequency of Reports.* (a) Each agency shall reduce by one-half the frequency of the regularly scheduled reports that the public is required, by rule or by policy, to provide to the Government (from quarterly to semiannually, from semiannually to annually, etc.), unless the department or agency head determines that such action is not legally permissible; would not adequately protect health, safety, or the environment; would be inconsistent with achieving regulatory flexibility or reducing regulatory burdens; or would impede the effective administration of the agency's program. The duty to make such determinations shall be nondelegable.

(b) Each agency shall, by June 15, 1995, submit a plan to the Director describing the actions it will take to implement the policies in paragraph 2(a), including a copy of any determination that certain reports are excluded.

B. *Application and Scope*: 1. The Director may issue further guidance as necessary to carry out the purposes of this memorandum.

2. This memorandum does not apply to matters related to law enforcement, national security, or foreign affairs, the importation or exportation of prohibited or restricted items, Government taxes, duties, fees, revenues, or receipts; nor does it apply to agencies (or components thereof) whose principal purpose is the collection, analysis, and dissemination of statistical information.

3. This memorandum is not intended, and should not be construed, to create any right or benefit, substantive or procedural, enforceable at law by a party against the United States, its agencies, its officers, or its employees.

4. The Director of the Office of Management and Budget is authorized and directed to publish this memorandum in the Federal Register.

WILLIAM J. CLINTON.

PLAIN LANGUAGE IN GOVERNMENT WRITING

Memorandum of President of the United States, June 1, 1998, 63 F.R. 31885, provided:

Memorandum for the Heads of Executive Departments and Agencies

The Vice President and I have made reinventing the Federal Government a top priority of my Administration. We are determined to make the Government more responsive, accessible, and understandable in its communications with the public.

The Federal Government's writing must be in plain language. By using plain language, we send a clear message about what the Government is doing, what it requires, and what services it offers. Plain language saves the Government and the private sector time, effort, and money.

Plain language requirements vary from one document to another, depending on the intended audience. Plain language documents have logical organization, easy-to-read design features, and use:

- common, everyday words, except for necessary technical terms;
- "you" and other pronouns;
- the active voice; and
- short sentences.

To ensure the use of plain language, I direct you to do the following:

- By October 1, 1998, use plain language in all new documents, other than regulations, that explain how to obtain a benefit or service or how to comply with a requirement you administer or enforce. For example, these documents may include letters, forms, notices, and instructions. By January 1, 2002, all such documents created prior to October 1, 1998, must also be in plain language.
- By January 1, 1999, use plain language in all proposed and final rulemaking documents published in the Federal Register, unless you proposed the rule before that date. You should consider rewriting existing regulations in plain language when you have the opportunity and resources to do so.

The National Partnership for Reinventing Government will issue guidance to help you comply with these directives and to explain more fully the elements of plain language. You should also use customer feedback and common sense to guide your plain language efforts.

I ask the independent agencies to comply with these directives.

This memorandum does not confer any right or benefit enforceable by law against the United States or its representatives. The Director of the Office of Management and Budget will publish this memorandum in the Federal Register.

WILLIAM J. CLINTON.

EX. ORD. NO. 13132. FEDERALISM

Ex. Ord. No. 13132, Aug. 4, 1999, 64 F.R. 43255, provided:

By the authority vested in me as President by the Constitution and the laws of the United States of America, and in order to guarantee the division of governmental responsibilities between the national government and the States that was intended by the Framers of the Constitution, to ensure that the principles of federalism established by the Framers guide the executive departments and agencies in the formulation and implementation of policies, and to further the policies of the Unfunded Mandates Reform Act [of 1995, Pub. L. 104–4, see Tables for classification], it is hereby ordered as follows:

SECTION 1. *Definitions.* For purposes of this order:

(a) "Policies that have federalism implications" refers to regulations, legislative comments or proposed legislation, and other policy statements or actions that have substantial direct effects on the States, on the relationship between the national government and the States, or on the distribution of power and responsibilities among the various levels of government.

(b) "State" or "States" refer to the States of the United States of America, individually or collectively, and, where relevant, to State governments, including units of local government and other political subdivisions established by the States.

(c) "Agency" means any authority of the United States that is an "agency" under 44 U.S.C. 3502(1), other than those considered to be independent regulatory agencies, as defined in 44 U.S.C. 3502(5).

(d) "State and local officials" means elected officials of State and local governments or their representative national organizations.

SEC. 2. *Fundamental Federalism Principles.* In formulating and implementing policies that have federalism implications, agencies shall be guided by the following fundamental federalism principles:

(a) Federalism is rooted in the belief that issues that are not national in scope or significance are most appropriately addressed by the level of government closest to the people.

(b) The people of the States created the national government and delegated to it enumerated governmental powers. All other sovereign powers, save those expressly prohibited the States by the Constitution, are reserved to the States or to the people.

(c) The constitutional relationship among sovereign governments, State and national, is inherent in the very structure of the Constitution and is formalized in and protected by the Tenth Amendment to the Constitution.

(d) The people of the States are free, subject only to restrictions in the Constitution itself or in constitutionally authorized Acts of Congress, to define the moral, political, and legal character of their lives.

(e) The Framers recognized that the States possess unique authorities, qualities, and abilities to meet the needs of the people and should function as laboratories of democracy.

(f) The nature of our constitutional system encourages a healthy diversity in the public policies adopted by the people of the several States according to their own conditions, needs, and desires. In the search for enlightened public policy, individual States and communities are free to experiment with a variety of approaches to public issues. One-size-fits-all approaches to public policy problems can inhibit the creation of effective solutions to those problems.

(g) Acts of the national government—whether legislative, executive, or judicial in nature—that exceed the enumerated powers of that government under the Constitution violate the principle of federalism established by the Framers.

(h) Policies of the national government should recognize the responsibility of—and should encourage opportunities for—individuals, families, neighborhoods, local governments, and private associations to achieve their personal, social, and economic objectives through cooperative effort.

(i) The national government should be deferential to the States when taking action that affects the policymaking discretion of the States and should act only with the greatest caution where State or local governments have identified uncertainties regarding the constitutional or statutory authority of the national government.

SEC. 3. *Federalism Policymaking Criteria.* In addition to adhering to the fundamental federalism principles set forth in section 2, agencies shall adhere, to the extent permitted by law, to the following criteria when formulating and implementing policies that have federalism implications:

(a) There shall be strict adherence to constitutional principles. Agencies shall closely examine the constitutional and statutory authority supporting any action that would limit the policymaking discretion of the States and shall carefully assess the necessity for such action. To the extent practicable, State and local offi-

cials shall be consulted before any such action is implemented. Executive Order 12372 of July 14, 1982 ("Intergovernmental Review of Federal Programs") [31 U.S.C. 6506 note] remains in effect for the programs and activities to which it is applicable.

(b) National action limiting the policymaking discretion of the States shall be taken only where there is constitutional and statutory authority for the action and the national activity is appropriate in light of the presence of a problem of national significance. Where there are significant uncertainties as to whether national action is authorized or appropriate, agencies shall consult with appropriate State and local officials to determine whether Federal objectives can be attained by other means.

(c) With respect to Federal statutes and regulations administered by the States, the national government shall grant the States the maximum administrative discretion possible. Intrusive Federal oversight of State administration is neither necessary nor desirable.

(d) When undertaking to formulate and implement policies that have federalism implications, agencies shall:

(1) encourage States to develop their own policies to achieve program objectives and to work with appropriate officials in other States;

(2) where possible, defer to the States to establish standards;

(3) in determining whether to establish uniform national standards, consult with appropriate State and local officials as to the need for national standards and any alternatives that would limit the scope of national standards or otherwise preserve State prerogatives and authority; and

(4) where national standards are required by Federal statutes, consult with appropriate State and local officials in developing those standards.

SEC. 4. *Special Requirements for Preemption.* Agencies, in taking action that preempts State law, shall act in strict accordance with governing law.

(a) Agencies shall construe, in regulations and otherwise, a Federal statute to preempt State law only where the statute contains an express preemption provision or there is some other clear evidence that the Congress intended preemption of State law, or where the exercise of State authority conflicts with the exercise of Federal authority under the Federal statute.

(b) Where a Federal statute does not preempt State law (as addressed in subsection (a) of this section), agencies shall construe any authorization in the statute for the issuance of regulations as authorizing preemption of State law by rulemaking only when the exercise of State authority directly conflicts with the exercise of Federal authority under the Federal statute or there is clear evidence to conclude that the Congress intended the agency to have the authority to preempt State law.

(c) Any regulatory preemption of State law shall be restricted to the minimum level necessary to achieve the objectives of the statute pursuant to which the regulations are promulgated.

(d) When an agency foresees the possibility of a conflict between State law and Federally protected interests within its area of regulatory responsibility, the agency shall consult, to the extent practicable, with appropriate State and local officials in an effort to avoid such a conflict.

(e) When an agency proposes to act through adjudication or rulemaking to preempt State law, the agency shall provide all affected State and local officials notice and an opportunity for appropriate participation in the proceedings.

SEC. 5. *Special Requirements for Legislative Proposals.* Agencies shall not submit to the Congress legislation that would:

(a) directly regulate the States in ways that would either interfere with functions essential to the States' separate and independent existence or be inconsistent with the fundamental federalism principles in section 2;

(b) attach to Federal grants conditions that are not reasonably related to the purpose of the grant; or

(c) preempt State law, unless preemption is consistent with the fundamental federalism principles set forth in section 2, and unless a clearly legitimate national purpose, consistent with the federalism policy-making criteria set forth in section 3, cannot otherwise be met.

SEC. 6. *Consultation.*

(a) Each agency shall have an accountable process to ensure meaningful and timely input by State and local officials in the development of regulatory policies that have federalism implications. Within 90 days after the effective date of this order, the head of each agency shall designate an official with principal responsibility for the agency's implementation of this order and that designated official shall submit to the Office of Management and Budget a description of the agency's consultation process.

(b) To the extent practicable and permitted by law, no agency shall promulgate any regulation that has federalism implications, that imposes substantial direct compliance costs on State and local governments, and that is not required by statute, unless:

(1) funds necessary to pay the direct costs incurred by the State and local governments in complying with the regulation are provided by the Federal Government; or

(2) the agency, prior to the formal promulgation of the regulation,

(A) consulted with State and local officials early in the process of developing the proposed regulation;

(B) in a separately identified portion of the preamble to the regulation as it is to be issued in the Federal Register, provides to the Director of the Office of Management and Budget a federalism summary impact statement, which consists of a description of the extent of the agency's prior consultation with State and local officials, a summary of the nature of their concerns and the agency's position supporting the need to issue the regulation, and a statement of the extent to which the concerns of State and local officials have been met; and

(C) makes available to the Director of the Office of Management and Budget any written communications submitted to the agency by State and local officials.

(c) To the extent practicable and permitted by law, no agency shall promulgate any regulation that has federalism implications and that preempts State law, unless the agency, prior to the formal promulgation of the regulation,

(1) consulted with State and local officials early in the process of developing the proposed regulation;

(2) in a separately identified portion of the preamble to the regulation as it is to be issued in the Federal Register, provides to the Director of the Office of Management and Budget a federalism summary impact statement, which consists of a description of the extent of the agency's prior consultation with State and local officials, a summary of the nature of their concerns and the agency's position supporting the need to issue the regulation, and a statement of the extent to which the concerns of State and local officials have been met; and

(3) makes available to the Director of the Office of Management and Budget any written communications submitted to the agency by State and local officials.

SEC. 7. *Increasing Flexibility for State and Local Waivers.*

(a) Agencies shall review the processes under which State and local governments apply for waivers of statutory and regulatory requirements and take appropriate steps to streamline those processes.

(b) Each agency shall, to the extent practicable and permitted by law, consider any application by a State for a waiver of statutory or regulatory requirements in connection with any program administered by that agency with a general view toward increasing opportunities for utilizing flexible policy approaches at the State or local level in cases in which the proposed waiver is consistent with applicable Federal policy objectives and is otherwise appropriate.

(c) Each agency shall, to the extent practicable and permitted by law, render a decision upon a complete application for a waiver within 120 days of receipt of such application by the agency. If the application for a waiver is not granted, the agency shall provide the applicant with timely written notice of the decision and the reasons therefor.

(d) This section applies only to statutory or regulatory requirements that are discretionary and subject to waiver by the agency.

SEC. 8. *Accountability.*

(a) In transmitting any draft final regulation that has federalism implications to the Office of Management and Budget pursuant to Executive Order 12866 of September 30, 1993 [set out above], each agency shall include a certification from the official designated to ensure compliance with this order stating that the requirements of this order have been met in a meaningful and timely manner.

(b) In transmitting proposed legislation that has federalism implications to the Office of Management and Budget, each agency shall include a certification from the official designated to ensure compliance with this order that all relevant requirements of this order have been met.

(c) Within 180 days after the effective date of this order, the Director of the Office of Management and Budget and the Assistant to the President for Intergovernmental Affairs shall confer with State and local officials to ensure that this order is being properly and effectively implemented.

SEC. 9. *Independent Agencies.* Independent regulatory agencies are encouraged to comply with the provisions of this order.

SEC. 10. *General Provisions.*

(a) This order shall supplement but not supersede the requirements contained in Executive Order 12372 ("Intergovernmental Review of Federal Programs") [31 U.S.C. 6506 note], Executive Order 12866 ("Regulatory Planning and Review") [set out above], Executive Order 12988 ("Civil Justice Reform" [28 U.S.C. 519 note]), and OMB Circular A–19.

(b) Executive Order 12612 ("Federalism"), Executive Order 12875 ("Enhancing the Intergovernmental Partnership"), Executive Order 13083 ("Federalism"), and Executive Order 13095 ("Suspension of Executive Order 13083") are revoked.

(c) This order shall be effective 90 days after the date of this order.

SEC. 11. *Judicial Review.* This order is intended only to improve the internal management of the executive branch, and is not intended to create any right or benefit, substantive or procedural, enforceable at law by a party against the United States, its agencies, its officers, or any person.

WILLIAM J. CLINTON.

SECTION REFERRED TO IN OTHER SECTIONS

This section is referred to in sections 504, 611 of this title; title 2 section 658; title 28 section 2412; title 44 section 3506.

§ 602. Regulatory agenda

(a) During the months of October and April of each year, each agency shall publish in the Federal Register a regulatory flexibility agenda which shall contain—

(1) a brief description of the subject area of any rule which the agency expects to propose or promulgate which is likely to have a significant economic impact on a substantial number of small entities;

(2) a summary of the nature of any such rule under consideration for each subject area listed in the agenda pursuant to paragraph (1), the objectives and legal basis for the issuance of the rule, and an approximate schedule for completing action on any rule for which the agency has issued a general notice of proposed rulemaking,[1] and

(3) the name and telephone number of an agency official knowledgeable concerning the items listed in paragraph (1).

(b) Each regulatory flexibility agenda shall be transmitted to the Chief Counsel for Advocacy of the Small Business Administration for comment, if any.

(c) Each agency shall endeavor to provide notice of each regulatory flexibility agenda to small entities or their representatives through direct notification or publication of the agenda in publications likely to be obtained by such small entities and shall invite comments upon each subject area on the agenda.

(d) Nothing in this section precludes an agency from considering or acting on any matter not included in a regulatory flexibility agenda, or requires an agency to consider or act on any matter listed in such agenda.

(Added Pub. L. 96–354, §3(a), Sept. 19, 1980, 94 Stat. 1166.)

SECTION REFERRED TO IN OTHER SECTIONS

This section is referred to in section 605 of this title.

§ 603. Initial regulatory flexibility analysis

(a) Whenever an agency is required by section 553 of this title, or any other law, to publish general notice of proposed rulemaking for any proposed rule, or publishes a notice of proposed rulemaking for an interpretative rule involving the internal revenue laws of the United States, the agency shall prepare and make available for public comment an initial regulatory flexibility analysis. Such analysis shall describe the impact of the proposed rule on small entities. The initial regulatory flexibility analysis or a summary shall be published in the Federal Register at the time of the publication of general notice of proposed rulemaking for the rule. The agency shall transmit a copy of the initial regulatory flexibility analysis to the Chief Counsel for Advocacy of the Small Business Administration. In the case of an interpretative rule involving the internal revenue laws of the United States, this chapter applies to interpretative rules published in the Federal Register for codification in the Code of Federal Regulations, but only to the extent that such interpretative rules impose on small entities a collection of information requirement.

(b) Each initial regulatory flexibility analysis required under this section shall contain—

(1) a description of the reasons why action by the agency is being considered;

(2) a succinct statement of the objectives of, and legal basis for, the proposed rule;

(3) a description of and, where feasible, an estimate of the number of small entities to which the proposed rule will apply;

(4) a description of the projected reporting, recordkeeping and other compliance requirements of the proposed rule, including an estimate of the classes of small entities which will be subject to the requirement and the type of professional skills necessary for preparation of the report or record;

(5) an identification, to the extent practicable, of all relevant Federal rules which may duplicate, overlap or conflict with the proposed rule.

(c) Each initial regulatory flexibility analysis shall also contain a description of any significant alternatives to the proposed rule which accomplish the stated objectives of applicable statutes and which minimize any significant economic impact of the proposed rule on small entities. Consistent with the stated objectives of applicable statutes, the analysis shall discuss significant alternatives such as—

(1) the establishment of differing compliance or reporting requirements or timetables that take into account the resources available to small entities;

(2) the clarification, consolidation, or simplification of compliance and reporting requirements under the rule for such small entities;

(3) the use of performance rather than design standards; and

(4) an exemption from coverage of the rule, or any part thereof, for such small entities.

(Added Pub. L. 96–354, §3(a), Sept. 19, 1980, 94 Stat. 1166; amended Pub. L. 104–121, title II, §241(a)(1), Mar. 29, 1996, 110 Stat. 864.)

REFERENCES IN TEXT

The internal revenue laws, referred to in subsec. (a), are classified generally to Title 26, Internal Revenue Code.

AMENDMENTS

1996—Subsec. (a). Pub. L. 104–121, §241(a)(1)(B), inserted at end "In the case of an interpretative rule involving the internal revenue laws of the United States, this chapter applies to interpretative rules published in the Federal Register for codification in the Code of Federal Regulations, but only to the extent that such interpretative rules impose on small entities a collection of information requirement."

Pub. L. 104–121, §241(a)(1)(A), which directed the insertion of ", or publishes a notice of proposed rulemaking for an interpretative rule involving the internal revenue laws of the United States" after "proposed rule" was executed by making the insertion where those words appeared in first sentence to reflect the probable intent of Congress.

EFFECTIVE DATE OF 1996 AMENDMENT

Amendment by Pub. L. 104–121 effective on expiration of 90 days after Mar. 29, 1996, but inapplicable to interpretative rules for which a notice of proposed rulemaking was published prior to Mar. 29, 1996, see section 245 of Pub. L. 104–121, set out as a note under section 601 of this title.

SECTION REFERRED TO IN OTHER SECTIONS

This section is referred to in sections 604, 605, 606, 607, 608, 609, 801 of this title; title 42 section 1302.

§ 604. Final regulatory flexibility analysis

(a) When an agency promulgates a final rule under section 553 of this title, after being re-

---

[1] So in original. The comma probably should be a semicolon.

quired by that section or any other law to publish a general notice of proposed rulemaking, or promulgates a final interpretative rule involving the internal revenue laws of the United States as described in section 603(a), the agency shall prepare a final regulatory flexibility analysis. Each final regulatory flexibility analysis shall contain—

(1) a succinct statement of the need for, and objectives of, the rule;

(2) a summary of the significant issues raised by the public comments in response to the initial regulatory flexibility analysis, a summary of the assessment of the agency of such issues, and a statement of any changes made in the proposed rule as a result of such comments;

(3) a description of and an estimate of the number of small entities to which the rule will apply or an explanation of why no such estimate is available;

(4) a description of the projected reporting, recordkeeping and other compliance requirements of the rule, including an estimate of the classes of small entities which will be subject to the requirement and the type of professional skills necessary for preparation of the report or record; and

(5) a description of the steps the agency has taken to minimize the significant economic impact on small entities consistent with the stated objectives of applicable statutes, including a statement of the factual, policy, and legal reasons for selecting the alternative adopted in the final rule and why each one of the other significant alternatives to the rule considered by the agency which affect the impact on small entities was rejected.

(b) The agency shall make copies of the final regulatory flexibility analysis available to members of the public and shall publish in the Federal Register such analysis or a summary thereof.

(Added Pub. L. 96–354, § 3(a), Sept. 19, 1980, 94 Stat. 1167; amended Pub. L. 104–121, title II, § 241(b), Mar. 29, 1996, 110 Stat. 864.)

REFERENCES IN TEXT

The internal revenue laws, referred to in subsec. (a), are classified generally to Title 26, Internal Revenue Code.

AMENDMENTS

1996—Subsec. (a). Pub. L. 104–121, § 241(b)(1), amended subsec. (a) generally. Prior to amendment, subsec. (a) read as follows: "When an agency promulgates a final rule under section 553 of this title, after being required by that section or any other law to publish a general notice of proposed rulemaking, the agency shall prepare a final regulatory flexibility analysis. Each final regulatory flexibility analysis shall contain—

"(1) a succinct statement of the need for, and the objectives of, the rule;

"(2) a summary of the issues raised by the public comments in response to the initial regulatory flexibility analysis, a summary of the assessment of the agency of such issues, and a statement of any changes made in the proposed rule as a result of such comments; and

"(3) a description of each of the significant alternatives to the rule consistent with the stated objectives of applicable statutes and designed to minimize any significant economic impact of the rule on small

entities which was considered by the agency, and a statement of the reasons why each one of such alternatives was rejected."

Subsec. (b). Pub. L. 104–121, § 241(b)(2), substituted "such analysis or a summary thereof." for "at the time of publication of the final rule under section 553 of this title a statement describing how the public may obtain such copies."

EFFECTIVE DATE OF 1996 AMENDMENT

Amendment by Pub. L. 104–121 effective on expiration of 90 days after Mar. 29, 1996, but inapplicable to interpretative rules for which a notice of proposed rulemaking was published prior to Mar. 29, 1996, see section 245 of Pub. L. 104–121, set out as a note under section 601 of this title.

SECTION REFERRED TO IN OTHER SECTIONS

This section is referred to in sections 605, 606, 607, 608, 611, 801 of this title; title 42 section 1302.

§ 605. Avoidance of duplicative or unnecessary analyses

(a) Any Federal agency may perform the analyses required by sections 602, 603, and 604 of this title in conjunction with or as a part of any other agenda or analysis required by any other law if such other analysis satisfies the provisions of such sections.

(b) Sections 603 and 604 of this title shall not apply to any proposed or final rule if the head of the agency certifies that the rule will not, if promulgated, have a significant economic impact on a substantial number of small entities. If the head of the agency makes a certification under the preceding sentence, the agency shall publish such certification in the Federal Register at the time of publication of general notice of proposed rulemaking for the rule or at the time of publication of the final rule, along with a statement providing the factual basis for such certification. The agency shall provide such certification and statement to the Chief Counsel for Advocacy of the Small Business Administration.

(c) In order to avoid duplicative action, an agency may consider a series of closely related rules as one rule for the purposes of sections 602, 603, 604 and 610 of this title.

(Added Pub. L. 96–354, § 3(a), Sept. 19, 1980, 94 Stat. 1167; amended Pub. L. 104–121, title II, § 243(a), Mar. 29, 1996, 110 Stat. 866.)

AMENDMENTS

1996—Subsec. (b). Pub. L. 104–121 amended subsec. (b) generally. Prior to amendment, subsec. (b) read as follows: "Sections 603 and 604 of this title shall not apply to any proposed or final rule if the head of the agency certifies that the rule will not, if promulgated, have a significant economic impact on a substantial number of small entities. If the head of the agency makes a certification under the preceding sentence, the agency shall publish such certification in the Federal Register, at the time of publication of general notice of proposed rulemaking for the rule or at the time of publication of the final rule, along with a succinct statement explaining the reasons for such certification, and provide such certification and statement to the Chief Counsel for Advocacy of the Small Business Administration."

EFFECTIVE DATE OF 1996 AMENDMENT

Amendment by Pub. L. 104–121 effective on expiration of 90 days after Mar. 29, 1996, but inapplicable to interpretative rules for which a notice of proposed rulemaking was published prior to Mar. 29, 1996, see section 245 of Pub. L. 104–121, set out as a note under section 601 of this title.

SECTION REFERRED TO IN OTHER SECTIONS

This section is referred to in sections 608, 609, 611, 801 of this title.

§ 606. Effect on other law

The requirements of sections 603 and 604 of this title do not alter in any manner standards otherwise applicable by law to agency action.

(Added Pub. L. 96–354, § 3(a), Sept. 19, 1980, 94 Stat. 1168.)

§ 607. Preparation of analyses

In complying with the provisions of sections 603 and 604 of this title, an agency may provide either a quantifiable or numerical description of the effects of a proposed rule or alternatives to the proposed rule, or more general descriptive statements if quantification is not practicable or reliable.

(Added Pub. L. 96–354, § 3(a), Sept. 19, 1980, 94 Stat. 1168.)

SECTION REFERRED TO IN OTHER SECTIONS

This section is referred to in sections 611, 801 of this title.

§ 608. Procedure for waiver or delay of completion

(a) An agency head may waive or delay the completion of some or all of the requirements of section 603 of this title by publishing in the Federal Register, not later than the date of publication of the final rule, a written finding, with reasons therefor, that the final rule is being promulgated in response to an emergency that makes compliance or timely compliance with the provisions of section 603 of this title impracticable.

(b) Except as provided in section 605(b), an agency head may not waive the requirements of section 604 of this title. An agency head may delay the completion of the requirements of section 604 of this title for a period of not more than one hundred and eighty days after the date of publication in the Federal Register of a final rule by publishing in the Federal Register, not later than such date of publication, a written finding, with reasons therefor, that the final rule is being promulgated in response to an emergency that makes timely compliance with the provisions of section 604 of this title impracticable. If the agency has not prepared a final regulatory analysis pursuant to section 604 of this title within one hundred and eighty days from the date of publication of the final rule, such rule shall lapse and have no effect. Such rule shall not be repromulgated until a final regulatory flexibility analysis has been completed by the agency.

(Added Pub. L. 96–354, § 3(a), Sept. 19, 1980, 94 Stat. 1168.)

SECTION REFERRED TO IN OTHER SECTIONS

This section is referred to in section 611 of this title.

§ 609. Procedures for gathering comments

(a) When any rule is promulgated which will have a significant economic impact on a substantial number of small entities, the head of the agency promulgating the rule or the official of the agency with statutory responsibility for the promulgation of the rule shall assure that small entities have been given an opportunity to participate in the rulemaking for the rule through the reasonable use of techniques such as—

(1) the inclusion in an advanced notice of proposed rulemaking, if issued, of a statement that the proposed rule may have a significant economic effect on a substantial number of small entities;

(2) the publication of general notice of proposed rulemaking in publications likely to be obtained by small entities;

(3) the direct notification of interested small entities;

(4) the conduct of open conferences or public hearings concerning the rule for small entities including soliciting and receiving comments over computer networks; and

(5) the adoption or modification of agency procedural rules to reduce the cost or complexity of participation in the rulemaking by small entities.

(b) Prior to publication of an initial regulatory flexibility analysis which a covered agency is required to conduct by this chapter—

(1) a covered agency shall notify the Chief Counsel for Advocacy of the Small Business Administration and provide the Chief Counsel with information on the potential impacts of the proposed rule on small entities and the type of small entities that might be affected;

(2) not later than 15 days after the date of receipt of the materials described in paragraph (1), the Chief Counsel shall identify individuals representative of affected small entities for the purpose of obtaining advice and recommendations from those individuals about the potential impacts of the proposed rule;

(3) the agency shall convene a review panel for such rule consisting wholly of full time Federal employees of the office within the agency responsible for carrying out the proposed rule, the Office of Information and Regulatory Affairs within the Office of Management and Budget, and the Chief Counsel;

(4) the panel shall review any material the agency has prepared in connection with this chapter, including any draft proposed rule, collect advice and recommendations of each individual small entity representative identified by the agency after consultation with the Chief Counsel, on issues related to subsections 603(b), paragraphs (3), (4) and (5) and 603(c);

(5) not later than 60 days after the date a covered agency convenes a review panel pursuant to paragraph (3), the review panel shall report on the comments of the small entity representatives and its findings as to issues related to subsections 603(b), paragraphs (3), (4) and (5) and 603(c), provided that such report shall be made public as part of the rulemaking record; and

(6) where appropriate, the agency shall modify the proposed rule, the initial regulatory flexibility analysis or the decision on whether an initial regulatory flexibility analysis is required.

(c) An agency may in its discretion apply subsection (b) to rules that the agency intends to certify under subsection 605(b), but the agency believes may have a greater than de minimis impact on a substantial number of small entities.

(d) For purposes of this section, the term "covered agency" means the Environmental Protection Agency and the Occupational Safety and Health Administration of the Department of Labor.

(e) The Chief Counsel for Advocacy, in consultation with the individuals identified in subsection (b)(2), and with the Administrator of the Office of Information and Regulatory Affairs within the Office of Management and Budget, may waive the requirements of subsections (b)(3), (b)(4), and (b)(5) by including in the rulemaking record a written finding, with reasons therefor, that those requirements would not advance the effective participation of small entities in the rulemaking process. For purposes of this subsection, the factors to be considered in making such a finding are as follows:

(1) In developing a proposed rule, the extent to which the covered agency consulted with individuals representative of affected small entities with respect to the potential impacts of the rule and took such concerns into consideration.

(2) Special circumstances requiring prompt issuance of the rule.

(3) Whether the requirements of subsection (b) would provide the individuals identified in subsection (b)(2) with a competitive advantage relative to other small entities.

(Added Pub. L. 96–354, § 3(a), Sept. 19, 1980, 94 Stat. 1168; amended Pub. L. 104–121, title II, § 244(a), Mar. 29, 1996, 110 Stat. 867.)

AMENDMENTS

1996—Pub. L. 104–121, § 244(a)(2), (3), designated existing provisions as subsec. (a) and inserted "including soliciting and receiving comments over computer networks" after "entities" in par. (4).

Pub. L. 104–121, § 244(a)(1), which directed insertion of "the reasonable use of" before "techniques," in introductory provisions, was executed by making the insertion in text which did not contain a comma after the word "techniques" to reflect the probable intent of Congress.

Subsecs. (b) to (e). Pub. L. 104–121, § 244(a)(4), added subsecs. (b) to (e).

EFFECTIVE DATE OF 1996 AMENDMENT

Amendment by Pub. L. 104–121 effective on expiration of 90 days after Mar. 29, 1996, but inapplicable to interpretative rules for which a notice of proposed rulemaking was published prior to Mar. 29, 1996, see section 245 of Pub. L. 104–121, set out as a note under section 601 of this title.

SMALL BUSINESS ADVOCACY CHAIRPERSONS

Section 244(b) of Pub. L. 104–121 provided that: "Not later than 30 days after the date of enactment of this Act [Mar. 29, 1996], the head of each covered agency that has conducted a final regulatory flexibility analysis shall designate a small business advocacy chairperson using existing personnel to the extent possible, to be responsible for implementing this section and to act as permanent chair of the agency's review panels established pursuant to this section."

SECTION REFERRED TO IN OTHER SECTIONS

This section is referred to in sections 611, 801 of this title.

§ 610. Periodic review of rules

(a) Within one hundred and eighty days after the effective date of this chapter, each agency shall publish in the Federal Register a plan for the periodic review of the rules issued by the agency which have or will have a significant economic impact upon a substantial number of small entities. Such plan may be amended by the agency at any time by publishing the revision in the Federal Register. The purpose of the review shall be to determine whether such rules should be continued without change, or should be amended or rescinded, consistent with the stated objectives of applicable statutes, to minimize any significant economic impact of the rules upon a substantial number of such small entities. The plan shall provide for the review of all such agency rules existing on the effective date of this chapter within ten years of that date and for the review of such rules adopted after the effective date of this chapter within ten years of the publication of such rules as the final rule. If the head of the agency determines that completion of the review of existing rules is not feasible by the established date, he shall so certify in a statement published in the Federal Register and may extend the completion date by one year at a time for a total of not more than five years.

(b) In reviewing rules to minimize any significant economic impact of the rule on a substantial number of small entities in a manner consistent with the stated objectives of applicable statutes, the agency shall consider the following factors—

(1) the continued need for the rule;

(2) the nature of complaints or comments received concerning the rule from the public;

(3) the complexity of the rule;

(4) the extent to which the rule overlaps, duplicates or conflicts with other Federal rules, and, to the extent feasible, with State and local governmental rules; and

(5) the length of time since the rule has been evaluated or the degree to which technology, economic conditions, or other factors have changed in the area affected by the rule.

(c) Each year, each agency shall publish in the Federal Register a list of the rules which have a significant economic impact on a substantial number of small entities, which are to be reviewed pursuant to this section during the succeeding twelve months. The list shall include a brief description of each rule and the need for and legal basis of such rule and shall invite public comment upon the rule.

(Added Pub. L. 96–354, § 3(a), Sept. 19, 1980, 94 Stat. 1169.)

REFERENCES IN TEXT

The effective date of this chapter, referred to in subsec. (a), is Jan. 1, 1981. See Effective Date note set out under section 601 of this title.

SECTION REFERRED TO IN OTHER SECTIONS

This section is referred to in sections 605, 611 of this title.

§ 611. Judicial review

(a)(1) For any rule subject to this chapter, a small entity that is adversely affected or aggrieved by final agency action is entitled to judicial review of agency compliance with the requirements of sections 601, 604, 605(b), 608(b), and 610 in accordance with chapter 7. Agency compliance with sections 607 and 609(a) shall be judicially reviewable in connection with judicial review of section 604.

(2) Each court having jurisdiction to review such rule for compliance with section 553, or under any other provision of law, shall have jurisdiction to review any claims of noncompliance with sections 601, 604, 605(b), 608(b), and 610 in accordance with chapter 7. Agency compliance with sections 607 and 609(a) shall be judicially reviewable in connection with judicial review of section 604.

(3)(A) A small entity may seek such review during the period beginning on the date of final agency action and ending one year later, except that where a provision of law requires that an action challenging a final agency action be commenced before the expiration of one year, such lesser period shall apply to an action for judicial review under this section.

(B) In the case where an agency delays the issuance of a final regulatory flexibility analysis pursuant to section 608(b) of this chapter, an action for judicial review under this section shall be filed not later than—

(i) one year after the date the analysis is made available to the public, or

(ii) where a provision of law requires that an action challenging a final agency regulation be commenced before the expiration of the 1-year period, the number of days specified in such provision of law that is after the date the analysis is made available to the public.

(4) In granting any relief in an action under this section, the court shall order the agency to take corrective action consistent with this chapter and chapter 7, including, but not limited to—

(A) remanding the rule to the agency, and

(B) deferring the enforcement of the rule against small entities unless the court finds that continued enforcement of the rule is in the public interest.

(5) Nothing in this subsection shall be construed to limit the authority of any court to stay the effective date of any rule or provision thereof under any other provision of law or to grant any other relief in addition to the requirements of this section.

(b) In an action for the judicial review of a rule, the regulatory flexibility analysis for such rule, including an analysis prepared or corrected pursuant to paragraph (a)(4), shall constitute part of the entire record of agency action in connection with such review.

(c) Compliance or noncompliance by an agency with the provisions of this chapter shall be subject to judicial review only in accordance with this section.

(d) Nothing in this section bars judicial review of any other impact statement or similar analysis required by any other law if judicial review of such statement or analysis is otherwise permitted by law.

(Added Pub. L. 96–354, § 3(a), Sept. 19, 1980, 94 Stat. 1169; amended Pub. L. 104–121, title II, § 242, Mar. 29, 1996, 110 Stat. 865.)

AMENDMENTS

1996—Pub. L. 104–121 amended section generally. Prior to amendment, section read as follows:

"(a) Except as otherwise provided in subsection (b), any determination by an agency concerning the applicability of any of the provisions of this chapter to any action of the agency shall not be subject to judicial review.

"(b) Any regulatory flexibility analysis prepared under sections 603 and 604 of this title and the compliance or noncompliance of the agency with the provisions of this chapter shall not be subject to judicial review. When an action for judicial review of a rule is instituted, any regulatory flexibility analysis for such rule shall constitute part of the whole record of agency action in connection with the review.

"(c) Nothing in this section bars judicial review of any other impact statement or similar analysis required by any other law if judicial review of such statement or analysis is otherwise provided by law."

EFFECTIVE DATE OF 1996 AMENDMENT

Amendment by Pub. L. 104–121 effective on expiration of 90 days after Mar. 29, 1996, but inapplicable to interpretative rules for which a notice of proposed rulemaking was published prior to Mar. 29, 1996, see section 245 of Pub. L. 104–121, set out as a note under section 601 of this title.

§ 612. Reports and intervention rights

(a) The Chief Counsel for Advocacy of the Small Business Administration shall monitor agency compliance with this chapter and shall report at least annually thereon to the President and to the Committees on the Judiciary and Small Business of the Senate and House of Representatives.

(b) The Chief Counsel for Advocacy of the Small Business Administration is authorized to appear as amicus curiae in any action brought in a court of the United States to review a rule. In any such action, the Chief Counsel is authorized to present his or her views with respect to compliance with this chapter, the adequacy of the rulemaking record with respect to small entities and the effect of the rule on small entities.

(c) A court of the United States shall grant the application of the Chief Counsel for Advocacy of the Small Business Administration to appear in any such action for the purposes described in subsection (b).

(Added Pub. L. 96–354, § 3(a), Sept. 19, 1980, 94 Stat. 1170; amended Pub. L. 104–121, title II, § 243(b), Mar. 29, 1996, 110 Stat. 866.)

AMENDMENTS

1996—Subsec. (a). Pub. L. 104–121, § 243(b)(1), which directed substitution of "the Committees on the Judiciary and Small Business of the Senate and House of Representatives" for "the committees on the Judiciary of the Senate and the House of Representatives, the Select Committee on Small Business of the Senate, and the Committee on Small Business of the House of Representatives", was executed by making the substitution for "the Committees on the Judiciary of the Senate and House of Representatives, the Select Committee on Small Business of the Senate, and the Committee on Small Business of the House of Representatives" to reflect the probable intent of Congress.

Subsec. (b). Pub. L. 104–121, § 243(b)(2), substituted "his or her views with respect to compliance with this chapter, the adequacy of the rulemaking record with respect to small entities and the" for "his views with respect to the".

EFFECTIVE DATE OF 1996 AMENDMENT

Amendment by Pub. L. 104–121 effective on expiration of 90 days after Mar. 29, 1996, but inapplicable to interpretative rules for which a notice of proposed rulemaking was published prior to Mar. 29, 1996, see section 245 of Pub. L. 104–121, set out as a note under section 601 of this title.

CHAPTER 7—JUDICIAL REVIEW

SHORT TITLE

The provisions of sections 551 to 559 of this title and this chapter were originally enacted by act June 11, 1946, ch. 423, 60 Stat. 237, popularly known as the "Administrative Procedure Act". That Act was repealed as part of the general revision of this title by Pub. L. 89–554 and its provisions incorporated into sections 551 to 559 of this title and this chapter.

CHAPTER REFERRED TO IN OTHER SECTIONS

This chapter is referred to in sections 559, 611, 8902, 8902a of this title; title 2 sections 501, 502; title 7 sections 136a, 1642, 6999; title 8 section 1421; title 10 section 2409; title 12 sections 1441a, 1467a, 1749bbb–17, 1786, 1787, 1815, 1818, 1821, 1959, 2266, 2268, 4583, 4634; title 15 sections 57a, 78dd–1, 78dd–2, 266, 687e, 1193, 1715, 2060, 2603, 2618, 2622, 3416, 5623, 6208; title 16 sections 460aa–3, 470q, 823b, 1374, 1536, 1855, 2404, 3636; title 17 sections 701, 908; title 18 sections 843, 3625; title 19 section 1337; title 20 sections 107d–2, 1683; title 21 sections 350b, 360e, 360g, 360kk; title 22 sections 277d–24, 1623, 1645n, 3794, 4140; title 23 sections 134, 135; title 25 sections 954, 1776b, 2713, 2714; title 26 section 9041; title 29 sections 214, 727, 792, 1137; title 30 sections 956, 1411, 1415, 1416; title 33 sections 524, 597; title 35 sections 135, 154; title 38 section 502; title 39 sections 404, 410, 3001, 3008, 3012, 3603; title 41 sections 43a, 265; title 42 sections 300j–6, 300j–9, 1395h, 1395oo, 1436c, 1437c–1, 2000d–2, 2022, 2231, 2236, 2239, 2282a, 2286f, 4104, 5405, 5851, 6105, 6303, 6306, 6973, 6976, 7276, 7525, 7607, 7622, 7920, 8412, 8433, 8441, 10132, 10155, 10244; title 44 section 2203; title 45 sections 1116, 1212; title 47 sections 303, 305, 310, 409; title 49 sections 5303, 31102, 31141, 70110; title 50 sections 835, 2011; title 50 App. sections 463, 2159, 2412.

§ 701. Application; definitions

(a) This chapter applies, according to the provisions thereof, except to the extent that—

(1) statutes preclude judicial review; or

(2) agency action is committed to agency discretion by law.

(b) For the purpose of this chapter—

(1) "agency" means each authority of the Government of the United States, whether or not it is within or subject to review by another agency, but does not include—

(A) the Congress;

(B) the courts of the United States;

(C) the governments of the territories or possessions of the United States;

(D) the government of the District of Columbia;

(E) agencies composed of representatives of the parties or of representatives of organizations of the parties to the disputes determined by them;

(F) courts martial and military commissions;

(G) military authority exercised in the field in time of war or in occupied territory; or

(H) functions conferred by sections 1738, 1739, 1743, and 1744 of title 12; chapter 2 of title 41; subchapter II of chapter 471 of title 49; or sections 1884, 1891–1902, and former section 1641(b)(2), of title 50, appendix; and

(2) "person", "rule", "order", "license", "sanction", "relief", and "agency action" have the meanings given them by section 551 of this title.

(Pub. L. 89–554, Sept. 6, 1966, 80 Stat. 392; Pub. L. 103–272, § 5(a), July 5, 1994, 108 Stat. 1373.)

HISTORICAL AND REVISION NOTES

Derivation	U.S. Code	Revised Statutes and Statutes at Large
(a)	5 U.S.C. 1009 (introductory clause).	June 11, 1946, ch. 324, § 10 (introductory clause), 60 Stat. 243.

In subsection (a), the words "This chapter applies, according to the provisions thereof," are added to avoid the necessity of repeating the introductory clause of former section 1009 in sections 702–706.

Subsection (b) is added on authority of section 2 of the Act of June 11, 1946, ch. 324, 60 Stat. 237, as amended, which is carried into section 551 of this title.

In subsection (b)(1)(G), the words "or naval" are omitted as included in "military".

In subsection (b)(1)(H), the words "functions which by law expire on the termination of present hostilities, within any fixed period thereafter, or before July 1, 1947" are omitted as executed. Reference to the "Selective Training and Service Act of 1940" is omitted as that Act expired on Mar. 31, 1947. Reference to the "Sugar Control Extension Act of 1947" is omitted as that Act expired on Mar. 31, 1948. References to the "Housing and Rent Act of 1947, as amended" and the "Veterans' Emergency Housing Act of 1946" have been consolidated as they are related. The reference to former section 1641(b)(2) of title 50, appendix, is retained notwithstanding its repeal by § 111(a)(1) of the Act of Sept. 21, 1961, Pub. L. 87–256, 75 Stat. 538, since § 111(c) of the Act provides that a reference in other Acts to a provision of law repealed by § 111(a) shall be considered to be a reference to the appropriate provisions of Pub. L. 87–256.

Standard changes are made to conform with the definitions applicable and the style of this title as outlined in the preface to the report.

REFERENCES IN TEXT

Sections 1891–1902 of title 50, appendix, referred to in subsec. (b)(1)(H), were omitted from the Code as executed.

AMENDMENTS

1994—Subsec. (b)(1)(H). Pub. L. 103–272 substituted "subchapter II of chapter 471 of title 49; or sections" for "or sections 1622,".

SECTION REFERRED TO IN OTHER SECTIONS

This section is referred to in title 2 sections 501, 502; title 7 sections 1508, 2143; title 16 section 839f; title 18 sections 843, 3625; title 20 section 1683; title 25 section 954; title 30 section 956; title 41 section 422; title 42 sections 5405, 6105, 6976; title 50 App. section 2412.

§ 702. Right of review

A person suffering legal wrong because of agency action, or adversely affected or aggrieved by agency action within the meaning of a relevant statute, is entitled to judicial review thereof. An action in a court of the United States seeking relief other than money damages and stating a claim that an agency or an officer or employee thereof acted or failed to act in an official capacity or under color of legal authority shall not be dismissed nor relief therein be denied on the ground that it is against the United States or that the United States is an indispensable party. The United States may be named as a defendant in any such action, and a judgment or decree may be entered against the United States: *Provided,* That any mandatory or injunctive decree shall specify the Federal officer or officers (by name or by title), and their successors in office, personally responsible for compliance. Nothing herein (1) affects other limitations on judicial review or the power or duty of the court to dismiss any action or deny relief on any other appropriate legal or equitable ground; or (2) confers authority to grant relief if any other statute that grants consent to suit expressly or impliedly forbids the relief which is sought.

(Pub. L. 89–554, Sept. 6, 1966, 80 Stat. 392; Pub. L. 94–574, § 1, Oct. 21, 1976, 90 Stat. 2721.)

HISTORICAL AND REVISION NOTES

Derivation	U.S. Code	Revised Statutes and Statutes at Large
....	5 U.S.C. 1009(a).	June 11, 1946, ch. 324, § 10(a), 60 Stat. 243.

Standard changes are made to conform with the definitions applicable and the style of this title as outlined in the preface to the report.

AMENDMENTS

1976—Pub. L. 94–574 removed the defense of sovereign immunity as a bar to judicial review of Federal administrative action otherwise subject to judicial review.

SECTION REFERRED TO IN OTHER SECTIONS

This section is referred to in title 2 sections 501, 502; title 7 section 2143; title 16 section 839f; title 18 sections 843, 3625; title 19 section 1677c; title 21 section 1906; title 25 section 954; title 28 section 2631; title 41 section 422; title 42 section 5405; title 43 section 1337; title 50 App. sections 16, 2412.

§ 703. Form and venue of proceeding

The form of proceeding for judicial review is the special statutory review proceeding relevant to the subject matter in a court specified by statute or, in the absence or inadequacy thereof, any applicable form of legal action, including actions for declaratory judgments or writs of prohibitory or mandatory injunction or habeas corpus, in a court of competent jurisdiction. If no special statutory review proceeding is applicable, the action for judicial review may be brought against the United States, the agency by its official title, or the appropriate officer. Except to the extent that prior, adequate, and exclusive opportunity for judicial review is provided by law, agency action is subject to judicial review in civil or criminal proceedings for judicial enforcement.

(Pub. L. 89–554, Sept. 6, 1966, 80 Stat. 392; Pub. L. 94–574, § 1, Oct. 21, 1976, 90 Stat. 2721.)

HISTORICAL AND REVISION NOTES

Derivation	U.S. Code	Revised Statutes and Statutes at Large
....	5 U.S.C. 1009(b).	June 11, 1946, ch. 324, § 10(b), 60 Stat. 243.

Standard changes are made to conform with the definitions applicable and the style of this title as outlined in the preface to the report.

AMENDMENTS

1976—Pub. L. 94–574 provided that if no special statutory review proceeding is applicable, the action for judicial review may be brought against the United States, the agency by its official title, or the appropriate officer as defendant.

SECTION REFERRED TO IN OTHER SECTIONS

This section is referred to in title 2 sections 501, 502; title 7 section 2143; title 16 section 839f; title 18 sections 843, 3625; title 25 section 954; title 41 section 422; title 42 section 5405; title 50 App. section 2412.

§ 704. Actions reviewable

Agency action made reviewable by statute and final agency action for which there is no other adequate remedy in a court are subject to judicial review. A preliminary, procedural, or intermediate agency action or ruling not directly reviewable is subject to review on the review of the final agency action. Except as otherwise expressly required by statute, agency action otherwise final is final for the purposes of this section whether or not there has been presented or determined an application for a declaratory order, for any form of reconsideration, or, unless the agency otherwise requires by rule and provides that the action meanwhile is inoperative, for an appeal to superior agency authority.

(Pub. L. 89–554, Sept. 6, 1966, 80 Stat. 392.)

HISTORICAL AND REVISION NOTES

Derivation	U.S. Code	Revised Statutes and Statutes at Large
....	5 U.S.C. 1009(c).	June 11, 1946, ch. 324, § 10(c), 60 Stat. 243.

Standard changes are made to conform with the definitions applicable and the style of this title as outlined in the preface of this report.

SECTION REFERRED TO IN OTHER SECTIONS

This section is referred to in title 2 sections 501, 502; title 7 section 2143; title 15 sections 78*l*, 78ccc; title 16 section 839f; title 18 sections 843, 3625; title 25 section 954; title 41 section 422; title 42 sections 5405, 7174, 7194; title 50 App. section 2412.

§ 705. Relief pending review

When an agency finds that justice so requires, it may postpone the effective date of action taken by it, pending judicial review. On such conditions as may be required and to the extent necessary to prevent irreparable injury, the reviewing court, including the court to which a case may be taken on appeal from or on application for certiorari or other writ to a reviewing court, may issue all necessary and appropriate process to postpone the effective date of an agency action or to preserve status or rights pending conclusion of the review proceedings.

(Pub. L. 89–554, Sept. 6, 1966, 80 Stat. 393.)

HISTORICAL AND REVISION NOTES

Derivation	U.S. Code	Revised Statutes and Statutes at Large
....	5 U.S.C. 1009(d).	June 11, 1946, ch. 324, § 10(d), 60 Stat. 243.

Standard changes are made to conform with the definitions applicable and the style of this title as outlined in the preface of this report.

SECTION REFERRED TO IN OTHER SECTIONS

This section is referred to in title 2 sections 501, 502; title 7 section 2143; title 15 sections 78y, 1262, 1474, 3416; title 16 sections 839f, 1855, 3636; title 18 sections 843, 3625; title 25 section 954; title 41 section 422; title 42 sections 5405, 7172; title 50 App. section 2412.

§ 706. Scope of review

To the extent necessary to decision and when presented, the reviewing court shall decide all relevant questions of law, interpret constitutional and statutory provisions, and determine the meaning or applicability of the terms of an agency action. The reviewing court shall—

(1) compel agency action unlawfully withheld or unreasonably delayed; and

(2) hold unlawful and set aside agency action, findings, and conclusions found to be—

(A) arbitrary, capricious, an abuse of discretion, or otherwise not in accordance with law;

(B) contrary to constitutional right, power, privilege, or immunity;

(C) in excess of statutory jurisdiction, authority, or limitations, or short of statutory right;

(D) without observance of procedure required by law;

(E) unsupported by substantial evidence in a case subject to sections 556 and 557 of this title or otherwise reviewed on the record of an agency hearing provided by statute; or

(F) unwarranted by the facts to the extent that the facts are subject to trial de novo by the reviewing court.

In making the foregoing determinations, the court shall review the whole record or those parts of it cited by a party, and due account shall be taken of the rule of prejudicial error.

(Pub. L. 89–554, Sept. 6, 1966, 80 Stat. 393.)

HISTORICAL AND REVISION NOTES

Derivation	U.S. Code	Revised Statutes and Statutes at Large
....	5 U.S.C. 1009(e).	June 11, 1946, ch. 324, § 10(e), 60 Stat. 243.

Standard changes are made to conform with the definitions applicable and the style of this title as outlined in the preface of this report.

ABBREVIATION OF RECORD

Pub. L. 85–791, Aug. 28, 1958, 72 Stat. 941, which authorized abbreviation of record on review or enforcement of orders of administrative agencies and review on the original papers, provided, in section 35 thereof, that: "This Act [enacting section 2112 of Title 28, Judiciary and Judicial Procedure, and amending sections 1036 and 1037(c) of former Title 5 [now sections 2346 and 2347(c) of Title 28], sections 8, 9, 193(c), 194(b)–(d), (h), 1115(c), 1599(c), 1600, and 1601 of Title 7, Agriculture, section 1848 of Title 12, Banks and Banking, sections 21,

45(b)–(d), 77i(a), 78y(a), 79x(a), 80a–42(a), 80b–13(a), and 717r(a), (b) of Title 15. Commerce and Trade, section 825l(a), (b) of Title 16, Conservation, sections 81r(c) and 1641(b) of Title 19, Customs Duties, section 277(b) of Title 20, Education, sections 346a(i)(2), (3), 371(f)(1), (3) of Title 21, Food and Drugs, section 1631f(b) of Title 22, Foreign Relations and Intercourse, section 204(h), Title 27, Intoxicating Liquors, sections 160(d)–(f) and 210(a) of Title 29, Labor, section 576 of former Title 39, The Postal Service, section 291j(b)(1), (2) of Title 42, Public Health and Welfare, section 315(f) of Title 45, Railroads, section 1181(b) of Title 46, Appendix, Shipping, section 402(d) of Title 47, Telegraphs, Telephones, and Radiotelegraphs, section 646(c) of former Title 49, Transportation, and sections 793(a), 820(e), 821(c), (d) of Title 50, War and National Defense] shall not be construed to repeal or modify any provision of the Administrative Procedure Act."

SECTION REFERRED TO IN OTHER SECTIONS

This section is referred to in section 7123 of this title; title 2 sections 501, 502, 1409, 1571; title 7 sections 252, 2143; title 8 section 1182; title 10 section 1508; title 11 section 1172; title 12 sections 1701q–1, 1723i, 1735f–14, 1735f–15, 3105; title 14 section 425; title 15 sections 57a, 78y, 1262, 1474, 2618, 5408, 6503, 6751; title 16 sections 773f, 839f, 973f, 1379, 1855, 1858, 2437, 3142, 3636, 5010, 5507; title 18 sections 843, 3625; title 19 section 1337; title 22 section 4140; title 25 section 954; title 28 sections 1491, 2640, 3902; title 29 sections 727, 1813, 1853; title 30 sections 956, 1462; title 39 section 3628; title 41 section 422; title 42 sections 300gg–22, 610, 3545, 5405, 5919, 6976, 7607, 9152; title 45 sections 726, 904, 915, 1105; title 47 section 402; title 49 sections 20104, 32904; title 50 App. section 2412.

CHAPTER 8—CONGRESSIONAL REVIEW OF AGENCY RULEMAKING

§ 801. Congressional review

(a)(1)(A) Before a rule can take effect, the Federal agency promulgating such rule shall submit to each House of the Congress and to the Comptroller General a report containing—

(i) a copy of the rule;

(ii) a concise general statement relating to the rule, including whether it is a major rule; and

(iii) the proposed effective date of the rule.

(B) On the date of the submission of the report under subparagraph (A), the Federal agency promulgating the rule shall submit to the Comptroller General and make available to each House of Congress—

(i) a complete copy of the cost-benefit analysis of the rule, if any;

(ii) the agency's actions relevant to sections 603, 604, 605, 607, and 609;

(iii) the agency's actions relevant to sections 202, 203, 204, and 205 of the Unfunded Mandates Reform Act of 1995; and

(iv) any other relevant information or requirements under any other Act and any relevant Executive orders.

(C) Upon receipt of a report submitted under subparagraph (A), each House shall provide copies of the report to the chairman and ranking member of each standing committee with jurisdiction under the rules of the House of Representatives or the Senate to report a bill to amend the provision of law under which the rule is issued.

(2)(A) The Comptroller General shall provide a report on each major rule to the committees of jurisdiction in each House of the Congress by the end of 15 calendar days after the submission or publication date as provided in section 802(b)(2). The report of the Comptroller General shall include an assessment of the agency's compliance with procedural steps required by paragraph (1)(B).

(B) Federal agencies shall cooperate with the Comptroller General by providing information relevant to the Comptroller General's report under subparagraph (A).

(3) A major rule relating to a report submitted under paragraph (1) shall take effect on the latest of—

(A) the later of the date occurring 60 days after the date on which—

(i) the Congress receives the report submitted under paragraph (1); or

(ii) the rule is published in the Federal Register, if so published;

(B) if the Congress passes a joint resolution of disapproval described in section 802 relating to the rule, and the President signs a veto of such resolution, the earlier date—

(i) on which either House of Congress votes and fails to override the veto of the President; or

(ii) occurring 30 session days after the date on which the Congress received the veto and objections of the President; or

(C) the date the rule would have otherwise taken effect, if not for this section (unless a joint resolution of disapproval under section 802 is enacted).

(4) Except for a major rule, a rule shall take effect as otherwise provided by law after submission to Congress under paragraph (1).

(5) Notwithstanding paragraph (3), the effective date of a rule shall not be delayed by operation of this chapter beyond the date on which either House of Congress votes to reject a joint resolution of disapproval under section 802.

(b)(1) A rule shall not take effect (or continue), if the Congress enacts a joint resolution of disapproval, described under section 802, of the rule.

(2) A rule that does not take effect (or does not continue) under paragraph (1) may not be reissued in substantially the same form, and a new rule that is substantially the same as such a rule may not be issued, unless the reissued or new rule is specifically authorized by a law enacted after the date of the joint resolution disapproving the original rule.

(c)(1) Notwithstanding any other provision of this section (except subject to paragraph (3)), a rule that would not take effect by reason of subsection (a)(3) may take effect, if the President makes a determination under paragraph (2) and submits written notice of such determination to the Congress.

(2) Paragraph (1) applies to a determination made by the President by Executive order that the rule should take effect because such rule is—

(A) necessary because of an imminent threat to health or safety or other emergency;

(B) necessary for the enforcement of criminal laws;

(C) necessary for national security; or

(D) issued pursuant to any statute implementing an international trade agreement.

(3) An exercise by the President of the authority under this subsection shall have no effect on the procedures under section 802 or the effect of a joint resolution of disapproval under this section.

(d)(1) In addition to the opportunity for review otherwise provided under this chapter, in the case of any rule for which a report was submitted in accordance with subsection (a)(1)(A) during the period beginning on the date occurring—

(A) in the case of the Senate, 60 session days, or

(B) in the case of the House of Representatives, 60 legislative days,

before the date the Congress adjourns a session of Congress through the date on which the same or succeeding Congress first convenes its next session, section 802 shall apply to such rule in the succeeding session of Congress.

(2)(A) In applying section 802 for purposes of such additional review, a rule described under paragraph (1) shall be treated as though—

(i) such rule were published in the Federal Register (as a rule that shall take effect) on—

(I) in the case of the Senate, the 15th session day, or

(II) in the case of the House of Representatives, the 15th legislative day,

after the succeeding session of Congress first convenes; and

(ii) a report on such rule were submitted to Congress under subsection (a)(1) on such date.

(B) Nothing in this paragraph shall be construed to affect the requirement under subsection (a)(1) that a report shall be submitted to Congress before a rule can take effect.

(3) A rule described under paragraph (1) shall take effect as otherwise provided by law (including other subsections of this section).

(e)(1) For purposes of this subsection, section 802 shall also apply to any major rule promulgated between March 1, 1996, and the date of enactment of this chapter.

(2) In applying section 802 for purposes of Congressional review, a rule described under paragraph (1) shall be treated as though—

(A) such rule were published in the Federal Register on the date of enactment of this chapter; and

(B) a report on such rule were submitted to Congress under subsection (a)(1) on such date.

(3) The effectiveness of a rule described under paragraph (1) shall be as otherwise provided by law, unless the rule is made of no force or effect under section 802.

(f) Any rule that takes effect and later is made of no force or effect by enactment of a joint resolution under section 802 shall be treated as though such rule had never taken effect.

(g) If the Congress does not enact a joint resolution of disapproval under section 802 respecting a rule, no court or agency may infer any intent of the Congress from any action or inaction of the Congress with regard to such rule, related statute, or joint resolution of disapproval.

(Added Pub. L. 104–121, title II, § 251, Mar. 29, 1996, 110 Stat. 868.)

REFERENCES IN TEXT

Sections 202, 203, 204, and 205 of the Unfunded Mandates Reform Act of 1995, referred to in subsec. (a)(1)(B)(iii), are classified to sections 1532, 1533, 1534, and 1535, respectively, of Title 2, The Congress.

The date of the enactment of this chapter, referred to in subsec. (e)(1), (2), is the date of the enactment of Pub. L. 104–121, which was approved Mar. 29, 1996.

EFFECTIVE DATE

Section 252 of Pub. L. 104–121 provided that: "The amendment made by section 351 [probably means section 251, enacting this chapter] shall take effect on the date of enactment of this Act [Mar. 29, 1996]."

TRUTH IN REGULATING

Pub. L. 106–312, Oct. 17, 2000, 114 Stat. 1248, provided that:

"SECTION 1. SHORT TITLE.

"This Act may be cited as the 'Truth in Regulating Act of 2000'.

"SEC. 2. PURPOSES.

"The purposes of this Act are to—

"(1) increase the transparency of important regulatory decisions;

"(2) promote effective congressional oversight to ensure that agency rules fulfill statutory requirements in an efficient, effective, and fair manner; and

"(3) increase the accountability of Congress and the agencies to the people they serve.

"SEC. 3. DEFINITIONS.

"In this Act, the term—

"(1) 'agency' has the meaning given such term under section 551(1) of title 5, United States Code;

"(2) 'economically significant rule' means any proposed or final rule, including an interim or direct final rule, that may have an annual effect on the economy of $100,000,000 or more or adversely affect in a material way the economy, a sector of the economy, productivity, competition, jobs, the environment, public health or safety, or State, local, or tribal governments or communities; and

"(3) 'independent evaluation' means a substantive evaluation of the agency's data, methodology, and assumptions used in developing the economically significant rule, including—

"(A) an explanation of how any strengths or weaknesses in those data, methodology, and assumptions support or detract from conclusions reached by the agency; and

"(B) the implications, if any, of those strengths or weaknesses for the rulemaking.

"SEC. 4. PILOT PROJECT FOR REPORT ON RULES.

"(a) IN GENERAL.—

"(1) REQUEST FOR REVIEW.—When an agency publishes an economically significant rule, a chairman or ranking member of a committee of jurisdiction of either House of Congress may request the Comptroller General of the United States to review the rule.

"(2) REPORT.—The Comptroller General shall submit a report on each economically significant rule selected under paragraph (4) to the committees of jurisdiction in each House of Congress not later than 180 calendar days after a committee request is received. The report shall include an independent evaluation of the economically significant rule by the Comptroller General.

"(3) INDEPENDENT EVALUATION.—The independent evaluation of the economically significant rule by the Comptroller General under paragraph (2) shall include—

"(A) an evaluation of the agency's analysis of the potential benefits of the rule, including any beneficial effects that cannot be quantified in monetary terms and the identification of the persons or entities likely to receive the benefits;

"(B) an evaluation of the agency's analysis of the potential costs of the rule, including any adverse effects that cannot be quantified in monetary terms and the identification of the persons or entities likely to bear the costs;

"(C) an evaluation of the agency's analysis of alternative approaches set forth in the notice of proposed rulemaking and in the rulemaking record, as well as of any regulatory impact analysis, federalism assessment, or other analysis or assessment prepared by the agency or required for the economically significant rule; and

"(D) a summary of the results of the evaluation of the Comptroller General and the implications of those results.

"(4) PROCEDURES FOR PRIORITIES OF REQUESTS.—The Comptroller General shall have discretion to develop procedures for determining the priority and number of requests for review under paragraph (1) for which a report will be submitted under paragraph (2).

"(b) AUTHORITY OF COMPTROLLER GENERAL.—Each agency shall promptly cooperate with the Comptroller General in carrying out this Act. Nothing in this Act is intended to expand or limit the authority of the General Accounting Office.

"SEC. 5. AUTHORIZATION OF APPROPRIATIONS.

"There are authorized to be appropriated to the General Accounting Office to carry out this Act $5,200,000 for each of fiscal years 2000 through 2002.

"SEC. 6. EFFECTIVE DATE AND DURATION OF PILOT PROJECT.

"(a) EFFECTIVE DATE.—This Act and the amendments made by this Act shall take effect 90 days after the date of enactment of this Act [Oct. 17, 2000].

"(b) DURATION OF PILOT PROJECT.—The pilot project under this Act shall continue for a period of 3 years, if in each fiscal year, or portion thereof included in that period, a specific annual appropriation not less than $5,200,000 or the pro-rated equivalent thereof shall have been made for the pilot project.

"(c) REPORT.—Before the conclusion of the 3-year period, the Comptroller General shall submit to Congress a report reviewing the effectiveness of the pilot project and recommending whether or not Congress should permanently authorize the pilot project."

SECTION REFERRED TO IN OTHER SECTIONS

This section is referred to in sections 802, 803, 808 of this title.

§ 802. Congressional disapproval procedure

(a) For purposes of this section, the term "joint resolution" means only a joint resolution introduced in the period beginning on the date on which the report referred to in section 801(a)(1)(A) is received by Congress and ending 60 days thereafter (excluding days either House of Congress is adjourned for more than 3 days during a session of Congress), the matter after the resolving clause of which is as follows: "That Congress disapproves the rule submitted by the ____ relating to ____, and such rule shall have no force or effect." (The blank spaces being appropriately filled in).

(b)(1) A joint resolution described in subsection (a) shall be referred to the committees in each House of Congress with jurisdiction.

(2) For purposes of this section, the term "submission or publication date" means the later of the date on which—

(A) the Congress receives the report submitted under section 801(a)(1); or

(B) the rule is published in the Federal Register, if so published.

(c) In the Senate, if the committee to which is referred a joint resolution described in subsection (a) has not reported such joint resolution (or an identical joint resolution) at the end of 20 calendar days after the submission or publication date defined under subsection (b)(2), such committee may be discharged from further consideration of such joint resolution upon a petition supported in writing by 30 Members of the Senate, and such joint resolution shall be placed on the calendar.

(d)(1) In the Senate, when the committee to which a joint resolution is referred has reported, or when a committee is discharged (under subsection (c)) from further consideration of a joint resolution described in subsection (a), it is at any time thereafter in order (even though a previous motion to the same effect has been disagreed to) for a motion to proceed to the consideration of the joint resolution, and all points of order against the joint resolution (and against consideration of the joint resolution) are waived. The motion is not subject to amendment, or to a motion to postpone, or to a motion to proceed to the consideration of other business. A motion to reconsider the vote by which the motion is agreed to or disagreed to shall not be in order. If a motion to proceed to the consideration of the joint resolution is agreed to, the joint resolution shall remain the unfinished business of the Senate until disposed of.

(2) In the Senate, debate on the joint resolution, and on all debatable motions and appeals in connection therewith, shall be limited to not more than 10 hours, which shall be divided equally between those favoring and those opposing the joint resolution. A motion further to limit debate is in order and not debatable. An amendment to, or a motion to postpone, or a motion to proceed to the consideration of other business, or a motion to recommit the joint resolution is not in order.

(3) In the Senate, immediately following the conclusion of the debate on a joint resolution described in subsection (a), and a single quorum call at the conclusion of the debate if requested in accordance with the rules of the Senate, the vote on final passage of the joint resolution shall occur.

(4) Appeals from the decisions of the Chair relating to the application of the rules of the Senate to the procedure relating to a joint resolution described in subsection (a) shall be decided without debate.

(e) In the Senate the procedure specified in subsection (c) or (d) shall not apply to the consideration of a joint resolution respecting a rule—

(1) after the expiration of the 60 session days beginning with the applicable submission or publication date, or

(2) if the report under section 801(a)(1)(A) was submitted during the period referred to in section 801(d)(1), after the expiration of the 60 session days beginning on the 15th session day after the succeeding session of Congress first convenes.

(f) If, before the passage by one House of a joint resolution of that House described in subsection (a), that House receives from the other House a joint resolution described in subsection (a), then the following procedures shall apply:

(1) The joint resolution of the other House shall not be referred to a committee.

(2) With respect to a joint resolution described in subsection (a) of the House receiving the joint resolution—

(A) the procedure in that House shall be the same as if no joint resolution had been received from the other House; but

(B) the vote on final passage shall be on the joint resolution of the other House.

(g) This section is enacted by Congress—

(1) as an exercise of the rulemaking power of the Senate and House of Representatives, respectively, and as such it is deemed a part of the rules of each House, respectively, but applicable only with respect to the procedure to be followed in that House in the case of a joint resolution described in subsection (a), and it supersedes other rules only to the extent that it is inconsistent with such rules; and

(2) with full recognition of the constitutional right of either House to change the rules (so far as relating to the procedure of that House) at any time, in the same manner, and to the same extent as in the case of any other rule of that House.

(Added Pub. L. 104–121, title II, § 251, Mar. 29, 1996, 110 Stat. 871.)

SECTION REFERRED TO IN OTHER SECTIONS

This section is referred to in sections 801, 803 of this title.

§ 803. Special rule on statutory, regulatory, and judicial deadlines

(a) In the case of any deadline for, relating to, or involving any rule which does not take effect (or the effectiveness of which is terminated) because of enactment of a joint resolution under section 802, that deadline is extended until the date 1 year after the date of enactment of the joint resolution. Nothing in this subsection shall be construed to affect a deadline merely by reason of the postponement of a rule's effective date under section 801(a).

(b) The term "deadline" means any date certain for fulfilling any obligation or exercising any authority established by or under any Federal statute or regulation, or by or under any court order implementing any Federal statute or regulation.

(Added Pub. L. 104–121, title II, § 251, Mar. 29, 1996, 110 Stat. 873.)

§ 804. Definitions

For purposes of this chapter—

(1) The term "Federal agency" means any agency as that term is defined in section 551(1).

(2) The term "major rule" means any rule that the Administrator of the Office of Infor-

mation and Regulatory Affairs of the Office of Management and Budget finds has resulted in or is likely to result in—

(A) an annual effect on the economy of $100,000,000 or more;

(B) a major increase in costs or prices for consumers, individual industries, Federal, State, or local government agencies, or geographic regions; or

(C) significant adverse effects on competition, employment, investment, productivity, innovation, or on the ability of United States-based enterprises to compete with foreign-based enterprises in domestic and export markets.

The term does not include any rule promulgated under the Telecommunications Act of 1996 and the amendments made by that Act.

(3) The term "rule" has the meaning given such term in section 551, except that such term does not include—

(A) any rule of particular applicability, including a rule that approves or prescribes for the future rates, wages, prices, services, or allowances therefor, corporate or financial structures, reorganizations, mergers, or acquisitions thereof, or accounting practices or disclosures bearing on any of the foregoing;

(B) any rule relating to agency management or personnel; or

(C) any rule of agency organization, procedure, or practice that does not substantially affect the rights or obligations of non-agency parties.

(Added Pub. L. 104–121, title II, § 251, Mar. 29, 1996, 110 Stat. 873.)

REFERENCES IN TEXT

The Telecommunications Act of 1996, referred to in par. (2), is Pub. L. 104–104, Feb. 8, 1996, 110 Stat. 56. For complete classification of this Act to the Code, see Short Title of 1996 Amendment note set out under section 609 of Title 47, Telegraphs, Telephones, and Radiotelegraphs, and Tables.

§ 805. Judicial review

No determination, finding, action, or omission under this chapter shall be subject to judicial review.

(Added Pub. L. 104–121, title II, § 251, Mar. 29, 1996, 110 Stat. 873.)

§ 806. Applicability; severability

(a) This chapter shall apply notwithstanding any other provision of law.

(b) If any provision of this chapter or the application of any provision of this chapter to any person or circumstance, is held invalid, the application of such provision to other persons or circumstances, and the remainder of this chapter, shall not be affected thereby.

(Added Pub. L. 104–121, title II, § 251, Mar. 29, 1996, 110 Stat. 873.)

§ 807. Exemption for monetary policy

Nothing in this chapter shall apply to rules that concern monetary policy proposed or implemented by the Board of Governors of the Fed-

eral Reserve System or the Federal Open Market Committee.

(Added Pub. L. 104–121, title II, § 251, Mar. 29, 1996, 110 Stat. 874.)

§ 808. Effective date of certain rules

Notwithstanding section 801—

(1) any rule that establishes, modifies, opens, closes, or conducts a regulatory program for a commercial, recreational, or subsistence activity related to hunting, fishing, or camping, or

(2) any rule which an agency for good cause finds (and incorporates the finding and a brief statement of reasons therefor in the rule issued) that notice and public procedure thereon are impracticable, unnecessary, or contrary to the public interest,

shall take effect at such time as the Federal agency promulgating the rule determines.

(Added Pub. L. 104–121, title II, § 251, Mar. 29, 1996, 110 Stat. 874.)

CHAPTER 9—EXECUTIVE REORGANIZATION

AMENDMENTS

1984—Pub. L. 98–614, § 3(e)(3), Nov. 8, 1984, 98 Stat. 3193, substituted "passage" for "disapproval" in item 912.

1977—Pub. L. 95–17, § 2, Apr. 6, 1977, 91 Stat. 29, reenacted chapter heading and items 901 to 903, 905 to 909, and 911 without change, substituted "plan" for "plans" in item 904 and "Introduction and reference of resolution" for "Reference of resolution to committee" in item 910, inserted "; vote on final disapproval" in item 912, and omitted item 913 "Decisions without debate on motion to postpone or proceed".

CHAPTER REFERRED TO IN OTHER SECTIONS

This chapter is referred to in title 7 section 5903; title 20 section 3463; title 42 sections 2000e–6, 3534, 7176, 8401, 8819; title 49 sections 103, 106, 703.

§ 901. Purpose

(a) The Congress declares that it is the policy of the United States—

(1) to promote the better execution of the laws, the more effective management of the executive branch and of its agencies and functions, and the expeditious administration of the public business;

(2) to reduce expenditures and promote economy to the fullest extent consistent with the efficient operation of the Government;

---

[1] So in original. Does not conform to section catchline.

(3) to increase the efficiency of the operations of the Government to the fullest extent practicable;

(4) to group, coordinate, and consolidate agencies and functions of the Government, as nearly as may be, according to major purposes;

(5) to reduce the number of agencies by consolidating those having similar functions under a single head, and to abolish such agencies or functions thereof as may not be necessary for the efficient conduct of the Government; and

(6) to eliminate overlapping and duplication of effort.

(b) Congress declares that the public interest demands the carrying out of the purposes of subsection (a) of this section and that the purposes may be accomplished in great measure by proceeding under this chapter, and can be accomplished more speedily thereby than by the enactment of specific legislation.

(c) It is the intent of Congress that the President should provide appropriate means for broad citizen advice and participation in restructuring and reorganizing the executive branch.

(d) The President shall from time to time examine the organization of all agencies and shall determine what changes in such organization are necessary to carry out any policy set forth in subsection (a) of this section.

(Pub. L. 89–554, Sept. 6, 1966, 80 Stat. 394; Pub. L. 92–179, §1, Dec. 10, 1971, 85 Stat. 574; Pub. L. 95–17, §2, Apr. 6, 1977, 91 Stat. 29.)

HISTORICAL AND REVISION NOTES

Derivation	U.S. Code	Revised Statutes and Statutes at Large
....	5 U.S.C. 133z.	June 20, 1949, ch. 226, §2, 63 Stat. 203.

In subsection (a), the words "from time to time examine" are substituted for "examine and from time to time reexamine" since the initial examination has been executed. The words "of the Government" following "agencies" are omitted as unnecessary in view of the definition of "agency" in section 902. In subsection (a)(1), the words "of the Government" following "executive branch" are omitted as unnecessary and to conform to the style of this title.

Standard changes are made to conform with the definitions applicable and the style of this title as outlined in the preface to the report.

CODIFICATION

Section 901(c) of former Title 5, Executive Departments and Government Officers and Employees, was transferred to section 60e–2(a) of Title 2, The Congress.

AMENDMENTS

1977—Subsecs. (a) to (d). Pub. L. 95–17 reenacted subsecs. (a) and (b) without change, added subsec. (c), and redesignated former subsec. (c) as (d).

1971—Subsec. (a). Pub. L. 92–179, §1(a), substituted "The Congress declares that it is the policy of the United States" for "The President shall from time to time examine the organization of all agencies and shall determine what changes therein are necessary to accomplish the following purposes" preceding par. (1).

Subsec. (c). Pub. L. 92–179, §1(b), added subsec. (c) consisting of provisions formerly set out preceding par. (1) of subsec. (a).

SHORT TITLE OF 1984 AMENDMENT

Pub. L. 98–614, §1, Nov. 8, 1984, 98 Stat. 3192, provided: "That this Act [amending sections 903 to 906 and 908 to 912 of this title] may be cited as the 'Reorganization Act Amendments of 1984'."

SHORT TITLE OF 1977 AMENDMENT

Section 1 of Pub. L. 95–17 provided: "That this Act [amending this chapter] may be cited as the 'Reorganization Act of 1977'."

NATIONAL COMMISSION ON EXECUTIVE ORGANIZATION

Pub. L. 100–527, §17, Oct. 25, 1988, 102 Stat. 2645, directed President, within 30 days after Mar. 15, 1989, to make a determination as to whether the national interest would be served by establishment of a National Commission on Executive Organization to review structural organization of executive branch of Federal Government, and stated that if President failed to transmit to Congress notification of his intent to establish such Commission section would cease to be effective 30 days after Mar. 15, 1989. [President did not transmit such notification to Cogress and thus section ceased to be effective 30 days after Mar. 15, 1989.]

EX. ORD. NO. 6166. REORGANIZATION OF EXECUTIVE AGENCIES GENERALLY

Ex. Ord. No. 6166, June 10, 1933, provided:

§1. PROCUREMENT

The function of determination of policies and methods of procurement, warehousing, and distribution of property, facilities, structures, improvements, machinery, equipment, stores, and supplies exercised by an agency is transferred to a Procurement Division in the Treasury Department, at the head of which shall be a Director of Procurement.

The Office of the Supervising Architect of the Treasury Department is transferred to the Procurement Division, except that the buildings of the Treasury Department shall be administered by the Treasury Department and the administration of post-office buildings is transferred to the Post Office Department. The General Supply Committee of the Treasury Department is abolished.

In respect of any kind of procurement, warehousing, or distribution for any agency the Procurement Division may, with the approval of the President, (a) undertake the performance of such procurement, warehousing, or distribution itself, or (b) permit such agency to perform such procurement, warehousing, or distribution, or (c) entrust such performance to some other agency, or (d) avail itself in part of any of these recourses, according as it may deem desirable in the interest of economy and efficiency. When the Procurement Division has prescribed the manner of procurement, warehousing, or distribution of any thing, no agency shall thereafter procure, warehouse, or distribute such thing in any manner other than so prescribed.

The execution of work now performed by the Corps of Engineers of the Army shall remain with said corps, subject to the responsibilities herein vested in the Procurement Division.

The Procurement Division shall also have control of all property, facilities, structures, machinery, equipment, stores, and supplies not necessary to the work of any agency; may have custody thereof or entrust custody to any other agency; and shall furnish the same to agencies as need therefor may arise.

The Fuel Yards of the Bureau of Mines of the Department of Commerce are transferred to the Procurement Office. (As amended by Ex. Ord. No. 6623 of Mar. 1, 1934.)

AMENDMENT OF SECTION BY EX. ORD. NO. 6623

Ex. Ord. No. 6623, Mar. 1, 1934, revoked a final paragraph of section 1 of Ex. Ord. No. 6166, which provided for the abolition of the Federal Employment Stabilization Board and the transfer of its functions to the Federal Emergency Administration of Public Works. Said Ex. Ord. No. 6623 also provided in part as follows:

"It is further ordered that the said Federal Employment Stabilization Board be, and it is hereby, abolished.

"There is hereby established in the Department of Commerce an office to be known as the 'Federal Employment Stabilization Office,' and there are hereby transferred to such office the functions of the Federal Employment Stabilization Board, together with its Director and other personnel, and records, supplies, equipment, and property of every kind.

"The unexpended balances of appropriations and/or allotments of appropriations of the Federal Employment Stabilization Board are hereby transferred to the Federal Employment Stabilization Office, Department of Commerce."

EFFECTIVE DATE

The effective date of Ex. Ord. No. 6166, § 1, as provided for in section 22, post, was extended to Dec. 31, 1933, by Ex. Ord. No. 6224, of July 27, 1933, and the effective date of the last paragraph, subsequently revoked by Ex. Ord. No. 6623, was deferred by Ex. Ord. No. 6624 of Mar. 1, 1934, until such revocation could become effective.

[Subsequent to the effective date of Ex. Ord. No. 6166, § 1, certain functions affected thereby were again transferred as follows: The Public Buildings Branch of the Procurement Division was transferred to Public Buildings Administration within the Federal Works Administration by 1939 Reorg. Plan No. 1, §§ 301, 303, 4 Fed. Reg. 2729; 53 Stat. 1426, 1427; the Federal Employment Stabilization Office, created by Ex. Ord. No. 6166, § 1, as amended by Ex. Ord. No. 6624, was abolished by 1939 Reorg. Plan No. 1, § 4, 4 Fed. Reg. 2727, 53 Stat. 1423, and its functions transferred to the Executive Office of the President.]

SUPERSEDURE OF PARS. 1, 3, AND 5

Section 602(b) of act June 30, 1949, ch. 288, title VI, 63 Stat. 401, eff. July 1, 1949, as renumbered from title V, section 502(b) of said act June 30, 1949 by act Sept. 5, 1950, ch. 849, §§ 6(a), (b), 7(e), 64 Stat. 583, provided that: "The provisions of the first, third, and fifth paragraphs of section 1 of Executive Order Numbered 6166 of June 10, 1933 [this Ex. Ord.], are hereby superseded, insofar as they relate to any function now administered by the Bureau of Federal Supply except functions with respect to standard contract forms."

§ 2. NATIONAL PARKS, BUILDINGS, AND RESERVATIONS

All functions of administration of public buildings, reservations, national parks, national monuments, and national cemeteries are consolidated in the National Park Service in the Department of the Interior, at the head of which shall be a Director of the National Park Service; except that where deemed desirable there may be excluded from this provision any public building or reservation which is chiefly employed as a facility in the work of a particular agency. This transfer and consolidation of functions shall include, among others, those of the former National Park Service of the Department of the Interior and the following National Cemeteries and Parks of the War Department which are located within the continental limits of the United States:

NATIONAL MILITARY PARKS

Chickamauga and Chattanooga National Military Park, Georgia and Tennessee.
Fort Donelson National Military Park, Tennessee.
Fredericksburg and Spotsylvania County Battle Fields Memorial, Virginia.
Gettysburg National Military Park, Pennsylvania.
Guilford Courthouse National Military Park, North Carolina.
Kings Mountain National Military Park, South Carolina.
Moores Creek National Military Park, North Carolina.

Petersburg National Military Park, Virginia.
Shiloh National Military Park, Tennessee.
Stones River National Military Park, Tennessee.
Vicksburg National Military Park, Mississippi.

NATIONAL PARKS

Abraham Lincoln National Park, Kentucky.
Fort McHenry National Park, Maryland.

BATTLEFIELD SITES

Antietam Battlefield, Maryland.
Appomattox, Virginia.
Brices Cross Roads, Mississippi.
Chalmette Monument and Grounds, Louisiana.
Cowpens, South Carolina.
Fort Necessity, Wharton County, Pennsylvania.
Kenesaw Mountain, Georgia.
Monocacy, Maryland.
Tupelo, Mississippi.
White Plains, New York.

NATIONAL MONUMENTS

Big Hole Battlefield, Beaverhead County, Montana.
Cabrillo Monument, Fort Rosecrans, California.
Castle Pinckney, Charleston, South Carolina.
Father Millet Cross, Fort Niagara, New York.
Fort Marion, St. Augustine, Florida.
Fort Matanzas, Florida.
Fort Pulaski, Georgia.
Meriwether Lewis, Hardin County, Tennessee.
Mound City Group, Chillicothe, Ohio.
Statue of Liberty, Fort Wood, New York.

MISCELLANEOUS MEMORIALS

Camp Blount Tablets, Lincoln County, Tennessee.
Kill Devil Hill Monument, Kitty Hawk, North Carolina.
New Echota Marker, Georgia.
Lee Mansion, Arlington National Cemetery, Virginia.

NATIONAL CEMETERIES

Custer Battlefield, National Cemetery in the State of Montana.
Battleground, District of Columbia.
Antietam (Sharpsburg), Maryland.
Vicksburg, Mississippi.
Gettysburg, Pennsylvania.
Chattanooga, Tennessee.
Fort Donelson (Dover), Tennessee.
Shiloh (Pittsburg Landing), Tennessee.
Stones River (Murfreesboro), Tennessee.
Fredericksburg, Virginia.
Poplar Grove (Petersburg), Virginia.
Yorktown, Virginia.

National cemeteries located in insular possessions under the jurisdiction of the War Department shall be administered by the Bureau of Insular Affairs of the War Department.

The functions of the following agencies are transferred to the National Park Service of the Department of the Interior, and the agencies are abolished:

Arlington Memorial Bridge Commission
Public Buildings Commission
Public Buildings and Public Parks of the National Capital
National Memorial Commission
Rock Creek and Potomac Parkway Commission

Expenditures by the Federal Government for the purposes of the Commission of Fine Arts, the George Rogers Clark Sesquicentennial Commission, and the Rushmore National Commission shall be administered by the Department of the Interior. (As amended by Ex. Ord. No. 6228 of July 28, 1933; Ex. Ord. No. 6614 of Feb. 26, 1934; Ex. Ord. No. 8428 of June 3, 1940, 5 F.R. 2132; and act Mar. 2, 1934. ch. 39, § 1, 48 Stat. 389.)

AMENDMENTS

The enumeration of the National Cemeteries and Parks of the War Department which were transferred to the Department of the Interior was added by Ex. Ord. No. 6228, § 1, of July 28, 1933, and Ex. Ord. No. 8428 of June 3, 1940.

A provision of this section transferring the administration of national cemeteries located in foreign countries to the State Department was revoked by Ex. Ord. No. 6614 of Feb. 26, 1934.

EFFECTIVE DATE

See section 22 of this Ex. Ord. The transfer of national cemeteries located in the insular possessions to the Bureau of Insular Affairs, as provided in this section, was postponed until further order by Ex. Ord. No. 6228, § 3, of July 28, 1933.

§ 3. INVESTIGATIONS

All functions now exercised by the Bureau of Prohibition of the Department of Justice with respect to the granting of permits under the national prohibition laws are transferred to the Division of Internal Revenue in the Treasury Department.

All functions now exercised by the Bureau of Prohibition with respect to investigations and all the functions now performed by the Bureau of Investigation of the Department of Justice are transferred to and consolidated in a Division of Investigation in the Department of Justice, at the head of which shall be a Director of Investigation.

All other functions now performed by the Bureau of Prohibition are transferred to such divisions in the Department of Justice as in the judgment of the Attorney General may be desirable.

§ 4. DISBURSEMENT

[Section, as amended by Ex. Ord. No. 6728, May 29, 1934; 1940 Reorg. Plan No. III, § 1(a)(1), eff. June 30, 1940, 5 F.R. 2107, 54 Stat. 1231; and 1940 Reorg. Plan No. IV, §§ 3, 4, eff. June 30, 1940, 5 F.R. 2421, 54 Stat. 1234, which provided that the function of disbursement of moneys of the United States exercised by any agency [except United States marshals; the Post Office Department; the Postmaster General; the Board of Trustees of the Postal Savings System; and those disbursement functions of the War Department, Navy Department (including the Marine Corps), and the Panama Canal, not pertaining to departmental salaries in the District of Columbia] were transferred to the [Fiscal Service of the] Treasury Department and, together with the Office of Disbursing Clerk of that department, was consolidated in a Division of Disbursement, at the head of which was a Chief Disbursing Officer, that the Division of Disbursement of the Treasury Department was authorized to establish local offices, or to delegate the exercise of its functions locally to officers or employees of other agencies, according as the interests of efficiency and economy might require, that the Division of Disbursement would disburse moneys only upon the certification of persons by law duly authorized to incur obligations upon behalf of the United States and that the function of accountability for improper certification would be transferred to such persons, and no disbursing officer would be held accountable therefor, was repealed and reenacted as section 3321 of Title 31, Money and Finance, by Pub. L. 97–258, Sept. 13, 1982, 96 Stat. 877, the first section of which enacted Title 31.]

AMENDMENTS

The bracketed provisions in the first sentence of section 4 of Ex. Ord. No. 6166 reflect the changes effected by 1940 Reorg. Plan No. IV, §§ 3, 4, eff. June 30, 1940, 5 F.R. 2421, 54 Stat. 1234, 1235, Ex. Ord. No. 6728, and 1940 Reorg. Plan No. III, § 1(a)(1), 5 F.R. 2107, 54 Stat. 1231, respectively.

EFFECTIVE DATE

The effective date of section 4 of Ex. Ord. No. 6166, originally fixed by section 22 of this Ex. Ord., was subsequently postponed as follows: to Dec. 31, 1933, by Ex. Ord. No. 6224 of July 27, 1933; to June 30, 1934 (insofar

as not already effected prior to Dec. 31, 1933), by Ex. Ord. No. 6540 of Dec. 28, 1933; to Dec. 31, 1934 (insofar as not already effected prior to June 30, 1934), by Ex. Ord. No. 6727 of May 29, 1934; to June 30, 1935, by Ex. Ord. No. 6927 of Dec. 31, 1934; to Dec. 31, 1935 (insofar as not already effected prior to June 30, 1934), by Ex. Ord. No. 7077 of June 15, 1935; to June 30, 1936 (insofar as not already effected prior to Dec. 31, 1935), by Ex. Ord. No. 7261 of Dec. 31, 1935. Each of these orders contained a provision that the changes therein delayed might be made sooner effective by order of the Secretary of the Treasury approved by the President.

§ 5. CLAIMS BY OR AGAINST THE UNITED STATES

The functions of prosecuting in the courts of the United States claims and demands by, and offenses against, the Government of the United States and of defending claims and demands against the Government, and of supervising the work of United States attorneys, marshals, and clerks in connection therewith, now exercised by any agency or officer, are transferred to the Department of Justice.

As to any case referred to the Department of Justice for prosecution or defense in the courts, the function of decision whether and in what manner to prosecute, or to defend, or to compromise, or to appeal, or to abandon prosecution or defense, now exercised by any agency or officer, is transferred to the Department of Justice.

For the exercise of such of his functions as are not transferred to the Department of Justice by the foregoing two paragraphs, the Solicitor of the Treasury is transferred from the Department of Justice to the Treasury Department.

Nothing in this section shall be construed to affect the function of any agency or officer with respect to cases at any stage prior to reference to the Department of Justice for prosecution or defense.

EFFECTIVE DATE

With regard to legal work performed by the Veterans' Administration in connection with suits against the United States arising under section 19 of the World War Veterans Act, 1924, the effective date of this section was postponed to Sept. 10, 1933, by Ex. Ord. No. 6222 of July 27, 1933.

The effective date of the first paragraph of this section, insofar as it affected the functions of the General Counsel for the Bureau of Internal Revenue, was postponed until Oct. 10, 1933, by Ex. Ord. No. 6244 of Aug. 8, 1933.

§ 6. INSULAR COURTS

The United States Court for China, the District Court of the United States for the Panama Canal Zone, and the District Court of the Virgin Islands of the United States are transferred to the Department of Justice.

EFFECTIVE DATE

Ex. Ord. No. 6243, Aug. 5, 1933, provided that "the effective date of the transfer to the Department of Justice of the District Court of the United States for the Panama Canal Zone is hereby postponed to October 4, 1933."

§ 7. SOLICITORS

The Solicitor for the Department of Commerce is transferred from the Department of Justice to the Department of Commerce.

The Solicitor for the Department of Labor is transferred from the Department of Justice to the Department of Labor.

§ 8. INTERNAL REVENUE

The Bureaus of Internal Revenue and or Industrial Alcohol of the Treasury Department are consolidated in a Division of Internal Revenue, at the head of which shall be a Commissioner of Internal Revenue.

EFFECTIVE DATE

The effective date of section 8 of Ex. Ord. No. 6166, originally fixed by section 22 of the same order, post, was subsequently postponed as follows: to Dec. 31, 1933, by Ex. Ord. No. 6224 of July 27, 1933; to June 30, 1934, by Ex. Ord. No. 6540 of Dec. 28, 1933. Said orders, however, contained a provision whereby the changes thereby delayed might be sooner effected by order of the Secretary of the Treasury approved by the President.

§ 9. ASSISTANT SECRETARY OF COMMERCE

The Assistant Secretary of Commerce for Aeronautics shall be an Assistant Secretary of Commerce and shall perform such functions as the Secretary of Commerce may designate.

§ 10. OFFICIAL REGISTER

The function of preparation of the Official Register is transferred from the Bureau of the Census to the Civil Service Commission.

§ 11. STATISTICS OF CITIES

The function of the Bureau of the Census of the Department of Commerce of compiling statistics of cities under 100,000 population is abolished for the period ending June 30, 1935.

§ 12. SHIPPING BOARD

The functions of the United States Shipping Board including those over and in respect to the United States Shipping Board Merchant Fleet Corporation are transferred to the Department of Commerce, and the United States Shipping Board is abolished.

§ 13. NATIONAL SCREW THREAD COMMISSION

The National Screw Thread Commission is abolished, and its records, property, facilities, equipment, and supplies are transferred to the Department of Commerce.

§ 14. IMMIGRATION AND NATURALIZATION

The Bureaus of Immigration and of Naturalization of the Department of Labor are consolidated as an Immigration and Naturalization Service of the Department of Labor, at the head of which shall be a Commissioner of Immigration and Naturalization.

§ 15. VOCATIONAL EDUCATION

The functions of the Federal Board for Vocational Education are transferred to the Department of the Interior, and the Board shall act in an advisory capacity without compensation.

§ 16. APPORTIONMENT OF APPROPRIATIONS

The functions of making, waiving, and modifying apportionments of appropriations are transferred to the Director of the Bureau of the Budget.

§ 17. COORDINATING SERVICE

The Federal Coordinating Service is abolished.

EFFECTIVE DATE

The effective date of this section originally fixed by section 22 of this Ex. Ord., was subsequently deferred to Oct. 10, 1933, by Ex. Ord. No. 6239 of Aug. 2, 1933.

§ 18. FUNCTIONS ABOLISHED

Section 18 of Ex. Ord. No. 6166, which provided for the partial abolition of cooperative vocational education payments for agricultural experiment stations; cooperative agricultural extension work; and endowment and maintenance of colleges for the benefit of agriculture and the mechanical arts, was revoked by Ex. Ord. No. 6536 of Feb. 6, 1934.

§ 19. GENERAL PROVISIONS

Each agency, all the functions of which are transferred to or consolidated with another agency, is abolished.

The records pertaining to an abolished agency or a function disposed of, disposition of which is not elsewhere herein provided for, shall be transferred to the successor. If there be no successor agency, and such abolished agency be within a department, said records shall be disposed of as the head of such department may direct.

The property, facilities, equipment, and supplies employed in the work of an abolished agency or the exercise of a function disposed of, disposition of which is not elsewhere herein provided for, shall, to the extent required, be transferred to the successor agency. Other such property, facilities, equipment, and supplies shall be transferred to the Procurement Division.

All personnel employed in connection with the work of an abolished agency or function disposed of shall be separated from the service of the United States, except that the head of any successor agency, subject to my approval, may, within a period of four months after transfer or consolidation, reappoint any of such personnel required for the work of the successor agency without reexamination or loss of civil-service status.

EFFECTIVE DATE

The effective date of the last paragraph of this section, originally fixed by section 22, post, was deferred as to employees separated from service under sections 2 and 15, ante, until Sept. 30, 1933, by Ex. Ord. No. 6227 of July 27, 1933. As to employees separated under section 12, ante, a similar deferment to Sept. 30, 1933, was made by Ex. Ord. No. 6245 of Aug. 9, 1933.

§ 20. APPROPRIATIONS

Such portions of the unexpended balances of appropriations for any abolished agency or function disposed of shall be transferred to the successor agency as the Director of the Budget shall deem necessary.

Unexpended balances of appropriations for an abolished agency or function disposed of, not so transferred by the Director of the Budget, shall, in accordance with law, be impounded and returned to the Treasury.

§ 21. DEFINITIONS

As used in this order—

"Agency" means any commission, independent establishment, board, bureau, division, service, or office in the executive branch of the Government.

"Abolished agency" means any agency which is abolished, transferred, or consolidated.

"Successor agency" means any agency to which is transferred some other agency or function, or which results from the consolidation of other agencies or functions.

"Function disposed of" means any function eliminated or transferred.

§ 22. EFFECTIVE DATE

In accordance with law, this order shall become effective 61 days from its date: *Provided*, That in case it shall appear to the President that the interests of economy require that any transfer, consolidation, or elimination be delayed beyond the date this order becomes effective, he may, in his discretion, fix a later date therefor, and he may for like cause further defer such date from time to time. (Promulgated June 10, 1933.)

[Postponements of effective date of certain transfers, etc., see notes under the various sections of this Executive Order effecting those transfers, etc.]

Executive Order No. 7261, promulgated December 31, 1935, provided that "except as hereinafter provided, the transfers, consolidations, and eliminations contemplated by section 4 of Executive Order No. 6166 of June 10, 1933, as amended, which are not effected prior to December 31, 1935, pursuant to Executive Order No. 6224 of July 27, 1933, Executive Order No. 6540 of December 28, 1933, Executive Order No. 6727 of May 29, 1934, Executive Order No. 6927 of December 21, 1934, and Executive Order No. 7077 of June 15, 1935, together with the operation of all other provisions of Executive Order

No. 6166 of June 10, 1933, as amended, in so far as they relate to said section 4, be further delayed until June 30, 1936: Provided, that any transfer, consolidation, or elimination, in whole or in part, under said section 4, including any other provisions of the said order of June 10, 1933, in so far as they relate to section 4 thereof, may be made operative and effective between December 31, 1935, and June 30, 1936, by order of the Secretary of the Treasury, approved by the President."

Executive Order No. 7980, promulgated September 29, 1938, provided: "That the transfers, consolidations, and eliminations contemplated by section 4 of Executive Order No. 6166 of June 10, 1933, as amended, together with the operation of all other provisions of Executive Order No. 6166 of June 10, 1933, as amended, so far as they relate to the said section 4, be further delayed until December 31, 1938, with respect to the function of disbursement now exercised by United States Marshals under the Department of Justice."

Functions relating to disbursement by United States marshals which would otherwise have become functions of Treasury Department on July 1, 1940, by virtue of Ex. Ord. No. 6166, as amended, were transferred to and vested in Department of Justice to be exercised by United States marshals under supervision of Attorney General in accordance with existing statutes pertaining to such functions, by Reorg. Plan No. IV of 1940, § 3, eff. June 30, 1940. See, also, sections 13–15 of said plan for provisions relating to transfer of functions of department heads, records, property, personnel, and funds.

Functions relating to disbursement of postal revenues and all other funds under jurisdiction of Post Office Department, Postmaster General, and Board of Trustees of Postal Savings System which would otherwise have become functions of Treasury Department on July 1, 1940, by virtue of Ex. Ord. No. 6166, as amended, set out in note under this section, were transferred to and vested in (a) said Board of Trustees as to postal savings disbursements, and (b) Post Office Department as to all other disbursements involved, such functions to be exercised by postmasters and other authorized disbursing agents of Post Office Department and of Postal Savings System in accordance with existing statutes pertaining to such functions, by Reorg. Plan No. IV of 1940, § 4, eff. June 30, 1940. See, also, sections 13–15 of said plan for provisions relating to transfer of functions of department heads, records, property, personnel, and funds.

Public Buildings Branch of Procurement Division and its functions and personnel were transferred to Public Buildings Administration, and functions of Secretary of Agriculture and Director of Procurement Division relating to administration thereof and to selection of sites for public buildings were transferred to Federal Works Administrator by Reorg. Plan No. I of 1939, §§ 301, 303, effective July 1, 1939. See also sections 307–310 of said plan for provisions relating to transfer of records, property, funds, and personnel.

EXECUTIVE ORDER NO. 11007

Ex. Ord. No. 11007, Feb. 27, 1962, 27 F.R. 1875, which related to regulations for formation and use of advisory committees, was superseded by Ex. Ord. No. 11671, June 5, 1972, 37 F.R. 11307.

EXECUTIVE ORDER NO. 11671

Ex. Ord. No. 11671, June 5, 1972, 37 F.R. 11307, which related to committee management, was superseded by Ex. Ord. No. 11686, Oct. 7, 1972, 37 F.R. 21421, set out in the Appendix to this title.

SECTION REFERRED TO IN OTHER SECTIONS

This section is referred to in section 903 of this title.

§ 902. Definitions

For the purpose of this chapter—
　(1) "agency" means—
　　(A) an Executive agency or part thereof; and

　　(B) an office or officer in the executive branch;

but does not include the General Accounting Office or the Comptroller General of the United States;
　(2) "reorganization" means a transfer, consolidation, coordination, authorization, or abolition, referred to in section 903 of this title; and
　(3) "officer" is not limited by section 2104 of this title.

(Pub. L. 89–554, Sept. 6, 1966, 80 Stat. 394; Pub. L. 90–83, § 1(98), Sept. 11, 1967, 81 Stat. 220; Pub. L. 95–17, § 2, Apr. 6, 1977, 91 Stat. 30.)

HISTORICAL AND REVISION NOTES
1966 ACT

Derivation	U.S. Code	Revised Statutes and Statutes at Large
(1)	5 U.S.C. 133z–5.	June 20, 1949, ch. 226, § 7, 63 Stat. 205.
(2)	5 U.S.C. 133z–6.	June 20, 1949, ch. 226, § 8, 63 Stat. 206.

In paragraph (1)(A), the words "an Executive agency or part thereof" are coextensive with and substituted for "any executive department, commission, council, independent establishment, Government corporation, board, bureau, division, service, . . . authority, administration, or other establishment, in the executive branch of the Government" and to conform to the definition in section 105.

In paragraph (1)(B), the words "an office or officer in the civil service or uniformed services in or under an Executive agency" are substituted for "office, officer, . . . in the executive branch of the Government" to conform to the definitions in sections 105, 2101, and 2104.

Standard changes are made to conform with the definitions applicable and the style of this title as outlined in the preface to the report.

1967 ACT

This section amends section 902 of title 5, United States Code, so as to preserve the application of the source statute for section 902 (sec. 7 of the Reorganization Act of 1949). In the codification of title 5 by Public Law 89–554, that application was inadvertently restricted due to the operation of section 2104 of title 5, providing a title-wide definition of "officer." Briefly, that section defines "officer" as a civil appointive officer of the Federal Government. In the Reorganization Act of 1949, the word "officer" was not defined, and has been construed to include not only civil appointive officers, but uniformed officers, the President, and officers of the government of the District of Columbia. Thus, this section amends section 902 of title 5 by inserting a paragraph providing that the title-wide definition of officer is inapplicable to chapter 9 of title 5. Also, paragraph (1)(B) of section 902 is amended so that the wording thereof is identical to that formerly appearing in section 7 of the Reorganization Act of 1949.

CODIFICATION

Section 902(a) of former Title 5, Executive Departments and Government Officers and Employees, was transferred to section 60e–2(b) of Title 2, The Congress.

AMENDMENTS

1977—Par. (1)(C). Pub. L. 95–17 struck out subpar. (C) which defined "agency" as any and all parts of the government of the District of Columbia other than the courts thereof.

EFFECTIVE DATE OF 1967 AMENDMENT

Amendment by Pub. L. 90–83 effective Sept. 6, 1966, for all purposes, see section 9(h) of Pub. L. 90–83, set out as a note under section 5102 of this title.

§ 903. Reorganization plans

(a) Whenever the President, after investigation, finds that changes in the organization of agencies are necessary to carry out any policy set forth in section 901(a) of this title, he shall prepare a reorganization plan specifying the reorganizations he finds are necessary. Any plan may provide for—

(1) the transfer of the whole or a part of an agency, or of the whole or a part of the functions thereof, to the jurisdiction and control of another agency;

(2) the abolition of all or a part of the functions of an agency, except that no enforcement function or statutory program shall be abolished by the plan;

(3) the consolidation or coordination of the whole or a part of an agency, or of the whole or a part of the functions thereof, with the whole or a part of another agency or the functions thereof;

(4) the consolidation or coordination of part of an agency or the functions thereof with another part of the same agency or the functions thereof;

(5) the authorization of an officer to delegate any of his functions; or

(6) the abolition of the whole or a part of an agency which agency or part does not have, or on the taking effect of the reorganization plan will not have, any functions.

The President shall transmit the plan (bearing an identification number) to the Congress together with a declaration that, with respect to each reorganization included in the plan, he has found that the reorganization is necessary to carry out any policy set forth in section 901(a) of this title.

(b) The President shall have a reorganization plan delivered to both Houses on the same day and to each House while it is in session, except that no more than three plans may be pending before the Congress at one time. In his message transmitting a reorganization plan, the President shall specify with respect to each abolition of a function included in the plan the statutory authority for the exercise of the function. The message shall also estimate any reduction or increase in expenditures (itemized so far as practicable), and describe any improvements in management, delivery of Federal services, execution of the laws, and increases in efficiency of Government operations, which it is expected will be realized as a result of the reorganizations included in the plan. In addition, the President's message shall include an implementation section which shall (1) describe in detail (A) the actions necessary or planned to complete the reorganization, (B) the anticipated nature and substance of any orders, directives, and other administrative and operational actions which are expected to be required for completing or implementing the reorganization, and (C) any preliminary actions which have been taken in the implementation process, and (2) contain a projected timetable for completion of the implementation process. The President shall also submit such further background or other information as the Congress may require for its consideration of the plan.

(c) Any time during the period of 60 calendar days of continuous session of Congress after the date on which the plan is transmitted to it, but before any resolution described in section 909 has been ordered reported in either House, the President may make amendments or modifications to the plan, consistent with sections 903–905 of this title, which modifications or revisions shall thereafter be treated as a part of the reorganization plan originally transmitted and shall not affect in any way the time limits otherwise provided for in this chapter. The President may withdraw the plan any time prior to the conclusion of 90 calendar days of continuous session of Congress following the date on which the plan is submitted to Congress.

(Pub. L. 89–554, Sept. 6, 1966, 80 Stat. 394; Pub. L. 90–83, § 1(99), Sept. 11, 1967, 81 Stat. 220; Pub. L. 92–179, § 2, Dec. 10, 1971, 85 Stat. 574; Pub. L. 95–17, § 2, Apr. 6, 1977, 91 Stat. 30; Pub. L. 98–614, §§ 3(b)(1), (2), 4, Nov. 8, 1984, 98 Stat. 3192, 3193.)

HISTORICAL AND REVISION NOTES
1966 ACT

Derivation	U.S. Code	Revised Statutes and Statutes at Large
....	5 U.S.C. 133z–1.	June 20, 1949, ch. 226, § 3, 63 Stat. 203.

In subsection (a)(5), the words "officer in the civil service or uniformed services" are substituted for "officer" to conform to the definitions in sections 2101 and 2104.

In subsection (b), the words "The President shall have a reorganization plan delivered" as substituted for "The delivery . . . shall be".

Standard changes are made to conform with the definitions applicable and the style of this title as outlined in the preface to the report.

1967 ACT

Section 1(99) amends section 903(a)(5) of title 5, United States Code, to conform to the wording formerly appearing in the source statute (sec. 3(5) of the Reorganization Act of 1949). In this regard, the explanation appearing in section 1(98) of this bill is equally applicable to this section.

AMENDMENTS

1984—Subsec. (b). Pub. L. 98–614, § 4, inserted "In addition, the President's message shall include an implementation section which shall (1) describe in detail (A) the actions necessary or planned to complete the reorganization, (B) the anticipated nature and substance of any orders, directives, and other administrative and operational actions which are expected to be required for completing or implementing the reorganization, and (C) any preliminary actions which have been taken in the implementation process, and (2) contain a projected timetable for completion of the implementation process. The President shall also submit such further background or other information as the Congress may require for its consideration of the plan."

Subsec. (c). Pub. L. 98–614, § 3(b)(1), (2), substituted "60 calendar days" for "thirty calendar days", and "90 calendar days" for "sixty calendar days".

1977—Subsec. (a)(2). Pub. L. 95–17 inserted provision that no enforcement function or statutory program shall be abolished by the plan.

Subsec. (b). Pub. L. 95–17 substituted provisions limiting to three the number of plans that may be pending before Congress at any one time for provisions limiting to one the number of plans that may be transmitted to Congress within any period of thirty consecutive days and provisions requiring that the President estimate any increase in expenditures and describe any improvements in management, delivery of Federal services, execution of laws, and increases in efficiency of Government operations expected as a result of the reorganizations included in the plan.

Subsec. (c). Pub. L. 95–17 added subsec. (c).

1971—Subsec. (a). Pub. L. 92–179, §2(a), restructured provisions covering requirements of findings of fact and certification by placing in a position preceding par. (1) provisions formerly set out following par. (6).

Subsec. (b). Pub. L. 92–179, §2(b), inserted provisions limiting to one plan within any period of thirty consecutive days the allowable number of plans submitted.

EFFECTIVE DATE OF 1967 AMENDMENT

Amendment by Pub. L. 90–83 effective Sept. 6, 1966, for all purposes, see section 9(h) of Pub. L. 90–83, set out as a note under section 5102 of this title.

SECTION REFERRED TO IN OTHER SECTIONS

This section is referred to in sections 902, 904, 905, 908, 909, 910 of this title.

§904. Additional contents of reorganization plan

A reorganization plan transmitted by the President under section 903 of this title—

(1) may, subject to section 905, change, in such cases as the President considers necessary, the name of an agency affected by a reorganization and the title of its head, and shall designate the name of an agency resulting from a reorganization and the title of its head;

(2) may provide for the appointment and pay of the head and one or more officers of any agency (including an agency resulting from a consolidation or other type of reorganization) if the President finds, and in his message transmitting the plan declares, that by reason of a reorganization made by the plan the provisions are necessary;

(3) shall provide for the transfer or other disposition of the records, property, and personnel affected by a reorganization;

(4) shall provide for the transfer of such unexpended balances of appropriations, and of other funds, available for use in connection with a function or agency affected by a reorganization, as the President considers necessary by reason of the reorganization for use in connection with the functions affected by the reorganization, or for the use of the agency which shall have the functions after the reorganization plan is effective; and

(5) shall provide for terminating the affairs of an agency abolished.

A reorganization plan transmitted by the President containing provisions authorized by paragraph (2) of this section may provide that the head of an agency be an individual or a commission or board with more than one member. In the case of an appointment of the head of such an agency, the term of office may not be fixed at more than four years, the pay may not be at a rate in excess of that found by the President to be applicable to comparable officers in the executive branch, and if the appointment is not to a position in the competitive service, it shall be by the President, by and with the advice and consent of the Senate. Any reorganization plan transmitted by the President containing provisions required by paragraph (4) of this section shall provide for the transfer of unexpended balances only if such balances are used for the purposes for which the appropriation was originally made.

(Pub. L. 89–554, Sept. 6, 1966, 80 Stat. 395; Pub. L. 92–179, §3, Dec. 10, 1971, 85 Stat. 575; Pub. L. 95–17, §2, Apr. 6, 1977, 91 Stat. 31; Pub. L. 98–614, §5(b), Nov. 8, 1984, 98 Stat. 3194.)

HISTORICAL AND REVISION NOTES

Derivation	U.S. Code	Revised Statutes and Statutes at Large
....	5 U.S.C. 133z–2.	June 20, 1949, ch. 226, §4, 63 Stat. 204.

In paragraph (1), the words "may change" are substituted for "shall change" in view of the discretionary grant of authority reflected by the words "in such cases as the President considers necessary".

In paragraph (2), the words "competitive service" are substituted for "classified civil service" to conform to the definition in section 2102.

Standard changes are made to conform with the definitions applicable and the style of this title as outlined in the preface to the report.

AMENDMENTS

1984—Par. (1). Pub. L. 98–614 inserted ", subject to section 905,".

1977—Pub. L. 95–17 struck out in provisions following par. (5) exception that, in the case of an officer of the government of the District of Columbia, the appointment of the head of an agency may be by the Commissioner or other body of that government designated in the plan.

1971—Pub. L. 92–179 revised the form of the provisions covering the elements which a reorganization plan contains by moving provisions formerly set out in par. (2) to a position following par. (5).

SECTION REFERRED TO IN OTHER SECTIONS

This section is referred to in section 903 of this title.

§905. Limitation on powers

(a) A reorganization plan may not provide for, and a reorganization under this chapter may not have the effect of—

(1) creating a new executive department or renaming an existing executive department, abolishing or transferring an executive department or independent regulatory agency, or all the functions thereof, or consolidating two or more executive departments or two or more independent regulatory agencies, or all the functions thereof;

(2) continuing an agency beyond the period authorized by law for its existence or beyond the time when it would have terminated if the reorganization had not been made;

(3) continuing a function beyond the period authorized by law for its exercise or beyond the time when it would have terminated if the reorganization had not been made;

(4) authorizing an agency to exercise a function which is not expressly authorized by law at the time the plan is transmitted to Congress;

(5) creating a new agency which is not a component or part of an existing executive department or independent agency;

(6) increasing the term of an office beyond that provided by law for the office; or

(7) dealing with more than one logically consistent subject matter.

(b) A provision contained in a reorganization plan may take effect only if the plan is transmitted to Congress (in accordance with section 903(b)) on or before December 31, 1984.

(Pub. L. 89–554, Sept. 6, 1966, 80 Stat. 396; Pub. L. 91–5, Mar. 27, 1969, 83 Stat. 6; Pub. L. 92–179, § 4, Dec. 10, 1971, 85 Stat. 576; Pub. L. 95–17, § 2, Apr. 6, 1977, 91 Stat. 31; Pub. L. 96–230, Apr. 8, 1980, 94 Stat. 329; Pub. L. 98–614, §§ 2(a), 5(a), Nov. 8, 1984, 98 Stat. 3192, 3193.)

HISTORICAL AND REVISION NOTES

Derivation	U.S. Code	Revised Statutes and Statutes at Large
(a)	5 U.S.C. 133z–3(a).	June 20, 1949, ch. 226, § 5(a), 63 Stat. 205. July 2, 1964, Pub. L. 88–351, § 2, 78 Stat. 240.
(b)	5 U.S.C. 133z–3(b).	June 20, 1949, ch. 226, § 5(b), 63 Stat. 205. Feb. 11, 1953, ch. 3, 67 Stat. 4. Mar. 25, 1955, ch. 16, 69 Stat. 14. Sept. 4, 1957, Pub. L. 85–286, § 1, 71 Stat. 611. Apr. 7, 1961, Pub. L. 87–18, 75 Stat. 41. July 2, 1964, Pub. L. 88–351, § 1, 78 Stat. 240. June 18, 1965, Pub. L. 89–43, 79 Stat. 135.

Standard changes are made to conform with the definitions applicable and the style of this title as outlined in the preface to the report.

AMENDMENTS

1984—Subsec. (a)(1). Pub. L. 98–614, § 5(a)(1), inserted "or renaming an existing executive department".

Subsec. (a)(5) to (7). Pub. L. 98–614, § 5(a)(2), added par. (5) and redesignated former pars. (5) and (6) as (6) and (7), respectively.

Subsec. (b). Pub. L. 98–614, § 2(a), substituted "(in accordance with section 903(b)) on or before December 31, 1984" for "within four years of the date of enactment of the Reorganization Act of 1977".

1980—Subsec. (b). Pub. L. 96–230 substituted "four years" for "three years".

1977—Subsec. (a)(1). Pub. L. 95–17 substituted "an executive department or independent regulatory agency," for "an Executive department" and "or more executive departments or two or more independent regulatory agencies," for "or more Executive departments".

Subsec. (a)(6), (7). Pub. L. 95–17 redesignated par. (7) as (6). Former par. (6), which related to limitation on reorganization plans that have effect of transferring to or consolidating with another agency the government of the District of Columbia or all the functions thereof which are subject to this chapter, or abolishing that government or all those functions, was struck out.

Subsec. (b). Pub. L. 95–17 substituted "within three years of the date of enactment of the Reorganization Act of 1977" for "before April 1, 1973".

1971—Subsec. (a)(7). Pub. L. 92–179, § 4(a), added par. (7).

Subsec. (b). Pub. L. 92–179, § 4(b), substituted "April 1, 1973" for "April 1, 1971".

1969—Subsec. (b). Pub. L. 91–5 substituted "April 1, 1971" for "December 31, 1968".

PLAN FOR TRANSPORTATION DEPARTMENT REORGANIZATION

Pub. L. 104–50, title III, § 335, Nov. 15, 1995, 109 Stat. 458, provided in part that: "notwithstanding 5 U.S.C. 905(b), the President may prepare and transmit to Congress not later than the date for transmittal to Congress of the Budget Request for Fiscal Year 1997, a reorganization plan pursuant to chapter 9 of title 5, United States Code, for the reorganization of the surface transportation activities of the Department of Transportation and the relationship of the Saint Lawrence Seaway Development Corporation to the Department."

SECTION REFERRED TO IN OTHER SECTIONS

This section is referred to in sections 903, 904 of this title; title 22 section 6601.

§ 906. Effective date and publication of reorganization plans

(a) Except as provided under subsection (c) of this section, a reorganization plan shall be effective upon approval by the President of a resolution (as defined in section 909) with respect to such plan, if such resolution is passed by the House of Representatives and the Senate, within the first period of 90 calendar days of continuous session of Congress after the date on which the plan is transmitted to Congress. Failure of either House to act upon such resolution by the end of such period shall be the same as disapproval of the resolution.

(b) For the purpose of this chapter—

(1) continuity of session is broken only by an adjournment of Congress sine die; and

(2) the days on which either House is not in session because of an adjournment of more than three days to a day certain are excluded in the computation of any period of time in which Congress is in continuous session.

(c) Under provisions contained in a reorganization plan, any provision thereof may be effective at a time later than the date on which the plan otherwise is effective.

(d) A reorganization plan which is effective shall be printed (1) in the Statutes at Large in the same volume as the public laws and (2) in the Federal Register.

(Pub. L. 89–554, Sept. 6, 1966, 80 Stat. 396; Pub. L. 95–17, § 2, Apr. 6, 1977, 91 Stat. 32; Pub. L. 98–614, § 3(a), Nov. 8, 1984, 98 Stat. 3192.)

HISTORICAL AND REVISION NOTES

Derivation	U.S. Code	Revised Statutes and Statutes at Large
(a)–(c)	5 U.S.C. 133z–4.	June 20, 1949, ch. 226, § 6, 63 Stat. 205. Sept. 4, 1957, Pub. L. 85–286, § 2, 71 Stat. 611.
(d)	5 U.S.C. 133z–9.	June 20, 1949, ch. 226, § 11, 63 Stat. 206.

Standard changes are made to conform with the definitions applicable and the style of this title as outlined in the preface to the report.

AMENDMENTS

1984—Subsec. (a). Pub. L. 98–614, § 3(a)(1), struck out "otherwise" before "provided under subsection (c)", substituted "shall be" for "is" before "effective", and substituted "upon approval by the President of a resolution (as defined in section 909) with respect to such plan, if such resolution is passed by the House of Representatives and the Senate, within the first period of 90 calendar days of continuous session of Congress after the date on which the plan is transmitted to Congress. Failure of either House to act upon such resolution by the end of such period shall be the same as disapproval of the resolution" for "at the end of the first period of sixty calendar days of continuous session of Congress after the date on which the plan is transmitted to it unless, between the date of transmittal and the end of the sixty-day period, either House passes a resolution stating in substance that the House does not favor the reorganization plan."

Subsec. (c). Pub. L. 98–614, § 3(a)(2), struck out before period at end "or, if both Houses of Congress have defeated a resolution of disapproval, may be effective at a time earlier than the expiration of the sixty-day period required by subsection (a)".

1977—Subsec. (a). Pub. L. 95–17 substituted "sixty" for "60" in two places.

Subsec. (b). Pub. L. 95–17 substituted in provisions preceding par. (1) "this chapter" for "subsection (a) of this section" and in par. (2) "any period of time in which Congress is in continuous session" for "the 60-day period".

Subsec. (c). Pub. L. 95–17 inserted provision that if both Houses of Congress have defeated a resolution of disapproval, the provision of a reorganization plan may be effective at a time earlier than the expiration of the sixty-day period required by subsec. (a).

Subsec. (d). Pub. L. 95–17 reenacted subsec. (d) without change.

RATIFICATION AND AFFIRMATION OF PRIOR REORGANIZATION PLANS AS LAW; ACTIONS TAKEN PURSUANT TO SUCH PLANS

Pub. L. 98–532, Oct. 19, 1984, 98 Stat. 2705, provided that:

"SECTION 1. The Congress hereby ratifies and affirms as law each reorganization plan that has, prior to the date of enactment of this Act [Oct. 19, 1984], been implemented pursuant to the provisions of chapter 9 of title 5, United States Code, or any predecessor Federal reorganization statute.

"SEC. 2. Any actions taken prior to the date of enactment of this Act [Oct. 19, 1984] pursuant to a reorganization plan that is ratified and affirmed by section 1 shall be considered to have been taken pursuant to a reorganization expressly approved by Act of Congress."

SECTION REFERRED TO IN OTHER SECTIONS

This section is referred to in title 22 section 5068.

§ 907. Effect on other laws, pending legal proceedings, and unexpended appropriations

(a) A statute enacted, and a regulation or other action made, prescribed, issued, granted, or performed in respect of or by an agency or function affected by a reorganization under this chapter, before the effective date of the reorganization, has, except to the extent rescinded, modified, superseded, or made inapplicable by or under authority of law or by the abolition of a function, the same effect as if the reorganization had not been made. However, if the statute, regulation, or other action has vested the functions in the agency from which it is removed under the reorganization plan, the function, insofar as it is to be exercised after the plan becomes effective, shall be deemed as vested in the agency under which the function is placed by the plan.

(b) For the purpose of subsection (a) of this section, "regulation or other action" means a regulation, rule, order, policy, determination, directive, authorization, permit, privilege, requirement, designation, or other action.

(c) A suit, action, or other proceeding lawfully commenced by or against the head of an agency or other officer of the United States, in his official capacity or in relation to the discharge of his official duties, does not abate by reason of the taking effect of a reorganization plan under this chapter. On motion or supplemental petition filed at any time within twelve months

after the reorganization plan takes effect, showing a necessity for a survival of the suit, action, or other proceeding to obtain a settlement of the questions involved, the court may allow the suit, action, or other proceeding to be maintained by or against the successor of the head or officer under the reorganization effected by the plan or, if there is no successor, against such agency or officer as the President designates.

(d) The appropriations or portions of appropriations unexpended by reason of the operation of the chapter may not be used for any purpose, but shall revert to the Treasury.

(Pub. L. 89–554, Sept. 6, 1966, 80 Stat. 396; Pub. L. 95–17, § 2, Apr. 6, 1977, 91 Stat. 32.)

HISTORICAL AND REVISION NOTES

Derivation	U.S. Code	Revised Statutes and Statutes at Large
(a)–(c)	5 U.S.C. 133z–7.	June 20, 1949, ch. 226, § 9, 63 Stat. 206.
(d)	5 U.S.C. 133z–8.	June 20, 1949, ch. 226, § 10, 63 Stat. 206.

In subsections (a) and (c), the words "the provisions of" in the phrase "under this chapter" are omitted as unnecessary.

In subsection (c), the words "the suit, action, or other proceeding" are substituted for "the same".

In subsection (d), the words "shall revert" are substituted for "shall be . . . returned", and the words "impounded and" are omitted as unnecessary.

Standard changes are made to conform with the definitions applicable and the style of this title as outlined in the preface to the report.

AMENDMENTS

1977—Subsecs. (a), (b). Pub. L. 95–17 reenacted subsecs. (a) and (b) without change.

Subsec. (c). Pub. L. 95–17 substituted "twelve months" for "12 months".

Subsec. (d). Pub. L. 95–17 reenacted subsec. (d) without change.

§ 908. Rules of Senate and House of Representatives on reorganization plans

Sections 909 through 912 of this title are enacted by Congress—

(1) as an exercise of the rulemaking power of the Senate and the House of Representatives, respectively, and as such they are deemed a part of the rules of each House, respectively, but applicable only with respect to the procedure to be followed in that House in the case of resolutions with respect to any reorganization plans transmitted to Congress (in accordance with section 903(b) of this chapter[1]) on or before December 31, 1984; and they supersede other rules only to the extent that they are inconsistent therewith; and

(2) with full recognition of the constitutional right of either House to change the rules (so far as relating to the procedure of that House) at any time, in the same manner and to the same extent as in the case of any other rule of that House.

(Pub. L. 89–554, Sept. 6, 1966, 80 Stat. 397; Pub. L. 95–17, § 2, Apr. 6, 1977, 91 Stat. 33; Pub. L. 98–614, § 2(b), Nov. 8, 1984, 98 Stat. 3192.)

---

[1] So in original. Probably should be "title".

HISTORICAL AND REVISION NOTES

Derivation	U.S. Code	Revised Statutes and Statutes at Large
....	5 U.S.C. 133z–10.	June 20, 1949, ch. 226, § 201, 63 Stat. 206.

The words "Sections 909–913 of this title" are substituted for "The following sections of this title" to reflect the codification of sections 202–206 of Title II of the Act of June 20, 1949.

Standard changes are made to conform with the definitions applicable and the style of this title as outlined in the preface to the report.

AMENDMENTS

1984—Par. (1). Pub. L. 98–614 substituted "with respect to any reorganization plans transmitted to Congress (in accordance with section 903(b) of this chapter) on or before December 31, 1984" for "described in section 909 of this title".

1977—Pub. L. 95–17 substituted "Sections 909 through 912 of this title" for "Sections 909–913 of this title" in provisions preceding par. (1).

SECTION REFERRED TO IN OTHER SECTIONS

This section is referred to in section 909 of this title.

§ 909. Terms of resolution

For the purpose of sections 908 through 912 of this title, "resolution" means only a joint resolution of the Congress, the matter after the resolving clause of which is as follows: "That the Congress approves the reorganization plan numbered   transmitted to the Congress by the President on   , 19   .", and includes such modifications and revisions as are submitted by the President under section 903(c) of this chapter. The blank spaces therein are to be filled appropriately. The term does not include a resolution which specifies more than one reorganization plan.

(Pub. L. 89–554, Sept. 6, 1966, 80 Stat. 397; Pub. L. 95–17, § 2, Apr. 6, 1977, 91 Stat. 33; Pub. L. 98–614, § 3(c), Nov. 8, 1984, 98 Stat. 3192.)

HISTORICAL AND REVISION NOTES

Derivation	U.S. Code	Revised Statutes and Statutes at Large
....	5 U.S.C. 133z–11.	June 20, 1949, ch. 226, § 202, 63 Stat. 207.

Standard changes are made to conform with the definitions applicable and the style of this title as outlined in the preface to the report.

REFERENCES IN TEXT

Section 903(c) of this chapter, referred to in text, means section 903(c) of this title.

AMENDMENTS

1984—Pub. L. 98–614 substituted "a joint resolution of the Congress" for "a resolution of either House of Congress", and "the Congress approves" for "the   does not favor".

1977—Pub. L. 95–17 substituted "sections 908 through 912 of this title" for "sections 908–913 of this title" and provision that the blank spaces are to be appropriately filled for provision that the first blank space is to be filled with the name of the resolving House and the other blank spaces are to be appropriately filled and inserted provision that "resolution" includes such modifications and revisions as are submitted by the President under section 903(c) of this chapter.

SECTION REFERRED TO IN OTHER SECTIONS

This section is referred to in sections 903, 906, 908, 910 of this title.

§ 910. Introduction and reference of resolution

(a) No later than the first day of session following the day on which a reorganization plan is transmitted to the House of Representatives and the Senate under section 903, a resolution, as defined in section 909, shall be introduced (by request) in the House by the chairman of the Government Operations Committee of the House, or by a Member or Members of the House designated by such chairman; and shall be introduced (by request) in the Senate by the chairman of the Governmental Affairs Committee of the Senate, or by a Member or Members of the Senate designated by such chairman.

(b) A resolution with respect to a reorganization plan shall be referred to the Committee on Governmental Affairs of the Senate and the Committee on Government Operations of the House (and all resolutions with respect to the same plan shall be referred to the same committee) by the President of the Senate or the Speaker of the House of Representatives, as the case may be. The committee shall make its recommendations to the House of Representatives or the Senate, respectively, within 75 calendar days of continuous session of Congress following the date of such resolution's introduction.

(Pub. L. 89–554, Sept. 6, 1966, 80 Stat. 397; Pub. L. 95–17, § 2, Apr. 6, 1977, 91 Stat. 33; Pub. L. 98–614, § 3(b)(3), Nov. 8, 1984, 98 Stat. 3192.)

HISTORICAL AND REVISION NOTES

Derivation	U.S. Code	Revised Statutes and Statutes at Large
....	5 U.S.C. 133z–12.	June 20, 1949, ch. 226, § 203, 63 Stat. 207.

Standard changes are made to conform with the definitions applicable and the style of this title as outlined in the preface to the report.

AMENDMENTS

1984—Subsec. (b). Pub. L. 98–614 substituted "75 calendar days" for "45 calendar days".

1977—Pub. L. 95–17 substituted "Introduction and reference of resolution" for "Reference of resolution to committee" in section catchline, designated existing provisions as subsec. (b), substituted "the Committee on Governmental Affairs of the Senate and the Committee on Government Operations of the House" for "a committee" and inserted requirement that the Committee shall make its recommendation to the House or Senate within 45 calendar days of continuous session of Congress following the date of a resolution's introduction, and added subsec. (a).

CHANGE OF NAME

Committee on Government Operations of House of Representatives treated as referring to Committee on Government Reform and Oversight of House of Representatives by section 1(a) of Pub. L. 104–14, set out as a note under section 21 of Title 2, The Congress. Committee on Government Reform and Oversight of House of Representatives changed to Committee on Government Reform of House of Representatives by House Resolution No. 5, One Hundred Sixth Congress, Jan. 6, 1999.

SECTION REFERRED TO IN OTHER SECTIONS

This section is referred to in sections 908, 909, 911 of this title.

§911. Discharge of committee considering resolution

If the committee to which is referred a resolution introduced pursuant to subsection (a) of section 910 (or, in the absence of such a resolution, the first resolution introduced with respect to the same reorganization plan) has not reported such resolution or identical resolution at the end of 75 calendar days of continuous session of Congress after its introduction, such committee shall be deemed to be discharged from further consideration of such resolution and such resolution shall be placed on the appropriate calendar of the House involved.

(Pub. L. 89–554, Sept. 6, 1966, 80 Stat. 397; Pub. L. 92–179, §5, Dec. 10, 1971, 85 Stat. 576; Pub. L. 95–17, §2, Apr. 6, 1977, 91 Stat. 34; Pub. L. 98–614, §3(b)(4), Nov. 8, 1984, 98 Stat. 3192.)

HISTORICAL AND REVISION NOTES

Derivation	U.S. Code	Revised Statutes and Statutes at Large
....	5 U.S.C. 133z–13.	June 20, 1949, ch. 226, §204, 63 Stat. 207.

In subsection (a), the words "at the end of 10 calendar days . . . it is" are substituted for "before the expiration of ten calendar days . . . it shall then (but not before) be".

In subsection (b), the words "A motion to discharge" are substituted for "Such motion".

Standard changes are made to conform with the definitions applicable and the style of this title as outlined in the preface to the report.

AMENDMENTS

1984—Pub. L. 98–614 substituted "75 calendar days" for "45 calendar days".

1977—Pub. L. 95–17 substituted provisions deeming the committee discharged from further consideration of a resolution where that committee has not reported the resolution within 45 days of continuous session of Congress after the resolution's introduction for provisions permitting a motion to discharge a committee where the committee considering a resolution has not reported the resolution within 20 calendar days after the resolution's introduction, provisions permitting a motion to discharge to be made only by an individual favoring the resolution and limiting debate to 1 hour, and provisions prohibiting a renewal of a motion to discharge where the original motion was agreed to or disagreed to or the making of another motion with respect to a resolution from the same reorganization plan.

1971—Subsec. (a). Pub. L. 92–179 substituted "20 calendar days" for "10 calendar days".

SECTION REFERRED TO IN OTHER SECTIONS

This section is referred to in sections 908, 909, 912 of this title.

§912. Procedure after report or discharge of committee; debate; vote on final passage

(a) When the committee has reported, or has been deemed to be discharged (under section 911) from further consideration of, a resolution with respect to a reorganization plan, it is at any time thereafter in order (even though a previous motion to the same effect has been disagreed to) for any Member of the respective House to move to proceed to the consideration of the resolution. The motion is highly privileged and is not debatable. The motion shall not be subject to amendment, or to a motion to postpone, or a motion to proceed to the consideration of other business. A motion to reconsider the vote by which the motion is agreed to or disagreed to shall not be in order. If a motion to proceed to the consideration of the resolution is agreed to, the resolution shall remain the unfinished business of the respective House until disposed of.

(b) Debate on the resolution, and on all debatable motions and appeals in connection therewith, shall be limited to not more than ten hours, which shall be divided equally between individuals favoring and individuals opposing the resolution. A motion further to limit debate is in order and not debatable. An amendment to, or a motion to postpone, or a motion to proceed to the consideration of other business, or a motion to recommit the resolution is not in order. A motion to reconsider the vote by which the resolution is passed or rejected shall not be in order.

(c) Immediately following the conclusion of the debate on the resolution with respect to a reorganization plan, and a single quorum call at the conclusion of the debate if requested in accordance with the rules of the appropriate House, the vote on final passage of the resolution shall occur.

(d) Appeals from the decisions of the Chair relating to the application of the rules of the Senate or the House of Representatives, as the case may be, to the procedure relating to a resolution with respect to a reorganization plan shall be decided without debate.

(e) If, prior to the passage by one House of a resolution of that House, that House receives a resolution with respect to the same reorganization plan from the other House, then—

(1) the procedure in that House shall be the same as if no resolution had been received from the other House; but

(2) the vote on final passage shall be on the resolution of the other House.

(Pub. L. 89–554, Sept. 6, 1966, 80 Stat. 398; Pub. L. 95–17, §2, Apr. 6, 1977, 91 Stat. 34; Pub. L. 98–614, §3(d), (e)(1), (2), Nov. 8, 1984, 98 Stat. 3193.)

HISTORICAL AND REVISION NOTES

Derivation	U.S. Code	Revised Statutes and Statutes at Large
....	5 U.S.C. 133z–14.	June 20, 1949, ch. 226, §205, 63 Stat. 207.

Standard changes are made to conform with the definitions applicable and the style of this title as outlined in the preface to the report.

AMENDMENTS

1984—Pub. L. 98–614, §3(e)(2), substituted "passage" for "disapproval" in section catchline.

Subsec. (b). Pub. L. 98–614, §3(d)(1), substituted "passed or rejected" for "agreed to or disagreed to".

Subsec. (c). Pub. L. 98–614, §3(d)(2), substituted "final passage" for "final approval".

Subsec. (e). Pub. L. 98–614, §3(e)(1), added subsec. (e).

1977—Pub. L. 95–17 inserted "; vote on final disapproval" after "debate" in section catchline.

Subsec. (a). Pub. L. 95–17 inserted provisions that a motion to discharge a committee is not subject to a motion to postpone or to a motion to proceed to the consideration of other business and that if a motion to proceed to the consideration of the resolution is agreed to, the resolution shall remain the unfinished business of the respective House until disposed of.

Subsec. (b). Pub. L. 95–17 inserted provisions that a motion to postpone or a motion to proceed to the consideration of other business is not in order.

Subsec. (c). Pub. L. 95–17 added subsec. (c).

Subsec. (d). Pub. L. 95–17 added subsec. (d) which provisions were formerly set out in section 913(b) of this title.

Section Referred to in Other Sections

This section is referred to in sections 908, 909 of this title; title 42 section 2941.

[§ 913. Omitted]

Codification

Section, Pub. L. 89–554, Sept. 6, 1966, 80 Stat. 398, providing for decision without debate with respect to motions to postpone, motions to proceed to the consideration of other business, and appeals from decisions of the Chair relating to the application of the rules of the Senate or the House of Representatives, was omitted in the general amendment of this chapter by Pub. L. 95–17, § 2, Apr. 6, 1977, 91 Stat. 29. See section 912 of this title.

PART II—CIVIL SERVICE FUNCTIONS AND RESPONSIBILITIES

Amendments

1992—Pub. L. 102–378, § 2(1), Oct. 2, 1992, 106 Stat. 1346, substituted "Employee" for "Individual" in item for chapter 12.

1989—Pub. L. 101–12, § 3(b)(1), Apr. 10, 1989, 103 Stat. 31, substituted ", Office of Special Counsel, and Individual Right of Action" for "and Special Counsel" in item for chapter 12.

1978—Pub. L. 95–454, title II, § 201(c)(1), Oct. 13, 1978, 92 Stat. 1121, substituted "CIVIL SERVICE FUNCTIONS AND RESPONSIBILITIES" for "THE UNITED STATES CIVIL SERVICE COMMISSION" in heading for Part II.

Pub. L. 95–454, title II, § 201(c)(2), Oct. 13, 1978, 92 Stat. 1121, substituted "Office of Personnel Management" for "Organization" in item for chapter 11.

Pub. L. 95–454, title II, § 202(d), Oct. 13, 1978, 92 Stat. 1131, added item for chapter 12.

CHAPTER 11—OFFICE OF PERSONNEL MANAGEMENT

Amendments

1978—Pub. L. 95–454, title II, § 201(a), Oct. 13, 1978, 92 Stat. 1119, substituted in chapter heading "OFFICE OF PERSONNEL MANAGEMENT" for "ORGANIZATION", in item 1101 "Office of Personnel Management" for "Appointment of Commissioners", in item 1102 "Director; Deputy Director; Associate Directors" for "Term of office; filling vacancies; removal", in item 1103 "Functions of the Director" for "Chairman; Vice Chairman; Executive Director", in item 1104 "Delegation of

authority for personnel management" for "Functions of Chairman", and in item 1105 "Administrative procedure" for "Boards of examiners".

§ 1101. Office of Personnel Management

The Office of Personnel Management is an independent establishment in the executive branch. The Office shall have an official seal, which shall be judicially noticed, and shall have its principal office in the District of Columbia, and may have field offices in other appropriate locations.

(Pub. L. 89–554, Sept. 6, 1966, 80 Stat. 398; Pub. L. 95–454, title II, § 201(a), Oct. 13, 1978, 92 Stat. 1119.)

Historical and Revision Notes

Derivation	U.S. Code	Revised Statutes and Statutes at Large
....	5 U.S.C. 632 (1st par.).	Jan. 16, 1883, ch. 27, § 1 (1st par.), 22 Stat. 403.

The words "official place under the United States" are changed to "another office or position in the Government" of the "United States" to conform to the present legislative use of "office" and "position".

Standard changes are made to conform with the definitions applicable and the style of this title as outlined in the preface to the report.

Amendments

1978—Pub. L. 95–454 substituted "Office of Personnel Management" for "Appointment of Commissioners" in section catchline, and in text provisions relating to the establishment, etc., of the Office of Personnel Management for provisions relating to the appointment of members to the United States Civil Service Commission.

Effective Date of 1978 Amendment

Section 907 of Pub. L. 95–454 provided that: "Except as otherwise expressly provided in this Act, the provisions of this Act [see Tables for classification] shall take effect 90 days after the date of the enactment of this Act [Oct. 13, 1978]."

Short Title of 1992 Amendment

Pub. L. 102–378, § 1(a), Oct. 2, 1992, 106 Stat. 1346, provided that: "This Act [see Tables for classification] may be cited as the 'Technical and Miscellaneous Civil Service Amendments Act of 1992'."

Short Title of 1984 Amendment

Pub. L. 98–224, § 1, Mar. 2, 1984, 98 Stat. 47, provided that: "This Act [amending sections 1304, 3323, 4108, 4109, 7104, and 7122 of this title] may be cited as the 'Civil Service Miscellaneous Amendments Act of 1983'."

Short Title of 1978 Amendment

Section 1 of Pub. L. 95–454 provided that: "This Act [see Tables for classification] may be cited as the 'Civil Service Reform Act of 1978'."

Combined Federal Campaign Brochure List and General Designation Option for International Agencies

Pub. L. 102–393, title V, § 532, Oct. 6, 1992, 106 Stat. 1763, provided that: "Notwithstanding any other provision of law, beginning October 1, 1992, and thereafter, no funds made available to the Office of Personnel Management may be used to prepare, promulgate, or implement any rules or regulations relating to the Combined Federal Campaign unless such rules or regulations include a Combined Federal Campaign brochure list and general designation option solely for international agencies, which list (listed by Federation in the case of affiliated agencies) and option shall include only those international agencies that elect in their annual application to be included under such list and option rather than under the national agencies list and option: *Provided*, That such limitation on the use of funds shall not apply to any activities related to the 1992 Combined Federal Campaign.''

REPORT ON PRODUCTIVITY OF FEDERAL WORKFORCE; DEADLINE

Pub. L. 101–509, title V, § 535, Nov. 5, 1990, 104 Stat. 1470, directed Office of Personnel Management to review and report to Congress, not later than 24 months after Nov. 5, 1990, on the productivity of the Federal workforce, such report to include recommendations with regard to (1) how productivity within the Federal workforce can be increased, the delivery of Government services improved, and the payroll costs of Government controlled through improved organization, training, advanced technology, and modern management practices, (2) the size, structure, and composition of the Federal workforce, (3) criteria for use by departments and agencies to determine the level of personnel necessary to accomplish their functions and goals, and (4) changes in Federal law, regulations, and administrative practices to promote economy, productivity, effectiveness, and managerial accountability within the Federal workforce.

FUNDS FOR PREPARATION, PROMULGATION, OR IMPLEMENTATION OF REGULATIONS RELATING TO COMBINED FEDERAL CAMPAIGN; ELIGIBILITY CRITERIA

Pub. L. 100–202, § 101(m) [title VI, § 618], Dec. 22, 1987, 101 Stat. 1329–390, 1329–423, provided that:

''(a) None of the funds appropriated by this Act, or any other Act in this or any fiscal year hereafter, may be used in preparing, promulgating, or implementing any regulations relating to the Combined Federal Campaign if such regulations are not in conformance with subsection (b).

''(b)(1)(A) Any requirements for eligibility to receive contributions through the Combined Federal Campaign shall not, to the extent that such requirements relate to litigation, public-policy advocacy, or attempting to influence legislation, be any more restrictive than any requirements established with respect to those subject matters under section 501(c)(3) or 501(h) of the Internal Revenue Code of 1986 [26 U.S.C. 501(c)(3), (h)].

''(B) Any requirements for eligibility to receive contributions through the Combined Federal Campaign shall, to the extent that such requirements relate to any subject matter other than one referred to in subparagraph (A), remain the same as the criteria in the 1984 regulations, except as otherwise provided in this section.

''(C) Notwithstanding any requirement referred to in subparagraph (A) or (B), for purposes of any Combined Federal Campaign—

''(i) any voluntary agency or federated group which was a named plaintiff as of September 1, 1987, in a case brought in the United States District Court for the District of Columbia, and designated as Civil Action No. 83–0928 or 86–1367, and

''(ii) The Federal Employee Education and Assistance Fund,

shall be considered to have national eligibility.

''(D) Public accountability standards shall remain similar to the standards which were by regulation established with respect to the 1984–1987 Combined Federal Campaigns, except that the Office of Personnel Management shall prescribe regulations under which a voluntary agency or federated group which does not exceed a certain size (as established under such regulations) may submit a copy of an appropriate Federal tax return, rather than complying with any independent auditing requirements which would otherwise apply.

''(2)(A) A voluntary agency or federated group shall, for purposes of any Combined Federal Campaign in any year, be considered to have national eligibility if such agency or group—

''(i) complies with all requirements for eligibility to receive contributions through the Combined Federal Campaign, without regard to any requirements relating to 'local presence'; and

''(ii) demonstrates that it provided services, benefits, or assistance, or otherwise conducted program activities, in—

''(I) 15 or more different States over the 3-year period immediately preceding the start of the year involved; or

''(II) several foreign countries or several parts of a foreign country.

For purposes of this subparagraph, an agency or federated group shall be considered to have conducted program activities in the required number of States, countries, or parts of a country, over the period of years involved, if such agency or group conducted program activities in such number of States, countries, or parts either in any single year during such period or in the aggregate over the course of such period, provided that no State, country, or part of a country is counted more than once.

''(B) Notwithstanding any other provisions, eligibility requirements relating to International Services Agencies shall remain at least as inclusive as existing requirements. Any voluntary agency or federated group which attains national eligibility under subparagraph (A), and any voluntary agency which is a member of the International Services Agencies, shall be considered to have satisfied any requirements relating to 'local presence'.

''(3)(A) If a federated group is eligible to receive donations in a Combined Federal Campaign, whether on a national level (pursuant to certification by the Office) or a local level (pursuant to certification by the local Federal coordinating committee), each voluntary agency which is a member of such group may, upon certification by the federated group, be considered eligible to participate on such national or local level, as the case may be.

''(B) Notwithstanding any provision of subparagraph (A)—

''(i) the Office may require a voluntary agency to provide information to support any certification submitted by a federated group with respect to such agency under subparagraph (A); and

''(ii) if a determination is made, in writing after notice and opportunity to submit written comments, that the information submitted by the voluntary agency does not satisfy the applicable eligibility requirements, such agency may be barred from participating in the Combined Federal Campaign on a national or local level, as the case may be, for a period not to exceed 1 campaign year.

''(4) The Office shall exercise oversight responsibility to ensure that—

''(A) regulations are uniformly and equitably implemented in all local combined Federal campaigns;

''(B) federated groups participating in a local combined Federal campaign are allowed to compete fairly for the role of principal combined fund organization;

''(C) federated groups participating in a local combined Federal campaign are afforded—

''(i) adequate opportunity to consult with the PCFO for the area involved before any plans are made final relating to the design or conduct of such campaign (including plans pertaining to any materials to be printed as part of the campaign);

''(ii) adequate opportunity to participate in campaign events and other related activities; and

''(iii) timely access to all reports, budgets, audits, and other records in the possession of, or under the control of, the PCFO for the areas involved; and

''(D) a federated group or voluntary agency found by the Office, by a written decision issued after notice and opportunity to submit written comments, to have violated the regulations may be barred from serving as a PCFO for not to exceed 1 campaign year.

"(5) The Office shall prescribe regulations to ensure that PCFOs do not make inappropriate delegations of decisionmaking authority.

"(6)(A) The Office shall, in consultation with federated groups, establish a formula under which any undesignated contributions received in a local combined Federal campaign shall be allocated in any year.

"(B) Under the formula for the 1990 Combined Federal Campaign, all undesignated contributions received in a local campaign shall be allocated as follows:

"(i) 82 percent shall be allocated to the United Way.

"(ii) 7 percent shall be allocated to the International Services Agencies.

"(iii) 7 percent shall be allocated to the National Voluntary Health Agencies.

"(iv) 4 percent shall, after fair and careful consideration of all eligible federated groups and agencies, be allocated by the local Federal coordinating committee among any or all of the following:

"(I) National federated groups (other than any identified in clauses (i), (ii), or (iii)), except that a national federated group shall not be eligible under this subclause unless there are at least 15 members of such group participating in the local campaign, unless the members of such group collectively receive at least 4 percent of the designated contributions in the local campaign, and unless such group was granted national eligibility status for the 1987, 1988, 1989, or 1990 Combined Federal Campaign.

"(II) Local federated groups.

"(III) Any local, non-affiliated voluntary agency which receives at least 4 percent of the designated contributions in the local campaign.

"(C) The formula set forth in subparagraph (B)—

"(i) shall be phased in over the course of the 1988 and 1989 Combined Federal Campaigns;

"(ii) shall be fully implemented with respect to the 1990 Combined Federal Campaigns [sic]; and

"(iii) shall, with respect to any Combined Federal Campaign thereafter, be adjusted based on the experience gained in the Combined Federal Campaigns referred to in clauses (i) and (ii).

"(D) Nothing in this paragraph shall apply with respect to any campaign conducted in a foreign country.

"(E) All appropriate steps shall be taken to encourage donors to make designated contributions.

"(7) The option for a donor to write in the name of a voluntary agency or federated group not listed in the campaign brochure to receive that individual's contribution in a local campaign shall be eliminated.

"(8) The name of any individual making a designated contribution in a campaign shall, upon request of the recipient voluntary agency or federated group, be released to such agency or group, unless the contributor indicates that his or her name is not to be released. Under no circumstance may the names of contributors be sold or otherwise released by such agency or group.

"(9)(A) The name of each participating voluntary agency and federated group, together with a brief description of their respective programs, shall be published in any information leaflet distributed to employees in a local combined Federal campaign. Agencies shall be arranged by federated group, with combined Federal campaign organization code numbers corresponding to each such agency and group.

"(B) The requirement under subparagraph (A) relating to the inclusion of program descriptions may, at the discretion of a local Federal coordinating committee, be waived for a local campaign in any year if, in the immediately preceding campaign year, contributions received through the local campaign totalled less than $100,000.

"(10) Employee coercion is not to be tolerated in the Combined Federal Campaign, and protections against employee coercion shall be strengthened and clarified.

"(11) The Office—

"(A) may not, after the date of the enactment of this Act [Dec. 22, 1987], grant national eligibility status to any federated group unless such group has at least 15 member voluntary agencies, each of which

meets the requirements for national eligibility under paragraph (2)(A); and

"(B) may withdraw federation status from any federated group for a period of not to exceed 1 campaign year if it is determined, on the record after opportunity for a hearing, that the federated group has not complied with the regulatory requirements.

"(12) The Office may bar from participation in the Combined Federal Campaign, for a period not to exceed 1 campaign year, any voluntary agency which the Office determines, in writing, and after notice and opportunity to submit written comments, did not comply with a reasonable request by the Office to furnish it with information relating to such agency's campaign accounting and auditing practices.

"(c) For purposes of this section, a voluntary agency or federated group having 'national eligibility' is one which is eligible to participate in each local domestic combined Federal campaign."

CIVIL SERVICE REFORM ACT OF 1978 FINDINGS AND STATEMENT OF PURPOSE

Section 3 of Pub. L. 95–454 provided that: "It is the policy of the United States that—

"(1) in order to provide the people of the United States with a competent, honest, and productive Federal work force reflective of the Nation's diversity, and to improve the quality of public service, Federal personnel management should be implemented consistent with merit system principles and free from prohibited personnel practices;

"(2) the merit system principles which shall govern in the competitive service and in the executive branch of the Federal Government should be expressly stated to furnish guidance to Federal agencies in carrying out their responsibilities in administering the public business, and prohibited personnel practices should be statutorily defined to enable Federal employees to avoid conduct which undermines the merit system principles and the integrity of the merit system;

"(3) Federal employees should receive appropriate protection through increasing the authority and powers of the Merit Systems Protection Board in processing hearings and appeals affecting Federal employees;

"(4) the authority and power of the Special Counsel should be increased so that the Special Counsel may investigate allegations involving prohibited personnel practices and reprisals against Federal employees for the lawful disclosure of certain information and may file complaints against agency officials and employees who engage in such conduct;

"(5) the function of filling positions and other personnel functions in the competitive service and in the executive branch should be delegated in appropriate cases to the agencies to expedite processing appointments and other personnel actions, with the control and oversight of this delegation being maintained by the Office of Personnel Management to protect against prohibited personnel practices and the use of unsound management practices by the agencies;

"(6) a Senior Executive Service should be established to provide the flexibility needed by agencies to recruit and retain the highly competent and qualified executives needed to provide more effective management of agencies and their functions, and the more expeditious administration of the public business;

"(7) in appropriate instances, pay increases should be based on quality of performance rather than length of service;

"(8) research programs and demonstration projects should be authorized to permit Federal agencies to experiment, subject to congressional oversight, with new and different personnel management concepts in controlled situations to achieve more efficient management of the Government's human resources and greater productivity in the delivery of service to the public;

"(9) the training program of the Government should include retraining of employees for positions in other agencies to avoid separations during reductions in force and the loss to the Government of the knowledge and experience that these employees possess; and

"(10) the right of Federal employees to organize, bargain collectively, and participate through labor organizations in decisions which affect them, with full regard for the public interest and the effective conduct of public business, should be specifically recognized in statute."

SAVINGS PROVISION

Section 902 of Pub. L. 95–454 provided that:

"(a) Except as otherwise provided in this Act [see Tables for classification], all executive orders, rules, and regulations affecting the Federal service shall continue in effect, according to their terms, until modified, terminated, superseded, or repealed by the President, the Office of Personnel Management, the Merit Systems Protection Board, the Equal Employment Opportunity Commission, or the Federal Labor Relations Authority with respect to matters within their respective jurisdictions.

"(b) No provision of this Act [see Tables for classification] shall affect any administrative proceedings pending at the time such provision takes effect. Orders shall be issued in such proceedings and appeals shall be taken therefrom as if this Act had not been enacted.

"(c) No suit, action, or other proceeding lawfully commenced by or against the Director of the Office of Personnel Management or the members of the Merit Systems Protection Board, or officers or employees thereof, in their official capacity or in relation to the discharge of their official duties, as in effect immediately before the effective date of this Act [see Effective Date of 1978 Amendment note above], shall abate by reason of the enactment of this Act [see Tables for classification]. Determinations with respect to any such suit, action, or other proceeding shall be made as if this Act had not been enacted."

POWERS OF PRESIDENT UNAFFECTED EXCEPT BY EXPRESS PROVISIONS

Section 904 of Pub. L. 95–454 provided that:

"Except as otherwise expressly provided in this Act [see Tables for classification], no provision of this Act shall be construed to—

"(1) limit, curtail, abolish, or terminate any function of, or authority available to, the President which the President had immediately before the effective date of this Act [see Effective Date of 1978 Amendment note above]; or

"(2) limit, curtail, or terminate the President's authority to delegate, redelegate, or terminate any delegation of functions."

REORGANIZATION PLANS NO. 1 AND 2 OF 1978 SUPERSEDED BY CIVIL SERVICE REFORM ACT OF 1978

Section 905 of Pub. L. 95–454 provided that: "Any provision in either Reorganization Plan Numbered 1 [set out in the Appendix to this title] or 2 [set out below] of 1978 inconsistent with any provision in this Act [see Tables for classification] is hereby superseded."

REORGANIZATION PLAN NO. 2 OF 1978

43 F.R. 36037, 92 Stat. 3783

Prepared by the President and transmitted to the Senate and the House of Representatives in Congress assembled, May 23, 1978,[1] pursuant to the provisions of Chapter 9 of Title 5 of the United States Code.

PART I. OFFICE OF PERSONNEL MANAGEMENT

SECTION 101. ESTABLISHMENT OF THE OFFICE OF PERSONNEL MANAGEMENT AND ITS DIRECTOR AND OTHER MATTERS

There is hereby established as an independent establishment in the Executive Branch, the Office of Personnel Management (the "Office"). The head of the Office shall be the Director of the Office of Personnel Management (the "Director"), who shall be appointed by the President, by and with the advice and consent of the Senate, and shall be compensated at the rate now or hereafter provided for level II of the Executive Schedule [5 U.S.C. 5313]. The position referred to in 5 U.S.C. 5109(b) is hereby abolished.

SEC. 102. TRANSFER OF FUNCTIONS

Except as otherwise specified in this Plan, all functions vested by statute in the United States Civil Service Commission, or the Chairman of said Commission, or the Boards of Examiners established by 5 U.S.C. 1105 are hereby transferred to the Director of the Office of Personnel Management.

SEC. 103. DEPUTY DIRECTOR AND ASSOCIATE DIRECTORS

(a) There shall be within the Office a Deputy Director who shall be appointed by the President by and with the advice and consent of the Senate and who shall be compensated at the rate now or hereafter provided for level III of the Executive Schedule [5 U.S.C. 5314]. The Deputy Director shall perform such functions as the Director may from time to time prescribe and shall act as Director during the absence or disability of the Director or in the event of a vacancy in the Office of the Director.

(b) There shall be within the Office not more than five Associate Directors, who shall be appointed by the Director in the excepted service, shall have such titles as the Director shall from time to time determine, and shall receive compensation at the rate now or hereafter provided for level IV of the Executive Schedule [5 U.S.C. 5315].

SEC. 104. FUNCTIONS OF THE DIRECTOR

The functions of the Director shall include, but not be limited to, the following:

(a) Aiding the President, as the President may request, in preparing such rules as the President prescribes, for the administration of civilian employment now within the jurisdiction of the United States Civil Service Commission;

(b) Advising the President, as the President may request, on any matters pertaining to civilian employment now within the jurisdiction of the United States Civil Service Commission;

(c) Executing, administering and enforcing the Civil Service rules and regulations of the President and the Office and the statutes governing the same, and other activities of the Office including retirement and classification activities except to the extent such functions remain vested in the Merit Systems Protection Board pursuant to Section 202 of this Plan, or are transferred to the Special Counsel pursuant to Section 204 of this Plan. The Director shall provide the public, where appropriate, a reasonable opportunity to comment and submit written views on the implementation and interpretation of such rules and regulations;

(d) Conducting or otherwise providing for studies and research for the purpose of assuring improvements in personnel management, and recommending to the President actions to promote an efficient Civil Service and a systematic application of the merit system principles, including measures relating to the selection, promotion, transfer, performance, pay, conditions of service, tenure, and separations of employees; and

(e) Performing the training responsibilities now performed by the United States Civil Service Commission as set forth in 5 U.S.C. Chapter 41.

SEC. 105. AUTHORITY TO DELEGATE FUNCTIONS

The Director may delegate, from time to time, to the head of any agency employing persons in the competitive service, the performance of all or any part of those functions transferred under this Plan to the Director which relate to employees, or applicants for employment, of such agency.

---

[1] As amended July 11, 1978.

PART II. MERIT SYSTEMS PROTECTION BOARD

Sec. 201. Merit Systems Protection Board

(a) The United States Civil Service Commission is hereby redesignated the Merit Systems Protection Board. The Commissioners of the United States Civil Service Commission are hereby redesignated as members of the Merit Systems Protection Board (the "Board").

(b) The Chairman of the Board shall be its chief executive and administrative officer. The position of Executive Director, established by 5 U.S.C. 1103(d), is hereby abolished.

Sec. 202. Functions of the Merit Systems Protection Board and Related Matters

(a) There shall remain with the Board the hearing, adjudication, and appeals functions of the United States Civil Service Commission specified in 5 U.S.C. 1104(b)(4) (except hearings, adjudications and appeals with respect to examination ratings), and also found in the following statutes:

(i) 5 U.S.C. 1504–1507, 7325, 5335, 7521, 7701 and 8347(d);

(ii) 38 U.S.C. 2023

(b) There shall remain with the Board the functions vested in the United States Civil Service Commission, or its Chairman, pursuant to 5 U.S.C. 1104(a)(5) and (b)(4) to enforce decisions rendered pursuant to the authorities described in Subsection (a) of this Section.

(c) Any member of the Board may request from the Director, in connection with a matter then pending before the Board for adjudication, an advisory opinion concerning interpretation of rules, regulations, or other policy directives promulgated by the Office of Personnel Management.

(d) Whenever the interpretation or application of a rule, regulation, or policy directive of the Office of Personnel Management is at issue in any hearing, adjudication, or appeal before the Board, the Board shall promptly notify the Director, and the Director shall have the right to intervene in such proceedings.

(e) The Board shall designate individuals to chair performance rating boards established pursuant to 5 U.S.C. 4305.

(f) The Chairman of the Board shall designate representatives to chair boards of review established pursuant to 5 U.S.C. 3383(b).

(g) The Board may from time to time conduct special studies relating to the Civil Service, and to other merit systems in the Executive Branch and report to the President and the Congress whether the public interest in a workforce free of personnel practices prohibited by law or regulations is being adequately protected. In carrying out this function the Board shall make such inquiries as may be necessary, and, to the extent permitted by law, shall have access to personnel records or information collected by the Office of Personnel Management and may require additional reports from other agencies as needed. The Board shall make such recommendations to the President and the Congress as it deems appropriate.

(h) The Board may delegate the performance of any of its administrative functions to any officer or employee of the Board.

(i) The Board shall have the authority to prescribe such regulations as may be necessary for the performance of its functions. The Board shall not issue advisory opinions. The Board may issue rules and regulations, consistent with statutory requirements, defining its review procedures, including the time limits within which an appeal must be filed and the rights and responsibilities of the parties to an appeal. All regulations of the Board shall be published in the Federal Register.

Sec. 203. Savings Provision

The Board shall accept appeals from agency actions effected prior to the effective date of this Plan. On the effective date of Part II of this Plan, proceedings then before the Federal Employee Appeals Authority shall continue before the Board; proceedings then before the Appeals Review Board and proceedings then before the United States Civil Service Commission on appeal from decisions of the Appeals Review Board shall continue before the Board; other employee appeals before boards or other bodies pursuant to law or regulation shall continue to be processed pursuant to those laws or regulations. Nothing in this section shall affect the right of a Federal employee to judicial review under applicable law.

Sec. 204. The Special Counsel

(a) There shall be a Special Counsel to the Board appointed for a term of four years by the President by and with the advice and consent of the Senate, who shall be compensated as now or hereafter provided for level IV of the Executive Schedule [5 U.S.C. 5315].

(b) There are hereby transferred to the Special Counsel all functions with respect to investigations relating to violations of 5 U.S.C. Chapter 15; 5 U.S.C. Subchapter III of Chapter 73 (Political Activities); and 5 U.S.C. 552(a)(4)(F) (public information).

(c) The Special Counsel may investigate, pursuant to 5 U.S.C. 1303, allegations of personnel practices which are prohibited by law or regulation.

(d) When in the judgment of the Special Counsel, such personnel practices exist, he shall report his findings and recommendations to the Chairman of the Merit Systems Protection Board, the agency affected, and to the Office of Personnel Management, and may report such findings to the President.

(e) When in the judgment of the Special Counsel, the results of an investigation would warrant the taking of disciplinary action against an employee who is within the jurisdiction of the Board, the Special Counsel shall prepare charges against such employee and present them with supporting documentation to the Board. Evidence supporting the need for disciplinary action against a Presidential appointee shall be submitted by the Special Counsel to the President.

(f) The Special Counsel may appoint personnel necessary to assist in the performance of his functions.

(g) The Special Counsel shall have the authority to prescribe rules and regulations relating to the receipt and investigation of matters under his jurisdiction. Such regulations shall be published in the Federal Register.

(h) The Special Counsel shall not issue advisory opinions.

PART III. FEDERAL LABOR RELATIONS AUTHORITY

Sec. 301. Establishment of the Federal Labor Relations Authority

(a) There is hereby established, as an independent establishment in the Executive Branch, the Federal Labor Relations Authority (the "Authority"). The Authority shall be composed of three members, one of whom shall be Chairman, not more than two of whom may be adherents of the same political party, and none of whom may hold another office or position in the Government of the United States except where provided by law or by the President.

(b) Members of the Authority shall be appointed by the President, by and with the advice and consent of the Senate. The President shall designate one member to serve as Chairman of the Authority, who shall be compensated at the rate now or hereafter provided for level III of the Executive Schedule [5 U.S.C. 5314]. The other members shall be compensated at the rate now or hereafter provided for level IV of the Executive Schedule [5 U.S.C. 5315].

(c) The initial members of the Authority shall be appointed as follows: one member for a term of two years; one member for a term of three years; and the Chairman for a term of four years. Thereafter, each member shall be appointed for a term of four years. An individual chosen to fill a vacancy shall be appointed for the unexpired term of the member replaced.

(d) The Authority shall make an annual report on its activities to the President for transmittal to Congress.

SEC. 302. ESTABLISHMENT OF THE GENERAL COUNSEL OF THE AUTHORITY

There shall be a General Counsel of the Authority, who shall be appointed by the President, by and with the advice and consent of the Senate for a term of four years, and who shall be compensated at the rate now or hereafter provided for level V of the Executive Schedule [5 U.S.C. 5316]. The General Counsel shall perform such duties as the Authority shall from time to time prescribe, including but not limited to the duty of determining and presenting facts required by the Authority in order to decide unfair labor practice complaints.

SEC. 303. THE FEDERAL SERVICE IMPASSES PANEL

The Federal Service Impasses Panel, established under Executive Order 11491, as amended [set out under 5 U.S.C. 7101], (the "Panel") shall continue, and shall be a distinct organizational entity within the Authority.

SEC. 304. FUNCTIONS

Subject to the provisions of Section 306, the following functions are hereby transferred:
(a) To the Authority—
(1) The functions of the Federal Labor Relations Council pursuant to Executive Order 11491, as amended [set out under 5 U.S.C. 7101];
(2) The functions of the Civil Service Commission under Sections 4(a) and 6(e) of Executive Order 11491, as amended;
(3) The functions of the Assistant Secretary of Labor for Labor-Management Relations, under Executive Order 11491, as amended, except for those functions related to alleged violations of the standards of conduct for labor organizations pursuant to Section 6(a)(4) of said Executive Order; and,
(b) to the Panel—the functions and authorities of the Federal Service Impasses Panel, pursuant to Executive Order 11491, as amended.

SEC. 305. AUTHORITY DECISIONS

The decisions of the Authority on any matter within its jurisdiction shall be final and not subject to judicial review.

SEC. 306. OTHER PROVISIONS

Unless and until modified, revised, or revoked, all policies, regulations, and procedures established, and decisions issued, under Executive Order 11491, as amended [set out under 5 U.S.C. 7101], shall remain in full force and effect. There is hereby expressly reserved to the President the power to modify the functions transferred to the Federal Labor Relations Authority and the Federal Service Impasses Panel pursuant to Section 304 of this Plan.

SEC. 307. SAVINGS PROVISION

All matters which relate to the functions transferred by Section 304 of this Plan, and which are pending on the effective date of the establishment of the Authority before the Federal Labor Relations Council, the Vice Chairman of the Civil Service Commission, or the Assistant Secretary of Labor for Labor-Management Relations shall continue before the Authority under such rules and procedures as the Authority shall prescribe. All such matters pending on the effective date of the establishment of the Authority before the Panel, shall continue before the Panel under such rules and procedures as the Panel shall prescribe.

PART IV. GENERAL PROVISIONS

SEC. 401. INCIDENTAL TRANSFER

So much of the personnel, property, records, and unexpended balances of appropriations, allocations and other funds employed, used, held, available, or to be made available in connection with the functions transferred under this Plan, as the Director of the Office of Management and Budget shall determine, shall be transferred to the appropriate agency, or component at such time or times as the Director of the Office of Management and Budget shall provide, except that no such unexpended balances transferred shall be used for purposes other than those for which the appropriation was originally made. The Director of the Office of Management and Budget shall provide for terminating the affairs of any agencies abolished herein and for such further measures and dispositions as such Director deems necessary to effectuate the purposes of this Reorganization Plan.

SEC. 402. INTERIM OFFICERS

(a) The President may authorize any persons who, immediately prior to the effective date of this Plan, held positions in the Executive Branch of the Government, to act as Director of the Office of Personnel Management, the Deputy Director of the Office of Personnel Management, the Special Counsel, the Chairman and other members of the Federal Labor Relations Authority, the Chairman and other members of the Federal Service Impasses Panel, or the General Counsel of the Authority, until those offices are for the first time filled pursuant to the provisions of this Reorganization Plan or by recess appointment, as the case may be.
(b) The President may authorize any such person to receive the compensation attached to the Office in respect of which that person so serves, in lieu of other compensation from the United States.

SEC. 403. EFFECTIVE DATE

The provisions of this Reorganization Plan shall become effective at such time or times, on or before January 1, 1979, as the President shall specify, but not sooner than the earliest time allowable under Section 906 of Title 5, United States Code.

[Pursuant to Ex. Ord. No. 12107, Dec. 28, 1978, 44 F.R. 1055, this Reorg. Plan is generally effective Jan. 1, 1979.]

MESSAGE OF THE PRESIDENT

To the Congress of the United States:

On March 2nd I sent to Congress a Civil Service Reform proposal to enable the Federal government to improve its service to the American people.

Today I am submitting another part of my comprehensive proposal to reform the Federal personnel management system through Reorganization Plan No. 2 of 1978. The plan will reorganize the Civil Service Commission and thereby create new institutions to increase the effectiveness of management and strengthen the protection of employee rights.

The Civil Service Commission has acquired inherently conflicting responsibilities: to help manage the Federal Government and to protect the rights of Federal employees. It has done neither job well. The Plan would separate the two functions.

OFFICE OF PERSONNEL MANAGEMENT

The positive personnel management tasks of the government—such as training, productivity programs, examinations, and pay and benefits administration—would be the responsibility of an Office of Personnel Management. Its Director, appointed by the President and confirmed by the Senate, would be responsible for administering Federal personnel matters except for Presidential appointments. The Director would be the government's principal representative in Federal labor relations matters.

MERIT SYSTEMS PROTECTION BOARD

The adjudication and prosecution responsibilities of the Civil Service Commission will be performed by the Merit Systems Protection Board. The Board will be headed by a bipartisan panel of three members appointed to six-year, staggered terms. This Board would be the first independent and institutionally impartial

Federal agency solely for the protection of Federal employees.

The Plan will create, within the Board, a Special Counsel to investigate and prosecute political abuses and merit system violations. Under the civil service reform legislation now being considered by the Congress, the Counsel would have power to investigate and prevent reprisals against employees who report illegal acts—the so-called "whistleblowers." The Council would be appointed by the President and confirmed by the Senate.

FEDERAL LABOR RELATIONS AUTHORITY

An Executive Order now vests existing labor-management relations in a part-time Federal Labor-Relations Council, comprised of three top government managers; other important functions are assigned to the Assistant Secretary of Labor for Labor-Management Relations. This arrangement is defective because the Council members are part-time, they come exclusively from the ranks of management and their jurisdiction is fragmented.

The Plan I submit today would consolidate the central policymaking functions in labor-management relations now divided between the Council and the Assistant Secretary into one Federal Labor Relations Authority. The Authority would be composed of three full-time members appointed by the President with the advice and consent of the Senate. Its General Counsel, also appointed by the President and confirmed by the Senate, would present unfair labor practice complaints. The Plan also provides for the continuance of the Federal Service Impasses Panel within the Authority to resolve negotiating impasses between Federal employee unions and agencies.

The cost of replacing the Civil Service Commission can be paid by our present resources. The reorganization itself would neither increase nor decrease the costs of personnel management throughout the government. But taken together with the substantive reforms I have proposed, this Plan will greatly improve the government's ability to manage programs, speed the delivery of Federal services to the public, and aid in executing other reorganizations I will propose to the Congress, by improving Federal personnel management.

Each of the provisions of this proposed reorganization would accomplish one or more of the purposes set forth in 5 U.S.C. 901(a). No functions are abolished by the Plan, but the offices referred to in 5 U.S.C. 5109(b) and 5 U.S.C. 1103(d) are abolished. The portions of the Plan providing for the appointment and pay for the head and one or more officers of the Office of Personnel Management, the Merit Systems Protection Board, the Federal Labor Relations Authority and the Federal Service Impasses Panel, are necessary to carry out the reorganization. The rates of compensation are comparable to those for similar positions within the Executive Branch.

I am confident that this Plan and the companion civil service reform legislation will both lead to more effective protection of Federal employees' legitimate rights and a more rewarding workplace. At the same time the American people will benefit from a better managed, more productive and more efficient Federal Government.

JIMMY CARTER.

THE WHITE HOUSE, May 23, 1978.

EXECUTIVE ORDER NO. 10729

Ex. Ord. No. 10729, Sept. 16, 1957, 22 F.R. 7449, which established the position of the Special Assistant to the President for Personnel Management, was revoked by Ex. Ord. No. 11205, Mar. 15, 1965, 30 F.R. 3513.

EX. ORD. NO. 11205. REVOCATION OF EXECUTIVE ORDER NO. 10729

Ex. Ord. No. 11205, Mar. 15, 1965, 30 F.R. 3513, provided:

By virtue of the authority vested in me as President of the United States, the position of Special Assistant to the President for Personnel Management, established by Executive Order No. 10729 of September 16, 1957, is abolished, and that Order is hereby revoked.

LYNDON B. JOHNSON.

EX. ORD. NO. 12107. IMPLEMENTATION OF REFORM OF PERSONNEL MANAGEMENT SYSTEM

Ex. Ord. No. 12107, Dec. 28, 1978, 44 F.R. 1055, as amended by Ex. Ord. No. 12126, Mar. 29, 1979, 44 F.R. 18923; Ex. Ord. No. 12128, Apr. 4, 1979, 44 F.R. 20625, provided:

By virtue of the authority vested in me as President by the Constitution and statutes of the United States of America, and by Section 403 of Reorganization Plan No. 2 of 1978 (43 FR 36037) [set out above], it is hereby ordered as follows:

SECTION 1

IMPLEMENTATION OF REORGANIZATION PLAN NO. 2 OF 1978

1–1. OFFICE OF PERSONNEL MANAGEMENT

1–101. *Establishment of Office of Personnel Management.* The establishment of the Office of Personnel Management and of the positions of Director, Deputy Director, and Associate Directors of that Office, as provided in Sections 101 and 103 of Reorganization Plan No. 2 of 1978, shall be effective on January 1, 1979.

1–102. *Transfer of Functions.* Section 102 of Reorganization Plan No. 2 of 1978, transferring functions to the Director of the Office of Personnel Management, shall be effective on January 1, 1979.

1–2. MERIT SYSTEMS PROTECTION BOARD

1–201. *Redesignation of Civil Service Commission.* The redesignation of the Civil Service Commission as the Merit Systems Protection Board and of the Commissioners as Members of the Board as provided in Section 201 of Reorganization Plan No. 2 of 1978 shall be effective on January 1, 1979.

1–202. *Functions of the Merit Systems Protection Board.* The functions of the Merit Systems Protection Board as provided in Section 202 and the savings provisions of Section 203 of Reorganization Plan No. 2 of 1978 shall be effective on January 1, 1979.

1–3. THE SPECIAL COUNSEL

1–301. *Establishment of the Office of Special Counsel.* The establishment of the Office of Special Counsel to the Merit Systems Protection Board as provided in Section 204(a) of Reorganization Plan No. 2 of 1978 shall be effective on January 1, 1979.

1–302. *Functions of the Special Counsel.* The transfer of functions provided for in Section 204(b) and the performance of functions set forth in Section 204(c)–(g) of Reorganization Plan No. 2 of 1978 shall be effective on January 1, 1979.

1–4. THE FEDERAL LABOR RELATIONS AUTHORITY

1–401. *The Establishment of the Federal Labor Relations Authority and the Office of General Counsel.* The establishment of the Federal Labor Relations Authority as provided in Section 301 and of the Office of General Counsel of the Authority as provided in Section 302 of Reorganization Plan No. 2 of 1978 shall be effective on January 1, 1979.

1–402. *The Federal Service Impasses Panel.* The continuation of the Federal Service Impasses Panel established under Executive Order No. 11491, as amended [set out as a note under section 7101 of this title], as a distinct organizational entity within the Federal Labor Relations Authority as provided in Section 303 of Reorganization Plan No. 2 of 1978, shall be effective on January 1, 1979.

1–403. *Functions of the Federal Labor Relations Authority, the General Counsel, and the Federal Service Impasses Panel.* The transfer of functions provided for in Section 304 of Reorganization Plan No. 2 of 1978 shall be effective on January 1, 1979.

1-5. GENERAL

1-501. *General Effective Date.* All other provisions of Reorganization Plan No. 2 of 1978 shall be effective on January 1, 1979.

SECTION 2

REDESIGNATIONS, AMENDMENTS TO RULES AND EXECUTIVE ORDERS AND GENERAL PROVISIONS

2-1. REDESIGNATIONS

2-101. *Office of Personnel Management.* Each of the Executive orders, as amended, listed in this Section under subsections (a) and (b), as applicable, and any other order which relates to functions or areas of responsibility delegated to the Office of Personnel Management, is amended and revised by substituting the words "Office of Personnel Management" for the words "Civil Service Commission" or "United States Civil Service Commission"; by substituting the word "Office" for the word "Commission" wherever the word "Commission" is used as a reference to United States Civil Service Commission; and by substituting the words "Director, Office of Personnel Management" for the words "Chairman, Civil Service Commission", "Chairman, United States Civil Service Commission", "Commissioners" or "Commissioner" wherever they appear.

(a) Executive orders relating to the Civil Service Rules, ethics and other matters of Presidential interest.

Executive Orders Numbered

8743
10577, as amended, except for
    Rules IV and V, as amended
    in this order,
10641
10717
10927
11183
11222
11315
11451
11570
11639
11648
11721
11935
12004
12014
12043

(b) Other Executive orders relating to Federal Personnel Management, and membership on Councils, Boards, and Committees.

Executive Orders Numbered

8744
9230
9712
9830
9932
9961
10000
10242
10422
10450
10459
10530
10549
10550
10552
10556
10647
10763
10774, except for Section 3(e)
10804
10826
10880
10903

10973
10982
11103
11171
11203
11219
11228
11264
11348
11355
11422
11434
11438
11490
11521
11552
11561
11579
11589
11603
11609
11639
11744
11817
11890
11895
11899
11938
11955
12008
12015
12027
12049
12067
12070
12089
12105

2-102. *Merit Systems Protection Board.* The provisions of Section 3(e) of Executive Order No. 10774 [set out as a note under section 2025 of Title 22, Foreign Relations and Intercourse], and Executive Order No. 11787 [formerly set out as a note under section 7701 of this title], are hereby amended and revised by substituting the words "Merit Systems Protection Board" for the words "Civil Service Commission" or "Commission" when used as a reference to the Civil Service Commission wherever such words appear.

2-103. *Amending the Civil Service Rules.* Section 101 of Executive Order No. 10577, as amended [set out as a note under section 3301 of this title], is further amended by substituting for Rule II—Appointment Through the Competitive System, a new Sec. 2.4 as follows:

"Sec. 2.4. *Probationary period.* Persons selected from registers of eligibles for career or career-conditional appointment and employees promoted, transferred, or otherwise assigned, for the first time, to supervisory or managerial positions shall be required to serve a probationary period under terms and conditions prescribed by the Office.";

by deleting the last sentence under Rule IV—Prohibited Practices, Sec. 4.3; and

by substituting for Rule V—Regulations, Investigations, and Enforcement, a new Rule V as follows:

"RULE V—REGULATIONS, INVESTIGATIONS, EVALUATION, AND ENFORCEMENT"

"Sec. 5.1. *Civil Service Regulations.* The Director, Office of Personnel Management, shall promulgate and enforce regulations necessary to carry out the provisions of the Civil Service Act and the Veterans' Preference Act, as reenacted in Title 5, United States Code, the Civil Service Rules, and all other statutes and Executive orders imposing responsibilities on the Office. The Director is authorized, whenever there are practical difficulties and unnecessary hardships in complying with the strict letter of the regulation, to grant a variation from the strict letter of the regulation if such a variation is within the spirit of the regulations, and the efficiency of the Government and the integrity of the competitive service are protected and promoted. Whenever a variation is granted the Director shall note the official record to show: (1) the particular practical difficulty or hardship involved, (2) what is permitted in place of what is required by regulation, (3) the circumstances which protect or promote the efficiency of the Government and the integrity of the competitive service, and (4) a statement limiting the application of the variation to the continuation of the conditions which gave rise to it. Like variations shall be granted whenever like conditions exist. All such decisions and information concerning variations noted in the official record shall be published promptly in a Federal Personnel Manual, Letter or Bulletin and in the Director's next annual report.

"Sec. 5.2. *Investigation and Evaluations.* The Director may secure effective implementation of the civil service laws, rules, and regulations, and all Executive orders imposing responsibilities on the Office by:

(a) Investigating the qualifications and suitability of applicants for positions in the competitive service. The Director may require appointments to be made subject to investigation to enable the Director to determine, after appointment, that the requirements of law or the civil service rules and regulations have been met.

(b) Evaluating the effectiveness of: (1) personnel policies, programs, and operations of Executive and other Federal agencies subject to the jurisdiction of the Office, including their effectiveness with regard to merit selection and employee development; (2) agency compliance with and enforcement of applicable laws, rules, regulations and office directives; and (3) agency personnel management evaluation systems.

(c) Investigating, or directing an agency to investigate and report on, apparent violations of applicable laws, rules, regulations, or directives requiring corrective action, found in the course of an evaluation.

(d) Requiring agencies to report, in a manner and at times as the Director may prescribe, personnel information the Director requests relating to civilian employees in the Executive branch of the Government, as defined by Section 311 of the Civil Service Reform Act of 1978 [set out as a note under section 3101 of this title], including positions and officers and employees in the competitive, excepted and Senior Executive services, whether permanent, career-conditional, temporary or emergency.

"Sec. 5.3. *Enforcement.*

(a) The Director is authorized to ensure enforcement of the civil service laws, rules, and regulations, and all applicable Executive orders, by:

(1) Instructing an agency to separate or take other action against an employee serving an appointment subject to investigation when the Director finds that the employee is disqualified for Federal employment. Where the employee or the agency appeals the Director's finding that a separation or other action is necessary, the Director may instruct the agency as to whether or not the employee should remain on duty and continue to receive pay pending adjudication of the appeal: *Provided,* That when an agency separates or takes other action against an employee pursuant to the Director's instructions, and the Director, on the basis of new evidence, subsequently reverses the initial decision as to the employee's qualifications and suitability, the agency shall, upon request of the Director, restore the employee to duty or otherwise reverse any action taken.

(2) Reporting the results of evaluation or investigations to the head of the agency concerned with instructions for any corrective action necessary, including cancellation of personnel actions where appropriate. The Director's findings resulting from evaluations or investigations are binding unless changed as a result of agency evidence and arguments against them. If, during the course of any evaluation or investigation under this Section, the Director finds evidence of matters which come within the investigative and prosecutorial jurisdiction of the Special Counsel of the Merit Systems Protection Board, the Director shall refer this evidence to the Special Counsel for appropriate disposition.

(b) Whenever the Director issues specific instructions as to separation or other corrective action with regard to an employee, including cancellation of a personnel action, the head of the agency concerned shall comply with the Director's instructions.

(c) If the agency head fails to comply with the specific instructions of the Director as to separation or other corrective action with regard to an employee, including cancellation of a personnel action, the Director may certify to the Comptroller General of the United States the agency's failure to act together with such additional information as the Comptroller General may require, and shall furnish a copy of such certification to the head of the agency concerned. The individual with respect to whom such separation or other corrective action was instructed shall be entitled thereafter to no pay or only to such pay as appropriate to effectuate the Director's instructions.

"Sec. 5.4. *Information and Testimony.* When required by the Office, the Merit Systems Protection Board, or the Special Counsel of the Merit Systems Protection Board, or by authorized representatives of these bodies, agencies shall make available to them, or to their authorized representatives, employees to testify in regard to matters inquired of under the civil service laws, rules, and regulations, and records pertinent to these matters. All such employees, and all applicants or eligibles for positions covered by these rules, shall give to the Office, the Merit Systems Protection Board, the Special Counsel, or to their authorized representatives, all information, testimony, documents, and material in regard to the above matters, the disclosure of which is not otherwise prohibited by law or regulation. These employees, applicants, and eligibles shall sign testimony given under oath or affirmation before an officer authorized by law to administer oaths. Employees are performing official duty when testifying or providing evidence pursuant to this section.".

2–104. *Effectiveness of Rule Changes.* The amendments to rules shall be effective on January 1, 1979, to the extent provided by law on that date.

2–2. REVOCATION OF EXECUTIVE ORDERS AND DELEGATION OF FUNCTIONS

2–201. *Revocation of Executive Orders and Delegation of Functions to the Director.* Executive Orders numbered 10540 and 10561 [set out as notes under sections 6301 and 1302, respectively, of this title] are revoked and the authority vested in the President by Section 202(c)(1)(C) of the Annual Sick Leave Act of 1951, as amended [section 6301(2)(XI) of this title], and the authority of the President, pursuant to the Civil Service Act of January 16, 1883, to designate official personnel folders in government agencies as records of the Office of Personnel Management and to prescribe regulations relating to the establishment, maintenance and transfers of official personnel folders, are delegated to the Director of the Office of Personnel Management. Any rules, regulations, directives, instructions or other actions taken pursuant to the authority delegated to the Director of the Office of Personnel Management shall remain in effect until amended, modified, or revoked pursuant to the delegations made by this Order.

2–202. *Savings Provision.* All personnel actions and decisions affecting employees or applicants for employment made on or before January 11, 1979 shall continue to be governed by the applicable Executive order, and the rules and regulations implementing that Order, to the same extent as if that Executive order had not been revoked effective January 11, 1979 unless amended, modified or revoked pursuant to this Order.

2–3. LABOR MANAGEMENT RELATIONS IN THE FEDERAL SERVICE

2–301. *Labor Management Relations.* Executive Order No. 11491 of October 29, 1969, as amended by Executive Orders numbered 11616, 11636, 11838, 11901, and 12027 [set out as a note under section 7101 of this title], relating to labor-management relations in the Federal service, is further amended as follows:

1. Subsections (g), (h) and (i) of Section 2 are amended and a new subsection (j) is added to read as follows:

"(g) 'Authority' means the Federal Labor Relations Authority;

"(h) 'Panel' means the Federal Service Impasses Panel;

"(i) 'Assistant Secretary' means the Assistant Secretary of Labor for Labor Management Relations; and

"(j) 'General Counsel' means the General Counsel of the Authority.".

2. Section 3(b) is amended—

(a) by substituting for paragraph (6) the following:

"(6) The Tennessee Valley Authority; or"; and

(b) by adding the following:

"(7) Personnel of the Federal Labor Relations Authority (including the Office of the General Counsel and the Federal Service Impasses Panel).".

3. Section (d) is amended to read as follows:

"(d) Employees engaged in administering a labor-management relations law or this Order who are otherwise authorized by this Order to be represented by a labor organization shall not be represented by a labor organization which also represents other groups of employees under the law or this Order, or which is affiliated directly or indirectly with an organization which represents such a group of employees.".

4. Section 4 is amended to read as follows:

"Sec. 4. *Powers and Duties of the Federal Labor Relations Authority.*

"(a) [Revoked].

"(b) The Authority shall administer and interpret this Order, decide major policy issues, and prescribe regulations.

"(c) The Authority shall, subject to its regulations:

(1) decide questions as to the appropriate unit for the purpose of exclusive recognition and related issues submitted for its considerations;

(2) supervise elections to determine whether a labor organization is the choice of a majority of the employees in an appropriate unit as their exclusive representative, and certify the results;

(3) decide questions as to the eligibility of labor organizations for national consultation rights;

(4) decide unfair labor practice complaints; and

(5) decide questions as to whether a grievance is subject to a negotiated grievance procedure or subject to arbitration under an agreement as provided in Section 13(d) of this Order.

"(d) The Authority may consider, subject to its regulations:

(1) appeals on negotiability issues as provided in Section 11(c) of this Order;

(2) exceptions to arbitration awards;

(3) appeals from decisions of the Assistant Secretary of Labor for Labor-Management Relations issued pursuant to Section 6(b) this Order; and

(4) other matters it deems appropriate to assure the effectuation of the purposes of this Order.

"(e) In any matters arising under subsection (c) and (d)(3) of this Section, the Authority may require an agency or a labor organization to cease and desist from violations of this Order and require it to take such affirmative action as the Authority considers appropriate to effectuate the policies of this Order.

"(f) In performing the duties imposed on it by this Section, the Authority may request and use the services and assistance of employees of other agencies in accordance with Section 1 of the Act of March 4, 1915 (38 Stat. 1084, as amended; 31 U.S.C. 686) [31 U.S.C. 1535].".

5. The caption of Section 5 is amended to read as follows:

"Sec. 5. *Powers and Duties of the Federal Service Impasses Panel.*"

6. Section 5(a) is amended:

(a) by substituting the words "a distinct organizational entity within the Authority" for the words "an agency within the Council" in the first sentence; and

(b) by substituting the word "Authority" for the word "Council" in the third sentence.

7. Section 6 is amended to read as follows:

"Sec. 6. *Powers and Duties of the Office of the General Counsel and the Assistant Secretary of Labor for Labor-Management Relations.*

"(a) The General Counsel is authorized, upon direction by the Authority, to:

(1) investigate complaints of violations of Section 19 of this Order;

(2) make final decisions as to whether to issue unfair labor practice complaints and prosecute such complaints before the Authority;

(3) direct and supervise all employees in the Office of General Counsel, including employees of the General Counsel in the regional office of the Authority;

(4) perform such other duties as the Authority may prescribe; and

(5) prescribe regulations needed to administer his functions under this Order.

"(b) The Assistant Secretary shall:

(1) decide alleged violations of the standards of conduct for labor organizations, established in Section 18 of this Order; and

(2) prescribe regulations needed to administer his functions under this Order.

"(c) In any matter arising under paragraph (b) of this Section, the Assistant Secretary may require a labor organization to cease and desist from violations of this Order and require it to take such affirmative action as he considers appropriate to effectuate the policies of this Order.

"(d) In performing the duties imposed on them by this Section, the General Counsel and the Assistant Secretary may request and use the services and assistance of employees of other agencies in accordance with Section 1 of the Act of March 4, 1915 (38 Stat. 1084, as amended; 31 U.S.C. 686) [31 U.S.C. 1535].".

8. Section 9 is amended:

(a) by substituting the word "Authority" for the word "Council" in the first sentence of subsection (a); and

(b) by substituting the word "Authority" for the words "Assistant Secretary" in subsection (c).

9. Section 10 is amended:

(a) by substituting the word "Authority" for the words "Assistant Secretary" in the last sentence of subsection (b); and

(b) by substituting the word "Authority" for the words "Assistant Secretary" and the word "it" for the word "him", in the first sentence of subsection (d).

10. Section 11 is amended:

(a) by substituting the word "Authority" for the word "Council" in the first sentence of subsection (a); and

(b) by substituting the word "Authority" for the word "Council" in paragraph (4) of subsection (c).

11. Section 11(d) is revoked.

12. Section 13 is amended:

(a) by substituting the word "Authority" for the word "Council" in the third sentence of subsection (b); and

(b) by substituting the word "Authority" for the words "Assistant Secretary" in the first and second sentence of subsection (d).

13. Section 19(d) is amended by substituting the word "Authority" for the words "Assistant Secretary" in the last sentence.

14. Section 21(a) is amended by substituting the words "Office of Personnel Management" for the words "Civil Service Commission" in the second sentence.

15. Section 22 is amended:

(a) by substituting the words "Office of Personnel Management" for the words "Civil Service Commission" in the first sentence and

(b) by substituting the words "Merit Systems Protection Board" for the words "Civil Service Commission" in the second and third sentences.

16. Section 25(a) is amended:

(a) by substituting the words "Office of Personnel Management" for the words "Civil Service Commission" in the first, second and third sentences; and

(b) by substituting the word "Authority" for the word "Council" in the third sentence.

17. Section 25(b) is amended by substituting the words "Office of Personnel Management" for the words "Department of Labor and Civil Service Commission.".

2-4. GENERAL PROVISIONS

2-401. *Study and Report Provisions.* The Director of the Office of Personnel Management is directed to conduct a study of Executive orders listed in Section 2-101(a) and (b) and to coordinate the study with such other agencies as may be named in or affected by these orders. The Director of Personnel Management and the Director of the Office of Management and Budget are directed to submit a report on or before July 1, 1981 to the President concerning the performance of functions specified in these Executive orders and any other Executive orders affecting the functions or responsibilities of the Office of Personnel Management. The report shall contain specific detailed recommendations for the continuation, modification, revision or revocation of each Executive order.

2-402. *Continuing Effect of this Order.* Except as required by the Civil Service Reform Act of 1978 [Pub. L. 95-454] as its provisions become effective, in accord with Section 7135 of Title 5, United States Code, as amended, and in accord with Section 902(a) of that Act [set out as a Savings Provisions note above], the provisions of this Order shall continue in effect, according to its terms, until modified, terminated or suspended.

2-403. *Transfers and Determinations.*

(a) The records, property, personnel and positions, and unexpended balances of appropriations or funds related to Civil Service Commission functions reassigned by this Order that are available, or to be made available, and necessary to finance or discharge the reassigned functions are transferred to the Director of the Office of Personnel Management, the Federal Labor Relations Authority, or the Federal Service Impasses Panel, as appropriate.

(b) The Director of the Office of Management and Budget shall make such determinations, issue such Orders and take all actions necessary or appropriate to effectuate the transfers or reassignments provided by this Order, including the transfer of funds, records, property and personnel.

2-404. *Effective Date.* Except as otherwise specifically provided in this Order, this Order shall be effective on January 1, 1979.

JIMMY CARTER.

EXECUTIVE ORDER NO. 12157

Ex. Ord. No. 12157, Sept. 14, 1979, 44 F.R. 54035, which related to the President's Management Improvement Council, was revoked by Ex. Ord. No. 12258, Dec. 31, 1980, 46 F.R. 1251, set out as a note under section 14 of the Appendix to this title.

§ 1102. Director; Deputy Director; Associate Directors

(a) There is at the head of the Office of Personnel Management a Director of the Office of Personnel Management appointed by the President, by and with the advice and consent of the Senate. The term of office of any individual appointed as Director shall be 4 years.

(b) There is in the Office a Deputy Director of the Office of Personnel Management appointed by the President, by and with the advice and consent of the Senate. The Deputy Director shall perform such functions as the Director may from time to time prescribe and shall act as Director during the absence or disability of the Director or when the office of Director is vacant.

(c) No individual shall, while serving as Director or Deputy Director, serve in any other office

or position in the Government of the United States except as otherwise provided by law or at the direction of the President. The Director and Deputy Director shall not recommend any individual for appointment to any position (other than Deputy Director of the Office) which requires the advice and consent of the Senate.

(d) There may be within the Office of Personnel Management not more than 5 Associate Directors, as determined from time to time by the Director. Each Associate Director shall be appointed by the Director.

(Pub. L. 89-554, Sept. 6, 1966, 80 Stat. 399; Pub. L. 95-454, title II, §201(a), Oct. 13, 1978, 92 Stat. 1119.)

HISTORICAL AND REVISION NOTES

Derivation	U.S. Code	Revised Statutes and Statutes at Large
....	5 U.S.C. 632 (2d-4th pars.).	Jan. 16, 1883, ch. 27, §1 (2d, 3d pars.), 22 Stat. 403. July 31, 1956, ch. 804, §201(a), 70 Stat. 742.

In subsection (a), the second sentence is substituted for original language concerning designation of Commissioners to serve six, four, and two years, respectively, as that provision is executed.

The section is reorganized to place the statutes relating to vacancies together, and redundancies are eliminated. Provisions relating to pay and travel expenses of Commissioners are omitted as superseded by the Act of Aug. 14, 1964, Pub. L. 88-426, §303(c)(18), (d)(66), 78 Stat. 417, 419, and Act of June 9, 1949, ch. 185, 63 Stat. 166, respectively, which are carried into this title.

Standard changes are made to conform with the definitions applicable and the style of this title as outlined in the preface to the report.

AMENDMENTS

1978—Pub. L. 95-454 substituted "Director; Deputy Director; Associate Directors" for "Term of office; filling vacancies; removal" in section catchline, and in text provisions relating to the Director, Deputy Director, and Associate Directors of the Office of Personnel Management for provisions relating to the term of office, vacancies, and removal of members of the United States Civil Service Commission.

EFFECTIVE DATE OF 1978 AMENDMENT

Amendment by Pub. L. 95-454 effective 90 days after Oct. 13, 1978, see section 907 of Pub. L. 95-454, set out as a note under section 1101 of this title.

§ 1103. Functions of the Director

(a) The following functions are vested in the Director of the Office of Personnel Management, and shall be performed by the Director, or subject to section 1104 of this title, by such employees of the Office as the Director designates:

(1) securing accuracy, uniformity, and justice in the functions of the Office;

(2) appointing individuals to be employed by the Office;

(3) directing and supervising employees of the Office, distributing business among employees and organizational units of the Office, and directing the internal management of the Office;

(4) directing the preparation of requests for appropriations for the Office and the use and expenditure of funds by the Office; and

(5) executing, administering, and enforcing—

(A) the civil service rules and regulations of the President and the Office and the laws governing the civil service; and

(B) the other activities of the Office including retirement and classification activities;

except with respect to functions for which the Merit Systems Protection Board or the Special Counsel is primarily responsible;

(6) reviewing the operations under chapter 87 of this title;

(7) aiding the President, as the President may request, in preparing such civil service rules as the President prescribes, and otherwise advising the President on actions which may be taken to promote an efficient civil service and a systematic application of the merit system principles, including recommending policies relating to the selection, promotion, transfer, performance, pay, conditions of service, tenure, and separation of employees;

(8) conducting, or otherwise providing for the conduct of, studies and research under chapter 47 of this title into methods of assuring improvements in personnel management; and

(9) incurring official reception and representation expenses of the Office subject to any limitation prescribed in any law.

(b)(1) The Director shall publish in the Federal Register general notice of any rule or regulation which is proposed by the Office and the application of which does not apply solely to the Office or its employees. Any such notice shall include the matter required under section 553(b)(1), (2), and (3) of this title.

(2) The Director shall take steps to ensure that—

(A) any proposed rule or regulation to which paragraph (1) of this subsection applies is posted in offices of Federal agencies maintaining copies of the Federal personnel regulations; and

(B) to the extent the Director determines appropriate and practical, exclusive representatives of employees affected by such proposed rule or regulation and interested members of the public are notified of such proposed rule or regulation.

(3) Paragraphs (1) and (2) of this subsection shall not apply to any proposed rule or regulation which is temporary in nature and which is necessary to be implemented expeditiously as a result of an emergency.

(4) Paragraphs (1) and (2) of this subsection and section 1105 of this title shall not apply to the establishment of any schedules or rates of basic pay or allowances under subpart D of part III of this title. The preceding sentence does not apply to the establishment of the procedures, methodology, or criteria used to establish such schedules, rates, or allowances.

(Pub. L. 89–554, Sept. 6, 1966, 80 Stat. 399; Pub. L. 95–454, title II, §201(a), Oct. 13, 1978, 92 Stat. 1119; Pub. L. 99–251, title III, §§301, 302, Feb. 27, 1986, 100 Stat. 26.)

HISTORICAL AND REVISION NOTES

Derivation	U.S. Code	Revised Statutes and Statutes at Large
....	[Uncodified].	1949 Reorg. Plan No. 5, §§1, 2(a) (35th through 46th words), 3, eff. Aug. 20, 1949, 63 Stat. 1067, 1069.
....	5 U.S.C. 632 (5th par.).	July 31, 1956, ch. 804, §201(b), 70 Stat. 742.

Standard changes are made to conform with the definitions applicable and the style of this title as outlined in the preface to the report.

AMENDMENTS

1986—Subsec. (a)(9). Pub. L. 99–251, §301, added par. (9).

Subsec. (b)(4). Pub. L. 99–251, §302, added par. (4).

1978—Pub. L. 95–454 substituted "Functions of the Director" for "Chairman; Vice Chairman; Executive Director" in section catchline, and in text provisions relating to the functions of the Director of the Office of Personnel Management for provisions relating to the Chairman, Vice Chairman, and Executive Director of the United States Civil Service Commission.

EFFECTIVE DATE OF 1978 AMENDMENT

Amendment by Pub. L. 95–454 effective 90 days after Oct. 13, 1978, see section 907 of Pub. L. 95–454, set out as a note under section 1101 of this title.

SECTION REFERRED TO IN OTHER SECTIONS

This section is referred to in sections 1105, 1204, 1212, 3133 of this title.

§ 1104. Delegation of authority for personnel management

(a) Subject to subsection (b)(3) of this section—

(1) the President may delegate, in whole or in part, authority for personnel management functions, including authority for competitive examinations, to the Director of the Office of Personnel Management; and

(2) the Director may delegate, in whole or in part, any function vested in or delegated to the Director, including authority for competitive examinations (except competitive examinations for administrative law judges appointed under section 3105 of this title, the cost of which examinations shall be reimbursed by payments from the agencies employing such judges to the revolving fund established under section 1304(e)), to the heads of agencies in the executive branch and other agencies employing persons in the competitive service.

(b)(1) The Office shall establish standards which shall apply to the activities of the Office or any other agency under authority delegated under subsection (a) of this section.

(2) The Office shall establish and maintain an oversight program to ensure that activities under any authority delegated under subsection (a) of this section are in accordance with the merit system principles and the standards established under paragraph (1) of this subsection.

(3) Nothing in subsection (a) of this section shall be construed as affecting the responsibility of the Director to prescribe regulations and to ensure compliance with the civil service laws, rules, and regulations.

(4) At the request of the head of an agency to whom a function has been delegated under sub-

section (a)(2), the Office may provide assistance to the agency in performing such function. Such assistance shall, to the extent determined appropriate by the Director of the Office, be performed on a reimbursable basis through the revolving fund established under section 1304(e).

(c) If the Office makes a written finding, on the basis of information obtained under the program established under subsection (b)(2) of this section or otherwise, that any action taken by an agency pursuant to authority delegated under subsection (a)(2) of this section is contrary to any law, rule, or regulation, or is contrary to any standard established under subsection (b)(1) of this section, the agency involved shall take any corrective action the Office may require.

(Pub. L. 89–554, Sept. 6, 1966, 80 Stat. 399; Pub. L. 90–83, § 1(2), Sept. 11, 1967, 81 Stat. 195; Pub. L. 95–454, title II, § 201(a), Oct. 13, 1978, 92 Stat. 1120; Pub. L. 104–52, title IV, § 1, Nov. 19, 1995, 109 Stat. 489.)

HISTORICAL AND REVISION NOTES
1966 ACT

Derivation	U.S. Code	Revised Statutes and Statutes at Large
....	[Uncodified].	1949 Reorg. Plan No. 5, § 2(a) (less 35th through 46th words), (b), eff. Aug. 20, 1949, 63 Stat. 1067.
....	5 U.S.C. 3013(a) (1st sentence, less 10th through 24th words).	Sept. 28, 1959, Pub. L. 86–382, § 14(a) (1st sentence, less 10th through 24th words), 73 Stat. 716.

In the first sentence, the word "officers" is omitted as included in "employees".

Subsection (a)(1) is added on authority of the words "to secure accuracy, uniformity, and justice in all their proceedings" in the first sentence of former section 635, which is carried into section 1105. The function in this paragraph was transferred from the chief examiner to the Chairman of the United States Civil Service Commission by 1949 Reorg. Plan No. 5, § 2(a)(2).

In subsection (a)(4), the words "requests for appropriations" are substituted for "budget estimates" on authority of the Act of Sept. 12, 1950, ch. 946, § 102(f), 64 Stat. 833; 31 U.S.C. 22.

In subsection (b)(2), the word "prescription" is substituted for "promulgation" and the words "now vested in the Commission" are omitted as surplusage.

In subsection (b)(4), the words "as is now authorized to be taken by the Commission" are omitted as surplusage.

In subsection (b)(5), the words "civil service" are substituted for "Federal service".

In subsection (b)(7), the words "submission of requests for appropriations" are substituted for "revision and submission . . . of budget estimates" on authority of the Act of Sept. 12, 1950, ch. 946, § 102(f), 64 Stat. 833; 31 U.S.C. 22.

Standard changes are made to conform with the definitions applicable and the style of this title as outlined in the preface to the report.

1967 ACT

Section of title 5	Source (U.S. Code)	Source (Statutes at Large)
1104(a)(6) ...	5:8713(a). [Uncodified].	[None.] 1965 Reorg. Plan No. 4, §§ 11(a), (e) (as applicable to (a)), 12 (as applicable to § 11(a)), 13 (as applicable to § 11(a)), eff. July 27, 1965, 79 Stat. 1322.

The paragraph added by this section is based on 5 U.S.C. 8713(a), and is restated to reflect the effect of sections 11–13 of 1965 Reorganization Plan No. 4, effective July 27, 1965.

AMENDMENTS

1995—Subsec. (a). Pub. L. 104–52, § 1(1)(B), struck out closing provisions which read as follows: "except that the Director may not delegate authority for competitive examinations with respect to positions that have requirements which are common to agencies in the Federal Government, other than in exceptional cases in which the interests of economy and efficiency require such delegation and in which such delegation will not weaken the application of the merit system principles."

Subsec. (a)(2). Pub. L. 104–52, § 1(1)(A), inserted ", the cost of which examinations shall be reimbursed by payments from the agencies employing such judges to the revolving fund established under section 1304(e)" after "title" and substituted period for semicolon at end.

Subsec. (b)(4). Pub. L. 104–52, § 1(2), added par. (4).

1978—Pub. L. 95–454 substituted "Delegation of authority for personnel management" for "Functions of Chairman" in section catchline, and in text provisions relating to the delegation of authority for personnel management for provisions relating to functions of the Chairman of the United States Civil Service Commission.

EFFECTIVE DATE OF 1978 AMENDMENT

Amendment by Pub. L. 95–454 effective 90 days after Oct. 13, 1978, see section 907 of Pub. L. 95–454, set out as a note under section 1101 of this title.

SECTION REFERRED TO IN OTHER SECTIONS

This section is referred to in sections 1103, 9501 of this title.

§ 1105. Administrative procedure

Subject to section 1103(b) of this title, in the exercise of the functions assigned under this chapter, the Director shall be subject to subsections (b), (c), and (d) of section 553 of this title, notwithstanding subsection (a) of such section 553.

(Pub. L. 89–554, Sept. 6, 1966, 80 Stat. 400; Pub. L. 95–454, title II, § 201(a), Oct. 13, 1978, 92 Stat. 1121.)

HISTORICAL AND REVISION NOTES

Derivation	U.S. Code	Revised Statutes and Statutes at Large
....	5 U.S.C. 635 (less last 24 words of 6th sentence, and less 7th sentence).	Jan. 16, 1883, ch. 27, § 3 (less last 24 words of 6th sentence, and less 7th sentence), 22 Stat. 404.
....	[Uncodified].	1949 Reorg. Plan No. 5, § 4, eff. Aug. 19, 1949, 63 Stat. 1069.

In subsection (a), the words "the District of Columbia" are substituted for "Washington". The words "at least three individuals in the service of the United States" are substituted for a "a suitable number of persons, not less than three, in the official service of the United States". So much of the first three sentences of former section 635 as related to the offices of the Chief Examiner and the Secretary are omitted because the offices were abolished by 1949 Reorg. Plan No. 5, § 4. So much of the first sentence as imposed a duty on the Chief Examiner, under the Commission's direction, to act with the examining boards to secure accuracy, uniformity, and justice in all their proceedings is restated in section 1104(a)(1). The fourth sentence of former section 635, authorizing the Commission to employ a stenographer and a messenger, is omitted as obsolete. The remainder is rewritten for clarity. The text of 1949 Reorg. Plan No. 5, §4, is omitted as executed.

In subsection (b), the words "Chairman, United States Civil Service Commission" are substituted for "chief examiner" on authority of 1949 Reorg. Plan No. 5, §2(a)(2). The words "at all times" are omitted as surplusage.

Standard changes are made to conform with the definitions applicable and the style of this title as outlined in the preface to the report.

AMENDMENTS

1978—Pub. L. 95–454 substituted "Administrative procedure" for "Boards of examiners" in section catchline, and in text provisions relating to administrative procedure applicable to administration of this chapter for provisions relating to boards of examiners for the United States Civil Service Commission.

EFFECTIVE DATE OF 1978 AMENDMENT

Amendment by Pub. L. 95–454 effective 90 days after Oct. 13, 1978, see section 907 of Pub. L. 95–454, set out as a note under section 1101 of this title.

SECTION REFERRED TO IN OTHER SECTIONS

This section is referred to in section 1103 of this title.

CHAPTER 12—MERIT SYSTEMS PROTECTION BOARD, OFFICE OF SPECIAL COUNSEL, AND EMPLOYEE RIGHT OF ACTION

AMENDMENTS

1989—Pub. L. 101–12, §3(b)(2), (3), Apr. 10, 1989, 103 Stat. 31, substituted ", OFFICE OF SPECIAL COUNSEL, AND EMPLOYEE RIGHT OF ACTION" for "AND SPECIAL COUNSEL" in chapter heading, and amended chapter analysis generally, inserting subchapter I heading, and in item 1204 substituting "Powers and functions of the Merit Systems Protection Board" for "Special Counsel; appointment and removal", in item 1205 substituting "Transmittal of information to Congress" for "Powers and functions of the Merit Systems Protec-

[1] So in original. Does not conform to section catchline.

tion Board and Special Counsel", in item 1206 substituting "Annual report" for "Authority and responsibilities of the Special Counsel", omitting items 1207 "Hearings and decisions on complaints filed by the Special Counsel", 1208 "Stays of certain personnel actions", and 1209 "Information", and inserting subchapters II and III headings and items 1211 to 1219, 1221, and 1222.

CHAPTER REFERRED TO IN OTHER SECTIONS

This chapter is referred to in sections 2302, 3352 of this title; title 3 section 401; title 22 section 4139.

SUBCHAPTER I—MERIT SYSTEMS PROTECTION BOARD

AMENDMENTS

1989—Pub. L. 101–12, §3(b)(4), Apr. 10, 1989, 103 Stat. 31, inserted subchapter heading.

§ 1201. Appointment of members of the Merit Systems Protection Board

The Merit Systems Protection Board is composed of 3 members appointed by the President, by and with the advice and consent of the Senate, not more than 2 of whom may be adherents of the same political party. The members of the Board shall be individuals who, by demonstrated ability, background, training, or experience are especially qualified to carry out the functions of the Board. No member of the Board may hold another office or position in the Government of the United States, except as otherwise provided by law or at the direction of the President. The Board shall have an official seal which shall be judicially noticed. The Board shall have its principal office in the District of Columbia and may have field offices in other appropriate locations.

(Added Pub. L. 95–454, title II, §202(a), Oct. 13, 1978, 92 Stat. 1121; amended Pub. L. 101–12, §3(a)(1), Apr. 10, 1989, 103 Stat. 16.)

AMENDMENTS

1989—Pub. L. 101–12 substituted "The members" for "The Chairman and members" in second sentence.

EFFECTIVE DATE OF 1989 AMENDMENT

Section 11 of Pub. L. 101–12 provided that: "This Act and the amendments made by this Act [see Short Title of 1989 Amendment note below] shall take effect 90 days following the date of enactment of this Act [Apr. 10, 1989]."

EFFECTIVE DATE

Subchapter effective 90 days after Oct. 13, 1978, see section 907 of Pub. L. 95–454, set out as an Effective Date of 1978 Amendment note under section 1101 of this title.

SHORT TITLE OF 1989 AMENDMENT

Section 1 of Pub. L. 101–12 provided that: "This Act [enacting subchapters II and III of this chapter and section 3352 of this title, amending this section and sections 1202 to 1206, 1209, 1211, 2302, 2303, 3393, 7502, 7512, 7521, 7542, 7701, and 7703 of this title and section 4139 of Title 22, Foreign Relations and Intercourse, repealing sections 1207 and 1208 of this title, and enacting provisions set out as notes under this section and sections 1211 and 5509 of this title] may be cited as the 'Whistleblower Protection Act of 1989'."

SAVINGS PROVISION

Section 7 of Pub. L. 101–12 provided that:
"(a) ORDERS, RULES, AND REGULATIONS.—All orders, rules, and regulations issued by the Merit Systems Pro-

tection Board or the Special Counsel before the effective date of this Act [see Effective Date of 1989 Amendment note above] shall continue in effect, according to their terms, until modified, terminated, superseded, or repealed.

"(b) ADMINISTRATIVE PROCEEDINGS.—No provision of this Act [see Short Title of 1989 Amendment note above] shall affect any administrative proceeding pending at the time such provisions take effect. Orders shall be issued in such proceedings, and appeals shall be taken therefrom, as if this Act had not been enacted.

"(c) SUITS AND OTHER PROCEEDINGS.—No suit, action, or other proceeding lawfully commenced by or against the members of the Merit Systems Protection Board, the Special Counsel, or officers or employees thereof, in their official capacity or in relation to the discharge of their official duties, as in effect immediately before the effective date of this Act [see Effective Date of 1989 Amendment note above], shall abate by reason of the enactment of this Act. Determinations with respect to any such suit, action, or other proceeding shall be made as if this Act had not been enacted."

WHISTLEBLOWER PROTECTION; CONGRESSIONAL STATEMENT OF FINDINGS AND PURPOSE

Section 2 of Pub. L. 101–12 provided that:
"(a) FINDINGS.—The Congress finds that—

"(1) Federal employees who make disclosures described in section 2302(b)(8) of title 5, United States Code, serve the public interest by assisting in the elimination of fraud, waste, abuse, and unnecessary Government expenditures;

"(2) protecting employees who disclose Government illegality, waste, and corruption is a major step toward a more effective civil service; and

"(3) in passing the Civil Service Reform Act of 1978 [Pub. L. 95–454, see Tables for classification], Congress established the Office of Special Counsel to protect whistleblowers (those individuals who make disclosures described in such section 2302(b)(8)) from reprisal.

"(b) PURPOSE.—The purpose of this Act [see Short Title of 1989 Amendment note above] is to strengthen and improve protection for the rights of Federal employees, to prevent reprisals, and to help eliminate wrongdoing within the Government by—

"(1) mandating that employees should not suffer adverse consequences as a result of prohibited personnel practices; and

"(2) establishing—

"(A) that the primary role of the Office of Special Counsel is to protect employees, especially whistleblowers, from prohibited personnel practices;

"(B) that the Office of Special Counsel shall act in the interests of employees who seek assistance from the Office of Special Counsel; and

"(C) that while disciplining those who commit prohibited personnel practices may be used as a means by which to help accomplish that goal, the protection of individuals who are the subject of prohibited personnel practices remains the paramount consideration."

TERMS OF OFFICE OF MEMBERS

Section 202(b) of Pub. L. 95–454 provided that: "Any term of office of any member of the Merit Systems Protection Board serving on the effective date of this Act [see Effective Date of 1978 Amendment note set out under section 1101 of this title] shall continue in effect until the term would expire under section 1102 of title 5, United States Code, as in effect immediately before the effective date of this Act, and upon expiration of the term, appointments to such office shall be made under sections 1201 and 1202 of title 5, United States Code (as added by this section)."

SECTION REFERRED TO IN OTHER SECTIONS

This section is referred to in section 1202 of this title.

§ 1202. Term of office; filling vacancies; removal

(a) The term of office of each member of the Merit Systems Protection Board is 7 years.

(b) A member appointed to fill a vacancy occurring before the end of a term of office of the member's predecessor serves for the remainder of that term. Any appointment to fill a vacancy is subject to the requirements of section 1201. Any new member serving only a portion of a seven-year term in office may continue to serve until a successor is appointed and has qualified, except that such member may not continue to serve for more than one year after the date on which the term of the member would otherwise expire, unless reappointed.

(c) Any member appointed for a 7-year term may not be reappointed to any following term but may continue to serve beyond the expiration of the term until a successor is appointed and has qualified, except that such member may not continue to serve for more than one year after the date on which the term of the member would otherwise expire under this section.

(d) Any member may be removed by the President only for inefficiency, neglect of duty, or malfeasance in office.

(Added Pub. L. 95–454, title II, § 202(a), Oct. 13, 1978, 92 Stat. 1122; amended Pub. L. 100–202, § 101(m) [title VI, § 620], Dec. 22, 1987, 101 Stat. 1329–390, 1329–427; Pub. L. 101–12, § 3(a)(2), (3), Apr. 10, 1989, 103 Stat. 17.)

AMENDMENTS

1989—Pub. L. 101–12, § 3(a)(2), substituted a semicolon for the comma after "office" in section catchline.

Subsec. (b). Pub. L. 101–12, § 3(a)(3), substituted "the member's" for "his" in first sentence and struck out "of this title" after "section 1201" in second sentence.

1987—Subsec. (b). Pub. L. 100–202 inserted provision permitting any new member serving portion of seven-year term to continue serving until successor is appointed and has qualified, with exception limiting duration of such service.

EFFECTIVE DATE OF 1989 AMENDMENT

Amendment by Pub. L. 101–12 effective 90 days following Apr. 10, 1989, see section 11 of Pub. L. 101–12, set out as a note under section 1201 of this title.

§ 1203. Chairman; Vice Chairman

(a) The President shall from time to time appoint, by and with the advice and consent of the Senate, one of the members of the Merit Systems Protection Board as the Chairman of the Board. The Chairman is the chief executive and administrative officer of the Board.

(b) The President shall from time to time designate one of the members of the Board as Vice Chairman of the Board. During the absence or disability of the Chairman, or when the office of Chairman is vacant, the Vice Chairman shall perform the functions vested in the Chairman.

(c) During the absence or disability of both the Chairman and the Vice Chairman, or when the offices of Chairman and Vice Chairman are vacant, the remaining Board member shall perform the functions vested in the Chairman.

(Added Pub. L. 95–454, title II, § 202(a), Oct. 13, 1978, 92 Stat. 1122; amended Pub. L. 101–12, § 3(a)(4), (5), Apr. 10, 1989, 103 Stat. 17.)

1989—Subsec. (a). Pub. L. 101–12, §3(a)(4), struck out the comma after "time" in first sentence.

Subsec. (c). Pub. L. 101–12, §3(a)(5), substituted "the Chairman and the Vice Chairman" for "the Chairman and Vice Chairman" after "both".

EFFECTIVE DATE OF 1989 AMENDMENT

Amendment by Pub. L. 101–12 effective 90 days following Apr. 10, 1989, see section 11 of Pub. L. 101–12, set out as a note under section 1201 of this title.

§ 1204. Powers and functions of the Merit Systems Protection Board

(a) The Merit Systems Protection Board shall—

(1) hear, adjudicate, or provide for the hearing or adjudication, of all matters within the jurisdiction of the Board under this title, chapter 43 of title 38, or any other law, rule, or regulation, and, subject to otherwise applicable provisions of law, take final action on any such matter;

(2) order any Federal agency or employee to comply with any order or decision issued by the Board under the authority granted under paragraph (1) of this subsection and enforce compliance with any such order;

(3) conduct, from time to time, special studies relating to the civil service and to other merit systems in the executive branch, and report to the President and to the Congress as to whether the public interest in a civil service free of prohibited personnel practices is being adequately protected; and

(4) review, as provided in subsection (f), rules and regulations of the Office of Personnel Management.

(b)(1) Any member of the Merit Systems Protection Board, any administrative law judge appointed by the Board under section 3105 of this title, and any employee of the Board designated by the Board may administer oaths, examine witnesses, take depositions, and receive evidence.

(2) Any member of the Board, any administrative law judge appointed by the Board under section 3105, and any employee of the Board designated by the Board may, with respect to any individual—

(A) issue subpoenas requiring the attendance and presentation of testimony of any such individual, and the production of documentary or other evidence from any place in the United States, any territory or possession of the United States, the Commonwealth of Puerto Rico, or the District of Columbia; and

(B) order the taking of depositions from, and responses to written interrogatories by, any such individual.

(3) Witnesses (whether appearing voluntarily or under subpoena) shall be paid the same fee and mileage allowances which are paid subpoenaed witnesses in the courts of the United States.

(c) In the case of contumacy or failure to obey a subpoena issued under subsection (b)(2)(A) or section 1214(b), upon application by the Board, the United States district court for the district in which the person to whom the subpoena is addressed resides or is served may issue an order requiring such person to appear at any designated place to testify or to produce documentary or other evidence. Any failure to obey the order of the court may be punished by the court as a contempt thereof.

(d) A subpoena referred to in subsection (b)(2)(A) may, in the case of any individual outside the territorial jurisdiction of any court of the United States, be served in such manner as the Federal Rules of Civil Procedure prescribe for service of a subpoena in a foreign country. To the extent that the courts of the United States can assert jurisdiction over such individual, the United States District Court for the District of Columbia shall have the same jurisdiction to take any action respecting compliance under this subsection by such individual that such court would have if such individual were personally within the jurisdiction of such court.

(e)(1)(A) In any proceeding under subsection (a)(1), any member of the Board may request from the Director of the Office of Personnel Management an advisory opinion concerning the interpretation of any rule, regulation, or other policy directive promulgated by the Office of Personnel Management.

(B)(i) The Merit Systems Protection Board may, during an investigation by the Office of Special Counsel or during the pendency of any proceeding before the Board, issue any order which may be necessary to protect a witness or other individual from harassment, except that an agency (other than the Office of Special Counsel) may not request any such order with regard to an investigation by the Office of Special Counsel from the Board during such investigation.

(ii) An order issued under this subparagraph may be enforced in the same manner as provided for under paragraph (2) with respect to any order under subsection (a)(2).

(2)(A) In enforcing compliance with any order under subsection (a)(2), the Board may order that any employee charged with complying with such order, other than an employee appointed by the President by and with the advice and consent of the Senate, shall not be entitled to receive payment for service as an employee during any period that the order has not been complied with. The Board shall certify to the Comptroller General of the United States that such an order has been issued and no payment shall be made out of the Treasury of the United States for any service specified in such order.

(B) The Board shall prescribe regulations under which any employee who is aggrieved by the failure of any other employee to comply with an order of the Board may petition the Board to exercise its authority under subparagraph (A).

(3) In carrying out any study under subsection (a)(3), the Board shall make such inquiries as may be necessary and, unless otherwise prohibited by law, shall have access to personnel records or information collected by the Office of Personnel Management and may require additional reports from other agencies as needed.

(f)(1) At any time after the effective date of any rule or regulation issued by the Director of the Office of Personnel Management in carrying out functions under section 1103, the Board shall review any provision of such rule or regulation—

(A) on its own motion;

(B) on the granting by the Board, in its sole discretion, of any petition for such review filed with the Board by any interested person, after consideration of the petition by the Board; or

(C) on the filing of a written complaint by the Special Counsel requesting such review.

(2) In reviewing any provision of any rule or regulation pursuant to this subsection, the Board shall declare such provision—

(A) invalid on its face, if the Board determines that such provision would, if implemented by any agency, on its face, require any employee to violate section 2302(b); or

(B) invalidly implemented by any agency, if the Board determines that such provision, as it has been implemented by the agency through any personnel action taken by the agency or through any policy adopted by the agency in conformity with such provision, has required any employee to violate section 2302(b).

(3) The Director of the Office of Personnel Management, and the head of any agency implementing any provision of any rule or regulation under review pursuant to this subsection, shall have the right to participate in such review.

(4) The Board shall require any agency—

(A) to cease compliance with any provisions of any rule or regulation which the Board declares under this subsection to be invalid on its face; and

(B) to correct any invalid implementation by the agency of any provision of any rule or regulation which the Board declares under this subsection to have been invalidly implemented by the agency.

(g) The Board may delegate the performance of any of its administrative functions under this title to any employee of the Board.

(h) The Board shall have the authority to prescribe such regulations as may be necessary for the performance of its functions. The Board shall not issue advisory opinions. All regulations of the Board shall be published in the Federal Register.

(i) Except as provided in section 518 of title 28, relating to litigation before the Supreme Court, attorneys designated by the Chairman of the Board may appear for the Board, and represent the Board, in any civil action brought in connection with any function carried out by the Board pursuant to this title or as otherwise authorized by law.

(j) The Chairman of the Board may appoint such personnel as may be necessary to perform the functions of the Board. Any appointment made under this subsection shall comply with the provisions of this title, except that such appointment shall not be subject to the approval or supervision of the Office of Personnel Management or the Executive Office of the President (other than approval required under section 3324 or subchapter VIII of chapter 33).

(k) The Board shall prepare and submit to the President, and, at the same time, to the appropriate committees of Congress, an annual budget of the expenses and other items relating to the Board which shall, as revised, be included as a separate item in the budget required to be transmitted to the Congress under section 1105 of title 31.

(l) The Board shall submit to the President, and, at the same time, to each House of the Congress, any legislative recommendations of the Board relating to any of its functions under this title.

(m)(1) Except as provided in paragraph (2) of this subsection, the Board, or an administrative law judge or other employee of the Board designated to hear a case arising under section 1215, may require payment by the agency involved of reasonable attorney fees incurred by an employee or applicant for employment if the employee or applicant is the prevailing party and the Board, administrative law judge, or other employee (as the case may be) determines that payment by the agency is warranted in the interest of justice, including any case in which a prohibited personnel practice was engaged in by the agency or any case in which the agency's action was clearly without merit.

(2) If an employee or applicant for employment is the prevailing party of a case arising under section 1215 and the decision is based on a finding of discrimination prohibited under section 2302(b)(1) of this title, the payment of attorney fees shall be in accordance with the standards prescribed under section 706(k) of the Civil Rights Act of 1964 (42 U.S.C. 2000e–5(k)).

(Added Pub. L. 95–454, title II, § 202(a), Oct. 13, 1978, 92 Stat. 1122, § 1205; amended Pub. L. 97–258, § 3(a)(2), Sept. 13, 1982, 96 Stat. 1063; renumbered § 1204 and amended Pub. L. 101–12, § 3(a)(7), Apr. 10, 1989, 103 Stat. 17; Pub. L. 102–568, title V, § 506(c)(4), Oct. 29, 1992, 106 Stat. 4341; Pub. L. 103–353, § 2(b)(2)(A), Oct. 13, 1994, 108 Stat. 3169; Pub. L. 103–424, § 2, Oct. 29, 1994, 108 Stat. 4361; Pub. L. 103–446, title XII, § 1203(c)(1), Nov. 2, 1994, 108 Stat. 4690.)

References in Text

The Federal Rules of Civil Procedure, referred to in subsec. (d), are set out in the Appendix to Title 28, Judiciary and Judicial Procedure.

Prior Provisions

A prior section 1204 was renumbered section 1211(b) of this title by Pub. L. 101–12, § 3(a)(6). Pub. L. 102–378, § 2(3), Oct. 2, 1992, 106 Stat. 1346, struck out section catchline of prior section 1204.

Amendments

1994—Subsec. (a)(1). Pub. L. 103–446, which directed the amendment of par. (1) by substituting "section 4303" for "section 4323" could not be executed because the phrase "section 4323" does not appear in text subsequent to the intervening amendment by Pub. L. 103–353 substituting "chapter 43" for "section 4323". See below.

Pub. L. 103–353 substituted "chapter 43" for "section 4323".

Subsec. (m). Pub. L. 103–424 added subsec. (m).

1992—Subsec. (a)(1). Pub. L. 102–568 substituted "4323" for "2023".

1989—Pub. L. 101–12, § 3(a)(7), renumbered section 1205 of this title as this section.

Pub. L. 101–12, § 3(a)(7)(A), struck out "and Special Counsel" after "Board" in section catchline.

Subsec. (a)(4). Pub. L. 101–12, § 3(a)(7)(A), (C), substituted "subsection (f)" for "subsection (e) of this section".

Subsec. (b)(1). Pub. L. 101–12, § 3(a)(7)(A), struck out "the Special Counsel," after "Board,".

Subsec. (b)(2). Pub. L. 101–12, § 3(a)(7)(D), amended par. (2) generally. Prior to amendment, par. (2) read as follows: "Any member of the Board, the Special Counsel, and any administrative law judge appointed by the Board under section 3105 of this title may—

"(A) issue subpenas requiring the attendance and testimony of witnesses and the production of documentary or other evidence from any place in the United States or any territory or possession thereof, the Commonwealth of Puerto Rico, or the District of Columbia; and

"(B) order the taking of depositions and order responses to written interrogatories."

Subsec. (b)(3). Pub. L. 101–12, § 3(a)(7)(B), substituted "subpoena" for "subpena" and "subpoenaed" for "subpenaed".

Subsec. (c). Pub. L. 101–12, § 3(a)(7)(B), (E), substituted "subpoena" for "subpena" in two places, "(b)(2)(A) or section 1214(b), upon application by the Board" for "(b)(2) of this section", and "for the district" for "for the judicial district".

Subsec. (d). Pub. L. 101–12, § 3(a)(7)(F), added subsec. (d). Former subsec. (d) redesignated (e).

Subsec. (e). Pub. L. 101–12, § 3(a)(7)(F), redesignated former subsec. (d) as (e). Former subsec. (e) redesignated (f).

Subsec. (e)(1). Pub. L. 101–12, § 3(a)(7)(A), (G)(i), designated existing provisions as subpar. (A), struck out "of this section" after "subsection (a)(1)", and added subpar. (B).

Subsec. (e)(2). Pub. L. 101–12, § 3(a)(7)(G)(ii), designated existing provisions as subpar. (A), struck out "of this section" after "subsection (a)(2)", and added subpar. (B).

Subsec. (e)(3). Pub. L. 101–12, § 3(a)(7)(A), (G)(iii), struck out "of this section" after "subsection (a)(3)" and inserted "of Personnel Management" after "Office".

Subsec. (f). Pub. L. 101–12, § 3(a)(7)(F), redesignated former subsec. (e) as (f). Former subsec. (f) redesignated (g).

Subsec. (f)(1). Pub. L. 101–12, § 3(a)(7)(H)(i), inserted "of the Office of Personnel Management" after "Director" and struck out "of this title" after "section 1103".

Subsec. (f)(2). Pub. L. 101–12, § 3(a)(7)(H)(ii), inserted comma after "subsection" and in subpars. (A) and (B) struck out "of this title" after "section 2302(b)".

Subsec. (f)(3), (4). Pub. L. 101–12, § 3(a)(7)(H)(iii), struck out "(A)" before "The Director", struck out subpar. (B) which provided that any review conducted by the Board be limited to determining the validity on its face of the provision under review and whether the provision under review has been validly implemented, and redesignated former subpar. (C) and cls. (i) and (ii) of former subpar. (C) as par. (4) and subpars. (A) and (B), respectively, of par. (4).

Subsecs. (g) to (i). Pub. L. 101–12, § 3(a)(7)(F), redesignated former subsecs. (f) to (h) as (g) to (i), respectively. Former subsec. (i) redesignated (j).

Subsec. (j). Pub. L. 101–12, § 3(a)(7)(F), (I), redesignated former subsec. (i) as (j) and substituted "chapter 33" for "chapter 33 of this title". Former subsec. (j) redesignated (k).

Subsecs. (k), (l). Pub. L. 101–12, § 3(a)(7)(F), redesignated former subsecs. (j) and (k) as (k) and (l), respectively.

1982—Subsec. (j). Pub. L. 97–258 substituted "section 1105 of title 31" for "section 201 of the Budget and Accounting Act, 1921 (31 U.S.C. 11)".

EFFECTIVE DATE OF 1994 AMENDMENTS

Section 14 of Pub. L. 103–424 provided that: "The provisions of this Act [amending this section and sections 1211, 1212, 1214, 1218, 1221, 2105, 2302, 4313, 7121, and 8348 of this title, enacting provisions set out as notes under sections 1212 and 1214 of this title and section 1441a of Title 12, Banks and Banking, and amending provisions set out as a note under section 5509 of this title] and

the amendments made by this Act shall be effective on and after the date of the enactment of this Act [Oct. 29, 1994]."

Amendment by Pub. L. 103–353 effective with respect to reemployments initiated on or after the first day after the 60-day period beginning Oct. 13, 1994, with transition rules, see section 8 of Pub. L. 103–353, set out as an Effective Date note under section 4301 of Title 38, Veterans' Benefits.

EFFECTIVE DATE OF 1989 AMENDMENT

Amendment by Pub. L. 101–12 effective 90 days following Apr. 10, 1989, see section 11 of Pub. L. 101–12, set out as a note under section 1201 of this title.

SECTION REFERRED TO IN OTHER SECTIONS

This section is referred to in sections 1212, 1221 of this title.

§ 1205. Transmittal of information to Congress

Notwithstanding any other provision of law or any rule, regulation or policy directive, any member of the Board, or any employee of the Board designated by the Board, may transmit to the Congress on the request of any committee or subcommittee thereof, by report, testimony, or otherwise, information and views on functions, responsibilities, or other matters relating to the Board, without review, clearance, or approval by any other administrative authority.

(Added Pub. L. 95–454, title II, § 202(a), Oct. 13, 1978, 92 Stat. 1131, § 1209(a); renumbered § 1205 and amended Pub. L. 101–12, § 3(a)(9), Apr. 10, 1989, 103 Stat. 18.)

PRIOR PROVISIONS

A prior section 1205 was renumbered section 1204 of this title.

AMENDMENTS

1989—Pub. L. 101–12 renumbered section 1209(a) of this title as this section and inserted section catchline.

EFFECTIVE DATE OF 1989 AMENDMENT

Amendment by Pub. L. 101–12 effective 90 days following Apr. 10, 1989, see section 11 of Pub. L. 101–12, set out as a note under section 1201 of this title.

§ 1206. Annual report

The Board shall submit an annual report to the President and the Congress on its activities, which shall include a description of significant actions taken by the Board to carry out its functions under this title. The report shall also review the significant actions of the Office of Personnel Management, including an analysis of whether the actions of the Office of Personnel Management are in accord with merit system principles and free from prohibited personnel practices.

(Added Pub. L. 95–454, title II, § 202(a), Oct. 13, 1978, 92 Stat. 1131, § 1209(b); renumbered § 1206 and amended Pub. L. 101–12, § 3(a)(10), Apr. 10, 1989, 103 Stat. 18.)

PRIOR PROVISIONS

A prior section 1206, added Pub. L. 95–454, title II, § 202(a), Oct. 13, 1978, 92 Stat. 1125, which related to authority and responsibilities of Special Counsel, was repealed by Pub. L. 101–12, §§ 3(a)(8), 11, Apr. 10, 1989, 103 Stat. 18, effective 90 days following Apr. 10, 1989. See section 1212 of this title.

AMENDMENTS

1989—Pub. L. 101–12 renumbered section 1209(b) of this title as this section and inserted section catchline.

EFFECTIVE DATE OF 1989 AMENDMENT

Amendment by Pub. L. 101–12 effective 90 days following Apr. 10, 1989, see section 11 of Pub. L. 101–12, set out as a note under section 1201 of this title.

TERMINATION OF REPORTING REQUIREMENTS

For termination, effective May 15, 2000, of provisions in first sentence of this section relating to annual reports to Congress (formerly 5 U.S.C. 1209(b)), see section 3003 of Pub. L. 104–66, as amended, set out as a note under section 1113 of Title 31, Money and Finance, and page 176 of House Document No. 103–7.

[§§ 1207, 1208. Repealed. Pub. L. 101–12, § 3(a)(8), Apr. 10, 1989, 103 Stat. 18]

Section 1207, added Pub. L. 95–454, title II, § 202(a), Oct. 13, 1978, 92 Stat. 1130, provided for hearings and decisions on complaints filed by Special Counsel. See section 1215(a)(2) to (5) of this title.

Section 1208, added Pub. L. 95–454, title II, § 202(a), Oct. 13, 1978, 92 Stat. 1130, related to stays of certain personnel actions. See section 1214(b) of this title.

EFFECTIVE DATE OF REPEAL

Repeal of sections effective 90 days following Apr. 10, 1989, see section 11 of Pub. L. 101–12, set out as an Effective Date of 1989 Amendment note under section 1201 of this title.

[§ 1209. Renumbered §§ 1205 and 1206]

CODIFICATION

Subsecs. (a) and (b) of this section were renumbered as sections 1205 and 1206, respectively, of this title by Pub. L. 101–12, § 3(a)(9), (10). Pub. L. 102–378, § 2(2), Oct. 2, 1992, 106 Stat. 1346, struck out section catchline of prior section 1209.

SUBCHAPTER II—OFFICE OF SPECIAL COUNSEL

SUBCHAPTER REFERRED TO IN OTHER SECTIONS

This subchapter is referred to in sections 1221, 4505a, 5754, 5755, 7121 of this title.

§ 1211. Establishment

(a) There is established the Office of Special Counsel, which shall be headed by the Special Counsel. The Office shall have an official seal which shall be judicially noticed. The Office shall have its principal office in the District of Columbia and shall have field offices in other appropriate locations.

(b) The Special Counsel shall be appointed by the President, by and with the advice and consent of the Senate, for a term of 5 years. The Special Counsel may continue to serve beyond the expiration of the term until a successor is appointed and has qualified, except that the Special Counsel may not continue to serve for more than one year after the date on which the term of the Special Counsel would otherwise expire under this subsection. The Special Counsel shall be an attorney who, by demonstrated ability, background, training, or experience, is especially qualified to carry out the functions of the position. A Special Counsel appointed to fill a vacancy occurring before the end of a term of office of the Special Counsel's predecessor serves for the remainder of the term. The Special

Counsel may be removed by the President only for inefficiency, neglect of duty, or malfeasance in office. The Special Counsel may not hold another office or position in the Government of the United States, except as otherwise provided by law or at the direction of the President.

(Added Pub. L. 101–12, § 3(a)(11), Apr. 10, 1989, 103 Stat. 19, § 1211(a), and Pub. L. 95–454, title II, § 202(a), Oct. 13, 1978, 92 Stat. 1122, § 1204; renumbered § 1211(b) and amended Pub. L. 101–12, § 3(a)(6), (12), Apr. 10, 1989, 103 Stat. 17, 19; Pub. L. 103–424, § 3(a), Oct. 29, 1994, 108 Stat. 4361.)

AMENDMENTS

1994—Subsec. (b). Pub. L. 101–424 inserted after first sentence "The Special Counsel may continue to serve beyond the expiration of the term until a successor is appointed and has qualified, except that the Special Counsel may not continue to serve for more than one year after the date on which the term of the Special Counsel would otherwise expire under this subsection."

1989—Subsec. (b). Pub. L. 101–12, § 3(a)(6), (12), renumbered section 1204 of this title as subsec. (b) of this section, substituted "Special Counsel shall be appointed by the President" for "Special Counsel of the Merit Systems Protection Board shall be appointed by the President from attorneys", substituted "The Special Counsel shall be an attorney who, by demonstrated ability, background, training, or experience, is especially qualified to carry out the functions of the position. A Special Counsel appointed to fill a vacancy occurring before the end of a term of office of the Special Counsel's predecessor serves for the remainder of the term." for "A Special Counsel appointed to fill a vacancy occurring before the end of a term of office of his predecessor serves for the remainder of the term.", and inserted at end "The Special Counsel may not hold another office or position in the Government of the United States, except as otherwise provided by law or at the direction of the President."

EFFECTIVE DATE

Subchapter effective 90 days following Apr. 10, 1989, see section 11 of Pub. L. 101–12, set out as a note under section 1201 of this title.

TRANSFER OF FUNDS

Section 8(c) of Pub. L. 101–12 provided that: "The personnel, assets, liabilities, contracts, property, records, and unexpended balances of appropriations, authorizations, allocations, and other funds employed, held, used, arising from, available or to be made available to the Special Counsel of the Merit Systems Protection Board are, subject to section 1531 of title 31, United States Code, transferred to the Special Counsel referred to in section 1211 of title 5, United States Code (as added by section 3(a) of this Act), for appropriate allocation."

SECTION REFERRED TO IN OTHER SECTIONS

This section is referred to in title 38 section 4324.

§ 1212. Powers and functions of the Office of Special Counsel

(a) The Office of Special Counsel shall—

(1) in accordance with section 1214(a) and other applicable provisions of this subchapter, protect employees, former employees, and applicants for employment from prohibited personnel practices;

(2) receive and investigate allegations of prohibited personnel practices, and, where appropriate—

(A) bring petitions for stays, and petitions for corrective action, under section 1214; and

(B) file a complaint or make recommendations for disciplinary action under section 1215;

(3) receive, review, and, where appropriate, forward to the Attorney General or an agency head under section 1213, disclosures of violations of any law, rule, or regulation, or gross mismanagement, a gross waste of funds, an abuse of authority, or a substantial and specific danger to public health or safety;

(4) review rules and regulations issued by the Director of the Office of Personnel Management in carrying out functions under section 1103 and, where the Special Counsel finds that any such rule or regulation would, on its face or as implemented, require the commission of a prohibited personnel practice, file a written complaint with the Board; and

(5) investigate and, where appropriate, bring actions concerning allegations of violations of other laws within the jurisdiction of the Office of Special Counsel (as referred to in section 1216).

(b)(1) The Special Counsel and any employee of the Office of Special Counsel designated by the Special Counsel may administer oaths, examine witnesses, take depositions, and receive evidence.

(2) The Special Counsel may—

(A) issue subpoenas; and

(B) order the taking of depositions and order responses to written interrogatories;

in the same manner as provided under section 1204.

(3)(A) In the case of contumacy or failure to obey a subpoena issued under paragraph (2)(A), the Special Counsel may apply to the Merit Systems Protection Board to enforce the subpoena in court pursuant to section 1204(c).

(B) A subpoena under paragraph (2)(A) may, in the case of any individual outside the territorial jurisdiction of any court of the United States, be served in the manner referred to in subsection (d) of section 1204, and the United States District Court for the District of Columbia may, with respect to any such individual, compel compliance in accordance with such subsection.

(4) Witnesses (whether appearing voluntarily or under subpoena) shall be paid the same fee and mileage allowances which are paid subpoenaed witnesses in the courts of the United States.

(c)(1) Except as provided in paragraph (2), the Special Counsel may as a matter of right intervene or otherwise participate in any proceeding before the Merit Systems Protection Board, except that the Special Counsel shall comply with the rules of the Board.

(2) The Special Counsel may not intervene in an action brought by an individual under section 1221, or in an appeal brought by an individual under section 7701, without the consent of such individual.

(d)(1) The Special Counsel may appoint the legal, administrative, and support personnel necessary to perform the functions of the Special Counsel.

(2) Any appointment made under this subsection shall be made in accordance with the provisions of this title, except that such appointment shall not be subject to the approval or supervision of the Office of Personnel Management or the Executive Office of the President (other than approval required under section 3324 or subchapter VIII of chapter 33).

(e) The Special Counsel may prescribe such regulations as may be necessary to perform the functions of the Special Counsel. Such regulations shall be published in the Federal Register.

(f) The Special Counsel may not issue any advisory opinion concerning any law, rule, or regulation (other than an advisory opinion concerning chapter 15 or subchapter III of chapter 73).

(g)(1) The Special Counsel may not respond to any inquiry or disclose any information from or about any person making an allegation under section 1214(a), except in accordance with the provisions of section 552a of title 5, United States Code, or as required by any other applicable Federal law.

(2) Notwithstanding the exception under paragraph (1), the Special Counsel may not respond to any inquiry concerning an evaluation of the work performance, ability, aptitude, general qualifications, character, loyalty, or suitability for any personnel action of any person described in paragraph (1)—

(A) unless the consent of the individual as to whom the information pertains is obtained in advance; or

(B) except upon request of an agency which requires such information in order to make a determination concerning an individual's having access to the information unauthorized disclosure of which could be expected to cause exceptionally grave damage to the national security.

(Added Pub. L. 101–12, §3(a)(13), Apr. 10, 1989, 103 Stat. 19; amended Pub. L. 103–424, §3(b), Oct. 29, 1994, 108 Stat. 4362.)

AMENDMENTS

1994—Subsec. (g)(1). Pub. L. 103–424, §3(b)(1) substituted "disclose any information from or about" for "provide information concerning".

Subsec. (g)(2). Pub. L. 103–424, §3(b)(2), substituted "an evaluation of the work performance, ability, aptitude, general qualifications, character, loyalty, or suitability for any personnel action of any" for "a matter described in subparagraph (A) or (B) of section 2302(b)(2) in connection with a".

POLICY STATEMENT REGARDING IMPLEMENTATION OF WHISTLEBLOWER PROTECTION ACT

Section 12(a) of Pub. L. 103–424 provided that: "No later than 6 months after the date of enactment of this Act [Oct. 29, 1994], the Special Counsel shall issue a policy statement regarding the implementation of the Whistleblower Protection Act of 1989 [see Short Title of 1989 Amendment note set out under section 1201 of this title]. Such policy statement shall be made available to each person alleging a prohibited personnel practice described under section 2302(b)(8) of title 5, United States Code, and shall include detailed guidelines identifying specific categories of information that may (or may not) be communicated to agency officials for an investigative purpose, or for the purpose of obtaining corrective action under section 1214 of title 5, United States Code, or disciplinary action under section 1215 of such title, the circumstances under which such information is likely to be disclosed, and whether or not the consent of any person is required in advance of any such communication."

ANNUAL SURVEY OF INDIVIDUALS SEEKING ASSISTANCE

Section 13 of Pub. L. 103–424 provided that:

"(a) IN GENERAL.—The Office of Special Counsel shall, after consulting with the Office of Policy and Evaluation of the Merit Systems Protection Board, conduct an annual survey of all individuals who contact the Office of Special Counsel for assistance. The survey shall—

"(1) determine if the individual seeking assistance was fully apprised of their rights;

"(2) determine whether the individual was successful either at the Office of Special Counsel or the Merit Systems Protection Board; and

"(3) determine if the individual, whether successful or not, was satisfied with the treatment received from the Office of Special Counsel.

"(b) REPORT.—The results of the survey conducted under subsection (a) shall be published in the annual report of the Office of Special Counsel."

SECTION REFERRED TO IN OTHER SECTIONS

This section is referred to in section 2105 of this title.

§ 1213. Provisions relating to disclosures of violations of law, gross mismanagement, and certain other matters

(a) This section applies with respect to—

(1) any disclosure of information by an employee, former employee, or applicant for employment which the employee, former employee, or applicant reasonably believes evidences—

(A) a violation of any law, rule, or regulation; or

(B) gross mismanagement, a gross waste of funds, an abuse of authority, or a substantial and specific danger to public health or safety;

if such disclosure is not specifically prohibited by law and if such information is not specifically required by Executive order to be kept secret in the interest of national defense or the conduct of foreign affairs; and

(2) any disclosure by an employee, former employee, or applicant for employment to the Special Counsel or to the Inspector General of an agency or another employee designated by the head of the agency to receive such disclosures of information which the employee, former employee, or applicant reasonably believes evidences—

(A) a violation of any law, rule, or regulation; or

(B) gross mismanagement, a gross waste of funds, an abuse of authority, or a substantial and specific danger to public health or safety.

(b) Whenever the Special Counsel receives information of a type described in subsection (a) of this section, the Special Counsel shall review such information and, within 15 days after receiving the information, determine whether there is a substantial likelihood that the information discloses a violation of any law, rule, or regulation, or gross mismanagement, gross waste of funds, abuse of authority, or substantial and specific danger to public health and safety.

(c)(1) Subject to paragraph (2), if the Special Counsel makes a positive determination under subsection (b) of this section, the Special Counsel shall promptly transmit the information with respect to which the determination was made to the appropriate agency head and require that the agency head—

(A) conduct an investigation with respect to the information and any related matters transmitted by the Special Counsel to the agency head; and

(B) submit a written report setting forth the findings of the agency head within 60 days after the date on which the information is transmitted to the agency head or within any longer period of time agreed to in writing by the Special Counsel.

(2) The Special Counsel may require an agency head to conduct an investigation and submit a written report under paragraph (1) only if the information was transmitted to the Special Counsel by—

(A) an employee, former employee, or applicant for employment in the agency which the information concerns; or

(B) an employee who obtained the information in connection with the performance of the employee's duties and responsibilities.

(d) Any report required under subsection (c) shall be reviewed and signed by the head of the agency and shall include—

(1) a summary of the information with respect to which the investigation was initiated;

(2) a description of the conduct of the investigation;

(3) a summary of any evidence obtained from the investigation;

(4) a listing of any violation or apparent violation of any law, rule, or regulation; and

(5) a description of any action taken or planned as a result of the investigation, such as—

(A) changes in agency rules, regulations, or practices;

(B) the restoration of any aggrieved employee;

(C) disciplinary action against any employee; and

(D) referral to the Attorney General of any evidence of a criminal violation.

(e)(1) Any such report shall be submitted to the Special Counsel, and the Special Counsel shall transmit a copy to the complainant, except as provided under subsection (f) of this section. The complainant may submit comments to the Special Counsel on the agency report within 15 days of having received a copy of the report.

(2) Upon receipt of any report of the head of an agency required under subsection (c) of this section, the Special Counsel shall review the report and determine whether—

(A) the findings of the head of the agency appear reasonable; and

(B) the report of the agency under subsection (c)(1) of this section contains the information required under subsection (d) of this section.

(3) The Special Counsel shall transmit any agency report received pursuant to subsection (c) of this section, any comments provided by the complainant pursuant to subsection (e)(1), and any appropriate comments or recommendations by the Special Counsel to the President and the congressional committees with jurisdiction over the agency which the disclosure involves.

(4) Whenever the Special Counsel does not receive the report of the agency within the time prescribed in subsection (c)(2) of this section, the Special Counsel shall transmit a copy of the information which was transmitted to the agency head to the President and the congressional committees with jurisdiction over the agency which the disclosure involves together with a statement noting the failure of the head of the agency to file the required report.

(f) In any case in which evidence of a criminal violation obtained by an agency in an investigation under subsection (c) of this section is referred to the Attorney General—

(1) the report shall not be transmitted to the complainant; and

(2) the agency shall notify the Office of Personnel Management and the Office of Management and Budget of the referral.

(g)(1) If the Special Counsel receives information of a type described in subsection (a) from an individual other than an individual described in subparagraph (A) or (B) of subsection (c)(2), the Special Counsel may transmit the information to the head of the agency which the information concerns. The head of such agency shall, within a reasonable time after the information is transmitted, inform the Special Counsel in writing of what action has been or is being taken and when such action shall be completed. The Special Counsel shall inform the individual of the report of the agency head. If the Special Counsel does not transmit the information to the head of the agency, the Special Counsel shall return any documents and other matter provided by the individual who made the disclosure.

(2) If the Special Counsel receives information of a type described in subsection (a) from an individual described in subparagraph (A) or (B) of subsection (c)(2), but does not make a positive determination under subsection (b), the Special Counsel may transmit the information to the head of the agency which the information concerns, except that the information may not be transmitted to the head of the agency without the consent of the individual. The head of such agency shall, within a reasonable time after the information is transmitted, inform the Special Counsel in writing of what action has been or is being taken and when such action will be completed. The Special Counsel shall inform the individual of the report of the agency head.

(3) If the Special Counsel does not transmit the information to the head of the agency under paragraph (2), the Special Counsel shall—

(A) return any documents and other matter provided by the individual who made the disclosure; and

(B) inform the individual of—

(i) the reasons why the disclosure may not be further acted on under this chapter; and

(ii) other offices available for receiving disclosures, should the individual wish to pursue the matter further.

(h) The identity of any individual who makes a disclosure described in subsection (a) may not be disclosed by the Special Counsel without such individual's consent unless the Special Counsel determines that the disclosure of the individual's identity is necessary because of an imminent danger to public health or safety or imminent violation of any criminal law.

(i) Except as specifically authorized under this section, the provisions of this section shall not be considered to authorize disclosure of any information by any agency or any person which is—

(1) specifically prohibited from disclosure by any other provision of law; or

(2) specifically required by Executive order to be kept secret in the interest of national defense or the conduct of foreign affairs.

(j) With respect to any disclosure of information described in subsection (a) which involves foreign intelligence or counterintelligence information, if the disclosure is specifically prohibited by law or by Executive order, the Special Counsel shall transmit such information to the National Security Advisor, the Permanent Select Committee on Intelligence of the House of Representatives, and the Select Committee on Intelligence of the Senate.

(Added Pub. L. 101–12, § 3(a)(13), Apr. 10, 1989, 103 Stat. 21; amended Pub. L. 104–316, title I, § 103(a), Oct. 19, 1996, 110 Stat. 3828.)

AMENDMENTS

1996—Subsec. (e)(3). Pub. L. 104–316, § 103(a)(1), substituted "President and" for "President," and struck out ", and the Comptroller General" before period at end.

Subsec. (e)(4). Pub. L. 104–316, § 103(a)(2), substituted "President and" for "President," and struck out ", and the Comptroller General" before "together with a".

SECTION REFERRED TO IN OTHER SECTIONS

This section is referred to in sections 1212, 1219, 2105 of this title.

§ 1214. Investigation of prohibited personnel practices; corrective action

(a)(1)(A) The Special Counsel shall receive any allegation of a prohibited personnel practice and shall investigate the allegation to the extent necessary to determine whether there are reasonable grounds to believe that a prohibited personnel practice has occurred, exists, or is to be taken.

(B) Within 15 days after the date of receiving an allegation of a prohibited personnel practice under paragraph (1), the Special Counsel shall provide written notice to the person who made the allegation that—

(i) the allegation has been received by the Special Counsel; and

(ii) shall include the name of a person at the Office of Special Counsel who shall serve as a contact with the person making the allegation.

(C) Unless an investigation is terminated under paragraph (2), the Special Counsel shall—

(i) within 90 days after notice is provided under subparagraph (B), notify the person who made the allegation of the status of the investigation and any action taken by the Office of the Special Counsel since the filing of the allegation;

(ii) notify such person of the status of the investigation and any action taken by the Office of the Special Counsel since the last notice, at least every 60 days after notice is given under clause (i); and

(iii) notify such person of the status of the investigation and any action taken by the Special Counsel at such time as determined appropriate by the Special Counsel.

(D) No later than 10 days before the Special Counsel terminates any investigation of a prohibited personnel practice, the Special Counsel shall provide a written status report to the person who made the allegation of the proposed findings of fact and legal conclusions. The person may submit written comments about the report to the Special Counsel. The Special Counsel shall not be required to provide a subsequent written status report under this subparagraph after the submission of such written comments.

(2)(A) If the Special Counsel terminates any investigation under paragraph (1), the Special Counsel shall prepare and transmit to any person on whose allegation the investigation was initiated a written statement notifying the person of—

(i) the termination of the investigation;

(ii) a summary of relevant facts ascertained by the Special Counsel, including the facts that support, and the facts that do not support, the allegations of such person;

(iii) the reasons for terminating the investigation; and

(iv) a response to any comments submitted under paragraph (1)(D).

(B) A written statement under subparagraph (A) may not be admissible as evidence in any judicial or administrative proceeding, without the consent of the person who received such statement under subparagraph (A).

(3) Except in a case in which an employee, former employee, or applicant for employment has the right to appeal directly to the Merit Systems Protection Board under any law, rule, or regulation, any such employee, former employee, or applicant shall seek corrective action from the Special Counsel before seeking corrective action from the Board. An employee, former employee, or applicant for employment may seek corrective action from the Board under section 1221, if such employee, former employee, or applicant seeks corrective action for a prohibited personnel practice described in section 2302(b)(8) from the Special Counsel and—

(A)(i) the Special Counsel notifies such employee, former employee, or applicant that an investigation concerning such employee, former employee, or applicant has been terminated; and

(ii) no more than 60 days have elapsed since notification was provided to such employee, former employee, or applicant for employment that such investigation was terminated; or

(B) 120 days after seeking corrective action from the Special Counsel, such employee, former employee, or applicant has not been notified by the Special Counsel that the Special Counsel shall seek corrective action on behalf of such employee, former employee, or applicant.

(4) If an employee, former employee, or applicant seeks a corrective action from the Board

under section 1221, pursuant to the provisions of paragraph (3)(B), the Special Counsel may continue to seek corrective action personal to such employee, former employee, or applicant only with the consent of such employee, former employee, or applicant.

(5) In addition to any authority granted under paragraph (1), the Special Counsel may, in the absence of an allegation, conduct an investigation for the purpose of determining whether there are reasonable grounds to believe that a prohibited personnel practice (or a pattern of prohibited personnel practices) has occurred, exists, or is to be taken.

(b)(1)(A)(i) The Special Counsel may request any member of the Merit Systems Protection Board to order a stay of any personnel action for 45 days if the Special Counsel determines that there are reasonable grounds to believe that the personnel action was taken, or is to be taken, as a result of a prohibited personnel practice.

(ii) Any member of the Board requested by the Special Counsel to order a stay under clause (i) shall order such stay unless the member determines that, under the facts and circumstances involved, such a stay would not be appropriate.

(iii) Unless denied under clause (ii), any stay under this subparagraph shall be granted within 3 calendar days (excluding Saturdays, Sundays, and legal holidays) after the date of the request for the stay by the Special Counsel.

(B) The Board may extend the period of any stay granted under subparagraph (A) for any period which the Board considers appropriate.

(C) The Board shall allow any agency which is the subject of a stay to comment to the Board on any extension of stay proposed under subparagraph (B).

(D) A stay may be terminated by the Board at any time, except that a stay may not be terminated by the Board—

(i) on its own motion or on the motion of an agency, unless notice and opportunity for oral or written comments are first provided to the Special Counsel and the individual on whose behalf the stay was ordered; or

(ii) on motion of the Special Counsel, unless notice and opportunity for oral or written comments are first provided to the individual on whose behalf the stay was ordered.

(2)(A)(i) Except as provided under clause (ii), no later than 240 days after the date of receiving an allegation of a prohibited personnel practice under paragraph (1), the Special Counsel shall make a determination whether there are reasonable grounds to believe that a prohibited personnel practice has occurred, exists, or is to be taken.

(ii) If the Special Counsel is unable to make the required determination within the 240-day period specified under clause (i) and the person submitting the allegation of a prohibited personnel practice agrees to an extension of time, the determination shall be made within such additional period of time as shall be agreed upon between the Special Counsel and the person submitting the allegation.

(B) If, in connection with any investigation, the Special Counsel determines that there are reasonable grounds to believe that a prohibited personnel practice has occurred, exists, or is to be taken which requires corrective action, the Special Counsel shall report the determination together with any findings or recommendations to the Board, the agency involved and to the Office of Personnel Management, and may report such determination, findings and recommendations to the President. The Special Counsel may include in the report recommendations for corrective action to be taken.

(C) If, after a reasonable period of time, the agency does not act to correct the prohibited personnel practice, the Special Counsel may petition the Board for corrective action.

(D) If the Special Counsel finds, in consultation with the individual subject to the prohibited personnel practice, that the agency has acted to correct the prohibited personnel practice, the Special Counsel shall file such finding with the Board, together with any written comments which the individual may provide.

(E) A determination by the Special Counsel under this paragraph shall not be cited or referred to in any proceeding under this paragraph or any other administrative or judicial proceeding for any purpose, without the consent of the person submitting the allegation of a prohibited personnel practice.

(3) Whenever the Special Counsel petitions the Board for corrective action, the Board shall provide an opportunity for—

(A) oral or written comments by the Special Counsel, the agency involved, and the Office of Personnel Management; and

(B) written comments by any individual who alleges to be the subject of the prohibited personnel practice.

(4)(A) The Board shall order such corrective action as the Board considers appropriate, if the Board determines that the Special Counsel has demonstrated that a prohibited personnel practice, other than one described in section 2302(b)(8), has occurred, exists, or is to be taken.

(B)(i) Subject to the provisions of clause (ii), in any case involving an alleged prohibited personnel practice as described under section 2302(b)(8), the Board shall order such corrective action as the Board considers appropriate if the Special Counsel has demonstrated that a disclosure described under section 2302(b)(8) was a contributing factor in the personnel action which was taken or is to be taken against the individual.

(ii) Corrective action under clause (i) may not be ordered if the agency demonstrates by clear and convincing evidence that it would have taken the same personnel action in the absence of such disclosure.

(c)(1) Judicial review of any final order or decision of the Board under this section may be obtained by any employee, former employee, or applicant for employment adversely affected by such order or decision.

(2) A petition for review under this subsection shall be filed with such court, and within such time, as provided for under section 7703(b).

(d)(1) If, in connection with any investigation under this subchapter, the Special Counsel determines that there is reasonable cause to believe that a criminal violation has occurred, the Special Counsel shall report the determination to the Attorney General and to the head of the

agency involved, and shall submit a copy of the report to the Director of the Office of Personnel Management and the Director of the Office of Management and Budget.

(2) In any case in which the Special Counsel determines that there are reasonable grounds to believe that a prohibited personnel practice has occurred, exists, or is to be taken, the Special Counsel shall proceed with any investigation or proceeding unless—

(A) the alleged violation has been reported to the Attorney General; and

(B) the Attorney General is pursuing an investigation, in which case the Special Counsel, after consultation with the Attorney General, has discretion as to whether to proceed.

(e) If, in connection with any investigation under this subchapter, the Special Counsel determines that there is reasonable cause to believe that any violation of any law, rule, or regulation has occurred other than one referred to in subsection (b) or (d), the Special Counsel shall report such violation to the head of the agency involved. The Special Counsel shall require, within 30 days after the receipt of the report by the agency, a certification by the head of the agency which states—

(1) that the head of the agency has personally reviewed the report; and

(2) what action has been or is to be taken, and when the action will be completed.

(f) During any investigation initiated under this subchapter, no disciplinary action shall be taken against any employee for any alleged prohibited activity under investigation or for any related activity without the approval of the Special Counsel.

(g) If the Board orders corrective action under this section, such corrective action may include—

(1) that the individual be placed, as nearly as possible, in the position the individual would have been in had the prohibited personnel practice not occurred; and

(2) reimbursement for attorney's fees, back pay and related benefits, medical costs incurred, travel expenses, and any other reasonable and foreseeable consequential damages.

(Added Pub. L. 101–12, § 3(a)(13), Apr. 10, 1989, 103 Stat. 23; amended Pub. L. 103–424, §§ 3(c), (d), 8(a), Oct. 29, 1994, 108 Stat. 4362, 4364.)

AMENDMENTS

1994—Subsec. (a)(1)(D). Pub. L. 103–424, § 3(c)(1), added subpar. (D).

Subsec. (a)(2)(A)(iv). Pub. L. 103–424, § 3(c)(2), added cl. (iv).

Subsec. (b)(2). Pub. L. 103–424, § 3(d), added subpars. (A) and (E) and redesignated former subpars. (A) to (C) as (B) to (D), respectively.

Subsec. (g). Pub. L. 103–424, § 8(a), added subsec. (g).

TERMINATION STATEMENT

Section 12(b) of Pub. L. 103–424 provided that: "The Special Counsel shall include in any letter terminating an investigation under section 1214(a)(2) of title 5, United States Code, the name and telephone number of an employee of the Special Counsel who is available to respond to reasonable questions from the person regarding the investigation or review conducted by the Special Counsel, the relevant facts ascertained by the

Special Counsel, and the law applicable to the person's allegations.''

SECTION REFERRED TO IN OTHER SECTIONS

This section is referred to in sections 1204, 1212, 1216, 1218, 1219, 1221, 2105, 2303, 7121 of this title; title 22 section 4139.

§ 1215. Disciplinary action

(a)(1) Except as provided in subsection (b), if the Special Counsel determines that disciplinary action should be taken against any employee for having—

(A) committed a prohibited personnel practice,

(B) violated the provisions of any law, rule, or regulation, or engaged in any other conduct within the jurisdiction of the Special Counsel as described in section 1216, or

(C) knowingly and willfully refused or failed to comply with an order of the Merit Systems Protection Board,

the Special Counsel shall prepare a written complaint against the employee containing the Special Counsel's determination, together with a statement of supporting facts, and present the complaint and statement to the employee and the Board, in accordance with this subsection.

(2) Any employee against whom a complaint has been presented to the Merit Systems Protection Board under paragraph (1) is entitled to—

(A) a reasonable time to answer orally and in writing, and to furnish affidavits and other documentary evidence in support of the answer;

(B) be represented by an attorney or other representative;

(C) a hearing before the Board or an administrative law judge appointed under section 3105 and designated by the Board;

(D) have a transcript kept of any hearing under subparagraph (C); and

(E) a written decision and reasons therefor at the earliest practicable date, including a copy of any final order imposing disciplinary action.

(3) A final order of the Board may impose disciplinary action consisting of removal, reduction in grade, debarment from Federal employment for a period not to exceed 5 years, suspension, reprimand, or an assessment of a civil penalty not to exceed $1,000.

(4) There may be no administrative appeal from an order of the Board. An employee subject to a final order imposing disciplinary action under this subsection may obtain judicial review of the order by filing a petition therefor with such court, and within such time, as provided for under section 7703(b).

(5) In the case of any State or local officer or employee under chapter 15, the Board shall consider the case in accordance with the provisions of such chapter.

(b) In the case of an employee in a confidential, policy-making, policy-determining, or policy-advocating position appointed by the President, by and with the advice and consent of the Senate (other than an individual in the Foreign Service of the United States), the complaint and statement referred to in subsection (a)(1), to-

gether with any response of the employee, shall be presented to the President for appropriate action in lieu of being presented under subsection (a).

(c)(1) In the case of members of the uniformed services and individuals employed by any person under contract with an agency to provide goods or services, the Special Counsel may transmit recommendations for disciplinary or other appropriate action (including the evidence on which such recommendations are based) to the head of the agency concerned.

(2) In any case in which the Special Counsel transmits recommendations to an agency head under paragraph (1), the agency head shall, within 60 days after receiving such recommendations, transmit a report to the Special Counsel on each recommendation and the action taken, or proposed to be taken, with respect to each such recommendation.

(Added Pub. L. 101–12, §3(a)(13), Apr. 10, 1989, 103 Stat. 27.)

SECTION REFERRED TO IN OTHER SECTIONS

This section is referred to in sections 1204, 1212, 1216, 1219, 1221, 2105, 2302, 3393, 7121, 7502, 7512, 7521, 7542 of this title.

§ 1216. Other matters within the jurisdiction of the Office of Special Counsel

(a) In addition to the authority otherwise provided in this chapter, the Special Counsel shall, except as provided in subsection (b), conduct an investigation of any allegation concerning—

(1) political activity prohibited under subchapter III of chapter 73, relating to political activities by Federal employees;

(2) political activity prohibited under chapter 15, relating to political activities by certain State and local officers and employees;

(3) arbitrary or capricious withholding of information prohibited under section 552, except that the Special Counsel shall make no investigation of any withholding of foreign intelligence or counterintelligence information the disclosure of which is specifically prohibited by law or by Executive order;

(4) activities prohibited by any civil service law, rule, or regulation, including any activity relating to political intrusion in personnel decisionmaking; and

(5) involvement by any employee in any prohibited discrimination found by any court or appropriate administrative authority to have occurred in the course of any personnel action.

(b) The Special Counsel shall make no investigation of any allegation of any prohibited activity referred to in subsection (a)(5), if the Special Counsel determines that the allegation may be resolved more appropriately under an administrative appeals procedure.

(c) If the Special Counsel receives an allegation concerning any matter under paragraph (1), (3), (4), or (5) of subsection (a), the Special Counsel may investigate and seek corrective action under section 1214 and disciplinary action under section 1215 in the same way as if a prohibited personnel practice were involved.

(Added Pub. L. 101–12, §3(a)(13), Apr. 10, 1989, 103 Stat. 28; amended Pub. L. 103–94, §3, Oct. 6, 1993, 107 Stat. 1004.)

AMENDMENTS

1993—Subsec. (c). Pub. L. 103–94 amended subsec. (c) generally. Prior to amendment, subsec. (c) read as follows:

"(1) If an investigation by the Special Counsel under subsection (a)(1) substantiates an allegation relating to any activity prohibited under section 7324, the Special Counsel may petition the Merit Systems Protection Board for any penalties provided for under section 7325.

"(2) If the Special Counsel receives an allegation concerning any matter under paragraph (3), (4), or (5) of subsection (a), the Special Counsel may investigate and seek corrective action under section 1214 in the same way as if a prohibited personnel practice were involved."

EFFECTIVE DATE OF 1993 AMENDMENT; SAVINGS PROVISION

Amendment by Pub. L. 103–94 effective 120 days after Oct. 6, 1993, but not to release or extinguish any penalty, forfeiture, or liability incurred under amended provision, which is to be treated as remaining in force for purpose of that penalty, forfeiture, or liability, and no provision of Pub. L. 103–94 to affect any proceedings with respect to which charges were filed on or before 120 days after Oct. 6, 1993, with orders to be issued in such proceedings and appeals taken therefrom as if Pub. L. 103–94 had not been enacted, see section 12 of Pub. L. 103–94, set out as an Effective Date; Savings Provision note under section 7321 of this title.

SECTION REFERRED TO IN OTHER SECTIONS

This section is referred to in sections 1212, 1215, 2105 of this title.

§ 1217. Transmittal of information to Congress

The Special Counsel or any employee of the Special Counsel designated by the Special Counsel, shall transmit to the Congress on the request of any committee or subcommittee thereof, by report, testimony, or otherwise, information and the Special Counsel's views on functions, responsibilities, or other matters relating to the Office. Such information shall be transmitted concurrently to the President and any other appropriate agency in the executive branch.

(Added Pub. L. 101–12, § 3(a)(13), Apr. 10, 1989, 103 Stat. 28.)

§ 1218. Annual report

The Special Counsel shall submit an annual report to the Congress on the activities of the Special Counsel, including the number, types, and disposition of allegations of prohibited personnel practices filed with it, investigations conducted by it, cases in which it did not make a determination whether there are reasonable grounds to believe that a prohibited personnel practice has occurred, exists, or is to be taken within the 240-day period specified in section 1214(b)(2)(A)(i), and actions initiated by it before the Merit Systems Protection Board, as well as a description of the recommendations and reports made by it to other agencies pursuant to this subchapter, and the actions taken by the agencies as a result of the reports or recommendations. The report required by this section shall include whatever recommendations for legislation or other action by Congress the Special Counsel may consider appropriate.

(Added Pub. L. 101–12, § 3(a)(13), Apr. 10, 1989, 103 Stat. 29; amended Pub. L. 103–424, § 3(e), Oct. 29, 1994, 108 Stat. 4363.)

AMENDMENTS

1994—Pub. L. 103–424 inserted "cases in which it did not make a determination whether there are reasonable grounds to believe that a prohibited personnel practice has occurred, exists, or is to be taken within the 240-day period specified in section 1214(b)(2)(A)(i)," after "investigations conducted by it,".

TERMINATION OF REPORTING REQUIREMENTS

For termination, effective May 15, 2000, of reporting provisions in this section, see section 3003 of Pub. L. 104–66, as amended, set out as a note under section 1113 of Title 31, Money and Finance, and page 188 of House Document No. 103–7.

§ 1219. Public information

(a) The Special Counsel shall maintain and make available to the public—

(1) a list of noncriminal matters referred to heads of agencies under subsection (c) of section 1213, together with reports from heads of agencies under subsection (c)(1)(B) of such section relating to such matters;

(2) a list of matters referred to heads of agencies under section 1215(c)(2);

(3) a list of matters referred to heads of agencies under subsection (e) of section 1214, together with certifications from heads of agencies under such subsection; and

(4) reports from heads of agencies under section 1213(g)(1).

(b) The Special Counsel shall take steps to ensure that any list or report made available to the public under this section does not contain any information the disclosure of which is prohibited by law or by Executive order requiring that information be kept secret in the interest of national defense or the conduct of foreign affairs.

(Added Pub. L. 101–12, § 3(a)(13), Apr. 10, 1989, 103 Stat. 29.)

SUBCHAPTER III—INDIVIDUAL RIGHT OF ACTION IN CERTAIN REPRISAL CASES

SUBCHAPTER REFERRED TO IN OTHER SECTIONS

This subchapter is referred to in section 7121 of this title; title 12 sections 1441a, 1831j.

§ 1221. Individual right of action in certain reprisal cases

(a) Subject to the provisions of subsection (b) of this section and subsection 1214(a)(3), an employee, former employee, or applicant for employment may, with respect to any personnel action taken, or proposed to be taken, against such employee, former employee, or applicant for employment, as a result of a prohibited personnel practice described in section 2302(b)(8), seek corrective action from the Merit Systems Protection Board.

(b) This section may not be construed to prohibit any employee, former employee, or applicant for employment from seeking corrective action from the Merit Systems Protection Board before seeking corrective action from the Special Counsel, if such employee, former employee, or applicant for employment has the right to appeal directly to the Board under any law, rule, or regulation.

(c)(1) Any employee, former employee, or applicant for employment seeking corrective action under subsection (a) may request that the Board order a stay of the personnel action involved.

(2) Any stay requested under paragraph (1) shall be granted within 10 calendar days (excluding Saturdays, Sundays, and legal holidays) after the date the request is made, if the Board determines that such a stay would be appropriate.

(3)(A) The Board shall allow any agency which would be subject to a stay under this subsection to comment to the Board on such stay request.

(B) Except as provided in subparagraph (C), a stay granted under this subsection shall remain in effect for such period as the Board determines to be appropriate.

(C) The Board may modify or dissolve a stay under this subsection at any time, if the Board determines that such a modification or dissolution is appropriate.

(d)(1) At the request of an employee, former employee, or applicant for employment seeking corrective action under subsection (a), the Board shall issue a subpoena for the attendance and testimony of any person or the production of documentary or other evidence from any person if the Board finds that the testimony or production requested is not unduly burdensome and appears reasonably calculated to lead to the discovery of admissible evidence.

(2) A subpoena under this subsection may be issued, and shall be enforced, in the same manner as applies in the case of subpoenas under section 1204.

(e)(1) Subject to the provisions of paragraph (2), in any case involving an alleged prohibited personnel practice as described under section 2302(b)(8), the Board shall order such corrective action as the Board considers appropriate if the employee, former employee, or applicant for employment has demonstrated that a disclosure described under section 2302(b)(8) was a contributing factor in the personnel action which was taken or is to be taken against such employee, former employee, or applicant. The employee may demonstrate that the disclosure was a contributing factor in the personnel action through circumstantial evidence, such as evidence that—

(A) the official taking the personnel action knew of the disclosure; and

(B) the personnel action occurred within a period of time such that a reasonable person could conclude that the disclosure was a contributing factor in the personnel action.

(2) Corrective action under paragraph (1) may not be ordered if the agency demonstrates by clear and convincing evidence that it would have taken the same personnel action in the absence of such disclosure.

(f)(1) A final order or decision shall be rendered by the Board as soon as practicable after the commencement of any proceeding under this section.

(2) A decision to terminate an investigation under subchapter II may not be considered in any action or other proceeding under this section.

(3) If, based on evidence presented to it under this section, the Merit Systems Protection Board determines that there is reason to believe that a current employee may have committed a prohibited personnel practice, the Board shall refer the matter to the Special Counsel to investigate and take appropriate action under section 1215.

(g)(1)(A) If the Board orders corrective action under this section, such corrective action may include—

(i) that the individual be placed, as nearly as possible, in the position the individual would have been in had the prohibited personnel practice not occurred; and

(ii) back pay and related benefits, medical costs incurred, travel expenses, and any other reasonable and foreseeable consequential changes.

(B) Corrective action shall include attorney's fees and costs as provided for under paragraphs (2) and (3).

(2) If an employee, former employee, or applicant for employment is the prevailing party before the Merit Systems Protection Board, and the decision is based on a finding of a prohibited personnel practice, the agency involved shall be liable to the employee, former employee, or applicant for reasonable attorney's fees and any other reasonable costs incurred.

(3) If an employee, former emloyee,[1] or applicant for employment is the prevailing party in an appeal from the Merit Systems Protection Board, the agency involved shall be liable to the employee, former employee, or applicant for reasonable attorney's fees and any other reasonable costs incurred, regardless of the basis of the decision.

(h)(1) An employee, former employee, or applicant for employment adversely affected or aggrieved by a final order or decision of the Board under this section may obtain judicial review of the order or decision.

(2) A petition for review under this subsection shall be filed with such court, and within such time, as provided for under section 7703(b).

(i) Subsections (a) through (h) shall apply in any proceeding brought under section 7513(d) if, or to the extent that, a prohibited personnel practice as defined in section 2302(b)(8) is alleged.

(j) In determining the appealability of any case involving an allegation made by an individual under the provisions of this chapter, neither the status of an individual under any retirement system established under a Federal statute nor any election made by such individual under any such system may be taken into account.

(Added Pub. L. 101–12, § 3(a)(13), Apr. 10, 1989, 103 Stat. 29; amended Pub. L. 103–424, §§ 4, 8(b), Oct. 29, 1994, 108 Stat. 4363, 4365.)

AMENDMENTS

1994—Subsec. (d)(1). Pub. L. 103–424, § 4(a), added par. (1) and struck out former par. (1) which read as follows: "At the request of an employee, former employee, or applicant for employment seeking corrective action under subsection (a), the Board may issue a subpoena for the attendance and testimony of any person or the production of documentary or other evidence from any person if the Board finds that such subpoena is necessary for the development of relevant evidence."

Subsec. (e)(1). Pub. L. 103–424, § 4(b), which directed the amendment of section 1221(e)(1), without specifying

---

[1] So in original. Probably should be "employee,".

the Code title to be amended, by inserting at end "The employee may demonstrate that the disclosure was a contributing factor in the personnel action through circumstantial evidence, such as evidence that—

"(A) the official taking the personnel action knew of the disclosure; and

"(B) the personnel action occurred within a period of time such that a reasonable person could conclude that the disclosure was a contributing factor in the personnel action.", was executed to subsec. (e)(1) of this section to reflect the probable intent of Congress.

Subsec. (f)(3). Pub. L. 103–424, § 4(c), added par. (3).

Subsec. (g). Pub. L. 103–424, § 8(b), added par. (1) and redesignated former pars. (1) and (2) as (2) and (3), respectively.

EFFECTIVE DATE

Subchapter effective 90 days following Apr. 10, 1989, see section 11 of Pub. L. 101–12, set out as an Effective Date of 1989 Amendment note under section 1201 of this title.

SECTION REFERRED TO IN OTHER SECTIONS

This section is referred to in sections 1212, 1214, 1222, 2105, 2303, 7121 of this title; title 22 section 4139.

§ 1222. Availability of other remedies

Except as provided in section 1221(i), nothing in this chapter or chapter 23 shall be construed to limit any right or remedy available under a provision of statute which is outside of both this chapter and chapter 23.

(Added Pub. L. 101–12, § 3(a)(13), Apr. 10, 1989, 103 Stat. 31.)

SECTION REFERRED TO IN OTHER SECTIONS

This section is referred to in section 2105 of this title.

CHAPTER 13—SPECIAL AUTHORITY

AMENDMENTS

1998—Pub. L. 105–362, title XIII, § 1302(b)(2)(A), Nov. 10, 1998, 112 Stat. 3293, struck out item 1308 "Annual reports".

1978—Pub. L. 95–251, § 2(c)(1), Mar. 27, 1978, 92 Stat. 183, substituted "Administrative law judges" for "Hearing examiners" in item 1305.

§ 1301. Rules

The Office of Personnel Management shall aid the President, as he may request, in preparing the rules he prescribes under this title for the administration of the competitive service.

(Pub. L. 89–554, Sept. 6, 1966, 80 Stat. 401; Pub. L. 95–454, title IX, § 906(a)(2), Oct. 13, 1978, 92 Stat. 1224.)

HISTORICAL AND REVISION NOTES

Derivation	U.S. Code	Revised Statutes and Statutes at Large
....	5 U.S.C. 633(1) (function of Civil Service Commission).	Jan. 16, 1883, ch. 27, § 2(1) (function of Civil Service Commission), 22 Stat. 403.

The authority of the President to prescribe rules is carried into sections 2951, 3302, 3304(a), 3306(a), 3321, 7152, 7153, 7321, and 7322 of this title.

Standard changes are made to conform with the definitions applicable and the style of this title as outlined in the preface to the report.

AMENDMENTS

1978—Pub. L. 95–454 substituted "Office of Personnel Management" for "Civil Service Commission".

EFFECTIVE DATE OF 1978 AMENDMENT

Amendment by Pub. L. 95–454 effective 90 days after Oct. 13, 1978, see section 907 of Pub. L. 95–454, set out as a note under section 1101 of this title.

§ 1302. Regulations

(a) The Office of Personnel Management, subject to the rules prescribed by the President under this title for the administration of the competitive service, shall prescribe regulations for, control, supervise, and preserve the records of, examinations for the competitive service.

(b) The Office shall prescribe and enforce regulations for the administration of the provisions of this title, and Executive orders issued in furtherance thereof, that implement the Congressional policy that preference shall be given to preference eligibles in certification for appointment, and in appointment, reinstatement, reemployment, and retention, in the competitive service in Executive agencies, permanent or temporary, and in the government of the District of Columbia.

(c) The Office shall prescribe regulations for the administration of the provisions of this title that implement the Congressional policy that preference shall be given to preference eligibles in certification for appointment, and in appointment, reinstatement, reemployment, and retention, in the excepted service in Executive agencies, permanent or temporary, and in the government of the District of Columbia.

(d) The Office may prescribe reasonable procedure and regulations for the administration of its functions under chapter 15 of this title.

(Pub. L. 89–554, Sept. 6, 1966, 80 Stat. 401; Pub. L. 95–454, title IX, § 906(a)(2), (3), Oct. 13, 1978, 92 Stat. 1224.)

HISTORICAL AND REVISION NOTES

Derivation	U.S. Code	Revised Statutes and Statutes at Large
(a)	5 U.S.C. 633(2)7 (last 17 words), (3) (less last 10 words).	Jan. 16, 1883, ch. 27, §§ 2(2)7 (last 17 words), (3) (less last 10 words), 22 Stat. 404.
(b)	5 U.S.C. 851 (1st 76 words), 868 (less proviso).	June 27, 1944, ch. 287, §§ 2 (1st 76 words), 19, 58 Stat. 387, 391.
(c)	5 U.S.C. 851 (1st 76 words), 860.	June 27, 1944, ch. 287, §§ 2 (1st 76 words), 11, 58 Stat. 387, 390.
(d)	5 U.S.C. 118k(d) (1st sentence).	July 19, 1940, ch. 640 § 4 "Sec. 12(d) (1st sentence)", 54 Stat. 769.

Subsection (a) is based on former section 633(3) (less last 10 words). The regulation-making power conferred by that section covers the power conferred by former section 633(2)7 (last 17 words) which is, therefore, omitted. The requirement of notice is preserved in section 3304. The words "through its members or the examiners" are omitted as unnecessary in view of section 1104. The authority of the President to prescribe rules, based on former section 633(1) is carried into sections 2951, 3302, 3304(a), 3306(a), 3321, 7152, 7153, 7321, and 7322 of this title.

In subsections (b)–(d), the word "rules" is omitted as included in "regulations".

The provisions of the Veterans' Preference Act of 1944 (former sections 851–869) to which the regulation-making authority of subsections (b) and (c) apply are carried into sections 2108, 3305(b), 3306(a)(2), 3308–3320, 3351, 3363, 3364, and 7701, subchapter I of chapter 35, and subchapter II of chapter 75 of this title. The first 76 words of former section 851 are added here to preserve the general statement of policy in the light of which the substantive provisions that formerly comprised the Veterans' Preference Act of 1944 are to be interpreted. See *Elder* v. *Brannan*, 241 U.S. 277, 286. In subsection (b), the words "in the competitive service in Executive agencies, permanent or temporary, and in the government of the District of Columbia", and in subsection (c) the words "in the excepted service in Executive agencies, permanent or temporary, and in the government of the District of Columbia" are coextensive with and substituted for "in civilian positions in all establishments, agencies, bureaus, administrations, projects, and departments of the Government, permanent or temporary, and in either (a) the classified civil service; (b) the unclassified civil service; (c) any temporary or emergency establishment, agency, bureau, administration, project, and department created by Acts of Congress or Presidential Executive order", in view of the exclusion of positions in the legislative and judicial branches by former section 869.

Standard changes are made to conform with the definitions applicable and the style of this title as outlined in the preface to the report.

AMENDMENTS

1978—Subsecs. (a) to (d). Pub. L. 95–454 substituted "Office of Personnel Management" for "Civil Service Commission" and "Office" for "Commission" wherever appearing.

EFFECTIVE DATE OF 1978 AMENDMENT

Amendment by Pub. L. 95–454 effective 90 days after Oct. 13, 1978, see section 907 of Pub. L. 95–454, set out as a note under section 1101 of this title.

EXECUTIVE ORDER NO. 10561

Ex. Ord. No. 10561, Sept. 13, 1954, 19 F.R. 5963, which related to official personnel folders, was revoked by section 2–201 of Ex. Ord. No. 12107, Dec. 28, 1978, 44 F.R. 1055, set out as a note under section 1101 of this title.

EXECUTIVE ORDER NO. 11397

Ex. Ord. No. 11397, Feb. 9, 1968, 33 F.R. 2833, formerly set out as a note under this section, which related to transitional appointments of veterans who served during the Vietnam Era, was revoked by Ex. Ord. No. 11521, Mar. 26, 1970, 35 F.R. 5311, set out as a note under section 3302 of this title.

SECTION REFERRED TO IN OTHER SECTIONS

This section is referred to in sections 1303, 2302 of this title; title 18 section 1917; title 22 section 1438.

§ 1303. Investigations; reports

The Office of Personnel Management, Merit Systems Protection Board, and Special Counsel may investigate and report on matters concerning—

(1) the enforcement and effect of the rules prescribed by the President under this title for the administration of the competitive service and the regulations prescribed by the Office of Personnel Management under section 1302(a) of this title; and

(2) the action of an examiner, a board of examiners, and other employees concerning the execution of the provisions of this title that relate to the administration of the competitive service.

(Pub. L. 89–554, Sept. 6, 1966, 80 Stat. 401; Pub. L. 95–454, title IX, § 906(a)(4), (11), Oct. 13, 1978, 92 Stat. 1225.)

HISTORICAL AND REVISION NOTES

Derivation	U.S. Code	Revised Statutes and Statutes at Large
....	5 U.S.C. 633(4).	Jan. 16, 1883, ch. 27, § 2(4), 22 Stat. 404.

The authority of the President to prescribe rules is carried into sections 2951, 3302, 3304(a), 3306(a), 3321, 7152, 7153, 7321, and 7322 of this title.

In paragraph (2), the words "in respect to the execution of this act" are changed to "concerning the execution of the provisions of this title that relate to the administration of the competitive service" to avoid having to refer in the text to the sections of this title into which the Civil Service Act, the act referred to, is codified. These sections are: 1101, 1102, 1105, 1302(a), 1303, 1307, 1308(a)(1), 2102, 2951, 3302, 3303, 3304(a), (d), 3305(a), 3306, 3318(a), 3319(a), 3321, 7152, 7153, 7321, 7322, and 7352. The words "the provisions of this title that relate to the administration of the competitive service" will include some of the sections derived from the Veterans' Preference Act of 1944 (former sections 851–869). They are based in part on former section 860 (codified in § 1302(c)). The authorization in that section to make and enforce regulations for the competitive service would include the authority to investigate and report. The words "and other employees" are substituted for "and its own subordinates, and those in the public service" in view of the definition of "employee" in section 2105.

Standard changes are made to conform with the definition applicable and the style of this title as outlined in the preface to the report.

AMENDMENTS

1978—Pub. L. 95–454 substituted in opening par. "Office of Personnel Management, Merit Systems Protection Board, and Special Counsel" for "Civil Service Commission" and in par. (1) "Office of Personnel Management" for "Commission".

EFFECTIVE DATE OF 1978 AMENDMENT

Amendment by Pub. L. 95–454 effective 90 days after Oct. 13, 1978, see section 907 of Pub. L. 95–454, set out as a note under section 1101 of this title.

§ 1304. Loyalty investigations; reports; revolving fund

(a) The Office of Personnel Management shall conduct the investigations and issue the reports required by the following statutes—

(1) sections 272b, 281b(e), and 290a of title 22;

(2) section 1874(c) of title 42; and

(3) section 1203(e) of title 6, District of Columbia Code.

(b) When an investigation under subsection (a) of this section develops data indicating that the loyalty of the individual being investigated is questionable, the Office shall refer the matter to the Federal Bureau of Investigation for a full field investigation, a report of which shall be furnished to the Office for its information and appropriate action.

(c) When the President considers it in the national interest, he may have the investigations of a group or class, which are required by subsection (a) of this section, made by the Federal Bureau of Investigation rather than the Office.

(d) The investigation and report required by subsection (a) of this section shall be made by the Federal Bureau of Investigation rather than the Office for those specific positions which the Secretary of State certifies are of a high degree of importance or sensitivity.

(e)(1) A revolving fund is available, to the Office without fiscal year limitation, for financing investigations, training, and such other functions as the Office is authorized or required to perform on a reimbursable basis, including personnel management services performed at the request of individual agencies (which would otherwise be the responsibility of such agencies), or at the request of nonappropriated fund instrumentalities. However, the functions which may be financed in any fiscal year by the fund are restricted to those functions which are covered by the budget estimates submitted to the Congress for that fiscal year. To the maximum extent feasible, each individual activity shall be conducted generally on an actual cost basis over a reasonable period of time.

(2) The capital of the fund consists of the aggregate of—

(A) appropriations made to provide capital for the fund, which appropriations are hereby authorized, and

(B) the sum of the fair and reasonable value of such supplies, equipment, and other assets as the Office from time to time transfers to the fund (including the amount of the unexpended balances of appropriations or funds relating to activities the financing of which is transferred to the fund) less the amount of related liabilities, the amount of unpaid obligations, and the value of accrued annual leave of employees, which are attributable to the activities the financing of which is transferred to the fund.

(3) The fund shall be credited with—

(A) advances and reimbursements from available funds of the Office or other agencies, or from other sources, for those services and supplies provided at rates estimated by the Office as adequate to recover expenses of operation (including provision for accrued annual leave of employees and depreciation of equipment); and

(B) receipts from sales or exchanges of property, and payments for loss of or damage to property, accounted for under the fund.

(4) Any unobligated and unexpended balances in the fund which the Office determines to be in excess of amounts needed for activities financed by the fund shall be deposited in the Treasury of the United States as miscellaneous receipts.

(5) The Office shall prepare a business-type budget providing full disclosure of the results of operations for each of the functions performed by the Office and financed by the fund, and such budget shall be transmitted to the Congress and considered, in the manner prescribed by law for wholly owned Government corporations.

(6) The Comptroller General of the United States shall, as a result of his periodic reviews of the activities financed by the fund, report and make such recommendations as he deems appropriate to the Committee on Governmental Affairs of the Senate and the Committee on Post Office and Civil Service of the House of Representatives.

(f) An agency may use available appropriations to reimburse the Office or the Federal Bureau of Investigation for the cost of investigations, training, and functions performed for them under this section, or to make advances toward their cost. These advances and reimbursements shall be credited directly to the applicable appropriations of the Office or the Federal Bureau of Investigation.

(g) This section does not affect the responsibility of the Federal Bureau of Investigation to investigate espionage, sabotage, or subversive acts.

(Pub. L. 89–554, Sept. 6, 1966, 80 Stat. 401; Pub. L. 91–189, §1, Dec. 30, 1969, 83 Stat. 851; Pub. L. 91–648, title V, §510, Jan. 5, 1971, 84 Stat. 1928; Pub. L. 95–454, title IX, §906(a)(2), (3), Oct. 13, 1978, 92 Stat. 1224; Pub. L. 96–60, title II, §203(a)(2), Aug. 15, 1979, 93 Stat. 398; Pub. L. 97–412, §1(a), Jan. 3, 1983, 96 Stat. 2047; Pub. L. 98–224, §5(b)(1), Mar. 2, 1984, 98 Stat. 48; Pub. L. 103–437, §3(a), Nov. 2, 1994, 108 Stat. 4581; Pub. L. 104–66, title II, §2182, Dec. 21, 1995, 109 Stat. 732; Pub. L. 104–208, div. A, title I, §101(f) [title IV, §421], Sept. 30, 1996, 110 Stat. 3009–314, 3009–343.)

HISTORICAL AND REVISION NOTES

Derivation	U.S. Code	Revised Statutes and Statutes at Large
(b)–(d)	5 U.S.C. 655.	Apr. 5, 1952, ch. 159, §1 (provisos), 66 Stat. 44. July 31, 1953, ch. 283, §9, 67 Stat. 241.
(e)	5 U.S.C. 657.	June 5, 1952, ch. 369, §701 (par. under "Civil Service Commission"), 66 Stat. 107.
(f)	[Uncodified].	Apr. 5, 1952, ch. 159, §4, 66 Stat. 44.
(g)	5 U.S.C. 656.	Apr. 5, 1952, ch. 159, §3, 66 Stat. 44.

Subsection (a) is based on section 1 of the Act of April 5, 1952, as amended, and is added for clarity. In subsection (a), the reference to section 10(b)(5)(B)(i) and (B)(ii) of the Act of August 1, 1946 (60 Stat. 766) is omitted because of the amendment of the Act of April 5, 1952, by the Act of July 31, 1953, ch. 283, 67 Stat. 240, and the reenactment of the provisions of the Act of April 5, 1952, insofar as they relate to the Atomic Energy Commission as section 145 of the Atomic Energy Act of 1954 (68 Stat. 942; 42 U.S.C. 2165). The references to section 1(2) of the Act of May 22, 1947 (61 Stat. 125), section 1 of the joint resolution of May 21, 1947 (61 Stat. 125), and section 110(c) of the Act of April 3, 1948 (62 Stat. 137) are omitted as these Acts were repealed by the Act of Aug. 26, 1954, ch. 937 §542(a) (1), (2), and (4), 68 Stat. 861. Reference to section 510 of the Mutual Security Act of 1951 (65 Stat. 381) is omitted because this section was replaced by section 531 of the Mutual Security Act of 1954 (68 Stat. 859) and the latter was repealed by the Act of Sept. 4, 1961, Pub. L. 87–195, §642(2), 75 Stat. 460.

In subsection (d), the references to section 10(b)(5)(B)(i) and (ii) of the Atomic Energy Act of 1946, section 510 of the Mutual Security Act of 1951, a majority of the members of the Atomic Energy Commission, and the Director of Mutual Security (which was changed to Director of the International Cooperation Administration on authority of section 8 of 1953 Reorg. Plan No. 7, 67 Stat. 641, and Executive Order 10610 of May 9, 1955) are omitted because of the disposition of the two sections as explained with reference to subsection (a).

In subsection (e), the words "There is established" are omitted as executed.

In subsection (g), the reference to statutes other than this section is omitted because nothing in those statutes affect the responsibility in question.

Standard changes are made to conform with the definitions applicable and the style of this title as outlined in the preface to the report.

REFERENCES IN TEXT

Section 1874(c) of title 42, referred to in subsec. (a)(2), which related to clearance of National Science Foundation personnel, was repealed by Pub. L. 96–516, §21(b)(1), Dec. 12, 1980, 94 Stat. 3010.

AMENDMENTS

1996—Subsec. (e)(1). Pub. L. 104–208 inserted ", including personnel management services performed at the request of individual agencies (which would otherwise be the responsibility of such agencies), or at the request of nonappropriated fund instrumentalities" before period at end of first sentence.

1995—Subsec. (e)(6). Pub. L. 104–66 struck out before period at end "at least once every three years".

1994—Subsec. (e)(6). Pub. L. 103–437 substituted "Committee on Governmental Affairs of the Senate and the Committee on Post Office and Civil Service of the House" for "Committees on Post Office and Civil Service of the Senate and House".

1984—Subsec. (e)(1). Pub. L. 98–224 struck out cl. (i) designation and struck out cl. (ii) which provided that participation fees imposed by the President's Commission on Executive Exchange for private sector participation in its Executive Exchange Program be collected and credited to the fund, and be available for the costs of education and related travel of exchanged executives, for printing without regard to section 501 of title 44, and, in such amounts as specified in appropriations Acts, for entertainment expenses. See section 4109(d) of this title.

1983—Subsec. (e)(1). Pub. L. 97–412 designated existing provisions as cl. (i) and added cl. (ii).

1979—Subsec. (a)(1). Pub. L. 96–60 struck out reference to section 1434 of title 22.

1978—Subsecs. (a) to (f). Pub. L. 95–454 substituted "Office of Personnel Management" for "Civil Service Commission" and "Office" for "Commission" wherever appearing.

1971—Subsec. (e). Pub. L. 91–648 struck out in par. (1) "of $4,000,000" after "revolving fund" and inserted in par. (2)(A) ", which appropriations are hereby authorized".

1969—Subsec. (e). Pub. L. 91–189, §1(a), increased the scope of reimbursable services for which the fund may be used, restricted reimbursement to services which were included in the budget estimates submitted to Congress for that fiscal year, inserted a list of components which comprise the fund, specifically listed those items that would be credited directly to the capital fund, required that a budget be prepared by the Commission, and directed the Comptroller General as a result of the activities financed to make recommendations to the committees on Post Office and Civil Service of the Senate and House of Representatives at least once every three years.

Subsec. (f). Pub. L. 91–189, §1(b), authorized an agency to use available appropriations to reimburse the Commission or the Federal Bureau of Investigation for the cost of training and functions performed.

EFFECTIVE DATE OF 1983 AMENDMENT

Section 1(b) of Pub. L. 97–412 provided that: "The authority granted in subsection (a) [amending this section] shall terminate on December 31, 1983."

EFFECTIVE DATE OF 1979 AMENDMENT

Amendment by Pub. L. 96–60 effective Oct. 1, 1979, see section 209 of Pub. L. 96–60, set out as a note under section 1471 of Title 22, Foreign Relations and Intercourse.

EFFECTIVE DATE OF 1978 AMENDMENT

Amendment by Pub. L. 95–454 effective 90 days after Oct. 13, 1978, see section 907 of Pub. L. 95–454, set out as a note under section 1101 of this title.

ABOLITION OF HOUSE COMMITTEE ON POST OFFICE AND CIVIL SERVICE

Committee on Post Office and Civil Service of House of Representatives abolished by House Resolution No. 6, One Hundred Fourth Congress, Jan. 4, 1995. References to Committee on Post Office and Civil Service treated as referring to Committee on Government Reform and Oversight, see section 1(b) of Pub. L. 104–14, set out as a note preceding section 21 of Title 2, The Congress. Committee on Government Reform and Oversight of House of Representatives changed to Committee on Government Reform of House of Representatives by House Resolution No. 5, One Hundred Sixth Congress, Jan. 6, 1999.

SECTION REFERRED TO IN OTHER SECTIONS

This section is referred to in section 1104 of this title.

§ 1305. Administrative law judges

For the purpose of sections 3105, 3344, 4301(2)(D), and 5372 of this title and the provisions of section 5335(a)(B) of this title that relate to administrative law judges, the Office of Personnel Management may, and for the purpose of section 7521 of this title, the Merit Systems Protection Board may investigate, prescribe regulations, appoint advisory committees as necessary, recommend legislation, subpena witnesses and records, and pay witness fees as established for the courts of the United States.

(Pub. L. 89–554, Sept. 6, 1966, 80 Stat. 402; Pub. L. 90–83, §1(3), Sept. 11, 1967, 81 Stat. 196; Pub. L. 95–251, §2(a)(1), (b)(1), Mar. 27, 1978, 92 Stat. 183; Pub. L. 95–454, title VIII, §801(a)(3)(B)(iii), title IX, §906(a)(12), Oct. 13, 1978, 92 Stat. 1221, 1225; Pub. L. 102–378, §2(4), Oct. 2, 1992, 106 Stat. 1346; Pub. L. 105–362, title XIII, §1302(a), Nov. 10, 1998, 112 Stat. 3293.)

HISTORICAL AND REVISION NOTES
1966 ACT

Derivation	U.S. Code	Revised Statutes and Statutes at Large
....	5 U.S.C. 1010 (5th sentence).	June 11, 1946, ch. 324, §11 (5th sentence), 60 Stat. 244.

Standard changes are made to conform with the definitions applicable and the style of this title as outlined in the preface to the report.

1967 ACT

This section amends 5 U.S.C. 1305 to correct a typographical error.

AMENDMENTS

1998—Pub. L. 105–362 struck out "require reports by agencies, issue reports, including an annual report to Congress," after "may investigate,".

1992—Pub. L. 102–378 substituted "sections 3105" for "section 3105".

1978—Pub. L. 95–454 substituted provisions respecting functions pursuant to specified sections of this title of the Office of Personnel Management and the Merit Systems Protection Board for provisions respecting the functions pursuant to specified sections of this title of the Civil Service Commission.

Pub. L. 95–251 substituted "Administrative law judges" for "Hearing examiners" in section catchline and "administrative law judges" for "hearing examiners" in text.

EFFECTIVE DATE OF 1978 AMENDMENT

Amendment by section 801(a)(3)(B)(iii) of Pub. L. 95–454 substituting "5372" for "5362" effective on first day of first applicable pay period beginning on or after the 90th day after Oct. 13, 1978, see section 801(a)(4) of Pub. L. 95–454, set out as an Effective Date note under section 5361 of this title.

Amendment by section 906(a)(12) of Pub. L. 95–454 respecting functions of the Office and the Board effective 90 days after Oct. 13, 1978, see section 907 of Pub. L. 95–454, set out as a note under section 1101 of this title.

EFFECTIVE DATE OF 1967 AMENDMENT

Amendment by Pub. L. 90–83 effective as of Sept. 6, 1966, for all purposes, see section 9(h) of Pub. L. 90–83, set out as a note under section 5102 of this title.

TERMINATION OF ADVISORY COMMITTEES

Advisory committees in existence on Jan. 5, 1973, excluding committees composed wholly of full-time officers or employees of the Federal Government, to terminate not later than the expiration of the 2-year period following Jan. 5, 1973, unless, in the case of a committee established by the President or an officer of the Federal Government, such committee is renewed by appropriate action prior to the expiration of such 2-year period, or in the case of a committee established by the Congress, its duration is otherwise provided for by law. See section 14 of Pub. L. 92–463, Oct. 6, 1972, 86 Stat. 776, set out in the Appendix to this title.

SECTION REFERRED TO IN OTHER SECTIONS

This section is referred to in section 559 of this title.

§ 1306. Oaths to witnesses

The Director of the Office of Personnel Management and authorized representatives of the Director may administer oaths to witnesses in matters pending before the Office.

(Pub. L. 89–554, Sept. 6, 1966, 80 Stat. 402; Pub. L. 95–454, title IX, § 906(a)(13), Oct. 13, 1978, 92 Stat. 1226.)

HISTORICAL AND REVISION NOTES

Derivation	U.S. Code	Revised Statutes and Statutes at Large
....	5 U.S.C. 634.	Aug. 23, 1912, ch. 350, § 1 (last par. under "Civil Service Commission"), 37 Stat. 372.
....	[Uncodified].	1949 Reorg. Plan No. 5, § 2(c), eff. Aug. 19, 1949, 63 Stat. 1069.

The section is rewritten to reflect expansion of authority of the Commission to include its Chairman under section 2(c) of 1949 Reorg. Plan No. 5.

Standard changes are made to conform with the definitions applicable and the style of this title as outlined in the preface to the report.

AMENDMENTS

1978—Pub. L. 95–454 substituted provisions respecting powers of the Director of the Office of Personnel Management in administering oaths in matters before the Office for provisions respecting powers of the Chairman of the Civil Service Commission and each Commissioner in administering oaths in matters before the Commission.

EFFECTIVE DATE OF 1978 AMENDMENT

Amendment by Pub. L. 95–454 effective 90 days after Oct. 13, 1978, see section 907 of Pub. L. 95–454, set out as a note under section 1101 of this title.

§ 1307. Minutes

The Civil Service Commission shall keep minutes of its proceedings.

(Pub. L. 89–554, Sept. 6, 1966, 80 Stat. 402.)

HISTORICAL AND REVISION NOTES

Derivation	U.S. Code	Revised Statutes and Statutes at Large
....	5 U.S.C. 633(3) (last 10 words).	Jan. 16, 1883, ch. 27, § 2(3) (last 10 words), 22 Stat. 404.

Standard changes are made to conform with the definitions applicable and the style of this title as outlined in the preface to the report.

TRANSFER OF FUNCTIONS

Functions vested by statute in United States Civil Service Commission transferred to Director of Office of Personnel Management (except as otherwise specified) by Reorg. Plan No. 2 of 1978, § 102, 43 F.R. 36037, 92 Stat. 3783, set out under section 1101 of this title, effective Jan. 1, 1979, as provided by section 1–102 of Ex. Ord. No. 12107, Dec. 28, 1978, 44 F.R. 1055, set out under section 1101 of this title.

[§ 1308. Repealed. Pub. L. 105–362, title XIII, § 1302(b)(1), Nov. 10, 1998, 112 Stat. 3293]

Section, Pub. L. 89–554, Sept. 6, 1966, 80 Stat. 402; Pub. L. 91–93, title I, § 104, Oct. 20, 1969, 83 Stat. 138; Pub. L. 93–156, Nov. 21, 1973, 87 Stat. 623; Pub. L. 95–454, title IX, § 906(a)(2), (3), Oct. 13, 1978, 92 Stat. 1224; Pub. L. 96–54, § 2(a)(3), Aug. 14, 1979, 93 Stat. 381; Pub. L. 96–470, title I, § 121, Oct. 19, 1980, 94 Stat. 2241, required annual reports on operation of subchapter III of chapter 83 of this title and chapters 87 and 89 of this title.

CHAPTER 15—POLITICAL ACTIVITY OF CERTAIN STATE AND LOCAL EMPLOYEES

AMENDMENTS

1974—Pub. L. 93–443, title IV, § 401(b)(2), Oct. 15, 1974, 88 Stat. 1290, substituted "candidacies" for "political activity" in item 1503.

CHAPTER REFERRED TO IN OTHER SECTIONS

This chapter is referred to in sections 1212, 1215, 1216, 1302, 4703 of this title; title 23 section 142; title 42 sections 2996e, 3056, 4728, 9851, 9918.

§ 1501. Definitions

For the purpose of this chapter—

(1) "State" means a State or territory or possession of the United States;

(2) "State or local agency" means the executive branch of a State, municipality, or other political subdivision of a State, or an agency or department thereof;

(3) "Federal agency" means an Executive agency or other agency of the United States, but does not include a member bank of the Federal Reserve System; and

(4) "State or local officer or employee" means an individual employed by a State or local agency whose principal employment is in

connection with an activity which is financed in whole or in part by loans or grants made by the United States or a Federal agency, but does not include—

(A) an individual who exercises no functions in connection with that activity; or

(B) an individual employed by an educational or research institution, establishment, agency, or system which is supported in whole or in part by a State or political subdivision thereof, or by a recognized religious, philanthropic, or cultural organization.

(Pub. L. 89–554, Sept. 6, 1966, 80 Stat. 403; Pub. L. 93–443, title IV, § 401(c), Oct. 15, 1974, 88 Stat. 1290.)

HISTORICAL AND REVISION NOTES

Derivation	U.S. Code	Revised Statutes and Statutes at Large
(1)	5 U.S.C. 118k–2.	July 19, 1940, ch. 640, § 4 "Sec. 19", 54 Stat. 772.
(2), (3)	5 U.S.C. 118k(f).	July 19, 1940, ch. 640, § 4 "Sec. 12(f)", 54 Stat. 770.
(4)	5 U.S.C. 118k(a) (1st 41 words), (e).	July 19, 1940, ch. 640, § 4 "Sec 12(a) (1st 41 words), (e)", 54 Stat. 767, 770.
	5 U.S.C. 118k–1 (as applicable to 5 U.S.C. 118k).	Oct. 24, 1942, ch. 620 "Sec. 21 (as applicable to § 12 of the Act of Aug. 2, 1939; added July 19, 1940, ch. 640, § 4, 54 Stat. 767)", 56 Stat. 986.
(5)	5 U.S.C. 118*l* (as applicable to 5 U.S.C. 118k).	July 19, 1940, ch. 640, § 4 "Sec. 15 (as applicable to § 12 of the Act of Aug. 2, 1939; added July 19, 1940, ch. 640, § 4, 54 Stat. 767)", 54 Stat. 771.

In paragraph (4)(B), the words "or by any Territory or Territorial possession of the United States" are omitted in view of the definition of "State" in paragraph (1).

In paragraph (5), the words "July 19, 1940" are substituted for "at the time this section takes effect".

Standard changes are made to conform with the definitions applicable and the style of this title as outlined in the preface to the report.

AMENDMENTS

1974—Par. (5). Pub. L. 93–443 struck out par. (5) which defined "an active part in political management or in political campaigns".

EFFECTIVE DATE OF 1974 AMENDMENT

Amendment by Pub. L. 93–443 effective Jan. 1, 1975, see section 410(a) of Pub. L. 93–443, set out as a note under section 431 of Title 2, The Congress.

§ 1502. Influencing elections; taking part in political campaigns; prohibitions; exceptions

(a) A State or local officer or employee may not—

(1) use his official authority or influence for the purpose of interfering with or affecting the result of an election or a nomination for office;

(2) directly or indirectly coerce, attempt to coerce, command, or advise a State or local officer or employee to pay, lend, or contribute anything of value to a party, committee, organization, agency, or person for political purposes; or

(3) be a candidate for elective office.

(b) A State or local officer or employee retains the right to vote as he chooses and to express his opinions on political subjects and candidates.

(c) Subsection (a)(3) of this section does not apply to—

(1) the Governor or Lieutenant Governor of a State or an individual authorized by law to act as Governor;

(2) the mayor of a city;

(3) a duly elected head of an executive department of a State or municipality who is not classified under a State or municipal merit or civil-service system; or

(4) an individual holding elective office.

(Pub. L. 89–554, Sept. 6, 1966, 80 Stat. 404; Pub. L. 93–443, title IV, § 401(a), Oct. 15, 1974, 88 Stat. 1290.)

HISTORICAL AND REVISION NOTES

Derivation	U.S. Code	Revised Statutes and Statutes at Large
....	5 U.S.C. 118k(a) (less 1st 41 words).	July 19, 1940, ch. 640, § 4 "Sec. 12(a) (less 1st 41 words)", 54 Stat. 767.

In subsection (a), the term "State or local officer or employee", defined in section 1501, is substituted for the first 41 words of former section 118k(a). The words "any part of his salary or compensation" are omitted as included in "anything of value".

Standard changes are made to conform with the definitions applicable and the style of this title as outlined in the preface to the report.

AMENDMENTS

1974—Subsec. (a)(3). Pub. L. 93–443 substituted "be a candidate for elective office" for "take an active part in political management or in political campaigns".

EFFECTIVE DATE OF 1974 AMENDMENT

Amendment by Pub. L. 93–443 effective Jan. 1, 1975, see section 410(a) of Pub. L. 93–443, set out as a note under section 431 of Title 2, The Congress.

SECTION REFERRED TO IN OTHER SECTIONS

This section is referred to in sections 1503, 1504, 1505, 1506 of this title; title 42 sections 9851, 9918.

§ 1503. Nonpartisan candidacies permitted

Section 1502(a)(3) of this title does not prohibit any State or local officer or employee from being a candidate in any election if none of the candidates is to be nominated or elected at such election as representing a party any of whose candidates for Presidential elector received votes in the last preceding election at which Presidential electors were selected.

(Pub. L. 89–554, Sept. 6, 1966, 80 Stat. 404; Pub. L. 93–443, title IV, § 401(b)(1), Oct. 15, 1974, 88 Stat. 1290.)

HISTORICAL AND REVISION NOTES

Derivation	U.S. Code	Revised Statutes and Statutes at Large
....	5 U.S.C. 118n (as applicable to 5 U.S.C. 118k(a)).	July 19, 1940, ch. 640, § 4 "Sec. 18 (as applicable to § 12 of the Act of Aug. 2, 1939; added July 19, 1940, ch. 640, § 4, 54 Stat. 767)", 54 Stat. 772.

Standard changes are made to conform with the definitions applicable and the style of this title as outlined in the preface to the report.

AMENDMENTS

1974—Pub. L. 93–443 substituted "candidacies" for "political activity" in section catchline and provision permitting nonpartisan candidacies for prior provision permitting political activity in connection with (1) an election and the preceding campaign if none of the candidates was to be nominated or elected at that election as representing a party any of whose candidates for presidential elector received votes in the last preceding election at which presidential electors were selected, or (2) a question which was not specifically identified with a National or State political party and deeming questions relating to constitutional amendments, referendums, approval of municipal ordinances, and others of a similar character as not specifically identified with a National or State political party.

EFFECTIVE DATE OF 1974 AMENDMENT

Amendment by Pub. L. 93–443 effective Jan. 1, 1975, see section 410(a) of Pub. L. 93–443, set out as a note under section 431 of Title 2, The Congress.

§ 1504. Investigations; notice of hearing

When a Federal agency charged with the duty of making a loan or grant of funds of the United States for use in an activity by a State or local officer or employee has reason to believe that the officer or employee has violated section 1502 of this title, it shall report the matter to the Special Counsel. On receipt of the report or on receipt of other information which seems to the Special Counsel to warrant an investigation, the Special Counsel shall investigate the report and such other information and present his findings and any charges based on such findings to the Merit Systems Protection Board, which shall—

(1) fix a time and place for a hearing; and

(2) send, by registered or certified mail, to the officer or employee charged with the violation and to the State or local agency employing him a notice setting forth a summary of the alleged violation and giving the time and place of the hearing.

The hearing may not be held earlier than 10 days after the mailing of the notice.

(Pub. L. 89–554, Sept. 6, 1966, 80 Stat. 405; Pub. L. 95–454, title IX, § 906(a)(7), Oct. 13, 1978, 92 Stat. 1225.)

HISTORICAL AND REVISION NOTES

Derivation	U.S. Code	Revised Statutes and Statutes at Large
....	5 U.S.C. 118k(b) (1st and 2d sentences, and 4th through 17th words of 3d sentence).	July 19, 1940, ch. 640 § 4 "Sec. 12(b) (1st and 2d sentences, and 4th through 17th words of 3d sentence)", 54 Stat. 768. June 11, 1960, Pub. L. 86–507, § 1(1), 74 Stat. 200.

Standard changes are made to conform with the definitions applicable and the style of this title as outlined in the preface to the report.

AMENDMENTS

1978—Pub. L. 95–454 substituted provisions respecting the functions of the Special Counsel and the Merit Systems Protection Board for provisions respecting the functions of the Civil Service Commission.

EFFECTIVE DATE OF 1978 AMENDMENT

Amendment by Pub. L. 95–454 effective 90 days after Oct. 13, 1978, see section 907 of Pub. L. 95–454, set out as a note under section 1101 of this title.

SECTION REFERRED TO IN OTHER SECTIONS

This section is referred to in sections 1505, 1508 of this title.

§ 1505. Hearings; adjudications; notice of determinations

Either the State or local officer or employee or the State or local agency employing him, or both, are entitled to appear with counsel at the hearing under section 1504 of this title, and be heard. After this hearing, the Merit Systems Protection Board shall—

(1) determine whether a violation of section 1502 of this title has occurred;

(2) determine whether the violation warrants the removal of the officer or employee from his office or employment; and

(3) notify the officer or employee and the agency of the determination by registered or certified mail.

(Pub. L. 89–554, Sept. 6, 1966, 80 Stat. 405; Pub. L. 95–454, title IX, § 906(a)(6), Oct. 13, 1978, 92 Stat. 1225.)

HISTORICAL AND REVISION NOTES

Derivation	U.S. Code	Revised Statutes and Statutes at Large
....	5 U.S.C. 118k(b) (3d sentence, less 4th, through 17th words, and 4th sentence).	July 19, 1940, ch. 640, § 4 "Sec. 12(b) (3d sentence, less 4th through 17th words, and 4th sentence)", 54 Stat. 768. June 11, 1960, Pub. L. 86–507, § 1(1), 74 Stat. 200.

Standard changes are made to conform with the definitions applicable and the style of this title as outlined in the preface to the report.

AMENDMENTS

1978—Pub. L. 95–454 substituted "Merit Systems Protection Board" for "Civil Service Commission".

EFFECTIVE DATE OF 1978 AMENDMENT

Amendment by Pub. L. 95–454 effective 90 days after Oct. 13, 1978, see section 907 of Pub. L. 95–454, set out as a note under section 1101 of this title.

SECTION REFERRED TO IN OTHER SECTIONS

This section is referred to in section 1508 of this title.

§ 1506. Orders; withholding loans or grants; limitations

(a) When the Merit Systems Protection Board finds—

(1) that a State or local officer or employee has not been removed from his office or employment within 30 days after notice of a determination by the Board that he has violated section 1502 of this title and that the violation warrants removal; or

(2) that the State or local officer or employee has been removed and has been appointed within 18 months after his removal to an office or employment in the same State in a State or local agency which does not receive loans or grants from a Federal agency;

the Board shall make and certify to the appropriate Federal agency an order requiring that agency to withhold from its loans or grants to the State or local agency to which notice was given an amount equal to 2 years' pay at the rate the officer or employee was receiving at the time of the violation. When the State or local agency to which appointment within 18 months after removal has been made is one that receives loans or grants from a Federal agency, the Board order shall direct that the withholding be made from that State or local agency.

(b) Notice of the order shall be sent by registered or certified mail to the State or local agency from which the amount is ordered to be withheld. After the order becomes final, the Federal agency to which the order is certified shall withhold the amount in accordance with the terms of the order. Except as provided by section 1508 of this title, a determination of order of the Board becomes final at the end of 30 days after mailing the notice of the determination or order.

(c) The Board may not require an amount to be withheld from a loan or grant pledged by a State or local agency as security for its bonds or notes if the withholding of that amount would jeopardize the payment of the principal or interest on the bonds or notes.

(Pub. L. 89–554, Sept. 6, 1966, 80 Stat. 405; Pub. L. 95–454, title IX, § 906(a)(6), Oct. 13, 1978, 92 Stat. 1225.)

HISTORICAL AND REVISION NOTES

Derivation	U.S. Code	Revised Statutes and Statutes at Large
....	5 U.S.C. 118k(b) (less 1st 4 sentences).	July 19, 1940, ch. 640, § 4 "Sec. 12(b) (less 1st 4 sentences)", 54 Stat. 768. June 11, 1960, Pub. L. 86–507, § 1(1), 74 Stat. 200.

Standard changes are made to conform with the definitions applicable and the style of this title as outlined in the preface to the report.

AMENDMENTS

1978—Subsec. (a). Pub. L. 95–454 substituted "Merit Systems Protection Board" for "Civil Service Commission" and "Board" for "Commission", respectively, wherever appearing.

Subsecs. (b), (c). Pub. L. 95–454 substituted "Board" for "Commission".

EFFECTIVE DATE OF 1978 AMENDMENT

Amendment by Pub. L. 95–454 effective 90 days after Oct. 13, 1978, see section 907 of Pub. L. 95–454, set out as a note under section 1101 of this title.

SECTION REFERRED TO IN OTHER SECTIONS

This section is referred to in section 1508 of this title.

§ 1507. Subpenas and depositions

(a) The Merit Systems Protection Board may require by subpena the attendance and testimony of witnesses and the production of documentary evidence relating to any matter before it as a result of this chapter. Any member of the Board may sign subpenas, and members of the Board and its examiners when authorized by the Board may administer oaths, examine witnesses, and receive evidence. The attendance of witnesses and the production of documentary evidence may be required from any place in the United States at the designated place of hearing. In case of disobedience to a subpena, the Board may invoke the aid of a court of the United States in requiring the attendance and testimony of witnesses and the production of documentary evidence. In case of contumacy or refusal to obey a subpena issued to a person, the United States District Court within whose jurisdiction the inquiry is carried on may issue an order requiring him to appear before the Board, or to produce documentary evidence if so ordered, or to give evidence concerning the matter in question; and any failure to obey the order of the court may be punished by the court as a contempt thereof.

(b) The Board may order testimony to be taken by deposition at any stage of a proceeding or investigation before it as a result of this chapter. Depositions may be taken before an individual designated by the Board and having the power to administer oaths. Testimony shall be reduced to writing by the individual taking the deposition, or under his direction, and shall be subscribed by the deponent. Any person may be compelled to appear and depose and to produce documentary evidence before the Board as provided by this section.

(c) A person may not be excused from attending and testifying or from producing documentary evidence or in obedience to a subpena on the ground that the testimony or evidence, documentary or otherwise required of him may tend to incriminate him or subject him to a penalty or forfeiture for or on account of any transaction, matter, or thing concerning which he is compelled to testify, or produce evidence, documentary or otherwise, before the Board in obedience to a subpena issued by it. A person so testifying is not exempt from prosecution and punishment for perjury committed in so testifying.

(Pub. L. 89–554, Sept. 6, 1966, 80 Stat. 406; Pub. L. 95–454, title IX, § 906(a)(6), Oct. 13, 1978, 92 Stat. 1225.)

HISTORICAL AND REVISION NOTES

Derivation	U.S. Code	Revised Statutes and Statutes at Large
....	5 U.S.C. 118k(d) (less 1st sentence).	July 19, 1940, ch. 640, § 4 "Sec. 12(d) (less 1st sentence)", 54 Stat. 769.

In subsection (a), the word "affirmation" is omitted as included in "oath" on authority of section 1 of title 1, United States Code. The title of the court is changed to conform to title 28.

In subsection (c), the prohibition is restated in positive form.

Standard changes are made to conform with the definitions applicable and the style of this title as outlined in the preface to the report.

AMENDMENTS

1978—Subsec. (a). Pub. L. 95–454 substituted "Merit Systems Protection Board" and "Board" for "Civil Service Commission" and "Commission", respectively, wherever appearing.

Subsecs. (b), (c). Pub. L. 95–454 substituted "Board" for "Commission" wherever appearing.

EFFECTIVE DATE OF 1978 AMENDMENT

Amendment by Pub. L. 95–454 effective 90 days after Oct. 13, 1978, see section 907 of Pub. L. 95–454, set out as a note under section 1101 of this title.

§ 1508. Judicial review

A party aggrieved by a determination or order of the Merit Systems Protection Board under section 1504, 1505, or 1506 of this title may, within 30 days after the mailing of notice of the determination or order, institute proceedings for review thereof by filing a petition in the United States District Court for the district in which the State or local officer or employee resides. The institution of the proceedings does not operate as a stay of the determination or order unless—

(1) the court specifically orders a stay; and

(2) the officer or employee is suspended from his office or employment while the proceedings are pending.

A copy of the petition shall immediately be served on the Board, and thereupon the Board shall certify and file in the court a transcript of the record on which the determination or order was made. The court shall review the entire record including questions of fact and questions of law. If application is made to the court for leave to adduce additional evidence, and it is shown to the satisfaction of the court that the additional evidence may materially affect the result of the proceedings and that there were reasonable grounds for failure to adduce this evidence in the hearing before the Board, the court may direct that the additional evidence be taken before the Board in the manner and on the terms and conditions fixed by the court. The Board may modify its findings of fact or its determination or order in view of the additional evidence and shall file with the court the modified findings, determination, or order; or the modified findings of fact, if supported by substantial evidence, are conclusive. The court shall affirm the determination or order, or the modified determination or order, if the court determines that it is in accordance with law. If the court determines that the determination or order, or the modified determination or order, is not in accordance with law, the court shall remand the proceeding to the Board with directions either to make a determination or order determined by the court to be lawful or to take such further proceedings as, in the opinion of the court, the law requires. The judgment and decree of the court are final, subject to review by the appropriate United States Court of Appeals as in other cases, and the judgment and decree of the court of appeals are final, subject to review by the Supreme Court of the United States on certiorari or certification as provided by section 1254 of title 28. If a provision of this section is held to be invalid as applied to a party by a determination or order of the Board, the determination or order becomes final and effective as to that party as if the provision had not been enacted.

(Pub. L. 89–554, Sept. 6, 1966, 80 Stat. 406; Pub. L. 95–454, title IX, § 906(a)(6), Oct. 13, 1978, 92 Stat. 1225.)

HISTORICAL AND REVISION NOTES

Derivation	U.S. Code	Revised Statutes and Statutes at Large
....	5 U.S.C. 118k(c).	July 19, 1940, ch. 640, § 4 "Sec. 12(c)", 54 Stat. 768.

Sections 346 and 347 of title 28 referred to in former section 118k(c) were repealed by the Act of June 25, 1948, ch. 646, § 39, 62 Stat. 862, and are now covered by section 1254 of title 28. The titles of the courts are changed to conform to title 28.

In the reference to filing a written petition, "written" is omitted as unnecessary.

Standard changes are made to conform with the definitions applicable and the style of this title as outlined in the preface to the report.

AMENDMENTS

1978—Pub. L. 95–454 substituted "Merit Systems Protection Board" and "Board" for "Civil Service Commission" and "Commission", respectively, wherever appearing.

EFFECTIVE DATE OF 1978 AMENDMENT

Amendment by Pub. L. 95–454 effective 90 days after Oct. 13, 1978, see section 907 of Pub. L. 95–454, set out as a note under section 1101 of this title.

SECTION REFERRED TO IN OTHER SECTIONS

This section is referred to in section 1506 of this title.

PART III—EMPLOYEES

Subpart A—General Provisions

AMENDMENTS

2000—Pub. L. 106–398, § 1 [[div. A], title X, § 1076(f)(1)(B)], Oct. 30, 2000, 114 Stat. 1654, 1654A–282, substituted "and Other Purposes" for "Purposes" in item for chapter 91.

Pub. L. 106–265, title I, § 1002(b), Sept. 19, 2000, 114 Stat. 769, added item for chapter 90.

1998—Pub. L. 105–206, title I, § 1201(b), July 22, 1998, 112 Stat. 719, added items for subpart I and chapter 95.

1993—Pub. L. 103–89, § 3(a)(2), Sept. 30, 1993, 107 Stat. 981, struck out item for chapter 54 "Performance Management and Recognition System".

1986—Pub. L. 99–335, title I, § 101(b), June 6, 1986, 100 Stat. 588, added item for chapter 84.

1985—Pub. L. 99–169, title VIII, § 801(b), Dec. 4, 1985, 99 Stat. 1010, added items for subpart H and chapter 91.

1984—Pub. L. 98–615, title II, § 201(b), Nov. 8, 1984, 98 Stat. 3214, substituted "Performance Management and Recognition System" for "Merit Pay and Cash Awards" in item for chapter 54.

1978—Pub. L. 95–454, title I, § 101(b)(1), title II, § 203(b), title V, § 503(i), title VI, § 601(b), title VII, § 703(b), title IX, § 906(c)(5), Oct. 13, 1978, 92 Stat. 1118, 1134, 1184, 1188, 1217, 1227, added items for chapters 23, 34, 47, 54, and 72, substituted in item for chapter 43 "Appraisal" for "Rating" and in item for chapter 71 "Labor-Management Relations" for "Policies", and inserted in heading of subpart F "Labor-Management and" before "Employee".

PART REFERRED TO IN OTHER SECTIONS

This part is referred to in title 28 section 996; title 42 section 3056b; title 44 section 2105; title 47 sections 154, 332.

Subpart A—General Provisions

CHAPTER 21—DEFINITIONS

AMENDMENTS

1980—Pub. L. 96–347, § 1(d), Sept. 12, 1980, 94 Stat. 1150, substituted "controller; Secretary" for "controller" in item 2109.

---

[1] So in original. Probably should be capitalized.

1978—Pub. L. 95–454, title IV, § 401(e), Oct. 13, 1978, 92 Stat. 1154, added item 2101a.

1972—Pub. L. 92–297, § 1(b), May 16, 1972, 86 Stat. 141, added item 2109.

CHAPTER REFERRED TO IN OTHER SECTIONS

This chapter is referred to in title 22 section 3664.

§ 2101. Civil service; armed forces; uniformed services

For the purpose of this title—

(1) the "civil service" consists of all appointive positions in the executive, judicial, and legislative branches of the Government of the United States, except positions in the uniformed services;

(2) "armed forces" means the Army, Navy, Air Force, Marine Corps, and Coast Guard; and

(3) "uniformed services" means the armed forces, the commissioned corps of the Public Health Service, and the commissioned corps of the National Oceanic and Atmospheric Administration.

(Pub. L. 89–554, Sept. 6, 1966, 80 Stat. 408; Pub. L. 90–83, § 1(4), Sept. 11, 1967, 81 Stat. 196; Pub. L. 96–54, § 2(a)(4), Aug. 14, 1979, 93 Stat. 381.)

HISTORICAL AND REVISION NOTES

1966 ACT

The section is supplied to establish basis of reference to employees in this title.

1967 ACT

This section amends various sections [§§ 2101, 4102, 4109, 5541, 8101] of title 5, United States Code, to reflect 1965 Reorganization Plan No. 2 (79 Stat. 1318), effective July 13, 1965, which consolidated the Coast and Geodetic Survey and the Weather Bureau to form a new agency in the Department of Commerce to be known as the Environmental Science Services Administration.

AMENDMENTS

1979—Par. (3). Pub. L. 96–54 substituted "National Oceanic and Atmospheric" for "Environmental Science Services".

EFFECTIVE DATE OF 1979 AMENDMENT

Amendment by Pub. L. 96–54 effective July 12, 1979, see section 2(b) of Pub. L. 96–54, set out as a note under section 305 of this title.

SHORT TITLE OF 1998 AMENDMENT

Pub. L. 105–339, § 1, Oct. 31, 1998, 112 Stat. 3182, provided that: "This Act [enacting sections 3330a to 3330c of this title, section 1316a of Title 2, The Congress, section 115 of Title 3, The President, and section 1354 of Title 31, Money and Finance, amending sections 2108, 2302, and 3304 of this title and section 4212 of Title 38, Veterans' Benefits, repealing section 1599c of Title 10, Armed Forces, enacting provisions set out as notes under section 2302 of this title and section 601 of Title 28, Judiciary and Judicial Procedure, and amending provisions set out as a note under section 106 of Title 49, Transportation] may be cited as the 'Veterans Employment Opportunities Act of 1998'."

SHORT TITLE OF 1994 AMENDMENT

Pub. L. 103–226, § 1, Mar. 30, 1994, 108 Stat. 111, provided that: "This Act [amending sections 3381, 4101, 4103, 4105, 4107, 4108, 4113, 4118, 5597, 8351, 8433 to 8435, 8437, 8440a to 8440d of this title and section 1206 of Title 45, Railroads, repealing sections 4106 and 4114 of this title, enacting provisions set out as notes under sections 3101, 3381, 5597, 8331, and 8351 of this title, and amending provisions set out as a note under section 403-4 of Title 50, War and National Defense] may be cited as the 'Federal Workforce Restructuring Act of 1994'."

SHORT TITLE OF 1990 AMENDMENT

Pub. L. 101-508, title VII, § 7202(a), Nov. 5, 1990, 104 Stat. 1388-335, provided that: "This section [amending sections 2105, 3502, 5334, 5335, 5365, 5551, 6308, 6312, 8331, 8347, 8401, 8461, and 8901 of this title and enacting provisions set out as notes under section 2105 of this title] may be cited as the 'Portability of Benefits for Nonappropriated Fund Employees Act of 1990'."

COORDINATION OF TITLE VII OF PUB. L. 101-508 WITH SECTION 909 OF TITLE 2

Pub. L. 101-508, title VII, § 7301, Nov. 5, 1990, 104 Stat. 1388-341, provided that: "For purposes of section 202 of the Balanced Budget and Emergency Deficit Reaffirmation Act of 1987 [probably means section 202 of the Balanced Budget and Emergency Deficit Control Reaffirmation Act of 1987, Pub. L. 100-119, which was formerly classified to section 909 of Title 2, The Congress], this title and the amendments made by this title [amending sections 552a, 2105, 3502, 5334, 5335, 5365, 5551, 6308, 6312, 8331, 8334, 8339, 8342, 8343a, 8347, 8348, 8401, 8420a, 8461, 8901, 8902, 8904, 8906, 8909, and 8910 of this title, enacting provisions set out as notes under this section and sections 552a, 2105, 8334, 8343a, 8348, 8902, 8904, and 8906 of this title, amending provisions set out as notes under sections 8343a and 8906 of this title, and repealing provisions set out as notes under sections 8343a and 8348 of this title] shall be considered an exception under subsection (b) of such section."

SECTION REFERRED TO IN OTHER SECTIONS

This section is referred to in title 18 section 207; title 22 section 3641; title 41 section 423.

§ 2101a. The Senior Executive Service

The "Senior Executive Service" consists of Senior Executive Service positions (as defined in section 3132(a)(2) of this title).

(Added Pub. L. 95-454, title IV, § 401(a), Oct. 13, 1978, 92 Stat. 1154.)

EFFECTIVE DATE

Section effective 9 months after Oct. 13, 1978, and congressional review of provisions of sections 401 through 412 of Pub. L. 95-454, see section 415 of Pub. L. 95-454, set out as a note under section 3131 of this title.

§ 2102. The competitive service

(a) The "competitive service" consists of—

(1) all civil service positions in the executive branch, except—

(A) positions which are specifically excepted from the competitive service by or under statute;

(B) positions to which appointments are made by nomination for confirmation by the Senate, unless the Senate otherwise directs; and

(C) positions in the Senior Executive Service;

(2) civil service positions not in the executive branch which are specifically included in the competitive service by statute; and

(3) positions in the government of the District of Columbia which are specifically included in the competitive service by statute.

(b) Notwithstanding subsection (a)(1)(B) of this section, the "competitive service" includes positions to which appointments are made by nomination for confirmation by the Senate when specifically included therein by statute.

(c) As used in other Acts of Congress, "classified civil service" or "classified service" means the "competitive service".

(Pub. L. 89-554, Sept. 6, 1966, 80 Stat. 408; Pub. L. 95-454, title IV, § 401(b), Oct. 13, 1978, 92 Stat. 1154.)

HISTORICAL AND REVISION NOTES

Derivation	U.S. Code	Revised Statutes and Statutes at Large
(a)	5 U.S.C. 638 (less applicability to appointment and promotion).	Jan. 16, 1883, ch. 27, § 7 (less applicability to appointment and promotion), 22 Stat. 406.

Subsection (a) is restated in the form of a definition.

Subsection (a)(1) is based on former section 638, which placed positions in the executive branch of the Government generally in the competitive service by the requirement that employment be predicated on passing an examination or being exempted from examination, and section 1 of the Act of Nov. 26, 1940, ch. 919, title I, 54 Stat. 1211 (see table III), which authorized the President, subject to certain exceptions, to place in the classified civil service positions in the Executive departments, independent establishments, and other agencies of the Government. In that Act the word "executive" has been construed to modify "departments", "independent establishments"; and "other agency". This construction is supported by the language of the Act of Jan. 16, 1883, and is embodied in Civil Service Rule I. Acting under this statute, the President has placed all but a comparatively few of the positions covered by the Act of Nov. 26, 1940, in the competitive service. The remainder are covered by the exceptions contained in the Civil Service Rules and Regulations. The authority of the President conferred by the Act of Nov. 26, 1940, has been superseded in part by exceptions created by statutes enacted after that date. The effect of these exceptions and the power conferred on the President by former section 633(2)8 (last sentence) to make exceptions to the Civil Service Rules are preserved by the words "positions which are specifically excepted from the competitive service by or under statute".

In subsection (a)(1)(B), the words "or to pass an examination" are omitted as covered by the exclusion from the "competitive service".

Subsection (a)(2) preserves the exception stated in former section 638 modified to recognize the several statutory exceptions to this exception that have been enacted. The language of former section 638 relative to examination is codified in sections 3304(b) and 3361. The reference to veterans' preference is omitted because the statute referred to, R.S. § 1754, was superseded by sections 3 and 21 of the Act of June 18, 1929, ch. 28, 46 Stat. 21. Section 3 of the Act of June 18, 1929, was superseded by the Act of June 27, 1944, ch. 287, 58 Stat. 387, as amended, which is carried into this title. Rights preserved by section 18 of the Act of June 27, 1944, are further preserved by technical section 8. The exception for laborers and workmen was superseded by the Act of Nov. 26, 1940.

Subsection (b) is added because of the provisions in section 3311 of title 39.

Subsection (c) is supplied for conformity inasmuch as the terms are coextensive by definition.

Standard changes are made to conform with the definitions applicable and the style of this title as outlined in the preface to the report.

AMENDMENTS

1978—Subsec. (a)(1)(C). Pub. L. 95-454 added cl. (C).

EFFECTIVE DATE OF 1978 AMENDMENT

Amendment by Pub. L. 95-454 effective 9 months after Oct. 13, 1978, and congressional review of provisions of sections 401 through 412 of Pub. L. 95–454, see section 415 of Pub. L. 95–454, set out as an Effective Date note under section 3131 of this title.

SECTION REFERRED TO IN OTHER SECTIONS

This section is referred to in sections 3132, 3304 of this title; title 10 sections 1744, 1792; title 16 section 3198; title 22 section 3641; title 28 section 569; title 36 section 2102; title 42 section 2000e; title 49 section 44506.

§ 2103. The excepted service

(a) For the purpose of this title, the "excepted service" consists of those civil service positions which are not in the competitive service or the Senior Executive Service.

(b) As used in other Acts of Congress, "unclassified civil service" or "unclassified service" means the "excepted service".

(Pub. L. 89–554, Sept. 6, 1966, 80 Stat. 408; Pub. L. 95–454, title IV, § 401(c), Oct. 13, 1978, 92 Stat. 1154.)

HISTORICAL AND REVISION NOTES

The section is supplied for convenience. The "excepted service" has come to mean all employees not in the competitive service, for whatever reason.

AMENDMENTS

1978—Subsec. (a). Pub. L. 95–454 inserted reference to Senior Executive Service.

EFFECTIVE DATE OF 1978 AMENDMENT

Amendment by Pub. L. 95–454 effective 9 months after Oct. 13, 1978, and congressional review of provisions of sections 401 through 412 of Pub. L. 95–454, see section 415 of Pub. L. 95–454, set out as an Effective Date note under section 3131 of this title.

SECTION REFERRED TO IN OTHER SECTIONS

This section is referred to in section 3304 of this title; title 10 sections 1614, 1744, 2164; title 49 section 44506.

§ 2104. Officer

(a) For the purpose of this title, "officer", except as otherwise provided by this section or when specifically modified, means a justice or judge of the United States and an individual who is—

(1) required by law to be appointed in the civil service by one of the following acting in an official capacity—

(A) the President;

(B) a court of the United States;

(C) the head of an Executive agency; or

(D) the Secretary of a military department;

(2) engaged in the performance of a Federal function under authority of law or an Executive act; and

(3) subject to the supervision of an authority named by paragraph (1) of this section, or the Judicial Conference of the United States, while engaged in the performance of the duties of his office.

(b) Except as otherwise provided by law, an officer of the United States Postal Service or of the Postal Rate Commission is deemed not an officer for purposes of this title.

(Pub. L. 89–554, Sept. 6, 1966, 80 Stat. 408; Pub. L. 91–375, § 6(c)(3), Aug. 12, 1970, 84 Stat. 775.)

HISTORICAL AND REVISION NOTES

The section is supplied for convenience.

AMENDMENTS

1970—Subsec. (a). Pub. L. 91–375, § 6(c)(3)(A), (B), designated existing provisions as subsec. (a) and inserted in introductory text "as otherwise provided by this section or" after "except".

Subsec. (b). Pub. L. 91–375, § 6(c)(3)(C), added subsec. (b).

EFFECTIVE DATE OF 1970 AMENDMENT

Amendment by Pub. L. 91–375 effective within 1 year after Aug. 12, 1970, on date established therefor by Board of Governors of United States Postal Service and published by it in Federal Register, see section 15(a) of Pub. L. 91–375, set out as an Effective Date note preceding section 101 of Title 39, Postal Service.

SECTION REFERRED TO IN OTHER SECTIONS

This section is referred to in section 902 of this title; title 18 section 202; title 41 section 423; title 42 section 14614; title 50 section 426.

§ 2105. Employee

(a) For the purpose of this title, "employee", except as otherwise provided by this section or when specifically modified, means an officer and an individual who is—

(1) appointed in the civil service by one of the following acting in an official capacity—

(A) the President;

(B) a Member or Members of Congress, or the Congress;

(C) a member of a uniformed service;

(D) an individual who is an employee under this section;

(E) the head of a Government controlled corporation; or

(F) an adjutant general designated by the Secretary concerned under section 709(c) of title 32;

(2) engaged in the performance of a Federal function under authority of law or an Executive act; and

(3) subject to the supervision of an individual named by paragraph (1) of this subsection while engaged in the performance of the duties of his position.

(b) An individual who is employed at the United States Naval Academy in the midshipmen's laundry, the midshipmen's tailor shop, the midshipmen's cobbler and barber shops, and the midshipmen's store, except an individual employed by the Academy dairy (if any), and whose employment in such a position began before October 1, 1996, and has been uninterrupted in such a position since that date is deemed an employee.

(c) An employee paid from nonappropriated funds of the Army and Air Force Exchange Service, Army and Air Force Motion Picture Service, Navy Ship's Stores Ashore, Navy exchanges, Marine Corps exchanges, Coast Guard exchanges, and other instrumentalities of the United States under the jurisdiction of the armed forces conducted for the comfort, pleasure, contentment, and mental and physical improvement of personnel of the armed forces is deemed not an employee for the purpose of—

(1) laws administered by the Office of Personnel Management, except—

(A) section 7204;

(B) as otherwise specifically provided in this title;

(C) the Fair Labor Standards Act of 1938;

(D) for the purpose of entering into an interchange agreement to provide for the noncompetitive movement of employees between such instrumentalities and the competitive service; or

(E) subchapter V of chapter 63, which shall be applied so as to construe references to benefit programs to refer to applicable programs for employees paid from nonappropriated funds; or

(2) subchapter I of chapter 81, chapter 84 (except to the extent specifically provided therein), and section 7902 of this title.

This subsection does not affect the status of these nonappropriated fund activities as Federal instrumentalities.

(d) A Reserve of the armed forces who is not on active duty or who is on active duty for training is deemed not an employee or an individual holding an office of trust or profit or discharging an official function under or in connection with the United States because of his appointment, oath, or status, or any duties or functions performed or pay or allowances received in that capacity.

(e) Except as otherwise provided by law, an employee of the United States Postal Service or of the Postal Rate Commission is deemed not an employee for purposes of this title.

(f) For purposes of sections 1212, 1213, 1214, 1215, 1216, 1221, 1222, 2302, and 7701, employees appointed under chapter 73 or 74 of title 38 shall be employees.

(Pub. L. 89–554, Sept. 6, 1966, 80 Stat. 409; Pub. L. 90–486, § 4, Aug. 13, 1968, 82 Stat. 757; Pub. L. 91–375, § 6(c)(4), Aug. 12, 1970, 84 Stat. 775; Pub. L. 92–392, § 2, Aug. 19, 1972, 86 Stat. 573; Pub. L. 95–454, title VII, § 703(c)(2), title IX, § 906(a)(2), Oct. 13, 1978, 92 Stat. 1217, 1224; Pub. L. 96–54, § 2(a)(5), (6), Aug. 14, 1979, 93 Stat. 381; Pub. L. 99–335, title II, § 207(a), June 6, 1986, 100 Stat. 594; Pub. L. 99–638, § 2(b)(1), Nov. 10, 1986, 100 Stat. 3536; Pub. L. 101–508, title VII, § 7202(b), Nov. 5, 1990, 104 Stat. 1388–335; Pub. L. 103–3, title II, § 201(b), Feb. 5, 1993, 107 Stat. 23; Pub. L. 103–424, § 7, Oct. 29, 1994, 108 Stat. 4364; Pub. L. 104–201, div. A, title III, § 370(b), Sept. 23, 1996, 110 Stat. 2499; Pub. L. 105–85, div. B, title XXVIII, § 2871(c)(2), Nov. 18, 1997, 111 Stat. 2015.)

HISTORICAL AND REVISION NOTES

Derivation	U.S. Code	Revised Statutes and Statutes at Large
(b)	[Uncodified].	Aug. 5, 1939, ch. 448, § 2, 53 Stat. 1210.
	[Uncodified].	Dec. 3, 1945, ch. 510, § 2, 59 Stat. 590.
	[Uncodified].	Dec. 28, 1945, ch. 593, § 2, 59 Stat. 660.
	[Uncodified].	Dec. 28, 1945, ch. 594, § 2, 59 Stat. 660.
	[Uncodified].	July 26, .1946, ch. 675, § 2 (last proviso), 60 Stat. 704.
(c)	5 U.S.C. 150k.	June 19, 1952, ch. 444, § 1, 66 Stat. 138.
(d)	5 U.S.C. 30r(d).	Aug. 10, 1956, ch. 1041, § 29(d), 70A Stat. 632.

Subsection (a) is supplied to avoid the necessity of defining "employee" each time it appears in this title. The subsection is based on a definition worked out independently by the Civil Service Commission and the Department of Labor and in use by both for more than a decade.

In subsection (b), the provisions of the source statutes which relate to credit for prior service and diminution of pay are executed, or, insofar as to be executed preserved by technical section 8.

In subsection (d), the words "officer or" are omitted as included within "employee".

Standard changes are made to conform with the definitions applicable and the style of this title as outlined in the preface to the report.

REFERENCES IN TEXT

The Fair Labor Standards Act of 1938, referred to in subsec. (c)(1)(C), is act June 25, 1938, ch. 676, 52 Stat. 1060, as amended, which is classified generally to chapter 8 (§ 201 et seq.) of Title 29, Labor. For complete classification of this Act to the Code, see section 201 of Title 29 and Tables.

AMENDMENTS

1997—Subsec. (b). Pub. L. 105–85 inserted "(if any)" after "Academy dairy".

1996—Subsec. (b). Pub. L. 104–201 inserted "who is" after "An individual" and "and whose employment in such a position began before October 1, 1996, and has been uninterrupted in such a position since that date" after "Academy dairy,".

1994—Subsec. (f). Pub. L. 103–424 added subsec. (f).

1993—Subsec. (c)(1)(E). Pub. L. 103–3 added subpar. (E).

1990—Subsec. (c)(1). Pub. L. 101–508, § 7202(b)(1), amended par. (1) generally. Prior to amendment, par. (1) read as follows: "laws (other than subchapter IV of chapter 53 of this title, subchapter III of chapter 83 of this title to the extent provided in section 8332(b)(16) of this title, and sections 5550 and 7204 of this title) administered by the Office of Personnel Management; or".

Subsec. (c)(2). Pub. L. 101–508, § 7202(b)(2), inserted "(except to the extent specifically provided therein)" after "chapter 84".

1986—Subsec. (c)(1). Pub. L. 99–638 inserted "of this title, subchapter III of chapter 83 of this title to the extent provided in section 8332(b)(16) of this title,".

Subsec. (c)(2). Pub. L. 99–335 substituted "chapter 81, chapter 84," for "chapter 81".

1979—Subsec. (a)(1)(F). Pub. L. 96–54, § 2(a)(5), substituted "an adjutant" for "the adjutants" and struck out ", United States Code" after "32".

Subsec. (c)(1). Pub. L. 96–54, § 2(a)(6), amended subsec. (c)(1) in same manner as amendment by section 703(c)(2) of Pub. L. 95–454. See 1978 Amendment note set out below.

1978—Subsec. (c)(1). Pub. L. 95–454 substituted "7204" for "7154", and "Office of Personnel Management" for "Civil Service Commission". Amendments by section 703(c)(1) and (c)(2) of Pub. L. 95–454 appear to have been inadvertently reversed. Subsec. (c)(1) purported to amend subsec. (c)(1) of this section, and subsec. (c)(2) purported to amend section 3302(2) of this title. However, the amendments specified by Pub. L. 95–454, § 703(c)(1) and (2), were impossible to execute literally. Thus, the amendment by Pub. L. 95–454, § 703(c)(2) was executed to this section, and the amendment by section 703(c)(1) was executed to section 3302(2) of this title as the probable intent of Congress.

1972—Subsec. (c)(1). Pub. L. 92–392 substituted "laws (other than subchapter IV of chapter 53 and sections 5550 and 7154 of this title)" for "laws".

1970—Subsec. (e). Pub. L. 91–375 added subsec. (e).

1968—Subsec. (a)(1)(F). Pub. L. 90–486 added subpar. (F).

EFFECTIVE DATE OF 1996 AMENDMENT

Section 370(e) of Pub. L. 104–201 provided that: "The amendments made by this section [amending this section and section 6971 of Title 10, Armed Forces, and repealing section 6970 of Title 10] shall take effect on October 1, 1996."

EFFECTIVE DATE OF 1993 AMENDMENT

Amendment by Pub. L. 103–3 effective 6 months after Feb. 5, 1993, see section 405(b)(1) of Pub. L. 103–3, set out as an Effective Date note under section 2601 of Title 29, Labor.

EFFECTIVE DATE OF 1990 AMENDMENT

Section 7202(m) of Pub. L. 101–508 provided that:

"(1) The amendments made by this section [amending this section and sections 3502, 5334, 5335, 5365, 5551, 6308, 6312, 8331, 8347, 8401, 8461, and 8901 of this title] shall apply with respect to any individual who, on or after January 1, 1987—

"(A) moves without a break in service of more than 3 days from employment in a nonappropriated fund instrumentality of the Department of Defense or the Coast Guard that is described in section 2105(c) of title 5, United States Code, to employment in the Department of Defense or the Coast Guard, respectively, that is not described in such section 2105(c); or

"(B) moves without a break in service from employment in the Department of Defense or the Coast Guard that is not described in such section 2105(c) to employment in a nonappropriated fund instrumentality of the Department of Defense or the Coast Guard, respectively, that is described in such section 2105(c).

"(2) The Secretary of Defense, the Secretary of Transportation, the Director of the Office of Personnel Management, and the Executive Director of the Federal Retirement Thrift Investment Board, as applicable, shall take such actions as may be practicable to ensure that each individual who has moved as described under paragraph (1) on or after January 1, 1987, and before the date of enactment of this Act [Nov. 5, 1990], receives the benefit of the amendments made by this section as if such amendments had been in effect at the time such individual so moved. Each such individual who wishes to make an election of retirement coverage under the amendments made by subsection (j) or (k) of this section [amending sections 8331, 8347, 8401, and 8461 of this title] shall complete such election within 180 days after the date of enactment of this Act."

EFFECTIVE DATE OF 1986 AMENDMENT

Amendment by Pub. L. 99–335 effective Jan. 1, 1987, see section 702(a) of Pub. L. 99–335, set out as an Effective Date note under section 8401 of this title.

EFFECTIVE DATE OF 1979 AMENDMENT

Amendment by Pub. L. 96–54 effective July 12, 1979, see section 2(b) of Pub. L. 96–54, set out as a note under section 305 of this title.

EFFECTIVE DATE OF 1978 AMENDMENT

Amendment by Pub. L. 95–454 effective 90 days after Oct. 13, 1978, see section 907 of Pub. L. 95–454, set out as a note under section 1101 of this title.

EFFECTIVE DATE OF 1972 AMENDMENT

Amendment by Pub. L. 92–392 effective on first day of first applicable pay period beginning on or after 90th day after Aug. 19, 1972, see section 15(a) of Pub. L. 92–392, set out as an Effective Date note under section 5341 of this title.

EFFECTIVE DATE OF 1970 AMENDMENT

Amendment by Pub. L. 91–375 effective within 1 year after Aug. 12, 1970, on date established therefor by Board of Governors of United States Postal Service and published by it in Federal Register, see section 15(a) of Pub. L. 91–375, set out as an Effective Date note preceding section 101 of Title 39, Postal Service.

EFFECTIVE DATE OF 1968 AMENDMENT

Amendment by Pub. L. 90–486 effective Jan. 1, 1968, except that no deductions or withholding from salary which result therefrom shall commence before the first day of the first pay period that begins on or after Jan.

1, 1968, see section 11 of Pub. L. 90–486, set out as a note under section 709 of Title 32, National Guard.

TREATMENT OF INDIVIDUALS ELECTING TO REMAIN SUBJECT TO THEIR FORMER RETIREMENT SYSTEM

Section 7202(n) of Pub. L. 101–508, as amended by Pub. L. 102–378, § 5(a)(2), Oct. 2, 1992, 106 Stat. 1358, provided that:

"(1) For the purpose of this section [amending this section and sections 3502, 5334, 5335, 5365, 5551, 6308, 6312, 8331, 8347, 8401, 8461, and 8901 of this title and enacting provisions set out as notes under this section and section 2101 of this title], the term 'nonappropriated fund instrumentality' means a nonappropriated fund instrumentality of the Department of Defense or the Coast Guard, described in section 2105(c) of title 5, United States Code.

"(2)(A) If an individual makes an election under section 8347(q)(1) of title 5, United States Code, to remain covered by subchapter III of chapter 83 of such title, any nonappropriated fund instrumentality thereafter employing such individual shall deduct from such individual's pay and contribute to the Thrift Savings Fund such sums as are required for such individual in accordance with section 8351 of such title.

"(B) Notwithstanding subsection (a) or (b) of section 8432 of title 5, United States Code, any individual who, as of the date of enactment of this Act [Nov. 5, 1990], becomes eligible to make an election under section 8347(q)(1) of such title may, within 30 days after such individual makes an election thereunder in accordance with subsection (m)(2) [set out as a note above], make any election described in section 8432(b)(1)(A) of such title.

"(3)(A) If an individual makes an election under section 8461(n)(1) of title 5, United States Code, to remain covered by chapter 84 of such title, any nonappropriated fund instrumentality thereafter employing such individual shall deduct from such individual's pay and shall contribute to the Thrift Savings Fund the funds deducted, together with such other sums as are required for such individual under subchapter III of such chapter.

"(B) Notwithstanding subsection (a) or (b) of section 8432 of title 5, United States Code, any individual who, as of the date of enactment of this Act, becomes eligible to make an election under section 8461(n)(1) of such title may, within 30 days after such individual makes an election thereunder in accordance with subsection (m)(2), make any election described in section 8432(b)(1)(A) of such title.

"(4) If an individual makes an election under section 8347(q)(2) or 8461(n)(2) of title 5, United States Code, to remain covered by a retirement system established for employees described in section 2105(c) of such title, any Government agency thereafter employing such individual shall, in lieu of any deductions or contributions for which it would otherwise be responsible with respect to such individual under chapter 83 or 84 of such title, make such deductions from pay and such contributions as would be required (under the retirement system for nonappropriated fund employees involved) if it were a nonappropriated fund instrumentality. Any such deductions and contributions shall be remitted to the Department of Defense or the Coast Guard, as applicable, for transmission to the appropriate retirement system."

[Amendment by Pub. L. 102–378 to section 7202(n) of Pub. L. 101–508, set out above, effective Nov. 5, 1990, see section 9(b)(6) of Pub. L. 102–378, set out as an Effective Date of 1992 Amendment note under section 6303 of this title.]

PROHIBITION OF DECREASE IN BASIC PAY RATE OF EMPLOYEES OF NONAPPROPRIATED FUND INSTRUMENTALITIES

Amendments by Pub. L. 92–392 not to decrease basic pay rate of subsec. (c) employees in service before effective date of the amendments as to such employees, see section 9(a)(2) of Pub. L. 92–392, set out as a note under section 5343 of this title.

SECTION REFERRED TO IN OTHER SECTIONS

This section is referred to in sections 3502, 5334, 5335, 5342, 5365, 5506, 5515, 5537, 5551, 5552, 5581, 5595, 5736, 5751, 5945, 5946, 6103, 6104, 6121, 6301, 6308, 6322, 6323, 6385, 7103, 7119, 7342, 7905, 8171, 8172, 8173, 8311, 8331, 8332, 8347, 8401, 8461, 8701, 8901, 9001 of this title; title 10 sections 975, 1587; title 18 section 202; title 19 section 2081; title 22 sections 3974, 4341, 4833; title 25 section 450i; title 26 section 7608; title 41 sections 419, 423; title 42 sections 3374, 14614; title 50 section 426.

§ 2106. Member of Congress

For the purpose of this title, "Member of Congress" means the Vice President, a member of the Senate or the House of Representatives, a Delegate to the House of Representatives, and the Resident Commissioner from Puerto Rico.

(Pub. L. 89–554, Sept. 6, 1966, 80 Stat. 409; Pub. L. 91–405, title II, § 204(b), Sept. 22, 1970, 84 Stat. 852; Pub. L. 96–54, § 2(a)(7), Aug. 14, 1979, 93 Stat. 381.)

HISTORICAL AND REVISION NOTES

The section is supplied to avoid the necessity of defining "Member of Congress" each time the term is used in this title.

AMENDMENTS

1979—Pub. L. 96–54 substituted "to the House of Representatives" for "from the District of Columbia".

1970—Pub. L. 91–405 included Delegate from District of Columbia.

EFFECTIVE DATE OF 1979 AMENDMENT

Amendment by Pub. L. 96–54 effective July 12, 1979, see section 2(b) of Pub. L. 96–54, set out as a note under section 305 of this title.

EFFECTIVE DATE OF 1970 AMENDMENT

Amendment by Pub. L. 91–405 effective Sept. 22, 1970, see section 206(b) of Pub. L. 91–405, set out as an Effective Date note under section 25a of Title 2, The Congress.

SECTION REFERRED TO IN OTHER SECTIONS

This section is referred to in sections 5520a, 7342, 8311, 8331, 8401, 8701, 8901 of this title.

§ 2107. Congressional employee

For the purpose of this title, "Congressional employee" means—

(1) an employee of either House of Congress, of a committee of either House, or of a joint committee of the two Houses;

(2) an elected officer of either House who is not a Member of Congress;

(3) the Legislative Counsel of either House and an employee of his office;

(4) a member of the Capitol Police;

(5) an employee of a Member of Congress if the pay of the employee is paid by the Secretary of the Senate or the Chief Administrative Officer of the House of Representatives;

[(6) Repealed. Pub. L. 90–83, § 1(5)(A), Sept. 11, 1967, 81 Stat. 196.]

(7) the Architect of the Capitol and an employee of the Architect of the Capitol;

(8) an employee of the Botanic Garden; and

(9) an employee of the Capitol Guide Service.

(Pub. L. 89–554, Sept. 6, 1966, 80 Stat. 409; Pub. L. 90–83, § 1(5), Sept. 11, 1967, 81 Stat. 196; Pub. L.

91–510, title IV, § 442(a), Oct. 26, 1970, 84 Stat. 1191; Pub. L. 104–186, title II, § 215(1), Aug. 20, 1996, 110 Stat. 1745.)

HISTORICAL AND REVISION NOTES

1966 ACT

The section is supplied to avoid the necessity of defining "Congressional employee" each time the term is used in this title.

1967 ACT

Section of title 5	Source (U.S. Code)	Source (Statutes at Large)
2107(6)	2:126–1.	July 27, 1965, Pub. L. 89–90, § 101 (proviso on p. 265), 79 Stat. 265.
2107(8)	5 App.: 2251(c).	Sept. 26, 1966, Pub. L. 89–604, § 1(a), 80 Stat. 846.

Paragraph (6), relating to Official Reporters of Debates of the Senate and their employees, is eliminated as unnecessary on authority of the act of July 27, 1965 (2 U.S.C. 126–1). Pursuant to that act, the Official Reporters and their employees became employees of the Senate; accordingly, they are now included within the definition of "Congressional employee" under paragraph (1).

In paragraph (8), based on the act of September 26, 1966 (5 App. U.S.C. 2251(c)), the word "officers" is omitted as included in "employees," and the words "United States" preceding the words "Botanic Garden" are omitted as unnecessary.

AMENDMENTS

1996—Par. (5). Pub. L. 104–186 substituted "Chief Administrative Officer" for "Clerk".

1970—Par. (9). Pub. L. 91–510 added par. (9).

EFFECTIVE DATE OF 1970 AMENDMENT

Amendment by Pub. L. 91–510 effective immediately prior to noon on June. 3, 1971, see section 601(1) of Pub. L. 91–510, set out as a note under section 72a of Title 2, The Congress.

SECTION REFERRED TO IN OTHER SECTIONS

This section is referred to in sections 5531, 8331, 8401, 8701, 8901 of this title; title 2 section 31b–5; title 22 section 3008; title 26 section 7448; title 31 section 774; title 38 section 7297.

§ 2108. Veteran; disabled veteran; preference eligible

For the purpose of this title—

(1) "veteran" means an individual who—

(A) served on active duty in the armed forces during a war, in a campaign or expedition for which a campaign badge has been authorized, or during the period beginning April 28, 1952, and ending July 1, 1955;

(B) served on active duty as defined by section 101(21) of title 38 at any time in the armed forces for a period of more than 180 consecutive days any part of which occurred after January 31, 1955, and before October 15, 1976, not including service under section 12103(d) of title 10 pursuant to an enlistment in the Army National Guard or the Air National Guard or as a Reserve for service in the Army Reserve, Naval Reserve, Air Force Reserve, Marine Corps Reserve, or Coast Guard Reserve; or

(C) served on active duty as defined by section 101(21) of title 38 in the armed forces during the period beginning on August 2, 1990, and ending on January 2, 1992;

and who has been separated from the armed forces under honorable conditions;

(2) "disabled veteran" means an individual who has served on active duty in the armed forces, has been separated therefrom under honorable conditions, and has established the present existence of a service-connected disability or is receiving compensation, disability retirement benefits, or pension because of a public statute administered by the Department of Veterans Affairs or a military department;

(3) "preference eligible" means, except as provided in paragraph (4) of this section—

(A) a veteran as defined by paragraph (1)(A) of this section;

(B) a veteran as defined by paragraph (1)(B) or (C) of this section;

(C) a disabled veteran;

(D) the unmarried widow or widower of a veteran as defined by paragraph (1)(A) of this section;

(E) the wife or husband of a service-connected disabled veteran if the veteran has been unable to qualify for any appointment in the civil service or in the government of the District of Columbia;

(F) the mother of an individual who lost his life under honorable conditions while serving in the armed forces during a period named by paragraph (1)(A) of this section, if—

(i) her husband is totally and permanently disabled;

(ii) she is widowed, divorced, or separated from the father and has not remarried; or

(iii) she has remarried but is widowed, divorced, or legally separated from her husband when preference is claimed; and

(G) the mother of a service-connected permanently and totally disabled veteran, if—

(i) her husband is totally and permanently disabled;

(ii) she is widowed, divorced, or separated from the father and has not remarried; or

(iii) she has remarried but is widowed, divorced, or legally separated from her husband when preference is claimed;

but does not include applicants for, or members of, the Senior Executive Service, the Defense Intelligence Senior Executive Service, the Senior Cryptologic Executive Service, or the Federal Bureau of Investigation and Drug Enforcement Administration Senior Executive Service;

(4) except for the purposes of chapters 43 and 75 of this title, "preference eligible" does not include a retired member of the armed forces unless—

(A) the individual is a disabled veteran; or

(B) the individual retired below the rank of major or its equivalent; and

(5) "retired member of the armed forces" means a member or former member of the armed forces who is entitled, under statute, to retired, retirement, or retainer pay on account of service as a member.

(Pub. L. 89–554, Sept. 6, 1966, 80 Stat. 410; Pub. L. 90–83, § 1(6), Sept. 11, 1967, 81 Stat. 196; Pub. L. 90–623, § 1(2), Oct. 22, 1968, 82 Stat. 1312; Pub. L. 92–187, § 1, Dec. 15, 1971, 85 Stat. 644; Pub. L. 94–502, title VII, § 702, Oct. 15, 1976, 90 Stat. 2405; Pub. L. 95–454, title III, § 307(a), title IV, § 401(d), Oct. 13, 1978, 92 Stat. 1147, 1154; Pub. L. 96–54, § 2(a)(8), (9)(A), Aug. 14, 1979, 93 Stat. 381; Pub. L. 96–191, § 8(a), Feb. 15, 1980, 94 Stat. 33; Pub. L. 97–89, title VIII, § 801, Dec. 4, 1981, 95 Stat. 1161; Pub. L. 100–325, § 2(a), May 30, 1988, 102 Stat. 581; Pub. L. 102–54, § 13(b)(1), June 13, 1991, 105 Stat. 274; Pub. L. 105–85, div. A, title XI, § 1102(a), (c), Nov. 18, 1997, 111 Stat. 1922; Pub. L. 105–339, § 4(a), Oct. 31, 1998, 112 Stat. 3185.)

HISTORICAL AND REVISION NOTES
1966 ACT

Derivation	U.S. Code	Revised Statutes and Statutes at Large
....	5 U.S.C. 851 (less 1st 76 words).	June 27, 1944, ch. 287, § 2 (less 1st 76 words), 58 Stat. 387. Jan. 19, 1948, ch. 1, § 1, 62 Stat. 3. July 2, 1948, ch. 816, 62 Stat. 1233. Aug. 26, 1949, ch. 513, 63 Stat. 666. Dec. 27, 1950, ch. 1151, § 1, 64 Stat. 1117. July 14, 1952, ch. 728, § 1, 66 Stat. 626.

In paragraph (2), the words "a military department" are substituted for "the War Department or Navy Department" (appearing in section 2 of the Act of June 27, 1944) because of the definition of "military department" in section 102. The Department of War was designated the Department of the Army by the Act of July 26, 1947, ch. 343, § 205, 61 Stat. 501. "Department of the Air Force" is included on authority of the Act of July 26, 1947, ch. 343, § 207 (a), (f), 61 Stat. 502.

Standard changes are made to conform with the definitions applicable and the style of this title as outlined in the preface to the report.

1967 ACT

Section of title 5	Source (U.S. Code)	Source (Statutes at Large)
2108	5 App.: 851.	Mar. 3, 1966, Pub. L. 89–358, § 11, 80 Stat. 28.

AMENDMENTS

1998—Par. (3). Pub. L. 105–339, in concluding provisions, substituted "or the Federal Bureau of Investigation and Drug Enforcement Administration Senior Executive Service;" for "the Federal Bureau of Investigation and Drug Enforcement Administration Senior Executive Service, or the General Accounting Office;".

1997—Par. (1)(B). Pub. L. 105–85, § 1102(c), substituted "October 15, 1976," for "the date of enactment of the Veterans' Education and Employment Assistance Act of 1976," and "12103(d) of title 10" for "511(d) of title 10".

Par. (1)(C). Pub. L. 105–85, § 1102(a)(1), added subpar. (C).

Par. (3)(B). Pub. L. 105–85, § 1102(a)(2), inserted "or (C)" after "paragraph (1)(B)".

1991—Par. (2). Pub. L. 102–54 substituted "Department of Veterans Affairs" for "Veterans' Administration".

1988—Par. (3). Pub. L. 100–325 inserted reference to Federal Bureau of Investigation and Drug Enforcement Administration Senior Executive Service in concluding provisions.

1981—Par. (3). Pub. L. 97–89 inserted reference to Defense Intelligence Senior Executive Service and Senior Cryptologic Executive Service in concluding provisions.

1980—Par. (3). Pub. L. 96–191 inserted reference to General Accounting Office in concluding provisions.

1979—Par. (3). Pub. L. 96–54, § 2(a)(8), inserted provision excepting applicants for, or members of, Senior Executive Service.

Par. (5). Pub. L. 96–54, § 2(a)(9)(A), struck out provision excepting applicants for, or members of, Senior Executive Service.

1978—Par. (2). Pub. L. 95–454, § 307(a)(1), struck out "and" at end.

Par. (3). Pub. L. 95–454, § 307(a)(2), (3), inserted ", except as provided in paragraph (4) of this section" after "means", and substituted a semicolon for the period at end.

Pars. (4), (5). Pub. L. 95–454, § 307(a)(4), added pars. (4) and (5) relating to retired members of the armed forces.

Par. (5). Pub. L. 95–454, § 401(d), inserted "; but does not include applicants for, or members of, the Senior Executive Service" before the period at end.

1976—Par. (1)(B). Pub. L. 94–502 substituted "any part of which occurred after January 31, 1955, and before the date of enactment of the Veterans' Education and Employment Assistance Act of 1976," for "after January 31, 1955,".

1971—Par. (3)(D). Pub. L. 92–187 inserted "or widower" after "unmarried widow".

Par. (3)(E). Pub. L. 92–187 inserted "or husband" after "the wife".

1968—Par. (3)(D). Pub. L. 90–623 inserted "as defined by paragraph (1)(A) of this section" after "veteran".

EFFECTIVE DATE OF 1981 AMENDMENT

Amendment by Pub. L. 97–89 effective Oct. 1, 1981, see section 806 of Pub. L. 97–89, set out as an Effective Date note under section 1621 of Title 10, Armed Forces.

EFFECTIVE DATE OF 1980 AMENDMENT

Amendment by Pub. L. 96–191 effective Oct. 1, 1980, see section 10(a) of Pub L. 96–191.

EFFECTIVE DATE OF 1979 AMENDMENT

Amendment by section 2(a)(8) of Pub. L. 96–54 effective July 12, 1979, see section 2(b) of Pub. L. 96–54, set out as a note under section 305 of this title.

Section 2(a)(9)(B) of Pub. L. 96–54 provided that: "The amendment made by subparagraph (A) [amending this section] shall take effect October 1, 1980".

EFFECTIVE DATE OF 1978 AMENDMENT

Section 307(a) of Pub. L. 95–454 provided that the amendment made by that section is effective Oct. 1, 1980.

Amendment by section 401(d) of Pub. L. 95–454 effective 9 months after Oct. 13, 1978, and congressional review of provisions of sections 401 through 412 of Pub. L. 95–454, see section 415 of Pub. L. 95–454, set out as an Effective Date note under section 3131 of this title.

EFFECTIVE DATE OF 1968 AMENDMENT

Amendment by Pub. L. 90–623 effective Sept. 11, 1967, for all purposes, see section 6 of Pub. L. 90–623, set out as a note under section 5334 of this title.

SECTION REFERRED TO IN OTHER SECTIONS

This section is referred to in sections 2302, 3305, 3309, 3312, 3318, 3352, 3502, 3504 of this title; title 2 section 1316a; title 3 section 115; title 10 sections 943, 1614; title 16 section 3198; title 22 sections 1438, 3941; title 32 section 709; title 38 sections 106, 5303A, 7281, 7802; title 39 section 1005; title 42 sections 2992a–1, 9839; title 49 section 47112.

§ 2109. Air traffic controller; Secretary

For the purpose of this title—

(1) "air traffic controller" or "controller" means a civilian employee of the Department of Transportation or the Department of Defense who, in an air traffic control facility or flight service station facility—

(A) is actively engaged—

(i) in the separation and control of air traffic; or

(ii) in providing preflight, inflight, or airport advisory service to aircraft operators; or

(B) is the immediate supervisor of any employee described in subparagraph (A); and

(2) "Secretary", when used in connection with "air traffic controller" or "controller", means the Secretary of Transportation with respect to controllers in the Department of Transportation, and the Secretary of Defense with respect to controllers in the Department of Defense.

(Added Pub. L. 92–297, § 1(a), May 16, 1972, 86 Stat. 141; amended Pub. L. 96–347, § 1(a), Sept. 12, 1980, 94 Stat. 1150; Pub. L. 99–335, title II, § 207(b), June 6, 1986, 100 Stat. 594.)

AMENDMENTS

1986—Par. (1). Pub. L. 99–335 amended par. (1) generally including within term "air traffic controller" or "controller" references to a flight service station facility and to employment providing preflight, inflight, or airport advisory service to aircraft operators and striking out provision that regulations prescribed by the Secretary be used in determining who is an air traffic controller.

1980—Pub. L. 96–347 substituted "controller; Secretary" for "controller" in section catchline, and in text included employees of the Department of Defense within the meaning of air traffic controller or controller and defined "Secretary" to mean Secretary of Transportation with respect to controllers in the Department of Transportation and Secretary of Defense with respect to controllers in the Department of Defense.

EFFECTIVE DATE OF 1986 AMENDMENT

Amendment by Pub. L. 99–335 effective Jan. 1, 1987, see section 702(a) of Pub. L. 99–335, set out as an Effective Date note under section 8401 of this title.

EFFECTIVE DATE OF 1980 AMENDMENT

Section 3 of Pub. L. 96–347 provided that: "This Act [amending this section and sections 3307, 3381 to 3385, and 8335 of this title and enacting provisions set out as a note under section 8335 of this title] shall take effect on the later of—

"(1) October 1, 1980, or

"(2) the ninetieth day after the date of the enactment of this Act [Sept. 12, 1980]."

EFFECTIVE DATE

Section effective on 90th day after May 16, 1972, see, section 10 of Pub. L. 92–297, set out as a note under section 3381 of this title.

SECTION REFERRED TO IN OTHER SECTIONS

This section is referred to in title 49 section 44506.

CHAPTER 23—MERIT SYSTEM PRINCIPLES

CHAPTER REFERRED TO IN OTHER SECTIONS

This chapter is referred to in sections 1222, 4703, 9501 of this title.

§ 2301. Merit system principles

(a) This section shall apply to—
(1) an Executive agency; and
(2) the Government Printing Office.

(b) Federal personnel management should be implemented consistent with the following merit system principles:

(1) Recruitment should be from qualified individuals from appropriate sources in an endeavor to achieve a work force from all segments of society, and selection and advancement should be determined solely on the basis of relative ability, knowledge, and skills, after fair and open competition which assures that all receive equal opportunity.

(2) All employees and applicants for employment should receive fair and equitable treatment in all aspects of personnel management without regard to political affiliation, race, color, religion, national origin, sex, marital status, age, or handicapping condition, and with proper regard for their privacy and constitutional rights.

(3) Equal pay should be provided for work of equal value, with appropriate consideration of both national and local rates paid by employers in the private sector, and appropriate incentives and recognition should be provided for excellence in performance.

(4) All employees should maintain high standards of integrity, conduct, and concern for the public interest.

(5) The Federal work force should be used efficiently and effectively.

(6) Employees should be retained on the basis of the adequacy of their performance, inadequate performance should be corrected, and employees should be separated who cannot or will not improve their performance to meet required standards.

(7) Employees should be provided effective education and training in cases in which such education and training would result in better organizational and individual performance.

(8) Employees should be—
(A) protected against arbitrary action, personal favoritism, or coercion for partisan political purposes, and
(B) prohibited from using their official authority or influence for the purpose of interfering with or affecting the result of an election or a nomination for election.

(9) Employees should be protected against reprisal for the lawful disclosure of information which the employees reasonably believe evidences—
(A) a violation of any law, rule, or regulation, or
(B) mismanagement, a gross waste of funds, an abuse of authority, or a substantial and specific danger to public health or safety.

(c) In administering the provisions of this chapter—
(1) with respect to any agency (as defined in section 2302(a)(2)(C) of this title), the President shall, pursuant to the authority otherwise available under this title, take any action, including the issuance of rules, regulations, or directives; and

(2) with respect to any entity in the executive branch which is not such an agency or part of such an agency, the head of such entity shall, pursuant to authority otherwise available, take any action, including the issuance of rules, regulations, or directives;

which is consistent with the provisions of this title and which the President or the head, as the case may be, determines is necessary to ensure that personnel management is based on and embodies the merit system principles.

(Added Pub. L. 95–454, title I, §101(a), Oct. 13, 1978, 92 Stat. 1113; amended Pub. L. 101–474, §5(c), Oct. 30, 1990, 104 Stat. 1099.)

AMENDMENTS

1990—Subsec. (a). Pub. L. 101–474 redesignated par. (3) as (2) and struck out former par. (2) which provided that this section is applicable to Administrative Office of United States Courts.

EFFECTIVE DATE

Chapter effective 90 days after Oct. 13, 1978, see section 907 of Pub. L. 95–454, set out as an Effective Date of 1978 Amendment note under section 1101 of this title.

SECTION REFERRED TO IN OTHER SECTIONS

This section is referred to in sections 2302, 4107, 4313, 5379 of this title; title 10 sections 1612, 1722; title 22 section 3902; title 31 section 732; title 41 section 433.

§ 2302. Prohibited personnel practices

(a)(1) For the purpose of this title, "prohibited personnel practice" means any action described in subsection (b).

(2) For the purpose of this section—
(A) "personnel action" means—
(i) an appointment;
(ii) a promotion;
(iii) an action under chapter 75 of this title or other disciplinary or corrective action;
(iv) a detail, transfer, or reassignment;
(v) a reinstatement;
(vi) a restoration;
(vii) a reemployment;
(viii) a performance evaluation under chapter 43 of this title;
(ix) a decision concerning pay, benefits, or awards, concerning education or training if the education or training may reasonably be expected to lead to an appointment, promotion, performance evaluation, or other action described in this subparagraph;
(x) a decision to order psychiatric testing or examination; and
(xi) any other significant change in duties, responsibilities, or working conditions;

with respect to an employee in, or applicant for, a covered position in an agency, and in the case of an alleged prohibited personnel practice described in subsection (b)(8), an employee or applicant for employment in a Government corporation as defined in section 9101 of title 31;

(B) "covered position" means, with respect to any personnel action, any position in the competitive service, a career appointee position in the Senior Executive Service, or a position in the excepted service, but does not include any position which is, prior to the personnel action—

(i) excepted from the competitive service because of its confidential, policy-determining, policy-making, or policy-advocating character; or

(ii) excluded from the coverage of this section by the President based on a determination by the President that it is necessary and warranted by conditions of good administration; and

(C) "agency" means an Executive agency and the Government Printing Office, but does not include—

(i) a Government corporation, except in the case of an alleged prohibited personnel practice described under subsection (b)(8);

(ii) the Federal Bureau of Investigation, the Central Intelligence Agency, the Defense Intelligence Agency, the National Imagery and Mapping Agency, the National Security Agency, and, as determined by the President, any Executive agency or unit thereof the principal function of which is the conduct of foreign intelligence or counter-intelligence activities; or

(iii) the General Accounting Office.

(b) Any employee who has authority to take, direct others to take, recommend, or approve any personnel action, shall not, with respect to such authority—

(1) discriminate for or against any employee or applicant for employment—

(A) on the basis of race, color, religion, sex, or national origin, as prohibited under section 717 of the Civil Rights Act of 1964 (42 U.S.C. 2000e–16);

(B) on the basis of age, as prohibited under sections 12 and 15 of the Age Discrimination in Employment Act of 1967 (29 U.S.C. 631, 633a);

(C) on the basis of sex, as prohibited under section 6(d) of the Fair Labor Standards Act of 1938 (29 U.S.C. 206(d));

(D) on the basis of handicapping condition, as prohibited under section 501 of the Rehabilitation Act of 1973 (29 U.S.C. 791); or

(E) on the basis of marital status or political affiliation, as prohibited under any law, rule, or regulation;

(2) solicit or consider any recommendation or statement, oral or written, with respect to any individual who requests or is under consideration for any personnel action unless such recommendation or statement is based on the personal knowledge or records of the person furnishing it and consists of—

(A) an evaluation of the work performance, ability, aptitude, or general qualifications of such individual; or

(B) an evaluation of the character, loyalty, or suitability of such individual;

(3) coerce the political activity of any person (including the providing of any political contribution or service), or take any action against any employee or applicant for employment as a reprisal for the refusal of any person to engage in such political activity;

(4) deceive or willfully obstruct any person with respect to such person's right to compete for employment;

(5) influence any person to withdraw from competition for any position for the purpose of improving or injuring the prospects of any other person for employment;

(6) grant any preference or advantage not authorized by law, rule, or regulation to any employee or applicant for employment (including defining the scope or manner of competition or the requirements for any position) for the purpose of improving or injuring the prospects of any particular person for employment;

(7) appoint, employ, promote, advance, or advocate for appointment, employment, promotion, or advancement, in or to a civilian position any individual who is a relative (as defined in section 3110(a)(3) of this title) of such employee if such position is in the agency in which such employee is serving as a public official (as defined in section 3110(a)(2) of this title) or over which such employee exercises jurisdiction or control as such an official;

(8) take or fail to take, or threaten to take or fail to take, a personnel action with respect to any employee or applicant for employment because of—

(A) any disclosure of information by an employee or applicant which the employee or applicant reasonably believes evidences—

(i) a violation of any law, rule, or regulation, or

(ii) gross mismanagement, a gross waste of funds, an abuse of authority, or a substantial and specific danger to public health or safety,

if such disclosure is not specifically prohibited by law and if such information is not specifically required by Executive order to be kept secret in the interest of national defense or the conduct of foreign affairs; or

(B) any disclosure to the Special Counsel, or to the Inspector General of an agency or another employee designated by the head of the agency to receive such disclosures, of information which the employee or applicant reasonably believes evidences—

(i) a violation of any law, rule, or regulation, or

(ii) gross mismanagement, a gross waste of funds, an abuse of authority, or a substantial and specific danger to public health or safety;

(9) take or fail to take, or threaten to take or fail to take, any personnel action against any employee or applicant for employment because of—

(A) the exercise of any appeal, complaint, or grievance right granted by any law, rule, or regulation;

(B) testifying for or otherwise lawfully assisting any individual in the exercise of any right referred to in subparagraph (A);

(C) cooperating with or disclosing information to the Inspector General of an agency, or the Special Counsel, in accordance with applicable provisions of law; or

(D) for refusing to obey an order that would require the individual to violate a law;

(10) discriminate for or against any employee or applicant for employment on the

basis of conduct which does not adversely affect the performance of the employee or applicant or the performance of others; except that nothing in this paragraph shall prohibit an agency from taking into account in determining suitability or fitness any conviction of the employee or applicant for any crime under the laws of any State, of the District of Columbia, or of the United States;

(11)(A) knowingly take, recommend, or approve any personnel action if the taking of such action would violate a veterans' preference requirement; or

(B) knowingly fail to take, recommend, or approve any personnel action if the failure to take such action would violate a veterans' preference requirement; or

(12) take or fail to take any other personnel action if the taking of or failure to take such action violates any law, rule, or regulation implementing, or directly concerning, the merit system principles contained in section 2301 of this title.

This subsection shall not be construed to authorize the withholding of information from the Congress or the taking of any personnel action against an employee who discloses information to the Congress.

(c) The head of each agency shall be responsible for the prevention of prohibited personnel practices, for the compliance with and enforcement of applicable civil service laws, rules, and regulations, and other aspects of personnel management, and for ensuring (in consultation with the Office of Special Counsel) that agency employees are informed of the rights and remedies available to them under this chapter and chapter 12 of this title. Any individual to whom the head of an agency delegates authority for personnel management, or for any aspect thereof, shall be similarly responsible within the limits of the delegation.

(d) This section shall not be construed to extinguish or lessen any effort to achieve equal employment opportunity through affirmative action or any right or remedy available to any employee or applicant for employment in the civil service under—

(1) section 717 of the Civil Rights Act of 1964 (42 U.S.C. 2000e–16), prohibiting discrimination on the basis of race, color, religion, sex, or national origin;

(2) sections 12 and 15 of the Age Discrimination in Employment Act of 1967 (29 U.S.C. 631, 633a), prohibiting discrimination on the basis of age;

(3) under section 6(d) of the Fair Labor Standards Act of 1938 (29 U.S.C. 206(d)), prohibiting discrimination on the basis of sex;

(4) section 501 of the Rehabilitation Act of 1973 (29 U.S.C. 791), prohibiting discrimination on the basis of handicapping condition; or

(5) the provisions of any law, rule, or regulation prohibiting discrimination on the basis of marital status or political affiliation.

(e)(1) For the purpose of this section, the term "veterans' preference requirement" means any of the following provisions of law:

(A) Sections 2108, 3305(b), 3309, 3310, 3311, 3312, 3313, 3314, 3315, 3316, 3317(b), 3318, 3320, 3351,

3352, 3363, 3501, 3502(b), 3504, and 4303(e) and (with respect to a preference eligible referred to in section 7511(a)(1)(B)) subchapter II of chapter 75 and section 7701.

(B) Sections 943(c)(2) and 1784(c) of title 10.

(C) Section 1308(b) of the Alaska National Interest Lands Conservation Act.

(D) Section 301(c) of the Foreign Service Act of 1980.

(E) Sections 106(f), 7281(e), and 7802(5) of title 38.

(F) Section 1005(a) of title 39.

(G) Any other provision of law that the Director of the Office of Personnel Management designates in regulations as being a veterans' preference requirement for the purposes of this subsection.

(H) Any regulation prescribed under subsection (b) or (c) of section 1302 and any other regulation that implements a provision of law referred to in any of the preceding subparagraphs.

(2) Notwithstanding any other provision of this title, no authority to order corrective action shall be available in connection with a prohibited personnel practice described in subsection (b)(11). Nothing in this paragraph shall be considered to affect any authority under section 1215 (relating to disciplinary action).

(Added Pub. L. 95–454, title I, § 101(a), Oct. 13, 1978, 92 Stat. 1114; amended Pub. L. 101–12, § 4, Apr. 10, 1989, 103 Stat. 32; Pub. L. 101–474, § 5(d), Oct. 30, 1990, 104 Stat. 1099; Pub. L. 102–378, § 2(5), Oct. 2, 1992, 106 Stat. 1346; Pub. L. 103–94, § 8(c), Oct. 6, 1993, 107 Stat. 1007; Pub. L. 103–359, title V, § 501(c), Oct. 14, 1994, 108 Stat. 3429; Pub. L. 103–424, § 5, Oct. 29, 1994, 108 Stat. 4363; Pub. L. 104–197, title III, § 315(b)(2), Sept. 16, 1996, 110 Stat. 2416; Pub. L. 104–201, div. A, title XI, § 1122(a)(1), title XVI, § 1615(b), Sept. 23, 1996, 110 Stat. 2687, 2741; Pub. L. 105–339, § 6(a), (b), (c)(2), Oct. 31, 1998, 112 Stat. 3187, 3188.)

REFERENCES IN TEXT

The civil service laws, referred to in subsec. (c), are set out in this title. See, particularly, section 3301 et seq. of this title.

Section 1308(b) of the Alaska National Interest Lands Conservation Act, referred to in subsec. (e)(1)(C), is classified to section 3198(b) of Title 16, Conservation.

Section 301(c) of the Foreign Service Act of 1980, referred to in subsec. (e)(1)(D), is classified to section 3941(c) of Title 22, Foreign Relations and Intercourse.

AMENDMENTS

1998—Subsec. (a)(1). Pub. L. 105–339, § 6(c)(2), amended par. (1) generally. Prior to amendment, par. (1) read as follows: "For purposes of this title, 'prohibited personnel practice' means the following:

"(A) Any action described in subsection (b) of this section.

"(B) Any action or failure to act that is designated as a prohibited personnel action under section 1599c(a) of title 10."

Subsec. (b)(10) to (12). Pub. L. 105–339, § 6(a), struck out "or" at end of par. (10), added par. (11), and redesignated former par. (11) as (12).

Subsec. (e). Pub. L. 105–339, § 6(b), added subsec. (e).

1996—Subsec. (a)(1). Pub. L. 104–201, § 1615(b), amended par. (1) generally. Prior to amendment, par. (1) read as follows: "For the purpose of this title, 'prohibited personnel practice' means any action described in subsection (b) of this section."

Subsec. (a)(2)(C)(ii). Pub. L. 104–201, §1122(a)(1), substituted "National Imagery and Mapping Agency" for "Central Imagery Office".

Subsec. (b)(2). Pub. L. 104–197 amended par. (2) generally. Prior to amendment, par. (2) read as follows: "solicit or consider any recommendation or statement, oral or written, with respect to any individual who requests or is under consideration for any personnel action except as provided under section 3303(f);".

1994—Subsec. (a)(2)(A). Pub. L. 103–424, §5(a)(3), in concluding provisions, inserted before semicolon ", and in the case of an alleged prohibited personnel practice described in subsection (b)(8), an employee or applicant for employment in a Government corporation as defined in section 9101 of title 31".

Subsec. (a)(2)(A)(x), (xi). Pub. L. 103–424, §5(a)(1), (2), added cls. (x) and (xi) and struck out former cl. (x) which read as follows: "any other significant change in duties or responsibilities which is inconsistent with the employee's salary or grade level;".

Subsec. (a)(2)(B). Pub. L. 103–424, §5(b), amended subpar. (B) generally. Prior to amendment, subpar. (B) read as follows: "'covered position' means any position in the competitive service, a career appointee position in the Senior Executive Service, or a position in the excepted service, but does not include—

"(i) a position which is excepted from the competitive service because of its confidential, policy-determining, policy-making, or policy-advocating character; or

"(ii) any position excluded from the coverage of this section by the President based on a determination by the President that it is necessary and warranted by conditions of good administration."

Subsec. (a)(2)(C)(i). Pub. L. 103–424, §5(c), inserted before semicolon ", except in the case of an alleged prohibited personnel practice described under subsection (b)(8)".

Subsec. (a)(2)(C)(ii). Pub. L. 103–359 inserted "the Central Imagery Office," after "Defense Intelligence Agency,".

Subsec. (c). Pub. L. 103–424, §5(d), inserted before period at end of first sentence ", and for ensuring (in consultation with the Office of Special Counsel) that agency employees are informed of the rights and remedies available to them under this chapter and chapter 12 of this title".

1993—Subsec. (b)(2). Pub. L. 103–94 amended par. (2) generally. Prior to amendment, par. (2) read as follows: "solicit or consider any recommendation or statement, oral or written, with respect to any individual who requests or is under consideration for any personnel action unless such recommendation or statement is based on the personal knowledge or records of the person furnishing it and consists of—

"(A) an evaluation of the work performance, ability, aptitude, or general qualifications of such individual; or

"(B) an evaluation of the character, loyalty, or suitability of such individual;".

1992—Subsec. (b)(8)(B). Pub. L. 102–378 substituted "Special Counsel" for "Special Counsel of the Merit Systems Protection Board".

1990—Subsec. (a)(2)(C). Pub. L. 101–474 struck out ", the Administrative Office of the United States Courts," after "means an Executive agency".

1989—Subsec. (b)(8). Pub. L. 101–12, §4(a), in introductory provision inserted ", or threaten to take or fail to take," after "fail to" and substituted "because of" for "as a reprisal for", in subpar. (A) substituted "any disclosure" for "a disclosure", in subpar. (A)(ii) inserted "gross" before "mismanagement", in subpar. (B) substituted "any disclosure" for "a disclosure", and in subpar. (B)(ii) inserted "gross" before "mismanagement".

Subsec. (b)(9). Pub. L. 101–12, §4(b), amended par. (9) generally. Prior to amendment, par. (9) read as follows: "take or fail to take any personnel action against any employee or applicant for employment as a reprisal for the exercise of any appeal right granted by any law, rule, or regulation;".

EFFECTIVE DATE OF 1996 AMENDMENTS

Amendment by section 1122(a)(1) of Pub. L. 104–201 effective Oct. 1, 1996, see section 1124 of Pub. L. 104–201, set out as a note under section 193 of Title 10, Armed Forces.

Section 315(c) of Pub. L. 104–197 provided that: "This section [amending this section and section 3303 of this title] shall take effect 30 days after the date of the enactment of this Act [Sept. 16, 1996]."

EFFECTIVE DATE OF 1993 AMENDMENT; SAVINGS PROVISION

Amendment by Pub. L. 103–94 effective 120 days after Oct. 6, 1993, but not to release or extinguish any penalty, forfeiture, or liability incurred under amended provision, which is to be treated as remaining in force for purpose of sustaining any proper proceeding or action for enforcement of that penalty, forfeiture, or liability, and no provision of Pub. L. 103–94 to affect any proceedings with respect to which charges were filed on or before 120 days after Oct. 6, 1993, with orders to be issued in such proceedings and appeals taken therefrom as if Pub. L. 103–94 had not been enacted, see section 12 of Pub. L. 103–94, set out as an Effective Date; Savings Provision note under section 7321 of this title.

EFFECTIVE DATE OF 1989 AMENDMENT

Amendment by Pub. L. 101–12 effective 90 days following Apr. 10, 1989, see section 11 of Pub. L. 101–12, set out as a note under section 1201 of this title.

SAVINGS PROVISION

Pub. L. 105–339, §6(d), Oct. 31, 1998, 112 Stat. 3188, provided that: "This section [amending this section and repealing section 1599c of Title 10, Armed Forces] shall be treated as if it had never been enacted for purposes of any personnel action (within the meaning of section 2302 of title 5, United States Code) preceding the date of enactment of this Act [Oct. 31, 1998]."

SECTION REFERRED TO IN OTHER SECTIONS

This section is referred to in sections 1204, 1212, 1214, 1221, 2105, 2301, 2303, 3352, 4505a, 4703, 5754, 5755, 7116, 7121, 7701 of this title; title 2 section 1371; title 7 sections 6932, 6962; title 10 section 1612; title 22 sections 3657, 3664, 3673, 3905, 4115; title 31 section 732; title 38 sections 4303, 4315, 4331; title 50 section 403q.

§ 2303. Prohibited personnel practices in the Federal Bureau of Investigation

(a) Any employee of the Federal Bureau of Investigation who has authority to take, direct others to take, recommend, or approve any personnel action, shall not, with respect to such authority, take or fail to take a personnel action with respect to any employee of the Bureau as a reprisal for a disclosure of information by the employee to the Attorney General (or an employee designated by the Attorney General for such purpose) which the employee or applicant reasonably believes evidences—

(1) a violation of any law, rule, or regulation, or

(2) mismanagement, a gross waste of funds, an abuse of authority, or a substantial and specific danger to public health or safety.

For the purpose of this subsection, "personnel action" means any action described in clauses (i) through (x) of section 2302(a)(2)(A) of this title with respect to an employee in, or applicant for, a position in the Bureau (other than a position of a confidential, policy-determining, policymaking, or policy-advocating character).

(b) The Attorney General shall prescribe regulations to ensure that such a personnel action shall not be taken against an employee of the Bureau as a reprisal for any disclosure of information described in subsection (a) of this section.

(c) The President shall provide for the enforcement of this section in a manner consistent with applicable provisions of sections 1214 and 1221 of this title.

(Added Pub. L. 95–454, title I, § 101(a), Oct. 13, 1978, 92 Stat. 1117; amended Pub. L. 101–12, § 9(a)(1), Apr. 10, 1989, 103 Stat. 34.)

AMENDMENTS

1989—Subsec. (c). Pub. L. 101–12 substituted "applicable provisions of sections 1214 and 1221" for "the provisions of section 1206".

EFFECTIVE DATE OF 1989 AMENDMENT

Amendment by Pub. L. 101–12 effective 90 days following Apr. 10, 1989, see section 11 of Pub. L. 101–12, set out as a note under section 1201 of this title.

DELEGATION OF RESPONSIBILITIES CONCERNING FBI EMPLOYEES UNDER THE CIVIL SERVICE REFORM ACT OF 1978

Memorandum of President of the United States, Apr. 14, 1997, 62 F.R. 23123, provided:

Memorandum for the Attorney General

By the authority vested in me by the Constitution and laws of the United States of America, including section 301 of title 3, United States Code, I hereby delegate to the Attorney General the functions concerning employees of the Federal Bureau of Investigation vested in the President by section 101(a) of the Civil Service Reform Act of 1978 (Public Law 95–454), as amended by the Whistleblower Protection Act of 1989 (Public Law 101–12), and codified at section 2303(c) of title 5, United States Code, and direct the Attorney General to establish appropriate processes within the Department of Justice to carry out these functions. Not later than March 1 of each year, the Attorney General shall provide a report to the President stating the number of allegations of reprisal received during the preceding calendar year, the disposition of each allegation resolved during the preceding calendar year, and the number of unresolved allegations pending as of the end of the calendar year.

All of the functions vested in the President by section 2303(c) of title 5, United States Code, and delegated to the Attorney General, may be redelegated, as appropriate, provided that such functions may not be redelegated to the Federal Bureau of Investigation.

You are authorized and directed to publish this memorandum in the Federal Register.

WILLIAM J. CLINTON.

§ 2304. Responsibility of the General Accounting Office

If requested by either House of the Congress (or any committee thereof), or if considered necessary by the Comptroller General, the General Accounting Office shall conduct audits and reviews to assure compliance with the laws, rules, and regulations governing employment in the executive branch and in the competitive service and to assess the effectiveness and soundness of Federal personnel management.

(Added Pub. L. 95–454, title I, § 101(a), Oct. 13, 1978, 92 Stat. 1118; amended Pub. L. 102–378, § 2(6), Oct. 2, 1992, 106 Stat. 1346; Pub. L. 104–66, title II, § 2181(e), Dec. 21, 1995, 109 Stat. 732.)

AMENDMENTS

1995—Pub. L. 104–66 struck out subsec. (a) designation before "If requested by" and struck out subsec. (b)

which read as follows: "The General Accounting Office shall prepare and submit an annual report to the President and the Congress on the activities of the Merit Systems Protection Board and the Office of Personnel Management. The report shall include a description of—

"(1) significant actions taken by the Board to carry out its functions under this title; and

"(2) significant actions of the Office of Personnel Management, including an analysis of whether or not the actions of the Office are in accord with merit system principles and free from prohibited personnel practices."

1992—Subsec. (b). Pub. L. 102–378 substituted "The" for "the" at beginning of first sentence.

§ 2305. Coordination with certain other provisions of law

No provision of this chapter, or action taken under this chapter, shall be construed to impair the authorities and responsibilities set forth in section 102 of the National Security Act of 1947 (61 Stat. 495; 50 U.S.C. 403), the Central Intelligence Agency Act of 1949 (63 Stat. 208; 50 U.S.C. 403a and following), the Act entitled "An Act to provide certain administrative authorities for the National Security Agency, and for other purposes", approved May 29, 1959 (73 Stat. 63; 50 U.S.C. 402 note), and the Act entitled "An Act to amend the Internal Security Act of 1950", approved March 26, 1964 (78 Stat. 168; 50 U.S.C. 831–835).

(Added Pub. L. 95–454, title I, § 101(a), Oct. 13, 1978, 92 Stat. 1118.)

REFERENCES IN TEXT

The Central Intelligence Agency Act of 1949 (63 Stat. 208; 50 U.S.C. 403a and following), referred to in text, is act June 20, 1949, ch. 227, 63 Stat. 208, as amended, which is classified generally to section 403a et seq. of Title 50, War and National Defense. For complete classification of this Act to the Code, see Short Title note set out under section 403a of Title 50 and Tables.

The Act entitled "An Act to provide certain administrative authorities for the National Security Agency, and for other purposes", approved May 29, 1959 (73 Stat. 63; 50 U.S.C. 402 note), referred to in text, is Pub. L. 86–36, May 29, 1959, 73 Stat. 63, as amended, and is set out as a note under section 402 of Title 50. For complete classification of this Act to the Code, see Tables.

The Act entitled "An Act to amend the Internal Security Act of 1950", approved March 26, 1964 (78 Stat. 168; 50 U.S.C. 831–835), referred to in text, is act Sept. 23, 1950, ch. 1024, title III, as added Mar. 26, 1964, Pub. L. 88–290, 78 Stat. 168, which is classified principally to subchapter III (§ 831 et seq.) of chapter 23 of Title 50. For complete classification of this Act to the Code, see Tables.

CHAPTER 29—COMMISSIONS, OATHS, RECORDS, AND REPORTS

SUBCHAPTER I—COMMISSIONS, OATHS, AND RECORDS

Sec.
2953.   Reports to Congress on additional employee requirements.
2954.   Information to committees of Congress on request.

AMENDMENTS

1978—Pub. L. 95–454, title IX, § 906(a)(16), Oct. 13, 1978, 92 Stat. 1226, substituted "Office of Personnel Management" for "Civil Service Commission" in item 2951.

SUBCHAPTER I—COMMISSIONS, OATHS, AND RECORDS

§ 2901. Commission of an officer

The President may make out and deliver, after adjournment of the Senate, the commission of an officer whose appointment has been confirmed by the Senate.

(Pub. L. 89–554, Sept. 6, 1966, 80 Stat. 411.)

HISTORICAL AND REVISION NOTES

Derivation	U.S. Code	Revised Statutes and Statutes at Large
....	5 U.S.C. 10.	R.S. § 1773.

The words "confirmed by" are substituted for "advised and consented to".

Standard changes are made to conform with the definitions applicable and the style of this title as outlined in the preface to the report.

§ 2902. Commission; where recorded

(a) Except as provided by subsections (b) and (c) of this section, the Secretary of State shall make out and record, and affix the seal of the United States to, the commission of an officer appointed by the President. The seal of the United States may not be affixed to the commission before the commission has been signed by the President.

(b) The commission of an officer in the civil service or uniformed services under the control of the Secretary of Agriculture, the Secretary of Commerce, the Secretary of Defense, the Secretary of a military department, the Secretary of the Interior, or the Secretary of the Treasury shall be made out and recorded in the department in which he is to serve under the seal of that department. The departmental seal may not be affixed to the commission before the commission has been signed by the President.

(c) The commissions of judicial officers and United States attorneys and marshals, appointed by the President, by and with the advice and consent of the Senate, and other commissions which before August 8, 1888, were prepared at the Department of State on the requisition of the Attorney General, shall be made out and recorded in the Department of Justice under the seal of that department and countersigned by the Attorney General. The departmental seal may not be affixed to the commission before the commission has been signed by the President.

(Pub. L. 89–554, Sept. 6, 1966, 80 Stat. 411; Pub. L. 94–183, § 2(3), Dec. 31, 1975, 89 Stat. 1057.)

HISTORICAL AND REVISION NOTES

Derivation	U.S. Code	Revised Statutes and Statutes at Large
(a)	4 U.S.C. 42 (as applicable to civil commissions).	[None.]

HISTORICAL AND REVISION NOTES—CONTINUED

Derivation	U.S. Code	Revised Statutes and Statutes at Large
(b)	5 U.S.C. 11.	Mar. 3, 1875, ch. 131, § 14, 18 Stat. 420. Mar. 28, 1896, ch. 73, 29 Stat. 75. Mar. 3, 1905, ch. 1422, 33 Stat. 990.
(c)	5 U.S.C. 12.	Aug. 8, 1888, ch. 786, 25 Stat. 387.

In subsection (a), the words "Except as provided by subsections (b) and (c) of this section," are added on authority of former sections 11 and 12, which are codified in subsections (b) and (c) of this section. The words "the commission of an officer" are substituted for "all civil commissions for officers of the United States" because of the definition of "officer" in section 2104. The words "by the President" are coextensive with and substituted for "by the President, by and with the advice and consent of the Senate, or by the President alone".

In subsection (b), the words "officer in the civil service or uniformed services" are substituted for "officer" because of the definition of "officer" in section 2104. The words "direction and" are omitted as included within "the control". The words "the Secretary of Defense" are added on authority of the Acts of July 26, 1947, ch. 343, § 305(a), 61 Stat. 508, and Aug. 10, 1949, ch. 412, § 12(g), 63 Stat. 591. The words "the Secretary of a military department" are substituted for "the Secretary of War, the Secretary of the Navy" (appearing in the Act of Mar. 28, 1896) because of the definition of "military department" in section 102. The title of the Secretary of War was changed to Secretary of the Army by the Act of July 26, 1947, ch. 343, § 205, 61 Stat. 501. "Secretary of the Air Force" is included on authority of the Act of July 26, 1947, ch. 343, § 207(a), (f), 61 Stat. 502. The words "Secretary of Commerce" are substituted for "Secretary of Commerce and Labor" on authority of the Act of Mar. 4, 1913, ch. 141, § 1, 37 Stat. 736. The words "under the departmental seal" are substituted for "and the departmental seal affixed thereto". The words "any laws to the contrary notwithstanding" are omitted as unnecessary. The last sentence of section 14 of the Act of Mar. 3, 1875, is omitted as executed.

In subsection (c), the words "and shall be" and "any laws to the contrary notwithstanding" are omitted as unnecessary.

Standard changes are made to conform with the definitions applicable and the style of this title as outlined in the preface to the report.

AMENDMENTS

1975—Subsec. (b). Pub. L. 94–183 struck out "the Postmaster General," after "under the control of".

SECTION REFERRED TO IN OTHER SECTIONS

This section is referred to in title 4 section 42.

§ 2903. Oath; authority to administer

(a) The oath of office required by section 3331 of this title may be administered by an individual authorized by the laws of the United States or local law to administer oaths in the State, District, or territory or possession of the United States where the oath is administered.

(b) An employee of an Executive agency designated in writing by the head of the Executive agency, or the Secretary of a military department with respect to an employee of his department, may administer—

(1) the oath of office required by section 3331 of this title, incident to entrance into the executive branch; or

(2) any other oath required by law in connection with employment in the executive branch.

(c) An oath authorized or required under the laws of the United States may be administered by—

(1) the Vice President; or

(2) an individual authorized by local law to administer oaths in the State, District, or territory or possession of the United States where the oath is administered.

(Pub. L. 89–554, Sept. 6, 1966, 80 Stat. 411.)

HISTORICAL AND REVISION NOTES

Derivation	U.S. Code	Revised Statutes and Statutes at Large
(a)	5 U.S.C. 18.	R.S. § 1758.
(b)	5 U.S.C. 16a(a) (less 1st 9 words after last comma).	June 26, 1943, ch. 145, § 206 (less 1st 9 words after last comma), 57 Stat. 196.
(c)	5 U.S.C. 16a(b).	Sept. 30, 1961, Pub. L. 87–322 (par. under "General Provision"), 75 Stat. 743.
	5 U.S.C. 92a.	July 3, 1926, ch. 752, 44 Stat. 830.

In subsection (b), the words "On and after June 26, 1943" are omitted as executed, and the word "officer" is omitted as included in "employee". The words "Executive agency" are coextensive with and substituted for "executive departments or independent establishments, including any agency the majority of the stock of which is owned by the Government of the United States" because of the definition of "Executive agency" in section 105. The words "or the Secretary of a military department with respect to an employee of his department" are inserted to preserve the application of the source law. Before enactment of the National Security Act Amendments of 1949 (63 Stat. 578), the Department of the Army, the Department of the Navy, and the Department of the Air Force were Executive departments. The National Security Act Amendments of 1949 established the Department of Defense as an Executive Department including the Department of the Army, the Department of the Navy, and the Department of the Air Force as military departments, not as Executive departments. However, the source law for this section, which was in effect in 1949, remained applicable to the Secretaries of the military departments by virtue of section 12(g) of the National Security Act Amendments of 1949 (63 Stat. 591), which is set out in the reviser's note for section 301. The words "of the Federal Government" and "and to have the same force and effect as oaths administered by officers having seals" are omitted as unnecessary.

In subsection (c), the word "Constitution" is omitted because "laws", as used in this title, encompasses the Constitution. In subsection (c)(1), the words "of the United States" are omitted as unnecessary. In subsection (c)(2), the words "an individual authorized by local law to administer oaths in the State, District, or territory, or possession of the United States where the oath is administered" are coextensive with and substituted for "notaries public duly appointed in any State, District, or Territory of the United States, by clerks and prothonotaries of courts of record of any such State, District, or Territory, by the deputies of such clerks and prothonotaries, and by all magistrates authorized by the laws of or pertaining to any such State, District, or Territory to administer oaths".

Standard changes are made to conform with the definitions applicable and the style of this title as outlined in the preface to the report.

SECTION REFERRED TO IN OTHER SECTIONS

This section is referred to in title 39 section 1011.

§ 2904. Oath; administered without fees

An employee of an Executive agency who is authorized to administer the oath of office required by section 3331 of this title, or any other oath required by law in connection with employment in the executive branch, may not charge or receive a fee or pay for administering the oath.

(Pub. L. 89–554, Sept. 6, 1966, 80 Stat. 412.)

HISTORICAL AND REVISION NOTES

Derivation	U.S. Code	Revised Statutes and Statutes at Large
....	5 U.S.C. 16a(a) (1st 9 words after last comma).	June 26, 1943, ch. 145, § 206 (1st 9 words after last comma), 57 Stat. 196. Sept. 30, 1961, Pub. L. 87–322 (so much of par. under "General Provision" as inserted "(a)"), 75 Stat. 743.
....	5 U.S.C. 20.	Aug. 29, 1890, ch. 820, § 1 (2d sentence under "Fourth Auditor's Office"), 26 Stat. 371.

The section is restated to combine former sections 16a(a) (1st 9 words after last comma) and 20. The prohibition is restated in positive form. The words "officer" and "clerk" are omitted as included in "employee". Reference to oaths taken on promotion is omitted as unnecessary.

Standard changes are made to conform with the definitions applicable and the style of this title as outlined in the preface to the report.

§ 2905. Oath; renewal

(a) An employee of an Executive agency or an individual employed by the government of the District of Columbia who, on original appointment, subscribed to the oath of office required by section 3331 of this title is not required to renew the oath because of a change in status so long as his service is continuous in the agency in which he is employed, unless, in the opinion of the head of the Executive agency, the Secretary of a military department with respect to an employee of his department, or the Commissioners of the District of Columbia, the public interest so requires.

(b) An individual who, on appointment as an employee of a House of Congress, subscribed to the oath of office required by section 3331 of this title is not required to renew the oath so long as his service as an employee of that House of Congress is continuous.

(Pub. L. 89–554, Sept. 6, 1966, 80 Stat. 412.)

HISTORICAL AND REVISION NOTES

Derivation	U.S. Code	Revised Statutes and Statutes at Large
(a)	5 U.S.C. 17b.	Aug. 14, 1937, ch. 624, 50 Stat. 640. Nov. 22, 1943, ch. 303, 57 Stat. 591.
(b)	5 U.S.C. 17c.	Mar. 28, 1955, ch. 17, 69 Stat. 14.

In subsection (a), the word "civilian" is omitted as unnecessary because of the definition of "employee" in section 2105. The words "Executive agency" are coextensive with and substituted for "executive departments and independent establishments of the United States" because of the definition of "Executive agency" in section 105. The words "the Secretary of a military department with respect to an employee of his department" are inserted to preserve the application of the source law. Before enactment of the National Security Act Amendments of 1949 (63 Stat. 578), the Department of the Army, the Department of the Navy, and the Department of the Air Force were Executive departments. The National Security Act Amendments of 1949 established the Department of Defense as an Executive Department including the Department of the Army, the Department of the Navy, and the Department of the Air Force as military departments, not as Executive departments. However, the source law for this section, which was in effect in 1949, remained applicable to the Secretaries of the military departments by virtue of section 12(g) of the National Security Act Amendments of 1949 (63 Stat. 591), which is set out in the reviser's note for section 301.

Standard changes are made to conform with the definitions applicable and the style of this title as outlined in the preface to the report.

§ 2906. Oath; custody

The oath of office taken by an individual under section 3331 of this title shall be delivered by him to, and preserved by, the House of Congress, agency, or court to which the office pertains.

(Pub. L. 89–554, Sept. 6, 1966, 80 Stat. 412.)

HISTORICAL AND REVISION NOTES

Derivation	U.S. Code	Revised Statutes and Statutes at Large
....	5 U.S.C. 21.	R.S. § 1759.

Standard changes are made to conform with the definitions applicable and the style of this title as outlined in the preface to the report.

SUBCHAPTER II—REPORTS

§ 2951. Reports to the Office of Personnel Management

The President may prescribe rules which shall provide, as nearly as conditions of good administration warrant, that—

(1) the appointing authority notify the Office of Personnel Management in writing of the following actions and their dates as to each individual selected for appointment in the competitive service from among those who have been examined—

(A) appointment and residence of appointee;

(B) separation during probation;

(C) transfer;

(D) resignation;

(E) removal; and

(2) the Office keep records of these actions.

(Pub. L. 89–554, Sept. 6, 1966, 80 Stat. 412; Pub. L. 95–454, title IX, § 906(a)(2), (3), (16), Oct. 13, 1978, 92 Stat. 1224, 1226.)

HISTORICAL AND REVISION NOTES

Derivation	U.S. Code	Revised Statutes and Statutes at Large
....	5 U.S.C. 633(2)8 (less last sentence).	Jan. 16, 1883, ch. 27, § 2(2)8 (less last sentence), 22 Stat. 404.

The authority of the President to prescribe rules is added on authority of former section 633(1), which is carried into section 3302.

In paragraph (1), the word "authority" is substituted for "power". The words "or employment" are omitted as included within "appointment".

In paragraph (1)(B), the words "separation during probation" are substituted for "of the rejection of any such person after probation". The words "rejection . . . after probation" refer to a rejection, i.e., separation, after a portion of the probationary period has been served but before the end of the probationary period. This is so because an individual can be rejected only during the probationary period. After he has completed the probationary period, he can be removed only under procedures governing removals from the competitive service, and removals of this nature are covered by paragraph (E).

Standard changes are made to conform with the definitions applicable and the style of this title as outlined in the preface to the report.

AMENDMENTS

1978—Pub. L. 95–454, § 906(a)(16), substituted "Office of Personnel Management" for "Civil Service Commission" in section catchline.

Pars. (1), (2). Pub. L. 95–454 substituted "Office of Personnel Management" for "Civil Service Commission" and "Office" for "Commission".

EFFECTIVE DATE OF 1978 AMENDMENT

Amendment by Pub. L. 95–454 effective 90 days after Oct. 13, 1978, see section 907 of Pub. L. 95–454, set out as a note under section 1101 of this title.

SECTION REFERRED TO IN OTHER SECTIONS

This section is referred to in section 3302 of this title.

§ 2952. Time of making annual reports

Except when a different time is specifically prescribed by statute, the head of each Executive department or military department shall make the annual reports, required to be submitted to Congress, at the beginning of each regular session of Congress. The reports shall cover the transactions of the preceding year.

(Pub. L. 89–554, Sept. 6, 1966, 80 Stat. 413.)

HISTORICAL AND REVISION NOTES

Derivation	U.S. Code	Revised Statutes and Statutes at Large
....	5 U.S.C. 106.	R.S. § 195.

The words "Executive department" are substituted for "department" as the definition of "department" applicable to this section is coextensive with the definition of "Executive department" in section 101.

The words "or military department" are inserted to preserve the application of the source law. Before enactment of the National Security Act Amendments of 1949 (63 Stat. 578), the Department of the Army, the Department of the Navy, and the Department of the Air Force were Executive departments. The National Security Act Amendments of 1949 established the Department of Defense as an Executive Department including the Department of the Army, the Department of the Navy, and the Department of the Air Force as military departments, not as Executive departments. However, the source law for this section, which was in effect in 1949, remained applicable to the Secretaries of the military departments by virtue of section 12(g) of the National Security Act Amendments of 1949 (63 Stat. 591), which is set out in the reviser's note for section 301.

This section was part of title IV of the Revised Statutes. The Act of July 26, 1947, ch. 343, 201(d), as added Aug. 10, 1949, ch. 412, § 4, 63 Stat. 579 (former 5 U.S.C. 171–1), which provides "Except to the extent inconsistent with the provisions of this Act [National Security Act of 1947], the provisions of title IV of the Revised

Statutes as now or hereafter amended shall be applicable to the Department of Defense" is omitted from this title but is not repealed.

Standard changes are made to conform with the definitions applicable and the style of this title as outlined in the preface to the report.

§ 2953. Reports to Congress on additional employee requirements

(a) Each report, recommendation, or other communication, of an official nature, of an Executive agency which—

(1) relates to pending or proposed legislation which, if enacted, will entail an estimated annual expenditure of appropriated funds in excess of $1,000,000;

(2) is submitted or transmitted to Congress or a committee thereof in compliance with law or on the initiative of the appropriate authority of the executive branch; and

(3) officially proposes or recommends the creation or expansion, either by action of Congress or by administrative action, of a function, activity, or authority of the Executive agency to be in addition to those functions, activities, and authorities thereof existing when the report, recommendation, or other communication is so submitted or transmitted;

shall contain a statement, concerning the Executive agency, for each of the first 5 fiscal years during which each additional or expanded function, activity, or authority so proposed or recommended is to be in effect, setting forth the following information—

(A) the estimated maximum additional—

(i) man-years of civilian employment, by general categories of positions;

(ii) expenditures for personal services; and

(iii) expenditures for all purposes other than personal services;

which are attributable to the function, activity, or authority and which will be required to be effected by the Executive agency in connection with the performance thereof; and

(B) such other statement, discussion, explanation, or other information as is considered advisable by the appropriate authority of the executive branch or that is required by Congress or a committee thereof.

(b) Subsection (a) of this section does not apply to—

(1) the Central Intelligence Agency;

(2) a Government controlled corporation; or

(3) the General Accounting Office.

(Pub. L. 89–554, Sept. 6, 1966, 80 Stat. 413.)

HISTORICAL AND REVISION NOTES

Derivation	U.S. Code	Revised Statutes and Statutes at Large
....	5 U.S.C. 642a.	July 25, 1956, ch. 730, §1, 70 Stat. 652.

In subsection (a), the words, "Executive agency" are substituted for "department, agency, or independent establishment of the executive branch of the Federal Government (including any corporation wholly owned by the United States)" in view of the definition of "Executive agency" in section 105. The exception of "a Government controlled corporation" is subsection (b)

(2) is added to preserve the application to corporations wholly owned by the United States.

The exception of "the General Accounting Office" in subsection (b)(3) is added to preserve application to the executive branch.

Standard changes are made to conform with the definitions applicable and the style of this title as outlined in the preface to the report.

§ 2954. Information to committees of Congress on request

An Executive agency, on request of the Committee on Government Operations of the House of Representatives, or of any seven members thereof, or on request of the Committee on Governmental Affairs of the Senate, or any five members thereof, shall submit any information requested of it relating to any matter within the jurisdiction of the committee.

(Pub. L. 89–554, Sept. 6, 1966, 80 Stat. 413; Pub. L. 103–437, §3(b), Nov. 2, 1994, 108 Stat. 4581.)

HISTORICAL AND REVISION NOTES

Derivation	U.S. Code	Revised Statutes and Statutes at Large
....	5 U.S.C. 105a.	May 29, 1928, ch. 901, §2, 45 Stat. 996.

The words "Executive agency" are substituted for "executive department and independent establishment" in view of the definition of "Executive agency" in section 105.

The words "Committee on Government Operations of the House of Representatives" are substituted for "Committee on Expenditures in the Executive Departments of the House of Representatives" on authority of H. Res. 647 of the 82d Congress, adopted July 3, 1952.

The words "Committee on Government Operations of the Senate" are substituted for "Committee on Expenditures in the Executive Departments of the Senate" on authority of S. Res. 280 of the 82d Congress, adopted Mar. 3, 1952.

Standard changes are made to conform with the definitions applicable and the style of this title as outlined in the preface to the report.

AMENDMENTS

1994—Pub. L. 103–437 substituted "Committee on Governmental Affairs of the Senate" for "Committee on Government Operations of the Senate".

CHANGE OF NAME

Committee on Government Operations of House of Representatives treated as referring to Committee on Government Reform and Oversight of House of Representatives by section 1(a) of Pub. L. 104–14, set out as a note under section 21 of Title 2, The Congress. Committee on Government Reform and Oversight of House of Representatives changed to Committee on Government Reform of House of Representatives by House Resolution No. 5, One Hundred Sixth Congress, Jan. 6, 1999.

Subpart B—Employment and Retention

CHAPTER 31—AUTHORITY FOR EMPLOYMENT

SUBCHAPTER I—EMPLOYMENT AUTHORITIES

Sec.
3101.   General authority to employ.
3102.   Employment of personal assistants for handicapped employees, including blind and deaf employees.

AMENDMENTS

2000—Pub. L. 106–398, § 1 [[div. A], title XI, § 1101(b)], Oct. 30, 2000, 114 Stat. 1654, 1654A–310, added subchapter IV heading and item 3161.

1997—Pub. L. 105–61, title VI, § 638(b), Oct. 10, 1997, 111 Stat. 1317, added item 3113.

1995—Pub. L. 104–66, title II, § 2181(a)(2), Dec. 21, 1995, 109 Stat. 732, struck out item 3135 "Biennial report".

1988—Pub. L. 100–325, § 1(b), May 30, 1988, 102 Stat. 581, added subchapter III heading and items 3151 and 3152.

1980—Pub. L. 96–523, § 1(b), Dec. 12, 1980, 94 Stat. 3040, substituted "personal assistants for handicapped employees, including blind and" for "reading assistants for blind employees and interpreting assistants for" in item 3102.

1978—Pub. L. 95–454, title III, §§ 301(b), 302(b)(1), 307(b)(3), title IV, § 402(c), Oct. 13, 1978, 92 Stat. 1145, 1146, 1148, 1160, added heading for subchapter I, substituted "reading assistants for blind employees and interpreting assistants for deaf employees" for "readers for blind employees" in item 3102, and added items 3111, 3112, heading for subchapter II, and items 3131 to 3136.

Pub. L. 95–251, § 2(c)(2), Mar. 27, 1978, 92 Stat. 184, substituted "administrative law judges" for "hearing examiners" in item 3105.

1967—Pub. L. 90–206, title II, § 221(b), Dec. 16, 1967, 81 Stat. 640, added item 3110.

SUBCHAPTER I—EMPLOYMENT AUTHORITIES

AMENDMENTS

1979—Pub. L. 96–54, § 2(a)(10), Aug. 14, 1979, 93 Stat. 381, added heading for subchapter I.

§ 3101. General authority to employ

Each Executive agency, military department, and the government of the District of Columbia may employ such number of employees of the various classes recognized by chapter 51 of this title as Congress may appropriate for from year to year.

(Pub. L. 89–554, Sept. 6, 1966, 80 Stat. 414.)

HISTORICAL AND REVISION NOTES

Derivation	U.S. Code	Revised Statutes and Statutes at Large
....	5 U.S.C. 43.	R.S. § 169. June 26, 1930, ch. 618, 46 Stat. 817.
....	5 U.S.C. 514d (2d par.).	Sept. 21, 1944, ch. 412, § 709, 58 Stat. 743.

The authorization is restated to conform to the style of this title. The word "Executive agency" are substituted for "executive department, independent establishment" in view of the definitions in sections 103, 104, and 105. The source statute (an act to authorize the appointment of employees in the executive branch etc.) applied to the entire executive branch, and government corporations as well as other agencies in the executive branch were included within the words "independent establishment". The words "or a military department" are inserted to preserve the application of the source statute. Before enactment of the National Security Act Amendments of 1949 (63 Stat. 578), the Department of the Army, the Department of the Navy, and the Department of the Air Force were Executive departments. The National Security Act Amendments of 1949 established the Department of Defense as an Executive department including the Department of the Army, the Department of the Navy, and the Department of the Air Force as military departments, not as Executive departments. However, the source statute for this subsection, which was in effect in 1949, remained applicable to the Secretaries of the military departments by virtue of section 12(g) of the National Security Act Amendments of 1949 (63 Stat. 591), which is set out in the reviser's note for section 301. The words "for services in the District of Columbia or elsewhere" are eliminated as surplusage. The reference to chapter 51 is substituted for the reference to the Classification Act of 1923 because the Act of Oct. 28, 1949, ch. 782, § 1106(a), 63 Stat. 972, amended the section to refer to the Classification Act of 1949, which is carried into this title. The proviso in former section 43 and former section 514d (2d par.) are omitted as superseded by former section 22a, which is carried into section 302. The last sentence of the Act of June 26, 1930, is omitted as executed.

This section was part of title IV of the Revised Statutes. The Act of July 26, 1947, ch. 343, § 201(d), as added Aug. 10, 1949, ch. 412, § 4, 63 Stat. 579 (former 5 U.S.C. 171–1), which provides "Except to the extent inconsistent with the provisions of this Act [National Security Act of 1947], the provisions of title IV of the Revised Statutes as now or hereafter amended shall be applicable to the Department of Defense" is omitted from this title but is not repealed.

Standard changes are made to conform with the definitions applicable and the style of this title as outlined in the preface to the report.

REDUCTION OF FEDERAL FULL-TIME EQUIVALENT POSITIONS

Pub. L. 103–226, § 5, Mar. 30, 1994, 108 Stat. 115, as amended by Pub. L. 103–329, title VI, § 631, Sept. 30, 1994, 108 Stat. 2424, provided that:

"(a) DEFINITION.—For the purpose of this section, the term 'agency' means an Executive agency (as defined by section 105 of title 5, United States Code), but does not include the General Accounting Office.

"(b) LIMITATIONS ON FULL-TIME EQUIVALENT POSITIONS.—The President, through the Office of Management and Budget (in consultation with the Office of Personnel Management), shall ensure that the total number of full-time equivalent positions in all agencies shall not exceed—

"(1) 2,084,600 during fiscal year 1994;
"(2) 2,043,300 during fiscal year 1995;
"(3) 2,003,300 during fiscal year 1996;
"(4) 1,963,300 during fiscal year 1997;
"(5) 1,922,300 during fiscal year 1998; and
"(6) 1,882,300 during fiscal year 1999.

"(c) MONITORING AND NOTIFICATION.—The Office of Management and Budget, after consultation with the Office of Personnel Management, shall—

"(1) continuously monitor all agencies and make a determination on the first date of each quarter of each applicable fiscal year of whether the requirements under subsection (b) are met; and

"(2) notify the President and the Congress on the first date of each quarter of each applicable fiscal year of any determination that any requirement of subsection (b) is not met.

"(d) COMPLIANCE.—If, at any time during a fiscal year, the Office of Management and Budget notifies the President and the Congress that any requirement under subsection (b) is not met, no agency may hire any employee for any position in such agency until the Office of Management and Budget notifies the President and the Congress that the total number of full-time equivalent positions for all agencies equals or is less than the applicable number required under subsection (b).

"(e) WAIVER.—

"(1) EMERGENCIES.—Any provision of this section may be waived upon a determination by the President that—

"(A) the existence of a state of war or other national security concern so requires; or

"(B) the existence of an extraordinary emergency threatening life, health, safety, property, or the environment so requires.

"(2) AGENCY EFFICIENCY OR CRITICAL MISSION.—

"(A) Subsection (d) may be waived, in the case of a particular position or category of positions in an agency, upon a determination of the President that the efficiency of the agency or the performance of a critical agency mission so requires.

"(B) Whenever the President grants a waiver pursuant to subparagraph (A), the President shall take all necessary actions to ensure that the overall limitations set forth in subsection (b) are not exceeded.

"(f) EMPLOYMENT BACKFILL PREVENTION.—

"(1) IN GENERAL.—The total number of funded employee positions in all agencies (excluding the Department of Defense and the Central Intelligence Agency) shall be reduced by one position for each vacancy created by the separation of any employee who has received, or is due to receive, a voluntary separation incentive payment under section 3(a)–(e) [5 U.S.C. 5597 note]. For purposes of this subsection, positions and vacancies shall be counted on a full-time-equivalent basis.

"(2) RELATED RESTRICTION.—No funds budgeted for and appropriated by any Act for salaries or expenses of positions eliminated under this subsection may be used for any purpose other than authorized separation costs.

"(3) APPLICABILITY OF BACKFILL PREVENTION PROVISIONS TO AGENCIES OTHERWISE EXEMPTED FROM FTE REDUCTION.—

"(A) IN GENERAL.—If any agency is otherwise exempted by any law from the limitations on full-time equivalent positions or the restrictions on hiring established by this section—

"(i) paragraph (1) shall apply to vacancies created in such agency; and

"(ii) the reductions required pursuant to clause (i) shall be made in the number of funded employee positions in such agency.

"(B) WAIVER AUTHORITY.—In the case of a particular position in an agency, subparagraph (A) may be waived upon a determination by the head of the agency that the performance of a critical agency mission requires the waiver.

"(C) RELATION TO OTHER LAW.—No law may be construed as suspending or modifying this paragraph unless such law specifically amends this paragraph.

"(g) LIMITATION ON PROCUREMENT OF SERVICE CONTRACTS.—The President shall take appropriate action to ensure that there is no increase in the procurement of service contracts by reason of the enactment of this Act [see Tables for classification], except in cases in which a cost comparison demonstrates such contracts would be to the financial advantage of the Federal Government."

LIMITATION ON NUMBER OF CIVILIAN EMPLOYEES IN EXECUTIVE BRANCH

Pub. L. 95–454, title III, § 311, Oct. 13, 1978, 92 Stat. 1153, which provided that the total number of civilian employees in the executive branch, on Sept. 30, 1979, on Sept. 30, 1980, and Sept. 30, 1981, shall not exceed the number of such employees on Sept. 30, 1977, terminated by its own terms on Jan. 31, 1981.

Pub. L. 91–47, title V, § 503, July 22, 1969, 83 Stat. 83, repealed section 201 of Pub. L. 90–364, title II, June 28, 1968, 82 Stat. 270, which provided for limitation on the number of civilian officers and employees in the executive branch and which was formerly set out under this section.

FREEZE ON HIRING OF FEDERAL CIVILIAN EMPLOYEES

Memorandum of the President of the United States, dated Jan. 20, 1981, 46 F.R. 9907, provided for a freeze on the hiring of Federal civilian employees in the executive branch.

CITIZENSHIP REQUIREMENT FOR EMPLOYEES COMPENSATED FROM APPROPRIATED FUNDS

Pub. L. 106–554, § 1(a)(3) [title VI, § 605], Dec. 21, 2000, 114 Stat. 2763, 2763A–155, provided that: "Unless otherwise specified during the current fiscal year, no part of any appropriation contained in this or any other Act shall be used to pay the compensation of any officer or employee of the Government of the United States (including any agency the majority of the stock of which is owned by the Government of the United States) whose post of duty is in the continental United States unless such person: (1) is a citizen of the United States; (2) is a person in the service of the United States on the date of the enactment of this Act [Dec. 21, 2000] who, being eligible for citizenship, has filed a declaration of intention to become a citizen of the United States prior to such date and is actually residing in the United States; (3) is a person who owes allegiance to the United States; (4) is an alien from Cuba, Poland, South Vietnam, the countries of the former Soviet Union, or the Baltic countries lawfully admitted to the United States for permanent residence; (5) is a South Vietnamese, Cambodian, or Laotian refugee paroled in the United States after January 1, 1975; or (6) is a national of the People's Republic of China who qualifies for adjustment of status pursuant to the Chinese Student Protection Act of 1992 [Pub. L. 102–404; 8 U.S.C. 1255 note]: *Provided*, That for the purpose of this section, an affidavit signed by any such person shall be considered prima facie evidence that the requirements of this section with respect to his or her status have been complied with: *Provided further*, That any person making a false affidavit shall be guilty of a felony, and, upon conviction, shall be fined no more than $4,000 or imprisoned for not more than 1 year, or both: *Provided further*, That the above penal clause shall be in addition to, and not in substitution for, any other provisions of existing law: *Provided further*, That any payment made to any officer or employee contrary to the provisions of this section shall be recoverable in action by the Federal Government. This section shall not apply to citizens of Ireland, Israel, or the Republic of the Philippines, or to nationals of those countries allied with the United States in a current defense effort, or to international broadcasters employed by the United States Information Agency, or to temporary employment of translators, or to temporary employment in the field service (not to exceed 60 days) as a result of emergencies."

[For abolition of United States Information Agency (other than Broadcasting Board of Governors and International Broadcasting Bureau), transfer of functions, and treatment of references thereto, see sections 6531, 6532, and 6551 of Title 22, Foreign Relations and Intercourse.]

Similar provisions were contained in the following prior appropriation acts:

Pub. L. 106–58, title VI, §605, Sept. 29, 1999, 113 Stat. 466.

Pub. L. 105–277, div. A, §101(h) [title VI, §606], Oct. 21, 1998, 112 Stat. 2681–480, 2681–513.

Pub. L. 105–61, title VI, §606, Oct. 10, 1997, 111 Stat. 1309.

Pub. L. 104–208, div. A, title I, §101(f) [title VI, §606], Sept. 30, 1996, 110 Stat. 3009–314, 3009–354.

Pub. L. 104–52, title VI, §606, Nov. 19, 1995, 109 Stat. 497.

Pub. L. 103–329, title VI, §606, Sept. 30, 1994, 108 Stat. 2416.

Pub. L. 103–123, title VI, §606, Oct. 28, 1993, 107 Stat. 1259.

Pub. L. 102–393, title VI, §607, Oct. 6, 1992, 106 Stat. 1766.

Pub. L. 102–141, title VI, §607, Oct. 28, 1991, 105 Stat. 868.

Pub. L. 101–509, title VI, §603, Nov. 5, 1990, 104 Stat. 1471.

Pub. L. 101–136, title VI, §603, Nov. 3, 1989, 103 Stat. 816.

Pub. L. 100–440, title VI, §603, Sept. 22, 1988, 102 Stat. 1751.

Pub. L. 100–202, §101(m) [title VI, §603], Dec. 22, 1987, 101 Stat. 1329–390, 1329–419.

Pub. L. 99–500, §101(m) [title VI, §603], Oct. 18, 1986, 100 Stat. 1783–308, 1783–328, and Pub. L. 99–591, §101(m) [title VI, §603], Oct. 30, 1986, 100 Stat. 3341–308, 3341–328.

Pub. L. 99–190, title I, §101(h) [H.R. 3036, title VI, §603], Dec. 19, 1985, 99 Stat. 1291.

Pub. L. 98–473, title I, §101(j) [H.R. 5798, title VI, §604], Oct. 12, 1984, 98 Stat. 1963.

Pub. L. 98–151, §101(f) [H.R. 4139, title VI, §603], Nov. 14, 1983, 97 Stat. 973.

Pub. L. 97–377, title I, §101(a) [incorporating H.R. 4121, title VI, §603, for FY 1982], Dec. 21, 1982, 96 Stat. 1830.

Pub. L. 97–92, §101(a) [H.R. 4121, title VI, §603], Dec. 15, 1981, 95 Stat. 1183.

Pub. L. 96–536, §101(a) [incorporating Pub. L. 96–74, title VI, §602], Dec. 16, 1980, 94 Stat. 3166.

Pub. L. 96–74, title VI, §602, Sept. 29, 1979, 93 Stat. 574.

Pub. L. 95–429, title VI, §602, Oct. 10, 1978, 92 Stat. 1015.

Pub. L. 95–81, title VI, §602, July 31, 1977, 91 Stat. 354.

Pub. L. 94–419, title VII, §750, Sept. 22, 1976, 90 Stat. 1299.

Pub. L. 94–363, title VI, §602, July 14, 1976, 90 Stat. 977.

Pub. L. 94–212, title VII, §753, Feb. 9, 1976, 90 Stat. 177.

Pub. L. 94–91, title VI, §602, Aug. 9, 1975, 89 Stat. 458.

Pub. L. 93–381, title VI, §602, Aug. 21, 1974, 88 Stat. 630.

Pub. L. 93–143, title VI, §602, Oct. 30, 1973, 87 Stat. 524.

Pub. L. 92–351, title VI, §602, July 13, 1972, 86 Stat. 487.

Pub. L. 92–49, title VI, §602, July 9, 1971, 85 Stat. 122.

Pub. L. 91–439, title V, §502, Oct. 7, 1970, 84 Stat. 902.

Pub. L. 91–144, title V, §502, Dec. 11, 1969, 83 Stat. 336.

Pub. L. 90–479, title V, §502, Aug. 12, 1968, 82 Stat. 717.

Pub. L. 90–147, title V, §502, Nov. 20, 1967, 81 Stat. 483.

Pub. L. 89–689, title V, §502, Oct. 15, 1966, 80 Stat. 1014.

Pub. L. 89–299, title V, §502, Oct. 28, 1965, 79 Stat. 1108.

Pub. L. 88–511, title V, §502, Aug. 30, 1964, 78 Stat. 693.

Pub. L. 88–257, title V, §502, Dec. 31, 1963, 77 Stat. 855.

Pub. L. 87–880, title V, §502, Oct. 24, 1962, 76 Stat. 1227.

Pub. L. 87–125, title V, §502, Aug. 3, 1961, 75 Stat. 282.

Pub. L. 86–642, title II, §202, July 12, 1960, 74 Stat. 476.

Pub. L. 86–79, title II, §202, July 8, 1959, 73 Stat. 165.

Pub. L. 85–468, title II, §202, June 25, 1958, 72 Stat. 224.

Pub. L. 85–48, title II, §202, June 5, 1957, 71 Stat. 53.

June 13, 1956, ch. 385, title II, §202, 70 Stat. 280.

June 29, 1955, ch. 226, title II, §202, 69 Stat. 195.

Aug. 26, 1954, ch. 935, Ch. XIII, §1302, 68 Stat. 828.

Aug. 7, 1953, ch. 340, Ch. XIII, §1302, 67 Stat. 435.

July 15, 1952, ch. 758, Ch. XIV, §1402, 66 Stat. 659.

Nov. 1, 1951, ch. 664, Ch. XIII, §1302, 65 Stat. 755.

Sept. 6, 1950, ch. 897, Ch. XII, §1202, 64 Stat. 763.

Aug. 24, 1949, ch. 506, title III, §302, 63 Stat. 661.

Apr. 20, 1948, ch. 219, title II, §202, 62 Stat. 193.

July 30, 1947, ch. 359, title II, §202, 61 Stat. 608.

Mar. 28, 1946, ch. 113, title II, §206, 60 Stat. 80.

May 3, 1945, ch. 106, title II, §206, 59 Stat. 132.

June 27, 1944, ch. 286, title II, §205, 58 Stat. 385.

June 26, 1943, ch. 145, title II, §205, 57 Stat. 196.

Citizenship requirement for permanent officers and employees of Census Bureau, see section 22 of Title 13, Census.

Exceptions to citizenship requirement for—

Department of Defense personnel, see section 1584 of Title 10, Armed Forces.

Department of State employees, see sections 2669, 2672 of Title 22, Foreign Relations and Intercourse.

Department of the Navy personnel, see section 7473 of Title 10.

Library of Congress positions, see section 169 of Title 2, The Congress.

National Aeronautics and Space Administration employees, see section 2473 of Title 42, The Public Health and Welfare.

EMPLOYMENT OF PERSONNEL DURING NATIONAL EMERGENCY PROCLAIMED ON DEC. 16, 1950

Section 1310 of act Nov. 1, 1951, ch. 664, Ch. XIII, 65 Stat. 757, as amended June 5, 1952, ch. 369, Ch. XIII, §1302, 66 Stat. 122; Sept. 1, 1954, ch. 1208, title VI, §602, 68 Stat. 1115; Oct. 11, 1962, Pub. L. 87–793, §717(b), 76 Stat. 858; Aug. 6, 1965, Pub. L. 89–114, 79 Stat. 448; Oct. 11, 1967, Pub. L. 90–105, §3, 81 Stat. 274; Apr. 21, 1976, Pub. L. 94–273, §4(5), 90 Stat. 377, provided that, upon the enactment of this Act [Nov. 1, 1951] and until termination of the national emergency proclaimed by the President on Dec. 16, 1950, agencies shall use their authority to require initial appointment be made on other than a permanent basis to limit the number of permanent employees, the Civil Service Commission facilitate the transfer of Federal employees from nondefense to defense activities with reemployment rights and make use of its authority to prohibit excessively rapid promotions, and agencies review certain positions annually and report to Congressional committees. All powers and authorities under section 1310 of act Nov. 1, 1951, as amended, terminated 2 years from Sept. 14, 1976, pursuant to Pub. L. 94–412, title I, §101, Sept. 14, 1976, 90 Stat. 1255 (50 U.S.C. 1601).

EX. ORD. NO. 12839. REDUCTION OF 100,000 FEDERAL POSITIONS

Ex. Ord. No. 12839, Feb. 10, 1993, 58 F.R. 8515, provided:

By the authority vested in me as President by the Constitution and the laws of the United States of America, including section 301 of title 3, United States Code, section 3301 of title 5, United States Code, and section 1111 of title 31, United States Code, it is hereby ordered as follows:

SECTION 1. *Limits on Hiring Civilian Personnel.* Each executive department or agency with over 100 employees shall eliminate not less than 4 percent of its civilian personnel positions (measured on a full-time equivalent (FTE) basis) over the next 3 fiscal years. The positions shall be vacated through attrition or early out programs established at the discretion of the department and agency heads. At least 10 percent of the reductions shall come from the Senior Executive Service, GS–15 and GS–14 levels or equivalent.

SEC. 2. *Coverage.* This order applies to all executive branch departments and agencies with over 100 employees (measured on a FTE basis).

SEC. 3. *Target Dates.* Each department and agency shall achieve 25 percent of its total reductions by the end of fiscal year 1993, 62.5 percent by the end of fiscal year 1994, and 100 percent by the end of fiscal year 1995.

SEC. 4. *Implementation.* The Director of the Office of Management and Budget shall issue detailed instructions regarding the implementation of this order, including exemptions necessary for the delivery of essential services and compliance with applicable law.

SEC. 5. *Independent Agencies.* All independent regulatory commissions and agencies are requested to comply with the provisions of this order.

WILLIAM J. CLINTON.

SECTION REFERRED TO IN OTHER SECTIONS

This section is referred to in title 3 section 107; title 10 section 10216; title 25 section 2a.

§ 3102. Employment of personal assistants for handicapped employees, including blind and deaf employees

(a) For the purpose of this section—
(1) "agency" means—
(A) an Executive agency;
(B) the Library of Congress; and
(C) an office, agency, or other establishment in the judicial branch;

(2) "handicapped employee" means an individual employed by an agency who is blind or deaf or who otherwise qualifies as a handicapped individual within the meaning of section 501 of the Rehabilitation Act of 1973 (29 U.S.C. 794); and

(3) "nonprofit organization" means an organization determined by the Secretary of the Treasury to be an organization described in section 501(c) of the Internal Revenue Code of 1986 (26 U.S.C. 501(c)) which is exempt from taxation under section 501(a) of such Code.

(b)(1) The head of each agency may employ one or more personal assistants who the head of the agency determines are necessary to enable a handicapped employee of that agency to perform the employee's official duties and who shall serve without pay from the agency without regard to—
(A) the provisions of this title governing appointment in the competitive service;
(B) chapter 51 and subchapter III of chapter 53 of this title; and
(C) section 1342 of title 31.

Such employment may include the employing of a reading assistant or assistants for a blind employee or an interpreting assistant or assistants for a deaf employee.

(2) A personal assistant, including a reading or interpreting assistant, employed under this subsection may receive pay for services performed by the assistant from the handicapped employee or a nonprofit organization, without regard to section 209 of title 18.

(c) The head of each agency may also employ or assign one or more personal assistants who the head of the agency determines are necessary to enable a handicapped employee of that agency to perform the employee's official duties. Such employment may include the employing of a reading assistant or assistants for a blind employee or an interpreting assistant or assistants for a deaf employee.

(d)(1) In the case of any handicapped employee (including a blind or deaf employee) traveling on official business, the head of the agency may authorize the payment to an individual to accompany or assist (or both) the handicapped employee for all or a portion of the travel period

involved. Any payment under this subsection to such an individual may be made either directly to that individual or by advancement or reimbursement to the handicapped employee.

(2) With respect to any individual paid to accompany or assist a handicapped employee under paragraph (1) of this subsection—
(A) the amount paid to that individual shall not exceed the limit or limits which the Office of Personnel Management shall prescribe by regulation to ensure that the payment does not exceed amounts (including pay and, if appropriate, travel expenses and per diem allowances) which could be paid to an employee assigned to accompany or assist the handicapped employee; and

(B) that individual shall be considered an employee, but only for purposes of chapter 81 of this title (relating to compensation for injury) and sections 2671 through 2680 of title 28 (relating to tort claims).

(e) This section may not be held or considered to prevent or limit in any way the assignment to a handicapped employee (including a blind or deaf employee) by an agency of clerical or secretarial assistance, at the expense of the agency under statutes and regulations currently applicable at the time, if that assistance normally is provided, or authorized to be provided, in that manner under currently applicable statutes and regulations.

(Pub. L. 89–554, Sept. 6, 1966, 80 Stat. 414; Pub. L. 90–623, §1(3), Oct. 22, 1968, 82 Stat. 1312; Pub. L. 95–454, title III, §302(a), (b)(2), Oct. 13, 1978, 92 Stat. 1145, 1146; Pub. L. 96–54, §2(a)(11), Aug. 14, 1979, 93 Stat. 382; Pub. L. 96–523, §1(a), Dec. 12, 1980, 94 Stat. 3039; Pub. L. 97–258, §3(a)(3), Sept. 13, 1982, 96 Stat. 1063; Pub. L. 99–514, §2, Oct. 22, 1986, 100 Stat. 2095; Pub. L. 106–518, title III, §311, Nov. 13, 2000, 114 Stat. 2421; Pub. L. 106–553, §1(a)(2) [title III, §307], Dec. 21, 2000, 114 Stat. 2762, 2762A–86.)

HISTORICAL AND REVISION NOTES

Derivation	U.S. Code	Revised Statutes and Statutes at Large
....	5 U.S.C. 43a.	Aug. 29, 1962, Pub. L. 87–614, 76 Stat. 408.

In subsection (a)(1), the word "agency" is substituted for "department". The words "Executive agency" are coextensive with and substituted for "each executive department of the Federal Government, each agency or independent establishment in the executive branch of such Government, each corporation wholly owned or controlled by such Government, and the General Accounting Office" in view of the definition of "Executive agency" in section 105.

In subsection (a)(3), the words "individual employed" are substituted for "employee" so as to include individuals employed by the government of the District of Columbia who are not employees as defined by section 2105.

In subsection (b), the word "may" is substituted for "is authorized" and the words "in his discretion" are omitted as unnecessary in view of the permissive nature of the authority. The words "in the provisions of this title governing appointment in the competitive service" are substituted for "the civil service rules". The words "section 209 of title 18" are substituted for "section 1914 of title 18" on authority of the Act of Oct. 24, 1962, Pub. L. 87–849, §2, 76 Stat. 1126.

Standard changes are made to conform with the definitions applicable and the style of this title as outlined in the preface to the report.

REFERENCES IN TEXT

Section 501 of the Rehabilitation Act of 1973, referred to in subsec. (a)(2), is classified to section 791 of Title 29, Labor, rather than to section 794 of Title 29 as shown in text.

AMENDMENTS

2000—Subsec. (a)(1)(C). Pub. L. 106–518 and Pub. L. 106–553 amended par. (1) identically, adding subpar. (C).

1986—Subsec. (a)(3). Pub. L. 99–514 substituted "Internal Revenue Code of 1986" for "Internal Revenue Code of 1954".

1982—Subsec. (b)(1)(C). Pub. L. 97–258 substituted "section 1342 of title 31" for "section 3679(b) of the Revised Statutes (31 U.S.C. 665(b))".

1980—Pub. L. 96–523 amended section generally and, among other changes, in section catchline substituted "personal assistants for handicapped employees, including blind and" for "reading assistants for blind employees and interpreting assistants for", in subsec. (a) substituted applicability to handicapped employees for applicability to blind and deaf employees omitted applicability to the government of the District of Columbia, in subsec. (b) substituted applicability to personal assistants for applicability to reading and interpreting assistants for blind and deaf employees, respectively, redesignated former subsec. (d) as (c) and made changes in phraseology, added subsec. (d), and redesignated former subsec. (c) as (e) and made changes in phraseology.

1979—Subsec. (a)(2). Pub. L. 96–54 substituted "Mayor" for "Commissioner".

1978—Pub. L. 95–454, § 302(b)(2), substituted "reading assistants for blind employees and interpreting assistants for deaf employees" for "readers for blind employees" in section catchline.

Subsec. (a)(4), (5). Pub. L. 95–454, § 302(a)(1), added par. (4) and redesignated former par. (4) as (5).

Subsec. (b). Pub. L. 95–454, § 302(a)(2), inserted provisions respecting applicability to employment and compensation for interpreting assistant or assistants for deaf employees.

Subsec. (c). Pub. L. 95–454, § 302(a)(3), inserted "or deaf" after "blind".

Subsec. (d). Pub. L. 95–454, § 302(a)(4), added subsec. (d).

1968—Subsec. (a)(2). Pub. L. 90–623 substituted "Commissioner" for "Board of Commissioners".

EFFECTIVE DATE OF 1980 AMENDMENT

Section 3 of Pub. L. 96–523 provided that: "The amendments made by this Act [amending this section, section 7 of the Federal Advisory Committee Act, set out in the Appendix to this title, section 604 of Title 28, Judiciary and Judicial Procedure, and section 410 of Title 39, Postal Service] shall take effect sixty days after the date of the enactment of this Act [Dec. 12, 1980]."

EFFECTIVE DATE OF 1979 AMENDMENT

Amendment by Pub. L. 96–54 effective July 12, 1979, see section 2(b) of Pub. L. 96–54, set out as a note under section 305 of this title.

EFFECTIVE DATE OF 1978 AMENDMENT

Amendment by Pub. L. 95–454 effective 90 days after Oct. 13, 1978, see section 907 of Pub. L. 95–454, set out as a note under section 1101 of this title.

EFFECTIVE DATE OF 1968 AMENDMENT

Amendment by Pub. L. 90–623 intended to restate without substantive change the law in effect on Oct. 22, 1968, see section 6 of Pub. L. 90–623, set out as a note under section 5334 of this title.

SECTION REFERRED TO IN OTHER SECTIONS

This section is referred to in title 28 section 604; title 38 section 7281; title 39 section 410.

§ 3103. Employment at seat of Government only for services rendered

An individual may be employed in the civil service in an Executive department at the seat of Government only for services actually rendered in connection with and for the purposes of the appropriation from which he is paid. An individual who violates this section shall be removed from the service.

(Pub. L. 89–554, Sept. 6, 1966, 80 Stat. 415.)

HISTORICAL AND REVISION NOTES

Derivation	U.S. Code	Revised Statutes and Statutes at Large
....	5 U.S.C. 46.	Aug. 5, 1882, ch. 389, § 4 (less 255th through 316th words), 22 Stat. 255. Sept. 23, 1950, ch. 1010, § 7, 64 Stat. 986.
....	5 U.S.C. 47 (so much as relates to removal).	Aug. 23, 1912, ch. 350, § 5 (so much as relates to removal), 37 Stat. 414.

The words "civil officer, draughtsman, copyist, messenger, assistant messenger, mechanic, watchman, laborer, or other employee" are omitted as obsolete language and "individual" is substituted therefor. The words "in the civil service" are added to preserve the application of former section 46 to civilian employees. The words "or subordinate bureaus or offices thereof" are omitted as surplusage. The words "and at the rate of pay usual and proper for the services" are omitted as surplusage since all pay rates are governed by statute.

All after the 75th words of section 4 of the Act of Aug. 5, 1882, as amended by section 7(b) of the Act of Sept. 23, 1950, except the 255th through 316th words, are omitted as executed. The 255th through 296th words are scheduled for repeal as superseded (see Table II–b), and the 297th through 316th words are codified in section 5501. The Act of Aug. 15, 1876, ch. 287, § 5, 19 Stat. 169, cited as authority for former section 46 was repealed by section 7(a) of the Act of Sept. 23, 1950.

In the last sentence, the word "removed" is substituted for "summarily removed" because of the provisions of the Lloyd-LaFollette Act, 37 Stat. 555, as amended, and the Veterans' Preference Act of 1944, 58 Stat. 387, as amended, which are carried into this title.

Standard changes are made to conform with the definitions applicable and the style of this title as outlined in the preface to the report.

SECTION REFERRED TO IN OTHER SECTIONS

This section is referred to in title 18 section 1916.

§ 3104. Employment of specially qualified scientific and professional personnel

(a) The Director of the Office of Personnel Management may establish, and from time to time revise, the maximum number of scientific or professional positions for carrying out research and development functions which require the services of specially qualified personnel which may be established outside of the General Schedule. Any such position may be established by action of the Director or, under such standards and procedures as the Office prescribes (including procedures under which the prior approval of the Director may be required), by agency action.

(b) The provisions of subsection (a) of this section shall not apply to any Senior Executive

Service position (as defined in section 3132(a) of this title).

(c) In addition to the number of positions authorized by subsection (a) of this section, the Librarian of Congress may establish, without regard to the second sentence of subsection (a) of this section, not more than 8 scientific or professional positions to carry out the research and development functions of the Library of Congress which require the services of specially qualified personnel.

(Pub. L. 89–554, Sept. 6, 1966, 80 Stat. 415; Pub. L. 90–83, §1(7), Sept. 11, 1967, 81 Stat. 196; Pub. L. 91–375, §6(c)(5), Aug. 12, 1970, 84 Stat. 776; Pub. L. 95–454, title IV, §414(a)(2)(B), (C), title VIII, §801(a)(3)(C), Oct. 13, 1978, 92 Stat. 1178, 1221; Pub. L. 99–386, title I, §101(b), Aug. 22, 1986, 100 Stat. 821; Pub. L. 102–378, §2(7), Oct. 2, 1992, 106 Stat. 1346.)

HISTORICAL AND REVISION NOTES
1966 ACT

Derivation	U.S. Code	Revised Statutes and Statutes at Large
(a)	5 U.S.C. 1161 (less 2d sentence of (g)).	Oct. 4, 1961, Pub. L. 87–367, §202 "Sec. 1", 75 Stat. 789. Oct. 11, 1962, Pub. L. 87–793, §1001(a)(2) "(g) (less 2d sentence)", 76 Stat. 863.
(b)	5 U.S.C. 1162(c).	Oct. 4, 1961, Pub. L. 87–367, §202 "Sec. 2(c)", 75 Stat. 790.
(c)	5 U.S.C. 1163.	Oct. 4, 1961, Pub. L. 87–367, §202 "Sec. 3", 75 Stat. 790.

In subsection (a), the authority to fix pay is omitted and carried into section 5361.

In subsection (b), the words "subsequent to February 1, 1958" appearing in former section 1162(c) are omitted as obsolete.

The Act of Aug. 1, 1947, ch. 433, 61 Stat. 715, as amended by the following Acts is omitted from the derivation and repealed (see Table II) as superseded by the Act of Oct. 4, 1961, Pub. L. 87–367, §202, 75 Stat. 789, which is carried into this section and sections 3325 and 5361:

June 24, 1948, ch. 624, 62 Stat. 604.
July 13, 1949, ch. 332, 63 Stat. 410.
July 31, 1956, ch. 804 §501(a), 70 Stat. 761.
Aug. 10, 1956, ch. 1041, §28, 70A Stat. 631.
June 20, 1958, Pub. L. 85–462, §12(a)–(d), 72 Stat. 213A.
Sept. 23, 1959, Pub. L. 86–370, §4, 73 Stat. 651.

Standard changes are made to conform with the definitions applicable and the style of this title as outlined in the preface to the report.

1967 ACT

Section of title 5	Source (U.S. Code)	Source (Statutes at Large)
3104(a)(5) ...	5 App.: 1161(e).	July 5, 1966, Pub. L. 89–492 §5, 80 Stat. 262.

The amendment to 5 U.S.C. 3104(a)(5) reflects Public Law 89–492, section 5.

The other amendments to 5 U.S.C. 3104 are based on section 302 of the act of July 20, 1958, Public Law 85–568 (72 Stat. 433), 42 U.S.C. 2453, and transfer plan, effective March 15, 1960, 25 Federal Register 2151, section (2)(a)(2), (b) of which in effect transferred from the Department of Defense to the National Aeronautics and Space Administration 12 of the 450 scientific and professional positions authorized by section 2 of Public Law 86–377 (10 U.S.C. 1581). Provisions relating to the date for reporting to Congress are based on 10 U.S.C. 1582.

AMENDMENTS

1992—Subsec. (a). Pub. L. 102–378 struck out "(not to exceed 517)" after "positions" in first sentence and amended second sentence generally, substituting provisions authorizing establishment of positions by Director and by agency action for provisions specifying that only Director may establish positions.

1986—Pub. L. 99–386 struck out subsec. (b) relating to reports to Congress, redesignated pars. (1), (2), and (3) of subsec. (a) as subsecs. (a), (b), and (c), respectively, and substituted "subsection (a) of this section" for "paragraph (1) of this subsection" wherever appearing in subsecs. (b) and (c) as redesignated.

1978—Subsec. (a). Pub. L. 95–454, §414(a)(2)(B), substituted provisions authorizing the Director to establish the maximum number of scientific or professional positions, excepting Senior Executive Service positions, and authorizing the Librarian to establish not more than 8 such positions for provisions authorizing the head of certain named agencies to establish a specified number of scientific or professional positions.

Subsec. (b). Pub. L. 95–454, §414(a)(2)(B), (C), struck out subsec. (b), redesignated subsec. (c) as (b), and substituted in subsec. (b), as redesignated, "to fix under section 5361 of this title the pay for positions established under this section" for "to establish and fix the pay of positions under this section and section 5361 of this title".

Pub. L. 95–454, §801(a)(3)(C), substituted in subsec. (b), as redesignated, "section 5371 of this title" for "section 5361 of this title".

Subsec. (c). Pub. L. 95–454, §414(a)(2)(C)(i), redesignated subsec. (c) as (b).

1970—Subsec. (a)(5). Pub. L. 91–375 repealed provision for employment in Post Office Department in scientific or professional positions of not more than 6 qualified individuals.

EFFECTIVE DATE OF 1978 AMENDMENT

Amendment by section 801(a)(3)(C) of Pub. L. 95–454 effective on first day of first applicable pay period beginning on or after 90th day after Oct. 13, 1978, see section 801(a)(4) of Pub. L. 95–454, set out as an Effective Date note under section 5361 of this title.

Amendment by section 414(a)(2)(B), (C) of Pub. L. 95–454 effective 180 days after Oct. 13, 1978, see section 415(a)(3) of Pub. L. 95–454, set out as an Effective Date note under section 3131 of this title.

EFFECTIVE DATE OF 1970 AMENDMENT

Amendment by Pub. L. 91–375 effective within 1 year after Aug. 12, 1970, on date established therefor by Board of Governors of United States Postal Service and published by it in Federal Register, see section 15(a) of Pub. L. 91–375, set out as an Effective Date note preceding section 101 of Title 39, Postal Service.

EXPERIMENTAL PERSONNEL PROGRAM FOR SCIENTIFIC AND TECHNICAL PERSONNEL

Pub. L. 105–261, div. A, title XI, §1101, Oct. 17, 1998, 112 Stat. 2139, as amended by Pub. L. 106–65, div. A, title X, §1067(3), Oct. 5, 1999, 113 Stat. 774; Pub. L. 106–398, §1 [[div. A] title X, §1087(d)(6), title XI, §1113], Oct. 30, 2000, 114 Stat. 1654, 1654A–293, 1654A–314, provided that:

"(a) PROGRAM AUTHORIZED.—During the program period specified in subsection (e)(1), the Secretary of Defense may carry out a program of experimental use of the special personnel management authority provided in subsection (b) in order to facilitate recruitment of eminent experts in science or engineering for research and development projects administered by the Defense Advanced Research Projects Agency and research and development projects administered by laboratories designated for the program by the Secretary from among the laboratories of each of the military departments.

"(b) SPECIAL PERSONNEL MANAGEMENT AUTHORITY.— Under the program, the Secretary may—

"(1) without regard to any provision of title 5, United States Code, governing the appointment of employees in the civil service, appoint scientists and engineers from outside the civil service and uniformed services (as such terms are defined in section 2101 of such title) to—

"(A) not more than 40 scientific and engineering positions in the Defense Advanced Research Projects Agency;

"(B) not more than 40 scientific and engineering positions in the designated laboratories of each of the military services; and

"(C) not more than a total of 10 scientific and engineering positions in the National Imagery and Mapping Agency and the National Security Agency;

"(2) prescribe the rates of basic pay for positions to which employees are appointed under paragraph (1) at rates not in excess of the maximum rate of basic pay authorized for senior-level positions under section 5376 of title 5, United States Code, as increased by locality-based comparability payments under section 5304 of such title, notwithstanding any provision of such title governing the rates of pay or classification of employees in the executive branch; and

"(3) pay any employee appointed under paragraph (1) payments in addition to basic pay within the limit applicable to the employee under subsection (d)(1).

"(c) LIMITATION ON TERM OF APPOINTMENT.—(1) Except as provided in paragraph (2), the service of an employee under an appointment under subsection (b)(1) may not exceed 4 years.

"(2) The Secretary may, in the case of a particular employee, extend the period to which service is limited under paragraph (1) by up to 2 years if the Secretary determines that such action is necessary to promote the efficiency of the Defense Advanced Research Projects Agency.

"(d) LIMITATIONS ON ADDITIONAL PAYMENTS.—(1) The total amount of the additional payments paid to an employee under subsection (b)(3) for any 12-month period may not exceed the least of the following amounts:

"(A) $25,000.

"(B) The amount equal to 25 percent of the employee's annual rate of basic pay.

"(C) The amount of the limitation that is applicable for a calendar year under section 5307(a)(1) of title 5, United States Code.

"(2) An employee appointed under subsection (b)(1) is not eligible for any bonus, monetary award, or other monetary incentive for service except for payments authorized under subsection (b)(3).

"(e) PERIOD OF PROGRAM.—(1) The period for carrying out the program authorized under this section begins on October 17, 1998, and ends on October 16, 2005.

"(2) After the termination of the program—

"(A) no appointment may be made under paragraph (1) of subsection (b);

"(B) a rate of basic pay prescribed under paragraph (2) of that subsection may not take effect for a position; and

"(C) no period of service may be extended under subsection (c)(2).

"(f) SAVINGS PROVISIONS.—In the case of an employee who, on the last day of the program period specified in subsection (e)(1), is serving in a position pursuant to an appointment under subsection (b)(1)—

"(1) the termination of the program does not terminate the employee's employment in that position before the expiration of the lesser of—

"(A) the period for which the employee was appointed; or

"(B) the period to which the employee's service is limited under subsection (c), including any extension made under paragraph (2) of that subsection before the termination of the program; and

"(2) the rate of basic pay prescribed for the position under subsection (b)(2) may not be reduced for so long (within the period applicable to the employee under paragraph (1)) as the employee continues to serve in the position without a break in service.

"(g) ANNUAL REPORT.—(1) Not later than October 15 of each year, beginning in 1999 and ending in 2006, the Secretary of Defense shall submit a report on the program to the Committee on Armed Services of the Senate and the Committee on Armed Services of the House of Representatives. The report submitted in a year shall cover the 12-month period ending on the day before the anniversary, in that year, of the date of the enactment of this Act.

"(2) The annual report shall contain, for the period covered by the report, the following:

"(A) A detailed discussion of the exercise of authority under this section.

"(B) The sources from which individuals appointed under subsection (b)(1) were recruited.

"(C) The methodology used for identifying and selecting such individuals.

"(D) Any additional information that the Secretary considers helpful for assessing the utility of the authority under this section."

FBI PERSONNEL MANAGEMENT SYSTEM FOR NON-SPECIAL AGENT EMPLOYEES; SECRETARY OF THE TREASURY

Pub. L. 105–119, title I, §122, Nov. 26, 1997, 111 Stat. 2469, as amended by Pub. L. 105–277, div. C, title I, §102, Oct. 21, 1998, 112 Stat. 2681–585, provided that during 3-year period beginning on Nov. 26, 1997, Director of the Federal Bureau of Investigation could, with approval of Attorney General, establish personnel management system providing for compensation and performance management of not more than 3,000 non-Special Agent employees to fill critical scientific, technical, engineering, intelligence analyst, language translator, and medical positions in Federal Bureau of Investigation, further authorized Secretary of the Treasury to establish, for period of three years from Nov. 26, 1997, personnel management demonstration project providing for compensation and performance management of not more than combined total of 950 employees who fill critical scientific, technical, engineering, intelligence analyst, language translator, and medical positions in Bureau of Alcohol, Tobacco and Firearms, United States Customs Service, and United States Secret Service, and further provided for submittal of reports to Congress and termination of demonstration project authority on Nov. 26, 2000.

TERMINATION OF AUTHORITY TO ESTABLISH SCIENTIFIC OR PROFESSIONAL POSITIONS OUTSIDE THE GENERAL SCHEDULE

Section 414(a)(2)(A) of Pub. L. 95–454 provided that: "Notwithstanding any other provision of law (other than section 3104 of title 5, United States Code), the authority granted to an agency (as defined in section 5102(a)(1) of such title 5) to establish scientific or professional positions outside of the General Schedule is hereby terminated."

Section 415(a)(3) of Pub. L. 95–454 provided that the provisions of section 414(a)(2)(A) take effect 180 days after Oct. 13, 1978.

LIMITATIONS ON EXECUTIVE POSITIONS NOT TO APPLY TO INDIVIDUALS OCCUPYING THOSE POSITIONS ON OCTOBER 12, 1978

Section 414(a)(3) of Pub. L. 95–454 provided that:

"(A) The provisions of paragraphs (1) and (2) of this subsection [amending sections 3104 and 5108 of this title] shall not apply with respect to any position so long as the individual occupying such position on the day before the date of the enactment of this Act [Oct. 13, 1978] continues to occupy such position.

"(B) The Director—

"(i) in establishing under section 5108 of title 5, United States Code, the maximum number of positions which may be placed in GS–16, 17, and 18 of the General Schedule, and

"(ii) in establishing under section 3104 of such title 5 the maximum number of scientific or professional positions which may be established,

shall take into account positions to which subparagraph (A) of this paragraph applies."

[Section 415(a)(3) of Pub. L. 95–454 provided that the provisions of section 414(a)(3) are effective 180 days after Oct. 13, 1978.]

[References in laws to rates of pay for GS–16, 17, or 18, or to maximum rates of pay under General Schedule, to be considered references to rates payable under specified sections of this title, see section 529 [title I, § 101(c)(1)] of Pub. L. 101–509, set out in a note under section 5376 of this title.]

SECTION REFERRED TO IN OTHER SECTIONS

This section is referred to in sections 3325, 5376, 5377 of this title; title 20 section 3461.

§ 3105. Appointment of administrative law judges

Each agency shall appoint as many administrative law judges as are necessary for proceedings required to be conducted in accordance with sections 556 and 557 of this title. Administrative law judges shall be assigned to cases in rotation so far as practicable, and may not perform duties inconsistent with their duties and responsibilities as administrative law judges.

(Pub. L. 89–554, Sept. 6, 1966, 80 Stat. 415; Pub. L. 95–251, § 2(a)(1), (b)(2), (d)(1), Mar. 27, 1978, 92 Stat. 183, 184.)

HISTORICAL AND REVISION NOTES

Derivation	U.S. Code	Revised Statutes and Statutes at Large
....	5 U.S.C. 1010 (1st sentence).	June 11, 1946, ch. 324, § 11 (1st sentence), 60 Stat. 244.

The words "Subject to the civil service" are omitted as unnecessary inasmuch as appointments are made subject to the civil service laws unless specifically excepted. The words "and other laws not inconsistent with this chapter" are omitted as unnecessary because of the organization of this title.

Standard changes are made to conform with the definitions applicable and the style of this title as outlined in the preface to the report.

AMENDMENTS

1978—Pub. L. 95–251 substituted references to administrative law judges for references to hearing examiners in section catchline and wherever appearing in text.

REFERENCES TO HEARING EXAMINER DEEMED REFERENCES TO ADMINISTRATIVE LAW JUDGE

Section 3 of Pub. L. 95–251 provided that: "Any reference in any law, regulation, or order to a hearing examiner appointed under section 3105 of title 5, United States Code, shall be deemed to be a reference to an administrative law judge."

HEARING EXAMINERS EMPLOYED BY DEPARTMENT OF AGRICULTURE

Functions vested by section 551 et seq. of this title in hearing examiners employed by Department of Agriculture not included in functions of officers, agencies, and employees of that Department transferred to Secretary of Agriculture by 1953 Reorg. Plan No. 2, § 1, eff. June 4, 1953, 18 F.R. 3219, 67 Stat. 633, set out in the Appendix to this title.

HEARING EXAMINERS EMPLOYED BY DEPARTMENT OF COMMERCE

Functions vested by section 551 et seq. of this title in hearing examiners employed by Department of Commerce not included in functions of officers, agencies, and employees of that Department transferred to Secretary of Commerce by 1950 Reorg. Plan No. 5, § 1, eff. May 24, 1950, 15 F.R. 3174, 64 Stat. 1263, set out in the Appendix to this title.

HEARING EXAMINERS EMPLOYED BY DEPARTMENT OF THE INTERIOR

Functions vested by section 551 et seq. of this title in hearing examiners employed by Department of the Interior not included in functions of officers, agencies, and employees of that Department transferred to Secretary of the Interior by 1950 Reorg. Plan No. 3, § 1, eff. May 24, 1950, 15 F.R. 3174, 64 Stat. 1262, transferred set out in the Appendix to this title.

HEARING EXAMINERS EMPLOYED BY DEPARTMENT OF JUSTICE

Functions vested by section 551 et seq. of this title in hearing examiners employed by Department of Justice not included in functions of officers, agencies, and employees of that Department transferred to Attorney General by 1950 Reorg. Plan No. 2, § 1, eff. May 24, 1950, 15 F.R. 3173, 64 Stat. 1261, set out in the Appendix to this title.

HEARING EXAMINERS EMPLOYED BY DEPARTMENT OF LABOR

Functions vested by section 551 et seq. of this title in hearing examiners employed by Department of Labor not included in functions of officers, agencies, and employees of Department transferred to Secretary of Labor by 1950 Reorg. Plan No. 6, § 1, eff. May 24, 1950, 15 F.R. 3174, 64 Stat. 1263, set out in the Appendix to this title.

HEARING EXAMINERS EMPLOYED BY DEPARTMENT OF THE TREASURY

Functions vested by section 551 et seq. of this title in hearing examiners employed by Department of the Treasury not included in functions of officers, agencies, and employees of Department transferred to Secretary of the Treasury by 1950 Reorg. Plan No. 26, § 1, eff. July 31, 1950, 15 F.R. 4935, 64 Stat. 1280, set out in the Appendix to this title.

HEARING EXAMINERS APPOINTED FOR INDIAN PROBATE WORK

Hearing examiners appointed for Indian probate work pursuant to former section 372–1 of Title 25, Indians, having met qualifications required for appointment pursuant to this section, deemed to have been appointed pursuant to this section, see section 12(b) of Pub. L. 101–301, set out as a Savings Provision note under former section 372–1 of Title 25.

SECTION REFERRED TO IN OTHER SECTIONS

This section is referred to in sections 554, 556, 559, 1104, 1204, 1215, 1305, 3132, 3323, 3344, 4301, 5102, 5304, 5372, 5372b, 7105, 7132, 7521, 7701 of this title; title 7 section 2023; title 15 sections 327, 1715; title 16 section 823b; title 19 section 1641; title 20 section 1234; title 29 sections 214, 661, 792; title 30 sections 804, 823, 932a; title 31 sections 3801, 6712, 6713, 6720; title 33 sections 873, 919; title 41 section 607; title 42 sections 2000e–4, 2282a, 3608, 3612, 6303, 8433; title 47 section 410; title 49 section 46104; title 50 App. section 2412.

§ 3106. Employment of attorneys; restrictions

Except as otherwise authorized by law, the head of an Executive department or military department may not employ an attorney or counsel for the conduct of litigation in which the United States, an agency, or employee thereof is a party, or is interested, or for the securing of evidence therefor, but shall refer the matter to the Department of Justice. This section does not apply to the employment and payment of counsel under section 1037 of title 10.

(Pub. L. 89–554, Sept. 6, 1966, 80 Stat. 415.)

HISTORICAL AND REVISION NOTES

Derivation	U.S. Code	Revised Statutes and Statutes at Large
....	5 U.S.C. 49.	R.S. § 189. Sept. 2, 1958, Pub. L. 85–861, § 7(a), 72 Stat. 1555.

HISTORICAL AND REVISION NOTES—CONTINUED

Derivation	U.S. Code	Revised Statutes and Statutes at Large
....	5 U.S.C. 314.	R.S. § 365. Sept. 2, 1958, Pub. L. 85–861, § 7(b), 72 Stat. 1555.

Sections 189 and 365 of the Revised Statutes, as amended, are combined and the section is revised to express the effect of the law since department heads have long employed, with the approval of Congress, attorneys to advise them in the conduct of their official duties. The law which concentrates the authority for the conduct of litigation in the Department of Justice is codified in section 516 of title 28 by this bill.

The words "Executive department" are substituted for "department" as the definition of "department" applicable to R.S. § 189 is coextensive with the definition of "Executive department" in section 101. The words "or military department" are inserted to preserve the application of the source law. Before enactment of the National Security Act Amendments of 1949 (63 Stat. 578), the Department of the Army, the Department of the Navy, and the Department of the Air Force were Executive departments. The National Security Act Amendments of 1949 established the Department of Defense as an Executive Department including the Department of the Army, the Department of the Navy, and the Department of the Air Force as military departments, not as Executive departments. However, the source law for this section, which was in effect in 1949, remained applicable to the Secretaries of the military departments by virtue of section 12(g) of the National Security Act Amendments of 1949 (63 Stat. 591), which is set out in the reviser's note for section 301.

R.S. § 189 was part of title IV of the Revised Statutes. The Act of July 26, 1947, ch. 343, § 201(d), as added Aug. 1, 1949, ch. 412, § 4, 63 Stat. 579 (former 5 U.S.C. 171–1), which provides "Except to the extent inconsistent with the provisions of this Act [National Security Act of 1947], the provisions of title IV of the Revised Statutes as now or hereafter amended shall be applicable to the Department of Defense" is omitted from this title but is not repealed.

Standard changes are made to conform with the definitions applicable and the style of this title as outlined in the preface to the report.

SECTION REFERRED TO IN OTHER SECTIONS

This section is referred to in title 22 section 2698.

§ 3107. Employment of publicity experts; restrictions

Appropriated funds may not be used to pay a publicity expert unless specifically appropriated for that purpose.

(Pub. L. 89–554, Sept. 6, 1966, 80 Stat. 416.)

HISTORICAL AND REVISION NOTES

Derivation	U.S. Code	Revised Statutes and Statutes at Large
....	5 U.S.C. 54.	Oct. 22, 1913, ch. 32, § 1 (last par. under "Interstate Commerce Commission"), 38 Stat. 212.

The prohibition is restated in positive form.

Standard changes are made to conform with the definitions applicable and the style of this title as outlined in the preface to the report.

§ 3108. Employment of detective agencies; restrictions

An individual employed by the Pinkerton Detective Agency, or similar organization, may not be employed by the Government of the United States or the government of the District of Columbia.

(Pub. L. 89–554, Sept. 6, 1966, 80 Stat. 416.)

HISTORICAL AND REVISION NOTES

Derivation	U.S. Code	Revised Statutes and Statutes at Large
....	5 U.S.C. 53.	Mar. 3, 1893, ch. 208 (5th par. under "Public Buildings"), 27 Stat. 591.

The prohibition is restated in positive form.

Standard changes are made to conform with the definitions applicable and the style of this title as outlined in the preface to the report.

§ 3109. Employment of experts and consultants; temporary or intermittent

(a) For the purpose of this section—

(1) "agency" has the meaning given it by section 5721 of this title; and

(2) "appropriation" includes funds made available by statute under section 9104 of title 31.

(b) When authorized by an appropriation or other statute, the head of an agency may procure by contract the temporary (not in excess of 1 year) or intermittent services of experts or consultants or an organization thereof, including stenographic reporting services. Services procured under this section are without regard to—

(1) the provisions of this title governing appointment in the competitive service;

(2) chapter 51 and subchapter III of chapter 53 of this title; and

(3) section 5 of title 41, except in the case of stenographic reporting services by an organization.

However, an agency subject to chapter 51 and subchapter III of chapter 53 of this title may pay a rate for services under this section in excess of the daily equivalent of the highest rate payable under section 5332 of this title only when specifically authorized by the appropriation or other statute authorizing the procurement of the services.

(c) Positions in the Senior Executive Service or the Federal Bureau of Investigation and Drug Enforcement Administration Senior Executive Service may not be filled under the authority of subsection (b) of this section.

(d) The Office of Personnel Management shall prescribe regulations necessary for the administration of this section. Such regulations shall include—

(1) criteria governing the circumstances in which it is appropriate to employ an expert or consultant under the provisions of this section;

(2) criteria for setting the pay of experts and consultants under this section; and

(3) provisions to ensure compliance with such regulations.

(e) Each agency shall report to the Office of Personnel Management on an annual basis with respect to—

(1) the number of days each expert or consultant employed by the agency during the period was so employed; and

(2) the total amount paid by the agency to each expert and consultant for such work during the period.

(Pub. L. 89–554, Sept. 6, 1966, 80 Stat. 416; Pub. L. 95–454, title IV, §402(b), Oct. 13, 1978, 92 Stat. 1160; Pub. L. 97–258, §3(a)(4), Sept. 13, 1982, 96 Stat. 1063; Pub. L. 100–325, §2(b), May 30, 1988, 102 Stat. 581; Pub. L. 102–378, §2(8), Oct. 2, 1992, 106 Stat. 1347.)

HISTORICAL AND REVISION NOTES

Derivation	U.S. Code	Revised Statutes and Statutes at Large
....	5 U.S.C. 55a.	Aug. 2, 1946, ch. 744, §15, 60 Stat. 810.

In subsection (a), the definitions of "agency" and "appropriation" are added on authority of the Act of Aug. 2, 1946, ch. 744, §18, 60 Stat. 811.

In subsection (b), the words "the provisions of this title governing appointment in the competitive service" are substituted for "the civil-service laws". The words "chapter 51 and subchapter III of chapter 53 of this title" are substituted for the reference to the classification laws which originally meant the Classification Act of 1923, as amended. Exception from the Classification Act of 1949 is based on sections 202(27) and 1106(a) of the Act of Oct. 28, 1949, ch. 782, 63 Stat. 956, 972.

Standard changes are made to conform with the definitions applicable and the style of this title as outlined in the preface to the report.

AMENDMENTS

1992—Subsecs. (d), (e). Pub. L. 102–378 added subsecs. (d) and (e).

1988—Subsec. (c). Pub. L. 100–325 inserted reference to Federal Bureau of Investigation and Drug Enforcement Administration Senior Executive Service.

1982—Subsec. (a)(2). Pub. L. 97–258 substituted "section 9104" for "section 849".

1978—Subsec. (c). Pub. L. 95–454 added subsec. (c).

EFFECTIVE DATE OF 1978 AMENDMENT

Amendment by Pub. L. 95–454 effective 9 months after Oct. 13, 1978, and congressional review of provisions of sections 401 through 412 of Pub. L. 95–454, see section 415 of Pub. L. 95–454, set out as an Effective Date note under section 3131 of this title.

APPROPRIATIONS RELATING TO LABOR, HEALTH AND HUMAN SERVICES, AND EDUCATION; PUBLIC DISCLOSURE OF CONSULTING SERVICE THROUGH PROCUREMENT CONTRACT

Pub. L. 102–394, title V, §501, Oct. 6, 1992, 106 Stat. 1825, provided that: "The expenditure of any appropriation under this Act or subsequent Departments of Labor, Health and Human Services, and Education, and Related Agencies Appropriations Acts for any consulting service through procurement contract, pursuant to 5 U.S.C. 3109, shall be limited to those contracts where such expenditures are a matter of public record and available for public inspection, except where otherwise provided under existing law, or under existing Executive order issued pursuant to existing law."

Similar provisions were contained in the following prior appropriation acts:

Pub. L. 102–170, title V, §501, Nov. 26, 1991, 105 Stat. 1140.

Pub. L. 101–517, title V, §501, Nov. 5, 1990, 104 Stat. 2220.

Pub. L. 101–166, title V, §501, Nov. 21, 1989, 103 Stat. 1189.

Pub. L. 100–202, §101(h) [title V, §501], Dec. 22, 1987, 101 Stat. 1329–256, 1329–287.

Pub. L. 99–500, §101(i) [H.R. 5233, title V, §501], Oct. 18, 1986, 100 Stat. 1783–287, and Pub. L. 99–591, §101(i) [H.R. 5233, title V, §501], Oct. 30, 1986, 100 Stat. 3341–287.

Pub. L. 99–178, title V, §501, Dec. 12, 1985, 99 Stat. 1132.

Pub. L. 98–619, title V, §501, Nov. 8, 1984, 98 Stat. 3332.

Pub. L. 98–139, title V, §501, Oct. 31, 1983, 97 Stat. 898.

Pub. L. 97–377, title I, §101(e)(1) [title V, §501], Dec. 21, 1982, 96 Stat. 1878, 1904.

AVAILABILITY OF APPROPRIATIONS FOR SERVICES

Pub. L. 102–394, title V, §503, Oct. 6, 1992, 106 Stat. 1825, provided that: "Appropriations contained in this Act or subsequent Departments of Labor, Health and Human Services, and Education, and Related Agencies Appropriations Acts, available for salaries and expenses, shall be available for services as authorized by 5 U.S.C. 3109 but at rates for individuals not to exceed the per diem rate equivalent to the maximum rate payable for senior-level positions under 5 U.S.C. 5376."

Similar provisions were contained in the following prior appropriation acts:

Pub. L. 102–170, title V, §503, Nov. 26, 1991, 105 Stat. 1140.

Pub. L. 101–517, title V, §503, Nov. 5, 1990, 104 Stat. 2221.

Pub. L. 101–166, title V, §503, Nov. 21, 1989, 103 Stat. 1189.

Pub. L. 100–202, §101(h) [title V, §503], Dec. 22, 1987, 101 Stat. 1329–256, 1329–287.

Pub. L. 99–500, §101(i) [H.R. 5233, title V, §503], Oct. 18, 1986, 100 Stat. 1783–287, and Pub. L. 99–591, §101(i) [H.R. 5233, title V, §503], Oct. 30, 1986, 100 Stat. 3341–287.

Pub. L. 99–178, title V, §503, Dec. 12, 1985, 99 Stat. 1132.

Pub. L. 98–619, title V, §503, Nov. 8, 1984, 98 Stat. 3333.

Pub. L. 98–139, title V, §503, Oct. 31, 1983, 97 Stat. 899.

Pub. L. 97–377, title I, §101(e)(1) [title V, §503], Dec. 21, 1982, 96 Stat. 1878, 1904.

APPROPRIATIONS RELATING TO ENERGY AND WATER DEVELOPMENT; PUBLIC DISCLOSURE OF CONSULTING SERVICE THROUGH PROCUREMENT CONTRACT

Pub. L. 102–377, title V, §504, Oct. 2, 1992, 106 Stat. 1342, provided that: "The expenditure of any appropriation under this Act or subsequent Energy and Water Development Appropriations Acts for any consulting service through procurement contract, pursuant to section 3109 of title 5, United States Code, hereafter shall be limited to those contracts where such expenditures are a matter of public record and available for public inspection, except where otherwise provided under existing law, or under existing Executive Order issued pursuant to existing law."

SECTION REFERRED TO IN OTHER SECTIONS

This section is referred to in sections 595, 3161, 5102, 7342, 8474 of this title; title 2 sections 136c, 179t, 1108, 1553, 1742; title 3 sections 105, 106, 107, 108; title 7 sections 16, 2225a, 5902; title 10 section 129b; title 12 section 2405; title 15 sections 205i, 634d, 636, 2206, 2218, 2451, 4105, 4805; title 16 sections 410cc–36, 410ww–24, 410yy–8, 410ccc–22, 460zz–2, 469b, 469j, 470m, 825q–1, 1052, 1406; title 18 sections 3153, 3168, 4204, 4352; title 19 sections 1331, 2171; title 20 sections 959, 1018a, 1087–2, 1098, 1505, 2012, 2106, 3413, 3425, 3462, 3463, 3702, 4355, 4414, 4513, 4710, 5608, 5708, 5826, 5933, 6031, 9252; title 21 sections 1305, 1703; title 22 sections 272a, 277d–3, 280b, 280i, 280k, 290b, 290f, 290h–5, 1469, 1474, 1622d, 2024, 2083, 2102, 2103, 2386, 2512, 2581, 2669, 2905, 3106, 4308, 4341, 4832, 6204, 6435a; title 25 sections 640d–11, 2707, 3505; title 26 section 7802; title 28 sections 602, 625, 994; title 29 sections 656, 671, 676, 783, 1302; title 30 section 1807; title 31 sections 332, 731, 1352, 5112; title 33 section 1123; title 36 section 2307; title 38 section 7281; title 40 sections 71a, 822, 873, 1106; title 41 section 422; title 42 sections 242b, 242l, 282, 285a–2, 285b–3, 290aa, 299c–5, 300v–2, 904, 1320b–9, 1962a–4, 1975b, 2286b, 2473, 3211, 3788, 4276, 4343, 5149, 5612, 5816, 5852, 6616, 7171, 7233, 10163, 10248, 10267, 10412, 11314, 12651f, 14196; title 43 section 377b; title 44 sections 2105, 2706, 3319; title 47 section 154; title 49 sections 106, 323, 1113, 40122, 45301; title 50 section 2402; title 50 App. section 2158.

§ 3110. Employment of relatives; restrictions

(a) For the purpose of this section—

(1) agency means—

(A) an Executive agency;

(B) an office, agency, or other establishment in the legislative branch;

(C) an office, agency, or other establishment in the judicial branch; and

(D) the government of the District of Columbia;

(2) "public official" means an officer (including the President and a Member of Congress), a member of the uniformed service, an employee and any other individual, in whom is vested the authority by law, rule, or regulation, or to whom the authority has been delegated, to appoint, employ, promote, or advance individuals, or to recommend individuals for appointment, employment, promotion, or advancement in connection with employment in an agency; and

(3) "relative" means, with respect to a public official, an individual who is related to the public official as father, mother, son, daughter, brother, sister, uncle, aunt, first cousin, nephew, niece, husband, wife, father-in-law, mother-in-law, son-in-law, daughter-in-law, brother-in-law, sister-in-law, stepfather, stepmother, stepson, stepdaughter, stepbrother, stepsister, half brother, or half sister.

(b) A public official may not appoint, employ, promote, advance, or advocate for appointment, employment, promotion, or advancement, in or to a civilian position in the agency in which he is serving or over which he exercises jurisdiction or control any individual who is a relative of the public official. An individual may not be appointed, employed, promoted, or advanced in or to a civilian position in an agency if such appointment, employment, promotion, or advancement has been advocated by a public official, serving in or exercising jurisdiction or control over the agency, who is a relative of the individual.

(c) An individual appointed, employed, promoted, or advanced in violation of this section is not entitled to pay, and money may not be paid from the Treasury as pay to an individual so appointed, employed, promoted, or advanced.

(d) The Office of Personnel Management may prescribe regulations authorizing the temporary employment, in the event of emergencies resulting from natural disasters or similar unforeseen events or circumstances, of individuals whose employment would otherwise be prohibited by this section.

(e) This section shall not be construed to prohibit the appointment of an individual who is a preference eligible in any case in which the passing over of that individual on a certificate of eligibles furnished under section 3317(a) of this title will result in the selection for appointment of an individual who is not a preference eligible.

(Added Pub. L. 90–206, title II, § 221(a), Dec. 16, 1967, 81 Stat. 640; amended Pub. L. 95–454, title IX, § 906(a)(2), Oct. 13, 1978, 92 Stat. 1224.)

AMENDMENTS

1978—Subsec. (d). Pub. L. 95–454 substituted "Office of Personnel Management" for "Civil Service Commission".

EFFECTIVE DATE OF 1978 AMENDMENT

Amendment by Pub. L. 95–454 effective 90 days after Oct. 13, 1978, see section 907 of Pub. L. 95–454, set out as a note under section 1101 of this title.

EFFECTIVE DATE

Section 220(a)(1) of title II of Pub. L. 90–206 provided, except as otherwise expressly provided, that: "This section [enacting provisions set out as a note under section 8704 of this title] and sections 201 [enacting provisions set out as Short Title note under section 5332 of this title], 207 [amending section 5303 of this title], 212 [enacting provisions set out as a note under section 5303 of this title], 218 [enacting provisions set out as a note under section 5332 of this title], 221 [enacting this section and provisions set out as a note under this section], 224(a) and (b) [amending sections 4101 and 8339 of this title], and 225 [enacting sections 351–361 of Title 2, The Congress] shall become effective on the date of enactment of this title [Dec. 16, 1967]."

RETROACTIVE EFFECT

Section 221(c) of Pub. L. 90–206 provided that: "The amendments made by this section [enacting this section] do not apply to an appointment, employment, advancement, or promotion made or advocated by a public official of any individual who is a relative of the public official if, prior to the effective date of this section [see Effective Date note above], the individual was appointed by the public official, or received an appointment advocated by the public official, and is serving under the appointment on such effective date."

[Section 221(c) of Pub. L. 90–206 effective Dec. 16, 1967, see section 220(a)(1) of Pub. L. 90–206, set out as an Effective Date note above.]

SECTION REFERRED TO IN OTHER SECTIONS

This section is referred to in section 2302 of this title; title 39 section 410.

§ 3111. Acceptance of volunteer service

(a) For the purpose of this section, "student" means an individual who is enrolled, not less than half-time, in a high school, trade school, technical or vocational institute, junior college, college, university, or comparable recognized educational institution. An individual who is a student is deemed not to have ceased to be a student during an interim between school years if the interim is not more than 5 months and if such individual shows to the satisfaction of the Office of Personnel Management that the individual has a bona fide intention of continuing to pursue a course of study or training in the same or different educational institution during the school semester (or other period into which the school year is divided) immediately after the interim.

(b) Notwithstanding section 1342 of title 31, the head of an agency may accept, subject to regulations issued by the Office, voluntary service for the United States if the service—

(1) is performed by a student, with the permission of the institution at which the student is enrolled, as part of an agency program established for the purpose of providing educational experiences for the student;

(2) is to be uncompensated; and

(3) will not be used to displace any employee.

(c)(1) Except as provided in paragraph (2), any student who provides voluntary service under subsection (b) of this section shall not be considered a Federal employee for any purpose other than for purposes of chapter 81 of this title (relating to compensation for injury) and sections 2671 through 2680 of title 28 (relating to tort claims).

(2) In addition to being considered a Federal employee for the purposes specified in paragraph (1), any student who provides voluntary service as part of a program established under subsection (b) of this section in the Internal Revenue Service, Department of the Treasury, shall be considered an employee of the Department of the Treasury for purposes of—

(A) section 552a of this title (relating to disclosure of records);

(B) subsections (a)(1), (h)(1), (k)(6), and (l)(4) of section 6103 of title 26 (relating to confidentiality and disclosure of returns and return information);

(C) sections 7213(a)(1) and 7431 of title 26 (relating to unauthorized disclosures of returns and return information by Federal employees and other persons); and

(D) section 7423 of title 26 (relating to suits against employees of the United States);

except that returns and return information (as defined in section 6103(b) of title 26) shall be made available to students under such program only to the extent that the Secretary of the Treasury or his designee determines that the duties assigned to such students so require.

(Added Pub. L. 95–454, title III, § 301(a), Oct. 13, 1978, 92 Stat. 1144; amended Pub. L. 97–258, § 3(a)(5), Sept. 13, 1982, 96 Stat. 1063; Pub. L. 97–437, Jan. 8, 1983, 96 Stat. 2285.)

Amendments

1983—Subsec. (c)(1). Pub. L. 97–437, § 1(1), substituted "(c)(1) Except as provided in par. (2), any" for "(c) Any".

Subsec. (c)(2). Pub. L. 97–437, § 1(2), added par. (2).

1982—Subsec. (b). Pub. L. 97–258 substituted "section 1342 of title 31" for "section 3679(b) of the Revised Statutes (31 U.S.C. 665(b))".

Effective Date

Section effective 90 days after Oct. 13, 1978, see section 907 of Pub. L. 95–454, set out as an Effective Date of 1978 Amendment note under section 1101 of this title.

§ 3112. Disabled veterans; noncompetitive appointment

Under such regulations as the Office of Personnel Management shall prescribe, an agency may make a noncompetitive appointment leading to conversion to career or career-conditional employment of a disabled veteran who has a compensable service-connected disability of 30 percent or more.

(Added Pub. L. 95–454, title III, § 307(b)(1), Oct. 13, 1978, 92 Stat. 1147.)

Effective Date

Section effective 90 days after Oct. 13, 1978, see section 907 of Pub. L. 95–454, set out as an Effective Date of 1978 Amendment note under section 1101 of this title.

§ 3113. Restriction on reemployment after conviction of certain crimes

An employee shall be separated from service and barred from reemployment in the Federal service, if—

(1) the employee is convicted of a violation of section 201(b) of title 18; and

(2) such violation related to conduct prohibited under section 1010(a) of the Controlled Substances Import and Export Act (21 U.S.C. 960(a)).

(Added Pub. L. 105–61, title VI, § 638(a), Oct. 10, 1997, 111 Stat. 1316.)

Effective Date

Section 638(c) of Pub. L. 105–61 provided that: "This section [enacting this section] shall apply during fiscal year 1998 and each fiscal year thereafter."

SUBCHAPTER II—THE SENIOR EXECUTIVE SERVICE

Subchapter Referred to in Other Sections

This subchapter is referred to in title 7 section 16; title 38 section 7425.

§ 3131. The Senior Executive Service

It is the purpose of this subchapter to establish a Senior Executive Service to ensure that the executive management of the Government of the United States is responsive to the needs, policies, and goals of the Nation and otherwise is of the highest quality. The Senior Executive Service shall be administered so as to—

(1) provide for a compensation system, including salaries, benefits, and incentives, and for other conditions of employment, designed to attract and retain highly competent senior executives;

(2) ensure that compensation, retention, and tenure are contingent on executive success which is measured on the basis of individual and organizational performance (including such factors as improvements in efficiency, productivity, quality of work or service, cost efficiency, and timeliness of performance and success in meeting equal employment opportunity goals);

(3) assure that senior executives are accountable and responsible for the effectiveness and productivity of employees under them;

(4) recognize exceptional accomplishment;

(5) enable the head of an agency to reassign senior executives to best accomplish the agency's mission;

(6) provide for severance pay, early retirement, and placement assistance for senior executives who are removed from the Senior Executive Service for nondisciplinary reasons;

(7) protect senior executives from arbitrary or capricious actions;

(8) provide for program continuity and policy advocacy in the management of public programs;

(9) maintain a merit personnel system free of prohibited personnel practices;

(10) ensure accountability for honest, economical, and efficient Government;

(11) ensure compliance with all applicable civil service laws, rules, and regulations, including those related to equal employment opportunity, political activity, and conflicts of interest;

(12) provide for the initial and continuing systematic development of highly competent senior executives;

(13) provide for an executive system which is guided by the public interest and free from improper political interference; and

(14) appoint career executives to fill Senior Executive Service positions to the extent practicable, consistent with the effective and efficient implementation of agency policies and responsibilities.

(Added Pub. L. 95–454, title IV, § 402(a), Oct. 13, 1978, 92 Stat. 1154.)

REFERENCES IN TEXT

The civil service laws, referred to in par. (11), are set out in this title. See, particularly, section 3301 et seq. of this title.

EFFECTIVE DATE

Section 415 of title IV of Pub. L. 95–454 provided that:
"(a)(1) The provisions of this title, other than sections 413 and 414(a) [enacting this subchapter and sections 2101a, 3391 to 3397, 3591 to 3595, 4311 to 4315, 4507, 5381 to 5385, 5752, and 7541 to 7543 of this title, amending sections 2102, 2103, 2108, 3109, 3501, 5311, 5331, 5504, 5541, 5595, 5723, 6304, 8336, and 8339 of this title, and enacting provisions set out as a note under section 5311 of this title], shall take effect 9 months after the date of the enactment of this Act [Oct. 13, 1978].

"(2) The provisions of section 413 of this title [set out as a note under section 3133 of this title] shall take effect on the date of the enactment of this Act [Oct. 13, 1978].

"(3) The provisions of section 414(a) of this title [amending sections 3104 and 5108 of this title and enacting provisions set out as notes under sections 3104 and 5108 of this title] shall take effect 180 days after the date of the enactment of this Act [Oct. 13, 1978].

"(b)(1) The amendments made by sections 401 through 412 of this title [enacting this subchapter and sections 2101a, 3391 to 3397, 3591 to 3595, 4311 to 4315, 4507, 5381 to 5385, 5752, and 7541 to 7543 of this title, amending sections 2102, 2103, 2108, 3109, 3501, 5311, 5331, 5504, 5541, 5595, 5723, 6304, 8336, and 8339 of this title] shall continue to have effect unless, during the first period of 60 calendar days of continuous session of the Congress beginning after 5 years after the effective date of such amendments, a concurrent resolution is introduced and adopted by the Congress disapproving the continuation of the Senior Executive Service. Such amendments shall cease to have effect on the first day of the first fiscal year beginning after the date of the adoption of such concurrent resolution.

"(2) The continuity of a session is broken only by an adjournment of the Congress sine die, and the days on which either House is not in session because of an adjournment of more than 3 days to a day certain are excluded in the computation of the 60-day period.

"(3) The provisions of subsections (d), (e), (f), (g), (h), (i), (j), and (k) of section 5305 of title 5, United States Code, shall apply with respect to any concurrent resolution referred to in paragraph (1) of this subsection, except that for the purpose of this paragraph the reference in such subsection (e) to 10 calendar days shall be considered a reference to 30 calendar days.

"(4) During the 5-year period referred to in paragraph (1) of this subsection, the Director of the Office of Personnel Management shall include in each report required under section 3135 of title 5, United States Code (as added by this title) an evaluation of the effectiveness of the Senior Executive Service and the manner in which such Service is administered."

CONGRESSIONAL FINDINGS RESPECTING CONTINUATION OF SENIOR EXECUTIVE SERVICE

Pub. L. 98–615, title III, § 301, Nov. 8, 1984, 98 Stat. 3217, provided that: "The Congress finds that the Senior Executive Service should be continued indefinitely."

SECTION REFERRED TO IN OTHER SECTIONS

This section is referred to in sections 3151, 3393a of this title; title 10 section 1606; title 31 section 733.

§ 3132. Definitions and exclusions

(a) For the purpose of this subchapter—

(1) "agency" means an Executive agency, except a Government corporation and the General Accounting Office, but does not include—

(A) any agency or unit thereof excluded from coverage by the President under subsection (c) of this section; or

(B) the Federal Bureau of Investigation, the Drug Enforcement Administration, the Central Intelligence Agency, the Defense Intelligence Agency, the National Imagery and Mapping Agency, the National Security Agency, Department of Defense intelligence activities the civilian employees of which are subject to section 1590 of title 10,,[1] and, as determined by the President, an Executive agency, or unit thereof, whose principal function is the conduct of foreign intelligence or counterintelligence activities;

(C) the Federal Election Commission; or

(D) the Office of the Comptroller of the Currency, the Office of Thrift Supervision, the Federal Housing Finance Board, the Resolution Trust Corporation, the Farm Credit Administration, the Office of Federal Housing Enterprise Oversight of the Department of Housing and Urban Development, and the National Credit Union Administration;

(2) "Senior Executive Service position" means any position in an agency which is classified above GS–15 pursuant to section 5108 or in level IV or V of the Executive Schedule, or an equivalent position, which is not required to be filled by an appointment by the President by and with the advice and consent of the Senate, and in which an employee—

(A) directs the work of an organizational unit;

(B) is held accountable for the success of one or more specific programs or projects;

(C) monitors progress toward organizational goals and periodically evaluates and makes appropriate adjustments to such goals;

(D) supervises the work of employees other than personal assistants; or

(E) otherwise exercises important policy-making, policy-determining, or other executive functions;

but does not include—

(i) any position in the Foreign Service of the United States; or

(ii) an administrative law judge position under section 3105 of this title;

(3) "senior executive" means a member of the Senior Executive Service;

(4) "career appointee" means an individual in a Senior Executive Service position whose appointment to the position or previous appointment to another Senior Executive Service position was based on approval by the Office of Personnel Management of the executive qualifications of such individual;

(5) "limited term appointee" means an individual appointed under a nonrenewable appointment for a term of 3 years or less to a

---

[1] So in original.

Senior Executive Service position the duties of which will expire at the end of such term;

(6) "limited emergency appointee" means an individual appointed under a nonrenewable appointment, not to exceed 18 months, to a Senior Executive Service position established to meet a bona fide, unanticipated, urgent need;

(7) "noncareer appointee" means an individual in a Senior Executive Service position who is not a career appointee, a limited term appointee, or a limited emergency appointee;

(8) "career reserved position" means a position which is required to be filled by a career appointee and which is designated under subsection (b) of this section; and

(9) "general position" means any position, other than a career reserved position, which may be filled by either a career appointee, noncareer appointee, limited emergency appointee, or limited term appointee.

(b)(1) For the purpose of paragraph (8) of subsection (a) of this section, the Office shall prescribe the criteria and regulations governing the designation of career reserved positions. The criteria and regulations shall provide that a position shall be designated as a career reserved position only if the filling of the position by a career appointee is necessary to ensure impartiality, or the public's confidence in the impartiality, of the Government. The head of each agency shall be responsible for designating career reserved positions in such agency in accordance with such criteria and regulations.

(2) The Office shall periodically review general positions to determine whether the positions should be designated as career reserved. If the Office determines that any such position should be so designated, it shall order the agency to make the designation.

(3) Notwithstanding the provisions of any other law, any position to be designated as a Senior Executive Service position (except a position in the Executive Office of the President) which—

(A) is under the Executive Schedule, or for which the rate of basic pay is determined by reference to the Executive Schedule, and

(B) on the day before the date of the enactment of the Civil Service Reform Act of 1978 was specifically required under section 2102 of this title or otherwise required by law to be in the competitive service,

shall be designated as a career reserved position if the position entails direct responsibility to the public for the management or operation of particular government programs or functions.

(4) Not later than March 1 of each year, the head of each agency shall publish in the Federal Register a list of positions in the agency which were career reserved positions during the preceding calendar year.

(c) An agency may file an application with the Office setting forth reasons why it, or a unit thereof, should be excluded from the coverage of this subchapter. The Office shall—

(1) review the application and stated reasons,

(2) undertake a review to determine whether the agency or unit should be excluded from the coverage of this subchapter, and

(3) upon completion of its review, recommend to the President whether the agency or unit should be excluded from the coverage of this subchapter.

If the Office recommends that an agency or unit thereof be excluded from the coverage of this subchapter, the President may, on written determination, make the exclusion for the period determined by the President to be appropriate.

(d) Any agency or unit which is excluded from coverage under subsection (c) of this section shall make a sustained effort to bring its personnel system into conformity with the Senior Executive Service to the extent practicable.

(e) The Office may at any time recommend to the President that any exclusion previously granted to an agency or unit thereof under subsection (c) of this section be revoked. Upon recommendation of the Office, the President may revoke, by written determination, any exclusion made under subsection (c) of this section.

(f) If—

(1) any agency is excluded under subsection (c) of this section, or

(2) any exclusion is revoked under subsection (e) of this section,

the Office shall, within 30 days after the action, transmit to the Congress written notice of the exclusion or revocation.

(Added Pub. L. 95–454, title IV, § 402(a), Oct. 13, 1978, 92 Stat. 1155; amended Pub. L. 96–54, § 2(a)(12), Aug. 14, 1979, 93 Stat. 382; Pub. L. 96–187, title II, § 203, Jan. 8, 1980, 93 Stat. 1368; Pub. L. 100–325, § 2(c), May 30, 1988, 102 Stat. 581; Pub. L. 101–73, title VII, § 742(c), Aug. 9, 1989, 103 Stat. 437; Pub. L. 101–509, title V, § 529 [title I, § 101(b)(9)(A)], Nov. 5, 1990, 104 Stat. 1427, 1441; Pub. L. 101–624, title XVIII, § 1841, Nov. 28, 1990, 104 Stat. 3835; Pub. L. 102–496, title IV, § 402(b), Oct. 24, 1992, 106 Stat. 3184; Pub. L. 102–550, title XIII, § 1351(b), Oct. 28, 1992, 106 Stat. 3969; Pub. L. 103–359, title V, § 501(d), Oct. 14, 1994, 108 Stat. 3429; Pub. L. 104–201, div. A, title XI, § 1122(a)(1), Sept. 23, 1996, 110 Stat. 2687.)

REFERENCES IN TEXT

Level IV or V of the Executive Schedule, referred to in subsec. (a)(2), are set out in sections 5315 and 5316 of this title.

The date of the enactment of the Civil Service Reform Act of 1978, referred to in subsec. (b)(3), is the date of the enactment of Pub. L. 95–454, which was approved Oct. 13, 1978.

AMENDMENTS

1996—Subsec. (a)(1)(B). Pub. L. 104–201 substituted "National Imagery and Mapping Agency" for "Central Imagery Office".

1994—Subsec. (a)(1)(B). Pub. L. 103–359 inserted "the Central Imagery Office," after "Defense Intelligence Agency,".

1992—Subsec. (a)(1)(B). Pub. L. 102–496 inserted ", Department of Defense intelligence activities the civilian employees of which are subject to section 1590 of title 10," after "National Security Agency".

Subsec. (a)(1)(D). Pub. L. 102–550 inserted "the Office of Federal Housing Enterprise Oversight of the Department of Housing and Urban Development," after "Farm Credit Administration,".

1990—Subsec. (a)(1)(D). Pub. L. 101–624 inserted reference to Farm Credit Administration.

Subsec. (a)(2). Pub. L. 101–509 substituted "classified above GS–15 pursuant to section 5108" for "in GS–16, 17, or 18 of the General Schedule".

1989—Subsec. (a)(1)(D). Pub. L. 101–73 added subpar. (D).

1988—Subsec. (a)(1)(B). Pub. L. 100–325, § 2(c)(1), inserted reference to Drug Enforcement Administration.

Subsec. (a)(2)(iii). Pub. L. 100–235, § 2(c)(2), struck out cl. (iii) which read as follows: "any position in the Drug Enforcement Administration which is excluded from the competitive service under section 201 of the Crime Control Act of 1976 (5 U.S.C. 5108 note; 90 Stat. 2425);".

1980—Subsec. (a)(1)(C). Pub. L. 96–187 added subpar. (C).

1979—Subsec. (a)(1)(B). Pub. L. 96–54 inserted "and," after "Security Agency,".

EFFECTIVE DATE OF 1996 AMENDMENT

Amendment by Pub. L. 104–201 effective Oct. 1, 1996, see section 1124 of Pub. L. 104–201, set out as a note under section 193 of Title 10, Armed Forces.

EFFECTIVE DATE OF 1990 AMENDMENT

Amendment by Pub. L. 101–509 effective on such date as the President shall determine, but not earlier than 90 days, and not later than 180 days, after Nov. 5, 1990, see section 529 [title III, § 305] of Pub. L. 101–509, set out as a note under section 5301 of this title.

EFFECTIVE DATE OF 1980 AMENDMENT

Amendment by Pub. L. 96–187 effective on Jan. 8, 1980, see section 301(a) of Pub. L. 96–187, set out as a note under section 431 of Title 2, The Congress.

EFFECTIVE DATE OF 1979 AMENDMENT

Amendment by Pub. L. 96–54 effective July 12, 1979, see section 2(b) of Pub. L. 96–54, set out as a note under section 305 of this title.

SECTION REFERRED TO IN OTHER SECTIONS

This section is referred to in sections 2101a, 3104, 3133, 3151, 3372, 3391, 3591, 4311, 4507, 4508, 5304, 5347, 5376, 5381, 5724, 7323, 8432, 9506 of this title; title 2 section 1316a; title 3 section 115; title 10 sections 1606, 1614, 3014, 5014, 8014; title 15 section 656; title 22 section 2664a; title 31 section 733; title 38 sections 308, 7281; title 42 section 904; title 44 section 2103; title 49 section 106.

§ 3133. Authorization of positions; authority for appointment

(a) During each even-numbered calendar year, each agency shall—

(1) examine its needs for Senior Executive Service positions for each of the 2 fiscal years beginning after such calendar year; and

(2) submit to the Office of Personnel Management a written request for a specific number of Senior Executive Service positions for each of such fiscal years.

(b) Each agency request submitted under subsection (a) of this section shall—

(1) be based on the anticipated type and extent of program activities and budget requests of the agency for each of the 2 fiscal years involved, and such other factors as may be prescribed from time to time by the Office; and

(2) identify, by position title, positions which are proposed to be designated as or removed from designation as career reserved positions, and set forth justifications for such proposed actions.

(c) The Office of Personnel Management, in consultation with the Office of Management and Budget, shall review the request of each agency and shall authorize, for each of the 2 fiscal years covered by requests required under subsection (a) of this section, a specific number of Senior Executive Service positions for each agency.

(d)(1) The Office of Personnel Management may, on a written request of an agency or on its own initiative, make an adjustment in the number of positions authorized for any agency. Each agency request under this paragraph shall be submitted in such form, and shall be based on such factors, as the Office shall prescribe.

(2) The total number of positions in the Senior Executive Service may not at any time during any fiscal year exceed 105 percent of the total number of positions authorized under subsection (c) of this section for such fiscal year.

(e)(1) Not later than July 1, 1979, and from time to time thereafter as the Director of the Office of Personnel Management finds appropriate, the Director shall establish, by rule issued in accordance with section 1103(b) of this title, the number of positions out of the total number of positions in the Senior Executive Service, as authorized by this section or section 413 of the Civil Service Reform Act of 1978, which are to be career reserved positions. Except as provided in paragraph (2) of this subsection, the number of positions required by this subsection to be career reserved positions shall not be less than the number of the positions then in the Senior Executive Service which before the date of such Act, were authorized to be filled only through competitive civil service examination.

(2) The Director may, by rule, designate a number of career reserved positions which is less than the number required by paragraph (1) of this subsection only if the Director determines such lesser number necessary in order to designate as general positions one or more positions (other than positions described in section 3132(b)(3) of this title) which—

(A) involve policymaking responsibilities which require the advocacy or management of programs of the President and support of controversial aspects of such programs;

(B) involve significant participation in the major political policies of the President; or

(C) require the senior executives in the positions to serve as personal assistants of, or advisers to, Presidential appointees.

The Director shall provide a full explanation for his determination in each case.

(Added Pub. L. 95–454, title IV, § 402(a), Oct. 13, 1978, 92 Stat. 1158.)

REFERENCES IN TEXT

Section 413 of the Civil Service Reform Act of 1978, referred to in subsec. (e)(1), is set out as a note below.

The date of such Act, referred to in subsec. (e)(1), probably means Oct. 13, 1978, the date of the enactment of the Civil Service Reform Act of 1978.

CONVERSION TO SENIOR EXECUTIVE SERVICE

Section 413 of Pub. L. 95–454 provided that:

"(a) For the purpose of this section, 'agency', 'Senior Executive Service position', 'career appointee', 'career reserved position', 'limited term appointee', 'noncareer appointee', and 'general position' have the meanings set forth in section 3132(a) of title 5, United States Code (as added by this title) and 'Senior Executive Service' has the meaning set forth in section 2101a of such title 5 (as added by this title).

"(b)(1) Under the guidance of the Office of Personnel Management, each agency shall—

"(A) designate those positions which it considers should be Senior Executive Service positions and designate which of those positions it considers should be career reserved positions; and

"(B) submit to the Office a written request for—

"(i) a specific number of Senior Executive Service positions; and

"(ii) authority to employ a specific number of noncareer appointees.

"(2) The Office of Personnel Management shall review the designations and requests of each agency under paragraph (1) of this subsection, and shall establish interim authorizations in accordance with sections 3133 and 3134 of title 5, United States Code (as added by this Act), and shall publish the titles of the authorized positions in the Federal Register.

"(c)(1) Each employee serving in a position at the time it is designated as a Senior Executive Service position under subsection (b) of this section shall elect to—

"(A) decline conversion and be appointed to a position under such employee's current type of appointment and pay system, retaining the grade, seniority, and other rights and benefits associated with such type of appointment and pay system; or

"(B) accept conversion and be appointed to a Senior Executive Service position in accordance with the provisions of subsections (d), (e), (f), (g), and (h) of this section.

The appointment of an employee in an agency because of an election under subparagraph (A) of this paragraph shall not result in the separation or reduction in grade of any other employee in such agency.

"(2) Any employee in a position which has been designated a Senior Executive Service position under this section shall be notified in writing of such designation, the election required under paragraph (1) of this subsection, and the provisions of subsections (d), (e), (f), (g), and (h) of this section. The employee shall be given 90 days from the date of such notification to make the election under paragraph (1) of this subsection.

"(d) Each employee who has elected to accept conversion to a Senior Executive Service position under subsection (c)(1)(B) of this section and who is serving under—

"(1) a career or career-conditional appointment; or

"(2) a similar type of appointment in an excepted service position, as determined by the Office;

in a position which is designated as a Senior Executive Service position shall be appointed as a career appointee to such Senior Executive Service position without regard to section 3393(b)–(e) of title 5, United States Code (as added by this title).

"(e) Each employee who has elected conversion to a Senior Executive Service position under subsection (c)(1)(B) of this section and who is serving under an excepted appointment in a position which is not designated a career reserved position in the Senior Executive Service, but is—

"(1) a position in Schedule C of subpart C of part 213 of title 5, Code of Federal Regulations;

"(2) a position filled by noncareer executive assignment under subpart F of part 305 of title 5, Code of Federal Regulations; or

"(3) a position in the Executive Schedule under subchapter II of chapter 53 of title 5, United States Code [section 5311 et seq. of this title], other than a career Executive Schedule position;

shall be appointed as a noncareer appointee to a Senior Executive Service position.

"(f) Each employee who has elected conversion to a Senior Executive Service position under subsection (c)(1)(B) of this section, who is serving in a position described in paragraph (1), (2), or (3) of subsection (e) of this section, and whose position is designated as a career reserved position under subsection (b) of this section shall be appointed as a noncareer appointee to an appropriate general position in the Senior Executive Service or shall be separated.

"(g) Each employee who has elected conversion to a Senior Executive Service position under subsection (c)(1)(B) of this section, who is serving in a position de-

scribed in paragraph (1), (2), or (3) of subsection (e) of this section, and whose position is designated as a Senior Executive Service position and who has reinstatement eligibility to a position in the competitive service, may, on request to the Office, be appointed as a career appointee to a Senior Executive Service position. The name of, and basis for reinstatement eligibility for, each employee appointed as a career appointee under this subsection shall be published in the Federal Register.

"(h) Each employee who has elected conversion to a Senior Executive Service position under subsection (c)(1)(B) of this section and who is serving under a limited executive assignment under subpart F of part 305 of title 5, Code of Federal Regulations, shall—

"(1) be appointed as a limited term appointee to a Senior Executive Service position if the position then held by such employee will terminate within 3 years of the date of such appointment;

"(2) be appointed as a noncareer appointee to a Senior Executive Service position if the position then held by such employee is designated as a general position; or

"(3) be appointed as a noncareer appointee to a general position if the position then held by such employee is designated as a career reserved position.

"(i) The rate of basic pay for any employee appointed to a Senior Executive Service position under this section shall be greater than or equal to the rate of basic pay payable for the position held by such employee at the time of such appointment.

"(j) Any employee who is aggrieved by any action by any agency under this section is entitled to appeal to the Merit Systems Protection Board under section 7701 of title 5, United States Code (as added by this title). An agency shall take any corrective action which the Board orders in its decision on an appeal under this subsection.

"(k) The Office shall prescribe regulations to carry out the purpose of this section."

Section 415(a)(2) of Pub. L. 95–454 provided that section 413 is effective Oct. 13, 1978.

SECTION REFERRED TO IN OTHER SECTIONS

This section is referred to in section 3392 of this title; title 42 section 904.

§ 3134. Limitations on noncareer and limited appointments

(a) During each calendar year, each agency shall—

(1) examine its needs for employment of noncareer appointees for the fiscal year beginning in the following year; and

(2) submit to the Office of Personnel Management, in accordance with regulations prescribed by the Office, a written request for authority to employ a specific number of noncareer appointees for such fiscal year.

(b) The number of noncareer appointees in each agency shall be determined annually by the Office on the basis of demonstrated need of the agency. The total number of noncareer appointees in all agencies may not exceed 10 percent of the total number of Senior Executive Service positions in all agencies.

(c) Subject to the 10 percent limitation of subsection (b) of this section, the Office may adjust the number of noncareer positions authorized for any agency under subsection (b) of this section if emergency needs arise that were not anticipated when the original authorizations were made.

(d) The number of Senior Executive Service positions in any agency which are filled by noncareer appointees may not at any time exceed the greater of—

(1) 25 percent of the total number of Senior Executive Service positions in the agency; or

(2) the number of positions in the agency which were filled on the date of the enactment of the Civil Service Reform Act of 1978 by—

(A) noncareer executive assignments under subpart F of part 305 of title 5, Code of Federal Regulations, as in effect on such date, or

(B) appointments to level IV or V of the Executive Schedule which were not required on such date to be made by and with the advice and consent of the Senate.

This subsection shall not apply in the case of any agency having fewer than 4 Senior Executive Service positions.

(e) The total number of limited emergency appointees and limited term appointees in all agencies may not exceed 5 percent of the total number of Senior Executive Service positions in all agencies.

(Added Pub. L. 95–454, title IV, § 402(a), Oct. 13, 1978, 92 Stat. 1159.)

REFERENCES IN TEXT

The date of enactment of the Civil Service Reform Act of 1978, referred to in subsec. (d)(2), is the date of enactment of Pub. L. 95–454, which was approved Oct. 13, 1978.

Level IV or V of the Executive Schedule, referred to in subsec. (d)(2)(B), are set out in sections 5315 and 5316 of this title.

SECTION REFERRED TO IN OTHER SECTIONS

This section is referred to in title 20 section 3461; title 38 section 709.

[§ 3135. Repealed. Pub. L. 104–66, title II, § 2181(a)(1), Dec. 21, 1995, 109 Stat. 732]

Section, added Pub. L. 95–454, title IV, § 402(a), Oct. 13, 1978, 92 Stat. 1159; amended Pub. L. 98–168, title III, § 301(b), Nov. 29, 1983, 97 Stat. 1112; Pub. L. 98–615, title III, § 306(a), Nov. 8, 1984, 98 Stat. 3219, directed Office of Personnel Management to submit reports to Congress relating to Senior Executive Service.

§ 3136. Regulations

The Office of Personnel Management shall prescribe regulations to carry out the purpose of this subchapter.

(Added Pub. L. 95–454, title IV, § 402(a), Oct. 13, 1978, 92 Stat. 1160.)

SUBCHAPTER III—THE FEDERAL BUREAU OF INVESTIGATION AND DRUG ENFORCEMENT ADMINISTRATION SENIOR EXECUTIVE SERVICE

§ 3151. The Federal Bureau of Investigation and Drug Enforcement Administration Senior Executive Service

(a) The Attorney General may by regulation establish a personnel system for senior personnel within the Federal Bureau of Investigation and the Drug Enforcement Administration to be known as the Federal Bureau of Investigation and Drug Enforcement Administration Senior Executive Service (hereinafter in this sub-

chapter referred to as the "FBI–DEA Senior Executive Service"). The regulations establishing the FBI–DEA Senior Executive Service shall—

(1) meet the requirements set forth in section 3131 for the Senior Executive Service;

(2) provide that positions in the FBI–DEA Senior Executive Service meet requirements that are consistent with the provisions of section 3132(a)(2);

(3) provide rates of pay for the FBI–DEA Senior Executive Service that are not in excess of the maximum rate or less than the minimum rate of basic pay established for the Senior Executive Service under section 5382 and that are adjusted at the same time and to the same extent as rates of basic pay for the Senior Executive Service are adjusted;

(4) provide a performance appraisal system for the FBI–DEA Senior Executive Service that conforms to the provisions of subchapter II of chapter 43;

(5) provide for—

(A) removal consistent with section 3592;

(B) reduction-in-force procedures consistent with section 3595(a), together with measures to ensure that a member of the FBI–DEA Senior Executive Service may not be removed due to a reduction in force unless reasonable efforts to place such member in another such position are first taken;

(C) procedures in accordance with which any furlough affecting the FBI–DEA Senior Executive Service shall be carried out;

(D) removal or suspension consistent with subsections (a), (b), and (c) of section 7543 (except that any hearing or appeal to which a member of the FBI–DEA Senior Executive Service is entitled shall be held or decided pursuant to procedures established by regulations of the Attorney General); and

(E) recertification consistent with section 3393a;

(6) permit the payment of performance awards to members of the FBI–DEA Senior Executive Service consistent with the provisions applicable to performance awards under section 5384; and

(7) provide that members of the FBI–DEA Senior Executive Service may be granted sabbatical leaves consistent with the provisions of section 3396(c).

(b)(1) Except as provided in subsection (a), the Attorney General may—

(A) make applicable to the FBI–DEA Senior Executive Service any of the provisions of this title applicable to applicants for or members of the Senior Executive Service; and

(B) appoint, promote, and assign individuals to positions established within the FBI–DEA Senior Executive Service without regard to the provisions of this title governing appointments and other personnel actions in the competitive service.

(2)(A) Notwithstanding any other provision of this section, an individual may not be selected for the FBI–DEA Senior Executive Service unless such individual is a career employee in the civil service.

(B) For the purpose of subparagraph (A), "career employee in the civil service" shall have such meaning as the Attorney General, in consultation with the Director of the Office of Personnel Management, by regulation prescribes.

(c) The President, based on the recommendations of the Attorney General, may award ranks to members of the FBI–DEA Senior Executive Service in a manner consistent with the provisions of section 4507.

(d) Notwithstanding any other provision of this section, the Attorney General may detail or assign any member of the FBI–DEA Senior Executive Service to serve in a position outside the Federal Bureau of Investigation or the Drug Enforcement Administration (as the case may be) in which the member's expertise and experience may be of benefit to the Federal Bureau of Investigation or the Drug Enforcement Administration (as the case may be) or another Government agency. Any such member shall not by reason of such detail or assignment lose any entitlement or status associated with membership in the FBI–DEA Senior Executive Service.

(e) The Attorney General shall each year submit to Congress, at the time the budget is submitted by the President to the Congress for the next fiscal year, a report on the FBI–DEA Senior Executive Service. The report shall include, in the aggregate and by agency—

(1) the number of FBI–DEA Senior Executive Service positions established as of the end of the preceding fiscal year;

(2) the number of individuals being paid at each rate of basic pay for the FBI–DEA Senior Executive Service as of the end of the preceding fiscal year;

(3) the number, distribution, and amount of awards paid to members of the FBI–DEA Senior Executive Service during the preceding fiscal year; and

(4) the number of individuals removed from the FBI–DEA Senior Executive Service during the preceding fiscal year—

(A) for less than fully successful performance;

(B) due to a reduction in force; or

(C) for any other reason.

(Added Pub. L. 100–325, § 1(a), May 30, 1988, 102 Stat. 579; amended Pub. L. 101–194, title V, § 506(b)(1), Nov. 30, 1989, 103 Stat. 1758.)

REFERENCES IN TEXT

Provisions of this title governing appointments and other personnel actions in the competitive service, referred to in subsec. (b)(1)(B), are classified generally to section 3301 et seq. of this title.

AMENDMENTS

1989—Subsec. (a)(5)(E). Pub. L. 101–194 added subpar. (E).

EFFECTIVE DATE OF 1989 AMENDMENT

Section 506(d) of Pub. L. 101–194 provided that: "The amendments made by this section [enacting section 3393a of this title and amending this section, sections 3393, 3592 to 3594, 7701, 8336, 8339, 8414, and 8421 of this title, section 1601 of Title 10, Armed Forces, section 3945 of Title 22, Foreign Relations and Intercourse, and provisions set out as a note under section 402 of Title 50, War and National Defense] shall take effect on January 1, 1991."

SECTION REFERRED TO IN OTHER SECTIONS

This section is referred to in sections 5304, 5376 of this title.

§ 3152. Limitation on pay

Members of the FBI–DEA Senior Executive Service shall be subject to the limitation under section 5307.

(Added Pub. L. 100–325, § 1(a), May 30, 1988, 102 Stat. 581; amended Pub. L. 102–378, § 2(9), Oct. 2, 1992, 106 Stat. 1347.)

AMENDMENTS

1992—Pub. L. 102–378 amended section generally. Prior to amendment, section read as follows: "Nothing in this subchapter shall be construed to allow the aggregate amount payable to a member of the FBI–DEA Senior Executive Service under this subchapter during any fiscal year to exceed the annual rate payable for positions at level I of the Executive Schedule in effect at the end of such year. This section shall be applied in a manner consistent with paragraphs (1) and (2) of section 5383(b)."

SUBCHAPTER IV—TEMPORARY ORGANIZATIONS ESTABLISHED BY LAW OR EXECUTIVE ORDER

§ 3161. Employment and compensation of employees

(a) DEFINITION OF TEMPORARY ORGANIZATION.—For the purposes of this subchapter, the term "temporary organization" means a commission, committee, board, or other organization that—

(1) is established by law or Executive order for a specific period not in excess of three years for the purpose of performing a specific study or other project; and

(2) is terminated upon the completion of the study or project or upon the occurrence of a condition related to the completion of the study or project.

(b) EMPLOYMENT AUTHORITY.—(1) Notwithstanding the provisions of chapter 51 of this title, the head of a temporary organization may appoint persons to positions of employment in a temporary organization in such numbers and with such skills as are necessary for the performance of the functions required of a temporary organization.

(2) The period of an appointment under paragraph (1) may not exceed three years, except that under regulations prescribed by the Office of Personnel Management the period of appointment may be extended for up to an additional two years.

(3) The positions of employment in a temporary organization are in the excepted service of the civil service.

(c) DETAIL AUTHORITY.—Upon the request of the head of a temporary organization, the head of any department or agency of the Government may detail, on a nonreimbursable basis, any personnel of the department or agency to that organization to assist in carrying out its duties.

(d) COMPENSATION.—(1) The rate of basic pay for an employee appointed under subsection (b) shall be established under regulations prescribed by the Office of Personnel Management without regard to the provisions of chapter 51 and subchapter III of chapter 53 of this title.

(2) The rate of basic pay for the chairman, a member, an executive director, a staff director, or another executive level position of a temporary organization may not exceed the maxi-

mum rate of basic pay established for the Senior Executive Service under section 5382 of this title.

(3) Except as provided in paragraph (4), the rate of basic pay for other positions in a temporary organization may not exceed the maximum rate of basic pay for grade GS–15 of the General Schedule under section 5332 of this title.

(4) The rate of basic pay for a senior staff position of a temporary organization may, in a case determined by the head of the temporary organization as exceptional, exceed the maximum rate of basic pay authorized under paragraph (3), but may not exceed the maximum rate of basic pay authorized for an executive level position under paragraph (2).

(5) In this subsection, the term "basic pay" includes locality pay provided for under section 5304 of this title.

(e) TRAVEL EXPENSES.—An employee of a temporary organization, whether employed on a full-time or part-time basis, may be allowed travel and transportation expenses, including per diem in lieu of subsistence, at rates authorized for employees of agencies under subchapter I of chapter 57 of this title, while traveling away from the employee's regular place of business in the performance of services for the temporary organization.

(f) BENEFITS.—An employee appointed under subsection (b) shall be afforded the same benefits and entitlements as are provided temporary employees under this title.

(g) RETURN RIGHTS.—An employee serving under a career or career conditional appointment or the equivalent in an agency who transfers to or converts to an appointment in a temporary organization with the consent of the head of the agency is entitled to be returned to the employee's former position or a position of like seniority, status, and pay without grade or pay retention in the agency if the employee—

(1) is being separated from the temporary organization for reasons other than misconduct, neglect of duty, or malfeasance; and

(2) applies for return not later than 30 days before the earlier of—

(A) the date of the termination of the employment in the temporary organization; or

(B) the date of the termination of the temporary organization.

(h) TEMPORARY AND INTERMITTENT SERVICES.— The head of a temporary organization may procure for the organization temporary and intermittent services under section 3109(b) of this title.

(i) ACCEPTANCE OF VOLUNTEER SERVICES.—(1) The head of a temporary organization may accept volunteer services appropriate to the duties of the organization without regard to section 1342 of title 31.

(2) Donors of voluntary services accepted for a temporary organization under this subsection may include the following:

(A) Advisors.
(B) Experts.
(C) Members of the commission, committee, board, or other temporary organization, as the case may be.
(D) A person performing services in any other capacity determined appropriate by the head of the temporary organization.

(3) The head of the temporary organization—

(A) shall ensure that each person performing voluntary services accepted under this subsection is notified of the scope of the voluntary services accepted;

(B) shall supervise the volunteer to the same extent as employees receiving compensation for similar services; and

(C) shall ensure that the volunteer has appropriate credentials or is otherwise qualified to perform in each capacity for which the volunteer's services are accepted.

(4) A person providing volunteer services accepted under this subsection shall be considered an employee of the Federal Government in the performance of those services for the purposes of the following provisions of law:

(A) Chapter 81 of this title, relating to compensation for work-related injuries.

(B) Chapter 171 of title 28, relating to tort claims.

(C) Chapter 11 of title 18, relating to conflicts of interest.

(Added Pub. L. 106–398, §1 [[div. A], title XI, §1101(a)], Oct. 30, 2000, 114 Stat. 1654, 1654A–308.)

CHAPTER 33—EXAMINATION, SELECTION, AND PLACEMENT

SUBCHAPTER I—EXAMINATION, CERTIFICATION, AND APPOINTMENT

AMENDMENTS

1998—Pub. L. 105–339, § 3(b), Oct. 31, 1998, 112 Stat. 3184, added items 3330a to 3330c.

Pub. L. 105–277, div. C, title I, § 151(c)(1), Oct. 21, 1998, 112 Stat. 2681–616, substituted "DETAILS, VACANCIES, AND APPOINTMENTS" for "DETAILS" in heading for subchapter III, "Acting officer" for "Details; to office of head of Executive agency or military department" in item 3345, "Time limitation" for "Details; to subordinate offices" in item 3346, "Exclusivity" for "Details; Presidential authority" in item 3347, "Vacant office" for "Details; limited in time" in item 3348, and "Reporting of vacancies" for "Details; to fill vacancies; restrictions" in item 3349 and added items 3349a to 3349d.

1996—Pub. L. 104–197, title III, § 315(b)(1), Sept. 16, 1996, 110 Stat. 2416, substituted "Competitive service; recommendations of Senators or Representatives" for "Political recommendations" in item 3303.

Pub. L. 104–106, div. A, title X, § 1037(b)(2), Feb. 10, 1996, 110 Stat. 432, which directed substitution of "3330. Government-wide list of vacant positions" for the item relating to section 3329, as added by section 4431(b) of Pub. L. 104–484, could not be executed because of the intervening amendment by Pub. L. 104–52, § 4(2). See 1995 Amendment note below.

1995—Pub. L. 104–52, title IV, § 4(2), Nov. 19, 1995, 109 Stat. 490, redesignated item 3329 "Government-wide list of vacant positions" as item 3330.

1993—Pub. L. 103–94, § 8(b), Oct. 6, 1993, 107 Stat. 1007, substituted "Political recommendations" for "Competitive service; recommendations of Senators or Representatives" in item 3303.

1992—Pub. L. 102–484, div. A, title V, § 544(b), div. D, title XLIV, § 4431(b), Oct. 23, 1992, 106 Stat. 2415, 2720, added two items 3329.

Pub. L. 102–378, § 2(13)(B), Oct. 2, 1992, 106 Stat. 1347, struck out item 3342 "Federal participants in executive exchange programs".

1990—Pub. L. 101–509, title V, § 529 [title I, § 101(b)(9)(C)(iii)], Nov. 5, 1990, 104 Stat. 1427, 1441, substituted "Appointments to positions classified above GS–15" for "Appointments at GS–16, 17, and 18" in item 3324.

Pub. L. 101–416, § 2(a)(2), Oct. 12, 1990, 104 Stat. 903, added item 3342.

1989—Pub. L. 101–194, title V, § 506(a)(2), Nov. 30, 1989, 103 Stat. 1758, added item 3393a.

Pub. L. 101–12, § 5(b), Apr. 10, 1989, 103 Stat. 33, added item 3352.

1988—Pub. L. 100–398, § 7(a)(3), Aug. 17, 1988, 102 Stat. 988, inserted "agency" after "Executive" in item 3345.

1985—Pub. L. 99–145, title XVI, § 1622(a)(2), Nov. 8, 1985, 99 Stat. 777, added item 3328.

1979—Pub. L. 96–54, § 2(a)(13), Aug. 14, 1979, 93 Stat. 382, struck out item 3315a "Registers; individuals receiving compensation for work injuries".

1978—Pub. L. 95–454, title III, §§ 303(b), 307(h)(2), 309(b), title IV, § 403(b), title IX, § 906(c)(4), Oct. 13, 1978, 92 Stat. 1146, 1149, 1152, 1165, 1227, substituted "probationary period" for "probation; period of" in item 3321, struck out item 3319 "Competitive service; selection; members of family restriction", added items 3327 and 3391 to 3397, and struck out items 3391 to 3398.

Pub. L. 95–437, § 3(b), Oct. 10, 1978, 92 Stat. 1058, added heading for subchapter VII and items 3391 to 3398.

Pub. L. 95–256, § 5(b)(2), Apr. 6, 1978, 92 Stat. 191, struck out item 3322 "Competitive service; temporary appointments after age 70".

Pub. L. 95–251, § 2(c)(3), Mar. 27, 1978, 92 Stat. 184, substituted "administrative law judges" for "hearing examiners" in item 3344.

---

[1] So in original. Does not conform to section catchline.

Pub. L. 95–228, § 2(a), Feb. 10, 1978, 92 Stat. 25, struck out item 3306 "Competitive service; departmental service; apportionment".

1975—Pub. L. 94–183, § 2(7), Dec. 31, 1975, 89 Stat. 1057, struck out item 3364 "Promotion; substitute employees in the postal field service".

1972—Pub. L. 92–297, §§ 2(b), 3(b), May 16, 1972, 86 Stat. 142, 144, substituted "maximum age entrance requirements, exceptions" for "maximum age requirement; restriction on use of appropriated funds" in item 3307, and added subchapter VII and items 3381 to 3385.

1971—Pub. L. 91–648, title IV, § 402(b), Jan. 5, 1971, 84 Stat. 1925, added heading for subchapter VI and items 3371 to 3376.

1970—Pub. L. 91–375, § 6(c)(7)(B), Aug. 12, 1970, 84 Stat. 776, struck out item 3327 "Postmasters; standards for determination of qualifications".

1967—Pub. L. 90–105, § 1(b), Oct. 11, 1967, 81 Stat. 273, added item 3304a.

Pub. L. 90–83, § 1(9)(B), Sept. 11, 1967, 81 Stat. 197, added item 3315a.

1966—Pub. L. 89–762, § 1(b), Nov. 5, 1966, 80 Stat. 1312, struck out item 3342 "Details; field to departmental service prohibited".

CHAPTER REFERRED TO IN OTHER SECTIONS

This chapter is referred to in title 20 section 1018; title 31 section 3801; title 35 section 3; title 36 sections 510, 151307, 151707, 152407; title 42 sections 290aa, 2297b–4.

SUBCHAPTER I—EXAMINATION, CERTIFICATION, AND APPOINTMENT

SUBCHAPTER REFERRED TO IN OTHER SECTIONS

This subchapter is referred to in section 9510 of this title; title 10 section 1744; title 16 section 3198; title 38 section 7403.

§ 3301. Civil service; generally

The President may—

(1) prescribe such regulations for the admission of individuals into the civil service in the executive branch as will best promote the efficiency of that service;

(2) ascertain the fitness of applicants as to age, health, character, knowledge, and ability for the employment sought; and

(3) appoint and prescribe the duties of individuals to make inquiries for the purpose of this section.

(Pub. L. 89–554, Sept. 6, 1966, 80 Stat. 417.)

HISTORICAL AND REVISION NOTES

Derivation	U.S. Code	Revised Statutes and Statutes at Large
....	5 U.S.C. 631 (less last 16 words).	R.S. § 1753 (less last 16 words).

The words "civil service in the executive branch" are substituted for "civil service of the United States" to confirm the grant of authority in view of the definition of "civil service" in section 2101. The word "will" is substituted for "may". The words "for the employment sought" are substituted for "for the branch of service into which he seeks to enter" as the latter are archaic since there are no "branches" within the executive branch. The word "applicant" is substituted for "candidate".

Standard changes are made to conform with the definitions applicable and the style of this title as outlined in the preface to the report.

SHORT TITLE OF 1998 AMENDMENT

Pub. L. 105–277, div. C, title I, § 151(a), Oct. 21, 1998, 112 Stat. 2681–611, provided that: "This section [enacting sections 3345 to 3349d of this title, repealing former sections 3345 to 3349 of this title, and enacting provisions set out as a note under section 3345 of this title] may be cited as the 'Federal Vacancies Reform Act of 1998'."

SHORT TITLE OF 1991 AMENDMENT

Pub. L. 102–175, § 1, Dec. 2, 1991, 105 Stat. 1222, provided that: "This Act [amending sections 3395, 3396, 5383, and 7701 of this title] may be cited as the 'Senior Executive Service Improvements Act'."

TEMPORARY MEASURES TO FACILITATE REEMPLOYMENT OF CERTAIN DISPLACED FEDERAL EMPLOYEES

Pub. L. 102–484, div. D, title XLIV, § 4432, Oct. 23, 1992, 106 Stat. 2720, provided that:

"(a) DEFINITIONS.—For the purpose of this section—

"(1) the term 'agency' means an Executive agency (as defined by section 105 of title 5, United States Code), excluding the General Accounting Office and the Department of Defense; and

"(2) the term 'displaced employee' means any individual who is—

"(A) an employee of the Department of Defense who has been given specific notice that such employee is to be separated due to a reduction in force; or

"(B) a former employee of the Department of Defense who was involuntarily separated therefrom due to a reduction in force.

"(b) METHOD OF CONSIDERATION.—In accordance with regulations which the Office of Personnel Management shall prescribe, consistent with otherwise applicable provisions of law, an agency shall, in filling a vacant position for which a qualified displaced employee has applied in timely fashion, give full consideration to the application of the displaced employee before selecting any candidate from outside the agency for the position.

"(c) LIMITATION.—A displaced employee is entitled to consideration in accordance with this section for the 24-month period beginning on the date such employee receives the specific notice referred to in subsection (a)(2)(A), except that, if the employee is separated pursuant to such notice, the right to such consideration shall continue through the end of the 24-month period beginning on the date of separation.

"(d) APPLICABILITY.—(1) This section shall apply to any individual who—

"(A) became a displaced employee within the 12-month period ending immediately before the date of the enactment of this Act [Oct. 23, 1992]; or

"(B) becomes a displaced employee on or after the date of the enactment of this Act and before October 1, 1997.

"(2) In the case of a displaced employee described in paragraph (1)(A), for purposes of computing any period of time under subsection (c), the date of the specific notice described in subsection (a)(2)(A) (or, if the employee was separated as described in subsection (a)(2)(B) before the date of enactment of this Act, the date of separation) shall be deemed to have occurred on such date of enactment.

"(3) Nothing in this section shall be considered to apply with respect to any position—

"(A) which has been filled as of the date of enactment of this Act; or

"(B) which has been excepted from the competitive service because of its confidential, policy-determining, policy-making or policy-advocating character."

NATIONAL ADVISORY COUNCIL ON THE PUBLIC SERVICE

Pub. L. 101–363, Aug. 14, 1990, 104 Stat. 424, provided that:

"SECTION 1. SHORT TITLE.

"This Act may be cited as the 'National Advisory Council on the Public Service Act of 1990'.

"SEC. 2. FINDINGS.

"The Congress finds that—

"(1) recognition of the services rendered by Federal employees (hereinafter in this Act referred to as 'national public service') should be accorded a high and continuing place on the national agenda;

"(2) the National Commission on the Public Service, through its good works, has documented the need for greater advocacy on behalf of those performing national public service;

"(3) although public service is an honorable profession, members of the public do not always perceive it favorably;

"(4) serious obstacles often hinder the Government's efforts to recruit and retain the best and the brightest for national public service;

"(5) just as the public has a right to expect Federal employees to adhere to the highest standards of excellence and ethicality, so Federal employees have a right to expect an atmosphere of trust and respect, and a sense of accomplishment from their work; and

"(6) an advisory council is needed to provide the President and the Congress with bipartisan, objective assessments of, and recommendations concerning, the Federal workforce.

"SEC. 3. ESTABLISHMENT.

"There shall be established a council to be known as the National Advisory Council on the Public Service (hereinafter in this Act referred to as the 'Council').

"SEC. 4. FUNCTIONS.

"The Council shall—

"(1) regularly assess the state of the Federal workforce;

"(2) in conjunction with the President, the Congress, and the Judiciary, seek to attract individuals of the highest caliber to careers involving national public service, and encourage them and others of similar distinction who are already part of the Federal workforce to make a continuing commitment to national public service;

"(3) promote better public understanding of the role of Federal employees in implementing Government programs and policies, and otherwise seek to improve the public perception of Federal employees;

"(4) encourage efforts to build student interest in performing national public service (whether those efforts are undertaken at the community level, in the classroom, or otherwise); and

"(5) develop methods for improving motivation and excellence among Federal employees.

"SEC. 5. MEMBERSHIP.

"(a) NUMBER AND APPOINTMENT.—The Council shall be composed of 15 members as follows:

"(1) 2 Members of the Senate, 1 of whom shall be appointed by the majority leader of the Senate and the other of whom shall be appointed by the minority leader of the Senate.

"(2) 2 Members of the House of Representatives, 1 of whom shall be appointed by the Speaker of the House of Representatives and the other of whom shall be appointed by the minority leader of the House of Representatives.

"(3) The Director of the Administrative Office of the United States Courts (or his delegate).

"(4) 10 individuals appointed by the President—

"(A) 4 of whom shall be chosen from among officers serving in the executive branch;

"(B) 1 of whom shall be chosen from among career employees in the civil service;

"(C) 1 of whom shall be a Federal employee who is a member of a labor organization (as defined by section 7103(a)(4) of title 5, United States Code); and

"(D) 4 of whom shall be chosen from among members of the public who do not hold any Government office or position.

"(b) CONTINUATION OF MEMBERSHIP.—If any member of the Council whose appointment is based on that individual's holding a Government office or position leaves such office or position, or if any member of the Council under subsection (a)(4)(D) is appointed or elected to a Government office or position, that individual may continue to serve as such a member for not longer than

the 90-day period beginning on the date of leaving that office or position, or entering into that office or position, as the case may be.

"(c) TERMS.—Members of the Council shall be appointed for the life of the Council.

"(d) VACANCIES.—A vacancy in the Council shall be filled in the manner in which the original appointment was made.

"(e) COMPENSATION.—(1) Members of the Council shall not be entitled to pay (or, in the case of members holding any Government office or position, pay in addition to any to which they are otherwise entitled for service in such office or position) by virtue of membership on the Council.

"(2) While serving away from their homes or regular places of business in the performance of duties for the Council, members shall be allowed travel expenses, including per diem in lieu of subsistence, in the same manner as authorized by section 5703 of title 5, United States Code, for persons employed intermittently in Government service.

"(f) QUORUM.—Eight members of the Council shall constitute a quorum.

"(g) CHAIRMAN.—The Chairman of the Council shall be designated by the President from among the members appointed under subsection (a)(4)(D).

"(h) MEETINGS.—The Council shall meet at the call of the Chairman or a majority of its members, and shall meet on at least a quarterly basis.

"SEC. 6. DIRECTOR AND STAFF; EXPERTS AND CONSULTANTS.

"(a) DIRECTOR.—With the approval of the Council, the Chairman may appoint a Director and fix the pay of such Director at a rate not to exceed the rate for level IV of the Executive Schedule [5 U.S.C. 5315]. The Director shall be a person who, by reason of demonstrated ability in the area of management, government, or public administration, is especially well qualified to serve.

"(b) STAFF.—With the approval of the Chairman, the Director may appoint and fix the pay of such personnel as may be necessary to carry out the functions of the Council. The staff of the Council shall be appointed subject to the provisions of title 5, United States Code, governing appointments in the competitive service, and shall be paid in accordance with the provisions of chapter 51 and subchapter III of chapter 53 of such title relating to classification and General Schedule pay rates.

"(c) EXPERTS AND CONSULTANTS.—The Council may procure temporary or intermittent services under section 3109(b) of title 5, United States Code, but at rates for individuals not to exceed the daily equivalent of the maximum rate payable under the General Schedule.

"(d) STAFF OF FEDERAL AGENCIES.—Upon the request of the Chairman, the head of a Federal agency may detail, on a reimbursable or nonreimbursable basis, any personnel of such agency to the Council to assist the Council in carrying out its functions under this Act.

"SEC. 7. POWERS.

"(a) MAILS.—The Council may use the United States mails in the same manner and under the same conditions as other Federal agencies.

"(b) ADMINISTRATIVE SUPPORT SERVICES.—The Administrator of General Services shall provide to the Council, on a reimbursable basis, such administrative support services as the Council may request.

"(c) OFFICIAL DATA.—The Council may secure directly from any Federal agency information necessary to carry out its functions under this Act. Each such agency is authorized and directed to furnish, to the extent permitted by law, any information requested by the Council.

"(d) GIFTS.—The Council—

"(1) may accept money and other property donated, bequeathed, or devised to the Council without condition or restriction (other than that it be used to carry out the work of the Council); and

"(2) may use, sell, or otherwise dispose of any such property to carry out its functions under this Act, except that, upon the termination of the Council, any such property shall be disposed of in accordance with applicable provisions of law governing the disposal of Federal property.

"SEC. 8. REPORTS.

"The Council shall transmit to the President and each House of the Congress—

"(1) within 1 and 2 years, respectively, after the date on which the Council first meets, reports containing its preliminary findings and recommendations; and

"(2) within 3 years after the date on which the Council first meets, a final report containing a detailed statement of the findings and conclusions of the Council, together with its recommendations for such legislation or administrative actions as it considers appropriate.

"SEC. 9. COMMENCEMENT; TERMINATION.

"(a) COMMENCEMENT.—Appointments under section 5 shall be made, and the Council shall first meet, within 90 days after the date of the enactment of this Act [Aug. 14, 1990].

"(b) TERMINATION.—The Council shall cease to exist upon transmitting its final report under section 8(2).

"SEC. 10. AUTHORIZATION.

"There is authorized to be appropriated such sums as may be necessary to carry out this Act."

EX. ORD. NO. 8743. EXTENDING THE CLASSIFIED CIVIL
SERVICE

Ex. Ord. No. 8743, Apr. 23, 1941, as amended by Ex. Ord. No. 9230, Aug. 20, 1942; Ex. Ord. No. 9678, Jan. 14, 1946; Ex. Ord. No. 9712, Apr. 13, 1946; Ex. Ord. No. 12107, Dec. 28, 1978, 44 F.R. 1055, provided:

By virtue of the authority vested in me by section 1 of the act of November 26, 1940, entitled "Extending the Classified Executive Civil Service of the United States" (54 Stat. 1211), by the Civil Service Act (22 Stat. 403), and by section 1753 of the Revised Statutes of the United States [sections 3301 and 7301 of this title], it is hereby ordered as follows:

SECTION 1. All offices and positions in the executive civil service of the United States except (1) those that are temporary, (2) those expressly excepted from the provisions of section 1 of the said act of November 26, 1940, (3) those excepted from the classified service under Schedules A and B of the Civil Service Rules, and (4) those which now have a classified status, are hereby covered into the classified civil service of the Government.

SECTION 2. Section 1 of this order shall become effective on January 1, 1942, except that as to positions affected thereby which are vacant at any time after June 30, 1941, and before January 1, 1942, it shall become effective when the vacancies first exist during such period, and appointments to such vacant positions shall be made in accordance with the Civil Service Rules as amended by section 3 of this order, unless prior express permission is given by the Office of Personnel Management for appointment without regard thereto.

SECTION 3. (a) Upon consideration of the report of the Committee on Civil Service Improvement (House Document No. 118, 77th Congress) appointed by Executive Order No. 8044 of January 31, 1939, it is hereby found and determined that the regulations and procedures hereinafter prescribed in this section with respect to attorney positions in the classified civil service are required by the conditions of good administration.

(b) There is hereby created in the Office of Personnel Management (hereinafter referred to as the Office) a board to be known as the Board of Legal Examiners (hereinafter referred to as the Board). The Board shall consist of the Solicitor General of the United States and the chief law officer of the Office of Personnel Management, as members *ex officio*, and nine members to be appointed by the President, four of whom shall be attorneys chosen from the chief officers of the Executive departments, agencies or corporate instrumentalities of the Government, two from the law-teaching profession, and three from attorneys engaged in private practice. The President shall designate the chairman of the Board. Five members shall constitute a quorum, and the Board may transact business notwithstanding vacancies thereon. Members of the Board shall receive no salary as such, but shall be entitled to necessary expenses incurred in the performance of their duties hereunder.

(c) It shall be the duty of the Board to promote the development of a merit system for the recruitment, selection, appointment, promotion, and transfer of attorneys in the classified civil service in accordance with the general procedures outlined in Plan A of the report of the Committee on Civil Service Improvement, appointed by Executive Order No. 8044 of January 31, 1939.

(d) The Board, in consultation with the Office, shall determine the regulations and procedures under this section governing the recruitment and examination of applicants for attorney positions, and the selection, appointment, promotion and transfer of attorneys, in the classified service.

(e) The Office shall in the manner determined by the Board establish a register or registers for attorney positions in the classified service and such positions shall thereafter be filled from such registers as are designated by the Board. Unless otherwise determined by the Board, any register so established shall not be in effect for a period longer than one year from the date of its establishment. Upon request of the Board, the Office shall appoint regional or local boards of examiners composed of persons approved by the Board, within or without the Federal service, to interview and examine applicants as the Board shall direct.

(f) The number of names to be placed upon any register of eligibles for attorney positions shall be limited to the number recommended by the Board; and such registers shall not be ranked according to the ratings received by the eligibles, except that persons entitled to veterans' preference as defined in section 1 of Civil Service Rule VI shall be appropriately designated thereon.

(g) Any person whose name has been placed upon three registers of eligibles covering positions of the same grade, and who has not been appointed therefrom, shall not thereafter be eligible for placement upon any subsequently established register covering positions of such grade.

(h) So far as practicable and consistent with good administration, the eligibles on any register for attorney positions and appointments for such register shall be apportioned among the several States and Territories and the District of Columbia upon the basis of population as ascertained in the last preceding census. The Office shall certify to the appointing officer for each vacancy all the eligibles on the appropriate register except those whose appointment would, in the determination of the Board, be inconsistent with the apportionment policy herein prescribed. The appointing officer shall make selections for any vacancy or vacancies in attorney positions from the register so certified, with sole reference to merit and fitness.

(i) Any position affected by this section may be filled before appropriate registers have been established pursuant to this section only by a person whose appointment is approved by the Board. The Board may require as a condition of its approval that persons thus proposed for appointment pass a noncompetitive examination and may designate examining committees composed of persons within or without the Federal service to conduct such examinations. Persons whose appointment was approved by the Board prior to March 16, 1942, and who pass a noncompetitive examination prescribed by the Board shall be eligible for a classified civil-service status after the expiration of six months from the date of appointment upon compliance with the provisions of Section 6 of Civil Service Rule II other than those provisions relating to examination. Effective March 16, 1942, all appointments to attorney and law clerk (trainee) positions shall be for the duration of the present war and for six months thereafter unless specifically limited to a shorter period.

(j) The incumbent of any attorney position covered into the classified service by section 1 of this order may acquire a classified civil-service status in accordance with the provisions of Section 2(a) of the act of November 26, 1940 (54 Stat. 1211) or, in the discretion of the Board and when applicable, Section 6, of Civil Service Rule II: *Provided,* That the noncompetitive examination required thereunder shall be prescribed by the Office with the approval of the Board.

(k) The Office with the approval of the Board shall appoint a competent person to act as Executive Secretary to the Board; and the Office shall furnish such further professionals, clerical, stenographic, and other assistants as may be necessary to carry out the provisions of this section.

(l) The Civil Service Rules are hereby amended to the extent necessary to give effect to the provisions of this section.

SECTION 4. The noncompetitive examinations prescribed pursuant to sections 3 and 6 of this order and section 2(a) of the said act of November 26, 1940, shall, among other things, require any person taking such examination to meet such reasonable standards of physical fitness and personal suitability as the Office of Personnel Management may prescribe.

SECTION 5. Persons who on the effective date of section 1 of this order are on furlough or leave without pay from any position covered into the classified service by that section may be recalled to duty within one year of the date that they are furloughed or given leave without pay, and may be continued in such positions thereafter but shall not thereby acquire a classified civil-service status. If they are not recalled to duty within the time specified herein, they shall be separated from the service.

SECTION 6. (a) Any person who, in order to perform active service with the military or naval forces of the United States, has left a position (other than a temporary position) which is covered into the classified civil service under section 1 of this order, shall be reinstated in such position or to a position of like seniority, status, and pay in the same department or agency, and may, upon reinstatement, acquire a classified civil-service status: *Provided,* (1) that he has been honorably discharged from the military or naval service, (2) that he makes application for reinstatement within 90 days after termination of his service with the armed forces or of hospitalization continuing after discharge for a period of not more than one year, and (3) that he qualifies in such suitable noncompetitive examination as the Office may prescribe.

(b) Any person who, in order to perform active service with the military or naval forces of the United States, has left a position in any department or agency (other than a temporary position) which is covered into the classified civil service under section 1 of this order, may, upon his applications and upon the request of the head of the same or any other department or agency, be reinstated in any position for which the Office finds he is qualified, and upon reinstatement shall acquire a classified civil-service status: *Provided,* (1) that he has been honorably discharged from the military or naval service, and (2) that he qualifies in such suitable noncompetitive examination as the Office may prescribe.

SECTION 7. Executive Order No. 8044 of January 31, 1939, is hereby revoked so far as it applies to positions covered into the classified civil service by this order.

EXECUTIVE ORDER No. 9367

Ex. Ord. No. 9367, Aug. 4, 1943, 8 F.R. 11017, which prohibited, with certain exceptions, instructions of applicants for civil service and foreign service examinations by officers or employees of the government, was revoked by Ex. Ord. No. 11408, Apr. 25, 1968, 33 F.R. 6459.

EX. ORD. No. 10577. CIVIL SERVICE RULES

Ex. Ord. No. 10577, Nov. 22, 1954, 19 F.R. 7521, eff. Jan. 23, 1955, as amended by Ex. Ord. No. 10641, Oct. 26, 1955, 20 F.R. 8137; Ex. Ord. No. 10675, Aug. 21, 1956, 21 F.R. 6327

Jan. 23, 1956; Ex. Ord. No. 10745, Dec. 12, 1957, 22 F.R. 10025; Ex. Ord. No. 10869, Mar. 9, 1960, 25 F.R. 2073; Ex. Ord. No. 11315, Nov. 17, 1966, 31 F.R. 14729; Ex. Ord. No. 11839, Feb. 15, 1975, 40 F.R. 7351; Ex. Ord. No. 11856, May 7, 1975, 40 F.R. 20259; Ex. Ord. No. 11887, Nov. 4, 1975, 40 F.R. 51411; Ex. Ord. No. 11935; Sept. 2, 1976, 41 F.R. 37301; Ex. Ord. No. 12021, Nov. 30, 1977, 42 F.R. 61237; Ex. Ord. No. 12043, Mar. 7, 1978, 43 F.R. 9773; Ex. Ord. No. 12107, Dec. 28, 1978, 44 F.R. 1055; Ex. Ord. No. 12125, Mar. 15, 1979, 44 F.R. 16879; Ex. Ord. No. 12148, July 20, 1979, 44 F.R. 43239; Ex. Ord. No. 12300, Mar. 23, 1981, 46 F.R. 18683; Ex. Ord. No. 12748, Feb. 1, 1991, 56 F.R. 4521; Ex. Ord. No. 12896, Feb. 3, 1994, 59 F.R. 5515; Ex. Ord. No. 12940, Nov. 28, 1994, 59 F.R. 61519; Ex. Ord. No. 13124, §2(b), June 4, 1999, 64 F.R. 31103, Ex. Ord. No. 13197, Jan. 18, 2001, 66 F.R. 7853; provided:

PART I—CIVIL SERVICE RULES

SECTION 101. The Civil Service Rules are hereby amended to read as follows:

RULE I—COVERAGE AND DEFINITIONS

§ 1.1. POSITIONS AND EMPLOYEES AFFECTED BY THESE RULES

These Rules shall apply to all positions in the competitive service and to all incumbents of such positions. Except as expressly provided in the Rule concerned, these Rules shall not apply to positions and employees in the excepted service.

§ 1.2. EXTENT OF THE COMPETITIVE SERVICE

The competitive service shall include: (a) All civilian positions in the executive branch of the Government unless specifically excepted therefrom by or pursuant to statute or by the Office of Personnel Management (hereafter referred to in these Rules as the Office) under section 6.1 of Rule VI; and (b) all positions in the legislative and judicial branches of the Federal Government and in the Government of the District of Columbia which are specifically made subject to the civil-service laws by statute. The Office is authorized and directed to determine finally whether a position is in the competitive service.

§ 1.3. DEFINITIONS

As used in these Rules:

(a) "Competitive service" shall have the same meaning as the words "classified service", or "classified (competitive) service", or "classified civil service" as defined in existing statutes and executive orders.

(b) "Competitive position" shall mean a position in the competitive service.

(c) "Competitive status" shall mean basic eligibility to be noncompetitively selected to fill a vacancy in a competitive position. A competitive status shall be acquired by career-conditional or career appointment through open competitive examination upon satisfactory completion of a probationary period, or may be granted by statute, executive order, or the Civil Service Rules without competitive examination. A person with competitive status may be promoted, transferred, reassigned, reinstated, or demoted without taking an open competitive examination, subject to the conditions prescribed by the Civil Service Rules and Regulations.

(d) An employee shall be considered as being in the competitive service when he has a competitive status and occupies a competitive position unless he is serving under a temporary appointment: *Provided,* That an employee who is in the competitive service at the time his position is first listed under Schedule A, B, or C shall be considered as continuing in the competitive service as long as he continues to occupy such position.

(e) "Tenure" shall mean the period of time an employee may reasonably expect to serve under his current appointment. Tenure shall be granted and governed by the type of appointment under which an employee is currently serving without regard to whether he has a competitive status or whether his appointment is to a competitive position or an excepted position.

§ 1.4. EXTENT OF THE EXCEPTED SERVICE

(a) The excepted service shall include all civilian positions in the executive branch of the Government which are specifically excepted from the requirements of the Civil Service Act or from the competitive service by or pursuant to statute or by the Office under section 6.1 of Rule VI.

(b) "Excepted service" shall have the same meaning as the words "unclassified service", or "unclassified civil service", or "positions outside the competitive civil service" as used in existing statutes and executive orders.

(c) "Excepted position" shall have the same meaning as "unclassified position", or "position excepted by law", or "position excepted by executive order", or "position excepted by Civil Service Rule", or "position outside the competitive service" as used in existing statutes and executive orders.

RULE II—APPOINTMENT THROUGH THE COMPETITIVE SYSTEM

§ 2.1. COMPETITIVE EXAMINATIONS AND ELIGIBLE REGISTERS

(a) The Office shall be responsible for open competitive examinations for admission to the competitive service which will fairly test the relative capacity and fitness of the persons examined for the position to be filled. The Office is authorized to establish standards with respect to citizenship, age, education, training and experience, suitability, and physical and mental fitness, and for residence or other requirements which applicants must meet to be admitted to or rated in examinations.

(b) In addition to the names of persons who qualify in competitive examinations, the names of persons who have lost eligibility on a career or career-conditional register because of service in the armed forces, and the names of persons who lost opportunity for certification or who have served under career or career-conditional appointment when the Office determines that they should be given certification, may also be entered at such places on appropriate registers and under such conditions as the Office may prescribe.

(c) Whenever the Office of Personnel Management (1) is unable to certify a sufficient number of names to permit the appointing officer to consider three eligibles for appointment to a fourth-class postmaster position in accordance with the regular procedure, or (2) finds that a particular rate of compensation for fourth-class postmaster positions is too low to warrant regular competitive examinations for such positions, it may authorize appointment to any such position or positions in accordance with such procedure as may be prescribed by the Office. Persons appointed under this subsection may acquire competitive status subject to satisfactory completion of a probationary period prescribed by the Office.

§ 2.2. APPOINTMENTS

(a) The Office shall establish and administer a career-conditional appointment system for positions subject to competitive examination which will permit adjustment of the career service to necessary fluctuations in Federal employment, and provide an equitable and orderly system for stabilizing the Federal work force. A competitive status shall be acquired by a career-conditional appointee upon satisfactory completion of a probationary period, but the appointee shall have career-conditional tenure for a period of service to be prescribed by regulation of the Office. When an employee has completed the required period of service his appointment shall be converted to a career appointment without time limitation: *Provided*, That his career-conditional appointment shall not be converted to a career appointment if the limitation on the number of permanent employees in the Federal civil service established under subsection (b) of this section would be exceeded thereby. Persons selected from competitive civil service registers for other than temporary appointment shall be given career-conditional appointments: *Provided*, That career appointments shall be given to the following classes of eligibles: (1) Persons whose appointments are required by statute to be made on a permanent basis; (2) employees serving under career appointments at the time of selections from such registers; (3) former employees who have eligibility for career appointments upon reinstatement; and (4) to the extent permitted by law, persons appointed to positions in the field service of the Post Office Department for which salary rates are fixed by the act of July 6, 1945, 59 Stat. 435, as heretofore or hereafter amended and supplemented.

(b) Under the career-conditional appointment system there shall be a limit on the number of permanent employees in the Federal civil service which shall be the ceiling established by section 1310 of the Supplemental Appropriation Act, 1952 (65 Stat. 757), as amended [set out as a note under section 3101 of this title]. In the event section 1310, supra, is repealed, the Office is authorized to fix such limitation on the number of permanent employees in the Federal civil service as it finds necessary to meet the needs of the service.

(c) The Office may determine the types, duration, and conditions of indefinite and temporary appointments, and may prescribe the method for replacing persons holding such appointments.

§ 2.3. APPORTIONMENT

Subject to such modifications as the Office finds to be necessary in the interest of good administration, appointments to positions in agencies' headquarters offices which are located within the metropolitan area of Washington, D.C., shall be made so as to maintain the apportionment of appointments among the several States, Territories, and the District of Columbia upon the basis of population.

§ 2.4. PROBATIONARY PERIOD

Persons selected from registers of eligibles for career or career-conditional appointment and employees promoted, transferred, or otherwise assigned, for the first time, to supervisory or managerial positions shall be required to serve a probationary period under terms and conditions prescribed by the Office.

RULE III—NONCOMPETITIVE ACQUISITION OF STATUS

§ 3.1. CLASSES OF PERSONS WHO MAY NONCOMPETITIVELY ACQUIRE STATUS

(a) Upon recommendation by the agency concerned, and subject to such noncompetitive examination, time limits, or other requirements as the Office may prescribe, the following classes of persons may acquire a competitive status without competitive examination:

(1) A person holding a permanent position when it is placed in the competitive service by statute or executive order or is otherwise made subject to competitive examination.

(2) A disabled veteran who, in a manner satisfactory to the Office, has completed a course of training in the executive branch of the Government prescribed by the Administrator of Veterans' Affairs in accordance with the act of March 24, 1943, 57 Stat. 43.

(3) An employee who has served at least two years in the immediate office of the President or on the White House Staff and who is transferred to a competitive position at the request of an agency.

(4) An employee who was serving when his name was reached for certification on a civil-service register appropriate for the position in which he was serving: *Provided*, That the recommendation for competitive status is made prior to expiration of the register on which his name appears or is made during a period of continuous

service since his name was reached: *Provided further,* That the register was being used for appointments conferring competitive status at the time his name was reached.

(b) Upon recommendation by the employing agency, and subject to such requirements as the Office of Personnel Management may prescribe, the following classes of handicapped employees may acquire competitive status without competitive examination:

(1) A severely physically handicapped employee who completes at least two years of satisfactory service in a position excepted from the competitive service.

(2) A mentally retarded employee who completes at least two years of satisfactory service in a position excepted from the competitive service.

(3) An employee with psychiatric disabilities who completes at least 2 years of satisfactory service in a position excepted from the competitive service.

§ 3.2. Appointments Without Competitive Examination in Rare Cases

Subject to receipt of satisfactory evidence of the qualifications of the person to be appointed, the Office may authorize an appointment in the competitive service without competitive examination whenever it finds that the duties or compensation of the position are such, or that qualified persons are so rare, that, in the interest of good civil-service administration, the position cannot be filled through open competitive examination. Any person heretofore or hereafter appointed under this section shall acquire a competitive status upon completion of at least one year of satisfactory service and compliance with such requirements as the Office may prescribe. Detailed statements of the reasons for the noncompetitive appointments made under this section shall be published in the Office's annual reports.

§ 3.3. Conversion of Appointments

Any person who acquires a competitive status under this Rule shall have his appointment converted to career-conditional appointment unless he meets the service requirement for career appointment prescribed under section 2.2 (a) of Rule II.

Rule IV—Prohibited Practices

§ 4.1. [Revoked by Ex. Ord. No. 12896, Feb. 3, 1994, 59 F.R. 5515.]

§ 4.2. Prohibition Against Racial, Political or Religious Discrimination

No person employed in the executive branch of the Federal Government who has authority to take or recommend any personnel action with respect to any person who is an employee in the competitive service or any eligible or applicant for a position in the competitive service shall make any inquiry concerning the race, political affiliation or religious beliefs of any such employee, eligible, or applicant. All disclosures concerning such matters shall be ignored, except as to such membership in political parties or organizations as constitutes by law a disqualification for Government employment. No discrimination shall be exercised, threatened, or promised by any person in the executive branch of the Federal Government against or in favor of any employee in the competitive service, or any eligible or applicant for a position in the competitive service because of his race, political affiliation or religious beliefs, except as may be authorized or required by law.

§ 4.3. Prohibition Against Securing Withdrawal From Competition

No person shall influence another person to withdraw from competition for any position in the competitive service for the purpose of either improving or injuring the prospects of any applicant for appointment.

Rule V—Regulations, Investigations, Evaluation, and Enforcement

§ 5.1. Civil Service Regulations

The Director, Office of Personnel Management, shall promulgate and enforce regulations necessary to carry out the provisions of the Civil Service Act and the Veterans' Preference Act, as reenacted in Title 5, United States Code [now covered by this chapter and chapter 35 of this title], the Civil Service Rules, and all other statutes and Executive orders imposing responsibilities on the Office. The Director is authorized, whenever there are practical difficulties and unnecessary hardships in complying with the strict letter of the regulation, to grant a variation from the strict letter of the regulation if such a variation is within the spirit of the regulations, and the efficiency of the Government and the integrity of the competitive service are protected and promoted. Whenever a variation is granted the Director shall note the official record to show: (1) the particular practical difficulty or hardship involved, (2) what is permitted in place of what is required by regulation, (3) the circumstances which protect or promote the efficiency of the Government and the integrity of the competitive service, and (4) a statement limiting the application of the variation to the continuation of the conditions which gave rise to it. Like variations shall be granted whenever like conditions exist. All such decisions and information concerning variations noted in the official record shall be published promptly in a Federal Personnel Manual, Letter or Bulletin and in the Director's next annual report.

§ 5.2. Investigation and Evaluations

The Director may secure effective implementation of the civil service laws, rules, and regulations, and all Executive orders imposing responsibilities on the Office by:

(a) Investigating the qualifications and suitability of applicants for positions in the competitive service. The Director may require appointments to be made subject to investigation to enable the Director to determine, after appointment, that the requirements of law or the civil service rules and regulations have been met.

(b) Evaluating the effectiveness of: (1) personnel policies, programs, and operations of Executive and other Federal agencies subject to the jurisdiction of the Office, including their effectiveness with regard to merit selection and employee development; (2) agency compliance with and enforcement of applicable laws, rules, regulations and office directives; and (3) agency personnel management evaluation systems.

(c) Investigating, or directing an agency to investigate and report on, apparent violations of applicable laws, rules, regulations, or directives requiring corrective action, found in the course of an evaluation.

§ 5.3. Enforcement

(a) The Director is authorized to ensure enforcement of the civil service laws, rules, and regulations, and all applicable Executive orders, by:

(1) Instructing an agency to separate or take other action against an employee serving an appointment subject to investigation when the Director finds that the employee is disqualified for Federal employment. Where the employee or the agency appeals the Director's finding that a separation or other action is necessary, the Director may instruct the agency as to whether or not the employee should remain on duty and continue to receive pay pending adjudication of the appeal: *Provided,* That when an agency separates or takes other action against an employee pursuant to the Director's instructions, and the Director, on the basis of new evidence, subsequently reverses the initial decision as to the employee's qualifications and suitability, the agency shall, upon request of the Director, restore the employee to duty or otherwise reverse any action taken.

(2) Reporting the results of evaluation or investigations to the head of the agency concerned with instruc-

tions for any corrective action necessary, including cancellation of personnel actions where appropriate. The Director's findings resulting from evaluations or investigations are binding unless changed as a result of agency evidence and arguments against them. If, during the course of any evaluation or investigation under this Section, the Director finds evidence of matters which come within the investigative and prosecutorial jurisdiction of the Special Counsel of the Merit Systems Protection Board, the Director shall refer this evidence to the Special Counsel for appropriate disposition.

(b) Whenever the Director issues specific instructions as to separation or other corrective action with regard to an employee, including cancellation of a personnel action, the head of the agency concerned shall comply with the Director's instructions.

(c) If the agency head fails to comply with the specific instructions of the Director as to separation or other corrective action with regard to an employee, including cancellation of a personnel action, the Director may certify to the Comptroller General of the United States the agency's failure to act together with such additional information as the Comptroller General may require, and shall furnish a copy of such certification to the head of the agency concerned. The individual with respect to whom such separation or other corrective action was instructed shall be entitled thereafter to no pay or only to such pay as appropriate to effectuate the Director's instructions.

§5.4. INFORMATION AND TESTIMONY

When required by the Office, the Merit Systems Protection Board, or the Special Counsel of the Merit Systems Protection Board, or by authorized representatives of these bodies, agencies shall make available to them, or to their authorized representatives, employees to testify in regard to matters inquired of under the civil service laws, rules, and regulations, and records pertinent to these matters. All such employees, and all applicants or eligibles for positions covered by these rules, shall give to the Office, the Merit Systems Protection Board, the Special Counsel, or to their authorized representatives, all information, testimony, documents, and material in regard to the above matters, the disclosure of which is not otherwise prohibited by law or regulation. These employees, applicants, and eligibles shall sign testimony given under oath or affirmation before an officer authorized by law to administer oaths. Employees are performing official duty when testifying or providing evidence pursuant to this section.

RULE VI—EXCEPTIONS FROM THE COMPETITIVE SERVICE

§6.1. AUTHORITY TO EXCEPT POSITIONS FROM THE COMPETITIVE SERVICE

(a) The Office may except positions from the competitive service when it determines that appointments thereto through competitive examination are not practicable. These positions shall be listed in the Office's annual report for the fiscal year in which the exceptions are made.

(b) The Office shall decide whether the duties of any particular position are such that it may be filled as an excepted position under the appropriate schedule.

(c) Notice of the Office's decision granting authority to make appointments to an excepted position under the appropriate schedule shall be published in the FEDERAL REGISTER.

§6.2. SCHEDULES OF EXCEPTED POSITIONS

The Office shall list positions that it excepts from the competitive service in Schedules A, B, and C, which schedules shall constitute parts of this Rule, as follows:

SCHEDULE A

Positions other than those of a confidential or policy-determining character for which it is not practicable to examine shall be listed in Schedule A.

SCHEDULE B

Positions other than those of a confidential or policy-determining character for which it is not practicable to hold a competitive examination shall be listed in Schedule B. Appointments to these positions shall be subject to such noncompetitive examinations as may be prescribed by the Office.

SCHEDULE C

Positions of a confidential or policy-determining character shall be listed in Schedule C.

§6.3. METHOD OF FILLING EXCEPTED POSITIONS AND STATUS OF INCUMBENTS

(a) The head of an agency may fill excepted positions by the appointment of persons without civil service eligibility or competitive status and such persons shall not acquire competitive status by reason of such appointment: *Provided*, That the Office, in its discretion, may by regulation prescribe conditions under which excepted positions may be filled in the same manner as competitive positions are filled and conditions under which persons so appointed may acquire a competitive status in accordance with the Civil Service Rules and Regulations.

(b) To the extent permitted by law and the provisions of this Rule, appointments and position changes in the excepted service shall be made in accordance with such regulations and practices as the head of the agency concerned finds necessary.

§6.4. REMOVAL OF INCUMBENTS OF EXCEPTED POSITIONS

Except as may be required by statute, the Civil Service Rules and Regulations shall not apply to removals from positions listed in Schedules A and C or from positions excepted from the competitive service by statute. The Civil Service Rules and Regulations shall apply to removals from positions listed in Schedule B of persons who have competitive status.

§6.5. ASSIGNMENT OF EXCEPTED EMPLOYEES

No person who is serving under an excepted appointment shall be assigned to the work of a position in the competitive service without prior approval of the Office.

§6.6. REVOCATION OF EXCEPTIONS

The Office may remove any position from or may revoke in whole or in part any provision of Schedule A, B, or C. Notice of the Office's decision making these changes shall be published in the FEDERAL REGISTER.

§6.7. MOVEMENT OF PERSONS BETWEEN THE CIVIL-SERVICE SYSTEM AND OTHER MERIT SYSTEMS

Whenever the Office and any Federal agency having an established merit system determine it to be in the interest of good administration and consistent with the intent of the civil-service laws and any other applicable laws, they may enter into an agreement prescribing conditions under which persons may be moved from one system to the other and defining the status and tenure that the persons affected shall acquire upon such movement.

§6.8. SPECIFIED EXCEPTIONS

(a) Positions in the Department of the Interior and in the Department of Commerce whose incumbents serve as the principal representative of the Secretary in their respective regions shall be listed in Schedule C for grades not exceeding grade GS-15 of the General Schedule, and shall be designated Noncareer Executive Assignments for positions graded higher than GS-15. Incumbents of these positions who are, on February 15, 1975, in the competitive service shall not be affected by the foregoing provisions of this Section.

(b) Positions in the Community Services Administration and ACTION [now Corporation for National and Community Service] whose incumbents serve as regional director or regional administrator shall be listed in Schedule C for grades not exceeding GS–15 of the General Schedule and shall be designated Noncareer Executive Assignments for positions graded higher than GS–15. Incumbents of these positions who are, on November 29, 1977, in the competitive service shall not be affected by the foregoing provisions of this subsection.

(c) Within the Department of Agriculture, positions the incumbents of which serve as State Executive Directors of the Consolidated Farm Service Agency and positions the incumbents of which serve as State Directors or State Directors-at-Large for Rural Economic and Community Development shall be listed in Schedule C for all grades of the General Schedule.

RULE VII—GENERAL PROVISIONS

§ 7.1. DISCRETION IN FILLING VACANCIES

In his discretion, an appointing officer may fill any position in the competitive service either by competitive appointment from a civil-service register or by noncompetitive selection of a present or former Federal employee, in accordance with the Civil Service Regulations. He shall exercise his discretion in all personnel actions solely on the basis of merit and fitness and without regard to political or religious affiliations, marital status, or race.

§ 7.2. REEMPLOYMENT RIGHTS

The Office, whenever it determines it to be necessary, shall prescribe regulations governing the release of employees (both within the competitive service and the excepted service) by any agency in the executive branch of the Government for employment in any other agency, and governing the establishment, granting, and exercise of rights to reemployment in the agencies from which employees are released.

§ 7.3. CITIZENSHIP

(a) No person shall be admitted to competitive examination unless such person is a citizen or national of the United States.

(b) No person shall be given any appointment in the competitive service unless such person is a citizen or national of the United States.

(c) The Office may, as an exception to this rule and to the extent permitted by law, authorize the appointment of aliens to positions in the competitive service when necessary to promote the efficiency of the service in specific cases or for temporary appointments.

RULE VIII—APPOINTMENTS TO OVERSEAS POSITIONS

§ 8.1. ADDITIONAL AUTHORITY OF THE OFFICE

In addition to authorizing the recruitment and appointment of persons to overseas positions under regulations issued under the preceding Rules, the Office may, by the regulations prescribed by it, authorize the recruitment and appointment of persons to such positions as provided in section 2 of this Rule. As used in this Rule, "overseas positions" means positions in foreign countries and in other areas beyond the continental limits of the United States, except as provided in section 8.4 hereof.

§ 8.2. APPOINTMENT OF UNITED STATES CITIZENS

United States citizens may be recruited overseas for appointment to overseas positions in the competitive service without regard to the competitive requirements of the Civil Service Act. Persons so recruited who meet the qualification standards and other requirements of the Office for overseas positions may be given appointments to be known as "overseas limited appointments." Such appointments shall be of temporary or indefinite duration, and shall not confer the right to acquire a competitive status. The Office may authorize overseas limited appointments for United States citizens recruited within the continental limits of the

United States whenever it determines that it is not feasible to appoint from a civil-service register. Persons serving under appointments made pursuant to this section are hereby excluded from the operation of the Civil Service Retirement Act of May 29, 1930, as amended [section 8301 et seq. of this title], unless eligible for retirement benefits by continuity of service or otherwise.

§ 8.3. APPOINTMENT OF PERSONS NOT CITIZENS OF THE UNITED STATES

Persons who are not citizens of the United States may be recruited overseas and appointed to overseas positions without regard to the Civil Service Act.

§ 8.4. POSITIONS EXCEPTED FROM THE APPLICATION OF THIS RULE

This Rule shall not apply to positions in Hawaii, Puerto Rico, the Virgin Islands, and Alaska, and on the Isthmus of Panama.

RULE IX—WORKFORCE INFORMATION

9.1 DEFINITION

As used in this rule, "Executive agency" means an Executive department, a Government corporation, and an independent establishment, as those terms are defined in chapter 1 of title 5, United States Code, but does not include the Federal Bureau of Investigation, the Central Intelligence Agency, the Defense Intelligence Agency, the National Imagery and Mapping Agency, the National Security Agency, and, as determined by the President, any Executive agency or unit within an Executive agency which has as its principal function the conduct of foreign intelligence or counterintelligence activities.

9.2 REPORTING WORKFORCE INFORMATION

The Director of the Office of Personnel Management may require all Executive agencies to report information relating to civilian employees, including positions and employees in the competitive, excepted, and Senior Executive services, in a manner and at times prescribed by the Director. The Director shall establish standards for workforce information submissions under this section, and agencies shall ensure that their submissions meet these standards consistent with the Privacy Act [5 U.S.C. 552a]. The Director may exempt from this section a specific agency or group of employees when the Director determines that an exemption is appropriate because of special circumstances.

RULE X—AGENCY ACCOUNTABILITY SYSTEMS; OPM AUTHORITY TO REVIEW PERSONNEL MANAGEMENT PROGRAMS

10.1 DEFINITIONS

For purposes of this rule—

(a) "agency" means an Executive agency as defined in Rule IX, but does not include a Government corporation or the General Accounting Office; and

(b) "merit system principles" means the principles for Federal personnel management that are set forth in section 2301(b) of title 5, United States Code.

10.2. ACCOUNTABILITY SYSTEMS

The Director of the Office of Personnel Management may require an agency to establish and maintain a system of accountability for merit system principles that (1) sets standards for applying the merit system principles, (2) measures the agency's effectiveness in meeting these standards, and (3) corrects any deficiencies in meeting these standards.

10.3. OPM AUTHORITY TO REVIEW PERSONNEL MANAGEMENT PROGRAMS AND PRACTICES

The Office of Personnel Management may review the human resources management programs and practices of any agency and report to the head of the agency and the President on the effectiveness of these programs and practices, including whether they are consistent with the merit system principles.

[Revoked by Ex. Ord. No. 12748, Feb. 1, 1991, 56 F.R. 4521.]

PART II—SPECIAL PROVISIONS FOR TRANSITION FROM INDEFINITE APPOINTMENT SYSTEM TO CAREER-CONDITIONAL APPOINTMENT SYSTEM

§ 201

(a) Under such conditions as the Office of Personnel Management may prescribe, all employees serving under indefinite appointments in the competitive service on the effective date of this order who were appointed by selection in regular order from appropriate competitive civil-service registers established subsequent to February 4, 1946, shall, as of the effective date of this order, have their appointments converted to career-conditional appointments if they have had less than three years of creditable service, and to career appointments if they have had three or more years of such service since they were appointed: *Provided*, That any such employees who left their positions prior to the effective date of this order to enter the armed forces of the United States and are reemployed in the competitive service after the effective date of this order pursuant to application for employment made within ninety days after honorable discharge, or after hospitalization continuing after discharge for not more than one year, shall have their former indefinite appointments converted to career-conditional or career appointments in accordance with this section: *Provided further*, That employees serving in excepted positions who would meet the conditions for career-conditional or career appointments if they were serving in competitive positions shall be granted competitive status upon completion of a probationary period.

(b) The Office may prescribe the conditions under which employees who are serving under indefinite appointments in the competitive service on the effective date of this order and who were not appointed by selection in regular order from competitive civil-service registers may be examined and have their names entered on existing competitive civil-service registers. When such employees are within reach for appointment from such registers they shall be eligible for career-conditional appointments if, since they were given indefinite appointments, they have had less than three years of creditable service, and for career appointments if they have had three or more years of such service.

(c) All employees in the competitive service who on the effective date of this order are serving under indefinite appointments made noncompetitively based upon prior service with a competitive status shall, as of the effective date of this order, have their appointments converted to career-conditional appointments if they have had less than three years of creditable service and to career appointments if they have had three or more years of such service under either permanent or indefinite appointment: *Provided*, That any such employees who left their positions prior to the effective date of this order to enter the armed forces of the United States and are reemployed in the competitive service after the effective date of this order pursuant to application for employment made within ninety days after honorable discharge, or after hospitalization continuing after discharge for not more than one year, shall have their former indefinite appointments converted to career-conditional or career appointments in accordance with this section: *Provided further*, That any such employees in the field service of the Post Office Department whose salary rates are fixed by the act of July 6, 1945, 59 Stat. 435, as heretofore or hereafter amended and supplemented, shall have their appointments converted to career appointments if they are serving in positions in the authorized complement of permanent positions (consisting of regular positions and positions within the authorized quota of substitutes).

(d) The Office shall define "creditable service" and shall prescribe the conditions for completion of the pe-

riod of creditable service required for career appointment.

(e) Except as provided in section 201(c) hereof, this section shall not apply to employees serving under indefinite appointments in the field service of the Post Office Department whose salary rates are fixed by the act of July 6, 1945, 59 Stat. 435, as heretofore or hereafter amended and supplemented.

§ 202

(a) Notwithstanding the provisions of section 201(a) of this order, and subject to such noncompetitive examination or other requirements as the Office may prescribe, any employee entitled to veteran preference who has a compensable service-connected disability of ten per centum or more may, upon recommendation of the agency concerned, noncompetitively acquire a competitive status subject to completion of a probationary period: *Provided*, That he is serving under an indefinite appointment, a temporary appointment pending establishment of a register, or a temporary appointment for job employment which has been continuous for more than one year: *Provided further*, That recommendation for acquisition of status under this section is made not later than December 31, 1957.

(b) Any employee who is recommended for noncompetitive acquisition of competitive status under section 202(a) hereof and who satisfies the noncompetitive examination and other requirements of the Office shall have the appointment under which he is serving converted to a career appointment if he has completed a probationary period or to a career-conditional appointment if he has not completed a probationary period. The career-conditional appointment of such an employee shall be converted to a career appointment upon completion of probation.

(c) An employee in the field service of the Post Office Department whose salary rate is fixed by the act of July 6, 1945, 59 Stat. 435, as heretofore or hereafter amended and supplemented, may not be recommended for competitive status under section 202(a) hereof unless he can be appointed to a vacancy in the authorized complement of permanent positions (consisting of regular positions and positions within the authorized quota of substitutes). When such an employee is recommended for noncompetitive acquisition of competitive status and satisfies the noncompetitive examination and other requirements of the Office, his appointment shall be converted to a career appointment subject to satisfactory completion of a probationary period.

§ 203

The career-conditional appointment of any employee entitled to veteran preference who has a compensable service-connected disability of ten per centum or more may be converted to a career appointment: *Provided*, That he received his career-conditional appointment prior to January 1, 1958, and that, not later than December 31, 1958, the agency in which he is employed recommends such conversion and certifies to the Office that he has satisfactorily completed a one-year probationary period: *Provided further*, That any such employee who is not certified for career appointment under this section shall have his career-conditional appointment converted to a career appointment when he has completed the service requirement for such appointment prescribed under section 2.2(a) of Civil Service Rule II.

§ 204

In order to effectuate the purposes of section 1310 of the Supplemental Appropriations Act, 1952 (65 Stat. 757), as amended [set out as a note under section 3101 of this title], the Office shall, after consultation with the agencies concerned, determine the division of allowable permanent appointments within and between the excepted service and the competitive service.

§ 205

The Office shall issue such regulations and instructions as may be necessary to effectuate the purposes of this part.

PART III

§ 301

The following-described executive orders and parts of executive orders are hereby revoked:

Part II of Executive Order No. 9830 of February 24, 1947, amending the Civil Service Rules: *Provided*, That the positions listed in Schedules A, B, and C as provided for in Civil Service Rule VI of that order, as amended, shall be considered as being listed in Schedules A, B, and C, respectively, as provided for in Civil Service Rule VI of this order, unless and until they are removed therefrom by the Office.

Executive Orders No. 9973 of June 28, 1948, No. 10440 of March 31, 1953, and No. 10463 of June 25, 1953, amending Civil Service Rule VI.

Executive Order No. 10180 of November 13, 1950, establishing special personnel procedures in the interest of national defense.

PART IV

§ 401

This order shall become effective on the first Sunday after the sixtieth day after the date hereof.

Executive Order No. 10590

Ex. Ord. No. 10590, Jan. 18, 1955, 20 F.R. 409, as amended by Ex. Ord. No. 10722, Aug. 7, 1957, 22 F.R. 6287; Ex. Ord. No. 10773, July 1, 1958, 23 F.R. 5061; Ex. Ord. No. 10782, Sept. 8, 1958, 23 F.R. 6971, which established the President's Committee on Government Employment Policy, was superseded by Ex. Ord. No. 11246, Sept. 24, 1965, 30 F.R. 12319, set out as a note under section 2000e of Title 42, The Public Health and Welfare.

Executive Order No. 10880

Ex. Ord. No. 10880, June 7, 1960, 25 F.R. 5131, as amended by Ex. Ord. No. 12107, Dec. 28, 1978, 44 F.R. 1055, which provided for conversion of indefinite or temporary appointments to career or career-conditional appointments, was revoked by Ex. Ord. No. 12608, Sept. 9, 1987, 52 F.R. 34617.

Executive Order No. 10925

Ex. Ord. No. 10925, Mar. 7, 1961, 26 F.R. 1977, as amended by Ex. Ord. No. 11114, June 24, 1963, 28 F.R. 6485; Ex. Ord. No. 11162, July 28, 1964, 29 F.R. 10563, which established the President's Committee on Equal Employment Opportunity, was superseded by Ex. Ord. No. 11246, Sept. 24, 1965, 30 F.R. 12319, set out as a note under section 2000e of Title 42, The Public Health and Welfare.

Executive Order No. 11114

Ex. Ord. No. 11114, June 24, 1963, 28 F.R. 6485, as amended by Ex. Ord. No. 11162, July 28, 1964, 29 F.R. 10563, which extended the authority of the President's Committee on Equal Employment Opportunity, was superseded by Ex. Ord. No. 11246, Sept. 24, 1965, 30 F.R. 12319, set out as a note under section 2000e of Title 42, The Public Health and Welfare.

Ex. Ord. No. 11141. Discrimination on the Basis of Age

Ex. Ord. No. 11141, Feb. 12, 1964, 29 F.R. 2477, provided:

WHEREAS the principle of equal employment opportunity is now an established policy of our Government and applies equally to all who wish to work and are capable of doing so; and

WHEREAS discrimination in employment because of age, except upon the basis of a *bona fide* occupational qualification, retirement plan, or statutory requirement, is inconsistent with that principle and with the social and economic objectives of our society; and

WHEREAS older workers are an indispensable source of productivity and experience which our Nation can ill afford to lose; and

WHEREAS President Kennedy, mindful that maximum national growth depends on the utilization of all manpower resources, issued a memorandum on March 14, 1963, reaffirming the policy of the Executive Branch of the Government of hiring and promoting employees on the basis of merit alone and emphasizing the need to assure that older people are not discriminated against because of their age and receive fair and full consideration for employment and advancement in Federal employment; and

WHEREAS, to encourage and hasten the acceptance of the principle of equal employment opportunity for older persons by all sectors of the economy, private and public, the Federal Government can and should provide maximum leadership in this regard by adopting that principle as an express policy of the Federal Government not only with respect to Federal employees but also with respect to persons employed by contractors and subcontractors engaged in the performance of Federal contracts:

NOW, THEREFORE, by virtue of the authority vested in me by the Constitution and statutes of the United States and as President of the United States, I hereby declare that it is the policy of the Executive Branch of the Government that (1) contractors and subcontractors engaged in the performance of Federal contracts shall not, in connection with the employment, advancement, or discharge of employees, or in connection with the terms, conditions, or privileges of their employment, discriminate against persons because of their age except upon the basis of a *bona fide* occupational qualification, retirement plan, or statutory requirement, and (2) that contractors and subcontractors, or persons acting on their behalf, shall not specify, in solicitations or advertisements for employees to work on Government contracts, a maximum age limit for such employment unless the specified maximum age limit is based upon a *bona fide* occupational qualification, retirement plan, or statutory requirement. The head of each department and agency shall take appropriate action to enunciate this policy, and to this end the Federal Procurement Regulations and the Armed Services Procurement Regulation shall be amended by the insertion therein of a statement giving continuous notice of the existence of the policy declared by this order.

Lyndon B. Johnson.

Executive Order No. 11162

Ex. Ord. No. 11162, July 28, 1964, 29 F.R. 10563, which related to membership of the President's Committee on Equal Employment Opportunity, was superseded by Ex. Ord. No. 11246, Sept. 24, 1965, 30 F.R. 12319, set out as a note under section 2000e of Title 42, The Public Health and Welfare.

Executive Order No. 11202

Ex. Ord. No. 11202, Mar. 5, 1965, 30 F.R. 3185, which established career or career-conditional appointments for student trainees, was revoked by Ex. Ord. No. 11813, Oct. 7, 1974, 39 F.R. 36317, formerly set out below.

Ex. Ord. No. 11203. Career Appointments to Certain Qualified Employees of Treasury Department

Ex. Ord No. 11203, Mar. 12, 1965; 30 F.R. 3417, as amended by Ex. Ord. No. 12107, Dec. 28, 1978, 44 F.R. 1055, provided:

By virtue of the authority vested in me by Section 2 of the Civil Service Act (22 Stat. 403) and Section 1753 of the Revised Statutes of the United States (5 U.S.C. 631) [sections 3301 and 7301 of this title] and as President of the United States, it is hereby ordered as follows—

Section 1. Any employee of the Treasury Department serving under an appointment under Schedule B of the Civil Service Rules in a position concerned with the protection of the life and safety of the President, members of his immediate family, or other persons for whom similar protective services are provided by law (which responsibility is hereinafter referred to as the protective function) may have his appointment converted to a career appointment if:

(1) he has completed at least three years of full-time continuous service in a position concerned with the protective function;

(2) The Secretary of the Treasury, or his designee, recommends the conversion of the employee's appointment within 90 days after the employee meets the service requirements of this section, or within 90 days after the date of this Order, whichever is later;

(3) he shall have passed a competitive examination appropriate for the position he is occupying or meets noncompetitive examination standards the Office of Personnel Management prescribes for his position; and

(4) he meets all other requirements prescribed by the Office pursuant to Section 5 of this Order.

SEC. 2. For the purposes of Section 1—

(1) "full-time continuous service" means service without a break of more than 30 calendar days;

(2) except as provided in paragraph (3) of this section, active service in the Armed Forces of the United States shall be deemed to be full-time continuous service in a position concerned with the protective function if the employee concerned shall have left a position concerned with the protective function to enter the Armed Forces and shall have been re-employed in a position concerned with the protective function within 120 days after he shall have been discharged from the Armed Forces under honorable conditions; and

(3) active service in the Armed Forces shall not be deemed to be full-time continuous service in a position concerned with the protective function if such active service exceeds a total of four years plus any period of additional service imposed pursuant to law.

SEC. 3. Any employee who shall have left a position concerned with the protective function to enter active service in the Armed Forces of the United States, who is re-employed in such a position within 120 days after his discharge under honorable conditions from such service, and who meets the requirements of Section 1 as the result of being credited with his period of active service in the Armed Forces pursuant to Section 2(2), may have his appointment converted if the Secretary of the Treasury or his designee, recommends that conversion within 90 days after his re-employment.

SEC. 4. Whenever the Secretary of the Treasury, or his designee, decides not to recommend conversion of the appointment of an employee under this Order or whenever the Secretary, or his designee, recommends conversion and the employee fails to qualify, the employee shall be separated by the date on which his current Schedule B appointment expires.

SEC. 5. The Office of Personnel Management shall prescribe such regulations as may be necessary to carry out the purposes of this Order.

EX. ORD. NO. 11219. APPOINTMENT IN COMPETITIVE SERVICE OF FOREIGN SERVICE OFFICERS AND EMPLOYEES

Ex. Ord. No. 11219, May 6, 1965, 30 F.R. 6381, as amended by Ex. Ord. No. 12107, Dec. 28, 1978, 44 F.R. 1055; Ex. Ord. No. 12292, Feb. 23, 1981, 46 F.R. 13967, provided:

By virtue of the authority vested in me by section 1753 of the Revised Statutes [sections 3301 and 7301 of this title] and the Civil Service Act (22 Stat. 403), and as President of the United States, it is hereby ordered as follows:

SECTION 1. Under regulations and conditions prescribed by the Office of Personnel Management, a present or former member of the Foreign Service may be appointed in the competitive service if he:

(a) Is qualified for the position in the competitive service;

(b) Was appointed in the Foreign Service under authority of the Foreign Service Act of 1946 as amended [former section 801 et seq. of Title 22, Foreign Relations and Intercourse], the Foreign Service Act of 1980 [section 3901 et seq. of Title 22], or legislation that supplements or replaces the latter Act;

(c) Served in the Foreign Service under an unlimited, career-type appointment and, immediately before his separation from that appointment, he completed at least one year of continuous service under one or more nontemporary appointments in the Foreign Service which may include the service that made him eligible for his career-type appointment; and

(d) Is appointed within 3 years after his separation from the Foreign Service, or he completed at least 3 years of substantially continuous service under one or more nontemporary appointments in the Foreign Service immediately before his separation from the unlimited, career-type appointment in that Service which may include the service that made him eligible for such appointment, or he is entitled to preference under section 2 of the Veterans' Preference Act of 1944, as amended [sections 1302 and 2108 of this title].

SEC. 2. (a) Except as provided in paragraph (b) of this section, a person appointed under Section 1 of this Order becomes a career conditional employee.

(b) A person appointed under Section 1 of this Order becomes a career employee when he:

(1) Has completed at least 3 years of substantially continuous service under one or more nontemporary appointments in the Foreign Service immediately before his separation from the unlimited, career-type appointment in that Service which may include the service that made him eligible for such appointment;

(2) Is appointed to a position in the competitive service required by law or Executive order to be filled on a permanent or career basis; or

(3) Has completed the service requirement for career tenure in the competitive service.

For the purpose of subparagraph (3) of this paragraph, service in the Foreign Service is creditable in meeting the service requirement only if the person concerned is appointed to a nontemporary position in the competitive service under Section 1 of this Order within 30 days after his separation from the Foreign Service.

SEC. 3. A person appointed to a nontemporary position in the competitive service under Section 1 of this Order acquires a competitive status automatically on appointment.

SEC. 4. Any law, Executive order, or regulation that would disqualify an applicant for appointment in the competitive service shall also disqualify a person for appointment under Section 1 of this Order.

SEC. 5. For the purpose of this Order, a person is deemed to be a member of the "Foreign Service" if he was appointed in any agency under authority of the Foreign Service Act of 1946, as amended [former section 801 et seq. of Title 22, Foreign Relations and Intercourse], the Foreign Service Act of 1980 [section 3901 et seq. of Title 22], or legislation that supplements or replaces the latter Act.

EX. ORD. NO. 11315. AMENDING THE CIVIL SERVICE RULES TO AUTHORIZE AN EXECUTIVE ASSIGNMENT SYSTEM FOR POSITIONS IN GRADES 16, 17, AND 18 OF THE GENERAL SCHEDULE

Ex. Ord. No. 11315, Nov. 17, 1966, 31 F.R. 14729, as amended by Ex. Ord. No. 12107, Dec. 28, 1978, 44 F.R. 1055, provided:

WHEREAS, the increasing complexities of Government require personnel of the highest attainable qualifications who are capable of assuming and discharging efficiently major and varied duties and responsibilities in the Executive Branch in response to present and future needs; and

WHEREAS, this need for high quality can best be met by the establishment of an executive assignment system for the top three grades of the General Schedule, extending and adapting merit principles in recruitment, selection, and development, combined with improvements in the identification, assignment and utilization of key personnel:

NOW, THEREFORE, by virtue of the authority vested in me by the Constitution of the United States, by 5 U.S.C. 3301 and 3302, and as President of the United States, it is ordered as follows:

PART I. CIVIL SERVICE RULES

SECTION 1. The Civil Service Rules are amended by the addition of Civil Service Rule IX reading as follows:

[Civil Service Rule IX, as established by Ex. Ord. No. 11315, as amended, was revoked by Ex. Ord. No. 12748, Feb. 1, 1991, 56 F.R. 4521. See Ex. Ord. No. 10577, as amended, set out above.]

CIVIL SERVICE RULE VI

SEC. 2. Civil Service Rule VI is amended in pertinent part as follows:

(a) Section 6.1(a) is amended to read as follows:

"(a) The Office may except positions from the competitive service when it determines that appointments thereto through competitive examination are not practicable. These positions shall be listed in the Office's annual report for the fiscal year in which the exceptions are made. The exception from the competitive service is effective on publication in the Federal Register."

(b) Section 6.6 is amended to read as follows:

"Section 6.6 *Revocation of exceptions.* The Office may remove any position from or may revoke in whole or in part any provision of Schedule A, B, or C. These changes are effective on publication in the Federal Register."

PART II. SPECIAL PROVISIONS FOR TRANSITION TO THE FULL ESTABLISHMENT OF EXECUTIVE ASSIGNMENTS UNDER RULE IX

SEC. 3. *Effective dates.* This order, except section 1, is effective upon filing for publication in the Federal Register. Section 1 of this order is effective not later than one year from the date of this order, or at such earlier dates as the Office of Personnel Management may specify for individual agencies or positions.

SEC. 4. *Interim appointments.* After the date of this order and before Civil Service Rule IX has become effective as to a position, an appointing officer may fill the position in accordance with the appointment system in effect on the day of the appointment.

SEC. 5. *Conversion of incumbents.* On the day Civil Service Rule IX becomes effective as to a position, the appointment of the incumbent of that position shall be changed as follows:

(a) If he is serving under a career or career-conditional appointment in the competitive service, he shall be converted to a Career Executive Assignment;

(b) If he is serving in the excepted service under a nontemporary appointment, he shall be converted to a Noncareer Executive Assignment;

(c) If he is serving in the competitive service under an indefinite or temporary appointment without definite time limit and:

(1) if he has served under this type of appointment for at least five years, he shall be:

(i) converted to a Career Executive Assignment, or appointed to a continuing position in the competitive service in grade GS–15, or below;

(ii) converted to a Noncareer Executive Assignment; or

(iii) separated from the service; or

(2) if he has served under this type of appointment for less than five years, he shall be:

(i) converted to a Noncareer Executive Assignment;

(ii) separated from the service; or

(iii) allowed to continue to serve until he has served five years, at which time the appointing officer shall take one of the actions provided for in subparagraph (1) of this paragraph.

An incumbent who is serving under any other type of appointment shall continue under that appointment until it is terminated.

PART III. ADMINISTRATION

SEC. 6. *Office responsibilities.* The Office of Personnel Management is responsible to the President for the effective implementation and administration of the executive assignment system established by this Order. The Office shall continuously review operations under this system, shall recommend promptly to the President any changes that are necessary to improve this system, and shall report periodically to the President any significant developments in the operation of the system. The Office shall recommend to the President a program of special honors and awards for the recognition of persons assigned to Career Executive Assignments and a program for the development and training of persons assigned to Career Executive Assignments. The training program shall include the establishment of special training and educational facilities, and provide for the relevant use of outside training facilities.

SEC. 7. *Responsibilities of the agencies.* The head of each agency in which there are positions covered by Civil Service Rule IX shall periodically review with the Office of Personnel Management his plans for staffing. The head of a newly established agency shall initially review with the Office his plans for staffing as soon as practicable after the establishment of the agency. The head of each agency shall cooperate fully with the Office in the establishment of special facilities and special boards and panels that are required under Civil Service Rule IX as a means of recruiting persons of the highest quality.

SEC. 8. *Regulations.* The Office of Personnel Management shall prescribe such regulations as may be necessary to carry out the purpose and intent of this Order.

EXECUTIVE ORDER NO. 11598

Ex. Ord. No. 11598, June 16, 1971, 36 F.R. 11711, formerly set out as a note under this section, which related to the listing of certain job vacancies by federal agencies and government contractors and subcontractors, was superseded by Ex. Ord. No. 11701, Jan. 24, 1973, 38 F.R. 2675, set out as a note under section 4212 of Title 38, Veterans' Benefits.

EXECUTIVE ORDER NO. 11813

Ex. Ord. No. 11813, Oct. 7, 1974, 39 F.R. 36317, which related to career or career-conditional appointments for cooperative education students, was revoked by Ex. Ord. No. 12015, Oct. 26, 1977, 42 F.R. 56947, set out below.

EX. ORD. NO. 11839. AMENDING THE CIVIL SERVICE RULES TO EXCEPT CERTAIN POSITIONS IN REGIONAL OFFICES FROM THE CAREER SERVICE

Ex. Ord. No. 11839, Feb. 15, 1975, 40 F.R. 7351, provided:

The program to decentralize Federal policy and decision making and to involve local governments and other interested parties in Federal, State, and local policy and program development requires a capability for deep involvement in the development and advocacy of Administration proposals and policies, and support of their controversial aspects, on the part of certain senior regional officials.

NOW, THEREFORE, by virtue of the authority vested in me by the Constitution of the United States and Sections 3301 and 3302 of Title 5 of the United States Code, and as President of the United States of America, it is hereby ordered as follows:

SECTION 1. Civil Service Rule VI is amended by adding the following Section:

"SECTION 6.8. SPECIFIED EXCEPTIONS

"Positions in the Department of the Interior whose incumbents serve as the principal representative of the Secretary in their respective regions shall be listed in Schedule C for grades not exceeding grade GS–15 of the General Schedule and shall be designated Noncareer Executive Assignments for positions graded higher than GS–15. Incumbents of these positions who are, on February 15, 1975, in the competitive service shall not be affected by the foregoing provisions of this Section."

SEC. 2. Civil Service Rule IX is amended by adding the following:

"Sec. 9.11. Specified Noncareer Executive Assignments

"The regional director, regional administrator, or the Secretary's principal regional representative positions in the Department of Health, Education, and Welfare, Housing and Urban Development, Transportation and Labor, and those positions in the Environmental Protection Agency shall be designated Noncareer Executive Assignments; and, the Limited Executive Assignments of any incumbents of these positions on February 15, 1975, are converted to Noncareer Executive Assignments. Incumbents of these positions serving in Career Executive Assignments on February 15, 1975, shall not be affected by the foregoing provisions of this Section."

GERALD R. FORD.

Ex. Ord. No. 11856. Amending the Civil Service Rules To Except Certain Positions in Regional Offices From the Career Service

Ex. Ord. No. 11856, May 7, 1975, 40 F.R. 20259, provided:

By virtue of the authority vested in me by the Constitution of the United States of America and Sections 3301 and 3302 of Title 5 of the United States Code, and as President of the United States of America, Section 9.11 of Civil Service Rule IX is amended by adding "and the Small Business Administration" after "Environmental Protection Agency."

GERALD R. FORD.

Ex. Ord. No. 11887. Amending the Civil Service Rules To Except Certain Positions From the Career Service

Ex. Ord. No. 11887, Nov. 4, 1975, 40 F.R. 51411, provided:

By virtue of the authority vested in me by the Constitution of the United States of America and Sections 3301 and 3302 of Title 5 of the United States Code, and as President of the United States of America, Section 6.8 of Civil Service Rule VI is amended by adding "and in the Department of Commerce" after "Department of the Interior".

GERALD R. FORD.

Ex. Ord. No. 11935. Amending the Civil Service Rules Concerning Citizenship Requirements for Federal Employment

Ex. Ord. No. 11935, Sept. 2, 1976, 41 F.R. 37301, as amended by Ex. Ord. No. 12107, Dec. 28, 1978, 44 F.R. 1055, provided:

By virtue of the authority vested in me by the Constitution and statutes of the United States of America, including Sections 3301 and 3302 of Title 5 of the United States Code, and as President of the United States of America, Civil Service Rule VII (5 CFR Part 7) is hereby amended by adding thereto the following new section:

"Section 7.4. Citizenship

"(a) No person shall be admitted to competitive examination unless such person is a citizen or national of the United States.

"(b) No person shall be given any appointment in the competitive service unless such person is a citizen or national of the United States.

"(c) The Office may, as an exception to this rule and to the extent permitted by law, authorize the appointment of aliens to positions in the competitive service when necessary to promote the efficiency of the service in specific cases or for temporary appointments.".

Ex. Ord. No. 11955. Career or Career-Conditional Appointment to Certain Qualified Employees of National Aeronautics and Space Administration

Ex. Ord. No. 11955, Jan. 10, 1977, 42 F.R. 2499, as amended by Ex. Ord. No. 12107, Dec. 28, 1978, 44 F.R. 1055, provided:

By virtue of the authority vested in me by section 3301 of title 5 of the United States Code [this section],

and as President of the United States of America, it is hereby ordered as follows:

SECTION 1. The appointment of a Command Pilot, Pilot or Mission Specialist candidate to a position in the Space Shuttle Astronaut Program of the National Aeronautics and Space Administration, which is listed under Schedule B of the Schedule of Excepted Positions, may be converted to career or career-conditional appointment if:

(a) the candidate has successfully completed two years of service as a candidate in an appropriate training program;

(b) the Administrator of the National Aeronautics and Space Administration, or the Administrator's designee, recommends the conversion of the candidate's appointment within ninety days of completion of the requirements of section 1(a);

(c) the candidate meets noncompetitive examination standards prescribed by the Office of Personnel Management; and

(d) the candidate meets all other requirements prescribed by the Office of Personnel Management pursuant to section 3 of this order.

SEC. 2. Whenever the Administrator of the National Aeronautics and Space Administration, or the Administrator's designee, decides not to recommend conversion of an appointment under this order or whenever the Administrator, or the Administrator's designee, recommends conversion and the candidate fails to qualify, the candidate shall be separated not later than the date of expiration of the current Schedule B appointment, unless the appointment can be converted through appropriate competitive examination or the candidate can be assigned to a suitable position under another excepted authority prior to the expiration date.

SEC. 3. The Office of Personnel Management shall prescribe such regulations as may be necessary to carry out the purpose of this order.

EXECUTIVE ORDER NO. 12008

Ex. Ord. No. 12008, Aug. 25, 1977, 42 F.R. 43373, as amended by Ex. Ord. No. 12107, Dec. 28, 1978, 44 F.R. 1055, which established a Presidential Management Intern Program, was revoked by Ex. Ord. No. 12364, May 24, 1982, 47 F.R. 22931, set out below.

Ex. Ord. No. 12015. Career or Career-Conditional Appointments in Competitive Service for Students Completing Approved Career-Related Work-Study Programs

Ex. Ord. No. 12015, Oct. 26, 1977, 42 F.R. 56947, as amended by Ex. Ord. No. 12107, Dec. 28, 1978, 44 F.R. 1055; Ex. Ord. No. 13024, Nov. 7, 1996, 61 F.R. 58125, provided:

By virtue of the authority vested in me by Sections 3301 and 3302 of Title 5 of the United States Code, and as President of the United States of America, it is hereby ordered as follows:

SECTION 1. As used in this order "career-related work-study programs" are those programs established by the Office of Personnel Management which provide for a formally-arranged schedule of periods of attendance at an accredited school combined with periods of career-related work in a Federal agency under a Schedule B appointment.

SEC. 2. The appointment of a student to a position in a career-related work-study program may be converted noncompetitively to a term, career, or career-conditional appointment if the student:

(a) has completed within the preceding 120 days an educational program that meets the provisions established by the Office of Personnel Management;

(b) has satisfied all course requirements leading to completion of the related curriculum at an accredited school;

(c) is recommended for such an appointment by the employing agency in which the career-related work was performed; and,

(d) satisfies such other requirements and conditions as the Office of Personnel Management may prescribe for term, career, or career-conditional appointment of an individual in career-related work-study programs.

SEC. 3. The Office of Personnel Management shall prescribe such regulations as it deems necessary to carry out the provisions of this order and to provide for the continuation of planning, implementation and evaluation of employment programs for students throughout the Government. These regulations shall provide for the periodic evaluation of the work of each student and require that each student's continuation in the program shall be dependent upon a finding of satisfactory performance.

SEC. 4. Students converted to term appointment under section 2 may subsequently be converted noncompetitively to a career or career-conditional appointment before the term appointment expires.

SEC. 5. Executive Order No. 11813 of October 7, 1974, is hereby revoked.

EX. ORD. NO. 12021. AMENDING THE CIVIL SERVICE RULES TO EXCEPT CERTAIN POSITIONS FROM THE CAREER SERVICE

Ex. Ord. No. 12021, Nov. 30, 1977, 42 F.R. 61237, provided:

By virtue of the authority vested in me by the Constitution of the United States of America, and Sections 3301 and 3302 of Title 5 of the United States Code, and as President of the United States of America, it is hereby ordered as follows:

SECTION 1. That portion of Section 6.8 of Civil Service Rule VI following the heading "Specified Exceptions." (5 C.F.R. 6.8) is designated subsection (a) and a new subsection (b) is added as follows:

"(b) Positions in the Community Services Administration and ACTION [now Corporation for National and Community Service] whose incumbents serve as regional director or regional administrator shall be listed in Schedule C for grades not exceeding GS–15 of the General Schedule and shall be designated Noncareer Executive Assignments for positions graded higher than GS–15. Incumbents of these positions who are, on November 29, 1977, in the competitive service shall not be affected by the foregoing provisions of this subsection.".

SEC. 2. That portion of Section 9.11 of Civil Service Rule IX following the heading "Career Executive Assignments; selection and assignment." (5 C.F.R. 9.11) is designated subsection (a) and a new subsection (b) is added as follows:

"(b) The regional director or regional administrator positions in the Defense Civil Preparedness Agency and the General Services Administration shall be designated as Noncareer Executive Assignments and the Limited Executive Assignments of any incumbents of these positions on November 29, 1977, are converted to Noncareer Executive Assignments. Incumbents of these positions who are, on November 29, 1977, serving in Career Executive Assignments shall not be affected by the foregoing provisions of this subsection.".

JIMMY CARTER.

EXECUTIVE ORDER NO. 12026

For provisions relating to eligibility for reinstatement in the competitive civil service of certain employees of the Energy Department, see Ex. Ord. No. 12026, Dec. 5, 1977, 42 F.R. 61849, set out as a note under section 7292 of Title 42, The Public Health and Welfare.

EX. ORD. NO. 12043. AMENDING THE CIVIL SERVICE RULES REGARDING NOTICE OF EXEMPTIONS FROM THE COMPETITIVE SERVICE

Ex. Ord. No. 12043, Mar. 7, 1978, 43 F.R. 9773, as amended by Ex. Ord. No. 12107, Dec. 28, 1978, 44 F.R. 1055, provided:

By virtue of the authority vested in me by the Constitution of the United States of America, and Sections 3301 and 3302 of Title 5 of the United States Code, and as President of the United States of America, it is hereby ordered as follows:

SECTION 1. Section 6.1 of Civil Service Rule VI (5 CFR 6.1) is amended by deleting the third sentence in subsection (a) thereof and by adding a new subsection (c) as follows:

"(c) Notice of the Office's decision granting authority to make appointments to an excepted position under the appropriate schedule shall be published in the FEDERAL REGISTER.".

SEC. 2. Section 6.6 of the Civil Service Rule VI (5 CFR 6.6) is amended by deleting the second sentence thereof and substituting "Notice of the Office's decision making these changes shall be published in the FEDERAL REGISTER.".

SEC. 3. Section 9.6 of the Civil Service Rule IX (5 CFR 9.6) is amended by adding a new subsection (c) as follows:

"(c) The Office shall include in its annual report a current listing, by agency, of all positions authorized to be filled by Limited Executive Assignment.".

SEC. 4. Section 9.20 of Civil Service Rule IX (5 CFR 9.20) is amended by adding a new subsection (f) as follows:

"(f) The Office shall include in its annual report a current listing, by agency, of all positions authorized to be filled by Noncareer Executive Assignment.".

JIMMY CARTER.

EX. ORD. NO. 12125. AMENDING THE CIVIL SERVICE RULES RELATING TO COMPETITIVE STATUS FOR HANDICAPPED FEDERAL EMPLOYEES

Ex. Ord. No. 12125, Mar. 15, 1979, 44 F.R. 16879, provided:

By the authority vested in me as President of the United States of America by Sections 3301 and 3302 of Title 5 of the United States Code, and in order to permit severely physically handicapped and mentally retarded individuals to obtain civil service competitive status, Civil Service Rule 3.1 (5 CFR 3.1) is hereby amended by adding the following new subsection:

"(b) Upon recommendation by the employing agency, and subject to such requirements as the Office of Personnel Management may prescribe, the following classes of handicapped employees may acquire competitive status without competitive examination:

"(1) A severely physically handicapped employee who completes at least two years of satisfactory service in a position excepted from the competitive service.

"(2) A mentally retarded employee who completes at least two years of satisfactory service in a position excepted from the competitive service.".

JIMMY CARTER.

EXECUTIVE ORDER NO. 12257

Ex. Ord. No. 12257, Dec. 18, 1980, 45 F.R. 84005, which provided for noncompetitive conversion of participants in the Comprehensive Employment and Training Act program to career or career-conditional Civil Service status, was revoked by Ex. Ord. No. 12553, Feb. 25, 1986, 51 F.R. 7237.

EXECUTIVE ORDER NO. 12300

Ex. Ord. No. 12300, Mar. 23, 1981, 46 F.R. 18683, which amended section 6.8 of Civil Service Rule VI by adding subsec. (c), excepting certain positions in Department of Agriculture from the competitive service, was superseded by Ex. Ord. No. 12940, Nov. 28, 1994, 59 F.R. 61519, set out below.

EXECUTIVE ORDER NO. 12362

Ex. Ord. No. 12362, May 12, 1982, 47 F.R. 21231, as amended by Ex. Ord. No. 12585, Mar. 3, 1987, 52 F.R. 6773, which related to appointment to competitive status of certain overseas employees upon return to the United States, was revoked by Ex. Ord. No. 12721, July 30, 1990, 55 F.R. 31349, set out below.

EX. ORD. NO. 12364. PRESIDENTIAL MANAGEMENT INTERN PROGRAM

Ex. Ord. No. 12364, May 24, 1982, 47 F.R. 22931, as amended by Ex. Ord. No. 12645, July 12, 1988, 53 F.R. 26750, provided:

By the authority vested in me as President by the Constitution and laws of the United States of America, including Sections 3301 and 3302 of Title 5 of the United States Code, and in order to provide for the recruitment and selection of outstanding employees for careers in public sector management, it is hereby ordered as follows:

SECTION 1. There is hereby reconstituted the Presidential Management Intern Program. The purpose of the Program is to attract to the Federal service outstanding men and women from a variety of academic disciplines who have a clear interest in, and commitment to, a career in the analysis and management of public policies and programs. Individuals selected for the Program will be known as Presidential Management Interns.

SEC. 2. Eligible individuals are those who have pursued a course of study at the graduate level which demonstrates both an exceptional ability and the commitment stated above. Such individuals at the time of application must have recently received or must expect to receive soon an appropriate advanced degree.

SEC. 3. (a) The Office of Personnel Management shall provide specific guidance as to what constitutes an appropriate advanced degree.

(b) The Office of Personnel Management shall develop appropriate procedures for the recruitment, nomination, screening, placement and continuing career development of outstanding individuals possessing the qualifications described above.

(c) In developing those procedures, the Office of Personnel Management shall be guided by the following principles and policies:

(1) The number of new Presidential Management Interns selected shall not exceed four hundred in any fiscal year.

(2) Final placement of Presidential Management Interns shall be made by the head of the department, agency, or component within the Executive Office of the President in which the Intern is to be employed, or by the designee thereof.

(3) Universities and colleges participating in the Program shall make nominations for the Program. In making nominations, they shall establish competitive selection processes and procedures to ensure that all applicants receive careful and thorough review.

(4) The procedures so developed shall provide for such affirmative actions as the Office of Personnel Management deems appropriate to assure equal employment opportunity. The procedures shall also provide for the application of appropriate veterans preference criteria.

SEC. 4. (a) Successful candidates shall be appointed as Presidential Management Interns to positions in Schedule A of the excepted service. The appointment shall not exceed two years unless extended by the Federal department or agency, with the concurrence of the Office of Personnel Management, for up to one additional year.

(b) Tenure for the Presidential Management Interns shall be governed by the following principles and policies:

(1) Assigned responsibilities shall be consistent with an Intern's educational background and career interests, and the purposes of this Program.

(2) Continuation in the Program shall be contingent upon satisfactory performance by the Interns throughout the internship period.

(3) Except as provided in subsection (4) of this Section, service as an Intern shall confer no rights to further Federal employment in either the competitive or excepted service upon the expiration of the internship period.

(4) Competitive civil service status may be granted to Interns who satisfactorily complete their internships and meet all other requirements prescribed by the Office of Personnel Management.

SEC. 5. Those individuals who are currently undergoing the process of selection, or who were selected or appointed under the provisions of Executive Order No. 12008 [formerly set out as a note above] and who have not at this time completed their scheduled period of excepted service, may continue their internships under the terms of this Order.

SEC. 6. The Office of Personnel Management shall prescribe such regulations as may be necessary to carry out the purposes of this Order.

SEC. 7. Executive Order No. 12008 of August 25, 1977 is revoked.

RONALD REAGAN.

EX. ORD. NO. 12505. CAREER APPOINTMENTS TO CERTAIN OFFICE OF MANAGEMENT AND BUDGET EMPLOYEES

Ex. Ord. No. 12505, Feb. 12, 1985, 50 F.R. 6151, provided:

By the authority vested in me as President by the laws of the United States of America, including Section 3301 and 3302 of Title 5, and Section 521 of Title 31 of the United States Code, it is hereby ordered as follows:

SECTION 1. No later than April 1, 1985, any employee of the Office of Management and Budget serving under an appointment under Schedule A in a position not limited to one year or less, concerned with implementation of the President's paperwork reduction and regulatory review and planning programs, may have his or her appointment converted to a career or career-conditional appointment if the Director of the Office of Management and Budget determines that:

(a) The employee has completed at least one year of full-time continuous service in a position concerned with the paperwork reduction and regulatory program;

(b) There is a continuing need for the position filled by the employee;

(c) The employee's past performance has been satisfactory and the employee possesses the qualifications necessary to continue in the position; and

(d) The employee meets the citizenship requirements and qualification standards appropriate for the position.

SEC. 2. If the Director determines not to convert an employee's appointment to career or career-conditional status under the preceding Section, the employee shall be separated not later than the date of expiration of the current appointment.

SEC. 3. Employees whose appointments are converted under this Order shall become career-conditional employees, or career employees if they have completed the service requirements for career tenure, and all converted employees shall acquire a competitive status.

RONALD REAGAN.

EXECUTIVE ORDER NO. 12596

Ex. Ord. No. 12596, May 7, 1987, 52 F.R. 17537, which provided for noncompetitive conversion to career status of certain employees in professional and administrative career positions, was revoked by Ex. Ord. No. 13162, July 6, 2000, 65 F.R. 43212, set out as a note below.

EX. ORD. NO. 12685. NONCOMPETITIVE CONVERSION OF PERSONAL ASSISTANTS TO EMPLOYEES WITH DISABILITIES

Ex. Ord. No. 12685, July 28, 1989, 54 F.R. 31796, provided:

By the authority vested in me as President by the Constitution and laws of the United States of America, including sections 3301 and 3302 of title 5, United States Code, it is hereby ordered as follows:

SECTION 1. Upon recommendation by the employing agency, and subject to qualifications and other requirements prescribed by the Office of Personnel Management, an employee in a position in the excepted service under 5 C.F.R. 213.3102(11) as a reader, interpreter, or personal assistant for a handicapped employee, whose employment in such position is no longer necessary and who has completed at least 1 year of satisfactory service in such position under a non-temporary appointment, may be converted noncompetitively to a career or career-conditional appointment.

SEC. 2. This order shall be effective upon publication in the Federal Register.

GEORGE BUSH.

Ex. Ord. No. 12718. President's Advisory Commission on the Public Service

Ex. Ord. No. 12718, June 29, 1990, 55 F.R. 27451, provided:

By the authority vested in me as President by the Constitution and laws of the United States of America, including the Federal Advisory Committee Act, as amended (5 U.S.C. App.), and in order to provide a continuing source of advice on the public service from outstanding leaders in various walks of private life, it is hereby ordered as follows:

Section 1. *Establishment*. The President's Advisory Commission on the Public Service ("Commission") is hereby established. The Commission shall be comprised of 13 members to be appointed by the President from among leading citizens in private life. The members shall be appointed for 2-year terms, except that initial appointments shall include six members appointed to serve 1-year terms. Any vacancy in the Commission shall be filled by an appointment for the remainder of the term for which the original appointment was made, and a member whose term has expired may serve until his or her successor has been appointed. The President shall designate one of the members of the Commission to serve as Chairperson.

Sec. 2. *Functions*. (a) The Commission shall meet from time to time at the request of the Chairperson and shall consider ways to enhance the public service in American life, including:

(1) improving the efficiency and attractiveness of the Federal civil service;

(2) increasing the interest among American students in pursuing careers in the public service; and

(3) strengthening the image of the public service in American life.

(b) The Commission shall submit a report on its activities to the Director of the Office of Personnel Management and the President each year.

Sec. 3. *Administrative Provisions*. (a) The members of the Commission shall serve without compensation, but may receive travel expenses, including per diem in lieu of subsistence, in accordance with sections 5702 and 5703 of title 5, United States Code.

(b) All executive agencies are directed, to the extent permitted by law, to provide such information, advice, and assistance to the Commission as the Commission may request.

(c) The Director of the Office of Personnel Management shall, to the extent permitted by law and subject to the availability of funds, provide the Commission with administrative services, staff support, and necessary expenses.

Sec. 4. *General*. Notwithstanding any other Executive order, the functions of the President under the Federal Advisory Committee Act, as amended [5 U.S.C. App.], except that of reporting to the Congress, which are applicable to the Commission, shall be performed by the Office of Personnel Management in accordance with the guidelines and procedures established by the Administrator of General Services.

GEORGE BUSH.

Ex. Ord. No. 12721. Eligibility of Overseas Employees for Noncompetitive Appointments

Ex. Ord. No. 12721, July 30, 1990, 55 F.R. 31349, provided:

By the authority vested in me as President by the Constitution and laws of the United States of America, including sections 3301 and 3302 of title 5 and section 301 of title 3 of the United States Code, and in order to permit certain overseas employees to acquire competitive status upon returning to the United States, it is hereby ordered as follows:

SECTION 1. A United States citizen who is a family member of a Federal civilian employee, of a nonappropriated fund employee, or of a member of a uniformed service and who meets the qualifications and other requirements established by the Director of the Office of Personnel Management, including an appro-

priate period of satisfactory service under one or more overseas appointments in the excepted or competitive civil service, may be appointed noncompetitively to a competitive service position in the executive branch within the United States (including Guam, Puerto Rico, and the Virgin Islands). The employing agency in the United States may waive a requirement for a written test for an individual appointed under this order if the agency determines that the duties and responsibilities of the position occupied overseas were similar enough to those of the position to which the individual is being appointed under this order to make the written test unnecessary.

SEC. 2. The Director of the Office of Personnel Management shall prescribe such regulations as may be necessary to implement this order.

SEC. 3. To the extent there is any conflict between this order and Civil Service Rule 8.2 (5 CFR 8.2) [set out above], the provisions of this order shall control.

SEC. 4. (a) Executive Order No. 12362 of May 12, 1982, as amended, and Executive Order No. 12585 of March 3, 1987, are revoked.

(b) Existing regulations prescribed by the Director of the Office of Personnel Management under Executive Order No. 12362, as amended, shall continue in effect until modified or superseded by the Director of the Office of Personnel Management.

SEC. 5. This order shall be effective upon publication in the Federal Register.

GEORGE BUSH.

Ex. Ord. No. 12940. Amendment to Civil Service Rule VI

Ex. Ord. No. 12940, Nov. 28, 1994, 59 F.R. 61519, provided:

By the authority vested in me as President by the Constitution and the laws of the United States of America, including sections 3301 and 3302 of title 5, United States Code, and having determined that it is necessary and warranted by conditions of good administration that certain positions in the Department of Agriculture continue to be excluded from the coverage of section 2302 of title 5, United States Code, and excepted from the competitive service because of their confidential, policy-determining, policy-making, or policy-advocating character, in order to ensure their deep involvement in the development and advocacy of Administration proposals and policies and to ensure their effective and vigorous implementation, and as a result of a reorganization of the Department of Agriculture carried out pursuant to Public Law 103–354 [7 U.S.C. 6901 et seq.], it is hereby ordered that subsection (c) of section 6.8 of Civil Service Rule VI (5 C.F.R. 6.8) is revised to read as follows:

"(c) Within the Department of Agriculture, positions the incumbents of which serve as State Executive Directors of the Consolidated Farm Service Agency and positions the incumbents of which serve as State Directors or State Directors-at-Large for Rural Economic and Community Development shall be listed in Schedule C for all grades of the General Schedule."

This order supersedes Executive Order No. 12300.

WILLIAM J. CLINTON.

Ex. Ord. No. 13124. Amending the Civil Service Rules Relating To Federal Employees With Psychiatric Disabilities

Ex. Ord. No. 13124, June 4, 1999, 64 F.R. 31103, provided:

By the authority vested in me as President by the Constitution and the laws of the United States of America, including sections 3301 and 3302 of title 5, United States Code, and in order to give individuals with psychiatric disabilities the same hiring opportunities as persons with severe physical disabilities or mental retardation under the Civil Service Rules, and to permit individuals with psychiatric disabilities to obtain Civil Service competitive status, it is hereby ordered as follows:

SECTION 1. *Policy*.

(a) It is the policy of the United States to assure equality of opportunity, full participation, independent living, and economic self-sufficiency for persons with disabilities. The Federal Government as an employer should serve as a model for the employment of persons with disabilities and utilize the full potential of these talented citizens.

(b) The Civil Service Rules governing appointment of persons with psychiatric disabilities were adopted years ago when attitudes about mental illness were different than they are today, which led to stricter standards for hiring persons with psychiatric disabilities than for persons with mental retardation or severe physical disabilities. The Civil Service Rules provide that persons with mental retardation, severe physical disabilities, or psychiatric disabilities may be hired under excepted appointing authorities. While persons with mental retardation or severe physical disabilities may be appointed for more than 2 years and may convert to competitive status after completion of 2 years of satisfactory service in their excepted position, people with psychiatric disabilities may not.

(c) The Office of Personnel Management (OPM) and the President's Task Force on Employment of Adults with Disabilities believe that the Federal Government could better benefit from the contributions of persons with psychiatric disabilities if they were given the same opportunities available to people with mental retardation or severe physical disabilities.

SEC. 2. *Implementation.*

(a) The Director of the Office of Personnel Management shall, consistent with OPM authority, provide that persons with psychiatric disabilities are subject to the same hiring rules as persons with mental retardation or severe physical disabilities.

(b) Civil Service Rule III (5 CFR Part 3) is amended by adding the following new paragraph to subsection (b) of section 3.1:

"(3) An employee with psychiatric disabilities who completes at least 2 years of satisfactory service in a position excepted from the competitive service."

SEC. 3. The Director of the Office of Personnel Management shall prescribe such regulations as may be necessary to implement this order.

WILLIAM J. CLINTON.

EX. ORD. NO. 13162. FEDERAL CAREER INTERN PROGRAM

Ex. Ord. No. 13162, July 6, 2000, 65 F.R. 43211, provided:

By the authority vested in me as President by the Constitution and the laws of the United States of America, including sections 3301 and 3302 of title 5, United States Code, and in order to provide for the recruitment and selection of exceptional employees for careers in the public sector, it is hereby ordered as follows:

SECTION 1. There is hereby constituted the Federal Career Intern Program (Program). The purpose of the Program is to attract exceptional men and women to the Federal workforce who have diverse professional experiences, academic training, and competencies, and to prepare them for careers in analyzing and implementing public programs. "Career Intern" is a generic term, and agencies may use occupational titles as appropriate.

SEC. 2. The Program is another step in the Administration's effort to recruit the highest caliber people to the Federal Government, develop their professional abilities, and retain them in Federal departments and agencies. Cabinet secretaries and agency administrators should view the Program as complementary to existing programs that provide career enhancement opportunities for Federal employees, and departments and agencies are encouraged to identify and make use of those programs, as well as the new Program, to meet department and agency needs.

SEC. 3. (a) The Office of Personnel Management (OPM) shall develop appropriate merit-based procedures for the recruitment, screening, placement, and continuing career development of Career Interns.

(b) In developing those procedures, the OPM shall provide for such actions as deemed appropriate to assure equal employment opportunity and the application of appropriate veterans' preference criteria.

SEC. 4. (a) A successful candidate shall be appointed to a position in Schedule B of the excepted service at the GS–5, 7, or 9 (and equivalent) or other trainee level appropriate for the Program, unless otherwise approved by the OPM. The appointment shall not exceed 2 years unless extended by the Federal department or agency, with the concurrence of the OPM, for up to 1 additional year.

(b) Tenure for a Career Intern shall be governed by the following principles and policies:

(1) Assigned responsibilities shall be consistent with a Career Intern's competencies and career interests, and the purposes of the Program.

(2) Continuation in the Program shall be contingent upon satisfactory performance by the Career Intern throughout the internship period.

(3) Except as provided in subsections (4) and (5) of this section, service as a Career Intern confers no rights to further Federal employment in either the competitive or excepted service upon the expiration of the internship period.

(4) Competitive civil service status may be granted to a Career Intern who satisfactorily completes the internship and meets all other requirements prescribed by the OPM.

(5) Within an agency, an employee who formerly held a career or career-conditional appointment immediately before entering the Career Intern Program, and who fails to complete the Career Intern Program for reasons unrelated to misconduct or suitability, shall be placed in a career or career-conditional position in the current agency at no lower grade or pay than the one the employee left to accept the position in the Career Intern Program.

SEC. 5. A Career Intern shall participate in a formal program of training and job assignments to develop competencies that the OPM identifies as core to the Program, and the employing agency identifies as appropriate to the agency's mission and needs.

SEC. 6. The OPM shall prescribe such regulations as it determines necessary to carry out the purpose of this order.

SEC. 7. The OPM shall provide oversight of the Program.

SEC. 8. Executive Order 12596 of May 7, 1987, is revoked.

SEC. 9. *Judicial Review.* This order is intended only to improve the internal management of the executive branch. It does not create any right or benefit, substantive or procedural, enforceable in law or equity, by a party against the United States, its agencies, its officers or employees, or any other person.

WILLIAM J. CLINTON.

SECTION REFERRED TO IN OTHER SECTIONS

This section is referred to in sections 3304, 3361 of this title; title 25 section 2a.

§ 3302. Competitive service; rules

The President may prescribe rules governing the competitive service. The rules shall provide, as nearly as conditions of good administration warrant, for—

(1) necessary exceptions of positions from the competitive service; and

(2) necessary exceptions from the provisions of sections 2951, 3304(a), 3321, 7202, and 7203 of this title.

Each officer and individual employed in an agency to which the rules apply shall aid in carrying out the rules.

(Pub. L. 89–554, Sept. 6, 1966, 80 Stat. 417; Pub. L. 95–228, §2(b), Feb. 10, 1978, 92 Stat. 25; Pub. L.

95–454, title VII, §703(c)(1), Oct. 13, 1978, 92 Stat. 1217; Pub. L. 96–54, §2(a)(16), Aug. 14, 1979, 93 Stat. 382; Pub. L. 103–94, §2(b)(1), Oct. 6, 1993, 107 Stat. 1004.)

HISTORICAL AND REVISION NOTES

Derivation	U.S. Code	Revised Statutes and Statutes at Large
....	5 U.S.C. 633(1) (less function of Civil Service Commission), (2)8 (last sentence).	Jan. 16, 1883, ch. 27, §2(1) (less function of Civil Service Commission), (2) 8 (last sentence), 22 Stat. 403, 404.

The reference to the competitive service is substituted for the reference to the Act creating that service. The reference to reasons for the exceptions is omitted as covered by section 1308 of this title. The words "provide for" are substituted for "provide and declare". Paragraph (1) is supplied to preserve the President's power to except positions from the competitive service, previously implied from the power to except from the first rule in former section 633(2). Authority to make exceptions to so much of former section 633(2) as is restated in this section and section 1302(a) is omitted as meaningless. Authority to make exceptions to so much of former section 633(2) as is restated in section 3318(a) is omitted as superseded by former section 857, which is carried into section 3318(a). In the last sentence, the words "Each officer and individual employed in an agency" are substituted for "officers of the United States in the departments and offices" because of the restrictive definition of "officer" in section 2104.

Standard changes are made to conform with the definitions applicable and the style of this title as outlined in the preface to the report.

AMENDMENTS

1993—Par. (2). Pub. L. 103–94 substituted "and 7203" for "7203, 7321, and 7322".

1979—Par. (2). Pub. L. 96–54 amended par. (2) in same manner as amendment by section 703(c)(1) of Pub. L. 95–454. See 1978 Amendment note below.

1978—Par. (2). Pub. L. 95–454 substituted "7202, 7203" for "7152, 7153".

Pub. L. 95–228 struck out reference to section 3306(a)(1) of this title. Amendments by section 703(c)(1) and (c)(2) of Pub. L. 95–454 appear to have been inadvertently reversed. Subsec. (c)(1) purported to amend subsec. (c)(1) of section 2105 of this title, and subsec. (c)(2) purported to amend par. (2) of this section. However, the amendments specified by Pub. L. 95–454, §703(c)(1) and (2), were impossible to execute literally. Thus, amendment by Pub. L. 95–454, §703(c)(2) was executed to section 2105 of this title, and amendment by section 703(c)(1) was executed to this section as the probable intent of Congress.

EFFECTIVE DATE OF 1993 AMENDMENT; SAVINGS PROVISION

Amendment by Pub. L. 103–94 effective 120 days after Oct. 6, 1993, but not to release or extinguish any penalty, forfeiture, or liability incurred under amended provision, which is to be treated as remaining in force for purpose of sustaining any proper proceeding or action for enforcement of that penalty, forfeiture, or liability, and no provision of Pub. L. 103–94 to affect any proceedings with respect to which charges were filed on or before 120 days after Oct. 6, 1993, with orders to be issued in such proceedings and appeals taken therefrom as if Pub. L. 103–94 had not been enacted, see section 12 of Pub. L. 103–94, set out as an Effective Date; Savings Provision note under section 7321 of this title.

EFFECTIVE DATE OF 1979 AMENDMENT

Amendment by Pub. L. 96–54 effective July 12, 1979, see section 2(b) of Pub. L. 96–54, set out as a note under section 305 of this title.

EFFECTIVE DATE OF 1978 AMENDMENT

Amendment by Pub. L. 95–454 effective 90 days after Oct. 13, 1978, see section 907 of Pub. L. 95–454, set out as a note under section 1101 of this title.

EX. ORD. NO. 11521. VETERANS READJUSTMENT APPOINTMENT FOR VETERANS OF VIETNAM ERA

Ex. Ord. No. 11521, Mar. 26, 1970, 35 F.R. 5311, as amended by Ex. Ord. No. 12107, Dec. 28, 1978, 44 F.R. 1055, provided:

WHEREAS this Nation has an obligation to assist veterans of the armed forces in readjusting to civilian life;

WHEREAS the Federal Government, as an employer, should reflect its recognition of this obligation in its personnel policies and practices;

WHEREAS veterans, by virtue of their military service, have lost opportunities to pursue education and training oriented toward civilian careers;

WHEREAS the Federal Government is continuously concerned with building an effective workforce, and veterans constitute a major recruiting source; and

WHEREAS the development of skills is most effectively achieved through a program combining employment with education or training:

NOW, THEREFORE, by virtue of the authority vested in me by the Constitution of the United States, by sections 3301 and 3302 of title 5, United States Code, and as President of the United States, it is ordered as follows:

SECTION 1. (a) Subject to paragraph (b) of this section, the head of an agency may make an excepted appointment, to be known as a "veterans readjustment appointment", to any position in the competitive service up to and including GS–5 or the equivalent thereof, of a veteran or disabled veteran as defined in section 2108(1), (2), of title 5, United States Code, who:

(1) served on active duty in the armed forces of the United States during the Vietnam era;

(2) at the time of his appointment has completed not more than fourteen years of education; and

(3) is found qualified to perform the duties of the position.

(b) Employment under paragraph (a) of this section is authorized only under a training or educational program developed by an agency in accordance with guidelines established by the Office of Personnel Management.

(c) An employee given a veterans readjustment appointment under paragraph (a) of this section shall serve subject to:

(1) the satisfactory performance of assigned duties; and

(2) participation in the training or educational program under which he is appointed.

(d) An employee who does not satisfactorily meet the conditions set forth in paragraph (c) of this section shall be removed in accordance with appropriate procedures.

(e) An employee serving under a veterans readjustment appointment may be promoted, reassigned, or transferred.

(f) An employee who completes the training or educational program and who has satisfactorily completed two years of substantially continuous service under a veterans readjustment appointment shall be converted to career-conditional or career employment. An employee converted under this paragraph shall automatically acquire a competitive status.

(g) In selecting an applicant for appointment under this section, an agency shall not discriminate because of race, color, religion, sex, national origin, or political affiliation.

SEC. 2. (a) A person eligible for appointment under section 1 of this order may be appointed only within one year after his separation from the armed forces, or one year following his release from hospitalization or treatment immediately following his separation from the armed forces, or one year after involuntary separation without cause from (i) a veterans readjustment appointment or (ii) a transitional appointment, or one year after the effective date of this order if he is serving under a transitional appointment.

(b) The Office of Personnel Management may determine the circumstances under which service under a transitional appointment may be deemed service under a veterans readjustment appointment for the purpose of paragraph (f) of section 1 of this order.

SEC. 3. Any law, Executive order, or regulation which would disqualify an applicant for appointment in the competitive service shall also disqualify a person otherwise eligible for appointment under section 1 of this order.

SEC. 4. For the purpose of this order:

(a) "agency" means a military department as defined in section 102 of title 5, United States Code, an executive agency (other than the General Accounting Office) as defined in section 105 of title 5, United States Code, and those portions of the legislative and judicial branches of the Federal Government and of the government of the District of Columbia having positions in the competitive service; and

(b) "Vietnam era" means the period beginning August 5, 1964, and ending on such date thereafter as may be determined by Presidential proclamation or concurrent resolution of the Congress.

SEC. 5. The Office of Personnel Management shall prescribe such regulations as may be necessary to carry out the provisions of this order.

SEC. 6. Executive Order No. 11397 of February 9, 1968, is revoked. Such revocation shall not affect the right of an employee to be converted to career-conditional or career employment if he meets the requirements of section 1(d) of Executive Order No. 11397 after the effective date of this order.

SEC. 7. This order is effective 14 days after its date.

SECTION REFERRED TO IN OTHER SECTIONS

This section is referred to in sections 3304, 3361 of this title; title 10 section 1784.

§ 3303. Competitive service; recommendations of Senators or Representatives

An individual concerned in examining an applicant for or appointing him in the competitive service may not receive or consider a recommendation of the applicant by a Senator or Representative, except as to the character or residence of the applicant.

(Pub. L. 89–554, Sept. 6, 1966, 80 Stat. 418; Pub. L. 103–94, § 8(a), Oct. 6, 1993, 107 Stat. 1006; Pub. L. 104–197, title III, § 315(a), Sept. 16, 1996, 110 Stat. 2416.)

HISTORICAL AND REVISION NOTES

Derivation	U.S. Code	Revised Statutes and Statutes at Large
....	5 U.S.C. 642.	Jan. 16, 1883, ch. 27, § 10, 22 Stat. 406.

The prohibition is restated in positive form. The words "An individual concerned in examining an applicant for or appointing him in the competitive service" are substituted for "any person concerned in making any examination or appointment under this act". The word "applicant" is substituted for "person who shall apply for office or place under the provisions of this act". The word "Representative" is substituted for "Member of the House of Representatives".

Standard changes are made to conform with the definitions applicable and the style of this title as outlined in the preface to the report.

AMENDMENTS

1996—Pub. L. 104–197 substituted "Competitive service; recommendations of Senators or Representatives"

for "Political recommendations" in section catchline and amended text generally, substituting provisions prohibiting receipt or consideration of recommendations of applicants in competitive service made by Senators or Representatives for provisions which directed that personnel actions be taken without solicitation of or regard to such recommendations from Members of Congress, congressional employees, any elected official of the government of any State (including D.C. and Puerto Rico) or subdivision thereof, or political party official, prohibited such persons from making such recommendations, prohibited employees or applicants from soliciting such recommendations and required notification of such prohibition, but allowed for certain exceptions regarding solicitation and consideration of recommendations if subject of recommendation was limited to factors pertinent to work performance, ability, aptitude, general qualifications, related to suitability or security standards, or furnished pursuant to law or regulation.

1993—Pub. L. 103–94 substituted "Political recommendations" for "Competitive service; recommendations of Senators or Representatives" as section catchline and amended text generally. Prior to amendment, text read as follows: "An individual concerned in examining an applicant for or appointing him in the competitive service may not receive or consider a recommendation of the applicant by a Senator or Representative, except as to the character or residence of the applicant."

EFFECTIVE DATE OF 1996 AMENDMENT

Amendment by Pub. L. 104–197 effective 30 days after Sept. 16, 1996, see section 315(c) of Pub. L. 104–197, set out as a note under section 2302 of this title.

EFFECTIVE DATE OF 1993 AMENDMENT; SAVINGS PROVISION

Amendment by Pub. L. 103–94 effective 120 days after Oct. 6, 1993, but not to release or extinguish any penalty, forfeiture, or liability incurred under amended provision, which is to be treated as remaining in force for purpose of sustaining any proper proceeding or action for enforcement of that penalty, forfeiture, or liability, and no provision of Pub. L. 103–94 to affect any proceedings with respect to which charges were filed on or before 120 days after Oct. 6, 1993, with orders to be issued in such proceedings and appeals taken therefrom as if Pub. L. 103–94 had not been enacted, see section 12 of Pub. L. 103–94, set out as an Effective Date; Savings Provision note under section 7321 of this title.

SECTION REFERRED TO IN OTHER SECTIONS

This section is referred to in title 38 section 7403.

§ 3304. Competitive service; examinations

(a) The President may prescribe rules which shall provide, as nearly as conditions of good administration warrant, for—

(1) open, competitive examinations for testing applicants for appointment in the competitive service which are practical in character and as far as possible relate to matters that fairly test the relative capacity and fitness of the applicants for the appointment sought; and

(2) noncompetitive examinations when competent applicants do not compete after notice has been given of the existence of the vacancy.

(b) An individual may be appointed in the competitive service only if he has passed an examination or is specifically excepted from examination under section 3302 of this title. This subsection does not take from the President any authority conferred by section 3301 of this title that is consistent with the provisions of this title governing the competitive service.

(c)(1) For the purpose of this subsection, the term "technician" has the meaning given such term by section 8337(h)(1) of this title.

(2) Notwithstanding a contrary provision of this title or of the rules and regulations prescribed under this title for the administration of the competitive service, an individual who served for at least 3 years as a technician acquires a competitive status for transfer to the competitive service if such individual—

(A) is involuntarily separated from service as a technician other than by removal for cause on charges of misconduct or delinquency;

(B) passes a suitable noncompetitive examination; and

(C) transfers to the competitive service within 1 year after separating from service as a technician.

(d) The Office of Personnel Management shall promulgate regulations on the manner and extent that experience of an individual in a position other than the competitive service, such as the excepted service (as defined under section 2103) in the legislative or judicial branch, or in any private or nonprofit enterprise, may be considered in making appointments to a position in the competitive service (as defined under section 2102). In promulgating such regulations OPM shall not grant any preference based on the fact of service in the legislative or judicial branch. The regulations shall be consistent with the principles of equitable competition and merit based appointments.

(e) Employees at any place outside the District of Columbia where the President or the Office of Personnel Management directs that examinations be held shall allow the reasonable use of public buildings for, and in all proper ways facilitate, holding the examinations.

(f)(1) Preference eligibles or veterans who have been separated from the armed forces under honorable conditions after 3 years or more of active service may not be denied the opportunity to compete for vacant positions for which the agency making the announcement will accept applications from individuals outside its own workforce under merit promotion procedures.

(2) If selected, a preference eligible or veteran described in paragraph (1) shall receive a career or career-conditional appointment, as appropriate.

(3) This subsection shall not be construed to confer an entitlement to veterans' preference that is not otherwise required by law.

(4) The area of consideration for all merit promotion announcements which include consideration of individuals of the Federal workforce shall indicate that preference eligibles and veterans who have been separated from the armed forces under honorable conditions after 3 years or more of active service are eligible to apply. The announcements shall be publicized in accordance with section 3327.

(5) The Office of Personnel Management shall prescribe regulations necessary for the administration of this subsection. The regulations shall ensure that an individual who has completed an initial tour of active duty is not excluded from the application of this subsection because of having been released from such tour of duty

shortly before completing 3 years of active service, having been honorably released from such duty.

(Pub. L. 89–554, Sept. 6, 1966, 80 Stat. 418; Pub. L. 95–454, title IX, § 906(a)(5), Oct. 13, 1978, 92 Stat. 1225; Pub. L. 99–586, Oct. 29, 1986, 100 Stat. 3325; Pub. L. 104–65, §§ 16(a), (b), 17(a), Dec. 19, 1995, 109 Stat. 703; Pub. L. 104–186, title II, § 215(2), Aug. 20, 1996, 110 Stat. 1745; Pub. L. 105–339, § 2, Oct. 31, 1998, 112 Stat. 3182; Pub. L. 106–117, title V, § 511(c), Nov. 30, 1999, 113 Stat. 1575.)

HISTORICAL AND REVISION NOTES

Derivation	U.S. Code	Revised Statutes and Statutes at Large
(a)	5 U.S.C. 633(2)1.	Jan. 16, 1883, ch. 27, § 2(2)1, 22 Stat. 403.
	5 U.S.C. 633(2)7 (less last 17 words).	Jan. 16, 1883, ch. 27, § 2(2)7 (less last 17 words), 22 Stat. 404.
(b)	5 U.S.C. 638 (as applicable to appointment).	Jan. 16, 1883, ch. 27, § 7 (as applicable to appointment), 22 Stat. 406.
(c)	5 U.S.C. 631b(b).	Nov. 26, 1940, ch. 919, § 2(b), 54 Stat. 1212. Feb. 12, 1946, ch. 3, 60 Stat. 3. May 29, 1958, Pub. L. 85–432, § 5, 72 Stat. 151.
	5 U.S.C. 631b(c).	June 24, 1952, ch. 456, 66 Stat. 155.
(d)	5 U.S.C. 635 (7th sentence).	Jan. 16, 1883, ch. 27, § 3 (7th sentence), 22 Stat. 404.

In subsection (a), the authority of the President to prescribe rules is added on authority of former section 633(1), which is carried into section 3302. The words "competitive service" are substituted for "public service" since the requirements do not apply to the excepted or uniformed service.

In subsection (b), the words "That after the expiration of six months from the passage of this act" are omitted as executed. The words "in the competitive service" are substituted for "in either of the said classes now existing, or that may be arranged hereunder pursuant to said rules" because of the definition of "competitive service" in section 2102. In the second sentence, the words "the provisions of this title governing the competitive service" are substituted for "this act".

In subsection (c), the provisions of former section 631b(b) and (c) are combined and restated for clarity. The words "From and after the effective date of this Act" and "From and after the date of approval of this Act" are omitted as executed. The words "competitive service" are substituted for "classified civil service" in view of the definition of "competitive service" in section 2102. The words "or as a clerical employee of the Senate or House of Representatives" are omitted as included in the reference to "an individual . . . in the legislative branch in a position in which he was paid by the Secretary of the Senate or the Clerk of the House of Representatives". The words "and nothing in this Act shall be construed to impair any right of retransfer provided for under civil service laws or regulations made thereunder" are omitted as unnecessary.

In subsection (d), the word "Employees" is substituted for "collector, postmaster, and other officers of the United States".

Standard changes are made to conform with the definitions applicable and the style of this title as outlined in the preface to the report.

AMENDMENTS

1999—Subsec. (f)(2), (3). Pub. L. 106–117, § 511(c)(2), (3), added par. (2) and redesignated former par. (2) as (3). Former par. (3) redesignated (4).

Subsec. (f)(4). Pub. L. 106–117, § 511(c)(1), (2), redesignated par. (3) as (4) and struck out former par. (4) which read as follows: "The Office of Personnel Management shall establish an appointing authority to appoint such preference eligibles and veterans."

Subsec. (f)(5). Pub. L. 106–117, §511(c)(4), added par. (5).

1998—Subsec. (f). Pub. L. 105–339 added subsec. (f).

1996—Subsec. (c)(1). Pub. L. 104–186 substituted "Chief Administrative Officer" for "Clerk".

1995—Subsec. (c). Pub. L. 104–65, §16(a), (b), redesignated subsec. (d) as (c) and struck out former subsec. (c) which read as follows: "Notwithstanding a contrary provision of this title or of the rules and regulations prescribed under this title for the administration of the competitive service, an individual who served—

"(1) for at least 3 years in the legislative branch in a position in which he was paid by the Secretary of the Senate or the Chief Administrative Officer of the House of Representatives; or

"(2) for at least 4 years as a secretary or law clerk, or both, to a justice or judge of the United States;

acquires a competitive status for transfer to the competitive service if he is involuntarily separated without prejudice from the legislative or judicial branch, passes a suitable noncompetitive examination, and transfers to the competitive service within 1 year of the separation from the legislative or judicial branch. For the purpose of this subsection, an individual who has served for at least 2 years in a position in the legislative branch described by paragraph (1) of this subsection and who is separated from that position to enter the armed forces is deemed to have held that position during his service in the armed forces."

Subsec. (d). Pub. L. 104–65, §17(a), which directed amendment of this section by adding subsec. (d) at the end thereof, was executed by adding subsec. (d) after subsec. (c) to reflect the probable intent of Congress.

Pub. L. 104–65, §16(b), redesignated subsec. (d) as (c).

1986—Subsecs. (d), (e). Pub. L. 99–586 added subsec. (d) and redesignated former subsec. (d) as (e).

1978—Subsec. (d). Pub. L. 95–454 substituted "the Office of Personnel Management" for "a Civil Service Commission board of examiners".

EFFECTIVE DATE OF 1999 AMENDMENT

Pub. L. 106–117, title V, §511(d)(2), Nov. 30, 1999, 113 Stat. 1576, provided that: "If pursuant to subsection (a) [113 Stat. 1575] the amendments specified in subsection (c) [amending this section] are made, those amendments shall take effect as of October 31, 1998, as if included in subsection (f) of section 3304 of title 5, United States Code, as enacted by section 2 of the Veterans Employment Opportunities Act of 1998 (Public Law 105–339; 112 Stat. 3182)."

EFFECTIVE DATE OF 1995 AMENDMENT

Section 16(c) of Pub. L. 104–65 provided that: "The repeal and amendment made by this section [amending this section] shall take effect 2 years after the date of the enactment of this Act [Dec. 19, 1995]."

Section 17(b) of Pub. L. 104–65 provided that: "The amendment made by this section [amending this section] shall take effect 2 years after the date of the enactment of this Act [Dec. 19, 1995], except the Office of Personnel Management shall—

"(1) conduct a study on excepted service considerations for competitive service appointments relating to such amendment; and

"(2) take all necessary actions for the regulations described under such amendment to take effect as final regulations on the effective date of this section."

EFFECTIVE DATE OF 1978 AMENDMENT

Amendment by Pub. L. 95–454 effective 90 days after Oct. 13, 1978, see section 907 of Pub. L. 95–454, set out as a note under section 1101 of this title.

SECTION REFERRED TO IN OTHER SECTIONS

This section is referred to in section 3302 of this title; title 22 section 3008; title 40 section 42.

§ 3304a. Competitive service; career appointment after 3 years' temporary service

(a) An individual serving in a position in the competitive service under an indefinite appointment or a temporary appointment pending establishment of a register (other than an individual serving under an overseas limited appointment, or in a position classified above GS–15 pursuant to section 5108) acquires competitive status and is entitled to have his appointment converted to a career appointment, without condition, when—

(1) he completes, without break in service of more than 30 days, a total of at least 3 years of service in such a position;

(2) he passes a suitable noncompetitive examination;

(3) the appointing authority (A) recommends to the Office of Personnel Management that the appointment of the individual be converted to a career appointment and (B) certifies to the Office that the work performance of the individual for the past 12 months has been satisfactory; and

(4) he meets Office qualification requirements for the position and is otherwise eligible for career appointment.

(b) The employing agency shall terminate the appointment of an individual serving in a position in the competitive service under an indefinite or temporary appointment described in subsection (a) of this section, not later than 90 days after he has completed the 3-year period referred to in subsection (a)(1) of this section, if, prior to the close of such 90-day period, such individual has not met the requirements and conditions of subparagraphs (2) to (4), inclusive, of subsection (a) of this section.

(c) In computing years of service under subsection (a)(1) of this section for an individual who leaves a position in the competitive service to enter the armed forces and is reemployed in such a position within 120 days after separation under honorable conditions, the period from the date he leaves his position to the date he is reemployed is included.

(d) The Office of Personnel Management may prescribe regulations necessary for the administration of this section.

(Added Pub. L. 90–105, §1(a), Oct. 11, 1967, 81 Stat. 273; amended Pub. L. 91–375, §6(c)(6), Aug. 12, 1970, 84 Stat. 776; Pub. L. 95–454, title IX, §906(a)(2), (3), Oct. 13, 1978, 92 Stat. 1224; Pub. L. 101–509, title V, §529 [title I, §101(b)(9)(B)], Nov. 5, 1990, 104 Stat. 1427, 1441.)

AMENDMENTS

1990—Subsec. (a). Pub. L. 101–509, which directed the substitution of "in a position classified above GS–15 pursuant to section 5108)" for "in GS–16, 17, or 18)", was executed by making the substitution for "in GS–16, GS–17, or GS–18)", as the probable intent of Congress.

1978—Subsec. (a). Pub. L. 95–454, §906(a)(2), (3), substituted "Office of Personnel Management" and "Office" for "Civil Service Commission" and "Commission", respectively, wherever appearing.

Subsec. (d). Pub. L. 95–454, §906(a)(2), substituted "Office of Personnel Management" for "Civil Service Commission".

1970—Subsec. (a). Pub. L. 91–375 struck out ", in the postal field service," after "limited appointment" in introductory parenthetical text.

EFFECTIVE DATE OF 1990 AMENDMENT

Amendment by Pub. L. 101–509 effective on such date as the President shall determine, but not earlier than 90 days, and not later than 180 days, after Nov. 5, 1990, see section 529 [title III, § 305] of Pub. L. 101–509, set out as a note under section 5301 of this title.

EFFECTIVE DATE OF 1978 AMENDMENT

Amendment by Pub. L. 95–454 effective 90 days after Oct. 13, 1978, see section 907 of Pub. L. 95–454, set out as a note under section 1101 of this title.

EFFECTIVE DATE OF 1970 AMENDMENT

Amendment by Pub. L. 91–375 effective within 1 year after Aug. 12, 1970, on date established therefor by Board of Governors of United States Postal Service and published by it in Federal Register, see section 15(a) of Pub. L. 91–375, set out as an Effective Date note preceding section 101 of Title 39, Postal Service.

EFFECTIVE DATE

Section 4 of Pub. L. 90–105 provided that:

"(a) This section and section 3 of this Act [amending provisions set out as a note under section 3101 of this title] shall become effective on the date of enactment of this Act [Oct. 11, 1967].

"(b) Subject to subsection (c) of this section, the first section and section 2 of this Act [enacting this section and section 3303 of former Title 39, The Postal Service] shall become effective on the one hundred and twentieth day following the date of enactment of this Act [Oct. 11, 1967].

"(c) For the purpose of the application of section 3304a(b) of title 5, United States Code, as enacted by this Act, in the case of an individual who, prior to the effective date prescribed by subsection (b) of this section, shall have completed the 3-year period referred to in such section 3304a(b), such individual shall be deemed to have completed such 3-year period on such effective date."

§ 3305. Competitive service; examinations; when held

(a) The Office of Personnel Management shall hold examinations for the competitive service at least twice a year in each State and territory or possession of the United States where there are individuals to be examined.

(b) The Office shall hold an examination for a position to which an appointment has been made within the preceding 3 years, on the application of an individual who qualifies as a preference eligible under section 2108(3)(C)–(G) of this title. The examination shall be held during the quarter following the application.

(Pub. L. 89–554, Sept. 6, 1966, 80 Stat. 418; Pub. L. 90–83, § 1(8), Sept. 11, 1967, 81 Stat. 197; Pub. L. 96–54, § 2(a)(14), (15), Aug. 14, 1979, 93 Stat. 382.)

HISTORICAL AND REVISION NOTES
1966 ACT

Derivation	U.S. Code	Revised Statutes and Statutes at Large
(a)	5 U.S.C. 635 (last 24 words of 6th sentence).	Jan. 16, 1883, ch. 27, § 3 (last 24 words of 6th sentence), 22 Stat. 404.
(b)	5 U.S.C. 859.	June 27, 1944, ch. 287, § 10, 58 Stat. 390. Jan. 19, 1948, ch. 1, § 3, 62 Stat. 3. Dec. 27, 1950, ch. 1151, § 2(b), 64 Stat. 1117.

Standard changes are made to conform with the definitions applicable and the style of this title as outlined in the preface to the report.

1967 ACT

This section amends various sections [§§ 3305, 3309, 3318] of title 5, United States Code, to reflect the redesignation of paragraphs (3)(B) through (F) of section 2108 of title 5 as paragraphs (3)(C) through (G) by section 1(6) of this bill.

AMENDMENTS

1979—Subsec. (a). Pub. L. 96–54, § 2(a)(14), substituted "Office of Personnel Management" for "Civil Service Commission".

Subsec. (b). Pub. L. 96–54, § 2(a)(15), substituted "Office" for "Commission".

EFFECTIVE DATE OF 1979 AMENDMENT

Amendment by Pub. L. 96–54 effective July 12, 1979, see section 2(b) of Pub. L. 96–54, set out as a note under section 305 of this title.

SECTION REFERRED TO IN OTHER SECTIONS

This section is referred to in section 2302 of this title; title 22 section 1438; title 40 section 42.

[§ 3306. Repealed. Pub. L. 95–228, § 1, Feb. 10, 1978, 92 Stat. 25]

Section, Pub. L. 89–554, Sept. 6, 1966, 80 Stat. 419, related to apportionment of appointments in the departmental service in the District of Columbia among the States, territories, etc.

§ 3307. Competitive service; maximum-age entrance requirements; exceptions

(a) Except as provided in subsections (b), (c), (d), (e), and (f) of this section appropriated funds may not be used to pay an employee who establishes a maximum-age requirement for entrance into the competitive service.

(b) The Secretary may, with the concurrence of such agent as the President may designate, determine and fix the maximum limit of age within which an original appointment to a position as an air traffic controller may be made.

(c) The Secretary of the Interior may determine and fix the minimum and maximum limits of age within which original appointments to the United States Park Police may be made.

(d) The head of any agency may determine and fix the minimum and maximum limits of age within which an original appointment may be made to a position as a law enforcement officer or firefighter, as defined by section 8331(20) and (21), respectively, of this title.

(e) The head of an agency may determine and fix the maximum age limit for an original appointment to a position as a firefighter or law enforcement officer, as defined by section 8401(14) or (17), respectively, of this title.

(f) The Secretary of Energy may determine and fix the maximum age limit for an original appointment to a position as a nuclear materials courier, as defined by section 8331(27) or 8401(33).

(Pub. L. 89–554, Sept. 6, 1966, 80 Stat. 419; Pub. L. 92–297, § 2(a), May 16, 1972, 86 Stat. 141; Pub. L. 93–350, § 1, July 12, 1974, 88 Stat. 355; Pub. L. 96–347, § 1(b), Sept. 12, 1980, 94 Stat. 1150; Pub. L. 100–238, title I, § 103(a)(1), Jan. 8, 1988, 101 Stat. 1744; Pub. L. 105–261, div. C, title XXXI, § 3154(a), Oct. 17, 1998, 112 Stat. 2254.)

Derivation	U.S. Code	Revised Statutes and Statutes at Large
....	5 U.S.C. 638b (less proviso).	June 27, 1956, ch. 452, §302 (less proviso), 70 Stat. 355.

The prohibition is restated in positive form. The word "officers" is omitted as included in "employees" in view of the definition of "employee" in section 2105.

Standard changes are made to conform with the definitions applicable and the style of this title as outlined in the preface to the report.

REFERENCES IN TEXT

For definition of Secretary, referred to in subsec. (b), see section 2109 of this title.

AMENDMENTS

1998—Subsec. (a). Pub. L. 105–261, §3154(a)(1), substituted "(d), (e), and (f)" for "and (d)".

Subsec. (f). Pub. L. 105–261, §3154(a)(2), added subsec. (f).

1988—Subsec. (d). Pub. L. 100–238, §103(a)(1)(A), substituted "may" for "may, with the concurrence of such agent as the President may designate,".

Subsec. (e). Pub. L. 100–238, §103(a)(1)(B), added subsec. (e).

1980—Subsec. (b). Pub. L. 96–347 substituted "Secretary" for "Secretary of Transportation".

1974—Subsec. (a). Pub. L. 93–350, §1(1), inserted reference to subsec. (d).

Subsec. (d). Pub. L. 93–350, §1(2), added subsec. (d).

1972—Pub. L. 92–297 designated existing provisions as subsec. (a) and added subsecs. (b) and (c).

EFFECTIVE DATE OF 1988 AMENDMENT

Section 103(f) of Pub. L. 100–238 provided that: "This section, and the amendments made by this section [amending this section and sections 8401 and 8704 of this title and enacting provisions set out as a note under section 8334 of this title], shall be effective as of January 1, 1987."

EFFECTIVE DATE OF 1980 AMENDMENT

Amendment by Pub. L. 96–347 effective on 90th day after Sept. 12, 1980, see section 3 of Pub. L. 96–347, set out as a note under section 2109 of this title.

EFFECTIVE DATE OF 1974 AMENDMENT

Section 7 of Pub. L. 93–350 provided that: "The amendments made by the first section [amending this section], and sections 2(b), 5, and 6 [amending sections 8331, 8336, and 8339 of this title], of this Act shall become effective on the date of enactment of this Act [July 12, 1974]. The amendments made by sections 2(a) and 3 [amending sections 8331 and 8334 of this title] of this Act shall become effective at the beginning of the first applicable pay period which begins after December 31, 1974. The amendment made by section 4 of this Act [amending section 8335 of this title] shall become effective on January 1, 1978."

EFFECTIVE DATE OF 1972 AMENDMENT

Amendment by Pub. L. 92–297 effective on 90th day after May 16, 1972, see section 10 of Pub. L. 92–297, set out as an Effective Date note under section 3381 of this title.

UNITED STATES PARK POLICE; AGE LIMITS FOR ORIGINAL APPOINTMENTS

Pub. L. 91–73, Sept. 26, 1969, 83 Stat. 116, which provided for age limits for appointments to the United States Park Police, was repealed by Pub. L. 92–297, §11, May 16, 1972, 86 Stat. 145, effective at the end of the 89th day after May 16, 1972. The Secretary of the Interior may fix age limits for appointment under subsec. (c) of this section.

EX. ORD. NO. 11817. OFFICE OF PERSONNEL MANAGEMENT DESIGNATED AGENT TO CONCUR WITH AGENCY DETERMINATION FIXING AGE LIMITS FOR MAKING ORIGINAL APPOINTMENTS RESPECTING LAW ENFORCEMENT OFFICER AND FIREFIGHTER POSITIONS

Ex. Ord. No. 11817, Nov. 5, 1974, 39 F.R. 39427, as amended by Ex. Ord. No. 12107, Dec. 28, 1978, 44 F.R. 1055, provided:

By virtue of the authority vested in me by section 3307(d) of title 5 of the United States Code, as added by the first section of the Act of July 12, 1974 (Public Law 93–350; 88 Stat. 355), I hereby designate the Office of Personnel Management as the agency to concur with determinations made by agencies to fix the minimum and maximum limits of age within which an original appointment may be made to a position as a law enforcement officer or firefighter, as defined by section 8331(20) and (21), respectively, of title 5 of the United States Code. The designation made by this order shall be effective as of October 15, 1974.

§ 3308. Competitive service; examinations; educational requirements prohibited; exceptions

The Office of Personnel Management or other examining agency may not prescribe a minimum educational requirement for an examination for the competitive service except when the Office decides that the duties of a scientific, technical, or professional position cannot be performed by an individual who does not have a prescribed minimum education. The Office shall make the reasons for its decision under this section a part of its public records.

(Pub. L. 89–554, Sept. 6, 1966, 80 Stat. 419; Pub. L. 95–454, title IX, §906(a)(2), (3), Oct. 13, 1978, 92 Stat. 1224.)

HISTORICAL AND REVISION NOTES

Derivation	U.S. Code	Revised Statutes and Statutes at Large
....	5 U.S.C. 854 (less 1st 2 sentences).	June 27, 1944, ch. 287, §5 (less 1st 2 sentences), 58 Stat. 388.

The prohibition is restated in positive form. The words "The Civil Service Commission or other examining agency" are added because these are the only agencies to which the prohibition could apply.

Standard changes are made to conform with the definitions applicable and the style of this title as outlined in the preface to the report.

AMENDMENTS

1978—Pub. L. 95–454 substituted "Office of Personnel Management" and "Office" for "Civil Service Commission" and "Commission", respectively, wherever appearing.

EFFECTIVE DATE OF 1978 AMENDMENT

Amendment by Pub. L. 95–454 effective 90 days after Oct. 13, 1978, see section 907 of Pub. L. 95–454, set out as a note under section 1101 of this title.

SECTION REFERRED TO IN OTHER SECTIONS

This section is referred to in section 3320 of this title; title 22 section 1438.

§ 3309. Preference eligibles; examinations; additional points for

A preference eligible who receives a passing grade in an examination for entrance into the competitive service is entitled to additional points above his earned rating, as follows—

(1) a preference eligible under section 2108(3)(C)–(G) of this title—10 points; and

(2) a preference eligible under section 2108(3)(A)–(B) of this title—5 points.

(Pub. L. 89–554, Sept. 6, 1966, 80 Stat. 419; Pub. L. 90–83, §1(8), Sept. 11, 1967, 81 Stat. 197; Pub. L. 105–85, div. A, title XI, §1102(b), Nov. 18, 1997, 111 Stat. 1922.)

HISTORICAL AND REVISION NOTES

Derivation	U.S. Code	Revised Statutes and Statutes at Large
....	5 U.S.C. 852 (1st sentence).	June 27, 1944, ch. 287, §3 (less proviso), 58 Stat. 388. Jan. 19, 1948, ch. 1, §2, 62 Stat. 3. Dec. 27, 1950, ch. 1151, §2(a), 64 Stat. 1117. July 14, 1952, ch. 728, §2, 66 Stat. 627. Aug. 14, 1953, ch. 485, §1(a) "Sec. 3 (1st sentence)", 67 Stat. 581.

The word "competitive" is added before "service" for clarity. Application of this section to the excepted service in the executive branch and to the government of the District of Columbia, as provided in former section 858, is carried into section 3320.

Standard changes are made to conform with the definitions applicable and the style of this title as outlined in the preface to the report.

AMENDMENTS

1997—Par. (2). Pub. L. 105–85 substituted "section 2108(3)(A)–(B)" for "section 2108(3)(A)".

1967—Cl. (1). Pub. L. 90–83 substituted "section 2108(3)(C)–(G)" for "section 2108(3)(B)–(F)." See Historical and Revision Notes under section 3305 of this title.

SECTION REFERRED TO IN OTHER SECTIONS

This section is referred to in sections 2302, 3313, 3320 of this title; title 2 section 1316a; title 3 section 115; title 22 section 1438.

§ 3310. Preference eligibles; examinations; guards, elevator operators, messengers, and custodians

In examinations for positions of guards, elevator operators, messengers, and custodians in the competitive service, competition is restricted to preference eligibles as long as preference eligibles are available.

(Pub. L. 89–554, Sept. 6, 1966, 80 Stat. 420.)

HISTORICAL AND REVISION NOTES

Derivation	U.S. Code	Revised Statutes and Statutes at Large
....	5 U.S.C. 852 (2d sentence).	June 27, 1944, ch. 287, §3 (proviso), 58 Stat. 388. Aug. 14, 1953, ch. 485, §1(a) "Sec. 3 (2d sentence)", 67 Stat. 581.

The words "in the competitive service" are added for clarity. The reference to "examinations held prior to December 31, 1954, for positions of apprentices" is omitted as obsolete. Application of this section to the excepted service in the executive branch and to the government of the District of Columbia, as provided in former section 858, is carried into section 3320.

Standard changes are made to conform with the definitions applicable and the style of this title as outlined in the preface to the report.

SECTION REFERRED TO IN OTHER SECTIONS

This section is referred to in sections 2302, 3320 of this title; title 2 section 1316a; title 3 section 115; title 22 section 1438.

§ 3311. Preference eligibles; examinations; crediting experience

In examinations for the competitive service in which experience is an element of qualification, a preference eligible is entitled to credit—

(1) for service in the armed forces when his employment in a similar vocation to that for which examined was interrupted by the service; and

(2) for all experience material to the position for which examined, including experience gained in religious, civic, welfare, service, and organizational activities, regardless of whether he received pay therefor.

(Pub. L. 89–554, Sept. 6, 1966, 80 Stat. 420.)

HISTORICAL AND REVISION NOTES

Derivation	U.S. Code	Revised Statutes and Statutes at Large
....	5 U.S.C. 853.	June 27, 1944, ch. 287, §4, 58 Stat. 388.

The words "for the competitive service" are added after "examinations" for clarity. Application of this section to the excepted service in the executive branch and to the government of the District of Columbia, as provided in former section 858, is carried into section 3320.

In paragraph (1), the words "service in the armed forces" are substituted for "in the military or naval service of the United States" on authority of the Act of July 26, 1947, ch. 343, §305(a), 61 Stat. 508. The word "actual" is omitted as surplusage.

In paragraph (2), the words "material to the position for which examined" are substituted for "valuable" for clarity.

Standard changes are made to conform with the definitions applicable and the style of this title as outlined in the preface to the report.

SECTION REFERRED TO IN OTHER SECTIONS

This section is referred to in sections 2302, 3320 of this title; title 2 section 1316a; title 3 section 115; title 22 section 1438.

§ 3312. Preference eligibles; physical qualifications; waiver

(a) In determining qualifications of a preference eligible for examination for, appointment in, or reinstatement in the competitive service, the Office of Personnel Management or other examining agency shall waive—

(1) requirements as to age, height, and weight, unless the requirement is essential to the performance of the duties of the position; and

(2) physical requirements if, in the opinion of the Office or other examining agency, after considering the recommendation of an accredited physician, the preference eligible is physically able to perform efficiently the duties of the position.

(b) If an examining agency determines that, on the basis of evidence before it, a preference eligible under section 2108(3)(C) of this title who has a compensable service-connected disability of 30 percent or more is not able to fulfill the physical requirements of the position, the examining agency shall notify the Office of the determination and, at the same time, the examining agency shall notify the preference eligible of the reasons for the determination and of the right to respond, within 15 days of the date of the notification, to the Office. The Office shall require a demonstration by the appointing authority that the notification was timely sent to the preference eligible's last known address and shall, before the selection of any other person for the position, make a final determination on the physical ability of the preference eligible to perform the duties of the position, taking into account any additional information provided in any such response. When the Office has completed its review of the proposed disqualification on the basis of physical disability, it shall send its findings to the appointing authority and the preference eligible. The appointing authority shall comply with the findings of the Office. The functions of the Office under this subsection may not be delegated.

(Pub. L. 89–554, Sept. 6, 1966, 80 Stat. 420; Pub. L. 95–454, title III, § 307(c), title IX, § 906(a)(2), (3), Oct. 13, 1978, 92 Stat. 1148, 1224.)

HISTORICAL AND REVISION NOTES

Derivation	U.S. Code	Revised Statutes and Statutes at Large
....	5 U.S.C. 854 (1st 2 sentences, less so much as relates to promotion, retention, and transfer).	June 27, 1944, ch. 287, § 5 (1st 2 sentences, less so much as relates to promotion, retention, and transfer), 58 Stat. 388.

The section is restated for clarity and conciseness. The words "for which examination is given" and "for which the examination is given" are omitted as surplusage. The application of this section to the excepted service in the executive branch and the government of the District of Columbia is preserved by section 3320.

Standard changes are made to conform with the definitions applicable and the style of this title as outlined in the preface to the report.

AMENDMENTS

1978—Pub. L. 95–454 designated existing provisions as subsec. (a), substituted "Office of Personnel Management" and "Office" for "Civil Service Commission" and "Commission", respectively, and added subsec. (b).

EFFECTIVE DATE OF 1978 AMENDMENT

Amendment by Pub. L. 95–454 effective 90 days after Oct. 13, 1978, see section 907 of Pub. L. 95–454, set out as a note under section 1101 of this title.

SECTION REFERRED TO IN OTHER SECTIONS

This section is referred to in sections 2302, 3320 of this title; title 2 section 1316a; title 3 section 115; title 22 section 1438.

§ 3313. Competitive service; registers of eligibles

The names of applicants who have qualified in examinations for the competitive service shall be entered on appropriate registers or lists of eligibles in the following order—

(1) for scientific and professional positions in GS–9 or higher, in the order of their ratings, including points added under section 3309 of this title; and

(2) for all other positions—

(A) disabled veterans who have a compensable service-connected disability of 10 percent or more, in order of their ratings, including points added under section 3309 of this title; and

(B) remaining applicants, in the order of their ratings, including points added under section 3309 of this title.

The names of preference eligibles shall be entered ahead of others having the same rating.

(Pub. L. 89–554, Sept. 6, 1966, 80 Stat. 420.)

HISTORICAL AND REVISION NOTES

Derivation	U.S. Code	Revised Statutes and Statutes at Large
....	5 U.S.C. 856.	June 27, 1944, 287, § 7, 58 Stat. 389. Aug. 14, 1953, ch. 485, § 1(b), 67 Stat. 581.

The section is restated for clarity and conciseness. The words "for the competitive service" are added for clarity. Application of this section to the excepted service in the executive branch and to the government of the District of Columbia is carried into section 3320. The words "employment lists" are omitted as included in "appropriate registers or lists of eligibles".

In paragraph (1), the words "in GS–9 or higher" are substituted for "in grade 9 or higher of the General Schedule of the Classification Act of 1949, as amended" in view of the codification of the Act in this title, and, in specific sections 5104 and 5332.

In paragraph (2)(A), the term "disabled veterans" is substituted for "preference eligibles" in view of the definition of "disabled veteran" in section 2108(2).

Standard changes are made to conform with the definitions applicable and the style of this title as outlined in the preface to the report.

SECTION REFERRED TO IN OTHER SECTIONS

This section is referred to in sections 2302, 3314, 3315, 3320 of this title; title 22 section 1438.

§ 3314. Registers; preference eligibles who resigned

A preference eligible who resigns, on request to the Office of Personnel Management, is entitled to have his name placed again on all registers for which he may have been qualified, in the order named by section 3313 of this title.

(Pub. L. 89–554, Sept. 6, 1966, 80 Stat. 420; Pub. L. 95–454, title IX, § 906(a)(2), Oct. 13, 1978, 92 Stat. 1224.)

HISTORICAL AND REVISION NOTES

Derivation	U.S. Code	Revised Statutes and Statutes at Large
....	5 U.S.C. 865.	June 27, 1944, ch. 287, § 16, 58 Stat. 391.

The last 28 words of former section 865 relating to recertification and reappointments are omitted since under sections 3317 and 3318(a) certification and appointment follow from placing on registers.

Standard changes are made to conform with the definitions applicable and the style of this title as outlined in the preface to the report.

AMENDMENTS

1978—Pub. L. 95–454 substituted "Office of Personnel Management" for "Civil Service Commission".

EFFECTIVE DATE OF 1978 AMENDMENT

Amendment by Pub. L. 95–454 effective 90 days after Oct. 13, 1978, see section 907 of Pub. L. 95–454, set out as a note under section 1101 of this title.

SECTION REFERRED TO IN OTHER SECTIONS

This section is referred to in sections 2302, 3320 of this title; title 22 section 1438.

§ 3315. Registers; preference eligibles furloughed or separated

(a) A preference eligible who has been separated or furloughed without delinquency or misconduct, on request, is entitled to have his name placed on appropriate registers and employment lists for every position for which his qualifications have been established, in the order named by section 3313 of this title. This subsection applies to registers and employment lists maintained by the Office of Personnel Management, an Executive agency, or the government of the District of Columbia.

(b) The Office may declare a preference eligible who has been separated or furloughed without pay under section 7512 of this title to be entitled to the benefits of subsection (a) of this section.

(Pub. L. 89–554, Sept. 6, 1966, 80 Stat. 420; Pub. L. 96–54, § 2(a)(14), (15), Aug. 14, 1979, 93 Stat. 382.)

HISTORICAL AND REVISION NOTES

Derivation	U.S. Code	Revised Statutes and Statutes at Large
(a)	5 U.S.C. 864 (1st sentence).	June 27, 1944, ch. 287 § 15 (1st sentence), 58 Stat. 391.
(b)	5 U.S.C. 863 (2d proviso).	June 27, 1944, ch. 287, § 14 (2d proviso), 58 Stat. 391.

In subsection (a), the term "Executive agency" is substituted for "any agency or project of the Federal Government" on authority of former section 869. The last 28 words of the 1st sentence of former section 864 relating to recertification and reappointment are omitted since under sections 3317 and 3318(a) certification and appointment follow from placing on registers.

Standard changes are made to conform with the definitions applicable and the style of this title as outlined in the preface to the report.

AMENDMENTS

1979—Subsec. (a). Pub. L. 96–54, § 2(a)(14), substituted "Office of Personnel Management" for "Civil Service Commission".

Subsec. (b). Pub. L. 96–54, § 2(a)(15), substituted "Office" for "Commission".

EFFECTIVE DATE OF 1979 AMENDMENT

Amendment by Pub. L. 96–54 effective July 12, 1979, see section 2(b) of Pub. L. 96–54, set out as a note under section 305 of this title.

SECTION REFERRED TO IN OTHER SECTIONS

This section is referred to in sections 2302, 3320 of this title; title 22 section 1438.

[§ 3315a. Repealed. Pub. L. 93–416, § 22(c), Sept. 7, 1974, 88 Stat. 1150]

Section, added Pub. L. 90–83 § 1(9)(A), Sept. 11, 1967, 81 Stat. 197, related to registration by Civil Service Commission of employees receiving compensation for injuries for certification for appointment to vacant positions.

§ 3316. Preference eligibles; reinstatement

On request of an appointing authority, a preference eligible who has resigned or who has been dismissed or furloughed may be certified for, and appointed to, a position for which he is eligible in the competitive service, an Executive agency, or the government of the District of Columbia.

(Pub. L. 89–554, Sept. 6, 1966, 80 Stat. 421.)

HISTORICAL AND REVISION NOTES

Derivation	U.S. Code	Revised Statutes and Statutes at Large
....	5 U.S.C. 862.	June 27, 1944, ch. 287, § 13, 58 Stat. 390.

The word "authority" is substituted for "officer" in recognition of the several appointing authorities named in section 2105(a)(1).

The words "in the competitive service, an Executive agency, or the government of the District of Columbia" are substituted for "in the civil service, Federal, or District of Columbia, or in any establishment, agency, bureau, administration, project, or department, temporary or permanent" on authority of former section 869.

Standard changes are made to conform with the definitions applicable and the style of this title as outlined in the preface to the report.

SECTION REFERRED TO IN OTHER SECTIONS

This section is referred to in sections 2302, 3320 of this title; title 22 section 1438.

§ 3317. Competitive service; certification from registers

(a) The Office of Personnel Management shall certify enough names from the top of the appropriate register to permit a nominating or appointing authority who has requested a certificate of eligibles to consider at least three names for appointment to each vacancy in the competitive service.

(b) When an appointing authority, for reasons considered sufficient by the Office, has three times considered and passed over a preference eligible who was certified from a register, certification of the preference eligible for appointment may be discontinued. However, the preference eligible is entitled to advance notice of discontinuance of certification.

(Pub. L. 89–554, Sept. 6, 1966, 80 Stat. 421; Pub. L. 95–454, title IX, § 906(a)(3), Oct. 13, 1978, 92 Stat. 1224; Pub. L. 96–54, § 2(a)(14), (15), Aug. 14, 1979, 93 Stat. 382.)

HISTORICAL AND REVISION NOTES

Derivation	U.S. Code	Revised Statutes and Statutes at Large
....	5 U.S.C. 857 (1st sentence and 2d proviso).	June 27, 1944, ch. 287, § 8 (1st sentence and 2d proviso), 58 Stat. 389.

In subsection (a), the word "authority" is substituted for "officer" in recognition of the several appointing authorities named in section 2105(a)(1). The words "in the competitive service" have been added for clarity. Application of the section to the excepted service in the executive branch and to the government of the District of Columbia, as provided in former section 858, is carried into section 3320.

In subsection (b), the word "thereafter" is omitted as unnecessary.

Standard changes are made to conform with the definitions applicable and the style of this title as outlined in the preface to the report.

AMENDMENTS

1979—Subsec. (a). Pub. L. 96–54, § 2(a)(14), substituted "Office of Personnel Management" for "Civil Service Commission".

Subsec. (b). Pub. L. 96–54, § 2(a)(15), amended subsec. (b) in same manner as amendment by Pub. L. 95–454. See 1978 Amendment note set out below.

1978—Subsec. (b). Pub. L. 95–454 which purported to amend section 3317b of this title by substituting "Office" for "Commission" was executed to subsec. (b) of this section as the probable intent of Congress.

EFFECTIVE DATE OF 1979 AMENDMENT

Amendment by Pub. L. 96–54 effective July 12, 1979, see section 2(b) of Pub. L. 96–54, set out as a note under section 305 of this title.

EFFECTIVE DATE OF 1978 AMENDMENT

Amendment by Pub. L. 95–454 effective 90 days after Oct. 13, 1978, see section 907 of Pub. L. 95–454, set out as a note under section 1101 of this title.

SECTION REFERRED TO IN OTHER SECTIONS

This section is referred to in sections 2302, 3110, 3318, 3320, 9510 of this title; title 22 section 1438.

§ 3318. Competitive service; selection from certificates

(a) The nominating or appointing authority shall select for appointment to each vacancy from the highest three eligibles available for appointment on the certificate furnished under section 3317(a) of this title, unless objection to one or more of the individuals certified is made to, and sustained by, the Office of Personnel Management for proper and adequate reason under regulations prescribed by the Office.

(b)(1) If an appointing authority proposes to pass over a preference eligible on a certificate in order to select an individual who is not a preference eligible, such authority shall file written reasons with the Office for passing over the preference eligible. The Office shall make the reasons presented by the appointing authority part of the record of the preference eligible and may require the submission of more detailed information from the appointing authority in support of the passing over of the preference eligible. The Office shall determine the sufficiency or insufficiency of the reasons submitted by the appointing authority, taking into account any response received from the preference eligible under paragraph (2) of this subsection. When the Office has completed its review of the proposed passover, it shall send its findings to the appointing authority and to the preference eligible. The appointing authority shall comply with the findings of the Office.

(2) In the case of a preference eligible described in section 2108(3)(C) of this title who has a compensable service-connected disability of 30 percent or more, the appointing authority shall at the same time it notifies the Office under paragraph (1) of this subsection, notify the preference eligible of the proposed passover, of the reasons therefor, and of his right to respond to such reasons to the Office within 15 days of the date of such notification. The Office shall, before completing its review under paragraph (1) of this subsection, require a demonstration by the appointing authority that the passover notification was timely sent to the preference eligible's last known address.

(3) A preference eligible not described in paragraph (2) of this subsection, or his representative, shall be entitled, on request, to a copy of—

(A) the reasons submitted by the appointing authority in support of the proposed passover, and

(B) the findings of the Office.

(4) In the case of a preference eligible described in paragraph (2) of this subsection, the functions of the Office under this subsection may not be delegated.

(c) When three or more names of preference eligibles are on a reemployment list appropriate for the position to be filled, a nominating or appointing authority may appoint from a register of eligibles established after examination only an individual who qualifies as a preference eligible under section 2108(3)(C)–(G) of this title.

(Pub. L. 89–554, Sept. 6, 1966, 80 Stat. 421; Pub. L. 90–83, §1(8), Sept. 11, 1967, 81 Stat. 197; Pub. L. 95–454, title III, §307(d), title IX, §906(a)(2), (3), Oct. 13, 1978, 92 Stat. 1148, 1224.)

HISTORICAL AND REVISION NOTES

Derivation	U.S. Code	Revised Statutes and Statutes at Large
(a), (b)	5 U.S.C. 633(2)2.	Jan. 16, 1883, ch. 27, §2(2)2, 22 Stat. 404.
	5 U.S.C. 857 (less 1st sentence, 2d proviso, and last sentence).	June 27, 1944, ch. 287, §8 (less 1st sentence, 2d proviso, and last sentence), 58 Stat. 389. Aug. 14, 1953, ch. 485, §2, 67 Stat. 582.
(c)	5 U.S.C. 864 (less 1st sentence).	June 27, 1944, ch. 287, §15 (less 1st sentence), 58 Stat. 391.

The word "authority" is substituted for "officer" in recognition of the several appointing authorities named in section 2105(a)(1).

In subsection (a), the provisions of former section 633(2)2 are merged in the requirement of former section 857, since the certificate must be of the three highest on the register and the nominating or appointing employee may select one of the three.

In subsection (c), the prohibition in former section 864 is restated in positive form. The words "an individual who qualifies as a preference eligible under section 2108(3)(B)–(F)" are substituted for "ten-point preference eligibles".

Standard changes are made to conform with the definitions applicable and the style of this title as outlined in the preface to the report.

AMENDMENTS

1978—Subsec. (a). Pub. L. 95–454, §906(a)(2), (3), substituted "Office of Personnel Management" and "Office" for "Civil Service Commission" and "Commission", respectively.

Subsec. (b). Pub. L. 95–454, §307(d), designated existing provisions as par. (1), substituted provisions respecting authority of the Office with respect to the selection procedures applicable, for provisions respecting authority of the Commission with respect to the selection procedures applicable, and added pars. (2) to (4).

1967—Subsec. (c). Pub. L. 90–83 substituted "section 2108(3)(C)–(G)" for "section 2108(3)(B)–(F)." See Historical and Revision Notes under section 3305 of this title.

EFFECTIVE DATE OF 1978 AMENDMENT

Amendment by Pub. L. 95–454 effective 90 days after Oct. 13, 1978, see section 907 of Pub. L. 95–454, set out as a note under section 1101 of this title.

SECTION REFERRED TO IN OTHER SECTIONS

This section is referred to in sections 2302, 3320, 9510 of this title; title 22 section 1438.

[§ 3319. Repealed. Pub. L. 95–454, title III, § 307(h)(1), Oct. 13, 1978, 92 Stat. 1149]

Section, Pub. L. 89–554, Sept. 6, 1966, 80 Stat. 421, related to prohibitions on employment of members of same family in the competitive service.

EFFECTIVE DATE OF REPEAL

Repeal effective 90 days after Oct. 13, 1978, see section 907 of Pub. L. 95–454, set out as an Effective Date of 1978 Amendment note under section 1101 of this title.

§ 3320. Excepted service; government of the District of Columbia; selection

The nominating or appointing authority shall select for appointment to each vacancy in the excepted service in the executive branch and in the government of the District of Columbia from the qualified applicants in the same manner and under the same conditions required for the competitive service by sections 3308–3318 of this title. This section does not apply to an appointment required by Congress to be confirmed by, or made with the advice and consent of, the Senate.

(Pub. L. 89–554, Sept. 6, 1966, 80 Stat. 422.)

HISTORICAL AND REVISION NOTES

Derivation	U.S. Code	Revised Statutes and Statutes at Large
....	5 U.S.C. 858.	June 27, 1944, ch. 287, § 9, 58 Stat. 389.
....	5 U.S.C. 869.	June 27, 1944, ch. 287, § 20, 58 Stat. 391.

Former sections 858 and 869 are combined and restated for clarity and to conform to section 3318(a). The word "authority" is substituted for "officer" in recognition of the several appointing authorities named in section 2105(a)(1). The words "shall select for appointment to each vacancy in the expected service in the executive branch and in the government of the District of Columbia from the qualified applicants in the same manner and under the same conditions required for the competitive service by sections 3308–3318 of this title" are substituted for "In the unclassified Federal, and District of Columbia, civil service, and in all other positions and employment hereinbefore referred to in (c) of section 851 of this title . . . shall make selection from the qualified applicants in accordance with the provisions of this chapter". The reference to the excepted service "in the executive branch" is substituted for the exception of the legislative and judicial branches in former section 869. Former section 869 did not prohibit the application of those provisions of the Act of June 27, 1944, which relate to the competitive service in the legislative or judicial branch by reason of the specific provisions of section 311 of the Act of June 10, 1921, as amended (31 U.S.C. 52); 28 U.S.C. 602; and Executive Order No. 67 of June 13, 1895. The reference to appointments of postmasters is omitted from this section since those referred to are in the competitive service. The application of former section 869 to the remainder of the Act of June 27, 1944, is covered by the sections into which the remainder is carried (see Table I).

This section merely continues, and does not in any way change, the requirements in former section 858 relative to the selection of applicants for positions in the excepted service. Under this section, the Federal Bureau of Investigation and other agencies having positions in the excepted service will continue to fill those positions in the same manner that they have been filled under former section 858. Such excepted appointments are appointments authorized to be made without regard to the statutes, rules, and regulations governing appointments in the competitive service and this is not changed.

Standard changes are made to conform with the definitions applicable and the style of this title as outlined in the preface to the report.

ASSISTANCE OF UNITED STATES CIVIL SERVICE COMMISSION IN DEVELOPING MERIT SYSTEM FOR DISTRICT OF COLUMBIA

Pub. L. 93–198, title VII, § 734, Dec. 24, 1973, 87 Stat. 823, authorized the United States Civil Service Commission to advise and assist the District of Columbia Mayor and Council in the further development of the merit system or systems required by the District of Columbia charter, which was approved on May 7, 1974, and authorized the Commission to enter into agreements with the District government to make available its registers of eligibles as a recruiting source to fill District positions as needed, with the costs of any specific services furnished by the Civil Service Commission to be compensated for under the provisions of section 685a of former Title 31, Money and Finance [31 U.S.C. 1537].

SECTION REFERRED TO IN OTHER SECTIONS

This section is referred to in section 2302 of this title; title 22 section 1438.

§ 3321. Competitive service; probationary period

(a) The President may take such action, including the issuance of rules, regulations, and directives, as shall provide as nearly as conditions of good administration warrant for a period of probation—

   (1) before an appointment in the competitive service becomes final; and

   (2) before initial appointment as a supervisor or manager becomes final.

(b) An individual—

   (1) who has been transferred, assigned, or promoted from a position to a supervisory or managerial position, and

   (2) who does not satisfactorily complete the probationary period under subsection (a)(2) of this section,

shall be returned to a position of no lower grade and pay than the position from which the individual was transferred, assigned, or promoted. Nothing in this section prohibits an agency from taking an action against an individual serving a probationary period under subsection (a)(2) of this section for cause unrelated to supervisory or managerial performance.

(c) Subsections (a) and (b) of this section shall not apply with respect to appointments in the Senior Executive Service or the Federal Bureau of Investigation and Drug Enforcement Administration Senior Executive Service.

(Pub. L. 89–554, Sept. 6, 1966, 80 Stat. 422; Pub. L. 95–454, title III, § 303(a), Oct. 13, 1978, 92 Stat. 1146; Pub. L. 100–325, § 2(d), May 30, 1988, 102 Stat. 581.)

HISTORICAL AND REVISION NOTES

Derivation	U.S. Code	Revised Statutes and Statutes at Large
....	5 U.S.C. 633(2)4.	Jan. 16, 1883, ch. 27. § 2(2)4, 22 Stat. 404.

The authority of the President to prescribe rules is added on authority of former section 633(1), which is carried into section 3302. Wording is changed because in practice an appointment is not made after probation. The words "or employment" are omitted as included within "appointment".

Standard changes are made to conform with the definitions applicable and the style of this title as outlined in the preface to the report.

1988—Subsec. (c). Pub. L. 100–325 inserted reference to Federal Bureau of Investigation and Drug Enforcement Administration Senior Executive Service.

1978—Pub. L. 95–454 substituted "probationary period" for "probation; period of" in section catchline, designated existing provisions as subsec. (a), substituted provisions authorizing the President to take necessary action, for provisions authorizing the President to prescribe rules, and added subsecs. (b) and (c).

EFFECTIVE DATE OF 1978 AMENDMENT

Amendment by Pub. L. 95–454 effective 90 days after Oct. 13, 1978, see section 907 of Pub. L. 95–454, set out as a note under section 1101 of this title.

SECTION REFERRED TO IN OTHER SECTIONS

This section is referred to in sections 3302, 4303, 7512, 9510 of this title.

[§ 3322. Repealed. Pub. L. 95–256, § 5(b)(1), Apr. 6, 1978, 92 Stat. 191]

Section, Pub. L. 89–554, Sept. 6, 1966, 80 Stat. 422, related to temporary appointments after age 70 in the competitive service.

EFFECTIVE DATE OF REPEAL

Repeal effective Sept. 30, 1978, see section 5(f) of Pub. L. 95–256, set out as an Effective Date of 1978 Amendment note under section 633a of Title 29, Labor.

§ 3323. Automatic separations; reappointment; reemployment of annuitants

(a) An individual who reaches the retirement age prescribed for automatic separation applicable to him may not be continued in the civil service or in the government of the District of Columbia. An individual separated on account of age under a statute or regulation providing for retirement on account of age is not eligible for appointment in the civil service or in the government of the District of Columbia. The President, when in his judgment the public interest so requires, may except an individual from this subsection by Executive order. This subsection does not apply to an individual named by a statute providing for the continuance of the individual in the civil service or in the government of the District of Columbia.

(b)(1) Notwithstanding other statutes, an annuitant, as defined by section 8331 or 8401, receiving annuity from the Civil Service Retirement and Disability Fund is not barred by reason of his retired status from employment in an appointive position for which the annuitant is qualified. An annuitant so reemployed, other than an annuitant reappointed under paragraph (2) of this subsection, serves at the will of the appointing authority.

(2) Subject to such regulations as the Director of the Office of Personnel Management may prescribe, any annuitant to whom the first sentence of paragraph (1) of this subsection applies and who has served as an administrative law judge pursuant to an appointment under section 3105 of this title may be reappointed an administrative law judge under such section for a specified period or for such period as may be necessary for such administrative law judge to conduct and complete the hearing and disposition of one or more specified cases. The provisions of this title that apply to or with respect to administrative law judges appointed under section 3105 of this title shall apply to or with respect to administrative law judges reappointed under such section pursuant to the first sentence of this paragraph.

(c) Notwithstanding subsection (a) of this section, a member of the Foreign Service retired under section 812 of the Foreign Service Act of 1980 is not barred by reason of his retired status from employment in a position in the civil service for which he is qualified. An annuitant so reemployed serves at the will of the appointing authority.

(d) Notwithstanding subsection (a) of this section, the Chief of Engineers of the Army, under section 569a of title 33, may employ a retired employee whose expert assistance is needed in connection with river and harbor or flood control works. There shall be deducted from the pay of an employee so reemployed an amount equal to the annuity or retired pay allocable to the period of actual employment.

(Pub. L. 89–554, Sept. 6, 1966, 80 Stat. 422; Pub. L. 96–465, title II, § 2314(a), Oct. 17, 1980, 94 Stat. 2167; Pub. L. 98–224, § 2, Mar. 2, 1984, 98 Stat. 47; Pub. L. 102–378, § 2(10), Oct. 2, 1992, 106 Stat. 1347.)

HISTORICAL AND REVISION NOTES

Derivation	U.S. Code	Revised Statutes and Statutes at Large
(a)	5 U.S.C. 715a.	June 30, 1932, ch. 314, § 204, 47 Stat. 404.
(b)	5 U.S.C. 2263(a).	July 31, 1956, ch. 804, § 401 "Sec. 13(a)", 70 Stat. 757.
(c)	22 U.S.C. 915(c).	Sept. 8, 1960, Pub. L. 86–723, § 10(d), 74 Stat. 832.
(d)	33 U.S.C. 544a, 701l.	June 20, 1938, ch. 535, § 5, 52 Stat. 805.

In subsection (a), the words "On and after July 1, 1932" are omitted as executed. The words "heretofore or hereafter" are omitted as unnecessary. The words "in the civil service" are substituted for "civilian service in any branch or service of the United States Government" and "to any appointive office, position, or employment under the United States" in view of the definition of "civil service" in section 2101.

In subsection (b), the words "receiving annuity from the Civil Service Retirement and Disability Fund" are substituted for "heretofore or hereafter retired under this chapter". The word "authority" is substituted for "officer" in recognition of the several appointing authorities named in section 2105(a)(1).

In subsection (c), the words "Notwithstanding subsection (a) of this section" are substituted for "Notwithstanding the provisions of sections 62 and 715a of title 5" to reflect the codification of former section 715a in subsection (a) of this section and in view of the repeal of section 62 of title 5 by § 402(a)(7) of the Act of Aug. 19, 1964, Pub. L. 88–448, 78 Stat. 492. The words "heretofore or hereafter" and "hereafter" are omitted as unnecessary. The words "in a position in the civil service" are substituted for "in Federal Government service in any appointive position" in view of the definition of "civil service" in section 2101. The word "authority" is substituted for "officer" in recognition of the several appointing authorities named in section 2105(a)(1).

In subsection (d), the words "Notwithstanding subsection (a) of this section" are substituted for "The provisions of section 715a of title 5 shall not be so construed as to prevent" to reflect the codification of former section 715a in subsection (a) of this section, and to conform to the style of this section. The words "under section 569a of title 33" are substituted for "under agreement as authorized by sections 569a, 584a and 607a of title 33'' on authority of the provision contained in section 569a of title 33. The word ''employee'' is coextensive with and substituted for ''civilian employee'' in view of the definition of ''employee'' in section 2105. The last sentence is restated for clarity.

Standard changes are made to conform with the definitions applicable and the style of this title as outlined in the preface to the report.

REFERENCES IN TEXT

Section 812 of the Foreign Service Act of 1980, referred to in subsec. (c), is classified to section 4052 of Title 22, Foreign Relations and Intercourse.

AMENDMENTS

1992—Subsec. (b)(1). Pub. L. 102–378 substituted ''annuitant, as defined by section 8331 or 8401,'' for ''annuitant as defined by section 8331 of this title''.

1984—Subsec. (b). Pub. L. 98–224 designated existing provisions as par. (1), substituted ''the annuitant'' for ''he'' and inserted '', other than an annuitant reappointed under paragraph (2) of this subsection,'', and added par. (2).

1980—Subsec. (c). Pub. L. 96–465 substituted ''member of the Foreign Service retired under section 812 of the Foreign Service Act of 1980'' for ''Foreign Service officer retired under section 1001 or 1002 of title 22 or a Foreign Service staff officer or employee retired under section 1063 of title 22''.

EFFECTIVE DATE OF 1980 AMENDMENT

Amendment by Pub. L. 96–465 effective Feb. 15, 1981, except as otherwise provided, see section 2403 of Pub. L. 96–465, set out as an Effective Date note under section 3901 of Title 22, Foreign Relations and Intercourse.

SECTION REFERRED TO IN OTHER SECTIONS

This section is referred to in title 22 sections 2386, 2512.

§ 3324. Appointments to positions classified above GS–15

(a) An appointment to a position classified above GS–15 pursuant to section 5108 may be made only on approval of the qualifications of the proposed appointee by the Office of Personnel Management. This section does not apply to a position—

(1) to which appointment is made by the Chief Judge of the United States Tax Court;

(2) to which appointment is made by the President;

(3) to which appointment is made by the Librarian of Congress; or

(4) the incumbent of which is paid from—

(A) appropriations for the Executive Office of the President under the heading ''The White House Office'', ''Special Projects'', ''Council of Economic Advisers'', or ''National Security Council''; or

(B) funds appropriated to the President under the heading ''Emergency Fund for the President'' by the Treasury, Post Office, and Executive Office Appropriation Act, 1966, or a later statute making appropriations for the same purpose.

(b) The Office may prescribe regulations necessary for the administration of this section.

(Pub. L. 89–554, Sept. 6, 1966, 80 Stat. 422; Pub. L. 90–83, § 1(10), Sept. 11, 1967, 81 Stat. 197; Pub. L. 95–454, title IX, § 906(a)(2), (3), Oct. 13, 1978, 92 Stat. 1224; Pub. L. 96–54, § 2(a)(17), Aug. 14, 1979, 93 Stat. 382; Pub. L. 101–509, title V, § 529 [title I,

§ 101(b)(9)(C)(i), (ii)], Nov. 5, 1990, 104 Stat. 1427, 1441; Pub. L. 102–378, § 2(11), Oct. 2, 1992, 106 Stat. 1347.)

HISTORICAL AND REVISION NOTES
1966 ACT

Derivation	U.S. Code	Revised Statutes and Statutes at Large
....	5 U.S.C. 1105(i).	June 20, 1958, Pub. L. 85–462, § 10 ''(i)'', 72 Stat. 213. Sept. 13, 1960, Pub. L. 86–768, 74 Stat. 910.

In subsection (a), the words ''in GS–16, 17, and 18'' are substituted for ''in grades 16, 17, and 18 of the General Schedule''.

In subsection (a)(2), the words ''by the President'' are coextensive with and substituted for ''by the President alone or by the President by and with the advice and consent of the Senate''.

In subsection (a)(4)(A), the words ''Office of Emergency Planning'' are substituted for ''Office of Defense Mobilization'' on authority of 1958 Reorg. Plan No. 1, § 2(a), effective July 1, 1958, 72 Stat. 1799, as amended Aug. 26, 1958, Pub. L. 85–763, 72 Stat. 861, and Sept. 22, 1961, Pub. L. 87–296, 75 Stat. 630. Reference to ''President's Advisory Committee on Government Organization'' is omitted since the Committee was abolished by Executive Order No. 10917, February 10, 1961.

In subsection (a)(4)(B), the words '' 'Emergency Fund for the President' by the Treasury, Post Office, and Executive Office Appropriation Act, 1966'' are substituted for '' 'Emergency Fund for the President, National Defense' by the General Government Matters Appropriation Act, 1959'' to reflect the heading and title of the current appropriation Act.

Subsection (b) is added on authority of former sections 1072 and 1072a, which are carried into section 5115.

Standard changes are made to conform with the definitions applicable and the style of this title as outlined in the preface to the report.

1967 ACT

This section amends 5 U.S.C. 3324(a)(4)(A) to correct typographical errors.

REFERENCES IN TEXT

The Treasury, Post Office, and Executive Office Appropriation Act, 1966, referred to in subsec. (a)(4)(B), is Pub. L. 89–57, June 30, 1965, 79 Stat. 196. For classification of this Act to the Code, see Tables.

AMENDMENTS

1992—Pub. L. 102–378, § 2(11)(A), substituted ''GS–15'' for ''GA–15'' in section catchline.

Subsec. (a)(1). Pub. L. 102–378, § 2(11)(B), amended par. (1) generally. Prior to amendment, par. (1) read as follows: ''provided for in section 5108(c)(2) of this title;''.

1990—Pub. L. 101–509, § 529 [title I, § 101(b)(9)(C)(ii)], which directed that ''to positions classified above GA–15'' be substituted for ''at GS–16, 17, or 18'' in section catchline, was executed by making the substitution for ''at GS–16, 17, and 18'', as the probable intent of Congress.

Subsec. (a). Pub. L. 101–509, § 529 [title I, § 101(b)(9)(C)(i)], substituted ''classified above GS–15 pursuant to section 5108'' for ''in GS–16, 17, or 18''.

1979—Subsec. (a)(4)(A). Pub. L. 96–54 struck out reference to Office of Emergency Planning.

1978—Subsecs. (a), (b). Pub. L. 95–454 substituted ''Office of Personnel Management'' for ''Civil Service Commission'' and ''Office'' for ''Commission''.

EFFECTIVE DATE OF 1992 AMENDMENT

Amendment by Pub. L. 102–378 effective May 4, 1991, see section 9(b)(4) of Pub. L. 102–378, set out as a note under section 6303 of this title.

Amendment by Pub. L. 101–509 effective on such date as the President shall determine, but not earlier than 90 days, and not later than 180 days, after Nov. 5, 1990, see section 529 [title III, § 305] of Pub. L. 101–509, set out as a note under section 5301 of this title.

EFFECTIVE DATE OF 1979 AMENDMENT

Amendment by Pub. L. 96–54 effective July 12, 1979, see section 2(b) of Pub. L. 96–54, set out as a note under section 305 of this title.

EFFECTIVE DATE OF 1978 AMENDMENT

Amendment by Pub. L. 95–454 effective 90 days after Oct. 13, 1978, see section 907 of Pub. L. 95–454, set out as a note under section 1101 of this title.

EFFECTIVE DATE OF 1967 AMENDMENT

Amendment by Pub. L. 90–83 effective as of Sept. 6, 1966, for all purposes, see section 9(h) of Pub. L. 90–83, set out as a note under section 5102 of this title.

SECTION REFERRED TO IN OTHER SECTIONS

This section is referred to in sections 1204, 1212, 7204 of this title; title 10 sections 4540, 7212, 9540; title 20 section 3461; title 42 section 7231.

§ 3325. Appointments to scientific and professional positions

(a) Positions established under section 3104 of this title are in the competitive service. However, appointments to the positions are made without competitive examination on approval of the qualifications of the proposed appointee by the Office of Personnel Management or its designee for this purpose.

(b) This section does not apply to positions established under section 3104(c).

(Pub. L. 89–554, Sept. 6, 1966, 80 Stat. 423; Pub. L. 95–454, title IX, § 906(a)(2), Oct. 13, 1978, 92 Stat. 1224; Pub. L. 102–378, § 2(12), Oct. 2, 1992, 106 Stat. 1347.)

HISTORICAL AND REVISION NOTES

Derivation	U.S. Code	Revised Statutes and Statutes at Large
(a)	5 U.S.C. 1162(a).	Oct. 4, 1961, Pub. L. 87–367, § 202 "Sec. 2(a)", 75 Stat. 790.
(b)	5 U.S.C. 1161 (g) (2d sentence).	Oct. 11, 1962, Pub. L. 87–793, § 1001(a)(2) "(g) (2d sentence)", 76 Stat. 863.

In subsection (a), the words "or its designee" are substituted for "or such officers or agents as the Commission may designate".

For repeal of the Act of Aug. 1, 1947, ch. 433, 61 Stat. 715, as amended, see revision note for section 3104.

Standard changes are made to conform with the definitions applicable and the style of this title as outlined in the preface to the report.

AMENDMENTS

1992—Subsec. (b). Pub. L. 102–378 substituted "section 3104(c)" for "section 3104(a)(7) of this title".

1978—Subsec. (a). Pub. L. 95–454 substituted "Office of Personnel Management" for "Civil Service Commission".

EFFECTIVE DATE OF 1978 AMENDMENT

Amendment by Pub. L. 95–454 effective 90 days after Oct. 13, 1978, see section 907 of Pub. L. 95–454, set out as a note under section 1101 of this title.

§ 3326. Appointments of retired members of the armed forces to positions in the Department of Defense

(a) For the purpose of this section, "member" and "Secretary concerned" have the meanings given them by section 101 of title 37.

(b) A retired member of the armed forces may be appointed to a position in the civil service in or under the Department of Defense (including a nonappropriated fund instrumentality under the jurisdiction of the armed forces) during the period of 180 days immediately after his retirement only if—

(1) the proposed appointment is authorized by the Secretary concerned or his designee for the purpose, and, if the position is in the competitive service, after approval by the Office of Personnel Management;

(2) the minimum rate of basic pay for the position has been increased under section 5305 of this title; or

(3) a state of national emergency exists.

(c) A request by appropriate authority for the authorization, or the authorization and approval, as the case may be, required by subsection (b)(1) of this section shall be accompanied by a statement which shows the actions taken to assure that—

(1) full consideration, in accordance with placement and promotion procedures of the department concerned, was given to eligible career employees;

(2) when selection is by other than certification from an established civil service register, the vacancy has been publicized to give interested candidates an opportunity to apply;

(3) qualification requirements for the position have not been written in a manner designed to give advantage to the retired member; and

(4) the position has not been held open pending the retirement of the retired member.

(Pub. L. 89–554, Sept. 6, 1966, 80 Stat. 423; Pub. L. 96–54, § 2(a)(14), Aug. 14, 1979, 93 Stat. 382; Pub. L. 101–509, title V, § 529 [title I, § 101(b)(3)(A)], Nov. 5, 1990, 104 Stat. 1427, 1439.)

HISTORICAL AND REVISION NOTES

Derivation	U.S. Code	Revised Statutes and Statutes at Large
(a)	5 U.S.C. 3101 (as applicable to 5 U.S.C. 3103).	Aug. 19, 1964, Pub. L. 88–448, § 101 (as applicable to § 204), 78 Stat. 484.
(b), (c)	5 U.S.C. 3103.	Aug. 19, 1964, Pub. L. 88–448, § 204, 78 Stat. 487.

In subsection (a), the definition of "armed forces" is omitted as unnecessary in view of the definition in section 2101.

In subsection (b), the words "position in the civil service" are substituted for "civilian office" in view of the definition of "civil service" in section 2101. The words "(including a nonappropriated fund instrumentality under the jurisdiction of the armed forces)" are added on authority of former section 3101(3).

Standard changes are made to conform with the definitions applicable and the style of this title as outlined in the preface to the report.

AMENDMENTS

1990—Subsec. (b)(2). Pub. L. 101–509 substituted "5305" for "5303".

1979—Subsec. (b)(1). Pub. L. 96–54 substituted "Office of Personnel Management" for "Civil Service Commission".

SUSPENSION OF SECTION

Pub. L. 101–510, div. A, title XII, §1206(f), Nov. 5, 1990, 104 Stat. 1661, provided that: "Section 3326 of title 5, United States Code, shall not be in effect for the period beginning on the date of the enactment of this Act [Nov. 5, 1990] and ending two years after such date."

EFFECTIVE DATE OF 1990 AMENDMENT

Amendment by Pub. L. 101–509 effective on such date as the President shall determine, but not earlier than 90 days, and not later than 180 days, after Nov. 5, 1990, see section 529 [title III, §305] of Pub. L. 101–509, set out as a note under section 5301 of this title.

EFFECTIVE DATE OF 1979 AMENDMENT

Amendment by Pub. L. 96–54 effective July 12, 1979, see section 2(b) of Pub. L. 96–54, set out as a note under section 305 of this title.

§ 3327. Civil service employment information

(a) The Office of Personnel Management shall provide that information concerning opportunities to participate in competitive examinations conducted by, or under authority delegated by, the Office of Personnel Management shall be made available to the employment offices of the United States Employment Service.

(b) Subject to such regulations as the Office may issue, each agency shall promptly notify the Office and the employment offices of the United States Employment Service of—

(1) each vacant position in the agency which is in the competitive service or the Senior Executive Service and for which the agency seeks applications from persons outside the Federal service, and

(2) the period during which applications will be accepted.

As used in this subsection, "agency" means an agency as defined in section 5102(a)(1) of this title other than an agency all the positions in which are excepted by statute from the competitive service.

(Added Pub. L. 95–454, title III, §309(a), Oct. 13, 1978, 92 Stat. 1151.)

PRIOR PROVISIONS

A prior section 3327, Pub. L. 89–554, Sept. 6, 1966, 80 Stat. 424, which prescribed standards for determination of qualifications of postmasters, including experience in postal field service, seniority, length of service, level of difficulty and responsibility of work, attendance, awards and commendations, and performance rating, was repealed by Pub. L. 91–375, §6(c)(7)(A), Aug. 12, 1970, 84 Stat. 776. See section 1001 of Title 39, Postal Service.

EFFECTIVE DATE

Section effective 90 days after Oct. 13, 1978, see section 907 of Pub. L. 95–454, set out as an Effective Date of 1978 Amendment note under section 1101 of this title.

SECTION REFERRED TO IN OTHER SECTIONS

This section is referred to in sections 3304, 3330 of this title.

§ 3328. Selective Service registration

(a) An individual—

(1) who was born after December 31, 1959, and is or was required to register under section 3 of the Military Selective Service Act (50 U.S.C. App. 453); and

(2) who is not so registered or knowingly and willfully did not so register before the requirement terminated or became inapplicable to the individual,

shall be ineligible for appointment to a position in an Executive agency.

(b) The Office of Personnel Management, in consultation with the Director of the Selective Service System, shall prescribe regulations to carry out this section. Such regulations shall include provisions prescribing procedures for the adjudication of determinations of whether a failure to register was knowing and willful. Such procedures shall require that such a determination may not be made if the individual concerned shows by a preponderance of the evidence that the failure to register was neither knowing nor willful. Such procedures may provide that determinations of eligibility under the requirements of this section shall be adjudicated by the Executive agency making the appointment for which the eligibility is determined.

(Added Pub. L. 99–145, title XVI, §1622(a)(1), Nov. 8, 1985, 99 Stat. 777; amended Pub. L. 100–180, div. A, title XII, §1249, Dec. 4, 1987, 101 Stat. 1167.)

AMENDMENTS

1987—Subsec. (b). Pub. L. 100–180 struck out "within the Office" after "for the adjudication" in second sentence and inserted at end "Such procedures may provide that determinations of eligibility under the requirements of this section shall be adjudicated by the Executive agency making the appointment for which the eligibility is determined."

SECTION REFERRED TO IN OTHER SECTIONS

This section is referred to in title 38 section 7403.

§ 3329. Appointments of military reserve technicians to positions in the competitive service

(a) For the purpose of this section, the term "military reserve technician" has the meaning given the term "military technician (dual status)" by section 8401(30).

(b) The Secretary of Defense shall take such steps as may be necessary to ensure that, except as provided in subsection (d), any military reserve technician who is involuntarily separated from technician service, after completing at least 15 years of such service and 20 years of service creditable under section 12732 of title 10, by reason of ceasing to satisfy the condition described in section 8401(30)(B)[1] shall, if appropriate written application is submitted within 1 year after the date of separation, be provided placement consideration in a position described in subsection (c) through a priority placement program of the Department of Defense.

(c)(1) The position for which placement consideration shall be provided to a former military technician under subsection (b) shall be a position—

(A) in either the competitive service or the excepted service;

(B) within the Department of Defense; and

(C) in which the person is qualified to serve, taking into consideration whether the em-

[1] See References in Text note below.

ployee in that position is required to be a member of a reserve component of the armed forces as a condition of employment.

(2) To the maximum extent practicable, the position shall also be in a pay grade or other pay classification sufficient to ensure that the rate of basic pay of the former military technician, upon appointment to the position, is not less than the rate of basic pay last received by the former military technician for technician service before separation.

(d) This section shall not apply in the case of—

(1) an involuntary separation for cause on charges of misconduct or delinquency; or

(2) a technician who, as of the date of application under this section, is eligible for immediate (including for disability) or early retirement under subchapter III of chapter 83 or under chapter 84.

(e) The Secretary of Defense shall, in consultation with the Director of the Office of Personnel Management, prescribe such regulations as may be necessary to carry out this section.

(Added Pub. L. 102–484, div. A, title V, § 544(a), Oct. 23, 1992, 106 Stat. 2415; amended Pub. L. 104–106, div. A, title X, § 1037(a), Feb. 10, 1996, 110 Stat. 431; Pub. L. 105–85, div. A, title XI, § 1103, Nov. 18, 1997, 111 Stat. 1923; Pub. L. 106–398, § 1 [[div. A], title X, § 1087(f)(1)], Oct. 30, 2000, 114 Stat. 1654, 1654A–293.)

REFERENCES IN TEXT

Section 8401(30) of this title, referred to in subsecs. (a) and (b), was amended generally by Pub. L. 106–65, div. A, title V, § 522(c)(2), Oct. 5, 1999, 113 Stat. 597, and, as so amended, no longer contains a subpar. (B).

CODIFICATION

Another section 3329 was renumbered section 3330 of this title.

AMENDMENTS

2000—Subsec. (a). Pub. L. 106–398, § 1 [[div. A], title X, § 1087(f)(1)(A)], substituted "the term 'military technician (dual status)'" for "such term".

Subsec. (b). Pub. L. 106–398, § 1 [[div. A], title X, § 1087(f)(1)(B)], substituted "section 12732 of title 10" for "section 1332 of title 10".

1997—Subsec. (b). Pub. L. 105–85 struck out "a position described in subsection (c) not later than 6 months after the date of the application" after "program of the Department of Defense".

1996—Subsec. (b). Pub. L. 104–106, § 1037(a)(1), substituted "be provided placement consideration in a position described in subsection (c) through a priority placement program of the Department of Defense" for "be offered".

Subsec. (c). Pub. L. 104–106, § 1037(a)(2), added subsec. (c) and struck out former subsec. (c) which read as follows: "The position to be offered shall be a position—

"(1) in the competitive service;

"(2) within the Department of Defense;

"(3) for which the individual is qualified; and

"(4) the rate of basic pay for which is not less than the rate last received for technician service before separation."

§ 3330. Government-wide list of vacant positions

(a) For the purpose of this section, the term "agency" means an Executive agency, excluding the General Accounting Office and any agency (or unit thereof) whose principal function is the conduct of foreign intelligence or counter-

intelligence activities, as determined by the President.

(b) The Office of Personnel Management shall establish and keep current a comprehensive list of all announcements of vacant positions in the competitive service within each agency that are to be filled by appointment for more than one year and for which applications are being (or will soon be) accepted from outside the agency's work force.

(c) Included for any position listed shall be—

(1) a brief description of the position, including its title, tenure, location, and rate of pay;

(2) application procedures, including the period within which applications may be submitted and procedures for obtaining additional information; and

(3) any other information which the Office considers appropriate.

(d) The list shall be available to members of the public.

(e) The Office shall prescribe such regulations as may be necessary to carry out this section. Any requirement under this section that agencies notify the Office as to the availability of any vacant positions shall be designed so as to avoid any duplication of information otherwise required to be furnished under section 3327 of this title or any other provision of law.

(f) The Office may, to the extent it determines appropriate, charge such fees to agencies for services provided under this section and for related Federal employment information. The Office shall retain such fees to pay the costs of providing such services and information.

(Added Pub. L. 102–484, div. D, title XLIV, § 4431(a), Oct. 23, 1992, 106 Stat. 2719, § 3329; renumbered § 3330 and amended Pub. L. 104–52, title IV, § 4(1), Nov. 19, 1995, 109 Stat. 490; Pub. L. 104–106, div. A, title X, § 1037(b)(1), Feb. 10, 1996, 110 Stat. 432.)

AMENDMENTS

1996—Pub. L. 104–106, which directed renumbering of the section 3329 of this title that was added by Pub. L. 102–484, § 4431, as section 3330 of this title, could not be executed because of the intervening renumbering of that section by Pub. L. 104–52, § 4(1)(A). See 1995 Amendment note below.

1995—Pub. L. 104–52, § 4(1)(A), renumbered section 3329 of this title, relating to government-wide list of vacant positions, as this section.

Subsec. (f). Pub. L. 104–52, § 4(1)(B), added subsec. (f).

§ 3330a. Preference eligibles; administrative redress

(a)(1) A preference eligible who alleges that an agency has violated such individual's rights under any statute or regulation relating to veterans' preference may file a complaint with the Secretary of Labor.

(2)(A) A complaint under this subsection must be filed within 60 days after the date of the alleged violation.

(B) Such complaint shall be in writing, be in such form as the Secretary may prescribe, specify the agency against which the complaint is filed, and contain a summary of the allegations that form the basis for the complaint.

(3) The Secretary shall, upon request, provide technical assistance to a potential complainant

with respect to a complaint under this subsection.

(b)(1) The Secretary of Labor shall investigate each complaint under subsection (a).

(2) In carrying out any investigation under this subsection, the Secretary's duly authorized representatives shall, at all reasonable times, have reasonable access to, for purposes of examination, and the right to copy and receive, any documents of any person or agency that the Secretary considers relevant to the investigation.

(3) In carrying out any investigation under this subsection, the Secretary may require by subpoena the attendance and testimony of witnesses and the production of documents relating to any matter under investigation. In case of disobedience of the subpoena or contumacy and on request of the Secretary, the Attorney General may apply to any district court of the United States in whose jurisdiction such disobedience or contumacy occurs for an order enforcing the subpoena.

(4) Upon application, the district courts of the United States shall have jurisdiction to issue writs commanding any person or agency to comply with the subpoena of the Secretary or to comply with any order of the Secretary made pursuant to a lawful investigation under this subsection and the district courts shall have jurisdiction to punish failure to obey a subpoena or other lawful order of the Secretary as a contempt of court.

(c)(1)(A) If the Secretary of Labor determines as a result of an investigation under subsection (b) that the action alleged in a complaint under subsection (a) occurred, the Secretary shall attempt to resolve the complaint by making reasonable efforts to ensure that the agency specified in the complaint complies with applicable provisions of statute or regulation relating to veterans' preference.

(B) The Secretary of Labor shall make determinations referred to in subparagraph (A) based on a preponderance of the evidence.

(2) If the efforts of the Secretary under subsection (b) with respect to a complaint under subsection (a) do not result in the resolution of the complaint, the Secretary shall notify the person who submitted the complaint, in writing, of the results of the Secretary's investigation under subsection (b).

(d)(1) If the Secretary of Labor is unable to resolve a complaint under subsection (a) within 60 days after the date on which it is filed, the complainant may elect to appeal the alleged violation to the Merit Systems Protection Board in accordance with such procedures as the Merit Systems Protection Board shall prescribe, except that in no event may any such appeal be brought—

(A) before the 61st day after the date on which the complaint is filed; or

(B) later than 15 days after the date on which the complainant receives written notification from the Secretary under subsection (c)(2).

(2) An appeal under this subsection may not be brought unless—

(A) the complainant first provides written notification to the Secretary of such complainant's intention to bring such appeal; and

(B) appropriate evidence of compliance with subparagraph (A) is included (in such form and manner as the Merit Systems Protection Board may prescribe) with the notice of appeal under this subsection.

(3) Upon receiving notification under paragraph (2)(A), the Secretary shall not continue to investigate or further attempt to resolve the complaint to which the notification relates.

(e)(1) This section shall not be construed to prohibit a preference eligible from appealing directly to the Merit Systems Protection Board from any action which is appealable to the Board under any other law, rule, or regulation, in lieu of administrative redress under this section.

(2) A preference eligible may not pursue redress for an alleged violation described in subsection (a) under this section at the same time the preference eligible pursues redress for such violation under any other law, rule, or regulation.

(Added Pub. L. 105–339, § 3(a), Oct. 31, 1998, 112 Stat. 3182.)

SECTION REFERRED TO IN OTHER SECTIONS

This section is referred to in sections 3330b, 3330c of this title.

§ 3330b. Preference eligibles; judicial redress

(a) In lieu of continuing the administrative redress procedure provided under section 3330a(d), a preference eligible may elect, in accordance with this section, to terminate those administrative proceedings and file an action with the appropriate United States district court not later than 60 days after the date of the election.

(b) An election under this section may not be made—

(1) before the 121st day after the date on which the appeal is filed with the Merit Systems Protection Board under section 3330a(d); or

(2) after the Merit Systems Protection Board has issued a judicially reviewable decision on the merits of the appeal.

(c) An election under this section shall be made, in writing, in such form and manner as the Merit Systems Protection Board shall by regulation prescribe. The election shall be effective as of the date on which it is received, and the administrative proceeding to which it relates shall terminate immediately upon the receipt of such election.

(Added Pub. L. 105–339, § 3(a), Oct. 31, 1998, 112 Stat. 3184.)

SECTION REFERRED TO IN OTHER SECTIONS

This section is referred to in section 3330c of this title.

§ 3330c. Preference eligibles; remedy

(a) If the Merit Systems Protection Board (in a proceeding under section 3330a) or a court (in a proceeding under section 3330b) determines that an agency has violated a right described in section 3330a, the Board or court (as the case may be) shall order the agency to comply with such provisions and award compensation for any loss of wages or benefits suffered by the individual by reason of the violation involved. If the Board or court determines that such violation was willful, it shall award an amount equal to backpay as liquidated damages.

(b) A preference eligible who prevails in an action under section 3330a or 3330b shall be awarded reasonable attorney fees, expert witness fees, and other litigation expenses.

(Added Pub. L. 105–339, §3(a), Oct. 31, 1998, 112 Stat. 3184.)

SUBCHAPTER II—OATH OF OFFICE

§ 3331. Oath of office

An individual, except the President, elected or appointed to an office of honor or profit in the civil service or uniformed services, shall take the following oath: "I, AB, do solemnly swear (or affirm) that I will support and defend the Constitution of the United States against all enemies, foreign and domestic; that I will bear true faith and allegiance to the same; that I take this obligation freely, without any mental reservation or purpose of evasion; and that I will well and faithfully discharge the duties of the office on which I am about to enter. So help me God." This section does not affect other oaths required by law.

(Pub. L. 89–554, Sept. 6, 1966, 80 Stat. 424.)

HISTORICAL AND REVISION NOTES

Derivation	U.S. Code	Revised Statutes and Statutes at Large
....	5 U.S.C. 16.	R.S. §1757. May 13, 1884, ch. 46, §§2, 3, 23 Stat. 22.

All but the quoted language in R.S. §1757 is omitted as obsolete since R.S. §1757 was originally an alternative oath to the oath prescribed in R.S. §1756 which oath was repealed by the Act of May 13, 1884, ch. 46, §2, 23 Stat. 22. The words "An individual, except the President, . . . in the civil service or uniformed services" are substituted for "any person . . . either in the civil, military, or naval service, except the President of the United States". The second sentence of former section 16 is changed to read, "This section does not affect other oaths required by law.".

Standard changes are made to conform with the definitions applicable and the style of this title as outlined in the preface to the report.

SECTION REFERRED TO IN OTHER SECTIONS

This section is referred to in sections 2903, 2904, 2905, 2906, 3332 of this title; title 2 section 64–1; title 10 sections 578, 603, 626, 12201, 14309; title 14 sections 273, 735; title 22 section 2504; title 33 section 854a–2; title 42 sections 1971, 4954.

§ 3332. Officer affidavit; no consideration paid for appointment

An officer, within 30 days after the effective date of his appointment, shall file with the oath of office required by section 3331 of this title an affidavit that neither he nor anyone acting in his behalf has given, transferred, promised, or paid any consideration for or in the expectation or hope of receiving assistance in securing the appointment.

(Pub. L. 89–554, Sept. 6, 1966, 80 Stat. 424.)

HISTORICAL AND REVISION NOTES

Derivation	U.S. Code	Revised Statutes and Statutes at Large
....	5 U.S.C. 21a.	Dec. 11, 1926, ch. 4, §1, 44 Stat. 918. Mar. 2, 1927, ch. 284, 44 Stat. 1346. Sept. 23, 1950, ch. 1010, §10, 64 Stat. 987.

The section is restated for clarity and conciseness. The term "officer" is coextensive with and substituted for "Each individual appointed hereafter as a civil officer of the United States by the President, by and with the advice and consent of the Senate, or by the President alone, or by a court of law, or by the head of a department" in view of the definition of "officer" in section 2104.

Standard changes are made to conform with the definitions applicable and the style of this title as outlined in the preface to the report.

SECTION REFERRED TO IN OTHER SECTIONS

This section is referred to in section 5507 of this title; title 22 section 4001; title 42 section 211.

§ 3333. Employee affidavit; loyalty and striking against the Government

(a) Except as provided by subsection (b) of this section, an individual who accepts office or employment in the Government of the United States or in the government of the District of Columbia shall execute an affidavit within 60 days after accepting the office or employment that his acceptance and holding of the office or employment does not or will not violate section 7311 of this title. The affidavit is prima facie evidence that the acceptance and holding of office or employment by the affiant does not or will not violate section 7311 of this title.

(b) An affidavit is not required from an individual employed by the Government of the United States or the government of the District of Columbia for less than 60 days for sudden emergency work involving the loss of human life or the destruction of property. This subsection does not relieve an individual from liability for violation of section 7311 of this title.

(Pub. L. 89–554, Sept. 6, 1966, 80 Stat. 424.)

HISTORICAL AND REVISION NOTES

Derivation	U.S. Code	Revised Statutes and Statutes at Large
....	5 U.S.C. 118q.	Aug. 9, 1955, ch. 690, §2, 69 Stat. 624.
....	[Uncodified].	June 29, 1956, ch. 479, §3 (as applicable to the Act of Aug. 9, 1955, ch. 690, §2, 69 Stat. 624), 70 Stat. 453.

The section is restated for clarity and to conform to the style of section 3332.

In subsection (a), the words "after August 9, 1955" are omitted as executed. The words "if the affidavit is executed prior to acceptance of such office or employment" are omitted as unnecessary. The words "From and after July 1, 1956", appearing in the Act of June 29, 1956, are omitted as executed.

Standard changes are made to conform with the definitions applicable and the style of this title as outlined in the preface to the report.

SECTION REFERRED TO IN OTHER SECTIONS

This section is referred to in title 22 section 4001; title 39 section 410.

SUBCHAPTER III—DETAILS, VACANCIES, AND APPOINTMENTS

AMENDMENTS

1998—Pub. L. 105–277, div. C, title I, §151(c)(2), Oct. 21, 1998, 112 Stat. 2681–616, substituted "DETAILS, VACANCIES, AND APPOINTMENTS" for "DETAILS" as subchapter heading.

ANNUAL REPORT TO CONGRESS ON EMPLOYEES OR MEMBERS OF ARMED SERVICES DETAILED TO EXECUTIVE AGENCIES; EXEMPTIONS

Pub. L. 103–329, title VI, §619, Sept. 30, 1993, 108 Stat. 2420, which directed each Executive agency detailing personnel submit an annual report to Senate and House Committees on Appropriations on all employees or members of armed services detailed to Executive agencies, listing grade, position, and offices of each person detailed and agency to which each such person was detailed, with exemptions for certain intelligence agencies, terminated, effective May 15, 2000, see section 3003 of Pub. L. 104–66, as amended, set out as a note under section 1113 of Title 31, Money and Finance, and page 151 of House Document No. 103–7. Similar provisions were contained in the following prior appropriations acts:

Pub. L. 103–123, title VI, §617, Oct. 28, 1993, 107 Stat. 1263.

Pub. L. 102–393, title VI, §619, Oct. 6, 1992, 106 Stat. 1769; repealed by Pub. L. 104–66, title III, §3001(h), Dec. 21, 1995, 109 Stat. 734.

Pub. L. 102–141, title VI, §619, Oct. 28, 1991, 105 Stat. 871.

Pub. L. 101–509, title VI, §616, Nov. 5, 1990, 104 Stat. 1474.

Pub. L. 101–136, title VI, §616, Nov. 3, 1989, 103 Stat. 819.

Pub. L. 100–440, title VI, §616, Sept. 22, 1988, 102 Stat. 1754.

Pub. L. 100–202, §101(m) [title VI, §621], Dec. 22, 1987, 101 Stat. 1329–390, 1329–427.

SUBCHAPTER REFERRED TO IN OTHER SECTIONS

This subchapter is referred to in title 42 section 6635.

§ 3341. Details; within Executive or military departments

(a) The head of an Executive department or military department may detail employees among the bureaus and offices of his department, except employees who are required by law to be exclusively engaged on some specific work.

(b)(1) Details under subsection (a) of this section may be made only by written order of the head of the department, and may be for not more than 120 days. These details may be renewed by written order of the head of the department, in each particular case, for periods not exceeding 120 days.

(2) The 120-day limitation in paragraph (1) for details and renewals of details does not apply to the Department of Defense in the case of a detail—

(A) made in connection with the closure or realignment of a military installation pursuant to a base closure law or an organizational restructuring of the Department as part of a reduction in the size of the armed forces or the civilian workforce of the Department; and

(B) in which the position to which the employee is detailed is eliminated on or before the date of the closure, realignment, or restructuring.

(c) For purposes of this section—

(1) the term "base closure law" means—
(A) section 2687 of title 10;
(B) title II of the Defense Authorization Amendments and Base Closure and Realignment Act (10 U.S.C. 2687 note); and
(C) the Defense Base Closure and Realignment Act of 1990 (10 U.S.C. 2687 note); and

(2) the term "military installation"—
(A) in the case of an installation covered by section 2687 of title 10, has the meaning given such term in subsection (e)(1) of such section;
(B) in the case of an installation covered by the Act referred to in subparagraph (B) of paragraph (1), has the meaning given such term in section 209(6) of such Act; and
(C) in the case of an installation covered by the Act referred to in subparagraph (C) of that paragraph, has the meaning given such term in section 2910(4) of such Act.

(Pub. L. 89–554, Sept. 6, 1966, 80 Stat. 424; Pub. L. 104–106, div. A, title X, §1033(a), Feb. 10, 1996, 110 Stat. 429.)

HISTORICAL AND REVISION NOTES

Derivation	U.S. Code	Revised Statutes and Statutes at Large
....	5 U.S.C. 38.	R.S. §166. May 28, 1896, ch. 252, §3, 29 Stat. 179.

The words "Executive department" are substituted for "department" as the definition of "department" applicable to this section is coextensive with the definition of "Executive department" in section 101.

The words "or military department" are inserted to preserve the application of the source law. Before enactment of the National Security Act Amendments of 1949 (63 Stat. 578), the Department of the Army, the Department of the Navy, and the Department of the Air Force were Executive departments. The National Security Act Amendments of 1949 established the Department of Defense as an Executive Department including the Department of the Army, the Department of the Navy, and the Department of the Air Force as military departments, not as Executive departments. However, the source law for this section, which was in effect in 1949, remained applicable to the Secretaries of the military departments by virtue of section 12(g) of the National Security Act Amendments of 1949 (63 Stat. 591), which is set out in the reviser's note for section 301.

The word "detail" is coextensive with and is substituted for "alter the distribution". The word "clerks" is omitted as included in "employees". The words "as he may find it necessary and proper to do" and "from time to time" are omitted as surplusage.

This section was part of title IV of the Revised Statutes. The Act of July 26, 1947, ch. 343, §201(d), as added Aug. 10, 1949, ch. 412, §4, 63 Stat. 579 (former 5 U.S.C. 171–1), which provides "Except to the extent inconsistent with the provisions of this Act [National Security Act of 1947], the provisions of title IV of the Revised Statutes as now or hereafter amended shall be applicable to the Department of Defense" is omitted from this title but is not repealed.

Standard changes are made to conform with the definitions applicable and the style of this title as outlined in the preface to the report.

REFERENCES IN TEXT

Section 209(6) of such Act, referred to in subsec. (c)(2)(B), means section 209(6) of Pub. L. 100–526, which is set out as a note under section 2687 of Title 10, Armed Forces.

Section 2910(4) of such Act, referred to in subsec. (c)(2)(C), means section 2910(4) of Pub. L. 101–510, which is set out as a note under section 2687 of Title 10.

AMENDMENTS

1996—Subsec. (b). Pub. L. 104–106 designated existing provisions as par. (1) and added par. (2).

Subsec. (c). Pub. L. 104–106, § 1033(a)(2), added subsec. (c).

EFFECTIVE DATE OF 1996 AMENDMENT

Section 1033(b) of Pub. L. 104–106 provided that: "The amendments made by subsection (a) [amending this section] apply to details made before the date of the enactment of this Act [Feb. 10, 1996] but still in effect on that date and details made on or after that date."

TRANSFER OF APPROPRIATED FUNDS; FUNDING OF DETAILED EMPLOYEES

For restriction on availability of funds for salaries of employees reassigned on temporary detail basis to another position without independent approval by head of employing department or agency, see section 515(3) of Pub. L. 103–333, set out as a note under section 1301 of Title 31, Money and Finance.

SECTION REFERRED TO IN OTHER SECTIONS

This section is referred to in section 9510 of this title; title 15 section 652; title 42 section 5667g–2.

[§ 3342. Repealed. Pub. L. 102–378, § 2(13)(A), Oct. 2, 1992, 106 Stat. 1347]

Section, added Pub. L. 101–416, § 2(a)(1), Oct. 12, 1990, 104 Stat. 902, related to Federal participants in executive exchange programs.

A prior section 3342, Pub. L. 89–554, Sept. 6, 1966, 80 Stat. 425, which prohibited details of employees from field service to Executive department in District of Columbia except for temporary duty, details specifically provided for by law, or detailing of one employee from Bureau of Customs for duty in District of Columbia, was repealed by Pub. L. 89–762, § 1(a), Nov. 5, 1966, 80 Stat. 1312.

EFFECTIVE DATE OF REPEAL

Section repealed effective Oct. 1, 1991, see section 9(b)(3) of Pub. L. 102–378, set out as an Effective Date of 1992 Amendment note under section 6303 of this title.

§ 3343. Details; to international organizations

(a) For the purpose of this section—

(1) "agency", "employee", and "international organization" have the meanings given them by section 3581 of this title; and

(2) "detail" means the assignment or loan of an employee to an international organization without a change of position from the agency by which he is employed to an international organization.

(b) The head of an agency may detail, for a period of not more than 5 years, an employee of his agency to an international organization which requests services, except that under special circumstances, where the President determines it to be in the national interest, he may extend the 5-year period for up to an additional 3 years.

(c) An employee detailed under subsection (b) of this section is deemed, for the purpose of preserving his allowances, privileges, rights, seniority, and other benefits, an employee of the agency from which detailed, and he is entitled to pay, allowances, and benefits from funds available to that agency. The authorization and payment of these allowances and other benefits from appropriations available therefor is deemed to comply with section 5536 of this title.

(d) Details may be made under subsection (b) of this section—

(1) without reimbursement to the United States by the international organization; or

(2) with agreement by the international organization to reimburse the United States for all or part of the pay, travel expenses, and allowances payable during the detail, and the reimbursement shall be credited to the appropriation, fund, or account used for paying the amounts reimbursed.

(e) An employee detailed under subsection (b) of this section may be paid or reimbursed by an international organization for allowances or expenses incurred in the performance of duties required by the detail, without regard to section 209 of title 18.

(Pub. L. 89–554, Sept. 6, 1966, 80 Stat. 425; Pub. L. 91–175, pt. V, § 502(a), Dec. 30, 1969, 83 Stat. 825.)

HISTORICAL AND REVISION NOTES

Derivation	U.S. Code	Revised Statutes and Statutes at Large
(a)	5 U.S.C. 2331.	Aug. 28, 1958, Pub. L. 85–795, § 2, 72 Stat. 959.
(b)–(e)	5 U.S.C. 2332.	Aug. 28, 1958, Pub. L. 85–795, § 3, 72 Stat. 959.

In subsection (a)(2), the words "without a change of position from the agency by which he is employed to an international organization" are substituted for "without the employee's transfer from the Federal agency by which he is employed" to eliminate the necessity of carrying into this section the definition of "transfer" appearing in former section 2331(5).

In subsection (e), the words "section 209 of title 18" are substituted for "section 1914 of title 18" on authority of the Act of Oct. 23, 1962, Pub. L. 87–849, § 2, 76 Stat. 1126.

Other definitions appearing in former section 2331 are omitted from this section as inappropriate but are carried into section 3581.

Standard changes are made to conform with the definitions applicable and the style of this title as outlined in the preface to the report.

AMENDMENTS

1969—Subsec. (b). Pub. L. 91–175 substituted "5" for "3" and inserted provision enabling President, regarding an agency employee detailed to an international organization for 5 years, to extend the 5-year period for up to an additional 3 years.

DETAILS TO INTERNATIONAL ORGANIZATIONS

For provisions concerning the providing for details of Federal employees to international organizations and the delegation of Presidential authority, concerning the extension of a detail under this section, to the Secretary of State, see Ex. Ord. No. 11552, Aug. 24, 1970, 35 F.R. 13569, set out as a note under section 3584 of this title.

SECTION REFERRED TO IN OTHER SECTIONS

This section is referred to in section 3584 of this title; title 26 section 3121; title 42 section 410.

§ 3344. Details; administrative law judges

An agency as defined by section 551 of this title which occasionally or temporarily is insufficiently staffed with administrative law judges appointed under section 3105 of this title may use administrative law judges selected by the Office of Personnel Management from and with the consent of other agencies.

(Pub. L. 89–554, Sept. 6, 1966, 80 Stat. 425; Pub. L. 95–251, § 2(a)(1), (b)(2), Mar. 27, 1978, 92 Stat. 183;

Pub. L. 95–454, title IX, § 906(a)(2), Oct. 13, 1978, 92 Stat. 1224.)

HISTORICAL AND REVISION NOTES

Derivation	U.S. Code	Revised Statutes and Statutes at Large
....	5 U.S.C. 1010 (4th sentence).	June 11, 1946, ch. 324, §11 (4th sentence), 60 Stat. 244.

Standard changes are made to conform with the definitions applicable and the style of this title as outlined in the preface to the report.

AMENDMENTS

1978—Pub. L. 95–454 substituted "Office of Personnel Management" for "Civil Service Commission".

Pub. L. 95–251 substituted references to administrative law judges for references to hearing examiners in section catchline and wherever appearing in text.

EFFECTIVE DATE OF 1978 AMENDMENT

Amendment by Pub. L. 95–454 effective 90 days after Oct. 13, 1978, see section 907 of Pub. L. 95–454, set out as a note under section 1101 of this title.

SECTION REFERRED TO IN OTHER SECTIONS

This section is referred to in sections 559, 1305 of this title; title 15 sections 1541, 1715; title 29 section 661; title 30 section 823; title 31 section 3801; title 42 sections 2000e–4, 3608, 3787.

§ 3345. Acting officer

(a) If an officer of an Executive agency (including the Executive Office of the President, and other than the General Accounting Office) whose appointment to office is required to be made by the President, by and with the advice and consent of the Senate, dies, resigns, or is otherwise unable to perform the functions and duties of the office—

(1) the first assistant to the office of such officer shall perform the functions and duties of the office temporarily in an acting capacity subject to the time limitations of section 3346;

(2) notwithstanding paragraph (1), the President (and only the President) may direct a person who serves in an office for which appointment is required to be made by the President, by and with the advice and consent of the Senate, to perform the functions and duties of the vacant office temporarily in an acting capacity subject to the time limitations of section 3346; or

(3) notwithstanding paragraph (1), the President (and only the President) may direct an officer or employee of such Executive agency to perform the functions and duties of the vacant office temporarily in an acting capacity, subject to the time limitations of section 3346, if—

(A) during the 365-day period preceding the date of death, resignation, or beginning of inability to serve of the applicable officer, the officer or employee served in a position in such agency for not less than 90 days; and

(B) the rate of pay for the position described under subparagraph (A) is equal to or greater than the minimum rate of pay payable for a position at GS–15 of the General Schedule.

(b)(1) Notwithstanding subsection (a)(1), a person may not serve as an acting officer for an office under this section, if—

(A) during the 365-day period preceding the date of the death, resignation, or beginning of inability to serve, such person—

(i) did not serve in the position of first assistant to the office of such officer; or

(ii) served in the position of first assistant to the office of such officer for less than 90 days; and

(B) the President submits a nomination of such person to the Senate for appointment to such office.

(2) Paragraph (1) shall not apply to any person if—

(A) such person is serving as the first assistant to the office of an officer described under subsection (a);

(B) the office of such first assistant is an office for which appointment is required to be made by the President, by and with the advice and consent of the Senate; and

(C) the Senate has approved the appointment of such person to such office.

(c)(1) Notwithstanding subsection (a)(1), the President (and only the President) may direct an officer who is nominated by the President for reappointment for an additional term to the same office in an Executive department without a break in service, to continue to serve in that office subject to the time limitations in section 3346, until such time as the Senate has acted to confirm or reject the nomination, notwithstanding adjournment sine die.

(2) For purposes of this section and sections 3346, 3347, 3348, 3349, 3349a, and 3349d, the expiration of a term of office is an inability to perform the functions and duties of such office.

(Added Pub. L. 105–277, div. C, title I, § 151(b), Oct. 21, 1998, 112 Stat. 2681–611.)

REFERENCES IN TEXT

The General Schedule, referred to in subsec. (a)(3)(B), is set out under section 5332 of this title.

PRIOR PROVISIONS

A prior section 3345, Pub. L. 89–554, Sept. 6, 1966, 80 Stat. 425; Pub. L. 100–398, §7(a)(1), (2), Aug. 17, 1988, 102 Stat. 988, provided for details to office of head of Executive agency or military department, prior to repeal by Pub. L. 105–277, div. C, title I, §151(b), (d)(1), Oct. 21, 1998, 112 Stat. 2681–611, 2681–616, effective 30 days after Oct. 21, 1998.

EFFECTIVE DATE

Pub. L. 105–277, div. C, title I, §151(d), Oct. 21, 1998, 112 Stat. 2681–616, provided that:

"(1) EFFECTIVE DATE.—Subject to paragraph (2), this section [enacting this section and sections 3346 to 3349d of this title, repealing former sections 3345 to 3349 of this title, and enacting provisions set out as a note under section 3301 of this title] and the amendments made by this section shall take effect 30 days after the date of enactment of this section [Oct. 21, 1998].

"(2) APPLICATION.—

"(A) IN GENERAL.—This section shall apply to any office that becomes vacant after the effective date of this section.

"(B) IMMEDIATE APPLICATION OF TIME LIMITATION.—Notwithstanding subparagraph (A), for any office vacant on the effective date of this section, the time limitations under section 3346 of title 5, United States Code (as amended by this section) shall apply to such office. Such time limitations shall apply as though such office first became vacant on the effective date of this section.

"(C) CERTAIN NOMINATIONS.—If the President submits to the Senate the nomination of any person after the effective date of this section for an office for which such person had been nominated before such date, the next nomination of such person after such date shall be considered a first nomination of such person to that office for purposes of sections 3345 through 3349 and section 3349d of title 5, United States Code (as amended by this section)."

EX. ORD. NO. 10513. DESIGNATION OF OFFICERS TO ACT AS SECRETARY OF LABOR

Ex. Ord. No. 10513, Jan. 19, 1954, 19 F.R. 369, provided:

I hereby authorize and direct the Assistant Secretaries of Labor and the Solicitor of Labor, in the order designated as hereinafter provided, to perform the duties of the office of the Secretary of Labor in case of the absence, sickness, resignation, or death of both the Secretary of Labor and the Under [Deputy] Secretary of Labor.

The Assistant Secretaries of Labor and the Solicitor of Labor shall act as Secretary of Labor as herein provided (1) in such order as the Secretary of Labor (or the Under [Deputy] Secretary when acting as Secretary) may by order designate from time to time, or (2) if no such designation order is in effect at the time, in the order of the respective dates of their commissions, or in the event that two or more of their commissions bear the same date, in the order in which they shall have taken their oath of office.

This order supersedes Executive Order No. 9968 of June 17, 1948, entitled "Designation of Certain Officers To Act as Secretary of Labor."

DWIGHT D. EISENHOWER.

EX. ORD. NO. 11274. ORDER OF SUCCESSION—DEPARTMENT OF HOUSING AND URBAN DEVELOPMENT

Ex. Ord. No. 11274, Mar. 30, 1966, 31 F.R. 5243, as amended by Pub. L. 101–509, title V, § 529 [title I, § 112(c)], Nov. 5, 1990, 104 Stat. 1427, 1454, provided:

By virtue of the authority vested in me by Section 179 of the Revised Statutes (5 U.S.C. 6) and Section 301 of Title 3 of the United States Code, and as President of the United States, it is ordered as follows:

1. In the event of a vacancy in the Office of the Secretary of Housing and Urban Development or during the absence or disability of the Secretary, the Deputy Secretary shall act as Secretary of Housing and Urban Development.

2. During any period when, by reason of absence, disability, or vacancy in office, neither the Secretary nor the Deputy Secretary is available to exercise the powers or perform the duties of the Office of the Secretary, an Assistant Secretary or the General Counsel, in such order as the Secretary may from time to time prescribe, shall act as Secretary of Housing and Urban Development. If no such order of succession is in effect at that time, then they shall act in the order in which they shall have taken office as Assistant Secretaries or General Counsel.

EX. ORD. NO. 11487. DESIGNATION OF OFFICERS OF THE DEPARTMENT OF THE INTERIOR TO ACT AS SECRETARY OF THE INTERIOR

Ex. Ord. No. 11487, Oct. 6, 1969, 34 F.R. 15593, as amended by Pub. L. 101–509, title V, § 529 [title I, § 112(c)], Nov. 5, 1990, 104 Stat. 1427, 1454, provided:

By virtue of the authority vested in me by [former] section 3347 of title 5 of the United States Code and section 301 of title 3 of the United States Code, and as President of the United States, it is ordered as follows:

SECTION 1. During any period when by reason of absence, disability, or vacancy in office, neither the Secretary of the Interior nor the Deputy Secretary of the Interior is available to exercise the powers or perform the duties of the office of Secretary, an Assistant Secretary of the Interior or the Solicitor of the Department of the Interior, in such order as the Secretary of the Interior may from time to time prescribe, shall act as Secretary. If no such order of succession is in effect at that time, they shall act as Secretary in the order in which they shall have taken office as Assistant Secretaries or Solicitor.

SEC. 2. This order supersedes Executive Order No. 10753 of February 15, 1958, entitled "Designation of certain officers of the Department of the Interior to act as Secretary of the Interior."

EX. ORD. NO. 11822. DESIGNATION OF OFFICERS OF THE DEPARTMENT OF THE TREASURY TO ACT AS SECRETARY OF THE TREASURY

Ex. Ord. No. 11822, Dec. 10, 1974, 39 F.R. 43275, provided:

By virtue of the authority vested in me by [former] section 3347 of title 5 and section 301 of title 3 of the United States Code and as President of the United States, it is ordered as follows:

SECTION 1. During any period when, by reason of absence, disability, or vacancy in office, either the Secretary of the Treasury or his Deputy Secretary is not available to exercise the powers or perform the duties of the office of Secretary, an officer from the Department of the Treasury appointed by the President—by and with the advice and consent of the Senate, in such order as the Secretary of the Treasury may from time to time prescribe—shall act as Secretary until the absence or the disability of the incumbent shall cease, or until a successor is appointed. If no such order of succession is in effect at that time, then such officers shall act as Secretary in the descending order of rank, as established by their offices being listed in sections 5314, 5315 or 5316 of title 5 of the United States Code and, at each level of the Executive Schedule, in the order which they shall have taken the oath as such officers.

SEC. 2. Executive Order No. 11680 of August 21, 1972, entitled "Designation of Certain Officers to Act as Secretary of the Treasury" is hereby revoked.

GERALD R. FORD.

EX. ORD. NO. 11880. DESIGNATION OF OFFICERS OF THE DEPARTMENT OF COMMERCE TO ACT AS SECRETARY OF COMMERCE

Ex. Ord. No. 11880, Oct. 2, 1975, 40 F.R. 46089, as amended by Ex. Ord. No. 12608, Sept. 9, 1987, 52 F.R. 34617; Ex. Ord. No. 12998, Apr. 5, 1996, 61 F.R. 15873, provided:

By virtue of the authority vested in me by [former] section 3347 of Title 5 of the United States Code and section 301 of Title 3 of the United States Code, and as President of the United States, it is hereby ordered as follows:

SECTION 1. During any period when, by reason of absence, disability or vacancy in office, both the Secretary of Commerce and the Deputy Secretary of Commerce are not available to exercise the powers or perform the duties of the Office of Secretary, an Assistant Secretary of Commerce, the General Counsel of the Department of Commerce, or an officer of the Department of Commerce appointed by the President with the advice and consent of the Senate in such order as the Secretary of Commerce may from time to time prescribe, shall act as Secretary. If no such order of succession is in effect at that time, an Assistant Secretary or the General Counsel shall act as Secretary in the order in which they shall have taken office as Assistant Secretaries or General Counsel.

SEC. 2. The President may at any time, pursuant to law but without regard to the foregoing provisions of this order, direct that an officer, as defined in [former] 5 U.S.C. 3347, and specified by the President shall act as Secretary of Commerce.

SEC. 3. This Order supersedes Executive Order No. 11388 of January 15, 1968.

EX. ORD. NO. 11957. DESIGNATION OF CERTAIN OFFICERS OF THE DEPARTMENT OF AGRICULTURE TO ACT AS SECRETARY OF AGRICULTURE.

Ex. Ord. No. 11957, Jan. 13, 1977, 42 F.R. 3295, provided:

By virtue of the authority vested in me by [former] Section 3347 of Title 5 and section 301 of Title 3 of the United States Code, and as President of the United States of America, it is hereby ordered as follows:

SECTION 1. During any period when, by reason of absence, disability, or vacancy in office, both the Secretary of Agriculture and the Deputy Secretary of Agriculture are not available to exercise the powers or perform the duties of the Office of Secretary, the officers from the Department of Agriculture whose appointments are vested in the President, by and with the advice and consent of the Senate, shall act as Secretary in such order as the Secretary of Agriculture may from time to time prescribe. If no such order of succession is in effect at that time, then such officers shall act as Secretary in the descending order of rank, as established by the listing of their offices in Sections 5314, 5315 or 5316 of Title 5 of the United States Code and, at each level of the Executive Schedule, in the order in which they shall have taken oath as such officers.

SEC. 2. Executive Order No. 11793 of July 10, 1974, is hereby revoked.

GERALD R. FORD.

Ex. Ord. No. 12343. Designation of Certain Officers To Act as Secretary of State

Ex. Ord. No. 12343, Jan. 27, 1982, 47 F.R. 4225, provided:

By the authority vested in me as President of the United States of America by [former] Section 3347 of Title 5 and Section 301 of Title 3 of the United States Code, it is hereby ordered as follows:

SECTION 1. During any period when, by reason of absence, disability, or vacancy in office, neither the Secretary of State nor the Deputy Secretary of State, is available to exercise the powers or perform the duties of the Office of the Secretary, an officer from the Department of State who has been appointed by the President, by and with the advice and consent of the Senate, in such order as the Secretary of State may from time to time prescribe, shall act as Secretary. If no such order of succession is in effect at that time, then such officers shall act as Secretary in descending order of rank, as established by the listing of their offices in Sections 5314 or 5315 of Title 5 of the United States Code, and at each level of the Executive Schedule in the order in which they shall have taken the oath as such officers.

SEC. 2. The President may at any time, pursuant to law but without regard to the foregoing provisions of this Order, direct that an officer specified by the President shall act as Secretary of State.

SEC. 3. Executive Order No. 10839 is revoked.

RONALD REAGAN.

Ex. Ord. No. 12879. Order of Succession of Officers To Act as Secretary of the Navy

Ex. Ord. No. 12879, Nov. 8, 1993, 58 F.R. 59929, provided:

By the authority vested in me as President by the Constitution and the laws of the United States of America, including [former] section 3347 of title 5, United States Code, it is hereby ordered as follows:

SECTION 1. *Succession to the Authority of the Secretary of the Navy.*

(a) In the event of the death, permanent disability, or resignation of the Secretary of the Navy, the incumbents holding the positions designated below, in the order indicated, shall act for and exercise the powers of the Secretary of the Navy:

(1) The Under Secretary of the Navy.

(2) The Assistant Secretaries and General Counsel of the Navy, in the order fixed by their length of services as permanent appointees in such positions.

(3) The Chief of Naval Operations.

(4) The Commandant of the Marine Corps.

(b) In the event of the temporary absence or temporary disability of the Secretary of the Navy, the incumbents holding the Department of the Navy positions designated in paragraph (a) of this section, in the order indicated, shall act for and exercise the powers of the Secretary of the Navy.

(1) In these instances, the designation of an Acting Secretary of the Navy applies only for the duration of the Secretary's absence or disability, and does not affect the authority of the Secretary to resume the powers of his office upon his return.

(2) In the event that the Secretary of the Navy is merely absent from this position, the Secretary of the Navy may continue to exercise the powers and fulfill the duties of his office during his absence, notwithstanding the provisions of this order.

(c) Precedence among those officers designated in paragraph (a) of this section who have the same date of appointment shall be determined by the Secretary of the Navy at the time that such appointments are made.

(d) Notwithstanding paragraph (a) and (b) of this section, an officer shall not act for or exercise the powers of the Secretary of the Navy under this order if that officer serves only in an acting capacity in the position that would otherwise entitle him to do so.

SEC. 2. *Temporary Nature of Succession.* Succession to act for and exercise the powers of the Secretary of the Navy pursuant to this order shall be on a temporary or interim basis and shall not have the effect of vacating the statutory appointment held by the successor.

WILLIAM J. CLINTON.

Ex. Ord. No. 12908. Order of Succession of Officers To Act as Secretary of the Army

Ex. Ord. No. 12908, Apr. 22, 1994, 59 F.R. 21907, provided:

By the authority vested in me as President by the Constitution and the laws of the United States of America, including [former] section 3347 of title 5, United States Code, it is hereby ordered as follows:

SECTION 1. *Succession To Act as the Secretary of the Army.*

(a) In the event of the death, permanent disability, or resignation of the Secretary of the Army, the incumbents holding the positions designated below, in the order indicated, shall act for and exercise the powers of the Secretary of the Army:

(1) The Under Secretary of the Army.

(2) The Assistant Secretaries and General Counsel of the Army, in the order fixed by their length of service as permanent appointees in such positions.

(3) The Chief of Staff of the Army.

(b) In the event of the absence or temporary disability of the Secretary of the Army, the incumbents holding the Department of the Army positions designated in paragraph (a) of this section, in the order indicated, shall act for and exercise the powers of the Secretary of the Army.

(1) The designation of an Acting Secretary of the Army under this subsection applies only for the duration of the Secretary's absence or disability, and does not affect the authority of the Secretary to resume the powers of the Secretary's office.

(2) When the Secretary of the Army is temporarily absent from the position, the Secretary of the Army may continue to exercise the powers and fulfill the duties of his office during his absence, notwithstanding the provisions of this order.

(c) Precedence among those officers designated in paragraph (a) of this section who have the same date of appointment shall be determined by the Secretary of the Army at the time that such appointments are made.

(d) Notwithstanding paragraphs (a) and (b) of this section, an officer shall not act for or exercise the powers of the Secretary of the Army under this order if that officer serves only in an acting capacity in the position that would otherwise entitle him to do so.

SEC. 2. *Temporary Nature of Succession.* Succession to act for and exercise the powers of the Secretary of the Army pursuant to this order shall be on a temporary or interim basis and shall not have the effect of vacating the statutory appointment held by the successor.

WILLIAM J. CLINTON.

Ex. Ord. No. 12909. Order of Succession of Officers To Act as Secretary of the Air Force

Ex. Ord. No. 12909, Apr. 22, 1994, 59 F.R. 21909, provided:

By the authority vested in me as President by the Constitution and the laws of the United States of America, including [former] section 3347 of title 5, United States Code, it is hereby ordered as follows:

SECTION 1. *Succession To Act as the Secretary of the Air Force.*

(a) In the event of the death, permanent disability, or resignation of the Secretary of the Air Force, the incumbents holding the positions designated below, in the order indicated, shall act for and exercise the powers of the Secretary of the Air Force:

(1) The Under Secretary of the Air Force.

(2) The Assistant Secretaries and General Counsel of the Air Force, in the order fixed by their length of service as permanent appointees in such positions.

(3) The Chief of Staff of the Air Force.

(b) In the event of the absence or temporary disability of the Secretary of the Air Force, the incumbents holding the Department of the Air Force positions designated in paragraph (a) of this section, in the order indicated, shall act for and exercise the powers of the Secretary of the Air Force.

(1) The designation of an Acting Secretary of the Air Force applies only for the duration of the Secretary's absence or disability, and does not affect the authority of the Secretary to resume the powers of the Secretary's office.

(2) In the event that the Secretary of the Air Force is temporarily absent from the position, the Secretary of the Air Force may continue to exercise the powers and fulfill the duties of his office during the absence, notwithstanding the provisions of this order.

(c) Precedence among those officers designated in paragraph (a) of this section who have the same date of appointment shall be determined by the Secretary of the Air Force at the time that such appointments are made.

(d) Notwithstanding paragraphs (a) and (b) of this section, an officer shall not act for or exercise the powers of the Secretary of the Air Force under this order if that officer serves only in an acting capacity in the position that would otherwise entitle him to do so.

SEC. 2. *Temporary Nature of Succession.* Succession to act for and exercise the powers of the Secretary of the Air Force pursuant to this order shall be on a temporary or interim basis and shall not have the effect of vacating the statutory appointment held by the successor.

WILLIAM J. CLINTON.

Ex. Ord. No. 13000. Order of Succession of Officers To Act as Secretary of Defense

Ex. Ord. No. 13000, Apr. 24, 1996, 61 F.R. 18483, provided:

By the authority vested in me as President by the Constitution and the laws of the United States of America, including [former] section 3347 of title 5, United States Code, it is hereby ordered as follows:

SECTION 1. *Succession to Act as the Secretary of Defense.*

(a) In the event of the death, permanent disability, or resignation of the Secretary of Defense, the incumbents holding the Department of Defense positions designated below, in the order indicated, shall act for and exercise the powers of the Secretary of Defense as Acting Secretary of Defense:

(1) Deputy Secretary of Defense.

(2) Secretary of the Army.

(3) Secretary of the Navy.

(4) Secretary of the Air Force.

(5) Under Secretary of Defense for Acquisition and Technology [now Under Secretary of Defense for Acquisition, Technology, and Logistics].

(6) Under Secretary of Defense for Policy.

(7) Under Secretary of Defense (Comptroller).

(8) Under Secretary of Defense for Personnel and Readiness.

(9) Deputy Under Secretary of Defense for Acquisition and Technology.

(10) Deputy Under Secretary of Defense for Policy.

(11) Director of Defense Research and Engineering.

(12) The Assistant Secretaries of Defense, the Director of Operational Test and Evaluation, and the General Counsel of the Department of Defense, in the order fixed by their length of service as permanent appointees in such positions.

(13) Under Secretaries of the Army, the Navy, and the Air Force, in the order fixed by their length of service as permanent appointees in such positions.

(14) Assistant Secretaries of the Army, the Navy, and the Air Force whose appointments are vested in the President, and General Counsels of the Army, the Navy, and the Air Force, in the order fixed by their length of service as permanent appointees in such positions.

(b) In the event of the temporary absence or temporary disability of the Secretary of Defense, the incumbents holding the Department of Defense positions designated in paragraph (a) of this section, in the order indicated, shall act for and exercise the powers of the Secretary of Defense as Acting Secretary of Defense.

(1) In these instances, the designation of an Acting Secretary of Defense applies only for the duration of the Secretary's absence or disability, and does not affect the authority of the Secretary to resume the powers of his office upon his return.

(2) In the event that the Secretary of Defense is temporarily absent from his position, the Secretary may continue to exercise the powers and fulfill the duties of this office during his absence, notwithstanding the provisions of this order.

(c) Precedence among those officers designated in paragraphs (a)(12)–(14) of this section who have the same appointment date shall be determined by the Secretary of Defense at the time that such appointments are made.

(d) Notwithstanding paragraphs (a) and (b) of this section, an officer shall not act for or exercise the powers of the Secretary of Defense under this order if that officer serves only in an acting capacity in the position that would otherwise entitle him to do so.

SEC. 2. *Temporary Nature of Succession.* Succession to act for and exercise the powers of the Secretary of Defense pursuant to this order shall be on a temporary or interim basis and shall not have the effect of vacating the statutory appointment held by the successor.

SEC. 3. *Revocation of Prior Executive Order.* Executive Order No. 12787 of December 31, 1991, is hereby revoked.

WILLIAM J. CLINTON.

SECTION REFERRED TO IN OTHER SECTIONS

This section is referred to in sections 3346, 3347, 3348, 3349, 3349b, 3349c, 3349d, 5535 of this title; title 7 section 2211; title 28 section 508.

§ 3346. Time limitation

(a) Except in the case of a vacancy caused by sickness, the person serving as an acting officer as described under section 3345 may serve in the office—

(1) for no longer than 210 days beginning on the date the vacancy occurs; or

(2) subject to subsection (b), once a first or second nomination for the office is submitted to the Senate, from the date of such nomination for the period that the nomination is pending in the Senate.

(b)(1) If the first nomination for the office is rejected by the Senate, withdrawn, or returned to the President by the Senate, the person may continue to serve as the acting officer for no more than 210 days after the date of such rejection, withdrawal, or return.

(2) Notwithstanding paragraph (1), if a second nomination for the office is submitted to the Senate after the rejection, withdrawal, or return of the first nomination, the person serving as the acting officer may continue to serve—

(A) until the second nomination is confirmed; or

(B) for no more than 210 days after the second nomination is rejected, withdrawn, or returned.

(c) If a vacancy occurs during an adjournment of the Congress sine die, the 210-day period under subsection (a) shall begin on the date that the Senate first reconvenes.

(Added Pub. L. 105–277, div. C, title I, § 151(b), Oct. 21, 1998, 112 Stat. 2681–612.)

PRIOR PROVISIONS

A prior section 3346, Pub. L. 89–554, Sept. 6, 1966, 80 Stat. 426, provided for details to subordinate offices, prior to repeal by Pub. L. 105–277, div. C, title I, § 151(b), (d)(1), Oct. 21, 1998, 112 Stat. 2681–611, 2681–616, effective 30 days after Oct. 21, 1998. See section 3345 of this title.

EFFECTIVE DATE

Section effective 30 days after Oct. 21, 1998, and applicable to any office that becomes vacant after such effective date, with certain exceptions, see section 151(d) of Pub. L. 105–277, set out as a note under section 3345 of this title.

SECTION REFERRED TO IN OTHER SECTIONS

This section is referred to in sections 3345, 3347, 3348, 3349, 3349a, 3349b, 3349c, 3349d, 5535 of this title.

§ 3347. Exclusivity

(a) Sections 3345 and 3346 are the exclusive means for temporarily authorizing an acting official to perform the functions and duties of any office of an Executive agency (including the Executive Office of the President, and other than the General Accounting Office) for which appointment is required to be made by the President, by and with the advice and consent of the Senate, unless—

(1) a statutory provision expressly—

(A) authorizes the President, a court, or the head of an Executive department, to designate an officer or employee to perform the functions and duties of a specified office temporarily in an acting capacity; or

(B) designates an officer or employee to perform the functions and duties of a specified office temporarily in an acting capacity; or

(2) the President makes an appointment to fill a vacancy in such office during the recess of the Senate pursuant to clause 3 of section 2 of article II of the United States Constitution.

(b) Any statutory provision providing general authority to the head of an Executive agency (including the Executive Office of the President, and other than the General Accounting Office) to delegate duties statutorily vested in that agency head to, or to reassign duties among, officers or employees of such Executive agency, is not a statutory provision to which subsection (a)(1) applies.

(Added Pub. L. 105–277, div. C, title I, § 151(b), Oct. 21, 1998, 112 Stat. 2681–613; amended Pub. L. 106–31, title V, § 5011, May 21, 1999, 113 Stat. 112.)

PRIOR PROVISIONS

A prior section 3347, Pub. L. 89–554, Sept. 6, 1966, 80 Stat. 426, provided for Presidential authority relating to details, prior to repeal by Pub. L. 105–277, div. C, title I, § 151(b), (d)(1), Oct. 21, 1998, 112 Stat. 2681–611, 2681–616, effective 30 days after Oct. 21, 1998. See section 3345 of this title.

AMENDMENTS

1999—Subsec. (b). Pub. L. 106–31 substituted "subsection (a)(1)" for "subsection (a)(2)".

EFFECTIVE DATE

Section effective 30 days after Oct. 21, 1998, and applicable to any office that becomes vacant after such effective date, with certain exceptions, see section 151(d) of Pub. L. 105–277, set out as a note under section 3345 of this title.

SECTION REFERRED TO IN OTHER SECTIONS

This section is referred to in sections 3345, 3348, 3349, 3349b, 3349c, 3349d, 5535 of this title; title 10 sections 3017, 5017, 8017.

§ 3348. Vacant office

(a) In this section—

(1) the term "action" includes any agency action as defined under section 551(13); and

(2) the term "function or duty" means any function or duty of the applicable office that—

(A)(i) is established by statute; and

(ii) is required by statute to be performed by the applicable officer (and only that officer); or

(B)(i)(I) is established by regulation; and

(II) is required by such regulation to be performed by the applicable officer (and only that officer); and

(ii) includes a function or duty to which clause (i)(I) and (II) applies, and the applicable regulation is in effect at any time during the 180-day period preceding the date on which the vacancy occurs.

(b) Unless an officer or employee is performing the functions and duties in accordance with sections 3345, 3346, and 3347, if an officer of an Executive agency (including the Executive Office of the President, and other than the General Accounting Office) whose appointment to office is required to be made by the President, by and with the advice and consent of the Senate, dies, resigns, or is otherwise unable to perform the functions and duties of the office—

(1) the office shall remain vacant; and

(2) in the case of an office other than the office of the head of an Executive agency (including the Executive Office of the President, and other than the General Accounting Office), only the head of such Executive agency may perform any function or duty of such office.

(c) If the last day of any 210-day period under section 3346 is a day on which the Senate is not in session, the second day the Senate is next in session and receiving nominations shall be deemed to be the last day of such period.

(d)(1) An action taken by any person who is not acting under section 3345, 3346, or 3347, or as provided by subsection (b), in the performance of any function or duty of a vacant office to which this section and sections 3346, 3347, 3349, 3349a,

3349b, and 3349c apply shall have no force or effect.

(2) An action that has no force or effect under paragraph (1) may not be ratified.

(e) This section shall not apply to—

(1) the General Counsel of the National Labor Relations Board;

(2) the General Counsel of the Federal Labor Relations Authority;

(3) any Inspector General appointed by the President, by and with the advice and consent of the Senate;

(4) any Chief Financial Officer appointed by the President, by and with the advice and consent of the Senate; or

(5) an office of an Executive agency (including the Executive Office of the President, and other than the General Accounting Office) if a statutory provision expressly prohibits the head of the Executive agency from performing the functions and duties of such office.

(Added Pub. L. 105–277, div. C, title I, § 151(b), Oct. 21, 1998, 112 Stat. 2681–613.)

PRIOR PROVISIONS

A prior section 3348, Pub. L. 89–554, Sept. 6, 1966, 80 Stat. 426; Pub. L. 100–398, § 7(b), Aug. 17, 1988, 102 Stat. 988, provided for time limitations relating to details, prior to repeal by Pub. L. 105–277, div. C, title I, § 151(b), (d)(1), Oct. 21, 1998, 112 Stat. 2681–611, 2681–616, effective 30 days after Oct. 21, 1998. See section 3346 of this title.

EFFECTIVE DATE

Section effective 30 days after Oct. 21, 1998, and applicable to any office that becomes vacant after such effective date, with certain exceptions, see section 151(d) of Pub. L. 105–277, set out as a note under section 3345 of this title.

SECTION REFERRED TO IN OTHER SECTIONS

This section is referred to in sections 3345, 3349, 3349a, 3349b, 3349c, 3349d of this title.

§ 3349. Reporting of vacancies

(a) The head of each Executive agency (including the Executive Office of the President, and other than the General Accounting Office) shall submit to the Comptroller General of the United States and to each House of Congress—

(1) notification of a vacancy in an office to which this section and sections 3345, 3346, 3347, 3348, 3349a, 3349b, 3349c, and 3349d apply and the date such vacancy occurred immediately upon the occurrence of the vacancy;

(2) the name of any person serving in an acting capacity and the date such service began immediately upon the designation;

(3) the name of any person nominated to the Senate to fill the vacancy and the date such nomination is submitted immediately upon the submission of the nomination; and

(4) the date of a rejection, withdrawal, or return of any nomination immediately upon such rejection, withdrawal, or return.

(b) If the Comptroller General of the United States makes a determination that an officer is serving longer than the 210-day period including the applicable exceptions to such period under section 3346 or section 3349a, the Comptroller General shall report such determination immediately to—

(1) the Committee on Governmental Affairs of the Senate;

(2) the Committee on Government Reform and Oversight of the House of Representatives;

(3) the Committees on Appropriations of the Senate and House of Representatives;

(4) the appropriate committees of jurisdiction of the Senate and House of Representatives;

(5) the President; and

(6) the Office of Personnel Management.

(Added Pub. L. 105–277, div. C, title I, § 151(b), Oct. 21, 1998, 112 Stat. 2681–614.)

PRIOR PROVISIONS

A prior section 3349, Pub. L. 89–554, Sept. 6, 1966, 80 Stat. 426, provided for restrictions relating to details to fill vacancies, prior to repeal by Pub. L. 105–277, div. C, title I, § 151(b), (d)(1), Oct. 21, 1998, 112 Stat. 2681–611, 2681–616, effective 30 days after Oct. 21, 1998. See section 3347 of this title.

CHANGE OF NAME

Committee on Government Reform and Oversight of House of Representatives changed to Committee on Government Reform of House of Representatives by House Resolution No. 5, One Hundred Sixth Congress, Jan. 6, 1999.

EFFECTIVE DATE

Section effective 30 days after Oct. 21, 1998, and applicable to any office that becomes vacant after such effective date, with certain exceptions, see section 151(d) of Pub. L. 105–277, set out as a note under section 3345 of this title.

SECTION REFERRED TO IN OTHER SECTIONS

This section is referred to in sections 3345, 3348, 3349b, 3349c, 3349d of this title.

§ 3349a. Presidential inaugural transitions

(a) In this section, the term "transitional inauguration day" means the date on which any person swears or affirms the oath of office as President, if such person is not the President on the date preceding the date of swearing or affirming such oath of office.

(b) With respect to any vacancy that exists during the 60-day period beginning on a transitional inauguration day, the 210-day period under section 3346 or 3348 shall be deemed to begin on the later of the date occurring—

(1) 90 days after such transitional inauguration day; or

(2) 90 days after the date on which the vacancy occurs.

(Added Pub. L. 105–277, div. C, title I, § 151(b), Oct. 21, 1998, 112 Stat. 2681–615.)

EFFECTIVE DATE

Section effective 30 days after Oct. 21, 1998, and applicable to any office that becomes vacant after such effective date, with certain exceptions, see section 151(d) of Pub. L. 105–277, set out as a note under section 3345 of this title.

SECTION REFERRED TO IN OTHER SECTIONS

This section is referred to in sections 3345, 3348, 3349, 3349b, 3349c, 3349d of this title.

§ 3349b. Holdover provisions

Sections 3345 through 3349a shall not be construed to affect any statute that authorizes a person to continue to serve in any office—

(1) after the expiration of the term for which such person is appointed; and

(2) until a successor is appointed or a specified period of time has expired.

(Added Pub. L. 105–277, div. C, title I, §151(b), Oct. 21, 1998, 112 Stat. 2681–615.)

EFFECTIVE DATE

Section effective 30 days after Oct. 21, 1998, and applicable to any office that becomes vacant after such effective date, with certain exceptions, see section 151(d) of Pub. L. 105–277, set out as a note under section 3345 of this title.

SECTION REFERRED TO IN OTHER SECTIONS

This section is referred to in sections 3348, 3349, 3349c, 3349d of this title.

§ 3349c. Exclusion of certain officers

Sections 3345 through 3349b shall not apply to—

(1) any member who is appointed by the President, by and with the advice and consent of the Senate to any board, commission, or similar entity that—

(A) is composed of multiple members; and

(B) governs an independent establishment or Government corporation;

(2) any commissioner of the Federal Energy Regulatory Commission;

(3) any member of the Surface Transportation Board; or

(4) any judge appointed by the President, by and with the advice and consent of the Senate, to a court constituted under article I of the United States Constitution.

(Added Pub. L. 105–277, div. C, title I, §151(b), Oct. 21, 1998, 112 Stat. 2681–615.)

EFFECTIVE DATE

Section effective 30 days after Oct. 21, 1998, and applicable to any office that becomes vacant after such effective date, with certain exceptions, see section 151(d) of Pub. L. 105–277, set out as a note under section 3345 of this title.

SECTION REFERRED TO IN OTHER SECTIONS

This section is referred to in sections 3348, 3349, 3349d of this title.

§ 3349d. Notification of intent to nominate during certain recesses or adjournments

(a) The submission to the Senate, during a recess or adjournment of the Senate in excess of 15 days, of a written notification by the President of the President's intention to submit a nomination after the recess or adjournment shall be considered a nomination for purposes of sections 3345 through 3349c if such notification contains the name of the proposed nominee and the office for which the person is nominated.

(b) If the President does not submit a nomination of the person named under subsection (a) within 2 days after the end of such recess or adjournment, effective after such second day the notification considered a nomination under subsection (a) shall be treated as a withdrawn nomination for purposes of sections 3345 through 3349c.

(Added Pub. L. 105–277, div. C, title I, §151(b), Oct. 21, 1998, 112 Stat. 2681–615.)

EFFECTIVE DATE

Section effective 30 days after Oct. 21, 1998, and applicable to any office that becomes vacant after such effective date, with certain exceptions, see section 151(d) of Pub. L. 105–277, set out as a note under section 3345 of this title.

SECTION REFERRED TO IN OTHER SECTIONS

This section is referred to in sections 3345, 3349 of this title.

SUBCHAPTER IV—TRANSFERS

§ 3351. Preference eligibles; transfer; physical qualifications; waiver

In determining qualifications of a preference eligible for transfer to another position in the competitive service, an Executive agency, or the government of the District of Columbia, the Office of Personnel Management or other examining agency shall waive—

(1) requirements as to age, height, and weight, unless the requirement is essential to the performance of the duties of the position; and

(2) physical requirements if, in the opinion of the Office or other examining agency, after considering the recommendation of an accredited physician, the preference eligible is physically able to perform efficiently the duties of the position.

This section does not apply to an appointment required by Congress to be confirmed by, or made with the advice and consent of, the Senate.

(Pub. L. 89–554, Sept. 6, 1966, 80 Stat. 426; Pub. L. 94–183, §2(4), Dec. 31, 1975, 89 Stat. 1057; Pub. L. 95–454, title IX, §906(a)(2), (3), Oct. 13, 1978, 92 Stat. 1224.)

HISTORICAL AND REVISION NOTES

Derivation	U.S. Code	Revised Statutes and Statutes at Large
....	5 U.S.C. 854 (1st 2 sentences, so much as relates to transfer).	June 27, 1944, ch. 287, §5 (1st 2 sentences, so much as relates to transfer), 58 Stat. 388.

The section is restated to conform to section 3312.

The words "in the competitive service, an Executive agency, or the government of the District of Columbia" are added on authority of former sections 851, 858, and 869, which are carried into this title. The last sentence is added on authority of former section 869.

Standard changes are made to conform with the definitions applicable and the style of this title as outlined in the preface to the report.

AMENDMENTS

1978—Pub. L. 95–454 substituted "Office of Personnel Management" and "Office" for "Civil Service Commission" and "Commission", respectively.

1975—Pub. L. 94–183 struck out ", except an appointment made under section 3311 of title 39" after "or made with the advice and consent of, the Senate".

EFFECTIVE DATE OF 1978 AMENDMENT

Amendment by Pub. L. 95–454 effective 90 days after Oct. 13, 1978, see section 907 of Pub. L. 95–454, set out as a note under section 1101 of this title.

SECTION REFERRED TO IN OTHER SECTIONS

This section is referred to in section 2302 of this title; title 22 section 1438.

§ 3352. Preference in transfers for employees making certain disclosures

(a) Subject to the provisions of subsections (d) and (e), in filling a position within any Executive agency, the head of such agency may give preference to any employee of such agency, or any other Executive agency, to transfer to a position of the same status and tenure as the position of such employee on the date of applying for a transfer under subsection (b) if—

(1) such employee is otherwise qualified for such position;

(2) such employee is eligible for appointment to such position; and

(3) the Merit Systems Protection Board makes a determination under the provisions of chapter 12 that a prohibited personnel action described under section 2302(b)(8) was taken against such employee.

(b) An employee who meets the conditions described under subsection (a)(1), (2), and (3) may voluntarily apply for a transfer to a position, as described in subsection (a), within the Executive agency employing such employee or any other Executive agency.

(c) If an employee applies for a transfer under the provisions of subsection (b) and the selecting official rejects such application, the selecting official shall provide the employee with a written notification of the reasons for the rejection within 30 days after receiving such application.

(d) An employee whose application for transfer is rejected under the provisions of subsection (c) may request the head of such agency to review the rejection. Such request for review shall be submitted to the head of the agency within 30 days after the employee receives notification under subsection (c). Within 30 days after receiving a request for review, the head of the agency shall complete the review and provide a written statement of findings to the employee and the Merit Systems Protection Board.

(e) The provisions of subsection (a) shall apply with regard to any employee—

(1) for no more than 1 transfer;

(2) for a transfer from or within the agency such employee is employed at the time of a determination by the Merit Systems Protection Board that a prohibited personnel action as described under section 2302(b)(8) was taken against such employee; and

(3) no later than 18 months after such a determination is made by the Merit Systems Protection Board.

(f) Notwithstanding the provisions of subsection (a), no preference may be given to any employee applying for a transfer under subsection (b), with respect to a preference eligible (as defined under section 2108(3)) applying for the same position.

(Added Pub. L. 101–12, §5(a), Apr. 10, 1989, 103 Stat. 32.)

EFFECTIVE DATE

Section effective 90 days following Apr. 10, 1989, see section 11 of Pub. L. 101–12, set out as an Effective Date of 1989 Amendment note under section 1201 of this title.

SECTION REFERRED TO IN OTHER SECTIONS

This section is referred to in section 2302 of this title.

SUBCHAPTER V—PROMOTION

§ 3361. Promotion; competitive service; examination

An individual may be promoted in the competitive service only if he has passed an examination or is specifically excepted from examination under section 3302 of this title. This section does not take from the President any authority conferred by section 3301 of this title that is consistent with the provisions of this title governing the competitive service.

(Pub. L. 89–554, Sept. 6, 1966, 80 Stat. 426.)

HISTORICAL AND REVISION NOTES

Derivation	U.S. Code	Revised Statutes and Statutes at Large
....	5 U.S.C. 638 (as applicable to promotion).	Jan. 16, 1883, ch. 27, §7 (as applicable to promotion), 22 Stat. 406.

The words "That after the expiration of six months from the passage of this act" are omitted as executed. The words "in the competitive service" are substituted for "in either of the said classes now existing, or that may be arranged hereunder pursuant to said rules" because of the definition of "competitive service" in section 2102. In the second sentence, the words "the provisions of this title governing the competitive service" are substituted for "this act".

Standard changes are made to conform with the definitions applicable and the style of this title as outlined in the preface to the report.

§ 3362. Promotion; effect of incentive award

An agency, in qualifying and selecting an employee for promotion, shall give due weight to an incentive award under chapter 45 of this title. For the purpose of this section, "agency" and "employee" have the meanings given them by section 4501 of this title.

(Pub. L. 89–554, Sept. 6, 1966, 80 Stat. 426.)

HISTORICAL AND REVISION NOTES

Derivation	U.S. Code	Revised Statutes and Statutes at Large
....	5 U.S.C. 2123(f).	Sept. 1, 1954, ch. 1208, §304(f), 68 Stat. 1113.

The word "incentive" is added for clarification. The second sentence is added on authority of former section 2122, which is carried into section 4501.

Standard changes are made to conform with the definitions applicable and the style of this title as outlined in the preface to the report.

§ 3363. Preference eligibles; promotion; physical qualifications; waiver

In determining qualifications of a preference eligible for promotion to another position in the competitive service, an Executive agency, or the government of the District of Columbia, the Office of Personnel Management or other examining agency shall waive—

(1) requirements as to age, height, and weight, unless the requirement is essential to the performance of the duties of the position; and

(2) physical requirements if, in the opinion of the Office or other examining agency, after considering the recommendation of an accred-

ited physician, the preference eligible is physically able to perform efficiently the duties of the position.

This section does not apply to an appointment required by Congress to be confirmed by, or made with the advice and consent of, the Senate.

(Pub. L. 89–554, Sept. 6, 1966, 80 Stat. 427; Pub. L. 94–183, § 2(5), Dec. 31, 1975, 89 Stat. 1057; Pub. L. 95–454, title IX, § 906(a)(2), (3), Oct. 13, 1978, 92 Stat. 1224.)

HISTORICAL AND REVISION NOTES

Derivation	U.S. Code	Revised Statutes and Statutes at Large
....	5 U.S.C. 854 (1st 2 sentences, so much as relates to promotion).	June 27, 1944, ch. 287, § 5 (1st 2 sentences, so much as relates to promotion), 58 Stat. 388.

The section is restated to conform to section 3312.

The words "in the competitive service, an Executive agency, or the government of the District of Columbia" are added on authority of former sections 851, 858, and 869, which are carried into this title. The last sentence is added on authority of former section 869.

Standard changes are made to conform with the definitions applicable and the style of this title as outlined in the preface to the report.

AMENDMENTS

1978—Pub. L. 95–454 substituted "Office of Personnel Management" and "Office" for "Civil Service Commission" and "Commission", respectively.

1975—Pub. L. 94–183 struck out ", except an appointment made under section 3311 of title 39" after "or made with the advice and consent of, the Senate".

EFFECTIVE DATE OF 1978 AMENDMENT

Amendment by Pub. L. 95–454 effective 90 days after Oct. 13, 1978, see section 907 of Pub. L. 95–454, set out as a note under section 1101 of this title.

SECTION REFERRED TO IN OTHER SECTIONS

This section is referred to in section 2302 of this title; title 22 section 1438.

[§ 3364. Repealed. Pub. L. 94–183, § 2(6), Dec. 31, 1975, 89 Stat. 1057]

Section, Pub. L. 89–554, Sept. 6, 1966, 80 Stat. 427, related to promotion to regular force of substitute employees in postal field service.

SUBCHAPTER VI—ASSIGNMENTS TO AND FROM STATES

SUBCHAPTER REFERRED TO IN OTHER SECTIONS

This subchapter is referred to in title 22 sections 2514, 4081; title 41 section 419; title 42 section 11708.

§ 3371. Definitions

For the purpose of this subchapter—

(1) "State" means—

(A) a State of the United States, the District of Columbia, the Commonwealth of Puerto Rico, the Trust Territory of the Pacific Islands, and a territory or possession of the United States; and

(B) an instrumentality or authority of a State or States as defined in subparagraph (A) of this paragraph (1) and a Federal-State authority or instrumentality;

(2) "local government" means—

(A) any political subdivision, instrumentality, or authority of a State or States as defined in subparagraph (A) of paragraph (1);

(B) any general or special purpose agency of such a political subdivision, instrumentality, or authority; and

(C) any Indian tribe, band, nation, or other organized group or community, including any Alaska Native village as defined in the Alaska Native Claims Settlement Act (85 Stat. 688), which is recognized as eligible for the special programs and services provided by the United States to Indians because of their status as Indians and includes any tribal organization as defined in section 4 of the Indian Self-Determination and Education Assistance Act;

(3) "Federal agency" means an Executive agency, military department, a court of the United States, the Administrative Office of the United States Courts, the Library of Congress, the Botanic Garden, the Government Printing Office, the Congressional Budget Office, the United States Postal Service, the Postal Rate Commission, the Office of the Architect of the Capitol, the Office of Technology Assessment, and such other similar agencies of the legislative and judicial branches as determined appropriate by the Office of Personnel Management; and

(4) "other organization" means—

(A) a national, regional, State-wide, area-wide, or metropolitan organization representing member State or local governments;

(B) an association of State or local public officials;

(C) a nonprofit organization which has as one of its principal functions the offering of professional advisory, research, educational, or development services, or related services, to governments or universities concerned with public management; or

(D) a federally funded research and development center.

(Added Pub. L. 91–648, title IV, § 402(a), Jan. 5, 1971, 84 Stat. 1920; amended Pub. L. 93–638, title I, § 104(a), formerly § 105(a), Jan. 4, 1975, 88 Stat. 2208, renumbered § 104(a), Pub. L. 100–472, title II, § 203(a), Oct. 5, 1988, 102 Stat. 2290; Pub. L. 95–454, title VI, § 603(a), Oct. 13, 1978, 92 Stat. 1189; Pub. L. 100–472, title II, § 203(b), Oct. 5, 1988, 102 Stat. 2290; Pub. L. 101–301, § 2(c), May 24, 1990, 104 Stat. 207; Pub. L. 103–337, div. A, title X, § 1068(a), Oct. 5, 1994, 108 Stat. 2852.)

REFERENCES IN TEXT

The Alaska Native Claims Settlement Act, referred to in par. (2)(C), is Pub. L. 92–203, Dec. 18, 1971, 85 Stat. 688, as amended, which is classified generally to chapter 33 (§ 1601 et seq.) of Title 43, Public Lands. For complete classification of this Act to the Code, see Short Title note set out under section 1601 of Title 43 and Tables.

Section 4 of the Indian Self-Determination and Education Assistance Act, referred to in par. (2)(C), is classified to section 450b of Title 25, Indians.

AMENDMENTS

1994—Par. (4)(D). Pub. L. 103–337 added subpar. (D).

1990—Par. (2)(C). Pub. L. 101–301 substituted "section 4" for "section 4(m)".

1988—Par. (2)(C). Pub. L. 100–472, §203(b), amended Pub. L. 93–638, by substituting "section 4(m)" for "section 4(c)" in the provision it added as par. (2)(C) of this section. See 1975 Amendment note below.

1978—Par. (1)(A). Pub. L. 95–454, §603(a)(1), inserted reference to the Trust Territory of the Pacific Islands.

Pars. (3), (4). Pub. L. 95–454, §603(a)(2), added pars. (3) and (4).

1975—Par. (2)(C). Pub. L. 93–638, as amended by Pub. L. 100–472, §203(b), added par. (2)(C).

EFFECTIVE DATE OF 1978 AMENDMENT

Amendment by Pub. L. 95–454 effective 90 days after Oct. 13, 1978, see section 907 of Pub. L. 95–454, set out as a note under section 1101 of this title.

EFFECTIVE DATE

Section 404 of title IV of Pub. L. 91–648 provided that: "This title [enacting this subchapter and repealing sections 1881 to 1888 of Title 7, Agriculture, section 869b of Title 20, Education, and section 246(f) of Title 42, The Public Health and Welfare, (less applicability to commissioned officers of the Public Health Service)] shall become effective sixty days after the date of enactment of this Act [Jan. 5, 1971]."

TERMINATION OF TRUST TERRITORY OF THE PACIFIC ISLANDS

For termination of Trust Territory of the Pacific Islands, see note set out preceding section 1681 of Title 48, Territories and Insular Possessions.

DECLARATION OF PURPOSE

Section 401 of title IV of Pub. L. 91–648, as amended by Pub. L. 95–454, title VI, §602(b), Oct. 13, 1978, 92 Stat. 1189, provided that: "The purpose of this title [see Effective Date note above] is to provide for the temporary assignment of personnel between the Federal Government and State and local governments, institutions of higher education, and other organizations."

SECTION REFERRED TO IN OTHER SECTIONS

This section is referred to in section 3372 of this title; title 22 section 2124c.

§ 3372. General provisions

(a) On request from or with the concurrence of a State or local government, and with the consent of the employee concerned, the head of a Federal agency may arrange for the assignment of—

(1) an employee of his agency, other than a noncareer appointee, limited term appointee, or limited emergency appointee (as such terms are defined in section 3132(a) of this title) in the Senior Executive Service and an employee in a position which has been excepted from the competitive service by reason of its confidential, policy-determining, policy-making, or policy-advocating character, to a State or local government; and

(2) an employee of a State or local government to his agency;

for work of mutual concern to his agency and the State or local government that he determines will be beneficial to both. The period of an assignment under this subchapter may not exceed two years. However, the head of a Federal agency may extend the period of assignment for not more than two additional years. In the case of assignments made to Indian tribes or tribal organizations as defined in section 3371(2)(C) of this subchapter, the head of an executive agency may extend the period of assign-

ment for any period of time where it is determined that this will continue to benefit both the executive agency and the Indian tribe or tribal organization. If the assigned employee fails to complete the period of assignment and there is another employee willing and available to do so, the Secretary may assign the employee to complete the period of assignment and may execute an agreement with the tribal organization with respect to the replacement employee. That agreement may provide for a different period of assignment as may be agreed to by the Secretary and the tribal organization.

(b) This subchapter is authority for and applies to the assignment of—

(1) an employee of a Federal agency to an institution of higher education;

(2) an employee of an institution of higher education to a Federal agency;

(3) an employee of a Federal agency to any other organization; and

(4) an employee of an other organization to a Federal agency.

(c)(1) An employee of a Federal agency may be assigned under this subchapter only if the employee agrees, as a condition of accepting an assignment under this subchapter, to serve in the civil service upon the completion of the assignment for a period equal to the length of the assignment.

(2) Each agreement required under paragraph (1) of this subsection shall provide that in the event the employee fails to carry out the agreement (except for good and sufficient reason, as determined by the head of the Federal agency from which assigned) the employee shall be liable to the United States for payment of all expenses (excluding salary) of the assignment. The amount shall be treated as a debt due the United States.

(d) Where the employee is assigned to a tribal organization, the employee shall be eligible for promotions, periodic step-increases, and additional step-increases, as defined in chapter 53 of this title, on the same basis as other Federal employees.

(e) Under regulations prescribed pursuant to section 3376 of this title—

(1) an assignment of an employee of a Federal agency to an other organization or an institution of higher education, and an employee so assigned, shall be treated in the same way as an assignment of an employee of a Federal agency to a State or local government, and an employee so assigned, is treated under the provisions of this subchapter governing an assignment of an employee of a Federal agency to a State or local government, except that the rate of pay of an employee assigned to a federally funded research and development center may not exceed the rate of pay that such employee would be paid for continued service in the position in the Federal agency from which assigned; and

(2) an assignment of an employee of an other organization or an institution of higher education to a Federal agency, and an employee so assigned, shall be treated in the same way as an assignment of an employee of a State or local government to a Federal agency, and an employee so assigned, is treated under the pro-

visions of this subchapter governing an assignment of an employee of a State or local government to a Federal agency.

(Added Pub. L. 91–648, title IV, § 402(a), Jan. 5, 1971, 84 Stat. 1921; amended Pub. L. 93–638, title I, § 104(k), (*l*), as added Pub. L. 100–472, title II, § 203(f), Oct. 5, 1988, 102 Stat. 2290; Pub. L. 95–454, title VI, § 603(b), (c), Oct. 13, 1978, 92 Stat. 1190; Pub. L. 98–146, title II, Nov. 4, 1983, 97 Stat. 946; Pub. L. 103–89, § 3(b)(1)(A), Sept. 30, 1993, 107 Stat. 981; Pub. L. 103–337, div. A, title X, § 1068(b), Oct. 5, 1994, 108 Stat. 2852.)

Amendments

1994—Subsec. (e). Pub. L. 103–337 added subsec. (e).

1993—Subsec. (d). Pub. L. 103–89 substituted "and additional step-increases, as defined in chapter 53" for "additional step-increases, merit pay, and cash awards, as defined in chapters 53 and 54".

1988—Subsecs. (a), (d). Pub. L. 100–472 added Pub. L. 93–638, § 104(k), (*l*). See 1975 Amendment note below.

1983—Subsec. (a). Pub. L. 98–146 inserted sentence providing that, in the case of assignments made to Indian tribes or tribal organizations as defined in section 3371(2)(C) of this title, the head of an executive agency may extend the period of assignment for any period of time where it is determined that this will continue to benefit both the executive agency and the Indian tribe or tribal organization.

1978—Subsec. (a). Pub. L. 95–454, § 603(b), (c)(1), substituted "a Federal" for "an executive" wherever appearing, and in cl. (1) inserted provisions relating to a noncareer appointee, limited term appointee, or limited emergency appointee, and an employee excepted from the competitive service.

Subsec. (b). Pub. L. 95–454, § 603(b), (c)(2)–(4), in cls. (1) and (2) substituted "a Federal" for "an executive", and added cls. (3) and (4).

Subsec. (c). Pub. L. 95–454, § 603(c)(5), added subsec. (c).

1975—Subsec. (a). Pub. L. 93–638, § 104(k), as added by Pub. L. 100–472, inserted at end "If the assigned employee fails to complete the period of assignment and there is another employee willing and available to do so, the Secretary may assign the employee to complete the period of assignment and may execute an agreement with the tribal organization with respect to the replacement employee. That agreement may provide for a different period of assignment as may be agreed to by the Secretary and the tribal organization."

Subsec. (d). Pub. L. 93–638, § 104(*l*), as added by Pub. L. 100–472, added subsec. (d).

Effective Date of 1993 Amendment

Section 3(c) of Pub. L. 103–89 provided that: "The amendments made by this section [amending this section and sections 4501, 4502, 5302, 5332, 5334 to 5336, 5361 to 5363, 5948, and 8473 of this title, sections 1602, 1732, and 1733 of Title 10, Armed Forces, and section 731 of Title 31, Money and Finance, repealing sections 4302a and 5401 to 5410 of this title, and amending provisions set out as a note under section 5304 of this title] shall take effect as of November 1, 1993."

Effective Date of 1978 Amendment

Amendment by Pub. L. 95–454 effective 90 days after Oct. 13, 1978, see section 907 of Pub. L. 95–454, set out as a note under section 1101 of this title.

Section Referred to in Other Sections

This section is referred to in title 16 sections 1a–2, 471j; title 25 section 450i.

§ 3373. Assignment of employees to State or local governments

(a) An employee of a Federal agency assigned to a State or local government under this sub-chapter is deemed, during the assignment, to be either—

(1) on detail to a regular work assignment in his agency; or

(2) on leave without pay from his position in the agency.

An employee assigned either on detail or on leave without pay remains an employee of his agency. The Federal Tort Claims Act and any other Federal tort liability statute apply to an employee so assigned. The supervision of the duties of an employee on detail may be governed by agreement between the Federal agency and the State or local government concerned.

(b) The assignment of an employee of a Federal agency either on detail or on leave without pay to a State or local government under this subchapter may be made with or without reimbursement by the State or local government for the travel and transportation expenses to or from the place of assignment and for the pay, or supplemental pay, or a part thereof, of the employee during assignment. Any reimbursements shall be credited to the appropriation of the Federal agency used for paying the travel and transportation expenses or pay.

(c) For any employee so assigned and on leave without pay—

(1) if the rate of pay for his employment by the State or local government is less than the rate of pay he would have received had he continued in his regular assignment in the agency, he is entitled to receive supplemental pay from the agency in an amount equal to the difference between the State or local government rate and the agency rate;

(2) he is entitled to annual and sick leave to the same extent as if he had continued in his regular assignment in the agency; and

(3) he is entitled, notwithstanding other statutes—

(A) to continuation of his insurance under chapter 87 of this title, and coverage under chapter 89 of this title or other applicable authority, so long as he pays currently into the Employee's Life Insurance Fund and the Employee's Health Benefits Fund or other applicable health benefits system (through his employing agency) the amount of the employee contributions;

(B) to credit the period of his assignment under this subchapter toward periodic step-increases, retention, and leave accrual purposes, and, on payment into the Civil Service Retirement and Disability Fund or other applicable retirement system of the percentage of his State or local government pay, and of his supplemental pay, if any, that would have been deducted from a like agency pay for the period of the assignment and payment by the Federal agency into the fund or system of the amount that would have been payable by the agency during the period of the assignment with respect to a like agency pay, to treat his service during that period as service of the type performed in the agency immediately before his assignment; and

(C) for the purpose of subchapter I of chapter 85 of this title, to credit the service performed during the period of his assignment under this subchapter as Federal service, and to consider his State or local government pay (and his supplemental pay, if any) as Federal wages. To the extent that the service could also be the basis for entitlement to unemployment compensation under a State law, the employee may elect to claim unemployment compensation on the basis of the service under either the State law or subchapter I of chapter 85 of this title.

However, an employee or his beneficiary may not receive benefits referred to in subparagraphs (A) and (B) of this paragraph (3), based on service during an assignment under this subchapter for which the employee or, if he dies without making such an election, his beneficiary elects to receive benefits, under any State or local government retirement or insurance law or program, which the Office of Personnel Management determines to be similar. The Federal agency shall deposit currently in the Employee's Life Insurance Fund, the Employee's Health Benefits Fund or other applicable health benefits system, respectively, the amount of the Government's contributions on account of service with respect to which employee contributions are collected as provided in subparagraphs (A) and (B) of this paragraph (3).

(d)(1) An employee so assigned and on leave without pay who dies or suffers disability as a result of personal injury sustained while in the performance of his duty during an assignment under this subchapter shall be treated, for the purpose of subchapter I of chapter 81 of this title, as though he were an employee as defined by section 8101 of this title who had sustained the injury in the performance of duty. When an employee (or his dependents in case of death) entitled by reason of injury or death to benefits under subchapter I of chapter 81 of this title is also entitled to benefits from a State or local government for the same injury or death, he (or his dependents in case of death) shall elect which benefits he will receive. The election shall be made within one year after the injury or death, or such further time as the Secretary of Labor may allow for reasonable cause shown. When made, the election is irrevocable unless otherwise provided by law.

(2) An employee who elects to receive benefits from a State or local government may not receive an annuity under subchapter III of chapter 83 of this title and benefits from the State or local government for injury or disability to himself covering the same period of time. This provision does not—

(A) bar the right of a claimant to the greater benefit conferred by either the State or local government or subchapter III of chapter 83 of this title for any part of the same period of time;

(B) deny to an employee an annuity accruing to him under subchapter III of chapter 83 of this title on account of service performed by him; or

(C) deny any concurrent benefit to him from the State or local government on account of the death of another individual.

(Added Pub. L. 91–648, title IV, § 402(a), Jan. 5, 1971, 84 Stat. 1921; amended Pub. L. 95–454, title

VI, § 603(b), title IX, § 906(a)(2), Oct. 13, 1978, 92 Stat. 1190, 1224; Pub. L. 102–378, § 2(14), Oct. 2, 1992, 106 Stat. 1347.)

REFERENCES IN TEXT

The Federal Tort Claims Act, referred to in subsec. (a), is classified to sections 1346(b) and 2671 et seq. of Title 28, Judiciary and Judicial Procedure.

AMENDMENTS

1992—Pub. L. 102–378 substituted "or local" for "and local" in section catchline.
1978—Subsecs. (a), (b). Pub. L. 95–454, § 603(b), substituted "a Federal" for "an executive" and "Federal agency" for "executive agency".
Subsec. (c). Pub. L. 95–454, §§ 603(b), 906(a)(2), substituted "Federal agency" for "executive agency" wherever appearing, and "Office of Personnel Management" for "Civil Service Commission".

EFFECTIVE DATE OF 1978 AMENDMENT

Amendment by Pub. L. 95–454 effective 90 days after Oct. 13, 1978, see section 907 of Pub. L. 95–454, set out as a note under section 1101 of this title.

SECTION REFERRED TO IN OTHER SECTIONS

This section is referred to in section 3396 of this title.

§ 3374. Assignments of employees from State or local governments

(a) An employee of a State or local government who is assigned to a Federal agency under an arrangement under this subchapter may—

(1) be appointed in the Federal agency without regard to the provisions of this title governing appointment in the competitive service for the agreed period of the assignment; or

(2) be deemed on detail to the Federal agency.

(b) An employee given an appointment is entitled to pay in accordance with chapter 51 and subchapter III of chapter 53 of this title or other applicable law, and is deemed an employee of the Federal agency for all purposes except—

(1) subchapter III of chapter 83 of this title or other applicable retirement system;

(2) chapter 87 of this title; and

(3) chapter 89 of this title or other applicable health benefits system unless his appointment results in the loss of coverage in a group health benefits plan the premium of which has been paid in whole or in part by a State or local government contribution.

The above exceptions shall not apply to non-Federal employees who are covered by chapters 83, 87, and 89 of this title by virtue of their non-Federal employment immediately before assignment and appointment under this section.

(c) During the period of assignment, a State or local government employee on detail to a Federal agency—

(1) is not entitled to pay from the agency, except to the extent that the pay received from the State or local government is less than the appropriate rate of pay which the duties would warrant under the applicable pay provisions of this title or other applicable authority;

(2) is deemed an employee of the agency for the purpose of chapter 73 of this title, sections 203, 205, 207, 208, 209, 602, 603, 606, 607, 643, 654, 1905, and 1913 of title 18, sections 1343, 1344, and

1349(b) of title 31, and the Federal Tort Claims Act and any other Federal tort liability statute; and

(3) is subject to such regulations as the President may prescribe.

The supervision of the duties of such an employee may be governed by agreement between the Federal agency and the State or local government concerned. A detail of a State or local government employee to a Federal agency may be made with or without reimbursement by the Federal agency for the pay, or a part thereof, of the employee during the period of assignment, or for the contribution of the State or local government, or a part thereof, to employee benefit systems.

(d) A State or local government employee who is given an appointment in a Federal agency for the period of the assignment or who is on detail to a Federal agency and who suffers disability or dies as a result of personal injury sustained while in the performance of his duty during the assignment shall be treated, for the purpose of subchapter I of chapter 81 of this title, as though he were an employee as defined by section 8101 of this title who had sustained the injury in the performance of duty. When an employee (or his dependents in case of death) entitled by reason of injury or death to benefits under subchapter I of chapter 81 of this title is also entitled to benefits from a State or local government for the same injury or death, he (or his dependents in case of death) shall elect which benefits he will receive. The election shall be made within 1 year after the injury or death, or such further time as the Secretary of Labor may allow for reasonable cause shown. When made, the election is irrevocable unless otherwise provided by law.

(e) If a State or local government fails to continue the employer's contribution to State or local government retirement, life insurance, and health benefit plans for a State or local government employee who is given an appointment in a Federal agency, the employer's contributions covering the State or local government employee's period of assignment, or any part thereof, may be made from the appropriations of the Federal agency concerned.

(Added Pub. L. 91–648, title IV, § 402(a), Jan. 5, 1971, 84 Stat. 1923; amended Pub. L. 95–454, title VI, § 603(b), (d), Oct. 13, 1978, 92 Stat. 1190; Pub. L. 97–258, § 3(a)(6), Sept. 13, 1982, 96 Stat. 1063.)

REFERENCES IN TEXT

The Federal Tort Claims Act, referred to in subsec. (c)(2), is classified to sections 1346(b) and 2671 et seq. of Title 28, Judiciary and Judicial Procedure.

AMENDMENTS

1982—Subsec. (c)(2). Pub. L. 97–258 substituted "sections 1343, 1344, and 1349(b)" for "section 638a".

1978—Subsec. (a). Pub. L. 95–454, § 603(b), substituted "a Federal" for "an executive", and "Federal agency" for "executive agency" in two places.

Subsec. (b). Pub. L. 95–454, § 603(b), (d)(1), inserted provisions relating to nonapplicability of exceptions to non-Federal employees, and substituted "Federal" for "executive".

Subsec. (c). Pub. L. 95–454, § 603(b), (d)(2), (3), inserted provisions relating to pay received from the State or local government at less than the appropriate rate of

pay, and provisions relating to contributions to employee benefit systems, and substituted "a Federal" for "an executive" and "Federal agency" for "executive agency" wherever appearing.

Subsec. (d). Pub. L. 95–454, § 603(b), substituted "a Federal" for "an executive" in two places.

Subsec. (e). Pub. L. 95–454, § 603(b), substituted "a Federal" for "an executive" and "Federal" for "executive".

EFFECTIVE DATE OF 1978 AMENDMENT

Amendment by Pub. L. 95–454 effective 90 days after Oct. 13, 1978, see section 907 of Pub. L. 95–454, set out as a note under section 1101 of this title.

SECTION REFERRED TO IN OTHER SECTIONS

This section is referred to in title 21 section 878; title 25 section 2804.

§ 3375. Travel expenses

(a) Appropriations of a Federal agency are available to pay, or reimburse, a Federal or State or local government employee in accordance with—

(1) subchapter I of chapter 57 of this title, for the expenses of—

(A) travel, including a per diem allowance, to and from the assignment location;

(B) a per diem allowance at the assignment location during the period of the assignment; and

(C) travel, including a per diem allowance, while traveling on official business away from his designated post of duty during the assignment when the head of the Federal agency considers the travel in the interest of the United States;

(2) section 5724 of this title, for the expenses of transportation of his immediate family and of his household goods and personal effects to and from the assignment location;

(3) section 5724a(a) of this title, for the expenses of per diem allowances for the immediate family of the employee to and from the assignment location;

(4) section 5724a(c) of this title, for subsistence expenses of the employee and his immediate family while occupying temporary quarters at the assignment location and on return to his former post of duty;

(5) section 5724a(g) of this title, to be used by the employee for miscellaneous expenses related to change of station where movement or storage of household goods is involved; and

(6) section 5726(c) of this title, for the expenses of nontemporary storage of household goods and personal effects in connection with assignment at an isolated location.

(b) Expenses specified in subsection (a) of this section, other than those in paragraph (1)(C), may not be allowed in connection with the assignment of a Federal or State or local government employee under this subchapter, unless and until the employee agrees in writing to complete the entire period of his assignment or one year, whichever is shorter, unless separated or reassigned for reasons beyond his control that are acceptable to the Federal agency concerned. If the employee violates the agreement, the money spent by the United States for these expenses is recoverable from the employee as a debt due the United States. The head of the Federal agency concerned may waive in whole or in part a right of recovery under this subsection with respect to a State or local government employee on assignment with the agency.

(c) Appropriations of a Federal agency are available to pay expenses under section 5742 of this title with respect to a Federal or State or local government employee assigned under this subchapter.

(Added Pub. L. 91–648, title IV, §402(a), Jan. 5, 1971, 84 Stat. 1924; amended Pub. L. 95–454, title VI, §603(b), (e), Oct. 13, 1978, 92 Stat. 1190, 1191; Pub. L. 104–201, div. A, title XVII, §1723(a)(1)(A), Sept. 23, 1996, 110 Stat. 2758.)

AMENDMENTS

1996—Subsec. (a)(3). Pub. L. 104–201, §1723(a)(1)(A)(i), substituted "section 5724a(a)" for "section 5724a(a)(1)".
Subsec. (a)(4). Pub. L. 104–201, §1723(a)(1)(A)(ii), substituted "section 5724a(c)" for "section 5724a(a)(3)".
Subsec. (a)(5). Pub. L. 104–201, §1723(a)(1)(A)(iii), substituted "section 5724a(g)" for "section 5724a(b)".
1978—Subsec. (a). Pub. L. 95–454, §603(b), (e), substituted "a Federal agency" for "an executive agency" in introductory text, substituted "Federal" for "executive" in cl. (1), added cl. (5), and redesignated former cl. (5) as (6).
Subsec. (b). Pub. L. 95–454, §603(b), substituted "the Federal" for "the executive".
Subsec. (c). Pub. L. 95–454, §603(b), substituted "a Federal agency" for "an executive agency".

EFFECTIVE DATE OF 1996 AMENDMENT

Amendment by Pub. L. 104–201 effective 180 days after Sept. 23, 1996, see section 1725(a) of Pub. L. 104–201, set out as a note under section 5722 of this title.

EFFECTIVE DATE OF 1978 AMENDMENT

Amendment by Pub. L. 95–454 effective 90 days after Oct. 13, 1978, see section 907 of Pub. L. 95–454, set out as a note under section 1101 of this title.

SECTION REFERRED TO IN OTHER SECTIONS

This section is referred to in title 22 section 4081.

§ 3376. Regulations

The President may prescribe regulations for the administration of this subchapter.

(Added Pub. L. 91–648, title IV, §402(a), Jan. 5, 1971, 84 Stat. 1925.)

EX. ORD. NO. 11589. DELEGATION OF FUNCTIONS TO OFFICE OF PERSONNEL MANAGEMENT

Ex. Ord. No. 11589, Apr. 1, 1971, 36 F.R. 6343, as amended by Ex. Ord. No. 12107, Dec. 28, 1978, 44 F.R. 1055, provided:
By virtue of the authority vested in me by section 301 of title 3 of the United States Code, and as President of the United States, it is ordered as follows:
SECTION 1. The Office of Personnel Management is hereby designated and empowered to exercise, without the approval, ratification, or other action of the President, the following:
(a) The authority of the President under section 3376 of title 5 of the United States Code [this section] to prescribe regulations for the administration of subchapter VI, "Assignments to and from States," of chapter 33 of that title [this chapter].
(b) The authority of the President under section 205 (a)(4) of the Federal Civil Defense Act of 1950, as amended (50 U.S.C. App. 2286(a)(4)), and as affected by Reorganization Plan No. 1 of 1958 (72 Stat. 1799) [set out in the Appendix to this title], relating to the establishment and maintenance of personnel standards on the merit basis.

SEC. 2. To the extent that section 1(b) of this order is inconsistent with the provisions of Executive Order No. 10952 of July 20, 1961, as amended [formerly set out as a note under section 2271 of Title 50, Appendix, War and National Defense], section 1(b) shall control.

SECTION REFERRED TO IN OTHER SECTIONS

This section is referred to in section 3372 of this title.

SUBCHAPTER VII—AIR TRAFFIC CONTROLLERS

§ 3381. Training

(a) An air traffic controller with 5 years of service as a controller who is to be removed as a controller because the Secretary has determined—

(1) he is medically disqualified for duties as a controller;

(2) he is unable to maintain technical proficiency as a controller; or

(3) such removal is necessary for the preservation of the physical or mental health of the controller;

is entitled to not more than the full-time equivalent of 2 years of training.

(b) During a period of training under this section, a controller shall be—

(1) retained at his last assigned grade and rate of basic pay as a controller;

(2) entitled to each increase in rate of basic pay provided under law; and

(3) excluded from staffing limitations otherwise applicable.

(c) Upon completion of training under this section, a controller may be—

(1) assigned to other duties in the Executive agency in which the controller is employed;

(2) released for transfer to another Executive agency; or

(3) involuntarily separated from the service.

The involuntary separation of a controller under this subsection is not a removal for cause on charges of misconduct, delinquency, or inefficiency for purposes of section 5595 or section 8336 of this title.

(d) The Secretary, without regard to section 3324(a) and (b) of title 31, may pay, or reimburse a controller for, all or part of the necessary expenses of training provided under this section, including expenses authorized to be paid under chapter 41 and subchapter I of chapter 57 of this title, and the costs of other services or facilities directly related to the training of a controller.

(e) Except as provided by subsection (d) of this section, the provisions of chapter 41 of this title, other than sections 4105, 4107(a) and (b),[1] and 4111, shall not apply to training under this section.

(f) The provisions of this section shall not otherwise affect the authority of the Secretary to provide training under chapter 41 of this title or under any other provision of law.

(Added Pub. L. 92–297, §3(a), May 16, 1972, 86 Stat. 142; amended Pub. L. 96–347, §1(b), (c)(1), Sept. 12, 1980, 94 Stat. 1150; Pub. L. 97–258, §3(a)(7), Sept. 13, 1982, 96 Stat. 1063; Pub. L. 103–226, §2(b)(1), Mar. 30, 1994, 108 Stat. 112.)

---

[1] See References in Text note below.

REFERENCES IN TEXT

For definition of Secretary, referred to in subsec. (a), see section 2109 of this title.

Subsecs. (a) and (b) of section 4107 of this title, referred to in subsec. (e), were struck out, and subsecs. (c) and (d) of section 4107 were redesignated (a) and (b), respectively, by Pub. L. 103–226, § 2(a)(5)(B), Mar. 30, 1994, 108 Stat. 112.

AMENDMENTS

1994—Subsec. (e). Pub. L. 103–226 substituted "4105," for "4105(a),".

1982—Subsec. (d). Pub. L. 97–258 substituted "section 3324(a) and (b)" for "section 529".

1980—Subsec. (a). Pub. L. 96–347, § 1(b), substituted "Secretary" for "Secretary of Transportation".

Subsec. (c)(1). Pub. L. 96–347, § 1(c)(1), substituted "in the Executive agency in which the controller is employed" for "in the Department of Transportation".

EFFECTIVE DATE OF 1994 AMENDMENT

Section 2(c) of Pub. L. 103–226 provided that: "The amendments made by this section [amending this section and sections 4101, 4103, 4105, 4107, 4108, 4113, and 4118 of this title and repealing sections 4106 and 4114 of this title] shall become effective on the date of enactment of this Act [Mar. 30, 1994]."

EFFECTIVE DATE OF 1980 AMENDMENT

Amendment by Pub. L. 96–347 effective on 90th day after Sept. 12, 1980, see section 3 of Pub. L. 96–347, set out as a note under section 2109 of this title.

EFFECTIVE DATE

Section 10 of Pub. L. 92–297 provided that: "This Act [enacting this subchapter and section 2109 of this title, amending sections 3307, 8332, 8334 to 8336, 8339, 8341, 8344 of this title, enacting provisions set out as notes under this section and section 8335 of this title, and repealing provisions set out as a note under section 3307 of this title] shall become effective at the beginning of the ninetieth day after the date of enactment of this Act [May 16, 1972]."

REPORT TO CONGRESS

Section 9 of Pub. L. 92–297 directed the Secretary of Transportation to report to Congress no later than 5 years after May 16, 1972, concerning his operations under the amendments made by Pub. L. 92–297, including a detailed statement of the effectiveness of Pub. L. 92–297 in meeting the needs of the Air Traffic Controller career program and of the air traffic control system plus recommendations for the management of the program or the system.

SECTION REFERRED TO IN OTHER SECTIONS

This section is referred to in sections 3382, 3383 of this title.

§ 3382. Involuntary separation for retirement

An air traffic controller who is eligible for immediate retirement under section 8336 of this title may be separated involuntarily from the service if the Secretary determines that the separation of the controller is necessary in the interest of—

(1) aviation safety;

(2) the efficient control of air traffic; or

(3) the preservation of the physical or mental health of the controller.

Chapter 75 of this title does not apply to a determination or action under this section. Separation under this section shall not become final, without the consent of the controller, until the last day of the second month following the day the controller receives a notification of the determination by the Secretary under this section, or, if a review is requested under section 3383 of this title, the last day of the month in which a final decision is issued by a board of review under section 3383(c) of this title, whichever is later. A controller who is to be separated under this section is entitled to training under section 3381 of this title. Separation of such a controller who elects to receive training under section 3381 shall not become final until the last day of the month following the completion of his training.

(Added Pub. L. 92–297, § 3(a), May 16, 1972, 86 Stat. 142; amended Pub. L. 96–347, § 1(b), Sept. 12, 1980, 94 Stat. 1150.)

REFERENCES IN TEXT

For definition of Secretary, referred to in text, see section 2109 of this title.

AMENDMENTS

1980—Pub. L. 96–347 in provisions preceding par. (1) substituted "Secretary determines" for "Secretary of Transportation determines".

EFFECTIVE DATE OF 1980 AMENDMENT

Amendment by Pub. L. 96–347 effective on 90th day after Sept. 12, 1980, see section 3 of Pub. L. 96–347, set out as a note under section 2109 of this title.

EFFECTIVE DATE

Section effective on 90th day after May 16, 1972, see section 10 of Pub. L. 92–297, set out as a note under section 3381 of this title.

SECTION REFERRED TO IN OTHER SECTIONS

This section is referred to in section 3383 of this title.

§ 3383. Determinations; review procedures

(a) An air traffic controller subject to a determination by the Secretary under section 3381(a) or section 3382 of this title, shall be furnished a written notice of the determination and the reasons therefor, and a notification that the controller has 15 days after the receipt of the notification within which to file a written request for reconsideration of the determination. Unless the controller files such a request within the 15 days, or unless the determination is rescinded by the Secretary within the 15 days, the determination shall be final.

(b) If the Secretary does not rescind his determination within 15 days after his receipt of the written request filed by the controller under subsection (a) of this section, the Secretary shall immediately convene a board of review, consisting of—

(1) a person designated by the controller;

(2) a representative of the Executive agency in which the controller is employed designated by the Secretary; and

(3) a representative of the Merit Systems Protection Board, designated by the Chairman, who shall serve as chairman of the board of review.

(c) The board of review shall review evidence supporting and inconsistent with the determination of the Secretary and, within a period of 30 days after being convened, shall issue its findings and furnish copies thereof to the Secretary and the controller. The board may approve or rescind the determination of the Secretary. A decision by the board under this subsection is final. The Secretary shall take such action as may be necessary to carry out the decision of the board.

(d) Except as provided under section 3382 of this title, the review procedure of this section is in addition to any other review or appeal procedures provided under any other provision of law, but is the sole and exclusive administrative remedy available to a controller within the Executive agency in which such controller is employed.

(Added Pub. L. 92–297, § 3(a), May 16, 1972, 86 Stat. 143; amended Pub. L. 95–454, title IX, § 906(a)(6), Oct. 13, 1978, 92 Stat. 1225; Pub. L. 96–347, § 1(b), (c)(2), (3), Sept. 12, 1980, 94 Stat. 1150.)

References in Text

For definition of Secretary, referred to in text, see section 2109 of this title.

Amendments

1980—Subsec. (a). Pub. L. 96–347, § 1(b), substituted "Secretary under" for "Secretary of Transportation under".

Subsec. (b)(2). Pub. L. 96–347, § 1(c)(2), substituted "the Executive agency in which the controller is employed" for "the Department of Transportation".

Subsec. (d). Pub. L. 96–347, § 1(c)(3), substituted "within the Executive agency in which such controller is employed" for "within the Department of Transportation".

1978—Subsec. (b)(3). Pub. L. 95–454 substituted "Merit Systems Protection Board" for "Civil Service Commission".

Effective Date of 1980 Amendment

Amendment by Pub. L. 96–347 effective on 90th day after Sept. 12, 1980, see section 3 of Pub. L. 96–347, set out as a note under section 2109 of this title.

Effective Date of 1978 Amendment

Amendment by Pub. L. 95–454 effective 90 days after Oct. 13, 1978, see section 907 of Pub. L. 95–454, set out as a note under section 1101 of this title.

Effective Date

Section effective on 90th day after May 16, 1972, see section 10 of Pub. L. 92–297, set out as a note under section 3381 of this title.

Section Referred to in Other Sections

This section is referred to in section 3382 of this title.

§ 3384. Regulations

The Secretary is authorized to issue regulations to carry out the provisions of this subchapter.

(Added Pub. L. 92–297, § 3(a), May 16, 1972, 86 Stat. 143; amended Pub. L. 96–347, § 1(b), Sept. 12, 1980, 94 Stat. 1150.)

References in Text

For definition of Secretary, referred to in text, see section 2109 of this title.

Amendments

1980—Pub. L. 96–347 substituted "Secretary" for "Secretary of Transportation".

Effective Date of 1980 Amendment

Amendment by Pub. L. 96–347 effective on 90th day after Sept. 12, 1980, see section 3 of Pub. L. 96–347, set out as a note under section 2109 of this title.

Effective Date

Section effective on 90th day after May 16, 1972, see section 10 of Pub. L. 92–297, set out as a note under section 3381 of this title.

§ 3385. Effect on other authority

This subchapter shall not limit the authority of the Secretary to reassign temporarily an air traffic controller to other duties with or without notice, in the interest of the safe or efficient separation and control of air traffic or the physical or mental health of a controller; or to reassign permanently or separate a controller under any other provision of law.

(Added Pub. L. 92–297, § 3(a), May 16, 1972, 86 Stat. 143; amended Pub. L. 96–347, § 1(b), Sept. 12, 1980, 94 Stat. 1150.)

References in Text

For definition of Secretary, referred to in text, see section 2109 of this title.

Amendments

1980—Pub. L. 96–347 substituted "Secretary" for "Secretary of Transportation".

Effective Date of 1980 Amendment

Amendment by Pub. L. 96–347 effective on 90th day after Sept. 12, 1980, see section 3 of Pub. L. 96–347, set out as a note under section 2109 of this title.

Effective Date

Section effective on 90th day after May 16, 1972, see section 10 of Pub. L. 92–297, set out as a note under section 3381 of this title.

SUBCHAPTER VIII—APPOINTMENT, REASSIGNMENT, TRANSFER, AND DEVELOPMENT IN THE SENIOR EXECUTIVE SERVICE

Prior Provisions

A prior subchapter VIII, added Pub. L. 95–437, § 3(a), Oct. 10, 1978, 92 Stat. 1056, which related to part-time career employment opportunities, was redesignated as chapter 34 of this title by Pub. L. 95–454, title IX, § 906(c)(1)(A), Oct. 13, 1978, 92 Stat. 1226.

Subchapter Referred to in Other Sections

This subchapter is referred to in sections 1204, 1212 of this title; title 38 section 7425.

§ 3391. Definitions

For the purpose of this subchapter, "agency", "Senior Executive Service position", "senior executive", "career appointee", "limited term appointee", "limited emergency appointee", "non-career appointee", and "general position" have the meanings set forth in section 3132(a) of this title.

(Added Pub. L. 95–454, title IV, § 403(a), Oct. 13, 1978, 92 Stat. 1161.)

Prior Provisions

A prior section 3391, added Pub. L. 95–437, § 3(a), Oct. 10, 1978, 92 Stat. 1056, which related to definitions for part-time career employment opportunities, was renumbered as section 3401 of this title by Pub. L. 95–454, title IX, § 906(c)(1)(B), Oct. 13, 1978, 92 Stat. 1226.

Effective Date

Subchapter effective 9 months after Oct. 13, 1978, and congressional review of provisions of sections 401 through 412 of Pub. L. 95–454, see section 415(a)(1), (b) of Pub. L. 95–454, set out as an Effective Date note under section 3131 of this title.

§ 3392. General appointment provisions

(a) Qualification standards shall be established by the head of each agency for each Senior Executive Service position in the agency—

(1) in accordance with requirements established by the Office of Personnel Management, with respect to standards for career reserved positions, and

(2) after consultation with the Office, with respect to standards for general positions.

(b) Not more than 30 percent of the Senior Executive Service positions authorized under section 3133 of this title may at any time be filled by individuals who did not have 5 years of current continuous service in the civil service immediately preceding their initial appointment to the Senior Executive Service, unless the President certifies to the Congress that the limitation would hinder the efficiency of the Government. In applying the preceding sentence, any break in service of 3 days or less shall be disregarded.

(c)(1) If a career appointee is appointed by the President, by and with the advice and consent of the Senate, to a civilian position in the executive branch which is not in the Senior Executive Service, and the rate of basic pay payable for which is equal to or greater than the rate payable for level V of the Executive Schedule, the career appointee may elect (at such time and in such manner as the Office may prescribe) to continue to have the provisions of this title relating to basic pay, performance awards, awarding of ranks, severance pay, leave, and retirement apply as if the career appointee remained in the Senior Executive Service position from which he was appointed. Such provisions shall apply in lieu of the provisions which would otherwise apply—

(A) to the extent provided under regulations prescribed by the Office, and

(B) so long as the appointee continues to serve under such Presidential appointment.

(2) An election under paragraph (1) may also be made by any career appointee who is appointed to a civilian position in the executive branch—

(A) which is not in the Senior Executive Service; and

(B) which is covered by the Executive Schedule, or the rate of basic pay for which is fixed by statute at a rate equal to 1 of the levels of the Executive Schedule.

An election under this paragraph shall remain effective so long as the appointee continues to serve in the same position.

(d) Appointment or removal of a person to or from any Senior Executive Service position in an independent regulatory commission shall not be subject, directly or indirectly, to review or approval by any officer or entity within the Executive Office of the President.

(Added Pub. L. 95–454, title IV, § 403(a), Oct. 13, 1978, 92 Stat. 1161; amended Pub. L. 101–335, § 7(a), July 17, 1990, 104 Stat. 325.)

REFERENCES IN TEXT

The Executive Schedule, referred to in subsec. (c), is set out as section 5311 et seq. of this title.

PRIOR PROVISIONS

A prior section 3392, added Pub. L. 95–437, § 3(a), Oct. 10, 1978, 92 Stat. 1056, which related to the establishment of part-time career employment programs, was renumbered as section 3402 of this title by Pub. L. 95–454, title IX, § 906(c)(1)(B), Oct. 13, 1978, 92 Stat. 1226.

AMENDMENTS

1990—Subsec. (c). Pub. L. 101–335 designated existing provisions as par. (1), redesignated former pars. (1) and (2) as subpars. (A) and (B), respectively, and added par. (2).

EFFECTIVE DATE OF 1990 AMENDMENT

Section 7(b)(1) of Pub. L. 101–335 provided that: "The amendments made by this section [amending this section] shall take effect on the date of enactment of this Act [July 17, 1990]."

ELECTION BY PERSONS PREVIOUSLY APPOINTED; RETROACTIVE PERFORMANCE AWARDS

Section 7(b)(2), (3) of Pub. L. 101–335, as amended by Pub. L. 102–378, § 7(a), Oct. 2, 1992, 106 Stat. 1359, provided that:

"(2) ELECTION BY PERSONS PREVIOUSLY APPOINTED.— The Office of Personnel Management shall prescribe regulations (including procedures and deadlines) under which an election under section 3392(c)(2) of title 5, United States Code (as amended by this section) may be made by any individual who—

"(A) on the date of enactment of this Act [July 17, 1990], is serving in a civilian position in the executive branch which—

"(i) is not in the Senior Executive Service; and

"(ii) satisfies section 3392(c)(2)(B) of such title 5 (as so amended);

"(B) was appointed to that position on or after November 1, 1986, and has served continuously in such position since then;

"(C) was a career appointee (within the meaning of section 3132(a)(4) of such title 5) immediately before having been so appointed; and

"(D) was not, based on such individual's appointment to the position described in subparagraph (A), eligible to make an election under section 3392(c) of such title 5 (as then in effect).

An election under this paragraph shall be effective as of the date of appointment to the position described in subparagraph (A).

"(3) RETROACTIVE PERFORMANCE AWARDS.—If an individual elects under paragraph (2) to continue to be subject to performance awards, the head of the agency in which such individual is serving shall determine whether to grant retroactive performance awards for any fiscal years prior to fiscal year 1991 to such individual, and the amount of any such awards, without regard to the provisions of subsection (b) of section 5383 of title 5, United States Code, and subsections (b) and (c) of section 5384 of such title. Before granting an award, the head of the agency shall make a written determination that the individual's performance during the fiscal year for which the award is given was at least fully successful, and shall consider the recommendation of the agency's performance review board with respect to the award. No such award for performance during any fiscal year may be less than 5 percent nor more than 15 percent of the individual's rate of basic pay as of the end of such fiscal year."

[Pub. L. 102–378, § 7(b), Oct. 2, 1992, 106 Stat. 1359, provided that: "The amendment made by subsection (a) [enacting section 7(b)(3) of Pub. L. 101–335, set out above] shall be effective as if enacted as a part of section 7 of the Thrift Savings Plan Technical Amendments Act of 1990 [Pub. L. 101–335]."]

§ 3393. Career appointments

(a) Each agency shall establish a recruitment program, in accordance with guidelines which shall be issued by the Office of Personnel Management, which provides for recruitment of career appointees from—

(1) all groups of qualified individuals within the civil service; or

(2) all groups of qualified individuals whether or not within the civil service.

(b) Each agency shall establish one or more executive resources boards, as appropriate, the members of which shall be appointed by the head of the agency from among employees of the agency or commissioned officers of the uniformed services serving on active duty in such agency. The boards shall, in accordance with merit staffing requirements established by the Office, conduct the merit staffing process for career appointees, including—

(1) reviewing the executive qualifications of each candidate for a position to be filled by a career appointee; and

(2) making written recommendations to the appropriate appointing authority concerning such candidates.

(c)(1) The Office shall establish one or more qualifications review boards, as appropriate. It is the function of the boards to certify the executive qualifications of candidates for initial appointment as career appointees in accordance with regulations prescribed by the Office. Of the members of each board more than one-half shall be appointed from among career appointees. Appointments to such boards shall be made on a non-partisan basis, the sole selection criterion being the professional knowledge of public management and knowledge of the appropriate occupational fields of the intended appointee.

(2) The Office shall, in consultation with the various qualification review boards, prescribe criteria for establishing executive qualifications for appointment of career appointees. The criteria shall provide for—

(A) consideration of demonstrated executive experience;

(B) consideration of successful participation in a career executive development program which is approved by the Office; and

(C) sufficient flexibility to allow for the appointment of individuals who have special or unique qualities which indicate a likelihood of executive success and who would not otherwise be eligible for appointment.

(d) An individual's initial appointment as a career appointee shall become final only after the individual has served a 1-year probationary period as a career appointee.

(e) Each career appointee shall meet the executive qualifications of the position to which appointed, as determined in writing by the appointing authority.

(f) The title of each career reserved position shall be published in the Federal Register.

(g) A career appointee may not be removed from the Senior Executive Service or civil service except in accordance with the applicable provisions of sections 1215, 3393a, 3592, 3595, 7532, or 7543 of this title.

(Added Pub. L. 95–454, title IV, § 403(a), Oct. 13, 1978, 92 Stat. 1161; amended Pub. L. 97–35, title XVII, § 1704(c), Aug. 13, 1981, 95 Stat. 758; Pub. L. 98–615, title III, § 306(b)(1), Nov. 8, 1984, 98 Stat. 3220; Pub. L. 101–12, § 9(b), Apr. 10, 1989, 103 Stat. 35; Pub. L. 101–194, title V, § 506(b)(2), Nov. 30, 1989, 103 Stat. 1758; Pub. L. 101–280, § 6(d)(1), May 4, 1990, 104 Stat. 160.)

PRIOR PROVISIONS

A prior section 3393, added Pub. L. 95–437, § 3(a), Oct. 10, 1978, 92 Stat. 1057, which related to limitations concerning part-time career employment opportunities, was renumbered as section 3403 of this title by Pub. L. 95–454, title IX, § 906(c)(1)(B), Oct. 13, 1978, 92 Stat. 1226.

AMENDMENTS

1990—Subsec. (g). Pub. L. 101–280 made technical correction to directory language of Pub. L. 101–194, see 1989 Amendment below.

1989—Subsec. (g). Pub. L. 101–194, as amended by Pub. L. 101–280, inserted "3393a," after "1215,".

Pub. L. 101–12 substituted "1215" for "1207".

1984—Subsec. (b). Pub. L. 98–615 inserted provision referring to commissioned officers of the uniformed services serving on active duty in such agency in provisions preceding par. (1).

1981—Subsec. (g). Pub. L. 97–35 added subsec. (g).

EFFECTIVE DATE OF 1989 AMENDMENTS

Amendment by Pub. L. 101–194 effective Jan. 1, 1991, see section 506(d) of Pub. L. 101–194, set out as a note under section 3151 of this title.

Amendment by Pub. L. 101–12 effective 90 days following Apr. 10, 1989, see section 11 of Pub. L. 101–12, set out as a note under section 1201 of this title.

EFFECTIVE DATE OF 1984 AMENDMENT

Section 307 of title III of Pub. L. 98–615 provided that: "The amendments made by this title [enacting section 3595a of this title, amending this section and sections 3135, 3593 to 3595, 4312, 5383, and 5384 of this title, and enacting provisions set out as a note under section 3131 of this title] shall be effective following the expiration of the 90-day period beginning on the date of enactment of this Act [Nov. 8, 1984], except that the amendments made by section 304 [amending sections 3395, 3595, 7543, and 8336 of this title] shall be effective as of such date of enactment."

EFFECTIVE DATE OF 1981 AMENDMENT

Amendment by Pub. L. 97–35 effective June 1, 1981, with certain exceptions and conditions, see section 1704(e) of Pub. L. 97–35, set out as an Effective Date note under section 3595 of this title.

SECTION REFERRED TO IN OTHER SECTIONS

This section is referred to in sections 3393a, 3592, 3593, 3594, 3595, 7541 of this title.

§ 3393a. Recertification

(a)(1) In order to ensure that the performance of career appointees demonstrates the excellence needed to meet the goals of the Senior Executive Service, as set forth in section 3131, each career appointee shall be subject to recertification by the employing agency in accordance with the provisions of this section.

(2) Beginning in calendar year 1991, and recurring every third calendar year thereafter, the head of an agency shall determine a time during such calendar year when the performance of career appointees in the agency shall be subject to recertification. Recertification shall not be required of any career appointee who has not been

continuously employed as a senior executive for the 156 weeks preceding the time determined for the recertification. For the purposes of the previous sentence, a break in service of 6 months shall be deemed not to interrupt the 156 weeks of continuous employment.

(b) The supervising official of each career appointee shall submit to a performance review board established by the agency under section 4314 a recommendation as to whether the career appointee's performance justifies recertification as a senior executive, based on such factors as the career appointee's performance ratings for the 3 preceding years under section 4314, any award or other recognition received by the career appointee, any developmental activities of the career appointee, and any other relevant factors. The supervising official's recommendation shall reflect that official's view as to whether the career appointee's overall performance over the 3 preceding years has demonstrated the excellence expected of a senior executive in relation to the written performance requirements for the career appointee's senior executive position as established under section 4312(b). The career appointee may submit to the performance review board a statement of accomplishments and other documentation giving evidence of the quality of the career appointee's performance.

(c)(1) After considering the recommendation and other information received under subsection (b), the performance review board shall submit to the appointing authority a recommendation as to whether the career appointee should be recertified, conditionally recertified, or not recertified as a senior executive. If the board proposes to recommend conditional recertification or nonrecertification, then the affected appointee shall be so notified and shall have the opportunity to appear before the performance review board. If the board is recommending that the career appointee be recertified, the board may also recommend that the career appointee's rate of basic pay be increased to a higher rate established under section 5382. If the board is recommending that the career appointee be conditionally recertified, the board may recommend that the career appointee's pay be reduced to the next lower rate established under section 5382. The board shall also provide to the appointing authority the recommendation and other information received under subsection (b).

(2) More than one-half of the members of a performance review board under this section shall consist of career appointees. The requirement of the preceding sentence shall not apply in any case in which the Office of Personnel Management determines that there exists an insufficient number of career appointees available to comply with the requirement.

(d)(1) If the appointing authority determines that the career appointee's performance during the preceding 3 years demonstrates the excellence expected of a senior executive, the appointing authority shall recommend to the head of the agency that the career appointee be recertified as a senior executive.

(2) If the appointing authority determines that the career appointee's performance has not demonstrated the excellence expected of a senior ex-

ecutive, the appointing authority shall recommend to the head of the agency that the career appointee be conditionally recertified as a senior executive or not be recertified as a senior executive.

(e)(1) If the head of the agency decides that the career appointee's performance warrants recertification as a senior executive, the career appointee shall continue in the Senior Executive Service. If a career appointee is recertified as a senior executive, the career appointee's rate of basic pay may not be reduced at the time of recertification.

(2) If the head of the agency decides that the career appointee's performance does not warrant full recertification, but does warrant conditional recertification, the career appointee—

    (A) shall remain a career appointee in the Senior Executive Service;

    (B) shall be subject to continuing close review of the career appointee's performance by the supervising official in coordination with an executive resources board established under section 3393, in accordance with a performance improvement plan developed by the supervising official and subject to the approval of the executive resources board;

    (C) may, if the head of the agency so determines, be reduced to the next lower rate of basic pay established under section 5382; and

    (D) shall be removed from the Senior Executive Service if the career appointee is not recertified as a senior executive at the end of the 12-month period following the conditional recertification.

If, at the end of the 12-month period following the conditional recertification, the career appointee is recertified as a senior executive, any reduction that was made in the career appointee's rate of basic pay under subparagraph (C) shall be restored prospectively.

(3) If the head of the agency decides that the career appointee's performance does not demonstrate that the career appointee qualifies for recertification or conditional recertification as a senior executive, the career appointee shall be removed from the Senior Executive Service in accordance with section 3592.

(f) The Office of Personnel Management shall prescribe standards and procedures to ensure consistency and fairness for the process of recertification under this section.

(Added Pub. L. 101–194, title V, § 506(a)(1), Nov. 30, 1989, 103 Stat. 1756.)

EFFECTIVE DATE

Section effective Jan. 1, 1991, see section 506(d) of Pub. L. 101–194, set out as an Effective Date of 1989 Amendment note under section 3151 of this title.

SECTION REFERRED TO IN OTHER SECTIONS

This section is referred to in sections 3151, 3393, 3592, 3593, 3594, 7701, 8336, 8414 of this title; title 22 section 3945.

§ 3394. Noncareer and limited appointments

(a) Each noncareer appointee, limited term appointee, and limited emergency appointee shall meet the qualifications of the position to which appointed, as determined in writing by the appointing authority.

(b) An individual may not be appointed as a limited term appointee or as a limited emergency appointee without the prior approval of the exercise of such appointing authority by the Office of Personnel Management.

(Added Pub. L. 95–454, title IV, § 403(a), Oct. 13, 1978, 92 Stat. 1162.)

PRIOR PROVISIONS

A prior section 3394, added Pub. L. 95–437, § 3(a), Oct. 10, 1978, 92 Stat. 1057, which related to personnel ceilings, was renumbered as section 3404 of this title by Pub. L. 95–454, title IX, § 906(c)(1)(B), Oct. 13, 1978, 92 Stat. 1226.

SECTION REFERRED TO IN OTHER SECTIONS

This section is referred to in section 3395 of this title; title 20 section 3461.

§ 3395. Reassignment and transfer within the Senior Executive Service

(a)(1) A career appointee in an agency—

(A) may, subject to paragraph (2) of this subsection, be reassigned to any Senior Executive Service position in the same agency for which the appointee is qualified; and

(B) may transfer to a Senior Executive Service position in another agency for which the appointee is qualified, with the approval of the agency to which the appointee transfers.

(2)(A) Except as provided in subparagraph (B) of this paragraph, a career appointee may be reassigned to any Senior Executive Service position only if the career appointee receives written notice of the reassignment at least 15 days before the effective date of such reassignment.

(B)(i) A career appointee may not be reassigned to a Senior Executive Service position outside the career appointee's commuting area unless—

(I) before providing notice under subclause (II) of this clause (or seeking or obtaining the consent of the career appointee under clause (ii) of this subparagraph to waive such notice), the agency consults with the career appointee on the reasons for, and the appointee's preferences with respect to, the proposed reassignment; and

(II) the career appointee receives written notice of the reassignment, including a statement of the reasons for the reassignment, at least 60 days before the effective date of the reassignment.

(ii) Notice of reassignment under clause (i)(II) of this subparagraph may be waived with the written consent of the career appointee involved.

(b)(1) Notwithstanding section 3394(b) of this title, a limited emergency appointee may be reassigned to another Senior Executive Service position in the same agency established to meet a bona fide, unanticipated, urgent need, except that the appointee may not serve in one or more positions in such agency under such appointment in excess of 18 months.

(2) Notwithstanding section 3394(b) of this title, a limited term appointee may be reassigned to another Senior Executive Service position in the same agency the duties of which will expire at the end of a term of 3 years or less, except that the appointee may not serve in one or more positions in the agency under such appointment in excess of 3 years.

(c) A limited term appointee or a limited emergency appointee may not be appointed to, or continue to hold, a position under such an appointment if, within the preceding 48 months, the individual has served more than 36 months, in the aggregate, under any combination of such types of appointment.

(d) A noncareer appointee in an agency—

(1) may be reassigned to any general position in the agency for which the appointee is qualified; and

(2) may transfer to a general position in another agency with the approval of the agency to which the appointee transfers.

(e)(1) Except as provided in paragraph (2) of this subsection, a career appointee in an agency may not be involuntarily reassigned—

(A) within 120 days after an appointment of the head of the agency; or

(B) within 120 days after the appointment in the agency of the career appointee's most immediate supervisor who—

(i) is a noncareer appointee; and

(ii) has the authority to make an initial appraisal of the career appointee's performance under subchapter II of chapter 43.

(2) Paragraph (1) of this subsection does not apply with respect to—

(A) any reassignment under section 4314(b)(3) of this title; or

(B) any disciplinary action initiated before an appointment referred to in paragraph (1) of this subsection.

(3) For the purpose of applying paragraph (1) to a career appointee, any days (not to exceed a total of 60) during which such career appointee is serving pursuant to a detail or other temporary assignment apart from such appointee's regular position shall not be counted in determining the number of days that have elapsed since an appointment referred to in subparagraph (A) or (B) of such paragraph.

(Added Pub. L. 95–454, title IV, § 403(a), Oct. 13, 1978, 92 Stat. 1163; amended Pub. L. 98–615, title III, § 304(a), Nov. 8, 1984, 98 Stat. 3218; Pub. L. 102–175, § 3, Dec. 2, 1991, 105 Stat. 1222.)

PRIOR PROVISIONS

A prior section 3395, added Pub. L. 95–437, § 3(a), Oct. 10, 1978, 92 Stat. 1057, which related to nonapplicability of part-time career employment opportunities program was renumbered as section 3405 of this title by Pub. L. 95–454, title IX, § 906(c)(1)(B), Oct. 13, 1978, 92 Stat. 1226.

AMENDMENTS

1991—Subsec. (e)(1)(B)(ii). Pub. L. 102–175, § 3(1), amended cl. (ii) generally. Prior to amendment, cl. (ii) read as follows: "has the authority to reassign the career appointee."

Subsec. (e)(3). Pub. L. 102–175, § 3(2), added par. (3).

1984—Subsec. (a)(2). Pub. L. 98–615 designated existing provisions as subpar. (A), inserted exception relating to subpar. (B), and added subpar. (B).

EFFECTIVE DATE OF 1984 AMENDMENT

Amendment by Pub. L. 98–615 effective Nov. 8, 1984, see section 307 of Pub. L. 98–615, set out as a note under section 3393 of this title.

§ 3396. Development for and within the Senior Executive Service

(a) The Office of Personnel Management shall establish programs for the systematic development of candidates for the Senior Executive Service and for the continuing development of senior executives, or require agencies to establish such programs which meet criteria prescribed by the Office.

(b) The Office shall assist agencies in the establishment of programs required under subsection (a) of this section and shall monitor the implementation of the programs. If the Office finds that any agency's program under subsection (a) of this section is not in compliance with the criteria prescribed under such subsection, it shall require the agency to take such corrective action as may be necessary to bring the program into compliance with the criteria.

(c)(1) The head of an agency may grant a sabbatical to any career appointee for not to exceed 11 months in order to permit the appointee to engage in study or uncompensated work experience which will contribute to the appointee's development and effectiveness. A sabbatical shall not result in loss of, or reduction in, pay, leave to which the career appointee is otherwise entitled, credit for time or service, or performance or efficiency rating. The head of the agency may authorize in accordance with chapter 57 of this title such travel expenses (including per diem allowances) as the head of the agency may determine to be essential for the study or experience.

(2) A sabbatical under this subsection may not be granted to any career appointee—

(A) more than once in any 10-year period;

(B) unless the appointee has completed 7 years of service—

(i) in one or more positions in the Senior Executive Service;

(ii) in one or more other positions in the civil service the level of duties and responsibilities of which are equivalent to the level of duties and responsibilities of positions in the Senior Executive Service; or

(iii) in any combination of such positions, except that not less than 2 years of such 7 years of service must be in the Senior Executive Service; and

(C) if the appointee is eligible for voluntary retirement with a right to an immediate annuity under section 8336 of this title.

Any period of assignment under section 3373 of this title, relating to assignments of employees to State and local governments, shall not be considered a period of service for the purpose of subparagraph (B) of this paragraph.

(3)(A) Any career appointee in an agency may be granted a sabbatical under this subsection only if the appointee agrees, as a condition of accepting the sabbatical, to serve in the civil service upon the completion of the sabbatical for a period of 2 consecutive years.

(B) Each agreement required under subparagraph (A) of this paragraph shall provide that in the event the career appointee fails to carry out the agreement (except for good and sufficient reason as determined by the head of the agency who granted the sabbatical) the appointee shall be liable to the United States for payment of all expenses (including salary) of the sabbatical. The amount shall be treated as a debt due the United States.

(d)(1) The Office shall encourage and assist individuals to improve their skills and increase their contribution by service in a variety of agencies as well as by accepting temporary placements in State or local governments or in the private sector.

(2) In order to promote the professional development of career appointees and to assist them in achieving their maximum levels of proficiency, the Office shall, in a manner consistent with the needs of the Government provide appropriate informational services and otherwise encourage career appointees to take advantage of any opportunities relating to—

(A) sabbaticals;

(B) training; or

(C) details or other temporary assignments in other agencies, State or local governments, or the private sector.

(Added Pub. L. 95–454, title IV, § 403(a), Oct. 13, 1978, 92 Stat. 1163; amended Pub. L. 102–175, § 4, Dec. 2, 1991, 105 Stat. 1223.)

PRIOR PROVISIONS

A prior section 3396, added Pub. L. 95–437, § 3(a), Oct. 10, 1978, 92 Stat. 1057, which related to issuance of regulations, was renumbered as section 3406 of this title by Pub. L. 95–454, title IX, § 906(c)(1)(B), Oct. 13, 1978, 92 Stat. 1226.

AMENDMENTS

1991—Subsec. (d). Pub. L. 102–175 designated existing provisions as par. (1) and added par. (2).

SECTION REFERRED TO IN OTHER SECTIONS

This section is referred to in section 3151 of this title; title 10 section 1606; title 22 section 3984.

§ 3397. Regulations

The Office of Personnel Management shall prescribe regulations to carry out the purpose of this subchapter.

(Added Pub. L. 95–454, title IV, § 403(a), Oct. 13, 1978, 92 Stat. 1164.)

PRIOR PROVISIONS

A prior section 3397, added Pub. L. 95–437, § 3(a), Oct. 10, 1978, 92 Stat. 1058, which related to reports, was renumbered as section 3407 of this title by Pub. L. 95–454, title IX, § 906(c)(1)(B), Oct. 13, 1978, 92 Stat. 1226.

A prior section 3398, added Pub. L. 95–437, § 3(a), Oct. 10, 1978, 92 Stat. 1058, which related to representation by employee organizations of employees employed on a part-time career employment basis, was renumbered as section 3408 of this title by Pub. L. 95–454, title IX, § 906(c)(1)(B), Oct. 13, 1978, 92 Stat. 1226.

CHAPTER 34—PART-TIME CAREER EMPLOYMENT OPPORTUNITIES

AMENDMENTS

1995—Pub. L. 104–66, title III, § 3001(a)(2), Dec. 21, 1995, 109 Stat. 734, struck out item 3407 "Reports".

1978—Pub. L. 95–437, § 3(b), Oct. 10, 1978, 92 Stat. 1058, added items 3391 to 3398, which were renumbered 3401 to 3408 by Pub. L. 95–454, title IX, § 906(c)(1)(A), Oct. 13, 1978, 92 Stat. 1226, which section also substituted "CHAPTER 34" for "SUBCHAPTER VIII" in heading.

CHAPTER REFERRED TO IN OTHER SECTIONS

This chapter is referred to in title 38 section 7407.

§ 3401. Definitions

For the purpose of this chapter—

(1) "agency" means—

(A) an Executive agency;

(B) a military department;

(C) an agency in the judicial branch;

(D) the Library of Congress;

(E) the Botanic Garden; and

(F) the Office of the Architect of the Capitol; but does not include—

(i) a Government controlled corporation;

(ii) the Tennessee Valley Authority;

(iii) the Virgin Islands Corporation;

(iv) the Federal Bureau of Investigation, Department of Justice;

(v) the Central Intelligence Agency; and

(vi) the National Security Agency, Department of Defense; and

(2) "part-time career employment" means part-time employment of 16 to 32 hours a week (or 32 to 64 hours during a biweekly pay period in the case of a flexible or compressed work schedule under subchapter II of chapter 61 of this title) under a schedule consisting of an equal or varied number of hours per day, whether in a position which would be part-time without regard to this section or one established to allow job-sharing or comparable arrangements, but does not include employment on a temporary or intermittent basis.

(Added Pub. L. 95–437, § 3(a), Oct. 10, 1978, 92 Stat. 1056, § 3391; renumbered § 3401 and amended Pub. L. 95–454, title IX, § 906(c)(1)(B), (2)(A), Oct. 13, 1978, 92 Stat. 1226; Pub. L. 97–221, § 3, July 23, 1982, 96 Stat. 233; Pub. L. 97–468, title VI, § 615(b)(1)(B), Jan. 14, 1983, 96 Stat. 2578; Pub. L. 102–378, § 2(15), Oct. 2, 1992, 106 Stat. 1347; Pub. L. 104–201, div. C, title XXXV, § 3548(a)(1), Sept. 23, 1996, 110 Stat. 2868.)

AMENDMENTS

1996—Par. (1). Pub. L. 104–201, which directed amendment of par. (1) by striking cl. (v) and redesignating cls. (vi), (vii), and (viii) as (v), (vi), and (vii), respectively, was executed by striking cl. (iv), relating to the Panama Canal Company, and redesignating cls. (v), (vi), and (vii) as (iv), (v), and (vi), respectively, to reflect the probable intent of Congress, because par. (1) does not contain a cl. (viii) and the amendments were included in a series of conforming amendments relating to the Panama Canal.

1992—Par. (1)(iii). Pub. L. 102–378, which directed the amendment of cl. (iv) by substituting "Virgin Islands" for "Virgin Island", was executed by making the substitution in cl. (iii) to reflect the probable intent of Congress.

1983—Par. (1)(iii) to (viii). Pub. L. 97–468 struck out cl. (iii) which excluded the Alaska Railroad, and redesignated cls. (iv) to (viii) as (iii) to (vii), respectively.

1982—Par. (2). Pub. L. 97–221 inserted "(or 32 to 64 hours during a biweekly pay period in the case of a flexible or compressed work schedule under subchapter II of chapter 61 of this title)" after "week".

1978—Pub. L. 95–454, § 906(c)(1)(B), renumbered section 3391 of this title as this section.

Pub. L. 95–454, § 906(c)(2)(A), substituted "chapter" for "subchapter".

EFFECTIVE DATE OF 1983 AMENDMENT

Amendment by Pub. L. 97–468 effective on date of transfer of Alaska Railroad to the State [Jan. 5, 1985], pursuant to section 1203 of Title 45, Railroads, see section 615(b) of Pub. L. 97–468.

EFFECTIVE DATE OF 1978 AMENDMENT

Amendment by Pub. L. 95–454 effective 90 days after Oct. 13, 1978, see section 907 of Pub. L. 95–454, set out as a note under section 1101 of this title.

SHORT TITLE OF 1978 AMENDMENT

Section 1 of Pub. L. 95–437 provided that: "This Act [enacting this chapter, amending sections 8347, 8716, 8906, and 8913 of this title, and enacting provisions set out as notes under this section and sections 3407 and 8906 of this title] may be cited as the 'Federal Employees Part-Time Career Employment Act of 1978'."

CONGRESSIONAL FINDINGS AND PURPOSE

Section 2 of Pub. L. 95–437 provided that:

"(a) The Congress finds that—

"(1) many individuals in our society possess great productive potential which goes unused because they cannot meet the requirements of a standard workweek; and

"(2) part-time permanent employment—

"(A) provides older individuals with a gradual transition into retirement;

"(B) provides employment opportunities to handicapped individuals or others who require a reduced workweek;

"(C) provides parents opportunities to balance family responsibilities with the need for additional income;

"(D) benefits students who must finance their own education or vocational training;

"(E) benefits the Government, as an employer, by increasing productivity and job satisfaction, while lowering turnover rates and absenteeism, offering management more flexibility in meeting work requirements, and filling shortages in various occupations; and

"(F) benefits society by offering a needed alternative for those individuals who require or prefer shorter hours (despite the reduced income), thus increasing jobs available to reduce unemployment while retaining the skills of individuals who have training and experience.

"(b) The purpose of this Act [enacting this chapter, amending sections 8347, 8716, 8906, and 8913 of this title, and enacting provisions set out as notes under this section and sections 3407 and 8906 of this title] is to provide increased part-time career employment opportunities throughout the Federal Government."

SECTION REFERRED TO IN OTHER SECTIONS

This section is referred to in sections 6323, 8347, 8402, 8716, 8906, 8913 of this title.

§ 3402. Establishment of part-time career employment programs

(a)(1) In order to promote part-time career employment opportunities in all grade levels, the head of each agency, by regulation, shall establish and maintain a program for part-time career employment within such agency. Such regulations shall provide for—

(A) the review of positions which, after such positions become vacant, may be filled on a part-time career employment basis (including the establishment of criteria to be used in identifying such positions);

(B) procedures and criteria to be used in connection with establishing or converting positions for part-time career employment, subject to the limitations of section 3403 of this title;

(C) annual goals for establishing or converting positions for part-time career employment, and a timetable setting forth interim and final deadlines for achieving such goals;

(D) a continuing review and evaluation of the part-time career employment program established under such regulations; and

(E) procedures for notifying the public of vacant part-time positions in such agency, utilizing facilities and funds otherwise available to such agency for the dissemination of information.

(2) The head of each agency shall provide for communication between, and coordination of the activities of, the individuals within such agency whose responsibilities relate to the part-time career employment program established within that agency.

(3) Regulations established under paragraph (1) of this subsection may provide for such exceptions as may be necessary to carry out the mission of the agency.

(b)(1) The Office of Personnel Management, by regulation, shall establish and maintain a program under which it shall, on the request of an agency, advise and assist such agency in the establishment and maintenance of its part-time career employment program under this chapter.

(2) The Office shall conduct a research and demonstration program with respect to part-time career employment within the Federal Government. In particular, such program shall be directed to—

(A) determining the extent to which part-time career employment may be used in filling positions which have not traditionally been open for such employment on any extensive basis, such as supervisory, managerial, and professional positions;

(B) determining the extent to which job-sharing arrangements may be established for various occupations and positions; and

(C) evaluating attitudes, benefits, costs, efficiency, and productivity associated with part-time career employment, as well as its various sociological effects as a mode of employment.

(Added Pub. L. 95–437, § 3(a), Oct. 10, 1978, 92 Stat. 1056, § 3392; renumbered § 3402 and amended Pub. L. 95–454, title IX, § 906(c)(1)(B), (2)(B), Oct. 13, 1978, 92 Stat. 1226.)

AMENDMENTS

1978—Pub. L. 95–454, § 906(c)(1)(B), renumbered section 3392 of this title as this section.

Subsec. (a)(1)(B). Pub. L. 95–454, § 906(c)(2)(B)(i), substituted "3403" for "3393".

Subsec. (b)(1). Pub. L. 95–454, § 906(c)(2)(B)(ii), substituted "Office of Personnel Management" for "Civil Service Commission" and "chapter" for "subchapter".

Subsec. (b)(2). Pub. L. 95–454, § 906(c)(2)(B)(iii), substituted "Office" for "Commission".

EFFECTIVE DATE OF 1978 AMENDMENT

Amendment by Pub. L. 95–454 effective 90 days after Oct. 13, 1978, see section 907 of Pub. L. 95–454, set out as a note under section 1101 of this title.

§ 3403. Limitations

(a) An agency shall not abolish any position occupied by an employee in order to make the duties of such position available to be performed on a part-time career employment basis.

(b) Any person who is employed on a full-time basis in an agency shall not be required to accept part-time employment as a condition of continued employment.

(Added Pub. L. 95–437, § 3(a), Oct. 10, 1978, 92 Stat. 1057, § 3393; renumbered § 3403, Pub. L. 95–454, title IX, § 906(c)(1)(B), Oct. 13, 1978, 92 Stat. 1226.)

AMENDMENTS

1978—Pub. L. 95–454 renumbered section 3393 of this title as this section.

SECTION REFERRED TO IN OTHER SECTIONS

This section is referred to in section 3402 of this title.

§ 3404. Personnel ceilings

In administering any personnel ceiling applicable to an agency (or unit therein), an employee employed by such agency on a part-time career employment basis shall be counted as a fraction which is determined by dividing 40 hours into the average number of hours of such employee's regularly scheduled workweek. This section shall become effective on October 1, 1980.

(Added Pub. L. 95–437, § 3(a), Oct. 10, 1978, 92 Stat. 1057, § 3394; renumbered § 3404, Pub. L. 95–454, title IX, § 906(c)(1)(B), Oct. 13, 1978, 92 Stat. 1226.)

AMENDMENTS

1978—Pub. L. 95–454 renumbered section 3394 of this title as this section.

§ 3405. Nonapplicability

(a) If, on the date of enactment of this chapter, there is in effect with respect to positions within an agency a collective-bargaining agreement which establishes the number of hours of employment a week, then this chapter shall not apply to those positions.

(b) This chapter shall not require part-time career employment in positions the rate of basic pay for which is fixed at a rate equal to or greater than the minimum rate payable under section 5376.

(Added Pub. L. 95–437, § 3(a), Oct. 10, 1978, 92 Stat. 1057, § 3395; renumbered § 3405 and amended Pub. L. 95–454, title IX, § 906(c)(1)(B), (2)(C), Oct. 13, 1978, 92 Stat. 1226, 1227; Pub. L. 101–509, title V, § 529 [title I, § 101(b)(9)(D)], Nov. 5, 1990, 104 Stat. 1427, 1441.)

REFERENCES IN TEXT

The date of enactment of this chapter, referred to in subsec. (a), is the date of the enactment of Pub. L. 95–437, which was approved Oct. 10, 1978.

AMENDMENTS

1990—Subsec. (b). Pub. L. 101–509 substituted "payable under section 5376" for "fixed for GS–16 of the General Schedule".

1978—Pub. L. 95–454, § 906(c)(1)(B), renumbered section 3395 of this title as this section.

Subsecs. (a), (b). Pub. L. 95–454, § 906(c)(2)(C), substituted "chapter" for "subchapter" wherever appearing.

EFFECTIVE DATE OF 1990 AMENDMENT

Amendment by Pub. L. 101–509 effective on such date as the President shall determine, but not earlier than 90 days, and not later than 180 days, after Nov. 5, 1990, see section 529 [title III, § 305] of Pub. L. 101–509, set out as a note under section 5301 of this title.

EFFECTIVE DATE OF 1978 AMENDMENT

Amendment by Pub. L. 95–454 effective 90 days after Oct. 13, 1978, see section 907 of Pub. L. 95–454, set out as a note under section 1101 of this title.

§ 3406. Regulations

Before any regulation is prescribed under this chapter, a copy of the proposed regulation shall be published in the Federal Register and an opportunity provided to interested parties to present written comment and, where practicable, oral comment. Initial regulations shall be prescribed not later than 180 days after the date of the enactment of this chapter.

(Added Pub. L. 95–437, § 3(a), Oct. 10, 1978, 92 Stat. 1057, § 3396; renumbered § 3406 and amended Pub. L. 95–454, title IX, § 906(c)(1)(B), (2)(C), Oct. 13, 1978, 92 Stat. 1226, 1227.)

REFERENCES IN TEXT

The date of the enactment of this chapter, referred to in text, is the date of the enactment of Pub. L. 95–437, which was approved Oct. 10, 1978.

AMENDMENTS

1978—Pub. L. 95–453, § 901(c)(1)(B), renumbered section 3396 of this title as this section.

Pub. L. 95–454, § 906(c)(2)(C), substituted "chapter" for "subchapter" wherever appearing.

EFFECTIVE DATE OF 1978 AMENDMENT

Amendment by Pub. L. 95–454 effective 90 days after Oct. 13, 1978, see section 907 of Pub. L. 95–454, set out as a note under section 1101 of this title.

[§ 3407. Repealed. Pub. L. 104–66, title III, § 3001(a)(1), Dec. 21, 1995, 109 Stat. 733]

Section, added Pub. L. 95–437, § 3(a), Oct. 10, 1978, 92 Stat. 1058, § 3397; renumbered § 3407 and amended Pub. L. 95–454, title IX, § 906(c)(1)(B), (2)(D), (E), Oct. 13, 1978, 92 Stat. 1226, 1227, related to reports.

§ 3408. Employee organization representation

If an employee organization has been accorded exclusive recognition with respect to a unit within an agency, then the employee organization shall be entitled to represent all employees within that unit employed on a part-time career employment basis.

(Added Pub. L. 95–437, § 3(a), Oct. 10, 1978, 92 Stat. 1058, § 3398; renumbered § 3408, Pub. L. 95–454, title IX, § 906(c)(1)(B), Oct. 13, 1978, 92 Stat. 1226.)

AMENDMENTS

1978—Pub. L. 95–454 renumbered section 3398 of this title as this section.

CHAPTER 35—RETENTION PREFERENCE, RESTORATION, AND REEMPLOYMENT

SUBCHAPTER I—RETENTION PREFERENCE

AMENDMENTS

1994—Pub. L. 103–353, § 2(b)(2)(C), Oct. 13, 1994, 108 Stat. 3169, struck out item for subchapter II "RESTORATION AFTER ACTIVE DUTY OR TRAINING DUTY" and item 3551 "Restoration; Reserves and National Guardsmen".

1984—Pub. L. 98–615, title III, § 306(c)(2), Nov. 8, 1984, 98 Stat. 3220, added item 3595a.

1981—Pub. L. 97–35, title XVII, § 1704(a)(2), Aug. 13, 1981, 95 Stat. 757, redesignated item 3595 as 3596, and added item 3595.

1980—Pub. L. 96–465, title II, § 2301(b), Oct. 17, 1980, 94 Stat. 2164, added item for subchapter VI and item 3597.

1978—Pub. L. 95–454, title IV, § 404(c), Oct. 13, 1978, 92 Stat. 1167, added item for subchapter V and items 3591 to 3595.

SUBCHAPTER I—RETENTION PREFERENCE

SUBCHAPTER REFERRED TO IN OTHER SECTIONS

This subchapter is referred to in section 6302 of this title; title 2 section 1316a; title 22 sections 3964, 4010a; title 42 section 237.

§ 3501. Definitions; application

(a) For the purpose of this subchapter, except section 3504—

(1) "active service" has the meaning given it by section 101 of title 37;

(2) "a retired member of a uniformed service" means a member or former member of a uniformed service who is entitled, under statute, to retired, retirement, or retainer pay on account of his service as such a member; and

(3) a preference eligible employee who is a retired member of a uniformed service is considered a preference eligible only if—

(A) his retirement was based on disability—

(i) resulting from injury or disease received in line of duty as a direct result of armed conflict; or

(ii) caused by an instrumentality of war and incurred in the line of duty during a period of war as defined by sections 101 and 1101 of title 38;

(B) his service does not include twenty or more years of full-time active service, regardless of when performed but not including period of active duty for training; or

(C) on November 30, 1964, he was employed in a position to which this subchapter applies and thereafter he continued to be so employed without a break in service of more than 30 days.

(b) Except as otherwise provided by this subsection and section 3504 of this title, this subchapter applies to each employee in or under an Executive agency. This subchapter does not apply to an employee whose appointment is required by Congress to be confirmed by, or made with the advice and consent of, the Senate or to a member of the Senior Executive Service or the Federal Bureau of Investigation and Drug Enforcement Administration Senior Executive Service.

(Pub. L. 89–554, Sept. 6, 1966, 80 Stat. 428; Pub. L. 94–183, § 2(8), Dec. 31, 1975, 89 Stat. 1057; Pub. L. 95–454, title IV, § 404(a), Oct. 13, 1978, 92 Stat. 1165; Pub. L. 100–325, § 2(e), May 30, 1988, 102 Stat. 581; Pub. L. 102–83, § 5(c)(2), Aug. 6, 1991, 105 Stat. 406.)

HISTORICAL AND REVISION NOTES

Derivation	U.S. Code	Revised Statutes and Statutes at Large
(a)(1), (2) ...	5 U.S.C. 3101 (as applicable to 5 U.S.C. 861).	Aug. 19, 1964, Pub. L. 88–448, § 101 (as applicable to § 202), 78 Stat. 484.
(a)(3)	5 U.S.C. 861(b).	June 27, 1944, ch. 287, § 12(b); added Aug. 19, 1964, Pub. L. 88–448, § 202(4) ("(b)"), 78 Stat. 486.

In subsection (a), the definitions of "uniformed services" and "armed forces" are omitted as unnecessary in view of the definitions in section 2101. The definition of "civilian office" is omitted as unnecessary as subsection (b) of this section states the application of this subchapter.

In subsection (a)(3), the words "Notwithstanding any other provision of this Act" are omitted as unnecessary. The words "preference eligible employee" are coextensive with and substituted for "employee * * * included under section 2 of this Act" in view of the definition of preference eligible in section 2108. In paragraph (3)(C), the words "on November 30, 1964, he was employed in a position to which this subchapter applies and thereafter he continued to be so employed" are substituted for "immediately prior to the effective date of this subsection, he was employed in a civilian office to which this Act applies and, on and after such date, he continues to be employed in any such office".

Subsection (b) is supplied on authority of sections 2, 12, and 20 of the Act of June 27, 1944, ch. 287, 58 Stat. 387, 391, which are carried into this title.

Standard changes are made to conform with the definitions applicable and the style of this title as outlined in the preface to the report.

AMENDMENTS

1991—Subsec. (a)(3)(A)(ii). Pub. L. 102–83 substituted reference to section 1101 of title 38 for reference to section 301 of title 38.

1988—Subsec. (b). Pub. L. 100–325 inserted reference to Federal Bureau of Investigation and Drug Enforcement Administration Senior Executive Service.

1978—Subsec. (b). Pub. L. 95–454 inserted reference to a member of Senior Executive Service.

1975—Subsec. (b). Pub. L. 94–183 struck out ", except an employee whose appointment is made under section 3311 of title 39" after "or made with the advice and consent of, the Senate".

EFFECTIVE DATE OF 1978 AMENDMENT

Amendment by Pub. L. 95–454 effective 9 months after Oct. 13, 1978, and congressional review of provisions of sections 401 through 412 of Pub. L. 95–454, see section 415 of Pub. L. 95–454, set out as an Effective Date note under section 3131 of this title.

SECTION REFERRED TO IN OTHER SECTIONS

This section is referred to in sections 2302, 3502, 6303 of this title; title 10 sections 1586, 1610; title 22 sections 1438, 4010a; title 31 section 732.

§ 3502. Order of retention

(a) The Office of Personnel Management shall prescribe regulations for the release of competing employees in a reduction in force which give due effect to—

(1) tenure of employment;

(2) military preference, subject to section 3501(a)(3) of this title;

(3) length of service; and

(4) efficiency or performance ratings.

In computing length of service, a competing employee—

(A) who is not a retired member of a uniformed service is entitled to credit for the total length of time in active service in the armed forces;

(B) who is a retired member of a uniformed service is entitled to credit for—

(i) the length of time in active service in the armed forces during a war, or in a campaign or expedition for which a campaign badge has been authorized; or

(ii) the total length of time in active service in the armed forces if he is included under section 3501(a)(3)(A), (B), or (C) of this title; and

(C) is entitled to credit for—

(i) service rendered as an employee of a county committee established pursuant to section 8(b) of the Soil Conservation and Allotment Act or of a committee or association of producers described in section 10(b) of the Agricultural Adjustment Act; and

(ii) service rendered as an employee described in section 2105(c) if such employee moves or has moved, on or after January 1, 1966, without a break in service of more than 3 days, from a position in a nonappropriated fund instrumentality of the Department of Defense or the Coast Guard to a position in the Department of Defense or the Coast Guard, respectively, that is not described in section 2105(c).

(b) A preference eligible described in section 2108(3)(C) of this title who has a compensable service-connected disability of 30 percent or more and whose performance has not been rated unacceptable under a performance appraisal system implemented under chapter 43 of this title is entitled to be retained in preference to other preference eligibles.

(c) An employee who is entitled to retention preference and whose performance has not been rated unacceptable under a performance appraisal system implemented under chapter 43 of this title is entitled to be retained in preference to other competing employees.

(d)(1) Except as provided under subsection (e), an employee may not be released, due to a reduction in force, unless—

(A) such employee and such employee's exclusive representative for collective-bargaining purposes (if any) are given written notice, in conformance with the requirements of paragraph (2), at least 60 days before such employee is so released; and

(B) if the reduction in force would involve the separation of a significant number of employees, the requirements of paragraph (3) are met at least 60 days before any employee is so released.

(2) Any notice under paragraph (1)(A) shall include—

(A) the personnel action to be taken with respect to the employee involved;

(B) the effective date of the action;

(C) a description of the procedures applicable in identifying employees for release;

(D) the employee's ranking relative to other competing employees, and how that ranking was determined; and

(E) a description of any appeal or other rights which may be available.

(3) Notice under paragraph (1)(B)—

(A) shall be given to—

(i) the State or entity designated by the State to carry out rapid response activities under section 134(a)(2)(A) of the Workforce Investment Act of 1998; and

(ii) the chief elected official of such unit or each of such units of local government as may be appropriate; and

(B) shall consist of written notification as to—

(i) the number of employees to be separated from service due to the reduction in force (broken down by geographic area or on such other basis as may be required under paragraph (4));

(ii) when those separations will occur; and

(iii) any other matter which might facilitate the delivery of rapid response assistance or other services under title I of the Workforce Investment Act of 1998.

(4) The Office shall prescribe such regulations as may be necessary to carry out this subsection. The Office shall consult with the Secretary of Labor on matters relating to title I of the Workforce Investment Act of 1998.

(e)(1) Subject to paragraph (3), upon request submitted under paragraph (2), the President may, in writing, shorten the period of advance notice required under subsection (d)(1)(A) and (B), with respect to a particular reduction in force, if necessary because of circumstances not reasonably foreseeable.

(2) A request to shorten notice periods shall be submitted to the President by the head of the agency involved, and shall indicate the reduction in force to which the request pertains, the number of days by which the agency head requests that the periods be shortened, and the reasons why the request is necessary.

(3) No notice period may be shortened to less than 30 days under this subsection.

(f)(1) The Secretary of Defense or the Secretary of a military department may—

(A) separate from service any employee who volunteers to be separated under this subparagraph even though the employee is not otherwise subject to separation due to a reduction in force; and

(B) for each employee voluntarily separated under subparagraph (A), retain an employee in a similar position who would otherwise be separated due to a reduction in force.

(2) The separation of an employee under paragraph (1)(A) shall be treated as an involuntary separation due to a reduction in force.

(3) An employee with critical knowledge and skills (as defined by the Secretary concerned) may not participate in a voluntary separation under paragraph (1)(A) if the Secretary concerned determines that such participation would impair the performance of the mission of the Department of Defense or the military department concerned.

(4) The regulations prescribed under this section shall incorporate the authority provided in this subsection.

(5) No authority under paragraph (1) may be exercised after September 30, 2005.

(Pub. L. 89–554, Sept. 6, 1966, 80 Stat. 428; Pub. L. 90–367, § 3, June 29, 1968, 82 Stat. 278; Pub. L. 90–623, § 1(23), Oct. 22, 1968, 82 Stat. 1313; Pub. L. 95–454, title III, § 307(e), title IX, § 906(a)(2), Oct. 13, 1978, 92 Stat. 1149, 1224; Pub. L. 99–251, title III, § 306(a), Feb. 27, 1986, 100 Stat. 27; Pub. L. 101–508, title VII, § 7202(c), Nov. 5, 1990, 104 Stat. 1388–335; Pub. L. 102–484, div. D, title XLIV, § 4433(a)(1), Oct. 23, 1992, 106 Stat. 2721; Pub. L. 104–106, div. A, title X, §§ 1034, 1043(d)(1), Feb. 10, 1996, 110 Stat. 430, 438; Pub. L. 104–201, div. A, title XVI, § 1609, Sept. 23, 1996, 110 Stat. 2738; Pub. L. 105–277, div. A, § 101(f) [title VIII, § 405(d)(1), (f)(1)], Oct. 21, 1998, 112 Stat. 2681–337, 2681–417, 2681–429; Pub. L. 106–398, § 1 [[div. A], title XI, § 1103], Oct. 30, 2000, 114 Stat. 1654, 1654A–311.)

HISTORICAL AND REVISION NOTES

Derivation	U.S. Code	Revised Statutes and Statutes at Large
(a)	5 U.S.C. 861(a) (less 2d and 3d provisos), (c).	June 27, 1944, ch. 287, § 12 (less 2d and 3d provisos), 58 Stat. 390. Aug. 19, 1964, Pub. L. 88–448, § 202 (1)–(3), (4) ("(c)"), 78 78 Stat. 486.
(b)	5 U.S.C. 861(a) (2d proviso).	June 27, 1944, ch. 287, § 12 (2d proviso), 58 Stat. 390.

In subsection (a), the words "reduction in force" are substituted for "reduction in personnel". The words "in any civilian service of any Federal agency" are omitted as unnecessary because of the application stated in section 3501. In the second sentence, the word "total" in the phrase "length of service" is omitted for consistency with paragraph (3), and the words "subject to subsection (c) of this section" are omitted as unnecessary in view of the supplied distinction between a competing employee who is not a retired member of a uniformed service and such an employee who is a retired member of a uniformed service. In paragraph (A), the words "total length of time in active service" are substituted for "length of time spent in active service" for consistency with paragraph (B)(ii).

In subsections (a) and (b), the references to "performance" ratings and ratings of "satisfactory" are added on authority of former section 2005, which is carried into section 4304.

Standard changes are made to conform with the definitions applicable and the style of this title as outlined in the preface to the report.

REFERENCES IN TEXT

Section 8(b) of the Soil Conservation and Allotment Act, referred to in subsec. (a)(C)(i), probably means section 8(b) of the Soil Conservation and Domestic Allotment Act, which is classified to section 590h(b) of Title 16, Conservation.

Section 10(b) of the Agricultural Adjustment Act, referred to in subsec. (a)(C)(i), is classified to section 610(b) of Title 7, Agriculture.

The Workforce Investment Act of 1998, referred to in subsec. (d)(3), (4), is Pub. L. 105–220, Aug. 7, 1998, 112 Stat. 936, as amended. Title I of the Act is classified principally to chapter 30 (§ 2801 et seq.) of Title 29, Labor. Section 134(a)(2)(A) of the Act is classified to section 2864(a)(2)(A) of Title 29. For complete classification of this Act to the Code, see Short Title note set out under section 9201 of Title 20, Education, and Tables.

AMENDMENTS

2000—Subsec. (f)(5). Pub. L. 106–398 substituted "September 30, 2005" for "September 30, 2001".

1998—Subsec. (d)(3)(A)(i). Pub. L. 105–277, § 101(f) [title VIII, § 405(f)(1)(A)(i)], added cl. (i) and struck out former cl. (i) which read as follows: "the appropriate State dislocated worker unit or office (referred to in section 311(b)(2) of the Job Training Partnership Act), or the State or entity designated by the State to carry out rapid response activities under section 134(a)(2)(A) of the Workforce Investment Act of 1998; and".

Pub. L. 105–277, § 101(f) [title VIII, § 405(d)(1)(A)(i)], added cl. (i) and struck out former cl. (i) which read as follows: "the appropriate State dislocated worker unit or units (referred to in section 311(b)(2) of the Job Training Partnership Act); and".

Subsec. (d)(3)(B)(iii). Pub. L. 105–277, § 101(f) [title VIII, § 405(f)(1)(A)(ii)], struck out "under the Job Training Partnership Act or" before "under title I of".

Pub. L. 105–277, § 101(f) [title VIII, § 405(d)(1)(A)(ii)], substituted "other services under the Job Training Partnership Act or under title I of the Workforce Investment Act of 1998" for "other services under the Job Training Partnership Act".

Subsec. (d)(4). Pub. L. 105–277, § 101(f) [title VIII, § 405(f)(1)(B)], struck out "the Job Training Partnership Act or" before "title I of".

Pub. L. 105–277, § 101(f) [title VIII, § 405(d)(1)(B)], substituted "Secretary of Labor on matters relating to the Job Training Partnership Act or title I of the Workforce Investment Act of 1998" for "Secretary of Labor on matters relating to the Job Training Partnership Act".

1996—Subsec. (a)(C)(ii). Pub. L. 104–106, § 1043(d)(1), substituted "January 1, 1966" for "January 1, 1987".

Subsec. (f). Pub. L. 104–201 amended subsec. (f) generally. Prior to amendment, subsec. (f) read as follows:

"(f)(1) The Secretary of Defense or the Secretary of a military department may—

"(A) release in a reduction in force an employee who volunteers for the release even though the em-

ployee is not otherwise subject to release in the reduction in force under the criteria applicable under the other provisions of this section; and

"(B) for each employee voluntarily released in the reduction in force under subparagraph (A), retain an employee in a similar position who would otherwise be released in the reduction in force under such criteria.

"(2) A voluntary release of an employee in a reduction in force pursuant to paragraph (1) shall be treated as an involuntary release in the reduction in force.

"(3) An employee with critical knowledge and skills (as defined by the Secretary concerned) may not participate in a voluntary release under paragraph (1) if the Secretary concerned determines that such participation would impair the performance of the mission of the Department of Defense or the military department concerned.

"(4) The regulations prescribed under this section shall incorporate the authority provided in this subsection.

"(5) The authority under paragraph (1) may not be exercised after September 30, 1996."

Pub. L. 104–106, § 1034, added subsec. (f).

1992—Subsecs. (d), (e). Pub. L. 102–484 added subsecs. (d) and (e).

1990—Subsec. (a)(C). Pub. L. 101–508 amended subpar. (C) generally. Prior to amendment, subpar. (C) read as follows: "is entitled to credit for service rendered as an employee of a county committee established pursuant to section 590h(b) of title 16, or of a committee or an association of producers described in section 610(b) of title 7."

1986—Subsec. (a)(C). Pub. L. 99–251 struck out "who is an employee in or under the Department of Agriculture" before "is entitled to credit".

1978—Subsec. (a). Pub. L. 95–454, § 906(a)(2), substituted "Office of Personnel Management" for "Civil Service Commission".

Subsec. (b). Pub. L. 95–454, § 307(e), substituted provisions relating to retention of a preference eligible with a compensable service-connected disability of 30 percent or more, for provisions relating to retention of preference eligible employees on the basis of ratings.

Subsec. (c). Pub. L. 95–454, § 307(e), added subsec. (c).

1968—Subsec. (a). Pub. L. 90–623 made minor changes in form and punctuation in subpars. (A) and (B), and, in subpar. (C), substituted "section 590h(b) of title 16" and "section 610(b) of title 7" for "section 8(b) of the Soil Conservation and Domestic Allotment Act (16 U.S.C. 590h(b))" and "section 10(b) of the Agricultural Adjustment Act of May 12, 1933 (48 Stat. 37)" respectively.

Subsec. (a)(C). Pub. L. 90–367 added subsec. (a)(C).

EFFECTIVE DATE OF 1998 AMENDMENT

Pub. L. 105–277, div. A, § 101(f) [title VIII, § 405(g)], Oct. 21, 1998, 112 Stat. 2681–337, 2681–434, as amended by Pub. L. 106–400, § 2, Oct. 30, 2000, 114 Stat. 1675, provided that:

"(1) IMMEDIATELY EFFECTIVE AMENDMENTS.—The amendments made by subsections (a) through (d) [amending this section and sections 2014, 2015, and 2026 of Title 7, Agriculture, sections 1255a and 1613 of Title 8, Aliens and Nationality, sections 636, 1022a, 3116, and 3151 of Title 15, Commerce and Trade, section 79l of Title 16, Conservation, section 665 of Title 18, Crimes and Criminal Procedure, sections 2296 and 2311 of Title 19, Customs Duties, sections 1070d–2, 1087vv, 3443, 5934, 5938, 6365, 6434, 6453, and 6455 of Title 20, Education, section 5855 of Title 22, Foreign Relations and Intercourse, section 2102 of Title 29, Labor, section 6703 of Title 31, Money and Finance, sections 4102A, 4103A, and 4213 of Title 38, Veterans' Benefits, and sections 603, 1437u, 1474, 3013, 3056, 3056a, 3056h, 3796eee, 4368a, 4953, 4959, 6103, 6864, 6873, 7274h, 9806, 11302, 12637, 12653c, 12655m, 12899c, 12899e, and 13823 of Title 42, The Public Health and Welfare, amending provisions set out as notes under sections 1183a and 1522 of Title 8, sections 1143, 2391, 2501, 2701, and 2687 of Title 10, Armed Forces, section 3304 of Title 26, Internal Revenue Code, section 1721 of Title 29, and section 4101 of Title 38, and repealing provisions set out as notes under sections 1501 and 1551 of Title 29] shall take effect on the date of the enactment of this Act [Oct. 21, 1998].

"(2) SUBSEQUENTLY EFFECTIVE AMENDMENTS.—

"(A) MCKINNEY-VENTO HOMELESS ASSISTANCE ACT.— The amendments made by subsection (e) shall take effect on July 1, 1999.

"(B) JOB TRAINING PARTNERSHIP ACT.—The amendments made by subsection (f) [amending this section and sections 2014, 2015, and 2026 of Title 7, Agriculture, sections 1255a and 1613 of Title 8, Aliens and Nationality, sections 636 and 3116 of Title 15, Commerce and Trade, sections 2296 and 2311 of Title 19, Customs Duties, sections 1070d–2, 1087vv, 6365, 6434, 6453, and 6455 of Title 20, Education, section 2102 of Title 29, Labor, section 6703 of Title 31, Money and Finance, sections 4102A, 4103A, and 4213 of Title 38, Veterans' Benefits, and sections 603, 1437u, 1474, 3013, 3056, 3056a, 3056h, 3796ee, 4368a, 4953, 4959, 6864, 6873, 7274h, 9806, 11302, 12653c, 12655m, 12899c, and 13823 of Title 42, The Public Health and Welfare, and amending provisions set out as notes under sections 1183a and 1522 of Title 8, sections 1143, 2501, 2687, and 2701 of Title 10, Armed Forces, section 3304 of Title 26, Internal Revenue Code, section 1721 of Title 29, and section 4101 of Title 38] shall take effect on July 1, 2000."

EFFECTIVE DATE OF 1996 AMENDMENT

Section 1043(d)(2) of Pub. L. 104–106 provided that: "Notwithstanding any provision of subsection (c) [set out as a note under section 8347 of this title], the amendment made by paragraph (1) [amending this section] shall—

"(A) take effect on the date of the enactment of this Act [Feb. 10, 1996]; and

"(B) apply with respect to any reduction in force carried out on or after such date."

EFFECTIVE DATE OF 1992 AMENDMENT

Section 4433(a)(2) of Pub. L. 102–484 provided that: "The amendment made by paragraph (1) [amending this section] shall apply with respect to any personnel action taking effect on or after the last day of the 90-day period beginning on the date of enactment of this Act [Oct. 23, 1992]."

EFFECTIVE DATE OF 1990 AMENDMENT

Amendment by Pub. L. 101–508 applicable with respect to any individual who, on or after Jan. 1, 1987, moves from employment in nonappropriated fund instrumentality of Department of Defense or Coast Guard, that is described in section 2105(c) of this title, to employment in Department or Coast Guard, that is not described in section 2105(c), or who moves from employment in Department or Coast Guard, that is not described in section 2105(c), to employment in nonappropriated fund instrumentality of Department or Coast Guard, that is described in section 2105(c), see section 7202(m)(1) of Pub. L. 101–508, set out as a note under section 2105 of this title.

EFFECTIVE DATE OF 1978 AMENDMENT

Amendment by Pub. L. 95–454 effective 90 days after Oct. 13, 1978, see section 907 of Pub. L. 95–454, set out as a note under section 1101 of this title.

EFFECTIVE DATE OF 1968 AMENDMENT

Amendment by Pub. L. 90–623 intended to restate without substantive change the law in effect on Oct. 22, 1968, see section 6 of Pub. L. 90–623, set out as a note under section 5334 of this title.

REGULATIONS

For provisions relating to promulgation of regulations necessary to carry out amendment by section 1043(d)(1) of Pub. L. 104–106, see section 1043(b) of Pub. L. 104–106, set out as a Regulations; Effective Date of 1996 Amendment note under section 8347 of this title.

INTERAGENCY PLACEMENT PROGRAM FOR FEDERAL EMPLOYEES AFFECTED BY REDUCTIONS IN FORCE

Pub. L. 103–337, div. A, title X, § 1066, Oct. 5, 1994, 108 Stat. 2850, provided that:

"(a) STUDY AND REPORT.—(1) The Director of the Office of Personnel Management shall conduct a study on the feasibility of establishing a mandatory interagency placement program for Federal employees affected by reductions in force.

"(2) For purposes of paragraph (1), an interagency placement program is a program that provides a system to require the offering of a position in an agency to an employee of another agency affected by a reduction in force if—

"(A) the position cannot be filled through a placement program of the agency in which the position is located;

"(B) the employee to whom the offer is made is qualified for the offered position; and

"(C) the geographic location of the offered position is within the commuting area of—

"(i) the residence of the employee; or

"(ii) the employee's present or last-held position.

"(3) The Director shall carry out this subsection in consultation with the Secretary of Defense.

"(4) The Director shall seek comments from the heads of all appropriate Federal agencies in conducting the study required by paragraph (1).

"(5) Not later than six months after the date of the enactment of this Act [Oct. 5, 1994], the Director shall submit to Congress a report on the results of the study required by paragraph (1) and on any action taken by the Director under subsection (b).

"(b) AGREEMENTS TO ESTABLISH INTERAGENCY PLACEMENT PROGRAM.—(1) The Director may establish a Government-wide interagency placement program for Federal employees affected by reductions in force if, during the 6-month period beginning on the date of the enactment of this Act [Oct. 5, 1994], the Director, in consultation with the Secretary of Defense, determines that such a program is feasible. To carry out the program, the Director may enter into an agreement with the head of each agency that agrees to participate in the program. If the Director establishes a program under this subsection, it is not necessary that the program be an interagency placement program within the meaning of subsection (a)(2).

"(2) If the Director establishes a program pursuant to paragraph (1), the report required by subsection (a)(5) shall identify each agency that does not agree to participate in the program and the reasons of the head of that agency for not agreeing to participate.

"(c) DEFINITIONS.—For purposes of this section:

"(1) The term 'agency' means an Executive agency as defined in section 105 of title 5, United States Code, except that such term does not include the General Accounting Office.

"(2) The term 'Federal employees affected by reductions in force' means Federal employees who are separated, or are scheduled to be separated, from service under a reduction in force pursuant to—

"(A) regulations prescribed under section 3502 of title 5, United States Code; or

"(B) procedures established under section 3595 of such title."

SPECIAL RULE ON APPLICATION OF SUBSECTIONS (d) AND (e)

Section 4433(b) of Pub. L. 102–484, as amended by Pub. L. 103–337, div. A, title III, § 341(a), Oct. 5, 1994, 108 Stat. 2720, provided that:

"(1) The provisions of section 3502(d) and (e) of title 5, United States Code (as added by subsection (a)) shall apply to employees of the Department of Defense according to their terms, except that, with respect to any reduction in force within that agency that would involve the separation of a significant number of employees (as determined under paragraph (1)(B) of such section 3502(d)), any reference in such section 3502(d) to '60 days' shall, in the case of the employees described in paragraph (2), be deemed to read '120 days'.

"(2) The employees described in this paragraph are those employees of the Department of Defense who are to be separated, due to a reduction in force described in paragraph (1), effective on or after the last day of the 90-day period referred to in subsection (a)(2) [see Effective Date of 1992 Amendment note above] and before February 1, 2000.

"(3) Nothing in this subsection shall prevent the application of the amendment made by subsection (a) [amending this section] with respect to an employee if—

"(A) the preceding paragraphs of this subsection do not apply with respect to such employee; and

"(B) the amendment made by subsection (a) would otherwise apply with respect to such employee.

"(4) The Secretary of Defense shall prescribe such regulations as may be necessary to carry out this subsection."

INDIAN PREFERENCE LAWS APPLICABLE TO BUREAU OF INDIAN AFFAIRS AND INDIAN HEALTH SERVICE POSITIONS

Applicability of Indian preference laws to Bureau of Indian Affairs and Indian Health Service positions for purposes of reduction-in-force procedures under subsec. (a) of this section, see section 472a(a) of Title 25, Indians.

EX. ORD. NO. 12828. DELEGATION OF CERTAIN PERSONNEL MANAGEMENT AUTHORITIES

Ex. Ord. No. 12828, Jan. 5, 1993, 58 F.R. 2965, provided:

By the authority vested in me as President by the Constitution and the laws of the United States of America, including section 301 of title 3 of the United States Code and sections 3502(e), 4505a(e), and 5377(i)(2) of title 5 of the United States Code, it is hereby ordered as follows:

SECTION 1. The Office of Personnel Management is designated and empowered to exercise, without the approval, ratification, or other action of the President, the following:

(1) The authority of the President under 5 U.S.C. 3502(e), as added by section 4433 of Public Law 102–484, to shorten the period of advance notice otherwise required by law with respect to reductions in force.

(2) The authority of the President under 5 U.S.C. 4505a(e), as added by section 2(19) of Public Law 102–378, to permit performance-based cash awards to be paid to categories of employees who would not otherwise be eligible.

SEC. 2. The Director of the Office of Management and Budget is designated and empowered to exercise, without the approval, ratification, or other action of the President, the authority of the President under 5 U.S.C. 5377(i)(2), as added by section 2(34) of Public Law 102–378, to designate one or more categories of positions within an agency to be treated as critical positions within the meaning of 5 U.S.C. 5377(a)(2).

SEC. 3. This order shall be effective immediately.

GEORGE BUSH.

SECTION REFERRED TO IN OTHER SECTIONS

This section is referred to in sections 2302, 7512, 7521, 9508 of this title; title 10 sections 1586, 1610; title 22 section 1438; title 25 section 472a; title 31 section 732; title 32 section 709; title 42 sections 616, 7237.

§ 3503. Transfer of functions

(a) When a function is transferred from one agency to another, each competing employee in the function shall be transferred to the receiving agency for employment in a position for which he is qualified before the receiving agency may make an appointment from another source to that position.

(b) When one agency is replaced by another, each competing employee in the agency to be replaced shall be transferred to the replacing agency for employment in a position for which he is qualified before the replacing agency may make an appointment from another source to that position.

(Pub. L. 89–554, Sept. 6, 1966, 80 Stat. 429; Pub. L. 95–454, title III, § 307(f), Oct. 13, 1978, 92 Stat. 1149; Pub. L. 96–54, § 2(a)(18), Aug. 14, 1979, 93 Stat. 382.)

HISTORICAL AND REVISION NOTES

Derivation	U.S. Code	Revised Statutes and Statutes at Large
....	5 U.S.C. 861(a) (3d proviso).	June 27, 1944, ch. 287, § 12 (3d proviso), 58 Stat. 390.

In subsection (a), the words "a function" are substituted for "any or all of the functions". The word "receiving" is substituted for "replacing" in the phrase "receiving agency" to avoid confusion with subsection (b).

In subsections (a) and (b), the word "first" in the phrase "shall first be transferred" is omitted as redundant in view of the subsequent limitation imposed by the words following "before". The words "make an appointment from another source to that position" are substituted for "appoint additional employees from any other source for such position".

Standard changes are made to conform with the definitions applicable and the style of this title as outlined in the preface to the report.

AMENDMENTS

1979—Subsecs. (a), (b). Pub. L. 96–54 substituted "competing employee" for "preference eligible employed".

1978—Subsecs. (a), (b). Pub. L. 95–454 which directed the substitution of "competing employee" for "preference eligible employee" was impossible to execute literally because the text contained reference to "preference eligible employed". See 1979 Amendment note above.

EFFECTIVE DATE OF 1979 AMENDMENT

Amendment by Pub. L. 96–54 effective July 12, 1979, see section 2(b) of Pub. L. 96–54, set out as a note under section 305 of this title.

EFFECTIVE DATE OF 1978 AMENDMENT

Amendment by Pub. L. 95–454 effective 90 days after Oct. 13, 1978, see section 907 of Pub. L. 95–454, set out as a note under section 1101 of this title.

SECTION REFERRED TO IN OTHER SECTIONS

This section is referred to in section 3595 of this title; title 10 section 1586; title 16 section 460lll–47; title 22 section 1438; title 24 section 225d.

§ 3504. Preference eligibles; retention; physical qualifications; waiver

(a) In determining qualifications of a preference eligible for retention in a position in the competitive service, an Executive agency, or the government of the District of Columbia, the Office of Personnel Management or other examining agency shall waive—

(1) requirements as to age, height, and weight, unless the requirement is essential to the performance of the duties of the position; and

(2) physical requirements if, in the opinion of the Office or other examining agency, after considering the recommendation of an accred-

ited physician, the preference eligible is physically able to perform efficiently the duties of the position.

(b) If an examining agency determines that, on the basis of evidence before it, a preference eligible described in section 2108(3)(C) of this title who has a compensable service-connected disability of 30 percent or more is not able to fulfill the physical requirements of the position, the examining agency shall notify the Office of the determination and, at the same time, the examining agency shall notify the preference eligible of the reasons for the determination and of the right to respond, within 15 days of the date of the notification, to the Office. The Office shall require a demonstration by the appointing authority that the notification was timely sent to the preference eligible's last known address and shall, before the selection of any other person for the position, make a final determination on the physical ability of the preference eligible to perform the duties of the position, taking into account any additional information provided in the response. When the Office has completed its review of the proposed disqualification on the basis of physical disability, it shall send its findings to the appointing authority and the preference eligible. The appointing authority shall comply with the findings of the Office. The functions of the Office under this subsection may not be delegated.

(Pub. L. 89–554, Sept. 6, 1966, 80 Stat. 429; Pub. L. 95–454, title III, § 307(g), title IX, § 906(a)(2), (3), Oct. 13, 1978, 92 Stat. 1149, 1224.)

HISTORICAL AND REVISION NOTES

Derivation	U.S. Code	Revised Statutes and Statutes at Large
....	5 U.S.C. 854 (1st 2 sentences, so much as relates to retention).	June 27, 1944, ch. 287, § 5 (1st 2 sentences, so much as relates to retention), 58 Stat. 388.

The words "in the competitive service, an Executive agency, or the government of the District of Columbia" are added on authority of former sections 851, 858, and 869 which are carried into this title. The words "preference eligible" are substituted for "veteran".

Standard changes are made to conform with the definitions applicable and the style of this title as outlined in the preface to the report.

AMENDMENTS

1978—Pub. L. 95–454 designated existing provisions as subsec. (a), substituted "Office of Personnel Management" for "Civil Service Commission" and "Office" for "Commission", and added subsec. (b).

EFFECTIVE DATE OF 1978 AMENDMENT

Amendment by Pub. L. 95–454 effective 90 days after Oct. 13, 1978, see section 907 of Pub. L. 95–454, set out as a note under section 1101 of this title.

SECTION REFERRED TO IN OTHER SECTIONS

This section is referred to in sections 2302, 3501 of this title; title 22 section 1438.

[SUBCHAPTER II—REPEALED]

[§ 3551. Repealed. Pub. L. 103–353, § 2(b)(2)(B), Oct. 13, 1994, 108 Stat. 3169]

Section, Pub. L. 89–554, Sept. 6, 1966, 80 Stat. 429; Pub. L. 90–491, § 2, Aug. 17, 1968, 82 Stat. 791, provided that

employee of Federal or District of Columbia government, ordered to active duty or to duty under sections 502–505 of Title 32, National Guard, as a Reserve of the armed forces or member of National Guard, was entitled, on release from duty within time limits specified in section 459(g) of Title 50, Appendix, War and National Defense, to be restored to position held by him when ordered to duty, and provided that a Reserve or member of National Guard who left position for which salary was disbursed by Secretary of the Senate or Clerk of the House of Representatives was entitled on release to be restored only under the provisions of section 459 of Title 50, Appendix.

EFFECTIVE DATE OF REPEAL

Repeal effective with respect to reemployments initiated on or after first day after 60-day period beginning Oct. 13, 1994, with transition rules, see section 8 of Pub. L. 103–353, set out as an Effective Date note under section 4301 of Title 38, Veterans' Benefits.

SUBCHAPTER III—REINSTATEMENT OR RESTORATION AFTER SUSPENSION OR REMOVAL FOR NATIONAL SECURITY

§ 3571. Reinstatement or restoration; individuals suspended or removed for national security

An individual suspended or removed under section 7532 of this title may be restored to duty in the discretion of the head of the agency concerned.

(Pub. L. 89–554, Sept. 6, 1966, 80 Stat. 429.)

HISTORICAL AND REVISION NOTES

Derivation	U.S. Code	Revised Statutes and Statutes at Large
....	5 U.S.C. 22–1 (1st 31 words of 3d proviso).	Aug. 26, 1950, ch. 803, § 1 (1st 31 words of 3d proviso), 64 Stat. 477.

The words "suspended or removed under section 7532 of this title" are coextensive with and substituted for "whose employment is so suspended or terminated under the authority of said sections".

Standard changes are made to conform with the definitions applicable and the style of this title as outlined in the preface to the report.

SUBCHAPTER IV—REEMPLOYMENT AFTER SERVICE WITH AN INTERNATIONAL ORGANIZATION

§ 3581. Definitions

For the purpose of this subchapter—
　(1) "agency" means—
　　(A) an Executive agency;
　　(B) a military department; and
　　(C) an employing authority in the legislative branch;
　(2) "employee" means an employee in or under an agency;
　(3) "international organization" means a public international organization or international-organization preparatory commission in which the Government of the United States participates;
　(4) "transfer" means the change of position by an employee from an agency to an international organization; and
　(5) "reemployment" means—
　　(A) the reemployment of an employee under section 3582(b) of this title; or
　　(B) the reemployment of a Congressional employee within 90 days from his separation from an international organization;

following a term of employment not extending beyond the period named by the head of the agency at the time of consent to transfer or, in the absence of a named period, not extending beyond the first 5 consecutive years, or any extension thereof, after entering the employ of the international organization.

(Pub. L. 89–554, Sept. 6, 1966, 80 Stat. 429; Pub. L. 91–175, pt. V, § 502(b), Dec. 30, 1969, 83 Stat. 825; Pub. L. 94–183, § 2(9), Dec. 31, 1975, 89 Stat. 1057.)

HISTORICAL AND REVISION NOTES

Derivation	U.S. Code	Revised Statutes and Statutes at Large
....	5 U.S.C. 2331.	Aug. 28, 1958, Pub. L. 85–795, § 2, 72 Stat. 959.

In paragraphs (1)(A) and (B), the terms "Executive agency" and "military department" are coextensive with and substituted for "any department or agency in the executive branch of the United States Government including independent establishments and Government owned or controlled corporations" in view of the definitions in sections 105 and 102.

In paragraph (2), the word "employee" is substituted for "any civilian appointive officer or employee" in view of the definition of "employee" in section 2105. The words "in or under an agency" are substituted for "in or under the executive or the legislative branch of the United States Government".

The definition of "Congressional employee" in former section 2331(4) is omitted as unnecessary because the term "Congressional employee", defined for the purpose of this title in section 2107, is coextensive with the definition in former section 2331(4).

The definition of "Detail" in former section 2331(6) is omitted from this section as inappropriate but is carried into section 3343.

Standard changes are made to conform with the definitions applicable and the style of this title as outlined in the preface to the report.

AMENDMENTS

1975—Subsec. (5)(A). Pub. L. 94–183 substituted "3582(b)" for "3582(a)".

1969—Par. (5). Pub. L. 91–175 substituted "the first 5 consecutive years, or any extension thereof, after entering the employ of the international organization" for "the first 3 consecutive years after entering the employ of the international organization".

DELEGATION OF AUTHORITY

Authority of President to extend a transfer of an employee under this section delegated to Secretary of State, see section 3 of Ex. Ord. No. 11552, Aug. 24, 1970, 35 F.R. 13569, set out as a note under section 3584 of this title.

SECTION REFERRED TO IN OTHER SECTIONS

This section is referred to in section 3343 of this title; title 26 section 3121; title 42 section 410.

§ 3582. Rights of transferring employees

(a) An employee serving under an appointment not limited to 1 year or less who transfers to an international organization with the consent of the head of his agency is entitled—

(1) to retain coverage, rights, and benefits under any system established by law for the retirement of employees, if necessary employee deductions and agency contributions in payment for the coverage, rights, and benefits for the period of employment with the international organization are currently deposited in the system's fund or depository; and the period during which coverage, rights, and benefits are retained under this paragraph is deemed creditable service under the system, except that such service shall not be considered creditable service for the purpose of any retirement system for transferring personnel, if such service forms the basis, in whole or in part, for an annuity or pension under the retirement system of the international organization;

(2) to retain coverage, rights, and benefits under chapters 87 and 89 of this title, if necessary employee deductions and agency contributions in payment for the coverage, rights, and benefits for the period of employment with the international organization are currently deposited in the Employees' Life Insurance Fund and the Employees' Health Benefits Fund, as applicable, and the period during which coverage, rights, and benefits are retained under this paragraph is deemed service as an employee under chapters 87 and 89 of this title;

(3) to retain coverage, rights, and benefits under subchapter I of chapter 81 of this title, and for this purpose his employment with the international organization is deemed employment by the United States, but if he or his dependents receive from the international organization a payment, allowance, gratuity, payment under an insurance policy for which the premium is wholly paid by the international organization, or other benefit of any kind on account of the same injury or death, the amount thereof, is credited against disability or death compensation, as the case may be, payable under subchapter I of chapter 81 of this title; and

(4) to elect to retain to his credit all accumulated and current accrued annual leave to which entitled at the time of transfer which would otherwise be liquidated by a lump-sum payment. On his request at any time before reemployment, he shall be paid for the annual leave retained. If he receives a lump-sum payment and is reemployed within 6 months after transfer, he shall refund to the agency the amount of the lump-sum payment. This paragraph does not operate to cause a forfeiture of retained annual leave following reemployment or to deprive an employee of a lump-sum payment to which he would otherwise be entitled.

(b) An employee entitled to the benefits of subsection (a) of this section is entitled to be reemployed within 30 days of his application for reemployment in his former position or a position of like seniority, status, and pay in the agency from which he transferred, if—

(1) he is separated from the international organization within 5 years, or any extension thereof, after entering on duty with the international organization or within such shorter period as may be named by the head of the agency at the time of consent to transfer; and

(2) he applies for reemployment not later than 90 days after the separation.

On reemployment, an employee entitled to the benefits of subsection (a) is entitled to the rate of basic pay to which the employee would have been entitled had the employee remained in the civil service. On reemployment, the agency shall restore the sick leave account of the employee, by credit or charge, to its status at the time of transfer. The period of separation caused by the employment of the employee with the international organization and the period necessary to effect reemployment are deemed creditable service for all appropriate civil service employment purposes. This subsection does not apply to a congressional employee.

(c) This section applies only with respect to so much of a period of employment with an international organization as does not exceed 5 years, or any extension thereof, or such shorter period named by the head of the agency at the time of consent to transfer, except that for retirement and insurance purposes this section continues to apply during the period after separation from the international organization in which—

(1) an employee, except a Congressional employee, is properly exercising or could exercise the reemployment right established by subsection (b) of this section; or

(2) a Congressional employee is effecting or could effect a reemployment.

During that reemployment period, the employee is deemed on leave without pay for retirement and insurance purposes.

(d) During the employee's period of service with the international organization, the agency from which the employee is transferred shall make contributions for retirement and insurance purposes from the appropriations or funds of that agency so long as contributions are made by the employee.

(Pub. L. 89–554, Sept. 6, 1966, 80 Stat. 430; Pub. L. 91–175, pt. V, §502(c)–(f), Dec. 30, 1969, 83 Stat. 825, 826; Pub. L. 94–183, §2(10), Dec. 31, 1975, 89 Stat. 1057; Pub. L. 105–277, div. G, subdiv. B, title XXV, §2504(a), Oct. 21, 1998, 112 Stat. 2681–837.)

HISTORICAL AND REVISION NOTES

Derivation	U.S. Code	Revised Statutes and Statutes at Large
....	5 U.S.C. 2333 (less (c)).	Aug. 28, 1958, Pub. L. 85–795 §4 (less (c)), 72 Stat. 960.

In subsection (a), the words "Notwithstanding the provisions of any law, Executive order, or regulation" are omitted as unnecessary. In paragraph (2), the words "an employee under chapter 87 of this title" are substituted for "an officer or employee of the United States". In paragraph (4), the words "under no circumstances" are omitted as unnecessary.

Standard changes are made to conform with the definitions applicable and the style of this title as outlined in the preface to the report.

AMENDMENTS

1998—Subsec. (b). Pub. L. 105–277 inserted concluding provisions and struck out former concluding provisions which read as follows: "On reemployment, he is entitled to the rate of basic pay to which he would be entitled had he remained in the civil service. On reemployment, the agency shall restore his sick leave account, by credit or charge, to its status at the time of transfer. The period of separation caused by his employment with the international organization and the period necessary to effect reemployment are deemed creditable service for all appropriate civil service employment purposes. On reemployment, he is entitled to be paid, under such regulations as the President may prescribe

and from appropriations or funds of the agency from which transferred, an amount equal to the difference between the pay, allowances, post differential, and other monetary benefits paid by the international organization and the pay, allowances, post differential, and other monetary benefits that would have been paid by the agency had he been detailed to the international organization under section 3343 of this title. Such a payment shall be made to an employee who is unable to exercise his reemployment right because of disability incurred while on transfer to an international organization under this subchapter and, in the case of an employee who dies while on such a transfer or during the period after separation from the international organization in which he is properly exercising or could exercise his reemployment right, in accordance with subchapter VIII of chapter 55 of this title. This subsection does not apply to a congressional employee nor may any payment provided for in the preceding two sentences of this subsection be based on a period of employment with an international organization occurring before the first day of the first pay period which begins after December 29, 1969."

1975—Subsec. (b). Pub. L. 94–183 substituted "after December 29, 1969" for "on or after the date of enactment of the Foreign Assistance Act of 1969" in last sentence.

1969—Subsec. (a). Pub. L. 91–175, §502(c), inserted provision at end of cl. (1) excepting from creditable service, for the purpose of any retirement system, an agency employee who transfers to an international organization, if such service forms the basis for an annuity or pension under the retirement system of the international organization, and, in cl. (2), inserted references to chapter 89 and Employees' Health Benefits Fund.

Subsec. (b). Pub. L. 91–175, §502(d), struck out ", except a Congressional employee," in provisions preceding cl. (1), substituted "5 years or any extension thereof," for "3 years" in cl. (1), and, in provisions following cl. (2), inserted provision dealing with pay differentials to be received by former agency employee on reemployment with agency after service with international organization.

Subsec. (c). Pub. L. 91–175, §502(e), substituted "5 years, or any extension thereof," for "3 years".

Subsec. (d). Pub. L. 91–175, §502(f), made contributions for retirement and insurance purposes mandatory by the agency from which employee is transferred, during employee's period of service with international organization, so long as contributions are made by employee.

EFFECTIVE DATE OF 1998 AMENDMENT

Pub. L. 105–277, div. G, subdiv. B, title XXV, §2504(b), Oct. 21, 1998, 112 Stat. 2681–837, provided that: "The amendment made by subsection (a) [amending this section] shall apply with respect to transfers that take effect on or after the date of enactment of this Act [Oct. 21, 1998]."

DELEGATION OF AUTHORITY

Authority of President under subsec. (b) of this section delegated to Office of Personnel Management, and authority to define and specify pay, allowances, etc., to be paid by the agency, delegated to Secretary of State, see section 3 of Ex. Ord. No. 11552, Aug. 24, 1970, 35 F.R. 13569, set out as a note under section 3584 of this title.

SECTION REFERRED TO IN OTHER SECTIONS

This section is referred to in sections 3581, 8432c of this title; title 22 section 6103; title 26 section 3121; title 42 section 410.

§ 3583. Computations

A computation under this subchapter before reemployment is made in the same manner as if the employee had received basic pay, or basic pay plus additional pay in the case of a Congressional employee, at the rate at which it would have been payable had the employee continued in the position in which he was serving at the time of transfer.

(Pub. L. 89–554, Sept. 6, 1966, 80 Stat. 431.)

HISTORICAL AND REVISION NOTES

Derivation	U.S. Code	Revised Statutes and Statutes at Large
....	5 U.S.C. 2333(c).	Aug. 28, 1958, Pub. L. 85–795, §4(c), 72 Stat. 961.

Standard changes are made to conform with the definitions applicable and the style of this title as outlined in the preface to the report.

§ 3584. Regulations

The President may prescribe regulations necessary to carry out this subchapter and section 3343 of this title and to protect and assure the retirement, insurance, leave, and reemployment rights and such other similar civil service employment rights as he finds appropriate. The regulations may provide for the exclusion of employees from the application of this subchapter and section 3343 of this title on the basis of the nature and type of employment including excepted appointments of a confidential or policy-determining character, or conditions pertaining to the employment including short-term appointments, seasonal or intermittent employment, and part-time employment.

(Pub. L. 89–554, Sept. 6, 1966, 80 Stat. 431.)

HISTORICAL AND REVISION NOTES

Derivation	U.S. Code	Revised Statutes and Statutes at Large
....	5 U.S.C. 2334.	Aug. 28, 1958, Pub. L. 85–795, §5, 72 Stat. 961.

The words "civil service employment rights" are substituted for "Federal employment rights". The word "including" is substituted for "such as, but not limited to".

Standard changes are made to conform with the definitions applicable and the style of this title as outlined in the preface to the report.

EXECUTIVE ORDER NO. 10804

Ex. Ord. No. 10804, Feb. 12, 1959, 24 F.R. 1147, which delegated to the United States Civil Service Commission the authority vested in the President by section 5 of the Federal Employees International Organization Service Act (72 Stat. 961) [now this section], was revoked by Ex. Ord. No. 11552, Aug. 24, 1970, 35 F.R. 13569, set out below.

EX. ORD. NO. 11552. PROVIDING FOR DETAILS AND TRANSFERS OF FEDERAL EMPLOYEES TO INTERNATIONAL ORGANIZATIONS

Ex. Ord. No. 11552, Aug. 24, 1970, 35 F.R. 13569, as amended by Ex. Ord. No. 12107, Dec. 28, 1978, 44 F.R. 1055, provided:

By virtue of the authority vested in me by section 301 of title 3 and section 3584 of title 5 [this section], United States Code, and as President of the United States, it is ordered as follows:

SECTION 1. Leadership and coordination. The Secretary of State shall provide leadership and coordination for the effort of the Federal Government to increase and improve its participation in international organizations through transfers and details of well-qualified Federal employees, and shall develop policies, procedures, and programs consistent with this order to advance and encourage such participation.

SEC. 2. Federal agency cooperation. Each agency in the executive branch of the Federal Government shall to the maximum extent feasible and with due regard to its manpower requirements assist and encourage details and transfers of employees to international organizations by observing the following policies and procedures:

(1) Vacancies in international organizations shall be brought to the notice of well-qualified agency employees whose abilities and levels of responsibility in the Federal service are commensurate with those required to fill such vacancies.

(2) Subject to prior approval of his agency, no leave shall be charged an employee who is absent for a maximum of three days for interview for a proposed detail or transfer at the formal request of an international organization of a Federal official; an agency may approve official travel for necessary travel within the United States in connection with such an interview.

(3) An agency, upon request of an appropriate authority, shall provide international organizations with detailed assessments of the technical or professional qualifications of individual employees being formally considered for details and transfers to specific positions.

(4) Upon return of an employee to his agency, the agency shall give due consideration to the employee's overall qualifications, including those which may have been acquired during his service with the international organization, in determining the position and grade in which he is reemployed.

SEC. 3. Delegations. (a) Except as otherwise provided in this order, there is hereby delegated to the Office of Personnel Management the authority vested in the President by sections 3582(b) and 3584 of title 5, United States Code.

(b) The following are hereby delegated to the Secretary of State:

(1) The authority vested in the President by sections 3343 and 3581 of title 5, United States Code, to determine whether it is in the national interest to extend a detail or transfer of an employee beyond five years.

(2) The authority vested in the President by section 3582(b) of title 5, United States Code, to define and specify "pay, allowances, post differential, and other monetary benefits" to be paid by the agency upon reemployment, disability, or death.

SEC. 4. Revocation. Executive Order No. 10804 of February 12, 1959, is hereby revoked.

SUBCHAPTER V—REMOVAL, REINSTATEMENT, AND GUARANTEED PLACEMENT IN THE SENIOR EXECUTIVE SERVICE

SUBCHAPTER REFERRED TO IN OTHER SECTIONS

This subchapter is referred to in title 38 section 7425.

§ 3591. Definitions

For the purpose of this subchapter, "agency", "Senior Executive Service position", "senior executive", "career appointee", "limited term appointee", "limited emergency appointee", "noncareer appointee", and "general position" have the meanings set forth in section 3132(a) of this title.

(Added Pub. L. 95–454, title IV, §404(b), Oct. 13, 1978, 92 Stat. 1165.)

EFFECTIVE DATE

Subchapter effective 9 months after Oct. 13, 1978, and congressional review of provisions of sections 401 through 412 of Pub. L. 95–454, see section 415(a)(1), (b), of Pub. L. 95–454, set out as a note under section 3131 of this title.

§ 3592. Removal from the Senior Executive Service

(a) Except as provided in subsection (b) of this section, a career appointee may be removed from the Senior Executive Service to a civil service position outside of the Senior Executive Service—

(1) during the 1-year period of probation under section 3393(d) of this title,

(2) at any time for less than fully successful executive performance as determined under subchapter II of chapter 43 of this title, or

(3) if the career appointee is not recertified as a senior executive under section 3393a,

except that in the case of a removal under paragraph (2) of this subsection the career appointee shall, at least 15 days before the removal, be entitled, upon request, to an informal hearing before an official designated by the Merit Systems Protection Board at which the career appointee may appear and present arguments, but such hearing shall not give the career appointee the right to initiate an action with the Board under section 7701 of this title, nor need the removal action be delayed as a result of the granting of such hearing. In the case of a removal under paragraph (3) of this subsection, the career appointee shall have the right to appeal the removal from the Senior Executive Service to the Merit Systems Protection Board under section 7701.

(b)(1) Except as provided in paragraph (2) of this subsection, a career appointee in an agency may not be involuntarily removed—

(A) within 120 days after an appointment of the head of the agency; or

(B) within 120 days after the appointment in the agency of the career appointee's most immediate supervisor who—

(i) is a noncareer appointee; and

(ii) has the authority to remove the career appointee.

(2) Paragraph (1) of this subsection does not apply with respect to—

(A) any removal under section 4314(b)(3) of this title; or

(B) any disciplinary action initiated before an appointment referred to in paragraph (1) of this subsection.

(c) A limited emergency appointee, limited term appointee, or noncareer appointee may be removed from the service at any time.

(Added Pub. L. 95–454, title IV, § 404(b), Oct. 13, 1978, 92 Stat. 1165; amended Pub. L. 101–194, title V, § 506(b)(3), Nov. 30, 1989, 103 Stat. 1758.)

Amendments

1989—Subsec. (a). Pub. L. 101–194, § 506(b)(3)(D), inserted at end "In the case of a removal under paragraph (3) of this subsection, the career appointee shall have the right to appeal the removal from the Senior Executive Service to the Merit Systems Protection Board under section 7701."

Subsec. (a)(3). Pub. L. 101–194, § 506(b)(3)(A)–(C), added par. (3).

Effective Date of 1989 Amendment

Amendment by Pub. L. 101–194 effective Jan. 1, 1991, see section 506(d) of Pub. L. 101–194, set out as a note under section 3151 of this title.

Section Referred to in Other Sections

This section is referred to in sections 3151, 3393, 3393a, 7542 of this title; title 10 section 1606; title 31 section 733.

§ 3593. Reinstatement in the Senior Executive Service

(a) A former career appointee may be reinstated, without regard to section 3393(b) and (c) of this title, to any Senior Executive Service position for which the appointee is qualified if—

(1) the appointee has successfully completed the probationary period established under section 3393(d) of this title; and

(2) the appointee left the Senior Executive Service for reasons other than misconduct, neglect of duty, malfeasance, less than fully successful executive performance as determined under subchapter II of chapter 43 of this title, or failure to be recertified as a senior executive under section 3393a.

(b) A career appointee who is appointed by the President to any civil service position outside the Senior Executive Service and who leaves the position for reasons other than misconduct, neglect of duty, or malfeasance shall be entitled to be placed in the Senior Executive Service if the appointee applies to the Office of Personnel Management within 90 days after separation from the Presidential appointment.

(c)(1) A former career appointee shall be reinstated, without regard to section 3393(b) and (c) of this title, to any vacant Senior Executive Service position in an agency for which the appointee is qualified if—

(A) the individual was a career appointee on May 31, 1981;

(B) the appointee was removed from the Senior Executive Service under section 3595 of this title before October 1, 1984, due to a reduction in force in that agency;

(C) before the removal occurred, the appointee successfully completed the probationary period established under section 3393(d) of this title; and

(D) the appointee applies for that vacant position within one year after the Office receives certification regarding that appointee pursuant to section 3595(b)(3)(B) of this title.

(2) A career appointee is entitled to appeal to the Merit Systems Protection Board under section 7701 of this title any determination by the agency that the appointee is not qualified for a position for which the appointee applies under paragraph (1) of this subsection.

(Added Pub. L. 95–454, title IV, § 404(b), Oct. 13, 1978, 92 Stat. 1166; amended Pub. L. 97–35, title XVII, § 1704(b), Aug. 13, 1981, 95 Stat. 757; Pub. L. 98–615, title III, § 303(a), Nov. 8, 1984, 98 Stat. 3217; Pub. L. 101–194, title V, § 506(b)(4), Nov. 30, 1989, 103 Stat. 1758.)

Amendments

1989—Subsec. (a)(2). Pub. L. 101–194 struck out "or" after "malfeasance," and inserted ", or failure to be recertified as a senior executive under section 3393a" before period at end.

1984—Subsec. (c)(1)(B). Pub. L. 98–615 inserted "before October 1, 1984,".

1981—Subsec. (c). Pub. L. 97–35 added subsec. (c).

Effective Date of 1989 Amendment

Amendment by Pub. L. 101–194 effective Jan. 1, 1991, see section 506(d) of Pub. L. 101–194, set out as a note under section 3151 of this title.

EFFECTIVE DATE OF 1984 AMENDMENT

Amendment by Pub. L. 98–615 effective following expiration of 90-day period beginning on Nov. 8, 1984, see section 307 of Pub. L. 98–615, set out as a note under section 3393 of this title.

EFFECTIVE DATE OF 1981 AMENDMENT

Amendment by Pub. L. 97–35 effective June 1, 1981, with certain exceptions and conditions, see section 1704(e) of Pub. L. 97–35, set out as an Effective Date note under section 3595 of this title.

§ 3594. Guaranteed placement in other personnel systems

(a) A career appointee who was appointed from a civil service position held under a career or career-conditional appointment (or an appointment of equivalent tenure, as determined by the Office of Personnel Management) and who, for reasons other than misconduct, neglect of duty, or malfeasance, is removed from the Senior Executive Service during the probationary period under section 3393(d) of this title, shall be entitled to be placed in a civil service position (other than a Senior Executive Service position) in any agency.

(b) A career appointee who has completed the probationary period under section 3393(d) of this title, and who—

(1) is removed from the Senior Executive Service for less than fully successful executive performance as determined under subchapter II of chapter 43 of this title;

(2) is removed from the Senior Executive Service under paragraph (4) or (5) of section 3595(b) of this title; or

(3) is removed from the Senior Executive Service for failure to be recertified under section 3393a;

shall be entitled to be placed in a civil service position (other than a Senior Executive Service position) in any agency.

(c)(1) For purposes of subsections (a) and (b) of this section—

(A) the position in which any career appointee is placed under such subsections shall be a continuing position at GS–15 of the General Schedule or classified above GS–15 pursuant to section 5108, or an equivalent position, and, in the case of a career appointee referred to in subsection (a) of this section, the career appointee shall be entitled to an appointment of a tenure equivalent to the tenure of the appointment held in the position from which the career appointee was appointed;

(B) any career appointee placed under subsection (a) or (b) of this section shall be entitled to receive basic pay at the highest of—

(i) the rate of basic pay in effect for the position in which placed;

(ii) the rate of basic pay in effect at the time of the placement for the position the career appointee held in the civil service immediately before being appointed to the Senior Executive Service; or

(iii) the rate of basic pay in effect for the career appointee immediately before being placed under subsection (a) or (b) of this section; and

(C) the placement of any career appointee under subsection (a) or (b) of this section may not be made to a position which would cause the separation or reduction in grade of any other employee.

(2) An employee who is receiving basic pay under paragraph (1)(B)(ii) or (iii) of this subsection is entitled to have the basic pay rate of the employee increased by 50 percent of the amount of each increase in the maximum rate of basic pay for the grade of the position in which the employee is placed under subsection (a) or (b) of this section until the rate is equal to the rate in effect under paragraph (1)(B)(i) of this subsection for the position in which the employee is placed.

(Added Pub. L. 95–454, title IV, § 404(b), Oct. 13, 1978, 92 Stat. 1166; amended Pub. L. 98–615, title III, § 303(b), Nov. 8, 1984, 98 Stat. 3217; Pub. L. 101–194, title V, § 506(b)(5), Nov 30, 1989, 103 Stat. 1758; Pub. L. 101–509, title V, § 529 [title I, § 101(b)(9)(E)], Nov. 5, 1990, 104 Stat. 1427, 1441; Pub. L. 102–378, § 2(16), Oct. 2, 1992, 106 Stat. 1347.)

REFERENCES IN TEXT

GS–15 of the General Schedule, referred to in subsec. (c)(1)(A), is set out under section 5332 of this title.

AMENDMENTS

1992—Subsec. (c)(1)(A). Pub. L. 102–378 substituted "section 5108," for "section 5108,,".

1990—Subsec. (c)(1)(A). Pub. L. 101–509 substituted "at GS–15 of the General Schedule or classified above GS–15 pursuant to section 5108," for "at GS–15 or above of the General Schedule".

1989—Subsec. (b)(3). Pub. L. 101–194 added par. (3).

1984—Subsec. (b). Pub. L. 98–615 inserted provision relating to career appointees removed from the Senior Executive Service under section 3595(b)(4) or (5) of this title.

EFFECTIVE DATE OF 1990 AMENDMENT

Amendment by Pub. L. 101–509 effective on such date as the President shall determine, but not earlier than 90 days, and not later than 180 days, after Nov. 5, 1990, see section 529 [title III, § 305] of Pub. L. 101–509, set out as a note under section 5301 of this title.

EFFECTIVE DATE OF 1989 AMENDMENT

Amendment by Pub. L. 101–194 effective Jan. 1, 1991, see section 506(d) of Pub. L. 101–194, set out as a note under section 3151 of this title.

EFFECTIVE DATE OF 1984 AMENDMENT

Amendment by Pub. L. 98–615 effective following expiration of 90-day period beginning on Nov. 8, 1984, see section 307 of Pub. L. 98–615, set out as a note under section 3393 of this title.

§ 3595. Reduction in force in the Senior Executive Service

(a) An agency shall establish competitive procedures for determining who shall be removed from the Senior Executive Service in any reduction in force of career appointees within that agency. The competitive procedures shall be designed to assure that such determinations are primarily on the basis of performance, as determined under subchapter II of chapter 43 of this title.

(b)(1) This subsection applies to any career appointee who has successfully completed the probationary period prescribed under section 3393(d) of this title.

(2) Except as provided in paragraphs (4) and (5), a career appointee may not be removed from

the Senior Executive Service due to a reduction in force within an agency.

(3) A career appointee who, but for this subsection, would be removed from the Senior Executive Service due to a reduction in force within an agency—

(A) is entitled to be assigned by the head of that agency to a vacant Senior Executive Service position for which the career appointee is qualified; or

(B) if the agency head certifies, in writing, to the Office of Personnel Management that no such position is available in the agency, shall be placed by the Office in any agency in any vacant Senior Executive Service position unless the head of that agency determines that the career appointee is not qualified for that position.

The Office of Personnel Management shall take all reasonable steps to place a career appointee under subparagraph (B) and may require any agency to take any action which the Office considers necessary to carry out any such placement.

(4) A career appointee who is not assigned under paragraph (3)(A) may be removed from the Senior Executive Service due to a reduction in force if the career appointee declines a reasonable offer for placement in a Senior Executive Service position under paragraph (3)(B).

(5) A career appointee who is not assigned under paragraph (3)(A) may be removed from the Senior Executive Service due to a reduction in force if the career appointee is not placed in another Senior Executive Service position under paragraph (3)(B) within 45 days after the Office receives certification regarding that appointee under paragraph (3)(B).

(c) A career appointee is entitled to appeal to the Merit Systems Protection Board under section 7701 of this title whether the reduction in force complies with the competitive procedures required under subsection (a).

(d) For purposes of this section, "reduction in force" includes the elimination or modification of a position due to a reorganization, due to a lack of funds or curtailment of work, or due to any other factor.

(e) The Office shall prescribe regulations under which the rights accorded to a career appointee in the event of a transfer of function are comparable to the rights accorded to a competing employee under section 3503 of this title in the event of such a transfer.

(Added Pub. L. 97–35, title XVII, § 1704(a)(1), Aug. 13, 1981, 95 Stat. 756; amended Pub. L. 97–346, § 5(a), (b), Oct. 15, 1982, 96 Stat. 1650; Pub. L. 98–615, title III, §§ 303(c), (d), 304(b), Nov. 8, 1984, 98 Stat. 3218, 3219.)

PRIOR PROVISIONS

A prior section 3595, added Pub. L. 95–454, title IV, § 404(b), Oct. 13, 1978, 92 Stat. 1167, which related to prescribing regulations, was renumbered section 3596 by Pub. L. 97–35, title XVII, § 1704(a)(1), Aug. 13, 1981, 95 Stat. 756.

AMENDMENTS

1984—Subsec. (b)(3)(B). Pub. L. 98–615, § 303(c)(1), struck out the designation "(i)" before provisions relating to placement in any agency in any vacant Execu-

tive Service position, and struck out former cl. (ii), which had related to detailing by the Office of Personnel Management to any vacant Senior Executive Service position for which the Office deemed the employee to be qualified in any agency for a period not to exceed 60 days, and placement in such position by the Office after the period of such detail, unless the head of the agency determined that the career appointee was not qualified for such position.

Subsec. (b)(4). Pub. L. 98–615, § 303(c)(2), struck out "and the civil service" after "removed from the Senior Executive Service", struck out the designation "(A)" before "the career appointee declines", and substituted a period for the semicolon and "or" at the end thereof. Former subpar. (B) redesignated par. (5).

Subsec. (b)(5). Pub. L. 98–615, § 303(c)(2), redesignated former par. (4)(B) as (5), substituted "A career appointee who is not assigned under paragraph (3)(A) may be removed from the Senior Executive Service due to a reduction in force if" for "subject to paragraph (5),", substituted "45 days" for "120 days", and struck out former par. (5), which had provided that persons who were career appointees as of May 31, 1981, could only be removed from the Senior Executive Service and the civil service due to a reduction in force after the 120-day period if the Director of the Office of Personnel Management certified to certain Congressional committees that the Office had taken all reasonable steps to place the appointee but had been unable to do so due to the appointee's highly specialized skills and experience.

Subsec. (c). Pub. L. 98–615, § 303(d), struck out the designation "(1)" before "whether the reduction", and struck out pars. (2) and (3), which had provided, respectively, the right to appeal any removal under subsec. (b)(4)(A) and the right to appeal any nonappointment under subsec. (b)(3), and, in the event of such nonappointment, whether the Office of Personnel Management took all reasonable steps to achieve such placement and whether the agency correctly decided under subsec. (b)(3)(B) that the career appointee was not qualified for such placement.

Subsec. (e). Pub. L. 98–615, § 304(b), added subsec. (e).

1982—Subsec. (b)(3)(B). Pub. L. 97–346, § 5(a), designated as cl. (i) existing provisions relating to placement in any agency in any vacant Executive Service position, and added cl. (ii).

Subsec. (c)(3). Pub. L. 97–346, § 5(b), designated as subpar. (A) existing provisions relating to taking of all reasonable steps by Office of Personnel Management, and added subpar. (B).

EFFECTIVE DATE OF 1984 AMENDMENT

Amendment by section 303(c), (d) of Pub. L. 98–615 effective following expiration of 90-day period beginning on Nov. 8, 1984, and amendment by section 304(b) of Pub. L. 98–615 effective Nov. 8, 1984, see section 307 of Pub. L. 98–615, set out as a note under section 3393 of this title.

EFFECTIVE DATE OF 1982 AMENDMENT

Section 5(c) of Pub. L. 97–346 provided that:

"(1) Except as provided in paragraph (2), the amendments made by this section [amending this section] shall take effect on the date of the enactment of this Act [Oct. 15, 1982].

"(2) The amendments made by this section [amending this section] shall apply to an individual who is a career appointee on or after September 30, 1982, except that any individual who is a career appointee on September 30, 1982, and who is described in section 3595(b)(3) of title 5, United States Code, may not be removed before December 15, 1982, due to a reduction in force, unless the removal is under section 3595(b)(4)(A) of such title on the grounds the individual declined a reasonable placement offer."

EFFECTIVE DATE

Section 1704(e) of Pub. L. 97–35 provided that:

"(1) Subject to paragraph (2), the amendments made by this section [enacting this section, redesignating former section 3595 as section 3596 of this title, and amending sections 3393, 3593, 7542, and 7543 of this title] shall be effective as of June 1, 1981.

"(2)(A) Except as provided in subparagraph (B), the amendments made by this section shall apply to any career appointee removed from the civil service after May 31, 1981, and before the date of the enactment of this section [Aug. 13, 1981] if, not later than 14 days after such date of enactment, application therefor is made to the Office of Personnel Management and to the head of the Agency in which the appointee was employed.

"(B) The provisions of section 3595(a), as added by subsection (a)(1), shall take effect on the date of the enactment of this Act [Aug. 13, 1981].

"(3) The effectiveness of the amendments made by this section shall be subject to section 415(b) of the Civil Service Reform Act of 1978 [Pub. L. 95–454, title IV, Oct. 13, 1978, 92 Stat. 1154] (5 U.S.C. 3131 note) to the same extent and manner as the amendments made by title IV of that Act."

Section Referred to in Other Sections

This section is referred to in sections 3151, 3393, 3593, 3594, 6302, 7542 of this title; title 10 sections 1606, 1610; title 31 section 732; title 42 sections 616, 7237.

§ 3595a. Furlough in the Senior Executive Service

(a) For the purposes of this section, "furlough" means the placement of a senior executive in a temporary status in which the senior executive has no duties and is not paid when the placement in such status is by reason of insufficient work or funds or for other nondisciplinary reasons.

(b) An agency may furlough a career appointee only in accordance with regulations issued by the Office of Personnel Management.

(c) A career appointee who is furloughed is entitled to appeal to the Merit Systems Protection Board under section 7701 of this title.

(Added Pub. L. 98–615, title III, § 306(c)(1), Nov. 8, 1984, 98 Stat. 3220.)

Effective Date

Section effective following expiration of 90-day period beginning on Nov. 8, 1984, see section 307 of Pub. L. 98–615, set out as an Effective Date of 1984 Amendment note under section 3393 of this title.

§ 3596. Regulations

The Office of Personnel Management shall prescribe regulations to carry out the purpose of this subchapter.

(Added Pub. L. 95–454, title IV, § 404(b), Oct. 13, 1978, 92 Stat. 1167, § 3595; renumbered § 3596, Pub. L. 97–35, title XVII, § 1704(a)(1), Aug. 13, 1981, 95 Stat. 756.)

Amendments

1981—Pub. L. 97–35 renumbered section 3596 of this title as this section.

SUBCHAPTER VI—REEMPLOYMENT FOLLOWING LIMITED APPOINTMENT IN THE FOREIGN SERVICE

§ 3597. Reemployment following limited appointment in the Foreign Service

An employee of any agency who accepts, with the consent of the head of that agency, a limited appointment in the Foreign Service under section 309 of the Foreign Service Act of 1980 is entitled, upon the expiration of that appointment, to be reemployed in that employee's former position or in a corresponding or higher position in that agency. Upon reemployment under this section, an employee shall be entitled to any within-in-grade increases in pay which the employee would have received if the employee had remained in the former position in the agency.

(Added Pub. L. 96–465, title II, § 2301(a), Oct. 17, 1980, 94 Stat. 2164.)

References in Text

Section 309 of the Foreign Service Act of 1980, referred to in text, is classified to section 3949 of Title 22, Foreign Relations and Intercourse.

Effective Date

Section effective Feb. 15, 1981, except as otherwise provided, see section 2403 of Pub. L. 96–465, set out as a note under section 3901 of Title 22, Foreign Relations and Intercourse.

Section Referred to in Other Sections

This section is referred to in title 22 section 3950.

Subpart C—Employee Performance

CHAPTER 41—TRAINING

Amendments

1995—Pub. L. 104–66, title II, § 2181(c)(2), Dec. 21, 1995, 109 Stat. 732, struck out item 4113 "Agency review of training needs; annual program reports".

1994—Pub. L. 103–226, § 2(b)(2), Mar. 30, 1994, 108 Stat. 112, struck out item 4106 "Non-Government facilities; amount of training limited", substituted "Restriction on degree training" for "Non-Government facilities; restrictions" in item 4107, and struck out item 4114 "Non-Government facilities; review of training programs".

1982—Pub. L. 97–346, § 1(b), Oct. 15, 1982, 96 Stat. 1647, added item 4119.

Chapter Referred to in Other Sections

This chapter is referred to in section 3381 of this title; title 18 section 209; title 26 section 4941; title 38 section 3681.

§ 4101. Definitions

For the purpose of this chapter—

(1) "agency", subject to section 4102 of this title, means—

(A) an Executive department;

(B) an independent establishment;

(C) a Government corporation subject to chapter 91 of title 31;

(D) the Library of Congress;

(E) the Government Printing Office; and

(F) the government of the District of Columbia;

(2) "employee", subject to section 4102 of this title, means—

(A) an individual employed in or under an agency; and

(B) a commissioned officer of the Environmental Science Services Administration;

(3) "Government" means the Government of the United States and the government of the District of Columbia;

(4) "training" means the process of providing for and making available to an employee, and placing or enrolling the employee in, a planned, prepared, and coordinated program, course, curriculum, subject, system, or routine of instruction or education, in scientific, professional, technical, mechanical, trade, clerical, fiscal, administrative, or other fields which will improve individual and organizational performance and assist in achieving the agency's mission and performance goals;

(5) "Government facility" means property owned or substantially controlled by the Government and the services of any civilian and military personnel of the Government; and

(6) "non-Government facility" means—

(A) the government of a State or of a territory or possession of the United States including the Commonwealth of Puerto Rico, and an interstate governmental organization, or a unit, subdivision, or instrumentality of any of the foregoing;

(B) a foreign government or international organization, or instrumentality of either, which is designated by the President as eligible to provide training under this chapter;

(C) a medical, scientific, technical, educational, research, or professional institution, foundation, or organization;

(D) a business, commercial, or industrial firm, corporation, partnership, proprietorship, or other organization;

(E) individuals other than civilian or military personnel of the Government; and

(F) the services and property of any of the foregoing furnishing the training.

(Pub. L. 89–554, Sept. 6, 1966, 80 Stat. 432; Pub. L. 90–206, title II, § 224(a), Dec. 16, 1967, 81 Stat. 642; Pub. L. 97–258, § 3(a)(8), Sept. 13, 1982, 96 Stat. 1063; Pub. L. 103–226, § 2(a)(1), Mar. 30, 1994, 108 Stat. 111.)

HISTORICAL AND REVISION NOTES

Derivation	U.S. Code	Revised Statutes and Statutes at Large
....	5 U.S.C. 2302.	July 7, 1958, Pub. L. 85–507, § 3, 72 Stat. 328.

In paragraph (1), the word "agency" is substituted for "department". Reference to the "General Accounting Office" is omitted as included in "independent establishment" because of the definition in section 104.

In paragraph (2)(B), the words "in the Department of Commerce" are omitted as unnecessary.

In paragraph (6)(C), the word "agency" is omitted as unnecessary and to avoid confusion with the word "agency" defined by paragraph (1).

In paragraph (6)(E), the words "individuals other than civilian or military personnel of the Government" are substituted for "an individual not a civilian or military officer or employee of the Government of the United States or of the municipal government of the District of Columbia" to conform to paragraph (5).

The definition of "Commission" in former section 2302(4) is omitted as unnecessary as the title "Civil Service Commission" is fully set out the first time it is used in each section of this chapter.

Standard changes are made to conform with the definitions applicable and the style of this title as outlined in the preface to the report.

AMENDMENTS

1994—Par. (4). Pub. L. 103–226 substituted "fields which will improve individual and organizational performance and assist in achieving the agency's mission and performance goals;" for "fields which are or will be directly related to the performance by the employee of official duties for the Government, in order to increase the knowledge, proficiency, ability, skill, and qualifications of the employee in the performance of official duties;".

1982—Par. (1)(C). Pub. L. 97–258 substituted "chapter 91" for "sections 846–852 or 856–859".

1967—Par. (2)(B). Pub. L. 90–206 substituted "Environmental Science Services Administration" for "Coast and Geodetic Survey".

EFFECTIVE DATE OF 1967 AMENDMENT

Amendment by Pub. L. 90–206 effective Dec. 16, 1967, see section 220(a)(1) of Pub. L. 90–206, set out as an Effective Date note under section 3110 of this title.

TRANSFER OF FUNCTIONS

For transfer of Environmental Science Services Administration to National Oceanic and Atmospheric Administration, see Transfer of Functions note set out under section 5541 of this title.

DELEGATION OF FUNCTIONS

Functions of President under subsec. (6)(B) of this section delegated to head of each agency concerned, see section 402 of Ex. Ord. No. 11348, Apr. 20, 1967, 32 F.R. 6335, set out as a note under section 4103 of this title.

SECTION REFERRED TO IN OTHER SECTIONS

This section is referred to in section 5379 of this title.

§ 4102. Exceptions; Presidential authority

(a)(1) This chapter does not apply to—

(A) a corporation supervised by the Farm Credit Administration if private interests elect or appoint a member of the board of directors;

(B) the Tennessee Valley Authority; or

(C) an individual (except a commissioned officer of the National Oceanic and Atmospheric Administration) who is a member of a uniformed service during a period in which he is entitled to pay under section 204 of title 37.

(2) This chapter (except sections 4110 and 4111) does not apply to—

(A) the Foreign Service of the United States; or

(B) an individual appointed by the President, unless the individual is specifically designated by the President for training under this chapter.

(b) The President, at any time in the public interest, may—

(1) except an agency or part thereof, or an employee or group or class of employees therein, from this chapter or a provision thereof (except this section); and

(2) withdraw an exception made under this subsection.

However, the President may not except the Office of Personnel Management from a provision of this chapter which vests in or imposes on the Office a function, duty, or responsibility concerning any matter except the establishment, operation, and maintenance, in the same capacity as other agencies, of training programs and plans for its employees.

(Pub. L. 89–554, Sept. 6, 1966, 80 Stat. 433; Pub. L. 90–83, §1(4), Sept. 11, 1967, 81 Stat. 196; Pub. L. 94–183, §2(11), Dec. 31, 1975, 89 Stat. 1057; Pub. L. 95–454, title IX, §906(a)(2), Oct. 13, 1978, 92 Stat. 1224; Pub. L. 96–54, §2(a)(15), (19), Aug. 14, 1979, 93 Stat. 382.)

HISTORICAL AND REVISION NOTES

Derivation	U.S. Code	Revised Statutes and Statutes at Large
....	5 U.S.C. 2303.	July 7, 1958, Pub. L. 85–507, §4, 72 Stat. 329. May 26, 1959, Pub. L. 86–33, 73 Stat. 62. Aug. 2, 1962, Pub. L. 87–566, 76 Stat. 264.

In subsection (a)(1), the exception for the President and Vice President is omitted as surplusage as these elected officers are not employed in or under an agency and thus are not included in the definition of "employee" in section 4101(2).

In subsection (a)(1)(C), the words "as defined by section 231(a) of Title 37" are omitted as unnecessary in view of the definition of "uniformed services" in section 2101(b). The words "section 204 of title 37" are substituted for "sections 232–234, 235, 236, 237, 238, and 239 of Title 37" on authority of section 12(b) of the Act of Sept. 7, 1962, Pub. L. 87–649, 76 Stat. 497.

In subsection (a)(2)(B), the words "by the President" are coextensive with and substituted for "by the President by and with the advice and consent of the Senate or by the President alone".

In subsection (b)(1), reference to "section 21, and section 22" is omitted as unnecessary since the sections are not carried into this title, but are scheduled for repeal, see Table II.

Standard changes are made to conform with the definitions applicable and the style of this title as outlined in the preface to the report.

AMENDMENTS

1979—Subsec. (a)(1)(C). Pub. L. 96–54, §2(a)(19), substituted "National Oceanic and Atmospheric" for "Environmental Science Services".

Subsec. (b). Pub. L. 96–54, §2(a)(15), substituted "Office" for "Commission".

1978—Subsec. (b). Pub. L. 95–454 substituted "Office of Personnel Management" for "Civil Service Commission".

1975—Subsec. (a)(2)(B). Pub. L. 94–183 struck out "(except a Postmaster)" after "an individual appointed by the President".

1967—Subsec. (a)(1)(C). Pub. L. 90–83 substituted "Environmental Science Services Administration" for "Coast and Geodetic Survey." See Historical and Revision Notes under section 2101 of this title.

EFFECTIVE DATE OF 1979 AMENDMENT

Amendments by Pub. L. 96–54 effective July 12, 1979, see section 2(b) of Pub. L. 96–54, set out as a note under section 305 of this title.

EFFECTIVE DATE OF 1978 AMENDMENT

Amendment by Pub. L. 95–454 effective 90 days after Oct. 13, 1978, see section 907 of Pub. L. 95–454, set out as a note under section 1101 of this title.

DELEGATION OF FUNCTIONS

Functions of President under subsec. (b)(1) of this section delegated to Office of Personnel Management, see section 401(a) of Ex. Ord. No. 11348, Apr. 20, 1967, 32 F.R. 6335, set out as a note under section 4103 of this title.

EX. ORD. NO. 10805. CENTRAL INTELLIGENCE AGENCY

Ex. Ord. No. 10805, Feb. 18, 1959, 24 F.R. 1301, provided:
SECTION 1. The Central Intelligence Agency is hereby designated as excepted from the following-described provisions of the Government Employees Training Act [this chapter and section 1308 of this title]:

(a) Section 2(4), 6, 9(b)(1), 11, 12, 15, 16, and 18 [sections 4117, 4118, 4105(b)(1), 4108, 4106, 4114, 4115, and 1308(a)(4)(A)–(C), (b) and 4113(b) respectively of this title].

(b) The last sentence of section 5 [section 4113(a) of this title].

(c) That part of section 7 [section 4103(1) of this title] which reads "shall conform, on or after the effective date of the regulations prescribed by the Commission under section 6 of this Act [section 4118 of this title], to the principles, standards, and related requirements contained in such regulations then current,".

(d) That part of section 10 [section 4109(a) of this title] which reads "in accordance with regulations issued by the Commission under authority of section 6(a)(8) [section 4118(a)(8) of this title]."

SEC. 2. Section 2 of Executive Order No. 10800, of January 15, 1959, is hereby amended by deleting the reference to "section 5" and the reference to "section 5(b)" and by inserting in lieu thereof "section 4" and "section 4(b)", respectively.

EXECUTIVE ORDER NO. 11531

Ex. Ord. No. 11531, May 26, 1970, 35 F.R. 8337, which related to the delegation of Presidential authority to designate United States Marshals and United States Attorneys for training, was superseded by Ex. Ord. No. 11895, Jan. 6, 1976, 41 F.R. 1465, set out below.

EX. ORD. NO. 11895. DELEGATION OF PRESIDENTIAL AUTHORITY TO DESIGNATE INDIVIDUALS APPOINTED BY THE PRESIDENT TO RECEIVE TRAINING

Ex. Ord. No. 11895, Jan. 6, 1976, 41 F.R. 1465, as amended by Ex. Ord. No. 12107, Dec. 28, 1978, 44 F.R. 1055, provided:

By virtue of the authority vested in me by Section 301 of Title 3 of the United States Code, and as President of the United States, it is hereby ordered as follows:

SECTION 1. Except as provided in Section 2 of this Order, the Office of Personnel Management is hereby designated and empowered to exercise the authority vested in the President by Section 4102(a)(2)(B) of Title 5, United States Code, to designate individuals appointed by the President for training under Chapter 41 of Title 5, United States Code.

SEC. 2. The Attorney General is hereby designated and empowered to exercise the authority vested in the President by Section 4102(a)(2)(B) to designate individuals appointed by the President as United States Attorneys and United States Marshals for training under Chapter 41 of Title 5, United States Code.

SEC. 3. Executive Order No. 11531 of May 26, 1970, is hereby superseded.

SECTION REFERRED TO IN OTHER SECTIONS

This section is referred to in sections 4101, 4108 of this title.

§ 4103. Establishment of training programs

(a) In order to assist in achieving an agency's mission and performance goals by improving employee and organizational performance, the head of each agency, in conformity with this chapter, shall establish, operate, maintain, and evaluate a program or programs, and a plan or plans thereunder, for the training of employees in or under the agency by, in, and through Government facilities and non-Government facilities. Each program, and plan thereunder, shall—

(1) conform to the principles, standards, and related requirements contained in the regulations prescribed under section 4118 of this title;

(2) provide for adequate administrative control by appropriate authority;

(3) provide that information concerning the selection and assignment of employees for training and the applicable training limitations and restrictions be made available to employees of the agency; and

(4) provide for the encouragement of self-training by employees by means of appropriate recognition of resultant increases in proficiency, skill, and capacity.

Two or more agencies jointly may operate under a training program.

(b)(1) Notwithstanding any other provision of this chapter, an agency may train any employee of the agency to prepare the employee for placement in another agency if the head of the agency determines that such training would be in the interests of the Government.

(2) In selecting an employee for training under this subsection, the head of the agency shall consider—

(A) the extent to which the current skills, knowledge, and abilities of the employee may be utilized in the new position;

(B) the employee's capability to learn skills and acquire knowledge and abilities needed in the new position; and

(C) the benefits to the Government which would result from such training.

(Pub. L. 89–554, Sept. 6, 1966. 80 Stat. 433; Pub. L. 95–454, title III, § 304, Oct. 13, 1978, 92 Stat. 1146; Pub. L. 103–226, § 2(a)(2), Mar. 30, 1994, 108 Stat. 111.)

HISTORICAL AND REVISION NOTES

Derivation	U.S. Code	Revised Statutes and Statutes at Large
....	5 U.S.C. 2306.	July 7, 1958, Pub. L. 85–507, § 7, 72 Stat. 331.

The words "Within two hundred and seventy days after the date of enactment of this Act [July 7, 1958]" are omitted as obsolete.

In paragraph (1), reference to the effective date of the regulations is omitted as obsolete.

Standard changes are made to conform with the definitions applicable and the style of this title as outlined in the preface to the report.

AMENDMENTS

1994—Subsec. (a). Pub. L. 103–226, § 2(a)(2)(A)(i), in introductory provisions, substituted "In order to assist in achieving an agency's mission and performance goals by improving employee and organizational performance, the head of each agency, in conformity with this chapter, shall establish, operate, maintain, and evaluate" for "In order to increase economy and efficiency in the operations of the agency and to raise the standards of performance by employees of their official du-

ties to the maximum possible level of proficiency, the head of each agency, in conformity with this chapter, shall establish, operate, maintain, and maintain".

Subsec. (a)(3), (4). Pub. L. 103–226, § 2(a)(2)(A)(ii)–(iv), added par. (3) and redesignated former par. (3) as (4).

Subsec. (b)(1). Pub. L. 103–226, § 2(a)(2)(B)(i), substituted "determines that such training would be in the interests of the Government." for "determines that the employee will otherwise be separated under conditions which would entitle the employee to severance pay under section 5595 of this title."

Subsec. (b)(2). Pub. L. 103–226, § 2(a)(2)(B)(ii), (iii), redesignated par. (3) as (2), in subpar. (C) substituted "such training" for "retaining the employee in the Federal service", and struck out former par. (2) which read as follows: "Before undertaking any training under this subsection, the head of the agency shall obtain verification from the Office of Personnel Management that there exists a reasonable expectation of placement in another agency."

Subsec. (b)(3). Pub. L. 103–226, § 2(a)(2)(B)(ii), redesignated par. (3) as (2).

1978—Pub. L. 95–454 designated existing provisions as subsec. (a) and added subsec. (b).

EFFECTIVE DATE OF 1978 AMENDMENT

Amendment by Pub. L. 95–454 effective 90 days after Oct. 13, 1978, see section 907 of Pub. L. 95–454, set out as a note under section 1101 of this title.

OPTIONAL PARTICIPATION OF FEDERAL EMPLOYEES IN AIDS TRAINING PROGRAMS

Pub. L. 104–146, § 9, May 20, 1996, 110 Stat. 1373, provided that:

"(a) IN GENERAL.—Notwithstanding any other provision of law, a Federal employee may not be required to attend or participate in an AIDS or HIV training program if such employee refuses to consent to such attendance or participation, except for training necessary to protect the health and safety of the Federal employee and the individuals served by such employees. An employer may not retaliate in any manner against such an employee because of the refusal of such employee to consent to such attendance or participation.

"(b) DEFINITION.—As used in subsection (a), the term 'Federal employee' has the same meaning given the term 'employee' in section 2105 of title 5, United States Code, and such term shall include members of the armed forces."

EXPERIMENTAL PROGRAM RELATING TO ACCEPTANCE OF VOLUNTARY SERVICES FROM PARTICIPANTS IN EXECUTIVE EXCHANGE PROGRAM

Pub. L. 101–416, § 1, Oct. 12, 1990, 104 Stat. 902, authorized a 90-day extension of programs established under Pub. L. 99–424 for individuals who were participating in the program on the expiration date.

Pub. L. 99–424, Sept. 30, 1986, 100 Stat. 964, as amended by Pub. L. 101–87, Aug. 16, 1989, 103 Stat. 595, authorized President to establish an experimental program, to be conducted during fiscal years 1987 through 1990, under which voluntary services could be accepted by the Government, without regard to 31 U.S.C. 1342.

CENTRAL INTELLIGENCE AGENCY

Exception of Central Intelligence Agency from provisions of cl. (1) of this section and certain other provisions of this chapter, and section 1308 of this title, see Ex. Ord. No. 10805, Feb. 18, 1959, 24 F.R. 1301, set out as a note under section 4102 of this title.

EX. ORD. NO. 11348. FURTHER TRAINING OF GOVERNMENT EMPLOYEES

Ex. Ord. No. 11348, Apr. 20, 1967, 32 F.R. 6335, as amended by Ex. Ord. No. 12107, Dec. 28, 1978, 44 F.R. 1055, provided:

By virtue of the authority vested in me by section 301 of Title 3 of the United States Code and by section 2 of the Act of July 7, 1958 (72 Stat. 327), it is ordered as follows:

PART I—GENERAL

SECTION 101. (a) As used in this order, the terms "agency", "employee", "Government", and "training", have meanings given to those terms, respectively, by section 4101 of Title 5, United States Code.

(b) "Interagency training" means training provided by one agency for other agencies or shared by two or more agencies.

SEC. 102. It is the policy of the Government of the United States to develop its employees through the establishment and operation of progressive and efficient training programs, thereby improving public service, increasing efficiency and economy, building and retaining a force of skilled and efficient employees, and installing and using the best modern practices and techniques in the conduct of the Government's business.

SEC. 103. The Office of Personnel Management shall provide leadership and guidance to insure that the policy set forth in section 102 is carried out.

PART II—OFFICE OF PERSONNEL MANAGEMENT RESPONSIBILITIES

SEC. 201. The Office of Personnel Management shall plan and promote the development, improvement, coordination, and evaluation of training in accordance with chapter 41 of Title 5, United States Code, and with the policy set forth in section 102 of this order.

SEC. 202. In carrying out its responsibilities under chapter 41 of Title 5, United States Code, and section 201 of this order, the Office shall:

(a) Advise the President on means for furthering and strengthening programs of training;

(b) Counsel heads of agencies and other agency officials on the improvement of training;

(c) Assist agencies to develop sound programs and financial plans for training and provide advice, information, and assistance to agencies on planning, programming, budgeting, operating, and evaluating training programs;

(d) Identify functional areas in which new or expanded interagency training activity is needed and either conduct such training or arrange for agencies having the substantive competence to do so;

(e) Coordinate interagency training conducted by and for agencies (including agencies and portions of agencies excepted by section 4102(a) of Title 5, United States Code);

(f) Encourage agencies to make appropriate use of non-Government training resources;

(g) Develop, install, and maintain a system to provide the training data needed to carry out its own functions and to provide staff assistance to the President; and

(h) Provide for identification and dissemination of findings of research into training technology and undertake or assign to other agencies, such research projects as may be needed.

PART III—AGENCY RESPONSIBILITIES AND OPERATIONS

SEC. 301. The head of each agency shall plan, program, budget, operate, and evaluate training programs in accordance with chapter 41 of Title 5, United States Code, and with the policy set forth in section 102 of this order.

SEC. 302. The head of each agency shall:

(a) Foster employee self-development by creating a work environment in which self-development is encouraged, by assuring that opportunities for training and self-study materials are reasonably available, where the employee is stationed, and by recognizing self-initiated improvement in performance;

(b) Provide training for employees without regard to race, creed, color, national origin, sex, or other factors unrelated to the need for training;

(c) Establish and make full use of agency facilities for training employees;

(d) Extend agency training programs to employees of other agencies (including agencies and portions of agencies excepted by section 4102(a) of Title 5, United States Code) and assign his employees to interagency training whenever this will result in better training, improved service, or savings to the Government;

(e) Establish interagency training facilities in areas of substantive competence as arranged by the Office of Personnel Management; and

(f) Use non-Government training resources as appropriate.

SEC. 303. In carrying out his responsibilities, the head of each agency shall, consonant with chapter 41 of Title 5, United States Code, this order, and regulations of the Office of Personnel Management:

(a) Review periodically, but not less often than annually, the agency's program to identify training needed to bring about more effective performance at the least possible cost;

(b) Conduct periodic reviews of individual employee's training needs as related to program objectives;

(c) Conduct research related to training objectives and required for program improvement and effectiveness;

(d) Plan, program, and evaluate training for both short and longrange program needs by occupations, organizations, or other appropriate groups;

(e) Establish priorities for needed training, and provide for the use of funds and manhours in accordance with these priorities;

(f) Utilize the flexibility of work assignments to provide work experience which promotes growth leading to higher quality and greater quantity of work done;

(g) Establish training facilities and services as needed;

(h) Monitor the effectiveness with which self-development is encouraged and on-the-job training is provided at all levels; and

(i) Establish criteria for the selection of employees for training; and

(j) Approve the acceptance of any contributions, awards, or payments to employees authorized by section 401(b) of this order and regulations issued by the Office of Personnel Management.

PART IV—DELEGATIONS

SEC. 401. The following functions vested in the President are hereby delegated to the Office of Personnel Management:

(a) The authority under section 4102(b)(1) of Title 5, United States Code, to designate any agency or part thereof, or any employee or employees therein, as excepted from any provision of chapter 41, of Title 5, United States Code, other than sections 4102, 4111(b), and 4112; and to designate any such agency or part thereof, or any employee or employees therein previously excepted, as again subject to chapter 41 of Title 5, United States Code, or any provision of that chapter.

(b) The authority under section 4111(a) of Title 5, United States Code, to fix by regulation the extent to which the contributions, awards, and payments referred to in that section may be made to and accepted by employees.

SEC. 402. The authority vested in the President by section 4101(6)(B) of Title 5, United States Code, to designate a foreign government or international organization or instrumentality of either as eligible to provide training, is hereby delegated to the head of each agency for his employees except that each such designation shall be made only after the agency head concerned has obtained and given due consideration to the advice of the Department of State thereon prior to the first use of such training facility and thereafter periodically but not less often than once every three years.

PART V—REVOCATION OF PRIOR ORDER

SEC. 501. Executive Order No. 10800 of January 15, 1959, is hereby revoked.

EXECUTIVE ORDER NO. 11451

Ex. Ord. No. 11451, Jan. 19, 1969, 34 F.R. 921, as amended by Ex. Ord. No. 12107, Dec. 28, 1978, 44 F.R. 1055, which established the President's Commission on Personnel Interchange, was superseded by Ex. Ord. No. 12136, May 15, 1979, 44 F.R. 28771, formerly set out below.

EXECUTIVE ORDER NO. 12136

Ex. Ord. No. 12136, May 15, 1979, 44 F.R. 28771, which continued the President's Commission on Personnel Interchange and renamed it the President's Commission on Executive Exchange, was revoked by Ex. Ord. No. 12493, Dec. 5, 1984, 49 F.R. 47819, formerly set out below.

EXECUTIVE ORDER NO. 12493

Ex. Ord. No. 12493, Dec. 5, 1984, 49 F.R. 47819, as amended by Ex. Ord. No. 12516, May 21, 1985, 50 F.R. 21417; Ex. Ord. No. 12602, July 15, 1987, 52 F.R. 27187, which continued the President's Commission on Executive Exchange, was revoked by Ex. Ord. No. 12760, § 2, May 2, 1991, 56 F.R. 21062, set out below.

Ex. Ord. No. 12574. Establishing Experimental Program Within President's Commission on Executive Exchange

Ex. Ord. No. 12574, Nov. 20, 1986, 51 F.R. 42199, provided:

By the authority vested in me as President by the Constitution and statutes of the United States of America, including the Executive Exchange Program Voluntary Services Act of 1986 (5 U.S.C. 4103 note, 100 Stat. 964), it is hereby ordered as follows:

SECTION 1. *Establishment of the Program.* Effective October 1, 1986, there is established, within the Executive Exchange Program of the President's Commission on Executive Exchange, an experimental program under which Executive agencies of the government may accept voluntary services for the United States from private sector participants in the Executive Exchange Program.

SEC. 2. *Program Limits.* The experimental program shall be conducted during the fiscal years 1987 through 1989, and not more than ten individuals may commence participation in the program during any fiscal year. Acceptance of voluntary services from such individuals may not result in the displacement of any employee of the government.

SEC. 3. *Participant Restrictions.* An individual participating in the experimental program shall be considered an employee of the agency to which assigned for purposes of any laws, rules, and regulations of the United States, except that such individual shall not be covered by chapters 51, 53, 63, 83, 87, or 89 of title 5, United States Code, or any comparable provisions relating to classification, pay, leave, retirement, life insurance, or health benefits for employees of the government.

RONALD REAGAN.

Ex. Ord. No. 12760. President's Commission on Executive Exchange

Ex. Ord. No. 12760, May 2, 1991, 56 F.R. 21062, provided:

By the authority vested in me as President by the Constitution and the laws of the United States of America, it is hereby ordered as follows:

SECTION 1. The President's Commission on Executive Exchange is hereby abolished. The Director of the Office of Personnel Management shall be responsible for terminating the functions of the Commission, which shall be completed no later than September 30, 1991.

SEC. 2. Executive Order No. 12493 of December 5, 1984 is revoked.

GEORGE BUSH.

Ex. Ord. No. 13111. Using Technology To Improve Training Opportunities for Federal Government Employees

Ex. Ord. No. 13111, Jan. 12, 1999, 64 F.R. 2793, as amended by Ex. Ord. No. 13188, Jan. 12, 2001, 66 F.R. 5419, provided:

Advances in technology and increased skills needs are changing the workplace at an ever increasing rate.

These advances can make Federal employees more productive and provide improved service to our customers, the American taxpayers. We need to ensure that we continue to train Federal employees to take full advantage of these technological advances and to acquire the skills and learning needed to succeed in a changing workplace. A coordinated Federal effort is needed to provide flexible training opportunities to employees and to explore how Federal training programs, initiatives, and policies can better support lifelong learning through the use of learning technology.

To help us meet these goals, I am creating a task force on Federal training technology, directing Federal agencies to take certain steps to enhance employees' training opportunities through the use of training technology, and an advisory committee on the use of training technology, which also will explore options for financing the training and post-secondary education needed to upgrade skills and gain new knowledge.

Therefore, by the authority vested in me as President by the Constitution and the laws of the United States of America, including the Federal Advisory Committee Act, as amended (5 U.S.C. App.), and in furtherance of the purposes of Chapter 41 of title 5, United States Code, the Government Employees Training Act of 1958 (Public Law 85–507 [see Tables for classification]), as amended, and Executive Order 11348, "Providing for the Further Training of Government Employees," [set out above] and in order to make effective use of technology to improve training opportunities for Federal Government employees, it is ordered as follows:

SECTION 1. *Establishment of the President's Task Force on Federal Training Technology.* (a) The "President's Task Force on Federal Training Technology" (Task Force) is established. The Task Force shall provide leadership regarding the effective use of technology in training and education; make training opportunities an integral part of continuing employment in the Federal Government; and facilitate the ongoing coordination of Federal activities concerning the use of technology in training. The Task Force shall consist of the heads of the following departments and agencies or their representatives: the Departments of State, the Treasury, Defense, Justice, Interior, Agriculture, Commerce, Labor, Health and Human Services, Housing and Urban Development, Transportation, Energy, and Education; the Office of Personnel Management, General Services Administration, Environmental Protection Agency, National Aeronautics and Space and Administration, Small Business Administration, and Social Security Administration; a representative from the Small Agency Council; and representatives from other relevant agencies and related Federal councils, as determined by the Chair and Vice Chair of the Task Force.

(b) Within 30 days of the date of this order, the head of each agency or council shall designate a senior official to serve as a representative to the Task Force. The representative shall report directly to the agency head or the President's Management Council member on the agency's or council's activities under this order.

(c) The Director of the Office of Personnel Management (OPM) shall be the Chair and the representative from the Department of Labor shall be the Vice Chair of the Task Force.

(d) The Chair and Vice Chair shall appoint an Executive Director.

(e) The Task Force member agencies shall provide any required staffing and funding, as appropriate.

SEC. 2. *Duties of the Task Force.* (a) Within 18 months of the date of this order, the Task Force shall develop and recommend to the President, through the Assistant to the President for Economic Policy and the Assistant to the President for Science and Technology, a policy to make effective use of technology to improve training opportunities for Federal Government employees. The policy should promote and integrate the effective use of training technologies to create affordable and convenient training opportunities to improve Federal employee performance. The Task Force shall seek the views of experts from industry, academia, and State and local governments as the Task Force proceeds, as appropriate. Specifically, the Task Force shall:

(1) develop strategies to improve the efficiency and availability of training opportunities for Federal Government employees;

(2) form partnerships among key Federal agencies, State and local governments, businesses, universities, and other appropriate entities to promote the development and use of high-quality training opportunities;

(3) analyze the use of technology in existing training programs and policies of the Task Force member agencies to determine what changes, modifications, and innovations may be necessary to advance training opportunities;

(4) in consultation with the Department of Defense and the National Institute of Standards and Technology, recommend standards for training software and associated services purchased by Federal agencies and contractors. These standards should be consistent with voluntary industry consensus-based commercial standards. Agencies, where appropriate, should use these standards in procurements to promote reusable training component software and thereby reduce duplication in the development of courseware;

(5) evaluate and, where appropriate, coordinate and collaborate on, research and demonstration activities of Task Force member agencies related to Federal training technology;

(6) identify and support cross-agency training areas that would particularly benefit from new instructional technologies and facilitate multiagency procurement and use of training materials, where appropriate;

(7) in consultation with the General Services Administration, the Office of Personnel Management, and the Office of Federal Procurement Policy of the Office of Management and Budget (OFPP), promote existing and new procurement vehicles that allow agencies to provide innovative training opportunities for Federal employees;

(8) recommend changes that may be needed to existing procurement laws to further the objectives of this order and forward the recommendations to the Administrator of OFPP; and

(b) develop options and recommendations for establishing a Federal Individual Training Account for each Federal worker for training relevant to his or her Federal employment. To the extent permitted by law, such accounts may be established with the funds allocated to the agency for employee training. Approval for training would be within the discretion of the individual employee's manager. Options and recommendations shall be reported no later than 6 months from the date of this order.

SEC. 3. *Duties of All Federal Agencies.* (a) Each Federal agency shall, to the extent permitted by law:

(1) include as part of its annual budget process a set of goals to provide the highest quality and most efficient training opportunities possible to its employees, and a set of performance measures of the quality and availability of training opportunities possible to its employees. Such measures should be, where appropriate, based on outcomes related to performance rather than time allocation;

(2) identify the resources necessary to achieve the aforementioned goals and performance measures articulated in its annual performance plan;

(3) and, where practicable, use the standards recommended by the Task Force and published by the Office of Personnel Management for purchasing training software and associated services; and

(4) subject to the availability of appropriations, post training courses, information, and other learning opportunities on the Department of Labor's America's Learning Exchange (ALX), or other appropriate information dissemination vehicles as determined by the Task Force, to make information about Federal training courses, information, and other

learning opportunities widely available to Federal employees.

(b) Each Federal agency, to the extent permitted by law, is encouraged to consider how savings achieved through the efficient use of training technology can be reinvested in improved training for their employees.

SEC. 4. *Duties of Specific Federal Agencies.* (a) In light of the Office of Personnel Management's responsibility for developing Government-wide training policy, coordinating and managing training policy programs, and providing technical assistance to Federal agencies, the Office of Personnel Management or other appropriate agency as determined by the Task Force shall:

(1) in consultation with the Task Force, the Department of Defense, the National Institute of Standards and Technology, the Department of Labor, and other appropriate agencies as determined by OPM, publish the standards for training software and associated services recommended by the Task Force; and

(2) ensure that qualification standards for civil service positions, where appropriate, reflect standard industry certification practices.

(b) The Department of Labor or other appropriate agency as determined by the Task Force shall, subject to the availability of appropriations:

(1) establish a specialized database for Federal training within the framework of the Department of Labor's ALX, or other appropriate information dissemination vehicles determined by the Task Force, to make information about Federal training courses, information, and other learning opportunities widely available to Federal employees;

(2) establish and maintain a training technology website for agencies to post training needs and to foster communication among the agencies and between public and private sector organizations to identify and meet common needs; and

(3) establish a staffed help desk and technology resource center to support Federal agencies using training technology and to facilitate the development of online training courses.

(c) The Department of Defense or other appropriate agency as determined by the Task Force shall:

(1) in consultation with the National Institute of Standards and Technology, lead Federal participation in business and university organizations charged with developing consensus standards for training software and associated services and lead the Federal review of the standards; and

(2) provide guidance to Defense agencies and advise the civilian agencies, as appropriate, on how best to use these standards for large-scale development and implementation of efficient and effective distributed learning technologies.

(d) Each Executive department shall designate at least one subject area of training that it will use to demonstrate opportunities in technology-based training and assign an agency leader in the designated area. Leaders in these training technology experiments shall work closely with other agencies with similar training interests. Each Executive department shall develop a plan for measuring and evaluating the effectiveness, cost-effectiveness, and benefits to employees and the agency for each designated subject area.

SEC. 5. *Establishment of Advisory Committee on Expanding Training Opportunities.*
The Advisory Committee on Expanding Training Opportunities (Committee) is established. The Committee shall consist of not more that 20 members appointed by the President from outside the Federal Government, including representatives of the research, education, labor, and training communities, information technology sector, and representatives from other critical sectors. The President shall designate Co-Chairs from among the members of the Committee.

SEC. 6. *Functions of the Advisory Committee.* The Committee shall provide the President, through the Assistant to the President for Economic Policy and the Assistant to the President for Science and Technology (Assistants to the President), with: (a) an independent assessment of:

(1) progress made by the Federal Government in its use and integration of technology in training programs, particularly in the use of voluntary industry consensus-based commercial standards for training software and associated services;

(2) how Federal Government programs, initiatives, and policies can encourage or accelerate training technology to provide more accessible, more timely, and more cost-effective training opportunities for all Americans;

(3) mechanisms for the Federal Government to encourage private sector investment in the development of high-quality instructional software and wider deployment and utilization of technology-mediated instruction so that all Americans may take advantage of the opportunities provided by learning technology; and

(4) the appropriate Federal Government role in research and development for learning technologies and their applications in order to develop high-quality training and education opportunities for all Americans;

(b) an analysis of options for helping adult Americans finance the training and post-secondary education needed to upgrade skills and gain new knowledge. Options for financial mechanisms may include grants, tax incentives, low-interest loans, or other vehicles to make training and post-secondary education accessible to adults throughout their lifetimes; and

(c) advice on other issues regarding emerging technologies in government training and financing training and post-secondary education for adult Americans as specified by the Assistants to the President.

SEC. 7. *Administration of the Advisory Committee.* (a) To the extent permitted by law and subject to the availability of appropriations, the Office of Personnel Management shall provide the financial and administrative support for the Committee.

(b) The heads of Executive agencies shall, to the extent permitted by law, provide to the Committee such information as it may require for the purpose of carrying out its functions.

(c) The Committee Co-Chairs may, from time to time, invite experts to submit information to the Committee and may form subcommittees or working groups within the Committee to review specific issues.

(d) Members of the Committee shall serve without compensation but shall be allowed travel expenses, including per diem instead of subsistence, as authorized by law for persons serving intermittently in the Government service (5 U.S.C. 5701–5707).

(e) Notwithstanding any other Executive order, the functions of the President under the Federal Advisory Committee Act, as amended, that are applicable to the Committee, except that of reporting to the Congress, shall be performed by the Office of Personnel Management in accordance with guidelines that have been issued by the Administrator of General Services.

(f) The Committee shall terminate on January 11, 2003[,] unless extended by the President prior to such date.

SEC. 8. *Definitions.* (a) As used in this order, the terms "agency," "employee," "Government," and "training" have the meaning given to those terms, respectively, by section 4101 of title 5, United States Code.

(b) The term "technology," means any equipment or interconnected system or subsystem of equipment that is used in the automatic acquisition, storage, manipulation, management, movement, control, display, switching, interchange, transmission, or reception of data or information, including computers, ancillary equipment, software, firmware and similar procedures, services (including support services), and related resources. For purposes of the preceding sentence, equipment is used by an Executive agency if the equipment is used by the Executive agency directly or is used by a contractor under a contract with the Executive agency that requires the use of such equipment. The term "technology" does not include any equipment that is acquired by a Federal contractor incidental to a Federal contract.

SEC. 9. *Judicial Review.* This order does not create any enforceable rights against the United States, its agencies, its officers, or any person.

WILLIAM J. CLINTON.

§ 4104. Government facilities; use of

An agency program for the training of employees by, in, and through Government facilities under this chapter shall—

(1) provide for training, insofar as practicable, by, in, and through Government facilities under the jurisdiction or control of the agency; and

(2) provide for the making by the agency, to the extent necessary and appropriate, of agreements with other agencies in any branch of the Government, on a reimbursable basis when requested by the other agencies, for—

(A) use of Government facilities under the jurisdiction or control of the other agencies in any branch of the Government; and

(B) extension to employees of the agency of training programs of other agencies.

(Pub. L. 89–554, Sept. 6, 1966, 80 Stat. 434.)

HISTORICAL AND REVISION NOTES

Derivation	U.S. Code	Revised Statutes and Statutes at Large
....	5 U.S.C. 2307.	July 7, 1958, Pub. L. 85–507, §8, 72 Stat. 331.

In paragraph (2), the words "other agencies in any branch of the Government" and "the other agencies" are coextensive with and substituted for "other departments, and with other agencies in any branch of the Government" and "such other departments and agencies". This is so because "other agencies in any branch of the Government" is broader than "agency" as defined for the purpose of this chapter in section 4101(1).

Standard changes are made to conform with the definitions applicable and the style of this title as outlined in the preface to the report.

SECTION REFERRED TO IN OTHER SECTIONS

This section is referred to in title 7 section 5922.

§ 4105. Non-Government facilities; use of

The head of an agency, without regard to section 5 of title 41, may make agreements or other arrangements for the training of employees of the agency by, in, or through non-Government facilities under this chapter.

(Pub. L. 89–554, Sept. 6, 1966, 80 Stat. 434; Pub. L. 103–226, §2(a)(3), Mar. 30, 1994, 108 Stat. 111.)

HISTORICAL AND REVISION NOTES

Derivation	U.S. Code	Revised Statutes and Statutes at Large
....	5 U.S.C. 2308.	July 7, 1958, Pub. L. 85–507, §9, 72 Stat. 331.

In subsection (a), the word "appropriate" is omitted as unnecessary.

In subsection (b)(1), the words "by, in, and through non-Government facilities" are omitted as unnecessary in view of the previous reference in the subsection.

In subsection (b)(2), the word "appropriate" is omitted as unnecessary.

Standard changes are made to conform with the definitions applicable and the style of this title as outlined in the preface to the report.

1994—Pub. L. 103–226 struck out subsec. (a) designation and subsecs. (b) and (c), which read as follows:

"(b) An agency program for the training of employees by, in, and through non-Government facilities under this chapter shall—

"(1) provide that information concerning the selection and assignment of employees for training and the applicable training limitations and restrictions be made available to employees of the agency; and

"(2) give consideration to the needs and requirements of the agency in recruiting and retaining scientific, professional, technical, and administrative employees.

"(c) In order to protect the Government concerning payment and reimbursement of training expenses, each agency shall prescribe such regulations as it considers necessary to implement the regulations prescribed under section 4118(a)(8) of this title."

CENTRAL INTELLIGENCE AGENCY

Exception of Central Intelligence Agency from provisions of subsec. (b)(1) of this section and certain other provisions of this chapter, and section 1308 of this title, see Ex. Ord. No. 10805, Feb. 18, 1959, 24 F.R. 1301, set out as a note under section 4102 of this title.

SECTION REFERRED TO IN OTHER SECTIONS

This section is referred to in section 3381 of this title.

[§ 4106. Repealed. Pub. L. 103–226, § 2(a)(4), Mar. 30, 1994, 108 Stat. 112]

Section, Pub. L. 89–554, Sept. 6, 1966, 80 Stat. 434; Pub. L. 95–454, title IX, § 906(a)(2), (3), Oct. 13, 1978, 92 Stat. 1224, related to limitations on amount of training of employees through non-Government facilities.

§ 4107. Restriction on degree training

(a) Except as provided in subsections (b) and (c) of this section, this chapter does not authorize the selection and assignment of an employee for training, or the payment or reimbursement of the costs of training, for—

(1) the purpose of providing an opportunity to an employee to obtain an academic degree in order to qualify for appointment to a particular position for which the academic degree is a basic requirement; or

(2) the sole purpose of providing an opportunity to an employee to obtain one or more academic degrees.

(b)(1) The regulations prescribed under section 4118 of this title shall include provisions under which the head of an agency may provide training, or payment or reimbursement for the costs of any training, not otherwise allowable under subsection (a) or (c) of this section, if necessary to assist in the recruitment or retention of employees in occupations in which the Government has or anticipates a shortage of qualified personnel, especially in occupations involving critical skills (as defined under such regulations).

(2) In exercising any authority under this subsection, an agency shall, consistent with the merit system principles set forth in paragraphs (1) and (2) of section 2301(b) of this title, take into consideration the need to maintain a balanced workforce in which women and members of racial and ethnic minority groups are appropriately represented in Government service.

(3) No authority under this subsection may be exercised on behalf of any employee occupying or seeking to qualify for appointment to any position which is excepted from the competitive service because of its confidential, policy-determining, policy-making, or policy-advocating character.

(c) With respect to an employee of the Department of Defense—

(1) this chapter does not authorize, except as provided in subsection (b) of this section, the selection and assignment of the employee for training, or the payment or reimbursement of the costs of training, for—

(A) the purpose of providing an opportunity to the employee to obtain an academic degree in order to qualify for appointment to a particular position for which the academic degree is a basic requirement; or

(B) the sole purpose of providing an opportunity to the employee to obtain one or more academic degrees, unless such opportunity is part of a planned, systematic, and coordinated program of professional development endorsed by the Department of Defense; and

(2) any course of post-secondary education delivered through classroom, electronic, or other means shall be administered or conducted by an institution recognized under standards implemented by a national or regional accrediting body, except in a case in which such standards do not exist or the use of such standards would not be appropriate.

(Pub. L. 89–554, Sept. 6, 1966, 80 Stat. 435; Pub. L. 101–510, div. A, title XII, § 1206(a), Nov. 5, 1990, 104 Stat. 1659; Pub. L. 103–226, § 2(a)(5), Mar. 30, 1994, 108 Stat. 112; Pub. L. 106–398, § 1 [[div. A], title XI, § 1121], Oct. 30, 2000, 114 Stat. 1654, 1654A–315.)

HISTORICAL AND REVISION NOTES

Derivation	U.S. Code	Revised Statutes and Statutes at Large
(a)	5 U.S.C. 2313.	July 7, 1958, Pub. L. 85–507, § 14, 72 Stat. 334.
(b)	5 U.S.C. 2318(d).	July 7, 1958, Pub. L. 85–507, § 19(d), 72 Stat. 336.
(c)	5 U.S.C. 2312.	July 7, 1958, Pub. L. 85–507, § 13, 72 Stat. 334.

The prohibitions are restated in positive form.

In subsection (a)(2), the words "Executive order" are substituted for "Executive orders of the President".

In subsection (c), the words "under authority of this chapter" and "by the Government" are omitted as unnecessary.

Standard changes are made to conform with the definitions applicable and the style of this title as outlined in the preface to the report.

AMENDMENTS

2000—Subsec. (a). Pub. L. 106–398, § 1 [[div. A], title XI, § 1121(1)], substituted "subsections (b) and (c)" for "subsection (b)" in introductory provisions.

Subsec. (b)(1). Pub. L. 106–398, § 1 [[div. A], title XI, § 1121(2)], substituted "subsection (a) or (c)" for "subsection (a)".

Subsec. (c). Pub. L. 106–398, § 1 [[div. A], title XI, § 1121(3)], added subsec. (c).

1994—Pub. L. 103–226, § 2(a)(5)(A), substituted "Restriction on degree training" for "Non-Government facilities; restrictions" in section catchline.

Subsec. (a). Pub. L. 103–226, § 2(a)(5)(B), (C), redesignated subsec. (c) as (a), in introductory provisions substituted "subsection (b)" for "subsection (d)" and struck out "by, in, or through a non-Government facility" after "employee for training", and struck out former subsec. (a) which read as follows: "Appropriations or other funds available to an agency are not available for payment for training an employee—

"(1) by, in or through a non-Government facility which teaches or advocates the overthrow of the Government of the United States by force or violence; or

"(2) by or through an individual concerning whom determination has been made by a proper Government administrative or investigatory authority that, on the basis of information or evidence developed in investigations and procedures authorized by law or Executive order, there exists a reasonable doubt of his loyalty to the United States."

Subsec. (b). Pub. L. 103–226, §2(a)(5)(B), (D), redesignated subsec. (d) as (b), substituted "subsection (a)" for "subsection (c)" in par. (1), and struck out former subsec. (b) which read as follows: "This chapter does not authorize training an employee by, in, or through a non-Government facility a substantial part of the activities of which is—

"(1) carrying on propaganda, or otherwise attempting, to influence legislation; or

"(2) participating or intervening, including publishing or distributing statements, in a political campaign on behalf of a candidate for public office."

Subsecs. (c), (d). Pub. L. 103–226, §2(a)(5)(B), redesignated subsecs. (c) and (d) as (a) and (b), respectively.

1990—Subsec. (c). Pub. L. 101–510, §1206(a)(1), substituted "Except as provided in subsection (d) of this section, this" for "This" in introductory provisions.

Subsec. (d). Pub. L. 101–510, §1206(a)(2), added subsec. (d).

SECTION REFERRED TO IN OTHER SECTIONS

This section is referred to in section 3381 of this title; title 10 section 1745; title 41 section 433.

§ 4108. Employee agreements; service after training

(a) An employee selected for training for more than a minimum period prescribed by the head of the agency shall agree in writing with the Government before assignment to training that he will—

(1) continue in the service of his agency after the end of the training period for a period at least equal to three times the length of the training period unless he is involuntarily separated from the service of his agency; and

(2) pay to the Government the amount of the additional expenses incurred by the Government in connection with his training if he is voluntarily separated from the service of his agency before the end of the period for which he has agreed to continue in the service of his agency.

(b) The payment agreed to under subsection (a)(2) of this section may not be required of an employee who leaves the service of his agency to enter into the service of another agency in any branch of the Government unless the head of the agency that authorized the training notifies the employee before the effective date of his entrance into the service of the other agency that payment will be required under this section.

(c) If an employee, except an employee relieved of liability under subsection (b) of this section or section 4102(b) of this title, fails to fulfill his agreement to pay to the Government the additional expenses incurred by the Government in connection with his training, a sum equal to the amount of the additional expenses of training is recoverable by the Government from the employee or his estate by—

(1) setoff against accrued pay, compensation, amount of retirement credit, or other amount due the employee from the Government; and

(2) such other method as is provided by law for the recovery of amounts owing to the Government.

The head of the agency concerned, under the regulations prescribed under section 4118 of this title, may waive in whole or in part a right of recovery under this subsection, if it is shown that the recovery would be against equity and good conscience or against the public interest.

(d) For purposes of this section, "training" includes a private sector assignment of an employee participating in the Executive Exchange Program of the President's Commission on Executive Exchange.

(Pub. L. 89–554, Sept. 6, 1966, 80 Stat. 435; Pub. L. 98–224, §5(a), Mar. 2, 1984, 98 Stat. 48; Pub. L. 103–226, §2(a)(6), Mar. 30, 1994, 108 Stat. 112.)

HISTORICAL AND REVISION NOTES

Derivation	U.S. Code	Revised Statutes and Statutes at Large
....	5 U.S.C. 2310.	July 7, 1958, Pub. L. 85–507, §11, 72 Stat. 332.

In subsection (a), the last sentence of former section 2310(a) is omitted as included in the first sentence of the revised subsection.

In subsection (b), the words, "another agency in any branch of the Government" are coextensive with and substituted for "another department or of any other agency in any branch of the Government". This is so because "agency in any branch of the Government" is broader than "agency" as defined for the purpose of this chapter in section 4101(1).

Standard changes are made to conform with the definitions applicable and the style of this title as outlined in the preface to the report.

AMENDMENTS

1994—Subsec. (a). Pub. L. 103–226 substituted "for more than a minimum period prescribed by the head of the agency" for "by, in, or through a non-Government facility under this chapter".

1984—Subsec. (d). Pub. L. 98–224 added subsec. (d).

CENTRAL INTELLIGENCE AGENCY

Exception of Central Intelligence Agency from provisions of this section and certain other provisions of this chapter, see Ex. Ord. No. 10805, Feb. 18, 1959, 24 F.R. 1301, set out as a note under section 4102 of this title.

§ 4109. Expenses of training

(a) The head of an agency, under the regulations prescribed under section 4118(a)(8) of this title and from appropriations or other funds available to the agency, may—

(1) pay all or a part of the pay (except overtime, holiday, or night differential pay) of an employee of the agency selected and assigned for training under this chapter, for the period of training; and

(2) pay, or reimburse the employee for, all or a part of the necessary expenses of the training, without regard to section 3324(a) and (b) of title 31, including among the expenses the necessary costs of—

(A) travel and per diem instead of subsistence under subchapter I of chapter 57 of this title or, in the case of commissioned officers of the National Oceanic and Atmospheric Administration, sections 404 and 405 of title 37, and the Joint Travel Regulations for the Uniformed Services;

(B) transportation of immediate family, household goods and personal effects, packing, crating, temporarily storing, draying, and unpacking under section 5724 of this title or, in the case of commissioned officers of the National Oceanic and Atmospheric Administration, sections 406 and 409 of title 37, and the Joint Travel Regulations for the Uniformed Services, when the estimated costs of transportation and related services are less than the estimated aggregate per diem payments for the period of training;

(C) tuition and matriculation fees;

(D) library and laboratory services;

(E) purchase or rental of books, materials, and supplies; and

(F) other services or facilities directly related to the training of the employee.

(b) The expenses of training do not include membership fees except to the extent that the fee is a necessary cost directly related to the training itself or that payment of the fee is a condition precedent to undergoing the training.

(c) Notwithstanding subsection (a)(1) of this section, the Administrator, Federal Aviation Administration, may pay an individual training to be an air traffic controller of such Administration, and the Secretary of Defense may pay an individual training to be an air traffic controller of the Department of Defense, during the period of such training, at the applicable rate of basic pay for the hours of training officially ordered or approved in excess of forty hours in an administrative workweek.

(d) Notwithstanding subsection (a)(1), a firefighter who is subject to section 5545b of this title shall be paid basic pay and overtime pay for the firefighter's regular tour of duty while attending agency sanctioned training.

(Pub. L. 89–554, Sept. 6, 1966, 80 Stat. 436; Pub. L. 90–83, § 1(4), Sept. 11, 1967, 81 Stat. 196; Pub. L. 96–54, § 2(a)(19), Aug. 14, 1979, 93 Stat. 382; Pub. L. 97–258, § 3(a)(9), Sept. 13, 1982, 96 Stat. 1063; Pub. L. 97–276, § 151(a), Oct. 2, 1982, 96 Stat. 1200; Pub. L. 98–224, § 5(b)(2), Mar. 2, 1984, 98 Stat. 48; Pub. L. 98–525, title XV, § 1537(a), Oct. 19, 1984, 98 Stat. 2635; Pub. L. 102–378, § 2(17), Oct. 2, 1992, 106 Stat. 1347; Pub. L. 105–277, div. A, § 101(h) [title VI, § 628(c)], Oct. 21, 1998, 112 Stat. 2681–480, 2681–521.)

HISTORICAL AND REVISION NOTES

Derivation	U.S. Code	Revised Statutes and Statutes at Large
....	5 U.S.C. 2309.	July 7, 1958, Pub. L. 85–507, § 10, 72 Stat. 332.

In subsection (a)(1) and (2), the words "training under this chapter" and "the training" are substituted for "training by, in, or through Government facilities or non-Government facilities under authority of this chapter" and "such training", respectively.

In subsection (a)(2)(A), the words "and the Standardized Government Travel Regulations" are omitted as included by the reference to "subchapter I of chapter 57 of this title".

In subsection (a)(2)(A) and (B), the words "sections 404 and 405 of title 37" and "sections 406 and 409 of title

37'' are substituted for the references to "section 253 of title 37" on authority of section 12(b) of the Act of Sept. 7, 1962, Pub. L. 87–649, 76 Stat. 497.

In subsection (a)(2)(B), the words "under section 5724 of this title" are substituted for "in accordance with section 73b–1 of this title, and Executive Order Numbered 9805, as amended" to reflect the codification of former section 73b–1 in this title and in view of the revocation of Executive Order No. 9805 by Executive Order No. 11012 of Mar. 27, 1962. The reference only to section 5724 is sufficient since that section contains the applicable substantive law, including the authority of the President to prescribe regulations.

Standard changes are made to conform with the definitions applicable and the style of this title as outlined in the preface to the report.

AMENDMENTS

1998—Subsec. (d). Pub. L. 105–277 added subsec. (d).

1992—Subsec. (d). Pub. L. 102–378 struck out subsec. (d) which made revolving fund referred to in section 1304(e)(1) of this title available for costs of education and related travel of participants in such program, for printing, and for entertainment expenses, and which required crediting of participation fees to revolving fund.

1984—Subsec. (c). Pub. L. 98–525 inserted "and the Secretary of Defense may pay an individual training to be an air traffic controller of the Department of Defense,".

Subsec. (d). Pub. L. 98–224 added subsec. (d).

1982—Subsec. (a)(2). Pub. L. 97–258 substituted "section 3324(a) and (b)'' for "section 529".

Subsec. (c). Pub. L. 97–276 added subsec. (c).

1979—Subsec. (a)(2). Pub. L. 96–54 substituted "National Oceanic and Atmospheric" for "Environmental Science Services" in cls. (A) and (B).

1967—Subsec. (a)(2). Pub. L. 90–83 substituted "Environmental Science Services Administration" for "Coast and Geodetic Survey" in cls. (A) and (B). See Historical and Revision Notes under section 2101 of this title.

EFFECTIVE DATE OF 1998 AMENDMENT

Pub. L. 105–277, div. A, § 101(h) [title VI, § 628(e)], Oct. 21, 1998, 112 Stat. 2681–480, 2681–521, provided that: "The amendments made by this section [enacting section 5545b of this title and amending this section and sections 5542 and 8331 of this title] shall take effect on the first day of the first applicable pay period which begins on or after October 1, 1998."

EFFECTIVE DATE OF 1992 AMENDMENT

Amendment by Pub. L. 102–378 effective Oct. 1, 1991, see section 9(b)(3) of Pub. L. 102–378, set out as a note under section 6303 of this title.

EFFECTIVE DATE OF 1984 AMENDMENT

Section 1537(f) of Pub. L. 98–525 provided that: "The amendments made by this section [amending this section and sections 5532, 5546a, 5547, and 8344 of this title] shall take effect on October 1, 1984."

EFFECTIVE DATE OF 1982 AMENDMENT

Amendment by Pub. L. 97–276 effective on first day of first applicable pay period beginning after Oct. 2, 1982, see section 151(h)(2) of Pub. L. 97–276, set out as an Effective Date note under section 5546a of this title.

EFFECTIVE DATE OF 1979 AMENDMENT

Amendment by Pub. L. 96–54 effective July 12, 1979, see section 2(b) of Pub. L. 96–54, set out as a note under section 305 of this title.

CENTRAL INTELLIGENCE AGENCY

Exception of Central Intelligence Agency from introductory provisions of subsec. (a) of this section and certain other provisions of this chapter, and section 1308 of this title, see Ex. Ord. No. 10805, Feb. 18, 1959, 24 F.R. 1301, set out as a note under section 4102 of this title.

SECTION REFERRED TO IN OTHER SECTIONS

This section is referred to in sections 4118, 5946 of this title.

§4110. Expenses of attendance at meetings

Appropriations available to an agency for travel expenses are available for expenses of attendance at meetings which are concerned with the functions or activities for which the appropriation is made or which will contribute to improved conduct, supervision, or management of the functions or activities.

(Pub. L. 89–554, Sept. 6, 1966, 80 Stat. 436.)

HISTORICAL AND REVISION NOTES

Derivation	U.S. Code	Revised Statutes and Statutes at Large
....	5 U.S.C. 2318(b).	July 7, 1958, Pub. L. 85–507, §19(b), 72 Stat. 336.

Standard changes are made to conform with the definitions applicable and the style of this title as outlined in the preface to the report.

SECTION REFERRED TO IN OTHER SECTIONS

This section is referred to in sections 4102, 5946 of this title; title 33 section 540a.

§4111. Acceptance of contributions, awards, and other payments

(a) To the extent authorized by regulation of the President, contributions and awards incident to training in non-Government facilities, and payment of travel, subsistence, and other expenses incident to attendance at meetings, may be made to and accepted by an employee, without regard to section 209 of title 18, if the contributions, awards, and payments are made by an organization determined by the Secretary of the Treasury to be an organization described by section 501(c)(3) of title 26 which is exempt from taxation under section 501(a) of title 26.

(b) When a contribution, award, or payment, in cash or in kind, is made to an employee for travel, subsistence, or other expenses under subsection (a) of this section, an appropriate reduction, under regulations of the President, shall be made from payment by the Government to the employee for travel, subsistence, or other expenses incident to training in a non-Government facility or to attendance at a meeting.

(Pub. L. 89–554, Sept. 6, 1966, 80 Stat. 437; Pub. L. 96–54, §2(a)(2), Aug. 14, 1979, 93 Stat. 381.)

HISTORICAL AND REVISION NOTES

Derivation	U.S. Code	Revised Statutes and Statutes at Large
(a)	5 U.S.C. 2318(a).	July 7, 1958, Pub. L. 85–507, §19(a), 72 Stat. 336.
(b)	5 U.S.C. 2318(c).	July 7, 1958, Pub. L. 85–507, §19(c), 72 Stat. 336.

In subsection (a), the words "section 209 of title 18" are substituted for "section 1914 of title 18" on authority of the Act of Oct. 23, 1962, Pub. L. 87–849, §2, 76 Stat. 1126.

Standard changes are made to conform with the definitions applicable and the style of this title as outlined in the preface to the report.

AMENDMENTS

1979—Subsec. (b). Pub. L. 96–54 substituted "President" for "Director of the Bureau of the Budget".

EFFECTIVE DATE OF 1979 AMENDMENT

Amendment by Pub. L. 96–54 effective July 12, 1979, see section 2(b) of Pub. L. 96–54, set out as a note under section 305 of this title.

TRANSFER OF FUNCTIONS

Functions vested by law (including reorganization plan) in Bureau of the Budget or Director of Bureau of the Budget transferred to President by section 101 of 1970 Reorg. Plan No. 2, eff. July 1, 1970, 35 F.R. 7959, 84 Stat. 2085, set out in the Appendix to this title. Section 102 of 1970 Reorg. Plan No. 2, redesignated Bureau of the Budget as Office of Management and Budget.

DELEGATION OF FUNCTIONS

Functions of President under subsec. (a) of this section delegated to Office of Personnel Management, see section 401(b) of Ex. Ord. No. 11348, Apr. 20, 1967, 32 F.R. 6335, set out as a note under section 4103 of this title.

Functions of President under subsec. (b) of this section delegated to Director of Office of Management and Budget, see Ex. Ord. No. 12152, Aug. 14, 1979, 44 F.R. 48143, set out as a note under section 301 of Title 3, The President.

SECTION REFERRED TO IN OTHER SECTIONS

This section is referred to in sections 3381, 4102 of this title; title 31 section 1353; title 38 section 7423.

§4112. Absorption of costs within funds available

(a) The President, to the extent he considers practicable, shall provide by regulation for the absorption of the costs of the training programs and plans under this chapter by the respective agencies from applicable appropriations or funds available for each fiscal year.

(b) Subsection (a) of this section may not be held or considered to require—

(1) the separation of an individual from the service by reduction in force or other personnel action; or

(2) the placement of an individual in a leave-without-pay status.

(Pub. L. 89–554, Sept. 6, 1966, 80 Stat. 437; Pub. L. 96–54, §2(a)(2), Aug. 14, 1979, 93 Stat. 381.)

HISTORICAL AND REVISION NOTES

Derivation	U.S. Code	Revised Statutes and Statutes at Large
....	5 U.S.C. 2319.	July 7, 1958, Pub. L. 85–507, §23, 72 Stat. 338.

In subsection (a), the words "for each fiscal year" are substituted for "for the fiscal year in which this chapter is enacted and for each succeeding fiscal year".

In subsection (b), the prohibition is restated in positive form.

Standard changes are made to conform with the definitions applicable and the style of this title as outlined in the preface to the report.

AMENDMENTS

1979—Subsec. (a). Pub. L. 96–54 substituted "President" for "Director of the Bureau of the Budget".

EFFECTIVE DATE OF 1979 AMENDMENT

Amendment by Pub. L. 96–54 effective July 12, 1979, see section 2(b) of Pub. L. 96–54, set out as a note under section 305 of this title.

DELEGATION OF FUNCTIONS

Functions of President under subsec. (a) of this section delegated to Director of Office of Management and Budget, see Ex. Ord. No. 12152, Aug. 14, 1979, 44 F.R.

48143, set out as a note under section 301 of Title 3, The President.

[§4113. Repealed. Pub. L. 104–66, title II, §2181(c)(1), Dec. 21, 1995, 109 Stat. 732]

Section, Pub. L. 89–554, Sept. 6, 1966, 80 Stat. 437; Pub. L. 95–454, title IX, §906(a)(2), (3), Oct. 13, 1978, 92 Stat. 1224; Pub. L. 103–226, §2(a)(7), Mar. 30, 1994, 108 Stat. 112, related to agency review of training needs and annual program reports.

[§4114. Repealed. Pub. L. 103–226, §2(a)(8), Mar. 30, 1994, 108 Stat. 112]

Section, Pub. L. 89–554, Sept. 6, 1966, 80 Stat. 438; Pub. L. 95–454, title IX, §906(a)(2), (3), Oct. 13, 1978, 92 Stat. 1224, related to review of employee training programs at non-Government facilities.

§4115. Collection of training information

The Office of Personnel Management, to the extent it considers appropriate in the public interest, may collect information concerning training programs, plans, and the methods inside and outside the Government. The Office, on request, may make the information available to an agency and to Congress.

(Pub. L. 89–554, Sept. 6, 1966, 80 Stat. 438; Pub. L. 95–454, title IX, §906(a)(2), (3), Oct. 13, 1978, 92 Stat. 1224.)

HISTORICAL AND REVISION NOTES

Derivation	U.S. Code	Revised Statutes and Statutes at Large
....	5 U.S.C. 2315.	July 7, 1958, Pub. L. 85–507, §16, 72 Stat. 335.

In the first sentence, the words "from time to time" are omitted as unnecessary. In the second sentence, the word "appropriate" is omitted as unnecessary.

Standard changes are made to conform with the definitions applicable and the style of this title as outlined in the preface to the report.

AMENDMENTS

1978—Pub. L. 95–454 substituted "Office of Personnel Management" and "Office" for "Civil Service Commission" and "Commission", respectively.

EFFECTIVE DATE OF 1978 AMENDMENT

Amendment by Pub. L. 95–454 effective 90 days after Oct. 13, 1978, see section 907 of Pub. L. 95–454, set out as a note under section 1101 of this title.

CENTRAL INTELLIGENCE AGENCY

Exception of Central Intelligence Agency from provisions of this section and certain other provisions of this chapter and section 1308 of this title, see Ex. Ord. No. 10805, Feb. 18, 1959, 24 F.R. 1301, set out as a note under section 4102 of this title.

§4116. Training program assistance

The Office of Personnel Management, on request of an agency, shall advise and assist in the establishment, operation, and maintenance of the training programs and plans of the agency under this chapter, to the extent of its facilities and personnel available for that purpose.

(Pub. L. 89–554, Sept. 6, 1966, 80 Stat. 438; Pub. L. 95–454, title IX, §906(a)(2), Oct. 13, 1978, 92 Stat. 1224.)

HISTORICAL AND REVISION NOTES

Derivation	U.S. Code	Revised Statutes and Statutes at Large
....	5 U.S.C. 2316.	July 7, 1958, Pub. L. 85–507, §17, 72 Stat. 335.

Standard changes are made to conform with the definitions applicable and the style of this title as outlined in the preface to the report.

AMENDMENTS

1978—Pub. L. 95–454 substituted "Office of Personnel Management" for "Civil Service Commission".

EFFECTIVE DATE OF 1978 AMENDMENT

Amendment by Pub. L. 95–454 effective 90 days after Oct. 13, 1978, see section 907 of Pub. L. 95–454, set out as a note under section 1101 of this title.

§4117. Administration

The Office of Personnel Management has the responsibility and authority for effective promotion and coordination of the training programs under this chapter and training operations thereunder. The functions, duties, and responsibilities of the Office under this chapter are subject to supervision and control by the President and review by Congress.

(Pub. L. 89–554, Sept. 6, 1966, 80 Stat. 438; Pub. L. 95–454, title IX, §906(a)(2), (3), Oct. 13, 1978, 92 Stat. 1224.)

HISTORICAL AND REVISION NOTES

Derivation	U.S. Code	Revised Statutes and Statutes at Large
....	5 U.S.C. 2301(4).	July 7, 1958, Pub. L. 85–507, §2(4), 72 Stat. 328.
....	5 U.S.C. 2318(e).	July 7, 1958, Pub. L. 85–507, §19(e), 72 Stat. 336.

Former sections 2301(4) and 2318(e) are combined and restated for clarity.

Standard changes are made to conform with the definitions applicable and the style of this title as outlined in the preface to the report.

AMENDMENTS

1978—Pub. L. 95–454 substituted "Office of Personnel Management" and "Office" for "Civil Service Commission" and "Commission", respectively.

EFFECTIVE DATE OF 1978 AMENDMENT

Amendment by Pub. L. 95–454 effective 90 days after Oct. 13, 1978, see section 907 of Pub. L. 95–454, set out as a note under section 1101 of this title.

CENTRAL INTELLIGENCE AGENCY

Exception of Central Intelligence Agency from provisions of subd. (4) of this section and certain other provisions of this chapter and section 1308 of this title, see Ex. Ord. No. 10805, Feb. 18, 1959, 24 F.R. 1301, set out as a note under section 4102 of this title.

§4118. Regulations

(a) The Office of Personnel Management, after considering the needs and requirements of each agency for training its employees and after consulting with the agencies principally concerned, shall prescribe regulations containing the principles, standards, and related requirements for the programs, and plans thereunder, for the training of employees under this chapter, including requirements for coordination of and reasonable uniformity in the agency training programs and plans. The regulations shall provide for the maintenance of necessary information concerning the general conduct of the training activities of each agency, and such other information as is necessary to enable the President and Congress to discharge effectively their respective duties and responsibilities for supervision, control, and review of these training programs. The regulations also shall cover—

(1) requirements concerning the determination and continuing review by each agency of its training needs and requirements;

(2) the scope and conduct of the agency training programs and plans;

(3) the selection and assignment of employees of each agency for training;

(4) the use in each agency of the services of employees who have undergone training;

(5) the evaluation of the results and effects of the training programs and plans;

(6) the interchange of training information among the agencies;

(7) the submission of reports by the agencies on results and effects of training programs and plans and economies resulting therefrom, including estimates of costs of training;

(8) requirements and limitations necessary with respect to payments and reimbursements in accordance with section 4109 of this title; and

(9) other matters considered appropriate or necessary by the Office to carry out the provisions of this chapter.

(b) The Office, in accordance with this chapter, may revise, supplement, or abolish regulations prescribed under this section, and prescribe additional regulations.

(c) This section does not authorize the Office to prescribe the types and methods of intra-agency training or to regulate the details of intra-agency training programs.

(Pub. L. 89–554, Sept. 6, 1966, 80 Stat. 438; Pub. L. 95–454, title IX, § 906(a)(2), (3), Oct. 13, 1978, 92 Stat. 1224; Pub. L. 103–226, § 2(a)(9), Mar. 30, 1994, 108 Stat. 112.)

HISTORICAL AND REVISION NOTES

Derivation	U.S. Code	Revised Statutes and Statutes at Large
....	5 U.S.C. 2305.	July 7, 1958, Pub. L. 85–507, § 6, 72 Stat. 329.

In subsection (a), the word "appropriate" is omitted as unnecessary. The words "with respect to training by, in, and through Government facilities and non-Government facilities" are omitted as unnecessary.

In subsection (b)(2) and (3), the words "by, in, or through a non-Government facility" are omitted as unnecessary in view of the previous reference in the subsection.

In subsection (c), the words "From time to time" are omitted as unnecessary.

In subsection (d), the prohibition is restated in positive form.

Standard changes are made to conform with the definitions applicable and the style of this title as outlined in the preface to the report.

AMENDMENTS

1994—Subsec. (a)(7). Pub. L. 103–226, § 2(a)(9)(A), struck out before semicolon at end "by, in, and through non-Government facilities".

Subsecs. (b) to (d). Pub. L. 103–226, § 2(a)(9)(B), (C), redesignated subsecs. (c) and (d) as (b) and (c), respectively, and struck out former subsec. (b) which read as follows: "In addition to the matters set forth by subsection (a) of this section, the regulations, concerning training of employees by, in, or through non-Government facilities, shall—

"(1) prescribe general policies governing the selection of a non-Government facility to provide training;

"(2) authorize training of employees only after the head of the agency concerned determines that adequate training for employees by, in, or through a Government facility is not reasonably available, and that consideration has been given to the existing or reasonably foreseeable availability and use of fully trained employees; and

"(3) prohibit training an employee for the purpose of filling a position by promotion if there is in the agency concerned another employee, of equal ability and suitability, fully qualified to fill the position and available at, or within a reasonable distance from, the place where the duties of the position are to be performed."

1978—Subsecs. (a), (c), (d). Pub. L. 95–454 substituted "Office of Personnel Management" and "Office" for "Civil Service Commission" and "Commission", respectively, wherever appearing.

EFFECTIVE DATE OF 1978 AMENDMENT

Amendment by Pub. L. 95–454 effective 90 days after Oct. 13, 1978, see section 907 of Pub. L. 95–454, set out as a note under section 1101 of this title.

CENTRAL INTELLIGENCE AGENCY

Exception of Central Intelligence Agency from provisions of this section and certain other provisions of this chapter and section 1308 of this title, see Ex. Ord. No. 10805, Feb. 18, 1959, 24 F.R. 1301, set out as a note under section 4102 of this title.

SECTION REFERRED TO IN OTHER SECTIONS

This section is referred to in sections 4103, 4107, 4108, 4109 of this title.

§ 4119. Training for employees under the Office of the Architect of the Capitol and the Botanic Garden

(a) The Architect of the Capitol may, by regulation, make applicable such provisions of this chapter as the Architect determines necessary to provide for training of (1) individuals employed under the Office of the Architect of the Capitol and the Botanic Garden and (2) other congressional employees who are subject to the administrative control of the Architect. The regulations shall provide for training which, in the determination of the Architect, is consistent with the training provided by agencies under the preceding sections of this chapter.

(b) The Office of Personnel Management shall provide the Architect of the Capitol with such advice and assistance as the Architect may request in order to enable the Architect to carry out the purposes of this section.

(Added Pub. L. 97–346, § 1(a), Oct. 15, 1982, 96 Stat. 1647.)

CHAPTER 43—PERFORMANCE APPRAISAL

SUBCHAPTER I—GENERAL PROVISIONS

AMENDMENTS

1993—Pub. L. 103–89, §3(b)(1)(B)(ii), Sept. 30, 1993, 107 Stat. 981, struck out item 4302a "Establishment of performance appraisal systems for performance management and recognition system employees".

1984—Pub. L. 98–615, title II, §202(b), Nov. 8, 1984, 98 Stat. 3216, added item 4302a.

1978—Pub. L. 95–454, title II, §203(a), title IV, §405(b), Oct. 13, 1978, 92 Stat. 1131, 1170, in chapter heading substituted "APPRAISAL" for "RATING", added heading for subchapter I, in item 4302 substituted "Establishment of performance appraisal systems" for "Performance-rating plans; establishment of", in item 4303 substituted "Actions based on unacceptable performance" for "Performance-rating plans; requirements for", in item 4304 substituted "Responsibilities of Office of Personnel Management" for "Ratings for performance", in item 4305 substituted "Regulations" for "Review of ratings", struck out items 4306 to 4308 "Performance-rating plans; inspection of", "Other rating procedures prohibited", and "Regulations", respectively, and added item for subchapter II and items 4311 to 4315.

CHAPTER REFERRED TO IN OTHER SECTIONS

This chapter is referred to in sections 2108, 2302, 3502, 9508 of this title; title 21 section 1703; title 31 section 3801; title 42 section 237.

SUBCHAPTER I—GENERAL PROVISIONS

AMENDMENTS

1979—Pub. L. 96–54, §2(a)(20), Aug. 14, 1979, 93 Stat. 382, added heading for subchapter I.

§ 4301. Definitions

For the purpose of this subchapter—
(1) "agency" means—
(A) an Executive agency; and
(B) the Government Printing Office;
but does not include—
(i) a Government corporation;
(ii) the Central Intelligence Agency, the Defense Intelligence Agency, the National Imagery and Mapping Agency, the National Security Agency, or any Executive agency or unit thereof which is designated by the President and the principal function of which is the conduct of foreign intelligence or counterintelligence activities; or
(iii) the General Accounting Office;

(2) "employee" means an individual employed in or under an agency, but does not include—
(A) an employee outside the United States who is paid in accordance with local native prevailing wage rates for the area in which employed;

(B) an individual in the Foreign Service of the United States;
(C) a physician, dentist, nurse, or other employee in the Veterans Health Administration of the Department of Veterans Affairs whose pay is fixed under chapter 73 of title 38;
(D) an administrative law judge appointed under section 3105 of this title;
(E) an individual in the Senior Executive Service or the Federal Bureau of Investigation and Drug Enforcement Administration Senior Executive Service;
(F) an individual appointed by the President;
(G) an individual occupying a position not in the competitive service excluded from coverage of this subchapter by regulations of the Office of Personnel Management; or
(H) an individual who (i) is serving in a position under a temporary appointment for less than one year, (ii) agrees to serve without a performance evaluation, and (iii) will not be considered for a reappointment or for an increase in pay based in whole or in part on performance; and

(3) "unacceptable performance" means performance of an employee which fails to meet established performance standards in one or more critical elements of such employee's position.

(Pub. L. 89–554, Sept. 6, 1966, 80 Stat. 440; Pub. L. 91–375, §6(c)(8), Aug. 12, 1970, 84 Stat. 776; Pub. L. 95–251, §2(a)(1), Mar. 27, 1978, 92 Stat. 183; Pub. L. 95–454, title II, §203(a), Oct. 13, 1978, 92 Stat. 1131; Pub. L. 100–325, §2(f), May 30, 1988, 102 Stat. 581; Pub. L. 101–474, §5(e), Oct. 30, 1990, 104 Stat. 1100; Pub. L. 101–510, div. A, title XII, §1206(e), Nov. 5, 1990, 104 Stat. 1661; Pub. L. 102–54, §13(b)(2), June 13, 1991, 105 Stat. 274; Pub. L. 103–359, title V, §501(e), Oct. 14, 1994, 108 Stat. 3429; Pub. L. 104–201, div. A, title XI, §1122(a)(1), Sept. 23, 1996, 110 Stat. 2687.)

HISTORICAL AND REVISION NOTES

Derivation	U.S. Code	Revised Statutes and Statutes at Large
....	5 U.S.C. 2001.	Sept. 30, 1950, ch. 1123, §2, 64 Stat. 1098. Sept. 1, 1954, ch. 1208, §601(a), 68 Stat. 1115. June 17, 1957, Pub. L. 85–56, §2201(21), 71 Stat. 159. July 11, 1957, Pub. L. 85–101, 71 Stat. 293. Sept. 2, 1958, Pub. L. 85–857, §13(p), 72 Stat. 1266. Mar. 26, 1964, Pub. L. 88–290, "Sec. 306(b)", 78 Stat. 170.

In paragraph (1), the term "Executive agency" is substituted for the reference to "executive departments, the independent establishments and agencies in the executive branch, including corporations wholly owned by the United States" and "the General Accounting Office". The exception of "a Government controlled corporation" is added in subparagraph (vii) to preserve the application of this chapter to "corporations wholly owned by the United States". The exceptions for Production credit corporations and Federal intermediate credit banks in former section 2001(b)(5), (6) are omitted as they are no longer "corporations wholly owned by the United States". Under the Farm Credit Act of 1956, 70 Stat. 659, the production credit corporations were

---
[1] So in original. Does not conform to section catchline.

merged in the Federal intermediate credit banks, and pursuant to that Act the Federal intermediate credit banks have ceased to be corporations owned by the United States. The exceptions for Federal land banks and banks for cooperatives in former section 2001(b)(7), (8) are omitted as included within the exception of "a Government controlled corporation" in subparagraph (vii).

Paragraph (2) is supplied because the definition of "employee" in section 2105 does not encompass individuals employed by the government of the District of Columbia. The definition in paragraph (2) does not encompass members of the uniformed services as they are not "employed" in or under an agency.

Paragraph (2)(E) is based on the third and fifth sentences, respectively, of former sections 1010 and 1011, which are carried into sections 5362 and 559, respectively, and section 1106(a) of the Act of Oct. 28, 1949, ch. 782, 63 Stat. 972.

Standard changes are made to conform with the definitions applicable and the style of this title as outlined in the preface to the report.

AMENDMENTS

1996—Par. (1)(ii). Pub. L. 104–201 substituted "National Imagery and Mapping Agency" for "Central Imagery Office".

1994—Par. (1)(ii). Pub. L. 103–359 inserted "the Central Imagery Office," after "Defense Intelligence Agency,".

1991—Par. (2)(C). Pub. L. 102–54 substituted "Veterans Health Administration of the Department of Veterans Affairs" for "Department of Medicine and Surgery, Veterans' Administration".

1990—Par. (1). Pub. L. 101–474 redesignated subpar. (C) as (B) and struck out former subpar. (B) which included Administrative Office of United States Courts within definition of "agency".

Par. (2)(H). Pub. L. 101–510 added subpar. (H).

1988—Par. (2)(E). Pub. L. 100–325 inserted reference to Federal Bureau of Investigation and Drug Enforcement Administration Senior Executive Service.

1978—Pub. L. 95–454 substituted provisions defining "agency", "employee", and "unacceptable performance" for provisions defining "agency" and "employee".

Par. (2)(E). Pub. L. 95–251 substituted "administrative law judge" for "hearing examiner".

1970—Par. (1)(ii). Pub. L. 91–375 repealed cl. (ii) which excluded postal field service from definition of "agency".

EFFECTIVE DATE OF 1996 AMENDMENT

Amendment by Pub. L. 104–201 effective Oct. 1, 1996, see section 1124 of Pub. L. 104–201, set out as a note under section 193 of Title 10, Armed Forces.

EFFECTIVE DATE OF 1978 AMENDMENT

Amendment by Pub. L. 95–454 effective 90 days after Oct. 13, 1978, see section 907 of Pub. L. 95–454, set out as a note under section 1101 of this title.

EFFECTIVE DATE OF 1970 AMENDMENT

Amendment by Pub. L. 91–375 effective within 1 year after Aug. 12, 1970, on date established therefor by Board of Governors of United States Postal Service and published by it in Federal Register, see section 15(a) of Pub. L. 91–375, set out as an Effective Date note preceding section 101 of Title 39, Postal Service.

SECTION REFERRED TO IN OTHER SECTIONS

This section is referred to in sections 559, 1305 of this title.

§ 4302. Establishment of performance appraisal systems

(a) Each agency shall develop one or more performance appraisal systems which—

(1) provide for periodic appraisals of job performance of employees;

(2) encourage employee participation in establishing performance standards; and

(3) use the results of performance appraisals as a basis for training, rewarding, reassigning, promoting, reducing in grade, retaining, and removing employees.

(b) Under regulations which the Office of Personnel Management shall prescribe, each performance appraisal system shall provide for—

(1) establishing performance standards which will, to the maximum extent feasible, permit the accurate evaluation of job performance on the basis of objective criteria (which may include the extent of courtesy demonstrated to the public) related to the job in question for each employee or position under the system;

(2) as soon as practicable, but not later than October 1, 1981, with respect to initial appraisal periods, and thereafter at the beginning of each following appraisal period, communicating to each employee the performance standards and the critical elements of the employee's position;

(3) evaluating each employee during the appraisal period on such standards;

(4) recognizing and rewarding employees whose performance so warrants;

(5) assisting employees in improving unacceptable performance; and

(6) reassigning, reducing in grade, or removing employees who continue to have unacceptable performance but only after an opportunity to demonstrate acceptable performance.

(c) In accordance with regulations which the Office shall prescribe, the head of an agency may administer and maintain a performance appraisal system electronically.

(Pub. L. 89–554, Sept. 6, 1966, 80 Stat. 440; Pub. L. 95–454, title II, § 203(a), Oct. 13, 1978, 92 Stat. 1132; Pub. L. 102–378, § 2(18), Oct. 2, 1992, 106 Stat. 1347; Pub. L. 106–398, § 1 [[div. A], title XI, § 1104], Oct. 30, 2000, 114 Stat. 1654, 1654A–311.)

HISTORICAL AND REVISION NOTES

Derivation	U.S. Code	Revised Statutes and Statutes at Large
....	5 U.S.C. 2002.	Sept. 30, 1950, ch. 1123, § 3, 64 Stat. 1098.

Standard changes are made to conform with the definitions applicable and the style of this title as outlined in the preface to the report.

AMENDMENTS

2000—Subsec. (c). Pub. L. 106–398 added subsec. (c).

1992—Subsec. (a)(3). Pub. L. 102–378 substituted a period for semicolon at end.

1978—Pub. L. 95–454 substituted "Establishment of performance appraisal systems" for "Performance-rating plans; establishment of" in section catchline and in text substituted provisions relating to the establishment of a performance appraisal system, for provisions relating to the establishment of performance-rating plans.

EFFECTIVE DATE OF 1978 AMENDMENT

Amendment by Pub. L. 95–454 effective 90 days after Oct. 13, 1978, see section 907 of Pub. L. 95–454, set out as a note under section 1101 of this title.

SECTION REFERRED TO IN OTHER SECTIONS

This section is referred to in section 9508 of this title; title 12 section 1441a; title 31 section 732.

[§ 4302a. Repealed. Pub. L. 103–89, § 3(b)(1)(B)(i), Sept. 30, 1993, 107 Stat. 981]

Section, added Pub. L. 98–615, title II, § 202(a), Nov. 8, 1984, 98 Stat. 3214; amended Pub. L. 101–103, § 5(a), Sept. 30, 1989, 103 Stat. 671; Pub. L. 102–22, § 2(a), Mar. 28, 1991, 105 Stat. 71, related to the establishment of performance appraisal systems for performance management and recognition system employees.

EFFECTIVE DATE OF REPEAL

Repeal effective Nov. 1, 1993, see section 3(c) of Pub. L. 103–89, set out as an Effective Date of 1993 Amendment note under section 3372 of this title.

§ 4303. Actions based on unacceptable performance

(a) Subject to the provisions of this section, an agency may reduce in grade or remove an employee for unacceptable performance.

(b)(1) An employee whose reduction in grade or removal is proposed under this section is entitled to—

(A) 30 days' advance written notice of the proposed action which identifies—

(i) specific instances of unacceptable performance by the employee on which the proposed action is based; and

(ii) the critical elements of the employee's position involved in each instance of unacceptable performance;

(B) be represented by an attorney or other representative;

(C) a reasonable time to answer orally and in writing; and

(D) a written decision which—

(i) in the case of a reduction in grade or removal under this section, specifies the instances of unacceptable performance by the employee on which the reduction in grade or removal is based, and

(ii) unless proposed by the head of the agency, has been concurred in by an employee who is in a higher position than the employee who proposed the action.

(2) An agency may, under regulations prescribed by the head of such agency, extend the notice period under subsection (b)(1)(A) of this section for not more than 30 days. An agency may extend the notice period for more than 30 days only in accordance with regulations issued by the Office of Personnel Management.

(c) The decision to retain, reduce in grade, or remove an employee—

(1) shall be made within 30 days after the date of expiration of the notice period, and

(2) in the case of a reduction in grade or removal, may be based only on those instances of unacceptable performance by the employee—

(A) which occurred during the 1-year period ending on the date of the notice under subsection (b)(1)(A) of this section in connection with the decision; and

(B) for which the notice and other requirements of this section are complied with.

(d) If, because of performance improvement by the employee during the notice period, the employee is not reduced in grade or removed, and the employee's performance continues to be acceptable for 1 year from the date of the advance written notice provided under subsection (b)(1)(A) of this section, any entry or other notation of the unacceptable performance for which the action was proposed under this section shall be removed from any agency record relating to the employee.

(e) Any employee who is—

(1) a preference eligible;

(2) in the competitive service; or

(3) in the excepted service and covered by subchapter II of chapter 75,

and who has been reduced in grade or removed under this section is entitled to appeal the action to the Merit Systems Protection Board under section 7701.

(f) This section does not apply to—

(1) the reduction to the grade previously held of a supervisor or manager who has not completed the probationary period under section 3321(a)(2) of this title,

(2) the reduction in grade or removal of an employee in the competitive service who is serving a probationary or trial period under an initial appointment or who has not completed 1 year of current continuous employment under other than a temporary appointment limited to 1 year or less, or

(3) the reduction in grade or removal of an employee in the excepted service who has not completed 1 year of current continuous employment in the same or similar positions.

(Pub. L. 89–554, Sept. 6, 1966, 80 Stat. 440; Pub. L. 95–454, title II, § 203(a), Oct. 13, 1978, 92 Stat. 1133; Pub. L. 101–376, § 2(b), Aug. 17, 1990, 104 Stat. 462.)

HISTORICAL AND REVISION NOTES

Derivation	U.S. Code	Revised Statutes and Statutes at Large
....	5 U.S.C. 2004.	Sept. 30, 1950, ch. 1123, § 5, 64 Stat. 1098.

The words "required by this chapter" are omitted as unnecessary.

Standard changes are made to conform with the definitions applicable and the style of this title as outlined in the preface to the report.

AMENDMENTS

1990—Subsec. (e). Pub. L. 101–376 amended subsec. (e) generally. Prior to amendment, subsec. (e) read as follows: "Any employee who is a preference eligible or is in the competitive service and who has been reduced in grade or removed under this section is entitled to appeal the action to the Merit Systems Protection Board under section 7701 of this title."

1978—Pub. L. 95–454 substituted "Actions based on unacceptable performance" for "Performance-rating plans; requirements for" in section catchline and in text substituted provisions relating to actions based on unacceptable performance, for provisions relating to requirements for performance-rating plans.

EFFECTIVE DATE OF 1990 AMENDMENT

Section 2(c) of Pub. L. 101–376 provided that: "The amendments made by this section [amending this section and section 7511 of this title] shall apply with respect to any personnel action taking effect on or after the effective date of this Act [see below]."

Section 4 of Pub. L. 101–376 provided that: "This Act and the amendments made by this Act [amending this section, sections 7511 and 7701 of this title, and enacting provisions set out as notes under this section and section 7501 of this title] shall become effective on the date of the enactment of this Act [Aug. 17, 1990], and, except as provided in section 2(c) [set out above], shall apply with respect to any appeal or other proceeding brought on or after such date.''

EFFECTIVE DATE OF 1978 AMENDMENT

Amendment by Pub. L. 95–454 effective 90 days after Oct. 13, 1978, see section 907 of Pub. L. 95–454, set out as a note under section 1101 of this title.

SECTION REFERRED TO IN OTHER SECTIONS

This section is referred to in sections 2302, 7121, 7512, 7701, 9508 of this title; title 31 section 732.

§ 4304. Responsibilities of the Office of Personnel Management

(a) The Office of Personnel Management shall make technical assistance available to agencies in the development of performance appraisal systems.

(b)(1) The Office shall review each performance appraisal system developed by any agency under this section and determine whether the performance appraisal system meets the requirements of this subchapter.

(2) The Comptroller General shall from time to time review on a selected basis performance appraisal systems established under this subchapter to determine the extent to which any such system meets the requirements of this subchapter and shall periodically report its findings to the Office and to the Congress.

(3) If the Office determines that a system does not meet the requirements of this subchapter (including regulations prescribed under section 4305), the Office shall direct the agency to implement an appropriate system or to correct operations under the system, and any such agency shall take any action so required.

(Pub. L. 89–554, Sept. 6, 1966, 80 Stat. 440; Pub. L. 95–454, title II, § 203(a), Oct. 13, 1978, 92 Stat. 1134.)

HISTORICAL AND REVISION NOTES

Derivation	U.S. Code	Revised Statutes and Statutes at Large
....	5 U.S.C. 2005.	Sept. 30, 1950, ch. 1123, § 6, 64 Stat. 1099.

In subsection (a)(1), the words "corresponding to an efficiency rating of 'good' under the Veterans' Preference Act of 1944, as amended, and under laws superseded by this chapter" in clause (1) of former section 2005 are omitted, but are carried into section 3502.

Standard changes are made to conform with the definitions applicable and the style of this title as outlined in the preface to the report.

AMENDMENTS

1978—Pub. L. 95–454 substituted "Responsibilities of the Office of Personnel Management" for "Ratings for performance" in section catchline and in text substituted provisions relating to the responsibilities of the Office of Personnel Management under this subchapter, for provisions relating to ratings for performance.

EFFECTIVE DATE OF 1978 AMENDMENT

Amendment by Pub. L. 95–454 effective 90 days after Oct. 13, 1978, see section 907 of Pub. L. 95–454, set out as a note under section 1101 of this title.

SECTION REFERRED TO IN OTHER SECTIONS

This section is referred to in title 12 section 1441a.

§ 4305. Regulations

The Office of Personnel Management may prescribe regulations to carry out the purpose of this subchapter.

(Pub. L. 89–554, Sept. 6, 1966, 80 Stat. 441; Pub. L. 95–454, title II, § 203(a), Oct. 13, 1978, 92 Stat. 1134.)

HISTORICAL AND REVISION NOTES

Derivation	U.S. Code	Revised Statutes and Statutes at Large
....	5 U.S.C. 2006.	Sept. 30, 1950, ch. 1123, § 7, 64 Stat. 1099.

In subsection (c), the words "as a matter of right" are omitted as unnecessary.

In subsection (d), the words "are entitled" are substituted for "shall be afforded an opportunity". The word "considers" is substituted for "deems to be".

Standard changes are made to conform with the definitions applicable and the style of this title as outlined in the preface to the report.

AMENDMENTS

1978—Pub. L. 95–454 substituted "Regulations" for "Review of ratings" in section catchline and in text substituted provisions relating to regulations to carry out this subchapter, for provisions relating to review of ratings.

EFFECTIVE DATE OF 1978 AMENDMENT

Amendment by Pub. L. 95–454 effective 90 days after Oct. 13, 1978, see section 907 of Pub. L. 95–454, set out as a note under section 1101 of this title.

SECTION REFERRED TO IN OTHER SECTIONS

This section is referred to in section 4304 of this title.

[§§ 4306 to 4308. Omitted]

CODIFICATION

Sections 4306 to 4308, Pub. L. 89–554, Sept. 6, 1966, 80 Stat. 441, 442, were omitted in the general revision of this chapter by the Civil Service Reform Act of 1978, Pub. L. 95–454, § 203(a), Oct. 13, 1978, 92 Stat. 1131.

Section 4306 related to inspection of performance-rating plans.

Section 4307 related to prohibition of other rating procedures.

Section 4308 related to regulations for administration of the chapter, and is covered by revised section 4305.

SUBCHAPTER II—PERFORMANCE APPRAISAL IN THE SENIOR EXECUTIVE SERVICE

SUBCHAPTER REFERRED TO IN OTHER SECTIONS

This subchapter is referred to in sections 3151, 3395, 3592, 3593, 3594, 3595, 5384, 8336, 8414 of this title; title 10 section 1606; title 31 section 733; title 38 section 7425.

§ 4311. Definitions

For the purpose of this subchapter, "agency", "senior executive", and "career appointee" have the meanings set forth in section 3132(a) of this title.

(Added Pub. L. 95–454, title IV, § 405(a), Oct. 13, 1978, 92 Stat. 1167.)

EFFECTIVE DATE

Subchapter effective 9 months after Oct. 13, 1978, and congressional review of provisions of sections 401 through 412 of Pub. L. 95–454, see section 415(a)(1), (b), of Pub. L. 95–454, set out as a note under section 3131 of this title.

§ 4312. Senior Executive Service performance appraisal systems

(a) Each agency shall, in accordance with standards established by the Office of Personnel Management, develop one or more performance appraisal systems designed to—

(1) permit the accurate evaluation of performance in any position on the basis of criteria which are related to the position and which specify the critical elements of the position;

(2) provide for systematic appraisals of performance of senior executives;

(3) encourage excellence in performance by senior executives; and

(4) provide a basis for making eligibility determinations for retention in the Senior Executive Service and for Senior Executive Service performance awards.

(b) Each performance appraisal system established by an agency under subsection (a) of this section shall provide—

(1) that, on or before the beginning of each rating period, performance requirements for each senior executive in the agency are established in consultation with the senior executive and communicated to the senior executive;

(2) that written appraisals of performance are based on the individual and organizational performance requirements established for the rating period involved; and

(3) that each senior executive in the agency is provided a copy of the appraisal and rating under section 4314 of this title and is given an opportunity to respond in writing and have the rating reviewed by an employee, or (with the consent of the senior executive) a commissioned officer in the uniformed services serving on active duty, in a higher level in the agency before the rating becomes final.

(c)(1) The Office shall review each agency's performance appraisal system under this section, and determine whether the agency performance appraisal system meets the requirements of this subchapter.

(2) The Comptroller General shall from time to time review performance appraisal systems under this section to determine the extent to which any such system meets the requirements under this subchapter and shall periodically report its findings to the Office and to each House of the Congress.

(3) If the Office determines that an agency performance appraisal system does not meet the requirements under this subchapter (including regulations prescribed under section 4315), the agency shall take such corrective action as may be required by the Office.

(d) A senior executive may not appeal any appraisal and rating under any performance appraisal system under this section.

(Added Pub. L. 95–454, title IV, § 405(a), Oct. 13, 1978, 92 Stat. 1167; amended Pub. L. 98–615, title III, § 306(b)(2), Nov. 8, 1984, 98 Stat. 3220.)

AMENDMENTS

1984—Subsec. (b)(3). Pub. L. 98–615 inserted ", or (with the consent of the senior executive) a commissioned officer in the uniformed services serving on active duty," and directed that "executive" be struck out which was executed by striking "executive" only where it appeared before "level in the agency".

EFFECTIVE DATE OF 1984 AMENDMENT

Amendment by Pub. L. 98–615 effective following expiration of 90-day period beginning on Nov. 8, 1984, see section 307 of Pub. L. 98–615, set out as a note under section 3393 of this title.

SECTION REFERRED TO IN OTHER SECTIONS

This section is referred to in section 3393a of this title.

§ 4313. Criteria for performance appraisals

Appraisals of performance in the Senior Executive Service shall be based on both individual and organizational performance, taking into account such factors as—

(1) improvements in efficiency, productivity, and quality of work or service, including any significant reduction in paperwork;

(2) cost efficiency;

(3) timeliness of performance;

(4) other indications of the effectiveness, productivity, and performance quality of the employees for whom the senior executive is responsible; and

(5) meeting affirmative action goals, achievement of equal employment opportunity requirements, and compliance with the merit systems principles set forth under section 2301 of this title.

(Added Pub. L. 95–454, title IV, § 405(a), Oct. 13, 1978, 92 Stat. 1168; amended Pub. L. 103–424, § 6, Oct. 29, 1994, 108 Stat. 4364.)

AMENDMENTS

1994—Par. (5). Pub. L. 103–424 amended par. (5) generally. Prior to amendment, par. (5) read as follows: "meeting affirmative action goals and achievement of equal employment opportunity requirements."

§ 4314. Ratings for performance appraisals

(a) Each performance appraisal system shall provide for annual summary ratings of levels of performance as follows:

(1) one or more fully successful levels,

(2) a minimally satisfactory level, and

(3) an unsatisfactory level.

(b) Each performance appraisal system shall provide that—

(1) any appraisal and any rating under such system—

(A) are made only after review and evaluation by a performance review board established under subsection (c) of this section;

(B) are conducted at least annually, subject to the limitation of subsection (c)(3) of this section;

(C) in the case of a career appointee, may not be made within 120 days after the beginning of a new Presidential administration; and

(D) are based on performance during a performance appraisal period the duration of which shall be determined under guidelines established by the Office of Personnel Management, but which may be terminated in any case in which the agency making an appraisal determines that an adequate basis exists on which to appraise and rate the senior executive's performance;

(2) any career appointee receiving a rating at any of the fully successful levels under subsection (a)(1) of this section may be given a performance award under section 5384 of this title;

(3) any senior executive receiving an unsatisfactory rating under subsection (a)(3) of this section shall be reassigned or transferred within the Senior Executive Service, or removed from the Senior Executive Service, but any senior executive who receives 2 unsatisfactory ratings in any period of 5 consecutive years shall be removed from the Senior Executive Service; and

(4) any senior executive who twice in any period of 3 consecutive years receives less than fully successful ratings shall be removed from the Senior Executive Service.

(c)(1) Each agency shall establish, in accordance with regulations prescribed by the Office, one or more performance review boards, as appropriate. It is the function of the boards to make recommendations to the appropriate appointing authority of the agency relating to the performance of senior executives in the agency.

(2) The supervising official of the senior executive shall provide to the performance review board, an initial appraisal of the senior executive's performance. Before making any recommendation with respect to the senior executive, the board shall review any response by the senior executive to the initial appraisal and conduct such further review as the board finds necessary.

(3) Performance appraisals under this subchapter with respect to any senior executive shall be made by the appointing authority only after considering the recommendations by the performance review board with respect to such senior executive under paragraph (1) of this subsection.

(4) Members of performance review boards shall be appointed in such a manner as to assure consistency, stability, and objectivity in performance appraisal. Notice of the appointment of an individual to serve as a member shall be published in the Federal Register.

(5) In the case of an appraisal of a career appointee, more than one-half of the members of the performance review board shall consist of career appointees. The requirement of the preceding sentence shall not apply in any case in which the Office determines that there exists an insufficient number of career appointees available to comply with the requirement.

(Added Pub. L. 95–454, title IV, § 405(a), Oct. 13, 1978, 92 Stat. 1169; amended Pub. L. 104–66, title II, § 2181(b), Dec. 21, 1995, 109 Stat. 732.)

AMENDMENTS

1995—Subsec. (d). Pub. L. 104–66 struck out subsec. (d) which related to reports to Congress.

SECTION REFERRED TO IN OTHER SECTIONS

This section is referred to in sections 3393a, 3395, 3592, 4312, 5384 of this title.

§ 4315. Regulations

The Office of Personnel Management shall prescribe regulations to carry out the purpose of this subchapter.

(Added Pub. L. 95–454, title IV, § 405(a), Oct. 13, 1978, 92 Stat. 1170.)

SECTION REFERRED TO IN OTHER SECTIONS

This section is referred to in section 4312 of this title.

CHAPTER 45—INCENTIVE AWARDS

SUBCHAPTER I—AWARDS FOR SUPERIOR ACCOMPLISHMENTS

AMENDMENTS

1994—Pub. L. 103–425, § 2(b), Oct. 31, 1994, 108 Stat. 4370, added items 4508 and 4509.

1992—Pub. L. 102–487, § 1(b), Oct. 24, 1992, 106 Stat. 3134, struck out item 4514 "Expiration of authority".

1990—Pub. L. 101–509, title V, § 529 [title II, § 207(b), title IV, § 408(b)], Nov. 5, 1990, 104 Stat. 1427, 1458, 1468, added item 4505a and heading for subchapter III and items 4521 to 4523.

1988—Pub. L. 100–611, § 1(b), Nov. 5, 1988, 102 Stat. 3179, struck out "; reporting requirement" after "authority" in item 4514.

1985—Pub. L. 99–145, title XII, § 1225(b)(1)(B), Nov. 8, 1985, 99 Stat. 730, inserted "; reporting requirement" in item 4514.

1981—Pub. L. 97–35, title XVII, § 1703(b)(3), Aug. 13, 1981, 95 Stat. 756, added heading for subchapter I and subchapter II and items 4511 to 4514.

1978—Pub. L. 95–454, title IV, § 406(b), Oct. 13, 1978, 92 Stat. 1171, added item 4507.

CHAPTER REFERRED TO IN OTHER SECTIONS

This chapter is referred to in section 3362 of this title; title 10 section 1124; title 28 sections 995, 996.

SUBCHAPTER I—AWARDS FOR SUPERIOR ACCOMPLISHMENTS

AMENDMENTS

1981—Pub. L. 97–35, title XVII, § 1703(b)(1), Aug. 13, 1981, 95 Stat. 756, added heading for subchapter I.

---

[1] So in original. Probably should not be capitalized.
[2] So in original. Does not conform to subchapter heading.

SUBCHAPTER REFERRED TO IN OTHER SECTIONS

This subchapter is referred to in section 9508 of this title.

§ 4501. Definitions

For the purpose of this subchapter—

    (1) "agency" means—

        (A) an Executive agency;

        (B) the Library of Congress;

        (C) the Office of the Architect of the Capitol;

        (D) the Botanic Garden;

        (E) the Government Printing Office;

        (F) the government of the District of Columbia; and

        (G) the United States Sentencing Commission;

but does not include—

        (i) the Tennessee Valley Authority; or

        (ii) the Central Bank for Cooperatives;

    (2) "employee" means—

        (A) an employee as defined by section 2105; and

        (B) an individual employed by the government of the District of Columbia; and

    (3) "Government" means the Government of the United States and the government of the District of Columbia.

(Pub. L. 89–554, Sept. 6, 1966, 80 Stat. 442; Pub. L. 95–454, title V, § 503(a), Oct. 13, 1978, 92 Stat. 1183; Pub. L. 97–35, title XVII, § 1703(b)(2), Aug. 13, 1981, 95 Stat. 756; Pub. L. 98–615, title II, § 204(a)(1), Nov. 8, 1984, 98 Stat. 3216; Pub. L. 100–690, title VII, § 7106(a), Nov. 18, 1988, 102 Stat. 4418; Pub. L. 101–474, § 5(f), Oct. 30, 1990, 104 Stat. 1100; Pub. L. 103–89, § 3(b)(1)(C), Sept. 30, 1993, 107 Stat. 981.)

HISTORICAL AND REVISION NOTES

Derivation	U.S. Code	Revised Statutes and Statutes at Large
....	5 U.S.C. 2122.	Sept. 1, 1954, ch. 1208, § 303, 68 Stat. 1113. Aug. 18, 1959, Pub. L. 86–168, § 202(d), 73 Stat. 389.

In paragraph (1), the term "Executive agency" is co-extensive with and substituted for "executive department or independent agency in the executive branch of the Government including a Government-owned or controlled corporation" in view of the definition of "Executive agency" in section 105. Application to the General Accounting Office (included in the term "Executive agency") is based on former section 933a.

Paragraph (2) is supplied because the definition of "employee" in section 2105 does not encompass individuals employed by the government of the District of Columbia.

Paragraph (3) is supplied for clarity and convenience.

Standard changes are made to conform with the definitions applicable and the style of this title as outlined in the preface to the report.

AMENDMENTS

1993—Par. (2)(A). Pub. L. 103–89 amended subpar. (A) generally. Prior to amendment, subpar. (A) read as follows: "an employee as defined by section 2105 of this title, but does not include an employee covered by the performance management and recognition system established under chapter 54 of this title; and".

1990—Par. (1). Pub. L. 101–474 redesignated subpars. (C) to (H) as (B) to (G), respectively, and struck out former subpar. (B) which included Administrative Office of United States Courts within definition of "agency".

1988—Par. (1)(H). Pub. L. 100–690 added subpar. (H).

1984—Par. (2)(A). Pub. L. 98–615 substituted "the performance management and recognition system established under chapter 54" for "the merit pay system established under section 5402".

1981—Pub. L. 97–35 substituted "subchapter" for "chapter" in provision preceding par. (1).

1978—Par. (2)(A). Pub. L. 95–454 inserted reference to an employee covered by merit pay system established under section 5402 of this title.

EFFECTIVE DATE OF 1993 AMENDMENT

Amendment by Pub. L. 103–89 effective Nov. 1, 1993, see section 3(c) of Pub. L. 103–89, set out as a note under section 3372 of this title.

EFFECTIVE DATE OF 1984 AMENDMENT

Section 205 of Pub. L. 98–615 provided that amendment by Pub. L. 98–615 was effective Oct. 1, 1984, and applicable with respect to pay periods commencing on or after that date, with certain exceptions and qualifications.

EFFECTIVE DATE OF 1981 AMENDMENT

Section 1703(c) of Pub. L. 97–35 provided that: "The amendments made by this section [enacting subchapter II of this chapter, designating this section and sections 4502 to 4507 of this title as subchapter I, and amending this section and sections 4502, 4505, and 4506 of this title] shall take effect on October 1, 1981."

EFFECTIVE DATE OF 1978 AMENDMENT

Section 504(a) of Pub. L. 95–454 provided that amendment by Pub. L. 95–454 was effective on first day of first applicable pay period which began on or after Oct. 1, 1981, except it could take effect with respect to any category or categories of positions before such day to extent prescribed by Director of Office of Personnel Management.

EX. ORD. NO. 12976. COMPENSATION PRACTICES OF GOVERNMENT CORPORATIONS

Ex. Ord. No. 12976, Oct. 5, 1995, 60 F.R. 52829, provided:

By the authority vested in me as President by the Constitution and the laws of the United States of America, including section 301 of title 3, United States Code, and sections 1105, 1108, and 1111 of title 31, United States Code, it is hereby ordered as follows:

SECTION 1. *Statement of Presidential Principles.*

Government corporations subject to this order should not pay bonuses in excess of those authorized by sections 4501 through 4507 of title 5, United States Code, except as otherwise specifically provided by law.

SEC. 2. *Administration Review.* (a) Before taking action to approve any bonus in excess of those authorized in section 4502 of title 5, United States Code, each corporation subject to this section (as provided in section 6 of this order) shall submit information to the Director of the Office of Management and Budget (OMB) relating to such bonuses as provided in subsection (b). Such corporation shall refrain from approving any such bonus until the Director of OMB has had an opportunity to review the information provided by the corporation.

(b) The Director of OMB shall issue instructions to the corporations subject to this section specifying when information is to be submitted, and the content and form of such information.

SEC. 3. *Information Reporting Requirements.* (a) Government corporations subject to this order will provide information to the Director of OMB relating to the compensation practices for senior executives of such corporations as provided in subsection (c).

(b) Information submitted shall include the following with respect to senior executives of each corporation subject to this section:

(1) the compensation plan, procedures, and structure of such corporation;

(2) base salary levels, annual bonuses, and other compensation; and

(3) information supporting the senior executive compensation plan and levels.

(c) The Director of OMB shall issue instructions to the corporations subject to this section specifying when information is to be submitted, and the content and form of such information.

SEC. 4. *Review.* (a) OMB, in consultation with the Department of Labor, will review the information submitted pursuant to section 3, taking into consideration:

(1) consistency with statutory requirements;

(2) consistency with corporate mission;

(3) standards of Federal management and efficiency; and

(4) equivalent private sector compensation practices.

SEC. 5. *Public Dissemination Requirement.* Government corporations subject to this order shall make available through public dissemination the information submitted pursuant to section 3 of this order.

SEC. 6. *Coverage.* This order will apply to all mixed-ownership and wholly owned corporations listed in section 9101(2) and (3) of title 31, United States Code. Section 2 shall apply only to wholly owned corporations except such corporations that have specific authority to approve bonuses in excess of those authorized under sections 4501 through 4507 of title 5, United States Code.

SEC. 7. *Administration.* All corporations subject to this order shall provide any information in the manner and form, and at the time, requested pursuant to this order by the Director of OMB.

SEC. 8. This order is intended only to improve the internal management of the executive branch and is not intended to create any right or benefit, substantive or procedural, enforceable at law by a party against the United States, its agencies, its officers, or any other person.

WILLIAM J. CLINTON.

SECTION REFERRED TO IN OTHER SECTIONS

This section is referred to in section 3362 of this title.

§ 4502. General provisions

(a) Except as provided by subsection (b) of this section, a cash award under this subchapter may not exceed $10,000.

(b) When the head of an agency certifies to the Office of Personnel Management that the suggestion, invention, superior accomplishment, or other meritorious effort for which the award is proposed is highly exceptional and unusually outstanding, a cash award in excess of $10,000 but not in excess of $25,000 may be granted with the approval of the Office.

(c) A cash award under this subchapter is in addition to the regular pay of the recipient. Acceptance of a cash award under this subchapter constitutes an agreement that the use by the Government of an idea, method, or device for which the award is made does not form the basis of a further claim of any nature against the Government by the employee, his heirs, or assigns.

(d) A cash award to, and expense for the honorary recognition of, an employee may be paid from the fund or appropriation available to the activity primarily benefiting or the various activities benefiting. The head of the agency concerned determines the amount to be paid by each activity for an agency award under section 4503 of this title. The President determines the amount to be paid by each activity for a Presidential award under section 4504 of this title.

(e) The Office of Personnel Management may by regulation permit agencies to grant employees time off from duty, without loss of pay or charge to leave, as an award in recognition of superior accomplishment or other personal effort that contributes to the quality, efficiency, or economy of Government operations.

(f) The Secretary of Defense may grant a cash award under subsection (b) of this section without regard to the requirements for certification and approval provided in that subsection.

(Pub. L. 89–554, Sept. 6, 1966, 80 Stat. 442; Pub. L. 95–454, title V, § 503(b), (c), Oct. 13, 1978, 92 Stat. 1183; Pub. L. 97–35, title XVII, § 1703(b)(2), Aug. 13, 1981, 95 Stat. 756; Pub. L. 101–509, title V, § 529 [title II, § 201], Nov. 5, 1990, 104 Stat. 1427, 1455; Pub. L. 103–89, § 3(b)(1)(D), Sept. 30, 1993, 107 Stat. 981; Pub. L. 106–398, § 1 [[div. A], title XI, § 1132], Oct. 30, 2000, 114 Stat. 1654, 1654A–318.)

HISTORICAL AND REVISION NOTES

Derivation	U.S. Code	Revised Statutes and Statutes at Large
....	5 U.S.C. 2123(d), (e), (g).	Sept. 1, 1954, ch. 1208, § 304(d), (e), (g), 68 Stat. 1113.

In subsections (a) and (b), the words "cash award" are substituted for "monetary award" and "such award" to conform to the remainder of the chapter.

In subsection (c), the word "Government" is substituted for "Government of the United States or the government of the District of Columbia" in view of the definition of "Government" in section 4501.

Standard changes are made to conform with the definitions applicable and the style of this title as outlined in the preface to the report.

AMENDMENTS

2000—Subsec. (f). Pub. L. 106–398 added subsec. (f).

1993—Subsec. (e). Pub. L. 103–89 struck out par. (2) designation and struck out par. (1) which read as follows: "Notwithstanding section 4501(2), for the purpose of this subsection, 'employee' includes an employee covered by the performance management and recognition system established under chapter 54."

1990—Subsec. (e). Pub. L. 101–509 added subsec. (e).

1981—Subsecs. (a), (c). Pub. L. 97–35 substituted "subchapter" for "chapter".

1978—Subsec. (a). Pub. L. 95–454, § 503(b), substituted "$10,000" for "$5,000".

Subsec. (b). Pub. L. 95–454, § 503(c), substituted "Office of Personnel Management" for "Civil Service Commission", "$10,000" for "$5,000", and "Office" for "Commission".

EFFECTIVE DATE OF 1993 AMENDMENT

Amendment by Pub. L. 103–89 effective Nov. 1, 1993, see section 3(c) of Pub. L. 103–89, set out as a note under section 3372 of this title.

EFFECTIVE DATE OF 1990 AMENDMENT

Amendment by Pub. L. 101–509 effective on such date as the President shall determine, but not earlier than 90 days, and not later than 180 days, after Nov. 5, 1990, see section 529 [title III, § 305] of Pub. L. 101–509, set out as a note under section 5301 of this title.

EFFECTIVE DATE OF 1981 AMENDMENT

Amendment by Pub. L. 97–35 effective Oct. 1, 1981, see section 1703(c) of Pub. L. 97–35, set out as a note under section 4501 of this title.

EFFECTIVE DATE OF 1978 AMENDMENT

Section 504(a) of Pub. L. 95–454 provided that amendment by Pub. L. 95–454 was effective on first day of first applicable pay period which began on or after Oct. 1, 1981, except it could take effect with respect to any category or categories of positions before such day to extent prescribed by Director of Office of Personnel Management.

DELEGATION OF FUNCTIONS

Functions of President under former section 2123(e) [now subsec. (d)] of this section delegated to Director of Office of Personnel Management, see section 2 of Ex. Ord. No. 11228, June 14, 1965, 30 F.R. 7739, set out as a note under section 301 of Title 3, The President.

SECTION REFERRED TO IN OTHER SECTIONS

This section is referred to in section 9508 of this title; title 12 section 1441a.

§ 4503. Agency awards

The head of an agency may pay a cash award to, and incur necessary expense for the honorary recognition of, an employee who—

(1) by his suggestion, invention, superior accomplishment, or other personal effort contributes to the efficiency, economy, or other improvement of Government operations or achieves a significant reduction in paperwork; or

(2) performs a special act or service in the public interest in connection with or related to his official employment.

(Pub. L. 89–554, Sept. 6, 1966, 80 Stat. 443; Pub. L. 95–454, title V, §502(a), Oct. 13, 1978, 92 Stat. 1183.)

HISTORICAL AND REVISION NOTES

Derivation	U.S. Code	Revised Statutes and Statutes at Large
....	5 U.S.C. 2123(a).	Sept. 1, 1954, ch. 1208, §304(a), 68 Stat. 1113.

The word "employee" is substituted for "civilian officers and employees of the Government" in view of the definition of "employee" in section 4501.

Standard changes are made to conform with the definitions applicable and the style of this title as outlined in the preface to the report.

AMENDMENTS

1978—Par. (1). Pub. L. 95–454 inserted "or achieves a significant reduction in paperwork".

EFFECTIVE DATE OF 1978 AMENDMENT

Section 504(a) of Pub. L. 95–454 provided that amendment by Pub. L. 95–454 was effective on first day of first applicable pay period which began on or after Oct. 1, 1981, except it could take effect with respect to any category or categories of positions before such day to extent prescribed by Director of Office of Personnel Management.

SECTION REFERRED TO IN OTHER SECTIONS

This section is referred to in sections 4502, 4504 of this title; title 12 section 1441a; title 50 section 403e–1.

§ 4504. Presidential awards

The President may pay a cash award to, and incur necessary expense for the honorary recognition of, an employee who—

(1) by his suggestion, invention, superior accomplishment, or other personal effort contributes to the efficiency, economy, or other improvement of Government operations or achieves a significant reduction in paperwork; or

(2) performs an exceptionally meritorious special act or service in the public interest in connection with or related to his official employment.

A Presidential award may be in addition to an agency award under section 4503 of this title.

(Pub. L. 89–554, Sept. 6, 1966, 80 Stat. 443; Pub. L. 95–454, title V, §502(b), Oct. 13, 1978, 92 Stat. 1183.)

HISTORICAL AND REVISION NOTES

Derivation	U.S. Code	Revised Statutes and Statutes at Large
....	5 U.S.C. 2123(b).	Sept. 1, 1954, ch. 1208, §304(b), 68 Stat. 1113.

The words "In instances determined by the President to warrant such action" are omitted as surplusage. The word "employee" is substituted for "civilian officers and employees of the Government" in view of the definition of "employee" in section 4501.

Standard changes are made to conform with the definitions applicable and the style of this title as outlined in the preface to the report.

AMENDMENTS

1978—Par. (1). Pub. L. 95–454 inserted "or achieves a significant reduction in paperwork".

EFFECTIVE DATE OF 1978 AMENDMENT

Section 504(a) of Pub. L. 95–454 provided that amendment by Pub. L. 95–454 was effective on first day of first applicable pay period which began on or after Oct. 1, 1981, except it could take effect with respect to any category or categories of positions before such day to extent prescribed by Director of Office of Personnel Management.

DELEGATION OF FUNCTIONS

Functions vested in Director of Office of Personnel Management under this section insofar as it affects officers and employees in or under executive branch of Government to be performed without approval of President, see section 2 of Ex. Ord. No. 11228, June 14, 1965, 30 F.R. 7739, set out as a note under section 301 of Title 3, The President.

EX. ORD. NO. 9586. THE PRESIDENTIAL MEDAL OF FREEDOM

Ex. Ord. No. 9586, July 6, 1945, 10 F.R. 8523, as amended by Ex. Ord. No. 10336, Apr. 3, 1952, 17 F.R. 2957; Ex. Ord. No. 11085, Feb. 22, 1963, 28 F.R. 1759; Ex. Ord. No. 11515, Mar. 13, 1970, 35 F.R. 4543, provided:

By virtue of the authority vested in me as President of the United States and as Commander in Chief of the armed forces of the United States, it is ordered as follows:

SECTION 1. *Medal established.* The Medal of Freedom is hereby reestablished as the Presidential Medal of Freedom, with accompanying ribbons and appurtenances. The Presidential Medal of Freedom, hereinafter referred to as the Medal, shall be in two degrees.

SEC. 2. *Award of the Medal.* (a) The Medal may be awarded by the President as provided in this order to any person who has made an especially meritorious contribution to (1) the security or national interests of the United States, or (2) world peace, or (3) cultural or other significant public or private endeavors.

(b) The President may select for the award of the Medal any person recommended to the President for award of the Medal or any person selected by the President upon his own initiative.

(c) The principal announcement of awards of the Medal shall normally be made annually, on or about July 4 of each year; but such awards may be made at other times, as the President may deem appropriate.

(d) Subject to the provision of this Order, the Medal may be awarded posthumously.

SEC. 3. *Distinguished Civilian Service Awards Board.* (a) The Distinguished Civilian Service Awards Board, established by Executive Order No. 10717 of June 27, 1957, hereinafter referred to as the Board, is hereby expanded, for the purpose of carrying out the objectives of this Order, to include five additional members appointed by the President from outside the Executive Branch of the Government. The terms of service of the members of the Board appointed under this paragraph shall be five years, except that the first five members so appointed shall have terms of service expiring on the 31st day of July 1964, 1965, 1966, 1967, and 1968, respectively. Any person appointed to fill a vacancy occurring prior to the expiration of the term for which his predecessor was appointed shall serve for the remainder of such term.

(b) A chairman of the Board shall be designated by the President from time to time from among the membership of the Board appointed from the Executive Branch.

(c) For purposes of recommending to the President persons to receive the President's Award for Distinguished Federal Civilian Service, and to carry out the other purposes of Executive Order No. 10717, only the members of the Board from the Executive Branch will sit. The names of persons so recommended will be submitted to the President without reference to the other members of the Board.

SEC. 4. *Functions of the Board.* (a) Any individual or group may make recommendations to the Board with respect to the award of the Medal, and the Board shall consider such recommendations.

(b) With due regard for the provisions of Section 2 of this Order, the Board shall screen such recommendations and, on the basis of such recommendations or upon its own motion, shall from time to time submit to the President nominations of individuals for award of the Medal, in appropriate degrees.

SEC. 5. *Expenses.* Necessary administrative expenses of the Board incurred in connection with the recommendation of persons to receive the Presidential Medal of Freedom, including expenses of travel of members of the Board appointed under Section 3(a) of this Order, during the fiscal year 1963, may be paid from the appropriation provided under the heading "Special Projects" in the Executive Office Appropriation Act, 1963, 76 Stat. 315, and during subsequent fiscal years, to the extent permitted by law, from any corresponding or like appropriation made available for such fiscal years. Such payments shall be without regard to the provisions of section 3681 of the Revised Statutes and section 9 of the Act of March 4, 1909, 35 Stat. 1027 (31 U.S.C. 672 and 673) [31 U.S.C. 1346(a) and (c)]. Members of the Board appointed under Section 3(a) of this Order shall serve without compensation.

SEC. 6. *Design of the Medal.* The Army Institute of Heraldry shall prepare for the approval of the President a design of the Medal in each of its degrees.

EX. ORD. NO. 10717. PRESIDENT'S AWARD FOR
DISTINGUISHED FEDERAL CIVILIAN SERVICE

Ex. Ord. No. 10717, June 27, 1957, 22 F.R. 4632, as amended by Ex. Ord. No. 10979, Dec. 12, 1961, 26 F.R. 11937; Ex. Ord. No. 11085, Feb. 22, 1963, 28 F.R. 1759; Ex. Ord. No. 12014, Oct. 19, 1977, 42 F.R. 56105; Ex. Ord. No. 12107, Dec. 28, 1978, 44 F.R. 1055, provided:

SECTION 1. There is hereby established an honorary award for the recognition of distinguished service by civilian officers and employees of the Federal Government. The award shall be known as the President's Award for Distinguished Federal Civilian Service, and shall consist of a gold medal, the design of which accompanies and is hereby made a part of this order, suspended on a ribbon of appropriate material and color, and accompanying appurtenances. Each medal shall be suitably inscribed, and an appropriate citation shall accompany each award.

SEC. 2. (a) The President's Award for Distinguished Federal Civilian Service shall be presented by the President to civilian officers or employees of the Federal Government for the best achievements having current impact in improving Government operations or serving the public interest. These achievements shall exemplify one or more of the following:

(1) Imagination in developing creative solutions to problems of government.

(2) Courage in persevering against great odds and difficulties.

(3) High ability in accomplishing extraordinary scientific or technological achievement, in providing outstanding leadership in planning, organizing, or directing a major program of unusual importance and complexity, or in performing an extraordinary act of credit to the Government and the country.

(4) Long and distinguished career service.

(b) The importance of the achievements to the Government and to the public interest shall be so outstanding that the officer or employee is deserving of greater public recognition than that which can be accorded by the head of the department or agency in which he is employed. Generally, not more than five awards shall be made in any one year. Presentation of the award shall be made at such times as the President may determine.

SEC. 3. The Director of the Office of Personnel Management shall advise and assist the President in selecting persons to receive this award. In performing this function, the Director shall carefully review nominations submitted pursuant to the provisions of Section 4 of this Order and decide which of them, if any, warrant presentation to the President. The Director shall thereupon transmit to the President the names of those persons who, in the opinion of the Director, merit the award, together with a statement of the reasons therefor. Recipients for the award shall be selected by the President.

SEC. 4. The form and procedures for making nominations for this award shall be prescribed by the Director of the Office of Personnel Management, in accord with the following principles:

(a) The Director shall be guided in the performance of this function by the provisions of Section 4504 and 4505 of Title 5 of the United States Code, and by additional criteria which the Director may prescribe.

(b) The Director shall not recommend any person for the award without the concurrence of the head of the agency in which that person was employed at the time of the achievement for which the award is recommended.

(c) Persons appointed by the President are not eligible for this award unless, in the opinion of the Office, they are currently serving in a career position.

SECTION REFERRED TO IN OTHER SECTIONS

This section is referred to in section 4502 of this title; title 15 section 3710c.

§ 4505. Awards to former employees

An agency may pay or grant an award under this subchapter notwithstanding the death or separation from the service of the employee concerned, if the suggestion, invention, superior accomplishment, other personal effort, or special act or service in the public interest for which the award is proposed was made or performed while the employee was in the employ of the Government.

(Pub. L. 89–554, Sept. 6, 1966, 80 Stat. 443; Pub. L. 97–35, title XVII, § 1703(b)(2), Aug. 13, 1981, 95 Stat. 756.)

HISTORICAL AND REVISION NOTES

Derivation	U.S. Code	Revised Statutes and Statutes at Large
....	5 U.S.C. 2123(c).	Sept. 1, 1954, ch. 1208 § 304(c), 68 Stat. 1113.

The words "or grant" are added for clarity.

Standard changes are made to conform with the definitions applicable and the style of this title as outlined in the preface to the report.

AMENDMENTS

1981—Pub. L. 97–35 substituted "subchapter" for "chapter".

EFFECTIVE DATE OF 1981 AMENDMENT

Amendment by Pub. L. 97–35 effective Oct. 1, 1981, see section 1703(c) of Pub. L. 97–35, set as a note under section 4501 of this title.

§ 4505a. Performance-based cash awards

(a)(1) An employee whose most recent performance rating was at the fully successful level or higher (or the equivalent thereof) may be paid a cash award under this section.

(2)(A) A cash award under this section shall be equal to an amount determined appropriate by the head of the agency, but may not be more than 10 percent of the employee's annual rate of basic pay. Notwithstanding the preceding sentence, the agency head may authorize a cash award equal to an amount exceeding 10 percent of the employee's annual rate of basic pay if the agency head determines that exceptional performance by the employee justifies such an award, but in no case may an award under this section exceed 20 percent of the employee's annual rate of basic pay.

(B) For purposes of computing a percentage of a rate of basic pay under subparagraph (A), the rate of basic pay used shall be determined without taking into account any comparability payment under section 5304.

(b)(1) A cash award under this section shall be paid as a lump sum, and may not be considered to be part of the basic pay of an employee.

(2) The failure to pay a cash award under this section, or the amount of such an award, may not be appealed. The preceding sentence shall not be construed to extinguish or lessen any right or remedy under subchapter II of chapter 12, chapter 71, or any of the laws referred to in section 2302(d).

(c) The Office of Personnel Management shall prescribe such regulations as it considers necessary for the administration of subsections (a) and (b).

(d) The preceding provisions of this section shall be applicable with respect to any employee to whom subchapter III of chapter 53 applies, and to any category of employees provided for under subsection (e).

(e) At the request of the head of an Executive agency, the President may authorize the application of subsections (a) through (c) with respect to any category of employees within such agency who would not otherwise be covered by this section.

(Added Pub. L. 101–509, title V, § 529 [title II, § 207(a)], Nov. 5, 1990, 104 Stat. 1427, 1457; amended Pub. L. 102–378, § 2(19), Oct. 2, 1992, 106 Stat. 1347.)

AMENDMENTS

1992—Subsec. (b)(2). Pub. L. 102–378, § 2(19)(A), inserted reference to chapter 71.

Subsec. (c). Pub. L. 102–378, § 2(19)(B), inserted "of Personnel Management" after "Office".

Subsecs. (d), (e). Pub. L. 102–378, § 2(19)(C), added subsecs. (d) and (e) and struck out former subsec. (d) which read as follows: "At the request of the head of an Executive agency, the President may authorize the application of the preceding provisions of this section with respect to 1 or more categories of employees within such agency who would not otherwise be covered by this section (including authority under subsection (c) to prescribe any necessary regulations)."

EFFECTIVE DATE OF 1992 AMENDMENT

Amendment by Pub. L. 102–378 effective May 4, 1991, see section 9(b)(4) of Pub. L. 102–378, set out as a note under section 6303 of this title.

EFFECTIVE DATE

Section effective on such date as the President shall determine, but not earlier than 90 days, and not later than 180 days, after Nov. 5, 1990, see section 529 [title III, § 305] of Pub. L. 101–509, set out as an Effective Date of 1990 Amendment note under section 5301 of this title.

DELEGATION OF FUNCTIONS

Authority of President under subsec. (e) of this section delegated to Director of Office of Personnel Management by Ex. Ord. No. 12828, § 1(2), Jan. 5, 1993, 58 F.R. 2965, set out as a note under section 3502 of this title.

Authority of President under subsec. (d) [now (e)] of this section delegated to Office of Personnel Management by section 6(a) of Ex. Ord. No. 12748, Feb. 1, 1991, 56 F.R. 4521, eff. May 4, 1991, set out as a note under section 5301 of this title.

SECTION REFERRED TO IN OTHER SECTIONS

This section is referred to in title 12 section 1441a.

§ 4506. Regulations

The Office of Personnel Management shall prescribe regulations and instructions under which the agency awards program set forth by this subchapter shall be carried out.

(Pub. L. 89–554, Sept. 6, 1966, 80 Stat. 443; Pub. L. 95–454, title V, § 503(d), Oct. 13, 1978, 92 Stat. 1184; Pub. L. 97–35, title XVII, § 1703(b)(2), Aug. 13, 1981, 95 Stat. 756.)

HISTORICAL AND REVISION NOTES

Derivation	U.S. Code	Revised Statutes and Statutes at Large
....	5 U.S.C. 2121 (1st 29 words).	Sept. 1, 1954, ch. 1208, § 302 (1st 29 words), 68 Stat. 1112.

Standard changes are made to conform with the definitions applicable and the style of this title as outlined in the preface to the report.

AMENDMENTS

1981—Pub. L. 97–35 substituted "subchapter" for "chapter".

1978—Pub. L. 95–454 substituted "Office of Personnel Management shall" for "Civil Service Commission may".

EFFECTIVE DATE OF 1981 AMENDMENT

Amendment by Pub. L. 97–35 effective Oct. 1, 1981, see section 1703(c) of Pub. L. 97–35, set out as a note under section 4501 of this title.

EFFECTIVE DATE OF 1978 AMENDMENT

Section 504(a) of Pub. L. 95–454 provided that amendment by Pub. L. 95–454 was effective on first day of first applicable pay period which began on or after Oct. 1, 1981, except it could take effect with respect to any category or categories of positions before such day to extent prescribed by Director of Office of Personnel Management.

§ 4507. Awarding of ranks in the Senior Executive Service

(a) For the purpose of this section, "agency", "senior executive", and "career appointee" have the meanings set forth in section 3132(a) of this title.

(b) Each agency shall submit annually to the Office recommendations of career appointees in the agency to be awarded the rank of Meritorious Executive or Distinguished Executive. The recommendations may take into account the individual's performance over a period of years. The Office shall review such recommendations and provide to the President recommendations as to which of the agency recommended appointees should receive such rank.

(c) During any fiscal year, the President may, subject to subsection (d) of this section, award to any career appointee recommended by the Office the rank of—

(1) Meritorious Executive, for sustained accomplishment, or

(2) Distinguished Executive, for sustained extraordinary accomplishment.

A career appointee awarded a rank under paragraph (1) or (2) of this subsection shall not be entitled to be awarded that rank during the following 4 fiscal years.

(d) During any fiscal year—

(1) the number of career appointees awarded the rank of Meritorious Executive may not exceed 5 percent of the Senior Executive Service; and

(2) the number of career appointees awarded the rank of Distinguished Executive may not exceed 1 percent of the Senior Executive Service.

(e)(1) Receipt by a career appointee of the rank of Meritorious Executive entitles such individual to a lump-sum payment of an amount equal to 20 percent of annual basic pay, which shall be in addition to the basic pay paid under section 5382 of this title or any award paid under section 5384 of this title.

(2) Receipt by a career appointee of the rank of Distinguished Executive entitles the individual to a lump-sum payment of an amount equal to 35 percent of annual basic pay, which shall be in addition to the basic pay paid under section 5382 of this title or any award paid under section 5384 of this title.

(Added Pub. L. 95–454, title IV, § 406(a), Oct. 13, 1978, 92 Stat. 1170; amended Pub. L. 105–277, div. A, § 101(h) [title VI, § 631(a), (b)], Oct. 21, 1998, 112 Stat. 2681–480, 2681–523.)

AMENDMENTS

1998—Subsec. (e)(1). Pub. L. 105–277, § 101(h) [title VI, § 631(a)], substituted "an amount equal to 20 percent of annual basic pay" for "$10,000".

Subsec. (e)(2). Pub. L. 105–277, § 101(h) [title VI, § 631(b)], substituted "an amount equal to 35 percent of annual basic pay" for "$20,000".

EFFECTIVE DATE OF 1998 AMENDMENT

Pub. L. 105–277, div. A, § 101(h) [title VI, § 631(c)], Oct. 21, 1998, 112 Stat. 2681–480, 2681–523, provided that: "The amendments made by this section [amending this section] shall take effect on October 1, 1998, or the date of enactment of this Act [Oct. 21, 1998], whichever is later."

EFFECTIVE DATE

Section effective 9 months after Oct. 13, 1978, and congressional review of provisions of sections 401 through 412 of Pub. L. 95–454, see section 415(a)(1), (b), of Pub. L. 95–454, set out as a note under section 3131 of this title.

SECTION REFERRED TO IN OTHER SECTIONS

This section is referred to in sections 3151, 5384 of this title; title 10 section 1606; title 22 section 3965; title 31 section 733; title 38 sections 7404, 7425.

§ 4508. Limitation of awards during a Presidential election year

(a) For purposes of this section, the term—

(1) "Presidential election period" means any period beginning on June 1 in a calendar year in which the popular election of the President occurs, and ending on January 20 following the date of such election; and

(2) "senior politically appointed officer" means any officer who during a Presidential election period serves—

(A) in a Senior Executive Service position and is not a career appointee as defined under section 3132(a)(4); or

(B) in a position of a confidential or policy-determining character under schedule C of subpart C of part 213 of title 5 of the Code of Federal Regulations.

(b) No senior politically appointed officer may receive an award under the provisions of this subchapter during a Presidential election period.

(Added Pub. L. 103–425, § 2(a), Oct. 31, 1994, 108 Stat. 4369.)

§ 4509. Prohibition of cash award to Executive Schedule officers

No officer may receive a cash award under the provisions of this subchapter, if such officer—

(1) serves in—

(A) an Executive Schedule position under subchapter II of chapter 53; or

(B) a position for which the compensation is set in statute by reference to a section or level under subchapter II of chapter 53; and

(2) was appointed to such position by the President, by and with the advice and consent of the Senate.

(Added Pub. L. 103–425, § 2(a), Oct. 31, 1994, 108 Stat. 4370.)

SUBCHAPTER II—AWARDS FOR COST SAVINGS DISCLOSURES

AMENDMENTS

1981—Pub. L. 97–35, title XVII, § 1703(a), Aug. 13, 1981, 95 Stat. 755, added subchapter II.

§ 4511. Definition and general provisions

(a) For purposes of this subchapter, the term "agency" means any Executive agency.

(b) A cash award under this subchapter is in addition to the regular pay of the recipient. Acceptance of a cash award under this subchapter constitutes an agreement that the use by the Government of an idea, method, or device for which the award is made does not form the basis of a further claim of any nature against the Government by the employee, his heirs, or assigns.

(Added Pub. L. 97–35, title XVII, § 1703(a), Aug. 13, 1981, 95 Stat. 755.)

EFFECTIVE DATE

Subchapter effective Oct. 1, 1981, see section 1703(c) of Pub. L. 97–35, set out as an Effective Date of 1981 Amendment note under section 4501 of this title.

AUTHORITY TO MAKE AWARDS

Pub. L. 102–487, § 1(c), Oct. 24, 1992, 106 Stat. 3134, provided that: "Awards may be made under subchapter II of chapter 45 of title 5, United States Code, on and after the date of the enactment of this Act [Oct. 24, 1992]."

§ 4512. Agency awards for cost savings disclosures

(a) The Inspector General of an agency, or any other agency employee designated under subsection (b), may pay a cash award to any employee of such agency whose disclosure of fraud, waste, or mismanagement to the Inspector General of the agency, or to such other designated agency employee, has resulted in cost savings for the agency. The amount of an award under this section may not exceed the lesser of—

(1) $10,000; or

(2) an amount equal to 1 percent of the agency's cost savings which the Inspector General, or other employee designated under subsection (b), determines to be the total savings attributable to the employee's disclosure.

For purposes of paragraph (2), the Inspector General or other designated employee may take into account agency cost savings projected for subsequent fiscal years which will be attributable to such disclosure.

(b) In the case of an agency for which there is no Inspector General, the head of the agency shall designate an agency employee who shall have the authority to make the determinations and grant the awards permitted under this section.

(Added Pub. L. 97–35, title XVII, § 1703(a), Aug. 13, 1981, 95 Stat. 755; amended Pub. L. 99–145, title XII, § 1225(b)(2), Nov. 8, 1985, 99 Stat. 730.)

AMENDMENTS

1985—Subsec. (c). Pub. L. 99–145 struck out subsec. (c) which provided that the Inspector General, or other employee designated under subsection (b), shall submit to the Comptroller General documentation substantiating any award made under this section and that the Comptroller General shall, from time to time, review awards made under this section and procedures used in making such awards to verify the cost savings for which the awards were made.

§ 4513. Presidential awards for cost savings disclosures

The President may pay a cash award in the amount of $20,000 to any employee whose disclosure of fraud, waste, or mismanagement has resulted in substantial cost savings for the Government. In evaluating the significance of a cost savings disclosure made by an employee for pur-

poses of determining whether to make an award to such employee under this section, the President may take into account cost savings projected for subsequent fiscal years which will be attributable to the disclosure. During any fiscal year, the President may not make more than 50 awards under this section.

(Added Pub. L. 97–35, title XVII, § 1703(a), Aug. 13, 1981, 95 Stat. 755.)

[§ 4514. Repealed. Pub. L. 102–487, § 1(a), Oct. 24, 1992, 106 Stat. 3134]

Section, added Pub. L. 97–35, title XVII, § 1703(a), Aug. 13, 1981, 95 Stat. 756; amended Pub. L. 99–145, title XII, § 1225(b)(1)(A), Nov. 8, 1985, 99 Stat. 730; Pub. L. 100–611, § 1(a), Nov. 5, 1988, 102 Stat. 3179, provided that no award could be made under this subchapter after Sept. 30, 1990.

SUBCHAPTER III—AWARD TO LAW ENFORCEMENT OFFICERS FOR FOREIGN LANGUAGE CAPABILITIES

AMENDMENTS

1992—Pub. L. 102–378, § 2(20), Oct. 2, 1992, 106 Stat. 1348, substituted "OFFICERS" for "OFFICER".

SUBCHAPTER REFERRED TO IN OTHER SECTIONS

This subchapter is referred to in title 19 section 267a.

§ 4521. Definition

For the purpose of this subchapter, the term "law enforcement officer" means—

(1) a law enforcement officer within the meaning of section 5541(3) and to whom the provisions of chapter 51 apply;

(2) a member of the United States Secret Service Uniformed Division;

(3) a member of the United States Park Police;

(4) a special agent in the Diplomatic Security Service;

(5) a probation officer (referred to in section 3672 of title 18); and

(6) a pretrial services officer (referred to in section 3153 of title 18).

(Added Pub. L. 101–509, title V, § 529 [title IV, § 408(a)], Nov. 5, 1990, 104 Stat. 1427, 1467; amended Pub. L. 102–141, title VI, § 627, Oct. 28, 1991, 105 Stat. 874; Pub. L. 102–378, § 2(21), Oct. 2, 1992, 106 Stat. 1348.)

AMENDMENTS

1992—Pub. L. 102–378 amended section generally, substituting in par. (1) "section 5541(3)" for "section 8331(20) or section 8401(17)".

1991—Pub. L. 102–141 amended section generally. Prior to amendment, section read as follows: "For the purpose of this subchapter, the term 'law enforcement officer' has the same meaning as under section 5949(a)."

EFFECTIVE DATE

Section 529 [title IV, § 408(d)] of Pub. L. 101–509 provided that: "The amendments made by this section [enacting this subchapter and amending provisions set out as a note under section 5541 of this title] shall be effective on January 1, 1992."

SECTION REFERRED TO IN OTHER SECTIONS

This section is referred to in title 19 section 267a.

§ 4522. General provision

An award under this subchapter is in addition to the basic pay of the recipient.

(Added Pub. L. 101–509, title V, §529 [title IV, §408(a)], Nov. 5, 1990, 104 Stat. 1427, 1467.)

§ 4523. Award authority

(a) An agency may pay a cash award, up to 5 percent of basic pay, to any law enforcement officer employed in or under such agency who possesses and makes substantial use of 1 or more foreign languages in the performance of official duties.

(b) Awards under this section shall be paid under regulations prescribed by the head of the agency involved (or designee thereof). Regulations prescribed by an agency head (or designee) under this subsecton[1] shall include—

(1) procedures under which foreign language proficiency shall be ascertained;

(2) criteria for the selection of individuals for recognition under this section; and

(3) any other provisions which may be necessary to carry out the purposes of this subchapter.

(Added Pub. L. 101–509, title V, §529 [title IV, §408(a)], Nov. 5, 1990, 104 Stat. 1427, 1467.)

CHAPTER 47—PERSONNEL RESEARCH PROGRAMS AND DEMONSTRATION PROJECTS

AMENDMENTS

1998—Pub. L. 105–362, title XIII, §1302(b)(2)(B)(ii), Nov. 10, 1998, 112 Stat. 3293, added item 4705 and struck out former items 4705 "Reports" and 4706 "Regulations".

CHAPTER REFERRED TO IN OTHER SECTIONS

This chapter is referred to in sections 1103, 9507 of this title.

§ 4701. Definitions

(a) For the purpose of this chapter—

(1) "agency" means an Executive agency and the Government Printing Office, but does not include—

(A) a Government corporation;

(B) the Federal Bureau of Investigation, the Central Intelligence Agency, the Defense Intelligence Agency, the National Imagery and Mapping Agency, the National Security Agency, and, as determined by the President, any Executive agency or unit thereof which is designated by the President and which has as its principal function the conduct of foreign intelligence or counterintelligence activities; or

(C) the General Accounting Office;

(2) "employee" means an individual employed in or under an agency;

(3) "eligible" means an individual who has qualified for appointment in an agency and whose name has been entered on the appropriate register or list of eligibles;

(4) "demonstration project" means a project conducted by the Office of Personnel Manage-

ment, or under its supervision, to determine whether a specified change in personnel management policies or procedures would result in improved Federal personnel management; and

(5) "research program" means a planned study of the manner in which public management policies and systems are operating, the effects of those policies and systems, the possibilities for change, and comparisons among policies and systems.

(b) This chapter shall not apply to any position in the Drug Enforcement Administration which is excluded from the competitive service under section 201 of the Crime Control Act of 1976 (28 U.S.C. 509 note; 90 Stat. 2425).

(Added Pub. L. 95–454, title VI, §601(a), Oct. 13, 1978, 92 Stat. 1185; amended Pub. L. 96–54, §2(a)(21), Aug. 14, 1979, 93 Stat. 382; Pub. L. 101–474, §5(g), Oct. 30, 1990, 104 Stat. 1100; Pub. L. 103–359, title V, §501(f), Oct. 14, 1994, 108 Stat. 3429; Pub. L. 104–201, div. A, title XI, §1122(a)(1), Sept. 23, 1996, 110 Stat. 2687.)

AMENDMENTS

1996—Subsec. (a)(1)(B). Pub. L. 104–201 substituted "National Imagery and Mapping Agency" for "Central Imagery Office".

1994—Subsec. (a)(1)(B). Pub. L. 103–359 inserted "the Central Imagery Office," after "Defense Intelligence Agency,".

1990—Subsec. (a)(1). Pub. L. 101–474 struck out ", the Administrative Office of the United States Courts," after "means an Executive agency".

1979—Subsec. (b). Pub. L. 96–54 substituted "chapter" for "subchapter" and "28 U.S.C. 509" for "5 U.S.C. 5108".

EFFECTIVE DATE OF 1996 AMENDMENT

Amendment by Pub. L. 104–201 effective Oct. 1, 1996, see section 1124 of Pub. L. 104–201, set out as a note under section 193 of Title 10, Armed Forces.

EFFECTIVE DATE OF 1979 AMENDMENT

Amendment by Pub. L. 96–54 effective July 12, 1979, see section 2(b) of Pub. L. 96–54, set out as a note under section 305 of this title.

EFFECTIVE DATE

Chapter effective 90 days after Oct. 13, 1978, see section 907 of Pub. L. 95–454, set out as an Effective Date of 1978 Amendment note under section 1101 of this title.

SECTION REFERRED TO IN OTHER SECTIONS

This section is referred to in section 9507 of this title.

§ 4702. Research programs

The Office of Personnel Management shall—

(1) establish and maintain (and assist in the establishment and maintenance of) research programs to study improved methods and technologies in Federal personnel management;

(2) evaluate the research programs established under paragraph (1) of this section;

(3) establish and maintain a program for the collection and public dissemination of information relating to personnel management research and for encouraging and facilitating the exchange of information among interested persons and entities; and

(4) carry out the preceding functions directly or through agreement or contract.

---

[1] So in original. Probably should be "subsection".

(Added Pub. L. 95–454, title VI, § 601(a), Oct. 13, 1978, 92 Stat. 1185.)

§ 4703. Demonstration projects

(a) Except as provided in this section, the Office of Personnel Management may, directly or through agreement or contract with one or more agencies and other public and private organizations, conduct and evaluate demonstration projects. Subject to the provisions of this section, the conducting of demonstration projects shall not be limited by any lack of specific authority under this title to take the action contemplated, or by any provision of this title or any rule or regulation prescribed under this title which is inconsistent with the action, including any law or regulation relating to—

(1) the methods of establishing qualification requirements for, recruitment for, and appointment to positions;

(2) the methods of classifying positions and compensating employees;

(3) the methods of assigning, reassigning, or promoting employees;

(4) the methods of disciplining employees;

(5) the methods of providing incentives to employees, including the provision of group or individual incentive bonuses or pay;

(6) the hours of work per day or per week;

(7) the methods of involving employees, labor organizations, and employee organizations in personnel decisions; and

(8) the methods of reducing overall agency staff and grade levels.

(b) Before conducting or entering into any agreement or contract to conduct a demonstration project, the Office shall—

(1) develop a plan for such project which identifies—

(A) the purposes of the project;

(B) the types of employees or eligibles, categorized by occupational series, grade, or organizational unit;

(C) the number of employees or eligibles to be included, in the aggregate and by category;

(D) the methodology;

(E) the duration;

(F) the training to be provided;

(G) the anticipated costs;

(H) the methodology and criteria for evaluation;

(I) a specific description of any aspect of the project for which there is a lack of specific authority; and

(J) a specific citation to any provision of law, rule, or regulation which, if not waived under this section, would prohibit the conducting of the project, or any part of the project as proposed;

(2) publish the plan in the Federal Register;

(3) submit the plan so published to public hearing;

(4) provide notification of the proposed project, at least 180 days in advance of the date any project proposed under this section is to take effect—

(A) to employees who are likely to be affected by the project; and

(B) to each House of the Congress;

(5) obtain approval from each agency involved of the final version of the plan; and

(6) provide each House of the Congress with a report at least 90 days in advance of the date the project is to take effect setting forth the final version of the plan as so approved.

(c) No demonstration project under this section may provide for a waiver of—

(1) any provision of chapter 63 or subpart G of this title;

(2)(A) any provision of law referred to in section 2302(b)(1) of this title; or

(B) any provision of law implementing any provision of law referred to in section 2302(b)(1) of this title by—

(i) providing for equal employment opportunity through affirmative action; or

(ii) providing any right or remedy available to any employee or applicant for employment in the civil service;

(3) any provision of chapter 15 or subchapter III of chapter 73 of this title;

(4) any rule or regulation prescribed under any provision of law referred to in paragraph (1), (2), or (3) of this subsection; or

(5) any provision of chapter 23 of this title, or any rule or regulation prescribed under this title, if such waiver is inconsistent with any merit system principle or any provision thereof relating to prohibited personnel practices.

(d)(1) Each demonstration project shall—

(A) involve not more than 5,000 individuals other than individuals in any control groups necessary to validate the results of the project; and

(B) terminate before the end of the 5-year period beginning on the date on which the project takes effect, except that the project may continue beyond the date to the extent necessary to validate the results of the project.

(2) Not more than 10 active demonstration projects may be in effect at any time.

(e) Subject to the terms of any written agreement or contract between the Office and an agency, a demonstration project involving the agency may be terminated by the Office, or the agency, if either determines that the project creates a substantial hardship on, or is not in the best interests of, the public, the Federal Government, employees, or eligibles.

(f) Employees within a unit with respect to which a labor organization is accorded exclusive recognition under chapter 71 of this title shall not be included within any project under subsection (a) of this section—

(1) if the project would violate a collective bargaining agreement (as defined in section 7103(8) of this title) between the agency and the labor organization, unless there is another written agreement with respect to the project between the agency and the organization permitting the inclusion; or

(2) if the project is not covered by such a collective bargaining agreement, until there has been consultation or negotiation, as appropriate, by the agency with the labor organization.

(g) Employees within any unit with respect to which a labor organization has not been accorded exclusive recognition under chapter 71 of this title shall not be included within any project under subsection (a) of this section unless there has been agency consultation regarding the project with the employees in the unit.

(h) The Office shall provide for an evaluation of the results of each demonstration project and its impact on improving public management.

(i) Upon request of the Director of the Office of Personnel Management, agencies shall cooperate with and assist the Office, to the extent practicable, in any evaluation undertaken under subsection (h) of this section and provide the Office with requested information and reports relating to the conducting of demonstration projects in their respective agencies.

(Added Pub. L. 95–454, title VI, § 601(a), Oct. 13, 1978, 92 Stat. 1186.)

AUTHORITY OF EXPORT-IMPORT BANK TO CONDUCT DEMONSTRATION PROGRAM

Pub. L. 104–97, § 2, Jan. 11, 1996, 109 Stat. 984, provided that: "Notwithstanding section 4701(a)(1)(A) of title 5, United States Code, the Export-Import Bank of the United States may conduct a demonstration project in accordance with section 4703 of such title."

SECTION REFERRED TO IN OTHER SECTIONS

This section is referred to in sections 5392, 9507 of this title.

§ 4704. Allocation of funds

Funds appropriated to the Office of Personnel Management for the purpose of this chapter may be allocated by the Office to any agency conducting demonstration projects or assisting the Office in conducting such projects. Funds so allocated shall remain available for such period as may be specified in appropriation Acts. No contract shall be entered into under this chapter unless the contract has been provided for in advance in appropriation Acts.

(Added Pub. L. 95–454, title VI, § 601(a), Oct. 13, 1978, 92 Stat. 1188.)

§ 4705. Regulations

The Office of Personnel Management shall prescribe regulations to carry out the purpose of this chapter.

(Added Pub. L. 95–454, title VI, § 601(a), Oct. 13, 1978, 92 Stat. 1188, § 4706; renumbered § 4705, Pub. L. 105–362, title XIII, § 1302(b)(2)(B)(i), Nov. 10, 1998, 112 Stat. 3293.)

PRIOR PROVISIONS

A prior section 4705, added Pub. L. 95–454, title VI, § 601(a), Oct. 13, 1978, 92 Stat. 1188, required annual report on research programs and demonstration projects, prior to repeal by Pub. L. 105–362, title XIII, § 1302(b)(2)(B)(i), Nov. 10, 1998, 112 Stat. 3293.

[§ 4706. Renumbered § 4705]

Subpart D—Pay and Allowances

SUBPART REFERRED TO IN OTHER SECTIONS

This subpart is referred to in section 1103 of this title; title 10 section 1602.

CHAPTER 51—CLASSIFICATION

AMENDMENTS

1992—Pub. L. 102–378, § 2(22), Oct. 2, 1992, 106 Stat. 1348, substituted "above GS–15" for "at GS–16, 17, and 18" in item 5108.

1986—Pub. L. 99–386, title I, § 110(b), Aug. 22, 1986, 100 Stat. 822, struck out item 5114 "Reports; positions in GS–16, 17, and 18".

1978—Pub. L. 95–454, title IX, § 906(a)(17), Oct. 13, 1978, 92 Stat. 1226, substituted "Office of Personnel Management" for "Civil Service Commission" in item 5112.

CHAPTER REFERRED TO IN OTHER SECTIONS

This chapter is referred to in sections 3101, 3102, 3109, 3161, 3374, 4521, 5307, 5331, 5334, 5342, 5348, 5361, 5363, 5371, 5377, 5380, 5392, 5541, 5544, 5545, 7204, 9503, 9509 of this title; title 2 sections 60e–2, 60e–2a, 60e–2b, 60e–6, 162a, 166, 197, 293, 353, 356, 437c; title 4 section 142; title 7 sections 511m, 610, 1507, 1642, 1765a, 6981, 7317; title 10 sections 2903, 4540, 7212, 9540; title 12 sections 482, 1441a, 1462a, 1701c, 1766, 2245, 2405, 3012, 4515, 4703; title 13 section 23; title 14 section 432; title 15 sections 78d, 78s, 205i, 278, 278a, 327, 634d, 648, 714g, 714h, 715h, 717q, 1023, 2053, 2451; title 16 sections 81c, 410cc–36, 410pp–4, 410ww–24, 410ccc–22, 450jj–1, 450ss–3, 460m, 469j, 470m, 583j–1, 590d, 793, 825i, 832i, 833h, 916*l*, 3702, 4604; title 18 section 4001; title 20 sections 74, 75f, 76dd, 80g, 80g–4, 80*o*, 1018, 1067j, 1089, 1098, 1102, 1137, 1138b, 1145, 1221e, 1417, 2106, 3413, 3425, 4416, 5509, 5826, 5933, 6011, 9011, 9105, 9252; title 21 sections 393, 394, 1908; title 22 sections 272a, 277d–3, 277d–19, 280b, 280i, 280k, 287e, 287r, 289b, 290b, 2024, 2083, 2124c, 2421, 2454, 2581, 3008, 3981, 4154, 4606, 6204, 6432b; title 25 sections 2a, 305a, 633, 640d–11, 2012, 2707; title 26 sections 7471, 9010, 9040; title 28 sections 625, 626; title 29 sections 172, 661, 676, 762, 783, 1147; title 30 sections 556, 664, 823; title 31 section 3801; title 33 sections 569a, 939, 940, 984, 1325, 1374; title 35 sections 3, 7; title 36 sections 510, 2303, 151304, 151307, 151704, 151707, 152404, 152407; title 38 sections 4103, 7281, 7802; title 40 sections 13b, 166b–1f, 166b–3, 174j–8, 609, 873, 1106; title 41 sections 38, 46, 104, 422; title 42 sections 204, 217a, 237, 282, 290aa, 299c–1, 300v–2, 907a, 1320a–4, 1320b–9, 1563, 1731, 1855f, 1863, 1873, 1962a–4, 2000e–4, 2000g, 2201, 2473, 4276, 4365, 4372, 5149, 5667g–2, 6063, 7231, 7383, 10266, 12373, 12619, 12651f, 14196; title 43 sections 316n, 1731; title 44 section 2503; title 45 sections 154, 362; title 46 App. sections 1111, 1295e, 1295g; title 47 section 154; title 49 section 32306; title 50 sections 402, 404; title 50 App. sections 460, 1989b–5, 2001, 2153.

§ 5101. Purpose

It is the purpose of this chapter to provide a plan for classification of positions whereby—

(1) in determining the rate of basic pay which an employee will receive—

(A) the principle of equal pay for substantially equal work will be followed; and

(B) variations in rates of basic pay paid to different employees will be in proportion to substantial differences in the difficulty, responsibility, and qualification requirements of the work performed and to the contributions of employees to efficiency and economy in the service; and

(2) individual positions will, in accordance with their duties, responsibilities, and qualification requirements, be so grouped and identified by classes and grades, as defined by section 5102 of this title, and the various classes will be so described in published standards, as provided by section 5105 of this title, that the resulting position-classification system can be used in all phases of personnel administration.

(Pub. L. 89–554, Sept. 6, 1966, 80 Stat. 443.)

HISTORICAL AND REVISION NOTES

Derivation	U.S. Code	Revised Statutes and Statutes at Large
....	5 U.S.C. 1071.	Oct. 28, 1949, ch. 782, § 101, 63 Stat. 954.

The words "and for rates of basic compensation" are omitted as inapplicable to this chapter since the provisions of former chapter 21 relating to rates of basic compensation are carried into subchapter III of chapter 53. The word "officer" is omitted as included in "employee" is defined in section 5102.

Standard changes are made to conform with the definitions applicable and the style of this title as outlined in the preface of the report.

REFERENCES IN OTHER LAWS TO CHAPTER 51 AND SUBCHAPTER III OF CHAPTER 53

References in laws to fix pay in accordance with this chapter and subchapter III of chapter 53 of this title considered to include authority under section 5376 of this title, if applicable, but not to include any authority under section 5304 of this title or section 529 [title III, § 302] of Pub. L. 101–509, set out as a note under section 5304 of this title, see section 529 [title I, § 101(c)(2)] of Pub. L. 101–509, set out in a References in Other Laws to GS–16, 17, or 18 Pay Rates; Regulations note under section 5376 of this title.

§ 5102. Definitions; application

(a) For the purpose of this chapter—
  (1) "agency" means—
    (A) an Executive agency;
    (B) the Library of Congress;
    (C) the Botanic Garden;
    (D) the Government Printing Office;
    (E) the Office of the Architect of the Capitol; and
    (F) the government of the District of Columbia;

but does not include—
    (i) a Government controlled corporation;
    (ii) the Tennessee Valley Authority;
    (iii) the Virgin Islands Corporation;
    (iv) the Atomic Energy Commission;
    (v) the Central Intelligence Agency;
    (vi) the National Security Agency, Department of Defense;
    (vii) the General Accounting Office; or [1]
    (ix) [2] the Defense Intelligence Agency, Department of Defense; or
    (x) the National Imagery and Mapping Agency, Department of Defense. [3]

(2) "employee" means an individual employed in or under an agency;

(3) "position" means the work, consisting of the duties and responsibilities, assignable to an employee;

(4) "class" or "class of positions" includes all positions which are sufficiently similar, as to—
    (A) kind or subject-matter of work;
    (B) level of difficulty and responsibility; and
    (C) the qualification requirements of the work;

to warrant similar treatment in personnel and pay administration; and

(5) "grade" includes all classes of positions which, although different with respect to kind or subject-matter of work, are sufficiently equivalent as to—
    (A) level of difficulty and responsibility; and
    (B) level of qualification requirements of the work;

to warrant their inclusion within one range of rates of basic pay in the General Schedule.

(b) Except as provided by subsections (c) and (d) of this section, this chapter applies to all civilian positions and employees in or under an agency, including positions in local boards and appeal boards within the Selective Service System and employees occupying those positions.

(c) This chapter does not apply to—
  [(1) Repealed. Pub. L. 91–375, § 6(c)(9), Aug. 12, 1970, 84 Stat. 776;]

(2) members of the Foreign Service whose pay is fixed under the Foreign Service Act of 1980; and positions in or under the Department of State which are—
    (A) connected with the representation of the United States to international organizations; or
    (B) specifically exempted by statute from this chapter or other classification or pay statute;

(3) physicians, dentists, nurses, and other employees in the Veterans Health Administration of the Department of Veterans Affairs whose pay is fixed under chapter 73 of title 38;

(4) teachers, school officials, and employees of the Board of Education of the District of Columbia whose pay is fixed under chapter 15 of title 31, District of Columbia Code; the chief judges and the associate judges of the Superior Court of the District of Columbia and the District of Columbia Court of Appeals; and nonjudicial employees of the District of Columbia court system whose pay is fixed under title 11 of the District of Columbia Code;

(5) members of the Metropolitan Police, the Fire Department of the District of Columbia, the United States Park Police, and the Executive Protective Service; members of the police force of the National Zoological Park whose pay is fixed under section 5375 of this title; and members of the police forces of the Bureau of Engraving and Printing and the United States Mint whose pay is fixed under section 5378 of this title;

(6) lighthouse keepers and civilian employees on lightships and vessels of the Coast Guard whose pay is fixed under section 432(f) and (g) of title 14;

---

[1] So in original. The word "or" probably should not appear.
[2] So in original. Subsec. (a)(1) does not contain a cl. (viii).
[3] So in original. The period probably should be a semicolon.

(7) employees in recognized trades or crafts, or other skilled mechanical crafts, or in unskilled, semiskilled, or skilled manual-labor occupations, and other employees including foremen and supervisors in positions having trade, craft, or laboring experience and knowledge as the paramount requirement, and employees in the Bureau of Engraving and Printing whose duties are to perform or to direct manual or machine operations requiring special skill or experience, or to perform or direct the counting, examining, sorting, or other verification of the product of manual or machine operations;

(8) officers and members of crews of vessels;

(9) employees of the Government Printing Office whose pay is fixed under section 305 of title 44;

(10) civilian professors, instructors, and lecturers at a professional military education school (and, in the case of the George C. Marshall European Center for Security Studies, the Director and the Deputy Director) whose pay is fixed under section 1595, 4021, 7478, or 9021 of title 10; civilian professors, lecturers, and instructors at the Military Academy, the Naval Academy, and the Air Force Academy whose pay is fixed under sections 4338, 6952, and 9338, respectively, of title 10; senior professors, professors, associate and assistant professors, and instructors at the Naval Postgraduate School whose pay is fixed under section 7044 of title 10; the Academic Dean of the Postgraduate School of the Naval Academy whose pay is fixed under section 7043 of title 10; civilian professors, instructors, and lecturers in the defense acquisition university structure (including the Defense Systems Management College) whose pay is fixed under section 1746(b) of title 10;

(11) aliens or noncitizens of the United States who occupy positions outside the United States;

[(12) Repealed. Pub. L. 104–201, div. C, title XXXV, §3548(a)(2)(B), Sept. 23, 1996, 110 Stat. 3868;]

(13) employees who serve without pay or at nominal rates of pay;

(14) employees whose pay is not wholly from appropriated funds of the United States (other than employees of the Federal Retirement Thrift Investment Management System appointed under section 8474(c)(2) of this title), except that with respect to the Veterans' Canteen Service, Department of Veterans Affairs this paragraph applies only to employees necessary for the transaction of the business of the Service at canteens, warehouses, and storage depots whose employment is authorized by section 7802 of title 38;

(15) employees whose pay is fixed under a cooperative agreement between the United States and—

(A) a State or territory or possession of the United States, or political subdivision thereof; or

(B) an individual or organization outside the service of the Government of the United States;

(16) student nurses, medical or dental interns, residents-in-training, student dietitians, student physical therapists, student occupational therapists, and other student employees, assigned or attached to a hospital, clinic, or laboratory primarily for training purposes, whose pay is fixed under subchapter V of chapter 53 of this title or sections 7405 and 7406 of title 38;

(17) inmates, patients, or beneficiaries receiving care or treatment or living in Government agencies or institutions;

(18) experts or consultants, when employed temporarily or intermittently in accordance with section 3109 of this title;

(19) emergency or seasonal employees whose employment is of uncertain or purely temporary duration, or who are employed for brief periods at intervals;

(20) employees employed on a fee, contract, or piece work basis;

(21) employees who may lawfully perform their duties concurrently with their private profession, business, or other employment, and whose duties require only a portion of their time, when it is impracticable to ascertain or anticipate the proportion of time devoted to the service of the Government of the United States;

(22) "teachers" and "teaching positions" as defined by section 901 of title 20;

(23) administrative patent judges and designated administrative patent judges in the United States Patent and Trademark Office;

(24) temporary positions in the Bureau of the Census established under section 23 of title 13, and enumerator positions in the Bureau of the Census;

(25) positions for which rates of basic pay are individually fixed, or expressly authorized to be fixed, by other statute, at or in excess of the rate for level V of the Executive Schedule;

(26) civilian members of the faculty of the Coast Guard Academy whose pay is fixed under section 186 of title 14;

(27) members of the police of the Library of Congress whose pay is fixed under section 167 of title 2;

(28) civilian members of the faculty of the Air Force Institute of Technology whose pay is fixed under section 9314 of title 10;

(29) administrative law judges appointed under section 3105; or

(30) members of agency boards of contract appeals appointed under section 8 of the Contract Disputes Act of 1978.

(d) This chapter does not apply to an employee of the Office of the Architect of the Capitol whose pay is fixed by other statute. Subsection (c) of this section, except paragraph (7), does not apply to the Office of the Architect of the Capitol.

(Pub. L. 89–554, Sept. 6, 1966, 80 Stat. 444; Pub. L. 90–83, §1(11), Sept. 11, 1967, 81 Stat. 197; Pub. L. 90–610, §2, Oct. 21, 1968, 82 Stat. 1201; Pub. L. 91–34, §2(a), June 30, 1969, 83 Stat. 41; Pub. L. 91–358, title I, §172(f), July 29, 1970, 84 Stat. 591; Pub. L. 91–375, §6(c)(9), Aug. 12, 1970, 84 Stat. 776; Pub. L. 93–176, §1, Dec. 5, 1973, 87 Stat. 693; Pub. L. 94–183, §2(12), (13), Dec. 31, 1975, 89 Stat. 1057; Pub. L. 95–454, title VIII, §801(a)(3)(D), title IX, §906(a)(2), Oct. 13, 1978, 92 Stat. 1221, 1224; Pub. L.

96–54, §2(a)(22), Aug. 14, 1979, 93 Stat. 382; Pub. L. 96–70, title III, §3302(e)(1), (6), Sept. 27, 1979, 93 Stat. 498; Pub. L. 96–191, §8(b), Feb. 15, 1980, 94 Stat. 33; Pub. L. 96–465, title II, §2314(b), Oct. 17, 1980, 94 Stat. 2167; Pub. L. 97–468, title VI, §615(b)(1)(C), Jan. 14, 1983, 96 Stat. 2578; Pub. L. 98–618, title V, §502(a), Nov. 8, 1984, 98 Stat. 3302; Pub. L. 99–145, title V, §504(b), Nov. 8, 1985, 99 Stat. 622; Pub. L. 99–335, title II, §207(n), June 6, 1986, 100 Stat. 598; Pub. L. 100–135, §1(b)(2), Oct. 16, 1987, 101 Stat. 811; Pub. L. 101–189, div. A, title XI, §1124(e), Nov. 29, 1989, 103 Stat. 1560; Pub. L. 101–474, §5(h), Oct. 30, 1990, 104 Stat. 1100; Pub. L. 101–509, title V, §529 [title I, §§101(b)(9)(F), 104(d)(1), 109(a)(2)], Nov. 5, 1990, 104 Stat. 1427, 1441, 1447, 1451; Pub. L. 101–510, div. A, title XII, §1209(h)(2), Nov. 5, 1990, 104 Stat. 1667; Pub. L. 102–40, title IV, §403(c)(1), May 7, 1991, 105 Stat. 240; Pub. L. 102–54, §13(b)(1), (2), June 13, 1991, 105 Stat. 274; Pub. L. 103–160, div. A, title V, §533(c), title IX, §923(b), Nov. 30, 1993, 107 Stat. 1658, 1731; Pub. L. 103–359, title V, §501(g), Oct. 14, 1994, 108 Stat. 3429; Pub. L. 103–446, title XII, §1203(b), Nov. 2, 1994, 108 Stat. 4689; Pub. L. 104–201, div. A, title XI, §1122(a)(1), div. C, title XXXV, §3548(a)(2), Sept. 23, 1996, 110 Stat. 2687, 2868; Pub. L. 106–113, div. B, §1000(a)(9) [title IV, §4732(b)(3)], Nov. 29, 1999, 113 Stat. 1536, 1501A–583.)

HISTORICAL AND REVISION NOTES
1966 ACT

Derivation	U.S. Code	Revised Statutes and Statutes at Large
(a)(1)	5 U.S.C. 1081(a).	Oct. 28, 1949, ch. 782, §201(a), 63 Stat. 954.
	5 U.S.C. 1082(12)–(20), (32).	Oct. 28, 1949, ch. 782, §202 (12)–(20), 63 Stat. 954. May 29, 1959, Pub. L. 86–36, §1, 73 Stat. 63. Sept. 23, 1959, Pub. L. 86–370, §6(a) (less (4)), 73 Stat. 652.
(a)(3)–(5)	5 U.S.C. 1091.	Oct. 28, 1949, ch. 782, §301, 63 Stat. 957.
(b)	5 U.S.C. 1081(b).	Oct. 28, 1949, ch. 782, §201(b), 63 Stat. 954.
(c)	5 U.S.C. 1082(1)–(6), (7) (less provisos), (8) (less last 31 words), (9)–(11), (21)–(31), (33)–(35).	Oct. 28, 1949, ch. 782, §202 (1)–(6), (7) (less last 25 words), (8) (less last 31 words), (9)–(11), (21)–(31), 63 Stat. 954. Sept. 1, 1954, ch. 1208, §105(a) "(7) (less provisos)", 68 Stat. 1106. June 17, 1957, Pub. L. 85–56, §2201(20), 71 Stat. 159. July 25, 1958, Pub. L. 85–550, §16(a), (b)(1), 72 Stat. 411. Sept. 2, 1958, Pub. L. 85–857, §13(o), 72 Stat. 1266. July 17, 1959, Pub. L. 86–91, §3, 73 Stat. 213. Sept. 23, 1959, Pub. L. 86–370, §6(a)(4), 73 Stat. 652. Sept. 13, 1960, Pub. L. 86–769, §4, 74 Stat. 912.
(d)	5 U.S.C. 1084(b).	Oct. 28, 1949, ch. 782, §204(b), 63 Stat. 957.

The section is reorganized and restated for clarity.

In subsection (a)(1)(i), the exception of "a Government controlled corporation" is added to preserve the application of this chapter to "corporations wholly owned by the United States". This is necessary as the defined term "Executive agency" includes the defined term "Government corporation" and the latter includes both Government owned and controlled corporations. Thus the exclusion of Government controlled corporations, which are distinct from wholly owned corporations, operates to preserve the application of the chapter to wholly owned corporations.

In subsection (a)(1)(vii), the words "Panama Canal Company" are substituted for "Panama Railroad Company" on authority of the Act of Sept. 26, 1950, ch. 1049, §2(a)(2), 64 Stat. 1038.

The exception for the Inland Waterways Corporation in former section 1082(13) is omitted on authority of the Act of July 19, 1963, Pub. L. 88–67, 77 Stat. 81.

The exceptions for Production Credit Corporations and Federal Intermediate Credit Banks in former section 1082(18) and (19) are omitted as they are no longer "corporations wholly owned by the United States". Under the Farm Credit Act of 1956, 70 Stat. 659, the Production Credit Corporations were merged in the Federal Intermediate Credit Banks, and pursuant to that Act the Federal Intermediate Credit Banks have ceased to be corporations wholly owned by the United States.

Subsection (a)(2) is added for clarity. The reference to "an individual employed in or under an agency" includes both officers and employees of an agency.

In subsection (a)(5), the words "in the General Schedule" are substituted for the reference in former section 1091(3) to "as specified in subchapter V of this chapter".

In subsection (b), the reference to former section 1085 is omitted as unnecessary. Former section 1085 which exempted certain agencies from former sections 1151–1153 is carried into section 305.

In subsection (c)(1), the words "chapter 45 of title 39" are substituted for the reference in former section 1082(1) to "chapter 23 of title 39" on authority of the Act of July 10, 1955, ch. 137, §805, 69 Stat. 130, and the Act of Sept. 2, 1960, Pub. L. 86–682, §5, 74 Stat. 705.

In subsection (c)(2)(B), the words "this chapter" are substituted for the reference in former section 1082(2)(B) to "the Classification Act of 1923, as amended," on authority of section 1106 of the Act of Oct. 28, 1949, 63 Stat. 972, and technical section 7(b).

In subsection (c)(4), the words "chapter 15 of title 31, District of Columbia Code" are substituted for the reference in former section 1082(4) to "the District of Columbia Teachers Salary Act of 1947, as supplemented by Public Law 151, Eighty-first Congress, approved June 30, 1949" on authority of the provisions contained therein. The words "District of Columbia Court of General Sessions" and "District of Columbia Court of Appeals" are substituted for "Municipal Court for the District of Columbia" and "Municipal Court of Appeals for the District of Columbia", respectively, on authority of D.C. Code §§11–902 and 11–702. The exception for judges of the Juvenile Court of the District of Columbia is based on D.C. Code §11–1502.

In subsection (c)(5), the word "officers" is omitted as included in "member".

In subsection (c)(10), the words "sections 6952 and 7478 of title 10", "section 7044 of title 10", and "section 7043 of title 10" are substituted for the references in former section 1082(10) to "section 1071 of title 34", "sections 1076–1076f of title 34", and "section 1074 of title 34", respectively, on authority of the Act of Aug. 10, 1956, ch. 1041, §49(b), 70A Stat. 640.

In subsection (c)(11), the words "the United States" are substituted for "the several States and the District of Columbia".

In subsection (c)(14), the words "employees necessary for the transaction of the business of the Service at canteens, warehouses, and storage depots whose employment is authorized by section 4202 of title 38" are substituted for the reference in former section 1082(23) to "positions which are exempt from this chapter, pursuant to section 4202 of title 38".

In subsection (c)(16), the reference to "section 4114 of title 38" is substituted for the reference in former section 1082(25) to "section 4114(b) of title 38" to reflect the pay fixing authority contained in subsection (a)(1) of section 4114.

In subsection (c)(22), the words "as defined by section 901 of title 20" are substituted for "as defined in the Defense Department Overseas Teachers Pay and Personnel Practices Act" on authority of former section 2351, which is scheduled for transfer to section 901 of title 20.

In subsection (c)(25), the word "schedule" is omitted since section 603 of the Act of Oct. 11, 1962, Pub. L. 87–793, 76 Stat. 847, eliminated the necessity of referring to rates as scheduled or longevity. The words "for GS–18" are substituted for "of the highest grade established by this chapter".

The second sentence of subsection (d) is based on former section 1084(c), which is carried into section 5103.

Standard changes are made to conform with the definitions applicable and the style of this title as outlined in the preface to the report.

1967 ACT

Section of title 5	Source (U.S. Code)	Source (Statutes at Large)
5102(c)(26) ..	5 App.: 1082(36).	June 9, 1966, Pub. L. 89–444, §4, 80 Stat. 198.

The amendment to 5 U.S.C. 5102(c)(15) is made to correct a typographical error.

The amendment to 5 U.S.C. 5102(c)(26) reflects Public Law 89–444, section 4.

REFERENCES IN TEXT

The Foreign Service Act of 1980, referred to in subsec. (c)(2), is Pub. L. 96–465, Oct. 17, 1980, 94 Stat. 2071, as amended, which is classified principally to chapter 52 (§ 3901 et seq.) of Title 22, Foreign Relations and Intercourse. For complete classification of this Act to the Code, see Short Title note set out under section 3901 of Title 22 and Tables.

Level V of the Executive Schedule, referred to in subsec. (c)(25), is set out in section 5316 of this title.

Section 8 of the Contract Disputes Act of 1978, referred to in subsec. (c)(30), is classified to section 607 of Title 41, Public Contracts.

AMENDMENTS

1999—Subsec. (c)(23). Pub. L. 106–113 amended par. (23) generally. Prior to amendment, par. (23) read as follows: "examiners-in-chief and designated examiners-in-chief in the Patent and Trademark Office, Department of Commerce;".

1996—Subsec. (a)(1)(vi), (vii). Pub. L. 104–201, § 3548(a)(2)(A), redesignated cls. (vii) and (viii) as (vi) and (vii), respectively, and struck out former cl. (vi) which read as follows: "the Panama Canal Commission;".

Subsec. (a)(1)(viii). Pub. L. 104–201, § 3548(a)(2)(A)(ii), which directed redesignation of cl. (ix) as (viii) could not be executed because subsec. (a)(1) did not contain a cl. (ix). See 1983 Amendment note below. Former cl. (viii) redesignated (vii).

Subsec. (a)(1)(ix), (x). Pub. L. 104–201, § 3548(a)(2)(A)(ii), redesignated cls. (x) and (xi) as (ix) and (x), respectively.

Subsec. (a)(1)(xi). Pub. L. 104–201, § 3548(a)(2)(A)(ii), redesignated cl. (xi) as (x).

Pub. L. 104–201, § 1122(a)(1), substituted "National Imagery and Mapping Agency" for "Central Imagery Office".

Subsec. (c)(12). Pub. L. 104–201, § 3548(a)(2)(B), struck out par. (12) which read as follows: "any Executive agency to the extent of any election under section 1212(b)(2) (relating to the Panama Canal Employment System) of the Panama Canal Act of 1979;".

1994—Subsec. (a)(1)(ix) to (xi). Pub. L. 103–359 directed the amendment of cl. (ix) by striking "or" at end which could not be executed because par. (1) does not contain a cl. (ix), directed the substitution of "; or" for period at end of cl. (x) which was executed by inserting "or" at end of cl. (x) to reflect the probable intent of Congress because a semicolon already exists at end of cl. (x), and added cl. (xi).

Subsec. (c)(3). Pub. L. 103–446 struck out comma after "Department of Veterans Affairs".

1993—Subsec. (c)(10). Pub. L. 103–160, § 923(b), inserted "(and, in the case of the George C. Marshall European Center for Security Studies, the Director and the Deputy Director)" after "professional military education school".

Pub. L. 103–160, § 533(c), substituted "at the Military Academy, the Naval Academy, and the Air Force Academy whose pay is fixed under sections 4338, 6952, and 9338, respectively, of title 10" for "at the Naval Academy whose pay is fixed under section 6952 of title 10".

1991—Subsec. (c)(3). Pub. L. 102–54, § 13(b)(2), substituted "Veterans Health Administration of the Department of Veterans Affairs" for "Department of Medicine and Surgery, Veterans' Administration".

Subsec. (c)(14). Pub. L. 102–54, § 13(b)(1), substituted "Department of Veterans Affairs" for "Veterans' Administration".

Pub. L. 102–40, § 403(c)(1)(A), substituted "section 7802 of title 38" for "section 4202 of title 38".

Subsec. (c)(16). Pub. L. 102–40, § 403(c)(1)(B), substituted "sections 7405 and 7406" for "section 4114".

1990—Subsec. (a)(1). Pub. L. 101–474 redesignated subpars. (C) to (G) as (B) to (F), respectively, and struck out former subpar. (B) which included Administrative Office of United States Courts within definition of "agency".

Subsec. (c)(5). Pub. L. 101–509, § 529 [title I, § 109(a)(2)], substituted "members" for "and members" after "Protective Service;" and inserted at end "and members of the police forces of the Bureau of Engraving and Printing and the United States Mint whose pay is fixed under section 5378 of this title;".

Subsec. (c)(10). Pub. L. 101–510 struck out "and" before "the Academic Dean" and inserted at end "civilian professors, instructors, and lecturers in the defense acquisition university structure (including the Defense Systems Management College) whose pay is fixed under section 1746(b) of title 10;".

Subsec. (c)(25). Pub. L. 101–509, § 529 [title I, § 101(b)(9)(F)], substituted "rate for level V of the Executive Schedule" for "maximum rate for GS–18".

Subsec. (c)(29), (30). Pub. L. 101–509, § 529 [title I, § 104(d)(1)], added pars. (29) and (30).

1989—Subsec. (c)(10). Pub. L. 101–189 inserted "civilian professors, instructors, and lecturers at a professional military education school whose pay is fixed under section 1595, 4021, 7478, or 9021 of title 10;", struck out "the Naval War College and" after "instructors at," and substituted "section 6952" for "sections 6952 and 7478".

1987—Subsec. (c)(27). Pub. L. 100–135 substituted "police" for "special police force".

1986—Subsec. (c)(14). Pub. L. 99–335 inserted "(other than employees of the Federal Retirement Thrift Investment System appointed under section 8474(c)(2) of this title)".

Subsec. (c)(28). Pub. L. 99–145 added par. (28).

1985—Subsec. (c)(28). Pub. L. 99–145 added par. (28).

1984—Subsec. (a)(1)(viii) to (x). Pub. L. 98–618 struck out "or" at end of cl. (viii), inserted "or" at end of cl. (ix), and added cl. (x).

1983—Subsec. (a)(1)(iii) to (ix). Pub. L. 97–468, eff. Jan. 5, 1985, struck out cl. (iii) which excluded the Alaska Railroad and redesignated cls. (iv) to (ix) as (iii) to (viii), respectively. See Effective Date of 1983 Amendment note below.

1980—Subsec. (a)(1)(ix). Pub. L. 96–191 added cl. (ix).

Subsec. (c)(2). Pub. L. 96–465 substituted "members of the Foreign Service whose pay is fixed under the Foreign Service Act of 1980" for "employees in the Foreign Service of the United States whose pay is fixed under chapter 14 of title 22".

1979—Subsec. (a)(1)(vii). Pub. L. 96–70, § 3302(e)(1), substituted "Commission" for "Company".

Subsec. (c)(12). Pub. L. 96–70, § 3302(e)(6), substituted provisions relating to any Executive agency to the extent of any election under section 1212(b)(2) of the Panama Canal Act of 1979 for provisions relating to employees of an agency who are stationed in the Canal Zone or in the Republic of Panama.

Subsec. (c)(23). Pub. L. 96–54 inserted "and Trademark" after "Patent".

1978—Subsec. (c)(5). Pub. L. 95–454, § 801(a)(3)(D), substituted "5375" for "5365".

Subsec. (c)(12)(B). Pub. L. 95–454, § 906(a)(2), substituted "Office of Personnel Management" for "Civil Service Commission".

1975—Subsec. (c)(5). Pub. L. 94–183, § 2(12), substituted "Executive Protective Service" for "White House Police".

Subsec. (c)(9). Pub. L. 94–183, § 2(13), substituted "305" for "40".

1973—Subsec. (b). Pub. L. 93–176 extended this chapter to include positions in local boards and appeal boards within the Selective Service System and employees occupying those positions.

1970—Subsec. (c)(1). Pub. L. 91–375 repealed provision declaring this chapter inapplicable to employees in the postal field service whose pay is fixed under chapter 45 of title 39.

Subsec. (c)(4). Pub. L. 91–358 expanded reference to include chief judges, substituted reference to the Superior Court of the District of Columbia for references to the District of Columbia Court of General Sessions and the Juvenile Court of the District of Columbia, and provided that chapter not apply to nonjudicial employees of the District of Columbia court system whose pay is fixed under title 11 of the District of Columbia Code.

1969—Subsec. (c)(5). Pub. L. 91–34 extended provisions to include members of the National Zoological Park police force whose pay is fixed under section 5365 of this title.

1968—Subsec. (c). Pub. L. 90–610 inserted par. (27).

CHANGE OF NAME

Reference to Executive Protective Service held to refer to United States Secret Service Uniformed Division pursuant to Pub. L. 95–179, set out as a note under section 202 of Title 3, The President.

EFFECTIVE DATE OF 1999 AMENDMENT

Amendment by Pub. L. 106–113 effective 4 months after Nov. 29, 1999, see section 1000(a)(9) [title IV, § 4731] of Pub. L. 106–113, set out as a note under section 1 of Title 35, Patents.

EFFECTIVE DATE OF 1996 AMENDMENT

Amendment by section 1122(a)(1) of Pub. L. 104–201 effective Oct. 1, 1996, see section 1124 of Pub. L. 104–201, set out as a note under section 193 of Title 10, Armed Forces.

EFFECTIVE DATE OF 1990 AMENDMENT

Amendment by section 529 [title I, §§ 101(b)(9)(F), 104(d)(1)] of Pub. L. 101–509 effective on such date as the President shall determine, but not earlier than 90 days, and not later than 180 days, after Nov. 5, 1990, see section 529 [title III, § 305] of Pub. L. 101–509, set out as a note under section 5301 of this title.

Amendment by section 529 [title I, § 109(a)(2)] of Pub. L. 101–509 effective on first day of first applicable pay period beginning on or after the 30th day following Nov. 5, 1990, see section 529 [title I, § 109(c)] of Pub. L. 101–509, set out as an Effective Date note under section 5378 of this title.

EFFECTIVE DATE OF 1987 AMENDMENT

Amendment by Pub. L. 100–135 applicable with respect to pay periods beginning after Sept. 30, 1987, except that any pay increase for employees of Library of Congress, pursuant to such amendment, to be subject to appropriation and to be implemented in four approximately equal annual increments, so that pay parity with Capitol Police occurs beginning with first pay period beginning after Sept. 30, 1990, see section 3 of Pub. L. 100–135, set out as a note under section 167 of Title 2, The Congress.

EFFECTIVE DATE OF 1986 AMENDMENT

Amendment by Pub. L. 99–335 effective Jan. 1, 1987, see section 702(a) of Pub. L. 99–335, set out as an Effective Date note under section 8401 of this title.

EFFECTIVE DATE OF 1983 AMENDMENT

Amendment by Pub. L. 97–468 effective on date of transfer of Alaska Railroad to the State [Jan. 5, 1985], pursuant to section 1203 of Title 45, Railroads, see section 615(b) of Pub. L. 97–468.

EFFECTIVE DATE OF 1980 AMENDMENTS

Amendment by Pub. L. 96–465 effective Feb. 15, 1981, except as otherwise provided, see section 2403 of Pub. L. 96–465, set out as an Effective Date note under section 3901 of Title 22, Foreign Relations and Intercourse.

Amendment by Pub. L. 96–191 effective Oct. 1, 1980, see section 10(a) of Pub. L. 96–191.

EFFECTIVE DATE OF 1979 AMENDMENTS

Amendment by Pub. L. 96–70 effective Oct. 1, 1979, see section 3304 of Pub. L. 96–70, set out as an Effective Date note under section 3601 of Title 22, Foreign Relations and Intercourse.

Amendment by Pub. L. 96–54 effective July 12, 1979, see section 2(b) of Pub. L. 96–54, set out as a note under section 305 of this title.

EFFECTIVE DATE OF 1978 AMENDMENT

Amendment by section 801(a)(3)(D) of Pub. L. 95–454 effective on first day of first applicable pay period beginning on or after the 90th day after Oct. 13, 1978, see section 801(a)(4) of Pub. L. 95–454, set out as an Effective Date note under section 5361 of this title.

Amendment by section 906(2)(2) of Pub. L. 95–454 effective 90 days after Oct. 13, 1978, see section 907 of Pub. L. 95–454, set out as a note under section 1101 of this title.

EFFECTIVE DATE OF 1973 AMENDMENT

Amendment by Pub. L. 93–176 effective not later than beginning of first pay period which begins on or after 90th day following Dec. 5, 1973, see section 4 of Pub. L. 93–176, set out as a note under section 460 of the Appendix to Title 50, War and National Defense.

EFFECTIVE DATE OF 1970 AMENDMENTS

Amendment by Pub. L. 91–375 effective within 1 year after Aug. 12, 1970, on date established therefor by Board of Governors of United States Postal Service and published by it in Federal Register, see section 15(a) of Pub. L. 91–375, set out as an Effective Date note preceding section 101 of Title 39, Postal Service.

Amendment by Pub. L. 91–358 effective first day of seventh calendar month which begins after July 29, 1970, see section 199(a) of Pub. L. 91–358, set out as a note under section 1257 of Title 28, Judiciary and Judicial Procedure.

EFFECTIVE DATE OF 1969 AMENDMENT

Amendment by Pub. L. 91–34 effective at beginning of first pay period which commences on or after June 30, 1969, see section 3(a) of Pub. L. 91–34, set out as an Effective Date note under section 5375 of this title.

EFFECTIVE DATE OF 1968 AMENDMENT

Amendment by Pub. L. 90–610 effective on first day of first pay period which begins on or after Oct. 21, 1968, see section 3 of Pub. L. 90–610, set out as a note under section 167 of Title 2, The Congress.

EFFECTIVE DATE OF 1967 AMENDMENT

Section 9(h) of Pub. L. 90–83 provided that: "Section 1(3) [amending section 1305 of this title], (10) [amending section 3324 of this title], (11) [amending this section], (12) [amending section 5108 of this title], (22) [enacting section 5534a of this title], (23) [amending the analysis for chapter 55 of this title], (83)(a) and (d) [amending section 8344 of this title], (89) [amending section 8521 of this title], (98) [amending section 902 of this title], (99) [amending section 903 of this title], and (100) [amending section 8113 of this title] of this Act is effective as of September 6, 1966, for all purposes."

REPEALS

General repealer of provisions inconsistent with Pub. L. 92–392 as not repealing or affecting subsec. (d) of this section, see section 13 of Pub. L. 92–392, Aug. 19, 1972, 86 Stat. 575, set out as a note under section 5341 of this title.

ABOLITION OF ATOMIC ENERGY COMMISSION

Atomic Energy Commission abolished and functions transferred by sections 5814 and 5841 of Title 42, The Public Health and Welfare. See, also, Transfer of Functions notes set out under those sections.

DISSOLUTION OF VIRGIN ISLANDS CORPORATION

Virgin Islands Corporation established to have succession until June 30, 1969, unless sooner dissolved by Act of Congress, by act June 30, 1949, ch. 285, 63 Stat. 350, as amended (48 U.S.C. 1407 et seq.). Corporation terminated its program June 30, 1965, and dissolved July 1, 1966. Act June 30, 1949, was repealed by Pub. L. 97–357, title III, § 308(e), Oct. 19, 1982, 96 Stat. 1710.

CIVILIAN MEMBERS OF FACULTY OF AIR FORCE INSTITUTE OF TECHNOLOGY ON NOVEMBER 8, 1985

Section 504(c) of Pub. L. 99–145 provided that: "Section 9314(b)(2) of title 10, United States Code (as added by subsection (a)(1)(B)), and section 5102(c)(28) of title 5, United States Code (as added by subsection (b)), shall not apply to any person who on the date of the enactment of this Act [Nov. 8, 1985]—

"(1) is a civilian member of the faculty of the United States Air Force Institute of Technology;

"(2) is paid a rate of basic pay under the General Schedule; and

"(3) elects, under procedures prescribed by the Secretary of the Air Force, to continue to be paid under the General Schedule."

PROHIBITION OF DECREASE IN BASIC PAY RATE OF SUBSEC. (c)(7), (8), OR (14) EMPLOYEES

Amendments by Pub. L. 92–392 not to decrease basic pay rate of subsec. (c)(7), (8), or (14) employees in service before effective date of the amendments as to such employees, see section 9(a)(2) of Pub. L. 92–392, Aug. 19, 1972, 86 Stat. 574, set out as a note under section 5343 of this title.

REDUCTION OF BASIC PAY RATE

Rate of basic pay not to be reduced by reason of the enactment of Pub. L. 91–34, which amended this section, see section 3(b) of Pub. L. 91–34, set out as a note under section 5365 of this title.

SECTION REFERRED TO IN OTHER SECTIONS

This section is referred to in sections 3327, 5101, 5103, 5331, 5342, 5348, 5349, 5361, 5377, 5391, 5753, 5754, 5755, 7511 of this title; title 20 section 903; title 29 section 218.

§ 5103. Determination of applicability

The Office of Personnel Management shall determine finally the applicability of section 5102 of this title to specific positions and employees, except for positions and employees in the Office of the Architect of the Capitol.

(Pub. L. 89–554, Sept. 6, 1966, 80 Stat. 446; Pub. L. 95–454, title IX, § 906(a)(2), Oct. 13, 1978, 92 Stat. 1224.)

HISTORICAL AND REVISION NOTES

Derivation	U.S. Code	Revised Statutes and Statutes at Large
....	5 U.S.C. 1083.	Oct. 28, 1949, ch. 782, § 203, 63 Stat. 956.
....	5 U.S.C. 1084(c).	Oct. 28, 1949, ch. 782, § 204(c), 63 Stat. 957. Sept. 1, 1954, ch. 1208, § 105(b), 68 Stat. 1106.

Former sections 1083 and 1084(c) are combined and restated for clarity. The words "hereinafter referred to as the Commission" in former section 1083 are omitted as unnecessary. The exception from "section 1082 (except paragraph (7) thereof)" in former section 1084(c) is carried into section 5102(d).

Standard changes are made to conform with the definitions applicable and the style of this title as outlined in the preface to the report.

AMENDMENTS

1978—Pub. L. 95–454 substituted "Office of Personnel Management" for "Civil Service Commission".

EFFECTIVE DATE OF 1978 AMENDMENT

Amendment by Pub. L. 95–454 effective 90 days after Oct. 13, 1978, see section 907 of Pub. L. 95–454, set out as a note under section 1101 of this title.

SECTION REFERRED TO IN OTHER SECTIONS

This section is referred to in title 20 section 903.

§ 5104. Basis for grading positions

The General Schedule, the symbol for which is "GS", is the basic pay schedule for positions to which this chapter applies. The General Schedule is divided into grades of difficulty and responsibility of work, as follows:

(1) Grade GS–1 includes those classes of positions the duties of which are to perform, under immediate supervision, with little or no latitude for the exercise of independent judgment—

(A) the simplest routine work in office, business, or fiscal operations; or

(B) elementary work of a subordinate technical character in a professional, scientific, or technical field.

(2) Grade GS–2 includes those classes of positions the duties of which are—

(A) to perform, under immediate supervision, with limited latitude for the exercise of independent judgment, routine work in office, business, or fiscal operations, or comparable subordinate technical work of limited scope in a professional, scientific, or technical field, requiring some training or experience; or

(B) to perform other work of equal importance, difficulty, and responsibility, and requiring comparable qualifications.

(3) Grade GS–3 includes those classes of positions the duties of which are—

(A) to perform, under immediate or general supervision, somewhat difficult and responsible work in office, business, or fiscal operations, or comparable subordinate technical work of limited scope in a professional, scientific, or technical field, requiring in either case—

(i) some training or experience;

(ii) working knowledge of a special subject matter; or

(iii) to some extent the exercise of independent judgment in accordance with well-established policies, procedures, and techniques; or

(B) to perform other work of equal importance, difficulty, and responsibility, and requiring comparable qualifications.

(4) Grade GS–4 includes those classes of positions the duties of which are—

(A) to perform, under immediate or general supervision, moderately difficult and responsible work in office, business, or fiscal operations, or comparable subordinate technical work in a professional, scientific, or technical field, requiring in either case—

(i) a moderate amount of training and minor supervisory or other experience;

(ii) good working knowledge of a special subject matter or a limited field of office, laboratory, engineering, scientific, or other procedure and practice; and

(iii) the exercise of independent judgment in accordance with well-established policies, procedures, and techniques; or

(B) to perform other work of equal importance, difficulty, and responsibility, and requiring comparable qualifications.

(5) Grade GS–5 includes those classes of positions the duties of which are—

(A) to perform, under general supervision, difficult and responsible work in office, business, or fiscal administration, or comparable subordinate technical work in a professional, scientific, or technical field, requiring in either case—

(i) considerable training and supervisory or other experience;

(ii) broad working knowledge of a special subject matter or of office, laboratory, engineering, scientific, or other procedure and practice; and

(iii) the exercise of independent judgment in a limited field;

(B) to perform, under immediate supervision, and with little opportunity for the exercise of independent judgment, simple and elementary work requiring professional, scientific, or technical training; or

(C) to perform other work of equal importance, difficulty, and responsibility, and requiring comparable qualifications.

(6) Grade GS–6 includes those classes of positions the duties of which are—

(A) to perform, under general supervision, difficult and responsible work in office, business, or fiscal administration, or comparable subordinate technical work in a professional, scientific, or technical field, requiring in either case—

(i) considerable training and supervisory or other experience;

(ii) broad working knowledge of a special and complex subject matter, procedure, or practice, or of the principles of the profession, art, or science involved; and

(iii) to a considerable extent the exercise of independent judgment; or

(B) to perform other work of equal importance, difficulty, and responsibility, and requiring comparable qualifications.

(7) Grade GS–7 includes those classes of positions the duties of which are—

(A) to perform, under general supervision, work of considerable difficulty and responsibility along special technical or supervisory lines in office, business, or fiscal administration, or comparable subordinate

technical work in a professional, scientific, or technical field, requiring in either case—

(i) considerable specialized or supervisory training and experience;

(ii) comprehensive working knowledge of a special and complex subject matter; procedure, or practice, or of the principles of the profession, art, or science involved; and

(iii) to a considerable extent the exercise of independent judgment;

(B) under immediate or general supervision, to perform somewhat difficult work requiring—

(i) professional, scientific, or technical training; and

(ii) to a limited extent, the exercise of independent technical judgment; or

(C) to perform other work of equal importance, difficulty, and responsibility, and requiring comparable qualifications.

(8) Grade GS–8 includes those classes of positions the duties of which are—

(A) to perform, under general supervision, very difficult and responsible work along special technical or supervisory lines in office, business, or fiscal administration, requiring—

(i) considerable specialized or supervisory training and experience;

(ii) comprehensive and thorough working knowledge of a specialized and complex subject matter, procedure, or practice, or of the principles of the profession, art, or science involved; and

(iii) to a considerable extent the exercise of independent judgment; or

(B) to perform other work of equal importance, difficulty, and responsibility, and requiring comparable qualifications.

(9) Grade GS–9 includes those classes of positions the duties of which are—

(A) to perform, under general supervision, very difficult and responsible work along special technical, supervisory, or administrative lines in office, business, or fiscal administration, requiring—

(i) somewhat extended specialized training and considerable specialized, supervisory, or administrative experience which has demonstrated capacity for sound independent work;

(ii) thorough and fundamental knowledge of a special and complex subject matter, or of the profession, art, or science involved; and

(iii) considerable latitude for the exercise of independent judgment;

(B) with considerable latitude for the exercise of independent judgment, to perform moderately difficult and responsible work, requiring—

(i) professional, scientific, or technical training equivalent to that represented by graduation from a college or university of recognized standing; and

(ii) considerable additional professional, scientific, or technical training or experience which has demonstrated capacity for sound independent work; or

(C) to perform other work of equal importance, difficulty, and responsibility, and requiring comparable qualifications.

(10) Grade GS–10 includes those classes of positions the duties of which are—

(A) to perform, under general supervision, highly difficult and responsible work along special technical, supervisory, or administrative lines in office, business, or fiscal administration, requiring—

(i) somewhat extended specialized, supervisory, or administrative training and experience which has demonstrated capacity for sound independent work;

(ii) thorough and fundamental knowledge of a specialized and complex subject matter, or of the profession, art, or science involved; and

(iii) considerable latitude for the exercise of independent judgment; or

(B) to perform other work of equal importance, difficulty, and responsibility, and requiring comparable qualifications.

(11) Grade GS–11 includes those classes of positions the duties of which are—

(A) to perform, under general administrative supervision and with wide latitude for the exercise of independent judgment, work of marked difficulty and responsibility along special technical, supervisory, or administrative lines in office, business, or fiscal administration, requiring—

(i) extended specialized, supervisory, or administrative training and experience which has demonstrated important attainments and marked capacity for sound independent action or decision; and

(ii) intimate grasp of a specialized and complex subject matter, or of the profession, art, or science involved, or of administrative work of marked difficulty;

(B) with wide latitude for the exercise of independent judgment, to perform responsible work of considerable difficulty requiring somewhat extended professional, scientific, or technical training and experience which has demonstrated important attainments and marked capacity for independent work; or

(C) to perform other work of equal importance, difficulty, and responsibility, and requiring comparable qualifications.

(12) Grade GS–12 includes those classes of positions the duties of which are—

(A) to perform, under general administrative supervision, with wide latitude for the exercise of independent judgment, work of a very high order of difficulty and responsibility along special technical, supervisory, or administrative lines in office, business, or fiscal administration, requiring—

(i) extended specialized, supervisory, or administrative training and experience which has demonstrated leadership and attainments of a high order in specialized or administrative work; and

(ii) intimate grasp of a specialized and complex subject matter or of the profession, art, or science involved;

(B) under general administrative supervision, and with wide latitude for the exercise of independent judgment, to perform professional, scientific, or technical work of marked difficulty and responsibility requiring extended professional, scientific, or technical training and experience which has demonstrated leadership and attainments of a high order in professional, scientific, or technical research, practice, or administration; or

(C) to perform other work of equal importance, difficulty, and responsibility, and requiring comparable qualifications.

(13) Grade GS–13 includes those classes of positions the duties of which are—

(A) to perform, under administrative direction, with wide latitude for the exercise of independent judgment, work of unusual difficulty and responsibility along special technical, supervisory, or administrative lines, requiring extended specialized, supervisory, or administrative training and experience which has demonstrated leadership and marked attainments;

(B) to serve as assistant head of a major organization involving work of comparable level within a bureau;

(C) to perform, under administrative direction, with wide latitude for the exercise of independent judgment, work of unusual difficulty and responsibility requiring extended professional, scientific, or technical training and experience which has demonstrated leadership and marked attainments in professional, scientific, or technical research, practice, or administration; or

(D) to perform other work of equal importance, difficulty, and responsibility, and requiring comparable qualifications.

(14) Grade GS–14 includes those classes of positions the duties of which are—

(A) to perform, under general administrative direction, with wide latitude for the exercise of independent judgment, work of exceptional difficulty and responsibility along special technical, supervisory, or administrative lines which has demonstrated leadership and unusual attainments;

(B) to serve as head of a major organization within a bureau involving work of comparable level;

(C) to plan and direct or to plan and execute major professional, scientific, technical, administrative, fiscal, or other specialized programs, requiring extended training and experience which has demonstrated leadership and unusual attainments in professional, scientific, or technical research, practice, or administration, or in administrative, fiscal, or other specialized activities; or

(D) to perform consulting or other professional, scientific, technical, administrative, fiscal, or other specialized work of equal importance, difficulty, and responsibility, and requiring comparable qualifications.

(15) Grade GS–15 includes those classes of positions the duties of which are—

(A) to perform, under general administrative direction, with very wide latitude for the exercise of independent judgment, work of outstanding difficulty and responsibility along special technical, supervisory, or administrative lines which has demonstrated leadership and exceptional attainments;

(B) to serve as head of a major organization within a bureau involving work of comparable level;

(C) to plan and direct or to plan and execute specialized programs of marked difficulty, responsibility, and national significance, along professional, scientific, technical, administrative, fiscal, or other lines, requiring extended training and experience which has demonstrated leadership and unusual attainments in professional, scientific, or technical research, practice, or administration, or in administrative, fiscal, or other specialized activities; or

(D) to perform consulting or other professional, scientific, technical, administrative, fiscal, or other specialized work of equal importance, difficulty, and responsibility, and requiring comparable qualifications.

(Pub. L. 89–554, Sept. 6, 1966, 80 Stat. 446; Pub. L. 101–509, title V, § 529 [title I, § 102(b)(1)], Nov. 5, 1990, 104 Stat. 1427, 1443.)

HISTORICAL AND REVISION NOTES

Derivation	U.S. Code	Revised Statutes and Statutes at Large
....	5 U.S.C. 1111.	Oct. 28, 1949, ch. 782, § 601, 63 Stat. 959. Sept. 1, 1954, ch. 1208, § 107, 68 Stat. 1108.
....	5 U.S.C. 1112.	Oct. 28, 1949, ch. 782, § 602, 63 Stat. 959. Sept. 1, 1954, ch. 1208, § 108, 68 Stat. 1108. June 20, 1958, Pub. L. 85–462, § 13(a), 72 Stat. 214.

Former sections 1111 and 1112 are combined and restated.

Standard changes are made to conform with the definitions applicable and the style of this title as outlined in the preface to the report.

REFERENCES IN TEXT

The General Schedule, referred to in text, is set out under section 5332 of this title.

AMENDMENTS

1990—Pub. L. 101–509 struck out "18" before "grades" in introductory provisions and struck out pars. (16) to (18) which described grades GS–16 to GS–18.

EFFECTIVE DATE OF 1990 AMENDMENT

Amendment by Pub. L. 101–509 effective on such date as the President shall determine, but not earlier than 90 days, and not later than 180 days, after Nov. 5, 1990, see section 529 [title III, § 305] of Pub. L. 101–509, set out as a note under section 5301 of this title.

JOB EVALUATION POLICY ACT OF 1970

Pub. L. 91–216, May 17, 1970, 84 Stat. 72, provided: "That this Act may be cited as the 'Job Evaluation Policy Act of 1970'.

"TITLE I—CONGRESSIONAL FINDINGS WITH RESPECT TO JOB EVALUATION AND RANKING IN THE EXECUTIVE BRANCH

"SEC. 101. The Congress hereby finds that—

"(1) the tremendous growth required in the activities of the Federal Government in order to meet the country's needs during the past several decades has led to the need for employees in an ever-increasing and changing variety of occupations and professions, many of which did not exist when the basic principles of job evaluation and ranking were established by the Classification Act of 1923 [Act Mar. 4, 1923, ch. 265, 42 Stat. 1488]. The diverse and constantly changing nature of these occupations and professions requires that the Federal Government reassess its approach to job evaluation and ranking better to fulfill its role as an employer and assure efficient economical administration;

"(2) the large number and variety of job evaluation and ranking systems in the executive branch have resulted in significant inequities in selection, promotion, and pay of employees in comparable positions among these systems;

"(3) little effort has been made by Congress or the executive branch to consolidate or coordinate the various job evaluation and ranking systems, and there has been no progress toward the establishment of a coordinated system in which job evaluation and ranking, regardless of the methods used, is related to a unified set of principles providing coherence and equity throughout the executive branch;

"(4) within the executive branch, there has been no significant study of, or experimentation with the several recognized methods of job evaluation and ranking to determine which of those methods are most appropriate for use and application to meet the present and future needs of the Federal Government; and

"(5) notwithstanding the recommendations resulting from the various studies conducted during the last twenty years, the Federal Government has not taken the initiative to implement those recommendations with respect to the job evaluation and ranking systems within the executive branch, with the result that such systems have not, in many cases, been adapted or administered to meet the rapidly changing needs of the Federal Government.

"TITLE II—STATEMENT OF POLICY

"SEC. 201. It is the sense of Congress that—

"(1) the executive branch shall, in the interest of equity, efficiency, and good administration, operate under a coordinated job evaluation and ranking system for all civilian positions, to the greatest extent practicable;

"(2) the system shall be designed so as to utilize such methods of job evaluation and ranking as are appropriate for use in the executive branch, taking into account the various occupational categories of positions therein; and

"(3) the United States Civil Service Commission shall be authorized to exercise general supervision and control over such a system.

"TITLE III—PREPARATION OF A JOB EVALUATION AND RANKING PLAN BY THE CIVIL SERVICE COMMISSION AND REPORTS AND RECOMMENDATIONS TO CONGRESS

"SEC. 301. The Civil Service Commission, through such organizational unit which it shall establish within the Commission and which shall report directly to the Commission, shall prepare a comprehensive plan for the establishment of a coordinated system of job evaluation and ranking for civilian positions, in the executive branch. The plan shall include, among other things—

"(1) provision for the establishment of a method or methods for evaluating jobs and alining them by level;

"(2) a time schedule for the conversion of existing job evaluation and ranking systems into the coordinated system;

"(3) provision that the Civil Service Commission shall have general supervision of and control over the coordinated job evaluation and ranking system, including, if the Commission deems it appropriate, the authority to approve or disapprove the adoption, use and administration in the executive branch of the method or methods established under that system;

"(4) provision for the establishment of procedures for the periodic review by the Civil Service Commission of the effectiveness of the method or methods adopted for use under the system; and

"(5) provision for maintenance of the system to meet the changing needs of the executive branch in the future.

"SEC. 302. In carrying out its functions under section 301 of this Act, the Commission shall consider all recognized methods of job evaluation and ranking.

"SEC. 303. The Civil Service Commission is authorized to secure directly from any executive agency, as defined by section 105 of title 5, United States Code, or any bureau, office, or part thereof, information, suggestions, estimates, statistics, and technical assistance for the purposes of this Act; and each such executive agency or bureau, office, or part thereof is authorized and directed to furnish such information, suggestions, estimates, statistics, and technical assistance directly to the Civil Service Commission upon request by the Commission.

"SEC. 304. (a) Within one year after the date of enactment of this Act, the Commission shall submit to the President and the Congress an interim progress report on the current status and results of its activities under this Act, together with its current findings.

"(b) Within two years after the date of enactment of this Act [Mar. 17, 1970]—

"(1) the Civil Service Commission shall complete its functions under this Act and shall transmit to the President a comprehensive report of the result of its activities, together with its recommendations (including its draft of proposed legislation to carry out such recommendations), and

"(2) the President shall transmit that report (including the recommendations and draft of proposed legislation of the Commission) to the Congress, together with such recommendations as the President deems appropriate.

"(c) The Commission shall submit to the Committees on Post Office and Civil Service of the Senate and House of Representatives once each calendar month, or at such other intervals as may be directed by those committees, or either of them, an interim progress report on the then current status and results of the activities of the Commission under this Act, together with the then current findings of the Commission.

"(d) The Commission shall periodically consult with, and solicit the views of, appropriate employee and professional organizations.

"(e) The organizational unit established under section 301 of this Act shall cease to exist upon the submission of the report to the Congress under subsection (b) of this section."

SECTION REFERRED TO IN OTHER SECTIONS

This section is referred to in section 7201 of this title; title 10 section 1586; title 25 section 2802.

§ 5105. Standards for classification of positions

(a) The Office of Personnel Management, after consulting the agencies, shall prepare standards for placing positions in their proper classes and grades. The Office may make such inquiries or investigations of the duties, responsibilities, and qualification requirements of positions as it considers necessary for this purpose. The agencies, on request of the Office, shall furnish information for and cooperate in the preparation of the standards. In the standards, which shall be published in such form as the Office may determine, the Office shall—

(1) define the various classes of positions in terms of duties, responsibilities, and qualification requirements;

(2) establish the official class titles; and

(3) set forth the grades in which the classes have been placed by the Office.

(b) The Office, after consulting the agencies to the extent considered necessary, shall revise, supplement, or abolish existing standards, or prepare new standards, so that, as nearly as may be practicable, positions existing at any given time will be covered by current published standards.

(c) The official class titles established under subsection (a)(2) of this section shall be used for personnel, budget, and fiscal purposes. However, this requirement does not prevent the use of organizational or other titles for internal administration, public convenience, law enforcement, or similar purposes.

(Pub. L. 89–554, Sept. 6, 1966, 80 Stat. 452; Pub. L. 95–454, title IX, § 906(a)(2), (3), Oct. 13, 1978, 92 Stat. 1224.)

HISTORICAL AND REVISION NOTES

Derivation	U.S. Code	Revised Statutes and Statutes at Large
....	5 U.S.C. 1094.	Oct. 28, 1949, ch. 782, § 401, 63 Stat. 957.

The section is restated for clarity.

In subsection (b), the requirement that the Commission keep the standards up to date is omitted as included in the requirement that the Commission revise, supplement, or abolish existing standards, or prepare new standards so as to keep them current as nearly as practicable.

Standard changes are made to conform with the definitions applicable and the style of this title as outlined in the preface to the report.

AMENDMENTS

1978—Subsecs. (a), (b). Pub. L. 95–454 substituted "Office of Personnel Management" and "Office" for "Civil Service Commission" and "Commission", respectively, wherever appearing.

EFFECTIVE DATE OF 1978 AMENDMENT

Amendment by Pub. L. 95–454 effective 90 days after Oct. 13, 1978, see section 907 of Pub. L. 95–454, set out as a note under section 1101 of this title.

SECTION REFERRED TO IN OTHER SECTIONS

This section is referred to in section 5101 of this title.

§ 5106. Basis for classifying positions

(a) Each position shall be placed in its appropriate class. The basis for determining the appropriate class is the duties and responsibilities of the position and the qualifications required by the duties and responsibilities.

(b) Each class shall be placed in its appropriate grade. The basis for determining the appropriate grade is the level of difficulty, responsibility, and qualification requirements of the work of the class.

(c) Appropriated funds may not be used to pay an employee who places a supervisory position in a class and grade solely on the basis of the size of the organization unit or the number of subordinates supervised. These factors may be given effect only to the extent warranted by the work load of the organization unit and then only in combination with other factors, such as the kind, difficulty, and complexity of work supervised, the degree and scope of responsibility delegated to the supervisor, and the kind, degree, and character of the supervision exercised.

(Pub. L. 89–554, Sept. 6, 1966, 80 Stat. 453.)

HISTORICAL AND REVISION NOTES

Derivation	U.S. Code	Revised Statutes and Statutes at Large
(a), (b)	5 U.S.C. 1092.	Oct. 28, 1949, ch. 782, § 302, 63 Stat. 957.
(c)	5 U.S.C. 1093.	Oct. 28, 1949, ch. 782, § 303, 63 Stat. 957.

In subsection (c), the prohibition is restated in positive form. The words "to pay" are substituted for the words "to pay the compensation of". The words "the group, section, bureau" are omitted as included in the words "the organization unit". The word "actually" in the phrase "of the supervision exercised" is omitted as unnecessary.

Standard changes are made to conform with the definitions applicable and the style of this title as outlined in the preface to the report.

§ 5107. Classification of positions

Except as otherwise provided by this chapter, each agency shall place each position under its jurisdiction in its appropriate class and grade in conformance with standards published by the Office of Personnel Management or, if no published standards apply directly, consistently with published standards. When facts warrant, an agency may change a position which it has placed in a class or grade under this section from that class or grade to another class or grade. Subject to subchapter VI of chapter 53 of this title, these actions of an agency are the basis for pay and personnel transactions until changed by certificate of the Office.

(Pub. L. 89–554, Sept. 6, 1966, 80 Stat. 453; Pub. L. 95–454, title VIII, § 801(a)(3)(E), title IX, § 906(a)(2), (3), Oct. 13, 1978, 92 Stat. 1222, 1224.)

HISTORICAL AND REVISION NOTES

Derivation	U.S. Code	Revised Statutes and Statutes at Large
....	5 U.S.C. 1102(a).	Oct. 28, 1949, ch. 782, § 502(a), 63 Stat. 958.

The words "to which this chapter applies" are omitted as unnecessary in view of section 5102. The words "Subject to section 5337 of this title" are added to reflect the qualification imposed by that section.

Standard changes are made to conform with the definitions applicable and the style of this title as outlined in the preface to the report.

AMENDMENTS

1978—Pub. L. 95–454 substituted "Office of Personnel Management" for "Civil Service Commission", "Office" for "Commission", and "subchapter VI of chapter 53" for "section 5337".

EFFECTIVE DATE OF 1978 AMENDMENT

Amendment by section 803(a)(3)(E) of Pub. L. 95–454, substituting reference to subchapter VI of chapter 53 for reference to section 5337, effective on first day of first applicable pay period beginning on or after 90th day after Oct. 13, 1978, see section 801(a)(4) of Pub. L. 95–454, set out as an Effective Date note under section 5361 of this title.

Amendment by section 906(a)(2), (3) of Pub. L. 95–454, substituting reference to Office of Personnel Management for reference to Civil Service Commission, effec-

tive 90 days after Oct. 13, 1978, see section 907 of Pub. L. 95–454, set out as a note under section 1101 of this title.

SECTION REFERRED TO IN OTHER SECTIONS

This section is referred to in sections 5111, 5112 of this title; title 12 section 4523; title 36 sections 151304, 151704, 152404.

§ 5108. Classification of positions above GS–15

(a) The Office of Personnel Management may, for any Executive agency—

(1) establish, and from time to time revise, the maximum number of positions which may at any one time be classified above GS–15; and

(2) establish standards and procedures (including requiring agencies, where necessary in the judgment of the Office, to obtain the prior approval of the Office) in accordance with which positions may be classified above GS–15.

(b) The President, rather than the Office, shall exercise the authority under subsection (a) in the case of positions proposed to be placed in the Federal Bureau of Investigation and Drug Enforcement Administration Senior Executive Service.

(Pub. L. 89–554, Sept. 6, 1966, 80 Stat. 453; Pub. L. 89–632, § 1(a)–(d), Oct. 8, 1966, 80 Stat. 878; Pub. L. 90–83, § 1(12), Sept. 11, 1967, 81 Stat. 197; Pub. L. 91–187, § 1, Dec. 30, 1969, 83 Stat. 850; Pub. L. 91–206, § 5(a), Mar. 10, 1970, 84 Stat. 51; Pub. L. 91–596, § 30, Dec. 29, 1970, 84 Stat. 1619; Pub. L. 91–644, title I, § 11, Jan. 2, 1971, 84 Stat. 1889; Pub. L. 91–656, § 9, Jan. 8, 1971, 84 Stat. 1955; Pub. L. 91–261, § 12, Mar. 24, 1972, 86 Stat. 112; Pub. L. 90–351, title I, § 506(c), as added Pub. L. 93–83, § 2, Aug. 6, 1973, 87 Stat. 211; Pub. L. 93–282, title III, § 301, May 14, 1974, 88 Stat. 137; Pub. L. 93–406, title I, § 507(b), title II, § 1051(b)(2), title IV, § 4002(c), Sept. 2, 1974, 88 Stat. 894, 951, 1005; Pub. L. 93–415, title II, § 201(g), Sept. 7, 1974, 88 Stat. 1113; Pub. L. 93–463, title IV, § 410, Oct. 23, 1974, 88 Stat. 1414; Pub. L. 93–516, title II, § 208(b), Dec. 7, 1974, 88 Stat. 1629; Pub. L. 93–651, title II, § 208(b), Nov. 21, 1974, 89 Stat. 2–14; Pub. L. 94–183, § 2(14), (15), Dec. 31, 1975, 89 Stat. 1057; Pub. L. 94–233, § 13, Mar. 15, 1976, 90 Stat. 233; Pub. L. 94–503, title II, § 202(a), Oct. 15, 1976, 90 Stat. 2426; Pub. L. 95–91, title VII, § 710(b), Aug. 4, 1977, 91 Stat. 609; Pub. L. 95–190, § 11(a), Nov. 16, 1977, 91 Stat. 1398; Pub. L. 95–219, § 3(c), Dec. 28, 1977, 91 Stat. 1614; Pub. L. 95–251, § 1, Mar. 27, 1978, 92 Stat. 183; Pub. L. 95–454, title IV, § 414(a)(1)(A), (C), (D), Oct. 13, 1978, 92 Stat. 1177; Pub. L. 95–486, § 10, Oct. 20, 1978, 92 Stat. 1634; Pub. L. 95–563, § 14(g), Nov. 1, 1978, 92 Stat. 2390; Pub. L. 95–612, § 3(b), Nov. 8, 1978, 92 Stat. 3091; Pub. L. 95–624, § 22, Nov. 9, 1978, 92 Stat. 3466; Pub. L. 95–630, title V, § 502(c), Nov. 10, 1978, 92 Stat. 3681; Pub. L. 96–54, § 2(a)(23), Aug. 14, 1979, 93 Stat. 382; Pub. L. 96–191, § 8(c), Feb. 15, 1980, 94 Stat. 33; Pub. L. 100–325, § 2(g), May 30, 1988, 102 Stat. 581; Pub. L. 100–702, title I, § 104(c)(2), Nov. 19, 1988, 102 Stat. 4645; Pub. L. 101–474, § 5(i), Oct. 30, 1990, 104 Stat. 1100; Pub. L. 101–509, title V, § 529 [title I, § 102(b)(2)], Nov. 5, 1990, 104 Stat. 1427, 1443; Pub. L. 102–378, § 2(23), Oct. 2, 1992, 106 Stat. 1348.)

HISTORICAL AND REVISION NOTES
1966 ACT

Derivation	U.S. Code	Revised Statutes and Statutes at Large
(a), (b), (c) (1)–(7), (d).	5 U.S.C. 1105(a)–(h), (j)–(l).	Oct. 28, 1949, ch. 782, § 505, 63 Stat. 959.
		Sept. 1, 1954, ch. 1208, § 101(a), 68 Stat. 1105.
		June 28, 1955, ch. 189, § 12(a), 69 Stat. 179.
		July 31, 1956, ch. 804, § 502, 70 Stat. 762.
		Aug. 14, 1957, Pub. L. 85–136, 71 Stat. 352.
		June 20, 1958, Pub. L. 85–462, §§ 10 (less "(i)"), 11, 72 Stat. 213, 213A.
		Sept. 23, 1959, Pub. L. 86–370, § 2(a), (b), 73 Stat. 650.
		Sept. 23, 1959, Pub. L. 86–377, § 1(a), 73 Stat. 700.
		July 1, 1960, Pub. L. 86–568, § 203, 74 Stat. 305.
		Sept. 26, 1961, Pub. L. 87–322, § 1, 75 Stat. 685.
		Oct. 4, 1961, Pub. L. 87–367, §§ 102(a), (b), 103(1), 75 Stat. 786, 787.
		Oct. 11, 1962, Pub. L. 87–793, § 606, 76 Stat. 848.
		Aug. 14, 1964, Pub. L. 88–426, § 103(b), 78 Stat. 402.
(c)(8)	5 U.S.C. 298a.	July 7, 1955, ch. 279, § 201 (2d proviso on p. 273), 69 Stat. 273.
		Oct. 11, 1962, Pub. L. 87–793, § 607(b), 76 Stat. 850.
(c)(9)	45 U.S.C. 228j(b)(4) (4th sentence).	Sept. 6, 1958, Pub. L. 85–927, § 3, 72 Stat. 1781.

The section is reorganized for clarity.

In subsection (a)(2), the date "October 4, 1961" is substituted for "the date of enactment of this subparagraph".

Subsection (c)(6) is added on authority of section 302 of the Act of July 29, 1958, Pub. L. 85–568, 72 Stat. 433, 42 U.S.C. 2453, and Transfer Plan, effective March 15, 1960, 25 F.R. 2151, section 2(c) of which in effect transferred from the Department of Defense to the National Aeronautics and Space Administration 5 of the 372 positions authorized to be placed in GS–16, 17, and 18 pursuant to section 1(a) of the Act of Sept. 23, 1959, Pub. L. 86–377, 73 Stat. 700.

In subsection (c)(8), the words "on and after July 7, 1955" are omitted as obsolete.

In subsection (d), the words "subsequent to February 1, 1958" are omitted as obsolete and the words "of the Government" are omitted as unnecessary.

Standard changes are made to conform with the definitions applicable and the style of this title as outlined in the preface to the report.

1967 ACT

The amendment to 5 U.S.C. 5108(c)(5) corrects a typographical error and conforms to the source law (act of October 11, 1962, Public Law 87–793, section 606(b), 76 Stat. 849; former 5 U.S.C. 1105(j)).

AMENDMENTS

1992—Subsec. (a)(2). Pub. L. 102–378 substituted a period for semicolon at end.

1990—Pub. L. 101–509 amended section generally, substituting provisions relating to classification of positions above GS–15, consisting of subsecs. (a) and (b), for provisions relating to classification of provisions at GS–16, 17, and 18, consisting of subsecs. (a) to (c).

Subsec. (c). Pub. L. 101–474 redesignated pars. (2) and (3) as (1) and (2), respectively, and struck out former par. (1), which read as follows: "the Director of the Administrative Office of the United States Courts, subject to the standards and procedures prescribed by this chapter, may place a total of 17 positions in GS–16, 17, and 18; and".

1988—Subsec. (a). Pub. L. 100–325 added cl. (iii) and substituted "the Federal Bureau of Investigation and Drug Enforcement Administration Senior Executive Service" for "GS–16, 17, and 18 in the Federal Bureau of Investigation" in last sentence.

Subsec. (c)(1). Pub. L. 100–702 substituted "17 positions" for "15 positions".

1980—Subsec. (c). Pub. L. 96–191 struck out par. (1) which authorized Comptroller General, subject to procedures prescribed by this section, to place a total of 90 positions in General Accounting Office in GS–16, 17, and 18, and redesignated pars. (2) to (4) as (1) to (3), respectively.

1979—Subsec. (c)(4), (17). Pub. L. 96–54 redesignated par. (17), relating to executive departments or agencies in which boards of contracts appeals are established, as par. (4).

1978—Subsec. (a). Pub. L. 95–630 substituted "3,310" for "3,301".

Pub. L. 95–612 substituted "3362" for "3301".

Pub. L. 95–454, § 414(a)(1)(C), substituted provisions authorizing Director of Office of Personnel Management to establish the maximum number of positions, not to exceed 10,777, which may be placed in GS–16, 17, and 18, and the Senior Executive Service and to place positions in GS–16, 17, or 18, and requiring the President to carry out the Director's authority for proposed positions in the Federal Bureau of Investigation for provisions authorizing a majority of the Civil Service Commissioners to establish the maximum number of positions, not to exceed 3362 (in addition to certain specified positions), which may be placed in GS–16, 17, and 18, placing a percentage limitation on the number of positions placed in GS–17 and 18, and requiring the approval of a majority of the Commissioners to place positions in GS–16, 17, or 18.

Pub. L. 95–251 substituted "340 administrative law judge" for "240 hearing examiner".

Subsec. (c)(2). Pub. L. 95–454, § 414(a)(1)(A)(i), (D)(i), redesignated par. (3), relating to the Director of the Administrative Office of the United States, as (2) and repealed former par. (2) relating to the Federal Bureau of Investigation.

Subsec. (c)(3). Pub. L. 95–486 inserted provision subjecting the Director of the Administrative Office of the United States Courts to the standards and procedures prescribed by this chapter and substituted provision authorizing placement of 15 positions in GS–16, 17, and 18 for provision authorizing placement of 4 positions in GS–17.

Pub. L. 95–454, § 414(a)(1)(D), redesignated par. (12), relating to the Chief Judge of the United States Tax Court, as par. (3). Former par. (3) redesignated (2).

Subsec. (c)(4) to (11). Pub. L. 95–454, § 414(a)(1)(A)(i), repealed par. (4) relating to the Commissioner of Immigration and Naturalization, par. (5) relating to the Secretary of Defense, par. (6) relating to the Administrator of the National Aeronautics and Space Administration, pars. (7) and (8) relating to the Attorney General, par. (9) relating to the Railroad Retirement Board, par. (10) relating to the Secretary of Labor and the Occupational Safety and Health Review Commission, and par. (11) relating to the Law Enforcement Assistance Administration.

Subsec. (c)(8). Pub. L. 95–624 substituted "45" for "32".

Subsec. (c)(12). Pub. L. 95–454, § 414(a)(1)(D)(i), redesignated par. (12) relating to the Chief Judge of the United States Tax Court, as (3).

Subsec. (c)(13) to (16). Pub. L. 95–454, § 414(a)(1)(A)(i), repealed par. (13) relating to the Commodity Futures Trading Commission, par. (14) relating to the Secretary of Health, Education, and Welfare, par. (15) relating to the Chairman of the Equal Employment Opportunity Commission, and par. (16) relating to the Secretary of Health, Education, and Welfare.

Subsec. (c)(17). Pub. L. 95–563 added par. (17).

Subsec. (d). Pub. L. 95–454, § 414(a)(1)(A)(ii), repealed subsec. (d) which provided the order for reducing the positions authorized to be placed in grades GS–16, 17, and 18 under this section when a general authorization statute authorized additional positions in these grades.

Subsec. (e). Pub. L. 95–454, § 414(a)(1)(A)(ii), repealed subsec. (e) which authorized Commissioner of Internal Revenue to place 20 additional positions in grades GS–16 and 17.

Subsec. (f). Pub. L. 95–454, § 414(a)(1)(A)(ii), repealed subsec. (f) which authorized Secretary of Labor to place additional positions in grades GS–16, 17, and 18.

Subsec. (g). Pub. L. 95–454, § 414(a)(1)(A)(ii), repealed subsec. (g) which authorized Pension Benefit Guaranty Corporation to place additional positions in grades GS–16, 17, and 18.

1977—Subsec. (a). Pub. L. 95–219 substituted "3301" for "3293".

Pub. L. 95–190 substituted "3293" for "3243".

Pub. L. 95–91 substituted "3243" for "2754".

1976—Subsec. (c)(7). Pub. L. 94–233 restructured provisions and, as restructured, deleted authority relating to 8 positions of Member of the Board of Parole in GS–17.

Subsec. (c)(8). Pub. L. 94–503 substituted provision that the Attorney General, without regard to any other provision of this section, may place a total of 32 positions in GS–16, 17, and 18 for provision that the Attorney General, without regard to this chapter (except section 5114), may place 1 position in GS–16.

1975—Subsec. (c)(11). Pub. L. 94–183, § 2(14), increased to twenty-five the number of positions which the Law Enforcement Assistance Administration may place in GS–16, 17, and 18. The increase required no change in text in view of the 1974 amendment by Pub. L. 93–415, which called for an identical increase.

Subsec. (c)(13) to (16). Pub. L. 94–183, § 2(15), redesignated par. (12) relating to the Commodity Futures Trading Commission, par. (12) relating to the Secretary of Health, Education, and Welfare and the Office for the Blind and Visually Handicapped of the Rehabilitation Services Administration, par. (13) relating to the Chairman of the Equal Employment Opportunity Commission, and par. (14) relating to the Secretary of Health, Education, and Welfare and the National Institute on Alcohol Abuse and Alcoholism, as pars. (13) to (16), respectively.

1974—Subsec. (c)(11). Pub. L. 93–415 increased from twenty-two to twenty-five the number of positions which the Law Enforcement Assistance Administration may place in GS–16, 17, and 18. Amendment has been executed to subsec. (c)(11) as the probable intent of Congress notwithstanding direction in section 210 (g) of Pub. L. 93–415 that the amendment be executed to subsec. (c) (10).

Subsec. (c)(11) to (14). Pub. L. 93–282 redesignated par. (10) relating to Law Enforcement Assistance Administration, par. (10) relating to Chief Judge of the United States Tax Court, par. (11) relating to Chairman of the Equal Employment Opportunity Commission, as pars. (11) to (13), respectively, and added par. (14) relating to GS–16, 17, and 18 positions in the National Institute on Alcohol Abuse and Alcoholism.

Subsec. (c)(12). Pub. L. 93–651 and Pub. L. 93–516 amended section identically, adding par. (12) relating to Secretary of Health, Education, and Welfare and the Office for the Blind and Visually Handicapped of the Rehabilitation Services Administration.

Subsec. (c)(12). Pub. L. 93–463 added par. (12) relating to Commodity Futures Trading Commission.

Subsec. (e). Pub. L. 93–406, § 1051(b)(2), added subsec. (e).

Subsec. (f). Pub. L. 93–406, § 507(b), added subsec. (f).

Subsec. (g). Pub. L. 93–406, § 4002(c), added subsec. (g).

1973—Subsec. (c)(10). Pub. L. 93–83 substituted in par. (10) as added by Pub. L. 91–644 "twenty-two" for "twenty".

1972—Subsec. (c). Pub. L. 92–261 added par. (11).

1971—Subsec. (a). Pub. L. 91–656, § 9(b), substituted "2,754" for "2,734".

Subsec. (c)(10). Pub. L. 91–656, § 9(a), added par. (10) relating to Chief Judge of the United States Tax Court.

Pub. L. 91–644 added par. (10) relating to Law Enforcement Assistance Administration.

1970—Subsec. (a). Pub. L. 91–206 substituted "2,734" for "2,727".

Subsec. (c)(10). Pub. L. 91–596 added par. (10) relating to positions in the Department of Labor.

1969—Subsec. (a). Pub. L. 91–187, § 1(a), substituted "2,727" for "2,577".

Subsec. (b)(2). Pub. L. 91–187, § 1(b), increased number of positions in Library of Congress from 28 to 44.

Subsec. (c)(1). Pub. L. 91–187, § 1(c), increased number of positions in GAO from 64 to 90.

Subsec. (c)(2). Pub. L. 91–187, § 1(d), increased number of positions in FBI from 110 to 140.

1966—Subsec. (a). Pub. L. 89–632, § 1(a), increased number of positions authorized to be established from 2,400 to 2,577, struck out cl. (1) designation preceding the provision limiting number of positions to be placed in GS–17 and GS–18, and struck out cls. (2) to (5), which made positions available only for allocation as follows: 50, with Presidential approval, for an agency or function created after Oct. 4, 1961, 14 to the United States Arms Control and Disarmament Agency, 6 to the Immigration and Naturalization Service, and 4 to the Federal Home Loan Bank Board, respectively.

Subsec. (b). Pub. L. 89–632, § 1(b), designated existing provisions as par. (1) and added par. (2).

Subsec. (c)(1). Public L. 89–632, § 1(c), increased number of positions in GAO from 39 to 64.

Subsec. (c)(2). Pub. L. 89–632, § 1(d), increased number of positions in FBI from 75 to 110.

EFFECTIVE DATE OF 1990 AMENDMENT

Amendment by Pub. L. 101–509 effective on such date as the President shall determine, but not earlier than 90 days, and not later than 180 days, after Nov. 5, 1990, see section 529 [title III, § 305] of Pub. L. 101–509, set out as a note under section 5301 of this title.

EFFECTIVE DATE OF 1988 AMENDMENT

Amendment by Pub. L. 100–702 effective Jan. 1, 1989, see section 109 of title I of Pub. L. 100–702, set out as a Federal Courts Study Committee note under section 331 of Title 28, Judiciary and Judicial Procedure.

EFFECTIVE DATE OF 1980 AMENDMENT

Amendment by Pub. L. 96–191 effective Oct. 1, 1980, see section 10(a) of Pub. L. 96–191.

EFFECTIVE DATE OF 1979 AMENDMENT

Amendment by Pub. L. 96–54 effective July 12, 1979, see section 2(b) of Pub. L. 96–54, set out as a note under section 305 of this title.

EFFECTIVE DATE OF 1978 AMENDMENTS

Amendment by Pub. L. 95–630 effective on expiration of 120 days after Nov. 10, 1978, see section 509 of Pub. L. 95–630, set out as a note under section 1752 of Title 12, Banks and Banking.

Amendment by Pub. L. 95–612 effective Oct. 1, 1978, or some later date related to availability of funds under appropriation acts authorized by appropriations authorization, see section 7 of Pub. L. 95–612, set out as a note under section 276c–2 of Title 22, Foreign Relations and Intercourse.

Amendment by Pub. L. 95–563 effective with respect to contracts entered into 120 days after Nov. 1, 1978 and, at the election of the contractor, with respect to any claim pending at such time before the contracting officer or initiated thereafter, see section 16 of Pub. L. 95–563, set out as an Effective Date note under section 601 of Title 41, Public Contracts.

Amendment by Pub. L. 95–454 effective 180 days after Oct. 13, 1978, see section 415(a)(3) of Pub. L. 95–454, set out as an Effective Date note under section 3131 of this title.

EFFECTIVE DATE OF 1976 AMENDMENT

Amendment by Pub. L. 94–233 effective on sixtieth day following Mar. 15, 1976, see section 16(b) of Pub. L.

94–233, set out as an Effective Date note under section 4201 of Title 18, Crimes and Criminal Procedure.

EFFECTIVE DATE OF 1974 AMENDMENTS

Amendment by Pub. L. 93–463 effective Oct. 23, 1974, see section 418 of Pub. L. 93–463, set out as a note under section 2 of Title 7, Agriculture.

Amendment by Pub. L. 93–415 effective Sept. 7, 1974, see section 263(a) of Pub. L. 93–415, set out as an Effective Date note under section 5601 of Title 42, The Public Health and Welfare.

Amendment by Pub. L. 93–406, § 1051(b)(2), effective on 90th day after Sept. 2, 1974, see section 1051(d) of Pub. L. 93–406, set out as a note under section 7802 of Title 26, Internal Revenue Code.

Amendment by Pub. L. 93–406, § 4002(c), effective Sept. 2, 1974, see section 4082(a) of Pub. L. 93–406, which is classified to section 1461(a) of Title 29, Labor.

EFFECTIVE DATE OF 1973 AMENDMENT

Offices and salaries modified under amendment by Pub. L. 93–83, prospectively only, effective on and after Aug. 6, 1973, see section 3 of Pub. L. 93–83.

EFFECTIVE DATE OF 1967 AMENDMENT

Amendment by Pub. L. 90–83 effective as of Sept. 6, 1966, for all purposes, see section 9(h) of Pub. L. 90–83, set out as a note under section 5102 of this title.

REPEALS

Pub. L. 95–612, § 3(b), Nov. 8, 1978, 92 Stat. 3091, cited as a credit to this section, was repealed by Pub. L. 97–258, § 5(b), Sept. 13, 1982, 96 Stat. 1068.

ADDITIONAL GS–16, GS–17, AND GS–18 POSITIONS; SOURCE FOR APPOINTMENTS; ELIGIBILITY OF APPOINTEES; TERMINATION OF AUTHORITY ON LEAVING POSITIONS; DETERMINATION OF AGGREGATE NUMBER OF POSITIONS AUTHORIZED FOR PLACEMENT IN SUCH GRADES

Pub. L. 95–612, § 3(a), (c), Nov. 8, 1978, 92 Stat. 3091, 3092, relating to the appointment of GS–16, GS–17, and GS–18 positions, was repealed by Pub. L. 97–258, § 5(b), Sept. 13, 1982, 96 Stat. 1068.

TERMINATION OF AUTHORITY TO PLACE POSITIONS IN GS–16, 17, OR 18 OF THE GENERAL SCHEDULE

Section 414(a)(1)(B) of Pub. L. 95–454 provided that: "Notwithstanding any other provision of law (other than section 5108 of such title 5), the authority granted to an agency (as defined in section 5102(a)(1) of such title 5 under any such provision to place one or more positions in GS–16, 17, or 18 of the General Schedule, is hereby terminated."

LIMITATIONS ON EXECUTIVE POSITIONS NOT TO APPLY TO INDIVIDUALS OCCUPYING THOSE POSITIONS ON OCTOBER 12, 1978

Section 414(a)(3) of Pub. L. 95–454 provided that:

"(A) The provisions of paragraphs (1) and (2) of this subsection [amending sections 3104 and 5108 of this title] shall not apply with respect to any position so long as the individual occupying such position on the day before the date of the enactment of this Act [Oct. 13, 1978] continues to occupy such position.

"(B) The Director—

"(i) in establishing under section 5108 of title 5, United States Code, the maximum number of positions which may be placed in GS–16, 17, and 18 of the General Schedule, and

"(ii) in establishing under section 3104 of such title 5 the maximum number of scientific or professional positions which may be established,

shall take into account positions to which subparagraph (A) of this paragraph applies."

[References in laws to rates of pay for GS–16, 17, or 18, or to maximum rates of pay under General Schedule, to be considered references to rates payable under speci-

fied sections of this title, see section 529 [title I, § 101(c)(1)] of Pub. L. 101–509, set out in a note under section 5376 of this title.]

ADDITIONAL POSITIONS IN OFFICE OF MANAGEMENT AND BUDGET

Pub. L. 95–26, title I, May 4, 1977, 91 Stat. 94, authorizing the Director of the Office of Management and Budget to place a total of five positions on GS–16, 17, and 18 in addition to the positions authorized by section 5108 of this title, was repealed by Pub. L. 97–258, § 5(b), Sept. 13, 1982, 96 Stat. 1068.

PREFERENCE TO BLIND IN SELECTION OF PERSONNEL

Preference to be given to blind individuals in selection of additional personnel under subsec. (c)(12) of this section, see section 208(c) of Pub. L. 93–516, set out as a note under section 702 of Title 29, Labor.

SECTION REFERRED TO IN OTHER SECTIONS

This section is referred to in sections 3132, 3304, 3324, 3594, 5372b, 5376, 5723 of this title; title 2 section 166; title 15 section 2053; title 20 sections 1505, 3461, 9175; title 22 sections 2193, 2385, 2454, 6204; title 25 section 640d–11; title 29 sections 661, 1137; title 30 section 1211; title 42 section 7231; title 45 section 231f.

§ 5109. Positions classified by statute

(a) The position held by an employee of the Department of Agriculture while he, under section 450d of title 7, is designated and vested with a delegated regulatory function or part thereof shall be classified in accordance with this chapter, but not lower than GS–14.

(b)(1) The position held by a fully experienced and qualified railroad safety inspector of the Department of Transportation shall be classified in accordance with this chapter, but not lower than GS–12.

(2) The position held by a railroad safety specialist of the Department shall be classified in accordance with this chapter, but not lower than GS–13.

(Pub. L. 89–554, Sept. 6, 1966, 80 Stat. 455; Pub. L. 91–34, § 2(b), June 30, 1969, 83 Stat. 41; Pub. L. 93–406, title II, § 1051(b)(1), Sept. 2, 1974, 88 Stat. 951; Pub. L. 95–454, title IX, § 906(b), Oct. 13, 1978, 92 Stat. 1226; Pub. L. 99–514, § 2, Oct. 22, 1986, 100 Stat. 2095; Pub. L. 101–509, title V, § 529 [title I, § 101(b)(9)(G)], Nov. 5, 1990, 104 Stat. 1427, 1441; Pub. L. 103–272, § 4(b)(1), July 5, 1994, 108 Stat. 1361; Pub. L. 105–206, title I, § 1102(e)(2), July 22, 1998, 112 Stat. 704.)

HISTORICAL AND REVISION NOTES

Derivation	U.S. Code	Revised Statutes and Statutes at Large
(a)	5 U.S.C. 516b (3d sentence).	Apr. 4, 1940, ch. 75, § 2 (3d sentence), 54 Stat. 81.
(b)	5 U.S.C. 3013(a) (10th through 24th words of 1st sentence, and 2d sentence).	Sept. 28, 1959, Pub. L. 86–382, § 14(a) (10th through 24th words of 1st sentence, and 2d sentence), 73 Stat. 716.
(c)	40 U.S.C. 193w.	Sept. 23, 1959, Pub. L. 86–379, § 1, 73 Stat. 702.

In subsection (a), the words "section 450d of title 7" are substituted for "this section" to reflect the scheduled transfer of former section 516b to title 7.

In subsection (c), the words "Notwithstanding any other law" were omitted as unnecessary.

Standard changes are made to conform with the definitions applicable and the style of this title as outlined in the preface to the report.

AMENDMENTS

1998—Subsecs. (b), (c). Pub. L. 105–206 redesignated subsec. (c) as (b) and struck out former subsec. (b) which read as follows: "The position held by the employee appointed under section 7802(b) of the Internal Revenue Code of 1986 shall be considered a position classified above GS–15 pursuant to section 5108."

1994—Subsec. (c). Pub. L. 103–272 added subsec. (c).

1990—Subsec. (b). Pub. L. 101–509 substituted "shall be considered a position classified above GS–15 pursuant to section 5108" for "is classified at GS–18, and is in addition to the number of positions authorized by section 5108(a) of this title".

1986—Subsec. (b). Pub. L. 99–514 substituted "Internal Revenue Code of 1986" for "Internal Revenue Code of 1954".

1978—Subsecs. (b), (c). Pub. L. 95–454, § 906(b), redesignated subsec. (c) as (b). Former subsec. (c), which related to classification of position held by an employee appointed under section 1104(a)(2) of this title, was struck out.

1974—Subsec. (c). Pub. L. 93–406 added subsec. (c). A prior subsec. (c) was repealed by Pub. L. 91–34.

1969—Subsec. (c). Pub. L. 91–34 repealed subsec. (c) provisions classifying positions on National Zoological Park police force authorized pursuant to section 193n of title 40.

EFFECTIVE DATE OF 1990 AMENDMENT

Amendment by Pub. L. 101–509 effective on such date as the President shall determine, but not earlier than 90 days, and not later than 180 days, after Nov. 5, 1990, see section 529 [title III, § 305] of Pub. L. 101–509, set out as a note under section 5301 of this title.

EFFECTIVE DATE OF 1978 AMENDMENT

Amendment by Pub. L. 95–454 effective 90 days after Oct. 13, 1978, see section 907 of Pub. L. 95–454, set out as a note under section 1101 of this title.

EFFECTIVE DATE OF 1974 AMENDMENT

Amendment by Pub. L. 93–406 effective on 90th day after Sept. 2, 1974, see section 1051(d) of Pub. L. 93–406, set out as a note under section 7802 of Title 26, Internal Revenue Code.

EFFECTIVE DATE OF 1969 AMENDMENT

Amendment by Pub. L. 91–34 effective at beginning of first pay period which commences on or after June 30, 1969, see section 3(a) of Pub. L. 91–34, set out as an Effective Date note under section 5375 of this title.

REDUCTION OF BASIC PAY RATE

Rate of basic pay not to be reduced by reason of enactment of Pub. L. 91–34, which amended this section, see section 3(b) of Pub. L. 91–34, set out as a note under section 5365 of this title.

SECTION REFERRED TO IN OTHER SECTIONS

This section is referred to in section 5115 of this title.

§ 5110. Review of classification of positions

(a) The Office of Personnel Management, from time to time, shall review such number of positions in each agency as will enable the Office to determine whether the agency is placing positions in classes and grades in conformance with or consistently with published standards.

(b) When the Office finds under subsection (a) of this section that a position is not placed in its proper class and grade in conformance with published standards or that a position for which there is no published standard is not placed in the class and grade consistently with published standards, it shall, after consultation with appropriate officials of the agency concerned, place the position in its appropriate class and grade and shall certify this action to the agency. The agency shall act in accordance with the certificate, and the certificate is binding on all administrative, certifying, payroll, disbursing, and accounting officials.

(Pub. L. 89–554, Sept. 6, 1966, 80 Stat. 455; Pub. L. 95–454, title IX, § 906(a)(2), (3), Oct. 13, 1978, 92 Stat. 1224.)

HISTORICAL AND REVISION NOTES

Derivation	U.S. Code	Revised Statutes and Statutes at Large
(a)	5 U.S.C. 1102(b).	Oct. 28, 1949, ch. 782, § 502(b), 63 Stat. 958.
(b)	5 U.S.C. 1103.	Oct. 28, 1949, ch. 782, § 503, 63 Stat. 958.

In subsection (b), the words "to which this chapter applies" are omitted as unnecessary in view of section 5102. The words "appropriate officials" and "administrative, certifying, payroll, disbursing, and accounting officials" are substituted for "appropriate officers and employees" and "administrative, certifying, payroll, disbursing, and accounting officers", respectively, to preserve the application to members of the uniformed services who are excluded from the definition of "officer" and "employee".

Standard changes are made to conform with the definitions applicable and the style of this title as outlined in the preface to the report.

AMENDMENTS

1978—Subsecs. (a), (b). Pub. L. 95–454 substituted "Office of Personnel Management" and "Office" for "Civil Service Commission" and "Commission", respectively.

EFFECTIVE DATE OF 1978 AMENDMENT

Amendment by Pub. L. 95–454 effective 90 days after Oct. 13, 1978, see section 907 of Pub. L. 95–454, set out as a note under section 1101 of this title.

§ 5111. Revocation and restoration of authority to classify positions

(a) When the Office of Personnel Management finds that an agency is not placing positions in classes and grades in conformance with or consistently with published standards, it may revoke or suspend the authority granted to the agency by section 5107 of this title and require that prior approval of the Office be secured before an action placing a position in a class and grade becomes effective for payroll and other personnel purposes. The Office may limit the revocation or suspension to—

(1) the departmental or field service, or any part thereof;

(2) a geographic area;

(3) an organization unit or group of organization units;

(4) certain types of classification actions;

(5) classes in particular occupational groups or grades; or

(6) classes for which standards have not been published.

(b) After revocation or suspension, the Office may restore the authority to the extent that it is satisfied that later actions placing positions in classes and grades will be in conformance with or consistent with published standards.

(Pub. L. 89–554, Sept. 6, 1966, 80 Stat. 455; Pub. L. 95–454, title IX, § 906(a)(2), (3), Oct. 13, 1978, 92 Stat. 1224.)

HISTORICAL AND REVISION NOTES

Derivation	U.S. Code	Revised Statutes and Statutes at Large
....	5 U.S.C. 1104.	Oct. 28, 1949, ch. 782, § 504, 63 Stat. 959.

In subsection (a), the words "in whole or in part" are omitted as unnecessary in view of the specific authority to limit the revocation or suspension. The words "The Commission may limit the revocation or suspension to" are substituted for "Such revocations or suspensions may be limited, in the discretion of the Commission, to" to eliminate redundancy.

In subsection (b), the words "After revocation or suspension" are substituted for "After all or part of the authority of the department has been revoked or suspended". The words "may restore" are substituted for "may at any time restore" to eliminate redundancy.

Standard changes are made to conform with the definitions applicable and the style of this title as outlined in the preface to the report.

AMENDMENTS

1978—Subsecs. (a), (b). Pub. L. 95–454 substituted "Office of Personnel Management" and "Office" for "Civil Service Commission" and "Commission", respectively, wherever appearing.

EFFECTIVE DATE OF 1978 AMENDMENT

Amendment by Pub. L. 95–454 effective 90 days after Oct. 13, 1978, see section 907 of Pub. L. 95–454, set out as a note under section 1101 of this title.

§ 5112. General authority of the Office of Personnel Management

(a) Notwithstanding section 5107 of this title, the Office of Personnel Management may—

(1) ascertain currently the facts as to the duties, responsibilities, and qualification requirements of a position;

(2) place in an appropriate class and grade a newly created position or a position coming initially under this chapter;

(3) decide whether a position is in its appropriate class and grade; and

(4) change a position from one class or grade to another class or grade when the facts warrant.

The Office shall certify to the agency concerned its action under paragraph (2) or (4) of this subsection. The agency shall act in accordance with the certificate, and the certificate is binding on all administrative, certifying, payroll, disbursing, and accounting officials.

(b) An employee affected or an agency may request at any time that the Office exercise the authority granted to it by subsection (a) of this section and the Office shall act on the request.

(Pub. L. 89–554, Sept. 6, 1966, 80 Stat. 456; Pub. L. 95–454, title IX, § 906(a)(2), (3), (17), Oct. 13, 1978, 92 Stat. 1224, 1226.)

HISTORICAL AND REVISION NOTES

Derivation	U.S. Code	Revised Statutes and Statutes at Large
....	5 U.S.C. 1101.	Oct. 28, 1949, ch. 782, § 501, 63 Stat. 958.

In subsection (a), the words "which may be exercised at any time in its discretion" are omitted as redundant. The words "is binding on all administrative, certifying, payroll, disbursing, and accounting officials"

are substituted for "shall be binding on all administrative, certifying, payroll, disbursing, and accounting officers of the Government" to preserve the application to members of the uniformed services.

Standard changes are made to conform with the definitions applicable and the style of this title as outlined in the preface to the report.

AMENDMENTS

1978—Pub. L. 95–454, § 906(a)(17), substituted "Office of Personnel Management" for "Civil Service Commission" in section catchline.

Subsecs. (a), (b). Pub. L. 95–454, § 906(a)(2), (3), substituted "Office of Personnel Management" and "Office" for "Civil Service Commission" and "Commission", respectively, wherever appearing.

EFFECTIVE DATE OF 1978 AMENDMENT

Amendment by Pub. L. 95–454 effective 90 days after Oct. 13, 1978, see section 907 of Pub. L. 95–454, set out as a note under section 1101 of this title.

SECTION REFERRED TO IN OTHER SECTIONS

This section is referred to in section 5366 of this title.

§ 5113. Classification records

The Office of Personnel Management may—

(1) prescribe the form in which each agency shall record the duties and responsibilities of positions and the places where these records shall be maintained;

(2) examine these or other pertinent records of the agency; and

(3) interview employees of the agency who have knowledge of the duties and responsibilities of positions and information as to the reasons for placing a position in a class or grade.

(Pub. L. 89–554, Sept. 6, 1966, 80 Stat. 456; Pub. L. 95–454, title IX, § 906(a)(2), Oct. 13, 1978, 92 Stat. 1224.)

HISTORICAL AND REVISION NOTES

Derivation	U.S. Code	Revised Statutes and Statutes at Large
....	5 U.S.C. 1106.	Oct. 28, 1949, ch. 782, § 506, 63 Stat. 959.

In paragraph (1), the words "to which this chapter applies" are omitted as unnecessary in view of section 5102.

Standard changes are made to conform with the definitions applicable and the style of this title as outlined in the preface to the report.

AMENDMENTS

1978—Pub. L. 95–454 substituted "Office of Personnel Management" for "Civil Service Commission".

EFFECTIVE DATE OF 1978 AMENDMENT

Amendment by Pub. L. 95–454 effective 90 days after Oct. 13, 1978, see section 907 of Pub. L. 95–454, set out as a note under section 1101 of this title.

[§ 5114. Repealed. Pub. L. 99–386, title I, § 110(a), Aug. 22, 1986, 100 Stat. 822]

Section, Pub. L. 89–554, Sept. 6, 1966, 80 Stat. 456; Pub. L. 95–454, title IX, § 906(a)(2), (3), Oct. 13, 1978, 92 Stat. 1224, related to reports to Congress on positions in GS–16, 17, and 18.

§ 5115. Regulations

The Office of Personnel Management may prescribe regulations necessary for the administration of this chapter, except sections 5109 and 5114.[1]

(Pub. L. 89–554, Sept. 6, 1966, 80 Stat. 457; Pub. L. 95–454, title IX, § 906(a)(2), Oct. 13, 1978, 92 Stat. 1224.)

HISTORICAL AND REVISION NOTES

Derivation	U.S. Code	Revised Statutes and Statutes at Large
....	5 U.S.C. 1072.	Oct. 28, 1949, ch. 782, § 1101, 63 Stat. 971.
....	5 U.S.C. 1072a.	Sept. 1, 1954, ch. 1208, § 113, 68 Stat. 1108.

Former sections 1072 and 1072a are combined and restated for clarity. The remainder of the authority is carried into sections 3324, 5338, and 7154.

Standard changes are made to conform with the definitions applicable and the style of this title as outlined in the preface to the report.

REFERENCES IN TEXT

Section 5114, referred to in text, was repealed by Pub. L. 99–386, title I, § 110(a), Aug. 22, 1986, 100 Stat. 822.

AMENDMENTS

1978—Pub. L. 95–454 substituted "Office of Personnel Management" for "Civil Service Commission".

EFFECTIVE DATE OF 1978 AMENDMENT

Amendment by Pub. L. 95–454 effective 90 days after Oct. 13, 1978, see section 907 of Pub. L. 95–454, set out as a note under section 1101 of this title.

CHAPTER 53—PAY RATES AND SYSTEMS

AMENDMENTS

2000—Pub. L. 106–554, § 1(a)(3) [title VI, § 645(a)(3)], Dec. 21, 2000, 114 Stat. 2763, 2763A–170, added item 5372b.

1992—Pub. L. 102–378, § 8(a), Oct. 2, 1992, 106 Stat. 1359, repealed Pub. L. 100–510, § 1206(i)(2). See 1990 Amendment note below.

Pub. L. 102–378, § 2(24), Oct. 2, 1992, 106 Stat. 1348, substituted "repayments" for "repayment" in item 5379 and struck out "Sec." before item 5391.

1990—Pub. L. 101–510, div. A, title XII, § 1206(i)(2), Nov. 5, 1990, 104 Stat. 1663, which added item 5380 "Pay authority for critical positions", was repealed by Pub. L. 102–378, § 8(a), Oct. 2, 1992, 106 Stat. 1359, which provided that this title shall read as if such section 1206(i)(2) had not been enacted.

Pub. L. 101–510, div. A, title XII, § 1206(b)(2), Nov. 5, 1990, 104 Stat. 1661, added item 5379.

---

[1] See References in Text note below.

Pub. L. 101–509, title V, §529 [title I, §§101(a)(2), 102(a)(2), 103(b), 104(b), 105(a)(2), 109(a)(1)(B), title II, §§205(b), 211(b)(2)], Nov. 5, 1990, 104 Stat. 1427, 1439, 1443, 1445, 1446, 1448, 1451, 1457, 1461, struck out items 5301 "Policy", 5303 "Higher minimum rates; Presidential authority", 5304 "Presidential policies and regulations", 5305 "Annual pay reports and adjustments", 5306 "Advisory Committee on Federal Pay", 5307 "Pay fixed by administrative action", and 5308 "Pay limitation", and added items 5301 to 5307, struck out "; higher rates for supervisors of prevailing rate employees" after "appointments" in item 5333, substituted "Health care positions" for "Scientific and professional positions" in item 5371, and added items 5372a, 5376 to 5378, item for subchapter IX, and items 5391 and 5392.

Pub. L. 101–263, §1(b), Apr. 4, 1990, 104 Stat. 125, inserted "the" before "National" in item 5375.

1979—Pub. L. 96–54, §2(a)(26)(B), Aug. 14, 1979, 93 Stat. 382, substituted "prevailing rate" for "wage-board" in item 5333.

1978—Pub. L. 95–454, title IV, §407(b), title VIII, §801(a)(3)(B)(i), (ii), Oct. 13, 1978, 92 Stat. 1172, 1221, struck out items 5337 "Pay saving" and 5345 "Retained rate of pay on reduction in grade or reassignment", added item for subchapter VI and items 5361 to 5366, redesignated former item for subchapter VI and items 5361 to 5365 as subchapter VII and items 5371 to 5375, respectively, and added item for subchapter VIII and items 5381 to 5385.

Pub. L. 95–251, §2(c)(4), Mar. 27, 1978, 92 Stat. 184, substituted "Administrative law judges" for "Hearing examiners" in item 5362.

1975—Pub. L. 94–82, title II, §202(b)(6), Aug. 9, 1975, 89 Stat. 420, added item 5318.

1972—Pub. L. 92–392, §1(b), Aug. 19, 1972, 86 Stat. 572, substituted items 5341, 5343, 5344, and 5345 relating to "Policy", "Prevailing rate determinations; wage schedules; night differentials", "Effective date of wage increase; retroactive pay" and "Retained rate of pay on reduction in grade or reassignment", for such former items relating to "Trades and crafts", "Effective date of pay increase", "Retroactive pay" and "Position classification appeals", added items 5342, 5346, 5347, and 5349, and renumbered former item 5342 as 5348.

1971—Pub. L. 91–656, §§2(b)(2), 3(b), Jan. 8, 1971, 84 Stat. 1946, 1951, struck out item 5302 "Annual reports on pay comparability" and added items 5305–5308.

1969—Pub. L. 91–34, §1(b), June 30, 1969, 83 Stat. 41, added item 5365.

1967—Pub. L. 90–206, title II, §223(b), Dec. 16, 1967, 81 Stat. 642, added item 5345.

CHAPTER REFERRED TO IN OTHER SECTIONS

This chapter is referred to in sections 3372, 5363, 9503 of this title; title 10 section 9314; title 15 section 770; title 20 sections 1018, 3502; title 22 sections 2124c, 2385, 3963, 4606; title 35 section 3; title 38 sections 7404, 7451; title 40 section 166b–3b; title 42 sections 5872, 7292.

SUBCHAPTER I—PAY COMPARABILITY SYSTEM

SUBCHAPTER REFERRED TO IN OTHER SECTIONS

This subchapter is referred to in section 8340 of this title; title 22 sections 3963, 4606; title 31 section 325; title 42 section 7211; title 50 section 2131.

§ 5301. Policy

It is the policy of Congress that Federal pay fixing for employees under the General Schedule be based on the principles that—

(1) there be equal pay for substantially equal work within each local pay area;

(2) within each local pay area, pay distinctions be maintained in keeping with work and performance distinctions;

(3) Federal pay rates be comparable with non-Federal pay rates for the same levels of work within the same local pay area; and

(4) any existing pay disparities between Federal and non-Federal employees should be completely eliminated.

(Pub. L. 89–554, Sept. 6, 1966, 80 Stat. 458; Pub. L. 91–656, §2(a), Jan. 8, 1971, 84 Stat. 1946; Pub. L. 96–465, title II, §2314(c)(1), Oct. 17, 1980, 94 Stat. 2167; Pub. L. 101–509, title V, §529 [title I, §101(a)(1)], Nov. 5, 1990, 104 Stat. 1427, 1429.)

HISTORICAL AND REVISION NOTES

Derivation	U.S. Code	Revised Statutes and Statutes at Large
....	5 U.S.C. 1171.	Oct. 11, 1962, Pub. L. 87–793, §502, 76 Stat. 841.

The words "It is the policy of Congress" are substituted for "The Congress hereby declares". The words "whereas the functions of a Federal salary system are to fix salary rates for the services rendered by Federal employees so as to make possible the employment of persons well qualified to conduct the Government's programs and to control expenditures of public funds for personal services with equity to the employee and to the taxpayer, and whereas fulfillment of these functions is essential to the development and maintenance of maximum proficiency in the civilian services of Government, then, accordingly" are omitted as unnecessary.

In the last sentence, the words "and henceforth" are omitted as executed.

Standard changes are made to conform with the definitions applicable and the style of this title as outlined in the preface to the report.

AMENDMENTS

1990—Pub. L. 101–509 amended section generally. Prior to amendment, section read as follows:

"(a) It is the policy of Congress that Federal pay fixing for employees under statutory pay systems be based on the principles that—

"(1) there be equal pay for substantially equal work;

"(2) pay distinctions be maintained in keeping with work and performance distinctions;

"(3) Federal pay rates be comparable with private enterprise pay rates for the same levels of work; and

"(4) pay levels for the statutory pay systems be interrelated.

"(b) The pay rates of each statutory pay system shall be fixed and adjusted in accordance with the principles under subsection (a) of this section and the provisions of sections 5305, 5306, and 5308 of this title.

"(c) For the purpose of this subchapter, 'statutory pay system' means a pay system under—

"(1) subchapter III of this chapter, relating to the General Schedule;

"(2) section 403 of the Foreign Service Act of 1980, relating to the Foreign Service of the United States; or

"(3) chapter 73 of title 38, relating to the Department of Medicine and Surgery, Veterans' Administration."

1980—Subsec. (c)(2). Pub. L. 96–465 substituted "section 403 of the Foreign Service Act of 1980" for "subchapter IV of chapter 14 of title 22".

1971—Pub. L. 91–656 designated provisions of first sentence as subsec. (a), incorporating former cl. (1) in cls. (1) and (2), and former cl. (2) in cl. (3), and inserted "for employees under statutory pay systems" after "Federal pay fixing"; substituted subsec. (b) reading "The pay rates of each statutory pay system shall be fixed and adjusted in accordance with the principles under subsection (a) of this section and the provisions of sections 5305, 5306, and 5308 of this title" for former second sentence providing "Pay levels for the several Federal statutory pay systems shall be interrelated, and pay levels shall be set and adjusted in accordance with these principles"; and added subsec. (c).

EFFECTIVE DATE OF 1990 AMENDMENT

Section 529 [title III, § 305] of Pub. L. 101–509 provided that:

"(a) GENERALLY.—Except as otherwise provided in this Act, this Act and the amendments made by this Act [this Act means section 529 [titles I–III, §§ 1–306] of Pub. L. 101–509, but does not include section 529 [title IV, §§ 401–412] of Pub. L. 101–509, see Short Title of 1990 Amendment; Rules of Construction note below, and see Tables for classification] shall take effect on such date as the President shall determine [see Ex. Ord. No. 12748, Feb. 1, 1991, 56 F.R. 4521, set out below], but not earlier than 90 days, and not later than 180 days, after the date of enactment of this Act [Nov. 5, 1990].

"(b) SPECIAL RULE.—The first calendar year in which comparability payments under section 5304 of title 5, United States Code (as amended by this Act), are paid shall be the calendar year beginning on January 1, 1994."

EFFECTIVE DATE OF 1980 AMENDMENT

Amendment by Pub. L. 96–465 effective Feb. 15, 1981, except as otherwise provided, see section 2403 of Pub. L. 96–465, set out as an Effective Date note under section 3901 of Title 22, Foreign Relations and Intercourse.

SHORT TITLE OF 2000 AMENDMENT

Pub. L. 106–554, § 1(a)(4) [div. B, title IX, § 901], Dec. 21, 2000, 114 Stat. 2763, 2763A–303, provided that: "This title [enacting provisions set out as notes under sections 5304 and 5305 of this title and section 204 of Title 3, The President, and amending provisions set out as a note under section 5305 of this title] may be cited as the 'Law Enforcement Pay Equity Act of 2000'."

SHORT TITLE OF 1993 AMENDMENT

Pub. L. 103–89, § 1, Sept. 30, 1993, 107 Stat. 981, provided that: "This Act [amending sections 3372, 4501, 4502, 5302, 5332, 5334 to 5336, 5361 to 5363, 5410, 5948, and 8473 of this title, sections 1602, 1732, and 1733 of Title 10, Armed Forces, and section 731 of Title 31, Money and Finance, repealing sections 4302a and 5401 to 5410 of this title, enacting provisions set out as notes under sections 3372, 5335, 5401, and 5410 of this title, and amending provisions set out as a note under section 5304 of this title] may be cited as the 'Performance Management and Recognition System Termination Act'."

SHORT TITLE OF 1990 AMENDMENT; RULES OF CONSTRUCTION

Section 529 [§ 1] of Pub. L. 101–509 provided that:

"(a) SHORT TITLE.—This section, and the sections immediately following this section through section 412, inclusive [section 529 [§§ 1–412] of Pub. L. 101–509, see Tables for classification], may be cited as the 'Federal Employees Pay Comparability Act of 1990' (hereinafter in this section referred to as 'FEPCA').

"(b) RULES OF CONSTRUCTION.—(1) Except as otherwise expressly provided, any reference (actual or implicit) in FEPCA (outside of this section) to 'this Act' (or to any title, section, or other designated provision of 'this Act') shall be construed to be a reference to FEPCA (or the corresponding provision within FEPCA).

"(2) Except as otherwise expressly provided, any reference (actual or implicit) in any provision of this Act outside of FEPCA to 'this Act' (or to any title, section, or other designated provision of 'this Act'), and any reference made in any provision of law outside of this Act to the 'Treasury, Postal Service and General Government Appropriations Act, 1991' [Pub. L. 101–509] (or to any title, section, or other designated provision of such Act), shall be construed disregarding the provisions of FEPCA."

Section 529 [title III, § 306] of Pub. L. 101–509 provided that: "Notwithstanding section 1(b) [section 529 [§ 1(b)] of Pub. L. 101–509, set out above], a reference in any of the preceding provisions of this title [section 529 [title III, §§ 301–305] of Pub. L. 101–509, enacting section 237 of

Title 42, The Public Health and Welfare, amending section 212 of Title 42, and enacting provisions set out as notes under this section, section 5304 of this title, and section 212 of Title 42] to 'this Act' [section 529 of Pub. L. 101–509] (other than a reference in section 301) [section 529 [title III, § 301] of Pub. L. 101–509, set out below] shall not be considered to include any provision of title IV [section 529 [title IV, §§ 401–412] of Pub. L. 101–509, enacting sections 4521 to 4523 of this title, amending sections 5541, 5542, 5547, 8335, and 8425 of this title, enacting provisions set out as notes under sections 4521, 5305, 5541, and 8335 of this title, and amending provisions set out as a note under section 5541 of this title]."

SHORT TITLE

Section 1 of Pub. L. 91–656 provided that: "This Act [enacting sections 5305 to 5308 and 5947 of this title, amending this section, sections 5108 and 5942 of this title, and section 410 of Title 39, Postal Service, repealing section 5302 of this title, and enacting provisions set out as notes under sections 5303 and 5942 of this title, section 60a of Title 2, The Congress, and section 410 of Title 39] may be cited as the 'Federal Pay Comparability Act of 1970'."

PAY-FOR-PERFORMANCE LABOR-MANAGEMENT COMMITTEE

Section 529 [title I, § 111] of Pub. L. 101–509 provided that:

"(a) POLICY.—It is the policy of Congress that—

"(1) the Federal Government should institute systems for determining pay for its General Schedule employees under which the linkage between their performance and their pay will be strengthened;

"(2) the design of such systems should be developed by the Office of Personnel Management, in conjunction with the Pay-for-Performance Labor-Management Committee;

"(3) the systems should provide flexibility to adapt to the different needs of different agencies and organizational components in the Federal Government; and

"(4) any legislation needed to implement the systems should be enacted in a timely fashion so as to permit implementation of the system by October 1, 1993.

"(b) ESTABLISHMENT.—The Office of Personnel Management shall establish a Pay-for-Performance Labor-Management Committee to advise the Office on the design and establishment of systems for strengthening the linkage between the performance of General Schedule employees and their pay.

"(c) MEMBERSHIP.—The members of the Committee shall be—

"(1) a Chairman, who shall be appointed by the Director of the Office of Personnel Management on the basis of the appointee's education, training, and experience as an expert in compensation practices, and after consultation with the Committee on Governmental Affairs of the Senate and the Committee on Post Office and Civil Service of the House of Representatives, respectively;

"(2) an employee of the Office of Personnel Management, designated by the Director of such Office;

"(3) an employee of the Department of Defense, designated by the Secretary of Defense;

"(4) 3 individuals, each of whom shall be an employee designated by the head of each of 3 other departments or agencies selected by the Director of the Office of Personnel Management from among departments and agencies having substantial numbers of General Schedule employees; and

"(5) 6 individuals appointed by the Director of the Office of Personnel Management to serve as representatives of employee organizations which represent substantial numbers of General Schedule employees, and who shall be selected with due consideration to such factors as the relative numbers of General Schedule employees represented by the various organizations, except that not more than 3 members of the Committee at any one time shall be from a single employee organization, council, federation, alliance, association, or affiliation of employee organizations.

"(d) PAY FOR MEMBERS.—The Chairman shall be paid at a rate of basic pay for the Senior Executive Service, to be determined by the Director of the Office of Personnel Management. The members of the Committee who are otherwise employees of the Federal Government shall not receive any additional pay by reason of their service on the Committee. The members of the Committee who are not otherwise employees of the Federal Government shall not be paid for their service on the Committee and shall not be considered employees of the Federal Government for any purpose by reason of their service on the Committee.

"(e) ADMINISTRATIVE SUPPORT.—The Office of Personnel Management may provide staff and administrative support for the Committee.

"(f) FUNCTIONS.—The Committee shall review available reports and studies on performance evaluation and performance-based pay systems (including a report to be prepared by the National Academy of Sciences) and any other pertinent information.

"(g) REPORT TO THE OFFICE OF PERSONNEL MANAGEMENT.—No later than 1 year after the date of enactment of this Act [Nov. 5, 1990], the Committee shall submit a report to the Director of the Office of Personnel Management, which shall include recommendations as to—

"(1) the types of pay raises to be covered;

"(2) guidelines for pay-for-performance systems, including the criteria to be used in determining eligibility for and the amount of increases in basic pay above the midpoint of the pay range;

"(3) the role organization performance should play in pay-for-performance systems;

"(4) any differences in pay-for-performance systems for different categories of employees;

"(5) the role for employee organizations in the implementation and operation of pay-for-performance systems; and

"(6) whether demonstration projects on pay-for-performance are desirable."

BUDGET ACT COMPLIANCE

Section 529 [title III, § 301] of Pub. L. 101–509 provided that: "For purposes of the Congressional Budget Act of 1974 [titles I through IX, of Pub. L. 93–344, July 12, 1974, 88 Stat. 297, see Tables for classification], any authority to make payments under this Act or any amendment made by this Act [see Short Title of 1990 Amendment note above] shall be effective only to the extent provided for in advance in appropriation Acts."

PAY RATES FOR CURRENT EMPLOYEES

Section 529 [title III, § 303] of Pub. L. 101–509 provided that: "Nothing in this Act or in any amendment made by this Act [see Short Title of 1990 Amendment note above] shall have the effect of diminishing the rate of basic pay payable to any individual employed by the United States on the date of the enactment of this Act [Nov. 5, 1990] to a rate below the rate payable to such individual on such date, so long as that individual continues in such position without a break in service."

EX. ORD. NO. 12748. PROVIDING FOR FEDERAL PAY ADMINISTRATION

Ex. Ord. No. 12748, Feb. 1, 1991, 56 F.R. 4521, as amended by Ex. Ord. No. 12883, Nov. 29, 1993, 58 F.R. 63281; Ex. Ord. No. 13106, § 8, Dec. 7, 1998, 63 F.R. 68152, provided:

By the authority vested in me as President by the Constitution and the laws of the United States of America, including the Federal Employees Pay Comparability Act of 1990 (hereinafter "FEPCA"), as incorporated in section 529 of Public Law 101–509 [see Short Title of 1990 Amendment note above], and sections 3301 and 3302 of title 5, United States Code, it is hereby ordered as follows:

SECTION 1. *Annual Adjustments to Pay Schedules.* The following agencies are designated under section 5303(g) of title 5, United States Code, as amended by FEPCA, to prescribe conversion rules for the initial adjustment of rates of pay to be applied during each annual adjustment of pay schedules under section 5303 of title 5, United Stated Code:

(a) the Office of Personnel Management, for the General Schedule;

(b) the Department of State, for the Foreign Service Schedule; and

(c) the Department of Veterans Affairs, for the Veterans Health Services and Research Administration Schedules.

SEC. 2. *Locality-based Comparability Payments.* (a) The Secretary of Labor, the Director of the Office of Management and Budget, and the Director of the Office of Personnel Management are hereby designated under section 5304(d)(1) of title 5, United States Code, as amended by FEPCA, to serve jointly as the President's agent under section 5304 of title 5, United States Code, and shall be known in this capacity as the President's Pay Agent.

(b) The head of each executive agency employing personnel under a statutory pay system, as defined in section 5302(1) of title 5, United States Code, as amended by FEPCA, shall provide such information and assistance as may be requested by the President's Pay Agent in carrying out the provisions of section 5304 of title 5, United States Code.

(c) The President's Pay Agent, as designated in subsection (a), is hereby authorized and designated to exercise the authorities of the President under section 5304(g)–(h) [5 U.S.C. 5304(g), (h)] concerning the extension of locality-based comparability payments to certain categories of positions not otherwise covered.

SEC. 3. *Special Pay Authority.* (a) The Office of Personnel Management is hereby authorized and designated, pursuant to section 5305(a) of title 5, United States Code, as amended by section 101 of FEPCA, to exercise the authorities of the President under section 5305 of title 5, United States Code, concerning higher rates of pay.

(b) Before exercising the delegated authorities under subsection (a) regarding employees in positions other than those covered by the General Schedule, the Office of Personnel Management shall consult with the head of the agency employing such employees.

SEC. 4. *Previous Order Revoked.* Executive Order No. 11721, as amended, is revoked.

SEC. 5. *Advance Payments for New Appointees.* Section 2(b) of Executive Order No. 10982, as amended [5 U.S.C. 5527 note], is further amended to read as follows:

"(b) The Office of Personnel Management is hereby designated and empowered to perform the functions conferred upon the President by the provisions of section 5527 of title 5, United States Code, with respect to allotments and assignments authorized by section 5525 of title 5, United States Code, and advance payments to new appointees authorized by section 5524a of title 5, United States Code, as added by section 107(a) of the Federal Employees Pay Comparability Act of 1990, as incorporated in section 529 of Public Law 101–509."

SEC. 6. *Extension of Cash Awards, Recruitment and Relocation Bonuses, and Retention Allowances.* The Office of Personnel Management is hereby designated and empowered to exercise the authority of the President under:

(a) section 4505a(d) of title 5, United States Code, as added by section 207(a) of FEPCA, concerning the application of performance-based cash awards to noncovered categories of employees;

(b) section 5753(e) of title 5, United States Code, as added by section 208 of FEPCA, concerning the application of recruitment and relocation bonuses to noncovered categories of employees; and

(c) section 5754(e) of title 5, United States Code, as added by section 208 of FEPCA, concerning the application of retention allowances to noncovered categories of employees.

Sec. 7. *Staffing Differentials.* The Office of Personnel Management is hereby designated and empowered to exercise the authority of the President under section 209 of FEPCA [5 U.S.C. 5305 note] to establish staffing differentials.

Sec. 8. *Executive Assignment System.* (a) Civil Service Rule 9 (5 CFR Part 9), as established by Executive Order No. 11315, as amended [5 U.S.C. 3301 note], is revoked.

(b) The Office of Personnel Management shall take such actions as the Office may determine to be necessary to provide for the orderly termination of the Executive Assignment System.

Sec. 9. *Effective Dates.* (a) Except as otherwise provided by Public Law 101–509, the provisions of subchapter I of chapter 53 of title 5, United States Code, as amended by section 101 of FEPCA [this subchapter], and the provisions of sections 1 through 4 of this order shall take effect on February 3, 1991.

(b) Except as otherwise provided by Public Law 101–509, the remaining provisions of FEPCA and of this order shall take effect on May 4, 1991, except that the Office of Personnel Management may establish an earlier effective date, but not earlier than February 3, 1991, for any such provisions with respect to which the Office determines an earlier effective date is appropriate. [For effective dates of certain provisions of FEPCA as established by the Office of Personnel Management, see notices and rules issued by the Office of Personnel Management and published in the Federal Register at 56 F.R. 6212, 11059, 12833, 20339, and 20343.]

ACT REFERRED TO IN OTHER SECTIONS

The Federal Pay Comparability Act of 1970 is referred to in title 19 sections 2075, 2171.

SECTION REFERRED TO IN OTHER SECTIONS

This section is referred to in title 31 section 732; title 42 section 12651f.

§ 5302. Definitions

For the purpose of this subchapter—

(1) the term "statutory pay system" means a pay system under—

(A) subchapter III, relating to the General Schedule;

(B) section 403 of the Foreign Service Act of 1980, relating to the Foreign Service of the United States; or

(C) chapter 74 of title 38, relating to the Veterans Health Administration (other than a position subject to section 7451 of title 38);

(2) the term "ECI" means the Employment Cost Index (wages and salaries, private industry workers) published quarterly by the Bureau of Labor Statistics;

(3) the "base quarter" for any year is the 3-month period ending on September 30 of such year;

(4) the term "pay agent" means the agent designated by the President under section 5304(d)(1);

(5) the term "locality" or "pay locality" means any locality, as established or modified under section 5304;

(6) the term "pay disparity", as used with respect to a locality, means the extent to which rates of pay payable under the General Schedule are generally lower than the rates paid for the same levels of work by non-Federal workers in the same locality; except as otherwise required in this subchapter, a pay disparity shall be expressed as a single percentage which, if uniformly applied to employees within the locality who are receiving rates of pay under the General Schedule, would cause the rates payable to such employees to become substantially equal (when considered in the aggregate) to the rates paid to non-Federal workers for the same levels of work in the same locality;

(7) the term "comparability payment" means a payment payable under section 5304;

(8) the term "rates of pay under the General Schedule", "rates of pay for the General Schedule", or "scheduled rates of basic pay" means—

(A) the rates of basic pay set forth in the General Schedule; and

(B) in the case of an employee receiving a retained rate of basic pay under section 5363, the rate of basic pay payable under such section; and

(9) the term "General Schedule position" means any position to which subchapter III applies.

(Added Pub. L. 101–509, title V, §529 [title I, §101(a)(1)], Nov. 5, 1990, 104 Stat. 1427, 1429; amended Pub. L. 102–378, §2(25), Oct. 2, 1992, 106 Stat. 1348; Pub. L. 103–89, §3(b)(1)(E), Sept. 30, 1993, 107 Stat. 981.)

REFERENCES IN TEXT

Section 403 of the Foreign Service Act of 1980, referred to in par. (1)(B), is classified to section 3963 of Title 22, Foreign Relations and Intercourse.

PRIOR PROVISIONS

A prior section 5302, Pub. L. 89–554, Sept. 6, 1966, 80 Stat. 458, provided for annual reports on pay comparability, prior to repeal by Pub. L. 91–656, §2(b)(1), Jan. 8, 1971, 84 Stat. 1946.

AMENDMENTS

1993—Par. (8). Pub. L. 103–89, §3(b)(1)(E)(i), redesignated subpar. (C) as (B) and struck out former subpar. (B) which read as follows: "in the case of an employee covered by the performance management and recognition system, the rates of basic pay under chapter 54; and".

Par. (9). Pub. L. 103–89, §3(b)(1)(E)(ii), substituted "applies" for "applies (including any position under the performance management and recognition system)".

1992—Par. (1)(C). Pub. L. 102–378, §2(25)(A), amended subpar. (C) generally. Prior to amendment, subpar. (C) read as follows: "chapter 73 of title 38, relating to the Veterans Health Services and Research Administration;".

Par. (8)(C). Pub. L. 102–378, §2(25)(B), added subpar. (C).

EFFECTIVE DATE OF 1993 AMENDMENT

Amendment by Pub. L. 103–89 effective Nov. 1, 1993, see section 3(c) of Pub. L. 103–89, set out as a note under section 3372 of this title.

EFFECTIVE DATE OF 1992 AMENDMENT

Amendment by Pub. L. 102–378 effective Feb. 3, 1991, see section 9(b)(5) of Pub. L. 102–378, set out as a note under section 6303 of this title.

EFFECTIVE DATE

Section effective on such date as the President shall determine, but not earlier than 90 days, and not later than 180 days, after Nov. 5, 1990, see section 529 [title III, §305] of Pub. L. 101–509, set out as an Effective Date of 1990 Amendment note under section 5301 of this title.

This section is referred to in section 5304 of this title; title 2 section 906; title 18 section 207.

§ 5303. Annual adjustments to pay schedules

(a) Effective as of the first day of the first applicable pay period beginning on or after January 1 of each calendar year, the rates of basic pay for each statutory pay system shall be increased by the percentage (rounded to the nearest one-tenth of 1 percent) equal to one-half of 1 percentage point less than the percentage by which the ECI for the base quarter of the year before the preceding calendar year exceeds the ECI for the base quarter of the second year before the preceding calendar year (if at all).

(b)(1) If, because of national emergency or serious economic conditions affecting the general welfare, the President should consider the pay adjustment which would otherwise be required by subsection (a) in any year to be inappropriate, the President shall—

(A) prepare and transmit to Congress before September 1 of the preceding calendar year a plan for such alternative pay adjustments as he considers appropriate, together with the reasons therefor; and

(B) adjust the rates of pay of each statutory pay system, in accordance with such plan, effective on the same day as the increase under subsection (a) would otherwise take effect.

(2) In evaluating an economic condition affecting the general welfare under this subsection, the President shall consider pertinent economic measures including, but not limited to, the Indexes of Leading Economic Indicators, the Gross National Product, the unemployment rate, the budget deficit, the Consumer Price Index, the Producer Price Index, the Employment Cost Index, and the Implicit Price Deflator for Personal Consumption Expenditures.

(3) The President shall include in the report to Congress under paragraph (1)(A) his assessment of the impact that the alternative pay adjustments under this subsection will have on the Government's ability to recruit and retain well-qualified employees.

(c) The rates of basic pay that take effect under this section—

(1) shall modify, supersede, or render inapplicable, as the case may be, to the extent inconsistent therewith, any prior rates of basic pay under the statutory pay system involved (as last adjusted under this section or prior provisions of law); and

(2) shall be printed in the Federal Register and the Code of Federal Regulations.

(d) An increase in rates of basic pay that takes effect under this section is not an equivalent increase in pay within the meaning of section 5335.

(e) This section does not impair any authority pursuant to which rates of basic pay may be fixed by administrative action.

(f) Pay may not be paid, by reason of any provision of this section (disregarding any comparability payment payable), at a rate in excess of the rate of basic pay payable for level V of the Executive Schedule.

(g) Any rate of pay under this section shall be initially adjusted, effective on the effective date of the rate of pay, under conversion rules prescribed by the President or by such agency or agencies as the President may designate.

(Pub. L. 89–554, Sept. 6, 1966, 80 Stat. 458; Pub. L. 90–206, title II, §207, Dec. 16, 1967, 81 Stat. 631; Pub. L. 91–375, §6(c)(10), Aug. 12, 1970, 84 Stat. 776; Pub. L. 94–183, §2(16), Dec. 31, 1975, 89 Stat. 1057; Pub. L. 95–454, title IX, §906(a)(2), Oct. 13, 1978, 92 Stat. 1224; Pub. L. 96–465, title II, §2314(c)(2), Oct. 17, 1980, 94 Stat. 2167; Pub. L. 101–509, title V, §529 [title I, §101(a)(1)], Nov. 5, 1990, 104 Stat. 1427, 1430.)

HISTORICAL AND REVISION NOTES

Derivation	U.S. Code	Revised Statutes and Statutes at Large
....	5 U.S.C. 1173.	Oct. 11, 1962, Pub. L. 87–793, §504, 76 Stat. 842. Aug. 14, 1964, Pub. L. 88–426, §123, 78 Stat. 412.

In subsection (a), the words "the provisions of this title governing appointment in the competitive service" are substituted for "the civil service laws and regulations".

In subsections (a), (b), and (d), the word "agency" is substituted for "agency or agencies" because the singular imports the plural, see 1 U.S.C. 1.

In subsection (d), the word "officer" is omitted as included in "employee", "agency" is substituted for "department", and "rules" is omitted as included in "regulations".

Standard changes are made to conform with the definitions applicable and the style of this title as outlined in the preface to the report.

REFERENCES IN TEXT

Level V of the Executive Schedule, referred to in subsec. (f), is set out in section 5316 of this title.

AMENDMENTS

1990—Pub. L. 101–509 amended section generally, substituting provisions relating to annual adjustments to pay schedules for provisions relating to President's authority to set higher minimum rates of basic pay.

1980—Subsec. (a)(4). Pub. L. 96–465 substituted "section 403 of the Foreign Service Act of 1980" for "sections 867 and 870 of title 22".

1978—Subsec. (a). Pub. L. 95–454 substituted "Office of Personnel Management" for "Civil Service Commission".

1975—Subsec. (c). Pub. L. 94–183 struck out "and section 3552 of title 39" after "of section 5335(a) of this title".

1970—Subsec. (a)(2). Pub. L. 91–375 repealed cl. (2) making positions paid under provisions of part III of title 39 relating to employees in the postal field service subject to higher minimum rates established by the President.

1967—Subsec. (a). Pub. L. 90–206, §207(a), substituted "maximum pay rate" for "seventh pay rate".

Subsec. (d). Pub. L. 90–206, §207(b), inserted provisions that permitted an initial adjustment to be made to statutory increases which become effective prior to, on, or after the date of enactment of the statute.

EFFECTIVE DATE OF 1990 AMENDMENT

Amendment by Pub. L. 101–509 effective on such date as the President shall determine, but not earlier than 90 days, and not later than 180 days, after Nov. 5, 1990, see section 529 [title III, §305] of Pub. L. 101–509, set out as a note under section 5301 of this title.

EFFECTIVE DATE OF 1980 AMENDMENT

Amendment by Pub. L. 96–465 effective Feb. 15, 1981, except as otherwise provided, see section 2403 of Pub. L.

96–465, set out as an Effective Date note under section 3901 of Title 22, Foreign Relations and Intercourse.

EFFECTIVE DATE OF 1978 AMENDMENT

Amendment by Pub. L. 95–454 effective 90 days after Oct. 13, 1978, see section 907 of Pub. L. 95–454, set out as a note under section 1101 of this title.

EFFECTIVE DATE OF 1970 AMENDMENT

Amendment by Pub. L. 91–375 effective within 1 year after Aug. 12, 1970, on date established therefor by Board of Governors of United States Postal Service and published by it in Federal Register, see section 15(a) of Pub. L. 91–375, set out as an Effective Date note preceding section 101 of Title 39, Postal Service.

EFFECTIVE DATE OF 1967 AMENDMENT

Amendment by Pub. L. 90–206 effective Dec. 16, 1967, see section 220(a)(1) of Pub. L. 90–206, set out as an Effective Date note under section 3110 of this title.

DELEGATION OF FUNCTIONS

For designation of agencies to perform functions of President under subsec. (g) of this section, see Ex. Ord. No. 12748, § 1, Feb. 1, 1991, 56 F.R. 4521, eff. Feb. 3, 1991, set out as a note under section 5301 of this title.

PAY RAISES FOR PROGRAMS FUNDED BY ENERGY AND WATER DEVELOPMENT APPROPRIATIONS ACTS TO BE ABSORBED WITHIN SUCH ACTS

Pub. L. 102–377, title V, § 506, Oct. 2, 1992, 106 Stat. 1343, provided that: "Such sums as may be necessary for Federal employee pay raises for programs funded by this Act or subsequent Energy and Water Development Appropriations Acts hereafter shall be absorbed within the levels appropriated in such Acts."

SENSE OF CONGRESS

Section 529 [title I, § 101(e)] of Pub. L. 101–509 provided that: "It is the sense of the Congress that the total funds dedicated to adjustments under sections 5303 and 5304 [of this title] for any year be no less than the total funds that would have been dedicated to adjustments under such section 5303 for such year had the full change in the ECI been applied to pay rates for such year."

FEDERAL EMPLOYEE PAY ADJUSTMENTS

2000—Pub. L. 106–554, § 1(a)(4) [div. B, title I, § 140], Dec. 21, 2000, 114 Stat. 2763, 2763A–235, provided that:

"(a) The adjustment in rates of basic pay for the statutory pay systems that takes effect in fiscal year 2001 under sections 5303 and 5304 of title 5, United States Code, shall be an increase of 3.7 percent.

"(b) Funds used to carry out this section shall be paid from appropriations which are made to each applicable department or agency for salaries and expenses for fiscal year 2001."

1999—Pub. L. 106–58, title VI, § 646, Sept. 29, 1999, 113 Stat. 478, provided that:

"(a) The adjustment in rates of basic pay for the statutory pay systems that takes effect in fiscal year 2000 under sections 5303 and 5304 of title 5, United States Code, shall be an increase of 4.8 percent.

"(b) Funds used to carry out this section shall be paid from appropriations which are made to each applicable department or agency for salaries and expenses for fiscal year 2000."

1998—Pub. L. 105–277, div. A, § 101(h) [title VI, § 621], Oct. 21, 1998, 112 Stat. 2681–480, 2681–518, provided that: "For purposes of each provision of law amended by section 704(a)(2) of the Ethics Reform Act of 1989 [Pub. L. 101–194] (5 U.S.C. 5318 note), no adjustment under section 5303 of title 5, United States Code, shall be considered to have taken effect in fiscal year 1999 in the rates of basic pay for the statutory pay systems."

Pub. L. 105–277, div. A, § 101(h) [title VI, § 647], Oct. 21, 1998, 112 Stat. 2681–480, 2681–527, provided that:

"(a) The adjustment in rates of basic pay for the statutory pay systems that takes effect in fiscal year 1999 under sections 5303 and 5304 of title 5, United States Code, shall be an increase of 3.6 percent.

"(b) Funds used to carry out this section shall be paid from appropriations which are made to each applicable department or agency for salaries and expenses for fiscal year 1999."

1996—Pub. L. 104–208, div. A, title I, § 101(f) [title VI, § 637], Sept. 30, 1996, 110 Stat. 3009–314, 3009–364, provided that: "For purposes of each provision of law amended by section 704(a)(2) of the Ethics Reform Act of 1989 [Pub. L. 101–194] (5 U.S.C. 5318 note), no adjustment under section 5303 of title 5, United States Code, shall be considered to have taken effect in fiscal year 1997 in the rates of basic pay for the statutory pay systems."

1995—Pub. L. 104–52, title VI, § 633, Nov. 19, 1995, 109 Stat. 507, provided that: "For purposes of each provision of law amended by section 704(a)(2) of the Ethics Reform Act of 1989 [Pub. L. 101–194] (5 U.S.C. 5318 note), no adjustment under section 5303 of title 5, United States Code, shall be considered to have taken effect in fiscal year 1996 in the rates of basic pay for the statutory pay systems."

1994—Pub. L. 103–329, title VI, § 630(a), Sept. 30, 1994, 108 Stat. 2424, provided that:

"(1) The adjustment in rates of basic pay for the statutory pay systems that takes effect in fiscal year 1995 under section 5303 of title 5, United States Code, shall be an increase of 2 percent.

"(2) For purposes of each provision of law amended by section 704(a)(2) of the Ethics Reform Act of 1989 [Pub. L. 101–194] (5 U.S.C. 5318 note), no adjustment under section 5303 of title 5, United States Code, shall be considered to have taken effect in fiscal year 1995 in the rates of basic pay for the statutory pay systems.

"(3) For purposes of this subsection, the term 'statutory pay system' shall have the meaning given such term by section 5302(1) of title 5, United States Code."

1993—Pub. L. 103–123, title V, § 517B, Oct. 28, 1993, 107 Stat. 1253, provided that:

"(a) Any adjustment required by section 5303 of title 5, United States Code, to become effective in fiscal year 1994 in the rates of basic pay for the statutory pay systems shall not be made.

"(b) For the purpose of this section, the term 'statutory pay system' has the meaning given such term by section 5302(1) of title 5, United States Code."

1990—Pub. L. 101–509, title VI, § 618, Nov. 5, 1990, 104 Stat. 1475, provided that:

"(a) Notwithstanding any other provision of law, in the case of fiscal year 1991, the overall average percentage of the adjustment under section 5305 of title 5, United States Code, in the rates of pay under the General Schedule, and in the rates of pay under the other statutory pay systems (as defined by section 5301(c) of such title), shall be an increase of 4.1 percent.

"(b) Any increase in a pay rate or schedule which takes effect under such section 5305 in fiscal year 1991 (in accordance with subsection (a)) shall, to the maximum extent practicable, be of the same percentage, and shall take effect as of the first day of the first applicable pay period commencing on or after January 1, 1991."

Pub. L. 101–509, title VI, § 633, Nov. 5, 1990, 104 Stat. 633, provided that:

"(a) IN GENERAL.—Notwithstanding any other provision of law (including any provision of the Federal Employees Pay Comparability Act of 1990 [see Short Title of 1990 Amendment note set out under section 5301 of this title] and any provision of law amended by such Act), for purposes of any adjustment scheduled to take effect under section 5303 of title 5, United States Code (as amended by section 101 [section 529 [title I, § 101] of Pub. L. 101–509]) during the period beginning on October 1, 1991, and ending on September 30, 1994, the provisions of section 5303 of such title (as so amended) shall be applied in accordance with the following:

"(1) For purposes of the adjustment taking effect in each of fiscal years 1992 and 1993, respectively, deem subsection (a) to be amended by striking 'one-half of 1 percentage point less than'.

"(2) Deem subsection (b) to be amended as follows:

"(A) In paragraph (1), strike 'if' and all that follows thereafter through 'welfare,' and insert 'Subject to paragraph (2), if'.

"(B) Redesignate paragraphs (2) and (3) as paragraphs (3) and (4), respectively.

"(C) Insert after paragraph (1) the following:

"'(2) Authority to provide alternative pay adjustments under this subsection in any year may not be exercised except in accordance with the following:

"'(A) If the adjustment which (but for this subsection) would otherwise take effect under this section in a fiscal year would be 5 percent or less, no reduction may be made unless necessary because a state of war or severe economic conditions exist.

"'(B) If the adjustment which (but for this subsection) would otherwise take effect under this section in a fiscal year would be greater than 5 percent, no reduction may be made—

"'(i) to a level of 5 percent or greater, unless necessary because of national emergency or serious economic conditions affecting the general welfare; or

"'(ii) to a level of less than 5 percent, unless necessary because of either of the reasons set forth in subparagraph (A).'

"(D) Add after paragraph (4) (as so redesignated by subparagraph (B)) the following:

"'(5) For the purpose of this subsection, "severe economic conditions" shall be considered to exist relative to an adjustment scheduled to take effect on a given date if, during the 12-month period ending 2 calendar quarters before such date, there occurred 2 consecutive quarters of negative growth in the GNP.'

"(b) REFERENCES.—Notwithstanding any other provision of law (including any provision of the Federal Employees Pay Comparability Act of 1990 [see Short Title of 1990 Amendment note set out under section 5301 of this title] and any provision of law amended made by such Act), effective for purposes of any pay adjustment scheduled to take effect during the period described in subsection (a), any reference in a provision of law to section 5303 of title 5, United States Code, as amended by section 101 [section 529 [title I, §101] of Pub. L. 101–509] (or to the effective date of a pay adjustment, the size of an adjustment, a rate payable after an adjustment, or other related matter under such section 5303) shall be considered a reference to such section as applied in accordance with this section (or to the corresponding matter, as determined under such section 5303, as applied in accordance with this section)."

1989—Pub. L. 101–194, title VII, §702, Nov. 30, 1989, 103 Stat. 1767, provided that:

"(a) RESTORATION.—

"(1) IN GENERAL.—Effective for pay periods beginning on or after the date of enactment of this Act [Nov. 30, 1989], the rate of basic pay for any office or position in the executive, legislative, or judicial branch of the Government or in the government of the District of Columbia shall be determined as if the provisions of law cited in paragraph (2) had never been enacted.

"(2) CITATIONS.—The provisions of law referred to in paragraph (1) are as follows:

"(A) Section 620(b) of the Treasury, Postal Service and General Government Appropriations Act, 1989 (2 U.S.C. 5305 note) [Pub. L. 100–440, set out below].

"(B) Section 619(b) of the Treasury, Postal Service and General Government Appropriations Act, 1990 (Public Law 101–136) [set out below].

"(b) EXCEPTIONS.—Notwithstanding any other provision of this section, the rate of basic pay for a Senator, the President pro tempore of the Senate, and the majority leader and the minority leader of the Senate shall be determined as if subsection (a) had not been enacted.

"(c) SPECIFIC AUTHORITY.—For purposes of section 140 of Public Law 97–92 (28 U.S.C. 461 note), appropriate salary increases are hereby authorized for Federal judges and Justices of the Supreme Court pursuant to subsection (a).

"(d) SPECIAL RULE.—Notwithstanding any other provision of this section, no adjustment in any rate of pay shall become effective, as a result of the enactment of this section, before the first applicable pay period beginning on or after the date as of which the order issued by the President on October 16, 1989, pursuant to section 252 of the Balanced Budget and Emergency Deficit Control Act of 1985 [2 U.S.C. 901] is rescinded."

Pub. L. 101–194, title XI, §1101(a), Nov. 30, 1989, 103 Stat. 1781, provided that:

"(1) ADJUSTMENTS IN RATES OF PAY.—Notwithstanding any other provision of law (including any provision of this Act or amendment made by this Act), effective as provided in paragraph (2), the rate of pay of each office and position of United States Senator, the President pro tempore of the Senate, and the majority and minority leaders of the Senate shall be increased by—

"(A) the percentage increase that would have taken effect in fiscal year 1988 if the provisions of section 601(a)(2) of the Legislative Reorganization Act of 1946 (2 U.S.C. 31(2)) were applied to the rate of pay of each such office and position in effect on January 1, 1988 without regard to section 108 of the resolution entitled 'Joint resolution making further continuing appropriations for the fiscal year 1988, and for other purposes', approved December 22, 1987 [Pub. L. 100–202]; (101 Stat. 1329–434; 5 U.S.C. 5305 note [set out below]);

"(B) the percentage increase that would have taken effect in fiscal year 1989 if the provisions of section 601(a)(2) of the Legislative Reorganization Act of 1946 (2 U.S.C. 31(2)) were applied to the rate of pay of each such office and position in effect on January 1, 1989 (as adjusted under subparagraph (A) of this paragraph) without regard to subsection (b) of section 620 of the Treasury, Postal Service and General Government Appropriations Act, 1989 (Public Law 100–440; 102 Stat. 1756; 5 U.S.C. 5305 note [set out below]); and

"(C) the percentage increase that would take effect in fiscal year 1990 by the application of section 601(a)(2) of the Legislative Reorganization Act of 1946 (2 U.S.C. 31(2)) (as adjusted under subparagraphs (A) and (B) of this paragraph) without regard to subsection (b) of section 619 of the Treasury, Postal Service and General Government Appropriations Act, 1990 (Public Law 101–136) [set out below].

"(2) The increase in the rates of pay for each office and position described under paragraph (1) shall be effective on the first day of the first pay period beginning on or after January 1, 1990."

Pub. L. 101–136, title VI, §619, Nov. 3, 1989, 103 Stat. 820, provided that:

"(a)(1) Notwithstanding any other provision of law, in the case of fiscal year 1990, the overall average percentage of the adjustment under section 5305 of title 5, United States Code, in the rates of pay under the General Schedule, and in the rates of pay under the other statutory pay systems (as defined by section 5301(c) of such title), shall be an increase of 3.6 percent.

"(2) Each increase in a pay rate or schedule which takes effect pursuant to paragraph (1) shall, to the maximum extent practicable, be of the same percentage, and shall take effect as of the first day of the first applicable pay period commencing on or after January 1, 1990.

"(b)(1) Notwithstanding any other provision of this Act or any other law, no adjustment in rates of pay under section 5305 of title 5, United States Code, which becomes effective on or after October 1, 1989, and before October 1, 1990, shall have the effect of increasing the rate of salary or basic pay for any office or position in the legislative, executive, or judicial branch or in the government of the District of Columbia—

"(A) if the rate of salary or basic pay payable for that office or position as of September 30, 1989, was equal to or greater than the rate of basic pay described in paragraph (3); or

"(B) to a rate exceeding the rate of basic pay described in paragraph (3) if, as of September 30, 1989, the rate of salary or basic pay payable for that office or position was less than the rate described in such paragraph.

"(2) For purposes of paragraph (1), the rate of salary or basic pay payable as of September 30, 1989, for any office or position which was not in existence on such date shall be deemed to be the rate of salary or basic pay payable to individuals in comparable offices or positions on such date, as determined under regulations prescribed—

"(A) by the President, in the case of any office or position within the executive branch or in the government of the District of Columbia;

"(B) jointly by the Speaker of the House of Representatives and the President pro tempore of the Senate, in the case of any office or position within the legislative branch; or

"(C) by the Chief Justice of the United States, in the case of any office or position within the judicial branch.

"(3) The rate of basic pay described in this paragraph is the rate equal to the rate of basic pay payable for level III of the Executive Schedule under section 5314 of title 5, United States Code, as of September 30, 1989, increased by 3.6 percent."

1988—Pub. L. 100–440, title VI, § 620, Sept. 22, 1988, 102 Stat. 1756, provided that:

"(a)(1) Notwithstanding any other provision of law, in the case of fiscal year 1989, the overall percentage of the adjustment under section 5305 of title 5, United States Code, in the rates of pay under the General Schedule, and in the rates of pay under the other statutory pay systems (as defined by section 5301(c) of such title), shall be an increase of 4.1 percent.

"(2) Each increase in a pay rate or schedule which takes effect pursuant to paragraph (1) shall, to the maximum extent practicable, be of the same percentage, and shall take effect as of the first day of the first applicable pay period commencing on or after January 1, 1989.

"(b)(1) Notwithstanding any other provision of this Act or any other law, no adjustment in rates of pay under section 5305 of title 5, United States Code, which becomes effective on or after October 1, 1988, and before October 1, 1989, shall have the effect of increasing the rate of salary or basic pay for any office or position in the legislative, executive, or judicial branch or in the government of the District of Columbia—

"(A) if the rate of salary or basic pay payable for that office or position as of September 30, 1988, was equal to or greater than the rate of basic pay then payable for level III of the Executive Schedule under section 5314 of title 5, United States Code; or

"(B) to a rate exceeding the rate of basic pay payable for level III of the Executive Schedule under such section 5314 as of September 30, 1988, if, as of that date, the rate of salary or basic pay payable for that office or position was less than the rate of basic pay then payable for such level III.

"(2) For purposes of paragraph (1), the rate of salary or basic pay payable as of September 30, 1988, for any office or position which was not in existence on such date shall be deemed to be the rate of salary or basic pay payable to individuals in comparable offices or positions on such date, as determined under regulations prescribed—

"(A) by the President, in the case of any office or position within the executive branch or in the government of the District of Columbia;

"(B) jointly by the Speaker of the House of Representatives and the President pro tempore of the Senate, in the case of any office or position within the legislative branch; or

"(C) by the Chief Justice of the United States, in the case of any office or position within the judicial branch."

1987—Pub. L. 100–202, § 108, Dec. 22, 1987, 101 Stat. 1329–434, provided that:

"(a) Notwithstanding any other provision of this resolution or any other law, no adjustment in rates of pay under section 5305 of title 5, United States Code, which becomes effective on or after October 1, 1987, and before October 1, 1988, shall have the effect of increasing the rate of salary or basic pay for any office or position in the legislative, executive, or judicial branch or in the government of the District of Columbia—

"(1) if the rate of salary or basic pay payable for that office or position as of September 30, 1987, was equal to or greater than the rate of basic pay then payable for level V of the Executive Schedule under section 5316 of title 5, United States Code; or

"(2) to a rate exceeding the rate of basic pay payable for level V of the Executive Schedule under such section 5316 as of September 30, 1987, if, as of that date, the rate of salary or basic pay payable for that office or position was less than the rate of basic pay then payable for such level V.

"(b) For purposes of subsection (a), the rate of salary or basic pay payable as of September 30, 1987, for any office or position which was not in existence on such date shall be deemed to be the rate of salary or basic pay payable to individuals in comparable offices or positions on such date, as determined under regulations prescribed—

"(1) by the President, in the case of any office or position within the executive branch or in the government of the District of Columbia;

"(2) jointly by the Speaker of the House of Representatives and the President pro tempore of the Senate, in the case of any office or position within the legislative branch; or

"(3) by the Chief Justice of the United States, in the case of any office or position within the judicial branch."

Pub. L. 100–202, § 110(a), Dec. 22, 1987, 101 Stat. 1329–436, provided that:

"(1) TWO-PERCENT INCREASE.—Notwithstanding any other provision of law, in the case of fiscal year 1988, the overall percentage of the adjustment under section 5305 of title 5, United States Code, in the rates of pay under the General Schedule, and in the rates of pay under the other statutory pay systems (as defined by section 5301(c) of such title), shall be an increase of 2 percent.

"(2) UNIFORM ADJUSTMENTS; DELAYED EFFECTIVE DATE.—Each increase in a pay rate or schedule which takes effect pursuant to paragraph (1) shall, to the maximum extent practicable, be of the same percentage and shall take effect as of the beginning of the first applicable pay period beginning on or after January 1, 1988."

1986—Pub. L. 99–500, § 144(a), Oct. 18, 1986, 100 Stat. 1783–350, and Pub. L. 99–591, § 144(a), Oct. 30, 1986, 100 Stat. 3341–353, provided that:

"(1) Notwithstanding any other provision of law, in the case of fiscal year 1987, the overall percentage of the adjustment under section 5305 of title 5, United States Code, in the rates of pay under the General Schedule, and in the rates of pay under the other statutory pay systems, shall be an increase of 3 percent.

"(2) Each increase in a pay rate or schedule which takes effect pursuant to paragraph (1) shall, to the maximum extent practicable, be of the same percentage, and shall take effect as of the first day of the first applicable pay period commencing on or after January 1, 1987.

"(3)(A) Notwithstanding any other provision of law, determinations relating to amounts to be appropriated in order to provide for the adjustment described in paragraph (1) shall be made based on the assumption that the various departments and agencies of the Government will, in the aggregate, absorb 50 percent of the increase in total pay for fiscal year 1987.

"(B) Subparagraph (A) does not apply with respect to the Department of Defense or pay for employees of the Department of Defense.

"(4) For purposes of this subsection—

"(A) the term 'total pay' means, with respect to a fiscal year, the total amount of basic pay which will be payable to employees covered by statutory pay systems for service performed during such fiscal year;

"(B) the term 'increase in total pay' means, with respect to a fiscal year, that part of total pay for such year which is attributable to the adjustment taking effect under this section during such year; and

"(C) the term 'statutory pay system' has the meaning given such term by section 5301(c) of title 5, United States Code."

Pub. L. 99–272, title XV, §15201(a), Apr. 7, 1986, 100 Stat. 332, provided that:

"(1) The rates of pay under the General Schedule and the rates of pay under the other statutory pay systems referred to in section 5301(c) of title 5, United States Code, shall not be adjusted under section 5305 of such title during fiscal year 1986.

"(2)(A)(i) For fiscal years 1987 and 1988, the President shall provide for the adjustment of rates of pay under section 5305 of title 5, United States Code, as appropriate to reduce outlays, relating to pay of officers and employees of the Federal Government, by at least $746,000,000 in fiscal year 1987 and $1,264,000,000 in fiscal year 1988 (without regard to reductions in outlays which result by reason of subparagraph (B)(ii) of this paragraph, paragraph (1) of this subsection, subsection (b) of this section, and the application of section 1009 of title 37, United States Code), computed using the baseline used for the First Concurrent Resolution on the Budget for Fiscal Year 1986 (S. Con. Res. 32, 99th Congress), agreed to on August 1, 1985.

"(ii) Clause (i) of this subparagraph shall not be construed to suspend the requirements of section 5305 of title 5, United States Code, with respect to fiscal years 1987 and 1988.

"(B) Each adjustment in a pay rate or schedule which takes effect pursuant to subparagraph (A) of this paragraph—

"(i) shall, to the maximum extent practicable, be of the same percentage; and

"(ii) shall be effective with respect to pay periods beginning on or after January 1 of the fiscal year involved."

1984—Pub. L. 98–270, title II, §202(a), Apr. 18, 1984, 98 Stat. 158, provided that:

"(1) Notwithstanding any other provision of law, in the case of fiscal year 1984, the overall percentage of the adjustment under section 5305 of title 5, United States Code, in the rates of pay under the General Schedule, and in the rates of pay under the other statutory pay systems, shall be an increase of 4 percent.

"(2) Each increase in a pay rate or schedule which takes effect pursuant to paragraph (1) shall, to the maximum extent practicable, be of the same percentage, and shall take effect as of the first day of the first applicable pay period commencing on or after January 1 of such fiscal year."

1982—Pub. L. 97–253, title III, §310(a), Sept. 8, 1982, 96 Stat. 799, provided that:

"(1) Notwithstanding any other provision of law, if—

"(A) before September 1, 1982, the President transmits to the Congress pursuant to section 5305(c)(1) of title 5, United States Code, an alternative plan which provides for an overall percentage pay adjustment which is less than 4 percent, and

"(B) the alternative plan referred to in subparagraph (A) is disapproved pursuant to such section 5305,

the rates of pay under the General Schedule and the rates of pay under the other statutory pay systems shall be increased under the provisions of such section 5305 by 4 percent in the case of fiscal year 1983.

"(2) Each increase in a pay rate or schedule which takes effect pursuant to paragraph (1) shall, to the maximum extent practicable, be of the same percentage, and shall take effect on the first day of the first applicable pay period commencing on or after October 1 of such fiscal year."

1981—Pub. L. 97–35, title XVII, §1701(a), Aug. 13, 1981, 95 Stat. 753, provided that: "Notwithstanding any other provision of law, the overall percentage of the adjust-

ment of the rates of pay under the General Schedule or any other statutory pay system under section 5305 of title 5, United States Code, which is to become effective with the first applicable pay period commencing on or after October 1, 1981, shall not exceed 4.8 percent."

1978—Pub. L. 95–429, title VI, §614, Oct. 10, 1978, 92 Stat. 1018, provided that:

"(a) No part of any of the funds appropriated for the fiscal year ending September 30, 1979, by this Act or any other Act, may be used to pay the salary or pay of any individual in any office or position in an amount which exceeds the rate of salary or basic pay payable for such office or position on September 30, 1978, by more than 5.5 percent, as a result of any adjustments which take effect during such fiscal year under—

"(1) section 5305 of title 5, United States Code;

"(2) any other provision of law if such adjustment is determined by reference to such section 5305; or

"(3) section 5343 of title 5, United States Code, if such adjustment is granted pursuant to a wage survey (but only with respect to prevailing rate employees described in section 5342(a)(2)(A) of that title).

"(b) For the purpose of administering any provision of law, rule, or regulation which provides premium pay, retirement, life insurance, or other employee benefit, which requires any deduction or contribution, or which imposes any requirement or limitation, on the basis of a rate of salary or basic pay, the rate of salary or basic pay payable after the application of this section shall be treated as the rate of salary or basic pay."

1971—Pub. L. 92–210, §3, Dec. 22, 1971, 85 Stat. 753, provided that: "Notwithstanding any provision of section 3(c) of the Federal Pay Comparability Act of 1970 (Public Law 91–656), or of section 5305 of title 5, United States Code, as added by section 3(a) of Public Law 91–656, and the provisions of the alternative plan submitted by the President to the Congress pursuant thereto on August 31, 1971, such comparability adjustments in the rates of pay of each Federal statutory pay system as may be required under such sections 5305 and 3(c), based on the 1971 Bureau of Labor Statistics survey—

"(1) shall not be greater than the guidelines established for the wage and salary adjustments for the private sector that may be authorized under authority of any statute of the United States, including the Economic Stabilization Act of 1970 (Public Law 91–379; 84 Stat. 799), as amended [formerly set out as a note under section 1904 of Title 12, Banks and Banking], and that may be in effect on December 31, 1971; and

"(2) shall be placed into effect on the first day of the first pay period that begins on or after January 1, 1972.

Nothing in this section shall be construed to provide any adjustments in rates of pay of any Federal statutory pay system which are greater than the adjustments based on the 1971 Bureau of Labor Statistics survey."

Section 3(c) of Pub. L. 91–656 provided that: "The President may make the initial adjustment required by subchapter I of chapter 53 of title 5, United States Code, as amended by this Act, without regard to the provisions of such subchapter relating to the Advisory Committee on Federal Pay and the Federal Employees Pay Council. Notwithstanding any provision of such subchapter I prescribing an effective date of October 1 for any pay adjustment made by the President, the initial adjustment based on the 1970 Bureau of Labor Statistics survey and the adjustment based on the 1971 Bureau of Labor Statistics survey shall become effective on the first day of the first applicable pay period that begins on or after January 1, 1971, and January 1, 1972, respectively. Notwithstanding the provisions of such subchapter I, the President's agent for purposes of the 1971 and 1972 adjustments shall be the Director, Office of Management and Budget and the Chairman, United States Civil Service Commission. Adjustments under the provisions of such subchapter I shall not apply to employees of the Post Office Department whose basic pay is fixed under the General Schedule."

1967—Pub. L. 90–206, title II, § 212, Dec. 16, 1967, 81 Stat. 634, provided that: "In order to complete the implementation of the policy of the Congress set forth in paragraph (2) of section 5301 of title 5, United States Code, the President, after seeking the views of such employee organizations as he considers appropriate and in such manner as he may provide, shall—

"(1) effective on the first day of the first pay period beginning on or after July 1, 1968, adjust the rates of basic pay, basic compensation, and salary, as in effect by reason of the enactment of the provisions of this title [see Short Title note under section 5332 of this title] other than this section and sections 205, 210, 213, 214, 215, and 219—

"(A) by amounts equal, as nearly as may be practicable, to one-half of the amounts by which such rates are exceeded by rates of pay paid for the same levels of work in private enterprise as determined on the basis of the 1967 annual survey conducted by the Bureau of Labor Statistics in accordance with the provisions of section 5302 of title 5, United States Code, or

"(B) by 3 per centum,

whichever is greater; and

"(2) effective on the first day of the first pay period beginning on or after July 1, 1969, adjust the rates he has established under subparagraph (1) of this section, and the rates established by Postal Field Service Schedule II, and Rural Carrier Schedule II (contained in the amendments made by subsections (a) and (b) of section 205 [amending sections 3542 and 3543 of Title 39, Postal Service], by amounts equal, as nearly as may be practicable, to the amounts by which such rates are exceeded by rates of pay paid for the same levels of work in private enterprise as determined on the basis of the 1968 annual survey conducted by the Bureau of Labor Statistics in accordance with the provisions of section 5302 of title 5, United States Code.

Adjustments made by the President under this section shall have the force and effect of statute. The rates of pay of personnel subject to sections 210, 213 (except subsections (d) and (e)), and 214 of this title [see Short Title note under section 5332 of this title], and any minimum or maximum rate, limitation, or allowance applicable to any such personnel, shall be adjusted, by amounts which are equal, insofar as practicable and with such exceptions as may be necessary to provide for appropriate relationships between positions, to the amounts of the adjustments made by the President under subparagraphs (1) and (2) of this section, by the following authorities—

"(i) the President pro tempore of the Senate, with respect to the United States Senate;

"(ii) the Speaker of the House of Representatives with respect to the United States House of Representatives;

"(iii) the Architect of the Capitol, with respect to the Office of the Architect of the Capitol;

"(iv) the Director of the Administrative Office of the United States Courts, with respect to the judicial branch of the Government; and

"(v) the Secretary of Agriculture, with respect to persons employed by the county committees established pursuant to section 8(b) of the Soil Conservation and Domestic Allotment Act (16 U.S.C. 590h(b)).

Such adjustments shall be made in such manner as the appropriate authority concerned deems advisable and shall have the force and effect of statute. Nothing in this section shall impair any authority pursuant to which rates of pay may be fixed by administrative action." [Section 212 of Pub. L. 90–206 effective Dec. 16, 1967, see section 220(a)(1) of Pub. L. 90–206, set out as a note under section 3110 of this title.]

SECTION REFERRED TO IN OTHER SECTIONS

This section is referred to in sections 5304, 5304a, 5306, 5318, 5332, 5372, 5376, 5382, 5392 of this title; title 2 sections 31, 57a, 60a–1, 60a–1b, 60a–2, 60a–2a, 906; title 3 section 104; title 10 section 1076a; title 22 section 3963; title 28 section 461; title 31 section 325; title 37 section 1009; title 42 section 254*l*.

§ 5304. Locality-based comparability payments

(a) Pay disparities shall be identified and reduced as follows:

(1) Comparability payments shall be payable within each locality determined to have a pay disparity greater than 5 percent.

(2)(A) The localities having pay disparities, and the size of those disparities, shall, for purposes of any comparability payment scheduled to take effect in any calendar year, be determined in accordance with the appropriate report, as prepared and submitted to the President under subsection (d)(1) for purposes of such calendar year.

(B) Any computation necessary to determine the size of the comparability payment to become payable for any locality in a year (as well as any determination as to the size of any pay disparity remaining after that comparability payment is made) shall likewise be made using data contained in the appropriate report (described in subparagraph (A)) so prepared and submitted for purposes of such calendar year.

(3) Subject to paragraph (4), the amount of the comparability payments payable under this subsection in a calendar year within any locality in which a comparability payment is payable shall be computed using such percentage as the President determines for such locality under subsection (d)(2), except that—

(A) the percentage for the first calendar year in which any amounts are payable under this section may not be less than $\frac{1}{5}$ of the amount needed to reduce the pay disparity of the locality involved to 5 percent;

(B) the percentage for the second calendar year in which any amounts are payable under this section may not be less than $\frac{3}{10}$ of the amount needed to reduce the pay disparity of the locality involved to 5 percent;

(C) the percentage for the third calendar year in which any amounts are payable under this section may not be less than $\frac{2}{5}$ of the amount needed to reduce the pay disparity of the locality involved to 5 percent;

(D) the percentage for the fourth calendar year in which any amounts are payable under this section may not be less than $\frac{1}{2}$ of the amount needed to reduce the pay disparity of the locality involved to 5 percent;

(E) the percentage for the fifth calendar year in which any amounts are payable under this section may not be less than $\frac{3}{5}$ of the amount needed to reduce the pay disparity of the locality involved to 5 percent;

(F) the percentage for the sixth calendar year in which any amounts are payable under this section may not be less than $\frac{7}{10}$ of the amount needed to reduce the pay disparity of the locality involved to 5 percent;

(G) the percentage for the seventh calendar year in which any amounts are payable under this section may not be less than $\frac{4}{5}$ of the amount needed to reduce the pay disparity of the locality involved to 5 percent;

(H) the percentage for the eighth calendar year in which any amounts are payable under this section may not be less than %10 of the amount needed to reduce the pay disparity of the locality involved to 5 percent; and

(I) the percentage for the ninth calendar year in which any amounts are payable under this section, and any year thereafter, may not be less than the full amount necessary to reduce the pay disparity of the locality involved to 5 percent.

(4) Nothing in this section shall be considered to preclude the President, in his discretion, from adjusting comparability payments to a level higher than the minimum level otherwise required in a calendar year, including to the level necessary to eliminate a locality's pay disparity completely.

(b) After the ninth calendar year (referred to in subsection (a)(3)(I)), the level of comparability payments payable within such locality may be reduced for any subsequent calendar year, but only if, or to the extent that, the reduction would not immediately create another pay disparity in excess of 5 percent within the locality (taking into consideration any comparability payments remaining payable).

(c)(1) The amount of the comparability payment payable within any particular locality during a calendar year—

(A) shall be stated as a single percentage, which shall be uniformly applicable to General Schedule positions within the locality; and

(B) shall, for any employee entitled to receive a comparability payment, be computed by applying that percentage to such employee's scheduled rate of basic pay (or, if lower due to a limitation on the rate payable, the rate actually payable), subject to subsection (g).

(2) A comparability payment—

(A) shall be considered to be part of basic pay for purposes of retirement under chapter 83 or 84, as applicable, life insurance under chapter 87, and premium pay under subchapter V of chapter 55, and for such other purposes as may be expressly provided for by law or as the Office of Personnel Management may by regulation prescribe; and

(B) shall be paid in the same manner and at the same time as the basic pay payable to such employee pursuant to any provision of law outside of this section.

(3) Nothing in this subchapter shall be considered to permit or require that any portion of a comparability payment be taken into account for purposes of any adjustment under section 5303.

(4)(A) Only employees receiving scheduled rates of basic pay (subject to any pay limitation which may apply) shall be eligible for comparability payments under this section.

(B) Comparability payments shall not be payable for service performed in any position which may not, under subsection (f)(1)(A), be included within a pay locality.

(d) In order to carry out this section, the President shall—

(1) direct such agent as he considers appropriate to prepare and submit to him annually,

after considering such views and recommendations as may be submitted under subsection (e) (but not later than 13 months before the start of the calendar year for purposes of which it is prepared), a report that—

(A) compares the rates of pay under the General Schedule (disregarding any described in section 5302(8)(C))[1] with the rates of pay generally paid to non-Federal workers for the same levels of work within each pay locality, as determined on the basis of appropriate surveys that shall be conducted by the Bureau of Labor Statistics;

(B) based on data from such surveys, identifies each locality in which a pay disparity exists and specifies the size of each such pay disparity (before and after taking into consideration any comparability payments payable);

(C) makes recommendations for appropriate comparability payments, in conformance with applicable requirements of this section; and

(D) includes the views and recommendations submitted under subsection (e);

(2) after considering the report of his agent (including the views and recommendations referred to in subsection (e)(2)(C), provide for or adjust comparability payments in conformance with applicable requirements of this section, effective as of the beginning of the first applicable pay period commencing on or after January 1 of the applicable year; and

(3) transmit to Congress a report of the actions taken under paragraph (2) (together with a copy of the report submitted to him by his agent, including the views and recommendations referred to in subsection (e)(2)(C)) which shall—

(A) identify each pay locality;

(B) specify which localities have pay disparities in excess of 5 percent, and the size of the disparity existing in each of those localities, according to the pay agent's most recent report under paragraph (1) (before and after taking into consideration any comparability payments payable); and

(C) indicate the size of the respective comparability payments (expressed as percentages) which will be in effect under paragraph (2) for the various pay localities specified under subparagraph (B) for the applicable calendar year.

(e)(1) The President shall establish a Federal Salary Council of 9 members, of whom—

(A) 3 shall be chosen from among persons generally recognized for their impartiality, knowledge, and experience in the field of labor relations and pay policy; and

(B) 6 shall be representatives of employee organizations which represent substantial numbers of employees holding General Schedule positions, and who shall be selected giving due consideration to such factors as the relative numbers of employees represented by the various organizations, except that not more than 3 members of the Council at any one time shall be from a single employee organization,

---

[1] See References in Text note below.

council, federation, alliance, association, or affiliation of employee organizations.

Members of the Council shall not receive pay by reason of their service on the Council, nor shall members who are not otherwise employees of the United States be considered employees by reason of any such service. However, members under subparagraph (A) may be paid expenses in accordance with section 5703. The President shall designate one of the members to serve as Chairman of the Federal Salary Council. One of the 3 members under subparagraph (A) may be the Chairman of the Federal Prevailing Rate Advisory Committee, notwithstanding the restriction under section 5347(a)(1), and such individual may also be designated to serve as Chairman of the Federal Salary Council.

(2) The pay agent shall—

(A) provide for meetings with the Council and give thorough consideration to the views and recommendations of the Council and the individual views and recommendations, if any, of the members of the Council regarding—

(i) the establishment or modification of pay localities;

(ii) the coverage of the surveys of pay localities conducted by the Bureau of Labor Statistics under subsection (d)(1)(A) (including, but not limited to, the occupations, establishment sizes, and industries to be surveyed, and how pay localities are to be surveyed);

(iii) the process of comparing the rates of pay payable under the General Schedule with rates of pay for the same levels of work performed by non-Federal workers; and

(iv) the level of comparability payments that should be paid in order to eliminate or reduce pay disparities in accordance with the requirements of this section;

(B) give thorough consideration to the views and recommendations of employee organizations not represented on the Council regarding the subjects in subparagraph (A)(i)–(iv); and

(C) include in its report to the President the views and recommendations submitted as provided in this subsection by the Council, by any member of the Council, and by employee organizations not represented on the Council.

(f)(1) The pay agent may provide for such pay localities as the pay agent considers appropriate, except that—

(A) each General Schedule position (excluding any outside the continental United States, as defined in section 5701(6)) shall be included with a pay locality; and

(B) the boundaries of pay localities shall be determined based on appropriate factors which may include local labor market patterns, commuting patterns, and practices of other employers.

(2)(A) The establishment or modification of any such boundaries shall be effected by regulations which, notwithstanding subsection (a)(2) of section 553, shall be promulgated in accordance with the notice and comment requirements of such section.

(B) Judicial review of any regulation under this subsection shall be limited to whether or not it was promulgated in accordance with the requirements referred to in subparagraph (A).

(g)(1) Except as provided in paragraph (2), comparability payments may not be paid at a rate which, when added to the rate of basic pay otherwise payable to the employee involved, would cause the total to exceed the rate of basic pay payable for level IV of the Executive Schedule.

(2) The applicable maximum under this subsection shall be level III of the Executive Schedule for—

(A) positions under subparagraphs (A)–(E) of subsection (h)(1); and

(B) any positions under subsection (h)(1)(F) which the President may determine.

(h)(1) For the purpose of this subsection, the term "position" means—

(A) a position to which section 5376 applies (relating to certain senior-level positions);

(B) a Senior Executive Service position under section 3132;

(C) a position in the Federal Bureau of Investigation and Drug Enforcement Administration Senior Executive Service under section 3151;

(D) a position to which section 5372 applies (relating to administrative law judges appointed under section 3105);

(E) a position to which section 5372a applies (relating to contract appeals board members); and

(F) a position within an Executive agency not covered under the General Schedule or any of the preceding subparagraphs, the rate of basic pay for which is (or, but for this section, would be) no more than the rate payable for level IV of the Executive Schedule;

but does not include—

(i) a position to which subchapter IV applies (relating to prevailing rate systems);

(ii) a position as to which a rate of pay is authorized under section 5377 (relating to critical positions); or

(iii) a position to which subchapter II applies (relating to the Executive Schedule).

(2)(A) Notwithstanding subsection (c)(4) or any other provision of this section, but subject to subparagraph (B) and paragraph (3), upon the request of the head of an Executive agency with respect to 1 or more categories of positions, the President may provide that each employee of such agency who holds a position within such category, and within the particular locality involved, shall be entitled to receive comparability payments.

(B) A request by an agency head or exercise of authority by the President under subparagraph (A) shall cover—

(i) with respect to the positions under subparagraphs (A) through (E) of paragraph (1), all positions described in the subparagraph or subparagraphs involved (excluding any under clause (i) or (ii) of such paragraph); and

(ii) with respect to positions under paragraph (1)(F), such positions as may be considered appropriate (excluding any under clause (i) or (ii) of paragraph (1)).

(C) Notwithstanding subsection (c)(4) or any other provision of law, but subject to paragraph

(3), in the case of a category with positions that are in more than 1 Executive agency, the President may, on his own initiative, provide that each employee who holds a position within such category, and in the locality involved, shall be entitled to receive comparability payments. No later than 30 days before an employee receives comparability payments under this subparagraph, the President or the President's designee shall submit a detailed report to the Congress justifying the reasons for the extension, including consideration of recruitment and retention rates and the expense of extending locality pay.

(3) Comparability payments under this subsection—

(A) may be paid only in any calendar year in which comparability payments under the preceding provisions of this section are payable with respect to General Schedule positions within the same locality;

(B) shall take effect, within the locality involved, on the first day of the first applicable pay period commencing on or after such date as the President designates (except that no date may be designated which would require any retroactive payments), and shall remain in effect through the last day of the last applicable pay period commencing during that calendar year;

(C) shall be computed using the same percentage as is applicable, for the calendar year involved, with respect to General Schedule positions within the same locality; and

(D) shall be subject to the applicable limitation under subsection (g).

(i) The Office of Personnel Management may prescribe regulations, consistent with the provisions of this section, governing the payment of comparability payments to employees.

(Pub. L. 89–554, Sept. 6, 1966, 80 Stat. 459; Pub. L. 91–375, § 6(c)(11), Aug. 12, 1970, 84 Stat. 776; Pub. L. 95–454, title IX, § 906(a)(2), Oct. 13, 1978, 92 Stat. 1224; Pub. L. 96–465, title II, § 2314(c)(3), Oct. 17, 1980, 94 Stat. 2168; Pub. L. 101–509, title V, § 529 [title I, § 101(a)(1)], Nov. 5, 1990, 104 Stat. 1427, 1431; Pub. L. 102–378, § 2(26), Oct. 2, 1992, 106 Stat. 1348.)

Historical and Revision Notes

Derivation	U.S. Code	Revised Statutes and Statutes at Large
....	5 U.S.C. 1174.	Oct. 11, 1962, Pub. L. 87–793, § 505, 76 Stat. 842.

The words "agencies" and "regulations" are substituted for "departments" and "rules", respectively.

Standard changes are made to conform with the definitions applicable and the style of this title as outlined in the preface to the report.

References in Text

The General Schedule, referred to in text, is set out under section 5332 of this title.

Section 5302(8)(C), referred to in subsec. (d)(1)(A), was redesignated 5302(8)(B) of this title by Pub. L. 103–89, § 3(b)(1)(E)(i)(II), Sept. 30, 1993, 107 Stat. 981.

Levels III and IV of the Executive Schedule, referred to in subsecs. (g) and (h)(1)(F), are set out in sections 5314 and 5315, respectively, of this title.

Amendments

1992—Subsec. (a)(3). Pub. L. 102–378, § 2(26)(A)(i), substituted "Subject to paragraph (4)," for "Subject to

paragraphs (4) and (5)," and "a comparability payment" for "a comparative payment".

Subsec. (a)(3)(H). Pub. L. 102–378, § 2(26)(A)(ii), inserted "and" after semicolon at end.

Subsec. (a)(3)(I). Pub. L. 102–378, § 2(26)(A)(iii), substituted a period for semicolon at end.

Subsec. (d)(1)(A). Pub. L. 102–378, § 2(26)(B), inserted "(disregarding any described in section 5302(8)(C))" after "General Schedule" and struck out "annual" before "surveys".

Subsec. (e)(1). Pub. L. 102–378, § 2(26)(C)(i), inserted after second sentence "However, members under subparagraph (A) may be paid expenses in accordance with section 5703."

Subsec. (e)(2)(A)(ii). Pub. L. 102–378, § 2(26)(C)(ii), substituted "surveys of pay localities" for "annual survey" and "industries" for "industries,".

Subsec. (g)(2). Pub. L. 102–378, § 2(26)(D), amended par. (2) generally. Prior to amendment, par. (2) read as follows: "For positions under subparagraphs (A)–(E) of subsection (h)(1), the applicable maximum under this subsection shall be level III of the Executive Schedule."

Subsec. (h)(1)(F). Pub. L. 102–378, § 2(26)(E)(i)(I), amended subpar. (F) generally. Prior to amendment, subpar. (F) read as follows: "a position within an Executive agency not covered under any of the preceding subparagraphs, the rate of basic pay for which is (or, but for this section, would be) less than the rate payable for level V of the Executive Schedule;".

Subsec. (h)(1)(iii). Pub. L. 102–378, § 2(26)(E)(i)(II)–(IV), added cl. (iii).

Subsec. (h)(2)(C). Pub. L. 102–378, § 2(26)(E)(ii), added subpar. (C).

Subsec. (h)(3)(B). Pub. L. 102–378, § 2(26)(E)(iii), amended subpar. (B) generally. Prior to amendment, subpar. (B) read as follows: "shall be payable, within the locality involved, for the entirety of each calendar year for which authority is granted by the President;".

1990—Pub. L. 101–509 amended section generally, substituting provisions relating to locality-based comparability payments for provisions making functions, duties, and regulations of agencies and Office of Personnel Management with respect to this subchapter subject to Presidential policies and regulations.

1980—Pub. L. 96–465 substituted "the Foreign Service Act of 1980" for "chapter 14 of title 22" in provisions preceding par. (1).

1978—Pub. L. 95–454 substituted "Office of Personnel Management" for "Civil Service Commission".

1970—Pub. L. 91–375 struck out provisions making functions, duties and regulations of the agencies and the Civil Service Commission with respect to the provisions of part III of title 39 relating to employees in the postal field service subject to Presidential policies and regulations.

Effective Date of 1990 Amendment

Amendment by Pub. L. 101–509 effective on such date as the President shall determine, but not earlier than 90 days, and not later than 180 days, after Nov. 5, 1990, with provision that first calendar year in which comparability payments under this section are paid shall be calendar year beginning Jan. 1, 1994, see section 529 [title III, § 305] of Pub. L. 101–509, set out as a note under section 5301 of this title.

Effective Date of 1980 Amendment

Amendment by Pub. L. 96–465 effective Feb. 15, 1981, except as otherwise provided, see section 2403 of Pub. L. 96–465, set out an Effective Date note under section 3901 of Title 22, Foreign Relations and Intercourse.

Effective Date of 1978 Amendment

Amendment by Pub. L. 95–454 effective 90 days after Oct. 13, 1978, see section 907 of Pub. L. 95–454, set out as a note under section 1101 of this title.

Effective Date of 1970 Amendment

Amendment by Pub. L. 91–375 effective within 1 year after Aug. 12, 1970, on date established therefor by

Board of Governors of United States Postal Service and published by it in Federal Register, see section 15(a) of Pub. L. 91–375, set out as an Effective Date note preceding section 101 of Title 39, Postal Service.

DELEGATION OF FUNCTIONS

For designation of agents of President under subsecs. (d)(1) and (h) of this section, see Ex. Ord. No. 12748, § 2(a), Feb. 1, 1991, 56 F.R. 4521, eff. Feb. 3, 1991, set out as a note under section 5301 of this title.

COMPARABILITY PAYMENTS BETWEEN 2002 AND 2007; COMPARISONS AND RECOMMENDATIONS; REVISION OF METHODOLOGY

Pub. L. 106–554, § 1(a)(3) [title VI, § 637], Dec. 21, 2000, 114 Stat. 2763, 2763A–165, provided that:

"(a) For purposes of this section—

"(1) the term 'comparability payment' refers to a locality-based comparability payment under section 5304 of title 5, United States Code;

"(2) the term 'President's pay agent' refers to the pay agent described in section 5302(4) of such title; and

"(3) the term 'pay locality' has the meaning given such term by section 5302(5) of such title.

"(b) Notwithstanding any provision of section 5304 of title 5, United States Code, for purposes of determining appropriate pay localities and making comparability payment recommendations, the President's pay agent may, in accordance with succeeding provisions of this section, make comparisons of General Schedule pay and non-Federal pay within any of the metropolitan statistical areas described in subsection (d)(3), using—

"(1) data from surveys of the Bureau of Labor Statistics;

"(2) salary data sets obtained under subsection (c); or

"(3) any combination thereof.

"(c) To the extent necessary in order to carry out this section, the President's pay agent may obtain any salary data sets (referred to in subsection (b)) from any organization or entity that regularly compiles similar data for businesses in the private sector.

"(d)(1)(A) This paragraph applies with respect to the five metropolitan statistical areas described in paragraph (3) which—

"(i) have the highest levels of nonfarm employment (as determined based on data made available by the Bureau of Labor Statistics); and

"(ii) as of the date of the enactment of this Act [Dec. 21, 2000], have not previously been surveyed by the Bureau of Labor Statistics (as discrete pay localities) for purposes of section 5304 of title 5, United States Code.

"(B) The President's pay agent, based on such comparisons under subsection (b) as the pay agent considers appropriate, shall: (i) determine whether any of the five areas under subparagraph (A) warrants designation as a discrete pay locality; and (ii) if so, make recommendations as to what level of comparability payments would be appropriate during 2002 for each area so determined.

"(C)(i) Any recommendations under subparagraph (B)(ii) shall be included—

"(I) in the pay agent's report under section 5304(d)(1) of title 5, United States Code, submitted for purposes of comparability payments scheduled to become payable in 2002; or

"(II) if compliance with subclause (I) is impracticable, in a supplementary report which the pay agent shall submit to the President and the Congress no later than March 1, 2001.

"(ii) In the event that the recommendations are completed in time to be included in the report described in clause (i)(I), a copy of those recommendations shall be transmitted by the pay agent to the Congress contemporaneous with their submission to the President.

"(D) Each of the five areas under subparagraph (A) that so warrants, as determined by the President's pay

agent, shall be designated as a discrete pay locality under section 5304 of title 5, United States Code, in time for it to be treated as such for purposes of comparability payments becoming payable in 2002.

"(2) The President's pay agent may, at any time after the 180th day following the submission of the report under subsection (f), make any initial or further determinations or recommendations under this section, based on any pay comparisons under subsection (b), with respect to any area described in paragraph (3).

"(3) An area described in this paragraph is any metropolitan statistical area within the continental United States that (as determined based on data made available by the Bureau of Labor Statistics and the Office of Personnel Management, respectively) has a high level of nonfarm employment and at least 2,500 General Schedule employees whose post of duty is within such area.

"(e)(1) The authority under this section to make pay comparisons and to make any determinations or recommendations based on such comparisons shall be available to the President's pay agent only for purposes of comparability payments becoming payable on or after January 1, 2002, and before January 1, 2007, and only with respect to areas described in subsection (d)(3).

"(2) Any comparisons and recommendations so made shall, if included in the pay agent's report under section 5304(d)(1) of title 5, United States Code, for any year (or the pay agent's supplementary report, in accordance with subsection (d)(1)(C)(i)(II)), be considered and acted on as the pay agent's comparisons and recommendations under such section 5304(d)(1) for the area and the year involved.

"(f)(1) No later than March 1, 2001, the President's pay agent shall submit to the Committee on Government Reform of the House of Representatives, the Committee on Governmental Affairs of the Senate, and the Committees on Appropriations of the House of Representatives and of the Senate, a report on the use of pay comparison data, as described in subsection (b)(2) or (3) (as appropriate), for purposes of comparability payments.

"(2) The report shall include the cost of obtaining such data, the rationale underlying the decisions reached based on such data, and the relative advantages and disadvantages of using such data (including whether the effort involved in analyzing and integrating such data is commensurate with the benefits derived from their use). The report may include specific recommendations regarding the continued use of such data.

"(g)(1) No later than May 1, 2001, the President's pay agent shall prepare and submit to the committees specified in subsection (f)(1) a report relating to the ongoing efforts of the Office of Personnel Management, the Office of Management and Budget, and the Bureau of Labor Statistics to revise the methodology currently being used by the Bureau of Labor Statistics in performing its surveys under section 5304 of title 5, United States Code.

"(2) The report shall include a detailed accounting of any concerns the pay agent may have regarding the current methodology, the specific projects the pay agent has directed any of those agencies to undertake in order to address those concerns, and a time line for the anticipated completion of those projects and for implementation of the revised methodology.

"(3) The report shall also include recommendations as to how those ongoing efforts might be expedited, including any additional resources which, in the opinion of the pay agent, are needed in order to expedite completion of the activities described in the preceding provisions of this subsection, and the reasons why those additional resources are needed."

FREEZE OF CURRENT RATE FOR LOCALITY-BASED COMPARABILITY ADJUSTMENTS

Pub. L. 106–554, § 1(a)(4) [div. B, title IX, § 902(b)], Dec. 21, 2000, 114 Stat. 2763, 2763A–304, provided that: "Notwithstanding any other provision of law, including this title [enacting provisions set out as notes under sections 5301 and 5305 of this title and section 204 of Title 3, The President, and amending provisions set out as a note under section 5305 of this title], or any provision of law amended by this title, no officer or member of the United States Secret Service Uniformed Division or the United States Park Police may be paid locality pay under section 5304 or section 5304a of title 5, United States Code, at a percentage rate for the applicable locality in excess of the rate in effect for pay periods during calendar year 2000."

COMPARABILITY PAYMENTS IN 1994 AND 1995

Pub. L. 103–329, title VI, § 630(b), (c), Sept. 30, 1994, 108 Stat. 2424, provided that:

"(b) For purposes of any locality-based comparability payments taking effect in fiscal year 1995 under subchapter I of chapter 53 of title 5, United States Code (whether by adjustment or otherwise), section 5304(a) of such title shall be deemed to be without force or effect.

"(c) Notwithstanding section 5304(a)(3)(B) of title 5, United States Code, the annualized cost of pay adjustments made under section 5304 of such title in calendar year 1995 shall be equal to 0.6 percent of the estimated aggregate fiscal year 1995 executive branch civilian payroll—

"(1) as determined by the pay agent (within the meaning of section 5302 of such title); and

"(2) determined as if the rates of pay and comparability payments payable on September 30, 1994, had remained in effect."

Section 8(b) of Pub. L. 102–378 provided that: "Notwithstanding section 5304 of title 5, United States Code, for purposes of any comparability payments scheduled to take effect under such section during calendar years 1994 and 1995, respectively—

"(1) the report required by subsection (d)(1) of such section may be submitted not later than 1 month before the start of the calendar year for purposes of which it is prepared; and

"(2) the surveys conducted by the Bureau of Labor Statistics for use in preparing any such report may be other than annual surveys, and shall, to the greatest extent practicable, be completed not later than 4 months before the start of the calendar year for purposes of which the surveys are conducted."

INTERIM GEOGRAPHIC ADJUSTMENTS

Section 529 [title III, § 302] of Pub. L. 101–509, as amended by Pub. L. 102–378, § 3(4), Oct. 2, 1992, 106 Stat. 1356; Pub. L. 103–89, § 3(b)(2), Sept. 30, 1993, 107 Stat. 982, provided that:

"(a) DEFINITIONS.—For the purpose of this section—

"(1) the term 'area' means any consolidated metropolitan statistical area, primary metropolitan statistical area, or metropolitan statistical area, with at least 5,000 General Schedule employees; and

"(2) the term 'pay relative' shall have the meaning given such term under regulations prescribed by the Bureau of Labor Statistics.

"(b) AUTHORITY.—(1) The President may establish geographic adjustments of up to 8 percent of basic pay which may be paid to each General Schedule employee whose duty station is within any area where such adjustment is needed (as determined under paragraph (2)).

"(2) In determining areas where an interim geographic adjustment is needed, the President shall consider available evidence of significant pay disparities, including BLS information on pay relatives and relevant commercial surveys, and recruitment or retention problems.

"(c) ADMINISTRATION.—(1) An adjustment under this section shall be administered, to the extent practicable, in the same manner as locality-based comparability payments under subchapter I of chapter 53 of title 5, United States Code (as amended by this Act), including in terms of—

"(A) the basic pay to which a percentage is applied in computing an amount payable under this section;

"(B) the purposes for which any amount under this section is to be considered part of basic pay;

"(C) the time and manner in which amounts under this section are to be paid (including any maximum rate limitation); and

"(D) the authority of the President, upon request of an agency head, to extend this section to employees who would not otherwise be covered.

"(2) No amount payable under this section shall be taken into account in any survey or computation under, or for any other purpose in the administration of, section 5304 of title 5, United States Code (as so amended).

"(d) COMMENCEMENT AND TERMINATION RULES.—(1) The effective date of an adjustment under this section shall be as determined by the President, but not later than January 1, 1994.

"(2)(A) The size of any payments under this section may be reduced or terminated after the amendments made by section 101 of this Act [section 529 [title I, § 101] of Pub. L. 101–509, see Tables for classification] take effect [see Effective Date of 1990 Amendment note set out under section 5301 of this title], except that the reduction or termination of a payment under this section may not have the effect of reducing, for the individual involved, the total rate at which additional forms of basic pay (as defined in subparagraph (B)) are payable to such individual.

"(B) The total rate to which subparagraph (A) applies is the sum of—

"(i) the rate at which comparability payments (under section 5304 of title 5, United States Code, as amended by such Act), are payable; and

"(ii) the rate at which payments under this section are payable.

"(e) EMPLOYEES RECEIVING SPECIAL PAY RATES.—The President (or his designated agent) shall determine what, if any, geographic adjustment shall be payable under this section in the case of an employee whose rate of pay is fixed under section 5303 of title 5, United States Code (as in effect before the date of enactment of this Act [Nov. 5, 1990]), section 5305 of title 5, United States Code (as amended by section 101 of this Act), or any similar provision of law.

"(f) EFFECTIVE DATE.—This section shall take effect on the date of enactment of this Act [Nov. 5, 1990]."

[Amendment by Pub. L. 103–89 to section 529 [title III, § 302] of Pub. L. 101–509, set out above, effective Nov. 1, 1993, see section 3(c) of Pub. L. 103–89, set out as an Effective Date of 1993 Amendment note under section 3372 of this title.]

[Amendment by Pub. L. 102–378 to section 529 [title III, § 302] of Pub. L. 101–509, set out above, effective Nov. 5, 1990, see section 9(b)(6) of Pub. L. 102–378, set out as an Effective Date of 1992 Amendment note under section 6303 of this title.]

Interim geographic adjustments pursuant to section 529 [title III, § 302] of Pub. L. 101–509, set out above, were provided by the following executive orders, formerly set out as notes under section 5332 of this title, effective on the first day of first pay period beginning on or after the effective date shown:

Ex. Ord. No. 12944, Dec. 28, 1994, 60 F.R. 309, effective Jan. 1, 1995.

Ex. Ord. No. 12826, Dec. 30, 1992, 57 F.R. 62909, effective Jan. 1, 1993.

Ex. Ord. No. 12786, Dec. 26, 1991, 56 F.R. 67453, effective Jan. 1, 1992.

Ex. Ord. No. 12736, Dec. 12, 1990, 55 F.R. 51385, effective Jan. 1, 1991.

EXECUTIVE ORDER NO. 11073

Ex. Ord. No. 11073, Jan. 7, 1963, 28 F.R. 203, as amended by Ex. Ord. No. 11173, Aug. 20, 1964, 29 F.R. 11999, which provided for Federal salary administration, was superseded by Ex. Ord. No. 11721, May 23, 1973, 38 F.R. 13717, formerly set out below.

EXECUTIVE ORDER NO. 11721

Ex. Ord. No. 11721, May 23, 1973, 38 F.R. 13717, as amended by Ex. Ord. No. 12004, July 20, 1977, 42 F.R.

37527; Ex. Ord. No. 12107, Dec. 28, 1978, 44 F.R. 1055, which provided for administration of the Federal pay system, was revoked by Ex. Ord. No. 12748, Feb. 1, 1991, 56 F.R. 4521, eff. Feb. 3, 1991, set out under section 5301 of this title.

Ex. Ord. No. 12764. Federal Salary Council

Ex. Ord. No. 12764, June 5, 1991, 56 F.R. 26587, provided:

By the authority vested in me as President by the Constitution and the laws of the United States of America, including section 5304(e) of title 5, United States Code, as amended, and in order to establish, in accordance with the provisions of the Federal Advisory Committee Act, as amended (5 U.S.C. App.), an advisory committee on locality-based comparability payments for General Schedule employees, it is hereby ordered as follows:

Section 1. *Establishment.* There is established a Federal Salary Council (the "Council"). The Council shall be composed of nine members appointed by the President in accordance with section 5304(e)(1) of title 5, United States Code. The President shall designate one of the members to serve as Chairman of the Council and shall designate another member to serve as Vice Chairman of the Council. The Vice Chairman shall act as Chairman in the absence of the Chairman.

Sec. 2. *Function.* The Council shall meet with the President's Pay Agent, as designated under section 2(a) of Executive Order No. 12748 of February 1, 1991 [5 U.S.C. 5301 note], to provide views and recommendations regarding:

(a) the establishment or modification of pay localities;

(b) the coverage of annual surveys conducted by the Bureau of Labor Statistics under subsection 5304(d)(1)(A) of title 5, United States Code (including, but not limited to, the occupations, establishment sizes, and industries to be surveyed, and how pay localities are to be surveyed);

(c) the process of comparing the rates of pay payable under the General Schedule with rates of pay for the same levels of work performed by non-Federal workers; and

(d) the level of comparability payments that should be paid in order to eliminate or reduce pay disparities in accordance with the requirements of section 5304 of title 5, United States Coce.

Sec. 3. *Administration.* (a) Members of the Council shall receive no pay by reason of their service on the Council.

(b) To the extent permitted by law and subject to the availability of appropriations, the Office of Personnel Management (the "Office") shall provide such facilities and administrative support to the Council as the Director of the Office determines appropriate.

(c) Notwithstanding the provisions of any other Executive order, the functions of the President under the Federal Advisory Committee Act, as amended [5 App. U.S.C.], except that reporting to the Congress, which are applicable to the Council, shall be performed by the Director of the Office, in accordance with the guidelines and procedures established by the Administrator of General Services.

George Bush.

Locality-Based Comparability Payments

Ex. Ord. No. 13182, Dec. 23, 2000, 65 F.R. 82879, 66 F.R. 10057, set out as a note under section 5332 of this title, provided in part for payment of locality-based comparability payments effective on the first day of the first applicable pay period beginning on or after Jan. 1, 2001. See Schedule set out as follows:

Schedule 9

Locality-Based Comparability Payments

(Effective on the first day of the first applicable pay period beginning on or after January 1, 2001)

Locality Pay Area [1]	Rate
Atlanta, GA	8.66%

Schedule 9—Continued

Locality-Based Comparability Payments

Locality Pay Area [1]	Rate
Boston-Worcester-Lawrence, MA–NH–ME–CT–RI	12.13%
Chicago-Gary-Kenosha, IL–IN–WI	13.00%
Cincinnati-Hamilton, OH–KY–IN	10.76%
Cleveland-Akron, OH	9.17%
Columbus, OH	9.61%
Dallas-Fort Worth, TX	9.71%
Dayton-Springfield, OH	8.60%
Denver-Boulder-Greeley, CO	11.90%
Detroit-Ann Arbor-Flint, MI	13.14%
Hartford, CT	12.65%
Houston-Galveston-Brazoria, TX	16.66%
Huntsville, AL	8.12%
Indianapolis, IN	7.89%
Kansas City, MO–KS	8.32%
Los Angeles-Riverside-Orange County, CA	14.37%
Miami-Fort Lauderdale, FL	11.09%
Milwaukee-Racine, WI	8.91%
Minneapolis-St. Paul, MN–WI	10.30%
New York-Northern New Jersey-Long Island, NY–NJ–CT–PA	13.62%
Orlando, FL	7.71%
Philadelphia-Wilmington-Atlantic City, PA–NJ–DE–MD	10.80%
Pittsburgh, PA	8.54%
Portland-Salem, OR–WA	10.32%
Richmond-Petersburg, VA	8.60%
Sacramento-Yolo, CA	10.73%
St. Louis, MO–IL	8.00%
San Diego, CA	11.31%
San Francisco-Oakland-San Jose, CA	16.98%
Seattle-Tacoma-Bremerton, WA	10.45%
Washington-Baltimore, DC–MD–VA–WV	10.23%
Rest of U.S.	7.68%

[1] Locality Pay Areas are defined in 5 CFR 531.603.

Ex. Ord. No. 13144, Dec. 21, 1999, 64 F.R. 72237, which provided for payment of locality-based comparability payments effective Jan. 1, 2000, was superseded by Ex. Ord. No. 13182, Dec. 23, 2000, 65 F.R. 82879, set out as a note under section 5332 of this title.

Ex. Ord. No. 13106, Dec. 7, 1998, 63 F.R. 68151, which provided for payment of locality-based comparability payments effective Jan. 1, 1999, was substantially superseded by Ex. Ord. No. 13144, Dec. 21, 1999, 64 F.R. 72237, formerly set out as a note under section 5332 of this title.

Ex. Ord. No. 13071, Dec. 29, 1997, 62 F.R. 68521, which provided for payment of locality-based comparability payments effective Jan. 1, 1998, was superseded by Ex. Ord. No. 13106, Dec. 7, 1998, 63 F.R. 68151, formerly set out as a note under section 5332 of this title.

Ex. Ord. No. 13033, Dec. 27, 1996, 61 F.R. 68987, which provided for payment of locality-based comparability payments effective Jan. 1, 1997, was superseded by Ex. Ord. No. 13071, Dec. 29, 1997, 62 F.R. 68521, formerly set out as a note under section 5332 of this title.

Ex. Ord. No. 12984, Dec. 28, 1995, 61 F.R. 237, which provided for payment of locality-based comparability payments effective Jan. 1, 1996, was superseded by Ex. Ord. No. 13033, Dec. 27, 1996, 61 F.R. 68987, formerly set out as a note under section 5332 of this title.

Approval of locality-based comparability payments recommended by the Director of the Office of Personnel Management was contained in the following:

Memorandum of President of the United States, Nov. 30, 1994, 59 F.R. 62549.

Memorandum of President of the United States, Dec. 1, 1993, 58 F.R. 64097.

Section Referred to in Other Sections

This section is referred to in sections 3161, 4505a, 5302, 5304a, 5305, 5392, 5542, 5543, 5545, 5547, 5753, 5754, 5755 of this title; title 2 sections 609–1, 906; title 7 section 2009aa–1; title 20 section 1018; title 21 section 379h; title 22 section 3974; title 28 section 594; title 35 section 3; title 40 App. section 106.

§ 5304a. Authority to fix an alternative level of comparability payments

(a) If, because of national emergency or serious economic conditions affecting the general welfare, the President should consider the level of comparability payments which would otherwise be payable under section 5304 in any year to be inappropriate, the President shall—

(1) prepare and transmit to Congress, at least 1 month before those comparability payments (disregarding this section) would otherwise become payable, a report describing the alternative level of payments which the President instead intends to provide, including the reasons why such alternative level is considered necessary; and

(2) implement the alternative level of payments beginning on the same date as would otherwise apply, for the year involved, under section 5304.

(b) The requirements set forth in paragraphs (2) and (3), respectively, of section 5303(b) shall apply with respect to any decision to exercise any authority to fix an alternative level of comparability payments under this section.

(Added Pub. L. 101–509, title V, § 529 [title I, § 101(a)(1)], Nov. 5, 1990, 104 Stat. 1427, 1436.)

EFFECTIVE DATE

Section effective on such date as the President shall determine, but not earlier than 90 days, and not later than 180 days, after Nov. 5, 1990, see section 529 [title III, § 305] of Pub. L. 101–509, set out as an Effective Date of 1990 Amendment note under section 5301 of this title.

SPECIAL RULE RELATING TO COMPARABILITY PAYMENTS IN 1994

Section 634 of Pub. L. 101–509 provided that:

"Notwithstanding any other provision of law (including any provision of the Federal Employees Pay Comparability Act of 1990 [see Short Title of 1990 Amendment note set out under section 5301 of this title] and any provision of law amended by such Act), for purposes of any comparability payments scheduled to take effect under section 5304 of title 5, United States Code (as amended by such Act) during calendar year 1994—

"(1) deem section 5304a of such title (as so amended) to be amended as follows:

"(A) in subsection (a), strike 'If' and all that follows thereafter through 'welfare,' and insert 'Subject to subsection (c), if'; and

"(B) add after subsection (b) the following:

"'(c)(1) For the purpose of this section—

"'(A) the "threshold amount" is $1,800,000,000; and

"'(B) "severe economic conditions" shall be considered to exist relative to comparability payments scheduled to take effect on a given date if, during the 12-month period ending 2 calendar quarters before such date, there occurred 2 consecutive quarters of negative growth in the GNP.

"'(2) Authority under this section to provide an alternative level of comparability payments in any year may not be exercised except in accordance with the following:

"'(A) If the estimated cost of the comparability payments which (but for this section) would otherwise be payable in such year would be equal to the threshold amount or less, no alternative level may be fixed under this section unless necessary because a state of war or severe economic conditions exist.

"'(B) If the estimated cost of the comparability payments which (but for this section) would otherwise be payable in such year would be greater than the threshold amount, no alternative level may be fixed—

"'(i) at a level which would result in an estimated cost equal to or greater than the threshold amount, unless necessary because of national emergency or serious economic conditions affecting the general welfare; or

"'(ii) at a level which would result in an estimated cost less than the threshold amount, unless necessary because of either of the reasons set forth in subparagraph (A).

"'(d)(1) The President's agent (as referred to in section 5304(d)) shall develop and include in the appropriate report under section 5304(d)(1) the methodology for estimating any costs under this section, and any estimate under this section shall be in accordance with such methodology.

"'(2) In making any estimate under this section, costs attributable to any authority under section 5304(h) may not be taken into account.'; and

"(2) the President's pay agent (referred to in section 5304(d) of such title, as so amended) may use appropriate estimates in lieu of BLS survey data if such data is not available for use in preparing the agent's report with respect to comparability payments payable during calendar year 1994."

SECTION REFERRED TO IN OTHER SECTIONS

This section is referred to in title 2 section 60a–1.

§ 5305. Special pay authority

(a) Whenever the President finds that the Government's recruitment or retention efforts with respect to 1 or more occupations in 1 or more areas or locations are, or are likely to become, significantly handicapped, due to any of the circumstances described in subsection (b), he may establish for the areas or locations involved, with respect to individuals in positions paid under any of the pay systems referred to in subsection (c), higher minimum rates of basic pay for 1 or more grades or levels, occupational groups, series, classes, or subdivisions thereof, and may make corresponding increases in all step rates of the pay range for each such grade or level. However, a minimum rate so established may not exceed the maximum pay rate prescribed by statute for the grade or level by more than 30 percent, and no rate may be established under this section (disregarding any amount payable under subsection (g)) in excess of the rate of basic pay payable for level V of the Executive Schedule. The President may authorize the exercise of the authority conferred on him by this section by the Office of Personnel Management or, in the case of individuals not subject to the provisions of this title governing appointment in the competitive service, by such other agency as he may designate.

(b) The circumstances referred to in subsection (a) are—

(1) rates of pay offered by non-Federal employers being significantly higher than those payable by the Government within the area, location, occupational group, or other class of positions under the pay system involved;

(2) the remoteness of the area or location involved;

(3) the undesirability of the working conditions or the nature of the work involved (including exposure to toxic substances or other occupational hazards); or

(4) any other circumstances which the President (or an agency duly authorized or designated by the President in accordance with the last sentence of subsection (a)) considers appropriate.

(c) Authority under subsection (a) may be exercised with respect to positions paid under—

(1) a statutory pay system; or

(2) any other pay system established by or under Federal statute for civilian positions within the executive branch.

(d) Within the limitations applicable under the preceding provisions of this section, rates of pay established under this section may be revised from time to time by the President or by such agency as he may designate. The actions and revisions have the force and effect of statute.

(e) An increase in a rate of basic pay established under this section is not an equivalent increase in pay within the meaning of section 5335.

(f) The rate of basic pay established under this section and received by an individual immediately before a statutory increase, which becomes effective prior to, on, or after the date of enactment of the statute, in the pay schedule applicable to such individual of any pay system specified in subsection (c) of this section, shall be initially adjusted, effective on the effective date of the statutory increase, under conversion rules prescribed by the President or by such agency as the President may designate.

(g)(1) The benefit of any comparability payments under section 5304 shall be available to individuals receiving rates of basic pay established under this section to such extent as the President (or his designated agency) considers appropriate, subject to paragraph (2) and subsection (h).

(2) Payments under this subsection may not be made if, or to the extent that, when added to basic pay otherwise payable, such payments would cause the total to exceed the rate of basic pay payable for level IV of the Executive Schedule.

(h) The rate of basic pay payable to an individual under this section may not, at any time, be less than the rate which would then be payable to such individual (taking comparability payments under section 5304 into account) if this section had never been enacted.

(Added Pub. L. 91–656, § 3(a), Jan. 8, 1971, 84 Stat. 1946; amended Pub. L. 94–82, title II, § 202(c), Aug. 9, 1975, 89 Stat. 420; Pub. L. 101–509, title V, § 529 [title I, § 101(a)(1)], Nov. 5, 1990, 104 Stat. 1427, 1436.)

REFERENCES IN TEXT

Levels IV and V of the Executive Schedule, referred to in subsecs. (a) and (g)(2), are set out in sections 5315 and 5316, respectively, of this title.

The provisions of this title governing appointment in the competitive service, referred to in subsec. (a), are classified generally to section 3301 et seq. of this title.

AMENDMENTS

1990—Pub. L. 101–509 amended section generally, substituting provisions authorizing President to make special pay increases whenever recruitment or retention efforts are handicapped for provisions requiring annual pay reports and adjustments, authorizing alternative plan in years of emergency or when economic conditions affect the general welfare, and setting forth procedure where Congressional committee disapproves such alternative plan.

1975—Subsec. (a)(3). Pub. L. 94–82, § 202(c)(1), inserted provision relating to specification in the report to the Congress of the overall percentage of the adjustment in the rates of pay under the General Schedule and under other statutory pay systems.

Subsec. (c)(1). Pub. L. 94–82, § 202(c)(2), inserted provision relating to specification in the report to the Congress of the overall percentage of the adjustment in the rates of pay under the General Schedule and under other statutory pay systems.

EFFECTIVE DATE OF 1990 AMENDMENT

Amendment by Pub. L. 101–509 effective on such date as the President shall determine, but not earlier than 90 days, and not later than 180 days, after Nov. 5, 1990, see section 529 [title III, § 305] of Pub. L. 101–509, set out as a note under section 5301 of this title.

DELEGATION OF FUNCTIONS

For delegation of authorities of President under this section, see Ex. Ord. No. 12748, § 3, Feb. 1, 1991, 56 F.R. 4521, eff. Feb. 3, 1991, set out as a note under section 5301 of this title.

STAFFING DIFFERENTIALS

Section 529 [title II, § 209] of Pub. L. 101–509, as amended by Pub. L. 102–378, § 3(3), Oct. 2, 1992, 106 Stat. 1355, provided that:

"(a) IN GENERAL.—Effective on the first day of the first applicable pay period beginning on or after January 1, 1991, the President may establish staffing differentials equal to 5 percent of basic pay, which may be paid to each General Schedule employee whose position is in—

"(1) grade GS–5 or 7 of the General Schedule;

"(2) a 2-grade-interval occupational series, as determined by the Office of Personnel Management; or

"(3) any combination of classes of positions described in paragraph (1) or (2) for which the President determines a recruiting difficulty exists.

"(b) MANNER OF PAYMENT; REDUCTION OR ELIMINATION.—A staffing differential under this section—

"(1) shall be paid in the same manner and at the same time as the employee's basic pay is paid, but may not be considered to be part of basic pay for any purpose; and

"(2) may be reduced or eliminated by the Office of Personnel Management in its sole discretion as the amendments made by this Act take effect [see Effective Date of 1990 Amendment and Short Title of 1990 Amendment notes set out under section 5301 of this title], except that no such reduction or elimination shall have the effect of reducing the total amount of pay (determined by adding basic pay and staffing differential) which any employee is receiving."

[Authority of President under section 529 [title II, § 209] of Pub. L. 101–509, set out above, delegated to Office of Personnel Management by Ex. Ord. No. 12748, Feb. 1, 1991, 56 F.R. 4521, eff. May 4, 1991, set out as a note under section 5301 of this title.]

FEDERAL LAW ENFORCEMENT PAY REFORM

Pub. L. 106–554, § 1(a)(4) [div. B, title IX, § 907(a)], Dec. 21, 2000, 114 Stat. 2763, 2763A–309, provided that: "Beginning on the effective date of this Act [see section 1(a)(4) [div. B, title IX, § 909] of Pub. L. 106–554, set out in a Conversion to New Salary Schedule note under section 204 of Title 3, The President]—

"(1) no existing special salary rates shall be authorized for members of the United States Park Police under section 5305 of title 5, United States Code (or any previous similar provision of law); and

"(2) no special rates of pay or special pay adjustments shall be applicable to members of the United States Park Police pursuant to section 405 of the Federal Law Enforcement Pay Reform Act of 1990 [section 529 [title IV, § 405] of Pub. L. 101–509, set out in a note below]."

Section 529 [title IV, §§ 401–407] of Pub. L. 101–509, as amended by Pub. L. 102–378, § 3(5)–(9), Oct. 2, 1992, 106 Stat. 1356; Pub. L. 103–123, title VI, § 628, Oct. 28, 1993, 107 Stat. 1266; Pub. L. 103–178, title III, § 303(a), Dec. 3, 1993, 107 Stat. 2034; Pub. L. 105–61, title I, § 118(e), Oct. 10, 1997, 111 Stat. 1288; Pub. L. 106–554, § 1(a)(4) [div. B, title IX, §907(b)], Dec. 21, 2000, 114 Stat. 2763, 2763A–309, provided that:

"SEC. 401. SHORT TITLE.

"This title [section 529 [title IV, §§401–412] of Pub. L. 101–509, enacting sections 4521 to 4523 of this title, amending sections 5541, 5542, 5547, 8335, and 8425 of this title, enacting provisions set out as notes under this section and sections 4521, 5541, and 8335 of this title, and amending provisions set out as a note under section 5541 of this title] may be cited as the 'Federal Law Enforcement Pay Reform Act of 1990'.

"SEC. 402. DEFINITION.

"For the purposes of this title, except as otherwise provided, the term 'law enforcement officer' means any law enforcement officer within the meaning of section 5541(3) of title 5, United States Code, with respect to whom the provisions of chapter 51 of such title apply.

"SEC. 403. SPECIAL RATES FOR LAW ENFORCEMENT OFFICERS.

"(a) Notwithstanding the procedures of section 5305 of title 5, United States Code, as amended by section 101 of this Act, or similar provision of law, higher minimum rates and corresponding increases in all step rates of each designated General Schedule grade shall be established for law enforcement officers in accordance with the provisions of this section.

"(b)(1) Effective on the first day of the first applicable pay period beginning on or after January 1, 1992, the higher minimum rates to be established are as follows:

"GS–3 .... Step 4
"GS–4 .... Step 4
"GS–5 .... Step 4
"GS–6 .... Step 3
"GS–7 .... Step 3
"GS–8 .... Step 3
"GS–9 .... Step 2
"GS–10 .... Step 2

"(2) Effective on the first day of the first applicable pay period beginning on or after January 1, 1993, the higher minimum rates to be established are as follows:

"GS–3 .... Step 7
"GS–4 .... Step 7
"GS–5 .... Step 8
"GS–6 .... Step 6
"GS–7 .... Step 5
"GS–8 .... Step 3
"GS–9 .... Step 2
"GS–10 .... Step 2

"(c) The higher minimum rates and corresponding higher rates for each step rate of each designated grade shall apply to every law enforcement officer in the designated grades (except in the case of any law enforcement officer for whom a higher rate is authorized under section 5305 of title 5, United States Code, as amended by section 101 of this Act, or similar provision of law) in the same manner as rates established under section 5305 of such title, as so amended, and may be increased in accordance with subsection (f) of such section 5305.

"(d) Any interim entry-level adjustment under section 209 of this Act [section 529 [title II, §209] of Pub. L. 101–509, set out as a note above] which a law enforcement officer is receiving shall be eliminated on the day before the effective date of the higher minimum rates under subsection (b)(1).

"SEC. 404. SPECIAL PAY ADJUSTMENTS FOR LAW ENFORCEMENT OFFICERS IN SELECTED CITIES.

"(a) A law enforcement officer shall be paid any applicable special pay adjustment in accordance with the provisions of this section, but such special pay adjustment shall be reduced by the amount of any applicable interim geographic adjustment under section 302 of this Act [section 529 [title III, §302] of Pub. L. 101–509, set out as a note under section 5304 of this title], any applicable locality-based comparability payment under section 5304 of title 5, United States Code, as amended by section 101 of this Act, and, to the extent determined appropriate by the Office of Personnel Management, any applicable special rate of pay under section 5305 of such title, as so amended, or any similar provision of law (other than section 403).

"(b)(1) Except as provided in subsection (a), effective on the first day of the first applicable pay period beginning on or after January 1, 1992, each law enforcement officer whose post of duty is in one of the following areas shall receive an adjustment, which shall be a percentage of the officer's rate of basic pay, as follows:

"Area	Differential
Boston-Lawrence-Salem, MA–NH Consolidated Metropolitan Statistical Area	16%
Chicago-Gary-Lake County, IL–IN–WI Consolidated Metropolitan Statistical Area	4%
Los Angeles-Anaheim-Riverside, CA Consolidated Metropolitan Statistical Area	16%
New York-Northern New Jersey-Long Island, NY–NJ–CT Consolidated Metropolitan Statistical Area	16%
Philadelphia-Wilmington-Trenton, PA–NJ–DE–MD Consolidated Metropolitan Statistical Area	4%
San Francisco-Oakland-San Jose, CA Consolidated Metropolitan Statistical Area	16%
San Diego, CA Metropolitan Statistical Area	8%
Washington-Baltimore DC–MD–VA–WV Consolidated Metropolitan Statistical Area	4%

"(2) In the case of any area specified in paragraph (1) that includes a portion, but not all, of a county, the Office of Personnel Management may, at the request of the head of 1 or more law enforcement agencies, extend the area specified in paragraph (1) to include, for the purposes of this section, the entire county, if the Office determines that such extension would be in the interests of good personnel administration. Any such extension shall be applicable to each law enforcement officer whose post of duty is in the area of the extension.

"(c)(1) A special pay adjustment under this section shall be administered, to the extent practicable, in the same manner as a locality-based comparability payment under section 5304 of title 5, United States Code, as amended by section 101 of this Act, and shall be considered part of basic pay to the same degree as such a locality-based comparability payment.

"(2) The Office of Personnel Management may prescribe such regulations as it considers necessary concerning the payment of special pay adjustments to law enforcement officers under this section.

"SEC. 405. SAME BENEFITS FOR OTHER LAW ENFORCEMENT OFFICERS.

"(a) The appropriate agency head (as defined in subsection (c)) shall prescribe regulations under which the purposes of sections 403, 404, and 407 shall be carried out with respect to individuals holding positions described in subsection (b).

"(b) This subsection applies with respect to any—

"(1) special agent within the Diplomatic Security Service;

"(2) probation officer (referred to in section 3672 of title 18, United States Code); or

"(3) pretrial services officer (referred to in section 3153 of title 18, United States Code).

"(c) For purposes of this section, the term 'appropriate agency head' means—

"(1) with respect to any individual under subsection (b)(1), the Secretary of State; or

"(2) with respect to any individual under subsection (b)(2) or (b)(3), the Director of the Administrative Office of the United States Courts.

"SEC. 406. FBI NEW YORK FIELD DIVISION.

"(a) The total pay of an employee of the Federal Bureau of Investigation assigned to the New York Field

Division before the date of September 29, 1993, in a position covered by the demonstration project conducted under section 601 of the Intelligence Authorization Act for Fiscal Year 1989 (Public Law 100–453) [102 Stat. 1911] shall not be reduced as a result of the termination of the demonstration project during the period that employee remains employed after that date in a position covered by the demonstration project.

"(b) Beginning on September 30, 1993, any periodic payment under section 601(a)(2) of the Intelligence Authorization Act for Fiscal Year 1989 [Pub. L. 100–453, 102 Stat. 1911] for any such employee shall be reduced by the amount of any increase in basic pay under title 5, United States Code, including the following provisions: an annual adjustment under section 5303, locality-based comparability payment under section 5304, initiation or increase in a special pay rate under section 5305, promotion under section 5334, periodic step increase under section 5335, merit increase under section 5404, or other increase to basic pay under any provision of law.

"SEC. 407. RELOCATION PAYMENTS.

"Notwithstanding section 5753(b)(1)(A) of title 5, United States Code, as added by this Act, a law enforcement officer whose rate of basic pay is less than $60,000 may receive a relocation payment of up to $15,000 under section 5753."

[Section 303(b) of Pub. L. 103–178 provided that: "The amendment made by subsection (a) [amending section 529 [title IV, § 406] of Pub. L. 101–509, set out above] shall take effect as of September 30, 1993, and shall apply to the pay of employees to whom the amendment applies that is earned on or after that date."]

[For effective dates of amendments by section 3(5)–(9) of Pub. L. 102–378 to section 529 [title IV, §§ 402, 403(d), 404(a), (b), 405(a)] of Pub. L. 101–509, set out above, see section 9(a), (b)(6), (9) of Pub. L. 102–378, set out as an Effective Date of 1992 Amendment note under section 6303 of this title.]

REPORTING REQUIREMENT

Section 529 [title IV, § 412] of Pub. L. 101–509 provided that: "Not later than January 1, 1993, the Office of Personnel Management, in consultation with Federal law enforcement agencies and law enforcement employee groups, shall submit to Congress, in writing, a plan to establish a separate pay and classification system for law enforcement officers and specifications for legislation to implement such plan."

SECTION REFERRED TO IN OTHER SECTIONS

This section is referred to in sections 3326, 5363, 5542, 5543, 5545, 5547 of this title; title 18 section 3006A; title 21 section 848; title 31 section 325; title 38 section 7451.

§ 5306. Pay fixed by administrative action

(a) Notwithstanding sections 1341, 1342, and 1349–1351 and subchapter II of chapter 15 of title 31—

(1) the rates of pay of—

(A) employees in the legislative, executive, and judicial branches of the Government of the United States (except employees whose pay is disbursed by the Secretary of the Senate or the Chief Administrative Officer of the House of Representatives) and of the government of the District of Columbia, whose rates of pay are fixed by administrative action under law and are not otherwise adjusted under this subchapter;

(B) employees under the Architect of the Capitol, whose rates of pay are fixed under section 166b–3a of title 40, and the Superintendent of Garages, House office buildings; and

(C) persons employed by the county committees established under section 590h(b) of title 16; and

(2) and minimum or maximum rate of pay (other than a maximum rate equal to or greater than the maximum rate then currently being paid under the General Schedule as a result of a pay adjustment under section 5303 (or prior corresponding provision of law)), and any monetary limitation on or monetary allowance for pay, applicable to employees described in subparagraphs (A), (B), and (C) of paragraph (1);

may be adjusted, by the appropriate authority concerned, effective at the beginning of the first applicable pay period commencing on or after the day on which a pay adjustment becomes effective under section 5303 (or prior provision of law), by whichever of the following methods the appropriate authority concerned considers appropriate—

(i) by an amount or amounts not in excess of the pay adjustment provided under section 5303 for corresponding rates of pay in the appropriate schedule or scale of pay;

(ii) if there are no corresponding rates of pay, by an amount or amounts equal or equivalent, insofar as practicable and with such exceptions and modifications as may be necessary to provide for appropriate pay relationships between positions, to the amount of the pay adjustment provided under section 5303; or

(iii) in the case of minimum or maximum rates of pay, or monetary limitations of allowances with respect to pay, by an amount rounded to the nearest $100 and computed on the basis of a percentage equal or equivalent, insofar as practicable and with such variations as may be appropriate, to the percentage of the pay adjustment provided under section 5303.

(b) An adjustment under subsection (a) in rates of pay, minimum or maximum rates of pay, the monetary limitations or allowances with respect to pay, shall be made in such manner as the appropriate authority concerned considers appropriate.

(c) This section does not authorize any adjustment in the rates of pay of employees whose rates of pay are fixed and adjusted from time to time as nearly as is consistent with the public interest in accordance with prevailing rates or practices.

(d) This section does not impair any authority under which rates of pay may be fixed by administrative action.

(e) Pay may not be paid, by reason of any exercise of authority under this section, at a rate in excess of the rate of basic pay payable for level V of the Executive Schedule.

(Added Pub. L. 91–656, § 3(a), Jan. 8, 1971, 84 Stat. 1949; amended Pub. L. 101–509, title V, § 529 [title I, § 101(a)(1)], Nov. 5, 1990, 104 Stat. 1427, 1437; Pub. L. 102–378, § 2(27), Oct. 2, 1992, 106 Stat. 1350; Pub. L. 104–186, title II, § 215(3), Aug. 20, 1996, 110 Stat. 1745.)

REFERENCES IN TEXT

The General Schedule, referred to in subsec. (a)(2), is set out under section 5332 of this title.

Level V of the Executive Schedule, referred to in subsec. (e), is set out in section 5316 of this title.

AMENDMENTS

1996—Subsec. (a)(1)(A). Pub. L. 104–186 substituted "Chief Administrative Officer" for "Clerk".

1992—Subsec. (a)(1)(B). Pub. L. 102–378 substituted "section 166b–3a" for "section 166b–3".

1990—Pub. L. 101–509 amended section generally, substituting provisions authorizing adjustments in rates of pay, minimum or maximum rates of pay, and monetary limitations or allowances with respect to pay of certain Federal employees for provisions establishing Advisory Committee on Federal Pay and setting forth its duties.

EFFECTIVE DATE OF 1990 AMENDMENT

Amendment by Pub. L. 101–509 effective on such date as the President shall determine, but not earlier than 90 days, and not later than 180 days, after Nov. 5, 1990, see section 529 [title III, § 305] of Pub. L. 101–509, set out as a note under section 5301 of this title.

SECTION REFERRED TO IN OTHER SECTIONS

This section is referred to in sections 5376, 5382 of this title; title 10 section 1602; title 40 section 174j–8.

§ 5307. Limitation on certain payments

(a)(1) Except as otherwise permitted by or under law, no allowance, differential, bonus, award, or other similar cash payment under this title may be paid to an employee in a calendar year if, or to the extent that, when added to the total basic pay paid or payable to such employee for service performed in such calendar year as an employee in the executive branch (or as an employee outside the executive branch to whom chapter 51 applies), such payment would cause the total to exceed the annual rate of basic pay payable for level I of the Executive Schedule, as of the end of such calendar year.

(2) This section shall not apply to any payment under—

(A) subchapter III or VII of chapter 55 or section 5596;

(B) chapter 57 (other than section 5753, 5754, or 5755); or

(C) chapter 59 (other than section 5925, 5928, 5941(a)(2), or 5948).

(b)(1) Any amount which is not paid to an employee in a calendar year because of the limitation under subsection (a) shall be paid to such employee in a lump sum at the beginning of the following calendar year.

(2) Any amount paid under this subsection in a calendar year shall be taken into account for purposes of applying[1] the limitations under subsection (a) with respect to such calendar year.

(c) The Office of Personnel Management shall prescribe such regulations as may be necessary to carry out this section, including regulations (consistent with section 5582) concerning how a lump-sum payment under subsection (b) shall be made with respect to any employee who dies before an amount payable to such employee under subsection (b) is made.

(Added Pub. L. 91–656, § 3(a), Jan. 8, 1971, 84 Stat. 1950; amended Pub. L. 97–258, § 3(a)(10), Sept. 13, 1982, 96 Stat. 1063; Pub. L. 101–509, title V, § 529 [title I, § 101(a)(1)], Nov. 5, 1990, 104 Stat. 1427, 1438; Pub. L. 102–77, § 2, July 26, 1991, 105 Stat. 369.)

REFERENCES IN TEXT

Level I of the Executive Schedule, referred to in subsec. (a)(1), is set out in section 5312 of this title.

[1] So in original. Probably should be "applying".

AMENDMENTS

1991—Subsec. (a). Pub. L. 102–77, § 2(1)–(3), designated existing provisions as par. (1), substituted "cause the" for "cause to the", and added par. (2).

Subsec. (b)(3). Pub. L. 102–77, § 2(4), struck out par. (3) which read as follows: "Paragraph (1) shall not apply to an amount if, or to the extent that, it is attributable to a payment the authority for which would derive from section 4505a(d), 5753(e), or 5754(e)."

1990—Pub. L. 101–509 amended section generally, substituting provisions prohibiting cash payments to employees in excess of annual rate of basic pay payable for level I of Executive Schedule in a calendar year, for provisions authorizing adjustments in rates of pay, minimum or maximum rates of pay, and monetary limitations or allowances with respect to pay of certain Federal employees.

1982—Subsec. (a). Pub. L. 97–258 substituted "sections 1341, 1342, and 1349–1351 and subchapter II of chapter 15" for "section 665".

EFFECTIVE DATE OF 1990 AMENDMENT

Amendment by Pub. L. 101–509 effective on such date as the President shall determine, but not earlier than 90 days, and not later than 180 days, after Nov. 5, 1990, see section 529 [title III, § 305] of Pub. L. 101–509, set out as a note under section 5301 of this title.

SECTION REFERRED TO IN OTHER SECTIONS

This section is referred to in sections 3152, 5383, 5948, 9501, 9502, 9505 of this title; title 15 section 78d; title 22 section 3965.

[§ 5308. Omitted]

CODIFICATION

Section, added Pub. L. 91–656, § 3(a), Jan. 8, 1971, 84 Stat. 1951, relating to pay limitation, was omitted in the general revision of this subchapter by Pub. L. 101–509.

SUBCHAPTER II—EXECUTIVE SCHEDULE PAY RATES

SUBCHAPTER REFERRED TO IN OTHER SECTIONS

This subchapter is referred to in sections 4509, 5304, 5374, 5377, 5380 of this title; title 7 section 2009aa–1; title 18 section 207; title 40 App. section 102; title 42 sections 3535, 4276; title 44 section 303.

§ 5311. The Executive Schedule

The Executive Schedule, which is divided into five pay levels, is the basic pay schedule for positions, other than Senior Executive Service positions and positions in the Federal Bureau of Investigation and Drug Enforcement Administration Senior Executive Service, to which this subchapter applies.

(Pub. L. 89–554, Sept. 6, 1966, 80 Stat. 459; Pub. L. 95–454, title IV, §§ 408(b)(1), 414(b)(1), Oct. 13, 1978, 92 Stat. 1173, 1178; Pub. L. 96–54, § 2(a)(24), Aug. 14, 1979, 93 Stat. 382; Pub. L. 100–325, § 2(h)(1), (2), May 30, 1988, 102 Stat. 582; Pub. L. 101–509, title V, § 529 [title I, § 104(c)], Nov. 5, 1990, 104 Stat. 1427, 1447.)

HISTORICAL AND REVISION NOTES

Derivation	U.S. Code	Revised Statutes and Statutes at Large
....	5 U.S.C. 2210.	Aug. 14, 1964, Pub. L. 88–426, § 302, 78 Stat. 415.

The words "There is hereby established" are omitted as executed. The word "offices" is omitted as included in "positions". The words "Executive Schedule" are substituted for "Federal Executive Salary Schedule".

Standard changes are made to conform with the definitions applicable and the style of this title as outlined in the preface to the report.

AMENDMENTS

1990—Pub. L. 101–509 struck out "(a)" before "The Executive Schedule, which" and struck out subsec. (b) which read as follows:

"(1) Not later than 180 days after the date of the enactment of the Civil Service Reform Act of 1978, the Director of the Office of Personnel Management shall determine the number and classification of executive level positions in existence in the executive branch on that date of enactment, and shall publish the determination in the Federal Register. Effective beginning on the date of the publication, the number of executive level positions within the executive branch may not exceed the number published under this subsection.

"(2) For the purpose of this subsection, 'executive level position' means—

"(A) any office or position in the civil service the rate of pay for which is equal to or greater than the rate of basic pay payable for positions under section 5316 of this title, or

"(B) any such office or position the rate of pay for which may be fixed by administrative action at a rate equal to or greater than the rate of basic pay payable for positions under section 5316 of this title;

but does not include any Senior Executive Service position (as defined in section 3132(a) of this title) or any position in the Federal Bureau of Investigation and Drug Enforcement Administration Senior Executive Service."

1988—Subsec. (a). Pub. L. 100–325, § 2(h)(1), inserted reference to positions in Federal Bureau of Investigation and Drug Enforcement Administration Senior Executive Service.

Subsec. (b)(2). Pub. L. 100–325, § 2(h)(2), substituted "(as defined in section 3132(a) of this title) or any position in the Federal Bureau of Investigation and Drug Enforcement Administration Senior Executive Service" for ", as defined in section 3132(a) of this title" in concluding provision.

1979—Subsec. (b)(1). Pub. L. 96–54 inserted "of the Office of Personnel Management" after "Director".

1978—Pub. L. 95–454, § 408(b)(1), inserted reference to Senior Executive Service positions.

Pub. L. 95–454, § 414(b)(1), designated existing provisions as subsec. (a) and added subsec. (b).

EFFECTIVE DATE OF 1990 AMENDMENT

Amendment by Pub. L. 101–509 effective on such date as the President shall determine, but not earlier than 90 days, and not later than 180 days, after Nov. 5, 1990, see section 529 [title III, § 305] of Pub. L. 101–509, set out as a note under section 5301 of this title.

EFFECTIVE DATE OF 1979 AMENDMENT

Amendment by Pub. L. 96–54 effective July 12, 1979, see section 2(b) of Pub. L. 96–54, set out as a note under section 305 of this title.

EFFECTIVE DATE OF 1978 AMENDMENT

Amendment by Pub. L. 95–454 effective 9 months after Oct. 13, 1978, and congressional review of provisions of sections 401 through 412 of Pub. L. 95–454, see section 415 of Pub. L. 95–454, set out as an Effective Date note under section 3131 of this title.

PLAN FOR AUTHORIZING EXECUTIVE LEVEL POSITIONS IN EXECUTIVE BRANCH; PRESIDENTIAL SUBMISSION TO CONGRESS

Section 414(b)(2) of Pub. L. 95–454 required President to transmit by Jan. 1, 1980, a plan to Congress for authorizing executive level positions in executive branch.

SECTION REFERRED TO IN OTHER SECTIONS

This section is referred to in title 21 section 1703; title 33 section 2309.

§ 5312. Positions at level I

Level I of the Executive Schedule applies to the following positions for which the annual rate of basic pay shall be the rate determined with respect to such level under chapter 11 of title 2, as adjusted by section 5318 of this title:

Secretary of State.
Secretary of the Treasury.
Secretary of Defense.
Attorney General.
Secretary of the Interior.
Secretary of Agriculture.
Secretary of Commerce.
Secretary of Labor.
Secretary of Health and Human Services.
Secretary of Housing and Urban Development.
Secretary of Transportation.
United States Trade Representative.
Secretary of Energy.
Secretary of Education.
Secretary of Veterans Affairs.
Director of the Office of Management and Budget.
Commissioner of Social Security, Social Security Administration.
Director of National Drug Control Policy.
Chairman, Board of Governors of the Federal Reserve System.

(Pub. L. 89–554, Sept. 6, 1966, 80 Stat. 460; Pub. L. 89–670, § 10(d)(1), Oct. 15, 1966, 80 Stat. 948; Pub. L. 91–375, § 6(c)(12), Aug. 12, 1970, 84 Stat. 776; Pub. L. 93–618, title I, § 141(b)(3)(A), Jan. 3, 1975, 88 Stat. 1999; Pub. L. 94–82, title II, § 202(b)(1), Aug. 9, 1975, 89 Stat. 419; Pub. L. 95–91, title VII, § 710(c), Aug. 4, 1977, 91 Stat. 609; Pub. L. 96–54, § 2(a)(25)(A), Aug. 14, 1979, 93 Stat. 382; Pub. L. 96–88, title V, § 508(c), (g), Oct. 17, 1979, 93 Stat. 692; Pub. L. 97–456, § 3(d)(1), (5), Jan. 12, 1983, 96 Stat. 2505; Pub. L. 99–198, title XI, § 1113(d), Dec. 23, 1985, 99 Stat. 1480; Pub. L. 99–260, § 4(c), Mar. 20, 1986, 100 Stat. 49; Pub. L. 100–527, § 13(c), Oct. 25, 1988, 102 Stat. 2643; Pub. L. 100–679, § 11(a), Nov. 17, 1988, 102 Stat. 4070; Pub. L. 100–690, title I, § 1003(a)(4)(A), Nov. 18, 1988, 102 Stat. 4182; Pub. L. 103–296, title I, § 108(e)(1), Aug. 15, 1994, 108 Stat. 1486; Pub. L. 105–277, div. C, title VII, § 713(a)(1), Oct. 21, 1998, 112 Stat. 2681–693; Pub. L. 106–569, title X, § 1002(a)(1), Dec. 27, 2000, 114 Stat. 3028.)

HISTORICAL AND REVISION NOTES

Derivation	U.S. Code	Revised Statutes and Statutes at Large
....	5 U.S.C. 2211(a).	Aug. 14, 1964, Pub. L. 88–426, § 303(a), 78 Stat. 416.

Standard changes are made to conform with the definitions applicable and the style of this title as outlined in the preface to the report.

CODIFICATION

Paragraph designation for the position added by Pub. L. 96–88 has been omitted in view of the deletion of all paragraph designations in this section by Pub. L. 96–54.

AMENDMENTS

2000—Pub. L. 106–569 inserted item relating to Chairman, Board of Governors of the Federal Reserve System.

1998—Pub. L. 105–277 inserted item relating to Director of National Drug Control Policy.

1994—Pub. L. 103–296 inserted item relating to Commissioner of Social Security, Social Security Administration.

1988—Pub. L. 100–690, §§ 1003(a)(4)(A), 1009, temporarily inserted item relating to Director of National Drug Control Policy. See Effective and Termination Dates of 1988 Amendments note below.

Pub. L. 100–679 inserted item relating to Director of Office of Management and Budget.

Pub. L. 100–527 inserted item relating to Secretary of Veterans Affairs.

1986—Pub. L. 99–260 struck out item relating to Special Assistant for Agricultural Trade and Food Aid.

1985—Pub. L. 99–198 inserted item relating to Special Assistant for Agricultural Trade and Food Aid.

1983—Pub. L. 97–456, § 3(d)(5), substituted "United States Trade Representative" for "Special Representative for Trade Negotiations".

1979—Pub. L. 96–88, § 508(g), substituted "Health and Human Services" for "Health, Education, and Welfare" in item relating to the Secretary of Health and Human Services.

Pars. (1) to (14). Pub. L. 96–54 struck out paragraph designations for positions listed herein.

Par. (15). Pub. L. 96–88, § 508(c), added par. (15) relating to Secretary of Education. See Codification note set out above.

1977—Par. (14). Pub. L. 95–91 added par. (14) relating to Secretary of Energy.

1975—Pub. L. 94–82 substituted provisions applying level I of Executive Schedule to positions for which annual rate of basic pay shall be rate determined with respect to such level under chapter 11 of title 2, as adjusted by section 5318 of this title for provisions applying such level I to positions for which annual rate of basic pay is $35,000.

Par. (13). Pub. L. 93–618 added par. (13) relating to Special Representative for Trade Negotiations.

1970—Par. (5). Pub. L. 91–375 struck out par. (5) relating to Postmaster General.

1966—Pub. L. 89–670 added par. (11) relating to Secretary of Housing and Urban Development, and par. (12) relating to Secretary of Transportation.

EFFECTIVE DATE OF 2000 AMENDMENT

Pub. L. 106–569, title X, § 1002(b), Dec. 27, 2000, 114 Stat. 3028, provided that: "This section [amending this section and sections 5313 and 5314 of this title] and the amendments made by this section shall take effect on the first day of the first pay period for the Chairman and Members of the Board of Governors of the Federal Reserve System beginning on or after the date of the enactment of this Act [Dec. 27, 2000]."

EFFECTIVE AND TERMINATION DATES OF 1988 AMENDMENTS

Amendment by Pub. L. 100–690 effective Jan. 21, 1989, and repealed on Sept. 30, 1997, see sections 1012 and 1009, respectively, of Pub. L. 100–690.

Section 11(e) of Pub. L. 100–679 provided that: "The amendments made by this section [amending sections 5312 to 5315 of this title] shall be effective on January 20, 1989."

Amendment by Pub. L. 100–527 effective Mar. 15, 1989, see section 18(a) of Pub. L. 100–527, set out as a Department of Veterans Affairs Act note under section 301 of Title 38, Veterans' Benefits.

EFFECTIVE DATE OF 1979 AMENDMENTS

Amendment by Pub. L. 96–88 effective May 4, 1980, with specified exceptions, see section 601 of Pub. L. 96–88, set out as an Effective Date note under section 3401 of Title 20, Education.

Section 2(a)(25)(B) of Pub. L. 96–54 provided that: The amendments made by subparagraph (A) [amending sections 5312 to 5316 of this title] shall take effect January 1, 1980".

EFFECTIVE DATE OF 1970 AMENDMENT

Amendment by Pub. L. 91–375 effective within 1 year after Aug. 12, 1970, on date established therefor by Board of Governors of United States Postal Service and published by it in Federal Register, see section 15(a) of Pub. L. 91–375, set out as an Effective Date note preceding section 101 of Title 39, Postal Service.

EFFECTIVE DATE OF 1966 AMENDMENT

Amendment by Pub. L. 89–670 effective 90 days after Secretary of Transportation first takes office, or on any earlier date after Oct. 15, 1966, as President prescribes and publishes in Federal Register, see section 16(a), formerly § 15(a), of Pub. L. 89–670.

SHORT TITLE OF 1975 AMENDMENT

Section 201 of title II of Pub. L. 94–82 provided that: "This title [enacting section 5318 of this title and section 461 of Title 28, Judiciary and Judicial Procedure, amending sections 5305, 5312, 5313, 5314, 5315 and 5316 of this title, sections 31, 60a note, 136a, 136a–1 and 356 of Title 2, The Congress, section 104 of Title 3, The President, section 68 of Title 11, Bankruptcy, sections 5, 44, 135, 173, 213, 252 and 792 of Title 28, sections 42a and 51a of former Title 31, Money and Finance, sections 162a and 166b of Title 40, Public Buildings, Property, and Works, and section 303 of Title 44, Public Printing and Documents, and enacting provisions set out as a note under section 356 of Title 2] may be cited as the 'Executive Salary Cost-of-Living Adjustment Act'."

SALARY INCREASES

2001—Salaries of positions at level I increased to $161,200 per annum, effective on the first day of the first pay period beginning on or after Jan. 1, 2001, as provided by Ex. Ord. No. 13182, Dec. 23, 2000, 65 F.R. 82879, 66 F.R. 10057, set out as a note under section 5332 of this title.

2000—Salaries of positions at level I increased to $157,000 per annum, effective on the first day of the first pay period beginning on or after Jan. 1, 2000, as provided by Ex. Ord. No. 13144, Dec. 21, 1999, 64 F.R. 72237.

1999—Salaries of positions at level I continued at $151,800 per annum by Ex. Ord. No. 13106, Dec. 7, 1998, 63 F.R. 68151.

1998—Salaries of positions at level I increased to $151,800 per annum, effective on the first day of the first pay period beginning on or after Jan. 1, 1998, as provided by Ex. Ord. No. 13071, Dec. 29, 1997, 62 F.R. 68521.

1997—Salaries of positions at level I continued at $148,400 per annum by Ex. Ord. No. 13033, Dec. 27, 1996, 61 F.R. 68987.

1996—Salaries of positions at level I continued at $148,400 per annum by Ex. Ord. No. 12984, Dec. 28, 1995, 61 F.R. 237.

1995—Salaries of positions at level I continued at $148,400 per annum by Ex. Ord. No. 12944, Dec. 28, 1994, 60 F.R. 309.

1993—Salaries of positions at level I increased to $148,400 per annum, effective on the first day of the first pay period beginning on or after Jan. 1, 1993, as provided by Ex. Ord. No. 12826, Dec. 30, 1992, 57 F.R. 62909.

1992—Salaries of positions at level I increased to $143,800 per annum, effective on the first day of the first pay period beginning on or after Jan. 1, 1992, as provided by Ex. Ord. No. 12786, Dec. 26, 1991, 56 F.R. 67453.

1991—Salaries of positions at level I increased to $138,900 per annum, effective on the first day of the first pay period beginning on or after Jan. 1, 1991, as provided by Ex. Ord. No. 12736, Dec. 12, 1990, 55 F.R. 51385.

1990—Salaries of positions at level I continued at $99,500 per annum, and increased to $107,300 per annum, effective on the first day of the first pay period beginning on or after Jan. 31, 1990, as provided by Ex. Ord. No. 12698, Dec. 23, 1989, 54 F.R. 53473.

1989—Salaries of positions at level I continued at $99,500 per annum, see Ex. Ord. No. 12663, Jan. 6, 1989, 54 F.R. 791.

1988—Salaries of positions at level I continued at $99,500 per annum by Ex. Ord. No. 12622, Dec. 31, 1987, 53 F.R. 222.

1987—Salaries of positions at level I increased to $99,500 per annum, on recommendation of the President of the United States, see note set out under section 358 of Title 2, The Congress.

Salaries of positions at level I increased to $88,800 per annum, effective on the first day of the first pay period beginning on or after Jan. 1, 1987, as provided by Ex. Ord. No. 12578, Dec. 31, 1986, 52 F.R. 505.

1985—Salaries of positions at level I increased to $86,200 per annum, effective on the first day of the first pay period beginning on or after Jan. 1, 1985, as provided by Ex. Ord. No. 12496, Dec. 28, 1984, 50 F.R. 211, as amended by Ex. Ord. No. 12540, Dec. 30, 1985, 51 F.R. 577.

1984—Salaries of positions at level I increased to $83,300 per annum, effective on the first day of the first pay period beginning on or after Jan. 1, 1984, as provided by Ex. Ord. No. 12456, Dec. 30, 1983, 49 F.R. 347, as amended Ex. Ord. No. 12477, May 23, 1984, 49 F.R. 22041; Ex. Ord. No. 12487, Sept. 14, 1984, 49 F.R. 36493.

1982—Salaries of positions at level I increased to $88,600 per annum, effective on the first day of the first pay period beginning on or after Oct. 1, 1982, as provided by Ex. Ord. No. 12387, Oct. 8, 1982, 47 F.R. 44981. Ex. Ord. No. 12387 further provided that pursuant to section 101(e) of Pub. L. 97–276 funds are not available to pay a salary at a rate which exceeds the rate in effect on Sept. 30, 1982, which was $69,630.00.

Maximum rate payable after Dec. 17, 1982, increased from $69,630.00 to $80,100.00, see Pub. L. 97–377, title I, § 129(b)–(d), Dec. 21, 1982, 96 Stat. 1914, set out as a note under section 5318 of this title.

Limitations on use of funds for fiscal year ending Sept. 30, 1983, appropriated by any Act to pay the salary or pay of any individual in legislative, executive, or judicial branch in position equal to or above level V of the Executive Schedule, see section 101(e) of Pub. L. 97–276, as amended, set out as a note under section 5318 of this title.

1981—Salaries of positions at level I increased to $85,200 per annum, effective on the first day of the first pay period beginning on or after Oct. 1, 1981, as provided by Ex. Ord. No. 12330, Oct. 15, 1981, 46 F.R. 50921. Ex. Ord. No. 12330 further provided that pursuant to section 101(c) of Pub. L. 97–51 funds are not available to pay a salary at a rate which exceeds the rate in effect on Sept. 30, 1981, which was $69,630.00.

Limitations on use of funds for fiscal year ending Sept. 30, 1982, appropriated by any Act to pay the salary or pay of any individual in legislative, executive, or judicial branch in position equal to or above level V of the Executive Schedule, see sections 101(g) and 141 of Pub. L. 97–92, set out as a note under section 5318 of this title.

1980—Salaries of positions at level I increased to $81,300 per annum, effective on the first day of the first pay period beginning on or after Oct. 1, 1980, as provided by Ex. Ord. No. 12248, Oct. 16, 1980, 45 F.R. 69199. Ex. Ord. No. 12248, further provided that pursuant to section 101(c) of Pub. L. 96–369, funds are not available to pay a salary at a rate which exceeds the rate in effect on Sept. 30, 1980, which was $69,630.

Limitations on use of funds for fiscal year ending Sept. 30, 1981, appropriated by any Act to pay the salary or pay of any individual in legislative, executive, or judicial branch in position equal to or above level V of the Executive Schedule, see section 101(c) of Pub. L. 96–536, as amended, set out as a note under section 5318 of this title.

1979—Salaries of positions at level I increased to $74,500 per annum, effective on the first day of the first pay period beginning on or after Oct. 1, 1979, as provided by Ex. Ord. No. 12165, Oct. 9, 1979, 44 F.R. 58671, as amended by Ex. Ord. No. 12200, Mar. 12, 1980, 45 F.R. 16443. Ex. Ord. No. 12165 further provided that pursuant to section 101(c) of Pub. L. 96–86 funds appropriated for fiscal year 1980 may not be used to pay a salary at a rate which exceeds an increase of 5.5 percent over the rate in effect on Sept. 30, 1978, which is a maximum rate payable of $69,630.

Applicability to funds appropriated by any Act for fiscal year ending Sept. 3, 1980, of limitation of section 304 of Pub. L. 95–391 on use of funds to pay the salary or pay of any individual in legislative, executive, or judicial branch in position equal to or above level V of the Executive Schedule, see section 101 of Pub. L. 96–86, set out as a note under section 5318 of this title.

1978—Salaries of positions at level I increased to $69,600 per annum, effective in the first pay period beginning on or after Oct. 1, 1978, as provided by Ex. Ord. No. 12087, Oct. 7, 1978, 43 F.R. 46823. Ex. Ord. No. 12087, further provided that pursuant to the Legislative Branch Appropriation Act, 1979, funds are not available to pay a salary at a rate which exceeds the rate in effect on Sept. 30, 1978, which was $66,000.

Limitations on use of funds for fiscal year ending Sept. 30, 1979, appropriated by any Act to pay the salary or pay of any individual in legislative, executive, or judicial branch in position equal or above level V of the Executive Schedule, see section 304 of Pub. L. 95–391 and section 613 of Pub. L. 95–429, set out as a note under section 5318 of this title.

1977—Salaries of positions at level I increased to $66,000 per annum, on recommendation of the President of the United States, see note set out under section 358 of Title 2, The Congress.

1976—Salaries of positions at level I increased to $66,000 per annum, effective on the first day of the first pay period beginning on or after Oct. 1, 1976, see Ex. Ord. No. 11941, Oct. 1, 1976, 41 F.R. 43889. Ex. Ord. No. 11941, further provided that pursuant to the Legislative Branch Appropriation Act, 1977, funds are not available to pay a salary at a rate which exceeds the rate in effect on Sept. 30, 1976, which was $63,000.

1975—Salaries of positions at level I increased to $63,000 per annum, effective on the first day of the first pay period beginning on or after Oct. 1, 1975, by Ex. Ord. No. 11883, Oct. 6, 1975, 40 F.R. 47091.

1969—Salaries of positions at level I increased from $35,000 to $60,000 per annum, commencing on the first day of the pay period which begins after February 14, 1969, on recommendation of the President of the United States, see note set out under section 358 of Title 2, The Congress.

COMPENSATION AND EMOLUMENTS OF SECRETARY OF THE TREASURY AT LEVEL IN EFFECT ON JANUARY 1, 1989

For provisions limiting compensation and emoluments of Secretary of the Treasury at levels in effect on Jan. 1, 1989, see section 1(a) of Pub. L. 103–2, set out as a note under section 301 of Title 31, Money and Finance.

COMPENSATION AND EMOLUMENTS OF SECRETARY OF STATE; FIXING AT LEVEL IN EFFECT ON JANUARY 1, 1977

Pub. L. 96–241, § 1, May 3, 1980, 94 Stat. 343, limited the compensation and other emoluments attached to the office of Secretary of State to those in effect Jan. 1, 1977, during the period beginning May 3, 1980, and ending on the date on which the first individual appointed to that office after May 3, 1980, ceases to hold that office.

COMPENSATION AND EMOLUMENTS OF ATTORNEY GENERAL; FIXING AT LEVEL IN EFFECT ON JANUARY 1, 1969

Provisions of Pub. L. 93–178, § 1, Dec. 10, 1973, 87 Stat. 697, which fixed the compensation and other emoluments attached to the Office of Attorney General at level in effect on Jan. 1, 1969, notwithstanding any other provision of law enacted or becoming effective during period from noon, Jan. 3, 1969, through noon, Jan. 2, 1975, were repealed by Pub. L. 94–2, Feb. 18, 1975, 89 Stat. 4, effective as of Feb. 4, 1975.

SECTION REFERRED TO IN OTHER SECTIONS

This section is referred to in sections 5315, 5377, 5380, 8432 of this title; title 2 section 362; title 10 sections 973, 1603; title 12 section 1723a; title 18 section 207; title 22 section 4606; title 26 sections 162, 3121, 7217; title 28 section 591; title 31 section 1344; title 38 section 7432; title 39 section 1003; title 42 sections 410, 7211, 7291; title 47 section 396; title 49 sections 106, 24315; title 50 App. section 2074.

§ 5313. Positions at level II

Level II of the Executive Schedule applies to the following positions, for which the annual rate of basic pay shall be the rate determined with respect to such level under chapter 11 of title 2, as adjusted by section 5318 of this title:

Deputy Secretary of Defense.
Deputy Secretary of State.
Deputy Secretary of State for Management and Resources.
Administrator, Agency for International Development.
Administrator of the National Aeronautics and Space Administration.
Deputy Secretary of Veterans Affairs.
Deputy Secretary of the Treasury.
Deputy Secretary of Transportation.
Chairman, Nuclear Regulatory Commission.
Chairman, Council of Economic Advisers.
Director of the Office of Science and Technology.
Director of Central Intelligence.
Secretary of the Air Force.
Secretary of the Army.
Secretary of the Navy.
Administrator, Federal Aviation Administration.
Director of the National Science Foundation.
Deputy Attorney General.
Deputy Secretary of Energy.
Deputy Secretary of Agriculture.
Director of the Office of Personnel Management.
Administrator, Federal Highway Administration.
Administrator of the Environmental Protection Agency.
Under Secretary of Defense for Acquisition, Technology, and Logistics.
Deputy Secretary of Labor.
Deputy Director of the Office of Management and Budget.
Independent Members, Thrift Depositor Protection Oversight Board.
Deputy Secretary of Health and Human Services.
Deputy Secretary of the Interior.
Deputy Secretary of Education.
Deputy Secretary of Housing and Urban Development.
Deputy Director for Management, Office of Management and Budget.
Director of the Office of Federal Housing Enterprise Oversight, Department of Housing and Urban Development.
Deputy Commissioner of Social Security, Social Security Administration.
Administrator of the Community Development Financial Institutions Fund.
Deputy Director of National Drug Control Policy.
Members, Board of Governors of the Federal Reserve System.

(Pub. L. 89–554, Sept. 6, 1966, 80 Stat. 460; Pub. L. 89–670, § 10(d)(2), Oct. 15, 1966, 80 Stat. 948; Pub. L. 90–83, § 1(13), Sept. 11, 1967, 81 Stat. 198; Pub. L. 90–407, § 15(a)(1), July 18, 1968, 82 Stat. 366; Pub. L. 91–644, title I, § 8(b), Jan. 2, 1971, 84 Stat. 1888; Pub. L. 92–255, title II, § 212(a), Mar. 21, 1972, 86 Stat. 69; Pub. L. 92–302, § 2(a), May 18, 1972, 86 Stat. 149; Pub. L. 92–352, title I, § 104(1), July 13, 1972, 86 Stat. 490; Pub. L. 92–596, § 6, Oct. 27, 1972, 86 Stat. 1318; Pub. L. 93–438, title III, § 310(1), Oct. 11, 1974, 88 Stat. 1252; Pub. L. 93–496, § 16(c), Oct. 28, 1974, 88 Stat. 1533; Pub. L. 94–82, title II, § 202(b)(2), Aug. 9, 1975, 89 Stat. 419; Pub. L. 94–237, § 4(c)(6), Mar. 19, 1976, 90 Stat. 244; Pub. L. 94–561, § 1(a), Oct. 19, 1976, 90 Stat. 2643; Pub. L. 95–91, title VII, § 710(d), Aug. 4, 1977, 91 Stat. 609; Pub. L. 95–140, § 3(d)(1), Oct. 21, 1977, 91 Stat. 1173; Pub. L. 95–454, title II, § 201(b)(1), Oct. 13, 1978, 92 Stat. 1121; Pub. L. 96–54, § 2(a)(25)(A), Aug. 14, 1979, 93 Stat. 382; Pub. L. 96–465, title II, § 2302, Oct. 17, 1980, 94 Stat. 2164; Pub. L. 97–449, §§ 3(1), 7(b), Jan. 12, 1983, 96 Stat. 2441, 2444; Pub. L. 98–80, § 2(a)(1), Aug. 23, 1983, 97 Stat. 485; Pub. L. 98–216, § 3(a)(1), Feb. 14, 1984, 98 Stat. 6; Pub. L. 99–348, title V, § 501(d)(1), July 1, 1986, 100 Stat. 708; Pub. L. 99–619, § 2(a)(2), Nov. 6, 1986, 100 Stat. 3491; Pub. L. 100–204, title I, § 178(a)(1), Dec. 22, 1987, 101 Stat. 1362; Pub. L. 100–527, § 13(d), Oct. 25, 1988, 102 Stat. 2643; Pub. L. 100–679, § 11(b), Nov. 17, 1988, 102 Stat. 4070; Pub. L. 101–73, title V, § 501(c), Aug. 9, 1989, 103 Stat. 394; Pub. L. 101–509, title V, § 529 [title I, § 112(b)], Nov. 5, 1990, 104 Stat. 1427, 1454; Pub. L. 101–576, title II, § 207(a), Nov. 15, 1990, 104 Stat. 2846; Pub. L. 102–233, title III, § 315(b), Dec. 12, 1991, 105 Stat. 1772; Pub. L. 102–550, title XIII, § 1351(a), Oct. 28, 1992, 106 Stat. 3969; Pub. L. 103–160, div. A, title IX, § 904(e)(1), Nov. 30, 1993, 107 Stat. 1728; Pub. L. 103–296, title I, § 108(e)(2), Aug. 15, 1994, 108 Stat. 1486; Pub. L. 103–325, title I, § 104(i), Sept. 23, 1994, 108 Stat. 2169; Pub. L. 105–277, div. C, title VII, § 713(a)(2), div. G, subdiv. A, title XII, § 1224(1), title XIII, § 1332(1), Oct. 21, 1998, 112 Stat. 2681–693, 2681–772, 2681–785; Pub. L. 106–65, div. A, title IX, § 911(e), Oct. 5, 1999, 113 Stat. 719; Pub. L. 106–553, § 1(a)(2) [title IV, § 404(b)], Dec. 21, 2000, 114 Stat. 2762, 2762A–96; Pub. L. 106–569, title X, § 1002(a)(2), Dec. 27, 2000, 114 Stat. 3028.)

HISTORICAL AND REVISION NOTES
1966 ACT

Derivation	U.S. Code	Revised Statutes and Statutes at Large
....	5 U.S.C. 2211(b) (less (15)).	Aug. 14, 1964, Pub. L. 88–426, § 303(b) (less (15)), 78 Stat. 416.

The proviso in paragraph (15) of former section 2211(b) is carried into section 5314. The remainder of paragraph (15) is omitted but not repealed, see table III. The part of paragraph (15) that is omitted but not repealed provides that the position of Director of the Federal Bureau of Investigation shall be in Level II of the Federal Executive Salary Schedule so long as the position is held by the incumbent of the position on August 14, 1964. The omission of this provision from title 5, without repealing the corresponding provision of the source statute, in effect leaves existing statute unchanged insofar as it relates to the present incumbent of the position of Director of the Federal Bureau of Investigation.

Standard changes are made to conform with the definitions applicable and the style of this title as outlined in the preface to the report.

1967 ACT

The deletion of paragraph (6) of 5 U.S.C. 5313 reflects the abolition of the position of "Administrator of the Housing and Home Finance Agency" by the act of September 9, 1965, Public Law 89–174, sections 5(a), 9(c), 79 Stat. 669, 671.

AMENDMENTS

2000—Pub. L. 106–569 struck out item relating to Chairman, Board of Governors of the Federal Reserve System and inserted item relating to Members, Board of Governors of the Federal Reserve System.

Pub. L. 106–553 inserted item relating to Deputy Secretary of State for Management and Resources.

1999—Pub. L. 106–65 substituted "Under Secretary of Defense for Acquisition, Technology, and Logistics" for "Under Secretary of Defense for Acquisition and Technology".

1998—Pub. L. 105–277, § 1332(1), struck out item relating to Director of the United States Information Agency.

Pub. L. 105–277, § 1224(1), struck out item relating to Director of the United States Arms Control and Disarmament Agency.

Pub. L. 105–277, § 713(a)(2), inserted item relating to Deputy Director of National Drug Control Policy.

1994—Pub. L. 103–325 inserted item relating to Administrator of the Community Development Financial Institutions Fund.

Pub. L. 103–296 inserted item relating to Deputy Commissioner of Social Security, Social Security Administration.

1993—Pub. L. 103–160 substituted "Under Secretary of Defense for Acquisition and Technology" for "Under Secretary of Defense for Acquisition".

1992—Pub. L. 102–550 inserted item relating to Director of the Office of Federal Housing Enterprise Oversight, Department of Housing and Urban Development.

1991—Pub. L. 102–233 substituted "Independent Members, Thrift Depositor Protection Oversight Board" for "Independent Members, Oversight Board, Resolution Trust Corporation".

1990—Pub. L. 101–576 inserted item relating to Deputy Director for Management, Office of Management and Budget.

Pub. L. 101–509 inserted items relating to Deputy Secretary of Health and Human Services, Deputy Secretary of the Interior, Deputy Secretary of Education, and Deputy Secretary of Housing and Urban Development.

1989—Pub. L. 101–73 inserted item relating to Independent Members, Oversight Board, Resolution Trust Corporation.

1988—Pub. L. 100–679 inserted item relating to Deputy Director of Office of Management and Budget and struck out item relating to Director of Office of Management and Budget.

Pub. L. 100–527 substituted "Deputy Secretary of Veterans Affairs" for "Administrator of Veterans' Affairs".

1987—Pub. L. 100–204 struck out item relating to Ambassadors at Large.

1986—Pub. L. 99–619 inserted item relating to Deputy Secretary of Labor.

Pub. L. 99–348 inserted item relating to Under Secretary of Defense for Acquisition.

1984—Pub. L. 98–216 substituted "Director of the Office of Management and Budget" for "Director of the Bureau of the Budget".

1983—Pub. L. 98–80 inserted item relating to Administrator of Environmental Protection Agency.

Pub. L. 97–499, § 3(1), inserted item relating to Administrator, Federal Highway Administration.

1980—Pub. L. 96–465 inserted item relating to Ambassadors at Large.

1979—Pars. (1)–(24). Pub. L. 96–54 struck out paragraph designations for positions listed herein.

1978—Par. (24). Pub. L. 95–454 added par. (24) relating to Director of Office of Personnel Management.

1977—Par. (1). Pub. L. 95–140 substituted "Deputy Secretary of Defense" for "Deputy Secretaries of Defense (2)".

Par. (22). Pub. L. 95–91 substituted "Deputy Secretary of Energy" for "Administrator of Energy Research and Development Administration".

1976—Par. (21). Pub. L. 94–237 struck out par. (21) relating to Director of Special Action Office for Drug Abuse Prevention.

Par. (23). Pub. L. 94–561 added par. (23) relating to Deputy Secretary of Agriculture.

1975—Pub. L. 94–82 substituted provisions applying level II of Executive Schedule to positions for which annual rate of basic pay shall be rate determined with respect to such level under chapter 11 of title 2, as adjusted by section 5318 of this title, for provisions applying such level II to positions for which annual rate of basic pay is $30,000.

1974—Par. (7). Pub. L. 93–496 substituted "Deputy Secretary of Transportation" for "Under Secretary for Transportation".

Par. (8). Pub. L. 93–438 substituted "Chairman, Nuclear Regulatory Commission" for "Chairman, Atomic Energy Commission".

Par. (22). Pub. L. 93–438 added par. (22) relating to Deputy Secretary of Energy.

1972—Par. (1). Pub. L. 92–596 substituted "Deputy Secretaries of Defense (2)" for "Deputy Secretary of Defense".

Par. (2). Pub. L. 92–352 substituted "Deputy Secretary of State" for "Under Secretary of State".

Par. (6). Pub. L. 92–302 added par. (6) relating to Deputy Secretary of the Treasury. A prior par. (6), "Administrator of the Housing and Home Finance Agency," was repealed by Pub. L. 90–83, § 1(13), Sept. 11, 1967, 81 Stat. 198.

Par. (21). Pub. L. 92–255 added par. (21) relating to Director of Special Action Office for Drug Abuse Prevention.

1971—Par. (20). Pub. L. 91–644 added par. (20) relating to position of Deputy Attorney General being formerly level III under former section 5314(1) of this title.

1968—Par. (19). Pub. L. 90–407 added par. (19) relating to Director of National Science Foundation.

1966—Pub. L. 89–670 substituted "Under Secretary of Transportation" for "Administrator of the Federal Aviation Agency" in item (7), and inserted item (19) relating to Administrator, Federal Aviation Administration.

EFFECTIVE DATE OF 2000 AMENDMENT

Amendment by Pub. L. 106–569 effective on the first day of the first pay period for the Chairman and Members of the Board of Governors of the Federal Reserve System beginning on or after Dec. 27, 2000, see section 1002(b) of Pub. L. 106–569, set out as a note under section 5312 of this title.

EFFECTIVE DATE OF 1998 AMENDMENT

Amendment by section 1224(1) of Pub. L. 105–277 effective Apr. 1, 1999, see section 1201 of Pub. L. 105–277, set out as an Effective Date note under section 6511 of Title 22, Foreign Relations and Intercourse.

Amendment by section 1332(1) of Pub. L. 105–277 effective Oct. 1, 1999, see section 1301 of Pub. L. 105–277, set out as an Effective Date note under section 6531 of Title 22, Foreign Relations and Intercourse.

EFFECTIVE DATE OF 1991 AMENDMENT

Amendment by Pub. L. 102–233 effective Feb. 1, 1992, see section 318 of Pub. L. 102–233, set out as a note under section 1441 of Title 12, Banks and Banking.

EFFECTIVE DATE OF 1990 AMENDMENT

Amendment by Pub. L. 101–509 effective on first day of first pay period beginning on or after Nov. 5, 1990, with continued service by incumbent Under Secretary of Health and Human Services, Under Secretary of the Interior, Under Secretary of Education, and Under Secretary of Housing and Urban Development, see section 529 [title I, § 112(e)] of Pub. L. 101–509, set out as a note under section 3404 of Title 20, Education.

EFFECTIVE DATE OF 1988 AMENDMENTS

Amendment by Pub. L. 100–679 effective Jan. 20, 1989, see section 11(e) of Pub. L. 100–679, set out as a note under section 5312 of this title.

Amendment by Pub. L. 100–527 effective Mar. 15, 1989, see section 18(a) of Pub. L. 100–527, set out as a Department of Veterans Affairs Act note under section 301 of Title 38, Veterans' Benefits.

EFFECTIVE DATE OF 1987 AMENDMENT

Section 178(b) of Pub. L. 100–204 provided that: "The amendments made by subsection (a) [amending sections 5313 and 5315 of this title] shall take effect 30 days after the date of enactment of this Act [Dec. 22, 1987] and shall not affect the salary of any individual holding the rank of Ambassador at Large immediately before the date of enactment of this Act during the period such individual continues to serve in such position."

EFFECTIVE DATE OF 1986 AMENDMENT

Amendment by Pub. L. 99–619 applicable to incumbent Under Secretary of Labor on Nov. 6, 1986, serving after such date, see section 2(f)(1) of Pub. L. 99–619, set out as a Present Incumbent note under section 552 of Title 29, Labor.

EFFECTIVE DATE OF 1980 AMENDMENT

Amendment by Pub. L. 96–465 effective Feb. 15, 1981, except as otherwise provided, see section 2403 of Pub. L. 96–465, set out as an Effective Date note under section 3901 of Title 22, Foreign Relations and Intercourse.

EFFECTIVE DATE OF 1979 AMENDMENT

Amendment by Pub. L. 96–54 effective Jan. 1, 1980, see section 2(a)(25)(B) of Pub. L. 96–54, set out as a note under section 5312 of this title.

EFFECTIVE DATE OF 1978 AMENDMENT

Amendment by Pub. L. 95–454 effective 90 days after Oct. 13, 1978, see section 907 of Pub. L. 95–454, set out as a note under section 1101 of this title.

EFFECTIVE DATE OF 1976 AMENDMENT

Section 5 of Pub. L. 94–561 provided that:

"(a) Except as otherwise provided in this section, this Act [enacting section 2212b of Title 7, Agriculture, amending sections 5313 to 5316 of this title, sections 2210 and 2211 of Title 7, and section 714g of Title 15, Commerce and Trade, and enacting provisions set out as a note under section 2210 of Title 7] shall take effect on its date of enactment [Oct. 19, 1976].

"(b) Subsection (b)(1) of section 3 of this Act [amending section 5316 of this title] shall take effect upon appointment of a Presidential appointee to fill the successor position created by section 2 of this Act [section 2212b of Title 7]."

EFFECTIVE DATE OF 1974 AMENDMENT

Amendment of Pub. L. 93–438 effective 120 days after Oct. 11, 1974, or on such earlier date as President may prescribe and publish in Federal Register, except that officers provided for in sections 5811 to 5820 of Title 42, The Public Health and Welfare, may be nominated and appointed at any time after Oct. 11, 1974, see section 312(a) of Pub. L. 93–438, set out as an Effective Date; Interim Appointments note under section 5801 of Title 42.

EFFECTIVE DATE OF 1972 AMENDMENT

Amendment by Pub. L. 92–302 effective May 18, 1972, see section 3 of Pub. L. 92–302, May 18, 1972, 86 Stat. 149.

EFFECTIVE DATE OF 1968 AMENDMENT

Section 15(a)(4) of Pub. L. 90–407 provided that: "The amendments made by this subsection [amending sections 5313, 5314, and 5316 of this title] (and the amendments made by sections 3 and 4 of this Act [amending section 1864 and enacting section 1864a of Title 42, The Public Health and Welfare] insofar as they relate to rates of basic pay) shall take effect on the first day of the first calendar month which begins on or after the date of the enactment of this Act [July 18, 1968]."

EFFECTIVE DATE OF 1966 AMENDMENT

Amendment by Pub. L. 89–670 effective April 1, 1967, see section 16(a), formerly § 15(a), of Pub. L. 89–670, and Ex. Ord. No. 11340, Mar. 30, 1967, 32 F.R. 5453.

TRANSFER OF FUNCTIONS

Office of Director of Office of Science and Technology abolished and functions vested by law in such office transferred to Director of the National Science Foundation by sections 2 and 3(a)(5) of 1973 Reorg. Plan No. 1, effective July 1, 1973, set out in the Appendix to this title.

SALARY INCREASES

2001—Salaries of positions at level II increased to $145,100 per annum, effective on the first day of the first pay period beginning on or after Jan. 1, 2001, as provided by Ex. Ord. No. 13182, Dec. 23, 2000, 65 F.R. 82879, 66 F.R. 10057, set out as a note under section 5332 of this title.

2000—Salaries of positions at level II increased to $141,300 per annum, effective on the first day of the first pay period beginning on or after Jan. 1, 2000, as provided by Ex. Ord. No. 13144, Dec. 21, 1999, 64 F.R. 72237.

1999—Salaries of positions at level II continued at $136,700 per annum by Ex. Ord. No. 13106, Dec. 7, 1998, 63 F.R. 68151.

1998—Salaries of positions at level II increased to $136,700 per annum, effective on the first day of the first pay period beginning on or after Jan. 1, 1998, as provided by Ex. Ord. No. 13071, Dec. 29, 1997, 62 F.R. 68521.

1997—Salaries of positions at level II continued at $133,600 per annum by Ex. Ord. No. 13033, Dec. 27, 1996, 61 F.R. 68987.

1996—Salaries of positions at level II continued at $133,600 per annum by Ex. Ord. No. 12984, Dec. 28, 1995, 61 F.R. 237.

1995—Salaries of positions at level II continued at $133,600 per annum by Ex. Ord. No. 12944, Dec. 28, 1994, 60 F.R. 309.

1993—Salaries of positions at level II increased to $133,600 per annum, effective on the first day of the first pay period beginning on or after Jan. 1, 1993, as provided by Ex. Ord. No. 12826, Dec. 30, 1992, 57 F.R. 62909.

1992—Salaries of positions at level II increased to $129,500 per annum, effective on the first day of the first pay period beginning on or after Jan. 1, 1992, as provided by Ex. Ord. No. 12786, Dec. 26, 1991, 56 F.R. 67453.

1991—Salaries of positions at level II increased to $125,100 per annum, effective on the first day of the first pay period beginning on or after Jan. 1, 1991, as provided by Ex. Ord. No. 12736, Dec. 12, 1990, 55 F.R. 51385.

1990—Salaries of positions at level II continued at $89,500 per annum, and increased to $96,600 per annum, effective on the first day of the first pay period beginning on or after Jan. 31, 1990, as provided by Ex. Ord. No. 12698, Dec. 23, 1989, 54 F.R. 53473.

1989—Salaries of positions at level II continued at $89,500 per annum, see Ex. Ord. No. 12663, Jan. 6, 1989, 54 F.R. 791.

1988—Salaries of positions at level II continued at $89,500 per annum by Ex. Ord. No. 12622, Dec. 31, 1987, 53 F.R. 222.

1987—Salaries of positions at level II increased to $89,500 per annum, on recommendation of the President of the United States, see note set out under section 358 of Title 2, The Congress.

Salaries of positions at level II increased to $77,400 per annum, effective on the first day of the first pay period beginning on or after Jan. 1, 1987, as provided by Ex. Ord. No. 12578, Dec. 31, 1986, 52 F.R. 505.

1985—Salaries of positions at level II increased to $75,100 per annum, effective on the first day of the first pay period beginning on or after Jan. 1, 1985, as provided by Ex. Ord. No. 12496, Dec. 28, 1984, 50 F.R. 211, as amended by Ex. Ord. No. 12540, Dec. 30, 1985, 51 F.R. 577.

1984—Salaries of positions at level II increased to $72,600 per annum, effective on the first day of the first pay period beginning on or after Jan. 1, 1984, as provided by Ex. Ord. No. 12456, Dec. 30, 1983, 49 F.R. 347, as amended Ex. Ord. No. 12477, May 23, 1984, 49 F.R. 22041; Ex. Ord. No. 12487, Sept. 14, 1984, 49 F.R. 36493.

1982—Salaries of positions at level II increased to $77,300 per annum, effective on the first day of the first pay period beginning on or after Oct. 1, 1982, as provided by Ex. Ord. No. 12387, Oct. 8, 1982, 47 F.R. 44981. Ex. Ord. No. 12387 further provided that pursuant to section 101(e) of Pub. L. 97-276 funds are not available to pay a salary at a rate which exceeds the rate in effect on Sept. 30, 1982, which was $60,662.50.

Maximum rate payable after Dec. 17, 1982, increased from $60,662.50 to $69,800.00, see Pub. L. 97-377, title I, § 129(b)–(d), Dec. 21, 1982, 96 Stat. 1914, set out as a note under section 5318 of this title.

Limitations on use of funds for fiscal year ending Sept. 30, 1983, appropriated by any Act to pay the salary or pay of any individual in legislative, executive, or judicial branch in position equal to or above level V of the Executive Schedule, see section 101(e) of Pub. L. 97-276, as amended, set out as a note under section 5318 of this title.

1981—Salaries of positions at level II increased to $74,300 per annum, effective on the first day of the first pay period beginning on or after Oct. 1, 1981, as provided by Ex. Ord. No. 12330, Oct. 15, 1981, 46 F.R. 50921. Ex. Ord. No. 12330 further provided that pursuant to section 101(c) of Pub. L. 97-51 funds are not available to pay a salary at a rate which exceeds the rate in effect on Sept. 30, 1981, which was $60,662.50.

Limitations on use of funds for fiscal year ending Sept. 30, 1982, appropriated by any Act to pay the salary or pay of any individual in legislative, executive, or judicial branch in position equal to or above level V of the Executive Schedule, see sections 101(g) and 141 of Pub. L. 97-92, set out as a note under section 5318 of this title.

1980—Salaries of positions at level II increased to $70,900 per annum, effective on the first day of the first pay period beginning on or after Oct. 1, 1980, as provided by Ex. Ord. No. 12248, Oct. 16, 1980, 45 F.R. 69199. Ex. Ord. No. 12248, further provided that pursuant to section 101(c) of Pub. L. 96-369, funds are not available to pay a salary at a rate which exceeds the rate in effect on Sept. 30, 1980, which was $60,662.50.

Limitations on use of funds for fiscal year ending Sept. 30, 1981, appropriated by any Act to pay the salary or pay of any individual in legislative, executive, or judicial branch in position equal to or above level V of the Executive Schedule, see section 101(c) of Pub. L. 96-536, as amended, set out as a note under section 5318 of this title.

1979—Salaries of positions at level II increased to $65,000 per annum, effective on the first day of the first pay period beginning on or after Oct. 1, 1979, as provided by Ex. Ord. No. 12165, Oct. 9, 1979, 44 F.R. 58671, as amended by Ex. Ord. No. 12200, Mar. 12, 1980, 45 F.R. 16443. Ex. Ord. No. 12165 further provided that pursuant to section 101(c) of Pub. L. 96-86 funds appropriated for fiscal year 1980 may not be used to pay a salary at a rate which exceeds an increase of 5.5 percent over the rate in effect on Sept. 30, 1978, which is a maximum rate payable of $60,662.50.

Applicability to funds appropriated by any Act for fiscal year ending Sept. 30, 1980, of limitation of section 304 of Pub. L. 95-391 on use of funds to pay the salary or pay of any individual in legislative, executive, or judicial branch in position equal or above level V of the Executive Schedule, see section 101 of Pub. L. 96-86, set out as a note under section 5318 of this title.

1978—Salaries of positions at level II increased to $60,700 per annum, effective in the first pay period beginning on or after Oct. 1, 1978, as provided by Ex. Ord. No. 12087, Oct. 7, 1978, 43 F.R. 46823. Ex. Ord. No. 12087, further provided that pursuant to the Legislative Branch Appropriation Act, 1979, funds are not available to pay a salary at a rate which exceeds the rate in effect on Sept. 30, 1978, which was $57,500.

Limitations on use of funds for fiscal year ending Sept. 30, 1979, appropriated by any Act to pay the salary or pay of any individual in legislative, executive, or judicial branch in position equal or above level V of the Executive Schedule, see section 304 of Pub. L. 95-391 and section 613 of Pub. L. 95-429, set out as a note under section 5318 of this title.

1977—Salaries of positions at level II increased to $57,500 per annum, on recommendation of the President of the United States, see note set out under section 358 of Title 2, The Congress.

1976—Salaries of positions at level II increased to $46,800 per annum, effective on the first day of the first pay period beginning on or after Oct. 1, 1976, see Ex. Ord. No. 11941, Oct. 1, 1976, 41 F.R. 43089. Ex. Ord. No. 11941, further provided that pursuant to the Legislative Branch Appropriation Act, 1977, funds are not available to pay a salary at a rate which exceeds the rate in effect on Sept. 30, 1976, which was $44,600.

1975—Salaries of positions at level II increased to $44,600 per annum, effective on the first day of the first pay period beginning on or after Oct. 1, 1975, by Ex. Ord. No. 11883, Oct. 6, 1975, 40 F.R. 47091.

1969—Salaries of positions at level II increased from $30,000 to $42,500 per annum, commencing on the first day of the pay period which begins after February 14, 1969, on recommendation of the President of the United States, see note set out under section 358 of Title 2, The Congress.

PAY INCREASE; EFFECTIVE DATE

Persons occupying a position under the Executive Schedule on May 18, 1972, and later appointed to a position created or authorized by Pub. L. 92-302, not eligible to an increase on basic pay until Jan. 21, 1973, see section 3(c) of Pub. L. 92-302, May 18, 1972, 86 Stat. 149.

DIRECTOR OF THE FEDERAL BUREAU OF INVESTIGATION, DEPARTMENT OF JUSTICE

Director of Federal Bureau of Investigation, Department of Justice to receive compensation at rate prescribed for level II of Federal Executive Salary Schedule [this section], effective as of day following date on which person holding such office on June 19, 1968, ceases to serve as Director, see section 1101(a) of Pub. L. 90-351, June 19, 1968, 82 Stat. 236, set out as a note under section 532 of Title 28, Judiciary and Judicial Procedure.

SECTION REFERRED TO IN OTHER SECTIONS

This section is referred to in sections 5315, 5377, 5380, 8432 of this title; title 2 sections 136a–2, 362; title 3 sections 105, 106, 108; title 10 section 973; title 18 section 207; title 22 section 3961; title 25 section 4042; title 26 section 3121; title 28 section 591; title 31 section 703; title 42 sections 210, 410, 1864, 4346, 5871, 5872, 6612, 7132, 7211, 7291, 7293; title 49 section 106.

§ 5314. Positions at level III

Level III of the Executive Schedule applies to the following positions, for which the annual rate of basic pay shall be the rate determined with respect to such level under chapter 11 of title 2, as adjusted by section 5318 of this title:

Solicitor General of the United States.

Under Secretary of Commerce, Under Secretary of Commerce for Economic Affairs, Under Secretary of Commerce for Export Administration, and Under Secretary of Commerce for Travel and Tourism.

Under Secretaries of State (6).

Under Secretaries of the Treasury (3).
Administrator of General Services.
Administrator of the Small Business Administration.
Deputy Administrator, Agency for International Development.
Chairman of the Merit Systems Protection Board.
Chairman, Federal Communications Commission.
Chairman, Board of Directors, Federal Deposit Insurance Corporation.
Chairman, Federal Energy Regulatory Commission.
Chairman, Federal Trade Commission.
Chairman, Surface Transportation Board.
Chairman, National Labor Relations Board.
Chairman, Securities and Exchange Commission.
Chairman, Board of Directors of the Tennessee Valley Authority.
Chairman, National Mediation Board.
Chairman, Railroad Retirement Board.
Chairman, Federal Maritime Commission.
Comptroller of the Currency.
Commissioner of Internal Revenue.
Under Secretary of Defense for Policy.
Under Secretary of Defense (Comptroller).
Under Secretary of Defense for Personnel and Readiness.
Deputy Administrator of the National Aeronautics and Space Administration.
Deputy Directors of Central Intelligence (2).
Director of the Office of Emergency Planning.
Director of the Peace Corps.
Deputy Director, National Science Foundation.
President of the Export-Import Bank of Washington.
Members, Nuclear Regulatory Commission.
Members, Defense Nuclear Facilities Safety Board.
Director of the Federal Bureau of Investigation, Department of Justice.
Administrator of the National Highway Traffic Safety Administration.
Administrator of the Federal Motor Carrier Safety Administration.
Administrator, Federal Railroad Administration.
Chairman, National Transportation Safety Board.
Chairman of the National Endowment for the Arts the incumbent of which also serves as Chairman of the National Council on the Arts.
Chairman of the National Endowment for the Humanities.
Director of the Federal Mediation and Conciliation Service.
Federal Transit Administrator.
President, Overseas Private Investment Corporation.
Chairman, Postal Rate Commission.
Chairman, Occupational Safety and Health Review Commission.
Governor of the Farm Credit Administration.
Chairman, Equal Employment Opportunity Commission.
Chairman, Consumer Product Safety Commission.

Under Secretaries of Energy (2).
Chairman, Commodity Futures Trading Commission.
Deputy United States Trade Representatives (3).
Chief Agricultural Negotiator.
Chairman, United States International Trade Commission.
Under Secretary of Commerce for Oceans and Atmosphere, the incumbent of which also serves as Administrator of the National Oceanic and Atmospheric Administration.
Associate Attorney General.
Chairman, Federal Mine Safety and Health Review Commission.
Chairman, National Credit Union Administration Board.
Deputy Director of the Office of Personnel Management.
Under Secretary of Agriculture for Farm and Foreign Agricultural Services.
Under Secretary of Agriculture for Food, Nutrition, and Consumer Services.
Under Secretary of Agriculture for Natural Resources and Environment.
Under Secretary of Agriculture for Research, Education, and Economics.
Under Secretary of Agriculture for Food Safety.
Under Secretary of Agriculture for Marketing and Regulatory Programs.
Director, Institute for Scientific and Technological Cooperation.
Under Secretary of Agriculture for Rural Development.
Administrator, Maritime Administration.
Executive Director Property Review Board.
Deputy Administrator of the Environmental Protection Agency.
Archivist of the United States.
Executive Director, Federal Retirement Thrift Investment Board.
Deputy Under Secretary of Defense for Acquisition and Technology.
Deputy Under Secretary of Defense for Logistics and Materiel Readiness.
Director, Trade and Development Agency.
Under Secretary of Commerce for Technology.
Under Secretary for Health, Department of Veterans Affairs.
Under Secretary for Benefits, Department of Veterans Affairs.
Under Secretary for Memorial Affairs, Department of Veterans Affairs.
Director of the Office of Government Ethics.
Administrator for Federal Procurement Policy.
Administrator, Office of Information and Regulatory Affairs, Office of Management and Budget.
Director of the Office of Thrift Supervision.
Chairperson of the Federal Housing Finance Board.
Executive Secretary, National Space Council.
Controller, Office of Federal Financial Management, Office of Management and Budget.
Administrator, Research and Special Programs Administration.
Deputy Director for Demand Reduction, Office of National Drug Control Policy.

Deputy Director for Supply Reduction, Office of National Drug Control Policy.

Deputy Director for State and Local Affairs, Office of National Drug Control Policy.

Under Secretary of Commerce for Intellectual Property and Director of the United States Patent and Trademark Office.

Register of Copyrights.

Commissioner of Customs, Department of the Treasury[1]

(Pub. L. 89–554, Sept. 6, 1966, 80 Stat. 460; Pub. L. 89–670, § 10(d)(3), (e), Oct. 15, 1966, 80 Stat. 948; Pub. L. 90–83, § 1(14), Sept. 11, 1967, 81 Stat. 198; Pub. L. 90–206, title II, § 215(a), Dec. 16, 1967, 81 Stat. 638; Pub. L. 90–351, title I, § 505, June 19, 1968, 82 Stat. 205, as amended Pub. L. 91–644, title I, § 7(1), Jan. 2, 1971, 84 Stat. 1887; Pub. L. 90–407, § 15(a)(2), July 18, 1968, 82 Stat. 367; Pub. L. 90–623, § 1(26), Oct. 22, 1968, 82 Stat. 1314; Pub. L. 91–175, pt. V, § 503(1), Dec. 30, 1969, 83 Stat. 826; Pub. L. 91–375, § 6(c)(13), Aug. 12, 1970, 84 Stat. 776; Pub. L. 91–596, § 12(c)(1), Dec. 29, 1970, 84 Stat. 1604; Pub. L. 91–644, title I, §§ 7(1), 8(a), Jan. 2, 1971, 84 Stat. 1887, 1888; Pub. L. 92–181, title V, § 5.41(a), formerly § 5.27(a), Dec. 10, 1971, 85 Stat. 625, as renumbered Pub. L. 99–205, title II, § 205(a)(2), Dec. 23, 1985, 99 Stat. 1703; Pub. L. 92–226, pt. IV, § 403, Feb. 7, 1972, 86 Stat. 34; Pub. L. 92–261, § 9(a), Mar. 24, 1972, 86 Stat. 110; Pub. L. 92–302, § 2(b), May 18, 1972, 86 Stat. 149; Pub. L. 92–352, title I, § 104(2), July 13, 1972, 86 Stat. 490; Pub. L. 92–573, § 4(h)(1), Oct. 27, 1972, 86 Stat. 1211; Pub. L. 93–83, § 2, Aug. 6, 1973, 87 Stat. 211; Pub. L. 93–438, title III, § 310(2), Oct. 11, 1974, 88 Stat. 1252; Pub. L. 93–463, title I, § 102(a), Oct. 23, 1974, 88 Stat. 1391; Pub. L. 93–618, title I, §§ 141(b)(3)(B), 172(c)(1), Jan. 3, 1975, 88 Stat. 1999, 2010; Pub. L. 94–82, title II, § 202(b)(3), Aug. 9, 1975, 89 Stat. 420; Pub. L. 94–123, § 2(c)(1), Oct. 22, 1975, 89 Stat. 670; Pub. L. 94–183, § 2(17), Dec. 31, 1975, 89 Stat. 1057; Pub. L. 92–255, title II, § 209(a), as added Pub. L. 94–237, § 4(b), Mar. 19, 1976, 90 Stat. 243; Pub. L. 94–461, § 4(a), Oct. 8, 1976, 90 Stat. 1969; Pub. L. 94–561, § 1(b), Oct. 19, 1976, 90 Stat. 2643; Pub. L. 95–91, title VII, § 710(e), Aug. 4, 1977, 91 Stat. 609; Pub. L. 95–139, § 3, Oct. 19, 1977, 91 Stat. 1171; Pub. L. 95–140, § 3(d)(2), Oct. 21, 1977, 91 Stat. 1173; Pub. L. 95–164, title III, § 302(c)(1), Nov. 9, 1977, 91 Stat. 1320; Pub. L. 95–426, title I, § 114(b)(1), Oct. 7, 1978, 92 Stat. 969; Pub. L. 95–454, title II, §§ 201(b)(2), 202(c)(1), Oct. 13, 1978, 92 Stat. 1121, 1131; Pub. L. 95–501, title V, § 501(b), Oct. 21, 1978, 92 Stat. 1691; Pub. L. 95–630, title V, § 502(d), Nov. 10, 1978, 92 Stat. 3681; Pub. L. 96–53, title IV, § 412(a), Aug. 14, 1979, 93 Stat. 377; Pub. L. 96–54, § 2(a)(25)(A), Aug. 14, 1979, 93 Stat. 382; Pub. L. 96–88, title V, § 508(d), (g), Oct. 17, 1979, 93 Stat. 692; Pub. L. 90–351, title I, § 808, as added Pub. L. 96–157, § 2, Dec. 27, 1979, 93 Stat. 1204; Pub. L. 96–355, § 3(b), Sept. 24, 1980, 94 Stat. 1173; Pub. L. 97–31, § 12(1)(A), Aug. 6, 1981, 95 Stat. 153; Pub. L. 97–63, § 4(a)(4), Oct. 16, 1981, 95 Stat. 1014; Pub. L. 97–195, § 1(b)(1), June 16, 1982, 96 Stat. 115; Pub. L. 97–377, title I, § 123, Dec. 21, 1982, 96 Stat. 1913; Pub. L. 97–449, § 3(2), Jan. 12, 1983, 96 Stat. 2441; Pub. L. 97–456, § 3(d)(1), (6), Jan. 12, 1983, 96 Stat. 2505, 2506; Pub. L. 98–80, § 2(b)(1), Aug. 23, 1983, 97 Stat. 485; Pub. L. 98–164, title I, § 125(b)(1), Nov. 22, 1983, 97 Stat. 1026; Pub. L. 98–216, § 3(a)(2), Feb. 14, 1984, 98 Stat. 6; Pub. L. 98–443, § 9(e), Oct. 4, 1984, 98 Stat. 1707; Pub. L. 98–473, title II, § 609J(a), Oct. 12, 1984, 98 Stat. 2102; Pub. L. 98–497, title I, § 107(h), Oct. 19, 1984, 98 Stat. 2292; Pub. L. 99–64, title I, § 116(b), July 12, 1985, 99 Stat. 153; Pub. L. 99–93, title I, § 116(b), title VII, § 704(a)(1), Aug. 16, 1985, 99 Stat. 412, 445; Pub. L. 99–335, title II, § 203, June 6, 1986, 100 Stat. 591; Pub. L. 99–348, title V, § 501(d)(2), July 1, 1986, 100 Stat. 708; Pub. L. 99–500, § 101(c) [title X, §§ 902(b), 903(b)(2)(A)], Oct. 18, 1986, 100 Stat. 1783–82, 1783–132, and Pub. L. 99–591, § 101(c) [title X, §§ 902(b), 903(b)(2)(A)], Oct. 30, 1986, 100 Stat. 3341–82, 3341–132; Pub. L. 99–619, § 2(a)(3), Nov. 6, 1986, 100 Stat. 3491; Pub. L. 99–659, title IV, § 407(e)(1), Nov. 14, 1986, 100 Stat. 3740; Pub. L. 99–661, div. A, title IX, formerly title IV, §§ 902(b), 903(b)(2)(A), Nov. 14, 1986, 100 Stat. 3911, 3912, as renumbered Pub. L. 100–26, § 3(5), Apr. 21, 1987, 101 Stat. 273; Pub. L. 100–418, title II, § 2204(d)(1), Aug. 23, 1988, 102 Stat. 1331; Pub. L. 100–456, div. A, title XIV, § 1441(b), Sept. 29, 1988, 102 Stat. 2084; Pub. L. 100–519, title II, § 201(d)(4), Oct. 24, 1988, 102 Stat. 2594; Pub. L. 100–527, § 13(e), Oct. 25, 1988, 102 Stat. 2643; Pub. L. 100–598, § 8, Nov. 3, 1988, 102 Stat. 3035; Pub. L. 100–679, § 11(c), Nov. 17, 1988, 102 Stat. 4070; Pub. L. 100–690, title I, §§ 1003(a)(4)(B), 1007(c)(3), Nov. 18, 1988, 102 Stat. 4182, 4188; Pub. L. 101–73, title VII, § 742(a)(1), Aug. 9, 1989, 103 Stat. 436; Pub. L. 101–328, § 3(b), July 8, 1990, 104 Stat. 308; Pub. L. 101–509, title V, § 529 [title I, § 112(d)], Nov. 5, 1990, 104 Stat. 1427, 1455; Pub. L. 101–576, title II, § 207(b), Nov. 15, 1990, 104 Stat. 2846; Pub. L. 102–103, title II, § 202, Aug. 17, 1991, 105 Stat. 498; Pub. L. 102–233, title III, § 315(c), Dec. 12, 1991, 105 Stat. 1772; Pub. L. 102–240, title III, § 3004(d)(1), Dec. 18, 1991, 105 Stat. 2088; Pub. L. 102–378, § 2(28), Oct. 2, 1992, 106 Stat. 1350; Pub. L. 102–405, title III, § 302(d), Oct. 9, 1992, 106 Stat. 1985; Pub. L. 102–508, title IV, § 401(c), Oct. 24, 1992, 106 Stat. 3310; Pub. L. 102–549, title II, § 202(d), Oct. 28, 1992, 106 Stat. 3658; Pub. L. 102–552, title II, § 201(b)(1), Oct. 28, 1992, 106 Stat. 4105; Pub. L. 103–160, div. A, title IX, §§ 901(b), 903(b), 904(e)(2), Nov. 30, 1993, 107 Stat. 1726, 1727, 1729; Pub. L. 103–204, § 5(b)(1), Dec. 17, 1993, 107 Stat. 2382; Pub. L. 103–211, title II, § 2003(b), Feb. 12, 1994, 108 Stat. 24; Pub. L. 103–236, title I, § 162(d)(1), Apr. 30, 1994, 108 Stat. 405; Pub. L. 103–337, div. A, title IX, § 903(c), Oct. 5, 1994, 108 Stat. 2823; Pub. L. 103–354, title II, §§ 225(e)(2), 231(f)(2), 241(e), 245(e), 251(e), 261(c), 285(e), Oct. 13, 1994, 108 Stat. 3214, 3219, 3222, 3223, 3226, 3227, as amended Pub. L. 105–277, div. A, § 101(a) [title X, § 1001(3)], Oct. 21, 1998, 112 Stat. 2681, 2681–41; Pub. L. 104–88, title III, § 301(a), Dec. 29, 1995, 109 Stat. 943; Pub. L. 104–105, title II, § 219(b)(1), Feb. 10, 1996, 110 Stat. 184; Pub. L. 104–127, title VII, § 794(b), Apr. 4, 1996, 110 Stat. 1155; Pub. L. 104–293, title VIII, § 812(a), Oct. 11, 1996, 110 Stat. 3482; Pub. L. 105–277, div. C, title VII, § 713(a)(3), div. G, subdiv. A, title XII, § 1224(2), subdiv. B, title XXIII, § 2305(a)(2), Oct. 21, 1998, 112 Stat. 2681–693, 2681–772, 2681–825; Pub. L. 105–304, title IV, § 401(a)(3), Oct. 28, 1998, 112 Stat. 2887; Pub. L. 105–368, title IV, § 403(b)(1), Nov. 11, 1998, 112 Stat. 3338; Pub. L. 106–65, div. A, title IX, § 911(b)(2), div. C, title XXXII, § 3293(a), Oct. 5, 1999, 113 Stat. 718, 969; Pub. L. 106–113, div. B, §§ 1000(a)(5) [title II, § 238(a)(2)], 1000(a)(9) [title

[1] So in original. Probably should be followed by a period.

IV, §4720(a)], Nov. 29, 1999, 113 Stat. 1536, 1501A–302, 1501A–581; Pub. L. 106–159, title I, §101(d)(1), Dec. 9, 1999, 113 Stat. 1751; Pub. L. 106–476, title II, §2002, Nov. 9, 2000, 114 Stat. 2175; Pub. L. 106–569, title X, §1002(a)(3), Dec. 27, 2000, 114 Stat. 3028.)

HISTORICAL AND REVISION NOTES
1966 ACT

Derivation	U.S. Code	Revised Statutes and Statutes at Large
(1)–(44)	5 U.S.C. 2211(c) (less (39) and (46)).	Aug. 14, 1964, Pub. L. 88–426, §303(c) (less (39) and (46)), 78 Stat. 416.
(45)	5 U.S.C. 2211(b)(15) (proviso).	Aug. 14, 1964, Pub. L. 88–426, §303(b)(15) (proviso), 78 Stat. 416.

The provisos in paragraphs (39) and (46) of former section 2211(c) are carried into section 5315. The remainders of paragraphs (39) and (46) are omitted but not repealed, see table III. The parts of paragraphs (39) and (46) that are omitted but not repealed provide that the positions of Director of Selective Service and Associate Director of the Federal Bureau of Investigation shall be in Level III so long as the positions are held by the incumbents of the positions on August 14, 1964. The omission of these provisions from title 5, without repealing the corresponding provisions of the source statute, in effect, leaves existing statute unchanged insofar as it relates to the present incumbents of the positions of Director of Selective Service and Associate Director of the Federal Bureau of Investigation.

Standard changes are made to conform with the definitions applicable and the style of this title as outlined in the preface to the report.

1967 ACT

Section of title 5	Source (U.S. Code)	Source (Statutes at Large)
5314(49)	20: 954(d) (2d sentence).	Sept. 29, 1965, Pub. L. 89–209, §5(d)(1) (2d sentence), 79 Stat. 847.
5314(50)	20:956(b)(1) (2d sentence).	Sept. 29, 1965, Pub. L. 89–209, §7(b)(1) (2d sentence), 79 Stat. 850.
5314(51)	5 App.: 2211(c)(47).	July 18, 1966, Pub. L. 89–504, §408(a), 80 Stat. 299.
5314(52)	42:3533(a) (as applicable to compensation of Under Secretary).	Sept. 9, 1965, Pub. L. 89–174, §4(a) (as applicable to compensation of Under Secretary), 79 Stat. 668.

The deletion of paragraph (41) of 5 U.S.C. 5314 reflects the abolition of the position of "Deputy Administrator of the Housing and Home Finance Agency" by the act of September 9, 1965, Public Law 89–174, sections 5(a), 9(c), 79 Stat. 669, 671.

In paragraph (49), the words "In lieu of receiving compensation at the rate prescribed by section 785(c) of this title" are omitted since the provisions of 20 U.S.C. 785(c) relating to compensation are repealed by this bill; also see table II. The wording further reflects the first sentence of 20 U.S.C. 954(d), and conforms to 5 U.S.C. 5314 which applies to positions rather than individuals.

CODIFICATION

Pub. L. 99–591 is a corrected version of Pub. L. 99–500.

Paragraph designation for the position added by Pub. L. 96–88 has been omitted in view of the deletion of all paragraph designations in this section by Pub. L. 96–54.

AMENDMENTS

2000—Pub. L. 106–569 struck out item relating to Members, Board of Governors of the Federal Reserve System.

Pub. L. 106–476 inserted item relating to Chief Agricultural Negotiator.

1999—Pub. L. 106–159 inserted item relating to Administrator of the Federal Motor Carrier Safety Administration.

Pub. L. 106–113, §1000(a)(9) [title IV, §4720(a)], substituted "Under Secretary of Commerce for Intellectual Property and Director of the United States Patent and Trademark Office." for "Assistant Secretary of Commerce and Commissioner of Patents and Trademarks."

Pub. L. 106–113, §1000(a)(5) [title II, §238(a)(2)], inserted item relating to Commissioner of Customs, Department of the Treasury.

Pub. L. 106–65, §3293(a), substituted "Under Secretaries of Energy (2)" for "Under Secretary, Department of Energy".

Pub. L. 106–65, §911(b)(2), inserted item relating to Deputy Under Secretary of Defense for Logistics and Materiel Readiness.

1998—Pub. L. 105–368 inserted item relating to Under Secretary for Memorial Affairs, Department of Veterans Affairs.

Pub. L. 105–304 inserted items relating to Assistant Secretary of Commerce and Commissioner of Patents and Trademarks and Register of Copyrights.

Pub. L. 105–277, §2305(a)(2), substituted "Under Secretaries of State (6)" for "Under Secretaries of State (5)".

Pub. L. 105–277, §1224(2), struck out item relating to Deputy Director of the United States Arms Control and Disarmament Agency.

Pub. L. 105–277, §713(a)(3), inserted items relating to Deputy Director for Demand Reduction, Office of National Drug Control Policy, Deputy Director for Supply Reduction, Office of National Drug Control Policy, and Deputy Director for State and Local Affairs, Office of National Drug Control Policy.

Pub. L. 105–277, §101(a) [title X, §1001(3)], added Pub. L. 103–354, §285(e). See 1994 Amendment note below.

1996—Pub. L. 104–293 substituted "Deputy Directors of Central Intelligence (2)" for "Deputy Director of Central Intelligence".

Pub. L. 104–127 substituted "Under Secretary of Agriculture for Rural Development" for "Under Secretary of Agriculture for Rural Economic and Community Development".

Pub. L. 104–105 struck out item relating to Chairperson, Board of Directors of the Farm Credit System Insurance Corporation.

1995—Pub. L. 104–88 substituted "Chairman, Surface Transportation Board" for "Chairman, Interstate Commerce Commission".

1994—Pub. L. 103–354, §285(e), as added by Pub. L. 105–277, §101(a) [title X, §1001(3)], inserted item relating to the Under Secretary of Agriculture for Marketing and Regulatory Programs.

Pub. L. 103–354 substituted "Under Secretary of Agriculture for Farm and Foreign Agricultural Services" for "Under Secretary of Agriculture for International Affairs and Commodity Programs", inserted items relating to Under Secretaries of Agriculture for Food, Nutrition, and Consumer Services; for Natural Resources and Environment; for Research, Education, and Economics; and for Food Safety, and substituted "Under Secretary of Agriculture for Rural Economic and Community Development" for "Under Secretary of Agriculture for Small Community and Rural Development".

Pub. L. 103–337 substituted "Under Secretary of Defense (Comptroller)" for "Comptroller of the Department of Defense".

Pub. L. 103–236 inserted item relating to Under Secretaries of State (5) and struck out items relating to Under Secretary of State for Political Affairs and Under Secretary of State for Economic and Agricultural Affairs and an Under Secretary of State for Coordinating Security Assistance Programs and Under Secretary of State for Management and Counselor of the Department of State.

Pub. L. 103–211 inserted item relating to Under Secretary of the Treasury (3) and struck out items relating to Under Secretary of the Treasury (or Counselor) and Under Secretary of the Treasury for Monetary Affairs.

1993—Pub. L. 103–204, which directed striking out of "chief executive officer of the Resolution Trust Corporation.", was executed by striking "chief executive officer, Resolution Trust Corporation." to reflect the probable intent of Congress.

Pub. L. 103–160 inserted items relating to Comptroller of the Department of Defense and Under Secretary of Defense for Personnel and Readiness and substituted "Deputy Under Secretary of Defense for Acquisition and Technology" for "Deputy Under Secretary of Defense for Acquisition".

1992—Pub. L. 102–552 inserted item relating to Chairperson, Board of Directors of the Farm Credit System Insurance Corporation.

Pub. L. 102–549 substituted "Director, Trade and Development Agency" for "Director, Trade and Development Program".

Pub. L. 102–508 inserted item relating to Administrator, Research and Special Programs Administration.

Pub. L. 102–405 substituted "Under Secretary for Health, Department of Veterans Affairs" for "Chief Medical Director, Department of Veterans Affairs" and "Under Secretary for Benefits, Department of Veterans Affairs" for "Chief Benefits Director, Department of Veterans Affairs".

Pub. L. 102–378 struck out each of the items relating to Under Secretary of Education, Under Secretary of Health and Human Services, Under Secretary of the Interior, and Under Secretary of Housing and Urban Development.

1991—Pub. L. 102–240 substituted "Federal Transit Administrator" for "Urban Mass Transportation Administrator".

Pub. L. 102–233 inserted item relating to chief executive officer, Resolution Trust Corporation.

Pub. L. 102–103 inserted item relating to Under Secretary of Education.

1990—Pub. L. 101–576 inserted item relating to Controller, Office of Federal Financial Management, Office of Management and Budget.

Pub. L. 101–509 directed the amendment of this section by striking the following:

"Under Secretary of Health and Human Services.

"Under Secretary of the Interior.

"Under Secretary of Education.

"Under Secretary of Housing and Urban Development.

Section did not contain the positions in the order referred to in Pub. L. 101–509. See 1992 Amendment note above for Pub. L. 102–378.

Pub. L. 101–328 inserted item relating to Executive Secretary, National Space Council.

1989—Pub. L. 101–73 inserted items relating to Director of the Office of Thrift Supervision and Chairperson of the Federal Housing Finance Board, and struck out item relating to Chairman of the Federal Home Loan Bank Board.

1988—Pub. L. 100–690, § 1007(c)(3), struck out item relating to Director of Office of Drug Abuse Policy.

Pub. L. 100–690, §§ 1003(a)(4)(B), 1009, temporarily inserted items relating to Deputy Director for Demand Reduction, Office of National Drug Control Policy, and Deputy Director for Supply Reduction, Office of National Drug Control Policy. See Effective and Termination Dates of 1988 Amendments note below.

Pub. L. 100–679 inserted items relating to Administrator for Federal Procurement Policy and to Administrator, Office of Information and Regulatory Affairs, Office of Management and Budget, and struck out item relating to Deputy Director of Office of Management and Budget.

Pub. L. 100–598 inserted item relating to Director of Office of Government Ethics.

Pub. L. 100–527 inserted items relating to Chief Medical Director, Department of Veterans Affairs, and Chief Benefits Director, Department of Veterans Affairs, and struck out item relating to Deputy Administrator of Veterans' Affairs.

Pub. L. 100–519 inserted item relating to Under Secretary of Commerce for Technology.

Pub. L. 100–456 inserted item relating to Members, Defense Nuclear Facilities Safety Board after item relating to Members, Nuclear Regulatory Commission.

Pub. L. 100–418 inserted item relating to Director, Trade and Development Program.

1986—Pub. L. 99–659 substituted "Under Secretary of Commerce for Oceans and Atmosphere, the incumbent of which also serves as Administrator of the National Oceanic and Atmospheric Administration" for "Administrator, National Oceanic and Atmospheric Administration".

Pub. L. 99–619 struck out item relating to Under Secretary of Labor.

Pub. L. 99–500, Pub. L. 99–591, and Pub. L. 99–661, amended section identically, inserting item relating to Deputy Under Secretary of Defense for Acquisition and striking out item relating to Director of Defense Research and Engineering.

Pub. L. 99–348 substituted "Under Secretary of Defense for Policy" for "Under Secretaries of Defense (2)" and inserted item relating to Director of Defense Research and Engineering.

Pub. L. 99–335 inserted item relating to Executive Director, Federal Retirement Thrift Investment Board.

1985—Pub. L. 99–93, § 116(b), substituted "Under Secretary of State for Economic and Agricultural Affairs" for "Under Secretary of State for Economic Affairs".

Pub. L. 99–93, § 704(a)(1), inserted item relating to Deputy Director of United States Arms Control and Disarmament Agency.

Pub. L. 99–64 inserted item relating to Under Secretary of Commerce for Export Administration.

1984—Pub. L. 98–497 inserted item relating to Archivist of United States.

Pub. L. 98–473 struck out item relating to Director of Office of Justice Assistance, Research, and Statistics.

Pub. L. 98–443 struck out item relating to Chairman of Civil Aeronautics Board.

Pub. L. 98–216 substituted "Deputy Director of the Office of Management and Budget" for "Deputy Director of the Bureau of the Budget".

1983—Pub. L. 98–164 inserted item relating to Counselor of Department of State.

Pub. L. 98–80 inserted item relating to Deputy Administrator of Environmental Protection Agency.

Pub. L. 97–456, § 3(d)(6), substituted "Deputy United States Trade Representatives (3)" for "Deputy Special Representatives for Trade Negotiations (2)".

Pub. L. 97–449 substituted "Administrator of the National Highway Traffic Safety Administration" for "Administrator, Federal Highway Administration".

1982—Pub. L. 97–377 inserted item relating to Executive Director of Property Review Board.

Pub. L. 97–195 substituted "Under Secretary of Commerce, Under Secretary of Commerce for Economic Affairs, and Under Secretary of Commerce for Travel and Tourism" for "Under Secretary of Commerce and Under Secretary of Commerce for Travel and Tourism".

1981—Pub. L. 97–63 substituted "Under Secretary of Commerce and Under Secretary of Commerce for Travel and Tourism" for "Under Secretary of Commerce".

Pub. L. 97–31 inserted item relating to Administrator, Maritime Administration.

1980—Pub. L. 96–355 inserted item relating to Under Secretary of Agriculture for Small Community and Rural Development.

1979—Pub. L. 96–157 inserted item relating to Director, Office of Justice Assistance, Research, and Statistics, and struck out item relating to Administrator of Law Enforcement Assistance.

Pub. L. 96–88, § 508(g), substituted "Health and Human Services" for "Health, Education, and Welfare" in item relating to Under Secretary of Health and Human Services.

Par. (5). Pub. L. 96–88, § 508(d), added par. (5) relating to Under Secretary of Education. See Codification note above.

Pars. (1) to (70). Pub. L. 96–54 struck out paragraph designations for positions listed herein.

Par. (70). Pub. L. 96–53 added par. (70) relating to Director, Institute for Scientific and Technological Cooperation.

1978—Par. (9). Pub. L. 95–426 inserted "and Under Secretary of State for Management".

Par. (17). Pub. L. 95–454, § 202(c)(1), substituted "Merit Systems Protection Board" for "United States Civil Service Commission".

Par. (66). Pub. L. 95–630 added par. (66) relating to Chairman, National Credit Union Administration Board.

Par. (68). Pub. L. 95–454, § 201(b)(2), added par. (68) relating to Deputy Director of Office of Personnel Management.

Par. (69). Pub. L. 95–501 added par. (69) relating to Under Secretary of Agriculture for International Affairs and Commodity Programs.

1977—Par. (21). Pub. L. 95–91 substituted "Federal Energy Regulatory Commission" for "Federal Power Commission".

Par. (32). Pub. L. 95–140 substituted "Under Secretaries of Defense (2)" for "Director of Defense Research and Engineering, Department of Defense".

Par. (60). Pub. L. 95–91 substituted "Under Secretary, Department of Energy" for "Deputy Administrator, Energy Research and Development Administration".

Par. (66). Pub. L. 95–164 added par. (66) relating to Chairman, Federal Mine Safety and Health Review Commission.

Pub. L. 95–139 added par. (66) relating to Associate Attorney General.

1976—Par. (3). Pub. L. 94–561 repealed par. (3) relating to Under Secretary of Agriculture.

Par. (64). Pub. L. 94–237 added par. (64) relating to Director of Office of Drug Abuse Policy.

Par. (65). Pub. L. 94–461 added par. (65) relating to Administrator, National Oceanic and Atmospheric Administration.

1975—Pub. L. 94–82 substituted provisions applying level III of Executive Schedule to positions for which annual rate of basic pay shall be rate determined with respect to such level under chapter 11 of title 2, as adjusted by section 5318 of this title, for provisions applying such level III to positions for which annual rate of basic pay is $29,500.

Par. (38). Pub. L. 94–123 repealed par. (38) relating to Chief Medical Director in Department of Medicine and Surgery, Veterans' Administration.

Par. (54). Pub. L. 94–183 redesignated par. (55), relating to Chairman, Postal Rate Commission, as par. (54).

Pars. (56), (57). Pub. L. 94–183 redesignated par. (57) relating to Chairman, Occupational Safety and Health Review Commission, and par. (58) relating to Governor of the Farm Credit Administration, as pars. (56) and (57), respectively.

Par. (60). Pub. L. 93–618, § 141(b)(3)(B), added par. (60) relating to Deputy Special Representative for Trade Negotiations. For renumbering by Pub. L. 94–183, see item relating to par. (62) hereunder.

Par. (61). Pub. L. 94–183 redesignated par. (60), relating to Chairman, Commodity Futures Trading Commission, as par. (61).

Pub. L. 93–618, § 172(c)(1), added par. (61). For renumbering by Pub. L. 94–183, see item relating to par. (63) hereunder.

Pars. (62), (63). Pub. L. 94–183 redesignated par. (60) relating to Deputy Special Representatives for Trade Negotiations, and par. (61) relating to Chairman, United States International Trade Commission, as pars. (62) and (63), respectively.

1974—Par. (42). Pub. L. 93–438 substituted "Members, Nuclear Regulatory Commission" for "Members, Atomic Energy Commission".

Par. (60). Pub. L. 93–463 added par. (60) relating to Chairman, Commodity Futures Trading Commission.

Pub. L. 93–438 added par. (60) relating to Deputy Administrator, Energy Research and Development Administration.

1973—Par. (55). Pub. L. 93–83 reenacted par. (55) relating to Administrator of Law Enforcement Assistance.

1972—Par. (9). Pub. L. 92–352 substituted "and" for "or", after "Political Affairs".

Pub. L. 92–226 included position of an Under Secretary of State for Coordinating Security Assistance Programs.

Par. (10). Pub. L. 92–302 substituted "Under Secretary of the Treasury (or Counselor)" for "Under Secretary of the Treasury".

Par. (58). Pub. L. 92–261 added par. (58) relating to Chairman, Equal Employment Opportunity Commission.

Par. (59). Pub. L. 92–573 added par. (59) relating to Chairman, Consumer Product Safety Commission.

1971—Pars. (1) to (54). Pub. L. 91–644, § 8(a), struck out par. (1) relating to Deputy Attorney General, now a level II position under section 5313 of this title, renumbered pars. (2) through (54) as (1) through (53), respectively.

Par. (55). Pub. L. 91–644, § 7(1), in amending section 505 of Pub. L. 90–351, renumbered par. (90) "Administrator of Law Enforcement Assistance" of section 5315 of this title as par. (55) of this section.

Par. (58). Pub. L. 92–181 added par. (58) relating to Governor of Farm Credit Administration.

1970—Par. (3). Pub. L. 91–375, § 6(c)(13)(A), struck out par. (3) relating to Deputy Postmaster General.

Par. (55). Pub. L. 91–375, § 6(c)(13)(B), added par. (55) relating to Chairman, Postal Rate Commission.

Par. (57). Pub. L. 91–596 added par. (57) relating to Chairman, Occupational Safety and Health Review Commission.

1969—Par. (54). Pub. L. 91–175 added par. (54) relating to President, Overseas Private Investment Corporation.

1968—Par. (40). Pub. L. 90–407 substituted "Deputy Director, National Science Foundation" for "Director of the National Science Foundation".

Par. (53). Pub. L. 90–623 added par. (53) relating to Urban Mass Transportation Administrator.

1967—Pub. L. 90–206 increased annual rate of basic pay from $28,500 to $29,500.

1966—Pub. L. 89–670 added pars. (46) to (48), relating to Administrator of Federal Highway Administration, Administrator of the Federal Railroad Administration, and Chairman of National Transportation Safety Board, respectively, and repealed par. (6) which provided for Under Secretary of Commerce for Transportation, subject to the provisions of section 1657 of former Title 49, Transportation.

CHANGE OF NAME

"Export-Import Bank of Washington", referred to in text, was changed to "Export-Import Bank of the United States" in the Export-Import Bank Act of 1945, section 635 et seq. of Title 12, Banks and Banking, as provided for in section 1(a) of Pub. L. 90–267, Mar. 13, 1968, 82 Stat. 47.

EFFECTIVE DATE OF 2000 AMENDMENT

Amendment by Pub. L. 106–569 effective on the first day of the first pay period for the Chairman and Members of the Board of Governors of the Federal Reserve System beginning on or after Dec. 27, 2000, see section 1002(b) of Pub. L. 106–569, set out as a note under section 5312 of this title.

EFFECTIVE DATE OF 1999 AMENDMENTS

Amendment by Pub. L. 106–159 effective Jan. 1, 2000, see section 107(a) of Pub. L. 106–159, set out as a note under section 104 of Title 49, Transportation.

Pub. L. 106–113, div. B, § 1000(a)(5) [title II, § 238(b)], Nov. 29, 1999, 113 Stat. 1536, 1501A–302, provided that: "The amendment made by this subsection [probably means this section, amending this section and section 5315 of this title] shall take effect on January 1, 2000."

Amendment by section 1000(a)(9) [title IV, § 4720(a)] of Pub. L. 106–113 effective 4 months after Nov. 29, 1999, see section 1000(a)(9) [title IV, § 4731] of Pub. L. 106–113, set out as a note under section 1 of Title 35, Patents.

Amendment by section 3293(a) of Pub. L. 106–65 effective Mar. 1, 2000, see section 3299 of Pub. L. 106–65, set out as an Effective Date note under section 2401 of Title 50, War and National Defense.

EFFECTIVE DATE OF 1998 AMENDMENT

Amendment by section 1224(2) of Pub. L. 105–277 effective Apr. 1, 1999, see section 1201 of Pub. L. 105–277, set out as an Effective Date note under section 6511 of Title 22, Foreign Relations and Intercourse.

EFFECTIVE DATE OF 1995 AMENDMENT

Amendment by Pub. L. 104–88 effective Jan. 1, 1996, see section 2 of Pub. L. 104–88, set out as an Effective Date note under section 701 of Title 49, Transportation.

EFFECTIVE DATE OF 1994 AMENDMENT

Amendment by Pub. L. 103–236 applicable with respect to officials, offices, and bureaus of Department of State when executive orders, regulations, or departmental directives implementing the amendments by sections 161 and 162 of Pub. L. 103–236 become effective, or 90 days after Apr. 30, 1994, whichever comes earlier, see section 161(b) of Pub. L. 103–236, as amended, set out as a note under section 2651a of Title 22, Foreign Relations and Intercourse.

EFFECTIVE DATE OF 1992 AMENDMENTS

Amendment by Pub. L. 102–552 effective Jan. 1, 1996, see section 201(c)(1) of Pub. L. 102–552, set out as an Effective Date of 1992 Amendment; Transitional Provision note under section 2277a–2 of Title 12, Banks and Banking.

Amendment by Pub. L. 102–378 effective as of the first day of the first applicable pay period beginning on or after Nov. 5, 1990, see section 9(b)(10) of Pub. L. 102–378, set out as a note under section 6303 of this title.

EFFECTIVE DATE OF 1991 AMENDMENTS

Amendment by Pub. L. 102–233 effective Feb. 1, 1992, see section 318 of Pub. L. 102–233, set out as a note under section 1441 of Title 12, Banks and Banking.

Amendment by Pub. L. 102–103 effective on first day of first pay period beginning on or after Aug. 17, 1991, see section 203 of Pub. L. 102–103, set out as a note under section 3412 of Title 20, Education.

EFFECTIVE DATE OF 1990 AMENDMENTS

Amendment by Pub. L. 101–509 effective on first day of first pay period beginning on or after Nov. 5, 1990, with continued service by incumbent Under Secretary of Health and Human Services, Under Secretary of the Interior, Under Secretary of Education, and Under Secretary of Housing and Urban Development, see section 529 [title I, §112(e)] of Pub. L. 101–509, set out as a note under section 3404 of Title 20, Education.

Section 6 of Pub. L. 101–328 provided that: "The provisions of this Act [amending this section and enacting provisions set out as notes under section 2471 of Title 42, The Public Health and Welfare] are effective as of October 1, 1989."

EFFECTIVE AND TERMINATION DATES OF 1988 AMENDMENTS

Amendment by Pub. L. 100–690 effective Jan. 21, 1989, and amendment by section 1003(a)(4)(B) of Pub. L. 100–690 repealed on Sept. 30, 1997, see sections 1012 and 1009, respectively, of Pub. L. 100–690.

Amendment by Pub. L. 100–679 effective Jan. 20, 1989, see section 11(e) of Pub. L. 100–679, set out as a note under section 5312 of this title.

Amendment by Pub. L. 100–527 effective Mar. 15, 1989, see section 18(a) of Pub. L. 100–527, set out as a Department of Veterans Affairs Act note under section 301 of Title 38, Veterans' Benefits.

EFFECTIVE DATE OF 1986 AMENDMENT

Amendment by Pub. L. 99–335 effective Jan. 1, 1987, see section 702(a) of Pub. L. 99–335, set out as an Effective Date note under section 8401 of this title.

EFFECTIVE DATE OF 1985 AMENDMENT

Section 116(d) of Pub. L. 99–64, as amended by Pub. L. 99–441, §5, Oct. 3, 1986, 100 Stat. 1118, provided that: "The provisions of section 15(a) of the Export Administration Act of 1979 [50 App. U.S.C. 2414(a)], as amended by subsection (a) of this section, and the amendments made by subsections (b) and (c) of this section [amending sections 5314 and 5315 of this title] shall take effect on October 1, 1987."

EFFECTIVE DATE OF 1984 AMENDMENTS

Amendment by Pub. L. 98–497 effective Apr. 1, 1985, see section 301 of Pub. L. 98–497, set out as a note under section 2102 of Title 44, Public Printing and Documents.

Amendment by section 609J of Pub. L. 98–473 effective Oct. 12, 1984, see section 609AA of Pub. L. 98–473, set out as an Effective Date note under section 3711 of Title 42, The Public Health and Welfare.

Section 9(v) of Pub. L. 98–443 provided that: "The amendments made by this section [amending sections 5314 and 5315 of this title, sections 1622 and 2145 of Title 7, Agriculture, sections 4746 and 9746 of Title 10, Armed Forces, sections 18, 21, 1607, 1681s, 1691c, and 1692l of Title 15, Commerce and Trade, section 18b of Title 16, Conservation, sections 47 and 7701 of Title 26, Internal Revenue Code, section 3726 of Title 31, Money and Finance, sections 3401, 5005, 5401, and 5402 of Title 39, Postal Service, section 3502 of Title 44, Public Printing and Documents, and sections 1159a, 1159b, 1301, 1305, 1377, 1382, 1388, 1389, and 1537 of former Title 49, Transportation] shall take effect on January 1, 1985."

EFFECTIVE DATE OF 1981 AMENDMENT

Amendment by Pub. L. 97–63 effective Oct. 1, 1981, see section 6 of Pub. L. 97–63, set out as a note under section 2121 of Title 22, Foreign Relations and Intercourse.

EFFECTIVE DATE OF 1980 AMENDMENT

Amendment by Pub. L. 96–355 effective Oct. 1, 1980, see section 10 of Pub. L. 96–355, set out as an Effective Date note under section 2204b of Title 7, Agriculture.

EFFECTIVE DATE OF 1979 AMENDMENTS

Amendment by Pub. L. 96–88 effective May 4, 1980, with specified exceptions, see section 601 of Pub. L. 96–88, set out as an Effective Date note under section 3401 of Title 20, Education.

Amendment by Pub. L. 96–54 effective Jan. 1, 1980, see section 2(a)(25)(B) of Pub. L. 96–54, set out as a note under section 5312 of this title.

Amendment by Pub. L. 96–53 effective Oct. 1, 1979, see section 512(a) of Pub. L. 96–53, set out as a note under section 2151 of Title 22, Foreign Relations and Intercourse.

EFFECTIVE DATE OF 1978 AMENDMENTS

Amendment by Pub. L. 95–630 effective on expiration of 120 days after Nov. 10, 1978, see section 509 of Pub. L. 95–630, set out as a note under section 1752 of Title 12, Banks and Banking.

Amendment by Pub. L. 95–454 effective 90 days after Oct. 13, 1978, see section 907 of Pub. L. 95–454, set out as a note under section 1101 of this title.

Section 114(c) of Pub. L. 95–426 provided that: "The amendments made by this section [amending sections 5314 and 5315 of this title and section 2652 of Title 22, Foreign Relations and Intercourse, and enacting provisions set out as a note under section 2652 of Title 22] shall take effect on October 1, 1978."

EFFECTIVE DATE OF 1977 AMENDMENT

Amendment by Pub. L. 95–164 effective 120 days after Nov. 9, 1977, except as otherwise provided, see section 307 of Pub. L. 95–164, set out as a note under section 801 of Title 30, Mineral Lands and Mining.

EFFECTIVE DATE OF 1975 AMENDMENT

Section 6(a), formerly section 6(a)(1), of Pub. L. 94–123, as renumbered Pub. L. 96–330, title I, §101, Aug.

26, 1980, 94 Stat. 1030, provided that: "The amendments made by section 2 of this Act [enacting former section 4118 of Title 38, Veterans' Benefits, amending this section, section 5315 of this title, and former section 4107 of Title 38, and enacting provisions set out as notes under former section 4118 of Title 38] shall become effective on October 12, 1975."

EFFECTIVE DATE OF 1974 AMENDMENTS

Amendment by Pub. L. 93–463 effective Oct. 23, 1974, see section 418 of Pub. L. 93–463, set out as a note under section 2 of Title 7, Agriculture.

Amendment by Pub. L. 93–438 effective 120 days after Oct. 11, 1974, or on such earlier date as President may prescribe and publish in Federal Register, except that officers provided for in sections 5811 to 5820 of Title 42, The Public Health and Welfare, may be nominated and appointed at any time after Oct. 11, 1974, see section 312(a) of Pub. L. 93–438, set out as an Effective Date; Interim Appointments note under section 5801 of Title 42.

EFFECTIVE DATE OF 1973 AMENDMENT

Offices and salaries modified under amendment by Pub. L. 93–83, prospectively only, effective on and after Aug. 6, 1973, see section 3 of Pub. L. 93–83, Aug. 6, 1973, 83 Stat. 218.

EFFECTIVE DATE OF 1972 AMENDMENT

Amendment by Pub. L. 92–302 effective May 18, 1972, see section 3 of Pub. L. 92–302, May 18, 1972, 86 Stat. 149.

EFFECTIVE DATE OF 1970 AMENDMENT

Amendment by Pub. L. 91–375 effective within 1 year after Aug. 12, 1970, on date established therefor by Board of Governors of United States Postal Service and published by it in Federal Register, see section 15(a) of Pub. L. 91–375, set out as an Effective Date note preceding section 101 of Title 39, Postal Service.

EFFECTIVE DATE OF 1968 AMENDMENTS

Amendment by Pub. L. 90–623 intended to restate without substantive change the law in effect on Oct. 22, 1968, see section 6 of Pub. L. 90–623, set out as a note under section 5334 of this title.

Amendment by Pub. L. 90–407 effective on first day of first calendar month which begins on or after July 18, 1968, see section 15 (a)(4) of Pub. L. 90–407, set out as a note under section 5313 of this title.

EFFECTIVE DATE OF 1967 AMENDMENT

Amendment by Pub. L. 90–206 effective at beginning of first pay period which begins on or after Dec. 16, 1967, see section 220(a)(3) of Pub. L. 90–206, set out as a note under section 603 of Title 28, Judiciary and Judicial Procedure.

EFFECTIVE DATE OF 1966 AMENDMENT

Amendment by Pub. L. 89–670 effective Apr. 1, 1967 as prescribed by President and published in Federal Register, see section 16(a), formerly § 15(a), of Pub. L. 89–670 and Ex. Ord. No. 11340, Mar. 30, 1967, 32 F.R. 5453.

TRANSFER OF FUNCTIONS

Office of Emergency Preparedness, including offices of Director, Deputy Director, Assistant Directors, and Regional Directors, abolished and functions vested by law in Office of Emergency Preparedness or Director of Office of Emergency Preparedness transferred to President by sections 1 and 3(a)(1) of 1973 Reorg. Plan No. 1, effective July 1, 1973, set out in the Appendix to this title.

SALARY INCREASES

2001—Salaries of positions at level III increased to $133,700 per annum, effective on the first day of the first pay period beginning on or after Jan. 1, 2001, as provided by Ex. Ord. No. 13182, Dec. 23, 2000, 65 F.R. 82879, 66 F.R. 10057, set out as a note under section 5332 of this title.

2000—Salaries of positions at level III increased to $130,200 per annum, effective on the first day of the first pay period beginning on or after Jan. 1, 2000, as provided by Ex. Ord. No. 13144, Dec. 21, 1999, 64 F.R. 72237.

1999—Salaries of positions at level III continued at $125,900 per annum by Ex. Ord. No. 13106, Dec. 7, 1998, 63 F.R. 68151.

1998—Salaries of positions at level III increased to $125,900 per annum, effective on the first day of the first pay period beginning on or after Jan. 1, 1998, as provided by Ex. Ord. No. 13071, Dec. 29, 1997, 62 F.R. 68521.

1997—Salaries of positions at level III continued at $123,100 per annum by Ex. Ord. No. 13033, Dec. 27, 1996, 61 F.R. 68987.

1996—Salaries of positions at level III continued at $123,100 per annum by Ex. Ord. No. 12984, Dec. 28, 1995, 61 F.R. 237.

1995—Salaries of positions at level III continued at $123,100 per annum by Ex. Ord. No. 12944, Dec. 28, 1994, 60 F.R. 309.

1993—Salaries of positions at level III increased to $123,100 per annum, effective on the first day of the first pay period beginning on or after Jan. 1, 1993, as provided by Ex. Ord. No. 12826, Dec. 30, 1992, 57 F.R. 62909.

1992—Salaries of positions at level III increased to $119,300 per annum, effective on the first day of the first pay period beginning on or after Jan. 1, 1992, as provided by Ex. Ord. No. 12786, Dec. 26, 1991, 56 F.R. 67453.

1991—Salaries of positions at level III increased to $115,300 per annum, effective on the first day of the first pay period beginning on or after Jan. 1, 1991, as provided by Ex. Ord. No. 12736, Dec. 12, 1990, 55 F.R. 51385.

1990—Salaries of positions at level III increased to $85,500 per annum, effective on the first day of the first pay period beginning on or after Jan. 1, 1990, and increased to $89,000 per annum, effective on the first day of the first pay period beginning on or after Jan. 31, 1990, as provided by Ex. Ord. No. 12698, Dec. 23, 1989, 54 F.R. 53473.

1989—Salaries of positions at level III continued at $82,500 per annum, see Ex. Ord. No. 12663, Jan. 6, 1989, 54 F.R. 791.

1988—Salaries of positions at level III continued at $82,500 per annum by Ex. Ord. No. 12622, Dec. 31, 1987, 53 F.R. 222.

1987—Salaries of positions at level III increased to $82,500 per annum, on recommendation of the President of the United States, see note set out under section 358 of Title 2, The Congress.

Salaries of positions at level III increased to $75,800 per annum, effective on the first day of the first pay period beginning on or after Jan. 1, 1987, as provided by Ex. Ord. No. 12578, Dec. 31, 1986, 52 F.R. 505.

1985—Salaries of positions at level III increased to $73,600 per annum, effective on the first day of the first pay period beginning on or after Jan. 1, 1985, as provided by Ex. Ord. No. 12496, Dec. 28, 1984, 50 F.R. 211, as amended by Ex. Ord. No. 12540, Dec. 30, 1985, 51 F.R. 577.

1984—Salaries of positions at level III increased to $71,100 per annum, effective on the first day of the first pay period beginning on or after Jan. 1, 1984, as provided by Ex. Ord. No. 12456, Dec. 30, 1983, 49 F.R. 347, as amended Ex. Ord. No. 12477, May 23, 1984, 49 F.R. 22041; Ex. Ord. No. 12487, Sept. 14, 1984, 49 F.R. 36493.

1982—Salaries of positions at level III increased to $70,500 per annum, effective on the first day of the first pay period beginning on or after Oct. 1, 1982, as provided by Ex. Ord. No. 12387, Oct. 8, 1982, 47 F.R. 44981. Ex. Ord. No. 12387 further provided that pursuant to section 101(e) of Pub. L. 97–276 funds are not available to pay a salary at a rate which exceeds the rate in effect on Sept. 30, 1982, which was $59,500.00.

Maximum rate payable after Dec. 17, 1982, increased from $59,500.00 to $68,400.00, see Pub. L. 97–377, title I, § 129(b)–(d), Dec. 21, 1982, 96 Stat. 1914, set out as a note under section 5318 of this title.

Limitations on use of funds for fiscal year ending Sept. 30, 1983, appropriated by any Act to pay the salary or pay of any individual in legislative, executive, or judicial branch in position equal to or above level V of the Executive Schedule, see section 101(e) of Pub. L. 97–276, as amended, set out as a note under section 5318 of this title.

1981—Salaries of positions at level III increased to $67,800 per annum, effective on the first day of the first pay period beginning on or after Oct. 1, 1981, as provided by Ex. Ord. No. 12330, Oct. 15, 1981, 46 F.R. 50921. Ex. Ord. No. 12330 further provided that pursuant to section 101(c) of Pub. L. 97–51 funds are not available to pay a salary at a rate which exceeds the rate in effect on Sept. 30, 1981, which was $55,387.50.

Limitations on use of funds for fiscal year ending Sept. 30, 1982, appropriated by any Act to pay the salary or pay of any individual in legislative, executive, or judicial branch in position equal to or above level V of the Executive Schedule, see sections 101(g) and 141 of Pub. L. 97–92, set out as a note under section 5318 of this title.

1980—Salaries of positions at level III increased to $64,700 per annum, effective on the first day of the first pay period beginning on or after Oct. 1, 1980, as provided by Ex. Ord. No. 12248, Oct. 16, 1980, 45 F.R. 69199. Ex. Ord. No. 12248, further provided that pursuant to section 101(c) of Pub. L. 96–369, funds are not available to pay a salary at a rate which exceeds the rate in effect on Sept. 30, 1980, which was $55,387.50.

Limitations on use of funds for fiscal year ending Sept. 30, 1981, appropriated by an Act to pay the salary or pay of any individual in legislative, executive, or judicial branch in position equal to or above level V of the Executive Schedule, see section 101(c) of Pub. L. 96–536, as amended, set out as a note under section 5318 of this title.

1979—Salaries of positions at level III increased to $59,300 per annum, effective on the first day of the first pay period beginning on or after Oct. 1, 1979, as provided by Ex. Ord. No. 12165, Oct. 9, 1979, 44 F.R. 58671, as amended by Ex. Ord. No. 12200, Mar. 12, 1980, 45 F.R. 16443. Ex. Ord. No. 12165 further provided that pursuant to section 101(c) of Pub. L. 96–86 funds appropriated for fiscal year 1980 may not be used to pay a salary at a rate which exceeds an increase of 5.5 percent over the rate in effect on Sept. 30, 1978, which is a maximum rate payable of $55,387.50.

Applicability to funds appropriated by any Act for fiscal year ending Sept. 30, 1980, of limitation of section 304 of Pub. L. 95–391 on use of funds to pay the salary or pay of any individual in legislative, executive, or judicial branch in position equal to or above level V of the Executive Schedule, see section 101 of Pub. L. 96–86, set out as a note under section 5318 of this title.

1978—Salaries of positions at level III increased to $55,400 per annum, effective in the first pay period beginning on or after Oct. 1, 1978, as provided by Ex. Ord. No. 12087, Oct. 7, 1978, 43 F.R. 46823. Ex. Ord. No. 12087, further provided that pursuant to the Legislative Branch Appropriation Act, 1979, funds are not available to pay a salary at a rate which exceeds the rate in effect on Sept. 30, 1978, which was $52,500.

Limitations on use of funds for fiscal year ending Sept. 30, 1979, appropriated by any Act to pay the salary or pay of any individual in legislative, executive, or judicial branch in position equal or above level V of the Executive Schedule, see section 304 of Pub. L. 95–391 and section 613 of Pub. L. 95–429, set out as a note under section 5318 of this title.

1977—Salaries of positions at level III increased to $52,500 per annum, on recommendation of the President of the United States, see note set out under section 358 of Title 2, The Congress.

1976—Salaries of positions at level III increased to $44,000 per annum, effective on the first day of the first pay period beginning on or after Oct. 1, 1976, see Ex. Ord. No. 11941, Oct. 1, 1976, 41 F.R. 43889, set out as a note under section 5332 of this title. Ex. Ord. No. 11941, further provided that pursuant to the Legislative Branch Appropriation Act, 1977, funds are not available to pay a salary at a rate which exceeds the rate in effect on Sept. 30, 1976, which was $42,000.

1975—Salaries of positions at level III increased to $42,000 per annum, effective on the first day of the first

pay period beginning on or after Oct. 1, 1975, by Ex. Ord. No. 11883, Oct. 6, 1975, 40 F.R. 47091.

1969—Salaries of positions at level III increased from $29,500 to $40,000 per annum, commencing on the first day of the pay period which begins after February 14, 1969, on recommendation of the President of the United States, see note set out under section 358 of Title 2, The Congress.

PAY INCREASE; EFFECTIVE DATE

Persons occupying a position under the Executive Schedule on May 18, 1972, and later appointed to a position created or authorized by Pub. L. 92–302, not eligible to an increase in basic pay until Jan. 21, 1973, see section 3(c) of Pub. L. 92–302, May 18, 1972, 86 Stat. 149.

DIRECTOR OF FEDERAL BUREAU OF INVESTIGATION, DEPARTMENT OF JUSTICE

Director of Federal Bureau of Investigation, Department of Justice to receive compensation at rate prescribed for level II of Federal Executive Salary Schedule [section 5313 of this title], effective as of day following date on which person holding such office on June 19, 1968 ceases to serve as Director, see section 1101(a) of Pub. L. 90–351, set out as a note under section 532 of Title 28, Judiciary and Judicial Procedure.

Position of Director of Federal Bureau of Investigation, referred to in text, placed temporarily in level II during incumbency of incumbent on Aug. 14, 1964, by Pub. L. 88–426, Aug. 14, 1964, § 303(b)(15), 78 Stat. 416.

Section 1101(a) of the Omnibus Crime Control and Safe Streets Act of 1968 (Pub. L. 90–351, June 19, 1968, 82 Stat. 236), which is set out as a note under section 532 of Title 28, Judiciary and Judicial Procedure, provided in part that when present incumbent of position of Director leaves office, his successors will be paid at rate prescribed for level II.

SECTION REFERRED TO IN OTHER SECTIONS

This section is referred to in sections 5315, 5377, 5380, 8432 of this title; title 2 sections 60a–1, 136a–2, 166, 282b, 288, 474, 1151; title 3 sections 105, 106, 107; title 10 section 973; title 12 sections 1422b, 2242, 2278a–2, 2278a–3; title 15 sections 205i, 1503b, 3704; title 17 section 701; title 18 section 207; title 19 section 2171; title 20 sections 4512, 9103; title 22 sections 2651a, 3505, 3961; title 26 section 3121; title 28 section 591; title 31 section 703; title 35 section 5; title 40 section 162a; title 42 sections 410, 1864a, 5871, 5872, 6612, 7132, 7134, 7211, 7291, 7293, 10242, 12651c; title 44 section 2103; title 49 sections 106, 701.

§ 5315. Positions at level IV

Level IV of the Executive Schedule applies to the following positions, for which the annual rate of basic pay shall be the rate determined with respect to such level under chapter 11 of title 2, as adjusted by section 5318 of this title:

Deputy Administrator of General Services.

Associate Administrator of the National Aeronautics and Space Administration.

Assistant Administrators, Agency for International Development (6).

Regional Assistant Administrators, Agency for International Development (4).

Under Secretary of the Air Force.

Under Secretary of the Army.

Under Secretary of the Navy.

Assistant Secretaries of Agriculture (2).

Assistant Secretaries of Commerce (11).

Assistant Secretaries of Defense (9).

Assistant Secretaries of the Air Force (4).

Assistant Secretaries of the Army (5).

Assistant Secretaries of the Navy (4).

Assistant Secretaries of Health and Human Services (6).

Assistant Secretaries of the Interior (6).

Assistant Attorneys General (10).

Assistant Secretaries of Labor (10), one of whom shall be the Assistant Secretary of Labor for Veterans' Employment and Training.

Assistant Secretaries of State (24) and 4 other State Department officials to be appointed by the President, by and with the advice and consent of the Senate.

Assistant Secretaries of the Treasury (7).

Members, United States International Trade Commission (5).

Assistant Secretaries of Education (10).

General Counsel, Department of Education.

Inspector General, Department of Education.

Director of Civil Defense, Department of the Army.

Deputy Director of the Office of Emergency Planning.

Deputy Director of the Office of Science and Technology.

Deputy Director of the Peace Corps.

Assistant Directors of the Office of Management and Budget (3).

General Counsel of the Department of Agriculture.

General Counsel of the Department of Commerce.

General Counsel of the Department of Defense.

General Counsel of the Department of Health and Human Services.

Solicitor of the Department of the Interior.

Solicitor of the Department of Labor.

General Counsel of the National Labor Relations Board.

General Counsel of the Department of the Treasury.

First Vice President of the Export-Import Bank of Washington.

Members, Council of Economic Advisers.

Members, Board of Directors of the Export-Import Bank of Washington.

Members, Federal Communications Commission.

Member, Board of Directors of the Federal Deposit Insurance Corporation.

Directors, Federal Housing Finance Board.

Members, Federal Energy Regulatory Commission.

Members, Federal Trade Commission.

Members, Surface Transportation Board.

Members, National Labor Relations Board.

Members, Securities and Exchange Commission.

Members, Board of Directors of the Tennessee Valley Authority.

Members, Merit Systems Protection Board.

Members, Federal Maritime Commission.

Members, National Mediation Board.

Members, Railroad Retirement Board.

Director of Selective Service.

Associate Director of the Federal Bureau of Investigation, Department of Justice.

Members, Equal Employment Opportunity Commission (4).

Director, Community Relations Service.

Members, National Transportation Safety Board.

General Counsel, Department of Transportation.

Deputy Administrator, Federal Aviation Administration.

Assistant Secretaries of Transportation (4).

Deputy Federal Highway Administrator.

Administrator of the Saint Lawrence Seaway Development Corporation.

Assistant Secretary for Science, Smithsonian Institution.

Assistant Secretary for History and Art, Smithsonian Institution.

Deputy Administrator of the Small Business Administration.

Assistant Secretaries of Housing and Urban Development (8).

General Counsel of the Department of Housing and Urban Development.

Commissioner of Interama.

Federal Insurance Administrator, Federal Emergency Management Agency.

Executive Vice President, Overseas Private Investment Corporation.

Members, National Credit Union Administration Board (2).

Members, Postal Rate Commission (4).

Members, Occupational Safety and Health Review Commission.

Deputy Under Secretaries of the Treasury (or Assistant Secretaries of the Treasury) (2).

Members, Consumer Product Safety Commission (4).

Members, Commodity Futures Trading Commission.

Director of Nuclear Reactor Regulation, Nuclear Regulatory Commission.

Director of Nuclear Material Safety and Safeguards, Nuclear Regulatory Commission.

Director of Nuclear Regulatory Research, Nuclear Regulatory Commission.

Executive Director for Operations, Nuclear Regulatory Commission.

President, Government National Mortgage Association, Department of Housing and Urban Development.

Assistant Secretary of Commerce for Oceans and Atmosphere, the incumbent of which also serves as Deputy Administrator of the National Oceanic and Atmospheric Administration.

Commissioner of Immigration and Naturalization, Department of Justice.

Director, Bureau of Prisons, Department of Justice.

Assistant Secretaries of Energy (6).

General Counsel of the Department of Energy.

Administrator, Economic Regulatory Administration, Department of Energy.

Administrator, Energy Information Administration, Department of Energy.

Inspector General, Department of Energy.

Director, Office of Science, Department of Energy.

Assistant Secretary of Labor for Mine Safety and Health.

Members, Federal Mine Safety and Health Review Commission.

President, National Consumer Cooperative Bank.

Inspector General, Department of Health and Human Services.

Inspector General, Department of Agriculture.

Special Counsel of the Merit Systems Protection Board.

Inspector General, Department of Housing and Urban Development.

Chairman, Federal Labor Relations Authority.

Inspector General, Department of Labor.

Inspector General, Department of Transportation.

Inspector General, Department of Veterans Affairs.

Deputy Director, Institute for Scientific and Technological Cooperation.

Director of the National Institute of Justice.

Director of the Bureau of Justice Statistics.

Chief Counsel for Advocacy, Small Business Administration.

Inspector General, Department of Defense.

Assistant Administrator for Toxic Substances, Environmental Protection Agency.

Assistant Administrator, Office of Solid Waste, Environmental Protection Agency.

Assistant Administrators, Environmental Protection Agency (8).

Director of Operational Test and Evaluation, Department of Defense.

Special Representatives of the President for arms control, nonproliferation, and disarmament matters, Department of State.

Administrator of the Health Care Financing Administration.

Director, National Institute of Standards and Technology, Department of Commerce.

Inspector General, Department of State.

Director of Defense Research and Engineering.

Ambassadors at Large.

Commissioner, National Center for Education Statistics.

Assistant Secretary of Commerce and Director General of the United States and Foreign Commercial Service.

Inspector General, Department of Commerce.

Inspector General, Department of the Interior.

Inspector General, Department of Justice.

Inspector General, Department of the Treasury.

Inspector General, Agency for International Development.

Inspector General, Environmental Protection Agency.

Inspector General, Federal Emergency Management Agency.

Inspector General, General Services Administration.

Inspector General, National Aeronautics and Space Administration.

Inspector General, Nuclear Regulatory Commission.

Inspector General, Office of Personnel Management.

Inspector General, Railroad Retirement Board.

Inspector General, Small Business Administration.

Inspector General, Tennessee Valley Authority.

Inspector General, Federal Deposit Insurance Corporation.

Assistant Secretaries, Department of Veterans Affairs (6).

General Counsel, Department of Veterans Affairs.

Commissioner of Food and Drugs, Department of Health and Human Services [1]

Chairman, Board of Veterans' Appeals.

Administrator, Office of Juvenile Justice and Delinquency Prevention.

Director, United States Marshals Service.

Inspector General, Resolution Trust Corporation.

Chairman, United States Parole Commission.

Director, Bureau of the Census, Department of Commerce.

Director of the Institute of Museum and Library Services.

Chief Financial Officer, Department of Agriculture.

Chief Financial Officer, Department of Commerce.

Chief Financial Officer, Department of Education.

Chief Financial Officer, Department of Energy.

Chief Financial Officer, Department of Health and Human Services.

Chief Financial Officer, Department of Housing and Urban Development.

Chief Financial Officer, Department of the Interior.

Chief Financial Officer, Department of Justice.

Chief Financial Officer, Department of Labor.

Chief Financial Officer, Department of State.

Chief Financial Officer, Department of Transportation.

Chief Financial Officer, Department of the Treasury.

Chief Financial Officer, Department of Veterans Affairs.

Chief Financial Officer, Environmental Protection Agency.

Chief Financial Officer, National Aeronautics and Space Administration.

Commissioner, Office of Navajo and Hopi Indian Relocation.

Inspector General, Central Intelligence Agency [1]

Deputy Under Secretary of Defense for Policy.

General Counsel of the Department of the Army.

General Counsel of the Department of the Navy.

General Counsel of the Department of the Air Force.

Liaison for Community and Junior Colleges, Department of Education.

Director of the Office of Educational Technology.

Director of the International Broadcasting Bureau.

Inspector General, Social Security Administration.

The [2] Commissioner of Labor Statistics, Department of Labor.

---

[1] So in original. Probably should be followed by a period.
[2] The word "The" probably should not appear.

Administrator, Rural Utilities Service, Department of Agriculture.

Executive Director of the Alternative Agricultural Research and Commercialization Corporation.

Chief Information Officer, Department of Agriculture.

Chief Information Officer, Department of Commerce.

Chief Information Officer, Department of Defense (unless the official designated as the Chief Information Officer of the Department of Defense is an official listed under section 5312, 5313, or 5314 of this title).

Chief Information Officer, Department of Education.

Chief Information Officer, Department of Energy.

Chief Information Officer, Department of Health and Human Services.

Chief Information Officer, Department of Housing and Urban Development.

Chief Information Officer, Department of the Interior.

Chief Information Officer, Department of Justice.

Chief Information Officer, Department of Labor.

Chief Information Officer, Department of State.

Chief Information Officer, Department of Transportation.

Chief Information Officer, Department of the Treasury.

Chief Information Officer, Department of Veterans Affairs.

Chief Information Officer, Environmental Protection Agency.

Chief Information Officer, National Aeronautics and Space Administration.

Chief Information Officer, Agency for International Development.

Chief Information Officer, Federal Emergency Management Agency.

Chief Information Officer, General Services Administration.

Chief Information Officer, National Science Foundation.

Chief Information Officer, Nuclear Regulatory Agency.

Chief Information Officer, Office of Personnel Management.

Chief Information Officer, Small Business Administration.

Inspector General, United States Postal Service.

Assistant Directors of Central Intelligence (3).

General Counsel of the Central Intelligence Agency.

Deputy Administrators of the National Nuclear Security Administration (3), but if the Deputy Administrator for Naval Reactors is an officer of the Navy on active duty, (2).

Deputy Under Secretary of Commerce for Intellectual Property and Deputy Director of the United States Patent and Trademark Office.

(Pub. L. 89–554, Sept. 6, 1966, 80 Stat. 461; Pub. L. 89–670, § 10(d)(4), (e), Oct. 15, 1966, 80 Stat. 948; Pub. L. 89–734, § 1(1), Nov. 2, 1966, 80 Stat. 1163; Pub. L. 89–779, § 8(c)(1), Nov. 6, 1966, 80 Stat. 1364;

Pub. L. 90–83, § 1(15), Sept. 11, 1967, 81 Stat. 198; Pub. L. 90–206, title II, § 215(b), Dec. 16, 1967, 81 Stat. 638; Pub. L. 90–351, title I, § 505, June 19, 1968, 82 Stat. 205; Pub. L. 90–448, title XI, § 1105(b), title XVII, § 1708(b), Aug. 1, 1968, 82 Stat. 567, 606; Pub. L. 90–623, § 1(4), Oct. 22, 1968, 82 Stat. 1312; Pub. L. 91–121, title IV, § 404(b), Nov. 19, 1969, 83 Stat. 207; Pub. L. 91–175, pt. V, § 503(2), Dec. 30, 1969, 83 Stat. 826; Pub. L. 91–206, § 5(b), Mar. 10, 1970, 84 Stat. 51; Pub. L. 91–375, § 6(c)(14), Aug. 12, 1970, 84 Stat. 776; Pub. L. 91–469, § 42(b), Oct. 21, 1970, 84 Stat. 1038; Pub. L. 91–477, § 3(b), Oct. 21, 1970, 84 Stat. 1072; Pub. L. 91–596, §§ 12(c)(2), 29(b), Dec. 29, 1970, 84 Stat. 1604, 1619; Pub. L. 91–611, title II, § 211(b), Dec. 31, 1970, 84 Stat. 1829; Pub. L. 91–644, title I, § 7 (1), (2), Jan. 2, 1971, 84 Stat. 1887; Pub. L. 92–22, § 2, June 1, 1971, 85 Stat. 76; Pub. L. 92–181, title V, § 5.41(a), formerly § 5.27(a), Dec. 10, 1971, 85 Stat. 625, renumbered Pub. L. 99–205, title II, § 205(a)(2), Dec. 23, 1985, 99 Stat. 1703; Pub. L. 92–215, § 2, Dec. 22, 1971, 85 Stat. 777; Pub. L. 92–255, title II, § 212(b), Mar. 21, 1972, 86 Stat. 69; Pub. L. 92–261, § 9(b), Mar. 24, 1972, 86 Stat. 110; Pub. L. 92–302, § 2(c), May 18, 1972, 86 Stat. 149; Pub. L. 92–352, title I, § 104(3), July 13, 1972, 86 Stat. 490; Pub. L. 92–419, title VI, § 604(b), Aug. 30, 1972, 86 Stat. 676; Pub. L. 92–573, § 4(h)(2), Oct. 27, 1972, 86 Stat. 1211; Pub. L. 92–603, title IV, § 404(b), Oct. 30, 1972, 86 Stat. 1488; Pub. L. 90–351, title I, § 506(a), as added Pub. L. 93–83, § 2, Aug. 6, 1973, 87 Stat. 211; Pub. L. 93–126, § 9(b), as added Pub. L. 93–312, § 9, June 8, 1974, 88 Stat. 238; Pub. L. 93–383, title VIII, § 818(c), Aug. 22, 1974, 88 Stat. 740; Pub. L. 93–400, § 13, Aug. 30, 1974, 88 Stat. 799; Pub. L. 93–438, title III, § 310(3), Oct. 11, 1974, 88 Stat. 1253; Pub. L. 93–463, title I, § 102(b), Oct. 23, 1974, 88 Stat. 1391; Pub. L. 93–618, title I, § 172(c)(2), Jan. 3, 1975, 88 Stat. 2010; Pub. L. 94–82, title II, § 202(b)(4), Aug. 9, 1975, 89 Stat. 420; Pub. L. 94–123, § 2(c)(2), Oct. 22, 1975, 89 Stat. 670; Pub. L. 94–183, § 2(18), Dec. 31, 1975, 89 Stat. 1057; Pub. L. 92–255, title II, § 209(b), as added Pub. L. 94–237, § 4(b), Mar. 19, 1976, 90 Stat. 243; Pub. L. 94–375, § 17(c), Aug. 3, 1976, 90 Stat. 1077; Pub. L. 94–461, § 4(b), Oct. 8, 1976, 90 Stat. 1969; Pub. L. 94–503, title II, § 202(b), Oct. 15, 1976, 90 Stat. 2426; Pub. L. 94–561, § 3(a), Oct. 19, 1976, 90 Stat. 2643; Pub. L. 95–88, title I, § 124(b), Aug. 3, 1977, 91 Stat. 542; Pub. L. 95–91, title VII, § 710(f), Aug. 4, 1977, 91 Stat. 609; Pub. L. 95–105, title I, § 109(d), Aug. 17, 1977, 91 Stat. 847; Pub. L. 95–108, § 2(b), Aug. 17, 1977, 91 Stat. 871; Pub. L. 95–164, title III, § 302(b), Nov. 9, 1977, 91 Stat. 1319; Pub. L. 95–173, § 9(b), Nov. 12, 1977, 91 Stat. 1360; Pub. L. 95–351, title III, § 302, Aug. 20, 1978, 92 Stat. 514; Pub. L. 95–426, title I, §§ 114(b)(2), 115(b)(1), Oct. 7, 1978, 92 Stat. 969; Pub. L. 95–452, § 10(a), Oct. 12, 1978, 92 Stat. 1108; Pub. L. 95–454, title II, §§ 202(c)(2), (3), title VII, § 703(d), Oct. 13, 1978, 92 Stat. 1131, 1217; Pub. L. 95–630, title V, § 502(e), Nov. 10, 1978, 92 Stat. 3681; Pub. L. 96–39, title XI, § 1106(c)(4), July 26, 1979, 93 Stat. 312; Pub. L. 96–53, title IV, § 412(b), Aug. 14, 1979, 93 Stat. 377; Pub. L. 96–54, § 2(a)(25)(A), Aug. 14, 1979, 93 Stat. 382; Pub. L. 96–88, title V, § 508(e), (g), Oct. 17, 1979, 93 Stat. 692; Pub. L. 96–107, title VIII, § 820(e)(1), Nov. 9, 1979, 93 Stat. 819; Pub. L. 96–132, § 5, Nov. 30, 1979, 93 Stat. 1045; Pub. L. 96–153, title VI, § 603(b), Dec. 21, 1979, 93 Stat. 1138; Pub. L. 90–351, title I, § 809, as added Pub. L. 96–157, § 2, Dec. 27, 1979, 93

Stat. 1204; Pub. L. 96–302, title IV, § 403, July 2, 1980, 94 Stat. 850; Pub. L. 96–511, § 4(d), Dec. 11, 1980, 94 Stat. 2826; Pub. L. 97–31, § 12(1)(B), Aug. 6, 1981, 95 Stat. 153; Pub. L. 97–35, title III, § 396(h)(4), Aug. 13, 1981, 95 Stat. 441; Pub. L. 97–98, title XIV, § 1414(b), Dec. 22, 1981, 95 Stat. 1303; Pub. L. 97–195, § 1(b)(2), June 16, 1982, 96 Stat. 115; Pub. L. 97–252, title XI, § 1117(d), Sept. 8, 1982, 96 Stat. 753; Pub. L. 97–325, § 8(b), Oct. 15, 1982, 96 Stat. 1605; Pub. L. 97–449, § 3(3), Jan. 12, 1983, 96 Stat. 2441; Pub. L. 98–80, § 2(c)(1), Aug. 23, 1983, 97 Stat. 485; Pub. L. 98–94, title XII, §§ 1211(b), 1212(d), Sept. 24, 1983, 97 Stat. 686, 687; Pub. L. 98–164, title I, § 125(b)(2), Nov. 22, 1983, 97 Stat. 1026; Pub. L. 98–202, § 6(b), Dec. 2, 1983, 97 Stat. 1382; Pub. L. 98–216, § 3(a)(3), Feb. 14, 1984, 98 Stat. 6; Pub. L. 98–369, title III, § 2332(b), July 18, 1984, 98 Stat. 1089; Pub. L. 98–443, § 9(e), Oct. 4, 1984, 98 Stat. 1707; Pub. L. 98–473, title II, §§ 609J(b), 1701(b), Oct. 12, 1984, 98 Stat. 2102, 2185; Pub. L. 98–594, § 1(b), Oct. 30, 1984, 98 Stat. 3129; Pub. L. 99–64, title I, § 116(c), July 12, 1985, 99 Stat. 153; Pub. L. 99–73, § 6(b)(1), July 29, 1985, 99 Stat. 173; Pub. L. 99–93, title I, § 115(b), title VII, § 704(a)(2), Aug. 16, 1985, 99 Stat. 411, 445; Pub. L. 99–399, title I, § 104(c), title IV, §§ 412(c), 413(e), formerly 413(a)(5), Aug. 27, 1986, 100 Stat. 856, 867, 868, as renumbered Pub. L. 100–204, title I, § 134(b), Dec. 22, 1987, 101 Stat. 1344; Pub. L. 99–500, § 101(c) [title X, § 903(b)(2)(B)], Oct. 18, 1986, 100 Stat. 1783–82, 1783–132, and Pub. L. 99–591, § 101(c) [title X, § 903(b)(2)(B)], Oct. 30, 1986, 100 Stat. 3341–82, 3341–132; Pub. L. 99–619, § 2(b)(2), Nov. 6, 1986, 100 Stat. 3491; Pub. L. 99–659, title IV, § 407(e)(2), Nov. 14, 1986, 100 Stat. 3740; Pub. L. 99–661, div. A, title IX, formerly title IV, § 903(b)(2)(B), Nov. 14, 1986, 100 Stat. 3912, as renumbered Pub. L. 100–26, § 3(5), Apr. 21, 1987, 101 Stat. 273; Pub. L. 100–204, title I, § 178(a)(2), Dec. 22, 1987, 101 Stat. 1362; Pub. L. 100–297, title III, § 3001(b)(2), Apr. 28, 1988, 102 Stat. 331; Pub. L. 100–418, title II, § 2301(i), formerly § 2301(h), title V, § 5112(c)(2), Aug. 23, 1988, 102 Stat. 1341, 1431, as renumbered Pub. L. 102–429, title II, § 203(b)(1), Oct. 21, 1992, 106 Stat. 2201; Pub. L. 100–485, title VI, § 603(b), Oct. 13, 1988, 102 Stat. 2409; Pub. L. 100–504, title I, § 103(a), Oct. 18, 1988, 102 Stat. 2521; Pub. L. 100–527, § 13(f), Oct. 25, 1988, 102 Stat. 2643; Pub. L. 100–607, title V, § 503(b)(2), Nov. 4, 1988, 102 Stat. 3121; Pub. L. 100–679, § 11(d), Nov. 17, 1988, 102 Stat. 4070; Pub. L. 100–687, div. A, title II, § 201(b)(1), Nov. 18, 1988, 102 Stat. 4109; Pub. L. 100–690, title I, §§ 1003(a)(4)(C), 1007(c)(4), title VII, §§ 7252(b)(3), 7608(e), Nov. 18, 1988, 102 Stat. 4182, 4188, 4436, 4517; Pub. L. 101–73, title V, § 501(b)(2)(A), title VII, § 742(a)(2), Aug. 9, 1989, 103 Stat. 393, 436; Pub. L. 101–189, div. A, title XI, § 1112, Nov. 29, 1989, 103 Stat. 1554; Pub. L. 101–319, § 3(a), July 3, 1990, 104 Stat. 290; Pub. L. 101–509, title V, § 529 [title I, § 113(2)], Nov. 5, 1990, 104 Stat. 1427, 1455; Pub. L. 101–512, title III, § 318 [title II, § 202(a)(2)], Nov. 5, 1990, 104 Stat. 1960, 1975; Pub. L. 101–576, title II, § 207(c), Nov. 15, 1990, 104 Stat. 2846; Pub. L. 102–138, title I, § 122(d)(1), Oct. 28, 1991, 105 Stat. 659; Pub. L. 102–180, § 3(g), Dec. 2, 1991, 105 Stat. 1231; Pub. L. 102–183, title IV, § 404, Dec. 4, 1991, 105 Stat. 1267; Pub. L. 102–190, div. A, title IX, §§ 901(b), 903(a)(1), div. C, title XXXV, § 3504(a), Dec. 5, 1991, 105 Stat. 1450, 1451, 1586; Pub. L. 102–325, title XV, § 1553(b), July 23, 1992, 106 Stat. 839; Pub. L. 102–359, § 2(b)(1), Aug. 26, 1992, 106 Stat. 962; Pub. L. 102–552, title II, § 201(b)(2), Oct. 28, 1992, 106 Stat. 4105; Pub. L. 103–123, title I, § 108(a)(2), Oct. 28, 1993, 107 Stat. 1234; Pub. L. 103–160, div. A, title IX, §§ 902(a)(2), 903(c)(2), Nov. 30, 1993, 107 Stat. 1727, 1728; Pub. L. 103–171, § 3(b)(1), Dec. 2, 1993, 107 Stat. 1991; Pub. L. 103–204, § 23(b), Dec. 17, 1993, 107 Stat. 2408; Pub. L. 103–227, title II, § 233(b), Mar. 31, 1994, 108 Stat. 155; Pub. L. 103–236, title I, § 162(d)(2), title III, § 307(b)(2), title VII, § 708(b), Apr. 30, 1994, 108 Stat. 405, 436, 494; Pub. L. 103–272, § 4(b)(2), July 5, 1994, 108 Stat. 1361; Pub. L. 103–296, title I, §§ 106(a)(7)(B), 108(e)(3), Aug. 15, 1994, 108 Stat. 1476, 1486; Pub. L. 103–333, title I, § 106, Sept. 30, 1994, 108 Stat. 2548; Pub. L. 103–337, div. A, title IX, § 901(b), Oct. 5, 1994, 108 Stat. 2822; Pub. L. 103–354, title II, §§ 218(d), 232(b)(3), Oct. 13, 1994, 108 Stat. 3212, 3219; Pub. L. 104–88, title III, § 301(b), Dec. 29, 1995, 109 Stat. 943; Pub. L. 104–105, title II, § 219(b)(2), Feb. 10, 1996, 110 Stat. 184; Pub. L. 104–106, div. A, title IX, § 902(b), div. E, title LI, § 5125(e), Feb. 10, 1996, 110 Stat. 401, 686; Pub. L. 104–127, title VII, § 723(b), Apr. 4, 1996, 110 Stat. 1119; Pub. L. 104–208, div. A, title I, § 101(e) [title VII, § 709(b)(1)], (f) [title VI, § 662(c)(1)], Sept. 30, 1996, 110 Stat. 3009–233, 3009–313, 3009–314, 3009–380; Pub. L. 104–293, title VIII, §§ 812(b), 813(c), Oct. 11, 1996, 110 Stat. 3482, 3483; Pub. L. 105–85, div. A, title X, § 1073(e)(1), div. C, title XXXV, § 3550(b), Nov. 18, 1997, 111 Stat. 1906, 2074; Pub. L. 105–245, title III, § 309(b)(2)(A), Oct. 7, 1998, 112 Stat. 1853; Pub. L. 105–261, div. A, title IX, § 901(b), Oct. 17, 1998, 112 Stat. 2091; Pub. L. 105–277, div. A, § 101(a) [title X, § 1003], div. G, subdiv. A, title XII, § 1224(3), title XIII, §§ 1314(c), 1332(2), subdiv. B, title XXIII, § 2305(b)(2), Oct. 21, 1998, 112 Stat. 2681, 2681–42, 2681–772, 2681–776, 2681–785, 2681–825; Pub. L. 105–368, title IV, § 403(b)(2), Nov. 11, 1998, 112 Stat. 3338; Pub. L. 106–65, div. C, title XXXII, §§ 3293(b), 3294(a)(1), Oct. 5, 1999, 113 Stat. 969, 970; Pub. L. 106–113, div. B, §§ 1000(a)(5) [title II, § 238(a)(1)], 1000(a)(9) [title IV, § 4720(b)], Nov. 29, 1999, 113 Stat. 1536, 1501A–302, 1501A–581; Pub. L. 106–422, § 1(c), Nov. 1, 2000, 114 Stat. 1872.)

HISTORICAL AND REVISION NOTES
1966 ACT

Derivation	U.S. Code	Revised Statutes and Statutes at Large
(1)–(69)	5 U.S.C. 2211(d).	Aug. 14, 1964, Pub. L. 88–426, § 303(d), 78 Stat. 417.
(70), (71)	5 U.S.C. 2211(c)(39) (proviso), (46) (proviso).	Aug. 14, 1964, Pub. L. 88–426, § 303(c)(39) (proviso), (46) (proviso), 78 Stat. 417.
(72)–(77)	5 U.S.C. 2211(g).	Aug. 14, 1964, Pub. L. 88–426, § 303(g), 78 Stat. 422.

Paragraphs (72)–(77) are added on authority of former section 2211(g) which authorized the President to place, from Aug. 15, 1964, to Feb. 1, 1965, not more than 30 positions in Levels IV and V of the Federal Executive Salary Schedule. Pursuant to this authority, the President by Executive Order No. 11189, Nov. 23, 1964, as amended by Executive Order No. 11195, Jan. 30, 1965, placed the positions listed in paragraphs (72)–(77) in Level IV.

Standard changes are made to conform with the definitions applicable and the style of this title as outlined in the preface to the report.

1967 ACT

Section of title 5	Source (U.S. Code)	Source (Statutes at Large)
5315(12)	5 App.: 2211(d)(12).	Aug. 26, 1965, Pub. L. 89–136, §601(b), 79 Stat. 569.
5315(17)	5 App.: 2211(d)(17).	Aug. 9, 1965, Pub. L. 89–115, §4(c) (words before semicolon), 79 Stat. 449.
		Oct. 2, 1965, Pub. L. 89–234, §1(b) (last sentence), 79 Stat. 903.
	[Uncodified].	1966 Reorg. Plan No. 2, §5(a), eff. May 10, 1966, 80 Stat. 1609.
5315(18)	[Uncodified].	1966 Reorg. Plan No. 2, §2 (last 20 words), eff. May 10, 1966, 80 Stat. 1609.
5315(21)	5 App.: 2211(d)(21).	July 5, 1966, Pub. L. 89–492, §3, 80 Stat. 262.
5315(30)	5 App.: 2211(d)(30).	July 18, 1966, Pub. L. 89–504, §408(b), 80 Stat. 299.
5315(87), (88).	42: 3533(a) (as applicable to compensation of four Assistant Secretaries and General Counsel).	Sept. 9, 1965, Pub. L. 89–174, §4(a) (as applicable to compensation of four Assistant Secretaries and General Counsel), 79 Stat. 668.
5315(89)	22: 2083(a) (1st sentence, less 1st 20 words).	Feb. 19, 1966, Pub. L. 89–355, §3(a) (1st sentence, less 1st 20 words), 80 Stat. 6.

The deletion of paragraphs (25)–(28) of 5 U.S.C. 5315 reflects the abolition of the positions of "Commissioner, Community Facilities Administration", "Commissioner, Federal Housing Administration", "Commissioner, Public Housing Administration", and "Commissioner, Urban Renewal Administration" by the act of September 9, 1965, Public Law 89–174, sections 5(a), 9(c), 79 Stat. 669, 671.

The redesignation of paragraphs (78) and (79), added by Public Law 89–734, and of paragraph (78), added by Public Law 89–779, as paragraphs "(84)", "(85)", and "(86)", respectively, reflects the addition of paragraphs (78)–(83) by section 10(d)(4) of Public Law 89–670.

CODIFICATION

Pub. L. 99–591 is a corrected version of Pub. L. 99–500.

The paragraph designation for the positions added or amended by Pub. L. 96–88 and Pub. L. 96–302 has been omitted in view of the deletion of all paragraph designations in this section by Pub. L. 96–54.

Amendment by Pub. L. 94–237 to formerly designated par. (95) of this section has been editorially made to formerly designated par. (96) of this section relating to the Deputy Director, Office of Drug Abuse Policy, in view of redesignation of par. (95) as (96) by Pub. L. 94–183 as the probable intent of Congress.

AMENDMENTS

2000—Pub. L. 106–422 inserted item relating to Inspector General, Tennessee Valley Authority.

1999—Pub. L. 106–113, §1000(a)(9) [title IV, §4720(b)], inserted item relating to Deputy Under Secretary of Commerce for Intellectual Property and Deputy Director of the United States Patent and Trademark Office.

Pub. L. 106–113, §1000(a)(5) [title II, §238(a)(1)], struck out "Commissioner of Customs, Department of the Treasury".

Pub. L. 106–65, §3294(a)(1), substituted "(6)" for "(8)" in item relating to Assistant Secretaries of Energy.

Pub. L. 106–65, §3293(b), inserted item relating to Deputy Administrators of the National Nuclear Security Administration.

1998—Pub. L. 105–368 struck out item relating to Director of the National Cemetery System.

Pub. L. 105–277, §2305(b)(2), which directed the substitution of "Assistant Secretaries of State (24)" for "Assistant Secretaries of State (20)", was executed by making the substitution for "20 Assistant Secretaries of State" in item relating to Assistant Secretaries of State and 4 other State Department officials to be appointed by the President, by and with the advice and consent of the Senate, to reflect the probable intent of Congress.

Pub. L. 105–277, §1332(2), struck out item relating to Deputy Director of the United States Information Agency and substituted "Director of the International Broadcasting Bureau." for "Director of the International Broadcasting Bureau, the United States Information Agency."

Pub. L. 105–277, §1314(c), struck out item relating to Inspector General, United States Information Agency.

Pub. L. 105–277, §1224(3), struck out item relating to Assistant Directors, United States Arms Control and Disarmament Agency (4) and substituted "Special Representatives of the President for arms control, nonproliferation, and disarmament matters, Department of State" for "Special Representatives of the President for arms control, nonproliferation, and disarmament matters, United States Arms Control and Disarmament Agency".

Pub. L. 105–277, §101(a) [title X, §1003], substituted "Assistant Secretaries of Agriculture (2)" for "Assistant Secretaries of Agriculture (3)".

Pub. L. 105–261 substituted "(9)" for "(10)" in item relating to Assistant Secretaries of Defense.

Pub. L. 105–245 substituted "Director, Office of Science, Department of Energy" for "Director, Office of Energy Research, Department of Energy".

1997—Pub. L. 105–85, §3550(b), struck out item relating to Administrator of the Panama Canal Commission.

Pub. L. 105–85, §1073(e)(1), inserted "the" before "Interior" in item relating to Chief Information Officer of Department of the Interior and before "Treasury" in item relating to Chief Information Officer of Department of the Treasury.

1996—Pub. L. 104–293 inserted items relating to Assistant Directors of Central Intelligence and General Counsel of Central Intelligence Agency.

Pub. L. 104–208, §101(f) [title VI, §662(c)(1)], inserted item relating to Inspector General, United States Postal Service.

Pub. L. 104–208, §101(e) [title VII, §709(b)(1)], substituted "Museum and Library Services" for "Museum Services" after "Director of the Institute of".

Pub. L. 104–127 inserted item relating to Executive Director of the Alternative Agricultural Research and Commercialization Corporation.

Pub. L. 104–106, §5125(e), inserted items relating to Chief Information Officer of Departments of Agriculture, Commerce, Defense, Education, Energy, Health and Human Services, Housing and Urban Development, Interior, Justice, Labor, State, Transportation, Treasury, and Veterans Affairs and Chief Information Officer of Environmental Protection Agency, National Aeronautics and Space Administration, Agency for International Development, Federal Emergency Management Agency, General Services Administration, National Science Foundation, Nuclear Regulatory Agency, Office of Personnel Management, and Small Business Administration.

Pub. L. 104–106, §902(b), substituted "(10)" for "(11)" in item relating to Assistant Secretaries of Defense.

Pub. L. 104–105 struck out item relating to Members, Board of Directors of the Farm Credit System Insurance Corporation.

1995—Pub. L. 104–88 substituted "Members, Surface Transportation Board" for "Members, Interstate Commerce Commission".

1994—Pub. L. 103–354 substituted "(3)" for "(7)" in item relating to Assistant Secretaries of Agriculture and inserted item relating to Administrator, Rural Utilities Service, Department of Agriculture.

Pub. L. 103–337 substituted "(11)" for "(10)" in item relating to Assistant Secretaries of Defense.

Pub. L. 103–333 inserted item relating to Commissioner of Labor Statistics, Department of Labor.

Pub. L. 103–296, §108(e)(3), inserted item relating to Inspector General, Social Security Administration.

Pub. L. 103–296, §106(a)(7)(B), struck out item relating to Commissioner of Social Security, Department of Health and Human Services.

Pub. L. 103–272 substituted "Saint" for "St." in item relating to Administrator of Saint Lawrence Seaway Development Corporation.

Pub. L. 103–236, § 708(b), substituted "Special Representatives of the President for arms control, nonproliferation, and disarmament matters, United States Arms Control and Disarmament Agency" for "Special Representatives for Arms Control and Disarmament Negotiations, United States Arms Control and Disarmament Agency (2)".

Pub. L. 103–236, § 307(b)(2), inserted item relating to Director of the International Broadcasting Bureau, United States Information Agency.

Pub. L. 103–236, § 162(d)(2), directed insertion of item relating to 20 Assistant Secretaries of State and 4 other State Department Officials to be appointed by the President, and struck out "Assistant Secretaries of State (15).", "Legal Adviser of the Department of State.", "Chief of Protocol, Department of State.", "Assistant Secretary for Oceans and International Environmental and Scientific Affairs, Department of State.", "Assistant Secretary for International Narcotics Matters, Department of State.", and "Assistant Secretary for South Asian Affairs, Department of State." New item was inserted in lieu of "Assistant Secretaries of State (15)." to reflect the probable intent of Congress.

Pub. L. 103–227 inserted item relating to Director of the Office of Educational Technology.

1993—Pub. L. 103–204 inserted item relating to Inspector General, Federal Deposit Insurance Corporation.

Pub. L. 103–171 substituted "(6)" for "(5)" in item relating to Assistant Secretaries of Health and Human Services.

Pub. L. 103–160 substituted "(10)" for "(11)" in item relating to Assistant Secretaries of Defense and struck out item relating to Chief Financial Officer, Department of Defense.

Pub. L. 103–123 inserted item relating to Commissioner of Customs, Department of the Treasury.

1992—Pub. L. 102–552 inserted item relating to Members, Board of Directors of the Farm Credit System Insurance Corporation.

Pub. L. 102–359 substituted "(10)" for "(6)" in item relating to Assistant Secretaries of Education.

Pub. L. 102–325 inserted item relating to Liaison for Community and Junior Colleges, Department of Education.

1991—Pub. L. 102–190, § 3504(a), inserted item relating to Administrator of the Panama Canal Commission.

Pub. L. 102–190, § 903(a)(1), inserted items relating to General Counsels of the Departments of the Army, Navy, and Air Force.

Pub. L. 102–190, § 901(b), inserted item relating to Deputy Under Secretary of Defense for Policy.

Pub. L. 102–183 inserted item relating to Inspector General of Central Intelligence Agency.

Pub. L. 102–180 inserted item relating to Commissioner, Office of Navajo and Hopi Indian Relocation.

Pub. L. 102–138 inserted item relating to Assistant Secretary for South Asian Affairs, Department of State.

1990—Pub. L. 101–576 inserted items relating to Chief Financial Officer of Departments of Agriculture, Commerce, Defense, Education, Energy, Health and Human Services, Housing and Urban Development, the Interior, Justice, Labor, State, Transportation, the Treasury, and Veterans Affairs and Chief Financial Officers of Environmental Protection Agency and National Aeronautics and Space Administration.

Pub. L. 101–512 inserted item relating to Director of the Institute of Museum Services.

Pub. L. 101–509 inserted item relating to Director, Bureau of the Census, Department of Commerce.

Pub. L. 101–319 inserted item relating to Chairman, United States Parole Commission.

1989—Pub. L. 101–189 substituted "(4)" for "(3)" in item relating to Assistant Secretaries of the Air Force.

Pub. L. 101–73, § 742(a)(2), substituted "Directors, Federal Housing Finance Board" for "Members, Federal Home Loan Bank Board".

Pub. L. 101–73, § 501(b)(2)(A), inserted item relating to Inspector General, Resolution Trust Corporation.

1988—Pub. L. 100–690, § 7608(e), inserted item relating to Director, United States Marshals Service.

Pub. L. 100–690, § 7252(b)(3), inserted item relating to Administrator, Office of Juvenile Justice and Delinquency Prevention.

Pub. L. 100–690, § 1007(c)(4), struck out item relating to Deputy Director of Office of Drug Abuse Policy.

Pub. L. 100–690, §§ 1003(a)(4)(C), 1009, temporarily inserted item relating to Associate Director for National Drug Control Policy, Office of National Drug Control Policy. See Effective and Termination Dates of 1988 Amendments note below.

Pub. L. 100–687 inserted item relating to Chairman, Board of Veterans' Appeals.

Pub. L. 100–679 struck out items relating to Administrator for Federal Procurement Policy and Administrator, Office of Information and Regulatory Affairs, Office of Management and Budget.

Pub. L. 100–607 inserted item relating to Commissioner of Food and Drugs, Department of Health and Human Services.

Pub. L. 100–527 substituted "Inspector General, Department of Veterans Affairs" for "Inspector General, Veterans' Administration" and inserted items relating to Assistant Secretaries, Department of Veterans Affairs (6), General Counsel, Department of Veterans Affairs, and Director of the National Cemetery System.

Pub. L. 100–504 inserted items relating to Inspector General for Departments of Commerce, Interior, Justice, and Treasury and for following agencies: Agency for International Development, Environmental Protection Agency, Federal Emergency Management Agency, General Services Administration, National Aeronautics and Space Administration, Nuclear Regulatory Commission, Office of Personnel Management, Railroad Retirement Board, and Small Business Administration.

Pub. L. 100–485 substituted "(5)" for "(4)" in item relating to Assistant Secretaries of Health and Human Services.

Pub. L. 100–418, § 5112(c)(2), substituted "Director, National Institute of Standards and Technology, Department of Commerce" for "Director, National Bureau of Standards, Department of Commerce".

Pub. L. 100–418, § 2301(h), inserted item relating to Assistant Secretary of Commerce and Director General of United States and Foreign Commercial Service.

Pub. L. 100–297 inserted item relating to Commissioner, National Center for Education Statistics.

1987—Pub. L. 100–204 inserted item relating to Ambassadors at Large.

1986—Pub. L. 99–619 substituted "Assistant Secretaries of Labor (10), one of whom shall be the Assistant Secretary of Labor for Veterans' Employment and Training" for "Assistant Secretaries of Labor (5)".

Pub. L. 99–659 substituted "Assistant Secretary of Commerce for Oceans and Atmosphere, the incumbent of which also serves as Deputy Administrator of the National Oceanic and Atmospheric Administration" for "Deputy Administrator, National Oceanic and Atmospheric Administration" and struck out item relating to Associate Administrator, National Oceanic and Atmospheric Administration.

Pub. L. 99–500, Pub. L. 99–591, and Pub. L. 99–661, amended section identically, inserting item relating to Director of Defense Research and Engineering.

Pub. L. 99–399, § 104(c), substituted "(15)" for "(14)" in item relating to Assistant Secretaries of State.

Pub. L. 99–399, §§ 412(c), 413(e), formerly § 413(a)(5), as renumbered by Pub. L. 100–204, § 134(b), inserted items relating to Inspector General, United States Information Agency, and Inspector General, Department of State.

1985—Pub. L. 99–93, § 704(a)(2)(A), struck out item relating to Deputy Director of United States Arms Control and Disarmament Agency.

Pub. L. 99–93, § 704(a)(2)(B), inserted item relating to Assistant Directors, United States Arms Control and Disarmament Agency (4).

Pub. L. 99–93, § 115(b)(1), struck out item relating to Director, Bureau of Intelligence and Research, Department of State.

Pub. L. 99–93, § 115(b)(2), substituted "(14)" for "(13)" in item relating to Assistant Secretaries of State.

Pub. L. 99–73 inserted item relating to Director, National Bureau of Standards, Department of Commerce.

Pub. L. 99–64 substituted "(11)" for "(8)" in item relating to Assistant Secretaries of Commerce.

1984—Pub. L. 98–594 substituted "(7)" for "(5)" in item relating to Assistant Secretaries of the Treasury.

Pub. L. 98–473, § 1701(b), struck out items relating to United States Attorney for Southern District of New York, United States Attorney for District of Columbia, United States Attorney for Northern District of Illinois, and United States Attorney for Central District of California.

Pub. L. 98–473, § 609J(b), struck out item relating to Administrator of Law Enforcement Assistance.

Pub. L. 98–443 struck out item relating to members of Civil Aeronautics Board.

Pub. L. 98–369 inserted item relating to Administrator of Health Care Financing Administration.

Pub. L. 98–216 substituted "Assistant Directors of Office of Management and Budget (3)" for "Assistant Directors of the Bureau of the Budget (3)".

1983—Pub. L. 98–202, § 6(b)(1), inserted item relating to two Special Representatives for Arms Control and Disarmament Negotiations, United States Arms Control and Disarmament Agency.

Pub. L. 98–202, § 6(b)(2), struck out item relating to Special Representative for Arms Control and Disarmament Negotiations, United States Arms Control and Disarmament Agency.

Pub. L. 98–164 struck out item relating to Counselor of Department of State.

Pub. L. 98–94, § 1212(d)(1), substituted "(11)" for "(7)" in item relating to Assistant Secretaries of Defense.

Pub. L. 98–94, § 1212(d)(2), substituted "(5)" for "(4)" in item relating to Assistant Secretaries of the Army.

Pub. L. 98–94, § 1212(d)(3), substituted "(4)" for "(3)" in item relating to Assistant Secretaries of the Navy.

Pub. L. 98–94, § 1211(b), inserted item relating to Director of Operational Test and Evaluation, Department of Defense.

Pub. L. 98–80 inserted items relating to Assistant Administrator for Toxic Substances, Environmental Protection Agency, Assistant Administrator, Office of Solid Waste, Environmental Protection Agency, and eight Assistant Administrators, Environmental Protection Agency.

Pub. L. 97–449 substituted "Deputy Federal Highway Administrator" for "Director of Public Roads".

1982—Pub. L. 97–325 substituted "(7)" for "(6)" in item relating to Assistant Secretaries of Agriculture.

Pub. L. 97–252 inserted item relating to Inspector General, Department of Defense.

Pub. L. 97–195 substituted "(8)" for "(7)" in item relating to Assistant Secretaries of Commerce.

1981—Pub. L. 97–98 substituted "(6)" for "(5)" in item relating to Assistant Secretaries of Agriculture.

Pub. L. 97–35 struck out item relating to Director, Office of Self-Help Development and Technical Assistance, National Consumer Cooperative Bank.

Pub. L. 97–31 substituted "(7)" for "(8)" in item relating to Assistant Secretaries of Commerce.

1980—Pub. L. 96–511 inserted item relating to Administrator, Office of Information and Regulatory Affairs, Office of Management and Budget.

Pub. L. 96–302 inserted item relating to Chief Counsel for Advocacy, Small Business Administration.

1979—Pub. L. 96–157 inserted items relating to Administrator of Law Enforcement Assistance, Director of National Institute of Justice, and Director of Bureau of Justice Statistics, and struck out items relating to Deputy Administrator for Policy Development and Deputy Administrator for Administration of Law Enforcement Assistance Administration.

Pub. L. 96–88, § 508(g), substituted "Health and Human Services" for "Health, Education, and Welfare" in

items relating to General Counsel of Department of Health and Human Services, Commissioner of Social Security, Department of Health and Human Services, and Inspector General, Department of Health and Human Services.

Pars. (1) to (128). Pub. L. 96–54 struck out paragraph designations for positions listed herein.

Pars. (13) to (16). Pub. L. 96–107 in par. (13), relating to Assistant Secretaries of Defense, substituted "(7)" for "(9)", par. (14), relating to Assistant Secretaries of the Air Force, "(3)" for "(4)", par. (15), relating to Assistant Secretaries of the Army, "(4)" for "(5)", and par. (16), relating to Assistant Secretaries of the Navy, "(3)" for "(4)".

Par. (17). Pub. L. 96–88, § 508(e)(1), substituted "(4)" for "(5)" and "Health and Human Services" for "Health, Education, and Welfare" in par. (17) relating to Assistant Secretaries of Health and Human Services. See Codification note above.

Par. (19). Pub. L. 96–132 in par. (19), relating to Assistant Attorneys General, increased authorized number from nine to ten.

Par. (24). Pub. L. 96–39 inserted "(5)" at end of par. (24) relating to Members, United States International Trade Commission.

Pars. (25) to (27). Pub. L. 96–88, § 508(e)(2), added pars. (25) to (27) relating to Assistant Secretaries of Education (6), General Counsel, Department of Education, and Inspector General, Department of Education, respectively. See Codification note above.

Par. (91). Pub. L. 96–153 substituted "Federal Emergency Management Agency" for "Department of Housing and Urban Development" in par. (91), relating to Federal Insurance Administrator, Federal Emergency Management Agency.

Par. (128). Pub. L. 96–53 added par. (128) relating to Deputy Director, Institute for Scientific and Technological Cooperation.

1978—Par. (10). Pub. L. 95–426, § 114(b)(2), struck out par. (10) relating to Deputy Under Secretary of State.

Par. (66). Pub. L. 95–454, § 202(c)(2), substituted "Merit Systems Protection Board" for "United States Civil Service Commission".

Par. (93). Pub. L. 95–630 substituted "Members, National Credit Union Administration Board (2)" for "Administrator of the National Credit Union Administration".

Par. (122). Pub. L. 95–452 added par. (122) relating to Inspector General, Department of Health, Education, and Welfare.

Pub. L. 95–426, § 115(b)(1), added par. (122) relating to Assistant Secretary for International Narcotics Matters, Department of State.

Pub. L. 95–351 added par. (122) relating to President, National Consumer Cooperative Bank.

Par. (123). Pub. L. 95–454, § 202(c)(3), added par. (123) relating to Special Counsel of Merit Systems Protection Board.

Pub. L. 95–452 added par. (123) relating to Inspector General, Department of Agriculture.

Pub. L. 95–351 added par. (123) relating to Director, Office of Self-Help Development and Technical Assistance, National Consumer Cooperative Bank.

Par. (124). Pub. L. 95–454, § 703(d), added par. (124) relating to Chairman of Federal Labor Relations Authority.

Pub. L. 95–452 added par. (124) relating to Inspector General, Department of Housing and Urban Development.

Pars. (125) to (127). Pub. L. 95–452 added pars. (125) to (127) relating to Inspectors General for Department of Labor, Department of Transportation, and Veterans' Administration, respectively.

1977—Par. (1). Pub. L. 95–105, § 109(d)(1), struck out par. (1) relating to Administrator, Bureau of Security and Consular Affairs, Department of State.

Par. (12). Pub. L. 95–173 substituted "(8)" for "(6)" in par. (12) relating to Assistant Secretaries of Commerce.

Par. (22). Pub. L. 95–105, § 109(d)(2), substituted "(13)" for "(11)" in par. (22) relating to Assistant Secretaries of State.

Par. (50). Pub. L. 95–108 added par. (50) relating to Special Representative for Arms Control and Disarmament Negotiations, United States Arms Control and Disarmament Agency. A prior par. (50), relating to General Manager of Atomic Energy Commission, was repealed by Pub. L. 93–438, title III, § 310(3), Oct. 11, 1974, 88 Stat. 1253.

Pars. (52), (53). Pub. L. 95–88 struck out par. (52) relating to Inspector General, Foreign Assistance, and par. (53) relating to Deputy Inspector General, Foreign Assistance.

Par. (60). Pub. L. 95–91 substituted "Federal Energy Regulatory Commission" for "Federal Power Commission" in par. (60) relating to Members, Federal Energy Regulatory Commission.

Par. (102). Pub. L. 95–91 struck out par. (102) relating to Assistant Administrators, Energy Research and Development Administration (6).

Pars. (114) to (119). Pub. L. 95–91 added pars. (114) to (119) relating to Assistant Secretaries of Energy (8), General Counsel of Department of Energy, Administrator, Economic Regulatory Administration, Department of Energy, Administrator, Energy Information Administration, Department of Energy, Inspector General, Department of Energy, and Director, Office of Energy Research, Department of Energy, respectively.

Pars. (120), (121). Pub. L. 95–164 added pars. (120) and (121) relating to Assistant Secretary of Labor for Mine Safety and Health and Members, Federal Mine Safety and Health Review Commission, respectively.

1976—Par. (11). Pub. L. 94–561 substituted "(5)" for "(4)" in par. (11) relating to Assistant Secretaries of Agriculture.

Par. (96). Pub. L. 94–237 substituted "Deputy Director of the Office of Drug Abuse Policy" for "Deputy Director of the Special Action Office for Drug Abuse Prevention".

Par. (108). Pub. L. 94–375 added par. (108) relating to President, Government National Mortgage Association, Department of Housing and Urban Development.

Par. (109). Pub. L. 94–461 added par. (109) relating to Deputy Administrator, National Oceanic and Atmospheric Administration.

Pub. L. 94–503 added par. (109) relating to Commissioner of Immigration and Naturalization.

Par. (110). Pub. L. 94–461 added par. (110) relating to Associate Administrator, National Oceanic and Atmospheric Administration.

Pub. L. 94–503 added par. (110) relating to United States Attorney for Northern District of Illinois.

Pars. (111) to (113). Pub. L. 94–503 added pars. (111) to (113) relating to United States Attorney for Central District of California, Director, Bureau of Prisons, Department of Justice, and Deputy Administrator for Administration of the Law Enforcement Assistance Administration, respectively.

1975—Pub. L. 94–82 substituted provisions applying level IV of Executive Schedule to positions for which annual rate of basic pay shall be rate determined with respect to such level under chapter 11 of title 2, as adjusted by section 5318 of this title, for provisions applying such level IV to positions for which annual rate of basic pay is $28,750.

Par. (24). Pub. L. 93–618 substituted "Members, United States International Trade Commission" for "Chairman of the United States Tariff Commission".

Par. (31). Pub. L. 94–123 repealed par. (31) relating to Deputy Chief Medical Director in Department of Medicine and Surgery, Veterans' Administration.

Pars. (93) to (107). Pub. L. 94–183 redesignated par. (92) Administrator of the National Credit Union Administration, par. (93) Members, Postal Rate Commission, par. (94) Members, Occupational Safety and Health Review Commission, par. (95) Deputy Director of the Special Action Office for Drug Abuse Prevention, par. (96) Deputy Under Secretaries of the Treasury (or Assistant Secretaries of the Treasury), par. (97) Members, Consumer Product Safety Commission, par. (97) Commissioner of Social Security, Department of Health, Education, and Welfare, par. (99) Assistant Secretary for Oceans and International Environmental and Scientific Affairs, Department of State, par. (100) Administrator for Federal Procurement Policy, par. (100) Assistant Administrators, Energy Research and Development Administration, par. (100) Members, Commodity Futures Trading Commission, par. (101) Director of Nuclear Reactor Regulation, Nuclear Regulatory Commission, par. (102) Director of Nuclear Material Safety and Safeguards, Nuclear Regulatory Commission, par. (103) Director of Nuclear Regulatory Research, Nuclear Regulatory Commission, par. (104) Executive Director for Operations, Nuclear Regulatory Commission, as pars. (93) to (107), respectively.

1974—Par. (50). Pub. L. 93–438 struck out par. (50) relating to General Manager of Atomic Energy Commission.

Par. (87). Pub. L. 93–383 increased number of Assistant Secretaries of Housing and Urban Development from 6 to 8.

Par. (99). Pub. L. 93–126, § 9(b), as added by Pub. L. 93–312, added par. (99) relating to Assistant Secretary for Oceans and International Environmental and Scientific Affairs, Department of State.

Par. (100). Pub. L. 93–463 added par. (100) relating to Members, Commodity Futures Trading Commission.

Pub. L. 93–438 added par. (100) relating to Assistant Administrators, Energy Research and Development Administration.

Pub. L. 93–400 added par. (100) relating to Administrator for Federal Procurement Policy.

Pars. (101) to (104). Pub. L. 93–438 added pars. (101) to (104) relating to Director of Nuclear Reactor Regulation, Director of Nuclear Material Safety and Safeguards, Director of Nuclear Regulatory Research, and Executive Director for Operations, respectively, of Nuclear Regulatory Commission.

1973—Par. (90). Pub. L. 93–83 substituted "Deputy Administrator for Policy Development of the Law Enforcement Assistance Administration" for "Associate Administrator of Law Enforcement Assistance (2)".

1972—Par. (10). Pub. L. 92–352 substituted "Secretary of State" for "Secretaries of State (2)".

Par. (11). Pub. L. 92–419 substituted "(4)" for "(3)" in par. (11) relating to Assistant Secretaries of Agriculture.

Par. (23). Pub. L. 92–302, § 2(c)(1), substituted "(5)" for "(4)" in par. (23) relating to Assistant Secretaries of the Treasury.

Par. (72). Pub. L. 92–261 substituted "Members, Equal Employment Opportunity Commission (4)" for "Chairman, Equal Employment Opportunity Commission".

Par. (95). Pub. L. 92–255 added par. (95) relating to Deputy Director of Special Action Office for Drug Abuse Prevention.

Par. (96). Pub. L. 92–302, § 2(c)(2), added par. (96) relating to Deputy Under Secretaries of the Treasury (or Assistant Secretaries of the Treasury) (2).

Par. (97). Pub. L. 92–603 added par. (97) relating to Commissioner of Social Security, Department of Health, Education, and Welfare.

Pub. L. 92–573 added par. (97) relating to Members, Consumer Product Safety Commission (4).

1971—Par. (13). Pub. L. 92–215 substituted "(9)" for "(8)" in par. (13) relating to Assistant Secretaries of Defense.

Par. (18). Pub. L. 92–22 substituted "(6)" for "(5)" in par. (18) relating to Assistant Secretaries of the Interior.

Par. (51). Pub. L. 92–181 struck out par. (51) relating to Governor of Farm Credit Administration.

Par. (90). Pub. L. 91–644, § 7(1), (2), in amending section 505 of Pub. L. 90–351, struck out par. (90) "Administrator of Law Enforcement Assistance", renumbered as par. (55) of section 5314 of this title, and renumbered par. (126) "Associate Administrator of Law Enforcement Assistance (2)" of section 5316 of this title as par. (90) of this section, respectively.

1970—Par. (12). Pub. L. 91–477 substituted "(6)" for "(5)" in par. (12) relating to Assistant Secretaries of Commerce. Pub. L. 91–469 also substituted "(6)" for

"(5)" in par. (12). Thus, the correct figure in par. (12) presumably should be seven. See amendment of par. (12) by Pub. L. 95–173 above.

Par. (15). Pub. L. 91–611 substituted "(5)" for "(4)" in par. (15) relating to Assistant Secretaries of the Army.

Par. (20). Pub. L. 91–596, § 29(b), substituted "(5)" for "(4)" in par. (20) relating to Assistant Secretaries of Labor.

Pars. (21), (45). Pub. L. 91–375, § 6(c)(14)(A), struck out pars. (21) and (45) relating to Assistant Postmasters General (6) and General Counsel of Post Office Department, respectively.

Par. (92). Pub. L. 91–206 added par. (92) relating to Administrator of National Credit Union Administration.

Par. (93). Pub. L. 91–375, § 6(c)(14)(B), added par. (93) relating to Members, Postal Rate Commission (4).

Par. (94). Pub. L. 91–596, § 12(c)(2), added par. (94) relating to Members, Occupational Safety and Health Review Commission.

1969—Par. (13). Pub. L. 91–121 substituted "(8)" for "(7)" in par. (13) relating to Assistant Secretaries of Defense.

Par. (92). Pub. L. 91–175 added par. (92) relating to Executive Vice President, Overseas Private Investment Corporation.

1968—Pars. (14) to (16). Pub. L. 90–623 substituted "(4)" for "(3)" in pars. (14) to (16) relating to Assistant Secretaries of Air Force, Army, and Navy respectively.

Par. (87). Pub. L. 90–448, § 1708(b), substituted "(6)" for "(4)" in par. (87) relating to Assistant Secretaries of Housing and Urban Development.

Par. (90). Pub. L. 90–351 added par. (90) relating to Administrator of Law Enforcement Assistance.

Par. (91). Pub. L. 90–448, § 1105(b), added par. (91) relating to Federal Insurance Administrator, Department of Housing and Urban Development.

1967—Pub. L. 90–206 increased annual rate of basic pay from $27,000 to $28,750.

1966—Pub. L. 89–779 added par. (78) relating to Deputy Administrator of Small Business Administration.

Pub. L. 89–734 added par. (78) relating to Assistant Secretary for Science, Smithsonian Institution, and par. (79) relating to Assistant Secretary for History and Art, Smithsonian Institution.

Pub. L. 89–670 added par. (78) relating to Members, National Transportation Safety Board, par. (79) relating to General Counsel, Department of Transportation, and pars. (80) to (83), and repealed par. (2) which provided for Deputy Administrator of Federal Aviation Agency, subject to the provisions of section 1657 of former Title 49, Transportation.

CHANGE OF NAME

"Export-Import Bank of Washington", referred to in items relating to First Vice President and Members, was changed to "Export-Import Bank of the United States" in the Export-Import Bank Act of 1945, section 635 et seq. of Title 12, Banks and Banking, as provided for in section 1(a) of Pub. L. 90–267, Mar. 13, 1968, 82 Stat. 47.

EFFECTIVE DATE OF 2000 AMENDMENT

Amendment by Pub. L. 106–422 effective 30 days after Nov. 1, 2000, see section 1(d)(1) of Pub. L. 106–422, set out as a note under section 8G of Pub. L. 95–452 [Inspector General Act of 1978] in the Appendix to this title.

EFFECTIVE DATE OF 1999 AMENDMENTS

Amendment by section 1000(a)(5) [title II, § 238(a)(1)] of Pub. L. 106–113 effective Jan. 1, 2000, see section 1000(a)(5) [title II, § 238(b)] of Pub. L. 106–113, set out as a note under section 5314 of this title.

Amendment by section 1000(a)(9) [title IV, § 4720(b)] of Pub. L. 106–113 effective 4 months after Nov. 29, 1999, see section 1000(a)(9) [title IV, § 4731] of Pub. L. 106–113, set out as a note under section 1 of Title 35, Patents.

Amendment by Pub. L. 106–65 effective Mar. 1, 2000, see section 3299 of Pub. L. 106–65, set out as an Effective Date note under section 2401 of Title 50, War and National Defense.

EFFECTIVE DATE OF 1998 AMENDMENT

Amendment by section 1224(3) of Pub. L. 105–277 effective Apr. 1, 1999, see section 1201 of Pub. L. 105–277, set out as an Effective Date note under section 6511 of Title 22, Foreign Relations and Intercourse.

Amendment by sections 1314(c) and 1332(2) of Pub. L. 105–277 effective Oct. 1, 1999, see section 1301 of Pub. L. 105–277, set out as an Effective Date note under section 6531 of Title 22, Foreign Relations and Intercourse.

EFFECTIVE DATE OF 1996 AMENDMENT

Amendment by section 5125(e) of Pub. L. 104–106 effective 180 days after Feb. 10, 1996, see section 5701 of Pub. L. 104–106, set out as an Effective Date note under section 1401 of Title 40, Public Buildings, Property, and Works.

EFFECTIVE DATE OF 1995 AMENDMENT

Amendment by Pub. L. 104–88 effective Jan. 1, 1996, see section 2 of Pub. L. 104–88, set out as an Effective Date note under section 701 of Title 49, Transportation.

EFFECTIVE DATE OF 1994 AMENDMENT

Amendment by section 162(d)(2) of Pub. L. 103–236 applicable with respect to officials, offices, and bureaus of Department of State when executive orders, regulations, or departmental directives implementing the amendments by sections 161 and 162 of Pub. L. 103–236 become effective, or 90 days after Apr. 30, 1994, whichever comes earlier, see section 161(b) of Pub. L. 103–236, as amended, set out as a note under section 2651a of Title 22, Foreign Relations and Intercourse.

EFFECTIVE DATE OF 1993 AMENDMENT

Section 108(b) of Pub. L. 103–123 provided that: "The amendments made by this section [amending this section and section 5316 of this title] shall take effect on the first applicable pay period after enactment [Oct. 28, 1993]."

EFFECTIVE DATE OF 1992 AMENDMENTS

Amendment by Pub. L. 102–552 effective Jan. 1, 1996, see section 201(c)(1) of Pub. L. 102–552, set out as an Effective Date of 1992 Amendment; Transitional Provision note under section 2277a–2 of Title 12, Banks and Banking.

Section 2(b)(3) of Pub. L. 102–359 provided that: "The amendments made by paragraphs (1) and (2) [amending this section and section 5316 of this title] shall take effect on the first day of the first pay period that begins on or after the date of the enactment of this Act [Aug. 26, 1992]."

Amendment by Pub. L. 102–325 effective Oct. 1, 1992, see section 2 of Pub. L. 102–325, set out as a note under section 1001 of Title 20, Education.

EFFECTIVE DATE OF 1991 AMENDMENT

Section 122(d)(2) of Pub. L. 102–138 provided that: "The amendment made by paragraph (1) [amending this section] shall take effect on October 1, 1991."

EFFECTIVE DATE OF 1990 AMENDMENTS

Amendment by Pub. L. 101–512 effective Oct. 1, 1990, see section 318 [title IV, § 403(a)] of Pub. L. 101–512, set out as a note under section 951 of Title 20, Education.

Amendment by Pub. L. 101–509 effective on such date as the President shall determine, but not earlier than 90 days, and not later than 180 days, after Nov. 5, 1990, see section 529 [title III, § 305] of Pub. L. 101–509, set out as a note under section 5301 of this title.

EFFECTIVE AND TERMINATION DATES OF 1988 AMENDMENTS

Amendment by sections 1003(a)(4)(C) and 1007(c)(4) of Pub. L. 100–690 effective Jan. 21, 1989, and amendment by section 1003(a)(4)(C) of Pub. L. 100–690 repealed on Sept. 30, 1997, see sections 1012 and 1009, respectively, of Pub. L. 100–690.

Amendment by section 7252(b)(3) of Pub. L. 100–690 effective Oct. 1, 1988, see section 7296(a) of Pub. L. 100–690, set out as a note under section 5601 of Title 42, The Public Health and Welfare.

Section 201(b)(2) of Pub. L. 100–687 provided that: "The amendment made by paragraph (1) [amending this section] shall take effect when the President first appoints an individual as Chairman of the Board of Veterans' Appeals under section 4001(b)(1) [now 7101(b)(1)] of title 38, United States Code (as amended by subsection (a))."

Amendment by Pub. L. 100–679 effective Jan. 20, 1989, see section 11(e) of Pub. L. 100–679, set out as a note under section 5312 of this title.

Amendment by Pub. L. 100–527 effective Mar. 15, 1989, see section 18(a) of Pub. L. 100–527, set out as a Department of Veterans Affairs Act note under section 301 of Title 38, Veterans' Benefits.

Amendment by Pub. L. 100–504 effective 180 days after Oct. 18, 1988, see section 113 of Pub. L. 100–504, set out as a note under section 5 of Pub. L. 95–452 [Inspector General Act of 1978] in the Appendix to this title.

Section 603(c) of Pub. L. 100–485 provided that: "The amendments made by this section [amending this section and enacting section 617 of Title 42, The Public Health and Welfare] shall become effective on February 1, 1989."

Amendment by Pub. L. 100–297 effective July 1, 1988, but with amendments authorizing appropriations for fiscal year 1988 effective Apr. 28, 1988, see section 6303 of Pub. L. 100–297, set out as an Effective Date of 1988 Amendment note under section 1071 of Title 20, Education.

EFFECTIVE DATE OF 1987 AMENDMENT

Amendment by Pub. L. 100–204 effective 30 days after Dec. 22, 1987, but not to affect salary of any individual holding rank of Ambassador at Large immediately before Dec. 22, 1987, during the period such individual continues to serve in such position, see section 178(b) of Pub. L. 100–204, set out as a note under section 5313 of this title.

EFFECTIVE DATE OF 1986 AMENDMENT

Amendment by Pub. L. 99–619 applicable to incumbent Assistant Secretary of Labor for Veterans' Employment on Nov. 6, 1986, serving after such date, see section 2(f)(2) of Pub. L. 99–619, set out as a Present Incumbent note under section 553 of Title 29, Labor.

EFFECTIVE DATE OF 1985 AMENDMENTS

Section 6(c) of Pub. L. 99–73 provided that: "The amendments made by this section [amending this section and section 5316 of this title and section 274 of Title 15, Commerce and Trade] shall be effective October 1, 1985."

Amendment by Pub. L. 99–64 effective Oct. 1, 1987, see section 116(d) of Pub. L. 99–64, set out as a note under section 5314 of this title.

EFFECTIVE DATE OF 1984 AMENDMENTS

Amendment by section 609J of Pub. L. 98–473 effective Oct. 12, 1984, see section 609AA of Pub. L. 98–473, set out as an Effective Date note under section 3711 of Title 42, The Public Health and Welfare.

Amendment by Pub. L. 98–443 effective Jan. 1, 1985, see section 9(v) of Pub. L. 98–443, set out as a note under section 5314 of this title.

Amendment by Pub. L. 98–369 applicable to appointments made after July 18, 1984, see section 2332(c) of Pub. L. 98–369, set out as an Effective Date note under section 1317 of Title 42, The Public Health and Welfare.

EFFECTIVE DATE OF 1983 AMENDMENT

Amendment by section 1211(b) of Pub. L. 98–94 effective Nov. 1, 1983, see section 1211(c) of Pub. L. 98–94, set out as an Effective Date note under section 139 of Title 10, Armed Forces.

Amendment by section 1212(d) of Pub. L. 98–94 effective Oct. 1, 1983, see section 1212(e) of Pub. L. 98–94, set out as a note under section 138 of Title 10.

EFFECTIVE DATE OF 1982 AMENDMENT

Amendment by Pub. L. 97–325 effective Oct. 15, 1982, see section 8(e) of Pub. L. 97–325.

EFFECTIVE DATE OF 1981 AMENDMENTS

Amendment by Pub. L. 97–98 effective Dec. 22, 1981, see section 1801 of Pub. L. 97–98, set out as an Effective Date note under section 4301 of Title 7, Agriculture.

Amendment by Pub. L. 97–35 effective on day after Final Government Equity Redemption Date, see section 396(i) of Pub. L. 97–35, set out as a note under section 3011 of Title 12, Banks and Banking.

EFFECTIVE DATE OF 1980 AMENDMENTS

Amendment by Pub. L. 96–511 effective Apr. 1, 1981, see section 5 of Pub. L. 96–511, set out as a note under section 2904 of Title 44, Public Printing and Documents.

Amendment by Pub. L. 96–302 effective Oct. 1, 1980, see section 507 of Pub. L. 96–302, set out as a note under section 631 of Title 15, Commerce and Trade.

EFFECTIVE DATE OF 1979 AMENDMENTS

Amendment by Pub. L. 96–88 effective May 4, 1980, with specified exceptions, see section 601 of Pub. L. 96–88, set out as an Effective Date note under section 3401 of Title 20, Education.

Amendment by Pub. L. 96–54 effective Jan. 1, 1980, see section 2(a)(25)(B) of Pub. L. 96–54, set out as a note under section 5312 of this title.

Amendment by Pub. L. 96–53 effective Oct. 1, 1979, see section 512(a) of Pub. L. 96–53, set out as a note under section 2151 of Title 22, Foreign Relations and Intercourse.

Amendment by Pub. L. 96–39 effective July 26, 1979, see section 1114 of Pub. L. 96–39, set out as an Effective Date note under section 2581 of Title 19, Customs Duties.

EFFECTIVE DATE OF 1978 AMENDMENTS

Amendment by Pub. L. 95–630 effective on expiration of 120 days after Nov. 10, 1978, see section 509 of Pub. L. 95–630, set out as a note under section 1752 of Title 12, Banks and Banking.

Amendment by Pub. L. 95–454 effective 90 days after Oct. 13, 1978, see section 907 of Pub. L. 95–454, set out as a note under section 1101 of this title.

Amendment by Pub. L. 95–452 effective Oct. 1, 1978, see section 12 of Pub. L. 95–452 set out in the Appendix to this title.

Amendment by section 114(b)(2) of Pub. L. 95–426 effective Oct. 1, 1978, see section 114(c) of Pub. L. 95–426, set out as a note under section 5314 of this title.

Section 115(b)(2) of Pub. L. 95–426 provided that: "The amendment made by paragraph (1) of this subsection [amending this section] shall take effect on October 1, 1978."

EFFECTIVE DATE OF 1977 AMENDMENTS

Amendment by Pub. L. 95–164 effective 120 days after Nov. 9, 1977, except as otherwise provided, see section 307 of Pub. L. 95–164, set out as a note under section 801 of Title 30, Mineral Lands and Mining.

Amendment by Pub. L. 95–88 effective July 1, 1978, see section 124(c) of Pub. L. 95–88, set out as a note under section 2384 of Title 22, Foreign Relations and Intercourse.

EFFECTIVE DATE OF 1975 AMENDMENT

Amendment by Pub. L. 94–123 effective Oct. 12, 1975, see section 6(a) of Pub. L. 94–123, set out as a note under section 5314 of this title.

EFFECTIVE DATE OF 1974 AMENDMENTS

Amendment by Pub. L. 93–463 effective Oct. 23, 1974, see section 418 of Pub. L. 93–463, set out as a note under section 2 of Title 7, Agriculture.

Amendment by Pub. L. 93–438 effective 120 days after Oct. 11, 1974, or on such earlier date as President may prescribe and publish in Federal Register, except that officers provided for in sections 5811–5820 of Title 42, The Public Health and Welfare, may be nominated and appointed at any time after Oct. 11, 1974, see section 312(a) of Pub. L. 93–438, set out as an Effective Date; Interim Appointments note under section 5801 of Title 42.

EFFECTIVE DATE OF 1973 AMENDMENT

Offices and salaries modified under amendment by Pub. L. 93–83, prospectively only, effective on and after Aug. 6, 1973, see section 3 of Pub. L. 93–83, Aug. 6, 1973, 83 Stat. 218.

EFFECTIVE DATE OF 1972 AMENDMENTS

Section 404(c) of Pub. L. 92–603 provided that: "The amendments made by the preceding provisions of this section [amending this section and section 5316 of this title] shall take effect on the first day of the first pay period of the Commissioner of Social Security, Department of Health, Education, and Welfare, which commences on or after the first day of the month which follows the month in which this Act is enacted [Oct. 30, 1972]."

Amendment by Pub. L. 92–302 effective May 18, 1972, see section 3 of Pub. L. 92–302, May 18, 1972, 86 Stat. 149.

EFFECTIVE DATE OF 1970 AMENDMENT

Amendment by Pub. L. 91–375 effective within 1 year after Aug. 12, 1970, on date established therefor by Board of Governors of United States Postal Service and published by it in Federal Register, see section 15(a) of Pub. L. 91–375, set out as an Effective Date note preceding section 101 of Title 39, Postal Service.

EFFECTIVE DATE OF 1968 AMENDMENT

Amendment by Pub. L. 90–623 intended to restate without substantive change the law in effect on Oct. 22, 1968, see section 6 of Pub. L. 90–623, set out as a note under section 5334 of this title.

EFFECTIVE DATE OF 1967 AMENDMENT

Amendment by Pub. L. 90–206 effective at beginning of first pay period which begins on or after Dec. 16, 1967, see section 220(a)(3) of Pub. L. 90–206, set out as a note under section 603 of Title 28, Judiciary and Judicial Procedure.

EFFECTIVE DATE OF 1966 AMENDMENT

Amendment by Pub. L. 89–670 effective Apr. 1, 1967, as prescribed by President and published in Federal Register, see section 16(a), formerly § 15(a), of Pub. L. 89–670 and Ex. Ord. No. 11340, Mar. 30, 1967, 32 F.R. 5453.

REPEALS

Pub. L. 93–496, § 16(c), Oct. 28, 1974, 88 Stat. 1533, cited as a credit to this section, was repealed by Pub. L. 97–449, § 7(b), Jan. 12, 1983, 96 Stat. 2444.

TRANSFER OF FUNCTIONS

Office of Emergency Preparedness, including offices of Director, Deputy Director, Assistant Directors, and Regional Directors, abolished and functions, vested by law in Office of Emergency Preparedness or Director of Office of Emergency Preparedness transferred to President by sections 1 and 3(a)(1) of 1973 Reorg. Plan No. 1, effective July 1, 1973, set out in the Appendix to this title.

Office of Deputy Director of Office of Science and Technology abolished and functions vested by law in such office transferred to Director of National Science Foundation by sections 2 and 3(a)(5) of 1973 Reorg. Plan No. 1, effective July 1, 1973, set out in the Appendix to this title.

ABOLITION OF ONE POSITION OF ASSISTANT ADMINISTRATOR, AGENCY FOR INTERNATIONAL DEVELOPMENT

One of the 6 positions of Assistant Administrator, Agency for International Development, provided for in this section, was abolished by Reorg. Plan No. 2 of 1979, § 7, 44 F.R. 41165, 93 Stat. 1378, set out in the Appendix to this title.

INSPECTOR GENERAL, UNITED STATES POSTAL SERVICE

Section 101(f) [title VI, § 662(c)(1)] of Pub. L. 104–208 provided in part that: "The amendment made by the preceding sentence [amending this section] shall apply notwithstanding section 410 or any other provision of title 39, United States Code."

COMPENSATION OF DEPUTY ADMINISTRATOR OF DRUG ENFORCEMENT ADMINISTRATION

Section 6153(c) of Pub. L. 100–690 provided that: "The Deputy Administrator of the Drug Enforcement Administration shall receive compensation at the rate now or hereafter prescribed by law for positions of Level IV of the Executive Schedule Pay Rate (5 U.S.C. 5315)."

TEMPORARY INCREASE IN NUMBER OF ASSISTANT SECRETARIES OF DEFENSE

Number of Assistant Secretaries of Defense authorized at level IV of Executive Schedule under this section to be increased by one (to a total of 12) until Jan. 20, 1989, see section 1311 of Pub. L. 100–180, set out as a note under section 138 of Title 10, Armed Forces.

ASSOCIATE DIRECTOR OF FEDERAL BUREAU OF INVESTIGATION

Position of Associate Director of Federal Bureau of Investigation placed temporarily in level III during incumbency of incumbent on Aug. 14, 1964, by Pub. L. 88–426, Aug. 14, 1964, § 303(c)(46), 78 Stat. 417.

SALARY INCREASES

2001—Salaries of positions at level IV increased to $125,700 per annum, effective on the first day of the first pay period beginning on or after Jan. 1, 2001, as provided by Ex. Ord. No. 13182, Dec. 23, 2000, 65 F.R. 82879, 66 F.R. 10057, set out as a note under section 5332 of this title.

2000—Salaries of positions at level IV increased to $122,400 per annum, effective on the first day of the first pay period beginning on or after Jan. 1, 2000, as provided by Ex. Ord. No. 13144, Dec. 21, 1999, 64 F.R. 72237.

1999—Salaries of positions at level IV continued at $118,400 per annum by Ex. Ord. No. 13106, Dec. 7, 1998, 63 F.R. 68151.

1998—Salaries of positions at level IV increased to $118,400 per annum, effective on the first day of the first pay period beginning on or after Jan. 1, 1998, as provided by Ex. Ord. No. 13071, Dec. 29, 1997, 62 F.R. 68521.

1997—Salaries of positions at level IV continued at $115,700 per annum by Ex. Ord. No. 13033, Dec. 27, 1996, 61 F.R. 68987.

1996—Salaries of positions at level IV continued at $115,700 per annum by Ex. Ord. No. 12984, Dec. 28, 1995, 61 F.R. 237.

1995—Salaries of positions at level IV continued at $115,700 per annum by Ex. Ord. No. 12944, Dec. 28, 1994, 60 F.R. 309.

1993—Salaries of positions at level IV increased to $115,700 per annum, effective on the first day of the first pay period beginning on or after Jan. 1, 1993, as provided by Ex. Ord. No. 12826, Dec. 30, 1992, 57 F.R. 62909.

1992—Salaries of positions at level IV increased to $112,100 per annum, effective on the first day of the first pay period beginning on or after Jan. 1, 1992, as provided by Ex. Ord. No. 12786, Dec. 26, 1991, 56 F.R. 67453.

1991—Salaries of positions at level IV increased to $108,300 per annum, effective on the first day of the first pay period beginning on or after Jan. 1, 1991, as provided by Ex. Ord. No. 12736, Dec. 12, 1990, 55 F.R. 51385.

1990—Salaries of positions at level IV increased to $83,600 per annum, effective on the first day of the first pay period beginning on or after Jan. 1, 1990, and continued at that rate by Ex. Ord. No. 12698, Dec. 23, 1989, 54 F.R. 53473.

1989—Salaries of positions at level IV increased to $80,700 per annum, effective on the first day of the first pay period beginning on or after Jan. 1, 1989, see Ex. Ord. No. 12663, Jan. 6, 1989, 54 F.R. 791.

1988—Salaries of positions at level IV continued at $77,500 per annum by Ex. Ord. No. 12622, Dec. 31, 1987, 53 F.R. 222.

1987—Salaries of positions at level IV increased to $77,500 per annum, on recommendation of the President of the United States, see note set out under section 358 of Title 2, The Congress.

Salaries of positions at level IV increased to $74,500 per annum, effective on the first day of the first pay period beginning on or after Jan. 1, 1987, as provided by Ex. Ord. No. 12578, Dec. 31, 1986, 52 F.R. 505.

1985—Salaries of positions at level IV increased to $72,300 per annum, effective on the first day of the first pay period beginning on or after Jan. 1, 1985, as provided by Ex. Ord. No. 12496, Dec. 28, 1984, 50 F.R. 211, as amended by Ex. Ord. No. 12540, Dec. 30, 1985, 51 F.R. 577.

1984—Salaries of positions at level IV increased to $69,900 per annum, effective on the first day of the first pay period beginning on or after Jan. 1, 1984, as provided by Ex. Ord. No. 12456, Dec. 30, 1983, 49 F.R. 347, as amended Ex. Ord. No. 12477, May 23, 1984, 49 F.R. 22041; Ex. Ord. No. 12487, Sept. 14, 1984, 49 F.R. 36493.

1982—Salaries of positions at level IV increased to $67,200 per annum, effective on the first day of the first pay period beginning on or after Oct. 1, 1982, as provided by Ex. Ord. No. 12387, Oct. 8, 1982, 47 F.R. 44981. Ex. Ord. No. 12387 further provided that pursuant to section 101(e) of Pub. L. 97–276 funds are not available to pay a salary at a rate which exceeds the rate in effect on Sept. 30, 1982, which was $58,500.00

Maximum rate payable after Dec. 17, 1982, increased from $58,500.00 to $67,200.00, see Pub. L. 97–377, title I, § 129(b)–(d), Dec. 21, 1982, 96 Stat. 1914, set out as a note under section 5318 of this title.

Limitations on use of funds for fiscal year ending Sept. 30, 1983, appropriated by any Act to pay the salary or pay of any individual in legislative, executive, or judicial branch in position equal to or above level V of the Executive Schedule, see section 101(e) of Pub. L. 97–276, as amended, set out as a note under section 5318 of this title.

1981—Salaries of positions at level IV increased to $64,600 per annum, effective on the first day of the first pay period beginning on or after Oct. 1, 1981, as provided by Ex. Ord. No. 12330, Oct. 15, 1981, 46 F.R. 50921. Ex. Ord. No. 12330 further provided that pursuant to section 101(c) of Pub. L. 97–51 funds are not available to pay a salary at a rate which exceeds the rate in effect on Sept. 30, 1981, which was $52,750.00.

Limitations on use of funds for fiscal year ending Sept. 30, 1982, appropriated by any Act to pay the salary or pay of any individual in legislative, executive, or judicial branch in position equal to or above level V of the Executive Schedule, see sections 101(g) and 141 of Pub. L. 97–92, set out as a note under section 5318 of this title.

1980—Salaries of positions at level IV increased to $61,600 per annum, effective on the first day of the first pay period beginning on or after Oct. 1, 1980, as provided by Ex. Ord. No. 12248, Oct. 16, 1980, 45 F.R. 69199. Ex. Ord. No. 12248, further provided that pursuant to section 101(c) of Pub. L. 96–369, funds are not available to pay a salary at a rate which exceeds the rate in effect on Sept. 30, 1980, which was $52,750.

Limitations on use of funds for fiscal year ending Sept. 30, 1981, appropriated by any Act to pay the salary or pay of any individual in legislative, executive, or judicial branch in position equal to or above level V of the Executive Schedule, see section 101(c) of Pub. L. 96–536, as amended, set out as a note under section 5318 of this title.

1979—Salaries of positions at level IV increased to $56,500 per annum, effective on the first day of the first pay period beginning on or after Oct. 1, 1979, as provided by Ex. Ord. No. 12165, Oct. 9, 1979, 44 F.R. 58671, as amended by Ex. Ord. No. 12200, Mar. 12, 1980, 45 F.R. 16443. Ex. Ord. No. 12165 further provided that pursuant to section 101(c) of Pub. L. 96–86 funds appropriated for

fiscal year 1980 may not be used to pay a salary at a rate which exceeds an increase of 5.5 percent over the rate in effect on Sept. 30, 1978, which is a maximum rate payable of $52,750.

Applicability to funds appropriated by any Act for fiscal year ending Sept. 30, 1980, of limitation of section 304 of Pub. L. 95–391 on use of funds to pay the salary or pay of any individual in legislative, executive, or judicial branch in position equal to or above level V of the Executive Schedule, see section 101 of Pub. L. 96–86, set out as a note under section 5318 of this title.

1978—Salaries of positions at level IV increased to $52,800 per annum, effective in the first pay period beginning on or after Oct. 1, 1978, as provided by Ex. Ord. No. 12087, Oct. 7, 1978, 43 F.R. 46823. Ex. Ord. No. 12087, further provided that pursuant to the Legislative Branch Appropriation Act, 1979, funds are not available to pay a salary at a rate which exceeds the rate in effect on Sept. 30, 1978, which was $50,000.

Limitations on use of funds for fiscal year ending Sept. 30, 1979, appropriated by any Act to pay the salary or pay of any individual in legislative, executive, or judicial branch in position equal or above level V of the Executive Schedule, see section 304 of Pub. L. 95–391 and section 613 of Pub. L. 95–429, set out as a note under section 5318 of this title.

1977—Salaries of positions at level IV increased to $50,000 per annum, on recommendation of the President of the United States, see note set out under section 358 of Title 2, The Congress.

1976—Salaries of positions at level IV increased to $41,800 per annum, effective on the first day of the first pay period beginning on or after Oct. 1, 1976, see Ex. Ord. No. 11941, Oct. 1, 1976, 41 F.R. 43889. Ex. Ord. No. 11941, further provided that pursuant to the Legislative Branch Appropriation Act, 1977, funds are not available to pay a salary at a rate which exceeds the rate in effect on Sept. 30, 1976, which was $39,900.

1975—Salaries of positions at level IV increased to $39,900 per annum, effective on the first day of the first pay period beginning on or after Oct. 1, 1975, by Ex. Ord. No. 11883, Oct. 6, 1975, 40 F.R. 47091.

1969—Salaries of positions at level IV increased from $28,750 to $38,000 per annum, commencing on the first day of the pay period which begins after February 14, 1969, on recommendation of the President of the United States, see note set out under section 358 of Title 2, The Congress.

PAY INCREASE; EFFECTIVE DATE

Persons occupying a position under the Executive Schedule on May 18, 1972, and later appointed to a position created or authorized by Pub. L. 92–302, not eligible to an increase in basic pay until Jan. 21, 1973, see section 3(c) of Pub. L. 92–302, May 18, 1972, 86 Stat. 149.

SECTION REFERRED TO IN OTHER SECTIONS

This section is referred to in sections 5317, 5377, 5380, 8432 of this title; title 2 sections 61d, 285e, 288, 437c, 474; title 7 section 5903; title 10 sections 973, 2359; title 12 sections 1422b, 2242; title 15 sections 274, 790b, 1507c, 2204; title 16 section 3181; title 18 section 207; title 19 section 2171; title 20 sections 76k, 929, 2103, 3501, 3503, 5603, 5608, 9001, 9002; title 21 section 1908; title 22 sections 286a, 290f, 290h–5, 2651a, 3506, 3862, 3961, 6203, 6207; title 25 sections 2704, 3505; title 26 section 3121; title 28 sections 332, 548, 587, 594, 603; title 29 section 792; title 30 sections 1121, 1211; title 31 section 731; title 38 section 7404; title 40 section 206–1; title 42 sections 293l, 294f, 297t, 299c, 300aa–12, 410, 1395b–6, 1975b, 3191, 4346, 5553, 5871, 5872, 7132, 7133, 7134, 7135, 7136, 7139, 7141, 7211, 7291, 7293, 8820, 10224, 12651e, 12651f; title 44 section 303; title 49 section 106.

§ 5316. Positions at level V

Level V of the Executive Schedule applies to the following positions, for which the annual rate of basic pay shall be the rate determined with respect to such level under chapter 11 of title 2, as adjusted by section 5318 of this title:

Administrator, Bonneville Power Administration, Department of the Interior.

Administrator of the National Capital Transportation Agency.

Associate Administrators of the Small Business Administration (4).

Associate Administrators, National Aeronautics and Space Administration (7).

Associate Deputy Administrator, National Aeronautics and Space Administration.

Deputy Associate Administrator, National Aeronautics and Space Administration.

Archivist of the United States.

Assistant Secretary of Health and Human Services for Administration.

Assistant Attorney General for Administration.

Assistant and Science Adviser to the Secretary of the Interior.

Chairman, Foreign Claims Settlement Commission of the United States, Department of Justice.

Assistant to the Secretary of Defense for Nuclear and Chemical and Biological Defense Programs, Department of Defense.

Chairman of the Renegotiation Board.

Chairman of the Subversive Activities Control Board.

Chief Counsel for the Internal Revenue Service, Department of the Treasury.

Commissioner, Federal Supply Service, General Services Administration.

Director, United States Fish and Wildlife Service, Department of the Interior.

Commissioner of Indian Affairs, Department of the Interior.

Commissioners, Indian Claims Commission (5).

Commissioner, Public Buildings Service, General Services Administration.

Commissioner of Reclamation, Department of the Interior.

Commissioner of Vocational Rehabilitation, Department of Health and Human Services.

Commissioner of Welfare, Department of Health and Human Services.

Director, Defense Advanced Research Projects Agency, Department of Defense.

Director, Bureau of Mines, Department of the Interior.

Director, Geological Survey, Department of the Interior.

Deputy Commissioner of Internal Revenue, Department of the Treasury.

Deputy General Counsel, Department of Defense.

Associate Director of the Federal Mediation and Conciliation Service.

Associate Director for Volunteers, Peace Corps.

Associate Director for Program Development and Operations, Peace Corps.

Assistants to the Director of the Federal Bureau of Investigation, Department of Justice (2).

Assistant Directors, Office of Emergency Planning (3).

Fiscal Assistant Secretary of the Treasury.

General Counsel of the Agency for International Development.

General Counsel of the Nuclear Regulatory Commission.

General Counsel of the National Aeronautics and Space Administration.

Manpower Administrator, Department of Labor.

Members, Renegotiation Board.

Members, Subversive Activities Control Board.

Deputy Under Secretaries of Defense for Research and Engineering, Department of Defense (4).

Assistant Administrator of General Services.

Director, United States Travel Service, Department of Commerce.

Administrator, Wage and Hour and Public Contracts Division, Department of Labor.

Assistant Director (Program Planning, Analysis and Research), Office of Economic Opportunity.

Deputy Director, National Security Agency.

Director, Bureau of Land Management, Department of the Interior.

Director, National Park Service, Department of the Interior.

National Export Expansion Coordinator, Department of Commerce.

Special Assistant to the Secretary of Defense.

Staff Director, Commission on Civil Rights.

Assistant Secretary for Administration, Department of Transportation.

Director, United States National Museum, Smithsonian Institution.

Director, Smithsonian Astrophysical Observatory, Smithsonian Institution.

Administrator of the Environmental Science Services Administration.

Associate Directors of the Office of Personnel Management (5).

Assistant Federal Highway Administrator.

Deputy Administrator of the National Highway Traffic Safety Administration.

Deputy Administrator of the Federal Motor Carrier Safety Administration.

Assistant Federal Motor Carrier Safety Administrator.

Director, Bureau of Narcotics and Dangerous Drugs, Department of Justice.

Vice Presidents, Overseas Private Investment Corporation (3).

Deputy Administrator, Federal Transit Administration, Department of Transportation.

General Counsel of the Equal Employment Opportunity Commission.

Executive Director, Advisory Council on Historic Preservation.

Additional Officers, Department of Energy (14).

General Counsel, Commodity Futures Trading Commission.

Additional officers, Nuclear Regulatory Commission (5).

Executive Director, Commodity Futures Trading Commission.

Assistant Administrator for Coastal Zone Management, National Oceanic and Atmospheric Administration.

Assistant Administrator for Fisheries, National Oceanic and Atmospheric Administration.

Assistant Administrators (3), National Oceanic and Atmospheric Administration.

General Counsel, National Oceanic and Atmospheric Administration.

Members, Federal Labor Relations Authority (2) and its General Counsel.

Additional officers, Institute for Scientific and Technological Cooperation (2).

Additional officers, Office of Management and Budget (6).

Associate Deputy Secretary, Department of Transportation.

Chief Scientist, National Oceanic and Atmospheric Administration.

Director, Indian Health Service, Department of Health and Human Services.

Commissioners, United States Parole Commission (8).

Commissioner, Administration on Children, Youth, and Families.

Director, Bureau of Transportation Statistics.

(Pub. L. 89–554, Sept. 6, 1966, 80 Stat. 463; Pub. L. 89–670, § 10(d)(5), (e), Oct. 15, 1966, 80 Stat. 948; Pub. L. 89–734, § 1(2), Nov. 2, 1966, 80 Stat. 1163; Pub. L. 89–779, § 8(c)(2), Nov. 6, 1966, 80 Stat. 1364; Pub. L. 90–9, § 6, Apr. 10, 1967, 81 Stat. 12; Pub. L. 90–83, § 1(16), Sept. 11, 1967, 81 Stat. 198; Pub. L. 90–206, title II, § 215(c), Dec. 16, 1967, 81 Stat. 638; Pub. L. 90–351, title I, § 506, June 19, 1968, 82 Stat. 205; Pub. L. 90–407, § 15(a)(3), July 18, 1968, 82 Stat. 367; Pub. L. 90–623, § 1(4), (5), Oct. 22, 1968, 82 Stat. 1312; Pub. L. 91–175, pt. V, § 503(3), Dec. 30, 1969, 83 Stat. 826; Pub. L. 91–375, § 6(c)(15), Aug. 12, 1970, 84 Stat. 776; Pub. L. 91–453, § 12, Oct. 15, 1970, 84 Stat. 968; Pub. L. 91–644, title I, § 7(2), Jan. 2, 1971, 84 Stat. 1887; Pub. L. 92–22, § 3, June 1, 1971, 85 Stat. 76; Pub. L. 92–255, title II, § 212(c), Mar. 21, 1972, 86 Stat. 69; Pub. L. 92–261, § 9(c), (d), Mar. 24, 1972, 86 Stat. 110; Pub. L. 92–302, § 2(d), May 18, 1972, 86 Stat. 149; Pub. L. 92–603, title IV, § 404(a), Oct. 30, 1972, 86 Stat. 1488; Pub. L. 93–43, § 2(c), June 18, 1973, 87 Stat. 78; Pub. L. 93–74, § 8, July 23, 1973, 87 Stat. 175; Pub. L. 90–351, title I, § 506(b), as added Pub. L. 93–83, § 2, Aug. 6, 1973, 87 Stat. 211; Pub. L. 93–271, § 2, Apr. 22, 1974, 88 Stat. 92; Pub. L. 93–126, § 9(c), as added Pub. L. 93–312, § 9, June 8, 1974, 88 Stat. 238; Pub. L. 93–383, title VIII, § 818(b), Aug. 22, 1974, 88 Stat. 740; Pub. L. 93–438, title III, § 310(4), Oct. 11, 1974, 88 Stat. 1253; Pub. L. 93–463, title I, § 102(c), Oct. 23, 1974, 88 Stat. 1392; Pub. L. 93–618, title I, § 172(c)(3), Jan. 3, 1975, 88 Stat. 2010; Pub. L. 94–82, title II, § 202(b)(5), Aug. 9, 1975, 89 Stat. 420; Pub. L. 94–183, § 2(19), Dec. 31, 1975, 89 Stat. 1058; Pub. L. 94–237, § 4(c)(6), Mar. 19, 1976, 90 Stat. 244; Pub. L. 94–307, § 7, June 4, 1976, 90 Stat. 681; Pub. L. 94–370, § 15(b), July 26, 1976, 90 Stat. 1032; Pub. L. 94–422, title II, § 202, Sept. 28, 1976, 90 Stat. 1323; Pub. L. 94–503, title II, § 202(c), Oct. 15, 1976, 90 Stat. 2427; Pub. L. 94–561, § 3(b), Oct. 19, 1976, 90 Stat. 2643; Pub. L. 94–582, § 26, Oct. 21, 1976, 90 Stat. 2889; Pub. L. 95–89, title II, § 209, Aug. 4, 1977, 91 Stat. 558; Pub. L. 95–91, title VII, § 710(g), Aug. 4, 1977, 91 Stat. 609; Pub. L. 95–115, § 3(a)(6), Oct. 3, 1977, 91 Stat. 1049; Pub. L. 95–219, § 3(b), Dec. 28, 1977, 91 Stat. 1614; Pub. L. 95–452, § 10(b), Oct. 12, 1978, 92 Stat. 1108; Pub. L. 95–454, title II, §§ 201(b)(3), 202(c)(4), title VII, § 703(e), Oct. 13, 1978, 92 Stat. 1121, 1131, 1217; Pub. L. 95–521, title IV, § 406, Oct. 26, 1978, 92 Stat. 1864;

Pub. L. 96–53, title IV, § 412(c), Aug. 14, 1979, 93 Stat. 377; Pub. L. 96–54, § 2(a)(25)(A), Aug. 14, 1979, 93 Stat. 382; Pub. L. 96–70, title III, § 3302(e)(11), Sept. 27, 1979, 93 Stat. 499; Pub. L. 96–88, title V, § 508(f), (g), Oct. 17, 1979, 93 Stat. 692; Pub. L. 96–107, title VIII, § 820(e)(2), Nov. 9, 1979, 93 Stat. 819; Pub. L. 96–209, title I, § 109, Mar. 14, 1980, 94 Stat. 97; Pub. L. 96–466, title V, § 504(d), Oct. 17, 1980, 94 Stat. 2203; Pub. L. 97–31, § 12(1)(C), Aug. 6, 1981, 95 Stat. 153; Pub. L. 97–113, title VII, § 705(b)(3), Dec. 29, 1981, 95 Stat. 1545; Pub. L. 97–258, § 2(a), Sept. 13, 1982, 96 Stat. 1052; Pub. L. 97–325, § 8(c), Oct. 15, 1982, 96 Stat. 1605; Pub. L. 97–449, § 3(4), (5), Jan. 12, 1983, 96 Stat. 2441; Pub. L. 98–557, § 26(b), Oct. 30, 1984, 98 Stat. 2873; Pub. L. 99–73, § 6(b)(2), July 29, 1985, 99 Stat. 173; Pub. L. 99–93, title VII, § 704(a)(3), Aug. 16, 1985, 99 Stat. 446; Pub. L. 99–145, title XII, § 1204(c), Nov. 8, 1985, 99 Stat. 721; Pub. L. 99–383, § 7(b)(2), Aug. 21, 1986, 100 Stat. 814; Pub. L. 99–619, § 2(c)(2), (d), Nov. 6, 1986, 100 Stat. 3491; Pub. L. 99–659, title IV, § 407(e)(3), Nov. 14, 1986, 100 Stat. 3740; Pub. L. 100–180, div. A, title XII, § 1245(c), Dec. 4, 1987, 101 Stat. 1165; Pub. L. 100–504, title I, § 103(b), Oct. 18, 1988, 102 Stat. 2522; Pub. L. 100–527, § 13(g), Oct. 25, 1988, 102 Stat. 2643; Pub. L. 100–598, § 8, Nov. 3, 1988, 102 Stat. 3035; Pub. L. 100–607, title V, § 503(b)(1), Nov. 4, 1988, 102 Stat. 3121; Pub. L. 100–690, title VII, § 7252(b)(4), Nov. 18, 1988, 102 Stat. 4436; Pub. L. 100–713, title VI, § 601(d), Nov. 23, 1988, 102 Stat. 4826; Pub. L. 101–319, §§ 3(b), 4, July 3, 1990, 104 Stat. 290, 291; Pub. L. 101–501, title IX, § 915(b)(1)(B), Nov. 3, 1990, 104 Stat. 1263; Pub. L. 101–509, title V, § 529 [title I, § 113(1)], Nov. 5, 1990, 104 Stat. 1427, 1455; Pub. L. 102–190, div. A, title IX, § 903(a)(2), div. C, title XXXV, § 3504(b), Dec. 5, 1991, 105 Stat. 1451, 1586; Pub. L. 102–240, title III, § 3004(d)(2), title VI, § 6006(d), Dec. 18, 1991, 105 Stat. 2088, 2174; Pub. L. 102–359, § 2(b)(2), Aug. 26, 1992, 106 Stat. 962; Pub. L. 103–123, title I, § 108(a)(1), Oct. 28, 1993, 107 Stat. 1234; Pub. L. 103–333, title I, § 106, Sept. 30, 1994, 108 Stat. 2549; Pub. L. 103–354, title II, § 294, Oct. 13, 1994, 108 Stat. 3237; Pub. L. 104–106, div. A, title IX, § 904(b)(2), Feb. 10, 1996, 110 Stat. 403; Pub. L. 104–201, div. A, title X, § 1073(e)(1)(A), Sept. 23, 1996, 110 Stat. 2658; Pub. L. 105–85, div. A, title X, § 1073(e)(2), Nov. 18, 1997, 111 Stat. 1906; Pub. L. 105–277, div. G, subdiv. A, title XII, § 1224(4), title XIII, § 1332(3), Oct. 21, 1998, 112 Stat. 2681–772, 2681–785; Pub. L. 105–393, title I, § 103, Nov. 13, 1998, 112 Stat. 3617; Pub. L. 106–44, § 2(b), Aug. 5, 1999, 113 Stat. 223; Pub. L. 106–113, div. B, § 1000(a)(9) [title IV, § 4732(b)(4)], Nov. 29, 1999, 113 Stat. 1536, 1501A–583; Pub. L. 106–159, title I, § 101(d)(2), Dec. 9, 1999, 113 Stat. 1751.)

HISTORICAL AND REVISION NOTES
1966 ACT

Derivation	U.S. Code	Revised Statutes and Statutes at Large
(1)–(99)	5 U.S.C. 2211(e).	Aug. 14, 1964, Pub. L. 88–426, § 303(e), 78 Stat. 419.
(100)–(116) ..	5 U.S.C. 2211(g).	Aug. 14, 1964, Pub. L. 88–426, § 303(g), 78 Stat. 422.

Paragraphs (100)–(116) are added on authority of former section 2211(g) which authorized the President to place, from Aug. 15, 1964, to Feb. 1, 1965, not more than 30 positions in Levels IV and V of the Federal Executive Salary Schedule. Pursuant to this authority, the President by Executive Order No. 11189, Nov. 23,

1964, as amended by Executive Order No. 11195, Jan. 30, 1965, placed the positions listed in paragraphs (100)–(116) in Level V.

Standard changes are made to conform with the definitions applicable and the style of this title as outlined in the preface to the report.

1967 ACT

Section of title 5	Source (U.S. Code)	Source (Statutes at Large)
5316(60)	5 App.: 2211(e)(60).	July 5, 1966, Pub. L. 89–492, § 4(1), 80 Stat. 262.
5316(94)	5 App.: 2211(e)(94).	Sept. 9, 1965, Pub. L. 89–174, § 5(b)(as applicable to § 303(e)(94) of the Federal Executive Salary Act of 1964), 79 Stat. 669.
5316(95)	5 App.: 2211(e)(95).	Aug. 9, 1965, Pub. L. 89–115, § 4(c)(words after semicolon), 79 Stat. 449.
5316(120)	5 App.: 2211(e)(100).	Aug. 26, 1965, Pub. L. 89–136, § 601(c), 79 Stat. 570.
5316(121)	[Uncodified].	1965 Reorg. Plan No. 2, § 4(a)(2d sentence, less 1st 18 words), eff. July 13, 1965, 79 Stat. 1318.
5316(122)	42:3533(b) (last 29 words).	Sept. 9, 1965, Pub. L. 89–174, § 4(b)(last 29 words), 79 Stat. 668.
5316(123)	5 App.: 2211(e)(101).	July 5, 1966, Pub. L. 89–492, § 4(2), 80 Stat. 262.
5316(124)	49: 1652(f)(2) (last 15 words in 2d sentence).	Oct. 15, 1966, Pub. L. 89–670, § 3(f)(2)(last 15 words in 2d sentence), 80 Stat. 932.
5316(125)	49: 1652(f)(1) (last 15 words in 2d sentence).	Oct. 15, 1966, Pub. L. 89–670, § 3(f)(1)(last 15 words in 2d sentence), 80 Stat. 932.

The deletion of paragraphs (22), (38), and (83) of 5 U.S.C. 5316 reflects (1) the termination, effective June 30, 1965, of the position of "Area Redevelopment Administrator, Department of Commerce" pursuant to Public Law 87–27 (sec. 29, 75 Stat. 63; 42 U.S.C. 2525); (2) the abolition of the position of "Chief, Weather Bureau, Department of Commerce" by 1965 Reorganization Plan No. 2 (sec. 2(a), 79 Stat. 1318); and (3) the abolition of the position of "General Counsel of the Housing and Home Finance Agency" by Public Law 89–174 (sec. 5(a), 9(c), 79 Stat. 669, 671).

The redesignation of paragraphs (117) and (118) as paragraphs "(118)" and "(119)", respectively, eliminates duplicate paragraph numbering effected by section 10(d)(5) of Public Law 89–670 and section 1(2) of Public Law 89–734.

CODIFICATION

The paragraph designations for the positions added by Pub. L. 96–88 have been omitted in view of the deletion of all paragraph designations in this section by Pub. L. 96–54.

AMENDMENTS

1999—Pub. L. 106–159 inserted items relating to Deputy Administrator of the Federal Motor Carrier Safety Administration and Assistant Federal Motor Carrier Safety Administrator.

Pub. L. 106–113 which directed amendment of this section by striking out items relating to Commissioner of Patents, Department of Commerce, Deputy Commissioner of Patents and Trademarks, Assistant Commissioner for Patents, and Assistant Commissioner for Trademarks, was executed by striking out items relating to Deputy Commissioner of Patents and Trademarks, Assistant Commissioner for Patents, and Assistant Commissioner for Trademarks to reflect the probable intent of Congress and the intervening amendment by Pub. L. 106–44, § 2(b), which struck out item relating to Commissioner of Patents, Department of Commerce. See below.

Pub. L. 106–44 struck out item relating to Commissioner of Patents, Department of Commerce.

1998—Pub. L. 105–393 struck out item relating to Administrator for Economic Development.

Pub. L. 105–277, § 1332(3), struck out items relating to Deputy Director, Policy and Plans, United States Information Agency, and Associate Director (Policy and Plans), United States Information Agency.

Pub. L. 105–277, § 1224(4), struck out item relating to General Counsel of the United States Arms Control and Disarmament Agency.

1997—Pub. L. 105–85 substituted "Nuclear and Chemical and Biological Defense Programs" for "Atomic Energy".

1996—Pub. L. 104–201 inserted "Defense" before "Advanced Research Projects Agency".

Pub. L. 104–106, which directed amendment of section by substituting "Assistant to the Secretary of Defense for Nuclear and Chemical and Biological Defense Programs, Department of Defense." for "The Assistant to the Secretary of Defense for Atomic Energy, Department of Defense.", could not be executed because the words to be substituted for did not appear.

1994—Pub. L. 103–354 struck out following items relating to Department of Agriculture: Administrator, Agricultural Marketing Service, Administrator, Agricultural Research Service, Administrator, Agricultural Stabilization and Conservation Service, Administrator, Farmers Home Administration, Administrator, Foreign Agricultural Service, Administrator, Rural Electrification Administration, Administrator, Soil Conservation Service, Chief Forester of the Forest Service, Director of Science and Education, Administrator, Animal and Plant Health Inspection Service, and Administrator, Federal Grain Inspection Service.

Pub. L. 103–333 struck out item relating to Commissioner of Labor Statistics, Department of Labor.

1993—Pub. L. 103–123 struck out item relating to Commissioner of Customs, Department of the Treasury.

1992—Pub. L. 102–359 struck out item relating to Additional Officers, Department of Education.

1991—Pub. L. 102–240, § 6006(d), inserted item relating to Director, Bureau of Transportation Statistics.

Pub. L. 102–240, § 3004(d)(2), substituted "Deputy Administrator, Federal Transit Administration" for "Deputy Administrator, Urban Mass Transportation Administration".

Pub. L. 102–190, § 3504(b), struck out item relating to Administrator of the Panama Canal Commission.

Pub. L. 102–190, § 903(a)(2), struck out items relating to General Counsels of the Departments of the Air Force, Army, and Navy.

1990—Pub. L. 101–509 struck out item relating to Director, Bureau of the Census, Department of Commerce.

Pub. L. 101–501 inserted item relating to Commissioner, Administration on Children, Youth, and Families.

Pub. L. 101–319, § 4, inserted items relating to Deputy Commissioner of Patents and Trademarks, Assistant Commissioner for Patents, and Assistant Commissioner for Trademarks.

Pub. L. 101–319, § 3(b), inserted item relating to Commissioners, United States Parole Commission.

1988—Pub. L. 100–713 inserted item relating to Director, Indian Health Service, Department of Health and Human Services.

Pub. L. 100–690 struck out item relating to Associate Administrator, Office of Juvenile Justice and Delinquency Prevention of Law Enforcement Assistance Administration.

Pub. L. 100–607 struck out item relating to Commissioner of Food and Drugs, Department of Health and Human Services.

Pub. L. 100–598 struck out item relating to Director of Office of Government Ethics.

Pub. L. 100–527 struck out items relating to Associate Deputy Administrator of Veterans' Affairs, Chief Benefits Director, Veterans' Administration, General Counsel of the Veterans' Administration, and Director, National Cemetery System, Veterans' Administration.

Pub. L. 100–504 struck out items relating to Inspectors General for Departments of Commerce and Interior and for Agency for International Development, Community Services Administration, Environmental Protection Agency, General Services Administration, National Aeronautics and Space Administration, and Small Business Administration and relating to Deputy Inspectors General for Departments of Energy and Health and Human Services.

1987—Pub. L. 100–180 substituted "Assistant to the Secretary of Defense for Atomic Energy, Department of Defense" for "Chairman of the Military Liaison Committee to the Atomic Energy Commission, Department of Defense".

1986—Pub. L. 99–659 inserted item relating to Chief Scientist, National Oceanic and Atmospheric Administration.

Pub. L. 99–619, § 2(c)(2), struck out item relating to Assistant Secretary of Labor for Administration.

Pub. L. 99–619, § 2(d), struck out item relating to Assistant Secretary of Labor for Veterans' Employment.

Pub. L. 99–383 struck out item relating to Assistant Directors, National Science Foundation (4).

1985—Pub. L. 99–145 struck out item relating to Administrator of Education for Overseas Dependents, Department of Education.

Pub. L. 99–93 struck out item relating to Assistant Directors, United States Arms Control and Disarmament Agency (4).

Pub. L. 99–73 struck out item relating to Director, National Bureau of Standards, Department of Commerce.

1984—Pub. L. 98–557 inserted item relating to Associate Deputy Secretary, Department of Transportation.

1983—Pub. L. 97–449, § 3(4), substituted "Assistant Federal Highway Administrator" for "Director, National Highway Safety Bureau".

Pub. L. 97–449, § 3(5), substituted "Deputy Administrator of the National Highway Traffic Safety Administration" for "Director, National Traffic Safety Bureau".

1982—Pub. L. 97–325 struck out item relating to Assistant Secretary of Agriculture for Administration.

Pub. L. 97–258 inserted item relating to Additional officers, Office of Management and Budget (6).

1981—Pub. L. 97–113 substituted "Inspector General, Agency for International Development" for "Auditor General of the Agency for International Development".

Pub. L. 97–31 purported to strike out "Maritime Administration, Department of Commerce" which was executed by striking out "Maritime Administrator, Department of Commerce." as the probable intent of Congress.

1980—Pub. L. 96–466 inserted item relating to Assistant Secretary of Labor for Veterans' Employment.

Pub. L. 96–209, § 109(1), which provided for striking out par. (31) and inserting in lieu thereof "(31) Chairman, Foreign Claims Settlement Commission of the United States, Department of Justice." was executed by striking out the item relating to the Chairman, Foreign Claims Settlement Commission of the United States which was designated par. (31) prior to amendment of this section by Pub. L. 96–54 and inserting the item relating to the Chairman, Foreign Claims Settlement Commission of the United States, Department of Justice. See 1979 Amendment note below.

Pub. L. 96–209, § 109(2), which provided for striking out par. (90) was executed by striking out item relating to Members, Foreign Claims Settlement Commission of United States which was designated par. (90) prior to amendment of this section by Pub. L. 96–54. See 1979 Amendment note below.

1979—Pub. L. 96–88, § 508(f)(1), which provided for striking out par. (41) was executed by striking out item relating to Commissioner of Education, Department of Health, Education, and Welfare which was designated par. (41) prior to amendment of this section by Pub. L. 96–54. See 1979 Amendment note below.

Pub. L. 96–88, § 508(g), substituted "Health and Human Services" for "Health, Education, and Welfare" in items relating to the Assistant Secretary of Health and Human Services for Administration, the Commissioner of Food and Drugs, the Commissioner of Vocational Rehabilitation, the Commissioner of Welfare, and the Deputy Inspector General of the Department of Health and Human Services.

Pars. (1) to (152). Pub. L. 96–54 struck out paragraph designations for positions listed herein.

Pars. (37), (38). Pub. L. 96–88, § 508(f)(2), added pars. (37) and (38) relating to additional officers and Administrator of Education for Overseas Dependents in Department of Education, respectively. See Codification note set out above.

Par. (87). Pub. L. 96–70 substituted "Administrator of the Panama Canal Commission" for "Governor of the Canal Zone".

Par. (96). Pub. L. 96–107 substituted "Deputy Under Secretaries of Defense for Research and Engineering, Department of Defense" for "Deputy Directors of Defense Research and Engineering, Department of Defense".

Par. (152). Pub. L. 96–53 added par. (152) relating to two additional officers in Institute for Scientific and Technological Cooperation.

1978—Par. (99). Pub. L. 95–454, § 202(c)(4), struck out par. (99) relating to Executive Director of United States Civil Service Commission.

Par. (122). Pub. L. 95–454, § 201(b)(3), added par. (122) relating to five Associate Directors of Office of Personnel Management.

Par. (144). Pub. L. 95–452, § 10(b), added par. (144) relating to Deputy Inspector General, Department of Health, Education, and Welfare.

Par. (145). Pub. L. 95–454, § 703(e), added par. (145) relating to Members and General Counsel of Federal Labor Relations Authority.

Pub. L. 95–452 added par. (145) relating to Inspector General, Department of Commerce.

Par. (146). Pub. L. 95–521 added par. (146) relating to Director of Office of Government Ethics.

Pub. L. 95–452 added par. (146) relating to Inspector General, Department of the Interior.

Pars. (147) to (151). Pub. L. 95–452 added pars. (147) to (151) relating to Inspector General, Community Services Administration, Inspector General, Environmental Protection Agency, Inspector General, General Services Administration, Inspector General, National Aeronautics and Space Administration, and Inspector General, Small Business Administration, respectively.

1977—Par. (11). Pub. L. 95–89 substituted "(4)" for "(3)" in par. (11) relating to Associate Administrators of the Small Business Administration.

Par. (135). Pub. L. 95–91 substituted "Deputy Inspector General, Department of Energy" for "General Counsel, Energy Research and Development Administration", covered in section 5315 by item relating to General Counsel of the Department of Energy.

Par. (136). Pub. L. 95–91 substituted "Department of Energy (14)" for "Energy Research and Development Administration (8)".

Par. (140). Pub. L. 95–219 substituted "Assistant" for "Associate", relating to Assistant Administrator for Coastal Zone Management, National Oceanic and Atmospheric Administration.

Par. (141). Pub. L. 95–219 added par. (141) relating to Assistant Administrator for Fisheries.

Pub. L. 95–115 added par. (141) relating to Associate Administrator Office of Juvenile Justice and Delinquency Prevention.

Pars. (142), (143). Pub. L. 95–219 added pars. (142) and (143) relating to three Assistant Administrators, National Oceanic and Atmospheric Administration and General Counsel, National Oceanic and Atmospheric Administration, respectively.

1976—Par. (15). Pub. L. 94–307 substituted "(7)" for "(6)" in par. (15) relating to Associate Administrators, National Aeronautics and Space Administration.

Par. (44). Pub. L. 94–503 struck out par. (44) relating to Commissioner of Immigration and Naturalization, Department of Justice.

Par. (55). Pub. L. 94–561, § 3(b)(1), struck out par. (55) relating to Director of Agricultural Economics, Department of Agriculture.

Par. (58). Pub. L. 94–503 struck out par. (58) relating to Director, Bureau of Prisons, Department of Justice.

Pars. (115), (116). Pub. L. 94–503 struck out par. (115) relating to United States Attorney for Northern District of Illinois, and par. (116) relating to United States Attorney for Southern District of California.

Par. (131). Pub. L. 94–237 struck out par. (131) relating to Assistant Directors, Special Action Office for Drug Abuse Prevention (6).

Par. (134). Pub. L. 94–503 struck out par. (134) relating to Deputy Administrator for Administration of Law Enforcement Assistance Administration.

Par. (135). Pub. L. 94–422 added par. (135) relating to Executive Director, Advisory Council on Historic Preservation.

Par. (137). Pub. L. 94–582 added par. (137) relating to Administrator, Federal Grain Inspection Service, Department of Agriculture.

Pub. L. 94–561 added par. (137) relating to Administrator, Animal and Plant Health Inspection Service, Department of Agriculture.

Par. (140). Pub. L. 94–370 added par. (140) relating to Associate Administrator for Coastal Zone Management, National Oceanic and Atmospheric Administration.

1975—Pub. L. 94–82 substituted provisions applying level V of Executive Schedule to positions for which annual rate of basic pay shall be rate determined with respect to such level under chapter 11 of title 2, as adjusted by section 5318 of this title, for provisions applying such level V to positions for which annual rate of basic pay is $28,000.

Par. (93). Pub. L. 93–613 struck out par. (93) relating to Members, United States Tariff Commission.

Pars. (134) to (139). Pub. L. 94–183 redesignated par. (133), Deputy Administrator for Administration of the Law Enforcement Assistance Administration, par. (134), General Counsel, Energy Research and Development Administration, par. (135), Additional officers, Energy Research and Development Administration (8), par. (135), General Counsel, Commodity Futures Trading Commission, par. (136), Additional officers, Nuclear Regulatory Commission (5), and par. (136), Executive Director, Commodity Futures Trading Commission, as pars. (134) to (139), respectively.

1974—Par. (29). Pub. L. 93–438 struck out par. (29) relating to Assistant General Manager, Atomic Energy Commission.

Par. (42). Pub. L. 93–271, § 2, substituted "Director, United States Fish and Wildlife" for "Commissioner of Fish and Wildlife".

Par. (62). Pub. L. 93–438 struck out par. (62) relating to Director of Regulation, Atomic Energy Commission. See section 5315 of this title.

Par. (69). Pub. L. 93–438 struck out par. (69) relating to Deputy General Manager, Atomic Energy Commission.

Par. (81). Pub. L. 93–438 substituted "General Counsel of the Nuclear Regulatory Commission" for "General Counsel of the Atomic Energy Commission".

Par. (102). Pub. L. 93–438 struck out par. (102) relating to Assistant General Managers, Atomic Energy Commission (2).

Par. (109). Pub. L. 93–126, § 9(c), as added by Pub. L. 93–312, repealed par. (109) relating to Director of International Scientific Affairs, Department of State.

Par. (122). Pub. L. 93–383 struck out par. (122) relating to Assistant Secretary of Housing and Urban Development for Administration.

Par. (134). Pub. L. 93–438 added par. (134) relating to General Counsel, Energy Research and Development Administration.

Pars. (135), (136), Pub. L. 93–463 added pars. (135) and (136) relating, respectively, to General Counsel, Commodity Futures Trading Commission, and Executive Director, Commodity Futures Trading Commission.

Pub. L. 93–438 added pars. (135) and (136) relating, respectively, to additional officers, Nuclear Regulatory Commission, and additional officers, Energy Research and Development Administration.

1973—Pars. (15) to (17). Pub. L. 93–74 added par. (15), Associate Administrators, National Aeronautics and Space Administration (6), and repealed provisions of former pars. (15) for an Associate Administrator for Advanced Research and Technology, (16) for Associate Administrator for Space Science and Applications, and (17) for Associate Administrator for Manned Space Flight, National Aeronautics and Space Administration.

Pars. (131) to (133). Pub. L. 93–43 redesignated par. (131) relating to General Counsel of the Equal Employment Opportunity Commission as par. (132), and added par. (133) relating to Director, National Cemetery System.

Par. (133). Pub. L. 93–83 added par. (133) relating to Deputy Administrator for Administration of the Law Enforcement Assistance Administration.

1972—Pars. (28), (64). Pub. L. 92–302 struck out pars. (28) and (64) relating to an Assistant Secretary of the Treasury for Administration and a Deputy Under Secretary for Monetary Affairs, Department of the Treasury, respectively.

Par. (51). Pub. L. 92–603 struck out par. (51) relating to Commissioner of Social Security, Department of Health, Education, and Welfare. See section 5315 of this title.

Par. (111). Pub. L. 92–261, § 9(c), struck out par. (111) relating to Members, Equal Employment Opportunity Commission (4). See section 5315 of this title.

Par. (131). Pub. L. 92–261, § 9(d), added par. (131) relating to General Counsel of the Equal Employment Opportunity Commission.

Pub. L. 92–255 added par. (131) relating to Assistant Directors, Special Action Office for Drug Abuse Prevention.

1971—Par. (25). Pub. L. 92–22 struck out position of Assistant Secretary of the Interior for Administration. See section 1453a of Title 43 and section 5315 of this title.

Par. (126). Pub. L. 91–644 struck out par. (126) relating to Associate Administrator of Law Enforcement Assistance (2). See section 5315 of this title.

1970—Pars. (37), (60), (123). Pub. L. 91–375 struck out pars. (37), (60), and (123) relating to Chief Postal Inspector; Director, Research and Development; and Director, Construction Engineering, respectively.

Par. (130). Pub. L. 91–453 added par. (130) relating to Deputy Administrator, Urban Mass Transportation Administration, Department of Transportation.

1969—Pars. (128), (129). Pub. L. 91–175 added pars. (128) and (129) relating to Auditor-General of the Agency for International Development, and Vice Presidents, Overseas Private Investment Corporation (3), respectively.

1968—Par. (66). Pub. L. 90–407 substituted "Assistant Directors, National Science Foundation (4)" for "Deputy Director, National Science Foundation".

Par. (126). Pub. L. 90–623, § 1(4), inserted "(2)" at end of par. (126) relating to Associate Administrator of Law Enforcement Assistance.

Pub. L. 90–351 added par. (126) relating to Associate Administrator of Law Enforcement Assistance.

Par. (127). Pub. L. 90–623, § 1(5), added par. (127) relating to Director, Bureau of Narcotics and Dangerous Drugs, Department of Justice.

1967—Pub. L. 90–206 increased annual rate of basic pay from $26,000 to $28,000.

Pars. (46), (47). Pub. L. 90–9 struck out par. (46) relating to Chief Commissioner, Indian Claims Commission, and substituted "Commissioners, Indian Claims Commission (5)" for "Associate Commissioners, Indian Claims Commission (2)" in par. (47).

1966—Pub. L. 89–779 substituted "Associate Administrators of the Small Business Administration (3)" for "Deputy Administrators of the Small Business Administration (4)" in par. (11).

Pub. L. 89–734 added par. (117) relating to Director, United States National Museum, Smithsonian Institution, and par. (118).

Pub. L. 89–670 added par. (117) relating to Assistant Secretary for Administration, Department of Transportation, and struck out pars. (10) Administrator of the Saint Lawrence Seaway Development Corporation, (12) Associate Administrator for Administration, Federal Aviation Agency, (13) Associate Administrator for Development, Federal Aviation Agency, (14) Associate Administrator for Programs, Federal Aviation Agency, (76) Federal Highway Administrator, Department of Commerce, and (82) General Counsel of the Federal Aviation Agency, subject to the provisions of section 1657 of former Title 49, Transportation.

CHANGE OF NAME

Bureau of Mines redesignated United States Bureau of Mines by section 10(b) of Pub. L. 102–285, set out as a note under section 1 of Title 30, Mineral Lands and Mining.

Geological Survey redesignated United States Geological Survey by provision of title I of Pub. L. 102–154, set out as a note under section 31 of Title 43, Public Lands.

EFFECTIVE DATE OF 1999 AMENDMENTS

Amendment by Pub. L. 106–159 effective Jan. 1, 2000, see section 107(a) of Pub. L. 106–159, set out as a note under section 104 of Title 49, Transportation.

Amendment by Pub. L. 106–113 effective 4 months after Nov. 29, 1999, see section 1000(a)(9) [title IV, § 4731] of Pub. L. 106–113, set out as a note under section 1 of Title 35, Patents.

EFFECTIVE DATE OF 1998 AMENDMENTS

Amendment by Pub. L. 105–393 effective on date determined by Secretary of Commerce, but not later than 90 days after Nov. 13, 1998, see section 105 of Pub. L. 105–393, set out as an Effective Date note under section 3121 of Title 42, The Public Health and Welfare.

Amendment by section 1224(4) of Pub. L. 105–277 effective Apr. 1, 1999, see section 1201 of Pub. L. 105–277, set out as an Effective Date note under section 6511 of Title 22, Foreign Relations and Intercourse.

Amendment by section 1332(3) of Pub. L. 105–277 effective Oct. 1, 1999, see section 1301 of Pub. L. 105–277, set out as an Effective Date note under section 6531 of Title 22, Foreign Relations and Intercourse.

EFFECTIVE DATE OF 1993 AMENDMENT

Amendment by Pub. L. 103–123 effective on first applicable pay period after Oct. 28, 1993, see section 108(b) of Pub. L. 103–123, set out as a note under section 5315 of this title.

EFFECTIVE DATE OF 1992 AMENDMENT

Amendment by Pub. L. 102–359 effective on first day of first pay period that begins on or after Aug. 26, 1992, see section 2(b)(3) of Pub. L. 102–359, set out as a note under section 5315 of this title.

EFFECTIVE DATE OF 1990 AMENDMENTS

Amendment by Pub. L. 101–509 effective on such date as the President shall determine, but not earlier than 90 days, and not later than 180 days, after Nov. 5, 1990, see section 529 [title III, § 305] of Pub. L. 101–509, set out as a note under section 5301 of this title.

Amendment by Pub. L. 101–501 effective Oct. 1, 1990, see section 1001(a) of Pub. L. 101–501, set out as a note under section 8621 of Title 42, The Public Health and Welfare.

EFFECTIVE DATE OF 1988 AMENDMENTS

Amendment by Pub. L. 100–690 effective Oct. 1, 1988, see section 7296(a) of Pub. L. 100–690, set out as a note under section 5601 of Title 42, The Public Health and Welfare.

Amendment by Pub. L. 100–527 effective Mar. 15, 1989, see section 18(a) of Pub. L. 100–527, set out as a Department of Veterans Affairs Act note under section 301 of Title 38, Veterans' Benefits.

Amendment by Pub. L. 100–504 effective 180 days after Oct. 18, 1988, see section 113 of Pub. L. 100–504, set out

as a note under section 5 of Pub. L. 95–452 [Inspector General Act of 1978] in the Appendix to this title.

EFFECTIVE DATE OF 1986 AMENDMENT

Section 2(e) of Pub. L. 99–619 provided that: "Subsection (c) of this section [amending this section and Reorg. Plan No. 6 of 1950, set out in the Appendix to this title] shall become effective on the day upon which the individual who is the incumbent of the position abolished by such subsection, as of the date of enactment [Nov. 6, 1986], ceases to hold the position."

EFFECTIVE DATE OF 1985 AMENDMENT

Amendment by Pub. L. 99–73 effective Oct. 1, 1985, see section 6(c) of Pub. L. 99–73, set out as a note under section 5315 of this title.

EFFECTIVE DATE OF 1982 AMENDMENT

Amendment by Pub. L. 97–325 to take effect on the appointment of a person to fill successor position created by section 2212c of Title 7, Agriculture, see section 8(e) of Pub. L. 97–325.

EFFECTIVE DATE OF 1980 AMENDMENTS

Amendment by Pub. L. 96–466 effective Oct. 1, 1980, see section 802(e) of Pub. L. 96–466, set out as a note under section 4101 of Title 38, Veterans' Benefits.

Amendment by Pub. L. 96–209 effective Mar. 14, 1980, see title VI of Pub. L. 96–209, set out as an Effective Date note under section 1622a of Title 22, Foreign Relations and Intercourse.

EFFECTIVE DATE OF 1979 AMENDMENTS

Amendment by Pub. L. 96–88 effective May 4, 1980, with specified exceptions, see section 601 of Pub. L. 96–88, set out as an Effective Date note under section 3401 of Title 20, Education.

Amendment by Pub. L. 96–70 effective Oct. 1, 1979, see section 3304 of Pub. L. 96–70, set out as an Effective Date note under section 3601 of Title 22, Foreign Relations and Intercourse.

Amendment by Pub. L. 96–54 effective Jan. 1, 1980, see section 2(a)(25)(B) of Pub. L. 96–54, set out as a note under section 5312 of this title.

Amendment by Pub. L. 96–53 effective Oct. 1, 1979, see section 512(a) of Pub. L. 96–53, set out as a note under section 2151 of Title 22, Foreign Relations and Intercourse.

EFFECTIVE DATE OF 1978 AMENDMENTS

Amendment by Pub. L. 95–454 effective 90 days after Oct. 13, 1978, see section 907 of Pub. L. 95–454, set out as a note under section 1101 of this title.

Amendment by Pub. L. 95–452 effective Oct. 1, 1978, see section 12 of Pub. L. 95–452 set out in the Appendix to this title.

EFFECTIVE DATE OF 1977 AMENDMENT

Amendment by Pub. L. 95–115 effective Oct. 1, 1977, see section 263(c) of Pub. L. 93–415, as added by Pub. L. 95–115, set out as a note under section 5601 of Title 42, The Public Health and Welfare.

EFFECTIVE DATE OF 1976 AMENDMENT

Amendment by Pub. L. 94–582 effective 30 days after Oct. 21, 1976, see section 27 of Pub. L. 94–582, as amended, set out as a note under section 74 of Title 7, Agriculture.

EFFECTIVE DATE OF 1974 AMENDMENTS

Amendment by Pub. L. 93–463 effective Oct. 23, 1974, see section 418 of Pub. L. 93–463, set out as a note under section 2 of Title 7, Agriculture.

Amendment by Pub. L. 93–438 effective 120 days after Oct. 11, 1974, or on such earlier date as President may prescribe and publish in Federal Register, except that officers provided for in sections 5811–5820 of Title 42, The Public Health and Welfare, may be nominated and appointed at any time after Oct. 11, 1974, see section 312(a) of Pub. L. 93–438, set out as an Effective Date; Interim Appointments note under section 5801 of Title 42.

Amendment by Pub. L. 93–271 effective July 1, 1974, see section 3 of Pub. L. 93–271, set out as a note under section 742b of Title 16, Conservation.

EFFECTIVE DATE OF 1973 AMENDMENTS

Offices and salaries modified under amendment by Pub. L. 93–83, prospectively only, effective on and after Aug. 6, 1973, see section 3 of Pub. L. 93–83, Aug. 6, 1973, 83 Stat. 218.

Amendment by Pub. L. 93–43 effective June 18, 1973, see section 10(a) of Pub. L. 93–43, set out as an Effective Date note under section 2400 of Title 38, Veterans' Benefits.

EFFECTIVE DATE OF 1972 AMENDMENTS

Amendment by Pub. L. 92–603 effective on first day of first pay period of Commissioner of Social Security, Department of Health, Education, and Welfare, which commences on or after first day of month which follows month in which Pub. L. 92–603 was enacted, see section 404(c) of Pub. L. 92–603, set out as a note under section 5315 of this title.

Amendment by Pub. L. 92–302, abolishing offices of Assistant Secretary of the Treasury for Administration and Deputy Under Secretary for Monetary Affairs, Department of the Treasury, effective on confirmation by Senate of Presidential appointees to fill the successor positions created by Pub. L. 92–302, see, section 3(b) of Pub. L. 92–302, May 18, 1972, 86 Stat. 149.

EFFECTIVE DATE OF 1971 AMENDMENT

Amendment by Pub. L. 92–22 effective on Senate confirmation of Presidential appointment under section 1453a of Title 43 and section 5315(18) of this title, see note set out under section 1453a of Title 43, Public Lands.

EFFECTIVE DATE OF 1970 AMENDMENT

Amendment by Pub. L. 91–375 effective within 1 year after Aug. 12, 1970, on date established therefor by Board of Governors of United States Postal Service and published by it in Federal Register, see section 15(a) of Pub. L. 91–375, set out as an Effective Date note preceding section 101 of Title 39, Postal Service.

EFFECTIVE DATE OF 1968 AMENDMENTS

Amendment by Pub. L. 90–623 intended to restate without substantive change the law in effect on Oct. 22, 1968, see section 6 of Pub. L. 90–623, set out as a note under section 5334 of this title.

Amendment by Pub. L. 90–407 effective on first day of first calendar month which begins on or after July 18, 1968, see section 15(a)(4) of Pub. L. 90–407, set out as a note under section 5313 of this title.

EFFECTIVE DATE OF 1967 AMENDMENT

Amendment by Pub. L. 90–206 effective as of beginning of first pay period which begins on or after Dec. 16, 1967, see section 220(a)(3) of Pub. L. 90–206, set out as a note under section 603 of Title 28, Judiciary and Judicial Procedure.

EFFECTIVE DATE OF 1966 AMENDMENT

Amendment by Pub. L. 89–670 effective Apr. 1, 1967, as prescribed by President and published in Federal Register, see section 16(a), formerly §15(a), of Pub. L. 89–670 and Ex. Ord. No. 11340, Mar. 30, 1967, 32 F.R. 5453.

TRANSFER OF FUNCTIONS

Office of Emergency Preparedness, including offices of Director, Deputy Director, Assistant Directors, and Regional Directors, abolished and functions vested by law in Office of Emergency Preparedness or Director of Office of Emergency Preparedness transferred to President by sections 1 and 3(a)(1) of 1973 Reorg. Plan No. 1, set out in the Appendix to this title.

Environmental Science Services Administration in Department of Commerce, including offices of Administrator and Deputy Administrator thereof, abolished by Reorg. Plan No. 4 of 1970, eff. Oct. 3, 1970, 35 F.R. 15627, 84 Stat. 2090, set out in the Appendix to this title, which created National Oceanic and Atmospheric Administration in Department of Commerce and transferred personnel, property, records, and unexpended balances of funds of Environmental Science Services Administration to such newly created National Oceanic and Atmospheric Administration. Components of Environmental Science Services Administration thus transferred included Weather Bureau [now National Weather Service], Coast and Geodetic Survey [now National Ocean Survey], Environmental Data Service, National Environmental Satellite Center, and ESSA Research Laboratories.

Bureau of Narcotics and Dangerous Drugs, including office of Director thereof, in Department of Justice abolished by 1973 Reorg. Plan No. 2, eff. July 1, 1973, 38 FR 15932, 87 Stat. 1091, set out in the Appendix to this title, 1973 Reorg. Plan No. 2 also created in Department of Justice an agency to be known as Drug Enforcement Administration, with an Administrator and Deputy Administrator appointed by President with advice and consent of Senate.

INDIAN CLAIMS COMMISSION

Indian Claims Commission terminated on Sept. 30, 1978, pursuant to Pub. L. 94–465, §2, Oct. 8, 1976, 90 Stat. 1990.

COMMISSIONER OF PATENTS

Commissioner of Patents redesignated Commissioner of Patents and Trademarks by Pub. L. 93–596, §3, Jan. 2, 1975, 88 Stat. 1949, set out as a note under section 1 of Title 35, Patents.

ADMINISTRATOR OF BONNEVILLE POWER ADMINISTRATION

Bonneville Power Administration transferred to Department of Energy by section 7152 of Title 42, The Public Health and Welfare.

GENERAL COUNSEL OF MILITARY DEPARTMENTS

Pub. L. 100–456, div. A, title VII, §703(b), Sept. 29, 1988, 102 Stat. 1996, which provided that, notwithstanding this section, the General Counsel of each of the military departments was to be paid at the highest rate of basic pay payable under section 5382 of this title, to a member of the Senior Executive Service, was repealed by Pub. L. 102–190, div. A, title IX, §903(b), Dec. 5, 1991, 105 Stat. 1451.

COMPENSATION OF DEPUTY ASSISTANT SECRETARY OF COMMERCE FOR COMMUNICATIONS AND INFORMATION

Pub. L. 95–567, title I, §106(c), Nov. 2, 1978, 92 Stat. 2409, provided that: "The position of Deputy Assistant Secretary of Commerce for Communications and Information, established in Department of Commerce Organization Order Numbered 10–10 (effective March 26, 1978), shall be compensated at the rate of pay in effect from time to time for level V of the Executive Schedule under section 5316 of title 5, United States Code."

SUBVERSIVE ACTIVITIES CONTROL BOARD

Subversive Activities Control Board, Chairman and Members of which were compensated under this section, ceased operation on June 3, 1973, as unfunded by Congress.

SALARY INCREASES

2001—Salaries of positions at level V increased to $117,600 per annum, effective on the first day of the first pay period beginning on or after Jan. 1, 2001, as provided by Ex. Ord. No. 13182, Dec. 23, 2000, 65 F.R. 82879, 66 F.R. 10057, set out as a note under section 5332 of this title.

2000—Salaries of positions at level V increased to $114,500 per annum, effective on the first day of the first pay period beginning on or after Jan. 1, 2000, as provided by Ex. Ord. No. 13144, Dec. 21, 1999, 64 F.R. 72237.

1999—Salaries of positions at level V continued at $110,700 per annum by Ex. Ord. No. 13106, Dec. 7, 1998, 63 F.R. 68151.

1998—Salaries of positions at level V increased to $110,700 per annum, effective on the first day of the first pay period beginning on or after Jan. 1, 1998, as provided by Ex. Ord. No. 13071, Dec. 29, 1997, 62 F.R. 68521.

1997—Salaries of positions at level V continued at $108,200 per annum by Ex. Ord. No. 13033, Dec. 27, 1996, 61 F.R. 68987.

1996—Salaries of positions at level V continued at $108,200 per annum by Ex. Ord. No. 12984, Dec. 28, 1995, 61 F.R. 237.

1995—Salaries of positions at level V continued at $108,200 per annum by Ex. Ord. No. 12944, Dec. 28, 1994, 60 F.R. 309.

1993—Salaries of positions at level V increased to $108,200 per annum, effective on the first day of the first pay period beginning on or after Jan. 1, 1993, as provided by Ex. Ord. No. 12826, Dec. 30, 1992, 57 F.R. 62909.

1992—Salaries of positions at level V increased to $104,800 per annum, effective on the first day of the first pay period beginning on or after Jan. 1, 1992, as provided by Ex. Ord. No. 12786, Dec. 26, 1991, 56 F.R. 67453.

1991—Salaries of positions at level V increased to $101,300 per annum, effective on the first day of the first pay period beginning on or after Jan. 1, 1991, as provided by Ex. Ord. No. 12736, Dec. 12, 1990, 55 F.R. 51385.

1990—Salaries of positions at level V increased to $78,200 per annum, effective on the first day of the first pay period beginning on or after Jan. 1, 1990, and continued at that rate by Ex. Ord. No. 12698, Dec. 23, 1989, 54 F.R. 53473.

1989—Salaries of positions at level V increased to $75,500 per annum, effective on the first day of the first pay period beginning on or after Jan. 1, 1989, as provided by Ex. Ord. No. 12663, Jan. 6, 1989, 54 F.R. 791.

1988—Salaries of positions at level V continued at $72,500 per annum by Ex. Ord. No. 12622, Dec. 31, 1987, 53 F.R. 222.

1987—Salaries of positions at level V increased to $72,500 per annum, on recommendation of the President of the United States, see note set out under section 358 of Title 2, The Congress.

Salaries of positions at level V increased to $70,800 per annum, effective on the first day of the first pay period beginning on or after Jan. 1, 1987, as provided by Ex. Ord. No. 12578, Dec. 31, 1986, 52 F.R. 505.

1985—Salaries of positions at level V increased to $68,700 per annum, effective on the first day of the first pay period beginning on or after Jan. 1, 1985, as provided by Ex. Ord. No. 12496, Dec. 28, 1984, 50 F.R. 211, as amended by Ex. Ord. No. 12540, Dec. 30, 1985, 51 F.R. 577.

1984—Salaries of positions at level V increased to $66,400 per annum, effective on the first day of the first pay period beginning on or after Jan. 1, 1984, as provided by Ex. Ord. No. 12456, Dec. 30, 1983, 49 F.R. 347, as amended Ex. Ord. No. 12477, May 23, 1984, 49 F.R. 22041; Ex. Ord. No. 12487, Sept. 14, 1984, 49 F.R. 36493.

1982—Salaries of positions at level V increased to $63,800 per annum, effective on the first day of the first pay period beginning on or after Oct. 1, 1982, as provided by Ex. Ord. No. 12387, Oct. 8, 1982, 47 F.R. 44981. Ex. Ord. No. 12387 further provided that pursuant to section 101(e) of Pub. L. 97–276 funds are not available to pay a salary at a rate which exceeds the rate in effect on Sept. 30, 1982, which was $57,500.00.

Maximum rate payable after Dec. 17, 1982, increased from $57,500.00 to $63,800.00, see Pub. L. 97–377, title I, § 129(b)–(d), Dec. 21, 1982, 96 Stat. 1914, set out as a note under section 5318 of this title.

Limitations on use of funds for fiscal year ending Sept. 30, 1983, appropriated by any Act to pay the salary or pay of any individual in legislative, executive, or judicial branch in position equal to or above level V of the Executive Schedule, see section 101(e) of Pub. L. 97–276, as amended, set out as a note under section 5318 of this title.

1981—Salaries of positions at level V increased to $61,300 per annum, effective on the first day of the first pay period beginning on or after Oct. 1, 1981, as provided by Ex. Ord. No. 12330, Oct. 15, 1981, 46 F.R. 50921. Ex. Ord. No. 12330 further provided that pursuant to section 101(c) of Pub. L. 97–51 funds are not available to pay a salary at a rate which exceeds the rate in effect on Sept. 30, 1981, which was $50,112.50.

Limitations on use of funds for fiscal year ending Sept. 30, 1982, appropriated by any Act to pay the salary or pay of any individual in legislative, executive, or judicial branch in position equal to or above level V of the Executive Schedule, see sections 101(g) and 141 of Pub. L. 97–92, set out as a note under section 5318 of this title.

1980—Salaries of positions at level V increased to $58,500 per annum, effective on the first day of the first pay period beginning on or after Oct. 1, 1980, as provided by Ex. Ord. No. 12248, Oct. 16, 1980, 45 F.R. 69199. Ex. Ord. No. 12248, further provided that pursuant to section 101(c) of Pub. L. 96–369, funds are not available to pay a salary at a rate which exceeds the rate in effect on Sept. 30, 1980, which was $50,112.50.

Limitations on use of funds for fiscal year ending Sept. 30, 1981, appropriated by any Act to pay the salary or pay of any individual in legislative, executive, or judicial branch in position equal to or above level V of the Executive Schedule, see section 101(c) of Pub. L. 96–536, as amended, set out as a note under section 5318 of this title.

1979—Salaries of positions at level V increased to $53,600 per annum, effective on the first day of the first pay period beginning on or after Oct. 1, 1979, as provided by Ex. Ord. No. 12165, Oct. 9, 1979, 44 F.R. 58671, as amended by Ex. Ord. No. 12200, Mar. 12, 1980, 45 F.R. 16443. Ex. Ord. No. 12165 further provided that pursuant to section 101(c) of Pub. L. 96–86 funds appropriated for fiscal year 1980 may not be used to pay a salary at a rate which exceeds an increase of 5.5 percent over the rate in effect on Sept. 30, 1978, which is a maximum rate payable of $50,112.50.

Applicability to funds appropriated by any Act for fiscal year ending Sept. 30, 1980, of limitation of section 304 of Pub. L. 95–391 on use of funds to pay the salary or pay of any individual in legislative, executive, or judicial branch in position equal to or above level V of the Executive Schedule, see section 101 of Pub. L. 96–86, set out as a note under section 5318 of this title.

1978—Salaries of positions at level V increased to $50,100 per annum, effective in the first pay period beginning on or after Oct. 1, 1978, as provided by Ex. Ord. No. 12087, Oct. 7, 1978, 43 F.R. 46823. Ex. Ord. No. 12087, further provided that pursuant to the Legislative Branch Appropriation Act, 1979, funds are not available to pay a salary at a rate which exceeds the rate in effect on Sept. 30, 1978, which was $47,500.

Limitations on use of funds for fiscal year ending Sept. 30, 1979, appropriated by any Act to pay the salary or pay of any individual in legislative, executive, or judicial branch in position equal or above level V of the Executive Schedule, see section 304 of Pub. L. 95–391 and section 613 of Pub. L. 95–429, set out as a note under section 5318 of this title.

1977—Salaries of positions at level V increased to $47,500 per annum, on recommendation of the President of the United States, see note set out under section 358 of Title 2, The Congress.

1976—Salaries of positions at level V increased to $39,600 per annum, effective on the first day of the first pay period beginning on or after Oct. 1, 1976, see Ex. Ord. No. 11941, Oct. 1, 1976, 41 F.R. 43889. Ex Ord. No. 11941, further provided that pursuant to the Legislative Branch Appropriation Act, 1977, funds are not available to pay a salary at a rate which exceeds the rate in effect on Sept. 30, 1976, which was $37,800.

1975—Salaries of positions at level V increased to $37,800 per annum, effective on the first day of the first pay period beginning on or after Oct. 1, 1975, by Ex. Ord. No. 11883, Oct. 6, 1975, 40 F.R. 47091.

1969—Salaries of positions at level V increased from $28,000 to $36,000 per annum, commencing on the first day of the pay period which begins after February 14, 1969, on recommendation of the President of the United States, see note set out under section 358 of Title 2, The Congress.

This section is referred to in sections 5317, 5377, 5380, 8432 of this title; title 2 sections 60a–2, 74a–3, 282b, 288, 353, 437c, 1381, 1382; title 3 section 113; title 10 section 973; title 12 sections 1723a, 4703; title 15 section 2204; title 18 section 207; title 20 sections 1221e, 3501, 3503, 5826, 5848, 5933, 6021; title 21 sections 1305, 1908; title 22 sections 286a, 1465c, 1622c, 3506, 3612, 3961, 4106, 5510, 6432b; title 25 section 3505; title 26 sections 3121, 6103; title 28 sections 537, 548, 625; title 31 section 731; title 38 sections 7404, 7451; title 39 section 206; title 41 section 422; title 42 sections 300aa–12, 410, 907a, 1108, 1320b–9, 2996d, 3015, 5871, 5872, 7211, 7232, 7291, 7293, 7383, 10704, 11314; title 44 sections 303, 3319; title 47 section 155; title 49 section 106.

§ 5317. Presidential authority to place positions at levels IV and V

In addition to the positions listed in sections 5315 and 5316 of this title, the President, from time to time, may place in levels IV and V of the Executive Schedule positions held by not to exceed 34 individuals when he considers that action necessary to reflect changes in organization, management responsibilities, or workload in an Executive agency. Such an action with respect to a position to which appointment is made by the President by and with the advice and consent of the Senate is effective only at the time of a new appointment to the position. Notice of each action taken under this section shall be published in the Federal Register, except when the President determines that the publication would be contrary to the interest of national security. The President may not take action under this section with respect to a position the pay for which is fixed at a specific rate by this subchapter or by statute enacted after August 14, 1964.

(Pub. L. 89–554, Sept. 6, 1966, 80 Stat. 467; Pub. L. 89–670, § 10(d)(6), Oct. 15, 1966, 80 Stat. 948; Pub. L. 90–83, § 1(17), Sept. 11, 1967, 81 Stat. 199.)

HISTORICAL AND REVISION NOTES
1966 ACT

Derivation	U.S. Code	Revised Statutes and Statutes at Large
....	5 U.S.C. 2211(f).	Aug. 14, 1964, Pub. L. 88–426, § 303(f), 78 Stat. 421.

The word "offices" is omitted as included in "positions". The term "Executive agency" is substituted for "Federal department or agency" in view of the definition in section 105. The words "after August 14, 1964" are substituted for "subsequent to the date of enactment of this Act".

Standard changes are made to conform with the definitions applicable and the style of this title as outlined in the preface to the report.

1967 ACT

The amendment to 5 U.S.C. 5317 conforms to the style of title 5.

AMENDMENTS

1966—Pub. L. 89–670 increased from thirty to thirty-four the number of additional level IV and V positions authorized when necessary.

EFFECTIVE DATE OF 1966 AMENDMENT

Amendment by Pub. L. 89–670 effective Apr. 1, 1967, as prescribed by President and published in Federal Register, see section 16(a), formerly § 15(a), of Pub. L. 89–670 and Ex. Ord. No. 11340, Mar. 30, 1967, 32 F.R. 5453.

EXECUTIVE ORDER NO. 11189

Ex. Ord. No. 11189, Nov. 23, 1964, 29 F.R. 15855, which placed certain positions in levels IV and V of the Executive Schedule, was revoked by Ex. Ord. No. 12060, May 15, 1978, 43 F.R. 21315.

EXECUTIVE ORDER NO. 11195

Ex. Ord. No. 11195, Jan. 30, 1965, 30 F.R. 1169, which placed certain positions in levels IV and V of the Executive Schedule, was revoked by Ex. Ord. No. 12060, May 15, 1978, 43 F.R. 21315.

EXECUTIVE ORDER NO. 11861

Ex. Ord. 11861, May 21, 1975, 40 F.R. 22531, as amended by Ex. Ord. No. 11864, June 13, 1975, 40 F.R. 25579; Ex. Ord. No. 11872, July 21, 1975, 40 F.R. 30619; Ex. Ord. No. 11877, Sept. 2, 1975, 40 F.R. 40797; Ex. Ord. No. 11885, Oct. 15, 1975, 40 F.R. 48491; Ex. Ord. No. 11893, Dec. 31, 1975, 41 F.R. 1040; Ex. Ord. No. 11898, Jan. 14, 1976, 41 F.R. 2365; Ex. Ord. No. 11908, Mar. 18, 1976, 41 F.R. 11805; Ex. Ord. No. 11927, July 22, 1976, 41 F.R. 30583; Ex. Ord. No. 11976, Mar. 11, 1977, 42 F.R. 14081; Ex. Ord. No. 11983, May 4, 1977, 42 F.R. 23127; Ex. Ord. No. 11986, May 20, 1977, 42 F.R. 26407; Ex. Ord. No. 11995, June 8, 1977, 42 F.R. 29841; Ex. Ord. No. 11999, June 27, 1977, 42 F.R. 33255; Ex. Ord. No. 12025, Dec. 1, 1977, 42 F.R. 61447; Ex. Ord. No. 12035, Jan. 20, 1978, 43 F.R. 3073; Ex. Ord. No. 12060, May 15, 1978, 43 F.R. 21315; Ex. Ord. No. 12069, June 30, 1978, 43 F.R. 28973, which related to the placement of certain positions in levels IV and V, was revoked by Ex. Ord. No. 12076, Aug. 18, 1978, 43 F.R. 37161, formerly set out below.

EXECUTIVE ORDER NO. 11864

Ex. Ord. No. 11864, June 13, 1975, 40 F.R. 25579, which placed the position of Adviser to the Secretary (Counselor, Economic Policy Board), Department of the Treasury, to terminate effective August 1, 1975, in level IV of the Executive Schedule was superseded by Ex. Ord. No. 11877, Sept. 2, 1975, 40 F.R. 40797.

EXECUTIVE ORDER NO. 11995

Ex. Ord. No. 11995, June 8, 1977, 42 F.R. 29841, which placed the position of Executive Director, Federal Personnel Management Systems Study, United States Civil Service Commission, in level V of the Executive Schedule, was revoked by Ex. Ord. No. 12060, May 15, 1978, 43 F.R. 21315.

EXECUTIVE ORDER NO. 12076

Ex. Ord. No. 12076, Aug. 18, 1978, 43 F.R. 37161, as amended by Ex. Ord. No. 12099, Nov. 17, 1978, 43 F.R. 54191; Ex. Ord. No. 12111, Jan. 2, 1979, 44 F.R. 1071; Ex. Ord. No. 12119, Feb. 14, 1979, 44 F.R. 10039, which related to the placement of positions in levels IV and V of the Federal Executive Salary Schedule, was revoked by Ex. Ord. No. 12154, Sept. 4, 1979, 44 F.R. 51965, set out below.

EX. ORD. NO. 12154. PLACEMENT OF POSITIONS IN LEVELS IV AND V

Ex. Ord. No. 12154, Sept. 4, 1979, 44 F.R. 51965, as amended by Ex. Ord. No. 12199, Mar. 12, 1980, 45 F.R. 16441; Ex. Ord. No. 12236, Sept. 3, 1980, 45 F.R. 58805; Ex. Ord. No. 12237, Sept. 3, 1980, 45 F.R. 58807; Ex. Ord. No. 12422, May 20, 1983, 48 F.R. 23157; Ex. Ord. No. 12431, July 8, 1983, 48 F.R. 31849; Ex. Ord. No. 12608, Sept. 9, 1987, 52 F.R. 34617; Ex. Ord. No. 12678, Apr. 28, 1989, 54 F.R. 18872; Ex. Ord. No. 12679, June 23, 1989, 54 F.R. 27149; Ex. Ord. No. 12749, Feb. 4, 1991, 56 F.R. 4711; Ex. Ord. No. 12758, Apr. 5, 1991, 56 F.R. 14631; Ex. Ord. No. 12814, Sept. 10, 1992, 57 F.R. 42483; Ex. Ord. No. 12833, Jan. 19, 1993, 58 F.R. 5907; Ex. Ord. No. 12841, Mar. 9, 1993, 58 F.R. 13529;

Ex. Ord. No. 12942, Dec. 12, 1994, 59 F.R. 64551; Ex. Ord. No. 13063, Sept. 30, 1997, 62 F.R. 51757, provided:

By the authority vested in me as President by Section 5317 of Title 5 of the United States Code it is hereby ordered as follows:

1-1. EXECUTIVE SCHEDULE POSITIONS

1-101. The following positions are placed in level IV of the Executive Schedule:

(a) Counselor to the Secretary, Department of the Treasury.

(b) Deputy Under Secretary for International Labor Affairs, Department of Labor.

(c) Administrator, Alcohol, Drug Abuse and Mental Health Administration, Department of Health and Human Services.

(d) Executive Secretary of the National Security Council.

(e) Administrator, Office of Juvenile Justice and Delinquency Prevention, Department of Justice.

(f) Comptroller of the Department of Defense [now Under Secretary of Defense (Comptroller)].

(g) Assistant Secretary of the Air Force (1).

(h) Director, Office for Victims of Crime, Department of Justice.

(i) Director, Bureau of Justice Assistance, Department of Justice.

(j) Director of the National Institutes of Health.

(k) Members, Chemical Safety and Hazard Investigation Board (5).

(k)[(l)] Commissioner on Aging [now Assistant Secretary for Aging], Department of Health and Human Services[.]

1-102. The following positions are placed in level V of the Executive Schedule:

(a) Deputy Assistant Secretary of Defense for Reserve Affairs, Department of Defense.

(b) Executive Assistant and Counselor to the Secretary of Labor, Department of Labor.

(c) Deputy Under Secretary for Education, Department of Education.

(d) Deputy Under Secretary for Education, Department of Education.

(e) Commissioner, Administration for Native Americans[.]

1-2. GENERAL PROVISIONS

1-201. Nothing in this Order shall be deemed to terminate or otherwise affect the appointment, or to require the reappointment, of any occupant of any position listed in Section 1-1 of this Order who was the occupant of that position immediately prior to the issuance of this Order.

1-202. Executive Order No. 12076, as amended, is hereby revoked.

SECTION REFERRED TO IN OTHER SECTIONS

This section is referred to in sections 5377, 5380, 8432 of this title; title 10 section 973; title 26 section 3121; title 28 sections 548, 587; title 42 section 410.

§ 5318. Adjustments in rates of pay

(a) Subject to subsection (b), effective at the beginning of the first applicable pay period commencing on or after the first day of the month in which an adjustment takes effect under section 5303 of this title in the rates of pay under the General Schedule, the annual rate of pay for positions at each level of the Executive Schedule shall be adjusted by an amount, rounded to the nearest multiple of $100 (or if midway between multiples of $100, to the next higher multiple of $100), equal to the percentage of such annual rate of pay which corresponds to the most recent percentage change in the ECI (relative to the date described in the next sentence), as determined under section 704(a)(1) of the Ethics

Reform Act of 1989. The appropriate date under this sentence is the first day of the fiscal year in which such adjustment in the rates of pay under the General Schedule takes effect.

(b) In no event shall the percentage adjustment taking effect under subsection (a) in any calendar year (before rounding), in any rate of pay, exceed the percentage adjustment taking effect in such calendar year under section 5303 in the rates of pay under the General Schedule.

(Added Pub. L. 94-82, title II, §202(a), Aug. 9, 1975, 89 Stat. 419; amended Pub. L. 101-194, title VII, §704(a)(2)(A), Nov. 30, 1989, 103 Stat. 1769; Pub. L. 101-509, title V, §529 [title I, §101(b)(4)(A)], Nov. 5, 1990, 104 Stat. 1427, 1439; Pub. L. 103-356, title I, §101(3), Oct. 13, 1994, 108 Stat. 3411.)

REFERENCES IN TEXT

The General Schedule, referred to in text, is set out under section 5332 of this title.

Section 704(a)(1) of the Ethics Reform Act of 1989, referred to in subsec. (a), is section 704(a)(1) of Pub. L. 101-194, which is set out below.

AMENDMENTS

1994—Pub. L. 103-356 designated existing provisions as subsec. (a), substituted "Subject to subsection (b), effective" for "Effective", and added subsec. (b).

1990—Pub. L. 101-509 substituted "5303" for "5305".

1989—Pub. L. 101-194 substituted "corresponds to the most recent percentage change in the ECI (relative to the date described in the next sentence), as determined under section 704(a)(1) of the Ethics Reform Act of 1989. The appropriate date under this sentence is the first day of the fiscal year in which such adjustment in the rates of pay under the General Schedule takes effect" for "corresponds to the overall average percentage (as set forth in the report transmitted to the Congress under such section 5305) of the adjustment in the rates of pay under the General Schedule".

EFFECTIVE DATE OF 1994 AMENDMENT

Section 101 of Pub. L. 103-356 provided that the amendment made by that section is effective as of Dec. 31, 1994.

EFFECTIVE DATE OF 1990 AMENDMENT

Amendment by Pub. L. 101-509 effective on such date as the President shall determine, but not earlier than 90 days, and not later than 180 days, after Nov. 5, 1990, see section 529 [title III, §305] of Pub. L. 101-509, set out as a note under section 5301 of this title.

EFFECTIVE DATE OF 1989 AMENDMENT

Section 704(b) of Pub. L. 101-194 provided that: "This section and the amendments made by this section [amending this section, section 31 of Title 2, The Congress, section 104 of Title 3, The President, and section 461 of Title 28, Judiciary and Judicial Procedure, and enacting provisions set out as a note under this section] shall take effect on January 1, 1991."

SALARY LEVELS OF SENIOR GOVERNMENT OFFICIALS

Pub. L. 102-90, title I, §6(a), Aug. 14, 1991, 105 Stat. 450, provided that: "The rate of pay for the offices referred to under section 703(a)(2)(B) of the Ethics Reform Act of 1989 [Pub. L. 101-194] (5 U.S.C. 5318 note) shall be the rate of pay that would be payable for each such office if the provisions of sections 703(a)(2)(B) and 1101(a)(1)(A) of such Act (5 U.S.C. 5318 note and 5305 note) had not been enacted."

Section 703 of Pub. L. 101-194 provided that:

"(a) SALARY LEVELS.—

"(1) EXECUTIVE POSITIONS.—Effective the first day of the first applicable pay period that begins on or after January 1, 1991, the rate of basic pay for positions in the Executive Schedule shall be increased in the amount of 25 percent of their respective rates (as last in effect before the increase), rounded to the nearest multiple of $100 (or, if midway between multiples of $100, to the next higher multiple of $100).

"(2) LEGISLATIVE POSITIONS; OFFICE OF THE VICE PRESIDENT.—

"(A) GENERALLY.—Effective the first day of the first applicable pay period that begins on or after January 1, 1991, the rate of basic pay for the offices and positions under subparagraphs (A) and (B) of section 225(f) of the Federal Salary Act of 1967 (2 U.S.C. 356(A) and (B)) shall be increased in the amount of 25 percent of their respective rates (as last in effect before the increase), rounded to the nearest multiple of $100 (or, if midway between multiples of $100, to the next higher multiple of $100), except as provided in subparagraph (B).

"(B) EXCEPTIONS.—Nothing in subparagraph (A) shall affect the rate of basic pay for a Senator, the President pro tempore of the Senate, or the majority leader or the minority leader of the Senate.

"(3) JUDICIAL POSITIONS.—Effective the first day of the first applicable pay period that begins on or after January 1, 1991, the rate of basic pay for the Chief Justice of the United States, an associate justice of the Supreme Court of the United States, a judge of a United States circuit court, a judge of a district court of the United States, and a judge of the United States Court of International Trade shall be increased in the amount of 25 percent of their respective rates (as last in effect before the increase), rounded to the nearest multiple of $100 (or, if midway between multiples of $100, to the next higher multiple of $100).

"(b) COORDINATION RULE.—If a pay adjustment under subsection (a) is to be made for an office or position as of the same date as any other pay adjustment affecting such office or position, the adjustment under subsection (a) shall be made first."

REVISION IN METHOD BY WHICH ANNUAL PAY ADJUSTMENTS FOR CERTAIN EXECUTIVE, LEGISLATIVE, AND JUDICIAL POSITIONS ARE TO BE MADE

Section 704(a) of Pub. L. 101–194 provided that:

"(a) PERCENT CHANGE IN THE EMPLOYMENT COST INDEX.—

"(1) METHOD FOR COMPUTING PERCENT CHANGE IN THE ECI.—

"(A) DEFINITIONS.—For purposes of this paragraph—

"(i) the term 'Employment Cost Index' or 'ECI' means the Employment Cost Index (wages and salaries, private industry workers) published quarterly by the Bureau of Labor Statistics; and

"(ii) the term 'base quarter' means the 3-month period ending on December 31 of a year.

"(B) METHOD.—For purposes of the provisions of law amended by paragraph (2), the 'most recent percentage change in the ECI', as of any date, shall be one-half of 1 percent less than the percentage (rounded to the nearest one-tenth of 1 percent) derived by—

"(i) reducing—

"(I) the ECI for the last base quarter prior to that date, by

"(II) the ECI for the second to last base quarter prior to that date,

"(ii) dividing the difference under clause (i) by the ECI for the base quarter referred to in clause (i)(II), and

"(iii) multiplying the quotient under clause (ii) by 100, except that no percentage change determined under this paragraph shall be—

"(I) less than zero; or

"(II) greater than 5 percent.

"(2) PROVISIONS THROUGH WHICH NEW METHOD IS TO BE IMPLEMENTED.—

"(A) AMENDMENT TO TITLES 3, 5, AND 28 OF THE UNITED STATES CODE.—Section 104 of title 3, United

States Code, section 5318 of title 5, United States Code, and section 461(a) of title 28, United States Code, are amended by striking 'corresponds to' and all that follows thereafter through the period, and inserting the following:

'corresponds to the most recent percentage change in the ECI (relative to the date described in the next sentence), as determined under section 704(a)(1) of the Ethics Reform Act of 1989. The appropriate date under this sentence is the first day of the fiscal year in which such adjustment in the rates of pay under the General Schedule takes effect.'.

"(B) AMENDMENT TO THE LEGISLATIVE REORGANIZATION ACT OF 1946.—Section 601(a)(2) of the Legislative Reorganization Act of 1946 (2 U.S.C. 31(2)) is amended by striking 'corresponds to' and all that follows thereafter through the period and inserting the following:

'corresponds to the most recent percentage change in the ECI (relative to the date described in the next sentence), as determined under section 704(a)(1) of the Ethics Reform Act of 1989. The appropriate date under this sentence is the first day of the fiscal year in which such adjustment in the rates of pay under the General Schedule takes effect.'.''

REDUCTION OF RATE OF SALARY OR BASIC PAY OF OFFICES OR POSITIONS IN THE EXECUTIVE, LEGISLATIVE, AND JUDICIAL BRANCHES TO THE SALARY OR BASIC PAY RATE PAYABLE AS OF JULY 14, 1983

Pub. L. 98–51, title III, § 304, July 14, 1983, 97 Stat. 279, provided that:

"(a) Except as provided in subsection (b), the rate of salary or basic pay prescribed by law as of the date of the enactment of this Act [July 14, 1983] shall be reduced to the salary or basic pay rate payable as of such date in the case of—

"(1) any office or position at level I, II, or III of the Executive Schedule,

"(2) any Member of Congress, and

"(3) any other office or position in the legislative, executive, or judicial branch, or in the government of the District of Columbia, for which the rate of salary or basic pay that is payable on such date of enactment is less than the rate then prescribed by law.

"(b) In the case of any office or position in the legislative, executive, or judicial branch, or in the government of the District of Columbia, for which the maximum rate of salary or basic pay that is payable on the date of the enactment of this Act [July 14, 1983] is less than the maximum rate then prescribed by law, the maximum rate prescribed by law as of such date of enactment shall be reduced to the maximum rate payable as of such date.

"(c) In determining the amount of the reduction under this section in the case of any Senator, the provisions of section 129, of Public Law 97–377 [set out as a note below] shall be applied without regard to subsection (c) of such section."

LIMITATION ON MAXIMUM RATE OF SALARY INCREASES FOR SENIOR EXECUTIVE, JUDICIAL, AND LEGISLATIVE POSITIONS (INCLUDING MEMBERS OF CONGRESS); SERVICES PERFORMED AFTER DECEMBER 17, 1982; APPLICABILITY TO SENATORS; CONSTRUCTION WITH PROVISIONS RELATING TO ANNUAL RATES OF COMPENSATION OF OFFICERS AND EMPLOYEES OF THE SENATE

Pub. L. 97–377, title I, § 129(b)–(d), Dec. 21, 1982, 96 Stat. 1914, provided that:

"(b) In lieu of payment of salary increases of up to 27.2 percent as authorized by law for senior executive, judicial, and legislative positions (including Members of Congress), it is the purpose of this section [enacting this provision and amending section 101(e) of Pub. L. 97–276, set out below] to limit such increases to 15 percent. Notwithstanding the provisions of section 306 of S. 2939 [set out below] made applicable by subsection (a) of this section, nothing in subsection (a) shall (or be construed to) require that the rate of salary or pay payable to any individual for or on account of services performed after December 17, 1982, be limited to an amount less than the rate (or maximum rate, if higher) of salary or pay payable as of such date for the position involved increased by 15 percent and rounded in accordance with section 5318 of title 5, United States Code.

"(c) Subsection (b) shall not apply to Senators.

"(d) For the purposes of any rule, regulation, or order having the force and effect of law and limiting the annual rates of compensation of officers and employees of the Senate by reference to the annual rate of pay of Senators, the annual rate of pay of Senators shall be deemed to be the annual rate of pay that would be payable to Senators without regard to subsection (c) of this section."

FISCAL YEAR 1983 LIMITATION ON USE OF FUNDS FOR PAY ADJUSTMENTS FOR CERTAIN POSITIONS

Pub. L. 97–276, § 101(e), Oct. 2, 1982, 96 Stat. 1189, as amended by Pub. L. 97–377, title I, § 129(a), Dec. 21, 1982, 96 Stat. 1914, provided in part that: "the provisions of section 306(a), (b), and (d) of S. 2939 [Ninety-seventh Congress, 2nd Session, as reported Sept. 22, 1982] shall apply to any appropriation, fund, or authority made available for the period October 1, 1982, through September 30, 1983, by this or any other Act." Section 306(a), (b), and (d) of S. 2939, Ninety-seventh Congress, 2nd Session, as reported Sept. 22, 1982, provided that:

"(a) No part of the funds appropriated for the fiscal year ending September 30, 1983, by this Act or any other Act may be used to pay the salary or pay of any individual in an office or position in the legislative, executive, or judicial branch, or in the government of the District of Columbia, at a rate which exceeds the rate (or maximum rate, if higher) of salary or basic pay payable for such office or position for September 30, 1982, if the rate of salary or basic pay for that office or position is—

"(1) fixed at a rate which is equal to or greater than the rate of basic pay for level V of the Executive Schedule under section 5316 of title 5, United States Code, or

"(2) limited to a maximum rate which is equal to or greater than the rate of basic pay for such level V (or to a percentage of such a maximum rate) by reason of section 5308 of title 5, United States Code, or any other provision of law or congressional resolution.

"(b) For purposes of subsection (a), the rate or maximum rate (as the case may be) of salary or basic pay payable for September 30, 1982, for any office or position which was not in existence on such date shall be deemed to be the rate or maximum rate (as the case may be) of salary or basic pay payable to individuals in comparable offices or positions for such date, as determined under regulations prescribed—

"(1) by the President, in the case of any office or position within the executive branch or in the government of the District of Columbia;

"(2) jointly by the Speaker of the House of Representatives and the President pro tempore of the Senate, in the case of any office or position within the legislative branch; or

"(3) by the Chief Justice of the United States, in the case of any office or position within the judicial branch.

"(d) For purposes of administering any provisions of law, rule, or regulation which provides retirement, life insurance, or other employee benefit, which requires any deduction or contribution, or which imposes any requirement or limitation, on the basis of a rate of salary or basic pay, the rate of salary or basic pay payable after the application of this section shall be treated as the rate of salary or basic pay."

FISCAL YEAR 1982 LIMITATION ON USE OF FUNDS FOR PAY ADJUSTMENTS FOR CERTAIN POSITIONS

Pub. L. 97–92, § 101(g), Dec. 15, 1981, 95 Stat. 1190, provided that: "The provisions of section 305(a), (b), and (d) of H.R. 4120, entitled the Legislative Branch Appropria-

tion Act, 1982, shall apply to any appropriation, fund, or authority made available for the period October 1, 1981, through September 30, 1982, by this or any other Act." Section 305(a), (b), and (d) of H.R. 4120, as reported July 9, 1981, provided that:

"(a) No part of the funds appropriated for the fiscal year ending September 30, 1982, by this Act or any other Act may be used to pay the salary or pay of any individual in any office or position in the legislative, executive, or judicial branch, or in the government of the District of Columbia, at a rate which exceeds the rate (or maximum rate, if higher) of salary or basic pay payable for such office or position for September 30, 1981, if the rate of salary or basic pay for that office or position is—

"(1) fixed at a rate which is equal to or greater than the rate of basic pay for level V of the executive Schedule under section 5316 of title 5, United States Code, or

"(2) limited to a maximum rate which is equal to or greater than the rate of basic pay for such level V (or to a percentage of such a maximum rate) by reason of section 5308 of title 5, United States Code, or any other provision of law or congressional resolution.

"(b) For purposes of subsection (a), the rate or maximum rate (as the case may be) of salary or basic pay payable for September 30, 1981, for any office or position which was not in existence on such date shall be deemed to be the rate or maximum rate (as the case may be) of salary or basic pay payable to individuals in comparable offices or positions for such date, as determined under regulations prescribed—

"(1) by the President, in the case of any office or position within the executive branch or in the government of the District of Columbia;

"(2) jointly by the Speaker of the House of Representatives and the President pro tempore of the Senate, in the case of any office or position within the legislative branch; or

"(3) by the Chief Justice of the United States, in the case of any office or position within the judicial branch.

"(d) For purposes of administering any provision of law, rule, or regulation which provides retirement, life insurance, or other employee benefit, which requires any deduction or contribution, or which imposes any requirement or limitation, on the basis of a rate of salary or basic pay, the rate of salary or basic pay payable after the application of this section shall be treated as the rate of salary or basic pay."

Similar provisions were contained in Pub. L. 97–51, § 101(c), Oct. 1, 1981, 95 Stat. 959, as amended Pub. L. 97–85, Nov. 23, 1981, 95 Stat. 1098.

Pub. L. 97–92, § 141, Dec. 15, 1981, 95 Stat. 1200, provided that:

"(a) Notwithstanding the provisions of section 305 of H.R. 4120 made applicable by section 101(g) of this joint resolution [set out above], but subject to subsection (b) of this section, nothing in section 101(g) shall (or shall be construed to) require that the rate of salary or basic pay, payable to any individual for or on account of services performed after December 31, 1981, be limited to or reduced to an amount which is less than—

"(1) $59,500, if such individual has an office or position the salary or pay for which corresponds to the rate of basic pay for level III of the Executive Schedule under section 5314 of title 5, United States Code;

"(2) $58,500, if such individual has an office or position the salary or pay for which corresponds to the rate of basic pay for level IV of the Executive Schedule under section 5315 of title 5, United States Code; or

"(3) $57,500, if such individual has an office or position the salary or pay for which corresponds to the rate of basic pay for level V of the Executive Schedule under section 5316 of title 5, United States Code.

"(b)(1) For purposes of subsection (a), any rate of salary or pay shall be considered to correspond to the basic pay for a level of the Executive Schedule if the rate of salary or pay for that office or position is (i) fixed at a rate which is equal to or greater than the rate of basic pay for that level of the Executive Schedule or (ii) limited to a maximum rate which is equal to or greater than the rate of basic pay for such level (or to a percentage of such a maximum rate) by reason of section 5308 of title 5, United States Code, or any other provision of law (other than the provisions of such section 305, as made applicable by section 101(g) of this joint resolution) or congressional resolution.

"(2) In applying subsection (a) for any office or position for which the rate of salary or basic pay is limited to a percentage of such a maximum rate, there shall be substituted, in lieu of the amount specified in subsection (a) for that office or position, an amount equal to such percentage of the specified amount.

"(c) Any adjustment pursuant to this section made to the pay of any employee or class of employees whose pay is disbursed by the Clerk of the House should be of such amount as to assure, to the maximum extent practicable, that such employees are not paid at rates at less than employees or classes of employees whose pay is disbursed by the Secretary of the Senate and who hold equivalent positions."

FISCAL YEAR 1981 LIMITATION ON USE OF FUNDS FOR PAY ADJUSTMENTS FOR CERTAIN POSITIONS

Pub. L. 96-536, §101(c), Dec. 16, 1980, 94 Stat. 3167, as amended by Pub. L. 97-12, title IV, §401, June 5, 1981, 95 Stat. 95, making further continuing appropriations for fiscal year 1981, provided in part that: "the provisions of section 306(a), (b), and (d) of H.R. 7593 (providing salary pay cap limitations for executive, legislative, and judicial employees and officials) [as passed the House of Representatives, July 21, 1980] shall apply to any appropriation, fund, or authority made available for the period October 1, 1980, through September 30, 1981, by this or any other Act." Section 306(a), (b), and (d) of H.R. 7593, as passed the House of Representatives on July 21, 1980, provided that:

"(a) No part of the funds appropriated for the fiscal year ending September 30, 1981, by this Act or any other Act may be used to pay the salary or pay of any individual in any office or position in the legislative, executive, or judicial branch, or in the government of the District of Columbia, at a rate which exceeds the rate (or maximum rate, if higher) of salary or basic pay payable for such office or position for September 30, 1980, if the rate of salary or basic pay for that office or position is—

"(1) fixed at a rate which is equal to or greater than the rate of basic pay for level V of the Executive Schedule under section 5316 of title 5, United States Code, or

"(2) limited to a maximum rate which is equal to or greater than the rate of basic pay for such level V (or to a percentage of such a maximum rate) by reason of section 5308 of title 5, United States Code, or any other provision of law or congressional resolution.

"(b) For purposes of subsection (a), the rate or maximum rate (as the case may be) of salary or basic pay payable for September 3, 1980, for any office or position which was not in existence on such date shall be deemed to be the rate or maximum rate (as the case may be) of salary or basic pay payable to individuals in comparable offices or positions for such date, as determined under regulations prescribed—

"(1) by the President, in the case of any office or position within the executive branch or in the government of the District of Columbia;

"(2) jointly by the Speaker of the House of Representatives and the President pro tempore of the Senate, in the case of any office or position within the legislative branch; or

"(3) by the Chief Justice of the United States, in the case of any office or position within the judicial branch.

"(d) For purposes of administering any provision of law, rule, or regulation which provides retirement, life insurance, or other employee benefit, which requires any deduction or contribution, or which imposes any

requirement or limitation, on the basis of a rate of salary or basic pay, the rate of salary or basic pay payable after the application of this section shall be treated as the rate of salary or basic pay."

Similar provisions were contained in Pub. L. 96-369, §101(c), Oct. 1, 1980, 94 Stat. 1352.

FISCAL YEAR 1980 LIMITATION ON USE OF FUNDS FOR PAY ADJUSTMENTS FOR CERTAIN POSITIONS

Pub. L. 96-86, §101(c), Oct. 12, 1979, 93 Stat. 657, provided in part that:

"For the fiscal year 1980, funds available for payment to executive employees, which includes Members of Congress, who under existing law are entitled to approximately 12.9 percent increase in pay, shall not be used to pay any such employee or elected or appointed official any sum in excess of 5.5 percent increase in existing pay and such sum if accepted shall be in lieu of the 12.9 percent due for such fiscal year.

"*Provided, further*, That for the purpose of carrying out this provision and notwithstanding the provisions of the Federal Pay Comparability Act of 1970 [Pub. L. 91-656], the Executive Salary Cost-Of-Living Adjustment Act [Pub. L. 94-82], or any other related provision of law, which would provide an approximate 12.9 percent increase in pay for certain Federal officials for pay periods beginning on or after October 1, 1979, and notwithstanding section 102 of this joint resolution, the provisions of section 304 of the Legislative Branch Appropriation Act, 1979 [set out below], which limit the pay for certain Federal offices and positions, shall apply to funds appropriated by this joint resolution or any Act for the fiscal year 1980, except that in applying such limitation the term 'at a rate which exceeds by more than 5.5 percent the rate' shall be substituted for the term 'at a rate which exceeds the rate' where it appears in subsection (a) of such section for the purpose of limiting pay increases to 5.5 percent."

FISCAL YEAR 1979 LIMITATION ON USE OF FUNDS FOR PAY ADJUSTMENTS FOR CERTAIN POSITIONS

Pub. L. 95-429, title VI, §613, Oct. 10, 1978, 92 Stat. 1017, provided that:

"(a) No part of the funds appropriated for the fiscal year ending September 30, 1979, by this Act or any other Act may be used to pay the salary or pay of any individual in any office or position in the legislative, executive, or judicial branch, or in the government of the District of Columbia, at a rate which exceeds the rate (or maximum rate, if higher) of salary or basic pay payable for such office or position for September 30, 1978, if the rate of salary or basic pay for such office or position is—

"(1) fixed at a rate which is equal to or greater than the rate of basic pay for level V of the Executive Schedule under section 5316 of title 5, United States Code, or

"(2) limited to a maximum rate which is equal to or greater than the rate of basic pay for such level V (or to a percentage of such a maximum rate) by reason of section 5308 of title 5, United States Code or any other provision of law or congressional resolution.

"(b) For purposes of subsection (a), the rate or maximum rate (as the case may be) of salary or basic pay payable for September 30, 1978, for any office or position which was not in existence on such date shall be deemed to be the rate or maximum rate (as the case may be) of salary or basic pay payable to individuals in comparable offices or positions for such date, as determined under regulations prescribed—

"(1) by the President, in the case of any office or position within the executive branch or in the government of the District of Columbia;

"(2) jointly by the Speaker of the House and the President pro tempore of the Senate, in the case of any office or position within the legislative branch; or

"(3) by the Chief Justice of the United States, in the case of any office or position within the judicial branch.

"(c) For purposes of administering any provision of law, rule, or regulation which provides retirement, life insurance, or other employee benefit, which requires any deduction or contribution, or which imposes any requirement or limitation, on the basis of a rate of salary or basic pay, the rate of salary or basic pay payable after the application of this section shall be treated as the rate of salary or basic pay."

Identical provisions were enacted by Pub. L. 95–391, title III, § 304, Sept. 30, 1978, 92 Stat. 788.

1977 COMPARABILITY ADJUSTMENT NOT EFFECTIVE FOR CERTAIN POSITIONS

Pub. L. 95–66, July 11, 1977, 91 Stat. 270, provided that: "The first adjustment which, but for this Act, would be made after the date of enactment of this Act under the following provisions of law in the salary or rate of pay of positions or individuals to which such provisions apply, shall not take effect:

"(1) the second sentence of section 104 of title 3, United States Code, relating to comparability adjustments in the salary of the Vice President of the United States;

"(2) paragraph (2) of section 601(a) of the Legislative Reorganization Act of 1946 (2 U.S.C. 31), relating to comparability adjustments in the annual rate of pay of Members of Congress;

"(3) section 461 of title 28, United States Code, relating to comparability adjustments in the salary and rate of pay of justices, judges, commissioners, and referees; and

"(4) section 5318 of title 5, United States Code, relating to comparability adjustments in the annual rate of pay for positions in the Executive Schedule."

FISCAL YEAR 1977 LIMITATION ON USE OF FUNDS FOR PAY ADJUSTMENTS FOR CERTAIN POSITIONS

Pub. L. 94–440, title II, § 100, Oct. 1, 1976, 90 Stat. 1446, provided that: "No part of the funds appropriated in this Act or any other Act shall be used to pay the salary of an individual in a position or office referred to in section 225(f) of the Federal Salary Act of 1967, as amended (2 U.S.C. 356), including a Delegate to the House of Representatives, at a rate which exceeds the salary rate in effect on September 30, 1976, for such position or office except increases submitted by the President pursuant to section 225 of the Federal Salary Act of 1967."

SECTION REFERRED TO IN OTHER SECTIONS

This section is referred to in sections 5312, 5313, 5314, 5315, 5316 of this title.

SUBCHAPTER III—GENERAL SCHEDULE PAY RATES

SUBCHAPTER REFERRED TO IN OTHER SECTIONS

This subchapter is referred to in sections 3102, 3109, 3161, 3374, 4505a, 5302, 5392, 5541, 5544, 5545, 5753, 5754, 5755, 7204, 9509 of this title; title 2 sections 60e–2, 60e–2a, 60e–2b, 60e–6, 162a, 166, 197, 293, 353, 356, 437c; title 4 section 142; title 7 sections 511m, 610, 1507, 1642, 1765a, 6981, 7317; title 10 sections 1464, 2006, 2903, 4540, 7212, 9540; title 12 sections 482, 1441a, 1462a, 1701c, 1766, 2245, 2405, 3012, 4515, 4703; title 13 section 23; title 14 section 432; title 15 sections 78d, 78s, 205i, 278e, 327, 634d, 648, 714g, 714h, 715h, 717q, 1023, 2451, 4105; title 16 sections 18c, 410cc–36, 410pp–4, 410ww–24, 410ccc–22, 450jj–1, 450ss–3, 469j, 470m, 583j–1, 590d, 793, 825i, 832i, 833h, 916*l*, 3702, 4604; title 18 section 4001; title 20 sections 74, 75f, 76dd, 80g, 80*o*, 80q–4, 1018, 1067j, 1089, 1098, 1102, 1137, 1138b, 1145, 1221e, 1417, 2106, 3413, 3425, 4512, 5509, 5826, 5933, 6011, 9011, 9105, 9252; title 21 sections 393, 1908; title 22 sections 272a, 277d–3, 277d–19, 280b, 280i, 280k, 287e, 287r, 289b, 290b, 2024, 2083, 2421, 2454, 2581, 3008, 4154, 4606, 6204, 6432b; title 25 sections 2a, 305a, 633, 640d–11, 2012, 2707; title 26 sections 7471, 9010, 9040; title 28 sections 625, 626; title 29 sections 172, 661, 676, 762, 783, 1147; title 30 sections 556, 664, 823; title 31 section 3801; title 33 sections

569a, 984, 1325, 1374; title 35 sections 3, 7; title 36 sections 510, 2303, 151304, 151307, 151704, 151707, 152404, 152407; title 38 sections 4103, 7281, 7631, 7802; title 40 sections 13b, 166b–1f, 166b–3, 174j–8, 609, 873, 1106; title 40 App. section 109; title 41 sections 38, 46, 104, 422; title 42 sections 204, 217a, 237, 282, 290aa, 299c–1, 300v–2, 907a, 1320a–4, 1320b–9, 1563, 1731, 1855f, 1873, 1962a–4, 2000e–4, 2000g, 2201, 2473, 4276, 4365, 4372, 5149, 5667g–2, 6063, 7383, 10266, 12373, 12619, 12651f, 14196; title 43 sections 316n, 1731; title 45 sections 154, 362; title 46 App. sections 1111, 1295e, 1295g; title 47 section 154; title 49 section 32306; title 50 sections 402, 404; title 50 App. sections 460, 1989b–5, 2001, 2153.

§ 5331. Definitions; application

(a) For the purpose of this subchapter, "agency", "employee", "position", "class", and "grade" have the meanings given them by section 5102 of this title.

(b) This subchapter applies to employees and positions to which chapter 51 applies, other than Senior Executive Service positions, positions in the Federal Bureau of Investigation and Drug Enforcement Administration Senior Executive Service, and positions to which section 5376 applies.

(Pub. L. 89–554, Sept. 6, 1966, 80 Stat. 467; Pub. L. 95–454, title IV, § 408(b)(2), Oct. 13, 1978, 92 Stat. 1173; Pub. L. 100–325, § 2(h)(3), May 30, 1988, 102 Stat. 582; Pub. L. 101–509, title V, § 529 [title I, § 102(c)], Nov. 5, 1990, 104 Stat. 1427, 1444.)

HISTORICAL AND REVISION NOTES

The section is added on authority of former sections 1081, 1082, 1084, and 1091, which are carried into section 5102.

AMENDMENTS

1990—Subsec. (b). Pub. L. 101–509 amended subsec. (b) generally. Prior to amendment, subsec. (b) read as follows: "This subchapter applies to employees and positions, other than Senior Executive Service positions and positions in the Federal Bureau of Investigation and Drug Enforcement Administration Senior Executive Service, to which chapter 51 of this title applies."

1988—Subsec. (b). Pub. L. 100–325 inserted reference to positions in Federal Bureau of Investigation and Drug Enforcement Administration Senior Executive Service.

1978—Subsec. (b). Pub. L. 95–454 inserted reference to Senior Executive Service positions.

EFFECTIVE DATE OF 1990 AMENDMENT

Amendment by Pub. L. 101–509 effective on such date as the President shall determine, but not earlier than 90 days, and not later than 180 days, after Nov. 5, 1990, see section 529 [title III, § 305] of Pub. L. 101–509, set out as a note under section 5301 of this title.

EFFECTIVE DATE OF 1978 AMENDMENT

Amendment by Pub. L. 95–454 effective 9 months after Oct. 13, 1978, and congressional review of provisions of sections 401 through 412 of Pub. L. 95–454, see section 415 of Pub. L. 95–454, set out as an Effective Date note under section 3131 of this title.

REFERENCES IN OTHER LAWS TO CHAPTER 51 AND SUBCHAPTER III OF CHAPTER 53

References in laws to fix pay in accordance with this subchapter and chapter 51 of this title considered to include authority under section 5376 of this title, if applicable, but not to include any authority under section 5304 of this title or section 529 [title III, § 302] of Pub. L. 101–509, set out as a note under section 5304 of this title, see section 529 [title I, § 101(c)(2)] of Pub. L. 101–509, set out in a References in Other Laws to GS–16, 17, or 18 Pay Rates; Regulations note under section 5376 of this title.

SECTION REFERRED TO IN OTHER SECTIONS

This section is referred to in title 50 App. section 2153.

§ 5332. The General Schedule

(a)(1) The General Schedule, the symbol for which is "GS", is the basic pay schedule for positions to which this subchapter applies. Each employee to whom this subchapter applies is entitled to basic pay in accordance with the General Schedule.

(2) The General Schedule is a schedule of annual rates of basic pay, consisting of 15 grades, designated "GS-1" through "GS-15", consecutively, with 10 rates of pay for each such grade. The rates of pay of the General Schedule are adjusted in accordance with section 5303.

(b) When payment is made on the basis of an hourly, daily, weekly, or biweekly rate, the rate is computed from the appropriate annual rate of basic pay named by subsection (a) of this section in accordance with the rules prescribed by section 5504(b) of this title.

(Pub. L. 89–554, Sept. 6, 1966, 80 Stat. 467; Pub. L. 90–83, §1(18), Sept. 11, 1967, 81 Stat. 199; Pub. L. 90–206, title II, §202(a), Dec. 16, 1967, 81 Stat. 624; Pub. L. 95–454, title V, §503(e), Oct. 13, 1978, 92 Stat. 1184; Pub. L. 98–615, title II, §204(a)(1), Nov. 8, 1984, 98 Stat. 3216; Pub. L. 102–378, §2(29), Oct. 2, 1992, 106 Stat. 1350; Pub. L. 103–89, §3(b)(1)(F), Sept. 30, 1993, 107 Stat. 982.)

HISTORICAL AND REVISION NOTES
1966 ACT

Derivation	U.S. Code	Revised Statutes and Statutes at Large
(a)	5 U.S.C. 1113 (less (c)).	Oct. 28, 1949, ch. 782, §603 (less (d)), 63 Stat. 965. Oct. 24, 1951, ch. 554, §1(a), 65 Stat. 612. Sept. 1, 1954, ch. 1208, §109 (less (c)), 68 Stat. 1108. June 28, 1955, ch. 189, §2(a), 69 Stat. 172. June 20, 1958, Pub. L. 85–462, §2(a), 72 Stat. 203. July 1, 1960, Pub. L. 86–568, §112(a), 74 Stat. 298. Oct. 11, 1962, Pub. L. 87–793, §602(a), 76 Stat. 843. Aug. 14, 1964, Pub. L. 88–426, §102(a), 78 Stat. 400.
(b)	5 U.S.C. 1113(c).	Oct. 28, 1949, ch. 782, §603 (d), 63 Stat. 965. Sept. 1, 1954, ch. 1208, §109(c), 68 Stat. 1108.

In subsection (a), the words "the symbol for which is 'GS'" are added on authority of former section 1111 which is carried into section 5104. So much as related to the Crafts, Protective, and Custodial Schedule is omitted as repealed effective not later than Sept. 11, 1955, by the Act of Sept. 1, 1954, §§109(b), 110(b), 68 Stat. 1108.

In subsection (b), reference to payment made on the basis of a "monthly" rate is omitted since section 5504(b), former section 944(c), no longer provides for converting a basic annual rate to a basic monthly rate.

Standard changes are made to conform with the definitions applicable and the style of this title as outlined in the preface to the report.

1967 ACT

Section of title 5	Source (U.S. Code)	Source (Statutes at Large)
5332(a)	5 App.: 1113(b).	Oct. 29, 1965, Pub. L. 89–301, §2(a), 79 Stat. 1111. July 18, 1966, Pub. L. 89–504, §102(a), 80 Stat. 288.

AMENDMENTS

1993—Subsec. (a)(1). Pub. L. 103–89 struck out ", except an employee covered by the performance management and recognition system established under chapter 54," after "whom this subchapter applies".

1992—Subsec. (a). Pub. L. 102–378 amended subsec. (a) generally. Prior to amendment, subsec. (a) read as follows: "The General Schedule, the symbol for which is 'GS', is the basic pay schedule for positions to which this subchapter applies. Each employee to whom this subchapter applies, except an employee covered by the performance management and recognition system established under chapter 54 of this title, is entitled to basic pay in accordance with the General Schedule."

1984—Subsec. (a). Pub. L. 98–615 substituted "the performance management and recognition system established under chapter 54" for "the merit pay system established under section 5402".

1978—Subsec. (a). Pub. L. 95–454 inserted in second sentence reference to an employee covered by the merit pay system established under section 5402 of this title.

1967—Subsec. (a). Pub. L. 90–206 increased the compensation in each step of each grade.

EFFECTIVE DATE OF 1993 AMENDMENT

Amendment by Pub. L. 103–89 effective Nov. 1, 1993, see section 3(c) of Pub. L. 103–89, set out as a note under section 3372 of this title.

EFFECTIVE DATE OF 1992 AMENDMENT

Amendment by Pub. L. 102–378 effective May 4, 1991, see section 9(b)(4) of Pub. L. 102–378, set out as a note under section 6303 of this title.

EFFECTIVE DATE OF 1984 AMENDMENT

Section 205 of Pub. L. 98–615 provided that amendment by Pub. L. 98–615 was effective Oct. 1, 1984, and applicable with respect to pay periods commencing on or after that date, with certain exceptions and qualifications.

EFFECTIVE DATE OF 1978 AMENDMENT

Section 504(a) of Pub. L. 95–454 provided that amendment by Pub. L. 95–454 was effective on first day of first applicable pay period which began on or after Oct. 1, 1981, except it could take effect with respect to any category or categories of positions before such day to extent prescribed by Director of Office of Personnel Management.

EFFECTIVE DATE OF 1967 AMENDMENT

Section 220(a)(2) of Pub. L. 90–206 provided, except as otherwise expressly provided, that: "Sections 202 [amending this section and enacting provisions set out as a note under this section], 203 [amending section 3301 of Title 39, The Postal Service], 204 [enacting section 3512A of Title 39, amending sections 3512, and 3513–3531 of Title 39, and enacting provisions set out as a note under section 3512A of Title 39], 205 [amending sections 3542–3544 of Title 39, and enacting provisions set out as notes under sections 3542, 3544, 3552, and 3560 of Title 39], 206 [amending sections 3560, 3573, and 3575 of Title 39, and enacting provisions set out as a note under section 3542 of Title 39], 208 [amending former section 4107 of Title 38, Veterans' Benefits], 209 [amending sections 867 and 870 of Title 22, Foreign Relations and Intercourse, and enacting provisions set out as a note under section 867 of Title 22], 210 [enacting provisions set out as a note under section 590h of Title 16, Conservation],

211 [enacting provisions set out as a note under this section and section 548 of Title 28, Judiciary and Judicial Procedure], 213 (except subsections (d) and (e)) [enacting provisions set out as notes under sections 603, 604, and 753 of Title 28], 214 (except subsections (j), (k), (l), (n), and (o)) [enacting sections 60e–14, 61–2, 74a–2, and 293c of Title 2, The Congress, amending section 166b–3 of Title 40, Public Buildings, Property and Works and enacting provisions set out as a note under section 8339 of this title], and 216 [enacting provisions set out as a note under section 60e–14 of Title 2] shall become effective as of the beginning of the first pay period which began on or after October 1, 1967."

SHORT TITLE

Section 1 of Pub. L. 90–206 provided: "That this Act [see Tables for classification] may be cited as the 'Postal Revenue and Federal Salary Act of 1967'."

Section 201 of title II of Pub. L. 90–206 provided that: "This title [see Tables for classification] may be cited as the 'Federal Salary Act of 1967'."

ADJUSTMENT OF PAY RATES EFFECTIVE OCTOBER 1, 1972

Pub. L. 93–549, Dec. 26, 1974, 88 Stat. 1743, provided: "That notwithstanding the provisions of any other law or any regulation issued thereunder, no officer or employee of the United States shall have his pay reduced by reason of Executive Order 11777, dated April 12, 1974, relating to the effective date of the 1972 Federal pay comparability adjustment.

"SEC. 2. The Civil Service Commission shall issue regulations necessary to implement this Act."

1970 INCREASE IN PAY RATES

Pub. L. 91–231, Apr. 15, 1970, 84 Stat. 195, provided that:

"SEC. 1. [Short Title]. This Act may be cited as the 'Federal Employees Salary Act of 1970'."

"SEC. 2. [Adjustment of Pay Rates]. (a) (1) The President shall increase the rates of basic pay, basic compensation, and salaries (as such rates were increased by Executive Order Numbered 11474, dated June 16, 1969) [formerly set out as a note under this section] contained in the schedules listed in paragraph (2) of this subsection by amounts equal, as nearly as may be practicable and with regard to maintaining approximately equal increments within any grade, level, or class of any such schedule, to 6 percent.

"(2) The schedules referred to in paragraph (1) of this subsection are as follows: the General Schedule contained in section 5332(a) of title 5, United States Code [subsec. (a) of this section]; the Postal Field Service Schedule and the Rural Carrier Schedule contained in sections 3542(a) and 3543(a), respectively, of title 39, United States Code; the schedules relating to certain positions within the Department of Medicine and Surgery of the Veterans' Administration and contained in [former] section 4107 of title 38, United States Code; and the Foreign Service schedules contained in sections 412 and 415 of the Foreign Service Act of 1946 [sections 867 and 870, respectively, of Title 22, Foreign Relations and Intercourse].

"(b) Rates of basic pay, basic compensation, and salaries of officers and employees paid under the schedules referred to in subsection (a) of this section shall be increased initially under conversion rules prescribed by the President or by such agency as the President may designate.

"(c) The increases made by the President under this section shall have the force and effect of law and shall be printed in (1) the Statutes at Large in the same volume as public laws, (2) the Federal Register, and (3) the Code of Federal Regulations.

"SEC. 3. [Employees of ASCS County Committees, Legislative and Judicial Branches; United States Attorneys: Salaries Fixed by Administrative Action]. (a) The rates of pay of personnel subject to sections 210 and 214 of the Federal Salary Act of 1967 (81 Stat. 633,

635; Public Law 90–206) [which, respectively, were set out as a note under section 590h of Title 16, Conservation, and amended sections 60e–14, 60j, 61–1, 61–2, 74a–2, 84–1, 84–2, and 293c of Title 2, The Congress, sections 5533 and 8339 note of this title, and section 166b–3 of Title 40, Public Buildings, Property and Works], relating to Agricultural Stabilization and Conservation County Committee employees and to certain employees of the legislative branch of the Government, respectively, and any minimum or maximum rate, limitation, or allowance applicable to any such personnel, shall be adjusted, effective on the first day of the first pay period which begins on or after December 27, 1969, by amounts which are identical, insofar as practicable, to the amounts of the adjustments under section 2 of this Act for corresponding rates of pay for employees subject to the General Schedule, by the following authorities—

"(1) the Secretary of Agriculture, with respect to individuals employed by the county committees established under section 590h(b) of title 16;

"(2) the President pro tempore of the Senate, with respect to the United States Senate;

"(3) the Finance Clerk of the House of Representatives, with respect to the United States House of Representatives; and

"(4) the Architect of the Capitol, with respect to the Office of the Architect of the Capitol.

The provisions of this section shall not be construed to allow adjustments in the rates of pay of the following officers of the United States House of Representatives: Parliamentarian, Chaplain, Clerk, Sergeant at Arms, Doorkeeper, Postmaster, and the four Floor Assistants to the Minority whose position titles formerly were Minority Clerk, Minority Sergeant at Arms, Minority Doorkeeper, and Minority Postmaster.

"(b) Notwithstanding section 665 of title 31 [sections 1341, 1342, and 1349–1351 and subchapter II of chapter 15 of Title 31, Money and Finance], the rates of pay of employees in and under the judicial branch of the Government, whose rates of pay are fixed by administrative action pursuant to law and are not otherwise adjusted under this section may be adjusted, effective on the first day of the first pay period which begins on or after December 27, 1969, by amounts not to exceed the amounts of the adjustments under section 2(a) of this Act for corresponding rates of pay. The limitations fixed by law with respect to the aggregate salaries payable to secretaries and law clerks of circuit and district judges shall be adjusted, effective on the first day of the first pay period which begins on or after the date on which adjustments become effective under this section, by amounts not to exceed the amounts of the adjustments under this section for corresponding rates of pay.

"(c) The rates of pay of the United States attorneys and assistant United States attorneys whose annual salaries are fixed pursuant to section 548 of title 28, United States Code, shall be increased, effective on the first day of the first pay period which begins on or after December 27, 1969, by amounts equal, as nearly as may be practicable, to the increases provided pursuant to section 2 of this Act for corresponding rates of pay.

"(d) Notwithstanding section 665 of title 31 [sections 1341, 1342, and 1349–1351 and subchapter II of chapter 15 of Title 31, Money and Finance], the rates of pay of employees of the Federal Government and of the government of the District of Columbia whose rates of pay are fixed by administrative action pursuant to law and are not otherwise increased pursuant to this section are hereby authorized to be increased, effective on the first day of the first pay period which begins on or after December 27, 1969, by amounts not to exceed the increases provided pursuant to section 2 of this Act for corresponding rates of pay in the appropriate schedule or scale of pay.

"SEC. 4. [Stop Increases; Administrative Action; Level V Limitations]. (a) An increase in pay, compensation, or salary which becomes effective under section 2 of this Act is not an equivalent increase in pay within the meaning of section 5335 of title 5, United States Code, or section 3552 of title 39, United States Code.

"(b) Nothing in this Act shall impair any authority pursuant to which rates of pay, compensation, or salary may be fixed by administrative action.

"(c) Notwithstanding any provisions other than section 6 of this Act—

"(1) any officer or employee of the United States Government receiving pay, compensation, or salary which is less than the basic pay for level V of the Executive Schedule in section 5316 of title 5, United States Code, in effect on the date of enactment of this Act [Apr. 15, 1970], shall not have his pay, compensation, or salary increased, by reason of the enactment of this Act, to a rate in excess of the basic pay for such level V; and

"(2) any officer or employee of the United States Government receiving pay, compensation, or salary equal to or in excess of the basic pay for such level V shall not have his pay, compensation, or salary increased.

"SEC. 5. [Retroactive Pay]. (a) Retroactive pay, compensation, or salary shall be paid by reason of this Act only in the case of an individual in the service of the United States (including service in the Armed Forces of the United States) or the municipal government of the District of Columbia on the date of enactment of this Act [Apr. 15, 1970], except that such retroactive pay, compensation, or salary shall be paid—

"(1) to an officer or employee who retired, during the period beginning on the first day of the first pay period which began on or after December 27, 1969, and ending on the date of enactment of this Act [Apr. 15, 1970], for services rendered during such period; and

"(2) in accordance with subchapter VIII of chapter 55 of title 5, United States Code, relating to settlement of accounts, for services rendered, during the period beginning on the first day of the first pay period which began on or after December 27, 1969, and ending on the date of enactment of this Act [Apr. 15, 1970], by an officer or employee who died during such period.

Such retroactive pay, compensation, or salary shall not be considered as basic pay for the purposes of subchapter III of chapter 83 of title 5, United States Code, relating to civil service retirement, or any other retirement law or retirement system, in the case of any such retired or deceased officer or employee.

"(b) For the purposes of this section, service in the Armed Forces of the United States, in the case of an individual relieved from training and service in the Armed Forces of the United States or discharged from hospitalization following such training and service, shall include the period provided by law for the mandatory restoration of such individual to a position in or under the United States Government or the municipal government of the District of Columbia.

"SEC. 6. [District of Columbia Judges; Board of Tax Appeals]. [Section amended sections 11–702(d), 11–902 (d), and 47–2402 of the District of Columbia Code and is therefore not set out herein.]

"SEC. 7. [Former Presidents' Staffs] [Section amended section 1(b) of Pub. L. 85–745, Aug. 25, 1958, 72 Stat. 838, as amended, which is set out as a note under section 102 of Title 3, The President. This section is therefore not set out herein.]

"SEC. 8. [Premium Pay]. [Section amended section 5545(c)(2) of this title, and is therefore not set out herein.]

"SEC. 9. [Effective Date]. (a) Sections 1 to 6, inclusive, of this Act shall become effective on the first day of the first pay period which begins on or after December 27, 1969.

"(b) This section and sections 7 and 8 of this Act shall become effective on the date of enactment of this Act [Apr. 15, 1970].

"(c) For purposes of determining the amount of insurance for which an individual is eligible under chapter 87 of title 5, United States Code, relating to group life insurance for Government employees, all changes in rates of pay, compensation, and salary which result from the enactment of this Act shall be held and considered to become effective as of the date of such enactment [Apr. 15, 1970].

"(d) Any deduction to be made as the result of the enactment of this Act from the pay, compensation, or salary of an officer or employee enrolled in a retirement system of the United States Government, and the contribution of the agency employing the officer or employee, shall be made at the rates of deductions and contributions in effect for that system on the date of such enactment [Apr. 15, 1970]."

INITIAL ADJUSTMENT OF 1967 PAY INCREASES

Section 202(b) of Pub. L. 90–206 provided that: "Except as provided in section 5303 of title 5, United States Code [section 5303 of this title], the rates of basic pay of officers and employees to whom the General Schedule set forth in the amendment made by subsection (a) of this section [amending this section] applies shall be initially adjusted as of the effective date of this section, as follows:

"(1) If the officer or employee is receiving basic pay immediately prior to the effective date of this section [see Effective Date of 1967 Amendment note under this section] at one of the rates of a grade in the General Schedule, he shall receive a rate of basic pay at the corresponding rate in effect on and after such date.

"(2) If the officer or employee is receiving basic pay immediately prior to the effective date of this section [see Effective Date of 1967 Amendment note under this section] at a rate between two rates of a grade in the General Schedule, he shall receive a rate of basic pay at the higher of the two corresponding rates in effect on and after such date.

"(3) If the officer or employee is receiving basic pay immediately prior to the effective date of this section [see Effective Date of 1967 Amendment note under this section] at a rate in excess of the maximum rate for his grade, he shall receive (A) the maximum rate for his grade in the new schedule, or (B) his existing rate of basic pay increased by 4.5 per centum, rounded to the next highest dollar, if such existing rate as so increased is higher.

"(4) If the officer or employee, immediately prior to the effective date of this section [see Effective Date of 1967 Amendment note under this section], is receiving, pursuant to section 2(b)(4) of the Federal Employees Salary Increase Act of 1955, an existing aggregate rate of pay determined under section 208(b) of the Act of September 1, 1954, (68 Stat. 1111), plus subsequent increases authorized by law, he shall receive an aggregate rate of pay equal to the sum of his existing aggregate rate of pay on the day preceding the effective date of this section, plus the amount of increase made by this section in the maximum rate of his grade, until (i) he leaves his position, or (ii) he is entitled to receive aggregate pay at a higher rate by reason of the operation of this Act or any other provision of law; but, when such position becomes vacant, the aggregate rate of pay of any subsequent appointee thereto shall be fixed in accordance with applicable provisions of law. Subject to clauses (i) and (ii) of the immediately preceding sentence of this subparagraph, the amount of the increase provided by this section shall be held and considered for the purposes of section 208(b) of the Act of September 1, 1954, to constitute a part of the existing rate of pay of the employee.

"(5) If the officer or employee, at any time during the period beginning on the effective date of this section [see Effective Date of 1967 Amendment note under this section], and ending on the date of enactment of this title [Dec. 16, 1967], was promoted from one grade under the General Schedule contained in section 5332(a) of title 5, United States Code [subsec. (a) of this section] to another such grade at a rate which is above the minimum rate thereof, his rate of basic pay shall be adjusted retroactively from the effective date of this section to the date on which he was so promoted, on the basis of the rate which he was receiving during the period from such effective date to the date of such promotion and, from the date of such promotion, on the basis of the rate for that step of the appropriate grade of the General Schedule contained in the amendment made by subsection (a) of this section [amending the section] which corresponds numerically to the step of the grade of the General Schedule to which such officer or employee was promoted as in effect (without regard to this title) at the time of such promotion.

"(6) If the officer or employee, at any time during the period beginning on the effective date of this section and ending on the date of enactment of this title [Dec. 16, 1967] became subject to the General Schedule and his rate of basic pay was set above the minimum rate of the grade on the basis of a previously earned rate above such minimum rate, his rate of basic pay shall be adjusted retroactively to the date on which he became subject to the General Schedule on the basis of the rate of the appropriate grade of the General Schedule contained in this section which corresponds numerically to the rate of the grade at which the pay of such officer or employee was set at the time he became subject to the General Schedule."

Section 202(b) of Pub. L. 90–206 effective as of the beginning of the first pay period which begins on or after Oct. 1, 1967, see section 220(a)(2) of Pub. L. 90–206, set out as a note under this section.

1967 SALARY INCREASE FOR PERSONS WHOSE COMPENSATION RATES ARE FIXED BY ADMINISTRATIVE ACTION

Section 211(b)–(d) of Pub. L. 90–206 provided that:

"(b) Notwithstanding section 3679 of the Revised Statutes, as amended (31 U.S.C. 665) [sections 1341, 1342, and 1349–1351 and subchapter II of chapter 15 of Title 31, Money and Finance], the rates of pay of officers and employees of the Federal Government and of the municipal government of the District of Columbia whose rates of pay are fixed by administrative action pursuant to law and are not otherwise increased by this title are hereby authorized to be increased, effective on the effective date of section 202 of this title [see Effective Date of 1967 Amendment note under this section], by amounts not to exceed the increases provided by this title for corresponding rates of pay in the appropriate schedule or scale of pay.

"(c) Nothing contained in this section shall be held or considered to authorize any increase in the rates of pay of officers and employees whose rates of pay are fixed and adjusted from time to time as nearly as is consistent with the public interest in accordance with prevailing rates or practices.

"(d) Nothing contained in this section shall affect the authority contained in any law pursuant to which rates of pay may be fixed by administrative action."

Sections 211(b)–(d) of Pub. L. 90–206 effective as of the beginning of the first pay period which begins on or after Oct. 1, 1967, see section 220(a)(2) of Pub. L. 90–206, set out as a note under this section.

RETROACTIVE COMPENSATION UNDER 1967 PAY INCREASES

Section 218 of Pub. L. 90–206 provided that:

"(a) Retroactive pay, compensation, or salary shall be paid by reason of this title only in the case of an individual in the service of the United States (including service in the Armed Forces of the United States) or the municipal government of the District of Columbia on the date of enactment of this title [Dec. 16, 1967] except that such retroactive pay, compensation, or salary shall be paid—

"(1) to an officer or employee who retired, during the period beginning on the first day of the first pay period which began on or after October 1, 1967, and ending on the date of enactment of this title [Dec. 16, 1967], for services rendered during such period, and

"(2) in accordance with subchapter VIII of chapter 55 of title 5, United States Code, relating to settlement of accounts, for services rendered, during the period beginning on the first day of the first pay period which began on or after October 1, 1967, and ending on the date of enactment of this title [Dec. 16, 1967], by an officer or employee who died during such period.

Such retroactive pay, compensation, or salary shall not be considered as basic pay for the purposes of subchapter III of chapter 83 of title 5, United States Code, relating to civil service retirement, or any other retirement law or retirement system, in the case of any such retired or deceased officer or employee.

"(b) For the purposes of this section, service in the Armed Forces of the United States, in the case of an individual relieved from training and service in the Armed Forces of the United States or discharged from hospitalization following such training and service, shall include the period provided by law for the mandatory restoration of such individual to a position in or under the Federal Government or the municipal government of the District of Columbia."

Section 218 of Pub. L. 90–206 effective Dec. 16, 1967, see section 220(a)(1) of Pub. L. 90–206, set out as a note under section 3110 of this title.

EXECUTIVE ORDER NO. 11413

Ex. Ord. No. 11413, June 11, 1968, 33 F.R. 8641, which provided for adjustment of pay rates effective July 1, 1968, was superseded by Ex. Ord. No. 11811, Oct. 7, 1974, 39 F.R. 36302, formerly set out below.

EXECUTIVE ORDER NO. 11474

Ex. Ord. No. 11474, June 16, 1969, 34 F.R. 9605, which provided for adjustment of pay rates effective July 1, 1969, was superseded by Ex. Ord. No. 11811, Oct. 7, 1974, 39 F.R. 36302, formerly set out below.

EXECUTIVE ORDER NO. 11524

Ex. Ord. No. 11524, Apr. 15, 1970, 35 F.R. 6247, which provided for adjustment of pay rates effective first pay period on or after Dec. 27, 1969, was superseded by Ex. Ord. No. 11811, Oct. 7, 1974, 39 F.R. 36302, formerly set out below.

EXECUTIVE ORDER NO. 11576

Ex. Ord. No. 11576, Jan. 8, 1971, 36 F.R. 347, which provided for adjustment of pay rates effective Jan. 1, 1971, was superseded by Ex. Ord. No. 11811, Oct. 7, 1974, 39 F.R. 36302, formerly set out below.

EXECUTIVE ORDER NO. 11637

Ex. Ord. No. 11637, Dec. 22, 1971, 36 F.R. 24911, which provided for adjustment of pay rates effective Jan. 1, 1972, was superseded by Ex. Ord. No. 11811, Oct. 7, 1974, 39 F.R. 36302, formerly set out below.

EXECUTIVE ORDER NO. 11691

Ex. Ord. No. 11691, Dec. 15, 1972, 37 F.R. 27607, as amended by Ex. Ord. No. 11777, Apr. 12, 1974, 39 F.R. 13519, which provided for adjustment of pay rates effective Oct. 1, 1972, was superseded by Ex. Ord. No. 11811, Oct. 7, 1974, 39 F.R. 36302, formerly set out below.

EXECUTIVE ORDER NO. 11739

Ex. Ord. No. 11739, Oct. 3, 1973, 38 F.R. 27581, which provided for adjustment of pay rates effective Oct. 1, 1973, was superseded by Ex. Ord. No. 11811, Oct. 7, 1974, 39 F.R. 36302, formerly set out below.

EXECUTIVE ORDER NO. 11811

Ex. Ord. No. 11811, Oct. 7, 1974, 39 F.R. 36302, which provided for adjustment of pay rates effective Oct. 1, 1974, was superseded by Ex. Ord. No. 11883, Oct. 6, 1975, 40 F.R. 47091, formerly set out below.

EXECUTIVE ORDER NO. 11883

Ex. Ord. No. 11883, Oct. 6, 1975, 40 F.R. 47091, which provided for adjustment of pay rates effective Oct. 1,

1975, was superseded by Ex. Ord. No. 11941, Oct. 1, 1976, 41 F.R. 43889, formerly set out below.

EXECUTIVE ORDER NO. 11941

Ex. Ord. No. 11941, Oct. 1, 1976, 41 F.R. 43899, as amended by Ex. Ord. No. 11943, Oct. 25, 1976, 41 F.R. 47213, which provided for adjustment of pay rates effective Oct. 1, 1976, was superseded by Ex. Ord. No. 12010, Sept. 28, 1977, 42 F.R. 52365, formerly set out below.

EXECUTIVE ORDER NO. 12010

Ex. Ord. No. 12010, Sept. 28, 1977, 42 F.R. 52365, which provided for adjustment of pay rates effective Oct. 1, 1977, was superseded by Ex. Ord. No. 12087, Oct. 7, 1978, 43 F.R. 46823, formerly set out below.

EXECUTIVE ORDER NO. 12087

Ex. Ord. No. 12087, Oct. 7, 1978, 43 F.R. 46823, which provided for adjustment of pay rates effective Oct. 1, 1978, was superseded by Ex. Ord. No. 12165, Oct. 9, 1979, 44 F.R. 58671, formerly set out below.

EXECUTIVE ORDER NO. 12165

Ex. Ord. No. 12165, Oct. 9, 1979, 44 F.R. 58671, as amended by Ex. Ord. No. 12200, Mar. 12, 1980, 44 F.R. 16443, which provided for adjustment of pay rates effective Oct. 1, 1979, was superseded by Ex. Ord. No. 12248, Oct. 16, 1980, 45 F.R. 69199, formerly set out below.

EXECUTIVE ORDER NO. 12248

Ex. Ord. No. 12248, Oct. 16, 1980, 45 F.R. 69199, which provided for adjustment of pay rates effective Oct. 1, 1980, was superseded by Ex. Ord. No. 12330, Oct. 15, 1981, 46 F.R. 50921, formerly set out below.

EXECUTIVE ORDER NO. 12330

Ex. Ord. No. 12330, Oct. 15, 1981, 46 F.R. 50921, which provided for adjustment of pay rates effective Oct. 1, 1981, was superseded by Ex. Ord. No. 12387, Oct. 8, 1982, 47 F.R. 44981, formerly set out below.

EXECUTIVE ORDER NO. 12387

Ex. Ord. No. 12387, Oct. 8, 1982, 47 F.R. 44981, which provided for adjustment of pay rates effective Oct. 1, 1982, was superseded by Ex. Ord. No. 12456, Dec. 30, 1983, 49 F.R. 347, as amended by Ex. Ord. No. 12477, May 23, 1984, 49 F.R. 22041, formerly set out below.

EXECUTIVE ORDER NO. 12456

Ex. Ord. No. 12456, Dec. 30, 1983, 49 F.R. 347, as amended by Ex. Ord. No. 12477, May 23, 1984, 49 F.R. 22041; Ex. Ord. No. 12487, Sept. 14, 1984, 49 F.R. 36493, which provided for adjustment of pay rates effective Jan. 1, 1984, was superseded by Ex. Ord. No. 12496, Dec. 28, 1984, 50 F.R. 211, as amended by Ex. Ord. No. 12540, Dec. 30, 1985, 51 F.R. 577, formerly set out below.

EXECUTIVE ORDER NO. 12496

Ex. Ord. No. 12496, Dec. 28, 1984, 50 F.R. 211, as amended by Ex. Ord. No. 12540, Dec. 30, 1985, 51 F.R. 577, which provided for adjustment of pay rates effective Jan. 1, 1985, was superseded by Ex. Ord. No. 12578, Dec. 31, 1986, 52 F.R. 505, formerly set out below.

EXECUTIVE ORDER NO. 12578

Ex. Ord. No. 12578, Dec. 31, 1986, 52 F.R. 505, which provided for adjustment of pay rates effective Jan. 1, 1987, was superseded by Ex. Ord. No. 12622, Dec. 31, 1987, 53 F.R. 222, formerly set out below.

EXECUTIVE ORDER NO. 12622

Ex. Ord. No. 12622, Dec. 31, 1987, 53 F.R. 222, which provided for adjustment of pay rates effective Jan. 1, 1988, was superseded by Ex. Ord. No. 12663, Jan. 6, 1989, 54 F.R. 791, formerly set out below.

EXECUTIVE ORDER NO. 12663

Ex. Ord. No. 12663, Jan. 6, 1989, 54 F.R. 791, which provided for adjustment of pay rates effective Jan. 1, 1989,

was superseded by Ex. Ord. No. 12698, Dec. 23, 1989, 54 F.R. 53473, formerly set out below.

EXECUTIVE ORDER NO. 12698

Ex. Ord. No. 12698, Dec. 23, 1989, 54 F.R. 53473, which provided for adjustment of pay rates effective Jan. 1 and 31, 1990, was superseded by Ex. Ord. No. 12736, Dec. 12, 1990, 55 F.R. 51385, formerly set out below.

EXECUTIVE ORDER NO. 12736

Ex. Ord. No. 12736, Dec. 12, 1990, 55 F.R. 51385, which provided for adjustment of pay rates effective Jan. 1, 1991, was superseded by Ex. Ord. No. 12786, Dec. 26, 1991, 56 F.R. 67453, formerly set out below.

EXECUTIVE ORDER NO. 12786

Ex. Ord. No. 12786, Dec. 26, 1991, 56 F.R. 67453, which provided for adjustment of pay rates effective Jan. 1, 1992, was superseded by Ex. Ord. No. 12826, Dec. 30, 1992, 57 F.R. 62909, formerly set out below.

EXECUTIVE ORDER NO. 12826

Ex. Ord. No. 12826, Dec. 30, 1992, 57 F.R. 62909, as amended by Ex. Ord. No. 12886, §3, Dec. 23, 1993, 58 F.R. 68709, which provided for adjustment of pay rates effective Jan. 1, 1993, was superseded by Ex. Ord. No. 12944, Dec. 28, 1994, 60 F.R. 309, formerly set out below.

EXECUTIVE ORDER NO. 12886

Ex. Ord. No. 12886, Dec. 23, 1993, 58 F.R. 68709, which provided for adjustment of pay rates for the uniformed services effective Jan. 1, 1994, was superseded by Ex. Ord. No. 12944, Dec. 28, 1994, 60 F.R. 309, formerly set out below.

EXECUTIVE ORDER NO. 12944

Ex. Ord. No. 12944, Dec. 28, 1994, 60 F.R. 309, which provided for adjustment of pay rates effective Jan. 1, 1995, was superseded by Ex. Ord. No. 12984, Dec. 28, 1995, 61 F.R. 237, formerly set out below.

EXECUTIVE ORDER NO. 12984

Ex. Ord. No. 12984, Dec. 28, 1995, 61 F.R. 237, as amended by Ex. Ord. No. 12990, §3, Feb. 29, 1996, 61 F.R. 8467, which provided for adjustment of pay rates effective Jan. 1, 1996, was superseded by Ex. Ord. No. 13033, Dec. 27, 1996, 61 F.R. 68987, formerly set out below.

EXECUTIVE ORDER NO. 12990

Ex. Ord. No. 12990, Feb. 29, 1996, 61 F.R. 8467, which provided for adjustment of pay rates for the uniformed services effective Jan. 1, 1996, was superseded by Ex. Ord. No. 13033, Dec. 27, 1996, 61 F.R. 68987, formerly set out below.

EXECUTIVE ORDER NO. 13033

Ex. Ord. No. 13033, Dec. 27, 1996, 61 F.R. 68987, which provided for adjustment of pay rates effective Jan. 1, 1997, was superseded by Ex. Ord. No. 13071, Dec. 29, 1997, 62 F.R. 68521, formerly set out below.

EXECUTIVE ORDER NO. 13071

Ex. Ord. No. 13071, Dec. 29, 1997, 62 F.R. 68521, which provided for adjustment of pay rates effective Jan. 1, 1998, was superseded by Ex. Ord. No. 13106, Dec. 7, 1998, 63 F.R. 68151, formerly set out below.

EXECUTIVE ORDER NO. 13106

Ex. Ord. No. 13106, Dec. 7, 1998, 63 F.R. 68151, as amended by Ex. Ord. No. 13144, §8, Dec. 21, 1999, 64 F.R. 72238, provided for adjustment of pay rates effective Jan. 1, 1999, and amendment of Ex. Ord. No. 12748 (5 U.S.C. 5301 note).

EXECUTIVE ORDER NO. 13144

Ex. Ord. No. 13144, Dec. 21, 1999, 64 F.R. 72237, which provided for adjustment of pay rates effective Jan. 1,

2000, was superseded by Ex. Ord. No. 13182, Dec. 23, 2000, 65 F.R. 82879, set out below.

Ex. Ord. No. 13182. Adjustments of Certain Rates of Pay

Ex. Ord. No. 13182, Dec. 23, 2000, 65 F.R. 82879, 66 F.R. 10057, provided:

By the authority vested in me as President by the Constitution and the laws of the United States of America, including the laws cited herein, it is hereby ordered as follows:

Section 1. *Statutory Pay Systems.* The rates of basic pay or salaries of the statutory pay systems (as defined in 5 U.S.C. 5302(1)), as adjusted under 5 U.S.C. 5303(a), are set forth on the schedules attached hereto and made a part hereof:

(a) The General Schedule (5 U.S.C. 5332(a)) at Schedule 1;

(b) The Foreign Service Schedule (22 U.S.C. 3963) at Schedule 2; and

(c) The schedules for the Veterans Health Administration of the Department of Veterans Affairs (38 U.S.C. 7306, 7404; section 301(a) of Public Law 102–40 [enacting provisions set out as a note under section 7451 of Title 38, Veterans' Benefits]) at Schedule 3.

Sec. 2. *Senior Executive Service.* The rates of basic pay for senior executives in the Senior Executive Service, as adjusted under 5 U.S.C. 5382, are set forth on Schedule 4 attached hereto and made a part hereof.

Sec. 3. *Executive Salaries.* The rates of basic pay or salaries for the following offices and positions are set forth on the schedules attached hereto and made a part hereof:

(a) The Executive Schedule (5 U.S.C. 5312–5318) at Schedule 5;

(b) The Vice President (3 U.S.C. 104) and the Congress (2 U.S.C. 31) at Schedule 6; and

(c) Justices and judges (28 U.S.C. 5, 44(d), 135, 252, and 461(a)) at Schedule 7.

Sec. 4. *Uniformed Services.* Pursuant to section 601 of Public Law 106–398 [enacting provisions set out as a note under section 1009 of Title 37, Pay and Allowances of the Uniformed Services], the rates of monthly basic pay (37 U.S.C. 203(a)) for members of the uniformed services and the rate of monthly cadet or midshipman pay (37 U.S.C. 203(c)) are set forth on Schedule 8 attached hereto and made a part hereof.

Sec. 5. *Locality-Based Comparability Payments.* (a) Pursuant to sections 5304 and 5304a of title 5, United States Code, locality-based comparability payments shall be paid in accordance with Schedule 9 attached hereto and made a part hereof.

(b) The Director of the Office of Personnel Management shall take such actions as may be necessary to implement these payments and to publish appropriate notice of such payments in the Federal Register.

Sec. 6. *Administrative Law Judges.* The rates of basic pay for administrative law judges, as adjusted under 5 U.S.C. 5372(b)(4), are set forth on Schedule 10 attached hereto and made a part hereof.

Sec. 7. *Effective Dates.* Schedule 8 is effective on January 1, 2001. The other schedules contained herein are effective on the first day of the first applicable pay period beginning on or after January 1, 2001.

Sec. 8. *Prior Order Superseded.* Executive Order 13144 of December 21, 1999, is superseded.

WILLIAM J. CLINTON.

SCHEDULE 1

General Schedule

(Effective on the first day of the first applicable pay period beginning on or after January 1, 2001)

	1	2	3	4	5	6	7	8	9	10
GS–1	$14,244	$14,719	$15,193	$15,664	$16,139	$16,418	$16,884	$17,356	$17,375	$17,819
GS–2	16,015	16,395	16,926	17,375	17,571	18,088	18,605	19,122	19,639	20,156
GS–3	17,474	18,056	18,638	19,220	19,802	20,384	20,966	21,548	22,130	22,712
GS–4	19,616	20,270	20,924	21,578	22,232	22,886	23,540	24,194	24,848	25,502
GS–5	21,947	22,679	23,411	24,143	24,875	25,607	26,339	27,071	27,803	28,535
GS–6	24,463	25,278	26,093	26,908	27,723	28,538	29,353	30,168	30,983	31,798
GS–7	27,185	28,091	28,997	29,903	30,809	31,715	32,621	33,527	34,433	35,339
GS–8	30,107	31,111	32,115	33,119	34,123	35,127	36,131	37,135	38,139	39,143
GS–9	33,254	34,362	35,470	36,578	37,686	38,794	39,902	41,010	42,118	43,226
GS–10	36,621	37,842	39,063	40,284	41,505	42,726	43,947	45,168	46,389	47,610
GS–11	40,236	41,577	42,918	44,259	45,600	46,941	48,282	49,623	50,964	52,305
GS–12	48,223	49,830	51,437	53,044	54,651	56,258	57,865	59,472	61,079	62,686
GS–13	57,345	59,257	61,169	63,081	64,993	66,905	68,817	70,729	72,641	74,553
GS–14	67,765	70,024	72,283	74,542	76,801	79,060	81,319	83,578	85,837	88,096
GS–15	79,710	82,367	85,024	87,681	90,338	92,995	95,652	98,309	100,966	103,623

SCHEDULE 2

Foreign Service Schedule

(Effective on the first day of the first applicable pay period beginning on or after January 1, 2001)

Step	Class 1	Class 2	Class 3	Class 4	Class 5	Class 6	Class 7	Class 8	Class 9
1	$79,710	$64,588	$52,335	$42,407	$34,362	$30,719	$27,462	$24,550	$21,947
2	82,101	66,526	53,905	43,679	35,393	31,641	28,286	25,287	22,605
3	84,564	68,521	55,522	44,990	36,455	32,590	29,134	26,045	23,284
4	87,101	70,577	57,188	46,339	37,548	33,567	30,008	26,826	23,982
5	89,714	72,694	58,904	47,729	38,675	34,575	30,909	27,631	24,702
6	92,406	74,875	60,671	49,161	39,835	35,612	31,836	28,460	25,443
7	95,178	77,121	62,491	50,636	41,030	36,680	32,791	29,314	26,206
8	98,033	79,435	64,365	52,155	42,261	37,780	33,775	30,193	26,992
9	100,974	81,818	66,296	53,720	43,529	38,914	34,788	31,099	27,802
10	103,623	84,273	68,285	55,332	44,835	40,081	35,832	32,032	28,636
11	103,623	86,801	70,334	56,991	46,180	41,284	36,907	32,993	29,495
12	103,623	89,405	72,444	58,701	47,565	42,522	38,014	33,983	30,380
13	103,623	92,087	74,617	60,462	48,992	43,798	39,154	35,002	31,291
14	103,623	94,850	76,856	62,276	50,462	45,112	40,329	36,053	32,230

SCHEDULE 3

Veterans Health Administration Schedules, Department of Veterans Affairs

(Effective on the first day of the first applicable pay period beginning on or after January 1, 2001)

Schedule for the Office of the Under Secretary for Health (38 U.S.C. 7306)[1]

Deputy Under Secretary for Health	[2]$135,370
Associate Deputy Under Secretary for Health	[3]129,659
Assistant Under Secretaries for Health	[3]125,837

SCHEDULE 3—Continued

Veterans Health Administration Schedules, Department of Veterans Affairs

	Minimum	Maximum
Medical Directors	$107,365	[3]$121,683
Service Directors	93,486	116,102
Director, National Center for Preventive Health	79,710	116,102
Physician and Dentist Schedule		
Director Grade	$93,486	$116,102
Executive Grade	86,324	110,017

SCHEDULE 3—Continued

Veterans Health Administration Schedules, Department of Veterans Affairs

Chief Grade	79,710	103,623
Senior Grade	67,765	88,096
Intermediate Grade	57,345	74,553
Full Grade	48,223	62,686
Associate Grade	40,236	52,305

Clinical Podiatrist and Optometrist Schedule

Chief Grade	$79,710	$103,623
Senior Grade	67,765	88,096
Intermediate Grade	57,345	74,553
Full Grade	48,223	62,686
Associate Grade	40,236	52,305

Physician Assistant and Expanded-Function Dental Auxiliary Schedule[4]

Director Grade	$79,710	$103,623
Assistant Director Grade	67,765	88,096
Chief Grade	57,345	74,553
Senior Grade	48,223	62,686
Intermediate Grade	40,236	52,305
Full Grade	33,254	43,226
Associate Grade	28,616	37,202
Junior Grade	24,463	31,798

[1] This schedule does not apply to the Assistant Under Secretary for Nursing Programs or the Director of Nursing Services. Pay for these positions is set by the Under Secretary for Health under 38 U.S.C. 7451.

[2] Pursuant to section 7404(d)(1) of title 38, United States Code, the rate of basic pay payable to this employee is limited to the rate for level IV of the Executive Schedule, which is $125,700.

[3] Pursuant to section 7404(d)(2) of title 38, United States Code, the rate of basic pay payable to these employees is limited to the rate for level V of the Executive Schedule, which is $117,600.

[4] Pursuant to section 301(a) of Public Law 102–40, these positions are paid according to the Nurse Schedule in 38 U.S.C. 4107(b) [former section 4107(b) of Title 38, Veterans' Benefits] as in effect on August 14, 1990, with subsequent adjustments.

SCHEDULE 4

Senior Executive Service

(Effective on the first day of the first applicable pay period beginning on or after January 1, 2001)

ES–1	$109,100
ES–2	114,200
ES–3	119,400
ES–4	125,500
ES–5	125,700
ES–6	125,700

SCHEDULE 5

Executive Schedule

(Effective on the first day of the first applicable pay period beginning on or after January 1, 2001)

level I	$161,200
level II	145,100
level III	133,700
level IV	125,700
level V	117,600

SCHEDULE 6

Vice President and Members of Congress

(Effective on the first day of the first applicable pay period beginning on or after January 1, 2001)

Vice President	$186,300
Senators	145,100
Members of the House of Representatives	145,100
Delegates to the House of Representatives	145,100
Resident Commissioner from Puerto Rico	145,100
President pro tempore of the Senate	161,200
Majority leader and minority leader of the Senate	161,200
Majority leader and minority leader of the House of Representatives	161,200
Speaker of the House of Representatives	186,300

SCHEDULE 7

Judicial Salaries

(Effective on the first day of the first applicable pay period beginning on or after January 1, 2001)

Chief Justice of the United States	$186,300

SCHEDULE 7

Associate Justices of the Supreme Court	178,300
Circuit Judges	153,900
District Judges	145,100
Judges of the Court of International Trade	145,100

SCHEDULE 8

Pay of the Uniformed Services

(Effective on January 1, 2001)

PART I—MONTHLY BASIC PAY

Years of Service (computed under 37 U.S.C. 205)

Commissioned Officers

Pay Grade	2 or less	Over 2	Over 3	Over 4	Over 6
O–10[1]	$8,518.80	$8,818.50	$8,818.50	$8,818.50	$8,818.50
O–9	7,550.10	7,747.80	7,912.80	7,912.80	7,912.80
O–8	6,838.20	7,062.30	7,210.50	7,252.20	7,437.30
O–7	5,682.30	6,068.40	6,068.40	6,112.50	6,340.80
O–6	4,211.40	4,626.60	4,930.20	4,930.20	4,949.10
O–5	3,368.70	3,954.90	4,228.80	4,280.40	4,450.50
O–4	2,839.20	3,457.20	4,687.90	3,739.50	3,953.40
O–3[2]	2,638.20	2,991.00	3,228.00	3,489.30	3,656.40
O–2[2]	2,301.00	2,620.80	3,018.60	3,120.30	3,184.80
O–1[2]	1,997.70	2,079.00	2,512.80	2,512.80	2,512.80

Pay Grade	Over 8	Over 10	Over 12	Over 14	Over 16
O–10[1]	$9,156.90	$9,156.90	$9,664.20	$9,664.20	$10,356.00
O–9	8,114.10	8,114.10	8,451.60	8,451.60	9,156.90
O–8	7,747.80	7,819.80	8,114.10	8,198.70	8,451.60
O–7	6,514.50	6,715.50	6,915.90	7,116.90	7,747.80
O–6	5,160.90	5,189.10	5,189.10	5,360.70	6,005.40
O–5	4,450.50	4,584.30	4,831.80	5,155.80	5,481.60
O–4	4,127.70	4,409.70	4,629.30	4,781.70	4,935.00
O–3[2]	3,839.70	3,992.70	4,189.80	4,292.10	4,292.10
O–2[2]	3,184.80	3,184.80	3,184.80	3,184.80	3,184.80
O–1[2]	2,512.80	2,512.80	2,512.80	2,512.80	2,512.80

Pay Grade	Over 18	Over 20	Over 22	Over 24	Over 26
O–10[1]	$10,356.00	$11,049.30	$11,103.90	$11,334.60	*$11,737.20
O–9	9,156.90	9,664.20	9,803.40	10,004.70	10,356.00
O–8	8,818.50	9,156.90	9,382.80	9,382.80	9,382.80
O–7	8,280.90	8,280.90	8,280.90	8,280.90	8,322.60
O–6	6,311.40	6,617.40	6,791.40	6,967.80	7,309.80
O–5	5,637.00	5,790.30	5,964.60	5,964.60	5,964.60
O–4	4,986.60	4,986.60	4,986.60	4,986.60	4,986.60
O–3[2]	4,292.10	4,292.10	4,292.10	4,292.10	4,292.10
O–2[2]	3,184.80	3,184.80	3,184.80	3,184.80	3,184.80
O–1[2]	2,512.80	2,512.80	2,512.80	2,512.80	2,512.80

[1] For officers serving as Chairman or Vice Chairman of the Joint Chiefs of Staff, Chief of Staff of the Army, Chief of Naval Operations, Chief of Staff of the Air Force, Commandant of the Marine Corps, or Commandant of the Coast Guard, basic pay for this grade is calculated to be $12,950.70 per month, regardless of cumulative years of service computed under section 205 of title 37, United States Code. Nevertheless, actual basic pay for these officers is limited to the rate of basic pay for level III of the Executive Schedule, which is $11,141.70 per month.

[2] Does not apply to commissioned officers who have been credited with over 4 years of active duty service as an enlisted member or warrant officer.

* Basic pay for these officers is limited to the rate of basic pay for level III of the Executive Schedule, which is $11,141.70 per month.

Commissioned officers with over 4 years of active duty service as an enlisted member or warrant officer

Pay Grade	Over 4	Over 6	Over 8	Over 10
O–3E	$3,489.30	$3,656.40	$3,839.70	$3,992.70
O–2E	3,120.30	3,184.80	3,285.90	3,457.20
O–1E	2,512.80	2,684.10	2,783.10	2,884.20

Pay Grade	Over 12	Over 14	Over 16	Over 18
O–3E	$4,189.80	$4,355.70	$4,450.50	$4,580.40
O–2E	3,589.50	3,687.90	3,687.90	3,687.90
O–1E	2,984.10	3,120.30	3,120.30	3,120.30

Pay Grade	Over 20	Over 22	Over 24	Over 26
O–3E	$4,580.40	$4,580.40	$4,580.40	$4,580.40
O–2E	3,687.90	3,687.90	3,687.90	3,687.90
O–1E	3,120.30	3,120.30	3,120.30	3,120.30

Warrant Officers

Pay Grade	2 or less	Over 2	Over 3	Over 4	Over 6
W–5	....	....	....	....	....
W–4	$2,688.00	$2,891.70	$2,974.80	$3,056.70	$3,197.40
W–3	2,443.20	2,649.90	2,649.90	2,684.10	2,793.90
W–2	2,139.60	2,315.10	2,315.10	2,391.00	2,512.80

Warrant Officers—Continued

Pay Grade	2 or less	Over 2	Over 3	Over 4	Over 6
W-1	1,782.60	2,043.90	2,043.90	2,214.60	2,315.10

Pay Grade	Over 8	Over 10	Over 12	Over 14	Over 16
W-5	....	....	....	....	....
W-4	$3,336.30	$3,477.00	$3,614.10	$3,756.30	$3,892.50
W-3	2,919.00	3,084.30	3,184.80	3,294.60	3,420.30
W-2	2,649.90	2,750.70	2,851.50	2,949.60	3,058.20
W-1	2,419.20	2,523.30	2,626.80	2,731.50	2,835.90

Pay Grade	Over 18	Over 20	Over 22	Over 24	Over 26
W-5	....	$4,640.70	$4,800.00	$4,959.90	$5,120.10
W-4	$4,032.00	4,168.20	4,309.50	4,448.40	4,590.90
W-3	3,545.10	3,669.90	3,794.70	3,919.80	4,045.20
W-2	3,169.50	3,280.80	3,391.80	3,503.40	3,503.40
W-1	2,940.00	3,018.60	3,018.60	3,018.60	3,018.60

Enlisted Members

Pay Grade	2 or less	Over 2	Over 3	Over 4	Over 6
E-9 [1] ...	....	....	....	....	....
E-8	....	....	....	....	....
E-7	$1,831.20	$1,999.20	$2,075.10	$2,149.80	$2,227.20
E-6	1,575.00	1,740.30	1,817.40	1,891.80	1,969.50
E-5	1,381.80	1,549.20	1,623.90	1,701.00	1,777.80
E-4	1,288.80	1,423.80	1,500.60	1,576.20	1,653.00
E-3	1,214.70	1,307.10	1,383.60	1,385.40	1,385.40
E-2	1,169.10	1,169.10	1,169.10	1,169.10	1,169.10
E-1 [2] ...	1,042.80	1,042.80	1,042.80	1,042.80	1,042.80
E-1 [3] ...	964.80	....	....	....	....

Pay Grade	Over 8	Over 10	Over 12	Over 14	Over 16
E-9 [1] ...	....	$3,126.90	$3,197.40	$3,287.10	$3,392.40
E-8	$2,622.00	2,697.90	2,768.40	2,853.30	2,945.10
E-7	2,303.10	2,379.00	2,454.90	2,529.60	2,607.00
E-6	2,046.00	2,122.80	2,196.90	2,272.50	2,327.70
E-5	1,855.80	1,930.50	2,007.90	2,007.90	2,007.90
E-4	1,653.00	1,653.00	1,653.00	1,653.00	1,653.00
E-3	1,385.40	1,385.40	1,385.40	1,385.40	1,385.40
E-2	1,169.10	1,169.10	1,169.10	1,169.10	1,169.10
E-1 [2] ...	1,042.80	1,042.80	1,042.80	1,042.80	1,042.80
E-1 [3] ...	....	....	....	....	....

Pay Grade	Over 18	Over 20	Over 22	Over 24	Over 26
E-9 [1] ...	$3,498.00	$3,601.80	$3,742.80	$3,882.60	$4,060.80
E-8	3,041.10	3,138.00	3,278.10	3,417.30	3,612.60
E-7	2,683.80	2,758.80	2,890.80	3,034.50	3,250.50
E-6	2,367.90	2,367.90	2,370.30	2,370.30	2,370.30
E-5	2,007.90	2,007.90	2,007.90	2,007.90	2,007.90
E-4	1,653.00	1,653.00	1,653.00	1,653.00	1,653.00
E-3	1,385.40	1,385.40	1,385.40	1,385.40	1,385.40
E-2	1,169.10	1,169.10	1,169.10	1,169.10	1,169.10
E-1 [2] ...	1,042.80	1,042.80	1,042.80	1,042.80	1,042.80
E-1 [3] ...	....	....	....	....	....

[1] For noncommissioned officers serving as Sergeant Major of the Army, Master Chief Petty Officer of the Navy or Coast Guard, Chief Master Sergeant of the Air Force, or Sergeant Major of the Marine Corps, basic pay for this grade is $4,893.60 per month, regardless of cumulative years of service under section 205 of title 37, United States Code.

[2] Applies to personnel who have served 4 months or more on active duty.

[3] Applies to personnel who have served less than 4 months on active duty.

PART II—RATE OF MONTHLY CADET OR MIDSHIPMAN PAY

The rate of monthly cadet or midshipman pay authorized by section 203(c) of title 37, United States Code, is $600.00.

NOTE: As a result of the enactment of sections 602–604 of Public Law 105–85 [see Tables for classification], the National Defense Authorization Act for Fiscal Year 1998, the Secretary of Defense now has the authority to adjust the rates of basic allowances for subsistence and housing. Therefore, these allowances are no longer adjusted by the President in conjunction with the adjustment of basic pay for members of the uniformed services. Accordingly, the tables of allowances included in previous orders are not included here.

SCHEDULE 9

Locality-Based Comparability Payments

(Effective on the first day of the first applicable pay period beginning on or after January 1, 2001)

Locality Pay Area [1]	Rate
Atlanta, GA	8.66%

SCHEDULE 9—Continued

Locality-Based Comparability Payments

Locality Pay Area [1]	Rate
Boston-Worcester-Lawrence, MA–NH–ME–CT–RI	12.13%
Chicago-Gary-Kenosha, IL–IN–WI	13.00%
Cincinnati-Hamilton, OH–KY–IN	10.76%
Cleveland-Akron, OH	9.17%
Columbus, OH	9.61%
Dallas-Fort Worth, TX	9.71%
Dayton-Springfield, OH	8.60%
Denver-Boulder-Greeley, CO	11.90%
Detroit-Ann Arbor-Flint, MI	13.14%
Hartford, CT	12.65%
Houston-Galveston-Brazoria, TX	16.66%
Huntsville, AL	8.12%
Indianapolis, IN	7.89%
Kansas City, MO–KS	8.32%
Los Angeles-Riverside-Orange County, CA	14.37%
Miami-Fort Lauderdale, FL	11.09%
Milwaukee-Racine, WI	8.91%
Minneapolis-St. Paul, MN–WI	10.30%
New York-Northern New Jersey-Long Island, NY–NJ–CT–PA ..	13.62%
Orlando, FL	7.71%
Philadelphia-Wilmington-Atlantic City, PA–NJ–DE–MD	10.80%
Pittsburgh, PA	8.54%
Portland-Salem, OR–WA	10.32%
Richmond-Petersburg, VA	8.60%
Sacramento-Yolo, CA	10.73%
St. Louis, MO–IL	8.00%
San Diego, CA	11.31%
San Francisco-Oakland-San Jose, CA	16.98%
Seattle-Tacoma-Bremerton, WA	10.45%
Washington-Baltimore, DC–MD–VA–WV	10.23%
Rest of U.S.	7.68%

[1] Locality Pay Areas are defined in 5 CFR 531.603.

SCHEDULE 10

Administrative Law Judges

(Effective on the first day of the first applicable pay period beginning on or after January 1, 2001)

AL–3/A	$82,100
AL–3/B	88,300
AL–3/C	94,700
AL–3/D	101,000
AL–3/E	107,300
AL–3/F	113,600
AL–2	120,000
AL–1	125,700

SECTION REFERRED TO IN OTHER SECTIONS

This section is referred to in sections 595, 3109, 3161, 5374, 5948, 6301, 8141, 8143 of this title; title 2 sections 60a–1, 60a–2, 166, 353, 437c, 476, 601, 1107, 1108; title 3 sections 105, 106, 107, 113, 114; title 7 sections 16, 1505, 1765a, 3127; title 8 section 1324b; title 10 sections 1482a, 1504, 2195; title 12 sections 634, 636, 1749bbb–1, 2405, 3013; title 15 sections 205h, 205i, 278, 1275, 2218, 2412, 2451, 4102; title 16 sections 79l, 469j, 470m, 825q–1, 1401, 1403; title 17 section 701; title 18 sections 207, 3153, 4202, 4204, 4351, 4352; title 19 sections 1331, 2171; title 20 sections 80q–10, 955, 957, 1102, 1505, 2011, 2012, 3413, 3462, 4512, 4513, 4710, 5608, 9105; title 21 sections 113a, 376, 379h; title 22 sections 290n–3, 1469, 1622d, 2385, 2386, 2456, 2511, 2512, 2669, 2903, 2905, 3507, 3508, 3963, 4110, 4135, 4155, 4356, 4605; title 25 section 2707; title 26 section 4946; title 28 sections 548, 602, 625; title 29 sections 183, 656, 661, 676; title 30 sections 812, 1229, 1315; title 31 section 731; title 32 section 509; title 33 sections 1320, 1325, 1374; title 37 section 1009; title 38 section 7455; title 41 section 351; title 42 sections 242q–1, 294o, 300j–10, 1320a–1, 1320c–2, 1395oo, 1395ww, 1873, 1962a–4, 1962b–4, 1975b, 3788, 4365, 4372, 4845, 5055, 5841, 6614, 6616, 6632, 7211, 7213, 7231, 7233, 8103, 10248, 11221, 12374, 12651f; title 44 sections 2706, 3319; title 46 sections 4508, 9307; title 50 sections 405, 2051; title 50 App. section 1989b–5.

§ 5333. Minimum rate for new appointments

New appointments shall be made at the minimum rate of the appropriate grade. However, under regulations prescribed by the Office of

Personnel Management which provide for such considerations as the existing pay or unusually high or unique qualifications of the candidate, or a special need of the Government for his services, the head of an agency may appoint, with the approval of the Office in each specific case, an individual to a position at such a rate above the minimum rate of the appropriate grade as the Office may authorize for this purpose. The approval of the Office in each specific case is not required with respect to an appointment made by the Librarian of Congress.

(Pub. L. 89–554, Sept. 6, 1966, 80 Stat. 467; Pub. L. 90–83, §1(19), Sept. 11, 1967, 81 Stat. 199; Pub. L. 95–454, title IX, §906(a)(2), (3), Oct. 13, 1978, 92 Stat. 1224; Pub. L. 96–54, §2(a)(26)(A), Aug. 14, 1979, 93 Stat. 382; Pub. L. 101–509, title V, §529 [title I, §106, title II, §211(b)(1)], Nov. 5, 1990, 104 Stat. 1427, 1449, 1461.)

HISTORICAL AND REVISION NOTES
1966 ACT

Derivation	U.S. Code	Revised Statutes and Statutes at Large
(a)	5 U.S.C. 1131.	Oct. 28, 1949, ch. 782, §801, 63 Stat. 969. Aug. 14, 1964, Pub. L. 88–426, §103(a), 78 Stat. 401.
(b)	5 U.S.C. 1133.	Oct. 28, 1949, ch. 782, §803, 63 Stat. 970. Sept. 1, 1954, ch. 1208, §104, 68 Stat. 1106. Oct. 11, 1962, Pub. L. 87–793, §604(c), 76 Stat. 848.

In subsection (b), the word "scheduled" is omitted since section 603 of the Act of Oct. 11, 1962, Pub. L. 87–793, 76 Stat. 847, eliminated the necessity of referring to rates as scheduled or longevity.

Standard changes are made to conform with the definitions applicable and the style of this title as outlined in the preface to the report.

1967 ACT

Section of title 5	Source (U.S. Code)	Source (Statutes at Large)
5333(a)	5 App.: 1131.	July 18, 1966, Pub. L. 89–504, §103, 80 Stat. 289.

AMENDMENTS

1990—Pub. L. 101–509 struck out "; higher rates for supervisors of prevailing rate employees" after "appointments" in section catchline, struck out "(a)" before "New appointments shall", struck out "in GS–11 or above" after "individual to a position", and struck out subsec. (b) which read as follows: "Under regulations prescribed by the Office of Personnel Management, an employee in a position to which this subchapter applies, who regularly has responsibility for supervision (including supervision over the technical aspects of the work concerned) over employees whose pay is fixed and adjusted from time to time by wage boards or similar administrative authority as nearly as is consistent with the public interest in accordance with prevailing rates, may be paid at one of the rates for his grade which is above the highest rate of basic pay being paid to any such prevailing-rate employee regularly supervised, or at the maximum rate for his grade, as provided by the regulations."

1979—Pub. L. 96–54 substituted "prevailing rate" for "wage-board" in section catchline.

1978—Subsecs. (a), (b). Pub. L. 95–454 substituted "Office of Personnel Management" and "Office" for "Civil Service Commission" and "Commission", respectively, wherever appearing.

EFFECTIVE DATE OF 1990 AMENDMENT

Amendment by Pub. L. 101–509 effective on such date as the President shall determine, but not earlier than 90 days, and not later than 180 days, after Nov. 5, 1990, see section 529 [title III, §305] of Pub. L. 101–509, set out as a note under section 5301 of this title.

EFFECTIVE DATE OF 1979 AMENDMENT

Amendment by Pub. L. 96–54 effective July 12, 1979, see section 2(b) of Pub. L. 96–54, set out as a note under section 305 of this title.

EFFECTIVE DATE OF 1978 AMENDMENT

Amendment by Pub. L. 95–454 effective 90 days after Oct. 13, 1978, see section 907 of Pub. L. 95–454, set out as a note under section 1101 of this title.

SECTION REFERRED TO IN OTHER SECTIONS

This section is referred to in title 7 section 84.

§ 5334. Rate on change of position or type of appointment; regulations

(a) The rate of basic pay to which an employee is entitled is governed by regulations prescribed by the Office of Personnel Management in conformity with this subchapter and chapter 51 of this title when—

(1) he is transferred from a position in the legislative, judicial, or executive branch to which this subchapter does not apply;

(2) he is transferred from a position in the legislative, judicial, or executive branch to which this subchapter applies to another such position;

(3) he is demoted to a position in a lower grade;

(4) he is reinstated, reappointed, or reemployed in a position to which this subchapter applies following service in any position in the legislative, judicial, or executive branch;

(5) his type of appointment is changed;

(6) his employment status is otherwise changed; or

(7) his position is changed from one grade to another grade.

For the purpose of this subsection, an individual employed by the Appalachian Regional Commission under section 106(2) of the Appalachian Regional Development Act of 1965 (40 U.S.C. App.), who was a Federal employee immediately prior to such employment by a commission and within 6 months after separation from such employment is employed in a position to which this subchapter applies, shall be treated as if transferred from a position in the executive branch to which this subchapter does not apply.

(b) An employee who is promoted or transferred to a position in a higher grade is entitled to basic pay at the lowest rate of the higher grade which exceeds his existing rate of basic pay by not less than two step-increases of the grade from which he is promoted or transferred. If, in the case of an employee so promoted or transferred who is receiving basic pay at a rate in excess of the maximum rate of his grade, there is no rate in the higher grade which is at least two step-increases above his existing rate of basic pay, he is entitled to—

(1) the maximum rate of the higher grade; or

(2) his existing rate of basic pay, if that rate is the higher.

If an employee so promoted or transferred is receiving basic pay at a rate saved to him under subchapter VI of this chapter on reduction in grade, he is entitled to—

    (A) basic pay at a rate two steps above the rate which he would be receiving if subchapter VI of this chapter were not applicable to him; or

    (B) his existing rate of basic pay, if that rate is the higher.

(c) An employee in the legislative branch who is paid by the Secretary of the Senate or the Chief Administrative Officer of the House of Representatives, and who has completed two or more years of service as such an employee, and a Member of the Senate or House of Representatives who has completed two or more years of service as such a Member, may, on appointment to a position to which this subchapter applies, have his initial rate of pay fixed—

    (1) at the minimum rate of the appropriate grade; or

    (2) at a step of the appropriate grade that does not exceed the highest previous rate of pay received by him during that service in the legislative branch.

(d) The rate of pay established for a teaching position as defined by section 901 of title 20 held by an individual who becomes subject to subsection (a) of this section is deemed increased by an amount determined under regulations which the Secretary of Defense shall prescribe for the determination of the yearly rate of pay of the position. The amount by which a rate of pay is increased under the regulations may not exceed the amount equal to 20 percent of that rate of pay.

(e) An employee of a county committee established pursuant to section 590h(b) of title 16 may, upon appointment to a position subject to this subchapter, have his initial rate of basic pay fixed at the minimum rate of the appropriate grade, or at any step of such grade that does not exceed the highest previous rate of basic pay received by him during service with such county committee.

(f) An employee of a nonappropriated fund instrumentality of the Department of Defense or the Coast Guard described in section 2105(c) who moves, without a break in service of more than 3 days, to a position in the Department of Defense or the Coast Guard, respectively, that is subject to this subchapter, may have such employee's initial rate of basic pay fixed at the minimum rate of the appropriate grade or at any step of such grade that does not exceed the highest previous rate of basic pay received by that employee during the employee's service described in section 2105(c). In the case of a nonappropriated fund employee who is moved involuntarily from such nonappropriated fund instrumentality without a break in service of more than 3 days and without substantial change in duties to a position that is subject to this subchapter, the employee's pay shall be set at a rate (not above the maximum for the grade, except as may be provided for under section 5365) that is not less than the employee's rate of basic pay under the nonappropriated fund instrumentality immediately prior to so moving.

(Pub. L. 89–554, Sept. 6, 1966, 80 Stat. 468; Pub. L. 90–103, title I, § 105, Oct. 11, 1967, 81 Stat. 257; Pub. L. 90–367, § 1, June 29, 1968, 82 Stat. 277; Pub L. 90–623, § 1(6), (24), Oct. 22, 1968, 82 Stat. 1312, 1314; Pub. L. 95–454, title V, § 503(f), title VIII, § 801(a)(2), (3)(F), (G), title IX, § 906(a)(2), Oct. 13, 1978, 92 Stat. 1184, 1221, 1222, 1224; Pub. L. 96–54, § 2(a)(27), Aug. 14, 1979, 93 Stat. 383; Pub. L. 98–615, title II, § 204(a)(1), Nov. 8, 1984, 98 Stat. 3216; Pub. L. 99–251, title III, § 306(b), Feb. 27, 1986, 100 Stat. 27; Pub. L. 101–508, title VII, § 7202(d), Nov. 5, 1990, 104 Stat. 1388–335; Pub. L. 103–89, § 3(b)(1)(G), Sept. 30, 1993, 107 Stat. 982; Pub. L. 104–186, title II, § 215(4), Aug. 20, 1996, 110 Stat. 1745; Pub. L. 105–85, div. A, title XI, § 1104(a), Nov. 18, 1997, 111 Stat. 1923; Pub. L. 105–393, title II, § 223, Nov. 13, 1998, 112 Stat. 3626.)

HISTORICAL AND REVISION NOTES

Derivation	U.S. Code	Revised Statutes and Statutes at Large
(a)–(d)	5 U.S.C. 1132.	Oct. 28, 1949, ch. 782, § 802, 63 Stat. 969. Sept. 1, 1954, ch. 1208, § 112 (as applicable to § 802(b)), 68 Stat. 1108. May 29, 1958, Pub. L. 85–432, § 4(a), (b), 72 Stat. 151. July 31, 1959, Pub. L. 86–122, § 2(a), 73 Stat. 268. Oct. 11, 1962, Pub. L. 87–793, § 604(a), (b), 76 Stat. 847.
(e)	5 U.S.C. 2357.	July 17, 1959, Pub. L. 86–91. § 9, 73 Stat. 216.

In subsection (b), the words "under any provision of law" are omitted from the second sentence as unnecessary.

In subsection (e), the words "as defined by section 901 of title 20" are added on authority of former section 2351, which section is scheduled for transfer to section 901 of title 20.

Standard changes are made to conform with the definitions applicable and the style of this title as outlined in the preface to the report.

AMENDMENTS

1998—Subsec. (a). Pub. L. 105–393 substituted "the Appalachian Regional Development Act of 1965 (40 U.S.C. App.)" for "title 40, appendix, or by a regional commission established pursuant to section 3182 of title 42, under section 3186(a)(2) of that title".

1997—Subsec. (d). Pub. L. 105–85 substituted "an amount determined under regulations which the Secretary of Defense shall prescribe for the determination of the yearly rate of pay of the position. The amount by which a rate of pay is increased under the regulations may not exceed the amount equal to 20 percent of that rate of pay." for "20 percent to determine the yearly rate of pay of the position."

1996—Subsec. (c). Pub. L. 104–186 substituted "Chief Administrative Officer" for "Clerk".

1993—Subsec. (c)(2). Pub. L. 103–89, § 3(b)(1)(G)(i), substituted "step" for "step, or for an employee appointed to a position covered by the performance management and recognition system established under chapter 54 of this title, any dollar amount,".

Subsecs. (f), (g). Pub. L. 103–89, § 3(b)(1)(G)(ii), redesignated subsec. (g) as (f) and struck out former subsec. (f) which read as follows: "In the case of an employee covered by the performance management and recognition system established under chapter 54 of this title, all references in this section to 'two steps' or 'two step-increases' shall be deemed to mean 6 percent."

1990—Subsec. (g). Pub. L. 101–508 added subsec. (g).

1986—Subsec. (e). Pub. L. 99–251 substituted "may, upon appointment to a position" for "may upon appointment to a position under the Department of Agriculture,".

1984—Subsecs. (c)(2), (f). Pub. L. 98–615 substituted "the performance management and recognition system established under chapter 54" for "the merit pay system established under section 5402".

1979—Subsec. (a). Pub. L. 96–54 substituted "106(2)" for "106(a)" and "3186(a)(2)" for "3186(2)".

1978—Subsec. (a). Pub. L. 95–454, § 906(a)(2), substituted "Office of Personnel Management" for "Civil Service Commission".

Subsec. (b). Pub. L. 95–454, § 801(a)(3)(F), substituted "subchapter VI of this chapter" for "section 5337 of this title" wherever appearing.

Subsec. (c). Pub. L. 95–454, § 503(f)(1), in par. (2) inserted reference to an employee appointed to a position covered by the merit pay system established under section 5402 of this title.

Subsecs. (d) to (f). Pub. L. 95–454, § 801(a)(2), (3)(G), redesignated subsecs. (e) and (f) as (d) and (e), respectively. Former subsec. (d), which related to regulations governing the retention of the rate of basic pay of an employee and his position covered by this subchapter and chapter 51 of this title, was struck out.

Pub. L. 95–454, § 503(f)(2), added a new subsec. (f).

1968—Subsec. (a). Pub. L. 90–623, § 1(6), substituted "title 40, appendix" for "the Appalachian Regional Development Act of 1965", "section 3182 of title 42, under section 3186(2) of that title" for "section 502 of the Public Works and Economic Development Act of 1965, under section 506(2) of such Act", and "6" for "six".

Subsec. (f). Pub. L. 90–623, § 1(24), substituted "section 590h(b) of title 16" for "section 8(b) of the Soil Conservation and Domestic Allotment Act (16 U.S.C. 590h(b))".

Pub. L. 90–367 added subsec. (f).

1967—Subsec. (a). Pub. L. 90–103 provided for treatment as a transfer from a position in the executive branch to which this subchapter does not apply of certain regional commission employees who were Federal employees immediately prior to employment by a commission and were employed within six months after separation from the commission in a position subject to this subchapter.

EFFECTIVE DATE OF 1997 AMENDMENT

Section 1104(b) of Pub. L. 105–85 provided that:

"(1) The amendment made by subsection (a) [amending this section] shall take effect 180 days after the date of the enactment of this Act [Nov. 18, 1997].

"(2) In the case of a person who is employed in a teaching position referred to in section 5334(d) of title 5, United States Code, on the day before the effective date under paragraph (1), the rate of pay of that person determined under that section (as in effect on that day) may not be reduced by reason of the amendment made by subsection (a) for so long as the person continues to serve in that position or another such position without a break in service of more than three days on or after that day."

EFFECTIVE DATE OF 1993 AMENDMENT

Amendment by Pub. L. 103–89 effective Nov. 1, 1993, see section 3(c) of Pub. L. 103–89, set out as a note under section 3372 of this title.

EFFECTIVE DATE OF 1990 AMENDMENT

Amendment by Pub. L. 101–508 applicable with respect to any individual who, on or after Jan. 1, 1987, moves from employment in nonappropriated fund instrumentality of Department of Defense or Coast Guard, that is described in section 2105(c) of this title, to employment in Department or Coast Guard, that is not described in section 2105(c), or who moves from employment in Department or Coast Guard, that is not described in section 2105(c), to employment in nonappropriated fund instrumentality of Department or Coast Guard, that is described in section 2105(c), see section 7202(m)(1) of Pub. L. 101–508, set out as a note under section 2105 of this title.

EFFECTIVE DATE OF 1984 AMENDMENT

Section 205 of Pub. L. 98–615 provided that amendment by Pub. L. 98–615 was effective Oct. 1, 1984, and ap-

plicable with respect to pay periods commencing on or after that date, with certain exceptions and qualifications.

EFFECTIVE DATE OF 1979 AMENDMENT

Amendment by Pub. L. 96–54 effective July 12, 1979, see section 2(b) of Pub. L. 96–54, set out as a note under section 305 of this title.

EFFECTIVE DATE OF 1978 AMENDMENT

Section 504(a) of Pub. L. 95–454 provided that amendment by section 503(f) of Pub. L. 95–454 was effective on first day of first applicable pay period which began on or after Oct. 1, 1981, except it could take effect with respect to any category or categories of positions before such day to extent prescribed by Director of Office of Personnel Management.

Amendment by section 801(a)(2), (3)(F), (G) of Pub. L. 95–454 effective on first day of first applicable pay period beginning on or after 90th day after Oct. 13, 1978, see section 801(a)(4) of Pub. L. 95–454, set out as an Effective Date note under section 5361 of this title.

Amendment by section 906(a)(2) of Pub. L. 95–454 effective 90 days after Oct. 13, 1978, see section 907 of Pub. L. 95–454, set out as a note under section 1101 of this title.

EFFECTIVE DATE OF 1968 AMENDMENT

Section 6 of Pub. L. 90–623 provided that:

"(a) Sections 1–5 of this Act [amending this section, sections 559, 2108, 3102, 3502, 5314, 5315, 5316, 5352, 5353, 5516, 5521, 5527, 5537, 5546, 5724, 6104, 6305, 6312, 6323, 6324, 8143, 8191, 8331, and 8347 of this title, sections 101, 510 [now 12102], 815, 1124, 3534, 4342, 5149, 6483, 6954, and 9342 of Title 10, Armed Forces, sections 101, 212, 205, 305, 306, 307, 308, 311, 406, 417, 554, 703, 904, 1001, and 1006 of Title 37, Pay and Allowances of the Uniformed Services, and sections 2727 and 2994b of Title 42, The Public Health and Welfare, and repealing section 8339 note of this title] restate, without substantive change, the laws replaced by those sections on the effective date of this Act. Laws effective after June 30, 1968, that are inconsistent with this Act [Oct. 22, 1968] supersede it to the extent of the inconsistency.

"(b) References made by other laws, regulations, and orders to the laws restated by this Act are deemed to refer to the corresponding provisions of this Act.

"(c) Actions taken under the laws restated by this Act are deemed to have been taken under the corresponding provisions of this Act.

"(d) Sections 1(2) and 1(14) of this Act [amending sections 2108 and 5724 of this title] are effective as of September 11, 1967, for all purposes.

"(e) Sections 1(13)(B) and 1(17) of this Act [amending sections 5546 and 6323 of this title] are effective as of September 6, 1966, for all purposes."

SECTION REFERRED TO IN OTHER SECTIONS

This section is referred to in title 40 App. section 109.

§ 5335. Periodic step-increases

(a) An employee paid on an annual basis, and occupying a permanent position within the scope of the General Schedule, who has not reached the maximum rate of pay for the grade in which his position is placed, shall be advanced in pay successively to the next higher rate within the grade at the beginning of the next pay period following the completion of—

(1) each 52 calendar weeks of service in pay rates 1, 2, and 3;

(2) each 104 calendar weeks of service in pay rates 4, 5, and 6; or

(3) each 156 calendar weeks of service in pay rates 7, 8, and 9;

subject to the following conditions:

(A) the employee did not receive an equivalent increase in pay from any cause during that period; and

(B) the work of the employee is of an acceptable level of competence as determined by the head of the agency.

(b) Under regulations prescribed by the Office of Personnel Management, the benefit of successive step-increases shall be preserved for employees whose continuous service is interrupted in the public interest by service with the armed forces or by service in essential non-Government civilian employment during a period of war or national emergency.

(c) When a determination is made under subsection (a) of this section that the work of an employee is not of an acceptable level of competence, the employee is entitled to prompt written notice of that determination and an opportunity for reconsideration of the determination within his agency under uniform procedures prescribed by the Office of Personnel Management. If the determination is affirmed on reconsideration, the employee is entitled to appeal to the Merit Systems Protection Board. If the reconsideration or appeal results in a reversal of the earlier determination, the new determination supersedes the earlier determination and is deemed to have been made as of the date of the earlier determination. The authority of the Office to prescribe procedures and the entitlement of the employee to appeal to the Board do not apply to a determination of acceptable level of competence made by the Librarian of Congress.

(d) An increase in pay granted by statute is not an equivalent increase in pay within the meaning of subsection (a) of this section.

(e) This section does not apply to the pay of an individual appointed by the President, by and with the advice and consent of the Senate.

(f) In computing periods of service under subsection (a) in the case of an employee who moves without a break in service of more than 3 days from a position under a nonappropriated fund instrumentality of the Department of Defense or the Coast Guard described in section 2105(c) to a position under the Department of Defense or the Coast Guard, respectively, that is subject to this subchapter, service under such instrumentality shall, under regulations prescribed by the Office, be deemed service in a position subject to this subchapter.

(Pub. L. 89–554, Sept. 6, 1966, 80 Stat. 469; Pub. L. 90–83, §1(20), Sept. 11, 1967, 81 Stat. 199; Pub. L. 95–251, §2(a)(1), Mar. 27, 1978, 92 Stat. 183; Pub. L. 95–454, title V, §503(g), title IX, §906(a)(2), (8), Oct. 13, 1978, 92 Stat. 1184, 1224, 1225; Pub. L. 96–54, §2(a)(28), Aug. 14, 1979, 93 Stat. 383; Pub. L. 98–615, title II, §§203, 204(a)(1), Nov. 8, 1984, 98 Stat. 3216; Pub. L. 101–508, title VII, §7202(e), Nov. 5, 1990, 104 Stat. 1388–336; Pub. L. 101–509, title V, §529 [title I, §104(d)(2)], Nov. 5, 1990, 104 Stat. 1427, 1447; Pub. L. 103–89, §3(b)(1)(H), Sept. 30, 1993, 107 Stat. 982.)

HISTORICAL AND REVISION NOTES
1966 ACT

Derivation	U.S. Code	Revised Statutes and Statutes at Large
(a)–(c)	5 U.S.C. 1121.	Oct. 11, 1962, Pub. L. 87–793, §603 "Sec. 701", 76 Stat. 847.
(d)	5 U.S.C. 1123 (as applicable to 5 U.S.C. 1121).	Oct. 11, 1962, Pub. L. 87–793, §603 "Sec. 703 (as applicable to §701)", 76 Stat. 847.

In subsection (a), the words "General Schedule" are substituted for "compensation schedules fixed by this chapter" since the General Schedule is now the only compensation schedule in that chapter. The word "scheduled" is omitted since section 603 of the Act of Oct. 11, 1962, Pub. L. 87–793, 76 Stat. 847, eliminated the necessity of referring to rates as scheduled or longevity.

In subsection (a)(B), the words "except a hearing examiner appointed under section 3105 of this title" are added on authority of the third sentence of former section 1010 and the fifth sentence of former section 1011, which are carried into sections 5362 and 559, respectively, and of section 1106(a) of the Act of Oct. 28, 1949, ch. 782, 63 Stat. 972.

Title VII (sections 701–705) of the Act of Oct. 28, 1949, ch. 782, 63 Stat. 967–969, as amended by the following Acts is omitted from the derivation and repealed (see Table II) as superseded by the Act of Oct. 11, 1962, Pub. L. 87–793, §603, 76 Stat. 847, which is carried into this section and section 5336:

June 28, 1950, ch. 382, §2, 64 Stat. 262.
Sept. 30, 1950, ch. 1123, §§9, 10, 64 Stat. 1100.
Oct. 24, 1951, ch. 554, §1(e), 65 Stat. 613.
Sept. 1, 1954, ch. 1208, §§102(a), 103(a), 112 (less applicability to §802(b)), 305(a), 68 Stat. 1105, 1108, 1113.
June 28, 1955, ch. 189, §2(e), 69 Stat. 175.

Standard changes are made to conform with the definitions applicable and the style of this title as outlined in the preface to the report.

1967 ACT

Section of title 5	Source (U.S. Code)	Source (Statutes at Large)
5335(c)	5 App.: 1121(c).	Oct. 29, 1965, Pub. L. 89–301, §3, 79 Stat. 1112.

The word "officer" is omitted as included in "employee", and the word "agency" is substituted for "department" to conform to the definition in 5 U.S.C. 5331.

AMENDMENTS

1993—Subsec. (e). Pub. L. 103–89, §3(b)(1)(H)(i), struck out "covered by the performance management and recognition system established under chapter 54 of this title, or," after "individual".

Subsecs. (f), (g). Pub. L. 103–89, §3(b)(1)(H)(ii), redesignated subsec. (g) as (f) and struck out former subsec. (f) which read as follows: "Notwithstanding subsection (b) or (e) of this section, an increase in pay granted under section 5404 of this title is an equivalent increase in pay within the meaning of subsection (a) of this section and shall be taken into account in the case of any employee who, before becoming subject to this section, was granted such an increase while covered by the performance management and recognition system established under chapter 54 of this title."

1990—Subsec. (a)(B). Pub. L. 101–509 struck out ", except an administrative law judge appointed under section 3105 of this title," after "work of the employee".

Subsec. (g). Pub. L. 101–508 added subsec. (g).

1984—Subsec. (e). Pub. L. 98–615, §204(a)(1), substituted "the performance management and recognition system established under chapter 54" for "the merit pay system established under section 5402".

Subsec. (f). Pub. L. 98–615, §203, added subsec. (f).

1979—Subsec. (a)(3)(B). Pub. L. 96–54 substituted "an administrative law judge" for "a administrative law judge".

1978—Subsec. (a). Pub. L. 95–251 substituted "administrative law judge" for "hearing examiner".

Subsec. (b). Pub. L. 95–454, § 906(a)(2), substituted "Office of Personnel Management" for "Civil Service Commission".

Subsec. (c). Pub. L. 95–454, § 906(a)(8), substituted references to Office of Personnel Management and Merit Systems Protection Board and Office and Board, respectively, for references to Civil Service Commission wherever appearing in text.

Subsec. (e). Pub. L. 95–454, § 503(g), inserted reference to merit pay system established under section 5402 of this title.

EFFECTIVE DATE OF 1993 AMENDMENT

Amendment by Pub. L. 103–89 effective Nov. 1, 1993, see section 3(c) of Pub. L. 103–89, set out as a note under section 3372 of this title.

EFFECTIVE DATE OF 1990 AMENDMENTS

Amendment by Pub. L. 101–509 effective on such date as the President shall determine, but not earlier than 90 days, and not later than 180 days, after Nov. 5, 1990, see section 529 [title III, § 305] of Pub. L. 101–509, set out as a note under section 5301 of this title.

Amendment by Pub. L. 101–508 applicable with respect to any individual who, on or after Jan. 1, 1987, moves from employment in nonappropriated fund instrumentality of Department of Defense or Coast Guard, that is described in section 2105(c) of this title, to employment in Department or Coast Guard, that is not described in section 2105(c), or who moves from employment in Department or Coast Guard, that is not described in section 2105(c), to employment in nonappropriated fund instrumentality of Department or Coast Guard, that is described in section 2105(c), see section 7202(m)(1) of Pub. L. 101–508, set out as a note under section 2105 of this title.

EFFECTIVE DATE OF 1984 AMENDMENT

Section 205 of Pub. L. 98–615 provided that amendment by Pub. L. 98–615 was effective Oct. 1, 1984, and applicable with respect to pay periods commencing on or after that date, with certain exceptions and qualifications.

EFFECTIVE DATE OF 1979 AMENDMENT

Amendment by Pub. L. 96–54 effective July 12, 1979, see section 2(b) of Pub. L. 96–54, set out as a note under section 305 of this title.

EFFECTIVE DATE OF 1978 AMENDMENT

Section 504(a) of Pub. L. 95–454 provided that amendment by section 503(g) of Pub. L. 95–454 was effective on first day of first applicable pay period which began on or after Oct. 1, 1981, except it could take effect with respect to any category or categories of positions before such day to extent prescribed by Director of Office of Personnel Management.

Amendment by section 906(a)(2), (8) of Pub. L. 95–454 effective 90 days after Oct. 13, 1978, see section 907 of Pub. L. 95–454, set out as a note under section 1101 of this title.

PAY INCREASES DEEMED EQUIVALENT INCREASES IN PAY

Section 5(a) of Pub. L. 103–89 provided that: "Notwithstanding the amendment made by section 3(b)(1)(H)(ii) [amending this section], an increase in pay granted under section 5404 of title 5, United States Code, before November 1, 1993, shall be deemed to be an equivalent increase in pay within the meaning of section 5335(a) of such title."

SECTION REFERRED TO IN OTHER SECTIONS

This section is referred to in sections 559, 1305, 5303, 5305, 5336, 9508 of this title; title 13 section 24.

§ 5336. Additional step-increases

(a) Within the limit of available appropriations and under regulations prescribed by the Office of Personnel Management, the head of each agency may grant additional step-increases in recognition of high quality performance above that ordinarily found in the type of position concerned. However, an employee is eligible under this section for only one additional step-increase within any 52-week period.

(b) A step-increase under this section is in addition to those under section 5335 of this title and is not an equivalent increase in pay within the meaning of section 5335(a) of this title.

(c) This section does not apply to the pay of an individual appointed by the President, by and with the advice and consent of the Senate.

(Pub. L. 89–554, Sept. 6, 1966, 80 Stat. 469; Pub. L. 95–454, title V, § 503(h), title IX, § 906(a)(2), Oct. 13, 1978, 92 Stat. 1184, 1224; Pub. L. 98–615, title II, § 204(a)(1), Nov. 8, 1984, 98 Stat. 3216; Pub. L. 103–89, § 3(b)(1)(I), Sept. 30, 1993, 107 Stat. 982.)

HISTORICAL AND REVISION NOTES

Derivation	U.S. Code	Revised Statutes and Statutes at Large
(a), (b)	5 U.S.C. 1122.	Oct. 11, 1962, Pub. L. 87–793, § 603 "Sec. 702", 76 Stat. 847.
(c)	5 U.S.C. 1123 (less applicability to 5 U.S.C. 1121).	Oct. 11, 1962, Pub. L. 87–793, § 603 "Sec. 703 (less applicability to § 701)", 76 Stat. 847.

For repeal of Title VII (sections 701–705) of the Act of Oct. 28, 1949, ch. 782, 63 Stat. 967–969, as amended, see revision note for section 5335.

Standard changes are made to conform with the definitions applicable and the style of this title as outlined in the preface to the report.

AMENDMENTS

1993—Subsec. (c). Pub. L. 103–89 struck out "covered by the performance management and recognition system established under chapter 54 of this title, or," after "individual".

1984—Subsec. (c). Pub. L. 98–615 substituted "the performance management and recognition system established under chapter 54" for "the merit pay system established under section 5402".

1978—Subsec. (a). Pub. L. 95–454, § 906(a)(2), substituted "Office of Personnel Management" for "Civil Service Commission".

Subsec. (c). Pub. L. 95–454, § 503(h), inserted reference to merit pay system established under section 5402 of this title.

EFFECTIVE DATE OF 1993 AMENDMENT

Amendment by Pub. L. 103–89 effective Nov. 1, 1993, see section 3(c) of Pub. L. 103–89, set out as a note under section 3372 of this title.

EFFECTIVE DATE OF 1984 AMENDMENT

Section 205 of Pub. L. 98–615 provided that amendment by Pub. L. 98–615 was effective Oct. 1, 1984, and applicable with respect to pay periods commencing on or after that date, with certain exceptions and qualifications.

EFFECTIVE DATE OF 1978 AMENDMENT

Section 504(a) of Pub. L. 95–454 provided that amendment by section 503(h) of Pub. L. 95–454 was effective on first day of first applicable pay period which began on or after Oct. 1, 1981, except it could take effect with respect to any category or categories of positions before such day to extent prescribed by Director of Office of Personnel Management.

Amendment by section 906(a)(2) of Pub. L. 95–454 effective 90 days after Oct. 13, 1978, see section 907 of Pub. L. 95–454, set out as a note under section 1101 of this title.

SECTION REFERRED TO IN OTHER SECTIONS

This section is referred to in title 13 section 24.

[§ 5337. Repealed. Pub. L. 95–454, title VIII, § 801(a)(2), Oct. 13, 1978, 92 Stat. 1221]

Section, Pub. L. 89–554, Sept. 6, 1966, 80 Stat. 470; Pub. L. 92–392, §3, Aug. 19, 1972, 86 Stat. 573, set forth provisions relating to pay saving for employees reduced in grade from a grade in the General Schedule. See section 5361 et seq. of this title.

EFFECTIVE DATE OF REPEAL

Repeal effective on first day of first applicable pay period beginning on or after 90th day after Oct. 13, 1978, and an employee receiving pay on day before such effective date not to have such pay reduced or terminated and, unless section 5362 applies, employee is entitled to continuation of such pay, etc., see section 801(a)(4) of Pub. L. 95–454, set out as an Effective Date note under section 5361 of this title.

§ 5338. Regulations

The Office of Personnel Management may prescribe regulations necessary for the administration of this subchapter.

(Pub. L. 89–554, Sept. 6, 1966, 80 Stat. 470; Pub. L. 95–454, title IX, §906(a)(2), Oct. 13, 1978, 92 Stat. 1224.)

HISTORICAL AND REVISION NOTES

The section is added on authority of former sections 1072 and 1072a, which are carried into section 5115.

AMENDMENTS

1978—Pub. L. 95–454 substituted "Office of Personnel Management" for "Civil Service Commission".

EFFECTIVE DATE OF 1978 AMENDMENT

Amendment by Pub. L. 95–454 effective 90 days after Oct. 13, 1978, see section 907 of Pub. L. 95–454, set out as a note under section 1101 of this title.

SUBCHAPTER IV—PREVAILING RATE SYSTEMS

SUBCHAPTER REFERRED TO IN OTHER SECTIONS

This subchapter is referred to in sections 5304, 5361, 5541, 7201, 7204, 9509 of this title; title 10 sections 4540, 7212, 9540; title 31 section 1515; title 40 section 174j–8.

§ 5341. Policy

It is the policy of Congress that rates of pay of prevailing rate employees be fixed and adjusted from time to time as nearly as is consistent with the public interest in accordance with prevailing rates and be based on principles that—

(1) there will be equal pay for substantially equal work for all prevailing rate employees who are working under similar conditions of employment in all agencies within the same local wage area;

(2) there will be relative differences in pay within a local wage area when there are substantial or recognizable differences in duties, responsibilities, and qualification requirements among positions;

(3) the level of rates of pay will be maintained in line with prevailing levels for comparable work within a local wage area; and

(4) the level of rates of pay will be maintained so as to attract and retain qualified prevailing rate employees.

(Added Pub. L. 92–392, §1(a), Aug. 19, 1972, 86 Stat. 564.)

PRIOR PROVISIONS

A prior section 5341, Pub. L. 89–554, Sept. 6, 1966, 80 Stat. 471; Pub. L. 90–83, §1(97), Sept. 11, 1967, 81 Stat. 220; Pub. L. 90–560, §4, Oct. 12, 1968, 82 Stat. 997, provided prevailing rate system for trades and crafts and is covered by sections 5343(c), (d) and 5349(a) of this title.

EFFECTIVE DATE

Section 15(a) of Pub. L. 92–392 provided that: "The provisions of this Act [enacting this subchapter and section 5550 of this title, amending sections 2105, 5337, 5541, 5544, 5548, 6101, 7154, and 8704 of this title, repealing section 6102 of this title, and enacting provisions set out as notes under sections 5341 and 5343 of this title and sections 60a–1 and 60a–2 of Title 2, The Congress] are effective on the first day of the first applicable pay period which begins on or after the ninetieth day after the date of enactment of this Act [Aug. 19, 1972], except that, in the case of those employees referred to in section 5342(a)(2)(B) and (C) of title 5, United States Code (as amended by the first section of this Act), such provisions are effective on the first day of the first applicable pay period which begins on or after the one hundred and eightieth day after such date of enactment or on such earlier date (not earlier than the ninetieth day after such date of enactment) as the Civil Service Commission may prescribe. Notwithstanding the provisions of this subsection, section 5343(e)(1)(D) and (E) and (e)(2)(C), as enacted by the first section of this Act, shall not be effective until the first day of the first pay period commencing after (1) the date on which the President ceases to exercise his authority under the Economic Stabilization Act of 1970 [formerly set out as a note under section 1904 of Title 12, Banks and Banking] to stabilize wages and salaries, or (2) April 30, 1973, whichever occurs first."

REPEALS

Section 13 of Pub. L. 92–392 provided that:

"(a) All laws or parts of laws inconsistent with this Act [see Effective Date note above] are hereby repealed to the extent of such inconsistency.

"(b) Subsection (a) of this section does not repeal or otherwise affect section 5102(d) of title 5, United States Code, section 305 of title 44 of such Code, or the provisions contained in section 180 of former title 31, United States Code."

SECTION REFERRED TO IN OTHER SECTIONS

This section is referred to in title 10 section 1602; title 41 section 351.

§ 5342. Definitions; application

(a) For the purpose of this subchapter—

(1) "agency" means an Executive agency; but does not include—

(A) a Government controlled corporation;

(B) the Tennessee Valley Authority;

(C) the Virgin Islands Corporation;

(D) the Atomic Energy Commission;

(E) the Central Intelligence Agency;

(F) the National Security Agency, Department of Defense;

(G) the Bureau of Engraving and Printing, except for the purposes of section 5349 of this title;

(H) the General Accounting Office; or[1]

(J)[2] the Defense Intelligence Agency, Department of Defense; or

(K) the National Imagery and Mapping Agency, Department of Defense;

(2) "prevailing rate employee" means—

(A) an individual employed in or under an agency in a recognized trade or craft, or other skilled mechanical craft, or in an unskilled, semiskilled, or skilled manual labor occupation, and any other individual, including a foreman and a supervisor, in a position having trade, craft, or laboring experience and knowledge as the paramount requirement;

(B) an employee of a nonappropriated fund instrumentality described by section 2105(c) of this title who is employed in a recognized trade or craft, or other skilled mechanical craft, or in an unskilled, semiskilled, or skilled manual labor occupation, and any other individual, including a foreman and a supervisor, in a position having trade, craft, or laboring experience and knowledge as the paramount requirement; and

(C) an employee of the Veterans' Canteen Service, Department of Veterans Affairs, excepted from chapter 51 of this title by section 5102 (c)(14) of this title who is employed in a recognized trade or craft, or other skilled mechanical craft, or in an unskilled, semiskilled, or skilled manual labor occupation, and any other individual, including a foreman and a supervisor, in a position having trade, craft, or labor experience and knowledge as the paramount requirement; and

(3) "position" means the work, consisting of duties and responsibilities, assignable to a prevailing rate employee.

(b)(1) Except as provided by paragraphs (2) and (3) of this subsection, this subchapter applies to all prevailing rate employees and positions in or under an agency.

(2) This subchapter does not apply to employees and positions described by section 5102(c) of this title other than by—

(A) paragraph (7) of that section to the extent that such paragraph (7) applies to employees and positions other than employees and positions of the Bureau of Engraving and Printing; and

(B) paragraph (14) of that section.

(3) This subchapter, except section 5348, does not apply to officers and members of crews of vessels excepted from chapter 51 of this title by section 5102(c)(8) of this title.

(c) Each prevailing rate employee employed within any of the several States or the District of Columbia shall be a United States citizen or a bona fide resident of one of the several States or the District of Columbia unless the Secretary of Labor certifies that no United States citizen or bona fide resident of one of the several States or the District of Columbia is available to fill the particular position.

(Added Pub. L. 92–392, §1(a), Aug. 19, 1972, 86 Stat. 564; amended Pub. L. 96–70, title III, §3302(e)(1), Sept. 27, 1979, 93 Stat. 498; Pub. L. 96–191, §8(d), Feb. 15, 1980, 94 Stat. 33; Pub. L. 97–468, title VI, §615(b)(1)(D), Jan. 14, 1983, 96 Stat. 2578; Pub. L. 98–618, title V, §502(b), Nov. 8, 1984, 98 Stat. 3303; Pub. L. 102–54, §13(b)(1), June 13, 1991, 105 Stat. 274; Pub. L. 103–359, title V, §501(h), Oct. 14, 1994, 108 Stat. 3429; Pub. L. 104–201, div. A, title XI, §1122(a)(1), div. C, title XXXV, §3548(a)(3)(A), Sept. 23, 1996, 110 Stat. 2687, 2868.)

PRIOR PROVISIONS

A prior section 5342, Pub. L. 89–554, Sept. 6, 1966, 80 Stat. 471, provided for crews of vessels.

Provisions similar to those comprising subsec. (b) of this section were contained in Pub. L. 89–554, Sept. 6, 1966, 80 Stat. 471 (formerly classified to section 5342 of this title) prior to the general amendment of this subchapter by section 1(a) of Pub. L. 92–392.

AMENDMENTS

1996—Subsec. (a)(1). Pub. L. 104–201, §3548(a)(3)(A), which directed amendment of subsec. (a)(1) by striking subpar. (G) and redesignating subpars. (H), (I), (J), (K), and (L) as (G), (H), (I), (J), and (K), respectively, was executed by striking subpar. (F), relating to the Panama Canal Commission, and redesignating subpars. (G), (H), (I), (K), and (L) as (F), (G), (H), (J), and (K), respectively, to reflect the probable intent of Congress, because subsec. (a)(1) does not contain a subpar. (J) and the amendments were included in a series of conforming amendments relating to the Panama Canal.

Subsec. (a)(1)(L). Pub. L. 104–201, §1122(a)(1), substituted "National Imagery and Mapping Agency" for "Central Imagery Office".

1994—Subsec. (a)(1)(J) to (L). Pub. L. 103–359 directed the amendment of subpar. (J) by striking out "or" at end which could not be executed because par. (1) does not contain a subpar. (J), added "or" at end of subpar. (K), and added subpar. (L).

1991—Subsec. (a)(2)(C). Pub. L. 102–54 substituted "Department of Veterans Affairs" for "Veterans' Administration".

1984—Subsec. (a)(1)(I) to (K). Pub. L. 98–618 struck out "or" at end of subpar. (I), inserted "or" at end of subpar. (J), and added subpar. (K).

1983—Subsec. (a)(1)(C) to (J). Pub. L. 97–468, eff. Jan. 5, 1985, struck out subpar. (C) which excluded the Alaska Railroad and redesignated subpars. (D) to (J) as (C) to (I), respectively. See Effective Date of 1983 Amendment note below.

1980—Subsec. (a)(1)(J). Pub. L. 96–191 added subpar. (J).

1979—Subsec. (a)(1)(G). Pub. L. 96–70 substituted "Commission" for "Company".

EFFECTIVE DATE OF 1996 AMENDMENT

Amendment by section 1122(a)(1) of Pub. L. 104–201 effective Oct. 1, 1996, see section 1124 of Pub. L. 104–201, set out as a note under section 193 of Title 10, Armed Forces.

EFFECTIVE DATE OF 1983 AMENDMENT

Amendment by Pub. L. 97–468 effective on date of transfer of Alaska Railroad to the State [Jan. 5, 1985], pursuant to section 1203 of Title 45, Railroads, see section 615(b) of Pub. L. 97–468.

EFFECTIVE DATE OF 1980 AMENDMENT

Amendment by Pub. L. 96–191 effective Oct. 1, 1980, see section 10(a) of Pub. L. 96–191.

EFFECTIVE DATE OF 1979 AMENDMENT

Amendment by Pub. L. 96–70 effective Oct. 1, 1979, see section 3304 of Pub. L. 96–70, set out as an Effective

Date note under section 3601 of Title 22, Foreign Relations and Intercourse.

EFFECTIVE DATE

Section effective on first day of first applicable pay period beginning on or after 90th day after Aug. 19, 1972, except that in the case of employees referred to in subsec. (a)(2)(B) and (C) section effective on first day of first applicable pay period beginning on or after 180th day after Aug. 19, 1972, or on such earlier date (not earlier than 90th day after Aug. 19, 1972) as Civil Service Commission may prescribe, see section 15(a) of Pub. L. 92–392, set out as a note under section 5341 of this title.

ABOLITION OF ATOMIC ENERGY COMMISSION

Atomic Energy Commission abolished and functions transferred by sections 5814 and 5841 of Title 42, The Public Health and Welfare. See, also, Transfer of Functions notes set out under those sections.

DISSOLUTION OF VIRGIN ISLANDS CORPORATION

Virgin Islands Corporation established to have succession until June 30, 1969, unless sooner dissolved by Act of Congress, by act June 30, 1949, ch. 285, 63 Stat. 350, as amended (48 U.S.C. 1407 et seq.). Corporation terminated its program June 30, 1965, and dissolved July 1, 1966. Act June 30, 1949, was repealed by Pub. L. 97–357, title III, § 308(e), Oct. 19, 1982, 96 Stat. 1710.

SECTION REFERRED TO IN OTHER SECTIONS

This section is referred to in sections 5343, 5361, 5544 of this title; title 10 section 1602.

§ 5343. Prevailing rate determinations; wage schedules; night differentials

(a) The pay of prevailing rate employees shall be fixed and adjusted from time to time as nearly as is consistent with the public interest in accordance with prevailing rates. Subject to section 213(f) of title 29, the rates may not be less than the appropriate rates provided by section 206(a)(1) of title 29. To carry out this subsection—

(1) the Office of Personnel Management shall define, as appropriate—

(A) with respect to prevailing rate employees other than prevailing rate employees under paragraphs (B) and (C) of section 5342(a)(2) of this title, the boundaries of—

(i) individual local wage areas for prevailing rate employees having regular wage schedules and rates; and

(ii) wage areas for prevailing rate employees having special wage schedules and rates;

(B) with respect to prevailing rate employees under paragraphs (B) and (C) of section 5342(a)(2) of this title, the boundaries of—

(i) individual local wage areas for prevailing rate employees under such paragraphs having regular wage schedules and rates (but such boundaries shall not extend beyond the immediate locality in which the particular prevailing rate employees are employed); and

(ii) wage areas for prevailing rate employees under such paragraphs having special wage schedules and rates;

(2) the Office of Personnel Management shall designate a lead agency for each wage area;

(3) subject to paragraph (5) of this subsection, and subsections (c)(1)–(3) and (d) of this section, a lead agency shall conduct wage surveys, analyze wage survey data, and develop and establish appropriate wage schedules and rates for prevailing rate employees;

(4) the head of each agency having prevailing rate employees in a wage area shall apply, to the prevailing rate employees of that agency in that area, the wage schedules and rates established by the lead agency, or by the Office of Personnel Management, as appropriate, for prevailing rate employees in that area; and

(5) the Office of Personnel Management shall establish wage schedules and rates for prevailing rate employees who are United States citizens employed in any area which is outside the several States, the District of Columbia, the Commonwealth of Puerto Rico, the territories and possessions of the United States, and the Trust Territory of the Pacific Islands.

(b) The Office of Personnel Management shall schedule full-scale wage surveys every 2 years and shall schedule interim surveys to be conducted between each 2 consecutive full-scale wage surveys. The Office may schedule more frequent surveys when conditions so suggest.

(c) The Office of Personnel Management, by regulation, shall prescribe practices and procedures for conducting wage surveys, analyzing wage survey data, developing and establishing wage schedules and rates, and administering the prevailing rate system. The regulations shall provide—

(1) that, subject to subsection (d) of this section, wages surveyed be those paid by private employers in the wage area for similar work performed by regular full-time employees, except that, for prevailing rate employees under paragraphs (B) and (C) of section 5342(a)(2) of this title, the wages surveyed shall be those paid by private employers to full-time employees in a representative number of retail, wholesale, service, and recreational establishments similar to those in which such prevailing rate employees are employed;

(2) for participation at all levels by representatives of organizations accorded recognition as the representatives of prevailing rate employees in every phase of providing an equitable system for fixing and adjusting the rates of pay for prevailing rate employees, including the planning of the surveys, the drafting of specifications, the selection of data collectors, the collection and the analysis of the data, and the submission or recommendations to the head of the lead agency for wage schedules and rates and for special wage schedules and rates where appropriate;

(3) for requirements for the accomplishment of wage surveys and for the development of wage schedules and rates for prevailing rate employees, including, but not limited to—

(A) nonsupervisory and supervisory prevailing rate employees paid under regular wage schedules and rates;

(B) nonsupervisory and supervisory prevailing rate employees paid under special wage schedules and rates; and

(C) nonsupervisory and supervisory prevailing rate employees described under paragraphs (B) and (C) of section 5342(a)(2) of this title;

(4) for proper differentials, as determined by the Office, for duty involving unusually severe working conditions or unusually severe hazards;

(5) rules governing the administration of pay for individual employees on appointment, transfer, promotion, demotion, and other similar changes in employment status; and

(6) for a continuing program of maintenance and improvement designed to keep the prevailing rate system fully abreast of changing conditions, practices, and techniques both in and out of the Government of the United States.

(d)(1) A lead agency, in making a wage survey, shall determine whether there exists in the local wage area a number of comparable positions in private industry sufficient to establish wage schedules and rates for the principal types of positions for which the survey is made. The determination shall be in writing and shall take into consideration all relevant evidence, including evidence submitted by employee organizations recognized as representative of prevailing rate employees in that area.

(2) When the lead agency determines that there is a number of comparable positions in private industry insufficient to establish the wage schedules and rates, such agency shall—

(A) establish the wage schedules and rates to be applicable to prevailing rate employees other than prevailing rate employees of the Department of Defense on the basis of—

(i) local private industry rates; and

(ii) rates paid for comparable positions in private industry in the nearest wage area that such agency determines is most similar in the nature of its population, employment, manpower, and industry to the local wage area for which the wage survey is being made; and

(B) establish the wage schedules and rates to be applicable to prevailing rate employees of the Department of Defense only on the basis of local private industry rates.

(e)(1) Each grade of a regular wage schedule for nonsupervisor prevailing rate employees shall have 5 steps with—

(A) the first step at 96 percent of the prevailing rate;

(B) the second step at 100 percent of the prevailing rate;

(C) the third step at 104 percent of the prevailing rate;

(D) the fourth step at 108 percent of the prevailing rate; and

(E) the fifth step at 112 percent of the prevailing rate.

(2) A prevailing rate employee under a regular wage schedule who has a work performance rating of satisfactory or better, as determined by the head of the agency, shall advance automatically to the next higher step within the grade at the beginning of the first applicable pay period following his completion of—

(A) 26 calendar weeks of service in step 1;

(B) 78 calendar weeks of service in step 2; and

(C) 104 calendar weeks of service in each of steps 3 and 4.

(3) Under regulations prescribed by the Office of Personnel Management, the benefits of successive step increases shall be preserved for prevailing rate employees under a regular wage schedule whose continuous service is interrupted in the public interest by service with the armed forces or by service in essential non-Government civilian employment during a period of war or national emergency.

(4) Supervisory wage schedules and special wage schedules authorized under subsection (c)(3) of this section may have single or multiple rates or steps according to prevailing practices in the industry on which the schedule is based.

(f) A prevailing rate employee is entitled to pay at his scheduled rate plus a night differential—

(1) amounting to 7½ percent of that scheduled rate for regularly scheduled nonovertime work a majority of the hours of which occur between 3 p.m. and midnight; and

(2) amounting to 10 percent of that scheduled rate for regularly scheduled nonovertime work a majority of the hours of which occur between 11 p.m. and 8 a.m.

A night differential under this subsection is a part of basic pay.

(Added Pub. L. 92–392, § 1(a), Aug. 19, 1972, 86 Stat. 566; amended Pub. L. 95–454, title IX, § 906(a)(2), (3), Oct. 13, 1978, 92 Stat. 1224; Pub. L. 96–70, title III, § 3302(e)(10), Sept. 27, 1979, 93 Stat. 499; Pub. L. 99–145, title XII, § 1242(a), Nov. 8, 1985, 99 Stat. 735; Pub. L. 104–201, div. C, title XXXV, § 3548(a)(3)(B), Sept. 23, 1996, 110 Stat. 2868.)

PRIOR PROVISIONS

A prior section 5343, Pub. L. 89–554, Sept. 6, 1966, 80 Stat. 471, related to effective date of pay increases and is covered by section 5344(a) of this title.

Provisions similar to those comprising part of first sentence of subsec. (c) and subsec. (d) of this section were contained in Pub. L. 90–560, § 4, Oct. 12, 1968, 82 Stat. 997 (formerly classified to section 5341(c) of this title) prior to the general amendment of this subchapter by section 1(a) of Pub. L. 92–392.

AMENDMENTS

1996—Subsec. (a)(5). Pub. L. 104–201 struck out "the areas and installations in the Republic of Panama made available to the United States pursuant to the Panama Canal Treaty of 1977 and related agreements (as described in section 3(a) of the Panama Canal Act of 1979)," after "Puerto Rico,".

1985—Subsec. (d)(2). Pub. L. 99–145 amended par. (2) generally, designating existing provisions as subpar. (A), inserting "to be applicable to prevailing rate employees other than prevailing rate employees of the Department of Defense", redesignating as cls. (i) and (ii) provisions previously designated subpars. (A) and (B), and adding subpar. (B).

1979—Subsec. (a)(5). Pub. L. 96–70 substituted "areas and installations in the Republic of Panama made available to the United States pursuant to the Panama Canal Treaty of 1977 and related agreements (as described in section 3(a) of the Panama Canal Act of 1979)" for "Canal Zone".

1978—Subsecs. (a) to (c), (e)(3). Pub. L. 95–454 substituted "Office of Personnel Management" for "Civil Service Commission" and "Office" for "Commission" wherever appearing.

EFFECTIVE DATE OF 1985 AMENDMENT

Section 1242(b) of Pub. L. 99–145 provided that: "The rate of pay payable to a prevailing rate employee employed by the Department of Defense on the day before the date of enactment of this Act [Nov. 8, 1985] may not be reduced by reason of the amendment made by subsection (a) [amending this section]."

EFFECTIVE DATE OF 1979 AMENDMENT

Amendment by Pub. L. 96–70 effective Oct. 1, 1979, see section 3304 of Pub. L. 96–70, set out as an Effective Date note under section 3601 of Title 22, Foreign Relations and Intercourse.

EFFECTIVE DATE OF 1978 AMENDMENT

Amendment by Pub. L. 95–454 effective 90 days after Oct. 13, 1978, see section 907 of Pub. L. 95–454, set out as a note under section 1101 of this title.

EFFECTIVE DATE

Section other than subsec. (e)(1)(D), (E), (2)(C) of this section effective on first day of first applicable pay period beginning on or after 90th day after Aug. 19, 1972, and such subsec. (a)(1)(D), (E), (2)(C) not effective until first day of first pay period commencing after date on which President ceases to exercise his authority under Economic Stabilization Act of 1970 to stabilize wages and salaries, or Apr. 30, 1973, whichever occurs first, see section 15(a) of Pub. L. 92–392, set out as a note under section 5341 of this title.

TERMINATION OF TRUST TERRITORY OF THE PACIFIC ISLANDS

For termination of Trust Territory of the Pacific Islands, see note set out preceding section 1681 of Title 48, Territories and Insular Possessions.

LIMITATION ON PAY ADJUSTMENTS FOR PREVAILING RATE EMPLOYEES AND CREWS OF VESSELS

Pub. L. 106–554, §1(a)(3) [title VI, §613], Dec. 21, 2000, 114 Stat. 2763, 2763A–157, provided that:

"(a) Notwithstanding any other provision of law, and except as otherwise provided in this section, no part of any of the funds appropriated for fiscal year 2001, by this or any other Act, may be used to pay any prevailing rate employee described in section 5342(a)(2)(A) of title 5, United States Code—

"(1) during the period from the date of expiration of the limitation imposed by section 613 of the Treasury and General Government Appropriations Act, 2000 [Pub. L. 106–58, 113 Stat. 468], until the normal effective date of the applicable wage survey adjustment that is to take effect in fiscal year 2001, in an amount that exceeds the rate payable for the applicable grade and step of the applicable wage schedule in accordance with such section 613; and

"(2) during the period consisting of the remainder of fiscal year 2001, in an amount that exceeds, as a result of a wage survey adjustment, the rate payable under paragraph (1) by more than the sum of—

"(A) the percentage adjustment taking effect in fiscal year 2001 under section 5303 of title 5, United States Code, in the rates of pay under the General Schedule; and

"(B) the difference between the overall average percentage of the locality-based comparability payments taking effect in fiscal year 2001 under section 5304 of such title (whether by adjustment or otherwise), and the overall average percentage of such payments which was effective in fiscal year 2000 under such section.

"(b) Notwithstanding any other provision of law, no prevailing rate employee described in subparagraph (B) or (C) of section 5342(a)(2) of title 5, United States Code, and no employee covered by section 5348 of such title, may be paid during the periods for which subsection (a) is in effect at a rate that exceeds the rates that would be payable under subsection (a) were subsection (a) applicable to such employee.

"(c) For the purposes of this section, the rates payable to an employee who is covered by this section and who is paid from a schedule not in existence on Sep-

tember 30, 2000, shall be determined under regulations prescribed by the Office of Personnel Management.

"(d) Notwithstanding any other provision of law, rates of premium pay for employees subject to this section may not be changed from the rates in effect on September 30, 2000, except to the extent determined by the Office of Personnel Management to be consistent with the purpose of this section.

"(e) This section shall apply with respect to pay for service performed after September 30, 2000.

"(f) For the purpose of administering any provision of law (including any rule or regulation that provides premium pay, retirement, life insurance, or any other employee benefit) that requires any deduction or contribution, or that imposes any requirement or limitation on the basis of a rate of salary or basic pay, the rate of salary or basic pay payable after the application of this section shall be treated as the rate of salary or basic pay.

"(g) Nothing in this section shall be considered to permit or require the payment to any employee covered by this section at a rate in excess of the rate that would be payable were this section not in effect.

"(h) The Office of Personnel Management may provide for exceptions to the limitations imposed by this section if the Office determines that such exceptions are necessary to ensure the recruitment or retention of qualified employees."

Similar provisions were contained in the following prior acts:

Pub. L. 106–58, title VI, §613, Sept. 29, 1999, 113 Stat. 468.

Pub. L. 105–277, div. A, §101(h) [title VI, §614], Oct. 21, 1998, 112 Stat. 2681–480, 2681–515.

Pub. L. 105–61, title VI, §614, Oct. 10, 1997, 111 Stat. 1311.

Pub. L. 104–208, div. A, title I, §101(f) [title VI, §616], Sept. 30, 1996, 110 Stat. 3009–314, 3009–356.

Pub. L. 104–52, title VI, §616, Nov. 19, 1995, 109 Stat. 500, as amended by Pub. L. 104–208, div. A, title I, §101(f) [title VI, §659 [title II, §206(b)(3)]], Sept. 30, 1996, 110 Stat. 3009–314, 3009–372, 3009–378.

Pub. L. 103–329, title VI, §617, Sept. 30, 1994, 108 Stat. 2419.

Pub. L. 103–123, title VI, §615, Oct. 28, 1993, 107 Stat. 1261.

Pub. L. 102–393, title VI, §616, Oct. 6, 1992, 106 Stat. 1768.

Pub. L. 102–141, title VI, §616, Oct. 28, 1991, 105 Stat. 870.

Pub. L. 101–509, title VI, §612, Nov. 5, 1990, 104 Stat. 1473.

Pub. L. 101–136, title VI, §612, Nov. 3, 1989, 103 Stat. 818.

Pub. L. 100–440, title VI, §612, Sept. 22, 1988, 102 Stat. 1753.

Pub. L. 100–202, §101(m) [title VI, §613], Dec. 22, 1987, 101 Stat. 1329–390, 1329–421.

Pub. L. 99–500, §101(m) [title VI, §613], Oct. 18, 1986, 100 Stat. 1783–308, 1783–330, and Pub. L. 99–591, §101(m) [title VI, §613], Oct. 30, 1986, 100 Stat. 3341–308, 3341–330.

Pub. L. 99–272, title XV, §15201(b), Apr. 7, 1986, 100 Stat. 332.

Pub. L. 99–190, §101(h) [H.R. 3036, title VI, §613], Dec. 19, 1985, 99 Stat. 1291.

Pub. L. 98–473, §101(j) [H.R. 5798, title VI, §616], Oct. 12, 1984, 98 Stat. 1963.

Pub. L. 98–369, div. B, title II, §2202, July 18, 1984, 98 Stat. 1058.

Pub. L. 98–270, title II, §202(b), Apr. 18, 1984, 98 Stat. 158.

Pub. L. 98–151, §101(f) [H.R. 4139, title VI, §616], Nov. 14, 1983, 97 Stat. 973.

Pub. L. 98–107, §110, Oct. 1, 1983, 97 Stat. 741.

Pub. L. 97–377, title I, §107, Dec. 21, 1982, 96 Stat. 1909.

Pub. L. 97–276, §109, Oct. 2, 1982, 96 Stat. 1191.

Pub. L. 97–35, title XVII, §1701(b), Aug. 13, 1981, 95 Stat. 754.

Pub. L. 96–536, §101(a) [incorporating Pub. L. 96–74, title VI, §613], Dec. 16, 1980, 94 Stat. 3166.

Pub. L. 96–369, § 114, Oct. 1, 1980, 94 Stat. 1356.
Pub. L. 96–74, title VI, § 613, Sept. 29, 1979, 93 Stat. 576.
Pub. L. 95–429, title VI, § 614, Oct. 10, 1978, 92 Stat. 1018.

WAGE RATE FOR CERTAIN CORPS OF ENGINEERS EMPLOYEES

Pub. L. 99–661, div. A, title XIII, § 1358, Nov. 14, 1986, 100 Stat. 3999, provided that:

"(a) WAGE DETERMINATIONS.—Notwithstanding any other provision of law, in the administration of the last undesignated paragraph preceding chapter 6 of title I of Public Law 97–257 (96 Stat. 832) [set out below], the individuals described in subsection (b) shall be paid wages determined in the same manner as that established in such undesignated paragraph with respect to United States Army Corps of Engineers employees paid from Corps of Engineers Special Power Rate Schedules.

"(b) COVERED INDIVIDUALS.—The individuals described in subsection (a) are electric powerplant controllers and powerplant shift operators (as defined under regulations prescribed by the Secretary of Defense) assigned to the Soo Locks Power Plant in the Detroit District in the North Central Region of the United States Army Corps of Engineers.

"(c) EFFECTIVE DATE.—Subsection (a) applies with respect to pay periods commencing on or after the date of the enactment of this Act [Nov. 14, 1986]."

EMPLOYEES OF UNITED STATES CORPS OF ENGINEERS PAID FROM CORPS OF ENGINEERS SPECIAL POWER RATE SCHEDULES; CONSISTENCY OF WAGES WITH WAGES OF ENERGY AND INTERIOR DEPARTMENT EMPLOYEES

Pub. L. 97–257, title I, § 100, Sept. 10, 1982, 96 Stat. 832, provided in part that: "Without regard to any other provision of law limiting the amounts payable to prevailing wage rate employees, United States Army Corps of Engineers employees paid from Corps of Engineers Special Power Rate Schedules shall be paid, beginning the effective date of each annual wage survey in the region after the date of enactment of this Act [Sept. 10, 1982], wages as determined by the Department of Defense Wage Fixing Authority to be consistent with wages of the Department of Energy and the Department of the Interior employees performing similar work in the corresponding area whose wage rates are established in accordance with section 9(b) of Public Law 92–392 or section 704 of Public Law 95–454 [set out as notes under this section]."

NEGOTIATING REQUIREMENTS FOR LABOR CONTRACTS, ETC., ON AND AFTER OCTOBER 13, 1978, AND NEGOTIATED UNDER PREVAILING RATES AND PRACTICES PRIOR TO AUGUST 19, 1972

Section 704 of Pub. L. 95–454 provided that:

"(a) Those terms and conditions of employment and other employment benefits with respect to Government prevailing rate employees to whom section 9(b) of Public Law 92–392 [set out as a note under this section] applies which were the subject of negotiation in accordance with prevailing rates and practices prior to August 19, 1972, shall be negotiated on and after the date of the enactment of this Act [Oct. 13, 1978] in accordance with the provisions of section 9(b) of Public Law 92–392 without regard to any provision of chapter 71 of title 5, United States Code (as amended by this title [title VII of Pub. L. 95–454]), to the extent that any such provision is inconsistent with this paragraph.

"(b) The pay and pay practices relating to employees referred to in paragraph (1) of this subsection shall be negotiated in accordance with prevailing rates and pay practices without regard to any provision of—

"(A) chapter 71 of title 5, United States Code (as amended by this title), to the extent that any such provision is inconsistent with this paragraph;

"(B) subchapter IV of chapter 53 and subchapter V of chapter 55 of title 5, United States Code; or

"(C) any rule, regulation, decision, or order relating to rates of pay or pay practices under subchapter IV of chapter 53 or subchapter V of chapter 55 of title 5, United States Code."

CONVERSION RULES FOR WAGE SCHEDULE; SERVICE FOR ONE STEP INCREASE; PROHIBITION OF DECREASE IN BASIC PAY RATE; RETAINED PAY CONTINUED

Section 9(a) of Pub. L. 92–392 provided that:

"(1) Except as provided by this subsection, an employee's initial rate of pay on conversion to a wage schedule established pursuant to the amendments made by this Act [see Effective Date note under section 5341 of this title] shall be determined under conversion rules prescribed by the Civil Service Commission. Service by an employee in a grade of a wage schedule performed before the effective date of the conversion of the employee to a wage schedule established pursuant to the amendments made by this Act shall be counted toward not to exceed one step increase under the time in step provisions of section 5343(e)(2) of title 5, United States Code, as amended by the first section of this Act [subsec. (e)(2) of this section].

"(2) In the case of any employee described in section 2105(c), 5102(c)(7), (8), or (14) of title 5, United States Code, who is in the service as such an employee immediately before the effective date, with respect to him, of the amendments made by this Act [see Effective Date note under section 5341 of this title], such amendments shall not be construed to decrease his rate of basic pay in effect immediately before the date [see Effective Date note under section 5341 of this title] on which such amendments become effective with respect to him. In addition, if an employee is receiving retained pay by virtue of law or agency policy immediately before the date on which the first wage schedule applicable to him under this Act is effective, he shall continue to retain that pay in accordance with the specific instructions under which the retained pay was granted until he leaves his position or until he becomes entitled to a higher rate."

LABOR CONTRACTS PERTAINING TO WAGES, TERMS AND CONDITIONS OF EMPLOYMENT, AND OTHER EMPLOYMENT BENEFITS

Section 9(b) of Pub. L. 92–392 provided that: "The amendments made by this Act [enacting this subchapter and section 5550 of this title, amending sections 2105(c)(1), 5337, 5541(2)(xi), 5544(a), 5548, 6101(a)(1), 7154(b), and 8704(d)(2) of this title, repealing section 6102 of this title, and enacting provisions set out as notes under sections 5341 and 5343 of this title and section 60a of Title 2, The Congress] shall not be construed to—

"(1) abrogate, modify, or otherwise affect in any way the provisions of any contract in effect on the date of enactment of this Act [Aug. 19, 1972] pertaining to the wages, the terms and conditions of employment, and other employment benefits, or any of the foregoing matters, for Government prevailing rate employees and resulting from negotiations between Government agencies and organizations of Government employees;

"(2) nullify, curtail, or otherwise impair in any way the right of any party to such contract to enter into negotiations after the date of enactment of this Act [Aug. 19, 1972] for the renewal, extension, modification, or improvement of the provisions of such contract or for the replacement of such contract with a new contract; or

"(3) nullify, change, or otherwise affect in any way after such date of enactment [Aug. 19, 1972] any agreement, arrangement, or understanding in effect on such date [Aug. 19, 1972] with respect to the various items of subject matter of the negotiations on which any such contract in effect on such date [Aug. 19, 1972] is based or prevent the inclusion of such items of subject matter in connection with the renegotiation of any such contract, or the replacement of such contract with a new contract, after such date [Aug. 19, 1972]."

WAGE SURVEY

Section 15(b) of Pub. L. 92–392 provided that: "A wage survey conducted by an agency before the effective date (with respect to employees covered by that wage survey) of this Act [see note under section 5341 of this title], for a wage schedule which becomes effective after that effective date [Aug. 19, 1972], is deemed to meet the requirement in this Act for a survey by a lead agency."

EQUITABLE WAGE ADJUSTMENTS FOR CERTAIN
PREVAILING RATE EMPLOYEES

Pub. L. 92–298, §§1, 2, May 17, 1972, 86 Stat. 146, provided: "That this Act [enacting this note and amending sections 60a–1 and 60a–2 of Title 2, The Congress] may be cited as the 'Prevailing Rate Equalization Adjustment Act of 1972'.

"SEC. 2. (a) Notwithstanding any other provision of law or any provision of an Executive order or regulation, a wage schedule adjustment for employees of the Government of the United States whose pay is fixed and adjusted from time to time in accordance with prevailing rates—

"(1) if based on a wage survey ordered to be made on or after August 15, 1971, but not placed into effect before November 14, 1971, by reason of the provisions of Executive Order 11615 or Executive Order 11627 [formerly set out as notes under section 1904 of Title 12]; or

"(2) if based on a wage survey which had been scheduled to be made during the period beginning on September 1, 1971, and ending on January 12, 1972, and which was ordered to be made on or after January 23, 1972;

shall be effective on the date on which such wage schedule adjustment would have been effective under section 5343 of title 5, United States (Code), had the fiscal year 1972 schedule for wage surveys for such employees been followed.

"(b) Retroactive pay made under the provisions of this section will be made in accordance with section 5344 of title 5, United States Code."

SECTION REFERRED TO IN OTHER SECTIONS

This section is referred to in sections 5361, 5544, 6101, 6123 of this title.

§ 5344. Effective date of wage increase; retroactive pay

(a) Each increase in rates of basic pay granted, pursuant to a wage survey, to prevailing rate employees is effective not later than the first day of the first pay period which begins on or after the 45th day, excluding Saturdays and Sundays, following the date the wage survey is ordered to be made.

(b) Retroactive pay is payable by reason of an increase in rates of basic pay referred to in subsection (a) of this section only when—

(1) the individual is in the service of the Government of the United States, including service in the armed forces, or the government of the District of Columbia on the date of the issuance of the order granting the increase; or

(2) the individual retired or died during the period beginning on the effective date of the increase and ending on the date of issuance of the order granting the increase, and only for services performed during that period.

For the purpose of this subsection, service in the armed forces includes the period provided by statute for the mandatory restoration of the individual to a position in or under the Government of the United States or the government of the District of Columbia after he is relieved from training and service in the armed forces or discharged from hospitalization following that training and service.

(Added Pub. L. 92–392, §1(a), Aug. 19, 1972, 86 Stat. 568.)

PRIOR PROVISIONS

Provisions similar to those comprising subsec. (a) of this section were contained in Pub. L. 89–554, Sept. 6, 1966, 80 Stat. 471 (formerly classified to section 5343 of this title) prior to the general amendment of this subchapter by section 1(a) of Pub. L. 92–392.

SECTION REFERRED TO IN OTHER SECTIONS

This section is referred to in sections 5349, 5581, 8331, 8704 of this title.

[§ 5345. Repealed. Pub. L. 95–454, title VIII, § 801(a)(2), Oct. 13, 1978, 92 Stat. 1221]

Section, added Pub. L. 92–392, §1(a), Aug. 19, 1972, 86 Stat. 569, related to retained rate of pay on reduction in grade or reassignment.

A prior section 5345, added Pub. L. 90–206, title II, §223(a), Dec. 16, 1967, 81 Stat. 641, which provided for position classification appeals, was omitted in the general amendment of this subchapter, and is covered by section 5346(c) of this title.

EFFECTIVE DATE OF REPEAL

Repeal effective on first day of first applicable pay period beginning on or after 90th day after Oct. 13, 1978, and an employee receiving pay on day before such effective date not to have such pay reduced or terminated and, unless section 5362 applies, employee is entitled to continuation of such pay, etc., see section 801(a)(4) of Pub. L. 95–454, set out as an Effective Date note under section 5361 of this title.

§ 5346. Job grading system

(a) The Office of Personnel Management, after consulting with the agencies and with employee organizations, shall establish and maintain a job grading system for positions to which this subchapter applies. In carrying out this subsection, the Office shall—

(1) establish the basic occupational alinement and grade structure or structures for the job grading system;

(2) establish and define individual occupations and the boundaries of each occupation;

(3) establish job titles within occupations;

(4) develop and publish job grading standards; and

(5) provide a method to assure consistency in the application of job standards.

(b) The Office, from time to time, shall review such numbers of positions in each agency as will enable the Office to determine whether the agency is placing positions in occupations and grades in conformance with or consistently with published job standards. When the Office finds that a position is not placed in its proper occupation and grade in conformance with published standards or that a position for which there is no published standard is not placed in the occupation and grade consistently with published standards, it shall, after consultation with appropriate officials of the agency concerned, place the position in its appropriate occupation and grade and shall certify this action to the agency. The agency shall act in accordance with the certificate, and the certificate is binding on all administrative, certifying, payroll, disbursing, and accounting officials.

(c) On application, made in accordance with regulations prescribed by the Office, by a prevailing rate employee for the review of the action of an employing agency in placing his position in an occupation and grade for pay purposes, the Office shall—

(1) ascertain currently the facts as to the duties, responsibilities, and qualification requirements of the position;

(2) decide whether the position has been placed in the proper occupation and grade; and

(3) approve, disapprove, or modify, in accordance with its decision, the action of the employing agency in placing the position in an occupation and grade.

The Office shall certify to the agency concerned its action under paragraph (3) of this subsection. The agency shall act in accordance with the certificate, and the certificate is binding on all administrative, certifying, payroll, disbursing, and accounting officials.

(Added Pub. L. 90–206, title II, § 223(a), Dec. 16, 1967, 81 Stat. 641, § 5345; renumbered § 5346 and amended Pub. L. 92–392, § 1(a), Aug. 19, 1972, 86 Stat. 570; Pub. L. 95–454, title IX, § 906(a)(2), (3), Oct. 13, 1978, 92 Stat. 1224.)

AMENDMENTS

1978—Subsecs. (a) to (c). Pub. L. 95–454 substituted "Office of Personnel Management" and "Office" for "Civil Service Commission" and "Commission", respectively, wherever appearing.

1972—Subsecs. (a), (b). Pub. L. 92–392 added subsecs. (a) and (b).

Subsec. (c). Pub. L. 92–392 designated existing provisions as subsec. (c) and substituted in introductory text "Commission", "a prevailing rate of employee" and "in placing his position in an occupation and grade" for "Civil Service Commission", "an employee subject to section 5341(a) of this title" and "in classifying his position", respectively, in par. (2) "placed in the proper occupation and grade" for "properly classified", in par. (3) "in placing the position in an occupation and grade" for "in classifying the position" and in last sentence "subsection" for "section".

EFFECTIVE DATE OF 1978 AMENDMENT

Amendment by Pub. L. 95–454 effective 90 days after Oct. 13, 1978, see section 907 of Pub. L. 95–454, set out as a note under section 1101 of this title.

EFFECTIVE DATE OF 1972 AMENDMENT

Amendment by Pub. L. 92–392 effective on first day of first applicable pay period beginning on or after 90th day after Aug. 19, 1972, see section 15(a) of Pub. L. 92–392, set out as an Effective Date note under section 5341 of this title.

SECTION REFERRED TO IN OTHER SECTIONS

This section is referred to in section 5366 of this title.

§ 5347. Federal Prevailing Rate Advisory Committee

(a) There is established a Federal Prevailing Rate Advisory Committee composed of—

(1) the Chairman, who shall not hold any other office or position in the Government of the United States or the government of the District of Columbia, and who shall be appointed by the Director of the Office of Personnel Management for a 4-year term;

(2) one member from the Office of the Secretary of Defense, designated by the Secretary of Defense;

(3) two members from the military departments, designated by the Director of the Office of Personnel Management;

(4) one member, designated by the Director of the Office of Personnel Management from time to time from an agency (other than the Department of Defense, a military department, and the Office of Personnel Management);

(5) an employee of the Office of Personnel Management, designated by the Director of the Office of Personnel Management; and

(6) five members, designated by the Director of the Office of Personnel Management, from among the employee organizations representing, under exclusive recognition of the Government of the United States, the largest numbers of prevailing rate employees.

(b) In designating members from among employee organizations under subsection (a)(6) of this section, the Director of the Office of Personnel Management shall designate, as nearly as practicable, a number of members from a particular employee organization in the same proportion to the total number of employee representatives appointed to the Committee under subsection (a)(6) of this section as the number of prevailing rate employees represented by such organization is to the total number of prevailing rate employees. However, there shall not be more than two members from any one employee organization nor more than four members from a single council, federation, alliance, association, or affiliation of employee organizations.

(c) Every 2 years the Director of the Office of Personnel Management shall review employee organization representation to determine adequate or proportional representation under the guidelines of subsection (b) of this section.

(d) The members from the employee organizations serve at the pleasure of the Director of the Office of Personnel Management.

(e) The Committee shall study the prevailing rate system and other matters pertinent to the establishment of prevailing rates under this subchapter and, from time to time, advise the Office of Personnel Management thereon. Conclusions and recommendations of the Committee shall be formulated by majority vote. The Chairman of the Committee may vote only to break a tie vote of the Committee.

(f) The Committee shall meet at the call of the Chairman. However, a special meeting shall be called by the Chairman if 5 members make a written request to the Chairman to call a special meeting to consider matters within the purview of the Committee.

(g)(1) Except as provided in paragraph (2), members of the Committee described in paragraphs (2)–(5) of subsection (a) of this section serve without additional pay. Members who represent employee organizations are not entitled to pay from the Government of the United States for services rendered to the Committee.

(2) The position of Chairman shall be considered to be a Senior Executive Service position within the meaning of section 3132(a), and shall be subject to all provisions of this title relating

to Senior Executive Service positions, including section 5383.

(h) The Office of Personnel Management shall provide such clerical and professional personnel as the Chairman of the Committee considers appropriate and necessary to carry out its functions under this subchapter. Such personnel shall be responsible to the Chairman of the Committee.

(Added Pub. L. 92–392, §1(a), Aug. 19, 1972, 86 Stat. 571; amended Pub. L. 95–454, title IX, §906(a)(1), (2), Oct. 13, 1978, 92 Stat. 1224; Pub. L. 96–54, §2(a)(15), Aug. 14, 1979, 93 Stat. 382; Pub. L. 102–378, §2(30), Oct. 2, 1992, 106 Stat. 1350; Pub. L. 104–66, title II, §2181(d), Dec. 21, 1995, 109 Stat. 732.)

AMENDMENTS

1995—Subsec. (e). Pub. L. 104–66 struck out at end "The Committee shall make an annual report to the Office and the President for transmittal to Congress, including recommendations and other matters considered appropriate. Any member of the Committee may include in the annual report recommendations and other matters he considers appropriate."

1992—Subsec. (g). Pub. L. 102–378 designated existing provisions as par. (1), substituted "Except as provided in paragraph (2), members" for "Members", struck out second sentence which read as follows: "The Chairman is entitled to a rate of pay equal to the maximum rate currently paid, from time to time, under the General Schedule.", and added par. (2).

1979—Subsec. (e). Pub. L. 96–54 substituted "Office" for "Commission".

1978—Subsecs. (a) to (e), (h). Pub. L. 95–454 substituted "Director of the Office of Personnel Management" for "Chairman of the Civil Service Commission" and "Office of Personnel Management" for "Civil Service Commission", wherever appearing.

EFFECTIVE DATE OF 1979 AMENDMENT

Amendment by Pub. L. 96–54 effective July 12, 1979, see section 2(b) of Pub. L. 96–54, set out as a note under section 305 of this title.

EFFECTIVE DATE OF 1978 AMENDMENT

Amendment by Pub. L. 95–454 effective 90 days after Oct. 13, 1978, see section 907 of Pub. L. 95–454, set out as a note under section 1101 of this title.

EFFECTIVE DATE

Section effective on first day of first applicable pay period beginning on or after 90th day after Aug. 19, 1972, see section 15(a) of Pub. L. 92–392, set out as a note under section 5341 of this title.

SECTION REFERRED TO IN OTHER SECTIONS

This section is referred to in section 5304 of this title.

§ 5348. Crews of vessels

(a) Except as provided by subsection (b) of this section, the pay of officers and members of crews of vessels excepted from chapter 51 of this title by section 5102(c)(8) of this title shall be fixed and adjusted from time to time as nearly as is consistent with the public interest in accordance with prevailing rates and practices in the maritime industry.

(b) Vessel employees in an area where inadequate maritime industry practice exists and vessel employees of the Corps of Engineers shall have their pay fixed and adjusted under the provisions of this subchapter other than this section, as appropriate.

(Pub. L. 89–544, Sept. 6, 1966, 80 Stat. 471, §5348, formerly §5342; renumbered and amended Pub. L. 92–392, §1(a), Aug. 19, 1972, 86 Stat. 572; Pub. L. 96–70, title III, §3302(e)(1), Sept. 27, 1979, 93 Stat. 498; Pub. L. 104–201, div. C, title XXXV, §3548(a)(3)(C), Sept. 23, 1996, 110 Stat. 2868.)

AMENDMENTS

1996—Subsec. (a). Pub. L. 104–201, §3548(a)(3)(C)(iii), substituted "subsection (b)" for "subsections (b) and (c)".

Subsecs. (b), (c). Pub. L. 104–201, §3548(a)(3)(C)(i), (ii), redesignated subsec. (c) as (b) and struck out former subsec. (b) which read as follows: "Vessel employees of the Panama Canal Commission may be paid in accordance with the wage practices of the maritime industry."

1979—Subsec. (b). Pub. L. 96–70 substituted "Commission" for "Company".

1972—Subsec. (a). Pub. L. 92–392 inserted reference to subsection (c) of this section.

Subsec. (c). Pub. L. 92–392 added subsec. (c).

EFFECTIVE DATE OF 1979 AMENDMENT

Amendment by Pub. L. 96–70 effective Oct. 1, 1979, see section 3304 of Pub. L. 96–70, set out as an Effective Date note under section 3601 of Title 22, Foreign Relations and Intercourse.

EFFECTIVE DATE OF 1972 AMENDMENT

Amendment by Pub. L. 92–392 effective on first day of first applicable pay period beginning on or after 90th day after Aug. 19, 1972, see section 15(a) of Pub. L. 92–392, set out as an Effective Date note under section 5341 of this title.

LIMITATION ON PAY ADJUSTMENTS

For provisions limiting the adjustment of salary or basic pay of employees covered by this section, see provisions set out as notes under section 5343 of this title.

SECTION REFERRED TO IN OTHER SECTIONS

This section is referred to in section 5342 of this title.

§ 5349. Prevailing rate employees; legislative, judicial, Bureau of Engraving and Printing, and government of the District of Columbia

(a) The pay of employees, described under section 5102(c)(7) of this title, in the Library of Congress, the Botanic Garden, the Government Printing Office, the General Accounting Office, the Office of the Architect of the Capitol, the Bureau of Engraving and Printing, and the government of the District of Columbia, shall be fixed and adjusted from time to time as nearly as is consistent with the public interest in accordance with prevailing rates and in accordance with such provisions of this subchapter, including the provisions of section 5344, relating to retroactive pay, and subchapter VI of this chapter, relating to grade and pay retention, as the pay-fixing authority of each such agency may determine. Subject to section 213(f) of title 29, the rates may not be less than the appropriate rates provided for by section 206(a)(1) of title 29. If the pay-fixing authority concerned determines that the provisions of subchapter VI of this chapter should apply to any employee under his jurisdiction, then the employee concerned shall be deemed to have satisfied the requirements of section 5361(1) of this title if the tenure of his appointment is substantially equivalent to the tenure of any appointment referred to in such paragraph.

(b) Subsection (a) of this section does not modify or otherwise affect section 5102(d) of this title, section 305 of title 44, and section 5141 of title 31.

(Added Pub. L. 92–392, §1(a), Aug. 19, 1972, 86 Stat. 572; amended Pub. L. 95–454, title VIII, §801(a)(3)(H), Oct. 13, 1978, 92 Stat. 1222; Pub. L. 97–258, §3(a)(11), Sept. 13, 1982, 96 Stat. 1063; Pub. L. 100–426, title III, §301, Sept. 9, 1988, 102 Stat. 1602; Pub. L. 101–474, §5(j), Oct. 30, 1990, 104 Stat. 1100.)

PRIOR PROVISIONS

Provisions similar to those comprising subsec. (a) of this section were contained in Pub. L. 89–554, Sept. 6, 1966, 80 Stat. 471; Pub. L. 90–83, §1(97), Sept. 11, 1967, 81 Stat. 220 (formerly classified to section 5341(a) of this title) prior to the general amendment of this subchapter by section 1(a) of Pub. L. 92–392.

AMENDMENTS

1990—Subsec. (a). Pub. L. 101–474 struck out "the Administrative Office of the United States Courts," before "the Library of Congress".

1988—Subsec. (a). Pub. L. 100–426 inserted reference to General Accounting Office.

1982—Subsec. (b). Pub. L. 97–258 substituted "section 5141" for "section 180".

1978—Subsec. (a). Pub. L. 95–454 substituted "subchapter VI of this chapter, relating to grade and pay retention," for "section 5345, relating to retention of pay,", "subchapter VI of this chapter" for "section 5345 of this title", and "section 5361(1)" for "paragraph (2) of section 5345(a)".

EFFECTIVE DATE OF 1978 AMENDMENT

Amendment by Pub. L. 95–454 effective on first day of first applicable pay period beginning on or after 90th day after Oct. 13, 1978, see section 801(a)(4) of Pub. L. 95–454, set out as an Effective Date note under section 5361 of this title.

EFFECTIVE DATE

Section effective on first day of first applicable pay period beginning on or after 90th day after Aug. 19, 1972, see section 15(a) of Pub. L. 92–392, set out as a note under section 5341 of this title.

SECTION REFERRED TO IN OTHER SECTIONS

This section is referred to in sections 5342, 5544, 6101, 8704 of this title; title 31 section 732.

SUBCHAPTER V—STUDENT-EMPLOYEES

SUBCHAPTER REFERRED TO IN OTHER SECTIONS

This subchapter is referred to in section 5102 of this title.

§ 5351. Definitions

For the purpose of this subchapter—
(1) "agency" means an Executive agency, a military department, and the government of the District of Columbia; and
(2) "student-employee" means—
(A) a student nurse, medical or dental intern, resident-in-training, student dietitian, student physical therapist, and student occupational therapist, assigned or attached to a hospital, clinic, or medical or dental laboratory operated by an agency; and
(B) any other student-employee, assigned or attached primarily for training purposes to a hospital, clinic, or medical or dental laboratory operated by an agency, who is

designated by the head of the agency with the approval of the Office of Personnel Management.

(Pub. L. 89–554, Sept. 6, 1966, 80 Stat. 472; Pub. L. 95–454, title IX, §906(a)(2), Oct. 13, 1978, 92 Stat. 1224.)

HISTORICAL AND REVISION NOTES

Derivation	U.S. Code	Revised Statutes and Statutes at Large
....	5 U.S.C. 1052.	Aug. 4, 1947, ch. 452, §2, 61 Stat. 727.

The section is restated in definition form. In paragraph (1), the words "an Executive agency, a military department" are coextensive with and substituted for "department, agency, or instrumentality of the Federal Government" in view of the definitions in sections 105 and 102.

The exception from the Classification Act of 1923, as amended, is omitted as obsolete and superseded by the Classification Act of 1949, as amended, which is carried into this title. The present exception from the Classification Act of 1949, as amended, is carried into section 5102(c)(16).

Standard changes are made to conform with the definitions applicable and the style of this title as outlined in the preface to the report.

AMENDMENTS

1978—Par. (2)(B). Pub. L. 95–454 substituted "Office of Personnel Management" for "Civil Service Commission".

EFFECTIVE DATE OF 1978 AMENDMENT

Amendment by Pub. L. 95–454 effective 90 days after Oct. 13, 1978, see section 907 of Pub. L. 95–454, set out as a note under section 1101 of this title.

SECTION REFERRED TO IN OTHER SECTIONS

This section is referred to in sections 5541, 8144, 8331, 8332, 8501 of this title; title 26 section 3121; title 42 section 410.

§ 5352. Stipends

The head of each agency, and the District of Columbia Council with respect to the government of the District of Columbia, shall fix the stipends of its student-employees. The stipend may not exceed the applicable maximum prescribed by the Office of Personnel Management.

(Pub. L. 89–554, Sept. 6, 1966, 80 Stat. 472; Pub. L. 90–623, §1(7), Oct. 22, 1968, 82 Stat. 1312; Pub. L. 95–454, title IX, §906(a)(2), Oct. 13, 1978, 92 Stat. 1224.)

HISTORICAL AND REVISION NOTES

Derivation	U.S. Code	Revised Statutes and Statutes at Large
....	5 U.S.C. 1051 (1st sentence).	Aug. 4, 1947, ch. 452, §3 (1st sentence), 61 Stat. 727.

Standard changes are made to conform with the definitions applicable and the style of this title as outlined in the preface to the report.

AMENDMENTS

1978—Pub. L. 95–454 substituted "Office of Personnel Management" for "Civil Service Commission".

1968—Pub. L. 90–623 inserted ", and the District of Columbia Council with respect to the government of the District of Columbia," after "head of each agency" and substituted "its" for "his".

EFFECTIVE DATE OF 1978 AMENDMENT

Amendment by Pub. L. 95–454 effective 90 days after Oct. 13, 1978, see section 907 of Pub. L. 95–454, set out as a note under section 1101 of this title.

EFFECTIVE DATE OF 1968 AMENDMENT

Amendment by Pub. L. 90–623 intended to restate without substantive change the law in effect on Oct. 22, 1968, see section 6 of Pub. L. 90–623, set out as a note under section 5334 of this title.

TRANSFER OF FUNCTIONS

District of Columbia Council, as established by Reorg. Plan No. 3 of 1967, abolished as of noon Jan. 2, 1975, by Pub. L. 93–198, title VII, §711, Dec. 24, 1973, 87 Stat. 818, and replaced by Council of District of Columbia, as provided by section 401 of Pub. L. 93–198.

§ 5353. Quarters, subsistence, and laundry

An agency may provide living quarters, subsistence, and laundering to student-employees while at the hospitals, clinics, or laboratories. The reasonable value of the accommodations, when furnished, shall be deducted from the stipend of the student-employee. The head of the agency concerned, and the District of Columbia Council with respect to the government of the District of Columbia, shall fix the reasonable value of the accommodations at an amount not less than the lowest deduction applicable to regular employees at the same hospital, clinic, or laboratory for similar accommodations.

(Pub. L. 89–554, Sept. 6, 1966, 80 Stat. 472; Pub. L. 90–623, §1(8), Oct. 22, 1968, 82 Stat. 1312.)

HISTORICAL AND REVISION NOTES

Derivation	U.S. Code	Revised Statutes and Statutes at Large
....	5 U.S.C. 1051 (less 1st sentence).	Aug. 4, 1947, ch. 452, §3 (less 1st sentence), 61 Stat. 727.

The section is restated for clarity.

Standard changes are made to conform with the definitions applicable and the style of this title as outlined in the preface to the report.

AMENDMENTS

1968—Pub. L. 90–623 inserted ", and the District of Columbia Council with respect to the government of the District of Columbia," after "head of the agency concerned".

EFFECTIVE DATE OF 1968 AMENDMENT

Amendment by Pub. L. 90–623 intended to restate without substantive change the law in effect on Oct. 22, 1968, see section 6 of Pub. L. 90–623, set out as a note under section 5334 of this title.

TRANSFER OF FUNCTIONS

District of Columbia Council, as established by Reorg. Plan No. 3 of 1967, abolished as of noon Jan. 2, 1975, by Pub. L. 93–198, title VII, §711, Dec. 24, 1973, 87 Stat. 818, and replaced by Council of District of Columbia, as provided by section 401 of Pub. L. 93–198.

§ 5354. Effect of detail or affiliation; travel expenses

(a) Status as a student-employee is not terminated by a temporary detail to, or affiliation with another Government or non-Government institution to procure necessary supplementary training or experience pursuant to an order of the head of the agency. A student-employee may receive his stipend and other perquisites provided under this subchapter from the hospital, clinic, or laboratory to which he is assigned or attached for not more than 60 days of a detail or affiliation for each training year, as defined by the head of the agency.

(b) When the detail or affiliation under subsection (a) of this section is to or with another Federal institution, the student-employee is entitled to necessary expenses of travel to and from the institution in accordance with subchapter I of chapter 57 of this title.

(Pub. L. 89–554, Sept. 6, 1966, 80 Stat. 472.)

HISTORICAL AND REVISION NOTES

Derivation	U.S. Code	Revised Statutes and Statutes at Large
....	5 U.S.C. 1055.	Aug. 4, 1947, ch. 452, §6, 61 Stat. 728.

In subsection (b), the reference to "subchapter I of chapter 57 of this title" is substituted for the reference to "the Standardized Government Travel Regulations and the provisions of the Subsistence Expense Act of 1926, as amended" as the Subsistence Expense Act of 1926 was repealed by section 9(a) of the Travel Expense Act of 1949, 63 Stat. 167, part of which appeared in former section 842 and is carried into section 5708, and as the authority for the Standardized Government Travel Regulations in former section 840 is carried into section 5707 of subchapter I of chapter 57.

Standard changes are made to conform with the definitions applicable and the style of this title as outlined in the preface to the report.

§ 5355. Effect on other statutes

This subchapter does not limit the authority conferred on the Secretary of Veterans Affairs by chapter 73 of title 38.

(Pub. L. 89–554, Sept. 6, 1966, 80 Stat. 472; Pub. L. 102–54, §13(b)(3), June 13, 1991, 105 Stat. 274.)

HISTORICAL AND REVISION NOTES

Derivation	U.S. Code	Revised Statutes and Statutes at Large
....	5 U.S.C. 1057.	Aug. 4, 1947, ch. 452, §8, 61 Stat. 728. June 17, 1957, Pub. L. 85–56, §2201(19), 71 Stat. 159. Sept. 2, 1958, Pub. L. 85–857, §13(m), 72 Stat. 1265.

The prohibition is restated in positive form.

Standard changes are made to conform with the definitions applicable and the style of this title as outlined in the preface to the report.

AMENDMENTS

1991—Pub. L. 102–54 substituted "Secretary of Veterans Affairs" for "Administrator of Veterans' Affairs".

§ 5356. Appropriations

Funds appropriated to an agency for expenses of its hospitals, clinics, and laboratories to which student-employees are assigned or attached are available to carry out the provisions of this subchapter.

(Pub. L. 89–554, Sept. 6, 1966, 80 Stat. 472.)

HISTORICAL AND REVISION NOTES

Derivation	U.S. Code	Revised Statutes and Statutes at Large
....	5 U.S.C. 1058.	Aug. 4, 1947, ch. 452, § 9, 61 Stat. 728.

Standard changes are made to conform with the definitions applicable and the style of this title as outlined in the preface to the report.

SUBCHAPTER VI—GRADE AND PAY RETENTION

PRIOR PROVISIONS

A prior subchapter VI was renumbered VII by Pub. L. 95–454, title VIII, § 801(a)(3)(A)(i), Oct. 13, 1978, 92 Stat. 1221.

SUBCHAPTER REFERRED TO IN OTHER SECTIONS

This subchapter is referred to in sections 5107, 5334, 5349, 8704, 9509 of this title; title 10 sections 4540, 7212, 9540; title 22 section 3964; title 31 section 732.

§ 5361. Definitions

For the purpose of this subchapter—

(1) "employee" means an employee to whom chapter 51 of this title applies, and a prevailing rate employee, as defined by section 5342(a)(2) of this title, whose employment is other than on a temporary or term basis;

(2) "agency" has the meaning given it by section 5102 of this title;

(3) "retained grade" means the grade used for determining benefits to which an employee to whom section 5362 of this title applies is entitled;

(4) "rate of basic pay" means, in the case of a prevailing rate employee, the scheduled rate of pay determined under section 5343 of this title;

(5) "covered pay schedule" means the General Schedule, any prevailing rate schedule established under subchapter IV of this chapter, or a special occupational pay system under subchapter IX;

(6) "position subject to this subchapter" means any position under a covered pay schedule; and

(7) "reduction-in-force procedures" means procedures applied in carrying out any reduction in force due to a reorganization, due to lack of funds or curtailment of work, or due to any other factor.

(Added Pub. L. 95–454, title VIII, § 801(a)(1), Oct. 13, 1978, 92 Stat. 1218; amended Pub. L. 98–615, title II, § 204(a)(2), Nov. 8, 1984, 98 Stat. 3216; Pub. L. 101–509, title V, § 529 [title I, § 105(b)(1)], Nov. 5, 1990, 104 Stat. 1427, 1448; Pub. L. 103–89, § 3(b)(1)(J), Sept. 30, 1993, 107 Stat. 982.)

PRIOR PROVISIONS

A prior section 5361, Pub. L. 89–554, Sept. 6, 1966, 80 Stat. 473, which related to scientific and professional positions, was renumbered section 5371 of this title by Pub. L. 95–454, title VIII, § 801(a)(3)(A)(ii), Oct. 13, 1978, 92 Stat. 1221.

AMENDMENTS

1993—Par. (5). Pub. L. 103–89 substituted "or a special occupational pay system under subchapter IX" for "a special occupational pay system under subchapter IX, or the performance management and recognition system under chapter 54 of this title".

1990—Par. (5). Pub. L. 101–509 inserted "a special occupational pay system under subchapter IX," before "or the performance".

1984—Par. (5). Pub. L. 98–615 substituted "performance management and recognition system" for "merit pay system".

EFFECTIVE DATE OF 1993 AMENDMENT

Amendment by Pub. L. 103–89 effective Nov. 1, 1993, see section 3(c) of Pub. L. 103–89, set out as a note under section 3372 of this title.

EFFECTIVE DATE OF 1990 AMENDMENT

Amendment by Pub. L. 101–509 effective on such date as the President shall determine, but not earlier than 90 days, and not later than 180 days, after Nov. 5, 1990, see section 529 [title III, § 305] of Pub. L. 101–509, set out as a note under section 5301 of this title.

EFFECTIVE DATE OF 1984 AMENDMENT

Section 205 of Pub. L. 98–615 provided that amendment by Pub. L. 98–615 was effective Oct. 1, 1984, and applicable with respect to pay periods commencing on or after that date, with certain exceptions and qualifications.

EFFECTIVE DATE

Section 801(a)(4) of Pub. L. 95–454 provided that:

"(A) The amendments made by this subsection [enacting sections 5361 to 5366 of this title and redesignating former sections 5361 to 5366 as sections 5371 to 5375 of this title, amending sections 559, 1305, 3104, 5102, 5107, 5334, 5349, and 8704 of this title, sections 4540, 7212, and 9540 of Title 10, Armed Forces, section 1715 of Title 15, Commerce and Trade, and section 3608 of Title 42, The Public Health and Welfare, and repealing sections 5337 and 5345 of this title] shall take effect on the first day of the first applicable pay period beginning on or after the 90th day after the date of the enactment of this Act [Oct. 13, 1978].

"(B) An employee who was receiving pay under the provisions of section 5334(d), 5337, or 5345 of title 5, United States Code, on the day before the effective date prescribed in subparagraph (A) of this paragraph shall not have such pay reduced or terminated by reason of the amendments made by this subsection and, unless section 5362 of such title 5 (as amended by subsection (a)(1) of this section) applies, such an employee is entitled to continue to receive pay as authorized by those provisions (as in effect on such date)."

SECTION REFERRED TO IN OTHER SECTIONS

This section is referred to in section 5349 of this title.

§ 5362. Grade retention following a change of positions or reclassification

(a) Any employee—

(1) who is placed as a result of reduction-in-force procedures from a position subject to this subchapter to another position which is subject to this subchapter and which is in a lower grade than the previous position, and

(2) who has served for 52 consecutive weeks or more in one or more positions subject to this subchapter at a grade or grades higher than that of the new position,

is entitled, to the extent provided in subsection (c) of this section, to have the grade of the position held immediately before such placement be considered to be the retained grade of the employee in any position he holds for the 2-year period beginning on the date of such placement.

(b)(1) Any employee who is in a position subject to this subchapter and whose position has been reduced in grade is entitled, to the extent provided in subsection (c) of this section, to have the grade of such position before reduction be treated as the retained grade of such employee for the 2-year period beginning on the date of the reduction in grade.

(2) The provisions of paragraph (1) of this subsection shall not apply with respect to any reduction in the grade of a position which had not been classified at the higher grade for a continuous period of at least one year immediately before such reduction.

(c) For the 2-year period referred to in subsections (a) and (b) of this section, the retained grade of an employee under such subsection (a) or (b) shall be treated as the grade of the employee's position for all purposes (including pay and pay administration under this chapter and chapter 55 of this title, retirement and life insurance under chapters 83, 84, and 87 of this title, and eligibility for training and promotion under this title) except—

(1) for purposes of subsection (a) of this section,

(2) for purposes of applying any reduction-in-force procedures, or

(3) for such other purposes as the Office of Personnel Management may provide by regulation.

(d) The foregoing provisions of this section shall cease to apply to an employee who—

(1) has a break in service of one workday or more;

(2) is demoted (determined without regard to this section) for personal cause or at the employee's request;

(3) is placed in, or declines a reasonable offer of, a position the grade of which is equal to or higher than the retained grade; or

(4) elects in writing to have the benefits of this section terminate.

(Added Pub. L. 95–454, title VIII, §801(a)(1), Oct. 13, 1978, 92 Stat. 1219; amended Pub. L. 98–615, title II, §204(a)(1), Nov. 8, 1984, 98 Stat. 3216; Pub. L. 103–89, §3(b)(1)(K), Sept. 30, 1993, 107 Stat. 982.)

Prior Provisions

A prior section 5362, Pub. L. 89–554, Sept. 6, 1966, 80 Stat. 473, Pub. L. 95–251, §2(a)(1), (b)(1), Mar. 27, 1978, 92 Stat. 183, which related to hearing examiners, was renumbered section 5372 of this title by Pub. L. 95–454, title VIII, §801(a)(3)(A)(ii), Oct. 13, 1978, 92 Stat. 1221.

Amendments

1993—Subsec. (c). Pub. L. 103–89 substituted "chapter 55 of this title, retirement and life insurance under chapters 83, 84, and 87" for "chapters 54 and 55 of this title, retirement and life insurance under chapters 83 and 87" in introductory provisions, redesignated par. (4) as (3), and struck out former par. (3) which read as follows: "for purposes of determining whether the employee is covered by the performance management and recognition system established under chapter 54 of this title, or".

1984—Subsec. (c)(3). Pub. L. 98–615 substituted "performance management and recognition system established under chapter 54" for "merit pay system established under section 5402".

Effective Date of 1993 Amendment

Amendment by Pub. L. 103–89 effective Nov. 1, 1993, see section 3(c) of Pub. L. 103–89, set out as a note under section 3372 of this title.

Effective Date of 1984 Amendment

Section 205 of Pub. L. 98–615 provided that amendment by Pub. L. 98–615 was effective Oct. 1, 1984, and applicable with respect to pay periods commencing on or after that date, with certain exceptions and qualifications.

Additional Pay and Benefits for Employees Reduced in Grade On or After January 1, 1977, Etc.

Section 801(b) of Pub. L. 95–454 provided that:

"(1) Under regulations prescribed by the Office of Personnel Management, any employee—

"(A) whose grade was reduced on or after January 1, 1977, and before the effective date of the amendments made by subsection (a) of this section [see Effective Date note set out under section 5361 of this title] under circumstances which would have entitled the employee to coverage under the provisions of section 5362 of title 5, United States Code (as amended by subsection (a) of this section) if such amendments had been in effect at the time of the reduction; and

"(B) who has remained employed by the Federal Government from the date of the reduction in grade to the effective date of the amendments made by subsection (a) of this section without a break in service of one workday or more;

shall be entitled—

"(i) to receive the additional pay and benefits which such employee would have been entitled to receive if the amendments made by subsection (a) of this section had been in effect during the period beginning on the effective date of such reduction in grade and ending on the day before the effective date of such amendments, and

"(ii) to have the amendments made by subsection (a), of this section apply to such employee as if the reduction in grade had occurred on the effective date of such amendments.

"(2) No employee covered by this subsection whose reduction in grade resulted in an increase in pay shall have such pay reduced by reason of the amendments made by subsection (a) of this section.

"(3)(A) For purposes of this subsection, the requirements under paragraph (1)(B) of this subsection, relating to continuous employment following reduction in grade, shall be considered to be met in the case of any employee—

"(i) who separated from service with a right to an immediate annuity under chapter 83 of title 5, United States Code, or under another retirement system for Federal employees; or

"(ii) who died.

"(B) Amounts payable by reason of subparagraph (A) of this paragraph in the case of the death of an employee shall be paid in accordance with the provisions of subchapter VIII of chapter 55 of title 5, United States Code, relating to settlement of accounts in the case of deceased employees.

"(4) The Office of Personnel Management shall have the same authority to prescribe regulations under this subsection as it has under section 5365 of title 5, United States Code, with respect to subchapter VI of chapter 53 of such title, as added by subsection (a) of this section."

Section Referred to in Other Sections

This section is referred to in sections 5361, 5363, 5364 of this title.

§ 5363. Pay retention

(a) Any employee—

(1) who ceases to be entitled to the benefits of section 5362 of this title by reason of the expiration of the 2-year period of coverage provided under such section;

(2) who is in a position subject to this subchapter and who is subject to a reduction or

termination of a special rate of pay established under section 5305 of this title (or corresponding prior provision of this title);

(3) who is in a position subject to this subchapter and who (but for this section) would be subject to a reduction in pay under circumstances prescribed by the Office of Personnel Management by regulation to warrant the application of this section; or

(4) who is in a position subject to this subchapter and who is subject to a reduction or termination of a rate of pay established under subchapter IX of chapter 53;

is entitled to basic pay at a rate equal to (A) the employee's allowable former rate of basic pay, plus (B) 50 percent of the amount of each increase in the maximum rate of basic pay payable for the grade of the employee's position immediately after such reduction in pay if such allowable former rate exceeds such maximum rate for such grade.

(b) For the purpose of subsection (a) of this section, "allowable former rate of basic pay" means the lower of—

(1) the rate of basic pay payable to the employee immediately before the reduction in pay; or

(2) 150 percent of the maximum rate of basic pay payable for the grade of the employee's position immediately after such reduction in pay.

(c) The preceding provisions of this section shall cease to apply to an employee who—

(1) has a break in service of one workday or more;

(2) is entitled by operation of this subchapter or chapter 51 or 53 of this title to a rate of basic pay which is equal to or higher than, or declines a reasonable offer of a position the rate of basic pay for which is equal to or higher than, the rate to which the employee is entitled under this section; or

(3) is demoted for personal cause or at the employee's request.

(Added Pub. L. 95–454, title VIII, §801(a)(1), Oct. 13, 1978, 92 Stat. 1219; amended Pub. L. 101–509, title V, §529 [title I, §§101(b)(3)(B), 105(b)(2)], Nov. 5, 1990, 104 Stat. 1427, 1439, 1448; Pub. L. 103–89, §3(b)(1)(L), Sept. 30, 1993, 107 Stat. 982.)

A prior section 5363, Pub. L. 89–554, Sept. 6, 1966, 80 Stat. 473, which related to limitation on pay fixed by administrative action, was renumbered section 5373 of this title by Pub. L. 95–454, title VIII, §801(a)(3)(A)(ii), Oct. 13, 1978, 92 Stat. 1221.

AMENDMENTS

1993—Subsec. (c)(2). Pub. L. 103–89 substituted "chapter 51 or 53" for "chapter 51, 53, or 54".

1990—Subsec. (a)(2) to (4). Pub. L. 101–509 substituted "5305 of this title (or corresponding prior provision of this title);" for "5303 of this title; or" in par. (2), inserted "or" at end of par. (3), and added par. (4).

EFFECTIVE DATE OF 1993 AMENDMENT

Amendment by Pub. L. 103–89 effective Nov. 1, 1993, see section 3(c) of Pub. L. 103–89, set out as a note under section 3372 of this title.

EFFECTIVE DATE OF 1990 AMENDMENT

Amendment by Pub. L. 101–509 effective on such date as the President shall determine, but not earlier than 90 days, and not later than 180 days, after Nov. 5, 1990, see section 529 [title III, §305] of Pub. L. 101–509, set out as a note under section 5301 of this title.

SECTION REFERRED TO IN OTHER SECTIONS

This section is referred to in sections 5302, 5364 of this title.

§ 5364. Remedial actions

Under regulations prescribed by the Office of Personnel Management, the Office may require any agency—

(1) to report to the Office information with respect to vacancies (including impending vacancies);

(2) to take such steps as may be appropriate to assure employees receiving benefits under section 5362 or 5363 of this title have the opportunity to obtain necessary qualifications for the selection to positions which would minimize the need for the application of such sections;

(3) to establish a program under which employees receiving benefits under section 5362 or 5363 of this title are given priority in the consideration for or placement in positions which are equal to their retained grade or pay; and

(4) to place certain employees, notwithstanding the fact their previous position was in a different agency, but only in circumstances in which the Office determines the exercise of such authority is necessary to carry out the purpose of this section.

(Added Pub. L. 95–454, title VIII, §801(a)(1), Oct. 13, 1978, 92 Stat. 1220.)

A prior section 5364, Pub. L. 89–554, Sept. 6, 1966, 80 Stat. 473, which related to miscellaneous positions in the executive branch, was renumbered section 5374 of this title by Pub. L. 95–454, title VIII, §801(a)(3)(A)(ii), Oct. 13, 1978, 92 Stat. 1221.

§ 5365. Regulations

(a) The Office of Personnel Management shall prescribe regulations to carry out the purpose of this subchapter.

(b) Under such regulations, the Office may provide for the application of all or portions of the provisions of this subchapter—

(1) to any individual reduced to a grade of a covered pay schedule from a position not subject to this subchapter;

(2) to individuals to whom such provisions do not otherwise apply; and

(3) to situations the application to which is justified for purposes of carrying out the mission of the agency or agencies involved.

Individuals with respect to whom authority under paragraph (2) may be exercised include individuals who are moved without a break in service of more than 3 days from employment in nonappropriated fund instrumentalities of the Department of Defense or the Coast Guard described in section 2105(c) to employment in the Department of Defense or the Coast Guard, respectively, that is not described in section 2105(c).

(Added Pub. L. 95–454, title VIII, §801(a)(1), Oct. 13, 1978, 92 Stat. 1220; amended Pub. L. 101–508, title VII, §7202(f), Nov. 5, 1990, 104 Stat. 1388–336.)

A prior section 5365, added Pub. L. 91–34, § 1(a), June 30, 1969, 83 Stat. 41; amended Pub. L. 94–183, § 2(20), Dec. 31, 1975, 89 Stat. 1058, which related to the police force of National Zoological Park, was renumbered section 5375 of this title by Pub. L. 95–454, title VIII, § 801(a)(3)(A)(ii), Oct. 13, 1978, 92 Stat. 1221.

AMENDMENTS

1990—Subsec. (b). Pub. L. 101–508 inserted at end "Individuals with respect to whom authority under paragraph (2) may be exercised include individuals who are moved without a break in service of more than 3 days from employment in nonappropriated fund instrumentalities of the Department of Defense or the Coast Guard described in section 2105(c) to employment in the Department of Defense or the Coast Guard, respectively, that is not described in section 2105(c)."

EFFECTIVE DATE OF 1990 AMENDMENT

Amendment by Pub. L. 101–508 applicable with respect to any individual who, on or after Jan. 1, 1987, moves from employment in nonappropriated fund instrumentality of Department of Defense or Coast Guard, that is described in section 2105(c) of this title, to employment in Department or Coast Guard, that is not described in section 2105(c), or who moves from employment in Department or Coast Guard, that is not described in section 2105(c), to employment in nonappropriated fund instrumentality of Department or Coast Guard, that is described in section 2105(c), see section 7202(m)(1) of Pub. L. 101–508, set out as a note under section 2105 of this title.

SECTION REFERRED TO IN OTHER SECTIONS

This section is referred to in section 5334 of this title.

§ 5366. Appeals

(a)(1) In the case of the termination of any benefits available to an employee under this subchapter on the grounds such employee declined a reasonable offer of a position the grade or pay of which was equal to or greater than his retained grade or pay, such termination may be appealed to the Office of Personnel Management under procedures prescribed by the Office.

(2) Nothing in this subchapter shall be construed to affect the right of any employee to appeal—

(A) under section 5112(b) or 5346(c) of this title, or otherwise, any reclassification of a position; or

(B) under procedures prescribed by the Office of Personnel Management, any reduction-in-force action.

(b) For purposes of any appeal procedures (other than those described in subsection (a) of this section) or any grievance procedure negotiated under the provisions of chapter 71 of this title—

(1) any action which is the basis of an individual's entitlement to benefits under this subchapter, and

(2) any termination of any such benefits under this subchapter,

shall not be treated as appealable under such appeals procedures or grievable under such grievance procedure.

(Added Pub. L. 95–454, title VIII, § 801(a)(1), Oct. 13, 1978, 92 Stat. 1221.)

SUBCHAPTER VII—MISCELLANEOUS PROVISIONS

AMENDMENTS

1978—Pub. L. 95–454, title VIII, § 801(a)(3)(A)(i), Oct. 13, 1978, 92 Stat. 1221, redesignated former subchapter VI as VII.

SUBCHAPTER REFERRED TO IN OTHER SECTIONS

This subchapter is referred to in title 42 section 1320a–4.

§ 5371. Health care positions

(a) For the purposes of this section, "health care" means direct patient-care services or services incident to direct patient-care services.

(b) The Office of Personnel Management may, with respect to any employee described in subsection (c), provide that 1 or more provisions of chapter 74 of title 38 shall apply—

(1) in lieu of any provision of chapter 51 or 61, subchapter V of chapter 55, or any other provision of this chapter; or

(2) notwithstanding any lack of specific authority for a matter with respect to which chapter 51 or 61, subchapter V of chapter 55, or this chapter, relates.

(c) Authority under subsection (b) may be exercised with respect to any employee holding a position—

(1) to which chapter 51 applies, excluding any Senior Executive Service position and any position in the Federal Bureau of Investigation and Drug Enforcement Administration Senior Executive Service; and

(2) which involves health care responsibilities.

(Pub. L. 89–554, Sept. 6, 1966, 80 Stat. 473, § 5361; renumbered § 5371 and amended Pub. L. 95–454, title VIII, § 801(a)(3)(A)(ii), title IX, § 906(a)(2), Oct. 13, 1978, 92 Stat. 1221, 1224; Pub. L. 101–509, title V, § 529 [title II, § 205(A)], Nov. 5, 1990, 104 Stat. 1427, 1456; Pub. L. 102–378, § 2(31), Oct. 2, 1992, 106 Stat. 1350.)

HISTORICAL AND REVISION NOTES

Derivation	U.S. Code	Revised Statutes and Statutes at Large
....	5 U.S.C. 1162(b).	Oct. 4, 1961, Pub. L. 87–367, § 202 "Sec. 2(b)", 75 Stat. 790. Oct. 11, 1962, Pub. L. 87–793, § 1001(a)(1), 76 Stat. 863.

The authority to fix rates of pay is added on authority of former section 1161, which is carried into section 3104.

For repeal of the Act of Aug. 1, 1947, ch. 433, 61 Stat. 715, as amended, see revision note for section 3104.

Standard changes are made to conform with the definitions applicable and the style of this title as outlined in the preface to the report.

AMENDMENTS

1992—Subsec. (b). Pub. L. 102–378 substituted "chapter 74" for "chapter 73" in introductory provisions and inserted "subchapter V of chapter 55," after "61," in pars. (1) and (2).

1990—Pub. L. 101–509 amended section generally, substituting designated provisions directing that Office of Personnel Management may provide that chapter 73 of title 38 provisions apply to certain health care professionals for undesignated text authorizing agency heads to fix pay rates for scientific and professional positions at between GS–16 and GS–18 rates.

1978—Pub. L. 95–454, § 906(a)(2), substituted "Office of Personnel Management" for "Civil Service Commission".

EFFECTIVE DATE OF 1990 AMENDMENT

Amendment by Pub. L. 101–509 effective on such date as the President shall determine, but not earlier than 90 days, and not later than 180 days, after Nov. 5, 1990, see section 529 [title III, § 305] of Pub. L. 101–509, set out as a note under section 5301 of this title.

EFFECTIVE DATE OF 1978 AMENDMENT

Amendment by section 906(a)(2) of Pub. L. 95–454 effective 90 days after Oct. 13, 1978, see section 907 of Pub. L. 95–454, set out as a note under section 1101 of this title.

SECTION REFERRED TO IN OTHER SECTIONS

This section is referred to in section 5948 of this title.

§ 5372. Administrative law judges

(a) For the purposes of this section, the term "administrative law judge" means an administrative law judge appointed under section 3105.

(b)(1)(A) There shall be 3 levels of basic pay for administrative law judges (designated as AL–1, 2, and 3, respectively), and each such judge shall be paid at 1 of those levels, in accordance with the provisions of this section.

(B) Within level AL–3, there shall be 6 rates of basic pay, designated as AL–3, rates A through F, respectively. Level AL–2 and level AL–1 shall each have 1 rate of basic pay.

(C) The rate of basic pay for AL–3, rate A, may not be less than 65 percent of the rate of basic pay for level IV of the Executive Schedule, and the rate of basic pay for AL–1 may not exceed the rate for level IV of the Executive Schedule.

(2) The Office of Personnel Management shall determine, in accordance with procedures which the Office shall by regulation prescribe, the level in which each administrative-law-judge position shall be placed and the qualifications to be required for appointment to each level.

(3)(A) Upon appointment to a position in AL–3, an administrative law judge shall be paid at rate A of AL–3, and shall be advanced successively to rates B, C, and D of that level at the beginning of the next pay period following completion of 52 weeks of service in the next lower rate, and to rates E and F of that level at the beginning of the next pay period following completion of 104 weeks of service in the next lower rate.

(B) The Office of Personnel Management may provide for appointment of an administrative law judge in AL–3 at an advanced rate under such circumstances as the Office may determine appropriate.

(4) Subject to paragraph (1), effective at the beginning of the first applicable pay period commencing on or after the first day of the month in which an adjustment takes effect under section 5303 in the rates of basic pay under the General Schedule, each rate of basic pay for administrative law judges shall be adjusted by an amount determined by the President to be appropriate.

(c) The Office of Personnel Management shall prescribe regulations necessary to administer this section.

(Pub. L. 89–554, Sept. 6, 1966, 80 Stat. 473, § 5362; Pub. L. 95–251, § 2(a)(1), (b)(1), Mar. 27, 1978, 92 Stat. 183; renumbered § 5372 and amended Pub. L. 95–454, title VIII, § 801(a)(3)(A)(ii), title IX, § 906(a)(2), Oct. 13, 1978, 92 Stat. 1221, 1224; Pub. L. 101–509, title V, § 529 [title I, § 104(a)(1)], Nov. 5, 1990, 104 Stat. 1427, 1445; Pub. L. 102–378, § 2(32), Oct. 2, 1992, 106 Stat. 1350; Pub. L. 106–97, § 1, Nov. 12, 1999, 113 Stat. 1322.)

HISTORICAL AND REVISION NOTES

Derivation	U.S. Code	Revised Statutes and Statutes at Large
....	5 U.S.C. 1010 (3d sentence).	June 10, 1946, ch. 324, § 11 (3d sentence), 60 Stat. 244.

The exception from the operation of the efficiency rating system is omitted as covered by sections 4301(2)(E) and 5335(a)(B). The reference to "subchapter III of this chapter and chapter 51 of this title" is substituted for "the Classification Act of 1923, as amended" on authority of section 1106(a) of the Act of Oct. 28, 1949, ch. 782, 63 Stat. 972.

Standard changes are made to conform with the definitions applicable and the style of this title as outlined in the preface to the report.

REFERENCES IN TEXT

Level IV of the Executive Schedule, referred to in subsec. (b)(1)(C), is set out in section 5315 of this title.

The General Schedule, referred to in subsec. (b)(4), is set out under section 5332 of this title.

AMENDMENTS

1999—Subsec. (b)(1). Pub. L. 106–97, § 1(1), designated first sentence as subpar. (A) and struck out after first sentence the following: "The rates of basic pay for those levels shall be as follows:

AL–3, rate A ..... 65 percent of the rate of basic pay for level IV of the Executive Schedule.

AL–3, rate B ..... 70 percent of the rate of basic pay for level IV of the Executive Schedule.

AL–3, rate C ..... 75 percent of the rate of basic pay for level IV of the Executive Schedule.

AL–3, rate D ..... 80 percent of the rate of basic pay for level IV of the Executive Schedule.

AL–3, rate E ..... 85 percent of the rate of basic pay for level IV of the Executive Schedule.

AL–3, rate F ..... 90 percent of the rate of basic pay for level IV of the Executive Schedule.

AL–2 .... 95 percent of the rate of basic pay for level IV of the Executive Schedule.

AL–1 .... The rate of basic pay for level IV of the Executive Schedule."

Subsec. (b)(1)(B), (C). Pub. L. 106–97, § 1(1), added subpars. (B) and (C).

Subsec. (b)(3)(A). Pub. L. 106–97, § 1(2), substituted "at the beginning of the next pay period following" for "upon" in two places.

Subsec. (b)(4). Pub. L. 106–97, § 1(3), added par. (4).

1992—Subsec. (c). Pub. L. 102–378 substituted "shall" for "shall,".

1990—Pub. L. 101–509 amended section generally. Prior to amendment, section read as follows: "Administrative law judges appointed under section 3105 of this title are entitled to pay prescribed by the Office of Personnel Management independently of agency recommendations or ratings and in accordance with subchapter III of this chapter and chapter 51 of this title."

1978—Pub. L. 95–454, § 906(a)(2), substituted "Office of Personnel Management" for "Civil Service Commission".

Pub. L. 95–251 substituted "Administrative law judges" for "Hearing examiners" in section catchline and text.

EFFECTIVE DATE OF 1990 AMENDMENT

Amendment by Pub. L. 101–509 effective on such date as the President shall determine, but not earlier than

90 days, and not later than 180 days, after Nov. 5, 1990, see section 529 [title III, §305] of Pub. L. 101–509, set out as a note under section 5301 of this title.

EFFECTIVE DATE OF 1978 AMENDMENT

Amendment by section 906(a)(2) of Pub. L. 95–454 effective 90 days after Oct. 13, 1978, see section 907 of Pub. L. 95–454, set out as a note under section 1101 of this title.

CONVERSION RULE FOR ADMINISTRATIVE LAW JUDGES

Section 529 [title I, §104(e)] of Pub. L. 101–509 provided that: "In making initial pay adjustments for administrative law judges after this section and the amendments made by this section [enacting section 5372a of this title, amending this section, sections 5102, 5311, and 5335 of this title, section 938 of Title 30, Mineral Lands and Mining, and section 607 of Title 41, Public Contracts] take effect [see Effective Date of 1990 Amendment note set out under section 5301 of this title], the rate of basic pay for any such judge shall, upon conversion to the new pay system, be at least equal to the rate which was payable to that individual immediately before such conversion."

PAY INCREASES

2001—The President, under Ex. Ord. No. 13182, Dec. 23, 2000, 65 F.R. 82879, 66 F.R. 10057, set out as a note under section 5332 of this title, adjusted the rates of basic pay for administrative law judges effective on the first day of the first applicable pay period beginning on or after Jan. 1, 2001, as follows:

AL–3/A	$82,100
AL–3/B	88,300
AL–3/C	94,700
AL–3/D	101,000
AL–3/E	107,300
AL–3/F	113,600
AL–2	120,000
AL–1	125,700

2000—Ex. Ord. No. 13144, Dec. 21, 1999, 64 F.R. 72237, which provided for adjustment of pay rates effective Jan. 1, 2000, was superseded by Ex. Ord. No. 13182, Dec. 23, 2000, 65 F.R. 82879, 66 F.R. 10057, set out as a note under section 5332 of this title.

SECTION REFERRED TO IN OTHER SECTIONS

This section is referred to in sections 559, 1305, 5304, 5372b, 5377, 5380, 7323 of this title; title 15 section 1715; title 29 section 661; title 30 section 938; title 38 section 7101A; title 42 sections 2000e–4, 3608.

§ 5372a. Contract appeals board members

(a) For the purpose of this section—
(1) the term "contract appeals board member" means a member of an agency board of contract appeals appointed under section 8 of the Contract Disputes Act of 1978; and
(2) the term "appeals board" means an agency board of contract appeals established pursuant to section 8 of the Contract Disputes Act of 1978.

(b) Rates of basic pay for contract appeals board members shall be as follows:
(1) Chairman of an appeals board—the rate of basic pay payable for level IV of the Executive Schedule.
(2) Vice chairman of an appeals board—97 percent of the rate under paragraph (1).
(3) Other members of an appeals board—94 percent of the rate under paragraph (1).

(c) Rates of pay taking effect under this section shall be printed in the Federal Register and the Code of Federal Regulations.

(Added Pub. L. 101–509, title V, §529 [title I, §104(a)(2)], Nov. 5, 1990, 104 Stat. 1427, 1446.)

REFERENCES IN TEXT

Section 8 of the Contract Disputes Act of 1978, referred to in subsec. (a), is classified to section 607 of Title 41, Public Contracts.

Level IV of the Executive Schedule, referred to in subsec. (b)(1), is set out in section 5315 of this title.

EFFECTIVE DATE

Section effective on such date as the President shall determine, but not earlier than 90 days, and not later than 180 days, after Nov. 5, 1990, see section 529 [title III, §305] of Pub. L. 101–509, set out as an Effective Date of 1990 Amendment note under section 5301 of this title.

SECTION REFERRED TO IN OTHER SECTIONS

This section is referred to in sections 5304, 5377, 5380, 7323 of this title; title 41 section 607.

§ 5372b. Administrative appeals judges

(a) For the purpose of this section—
(1) the term "administrative appeals judge position" means a position the duties of which primarily involve reviewing decisions of administrative law judges appointed under section 3105; and
(2) the term "agency" means an Executive agency, as defined by section 105, but does not include the General Accounting Office.

(b) Subject to such regulations as the Office of Personnel Management may prescribe, the head of the agency concerned shall fix the rate of basic pay for each administrative appeals judge position within such agency which is not classified above GS–15 pursuant to section 5108.

(c) A rate of basic pay fixed under this section shall be—
(1) not less than the minimum rate of basic pay for level AL–3 under section 5372; and
(2) not greater than the maximum rate of basic pay for level AL–3 under section 5372.

(Added Pub. L. 106–554, §1(a)(3) [title VI, §645(a)(1)], Dec. 21, 2000, 114 Stat. 2763, 2763A–169.)

REFERENCES IN TEXT

GS–15, referred to in subsec. (b), is contained in the General Schedule which is set out under section 5332 of this title.

EFFECTIVE DATE

Pub. L. 106–554, §1(a)(3) [title VI, §645(b)], Dec. 21, 2000, 114 Stat. 2763, 2763A–170, provided that: "The amendment made by subsection (a)(1) [enacting this section] shall apply with respect to pay for service performed on or after the first day of the first applicable pay period beginning on or after—
"(1) the 120th day after the date of the enactment of this Act [Dec. 21, 2000]; or
"(2) if earlier, the effective date of regulations prescribed by the Office of Personnel Management to carry out such amendment."

SECTION REFERRED TO IN OTHER SECTIONS

This section is referred to in section 7323 of this title.

§ 5373. Limitation on pay fixed by administrative action

(a) Except as provided in subsection (b) and by the Government Employees Salary Reform Act of 1964 (78 Stat. 400) and notwithstanding the provisions of other statutes, the head of an Executive agency or military department who is authorized to fix by administrative action the annual rate of basic pay for a position or employee may not fix the rate at more than the rate for level IV of the Executive Schedule. This section does not impair the authorities provided by—

(1) sections 248, 482, 1766, and 1819 of title 12, section 206 of the Bank Conservation Act, sections 2B(b) and 21A(e)(4) of the Federal Home Loan Bank Act, section 2A(i)[1] of the Home Owners' Loan Act, and sections 5.11 and 5.58 of the Farm Credit Act of 1971;

(2) section 831b of title 16; or

(3) sections 403a–403c, 403e–403h, and 403j of title 50.

(b) Subsection (a) shall not affect the authority of the Secretary of Defense or the Secretary of a military department to fix the pay of a civilian employee paid from nonappropriated funds, except that the annual rate of basic pay (including any portion of such pay attributable to comparability with private-sector pay in a locality) of such an employee may not be fixed at a rate greater than the rate for level III of the Executive Schedule.

(Pub. L. 89–554, Sept. 6, 1966, 80 Stat. 473, § 5363; renumbered § 5373, Pub. L. 95–454, title VIII, § 801(a)(3)(A)(ii), Oct. 13, 1978, 92 Stat. 1221; Pub. L. 96–70, title III, § 3302(e)(4), Sept. 27, 1979, 93 Stat. 498; Pub. L. 101–73, title VII, § 742(b), title XII, § 1209, Aug. 9, 1989, 103 Stat. 437, 523; Pub. L. 101–509, title V, § 529 [title I, § 101(b)(9)(H)], Nov. 5, 1990, 104 Stat. 1427, 1441; Pub. L. 104–201, div. C, title XXXV, § 3548(a)(4), Sept. 23, 1996, 110 Stat. 2868; Pub. L. 106–65, div. A, title XI, § 1102, Oct. 5, 1999, 113 Stat. 776.)

HISTORICAL AND REVISION NOTES

Derivation	U.S. Code	Revised Statutes and Statutes at Large
....	5 U.S.C. 2212.	Aug. 14, 1964, Pub. L. 88–426, § 308, 78 Stat. 432. Oct. 6, 1964, Pub. L. 88–631, § 3(e), 78 Stat. 1008.

The words "head of an Executive agency or military department" are coextensive with and substituted for "head of any executive department, independent establishment, or agency in the executive branch" because of the definitions in sections 102 and 105.

Standard changes are made to conform to the definitions applicable and the style of this title as outlined in the preface to the report.

REFERENCES IN TEXT

The Government Employees Salary Reform Act of 1964 (78 Stat. 400), referred to in subsec. (a), is Pub. L. 88–426, Aug. 14, 1964, 78 Stat. 400, as amended. For complete classification of this Act to the Code, see Tables.

Level IV of the Executive Schedule, referred to in subsec. (a), is set out in section 5315 of this title.

Section 206 of the Bank Conservation Act, referred to in subsec. (a)(1), is classified to section 206 of Title 12, Banks and Banking.

Sections 2B(b) and 21A(e)(4) of the Federal Home Loan Bank Act, referred to in subsec. (a)(1), are classified to sections 1422b(b) and 1441a(e)(4), respectively, of Title 12, Banks and Banking.

Section 2A(i) of the Home Owners' Loan Act, referred to in subsec. (a)(1), probably should be a reference to section 3(g) of the Home Owners' Loan Act, act June 13, 1933, ch. 64, as amended by Pub. L. 101–73, title III, § 301, Aug. 9, 1989, 103 Stat. 278, which is classified to section 1462a(g) of Title 12, Banks and Banking.

---

[1] See References in Text note below.

Sections 5.11 and 5.58 of the Farm Credit Act of 1971, referred to in subsec. (a)(1), are classified to sections 2245 and 2277a–7, respectively, of Title 12, Banks and Banking.

Sections 403a–403c, 403e–403h, and 403j of title 50, referred to in subsec. (a)(3), was in the original (78 Stat. 432) a reference to "the Central Intelligence Agency Act of 1949, as amended (50 U.S.C. 403a and the following". Subsequent to the enactment of Title 5, Government Organization and Employees, by Pub. L. 89–554, additional sections have been added to the 1949 Act and are classified to sections 403k to 403r, and 403s to 403v of Title 50, War and National Defense.

Level III of the Executive Schedule, referred to in subsec. (b), is set out in section 5314 of this title.

AMENDMENTS

1999—Pub. L. 106–65 designated existing provisions as subsec. (a), substituted "(a) Except as provided in subsection (b) and" for "Except as provided", and added subsec. (b).

1996—Pub. L. 104–201 redesignated pars. (2) to (4) as (1) to (3), respectively, and struck out former par. (1) which read as follows: "section 1202 of the Panama Canal Act of 1979;".

1990—Pub. L. 101–509 substituted "rate for level IV of the Executive Schedule." for "maximum rate for GS–18."

1989—Par. (2). Pub. L. 101–73, § 1209, amended par. (2) generally. Prior to amendment, par. (2) read as follows: "sections 248, 481, 1437, 1439, and 1819 of title 12;".

Pub. L. 101–73, § 742(b), inserted references to sections 1437 and 1439 of title 12.

1979—Par. (1). Pub. L. 96–70 substituted "section 1202 of the Panama Canal Act of 1979" for "section 121 of title 2, Canal Zone Code (76A Stat. 15)".

EFFECTIVE DATE OF 1990 AMENDMENT

Amendment by Pub. L. 101–509 effective on such date as the President shall determine, but not earlier than 90 days, and not later than 180 days, after Nov. 5, 1990, see section 529 [title III, § 305] of Pub. L. 101–509, set out as a note under section 5301 of this title.

EFFECTIVE DATE OF 1979 AMENDMENT

Amendment by Pub. L. 96–70 effective Oct. 1, 1979, see section 3304 of Pub. L. 96–70, set out as an Effective Date note under section 3601 of Title 22, Foreign Relations and Intercourse.

SECTION REFERRED TO IN OTHER SECTIONS

This section is referred to in sections 5376, 5382 of this title; title 10 sections 2113, 9314; title 38 section 7281.

§ 5374. Miscellaneous positions in the executive branch

The head of the agency concerned shall fix the annual rate of basic pay for each position in the executive branch specifically referred to in, or covered by, a conforming change in statute made by section 305 of the Government Employees Salary Reform Act of 1964 (78 Stat. 422), or other position in the executive branch for which the annual pay is fixed at a rate of $18,500 or more under special provision of statute enacted before August 14, 1964, which is not placed in a level of the Executive Schedule set forth in subchapter II of this chapter, at a rate equal to the pay rate of a grade and step of the General Schedule set forth in section 5332 of this title. The head of the agency concerned shall report each action taken under this section to the Office of Personnel Management and publish a notice thereof in the Federal Register, except when the President determines that the report and publication would be contrary to the interest of national security.

(Pub. L. 89–554, Sept. 6, 1966, 80 Stat. 473, §5364; renumbered §5374 and amended Pub. L. 95–454, title VIII, §801(a)(3)(A)(ii), title IX, §906(a)(2), Oct. 13, 1978, 92 Stat. 1221, 1224.)

Historical and Revision Notes

Derivation	U.S. Code	Revised Statutes and Statutes at Large
....	5 U.S.C. 2213.	Aug. 14, 1964, Pub. L. 88–426, §309, 78 Stat. 433.

The word "office" is omitted as included in "position". The words "before August 14, 1964" are substituted for "prior to the date of enactment of this Act". The words "pursuant to section 303 of this Act" are omitted as surplusage.

Standard changes are made to conform to the definitions applicable and the style of this title as outlined in the preface to the report.

References in Text

Section 305 of the Government Employees Salary Reform Act of 1964, referred to in text, means section 305 of Pub. L. 88–426, Aug. 14, 1964. For complete classification of this section to the Code, see Tables.

Amendments

1978—Pub. L. 95–454, §906(a)(2), substituted "Office of Personnel Management" for "Civil Service Commission".

Effective Date of 1978 Amendment

Amendment by section 906(a)(2) of Pub. L. 95–454 effective 90 days after Oct. 13, 1978, see section 907 of Pub. L. 95–454, set out as a note under section 1101 of this title.

§ 5375. Police force of the National Zoological Park

The Secretary of the Smithsonian Institution shall fix the annual rates of basic pay for positions on the police force of the National Zoological Park as follows:

(1) Private, not more than the maximum annual rate of basic pay payable for grade GS–7 of the General Schedule.

(2) Sergeant, not more than the maximum annual rate of basic pay payable for grade GS–8 of the General Schedule.

(3) Lieutenant, not more than the maximum annual rate of basic pay payable for grade GS–9 of the General Schedule.

(4) Captain, not more than the maximum annual rate of basic pay payable for grade GS–10 of the General Schedule.

(Added Pub. L. 91–34, §1(a), June 30, 1969, 83 Stat. 41, §5365; amended Pub. L. 94–183, §2(20), Dec. 31, 1975, 89 Stat. 1058; renumbered §5375, Pub. L. 95–454, title VIII, §801(a)(3)(A)(ii), Oct. 13, 1978, 92 Stat. 1221; Pub. L. 101–263, §1(a), Apr. 4, 1990, 104 Stat. 125; Pub. L. 102–378, §2(33), Oct. 2, 1992, 106 Stat. 1350.)

References in Text

General Schedule, referred to in text, is set out under section 5332 of this title.

Amendments

1992—Par. (2). Pub. L. 102–378 substituted "GS–8" for "GS–8,".

1990—Pub. L. 101–263 inserted "the" before "National" in section catchline and amended text generally. Prior to amendment, text read as follows: "The Secretary of the Smithsonian Institution shall fix the per annum rates of basic pay of positions on the police force of the National Zoological Park in accordance with the following provisions:

"(1) Private—not more than the rate for GS–7, Step 5;

"(2) Sergeant—not more than the rate for GS–8, Step 5;

"(3) Lieutenant—not more than the rate for GS–9, Step 5;

"(4) Captain—not more than the rate for GS–10, Step 5."

1975—Pub. L. 94–183 struck out designation "(a)" at beginning.

Effective Date of 1990 Amendment

Section 2 of Pub. L. 101–263 provided that: "The amendments made by section 1 [amending this section] shall apply with respect to pay periods beginning after the date of the enactment of this Act [Apr. 4, 1990]."

Effective Date

Section 3(a) of Pub. L. 91–34 provided that: "The foregoing provisions of this Act [enacting this section and amending sections 5102 and 5109 of this title and section 193n of Title 40, Public Buildings, Property, and Works] shall become effective at the beginning of the first pay period which commences on or after the date of enactment of this Act [June 30, 1969]."

Reduction of Basic Pay Rate

Section 3(b) of Pub. L. 91–34 provided that: "No rate of basic pay shall be reduced by reason of the enactment of this Act [enacting this section and amending sections 5102 and 5109 of this title and section 193n of Title 40, Public Buildings, Property, and Works]."

Section Referred to in Other Sections

This section is referred to in section 5102 of this title; title 40 section 193n.

§ 5376. Pay for certain senior-level positions

(a) This section applies to—

(1) positions that are classified above GS–15 pursuant to section 5108; and

(2) scientific or professional positions established under section 3104;

but does not apply to—

(A) any Senior Executive Service position under section 3132; or

(B) any position in the Federal Bureau of Investigation and Drug Enforcement Administration Senior Executive Service under section 3151.

(b)(1) Subject to such regulations as the Office of Personnel Management prescribes, the head of the agency concerned shall fix the rate of basic pay for any position within such agency to which this section applies. A rate fixed under this section shall be—

(A) not less than 120 percent of the minimum rate of basic pay payable for GS–15 of the General Schedule; and

(B) not greater than the rate of basic pay payable for level IV of the Executive Schedule.

The payment of a rate of basic pay under this section shall not be subject to the pay limitation of section 5306(e) or 5373.

(2) Subject to paragraph (1), effective at the beginning of the first applicable pay period commencing on or after the first day of the month in which an adjustment takes effect under section 5303 in the rates of pay under the General

Schedule, each rate of pay established under this section for positions within an agency shall be adjusted by such amount as the head of such agency considers appropriate.

(Added Pub. L. 101–509, title V, § 529 [title I, § 102(a)(1)], Nov. 5, 1990, 104 Stat. 1427, 1443.)

REFERENCES IN TEXT

The General Schedule, referred to in subsec. (b), is set out under section 5332 of this title.

Level IV of the Executive Schedule, referred to in subsec. (b)(1)(B), is set out in section 5315 of this title.

EFFECTIVE DATE

Section effective on such date as the President shall determine, but not earlier than 90 days, and not later than 180 days, after Nov. 5, 1990, see section 529 [title III, § 305] of Pub. L. 101–509, set out as an Effective Date of 1990 Amendment note under section 5301 of this title.

REFERENCES IN OTHER LAWS TO GS–16, 17, OR 18 PAY RATES; REGULATIONS

Section 529 [title I, § 101(c), (d)] of Pub. L. 101–509 provided that:

"(c) OTHER REFERENCES.—Until otherwise provided by law—

"(1) any reference in a provision of law (which is outside title 5, United States Code, and in effect immediately before this section takes effect [see Effective Date of 1990 Amendment note set out under section 5301 of this title], excluding any reference in a provision of law amended by this Act [see Short Title of 1990 Amendment note set out under section 5301 of this title])—

"(A)(i) to the rate of pay for grade GS–18 of the General Schedule, or to the maximum rate of pay under the General Schedule, shall be considered a reference to the maximum rate payable under section 5376 of such title (as amended by section 102(a));

"(ii) to the minimum rate of pay for grade GS–16 of the General Schedule shall be considered a reference to the minimum rate payable under section 5376 of such title (as amended by section 102(a)); and

"(iii) to a rate of pay for grade GS–16 or 17 of the General Schedule shall (except as provided in clause (ii)) be considered a reference to a rate of pay for a position classified above GS–15 pursuant to section 5108 of such title (as amended by section 102(b)(2)); and

"(B) to a rate of pay under the General Schedule shall not include any comparability payment payable under section 5304 of such title (as amended by this section) or any geographic adjustment payable under section 302 [section 529 [title III, § 302] of Pub. L. 101–509, set out as a note under section 5304 of this title]; and

"(2) any authority granted by a provision of law (which is outside such title, and in effect immediately before this section takes effect) to fix pay in accordance with chapter 51 and subchapter III of chapter 53 of such title—

"(A) shall not be considered to include any authority under section 5304 of such title (as amended by this section) or section 302; but

"(B) shall be considered to include authority under section 5376 of such title (as amended by section 102(a)), if applicable.

"(d) REGULATIONS.—The Office of Personnel Management may prescribe regulations, consistent with subsection (c)(1)(B) and section 303 [section 529 [title III, § 303] of Pub. L. 101–509, set out as a note under section 5301 of this title], governing the conversion or adjustment of rates of pay, where necessary because of the abolishment of grades GS–16, 17, and 18 of the General Schedule."

SECTION REFERRED TO IN OTHER SECTIONS

This section is referred to in sections 3405, 5304, 5331, 5382, 5595, 5948, 9509 of this title; title 7 section 7317; title 10 section 180; title 20 section 6011; title 33 sections 1123, 1128; title 36 sections 2302, 2303, 2307; title 42 sections 1863, 1864, 5612, 5651.

§ 5377. Pay authority for critical positions

(a) For the purpose of this section—

(1) the term "agency" has the meaning given it by section 5102; and

(2) the term "position" means—

(A) a position to which chapter 51 applies, including a position in the Senior Executive Service or the Federal Bureau of Investigation and Drug Enforcement Administration Senior Executive Service;

(B) a position under the Executive Schedule under sections 5312–5317;

(C) a position to which section 5372 applies (or would apply, but for this section);

(D) a position to which section 5372a applies (or would apply, but for this section);

(E) a position established under section 3104; and

(F) a position in a category as to which a designation is in effect under subsection (i).

(b) Authority under this section—

(1) may be granted or exercised only with respect to a position—

(A) which requires expertise of an extremely high level in a scientific, technical, professional, or administrative field; and

(B) which is critical to the agency's successful accomplishment of an important mission; and

(2) may be granted or exercised only to the extent necessary to recruit or retain an individual exceptionally well qualified for the position.

(c) The Office of Management and Budget, in consultation with the Office of Personnel Management, may, upon the request of the head of an agency, grant authority to fix the rate of basic pay for 1 or more positions in such agency in accordance with this section.

(d)(1) The rate of basic pay fixed under this section by an agency head may not be less than the rate of basic pay (including any comparability payments) which would then otherwise be payable for the position involved if this section had never been enacted.

(2) Basic pay may not be fixed under this section at a rate greater than the rate payable for level I of the Executive Schedule, except upon written approval of the President.

(e) The authority to fix the rate of basic pay under this section for a position shall terminate—

(1) whenever the Office of Management and Budget determines (in accordance with such procedures and subject to such terms or conditions as such Office by regulation prescribes) that 1 or more of the requirements of subsection (b) are no longer met; or

(2) as of such date as such Office may otherwise specify, except that termination under this paragraph may not take effect before the authority has been available for such position for at least 1 calendar year.

(f) The Office of Management and Budget may not authorize the exercise of authority under this section with respect to more than 800 positions at any time, of which not more than 30 may, at any such time, be positions the rate of basic pay for which would otherwise be determined under subchapter II.

(g) The Office of Management and Budget shall consult with the Office of Personnel Management before prescribing regulations under this section or making any decision to grant or terminate any authority under this section.

(h) The Office of Management and Budget shall report to the Committee on Post Office and Civil Service of the House of Representatives and the Committee on Governmental Affairs of the Senate each year, in writing, on the operation of this section. Each report under this subsection shall include—

(1) the number of positions, in the aggregate and by agency, for which higher rates of pay were authorized or paid under this section during any part of the period covered by such report; and

(2) the name of each employee to whom a higher rate of pay was paid under this section during any portion of the period covered by such report, the rate on rates paid under this section during such period, the dates between which each such higher rate was paid, and the rate or rates that would have been paid but for this section.

(i)(1) For the purpose of this subsection, the term "position" means the work, consisting of the duties and responsibilities, assignable to an employee, except that such term does not include any position under subsection (a)(2)(A)–(E).

(2) At the request of an agency head, the President may designate 1 or more categories of positions within such agency to be treated, for purposes of this section, as positions within the meaning of subsection (a)(2).

(Added Pub. L. 101–509, title V, §529 [title I, §103(a)], Nov. 5, 1990, 104 Stat. 1427, 1444; amended Pub. L. 102–378, §2(34), Oct. 2, 1992, 106 Stat. 1350.)

REFERENCES IN TEXT

Level I of the Executive Schedule, referred to in subsec. (d)(2), is set out in section 5312 of this title.

AMENDMENTS

1992—Subsec. (a)(2)(E), (F). Pub. L. 102–378, §2(34)(A), added subpars. (E) and (F).
Subsec. (i). Pub. L. 102–378, §2(34)(B), added subsec. (i).

EFFECTIVE DATE

Section effective on such date as the President shall determine, but not earlier than 90 days, and not later than 180 days, after Nov. 5, 1990, see section 529 [title III, §305] of Pub. L. 101–509, set out as an Effective Date of 1990 Amendment note under section 5301 of this title.

ABOLITION OF HOUSE COMMITTEE ON POST OFFICE AND CIVIL SERVICE

Committee on Post Office and Civil Service of House of Representatives abolished by House Resolution No. 6, One Hundred Fourth Congress, Jan. 4, 1995. References to Committee on Post Office and Civil Service treated as referring to Committee on Government Reform and Oversight, see section 1(b) of Pub. L. 104–14, set out as a note preceding section 21 of Title 2, The Congress. Committee on Government Reform and Over-

sight of House of Representatives changed to Committee on Government Reform of House of Representatives by House Resolution No. 5, One Hundred Sixth Congress, Jan. 6, 1999.

DELEGATION OF FUNCTIONS

Authority of President under subsec. (i)(2) of this section delegated to Director of Office of Management and Budget by Ex. Ord. No. 12828, §2, Jan. 5, 1993, 58 F.R. 2965, set out as a note under section 3502 of this title.

SECTION REFERRED TO IN OTHER SECTIONS

This section is referred to in sections 5304, 5948, 9502 of this title; title 42 section 237.

§ 5378. Police forces of the Bureau of Engraving and Printing and the United States Mint

(a) The Secretary of the Department of the Treasury, or his designee, in his sole discretion shall fix the rates of basic pay for positions within the police forces of the United States Mint and the Bureau of Engraving and Printing without regard to the pay provisions of title 5, United States Code, except that no entry-level police officer shall receive basic pay for a calendar year that is less than the basic rate of pay for General Schedule GS–7 and no executive security official shall receive basic compensation for a calendar year that exceeds the basic rate of pay for General Schedule GS–15.

(b) For the purpose of this section, the term "police forces of the Bureau of Engraving and Printing and the United States Mint" means the employees of the Department of the Treasury who are appointed, under the authority of the Secretary of the Treasury, as police officers for the protection of the Bureau of Engraving and Printing and the United States Mint buildings and property.

(Added Pub. L. 101–509, title V, §529 [title I, §109(a)(1)(A)], Nov. 5, 1990, 104 Stat. 1427, 1451; amended Pub. L. 104–52, title V, §521, Nov. 19, 1995, 109 Stat. 494; Pub. L. 105–61, title I, §121, Oct. 10, 1997, 111 Stat. 1289.)

REFERENCES IN TEXT

The General Schedule, referred to in subsec. (a), is set out under section 5332 of this title.

AMENDMENTS

1997—Subsec. (a). Pub. L. 105–61 amended subsec. (a) generally. Prior to amendment, subsec. (a) consisted of pars. (1) to (8) providing maximum levels of General Schedule at which Secretary of the Treasury was to set basic rates of pay for positions in police forces of Bureau of Engraving and Printing and United States Mint.
1995—Subsec. (a)(8). Pub. L. 104–52, which directed amendment of this section by adding par. (8), was executed by adding par. (8) at end of subsec. (a) to reflect the probable intent of Congress.

EFFECTIVE DATE; CONVERSION AND SAVINGS PROVISIONS

Section 529 [title I, §109(c)] of Pub. L. 101–509 provided that:
"(1) This section and the amendments made by this section [enacting this section, amending section 5102 of this title, and enacting provisions set out as a note below] shall become effective on the first day of the first applicable pay period beginning on or after the 30th day following the date of enactment of this Act [Nov. 5, 1990].
"(2)(A) A special pay rate (as defined in subparagraph (B)) shall apply to an individual holding a position if—

"(i) as a result of the initial exercise of authority with respect to such position under the amendment made by subsection (a)(1)(A) [enacting this section], such individual would (but for this paragraph) be paid—

"(I) at the step of the grade for which such special pay rate is then in effect; or

"(II) at a level which is between steps for which special pay rates are then in effect; and

"(ii) such position is within the area or location with respect to which that special pay rate or those special pay rates, as applicable, are then in effect.

The Secretary of the Treasury shall prescribe regulations for determining which special pay rate shall apply in a situation described in clause (i)(II).

"(B) For the purpose of this paragraph, the term 'special pay rate' means a rate which—

"(i) is established under section 5303 of title 5, United States Code (or a succeeding provision of law);

"(ii) is applicable to positions within the police forces of the Bureau of Engraving and Printing and the United States Mint; and

"(iii) has been in effect (including any adjustments under section 5303(d) of such title) since on or before the effective date of this section.

"(3) No rate of basic pay in effect immediately before this section takes effect shall be reduced by reason of the enactment of this section."

SPECIAL PAY RATES NOT AFFECTED

Section 529 [title I, § 109(b)] of Pub. L. 101–509, as amended by Pub. L. 102–378, § 3(1), Oct. 2, 1992, 106 Stat. 1355, provided that: "Nothing in this section or in any amendment made by this section [enacting this section, amending section 5102 of this title, and enacting provisions set out as a note above] shall—

"(1) affect any special pay rate under section 5303 of title 5, United States Code, established before this section takes effect; or

"(2) impair any authority to fix or adjust special pay rates under such section 5303 (or a succeeding provision of law) for positions within the police forces of the Bureau of Engraving and Printing and the United States Mint."

[Amendment by Pub. L. 102–378 to section 529 [title I, § 109(b)] of Pub. L. 101–509, set out above, effective Nov. 5, 1990, see section 9(b)(6) of Pub. L. 102–378, set out as an Effective Date of 1992 Amendment note under section 6303 of this title.]

SECTION REFERRED TO IN OTHER SECTIONS

This section is referred to in section 5102 of this title.

§ 5379. Student loan repayments

(a)(1) For the purpose of this section—

(A) the term "agency" means an agency under subparagraph (A), (B), (C), (D), or (E) of section 4101(1) of this title; and

(B) the term "student loan" means—

(i) a loan made, insured, or guaranteed under part B of title IV of the Higher Education Act of 1965 (20 U.S.C. 1071 et seq.);

(ii) a loan made under part D or E of title IV of the Higher Education Act of 1965 (20 U.S.C. 1087a et seq., 1087aa et seq.); and

(iii) a health education assistance loan made or insured under part A of title VII of the Public Health Service Act (42 U.S.C. 292 et seq.) or under part E of title VIII of such Act (42 U.S.C. 297a et seq.).

(2) An employee shall be ineligible for benefits under this section if the employee occupies a position that is excepted from the competitive service because of its confidential, policy-determining, policy-making, or policy-advocating character.

(b)(1) The head of an agency may, in order to recruit or retain highly qualified personnel, establish a program under which the agency may agree to repay (by direct payments on behalf of the employee) any student loan previously taken out by such employee.

(2) Payments under this section shall be made subject to such terms, limitations, or conditions as may be mutually agreed to by the agency and employee concerned, except that the amount paid by an agency under this section may not exceed—

(A) $6,000 for any employee in any calendar year; or

(B) a total of $40,000 in the case of any employee.

(3) Nothing in this section shall be considered to authorize an agency to pay any amount to reimburse an employee for any repayments made by such employee prior to the agency's entering into an agreement under this section with such employee.

(c)(1) An employee selected to receive benefits under this section must agree in writing, before receiving any such benefit, that the employee will—

(A) remain in the service of the agency for a period specified in the agreement (not less than 3 years), unless involuntarily separated; and

(B) if separated involuntarily on account of misconduct, or voluntarily, before the end of the period specified in the agreement, repay to the Government the amount of any benefits received by such employee from that agency under this section.

(2) The payment agreed to under paragraph (1)(B) of this subsection may not be required of an employee who leaves the service of such employee's agency voluntarily to enter into the service of any other agency unless the head of the agency that authorized the benefits notifies the employee before the effective date of such employee's entrance into the service of the other agency that payment will be required under this subsection.

(3) If an employee who is involuntarily separated on account of misconduct or who (excluding any employee relieved of liability under paragraph (2) of this subsection) is voluntarily separated before completing the required period of service fails to repay the amount agreed to under paragraph (1)(B) of this subsection, a sum equal to the amount outstanding is recoverable by the Government from the employee (or such employee's estate, if applicable) by—

(A) setoff against accrued pay, compensation, amount of retirement credit, or other amount due the employee from the Government; and

(B) such other method as is provided by law for the recovery of amounts owing to the Government.

The head of the agency concerned may waive, in whole or in part, a right of recovery under this subsection if it is shown that recovery would be against equity and good conscience or against the public interest.

(4) Any amount repaid by, or recovered from, an individual (or an estate) under this sub-

section shall be credited to the appropriation account from which the amount involved was originally paid. Any amount so credited shall be merged with other sums in such account and shall be available for the same purposes and period, and subject to the same limitations (if any), as the sums with which merged.

(d) An employee receiving benefits under this section from an agency shall be ineligible for continued benefits under this section from such agency if the employee—

(1) separates from such agency; or

(2) does not maintain an acceptable level of performance, as determined under standards and procedures which the agency head shall by regulation prescribe.

(e) In selecting employees to receive benefits under this section, an agency shall, consistent with the merit system principles set forth in paragraphs (1) and (2) of section 2301(b) of this title, take into consideration the need to maintain a balanced workforce in which women and members of racial and ethnic minority groups are appropriately represented in Government service.

(f) Any benefit under this section shall be in addition to basic pay and any other form of compensation otherwise payable to the employee involved.

(g) The Director of the Office of Personnel Management, after consultation with heads of a representative number and variety of agencies and any other consultation which the Director considers appropriate, shall prescribe regulations containing such standards and requirements as the Director considers necessary to provide for reasonable uniformity among programs under this section.

(h)(1) Each head of an agency shall maintain, and annually submit to the Director of the Office of Personnel Management, information with respect to the agency on—

(A) the number of Federal employees selected to receive benefits under this section;

(B) the job classifications for the recipients; and

(C) the cost to the Federal Government of providing the benefits.

(2) The Director of the Office of Personnel Management shall prepare, and annually submit to Congress, a report containing the information submitted under paragraph (1), and information identifying the agencies that have provided benefits under this section.

(Added Pub. L. 101–510, div. A, title XII, § 1206(b)(1), Nov. 5, 1990, 104 Stat. 1659; amended Pub. L. 106–398, § 1 [[div. A], title XI, § 1122(a), (b), (d)], Oct. 30, 2000, 114 Stat. 1654, 1654A–316.)

REFERENCES IN TEXT

The Higher Education Act of 1965, referred to in subsec. (a)(1)(B)(i), (ii), is Pub. L. 89–329, Nov. 8, 1965, 79 Stat. 1219, as amended. Parts B, D, and E of title IV of the Act are classified to parts B (§ 1071 et seq.), C (§ 1087a et seq.), and D (§ 1087aa et seq.), respectively, of subchapter IV of chapter 28 of Title 20, Education. For complete classification of this Act to the Code, see Short Title note set out under section 1001 of Title 20 and Tables.

The Public Health Service Act, referred to in subsec. (a)(1)(B)(iii), is act July 1, 1944, ch. 373, 58 Stat. 682, as

amended. Part A of title VII of the Act is classified generally to part A (§ 292 et seq.) of subchapter V of chapter 6A of Title 42, The Public Health and Welfare. Part E of title VIII of the Act is classified generally to part E (§ 297a et seq.) of subchapter VI of chapter 6A of Title 42. For complete classification of this Act to the Code, see Short Title note set out under section 201 of Title 42 and Tables.

AMENDMENTS

2000—Subsec. (a)(1)(B)(i). Pub. L. 106–398, § 1 [[div. A], title XI, § 1122(a)(1)], inserted "(20 U.S.C. 1071 et seq.)" before semicolon.

Subsec. (a)(1)(B)(ii). Pub. L. 106–398, § 1 [[div. A], title XI, § 1122(a)(2)], substituted "part D or E of title IV of the Higher Education Act of 1965 (20 U.S.C. 1087a et seq., 1087aa et seq.)" for "part E of title IV of the Higher Education Act of 1965".

Subsec. (a)(1)(B)(iii). Pub. L. 106–398, § 1 [[div. A], title XI, § 1122(a)(3)], substituted "part A of title VII of the Public Health Service Act (42 U.S.C. 292 et seq.) or under part E of title VIII of such Act (42 U.S.C. 297a et seq.)" for "part C of title VII of Public Health Service Act or under part B of title VIII of such Act".

Subsec. (a)(2). Pub. L. 106–398, § 1 [[div. A], title XI, § 1122(b)(1)], amended par. (2) generally. Prior to amendment, par. (2) read as follows: "An employee shall be ineligible for benefits under this section if such employee occupies a position which—

"(A) is excepted from the competitive service because of its confidential, policy-determining, policy-making, or policy-advocating character; or

"(B) is not subject to subchapter III of this chapter."

Subsec. (b)(1). Pub. L. 106–398, § 1 [[div. A], title XI, § 1122(b)(2)], struck out "professional, technical, or administrative" after " highly qualified".

Subsec. (h). Pub. L. 106–398, § 1 [[div. A], title XI, § 1122(d)], added subsec. (h).

REGULATIONS

Pub. L. 106–398, § 1 [[div. A], title XI, § 1122(c)], Oct. 30, 2000, 114 Stat. 1654, 1654A–316, provided that:

"(1) Not later than 60 days after the date of the enactment of this Act [Oct. 30, 2000], the Director of the Office of Personnel Management shall issue proposed regulations under section 5379(g) of title 5, United States Code. The Director shall provide for a period of not less than 60 days for public comment on the regulations.

"(2) Not later than 240 days after the date of the enactment of this Act [Oct. 30, 2000], the Director shall issue final regulations."

SECTION REFERRED TO IN OTHER SECTIONS

This section is referred to in title 10 section 1745.

[§ 5380. Repealed. Pub. L. 102–378, § 8(a), Oct. 2, 1992, 106 Stat. 1359]

Section, added Pub. L. 101–510, div. A, title XII, § 1206(i)(1), Nov. 5, 1990, 104 Stat. 1662, related to pay authority for critical positions. See section 5377 of this title. Pub. L. 102–378, § 8(a), repealed Pub. L. 101–510, § 1206(i)(1), and provided that this title shall read as if section 1206(i)(1) had not been enacted.

Pub. L. 101–510, § 1206(i)(3), provided that (A) unless section 5380 of this title did not take effect as provided in subpar. (B), such section would cease to be in effect on the earlier of Oct. 1, 1992, or the date of the enactment of the Federal Employees Pay Comparability Act of 1990 [Nov. 5, 1990], and (B) section 5380 of this title would not take effect if the Federal Employees Pay Comparability Act of 1990 [Pub. L. 101–509] was enacted before the date of the enactment of this Act [Nov. 5, 1990]. Pub. L. 102–378, § 8(a), repealed Pub. L. 101–510, § 1206(i)(3), and provided that this title shall read as if section 1206(i)(3) had not been enacted.

EFFECTIVE DATE OF REPEAL

Repeal effective Nov. 5, 1990, see section 9(b)(6) of Pub. L. 102–378, set out as an Effective Date of 1992 Amendment note under section 6303 of this title.

SUBCHAPTER VIII—PAY FOR THE SENIOR EXECUTIVE SERVICE

SUBCHAPTER REFERRED TO IN OTHER SECTIONS

This subchapter is referred to in section 5948 of this title; title 38 section 7425.

§ 5381. Definitions

For the purpose of this subchapter, "agency", "Senior Executive Service position", "career appointee", and "senior executive" have the meanings set forth in section 3132(a) of this title.

(Added Pub. L. 95–454, title IV, § 407(a), Oct. 13, 1978, 92 Stat. 1171; amended Pub. L. 101–136, title VI, § 625(b), Nov. 3, 1989, 103 Stat. 823.)

AMENDMENTS

1989—Pub. L. 101–136 inserted "'career appointee'," before "and".

EFFECTIVE DATE

Subchapter effective 9 months after Oct. 13, 1978, and congressional review of provisions of sections 401 through 412 of Pub. L. 95–454, see section 415(a)(1), (b) of Pub. L. 95–454, set out as a note under section 3131 of this title.

§ 5382. Establishment and adjustment of rates of pay for the Senior Executive Service

(a) There shall be 5 or more rates of basic pay for the Senior Executive Service, and each senior executive shall be paid at one of the rates. The rates of basic pay shall be initially established and thereafter adjusted by the President subject to subsection (b) of this section.

(b) In setting rates of basic pay, the lowest rate for the Senior Executive Service shall not be less than the minimum rate of basic pay payable under section 5376 and the highest rate shall not exceed the rate for level IV of the Executive Schedule. The payment of the rates shall not be subject to the pay limitation of section 5306(e) or 5373 of this title.

(c) Subject to subsection (b) of this section, effective at the beginning of the first applicable pay period commencing on or after the first day of the month in which an adjustment takes effect under section 5303 of this title in the rates of pay under the General Schedule, each rate of basic pay for the Senior Executive Service shall be adjusted by an amount determined by the President to be appropriate.

(d) The rates of basic pay that are established and adjusted under this section shall be printed in the Federal Register and shall supersede any prior rates of basic pay for the Senior Executive Service.

(Added Pub. L. 95–454, title IV, § 407(a), Oct. 13, 1978, 92 Stat. 1171; amended Pub. L. 101–509, title V, § 529 [title I, § 101(b)(4)(B), (6)(A), (9)(I)], Nov. 5, 1990, 104 Stat. 1427, 1439, 1440, 1442.)

REFERENCES IN TEXT

Level IV of the Executive Schedule, referred to in subsec. (b), is set out in section 5315 of this title.

The General Schedule, referred to in subsec. (c), is set out under section 5332 of this title.

AMENDMENTS

1990—Subsec. (b). Pub. L. 101–509, § 529 [title I, § 101(b)(6)(A), (9)(I)], substituted "under section 5376" for "for GS–16 of the General Schedule" and "5306(e)" for "5308".

Subsec. (c). Pub. L. 101–509, § 529 [title I, § 101(b)(4)(B)], substituted "5303" for "5305" and struck out at end "The adjusted rates of basic pay for the Senior Executive Service shall be included in the report transmitted to the Congress by the President under section 5305(a)(3) or (c)(1) of this title."

EFFECTIVE DATE OF 1990 AMENDMENT

Amendment by Pub. L. 101–509 effective on such date as the President shall determine, but not earlier than 90 days, and not later than 180 days, after Nov. 5, 1990, see section 529 [title III, § 305] of Pub. L. 101–509, set out as a note under section 5301 of this title.

PAY INCREASES

2001—The President, under Ex. Ord. No. 13182, Dec. 23, 2000, 65 F.R. 82879, 66 F.R. 10057, set out as a note under section 5332 of this title, adjusted the rates of basic pay for the Senior Executive Service effective on the first day of the first applicable pay period beginning on or after Jan. 1, 2001, as follows:

ES–1	$109,100
ES–2	114,200
ES–3	119,400
ES–4	125,500
ES–5	125,700
ES–6	125,700

2000—Ex. Ord. No. 13144, Dec. 21, 1999, 64 F.R. 72237, which provided for adjustment of pay rates effective Jan. 1, 2000, was superseded by Ex. Ord. No. 13182, Dec. 23, 2000, 65 F.R. 82879, 66 F.R. 10057, set out as a note under section 5332 of this title.

1999—Ex. Ord. No. 13106, Dec. 7, 1998, 63 F.R. 68151, which provided for adjustment of pay rates effective Jan. 1, 1999, was substantially superseded by Ex. Ord. No. 13144, Dec. 21, 1999, 64 F.R. 72237.

1998—Ex. Ord. No. 13071, Dec. 29, 1997, 62 F.R. 68521, which provided for adjustment of pay rates effective Jan. 1, 1998, was superseded by Ex. Ord. No. 13106, Dec. 7, 1998, 63 F.R. 68151.

1997—Ex. Ord. No. 13033, Dec. 27, 1996, 61 F.R. 68987, which provided for adjustment of pay rates effective Jan. 1, 1997, was superseded by Ex. Ord. No. 13071, Dec. 29, 1997, 62 F.R. 68521.

1996—Ex. Ord. No. 12984, Dec. 28, 1995, 61 F.R. 237, which provided for adjustment of pay rates effective Jan. 1, 1996, was superseded by Ex. Ord. No. 13033, Dec. 27, 1996, 61 F.R. 68987.

1995—Ex. Ord. No. 12944, Dec. 28, 1994, 60 F.R. 309, which continued pay rates, was superseded by Ex. Ord. No. 12984, Dec. 28, 1995, 61 F.R. 237.

1993—Ex. Ord. No. 12826, Dec. 30, 1992, 57 F.R. 62909, which provided for adjustment of pay rates effective Jan. 1, 1993, was superseded by Ex. Ord. No. 12944, Dec. 28, 1994, 60 F.R. 309.

1992—Ex. Ord. No. 12786, Dec. 26, 1991, 56 F.R. 67453, which provided for adjustment of pay rates effective Jan. 1, 1992, was superseded by Ex. Ord. No. 12826, Dec. 30, 1992, 57 F.R. 62909.

1991—Ex. Ord. No. 12736, Dec. 12, 1990, 55 F.R. 51385, which provided for adjustment of pay rates effective Jan. 1, 1991, was superseded by Ex. Ord. No. 12786, Dec. 26, 1991, 56 F.R. 67453.

1990—Ex. Ord. No. 12698, Dec. 23, 1989, 54 F.R. 53473, which provided for adjustment of pay rates effective Jan. 1, 1990, was superseded by Ex. Ord. No. 12736, Dec. 12, 1990, 55 F.R. 51385.

1989—Ex. Ord. No. 12663, Jan. 6, 1989, 54 F.R. 791, which provided for adjustment of pay rates effective Jan. 1, 1989, was superseded by Ex. Ord. No. 12698, Dec. 23, 1989, 54 F.R. 53473.

1988—Ex. Ord. No. 12622, Dec. 31, 1987, 53 F.R. 222, which provided for adjustment of pay rates effective Jan. 1, 1988, was superseded by Ex. Ord. No. 12663, Jan. 6, 1989, 54 F.R. 791.

1987—Ex. Ord. No. 12578, Dec. 31, 1986, 52 F.R. 505, which provided for adjustment of pay rates effective

Jan. 1, 1987, was superseded by Ex. Ord. No. 12622, Dec. 31, 1987, 53 F.R. 222.

1985—Ex. Ord. No. 12496, Dec. 28, 1984, 50 F.R. 211, as amended by Ex. Ord. No. 12540, Dec. 30, 1985, 51 F.R. 577, which provided for adjustment of pay rates effective Jan. 1, 1985, was superseded by Ex. Ord. No. 12578, Dec. 31, 1986, 52 F.R. 505.

1984—Ex. Ord. No. 12456, Dec. 30, 1983, 49 F.R. 347, as amended by Ex. Ord. No. 12477, May 23, 1984, 49 F.R. 22041; Ex. Ord. No. 12487, Sept. 14, 1984, 49 F.R. 36493, which provided for adjustment of pay rates effective Jan. 1, 1984, was superseded by Ex. Ord. No. 12496, Dec. 28, 1984, 50 F.R. 211, as amended by Ex. Ord. No. 12540, Dec. 30, 1985, 51 F.R. 577.

1982—Ex. Ord. No. 12387, Oct. 8, 1982, 47 F.R. 44981, which provided for adjustment of pay rates effective Oct. 1, 1982, was superseded by Ex. Ord. No. 12456, Dec. 30, 1983, 49 F.R. 347, as amended Ex. Ord. No. 12477, May 23, 1984, 49 F.R. 22041; Ex. Ord. No. 12487, Sept. 14, 1984, 49 F.R. 36493.

Maximum rate payable after Dec. 17, 1982, increased from $58,500 to $67,200, see Pub. L. 97–377, title I, §129(b)–(d), set out as a note under section 5318 of this title.

Limitations on use of funds for fiscal year ending Sept. 30, 1983, appropriated by any Act to pay salary or pay of any individual in legislative, executive, or judicial branch in position equal to or above level V of Executive Schedule, see section 101(e) of Pub. L. 97–276, as amended, set out as a note under section 5318 of this title.

1981—Ex. Ord. No. 12330, Oct. 15, 1981, 46 F.R. 50921, which provided for adjustment of pay rates effective Oct. 1, 1981, was superseded by Ex. Ord. No. 12387, Oct. 8, 1982, 47 F.R. 44981.

Limitations on use of funds for fiscal year ending Sept. 30, 1982, appropriated by any Act to pay salary or pay of any individual in legislative, executive, or judicial branch in position equal to or above level V of Executive Schedule, see sections 101(g) and 141 of Pub. L. 97–92, set out as a note under section 5318 of this title.

1980—Ex. Ord. No. 12248, Oct. 16, 1980, 45 F.R. 69199, which provided for adjustment of pay rates effective Oct. 1, 1980, was superseded by Ex. Ord. No. 12330, Oct. 15, 1981, 46 F.R. 50921.

Limitations on use of funds for fiscal year ending Sept. 30, 1981, appropriated by any Act to pay salary or pay of any individual in legislative, executive, or judicial branch in position equal to or above level V of Executive Schedule, see section 101(c) of Pub. L. 96–536, as amended, set out as a note under section 5318 of this title.

1979—Ex. Ord. No. 12165, Oct, 9, 1979, 44 F.R. 58671, as amended by Ex. Ord. No. 12200, Mar. 12, 1980, 45 F.R. 16443, which provided for adjustment of pay rates effective Oct. 1, 1979, was superseded by Ex. Ord. No. 12248, Oct. 16, 1980, 45 F.R. 69199.

Applicability to funds appropriated by any Act for fiscal year ending Sept. 30, 1980, of limitation of section 304 of Pub. L. 95–391 on use of funds to pay salary or pay of any individual in legislative, executive, or judicial branch in position equal to or above level V of Executive Schedule, see section 101 of Pub. L. 96–86, set out as a note under section 5318 of this title.

EXECUTIVE ORDER NO. 12592

Ex. Ord. No. 12592, Apr. 10, 1987, 52 F.R. 13417, as amended by Ex. Ord. No. 12609, Sept. 23, 1987, 52 F.R. 36211, which related to the establishment, functions, administration, and termination of the President's Commission on Compensation of Career Federal Executives, was revoked by Ex. Ord. No. 12692, Sept. 29, 1989, 54 F.R. 40627, formerly set out as a note under section 14 of the Federal Advisory Committee Act in the Appendix to this title.

SECTION REFERRED TO IN OTHER SECTIONS

This section is referred to in sections 3151, 3161, 3393a, 4507, 5383, 5384 of this title; title 3 section 115; title 7 section 2009aa–1; title 10 section 1602; title 15 section 1511e; title 20 section 1018; title 22 sections 3962, 4154; title 26 section 7803; title 28 sections 594, 995; title 29 sections 715, 772, 782, 783, 792, 794b; title 31 sections 325, 733; title 35 section 3; title 40 App. section 106; title 42 sections 902, 903, 1317, 14196.

§ 5383. Setting individual senior executive pay

(a) Each appointing authority shall determine, in accordance with criteria established by the Office of Personnel Management, which of the rates established under section 5382 of this title shall be paid to each senior executive under such appointing authority.

(b) Members of the Senior Executive Service shall be subject to the limitation under section 5307.

(c) Except for any pay adjustment under section 5382 of this title, the rate of basic pay for any senior executive may not be adjusted more than once during any 12-month period.

(d) The rate of basic pay for any career appointee may be reduced from any rate of basic pay to any lower rate of basic pay only if the career appointee receives a written notice of the reduction at least 15 days in advance of the reduction.

(e)(1) This subsection applies to—

(A) any individual who, after serving at least 5 years of current continuous service in 1 or more positions in the competitive service, is appointed, without any break in service, as a career appointee; and

(B) any individual who—

(i) holds a position which is converted from the competitive service to a career reserved position in the Senior Executive Service; and

(ii) as of the conversion date, has at least 5 years of current continuous service in 1 or more positions in the competitive service.

(2)(A) The initial rate of pay for a career appointee who is appointed under the circumstances described in paragraph (1)(A) may not be less than the rate of basic pay last payable to that individual immediately before being so appointed.

(B) The initial rate of pay for a career appointee following the position's conversion (as described in paragraph (1)(B)) may not be less than the rate of basic pay last payable to that individual immediately before such position's conversion.

(Added Pub. L. 95–454, title IV, §407(a), Oct. 13, 1978, 92 Stat. 1171; amended Pub. L. 96–166, §3, Dec. 29, 1979, 93 Stat. 1273; Pub. L. 98–615, title III, §305, Nov. 8, 1984, 98 Stat. 3219; Pub. L. 101–509, title V, §529 [title I, §101(b)(7)], Nov. 5, 1990, 104 Stat. 1427, 1440; Pub. L. 102–175, §2, Dec. 2, 1991, 105 Stat. 1222; Pub. L. 102–378, §2(35), Oct. 2, 1992, 106 Stat. 1351.)

AMENDMENTS

1992—Subsec. (b). Pub. L. 102–378 amended subsec. (b) generally. Prior to amendment, subsec. (b) read as follows:

"(1) In no event may the aggregate amount paid to a senior executive during any fiscal year under sections 4507, 5382, 5384, and 5948 of this title exceed the annual rate payable for positions at level I of the Executive Schedule in effect at the end of such fiscal year.

"(2)(A) Any amount which is not paid to a senior executive during a fiscal year because of the limitation under paragraph (1) of this subsection shall be paid to that individual in a lump sum at the beginning of the following fiscal year.

"(B) Any amount paid under this paragraph during a fiscal year shall be taken into account for purposes of applying the limitation under paragraph (1) of this subsection with respect to such fiscal year.

"(C) The Office of Personnel Management shall prescribe regulations, consistent with section 5582 of this title, under which payment under this paragraph shall be made in the case of any individual whose death precludes payment under subparagraph (A) of this paragraph."

1991—Subsec. (e). Pub. L. 102–175 added subsec. (e).

1990—Subsec. (b)(1). Pub. L. 101–509, which directed that "5304(j)," be struck out after the reference to section 4507, could not be executed because "5304(j)," does not appear in text.

1984—Subsec. (b). Pub. L. 98–615 designated existing provisions as par. (1) and added par. (2).

1979—Subsec. (b). Pub. L. 96–166 inserted reference to section 5948.

EFFECTIVE DATE OF 1984 AMENDMENT

Amendment by Pub. L. 98–615 effective following expiration of 90-day period beginning on Nov. 8, 1984, see section 307 of Pub. L. 98–615, set out as a note under section 3393 of this title.

SENIOR EXECUTIVE SERVICE; MAXIMUM AGGREGATE AMOUNT PAYABLE, ETC.; REPORT

Pub. L. 98–168, title III, §301(a), Nov. 29, 1983, 97 Stat. 1112, required Office of Personnel Management to study and, within 12 months after Nov. 29, 1983, submit to each House of Congress a report on effect which 5 U.S.C. 5383(b) (relating to maximum aggregate amount payable to a member of Senior Executive Service in a fiscal year) has had with respect to recruitment, retention, and morale of career appointees in Senior Executive Service.

SECTION REFERRED TO IN OTHER SECTIONS

This section is referred to in section 5347 of this title; title 20 section 4709.

§ 5384. Performance awards in the Senior Executive Service

(a)(1) To encourage excellence in performance by career appointees, performance awards shall be paid to career appointees in accordance with the provisions of this section.

(2) Such awards shall be paid in a lump sum and shall be in addition to the basic pay paid under section 5382 of this title or any award paid under section 4507 of this title.

(b)(1) No performance award under this section shall be paid to any career appointee whose performance was determined to be less than fully successful at the time of the appointee's most recent performance appraisal and rating under subchapter II of chapter 43 of this title.

(2) The amount of a performance award under this section shall be determined by the agency head but may not be less than 5 percent nor more than 20 percent of the career appointee's rate of basic pay.

(3) The aggregate amount of performance awards paid under this section by an agency during any fiscal year may not exceed the greater of—

(A) an amount equal to 10 percent of the aggregate amount of basic pay paid to career appointees in such agency during the preceding fiscal year; or

(B) an amount equal to 20 percent of the average of the annual rates of basic pay paid to career appointees in such agency during the preceding fiscal year.

(c)(1) Performance awards paid by any agency under this section shall be based on recommendations by performance review boards established by such agency under section 4314 of this title.

(2) not[1] less than a majority of the members of any review board referred to in paragraph (1) shall be career appointees whenever making recommendations under such paragraph with respect to a career appointee. The requirement of the preceding sentence shall not apply in any case in which the Office of Personnel Management determines that there exists an insufficient number of career appointees available to comply with the requirement.

(d) The Office of Personnel Management may issue guidance to agencies concerning the proportion of Senior Executive Service salary expenses that may be appropriately applied to payment of performance awards and the distribution of awards.

(Added Pub. L. 95–454, title IV, §407(a), Oct. 13, 1978, 92 Stat. 1172; amended Pub. L. 98–615, title III, §302, Nov. 8, 1984, 98 Stat. 3217; Pub. L. 101–136, title VI, §625(a), Nov. 3, 1989, 103 Stat. 822; Pub. L. 105–277, div. A, §101(h) [title VI, §632(a)], Oct. 21, 1998, 112 Stat. 2681–480, 2681–523.)

AMENDMENTS

1998—Subsec. (b)(3). Pub. L. 105–277 substituted "10 percent" for "3 percent" in subpar. (A) and substituted "20 percent" for "15 percent" in subpar. (B).

1989—Subsec. (c). Pub. L. 101–136 designated existing provisions as par. (1) and added par. (2).

1984—Subsec. (b)(2). Pub. L. 98–615, §302(1), substituted "but may not be less than 5 percent nor more than 20 percent" for "but may not exceed 20 percent".

Subsec. (b)(3). Pub. L. 98–615, §302(2), substituted provisions limiting the aggregate amount of performance awards paid under this section by an agency during any fiscal year to the greater of 3 percent of the aggregate basic pay of career appointees in that agency during the preceding fiscal year or 15 percent of the average of the annual rates of basic pay of such appointees during such fiscal year for provisions limiting the number of career appointees paid performance awards under this section during any fiscal year to 50 percent of the number of Senior Executive Service positions in such agency, except for an agency having less than 4 such positions.

EFFECTIVE DATE OF 1998 AMENDMENT

Pub. L. 105–277, div. A, §101(h) [title VI, §632(b)], Oct. 21, 1998, 112 Stat. 2681–480, 2681–523, provided that: "The amendments made by this section [amending this section] shall take effect on October 1, 1998, or the date of enactment of this Act [Oct. 21, 1998], whichever is later."

EFFECTIVE DATE OF 1984 AMENDMENT

Amendment by Pub. L. 98–615 effective following expiration of 90-day period beginning on Nov. 8, 1984, see section 307 of Pub. L. 98–615, set out as a note under section 3393 of this title.

LIMITATION ON NUMBER OF PERFORMANCE AWARDS FOR CAREER APPOINTEES

Section 306(c) of S. 2939, Ninety-seventh Congress, 2nd Session, as reported Sept. 22, 1982, and incorporated by

---

[1] So in original. Probably should be capitalized.

reference in Pub. L. 97–276, § 101(e), Oct. 2, 1982, 96 Stat. 1189, to be effective as if enacted into law, provided that: "None of the funds appropriated by this Act or any other Act shall be used by any agency to pay performance awards in fiscal year 1983 under section 5384 of title 5, United States Code, or any comparable personnel system established on or after October 13, 1978, to more than 20 per centum of the number of Senior Executive Service or comparable personnel system positions in such agency: *Provided,* That an agency with less than five Senior Executive Service employees or equivalent positions may grant one such performance award."

Similar provisions were contained in the following acts:

Pub. L. 97–51, §§ 101(c), 124, Oct. 1, 1981, 95 Stat. 959, 965.

Pub. L. 96–536, § 101(c), Dec. 16, 1980, 94 Stat. 3167.

Pub. L. 96–369, § 101(c), Oct. 1, 1980, 94 Stat. 1352.

Pub. L. 96–304, title III, § 303, July 8, 1980, 94 Stat. 927.

SECTION REFERRED TO IN OTHER SECTIONS

This section is referred to in sections 3151, 4314, 4507, 9505 of this title; title 10 section 1606; title 22 section 3965; title 31 section 733; title 38 section 7404.

§ 5385. Regulations

The Office of Personnel Management shall prescribe regulations to carry out the purpose of this subchapter.

(Added Pub. L. 95–454, title IV, § 407(a), Oct. 13, 1978, 92 Stat. 1172.)

SUBCHAPTER IX—SPECIAL OCCUPATIONAL PAY SYSTEMS

AMENDMENTS

1992—Pub. L. 102–378, § 2(36), Oct. 2, 1992, 106 Stat. 1351, struck out subchapter analysis, consisting of item 5391 "Definitions" and item 5392 "Establishment of special occupational pay systems".

SUBCHAPTER REFERRED TO IN OTHER SECTIONS

This subchapter is referred to in sections 5361, 5363, 5948 of this title.

§ 5391. Definitions

For the purposes of this subchapter, "agency", "employee", and "position" have the meanings given them by section 5102.

(Added Pub. L. 101–509, title V, § 529 [title I, § 105(a)(1)], Nov. 5, 1990, 104 Stat. 1427, 1447.)

EFFECTIVE DATE

Subchapter effective on such date as the President shall determine, but not earlier than 90 days, and not later than 180 days, after Nov. 5, 1990, see section 529 [title III, § 305] of Pub. L. 101–509, set out as an Effective Date of 1990 Amendment note under section 5301 of this title.

§ 5392. Establishment of special occupational pay systems

(a) Authority under this section may be exercised with respect to any occupation or group of occupations to which subchapter III applies (or would apply but for this section).

(b) Subject to subsection (a), the President's pay agent (as referred to in section 5304(d)) may establish one or more special occupational pay systems for any positions within occupations or groups of occupations that the pay agent determines, for reasons of good administration,

should not be classified under chapter 51 or subject to subchapter III.

(c) In establishing special occupational pay systems, the pay agent shall—

(1) identify occupations or groups of occupations for which chapter 51 and subchapter III do not function adequately;

(2) consider alternative approaches for determining the pay for employees in positions in such occupations or groups of occupations;

(3) give thorough consideration to the views of agencies employing such employees and labor organizations representing such employees, as well as other interested parties;

(4) publish a proposed plan for determining the pay of such employees in the Federal Register;

(5) conduct one or more public hearings;

(6) provide each House of Congress with a report at least 90 days in advance of the date the system is to take effect setting forth the details of the proposed plan; and

(7) not later than 30 days before the date the system is to take effect, publish in the Federal Register the details of the final plan for the special occupational pay system.

(d) A special occupational pay system may not—

(1) provide for a waiver of any law, rule, or regulation that could not be waived under section 4703(c); or

(2) provide a rate of basic pay for any employee in excess of the rate payable for level V of the Executive Schedule.

(e) Subject to subsection (d)(2), effective at the beginning of the first applicable pay period commencing on or after the first day of the month in which an adjustment takes effect under section 5303 in the rates of pay under the General Schedule, each rate of pay established under this section shall be adjusted by such amount as the Office considers appropriate.

(Added Pub. L. 101–509, title V, § 529 [title I, § 105(a)(1)], Nov. 5, 1990, 104 Stat. 1427, 1448.)

REFERENCES IN TEXT

Level V of the Executive Schedule, referred to in subsec. (d)(2), is set out in section 5316 of this title.

The General Schedule, referred to in subsec. (e), is set out under section 5332 of this title.

[CHAPTER 54—REPEALED]

[§§ 5401 to 5410. Repealed. Pub. L. 103–89, § 3(a)(1), Sept. 30, 1993, 107 Stat. 981]

Section 5401, added Pub. L. 95–454, title V, § 501, Oct. 13, 1978, 92 Stat. 1180; amended Pub. L. 97–346, § 2, Oct. 15, 1982, 96 Stat. 1647; Pub. L. 98–615, title II, § 201(a), Nov. 8, 1984, 98 Stat. 3208; Pub. L. 102–378, § 2(37), Oct. 2, 1992, 106 Stat. 1351, stated purpose of chapter to provide a performance management and recognition system.

Section 5402, added Pub. L. 95–454, title V, § 501, Oct. 13, 1978, 92 Stat. 1181; amended Pub. L. 98–615, title II, § 201(a), Nov. 8, 1984, 98 Stat. 3208, related to applicability of chapter.

Section 5403, added Pub. L. 95–454, title V, § 501, Oct. 13, 1978, 92 Stat. 1182; amended Pub. L. 98–615, title II, § 201(a), Nov. 8, 1984, 98 Stat. 3209; Pub. L. 101–509, title V, § 529 [title I, § 101(b)(4)(C)], Nov. 5, 1990, 104 Stat. 1427, 1439; Pub. L. 102–378, § 2(38), Oct. 2, 1992, 106 Stat. 1351, related to general pay increases.

Section 5404, added Pub. L. 95–454, title V, § 501, Oct. 13, 1978, 92 Stat. 1183; amended Pub. L. 98–615, title II,

§201(a), Nov. 8, 1984, 98 Stat. 3210; Pub. L. 101–103, §3(a), Sept. 30, 1989, 103 Stat. 670, related to merit increases.

Section 5405, added Pub. L. 95–454, title V, §501, Oct. 13, 1978, 92 Stat. 1183; amended Pub. L. 98–615, title II, §201(a), Nov. 8, 1984, 98 Stat. 3211; Pub. L. 101–509, title V, §529 [title I, §101(b)(3)(C)], Nov. 5, 1990, 104 Stat. 1427, 1439, related to pay administration.

Section 5406, added Pub. L. 98–615, title II, §201(a), Nov. 8, 1984, 98 Stat. 3211; amended Pub. L. 101–103, §4, Sept. 30, 1989, 103 Stat. 671; Pub. L. 102–22, §2(b), Mar. 28, 1991, 105 Stat. 71, related to performance awards.

Section 5407, added Pub. L. 98–615, title II, §201(a), Nov. 8, 1984, 98 Stat. 3213, related to cash award program.

Section 5408, added Pub. L. 98–615, title II, §201(a), Nov. 8, 1984, 98 Stat. 3214, required annual reports by Office of Personnel Management.

Section 5409, added Pub. L. 98–615, title II, §201(a), Nov. 8, 1984, 98 Stat. 3214, directed Office of Personnel Management to prescribe regulations.

Section 5410, added Pub. L. 98–615, title II, §201(a), Nov. 8, 1984, 98 Stat. 3214; amended Pub. L. 101–103, §2, Sept. 30, 1989, 103 Stat. 670; Pub. L. 102–22, §2(c), Mar. 28, 1991, 105 Stat. 71; Pub. L. 103–89, §2, Sept. 30, 1993, 107 Stat. 981, related to termination of chapter and accompanying regulations.

EFFECTIVE DATE OF REPEAL

Repeal effective Nov. 1, 1993, see section 3(c) of Pub. L. 103–89, set out as an Effective Date of 1993 Amendment note under section 3372 of this title.

TREATMENT OF EMPLOYEES COVERED BY SYSTEM AS OF TERMINATION DATE

Section 4 of Pub. L. 103–89 provided that:

"(a) DEFINITIONS.—For purposes of this section—

"(1) the term 'employee' means an individual employed by an agency (within the meaning of section 7103(a)(3) of title 5, United States Code);

"(2) the term 'performance management and recognition system' means the performance management and recognition system under chapter 54 of title 5, United States Code;

"(3) the term 'basic pay' does not include any amount payable under section 302 [set out as a note under section 5304 of this title] or title IV [see Short Title set out in a note under section 5305 of this title] of FEPCA or section 5304 or 5304a of title 5, United States Code;

"(4) the term 'pay rate', as used in clauses (iii) through (v) of subsection (c)(2)(B), is used in the same way as such term is used under section 5335(a) of title 5, United States Code; and

"(5) the term 'FEPCA' means the Federal Employees Pay Comparability Act of 1990 [section 529 [§§1–412] of Pub. L. 101–509, see Short Title of 1990 Amendment; Rules of Construction note set out under section 5301 of this title] (contained in the Treasury, Postal Service and General Government Appropriations Act, 1991 (Public Law 101–509; 104 Stat. 1427)).

"(b)   APPLICABILITY.—Notwithstanding section 5332(a)(1) of title 5, United States Code (as amended by section 3(b)(1)(F)), or any other provision of law, the rate of basic pay for an employee covered by the performance management and recognition system on October 31, 1993, shall be determined in accordance with this section so long as such employee continues, without a break in service of more than 3 days, to occupy any position—

"(1) which is in the same grade of the General Schedule, and the same agency, as the position which such employee occupied on October 31, 1993; and

"(2) to which the provisions of chapter 54 of title 5, United States Code (as in effect on October 31, 1993) would apply if such provisions had remained in effect.

"(c) SPECIAL RULES.—

"(1) IN GENERAL.—The rate of basic pay for an employee who is subject to this section shall be the rate payable to such employee on October 31, 1993, subject to paragraph (2).

"(2) ADJUSTMENTS.—Adjustments in the rate of basic pay for an employee who is subject to this section shall be made in accordance with the relevant provisions of title 5, United States Code, or otherwise applicable provisions of law, subject to the following:

"(A) DEEM RATES AND POSITIONS TO BE UNDER THE GENERAL SCHEDULE.—For purposes of applying subchapters I and III of chapter 53 of such title (and the provisions of section 302 [set out as a note under section 5304 of this title] and title IV [see Short Title set out in a note under section 5305 of this title] of FEPCA with respect to any payment under any of those provisions)—

"(i) the rate of basic pay determined under this section for an employee shall be treated as a rate of basic pay described in section 5302(8) of such title;

"(ii) the position then currently occupied by an employee who is subject to this section shall be deemed to be a 'General Schedule position' within the meaning of section 5302(9) of such title; and

"(iii) any employee who is subject to this section shall be considered to be a 'General Schedule employee' (as referred to in section 302(b) of FEPCA).

"(B) SPECIAL RULES RELATING TO PROVISIONS GOVERNING STEP-INCREASES.—For purposes of applying the provisions of sections 5335 and 5336 of title 5, United States Code, with respect to any employee who is subject to this section—

"(i) any reference in such provisions to a 'step-increase' shall be considered to mean an increase equal to one-ninth of the difference between the minimum and maximum rates of pay for the applicable grade of the General Schedule;

"(ii) any reference in such provisions to the 'next higher rate within the grade' shall be considered to mean the rate of basic pay which exceeds such employee's then current rate of basic pay by the amount of a step-increase;

"(iii) if the employee's rate of basic pay is less than the rate for pay rate 4 of the applicable grade, such employee's rate of basic pay shall be governed by paragraph (1) of section 5335(a) of such title;

"(iv) if the employee's rate of basic pay is equal to or greater than the rate for pay rate 4 but less than the rate for pay rate 7 of the applicable grade, such employee's rate of basic pay shall be governed by paragraph (2) of section 5335(a) of such title; and

"(v) if the employee's rate of basic pay is equal to or greater than the rate for pay rate 7 but less than the maximum rate of the applicable grade, such employee's rate of basic pay shall be governed by paragraph (3) of section 5335(a) of such title.

No rate of basic pay for an employee may be increased, as a result of this subparagraph (or any provision of law to which any clause of this subparagraph relates), if or to the extent that the resulting rate would exceed the maximum rate for the grade of the position occupied by such employee.

"(d) REGULATIONS.—The Office of Personnel Management shall prescribe any regulations which may be necessary for the administration of this section."

PERFORMANCE AWARDS FOR FISCAL YEAR 1994

Section 5(b) of Pub. L. 103–89 provided that: "Notwithstanding section 2 [amending former section 5410 of this title to extend termination date of this chapter], for purposes of applying section 5406 of title 5, United States Code, the amount under subsection (c)(1)(A)(ii) of such section 5406 with respect to awards for work performed during fiscal year 1994 shall, for each agency subject to such section 5406, be deemed to be zero."

CHAPTER 55—PAY ADMINISTRATION

AMENDMENTS

1999—Pub. L. 106–65, div. A, title VI, §651(a)(2), Oct. 5, 1999, 113 Stat. 664, struck out item 5532 "Employment of retired members of the uniformed services; reduction in retired or retainer pay."

1998—Pub. L. 105–277, div. A, §101(h) [title VI, §628(b)], Oct. 21, 1998, 112 Stat. 2681–480, 2681–521, added item 5545b.

1994—Pub. L. 103–329, title VI, §633(b)(3), Sept. 30, 1994, 108 Stat. 2427, added item 5545a.

1993—Pub. L. 103–94, §9(b)(1), Oct. 6, 1993, 107 Stat. 1010, which directed amendment of table of chapters for chapter 55 of this title by adding item 5520a, was executed by adding item 5520a to table of sections for this chapter to reflect the probable intent of Congress.

1992—Pub. L. 102–484, div. D, title XLIV, §4436(a)(2), Oct. 23, 1992, 106 Stat. 2724, added item 5597.

Pub. L. 102–378, §2(44)(B), (45)(B), Oct. 2, 1992, 106 Stat. 1352, 1353, struck out item 5550 "Pay for Sunday and overtime work; employees of nonappropriated fund instrumentalities" and added item 5553.

1990—Pub. L. 101–509, title V, §529 [title I, §107(b)], Nov. 5, 1990, 104 Stat. 1427, 1449, added item 5524a.

---

[1] Section catchline amended by Pub. L. 97–365 without corresponding amendment of chapter analysis.

1986—Pub. L. 99–399, title VIII, § 803(b), Aug. 27, 1986, 100 Stat. 883, added items 5569 and 5570.

1985—Pub. L. 99–224, § 1(b), Dec. 28, 1985, 99 Stat. 1741, substituted "and of travel, transportation and relocation expenses and allowances" for "other than travel and transportation expenses and allowances and relocation expenses" in item 5584.

1984—Pub. L. 98–525, title XV, § 1537(c)(6)(B), Oct. 19, 1984, 98 Stat. 2636, inserted "and the Department of Defense" in item 5546a.

1982—Pub. L. 97–276, § 151(c)(2), Oct. 2, 1982, 96 Stat. 1201, added item 5546a.

1978—Pub. L. 95–454, title III, § 308(f)(2), Oct. 13, 1978, 92 Stat. 1151, substituted "members of the uniformed services; reduction in retired or retainer pay" for "officers of the uniformed services; reduction in retired or retirement pay; exceptions" in item 5532.

Pub. L. 95–390, title IV, § 401(b), Sept. 29, 1978, 92 Stat. 762, added item 5550a.

1977—Pub. L. 95–30, title IV, § 408(b), May 23, 1977, 91 Stat. 157, substituted "city or county" for "city" in item 5520.

1975—Pub. L. 94–183, § 2(24), Dec. 31, 1975, 89 Stat. 1058, struck out "Sunday," after "Night," in item 5545.

1974—Pub. L. 93–340, § 1(b), July 10, 1974, 88 Stat. 294, added item 5520.

1972—Pub. L. 92–453, § 3(2), Oct. 2, 1972, 86 Stat. 760, substituted "overpayment of pay and allowances, other than travel and transportation expenses and allowances and relocation expenses" for "overpayment of pay" in item 5584.

Pub. L. 92–392, § 10(b), Aug. 19, 1972, 86 Stat. 574, added item 5550.

1970—Pub. L. 91–563, §§ 2(b), 3(b), Dec. 19, 1970, 84 Stat. 1477, substituted "jury or witness service" for "jury service in State courts" in item 5515, and "jury and witness service" for "jury service in courts of the United States" in item 5537.

1968—Pub. L. 90–616, § 1(b), Oct. 21, 1968, 82 Stat. 1212, added item 5584.

Pub. L. 90–588, § 2(c), Oct. 17, 1968, 82 Stat. 1152, added item 5519.

1967—Pub. L. 90–83, § 1(23), (26)(B), (28), (30), (35), Sept. 11, 1967, 81 Stat. 200, 201, 203, inserted items 5534a, 5595 and 5596, included Sunday rates in item 5544, Sunday and hazardous duty differential in item 5545 and Sundays in item 5546, substituted "Severance Pay and Back Pay" for "Back Pay" in heading of subchapter IX, and struck out items 5591 to 5594.

CHAPTER REFERRED TO IN OTHER SECTIONS

This chapter is referred to in section 5362 of this title.

SUBCHAPTER I—GENERAL PROVISIONS

§ 5501. Disposition of money accruing from lapsed salaries or unused appropriations for salaries

Money accruing from lapsed salaries or from unused appropriations for salaries shall be covered into the Treasury of the United States. An individual who violates this section shall be removed from the service.

(Pub. L. 89–554, Sept. 6, 1966, 80 Stat. 475.)

HISTORICAL AND REVISION NOTES

Derivation	U.S. Code	Revised Statutes and Statutes at Large
....	5 U.S.C. 50 (1st sentence; and 2d sentence, so much as relates to removal).	Aug. 5, 1882, ch. 389, § 4 (297th through 316th words), 22 Stat. 255. Aug. 23, 1912, ch. 350, § 5 (so much as relates to removal), 37 Stat. 414.

In the last sentence, the word "removed" is substituted for "summarily removed" because of the pro-

visions of the Lloyd-LaFollette Act 37 Stat. 555, as amended, and the Veterans' Preference Act of 1944, 58 Stat. 387, as amended, which are carried into this title.

Standard changes are made to conform with the definitions applicable and the style of this title as outlined in the preface to the report.

SECTION REFERRED TO IN OTHER SECTIONS

This section is referred to in title 18 section 1916.

§ 5502. Unauthorized office; prohibition on use of funds

(a) Payment for services may not be made from the Treasury of the United States to an individual acting or assuming to act as an officer in the civil service or uniformed services in an office which is not authorized by existing law, unless the office is later sanctioned by law.

(b) Except as otherwise provided by statute, public money and appropriations may not be used for pay or allowance for an individual employed by an official of the United States retired from active service.

(Pub. L. 89–554, Sept. 6, 1966, 80 Stat. 475.)

HISTORICAL AND REVISION NOTES

Derivation	U.S. Code	Revised Statutes and Statutes at Large
(a)	5 U.S.C. 52.	R.S. § 1760.
(b)	5 U.S.C. 85.	July 1, 1898, ch. 546, § 1 (3d proviso on p. 644), 30 Stat. 644.

In subsection (a), the words "in the civil service or uniformed services" are substituted for "civil, military, or naval".

In subsection (b), the words "Except as otherwise provided by statute" are added in recognition of the Act of Aug. 25, 1958, Pub. L. 85–745, 72 Stat. 838, which authorizes an office staff for former Presidents. The reference to "public money and appropriations" is added for clarity.

Standard changes are made to conform with the definitions applicable and the style of this title as outlined in the preface to the report.

§ 5503. Recess appointments

(a) Payment for services may not be made from the Treasury of the United States to an individual appointed during a recess of the Senate to fill a vacancy in an existing office, if the vacancy existed while the Senate was in session and was by law required to be filled by and with the advice and consent of the Senate, until the appointee has been confirmed by the Senate. This subsection does not apply—

(1) if the vacancy arose within 30 days before the end of the session of the Senate;

(2) if, at the end of the session, a nomination for the office, other than the nomination of an individual appointed during the preceding recess of the Senate, was pending before the Senate for its advice and consent; or

(3) if a nomination for the office was rejected by the Senate within 30 days before the end of the session and an individual other than the one whose nomination was rejected thereafter receives a recess appointment.

(b) A nomination to fill a vacancy referred to by paragraph (1), (2), or (3) of subsection (a) of this section shall be submitted to the Senate not later than 40 days after the beginning of the next session of the Senate.

(Pub. L. 89–554, Sept. 6, 1966, 80 Stat. 475.)

HISTORICAL AND REVISION NOTES

Derivation	U.S. Code	Revised Statutes and Statutes at Large
....	5 U.S.C. 56.	R.S. §1761. July 11, 1940, ch. 580, 54 Stat. 751.

Standard changes are made to conform with the definitions applicable and the style of this title as outlined in the preface to the report.

§ 5504. Biweekly pay periods; computation of pay

(a) The pay period for an employee covers two administrative workweeks. For the purpose of this subsection, "employee" means—

(1) an employee in or under an Executive agency;

(2) an employee in or under the Office of the Architect of the Capitol, the Botanic Garden, and the Library of Congress, for whom a basic administrative workweek is established under section 6101(a)(5) of this title; and

(3) an individual employed by the government of the District of Columbia;

but does not include—

(A) an employee on the Isthmus of Panama in the service of the Panama Canal Commission; or

(B) an employee or individual excluded from the definition of employee in section 5541(2) of this title other than an employee or individual excluded by section 5541(2)(xvi) of this title.

(b) When, in the case of an employee, it is necessary for computation of pay under this subsection to convert an annual rate of basic pay to a basic hourly, daily, weekly, or biweekly rate, the following rules govern:

(1) To derive an hourly rate, divide the annual rate by 2,087.

(2) To derive a daily rate, multiply the hourly rate by the number of daily hours of service required.

(3) To derive a weekly or biweekly rate, multiply the hourly rate by 40 or 80, as the case may be.

Rates are computed to the nearest cent, counting one-half and over as a whole cent. For the purpose of this subsection, "employee" means—

(A) an employee in or under an Executive agency;

(B) an employee in or under the judicial branch;

(C) an employee in or under the Office of the Architect of the Capitol, the Botanic Garden, and the Library of Congress, for whom a basic administrative workweek is established under section 6101(a)(5) of this title; and

(D) an individual employed by the government of the District of Columbia;

but does not include an employee or individual excluded from the definition of employee in section 5541(2) of this title other than an employee or individual excluded by section 5541(2)(xvi) of this title.

(c) The Office of Personnel Management may prescribe regulations, subject to the approval of the President, necessary for the administration of this section insofar as this section affects employees in or under an Executive agency.

(Pub. L. 89–554, Sept. 6, 1966, 80 Stat. 475; Pub. L. 90–83, §1(21), Sept. 11, 1967, 81 Stat. 199; Pub. L. 95–454, title IV, §408(a)(1), title IX, §906(a)(2), Oct. 13, 1978, 92 Stat. 1173, 1224; Pub. L. 96–54, §2(a)(29), Aug. 14, 1979, 93 Stat. 383; Pub. L. 96–70, title III, §3302(e)(2), Sept. 27, 1979, 93 Stat. 498; Pub. L. 99–272, title XV, §15203(a), Apr. 7, 1986, 100 Stat. 334.)

HISTORICAL AND REVISION NOTES
1966 ACT

Derivation	U.S. Code	Revised Statutes and Statutes at Large
(a)	5 U.S.C. 944(b), (d) (last 27 words, as applicable to subsection (b)).	June 30, 1945, ch. 212, §604(b), (e) (last 27 words, as applicable to subsection (b)), 59 Stat. 303, 304. July 31, 1959, Pub. L. 86–122, §1, 73 Stat. 268.
(b)	5 U.S.C. 944(c), (d) (last 27 words, less applicability to subsection (b)).	June 30, 1945, ch. 212, §604(d), (e) (last 27 words, less applicability to subsection (b)), 59 Stat. 303, 304. Oct. 28, 1949, ch. 782, §1203, 63 Stat. 973. June 20, 1958, Pub. L. 85–462, §15, 72 Stat. 214. Aug. 14, 1964, Pub. L. 88–426, §103(c), 78 Stat. 402.

In subsection (a), the words "Beginning not later than October 1, 1945" are omitted as executed. Paragraphs (1) and (3) are substituted for the words "all officers and employees of the organizations referred to in subsection (a) of this section". In paragraph (A), the words "Canal Zone Government" and "Panama Canal Company" are substituted for "The Panama Canal" and "Panama Railroad Company" on authority of the Act of Sept. 26, 1950, ch. 1049, §2(a), 64 Stat. 1038. Paragraph (B) is added on authority of former section 902, which is carried into section 5541.

In subsection (b), the exception in the last sentence is added on authority of former section 902, which is carried into section 5541.

Subsection (c) is added on authority of former section 945, which is carried into section 5548. The words "an Executive agency" are substituted for "the executive branch of the Government" to conform to the definition in section 105. Applicability of this section to employees of the General Accounting Office is based on former section 933a.

Standard changes are made to conform with the definitions applicable and the style of this title as outlined in the preface to the report.

1967 ACT

This section amends 5 U.S.C. 5504 to reflect the amendment to 5 U.S.C. 6101 by section 1(43) of this bill.

AMENDMENTS

1986—Subsec. (b). Pub. L. 99–272 struck out first sentence which provided that for pay computation purposes affecting an employee, the annual rate of basic pay established by or under statute is deemed payment for employment during 52 basic administrative workweeks of 40 hours, inserted ", in the case of an employee," after "When" in second sentence, substituted "2,087" for "2,080" in par. (1), and inserted "other than an employee or individual excluded by section 5541(2)(xvi) of this title" at end of last sentence.

1979—Subsec. (a)(A). Pub. L. 96–70 substituted "Panama Canal Commission" for "Canal Zone Government or the Panama Canal Company".

Subsec. (a)(B). Pub. L. 96–54 substituted "(xvi) of this title" for "(xvi) of this section".

1978—Subsec. (a). Pub. L. 95–454, § 408(a)(1), in par. (B) inserted reference to an employee or individual excluded by section 5541(2)(xvi).

Subsec. (c). Pub. L. 95–454, § 906(a)(2), substituted "Office of Personnel Management" for "Civil Service Commission".

Effective Date of 1986 Amendment

Section 15203(b) of Pub. L. 99–272 provided that: "The amendments made by subsection (a) [amending this section] shall be effective with respect to pay periods commencing on or after March 1, 1986."

Effective Date of 1979 Amendments

Amendment by Pub. L. 96–70 effective Oct. 1, 1979, see section 3304 of Pub. L. 96–70, set out as an Effective Date note under section 3601 of Title 22, Foreign Relations and Intercourse.

Amendment by Pub. L. 96–54 effective July 12, 1979, see section 2(b) of Pub. L. 96–54, set out as a note under section 305 of this title.

Effective Date of 1978 Amendment

Amendment by section 408(a)(1) of Pub. L. 95–454 effective 9 months after Oct. 13, 1978, and congressional review of provisions of sections 401 through 415 of Pub. L. 95–454, see section 415 of Pub. L. 95–454, set out as an Effective Date note under section 3131 of this title.

Amendment by section 906(a)(2) of Pub. L. 95–454 effective 90 days after Oct. 13, 1978, see section 907 of Pub. L. 95–454, set out as a note under section 1101 of this title.

Delegation of Functions

Functions vested in Office of Personnel Management under this section insofar as it affects officers and employees in or under executive branch of government to be performed without approval of President, see section 1(1) of Ex. Ord. No. 11228, June 14, 1965, 30 F.R. 7739, set out as a note under section 301 of Title 3, The President.

Determination of Hourly Rate

Pub. L. 97–253, title III, § 310(b), Sept. 8, 1982, 96 Stat. 799, as amended by Pub. L. 97–346, § 3(l), Oct. 15, 1982, 96 Stat. 1649; Pub. L. 98–117, § 1, Oct. 11, 1983, 97 Stat. 802, provided that:

"(1) Notwithstanding any other provision of law, effective with respect to pay periods beginning in fiscal years 1984 and 1985, and applicable in the case of an employee as defined in section 5504(b) of title 5, United States Code [subsection (b) of this section], any hourly rate derived under section 5504(b)(1) of title 5, United States Code, shall be derived by dividing the annual rate of basic pay by 2,087.

"(2) Paragraph (1) shall not apply in determining basic pay for purposes of subchapter III of chapter 83 of title 5, United States Code.

"(3) The Office of Personnel Management may prescribe regulations necessary for the administration of this subsection insofar as this subsection affects employees in or under an Executive agency.

"(4) Notwithstanding any other provision of this subsection, paragraph (1) shall not be effective with respect to pay periods beginning before the effective date of any increase under section 5305 of title 5, United States Code, in the rates of pay under the General Schedule and the rates of pay under the other statutory pay systems for fiscal year 1984."

[Section 2 of Pub. L. 98–117 provided that: "The amendment made by this Act [enacting par. (4) of this note] shall be effective as of October 1, 1983."]

Section Referred to in Other Sections

This section is referred to in sections 5332, 5505, 5545b of this title; title 2 sections 142e, 142f, 142g, 142l; title 38 section 7423; title 40 sections 166b–1d, 166b–1e.

§ 5505. Monthly pay periods; computation of pay

The pay period for an individual in the service of the United States whose pay is monthly or annual covers one calendar month, and the following rules for division of time and computation of pay for services performed govern:

(1) A month's pay is one-twelfth of a year's pay.

(2) A day's pay is one-thirtieth of a month's pay.

(3) The 31st day of a calendar month is ignored in computing pay, except that one day's pay is forfeited for one day's unauthorized absence on the 31st day of a calendar month.

(4) For each day of the month elapsing before entering the service, one day's pay is deducted from the first month's pay of the individual.

This section does not apply to an employee whose pay is computed under section 5504(b) of this title.

(Pub. L. 89–554, Sept. 6, 1966, 80 Stat. 476.)

Historical and Revision Notes

Derivation	U.S. Code	Revised Statutes and Statutes at Large
....	5 U.S.C. 84.	June 30, 1906, ch. 3914, § 6, 34 Stat. 763. June 30, 1945, ch. 212, § 604(c) (2d sentence), 59 Stat. 303.

Standard changes are made to conform with the definitions applicable and the style of this title as outlined in the preface to the report.

Section Referred to in Other Sections

This section is referred to in title 2 section 142e; title 26 section 7443.

§ 5506. Computation of extra pay based on standard or daylight saving time

When an employee as defined by section 2105 of this title or an individual employed by the government of the District of Columbia is entitled to extra pay for services performed between or after certain named hours of the day or night, the extra pay is computed on the basis of either standard or daylight saving time, depending on the time observed by law, custom, or practice where the services are performed.

(Pub. L. 89–554, Sept. 6, 1966, 80 Stat. 476.)

Historical and Revision Notes

Derivation	U.S. Code	Revised Statutes and Statutes at Large
....	5 U.S.C. 914.	Sept. 7, 1949, ch. 538, § 2, 63 Stat. 690.

Standard changes are made to conform with the definitions applicable and the style of this title as outlined in the preface to the report.

§ 5507. Officer affidavit; condition to pay

An officer required by section 3332 of this title to file an affidavit may not be paid until the affidavit has been filed.

(Pub. L. 89–554, Sept. 6, 1966, 80 Stat. 477.)

Historical and Revision Notes

Derivation	U.S. Code	Revised Statutes and Statutes at Large
....	5 U.S.C. 21b.	Dec. 11, 1926, ch. 4, § 2, 44 Stat. 919.

Standard changes are made to conform with the definitions applicable and the style of this title as outlined in the preface to the report.

§ 5508. Officer entitled to leave; effect on pay status

An officer in the executive branch and an officer of the government of the District of Columbia to whom subchapter I of chapter 63 of this title applies are not entitled to the pay of their offices solely because of their status as officers.

(Pub. L. 89–554, Sept. 6, 1966, 80 Stat. 477.)

HISTORICAL AND REVISION NOTES

Derivation	U.S. Code	Revised Statutes and Statutes at Large
....	5 U.S.C. 2061(c)(1) (last sentence).	July 2, 1953, ch. 178, § 1 "(c)(1) (last sentence)", 67 Stat. 136.

The words "including an officer of a corporation wholly owned or controlled by the United States" are omitted as unnecessary in view of the definition of "officer" in section 2104.

Standard changes are made to conform with the definitions applicable and the style of this title as outlined in the preface to the report.

§ 5509. Appropriations

There are authorized to be appropriated sums necessary to carry out the provisions of this title.

(Pub. L. 89–554, Sept. 6, 1966, 80 Stat. 477.)

HISTORICAL AND REVISION NOTES

Derivation	U.S. Code	Revised Statutes and Statutes at Large
....	[Uncodified].	June 30, 1945, ch. 212, § 609, 59 Stat. 306.
....	[Uncodified].	Oct. 28, 1949, ch. 782, § 1107, 63 Stat. 972.
....	[Uncodified].	Sept. 30, 1950, ch. 1123, § 13, 64 Stat. 1100.
....	42 U.S.C. 1370.	Sept. 1, 1954, ch. 1212, § 4(a) "Sec. 1510", 68 Stat. 1135.
....	[Uncodified].	Sept. 6, 1960, Pub. L. 86–707, § 501(a), 74 Stat. 800.

The remainder of the authority for this section is implied from the statutes from which this title is derived.

MERIT SYSTEMS PROTECTION BOARD AND OFFICE OF SPECIAL COUNSEL; AUTHORIZATION OF APPROPRIATIONS; RESTRICTION ON APPROPRIATIONS

Pub. L. 101–12, § 8(a), (b), Apr. 10, 1989, 103 Stat. 34, as amended by Pub. L. 103–424, § 1, Oct. 29, 1994, 108 Stat. 4361; Pub. L. 104–208, div. A, title I, § 101(f) [title VI, §§ 641(a), 642(a)], Sept. 30, 1996, 110 Stat. 3009–314, 3009–365, provided that:

"(a) AUTHORIZATION OF APPROPRIATIONS.—There are authorized to be appropriated, out of any moneys in the Treasury not otherwise appropriated—

"(1) for each of fiscal years 1998, 1999, 2000, 2001, and 2002[,] such sums as necessary to carry out subchapter I of chapter 12 of title 5, United States Code (as amended by this Act); and

"(2) for each of fiscal years 1993, 1994, 1995, 1996, and 1997, such sums as necessary to carry out subchapter II of chapter 12 of title 5, United States Code (as amended by this Act).

"(b) RESTRICTION RELATING TO APPROPRIATIONS UNDER THE CIVIL SERVICE REFORM ACT OF 1978.—No funds may be appropriated to the Merit Systems Protection Board or the Office of Special Counsel pursuant to section 903 of the Civil Service Reform Act of 1978 [Pub. L. 95–454] (5 U.S.C. 5509 note)."

[Pub. L. 104–208, div. A, title I, § 101(f) [title VI, §§ 641(b), 642(b)], Sept. 30, 1996, 110 Stat. 3009–314, 3009–365, provided that the amendments made by section 101(f) [title VI, §§ 641(a), 642(a)] of Pub. L. 104–208 [amending provisions set out above] were to be effective on Oct. 1, 1998.]

AUTHORIZATION OF APPROPRIATIONS

Pub. L. 95–454, title IX, § 903, Oct. 13, 1978, 92 Stat. 1224, provided that: "There are authorized to be appropriated, out of any moneys in the Treasury not otherwise appropriated, such sums as may be necessary to carry out the provisions of this Act [For classification of Pub. L. 95–454, see Tables]."

SUBCHAPTER II—WITHHOLDING PAY

SUBCHAPTER REFERRED TO IN OTHER SECTIONS

This subchapter is referred to in title 15 section 78d.

§ 5511. Withholding pay; employees removed for cause

(a) Except as provided by subsection (b) of this section, the earned pay of an employee removed for cause may not be withheld or confiscated.

(b) If an employee indebted to the United States is removed for cause, the pay accruing to the employee shall be applied in whole or in part to the satisfaction of any claim or indebtedness due the United States.

(Pub. L. 89–554, Sept. 6, 1966, 80 Stat. 477.)

HISTORICAL AND REVISION NOTES

Derivation	U.S. Code	Revised Statutes and Statutes at Large
....	5 U.S.C. 46a.	Feb. 24, 1931, ch. 287, 46 Stat. 1415.

In subsection (a), the words "From and after February 24, 1931" are omitted as executed. The word "employee" is coextensive with and substituted for "civil employee of the United States" in view of the definition of "employee" in section 2105.

Standard changes are made to conform with the definitions applicable and the style of this title as outlined in the preface to the report.

§ 5512. Withholding pay; individuals in arrears

(a) The pay of an individual in arrears to the United States shall be withheld until he has accounted for and paid into the Treasury of the United States all sums for which he is liable.

(b) When pay is withheld under subsection (a) of this section, the employing agency, on request of the individual, his agent, or his attorney, shall report immediately to the Attorney General the balance due; and the Attorney General, within 60 days, shall order suit to be commenced against the individual.

(Pub. L. 89–554, Sept. 6, 1966, 80 Stat. 477; Pub. L. 92–310, title II, § 202, June 6, 1972, 86 Stat. 202; Pub. L. 104–316, title I, § 103(b), Oct. 19, 1996, 110 Stat. 3828.)

HISTORICAL AND REVISION NOTES

Derivation	U.S. Code	Revised Statutes and Statutes at Large
....	5 U.S.C. 82.	R.S. § 1766.

In subsection (b), reference to the "General Accounting Office" is substituted for "accounting officers of the Treasury" on authority of the Act of June 10, 1921, ch. 18, title III, 42 Stat. 23. The words "on request of" are substituted for "if required to do so by" as more accurately reflecting the intent. Reference to the "Attorney General" is substituted for "Solicitor of the Treasury" and "Solicitor" on authority of section 16 of the Act of March 3, 1933, ch. 212, 47 Stat. 1517; section 5 of E.O. 6166, June 10, 1933; and section 1 of 1950 Reorg. Plan No. 2, 64 Stat. 1261.

Standard changes are made to conform with the definitions applicable and the style of this title as outlined in the preface to the report.

AMENDMENTS

1996—Subsec. (b). Pub. L. 104–316 substituted "employing agency" for "General Accounting Office".

1972—Subsec. (b). Pub. L. 92–310 struck out "and his sureties" after "against the individual".

SECTION REFERRED TO IN OTHER SECTIONS

This section is referred to in title 37 section 1007.

§ 5513. Withholding pay; credit disallowed or charge raised for payment

When the General Accounting Office, on a statement of the account of a disbursing or certifying official of the United States, disallows credit or raises a charge for a payment to an individual in or under an Executive agency otherwise entitled to pay, the pay of the payee shall be withheld in whole or in part until full reimbursement is made under regulations prescribed by the head of the Executive agency from which the payee is entitled to receive pay. This section does not repeal or modify existing statutes relating to the collection of the indebtedness of an accountable, certifying, or disbursing official.

(Pub. L. 89–554, Sept. 6, 1966, 80 Stat. 477.)

HISTORICAL AND REVISION NOTES

Derivation	U.S. Code	Revised Statutes and Statutes at Large
....	5 U.S.C. 46b.	May 26, 1936, ch. 452, 49 Stat. 1374. Aug. 3, 1950, ch. 515, 64 Stat. 393.

The words "On and after May 26, 1936" are omitted as executed. The word "official" is substituted for "officer" and "officers" as the definition of "officer" in section 2104 excludes a member of a uniformed service. The words "from the United States or from an agency or instrumentality thereof" are omitted as unnecessary.

Standard changes are made to conform with the definitions applicable and the style of this title as outlined in the preface to the report.

§ 5514. Installment deduction for indebtedness to the United States

(a)(1) When the head of an agency or his designee determines that an employee, member of the Armed Forces or Reserve of the Armed Forces, is indebted to the United States for debts to which the United States is entitled to be repaid at the time of the determination by the head of an agency or his designee, or is notified of such a debt by the head of another agency or his designee the amount of indebtedness may be collected in monthly installments, or at officially established pay intervals, by deduction from the current pay account of the individual. The deductions may be made from basic pay, special pay, incentive pay, retired pay, retainer pay, or, in the case of an individual not entitled to basic pay, other authorized pay. The amount deducted for any period may not exceed 15 percent of disposable pay, except that a greater percentage may be deducted upon the written consent of the individual involved. If the individual retires or resigns, or if his employment or period of active duty otherwise ends, before collection of the amount of the indebtedness is completed, deduction shall be made from subsequent payments of any nature due the individual from the agency concerned. All Federal agencies to which debts are owed and which have outstanding delinquent debts shall participate in a computer match at least annually of their delinquent debt records with records of Federal employees to identify those employees who are delinquent in repayment of those debts. The preceding sentence shall not apply to any debt under the Internal Revenue Code of 1986. Matched Federal employee records shall include, but shall not be limited to, records of active Civil Service employees government-wide, military active duty personnel, military reservists, United States Postal Service employees, employees of other government corporations, and seasonal and temporary employees. The Secretary of the Treasury shall establish and maintain an interagency consortium to implement centralized salary offset computer matching, and promulgate regulations for this program. Agencies that perform centralized salary offset computer matching services under this subsection are authorized to charge a fee sufficient to cover the full cost for such services.

(2) Except as provided in paragraph (3) of this subsection, prior to initiating any proceedings under paragraph (1) of this subsection to collect any indebtedness of an individual, the head of the agency holding the debt or his designee, shall provide the individual with—

(A) a minimum of thirty days written notice, informing such individual of the nature and amount of the indebtedness determined by such agency to be due, the intention of the agency to initiate proceedings to collect the debt through deductions from pay, and an explanation of the rights of the individual under this subsection;

(B) an opportunity to inspect and copy Government records relating to the debt;

(C) an opportunity to enter into a written agreement with the agency, under terms agreeable to the head of the agency or his designee, to establish a schedule for the repayment of the debt; and

(D) an opportunity for a hearing on the determination of the agency concerning the existence or the amount of the debt, and in the case of an individual whose repayment schedule is established other than by a written agreement pursuant to subparagraph (C), concerning the terms of the repayment schedule.

A hearing, described in subparagraph (D), shall be provided if the individual, on or before the fifteenth day following receipt of the notice described in subparagraph (A), and in accordance with such procedures as the head of the agency may prescribe, files a petition requesting such a hearing. The timely filing of a petition for hearing shall stay the commencement of collection proceedings. A hearing under subparagraph (D) may not be conducted by an individual under the supervision or control of the head of the agency, except that nothing in this sentence shall be construed to prohibit the appointment of an administrative law judge. The hearing official shall issue a final decision at the earliest practicable date, but not later than sixty days after the filing of the petition requesting the hearing.

(3) Paragraph (2) shall not apply to routine intra-agency adjustments of pay that are attributable to clerical or administrative errors or delays in processing pay documents that have occurred within the four pay periods preceding the adjustment and to any adjustment that amounts to $50 or less, if at the time of such adjustment, or as soon thereafter as practical, the individual is provided written notice of the nature and the amount of the adjustment and a point of contact for contesting such adjustment.

(4) The collection of any amount under this section shall be in accordance with the standards promulgated pursuant to sections 3711 and 3716–3718 of title 31 or in accordance with any other statutory authority for the collection of claims of the United States or any agency thereof.

(5) For purposes of this subsection—

(A) "disposable pay" means that part of pay of any individual remaining after the deduction from those earnings of any amounts required by law to be withheld; and

(B) "agency" includes executive departments and agencies, the United States Postal Service, the Postal Rate Commission, the United States Senate, the United States House of Representatives, and any court, court administrative office, or instrumentality in the judicial or legislative branches of the Government, and government corporations.

(b)(1) The head of each agency shall prescribe regulations, subject to the approval of the President, to carry out this section and section 3530(d) of title 31. Regulations prescribed by the Secretaries of the military departments shall be uniform for the military services insofar as practicable.

(2) For purposes of section 7117(a) of this title, no regulation prescribed to carry out subsection (a)(2) of this section shall be considered to be a Government-wide rule or regulation.

(c) Subsection (a) of this section does not modify existing statutes which provide for forfeiture of pay or allowances. This section and section 3530(d) of title 31 do not repeal, modify, or amend section 4837(d) or 9837(d) of title 10 or section 1007(b), (c) of title 37.

(d) A levy pursuant to the Internal Revenue Code of 1986 shall take precedence over other deductions under this section.

(Pub. L. 89–554, Sept. 6, 1966, 80 Stat. 477; Pub. L. 96–54, §2(a)(2), Aug. 14, 1979, 93 Stat. 381; Pub. L. 97–258, §3(a)(12), Sept. 13, 1982, 96 Stat. 1063; Pub. L. 97–365, §5, Oct. 25, 1982, 96 Stat. 1751; Pub. L. 97–452, §2(a)(2), Jan. 12, 1983, 96 Stat. 2478; Pub. L. 98–216, §3(a)(4), Feb. 14, 1984, 98 Stat. 6; Pub. L. 104–134, title III, §31001(h), Apr. 26, 1996, 110 Stat. 1321–363.)

HISTORICAL AND REVISION NOTES

Derivation	U.S. Code	Revised Statutes and Statutes at Large
....	5 U.S.C. 46d.	July 15, 1954, ch. 509, §§1, 2, 4, 68 Stat. 482, 483.
....	5 U.S.C. 46e.	

In subsection (a), the words "head of the agency concerned" are substituted for "Secretary of the department concerned or the head of the agency or independent establishment concerned, or one of their designees". The words "an employee, a member of the armed forces, or a Reserve of the armed forces" are co-extensive with and substituted for "an employee of the United States or any member of the Army, Navy, Air Force, Marine Corps, or Coast Guard, or a reserve component thereof" in view of the definitions in sections 2101 and 2105. The words "basic compensation" are omitted as included in "basic pay".

In subsection (b), the words "head of each agency" are substituted for "Each Secretary of a department, or head of an agency or independent establishment, as appropriate". The words "Secretaries of the military departments" are substituted for "Secretaries of the Army, Navy, and Air Force" to conform to the definition of "military department" in section 102.

In subsection (c), the words "section 4837(d) or 9837(d) of title 10 or section 1007(b), (c) of title 37" are substituted for "the provisions of the Act of May 22, 1928 (ch. 676, 45 Stat. 698)" in section 4 of the Act of July 15, 1954, on authority of the Acts of Aug. 10, 1956, ch. 1041, §49(b), 70A Stat. 640, and Sept. 7, 1962, Pub. L. 87–649, §12(b), 76 Stat. 497.

REFERENCES IN TEXT

The Internal Revenue Code of 1986, referred to in subsecs. (a)(1) and (d), is classified generally to Title 26, Internal Revenue Code.

AMENDMENTS

1996—Subsec. (a)(1). Pub. L. 104–134, §31001(h)(A)(i), inserted at end "All Federal agencies to which debts are owed and which have outstanding delinquent debts shall participate in a computer match at least annually of their delinquent debt records with records of Federal employees to identify those employees who are delinquent in repayment of those debts. The preceding sentence shall not apply to any debt under the Internal Revenue Code of 1986. Matched Federal employee records shall include, but shall not be limited to, records of active Civil Service employees government-wide, military active duty personnel, military reservists, United States Postal Service employees, employees of other government corporations, and seasonal and temporary employees. The Secretary of the Treasury shall establish and maintain an interagency consortium to implement centralized salary offset computer matching, and promulgate regulations for this program. Agencies that perform centralized salary offset computer matching services under this subsection are authorized to charge a fee sufficient to cover the full cost for such services."

Subsec. (a)(3), (4). Pub. L. 104–134, §31001(h)(A)(ii), (iii), added par. (3) and redesignated former pars. (3) and (4) as (4) and (5), respectively.

Subsec. (a)(5). Pub. L. 104–134, §31001(h)((A)(ii), redesignated par. (4) as (5).

Subsec. (a)(5)(B). Pub. L. 104–134, §31001(h)(A)(iv), amended subpar. (B) generally. Prior to amendment, subpar. (B) read as follows: "'agency' includes the United States Postal Service and the Postal Rate Commission."

Subsec. (d). Pub. L. 104–134, §31001(h)(B), added subsec. (d).

1984—Subsec. (c). Pub. L. 98–216 substituted "section 3530(d)" for "section 581d".

1983—Subsec. (a)(3). Pub. L. 97–452 substituted "sections 3711 and 3716–3718 of title 31" for "the Federal Claims Collection Act of 1966 (31 U.S.C. 951 et seq.)".

1982—Pub. L. 97–365, §5(c), substituted "indebtedness to the United States" for "indebtedness because of erroneous payment" in section catchline.

Subsec. (a). Pub. L. 97–365, §5(a), designated existing provisions as par. (1), in par. (1) as so designated substituted provisions relating to debts to which the United States is entitled to be repaid for provisions which had related to an indebtedness to the United States because of an erroneous payment made by an agency to or on behalf of an individual, inserted provisions relating to the notification of a debt by the head of another agency or his designee, substituted provisions authorizing the deduction of not to exceed 15 percent of disposable pay for provisions which had authorized the deduction of not to exceed two-thirds of the pay from which the deduction was made, and added pars. (2), (3), and (4).

Subsec. (b). Pub. L. 97–365, §5(b), designated existing provisions as par. (1) and added par. (2).

Pub. L. 97–258 substituted "section 3530(d)" for "section 581d".

1979—Subsec. (b). Pub. L. 96–54 substituted "President" for "Director of the Bureau of the Budget".

Effective Date of 1979 Amendment

Amendment by Pub. L. 96–54 effective July 12, 1979, see section 2(b) of Pub. L. 96–54, set out as a note under section 305 of this title.

Short Title of 1982 Amendment

Section 1 of Pub. L. 97–365 provided: "That this Act [enacting sections 954 and 955 of former Title 31, Money and Finance, amending this section and section 552a of this title, section 1114 of Title 18, Crimes and Criminal Procedure, sections 6103 and 7213 of Title 26, Internal Revenue Code, section 2415 of Title 28, Judiciary and Judicial Procedure, and sections 484, 951, and 952 of former Title 31, and enacting provisions set out as notes under this section and section 6103 of Title 26] may be cited as the 'Debt Collection Act of 1982'."

Delegation of Functions

Authority of President under subsec. (b) of this section to approve regulations prescribed by head of each agency to carry out this section and section 581d of Title 31, Money and Finance [31 U.S.C. 3530(d)], relating to installment deductions from pay for indebtedness because of erroneous payment, delegated to Office of Personnel Management, see section 8(1) of Ex. Ord. No. 11609, July 22, 1971, 36 F.R. 13747, set out as a note under section 301 of Title 3, The President.

Improvements in Debt Collection Procedures Under 1982 Amendments as Contained in Debt Collection Act of 1982 Inapplicable to Claims or Indebtedness Under Internal Revenue Code, Social Security Act, or Tariff Laws

Section 8(e) of Pub. L. 97–365, as amended by Pub. L. 99–514, §2, Oct. 22, 1986, 100 Stat. 2095, provided that: "Except as otherwise provided in section 4 or 7 or the foregoing provisions of this section [amending sections 6103 and 7213 of Title 26, Internal Revenue Code, and enacting provisions set out as notes under section 6103 of Title 26], nothing in this Act (or in the amendments made by this Act) [see Short Title of 1982 Amendment note above] shall apply to claims or indebtedness arising under, or amounts payable under, the Internal Revenue Code of 1986 [Title 26], the Social Security Act [section 301 et seq. of Title 42, The Public Health and Welfare], or the tariff laws of the United States [Title 19, Customs Duties]."

Collection of Indebtedness of Employees of Federal Government Resulting From Action or Suit Brought Against Employee by United States

Pub. L. 97–276, §124, Oct. 2, 1982, 96 Stat. 1195, provided that: "Notwithstanding any other provision of this joint resolution [Pub. L. 97–276], in the case of any employee of the Federal Government who is indebted to the United States, as determined by a court of the United States in an action or suit brought against such employee by the United States, the amount of the indebtedness may be collected in monthly installments, or at officially established regular pay period intervals, by deduction in reasonable amounts from the current pay account of the individual. The deductions may be made only from basic pay, special pay, incentive pay, or, in the case of an individual not entitled to basic pay, other authorized pay. Collection shall be made over a period not greater than the anticipated period of employment. The amount deducted for any period may not exceed one-fourth of the pay from which the deduction is made, unless the deduction of a greater amount is necessary to make the collection within the period of anticipated employment. If the individual retires or resigns, or if his employment otherwise ends, before collection of the amount of the indebtedness is completed, deduction shall be made from later payments of any nature due to the individual from the United States Treasury."

Section Referred to in Other Sections

This section is referred to in title 7 sections 2020, 2022; title 10 section 1055; title 16 section 470m; title 22 section 3664; title 42 sections 292r, 297b, 404.

§ 5515. Crediting amounts received for jury or witness service

An amount received by an employee as defined by section 2105 of this title (except an individual whose pay is disbursed by the Secretary of the Senate or the Chief Administrative Officer of the House of Representatives) or an individual employed by the government of the District of Columbia for service as a juror or witness during a period for which he is entitled to leave under section 6322(a) of this title, or is performing official duty under section 6322(b) of this title, shall be credited against pay payable to him by the United States or the District of Columbia with respect to that period.

(Pub. L. 89–554, Sept. 6, 1966, 80 Stat. 478; Pub. L. 91–563, §2(a), Dec. 19, 1970, 84 Stat. 1476; Pub. L. 104–186, title II, §215(5), Aug. 20, 1996, 110 Stat. 1745.)

Historical and Revision Notes

Derivation	U.S. Code	Revised Statutes and Statutes at Large
....	5 U.S.C. 30p.	June 29, 1940, ch. 446, §3, 54 Stat. 689.

Standard changes are made to conform with the definitions applicable and the style of this title as outlined in the preface to the report.

Amendments

1996—Pub. L. 104–186 substituted "Chief Administrative Officer" for "Clerk".

1970—Pub. L. 91–563 substituted "jury or witness service" for "jury service in State courts" in section catchline.

Pub. L. 91–563 authorized crediting of amounts received for jury service in courts in the District of Columbia and in territories or possessions of the United States, included amounts received for service as a witness or when performing official duty under section 6322(b) of this title, and excepted individuals whose pay is disbursed by the Secretary of the Senate or the Clerk of the House of Representatives.

§ 5516. Withholding District of Columbia income taxes

(a) The Secretary of the Treasury, under regulations prescribed by the President, shall enter into an agreement with the Mayor of the District of Columbia within 120 days of a request for agreement from the Mayor. The agreement shall provide that the head of each agency of the United States shall comply with the requirements of subchapter II of chapter 15 of title 47, District of Columbia Code, in the case of employees of the agency who are subject to income taxes imposed by that subchapter and whose regular place of employment is within the District of Columbia. The agreement may not apply to pay of an employee who is not a resident of the District of Columbia as defined in subchapter II of chapter 15 of title 47, District of Columbia Code. In the case of pay for service as a member of the armed forces, the second sentence of this subsection shall be applied by substituting "who are residents of the District of Columbia" for "whose regular place of employment is within the District of Columbia". For the purpose of this subsection, "employee" has the meaning given it by section 1551c(z) of title 47, District of Columbia Code.

(b) This section does not give the consent of the United States to the application of a statute which imposes more burdensome requirements on the United States than on other employers, or which subjects the United States or its employees to a penalty or liability because of this section.

(Pub. L. 89–554, Sept. 6, 1966, 80 Stat. 478; Pub. L. 90–623, §1(9), Oct. 22, 1968, 82 Stat. 1312; Pub. L. 94–455, title XII, §1207(a)(2), Oct. 4, 1976, 90 Stat. 1705; Pub. L. 96–54, §2(a)(30), Aug. 14, 1979, 93 Stat. 383.)

HISTORICAL AND REVISION NOTES

Derivation	U.S. Code	Revised Statutes and Statutes at Large
....	[Uncodified].	Mar. 31, 1956, ch. 154, §11 "(k)", 70 Stat. 77.

Section 2(c) "(z)" of the Act of Mar. 31, 1956, 70 Stat. 68 (section 1551c(z) of title 47, District of Columbia Code) contains a definition of "employee" that is applicable to this section. Accordingly, the last sentence of subsection (a) is added to preserve the application of the source law.

Standard changes are made to conform with the definitions applicable and the style of this title as outlined in the preface to the report.

AMENDMENTS

1979—Subsec. (a). Pub. L. 96–54 substituted "Mayor" for "Commissioner" wherever appearing.

1976—Pub. L. 94–455 struck out "pay for service as a member of the armed forces, or to" after "The agreement may not apply to" and inserted provision that in the case of service as a member of the armed forces, the second sentence shall be applied by substituting "who are residents of the District of Columbia" for "whose regular place of employment is within the District of Columbia".

1968—Subsec. (a). Pub. L. 90–623 substituted "Commissioner" for "Commissioners" in two places.

EFFECTIVE DATE OF 1979 AMENDMENT

Amendment by Pub. L. 96–54 effective July 12, 1979, see section 2(b) of Pub. L. 96–54, set out as a note under section 305 of this title.

EFFECTIVE DATE OF 1976 AMENDMENT

Section 1207(f)(1) of Pub. L. 94–455 provided that: "The amendments made by subsection (a) [amending this

section and section 5517 of this title] shall apply to wages withheld after the 120-day period following any request for an agreement after the date of the enactment of this Act [Oct. 4, 1976]."

EFFECTIVE DATE OF 1968 AMENDMENT

Amendment by Pub. L. 90–623 intended to restate without substantive change the law in effect on Oct. 22, 1968, see section 6 of Pub. L. 90–623, set out as a note under section 5334 of this title.

SECTION REFERRED TO IN OTHER SECTIONS

This section is referred to in section 5517 of this title.

§ 5517. Withholding State income taxes

(a) When a State statute—

(1) provides for the collection of a tax either by imposing on employers generally the duty of withholding sums from the pay of employees and making returns of the sums to the State, or by granting to employers generally the authority to withhold sums from the pay of employees if any employee voluntarily elects to have such sums withheld; and

(2) imposes the duty or grants the authority to withhold generally with respect to the pay of employees who are residents of the State;

the Secretary of the Treasury, under regulations prescribed by the President, shall enter into an agreement with the State within 120 days of a request for agreement from the proper State official. The agreement shall provide that the head of each agency of the United States shall comply with the requirements of the State withholding statute in the case of employees of the agency who are subject to the tax and whose regular place of Federal employment is within the State with which the agreement is made. In the case of pay for service as a member of the armed forces, the preceding sentence shall be applied by substituting "who are residents of the State with which the agreement is made" for "whose regular place of Federal employment is within the State with which the agreement is made".

(b) This section does not give the consent of the United States to the application of a statute which imposes more burdensome requirements on the United States than on other employers, or which subjects the United States or its employees to a penalty or liability because of this section. An agency of the United States may not accept pay from a State for services performed in withholding State income taxes from the pay of the employees of the agency.

(c) For the purpose of this section, "State" means a State, territory, possession, or commonwealth of the United States.

(d) For the purpose of this section and sections 5516 and 5520, the terms "serve as a member of the armed forces" and "service as a member of the Armed Forces" include—

(1) participation in exercises or the performance of duty under section 502 of title 32, United States Code, by a member of the National Guard; and

(2) participation in scheduled drills or training periods, or service on active duty for training, under section 10147 of title 10, United States Code, by a member of the Ready Reserve.

(Pub. L. 89–554, Sept. 6, 1966, 80 Stat. 478; Pub. L. 94–455, title XII, § 1207(a)(1), (b), (c), Oct. 4, 1976, 90 Stat. 1704, 1705; Pub. L. 100–180, div. A, title V, § 505(1), Dec. 4, 1987, 101 Stat. 1086; Pub. L. 103–337, div. A, title XVI, § 1677(a)(1), Oct. 5, 1994, 108 Stat. 3019; Pub. L. 105–34, title XIV, § 1462(a), Aug. 5, 1997, 111 Stat. 1057.)

HISTORICAL AND REVISION NOTES

Derivation	U.S. Code	Revised Statutes and Statutes at Large
....	5 U.S.C. 84b.	July 17, 1952, ch. 940, § 1, 66 Stat. 765. Sept. 23, 1959, Pub. L. 86–371 "Sec. 1", 73 Stat. 653.
....	5 U.S.C. 84c.	July 17, 1952, ch. 940, § 2, 66 Stat. 766. Sept. 23, 1959, Pub. L. 86–371 "Sec. 2", 73 Stat. 653.

In subsection (b), the words "after March 31, 1959" are omitted as executed.

Standard changes are made to conform with the definitions applicable and the style of this title as outlined in the preface to the report.

AMENDMENTS

1997—Subsec. (c). Pub. L. 105–34 substituted ", territory, possession, or commonwealth" for "or territory or possession".

1994—Subsec. (d)(2). Pub. L. 103–337 substituted "section 10147" for "section 270(a)".

1987—Subsec. (d). Pub. L. 100–180 struck out "do not" before "include".

1976—Subsec. (a). Pub. L. 94–455, § 1207(a)(1), (c), inserted in par. (1) provision relating to the grant to employers of the authority to withhold sums from the pay of employees if any employee voluntarily elects to have such sums withheld, inserted in par. (2) "or grants the authority" after "imposes the duty", and substituted in text following par. (2) provisions that in the case of pay for service as a member of the armed forces, the preceding sentence shall be applied by substituting "who are residents of the State with which the agreement is made" for "whose regular place of Federal employment is within the State with which the agreement is made" for provision that the agreement may not apply to pay for service as a member of the armed forces.

Subsec. (d). Pub. L. 94–455, § 1207(b), added subsec. (d).

EFFECTIVE DATE OF 1997 AMENDMENT

Section 1462(b) of Pub. L. 105–34 provided that: "The amendment made by subsection (a) [amending this section] shall take effect on January 1, 1998."

EFFECTIVE DATE OF 1994 AMENDMENT

Amendment by Pub. L. 103–337 effective Dec. 1, 1994, except as otherwise provided, see section 1691 of Pub. L. 103–337, set out as an Effective Date note under section 10001 of Title 10, Armed Forces.

EFFECTIVE DATE OF 1976 AMENDMENT

Amendment by section 1207(a)(1) of Pub. L. 94–455 applicable to wages withheld after the 120-day period following any request for an agreement after Oct. 4, 1976, see section 1207(f)(1) of Pub. L. 94–455, set out as a note under section 5516 of this title.

Section 1207(f)(2) of Pub. L. 94–455 provided that: "The amendments made by subsections (b) and (c) [amending this section] shall apply to wages withheld after the 120-day period following the date of the enactment of this Act [Oct. 4, 1976]."

EXECUTIVE ORDER NO. 10407

Ex. Ord. No. 10407, Nov. 7, 1952, 17 F.R. 10132, which related to regulations governing agreements concerning withholding of state or territorial income taxes, was

revoked by Ex. Ord. No. 11968, Jan. 31, 1977, 42 F.R. 6787, formerly set out as a note under section 5520 of this title.

SECTION REFERRED TO IN OTHER SECTIONS

This section is referred to in section 5520 of this title.

§ 5518. Deductions for State retirement systems; National Guard employees

When—

(1) a State statute provides for the payment of employee contributions to a State employee retirement system or to a State sponsored plan providing retirement, disability, or death benefits, by withholding sums from the pay of State employees and making returns of the sums withheld to State authorities or to the person or organization designated by State authorities to receive sums withheld for the program; and

(2) individuals employed by the Army National Guard and the Air National Guard, except employees of the National Guard Bureau, are eligible for membership in a State employee retirement system or other State sponsored plan;

the Secretary of Defense, under regulations prescribed by the President, shall enter into an agreement with the State within 120 days of a request for agreement from the proper State official. The agreement shall provide that the Department of Defense shall comply with the requirements of State statute as to the individuals named by paragraph (2) of this section who are eligible for membership in the State employee retirement system. The disbursing officials paying these individuals shall withhold and pay to the State employee retirement system or to the person or organization designated by State authorities to receive sums withheld for the program the employee contributions for these individuals. For the purpose of this section, "State" means a State or territory or possession of the United States including the Commonwealth of Puerto Rico.

(Pub. L. 89–554, Sept. 6, 1966, 80 Stat. 479.)

HISTORICAL AND REVISION NOTES

Derivation	U.S. Code	Revised Statutes and Statutes at Large
....	5 U.S.C. 84d.	June 15, 1956, ch. 390, 70 Stat. 283. Sept. 13, 1961, Pub. L. 87–224, § 1, 75 Stat. 496.

The words "individuals employed by" and the word "individuals" are substituted for "civilian employees of" and "employees", respectively, in view of the definition of "employee" in section 2105 which is limited to those employed by the Government of the United States. The word "civilian" is omitted as unnecessary as military personnel are not "employed". The words "disbursing officials" are substituted for "disbursing officers" as the definition of "officer" in section 2104 excludes a member of a uniformed service.

Standard changes are made to conform with the definitions applicable and the style of this title as outlined in the preface to the report.

EX. ORD. NO. 10996. WITHHOLDING OF COMPENSATION FOR STATE AND STATE-SPONSORED EMPLOYEE RETIREMENT, DISABILITY, OR DEATH BENEFITS PROGRAMS

Ex. Ord. No. 10996, Feb. 16, 1962, 27 F.R. 1521, provided:

By virtue of the authority vested in me by the act of June 15, 1956, as amended, 75 Stat. 496 (5 U.S.C. 84d) [now this section], and by section 301 of title 3 of the United States Code, and as President of the United States, it is ordered as follows:

SECTION 1. As used in this order, the term:

(a) "Employees" means civilian employees of the Army National Guard or Air National Guard of a State who are employed pursuant to section 709 of title 32 of the United States Code, and paid from Federal, appropriated funds.

(b) "State" means one of the United States, the Commonwealth of Puerto Rico, and any territory of the United States.

SEC. 2. Each agreement between the Secretary of Defense and the Governor or other proper official of a State, pursuant to the provisions of the act of June 15, 1956, as amended, with respect to withholding of compensation of certain civilian employees of the Army National Guard and the Air National Guard for purposes of State or State-sponsored employee retirement, disability, or death benefits systems, shall be entered into by the Secretary of Defense within one hundred and twenty days of the receipt of a request therefor by the Secretary from the Governor or any other proper official of any State; *Provided*, that—

(a) the law of such State provides for the payment of employee contributions to such State or State-sponsored employee retirement, disability, or death benefits systems by withholding sums from the compensation of such State employees and making returns of such sums to officials of such State or organization designated by such officials to receive sums withheld for such programs;

(b) civilian employees of the Army National Guard and the Air National Guard, other than those employed by the National Guard Bureau, are eligible for membership in a State retirement, disability, or death benefits system; and

(c) each such agreement is consistent with the provisions of the said act of June 15, 1956, as amended, and of rules and regulations issued thereunder, and contains a clause that it shall be subject to any amendments of the said act, including amendments occurring after the effective date of such agreement.

SEC. 3. Each such agreement shall:

(a) Provide that the Secretary of the Army with respect to civilian employees of the Army National Guard, and the Secretary of the Air Force with respect to civilian employees of the Air National Guard, shall comply with the requirements of such State law in the case of employee subject to the said act of June 15, 1956, as amended, who are eligible for membership in such retirement, disability, or death benefits system for State employees;

(b) Specify when the withholding of sums from the compensation of such State employees shall commence; and

(c) Provide for procedures for the withholding, the filing of the returns, and the payment of the sums withheld from compensation to the officials of the State, or organization designated by such officials to receive sums withheld for such programs, which procedures shall conform, so far as practicable, to the usual fiscal practices of the Department of the Army and the Department of the Air Force, respectively.

SEC. 4. The Secretary of the Army with respect to civilian employees of the Army National Guard, and the Secretary of the Air Force with respect to civilian employees of the Air National Guard, shall designate, or provide for the designation of, the officers or employees whose duty it shall be to withhold sums from compensation, file required returns, and direct the payment of sums so withheld, in accordance with the terms of the agreements entered into between the Secretary of Defense and the States.

SEC. 5. Nothing in this order, or in rules or regulations issued thereunder, or in any agreement entered into pursuant thereto, shall be construed as giving consent to the application of any provision of law of any State which has the effect of imposing more burdensome requirements upon the United States than it imposes upon departments, agencies, or political subdivisions of the State concerned, with respect to employees thereof who are members of the State or State-sponsored retirement, disability, or death benefits system, or which has the effect of subjecting the United States or any of its officers or employees to any penalty or liability.

SEC. 6. I hereby delegate to the Secretary of Defense authority to prescribe such rules and regulations, not inconsistent herewith, as may be necessary to effectuate further the provisions of the said act of June 15, 1956, as amended, or of this order.

SEC. 7. Except to the extent that they may be inconsistent with this order, all determinations, authorizations, regulations, rulings, certificates, orders, directives, contracts, agreements, and other actions made, issued, or entered into with respect to any function affected by this order and not revoked, superseded, or otherwise made inapplicable before the date of this order, shall continue in full force and effect until amended, modified, or terminated by appropriate authority.

SEC. 8. This order supersedes Executive Order No. 10679 of September 20, 1956.

JOHN F. KENNEDY.

§ 5519. Crediting amounts received for certain Reserve or National Guard service

An amount (other than a travel, transportation, or per diem allowance) received by an employee or individual for military service as a member of the Reserve or National Guard for a period for which he is granted military leave under section 6323(b) or (c) shall be credited against the pay payable to the employee or individual with respect to his civilian position for that period.

(Added Pub. L. 90–588, § 2(b), Oct. 17, 1968, 82 Stat. 1152; amended Pub. L. 102–378, § 2(39), Oct. 2, 1992, 106 Stat. 1351; Pub. L. 104–106, div. A, title V, § 516(b), Feb. 10, 1996, 110 Stat. 309.)

AMENDMENTS

1996—Pub. L. 104–106 substituted "granted military leave" for "entitled to leave".

1992—Pub. L. 102–378 substituted "6323(b) or (c)" for "6323(c) or (d) of this title".

SECTION REFERRED TO IN OTHER SECTIONS

This section is referred to in section 6323 of this title.

§ 5520. Withholding of city or county income or employment taxes

(a) When a city or county ordinance—

(1) provides for the collection of a tax by imposing on employers generally the duty of withholding sums from the pay of employees and making returns of the sums to a designated city or county officer, department, or instrumentality; and

(2) imposes the duty to withhold generally on the payment of compensation earned within the jurisdiction of the city or county in the case of employees whose regular place of employment is within such jurisdiction;

the Secretary of the Treasury, under regulations prescribed by the President, shall enter into an agreement with the city or county within 120 days of a request for agreement by the proper city or county official. The agreement shall provide that the head of each agency of the United

States shall comply with the requirements of the city or county ordinance in the case of any employee of the agency who is subject to the tax and (i) whose regular place of Federal employment is within the jurisdiction of the city or county with which the agreement is made or (ii) is a resident of such city or county. The agreement may not apply to pay for service as a member of the Armed Forces (other than service described in section 5517(d) of this title). The agreement may not permit withholding of a city or county tax from the pay of an employee who is not a resident of, or whose regular place of Federal employment is not within, the State in which that city or county is located unless the employee consents to the withholding.

(b) This section does not give the consent of the United States to the application of an ordinance which imposes more burdensome requirements on the United States than on other employers or which subjects the United States or its employees to a penalty or liability because of this section. An agency of the United States may not accept pay from a city or county for services performed in withholding city or county income or employment taxes from the pay of employees of the agency.

(c) For the purpose of this section—

(1) "city" means any unit of general local government which—

(A) is classified as a municipality by the Bureau of the Census, or

(B) is a town or township which, in the determination of the Secretary of the Treasury—

(i) possesses powers and performs functions comparable to those associated with municipalities,

(ii) is closely settled, and

(iii) contains within its boundaries no incorporated places, as defined by the Bureau of the Census,

within the political boundaries of which 500 or more persons are regularly employed by all agencies of the Federal Government;

(2) "county" means any unit of local general government which is classified as a county by the Bureau of the Census and within the political boundaries of which 500 or more persons are regularly employed by all agencies of the Federal Government;

(3) "ordinance" means an ordinance, order, resolution, or similar instrument which is duly adopted and approved by a city or county in accordance with the constitution and statutes of the State in which it is located and which has the force of law within such city or county; and

(4) "agency" means—

(A) an Executive agency;

(B) the judicial branch; and

(C) the United States Postal Service.

(Added Pub. L. 93–340, § 1(a), July 10, 1974, 88 Stat. 294; amended Pub. L. 94–358, § 1, July 12, 1976, 90 Stat. 910; Pub. L. 95–30, title IV, § 408(a), May 23, 1977, 91 Stat. 157; Pub. L. 95–365, § 1, Sept. 15, 1978, 92 Stat. 599; Pub. L. 100–180, div. A, title V, § 505(2), Dec. 4, 1987, 101 Stat. 1086.)

AMENDMENTS

1987—Subsec. (a). Pub. L. 100–180 inserted "(other than service described in section 5517(d) of this title)" after "Armed Forces" in penultimate sentence.

1978—Subsec. (a). Pub. L. 95–365 designated existing provisions as cl. (i), inserted ", or whose regular place of Federal employment is not within," after "not a resident of", and added cl. (ii).

1977—Pub. L. 95–30, § 408(a)(1), inserted "or county" after "city" in section catchline.

Subsec. (a). Pub. L. 95–30, § 408(a)(2), (3), substituted "city or county" for "city" in introductory provisions preceding par. (1), in par. (2), and in provisions following par. (2), and, in par. (1), substituted "a designated city or county officer, department, or instrumentality" for "the city".

Subsec. (b). Pub. L. 95–30, § 408(a)(2), substituted "city or county" for "city".

Subsec. (c). Pub. L. 95–30, § 408(a)(4), (5), added pars. (2) and (3) and redesignated former par. (2) as (4).

1976—Subsec. (c)(1). Pub. L. 94–358 substituted provision defining a city, for purposes of this section, as any unit of general local government which is classified a municipality by the Bureau of the Census, or is a town or township which in the opinion of the Secretary of the Treasury possesses powers and performs functions comparable to those associated with municipalities, is closely settled, and contains within its boundaries no incorporated places, as defined by the Bureau of the Census, within the political boundaries of which five hundred or more persons are regularly employed by all agencies of the Federal Government, for provision defining a city, for purposes of this section, as a city which is duly incorporated under the laws of a State and within the political boundaries of which five hundred or more persons are regularly employed by all agencies of the Federal Government.

EFFECTIVE DATE OF 1978 AMENDMENT

Section 2 of Pub. L. 95–365 provided that: "The amendments made by the first section of this Act [amending this section] shall take effect on the 90th day after the date of the enactment of this Act [Sept. 15, 1978]."

EFFECTIVE DATE OF 1977 AMENDMENT

Section 408(c) of Pub. L. 95–30 provided that: "The amendments made by this section [amending this section] shall take effect on the date of enactment of this Act [May 23, 1977]."

EFFECTIVE DATE OF 1976 AMENDMENT

Section 2 of Pub. L. 94–358 provided that: "The amendment made by the first section of this Act [amending this section] shall take effect on the date of the enactment of this Act [July 12, 1976]."

EFFECTIVE DATE

Section 3 of Pub. L. 93–340 provided that: "This section shall become effective on the date of enactment of this Act [July 10, 1974]. The provisions of the first section and section 2 of this Act [enacting this section and amending section 410 of Title 39, Postal Service] shall become effective on the ninetieth day following the date of enactment."

EXECUTIVE ORDER NO. 11833

Ex. Ord. No. 11833, Jan. 13, 1975, 40 F.R. 2673, which related to the withholding of city income or employment taxes by Federal agencies, was revoked by Ex. Ord. No. 11863, June 12, 1975, 40 F.R. 25413, formerly set out below.

EXECUTIVE ORDER NO. 11863

Ex. Ord. No. 11863, June 12, 1975, 40 F.R. 25431, which related to the withholding of city income or employment taxes by Federal agencies, was revoked by Ex. Ord. No. 11968, Jan. 31, 1977, 42 F.R. 6787, formerly set out below.

EXECUTIVE ORDER No. 11968

Ex. Ord. No. 11968, Jan. 31, 1977, 42 F.R. 6787, which related to the withholding of District of Columbia, State and city income or employment taxes, was revoked by Ex. Ord. No. 11997, June 22, 1977, 42 F.R. 31759, set out below.

EX. ORD. No. 11997. WITHHOLDING OF DISTRICT OF COLUMBIA, STATE, CITY AND COUNTY INCOME OR EMPLOYMENT TAXES

Ex. Ord. No. 11997, June 22, 1977, 42 F.R. 31759, provided:

By virtue of the authority vested in me by Sections 5516, 5517 and 5520 of Title 5 of the United States Code, and Section 301 of Title 3 of the United States Code, and as President of the United States of America, in order to authorize the Secretary of the Treasury to provide for the withholding of county income or employment taxes as authorized by Section 5520 of Title 5 of the United States Code as amended by Section 408 of Public Law 95–30, as well as to provide for the withholding of District of Columbia, State and city income or employment taxes, it is hereby ordered as follows:

SECTION 1. Whenever the Secretary of the Treasury enters into an agreement pursuant to Sections 5516, 5517 or 5520 of Title 5 of the United States Code, with the District of Columbia, a State, a city or a county, as the case may be, with regard to the withholding, by an agency of the United States, hereinafter referred to as an agency, of income or employment taxes from the pay of Federal employees or members of the Armed Forces, the Secretary of the Treasury shall ensure that each agreement is consistent with those sections and regulations, including this Order, issued thereunder.

SEC. 2. Each agreement shall provide (a) when tax withholding shall begin, (b) that the head of an agency may rely on the withholding certificate of an employee or a member of the Armed Forces in withholding taxes, (c) that the method for calculating the amount to be withheld for District of Columbia, State, city or county income or employment taxes shall produce approximately the tax required to be withheld by the District of Columbia or State law; or city or county ordinance, whichever is applicable, and (d) that procedures for the withholding, filing of returns, and payment of the withheld taxes to the District of Columbia, a State, a city or a county shall conform to the usual fiscal practices of agencies. Any agreement affecting members of the Armed Forces shall also provide that the head of an agency may rely on the certificate of legal residence of a member of the Armed Forces in determining his or her residence for tax withholding purposes. No agreement shall require the collection by an agency of delinquent tax liabilities of an employee or a member of the Armed Forces.

SEC. 3. The head of each agency shall designate, or provide for the designation of, the officers or employees whose duty it shall be to withhold taxes, file required returns, and direct payment of the taxes withheld, in accordance with this Order, any regulations prescribed by the Secretary of the Treasury, and the new applicable agreement.

SEC. 4. The Secretary of the Treasury is authorized to prescribe additional regulations to implement Sections 5516, 5517 and 5520 of Title 5 of the United States Code, and this Order.

SEC. 5. Executive Order No. 11968 of January 31, 1977, is hereby revoked. However, all actions heretofore taken by the President or his delegates in respect of the matters affected by this Order and in force at the time of the issuance of this Order, including any regulations prescribed or approved by the President or his delegates in respect of such matters and any existing agreements approved by his delegates, shall, except as they may be inconsistent with the provisions of this Order, remain in effect until amended, modified, or revoked pursuant to the authority conferred by this Order, unless sooner terminated by operation of law.

JIMMY CARTER.

SECTION REFERRED TO IN OTHER SECTIONS

This section is referred to in section 5517 of this title; title 39 section 410.

§ 5520a. Garnishment of pay

(a) For purposes of this section—

(1) "agency" means each agency of the Federal Government, including—

(A) an executive agency, except for the General Accounting Office;

(B) the United States Postal Service and the Postal Rate Commission;

(C) any agency of the judicial branch of the Government; and

(D) any agency of the legislative branch of the Government, including the General Accounting Office, each office of a Member of Congress, a committee of the Congress, or other office of the Congress;

(2) "employee" means an employee of an agency (including a Member of Congress as defined under section 2106);

(3) "legal process" means any writ, order, summons, or other similar process in the nature of garnishment, that—

(A) is issued by a court of competent jurisdiction within any State, territory, or possession of the United States, or an authorized official pursuant to an order of such a court or pursuant to State or local law; and

(B) orders the employing agency of such employee to withhold an amount from the pay of such employee, and make a payment of such withholding to another person, for a specifically described satisfaction of a legal debt of the employee, or recovery of attorney's fees, interest, or court costs; and

(4) "pay" means—

(A) basic pay, premium pay paid under subchapter V, any payment received under subchapter VI, VII, or VIII, severance and back pay paid under subchapter IX, sick pay, incentive pay, and any other compensation paid or payable for personal services, whether such compensation is denominated as wages, salary, commission, bonus pay or otherwise; and

(B) does not include awards for making suggestions.

(b) Subject to the provisions of this section and the provisions of section 303 of the Consumer Credit Protection Act (15 U.S.C. 1673) pay from an agency to an employee is subject to legal process in the same manner and to the same extent as if the agency were a private person.

(c)(1) Service of legal process to which an agency is subject under this section may be accomplished by certified or registered mail, return receipt requested, or by personal service, upon—

(A) the appropriate agent designated for receipt of such service of process pursuant to the regulations issued under this section; or

(B) the head of such agency, if no agent has been so designated.

(2) Such legal process shall be accompanied by sufficient information to permit prompt identification of the employee and the payments involved.

(d) Whenever any person, who is designated by law or regulation to accept service of process to which an agency is subject under this section, is effectively served with any such process or with interrogatories, such person shall respond thereto within thirty days (or within such longer period as may be prescribed by applicable State law) after the date effective service thereof is made, and shall, as soon as possible but not later than fifteen days after the date effective service is made, send written notice that such process has been so served (together with a copy thereof) to the affected employee at his or her duty station or last-known home address.

(e) No employee whose duties include responding to interrogatories pursuant to requirements imposed by this section shall be subject to any disciplinary action or civil or criminal liability or penalty for, or on account of, any disclosure of information made by such employee in connection with the carrying out of any of such employee's duties which pertain directly or indirectly to the answering of any such interrogatory.

(f) Agencies affected by legal process under this section shall not be required to vary their normal pay and disbursement cycles in order to comply with any such legal process.

(g) Neither the United States, an agency, nor any disbursing officer shall be liable with respect to any payment made from payments due or payable to an employee pursuant to legal process regular on its face, provided such payment is made in accordance with this section and the regulations issued to carry out this section. In determining the amount of any payment due from, or payable by, an agency to an employee, there shall be excluded those amounts which would be excluded under section 462(g) of the Social Security Act (42 U.S.C. 662(g)).

(h)(1) Subject to the provisions of paragraph (2), if an agency is served under this section with more than one legal process with respect to the same payments due or payable to an employee, then such payments shall be available, subject to section 303 of the Consumer Credit Protection Act (15 U.S.C. 1673), to satisfy such processes in priority based on the time of service, with any such process being satisfied out of such amounts as remain after satisfaction of all such processes which have been previously served.

(2) A legal process to which an agency is subject under section 459 of the Social Security Act (42 U.S.C. 659) for the enforcement of the employee's legal obligation to provide child support or make alimony payments, shall have priority over any legal process to which an agency is subject under this section.

(i) The provisions of this section shall not modify or supersede the provisions of section 459 of the Social Security Act (42 U.S.C. 659) concerning legal process brought for the enforcement of an individual's legal obligations to provide child support or make alimony payments.

(j)(1) Regulations implementing the provisions of this section shall be promulgated—

(A) by the President or his designee for each executive agency, except with regard to employees of the United States Postal Service, the President or, at his discretion, the Postmaster General shall promulgate such regulations;

(B) jointly by the President pro tempore of the Senate and the Speaker of the House of Representatives, or their designee, for the legislative branch of the Government; and

(C) by the Chief Justice of the United States or his designee for the judicial branch of the Government.

(2) Such regulations shall provide that an agency's administrative costs in executing a garnishment action may be added to the garnishment, and that the agency may retain costs recovered as offsetting collections.

(k)(1) No later than 180 days after the date of the enactment of this Act, the Secretaries of the Executive departments concerned shall promulgate regulations to carry out the purposes of this section with regard to members of the uniformed services.

(2) Such regulations shall include provisions for—

(A) the involuntary allotment of the pay of a member of the uniformed services for indebtedness owed a third party as determined by the final judgment of a court of competent jurisdiction, and as further determined by competent military or executive authority, as appropriate, to be in compliance with the procedural requirements of the Soldiers' and Sailors' Civil Relief Act of 1940 (50 App. U.S.C. 501 et seq.); and

(B) consideration for the absence of a member of the uniformed service from an appearance in a judicial proceeding resulting from the exigencies of military duty.

(3) The Secretaries of the Executive departments concerned shall promulgate regulations under this subsection that are, as far as practicable, uniform for all of the uniformed services. The Secretary of Defense shall consult with the Secretary of Transportation with regard to the promulgation of such regulations that might affect members of the Coast Guard when the Coast Guard is operating as a service in the Navy.

(Added Pub. L. 103–94, §9(a), Oct. 6, 1993, 107 Stat. 1007; amended Pub. L. 104–106, div. A, title VI, §643, Feb. 10, 1996, 110 Stat. 368; Pub. L. 104–193, title III, §362(b)(2), Aug. 22, 1996, 110 Stat. 2246; Pub. L. 105–85, div. A, title XI, §1105, Nov. 18, 1997, 111 Stat. 1923.)

REFERENCES IN TEXT

The date of the enactment of this Act, referred to in subsec. (k)(1), probably means the date of enactment of Pub. L. 103–94, which enacted this section and was approved Oct. 6, 1993.

The Soldiers' and Sailors' Relief Act of 1940, referred to in subsec. (k)(2)(A), is act Oct. 17, 1940, ch. 888, 54 Stat. 1178, as amended, which is classified to section 501 et seq. of Title 50, Appendix, War and National Defense. For complete classification of this Act to the Code, see section 501 of Title 50, Appendix, and Tables.

AMENDMENTS

1997—Subsec. (j)(2). Pub. L. 105–85, §1105(1), added par. (2) and struck out former par. (2) which read as follows: "Such regulations shall provide that an agency's administrative costs incurred in executing legal process to which the agency is subject under this section shall be deducted from the amount withheld from the pay of the employee concerned pursuant to the legal process."

Subsec. (k)(3), (4). Pub. L. 105–85, §1105(2), redesignated par. (4) as (3) and struck out former par. (3) which read as follows: "Regulations under this subsection may also provide that the administrative costs incurred in establishing and maintaining an involuntary allotment be deducted from the amount withheld from the pay of the member of the uniformed services concerned pursuant to such regulations."

Subsec. (*l*). Pub. L. 105–85, §1105(3), struck out subsec. (*l*) which read as follows: "The amount of an agency's administrative costs deducted under regulations prescribed pursuant to subsection (j)(2) or (k)(3) shall be credited to the appropriation, fund, or account from which such administrative costs were paid."

1996—Subsecs. (h)(2), (i). Pub. L. 104–193 substituted "section 459 of the Social Security Act (42 U.S.C. 659)" for "sections 459, 461, and 462 of the Social Security Act (42 U.S.C. 659, 661, and 662)".

Subsec. (j)(2). Pub. L. 104–106, §643(a), added par. (2) and struck out former par. (2) which read as follows: "Such regulations shall provide that an agency's administrative costs in executing a garnishment action may be added to the garnishment, and that the agency may retain costs recovered as offsetting collections."

Subsec. (k)(3), (4). Pub. L. 104–106, §643(b), added par. (3) and redesignated former par. (3) as (4).

Subsec. (*l*). Pub. L. 104–106, §643(c), added subsec. (*l*).

EFFECTIVE DATE OF 1996 AMENDMENT

Amendment by Pub. L. 104–193 effective six months after Aug. 22, 1996, see section 362(d) of Pub. L. 104–193, set out as a note under section 659 of Title 42, The Public Health and Welfare.

For provisions relating to effective date of title III of Pub. L. 104–193, see section 395(a)–(c) of Pub. L. 104–193, set out as a note under section 654 of Title 42, The Public Health and Welfare.

EFFECTIVE DATE; SAVINGS PROVISION

Section effective 120 days after Oct. 6, 1993, and not to affect any proceedings with respect to which charges were filed on or before 120 days after Oct. 6, 1993, with orders to be issued in such proceedings and appeals taken therefrom as if Pub. L. 103–94 had not been enacted, see section 12 of Pub. L. 103–94, set out as a note under section 7321 of this title.

PILOT PROGRAM ON ALTERNATIVE NOTICE OF RECEIPT OF LEGAL PROCESS FOR GARNISHMENT OF FEDERAL PAY FOR CHILD SUPPORT AND ALIMONY

Pub. L. 105–261, div. A, title X, §1061, Oct. 17, 1998, 112 Stat. 2128, provided that:

"(a) PROGRAM REQUIRED.—The Secretary of Defense shall conduct a pilot program on alternative notice procedures for withholding or garnishment of pay for the payment of child support and alimony under section 459 of the Social Security Act (42 U.S.C. 659).

"(b) PURPOSE.—The purpose of the pilot program is to test the efficacy of providing notice in accordance with subsection (c) to the person whose pay is to be withheld or garnished.

"(c) AUTHORIZATION OF ALTERNATIVE TO PROVIDING COPY OF NOTICE OR SERVICE RECEIVED BY THE SECRETARY.—(1) Under the pilot program, whenever the Secretary of Defense (acting through the DOD section 459 agent) provides a section 459 notice to an individual, the Secretary may include as part of that notice the information specified in subsection (e) in lieu of sending with that notice a copy (otherwise required pursuant to the parenthetical phrase in section 459(c)(2)(A) of the Social Security Act) of the notice or service received by the DOD section 459 agent with respect to that individual's child support or alimony payment obligations.

"(2) Under the pilot program, whenever the Secretary of Defense (acting through the DOD section 5520a agent) provides a section 5520a notice to an individual, the Secretary may include as part of that notice the information specified in subsection (e) in lieu of sending with that notice a copy (otherwise required pursuant to the second parenthetical phrase in section 5520a(c) of title 5, United States Code) of the legal process re-

ceived by the DOD section 5520a agent with respect to that individual.

"(d) DEFINITIONS.—For purposes of this section:

"(1) DOD SECTION 459 AGENT.—The term 'DOD section 459 agent' means the agent or agents designated by the Secretary of Defense under subsection (c)(1)(A) of section 459 of the Social Security Act (42 U.S.C. 659) to receive orders and accept service of process in matters related to child support or alimony.

"(2) SECTION 459 NOTICE.—The term 'section 459 notice' means, with respect to the Department of Defense, the notice required by subsection (c)(2)(A) of section 459 of the Social Security Act (42 U.S.C. 659) to be sent to an individual in writing upon the receipt by the DOD section 459 agent of notice or service with respect to the individual's child support or alimony payment obligations.

"(3) DOD SECTION 5520A AGENT.—The term 'DOD section 5520a agent' means a person who is designated by law or regulation to accept service of process to which the Department of Defense is subject under section 5520a of title 5, United States Code (including the regulations promulgated under subsection (k) of that section).

"(4) SECTION 5520A NOTICE.—The term 'section 5520a notice' means, with respect to the Department of Defense, the notice required by subsection (c) of section 5520a of title 5, United States Code, to be sent in writing to an employee (or, pursuant to the regulations promulgated under subsection (k) of that section, to a member of the Armed Forces) upon the receipt by the DOD section 5520a agent of legal process covered by that section.

"(e) ALTERNATIVE REQUIREMENTS.—The information referred to in subsection (c) that is to be included as part of a section 459 notice or section 5520a notice sent to an individual (in lieu of sending with that notice a copy of the notice or service received by the DOD section 459 agent or the DOD section 5520a agent) is the following:

"(1) A description of the pertinent court order, notice to withhold, or other order, process, or interrogatory received by the DOD section 459 agent or the DOD section 5520a agent.

"(2) The identity of the court or judicial forum involved and (in the case of a notice or process concerning the ordering of a support or alimony obligation) the case number, the amount of the obligation, and the name of the beneficiary.

"(3) Information on how the individual may obtain from the Department of Defense a copy of the notice, service, or legal process, including an address and telephone number that the individual may be contacted for the purpose of obtaining such a copy.

"(f) PERIOD OF PILOT PROGRAM.—The Secretary shall commence the pilot program not later than 90 days after the date of the enactment of this Act [Oct. 17, 1998]. The pilot program shall terminate on September 30, 2001.

"(g) REPORT.—Not later than January 1, 2001, the Secretary shall submit to Congress a report describing the experience of the Department of Defense under the authority provided by this section. The report shall include the following:

"(1) The number of section 459 notices provided by the DOD section 459 agent during the period the authority provided by this section was in effect.

"(2) The number of individuals who requested the DOD section 459 agent to provide to them a copy of the actual notice or service.

"(3) Any complaint the Secretary received by reason of not having provided the actual notice or service in the section 459 notice.

"(4) The number of section 5520a notices provided by the DOD section 5520a agent during the period the authority provided by this section was in effect.

"(5) The number of individuals who requested the DOD section 5520a agent to provide to them a copy of the actual legal process.

"(6) Any complaint the Secretary received by reason of not having provided the actual legal process in the section 5520a notice."

Ex. Ord. No. 12897. Garnishment of Federal Employees' Pay

Ex. Ord. No. 12897, Feb. 3, 1994, 59 F.R. 5517, provided:

By the authority vested in me as President by the Constitution and the laws of the United States of America, including section 5520a(j)(1)(A) of title 5, United States Code, as added by section 9 of Public Law 103–94, it is hereby ordered as follows:

Section 1. The Office of Personnel Management, in consultation with the Attorney General, is designated to promulgate regulations for the implementation of section 5520a of title 5, United States Code, with respect to civilian employees and agencies in the executive branch, except as provided in section 2 of this order.

Sec. 2. The Postmaster General is designated to promulgate regulations for the implementation of section 5520a of title 5, United States Code, with respect to employees of the United States Postal Service.

William J. Clinton.

Section Referred to in Other Sections

This section is referred to in title 22 sections 3612a, 3664; title 39 section 410.

SUBCHAPTER III—ADVANCEMENT, ALLOTMENT, AND ASSIGNMENT OF PAY

Subchapter Referred to in Other Sections

This subchapter is referred to in sections 5307, 5527 of this title; title 15 section 78d.

§ 5521. Definitions

For the purpose of this subchapter—

(1) "agency" means—

(A) an Executive agency;

(B) the judicial branch;

(C) the Library of Congress;

(D) the Government Printing Office; and

(E) the government of the District of Columbia;

(2) "employee" means an individual employed in or under an agency;

(3) "head of each agency" means—

(A) the Director of the Administrative Office of the United States Courts with respect to the judicial branch; and

(B) the Mayor of the District of Columbia with respect to the government of the District of Columbia; and

(4) "United States", when used in a geographical sense, means the several States and the District of Columbia.

(Pub. L. 89–554, Sept. 6, 1966, 80 Stat. 479; Pub. L. 90–623, §1(10), Oct. 22, 1968, 82 Stat. 1312; Pub. L. 96–54, §2(a)(31), Aug. 14, 1979, 93 Stat. 383.)

Historical and Revision Notes

Derivation	U.S. Code	Revised Statutes and Statutes at Large
....	5 U.S.C. 3071.	Sept. 26, 1961, Pub. L. 87–304, §1, 75 Stat. 662. June 24, 1965, Pub. L. 89–47, 79 Stat. 171.

In paragraph (1), the word "agency" is substituted for "department". The term "Executive agency" is substituted for the reference to "each executive department of the Government of the United States of America; each agency or independent establishment in the executive branch of such Government; each corporation wholly owned or controlled by such Government" in former section 3071(1)(A)–(C).

Paragraph (2) is added for clarity and in view of the fact that the definition of "employee" in section 2105 does not include individuals employed by the government of the District of Columbia.

In paragraph (3), the term "department head" is omitted as unnecessary.

In paragraph (4), the words "of the United States of America" are omitted as unnecessary.

Standard changes are made to conform with the definitions applicable and the style of this title as outlined in the preface to the report.

Amendments

1979—Par. (3)(B). Pub. L. 96–54 substituted "Mayor" for "Commissioner".

1968—Par. (3)(B). Pub. L. 90–623 substituted "Commissioner" for "Board of Commissioners".

Effective Date of 1979 Amendment

Amendment by Pub. L. 96–54 effective July 12, 1979, see section 2(b) of Pub. L. 96–54, set out as a note under section 305 of this title.

Effective Date of 1968 Amendment

Amendment by Pub. L. 90–623 intended to restate without substantive change the law in effect on Oct. 22, 1968, see section 6 of Pub. L. 90–623, set out as a note under section 5334 of this title.

§ 5522. Advance payments; rates; amounts recoverable

(a) The head of each agency may provide for the advance payment of the pay, allowances, and differentials, or any of them, covering a period of not more than 30 days, to or for the account of each employee of the agency (or, under emergency circumstances and on a reimbursable basis, an employee of another agency) whose departure (or that of his dependents or immediate family, as the case may be) from a place inside or outside the United States is officially authorized or ordered—

(1) from a place outside the United States from which the Secretary of State determines it is in the national interest to require the departure of some or all employees, their dependents, or both; or

(2) from any place where there is imminent danger to the life of the employee or the lives of the dependents or immediate family of the employee.

(b) Subject to adjustment of the account of an employee under section 5524 of this title and other applicable statute, the advance payment of pay, allowances, and differentials is at rates currently authorized with respect to the employee on the date the advance payment is made under agency procedures governing advance payments under this subsection. The rates so authorized may not exceed the rates to which the employee was entitled immediately before issuance of the departure order.

(c) An advance of funds under subsection (a) of this section is recoverable by the Government of the United States or the government of the District of Columbia, as the case may be, from the employee or his estate by—

(1) setoff against accrued pay, amount of retirement credit, or other amount due to the employee from the Government of the United States or the government of the District of Columbia; and

(2) such other method as is provided by law.

The head of the agency concerned may waive in whole or in part a right of recovery of an advance of funds under subsection (a) of this section, if it is shown that the recovery would be against equity and good conscience or against the public interest.

(Pub. L. 89–554, Sept. 6, 1966, 80 Stat. 480; Pub. L. 96–465, title II § 2303(a), (b), Oct. 17, 1980, 94 Stat. 2164, 2165.)

HISTORICAL AND REVISION NOTES

Derivation	U.S. Code	Revised Statutes and Statutes at Large
....	5 U.S.C. 3072.	Sept. 26, 1961, Pub. L. 87–304, § 2, 75 Stat. 662.

Standard changes are made to conform with the definitions applicable and the style of this title as outlined in the preface to the report.

AMENDMENTS

1980—Subsec. (a). Pub. L. 96–465, § 2303(a), substituted "departure" for "evacuation", substituted "is officially authorized or ordered" for "is ordered for military or other reasons which create imminent danger to the life or lives of the employee or of his dependents or immediate family", and added pars. (1) and (2).

Subsec. (b). Pub. L. 96–465, § 2303(b), substituted "departure" for "evacuation" after "issuance of the".

EFFECTIVE DATE OF 1980 AMENDMENT

Amendment by Pub. L. 96–465 effective Feb. 15, 1981, except as otherwise provided, see section 2403 of Pub. L. 96–465, set out as an Effective Date note under section 3901 of Title 22, Foreign Relations and Intercourse.

SECTION REFERRED TO IN OTHER SECTIONS

This section is referred to in sections 5523, 5524 of this title; title 31 section 3721.

§ 5523. Duration of payments; rates; active service period

(a) The head of each agency may provide for—

(1) the payment of monetary amounts covering a period of not more than 60 days to or for the account of each employee of the agency (or, under emergency circumstances and on a reimbursable basis, an employee of another agency) whose departure (or that of the employee's dependents or immediate family, as the case may be) is authorized or ordered under section 5522(a); and

(2) the termination of payment of the monetary amounts.

The President, with respect to the Executive agencies, may extend the 60-day period for not more than 120 additional days if he determines that the extension of the period is in the interest of the United States.

(b) Subject to adjustment of the account of an employee under section 5524 of this title and other applicable statute, each payment under this section is at rates of pay, allowances, and differentials, or any of them, currently authorized with respect to the employee on the date payment is made under agency procedures governing payments under this section. The rates so authorized may not exceed the rates to which the employee was entitled immediately before issuance of the departure order. An employee in an Executive agency may be granted such additional allowance payments as the President determines necessary to offset the direct added expenses incident to the departure.

(c) Each period for which payment of amounts is made under this section to or for the account of an employee is deemed, for all purposes with respect to the employee, a period of active service, without break in service, performed by the employee in the employment of the Government of the United States or the government of the District of Columbia.

(Pub. L. 89–554, Sept. 6, 1966, 80 Stat. 480; Pub. L. 96–465, title II, § 2303(c), (d), Oct. 17, 1980, 94 Stat. 2165; Pub. L. 102–138, title I, § 147(a), Oct. 28, 1991, 105 Stat. 669.)

HISTORICAL AND REVISION NOTES

Derivation	U.S. Code	Revised Statutes and Statutes at Large
....	5 U.S.C. 3073.	Sept. 26, 1961, Pub. L. 87–304, § 3, 75 Stat. 663.

Standard changes are made to conform with the definitions applicable and the style of this title as outlined in the preface to the report.

AMENDMENTS

1991—Subsec. (a)(1). Pub. L. 102–138 substituted "agency) whose departure (or that of the employee's dependents or immediate family, as the case may be) is authorized or ordered under section 5522(a); and" for "agency)—

"(A) whose departure is authorized or ordered under section 5522(a) of this title; and

"(B) who is prevented, by circumstances beyond his control and beyond the control of the Government of the United States or the government of the District of Columbia, or both, as the case may be, from performing the duties of the position which he held immediately before issuance of the departure order; and".

1980—Subsec. (a)(1). Pub. L. 96–465, § 2303(c), in subpar. (A) substituted "whose departure is authorized or ordered under section 5522(a) of this title; and" for "whose evacuation from a place inside or outside the United States is ordered for military or other reasons which create imminent danger to the life of the employee; and", and in subpar. (B) substituted "departure" for "evacuation" after "issuance of the".

Subsec. (b). Pub. L. 96–465, § 2303(d), substituted "departure" for "evacuation" in two places.

EFFECTIVE DATE OF 1980 AMENDMENT

Amendment by Pub. L. 96–465 effective Feb. 15, 1981, except as otherwise provided, see section 2403 of Pub. L. 96–465, set out as an Effective Date note under section 3901 of Title 22, Foreign Relations and Intercourse.

SECTION REFERRED TO IN OTHER SECTIONS

This section is referred to in section 5524 of this title.

§ 5524. Review of accounts

The head of each agency shall provide for—

(1) the review of the account of each employee of the agency in receipt of payments under section 5522 or 5523 of this title, or both, as the case may be; and

(2) the adjustment of the amounts of the payments on the basis of—

(A) the rates of pay, allowances, and differentials to which the employee would have been entitled under applicable statute other than this subchapter for the respective periods covered by the payments, if he had performed active service under the terms of his appointment during each period in the position he held immediately before the issuance of the applicable evacuation order; and

(B) such additional amounts as the employee is authorized to receive in accordance with a determination of the President under section 5523(b) of this title.

(Pub. L. 89–554, Sept. 6, 1966, 80 Stat. 481.)

HISTORICAL AND REVISION NOTES

Derivation	U.S. Code	Revised Statutes and Statutes at Large
....	5 U.S.C. 3074.	Sept. 26, 1961, Pub. L. 87–304, § 4, 75 Stat. 663.

Standard changes are made to conform with the definitions applicable and the style of this title as outlined in the preface to the report.

SECTION REFERRED TO IN OTHER SECTIONS

This section is referred to in sections 5522, 5523 of this title.

§ 5524a. Advance payments for new appointees

(a) The head of each agency may provide for the advance payment of basic pay, covering not more than 2 pay periods, to any individual who is newly appointed to a position in the agency.

(b)(1) Subject to adjustment of the account of an employee under paragraph (2) and other applicable statutes, the advance payment of basic pay shall be made, under agency procedures governing advance payments under this section, at the initial rate of basic pay to be payable to the employee upon the commencement of service in the position to which appointed.

(2) The head of each agency shall provide for—

(A) the review of the account of each employee of the agency in receipt of any payment under this section; and

(B) the adjustment of the amount of any such payment on the basis of the rate of basic pay to which the employee would have been entitled under applicable statute other than this section for the respective periods covered by the payments, if the employee had performed active service under the terms of such employee's appointment during each period in the position to which appointed.

(c) An advance payment under this section is recoverable by the Government of the United States or the government of the District of Columbia, as the case may be, from the employee or such employee's estate by—

(1) setoff against accrued pay, amount of retirement credit, or other amount due to the employee from the Government of the United States or the government of the District of Columbia; and

(2) such other method as is provided by law.

The head of the agency concerned may waive in whole or in part a right of recovery of an advance payment under this section if it is shown that the recovery would be against equity and good conscience or against the public interest.

(Added Pub. L. 101–509, title V, § 529 [title I, § 107(a)], Nov. 5, 1990, 104 Stat. 1427, 1449.)

EFFECTIVE DATE

Section effective on such date as the President shall determine, but not earlier than 90 days, and not later than 180 days, after Nov. 5, 1990, see section 529 [title III, § 305] of Pub. L. 101–509, set out as an Effective Date of 1990 Amendment note under section 5301 of this title.

SECTION REFERRED TO IN OTHER SECTIONS

This section is referred to in section 8906 of this title; title 38 section 7410.

§ 5525. Allotment and assignment of pay

The head of each agency may establish procedures under which each employee of the agency is permitted to make allotments and assignments of amounts out of his pay for such purpose as the head of the agency considers appropriate.

(Pub. L. 89–554, Sept. 6, 1966, 80 Stat. 481.)

HISTORICAL AND REVISION NOTES

Derivation	U.S. Code	Revised Statutes and Statutes at Large
....	5 U.S.C. 3075.	Sept. 26, 1961, Pub. L. 87–304, § 5, 75 Stat. 663.

Standard changes are made to conform with the definitions applicable and the style of this title as outlined in the preface to the report.

§ 5526. Funds available on reimbursable basis

Funds available to an agency for payment of pay, allowances, and differentials to or for the accounts of employees of the agency are available on a reimbursable basis for payment of pay, allowances, and differentials to or for the accounts of employees of another agency under this subchapter.

(Pub. L. 89–554, Sept. 6, 1966, 80 Stat. 481.)

HISTORICAL AND REVISION NOTES

Derivation	U.S. Code	Revised Statutes and Statutes at Large
....	5 U.S.C. 3078.	Sept. 26, 1961, Pub. L. 87–304, § 8, 75 Stat. 664.

The word "civilian" is omitted as unnecessary in view of the definition of "employee" in section 5521(2), and the fact that military personnel are not "employed".

Standard changes are made to conform with the definitions applicable and the style of this title as outlined in the preface to the report.

§ 5527. Regulations

(a) To the extent practicable in the public interest, the President shall coordinate the policies and procedures of the respective Executive agencies under this subchapter.

(b) The President, with respect to the Executive agencies, the head of the agency concerned, with respect to the appropriate agency outside the executive branch, and the District of Columbia Council, with respect to the government of the District of Columbia, shall prescribe and issue, or provide for the formulation and issuance of, regulations necessary and appropriate to carry out the provisions, accomplish the purposes, and govern the administration of this subchapter.

(c) The head of each Executive agency may prescribe and issue regulations, not inconsistent with the regulations of the President issued under subsection (b) of this section, necessary and appropriate to carry out his functions under this subchapter.

(Pub. L. 89–554, Sept. 6, 1966, 80 Stat. 481; Pub. L. 90–623, §1(11), Oct. 22, 1968, 82 Stat. 1312.)

HISTORICAL AND REVISION NOTES

Derivation	U.S. Code	Revised Statutes and Statutes at Large
....	5 U.S.C. 3076.	Sept. 26, 1961, Pub. L. 87–304, §6, 75 Stat. 664.

In subsection (b), the last sentence of former section 3076, which provided for the issuance of the regulations not later than December 25, 1961, and the effective date of the regulations as not later than March 25, 1962, is omitted as executed.

Standard changes are made to conform with the definitions applicable and the style of this title as outlined in the preface to the report.

AMENDMENTS

1968—Subsec. (b). Pub. L. 90–623 inserted reference to the District of Columbia Council, with respect to the government of the District of Columbia.

EFFECTIVE DATE OF 1968 AMENDMENT

Amendment by Pub. L. 90–623 intended to restate without substantive change the law in effect on Oct. 22, 1968, see section 6 of Pub. L. 90–623, set out as a note under section 5334 of this title.

TRANSFER OF FUNCTIONS

District of Columbia Council, as established by Reorg. Plan No. 3 of 1967, abolished as of noon Jan. 2, 1975, by Pub. L. 93–198, title VII, §711, Dec. 24, 1973, 87 Stat. 818, and replaced by Council of District of Columbia, as provided by section 401 of Pub. L. 93–198.

EX. ORD. NO. 10982. ADMINISTRATION OF PROVISIONS OF CHAPTER

Ex. Ord. No. 10982, Dec. 25, 1961, 27 F.R. 3, as amended by Ex. Ord. No. 12107, Dec. 28, 1978, 44 F.R. 1055; Ex. Ord. No. 12748, Feb. 1, 1991, 56 F.R. 4521, provided:

By virtue of the authority vested in me by the act of September 26, 1961 (75 Stat. 662) [this subchapter] and by section 301 of title 3 of the United States Code, and as President of the United States, it is ordered as follows:

SECTION 1. As used in this order:

(a) The term "the act" means the act of September 26, 1961 (Public Law 87–304), 75 Stat. 662 [now this subchapter].

(b) The term "Federal agency" means any executive department of the Government of the United States of America, any agency or independent establishment in the executive branch of the Government, and any corporation wholly owned or controlled by the Government.

(c) The term "foreign area" means any area (including the Trust Territory of the Pacific Islands) situated outside (1) the United States (including the District of Columbia), (2) the Commonwealth of Puerto Rico, (3) the Canal Zone, and (4) any territory or possession of the United States.

SEC. 2. (a) Except as otherwise provided by section 2(b) and section 3(c) of this order, the Secretary of State in respect of civilian employees of Federal agencies who are located in foreign areas immediately prior to an emergency evacuation, and the Office of Personnel Management in respect of all other civilian employees of Federal agencies, are hereby designated and empowered, without the approval, ratification, or other action of the President, to perform the functions conferred upon the President by section 3(a), section 3(b), and section 6(a) of the act [sections 5523(a), 5523(b), and 5527(a) of this title].

(b) The Office of Personnel Management is hereby designated and empowered to perform the functions conferred upon the President by the provisions of section 5527 of title 5, United States Code, with respect to allotments and assignments authorized by section 5525 of title 5, United States Code, and advance payments to new appointees authorized by section 5524a of title 5, United States Code, as added by section 107(a) of the Federal Employees Pay Comparability Act of 1990, as incorporated in section 529 of Public Law 101–509.

SEC. 3. The following regulations are hereby prescribed as necessary and appropriate to carry out the provisions, accomplish the purposes, and govern the administration of the act:

(a) To the maximum extent practicable, the Secretary of State, the Office of Personnel Management, and the heads of other Federal agencies shall exercise their authority under the act and this order so that employees of different Federal agencies evacuated from the same geographic area under the same general circumstances may be treated uniformly.

(b) Advance payments of compensation, allowances, and differentials, as authorized by section 2 of the act [section 5522 of this title], shall be held to the minimum period during which the order for evacuation is anticipated to continue, and shall in no event be made for a period of more than thirty days.

(c) It is hereby determined to be in the interest of the United States that payments of monetary amounts as authorized by section 3 of the act [section 5523 of this title] to and for the account of an employee whose evacuation is ordered and who is prevented from performing the duties of his position, under the circumstances set forth in section 3 of the act, should be extended beyond sixty days for not more than one hundred and twenty additional days only upon determination, pursuant to regulations of the head of the Federal agency concerned, that such additional payments are reasonably necessary to maintain a civilian staff available for performance of duty. Such payments of monetary amounts under the authority of section 3 of the act shall be terminated as of such dates as may be determined by the Secretary of State or the Office of Personnel Management, as appropriate, but not later than the date on which an employee resumes his duties at the post from which he has been evacuated or is assigned to another position.

SEC. 4. (a) The head of each Federal agency shall issue as soon as practicable such regulations as may be necessary and appropriate to carry out his functions under the act and this order.

(b) In order to coordinate the policies and procedures of the executive branch of the Government, all regulations of any Federal agency prepared for issuance under the provisions of section 6(c) of the act [section 5527(c) of this title] and section 4(a) of this order shall be submitted for prior approval to the Secretary of State, or to the Office of Personnel Management, as may be appropriate, under section 2 of this order. The Secretary of State and the Office of Personnel Management shall review such regulations for conformance with the purpose and intent of the act and of the regulations contained in section 3 of this order. No Federal agency shall make any payment under the provisions of the act or this order until such regulations have been approved by the Secretary of State, or the Office of Personnel Management, as appropriate.

SUBCHAPTER IV—DUAL PAY AND DUAL EMPLOYMENT

§ 5531. Definitions

For the purpose of section 5533 of this title—

(1) "member" has the meaning given such term by section 101(23) of title 37;

(2) "position" means a civilian office or position (including a temporary, part-time, or intermittent position), appointive or elective, in the legislative, executive, or judicial branch of the Government of the United States (in-

cluding a Government corporation and a non-appropriated fund instrumentality under the jurisdiction of the armed forces) or in the government of the District of Columbia;

(3) "retired or retainer pay" means retired pay, as defined in section 8311(3) of this title, determined without regard to subparagraphs (B) through (D) of such section 8311(3); except that such term does not include an annuity payable to an eligible beneficiary of a member or former member of a uniformed service under chapter 73 of title 10;

(4) "agency in the legislative branch" means the General Accounting Office, the Government Printing Office, the Library of Congress, the Office of Technology Assessment, the Office of the Architect of the Capitol, the United States Botanic Garden, and the Congressional Budget Office;

(5) "employee of the House of Representatives" means a congressional employee whose pay is disbursed by the Chief Administrative Officer of the House of Representatives;

(6) "employee of the Senate" means a congressional employee whose pay is disbursed by the Secretary of the Senate; and

(7) "congressional employee" has the meaning given that term by section 2107 of this title, excluding an employee of an agency in the legislative branch.

(Pub. L. 89–554, Sept. 6, 1966, 80 Stat. 482; Pub. L. 95–454, title III, § 308(b), Oct. 13, 1978, 92 Stat. 1150; Pub. L. 102–190, div. A, title VI, § 655(a)(2), Dec. 5, 1991, 105 Stat. 1391; Pub. L. 104–186, title II, § 215(6), Aug. 20, 1996, 110 Stat. 1745; Pub. L. 106–398, § 1 [[div. A], title X, § 1087(f)(2)], Oct. 30, 2000, 114 Stat. 1654, 1654A–293.)

HISTORICAL AND REVISION NOTES

Derivation	U.S. Code	Revised Statutes and Statutes at Large
....	5 U.S.C. 3101 (as applicable to 5 U.S.C. 3102(a)–(e) and 3105 (less (e))).	Aug. 19, 1964, Pub. L. 88–448, § 101 (as applicable to §§ 201(a)–(e) and 301 (less (e))), 78 Stat. 484.

In paragraph (2), the defined word "position" is substituted for "civilian office." The words "Government corporation" are substituted for "corporation owned or controlled by such Government" in view of the definition in section 103.

The definitions of "uniformed services" and "armed forces" are omitted as unnecessary in view of the definitions in section 2101.

Standard changes are made to conform with the definitions applicable and the style of this title as outlined in the preface to the report.

AMENDMENTS

2000—Pub. L. 106–398 substituted "section" for "sections 5532 and" in introductory provisions.

1996—Par. (5). Pub. L. 104–186 substituted "Chief Administrative Officer" for "Clerk".

1991—Pars. (4) to (7). Pub. L. 102–190 added pars. (4) to (7).

1978—Pub. L. 95–454 substituted " 'member' " for " 'officer' " in par. (1) and added par. (3).

EFFECTIVE DATE OF 1978 AMENDMENT

Amendment by Pub. L. 95–454 effective 90 days after Oct. 13, 1978, see section 907 of Pub. L. 95–454, set out as a note under section 1101 of this title.

DUAL PAY REQUIREMENTS FOR PAY PERIODS SUBSEQUENT TO ENACTMENT OF CIVIL SERVICE ACT OF 1978

Pub. L. 95–454, title III, § 308(g), Oct. 13, 1978, 92 Stat. 1151, provided that:

"(1) Except as provided in paragraph (2) of this subsection, the amendments made by this section [amending this section and section 5532 of this title] shall apply only with respect to pay periods beginning after the effective date of this Act [see Effective Date note set out under section 1101 of this title] and only with respect to members of the uniformed services who first receive retired or retainer pay (as defined in section 5531(3) of title 5, United States Code (as amended by this section)), after the effective date of this Act.

"(2) Such amendments shall not apply to any individual employed in a position on the date of the enactment of this Act [Oct. 13, 1978] so long as the individual continues to hold any such position (disregarding any break in service of 3 days or less) if the individual, on that date, would have been entitled to retired or retainer pay but for the fact the individual does not satisfy any applicable age requirement.

"(3) The provisions of section 5532 of title 5, United States Code, as in effect immediately before the effective date of this Act, shall apply with respect to any retired officer of a regular component of the uniformed services who is receiving retired pay on or before such date, or any individual to whom paragraph (2) applies, in the same manner and to the same extent as if the preceding subsections of this section had not been enacted."

SECTION REFERRED TO IN OTHER SECTIONS

This section is referred to in sections 8344, 8468 of this title; title 22 section 3664; title 24 section 421.

[§ 5532. Repealed. Pub. L. 106–65, div. A, title VI, § 651(a)(1), Oct. 5, 1999, 113 Stat. 664]

Section, Pub. L. 89–554, Sept. 6, 1966, 80 Stat. 482; Pub. L. 95–454, title III, § 308(a), (c)–(f)(1), Oct. 13, 1978, 92 Stat. 1149–1151; Pub. L. 97–276, § 151(b), Oct. 2, 1982, 96 Stat. 1200; Pub. L. 98–396, title III, § 306, Aug. 22, 1984, 98 Stat. 1424; Pub. L. 98–525, title XV, § 1537(b), Oct. 19, 1984, 98 Stat. 2635; Pub. L. 99–88, title I, § 100, Aug. 15, 1985, 99 Stat. 351; Pub. L. 99–500, § 101(*l*), Oct. 18, 1986, 100 Stat. 1783–308, and Pub. L. 99–591, § 101(*l*), Oct. 30, 1986, 100 Stat. 3341–308; Pub. L. 100–202, §§ 101(*l*) [title I, § 101], 106, Dec. 22, 1987, 101 Stat. 1329–358, 1329–362, 1329–433; Pub. L. 100–457, title I, Sept. 30, 1988, 102 Stat. 2129; Pub. L. 101–509, title V, § 529 [title I, § 108(a)], Nov. 5, 1990, 104 Stat. 1427, 1449; Pub. L. 101–510, div. A, title XII, § 1206(j)(1), Nov. 5, 1990, 104 Stat. 1663; Pub. L. 102–83, § 5(c)(2), Aug. 6, 1991, 105 Stat. 406; Pub. L. 102–190, div. A, title VI, § 655(a)(1), Dec. 5, 1991, 105 Stat. 1390; Pub. L. 102–378, § 8(a), Oct. 2, 1992, 106 Stat. 1359; Pub. L. 105–55, title I, § 107, Oct. 7, 1997, 111 Stat. 1184, related to employment of retired members of uniformed services and reduction in retired or retainer pay.

EFFECTIVE DATE OF REPEAL

Repeal effective Oct. 1, 1999, see section 651(c) of Pub. L. 106–65, set out as an Effective Date of 1999 Amendment note under section 1466 of Title 10, Armed Forces.

§ 5533. Dual pay from more than one position; limitations; exceptions

(a) Except as provided by subsections (b), (c), and (d) of this section, an individual is not entitled to receive basic pay from more than one position for more than an aggregate of 40 hours of work in one calendar week (Sunday through Saturday).

(b) Except as otherwise provided by subsection (c) of this section, the Office of Personnel Management, subject to the supervision and control of the President, may prescribe regulations under which exceptions may be made to the restrictions in subsection (a) of this section when appropriate authority determines that the exceptions are warranted because personal services otherwise cannot be readily obtained.

(c)(1) Unless otherwise authorized by law and except as otherwise provided by paragraph (2) or (4) of this subsection, appropriated funds are not available for payment to an individual of pay from more than one position if the pay of one of the positions is paid by the Secretary of the Senate or the Chief Administrative Officer of the House of Representatives, or one of the positions is under the Office of the Architect of the Capitol, and if the aggregate gross pay from the positions exceeds $7,724 a year ($10,540, in the case of pay disbursed by the Secretary of the Senate).

(2) Notwithstanding paragraph (1) of this subsection, appropriated funds are not available for payment to an individual of pay from more than one position, for each of which the pay is disbursed by the Chief Administrative Officer of the House of Representatives, if the aggregate gross pay from those positions exceeds the maximum per annum gross rate of pay authorized to be paid to an employee out of the clerk hire allowance of a Member of the House.

(3) For the purposes of this subsection, "gross pay" means the annual rate of pay (or equivalent thereof in the case of an individual paid on other than an annual basis) received by an individual.

(4) Paragraph (1) of this subsection does not apply to pay on a when-actually-employed basis received from more than one consultant or expert position if the pay is not received for the same day.

(d) Subsection (a) of this section does not apply to—

(1) pay on a when-actually-employed basis received from more than one consultant or expert position if the pay is not received for the same hours of the same day;

(2) pay consisting of fees paid on other than a time basis;

(3) pay received by a teacher of the public schools of the District of Columbia for employment in a position during the summer vacation period;

(4) pay paid by the Tennessee Valley Authority to an employee performing part-time or intermittent work in addition to his normal duties when the Authority considers it to be in the interest of efficiency and economy;

(5) pay received by an individual holding a position—

(A) the pay of which is paid by the Secretary of the Senate or the Chief Administrative Officer of the House of Representatives; or

(B) under the Architect of the Capitol;

(6) pay paid by the United States Coast Guard to an employee occupying a part-time position of lamplighter; and

(7) pay within the purview of any of the following statutes:

(A) section 162 of title 2;

(B) section 23(b) of title 13;

(C) section 327 of title 15;

(D) section 907 of title 20;

(E) section 873 of title 33; or

(F) section 631 or 631a of title 31, District of Columbia Code.

[(G) Repealed. Pub. L. 96–70, title III, § 3302(e)(8), Sept. 27, 1979, 93 Stat. 498.]

(e)(1) This section does not apply to an individual employed under sections 174j–1 to 174j–7 or 174k of title 40.

(2) Subsection (c) of this section does not apply to pay received by a teacher of the public schools of the District of Columbia for employment in a position during the summer vacation period.

(Pub. L. 89–554, Sept. 6, 1966, 80 Stat. 483; Pub. L. 90–57, § 105(h), July 28, 1967, 81 Stat. 143; Pub. L. 90–206, title II, § 214(o), Dec. 16, 1967. 81 Stat. 637; Pub. L. 91–510, title IV, § 477(d), Oct. 26, 1970, 84 Stat. 1195; Pub. L. 93–140, § 23, Oct. 26, 1973, 87 Stat. 508; Pub. L. 93–145, § 101, Nov. 1, 1973, 87 Stat. 532; Pub. L. 94–183, § 2(21), Dec. 31, 1975, 89 Stat. 1058; Pub. L. 94–440, title I, § 103, Oct. 1, 1976, 90 Stat. 1443; Pub. L. 95–454, title IX, § 906(a)(2), Oct. 13, 1978, 92 Stat. 1224; Pub. L. 96–70, title III, § 3302(e)(8), Sept. 27, 1979, 93 Stat. 498; Pub. L. 104–186, title II, § 215(7), Aug. 20, 1996, 110 Stat. 1745.)

HISTORICAL AND REVISION NOTES

Derivation	U.S. Code	Revised Statutes and Statutes at Large
....	5 U.S.C. 3105 (less (e)).	Aug. 19, 1964, Pub. L. 88–448, § 301 (less (e)), 78 Stat. 488.

In subsection (a), the words "an individual" are substituted for "civilian personnel".

In subsection (b), the words "and issue" are omitted as surplusage.

In subsection (c), the words "appropriated funds are not" are substituted for "no funds appropriated by any Act shall be". The words "$2,000 a year" are substituted for "the sum of $2,000 per annum".

In subsection (d)(7)(D), reference to "section 907 of title 20" is substituted for 5 U.S.C. 3105(d)(7)(F) to reflect the scheduled transfer of 5 U.S.C. 2358(b) to title 20.

In subsection (d)(7)(H), the words "of chapter 7" are omitted as surplusage.

Standard changes are made to conform with the definitions applicable and the style of this title as outlined in the preface to the report.

AMENDMENTS

1996—Subsecs. (c)(1), (2), (d)(5)(A). Pub. L. 104–186 substituted "Chief Administrative Officer" for "Clerk".

1979—Subsec. (d)(7). Pub. L. 96–70 struck out subpar. (G) which made reference to section 102 of title 2, Canal Zone Code.

1978—Subsec. (b). Pub. L. 95–454 substituted "Office of Personnel Management" for "Civil Service Commission".

1976—Subsec. (c)(1). Pub. L. 94–440 inserted "($10,540, in the case of pay disbursed by the Secretary of the Senate)" after "exceeds $7,724 a year".

1975—Subsec. (d)(7). Pub. L. 94–183 struck out subpar. (F) relating to section 3335 (a) or (c) of title 39, and redesignated subpars. (G) and (H) as (F) and (G), respectively.

1973—Subsec. (c)(1), (4). Pub. L. 93–145 inserted reference to par. (4) in par. (1) and added par. (4).

Subsec. (e). Pub. L. 93–140 designated existing provisions as par. (1) and added par. (2).

1970—Subsec. (c)(1). Pub. L. 91–510 inserted "and except as otherwise provided by paragraph (2) of this section" after "authorized by law" and substituted "if the aggregate gross pay from the positions exceeds $7,724 a year" for "if—

"(A) the pay of one or more of the positions is fixed at a single gross per annum rate, and the aggregate gross pay from the positions exceeds $6,256 a year, or

"(B) the pay of each such position is fixed at a basic rate plus additional compensation authorized by law, and the aggregate basic pay of the positions exceeds $2,000 a year".

Subsec. (c)(2). Pub. L. 91–510 substituted provision making appropriated funds unavailable for payment to an individual of pay from more than one position, for each of which pay is disbursed by the Clerk of the House, if the aggregate gross pay from those positions exceeds the maximum per annum gross rate of pay authorized to be paid to an employee out of clerk hire allowance of a Member of the House for definition of "gross pay", now incorporated in cl. (3).

Subsec. (c)(3). Pub. L. 91–510 redesignated former cl. (2) as (3) and deleted provision which included in gross pay of an individual receiving basic pay plus additional compensation provided by law the aggregate amount received as basic and additional compensation, but excluded sums received as premium pay under subchapter V of this chapter.

1967—Subsec. (c). Pub. L. 90–206 provided for an increase in the aggregate gross pay allowed to certain specified congressional employees on two payrolls as dual office compensation.

Pub. L. 90–57 designated existing dual pay limitation provisions relating to basic compensation as par. (1), redesignated cls. (1) and (2) as (A) and (B), eliminated from cl. (A) provision for pay for one of the positions by the Secretary of the Senate and restricted such cl. (A) to payments in case of employees receiving basic rates of compensation and added par. (2) dual pay limitations applicable to aggregate gross compensation of employees receiving single per annum rates of compensation.

EFFECTIVE DATE OF 1979 AMENDMENT

Amendment by Pub. L. 96–70 effective Oct. 1, 1979, see section 3304 of Pub. L. 96–70, set out as an Effective Date note under section 3601 of Title 22, Foreign Relations and Intercourse.

EFFECTIVE DATE OF 1978 AMENDMENT

Amendment by Pub. L. 95–454 effective 90 days after Oct. 13, 1978, see section 907 of Pub. L. 95–454, set out as a note under section 1101 of this title.

EFFECTIVE DATE OF 1970 AMENDMENT

Amendment by Pub. L. 91–510 effective immediately prior to noon on Jan. 3, 1971, see section 601(1) of Pub. L. 91–510, set out as a note under section 72a of Title 2, The Congress.

EFFECTIVE DATE OF 1967 AMENDMENTS

Amendment by Pub. L. 90–206 effective at beginning of first pay period which begins on or after Dec. 16, 1967, see section 220(a)(3) of Pub. L. 90–206, set out as a note under section 603 of Title 28, Judiciary and Judicial Procedure.

Amendment by Pub. L. 90–57, effective Aug. 1, 1967, see section 105(k) of Pub. L. 90–57, set out as an Effective Date note under section 61–1 of Title 2, The Congress.

INCREASE IN COMPENSATION OF INDIVIDUALS WHOSE PAY IS DISBURSED BY SECRETARY OF SENATE

2001—The figure "$25,362" in subsec. (c)(1) of this section to be deemed to refer, effective Jan. 1, 2001, to the figure "$26,329", see section 9 of Salary Directive of President pro tempore of the Senate, Dec. 20, 2000, set out as a note under section 60a–1 of Title 2, The Congress.

2000—The figure "$10,540" in subsec. (c)(1) of this section to be deemed to refer, effective Jan. 1, 2000, to the figure "$25,362", see section 9 of Salary Directive of

President pro tempore of the Senate, Dec. 12, 1999, formerly set out as a note under section 60a–1 of Title 2.

1999—The figure "$10,540" in subsec. (c)(1) of this section to be deemed to refer, effective Jan. 1, 1999, to the figure "$24,433", see section 9 of Salary Directive of President pro tempore of the Senate, Dec. 16, 1998, formerly set out as a note under section 60a–1 of Title 2.

1998—The figure "$10,540" in subsec. (c)(1) of this section to be deemed to refer, effective Jan. 1, 1998, to the figure "$23,698", see section 9 of Salary Directive of President pro tempore of the Senate, Dec. 19, 1997, formerly set out as a note under section 60a–1 of Title 2.

1997—The figure "$10,540" in subsec. (c)(1) of this section to be deemed to refer, effective Jan. 1, 1997, to the figure "$23,165", see section 9 of Salary Directive of President pro tempore of the Senate, Dec. 18, 1996, formerly set out as a note under section 60a–1 of Title 2.

1995—The figure "$10,540" in subsec. (c)(1) of this section to be deemed to refer, effective Jan. 1, 1995, to the figure "$22,200", see section 9 of Salary Directive of President pro tempore of the Senate, Dec. 28, 1994, formerly set out as a note under section 60a–1 of Title 2.

1993—The figure "$10,540" in subsec. (c)(1) of this section to be deemed to refer, effective Jan. 1, 1993, to the figure "$21,764", see section 9 of Salary Directive of President pro tempore of the Senate, Dec. 17, 1992, formerly set out as a note under section 60a–1 of Title 2.

1992—The figure "$10,540" in subsec. (c)(1) of this section to be deemed to refer, effective Jan. 1, 1992, to the figure "$20,987", see section 9 of Salary Directive of President pro tempore of the Senate, Dec. 18, 1991, formerly set out as a note under section 60a–1 of Title 2.

1991—The figure "$10,540" in subsec. (c)(1) of this section to be deemed to refer, effective Jan. 1, 1991, to the figure "$20,141", see section 9 of Salary Directive of President pro tempore of the Senate, Dec. 20, 1990, formerly set out as a note under section 60a–1 of Title 2.

1990—The figure "$10,540" in subsec. (c)(1) of this section to be deemed to refer, effective Jan. 1, 1990, to the figure "$19,347", see section 9 of Salary Directive of President pro tempore of the Senate, Dec. 21, 1989, formerly set out as a note under section 60a–1 of Title 2.

1989—The figure "$10,540" in subsec. (c)(1) of this section to be deemed to refer, effective Jan. 1, 1989, to the figure "$18,674", see section 9 of Salary Directive of President pro tempore of the Senate, Dec. 9, 1988, formerly set out as a note under section 60a–1 of Title 2.

1988—The figure "$10,540" in subsec. (c)(1) of this section to be deemed to refer, effective Jan. 1, 1988, to the figure "$17,938", see section 9 of Salary Directive of President pro tempore of the Senate, Jan. 4, 1988, formerly set out as a note under section 60a–1 of Title 2.

1987—The figure "$10,540" in subsec. (c)(1) of this section to be deemed to refer, effective Jan. 1, 1987, to the figure "$17,586", see section 9 of Salary Directive of President pro tempore of the Senate, Dec. 19, 1986, formerly set out as a note under section 60a–1 of Title 2.

1985—The figure "$10,540" in subsec. (c)(1) of this section to be deemed to refer, effective Jan. 1, 1985, to the figure "$17,073", see section 9 of Salary Directive of President pro tempore of the Senate, Jan. 4, 1985, formerly set out as a note under section 60a–1 of Title 2.

1984—The figure "$10,540" in subsec. (c)(1) of this section to be deemed to refer, effective Jan. 1, 1984, to the figure "$16,495", see section 9 of Salary Directive of President pro tempore of the Senate, Dec. 20, 1983, formerly set out as a note under section 60a–1 of Title 2.

1982—The figure "$10,540" in subsec. (c)(1) of this section to be deemed to refer, effective Oct. 1, 1982, to the figure "$15,860", see section 9 of Salary Directive of President pro tempore of the Senate, Oct. 1, 1982, formerly set out as a note under section 60a–1 of Title 2.

1980—The figure "$10,540" in subsec. (c)(1) of this section to be deemed to refer, effective Oct. 1, 1980, to the figure "$14,551", see section 9 of Salary Directive of President pro tempore of the Senate, Oct. 1, 1980, formerly set out as a note under section 60a–1 of Title 2.

1979—The figure "$10,540" in subsec. (c)(1) of this section to be deemed to refer, effective Oct. 1, 1979, to the figure "$13,337", see section 9 of Salary Directive of

President pro tempore of the Senate, Oct. 13, 1979, formerly set out as a note under section 60a–1 of Title 2.

1978—The figure "$10,540" in subsec. (c)(1) of this section to be deemed to refer, effective Oct. 1, 1978, to the figure "$12,480", see section 9 of Salary Directive of President pro tempore of the Senate, Oct. 9, 1978, formerly set out as a note under section 60a–1 of Title 2.

1977—The figure "$10,540" in subsec. (c)(1) of this section to be deemed to refer, effective Oct. 1, 1977, to the figure "$11,830", see section 9 of Salary Directive of President pro tempore of the Senate, Sept. 27, 1977, formerly set out as a note under section 60a–1 of Title 2.

1976—The figure "$10,540" in subsec. (c)(1) of this section to be deemed to refer, effective Oct. 1, 1976, to the figure "$11,050", see section 9 of Salary Directive of President pro tempore of the Senate, Oct. 8, 1976, formerly set out as a note under section 60a–1 of Title 2.

1973—The figure "7,724" in subsection (c)(1) of this section, deemed to refer, effective Jan. 1, 1973, to the figure "9,080", see section 9 of Salary Directive of President pro tempore of the Senate, Dec. 16, 1972, formerly set out as a note under section 60a–1 of Title 2.

1972—The figure "7,724" in subsection (c)(1) of this section, deemed to refer, effective Jan. 1, 1972, to the figure "8,637", see section 9 of Salary Directive of President pro tempore of the Senate, Dec. 23, 1971, formerly set out as a note under section 60a–1 of Title 2.

1971—The figure "7,724" in subsection (c)(1) of this section, deemed to refer, effective Feb. 1, 1971, to the figure "8,187", see section 9 of Salary Directive of President pro tempore of the Senate, Jan. 15, 1971, formerly set out as a note under section 60a–1 of Title 2.

1970—Adjustment by President pro tempore of the Senate with respect to Senate, by Finance Clerk of House with respect to House of Representatives, and by Architect of Capitol with respect to Office of Architect of Capitol, effective on the first day of the first pay period which begins on or after Dec. 27, 1969, of rates of pay of employees of legislative branch subject to section 214 of Pub. L. 90–206 with certain exceptions, by amounts of adjustment for corresponding rates for employees subject to the General Schedule, set out in section 5332 of this title, which had been made by section 2 of Pub. L. 91–231 raising such rates by 6 percent, see Pub. L. 91–231, set out as a note under section 5332 of this title.

1969—The figure "6,662" in subsection (c)(1)(A) of this section, as increased by Order of June 12, 1968, deemed, on and after July 1, 1969, to refer to the figure "7,287", see section 4(d) of Salary Directive of President pro tempore of the Senate, June 17, 1969, formerly set out as a note under section 60a–1 of Title 2.

1968—The figure "6,256" in subsection (c)(1)(A) of this section deemed to refer, on and after July 1, 1968, to the figure "6,622", see section 1(i) of Salary Directive of President pro tempore of the Senate, June 12, 1968, formerly set out as a note under section 60a–1 of Title 2.

SECTION REFERRED TO IN OTHER SECTIONS

This section is referred to in section 5531 of this title; title 2 section 162; title 13 section 23; title 15 section 327; title 20 section 907; title 22 sections 2396, 3664; title 25 section 2012; title 33 section 873; title 39 section 1001.

§ 5534. Dual employment and pay of Reserves and National Guardsmen

A Reserve of the armed forces or member of the National Guard may accept a civilian office or position under the Government of the United States or the government of the District of Columbia, and he is entitled to receive the pay of that office or position in addition to pay and allowances as a Reserve or member of the National Guard.

(Pub. L. 89–554, Sept. 6, 1966, 80 Stat. 484.)

HISTORICAL AND REVISION NOTES

Derivation	U.S. Code	Revised Statutes and Statutes at Large
....	5 U.S.C. 30r(c) (1st sentence).	Aug. 10, 1956, ch. 1041, § 29(c) (1st sentence), 70A Stat. 632.

Standard changes are made to conform with the definitions applicable and the style of this title as outlined in the preface to the report.

SECTION REFERRED TO IN OTHER SECTIONS

This section is referred to in title 22 section 3664.

§ 5534a. Dual employment and pay during terminal leave from uniformed services

A member of a uniformed service who has performed active service and who is on terminal leave pending separation from, or release from active duty in, that service under honorable conditions may accept a civilian office or position in the Government of the United States, its territories or possessions, or the government of the District of Columbia, and he is entitled to receive the pay of that office or position in addition to pay and allowances from the uniformed service for the unexpired portion of the terminal leave.

(Added Pub. L. 90–83, § 1(22), Sept. 11, 1967, 81 Stat. 199.)

HISTORICAL AND REVISION NOTES

This section amends chapter 55 of title 5, United States Code, by inserting a new section 5534a. This section is based on subsections (a) and (f) of former 5 U.S.C. 61a–1 the source statute for which (act of Nov. 21, 1945, ch. 489, 59 Stat. 584) was repealed by the act of September 6, 1966, Public Law 89–554 (sec. 8, 80 Stat. 653). Senate Report 1380, 89th Congress, second session, pages 449, 511, explains that the source was repealed since it had been rendered obsolete by section 4(c) of the Armed Forces Leave Act of 1946, as amended (37 U.S.C. 501), and section 219(c) of the Public Health Service Act, as added August 9, 1950 (ch. 654, sec. 2, 64 Stat. 426; 42 U.S.C. 210–1(c)), and that any existing rights are preserved by section 8 of Public Law 89–554.

At the time of enactment of the act of November 21, 1945, there was no authority to make lump-sum leave payments to members of the uniformed services who were being separated from or released from active duty in the uniformed services. Accordingly, they were placed on terminal leave until the expiration of the unused portion of their accumulated and current accrued leave, and only then separated or released. The act of November 21, 1945, in part, authorized the employment of these members during terminal leave and provided they were entitled to receive, in addition to the payment from the employment, military pay and allowances for the unexpired portion of the terminal leave. The Armed Forces Leave Act of 1946 authorized lump-sum leave payments of unused accumulated and current accrued leave. Generally, thereafter, members of the uniformed services were not placed on terminal leave, but were separated and paid a lump-sum leave payment. However, in certain instances a member may be placed on terminal leave. Such a case was considered recently by the Comptroller General of the United States (see B–157500, Oct. 13, 1965, 45 Comp. Gen. 180. In view of the foregoing, it is concluded that subsection (a) of former 5 U.S.C. 61a–1 had prospective effect and should have been reenacted in title 5, U.S.C., by Public Law 89–554.

In section 5534a, the words "A member of a uniformed service who has performed active service" are substituted for "Any person, who, shall have performed active service in the Armed Forces'' to conform to the style of title 5 and the definition of "uniformed services" in 5 U.S.C. 2101 which is coextensive with the definition of "armed forces" in subsection (f) of former 5 U.S.C. 61a–1. Reorganization Plan No. 2 of 1965 (79 Stat. 1318), effective July 13, 1965, consolidated the Coast and Geodetic Survey and the Weather Bureau to form a new agency in the Department of Commerce to be known as the Environmental Science Services Administration. The words "subsequent to May 1, 1940" are omitted as executed. The word "territories" is substituted for "Territories" inasmuch as there now are no incorporated territories. The words "(including any corporation created under authority of an act of Congress which is either wholly controlled or wholly owned by the Government of the United States, or any department, agency, or establishment thereof, whether or not the employees thereof are paid from funds appropriated by Congress)" are omitted as included in "a civilian office or position in the Government of the United States". The word "pay" is substituted for "compensation."

EFFECTIVE DATE

Section effective Sept. 6, 1966, for all purposes, see section 9(h) of Pub. L. 90–83, set out as an Effective Date of 1967 Amendment note under section 5102 of this title.

SECTION REFERRED TO IN OTHER SECTIONS

This section is referred to in title 22 section 3664.

§ 5535. Extra pay for details prohibited

(a) An officer may not receive pay in addition to the pay for his regular office for performing the duties of a vacant office as authorized by sections 3345–3347 of this title.

(b) An employee may not receive—

(1) additional pay or allowances for performing the duties of another employee; or

(2) pay in addition to the regular pay received for employment held before his appointment or designation as acting for or instead of an occupant of another position or employment.

This subsection does not prevent a regular and permanent appointment by promotion from a lower to a higher grade of employment.

(Pub. L. 89–554, Sept. 6, 1966, 80 Stat. 484.)

HISTORICAL AND REVISION NOTES

Derivation	U.S. Code	Revised Statutes and Statutes at Large
(a)	5 U.S.C. 9.	R.S. § 182.
(b)	5 U.S.C. 69 (1st 34 words).	R.S. § 1764 (1st 34 words).
	5 U.S.C. 72.	Aug. 1, 1914, ch. 223, § 12, 38 Stat. 680.

Subsection (a) was part of title IV of the Revised Statutes. The Act of July 26, 1947, ch. 343, § 201(d), as added Aug. 10, 1949, ch. 412, § 4, 63 Stat. 579 (former 5 U.S.C. 171–1), which provides "Except to the extent inconsistent with the provisions of this Act [National Security Act of 1947], the provisions of title IV of the Revised Statutes as now or hereafter amended shall be applicable to the Department of Defense" is omitted from this title but is not repealed.

In subsection (a), the words "regular office" are coextensive with and substituted for "proper office".

In subsection (b), former sections 69 (1st 34 words) and 72 are combined and restated for clarity and conciseness. The word "employee" is coextensive with and substituted for "officer or clerk", "officer or clerk in the same or any other department", and "person em-

ployed in the service of the United States". The words "under any general or lump-sum appropriation" are omitted as unnecessary.

Standard changes are made to conform with the definitions applicable and the style of this title as outlined in the preface to the report.

SECTION REFERRED TO IN OTHER SECTIONS

This section is referred to in title 22 sections 3664, 3971; title 39 section 1001.

§ 5536. Extra pay for extra services prohibited

An employee or a member of a uniformed service whose pay or allowance is fixed by statute or regulation may not receive additional pay or allowance for the disbursement of public money or for any other service or duty, unless specifically authorized by law and the appropriation therefor specifically states that it is for the additional pay or allowance.

(Pub. L. 89–554, Sept. 6, 1966, 80 Stat. 484.)

HISTORICAL AND REVISION NOTES

Derivation	U.S. Code	Revised Statutes and Statutes at Large
....	5 U.S.C. 51.	R.S. § 170.
....	5 U.S.C. 69 (less 1st 34 words).	R.S. § 1764 (less 1st 34 words).
....	5 U.S.C. 70.	R.S. § 1765.
....	5 U.S.C. 71.	June 20, 1874, ch. 328, § 3, 18 Stat. 109. Sept. 3, 1954, ch. 1263, § 7, 68 Stat. 1228.

Sections are consolidated as R.S. § 1765 includes the scope of R.S. § 170, R.S. § 1764, and the Act of June 20, 1874, as amended. So much of R.S. § 1764 as relates to details is covered by section 5535.

R.S. § 170 was part of title IV of the Revised Statutes. The Act of July 26, 1947, ch. 343, § 201(d), as added Aug. 10, 1949, ch. 412, § 4, 63 Stat. 579 (former 5 U.S.C. 171–1), which provides "Except to the extent inconsistent with the provisions of this Act [National Security Act of 1947], the provisions of title IV of the Revised Statutes as now or hereafter amended shall be applicable to the Department of Defense" is omitted from his title but is not repealed.

Standard changes are made to conform with the definitions applicable and the style of this title as outlined in the preface to the report.

SECTION REFERRED TO IN OTHER SECTIONS

This section is referred to in section 5942a of this title; title 22 sections 3971, 4085, 6104; title 39 section 1001; title 50 section 403e–1.

§ 5537. Fees for jury and witness service

(a) An employee as defined by section 2105 of this title (except an individual whose pay is disbursed by the Secretary of the Senate or the Chief Administrative Officer of the House of Representatives) or an individual employed by the government of the District of Columbia may not receive fees for service—

(1) as a juror in a court of the United States or the District of Columbia; or

(2) as a witness on behalf of the United States or the District of Columbia.

(b) An official of a court of the United States or the District of Columbia may not receive witness fees for attendance before a court, commissioner, or magistrate judge where he is officiating.

(c) For the purpose of this section, "court of the United States" has the meaning given it by section 451 of title 28 and includes the District Court of Guam and the District Court of the Virgin Islands.

(Pub. L. 89–554, Sept. 6, 1966, 80 Stat. 484; Pub. L. 90–623, § 1(12), Oct. 22, 1968, 82 Stat. 1312; Pub. L. 91–563, § 3(a), Dec. 19, 1970, 84 Stat. 1477; Pub. L. 101–650, title III, § 321, Dec. 1, 1990, 104 Stat. 5117; Pub. L. 104–186, title II, § 215(8), Aug. 20, 1996, 110 Stat. 1746; Pub. L. 104–201, div. C, title XXXV, § 3548(a)(5), Sept. 23, 1996, 110 Stat. 2868.)

HISTORICAL AND REVISION NOTES

Derivation	U.S. Code	Revised Statutes and Statutes at Large
....	5 U.S.C. 30o.	June 29, 1940, ch. 446, § 2, 54 Stat. 689.

The words "fees for jury service" are coextensive with and substituted for "compensation for such service".

Standard changes are made to conform with the definitions applicable and the style of this title as outlined in the preface to the report.

AMENDMENTS

1996—Subsec. (a). Pub. L. 104–186 substituted "Chief Administrative Officer" for "Clerk" in introductory provisions.

Subsec. (c). Pub. L. 104–201 substituted "the District Court of Guam and the District Court of the Virgin Islands" for "the United States District Court for the District of the Canal Zone, the District Court of Guam, and the District Court of the Virgin Islands".

1970—Pub. L. 91–563 substituted "jury and witness service" for "jury service in courts of the United States" in section catchline, designated existing provisions as subsec. (a), inserted provisions prohibiting payment of fees for jury service in a court of the District of Columbia or for service as a witness on behalf of the United States or the District of Columbia and excepting employees whose pay is disbursed by the Secretary of the Senate or the Clerk of the House of Representatives, and added subsecs. (b) and (c).

1968—Pub. L. 90–623 inserted ", who is entitled to leave under section 6322 of this title," after "individual employed by the government of the District of Columbia".

CHANGE OF NAME

Words "magistrate judge" substituted for "magistrate" in subsec. (b) pursuant to section 321 of Pub. L. 101–650, set out as a note under section 631 of Title 28, Judiciary and Judicial Procedure.

EFFECTIVE DATE OF 1968 AMENDMENT

Amendment by Pub. L. 90–623 intended to restate without substantive change the law in effect on Oct. 22, 1968, see section 6 of Pub. L. 90–623, set out as a note under section 5334 of this title.

SUBCHAPTER V—PREMIUM PAY

SUBCHAPTER REFERRED TO IN OTHER SECTIONS

This subchapter is referred to in sections 5304, 5371, 5520a, 5926 of this title; title 10 sections 4338, 6952, 9338; title 22 section 3972.

§ 5541. Definitions

For the purpose of this subchapter—

(1) "agency" means—
(A) an Executive agency;
(B) a military department;
(C) an agency in the judicial branch;
(D) the Library of Congress;
(E) the Botanic Garden;
(F) the Office of the Architect of the Capitol; and
(G) the government of the District of Columbia;

(2) "employee" means—
(A) an employee in or under an Executive agency;
(B) an individual employed by the government of the District of Columbia; and
(C) an employee in or under the judicial branch, the Library of Congress, the Botanic Garden, and the Office of the Architect of the Capitol, who occupies a position subject to chapter 51 and subchapter III of chapter 53 of this title;

but does not include—
(i) a justice or judge of the United States;
(ii) the head of an agency other than the government of the District of Columbia;
(iii) a teacher, school official, or employee of the Board of Education of the District of Columbia, whose pay is fixed under chapter 15 of title 31, District of Columbia Code;
(iv) a member of—
(I) the Metropolitan Police or the Fire Department of the District of Columbia; or
(II) a member of the United States Secret Service Uniformed Division, a member of the United States Park Police, other than for purposes of section[1] 5545(a) and 5546;

(v) a student-employee as defined by section 5351 of this title;
[(vi) Repealed. Pub. L. 91–375, § 6(c)(16), Aug. 12, 1970, 84 Stat. 776;]
(vii) an employee outside the continental United States or in Alaska who is paid in accordance with local native prevailing wage rates for the area in which employed;
(viii) an employee of the Tennessee Valley Authority;
(ix) an individual to whom section 1291(a) of title 50, appendix, applies;
(x) an employee of a Federal land bank, a Federal intermediate credit bank, or a bank for cooperatives;
(xi) an employee whose pay is fixed and adjusted from time to time in accordance with prevailing rates under subchapter IV of chapter 53 of this title, or by a wage board or similar administrative authority serving the same purpose, except as provided by section 5544 of this title;
(xii) an employee of the Transportation Corps of the Army on a vessel operated by the United States, a vessel employee of the Environmental Science Services Administration, or a vessel employee of the Department of the Interior;
(xiii) a "teacher" or an individual holding a "teaching position" as defined by section 901 of title 20;
(xiv) a Foreign Service officer;
(xv) a member of the Senior Foreign Service;
(xvi) member of the Senior Executive Service; or
(xvii) a member of the Federal Bureau of Investigation and Drug Enforcement Administration Senior Executive Service; and

---

[1] So in original. Probably should be "sections".

(3) "law enforcement officer" means an employee who—

(A) is a law enforcement officer within the meaning of section 8331(20) or 8401(17);

(B) in the case of an employee who holds a supervisory or administrative position and is subject to subchapter III of chapter 83, but who does not qualify to be considered a law enforcement officer within the meaning of section 8331(20), would so qualify if such employee had transferred directly to such position after serving as a law enforcement officer within the meaning of such section;

(C) in the case of an employee who holds a supervisory or administrative position and is subject to chapter 84, but who does not qualify to be considered a law enforcement officer within the meaning of section 8401(17), would so qualify if such employee had transferred directly to such position after performing duties described in section 8401(17)(A) and (B) for at least 3 years; and

(D) in the case of an employee who is not subject to subchapter III of chapter 83 or chapter 84—

(i) holds a position that the Office of Personnel Management determines would satisfy subparagraph (A), (B), or (C) if the employee were subject to subchapter III of chapter 83 or chapter 84; or

(ii) is a special agent in the Diplomatic Security Service.

(Pub. L. 89–554, Sept. 6, 1966, 80 Stat. 485; Pub. L. 90–83, § 1(4), Sept. 11, 1967, 81 Stat. 196; Pub. L. 91–375, § 6(c)(16), Aug. 12, 1970, 84 Stat. 776; Pub. L. 92–392, § 4, Aug. 14, 1972, 86 Stat. 573; Pub. L. 94–183, § 2(22), Dec. 31, 1975, 89 Stat. 1058; Pub. L. 95–105, title IV, § 412(a)(1), Aug. 17, 1977, 91 Stat. 855; Pub. L. 95–426, title II, § 204(b)(5)(B), Oct. 7, 1978, 92 Stat. 974; Pub. L. 95–454, title IV, § 408(a)(2), Oct. 13, 1978, 92 Stat. 1173; Pub. L. 96–70, title III, § 3302(e)(1), Sept. 27, 1979, 93 Stat. 498; Pub. L. 96–465, title II, § 2304, Oct. 17, 1980, 94 Stat. 2165; Pub. L. 100–325, § 2(i)(1), May 30, 1988, 102 Stat. 582; Pub. L. 101–509, title V, § 529 [title IV, § 411(a)], Nov. 5, 1990, 104 Stat. 1427, 1469; Pub. L. 102–378, § 2(40)(A)–(C), Oct. 2, 1992, 106 Stat. 1351; Pub. L. 104–201, div. C, title XXXV, § 3548(a)(6), Sept. 23, 1996, 110 Stat. 2869.)

HISTORICAL AND REVISION NOTES

Derivation	U.S. Code	Revised Statutes and Statutes at Large
....	5 U.S.C. 901(a), (d), (e).	June 30, 1945, ch. 212 § 101(a), (d), (e), 59 Stat. 295, 296. Sept. 1, 1954, ch. 1208, § 202(a), 68 Stat. 1109.
....	5 U.S.C. 902 (less clause (1) and last sentence of (a)).	June 30, 1945, ch. 212, § 102 (less clause (1) and last sentence of (a)), 59 Stat. 296. May 24, 1946, ch. 270, § 8(a), 60 Stat. 218. Aug. 4, 1947, ch. 452, § 1, 61 Stat. 727. Aug. 18, 1959, Pub. L. 86–168, § 202(c) 73 Stat. 389.
....	5 U.S.C. 2358(a) (as applicable to the Federal Employees Pay Act of 1945, as amended).	July 17, 1959, Pub. L. 86–91, § 10(a) (as applicable to the Federal Employees Pay Act of 1945, as amended), 73 Stat. 217.

The section is revised as a definition section. The provisions of former section 901(d) are omitted as unnecessary because the sections referred to state their application and there is no need to restate the application here.

In paragraph (1), the terms "Executive agency" and "military department" are substituted for the references in former section 901(a) and (e) to the executive branch, including Government-owned or controlled corporations, and the General Accounting Office in view of the definitions in sections 105 and 102.

In paragraph (2)(iii), the words "chapter 15 of title 31, District of Columbia Code" are substituted for the reference in former section 902(a)(4) to "the Teachers Salary Act of June 4, 1924, as amended" on authority of the provisions contained therein. Enumeration of the individuals to which the provisions apply are added.

In paragraph (2)(iv), the provisions of former section 902(a)(5) and (b)(6) are combined.

In paragraph (2)(v), the words "student-employee as defined by section 5351 of this title" are coextensive with and substituted for the enumeration of the employees in former section 902(a)(6).

In paragraph (2)(iv), (vi), (vii), (viii), (ix), (xi), and (xii), the reference to former section 947 is omitted as that section was repealed by the Act of Sept. 12, 1950, ch. 946, § 301(85), 64 Stat. 843.

In paragraph (2)(xii), the reference to former section 946 is omitted as unnecessary since that section is not carried into this subchapter. The words "Panama Canal Company" are substituted for "Panama Railroad Company" on authority of the Act of Sept. 2, 1950, ch. 1049, § 2(a)(2), 64 Stat. 1038.

In paragraph (2)(xiii), the words "as defined by section 901 of title 20" are added on authority of former section 2351, which section is scheduled for transfer to section 901 of title 20.

The exception for officers and employees of the Inland Waterways Corporation in former section 902(b)(3) is omitted on authority of the Act of July 19, 1963, Pub. L. 88–67, 77 Stat. 81.

Standard changes are made to conform with the definitions applicable and the style of this title as outlined in the preface to the report.

AMENDMENTS

1996—Par. (2)(xii). Pub. L. 104–201 inserted "or" after "Services Administration," and struck out ", or a vessel employee of the Panama Canal Commission" after "Interior".

1992—Par. (3). Pub. L. 102–378 added par. (3).

1990—Par. (2)(iv). Pub. L. 101–509 amended cl. (iv) generally. Prior to amendment, cl. (iv) read as follows: "a member of the Metropolitan Police, the Fire Department of the District of Columbia, the United States Park Police, or the Executive Protective Service;".

1988—Par. (2)(xvii). Pub. L. 100–325 added cl. (xvii).

1980—Par. (2)(xiv). Pub. L. 96–465 struck out "within the meaning of section 401 of the Foreign Service Act of 1946" after "officer".

Par. (2)(xv). Pub. L. 96–465 substituted "a member of the Senior Foreign Service" for "a 'Foreign Service information officer' as provided for by the first section of the Act entitled 'An Act to promote the foreign policy of the United States by strengthening and improving the Foreign Service personnel system of the International Communication Agency through establishment of a Foreign Service Information Officer Corps', approved August 20, 1968".

1979—Par. (2)(xii). Pub. L. 96–70 substituted "Commission" for "Company".

1978—Par. (2)(xvi). Pub. L. 95–454 added cl. (xvi).

Par. (2)(xv). Pub. L. 95–426 substituted "International Communication Agency" for "United States Information Agency".

1977—Par. (2)(xiv), (xv). Pub. L. 95–105 added cls. (xiv) and (xv).

1975—Par. (2)(iv). Pub. L. 94–183 substituted "Executive Protective Service" for "White House Police".

1972—Par. (2)(xi). Pub. L. 92–392 substituted "pay" for "basic pay" and provided for determination of pay under subchapter IV of chapter 53 of this title.

1970—Par. (2)(vi). Pub. L. 91–375 repealed cl. (vi) which excluded an employee in the postal field service from definition of "employee".

1967—Par. (2)(xii). Pub. L. 90–83 substituted "Environmental Science Services Administration" for "Coast and Geodetic Survey". See Historical and Revision Notes under section 2101 of this title.

EFFECTIVE DATE OF 1992 AMENDMENT

Amendment by Pub. L. 102–378 effective as of first day of first applicable pay period beginning on or after Oct. 2, 1992, see section 9(b)(9) of Pub. L. 102–378, set out as a note under section 6303 of this title.

EFFECTIVE DATE OF 1990 AMENDMENT

Section 529 [title IV, § 411(b)] of Pub. L. 101–509 provided that: "The amendment made by this section [amending this section] shall be effective on January 1, 1992."

EFFECTIVE DATE OF 1980 AMENDMENT

Amendment by Pub. L. 96–465 effective Feb. 15, 1981, except as otherwise provided, see section 2403 of Pub. L. 96–465, set out as an Effective Date note under section 3901 of Title 22, Foreign Relations and Intercourse.

EFFECTIVE DATE OF 1979 AMENDMENT

Amendment by Pub. L. 96–70 effective Oct. 1, 1979, see section 3304 of Pub. L. 96–70, set out as an Effective Date note under section 3601 of Title 22, Foreign Relations and Intercourse.

EFFECTIVE DATE OF 1978 AMENDMENTS

Amendment by Pub. L. 95–454 effective 9 months after Oct. 13, 1978, and congressional review of provisions of sections 401 through 412 of Pub. L. 95–454, see section 415 of Pub. L. 95–454, set out as an Effective Date note under section 3131 of this title.

Section 204(b)(5)(B) of Pub. L. 95–426 provided that the amendment made by such section 204(b)(5)(B) is effective Oct. 1, 1978.

EFFECTIVE DATE OF 1977 AMENDMENT

Section 412(a)(2) of Pub. L. 95–105 provided that: "The amendments made by paragraph (1) [amending this section] shall take effect on October 1, 1978."

EFFECTIVE DATE OF 1972 AMENDMENT

Amendment by Pub. L. 92–392 effective on first day of first applicable pay period beginning on or after 90th day after Aug. 19, 1972, see section 15(a) of Pub. L. 92–392, set out as an Effective Date note under section 5341 of this title.

EFFECTIVE DATE OF 1970 AMENDMENT

Amendment by Pub. L. 91–375 effective within 1 year after Aug. 12, 1970, on date established therefor by Board of Governors of United States Postal Service and published by it in Federal Register, see section 15(a) of Pub. L. 91–375, set out as an Effective Date note preceding section 101 of Title 39, Postal Service.

SHORT TITLE OF 1994 AMENDMENT

Pub. L. 103–329, title VI, § 633(a), Sept. 30, 1994, 108 Stat. 2425, provided that: "This section [enacting section 5545a of this title, amending sections 5542 and 5547 of this title and section 213 of Title 29, Labor, and enacting provisions set out as notes under section 5545a of this title] may be cited as the 'Law Enforcement Availability Pay Act of 1994'."

TRANSFER OF FUNCTIONS

Environmental Science Services Administration in Department of Commerce, including offices of Administrator and Deputy Administrator thereof, abolished by Reorg. Plan No. 4 of 1970, eff. Oct. 3, 1970, 35 F.R. 15627, 84 Stat. 2090, set out in the Appendix to this title, which created National Oceanic and Atmospheric Administration in Department of Commerce and transferred personnel, property, records, and unexpended balances of funds of Environmental Science Services Administration to such newly created National Oceanic and Atmospheric Administration. Components of Environmental Science Services Administration thus transferred included Weather Bureau [now National Weather Service], Coast and Geodetic Survey [now National Ocean Survey], Environmental Data Service, National Environmental Satellite Center, and ESSA Research Laboratories.

AVAILABILITY OF PREMIUM PAY FOR ATTORNEYS EMPLOYED IN DEPARTMENT OF JUSTICE

Pub. L. 106–113, div. B, § 1000(a)(1) [title I, § 115], Nov. 29, 1999, 113 Stat. 1535, 1501A–21, provided that:

"(a) None of the funds made available by this or any other Act may be used to pay premium pay under title 5, United States Code, sections 5542–5549, to any individual employed as an attorney, including an Assistant United States Attorney, in the Department of Justice for any work performed on or after the date of the enactment of this Act [Nov. 29, 1999].

"(b) Notwithstanding any other provision of law, neither the United States nor any individual or entity acting on its behalf shall be liable for premium pay under title 5, United States Code, sections 5542–5549, for any work performed on or after the date of the enactment of this Act [Nov. 29, 1999] by any individual employed as an attorney in the Department of Justice, including an Assistant United States Attorney."

[Pub. L. 106–553, § 1(a)(2) [title I, § 111], Dec. 21, 2000, 114 Stat. 2762, 2762A–68, provided that: "Section 115 of the Departments of Commerce, Justice, and State, the Judiciary, and Related Agencies Appropriations Act, 2000 (as enacted into law by section 1000(a)(1) of Public Law 106–113) [set out above] shall apply hereafter."]

SENSE OF CONGRESS RELATING TO LAW ENFORCEMENT OFFICER PROVISIONS

Section 2(40)(D) of Pub. L. 102–378 provided that: "It is the sense of the Congress that—

"(i) the provisions of section 5541(3) of title 5, United States Code (as added by section 2(40)(C) of this Act)—

"(I) are enacted only for the purposes of pay and not for the purposes of retirement;

"(II) do not reflect any intent of the Congress to change retirement eligibility standards for law enforcement officers; and

"(ii) law enforcement officers in primary positions have different retirement eligibility standards than employees in supervisory or administrative positions because of the different requirements in their responsibilities."

PAYMENT OF BONUSES FOR FOREIGN LANGUAGE CAPABILITIES

Pub. L. 100–690, title VI, § 6401, Nov. 18, 1988, 102 Stat. 4370, as amended by Pub. L. 101–509, title V, § 529 [title IV, § 408(c)], Nov. 5, 1990, 104 Stat. 1427, 1468, provided that:

"(a) IN GENERAL.—Notwithstanding any other provision of law, the Drug Enforcement Administration and the Federal Bureau of Investigation are authorized on and after October 1, 1988, to pay bonuses up to 25 percent of base pay to employees of the Drug Enforcement Administration and the Federal Bureau of Investigation who possess and make substantial use of one or more languages, other than English, in the performance of their official duties. The Administrator of the Drug Enforcement Administration and the Director of the Federal Bureau of Investigation shall develop such policies as necessary to implement the payment of these bonuses.

"(b) LIMITATION.—The provisions of this section shall apply only to an employee who has received a bonus under this section before January 1, 1992. The provisions of subchapter III of chapter 45 of title 5, United States Code, shall apply to any employee who would otherwise be eligible to receive a bonus under this section, on and after such date."

SECTION REFERRED TO IN OTHER SECTIONS

This section is referred to in sections 4521, 5504, 5545a, 5550a, 6101 of this title; title 2 section 1371.

§ 5542. Overtime rates; computation

(a) For full-time, part-time and intermittent tours of duty, hours of work officially ordered or approved in excess of 40 hours in an administrative workweek, or (with the exception of an employee engaged in professional or technical engineering or scientific activities for whom the first 40 hours of duty in an administrative workweek is the basic workweek and an employee whose basic pay exceeds the minimum rate for GS–10 (including any applicable locality-based comparability payment under section 5304 or similar provision of law and any applicable special rate of pay under section 5305 or similar provision of law) for whom the first 40 hours of duty in an administrative workweek is the basic workweek) in excess of 8 hours in a day, performed by an employee are overtime work and shall be paid for, except as otherwise provided by this subchapter, at the following rates:

(1) For an employee whose basic pay is at a rate which does not exceed the minimum rate of basic pay for GS–10 (including any applicable locality-based comparability payment under section 5304 or similar provision of law and any applicable special rate of pay under section 5305 or similar provision of law), the overtime hourly rate of pay is an amount equal to one and one-half times the hourly rate of basic pay of the employee, and all that amount is premium pay.

(2) For an employee whose basic pay is at a rate which exceeds the minimum rate of basic pay for GS–10 (including any applicable locality-based comparability payment under section 5304 or similar provision of law and any applicable special rate of pay under section 5305 or similar provision of law), the overtime hourly rate of pay is an amount equal to one and one-half times the hourly rate of the minimum rate of basic pay for GS–10 (including any applicable locality-based comparability payment under section 5304 or similar provision of law and any applicable special rate of pay under section 5305 or similar provision of law), and all that amount is premium pay.

(3) Notwithstanding paragraphs (1) and (2) of this subsection for an employee of the Department of Transportation who occupies a non-managerial position in GS–14 or under and, as determined by the Secretary of Transportation,

(A) the duties of which are critical to the immediate daily operation of the air traffic control system, directly affect aviation safety, and involve physical or mental strain or hardship;

(B) in which overtime work is therefore unusually taxing; and

(C) in which operating requirements cannot be met without substantial overtime work;

the overtime hourly rate of pay is an amount equal to one and one-half times the hourly rate of basic pay of the employee, and all that amount is premium pay.

(4) Notwithstanding paragraph (2) of this subsection, for an employee who is a law enforcement officer, and whose basic pay is at a rate which exceeds the minimum rate of basic pay for GS–10 (including any applicable locality-based comparability payment under section 5304 or similar provision of law and any applicable special rate of pay under section 5305 or similar provision of law), the overtime hourly rate of pay is an amount equal to the greater of—

(A) one and one-half times the minimum hourly rate of basic pay for GS–10 (including any applicable locality-based comparability payment under section 5304 or similar provision of law and any applicable special rate of pay under section 5305 or similar provision of law); or

(B) the hourly rate of basic pay of the employee,

and all that amount is premium pay.

(5) Notwithstanding paragraphs (1) and (2), for an employee of the Department of the Interior or the United States Forest Service in the Department of Agriculture engaged in emergency wildland fire suppression activities, the overtime hourly rate of pay is an amount equal to one and one-half times the hourly rate of basic pay of the employee, and all that amount is premium pay.

(b) For the purpose of this subchapter—

(1) unscheduled overtime work performed by an employee on a day when work was not scheduled for him, or for which he is required to return to his place of employment, is deemed at least 2 hours in duration; and

(2) time spent in a travel status away from the official-duty station of an employee is not hours of employment unless—

(A) the time spent is within the days and hours of the regularly scheduled administrative workweek of the employee, including regularly scheduled overtime hours; or

(B) the travel (i) involves the performance of work while traveling, (ii) is incident to travel that involves the performance of work while traveling, (iii) is carried out under arduous conditions, or (iv) results from an event which could not be scheduled or controlled administratively, including travel by an employee to such an event and the return of such employee from such event to his or her official-duty station.

(c) Subsection (a) shall not apply to an employee who is subject to the overtime pay provisions of section 7 of the Fair labor[1] Standards Act of 1938. In the case of an employee who would, were it not for the preceding sentence, be subject to this section, the Office of Personnel Management shall by regulation prescribe what hours shall be deemed to be hours of work and what hours of work shall be deemed to be overtime hours for the purpose of such section 7 so

---

[1] So in original. Probably should be capitalized.

as to ensure that no employee receives less pay by reason of the preceding sentence.

(d) In applying subsection (a) of this section with respect to any criminal investigator who is paid availability pay under section 5545a—

(1) such investigator shall be compensated under such subsection (a), at the rates there provided, for overtime work which is scheduled in advance of the administrative workweek—

(A) in excess of 10 hours on a day during such investigator's basic 40 hour workweek; or

(B) on a day outside such investigator's basic 40 hour workweek; and

(2) such investigator shall be compensated for all other overtime work under section 5545a.

(e) Notwithstanding subsection (d)(1) of this section, all hours of overtime work scheduled in advance of the administrative workweek shall be compensated under subsection (a) if that work involves duties as authorized by section 3056(a) of title 18 or section 37(a)(3) of the State Department Basic Authorities Act of 1956, and if the investigator performs, on that same day, at least 2 hours of overtime work not scheduled in advance of the administrative workweek.

(f) In applying subsection (a) of this section with respect to a firefighter who is subject to section 5545b—

(1) such subsection shall be deemed to apply to hours of work officially ordered or approved in excess of 106 hours in a biweekly pay period, or, if the agency establishes a weekly basis for overtime pay computation, in excess of 53 hours in an administrative workweek; and

(2) the overtime hourly rate of pay is an amount equal to one and one-half times the hourly rate of basic pay under section 5545b(b)(1)(A) or (c)(1)(B), as applicable, and such overtime hourly rate of pay may not be less than such hourly rate of basic pay in applying the limitation on the overtime rate provided in paragraph (2) of such subsection (a).

(Pub. L. 89–554, Sept. 6, 1966, 80 Stat. 485; Pub. L. 90–83, §1(24), Sept. 11, 1967, 81 Stat. 200; Pub. L. 90–206, title II, §222(a), Dec. 16, 1967, 81 Stat. 641; Pub. L. 90–556, §1, Oct. 10, 1968, 82 Stat. 969; Pub. L. 92–194, Dec. 15, 1971, 85 Stat. 648; Pub. L. 98–473, title I, §101(c) [title III, §322], Oct. 12, 1984, 98 Stat. 1837, 1874; Pub. L. 101–509, title V, §529 [title I, §101(b)(3)(E), title II, §210(1), title IV, §410(a)], Nov. 5, 1990, 104 Stat. 1427, 1439, 1460, 1468; Pub. L. 102–378, §2(41), Oct. 2, 1992, 106 Stat. 1352; Pub. L. 103–329, title VI, §633(c), Sept. 30, 1994, 108 Stat. 2427; Pub. L. 104–52, title V, §531, Nov. 19, 1995, 109 Stat. 496; Pub. L. 105–277, div. A, §101(b) [title IV, §407(c)(2)], (h) [title VI, §628(a)(1)], div. G, subdiv. B, title XXIII, §2316(c)(2), Oct. 21, 1998, 112 Stat. 2681–50, 2681–102, 2681–480, 2681–519, 2681–829; Pub. L. 106–558, §2(a), Dec. 21, 2000, 114 Stat. 2776.)

HISTORICAL AND REVISION NOTES
1966 ACT

Derivation	U.S. Code	Revised Statutes and Statutes at Large
(a)	5 U.S.C. 911.	June 30, 1945, ch. 212, §201, 59 Stat. 296. Sept. 1, 1954, ch. 1208, §203, 68 Stat. 1109.
(b)	5 U.S.C. 912a. 5 U.S.C. 912b.	Sept. 1, 1954, ch. 1208, §205(b), 68 Stat. 1110.

In subsection (a)(1), and (2), the word "officer" is omitted as included in "employee". The word "scheduled" is omitted since section 603 of the Act of Oct. 11, 1962, Pub. L. 87–793, 76 Stat. 847, eliminated the necessity of referring to rates as scheduled or longevity. References to the "Classification Act of 1949, as amended" are omitted as unnecessary.

In subsection (b), former sections 912a and 912b are combined and restated.

Standard changes are made to conform with the definitions applicable and the style of this title as outlined in the preface to the report.

1967 ACT

Section of title 5	Source (U.S. Code)	Source (Statutes at Large)
5542(a)	5 App.: 911.	July 18, 1966, Pub. L. 89–504, §404(a), 80 Stat. 297.

The words "of the Classification Act of 1949, as amended" are omitted as unnecessary.

REFERENCES IN TEXT

GS–10 and GS–14, referred to in subsec. (a), are contained in the General Schedule which is set out under section 5332 of this title.

Section 7 of the Fair Labor Standards Act of 1938, referred to in subsec. (c), is classified to section 207 of Title 29, Labor.

Section 37(a)(3) of the State Department Basic Authorities Act of 1956, referred to in subsec. (e), is classified to section 2709(a)(3) of Title 22, Foreign Relations and Intercourse.

AMENDMENTS

2000—Subsec. (a)(5). Pub. L. 106–558 added par. (5).

1998—Subsec. (e). Pub. L. 105–277, §101(b) [title IV, §407(c)(2)] and §2316(c)(2), amended subsec. (e) identically, substituting "title 18 or section 37(a)(3) of the State Department Basic Authorities Act of 1956," for "title 18, United States Code,".

Subsec. (f). Pub. L. 105–277, §101(h) [title VI, §628(a)(1)], added subsec. (f).

1995—Subsec. (e). Pub. L. 104–52 added subsec. (e).

1994—Subsec. (d). Pub. L. 103–329 added subsec. (d).

1992—Subsec. (a)(4). Pub. L. 102–378, §2(41)(A), substituted "officer," for "officer (within the meaning of section 8331(20) or 8401(17))," and realigned margin of closing provision.

Subsec. (c). Pub. L. 102–378, §2(41)(B), amended second sentence generally. Prior to amendment, second sentence read as follows: "In the case of an employee who would, were it not for the preceding sentence, be subject to this section, hours of work in excess of 8 hours in a day shall be deemed to be overtime hours for the purposes of such section 7 and hours in a paid nonwork status shall be deemed to be hours of work."

1990—Subsec. (a). Pub. L. 101–509, §529 [title I, §101(b)(3)(E)], inserted "(including any applicable locality-based comparability payment under section 5304 or similar provision of law and any applicable special rate of pay under section 5305 or similar provision of law)" after "GS–10" wherever appearing.

Subsec. (a)(4). Pub. L. 101–509, §529 [title IV, §410(a)], added par. (4).

Subsec. (c). Pub. L. 101–509, §529 [title II, §210(1)], added subsec. (c).

1984—Subsec. (b)(2)(B)(iv). Pub. L. 98–473 inserted '', including travel by an employee to such an event and the return of such employee from such event to his or her official-duty station''.

1971—Subsec. (a). Pub. L. 92–194 substituted ''For full-time, part-time and intermittent tours of duty, hours'' for ''Hours''.

1968—Subsec. (a)(3). Pub. L. 90–556 added par. (3).

1967—Subsec. (b)(2)(B). Pub. L. 90–206 designated existing provisions as cls. (i) and (iii) and added cls. (ii) and (iv).

EFFECTIVE DATE OF 2000 AMENDMENT

Pub. L. 106–558, § 2(b), Dec. 21, 2000, 114 Stat. 2777, provided that: ''The amendments made by this section [amending this section] shall take effect on the first day of the first applicable pay period beginning on or after the end of the 30-day period beginning on the date of the enactment of this Act [Dec. 21, 2000], and shall apply only to funds appropriated after the date of the enactment of this Act.''

EFFECTIVE DATE OF 1998 AMENDMENT

Pub. L. 105–277, div. A, § 101(b) [title IV, § 407(d)], div. G, subdiv. B, title XXIII, § 2316(d), Oct. 21, 1998, 112 Stat. 2681–50, 2681–102, 2681–829, provided that: ''The amendments made by this section [amending this section and section 5545a of this title] shall take effect on the first day of the first applicable pay period—

''(1) which begins on or after the 90th day following the date of the enactment of this Act [Oct. 21, 1998]; and

''(2) on which date all regulations necessary to carry out such amendments are (in the judgment of the Director of the Office of Personnel Management and the Secretary of State) in effect.'' [Jan. 29, 1999, see 64 F.R. 4517.]

Amendment by section 101(h) [title VI, § 628(a)(1)] of Pub. L. 105–277 effective on first day of first applicable pay period which begins on or after Oct. 1, 1998, see section 101(h) [title VI, § 628(e)] of Pub. L. 105–277, set out as a note under section 4109 of this title.

EFFECTIVE DATE OF 1994 AMENDMENT

Amendment by Pub. L. 103–329 effective first day of first applicable pay period beginning on or after 30th day following Sept. 30, 1994, with exceptions relating to criminal investigators employed in Offices of Inspectors General, see section 633(e) of Pub. L. 103–329, set out as an Effective Date note under section 5545a of this title.

EFFECTIVE DATE OF 1992 AMENDMENT

Amendment by Pub. L. 102–378 effective as of first day of first applicable pay period beginning on or after Oct. 2, 1992, see section 9(b)(9) of Pub. L. 102–378, set out as a note under section 6303 of this title.

EFFECTIVE DATE OF 1990 AMENDMENT

Amendment by section 529 [title I, § 101(b)(3)(E), title II, § 210(1)] of Pub. L. 101–509 effective on such date as the President shall determine, but not earlier than 90 days, and not later than 180 days, after Nov. 5, 1990, see section 529 [title III, § 305] of Pub. L. 101–509, set out as a note under section 5301 of this title.

EFFECTIVE DATE OF 1968 AMENDMENT

Section 3 of Pub. L. 90–556 provided that: ''The amendments made by this Act [amending this section and section 5545 of this title] shall take effect on the first day of the first pay period which begins on or after the thirtieth day after the date of enactment of this Act [Oct. 10, 1968].''

EFFECTIVE DATE OF 1967 AMENDMENT

Section 220(a)(4) of title II of Pub. L. 90–206 provided that, except as otherwise expressly provided: ''Sections 222 [enacting section 5733 of this title and amending

this section, section 5544 of this title, section 3571 of Title 39, The Postal Service], and 223 [enacting section 5345 of this title] shall become effective thirty days after the date of enactment of this title [Dec. 16, 1967].''

SECTION REFERRED TO IN OTHER SECTIONS

This section is referred to in sections 5543, 5545, 5545a, 5545b, 5546, 5547, 6123, 6128 of this title; title 2 section 1371; title 14 section 432; title 15 section 278e; title 32 section 709.

§ 5543. Compensatory time off

(a) The head of an agency may—

(1) on request of an employee, grant the employee compensatory time off from his scheduled tour of duty instead of payment under section 5542 or section 7 of the Fair Labor Standards Act of 1938 for an equal amount of time spent in irregular or occasional overtime work; and

(2) provide that an employee whose rate of basic pay is in excess of the maximum rate of basic pay for GS–10 (including any applicable locality-based comparability payment under section 5304 or similar provision of law and any applicable special rate of pay under section 5305 or similar provision of law) shall be granted compensatory time off from his scheduled tour of duty equal to the amount of time spent in irregular or occasional overtime work instead of being paid for that work under section 5542 of this title.

(b) The head of an agency may, on request of an employee, grant the employee compensatory time off from the employee's scheduled tour of duty instead of payment under section 5544 or section 7 of the Fair Labor Standards Act of 1938 for an equal amount of time spent in irregular or occasional overtime work. An agency head may not require an employee to be compensated for overtime work with an equivalent amount of compensatory time-off from the employee's tour of duty.

(c) The Architect of the Capitol may grant an employee paid on an annual basis compensatory time off from duty instead of overtime pay for overtime work.

(Pub. L. 89–554, Sept. 6, 1966, 80 Stat. 486; Pub. L. 90–83, § 1(25), Sept. 11, 1967, 81 Stat. 200; Pub. L. 101–509, title V, § 529 [title I, § 101(b)(3)(E), title II, § 210(2)], Nov. 5, 1990, 104 Stat. 1427, 1439, 1460; Pub. L. 104–201, div. A, title XVI, § 1610(a), Sept. 23, 1996, 110 Stat. 2738.)

HISTORICAL AND REVISION NOTES
1966 ACT

Derivation	U.S. Code	Revised Statutes and Statutes at Large
....	5 U.S.C. 912.	June 30, 1945, ch. 212, § 202, 59 Stat. 297. May 24, 1946, ch. 270, § 9, 60 Stat. 218. Sept. 1, 1954, ch. 1208, § 204, 68 Stat. 1109.

In subsection (a), the words ''head of an agency'' are substituted for ''head of any department, independent establishment, or agency, including Government-owned or controlled corporations, or of the municipal government of the District of Columbia, or the head of any legislative or judicial agency to which this subchapter applies'' because of the definition of ''agency'' and the application stated in section 5541.

In subsection (a)(1), the word "officer" is omitted as included in "employee".

In subsection (a)(2), the words "at his own discretion" are omitted as unnecessary in view of the permissive nature of the authority. The word "officer" is omitted as included in "employee". The word "scheduled" is omitted since section 603 of the Act of Oct. 11, 1962, Pub. L. 87–793, 76 Stat. 847, eliminated the necessity of referring to rates as scheduled or longevity. Reference to the "Classification Act of 1949, as amended" is omitted as unnecessary.

In subsection (b), the words "in his discretion" are omitted as unnecessary in view of the permissive nature of the authority. The words "overtime work" are substituted for "any work in excess of forty hours in any regularly scheduled administrative workweek" because of the definition of "overtime work" in section 5542(a).

Standard changes are made to conform with the definitions applicable and the style of this title as outlined in the preface to the report.

1967 ACT

Section of title 5	Source (U.S. Code)	Source (Statutes at Large)
5543(a)(2) ...	5 App.: 912.	July 18, 1966, Pub. L. 89–504, §404(b), 80 Stat. 297.

REFERENCES IN TEXT

Section 7 of the Fair Labor Standards Act of 1938, referred to in subsecs. (a)(1) and (b), is classified to section 207 of Title 29, Labor.

GS–10, referred to in subsec. (a)(2), is contained in the General Schedule which is set out under section 5332 of this title.

AMENDMENTS

1996—Subsecs. (b), (c). Pub. L. 104–201 added subsec. (b) and redesignated former subsec. (b) as (c).

1990—Subsec. (a)(1). Pub. L. 101–509, §529 [title II, §210(2)], inserted "under section 5542 or section 7 of the Fair Labor Standards Act of 1938" after "payment".

Subsec. (a)(2). Pub. L. 101–509, §529 [title I, §101(b)(3)(E)], inserted "(including any applicable locality-based comparability payment under section 5304 or similar provision of law and any applicable special rate of pay under section 5305 or similar provision of law)" after "GS–10".

EFFECTIVE DATE OF 1990 AMENDMENT

Amendment by Pub. L. 101–509 effective on such date as the President shall determine, but not earlier than 90 days, and not later than 180 days, after Nov. 5, 1990, see section 529 [title III, §305] of Pub. L. 101–509, set out as a note under section 5301 of this title.

SECTION REFERRED TO IN OTHER SECTIONS

This section is referred to in sections 5544, 6123 of this title; title 2 section 1371; title 14 section 432; title 15 section 278e; title 32 section 709.

§ 5544. Wage-board overtime and Sunday rates; computation

(a) An employee whose pay is fixed and adjusted from time to time in accordance with prevailing rates under section 5343 or 5349 of this title, or by a wage board or similar administrative authority serving the same purpose, is entitled to overtime pay for overtime work in excess of 8 hours a day or 40 hours a week. However, an employee subject to this subsection who regularly is required to remain at or within the confines of his post of duty in excess of 8 hours a day in a standby or on-call status is entitled to overtime pay only for hours of duty, exclusive of eating and sleeping time, in excess of 40 a week. The overtime hourly rate of pay is computed as follows:

(1) If the basic rate of pay of the employee is fixed on a basis other than an annual or monthly basis, multiply the basic hourly rate of pay by not less than one and one-half.

(2) If the basic rate of pay of the employee is fixed on an annual basis, divide the basic annual rate of pay by 2,087, and multiply the quotient by one and one-half.

(3) If the basic rate of pay of the employee is fixed on a monthly basis, multiply the basic monthly rate of pay by 12 to derive a basic annual rate of pay, divide the basic annual rate of pay by 2,087, and multiply the quotient by one and one-half.

An employee subject to this subsection whose regular work schedule includes an 8-hour period of service a part of which is on Sunday is entitled to additional pay at the rate of 25 percent of his hourly rate of basic pay for each hour of work performed during that 8-hour period of service. For employees serving outside the United States in areas where Sunday is a routine workday and another day of the week is officially recognized as the day of rest and worship, the Secretary of State may designate the officially recognized day of rest and worship as the day with respect to which the preceding sentence shall apply instead of Sunday. Time spent in a travel status away from the official duty station of an employee subject to this subsection is not hours of work unless the travel (i) involves the performance of work while traveling, (ii) is incident to travel that involves the performance of work while traveling, (iii) is carried out under arduous conditions, or (iv) results from an event which could not be scheduled or controlled administratively. The first and third sentences of this subsection shall not be applicable to an employee who is subject to the overtime pay provisions of section 7 of the Fair Labor Standards Act of 1938. In the case of an employee who would, were it not for the preceding sentence, be subject to the first and third sentences of this subsection, the Office of Personnel Management shall by regulation prescribe what hours shall be deemed to be hours of work and what hours of work shall be deemed to be overtime hours for the purpose of such section 7 so as to ensure that no employee receives less pay by reason of the preceding sentence.

(b) An employee under the Office of the Architect of the Capitol who is paid on a daily or hourly basis and who is not subject to chapter 51 and subchapter III of chapter 53 of this title is entitled to overtime pay for overtime work in accordance with subsection (a) of this section. The overtime hourly rate of pay is computed in accordance with subsection (a)(1) of this section.

(c) The provisions of this section, including the last two sentences of subsection (a) and the provisions of section 5543(b), shall apply to a prevailing rate employee described in section 5342(a)(2)(B).

(Pub. L. 89–554, Sept. 6, 1966, 80 Stat. 486; Pub. L. 90–83, §1(26)(A), Sept. 11, 1967, 81 Stat. 200; Pub. L. 90–206, title II, §222(d), Dec. 16, 1967, 81 Stat. 641; Pub. L. 92–392, §5, Aug. 19, 1972, 86 Stat. 573;

Pub. L. 101–509, title V, § 529 [title II, § 210(3)], Nov. 5, 1990, 104 Stat. 1427, 1460; Pub. L. 102–378, § 2(42), Oct. 2, 1992, 106 Stat. 1352; Pub. L. 104–201, div. A, title XVI, § 1610(b), Sept. 23, 1996, 110 Stat. 2738; Pub. L. 105–277, div. G, subdiv. B, title XXIII, § 2317(1), Oct. 21, 1998, 112 Stat. 2681–829.)

HISTORICAL AND REVISION NOTES
1966 ACT

Derivation	U.S. Code	Revised Statutes and Statutes at Large
(a)	5 U.S.C. 673c (2d proviso).	Mar. 28, 1934, ch. 102, § 23 (proviso), 48 Stat. 522. Aug. 13, 1962, Pub. L. 87–581, § 201 (2d proviso), 76 Stat. 360.
	5 U.S.C. 913.	June 30, 1945, ch. 212, § 203, 59 Stat. 297. Sept. 1, 1954, ch. 1208, § 205(a), 68 Stat. 1109.
(b)	5 U.S.C. 933 (as applicable to 5 U.S.C. 673c).	June 30, 1945, ch. 212, § 503 (as applicable to § 23 of the Act of Mar. 28, 1934, ch. 102, 48 Stat. 522, as amended), 59 Stat. 301.

In subsection (a), former sections 673c (2d proviso) and 913 are combined and restated for clarity and conciseness. The last 28 words of section 205(a) of the Act of Sept. 1, 1954, 68 Stat. 1109, are omitted as executed and covered by technical section 8.

Subsection (b) is restated to conform to subsection (a). In former section 933, the words "Classification Act of 1949" were substituted for "Classification Act of 1923" on authority of section 1106(a) of the Act of Oct. 28, 1949, ch. 782, 63 Stat. 972.

Standard changes are made to conform with the definitions applicable and the style of this title as outlined in the preface to the report.

1967 ACT

Section of title 5	Source (U.S. Code)	Source (Statutes at Large)
5544(a)	5 App.: 673c (last proviso of 1st par.).	July 18, 1966, Pub. L. 89–504, § 405(f), 80 Stat. 298.

The words "a part of which is on Sunday" are coextensive with and substituted for "any part of which is within the period commencing at midnight Saturday and ending at midnight Sunday." The words "is entitled to additional pay" are coextensive with and substituted for "shall be paid extra compensation."

REFERENCES IN TEXT

Section 7 of the Fair Labor Standards Act of 1938, referred to in subsec. (a), is classified to section 207 of Title 29, Labor.

AMENDMENTS

1998—Subsec. (a). Pub. L. 105–277, which directed the amendment of subsec. (a) by inserting after the fourth sentence "For employees serving outside the United States in areas where Sunday is a routine workday and another day of the week is officially recognized as the day of rest and worship, the Secretary of State may designate the officially recognized day of rest and worship as the day with respect to which the preceding sentence shall apply instead of Sunday.", was executed by making the insertion after the first sentence of the concluding provisions, to reflect the probable intent of Congress.

1996—Subsec. (c). Pub. L. 104–201 inserted "and the provisions of section 5543(b)" after "the last two sentences of subsection (a)".

1992—Subsec. (a). Pub. L. 102–378, § 2(42)(B), amended last two sentences generally. Prior to amendment, last two sentences read as follows: "This section, other

than the sixth sentence, shall not be applicable to an employee who is subject to the overtime pay provisions of section 7 of the Fair Labor Standards Act of 1938. In the case of an employee who would, were it not for the preceding sentence, be subject to this section, hours of work in excess of 8 hours in a day shall be deemed to be overtime hours for the purposes of such section 7 and hours in a paid nonwork status shall be deemed to be hours of work."

Subsec. (a)(2), (3). Pub. L. 102–378, § 2(42)(A), substituted "2,087" for "2,080".

Subsec. (c). Pub. L. 102–378, § 2(42)(C), added subsec. (c).

1990—Subsec. (a). Pub. L. 101–509 inserted at end "This section, other than the sixth sentence, shall not be applicable to an employee who is subject to the overtime pay provisions of section 7 of the Fair Labor Standards Act of 1938. In the case of an employee who would, were it not for the preceding sentence, be subject to this section, hours of work in excess of 8 hours in a day shall be deemed to be overtime hours for the purposes of such section 7 and hours in a paid nonwork status shall be deemed to be hours of work."

1972—Subsec. (a). Pub. L. 92–392 substituted "pay" for "basic pay" and provided for determination of pay under section 5343 or 5349 of this title.

1967—Subsec. (a). Pub. L. 90–206 provided that time spent in a travel status away from the official duty station could not qualify as hours of work unless the travel involved the performance of work while traveling, was incident to travel involving the performance of work while traveling, carried out under arduous conditions, or resulting from an event which could not be scheduled or controlled administratively.

EFFECTIVE DATE OF 1992 AMENDMENT

Amendment by Pub. L. 102–378 effective as of first day of first applicable pay period beginning on or after Oct. 2, 1992, see section 9(b)(9) of Pub. L. 102–378, set out as a note under section 6303 of this title.

EFFECTIVE DATE OF 1990 AMENDMENT

Amendment by Pub. L. 101–509 effective on such date as the President shall determine, but not earlier than 90 days, and not later than 180 days, after Nov. 5, 1990, see section 529 [title III, § 305] of Pub. L. 101–509, set out as a note under section 5301 of this title.

EFFECTIVE DATE OF 1972 AMENDMENT

Amendment by Pub. L. 92–392 effective on first day of first applicable pay period beginning on or after 90th day after Aug. 19, 1972, see section 15(a) of Pub. L. 92–392, set out as an Effective Date note under section 5341 of this title.

EFFECTIVE DATE OF 1967 AMENDMENT

Amendment by Pub. L. 90–206 effective thirty days after Dec. 16, 1967, see section 220(a)(4) of Pub. L. 90–206, set out as a note under section 5542 of this title.

CANAL ZONE EMPLOYEES

Section 17(3) of Pub. L. 85–550, July 25, 1958, 72 Stat. 411, provided that nothing in Pub. L. 85–550, which related to wage and employment practices of the Government of the United States in the Canal Zone, should affect the applicability of former sections 673c and 913 of this title [covered by this section] to those classes of employees, within the scope of former sections 673c and 913 of this title [covered by this section] on July 25, 1958.

SECTION REFERRED TO IN OTHER SECTIONS

This section is referred to in sections 5541, 5543, 6123, 6128 of this title; title 2 sections 60e–2b, 1371; title 14 section 432; title 15 section 278e; title 32 section 709.

§ 5545. Night, standby, irregular, and hazardous duty differential

(a) Except as provided by subsection (b) of this section, nightwork is regularly scheduled work between the hours of 6:00 p.m. and 6:00 a.m., and includes—

(1) periods of absence with pay during these hours due to holidays; and

(2) periods of leave with pay during these hours if the periods of leave with pay during a pay period total less than 8 hours.

Except as otherwise provided by subsection (c) of this section, an employee is entitled to pay for nightwork at his rate of basic pay plus premium pay amounting to 10 percent of that basic rate. This subsection and subsection (b) of this section do not modify section 5141 of title 31, or other statute authorizing additional pay for nightwork.

(b) The head of an agency may designate a time after 6:00 p.m. and a time before 6:00 a.m. as the beginning and end, respectively, of nightwork for the purpose of subsection (a) of this section, at a post outside the United States where the customary hours of business extend into the hours of nightwork provided by subsection (a) of this section.

(c) The head of an agency, with the approval of the Office of Personnel Management, may provide that—

(1) an employee in a position requiring him regularly to remain at, or within the confines of, his station during longer than ordinary periods of duty, a substantial part of which consists of remaining in a standby status rather than performing work, shall receive premium pay for this duty on an annual basis instead of premium pay provided by other provisions of this subchapter, except for irregular, unscheduled overtime duty in excess of his regularly scheduled weekly tour. Premium pay under this paragraph is determined as an appropriate percentage, not in excess of 25 percent, of such part of the rate of basic pay for the position as does not exceed the minimum rate of basic pay for GS–10 (including any applicable locality-based comparability payment under section 5304 or similar provision of law and any applicable special rate of pay under section 5305 or similar provision of law) (or, for a position described in section 5542(a)(3) of this title, of the basic pay of the position), by taking into consideration the number of hours of actual work required in the position, the number of hours required in a standby status at or within the confines of the station, the extent to which the duties of the position are made more onerous by night, Sunday, or holiday work, or by being extended over periods of more than 40 hours a week, and other relevant factors; or

(2) an employee in a position in which the hours of duty cannot be controlled administratively, and which requires substantial amounts of irregular, unscheduled overtime duty with the employee generally being responsible for recognizing, without supervision, circumstances which require the employee to remain on duty, shall receive premium pay for this duty on an annual basis instead of premium pay provided by other provisions of this subchapter, except for regularly scheduled overtime, night, and Sunday duty, and for holiday duty. Premium pay under this paragraph is an appropriate percentage, not less than 10 percent nor more than 25 percent, of the rate

of basic pay for the position, as determined by taking into consideration the frequency and duration of irregular, unscheduled overtime duty required in the position.

(d) The Office shall establish a schedule or schedules of pay differentials for duty involving unusual physical hardship or hazard. Under such regulations as the Office may prescribe, and for such minimum periods as it determines appropriate, an employee to whom chapter 51 and subchapter III of chapter 53 of this title applies is entitled to be paid the appropriate differential for any period in which he is subjected to physical hardship or hazard not usually involved in carrying out the duties of his position. However, the pay differential—

(1) does not apply to an employee in a position the classification of which takes into account the degree of physical hardship or hazard involved in the performance of the duties thereof, except in such circumstances as the Office may by regulation prescribe; and

(2) may not exceed an amount equal to 25 percent of the rate of basic pay applicable to the employee.

(Pub. L. 89–554, Sept. 6, 1966, 80 Stat. 487; Pub. L. 90–83, §1(27), Sept. 11, 1967, 81 Stat. 200; Pub. L. 90–206, title II, §217, Dec. 16, 1967, 81 Stat. 638; Pub. L. 90–556, §2, Oct. 10, 1968, 82 Stat. 969; Pub. L. 91–231, §8, Apr. 15, 1970, 84 Stat. 198; Pub. L. 94–183, §2(23), Dec. 31, 1975, 89 Stat. 1058; Pub. L. 95–454, title IX, §906(a)(2), (3), Oct. 13, 1978, 92 Stat. 1224; Pub. L. 96–54, §2(a)(32), Aug. 14, 1979, 93 Stat. 383; Pub. L. 97–258, §3(a)(13), Sept. 13, 1982, 96 Stat. 1063; Pub. L. 101–173, §1(a), Nov. 27, 1989, 103 Stat. 1292; Pub. L. 101–509, title V, §529 [title I, §101(b)(3)(E), title II, §203], Nov. 5, 1990, 104 Stat. 1427, 1439, 1456; Pub. L. 102–378, §3(2), Oct. 2, 1992, 106 Stat. 1355.)

HISTORICAL AND REVISION NOTES
1966 ACT

Derivation	U.S. Code	Revised Statutes and Statutes at Large
(a), (b)	5 U.S.C. 921.	June 30, 1945, ch. 212, §301, 59 Stat. 298. May 24, 1946, ch. 270, §10, 60 Stat. 218. Sept. 1, 1954, ch. 1208, §206, 68 Stat. 1110.
(c)	5 U.S.C. 926.	Sept. 1, 1954, ch. 1208, §208(a), 68 Stat. 1111. July 18, 1958, Pub. L. 85–525, 72 Stat. 363.

In subsection (b), the words "head of an agency" are substituted for "head of any department, independent establishment, or agency, including Government-owned or controlled corporations" because of the definition of "agency" and the application stated in section 5541. The words "the United States" are substituted for "the several States and the District of Columbia".

In subsection (c), the words "head of an agency" are substituted for "head of any department, independent establishment, or agency, including Government-owned or controlled corporations, or of the municipal government of the District of Columbia" because of the definition of "agency" and the application stated in section 5541. The word "officer" is omitted as included in "employee". The word "scheduled" is omitted since section 603 of the Act of Oct. 11, 1962, Pub. L. 87–793, 76 Stat. 847, eliminated the necessity of referring to rates as scheduled or longevity. Reference to the "Classification Act of 1949, as amended" is omitted as unnecessary.

Standard changes are made to conform with the definitions applicable and the style of this title as outlined in the preface to the report.

1967 ACT

Section of title 5	Source (U.S. Code)	Source (Statutes at Large)
5545(c)	5 App.: 926.	July 18, 1966, Pub. L. 89–504 §§ 404(c), 405(d), (e), 80 Stat. 297, 298.
5545(d)	5 App.: 1134.	July 19, 1966, Pub. L. 89–512, § 1, 80 Stat. 318.

In the second sentence of subsection (d), the words "Under such regulations as the Commission may prescribe, and for such minimum periods as it determines appropriate" are substituted for clauses (3) and (4) of the third sentence of 5 App. U.S.C. 1134. That requirement in clause (4) that the Commission prescribe regulations is codified in 5 U.S.C. 5548(b) by section 1 (32) of this bill. The words "an employee to whom chapter 51 and subchapter III of chapter 53 of this title applies is entitled to be paid the appropriate differential" are substituted for "The appropriate differential shall be paid to any officer or employee to whom this Act applies" to reflect the codification of that act (Classification Act of 1949) in title 5, United States Code, and to conform with the definitions applicable.

In subsection (d)(1), the words "does not apply to an employee" are substituted for "shall not be applicable with respect to any officer or employee."

In subsection (d)(2), the words "may not . . . applicable to the employee" are substituted for "shall not . . . applicable with respect to such officer or employee".

REFERENCES IN TEXT

GS–10, referred to in subsec. (c)(1), is contained in the General Schedule which is set out under section 5332 of this title.

AMENDMENTS

1992—Subsec. (d). Pub. L. 102–378 made technical correction to directory language of Pub. L. 101–509, § 529 [title II, § 203]. See 1990 Amendment note below.

1990—Subsec. (c)(1). Pub. L. 101–509, § 529 [title I, § 101(b)(3)(E)], inserted "(including any applicable locality-based comparability payment under section 5304 or similar provision of law and any applicable special rate of pay under section 5305 or similar provision of law)" after "GS–10".

Subsec. (d). Pub. L. 101–509, § 529 [title II, § 203], as amended by Pub. L. 102–378, struck out "irregular or intermittent" before "duty involving unusual" in first sentence and inserted ", except in such circumstances as the Office may by regulation prescribe" after "thereof" in par. (1).

1989—Subsec. (c)(2). Pub. L. 101–173 amended par. (2) generally. Prior to amendment, par. (2) read as follows: "an employee in a position in which the hours of duty cannot be controlled administratively, and which requires substantial amounts of irregular, unscheduled, overtime duty with the employee generally being responsible for recognizing, without supervision, circumstances which require him to remain on duty, shall receive premium pay for this duty on an annual basis instead of premium pay provided by other provisions of this subchapter, except for regularly scheduled overtime, night, and Sunday duty, and for holiday duty. Premium pay under this paragraph is determined as an appropriate percentage, not less than 10 percent nor more than 25 percent, of such part of the rate of basic pay for the position as does not exceed the minimum rate of basic pay for GS–10, by taking into consideration the frequency and duration of irregular unscheduled overtime duty required in the position."

1982—Subsec. (a). Pub. L. 97–258 substituted "section 5141" for "section 180".

1979—Subsec. (c)(2). Pub. L. 96–54 substituted "percent" for "per centum" wherever appearing.

1978—Subsecs. (c), (d). Pub. L. 95–454 substituted "Office of Personnel Management" for "Civil Service Commission" and "Office" for "Commission" wherever appearing.

1975—Pub. L. 94–183 struck out "Sunday," after "Night," in section catchline.

1970—Subsec. (c)(2). Pub. L. 91–231 corrected the system of premium compensation of employees whose work schedules cannot be administratively controlled by providing for separate treatment for irregular, unscheduled, and overtime duty on one hand and for duty at night, on Sundays, and on holidays on the other.

1968—Subsec. (c)(1). Pub. L. 90–556 inserted "(or, for a position described in section 5542(a)(3) of this title, of the basic pay of the position)" after "GS–10".

1967—Subsec. (e)(2). Pub. L. 90–206 substituted "not less than 10 percent nor more than 25 percent" for "not in excess of 15 percent".

EFFECTIVE DATE OF 1990 AMENDMENT

Amendment by Pub. L. 101–509 effective on such date as the President shall determine, but not earlier than 90 days, and not later than 180 days, after Nov. 5, 1990, see section 529 [title III, § 305] of Pub. L. 101–509, set out as a note under section 5301 of this title.

EFFECTIVE DATE OF 1989 AMENDMENT

Section 1(b) of Pub. L. 101–173 provided that: "The amendment made by subsection (a) [amending this section] shall apply with respect to overtime duty performed on or after the first day of the first applicable pay period beginning after September 30, 1990."

EFFECTIVE DATE OF 1979 AMENDMENT

Amendment by Pub. L. 96–54 effective July 12, 1979, see section 2(b) of Pub. L. 96–54, set out as a note under section 305 of this title.

EFFECTIVE DATE OF 1978 AMENDMENT

Amendment by Pub. L. 95–454 effective 90 days after Oct. 13, 1978, see section 907 of Pub. L. 95–454, set out as a note under section 1101 of this title.

EFFECTIVE DATE OF 1970 AMENDMENT

Amendment by Pub. L. 91–231 effective Apr. 15, 1970, see section 9(b) of Pub. L. 91–231, set out in a 1970 Increase in Pay Rates note under section 5332 of this title.

EFFECTIVE DATE OF 1968 AMENDMENT

Amendment by Pub. L. 90–556 effective on first day of first pay period beginning on or after thirtieth day after Oct. 10, 1968, see section 3 of Pub. L. 90–556, set out as a note under section 5542 of this title.

EFFECTIVE DATE OF 1967 AMENDMENT

Amendment by Pub. L. 90–206 effective at beginning of first pay period which begins on or after Dec. 16, 1967, see section 220(a)(3) of Pub. L. 90–206, set out as a note under section 603 of Title 28, Judiciary and Judicial Procedure.

SECTION REFERRED TO IN OTHER SECTIONS

This section is referred to in sections 5541, 5545a, 5546, 5547, 5548, 5595, 6123, 8114, 8331, 8704 of this title; title 2 section 1371; title 14 section 432; title 15 section 278e; title 38 section 7457.

§ 5545a. Availability pay for criminal investigators

(a) For purposes of this section—

(1) the term "available" refers to the availability of a criminal investigator and means that an investigator shall be considered generally and reasonably accessible by the agency employing such investigator to perform un-

scheduled duty based on the needs of an agency;

(2) the term "criminal investigator" means a law enforcement officer as defined under section 5541(3) (other than an officer occupying a position under title II of Public Law 99–399, subject to subsection (k)) who is required to—

(A) possess a knowledge of investigative techniques, laws of evidence, rules of criminal procedure, and precedent court decisions concerning admissibility of evidence, constitutional rights, search and seizure, and related issues;

(B) recognize, develop, and present evidence that reconstructs events, sequences and time elements for presentation in various legal hearings and court proceedings;

(C) demonstrate skills in applying surveillance techniques, undercover work, and advising and assisting the United States Attorney in and out of court;

(D) demonstrate the ability to apply the full range of knowledge, skills, and abilities necessary for cases which are complex and unfold over a long period of time (as distinguished from certain other occupations that require the use of some investigative techniques in short-term situations that may end in arrest or detention);

(E) possess knowledge of criminal laws and Federal rules of procedure which apply to cases involving crimes against the United States, including—

(i) knowledge of the elements of a crime;
(ii) evidence required to prove the crime;
(iii) decisions involving arrest authority;
(iv) methods of criminal operations; and
(v) availability of detection devices; and

(F) possess the ability to follow leads that indicate a crime will be committed rather than initiate an investigation after a crime is committed;

(3) the term "unscheduled duty" means hours of duty a criminal investigator works, or is determined to be available for work, that are not—

(A) part of the 40 hours in the basic work week of the investigator; or
(B) overtime hours paid under section 5542; and

(4) the term "regular work day" means each day in the investigator's basic work week during which the investigator works at least 4 hours that are not overtime hours paid under section 5542 or hours considered part of section 5545a.

(b) The purpose of this section is to provide premium pay to criminal investigators to ensure the availability of criminal investigators for unscheduled duty in excess of a 40 hour work week based on the needs of the employing agency.

(c) Each criminal investigator shall be paid availability pay as provided under this section. Availability pay shall be paid to ensure the availability of the investigator for unscheduled duty. The investigator is generally responsible for recognizing, without supervision, circumstances which require the investigator to be on duty or be available for unscheduled duty based

on the needs of the agency. Availability pay provided to a criminal investigator for such unscheduled duty shall be paid instead of premium pay provided by other provisions of this subchapter, except premium pay for regularly scheduled overtime work as provided under section 5542, night duty, Sunday duty, and holiday duty.

(d)(1) A criminal investigator shall be paid availability pay, if the average of hours described under paragraph (2)(A) and (B) is equal to or greater than 2 hours.

(2) The hours referred to under paragraph (1) are—

(A) the annual average of unscheduled duty hours worked by the investigator in excess of each regular work day; and

(B) the annual average of unscheduled duty hours such investigator is available to work on each regular work day upon request of the employing agency.

(3) Unscheduled duty hours which are worked by an investigator on days that are not regular work days shall be considered in the calculation of the annual average of unscheduled duty hours worked or available for purposes of certification.

(4) An investigator shall be considered to be available when the investigator cannot reasonably and generally be accessible due to a status or assignment which is the result of an agency direction, order, or approval as provided under subsection (f)(1).

(e)(1) Each criminal investigator receiving availability pay under this section and the appropriate supervisory officer, to be designated by the head of the agency, shall make an annual certification to the head of the agency that the investigator has met, and is expected to meet, the requirements of subsection (d). The head of a law enforcement agency may prescribe regulations necessary to administer this subsection.

(2) Involuntary reduction in pay resulting from a denial of certification under paragraph (1) shall be a reduction in pay for purposes of section 7512(4) of this title.

(f)(1) A criminal investigator who is eligible for availability pay shall receive such pay during any period such investigator is—

(A) attending agency sanctioned training;
(B) on agency approved sick leave or annual leave;
(C) on agency ordered travel status; or
(D) on excused absence with pay for relocation purposes.

(2) Notwithstanding paragraph (1)(A), agencies or departments may provide availability pay to investigators during training which is considered initial, basic training usually provided in the first year of service.

(3) Agencies or departments may provide availability pay to investigators when on excused absence with pay, except as provided in paragraph (1)(D).

(g) Section 5545(c) shall not apply to any criminal investigator who is paid availability pay under this section.

(h) Availability pay under this section shall be—

(1) 25 percent of the rate of basic pay for the position; and

(2) treated as part of the basic pay for purposes of—

(A) sections 5595(c), 8114(e), 8331(3), and 8704(c); and

(B) such other purposes as may be expressly provided for by law or as the Office of Personnel Management may by regulation prescribe.

(i) The provisions of subsections (a)–(h) providing for availability pay shall apply to a pilot employed by the United States Customs Service who is a law enforcement officer as defined under section 5541(3). For the purpose of this section, section 5542(d) of this title, and section 13(a)(16) and (b)(30) of the Fair Labor Standards Act of 1938 (29 U.S.C. 213(a)(16) and (b)(30)), such pilot shall be deemed to be a criminal investigator as defined in this section. The Office of Personnel Management may prescribe regulations to carry out this subsection.

(j) Notwithstanding any other provision of this section, any Office of Inspector General which employs fewer than 5 criminal investigators may elect not to cover such criminal investigators under this section.

(k)(1) For purposes of this section, the term "criminal investigator" includes a special agent occupying a position under title II of Public Law 99–399 if such special agent—

(A) meets the definition of such term under paragraph (2) of subsection (a) (applied disregarding the parenthetical matter before subparagraph (A) thereof); and

(B) such special agent satisfies the requirements of subsection (d) without taking into account any hours described in paragraph (2)(B) thereof.

(2) In applying subsection (h) with respect to a special agent under this subsection—

(A) any reference in such subsection to "basic pay" shall be considered to include amounts designated as "salary";

(B) paragraph (2)(A) of such subsection shall be considered to include (in addition to the provisions of law specified therein) sections 609(b)(1), 805, 806, and 856 of the Foreign Service Act of 1980; and

(C) paragraph (2)(B) of such subsection shall be applied by substituting for "Office of Personnel Management" the following: "Office of Personnel Management or the Secretary of State (to the extent that matters exclusively within the jurisdiction of the Secretary are concerned)".

(Added Pub. L. 103–329, title VI, § 633(b)(1), Sept. 30, 1994, 108 Stat. 2425; amended Pub. L. 104–19, title I, §§ 901, 902(a), July 27, 1995, 109 Stat. 230; Pub. L. 104–208, div. A, title I, § 101(f) [title VI, § 659 [title II, § 206(b)(2)]], Sept. 30, 1996, 110 Stat. 3009–314, 3009–372, 3009–378; Pub. L. 105–277, div. A, § 101(b) [title IV, § 407(a), (c)(1)], div. G, subdiv. B, title XXIII, § 2316(a), (c)(1), Oct. 21, 1998, 112 Stat. 2681–50, 2681–101, 2681–102, 2681–828.)

REFERENCES IN TEXT

Title II of Public Law 99–399, referred to in subsecs. (a)(2) and (k)(1), is title II of Pub. L. 99–399, Aug. 27, 1986, 100 Stat. 858, as amended, which is classified generally to subchapter II (§ 4821 et seq.) of chapter 58 of Title 22, Foreign Relations and Intercourse. For complete classification of this Act to the Code, see Short Title note set out under section 4801 of Title 22 and Tables.

Sections 609(b)(1), 805, 806, and 856 of the Foreign Service Act of 1980, referred to in subsec. (k)(2)(B), are classified to sections 4009(b)(1), 4045, 4046, and 4071e, respectively, of Title 22, Foreign Relations and Intercourse.

AMENDMENTS

1998—Subsec. (a)(2). Pub. L. 105–277, § 101(b) [title IV, § 407(c)(1)] and § 2316(c)(1), amended subsec. (a)(2) identically, substituting "Public Law 99–399, subject to subsection (k))" for "Public Law 99–399)" in introductory provisions.

Subsec. (k). Pub. L. 105–277, § 101(b) [title IV, § 407(a)] and § 2316(a), amended section identically, adding subsec. (k).

1996—Subsec. (h)(2)(A). Pub. L. 104–208 struck out "8431," after "8331(3),".

1995—Subsec. (a)(2). Pub. L. 104–19, § 901(1)(A), inserted "who" before "is required to" in introductory provisions.

Subsec. (a)(2)(E)(v). Pub. L. 104–19, § 901(1)(B), inserted "and" at end.

Subsec. (i). Pub. L. 104–19, § 902(a), added subsec. (i).

Subsec. (j). Pub. L. 104–19, § 901(2), added subsec. (j).

EFFECTIVE DATE OF 1998 AMENDMENT

For effective date of amendment by Pub. L. 105–277, see section 101(b) [title IV, § 407(d)] and section 2316(d) of Pub. L. 105–277, set out as a note under section 5542 of this title.

EFFECTIVE DATE OF 1996 AMENDMENT

Section 101(f) [title VI, § 659 [title II, § 207]] of Pub. L. 104–208 provided that: "This title [title II (§§ 201–207) of section 659 of section 101(f) of Pub. L. 104–208, amending this section and sections 8351, 8401, 8433, 8435, and 8440a to 8440c of this title, repealing section 8431 of this title, enacting provisions set out as notes under sections 8401 and 8433 of this title, and amending provisions set out as a note under section 5343 of this title] shall take effect on the date of the enactment of this Act [Sept. 30, 1996] and withdrawals and elections as provided under the amendments made by this title shall be made at the earliest practicable date as determined by the Executive Director in regulations."

EFFECTIVE DATE OF 1995 AMENDMENT

Section 902(b) of Pub. L. 104–19 provided that: "The amendment made by subsection (a) of this section [amending this section] shall take effect on the first day of the first applicable pay period which begins on or after the 30th day following the date of enactment of this Act [July 27, 1995]."

EFFECTIVE DATE

Section 633(e) of Pub. L. 103–329 provided that: "The amendments made by this section [enacting this section and amending sections 5542 and 5547 of this title and section 213 of Title 29, Labor] shall take effect on the first day of the first applicable pay period which begins on or after the later of October 1, 1994, or the 30th day following the date of enactment of this Act [Sept. 30, 1994], except that:

"(1) Criminal investigators, employed in Offices of Inspectors General, who are not receiving administratively uncontrollable overtime compensation or who are receiving such premium pay at a rate less than 25 percent prior to the date of enactment of this Act, may implement availability pay at any time prior to September 30, 1995, after which date availability pay as authorized under this section shall be provided to such criminal investigators.

"(2) Criminal investigators, employed by Offices of Inspectors General, who are receiving administratively uncontrollable overtime at a rate less than 25 percent, shall continue to receive this compensation at the same rate or higher until availability pay compensation is provided, which shall be no later than the last pay period ending on or before September 30, 1995.''

IMPLEMENTATION

Pub. L. 105–277, div. A, § 101(b) [title IV, § 407(b)], div. G, subdiv. B, title XXIII, § 2316(b), Oct. 21, 1998, 112 Stat. 2681–50, 2681–102, 2681–828, provided that: ''Not later than the date on which the amendments made by this section [amending this section and section 5542 of this title] take effect [see Effective Date of 1998 Amendment note set out above], each special agent of the Diplomatic Security Service who satisfies the requirements of subsection (k)(1) of section 5545a of title 5, United States Code, as amended by this section, and the appropriate supervisory officer, to be designated by the Secretary of State, shall make an initial certification to the Secretary of State that the special agent is expected to meet the requirements of subsection (d) of such section 5545a. The Secretary of State may prescribe procedures necessary to administer this subsection.''

CERTIFICATION OF CRIMINAL INVESTIGATORS

Section 633(f) of Pub. L. 103–329 provided that: ''Not later than the effective date of this section [see Effective Date note above], each criminal investigator under section 5545a of title 5, United States Code, as added by this section, and the appropriate supervisory officer, to be designated by the head of the agency, shall make an initial certification to the head of the agency that the criminal investigator is expected to meet the requirements of subsection (d) of such section 5545a. The head of a law enforcement agency may prescribe procedures necessary to administer this paragraph.''

SECTION REFERRED TO IN OTHER SECTIONS

This section is referred to in sections 5542, 5547, 8331 of this title; title 2 section 1371; title 29 section 213.

§ 5545b. Pay for firefighters

(a) This section applies to an employee whose position is classified in the firefighter occupation in conformance with the GS–081 standard published by the Office of Personnel Management, and whose normal work schedule, as in effect throughout the year, consists of regular tours of duty which average at least 106 hours per biweekly pay period.

(b)(1) If the regular tour of duty of a firefighter subject to this section generally consists of 24-hour shifts, rather than a basic 40-hour workweek (as determined under regulations prescribed by the Office of Personnel Management), section 5504(b) shall be applied as follows in computing pay—

(A) paragraph (1) of such section shall be deemed to require that the annual rate be divided by 2756 to derive the hourly rate; and

(B) the computation of such firefighter's daily, weekly, or biweekly rate shall be based on the hourly rate under subparagraph (A);

(2) For the purpose of sections 5595(c), 5941, 8331(3), and 8704(c), and for such other purposes as may be expressly provided for by law or as the Office of Personnel Management may by regulation prescribe, the basic pay of a firefighter subject to this subsection shall include an amount equal to the firefighter's basic hourly rate (as computed under paragraph (1)(A)) for all hours in such firefighter's regular tour of duty (including overtime hours).

(c)(1) If the regular tour of duty of a firefighter subject to this section includes a basic

40-hour workweek (as determined under regulations prescribed by the Office of Personnel Management), section 5504(b) shall be applied as follows in computing pay—

(A) the provisions of such section shall apply to the hours within the basic 40-hour workweek;

(B) for hours outside the basic 40-hour workweek, such section shall be deemed to require that the hourly rate be derived by dividing the annual rate by 2756; and

(C) the computation of such firefighter's daily, weekly, or biweekly rate shall be based on subparagraphs (A) and (B), as each applies to the hours involved.

(2) For purposes of sections 5595(c), 5941, 8331(3), and 8704(c), and for such other purposes as may be expressly provided for by law or as the Office of Personnel Management may by regulation prescribe, the basic pay of a firefighter subject to this subsection shall include—

(A) an amount computed under paragraph (1)(A) for the hours within the basic 40-hour workweek; and

(B) an amount equal to the firefighter's basic hourly rate (as computed under paragraph (1)(B)) for all hours outside the basic 40-hour workweek that are within such firefighter's regular tour of duty (including overtime hours).

(d)(1) A firefighter who is subject to this section shall receive overtime pay in accordance with section 5542, but shall not receive premium pay provided by other provisions of this subchapter.

(2) For the purpose of applying section 7(k) of the Fair Labor Standards Act of 1938 to a firefighter who is subject to this section, no violation referred to in such section 7(k) shall be deemed to have occurred if the requirements of section 5542(a) are met, applying section 5542(a) as provided in subsection (f) of that section: Provided, That the overtime hourly rate of pay for such firefighter shall in all cases be an amount equal to one and one-half times the firefighter's hourly rate of basic pay under subsection (b)(1)(A) or (c)(1)(B) of this section, as applicable.

(3) The Office of Personnel Management may prescribe regulations, with respect to firefighters subject to this section, that would permit an agency to reduce or eliminate the variation in the amount of firefighters' biweekly pay caused by work scheduling cycles that result in varying hours in the regular tours of duty from pay period to pay period. Under such regulations, the pay that a firefighter would otherwise receive for regular tours of duty over the work scheduling cycle shall, to the extent practicable, remain unaffected.

(4) Notwithstanding section 8114(e)(1), overtime pay for a firefighter subject to this section for hours in a regular tour of duty shall be included in any computation of pay under section 8114.

(Added Pub. L. 105–277, div. A, § 101(h) [title VI, § 628(a)(2)], Oct. 21, 1998, 112 Stat. 2681–480, 2681–519; amended Pub. L. 106–554, § 1(a)(3) [title VI, § 641(a)], Dec. 21, 2000, 114 Stat. 2763, 2763A–169.)

REFERENCES IN TEXT

Section 7(k) of the Fair Labor Standards Act of 1938, referred to in subsec. (d)(2), is classified to section 207(k) of Title 29, Labor.

AMENDMENTS

2000—Subsec. (d)(4). Pub. L. 106–554 added par. (4).

EFFECTIVE DATE OF 2000 AMENDMENT

Pub. L. 106–554, § 1(a)(3) [title VI, § 641(b)], Dec. 21, 2000, 114 Stat. 2763, 2763A–169, provided that: "The amendment in subsection (a) [amending this section] shall be effective as if it had been enacted as part of the Federal Firefighters Overtime Pay Reform Act of 1998 [Pub. L. 105–277, div A, § 101(h) [title VI, § 628]] (112 Stat. 2681–519)."

EFFECTIVE DATE

Section effective on first day of first applicable pay period which begins on or after Oct. 1, 1998, see section 101(h) [title VI, § 628(e)] of Pub. L. 105–277, set out as an Effective Date of 1998 Amendment note under section 4109 of this title.

REGULATIONS

Pub. L. 105–277, div. A, § 101(h) [title VI, § 628(f)], Oct. 21, 1998, 112 Stat. 2681–480, 2681–521, provided that: "Under regulations prescribed by the Office of Personnel Management, a firefighter subject to section 5545b of title 5, United States Code, as added by this section, whose regular tours of duty average 60 hours or less per workweek and do not include a basic 40-hour workweek, shall, upon implementation of this section, be granted an increase in basic pay equal to 2 step-increases of the applicable General Schedule grade, and such increase shall not be an equivalent increase in pay. If such increase results in a change to a longer waiting period for the firefighter's next step increase, the firefighter shall be credited with an additional year of service for the purpose of such waiting period. If such increase results in a rate of basic pay which is above the maximum rate of the applicable grade, such resulting pay rate shall be treated as a retained rate of basic pay in accordance with section 5363 of title 5, United States Code."

ELIGIBILITY FOR PAY INCREASE

Pub. L. 106–31, title III, § 3032, May 21, 1999, 113 Stat. 104, provided that:

"(a) The treatment provided to firefighters under section 628(f) of the Treasury and General Government Appropriations Act, 1999 (as included in section 101(h) of division A of the Omnibus Consolidated and Emergency Supplemental Appropriations Act, 1999 (Public Law 105–277)) [set out as a note above] shall be provided to any firefighter who—

"(1) on the effective date of section 5545b of title 5, United States Code [see Effective Date note above]—

"(A) was subject to such section; and

"(B) had a regular tour of duty that averaged more than 60 hours per week; and

"(2) before December 31, 1999, is involuntarily moved without a break in service from the regular tour of duty under paragraph (1) to a regular tour of duty that—

"(A) averages 60 hours or less per week; and

"(B) does not include a basic 40-hour workweek.

"(b) Subsection (a) shall apply to firefighters described under that subsection as of the effective date of section 5545b of title 5, United States Code.

"(c) The Office of Personnel Management may prescribe regulations necessary to implement this section."

NO REDUCTION IN REGULAR PAY

Pub. L. 105–277, div. A, § 101(h) [title VI, § 628(g)], Oct. 21, 1998, 112 Stat. 2681–480, 2681–521, provided that: "Under regulations prescribed by the Office of Person-

nel Management, the regular pay (over the established work scheduling cycle) of a firefighter subject to section 5545b of title 5, United States Code, as added by this section, shall not be reduced as a result of the implementation of this section."

SECTION REFERRED TO IN OTHER SECTIONS

This section is referred to in sections 4109, 5542, 8331 of this title.

§ 5546. Pay for Sunday and holiday work

(a) An employee who performs work during a regularly scheduled 8-hour period of service which is not overtime work as defined by section 5542(a) of this title a part of which is performed on Sunday is entitled to pay for the entire period of service at the rate of his basic pay, plus premium pay at a rate equal to 25 percent of his rate of basic pay. For employees serving outside the United States in areas where Sunday is a routine workday and another day of the week is officially recognized as the day of rest and worship, the Secretary of State may designate the officially recognized day of rest and worship as the day with respect to which the preceding sentence shall apply instead of Sunday.

(b) An employee who performs work on a holiday designated by Federal Statute, Executive order, or with respect to an employee of the government of the District of Columbia, by order of the District of Columbia Council, is entitled to pay at the rate of his basic pay, plus premium pay at a rate equal to the rate of his basic pay, for that holiday work which is not—

(1) in excess of 8 hours; or

(2) overtime work as defined by section 5542(a) of this title.

(c) An employee who is required to perform any work on a designated holiday is entitled to pay for at least 2 hours of holiday work.

(d) An employee who performs overtime work as defined by section 5542(a) of this title on a Sunday or a designated holiday is entitled to pay for that overtime work in accordance with section 5542(a) of this title.

(e) Premium pay under this section is in addition to premium pay which may be due for the same work under section 5545(a) and (b) of this title, providing premium pay for nightwork.

(Pub. L. 89–554, Sept. 6, 1966, 80 Stat. 488; Pub. L. 90–83, § 1(29), Sept. 11, 1967, 81 Stat. 201; Pub. L. 90–623, § 1(13), Oct. 22, 1968, 82 Stat. 1312; Pub. L. 105–277, div. G, subdiv. B, title XXIII, § 2317(2), Oct. 21, 1998, 112 Stat. 2681–829.)

HISTORICAL AND REVISION NOTES
1966 ACT

Derivation	U.S. Code	Revised Statutes and Statutes at Large
....	5 U.S.C. 922.	June 30, 1945, ch. 212, § 302, 59 Stat. 298. May 24, 1946, ch. 270, § 11, 60 Stat. 218. Sept. 1, 1954, ch. 1208, § 207, 68 Stat. 1110. July 18, 1958, Pub. L. 85–533, § 1, 72 Stat. 377.

In subsections (a) and (b), the word "officer" is omitted as included in "employee".

In subsections (b) and (c), the word "designated" is substituted for "such a" and "such" in former section

922(b) and (c) to identify the holiday as one designated by statute, Executive order, or the Board of Commissioners of the District of Columbia.

Standard changes are made to conform with the definitions applicable and the style of this title as outlined in the preface to the report.

1967 ACT

Section of title 5	Source (U.S. Code)	Source (Statutes at Large)
5546(a)	5 App.: 921a.	July 18, 1966, Pub. L. 89–504, § 405(b)(1), (c), 80 Stat. 297.

In subsection (a), the words "An employee who performs work . . . is entitled to pay . . . at the rate of his basic pay" are coextensive with and substituted for "Any . . . service . . . performed . . . shall be compensated . . . at the rate of basic compensation of the officer or employee performing such work." The words "section 5542(a) of this title" are substituted for "section 201 of this Act" to reflect the codification of that section in title 5, United States Code. The words "between midnight Saturday and midnight Sunday" are coextensive with and substituted for "within the period commencing at midnight Saturday and ending at midnight Sunday".

AMENDMENTS

1998—Subsec. (a). Pub. L. 105–277 inserted at end "For employees serving outside the United States in areas where Sunday is a routine workday and another day of the week is officially recognized as the day of rest and worship, the Secretary of State may designate the officially recognized day of rest and worship as the day with respect to which the preceding sentence shall apply instead of Sunday."

1968—Subsec. (b). Pub. L. 90–623, § 1(13)(A), substituted "District of Columbia Council" for "Board of Commissioners of the District of Columbia".

Subsec. (d). Pub. L. 90–623, § 1(13)(B), substituted "5542(a)" for "5442(a)".

EFFECTIVE DATE OF 1968 AMENDMENT

Amendment by Pub. L. 90–623 intended to restate without substantive change the law in effect on Oct. 22, 1968, but amendment of subsec. (d) of this section by section 1(13)(B) of Pub. L. 90–623 effective as of Sept. 6, 1966, for all purposes, see section 6 of Pub. L. 90–623, set out as a note under section 5334 of this title.

TRANSFER OF FUNCTIONS

District of Columbia Council, as established by Reorg. Plan No. 3 of 1967, abolished as of noon Jan. 2, 1975, by Pub. L. 93–198, title VII, § 711, Dec. 24, 1973, 87 Stat. 818, and replaced by Council of District of Columbia, as provided by section 401 of Pub. L. 93–198.

CONDITION OF PERFORMANCE

Pub. L. 105–277, div. A, § 101(h) [title VI, § 624], Oct. 21, 1998, 112 Stat. 2681–480, 2681–518, provided that: "Notwithstanding any other provision of law, no part of any funds provided by this Act or any other Act beginning in fiscal year 1999 and thereafter shall be available for paying Sunday premium pay to any employee unless such employee actually performed work during the time corresponding to such premium pay."

Similar provisions were contained in the following prior appropriations act:

Pub. L. 105–61, title VI, § 636, Oct. 10, 1997, 111 Stat. 1316.

SECTION REFERRED TO IN OTHER SECTIONS

This section is referred to in sections 5541, 5547, 6128 of this title; title 2 section 1371; title 14 section 432; title 15 section 278e.

§ 5546a. Differential pay for certain employees of the Federal Aviation Administration and the Department of Defense

(a) The Administrator of the Federal Aviation Administration (hereafter in this section referred to as the "Administrator") and the Secretary of Defense (hereafter in this section referred to as the "Secretary") may pay premium pay at the rate of 5 per centum of the applicable rate of basic pay to—

(1) any employee of the Federal Aviation Administration or the Department of Defense who is—

(A) occupying a position in the air traffic controller series classified not lower than GS–9 and located in an air traffic control center or terminal or in a flight service station;

(B) assigned to a position classified not lower than GS–09 or WG–10 located in an airway facilities sector; or

(C) assigned to a flight inspection crewmember position classified not lower than GS–11 located in a flight inspection field office,

the duties of whose position are determined by the Administrator or the Secretary to be directly involved in or responsible for the operation and maintenance of the air traffic control system; and

(2) any employee of the Federal Aviation Administration or the Department of Defense who is assigned to a flight test pilot position classified not lower than GS–12 located in a region or center, the duties of whose position are determined by the Administrator or the Secretary to be unusually taxing, physically or mentally, and to be critical to the advancement of aviation safety; and

(3) any employee of the Federal Aviation Administration who occupies a position at the Federal Aviation Administration Academy, Oklahoma City, Oklahoma, the duties of which are determined by the Administrator to require the individual to be actively engaged in or directly responsible for training employees to perform the duties of a position described in subparagraph (a); (b); or (c) or paragraph (1) of this subsection, and who, immediately prior to assuming such position at such Academy, occupied a position referred to in subparagraph (a), (b), or (c) of paragraph (1) of this subsection.

(b) The premium pay payable under any subsection of this section is in addition to basic pay and to premium pay payable under any other subsection of this section and any other provision of this subchapter.

(c)(1) The Administrator or the Secretary may pay premium pay to any employee of the Federal Aviation Administration or the Department of Defense who—

(A) is an air traffic controller located in an air traffic control center or terminal;

(B) is not required as a condition of employment to be certified by the Administrator or the Secretary as proficient and medically qualified to perform duties including the separation and control of air traffic; and

(C) is so certified.

(2) Premium pay paid under paragraph (1) of this subsection shall be paid at the rate of 1.6 per centum of the applicable rate of basic pay for so long as such employee is so certified.

(d)(1) The Administrator or the Secretary may pay premium pay to any air traffic controller of the Federal Aviation Administration or the Department of Defense who is assigned by the Administrator or the Secretary to provide on-the-job training to another air traffic controller while such other air traffic controller is directly involved in the separation and control of live air traffic.

(2) Premium pay paid under paragraph (1) of this subsection shall be paid at the rate of 10 per centum of the applicable hourly rate of basic pay times the number of hours and portion of an hour during which the air traffic controller of the Federal Aviation Administration or the Department of Defense provides on-the-job training.

(e)(1) The Administrator or the Secretary may pay premium pay to any air traffic controller or flight service station specialist of the Federal Aviation Administration or the Department of Defense who, while working a regularly scheduled eight-hour period of service, is required by his supervisor to work during the fourth through sixth hour of such period without a break of thirty minutes for a meal.

(2) Premium pay paid under paragraph (1) of this subsection shall be paid at the rate of 50 per centum of one-half of the applicable hourly rate of basic pay.

(f)(1) The Administrator or the Secretary shall prescribe standards for determining which air traffic controllers and other employees of the Federal Aviation Administration or the Department of Defense are to be paid premium pay under this section.

(2) The Administrator and the Secretary may prescribe such rules as he determines are necessary to carry out the provisions of this section.

(Added Pub. L. 97–276, §151(c)(1), (d), Oct. 2, 1982, 96 Stat. 1200, 1201; amended Pub. L. 97–377, title I, §145(a), formerly §145, Dec. 21, 1982, 96 Stat. 1917, renumbered Pub. L. 98–78, title III, §320(1), Aug. 15, 1983, 97 Stat. 473; Pub. L. 98–525, title XV, §1537(c)(1)–(6)(A), Oct. 19, 1984, 98 Stat. 2635, 2636.)

AMENDMENTS

1984—Pub. L. 98–525, §1537(c)(6)(A), inserted "and the Department of Defense" in section catchline.

Subsec. (a). Pub. L. 98–525, §1537(c)(1)(A), inserted "and the Secretary of Defense (hereafter in this section referred to as the 'Secretary')" in provisions preceding par. (1).

Subsec. (a)(1). Pub. L. 98–525, §1537(c)(1)(B), inserted "or the Department of Defense" in provisions preceding subpar. (A) and "or the Secretary" in provisions following subpar. (C).

Subsec. (a)(2). Pub. L. 98–525, §1537(c)(1)(C), inserted "or the Department of Defense" and "or the Secretary".

Subsecs. (c)(1), (d), (e)(1), (f)(1). Pub. L. 98–525, §1537(c)(2)–(5)(A), inserted "or the Secretary" after "Administrator" wherever appearing, and "or the Department of Defense" after "Administration" wherever appearing.

Subsec. (f)(2). Pub. L. 98–525, §1537(c)(5)(B), inserted "and the Secretary".

1982—Subsec. (a)(3). Pub. L. 97–377 added par. (3).

EFFECTIVE DATE OF 1984 AMENDMENT

Amendment by Pub. L. 98–525 effective Oct. 1, 1984, see section 1537(f) of Pub. L. 98–525, set out as a note under section 4109 of this title.

EFFECTIVE DATE OF 1982 AMENDMENT

Section 145(b) of Pub. L. 97–377, as added by Pub. L. 98–78, title III, §320(2), Aug. 15, 1983, 97 Stat. 473, provided that: "The amendment made by subsection (a) of this section [amending this section] shall be effective as of 5 o'clock ante meridian eastern daylight time, August 3, 1981."

EFFECTIVE DATE

Section 151(h)(1), (2) of Pub. L. 97–276 provided that: "(1) The amendments made by subsections 152 [151] (b), (c), (e), and (g) of this joint resolution [enacting subsecs. (a) and (b) of this section and amending sections 5532, 5547, and 8344 of this title] shall take effect at 5 o'clock ante meridian eastern daylight time, August 3, 1981.

"(2) The amendments made by subsection 152 [151] (a) and subsection 152 [151] (d) of this joint resolution [enacting subsecs. (c)–(f) of this section and amending section 4109 of this title] shall take effect on the first day of the first applicable pay period beginning after the date of the enactment of this joint resolution [Oct. 2, 1982]."

SECTION REFERRED TO IN OTHER SECTIONS

This section is referred to in section 5547 of this title; title 2 section 1371.

§ 5547. Limitation on premium pay

(a) An employee may be paid premium pay under sections 5542, 5545(a), (b), and (c), 5545a, and 5546(a) and (b) of this title only to the extent that the payment does not cause his aggregate rate of pay for any pay period to exceed the maximum rate for GS–15 (including any applicable locality-based comparability payment under section 5304 or similar provision of law and any applicable special rate of pay under section 5305 or similar provision of law). The first sentence of this subsection shall not apply to any employee of the Federal Aviation Administration or the Department of Defense who is paid premium pay under section 5546a of this title.

(b)(1) Subject to regulations prescribed by the Office of Personnel Management, the first sentence of subsection (a) shall not apply to an employee who is paid premium pay by reason of work in connection with an emergency which involves a direct threat to life or property, including a forest wildfire emergency.

(2) Notwithstanding paragraph (1), no employee referred to in such paragraph may be paid premium pay under the provisions of law cited in the first sentence of subsection (a) if, or to the extent that, the aggregate of such employee's basic pay and premium pay under those provisions would, in any calendar year, exceed the maximum rate payable for GS–15 in effect at the end of such calendar year.

(c)(1) Subsections (a) and (b) shall not apply to a law enforcement officer.

(2) A law enforcement officer may be paid premium pay under the provisions of law cited in the first sentence of subsection (a) only to the extent that the payment does not cause the offi-

cer's aggregate rate of pay for any pay period to exceed the lesser of—

(A) 150 percent of the minimum rate payable for GS–15 (including any applicable locality-based comparability payment under section 5304 or similar provision of law and any applicable special rate of pay under section 5305 or similar provision of law); or

(B) the rate payable for level V of the Executive Schedule.

(Pub. L. 89–554, Sept. 6, 1966, 80 Stat. 488; Pub. L. 90–83, § 1(31), Sept. 11, 1967, 81 Stat. 201; Pub. L. 97–276, § 151(e), Oct. 2, 1982, 96 Stat. 1201; Pub. L. 98–525, title XV, § 1537(d), Oct. 19, 1984, 98 Stat. 2636; Pub. L. 100–523, § 2, Oct. 24, 1988, 102 Stat. 2605; Pub. L. 101–509, title V, § 529 [title II, § 204, title IV, § 410(b)], Nov. 5, 1990, 104 Stat. 1427, 1456, 1469; Pub. L. 102–378, § 2(43), Oct. 2, 1992, 106 Stat. 1352; Pub. L. 103–329, title VI, § 633(b)(2), Sept. 30, 1994, 108 Stat. 2427.)

HISTORICAL AND REVISION NOTES
1966 ACT

Derivation	U.S. Code	Revised Statutes and Statutes at Large
....	5 U.S.C. 943.	June 30, 1945, ch. 212, § 603, 59 Stat. 302. May 24, 1946, ch. 270, § 7(a), 60 Stat. 218. July 3, 1948, ch. 830, § 303(a), 62 Stat. 1268. Sept. 1, 1954, ch. 1208, § 209, 68 Stat. 1112.

Former section 943(a), (b) is combined and restated for clarity and conciseness. The word "officer" is omitted as included in "employee". The word "scheduled" is omitted since section 603 of the Act of Oct. 11, 1962, Pub. L. 87–793, 76 Stat. 847, eliminated the necessity of referring to rates as scheduled or longevity. Reference to the "Classification Act of 1949, as amended" is omitted as unnecessary.

Standard changes are made to conform with the definitions applicable and the style of this title as outlined in the preface to the report.

1967 ACT

In the codification of 5 U.S.C. 5547, the words "premium pay under this subchapter" were substituted for "premium compensation provided by this Act" appearing in the source statute—section 603 of the Federal Employees Pay Act of 1945, as amended (former 5 U.S.C. 943). This amendment of 5 U.S.C. 5547 is made for clarity and precision of reference and in recognition that the source statutes for certain sections of subchapter V of chapter 55 of title 5 include statutes that were not a part of the Federal Employees Pay Act of 1949. Specifically, 5 U.S.C. 5544(a) is based in part on section 23 (2d proviso) of the act of March 28, 1934, as amended by 76 Stat. 360; and 5 U.S.C. 5545(d) is based on section 804 of the Classification Act of 1949, as added by Public Law 89–512, 80 Stat. 318. Also, 5 U.S.C. 5541(2)(xi) in effect excludes employees subject to 5 U.S.C. 5544 from the operation of 5 U.S.C. 5547.

REFERENCES IN TEXT

GS–15, referred to in subsecs. (a), (b)(2), and (c)(2)(A), is contained in the General Schedule which is set out under section 5332 of this title.

Level V of the Executive Schedule, referred to in subsec. (c)(2)(B), is set out in section 5316 of this title.

AMENDMENTS

1994—Subsec. (a). Pub. L. 103–329 inserted "5545a," after "5545(a), (b), and (c),".

1992—Subsec. (c)(3). Pub. L. 102–378 struck out par. (3) which read as follows: "For the purposes of this sub-

section, 'law enforcement officer' means any law enforcement officer within the meaning of section 8331(20) or section 8401(17)."

1990—Subsec. (a). Pub. L. 101–509, § 529 [title II, § 204(1)], inserted "(including any applicable locality-based comparability payment under section 5304 or similar provision of law and any applicable special rate of pay under section 5305 or similar provision of law)" after "GS–15".

Subsec. (b). Pub. L. 101–509, § 529 [title II, § 204(2)], amended subsec. (b) generally, substituting present provisions for former provisions consisting of pars. (1) to (3) that related to pay of forest firefighters working on forest wildfire emergencies.

Subsec. (c). Pub. L. 101–509, § 529 [title IV, § 410(b)], added subsec. (c).

1988—Pub. L. 100–523 amended section generally, designating existing provisions as subsec. (a) and adding subsec. (b).

1984—Pub. L. 98–525 inserted "or the Department of Defense".

1982—Pub. L. 97–276 inserted provision directing that first sentence of this section not apply to any employee of Federal Aviation Administration who is paid premium pay under section 5546a of this title.

EFFECTIVE DATE OF 1994 AMENDMENT

Amendment by Pub. L. 103–329 effective first day of first applicable pay period beginning on or after 30th day following Sept. 30, 1994, with exceptions relating to criminal investigators employed in Offices of Inspectors General, see section 633(e) of Pub. L. 103–329, set out as an Effective Date note under section 5545a of this title.

EFFECTIVE DATE OF 1992 AMENDMENT

Amendment by Pub. L. 102–378 effective as of first day of first applicable pay period beginning on or after Oct. 2, 1992, see section 9(b)(9) of Pub. L. 102–378, set out as a note under section 6303 of this title.

EFFECTIVE DATE OF 1990 AMENDMENT

Amendment by section 529 [title II, § 204] of Pub. L. 101–509 effective on such date as the President shall determine, but not earlier than 90 days, and not later than 180 days, after Nov. 5, 1990, see section 529 [title III, § 305] of Pub. L. 101–509, set out as a note under section 5301 of this title.

EFFECTIVE DATE OF 1984 AMENDMENT

Amendment by Pub. L. 98–525 effective Oct. 1, 1984, see section 1537(f) of Pub. L. 98–525, set out as a note under section 4109 of this title.

EFFECTIVE DATE OF 1982 AMENDMENT

Amendment by Pub. L. 97–276 effective at 5 o'clock ante meridian eastern daylight time, Aug. 3, 1981, see section 151(h)(1) of Pub. L. 97–276, set out as an Effective Date note under section 5546a of this title.

SHORT TITLE OF 1988 AMENDMENT

Section 1 of Pub. L. 100–523 provided: "That this Act [amending this section] may be cited as the 'Forest Wildfire Emergency Pay Equity Act of 1988'."

PREMIUM PAY FOR PROTECTIVE SERVICES OF UNITED STATES SECRET SERVICE

Pub. L. 106–554, § 1(a)(3) [title I, § 118], Dec. 21, 2000, 114 Stat. 2763, 2763A–134, provided that: "Hereafter, funds made available by this or any other Act may be used to pay premium pay for protective services authorized by section 3056(a) of title 18, United States Code, without regard to the limitation on the rate of pay payable during a pay period contained in section 5547(c)(2) of title 5, United States Code, except that such premium pay shall not be payable to an employee to the extent that the aggregate of the employee's basic and premium pay for the year would otherwise exceed the annual equivalent of that limitation. The term premium pay refers to the provisions of law cited in the first sentence of section 5547(a) of title 5, United States Code. Payment of additional premium pay payable under this section may be made in a lump sum on the last payday of the calendar year.''

Similar provisions were contained in Pub. L. 106–58, title I, § 118, Sept. 29, 1999, 113 Stat. 441.

SECTION REFERRED TO IN OTHER SECTIONS

This section is referred to in title 2 section 1371.

§ 5548. Regulations

(a) The Office of Personnel Management may prescribe regulations, subject to the approval of the President, necessary for the administration of this subchapter, except section 5545(d) insofar as this subchapter affects employees in or under an Executive agency.

(b) The Office shall prescribe regulations necessary for the administration of section 5545(d).

(Pub. L. 89–554, Sept. 6, 1966, 80 Stat. 488; Pub. L. 90–83, § 1(32), Sept. 11, 1967, 81 Stat. 201; Pub. L. 92–392, § 12, Aug. 19, 1972, 86 Stat. 575; Pub. L. 95–454, title IX, § 906(a)(2), (3), Oct. 13, 1978, 92 Stat. 1224; Pub. L. 102–378, § 2(44)(C), Oct. 2, 1992, 106 Stat. 1352.)

HISTORICAL AND REVISION NOTES
1966 ACT

Derivation	U.S. Code	Revised Statutes and Statutes at Large
....	5 U.S.C. 945.	June 30, 1945, ch. 212, § 605, 59 Stat. 304.

The words "an Executive agency" are substituted for "the executive branch of the Government" to conform to the definition in section 105. Applicability of this section to employees of the General Accounting Office is based on former section 933a.

The remainder of the authority is covered by sections 5504 and 6101.

Standard changes are made to conform with the definitions applicable and the style of this title as outlined in the preface to the report.

1967 ACT

Section of title 5	Source (U.S. Code)	Source (Statutes at Large)
5548(b)	5 App.: 1072 (as applicable to 5 App.: 1134.)	Oct. 28, 1949, ch. 782, § 1101 (as applicable to § 804, added July 19, 1966, Pub. L. 89–512, § 1, 80 Stat. 318), 63 Stat. 971.
	5 App.: 1134(4) (6th through 9th words).	July 19, 1966, Pub. L. 89–512, § 1 "Sec. 804(4) (6th through 9th words)", 80 Stat. 318.

This section consolidates into 5 U.S.C. 5548(b) general regulatory authority granted to the Civil Service Commission by section 1101 of the Classification Act of 1949 (as applicable to sec. 804 of that act, added by Public Law 89–512) and the specific requirement in section 804(4) of that act that the Commission prescribe regulations.

AMENDMENTS

1992—Subsec. (b). Pub. L. 102–378 substituted "section 5545(d)" for "sections 5545(d) and 5550 of this title".

1978—Subsecs. (a), (b). Pub. L. 95–454 substituted "Office of Personnel Management" for "Civil Service Commission" and "Office" for "Commission".

1972—Subsec. (a). Pub. L. 92–392, § 12(a), struck out reference to section 5544 of this title.

Subsec. (b). Pub. L. 92–392, § 12(b), inserted reference to section 5550 of this title.

EFFECTIVE DATE OF 1978 AMENDMENT

Amendment by Pub. L. 95–454 effective 90 days after Oct. 13, 1978, see section 907 of Pub. L. 95–454, set out as a note under section 1101 of this title.

EFFECTIVE DATE OF 1972 AMENDMENT

Amendment by Pub. L. 92–392 effective on first day of first applicable pay period beginning on or after 90th day after Aug. 19, 1972, see section 15(a) of Pub. L. 92–392, set out as an Effective Date note under section 5341 of this title.

DELEGATION OF FUNCTIONS

Function vested in Office of Personnel Management under this section to be performed without approval of President, see section 1(1) of Ex. Ord. No. 11228, June 14, 1965, 30 F.R. 7739, set out as a note under section 301 of Title 3, The President.

SECTION REFERRED TO IN OTHER SECTIONS

This section is referred to in title 2 section 1371.

§ 5549. Effect on other statutes

This subchapter does not prevent payment for overtime services or for Sunday or holiday work under any of the following statutes—

　(1) section 394 of title 7;
　(2) sections 1353a and 1353b of title 8;
　(3) sections 261,[1] 267, 1450, 1451, 1451a,[1] and 1452 of title 19;
　(4) sections 2111 and 2112 of title 46; and
　(5) section 154(f)(3) of title 47.

However, an employee may not receive premium pay under this subchapter for the same services for which he is paid under one of these statutes.

(Pub. L. 89–554, Sept. 6, 1966, 80 Stat. 488; Pub. L. 98–89, § 3(a), Aug. 26, 1983, 97 Stat. 599.)

HISTORICAL AND REVISION NOTES

Derivation	U.S. Code	Revised Statutes and Statutes at Large
....	5 U.S.C. 941.	June 30, 1945, ch. 212, § 601, 59 Stat. 302.

In paragraph (2), the words "sections 1353a and 1353b of title 8" are substituted for "sections 342c and 342d of this title" to reflect the scheduled transfer of those sections to title 8.

In paragraph (5), the words "section 154(f)(3) of title 47" are substituted for "section 154(f)(2) of title 47" on authority of the Act of July 16, 1952, ch. 879, § 3(b), 66 Stat. 711, which redesignated subsection (f)(2) as (f)(3).

Standard changes are made to conform with the definitions applicable and the style of this title as outlined in the preface to the report.

REFERENCES IN TEXT

Section 261 of title 19, referred to in par. (3), was omitted from the Code in the general revision of section 5 of act Feb. 13, 1911, ch. 46, by Pub. L. 103–66, title XIII, § 13811(a), Aug. 10, 1993, 107 Stat. 668.

Section 1451a of title 19, referred to in par. (3), was repealed by Pub. L. 103–66, title XIII, § 13811(b)(1), Aug. 10, 1993, 107 Stat. 670.

AMENDMENTS

1983—Par. (4). Pub. L. 98–89 substituted "sections 2111 and 2112 of title 46" for "section 382b of title 46".

SECTION REFERRED TO IN OTHER SECTIONS

This section is referred to in title 2 section 1371.

---

[1] See References in Text note below.

[§ 5550. Repealed. Pub. L. 102–378, § 2(44)(A), Oct. 2, 1992, 106 Stat. 1352]

Section, added Pub. L. 92–392, § 10(a), Aug. 19, 1972, 86 Stat. 574, related to pay for Sunday and overtime work for employees of nonappropriated fund instrumentalities.

§ 5550a. Compensatory time off for religious observances

(a) Not later than 30 days after the date of the enactment of this section, the Office of Personnel Management shall prescribe regulations providing for work schedules under which an employee whose personal religious beliefs require the abstention from work during certain periods of time, may elect to engage in overtime work for time lost for meeting those religious requirements. Any employee who so elects such overtime work shall be granted equal compensatory time off from his scheduled tour of duty (in lieu of overtime pay) for such religious reasons, notwithstanding any other provision of law.

(b) In the case of any agency described in subparagraphs (C) through (G) of section 5541(1) of this title, the head of such agency (in lieu of the Office) shall prescribe the regulations referred to in subsection (a) of this section.

(c) Regulations under this section may provide for such exceptions as may be necessary to efficiently carry out the mission of the agency or agencies involved.

(Added Pub. L. 95–390, title IV, § 401(a), Sept. 29, 1978, 92 Stat. 762; amended Pub. L. 96–54, § 2(a)(14), (15), Aug. 14, 1979, 93 Stat. 382.)

REFERENCES IN TEXT

The date of enactment of this section, referred to in subsec. (a), is the date of enactment of Pub. L. 95–390, which was approved Sept. 29, 1978.

AMENDMENTS

1979—Subsecs. (a), (b). Pub. L. 96–54 substituted "Office of Personnel Management" for "Civil Service Commission" and "Office" for "Commission".

EFFECTIVE DATE OF 1979 AMENDMENT

Amendment by Pub. L. 96–54 effective July 12, 1979, see section 2(b) of Pub. L. 96–54, set out as a note under section 305 of this title.

SECTION REFERRED TO IN OTHER SECTIONS

This section is referred to in title 2 section 1371.

SUBCHAPTER VI—PAYMENT FOR ACCUMULATED AND ACCRUED LEAVE

SUBCHAPTER REFERRED TO IN OTHER SECTIONS

This subchapter is referred to in sections 5520a, 5948, 8331 of this title; title 22 section 3664; title 38 section 7453.

§ 5551. Lump-sum payment for accumulated and accrued leave on separation

(a) An employee as defined by section 2105 of this title or an individual employed by the government of the District of Columbia, who is separated from the service, is transferred to a position described under section 6301(2)(B)(xiii) of this title, or elects to receive a lump-sum payment for leave under section 5552 of this title, is entitled to receive a lump-sum payment for accumulated and current accrued annual or vacation leave to which he is entitled by statute. The lump-sum payment shall equal the pay (excluding any differential under section 5925 and any allowance under section 5928) the employee or individual would have received had he remained in the service until expiration of the period of the annual or vacation leave. The lump-sum payment is considered pay for taxation purposes only. The period of leave used for calculating the lump-sum payment shall not be extended due to any holiday occurring after separation. For the purposes of this subsection, movement to employment described in section 2105(c) shall not be deemed separation from the service in the case of an employee whose annual leave is transferred under section 6308(b).

(b) The accumulated and current accrued annual leave to which an officer excepted from subchapter I of chapter 63 of this title by section 6301(2)(x)–(xiii) of this title, is entitled immediately before the date he is excepted under that section shall be liquidated by a lump-sum payment in accordance with subsection (a) of this section or subchapter VIII of this chapter, except that the payment is based on the rate of pay which he was receiving, immediately before the date on which section 6301(2)(x)–(xiii) of this title became applicable to him.

(c)(1) Annual leave that is restored to an employee of the Department of Defense under section 6304(d) of this title by reason of the operation of paragraph (3) of such section and remains unused upon the transfer of the employee to a position described in paragraph (2) shall be liquidated by payment of a lump-sum for such leave to the employee upon the transfer.

(2) A position referred to in paragraph (1) is a position in a department or agency of the Federal Government outside the Department of Defense or a Department of Defense position that is not located at a Department of Defense installation being closed or realigned as described in section 6304(d)(3) of this title.

(Pub. L. 89–554, Sept. 6, 1966, 80 Stat. 488; Pub. L. 93–181, § 1, Dec. 14, 1973, 87 Stat. 705; Pub. L. 95–519, § 2, Oct. 25, 1978, 92 Stat. 1819; Pub. L. 96–499, title IV, § 402(a), Dec. 5, 1980, 94 Stat. 2605; Pub. L. 101–508, title VII, § 7202(g), Nov. 5, 1990, 104 Stat. 1388–336; Pub. L. 102–138, title I, § 147(b)(1), Oct. 28, 1991, 105 Stat. 669; Pub. L. 104–201, div. A, title XVI, § 1611(a), Sept. 23, 1996, 110 Stat. 2738; Pub. L. 106–518, title III, § 310, Nov. 13, 2000, 114 Stat. 2420.)

HISTORICAL AND REVISION NOTES

Derivation	U.S. Code	Revised Statutes and Statutes at Large
(a)	5 U.S.C. 61b (1st, 2d, and 6th sentences).	Dec. 21, 1944, ch. 632, § 1 (less 1st proviso, and less so much of last sentence as precedes 2d proviso), 58 Stat. 845. July 2, 1953, ch. 178, § 4(a) (1st and 5th sentences), 67 Stat. 137.
(b)	5 U.S.C. 2061a(a).	July 2, 1953, ch. 178, § 2(a), 67 Stat. 136.

In subsection (a), the words "An employee as defined by section 2105 of this title" are coextensive with and substituted for "civilian officer or employee of the Federal Government". Reference to "section 1474 of Appendix to Title 50, is omitted in view of the repeal of that section by the Act of July 24, 1956, ch. 671, § 5(a)(3), 70 Stat. 606. The words "and shall not be subject to retirement deductions" are omitted and carried into section 8331(3).

In subsection (b)(2), reference to the limitation imposed by section 5 of the Act of July 2, 1953, ch. 178, 67 Stat. 138, is omitted as obsolete since the limitation was eliminated by the Act of Sept. 2, 1958, Pub. L. 85–914, § 1, 72 Stat. 1761.

Standard changes are made to conform with the definitions applicable and the style of this title as outlined in the preface to the report.

AMENDMENTS

2000—Subsec. (a). Pub. L. 106–518 substituted ", is transferred to a position described under section 6301(2)(B)(xiii) of this title, or elects" for "or elects" in first sentence.

1996—Subsec. (c). Pub. L. 104–201 added subsec. (c).

1991—Subsec. (a). Pub. L. 102–138 inserted "(excluding any differential under section 5925 and any allowance under section 5928)" after "pay" in second sentence.

1990—Subsec. (a). Pub. L. 101–508 inserted at end "For the purposes of this subsection, movement to employment described in section 2105(c) shall not be deemed separation from the service in the case of an employee whose annual leave is transferred under section 6308(b)."

1980—Subsec. (a). Pub. L. 96–499 provided that the period of leave used for calculating the lump-sum payment was not to be extended due to any holiday occurring after separation.

1978—Subsec. (b). Pub. L. 95–519 substituted "6301(2)(x)–(xiii)" for "6301(2)(x)–(xii)" in two places.

1973—Subsec. (a). Pub. L. 93–181 struck out exception clause that the lump-sum payment may not exceed pay for a period of annual or vacation leave in excess of 30 days or the number of days carried over to his credit at the beginning of the leave year in which entitlement to payment occurs, whichever is greater.

Subsec. (b). Pub. L. 93–181 struck out second exception clause that the payment is made without regard to the limitation in subsec. (a) of this section on the amount of leave compensable.

EFFECTIVE DATE OF 1996 AMENDMENT

Section 1611(b) of Pub. L. 104–201 provided that: "Subsection (c) of section 5551 of title 5, United States Code (as added by subsection (a)), shall apply with respect to transfers described in such subsection (c) that take effect on or after the date of the enactment of this Act [Sept. 23, 1996]."

EFFECTIVE DATE OF 1991 AMENDMENT

Section 147(b)(2) of Pub. L. 102–138 provided that: "The amendment made by paragraph (1) [amending this section] shall apply with respect to service as part of a tour of duty or extension thereof commencing on or after the date of enactment of this Act [Oct. 28, 1991]."

EFFECTIVE DATE OF 1990 AMENDMENT

Amendment by Pub. L. 101–508 applicable with respect to any individual who, on or after Jan. 1, 1987, moves from employment in nonappropriated fund instrumentality of Department of Defense or Coast Guard, that is described in section 2105(c) of this title, to employment in Department or Coast Guard, that is not described in section 2105(c), or who moves from employment in Department or Coast Guard, that is not described in section 2105(c), to employment in nonappropriated fund instrumentality of Department or Coast Guard, that is described in section 2105(c), see section 7202(m)(1) of Pub. L. 101–508, set out as a note under section 2105 of this title.

EFFECTIVE DATE OF 1980 AMENDMENT

Section 402(b) of Pub. L. 96–499 provided that: "The amendment made by subsection (a) [amending this section] shall take effect on the date of the enactment of this Act [Dec. 5, 1980] and shall apply to employees separating from the service on or after such date."

EFFECTIVE DATE OF 1978 AMENDMENT

Section 4 of Pub. L. 95–519 provided that:

"(a) The amendments made by the first section and section 2 of this Act [amending this section and sections 6301, 6302, and 6306 of this title] shall take effect beginning on the first day of the first applicable pay period beginning on or after the date of the enactment of this Act [Oct. 25, 1978].

"(b) The amendment made by section 3 of this Act [amending section 8339 of this title] shall apply only with respect to employees who retire or die on or after the date of the enactment of this Act [Oct. 25, 1978]."

SECTION REFERRED TO IN OTHER SECTIONS

This section is referred to in sections 5552, 5596, 6304, 6306, 6335, 6368, 8344, 8468 of this title; title 15 section 2081; title 20 sections 904, 4416; title 25 section 2012; title 38 section 7458; title 45 section 1206.

§ 5552. Lump-sum payment for accumulated and accrued leave on entering active duty; election

An employee as defined by section 2105 of this title or an individual employed by a territory or possession of the United States or the government of the District of Columbia who enters on active duty in the armed forces is entitled to—

(1) receive, in addition to his pay and allowances from the armed forces, a lump-sum payment for accumulated and current accrued annual or vacation leave in accordance with section 5551 of this title; or

(2) elect to have the leave remain to his credit until his return from active duty.

(Pub. L. 89–554, Sept. 6, 1966, 80 Stat. 489.)

HISTORICAL AND REVISION NOTES

Derivation	U.S. Code	Revised Statutes and Statutes at Large
....	5 U.S.C. 61a.	Aug. 1, 1941, ch. 348, 55 Stat. 616. Apr. 7, 1942, ch. 220, 56 Stat. 200.

The words "An employee as defined by section 2105 of this title" are coextensive with and substituted for "Employees of the United States Government, . . . (including employees of any corporation created under authority of an Act of Congress which is either wholly controlled or wholly owned by the United States Government, or any corporation, all the stock of which is owned or controlled by the United States Government, or any department, agency, or establishment thereof, whether or not the employees thereof are paid from funds appropriated by Congress)".

The words "subsequent to May 1, 1940" are omitted as obsolete. The words "active duty in the armed forces" and "active duty" are substituted for "active military or naval service in the land or naval forces of the United States" and "active military or naval service", respectively, on authority of the National Security Act of 1947, 61 Stat. 495, as amended. The words "by voluntary enlistment or otherwise" are omitted as unnecessary.

In paragraph (1), the words "in accordance with section 5551 of this title" are added on authority of former section 61b, which is carried into section 5551.

Standard changes are made to conform with the definitions applicable and the style of this title as outlined in the preface to the report.

SECTION REFERRED TO IN OTHER SECTIONS

This section is referred to in sections 5551, 5596, 6304, 6335, 6368 of this title; title 38 section 7458.

§ 5553. Regulations

The Office of Personnel Management may prescribe regulations necessary for the administration of this subchapter.

(Added Pub. L. 102–378, § 2(45)(A), Oct. 2, 1992, 106 Stat. 1353.)

SUBCHAPTER VII—PAYMENTS TO MISSING EMPLOYEES

SUBCHAPTER REFERRED TO IN OTHER SECTIONS

This subchapter is referred to in sections 5307, 5520a of this title; title 10 section 1511; title 18 section 1923; title 22 section 3970; title 50 App. section 1291.

§ 5561. Definitions

For the purpose of this subchapter—

(1) "agency" means an Executive agency and a military department;

(2) "employee" means an employee in or under an agency who is a citizen or national of the United States or an alien admitted to the United States for permanent residence, but does not include a part-time or intermittent employee or native labor casually hired on an hourly or daily basis. However, such an employee who enters a status listed in paragraph (5)(A)–(E) of this section—

(A) inside the continental United States; or

(B) who is a resident at or in the vicinity of his place of employment in a territory or possession of the United States or in a foreign country and who was not living there solely as a result of his employment;

is an employee for the purpose of this subchapter only on a determination by the head of the agency concerned that this status is the proximate result of employment by the agency;

(3) "dependent" means—

(A) a wife;

(B) an unmarried child (including an unmarried dependent stepchild or adopted child) under 21 years of age;

(C) a dependent mother or father;

(D) a dependent designated in official records; and

(E) an individual determined to be dependent by the head of the agency concerned or his designee;

(4) "active service" means active Federal service by an employee;

(5) "missing status" means the status of an employee who is in active service and is officially carried or determined to be absent in a status of—

(A) missing;

(B) missing in action;

(C) interned in a foreign country;

(D) captured, beleaguered, or besieged by a hostile force; or

(E) detained in a foreign country against his will;

but does not include the status of an employee for a period during which he is officially determined to be absent from his post of duty without authority; and

(6) "pay and allowances" means—

(A) basic pay;

(B) special pay;

(C) incentive pay;

(D) basic allowance for housing;

(E) basic allowance for subsistence; and

(F) station per diem allowances for not more than 90 days.

(Pub. L. 89–554, Sept. 6, 1966, 80 Stat. 489; Pub. L. 105–85, div. A, title VI, § 603(d)(3), Nov. 18, 1997, 111 Stat. 1783.)

HISTORICAL AND REVISION NOTES

Derivation	U.S. Code	Revised Statutes and Statutes at Large
(1)–(4)	50A U.S.C. 1001.	Mar. 7, 1942, ch. 166, § 1, 56 Stat. 143. July 1, 1944, ch. 371, § 1, 58 Stat. 679. May 16, 1947, ch. 70, § 1, 61 Stat. 96. Aug. 29, 1957, Pub. L. 85–217, § 1(a), 71 Stat. 491. Aug. 14, 1964, Pub. L. 88–428, § 1(1), (2), 78 Stat. 437.
(5)	50A U.S.C. 1002(a) (3d through 66th words of 1st sentence, and 1st 28 words of 3d sentence, for definition purposes).	Mar. 7, 1942, ch. 166, § 2(a) (3d through 66th words and 96th through 120th words of 1st sentence, and 1st 28 words of 3d sentence, for definition purposes); added July 1, 1944, ch. 371, § 2, 58 Stat. 679. Apr. 4, 1953, ch. 17, § 1(a), 67 Stat. 21. Aug. 29, 1957, Pub. L. 85–217, § 1(b) (1st par.), 71 Stat. 491. Aug. 14, 1964, Pub. L. 88–428, § 1(3)(A), (C), 78 Stat. 437.
(5)	50A U.S.C. 1014 (as applicable to § 1002(a) (1st sentence)).	Mar. 7, 1942, ch. 166, § 14 (as applicable to § 2(a) (1st sentence)), 56 Stat. 147. Apr. 4, 1953, ch. 17, § 1(e), 67 Stat. 21.
(6)	50A U.S.C. 1002(a) (96th through 120th words of 1st sentence, for definition purposes).	

Only that portion of the source law which is applicable to civilian officers and employees and their dependents is codified in this section.

In paragraph (1), the word "agency" is substituted for "department". The words "including such term when used in the amendment made by section 16" are omitted as surplusage. The words "an Executive agency and a military department" are coextensive with and substituted for "any executive department, independent establishment, or agency (including corporations) in the executive branch of the Federal Government" in view of the definitions in sections 105 and 102, and on authority of 5 U.S.C. 933a which provides that general legislation governing employment, compensation, and the status of employees of the United States applies to employees of the General Accounting Office in the same manner as if they were in the executive branch.

In paragraph (3)(A), the word "lawful" is omitted as unnecessary in view of the accepted recognition of the fact that the word "wife" means a lawful wife. In paragraph (3)(E), the words "head of the agency concerned or his designee" are substituted for "head of the department concerned, or subordinate designated by him".

The definitions in paragraphs (5) and (6), which do not appear in, but are based on, the source law are created for legislative convenience.

Standard changes are made to conform with the definitions applicable and the style of this title as outlined in the preface to the report.

AMENDMENTS

1997—Par. (6)(D). Pub. L. 105–85 substituted "housing" for "quarters".

EFFECTIVE DATE OF 1997 AMENDMENT

Section 603(e) of Pub. L. 105–85 provided that: "This section [amending this section, sections 708, 2830, 2882, 7572, and 7573 of Title 10, Armed Forces, section 107 of Title 32, National Guard, sections 101, 403, 405, 406, 420, 427, 551, and 1014 of Title 37, Pay and Allowances of the Uniformed Services, and section 454 of Title 50, Appendix, War and National Defense, repealing section 403a of Title 37, and enacting provisions set out as a note under section 403 of Title 37] and the amendments made by this section shall take effect on January 1, 1998."

ACCOUNTING FOR CIVILIAN EMPLOYEES AND
CONTRACTORS OF UNITED STATES

Pub. L. 104–106, div. A, title V, § 569(e), Feb. 10, 1996, 110 Stat. 352, directed Secretary of State to carry out comprehensive study of provisions of this subchapter and any other law or regulation establishing procedures for accounting for civilian employees of the United States or contractors of the United States who serve with or accompany the Armed Forces in the field to determine the means, if any, by which those procedures may be improved, and further provided for submission of report to Congress not later than one year after Feb. 10, 1996, on results of study.

BENEFITS FOR UNITED STATES HOSTAGES IN IRAQ AND
KUWAIT AND UNITED STATES HOSTAGES CAPTURED IN
LEBANON

Pub. L. 101–513, title V, § 599C, Nov. 5, 1990, 104 Stat. 2064, as amended by Pub. L. 102–138, title III, § 302(a), Oct. 28, 1991, 105 Stat. 707; Pub. L. 102–499, § 5(a), Oct. 24, 1992, 106 Stat. 3266, provided for payment of benefits during fiscal year 1991 and thereafter for United States hostages in Iraq and Kuwait and United States hostages captured in Lebanon.

HOSTAGE RELIEF

Pub. L. 96–449, Oct. 14, 1980, 94 Stat. 1967, as amended by Pub. L. 99–514, § 2, Oct. 22, 1986, 100 Stat. 2095; Pub. L. 102–83, § 5(c)(2), Aug. 6, 1991, 105 Stat. 406, known as the "Hostage Relief Act of 1980", provided for benefits for United States civil service and uniformed service personnel who were placed in a captive status during a hostage period beginning on Nov. 4, 1979, due to the seizure of the United States Embassy in Iran.

EXECUTIVE ORDER NO. 12268

Ex. Ord. No. 12268, Jan. 15, 1981, 46 F.R. 4671, provided for the implementation of the Hostage Relief Act of 1980 (Pub. L. 96–449).

EXECUTIVE ORDER NO. 12313

Ex. Ord. No. 12313, July 13, 1981, 46 F.R. 36689, designated Jan. 11, 1981, as date on which all citizens and resident aliens of the United States who had been placed in captive status as a result of seizure of United States Embassy in Iran were returned to United States or otherwise accounted for and were no longer under foreign control.

SECTION REFERRED TO IN OTHER SECTIONS

This section is referred to in sections 5564, 5569 of this title; title 10 sections 4342, 6954, 9342; title 26 sections 112, 6013.

§ 5562. Pay and allowances; continuance while in a missing status; limitations

(a) An employee in a missing status is entitled to receive or have credited to his account, for the period he is in that status, the same pay and allowances to which he was entitled at the beginning of that period or may become entitled thereafter. Notwithstanding any other provision of law, an employee in a missing status on or after January 1, 1965, is entitled—

(1) to payment for annual leave which accrued to his account on or after January 1, 1965, but which was forfeited under section 6304 of this title because he was unable to use that leave by virtue of his missing status; or

(2) to have all of that leave restored to him and credited to a separate leave account in accordance with the provisions of section 6304(d)(2) of this title.

An employee shall elect in writing, within 90 days immediately following December 14, 1973, or within 90 days immediately following the termination of his missing status, whichever is later, whether he desires payment for the leave under clause (1) of this subsection or credit of the leave under clause (2) of this subsection. Payment under clause (1) of this subsection shall be at the employee's rate of basic pay in effect at the time the leave was forfeited.

(b) Entitlement to pay and allowances under subsection (a) of this section ends on the date of—

(1) receipt by the head of the agency concerned of evidence that the employee is dead; or

(2) death prescribed or determined under section 5565 of this title.

That entitlement does not end—

(A) on the expiration of the term of service or employment of an employee while he is in a missing status; or

(B) earlier than the dates prescribed in paragraphs (1) and (2) of this subsection if the employee dies while he is in a missing status.

(c) An employee who is officially determined to be absent from his post of duty without authority is indebted to the United States for payments of amounts credited to his account under subsection (a) of this section for the period of that absence.

(d) When an employee in a missing status is continued in that status under section 5565 of this title, he continues to be entitled to have pay and allowances credited under subsection (a) of this section.

(Pub. L. 89–554, Sept. 6, 1966, 80 Stat. 490; Pub. L. 93–181, § 7(a), Dec. 14, 1973, 87 Stat. 707; Pub. L. 96–54, § 2(a)(33), Aug. 14, 1979, 93 Stat. 383.)

HISTORICAL AND REVISION NOTES

Derivation	U.S. Code	Revised Statutes and Statutes at Large
(a)	50A U.S.C. 1002(a) (1st sentence, less last 46 words).	Mar. 7, 1942, ch. 166, § 2(a) (1st 2 sentences and 3d sentence, less 1st 28 words); added July 1, 1944, ch. 371, § 2, 58 Stat. 679. Apr. 4, 1953, ch. 17, § 1(a), 67 Stat. 21. Aug. 29, 1957, Pub. L. 85–217, § 1(b), 71 Stat. 491. Aug. 14, 1964, Pub. L. 88–428, § 1(3)(A), (B), 78 Stat. 437.
	50A U.S.C. 1014 (as applicable to § 1002(a) (1st sentence)).	Mar. 7, 1942, ch. 166, § 14 (as applicable to § 2(a) (1st sentence)), 56 Stat. 147. Apr. 4, 1953, ch. 17, § 1(e), 67 Stat. 21.

Derivation	U.S. Code	Revised Statutes and Statutes at Large
(b)	50A U.S.C. 1002(a) (last 46 words of 1st sentence, and 2d sentence).	
(c)	50A U.S.C. 1002(a) (3d sentence, less 1st 28 words).	
(d)	50A U.S.C. 1006 (2d sentence, as applicable to pay and allowances).	Mar. 7, 1942, ch. 166, §6 (2d sentence, as applicable to pay and allowances); added Dec. 24, 1942, ch. 828, §1 (4th par.), 56 Stat. 1093. Aug. 14, 1964, Pub. L. 88–428, §1(5)(B), 78 Stat. 437.

Only that portion of the source law which is applicable to civilian officers and employees and their dependents is codified in this section.

In subsection (a), the words "An employee in a missing status" are substituted for the first 66 words of 50A U.S.C. 1002(a) to conform to the definitions in section 5561(2) and (5). The words "pay and allowances" are substituted for the enumeration of pay and allowances in the first sentence of 50A U.S.C. 1002(a) to conform to the definition in sections 5561(6). The words "or is performing full-time training duty, other full-time duty, or inactive duty training" and "except that the pay and allowances for a person who is performing full-time training duty or other full-time duty without pay, or inactive duty training with or without pay, shall be that to which he would have been entitled if he had been performing full-time active duty with pay;" are omitted as inapplicable to civilian officers and employees.

In subsection (b), the words "under subsection (a) of this section" are inserted for clarity.

In subsection (c), the words "United States" are substituted for "Government" to conform to the style of this title. The words "under subsection (a) of this section" are inserted for clarity.

In subsection (d), the words "an employee in a missing status" are substituted for "a person missing under the conditions specified in section 2 of this Act" to conform to the definitions in section 5561(2) and (5).

Standard changes are made to conform with the definitions applicable and the style of this title as outlined in the preface to the report.

AMENDMENTS

1979—Subsec. (a). Pub. L. 96–54 substituted "December 14, 1973," for "the date of enactment of this sentence".

1973—Subsec. (a). Pub. L. 93–181 inserted provisions relating to employees in missing status on or after January 1, 1965.

EFFECTIVE DATE OF 1979 AMENDMENT

Amendment by Pub. L. 96–54 effective July 12, 1979, see section 2(b) of Pub. L. 96–54, set out as a note under section 305 of this title.

FORMER EMPLOYEES OR THEIR BENEFICIARIES

Section 7(b) of Pub. L. 93–181 provided that: "The amendment made by subsection (a) of this section [amending subsec. (a) of this section] shall apply to former employees or their beneficiaries."

SECTION REFERRED TO IN OTHER SECTIONS

This section is referred to in sections 5563, 5567, 5569, 6304 of this title; title 26 section 6013.

§ 5563. Allotments; continuance, suspension, initiation, resumption, or increase while in a missing status; limitations

(a) An allotment (including one for the purchase of United States savings bonds) made by an employee before he was in a missing status may be continued for the period he is in that status, notwithstanding the end of the period for which the allotment was made.

(b) In the absence of an allotment or when an allotment is insufficient for a purpose authorized by the head of the agency concerned, he or his designee may authorize such a new or increased allotment as circumstances warrant, which is payable for the period the employee concerned is in a missing status.

(c) All allotments from the pay and allowances of an employee in a missing status may not total more than the amount of pay and allowances he is permitted to allot under regulations prescribed by the head of the agency concerned.

(d) A premium paid by the United States on insurance issued on the life of an employee, which is unearned because it covers a period after his death, reverts to the appropriation of the agency concerned.

(e) Subject to subsections (f) and (g) of this section, the head of the agency concerned or his designee may direct the initiation, continuance, discontinuance, increase, decrease, suspension, or resumption of an allotment from the pay and allowances of an employee in a missing status when that action is in the interests of the employee, his dependents, or the United States.

(f) When the head of the agency concerned officially reports that an employee in a missing status is alive, an allotment under subsections (a)–(d) of this section may be paid, subject to section 5562 of this title, until the date the head of the agency concerned receives evidence that the employee is dead or has returned to the controllable jurisdiction of the agency concerned.

(g) When an employee in a missing status is continued in that status under section 5565 of this title, an allotment under subsections (a)–(d) of this section may be continued, increased, or initiated.

(h) When the head of the agency concerned considers it essential for the well-being and protection of the dependents of an employee in active service (other than an employee in a missing status), he may, with or without the consent of the employee and subject to termination on specific request of the employee—

(1) direct the payment of a new allotment from the pay of the employee;

(2) increase or decrease the amount of an allotment made by the employee; and

(3) continue payment of an allotment of the employee which has expired.

(Pub. L. 89–554, Sept. 6, 1966, 80 Stat. 490.)

HISTORICAL AND REVISION NOTES

Derivation	U.S. Code	Revised Statutes and Statutes at Large
(a)	50A U.S.C. 1003 (1st sentence).	Mar. 7, 1942, ch. 166, §3, 56 Stat. 144. Dec. 24, 1942, ch. 828, §1 (1st par.), 56 Stat. 1092. July 1, 1944, ch. 371, §3, 58 Stat. 680.
(b)	50A U.S.C. 1003 (2d sentence, less proviso).	
(c)	50A U.S.C. 1003 (1st proviso of 2d sentence).	
(d)	50A U.S.C. 1003 (2d proviso of 2d sentence).	

Derivation	U.S. Code	Revised Statutes and Statutes at Large
(e)	50A U.S.C. 1004	Mar. 7, 1942, ch. 166, § 4, 56 Stat. 144. Dec. 24, 1942, ch. 828, § 1 (2d par.), 56 Stat. 1093. July 1, 1944, ch. 371, § 4, 58 Stat. 680.
(f)	50A U.S.C. 1006 (1st sentence).	Mar. 7, 1942, ch. 166, § 6 (1st sentence and 2d sentence, as applicable to allotments); added Dec. 24, 1942, ch. 828, § 1 (4th par.), 56 Stat. 1093. Apr. 4, 1953, ch. 17, § 1(b), 67 Stat. 21. Aug. 14, 1964, Pub. L. 88–428, § 1(5), 78 Stat. 437.
	50A U.S.C. 1014 (as applicable to § 1006 (1st sentence)).	Mar. 7, 1942, ch. 166, § 14 (as applicable to § 6 (1st sentence)), 56 Stat. 147. Apr. 4, 1953, ch. 17, § 1(e), 67 Stat. 21.
(g)	50A U.S.C. 1006 (2d sentence, as applicable to allotments).	
(h)	50A U.S.C. 1007.	Mar. 7, 1942, ch. 166 § 7, 56 Stat. 145. Aug. 14, 1964, Pub. L. 88–428, § 1(6), 78 Stat. 437.

Only that portion of the source law which is applicable to civilian officers and employees and their dependents is codified in this section.

In subsection (a), the words "employee . . . in a missing status" are substituted for the reference to "person . . . entitled under section 2 of this Act to receive or be credited with pay and allowances" to conform to the definitions in section 5561(2) and (5). The words "except as otherwise provided herein" are omitted as unnecessary.

In subsection (b), the words "head of the agency concerned, he or his designee" are substituted for "head of the department concerned . . . head of the department concerned, or such subordinate as he may designate". The word "employee" is substituted for "person" to conform to the definition in section 5561(2).

In subsection (c), the words "in effect" are omitted as surplusage. The words "employee in a missing status" are substituted for "absent person" to conform to the definitions in section 5561(2) and (5).

In subsection (d), the words "United States" are substituted for "Government" to conform to the style of this title. The word "employee" is substituted for "person" to conform to the definition in section 5561(2).

In subsection (e), the words "head of the agency concerned or his designee" are substituted for "head of the department concerned, or such subordinates as he may designate". The words "employee in a missing status" are substituted for "person entitled to receive or be credited with pay and allowances under section 2 of this Act" to conform to the definitions in section 5561(2) and (5). The words "United States" are substituted for "Government" to conform to the style of this title.

In subsections (f) and (g), the words "employee in a missing status" are substituted for "person missing under the conditions specified in section 2 of this Act" to conform to the definitions in section 5561(2) and (5).

In subsection (h), the words "employee in a missing status" are substituted for "persons entitled under section 2 or 14 of this Act to receive pay and allowances" to conform to the definitions in section 5561(2) and (5). In paragraph (2), the words "heretofore or hereafter" are omitted as unnecessary.

Standard changes are made to conform with the definitions applicable and the style of this title as outlined in the preface to the report.

This section is referred to in sections 5567, 5569 of this title.

§ 5564. Travel and transportation; dependents; household and personal effects; motor vehicles; sale of bulky items; claims for proceeds; appropriation chargeable

(a) For the purpose of this section, "household and personal effects" and "household effects" may include, in addition to other authorized weight allowances, one privately owned motor vehicle which may be shipped at United States expense.

(b) Transportation (including packing, crating, draying, temporarily storing, and unpacking of household and personal effects) may be provided for the dependents and household and personal effects of an employee in active service (without regard to pay grade) who is officially reported as dead, injured, or absent for more than 29 days in a status listed in section 5561(5) (A)–(E) of this title to—

(1) the official residence of record for the employee;

(2) the residence of his dependent, next of kin, or other person entitled to the effects under regulations prescribed by the head of the agency concerned; or

(3) another location determined in advance or later approved by the head of the agency concerned or his designee on request of the employee (if injured) or his dependent, next of kin, or other person described in paragraph (2) of this subsection.

(c) When an employee described in subsection (b) of this section is in an injured status, transportation of dependents and household and personal effects may be provided under this section only when prolonged hospitalization or treatment is anticipated.

(d) Transportation on request of a dependent may be authorized under this section only when there is a reasonable relationship between the circumstances of the dependent and the destination requested.

(e) Instead of providing transportation for dependents under this section, when the travel has been completed the head of the agency concerned may authorize—

(1) reimbursement for the commercial cost of the transportation; or

(2) a monetary allowance, instead of transportation, as authorized by statute for the whole or that part of the travel for which transportation in kind was not furnished.

(f) The head of the agency concerned may store the household and personal effects of an employee described in subsection (b) of this section until proper disposition can be made. The cost of the storage and transportation (including packing, crating, draying, temporarily storing, and unpacking) of household and personal effects shall be charged against appropriations currently available.

(g) When the head of the agency concerned determines that an emergency exists and that a sale would be in the best interests of the United States, he may provide for the public or private sale of motor vehicles and other bulky items of the household and personal effects of an employee described in subsection (b) of this section. Before a sale, and if practicable, a reasonable effort shall be made to determine the desires of interested persons. The net proceeds from the sale shall be sent to the owner or other person entitled thereto under regulations prescribed by the head of the agency concerned. If there is no owner or other person entitled thereto, or if the owner or other person or their addresses are not ascertained within 1 year from the date of sale, the net proceeds may be covered into the Treasury of the United States as miscellaneous receipts.

(h) A claim for net proceeds covered into the Treasury under subsection (g) of this section may be filed with the Administrator of General Services by the owner, his heir or next of kin, or his legal representative at any time before the end of 5 years from the date the proceeds are covered into the Treasury. When a claim is filed, the Administrator of General Services shall allow or disallow it. A claim that is allowed shall be paid from the appropriation for refunding money erroneously received and covered. If a claim is not filed before the end of 5 years from the date the proceeds are covered into the Treasury, it is barred from being acted on by the Administrator of General Services or the courts.

(i) This section does not amend or repeal—

    (1) section 2575, 2733, 4712, 6522, or 9712 of title 10;

    (2) section 507 of title 14; or

    (3) chapter 171 of title 28.

(Pub. L. 89–554, Sept. 6, 1966, 80 Stat. 491; Pub. L. 90–83, § 1(33), Sept. 11, 1967, 81 Stat. 201; Pub. L. 102–190, div. A, title X, § 1063(a), Dec. 5, 1991, 105 Stat. 1476; Pub. L. 104–316, title II, § 202(a), Oct. 19, 1996, 110 Stat. 3842.)

HISTORICAL AND REVISION NOTES
1966 ACT

Derivation	U.S. Code	Revised Statutes and Statutes at Large
(a)	50A U.S.C. 1012 (14th sentence).	Mar. 7, 1942, ch. 166, § 12, 56 Stat. 146. Feb. 12, 1946, ch. 6, § 1(a), 60 Stat. 5. Aug. 29, 1951, ch. 356, § 1, 65 Stat. 207. Apr. 4, 1953, ch. 17, § 1(d), 67 Stat. 21. Aug. 29, 1957, Pub. L. 85–217, § 1(d), 71 Stat. 492.
(b)	50A U.S.C. 1012 (1st sentence). 50A U.S.C. 1014 (as applicable to § 1012 (1st sentence)).	Aug. 14, 1964, Pub. L. 88–428, § 1(8), 78 Stat. 437. Mar. 7, 1942, ch. 166, § 14 (as applicable to § 12 (1st sentence)), 56 Stat. 147. Apr. 4, 1953, ch. 17, § 1(e), 67 Stat. 21.
(c)	50A U.S.C. 1012 (12th sentence).	
(d)	50A U.S.C. 1012 (13th sentence).	
(e)	50A U.S.C. 1012 (11th sentence).	
(f)	50A U.S.C. 1012 (9th and 10th sentences).	
(g)	50A U.S.C. 1012 (2d–4th sentences).	
(h)	50A U.S.C. 1012 (5th–7th sentences).	
(i)	50A U.S.C. 1012 (8th sentence).	

Only that portion of the source law which is applicable to civilian officers and employees and their dependents is codified in this section.

In subsection (a), the words "Beginning June 25, 1950, and" are omitted as executed. The words "not to exceed" are omitted as unnecessary. The words "outside the United States, or in Alaska or Hawaii" are substituted for "outside the continental limits of the United States or in Alaska".

In subsection (b), the words "Transportation . . . may be provided" are substituted for "may be moved". The words "an employee . . . for more than 28 days in a status listed in section 5561(5)(A)–(E) of this title" are substituted for "person . . . for a period of thirty days or more in any status listed in section 2 of this Act" for clarity and to conform to the definitions in section 5561(2) and (5). In paragraph (1), the words "the employee" are substituted for "any such person". In paragraph (3), the words "head of the agency concerned or his designee" are substituted for "head of the department concerned or by such person as he may designate".

In subsection (c), the word "employee" is substituted for "person". The words "transportation . . . may be provided under this section only when" are substituted for "movement . . . provided for herein may be authorized only in cases where".

In subsection (d), the words "on request of a dependent may be provided under . . . only" are substituted for "No . . . shall be authorized pursuant to . . . upon application by dependents unless". The words "condition and" are omitted as surplusage.

In subsection (e)(1), the words "reimbursement for" are substituted for "the payment in money of amounts equal to".

In subsection (f), the word "employee" is substituted for "person". The words "such time as" are omitted as surplusage.

In subsection (g), the words "United States" are substituted for "Government" to conform to the style of this title. The word "employee" is substituted for "person". The words "under . . . prescribed" are substituted for "in accordance with . . . issued".

In subsection (h), the words "under subsection (g) of this section" are substituted for "under authority of this section".

In subsection (i), the words "the provisions of" are omitted as surplusage. Paragraph (3) is substituted for "the Federal Tort Claims Act (60 Stat. 842–847), as amended;" to reflect the correct citation of that Act.

Standard changes are made to conform with the definitions applicable and the style of this title as outlined in the preface to the report.

1967 ACT

Section of title 5	Source (U.S. Code)	Source (Statutes at Large)
5564(a)	50 App.: 1012.	Oct. 19, 1965, Pub. L. 89–271, 79 Stat. 992.

Only that portion of the source law applicable to civilian officers and employees and their dependents is codified in this section. That portion of the source law applicable to members of the uniformed services and their dependents is codified in 37 U.S.C. 554(a) by section 5(2) of this bill.

AMENDMENTS

1996—Subsec. (h). Pub. L. 104–316 substituted "Administrator of General Services" for "General Accounting Office" wherever appearing.

1991—Subsec. (i)(1). Pub. L. 102–190 substituted "6522, or 9712" for "4713, 6522, 9712, or 9713".

§ 5565. Agency review

(a) When an employee has been in a missing status almost 12 months and no official report of his death or the circumstances of his continued absence has been received by the head of the agency concerned, he shall have the case fully reviewed. After that review and the end of 12 months in a missing status, or after any later review which shall be made when warranted by information received or other circumstances, the head of the agency concerned or his designee may—

(1) direct the continuance of his missing status, if there is a reasonable presumption that the employee is alive; or

(2) make a finding of death.

(b) When a finding of death is made under subsection (a) of this section, it shall include the date death is presumed to have occurred for the purpose of the ending of crediting pay and allowances and settlement of accounts. That date is—

(1) the day after the day on which the 12 months in a missing status ends; or

(2) a day determined by the head of the agency concerned or his designee when the missing status has been continued under subsection (a) of this section.

(c) For the purpose of determining status under this section, a dependent of an employee in active service is deemed an employee. A determination under this section made by the head of the agency concerned or his designee is conclusive on all other agencies of the United States. This section does not entitle a dependent to pay, allowances, or other compensation to which he is not otherwise entitled.

(Pub. L. 89–554, Sept. 6, 1966, 80 Stat. 492.)

HISTORICAL AND REVISION NOTES

Derivation	U.S. Code	Revised Statutes and Statutes at Large
(a)	50A U.S.C. 1005 (1st and 2d sentences).	Mar. 7, 1942, ch. 166, §5, 56 Stat. 145. Dec. 24, 1942, ch. 828, §1 (3d par.), 56 Stat. 1093. Aug. 14, 1964, Pub. L. 88–428, §1(4), 78 Stat. 437.
	50A U.S.C. 1014 (as applicable to §1005 (1st sentence)).	Mar. 7, 1942, ch. 166, §14 (as applicable to §5 (1st sentence)), 56 Stat. 147. Apr. 4, 1953, ch. 17, §1(e), 67 Stat. 21.
(b)	50A U.S.C. 1005 (less 1st and 2d sentences).	
(c)	50A U.S.C. 1009(b) (as applicable to §1005).	Mar. 7, 1942, ch. 166, §9(b) (as applicable to §5); added Aug. 29, 1957, Pub. L. 85–217, §1(c), 71 Stat. 492.

Only that portion of the source law which is applicable to civilian officers and employees and their dependents is codified in this section.

In subsection (a), the words "When an employee has been in a missing status almost 12 months" are substituted for "When the twelve months' period from the date of commencement of absence is about to expire in any case of a person entitled under section 2 of this Act to receive or be credited with pay and allowances" for clarity and to conform to the definitions in section 5561(2) and (5). For the same reasons, the words "the end of 12 months in a missing status" are substituted for "the twelve months' absence shall have expired". The words "or his designee" are supplied on authority of 50A U.S.C. 1009(a) which is codified in part in section 5566(a). In paragraph (1), the words "his" and "employee" are substituted for "person's" and "person". In subsection (b), the words "under subsection (a) of this section" are inserted for clarity. The words "and

payment of death gratuities" are omitted as inapplicable to civilian officers and employees. In paragraph (1), the words "the day on which the 12 months in a missing status ends" are substituted for "the day of expiration of an absence of twelve months" for consistency with subsection (a) of this section and in view of the definition in section 5561(5). In paragraph (2), the words "or his designee" are supplied on authority of 50A U.S.C. 1009(a) which is in part codified in section 5566(a). The words "under subsection (a) of this section" are substituted for "as hereinbefore authorized".

In subsection (c), the word "sole" is omitted as surplusage and in view of the provisions of section 5566(h). The word "deemed" is supplied to evidence the legal fiction provided by the words "is a 'person' under this Act" in 50A U.S.C. 1009(a). The words "or his designee" are supplied on authority of 50A U.S.C. 1009(a) which is in part codified in section 5566(a). The words "agencies of the United States" are substituted for "departments of the Government". The words "This section does not entitle" are substituted for "Provided, That nothing in this section shall be construed as conferring . . . any right".

Standard changes are made to conform with the definitions applicable and the style of this title as outlined in the preface to the report.

SECTION REFERRED TO IN OTHER SECTIONS

This section is referred to in sections 5562, 5563, 5566, 5567 of this title.

§ 5566. Agency determinations

(a) The head of the agency concerned or his designee may make any determination necessary to administer this subchapter, and when so made it is conclusive as to—

(1) death or finding of death;

(2) the fact of dependency under this subchapter;

(3) any other status covered by this subchapter;

(4) an essential date, including one on which evidence or information is received by the head of the agency concerned; and

(5) whether information received concerning an employee is to be construed and acted on as an official report of death.

(b) When the head of the agency concerned receives information that he considers to conclusively establish the death of an employee, he shall take action thereon as an official report of death, notwithstanding an earlier action relating to death or status of the employee. After the end of 12 months in a missing status prescribed by section 5565 of this title, the head of the agency concerned or his designee shall make a finding of death when he considers that the information received, or a lapse of time without information, establishes a reasonable presumption that an employee in a missing status is dead.

(c) The head of the agency concerned or his designee may determine the entitlement of an employee to pay and allowances under this subchapter, including credits and charges in his account, and that determination is conclusive. An account may not be charged or debited with an amount that an employee captured, beleaguered, or besieged by a hostile force may receive or be entitled to receive from, or have placed to his credit by, the hostile force as pay, allowances, or other compensation.

(d) When circumstances warrant the reconsideration of a determination made under this subchapter, the head of the agency concerned or his designee may change or modify it.

(e) When the account of an employee has been charged or debited with an allotment paid under this subchapter, the amount so charged or debited shall be recredited to the account of the employee if the head of the agency concerned or his designee determines that the payment was induced by fraud or misrepresentation to which the employee was not a party.

(f) Except an allotment for an unearned insurance premium, an allotment paid from the pay and allowances of an employee for the period he is in a missing status may not be collected from the allottee as an overpayment when payment was caused by delay in receiving evidence of death. An allotment paid for a period after the end, under this subchapter or otherwise, of entitlement to pay and allowances may not be collected from the allottee or charged against the pay of a deceased employee when payment was caused by delay in receiving evidence of death.

(g) The head of the agency concerned or his designee may waive the recovery of an erroneous payment or overpayment of an allotment to a dependent if he considers recovery is against equity and good conscience.

(h) For the purpose of determining status under this section, a dependent of an employee in active service is deemed an employee. A determination under this section made by the head of the agency concerned or his designee is conclusive on all other agencies of the United States. This section does not entitle a dependent to pay, allowances, or other compensation to which he is not otherwise entitled.

(Pub. L. 89–554, Sept. 6, 1966, 80 Stat. 493.)

HISTORICAL AND REVISION NOTES

Derivation	U.S. Code	Revised Statutes and Statutes at Large
(a)	50A U.S.C. 1009(a) (1st and 2d sentences).	Mar. 7, 1942, ch. 166, §9(a) (less 5th and last sentences); added July 1, 1944, ch. 371, §5, 58 Stat. 680. Apr. 4, 1953, ch. 17, §1(c), 67 Stat. 21. Aug. 29, 1957, Pub. L. 85–217, §1(c), 71 Stat. 492.
	50A U.S.C. 1010.	Mar. 7, 1942, ch. 166, §10, 56 Stat. 145. July 1, 1944, ch. 371, §6, 58 Stat. 681. Aug. 14, 1964, Pub. L. 88–428, §1(7), 78 Stat. 437.
(b)	50A U.S.C. 1009(a) (3d and 4th sentences).	
(c)	50A U.S.C. 1009(a) (6th sentence, less last proviso). 50A U.S.C. 1014 (as applicable to §1009(a) (1st proviso of 6th sentence)).	Mar. 7, 1942, ch. 166, §14 (as applicable to §9(a) (1st proviso of 6th sentence)), 56 Stat. 147. Apr. 4, 1953, ch. 17, §1(e), 67 Stat. 21.
(d)	50A U.S.C. 1009(a) (7th sentence).	
(e)	50A U.S.C. 1009(a) (last proviso of 6th sentence).	
(f)	50A U.S.C. 1009(a) (8th sentence).	
(g)	50A U.S.C. 1009(a) (9th sentence).	

HISTORICAL AND REVISION NOTES—CONTINUED

Derivation	U.S. Code	Revised Statutes and Statutes at Large
(h)	50A U.S.C. 1009(b) (as applicable to §1009).	Mar. 7, 1942, ch. 166, §9(b) (as applicable to §9); added Aug. 29, 1957, Pub. L. 85–217, §1(c), 71 Stat. 492.

Only that portion of the source law which is applicable to civilian officers and employees and their dependents is codified in this section.

In subsection (a), the words "head of the agency concerned or his designee" are substituted for "head of the department concerned, or such subordinate as he may designate". The words "for the purposes of this Act" are omitted as surplusage. The words "final and" in 50A U.S.C. 1010 are omitted as surplusage and for consistency with 50A U.S.C. 1009(a) (1st sentence). The words "the determination of the fact of dependency for the purpose of payment of all six months' death gratuities as authorized by law, and the determination of the fact of dependency under the provisions of any and all other laws providing for the payment of pay, allowances, or other emoluments to enlisted personnel in the Army, Navy, Air Force, Marine Corps, and Coast Guard of the United States where such payments are contingent upon dependency" in 50A U.S.C. 1010 are omitted as inapplicable to civilian officers and employees and their dependents. In paragraph (2), the words "under this subchapter" are substituted for "under the provisions of this Act". In paragraph (3), the words "covered by this subchapter" are substituted for "dealt with by this Act". In paragraph (4), the words "by the head of the agency concerned" are substituted for "in such department or by the head thereof". In paragraph (5), the word "employee" is substituted for "person".

In subsection (b), the words "head of the agency concerned" are substituted for "department concerned". The word "employee" is substituted for "person". In the second sentence, the words "the head of the agency concerned or his designee" are inserted for clarity. The words "is dead" are substituted for "is no longer alive" for consistency with references in this section to "death".

In subsection (c), the words "or his designee" are substituted for "or by such subordinate as he may designate". The words "captured, beleaguered, or besieged by a hostile force" are substituted for "in the hands of a hostile force" on authority of 50A U.S.C. 1014.

In subsection (d), the words "under this subchapter" are substituted for "authorized to be made by this Act". The words "or his designee" are substituted for "or such subordinate as he may designate".

In subsection (e), the words "an employee . . . allotment paid under this subchapter" are substituted for "any person . . . allotments paid pursuant to this Act". The words "the employee if the head of the agency concerned or his designee" are substituted for "such person's . . . in any case in which . . . the head of the department concerned, or such subordinate as he may designate."

In subsection (f), the words "may not be collected" are substituted for "shall not be subject to collection" in two places. The word "employee" is substituted for "person".

In subsection (g), the words "or his designee" are substituted for "or such subordinate as he may designate".

In subsection (h), the word "sole" is omitted as surplusage and in view of the provisions of section 5565(c). The word "deemed" is supplied to evidence the legal fiction provided by the words "is a 'person' under this Act" in 50A U.S.C. 1009(a). The words "or his designee" are supplied on authority of 50A U.S.C. 1009(a) which is codified in part in subsection (a) of this section. The words "agencies of the United States" are substituted for "departments of the Government". The words "This section does not entitle" are substituted for "Provided, That nothing in this section shall be construed as conferring . . . any right".

Standard changes are made to conform with the definitions applicable and the style of this title as outlined in the preface to the report.

SECTION REFERRED TO IN OTHER SECTIONS

This section is referred to in section 5569 of this title; title 26 section 2.

§ 5567. Settlement of accounts

(a) The head of the agency concerned or his designee may settle the accounts of—

(1) an employee for whose account payment has been made under sections 5562, 5563, and 5565 of this title; and

(2) a survivor of a casualty to a ship, station, or military installation which results in the loss or destruction of disbursing records.

That settlement is conclusive on the accounting officials of the United States in settling the accounts of disbursing officials.

(b) Payment or settlement of an account made pursuant to a report, determination, or finding of death may not be recovered or reopened because of a later report or determination which fixes a date of death. However, an account shall be reopened and settled on the basis of a date of death so fixed which is later than that used as a basis for earlier settlement.

(c) In settling the accounts of a disbursing official, he is entitled to credit for an erroneous payment or overpayment made by him in carrying out this subchapter, except section 5568, if there is no fraud or criminality by him. Recovery may not be made from an individual who authorizes a payment under this subchapter, except section 5568, if there is no fraud or criminality by him.

(Pub. L. 89–554, Sept. 6, 1966, 80 Stat. 494.)

HISTORICAL AND REVISION NOTES

Derivation	U.S. Code	Revised Statutes and Statutes at Large
(a)	50A U.S.C. 1011.	Mar. 7, 1942, ch. 166, §11, 56 Stat. 146.
(b)	50A U.S.C. 1009(a) (5th sentence).	Mar. 7, 1942, ch. 166, §9(a) (5th and last sentences); added July 1, 1944, ch. 371, §5, 58 Stat. 680. Aug. 29, 1957, Pub. L. 85–217, §1(c), 71 Stat. 492.
(c)	50A U.S.C. 1009(a) (last sentence).	

Only that portion of the source law which is applicable to civilian officers and employees and their dependents is codified in this section.

In subsection (a), the words "or his designee" are substituted for "or such person as he may designate". The word "employee" is substituted for "persons". The words "United States" are substituted for "Government" to conform to the style of this title.

In subsection (c), the words "in carrying out this subchapter, except section 5568" are substituted for "in carrying out the provisions of this Act, except sections 13, 16, 17, and 18", since sections 16 and 17 are scheduled for repeal (see Table II) and section 18 was previously repealed. The words "under this subchapter, except section 5568" are substituted for "under such provisions" for the reasons stated in the preceding sentence.

Standard changes are made to conform with the definitions applicable and the style of this title as outlined in the preface to the report.

§ 5568. Income tax deferment

Notwithstanding other statutes, any Federal income tax return of, or the payment of any Federal income tax by, an employee who, at the time the return or payment would otherwise become due, is in a missing status does not become due until the earlier of the following dates:

(1) the fifteenth day of the third month in which he ceased (except because of death or incompetency) being in a missing status, unless before the end of that fifteenth day he is again in a missing status; or

(2) the fifteenth day of the third month after the month in which an executor, administrator, or conservator of the estate of the taxpayer is appointed.

That due date is prescribed subject to the power of the Secretary of the Treasury or his delegate to extend the time for filing the return or paying the tax, as in other cases, and to assess and collect the tax as provided by sections 6851, 6861, and 6871 of title 26 in cases in which the assessment or collection is jeopardized and in cases of bankruptcy or receivership.

(Pub. L. 89–554, Sept. 6, 1966, 80 Stat. 494.)

HISTORICAL AND REVISION NOTES

Derivation	U.S. Code	Revised Statutes and Statutes at Large
....	50A U.S.C. 1013.	Mar. 7, 1942, ch. 166, §13, 56 Stat. 146. Aug. 8, 1947, ch. 515, §6, 61 Stat. 918. Aug. 14, 1964, Pub. L. 88–428, §1(9), 78 Stat. 437.

Only that portion of the source law which is applicable to civilian officers and employees and their dependents is codified in this section.

The words "in the case of any taxable year beginning after December 31, 1940" are omitted as unnecessary.

The words "an employee" are substituted for "any civilian officer or employee of any department" to conform to the definition in section 5561(2). The words "in a missing status" are substituted for "absent from his duty station under the conditions specified in section 2 of this Act" to conform to the definition in section 5561(5) and in view of the provisions of section 5562 establishing the entitlement of an employee in a missing status to receive pay and allowances or to have them credited to his account. Reference to "title 26" is substituted for "Internal Revenue Code of 1954".

Standard changes are made to conform with the definitions applicable and the style of this title as outlined in the preface to the report.

SECTION REFERRED TO IN OTHER SECTIONS

This section is referred to in section 5567 of this title.

§ 5569. Benefits for captives

(a) For the purpose of this section—

(1) "captive" means any individual in a captive status commencing while such individual is—

(A) in the Civil Service, or

(B) a citizen, national, or resident alien of the United States rendering personal service to the United States similar to the service of an individual in the Civil Service (other than as a member of the uniformed services);

(2) "captive status" means a missing status which, as determined by the President, arises

because of a hostile action and is a result of the individual's relationship with the Government;

(3) "missing status"—

(A) in the case of an employee, has the meaning provided under section 5561(5) of this title; and

(B) in the case of an individual other than an employee, has a similar meaning; and

(4) "family member", as used with respect to a person, means—

(A) any dependent of such person; and

(B) any individual (other than a dependent under subparagraph (A)) who is a member of such person's family or household.

(b)(1) The Secretary of the Treasury shall establish a savings fund to which the head of an agency may allot all or any portion of the pay and allowances of any captive to the extent that such pay and allowances are not subject to an allotment under section 5563 of this title or any other provision of law.

(2) Amounts so allotted to the savings fund shall bear interest at a rate which, for any calendar quarter, shall be equal to the average rate paid on United States Treasury bills with 3-month maturities issued during the preceding calendar quarter. Such interest shall be compounded quarterly.

(3) Amounts in the savings fund credited to a captive shall be considered as pay and allowances for purposes of section 5563 of this title and shall otherwise be subject to withdrawal under procedures which the Secretary of the Treasury shall establish.

(4) Any interest accruing under this subsection on—

(A) any amount for which an individual is indebted to the United States under section 5562(c) of this title shall be deemed to be part of the amount due under such section 5562(c); and

(B) any amount referred to in section 5566(f) of this title shall be deemed to be part of such amount for purposes of such section 5566(f).

(5) An allotment under this subsection may be made without regard to section 5563(c) of this title.

(c) The head of an agency shall pay (by advancement or reimbursement) any individual who is a captive, and any family member of such individual, for medical and health care, and other expenses related to such care, to the extent that such care—

(1) is incident to such individual being a captive; and

(2) is not covered—

(A) by any Government medical or health program; or

(B) by insurance.

(d)(1) Except as provided in paragraph (3), the President shall make a cash payment, computed under paragraph (2), to any individual who became or becomes a captive commencing on or after November 4, 1979. Such payment shall be made before the end of the one-year period beginning on the date on which the captive status of such individual terminates or, in the case of any individual whose status as a captive termi-

nated before the date of the enactment of the Victims of Terrorism Compensation Act, before the end of the one-year period beginning on such date.

(2) Except as provided in section 802 of the Victims of Terrorism Compensation Act, the amount of the payment under this subsection with respect to an individual held as a captive shall be not less than one-half of the amount of the world-wide average per diem rate under section 5702 of this title which was in effect for each day that individual was so held.

(3) The President—

(A) may defer a payment under this subsection in the case of any individual who, during the one-year period described in paragraph (1), is charged with an offense described in subparagraph (B), until final disposition of such charge; and

(B) may deny such payment in the case of any individual who is convicted of an offense described in subsection (b) or (c) of section 8312 of this title committed—

(i) during the period of captivity of such individual; and

(ii) related to the captive status of such individual.

(4) A payment under this subsection shall be in addition to any other amount provided by law.

(5) The provisions of subchapter VIII of this chapter (or, in the case of any person not covered by such subchapter, similar provisions prescribed by the President) shall apply with respect to any amount due an individual under paragraph (1) after such individual's death.

(6) Any payment made under paragraph (1) which is later denied under paragraph (3)(B) is a claim of the United States Government for purposes of section 3711 of title 31.

(e)(1) Under regulations prescribed by the President, the benefits provided by the Soldiers' and Sailors' Civil Relief Act of 1940, including the benefits provided by section 701 of such Act but excluding the benefits provided by sections 104, 105, 106, 400 through 408,[1] 501 through 512, and 514 of such Act, shall be provided in the case of any individual who is a captive.

(2) In applying such Act under this subsection—

(A) the term "person in the military service" is deemed to include any such captive;

(B) the term "period of military service" is deemed to include the period during which the individual is in a captive status; and

(C) references to the Secretary of the Army, the Secretary of the Navy, the Adjutant General of the Army, the Chief of Naval Personnel, and the Commandant, United States Marine Corps, are deemed, in the case of any captive, to be references to an individual designated for that purpose by the President.

(f)(1)(A) Under regulations prescribed by the President, the head of an agency shall pay (by advancement or reimbursement) a spouse or child of a captive for expenses incurred for subsistence, tuition, fees, supplies, books, and equipment, and other educational expenses, while attending an educational or training institution.

---

[1] See References in Text note below.

(B) Except as provided in subparagraph (C), payments shall be available under this paragraph for a spouse or child of an individual who is a captive for education or training which occurs—

(i) after that individual has been in captive status for 90 days or more, and

(ii) on or before—

(I) the end of any semester or quarter (as appropriate) which begins before the date on which the captive status of that individual terminates, or

(II) if the educational or training institution is not operated on a semester or quarter system, the earlier of the end of any course which began before such date or the end of the 16-week period following that date.

In order to respond to special circumstances, the appropriate agency head may specify a date for purposes of cessation of assistance under clause (ii) which is later than the date which would otherwise apply under such clause.

(C) In the event a captive dies and the death is incident to that individual being a captive, payments shall be available under this paragraph for a spouse or child of such individual for education or training which occurs after the date of such individual's death.

(D) The preceding provisions of this paragraph shall not apply with respect to any spouse or child who is eligible for assistance under chapter 35 of title 38 or similar assistance under any other provision of law.

(E) For the purpose of this paragraph, "child" means a dependent under section 5561(3)(B) of this title.

(2)(A) In order to respond to special circumstances, the head of an agency may pay (by advancement or reimbursement) a captive for expenses incurred for subsistence, tuition, fees, supplies, books, and equipment, and other educational expenses, while attending an educational or training institution.

(B) Payments shall be available under this paragraph for a captive for education or training which occurs—

(i) after the termination of that individual's captive status, and

(ii) on or before—

(I) the end of any semester or quarter (as appropriate) which begins before the date which is 10 years after the day on which the captive status of that individual terminates, or

(II) if the educational or training institution is not operated on a semester or quarter system, the earlier of the end of any course which began before such date or the end of the 16-week period following that date, and

shall be available only to the extent that such payments are not otherwise authorized by law.

(3) Assistance under this subsection—

(A) shall be discontinued for any individual whose conduct or progress is unsatisfactory under standards consistent with those established pursuant to section 3524 of title 38; and

(B) may not be provided for any individual for a period in excess of 45 months (or the equivalent thereof in other than full-time education or training).

(4) Regulations prescribed to carry out this subsection shall provide that the program under this subsection shall be consistent with the assistance program under chapters 35 and 36 of title 38.

(g) Any benefit provided under subsection (c) or (d) may, under regulations prescribed by the President, be provided to a family member of an individual if—

(1) such family member is held in captive status; and

(2) such individual is performing service for the United States as described in subsection (a)(1)(A) when the captive status of such family member commences.

(h) Except as provided in subsection (d), this section applies with respect to any individual in a captive status commencing after January 21, 1981.

(i) Notwithstanding any other provision of this subchapter, any determination by the President under subsection (a)(2) or (d) shall be conclusive and shall not be subject to judicial review.

(j) The President may prescribe regulations necessary to administer this section.

(k) Any benefit or payment pursuant to this section shall be paid out of funds available for salaries and expenses of the relevant agency of the United States.

(Added Pub. L. 99–399, title VIII, § 803(a), Aug. 27, 1986, 100 Stat. 879; amended Pub. L. 102–83, § 5(c)(2), Aug. 6, 1991, 105 Stat. 406.)

REFERENCES IN TEXT

The date of the enactment of the Victims of Terrorism Compensation Act [title VIII of Pub. L. 99–399], referred to in subsec. (d)(1), is Aug. 27, 1986.

Section 802 of the Victims of Terrorism Compensation Act [Pub. L. 99–399], referred to in subsec. (d)(2), is set out as a note below.

The Soldiers' and Sailors' Relief Act of 1940, referred to in subsec. (e)(1), is act Oct. 17, 1940, ch. 888, 54 Stat. 1178, as amended, which is classified to section 501 et seq. of the Appendix to Title 50, War and National Defense. Sections 104, 105, 106, 400 through 408, 501 through 512, 514, and 701 of the Act are classified to sections 514, 515, 516, 540 through 548, 561 through 572, 574, and 591, respectively, of the Appendix to Title 50. For complete classification of this Act to the Code, see section 501 of Appendix to Title 50 and Tables.

Section 408, referred to in subsec. (e)(1), is section 408 of act Oct. 17, 1940, ch. 888, 54 Stat. 1185, as amended, which was classified to section 548 of the Appendix to Title 50, War and National Defense, and was repealed by Pub. L. 102–12, § 9(18), Mar. 18, 1991, 105 Stat. 40.

AMENDMENTS

1991—Subsec. (f)(3)(A). Pub. L. 102–83 substituted "section 3524 of title 38" for "section 1724 of title 38".

SHORT TITLE

Section 801 of title VIII of Pub. L. 99–399 provided that: "This title [enacting this section, section 5570 of this title, sections 1051, 1095, and 2181 to 2185 of Title 10, Armed Forces, and sections 559 and 1013 of Title 37, Pay and Allowances of the Uniformed Services, amending section 6325 of this title, and enacting provisions set out as notes under this section, sections 1051, 1095, and 2181 of Title 10, and section 559 of Title 37] may be cited as the 'Victims of Terrorism Compensation Act'."

PAYMENT TO INDIVIDUALS HELD IN CAPTIVE STATUS BETWEEN NOVEMBER 4, 1979, AND JANUARY 21, 1981

Section 802 of title VIII of Pub. L. 99–399 provided that: "The amount of the payment for individuals in the Civil Service referred to in section 5569(d) of title 5, United States Code (as added by section 803 of this title), or for individuals in the uniformed services referred to in section 559(c) of title 37, United States Code (as added by section 806 of this title), as the case may be, shall be $50 for each day any such individual was held in captive status during a period commencing on or after November 4, 1979, and ending on or before January 21, 1981.''

TRANSITION PROVISIONS

Section 805 of title VIII of Pub. L. 99–399 provided that:

"(a) SAVINGS FUND.—(1) Amounts may be allotted to the savings fund under subsection (b) of section 5569 of title 5, United States Code (as added by section 803(a) of this Act) from pay and allowances for any pay period ending after January 21, 1981, and before the establishment of such fund.

"(2) Interest on amounts so allotted with respect to any such pay period shall be calculated as if the allotment had occurred at the end of such pay period.

"(b) MEDICAL AND HEALTH CARE; EDUCATIONAL EXPENSES.—Subsections (c) and (f) of such section 5569 (as so added) shall be carried out with respect to the period after January 21, 1981, and before the effective date of those subsections, under regulations prescribed by the President.

"(c) DEFINITION.—For the purpose of this subsection, 'pay and allowances' has the meaning provided under section 5561 of title 5, United States Code.''

REGULATIONS

Section 807 of title VIII of Pub. L. 99–399 provided that: "Any regulation required by this title or by any amendment made by this title [see Short Title note above] shall take effect not later than 6 months after the date of enactment of this Act [Aug. 27, 1986].''

EFFECTIVE DATE OF ENTITLEMENTS

Section 808 of title VIII of Pub. L. 99–399 provided that: "Provisions enacted by this title [see Short Title note above] which provide new spending authority described in section 401(c)(2)(C) of the Congressional Budget Act of 1974 [2 U.S.C. 651(c)(2)(C)] shall not be effective until October 1, 1986.''

EXECUTIVE ORDER NO. 12576

Ex. Ord. No. 12576, Dec. 2, 1986, 51 F.R. 43721, relating to victims of terrorism compensation, was superseded by Ex. Ord. No. 12598, June 17, 1987, 52 F.R. 23421, set out below.

EX. ORD. NO. 12598. VICTIMS OF TERRORISM COMPENSATION

Ex. Ord. No. 12598, June 17, 1987, 52 F.R. 23421, provided:

By the authority vested in me as President by the Constitution and laws of the United States of America, including Title VIII of the Omnibus Diplomatic Security and Antiterrorism Act of 1986 (Public Law 99–399, 100 Stat. 853) ("the Act") [see Short Title note set out above], and in order to provide for the implementation of that Act, it is hereby ordered as follows:

SECTION 1. The functions vested in the President by that part of section 803(a) of the Act to be codified at 5 U.S.C. 5569 are delegated to the Secretary of State.

SEC. 2. The functions vested in the President by that part of section 803(a) of the Act to be codified at 5 U.S.C. 5570 are delegated to the Secretary of State, to be exercised in consultation with the Secretary of Labor.

SEC. 3. The functions vested in the President by section 806(a) (to be codified at 37 U.S.C. 559), section 806(c) (to be codified at 10 U.S.C. 1095 [now 10 U.S.C. 1095a]), and section 806(d) (to be codified at 10 U.S.C. 2181–2185) are delegated to the Secretary of Defense.

SEC. 4. The functions vested in the President by section 806(b) (to be codified at 10 U.S.C. 1051 [now 10

U.S.C. 1032]) are delegated to the Secretary of Defense, to be exercised in consultation with the Secretary of Labor.

SEC. 5. The Secretaries of State and Defense shall consult with each other and with the heads of other appropriate Executive departments and agencies in carrying out their functions under this Order.

SEC. 6. Executive Order No. 12576 of December 2, 1986, is hereby superseded.

RONALD REAGAN.

SECTION REFERRED TO IN OTHER SECTIONS

This section is referred to in section 5570 of this title; title 37 section 559.

§ 5570. Compensation for disability or death

(a) For the purpose of this section—

(1) "employee" means—

(A) any individual in the Civil Service; and

(B) any individual rendering personal service to the United States similar to the service of an individual in the Civil Service (other than as a member of the uniformed services); and

(2) "family member", as used with respect to an employee, means—

(A) any dependent of such employee; and

(B) any individual (other than a dependent under subparagraph (A)) who is a member of the employee's family or household.

(b) The President shall prescribe regulations under which an agency head may pay compensation for the disability or death of an employee or a family member of an employee if, as determined by the President, the disability or death was caused by hostile action and was a result of the individual's relationship with the Government.

(c) Any compensation otherwise payable to an individual under this section in connection with any disability or death shall be reduced by any amounts payable to such individual under any other program funded in whole or in part by the United States (excluding any amount payable under section 5569(d) of this title) in connection with such disability or death, except that nothing in this subsection shall result in the reduction of any amount below zero.

(d) A determination by the President under subsection (b) shall be conclusive and shall not be subject to judicial review.

(e) Compensation under this section may include payment (whether by advancement or reimbursement) for any medical or health expenses relating to the death or disability involved to the extent that such expenses are not covered under subsection (c) of section 5569 of this title (other than because of paragraph (2) of such subsection).

(f) This section applies with respect to any disability or death resulting from an injury which occurs after January 21, 1981.

(g) Any benefit or payment pursuant to this section shall be paid out of funds available for salaries and expenses of the relevant agency of the United States.

(Added Pub. L. 99–399, title VIII, § 803(a), Aug. 27, 1986, 100 Stat. 882.)

DELEGATION OF FUNCTIONS

Functions of the President under this section delegated to the Secretary of State to be exercised in consultation with the Secretary of Labor, see Ex. Ord. No. 12598, June 17, 1987, 52 F.R. 23421, set out as a note under section 5569 of this title.

SUBCHAPTER VIII—SETTLEMENT OF ACCOUNTS

SUBCHAPTER REFERRED TO IN OTHER SECTIONS

This subchapter is referred to in sections 5520a, 5551, 5569 of this title; title 15 section 78d.

§ 5581. Definitions

For the purpose of this subchapter—

(1) "employee" means—

(A) an employee as defined by section 2105 of this title; and

(B) an individual employed by the government of the District of Columbia;

but does not include the employee of—

(i) a Federal land bank;

(ii) a Federal intermediate credit bank;

(iii) a regional bank for cooperatives; or

(iv) the Senate within the purview of section 36a of title 2; and

(2) "money due" means the pay and allowances due on account of the services of a deceased employee for the Government of the United States or the government of the District of Columbia. It includes, but is not limited to—

(A) per diem instead of subsistence, mileage, and amounts due in reimbursement of travel expenses, including incidental and miscellaneous expenses in connection therewith for which reimbursement is due;

(B) allowances on change of official station;

(C) quarters and cost-of-living allowances and overtime or premium pay;

(D) amounts due for payment of cash awards for employees' suggestions;

(E) amounts due as refund of pay deductions for United States savings bonds;

(F) payment for accumulated and current accrued annual or vacation leave equal to the pay the decreased employee would have received had he lived and remained in the service until the end of the period of annual or vacation leave;

(G) amounts of checks drawn for pay and allowances which were not delivered by the Government to the employee during his lifetime;

(H) amounts of unnegotiated checks returned to the Government because of the death of the employee; and

(I) retroactive pay under section 5344(a) (2) of this title.

It does not include benefits, refunds, or interest payable under subchapter III of chapter 83 of this title applicable to the service of the deceased employee, or amounts the disposition of which is otherwise expressly prescribed by Federal statute.

(Pub. L. 89–554, Sept. 6, 1966, 80 Stat. 495; Pub. L. 96–54, § 2(a)(34), Aug. 14, 1979, 93 Stat. 383.)

HISTORICAL AND REVISION NOTES

Derivation	U.S. Code	Revised Statutes and Statutes at Large
(1)	5 U.S.C. 61k.	Aug. 3, 1950, ch. 518, § 7, 64 Stat. 396.
		Apr. 30, 1954, ch. 177, § 2, 68 Stat. 65.
(2)	5 U.S.C. 61g.	Aug. 3, 1950, ch. 518, § 2, 64 Stat. 396.
		July 2, 1953, ch. 178, § 5, 67 Stat. 138.
		Sept. 1, 1954, ch. 1208, § 501, 68 Stat. 1115.
		Sept. 2, 1958, Pub. L. 85–914, § 1, 72 Stat. 1761.
	5 U.S.C. 61i.	Aug. 3, 1950, ch. 518, § 4, 64 Stat. 396.

Paragraph (1) is supplied for convenience and is based on the first 35 words of former section 61f, which is carried into section 5582, and former section 61k.

The exception for production credit corporations in section 7 of the Act of Aug. 3, 1950, is omitted as they were merged in the Federal intermediate credit banks by the Farm Credit Act of 1956, 70 Stat. 659.

The exception in paragraph (1)(iv) for employees of the Senate is added on authority of the Act of Jan. 6, 1951, ch. 1213, 64 Stat. 1124; 2 U.S.C. 36a.

In paragraph (2), the definition of "money due" is substituted for "unpaid compensation". Paragraph (2)(I) is added on authority of former section 1182(a)(2), which is carried into section 5344.

Standard changes are made to conform with the definitions applicable and the style of this title as outlined in the preface to the report.

REFERENCES IN TEXT

Section 5344 of this title, referred to in par. (2)(I), was amended generally by Pub. L. 92–392 and provisions relating to retroactive pay formerly contained in section 5344(a)(2) are contained in section 5344(b)(2).

AMENDMENTS

1979—Par. (1). Pub. L. 96–54 inserted "and" after cl. (iv).

EFFECTIVE DATE OF 1979 AMENDMENT

Amendment by Pub. L. 96–54 effective July 12, 1979, see section 2(b) of Pub. L. 96–54, set out as a note under section 305 of this title.

§ 5582. Designation of beneficiary; order of precedence

(a) The employing agency shall notify each employee of his right to designate a beneficiary or beneficiaries to receive money due, and of the disposition of money due if a beneficiary is not designated. An employee may change or revoke a designation at any time under regulations promulgated—

(1) by the Director of the Office of Personnel Management or his designee, in the case of an employee of an executive agency;

(2) jointly by the President pro tempore of the Senate and the Speaker of the House of Representatives, or their designee, in the case of an employee of the legislative branch; and

(3) by the Chief Justice of the United States or his or her designee, in the case of an employee of the judicial branch.

(b) In order to facilitate the settlement of the accounts of deceased employees, money due an employee at the time of his death shall be paid to the person or persons surviving at the date of death, in the following order of precedence, and the payment bars recovery by another person of amounts so paid:

First, to the beneficiary or beneficiaries designated by the employee in a writing received in the employing agency before his death.

Second, if there is no designated beneficiary, to the widow or widower of the employee.

Third, if none of the above, to the child or children of the employee and descendants of deceased children by representation.

Fourth, if none of the above, to the parents of the employee or the survivor of them.

Fifth, if none of the above, to the duly appointed legal representative of the estate of the employee.

Sixth, if none of the above, to the person or persons entitled under the laws of the domicile of the employee at the time of his death.

(Pub. L. 89–554, Sept. 6, 1966, 80 Stat. 495; Pub. L. 104–316, title I, § 103(c), Oct. 19, 1996, 110 Stat. 3828.)

HISTORICAL AND REVISION NOTES

Derivation	U.S. Code	Revised Statutes and Statutes at Large
(a)	5 U.S.C. 61j.	Aug. 3, 1950, ch. 518, § 5, 64 Stat. 396.
(b)	5 U.S.C. 61f.	Aug. 3, 1950, ch. 518, § 1, 64 Stat. 395.

Subsection (a) is restated for clarity. The word "officers" is omitted as included in "employee".

In subsection (b), so much of the first 35 words of former section 61f as states the application is carried into the definition of "employee" in section 5581(1). The word "officer" is omitted as included in "employee".

Standard changes are made to conform with the definitions applicable and the style of this title as outlined in the preface to the report.

AMENDMENTS

1996—Subsec. (a). Pub. L. 104–316 substituted "An employee may change or revoke a designation at any time under regulations promulgated—" for "An employee may change or revoke a designation at any time under such regulations as the Comptroller General of the United States may prescribe." in introductory provisions and added pars. (1) to (3).

SECTION REFERRED TO IN OTHER SECTIONS

This section is referred to in sections 5307, 5583, 5595 of this title; title 22 sections 2504, 3965; title 42 section 4955.

§ 5583. Payment of money due; settlement of accounts

(a) Under such regulations as the Director of the Office of Personnel Management may prescribe, the employing agency shall pay money due a deceased employee to the beneficiary designated by the employee under section 5582(b) of this title, or, if none, to the widow or widower of the employee.

(b) The Director may by regulation prescribe the method for settlement of accounts payable under subsection (a) of this section. However—

(1) accounts of employees of the government of the District of Columbia shall be paid by the District of Columbia; and

(2) accounts of employees of Government corporations or mixed ownership Government corporations may be paid by the corporations.

(Pub. L. 89–554, Sept. 6, 1966, 80 Stat. 496; Pub. L. 96–70, title III, § 3302(e)(7), Sept. 27, 1979, 93 Stat.

498; Pub. L. 104–316, title II, § 202(b), Oct. 19, 1996, 110 Stat. 3842.)

HISTORICAL AND REVISION NOTES

Derivation	U.S. Code	Revised Statutes and Statutes at Large
....	5 U.S.C. 61h.	Aug. 3, 1950, ch. 518, § 3, 64 Stat. 396. Apr. 30, 1954, ch. 177, § 1, 68 Stat. 64.

In subsection (a), the word "officer" is omitted as included in "employee".

Standard changes are made to conform with the definitions applicable and the style of this title as outlined in the preface to the report.

AMENDMENTS

1996—Subsec. (a). Pub. L. 104–316, § 202(b)(1), substituted "Director of the Office of Personnel Management" for "Comptroller General of the United States".

Subsec. (b). Pub. L. 104–316, § 202(b)(2), substituted "The Director may by regulation prescribe the method for settlement of accounts payable under subsection (a) of this section." for "Except as the Comptroller General may by regulation otherwise authorize or direct, accounts not payable under subsection (a) of this section are payable on settlement of the General Accounting Office."

1979—Subsec. (b). Pub. L. 96–70 struck out par. (2) providing that accounts of the employees of the Canal Zone Government be paid by the Canal Zone Government, and redesignated par. (3) as (2).

EFFECTIVE DATE OF 1979 AMENDMENT

Amendment by Pub. L. 96–70 effective Oct. 1, 1979, see section 3304 of Pub. L. 96–70, set out as an Effective Date note under section 3601 of Title 22, Foreign Relations and Intercourse.

§ 5584. Claims for overpayment of pay and allowances, and of travel, transportation and relocation expenses and allowances

(a) A claim of the United States against a person arising out of an erroneous payment of pay or allowances made on or after July 1, 1960, or arising out of an erroneous payment of travel, transportation or relocation expenses and allowances, to an employee of an agency, the collection of which would be against equity and good conscience and not in the best interests of the United States, may be waived in whole or in part by—

(1) the authorized official;

(2) the head of an agency when—

(A) the claim is in an amount aggregating not more than $1,500; and

(B) the waiver is made in accordance with standards which the authorized official shall prescribe; or

(3) the Director of the Administrative Office of the United States Courts when the claim is in an amount aggregating not more than $10,000 and involves an officer or employee of the Administrative Office of the United States Courts, the Federal Judicial Center, or any of the courts set forth in section 610 of title 28.

(b) The authorized official or the head of the agency, as the case may be, may not exercise his authority under this section to waive any claim—

(1) if, in his opinion, there exists, in connection with the claim, an indication of fraud,

misrepresentation, fault, or lack of good faith on the part of the employee or any other person having an interest in obtaining a waiver of the claim;

(2) except in the case of employees of the Government Printing Office, the Library of Congress, the Office of the Architect of the Capitol, or the Botanic Garden, if application for waiver is received in his office, after the expiration of three years immediately following the date on which the erroneous payment of pay was discovered or three years immediately following October 21, 1968, whichever is later;

(3) except in the case of employees of the Government Printing Office, the Library of Congress, the Office of the Architect of the Capitol, or the Botanic Garden, if application for waiver is received in his office after the expiration of three years immediately following the date on which the erroneous payment of allowances was discovered or three years immediately following October 2, 1972, whichever is later;

(4) in the case of employees of the Government Printing Office, the Library of Congress, the Office of the Architect of the Capitol, or the Botanic Garden, if application for waiver is received in his office after the expiration of 3 years immediately following the date on which the erroneous payment of pay or allowances was discovered or 3 years immediately following July 25, 1974, whichever is later; or

(5) in the case of a claim involving an erroneous payment of travel, transportation or relocation expenses and allowances, if application for waiver is received in his office after the expiration of 3 years immediately following the date on which the erroneous payment was discovered.

(c) A person who has repaid to the United States all or part of the amount of a claim, with respect to which a waiver is granted under this section, is entitled, to the extent of the waiver, to refund, by the employing agency at the time of the erroneous payment, of the amount repaid to the United States, if he applies to that employing agency for that refund within two years following the effective date of the waiver. The employing agency shall pay that refund in accordance with this section.

(d) In the audit and settlement of the accounts of any accountable official, full credit shall be given for any amounts with respect to which collection by the United States is waived under this section.

(e) An erroneous payment, the collection of which is waived under this section, is deemed a valid payment for all purposes.

(f) This section does not affect any authority under any other statute to litigate, settle, compromise, or waive any claim of the United States.

(g) For the purpose of this section, "agency" means—

(1) an Executive agency;
(2) the Government Printing Office;
(3) the Library of Congress;
(4) the Office of the Architect of the Capitol;
(5) the Botanic Garden; and
(6) the Administrative Office of the United States Courts, the Federal Judicial Center,

and any of the courts set forth in section 610 of title 28.

For purposes of this section, the Director of the Administrative Office of the United States Courts shall be the head of the agency in the case of those entities set forth in paragraph (6) of this subsection.

(g)[1] For the purpose of this section, the term "authorized official" means—

(1) the head of an agency, with respect to an agency or employee in the legislative branch; or

(2) the Director of the Office of Management and Budget, with respect to any other agency or employee.

(Added Pub. L. 90–616, §1(a), Oct. 21, 1968, 82 Stat. 1212; amended Pub. L. 92–453, §3(1), Oct. 2, 1972, 86 Stat. 760; Pub. L. 93–359, §1, July 25, 1974, 88 Stat. 393; Pub. L. 96–54, §2(a)(35), Aug. 14, 1979, 93 Stat. 383; Pub. L. 99–224, §1(a), Dec. 28, 1985, 99 Stat. 1741; Pub. L. 100–702, title X, §1009(a), Nov. 19, 1988, 102 Stat. 4667; Pub. L. 102–190, div. A, title VI, §657(a), Dec. 5, 1991, 105 Stat. 1393; Pub. L. 104–316, title I, §103(d), Oct. 19, 1996, 110 Stat. 3828.)

AMENDMENTS

1996—Subsec. (a). Pub. L. 104–316, §103(d)(1), in par. (1) substituted "authorized official" for "Comptroller General of the United States", and in par. (2) inserted "and" at end of subpar. (A), redesignated subpar. (C) as (B) and substituted "authorized official" for "Comptroller General", and struck out former subpar. (B) which read as follows: "the claim is not the subject of an exception made by the Comptroller General in the account of any accountable official; and".

Subsec. (b). Pub. L. 104–316, §103(d)(2), substituted "authorized official" for "Comptroller General" in introductory provisions.

Subsec. (g). Pub. L. 104–316, §103(d)(3), added subsec. (g) defining "authorized official".

1991—Subsec. (a)(2)(A). Pub. L. 102–190 substituted "$1,500" for "$500".

1988—Subsec. (a)(3). Pub. L. 100–702, §1009(a)(1), added par. (3).

Subsec. (g). Pub. L. 100–702, §1009(a)(2), added par. (6) and last sentence.

1985—Pub. L. 99–224, §1(a)(1), substituted "and of travel, transportation and relocation expenses and allowances" for "other than travel and transportation expenses and allowances and relocation expenses" in section catchline.

Subsec. (a). Pub. L. 99–224, §1(a)(2), substituted "made on or after July 1, 1960, or arising out of an erroneous payment of travel, transportation or relocation expenses and allowances" for ", other than travel and transportation expenses and allowances and relocation expenses payable under section 5724a of this title, on or after July 1, 1960".

Subsec. (b). Pub. L. 99–224, §1(a)(3), added par. (5).

1979—Subsec. (b)(4). Pub. L. 96–54 substituted "July 25, 1974" for "the date on which this clause (4) is enacted into law".

1974—Subsec. (a). Pub. L. 93–359, §1(1), substituted "agency" for "executive agency" in provisions preceding cl. (1) and in cl. (2) preceding subcl. (A).

Subsec. (b). Pub. L. 93–359, §1(1), substituted "agency" for "executive agency" in provisions preceding cl. (1), inserted "except in the case of employees of the Government Printing Office, the Library of Congress, the Office of the Architect of the Capitol, or the Botanic Garden," immediately following the designation "(2)" in cl. (2) and immediately following the des-

---

[1] So in original. Probably should be "(h)".

ignation "(3)" in cl. (3), struck out "or" at end of cl. (2), substituted "October 2, 1972, whichever is later; or" for "the effective date of the amendment authorizing the waiver of allowances, whichever is later" in cl. (3) and struck out the period at end of cl. (3), and added cl. (4).

Subsec. (g). Pub. L. 93–359, §1(5), added subsec. (g).

1972—Pub. L. 92–453 inserted "and allowances, other than travel and transportation expenses and allowances and relocation expenses" in section catchline, and substituted "payment of pay or allowances, other than travel and transportation expenses and allowances and relocation expenses payable under section 5724a of this title" for "payment of pay" in subsec. (a).

Subsec. (b)(2). Pub. L. 92–453 inserted "if application for waiver is received in his office" in cl. (2), and substituted "October 21, 1968" for "the effective date of this section."

Subsec. (b)(3). Pub. L. 92–453 added cl. (3).

EFFECTIVE DATE OF 1996 AMENDMENT

Amendment by Pub. L. 104–316 effective 60 days after Oct. 19, 1996, see section 101(e)(2) of Pub. L. 104–316, set out as a note under section 130c of Title 2, The Congress.

EFFECTIVE DATE OF 1988 AMENDMENT

Section 1009(b) of Pub. L. 100–702 provided that: "The amendments made by this section [amending this section] shall apply with respect to any claim arising before the date of the enactment of this Act [Nov. 19, 1988] which is pending on such date, and to any claim which arises on or after such date of enactment."

EFFECTIVE DATE OF 1985 AMENDMENT

Section 4 of Pub. L. 99–224 provided that: "The amendments made by section 1 of this Act [amending this section] shall apply to any claim arising out of an erroneous payment of travel, transportation, or relocation expenses and allowances made on or after the date of the enactment of this Act [Dec. 28, 1985]. The amendments made by sections 2 and 3 of this Act [amending section 2774 of Title 10, Armed Forces, and section 716 of Title 32, National Guard] shall apply to any claim arising out of an erroneous payment of travel and transportation allowances made on or after the date of the enactment of this Act."

EFFECTIVE DATE OF 1979 AMENDMENT

Amendment by Pub. L. 96–54 effective July 12, 1979, see section 2(b) of Pub. L. 96–54. set out as a note under section 305 of this title.

SECTION REFERRED TO IN OTHER SECTIONS

This section is referred to in sections 6302, 8118 of this title; title 22 section 2504; title 42 section 5055.

SUBCHAPTER IX—SEVERANCE PAY AND BACK PAY

AMENDMENTS

1967—Pub. L. 90–83, §1(34)(A), Sept. 11, 1967, 81 Stat. 201, inserted "SEVERANCE PAY AND" before "BACK PAY" in subchapter heading.

SUBCHAPTER REFERRED TO IN OTHER SECTIONS

This subchapter is referred to in section 5520a of this title; title 22 section 3664.

[§§ 5591 to 5594. Repealed. Pub. L. 90–83, § 1(34)(B), Sept. 11, 1967, 81 Stat. 201]

HISTORICAL AND REVISION NOTES

This section deletes sections 5591, 5592, 5593, and 5594 of title 5, United States Code, to reflect the repeal of the source statutes of those sections by the act of March 30, 1966, Public Law 89–380, section 5, 80 Stat. 95. [Sections, Pub. L. 89–554, Sept. 6, 1966, 80 Stat. 496, 497, related to back pay for individuals or preference

eligibles reinstated or restored, and are covered by section 5596 of this title.]

§ 5595. Severance pay

(a) For the purpose of this section—
  (1) "agency" means—
    (A) an Executive agency;
    (B) the Library of Congress;
    (C) the Government Printing Office;
    (D) the government of the District of Columbia;
    (E) the Administrative Office of the United States Courts, the Federal Judicial Center, and the courts named by section 610 of title 28; and
    (F) the Office of the Architect of the Capitol; and

  (2) "employee" means—
    (A) an individual employed in or under an agency; and
    (B) an individual employed by a county committee established under section 590h(b) of title 16;

but does not include—
  (i) an employee (other than a member of the Senior Executive Service or the Federal Bureau of Investigation and Drug Enforcement Administration Senior Executive Service, or an employee whose pay is fixed under section 5376) whose rate of basic pay is fixed at a rate provided for one of the levels of the Executive Schedule or is in excess of the minimum rate for the Executive Schedule;
  (ii) an employee serving under an appointment with a definite time limitation, except one so appointed for full-time employment without a break in service of more than 3 days following service under an appointment without time limitation;
  (iii) an alien employee who occupies a position outside the several States, the District of Columbia, and the areas and installations in the Republic of Panama made available to the United States pursuant to the Panama Canal Treaty of 1977 and related agreements (as described in section 3(a) of the Panama Canal Act of 1979);
  (iv) an employee who is subject to subchapter III of chapter 83 of this title or any other retirement statute or retirement system applicable to an employee as defined by section 2105 of this title or a member of a uniformed service and, who, at the time of separation from the service, has fulfilled the requirements for immediate annuity under such a statute or system;
  (v) an employee who, at the time of separation from the service, is receiving compensation under subchapter I of chapter 81 of this title, other than one receiving this compensation concurrently with pay or on account of the death of another individual;
  (vi) an employee who, at the time of separation from the service, is entitled to receive benefits under section 609(b)(1) of the Foreign Service Act of 1980 or any other severance pay from the Government;
  (vii) an employee of the Tennessee Valley Authority;
  (viii) an employee of the Office of the Architect of the Capitol, who is employed on a temporary when actually employed basis;

(ix) an employee of the Government Printing Office, who is employed on a temporary when actually employed basis; or

(x) such other employee as may be excluded by regulations of the President or such other officer or agency as he may designate.

(b) Under regulations prescribed by the President or such officer or agency as he may designate, an employee who—

(1) has been employed currently for a continuous period of at least 12 months; and

(2) is involuntarily separated from the service, not by removal for cause on charges of misconduct, delinquency, or inefficiency;

is entitled to be paid severance pay in regular pay periods by the agency from which separated. However, the Director of the Administrative Office of the United States Courts may prescribe regulations to effect the application and operation of this section to the agencies specified in subsection (a)(1)(E) of this section. The Architect of the Capitol may prescribe regulations to effect the application and operation of this section to the agency specified in subsection (a)(1)(F) of this section. The Public Printer may prescribe regulations to effect the application and operation of this section to the agency specified in subsection (a)(1)(C) of this section.

(c) Severance pay consists of—

(1) a basic severance allowance computed on the basis of 1 week's basic pay at the rate received immediately before separation for each year of civilian service up to and including 10 years for which severance pay has not been received under this or any other authority and 2 weeks' basic pay at that rate for each year of civilian service beyond 10 years for which severance pay has not been received under this or any other authority; and

(2) an age adjustment allowance computed on the basis of 10 percent of the total basic severance allowance for each year by which the age of the recipient exceeds 40 years at the time of separation.

Total severance pay under this section may not exceed 1 year's pay at the rate received immediately before separation. For the purpose of this subsection, "basic pay" includes premium pay under section 5545(c)(1) of this title.

(d) If an employee is reemployed by the Government of the United States or the government of the District of Columbia before the end of the period covered by payments of severance pay, the payments shall be discontinued beginning with the date of reemployment and the service represented by the unexpired portion of the period shall be recredited to the employee for use in any later computations of severance pay. For the purpose of subsection (b) (1) of this section, reemployment that causes severance pay to be discontinued is deemed employment continuous with that serving as the basis for severance pay.

(e) If the employee dies before the end of the period covered by payments of severance pay, the payments of severance pay with respect to the employee shall be continued as if the employee were living and shall be paid on a pay period basis to the survivor of the employee in accordance with section 5582(b) of this title.

(f) Severance pay under this section is not a basis for payment, and may not be included in the basis for computation, of any other type of United States or District of Columbia Government benefits. A period covered by severance pay is not a period of United States or District of Columbia Government service or employment.

(g) The Secretary of Agriculture shall prescribe regulations to effect the application and operation of this section to an individual named by subsection (a)(2)(B) of this section.

(h)(1) Severance pay under this section may not be paid to—

(A) a person described in paragraph (4)(A) during any period in which the person is employed in a defense nonappropriated fund instrumentality; or

(B) a person described in paragraph (4)(B) during any period in which the person is employed in a Coast Guard nonappropriated fund instrumentality.

(2)(A) Except as provided in subparagraph (B), payment of severance pay to a person referred to in paragraph (1) may be resumed upon any involuntary separation of the person from the position of employment in a nonappropriated fund instrumentality, not by removal for cause on charges of misconduct, delinquency, or inefficiency.

(B) Payment of severance pay may not be resumed under subparagraph (A) in the case of a person who, upon separation, is entitled to immediate payment of retired or retainer pay as a member or former member of the uniformed services or to an immediate annuity under—

(i) a retirement system for persons retiring from employment by a nonappropriated fund instrumentality;

(ii) subchapter III of chapter 83 of this title;

(iii) subchapter II of chapter 84 of this title; or

(iv) any other retirement system of the Federal Government for persons retiring from employment with the Federal Government.

(3) Upon resumption of payment of severance pay under paragraph (2)(A) in the case of a person separated as described in such paragraph, the amount of the severance pay so payable for a period shall be reduced (but not below zero) by the portion (if any) of the amount of any severance pay payable for such period to the person by the nonappropriated fund instrumentality that is attributable to credit for service taken into account under subsection (c) in the computation of the amount of the severance pay so resumed.

(4) Paragraph (1) applies to a person who, on or after January 1, 1987, moves without a break in service—

(A) from employment in the Department of Defense that is not employment in a defense nonappropriated fund instrumentality to employment in a defense nonappropriated fund instrumentality; or

(B) from employment in the Coast Guard that is not employment in a Coast Guard nonappropriated fund instrumentality to employment in a Coast Guard nonappropriated fund instrumentality.

(5) The Secretary of Defense, in consultation with the Secretary of Transportation, shall prescribe regulations to carry out this subsection.

(6) In this subsection:

(A) The term "defense nonappropriated fund instrumentality" means a nonappropriated fund instrumentality of the Department of Defense.

(B) The term "Coast Guard nonappropriated fund instrumentality" means a nonappropriated fund instrumentality of the Coast Guard.

(C) The term "nonappropriated fund instrumentality" means a nonappropriated fund instrumentality described in section 2105(c) of this title.

(i)(1) In the case of an employee of the Department of Defense who is entitled to severance pay under this section, the Secretary of Defense or the Secretary of the military department concerned may, upon application by the employee, pay the total amount of the severance pay to the employee in one lump sum.

(2)(A) If an employee paid severance pay in a lump sum under this subsection is reemployed by the Government of the United States or the government of the District of Columbia at such time that, had the employee been paid severance pay in regular pay periods under subsection (b), the payments of such pay would have been discontinued under subsection (d) upon such reemployment, the employee shall repay to the Department of Defense (for the military department that formerly employed the employee, if applicable) an amount equal to the amount of severance pay to which the employee was entitled under this section that would not have been paid to the employee under subsection (d) by reason of such reemployment.

(B) The period of service represented by an amount of severance pay repaid by an employee under subparagraph (A) shall be considered service for which severance pay has not been received by the employee under this section.

(C) Amounts repaid to an agency under this paragraph shall be credited to the appropriation available for the pay of employees of the agency for the fiscal year in which received. Amounts so credited shall be merged with, and shall be available for the same purposes and the same period as, the other funds in that appropriation.

(3) If an employee fails to repay to an agency an amount required to be repaid under paragraph (2)(A), that amount is recoverable from the employee as a debt due the United States.

(4) This subsection applies with respect to severance pay payable under this section for separations taking effect on or after February 10, 1996, and before October 1, 2003.

(j)(1) In the case of an employee of the Department of Energy who is entitled to severance pay under this section as a result of the establishment of the National Nuclear Security Administration, the Secretary of Energy may, upon application by the employee, pay the total amount of the severance pay to the employee in one lump sum.

(2)(A) If an employee paid severance pay in a lump sum under this subsection is reemployed by the Government of the United States or the government of the District of Columbia at such time that, had the employee been paid severance

pay in regular pay periods under subsection (b), the payments of such pay would have been discontinued under subsection (d) upon such reemployment, the employee shall repay to the Department of Energy an amount equal to the amount of severance pay to which the employee was entitled under this section that would not have been paid to the employee under subsection (d) by reason of such reemployment.

(B) The period of service represented by an amount of severance pay repaid by an employee under subparagraph (A) shall be considered service for which severance pay has not been received by the employee under this section.

(C) Amounts repaid to the Department of Energy under this paragraph shall be credited to the appropriation available for the pay of employees of the agency for the fiscal year in which received. Amounts so credited shall be merged with, and shall be available for the same purposes and the same period as, the other funds in that appropriation.

(3) If an employee fails to repay to the Department of Energy an amount required to be repaid under paragraph (2)(A), that amount is recoverable from the employee as a debt due the United States.

(Added Pub. L. 90–83, § 1(34)(C), Sept. 11, 1967, 81 Stat. 201; amended Pub. L. 95–454, title IV, § 408(a)(3), Oct. 13, 1978, 92 Stat. 1173; Pub. L. 96–70, title I, § 1231(d), Sept. 27, 1979, 93 Stat. 470; Pub. L. 96–465, title II, § 2305, Oct. 17, 1980, 94 Stat. 2165; Pub. L. 100–325, § 2(i)(2), May 30, 1988, 102 Stat. 582; Pub. L. 101–474, § 5(k), Oct. 30, 1990, 104 Stat. 1100; Pub. L. 101–509, title V, § 529 [title I, § 101(b)(9)(J)], Nov. 5, 1990, 104 Stat. 1427, 1442; Pub. L. 103–337, div. A, title III, § 343(a), Oct. 5, 1994, 108 Stat. 2721; Pub. L. 104–106, div. A, title X, § 1035, Feb. 10, 1996, 110 Stat. 430; Pub. L. 105–55, title III, § 310(a), Oct. 7, 1997, 111 Stat. 1199; Pub. L. 105–275, title III, §§ 308(a), 309(a), Oct. 21, 1998, 112 Stat. 2452, 2454; Pub. L. 106–31, title V, § 5006, May 21, 1999, 113 Stat. 112; Pub. L. 106–65, div. A, title XI, § 1104(a), div. C, title XXXII, § 3243, Oct. 5, 1999, 113 Stat. 777, 965.)

HISTORICAL AND REVISION NOTES

Section of title 5	Source (U.S. Code)	Source (Statutes at Large)
5595	5 App.: 1117.	Oct. 29, 1965, Pub. L. 89–301, § 9, 79 Stat. 1118. Nov. 2, 1966, Pub. L. 89–737, § 2, 80 Stat. 1164.

In subsection (a), subsections (a) and (b) of 5 App. U.S.C. 1117 are restated as definitions.

In subsection (a)(1)(A), the term "Executive agency" is substituted for "the executive branch of the Government of the United States, including each corporation wholly owned or controlled by the United States" and "the General Accounting Office" to conform to the definition in 5 U.S.C. 105.

The definition in subsection (a)(2) continues the application of the section to only civilian officers and employees, and does not encompass members of the uniformed services as they are not "employed" in or under an agency. Throughout the section, the word "officer", in the phrase "officer or employee", is omitted as included within "employee". The last 40 words of 5 App. U.S.C. 1117(a) are codified in subsection (g).

In subsection (a)(2)(i), the words "Executive Schedule" are substituted for "Federal Executive Salary Schedule" to reflect the provisions of 5 U.S.C. 5311. The words "of the General Schedule of the Classification Act of 1949, as amended" are omitted as unnecessary.

In subsection (a)(2)(ii), the words "without a break in service of more than 3 days" are coextensive with and substituted for "without a break in service or after a separation of three days or less".

In subsection (a)(2)(iv), the words "subchapter III of chapter 83 of this title" are substituted for "the Civil Service Retirement Act, as amended" to reflect the codification of the act in title 5 U.S.C. The words "employees as defined by section 2105 of this title" are coextensive with and substituted for "Federal officers and employees".

In subsection (a)(2)(v), the words "subchapter I of chapter 81 of this title" are substituted for "the Federal Employees' Compensation Act, as amended" to reflect the codification of the act in title 5, U.S.C.

In subsection (b) the word "agency" is substituted for "department, independent establishment, corporation, or other governmental unit" to conform to the definition in subsection (a)(1). Subsection (b)(1) is substituted for 5 App. U.S.C. 1117(e).

In subsection (e), the words "section 5582(b) of this title" are substituted for "the first section of the Act of August 3, 1950 (5 U.S.C. 61f)" to reflect the codification of the section in title 5, United States Code.

REFERENCES IN TEXT

The Executive Schedule, referred to in subsec. (a)(2)(i), is set out in section 5311 et seq. of this title.

Section 3(a) of the Panama Canal Act of 1979, referred to in subsec. (a)(2)(iii), is classified to section 3602(a) of Title 22, Foreign Relations and Intercourse.

Section 609(b)(1) of the Foreign Service Act of 1980, referred to in subsec. (a)(2)(vi), is classified to section 4009(b)(1) of Title 22.

AMENDMENTS

1999—Subsec. (b). Pub. L. 106–31 substituted "(a)(1)(C)" for "(a)(1)(G)" in last sentence.

Subsec. (i)(4). Pub. L. 106–65, §1104(a), substituted "February 10, 1996, and before October 1, 2003" for "the date of the enactment of the National Defense Authorization Act for Fiscal Year 1996 and before October 1, 1999".

Subsec. (j). Pub. L. 106–65, §3243, added subsec. (j).

1998—Subsec. (a)(1)(F). Pub. L. 105–275, §308(a)(1), struck out ", but only with respect to the United States Senate Restaurants" after "Capitol".

Subsec. (a)(2)(viii). Pub. L. 105–275, §§308(a)(2), 309(a)(1)(A), struck out "of the United States Senate Restaurants" after "an employee" and "or" after the semicolon.

Subsec. (a)(2)(ix), (x). Pub. L. 105–275, §309(a)(1)(B), added cl. (ix) and redesignated former cl. (ix) as (x).

Subsec. (b). Pub. L. 105–275, §309(a)(2), inserted at end "The Public Printer may prescribe regulations to effect the application and operation of this section to the agency specified in subsection (a)(1)(G) of this section."

1997—Subsec. (a)(1)(F). Pub. L. 105–55, §310(a)(1), added subpar. (F).

Subsec. (a)(2)(viii), (ix). Pub. L. 105–55, §310(a)(2), added cl. (viii) and redesignated former cl. (viii) as (ix).

Subsec. (b). Pub. L. 105–55, §310(a)(3), inserted at end "The Architect of the Capitol may prescribe regulations to effect the application and operation of this section to the agency specified in subsection (a)(1)(F) of this section."

1996—Subsec. (i). Pub. L. 104–106 added subsec. (i).

1994—Subsec. (h). Pub. L. 103–337 added subsec. (h).

1990—Subsec. (a)(1)(E). Pub. L. 101–474, §5(k)(1), added subpar. (E).

Subsec. (a)(2)(i). Pub. L. 101–509 substituted "employee (other" for "employee, other", inserted "or an employee whose pay is fixed under section 5376)" before "whose rate", and substituted "the Executive Schedule" for "GS–18".

Subsec. (b). Pub. L. 101–474, §5(k)(2), inserted at end "However, the Director of the Administrative Office of

the United States Courts may prescribe regulations to effect the application and operation of this section to the agencies specified in subsection (a)(1)(E) of this section."

1988—Subsec. (a)(2)(i). Pub. L. 100–325 inserted reference to Federal Bureau of Investigation and Drug Enforcement Administration Senior Executive Service.

1980—Subsec. (a)(2)(vi). Pub. L. 96–465 inserted "benefits under section 609(b)(1) of the Foreign Service Act of 1980 or any" after "to receive".

1979—Subsec. (a)(2)(iii). Pub. L. 96–70 substituted "areas and installations in the Republic of Panama made available to the United States pursuant to the Panama Canal Treaty of 1977 and related agreements (as described in section 3(a) of the Panama Canal Act of 1979)" for "Canal Zone".

1978—Subsec. (a)(2)(i). Pub. L. 95–454 inserted reference to a member of the Senior Executive Service.

EFFECTIVE DATE OF 1999 AMENDMENT

Amendment by section 3243 of Pub. L. 106–65 effective Mar. 1, 2000, see section 3299 of Pub. L. 106–65, set out as an Effective Date note under section 2401 of Title 50, War and National Defense.

EFFECTIVE DATE OF 1994 AMENDMENT

Section 343(b) of Pub. L. 103–337 provided that: "Subsection (h) of section 5595 of title 5, United States Code, as added by subsection (a), shall apply with respect to pay periods that begin on or after the date of the enactment of this Act [Oct. 5, 1994]."

EFFECTIVE DATE OF 1990 AMENDMENT

Amendment by Pub. L. 101–509 effective on such date as the President shall determine, but not earlier than 90 days, and not later than 180 days, after Nov. 5, 1990, see section 529 [title III, §305] of Pub. L. 101–509, set out as a note under section 5301 of this title.

EFFECTIVE DATE OF 1980 AMENDMENT

Amendment by Pub. L. 96–465 effective Feb. 15, 1981, except as otherwise provided, see section 2403 of Pub. L. 96–465, set out as an Effective Date note under section 3901 of Title 22, Foreign Relations and Intercourse.

EFFECTIVE DATE OF 1979 AMENDMENT

Amendment by Pub. L. 96–70 effective Oct. 1, 1979, see section 3304 of Pub. L. 96–70, set out as an Effective Date note under section 3601 of Title 22, Foreign Relations and Intercourse.

EFFECTIVE DATE OF 1978 AMENDMENT

Amendment by Pub. L. 95–454 effective 9 months after Oct. 13, 1978, and congressional review of provisions of sections 401 through 412 of Pub. L. 95–454, see section 415 of Pub. L. 95–454, set out as a note under section 3131 of this title.

SECTION REFERRED TO IN OTHER SECTIONS

This section is referred to in sections 3381, 5545a, 5545b, 5597, 5948 of this title; title 15 section 2081; title 22 section 3691; title 38 sections 7453, 7458.

§ 5596. Back pay due to unjustified personnel action

(a) For the purpose of this section, "agency" means—

  (1) an Executive agency;

  (2) the Administrative Office of the United States Courts, the Federal Judicial Center, and the courts named by section 610 of title 28;

  (3) the Library of Congress;

  (4) the Government Printing Office; and

  (5) the government of the District of Columbia.

(b)(1) An employee of an agency who, on the basis of a timely appeal or an administrative determination (including a decision relating to an unfair labor practice or a grievance) is found by appropriate authority under applicable law, rule, regulation, or collective bargaining agreement, to have been affected by an unjustified or unwarranted personnel action which has resulted in the withdrawal or reduction of all or part of the pay, allowances, or differentials of the employee—

(A) is entitled, on correction of the personnel action, to receive for the period for which the personnel action was in effect—

(i) an amount equal to all or any part of the pay, allowances, or differentials, as applicable which the employee normally would have earned or received during the period if the personnel action had not occurred, less any amounts earned by the employee through other employment during that period; and

(ii) reasonable attorney fees related to the personnel action which, with respect to any decision relating to an unfair labor practice or a grievance processed under a procedure negotiated in accordance with chapter 71 of this title, or under chapter 11 of title I of the Foreign Service Act of 1980, shall be awarded in accordance with standards established under section 7701(g) of this title; and

(B) for all purposes, is deemed to have performed service for the agency during that period, except that—

(i) annual leave restored under this paragraph which is in excess of the maximum leave accumulation permitted by law shall be credited to a separate leave account for the employee and shall be available for use by the employee within the time limits prescribed by regulations of the Office of Personnel Management, and

(ii) annual leave credited under clause (i) of this subparagraph but unused and still available to the employee under regulations prescribed by the Office shall be included in the lump-sum payment under section 5551 or 5552(1) of this title but may not be retained to the credit of the employee under section 5552(2) of this title.

(2)(A) An amount payable under paragraph (1)(A)(i) of this subsection shall be payable with interest.

(B) Such interest—

(i) shall be computed for the period beginning on the effective date of the withdrawal or reduction involved and ending on a date not more than 30 days before the date on which payment is made;

(ii) shall be computed at the rate or rates in effect under section 6621(a)(1) of the Internal Revenue Code of 1986 during the period described in clause (i); and

(iii) shall be compounded daily.

(C) Interest under this paragraph shall be paid out of amounts available for payments under paragraph (1) of this subsection.

(3) This subsection does not apply to any reclassification action nor authorize the setting aside of an otherwise proper promotion by a selecting official from a group of properly ranked and certified candidates.

(4) The pay, allowances, or differentials granted under this section for the period for which an unjustified or unwarranted personnel action was in effect shall not exceed that authorized by the applicable law, rule, regulations, or collective bargaining agreement under which the unjustified or unwarranted personnel action is found, except that in no case may pay, allowances, or differentials be granted under this section for a period beginning more than 6 years before the date of the filing of a timely appeal or, absent such filing, the date of the administrative determination.

(5) For the purpose of this subsection, "grievance" and "collective bargaining agreement" have the meanings set forth in section 7103 of this title and (with respect to members of the Foreign Service) in sections 1101 and 1002 of the Foreign Service Act of 1980, "unfair labor practice" means an unfair labor practice described in section 7116 of this title and (with respect to members of the Foreign Service) in section 1015 of the Foreign Service Act of 1980, and "personnel action" includes the omission or failure to take an action or confer a benefit.

(c) The Office of Personnel Management shall prescribe regulations to carry out this section. However, the regulations are not applicable to the Tennessee Valley Authority and its employees, or to the agencies specified in subsection (a)(2) of this section.

(Added Pub. L. 90–83, §1(34)(C), Sept. 11, 1967, 81 Stat. 203; amended Pub. L. 94–172, §1(a), Dec. 23, 1975, 89 Stat. 1025; Pub. L. 95–454, title VII, §702, Oct. 13, 1978, 92 Stat. 1216; Pub. L. 96–54, §2(a)(14), Aug. 14, 1979, 93 Stat. 382; Pub. L. 96–465, title II, §2306, Oct. 17, 1980, 94 Stat. 2165; Pub. L. 100–202, §101(m) [title VI, §623(a)], Dec. 22, 1987, 101 Stat. 1329–390, 1329–428; Pub. L. 101–474, §5(l), Oct. 30, 1990, 104 Stat. 1100; Pub. L. 105–261, div. A, title XI, §1104(a), Oct. 17, 1998, 112 Stat. 2141.)

HISTORICAL AND REVISION NOTES

Section of title 5	Source (U.S. Code)	Source (Statutes at Large)
5596(a)	5 App.: 652a.	Mar. 30, 1966, Pub. L. 89–380, §§2–4, 80 Stat. 94, 95.
5596(b)	5 App.: 652b.	
5596(c)	5 App.: 652c.	

In subsection (a)(1), the term "an Executive agency" is substituted for "executive department of the Government of the United States", "agency or independent establishment in the executive branch of such Government", "corporation owned or controlled by such Government", and "the General Accounting Office" to conform to the definition in 5 U.S.C. 105.

In subsection (b), the word "employee" is substituted for "civilian officer or employee" and "such officer or employee" to conform to the definition in 5 U.S.C. 2105. The words "on or after the date of enactment of this Act" and "taken prior to, on, or after the date of enactment of his Act" are omitted as executed and unnecessary, since title 5 is restated prospectively and as any existing rights are preserved by section 7 of this bill.

In subsection (c), the word "employees" is substituted for "officers and employees" to conform to the definition in 5 U.S.C. 2105.

REFERENCES IN TEXT

The Foreign Service Act of 1980, referred to in subsec. (b)(1)(A)(ii), is Pub. L. 96–465, Oct. 17, 1980, 94 Stat. 2071. Chapter 11 of title I of the Act is classified generally to subchapter XI (§4131 et seq.) of chapter 52 of Title 22,

Foreign Relations and Intercourse. For complete classification of this Act to the Code, see Short Title note set out under section 3901 of Title 22 and Tables.

Section 6621(a)(1) of the Internal Revenue Code of 1986, referred to in subsec. (b)(2)(B)(ii), is classified to section 6621(a)(1) of Title 26, Internal Revenue Code.

Sections 1101, 1002, and 1015 of the Foreign Service Act of 1980, referred to in subsec. (b)(5), are classified to sections 4131, 4102, and 4115, respectively, of Title 22, Foreign Relations and Intercourse.

AMENDMENTS

1998—Subsec. (b)(4), (5). Pub. L. 105–261 added par. (4) and redesignated former par. (4) as (5).

1990—Subsec. (a)(2). Pub. L. 101–474, §5(l)(1), substituted "Courts, the Federal Judicial Center, and the courts named by section 610 of title 28" for "Courts".

Subsec. (c). Pub. L. 101–474, §5(l)(2), substituted "employees, or to the agencies specified in subsection (a)(2) of this section" for "employees".

1987—Subsec. (b)(2) to (4). Pub. L. 100–202 added par. (2) and redesignated former pars. (2) and (3) as (3) and (4), respectively.

1980—Subsec. (b)(1). Pub. L. 96–465, §2306(1), inserted in subpar. (A)(ii) "or under chapter 11 of title I of the Foreign Service Act of 1980" after "chapter 71 of this title,".

Subsec. (b)(3). Pub. L. 96–465, §2306(2), inserted "and (with respect to members of the Foreign Service) in sections 1101 and 1002 of the Foreign Service Act of 1980" after "section 7103 of this title", and "and (with respect to members of the Foreign Service) in section 1015 of the Foreign Service Act of 1980" after "section 7116 of this title".

1979—Subsec. (c). Pub. L. 96–54 substituted "Office of Personnel Management" for "Civil Service Commission".

1978—Subsec. (b). Pub. L. 95–454 substituted provisions relating to corrective measures applicable to an employee who, on the basis of a timely appeal or an administrative determination, including a decision relative to an unfair labor practice or grievance, is found by an appropriate authority under applicable law, rule, regulation, or collective bargaining agreement to have been affected by an unjustified or unwarranted personnel action, for provisions relating to corrective measures applicable to an employee who, on the basis of an administrative determination or a timely appeal, is found by an appropriate authority under applicable law or regulation to have undergone an unjustified or unwarranted personnel action.

1975—Subsec. (b)(2). Pub. L. 94–172 struck out in introductory clause provision relating to prohibition on leave credit cumulated in excess of maximum allowed under law or regulations, and added subpars. (A) and (B).

EFFECTIVE DATE OF 1987 AMENDMENT

Section 101(m) [title VI, §623(b)] of Pub. L. 100–202 provided that:

"(1) GENERALLY.—Except as provided in paragraph (2), the amendments made by subsection (a) [amending this section] shall take effect on the date of the enactment of this Act [Dec. 22, 1987], and shall apply with respect to any employee found, in a final judgment entered or a final decision otherwise rendered on or after such date, to have been the subject of an unjustified or unwarranted personnel action, the correction of which entitles such employee to an amount under section 5596(b)(1)(A)(i) of title 5, United States Code.

"(2) EXCEPTION.—

"(A) CASES IN WHICH A RIGHT TO INTEREST WAS RESERVED.—The amendments made by subsection (a) [amending this section] shall also apply with respect to any claim which was brought under section 5596 of title 5, United States Code, and with respect to which a final judgment was entered or a final decision was otherwise rendered before the date of the enactment of this Act [Dec. 22, 1987], if, under terms of such judgment or decision, a right to interest was specifically reserved, contingent on the enactment of a statute authorizing the payment of interest on claims brought under such section 5596.

"(B) METHOD OF COMPUTING INTEREST.—The amount of interest payable under this paragraph with respect to a claim shall be determined in accordance with section 5596(b)(2)(B) of title 5, United States Code (as amended by this section).

"(C) SOURCE.—An amount payable under this paragraph shall be paid from the appropriation made by section 1304 of title 31, United States Code, notwithstanding section 5596(b)(2)(C) of title 5, United States Code (as amended by this section) or any other provision of law.

"(D) DEADLINE.—An application for a payment under this paragraph shall be ineffective if it is filed after the end of the 1-year period beginning on the date of the enactment of this Act [Dec. 22, 1987].

"(E) LIMITATION ON PAYMENTS.—Payments under this paragraph may not be made before October 1, 1988, except that interest shall continue to accrue in accordance with [section] 5596(b)(2)(B) of title 5, United States Code."

EFFECTIVE DATE OF 1980 AMENDMENT

Amendment by Pub. L. 96–465 effective Feb. 15, 1981, except as otherwise provided, see section 2403 of Pub. L. 96–465, set out as an Effective Date note under section 3901 of Title 22, Foreign Relations and Intercourse.

EFFECTIVE DATE OF 1979 AMENDMENT

Amendment by Pub. L. 96–54 effective July 12, 1979, see section 2(b) of Pub. L. 96–54, set out as a note under section 305 of this title.

EFFECTIVE DATE OF 1978 AMENDMENT

Amendment by Pub. L. 95–454 effective 90 days after Oct. 13, 1978, see section 907 of Pub. L. 95–454, set out as an Effective Date note under section 1101 of this title.

EFFECTIVE DATE OF 1975 AMENDMENT

Section 1(b) of Pub. L. 94–172 provided that: "The amendment made by subsection (a) [amending this section] shall apply to any employee found, on or after March 30, 1966, to have undergone an unjustified or unwarranted personnel action the correction of which entitled or entitles such employee to the benefits provided under section 5596 of title 5, United States Code."

LUMP-SUM PAYMENTS FOR FORMER EMPLOYEES NOT ON THE ROLLS ON DECEMBER 23, 1975

Section 2 of Pub. L. 94–172 provided that: "With respect to former employee (except a former employee referred to in section 3 of this Act) [set out as a note below] who is not on the rolls on the date of the enactment of this Act [Dec. 23, 1975], annual leave, which was not credited under section 5596 of title 5, United States Code, because it was in an amount that would have caused the amount of leave to the employee's credit to exceed the maximum amount of the leave authorized for the employee by law or regulation, is subject to credit and liquidation by lump-sum payment only if a claim therefor is filed within three years immediately following the date of the enactment of this Act with the agency by which the employee was employed when the lump-sum payment provisions of section 5551 of title 5, United States Code, last became applicable to such employee. Payment shall be by that agency at the salary rate in effect on the date the lump-sum payment provisions became applicable."

LUMP-SUM PAYMENTS FOR POSTAL EMPLOYEES NOT ON THE ROLLS ON DECEMBER 23, 1975

Section 3 of Pub. L. 94–172 provided that:

"(a) With respect to a former employee of the Post Office Department or a former employee of the United States Postal Service who had prior civilian service with the Post Office Department or other Federal agency, who is not on the rolls on the date of the enactment of this Act [Dec. 23, 1975], annual leave which was accrued before July 1, 1971, but was not credited under section 5596 of title 5, United States Code, because it was in an amount that would have caused the amount of leave to his credit to exceed the maximum amount of the leave authorized for the employee by law or regulation, is subject to credit and, liquidation by lump-sum payment only if a claim therefor is filed within 3 years immediately following the date of enactment of this Act with the Postal Service. Payment shall be by the Postal Service at the salary rate in effect on the date the lump-sum payment provisions of section 5551 of title 5, United States Code, or comparable provisions of regulations of the Postal Service, as appropriate, last became applicable to the former employee.

"(b) With respect to a present employee of the Postal Service who had prior Federal civilian service with the Post Office Department or other Federal agency, annual leave which was accrued before July 1, 1971, but was not credited under section 5596 of title 5, United States Code, because it was in an amount that would have caused the amount of leave to the employee's credit to exceed the maximum amount of the leave authorized for the employee by law or regulation, is subject to credit and liquidation by lump-sum payment only if a claim therefor is filed with the Postal Service within three years immediately following the date of the enactment of this Act [Dec. 23, 1975]. Payment shall be by the Postal Service at the salary rate in effect on the date of the enactment of this Act."

SECTION REFERRED TO IN OTHER SECTIONS

This section is referred to in sections 5307, 7118, 7121, 7122, 7371 of this title; title 22 sections 4116, 4137.

§ 5597. Separation pay

(a) For the purpose of this section—

(1) the term "Secretary" means the Secretary of Defense;

(2) the term "defense agency" means an agency of the Department of Defense, as further defined under regulations prescribed by the Secretary; and

(3) the term "employee" means an employee of a defense agency, serving under an appointment without time limitation, who has been currently employed for a continuous period of at least 12 months, except that such term does not include—

(A) a reemployed annuitant under subchapter III of chapter 83, chapter 84, or another retirement system for employees of the Government; or

(B) an employee having a disability on the basis of which such employee is or would be eligible for disability retirement under any of the retirement systems referred to in subparagraph (A).

(b) In order to avoid or minimize the need for involuntary separations due to a reduction in force, base closure, reorganization, transfer of function, workforce restructuring (to meet mission needs, achieve one or more strength reductions, correct skill imbalances, or reduce the number of high-grade, managerial, or supervisory positions), or other similar action affecting 1 or more defense agencies, the Secretary shall establish a program under which separation pay may be offered to encourage eligible employees to separate from service voluntarily (whether by retirement or resignation).

(c) Under the program, separation pay may be offered by a defense agency only—

(1) with the prior consent, or on the authority, of the Secretary; and

(2) to employees within such occupational groups or geographic locations, or subject to such other similar objective and nonpersonal limitations or conditions, as the Secretary may require.

A determination of which employees are within the scope of an offer of separation pay shall be made only on the basis of consistent and well-documented application of the relevant criteria.

(d) Such separation pay—

(1) shall be paid in a lump-sum or in installments;

(2) shall be equal to the lesser of—

(A) an amount equal to the amount the employee would be entitled to receive under section 5595(c) if the employee were entitled to payment under such section; or

(B) $25,000;

(3) shall not be a basis for payment, and shall not be included in the computation, of any other type of Government benefit;

(4) shall not be taken into account for purposes of determining the amount of any severance pay to which an individual may be entitled under section 5595 based on any other separation; and

(5) if paid in installments, shall cease to be paid upon the recipient's acceptance of employment by the Federal Government, or commencement of work under a personal services contract, as described in subsection (g)(1).

(e) No amount shall be payable under this section based on any separation occurring after September 30, 2003.

(f) The Secretary shall prescribe such regulations as may be necessary to carry out this section.

(g)(1) An employee who receives separation pay under this section on the basis of a separation occurring on or after the date of the enactment of the Federal Workforce Restructuring Act of 1994 and accepts employment with the Government of the United States, or who commences work for an agency of the United States through a personal services contract with the United States, within 5 years after the date of the separation on which payment of the separation pay is based shall be required to repay the entire amount of the separation pay to the defense agency that paid the separation pay.

(2) If the employment is with an Executive agency, the Director of the Office of Personnel Management may, at the request of the head of the agency, waive the repayment if the individual involved possesses unique abilities and is the only qualified applicant available for the position.

(3) If the employment is with an entity in the legislative branch, the head of the entity or the appointing official may waive the repayment if the individual involved possesses unique abilities and is the only qualified applicant available for the position.

(4) If the employment is with the judicial branch, the Director of the Administrative Office of the United States Courts may waive the repayment if the individual involved possesses unique abilities and is the only qualified applicant available for the position.

(5) If the employment is without compensation, the appointing official may waive the repayment.

(h)(1)(A) In addition to any other payment that it is required to make under subchapter III of chapter 83 or chapter 84, the Department of Defense shall remit to the Office of Personnel Management an amount equal to 15 percent of the final basic pay of each covered employee.

(B) If the employee is one with respect to whom a remittance would otherwise be required under section 4(a) of the Federal Workforce Restructuring Act of 1994 based on the separation involved, the remittance under this subsection shall be instead of the remittance otherwise required under such section 4(a).

(2) Amounts remitted under paragraph (1) shall be deposited in the Treasury of the United States to the credit of the Civil Service Retirement and Disability Fund.

(3) For the purposes of this subsection—

(A) the term "covered employee" means an employee who is subject to subchapter III of chapter 83 or chapter 84 and to whom a voluntary separation incentive has been paid under this section on the basis of a separation occurring on or after October 1, 1997; and

(B) the term "final basic pay" has the meaning given such term in section 4(a)(2) of the Federal Workforce Restructuring Act of 1994.

(i)(1) Notwithstanding any other provision of this section, during fiscal year 2001, separation pay may be offered under the program carried out under this section with respect to workforce restructuring only to persons who, upon separation, are entitled to an immediate annuity under section 8336, 8412, or 8414 of this title and are otherwise eligible for the separation pay under this section.

(2) In the administration of the program under this section during fiscal year 2001, the Secretary shall ensure that not more than 1,000 employees are, as a result of workforce restructuring, separated from service in that fiscal year entitled to separation pay under this section.

(3) Separation pay may not be offered as a result of workforce restructuring under the program carried out under this section after fiscal year 2003.

(Added Pub. L. 102–484, div. D, title XLIV, § 4436(a)(1), Oct. 23, 1992, 106 Stat. 2723; amended Pub. L. 103–226, § 8(a), Mar. 30, 1994, 108 Stat. 118; Pub. L. 103–337, div. A, title III, § 341(b)(1), Oct. 5, 1994, 108 Stat. 2720; Pub. L. 104–201, div. A, title XVI, § 1612(a), Sept. 23, 1996, 110 Stat. 2739; Pub. L. 105–85, div. A, title XI, § 1106(a), (b)(1), Nov. 18, 1997, 111 Stat. 1923, 1924; Pub. L. 106–65, div. A, title XI, § 1104(b), Oct. 5, 1999, 113 Stat. 777; Pub. L. 106–398, § 1 [[div. A], title XI, §§ 1151, 1153(a)], Oct. 30, 2000, 114 Stat. 1654, 1654A–319, 1654A–323.)

REFERENCES IN TEXT

The date of the enactment of the Federal Workforce Restructuring Act of 1994, referred to in subsec. (g)(1), is the date of enactment of Pub. L. 103–226, which was approved Mar. 30, 1994.

Section 4(a) of the Federal Workforce Restructuring Act of 1994, referred to in subsec. (h)(1)(B), (3)(B), is section 4(a) of Pub. L. 103–226, as amended, which is set out as a note under section 8331 of this title.

AMENDMENTS

2000—Subsec. (b). Pub. L. 106–398, § 1 [[div. A], title XI, § 1151(a)], inserted "workforce restructuring (to meet mission needs, achieve one or more strength reductions, correct skill imbalances, or reduce the number of high-grade, managerial, or supervisory positions)," after "transfer of function,".

Subsec. (c). Pub. L. 106–398, § 1 [[div. A], title XI, § 1151(b)(2)], inserted concluding provisions.

Subsec. (c)(2). Pub. L. 106–398, § 1 [[div. A], title XI, § 1151(b)(1)], inserted "objective and nonpersonal" after "similar".

Subsec. (d)(1). Pub. L. 106–398, § 1 [[div. A], title XI, § 1151(c)(1)], added par. (1) and struck out former par. (1) which read as follows: "shall be paid in a lump sum;".

Subsec. (d)(5). Pub. L. 106–398, § 1 [[div. A], title XI, § 1151(c)(2)–(4)], added par. (5).

Subsec. (g)(1). Pub. L. 106–398, § 1 [[div. A], title XI, § 1151(d)], inserted ", or who commences work for an agency of the United States through a personal services contract with the United States," after "employment with the Government of the United States".

Subsec. (i). Pub. L. 106–398, § 1 [[div. A], title XI, § 1153(a)], added subsec. (i).

1999—Subsec. (e). Pub. L. 106–65 substituted "September 30, 2003" for "September 30, 2001".

1997—Subsec. (e). Pub. L. 105–85, § 1106(b)(1), substituted "September 30, 2001" for "September 30, 1999".

Subsec. (h). Pub. L. 105–85, § 1106(a), added subsec. (h).

1996—Subsec. (g)(5). Pub. L. 104–201 added par. (5).

1994—Subsec. (e). Pub. L. 103–337 substituted "September 30, 1999" for "September 30, 1997".

Subsec. (g). Pub. L. 103–226 added subsec. (g).

EFFECTIVE DATE OF 1996 AMENDMENT

Section 1612(b) of Pub. L. 104–201 provided that: "The amendment made by subsection (a) [amending this section] shall apply with respect to employment accepted on or after the date of the enactment of this Act [Sept. 23, 1996]."

LIMITATIONS FOR FISCAL YEARS 2002 AND 2003 ON VSIP AND VERA

Pub. L. 106–398, § 1 [[div. A], title XI, § 1153(b)], Oct. 30, 2000, 114 Stat. 1654, 1654A–323, provided that:

"(1) Subject to paragraph (2), the Secretary of Defense shall ensure that, in each of fiscal years 2002 and 2003, not more than 4,000 employees of the Department of Defense are, as a result of workforce restructuring, separated from service entitled to one or more of the following benefits:

"(A) Voluntary separation incentive pay under section 5597 of title 5, United States Code.

"(B) Immediate annuity under section 8336(*o*) or 8414(d) of such title.

"(2) Notwithstanding sections 5597(e), 8336(*o*), and 8414(d) of title 5, United States Code, the Secretary of Defense may carry out the programs authorized in those sections during fiscal years 2002 and 2003 with respect to workforce restructuring only to the extent provided in a law enacted by the One Hundred Seventh Congress."

VOLUNTARY SEPARATION INCENTIVES

Pub. L. 106–303, § 2, Oct. 13, 2000, 114 Stat. 1064, authorized the Comptroller General to provide voluntary separation incentive payments with respect to employees of the General Accounting Office during the period from Oct. 13, 2000 to Dec. 31, 2003 and specified terms and conditions of such incentive payments, required additional contribution to the Retirement Fund, defined pertinent terms, specified a numerical percentage limitation of the workforce permitted to receive such incentive payments, and authorized the Comptroller General to prescribe regulations to implement these provisions.

Pub. L. 106–117, title XI, Nov. 30, 1999, 113 Stat. 1595, as amended by Pub. L. 106–419, title II, § 207, Nov. 1, 2000, 114 Stat. 1842, known as the "Department of Veterans Affairs Employment Reduction Assistance Act of 1999", authorized the Secretary of Veterans Affairs to submit a plan to the Director of the Office of Management and Budget for the payment of voluntary separation incentive payments, and upon approval thereof to pay voluntary separation incentive payments to eligible employees of the Department of Veterans Affairs only to the extent necessary to reduce or restructure the positions and functions identified by the plan, provided that the employees separate from service with the Department through Dec. 31, 2002, whether by retirement or resignation, defined "employee" for separation incentive purposes, and provided for additional contributions to the Retirement Fund, effect of subsequent employment with the Federal Government, and effect on agency employment levels.

Pub. L. 106–113, div. B, § 1000(a)(2) [title V, § 579], Nov. 29, 1999, 113 Stat. 1535, 1501A–113, as amended by Pub. L. 106–429, § 101(a) [title V, § 584], Nov. 6, 2000, 114 Stat. 1900, 1900A–56, authorized voluntary separation incentives for employees of the United States Agency for International Development who voluntarily separated (whether by retirement or resignation) on or before Dec. 31, 2001, and defined pertinent terms, provided for the development of an agency strategic plan and the approval of such plan by the Director of the Office of Management and Budget, required additional agency contributions to the Retirement Fund, specified the effect of subsequent employment with the Federal Government, mandated a reduction of agency employment levels, and authorized the Office of Personnel Management to prescribe regulations to implement these provisions.

Pub. L. 106–58, title I, § 116, Sept. 29, 1999, 113 Stat. 439, authorized the Treasury Inspector General for Tax Administration, during the period from Oct. 1, 1999 through Jan. 1, 2003, to offer voluntary separation incentives in order to provide the necessary flexibility to carry out the plan to establish and reorganize the Office of the Treasury Inspector General for Tax Administration, defined "employee" for separation incentive purposes, and provided for authority to provide separation incentive payments, additional contributions to the Retirement Fund, effect of subsequent employment with the Federal Government, and effect on agency employment levels.

Pub. L. 106–58, title I, § 119, Sept. 29, 1999, 113 Stat. 441, authorized the Commissioner of the Financial Management Services of the Department of the Treasury, during the period from Oct. 1, 1999 through Jan. 31, 2000, to offer voluntary separation incentives in order to provide the necessary flexibility to carry out the closure of the Chicago Financial Center (CFC) in a manner which the Commissioner deemed most efficient, equitable to employees, and cost effective to the Government, defined "employee" for separation incentive purposes, and provided for an agency plan, authority to provide separation incentive payments, eligibility requirements, effect on subsequent employment with the Federal Government, contributions to the Retirement Fund, and reduction of agency employment levels.

Pub. L. 106–58, title IV, § 411, Sept. 29, 1999, 113 Stat. 456, as amended by Pub. L. 106–554, § 1(a)(3) [title IV, § 408], Dec. 21, 2000, 114 Stat. 2763, 2763A–146, authorized the Administrator of General Services, during the period Oct. 1, 1999 through Apr. 30, 2002, to offer a voluntary separation incentive in order to provide the necessary flexibility to carry out the closing of the Federal Supply Service distribution centers, forward supply points, and associated programs in a manner which the Administrator deemed most efficient, equitable to all employees, and cost effective for the Government, defined "employee" for separation incentive purposes, and provided for agency strategic plan, authority to provide incentive payments, eligibility requirements, effect of subsequent employment with the Federal Government, contributions to the Retirement Fund, and reduction of agency employment levels.

Pub. L. 105–206, title I, § 1202, July 22, 1998, 112 Stat. 719, authorized Commissioner of Internal Revenue to pay voluntary separation incentive payments to any qualifying employee of the Internal Revenue Service who voluntarily separated (whether by retirement or resignation) before Jan. 1, 2003, provided for pertinent definitions, additional Internal Revenue Service contributions to the Retirement Fund, effect of subsequent employment with the Government, and effect on Internal Revenue Service employment levels.

Pub. L. 104–208, div. A, title I, § 101(e) [title V, § 520], Sept. 30, 1996, 110 Stat. 3009–233, 3009–272, as amended by Pub. L. 105–78, title V, § 517, Nov. 13, 1997, 111 Stat. 1519; Pub. L. 106–113, div. B, § 1000(a)(4) [title V, § 515], Nov. 29, 1999, 113 Stat. 1535, 1501A–276, authorized Railroad Retirement Board and Office of Inspector General of Railroad Retirement Board to provide voluntary separation incentive payments to any qualifying employee who voluntarily separated (whether by retirement or resignation) before Mar. 31, 2000, directed the Railroad Retirement Board, prior to obligating any resources for voluntary separation incentive payments, to submit to Congress a strategic plan outlining intended use of such incentive payments and a proposed organizational chart for agency once such incentive payments have been completed, and further provided for pertinent definitions, additional contributions to the Retirement Fund, effect of subsequent employment with the Government, reduction of agency employment levels, and that program would take effect Oct. 1, 1996.

Pub. L. 106–65, div. C, title XXXI, § 3161, Oct. 5, 1999, 113 Stat. 942, provided that notwithstanding section 101(f) [title VI, § 663(c)(2)(D)] of Public Law 104–208, set out below, Department of Energy could pay voluntary separation incentive payments under such section 663 to qualifying employees who voluntarily separated (whether by retirement or resignation) before Jan. 1, 2003, and that not later than Mar. 15, 2000, Secretary of Energy was to submit to Director of Office of Personnel Management and Congress a report describing how the Department has paid voluntary separation payments under such section 663.

Pub. L. 105–261, div. C, title XXXI, § 3156, Oct. 17, 1998, 112 Stat. 2257, provided that notwithstanding section 101(f) [title VI, § 663(c)(2)(D)] of Public Law 104–208, set out below, Department of Energy could pay voluntary separation incentive payments to qualifying employees who voluntarily separated (whether by retirement or resignation) before Jan. 1, 2001.

Pub. L. 104–208, div. A, title I, § 101(f) [title VI, § 663], Sept. 30, 1996, 110 Stat. 3009–314, 3009–383, authorized any Executive agency other than Executive agency previously authorized to provide voluntary separation incentive payments during all, or any part of, fiscal year 1997, to provide voluntary separation incentive payments to any qualifying employee who voluntarily separated (whether by retirement or resignation) before Dec. 31, 1997, only to extent necessary to eliminate positions and functions identified by strategic plan to be submitted to Congress outlining intended use of such incentive payments and proposed organizational chart for agency once such incentive payments have been completed, and further provided for amount and treatment of payments, definitions, additional agency contributions to the Retirement Fund, effect of subsequent employment with Government, reduction of agency employment levels, and that program would take effect Oct. 1, 1996.

Pub. L. 104–205, title III, § 349, Sept. 30, 1996, 110 Stat. 2976, authorized certain agencies of Department of Transportation to provide voluntary separation incentive payments to any qualifying employee, provided that no amount would be payable based on any separation occurring before Sept. 30, 1996, or after Sept. 30, 1997, directed agencies to submit to Congress a strategic plan outlining intended use of such incentive payments and proposed organization chart for agency once such incentive payments have been completed, and further provided for definitions, additional agency contributions to the Retirement Fund, effect of subsequent employment with the Government, reductions of agency employment levels, and that program would take effect Oct. 1, 1996.

Pub. L. 104–204, title IV, § 432, Sept. 26, 1996, 110 Stat. 2931, as amended by Pub. L. 106–377, § 1(a)(1) [title IV, § 428], Oct. 27, 2000, 114 Stat. 1441, 1441A–56, known as the "National Aeronautics and Space Administration Federal Employment Reduction Assistance Act of 1996", authorized the Administrator of the National Aeronautics and Space Administration (NASA), in order to avoid or minimize the need for involuntary separations due to a reduction in force, installation closure, reorganization, transfer of function, or other similar action affecting NASA, to establish a program under which voluntary separation pay, subject to the availability of appropriated funds, be offered to encourage eligible employees to separate from service by retirement or resignation up to Sept. 30, 2002, defined terms, provided for effect of subsequent employment with the Federal Government, required additional agency contributions to the Retirement Fund, reduced agency employment levels, and required an annual report on the program to be submitted to the Office of Personnel Management.

Pub. L. 104–190, § 1, Aug. 20, 1996, 110 Stat. 1932, authorized Agency for International Development to provide voluntary separation incentive payments to not more than 100 qualified employees of such agency who voluntarily separated (whether by retirement or resignation) before Feb. 1, 1997, and only to extent necessary to eliminate positions and functions identified by strategic plan to be submitted to Congress outlining intended use of such incentive payments and proposed organizational chart for agency once such incentive payments have been completed, and further provided for definitions, amount and treatment of payments, additional agency contributions to the Retirement Fund, effect of subsequent employment with the Government, and reduction of agency employment levels.

Pub. L. 104–180, title VII, § 735, Aug. 6, 1996, 110 Stat. 1604, authorized Department of Agriculture to provide voluntary separation incentive payments to qualified employees to extent necessary to eliminate positions and functions identified by strategic plan to be submitted to Congress outlining intended use of such incentive payments and proposed organizational chart for agency once such incentive payments have been completed, provided that no amount would be payable based on any separation occurring before Aug. 6, 1996, or after Sept. 30, 2000, and further provided for definitions, amount and treatment of payments, additional agency contributions to the Retirement Fund, effect of subsequent employment with the Government, reduction of agency employment levels, and that program would take effect Oct. 1, 1996.

Pub. L. 104–134, title I, § 101(c) [title III, § 339], Apr. 26, 1996, 110 Stat. 1321–156, 1321–210; renumbered title I, Pub. L. 104–140, § 1(a), May 2, 1996, 110 Stat. 1327, provided that, in order to avoid or minimize need for involuntary separations due to reduction in force, reorganization, transfer of function, or other similar action, Secretary of the Smithsonian Institution could pay, or authorize payment of, voluntary separation incentive payments to Smithsonian Institution employees who separated from Federal service voluntarily through Oct. 1, 1996 (whether by retirement or resignation).

Pub. L. 104–19, title I, § 702, July 27, 1995, 109 Stat. 221, provided that General Accounting Office could for such employees as it deemed appropriate authorize payment to employees who voluntarily separated before Oct. 1, 1995, whether by retirement or resignation, which payment would be paid in accordance with provisions of subsection (d) of this section.

Section 3 of Pub. L. 103–226 authorized Executive agencies (other than Department of Defense, Central Intelligence Agency, or General Accounting Office) to provide voluntary separation incentive payments to qualified employees of such agencies in order to avoid or minimize need for involuntary separations due to reduction in force, reorganization, transfer of function, or other similar action, provided that in order to receive incentive payment, employee must have separated from service with agency (whether by retirement or resignation) before Apr. 1, 1995, or, under certain circumstances, not later than Mar. 31, 1997, and further provided for definitions, amount and treatment of payments, effect of subsequent employment with the Government, regulations, and authority for Director of Administrative Office of the United States Courts to establish similar program for individuals serving in the judicial branch.

MONITORING AND REPORT RELATING TO VOLUNTARY
SEPARATION INCENTIVE PAYMENTS

Section 6 of Pub. L. 103–226 provided that: "No later than December 31st of each fiscal year, the Office of Personnel Management shall submit to the Committee on Governmental Affairs of the Senate and the Committee on Post Office and Civil Service of the House of Representatives a report which, with respect to the preceding fiscal year, shall include—

"(1) the number of employees who received a voluntary separation incentive payment under section 3 [set out above] during such preceding fiscal year;

"(2) the agency from which each such employee separated;

"(3) at the time of separation from service by each such employee—

"(A) such employee's grade or pay level; and

"(B) the geographic location of such employee's official duty station, by region, State, and city (or foreign nation, if applicable); and

"(4)(A) the number of waivers made (in the repayment upon subsequent employment) by each agency or other authority under section 3 [set out above] or the amendments made by section 8 [amending this section and provisions set out as a note under section 403–4 of Title 50, War and National Defense]; and

"(B) the title and the grade or pay level of the position filled by the employee to whom such waiver applied."

[Committee on Post Office and Civil Service of House of Representatives abolished by House Resolution No. 6, One Hundred Fourth Congress, Jan. 4, 1995. References to Committee on Post Office and Civil Service treated as referring to Committee on Government Reform and Oversight, see section 1(b) of Pub. L. 104–14, set out as a note preceding section 21 of Title 2, The Congress. Committee on Government Reform and Oversight of House of Representatives changed to Committee on Government Reform of House of Representatives by House Resolution No. 5, One Hundred Sixth Congress, Jan. 6, 1999.]

SOURCE OF PAYMENTS

Section 4436(b)(1) of Pub. L. 102–484 provided that: "For fiscal years after fiscal year 1993, separation pay shall be paid by an agency out of any funds or appropriations available for salaries and expenses of such agency."

REPORT

Section 4436(c) of Pub. L. 102–484 provided that: "At the end of each of fiscal years 1993 through 1998, the Secretary of Defense shall submit to the President, the Congress, and the Director of the Office of Personnel Management a report on the effectiveness and costs of carrying out the amendments made by this section [enacting this section]."

SECTION REFERRED TO IN OTHER SECTIONS

This section is referred to in title 10 section 1598.

CHAPTER 57—TRAVEL, TRANSPORTATION, AND SUBSISTENCE

SUBCHAPTER I—TRAVEL AND SUBSISTENCE
EXPENSES; MILEAGE ALLOWANCES

AMENDMENTS

1998—Pub. L. 105–264, §§ 4(b), 5(c), Oct. 19, 1998, 112 Stat. 2354, 2355, added items 5706c, 5710, and 5739.

1996—Pub. L. 104–201, div. A, title XVI, § 1605(a)(2), title XVII, § 1723(c), Sept. 23, 1996, 110 Stat. 2736, 2759, added items 5736 to 5738 and 5756.

1994—Pub. L. 103–337, div. A, title III, § 345(a)(2), Oct. 5, 1994, 108 Stat. 2724, added item 5735.

1992—Pub. L. 102–378, § 2(46), Oct. 2, 1992, 106 Stat. 1353, struck out "; manpower shortage positions" after "trainees" in item 5723 and added item 5755.

1990—Pub. L. 101–509, title V, § 529 [title II, §§ 206(a)(2), 208(b)], Nov. 5, 1990, 104 Stat. 1427, 1457, 1460, added items 5706b, 5753, and 5754.

Pub. L. 101–391, § 4(b), Sept. 25, 1990, 104 Stat. 750, added item 5707a.

1986—Pub. L. 99–234, title I, §§ 103(b), 106(b), Jan. 2, 1986, 99 Stat. 1758, 1759, added items 5706a and 5734.

1983—Pub. L. 98–151, § 118(a)(7)(A)(ii), Nov. 14, 1983, 97 Stat. 979, added items 5724b and 5724c.

1978—Pub. L. 95–454, title IV, § 409(c), Oct. 13, 1978, 92 Stat. 1173, added item 5752.

1975—Pub. L. 94–22, § 7, May 19, 1975, 89 Stat. 86, inserted "and reports" after "Regulations" in item 5707.

1970—Pub. L. 91–563, § 4(b), Dec. 19, 1970, 84 Stat. 1477, added heading of Subchapter IV and item 5751.

Pub. L. 91–481, § 1(2), Oct. 21, 1970, 84 Stat. 1081, added item 5709.

1967—Pub. L. 90–206, title II, § 222(c)(2), Dec. 16, 1967, 81 Stat. 641, added item 5733.

Pub. L. 90–83 § 1(37)(B), Sept. 11, 1967, 81 Stat. 205, added item 5724a.

CHAPTER REFERRED TO IN OTHER SECTIONS

This chapter is referred to in sections 3396, 5307 of this title; title 14 section 193; title 18 section 3168; title 22 section 3671; title 26 section 7471; title 42 section 5816; title 43 section 50d; title 49 section 106.

SUBCHAPTER I—TRAVEL AND SUBSISTENCE EXPENSES; MILEAGE ALLOWANCES

SUBCHAPTER REFERRED TO IN OTHER SECTIONS

This subchapter is referred to in sections 3161, 3375, 3381, 4109, 5354, 5723, 5737, 5751, 8476 of this title; title 2 sections 476, 1381, 1385; title 7 section 2229; title 10 sections 180, 9441; title 12 sections 635, 1441a, 2278a–2; title 15 sections 278g–4, 634, 657, 4632, 4804; title 16 sections 463, 916*l*, 961; title 19 section 2171; title 20 section 5933; title 21 sections 874, 1709; title 22 sections 290n–3, 1754, 2024, 2511, 2672, 4356, 4832, 6431; title 26 sections 7456, 7471, 7802; title 28 section 594; title 29 section 2911; title 33 sections 467f, 2309; title 38 section 4110; title 42 sections 293*l*, 294f, 297t, 1314a, 1395ww, 1975b, 2477, 4276, 4277, 5196, 7383, 9844, 11609, 12651b; title 44 section 2705; title 46 App. section 1717.

§ 5701. Definitions

Except as otherwise provided in section 5707(d),[1] for the purpose of this subchapter—

(1) "agency" means—

(A) an Executive agency;

(B) a military department;

(C) an office, agency, or other establishment in the legislative branch;

(D) an office, agency, or other establishment in the judicial branch; and

(E) the government of the District of Columbia;

but does not include—

---

[1] See References in Text note below.

(i) a Government controlled corporation;

(ii) a Member of Congress; or

(iii) an office or committee of either House of Congress or of the two Houses;

(2) "employee" means an individual employed in or under an agency including an individual employed intermittently in the Government service as an expert or consultant and paid on a daily when-actually-employed basis and an individual serving without pay or at $1 a year;

(3) "subsistence" means lodging, meals, and other necessary expenses for the personal sustenance and comfort of the traveler;

(4) "per diem allowance" means a daily payment instead of actual expenses for subsistence and fees or tips to porters and stewards;

(5) "Government" means the Government of the United States and the government of the District of Columbia; and

(6) "continental United States" means the several States and the District of Columbia, but does not include Alaska or Hawaii.

(Pub. L. 89–554, Sept. 6, 1966, 80 Stat. 498; Pub. L. 94–22, § 2(a), May 19, 1975, 89 Stat. 84; Pub. L. 99–234, title I, § 101, Jan. 2, 1986, 99 Stat. 1756; Pub. L. 101–391, § 5(a)(2), Sept. 25, 1990, 104 Stat. 751.)

HISTORICAL AND REVISION NOTES

Derivation	U.S. Code	Revised Statutes and Statutes at Large
(1)–(5)	5 U.S.C. 835.	June 9, 1949, ch. 185, § 2, 63 Stat. 166.
(6)	[Uncodified].	Aug. 14, 1961, Pub. L. 87–139, § 8(c), 75 Stat. 340.

In paragraph (1), the word "agency" is substituted for "departments and establishments". The terms "Executive agency" and "military department" are substituted for "any executive department, independent commission, board, bureau, office, agency, or other establishment in the executive branch of the Government, including wholly owned Government corporations" in view of the definitions in sections 105 and 102. The exception of "a Government controlled corporation" is added in subparagraph (i) to preserve the application of this subchapter to "wholly owned Government corporations".

Paragraph (2) is added for convenience and to eliminate the necessity of referring to "civilian officers and employees of the agencies" elsewhere in the text of the subchapter.

In paragraph (4), the words "for subsistence and fees or tips to porters and stewards" are added on authority of the words "in lieu of their actual expenses of subsistence and all fees or tips to porters and stewards" and "in lieu of subsistence" in former sections 836 and 73b–2, which are carried into sections 5702 and 5703, respectively.

Paragraph (5) is added for convenience and is based in part on former section 835(1)(A) and, insofar as concerns section 5703, on section 18 of the Act of Aug. 2, 1946, ch. 744, 60 Stat. 811.

Paragraph (6), insofar as concerns section 5703, is based in part on section 18 of the Act of Aug. 2, 1946, ch. 744, 60 Stat. 811.

The definition of "Member of Congress" in former section 835(4) is omitted as unnecessary in view of the definition of "Member of Congress" in section 2106.

Standard changes are made to conform with the definitions applicable and the style of this title as outlined in the preface to the report.

REFERENCES IN TEXT

Section 5707(d) of this title, referred to in text, was repealed by Pub. L. 104–201, div. A, title XVI, § 1614(a)(1), Sept. 23, 1996, 110 Stat. 2739.

AMENDMENTS

1990—Pub. L. 101–391 substituted "Except as otherwise provided in section 5707(d), for the purpose" for "For the purpose".

1986—Par. (4). Pub. L. 99–234 amended par. (4) generally, striking out "flat rate" before "payment".

1975—Par. (2). Pub. L. 94–22 redefined "employee" to include individuals employed intermittently as experts or consultants and paid on a daily when-actually-employed basis, and individuals serving without pay at $1 a year.

EFFECTIVE DATE OF 1986 AMENDMENT; REGULATIONS

Section 301 of Pub. L. 99–234 provided that:

"(a) The Administrator of General Services shall promulgate regulations implementing the amendments made by sections 101, 102, 103, 104, and 106 of this Act [enacting sections 5706a and 5734 of this title and amending this section and sections 5702 and 5707 of this title] not later than 150 days after the date of enactment of this Act [Jan. 2, 1986]. The amendments made by title I of this Act [enacting sections 5706a and 5734 of this title and amending this section, sections 5702, 5707, and 5724a of this title, section 476 of Title 2, The Congress, section 2396 of Title 22, Foreign Relations and Intercourse, section 4941 of Title 26, Internal Revenue Code, section 456 of Title 28, Judiciary and Judicial Procedure, section 326 of Title 31, Money and Finance, and section 2477 of Title 42, The Public Health and Welfare] shall take effect on the effective date of such regulations, or 180 days after the date of enactment of this Act [Jan. 2, 1986], whichever occurs first.

"(b) The amendments made by section 201 of this Act [enacting section 420 of Title 41, Public Contracts] shall take effect 30 days after the effective date of the amendments made by title I."

SHORT TITLE OF 1998 AMENDMENT

Pub. L. 105–264, § 1, Oct. 19, 1998, 112 Stat. 2350, provided that: "This Act [enacting sections 5706c, 5710, and 5739 of this title, amending sections 5721 to 5724, 5724a, 5725, 5727 to 5729, 5731, and 5732 of this title, section 3413 of Title 12, Banks and Banking, and sections 3322, 3528, and 3726 of Title 31, Money and Finance, and enacting provisions set out as notes under this section, section 5706c of this title, and section 3322 of Title 31] may be cited as the 'Travel and Transportation Reform Act of 1998'."

SHORT TITLE OF 1996 AMENDMENT

Pub. L. 104–201, div. A, title XVII, § 1701, Sept. 23, 1996, 110 Stat. 2752, provided that: "This title [enacting sections 5737, 5738, and 5756 of this title, amending sections 3375, 5722 to 5724c, 5726 to 5729, and 5731 of this title, section 1348 of Title 31, Money and Finance, section 707 of Title 38, Veterans' Benefits, and sections 290aa and 299c–4 of Title 42, The Public Health and Welfare, and enacting provisions set out as notes under section 5722 of this title] may be cited as the 'Federal Employee Travel Reform Act of 1996'."

SHORT TITLE OF 1986 AMENDMENT

Section 1 of Pub. L. 99–234 provided that: "This Act [enacting sections 5706a and 5734 of this title and section 420 of Title 41, Public Contracts, amending this section, sections 5702, 5707, and 5724a of this title, section 476 of Title 2, The Congress, section 2396 of Title 22, Foreign Relations and Intercourse, section 4941 of Title 26, Internal Revenue Code, section 456 of Title 28, Judiciary and Judicial Procedure, section 326 of Title 31, Money and Finance, and section 2477 of Title 42, The Public Health and Welfare, and enacting provisions set out as notes under this section and section 420 of Title

41] may be cited as the 'Federal Civilian Employee and Contractor Travel Expenses Act of 1985'."

Section 1 of Pub. L. 94–22 provided: "That this Act [amending this section, sections 5702, 5703, 5704, 5705, and 5707 of this title, and section 68b of Title 2, The Congress, and enacting provisions set out as a note under section 5707 of this title] may be cited as the "Travel Expense Amendments Act of 1975'."

Pub. L. 105–264, § 2, Oct. 19, 1998, 112 Stat. 2350, provided that:

"(a) IN GENERAL.—Under regulations issued by the Administrator of General Services after consultation with the Secretary of the Treasury, the Administrator shall require that Federal employees use the travel charge card established pursuant to the United States Travel and Transportation Payment and Expense Control System, or any Federal contractor-issued travel charge card, for all payments of expenses of official Government travel. The Administrator shall exempt any payment, person, type or class of payments, or type or class of personnel from any requirement established under the preceding sentence in any case in which—

"(1) it is in the best interest of the United States to do so;

"(2) payment through a travel charge card is impractical or imposes unreasonable burdens or costs on Federal employees or Federal agencies; or

"(3) the Secretary of Defense or the Secretary of Transportation (with respect to the Coast Guard) requests an exemption with respect to the members of the uniformed services.

"(b) AGENCY EXEMPTION.—The head of a Federal agency or the designee of such head may exempt any payment, person, type or class of payments, or type or class of agency personnel from subsection (a) if the agency head or the designee determines the exemption to be necessary in the interest of the agency. Not later than 30 days after granting such an exemption, the head of such agency or the designee shall notify the Administrator of General Services in writing of such exemption stating the reasons for the exemption.

"(c) LIMITATION ON RESTRICTION ON DISCLOSURE.—

"(1) IN GENERAL.—[Amended section 3413 of Title 12, Banks and Banking.]

"(2) EFFECTIVE DATE.—The amendment made by paragraph (1) is effective as of October 1, 1983, and applies to any records created pursuant to the United States Travel and Transportation Payment and Expense Control System or any Federal contractor-issued travel charge card issued for official Government travel.

"(d) COLLECTION OF AMOUNTS OWED.—

"(1) IN GENERAL.—Under regulations issued by the Administrator of General Services and upon written request of a Federal contractor, the head of any Federal agency or a disbursing official of the United States may, on behalf of the contractor, collect by deduction from the amount of pay owed to an employee of the agency any amount of funds the employee owes to the contractor as a result of delinquencies not disputed by the employee on a travel charge card issued for payment of expenses incurred in connection with official Government travel. The amount deducted from the pay owed to an employee with respect to a pay period may not exceed 15 percent of the disposable pay of the employee for that pay period, except that a greater percentage may be deducted upon the written consent of the employee.

"(2) DUE PROCESS PROTECTIONS.—Collection under this subsection shall be carried out in accordance with procedures substantially equivalent to the procedures required under section 3716(a) of title 31, United States Code.

"(3) DEFINITIONS.—For the purpose of this subsection:

"(A) AGENCY.—The term 'agency' has the meaning that term has under section 101 of title 31, United States Code.

"(B) EMPLOYEE.—The term 'employee' means an individual employed in or under an agency, including a member of any of the uniformed services. For purposes of this subsection, a member of one of the uniformed services is an employee of that uniformed service.

"(C) MEMBER; UNIFORMED SERVICE.—Each of the terms 'member' and 'uniformed service' has the meaning that term has in section 101 of title 37, United States Code.

"(e) REGULATIONS.—Within 270 days after the date of the enactment of this Act [Oct. 19, 1998], the Administrator of General Services shall promulgate regulations implementing this section, that—

"(1) make the use of the travel charge card established pursuant to the United States Travel and Transportation System and Expense Control System, or any Federal contractor-issued travel charge card, mandatory for all payments of expenses of official Government travel pursuant to this section;

"(2) specify the procedures for effecting under subsection (d) a deduction from pay owed to an employee, and ensure that the due process protections provided to employees under such procedures are no less than the protections provided to employees pursuant to section 3716 of title 31, United States Code;

"(3) provide that any deduction under subsection (d) from pay owed to an employee may occur only after reimbursement of the employee for the expenses of Government travel with respect to which the deduction is made; and

"(4) require agencies to promptly reimburse employees for expenses charged on a travel charge card pursuant to this section, and by no later than 30 days after the submission of a claim for reimbursement.

"(f) REPORTS.—

"(1) IN GENERAL.—The Administrator of General Services shall submit 2 reports to the Congress on agency compliance with this section and regulations that have been issued under this section.

"(2) TIMING.—The first report under this subsection shall be submitted before the end of the 180-day period beginning on the date of the enactment of this Act [Oct. 19, 1998], and the second report shall be submitted after that period and before the end of the 540-day period beginning on that date of enactment.

"(3) PREPARATION.—Each report shall be based on a sampling survey of agencies that expended more than $5,000,000 during the previous fiscal year on travel and transportation payments, including payments for employee relocation. The head of an agency shall provide to the Administrator the necessary information in a format prescribed by the Administrator and approved by the Director of the Office of Management and Budget.

"(g) REIMBURSEMENT OF TRAVEL EXPENSES.—In accordance with regulations prescribed by the Administrator of General Services, the head of an agency shall ensure that the agency reimburses an employee who submits a proper voucher for allowable travel expenses in accordance with applicable travel regulations within 30 days after submission of the voucher. If an agency fails to reimburse an employee who has submitted a proper voucher within 30 days after submission of the voucher, the agency shall pay the employee a late payment fee as prescribed by the Administrator."

This section is referred to in section 5304 of this title; title 2 section 68b; title 7 sections 3128, 5843; title 15 section 2224; title 16 sections 971a, 971b, 2443, 3608, 3641, 5608, 5709; title 22 section 1474; title 24 section 415; title 42 section 12653h.

§ 5702. Per diem; employees traveling on official business

(a)(1) Under regulations prescribed pursuant to section 5707 of this title, an employee, when traveling on official business away from the employee's designated post of duty, or away from the employee's home or regular place of business (if the employee is described in section 5703 of this title), is entitled to any one of the following:

(A) a per diem allowance at a rate not to exceed that established by the Administrator of General Services for travel within the continental United States, and by the President or his designee for travel outside the continental United States;

(B) reimbursement for the actual and necessary expenses of official travel not to exceed an amount established by the Administrator for travel within the continental United States or an amount established by the President or his designee for travel outside the continental United States; or

(C) a combination of payments described in subparagraphs (A) and (B) of this paragraph.

(2) Any per diem allowance or maximum amount of reimbursement shall be established, to the extent feasible, by locality.

(3) For travel consuming less than a full day, the payment prescribed by regulation shall be allocated in such manner as the Administrator may prescribe.

(b)(1) Under regulations prescribed pursuant to section 5707 of this title, an employee who is described in subsection (a) of this section and who abandons the travel assignment prior to its completion—

(A) because of an incapacitating illness or injury which is not due to the employee's own misconduct is entitled to reimbursement for expenses of transportation to the employee's designated post of duty, or home or regular place of business, as the case may be, and to payments pursuant to subsection (a) of this section until that location is reached; or

(B) because of a personal emergency situation (such as serious illness, injury, or death of a member of the employee's family, or an emergency situation such as fire, flood, or act of God), may be allowed, with the approval of an appropriate official of the agency concerned, reimbursement for expenses of transportation to the employee's designated post of duty, or home or regular place of business, as the case may be, and payments pursuant to subsection (a) of this section until that location is reached.

(2)(A) Under regulations prescribed pursuant to section 5707 of this title, an employee who is described in subsection (a) of this section and who, with the approval of an appropriate official of the agency concerned, interrupts the travel assignment prior to its completion for a reason specified in subparagraph (A) or (B) of paragraph (1) of this subsection, may be allowed (subject to the limitation provided in subparagraph (B) of this paragraph)—

(i) reimbursement for expenses of transportation to the location where necessary medical services are provided or the emergency situation exists,

(ii) payments pursuant to subsection (a) of this section until that location is reached, and

(iii) such reimbursement and payments for return to such assignment.

(B) The reimbursement which an employee may be allowed pursuant to subparagraph (A) of this paragraph shall be the employee's actual costs of transportation to the location where necessary medical services are provided or the emergency exists, and return to assignment from such location, less the costs of transportation which the employee would have incurred had such travel begun and ended at the employee's designated post of duty, or home or regular place of business, as the case may be. The payments which an employee may be allowed pursuant to subparagraph (A) of this paragraph shall be based on the additional time (if any) which was required for the employee's transportation as a consequence of the transportation's having begun and ended at a location on the travel assignment (rather than at the employee's designated post of duty, or home or regular place of business, as the case may be).

(3) Subject to the limitations contained in regulations prescribed pursuant to section 5707 of this title, an employee who is described in subsection (a) of this section and who interrupts the travel assignment prior to its completion because of an incapacitating illness or injury which is not due to the employee's own misconduct is entitled to payments pursuant to subsection (a) of this section at the location where the interruption occurred.

(c) This section does not apply to a justice or judge, except to the extent provided by section 456 of title 28.

(Pub. L. 89–554, Sept. 6, 1966, 80 Stat. 498; Pub. L. 91–114, §1, Nov. 10, 1969, 83 Stat. 190; Pub. L. 94–22, §3, May 19, 1975, 89 Stat. 84; Pub. L. 96–54, §2(a)(36), Aug. 14, 1979, 93 Stat. 383; Pub. L. 96–346, §1, Sept. 10, 1980, 94 Stat. 1148; Pub. L. 99–234, title I, §102, Jan. 2, 1986, 99 Stat. 1756; Pub. L. 102–378, §2(47), Oct. 2, 1992, 106 Stat. 1353.)

HISTORICAL AND REVISION NOTES

Derivation	U.S. Code	Revised Statutes and Statutes at Large
....	5 U.S.C. 836.	June 9, 1949, ch. 185, §3, 63 Stat. 166. Apr. 26, 1950, ch. 108, 64 Stat. 89. July 28, 1955, ch. 424, §1, 69 Stat. 393. Aug. 14, 1961, Pub. L. 87–139, §§1, 8(a), 75 Stat. 339, 340.

In subsection (a), the term "employee" is substituted for "civilian officers and employees of the departments and establishments" in view of the definition of "employee" in sections 5701 and 2105. The words "in lieu of their actual expenses for subsistence and all fees or tips to porters and stewards" are omitted as unnecessary in view of the definition of "per diem allowance" in section 5701(4).

In subsection (b), the words "Under regulations prescribed under section 5707 of this title" are substituted for "in accordance with regulations promulgated and approved under sections 835–842 of this title".

In subsection (c), the words "Under regulations prescribed under section 5707 of this title" are substituted for "in accordance with regulations promulgated by the Director, Bureau of the Budget, pursuant to section 840 of this title."

Standard changes are made to conform with the definitions applicable and the style of this title as outlined in the preface to the report.

AMENDMENTS

1992—Pub. L. 102–378 substituted "employees" for "employee" in section catchline.

1986—Subsec. (a). Pub. L. 99–234, § 102(a), amended subsec. (a) generally. Prior to amendment, subsec. (a) read as follows: "Under regulations prescribed under section 5707 of this title, an employee while traveling on official business away from his designated post of duty, or in the case of an individual described under section 5703 of this title, his home or regular place of business, is entitled to (1) a per diem allowance for travel inside the continental United States at a rate not to exceed $50, and (2) a per diem allowance for travel outside the continental United States, that may not exceed the rate established by the President, or his designee, for each locality where travel is to be performed. For travel consuming less than a full day, such rate may be allocated proportionately."

Subsec. (b). Pub. L. 99–234, § 102(a), amended subsec. (b) generally. Prior to amendment, subsec. (b) read as follows: "Under regulations prescribed under section 5707 of this title, an employee who, while traveling on official business away from his designated post of duty or, in the case of an individual described under section 5703 of this title, his home or regular place of business, becomes incapacitated by illness or injury not due to his own misconduct, is entitled to the per diem allowance and appropriate transportation expenses to his designated post of duty, or home or regular place of business, as the case may be."

Subsec. (c). Pub. L. 99–234, § 102, redesignated subsec. (e) as (c) and struck out former subsec. (c) which read as follows: "Under regulations prescribed under section 5707 of this title, the Administrator of General Services, or his designee, may prescribe conditions under which an employee may be reimbursed for the actual and necessary expenses of official travel when the maximum per diem allowance would be less than these expenses, except that such reimbursement shall not exceed $75 for each day in a travel status within the continental United States when the per diem otherwise allowable is determined to be inadequate (1) due to the unusual circumstances of the travel assignment, or (2) for travel to high rate geographical areas designated as such in regulations prescribed under section 5707 of this title."

Subsec. (d). Pub. L. 99–234, § 102(a), struck out subsec. (d) which read as follows: "Under regulations prescribed under section 5707 of this title, for travel outside the continental United States, the Administrator of General Services or his designee, may prescribe conditions under which an employee may be reimbursed for the actual and necessary expenses of official travel when the per diem allowance would be less than these expenses, except that such reimbursement shall not exceed $33 for each day in a travel status outside the continental United States plus the locality per diem rate prescribed for such travel."

Subsec. (e). Pub. L. 99–234, § 102(b), redesignated subsec. (e) as (c).

1980—Subsec. (a). Pub. L. 96–346, § 1(1), increased to $50 from $35 the maximum per diem allowance for travel inside the continental United States.

Subsec. (c). Pub. L. 96–346, § 1(2), increased to $75 from $50 the maximum reimbursement for actual and necessary expenses for travel within the continental United States.

Subsec. (d). Pub. L. 96–346, § 1(3), increased to $33 from $21 the maximum reimbursement for travel outside the continental United States.

1979—Subsec. (c). Pub. L. 96–54 substituted "(1)" for "(A)" and "(2)" for "(B)".

1975—Subsec. (a). Pub. L. 94–22 substituted provision relating to determination of per diem allowance under regulations prescribed under section 5707 for provision allowing for such determination by agency concerned, inserted provisions relating to an individual described under section 5703 and to proportionate allocation of rates for travel consuming less than a full day, struck out provision relating to Director of Bureau of Budget or another officer of Government of the United States as persons who may be designees, and raised maximum allowance from $25 to $35.

Subsec. (b). Pub. L. 94–22 inserted provision relating to an individual described under section 5703, inserted "appropriate" before "transportation", and "or home or regular place of business, as the case may be." after "expenses to his designated post of duty".

Subsec. (c). Pub. L. 94–22 substituted the Administrator of General Services, or his designee, for the head of the agency concerned, as the party who may prescribe conditions for reimbursement for actual and necessary expenses, raised from $40 to $50 the maximum reimbursement for travel within the continental United States when the rate otherwise allowable is inadequate due to unusual circumstances or due to travel to areas designated as high rate areas, and struck out a provision, now covered by subsec. (d), for a maximum allowance per day for travel outside the continental United States.

Subsecs. (d), (e). Pub. L. 94–22 transferred from subsec. (c) to (d) provisions for reimbursement for actual and necessary expenses for travel outside the continental United States and raised from $18 to $21 the maximum reimbursement for such expenses, and redesignated former subsec. (d) as (e).

1969—Subsec. (a). Pub. L. 91–114 increased the per diem allowance for travel inside the continental United States from not to exceed the rate of $16 to not to exceed the rate of $25.

Subsec. (c). Pub. L. 91–114 in cl. (1) increased the amount authorized to be named in the travel authorization for each day in a travel status inside the continental United States from not to exceed $30 to not to exceed $40, and in cl. (2) increased the amount authorized to be named in the travel authorization for each day in a travel status outside the continental United States from not to exceed the maximum per diem allowance plus $10 to not to exceed the maximum per diem allowance plus $18.

EFFECTIVE DATE OF 1986 AMENDMENT

Amendment by Pub. L. 99–234 effective (1) on effective date of regulations to be promulgated not later than 150 days after Jan. 2, 1986, or (2) 180 days after Jan. 2, 1986, whichever occurs first, see section 301(a) of Pub. L. 99–234, set out as a note under section 5701 of this title.

EFFECTIVE DATE OF 1979 AMENDMENT

Amendment by Pub. L. 96–54 effective July 12, 1979, see section 2(b) of Pub. L. 96–54, set out as a note under section 305 of this title.

DELEGATION OF FUNCTIONS

Authority of President under subsec. (a) of this section to establish maximum rates of per diem allowances to extent that such authority pertains to travel status of employees while enroute to, from, or between localities situated outside 48 contiguous States of United States and District of Columbia delegated to Administrator of General Services, see section 1(2) of Ex. Ord. No. 11609, July 22, 1971, 36 F.R. 13747, set out as a note under section 301 of Title 3, The President.

Authority of President under subsec. (a) of this section to establish maximum rates of per diem allowances and reimbursements for actual and necessary expenses of official travel for employees of Government to extent that such authority pertains to travel status in localities in Alaska, Hawaii, the Commonwealth of Puerto Rico, and possessions of United States delegated to Secretary of Defense, see section 1(h) of Ex. Ord. No. 10621, set out as a note under section 301 of Title 3.

COST SAVINGS FOR OFFICIAL TRAVEL

Pub. L. 103–355, title VI, § 6008, Oct. 13, 1994, 108 Stat. 3367, provided that:

"(a) GUIDELINES.—The Administrator of the General Services Administration shall issue guidelines to ensure that agencies promote, encourage, and facilitate the use of frequent traveler programs offered by airlines, hotels, and car rental vendors by Federal employees who engage in official air travel, for the purpose of realizing to the maximum extent practicable cost savings for official travel.

"(b) REQUIREMENT.—Any awards granted under such a frequent traveler program accrued through official travel shall be used only for official travel.

"(c) REPORT.—Not later than one year after the date of the enactment of this Act [Oct. 13, 1994], the Administrator shall report to Congress on efforts to promote the use of frequent traveler programs by Federal employees."

REPORTS TO CONGRESS OF PER DIEM AND MILEAGE ALLOWANCE PAYMENTS FOR FISCAL YEARS 1979 THROUGH 1981; RULES AND REGULATIONS

Section 3 of Pub. L. 96–346, for fiscal years 1979 to 1981, directed the Administrator of General Services to collect by fiscal year information with respect to agencies spending more than $5,000,000 annually on transportation of people, identifying general causes and purposes of travel and estimates of total payments, average cost and duration of trip, and identifying by specific agency of travel practices which appear to be inefficient and recommendations to Congress on the applicability of alternatives to travel as well as other techniques to improve use of travel in carrying out program objectives relating travel to mission.

EX. ORD. NO. 12561. DELEGATION OF FUNCTIONS RELATING TO TRAVEL OUTSIDE CONTINENTAL UNITED STATES

Ex. Ord. No. 12561, July 1, 1986, 51 F.R. 24299, provided:

By the authority vested in me as President by the Constitution and laws of the United States of America, including Section 102(a) of the Federal Civilian Employee and Contractor Travel Expenses Act of 1985 (Public Law 99–234) ("the Act") [amending this section] and Section 301 of Title 3 of the United States Code, it is ordered as follows:

SECTION 1. Section 1 of Executive Order No. 10621 of July 1, 1955, as amended [3 U.S.C. 301 note], is further amended by redesignating the current subsection (i) as subsection (g); by revoking the current subsection (o); and by adding the following new subsection (h):

"(h) The authority vested in the President by Section 102(a) of the Federal Civilian Employee and Contractor Travel Expenses Act of 1985, 5 U.S.C. 5702(a), to establish maximum rates of per diem allowances and reimbursements for the actual and necessary expenses of official travel for employees of the Government to the extent that such authority pertains to travel status in localities in Alaska, Hawaii, the Commonwealth of Puerto Rico, and possessions of the United States."

SEC. 2. There is hereby delegated to the Secretary of State the authority vested in the President by Section 102(a) of the Act (5 U.S.C. 5702(a)) to establish maximum rates of per diem allowances and reimbursements for the actual and necessary expenses of official travel for employees of the Government to the extent that such authority pertains to travel status in localities (including the Trust Territories of the Pacific Islands) in any area situated outside the United States, the Commonwealth of Puerto Rico, and possessions of the United States.

SEC. 3. Executive Order No. 11294 of August 4, 1966, is revoked.

RONALD REAGAN.

SECTION REFERRED TO IN OTHER SECTIONS

This section is referred to in sections 5569, 5707, 5724a, 8474 of this title; title 2 sections 476, 1723; title 7 sections 3128, 5843; title 12 section 1834a; title 15 sections 1341, 4603; title 16 sections 971a, 971b, 2443, 3608, 3641, 5608, 5709; title 18 section 4285; title 21 section 1544; title 22 sections 1474, 2396, 2704; title 24 section 415; title 25 sections 3006, 3505; title 26 section 4941; title 28 sections 456, 604, 1821; title 31 section 326; title 33 section 2732;

title 36 sections 2101, 152403; title 38 section 111; title 42 sections 1873, 2210, 2477, 7238, 10163, 10265, 11221, 13458, 14195.

§ 5703. Per diem, travel, and transportation expenses; experts and consultants; individuals serving without pay

An employee serving intermittently in the Government service as an expert or consultant and paid on a daily when-actually-employed basis, or serving without pay or at $1 a year, may be allowed travel or transportation expenses, under this subchapter, while away from his home or regular place of business and at the place of employment or service.

(Pub. L. 89–554, Sept. 6, 1966, 80 Stat. 499; Pub. L. 91–114, § 2, Nov. 10, 1969, 83 Stat. 190; Pub. L. 94–22, § 4, May 19, 1975, 89 Stat. 85.)

HISTORICAL AND REVISION NOTES

Derivation	U.S. Code	Revised Statutes and Statutes at Large
....	5 U.S.C. 73b–2.	Aug. 2, 1946, ch. 744, §5, 60 Stat. 808. July 28, 1955, ch. 424, §2, 69 Stat. 394. Aug. 14, 1961, Pub. L. 87–139, §§2, 8(b), 75 Stat. 339, 340.

Subsection (a) is added on authority of section 18 of the Act of Aug. 2, 1946, ch. 744, 60 Stat. 811.

In subsection (b), the words "in lieu of subsistence" are omitted as unnecessary in view of the definition of "per diem allowance" in section 5701(4). The words "this subchapter" are substituted for "the Standardized Government Travel Regulations, Subsistence Expense Act of 1926, as amended (5 U.S.C. 821–833) and the Act of February 14, 1931, as amended by this Act" as the Subsistence Expense Act of 1926 and the Act of February 14, 1931, were repealed by section 9(a) of the Travel Expense Act of 1949, 63 Stat. 167, part of which appeared in former section 842 and is carried into section 5708, and as the authority for the Standardized Government Travel Regulations in former section 840 is carried into section 5707.

In subsection (c), the words "this subchapter" are substituted for "said regulations and said Act of February 14, 1931, as so amended" as the Act of February 14, 1931, was repealed by section 9(a) of the Travel Expense Act of 1949, 63 Stat. 167, part of which appeared in former section 842 and is carried into section 5708, and as the authority for the Standardized Government Travel Regulations in former section 840 is carried into section 5707. The words "in lieu of subsistence" are omitted as unnecessary in view of the definition of "per diem allowance" in section 5701(4).

In subsection (d), the words "Under regulations prescribed under section 5707 of this title" are substituted for "in accordance with regulations promulgated by the Director, Bureau of the Budget, pursuant to section 840 of this title".

Standard changes are made to conform with the definitions applicable and the style of this title as outlined in the preface to the report.

AMENDMENTS

1975—Pub. L. 94–22 struck out separate provisions for per diem allowances of employees serving as experts, consultants, or serving without pay or at $1 a year.

1969—Subsec. (c)(1). Pub. L. 91–114 increased the per diem allowance for travel inside continental United States from not to exceed the rate of $16 to not to exceed the rate of $25.

Subsec. (d). Pub. L. 91–114 in cl. (1) increased amount authorized to be named in travel authorization for each day in a travel status inside continental United States from not to exceed $30 to not to exceed $40, and in cl. (2) increased amount authorized to be named in travel authorization for each day in a travel status outside continental United States from not to exceed maximum per diem allowance plus $10 to not to exceed the maximum per diem allowance plus $18.

Section Referred to in Other Sections

This section is referred to in sections 593, 5304, 5702, 7119, 8474 of this title; title 2 sections 175, 352, 475, 1108, 1723; title 7 sections 87j, 499t, 1388, 1505, 1736bb, 2233, 3128, 5331, 5843, 5853, 6204, 6518, 7317; title 10 sections 1464, 2006; title 12 sections 1701j–2, 1701y, 1749bbb–1, 1834a, 3013; title 15 sections 637, 652, 1275, 1341, 4102, 4105, 4603; title 16 sections 1a–2, 410cc–31, 410nn–3, 410pp–4, 410tt–4, 410ww–21, 410yy–8, 410bbb–5, 410ccc–22, 450jj–6, 460ss–2, 460ss–3, 460zz–2, 460kkk, 469j, 583j–1, 698u–5, 839b, 972a, 1105, 1157, 1401, 1403, 1447b, 1536, 1537a, 1604, 2443, 3181, 4004, 5404, 5803; title 18 section 4351; title 19 sections 1903, 2171; title 20 sections 80q–3, 80q–10, 929, 955, 957, 959, 1098, 1134a, 1505, 2012, 2106, 3602, 3701, 4412, 4414, 4513, 4710, 5508, 5608, 5708, 5822, 6031, 9105, 9175; title 21 sections 355, 360c, 360d, 360e, 360j, 379e, 679a, 1115, 1303, 1544, 1908; title 22 sections 287o, 287q, 290f, 290h–5, 1465c, 1471, 1474, 1622c, 2102, 2103, 2351, 2456, 2581, 2672b, 2903, 2905, 3106, 3507, 3617, 4110, 4605, 4902, 6203, 6204; title 24 section 415; title 25 sections 305, 3006, 3505; title 28 sections 594, 2077; title 29 sections 656, 765, 772, 774, 782, 792, 794b, 1142, 1302, 2634; title 30 sections 663, 812, 1315, 1903; title 31 section 751; title 33 sections 426, 857–16, 1320, 2073, 2251, 2732; title 35 section 5; title 36 sections 2101, 2302, 152403; title 40 sections 333, 486, 822, 872, 1106; title 41 sections 46, 422; title 42 sections 210, 242l, 242q–1, 254j, 300j–5, 300v, 300aa–19, 903, 1108, 1314, 1320a–1, 1870, 1873, 2210, 2473, 2495, 3015, 3211, 3535, 3609, 3788, 4025, 4768, 4914, 5404, 5651, 5661, 6007, 6614, 6632, 7234, 7417, 9511, 10163, 10265, 12314, 12374, 12619, 12851, 13458, 14195; title 44 sections 2104, 2503, 3318; title 46 sections 4508, 9307, 13110; title 46 App. section 1295b; title 47 section 394; title 49 sections 106, 325, 44508, 60115; title 50 section 98h–1; title 50 App. sections 1989b–5, 2160.

§ 5704. Mileage and related allowances

(a)(1) Under regulations prescribed under section 5707 of this title, an employee who is engaged on official business for the Government is entitled to a rate per mile established by the Administrator of General Services, instead of the actual expenses of transportation, for the use of a privately owned automobile when that mode of transportation is authorized or approved as more advantageous to the Government. In any year in which the Internal Revenue Service establishes a single standard mileage rate for optional use by taxpayers in computing the deductible costs of operating their automobiles for business purposes, the rate per mile established by the Administrator shall not exceed the single standard mileage rate established by the Internal Revenue Service.

(2) Under regulations prescribed under section 5707 of this title, an employee who is engaged on official business for the Government is entitled to a rate per mile established by the Administrator of General Services, instead of the actual expenses of transportation, for the use of a privately owned airplane or a privately owned motorcycle when that mode of transportation is authorized or approved as more advantageous to the Government.

(b) A determination that travel by a privately owned vehicle is more advantageous to the Government is not required under subsection (a) of this section when payment on a mileage basis is limited to the cost of travel by common carrier including per diem.

(c) Notwithstanding the provisions of subsections (a) and (b) of this section, in any case in which an employee who is engaged on official business for the Government chooses to use a privately owned vehicle in lieu of a Government vehicle, payment on a mileage basis is limited to the cost of travel by a Government vehicle.

(d) In addition to the rate per mile authorized under subsection (a) of this section, the employee may be reimbursed for—

(1) parking fees;
(2) ferry fees;
(3) bridge, road, and tunnel costs; and
(4) airplane landing and tie-down fees.

(Pub. L. 89–554, Sept. 6, 1966, 80 Stat. 499; Pub. L. 94–22, § 5, May 19, 1975, 89 Stat. 85; Pub. L. 96–346, § 2, Sept. 10, 1980, 94 Stat. 1148; Pub. L. 103–329, title VI, § 634(a), Sept. 30, 1994, 108 Stat. 2428.)

Historical and Revision Notes

Derivation	U.S. Code	Revised Statutes and Statutes at Large
....	5 U.S.C. 837.	June 9, 1949, ch. 185, § 4, 63 Stat. 166. July 28, 1955, ch. 424, § 4, 69 Stat. 394. Aug. 14, 1961, Pub. L. 87–139, §§ 3, 4, 75 Stat. 339, 340.

The word "employee" is substituted for "Civilian officers and employees of departments and establishments" in view of the definition of "employee" in sections 5701 and 2105.

In subsection (a), the words "Under regulations prescribed under section 5707 of this title" are substituted for "under regulations prescribed by the Director of the Bureau of the Budget".

Standard changes are made to conform with the definitions applicable and the style of this title as outlined in the preface to the report.

Amendments

1994—Pub. L. 103–329 amended text generally. Prior to amendment, text read as follows:

"(a) Under regulations prescribed under section 5707 of this title, an employee who is engaged on official business for the Government is entitled to not in excess of—

"(1) 20 cents a mile for the use of a privately owned motorcycle;
"(2) 25 cents a mile for the use of a privately owned automobile; or
"(3) 45 cents a mile for the use of a privately owned airplane;

instead of actual expenses of transportation when that mode of transportation is authorized or approved as more advantageous to the Government. A determination of such advantage is not required when payment on a mileage basis is limited to the cost of travel by common carrier including per diem. Notwithstanding the preceding provisions of this subsection, in any case in which an employee who is engaged on official business for the Government chooses to use a privately owned vehicle in lieu of a Government vehicle, payment on a mileage basis is limited to the cost of travel by a Government vehicle.

"(b) In addition to the mileage allowance authorized under subsection (a) of this section, the employee may be reimbursed for—

"(1) parking fees;
"(2) ferry fees;
"(3) bridge, road, and tunnel costs; and
"(4) airplane landing and tie-down fees."

1980—Subsec. (a)(1). Pub. L. 96–346, § 2(1), substituted "20 cents" for "11 cents".

Subsec. (a)(2). Pub. L. 96–346, § 2(2), substituted "25 cents" for "20 cents".

Subsec. (a)(3). Pub. L. 96–346, § 2(3), substituted "45 cents" for "24 cents".

1975—Subsec. (a). Pub. L. 94–22 struck out "or other individual performing services for the Government" after "employee", substituted "for the Government" for "inside or outside his designated post of duty or place of service", increased from 8 to 11 cents the allowance for use of a motorcycle, from 12 to 20 cents the allowance for use of an automobile, and from 12 to 24 cents the allowance for use of an airplane, and inserted provision relating to the limitation of an allowance to the cost of travel by Government vehicle when an employee chooses a privately owned vehicle in lieu of a Government vehicle.

Subsec. (b). Pub. L. 94–22 inserted "authorized" after "allowance", struck out "or other individual performing service for the Government" after "employee", and provided for reimbursement of airplane landing and tie-down fee.

SECTION REFERRED TO IN OTHER SECTIONS

This section is referred to in sections 5707, 5724 of this title; title 2 section 476; title 7 sections 3128, 5843; title 13 sections 24, 26; title 16 sections 971a, 971b, 2443, 3608, 3641, 5608, 5709; title 22 section 1474; title 24 section 415; title 28 section 1821; title 30 section 812; title 33 section 1320; title 37 section 404; title 38 section 111; title 42 section 2477.

§ 5705. Advancements and deductions

An agency may advance, through the proper disbursing official, to an employee entitled to per diem or mileage allowances under this subchapter, a sum considered advisable with regard to the character and probable duration of the travel to be performed. A sum advanced and not used for allowable travel expenses is recoverable from the employee or his estate by—

(1) setoff against accrued pay, retirement credit, or other amount due the employee;

(2) deduction from an amount due from the United States; and

(3) such other method as is provided by law.

(Pub. L. 89–554, Sept. 6, 1966, 80 Stat. 500; Pub. L. 94–22, § 2(b), May 19, 1975, 89 Stat. 84.)

HISTORICAL AND REVISION NOTES

Derivation	U.S. Code	Revised Statutes and Statutes at Large
....	5 U.S.C. 838.	June 9, 1949, ch. 185, § 5, 63 Stat. 166.

The words "disbursing official" are substituted for "disbursing officer" because of the definition of "officer" in section 2104 which excludes a member of a uniformed service. Application to section 5703 is based on former section 73b–2, which is carried into section 5703.

Standard changes are made to conform with the definitions applicable and the style of this title as outlined in the preface to the report.

AMENDMENTS

1975—Pub. L. 94–22 struck out "or individual" after "employee" wherever appearing.

SECTION REFERRED TO IN OTHER SECTIONS

This section is referred to in section 5724 of this title; title 7 sections 3128, 5843; title 16 sections 971a, 971b, 2443, 3608, 3641, 5608, 5709; title 22 section 1474; title 24 section 415.

§ 5706. Allowable travel expenses

Except as otherwise permitted by this subchapter or by statutes relating to members of the uniformed services, only actual and necessary travel expenses may be allowed to an individual holding employment or appointment under the United States.

(Pub. L. 89–554, Sept. 6, 1966, 80 Stat. 500.)

HISTORICAL AND REVISION NOTES

Derivation	U.S. Code	Revised Statutes and Statutes at Large
....	5 U.S.C. 839.	June 9, 1949, ch. 185, § 6, 63 Stat. 167.

The words "members of the uniformed services" are substituted for "military personnel".

Standard changes are made to conform with the definitions applicable and the style of this title as outlined in the preface to the report.

SECTION REFERRED TO IN OTHER SECTIONS

This section is referred to in title 7 sections 3128, 5843; title 16 sections 971a, 971b, 2443, 3608, 3641, 5608, 5709; title 22 section 1474; title 24 section 415.

§ 5706a. Subsistence and travel expenses for threatened law enforcement personnel

(a) Under regulations prescribed pursuant to section 5707 of this title, when the life of an employee who serves in a law enforcement, investigative, or similar capacity, or members of such employee's immediate family, is threatened as a result of the employee's assigned duties, the head of the agency concerned may approve appropriate subsistence payments for the employee or members of the employee's family (or both) while occupying temporary living accommodations at or away from the employee's designated post of duty.

(b) When a situation described in subsection (a) of this section requires the employee or members of the employee's family (or both) to be temporarily relocated away from the employee's designated post of duty, the head of the agency concerned may approve transportation expenses to and from such alternate location.

(Added Pub. L. 99–234, title I, § 103(a), Jan. 2, 1986, 99 Stat. 1757.)

EFFECTIVE DATE

Section effective (1) on effective date of regulations to be promulgated not later than 150 days after Jan. 2, 1986, or (2) 180 days after Jan. 2, 1986, whichever occurs first, see section 301(a) of Pub. L. 99–234, set out as an Effective Date of 1986 Amendment note under section 5701 of this title.

SECTION REFERRED TO IN OTHER SECTIONS

This section is referred to in section 5707 of this title; title 7 sections 3128, 5843; title 16 sections 971a, 971b, 2443, 3608, 3641, 5608, 5709; title 22 section 1474; title 24 section 415.

§ 5706b. Interview expenses

An individual being considered for employment by an agency may be paid travel or transportation expenses under this subchapter for travel to and from pre-employment interviews determined necessary by the agency.

(Added Pub. L. 101–509, title V, § 529 [title II, § 206(a)(1)], Nov. 5, 1990, 104 Stat. 1427, 1457.)

EFFECTIVE DATE

Section effective on such date as the President shall determine, but not earlier than 90 days, and not later than 180 days, after Nov. 5, 1990, see section 529 [title III, § 305] of Pub. L. 101–509, set out as an Effective Date of 1990 Amendment note under section 5301 of this title.

This section is referred to in title 7 sections 3128, 5843; title 16 sections 971a, 971b, 2443, 3608, 3641, 5608, 5709; title 22 section 1474; title 24 section 415; title 38 section 7410.

§ 5706c. Reimbursement for taxes incurred on money received for travel expenses

(a) Under regulations prescribed pursuant to section 5707 of this title, the head of an agency or department, or his or her designee, may use appropriations or other funds available to the agency for administrative expenses, for the reimbursement of Federal, State, and local income taxes incurred by an employee of the agency or by an employee and such employee's spouse (if filing jointly), for any travel or transportation reimbursement made to an employee for which reimbursement or an allowance is provided.

(b) Reimbursements under this section shall include an amount equal to all income taxes for which the employee and spouse, as the case may be, would be liable due to the reimbursement for the taxes referred to in subsection (a). In addition, reimbursements under this section shall include penalties and interest, for the tax years 1993 and 1994 only, as a result of agencies failing to withhold the appropriate amounts for tax liabilities of employees affected by the change in the deductibility of travel expenses made by Public Law 102–486.

(Added Pub. L. 105–264, § 4(a), Oct. 19, 1998, 112 Stat. 2354.)

REFERENCES IN TEXT

Public Law 102–486, referred to in subsec. (b), is Pub. L. 102–486, Oct. 24, 1992, 106 Stat. 2776, known as the Energy Policy Act of 1992. For complete classification of this Act to the Code, see Short Title note set out under section 13201 of Title 42, The Public Health and Welfare, and Tables.

EFFECTIVE DATE

Pub. L. 105–264, § 4(c), Oct. 19, 1998, 112 Stat. 2354, provided that: "This section [enacting this section] shall be effective as of January 1, 1993."

§ 5707. Regulations and reports

(a)(1) The Administrator of General Services shall prescribe regulations necessary for the administration of this subchapter, except that the Director of the Administrative Office of the United States Courts shall prescribe such regulations with respect to official travel by employees of the judicial branch of the Government.

(2) Regulations promulgated to implement section 5702 or 5706a of this title shall be transmitted to the appropriate committees of the Congress and shall not take effect until 30 days after such transmittal.

(b) The Administrator of General Services shall prescribe the mileage reimbursement rates for use on official business of privately owned airplanes, privately owned automobiles, and privately owned motorcycles while engaged on official business as provided for in section 5704 of this title as follows:

(1)(A) The Administrator of General Services, in consultation with the Secretary of Transportation, the Secretary of Defense, and representatives of organizations of employees of the Government, shall conduct periodic investigations of the cost of travel and the operation of privately owned vehicles to employees while engaged on official business, and shall report the results of such investigations to Congress at least once a year.

(B) In conducting the periodic investigations, the Administrator shall review and analyze among other factors—

(i) depreciation of original vehicle cost;

(ii) gasoline and oil (excluding taxes);

(iii) maintenance, accessories, parts, and tires;

(iv) insurance; and

(v) State and Federal taxes.

(2)(A) The Administrator shall issue regulations under this section which—

(i) shall prescribe a mileage reimbursement rate which reflects the current costs as determined by the Administrator of operating privately owned automobiles, and which shall not exceed, as provided in section 5704(a)(1) of this title, the single standard mileage rate established by the Internal Revenue Service, and

(ii) shall prescribe mileage reimbursement rates which reflect the current costs as determined by the Administrator of operating privately owned airplanes and motorcycles.

(B) At least once each year after the issuance of the regulations described in subparagraph (A) of this paragraph, the Administrator shall determine, based upon the results of the cost investigation, specific figures, each rounded to the nearest half cent, of the average, actual cost per mile during the period for the use of a privately owned airplane, automobile, and motorcycle.

(C) The Administrator shall report the specific figures to Congress not later than five working days after the Administrator makes the cost determination. Each such report shall be printed in the Federal Register.

(D) The mileage reimbursement rates contained in the regulations prescribed under this section shall be adjusted within thirty days following the submission of the report under subparagraph (C) of this paragraph.

(c) The Administrator of General Services shall periodically, but at least every 2 years, submit to the Director of the Office of Management and Budget an analysis of estimated total agency payments for such items as travel and transportation of people, average costs and duration of trips, and purposes of official travel; and of estimated total agency payments for employee relocation. This analysis shall be based on a sampling survey of agencies each of which spent more than $5,000,000 during the previous fiscal year on travel and transportation payments, including payments for employee relocation. Agencies shall provide to the Administrator the necessary information in a format prescribed by the Administrator and approved by the Director.

(Pub. L. 89–554, Sept. 6, 1966, 80 Stat. 500; Pub. L. 94–22, § 6(a), May 19, 1975, 89 Stat. 85; Pub. L.

99–234, title I, § 104, Jan. 2, 1986, 99 Stat. 1758; Pub. L. 101–391, § 5(a)(1), Sept. 25, 1990, 104 Stat. 750; Pub. L. 103–329, title VI, § 634(b), (c), Sept. 30, 1994, 108 Stat. 2429, 2430; Pub. L. 104–201, div. A, title XVI, § 1614(a)(1), Sept. 23, 1996, 110 Stat. 2739; Pub. L. 104–316, title I, § 103(e), Oct. 19, 1996, 110 Stat. 3829.)

HISTORICAL AND REVISION NOTES

Derivation	U.S. Code	Revised Statutes and Statutes at Large
....	5 U.S.C. 840.	June 9, 1949, ch. 185, § 7, 63 Stat. 167.

The first sentence is based in part on former sections 73b–2, 836, and 837, which are carried into this subchapter. Application of the second sentence to section 5703, and the third sentence, are based on former section 73b–2, which is carried into section 5703.

Standard changes are made to conform with the definitions applicable and the style of this title as outlined in the preface to the report.

AMENDMENTS

1996—Subsec. (b)(1)(A). Pub. L. 104–316 struck out "the Comptroller General of the United States," after "in consultation with".

Subsec. (d). Pub. L. 104–201 struck out subsec. (d) which provided that agencies ensure that their approved accommodation percentages be not less than specified percentages for fiscal years beginning 4 and 5 years after Sept. 25, 1990, and that their percentages be not less than 90 percent for fiscal years beginning 6 years after Sept. 25, 1990, and thereafter.

1994—Subsec. (b). Pub. L. 103–329, § 634(b), amended subsec. (b) generally, revising and restructuring text.

Subsec. (c). Pub. L. 103–329, § 634(c), redesignated par. (1) as entire subsec. and struck out par. (2) which read as follows: "The requirements of paragraph (1) of this subsection shall expire upon the Administrator's submission of the analysis that includes the fiscal year that ends September 30, 1991."

1990—Subsec. (d). Pub. L. 101–391 added subsec. (d).

1986—Subsec. (a). Pub. L. 99–234 designated existing provisions as par. (1) and added par. (2).

Subsec. (c). Pub. L. 99–234 added subsec. (c).

1975—Pub. L. 94–22 inserted "and reports" in section catchline, designated existing provisions as subsec. (a), substituted "Administrator of General Services" for "Director of the Bureau of the Budget", struck out provision for fixing, payment, advancement and recovery of travel allowances and expenses in accordance with the regulations and provision for the non-applicability of this section to per diem allowances under section 5703(c), and inserted provision for regulations for travel by employees of the judicial branch of the Government by the Director of the Administrative Office of the United States Courts, and added subsec. (b).

EFFECTIVE DATE OF 1986 AMENDMENT

Amendment by Pub. L. 99–234 effective (1) on effective date of regulations to be promulgated not later than 150 days after Jan. 2, 1986, or (2) 180 days after Jan. 2, 1986, whichever occurs first, see section 301(a) of Pub. L. 99–234, set out as a note under section 5701 of this title.

REGULATIONS; TIME FOR ISSUANCE

Section 6(b) of Pub. L. 94–22 provided that regulations required under the first sentence of subsec. (b)(2) of this section, as amended by subsec. (a) of section 6 of Pub. L. 94–22, were to be issued no later than 30 days after May 19, 1975.

TERMINATION OF REPORTING REQUIREMENTS

For termination, effective May 15, 2000, of provisions in subsection (b)(1) of this section relating to reporting results of investigations to Congress, see section 3003 of

Pub. L. 104–66, as amended, set out as a note under section 1113 of Title 31, Money and Finance, and page 174 of House Document No. 103–7.

REPORTS REGARDING FOREIGN TRAVEL

Pub. L. 105–277, div. G, subdiv. B, title XXV, § 2505, Oct. 21, 1998, 112 Stat. 2681–837, as amended by Pub. L. 106–113, div. B, § 1000(a)(7) [div. A, title VII, § 707], Nov. 29, 1999, 113 Stat. 1536, 1501A–461, provided that:

"(a) PROHIBITION.—Except as provided in subsection (e), none of the funds authorized to be appropriated for the Department of State for fiscal year 2000 or 2001 may be used to pay for the expenses of foreign travel by an officer or employee of an Executive branch agency to attend an international conference, or for the routine services that a United States diplomatic mission or consular post provides in support of foreign travel by such an officer or employee to attend an international conference, unless that officer or employee has submitted a preliminary report with respect to that foreign travel in accordance with subsection (b), and has not previously failed to submit a final report with respect to foreign travel to attend an international conference required by subsection (c).

"(b) PRELIMINARY REPORTS.—A preliminary report referred to in subsection (a) is a report by an officer or employee of an Executive branch agency with respect to proposed foreign travel to attend an international conference, submitted to the Director prior to commencement of the travel, setting forth—

"(1) the name and employing agency of the officer or employee;

"(2) the name of the official who authorized the travel; and

"(3) the purpose and duration of the travel.

"(c) FINAL REPORTS.—A final report referred to in subsection (a) is a report by an officer or employee of an Executive branch agency with respect to foreign travel to attend an international conference, submitted to the Director not later than 30 days after the conclusion of the travel—

"(1) setting forth the actual duration and cost of the travel; and

"(2) updating any other information included in the preliminary report.

"(d) REPORT TO CONGRESS.—The Director shall submit a report on January 31 of the years 2000 and 2001 and July 31 of the years 2000 and 2001, to the Committees on Foreign Relations and Appropriations of the Senate and the Committees on International Relations and Appropriations of the House of Representatives, setting forth with respect to each international conference for which reports described in subsection (c) were required to be submitted to the Director during the preceding six months—

"(1) the names and employing agencies of all officers and employees of Executive branch agencies who attended the international conference;

"(2) the names of all officials who authorized travel to the international conference, and the total number of officers and employees who were authorized to travel to the conference by each such official; and

"(3) the total cost of travel by officers and employees of Executive branch agencies to the international conference.

"(e) EXCEPTIONS.—This section shall not apply to travel by—

"(1) the President or the Vice President;

"(2) any officer or employee who is carrying out an intelligence or intelligence-related activity, who is performing a protective function, or who is engaged in a sensitive diplomatic mission; or

"(3) any officer or employee who travels prior to January 1, 1999.

"(f) DEFINITIONS.—In this section:

"(1) DIRECTOR.—The term 'Director' means the Director of the Office of International Conferences of the Department of State.

"(2) EXECUTIVE BRANCH AGENCY.—The terms 'Executive branch agency' and 'Executive branch agencies' mean—

"(A) an entity or entities, other than the General Accounting Office, defined in section 105 of title 5, United States Code; and

"(B) the Executive Office of the President (except as provided in subsection (e)).

"(3) INTERNATIONAL CONFERENCE.—The term 'international conference' means any meeting held under the auspices of an international organization or foreign government, at which representatives of more than two foreign governments are expected to be in attendance, and to which United States Executive branch agencies will send a total of ten or more representatives.

"(g) REPORT.—Not later than 180 days after the date of enactment of this Act [Oct. 21, 1998], and annually thereafter, the President shall submit to the appropriate congressional committees a report describing—

"(1) the total Federal expenditure of all official international travel in each Executive branch agency during the previous fiscal year; and

"(2) the total number of individuals in each agency who engaged in such travel."

REPORTING OF EMPLOYEE RELOCATION EXPENSES

Pub. L. 105–61, title VI, § 635, Oct. 10, 1997, 111 Stat. 1316, provided that: "No later than 30 days after the enactment of this Act [Oct. 10, 1997], the Director of the Office of Management and Budget shall require all Federal departments and agencies to report total obligations for the expenses of employee relocation. All obligations incident to employee relocation authorized under either chapter 57 of title 5, United States Code, or section 901 of the Foreign Service Act of 1980 (22 U.S.C. 4081; Public Law 96–465), shall be included. Such information for the past, current, and budget years shall be included in the agency budget submission to the President. The Director of the Office of Management and Budget shall prepare a table presenting obligations for the expenses of employee relocation for all departments and agencies, and such table shall be transmitted to Congress each year as part of the President's annual budget."

GAO AUDIT OF AGENCY COMPLIANCE

Section 5(b) of Pub. L. 101–391, which provided that not later than 6 months after the last day of the first fiscal year during which lodging expenses were subject to the requirements of former subsec. (d) of this section, and not later than 6 months after the last day of every fiscal year thereafter, the Comptroller General was to conduct an audit of the compliance of agencies with the requirements of such subsection, and was to submit a report to Congress describing the results of such audit, was repealed by Pub. L. 104–201, div. A, title XVI, § 1614(a)(2), Sept. 23, 1996, 110 Stat. 2739, and Pub. L. 104–316, title I, § 103(f), Oct. 19, 1996, 110 Stat. 3829.

SECTION REFERRED TO IN OTHER SECTIONS

This section is referred to in sections 5701, 5702, 5704, 5706a, 5706c, 5709 of this title; title 7 sections 3128, 5843; title 16 sections 971a, 971b, 2443, 3608, 3641, 5608, 5709; title 22 section 1474; title 24 section 415; title 28 section 456; title 40 section 872.

§ 5707a. Adherence to fire safety guidelines in establishing rates and discounts for lodging expenses

(a)(1) For the purpose of making payments under this chapter for lodging expenses incurred in a State, each agency shall ensure that not less than 90 percent of the commercial-lodging room nights for employees of that agency for a fiscal year are booked in approved places of public accommodation.

(2) Each agency shall establish explicit procedures to satisfy the percentage requirement of paragraph (1).

(3) An agency shall be considered to be in compliance with the percentage requirement of paragraph (1) until September 30, 2002, and after that date if travel arrangements of the agency, whether made for civilian employees, members of the uniformed services, or foreign service personnel, are made through travel management processes designed to book commercial lodging in approved places of public accommodation, whenever available.

(b) Studies or surveys conducted for the purposes of establishing per diem rates for lodging expenses under this chapter shall be limited to approved places of public accommodation. The provisions of this subsection shall not apply with respect to studies and surveys that are conducted in any jurisdiction that is not a State.

(c) The Administrator of General Services may not include in any directory which lists lodging accommodations any hotel, motel, or other place of public accommodation that is not an approved place of public accommodation.

(d) The Administrator of General Services shall include in each directory which lists lodging accommodations a description of the access and safety devices, including appropriate emergency alerting devices, which each listed place of public accommodation provides for guests who are hearing-impaired or visually or physically handicapped.

(e) The Administrator of General Services may take any additional actions the Administrator determines appropriate to facilitate the ability of employees traveling on official business to stay at approved places of public accommodation.

(f) For purposes of this section:

(1) The term "agency" does not include the government of the District of Columbia.

(2) The term "approved places of public accommodation" means hotels, motels, and other places of public accommodation that are listed by the Director of the Federal Emergency Management Agency as meeting the requirements of the fire prevention and control guidelines described in section 29 of the Federal Fire Prevention and Control Act of 1974 (15 U.S.C. 2225).

(3) The term "State" means any State, the District of Columbia, the Commonwealth of Puerto Rico, the Commonwealth of the Northern Mariana Islands, the Trust Territory of the Pacific Islands, the Virgin Islands, Guam, American Samoa, or any other territory or possession of the United States.

(Added Pub. L. 101–391, § 4(a), Sept. 25, 1990, 104 Stat. 749; amended Pub. L. 105–85, div. A, title XI, § 1107(a)–(c), Nov. 18, 1997, 111 Stat. 1924, 1925.)

AMENDMENTS

1997—Subsec. (a). Pub. L. 105–85, § 1107(a)(2), added subsec. (a). Former subsec. (a) redesignated (b).

Subsec. (b). Pub. L. 105–85, § 1107(c)(1), substituted "approved places of public accommodation" for "places of public accommodation that meet the requirements of the fire prevention and control guidelines described in section 29 of the Federal Fire Prevention and Control Act of 1974" and struck out "as defined in section 4 of the Federal Fire Prevention and Control Act of 1974" after "that is not a State".

Pub. L. 105–85, § 1107(a)(1), redesignated subsec. (a) as (b). Former subsec. (b) redesignated (c).

Subsec. (c). Pub. L. 105–85, § 1107(c)(2), substituted "is not an approved place of public accommodation" for "does not meet the requirements of the fire prevention and control guidelines described in section 29 of the Federal Fire Prevention and Control Act of 1974".

Pub. L. 105–85, § 1107(a)(1), redesignated subsec. (b) as (c). Former subsec. (c) redesignated (d).

Subsec. (d). Pub. L. 105–85, § 1107(a)(1), redesignated subsec. (c) as (d). Former subsec. (d) redesignated (e).

Subsec. (e). Pub. L. 105–85, § 1107(c)(3), substituted "facilitate the ability of" for "encourage" and "approved places of public accommodation" for "places of public accommodation that meet the requirements of the fire prevention and control guidelines described in section 29 of the Federal Fire Prevention and Control Act of 1974".

Pub. L. 105–85, § 1107(a)(1), redesignated subsec. (d) as (e).

Subsec. (f). Pub. L. 105–85, § 1107(b), added subsec. (f).

EFFECTIVE DATE

Section 4(c) of Pub. L. 101–391 provided that: "The amendments made by this section [enacting this section] shall take effect 60 days after the date of the publication in the Federal Register [Nov. 24, 1992, 57 F.R. 55314] of the master list of certified places of public accommodation maintained by the Director of the Federal Emergency Management Agency pursuant to section 28(b) of the Federal Fire Prevention and Control Act of 1974 [15 U.S.C. 2224(b)] (as added by section 3 of this Act)."

TERMINATION OF TRUST TERRITORY OF THE PACIFIC ISLANDS

For termination of Trust Territory of the Pacific Islands, see note set out preceding section 1681 of Title 48, Territories and Insular Possessions.

SECTION REFERRED TO IN OTHER SECTIONS

This section is referred to in title 16 sections 5608, 5709.

§ 5708. Effect on other statutes

This subchapter does not modify or repeal—

(1) any statute providing for the traveling expenses of the President;

(2) any statute providing for mileage allowances for Members of Congress;

(3) any statute fixing or permitting rates higher than the maximum rates established under this subchapter; or

(4) any appropriation statute item for examination of estimates in the field.

(Pub. L. 89–554, Sept. 6, 1966, 80 Stat. 500.)

HISTORICAL AND REVISION NOTES

Derivation	U.S. Code	Revised Statutes and Statutes at Large
(1), (2)	5 U.S.C. 841.	June 9, 1949, ch. 185, § 8, 63 Stat. 167.
(3), (4)	5 U.S.C. 842.	June 9, 1949, ch. 185, § 9, 63 Stat. 167.

In paragraph (2), the words "Members of Congress" are substituted for "the President of the Senate or Members of Congress" in view of the definition of "Member of Congress" in section 2106.

The first sentence of section 9 of the Act of June 9, 1949, which repealed the Subsistence Act of 1926 and the Auto Mileage Act of February 14, 1931, is omitted as executed.

The first proviso of former section 842, which related to appropriation Acts for the years 1949 and 1950, is omitted as obsolete. The remainder of former section 842, other than the parenthetical expressions, is omitted as executed and existing rights are preserved by technical section 8.

Standard changes are made to conform with the definitions applicable and the style of this title as outlined in the preface to the report.

SECTION REFERRED TO IN OTHER SECTIONS

This section is referred to in title 16 sections 971a, 971b, 2443, 3608, 3641, 5608, 5709; title 22 section 1474.

§ 5709. Air evacuation patients: furnished subsistence

Notwithstanding any other provision of law, and under regulations prescribed under section 5707 of this title, an employee and his dependents may be furnished subsistence without charge while being evacuated as a patient by military aircraft of the United States.

(Added Pub. L. 91–481, § 1(1), Oct. 21, 1970, 84 Stat. 1081.)

§ 5710. Authority for travel expenses test programs

(a)(1) Notwithstanding any other provision of this subchapter, under a test program which the Administrator of General Services determines to be in the interest of the Government and approves, an agency may pay through the proper disbursing official for a period not to exceed 24 months any necessary travel expenses in lieu of any payment otherwise authorized or required under this subchapter. An agency shall include in any request to the Administrator for approval of such a test program an analysis of the expected costs and benefits and a set of criteria for evaluating the effectiveness of the program.

(2) Any test program conducted under this section shall be designed to enhance cost savings or other efficiencies that accrue to the Government.

(3) Nothing in this section is intended to limit the authority of any agency to conduct test programs.

(b) The Administrator shall transmit a copy of any test program approved by the Administrator under this section to the appropriate committees of the Congress at least 30 days before the effective date of the program.

(c) An agency authorized to conduct a test program under subsection (a) shall provide to the Administrator and the appropriate committees of the Congress a report on the results of the program no later than 3 months after completion of the program.

(d) No more than 10 test programs under this section may be conducted simultaneously.

(e) The authority to conduct test programs under this section shall expire 7 years after the date of the enactment of the Travel and Transportation Reform Act of 1998.

(Added Pub. L. 105–264, § 5(a), Oct. 19, 1998, 112 Stat. 2354.)

REFERENCES IN TEXT

The date of the enactment of the Travel and Transportation Reform Act of 1998, referred to in subsec. (e), is the date of enactment of Pub. L. 105–264, which was approved Oct. 19, 1998.

SUBCHAPTER II—TRAVEL AND TRANSPORTATION EXPENSES; NEW APPOINTEES, STUDENT TRAINEES, AND TRANSFERRED EMPLOYEES

SUBCHAPTER REFERRED TO IN OTHER SECTIONS

This subchapter is referred to in title 8 section 1353; title 46 App. section 1717.

§ 5721. Definitions

For the purpose of this subchapter—

(1) "agency" means—

(A) an Executive agency;

(B) a military department;

(C) a court of the United States;

(D) the Administrative Office of the United States Courts;

(E) the Library of Congress;

(F) the Botanic Garden;

(G) the Government Printing Office; and

(H) the government of the District of Columbia;

but does not include a Government controlled corporation;

(2) "employee" means an individual employed in or under an agency;

(3) "continental United States" means the several States and the District of Columbia, but does not include Alaska or Hawaii;

(4) "Government" means the government of the United States and the government of the District of Columbia;

(5) "appropriation" includes funds made available by statute under section 9104 of title 31;

(6) "United States" means the several States, the District of Columbia, the Commonwealth of Puerto Rico, the Commonwealth of the Northern Mariana Islands, the territories and possessions of the United States, and the areas and installations in the Republic of Panama that are made available to the United States pursuant to the Panama Canal Treaty of 1977 and related agreements (as described in section 3(a) of the Panama Canal Act of 1979); and

(7) "Foreign Service of the United States" means the Foreign Service as constituted under the Foreign Service Act of 1980.

(Pub. L. 89–554, Sept. 6, 1966, 80 Stat. 500; Pub. L. 97–258, § 3(a)(14), Sept. 13, 1982, 96 Stat. 1063; Pub. L. 105–264, § 6(1), Oct. 19, 1998, 112 Stat. 2356.)

HISTORICAL AND REVISION NOTES

The section is based on sections 18 and 19 of the Act of Aug. 2, 1946, ch. 744, 60 Stat. 811, 812. Sections 18 and 19 of the Act of Aug. 2, 1946, are omitted from this title and transferred to other titles of the United States Code since such sections apply also to sections 9, 11, and 16(a) of the Act of Aug. 2, 1946, which sections appear in titles 31 and 41 of the United States Code.

Standard changes are made to conform with the definitions applicable and the style of this title as outlined in the preface to the report.

REFERENCES IN TEXT

Section 3(a) of the Panama Canal Act of 1979, referred to in par. (6), is classified to section 3602(a) of Title 22, Foreign Relations and Intercourse.

The Foreign Service Act of 1980, referred to in par. (7), is Pub. L. 96–465, Oct. 17, 1980, 94 Stat. 2071, as amended, which is classified principally to chapter 52

(§ 3901 et seq.) of Title 22, Foreign Relations and Intercourse. For complete classification of this Act to the Code, see Short Title note set out under section 3901 of Title 22 and Tables.

AMENDMENTS

1998—Pars. (6), (7). Pub. L. 105–264 added pars. (6) and (7).

1982—Par. (5). Pub. L. 97–258 substituted "section 9104" for "section 849".

SECTION REFERRED TO IN OTHER SECTIONS

This section is referred to in sections 302, 503, 3109, 5734, 5913 of this title; title 26 section 912; title 42 section 8241.

§ 5722. Travel and transportation expenses of new appointees; posts of duty outside the continental United States

(a) Under regulations prescribed under section 5738 of this title and subject to subsections (b) and (c) of this section, an agency may pay from its appropriations—

(1) travel expenses of a new appointee and transportation expenses of his immediate family and his household goods and personal effects from the place of actual residence at the time of appointment to the place of employment outside the continental United States;

(2) these expenses on the return of an employee from his post of duty outside the continental United States to the place of his actual residence at the time of assignment to duty outside the continental United States; and

(3) the expenses of transporting a privately owned motor vehicle as authorized under section 5727(c) of this title.

(b) An agency may pay expenses under subsection (a)(1) of this section only after the individual selected for appointment agrees in writing to remain in the Government service for a minimum period of—

(1) one school year as determined under chapter 25 of title 20, if selected for appointment to a teaching position, except as a substitute, in the Department of Defense under that chapter; or

(2) 12 months after his appointment, if selected for appointment to any other position;

unless separated for reasons beyond his control which are acceptable to the agency concerned. If the individual violates the agreement, the money spent by the Government for the expenses is recoverable from the individual as a debt due the Government.

(c) An agency may pay expenses under subsection (a)(2) of this section only after the individual has served for a minimum period of—

(1) one school year as determined under chapter 25 of title 20, if employed in a teaching position, except as a substitute, in the Department of Defense under that chapter; or

(2) not less than one nor more than 3 years prescribed in advance by the head of the agency, if employed in any other position;

unless separated for reasons beyond his control which are acceptable to the agency concerned. These expenses are payable whether the separation is for Government purposes or for personal convenience.

(d) This section does not apply to appropriations for the Foreign Service of the United States.

(Pub. L. 89–554, Sept. 6, 1966, 80 Stat. 501; Pub. L. 104–201, div. A, title XVII, §§ 1715(b)(1), 1723(b)(1), Sept. 23, 1996, 110 Stat. 2755, 2759; Pub. L. 105–264, § 6(2), Oct. 19, 1998, 112 Stat. 2356.)

HISTORICAL AND REVISION NOTES

Derivation	U.S. Code	Revised Statutes and Statutes at Large
....	5 U.S.C. 73b–3(a) (less 3d–6th proviso).	Aug. 2, 1946, ch. 744, § 7, 60 Stat. 808. Sept. 23, 1950, ch. 1010, § 2, 64 Stat. 985. Aug. 30, 1961, Pub. L. 87–172, § 2, 75 Stat. 409.

In subsections (b)(1) and (c)(1), the words "under chapter 25 of title 20" are substituted for "under the Defense Department Overseas Teachers Pay and Personnel Practices Act" to reflect the scheduled transfer of that Act from chapter 34 of title 5 to chapter 25 of title 20.

Standard changes are made to conform with the definitions applicable and the style of this title as outlined in the preface to the report.

AMENDMENTS

1998—Subsec. (a)(2). Pub. L. 105–264, § 6(2)(A), substituted "continental United States;" for "United States;".

Subsec. (b). Pub. L. 105–264, § 6(2)(B), substituted "Government" for "United States" in two places in concluding provisions.

1996—Subsec. (a). Pub. L. 104–201, § 1723(b)(1), in introductory provisions, substituted "Under regulations prescribed under section 5738 of this title" for "Under such regulations as the President may prescribe".

Subsec. (a)(3). Pub. L. 104–201, § 1715(b)(1), added par. (3).

EFFECTIVE DATE OF 1996 AMENDMENT

Section 1725(a) of title XVII of div. A of Pub. L. 104–201 provided that: "The amendments made by this title [enacting sections 5737, 5738, and 5756 of this title, amending this section, sections 3375, 5723 to 5724c, 5726 to 5729, and 5731 of this title, section 1348 of Title 31, Money and Finance, section 707 of Title 38, Veterans' Benefits, and sections 290aa and 299c–1 of Title 42, The Public Health and Welfare] shall take effect 180 days after the date of the enactment of this Act [Sept. 23, 1996]."

REGULATIONS

Section 1725(b) of title XVII of div. A of Pub. L. 104–201 provided that: "The Administrator of General Services shall, not later than the effective date set forth under subsection (a) [set out above], issue final regulations implementing the amendments made by this title [see Effective Date of 1996 Amendment note above]."

ASSESSMENT OF COST SAVINGS

Section 1724 of title XVII of div. A of Pub. L. 104–201 directed Comptroller General, not later than one year after the effective date set forth in section 1725(a) of Pub. L. 104–201, to submit to Congress an assessment of costs of Federal travel administration that were saved as a result of the amendments made by title XVII of div. A of Pub. L. 104–201 and the regulations prescribed to carry out the amendments.

SECTION REFERRED TO IN OTHER SECTIONS

This section is referred to in sections 5724, 5726, 5727 of this title.

§ 5723. Travel and transportation expenses of new appointees and student trainees

(a) Under regulations prescribed under section 5738 of this title and subject to subsections (b) and (c) of this section, an agency may pay from its appropriations—

(1) travel expenses (A) of a new appointee, or a student trainee when assigned on completion of college work, to any position, (B) of a new appointee to the Senior Executive Service or the Federal Bureau of Investigation and Drug Enforcement Administration Senior Executive Service, or (C) of any person appointed by the President to a position the rate of pay for which is equal to or higher than the minimum rate of pay payable for a position classified above GS–15 pursuant to section 5108;

(2) transportation expenses of his immediate family and his household goods and personal effects to the extent authorized by section 5724 of this title; and

(3) the expenses of transporting a privately owned motor vehicle as authorized under section 5727(c) of this title;

from his place of residence at the time of selection or assignment to his duty station. If the travel and transportation expenses of a student trainee were paid when he was appointed, they may not be paid when he is assigned after completion of college work. Travel expenses payable under this subsection may include the per diem and mileage allowances authorized for employees by subchapter I of this chapter. Advances of funds may be made for the expenses authorized by this subsection to the extent authorized by section 5724(f) of this title. In the case of an appointee described in paragraph (1) who has performed transition activities under section 3 of the Presidential Transition Act of 1963 (3 U.S.C. 102 note), the provisions of paragraphs (1) and (2) may apply to travel and transportation expenses from the place of residence of such appointee (at the time of relocation following the most recent general elections held to determine the electors of the President) to the assigned duty station of such appointee.

(b) An agency may pay travel and transportation expenses under subsection (a) of this section only after the individual selected or assigned agrees in writing to remain in the Government service for 12 months after his appointment or assignment, unless separated for reasons beyond his control which are acceptable to the agency concerned. If the individual violates the agreement, the money spent by the Government for the expenses is recoverable from the individual as a debt due the Government.

(c) An agency may pay travel and transportation expenses under subsection (a) of this section whether or not the individual selected has been appointed at the time of the travel. In the case of an appointee described in subsection (a)(1) who has performed transition activities under section 3 of the Presidential Transition Act of 1963 (3 U.S.C. 102 note), the travel or transportation shall take place at any time after the most recent general elections held to determine the electors of the President.

(d) This section does not impair or otherwise affect the authority of an agency under existing statute to pay travel and transportation expenses of individuals named by subsection (a) of this section.

(Pub. L. 89–554, Sept. 6, 1966, 80 Stat. 502; Pub. L. 95–454, title III, § 305, title IV, § 409(a), title IX, § 906(a)(2), (3), Oct. 13, 1978, 92 Stat. 1147, 1173, 1224; Pub. L. 98–151, § 118(a)(1), Nov. 14, 1983, 97 Stat. 977; Pub. L. 98–473, title I, § 120(a), Oct. 12, 1984, 98 Stat. 1968; Pub. L. 100–325, § 2(j), May 30, 1988, 102 Stat. 582; Pub. L. 100–398, § 6, Aug. 17, 1988, 102 Stat. 987; Pub. L. 101–509, title V, § 529 [title II, § 206(b)], Nov. 5, 1990, 104 Stat. 1427, 1457; Pub. L. 102–378, § 2(48), Oct. 2, 1992, 106 Stat. 1353; Pub. L. 104–201, div. A, title XVII, §§ 1715(b)(2), 1723(b)(1), Sept. 23, 1996, 110 Stat. 2755, 2759; Pub. L. 105–264, § 6(3), Oct. 19, 1998, 112 Stat. 2356.)

HISTORICAL AND REVISION NOTES

Derivation	U.S. Code	Revised Statutes and Statutes at Large
....	5 U.S.C. 73b–3 (less (a)).	Aug. 25, 1958, Pub. L. 85–749, 72 Stat. 843. July 5, 1960, Pub. L. 86–587, § 1, 74 Stat. 327. Oct. 16, 1963, Pub. L. 88–146, 77 Stat. 252.

Standard changes are made to conform with the definitions applicable and the style of this title as outlined in the preface to the report.

REFERENCES IN TEXT

Section 3 of the Presidential Transition Act of 1963, referred to in subsecs. (a) and (c), is section 3 of Pub. L. 88–277, which is set out as a note under section 102 of Title 3, The President.

AMENDMENTS

1998—Subsec. (b). Pub. L. 105–264 substituted "spent by the Government" for "spent by the United States" and "due the Government" for "due the United States".

1996—Subsec. (a). Pub. L. 104–201, § 1723(b)(1), in introductory provisions, substituted "Under regulations prescribed under section 5738 of this title" for "Under such regulations as the President may prescribe".

Subsec. (a)(3). Pub. L. 104–201, § 1715(b)(2), which directed amendment of subsec. (a) by adding par. (3) at the end, was executed by adding par. (3) after par. (2) to reflect the probable intent of Congress.

1992—Pub. L. 102–378, § 2(48)(A), struck out "; manpower shortage positions" after "trainees" in section catchline.

Subsecs. (d), (e). Pub. L. 102–378, § 2(48)(B), redesignated subsec. (e) as (d) and struck out former subsec. (d) which authorized Office to delegate its authority to determine positions for which there was a manpower shortage for purposes of this section.

1990—Subsec. (a)(1)(A). Pub. L. 101–509, § 529 [title II, § 206(b)(1)], substituted "any position" for "a position in the United States for which the Office of Personnel Management determines there is a manpower shortage".

Subsec. (a)(1)(C). Pub. L. 101–509, § 529 [title II, § 206(b)(2)], substituted "the minimum rate of pay payable for a position classified above GS–15 pursuant to section 5108; and" for "the minimum rate of pay prescribed for GS–16; and".

1988—Subsec. (a). Pub. L. 100–398, § 6(2), inserted at end "In the case of an appointee described in paragraph (1) who has performed transition activities under section 3 of the Presidential Transition Act of 1963 (3 U.S.C. 102 note), the provisions of paragraphs (1) and (2) may apply to travel and transportation expenses from the place of residence of such appointee (at the time of relocation following the most recent general elections held to determine the electors of the President) to the assigned duty station of such appointee."

Subsec. (a)(1). Pub. L. 100–398, § 6(1), which directed that par. (1) be amended by striking out "or (B)" and inserting "or (C)", could not be executed because phrase "or (B)" did not appear in par. (1) after the intervening amendment by Pub. L. 100–325, see below.

Pub. L. 100–325 inserted reference to Federal Bureau of Investigation and Drug Enforcement Administration Senior Executive Service in cl. (B) and redesignated a second cl. (B) as (C).

Subsec. (c). Pub. L. 100–398, § 6(3), inserted at end "In the case of an appointee described in subsection (a)(1) who has performed transition activities under section 3 of the Presidential Transition Act of 1963 (3 U.S.C. 102 note), the travel or transportation shall take place at any time after the most recent general elections held to determine the electors of the President."

1984—Subsec. (a)(1). Pub. L. 98–473 directed amendment of subpar. (C) by striking out ", by and with the advice and consent of the Senate," which was executed to second subpar. (B) by striking out that phrase following "appointed by the President", as probable intent of Congress.

1983—Subsec. (a)(1). Pub. L. 98–151, designated existing provisions as subpars. (A) and (B), and added a second subpar. (B) relating to any person appointed by President.

1978—Subsec. (a)(1). Pub. L. 95–454, § 906(a)(2), substituted "Office of Personnel Management" for "Civil Service Commission".

Pub. L. 95–454, § 409(a), inserted reference to a new appointee to the Senior Executive Service.

Subsec. (d). Pub. L. 95–454, §§ 305, 906(a)(3), struck out "not" before "delegate", and substituted "Office" for "Commission".

EFFECTIVE DATE OF 1996 AMENDMENT

Amendment by Pub. L. 104–201 effective 180 days after Sept. 23, 1996, see section 1725(a) of Pub. L. 104–201, set out as a note under section 5722 of this title.

EFFECTIVE DATE OF 1990 AMENDMENT

Amendment by Pub. L. 101–509 effective on such date as the President shall determine, but not earlier than 90 days, and not later than 180 days, after Nov. 5, 1990, see section 529 [title III, § 305] of Pub. L. 101–509, set out as a note under section 5301 of this title.

EFFECTIVE DATE OF 1983 AMENDMENT; REGULATIONS

Amendment by Pub. L. 98–151 and promulgation of regulations for amendments by Pub. L. 98–151 effective Nov. 14, 1983, see section 118(c) of Pub. L. 98–151, set out as a note under section 5724 of this title.

EFFECTIVE DATE OF 1978 AMENDMENT

Amendment by sections 305 and 906(a)(2), (3) of Pub. L. 95–454 effective 90 days after Oct. 13, 1978, see section 907 of Pub. L. 95–454, set out as a note under section 1101 of this title.

Amendment by section 409(a) of Pub. L. 95–454 effective 9 months after Oct. 13, 1978, and congressional review of provisions of sections 401 through 412 of Pub. L. 95–454, see section 415 of Pub. L. 95–454, set out as an Effective Date note under section 3131 of this title.

FUNDING OF AMENDMENTS BY PUB. L. 98–151

Amendments by Pub. L. 98–151 to be carried out by agencies by use of funds appropriated or otherwise available for administrative expenses of such agencies, and do not authorize appropriation of funds in amounts exceeding sums already authorized to be appropriated for such agencies, see section 118(b) of Pub. L. 98–151, set out as a note under section 5724 of this title.

SECTION REFERRED TO IN OTHER SECTIONS

This section is referred to in sections 5726, 5727, 9504 of this title; title 28 section 530; title 42 sections 1873, 7238.

§ 5724. Travel and transportation expenses of employees transferred; advancement of funds; reimbursement on commuted basis

(a) Under regulations prescribed under section 5738 of this title and when the head of the agency concerned or his designee authorizes or approves, the agency shall pay from Government funds—

(1) the travel expenses of an employee transferred in the interest of the Government from one official station or agency to another for permanent duty, and the transportation expenses of his immediate family, or a commutation thereof under section 5704 of this title;

(2) the expenses of transporting, packing, crating, temporarily storing, draying, and unpacking his household goods and personal effects not in excess of 18,000 pounds net weight; and

(3) upon the separation (or death in service) of a career appointee, as defined in section 3132(a)(4) of this title, the travel expenses of that individual (if applicable), the transportation expenses of the immediate family of such individual, and the expenses of moving (including transporting, packing, crating, temporarily storing, draying, and unpacking) the household goods of such individual and personal effects not in excess of eighteen thousand pounds net weight, to the place where the individual will reside (or, in the case of a career appointee who dies in service or who dies after separating but before the travel, transportation, and moving is completed, to the place where the family will reside) within the United States, if such individual—

(A) during or after the five years preceding eligibility to receive an annuity under subchapter III of chapter 83, or of chapter 84 of this title, has been transferred in the interest of the Government from one official station to another for permanent duty as a career appointee in the Senior Executive Service or as a director under section 4103(a)(8) of title 38 (as in effect on November 17, 1988); and

(B) is eligible to receive an annuity upon such separation (or, in the case of death in service, met the requirements for being considered eligible to receive an annuity, as of date of death) under the provisions of subchapter III of chapter 83 or chapter 84 of this title.

(b) Under regulations prescribed under section 5738 of this title, an employee who transports a house trailer or mobile dwelling inside the continental United States, inside Alaska, or between the continental United States and Alaska, for use as a residence, and who otherwise would be entitled to transportation of household goods and personal effects under subsection (a) of this section, is entitled, instead of that transportation, to—

(1) a reasonable allowance for transportation of the house trailer or mobile dwelling, if the trailer or dwelling is transported by the employee; or

(2) commercial transportation of the house trailer or mobile dwelling, at Government expense, or reimbursement to the employee therefor, including the payment of necessary tolls, charges, and permit fees, if the trailer or dwelling is not transported by the employee.

However, payment under this subsection may not exceed the maximum payment to which the employee otherwise would be entitled under subsection (a) of this section for transportation and temporary storage of his household goods and personal effects in connection with this transfer.

(c) Under regulations prescribed under section 5738 of this title, an employee who transfers between points inside the continental United States, instead of being paid for the actual expenses of transporting, packing, crating, temporarily storing, draying, and unpacking of household goods and personal effects, shall be reimbursed on a commuted basis at the rates per 100 pounds that are fixed by zones in the regulations. The reimbursement may not exceed the amount which would be allowable for the authorized weight allowance. However, under regulations prescribed under section 5738 of this title, payment of actual expenses may be made when the head of the agency determines that payment of actual expenses is more economical to the Government.

(d) When an employee transfers to a post of duty outside the continental United States, his expenses of travel and transportation to and from the post shall be allowed to the same extent and with the same limitations prescribed for a new appointee under section 5722 of this title.

(e) When an employee transfers from one agency to another, the agency to which he transfers pays the expenses authorized by this section. However, under regulations prescribed under section 5738 of this title, in a transfer from one agency to another because of a reduction in force or transfer of function, expenses authorized by this section and sections 5726(b) and 5727 of this title (other than expenses authorized in connection with a transfer to a foreign country) and by section 5724a(a) through (f) of this title may be paid in whole or in part by the agency from which the employee transfers or by the agency to which he transfers, as may be agreed on by the heads of the agencies concerned.

(f) An advance of funds may be made to an employee under regulations prescribed under section 5738 of this title with the same safeguards required under section 5705 of this title.

(g) The allowances authorized by this section do not apply to an employee transferred under the Foreign Service Act of 1980.

(h) When a transfer is made primarily for the convenience or benefit of an employee, including an employee in the Foreign Service of the United States, or at his request, his expenses of travel and transportation and the expenses of transporting, packing, crating, temporarily storing, draying, and unpacking of household goods and personal effects may not be allowed or paid from Government funds.

(i) An agency may pay travel and transportation expenses (including storage of household goods and personal effects) and other relocation allowances under this section and sections 5724a, 5724b, and 5726(c) of this title when an employee is transferred within the continental United States only after the employee agrees in writing to remain in the Government service for 12 months after his transfer, unless separated for reasons beyond his control that are acceptable to the agency concerned. If the employee violates the agreement, the money spent by the Government for the expenses and allowances is recoverable from the employee as a debt due the Government.

(j) The regulations prescribed under this section shall provide that the reassignment or transfer of any employee, for permanent duty, from one official station or agency to another which is outside the employee's commuting area shall take effect only after the employee has been given advance notice for a reasonable period. Emergency circumstances shall be taken into account in determining whether the period of advance notice is reasonable.

(Pub. L. 89–554, Sept. 6, 1966, 80 Stat. 502; Pub. L. 90–83, § 1(36), Sept. 11, 1967, 81 Stat. 204; Pub. L. 90–623, § 1(14), Oct. 22, 1968, 82 Stat. 1313; Pub. L. 96–465, title II, § 2314(d), Oct. 17 1980, 94 Stat. 2168; Pub. L. 98–151, § 118(a)(2)–(4), (7)(B), Nov. 14, 1983, 97 Stat. 977, 979; Pub. L. 100–440, title VI, § 629(a), Sept. 22, 1988, 102 Stat. 1758; Pub. L. 100–566, § 3, Oct. 31, 1988, 102 Stat. 2845; Pub. L. 102–378, § 2(49), Oct. 2, 1992, 106 Stat. 1353; Pub. L. 103–338, §§ 3(a), 4, Oct. 6, 1994, 108 Stat. 3114; Pub. L. 104–201, div. A, title XVII, § 1723(a)(1)(B), (b)(1), (2), Sept. 23, 1996, 110 Stat. 2759; Pub. L. 105–85, div. C, title XXXV, § 3550(c)(1), Nov. 18, 1997, 111 Stat. 2074; Pub. L. 105–264, § 6(4), Oct. 19, 1998, 112 Stat. 2356.)

HISTORICAL AND REVISION NOTES
1966 ACT

Derivation	U.S. Code	Revised Statutes and Statutes at Large
....	5 U.S.C. 73b–1(a), (b).	Aug. 2, 1946, ch. 744, § 1(a), (b), 60 Stat. 806. Sept. 23, 1950, ch. 1010, §§ 1(a), (b), 3(b), 64 Stat. 985, 986. Feb. 12, 1958, Pub. L. 85–326, 72 Stat. 14. Sept. 6, 1960, Pub. L. 86–707, § 301(c)(1), 74 Stat. 796. Oct. 9, 1962, Pub. L. 87–776, 76 Stat. 777.

In subsections (a)(1) and (f), the words "section 5704 of this title" and "section 5705 of this title", respectively, are substituted for "the Act of February 14, 1931 (5 U.S.C. 73a)" and "the Subsistence Expense Act of 1926 (5 U.S.C. 828)", respectively, on authority of sections 4, 5, and 9(a) of the Travel Expense Act of 1949, as amended, which are carried into sections 5704, 5705, and 5708.

Standard changes are made to conform with the definitions applicable and the style of this title as outlined in the preface to the report.

1967 ACT

Section of title 5	Source (U.S. Code)	Source (Statutes at Large)
5724(a)(2) ...	5 App.: 73b–1(a).	July 21, 1966, Pub. L. 89–516, § 1(a), 80 Stat. 323.
5724(c)	5 App.: 73b–1(b).	July 21, 1966, Pub. L. 89–516, § 1(b), 80 Stat. 323.
5724(e)	5 App.: 73b–4d.	July 21, 1966, Pub. L. 89–516, § 2 "Sec. 26", 80 Stat. 324.
5724(i)	5 App.: 73b–4f.	July 21, 1966, Pub. L. 89–516, § 2 "Sec. 28", 80 Stat. 325.

Subsection (a)(1), (3) of section 1 of the act of July 21, 1966, was effected in the codification of 5 U.S.C.

5724(a)(1), (f); accordingly, no further amendments to 5 U.S.C. 5724 are necessary.

In subsection (e), the word "However" is substituted for "and notwithstanding the provisions of the fourth proviso of section 1(a) of this Act" to reflect the codification of that proviso in 5 U.S.C. 5724(e). The words "agency" and "agencies" are substituted for "department" and "departments", respectively, to conform to the definition in 5 U.S.C. 5721(1). The words "this section and sections 5726(b) and 5727 of this title" and "section 5724a (a), (b) of this title" are substituted for "section 1, subsections (a) and (b) and subsections (e) and (f)" and "sections 23 and 24 of this Act", respectively, to reflect the codification of the cited sections in 5 U.S.C. The word "employee" is substituted for "officer or employee" to conform to the definitions in 5 U.S.C. 5721(2) and 2105.

In subsection (i), the words "An agency may pay * * * expenses * * * and allowances under this section and sections 5724a and 5726(c) of this title * * * only after" are substituted for "Notwithstanding the provisions of subsections (a) and (b) of section 1, and of sections 23, 24, 25, and 27 of this Act, the * * * expenses * * * and * * * allowances shall not be allowed thereunder * * * unless and until" for clarity and to conform to the style of 5 U.S.C., and to reflect the codification of the cited sections in 5 U.S.C. The word "employee" is substituted for "civilian officer or employee" and "such officer or employee" to conform to the definitions in 5 U.S.C. 5721(2) and 2105. The words "continental United States" are substituted for "continental United States, excluding Alaska" to conform to the definition in 5 U.S.C. 5721(3). The word "agency" is substituted for "department or agency" to conform to the definition in 5 U.S.C. 5721(1). In the last sentence, the words "money spent by the United States for the expenses and allowances" are substituted for "moneys expended by the United States under said sections of this act on account of such officer or employee."

REFERENCES IN TEXT

Section 4103 of title 38, referred to in subsec. (a)(3)(A), was repealed by Pub. L. 102–40, title IV, § 401(a)(3), May 7, 1991, 105 Stat. 210. See section 7306 of Title 38, Veterans' Benefits.

The Foreign Service Act of 1980, referred to in subsec. (g), is Pub. L. 96–465, Oct. 17, 1980, 94 Stat. 2071, which is classified principally to chapter 52 (§ 3901 et seq.) of Title 22, Foreign Relations and Intercourse. For complete classification of this Act to the Code, see Short Title note set out under section 3901 of Title 22 and Tables.

AMENDMENTS

1998—Subsec. (a)(3). Pub. L. 105–264, § 6(4)(A), struck out ", its territories or possessions, the Commonwealth of Puerto Rico, or the areas and installations in the Republic of Panama made available to the United States pursuant to the Panama Canal Treaty of 1977 and related agreements, as described in section 3(a) of the Panama Canal Act of 1979" after "United States".

Subsec. (i). Pub. L. 105–264, § 6(4)(B), substituted "Government" for "United States" in two places in last sentence.

1997—Subsec. (a)(3). Pub. L. 105–85, which directed the substitution of "or the Commonwealth of Puerto Rico" for ", the Commonwealth of Puerto Rico, or the areas and installations in the Republic of Panama made available to the United States pursuant to the Panama Canal Treaty of 1977 and related agreements, as described in section 3(a) of the Panama Canal Act of 1979", effective Jan. 1, 1999, could not be executed because such language did not appear in text subsequent to amendment by Pub. L. 105–264. See 1998 Amendment note above.

1996—Subsecs. (a), (b). Pub. L. 104–201, § 1723(b)(1), in introductory provisions, substituted "Under regulations prescribed under section 5738 of this title" for "Under such regulations as the President may prescribe".

Subsec. (c). Pub. L. 104–201, § 1723(b)(2)(A), substituted "under regulations prescribed under section 5738 of this title" for "under regulations prescribed by the President".

Pub. L. 104–201, § 1723(b)(1), substituted "Under regulations prescribed under section 5738 of this title" for "Under such regulations as the President may prescribe".

Subsec. (e). Pub. L. 104–201, § 1723(b)(2)(A), substituted "under regulations prescribed under section 5738 of this title" for "under regulations prescribed by the President".

Pub. L. 104–201, § 1723(a)(1)(B), substituted "section 5724a(a) through (f)" for "section 5724a(a), (b)".

Subsec. (f). Pub. L. 104–201, § 1723(b)(2)(B), substituted "under regulations prescribed under section 5738 of this title" for "under the regulations of the President".

1994—Subsec. (a)(3). Pub. L. 103–338, § 4, amended par. (3) generally. Prior to amendment, par. (3) read as follows: "upon the separation of a career appointee (as defined in section 3132(a)(4) of this title), the travel expenses of that individual, the transportation expenses of the immediate family of such individual, and the expenses of moving (including transporting, packing, crating, temporarily storing, draying, and unpacking) the household goods of such individual and personal effects not in excess of eighteen thousand pounds net weight, to the place where the individual will reside within the United States, its territories or possessions, the Commonwealth of Puerto Rico, or the areas and installations in the Republic of Panama made available to the United States pursuant to the Panama Canal Treaty of 1977 and related agreements, as described in section 3(a) of the Panama Canal Act of 1979 (or, if the individual dies before the travel, transportation, and moving is completed, to the place where the family will reside) if such individual—

"(A) during or after the five years preceding eligibility to receive an annuity under subchapter III of chapter 83, or of chapter 84 of this title, has been transferred in the interest of the Government from one official station to another for permanent duty as a career appointee in the Senior Executive Service or as a director under section 4103(a)(8) of title 38 (as in effect on November 17, 1988); and

"(B) is eligible to receive an annuity upon such separation under the provisions of subchapter III of chapter 83 or chapter 84 of this title."

Subsec. (a)(3)(A). Pub. L. 103–338, § 3(a), substituted "November 17, 1988" for "November 27, 1988".

1992—Subsec. (a)(3)(A). Pub. L. 102–378 substituted "Service or as a director under section 4103(a)(8) of title 38 (as in effect on November 27, 1988)" for "Service".

1988—Subsec. (a)(3). Pub. L. 100–440 added par. (3).

Subsec. (a)(3)(A). Pub. L. 100–566 substituted "during or after the five" for "during the five" and struck out ", and thereafter" after "of this title".

1983—Subsec. (a)(2). Pub. L. 98–151, § 118(a)(2), substituted "18,000" for "11,000".

Subsec. (b)(1). Pub. L. 98–151, § 118(a)(3), struck out "not in excess of 20 cents a mile" after "allowance".

Subsec. (i). Pub. L. 98–151, § 118(a)(7)(B), inserted reference to section 5724b of this title.

Subsec. (j). Pub. L. 98–151, § 118(a)(4), added subsec. (j).

1980—Subsec. (g). Pub. L. 96–465 substituted "the Foreign Service Act of 1980" for "chapter 14 of title 22".

1968—Subsec. (e). Pub. L. 90–623 substituted "section 5724a(a), (b)" for "section 5724a(a), (b)".

EFFECTIVE DATE OF 1997 AMENDMENT

Section 3550(c)(3) of Pub. L. 105–85 provided that: "The amendments made by this subsection [amending this section and section 5724a of this title] shall take effect on January 1, 1999."

EFFECTIVE DATE OF 1996 AMENDMENT

Amendment by Pub. L. 104–201 effective 180 days after Sept. 23, 1996, see section 1725(a) of Pub. L. 104–201, set out as a note under section 5722 of this title.

EFFECTIVE DATE OF 1994 AMENDMENT

Section 3(b) of Pub. L. 103–338 provided that: "The amendment made by subsection (a) [amending this section] shall take effect as if included in the Technical and Miscellaneous Civil Service Amendments Act of 1992 (Public Law 102–378; 106 Stat. 1346; 5 U.S.C. 1101 note)."

Section 5(a) of Pub. L. 103–338 provided that: "This Act [amending this section and enacting provisions set out as notes under this section] and the amendment made by this Act shall take effect on October 1, 1994, or, if later, the date of the enactment of this Act [Oct. 6, 1994]."

EFFECTIVE DATE OF 1992 AMENDMENT

Amendment by Pub. L. 102–378 applicable with respect to a separation that takes effect on or after Oct. 2, 1992, see section 9(b)(11) of Pub. L. 102–378, set out as a note under section 6303 of this title.

EFFECTIVE DATE OF 1983 AMENDMENT; PROMULGATION OF REGULATIONS

Section 118(c) of Pub. L. 98–151 provided that:

"(1) The amendments made by subsection (a) [enacting sections 5724b and 5724c of this title and amending this section and sections 5723, 5724a, and 5726 of this title] shall take effect on the date of the enactment of this joint resolution [Nov. 14, 1983]."

"(2) Not later than thirty days after the date of the enactment of this joint resolution, the President shall prescribe the regulations required under the amendments made by subsection (a). Such regulations shall take effect as of such date of enactment."

EFFECTIVE DATE OF 1980 AMENDMENT

Amendment by Pub. L. 96–465 effective Feb. 15, 1981, except as otherwise provided, see section 2403 of Pub. L. 96–465, set out as an Effective Date note under section 3901 of Title 22, Foreign Relations and Intercourse.

EFFECTIVE DATE OF 1968 AMENDMENT

Amendment by Pub. L. 90–623 effective as of Sept. 11, 1967, for all purposes, see section 6 of Pub. L. 90–623, set out as a note under section 5334 of this title.

MOVING EXPENSES FOR FAMILY OF CAREER APPOINTEES DYING IN SERVICE BETWEEN JANUARY 1, 1994, AND OCTOBER 6, 1994

Section 5(b) of Pub. L. 103–338 provided that:

"(1) IN GENERAL.—Under regulations prescribed by the President or his designee, an agency shall, as appropriate, pay or make reimbursement for any moving expenses which would be payable under the provisions of section 5724(a)(3) of title 5, United States Code, as amended by section 4 (but which would not have been payable under such provisions, as last in effect before being so amended).

"(2) APPLICABILITY.—The moving expenses to which this subsection applies are those incurred by the family of an individual who died—

"(i) before separating from Government service; and

"(ii) during the period beginning on January 1, 1994, and ending on the effective date of this Act [Oct. 6, 1994].

"(3) CONDITION.—Payment or reimbursement under this subsection may not be made except upon appropriate written application submitted within 12 months after the date on which the regulations referred to in paragraph (1) take effect."

FUNDING OF AMENDMENTS BY PUB. L. 100–440

Section 629(b) of Pub. L. 100–440 provided that: "The amendments made by subsection (a) [amending this section] shall be carried out by agencies by the use of funds appropriated or otherwise available for the administrative expenses of each of such respective agencies. The amendments made by such subsection do not authorize the appropriation of funds in amounts exceeding the sums otherwise authorized to be appropriated for such agencies."

FUNDING OF AMENDMENTS BY PUB. L. 98–151

Section 118(b) of Pub. L. 98–151 provided that: "The amendments made by subsection (a) [enacting sections 5724b and 5724c of this title and amending this section and sections 5723, 5724a, and 5726 of this title] shall be carried out by agencies by the use of funds appropriated or otherwise available for the administrative expenses of each of such respective agencies. The amendments made by such subsection do not authorize the appropriation of funds in amounts exceeding the sums already authorized to be appropriated for such agencies."

RATES OF REIMBURSEMENT

Administrator of General Services empowered to prescribe regulations relating to establishment of rates used in reimbursing civilian officers or employees of Government on a commuted basis in lieu of payment of actual expenses of transportation, etc., of their household goods and personal effects upon transfer from one official station to another, see Ex. Ord. No. 11012, Mar. 28, 1962, 27 F.R. 2983, set out as a note under section 301 of Title 3, The President.

SECTION REFERRED TO IN OTHER SECTIONS

This section is referred to in sections 3375, 4109, 5723, 5724a, 5724b, 5726, 5737 of this title; title 16 section 3378; title 42 sections 290aa, 299c–5; title 50 section 403e.

§ 5724a. Relocation expenses of employees transferred or reemployed

(a) Under regulations prescribed under section 5738, an agency shall pay to or on behalf of an employee who transfers in the interest of the Government, a per diem allowance or the actual subsistence expenses, or a combination thereof, of the immediate family of the employee for en route travel of the immediate family between the employee's old and new official stations.

(b)(1) Under regulations prescribed under section 5738, an agency may pay to or on behalf of an employee who transfers in the interest of the Government between official stations located within the United States—

   (A) the expenses of transportation of the employee and the employee's spouse for travel to seek permanent residence quarters at a new official station; and

   (B) either—

      (i) a per diem allowance or the actual subsistence expenses (or a combination of both); or

      (ii) an amount for subsistence expenses, that may not exceed a maximum amount determined by the Administrator of General Services.

(2) Expenses may be allowed under paragraph (1) only for one round trip in connection with each change of station of the employee.

(c)(1) Under regulations prescribed under section 5738, an agency may pay to or on behalf of an employee who transfers in the interest of the Government—

   (A) actual subsistence expenses of the employee and the employee's immediate family for a period of up to 60 days while the employee or family is occupying temporary quarters when the new official station is located within the United States; or

   (B) an amount for subsistence expenses, that may not exceed a maximum amount determined by the Administrator of General Services, instead of the actual subsistence expenses authorized in subparagraph (A) of this paragraph.

(2) The period authorized in paragraph (1) of this subsection for payment of expenses for residence in temporary quarters may be extended up to an additional 60 days if the head of the agency concerned or the designee of such head of the agency determines that there are compelling reasons for the continued occupancy of temporary quarters.

(3) The regulations implementing paragraph (1)(A) shall prescribe daily rates and amounts for subsistence expenses per individual.

(d)(1) Under regulations prescribed under section 5738, an agency shall pay to or on behalf of an employee who transfers in the interest of the Government, expenses of the sale of the residence (or the settlement of an unexpired lease) of the employee at the old official station and purchase of a residence at the new official station that are required to be paid by the employee, when the old and new official stations are located within the United States.

(2) Under regulations prescribed under section 5738, an agency shall pay to or on behalf of an employee who transfers in the interest of the Government from a post of duty located outside the United States to an official station within the United States (other than the official station within the United States from which the employee was transferred when assigned to the foreign tour of duty)—

   (A) expenses required to be paid by the employee of the sale of the residence (or the settlement of an unexpired lease) of the employee at the old official station from which the employee was transferred when the employee was assigned to the post of duty located outside the United States; and

   (B) expenses required to be paid by the employee of the purchase of a residence at the new official station within the United States.

(3) Reimbursement of expenses under paragraph (2) of this subsection shall not be allowed for any sale (or settlement of an unexpired lease) or purchase transaction that occurs prior to official notification that the employee's return to the United States would be to an official station other than the official station from which the employee was transferred when assigned to the post of duty outside the United States.

(4) Reimbursement for brokerage fees on the sale of the residence and other expenses under this subsection may not exceed those customarily charged in the locality where the residence is located.

(5) Reimbursement may not be made under this subsection for losses incurred by the employee on the sale of the residence.

(6) This subsection applies regardless of whether title to the residence or the unexpired lease is—

   (A) in the name of the employee alone;

   (B) in the joint names of the employee and a member of the employee's immediate family; or

(C) in the name of a member of the employee's immediate family alone.

(7)(A) In connection with the sale of the residence at the old official station, reimbursement under this subsection shall not exceed 10 percent of the sale price.

(B) In connection with the purchase of a residence at the new official station, reimbursement under this subsection shall not exceed 5 percent of the purchase price.

(8) Under regulations prescribed under section 5738, an agency may pay to or on behalf of an employee who transfers in the interest of the Government expenses of property management services, instead of expenses under paragraph (1) or (2) of this subsection for sale of the employee's residence, when the agency determines that such transfer is advantageous and cost-effective for the Government.

(e) Under regulations prescribed under section 5738, an agency may pay to or on behalf of an employee who transfers in the interest of the Government, the expenses of property management services when the employee transfers to a post of duty outside the United States. Such payment shall terminate upon return of the employee to an official station within the United States.

(f)(1) Under regulations prescribed under section 5738 and subject to paragraph (2), an employee who is reimbursed under subsections (a) through (e) of this section or section 5724(a) of this title is entitled to an amount for miscellaneous expenses—

(A) not to exceed two weeks' basic pay, if such employee has an immediate family; or

(B) not to exceed one week's basic pay, if such employee does not have an immediate family.

(2) Amounts paid under paragraph (1) may not exceed amounts determined at the maximum rate payable for a position at GS–13 of the General Schedule.

(g) A former employee separated by reason of reduction in force or transfer of function who within one year after the separation is reemployed by a nontemporary appointment at a different geographical location from that where the separation occurred, may be allowed and paid the expenses authorized by sections 5724, 5725, 5726(b), and 5727 of this title, and may receive the benefits authorized by subsections (a) through (f) of this section, in the same manner as though the employee had been transferred in the interest of the Government without a break in service to the location of reemployment from the location where separated.

(h) Payments for subsistence expenses, including amounts in lieu of per diem or actual subsistence expenses or a combination thereof, authorized under this section may not exceed the maximum payment allowed under regulations which implement section 5702 of this title.

(Added Pub. L. 90–83, § 1(37)(A), Sept. 11, 1967, 81 Stat. 204; amended Pub. L. 96–70, title I, § 1231(d), Sept. 27, 1979, 93 Stat. 470; Pub. L. 98–151, § 118(a)(5), (6), Nov. 14, 1983, 97 Stat. 977, 978; Pub. L. 99–234, title I, § 105, Jan. 2, 1986, 99 Stat. 1758; Pub. L. 100–202, § 101(m) [title VI, § 628(a)(1)], Dec. 22, 1987, 101 Stat. 1329–390, 1329–430; Pub. L.

101–510, div. A, title XII, § 1206(c), Nov. 5, 1990, 104 Stat. 1661; Pub. L. 104–201, div. A, title XVII, §§ 1711–1713(a), 1714, 1718, Sept. 23, 1996, 110 Stat. 2753–2755, 2757; Pub. L. 105–85, div. C, title XXXV, § 3550(c)(2), Nov. 18, 1997, 111 Stat. 2074; Pub. L. 105–264, §§ 6(5), 7, Oct. 19, 1998, 112 Stat. 2356, 2357.)

HISTORICAL AND REVISION NOTES

Section of title 5	Source (U.S. Code)	Source (Statutes at Large)
5724a(a)	5 App.: 73b–4a.	July 21, 1966, Pub. L. 89–516, § 2 "Sec. 23", 80 Stat. 323.
5724a(b)	5 App.: 73b–4b.	July 21, 1966, Pub. L. 89–516, § 2 "Sec. 24", 80 Stat. 324.
5724a(c)	5 App.: 73b–4e.	July 21, 1966, Pub. L. 89–516, § 2 "Sec. 27", 80 Stat. 325.

In subsection (a), the word "agency" is substituted for "department" to conform to the definition in 5 U.S.C. 5721(1). The word "employee" is substituted for "officers or employees" and "officer or employee" to conform to the definitions in 5 U.S.C. 5721(2) and 2105. The words "section 5724(a) of this title" and "section 5702 of this title" are substituted for "subsection (a) of section 1 of this Act" and "section 3 of the Travel Expense Act of 1949 (63 Stat. 166, as amended; 5 U.S.C. 836)" to reflect the codification of the cited acts in 5 U.S.C. In subsection (a)(2), the words "within the continental United States" are coextensive with and substituted for "within the continental United States, excluding Alaska" on authority of the definition of "continental United States" in 5 U.S.C. 5721(3).

In subsection (b), the words "this subchapter" and "subsection (a) of this section or section 5724(a) of this title" are substituted for "this Act" and "section 1(a) or section 23 of this Act", respectively, to reflect the codification of the act in 5 U.S.C. The word "officer" is omitted as included in "employee". The words "in the General Schedule of the Classification Act of 1949, as amended" are omitted as unnecessary.

In subsection (c), the word "officer" is omitted as included in "employee". The words "sections 5724, 5725, 5726(b), and 5727 of this title" and "subsections (a) and (b) of this section" are substituted for "section 1 of this Act" and "sections 23 and 24 of this Act", respectively, to reflect the codification of the act in title 5, United States Code.

REFERENCES IN TEXT

The General Schedule, referred to in subsec. (f)(2), is set out under section 5332 of this title.

AMENDMENTS

1998—Subsec. (a). Pub. L. 105–264, § 7(1), substituted "Under regulations prescribed under section 5738, an agency shall pay" for "An agency shall pay".

Subsec. (b)(1). Pub. L. 105–264, § 7(2), substituted "Under regulations prescribed under section 5738, an agency may pay" for "An agency may pay" in introductory provisions.

Subsec. (b)(1)(B)(ii). Pub. L. 105–264, § 7(3), amended cl. (ii) generally. Prior to amendment, cl. (ii) read as follows: "an amount for subsistence expenses."

Subsec. (c)(1). Pub. L. 105–264, § 7(2), substituted "Under regulations prescribed under section 5738, an agency may pay" for "An agency may pay" in introductory provisions.

Subsec. (c)(1)(B). Pub. L. 105–264, § 7(4), substituted "an amount for subsistence expenses, that may not exceed a maximum amount determined by the Administrator of General Services," for "an amount for subsistence expenses".

Subsec. (d)(1), (2). Pub. L. 105–264, § 7(1), substituted "Under regulations prescribed under section 5738, an agency shall pay" for "An agency shall pay".

Subsec. (d)(2)(A). Pub. L. 105–264, § 7(5), substituted "of the sale" for "for the sale".

Subsec. (d)(2)(B). Pub. L. 105–264, §7(6), substituted "of the purchase" for "for the purchase".

Subsec. (d)(8). Pub. L. 105–264, §7(2), (7), substituted "Under regulations prescribed under section 5738, an agency may pay" for "An agency may pay" and "paragraph (1) or (2)" for "paragraph (2) or (3)".

Subsec. (e). Pub. L. 105–264, §7(2), substituted "Under regulations prescribed under section 5738, an agency may pay" for "An agency may pay".

Subsec. (f)(1). Pub. L. 105–264, §7(8), substituted "Under regulations prescribed under section 5738 and subject to paragraph (2)," for "Subject to paragraph (2)," in introductory provisions.

Subsec. (i). Pub. L. 105–264, §7(9), struck out subsec. (i) which read as follows: "Subsections (a), (b), and (c) shall be implemented under regulations issued under section 5738 of this title."

Subsec. (j). Pub. L. 105–264, §6(5), struck out subsec. (j) which read as follows: "For purposes of subsections (c), (d), and (e), the term 'United States' includes the District of Columbia, the Commonwealth of Puerto Rico, the Commonwealth of the Northern Mariana Islands, the territories and possessions of the United States, and the areas and installations in the Republic of Panama that are made available to the United States pursuant to the Panama Canal Treaty of 1977 and related agreements (as described in section 3(a) of the Panama Canal Act of 1979 (22 U.S.C. 3602(a)))."

1997—Subsec. (j). Pub. L. 105–85, which directed the amendment of subsec. (j) by inserting "and" after "Northern Mariana Islands," and by substituting "United States." for "United States, and the areas and installations in the Republic of Panama that are made available to the United States pursuant to the Panama Canal Treaty of 1977 and related agreements (as described in section 3(a) of the Panama Canal Act of 1979 (22 U.S.C. 3602(a))).", effective Jan. 1, 1999, could not be executed because subsec. (j) did not appear subsequent to amendment by Pub. L. 105–264. See 1998 Amendment note above.

1996—Pub. L. 104–201, §1711, amended section generally, substituting subsecs. (a) and (b) for former subsecs. (a) to (c) which made funds available to pay certain expenses of employees for whom Government pays travel and transportation expenses under section 5724(a) of this title, provided for entitlement to certain amounts of basic pay to such employees, and provided for payment of expenses of certain former employees.

Subsec. (c). Pub. L. 104–201, §1712, added subsec. (c).

Subsec. (d). Pub. L. 104–201, §1713(a), added subsec. (d).

Subsec. (d)(8). Pub. L. 104–201, §1714(1), added par. (8).

Subsec. (e). Pub. L. 104–201, §1714(2), added subsec. (e).

Subsecs. (f) to (j). Pub. L. 104–201, §1718, added subsecs. (f) to (j).

1990—Subsec. (a)(2). Pub. L. 101–510 struck out "continental" before "United States" in second sentence.

1987—Subsec. (a)(4)(A). Pub. L. 100–202 inserted provisions authorizing reimbursement of expenses of selling residence of employee at official station from which employee was transferred when assigned to duty outside United States, its territories or possessions, Puerto Rico, or parts of Panama, provisions authorizing reimbursement of expenses of purchasing residence at new official station in United States, its territories or possessions, Puerto Rico, or parts of Panama, and provisions disallowing reimbursement of expenses in connection with transfers from a post of duty located outside the United States, its territories or possessions, Puerto Rico, or parts of Panama, for any transaction that occurs prior to official notification that employee's return to the United States would be to official station other than official station from which employee was transferred.

1986—Subsec. (a)(1). Pub. L. 99–234, §105(1), (2), substituted "allowance or" for "allowance instead of" and "maximum payment permitted under regulations which implement section 5702 of this title" for "maximum per diem rates prescribed by or under section 5702 of this title".

Subsec. (a)(2). Pub. L. 99–234, §105(1), (2), substituted "allowance or" for "allowance instead of" and "maxi-

mum payment permitted under regulations which implement section 5702 of this title" for "maximum per diem rates prescribed by or under section 5702 of this title".

Subsec. (a)(3). Pub. L. 99–234, §105(2), (3), substituted "maximum payment permitted under regulations which implement section 5702 of this title" for "maximum per diem rates prescribed by or under section 5702 of this title" and "daily rates and amounts" for "average daily rates".

1983—Subsec. (a)(3). Pub. L. 98–151, §118(a)(5)(A), in first sentence substituted "60 days" for "30 days".

Pub. L. 98–151, §118(a)(5)(B), substituted provisions authorizing extension for an additional 60 days if agency head or designee determines existence of compelling reasons for continued occupancy, for provisions authorizing extension for an additional 30 days if the employee moves to or from Alaska, Hawaii, the territories or possessions, etc., and struck out provisions relating to additional limitations on daily rates for reimbursement for subsistence expenses.

Subsec. (a)(4). Pub. L. 98–151, §118(a)(6), redesignated existing provisions as subpar. (A) and added subpar. (B).

1979—Subsec. (a)(3), (4). Pub. L. 96–70 substituted in pars. (3) and (4) "areas and installations in the Republic of Panama made available to the United States pursuant to the Panama Canal Treaty of 1977 and related agreements (as described in section 3(a) of the Panama Canal Act of 1979)" for "Canal Zone" wherever appearing.

EFFECTIVE DATE OF 1997 AMENDMENT

Amendment by Pub. L. 105–85 effective Jan. 1, 1999, see section 3550(c)(3) of Pub. L. 105–85, set out as a note under section 5724 of this title.

EFFECTIVE DATE OF 1996 AMENDMENT

Amendment by Pub. L. 104–201 effective 180 days after Sept. 23, 1996, see section 1725(a) of Pub. L. 104–201, set out as a note under section 5722 of this title.

EFFECTIVE DATE OF 1987 AMENDMENT

Section 101(m) [title VI, §628(a)(2)] of Pub. L. 100–202 provided that: "The amendments made by paragraph (2) [probably means par. (1) which amended this section] shall be applicable with respect to any employee transferred to or from a post of duty on or after 60 days after the date of enactment of this section [Dec. 22, 1987]."

EFFECTIVE DATE OF 1986 AMENDMENT

Amendment by Pub. L. 99–234 effective (1) on effective date of regulations to be promulgated not later than 150 days after Jan. 2, 1986, or (2) 180 days after Jan. 2, 1986, whichever occurs first, see section 301(a) of Pub. L. 99–234, set out as a note under section 5701 of this title.

EFFECTIVE DATE OF 1983 AMENDMENT; PROMULGATION OF REGULATIONS

Amendment by Pub. L. 98–151 and promulgation of regulations for amendments by Pub. L. 98–151 effective Nov. 14, 1983, see section 118(c) of Pub. L. 98–151, set out as a note under section 5724 of this title.

EFFECTIVE DATE OF 1979 AMENDMENT

Amendment by Pub. L. 96–70 effective Oct. 1, 1979, see section 3304 of Pub. L. 96–70, set out as an Effective Date note under section 3601 of Title 22, Foreign Relations and Intercourse.

EXTENSION OF PAYMENT OF RELOCATION EXPENSES TO PUERTO RICO, NORTHERN MARIANA ISLANDS, AND TERRITORIES AND POSSESSIONS OF THE UNITED STATES

Pub. L. 105–277, div. A, §101(b) [title I, §125], Oct. 21, 1998, 112 Stat. 2681–50, 2681–74, provided that: "Effective with the enactment of this Act [Oct. 21, 1998], and in any fiscal year hereafter, the Attorney General and the Secretary of the Treasury may, for their respective agencies, extend the payment of relocation expenses listed in section 5724a(b)(1) of Title 5 of the United States Code to include the Commonwealth of Puerto Rico, the Commonwealth of the Northern Mariana Islands, and the territories and possessions of the United States.''

FUNDING OF AMENDMENTS BY PUB. L. 98–151

Amendments by Pub. L. 98–151 to be carried out be agencies by use of funds appropriated or otherwise available for administrative expenses of such agencies, and do not authorize appropriation of funds in amounts exceeding sums already authorized to be appropriated for such agencies, see section 118(b) of Pub. L. 98–151, set out as a note under section 5724 of this title.

SECTION REFERRED TO IN OTHER SECTIONS

This section is referred to in sections 3375, 5724, 5724b, 5737, 9504 of this title; title 22 section 3691; title 38 section 707; title 42 sections 290aa, 299c–5; title 50 section 403e.

§ 5724b. Taxes on reimbursements for travel, transportation, and relocation expenses of employees transferred

(a) Under regulations prescribed under section 5738 of this title and to the extent considered necessary and appropriate, as provided therein, appropriations or other funds available to an agency for administrative expenses are available for the reimbursement of substantially all of the Federal, State, and local income taxes incurred by an employee, or by an employee and such employee's spouse (if filing jointly), for any moving or storage expenses furnished in kind, or for which reimbursement or an allowance is provided (but only to the extent of the expenses paid or incurred). Reimbursements under this subsection shall also include an amount equal to all income taxes for which the employee and spouse, as the case may be,[1] would be liable due to the reimbursement for the taxes referred to in the first sentence of this subsection.

(b) For the purposes of this section, ''moving or storage expenses'' means travel and transportation expenses (including storage of household goods and personal effects under section 5724 of this title) and other relocation expenses under sections 5724a and 5724c of this title.

(Added Pub. L. 98–151, § 118(a)(7)(A)(i), Nov. 14, 1983, 97 Stat. 978; amended Pub. L. 98–473, title I, § 120(b), Oct. 12, 1984, 98 Stat. 1969; Pub. L. 104–201, div. A, title XVII, § 1723(b)(1), Sept. 23, 1996, 110 Stat. 2759.)

CODIFICATION

Prior to amendment by Pub. L. 98–473, the words ''as the case may be'' were preceded by ''the employee, or the employee and spouse,''.

AMENDMENTS

1996—Subsec. (a). Pub. L. 104–201 substituted ''Under regulations prescribed under section 5738 of this title'' for ''Under such regulations as the President may prescribe''.

1984—Pub. L. 98–473 amended section generally, substituting ''reimbursement of substantially all of the Federal, State, and local income taxes'' for ''reimbursement of all or part of the Federal, State, and city income taxes'' and ''for which the employee and spouse, as the case may be'' for ''for which the employee, or the

employee and spouse, as the case may be'' in subsec. (a) and ''5724c'' for ''5726(c)'' in subsec. (b).

EFFECTIVE DATE OF 1996 AMENDMENT

Amendment by Pub. L. 104–201 effective 180 days after Sept. 23, 1996, see section 1725(a) of Pub. L. 104–201, set out as a note under section 5722 of this title.

EFFECTIVE DATE; PROMULGATION OF REGULATIONS

Enactment by Pub. L. 98–151 and promulgation of regulations for amendments by Pub. L. 98–151 effective Nov. 14, 1983, see section 118(c) of Pub. L. 98–151, set out as an Effective Date of 1983 Amendment; Promulgation of Regulations note under section 5724 of this title.

FUNDING OF AMENDMENTS BY PUB. L. 98–151

Amendments by Pub. L. 98–151 to be carried out by agencies by use of funds appropriated or otherwise available for administrative expenses of such agencies, and do not authorize appropriation of funds in amounts exceeding sums already authorized to be appropriated for such agencies, see section 118(b) of Pub. L. 98–151, set out as a note under section 5724 of this title.

SECTION REFERRED TO IN OTHER SECTIONS

This section is referred to in sections 5724, 5737, 5738 of this title.

§ 5724c. Relocation services

Under regulations prescribed under section 5738 of this title, each agency may enter into contracts to provide relocation services to agencies and employees for the purpose of carrying out this subchapter. An agency may pay a fee for such services. Such services include arranging for the purchase of a transferred employee's residence.

(Added Pub. L. 98–151, § 118(a)(7)(A)(i), Nov. 14, 1983, 97 Stat. 978; amended Pub. L. 98–473, title I, § 120(b), Oct. 12, 1984, 98 Stat. 1969; Pub. L. 104–201, div. A, title XVII, § 1713(b), Sept. 23, 1996, 110 Stat. 2754.)

AMENDMENTS

1996—Pub. L. 104–201 amended section generally. Prior to amendment, section read as follows: ''Under such regulations as the President may prescribe, each agency is authorized to enter into contracts to provide relocation services to agencies and employees for the purpose of carrying out the provisions of this subchapter. Such services include but need not be limited to arranging for the purchase of a transferred employee's residence.''

1984—Pub. L. 98–473 amended section generally, adding authority of the President to prescribe regulations.

EFFECTIVE DATE OF 1996 AMENDMENT

Amendment by Pub. L. 104–201 effective 180 days after Sept. 23, 1996, see section 1725(a) of Pub. L. 104–201, set out as a note under section 5722 of this title.

EFFECTIVE DATE; PROMULGATION OF REGULATIONS

Enactment by Pub. L. 98–151 and promulgation of regulations for amendments by Pub. L. 98–151 effective Nov. 14, 1983, see section 118(c) of Pub. L. 98–151, set out as an Effective Date of 1983 Amendment; Promulgation of Regulations note under section 5724 of this title.

FUNDING OF AMENDMENTS BY PUB. L. 98–151

Amendments by Pub. L. 98–151 to be carried out by agencies by use of funds appropriated or otherwise available for administrative expenses of such agencies, and do not authorize appropriation of funds in amounts exceeding sums already authorized to be appropriated for such agencies, see section 118(b) of Pub. L. 98–151, set out as a note under section 5724 of this title.

[1] See Codification note below.

SECTION REFERRED TO IN OTHER SECTIONS

This section is referred to in sections 5724b, 5756 of this title.

§ 5725. Transportation expenses; employees assigned to danger areas

(a) When an employee of the Government is on duty, or is transferred or assigned to duty, at a place designated by the head of the agency concerned as inside a zone—

(1) from which his immediate family should be evacuated; or

(2) to which they are not permitted to accompany him;

because of military or other reasons which create imminent danger to life or property, or adverse living conditions which seriously affect the health, safety, or accommodations of the immediate family, Government funds may be used to transport his immediate family and household goods and personal effects, under regulations prescribed by the head of the agency, to a location designated by the employee. When circumstances prevent the employee from designating a location, or it is administratively impracticable to determine his intent, the immediate family may designate the location. When the designated location is inside a zone to which movement of families is prohibited under this subsection, the employee or his immediate family may designate an alternate location.

(b) When the employee is assigned to a duty station from which his immediate family is not excluded by the restrictions in subsection (a) of this section, Government funds may be used to transport his immediate family and household goods and personal effects from the designated or alternate location to the duty station.

(Pub. L. 89–554, Sept. 6, 1966, 80 Stat. 503; Pub. L. 105–264, § 6(6), Oct. 19, 1998, 112 Stat. 2356.)

HISTORICAL AND REVISION NOTES

Derivation	U.S. Code	Revised Statutes and Statutes at Large
....	5 U.S.C. 73b–1(d).	Sept. 23, 1960, ch. 1010, § 1(c), 64 Stat. 985.

The word "employee" is substituted for "civilian officers and employees" in view of the definition of "employee" in sections 5721 and 2105.

Standard changes are made to conform with the definitions applicable and the style of this title as outlined in the preface to the report.

AMENDMENTS

1998—Subsec. (a). Pub. L. 105–264 substituted "Government" for "United States" in introductory provisions.

SECTION REFERRED TO IN OTHER SECTIONS

This section is referred to in section 5724a of this title.

§ 5726. Storage expenses; household goods and personal effects

(a) For the purpose of subsection (b) of this section, "household goods and personal effects" means such personal property of an employee and his dependents as authorized under regulations prescribed under section 5738 of this title to be transported or stored, including, in emergencies, motor vehicles authorized to be shipped at Government expense.

(b) Under regulations prescribed under section 5738 of this title, an employee, including a new appointee and a student trainee to the extent authorized by sections 5722 and 5723 of this title, assigned to a permanent duty station outside the continental United States may be allowed storage expenses and related transportation and other expenses for his household goods and personal effects when—

(1) the duty station is one to which he cannot take or at which he is unable to use his household goods and personal effects; or

(2) the head of the agency concerned authorizes storage of the household goods and personal effects in the public interest or for reasons of economy.

The weight of the household goods and personal effects stored under this subsection, together with the weight of property transported under section 5724(a), may not exceed 18,000 pounds net weight, excluding a motor vehicle described by subsection (a) of this section.

(c) Under regulations prescribed under section 5738 of this title, when an employee, including a new appointee and a student trainee to the extent authorized by section 5723 of this title, is assigned to a permanent duty station at an isolated location in the continental United States to which he cannot take or at which he is unable to use his household goods and personal effects because of the absence of residence quarters at the location, nontemporary storage expenses or storage at Government expense in Government-owned facilities (including related transportation and other expenses), whichever is more economical, may be allowed the employee under regulations prescribed by the head of the agency concerned. The weight of property stored under this subsection, together with the weight of property transported under sections 5723(a) and 5724(a) of this title, may not exceed the total maximum weight the employee would be entitled to have moved. The period of nontemporary storage under this subsection may not exceed 3 years.

(Pub. L. 89–554, Sept. 6, 1966, 80 Stat. 504; Pub. L. 90–83, § 1(38), Sept. 11, 1967, 81 Stat. 205; Pub. L. 98–151, § 118(a)(2), Nov. 14, 1983, 97 Stat. 977; Pub. L. 104–201, div. A, title XVII, § 1723(b)(1), (3), Sept. 23, 1996, 110 Stat. 2759.)

HISTORICAL AND REVISION NOTES
1966 ACT

Derivation	U.S. Code	Revised Statutes and Statutes at Large
....	5 U.S.C. 73b–1(e).	Sept. 6, 1960, Pub. L. 86–707, § 301(c)(2), (d) (as applicable to the Administrative Expenses Act of 1946, as amended), 74 Stat. 796.

The word "employee" is substituted for "civilian officer or employee" in view of the definition of "employee" in sections 5721 and 2105.

In subsection (b), the words "including a new appointee and a student trainee to the extent authorized by sections 5722 and 5723 of this title" are substituted for "including any new appointee in accordance with section 73b–3 of this title" for clarity and reflect the codification of former section 73b–3 in this title.

Standard changes are made to conform with the definitions applicable and the style of this title as outlined in the preface to the report.

1967 ACT

Section of title 5	Source (U.S. Code)	Source (Statutes at Large)
5726(c)	5 App.: 73b–4c.	July 21, 1966, Pub. L. 89–516, § 2 "Sec. 25", 80 Stat. 324.

The amendment of subsection (a) of 5 U.S.C. 5726 reflects the addition of a new subsection (c).

Subsection (b) of 5 U.S.C. 5726 was derived from subsection (e) of section 1 of the Administrative Expenses Act of 1946, as amended (74 Stat. 796). In the codification of subsection (e), the words "7,000 pounds net weight" were substituted for "the maximum weight limitation provided by subsection (a)". During the pendency of the codification bill, section 1(a)(2) of Public Law 89–516, amended subsection (a) of section 1 of the Administrative Expenses Act of 1946 to increase the maximum weight limitation from 7,000 to 11,000 pounds. Thus, the amendment of subsection (b) is necessary to reflect the current weight limitation applicable.

In subsection (c), the word "employee" is substituted for "civilian officer or employee" to conform to the definitions in 5 U.S.C. 5721(2) and 2105. The words "including a new appointee and a student trainee to the extent authorized by section 5723 of this title" are substituted for "including any new appointee in accordance with section 7(b) of this Act, as amended" for clarity and to reflect the codification of section 7(b) in 5 U.S.C. 5723. The words "continental United States" are coextensive with and substituted for "continental United States, excluding Alaska" on authority of the definition of "continental United States" in 5 U.S.C. 5721(3). The words "head of the agency concerned" are substituted for "head of the Executive Department or agency concerned" to conform to the definition in 5 U.S.C. 5721(1). In the penultimate sentence, the words "sections 5723(a) and 5724(a) of this title" are substituted for "section 1 or 7(b) of this Act" to reflect the codification of sections 1 and 7(b) in 5 U.S.C. 5723(a) and 5724(a); and the word "officer" is omitted as included in "employee". In the last sentence, the words "under this subsection" are inserted for clarity.

Subsection (b) of section 25 of the Administrative Expenses Act of 1946 (added by section 2 of Public Law 89–516) is omitted as executed.

AMENDMENTS

1996—Subsec. (a). Pub. L. 104–201, § 1723(b)(3), substituted "as authorized under regulations prescribed under section 5738 of this title" for "as the President may by regulation authorize".

Subsecs. (b), (c). Pub. L. 104–201, § 1723(b)(1), substituted "Under regulations prescribed under section 5738 of this title" for "Under such regulations as the President may prescribe".

1983—Subsec. (b). Pub. L. 98–151 substituted "18,000" for "11,000".

EFFECTIVE DATE OF 1996 AMENDMENT

Amendment by Pub. L. 104–201 effective 180 days after Sept. 23, 1996, see section 1725(a) of Pub. L. 104–201, set out as a note under section 5722 of this title.

EFFECTIVE DATE OF 1983 AMENDMENT; PROMULGATION OF REGULATIONS

Amendment by Pub. L. 98–151 and promulgation of regulations for amendments by Pub. L. 98–151 effective Nov. 14, 1983, see section 118(c) of Pub. L. 98–151, set out as a note under section 5724 of this title.

FUNDING OF AMENDMENTS BY PUB. L. 98–151

Amendments by Pub. L. 98–151 to be carried out by agencies by use of funds appropriated or otherwise available for administrative expenses of such agencies, and do not authorize appropriation of funds in amounts exceeding sums already authorized to be appropriated for such agencies, see section 118(b) of Pub. L. 98–151, set out as a note under section 5724 of this title.

SECTION REFERRED TO IN OTHER SECTIONS

This section is referred to in sections 3735, 5724, 5724a, 5737 of this title; title 26 section 912; title 42 sections 290aa, 299c–5.

§ 5727. Transportation of motor vehicles

(a) Except as specifically authorized by statute, an authorization in a statute or regulation to transport the effects of an employee or other individual at Government expense is not an authorization to transport an automobile.

(b) Under regulations prescribed under section 5738 of this title, the privately owned motor vehicle of an employee, including a new appointee and a student trainee to the extent authorized by sections 5722 and 5723 of this title, may be transported at Government expense to, from, and between the continental United States and a post of duty outside the continental United States, or between posts of duty outside the continental United States, when—

(1) the employee is assigned to the post of duty for other than temporary duty; and

(2) the head of the agency concerned determines that it is in the interest of the Government for the employee to have the use of a motor vehicle at the post of duty.

(c) Under regulations prescribed under section 5738 of this title, the privately owned motor vehicle or vehicles of an employee, including a new appointee or a student trainee for whom travel and transportation expenses are authorized under section 5723 of this title, may be transported at Government expense to a new official station of the employee when the agency determines that such transport is advantageous and cost-effective to the Government.

(d) An employee may transport only one motor vehicle under subsection (b) of this section during a 4-year period, except when the head of the agency concerned determines that replacement of the motor vehicle during the period is necessary for reasons beyond the control of the employee and is in the interest of the Government, and authorizes in advance the transportation under subsection (b) of this section of one additional privately owned motor vehicle as a replacement. When an employee has remained in continuous service outside the continental United States during the 4-year period after the date of transportation under subsection (b) of this section of his motor vehicle, the head of the agency concerned may authorize transportation under subsection (b) of this section of a replacement for that motor vehicle.

(e) When the head of an agency authorizes transportation under subsection (b) or (c) of this section of a privately owned motor vehicle, the transportation may be by—

(1) commercial means, if available at reasonable rates and under reasonable conditions; or

(2) Government means on a space-available basis.

(f)(1) This section, except subsection (a), does not apply to—

(A) the Foreign Service of the United States; or

(B) the Central Intelligence Agency.

(2) This section, except subsection (a), does not affect section 403e(4) of title 50.

(Pub. L. 89–554, Sept. 6, 1966, 80 Stat. 504; Pub. L. 96–465, title II, § 2314(e), Oct. 17, 1980, 94 Stat. 2168; Pub. L. 104–201, div. A, title XVII, §§ 1715(a), 1723(b)(1), Sept. 23, 1996, 110 Stat. 2755, 2759; Pub. L. 105–264, § 6(7), Oct. 19, 1998, 112 Stat. 2356.)

HISTORICAL AND REVISION NOTES

Derivation	U.S. Code	Revised Statutes and Statutes at Large
(a)	5 U.S.C. 73c.	June 30, 1932, ch. 314, § 209, 47 Stat. 405. Apr. 30, 1940, ch. 172, 54 Stat. 174. Aug. 13, 1946, ch. 957, § 1131(64), 60 Stat. Stat. 1040.
(b)–(e)	5 U.S.C. 73b–1(f).	Sept. 6, 1960, Pub. L. 86–707, § 321, 74 Stat. 797. Feb. 5, 1964, Pub. L. 88–266, 78 Stat. 8.

In subsection (a), the proviso in former section 73c is omitted as superseded by section 2634 of title 10, and by former section 73b–1(f), which is carried into subsections (b)–(e).

In subsection (b), the words "including a new appointee and a student trainee to the extent authorized by sections 5722 and 5723 of this title" are substituted for "including any new appointee, in accordance with section 73b–3 of this title" for clarity and reflect the codification of former section 73b–3 in this title. The words "at Government expense" are inserted for clarity.

The last sentence of subsection (f) of former section 73b–1 which provided that for the purposes of that subsection and subsection (e), which is carried into section 5726, Alaska shall be considered to be outside the continental limits of the United States is omitted as unnecessary in view of the definition of "continental United States" in section 5721(4).

Standard changes are made to conform with the definitions applicable and the style of this title as outlined in the preface to the report.

AMENDMENTS

1998—Subsec. (d). Pub. L. 105–264 substituted "continental United States" for "United States".

1996—Subsec. (b). Pub. L. 104–201, § 1723(b)(1), in introductory provisions, substituted "Under regulations prescribed under section 5738 of this title" for "Under such regulations as the President may prescribe".

Subsec. (c). Pub. L. 104–201, § 1715(a)(2), added subsec. (c). Former subsec. (c) redesignated (d).

Subsec. (d). Pub. L. 104–201, § 1715(a)(1), redesignated subsec. (c) as (d). Former subsec. (d) redesignated (e).

Subsec. (e). Pub. L. 104–201, § 1715(a)(3), inserted "or (c)" after "subsection (b)".

Pub. L. 104–201, § 1715(a)(1), redesignated subsec. (d) as (e). Former subsec. (e) redesignated (f).

Subsec. (f). Pub. L. 104–201, § 1715(a)(1), redesignated subsec. (e) as (f).

1980—Subsec. (e)(2). Pub. L. 96–465 substituted "section 403e(4) of title 50" for "(A) section 1138 of title 22; or" and struck out "(B) section 403e(4) of title 50".

EFFECTIVE DATE OF 1996 AMENDMENT

Amendment by Pub. L. 104–201 effective 180 days after Sept. 23, 1996, see section 1725(a) of Pub. L. 104–201, set out as a note under section 5722 of this title.

EFFECTIVE DATE OF 1980 AMENDMENT

Amendment by Pub. L. 96–465 effective Feb. 15, 1981, except as otherwise provided, see section 2403 of Pub. L.

96–465, set out as an Effective Date note under section 3901 of Title 22, Foreign Relations and Intercourse.

SECTION REFERRED TO IN OTHER SECTIONS

This section is referred to in sections 5722, 5723, 5724, 5724a, 5737 of this title; title 26 section 912.

§ 5728. Travel and transportation expenses; vacation leave

(a) Under regulations prescribed under section 5738 of this title, an agency shall pay from its appropriations the expenses of round-trip travel of an employee, and the transportation of his immediate family, but not household goods, from his post of duty outside the continental United States, Alaska, and Hawaii to the place of his actual residence at the time of appointment or transfer to the post of duty, after he has satisfactorily completed an agreed period of service outside the continental United States, Alaska, and Hawaii and is returning to his actual place of residence to take leave before serving another tour of duty at the same or another post of duty outside the continental United States, Alaska, and Hawaii under a new written agreement made before departing from the post of duty.

(b) Under regulations prescribed under section 5738 of this title, an agency shall pay from its appropriations the expenses of round-trip travel of an employee of the Government appointed by the President, by and with the advice and consent of the Senate, for a term fixed by statute, and of transportation of his immediate family, but not household goods, from his post of duty outside the continental United States, Alaska, and Hawaii to the place of his actual residence at the time of appointment to the post of duty, after he has satisfactorily completed each 2 years of service outside the continental United States, Alaska, and Hawaii and is returning to his actual place of residence to take leave before serving at least 2 more years of duty outside the continental United States, Alaska, and Hawaii.

(c)(1) Under regulations prescribed under section 5738 of this title, an agency may pay, subject to paragraph (3) of this subsection, the expenses described in paragraph (2) of this subsection in any case in which the head of the agency determines that the payment of such expenses is necessary for the purpose of recruiting or retaining an employee for service of a tour of duty at a post of duty in Alaska or Hawaii.

(2) The expenses payable under paragraph (1) of this subsection are the expenses of round-trip travel of an employee, and the transportation of his immediate family, but not household goods, from his post of duty in Alaska or Hawaii to the place of his actual residence at the time of appointment or transfer to the post of duty, incurred after he has satisfactorily completed an agreed period of service in Alaska or Hawaii and in returning to his actual place of residence to take leave before serving another tour of duty at the same or another post of duty in Alaska or Hawaii under a new written agreement made before departing from the post of duty.

(3) The payment of expenses of any employee and the transportation of his family under paragraph (1) of this subsection is limited to the expenses of travel and transportation incurred for

not more than two round trips commenced within 5 years after the date the employee first commences any period of consecutive tours of duty in Alaska or Hawaii.

(d) This section does not apply to appropriations for the Foreign Service of the United States.

(Pub. L. 89–554, Sept. 6, 1966, 80 Stat. 505; Pub. L. 97–253, title III, § 351(a), (b), Sept. 8, 1982, 96 Stat. 800; Pub. L. 104–201, div. A, title XVII, § 1723(b)(1), Sept. 23, 1996, 110 Stat. 2759; Pub. L. 105–264, § 6(8), Oct. 19, 1998, 112 Stat. 2356.)

HISTORICAL AND REVISION NOTES

Derivation	U.S. Code	Revised Statutes and Statutes at Large
(a)	5 U.S.C. 73b–3(a) (3d proviso).	Aug. 31, 1954, ch. 1155 (1st proviso), 68 Stat. 1008.
(b)	5 U.S.C. 73b–3(a) (4th proviso).	Sept. 2, 1958, Pub. L. 85–858, 72 Stat. 1274.

The first 14 words of subsections (a) and (b), and subsection (c), are added on authority of former section 73b–3(a) (less 3d–6th provisos), which is carried into section 5722.

Standard changes are made to conform with the definitions applicable and the style of this title as outlined in the preface to the report.

AMENDMENTS

1998—Subsec. (b). Pub. L. 105–264 substituted "an employee of the Government" for "an employee of the United States".

1996—Subsecs. (a) to (c)(1). Pub. L. 104–201, § 1723(b)(1), substituted "Under regulations prescribed under section 5738 of this title" for "Under such regulations as the President may prescribe".

1982—Subsecs. (a), (b). Pub. L. 97–253, § 351(a), inserted ", Alaska, and Hawaii" after "continental United States" wherever appearing.

Subsecs. (c), (d). Pub. L. 97–253, § 351(b), added subsec. (c) and redesignated former subsec. (c) as (d).

EFFECTIVE DATE OF 1996 AMENDMENT

Amendment by Pub. L. 104–201 effective 180 days after Sept. 23, 1996, see section 1725(a) of Pub. L. 104–201, set out as a note under section 5722 of this title.

EFFECTIVE DATE OF 1982 AMENDMENT

Section 351(c), (d) of Pub. L. 97–253, as amended by Pub. L. 97–346, § 3(m), Oct. 15, 1982, 96 Stat. 1649, provided that:

"(c)(1) Except as provided in paragraph (2), the amendments made by subsection (a) [amending this section] shall take effect with respect to expenses incurred after the date of enactment of this Act [Sept. 8, 1982] for round-trip travel (commenced after such date) of an employee or transportation of his immediate family from his post of duty to the place of his actual residence at the time of appointment or transfer to the post of duty.

"(2) The amendments made by this section [amending this section] shall not apply to any employee who is serving a tour of duty at a post of duty in Alaska or Hawaii on the date of the enactment of this Act [Sept. 8, 1982] during—

"(A) such tour of duty, and

"(B) any other consecutive tour of duty following such tour of duty.

"(d) For the purposes of subsection (c), the term 'employee' shall have the same meaning as provided in section 5721(2) of title 5, United States Code."

§ 5729. Transportation expenses; prior return of family

(a) Under regulations prescribed under section 5738 of this title, an agency shall pay from its appropriations, not more than once before the return to the United States of an employee whose post of duty is outside the continental United States, the expenses of transporting his immediate family and of shipping his household goods and personal effects from his post of duty to his actual place of residence when—

(1) he has acquired eligibility for that transportation; or

(2) the public interest requires the return of the immediate family for compelling personal reasons of a humanitarian or compassionate nature, such as may involve physical or mental health, death of a member of the immediate family, or obligation imposed by authority or circumstances over which the individual has no control.

(b) Under regulations prescribed under section 5738 of this title, an agency shall reimburse from its appropriations an employee whose post of duty is outside the continental United States for the proper transportation expenses of returning his immediate family and his household goods and personal effects to the United States, when—

(1) their return was made at the expense of the employee before his return and for other than reasons of public interest; and

(2) he acquires eligibility for those transportation expenses.

(c) This section does not apply to appropriations for the Foreign Service of the United States.

(Pub. L. 89–554, Sept. 6, 1966, 80 Stat. 505; Pub. L. 104–201, div. A, title XVII, § 1723(b)(1), Sept. 23, 1996, 110 Stat. 2759; Pub. L. 105–264, § 6(9), Oct. 19, 1998, 112 Stat. 2356.)

HISTORICAL AND REVISION NOTES

Derivation	U.S. Code	Revised Statutes and Statutes at Large
....	5 U.S.C. 73b–3(a) (5th and 6th provisos).	Aug. 31, 1954, ch. 1155 (less 1st proviso), 68 Stat. 1008.

The first 14 words of subsections (a) and (b), and subsection (c), are added on authority of former section 73b–3(a) (less 3d–6th provisos), which is carried into section 5722. The words "household effects" and "household goods" in the 5th and 6th provisos of former section 73b–3(a) are changed to "household goods and personal effects" for clarity and consistency in the use of the words elsewhere in this subchapter.

Standard changes are made to conform with the definitions applicable and the style of this title as outlined in the preface to the report.

AMENDMENTS

1998—Subsecs. (a), (b). Pub. L. 105–264 struck out "or its territories or possessions" after "to the United States".

1996—Subsecs. (a), (b). Pub. L. 104–201 substituted "Under regulations prescribed under section 5738 of this title" for "Under such regulations as the President may prescribe".

EFFECTIVE DATE OF 1996 AMENDMENT

Amendment by Pub. L. 104–201 effective 180 days after Sept. 23, 1996, see section 1725(a) of Pub. L. 104–201, set out as a note under section 5722 of this title.

§ 5730. Funds available

Funds available for travel expenses of an employee are available for expenses of transportation of his immediate family, and funds available for transportation of things are available for transportation of household goods and personal effects, as authorized by this subchapter.

(Pub. L. 89–554, Sept. 6, 1966, 80 Stat. 506.)

HISTORICAL AND REVISION NOTES

Derivation	U.S. Code	Revised Statutes and Statutes at Large
....	5 U.S.C. 73b–1(c).	Aug. 2, 1946, ch. 744, §1(c). 60 Stat. 807.

Standard changes are made to conform with the definitions applicable and the style of this title as outlined in the preface to the report.

§ 5731. Expenses limited to lowest first-class rate

(a) The allowance for actual expenses for transportation may not exceed the lowest first-class rate by the transportation facility used unless it is certified, in accordance with regulations prescribed under section 5738 of this title, that—

(1) lowest first-class accommodations are not available; or

(2) use of a compartment or other accommodation authorized or approved by the head of the agency concerned or his designee is required for security purposes.

(b) Instead of the maximum fixed by subsection (a) of this section, the allowance to an employee of the Government for actual expenses for transportation on an inter-island steamship in Hawaii may not exceed the rate for accommodations on the steamship that is equivalent as nearly as possible to the rate for the lowest first-class accommodations on trans-pacific steamships.

(Pub. L. 89–554, Sept. 6, 1966, 80 Stat. 506; Pub. L. 104–201, div. A, title XVII, §1723(b)(4), Sept. 23, 1996, 110 Stat. 2759; Pub. L. 105–264, §6(10), Oct. 19, 1998, 112 Stat. 2356.)

HISTORICAL AND REVISION NOTES

Derivation	U.S. Code	Revised Statutes and Statutes at Large
(a)	5 U.S.C. 73b.	Mar. 3, 1933, ch. 212, §10, 47 Stat. 1516. Aug. 2, 1946, ch. 744, §6, 60 Stat. 808.
(b)	5 U.S.C. 73e.	May 28, 1938, ch. 289, §811, 52 Stat. 577.

In subsection (a), the words "by or under authority of law" are omitted as surplusage.

In subsection (b), the words "by or under authority of law" are omitted as surplusage. The words "after the date of the enactment of this Act" are omitted as obsolete.

Standard changes are made to conform with the definitions applicable and the style of this title as outlined in the preface to the report.

AMENDMENTS

1998—Subsec. (b). Pub. L. 105–264 substituted "Government" for "United States".

1996—Subsec. (a). Pub. L. 104–201 substituted "in accordance with regulations prescribed under section 5738 of this title" for "in accordance with regulations prescribed by the President".

EFFECTIVE DATE OF 1996 AMENDMENT

Amendment by Pub. L. 104–201 effective 180 days after Sept. 23, 1996, see section 1725(a) of Pub. L. 104–201, set out as a note under section 5722 of this title.

SECTION REFERRED TO IN OTHER SECTIONS

This section is referred to in title 2 section 476; title 16 sections 916*l*, 961, 971a, 971b, 2443, 3608, 3641, 5608, 5709; title 22 sections 287e, 287r, 2024; title 42 sections 2477, 4277; title 50 section 403e.

§ 5732. General average contribution; payment or reimbursement

Under such regulations as the President may prescribe, appropriations chargeable for the transportation of baggage and household goods and personal effects of employees of the Government, volunteers as defined by section 8142(a) of this title, and members of the uniformed services are available for the payment or reimbursement of general average contributions required. Appropriations are not available for the payment or reimbursement of general average contributions—

(1) required in connection with and applicable to quantities of baggage and household goods and personal effects in excess of quantities authorized by statute or regulation to be transported;

(2) when the individual concerned is allowed under statute or regulation a commutation instead of actual transportation expenses; or

(3) when the individual concerned selected the means of shipment.

(Pub. L. 89–554, Sept. 6, 1966, 80 Stat. 506; Pub. L. 105–264, §6(11), Oct. 19, 1998, 112 Stat. 2356.)

HISTORICAL AND REVISION NOTES

Derivation	U.S. Code	Revised Statutes and Statutes at Large
....	5 U.S.C. 73b–5.	June 4, 1954, ch. 264, §4, 68 Stat. 176.
....	22 U.S.C. 2504(h) (as applicable to 5 U.S.C. 73b–5).	Dec. 13, 1963, Pub. L. 88–200, §2(e) (as applicable to the Act of June 4, 1954, ch. 264, §4 (5 U.S.C. 73b–5)), 77 Stat. 360.

The word "personal" is added before the word "effects" for clarity and to preserve consistency throughout this subchapter. The words "employees of the United States . . . and members of the uniformed services" are substituted for "military personnel and civilian employees of departments and agencies of the Federal Government". The words "a volunteer as defined by section 8142(a) of this title" are based on sections 2504(a), 2505, and 2507 (a) of title 22. The words "pursuant to law" are omitted as unnecessary.

Standard changes are made to conform with the definitions applicable and the style of this title as outlined in the preface to the report.

AMENDMENTS

1998—Pub. L. 105–264 substituted "Government" for "United States" in introductory provisions.

EX. ORD. NO. 10614. PAYMENT OF GENERAL-AVERAGE CONTRIBUTIONS IN CONNECTION WITH TRANSPORTATION OF EFFECTS

Ex. Ord. No. 10614, May 25, 1955, 20 F.R. 3699, provided:

SECTION 1. *Definitions.* As used in these regulations:

(a) The term "military personnel" means members and former and deceased members of the uniformed services as defined in section 102 of the Career Compensation Act of 1949 (63 Stat. 804) [37 U.S.C. 101].

(b) The term "civilian employees" means civilian officers and employees of a department, including Foreign Service personnel, and former and deceased civilian officers and employees.

(c) The terms "military personnel" and "civilian employees" shall also include those individuals enumerated under the term "person" as defined in section 1 of the Missing Persons Act, as amended [now section 5561 of this title].

(d) The term "department" means an executive department, independent establishment, or other agency of the Federal Government, including wholly-owned or controlled Government corporations.

(e) The term "general-average contribution" means the contribution by all parties to a sea venture (1) to make good the loss sustained by any one of their number on account of voluntary sacrifices made of part of the ship or cargo to save the residue or the lives of those on board from impending peril, or (2) for extraordinary expenses necessarily incurred for the common benefit and safety of all.

(f) The term "household goods" means such baggage, household goods, and effects, including privately-owned automobiles and professional books, papers, and equipment, of military personnel and civilian employees as are authorized to be transported at Government expense by law or regulations pursuant to law.

SEC. 2. *Allowance of general-average contributions.* Whenever military personnel or civilian employees of a department are liable for general-average contributions arising out of shipments of household goods (as defined in section 1 (f) hereof), authorized or approved under law or regulations pursuant to law, disbursements shall be made, under rules and regulations prescribed by the head of the department concerned, from appropriations chargeable for the transportation of baggage and household goods and effects (a) for the payment of the general-average contributions for which such military personnel or civilian employees are liable, or (b) for the reimbursement of such military personnel or civilian employees in the amounts of their general-average liability paid by them and for which receipts are furnished, subject to the limitations set forth in section 3 hereof.

SEC. 3. *Limitations.* The provisions of section 2 hereof shall not apply:

(a) In case the shipment of household goods is made under law or regulation pursuant to law which provides for reimbursement to the military person or civilian employee concerned on a commuted basis in lieu of payment by the Government of the actual costs of the shipment; or

(b) In case the military person or civilian employee concerned has himself selected the means of shipment; or

(c) To quantities of household goods (excluding automobiles) shipped in excess of quantities authorized to be transported by law or regulation pursuant to law. In any case of such excess shipment, the liability of the Government for the employee's general-average contribution shall not exceed the proportion that the applicable limitation, by weight or volume, bears to the total quantity, by weight or volume, of the household goods shipped.

SEC. 4. *Effective date.* This order shall be effective in any case in which the loss involved occurs, or has occurred, on or after June 4, 1954.

DWIGHT D. EISENHOWER.

SECTION REFERRED TO IN OTHER SECTIONS

This section is referred to in title 12 section 1701h; title 22 section 2504.

§ 5733. Expeditious travel

The travel of an employee shall be by the most expeditious means of transportation practicable and shall be commensurate with the nature and purpose of the duties of the employee requiring such travel.

(Added Pub. L. 90–206, title II, § 222(c)(1), Dec. 16, 1967, 81 Stat. 641.)

EFFECTIVE DATE

Section effective thirty days after Dec. 16, 1967, see section 220(a)(4) of Pub. L. 90–206, set out as an Effective Date of 1967 Amendment note under section 5542 of this title.

SECTION REFERRED TO IN OTHER SECTIONS

This section is referred to in title 16 section 2443.

§ 5734. Travel, transportation, and relocation expenses of employees transferred from the Postal Service

Notwithstanding the provisions of any other law, officers and employees of the United States Postal Service promoted or transferred under section 1006 of title 39, United States Code, from the Postal Service to an agency (as defined in section 5721 of this title), for permanent duty may be authorized travel, transportation, and relocation expenses and allowances under the same conditions and to the same extent authorized by this subchapter for other transferred employees within the meaning of this chapter.

(Added Pub. L. 99–234, title I, § 106(a), Jan. 2, 1986, 99 Stat. 1758.)

EFFECTIVE DATE

Section effective (1) on effective date of regulations to be promulgated not later than 150 days after Jan. 2, 1986, or (2) 180 days after Jan. 2, 1986, whichever occurs first, see section 301(a) of Pub. L. 99–234, set out as an Effective Date of 1986 Amendment note under section 5701 of this title.

§ 5735. Travel, transportation, and relocation expenses of employees transferring to the United States Postal Service

(a) IN GENERAL.—Notwithstanding any other provision of law, employees of the Department of Defense described in subsection (b) may be authorized travel, transportation, and relocation expenses and allowances in connection with appointments referred to in such subsection under the same conditions and to the same extent authorized by this subchapter for transferred employees.

(b) COVERED EMPLOYEES.—Subsection (a) applies to any employee of the Department of Defense who—

(1) is scheduled for separation from the Department, other than for cause;

(2) is selected for appointment to a continuing position with the United States Postal Service; and

(3) accepts the appointment.

(Added Pub. L. 103–337, div. A, title III, § 345(a)(1), Oct. 5, 1994, 108 Stat. 2723.)

EFFECTIVE DATE

Section 345(b) of Pub. L. 103–337 provided that: "The amendments made by subsection (a) [enacting this section] shall apply to persons separated from employment with the Department of Defense on or after the date of the enactment of this Act [Oct. 5, 1994]."

SECTION REFERRED TO IN OTHER SECTIONS

This section is referred to in section 5738 of this title.

§ 5736. Travel, transportation, and relocation expenses of certain nonappropriated fund employees

An employee of a nonappropriated fund instrumentality of the Department of Defense or the Coast Guard described in section 2105(c) of this title who moves, without a break in service of more than 3 days, to a position in the Department of Defense or the Coast Guard, respectively, may be authorized travel, transportation, and relocation expenses and allowances under the same conditions and to the same extent authorized by this subchapter for transferred employees.

(Added Pub. L. 104–201, div. A, title XVI, § 1605(a)(1), Sept. 23, 1996, 110 Stat. 2736.)

EFFECTIVE DATE

Section 1605(b) of Pub. L. 104–201 provided that: "Section 5736 of title 5, United States Code (as added by subsection (a)(1)), shall apply to moves between positions as described in such section that are effective on or after October 1, 1996."

§ 5737. Relocation expenses of an employee who is performing an extended assignment

(a) Under regulations prescribed under section 5738 of this title, an agency may pay to or on behalf of an employee assigned from the employee's official station to a duty station for a period of not less than six months and not greater than 30 months, the following expenses in lieu of payment of expenses authorized under subchapter I of this chapter:

(1) Travel expenses to and from the assignment location in accordance with section 5724 of this title.

(2) Transportation expenses of the immediate family and household goods and personal effects to and from the assignment location in accordance with section 5724 of this title.

(3) A per diem allowance for en route travel of the employee's immediate family to and from the assignment location in accordance with section 5724a(a) of this title.

(4) Travel and transportation expenses of the employee and spouse to seek new residence quarters at the assignment location in accordance with section 5724a(b) of this title.

(5) Subsistence expenses of the employee and the employee's immediate family while occupying temporary quarters upon commencement and termination of the assignment in accordance with section 5724a(c) of this title.

(6) An amount, in accordance with section 5724a(f), to be used by the employee for miscellaneous expenses of this title.[1]

(7) The expenses of transporting a privately owned motor vehicle or vehicles to the assignment location in accordance with section 5727 of this title.

(8) An allowance as authorized under section 5724b of this title for Federal, State, and local income taxes incurred on reimbursement of expenses paid under this section or on services provided in kind under this section.

(9) Expenses of nontemporary storage of household goods and personal effects as de-

fined in section 5726(a) of this title, subject to the limitation that the weight of the household goods and personal effects stored, together with the weight of property transported under section 5724(a) of this title, may not exceed the total maximum weight which could be transported in accordance with section 5724(a) of this title.

(10) Expenses of property management services.

(b) An agency shall not make payment under this section to or on behalf of the employee for expenses incurred after termination of the temporary assignment.

(Added Pub. L. 104–201, div. A, title XVII, § 1716, Sept. 23, 1996, 110 Stat. 2756.)

EFFECTIVE DATE

Section effective 180 days after Sept. 23, 1996, see section 1725(a) of Pub. L. 104–201, set out as an Effective Date of 1996 Amendment note under section 5722 of this title.

§ 5738. Regulations

(a)(1) Except as specifically provided in this subchapter, the Administrator of General Services shall prescribe regulations necessary for the administration of this subchapter.

(2) The Administrator of General Services shall include in the regulations authority for the head of an agency or his designee to waive any limitation of this subchapter or in any implementing regulation for any employee relocating to or from a remote or isolated location who would suffer hardship if the limitation were not waived. A waiver of a limitation under authority provided in the regulations pursuant to this paragraph shall be effective notwithstanding any other provision of this subchapter.

(b) In prescribing regulations for the implementation of section 5724b of this title, the Administrator of General Services shall consult with the Secretary of the Treasury.

(c) The Secretary of Defense shall prescribe regulations necessary for the implementation of section 5735 of this title.

(Added Pub. L. 104–201, div. A, title XVII, § 1722, Sept. 23, 1996, 110 Stat. 2758.)

EFFECTIVE DATE

Section effective 180 days after Sept. 23, 1996, see section 1725(a) of Pub. L. 104–201, set out as an Effective Date of 1996 Amendment note under section 5722 of this title.

SECTION REFERRED TO IN OTHER SECTIONS

This section is referred to in sections 5722, 5723, 5724, 5724a, 5724b, 5724c, 5726, 5727, 5728, 5729, 5731, 5737 of this title.

§ 5739. Authority for relocation expenses test programs

(a)(1) Notwithstanding any other provision of this subchapter, under a test program which the Administrator of General Services determines to be in the interest of the Government and approves, an agency may pay through the proper disbursing official for a period not to exceed 24 months any necessary relocation expenses in lieu of any payment otherwise authorized or re-

---

[1] So in original.

quired under this subchapter. An agency shall include in any request to the Administrator for approval of such a test program an analysis of the expected costs and benefits and a set of criteria for evaluating the effectiveness of the program.

(2) Any test program conducted under this section shall be designed to enhance cost savings or other efficiencies that accrue to the Government.

(3) Nothing in this section is intended to limit the authority of any agency to conduct test programs.

(b) The Administrator shall transmit a copy of any test program approved by the Administrator under this section to the appropriate committees of the Congress at least 30 days before the effective date of the program.

(c) An agency authorized to conduct a test program under subsection (a) shall provide to the Administrator and the appropriate committees of the Congress a report on the results of the program no later than 3 months after completion of the program.

(d) No more than 10 test programs under this section may be conducted simultaneously.

(e) The authority to conduct test programs under this section shall expire 7 years after the date of the enactment of the Travel and Transportation Reform Act of 1998.

(Added Pub. L. 105–264, § 5(b), Oct. 19, 1998, 112 Stat. 2355.)

REFERENCES IN TEXT

The date of the enactment of the Travel and Transportation Reform Act of 1998, referred to in subsec. (e), is the date of enactment of Pub. L. 105–264, which was approved Oct. 19, 1998.

SUBCHAPTER III—TRANSPORTATION OF REMAINS, DEPENDENTS, AND EFFECTS

§ 5741. General prohibition

Except as specifically authorized by statute, the head of an Executive department or military department may not authorize an expenditure in connection with the transportation of remains of a deceased employee.

(Pub. L. 89–554, Sept. 6, 1966, 80 Stat. 506.)

HISTORICAL AND REVISION NOTES

Derivation	U.S. Code	Revised Statutes and Statutes at Large
....	5 U.S.C. 103.	June 7, 1897, ch. 3, § 1 (last proviso on p. 86), 30 Stat. 86.

The words "a military department" are inserted to preserve the application of the source law. Before enactment of the National Security Act Amendments of 1949 (63 Stat. 578), the Department of the Army, the Department of the Navy, and the Department of the Air Force were Executive departments. The National Security Act Amendments of 1949 established the Department of Defense as an Executive Department including the Department of the Army, the Department of the Navy, and the Department of the Air Force as military departments, not as Executive departments. However, the source law for this section, which was in effect in 1949, remained applicable to the Secretaries of the military departments by virtue of section 12(g) of the National Security Act Amendments of 1949 (63 Stat. 591), which is set out in the reviser's note for section 301.

Standard changes are made to conform with the definitions applicable and the style of this title as outlined in the preface to the report.

§ 5742. Transportation of remains, dependents, and effects; death occurring away from official station or abroad

(a) For the purpose of this section, "agency" means—

(1) an Executive agency;
(2) a military department;
(3) an agency in the legislative branch; and
(4) an agency in the judicial branch.

(b) When an employee dies, the head of the agency concerned, under regulations prescribed by the President and, except as otherwise provided by law, may pay from appropriations available for the activity in which the employee was engaged—

(1) the expense of preparing and transporting the remains to the home or official station of the employee, or such other place appropriate for interment as is determined by the head of the agency concerned, if death occurred while the employee was in a travel status away from his official station in the United States or while performing official duties outside the continental United States or in transit thereto or therefrom;

(2) the expense of transporting his dependents, including expenses of packing, crating, draying, and transporting household effects and other personal property to his former home or such other place as is determined by the head of the agency concerned, if death occurred while the employee was performing official duties outside the continental United States or in transit thereto or therefrom; and

(3) the travel expenses of not more than 2 persons to escort the remains of a deceased employee, if death occurred while the employee was in travel status away from his official station in the United States or while performing official duties outside the United States or in transit thereto or therefrom, from the place of death to the home or official station of such person, or such other place appropriate for interment as is determined by the head of the agency concerned.

(c) When a dependent of an employee dies while residing with the employee performing official duties outside the continental United States or in Alaska or in transit thereto or therefrom, the head of the agency concerned may pay the necessary expenses of transporting the remains to the home of the dependent, or such other place appropriate for interment as is determined by the head of the agency concerned. If practicable, the agency concerned in respect of the deceased may furnish mortuary services and supplies on a reimbursable basis when—

(1) local commercial mortuary facilities and supplies are not available; or

(2) the cost of available mortuary facilities and supplies are prohibitive in the opinion of the head of the agency.

Reimbursement for the cost of mortuary services and supplies furnished under this subsection shall be collected and credited to current appropriations available for the payment of these costs.

(d) The benefits of this section may not be denied because the deceased was temporarily absent from duty when death occurred.

(e) Employees covered by this section include an employee who has been reassigned away from the employee's home of record pursuant to a mandatory mobility agreement executed as a condition of employment.

(Pub. L. 89–554, Sept. 6, 1966, 80 Stat. 507; Pub. L. 101–510, div. A, title XII, § 1206(d), Nov. 5, 1990, 104 Stat. 1661; Pub. L. 105–277, div. A, § 101(d) [title V, § 589(b)], Oct. 21, 1998, 112 Stat. 2681–150, 2681–210.)

HISTORICAL AND REVISION NOTES

Derivation	U.S. Code	Revised Statutes and Statutes at Large
(a)–(c)	5 U.S.C. 103a.	July 8, 1940, ch. 551, § 1, 54 Stat. 743.
		July 15, 1954, ch. 507, § 7(b), 68 Stat. 479.
(d)	5 U.S.C. 103b.	July 8, 1940, ch. 551, § 2, 54 Stat. 744.

Subsection (a) is based on the words "department, independent establishment, agency, or federally owned or controlled corporation, hereinafter called department" in former section 103a. The terms "Executive agency" and "military department" include a department, independent establishment, agency, or federally owned or controlled corporation in the executive branch because of the definitions in sections 105 and 102.

The words "a military department" are included to preserve the application of the source law. Before enactment of the National Security Act Amendments of 1949 (63 Stat. 578), the Department of the Army, the Department of the Navy, and the Department of the Air Force were Executive departments. The National Security Act Amendments of 1949 established the Department of Defense as an Executive Department including the Department of the Army, the Department of the Navy, and the Department of the Air Force, as military departments, not as Executive departments. However, the source law for this section, which was in effect in 1949, remained applicable to the Secretaries of the military departments by virtue of section 12(g) of the National Security Act Amendments of 1949 (63 Stat. 591), which is set out in the reviser's note for section 301.

Subsection (b) is restated for clarity and conciseness and to eliminate redundancy. In paragraphs (1) and (2), the words "outside the United States" are coextensive with and substituted for "in a Territory or possession of the United States or in a foreign country".

Standard changes are made to conform with the definitions applicable and the style of this title as outlined in the preface to the report.

AMENDMENTS

1998—Subsec. (b)(3). Pub. L. 105–277 added par. (3).
1990—Subsec. (b)(1), (2). Pub. L. 101–510, § 1206(d)(1), inserted "continental" after "outside the".
Subsec. (e). Pub. L. 101–510, § 1206(d)(2), added subsec. (e).

DELEGATION OF FUNCTIONS

Authority of President under subsec. (b) of this section to prescribe regulations with respect to payment of expenses when an employee dies delegated to Administrator of General Services, see section 1(13) of Ex. Ord. No. 11609, July 22, 1971, 36 F.R. 13747, set out as a note under section 301 of Title 3, The President.

Authority of President under subsec. (e) of this section delegated to Office of Personnel Management by section 6(b) of Ex. Ord. No. 12748, Feb. 1, 1991, 56 F.R. 4521, eff. May 4, 1991, set out as a note under section 5301 of this title.

SECTION REFERRED TO IN OTHER SECTIONS

This section is referred to in section 3375 of this title; title 10 section 1482a.

SUBCHAPTER IV—MISCELLANEOUS PROVISIONS

AMENDMENTS

1970—Pub. L. 91–563, § 4(a), Dec. 19, 1970, 84 Stat. 1477, added heading of Subchapter IV.

§ 5751. Travel expenses of witnesses

(a) Under such regulations as the Attorney General may prescribe, an employee as defined by section 2105 of this title (except an individual whose pay is disbursed by the Secretary of the Senate or the Chief Administrative Officer of the House of Representatives) summoned, or assigned by his agency, to testify or produce official records on behalf of the United States is entitled to travel expenses under subchapter I of this chapter. If the case involves the activity in connection with which he is employed, the travel expenses are paid from the appropriation otherwise available for travel expenses of the employee under proper certification by a certifying official of the agency concerned. If the case does not involve its activity, the employing agency may advance or pay the travel expenses of the employee, and later obtain reimbursement from the agency properly chargeable with the travel expenses.

(b) An employee as defined by section 2105 of this title (except an individual whose pay is disbursed by the Secretary of the Senate or the Chief Administrative Officer of the House of Representatives) summoned, or assigned by his agency, to testify in his official capacity or produce official records, on behalf of a party other than the United States, is entitled to travel expenses under subchapter I of this chapter, except to the extent that travel expenses are paid to the employee for his appearance by the court, authority, or party which caused him to be summoned.

(Added Pub. L. 91–563, § 4(a), Dec. 19, 1970, 84 Stat. 1477; amended Pub. L. 104–186, title II, § 215(9), Aug. 20, 1996, 110 Stat. 1746.)

AMENDMENTS

1996—Pub. L. 104–186 substituted "Chief Administrative Officer" for "Clerk" in subsecs. (a) and (b).

SECTION REFERRED TO IN OTHER SECTIONS

This section is referred to in title 2 section 1385.

§ 5752. Travel expenses of Senior Executive Service candidates

Employing agencies may pay candidates for Senior Executive Service positions travel expenses incurred incident to preemployment interviews requested by the employing agency.

(Added Pub. L. 95–454, title IV, § 409(b), Oct. 13, 1978, 92 Stat. 1173.)

EFFECTIVE DATE

Section effective 9 months after Oct. 13, 1978, and congressional review of provisions of sections 401 through 412 of Pub. L. 95–454, see section 415(a)(1), (b) of Pub. L. 95–454, set out as an Effective Date note under section 3131 of this title.

§ 5753. Recruitment and relocation bonuses

(a) The Office of Personnel Management may authorize the head of an agency to pay a bonus to an employee who is newly appointed to a position under the General Schedule, or to an employee under the General Schedule or under any other pay authority in the executive, legislative, or judicial branch who must relocate to accept a position under the General Schedule, if the Office determines that the agency would be likely, in the absence of such a bonus, to encounter difficulty in filling the position.

(b)(1)(A) The amount of a bonus under this section shall be determined by regulations of the Office, but may not exceed 25 percent of the annual rate of basic pay of the position to which the employee is being appointed or relocated.

(B) For purposes of computing a percentage of a rate of basic pay under subparagraph (A), the rate of basic pay used shall be determined without taking into account any comparability payment under section 5304.

(2) Payment of a bonus under this section shall be contingent upon the employee entering into an agreement with the agency to complete a period of employment with the agency, with the required period determined pursuant to regulations of the Office. If the employee voluntarily fails to complete such period of service or is separated from the service before completion of such period of service for cause on charges of misconduct or delinquency, the employee shall repay the bonus on a pro rata basis.

(3) A bonus under this section shall be paid as a lump sum, and may not be considered to be part of the basic pay of an employee.

(4) Under regulations of the Office, a recruitment bonus may be paid to a newly-hired employee before the employee enters on duty.

(c) For the purpose of this section—

　(1) the terms "agency" and "employee" have the meanings given them by section 5102; and

　(2) any reference to "a position under the General Schedule" or "an employee under the General Schedule" shall be considered to be a reference to any position or employee to which subchapter III of chapter 53 applies.

(d) The Office shall prescribe such regulations as it considers necessary for the administration of subsections (a) through (c).

(e) At the request of the head of an Executive agency, the President may authorize the application of the preceding provisions of this section with respect to 1 or more categories of employees within such agency who would not otherwise be covered by this section (including authority under subsection (d) to prescribe any necessary regulations).

(Added Pub. L. 101–509, title V, § 529 [title II, § 208(a)], Nov. 5, 1990, 104 Stat. 1427, 1458.)

EFFECTIVE DATE

Section effective on such date as the President shall determine, but not earlier than 90 days, and not later than 180 days, after Nov. 5, 1990, see section 529 [title III, § 305] of Pub. L. 101–509, set out as an Effective Date of 1990 Amendment note under section 5301 of this title.

SECTION REFERRED TO IN OTHER SECTIONS

This section is referred to in sections 5307, 9504 of this title; title 38 section 7410.

§ 5754. Retention allowances

(a) The Office of Personnel Management may authorize the head of an agency to pay an allowance to an employee under the General Schedule if—

　(1) the unusually high or unique qualifications of the employee or a special need of the agency for the employee's services makes it essential to retain the employee; and

　(2) the agency determines that the employee would be likely to leave in the absence of a retention allowance.

(b)(1) A retention allowance, which shall be stated as a percentage of the rate of basic pay (excluding any comparability payments under section 5304) of the employee, may not exceed 25 percent of such rate of basic pay.

(2) A retention allowance may not be considered to be part of the basic pay of an employee, and the reduction or elimination of a retention allowance may not be appealed. The preceding sentence shall not be construed to extinguish or lessen any right or remedy under subchapter II of chapter 12 or under any of the laws referred to in section 2302(d).

(3) A retention allowance shall be paid at the same time and in the same manner as the employee's basic pay is paid.

(c) For the purpose of this section—

　(1) the terms "agency" and "employee" have the meanings given them by section 5102; and

　(2) any reference to "an employee under the General Schedule" shall be considered to be a reference to any employee holding a position to which subchapter III of chapter 53 applies.

(d) The Office shall prescribe such regulations as it considers necessary for the administration of subsections (a) through (c).

(e) At the request of the head of an Executive agency, the President may authorize the application of the preceding provisions of this section with respect to 1 or more categories of employees within such agency who would not otherwise be covered by this section (including authority under subsection (d) to prescribe any necessary regulations).

(Added Pub. L. 101–509, title V, § 529 [title II, § 208(a)], Nov. 5, 1990, 104 Stat. 1427, 1459.)

EFFECTIVE DATE

Section effective on such date as the President shall determine, but not earlier than 90 days, and not later than 180 days, after Nov. 5, 1990, see section 529 [title III, § 305] of Pub. L. 101–509, set out as an Effective Date of 1990 Amendment note under section 5301 of this title.

DELEGATION OF FUNCTIONS

Authority of President under subsec. (e) of this section delegated to Office of Personnel Management by section 6(c) of Ex. Ord. No. 12748, Feb. 1, 1991, 56 F.R. 4521, eff. May 4, 1991, set out as a note under section 5301 of this title.

SECTION REFERRED TO IN OTHER SECTIONS

This section is referred to in sections 5307, 9504 of this title; title 38 section 7410.

§ 5755. Supervisory differentials

(a)(1) The Office of Personnel Management may authorize the head of an agency to pay a differential to an employee under the General Schedule who has supervisory responsibility for 1 or more employees not under the General Schedule, if 1 or more of the subordinate employees would, in the absence of such a differential, be paid more than the supervisory employee.

(2) For the purposes of comparing the pay of a supervisory employee under the General Schedule with the pay of a subordinate employee not under the General Schedule, comparability payments under section 5304, differentials, and allowances that are not a part of basic pay may be taken into consideration, as provided by regulations of the Office.

(b)(1) A supervisory differential, which shall be stated as a percentage of the supervisory employee's rate of basic pay (excluding any comparability payments under section 5304) or as a dollar amount, may not cause the supervisory employee's pay to exceed the pay of the highest paid subordinate employee by more than 3 percent.

(2) A supervisory differential may not be considered to be part of the basic pay of an employee, and the reduction or elimination of a supervisory differential may not be appealed. The preceding sentence shall not be construed to extinguish or lessen any right or remedy under subchapter II of chapter 12 or under any of the laws referred to in section 2302(d).

(3) A supervisory differential shall be paid in the same manner and at the same time as the employee's basic pay is paid.

(c) For the purpose of this section—

(1) the terms "agency" and "employee" have the meanings given them by section 5102; and

(2) any reference to "an employee under the General Schedule" shall be considered to be a reference to any employee holding a position to which subchapter III of chapter 53 applies.

(d) The Office shall prescribe such regulations as it considers necessary for the administration of this section.

(Added Pub. L. 101–509, title V, § 529 [title II, § 211(a)], Nov. 5, 1990, 104 Stat. 1427, 1461.)

EFFECTIVE DATE

Section effective on such date as the President shall determine, but not earlier than 90 days, and not later than 180 days, after Nov. 5, 1990, see section 529 [title III, § 305] of Pub. L. 101–509, set out as an Effective Date of 1990 Amendment note under section 5301 of this title.

SECTION REFERRED TO IN OTHER SECTIONS

This section is referred to in section 5307 of this title.

§ 5756. Home marketing incentive payment

(a) Under regulations prescribed under subsection (b), an agency may pay to an employee who transfers in the interest of the Government an amount to encourage the employee to aggressively market the employee's residence at the official station from which transferred when—

(1) the residence is entered into a relocation services program established under a contract in accordance with section 5724c of this title to arrange for the purchase of the residence;

(2) the employee finds a buyer who completes the purchase of the residence through the program; and

(3) the sale of the residence results in a reduced cost to the Government.

(b)(1) The Administrator of General Services shall prescribe regulations to carry out this section.

(2) The regulations shall include a limitation on the maximum amount payable with respect to an employee's residence. The Administrator shall establish the limitation in consultation with the Director of the Office of Management and Budget. For fiscal years 1997 and 1998, the maximum amount shall be the amount equal to five percent of the sale price of the residence.

(Added Pub. L. 104–201, div. A, title XVII, § 1717, Sept. 23, 1996, 110 Stat. 2757.)

EFFECTIVE DATE

Section effective 180 days after Sept. 23, 1996, see section 1725(a) of Pub. L. 104–201, set out as an Effective Date of 1996 Amendment note under section 5722 of this title.

CHAPTER 59—ALLOWANCES

SUBCHAPTER I—UNIFORMS

AMENDMENTS

1991—Pub. L. 102–190, div. A, title X, § 1092(a)(2), Dec. 5, 1991, 105 Stat. 1487, added item 5942a.

1983—Pub. L. 98–164, title I, § 127(b)(2), Nov. 22, 1983, 97 Stat. 1027, struck out item 5944 "Illness and burial expenses; native employees in foreign countries".

1980—Pub. L. 96–465, title II, §§ 2310(b), 2311(b), Oct. 17, 1980, 94 Stat. 2166, added items 5927 and 5928.

1978—Pub. L. 95–603, §2(b), Nov. 6, 1978, 92 Stat. 3020, added item 5948.

Pub. L. 95–426, title IV, §411(b), Oct. 7, 1978, 92 Stat. 981, added item 5926.

1971—Pub. L. 91–656, §§6(c), 7(b), Jan. 8, 1971, 84 Stat. 1954, substituted "duty at remote worksites" for "duty on California offshore islands or at Nevada Test Site" in item 5942 and added item 5947.

1967—Pub. L. 90–83, §1(40)(B), (42), Sept. 11, 1967, 81 Stat. 206, 207, added items 5902 and 5903, and inserted "or at Nevada Test Site" in item 5942.

CHAPTER REFERRED TO IN OTHER SECTIONS

This chapter is referred to in section 5307 of this title; title 22 section 3664.

SUBCHAPTER I—UNIFORMS

§ 5901. Uniform allowances

(a) There is authorized to be appropriated annually to each agency of the Government of the United States, including a Government owned corporation, and of the government of the District of Columbia, on a showing of necessity or desirability, such sums as may be necessary to carry out this subchapter. The head of the agency concerned, out of funds made available by the appropriation, shall—

(1) furnish to each of these employees a uniform at a cost not to exceed $400 a year (or such higher maximum amount as the Office of Personnel Management may establish under section 5902); or

(2) pay to each of these employees an allowance for a uniform not to exceed $400 a year (or such higher maximum amount as the Office of Personnel Management may establish under section 5902).

The allowance may be paid only at the times and in the amounts authorized by the regulations prescribed under section 5903 of this title. When the agency pays direct to the uniform vendor, the head of the agency may deduct a service charge of not more than 4 percent.

(b) When the furnishing of a uniform or the payment of a uniform allowance is authorized under another statute or regulation existing on September 1, 1954, the head of the agency concerned may continue the furnishing of the uniform or the payment of the uniform allowance under that statute or regulation, but in that event a uniform may not be furnished or allowance paid under this section.

(c) An allowance paid under this section is not wages within the meaning of section 409 of title 42 or chapters 21 and 24 of title 26.

(Pub. L. 89–554, Sept. 6, 1966, 80 Stat. 508; Pub. L. 90–83, §1(39), Sept. 11, 1967, 81 Stat. 206; Pub. L. 101–509, title V, §529 [title II, §202(a)], Nov. 5, 1990, 104 Stat. 1427, 1456; Pub. L. 102–378, §2(50), Oct. 2, 1992, 106 Stat. 1353.)

HISTORICAL AND REVISION NOTES
1966 ACT

Derivation	U.S. Code	Revised Statutes and Statutes at Large
(a), (b)	5 U.S.C. 2131.	Sept. 1, 1954, ch. 1208, §402, 68 Stat. 1114. May 13, 1955, ch. 40, 69 Stat. 49.
(c)	5 U.S.C. 2132 (less applicability to the Civil Service Retirement Act, as amended).	Sept. 1, 1954, ch. 1208, §403 (less applicability to the Civil Service Retirement Act, as amended), 68 Stat. 1115.

HISTORICAL AND REVISION NOTES—CONTINUED
1966 ACT

Derivation	U.S. Code	Revised Statutes and Statutes at Large
(d)	5 U.S.C. 2133.	Sept. 1, 1954, ch. 1208, §404, 68 Stat. 1115.

In subsection (a), the word "concerned" is substituted for "to which any such appropriation is made".

In subsection (b), the words "in his discretion" are omitted as unnecessary in view of the permissive nature of the authority.

In subsections (b) and (d), the word "rules" is omitted as covered by the word "regulations".

Standard changes are made to conform with the definitions applicable and the style of this title as outlined in the preface to the report.

1967 ACT

Section of title 5	Source (U.S. Code)	Source (Statutes at Large)
5901(a)	5 App.: 2131.	Oct. 29, 1965, Pub. L. 89–301 §13, 79 Stat. 1122. July 18, 1966, Pub. L. 89–504, §407(a), 80 Stat. 299.

The amendment to the third sentence of subsection (a) of 5 U.S.C. 5901, and the deletion of subsection (d) thereof, reflect the recodification of subsection (d) in 5 U.S.C. 5903 by section 1(40)(A) of this bill. In the last sentence of subsection (a), the words "When" and "pays" are substituted for "In those instances where" and "makes reimbursement", respectively.

AMENDMENTS

1992—Subsec. (a)(1), (2). Pub. L. 102–378 substituted "5902)" for "5902)."

1990—Subsec. (a). Pub. L. 101–509, §529 [title II, §202(a)(1)], substituted "such sums as may be necessary to carry out this subchapter." for "an amount not to exceed $125 multiplied by the number of employees of the agency who are required by regulation or statute to wear a prescribed uniform in the performance of official duties and who are not being furnished with the uniform."

Subsec. (a)(1), (2). Pub. L. 101–509, §529 [title II, §202(a)(2)], substituted "$400 a year (or such higher maximum amount as the Office of Personnel Management may establish under section 5902)." for "$125 a year".

EFFECTIVE DATE OF 1990 AMENDMENT

Amendment by Pub. L. 101–509 effective on such date as the President shall determine, but not earlier than 90 days, and not later than 180 days, after Nov. 5, 1990, see section 529 [title III, §305] of Pub. L. 101–509, set out as a note under section 5301 of this title.

AVAILABILITY OF APPROPRIATIONS FOR UNIFORMS AND UNIFORM ALLOWANCES

Pub. L. 102–394, title V, §504, Oct. 6, 1992, 106 Stat. 1825, provided that: "Appropriations contained in this Act or subsequent Departments of Labor, Health and Human Services, and Education, and Related Agencies Appropriations Acts, available for salaries and expenses, shall be available for uniforms or allowances therefor as authorized by law (5 U.S.C. 5901–5902)."

Similar provisions were contained in the following prior appropriation acts:

Pub. L. 102–170, title V, §504, Nov. 26, 1991, 105 Stat. 1141.

Pub. L. 101–517, title V, §504, Nov. 5, 1990, 104 Stat. 2221.

Pub. L. 101–166, title V, §504, Nov. 21, 1989, 103 Stat. 1189.

Pub. L. 100–202, §101(h) [title V, §504], Dec. 22, 1987, 101 Stat. 1329–256, 1329–287.

Pub. L. 99–500, § 101(i) [H.R. 5233, title V, § 504], Oct. 18, 1986, 100 Stat. 1783–287, and Pub. L. 99–591, § 101(i) [H.R. 5233, title V, § 504], Oct. 30, 1986, 100 Stat. 3341–287.

Pub. L. 99–178, title V, § 504, Dec. 12, 1985, 99 Stat. 1132.

Pub. L. 98–619, title V, § 504, Nov. 8, 1984, 98 Stat. 3333.

Pub. L. 98–139, title V, § 504, Oct. 31, 1983, 97 Stat. 889.

Pub. L. 97–377, title I, § 101(e)(1) [title V, § 504], Dec. 21, 1982, 96 Stat. 1878, 1904.

SECTION REFERRED TO IN OTHER SECTIONS

This section is referred to in sections 5902, 8331 of this title; title 10 sections 1593, 1622; title 16 sections 1a–4, 742j–2; title 25 section 2807; title 33 section 540a; title 37 sections 417, 418; title 38 section 903; title 43 section 1468.

§ 5902. Increase in maximum uniform allowance

The Office of Personnel Management may, from time to time, by regulation adjust the maximum amount for the cost of uniforms and the maximum allowance for uniforms under section 5901.

(Added Pub. L. 90–83, § 1(40)(A), Sept. 11, 1967, 81 Stat. 206; amended Pub. L. 101–509, title V, § 529 [title II, § 202(b)], Nov. 5, 1990, 104 Stat. 1427, 1456.)

HISTORICAL AND REVISION NOTES

Section of title 5	Source (U.S. Code)	Source (Statutes at Large)
5902	5 App.: 2134.	July 18, 1966, Pub. L. 89–504, § 407(b), 80 Stat. 299.

The words "any other provision of" following "Notwithstanding" are omitted as unnecessary. The words "section 5901 of this title" are substituted for "this title" in three places to reflect the codification of that title in title 5, United States Code.

AMENDMENTS

1990—Pub. L. 101–509 amended section generally. Prior to amendment, section read as follows: "Notwithstanding section 5901 of this title, each of the respective maximum uniform allowances in effect on April 1, 1966, for the respective categories of employees to whom uniform allowances are paid under section 5901 of this title are increased, subject to the maximum allowance authorized by section 5901 of this title, as follows:

"(1) If the maximum uniform allowance is $100 or more, it is increased by 25 percent.

"(2) If the maximum uniform allowance is $75 or more but less than $100, it is increased by 30 percent.

"(3) If the maximum uniform allowance is $50 or more but less than $75, it is increased by 35 percent.

"(4) If the maximum uniform allowance is less than $50, it is increased by 40 percent.

The maximum uniform allowances, as in effect on April 1, 1966, and as increased by this section, may not be reduced."

EFFECTIVE DATE OF 1990 AMENDMENT

Amendment by Pub. L. 101–509 effective on such date as the President shall determine, but not earlier than 90 days, and not later than 180 days, after Nov. 5, 1990, see section 529 [title III, § 305] of Pub. L. 101–509, set out as a note under section 5301 of this title.

SECTION REFERRED TO IN OTHER SECTIONS

This section is referred to in section 5901 of this title; title 33 section 540a.

§ 5903. Regulations

The Office of Personnel Management may prescribe such regulations as it considers necessary for the administration of this subchapter.

(Added Pub. L. 90–83, § 1(40)(A), Sept. 11, 1967, 81 Stat. 206; amended Pub. L. 96–54, § 2(a)(2), Aug. 14, 1979, 93 Stat. 381; Pub. L. 101–509, title V, § 529 [title II, § 202(b)], Nov. 5, 1990, 104 Stat. 1427, 1456.)

HISTORICAL AND REVISION NOTES

Section of title 5	Source (U.S. Code)	Source (Statutes at Large)
5903	5: 5901(d).	[None.]

The regulatory authority contained in 5 U.S.C. 5901(d), the source statute for which was section 404 of the act of September 1, 1954, ch. 1208, 68 Stat. 1115, applies also to section 405 of that act (added by section 407 of the act of July 18, 1966, Public Law 89–504, 80 Stat. 299). Section 405 is codified as 5 U.S.C. 5902 by this bill.

AMENDMENTS

1990—Pub. L. 101–509 amended section generally. Prior to amendment, section read as follows: "The President shall prescribe regulations necessary for the uniform administration of this subchapter."

1979—Pub. L. 96–54 substituted "President" for "Director of the Bureau of the Budget".

EFFECTIVE DATE OF 1990 AMENDMENT

Amendment by Pub. L. 101–509 effective on such date as the President shall determine, but not earlier than 90 days, and not later than 180 days, after Nov. 5, 1990, see section 529 [title III, § 305] of Pub. L. 101–509, set out as a note under section 5301 of this title.

EFFECTIVE DATE OF 1979 AMENDMENT

Amendment by Pub. L. 96–54 effective July 12, 1979, see section 2(b) of Pub. L. 96–54, set out as a note under section 305 of this title.

SECTION REFERRED TO IN OTHER SECTIONS

This section is referred to in section 5901 of this title.

SUBCHAPTER II—QUARTERS

§ 5911. Quarters and facilities; employees in the United States

(a) For the purpose of this section—

(1) "Government" means the Government of the United States;

(2) "agency" means an Executive agency, but does not include the Tennessee Valley Authority;

(3) "employee" means an employee of an agency;

(4) "United States" means the several States, the District of Columbia, and the territories and possessions of the United States including the Commonwealth of Puerto Rico;

(5) "quarters" means quarters owned or leased by the Government; and

(6) "facilities" means household furniture and equipment, garage space, utilities, subsistence, and laundry service.

(b) The head of an agency may provide, directly or by contract, an employee stationed in the United States with quarters and facilities, when conditions of employment or of availability of quarters warrant the action.

(c) Rental rates for quarters provided for an employee under subsection (b) of this section or occupied on a rental basis by an employee or member of a uniformed service under any other provision of statute, and charges for facilities made available in connection with the occupancy of the quarters, shall be based on the reasonable value of the quarters and facilities to the employee or member concerned, in the circumstances under which the quarters and facilities are provided, occupied, or made available. The amounts of the rates and charges shall be paid by, or deducted from the pay of, the employee or member of a uniformed service, or otherwise charged against him in accordance with law. The amounts of payroll deductions for the rates and charges shall remain in the applicable appropriation or fund. When payment of the rates and charges is made by other than payroll deductions, the amounts of payment shall be credited to the Government as provided by law.

(d) When, as an incidental service in support of a program of the Government, quarters and facilities are provided by appropriate authority of the Government to an individual other than an employee or member of a uniformed service, the rates and charges therefor shall be determined in accordance with this section. The amounts of payment of the rates and charges shall be credited to the Government as provided by law.

(e) The head of an agency may not require an employee or member of a uniformed service to occupy quarters on a rental basis, unless the agency head determines that necessary service cannot be rendered, or that property of the Government cannot adequately be protected, otherwise.

(f) The President may prescribe regulations governing the provision, occupancy, and availability of quarters and facilities, the determination of rates and charges therefor, and other related matters, necessary and appropriate to carry out this section. The head of each agency may prescribe regulations, not inconsistent with the regulations of the President, necessary and appropriate to carry out the functions of the agency head under this section.

(g) Subsection (c) of this section does not repeal or modify any provision of statute authorizing the provision of quarters or facilities, either without charge or at rates or charges specifically fixed by statute.

(h) A member of the uniformed service on a permanent change of duty station or temporary duty orders and occupying unaccompanied personnel housing—

(1) is exempt from the requirement of subsection (c) to pay a rental rate or charge based on the reasonable value of the quarters and facilities provided; and

(2) shall pay such lesser rate or charge as the Secretary of Defense establishes by regulation.

(Pub. L. 89–554, Sept. 6, 1966, 80 Stat. 508; Pub. L. 99–145, title VIII, § 809(c), Nov. 8, 1985, 99 Stat. 681.)

HISTORICAL AND REVISION NOTES

Derivation	U.S. Code	Revised Statutes and Statutes at Large
(a)	5 U.S.C. 3121.	Aug. 20, 1964, Pub. L. 88–459, § 1, 78 Stat. 557.
(b)	5 U.S.C. 3122.	Aug. 20, 1964, Pub. L. 88–459, § 2, 78 Stat. 557.
(c)	5 U.S.C. 3123.	Aug. 20, 1964, Pub. L. 88–459, § 3, 78 Stat. 557.

HISTORICAL AND REVISION NOTES—CONTINUED

Derivation	U.S. Code	Revised Statutes and Statutes at Large
(d)	5 U.S.C. 3124.	Aug. 20, 1964, Pub. L. 88–459, § 4, 78 Stat. 557.
(e)	5 U.S.C. 3125.	Aug. 20, 1964, Pub. L. 88–459, § 5, 78 Stat. 557.
(f)	5 U.S.C. 3126.	Aug. 20, 1964, Pub. L. 88–459, § 6, 78 Stat. 558.
(g)	5 U.S.C. 3127.	Aug. 20, 1964, Pub. L. 88–459, § 7, 78 Stat. 558.

In subsection (a)(2), the term "Executive agency" is coextensive with and substituted for "each executive department of the Government", "each agency or independent establishment in the executive branch of the Government", "each corporation owned or controlled by the Government", and "the General Accounting Office" in view of the definition of "Executive agency" in section 105.

In subsection (a)(3), the term "employee" is substituted for "civilian officer or employee" in view of the definition of "employee" in section 2105.

Subsection (a)(7) of former section 3121 is omitted as unnecessary in view of the definition of "uniformed services" in section 2101.

Standard changes are made to conform with the definitions applicable and the style of this title as outlined in the preface to the report.

AMENDMENTS

1985—Subsec. (h). Pub. L. 99–145 added subsec. (h).

EFFECTIVE DATE OF 1985 AMENDMENT

Amendment by Pub. L. 99–145 effective Oct. 1, 1985, see section 813 of Pub. L. 99–145, formerly set out in a Military Family Policy and Programs note under section 113 of Title 10, Armed Forces.

DELEGATION OF FUNCTIONS

Authority of President under subsec. (f) of this section to issue regulations provided for therein (relating to provision, occupancy, and availability of quarters and facilities, determination of rates and charges therefor, and other related matters, as are necessary and appropriate to carry out provisions of this section) delegated to Director of Office of Management and Budget, see section 9(1) of Ex. Ord. No. 11609, July 22, 1971, 36 F.R. 13747, set out as a note under section 301 of Title 3, The President.

DEPOSIT IN SPECIAL FUND OF RENTS AND CHARGES COLLECTED FOR USE OR OCCUPANCY OF QUARTERS

Pub. L. 98–473, title I, § 101(c) [title III, § 320], Oct. 12, 1984, 98 Stat. 1837, 1874, as amended by Pub. L. 100–446, title III, § 316, Sept. 27, 1988, 102 Stat. 1826; Pub. L. 101–121, title III, § 317, Oct. 23, 1989, 103 Stat. 745, provided that: "Notwithstanding title 5 of the United States Code or any other provision of law, after September 30, 1984, rents and charges collected by payroll deduction or otherwise for the use or occupancy of quarters of agencies funded by this Act [probably means Department of the Interior and Related Agencies Appropriation Act, 1985, as set forth in section 101(c) of Pub. L. 98–473] shall thereafter be deposited in a special fund in each agency, to remain available until expended, for the maintenance and operation of the quarters of that agency: *Provided*, That nothing contained herein shall prohibit an agreement between an Indian tribe or tribal organization and the Secretary of the Interior or the Secretary of Health and Human Services, pursuant to the Indian Self-Determination Act, as amended (25 U.S.C. 450 et seq.) [25 U.S.C. 450f et seq.], under which such tribe or tribal organization may retain rents and charges for the operation, maintenance, and repair of such quarters."

SECTION REFERRED TO IN OTHER SECTIONS

This section is referred to in title 16 sections 17o, 754; title 25 section 450j; title 42 section 12655n.

§ 5912. Quarters in Government owned or rented buildings; employees in foreign countries

Under regulations prescribed by the head of the agency concerned and approved by the President, an employee who is a citizen of the United States permanently stationed in a foreign country may be furnished, without cost to him, living quarters, including heat, fuel, and light, in a Government owned or rented building. The rented quarters may be furnished only within the limits of appropriations made therefor.

(Pub. L. 89–554, Sept. 6, 1966, 80 Stat. 509.)

HISTORICAL AND REVISION NOTES

Derivation	U.S. Code	Revised Statutes and Statutes at Large
....	5 U.S.C. 118a.	June 26, 1930, ch. 622, 46 Stat. 818. Sept. 6, 1960, Pub. L. 86–707, §511(c)(6), 74 Stat. 801.

The words "which appropriations are hereby authorized" are omitted as unnecessary in view of section 5509.

Standard changes are made to conform with the definitions applicable and the style of this title as outlined in the preface to the report.

SECTION REFERRED TO IN OTHER SECTIONS

This section is referred to in section 5922 of this title; title 20 section 905; title 22 sections 287e, 287r, 1474.

§ 5913. Official residence expenses

(a) For the purpose of this section, "agency" has the meaning given it by section 5721 of this title.

(b) Under such regulations as the President may prescribe, funds available to an agency for administrative expenses may be allotted to posts in foreign countries to defray the unusual expenses incident to the operation and maintenance of official residences suitable for—

(1) the chief representatives of the United States at the posts; and

(2) such other senior officials of the Government of the United States as the President may designate.

(Pub. L. 89–554, Sept. 6, 1966, 80 Stat. 510.)

HISTORICAL AND REVISION NOTES

Derivation	U.S. Code	Revised Statutes and Statutes at Large
....	5 U.S.C. 3039.	Aug. 2, 1946, ch. 744, §22, added Sept. 6, 1960, Pub. L. 86–707, §311(a), 74 Stat. 796.

The word "agency" is substituted for "department" and defined to conform to the definition of "department" in section 18 of the Act of Aug. 2, 1946, ch. 744, 60 Stat. 811.

Standard changes are made to conform with the definitions applicable and the style of this title as outlined in the preface to the report.

DELEGATION OF FUNCTIONS

Secretary of State empowered to prescribe regulations governing allotment to posts in foreign countries, for purpose stated in this section, of funds available to the departments for administrative expenses, and to designate senior officials of this Government in foreign countries, see section 1(c) of Ex. Ord. No. 10903, Jan. 11, 1961, 26 F.R. 217, set out as a note under section 5921 of this title.

SECTION REFERRED TO IN OTHER SECTIONS

This section is referred to in title 22 sections 287e, 287e–1, 2687; title 26 section 912.

SUBCHAPTER III—OVERSEAS DIFFERENTIALS AND ALLOWANCES

§ 5921. Definitions

For the purpose of this subchapter—

(1) "Government" means the Government of the United States;

(2) "agency" means an Executive agency and the Library of Congress, but does not include a Government controlled corporation;

(3) "employee" means an employee in or under an agency and more specifically defined by regulations prescribed by the President;

(4) "United States", when used in a geographical sense, means the several States and the District of Columbia;

(5) "continental United States" means the several States and the District of Columbia, but does not include Alaska or Hawaii; and

(6) "foreign area" means—

(A) the Trust Territory of the Pacific Islands; and

(B) any other area outside the United States, the Commonwealth of Puerto Rico, the Canal Zone, and territories and possessions of the United States.

(Pub. L. 89–554, Sept. 6, 1966, 80 Stat. 510.)

HISTORICAL AND REVISION NOTES

Derivation	U.S. Code	Revised Statutes and Statutes at Large
....	5 U.S.C. 3032.	Sept. 6, 1960, Pub. L. 86–707, §111, 74 Stat. 792.

In paragraph (1), the words "of America" are omitted as unnecessary.

In paragraph (2), the word "agency" is substituted for "Government agency". The term "Executive agency" is substituted for the reference to "each executive department of the Government, each independent establishment or agency in the executive branch of the Government, including each corporation wholly owned (either directly or through one or more corporations) by the Government". The exception of "a Government controlled corporation" is added to preserve the application of this subchapter to corporations wholly owned by the Government.

In paragraph (3), the word "employee" is substituted for "individual in the civilian service" in view of the definition of "employee" in section 2105. Reference to "ambassadors, ministers, and officers of the Foreign Service under the Department of State" is omitted as included in the definition of "employee".

In paragraph (4), the words "of the United States of America" are omitted as unnecessary.

Standard changes are made to conform with the definitions applicable and the style of this title as outlined in the preface to the report.

REFERENCES IN TEXT

For definition of Canal Zone, referred to in text, see section 3602(b) of Title 22, Foreign Relations and Intercourse.

TERMINATION OF TRUST TERRITORY OF THE PACIFIC ISLANDS

For termination of Trust Territory of the Pacific Islands, see note set out preceding section 1681 of Title 48, Territories and Insular Possessions.

LIMITATION ON HOUSING BENEFITS

Pub. L. 101–246, title I, § 156, Feb. 16, 1990, 104 Stat. 46, provided that:

"(a) IN GENERAL.—The Secretary of State shall establish and implement an appropriate housing policy and space standards in consultation with all agencies with employees outside the United States who are under the authority of the chief of mission or with other agencies or employees who participate in the overseas housing program. Such policy may not provide housing or related benefits based solely on the representational status of the employee, except if such individual is the ambassador, deputy chief of mission, permanent charge, or the consul general when serving as the principal officer.

"(b) WAIVER.—The Secretary of State may grant exceptions to the restriction on providing housing or related benefits on a representational basis under subsection (a) on a case-by-case basis where a documented need for such exception is established. The Secretary of State shall prepare a comprehensive list annually of all such exceptions granted under this subsection."

AMENDMENT, MODIFICATION, OR SUPERSEDURE OF PROVISIONS INCONSISTENT WITH THE OVERSEAS DIFFERENTIALS AND ALLOWANCES ACT

Section 511(b) of Pub. L. 86–707, Sept. 6, 1960, 74 Stat. 800, Overseas Differentials and Allowances Act, provided that: "Any provision of law which is not repealed by subsection (a) of this section but is inconsistent with any provision of this Act or of any amendment made by this Act [enacting chapter 37 of former title 5 (now covered by this subchapter), amending other sections as shown in the Tables, and enacting provisions set out as notes under this section and section 912 of Title 26, Internal Revenue Code] shall be held and considered to be amended, modified, or superseded to the extent necessary to carry out the purposes of and conform to such provision of this Act or of such amendment."

APPROPRIATIONS

Section 501(a) of Pub. L. 86–707, Sept. 6, 1960, 74 Stat. 800, Overseas Differentials and Allowances Act, provided that: "There are hereby authorized to be appropriated such sums as may be necessary to carry out the purposes of this Act and the amendments made by this Act [enacting chapter 37 of former title 5 (now covered by this subchapter), amending other sections as shown in the Tables, and enacting provisions set out as notes under this section and section 912 of Title 26, Internal Revenue Code]."

REFERENCES TO PROVISIONS AFFECTED BY THE OVERSEAS DIFFERENTIALS AND ALLOWANCES ACT

Section 521 of Pub. L. 86–707, Sept. 6, 1960, 74 Stat. 802, Overseas Differentials and Allowances Act, provided that: "Whenever reference is made in any other law or in any regulation to any provision of law which is repealed, modified, amended, or superseded by reason of section 511 of this Act [repealing sections 170g(b), 170r, and 170s of former title 5, sections 888, 1132, 1133 and 1136(9) of Title 22, Foreign Relations and Intercourse, and sections 403a(d) and 403e(b) of Title 50, War and National Defense, amending section 118a of former title 5, section 1131 of Title 22, and sections 403a(c) and 403e(1)(A), (3) (A–C) of Title 50, and enacting provisions set out as a note under this section], such reference, unless inconsistent with this Act shall be held and considered to refer to this Act or the appropriate provision of, or amendment made by, this Act."

TRANSITIONAL PROVISIONS FOR PAYMENT OF ALLOWANCES AND DIFFERENTIALS

Section 522 of Pub. L. 86–707, Sept. 6, 1960, 74 Stat. 802, Overseas Differentials and Allowances Act, provided that: "Notwithstanding any provision of this Act [enacting chapter 37 of former title 5 (now covered by this

subchapter), amending other sections as shown in the Tables, and enacting provisions set out as notes under this section and section 912 of Title 26, Internal Revenue Code] and until such time as regulations are issued under this Act, employees shall continue to be paid allowances and differentials in accordance with rules and regulations issued pursuant to the laws in effect immediately prior to the enactment of this Act [Sept. 6, 1960] and such rules and regulations may be amended or revoked in accordance with the provision of such laws."

EX. ORD. NO. 10903. DELEGATION OF REGULATORY AUTHORITY

Ex. Ord. No. 10903, Jan. 11, 1961, 26 F.R. 217, as amended by Ex. Ord. No. 11228, June 14, 1965, 30 F.R. 7739; Ex. Ord. No. 11230, June 28, 1965, 30 F.R. 8447; Ex. Ord. No. 11380, Nov. 8, 1967, 32 F.R. 15627; Ex. Ord. No. 12107, Dec. 28, 1978, 44 F.R. 1055; Ex. Ord. No. 12292, Feb. 23, 1981, 46 F.R. 13967; Ex. Ord. No. 12608, Sept. 9, 1987, 52 F.R. 34617, provided:

By virtue of the authority vested in me by section 301 of title 3 of the United States Code, and various provisions of law cited in the body of this order, and as President of the United States, it is hereby ordered as follows:

SECTION 1. The Secretary of State is hereby designated and empowered to perform the following-described functions without the approval, ratification, or other action of the President:

(a) The authority vested in the President by section 5921(3) of title 5, United States Code, to prescribe regulations defining the term "employee".

(b) The authority vested in the President by subchapter III of chapter 59 of title 5 of the United States Code, to prescribe regulations, including the regulations referred to in sections 5922(b), 5922(c), and 5924(4)(B) of that title (governing, respectively, (1) certain waivers of recovery, (2) the payment of allowances and differentials authorized by said subchapter and certain other matters, and (3) travel expenses for dependents of certain employees).

(c) The authority vested in the President by section 5913 of title 5 of the United States Code, (1) to prescribe regulations governing the allotment to posts in foreign countries, for the purpose stated in that section, of funds available to the departments for administrative expenses, and (2) to designate senior officials of this Government in foreign countries.

(d) The authority vested in the President by other provisions of law (including section 235(2) [now 707(a)(2)] of title 38 of the United States Code) to prescribe regulations governing representation allowances similar to those authorized by section 905 of the Foreign Service Act of 1980 (22 U.S.C. 4085).

(e) The authority vested in the President by section 5912 of title 5 of the United States Code to approve regulations prescribed by heads of agencies (under which employees who are citizens of the United States permanently stationed in foreign countries may be furnished, without cost to them, living quarters, including heat, fuel, and light, in government-owned or rented buildings).

(f) [Repealed by Ex. Ord. No. 12292, § 4(f), Feb. 23, 1981, 46 F.R. 13967]

(g) [Redesignated (e) by Ex. Ord. No. 12292, § 4(f), Feb. 23, 1981, 46 F.R. 13967]

SEC. 2. (1) [Superseded by Ex. Ord. No. 11230, § 2(8). June 28, 1965, 30 F.R. 8447]

SEC. 2. (2) [Superseded by Ex. Ord. No. 11228, § 3(5), June 14, 1965, 30 F.R. 7739]

SEC. 3. That portion of section 2 of Executive Order No. 10624 of July 28, 1955 [set out as a note under section 1762 of Title 7, Agriculture], which precedes the proviso thereof, is hereby amended to read as follows:

"SEC. 2. In addition to rules and regulations, pertaining to allowances and benefits, otherwise applicable to personnel assigned abroad under Title VI of the Act of August 28, 1954 [chapter 43 of Title 7, Agriculture], there shall be applicable to the personnel rules and regulations prescribed by the Secretary of State in pursuance of (1) so much of the authority vested in the President by Title II of the Overseas Differentials and Allowances Act [sections 5922–5925, of this title], or by any amendment thereof, as relates to quarters allowances of cost-of-living allowances, and (2) so much of the authority vested in the President and the Secretary of State by Title IX of the Foreign Service Act of 1946 [subchapter IX of chapter 14 of Title 22, Foreign Relations and Intercourse], or by any amendment thereof, as relates to allowances and benefits under the said Title IX [subchapter IX of chapter 14 of Title 22.]:"

SEC. 4. (a) Section 2 of Executive Order No. 10853 of November 27, 1959, is hereby amended to read as follows:

"SEC. 2. The Secretary of State is hereby authorized and directed to exercise the following-described statutory powers of the President:

"(a) That part of the functions vested in the President by section 7(a) of the Defense Department Overseas Teachers Pay and Personnel Practices Act (73 Stat. 216; 5 U.S.C. 2355(a)) [section 905(a) of Title 20, Education] which consists of authority to prescribe regulations relating to quarters and quarters allowance.

"(b) The authority vested in the President by section 8(a)(1) of the Defense Department Overseas and Teachers Pay and Personnel Practices Act (73 Stat. 216; 5 U.S.C. 2356(a)(1)) [section 906(a)(1) of Title 20, Education] to prescribe regulations relating to cost-of-living allowances.

"(c) The authority vested in the President by section 235(a) [now 707(a)(5)] of title 38 of the United States Code to prescribe rules and regulations with respect to allowances and benefits similar to those provided for in section 941 of the Foreign Service Act of 1946, as amended (22 U.S.C. 1156)."

(b) The reference in section 1 of Executive Order No. 10853 of November 27, 1959, to the regulations contained in Executive Order No. 10000 of September 16, 1948, shall be deemed to include a reference to the corresponding regulations prescribed in pursuance of the provisions of this order.

SEC. 5. (a) The following-described Executive order and parts thereof are hereby revoked, subject to the provisions of section 5(b) of this order:

1. Parts I, III, IV, and V of Executive Order No. 10000 of September 16, 1948.
2. Executive Order No. 10011 of October 22, 1948.
3. Executive Order No. 10085 of October 28, 1949.
4. Executive Order No. 10100 of January 28, 1950.
5. Executive Order No. 10187 of December 4, 1950.
6. Executive Order No. 10261 of June 27, 1951.
7. Executive Order No. 10313 of December 14, 1951.
8. Executive Order No. 10391 of September 3, 1952.
9. Executive Order No. 10503 of December 1, 1953.
10. Executive Order No. 10623 of July 23, 1955.
11. Section 1 and, to the extent that it pertains to Executive Order No. 10000, section 3 of Executive Order No. 10636 of September 16, 1955.

(b) Existing rules and regulations prescribed in or pursuant to the Executive order provisions revoked by section 5(a) of this order, other existing rules and regulations pertaining to allowances, differentials, and other benefits corresponding to those authorized by the provisions of law referred to in this order and actions heretofore taken in pursuance of any thereof shall remain in effect until hereafter superseded in pursuance of the provisions of this order.

SEC. 6. This order and such of the regulations prescribed by the Secretary of State, the Director of the Office of Management and Budget, and the Office of Personnel Management thereunder as the Secretary, Director, and Office shall, respectively, determine, shall be published in the Federal Register.

EX. ORD. NO. 11137. ALLOWANCES AND BENEFITS

Ex. Ord. No. 11137, Jan. 7, 1964, 29 F.R. 223, as amended by Ex. Ord. No. 11382, Nov. 28, 1967, 32 F.R. 16247; Pub. L. 99–514, § 2, Oct. 22, 1986, 100 Stat. 2095, provided:

By virtue of the authority vested in me by section 301 of title 3 of the United States Code and by the various provisions of law cited in the body of this order, and as President of the United States it is ordered as follows:

PART I—ALLOWANCES AND DIFFERENTIALS IN FOREIGN AREAS

SECTION 101. The term "employee", as defined in 5 U.S.C. 5921(3), is hereby further defined as including civilian employees, compensated from non-appropriated funds, of the instrumentalities of the United States under the jurisdiction of the armed forces covered by 5 U.S.C. 2105(c).

SEC. 102. The Secretary of each military department with respect to his department, and the Secretary of Transportation with respect to the Coast Guard when it is not operating as a service in the Navy, are hereby designated and empowered to exercise, without the approval, ratification, or other action of the President, the authority vested in the President by 5 U.S.C. 5922(c) to prescribe regulations governing payments of allowances and differentials in foreign areas to the extent that the said authority is in respect of employees referred to in section 101 of this order whose rates of basic compensation from nonappropriated funds are fixed in accordance with regulations prescribed by the Secretary concerned.

SEC. 103. Regulations prescribed under authority delegated by the provisions of Section 102 hereof:

(a) Shall, so far as practicable, be uniform.
(b) In the case of regulations prescribed by the Secretaries of the military departments, shall require the approval of the Secretary of Defense.
(c) Shall not, with respect to any locality, authorize allowances or differentials which exceed those prescribed under Executive Order No. 10903 of January 9, 1961, [set out as a note under this section], for other employees of the United States in the same locality.

SEC. 104. Executive Order No. 10903 of January 9, 1961, [set out as a note under this section], is hereby modified to the extent of the definition and the delegations of authority contained in Sections 101 and 102 hereof.

PART II—COST OF LIVING ALLOWANCES IN CERTAIN NON-FOREIGN AREAS

SEC. 201. The Secretary of Defense with respect to the military departments, and the Secretary of Transportation with respect to the Coast Guard when it is not operating as a service in the Navy, are hereby designated and empowered to exercise, without the approval, ratification, or other action of the President, the authority vested in the President by paragraph (2) of Section 912 of the Internal Revenue Code of 1986, as amended (26 U.S.C. 912(2)), to approve the regulations there contemplated to the extent that the said regulations are in respect of the payment of cost-of-living allowances to employees, compensated from nonappropriated funds, of instrumentalities of the United States under the jurisdiction of the armed forces covered by 5 U.S.C. 2105(c), who are stationed outside the continental United States or in Alaska.

SEC. 202. Regulations approved under authority delegated by the provisions of Section 201 hereof:

(a) Shall, so far as practicable, be uniform.
(b) Shall not apply to employees who are stationed in either the Canal Zone or in any "foreign area" as defined in 5 U.S.C. 5921(6).
(c) Shall be limited to employees whose rates of basic compensation are fixed in conformity with rates paid by the Government for work of a comparable level of difficulty and responsibility to employees stationed in the continental United States, exclusive of Alaska.
(d) Shall not, with respect to any locality, authorize allowances which exceed those prescribed under Executive Order No. 10000 of September 16, 1948, as amended, for other employees of the United States in the same locality.

PART III—GENERAL PROVISIONS

SEC. 301. All actions heretofore taken by the President or his delegate with respect to the matters affected by this order, and in effect at the time of the issuance of this order, including any regulations prescribed or approved by the President or his delegate with respect to such matters, shall, except as they are inconsistent with the provisions of this order, remain in effect until amended, modified, or revoked pursuant to appropriate authority.

SEC. 302. This order, and the regulations prescribed or approved under the authority thereof, shall be published in the Federal Register.

SECTION REFERRED TO IN OTHER SECTIONS

This section is referred to in section 5924 of this title; title 22 section 1474.

§ 5922. General provisions

(a) Notwithstanding section 5536 of this title and except as otherwise provided by this subchapter, the allowances and differentials authorized by this subchapter may be granted to an employee officially stationed in a foreign area—

(1) who is a citizen of the United States; and

(2) whose rate of basic pay is fixed by statute or, without taking into consideration the allowances and differentials provided by this subchapter, is fixed by administrative action pursuant to law or is fixed administratively in conformity with rates paid by the Government for work of a comparable level of difficulty and responsibility in the continental United States.

To the extent authorized by a provision of statute other than this subchapter, the allowances and differentials provided by this subchapter may be paid to an employee officially stationed in a foreign area who is not a citizen of the United States.

(b) Allowances granted under this subchapter may be paid in advance, or advance of funds may be made therefor, through the proper disbursing official in such sums as are considered advisable in consideration of the need and the period of time during which expenditures must be made in advance by the employee. An advance of funds not subsequently covered by allowances accrued to the employee under this subchapter is recoverable by the Government by—

(1) setoff against accrued pay, compensation, amount of retirement credit, or other amount due the employee from the Government; and

(2) such other method as is provided by law for the recovery of amounts owing to the Government.

The head of the agency concerned, under regulations of the President, may waive in whole or in part a right of recovery under this subsection, if it is shown that the recovery would be against equity and good conscience or against the public interest.

(c) The allowances and differentials authorized by this subchapter shall be paid under regulations prescribed by the President governing—

(1) payments of the allowances and differentials and the respective rates at which the payments are made;

(2) the foreign areas, the groups of positions, and the categories of employees to which the rates apply; and

(3) other related matters.

(d) When a quarters allowance or allowance related to education under this subchapter, or quarters furnished in Government-owned or controlled buildings under section 5912, would be furnished to an employee but for the death of the employee, such allowances or quarters may be furnished or continued for the purpose of allowing any child of the employee to complete the current school year at post or away from post notwithstanding the employee's death.

(e) When an allowance related to education away from post under this subchapter would be authorized with respect to an employee but for the evacuation or authorized departure status of the post, such an allowance may be furnished or continued for the purpose of allowing any dependent children of such employee to complete the current school year.

(f)(1) If an employee dies at post in a foreign area, a transfer allowance under section 5924(2)(B) may be granted to the spouse or dependents of such employee (or both) for the purpose of providing for their return to the United States.

(2) A transfer allowance under this subsection may not be granted with respect to the spouse or a dependent of the employee unless, at the time of death, such spouse or dependent was residing—

(A) at the employee's post of assignment; or

(B) at a place, outside the United States, for which a separate maintenance allowance was being furnished under section 5924(3).

(3) The President may prescribe any regulations necessary to carry out this subsection.

(Pub. L. 89–554, Sept. 6, 1966, 80 Stat. 510; Pub. L. 102–138, title I, §147(c), Oct. 28, 1991, 105 Stat. 669; Pub. L. 106–113, div. B, §1000(a)(7) [div. A, title III, §335], Nov. 29, 1999, 113 Stat. 1536, 1501A–441.)

HISTORICAL AND REVISION NOTES

Derivation	U.S. Code	Revised Statutes and Statutes at Large
(a)	5 U.S.C. 3033.	Sept. 6, 1960, Pub. L. 86–707, §201, 74 Stat. 793.
(b)	5 U.S.C. 3034.	Sept. 6, 1960, Pub. L. 86–707, §202, 74 Stat. 793.
(c) ....,	5 U.S.C. 3035.	Sept. 6, 1960, Pub. L. 86–707, §203, 74 Stat. 793.

In subsection (a), the word "only" is omitted as surplusage.

In subsection (b), the words "disbursing official" are substituted for "disbursing officer" because of the definition of "officer" in section 2104 which excludes a member of a uniformed service.

Standard changes are made to conform with the definitions applicable and the style of this title as outlined in the preface to the report.

AMENDMENTS

1999—Subsec. (f). Pub. L. 106–113 added subsec. (f).

1991—Subsecs. (d), (e). Pub. L. 102–138 added subsecs. (d) and (e).

DELEGATION OF FUNCTIONS

Secretary of State empowered to prescribe regulations, see section 1(b) of Ex. Ord. No. 10903, Jan. 11, 1961, 26 F.R. 217, set out as a note under section 5921 of this title.

SECTION REFERRED TO IN OTHER SECTIONS

This section is referred to in title 22 section 1474; title 26 section 912.

§ 5923. Quarters allowances

(a) When Government owned or rented quarters are not provided without charge for an employee in a foreign area, one or more of the following quarters allowances may be granted when applicable:

(1) A temporary subsistence allowance for the reasonable cost of temporary quarters (including meals and laundry expenses) incurred by the employee and his family—

(A) for a period not in excess of 90 days after first arrival at a new post of assignment in a foreign area or a period ending with the occupation of residence quarters, whichever is shorter; and

(B) for a period of not more than 30 days immediately before final departure from the post after the necessary evacuation of residence quarters.

(2) A living quarters allowance for rent, heat, light, fuel, gas, electricity, and water, without regard to section 3324(a) and (b) of title 31.

(3) Under unusual circumstances, payment or reimbursement for extraordinary, necessary, and reasonable expenses, not otherwise compensated for, incurred in initial repairs, alterations, and improvements to the privately leased residence of an employee at a post of assignment in a foreign area, if—

(A) the expenses are administratively approved in advance; and

(B) the duration and terms of the lease justify payment of the expenses by the Government.

(b) The 90-day period under subsection (a)(1)(A) and the 30-day period under subsection (a)(1)(B) may each be extended for not more than 60 additional days if the head of the agency concerned or his designee determines that there are compelling reasons beyond the control of the employee for the continued occupancy of temporary quarters.

(Pub. L. 89–554, Sept. 6, 1966, 80 Stat. 511; Pub. L. 97–258, §3(a)(15), Sept. 13, 1982, 96 Stat. 1063; Pub. L. 102–138, title I, §147(d), Oct. 28, 1991, 105 Stat. 669.)

HISTORICAL AND REVISION NOTES

Derivation	U.S. Code	Revised Statutes and Statutes at Large
....	5 U.S.C. 3036.	Sept. 6, 1960, Pub. L. 86–707, §211, 74 Stat. 793.

Standard changes are made to conform with the definitions applicable and the style of this title as outlined in the preface to the report.

AMENDMENTS

1991—Pub. L. 102–138 designated existing provisions as subsec. (a), substituted "subsistence" for "lodging" and inserted "(including meals and laundry expenses)" after "quarters" in par. (1), substituted "90 days" for "3 months" in par. (1)(A), substituted "30 days" for "1 month" in par. (1)(B), and added subsec. (b).

1982—Par. (2). Pub. L. 97–258 substituted "section 3324(a) and (b)" for "section 529".

SECTION REFERRED TO IN OTHER SECTIONS

This section is referred to in section 5924 of this title; title 22 sections 1474, 2506; title 26 section 912.

§ 5924. Cost-of-living allowances

The following cost-of-living allowances may be granted, when applicable, to an employee in a foreign area:

(1) A post allowance to offset the difference between the cost of living at the post of assignment of the employee in a foreign area and the cost of living in the District of Columbia, except that employees receiving the temporary subsistence allowance under section 5923(1) are ineligible for a post allowance under this paragraph.

(2) A transfer allowance for extraordinary, necessary, and reasonable subsistence and other relocation expenses (including unavoidable lease penalties), not otherwise compensated for, incurred by an employee incident to establishing himself at a post of assignment in—

(A) a foreign area (including costs incurred in the United States, its territories or possessions, the Commonwealth of Puerto Rico, the Commonwealth of the Northern Mariana Islands, or the areas and installations in the Republic of Panama made available to the United States pursuant to the Panama Canal Treaty of 1977 and related agreements prior to departure for a post of assignment in a foreign area); or

(B) the United States after the employee agrees in writing to remain in Government service for 12 months after transfer, unless separated for reasons beyond the control of the employee that are acceptable to the agency concerned.

(3) A separate maintenance allowance to assist an employee who is compelled or authorized, because of dangerous, notably unhealthful, or excessively adverse living conditions at the employee's post of assignment in a foreign area, or for the convenience of the Government, or who requests such an allowance because of special needs or hardship involving the employee or the employee's spouse or dependents, to meet the additional expenses of maintaining, elsewhere than at the post, the employee's spouse or dependents, or both.

(4) An education allowance or payment of travel costs to assist an employee with the extraordinary and necessary expenses, not otherwise compensated for, incurred because of his service in a foreign area or foreign areas in providing adequate education for his dependents (or, to the extent education away from post is involved, official assignment to service in such area or areas), as follows:

(A) An allowance not to exceed the cost of obtaining such kindergarten, elementary and secondary educational services as are ordinarily provided without charge by the public schools in the United States (including such educational services as are provided by the States under the Individuals with Disabilities Education Act), plus, in those cases when adequate schools are not available at the post of the employee, board and room, and periodic transportation between that post and the school chosen by the employee, not to exceed the total cost to the Government of the dependent attending an adequate school in the nearest locality where an adequate school is available, without regard to section 3324(a) and (b) of title 31. When travel from school to post is infeasible, travel may be allowed between the school attended and the home of a designated relative or family friend or to join a parent at any location, with the allowable travel expense not to exceed the cost of travel between the school and the post. The amount of the allowance granted shall be determined on the basis of the educational facility used.

(B) The travel expenses of dependents of an employee to and from a school in the United States (or to and from a school outside the United States if the dependent is attending that school for less than one year under a program approved by the school in the United States at which the dependent is enrolled, with the allowable travel expense not to exceed the cost of travel to and from the school in the United States) to obtain an American secondary or postsecondary educational institution education (other than a program of post-baccalaureate education), not to exceed one annual trip each way for each dependent. An allowance payment under subparagraph (A) of this paragraph (4) may not be made for a dependent during the 12 months following his arrival in the United States for secondary education under authority contained in this subparagraph (B). Notwithstanding section 5921(6) of this title, travel expenses, for the purpose of obtaining postsecondary educational institution education (other than a program of post-baccalaureate education), may be authorized under this subparagraph (B), under such regulations as the President may prescribe, for dependents of employees who are citizens of the United States stationed in the Canal Zone. For the purposes of this subparagraph, the term "educational institution" has the meaning defined under section 1701(a)(6)[1] of title 38.

(C) In those cases in which an adequate school is available at the post of the employee, if the employee chooses to educate the dependent at a school away from post, the education allowance which includes board and room, and periodic travel between the post and the school chosen, shall not exceed the total cost to the Government of the dependent attending an adequate school at the post of the employee.

(Pub. L. 89–554, Sept. 6, 1966, 80 Stat. 511; Pub. L. 92–187, §2, Dec. 15, 1971, 85 Stat. 644; Pub. L. 93–126, §12, Oct. 18, 1973, 87 Stat. 454; Pub. L. 93–475, §13, Oct. 26, 1974, 88 Stat. 1443; Pub. L. 94–141, title IV, §405, Nov. 29, 1975, 89 Stat. 770; Pub. L. 96–53, title V, §510, Aug. 14, 1979, 93 Stat. 380; Pub. L. 96–100, title V, §502, Nov. 2, 1979, 93 Stat. 734; Pub. L. 96–132, §4(h), Nov. 30, 1979, 93 Stat. 1045; Pub. L. 96–465, title II, §§2307, 2308, Oct. 17, 1980, 94 Stat. 2165; Pub. L. 97–258, §3(a)(15), Sept. 13, 1982, 96 Stat. 1063; Pub. L. 99–251, title III, §303, Feb. 27, 1986, 100 Stat. 26;

---

[1] See References in Text note below.

Pub. L. 101–510, div. A, title XII, §1206(h), Nov. 5, 1990, 104 Stat. 1662; Pub. L. 102–138, title I, §147(e), Oct. 28, 1991, 105 Stat. 670; Pub. L. 103–236, title I, §176, Apr. 30, 1994, 108 Stat. 413; Pub. L. 104–201, div. C, title XXXV, §3548(a)(7), Sept. 23, 1996, 110 Stat. 2869; Pub. L. 106–113, div. B, §1000(a)(7) [div. A, title III, §336], Nov. 29, 1999, 113 Stat. 1536, 1501A–442.)

HISTORICAL AND REVISION NOTES

Derivation	U.S. Code	Revised Statutes and Statutes at Large
....	5 U.S.C. 3037.	Sept. 6, 1960, Pub. L. 86–707, §221, 74 Stat. 794.

In paragraph (1), the word "Washington" is omitted as covered by "District of Columbia".

Standard changes are made to conform with the definitions applicable and the style of this title as outlined in the preface to the report.

REFERENCES IN TEXT

The Individuals with Disabilities Education Act, referred to in par. (4)(A), is title VI of Pub. L. 91–230, Apr. 13, 1970, 84 Stat. 175, as amended, which is classified generally to chapter 33 (§1400 et seq.) of Title 20, Education. For complete classification of this Act to the Code, see section 1400 of Title 20 and Tables.

Section 1701(a)(6) of title 38, referred to in par. (4)(B), was renumbered section 3501(a)(6) of title 38 by Pub. L. 102–83, §5(a), Aug. 6, 1991, 105 Stat. 406.

For definition of Canal Zone, referred to in par. (4)(B), see section 3602(b) of Title 22, Foreign Relations and Intercourse.

AMENDMENTS

1999—Par. (4). Pub. L. 106–113 substituted "between that post and the school chosen by the employee, not to exceed the total cost to the Government of the dependent attending an adequate school in the nearest locality where an adequate school is available," for "between that post and the nearest locality where adequate schools are available," in subpar. (A) and added subpar. (C).

1996—Par. (3). Pub. L. 104–201 struck out at end "Notwithstanding section 1217(d) of the Panama Canal Act of 1979 (22 U.S.C. 3657(d)), for the purposes of this paragraph, the term 'foreign area' includes the Republic of Panama."

1994—Par. (4)(A). Pub. L. 103–236, §176(a), inserted after first sentence "When travel from school to post is infeasible, travel may be allowed between the school attended and the home of a designated relative or family friend or to join a parent at any location, with the allowable travel expense not to exceed the cost of travel between the school and the post."

Par. (4)(B). Pub. L. 103–236, §176(b), inserted "(or to and from a school outside the United States if the dependent is attending that school for less than one year under a program approved by the school in the United States at which the dependent is enrolled, with the allowable travel expense not to exceed the cost of travel to and from the school in the United States)" after "in the United States".

1991—Par. (1). Pub. L. 102–138, §147(e)(1), substituted "Columbia, except that employees receiving the temporary subsistence allowance under section 5923(1) are ineligible for a post allowance under this paragraph" for "Columbia".

Par. (2). Pub. L. 102–138, §147(e)(2), in introductory provisions substituted "subsistence and other relocation expenses (including unavoidable lease penalties)" for "expenses", in subpar. (A) inserted "the Commonwealth of the Northern Mariana Islands," after "Puerto Rico," and in subpar. (B) substituted "after the employee agrees in writing to remain in Government service for 12 months after transfer, unless separated for reasons beyond the control of the employee that are acceptable to the agency concerned" for "between assignments to posts in foreign areas".

Par. (4). Pub. L. 102–138, §147(e)(3), in introductory provisions substituted "dependents (or, to the extent education away from post is involved, official assignment to service in such area or areas)" for "dependents", in subpar. (A) substituted "United States (including such educational services as are provided by the States under the Individuals with Disabilities Education Act)" for "United States", and in subpar. (B) substituted "postsecondary educational institution education (other than a program of post-baccalaureate education)" for "undergraduate college education" in two places and inserted at end provision defining "educational institution" for purposes of subpar. (B).

1990—Par. (3). Pub. L. 101–510 inserted at end "Notwithstanding section 1217(d) of the Panama Canal Act of 1979 (22 U.S.C. 3657(d)), for the purposes of this paragraph, the term 'foreign area' includes the Republic of Panama."

1986—Par. (2)(A). Pub. L. 99–251 inserted ", its territories or possessions, the Commonwealth of Puerto Rico, or the areas and installations in the Republic of Panama made available to the United States pursuant to the Panama Canal Treaty of 1977 and related agreements".

1982—Par. (4)(A). Pub. L. 97–258 substituted "section 3324(a) and (b)" for "section 529".

1980—Par. (3). Pub. L. 96–465, §2307, inserted "or authorized" after "compelled" and "or who requests such an allowance because of special needs or hardship involving the employee or the employee's spouse or dependents" after "of the Government,".

Par. (4)(B). Pub. L. 96–465, §2308, substituted "one annual trip each way for each dependent" for "(i) in the case of dependents traveling to obtain secondary education, one annual trip, or in the case of dependents traveling to obtain undergraduate college education, two annual trips, each way for each dependent of an employee of the Department of State, of the International Communication Agency, of the Department of Justice, of the Agency for International Development, of the Central Intelligence Agency, or of the National Security Agency, or (ii) or one trip each way for each dependent of any other employee, for the purpose of obtaining each type of education".

1979—Par. (4)(B). Pub. L. 96–132 inserted reference to the Department of Justice.

Pub. L. 96–100 inserted provisions relating to applicability to dependents of employees of the Central Intelligence Agency and the National Security Agency.

Pub. L. 96–53 substituted "(i) in the case of dependents traveling to obtain secondary education, one annual trip, or in the case of dependents traveling to obtain undergraduate college education, two annual trips, each way for each dependent of an employee of the Department of State, of the International Communication Agency, or of the Agency for International Development, or (ii)" for "one annual trip each way for each dependent of an employee of the Department of State or the United States Information Agency, or".

1975—Par. (2)(A). Pub. L. 94–141 expanded applicability to include costs incurred in the United States prior to departure for a post of assignment in a foreign area.

1974—Par. (4)(B). Pub. L. 93–475 substituted "one annual trip each way for each dependent of an employee of the Department of State or the United States Information Agency, or one trip each way for each dependent of any other employee," for "one trip each way for each dependent".

1973—Par. (4)(A). Pub. L. 93–126 inserted "kindergarten," before "elementary".

1971—Par. (3). Pub. L. 92–187 substituted "the employee's post" for "his post" and "the employee's spouse or" for "his wife or his".

EFFECTIVE DATE OF 1980 AMENDMENT

Amendment by Pub. L. 96–465 effective Feb. 15, 1981, except as otherwise provided, see section 2403 of Pub. L.

96–465, set out as an Effective Date note under section 3901 of Title 22, Foreign Relations and Intercourse.

EFFECTIVE DATE OF 1979 AMENDMENT

Amendment by Pub. L. 96–53 effective Oct. 1, 1979, see section 512(a) of Pub. L. 96–53, set out as a note under section 2151 of Title 22, Foreign Relations and Intercourse.

DELEGATION OF FUNCTIONS

Secretary of State empowered to prescribe regulations governing travel expenses for dependents of certain employees, see section 1(b) of Ex. Ord. No. 10903, Jan. 11, 1961, 26 F.R. 217, set out as a note under section 5921 of this title.

SECTION REFERRED TO IN OTHER SECTIONS

This section is referred to in sections 5922, 5941 of this title; title 10 section 1605; title 20 section 906; title 22 sections 1474, 2506, 4081; title 26 section 912; title 37 section 431.

§ 5925. Post differentials

(a) A post differential may be granted on the basis of conditions of environment which differ substantially from conditions of environment in the continental United States and warrant additional pay as a recruitment and retention incentive. A post differential may be granted to an employee officially stationed in the United States who is on extended detail in a foreign area. A post differential under this subsection may not exceed 25 percent of the rate of basic pay.

(b) Any employee granted a differential under subsection (a) of this section may be granted an additional differential for an assignment to a post determined to have especially adverse conditions of environment which warrant additional pay as a recruitment and retention incentive for the filling of positions at that post. An additional differential for any employee under this subsection—

(1) may be paid for each assignment to a post determined to have such conditions;

(2) may be paid periodically or in a lump sum; and

(3) may not exceed 15 percent of the rate of basic pay of that employee for the period served under that assignment.

(Pub. L. 89–554, Sept. 6, 1966, 80 Stat. 512; Pub. L. 96–465, title II, §2309, Oct. 17, 1980, 94 Stat. 2165.)

HISTORICAL AND REVISION NOTES

Derivation	U.S. Code	Revised Statutes and Statutes at Large
....	5 U.S.C. 3038.	Sept. 6, 1960, Pub. L. 86–707, §231, 74 Stat. 795.

In the last sentence, the words "Additional compensation paid as" are omitted as surplusage.

Standard changes are made to conform with the definitions applicable and the style of this title as outlined in the preface to the report.

AMENDMENTS

1980—Pub. L. 96–465 designated existing provisions as subsec. (a), inserted "under this subsection" before "may not exceed", and added subsec. (b).

EFFECTIVE DATE OF 1980 AMENDMENT

Amendment by Pub. L. 96–465 effective Feb. 15, 1981, except as otherwise provided, see section 2403 of Pub. L.

96–465, set out as an Effective Date note under section 3901 of Title 22, Foreign Relations and Intercourse.

EXTENSION OF FOREIGN POST DIFFERENTIALS TO CERTAIN FEDERAL EMPLOYEES WHO SERVED IN CONNECTION WITH OPERATION DESERT STORM

Pub. L. 102–190, div. A, title X, § 1093, Dec. 5, 1991, 105 Stat. 1487, provided that:

"(a) WAIVER OF REQUIREMENT THAT EMPLOYEE BE DETAILED TO A POST FOR AN 'EXTENDED' PERIOD.—An individual who performed service of a type described in subsection (b) shall, upon appropriate written application, be granted the total amount to which such individual would have been entitled for such service under section 5925(a) of title 5, United States Code, disregarding any eligibility requirement relating to the minimum period of time for which an individual must serve at, or be detailed to, a post.

"(b) DESCRIPTION OF SERVICE INVOLVED.—This section applies with respect to any period of service if, or to the extent that—

"(1) it was performed as an employee—
"(A) in connection with Operation Desert Storm;
"(B) during the Persian Gulf conflict;
"(C) at a post within the area designated by the President, in Executive Order 12744 [26 U.S.C. 112 note], as a 'combat zone' for purposes of section 112 of the Internal Revenue Code of 1986 [26 U.S.C. 112]; and
"(D) while a differential under section 5925(a) of title 5, United States Code, was authorized with respect to such post; and
"(2) no differential under such section 5925(a) was granted to such employee for such service.

"(c) REGULATIONS.—The President may prescribe any regulations necessary to carry out this section.

"(d) DEFINITIONS.—For the purpose of this section—
"(1) the term 'employee' has the meaning given such term by section 5921(3) of title 5, United States Code;
"(2) the term 'Operation Desert Storm' has the meaning given such term by section 3(1) of the Persian Gulf Conflict Supplemental Authorization and Personnel Benefits Act of 1991 [Pub. L. 102–25] (10 U.S.C. 101 note); and
"(3) the term 'Persian Gulf conflict' means the period beginning on August 2, 1990, and ending on June 2, 1991."

SECTION REFERRED TO IN OTHER SECTIONS

This section is referred to in sections 5307, 5551, 5928 of this title; title 22 sections 1474, 2506, 4057; title 26 section 912; title 50 section 2081.

§ 5926. Compensatory time off at certain posts in foreign areas

(a) Under regulations prescribed pursuant to this subchapter, and notwithstanding subchapter V of chapter 55 of this title or any other law, the head of an agency may, on request of an employee serving in a foreign area—

(1) at an isolated post performing functions required to be maintained on a substantially continuous basis, grant the employee compensatory time off for an equal amount of time spent in regularly scheduled overtime work; or

(2) at a post in a locality that customarily observes irregular hours of work or where other special conditions are present, in order to cope with those special circumstances, grant the employee compensatory time off for an equal amount of time spent in regularly scheduled overtime work for use during the pay period in which it is earned.

Credit for compensatory time off earned under paragraph (2) shall not form the basis for any additional compensation.

(b) Compensatory time earned under this section shall be for use only while the employee is assigned to the post where it is earned. Any such compensatory time not used at the time the employee is reassigned to another post shall be forfeited.

(Added Pub. L. 95–426, title IV, § 411(a), Oct. 7, 1978, 92 Stat. 980.)

SECTION REFERRED TO IN OTHER SECTIONS

This section is referred to in title 22 section 1474.

§ 5927. Advances of pay

(a) Up to three months' pay may be paid in advance—

(1) to an employee upon the assignment of the employee to a post in a foreign area;

(2) to an employee, other than an employee appointed under section 303 of the Foreign Service Act of 1980 (and employed under section 311 of such Act), who—

(A) is a citizen of the United States;
(B) is officially stationed or located outside the United States pursuant to Government authorization; and
(C) requires (or has a family member who requires) medical treatment outside the United States, in circumstances specified by the President in regulations; and

(3) to a foreign national employee appointed under section 303 of the Foreign Service Act of 1980, or a nonfamily member United States citizen appointed under such section 303 (and employed under section 311 of such Act) for service at such nonfamily member's post of residence, who—

(A) is located outside the country of employment of such foreign national employee or nonfamily member (as the case may be) pursuant to Government authorization; and
(B) requires medical treatment outside the country of employment of such foreign national employee or nonfamily member (as the case may be), in circumstances specified by the President in regulations.

(b) For the purpose of this section, the term "country of employment", as used with respect to an individual under subsection (a)(3), means the country (or other area) outside the United States where such individual is appointed (as described in subsection (a)(3)) by the Government.

(Added Pub. L. 96–465, title II, § 2310(a), Oct. 17, 1980, 94 Stat. 2166; amended Pub. L. 106–113, div. B, § 1000(a)(7) [div. A, title III, § 337], Nov. 29, 1999, 113 Stat. 1536, 1501A–442.)

REFERENCES IN TEXT

Sections 303 and 311 of the Foreign Service Act of 1980, referred to in subsec. (a)(2), (3), are classified to sections 3943 and 3951, respectively, of Title 22, Foreign Relations and Intercourse.

AMENDMENTS

1999—Pub. L. 106–113 reenacted section catchline without change and amended text generally. Prior to amendment, text read as follows: "Up to three months' pay may be paid in advance to an employee upon the assignment of the employee to a post in a foreign area."

EFFECTIVE DATE

Section effective Feb. 15, 1981, except as otherwise provided, see section 2403 of Pub. L. 96–465, set out as a note under section 3901 of Title 22, Foreign Relations and Intercourse.

SECTION REFERRED TO IN OTHER SECTIONS

This section is referred to in title 22 section 1474.

§ 5928. Danger pay allowance

An employee serving in a foreign area may be granted a danger pay allowance on the basis of civil insurrection, civil war, terrorism, or wartime conditions which threaten physical harm or imminent danger to the health or well-being of the employee. A danger pay allowance may not exceed 25 percent of the basic pay of the employee, except that if an employee is granted an additional differential under section 5925(b) of this title with respect to an assignment, the sum of that additional differential and any danger pay allowance granted to the employee with respect to that assignment may not exceed 25 percent of the basic pay of the employee. The presence of nonessential personnel or dependents shall not preclude payment of an allowance under this section. In each instance where an allowance under this section is initiated or terminated, the Secretary of State shall inform the Speaker of the House of Representatives and the Committee on Foreign Relations of the Senate of the action taken and the circumstances justifying it.

(Added Pub. L. 96–465, title II, §2311(a), Oct. 17, 1980, 94 Stat. 2166; amended Pub. L. 98–164, title I, §131, Nov. 22, 1983, 97 Stat. 1028.)

AMENDMENTS

1983—Pub. L. 98–164 inserted provision that presence of nonessential personnel or dependents shall not preclude payment of an allowance under this section, and that each instance where an allowance under this section is initiated or terminated, the Secretary of State shall inform the Speaker of the House of Representatives and the Committee on Foreign Relations of the Senate of action taken and circumstances justifying it.

EFFECTIVE DATE

Section effective Feb. 15, 1981, except as otherwise provided, see section 2403 of Pub. L. 96–465, set out as a note under section 3901 of Title 22, Foreign Relations and Intercourse.

DANGER PAY ALLOWANCE; DEA EMPLOYEE

Pub. L. 101–246, title I, §151, Feb. 16, 1990, 104 Stat. 42, provided that: "The Secretary of State may not deny a request by the Drug Enforcement Administration to authorize a danger pay allowance (under section 5928 of title 5, United States Code) for any employee of such agency."

GREATER UTILIZATION OF DANGER PAY ALLOWANCE

Pub. L. 98–533, title III, §304, Oct. 19, 1984, 98 Stat. 2711, provided that: "In recognition of the current epidemic of worldwide terrorist activity and the courage and sacrifice of employees of United States agencies overseas, civilian as well as military, it is the sense of Congress that the provisions of section 5928 of title 5, United States Code, relating to the payment of danger pay allowance, should be more extensively utilized at United States missions abroad."

SECTION REFERRED TO IN OTHER SECTIONS

This section is referred to in sections 5307, 5551 of this title; title 22 sections 1474, 4057; title 50 section 2081.

SUBCHAPTER IV—MISCELLANEOUS ALLOWANCES

ELIGIBILITY OF ADDITIONAL EMPLOYEES FOR REIMBURSEMENT FOR PROFESSIONAL LIABILITY INSURANCE

Pub. L. 106–567, title IV, §406, Dec. 27, 2000, 114 Stat. 2849, provided that:

"(a) IN GENERAL.—Notwithstanding any provision of title VI, section 636 of the Treasury, Postal Service, and General Government Appropriations Act, 1997 [Pub. L. 104–208, div. A, title I, §101(f)] (5 U.S.C. prec. 5941 note), the Director of Central Intelligence may—

"(1) designate as qualified employees within the meaning of subsection (b) of that section appropriate categories of employees not otherwise covered by that subsection; and

"(2) use appropriated funds available to the Director to reimburse employees within categories so designated for one-half of the costs incurred by such employees for professional liability insurance in accordance with subsection (a) of that section.

"(b) REPORTS.—The Director of Central Intelligence shall submit to the Select Committee on Intelligence of the Senate and the Permanent Select Committee of Intelligence of the House of Representatives a report on each designation of a category of employees under paragraph (1) of subsection (a), including the approximate number of employees covered by such designation and an estimate of the amount to be expended on reimbursement of such employees under paragraph (2) of that subsection."

Pub. L. 106–346, §101(a) [title III, §348], Oct. 23, 2000, 114 Stat. 1356, 1356A–33, provided that: "In addition to the authority provided in section 636 of the Treasury, Postal Service, and General Government Appropriations Act, 1997, as included in Public Law 104–208, title I, section 101(f), as amended [set out as a note below], beginning in fiscal year 2001 and thereafter, amounts appropriated for salaries and expenses for the Department of Transportation may be used to reimburse an employee whose position is that of safety inspector for not to exceed one-half the costs incurred by such employee for professional liability insurance. Any payment under this section shall be contingent upon the submission of such information or documentation as the Department may require."

REIMBURSEMENTS RELATING TO PROFESSIONAL LIABILITY INSURANCE

Pub. L. 104–208, div. A, title I, §101(f) [title VI, §636], Sept. 30, 1996, 110 Stat. 3009–314, 3009–363, as amended by Pub. L. 105–277, div. A, §101(h) [title VI, §644], Oct. 21, 1998, 112 Stat. 2681–480, 2681–526; Pub. L. 106–58, title VI, §642(a), Sept. 29, 1999, 113 Stat. 477, provided that:

"(a) AUTHORITY.—Notwithstanding any other provision of law, amounts appropriated by this Act (or any other Act for fiscal year 1997 or any fiscal year thereafter) for salaries and expenses shall be used to reimburse any qualified employee for not to exceed one-half the costs incurred by such employee for professional liability insurance. A payment under this section shall be contingent upon the submission of such information or documentation as the employing agency may require.

"(b) QUALIFIED EMPLOYEE.—For purposes of this section, the term 'qualified employee' means an agency employee whose position is that of—

"(1) a law enforcement officer; or

"(2) a supervisor or management official.

"(c) DEFINITIONS.—For purposes of this section—

"(1) the term 'agency' means an Executive agency, as defined by section 105 of title 5, United States Code, any agency or court in the Judicial Branch, and any agency of the Legislative Branch of Government including any office or committee of the Senate or the House of Representatives;

"(2) the term 'law enforcement officer' means an employee, the duties of whose position are primarily the investigation, apprehension, prosecution, detention, or supervision of individuals suspected or convicted of offenses against the criminal laws of the United States, including any law enforcement officer under section 8331(20) or 8401(17) of such title 5, or under section 4823 of title 22, United States Code;

"(3) the terms 'supervisor' and 'management official' have the respective meanings given them by section 7103(a) of such title 5, and, with regard to the Judicial Branch, mean a justice or judge of the United States as defined in 28 U.S.C. 451 in regular active service or retired from regular active service, other judicial officers as authorized by the Judicial Conference of the United States, and supervisors and managers within the Judicial Branch as authorized by the Judicial Conference of the United States, and

"(4) the term 'professional liability insurance' means insurance which provides coverage for—

"(A) legal liability for damages due to injuries to other persons, damage to their property, or other damage or loss to such other persons (including the expenses of litigation and settlement) resulting from or arising out of any tortious act, error, or omission of the covered individual (whether common law, statutory, or constitutional) while in the performance of such individual's official duties as a qualified employee; and

"(B) the cost of legal representation for the covered individual in connection with any administrative or judicial proceeding (including any investigation or disciplinary proceeding) relating to any act, error, or omission of the covered individual while in the performance of such individual's official duties as a qualified employee, and other legal costs and fees relating to any such administrative or judicial proceeding.

"(d) APPLICABILITY.—The amendments made by this section [this note] shall take effect on the date of the enactment of this Act [Sept. 30, 1996] and shall apply thereafter."

[Pub. L. 106–58, title VI, § 642(b), Sept. 29, 1999, 113 Stat. 477, provided that: "The amendment made by subsection (a) [amending section 101(f) [title VI, 3636] of Pub. L. 104–208, set out above] shall take effect on October 1, 1999, or the date of the enactment of this Act [Sept. 29, 1999], whichever is later."]

§ 5941. Allowances based on living costs and conditions of environment; employees stationed outside continental United States or in Alaska

(a) Appropriations or funds available to an Executive agency, except a Government controlled corporation, for pay of employees stationed outside the continental United States or in Alaska whose rates of basic pay are fixed by statute, are available for allowances to these employees. The allowance is based on—

(1) living costs substantially higher than in the District of Columbia;

(2) conditions of environment which differ substantially from conditions of environment in the continental United States and warrant an allowance as a recruitment incentive; or

(3) both of these factors.

The allowance may not exceed 25 percent of the rate of basic pay. Except as otherwise specifically authorized by statute, the allowance is paid only in accordance with regulations prescribed by the President establishing the rates and defining the area, groups of positions, and classes of employees to which each rate applies.

(b) An employee entitled to a cost-of-living allowance under section 5924 of this title may not be paid an allowance under subsection (a) of this section based on living costs substantially higher than in the District of Columbia.

(Pub. L. 89–554, Sept. 6, 1966, 80 Stat. 512.)

HISTORICAL AND REVISION NOTES

Derivation	U.S. Code	Revised Statutes and Statutes at Large
....	5 U.S.C. 118h.	Apr. 20, 1948, ch. 219, § 207, 62 Stat. 194. June 30, 1948, ch. 775, § 104, 62 Stat. 1205.

The section is reorganized and restated for clarity and conciseness.

The word "allowances" is substituted for "additional compensation" as a more apt term and for consistency.

In subsection (a), the words "Executive agency" are substituted for "executive departments, independent establishments, and wholly owned Government corporations" in view of the definition of "Executive agency" in section 105. The exception of a "Government controlled corporation" is added to preserve the application to "wholly owned Government corporation".

Subsection (b) is based on the second proviso of former section 118h and is restated to reflect the provisions of sections 511(b), (c)(7) and 521 of the Act of Sept. 6, 1960, Pub. L. 86–707, 74 Stat. 800–802. The reference to section 204 of the Act of Apr. 20, 1948, is omitted as obsolete, since the section was applicable only to fiscal year 1949.

The last proviso of former section 118h which provided the effective date of the section is omitted as executed.

Standard changes are made to conform with the definitions applicable and the style of this title as outlined in the preface to the report.

PROHIBITION OF REDUCTION OF ALLOWANCE; STUDY AND REPORT ON ADJUSTING CALCULATION OF GEOGRAPHIC FACTORS

Pub. L. 102–141, title IV, § 1, Oct. 28, 1991, 105 Stat. 861, as amended by Pub. L. 103–329, title V, § 532, Sept. 30, 1994, 108 Stat. 2413; Pub. L. 104–52, title IV, § 5, Nov. 19, 1995, 109 Stat. 490; Pub. L. 105–61, title V, § 515, Oct. 10, 1997, 111 Stat. 1306, provided that: "The allowances provided to employees at rates set under section 5941 of title 5, United States Code, and Executive Order Numbered 10000 [set out below] as in effect on the date of the enactment of this Act [Oct. 28, 1991] may not be reduced during the period beginning on the date of the enactment of this Act through December 31, 2000: Provided, That no later than March 1, 2000, the Office of Personnel Management shall conduct a study and submit a report to the Congress proposing appropriate changes in the method of fixing compensation for affected employees, including any necessary legislative changes. Such study shall include—

"(1) an examination of the pay practices of other employers in the affected areas;

"(2) a consideration of alternative approaches to dealing with the unusual and unique circumstances of the affected areas, including modifications to the current methodology for calculating allowances to take into account all cost of living in the geographic areas of the affected employee; and

"(3) an evaluation of the likely impact of the different approaches on the Government's ability to recruit and retain a well-qualified workforce.

For the purpose of conducting such study and preparing such report, the Office may accept and utilize (without regard to any restriction on unanticipated travel expenses imposed in an Appropriations Act) funds made available to the Office pursuant to court approval."

EX. ORD. NO. 10000. REGULATIONS GOVERNING ADDITIONAL COMPENSATION AND CREDIT GRANTED CERTAIN FEDERAL EMPLOYEES SERVING OUTSIDE THE UNITED STATES

Ex. Ord. No. 10000, Sept. 16, 1948, 13 F.R. 5453, as amended by Ex. Ord. No. 10636, Sept. 16, 1955, 20 F.R. 7025; Ex. Ord. No. 11938, Sept. 29, 1976, 41 F.R. 43383; Ex.

Ord. No. 12107, Dec. 28, 1978, 44 F.R. 1055; Ex. Ord. No. 12510, Apr. 17, 1985, 50 F.R. 15535, provided:

By virtue of the authority vested in me by section 207 of the Independent Offices Appropriation Act, 1949, approved April 20, 1948 (Public Law 491, 80th Congress), as amended by section 104 of the Supplemental Independent Offices Appropriation Act, 1949, approved June 30, 1948 (Public Law 862, 80th Congress), and by sections 303, 443, and 853 of the Foreign Service Act of 1946 (60 Stat. 1002, 1006, 1024), and as President of the United States, I hereby prescribe the following regulations (1) governing the payment of additional compensation to personnel of the United States employed outside the continental United States or in Alaska, under the provisions of the said section 207, as amended, (2) governing the payment of salary differentials to Foreign Service staff officers and employees serving at certain posts, pursuant to the said section 443, and (3) relating to unhealthful foreign posts, pursuant to the said section 853:

PART I—ADDITIONAL COMPENSATION IN FOREIGN AREAS

SECTION 101. DEFINITIONS. As used in this Part, (a) the words "foreign areas" mean all areas exclusive of (1) the forty-eight states of the United States, (2) the District of Columbia, and (3) non-foreign areas as defined in section 201 of this order, and (b) the words "section 207 of the Act" mean section 207 of the Independent Offices Appropriation Act, 1949, approved April 20, 1948, Public Law 491, 80th Congress, as amended by section 104 of the Supplemental Independent Offices Appropriation Act, 1949, approved June 30, 1948, Public Law 862, 80th Congress.

SEC. 102. ADDITIONAL COMPENSATION BY REASON OF ENVIRONMENT. The Secretary of State shall from time to time, subject to applicable law, (a) designate places in foreign areas having conditions of environment which differ substantially from conditions of environment in the United States and warrant additional compensation as a recruitment incentive, (b) fix for each such place the additional rate or rates of compensation to be paid by reason of such environment pursuant to section 207 of the Act, after giving due consideration to the degree of environmental difference, and (c) prescribe such further regulations, governing such compensation, as may be necessary. Additional compensation so fixed is hereafter in this Part referred to as "foreign post differential."

SEC. 103. BASIS FOR FOREIGN POST DIFFERENTIAL. The Secretary of State may establish a foreign post differential for any place when, and only when, the place involves any one or more of the following: (a) extraordinarily difficult living conditions, (b) excessive physical hardship, or (c) notably unhealthful conditions.

SEC. 104. AGENCIES COVERED. Subject to the provisions of section 207 of the Act and of this Part, every executive department, independent establishment, and wholly owned Government corporation shall pay a foreign post differential fixed under section 102 hereof to each of its employees whose basic compensation is fixed by statute and who is located at the post for which that differential has been fixed.

SEC. 105. PERSONS ELIGIBLE TO RECEIVE FOREIGN POST DIFFERENTIAL. (a) In order that an employee be eligible to receive a foreign post differential under this Part, (1) he shall be a citizen or national of the United States, (2) his residence in the place to which the foreign post differential applies, at the time of receipt thereof, shall be fairly attributable to his employment by the United States, and (3) his residence at such place over an appropriate prior period of time must not be fairly attributable to reasons other than employment by the United States or by United States firms, interests, or organizations.

(b) Subject to the provisions of section 105(a) hereof, the classes of persons eligible to receive the foreign post differentials fixed pursuant to section 102 hereof shall include:

(1) Persons recruited or transferred from the United States.

(2) Persons employed locally but (a) who were originally recruited from the United States and have been in substantially continuous employment by other Federal agencies, United States firms, interests, or organizations, international organizations in which the United States Government participates, or foreign governments, and whose conditions of employment provide for their return transportation to the United States, or (b) who were at the time of employment temporarily absent from the United States for purposes of travel or formal study and maintained residence in the United States during such temporary absence. When used in a geographical sense in section 105(b) hereof, "United States" includes the areas included within the definition of non-foreign areas as set forth in section 201 hereof.

(3) Persons who are not normally residents of the area concerned and who are discharged from the military service of the United States in such area to accept employment therein with an agency of the Federal Government.

SEC. 106. PAYMENT OF FOREIGN POST DIFFERENTIALS.

(a) The following regulations shall govern the payment of foreign post differentials under this Part:

(1) Payments shall begin as of the date of arrival at the post on assignment or transfer and shall end as of the date of departure from the post for separation or transfer, except that in case of local recruitment such payments shall begin and end as of the beginning and the end of employment, respectively.

(2) Payments for periods of leave and of detail shall begin and end as determined in regulations prescribed under section 102(c) hereof.

(3) Payments to persons serving on a part-time basis shall be pro-rated to cover only those periods of time for which such persons receive basic compensation.

(4) Payment shall not be made for any time for which an employee does not receive basic compensation.

SEC. 107. PERSONS SERVING UNDER CONTRACT. Any other provision of this Part notwithstanding, any person who would otherwise be eligible to receive a foreign post differential under this Part shall, if he is serving under contract, be compensated according to the terms of such contract for the period thereof and shall, during such period, be ineligible to receive a foreign post differential.

SEC. 108. PERIODIC REVIEW. The Secretary of State shall periodically, but at least annually, review the places designated, the rates fixed, and the regulations prescribed pursuant to section 102 hereof, with a view to making such changes therein as will insure that the payment of additional compensation under the provisions of this Part shall continue only during the continuance of conditions justifying such payment and shall not in any instance exceed the amount justified.

SEC. 109. ADDITIONAL LIVING COST COMPENSATION. No executive department, independent establishment, or wholly owned Government corporation shall pay, pursuant to section 207 of the Act, additional compensation to any employee located in any foreign area by reason of living costs which are substantially higher than those in the District of Columbia: *Provided*, That this section shall not be construed to prevent any payment, under section 204 of said Independent Offices Appropriation Act, 1949, or under other appropriate authority.

PART II—ADDITIONAL COMPENSATION IN NON-FOREIGN AREAS

SEC. 201. DEFINITION. As used in this Part, (a) the term "non-foreign areas" includes Alaska, Hawaii, the territories and possessions of the United States, the Trust Territory of the Pacific Islands, and such additional areas located outside the continental United States as the Secretary of State shall designate as being within the scope of the provisions of this Part, and (b) the words "section 207 of the Act" have the meaning set forth in section 101 hereof.

SEC. 202. ADDITIONAL COMPENSATION BY REASON OF ENVIRONMENT. The Office of Personnel Management shall from time to time, subject to applicable law, (a) designate places in non-foreign areas having conditions of environment which differ substantially from conditions of environment in the United States and warrant additional compensation as a recruitment incentive, (b) fix for each such place the additional rate or rates of compensation to be paid by reason of such environment pursuant to section 207 of the Act, after giving due consideration to the degree of environmental difference, and (c) prescribe such further regulations, governing such compensation, as may be necessary. Additional compensation so fixed is hereafter in this Part referred to as "non-foreign area post differential."

SEC. 203. BASIS FOR NON-FOREIGN AREA POST DIFFERENTIAL. The Office of Personnel Management may establish a non-foreign area post differential for any place in the non-foreign areas when, and only when, the place involves any one or more of the following: (a) extraordinarily difficult living conditions, (b) excessive physical hardship, or (c) notably unhealthful conditions.

SEC. 204. PERSONS ELIGIBLE TO RECEIVE NON-FOREIGN AREA POST DIFFERENTIAL. (a) In order that an employee be eligible to receive a non-foreign area post differential under this Part, (1) he shall be a citizen or national of the United States, (2) his residence in the place to which the non-foreign area post differential applies, at the time of receipt thereof, shall be fairly attributable to his employment by the United States, and (3) his residence at such place over an appropriate prior period of time must not be fairly attributable to reasons other than employment by the United States or by United States firms, interests, or organizations.

(b) Subject to the provisions of section 204(a) hereof, the classes of persons eligible to receive the non-foreign area post differentials fixed pursuant to section 202 hereof shall include:

(1) Persons recruited or transferred from outside the area concerned.

(2) Persons employed in the area concerned but (a) who were originally recruited from outside such area and have been in substantially continuous employment by other Federal agencies, contractors of Federal agencies, or international organizations in which the U. S. Government participates, and whose conditions of employment provide for their return transportation to places outside the area concerned, or (b) who were at the time of employment temporarily present in the area concerned for purposes of travel or formal study and maintained residence outside such area during the period so present.

(3) Persons who are not normally residents of the area concerned and who are discharged from the military service of the United States in such area to accept employment therein with an agency of the Federal Government.

SEC. 205. ADDITIONAL LIVING COST COMPENSATION. (a) The Office of Personnel Management shall from time to time, subject to applicable law, (1) designate places in non-foreign areas eligible to receive additional compensation by virtue of living costs that are substantially higher than in the Washington, D.C., area, (2) fix for each place so designated an additional rate or rates of compensation by reason of such higher living costs, and (3) prescribe by regulation such additional policies or procedures as may be necessary to administer such compensation. Additional compensation under this section is referred to as a "non-foreign area cost-of-living allowance".

(b) In fixing the non-foreign area cost-of-living allowances, the Office of Personnel Management shall make appropriate deductions when quarters or subsistence, or commissary or other purchasing privileges are furnished as a result of Federal civilian employment at a cost substantially lower than the prevailing costs in the allowance area concerned.

SEC. 206. COORDINATION. The Office of Personnel Management shall define the extent to which and the conditions under which an employee serving within the non-foreign areas may receive both a non-foreign area post differential and a non-foreign area cost-of-living allowance, pursuant to section 207 of the Act. In carrying out its functions under this Part the Office may take due notice if any special allowances, other than under section 207 of the act, granted to personnel employed by the United States in non-foreign areas.

SEC. 207. AGENCIES COVERED. Subject to the provisions of section 207 of the Act and of this Part, every Executive department, independent establishment, and wholly owned Government corporation shall pay (a) a non-foreign area post differential fixed under section 202 hereof to each of its employees whose basic compensation is fixed by statute and who is located at the post for which that differential has been fixed, and (b) a non-foreign area cost-of-living allowance fixed under section 205 hereof to each of its employees whose basic compensation is fixed by statute and who is located at the post for which that allowance has been fixed.

SEC. 208. PAYMENT OF NON-FOREIGN AREA POST DIFFERENTIALS AND COST-OF-LIVING ALLOWANCES.

(a) The following regulations shall govern the payment of non-foreign area post differentials and non-foreign area cost-of-living allowances under this Part:

(1) Payments shall begin as of the date of arrival at the post on assignment or transfer and shall end as of the date of departure from the post for separation or transfer, except that in case of local recruitment such payments shall begin and end as of the beginning and end of employment, respectively.

(2) Payments for periods of leave and of detail shall begin and end as determined in regulations prescribed under section 202(c) hereof.

(3) Payments to persons serving on a part-time basis shall be prorated to cover only those periods of time for which such persons receive basic compensation.

(4) Payment shall not be made for any time for which an employee does not receive basic compensation.

SEC. 209. PERSONS SERVING UNDER CONTRACT. Any other provision of this Part notwithstanding, any person who would otherwise be eligible to receive a non-foreign area post differential or a non-foreign area cost-of-living allowance under this Part shall, if he is serving under a contract, be compensated according to the terms of such contract for the period thereof and shall, during such period, be ineligible to receive said differential and allowance.

SEC. 210. PERIODIC REVIEW. The Office of Personnel Management shall periodically, but at least annually, review the places designated, the rates fixed, and the regulations prescribed pursuant to this Part, with a view to making such changes therein as will insure that payment of additional compensation under the provisions of this Part shall continue only during the continuance of conditions justifying such payment and shall not in any instance exceed the amount justified: *Provided,* That if program or methodology revisions would substantially reduce an established differential or allowance rate, then the rate of such additional compensation may be reduced gradually.

PART III—INTERIM ARRANGEMENTS

SEC. 301. TEMPORARY REGULATIONS. During the period commencing with the date of this order or the effective date of section 207 of the Act (as defined in section 101 hereof), whichever shall occur earlier, and ending on a date or dates fixed by the Secretary of State and the Office of Personnel Management, respectively, as the effective dates of the designation of places and of the fixing of additional rates of compensation, under Parts I and II of this order, but in no event later than January 1, 1949, and notwithstanding the provisions of Parts I and II of this order, the payment of salaries and compensation (including the payment of additional compensation) of persons subject to the provisions of said section 207 shall be governed by the regulations and practices in effect in the respective Executive departments, independent establishments, and wholly owned government corporations immediately prior to April 20, 1948. Executive Order No. 9962 of May 24, 1948 is hereby revoked.

PART IV—FOREIGN SERVICE SALARY DIFFERENTIALS

[Part IV relating to Foreign Service salary differentials terminated June 30, 1951, pursuant to section 404 of this Executive Order.]

PART V—UNHEALTHFUL POSTS

[Part V relating to Unhealthful Posts terminated June 30, 1951, pursuant to section 503 of this Executive Order.]

PART VI—GENERAL PROVISIONS

SEC. 601. PUBLICATION. This order, and the places designated, the rates fixed, and the regulations prescribed by the Secretary of State and the Office of Personnel Management pursuant to Parts I and II of this order, shall be published in the Federal Register.

EXECUTIVE ORDER NO. 12070

Ex. Ord. No. 12070, June 30, 1978, 43 F.R. 28977, as amended by Ex. Ord. No. 12107, Dec. 28, 1978, 44 F.R. 1055, which related to suspension of certain requirements in determination of cost of living allowance rates, was superseded by Ex. Ord. No. 12510, Apr. 17, 1985, 50 F.R. 15535.

SECTION REFERRED TO IN OTHER SECTIONS

This section is referred to in sections 5307, 5545b of this title; title 10 section 1603; title 20 section 906; title 22 section 2506; title 39 section 1005.

§ 5942. Allowance based on duty at remote worksites

(a) Notwithstanding section 5536 of this title, an employee of an Executive department or an independent establishment who is assigned to duty, except temporary duty, at a site so remote from the nearest established communities or suitable places of residence as to require an appreciable degree of expense, hardship, and inconvenience, beyond that normally encountered in metropolitan commuting, on the part of the employee in commuting to and from his residence and such worksite, is entitled, in addition to pay otherwise due him, to an allowance of not to exceed $10 a day. The allowance shall be paid under regulations prescribed by the President establishing the rates at which the allowance will be paid and defining and designating those sites, areas, and groups of positions to which the rates apply.

(b) Under procedures prescribed by the President, the maximum allowance specified in subsection (a) may be adjusted from time to time in the interest of recruiting and retaining employees for performance of duty at remote worksites.

(Pub. L. 89–554, Sept. 6, 1966, 80 Stat. 513; Pub. L. 90–83, § 1(41), Sept. 11, 1967, 81 Stat. 207; Pub. L. 91–656, § 6(a), Jan. 8, 1971, 84 Stat. 1953; Pub. L. 101–510, div. A, title XII, § 1206(g), Nov. 5, 1990, 104 Stat. 1662.)

HISTORICAL AND REVISION NOTES
1966 ACT

Derivation	U.S. Code	Revised Statutes and Statutes at Large
....	5 U.S.C. 70c.	Aug. 31, 1964, Pub. L. 88–538, § 1, 78 Stat. 745.

The words "of the United States" are omitted as unnecessary because of the definition of "employee" in section 2105.

Standard changes are made to conform with the definitions applicable and the style of this title as outlined in the preface to the report.

1967 ACT

Section of title 5	Source (U.S. Code)	Source (Statutes at Large)
5942	5 App.: 70c.	Mar. 31, 1966, Pub. L. 89–383, § 1, 80 Stat. 98.

AMENDMENTS

1990—Pub. L. 101–510 designated existing provisions as subsec. (a) and added subsec. (b).

1971—Pub. L. 91–656 substituted "duty at remote worksites" for "duty on California offshore islands or at Nevada Test Site" in section catchline and assignment to duty "at a site so remote from the nearest established communities or suitable places of residence as to require an appreciable degree of expense, hardship, and inconvenience, beyond that normally encountered in metropolitan commuting, on the part of the employee in commuting to and from his residence and such worksite" for assignment to duty "on one of the California offshore islands or at the United States Atomic Energy Commission Nevada Test Site, including the Nuclear Rocket Development Station", inserted reference to employee "of an Executive department or an independent establishment" and provision for designation by regulation of sites to which the rates apply.

EFFECTIVE DATE OF 1971 AMENDMENT

Section 6(b) of Pub. L. 91–656 provided that: "Notwithstanding section 5536 of title 5, United States Code, and the amendment made by subsection (a) of this section [amending this section], and until the effective date of regulations prescribed by the President under such amendment—

"(1) allowances may be paid to employees under section 5942 of title 5, United States Code, and the regulations prescribed by the President under such section, as in effect immediately prior to the effective date of this section [Jan. 8, 1971]; and

"(2) such regulations may be amended or revoked in accordance with such section 5942 as in effect immediately prior to the effective date of this section [Jan. 8, 1971]."

DELEGATION OF FUNCTIONS

Authority of President under this section to prescribe regulations establishing rates at which an allowance based on duty (except temporary duty) at remote worksites will be paid and defining and designating sites, areas, and groups of positions to which rates apply delegated to Office of Personnel Management, see section 8(3) of Ex. Ord. No. 11609, July 22, 1971, 36 F.R. 13747, set out as a note under section 301 of Title 3, The President.

§ 5942a. Separate maintenance allowance for duty at Johnston Island

(a) Notwithstanding section 5536 of this title, and under regulations prescribed by the President, an employee of an Executive agency (other than a Government corporation) who is assigned to a post of duty at Johnston Island, a possession of the United States in the Pacific Ocean, is entitled to receive a separate maintenance allowance if the head of the employing agency finds that—

(1) it is necessary for the employee to maintain the employee's spouse or dependents, or both, at a location other than Johnston Island—

(A) by reason of dangerous or adverse living conditions at Johnston Island; or

(B) for the convenience of the Federal Government; and

(2) the allowance is needed to help the employee meet the additional expenses involved

in maintaining the employee's spouse or dependents, or both, at such other location rather than at the post.

(b) The regulations prescribed by the President shall include provisions for determining the rate at which an allowance under this section shall be paid.

(Added Pub. L. 102–190, div. A, title X, §1092(a)(1), Dec. 5, 1991, 105 Stat. 1486.)

EFFECTIVE DATE

Section 1092(b) of Pub. L. 102–190 provided that: "The amendments made by subsection (a) [enacting this section] shall take effect on the first day of the first month beginning on or after the date of the enactment of this Act [Dec. 5, 1991]."

DELEGATION OF FUNCTIONS

Authority of President under this section to prescribe regulations delegated to the Office of Personnel Management by section 8(4) of Ex. Ord. No. 11609, set out as a note under section 301 of Title 3, The President.

§5943. Foreign currency appreciation allowances

(a) The President, under such regulations as he may prescribe, may meet losses sustained by employees and members of the uniformed services while serving in a foreign country due to the appreciation of foreign currency in its relation to the American dollar. Allowances and expenditures under this section are not subject to income taxes.

(b) Annual appropriations are authorized to carry out subsection (a) of this section and to cover any deficiency in the accounts of the Secretary of the Treasury, including interest, arising out of the arrangement approved by the President on July 27, 1933, for the conversion into foreign currency of checks and drafts of employees and members of the uniformed services for pay and expenses.

(c) Payment under subsection (a) of this section may not be made to an employee or member of a uniformed service for a period during which his check or draft was converted into foreign currency under the arrangement referred to by subsection (b) of this section.

(d) The President shall report annually to Congress all expenditures made under this section.

(Pub. L. 89–554, Sept. 6, 1966, 80 Stat. 513; Pub. L. 96–54, §2(a)(37), Aug. 14, 1979, 93 Stat. 383.)

HISTORICAL AND REVISION NOTES

Derivation	U.S. Code	Revised Statutes and Statutes at Large
....	5 U.S.C. 118c.	Mar. 26, 1934, ch. 87, 48 Stat. 466. Aug. 14, 1937, ch. 627, 50 Stat. 641. Sept. 12, 1950, ch. 946, §301(87), 64 Stat. 843.

The section is reorganized and restated for clarity and conciseness.

In subsection (a), the words "notwithstanding the provisions of any other Act" are omitted as unnecessary. The words "Secretary of the Treasury" are substituted for "Treasurer of the United States" on authority of 1950 Reorg. Plan No. 26 §§1, 2, eff. July 31, 1950, 64 Stat. 1280. The words "Provided, That such action as the President may take shall be binding upon

all executive officers of the Government" are omitted as surplusage.

Standard changes are made to conform with the definitions applicable and the style of this title as outlined in the preface to the report.

AMENDMENTS

1979—Subsec. (a). Pub. L. 96–54, §2(a)(37)(A), struck out provision relating to recommendation of the Director of the Bureau of the Budget to the President.

Subsec. (d). Pub. L. 96–54, §2(a)(37)(B), substituted "President" for "Director of the Bureau of the Budget".

EFFECTIVE DATE OF 1979 AMENDMENT

Amendment by Pub. L. 96–54 effective July 12, 1979, see section 2(b) of Pub. L. 96–54, set out as a note under section 305 of this title.

DELEGATION OF FUNCTIONS

Authority of President under subsec. (a) of this section to make recommendations concerning meeting of losses sustained by employees and members of uniformed services while serving in a foreign country due to appreciation of foreign currency in its relation to American dollar and under subsec. (d) of this section to report annually to Congress on expenditures made under subsec. (d) of this section, delegated to Secretary of the Treasury, see section 2 of Ex. Ord. No. 11609, July 22, 1971, 36 F.R. 13747, set out as a note under section 301 of Title 3, The President.

SECTION REFERRED TO IN OTHER SECTIONS

This section is referred to in title 26 section 139.

[§5944. Repealed. Pub. L. 98–164, title I, §127(b)(1), Nov. 22, 1983, 97 Stat. 1027]

Section, Pub. L. 89–554, Sept. 6, 1966, 80 Stat. 513, authorized head of Executive department or military department which maintained a permanent staff of employees in foreign countries to pay burial expenses and expenses in connection with last illness and death of a native employee of his department in a country in which Secretary of State determined it was customary for employers to pay these expenses, and in foreign countries in which custom did not exist, on finding that immediate family of deceased was destitute, he could pay such of expenses as employee in charge of the office abroad in which deceased was employed considered proper. See section 3968(a)(1) of Title 22, Foreign Relations and Intercourse.

§5945. Notary public commission expenses

An employee as defined by section 2105 of this title or an individual employed by the government of the District of Columbia who is required to serve as a notary public in connection with the performance of official business is entitled to an allowance, established by the agency concerned, not in excess of the expense required to obtain the commission. Funds available to an agency concerned for personal services or general administrative expenses are available to carry out this section.

(Pub. L. 89–554, Sept. 6, 1966, 80 Stat. 514.)

HISTORICAL AND REVISION NOTES

Derivation	U.S. Code	Revised Statutes and Statutes at Large
....	5 U.S.C. 70a.	July 11, 1956, ch. 554, §1, 70 Stat. 519.
....	5 U.S.C. 70b.	July 11, 1956, ch. 554, §2, 70 Stat. 520.

In the first sentence, the words "to be incurred by them in order" are omitted as surplusage. The words "from and after January 1, 1955" are omitted as obsolete.

Standard changes are made to conform with the definitions applicable and the style of this title as outlined in the preface to the report.

§ 5946. Membership fees; expenses of attendance at meetings; limitations

Except as authorized by a specific appropriation, by express terms in a general appropriation, or by sections 4109 and 4110 of this title, appropriated funds may not be used for payment of—

(1) membership fees or dues of an employee as defined by section 2105 of this title or an individual employed by the government of the District of Columbia in a society or association; or

(2) expenses of attendance of an individual at meetings or conventions of members of a society or association.

This section does not prevent the use of appropriations for the Department of Agriculture for expenses incident to the delivery of lectures, the giving of instructions, or the acquiring of information at meetings by its employees on subjects relating to the authorized work of the Department.

(Pub. L. 89–554, Sept. 6, 1966, 80 Stat. 514.)

HISTORICAL AND REVISION NOTES

Derivation	U.S. Code	Revised Statutes and Statutes at Large
....	5 U.S.C. 83.	June 26, 1912, ch. 182, § 8, 37 Stat. 184. Mar. 4, 1913, ch. 145 (3d full par. on p. 854), 37 Stat. 854.

The words "or by sections 4109 and 4110 of this title" are added on authority of former sections 2309 and 2318(b), which are carried into sections 4109 and 4110, respectively.

In the last sentence, the words "This section does not" are substituted for "That nothing contained in the Act making appropriations to provide for the expenses of the Government of the District of Columbia for the fiscal year ending June thirtieth, nineteen hundred and thirteen, and for other purposes, approved June twenty-sixth, nineteen hundred and twelve, shall be so construed as to" appearing in the Act of Mar. 4, 1913, 37 Stat. 854.

Standard changes are made to conform with the definitions applicable and the style of this title as outlined in the preface to the report.

SECTION REFERRED TO IN OTHER SECTIONS

This section is referred to in title 22 section 1474.

§ 5947. Quarters, subsistence, and allowances for employees of the Corps of Engineers, Department of the Army, engaged in floating plant operations

(a) An employee of the Corps of Engineers, Department of the Army, engaged in floating plant operations may be furnished quarters or subsistence, or both, on vessels, without charge, when the furnishing of the quarters or subsistence, or both, is determined to be equitable to the employee concerned, and necessary in the public interest, in connection with such operations.

(b) Notwithstanding section 5536 of this title, an employee entitled to the benefits of sub-

section (a) of this section while on a vessel, may be paid, in place of these benefits, an allowance for quarters or subsistence, or both, when—

(1) adverse weather conditions or similar circumstances beyond the control of the employee or the Corps of Engineers prevent transportation of the employee from shore to the vessel; or

(2) quarters or subsistence, or both, are not available on the vessel while it is undergoing repairs.

(c) The quarters or subsistence, or both, or allowance in place thereof, may be furnished or paid only under regulations prescribed by the Secretary of the Army.

(Added Pub. L. 91–656, § 7(a), Jan. 8, 1971, 84 Stat. 1954.)

§ 5948. Physicians comparability allowances

(a) Notwithstanding any other provision of law, and in order to recruit and retain highly qualified Government physicians, the head of an agency, subject to the provisions of this section, section 5307, and such regulations as the President or his designee may prescribe, may enter into a service agreement with a Government physician which provides for such physician to complete a specified period of service in such agency in return for an allowance for the duration of such agreement in an amount to be determined by the agency head and specified in the agreement, but not to exceed—

(1) $14,000 per annum if, at the time the agreement is entered into, the Government physician has served as a Government physician for twenty-four months or less, or

(2) $30,000 per annum if the Government physician has served as a Government physician for more than twenty-four months.

For the purpose of determining length of service as a Government physician, service as a physician under section 4104 or 4114[1] of title 38 or active service as a medical officer in the commissioned corps of the Public Health Service under Title II of the Public Health Service Act (42 U.S.C. ch. 6A) shall be deemed service as a Government physician.

(b) An allowance may not be paid pursuant to this section to any physician who—

(1) is employed on less than a half-time or intermittent basis,

(2) occupies an internship or residency training position,

(3) is a reemployed annuitant, or

(4) is fulfilling a scholarship obligation.

(c) The head of an agency, pursuant to such regulations, criteria, and conditions as the President or his designee may prescribe, shall determine categories of positions applicable to physicians in such agency with respect to which there is a significant recruitment and retention problem. Only physicians serving in such positions shall be eligible for an allowance pursuant to this section. The amounts of each such allowance shall be determined by the agency head, subject to such regulations, criteria, and conditions as the President or his designee may pre-

---

[1] See References in Text note below.

scribe, and shall be the minimum amount necessary to deal with the recruitment and retention problem for each such category of physicians.

(d) Any agreement entered into by a physician under this section shall be for a period of one year of service in the agency involved unless the physician requests an agreement for a longer period of service.

(e) Unless otherwise provided for in the agreement under subsection (f) of this section, an agreement under this section shall provide that the physician, in the event that such physician voluntarily, or because of misconduct, fails to complete at least one year of service pursuant to such agreement, shall be required to refund the total amount received under this section, unless the head of the agency, pursuant to such regulations as may be prescribed under this section by the President or his designee, determines that such failure is necessitated by circumstances beyond the control of the physician.

(f) Any agreement under this section shall specify, subject to such regulations as the President or his designee may prescribe, the terms under which the head of the agency and the physician may elect to terminate such agreement, and the amounts, if any, required to be refunded by the physician for each reason for termination.

(g) For the purpose of this section—

(1) "Government physician" means any individual employed as a physician or dentist who is paid under—

(A) section 5332 of this title, relating to the General Schedule;

(B) Subchapter VIII of chapter 53 of this title, relating to the Senior Executive Service;

(C) section 5371, relating to certain health care positions;

(D) section 3 of the Tennessee Valley Authority Act of 1933 (16 U.S.C. 831b), relating to the Tennessee Valley Authority;

(E) chapter 4 of title I of the Foreign Service Act of 1980 (22 U.S.C. 3961 and following), relating to the Foreign Service;

(F) section 10 of the Central Intelligence Agency Act of 1949 (50 U.S.C. 403j), relating to the Central Intelligence Agency;

(G) section 1202 of the Panama Canal Act of 1979, relating to the Panama Canal Commission;

(H) section 2 of the Act of May 29, 1959[2] (Public Law 86–36, as amended, 50 U.S.C. 402 note), relating to the National Security Agency;

(I) section 5376, relating to certain senior-level positions;

(J) section 5377, relating to critical positions; or

(K) subchapter IX of chapter 53, relating to special occupational pay systems; and

(2) "agency" means an Executive agency, as defined in section 105 of this title, the Library of Congress, and the District of Columbia government.

(h)(1) Any allowance paid under this section shall not be considered as basic pay for the pur-

poses of subchapter VI and section 5595 of chapter 55, chapter 81 or 87 of this title, or other benefits related to basic pay.

(2) Any allowance under this section for a Government physician shall be paid in the same manner and at the same time as the physician's basic pay is paid.

(i) Any regulations, criteria, or conditions that may be prescribed under this section by the President or his designee shall not be applicable to the Tennessee Valley Authority, and the Tennessee Valley Authority shall have sole responsibility for administering the provisions of this section with respect to Government physicians employed by the Authority.

(j) Not later than June 30 of each year, the President shall submit to each House of Congress a written report on the operation of this section. Each report shall include, with respect to the year covered by such report, information as to—

(1) which agencies entered into agreements under this section;

(2) the nature and extent of the recruitment or retention problems justifying the use of authority by each agency under this section;

(3) the number of physicians with whom agreements were entered into by each agency;

(4) the size of the allowances and the duration of the agreements entered into; and

(5) the degree to which the recruitment or retention problems referred to in paragraph (2) were alleviated under this section.

(Added Pub. L. 95–603, § 2(a), Nov. 6, 1978, 92 Stat. 3018; amended Pub. L. 96–166, § 2, Dec. 29, 1979, 93 Stat. 1273; Pub. L. 97–141, § 2, Dec. 29, 1981, 95 Stat. 1719; Pub. L. 98–168, title I, § 102(a), Nov. 29, 1983, 97 Stat. 1105; Pub. L. 98–615, title II, § 204(a)(3), Nov. 8, 1984, 98 Stat. 3216; Pub. L. 100–140, § 1, Oct. 26, 1987, 101 Stat. 830; Pub. L. 101–420, § 1, formerly § 1, Oct. 12, 1990, 104 Stat. 908, renumbered § 1(a), Pub. L. 103–114, § 1(b)(2)(A), Oct. 26, 1993, 107 Stat. 1115; Pub. L. 102–378, § 2(51), Oct. 2, 1992, 106 Stat. 1353; Pub. L. 103–89, § 3(b)(1)(M), Sept. 30, 1993, 107 Stat. 982; Pub. L. 103–114, §§ 1(a)(1), 2(a), Oct. 26, 1993, 107 Stat. 1115, 1116; Pub. L. 105–61, title V, § 517(a), Oct. 10, 1997, 111 Stat. 1307; Pub. L. 105–266, § 7(a), Oct. 19, 1998, 112 Stat. 2369; Pub. L. 106–554, § 1(a)(1) [title II, § 218(a)], Dec. 21, 2000, 114 Stat. 2763, 2763A–28; Pub. L. 106–571, §§ 2(a)(1), (b), 3(d), Dec. 28, 2000, 114 Stat. 3054, 3057.)

REFERENCES IN TEXT

Sections 4104 and 4114 of title 38, referred to in subsec. (a), were repealed by Pub. L. 102–40, title IV, § 401(a)(3), May 7, 1991, 105 Stat. 210, and a new section 4101 containing different subject matter was added. For provisions similar to those contained in sections 4104 and 4114 prior to repeal, see sections 7401 and 7405 to 7407 of Title 38, Veterans' Benefits.

The Public Health Service Act, referred to in subsec. (a), is act July 1, 1944, ch. 373, 58 Stat. 682, as amended. Title II of the Public Health Service Act is classified generally to subchapter I (§ 201 et seq.) of chapter 6A of Title 42, The Public Health and Welfare. For complete classification of this Act to the Code, see Short Title note set out under section 201 of Title 42 and Tables.

The Foreign Service Act of 1980, referred to in subsec. (g)(1)(E), is Pub. L. 96–465, Oct. 17, 1980, 94 Stat. 2071, as amended. Chapter 4 of title I of the Act is classified generally to subchapter IV (§ 3961 et seq.) of chapter 52 of Title 22, Foreign Relations and Intercourse. For

---

[2] See References in Text note below.

complete classification of this Act to the Code, see Short Title note set out under section 3901 of Title 22 and Tables.

Section 1202 of the Panama Canal Act of 1979, referred to in subsec. (g)(1)(G), is classified to section 3642 of Title 22, Foreign Relations and Intercourse.

Section 2 of the Act of May 29, 1959 (Public Law 86–36, as amended, 50 U.S.C. 402 note), referred to in subsec. (g)(1)(H), was repealed by Pub. L. 104–201, div. A, title XVI, §1633(b)(1), Sept. 23, 1996, 110 Stat. 2751.

AMENDMENTS

2000—Subsec. (d). Pub. L. 106–571, §2(a)(1), struck out second sentence which read as follows: "No agreement shall be entered into under this section later than September 30, 2005, nor shall any agreement cover a period of service extending beyond September 30, 2007."

Pub. L. 106–554 amended second sentence generally. Prior to amendment, second sentence read as follows: "No agreement shall be entered into under this section later than September 30, 2000, nor shall any agreement cover a period of service extending beyond September 30, 2002."

Subsec. (h)(1). Pub. L. 106–571, §3(d), substituted "chapter 81 or 87" for "chapter 81, 83, or 87".

Subsec. (j). Pub. L. 106–571, §2(b), in par. (1), substituted "(j)" for "(j)(1)", redesignated subpars. (A) to (E) as pars. (1) to (5), respectively, in par. (5), substituted "paragraph (2)" for "subparagraph (B)", and struck out former par. (2) which read as follows: "In addition to the information required under paragraph (1), the last report due under this subsection before the expiration of the authority to enter into agreements under this section shall include—

"(A) recommendations as to whether or not such authority should be continued beyond September 30, 2000, and, if so, by what period of time; and

"(B) the reasons for those recommendations."

1998—Subsec. (a)(2). Pub. L. 105–266 substituted "$30,000" for "$20,000".

1997—Subsec. (d). Pub. L. 105–61, §517(a)(1), substituted "No agreement shall be entered into under this section later than September 30, 2000, nor shall any agreement cover a period of service extending beyond September 30, 2002." for "No agreement shall be entered into under this section later than September 30, 1997, nor shall any agreement cover a period of service extending beyond September 30, 1999."

Subsec. (j)(2)(A). Pub. L. 105–61, §517(a)(2), substituted "September 30, 2000" for "September 30, 1997".

1993—Subsec. (d). Pub. L. 103–114, §1(a)(1), amended second sentence generally. Prior to amendment, second sentence read as follows: "No agreement shall be entered into under this section later than September 30, 1993, nor shall any agreement cover a period of service extending beyond September 30, 1995."

Subsec. (g)(1)(C) to (L). Pub. L. 103–89 redesignated subpars. (D) to (L) as (C) to (K), respectively, and struck out former subpar. (C) which read as follows: "chapter 54 of this title, relating to the performance management and recognition system;".

Subsec. (j). Pub. L. 103–114, §2(a), added subsec. (j).

1992—Subsec. (a). Pub. L. 102–378, §2(51)(A), inserted ", section 5307," after "provisions of this section" in first sentence.

Subsec. (g)(1)(D). Pub. L. 102–378, §2(51)(B)(i), amended subpar. (D) generally. Prior to amendment, subpar. (D) read as follows: "section 5371 of this title, or similar statutory authority, relating to administratively determined pay for certain specially qualified scientific or professional personnel;".

Subsec. (g)(1)(J) to (L). Pub. L. 102–378, §2(51)(B)(ii)–(iv), added subpars. (J) to (L).

1990—Subsec. (d). Pub. L. 101–420 added second sentence and struck out former second sentence which read as follows: "No agreement shall be entered into under this section later than September 30, 1990, nor shall any agreement cover a period of service extending beyond September 30, 1992."

1987—Subsec. (a). Pub. L. 100–140, §1(a)(3), inserted last sentence.

Subsec. (a)(1). Pub. L. 100–140, §1(a)(1), substituted "$14,000" for "$7,000".

Subsec. (a)(2). Pub. L. 100–140, §1(a)(2), substituted "$20,000" for "$10,000".

Subsec. (d). Pub. L. 100–140, §1(b), substituted "September 30, 1990" for "September 30, 1987" and "September 30, 1992" for "September 30, 1989".

1984—Subsec. (g)(1)(C). Pub. L. 98–615 substituted "performance management and recognition system" for "Merit Pay System".

1983—Subsec. (d). Pub. L. 98–168 substituted "1987" for "1983", and "1989" for "1985".

1981—Subsec. (d). Pub. L. 97–141, §2(1), substituted "September 30, 1983, nor shall any agreement cover a period of service extending beyond September 30, 1985" for "September 30, 1981, nor shall any agreement cover a period of service extending beyond September 30, 1983".

Subsec. (g)(1). Pub. L. 97–141, §2(2), (3), reenacted provisions preceding subpar. (A) without change, and in subpar. (F), substituted "chapter 4 of title I of the Foreign Service Act of 1980 (22 U.S.C. 3961 and following)" for "title 4 of the Foreign Service Act of 1946 (22 U.S.C. 861–890)".

1979—Subsec. (d). Pub. L. 96–166, §2(1), substituted "September 30, 1981" for "September 30, 1979" and "September 30, 1983" for "September 30, 1981".

Subsec. (g)(1). Pub. L. 96–166, §2(2)(A), directed the amendment of subsec. (g)(1) by inserting "or dentist" after "physician" which was executed by inserting the term after "employed as a physician" in introductory phrase as the probable intent of Congress.

Pub. L. 96–166, §2(2)(B)–(E), redesignated subpars. (B) through (G) as (D) through (I), respectively, added subpars. (B) and (C), substituted in subpar. (D) as redesignated, "5371" for "5361", and substituted in subpar. (H) as redesignated, "section 1202 of the Panama Canal Act of 1979, relating to the Panama Canal Commission; or" for "section 121 of title 2 of the Canal Zone Code, relating to the Canal Zone Government and the Panama Canal Company; or".

Subsec. (g)(2). Pub. L. 96–166, §2(3), inserted reference to the Library of Congress.

EFFECTIVE DATE OF 1997 AMENDMENT

Section 517(c) of Pub. L. 105–61 provided that: "The amendments made by this section [amending this section and provisions set out as a note under this section] shall take effect on the date of enactment of this Act [Oct. 10, 1997]."

EFFECTIVE DATE OF 1993 AMENDMENT

Amendment by Pub. L. 103–89 effective Nov. 1, 1993, see section 3(c) of Pub. L. 103–89, set out as a note under section 3372 of this title.

EFFECTIVE DATE OF 1984 AMENDMENT

Section 205 of Pub. L. 98–615 provided that amendment by Pub. L. 98–615 was effective Oct. 1, 1984, and applicable with respect to pay periods commencing on or after that date, with certain exceptions and qualifications.

EFFECTIVE DATE OF REPEAL

Section 3 of Pub. L. 95–603, as amended by Pub. L. 96–166, §4, Dec. 29, 1979, 93 Stat. 1273; Pub. L. 97–141, §3, Dec. 29, 1981, 95 Stat. 1719; Pub. L. 98–168, title I, §102(b), Nov. 29, 1983, 97 Stat. 1105; Pub. L. 100–140, §1(c), as added Pub. L. 103–114, §1(b)(1), Oct. 26, 1993, 107 Stat. 1115; Pub. L. 101–420, §1(b), as added Pub. L. 103–114, §1(b)(2)(B), Oct. 26, 1993, 107 Stat. 1115; Pub. L. 103–114, §1(a)(2), Oct. 26, 1993, 107 Stat. 1115; Pub. L. 105–61, title V, §517(b), Oct. 10, 1997, 111 Stat. 1307; Pub. L. 106–554, §1(a)(1) [title II, §218(b)], Dec. 21, 2000, 114 Stat. 2763, 2763A–28, which provided that this section would be repealed, unless specifically extended by Act of Congress, effective on Sept. 30, 2007, was repealed by Pub. L. 106–571, §2(a)(2), Dec. 28, 2000, 114 Stat. 3054.

SHORT TITLE OF 2000 AMENDMENT

Pub. L. 106–571, §1, Dec. 28, 2000, 114 Stat. 3054, provided that: "This Act [amending this section and sections 8331, 8339, 8401, and 8415 of this title] may be cited as the 'Federal Physicians Comparability Allowance Amendments of 2000'.''

SHORT TITLE OF 1983 AMENDMENT

Section 101 of title I of Pub. L. 98–168 provided that: ''This title [amending this section, enacting provisions set out below, and amending provisions set out as a note above] may be cited as the 'Federal Physicians Comparability Allowance Amendments of 1983'.''

SHORT TITLE OF 1981 AMENDMENT

Section 1 of Pub. L. 97–141 provided: ''That this Act [amending this section and section 8344 of this title and provisions set out below and enacting provisions set out as notes under this section and section 8344 of this title] may be cited as the 'Federal Physicians Comparability Allowance Amendments of 1981'.''

SHORT TITLE OF 1979 AMENDMENT

Section 1 of Pub. L. 96–166 provided: ''That this Act [amending this section and section 5383 of this title and provisions set out as a note under this section, and enacting provisions set out below] may be cited as the 'Federal Physicians Comparability Allowance Amendments of 1979'.''

SHORT TITLE

Section 1 of Pub. L. 95–603 provided: ''That this Act [enacting this section and provisions set out as notes under this section] may be cited as the 'Federal Physicians Comparability Allowance Act of 1978'.''

CONSTRUCTION OF 1998 AMENDMENT

Pub. L. 105–266, § 7(c), Oct. 19, 1998, 112 Stat. 2370, provided that: ''Nothing in this section [amending this section and enacting provisions set out as a note below] shall be considered to authorize additional or supplemental appropriations for the fiscal year in which occurs the date of the enactment of this Act [Oct. 19, 1998].''

CONSTRUCTION OF 1993 AMENDMENT

Section 1(a)(4) of Pub. L. 103–114 provided that: ''The amendments made by this subsection [amending this section and provisions set out above] shall not be construed to authorize additional or supplemental appropriations for the fiscal year ending September 30, 1993.''

Section 1(c) of Pub. L. 103–114 provided that: ''For purposes of applying the amendments made by this section [amending this section and enacting and amending provisions set out as notes above]—

''(1) the provisions of subsection (b)(1) [enacting and amending provisions set out as notes above] shall be treated as having been enacted immediately before the provisions of subsection (b)(2) [enacting and amending provisions set out as notes above]; and

''(2) the provisions of subsection (b)(2) shall be treated as having been enacted immediately before the provisions of subsection (a) [amending this section and enacting and amending provisions set out as notes above].''

MODIFICATION OF SERVICE AGREEMENTS IN EFFECT ON OCTOBER 19, 1998; LIMITATION

Pub. L. 105–266, § 7(b), Oct. 19, 1998, 112 Stat. 2369, provided that:

''(1) IN GENERAL.—Any service agreement under section 5948 of title 5, United States Code, which is in effect on the date of the enactment of this Act [Oct. 19, 1998] may, with respect to any period of service remaining in such agreement, be modified based on the amendment made by subsection (a) [amending this section].

''(2) LIMITATION.—A modification taking effect under this subsection in any year shall not cause an allowance to be increased to a rate which, if applied throughout such year, would cause the limitation under section 5948(a)(2) of such title (as amended by this section), or any other applicable limitation, to be exceeded.''

EFFECTIVENESS OF SERVICE AGREEMENTS LIMITED BY APPROPRIATION ACTS

Section 1(a)(3) of Pub. L. 103–114 provided that: ''Any service agreement entered into on or after the date of the enactment of this Act [Oct. 26, 1993] pursuant to section 5948 of title 5, United States Code, as amended by paragraph (1), shall be effective only to such extent or in such amounts as are provided in advance in appropriation Acts.''

DUE DATE FOR FIRST ANNUAL REPORT ON OPERATION OF SECTION

Section 2(b) of Pub. L. 103–114 provided that: ''The first report under section 5948(j) of title 5, United States Code, as amended by subsection (a), shall be due not later than June 30, 1994.''

PAY OF CERTAIN FEDERAL PHYSICIANS FOR FISCAL YEAR 1982

Section 103 of Pub. L. 98–168 provided that any individual whose aggregate pay for fiscal year 1982 exceeded the limitation set forth in section 5383(b) of this title is relieved of all liability to the United States for any amounts paid to such individual in excess of such limitation if, and to the extent that, such liability takes into account any allowance paid under this section, provided for repayment to individuals relieved from liability of amounts already paid, and defined the terms ''aggregate pay'', ''appropriate agency head'', and ''agency''.

SERVICE AGREEMENTS ENTERED INTO ON OR AFTER DECEMBER 29, 1981; ADVANCE AUTHORIZATION; FISCAL YEAR 1982

Section 4 of Pub. L. 97–141 provided that any service agreement entered into on or after Dec. 29, 1981, pursuant to this section, as amended by section 2 of Pub. L. 97–141, shall be effective only to such extent or in such amounts as are provided in advance in appropriation Acts, and that the amendments made by Pub. L. 97–141 shall not be construed to authorize additional or supplemental appropriations for the fiscal year ending Sept. 30, 1982.

SERVICE AGREEMENTS ENTERED INTO ON OR AFTER DECEMBER 29, 1979; ADVANCE AUTHORIZATION

Section 5 of Pub. L. 96–166 provided that any service agreement entered into on or after Dec. 29, 1979, pursuant to this section, as amended by section 2 of Pub. L. 96–166, shall be effective only to such extent or in such amounts as are provided in advance in appropriation Acts.

TIME OF ENTRY INTO ALLOWANCE AGREEMENTS AND FOR COMMENCEMENT OF ALLOWANCE

Section 2(c) of Pub. L. 95–603 provided that no agreement be entered into under this section before 60th day after Nov. 6, 1978, and that no agreement provide for payment of any allowance under such section for any pay period beginning before later of such 60th day, or Oct. 1, 1978.

EX. ORD. NO. 12109. DELEGATION OF AUTHORITY TO DIRECTOR OF OFFICE OF PERSONNEL MANAGEMENT

Ex. Ord. No. 12109, Dec. 28, 1978, 44 F.R. 1067, provided:

By the authority vested in me as President of the United States of America by Section 5948 of Title 5 and Section 301 of Title 3 of the United States Code, it is hereby ordered as follows:

1–101. The Director of the Office of Personnel Management is hereby designated and empowered to exercise, in consultation with the Director of the Office of Management and Budget, the authority of the President under Section 5948 of Title 5 of the United States Code, to prescribe regulations, criteria, and conditions with regard to the payment of comparability allowances to recruit and retain certain Federal physicians.

1–102. Until the Office of Personnel Management is established (on or before January 1, 1979), pursuant to Reorganization Plan No. 2 of 1978 (43 FR 36037) [set out under section 1101 of this title], the Civil Service Commission shall exercise the authority delegated under this Order to the Director of the Office of Personnel Management.

JIMMY CARTER.

SECTION REFERRED TO IN OTHER SECTIONS

This section is referred to in sections 5307, 8331, 8401 of this title; title 24 section 225e; title 42 section 1395b–6.

Subpart E—Attendance and Leave

CHAPTER 61—HOURS OF WORK

SUBCHAPTER I—GENERAL PROVISIONS

AMENDMENTS

1982—Pub. L. 97–221, § 2(b), July 23, 1982, 96 Stat. 233, inserted "SUBCHAPTER I—GENERAL PROVISIONS" before item 6101 and inserted "SUBCHAPTER II—FLEXIBLE AND COMPRESSED WORK SCHEDULES" and items 6120 to 6133 after item 6106.

1972—Pub. L. 92–392, § 7(b), Aug. 19, 1972, 86 Stat. 573, struck out item 6102 "Eight-hour day; 40-hour work week; wage-board employees".

CHAPTER REFERRED TO IN OTHER SECTIONS

This chapter is referred to in section 5371 of this title.

SUBCHAPTER I—GENERAL PROVISIONS

AMENDMENTS

1982—Pub. L. 97–221, § 2(a)(1), July 23, 1982, 96 Stat. 227, added subchapter I heading so as to designate existing provisions as "SUBCHAPTER I—GENERAL PROVISIONS".

§ 6101. Basic 40-hour workweek; work schedules; regulations

(a)(1) For the purpose of this subsection, "employee" includes an employee of the government of the District of Columbia and an employee whose pay is fixed and adjusted from time to time under section 5343 or 5349 of this title, or by a wage board or similar administrative authority serving the same purpose, but does not include an employee or individual excluded from the definition of employee in section 5541(2) of this title, except as specifically provided under this paragraph.

(2) The head of each Executive agency, military department, and of the government of the District of Columbia shall—

(A) establish a basic administrative workweek of 40 hours for each full-time employee in his organization; and

(B) require that the hours of work within that workweek be performed within a period of not more than 6 of any 7 consecutive days.

(3) Except when the head of an Executive agency, a military department, or of the government of the District of Columbia determines that his organization would be seriously handicapped in carrying out its functions or that costs would be substantially increased, he shall provide, with respect to each employee in his organization, that—

(A) assignments to tours of duty are scheduled in advance over periods of not less than 1 week

(B) the basic 40-hour workweek is scheduled on 5 days, Monday through Friday when possible, and the 2 days outside the basic workweek are consecutive;

(C) the working hours in each day in the basic workweek are the same;

(D) the basic nonovertime workday may not exceed 8 hours;

(E) the occurrence of holidays may not affect the designation of the basic workweek; and

(F) breaks in working hours of more than 1 hour may not be scheduled in a basic workday.

(4) Notwithstanding paragraph (3) of this subsection, the head of an Executive agency, a military department, or of the government of the District of Columbia may establish special tours of duty, of not less than 40 hours, to enable employees to take courses in nearby colleges, universities, or other educational institutions that will equip them for more effective work in the agency. Premium pay may not be paid to an employee solely because his special tour of duty established under this paragraph results in his working on a day or at a time of day for which premium pay is otherwise authorized.

(5) The Architect of the Capitol may apply this subsection to employees under the Office of the Architect of the Capitol or the Botanic Garden. The Librarian of Congress may apply this subsection to employees under the Library of Congress.

(b)(1) For the purpose of this subsection, "agency" and "employee" have the meanings given them by section 5541 of this title.

(2) To the maximum extent practicable, the head of an agency shall schedule the time to be spent by an employee in a travel status away from his official duty station within the regularly scheduled workweek of the employee.

(c) The Office of Personnel Management may prescribe regulations, subject to the approval of the President, necessary for the administration of this section insofar as this section affects employees in or under an Executive agency.

(Pub. L. 89–554, Sept. 6, 1966, 80 Stat. 514; Pub. L. 90–83, § 1(43), Sept. 11, 1967, 81 Stat. 207; Pub. L. 92–392, § 6, Aug. 19, 1972, 86 Stat. 573; Pub. L. 94–183, § 2(25), Dec. 31, 1975, 89 Stat. 1058; Pub. L. 95–454, title IX, § 906(a)(2), Oct. 13, 1978, 92 Stat. 1224.)

HISTORICAL AND REVISION NOTES
1966 ACT

Derivation	U.S. Code	Revised Statutes and Statutes at Large
(a), (b)	5 U.S.C. 944(a).	June 30, 1945, ch. 212, § 604(a), 59 Stat. 303. Sept. 1, 1954, ch. 1208, § 210, 68 Stat. 1112.
(c)	5 U.S.C. 944(d) (less last 27 words).	June 30, 1945, ch. 212, § 604(e) (less last 27 words), 59 Stat. 304.

In subsection (a), the words "in the departmental and the field services" are omitted as unnecessary.

In subsections (a) and (b), the words "an Executive agency, a military department" are coextensive with and substituted for "the several departments and independent establishments and agencies in the executive branch, including Government-owned or controlled corporations" and "such department, establishment, or agency" in view of the definitions in sections 105 and 102. The words "a military department" are included to preserve the application of the source law. Before enactment of the National Security Act Amendments of 1949 (63 Stat. 578), the Department of the Army, the Department of the Navy, and the Department of the Air Force were Executive departments. The National Security Act Amendments of 1949 established the Department of Defense as an Executive Department including the Department of the Army, the Department of the Navy, and the Department of the Air Force as military departments, not as Executive departments. However, the source law for this section which was in effect in 1949, remained applicable to the Secretaries of the military departments by virtue of section 12(g) of the National Security Act Amendments of 1949 (63 Stat. 591), which is set out in the reviser's note for section 301.

Subsection (d) is added on authority of former sections 901(d) and 2358(a) (as applicable to the Federal Employees Pay Act of 1945, as amended) which are carried into section 5541, and to include individuals employed by the government of the District of Columbia as they are not included in the definition of "employee" in section 2105.

Subsection (e) is added on authority of former section 945, which is carried into section 5548. The words "an Executive agency" are substituted for "the executive branch of the Government" to conform to the definition in section 105. Applicability of this section to employees of the General Accounting Office is based on former section 933a.

Standard changes are made to conform with the definitions applicable and the style of this title as outlined in the preface to the report.

1967 ACT

Section of title 5	Source (U.S. Code)	Source (Statutes at Large)
6101(a) (1)–(3), (5).	5:6101(a)–(d).	[None.]
6101(a)(4) ...	5 App.: 944(a)(3).	June 29, 1966, Pub. L. 89–478, 80 Stat. 231.
6101(b)	5 App.: 912b (last sentence).	Oct. 29, 1965, Pub. L. 89–301, § 16, 79 Stat. 1123.
6101(c)	5:6101(e).	[None.]

In subsection (a)(4), the words "without regard to the requirements of such paragraph" are omitted as redundant in view of the words "notwithstanding paragraph (3) of this subsection" at the beginning thereof. The words "an Executive agency, a military department" are coextensive with and substituted for "each such department, establishment, or agency" and to conform to subsections (a)(2) and (a)(3). The words "officers" and "officer" are omitted as included in "employees" and "employee". The word "pay" is substituted for "compensation" to conform to the style of title 5, United States Code.

Subsection (b)(1) is added on authority of former sections 901 and 902 of title 5, which are now codified in 5 U.S.C. 5541.

In subsection (b)(2), the words "head of an agency" are substituted for "head of any department, independent establishment, or agency, including Government-owned or controlled corporations, or of the municipal government of the District of Columbia, or the head of any legislative or judicial agency to which this title applies" to conform to the definition of "agency" in 5 U.S.C. 5541, which is made applicable to this subsection by subsection (b)(1). The word "officer" is omitted as included in "employee".

AMENDMENTS

1978—Subsec. (c). Pub. L. 95–454 substituted "Office of Personnel Management" for "Civil Service Commission".

1975—Subsec. (a)(4). Pub. L. 94–183 substituted "educational" for "education".

1972—Subsec. (a)(1). Pub. L. 92–392 defined "employee" to include an employee whose pay is fixed and adjusted from time to time under section 5343 or 5349 of this title or by a wage board or similar administrative authority serving the same purpose and exclude certain employees "except as specifically provided under this paragraph".

TERMINATION DATE OF 1982 AMENDMENT

Pub. L. 97–221, § 5, July 23, 1982, 96 Stat. 234, as amended by Pub. L. 99–69, July 22, 1985, 99 Stat. 167; Pub. L. 99–109, Sept. 30, 1985, 99 Stat. 482; Pub. L. 99–140, Oct. 31, 1985, 99 Stat. 563, which had provided that enactment of subchapter II of this chapter, amendment of sections 3401 and 6106 of this title, and enactment of provisions set out as notes under sections 6101 and 6106 of this title, should not be in effect after Dec. 31, 1985, was repealed by Pub. L. 99–190, § 140, Dec. 19, 1985, 99 Stat. 1324, and also by Pub. L. 99–196, Dec. 23, 1985, 99 Stat. 1350.

EFFECTIVE DATE OF 1978 AMENDMENT

Amendment by Pub. L. 95–454 effective 90 days after Oct. 13, 1978, see section 907 of Pub. L. 95–454, set out as a note under section 1101 of this title.

EFFECTIVE DATE OF 1972 AMENDMENT

Amendment by Pub. L. 92–392 effective on first day of first applicable pay period beginning on or after 90th day after Aug. 19, 1972, see section 15(a) of Pub. L. 92–392, set out as an Effective Date note under section 5341 of this title.

SHORT TITLE OF 1982 AMENDMENT

Pub. L. 97–221, § 1, July 23, 1982, 96 Stat. 227, provided: "That this Act [enacting subchapter II of this chapter, amending sections 3401 and 6106 of this title, and enacting provisions set out as notes under this section and section 6106 of this title] may be cited as the 'Federal Employees Flexible and Compressed Work Schedules Act of 1982'."

DELEGATION OF FUNCTIONS

Functions vested in Office of Personnel Management under this section insofar as it affects officers and employees in or under the executive branch of the government to be performed without approval of President, see section 1(1) of Ex. Ord. No. 11228, June 14, 1965, 30 F.R. 7739, set out as a note under section 301 of Title 3, The President.

FEDERAL EMPLOYEES FLEXIBLE AND COMPRESSED WORK
SCHEDULES

Pub. L. 95–390, §§ 1–306, Sept. 29, 1978, 92 Stat. 755–762,
as amended by Pub. L. 97–160, Mar. 26, 1982, 96 Stat. 21,
provided that:

"SHORT TITLE

"SECTION 1. This Act [enacting section 5550a of this
title and this note] may be cited as the 'Federal Employees Flexible and Compressed Work Schedules Act
of 1978'.

"CONGRESSIONAL FINDINGS

"SEC. 2. The Congress finds that new trends in the
usage of 4-day workweeks, flexible work hours, and
other variations in workday and workweek schedules in
the private sector appear to show sufficient promise to
warrant carefully designed, controlled, and evaluated
experimentation by Federal agencies to determine
whether and in what situations such varied work schedules can be successfully used by Federal agencies on a
permanent basis. The Congress also finds that there
should be sufficient flexibility in the work schedules of
Federal employees to allow such employees to meet the
obligations of their faith.

"DEFINITIONS

"SEC. 3. For purposes of this Act (other than title IV)
[this note]—
   "(1) the term 'agency' means an Executive agency
and a military department (as such terms are defined
in sections 105 and 102, respectively, of title 5, United
States Code);
   "(2) the term 'employ' has the meaning given it by
section 2105 of title 5, United States Code;
   "(3) the term 'Commission' means the United
States Civil Service Commission; and
   "(4) the term 'basic work requirement' means the
number of hours, excluding overtime hours, which an
employee is required to work or is required to account for by leave or otherwise.

"EXPERIMENTAL PROGRAMS

"SEC. 4. (a)(1) Within 180 days after the effective date
of this section, and subject to the requirements of section 302 and the terms of any written agreement referred to in section 302(a), the Commission shall establish a program which provides for the conducting of
experiments by the Commission under titles I and II of
this Act. Such experimental program shall cover a sufficient number of positions throughout the executive
branch, and a sufficient range of worktime alternatives, as to provide an adequate basis on which to
evaluate the effectiveness and desirability of permanently maintaining flexible or compressed work schedules within the executive branch.
   "(2) Each agency may conduct one or more experiments under titles I and II of this Act. Such experiments shall be subject to such regulations as the Commission may prescribe under section 305 of this Act.
   "(b) The Commission shall, not later than 90 days
after the effective date of this section, establish a master plan which shall contain guidelines and criteria by
which the Commission will study and evaluate experiments conducted under titles I and II of this Act. Such
master plan shall provide for the study and evaluation
of experiments within a sample of organizations of different size, geographic location, and functions and activities, sufficient to insure adequate evaluation of the
impact of varied work schedules on—
   "(1) the efficiency of Government operations;
   "(2) mass transit facilities and traffic;
   "(3) levels of energy consumption;
   "(4) service to the public;
   "(5) increased opportunities for full-time and part-
time employment; and
   "(6) individuals and families generally.
   "(c) The Commission shall provide educational material, and technical aids and assistance, for use by an

agency before and during the period such agency is conducting experiments under this Act [enacting section
5550a of this title and this note].
   "(d) If the head of an agency determines that the implementation of an experimental program referred to in
subsection (a) would substantially disrupt the agency
in carrying out its functions, such agency head shall
request the Commission to exempt such agency from
the requirements of any experiment conducted by the
Commission under subsection (a). Such request shall be
accompanied by a report detailing the reasons for such
determination. The Commission shall exempt an agency from such requirements only if it finds that including the agency within the experiment would not be in
the best interest of the public, the Government, or the
employees. The filing of such a request with the Commission shall exclude the agency from the experiment
until the Commission has made its determination or
until 180 days after the date the request is filed, whichever first occurs.

"TITLE I—FLEXIBLE SCHEDULING OF WORK
HOURS

"DEFINITIONS

"SEC. 101. For purposes of this title—
   "(1) the term 'credit hours' means any hours, within a flexible schedule established under this title,
which are in excess of an employee's basic work requirement and which the employee elects to work so
as to vary the length of a workweek or a workday;
and
   "(2) the term 'overtime hours' means all hours in
excess of 8 hours in a day or 40 hours in a week which
are officially ordered in advance, but does not include
credit hours.

"FLEXIBLE SCHEDULING EXPERIMENTS

"SEC. 102. (a) Notwithstanding section 6101 of title 5,
United States Code, experiments may be conducted in
agenices [agencies] to test flexible schedules which include—
   "(1) designated hours and days during which an employee on such a schedule must be present for work;
and
   "(2) designated hours during which an employee on
such a schedule may elect the time of such employee's arrival at and departure from work, solely for
such purpose or, if and to the extent permitted, for
the purpose of accumulating credit hours to reduce
the length of the workweek or another workday.
An election by an employee referred to in paragraph (2)
shall be subject to limitations generally prescribed to
ensure that the duties and requirements of the employee's position are fulfilled.
   "(b) Notwithstanding any other provision of this Act
[enacting section 5550a of this title and this note], but
subject to the terms of any written agreement under
section 302(a)—
   "(1) any experiment under subsection (a) of this
section may be terminated by the Commission if it
determines that the experiment is not in the best interest of the public, the Government, or the employees; or
   "(2) if the head of an agency determines that any
organization within the agency which is participating
in an experiment under subsection (a) is being substantially disrupted in carrying out its functions or
is incurring additional costs because of such participation, such agency head may—
      "(A) restrict the employees' choice of arrival and
departure time,
      "(B) restrict the use of credit hours, or
      "(C) exclude from such experiment any employee
or group of employees.
   "(c) Experiments under subsection (a) shall terminate not later than the first day of the second pay period beginning after July 4, 1982.

"COMPUTATION OF PREMIUM PAY

"SEC. 103. (a) For purposes of determining compensation for overtime hours in the case of an employee participating in an experiment under section 102—

"(1) the head of an agency may, on request of the employee, grant the employee compensatory time off in lieu of payment for such overtime hours, whether or not irregular or occasional in nature and notwithstanding the provisions of sections 5542(a), 5543(a)(1), 5544(a), and 5550 of title 5, United States Code, section 4107(e)(5) of title 38, United States Code section 7 of the Fair Labor Standards Act, as amended [section 207 of Title 29, Labor], or any other provision of law; or

"(2) the employee shall be compensated for such overtime hours in accordance with such provisions, as applicable.

"(b) Notwithstanding the provisions of law referred to in paragraph (1) of subsection (a), an employee shall not be entitled to be compensated for credit hours worked except to the extent authorized under section 106 or to the extent such employee is allowed to have such hours taken into account with respect to the employee's basic work requirement.

"(c)(1) Notwithstanding section 5545(a) of title 5, United States Code, premium pay for nightwork will not be paid to an employee otherwise subject to such section solely because the employee elects to work credit hours, or elects a time of arrival or departure, at a time of day from which such premium pay is otherwise authorized; except that—

"(A) if an employee is on a flexible schedule under which—

"(i) the number of hours during which such employee must be present for work, plus

"(ii) the number of hours during which such employee may elect to work credit hours or elect the time of arrival at and departure from work,

which occur outside of the night work hours designated in or under such section 5545(a) total less than 8 hours, such premium pay shall be paid for those hours which, when combined with such total, do not exceed 8 hours, and

"(B) if an employee is on a flexible schedule under which the hours that such employee must be present for work include any hours designated in or under such section 5545(a), such premium pay shall be paid for such hours so designated.

"(2) Notwithstanding section 5343(f) of title 5, United States Code, and 4107(e)(2) of title 38, United States Code, night differential will not be paid to any employee otherwise subject to either of such sections solely because such employee elects to work credit hours, or elects a time of arrival or departure, at a time of day for which night differential is otherwise authorized; except that such differential shall be paid to an employee on a flexible schedule under this title—

"(A) in the case of an employee subject to such section 5343(f), for which all or a majority of the hours of such schedule for any day fall between the hours specified in such section, or

"(B) in the case of an employee subject to such section 4107(e)(2), for which 4 hours of such schedule fall between the hours specified in such section.

"HOLIDAYS

"SEC. 104. Notwithstanding sections 6103 and 6104 of title 5, United States Code, if any employee on a flexible schedule under this title is relieved or prevented from working on a day designated as a holiday by Federal statute or Executive order, such employee is entitled to pay with respect to that day for 8 hours (or, in the case of a part-time employee, an appropriate portion of the employee's biweekly basic work requirement as determined under regulations prescribed by the Commission).

"TIME-RECORDING DEVICES

"SEC. 105. Notwithstanding section 6106 of title 5, United States Code, the Commission or an agency may use recording clocks as part of its experiments under this title.

"CREDIT HOURS; ACCUMULATION AND COMPENSATION

"SEC. 106. (a) Subject to any limitation prescribed by the Commission or the agency, a full-time employee on a flexible schedule can accumulate not more than 10 credit hours, and a part-time employee can accumulate not more than one-eighth of the hours in such employee's biweekly basic work requirement, for carryover from a biweekly pay period to a succeeding biweekly pay period for credit to the basic work requirement for such period.

"(b) Any employee who is on a flexible schedule experiment under this title and who is no longer subject to such an experiment shall be paid at such employee's then current rate of basic pay for—

"(1) in the case of a full-time employee, not more than 10 credit hours accumulated by such employee, or

"(2) in the case of a part-time employee, the number of credit hours (not in excess of one-eighth of the hours in such employee's biweekly basic work requirement) accumulated by such employee.

"TITLE II—4-DAY WEEK AND OTHER COMPRESSED WORK SCHEDULES

"DEFINITIONS

"SEC. 201. For purposes of this title—

"(1) the term 'compressed schedule' means—

"(A) in the case of a full-time employee, an 80-hour biweekly basic work requirement which is scheduled for less than 10 workdays, and

"(B) in the case of a part-time employee, a biweekly basic work requirement of less than 80 hours which is scheduled for less than 10 workdays; and

"(2) the term 'overtime hours' means any hours in excess of those specified hours which constitute the compressed schedule.

"COMPRESSED SCHEDULE EXPERIMENTS

"SEC. 202. (a) Notwithstanding section 6101 of title 5, United States Code, experiments may be conducted in agencies to test a 4-day work-week or other compressed schedule.

"(b)(1) An employee in a unit with respect to which an organization of Government employees has not been accorded exclusive recognition shall not be required to participate in any experiment under subsection (a) unless a majority of the employees in such unit who, but for this paragraph, would be included in such experiment have voted to be so included.

"(2) Upon written request to any agency by an employee, the agency, if it determines that participation in an experiment under subsection (a) would impose a personal hardship on such employee, shall—

"(A) except such employee from such experiment; or

"(B) reassign such employee to the first position within the agency—

"(i) which becomes vacant after such determination,

"(ii) which is not included within such experiment,

"(iii) for which such employee is qualified, and

"(iv) which is acceptable to the employee.

A determination by an agency under this paragraph shall be made not later than 10 days after the day on which a written request for such determination is received by the agency.

"(c) Notwithstanding any other provision of this Act [enacting section 5550a of this title and this note], but subject to the terms of any written agreement under section 302(a), any experiment under subsection (a) may be terminated by the Commission, or the agency, if it determines that the experiment is not in the best interest of the public, the Government, or the employees.

"(d) Experiments under subsection (a) shall terminate not later than the end of the first day of the second pay period beginning after July 4, 1982.

"COMPUTATION OF PREMIUM PAY

"SEC. 203. (a) The provisions of sections 5542(a), 5544(a), and 5550(2) of title 5, United States Code, section 4107(e)(5) of title 38, United States Code, section 7 of the Fair Labor Standards Act, as amended [section 207 of Title 29, Labor], or any other law, which relate to premium pay for overtime work, shall not apply to the hours which constitute a compressed schedule.

"(b) In the case of any full-time employee, hours worked in excess of the compressed schedule shall be overtime hours and shall be paid for as provided by whichever statutory provisions referred to in subsection (a) are applicable to the employee. In the case of any part-time employee on a compressed schedule, overtime pay shall begin to be paid after the same number of hours of work after which a full-time employee on a similar schedule would begin to receive overtime pay.

"(c) Notwithstanding section 5544(a), 5546(a), or 5550(1) of title 5, United States Code, or any other applicable provision of law, in the case of any full-time employee on a compressed schedule who performs work (other than overtime work) on a tour of duty for any workday a part of which is performed on a Sunday, such employee is entitled to pay for work performed during the entire tour of duty at the rate of such employee's basic pay, plus premium pay at a rate equal to 25 percent of such basic pay rate.

"(d) Notwithstanding section 5546(b) of title 5, United States Code, an employee on a compressed schedule who performs work on a holiday designated by Federal statute or Executive order is entitled to pay at the rate of such employee's basic pay, plus premium pay at a rate equal to such basic pay rate, for such work which is not in excess of the basic work requirement of such employee for such day. For hours worked on such a holiday in excess of the basic work requirement for such day, the employee is entitled to premium pay in accordance with the provisions of section 5542(a) or 5544(a) of title 5, United States Code, as applicable, or the provisions of section 7 of the Fair Labor Standards Act, as amended [section 207 of Title 29, Labor], whichever provisions are more beneficial to the employee.

"TITLE III—ADMINISTRATIVE PROVISIONS

"ADMINISTRATION OF LEAVE AND RETIREMENT PROVISIONS

"SEC. 301. For purposes of administering sections 6303(a), 6304, 6307(a) and (c), 6323, 6326, and 8339(m) of title 5, United States Code, in the case of an employee who is in any experiment under title I or II, references to a day or workday (or to multiples or parts thereof) contained in such sections shall be considered to be references to 8 hours (or to the respective multiples or parts thereof).

"APPLICATION OF EXPERIMENTS IN THE CASE OF NEGOTIATED CONTRACTS

"SEC. 302. (a) Employees within a unit with respect to which an organization of Government employees has been accorded exclusive recognition shall not be included within any experiment under title I or II of this Act except to the extent expressly provided under a written agreement between the agency and such organization.

"(b) The Commission or an agency may not participate in a flexible or compressed schedule experiment under a negotiated contract which contains premium pay provisions which are inconsistent with the provisions of section 103 or 203 of this Act, as applicable.

"PROHIBITION OF COERCION

"SEC. 303. (a) An employee may not directly or indirectly intimidate, threaten, or coerce, or attempt to intimidate, threaten, or coerce, any other employee for the purpose of interfering with—

"(1) such employee's rights under title I to elect a time of arrival or departure, to work or not to work credit hours, or to request or not to request compensatory time off in lieu of payment for overtime hours; or

"(2) such employee's right under section 202(b)(1) to vote whether or not to be included within a compressed schedule experiment or such employee's right to request an agency determination under section 202(b)(2).

For the purpose of the preceding sentence, the term 'intimidate, threaten, or coerce' includes, but is not limited to, promising to confer or conferring any benefit (such as appointment, promotion, or compensation), or effecting or threatening to effect any reprisal (such as deprivation of appointment, promotion, or compensation).

"(b) Any employee who violates the provisions of subsection (a) shall, upon a final order of the Commission, be—

"(1) removed from such employee's position, in which event that employee may not thereafter hold any position as an employee for such period as the Commission may prescribe;

"(2) suspended without pay from such employee's position for such period as the Commission may prescribe; or

"(3) disciplined in such other manner as the Commission shall deem appropriate.

The commission shall prescribe procedures to carry out this subsection under which an employee subject to removal, suspension, or other disciplinary action shall have rights comparable to the rights afforded an employee subject to removal or suspension under subchapter III of chapter 73 of title 5, United States Code, relating to certain prohibited political activities.

"REPORTS

"SEC. 304. Not later than 2½ years after the effective date of titles I and II of this Act, the Commission shall—

"(1) prepare an interim report containing recommendations as to what, if any, legislative or administrative action shall be taken based upon the results of experiments conducted under this Act [enacting section 5550a of this title and this note], and

"(2) submit copies of such report to the President, the Speaker of the House, and the President pro tempore of the Senate.

The Commission shall prepare a final report with regard to experiments conducted under this Act [enacting section 5550a of this title and this note] and shall submit copies of such report to the President, the Speaker of the House, and the President pro tempore of the Senate not later than 3 years after such effective date.

"REGULATIONS

"SEC. 305. The Commission shall prescribe regulations necessary for the administration of the foregoing provisions of this Act [enacting section 5550a of this title and this note].

"EFFECTIVE DATE

"SEC. 306. The provisions of section 4 and titles I and II of this Act shall take effect on the 180th day after—

"(1) the date of the enactment of this Act [Sept. 29, 1978], or

"(2) October 1, 1978,

whichever date is later."

SAVINGS PROVISIONS; 1982 AMENDMENT

Pub. L. 97–221, § 4, July 23, 1982, 96 Stat. 234, provided that:

"(a) Except as provided in subsection (b), each flexible or compressed work schedule established by any agency under the Federal Employees Flexible and Compressed Work Schedules Act of 1978 (5 U.S.C. 6101 note) in existence on the date of enactment of this Act [July 23, 1982] shall be continued by the agency concerned.

"(b)(1) During the 90-day period after the date of the enactment of this Act [July 23, 1982] any flexible or compressed work schedule referred to in subsection (a) may be reviewed by the agency concerned. If, in reviewing the schedule, the agency determines in writing that—

"(A) the schedule has reduced the productivity of the agency or the level of services to the public, or has increased the cost of the agency operations, and

"(B) termination of the schedule will not result in an increase in the cost of the agency operations (other than a reasonable administrative cost relating to the process of terminating a schedule),

the agency shall, notwithstanding any provision of a negotiated agreement, immediately terminate such schedule and such termination shall not be subject to negotiation or to administrative review (except as the President may provide) or to judicial review.

"(2) If a schedule established pursuant to a negotiated agreement is terminated under paragraph (1), either the agency or the exclusive representative concerned may, by written notice to the other party within 90 days after the date of such termination, initiate collective bargaining pertaining to the establishment of another flexible or compressed work schedule under subchapter II of chapter 61 of title 5, United States Code, which would be effective for the unexpired portion of the term of the negotiated agreement."

SECTION REFERRED TO IN OTHER SECTIONS

This section is referred to in sections 5504, 6122, 6127 of this title; title 10 sections 4338, 6952, 9338; title 32 section 709; title 40 sections 166b–1d, 166b–1e.

[§ 6102. Repealed. Pub. L. 92–392, § 7(a), Aug. 19, 1972, 86 Stat. 573]

Section, Pub. L. 89–554, Sept. 6, 1966, 80 Stat. 515, provided for eight-hour day and 40-hour workweek for wage-board employees. See sections 5544(a) and 6101(a)(1) of this title.

EFFECTIVE DATE OF REPEAL

Repeal effective on first day of first applicable pay period beginning on or after 90th day after Aug. 19, 1972, see section 15(a) of Pub. L. 92–392, set out as an Effective Date note under section 5341 of this title.

§ 6103. Holidays

(a) The following are legal public holidays:

New Year's Day, January 1.

Birthday of Martin Luther King, Jr., the third Monday in January.

Washington's Birthday, the third Monday in February.

Memorial Day, the last Monday in May.

Independence Day, July 4.

Labor Day, the first Monday in September.

Columbus Day, the second Monday in October.

Veterans Day, November 11.

Thanksgiving Day, the fourth Thursday in November.

Christmas Day, December 25.

(b) For the purpose of statutes relating to pay and leave of employees, with respect to a legal public holiday and any other day declared to be a holiday by Federal statute or Executive order, the following rules apply:

(1) Instead of a holiday that occurs on a Saturday, the Friday immediately before is a legal holiday for—

(A) employees whose basic workweek is Monday through Friday; and

(B) the purpose of section 6309[1] of this title.

(2) Instead of a holiday that occurs on a regular weekly non-workday of an employee whose basic workweek is other than Monday through Friday, except the regular weekly non-workday administratively scheduled for the employee instead of Sunday, the workday immediately before that regular weekly non-workday is a legal public holiday for the employee.

(3) Instead of a holiday that is designated under subsection (a) to occur on a Monday, for an employee at a duty post outside the United States whose basic workweek is other than Monday through Friday, and for whom Monday is a regularly scheduled workday, the legal public holiday is the first workday of the workweek in which the Monday designated for the observance of such holiday under subsection (a) occurs.

This subsection, except subparagraph (B) of paragraph (1), does not apply to an employee whose basic workweek is Monday through Saturday.

(c) January 20 of each fourth year after 1965, Inauguration Day, is a legal public holiday for the purpose of statutes relating to pay and leave of employees as defined by section 2105 of this title and individuals employed by the government of the District of Columbia employed in the District of Columbia, Montgomery and Prince Georges Counties in Maryland, Arlington and Fairfax Counties in Virginia, and the cities of Alexandria and Falls Church in Virginia. When January 20 of any fourth year after 1965 falls on Sunday, the next succeeding day selected for the public observance of the inauguration of the President is a legal public holiday for the purpose of this subsection.

(d)(1) For purposes of this subsection—

(A) the term "compressed schedule" has the meaning given such term by section 6121(5); and

(B) the term "adverse agency impact" has the meaning given such term by section 6131(b).

(2) An agency may prescribe rules under which employees on a compressed schedule may, in the case of a holiday that occurs on a regularly scheduled non-workday for such employees, and notwithstanding any other provision of law or the terms of any collective bargaining agreement, be required to observe such holiday on a workday other than as provided by subsection (b), if the agency head determines that it is necessary to do so in order to prevent an adverse agency impact.

(Pub. L. 89–554, Sept. 6, 1966, 80 Stat. 515; Pub. L. 90–363, § 1(a), June 28, 1968, 82 Stat. 250; Pub. L. 94–97, Sept. 18, 1975, 89 Stat. 479; Pub. L. 98–144, § 1, Nov. 2, 1983, 97 Stat. 917; Pub. L. 104–201, div. A, title XVI, § 1613, Sept. 23, 1996, 110 Stat. 2739; Pub. L. 105–261, div. A, title XI, § 1107, Oct. 17, 1998, 112 Stat. 2142.)

---

[1] See References in Text note below.

Derivation	U.S. Code	Revised Statutes and Statutes at Large
(a)	5 U.S.C. 87.	June 28, 1894, ch. 118, 28 Stat. 96.
	5 U.S.C. 87a.	May 13, 1938, ch. 210, 52 Stat. 351.
		June 1, 1954, ch. 250, 68 Stat. 168.
	5 U.S.C. 87b.	Dec. 26, 1941, ch. 631, 55 Stat. 862.
(b)	5 U.S.C. 87c.	Sept. 22, 1959, Pub. L. 86–362, §§1, 2, 73 Stat. 643, 644.
(c)	[Uncodified].	Jan. 11, 1957, Pub. L. 85–1, 71 Stat. 3.

In subsection (a), former sections 87, 87a, and 87b are combined and restated for clarity. The names of all holidays are inserted for ready reference in a like manner to that used in former section 87c.

In subsection (c), the year "1965" is substituted for "1957".

Standard changes are made to conform with the definitions applicable and the style of this title as outlined in the preface to the report.

REFERENCES IN TEXT

Section 6309 of this title, referred to in subsec. (b)(1)(B), was repealed by Pub. L. 94–183, §2(26), Dec. 31, 1975, 89 Stat. 1058.

AMENDMENTS

1998—Subsec. (b)(3). Pub. L. 105–261 added par. (3).

1996—Subsec. (d). Pub. L. 104–201 added subsec. (d).

1983—Subsec. (a). Pub. L. 98–144 inserted item relating to birthday of Martin Luther King, Jr.

1975—Subsec. (a). Pub. L. 94–97 changed Veterans Day from fourth Monday in October to November 11.

1968—Subsec. (a). Pub. L. 90–363 added Columbus Day, the second Monday in October, to the enumerated legal public holidays, and substituted provisions that Washington's Birthday, Memorial Day, and Veterans Day are to be celebrated on the third Monday in February, the last Monday in May, and the fourth Monday in October, respectively, for provisions that the above mentioned public holidays are to be celebrated on February 22, May 30, and November 11, respectively.

EFFECTIVE DATE OF 1983 AMENDMENT

Section 2 of Pub. L. 98–144 provided that: "The amendment made by the first section of this Act [amending this section] shall take effect on the first January 1 that occurs after the two-year period following the date of the enactment of this Act [Nov. 2, 1983]."

EFFECTIVE DATE OF 1975 AMENDMENT

Pub. L. 94–97 provided that the amendment made by Pub. L. 94–97 is effective Jan. 1, 1978.

EFFECTIVE DATE OF 1968 AMENDMENT

Section 2 of Pub. L. 90–363 provided that: "The amendment made by subsection (a) of the first section of this Act [amending this section] shall take effect on January 1, 1971."

REFERENCES IN LAWS OF THE UNITED STATES TO OBSERVANCES OF LEGAL PUBLIC HOLIDAYS

Section 1(b) of Pub. L. 90–363 provided that: "Any reference in a law of the United States (in effect on the effective date of the amendment made by subsection (a) of this section) [January 1, 1971] to the observance of a legal public holiday on a day other than the day prescribed for the observance of such holiday by section 6103(a) of title 5, United States Code, as amended by subsection (a), shall on and after such effective date be considered a reference to the day for the observance of such holiday prescribed in such amended section 6103(a)."

EXECUTIVE ORDER NO. 10358

Ex. Ord. No. 10358, June 9, 1952, 17 F.R. 1529, as amended by Ex. Ord. No. 11226, May 27, 1965, 30 F.R. 7213; Ex. Ord. No. 11272, Feb. 23, 1966, 31 F.R. 3111, which related to the observance of holidays, was revoked by Ex. Ord. No. 11582, Feb. 11, 1971, 36 F.R. 2957, set out below.

EX. ORD. NO. 11582. OBSERVANCE OF HOLIDAYS

Ex. Ord. No. 11582, Feb. 11, 1971, 36 F.R. 2957, provided:

By virtue of the authority vested in me as President of the United States, it is hereby ordered as follows:

SECTION 1. Except as provided in section 7, this order shall apply to all executive departments, independent agencies, and Government corporations, including their field services.

SEC. 2. As used in this order:

(a) *Holiday* means the first day of January, the third Monday of February, the last Monday of May, the fourth day of July, the first Monday of September, the second Monday of October, the fourth Monday of October, the fourth Thursday of November, the twenty-fifth day of December, or any other calendar day designated as a holiday by Federal statute or Executive order.

(b) *Workday* means those hours which comprise in sequence the employee's regular daily tour of duty within any 24-hour period, whether falling entirely within one calendar day or not.

SEC. 3. (a) Any employee whose basic workweek does not include Sunday and who would ordinarily be excused from work on a holiday falling within his basic workweek shall be excused from work on the next workday of his basic workweek whenever a holiday falls on Sunday.

(b) Any employee whose basic workweek includes Sunday and who would ordinarily be excused from work on a holiday falling within his basic workweek shall be excused from work on the next workday of his basic workweek whenever a holiday falls on a day that has been administratively scheduled as his *regular* weekly nonworkday in lieu of Sunday.

SEC. 4. The holiday for a full-time employee for whom the head of a department has established the first 40 hours of duty performed within a period of not more than six days of the administrative workweek as his basic workweek because of the impracticability of prescribing a regular schedule of definite hours of duty for each workday, shall be determined as follows:

(a) If a holiday occurs on Sunday, the head of the department shall designate in advance either Sunday or Monday as the employee's holiday and the employee's basic 40-hour tour of duty shall be deemed to include eight hours on the day designated as the employee's holiday.

(b) If a holiday occurs on Saturday, the head of the department shall designate in advance either the Saturday or the preceding Friday as the employee's holiday and the employee's basic 40-hour tour of duty shall be deemed to include eight hours on the day designated as the employee's holiday.

(c) If a holiday occurs on any other day of the week, that day shall be the employee's holiday, and the employee's basic 40-hour tour of duty shall be deemed to include eight hours on that day.

(d) When a holiday is less than a full day, proportionate credit will be given under paragraph (a), (b), or (c) of this section.

SEC. 5. Any employee whose workday covers portions of two calendar days and who would, except for this section, ordinarily be excused from work scheduled for the hours of any calendar day on which a holiday falls, shall instead be excused from work on his entire workday which commences on any such calendar day.

SEC. 6. In administering the provisions of law relating to pay and leave of absence, the workdays referred to in sections 3, 4, and 5 shall be treated as holidays in lieu of the corresponding calendar holidays.

SEC. 7. The provisions of this order shall apply to officers and employees of the Post Office Department and the United States Postal Service (except that sections

3, 4, 5, and 6 shall not apply to the Postal Field Service) until changed by the Postal Service in accordance with the Postal Reorganization Act.

SEC. 8. Executive Order No. 10358 of June 9, 1952, entitled *Observance of Holidays by Government Agencies* and amendatory Executive Orders No. 11226 of May 27, 1965, and No. 11272 of February 23, 1966, are revoked.

SEC. 9. This order is effective as of January 1, 1971.

RICHARD NIXON.

SECTION REFERRED TO IN OTHER SECTIONS

This section is referred to in sections 6104, 6124 of this title; title 12 section 3710; title 21 section 1053; title 29 section 1201; title 38 section 5120; title 42 section 909.

§ 6104. Holidays; daily, hourly, and piece-work basis employees

When a regular employee as defined by section 2105 of this title or an individual employed regularly by the government of the District of Columbia, whose pay is fixed at a daily or hourly rate, or on a piece-work basis, is relieved or prevented from working on a day—

(1) on which agencies are closed by Executive order, or, for individuals employed by the government of the District of Columbia, by order of the Mayor;

(2) by administrative order under regulations issued by the President, or, for individuals employed by the government of the District of Columbia, by the Council of the District of Columbia; or

(3) solely because of the occurrence of a legal public holiday under section 6103 of this title, or a day declared a holiday by Federal statute, Executive order, or, for individuals employed by the government of the District of Columbia, by order of the Mayor;

he is entitled to the same pay for that day as for a day on which an ordinary day's work is performed.

(Pub. L. 89–554, Sept. 6, 1966, 80 Stat. 516; Pub. L. 90–623, §1(15), Oct. 22, 1968, 82 Stat. 1313; Pub. L. 96–54, §2(a)(38), Aug. 14, 1979, 93 Stat. 383.)

HISTORICAL AND REVISION NOTES

Derivation	U.S. Code	Revised Statutes and Statutes at Large
....	5 U.S.C. 86a.	June 29, 1938, ch. 818, §1, 52 Stat. 1246. June 11, 1954, ch. 283, 68 Stat. 249. July 18, 1958, Pub. L. 85–533, §2, 72 Stat. 377.

The enumeration of holidays is eliminated as unnecessary in view of section 6103.

Standard changes are made to conform with the definitions applicable and the style of this title as outlined in the preface to the report.

AMENDMENTS

1979—Pub. L. 96–54 substituted "Mayor" for "Commissioner" in pars. (1) and (3), and "Council of the District of Columbia" for "District of Columbia Council" in par. (2).

1968—Pub. L. 90–623 substituted "Commissioner" for "Board of Commissioners" in pars. (1) and (3), and "District of Columbia Council" for "Board of Commissioners" in par. (2).

EFFECTIVE DATE OF 1979 AMENDMENT

Amendment by Pub. L. 96–54 effective July 12, 1979, see section 2(b) of Pub. L. 96–54, set out as a note under section 305 of this title.

EFFECTIVE DATE OF 1968 AMENDMENT

Amendment by Pub. L. 90–623 intended to restate without substantive change the law in effect on Oct. 22, 1968, see section 6 of Pub. L. 90–623, set out as a note under section 5334 of this title.

EX. ORD. NO. 10552. DELEGATION OF AUTHORITY TO PROMULGATE REGULATIONS

Ex. Ord. No. 10552, Aug. 10, 1954, 19 F.R. 5079, as amended by Ex. Ord. No. 12107, Dec. 28, 1978, 44 F.R. 1055, provided:

By virtue of the authority vested in me by section 301 of title 3 of the United States Code, 65 Stat. 713, it is declared that the Office of Personnel Management be, and it is hereby, designated and empowered to exercise, without the approval, ratification, or other action of the President, the authority vested in the President by the joint resolution of June 29, 1938, 52 Stat. 1246, as amended by the act of June 11, 1954, 68 Stat. 249 [this section], to promulgate regulations under which certain employees of the Government may be prevented or relieved from working by administrative order.

SECTION REFERRED TO IN OTHER SECTIONS

This section is referred to in section 6124 of this title.

§ 6105. Closing of Executive departments

An Executive department may not be closed as a mark to the memory of a deceased former official of the United States.

(Pub. L. 89–554, Sept. 6, 1966, 80 Stat. 516.)

HISTORICAL AND REVISION NOTES

Derivation	U.S. Code	Revised Statutes and Statutes at Large
....	5 U.S.C. 28.	Mar. 3, 1893, ch. 211, §4, 27 Stat. 715.

Standard changes are made to conform with the definitions applicable and the style of this title as outlined in the preface to the report.

§ 6106. Time clocks; restrictions

A recording clock may not be used to record time of an employee of an Executive department in the District of Columbia, except that the Bureau of Engraving and Printing may use such recording clocks.

(Pub. L. 89–554, Sept. 6, 1966, 80 Stat. 516; Pub. L. 97–221, §6(a), July 23, 1982, 96 Stat. 234.)

HISTORICAL AND REVISION NOTES

Derivation	U.S. Code	Revised Statutes and Statutes at Large
....	5 U.S.C. 27.	Feb. 24, 1899, ch. 187, §1 (14th par. on p. 864), 30 Stat. 864.

The words "District of Columbia" are substituted for "Washington" as a clearer statement.

Standard changes are made to conform with the definitions applicable and the style of this title as outlined in the preface to the report.

AMENDMENTS

1982—Pub. L. 97–221 substituted "District of Columbia, except that the Bureau of Engraving and Printing may use such recording clocks" for "District of Columbia".

EFFECTIVE DATE OF 1982 AMENDMENT

Section 6(b) of Pub. L. 97–221 provided that: "The amendment made by this section [amending this section] shall take effect October 1, 1982. Section 5 of this Act [set out in the Termination Date of 1982 Amendment note under section 6101 of this title] shall not apply to the amendment made by this section.''

SECTION REFERRED TO IN OTHER SECTIONS

This section is referred to in section 6125 of this title.

SUBCHAPTER II—FLEXIBLE AND COMPRESSED WORK SCHEDULES

AMENDMENTS

1982—Pub. L. 97–221, § 2(a)(2), July 23, 1982, 96 Stat. 227, added subchapter II heading as part of enactment of sections 6120 to 6133 of this title.

SUBCHAPTER REFERRED TO IN OTHER SECTIONS

This subchapter is referred to in section 3401 of this title; title 25 section 1616i.

§ 6120. Purpose

The Congress finds that the use of flexible and compressed work schedules has the potential to improve productivity in the Federal Government and provide greater service to the public.

(Added Pub. L. 97–221, § 2(a)(2), July 23, 1982, 96 Stat. 227.)

TELECOMMUTING IN EXECUTIVE AGENCIES

Pub. L. 106–346, § 101(a) [title III, § 359], Oct. 23, 2000, 114 Stat. 1356, 1356A–36, provided that: "Each executive agency shall establish a policy under which eligible employees of the agency may participate in telecommuting to the maximum extent possible without diminished employee performance. Not later than 6 months after the date of the enactment of this Act [Oct. 23, 2000], the Director of the Office of Personnel Management shall provide that the requirements of this section are applied to 25 percent of the Federal workforce, and to an additional 25 percent of such workforce each year thereafter."

EXPANDING FAMILY-FRIENDLY WORK ARRANGEMENTS IN EXECUTIVE BRANCH

Memorandum of President of the United States, July 11, 1994, 59 F.R. 36017, provided:

Memorandum for the Heads of Executive Departments and Agencies

In order to recruit and retain a Federal work force that will provide the highest quality of service to the American people, the executive branch must implement flexible work arrangements to create a "family-friendly" workplace. Broad use of flexible work arrangements to enable Federal employees to better balance their work and family responsibilities can increase employee effectiveness and job satisfaction, while decreasing turnover rates and absenteeism. I therefore adopt the National Performance Review's recommendation that a more family-friendly workplace be created by expanding opportunities for Federal workers to participate in flexible work arrangements, consistent with the mission of the executive branch to serve the public.

The head of each executive department or agency (hereafter collectively "agency" or "agencies") is hereby directed to establish a program to encourage and support the expansion of flexible family-friendly work arrangements, including: job sharing; career part-time employment; alternative work schedules; telecommuting and satellite work locations. Such a program shall include:

(1) identifying agency positions that are suitable for flexible work arrangements;

(2) adopting appropriate policies to increase the opportunities for employees in suitable positions to participate in such flexible work arrangements;

(3) providing appropriate training and support necessary to implement flexible work arrangements; and

(4) identifying barriers to implementing this directive and providing recommendations for addressing such barriers to the President's Management Council.

I direct the Director of the Office of Personnel Management ("OPM") and the Administrator of General Services ("GSA") to take all necessary steps to support and encourage the expanded implementation of flexible work arrangements. The OPM and GSA shall work in concert to promptly review and revise regulations that are barriers to such work arrangements and develop legislative proposals, as needed, to achieve the goals of this directive. The OPM and GSA also shall assist agencies, as requested, to implement this directive.

The President's Management Council, in conjunction with the Office of Management and Budget, shall ensure that any guidance necessary to implement the actions set forth in this directive is provided.

Independent agencies are requested to adhere to this directive to the extent permitted by law.

This directive is for the internal management of the executive branch and is not intended to, and does not, create any right or benefit, substantive or procedural, enforceable by a party against the United States, its agencies or instrumentalities, its officers or employees, or any other person.

The Director of the Office of Management and Budget is authorized and directed to publish this directive in the Federal Register.

WILLIAM J. CLINTON.

§ 6121. Definitions

For purposes of this subchapter—

(1) "agency" means any Executive agency, any military department, the Government Printing Office, and the Library of Congress;

(2) "employee" has the meaning given the term in subsection (a) of section 2105 of this title, except that such term also includes an employee described in subsection (c) of that section;

(3) "basic work requirement" means the number of hours, excluding overtime hours, which an employee is required to work or is required to account for by leave or otherwise;

(4) "credit hours" means any hours, within a flexible schedule established under section 6122 of this title, which are in excess of an employee's basic work requirement and which the employee elects to work so as to vary the length of a workweek or a workday;

(5) "compressed schedule" means—

(A) in the case of a full-time employee, an 80-hour biweekly basic work requirement which is scheduled for less than 10 workdays, and

(B) in the case of a part-time employee, a biweekly basic work requirement of less than 80 hours which is scheduled for less than 10 workdays;

(6) "overtime hours", when used with respect to flexible schedule programs under sections 6122 through 6126 of this title, means all hours in excess of 8 hours in a day or 40 hours in a week which are officially ordered in advance, but does not include credit hours;

(7) "overtime hours", when used with respect to compressed schedule programs under sections 6127 and 6128 of this title, means any hours in excess of those specified hours which constitute the compressed schedule; and

(8) "collective bargaining", "collective bargaining agreement", and "exclusive representative" have the same meanings given such terms—

(A) by section 7103(a)(12), (8), and (16) of this title, respectively, in the case of any unit covered by chapter 71 of this title; and

(B) in the case of any other unit, by the corresponding provisions applicable under the personnel system covering this unit.

(Added Pub. L. 97–221, §2(a)(2), July 23, 1982, 96 Stat. 227; amended Pub. L. 101–163, title III, §312, Nov. 21, 1989, 103 Stat. 1065; Pub. L. 104–106, div. A, title X, §1041, Feb. 10, 1996, 110 Stat. 433.)

AMENDMENTS

1996—Par. (2). Pub. L. 104–106 amended par. (2) generally. Prior to amendment, par. (2) read as follows: "'employee' has the meaning given it by section 2105 of this title;".

1989—Par. (1). Pub. L. 101–163 inserted "the Government Printing Office," after "military department,".

SECTION REFERRED TO IN OTHER SECTIONS

This section is referred to in section 6103 of this title.

§ 6122. Flexible schedules; agencies authorized to use

(a) Notwithstanding section 6101 of this title, each agency may establish, in accordance with this subchapter, programs which allow the use of flexible schedules which include—

(1) designated hours and days during which an employee on such a schedule must be present for work; and

(2) designated hours during which an employee on such a schedule may elect the time of such employee's arrival at and departure from work, solely for such purpose or, if and to the extent permitted, for the purpose of accumulating credit hours to reduce the length of the workweek or another workday.

An election by an employee referred to in paragraph (2) shall be subject to limitations generally prescribed to ensure that the duties and requirements of the employee's position are fulfilled.

(b) Notwithstanding any other provision of this subchapter, but subject to the terms of any written agreement referred to in section 6130(a) of this title, if the head of an agency determines that any organization within the agency which is participating in a program under subsection (a) is being substantially disrupted in carrying out its functions or is incurring additional costs because of such participation, such agency head may—

(1) restrict the employees' choice of arrival and departure time,

(2) restrict the use of credit hours, or

(3) exclude from such program any employee or group of employees.

(Added Pub. L. 97–221, §2(a)(2), July 23, 1982, 96 Stat. 228.)

SECTION REFERRED TO IN OTHER SECTIONS

This section is referred to in sections 6121, 6123, 6124, 6125, 6126, 6132 of this title.

§ 6123. Flexible schedules; computation of premium pay

(a) For purposes of determining compensation for overtime hours in the case of an employee participating in a program under section 6122 of this title—

(1) the head of an agency may, on request of the employee, grant the employee compensatory time off in lieu of payment for such overtime hours, whether or not irregular or occasional in nature and notwithstanding the provisions of sections 5542(a), 5543(a)(1) and section[1] 5544(a) of this title, section 7453(e) of title 38, section 7 of the Fair Labor Standards Act (29 U.S.C. 207), or any other provision of law; or

(2) the employee shall be compensated for such overtime hours in accordance with such provisions, as applicable.

(b) Notwithstanding the provisions of law referred to in subsection (a)(1) of this section, an employee shall not be entitled to be compensated for credit hours worked except to the extent authorized under section 6126 of this title or to the extent such employee is allowed to have such hours taken into account with respect to the employee's basic work requirement.

(c)(1) Notwithstanding section 5545(a) of this title, premium pay for nightwork will not be paid to an employee otherwise subject to such section solely because the employee elects to work credit hours, or elects a time of arrival or departure, at a time of day for which such premium pay is otherwise authorized, except that—

(A) if an employee is on a flexible schedule under which—

(i) the number of hours during which such employee must be present for work, plus

(ii) the number of hours during which such employee may elect to work credit hours or elect the time of arrival at and departure from work,

which occur outside of the nightwork hours designated in or under such section 5545(a) total less than 8 hours, such premium pay shall be paid for those hours which, when combined with such total, do not exceed 8 hours, and

(B) if an employee is on a flexible schedule under which the hours that such employee must be present for work include any hours designated in or under such section 5545(a), such premium pay shall be paid for such hours so designated.

(2) Notwithstanding section 5343(f) of this title, and section 7453(b) of title 38, night differential will not be paid to any employee otherwise subject to either of such sections solely because such employee elects to work credit hours, or elects a time of arrival or departure, at a time of day for which night differential is otherwise authorized, except that such differential shall be paid to an employee on a flexible schedule under this subchapter—

(A) in the case of an employee subject to subsection (f) of such section 5343, for which all or a majority of the hours of such schedule for any day fall between the hours specified in such subsection, or

(B) in the case of an employee subject to subsection (b) of such section 7453, for which 4 hours of such schedule fall between the hours specified in such subsection.

---

[1] So in original. The word "section" probably should not appear.

(Added Pub. L. 97–221, §2(a)(2), July 23, 1982, 96 Stat. 228; amended Pub. L. 102–40, title IV, §403(c)(2), May 7, 1991, 105 Stat. 240; Pub. L. 102–378, §2(44)(D), Oct. 2, 1992, 106 Stat. 1352.)

AMENDMENTS

1992—Subsec. (a)(1). Pub. L. 102–378 substituted "5543(a)(1) and section 5544(a)" for "5543(a)(1), 5544(a), and 5550".

1991—Subsec. (a)(1). Pub. L. 102–40, §403(c)(2)(A), substituted "section 7453(e)" for "section 4107(e)(5)".

Subsec. (c)(2). Pub. L. 102–40, §403(c)(2)(B), in introductory provisions substituted "section 7453(b)" for "section 4107(e)(2)" and in subpar. (B) substituted "subsection (b) of such section 7453" for "subsection (e)(2) of such section 4107".

SECTION REFERRED TO IN OTHER SECTIONS

This section is referred to in sections 6121, 6130, 6132 of this title.

§ 6124. Flexible schedules; holidays

Notwithstanding sections 6103 and 6104 of this title, if any employee on a flexible schedule under section 6122 of this title is relieved or prevented from working on a day designated as a holiday by Federal statute or Executive order, such employee is entitled to pay with respect to that day for 8 hours (or, in the case of a part-time employee, an appropriate portion of the employee's biweekly basic work requirement as determined under regulations prescribed by the Office of Personnel Management).

(Added Pub. L. 97–221, §2(a)(2), July 23, 1982, 96 Stat. 229.)

SECTION REFERRED TO IN OTHER SECTIONS

This section is referred to in sections 6121, 6132 of this title.

§ 6125. Flexible schedules; time-recording devices

Notwithstanding section 6106 of this title, the Office of Personnel Management or any agency may use recording clocks as part of programs under section 6122 of this title.

(Added Pub. L. 97–221, §2(a)(2), July 23, 1982, 96 Stat. 229.)

SECTION REFERRED TO IN OTHER SECTIONS

This section is referred to in sections 6121, 6132 of this title.

§ 6126. Flexible schedules; credit hours; accumulation and compensation

(a) Subject to any limitation prescribed by the Office of Personnel Management or the agency, a full-time employee on a flexible schedule can accumulate not more than 24 credit hours, and a part-time employee can accumulate not more than one-fourth of the hours in such employee's biweekly basic work requirement, for carryover from a biweekly pay period to a succeeding biweekly pay period for credit to the basic work requirement for such period.

(b) Any employee who is on a flexible schedule program under section 6122 of this title and who is no longer subject to such a program shall be paid at such employee's then current rate of basic pay for—

(1) in the case of a full-time employee, not more than 24 credit hours accumulated by such employee, or

(2) in the case of a part-time employee, the number of credit hours (not in excess of one-fourth of the hours in such employee's biweekly basic work requirement) accumulated by such employee.

(Added Pub. L. 97–221, §2(a)(2), July 23, 1982, 96 Stat. 230.)

SECTION REFERRED TO IN OTHER SECTIONS

This section is referred to in sections 6121, 6123, 6132 of this title.

§ 6127. Compressed schedules; agencies authorized to use

(a) Notwithstanding section 6101 of this title, each agency may establish programs which use a 4-day workweek or other compressed schedule.

(b)(1) An employee in a unit with respect to which an organization of Government employees has not been accorded exclusive recognition shall not be required to participate in any program under subsection (a) unless a majority of the employees in such unit who, but for this paragraph, would be included in such program have voted to be so included.

(2) Upon written request to any agency by an employee, the agency, if it determines that participation in a program under subsection (a) would impose a personal hardship on such employee, shall—

(A) except such employee from such program; or

(B) reassign such employee to the first position within the agency—

(i) which becomes vacant after such determination,

(ii) which is not included within such program,

(iii) for which such employee is qualified, and

(iv) which is acceptable to the employee.

A determination by an agency under this paragraph shall be made not later than 10 days after the day on which a written request for such determination is received by the agency.

(Added Pub. L. 97–221, §2(a)(2), July 23, 1982, 96 Stat. 230.)

SECTION REFERRED TO IN OTHER SECTIONS

This section is referred to in sections 6121, 6132 of this title.

§ 6128. Compressed schedules; computation of premium pay

(a) The provisions of sections 5542(a) and 5544(a) of this title, section 7453(e) of title 38, section 7 of the Fair Labor Standards Act (29 U.S.C. 207), or any other law, which relate to premium pay for overtime work, shall not apply to the hours which constitute a compressed schedule.

(b) In the case of any full-time employee, hours worked in excess of the compressed schedule shall be overtime hours and shall be paid for as provided by the applicable provisions referred to in subsection (a) of this section. In the case of any part-time employee on a compressed schedule, overtime pay shall begin to be paid after the same number of hours of work after which a full-time employee on a similar schedule would begin to receive overtime pay.

(c) Notwithstanding section 5544(a) or 5546(a) of this title, or any other applicable provision of law, in the case of any full-time employee on a compressed schedule who performs work (other than overtime work) on a tour of duty for any workday a part of which is performed on a Sunday, such employee is entitled to pay for work performed during the entire tour of duty at the rate of such employee's basic pay, plus premium pay at a rate equal to 25 percent of such basic pay rate.

(d) Notwithstanding section 5546(b) of this title, an employee on a compressed schedule who performs work on a holiday designated by Federal statute or Executive order is entitled to pay at the rate of such employee's basic pay, plus premium pay at a rate equal to such basic pay rate, for such work which is not in excess of the basic work requirement of such employee for such day. For hours worked on such a holiday in excess of the basic work requirement for such day, the employee is entitled to premium pay in accordance with the provisions of section 5542(a) or 5544(a) of this title, as applicable, or the provisions of section 7 of the Fair Labor Standards Act (29 U.S.C. 207) whichever provisions are more beneficial to the employee.

(Added Pub. L. 97–221, § 2(a)(2), July 23, 1982, 96 Stat. 230; amended Pub. L. 102–40, title IV, § 403(c)(3), May 7, 1991, 105 Stat. 240; Pub. L. 102–378, § 2(44)(E), Oct. 2, 1992, 106 Stat. 1352.)

AMENDMENTS

1992—Subsec. (a). Pub. L. 102–378, § 2(44)(E)(i), substituted "5542(a) and 5544(a)" for "5542(a), 5544(a), and 5550(2)".

Subsec. (c). Pub. L. 102–378, § 2(44)(E)(ii), substituted "5544(a) or 5546(a)" for "5544(a), 5546(a), or 5550(1)".

1991—Subsec. (a). Pub. L. 102–40 substituted "section 7453(e)" for "section 4107(e)(5)".

SECTION REFERRED TO IN OTHER SECTIONS

This section is referred to in sections 6121, 6130 of this title.

§ 6129. Administration of leave and retirement provisions

For purposes of administering sections 6303(a), 6304, 6307(a) and (d), 6323, 6326, 6327, and 8339(m) of this title, in the case of an employee who is in any program under this subchapter, references to a day or workday (or to multiples or parts thereof) contained in such sections shall be considered to be references to 8 hours (or to the respective multiples or parts thereof).

(Added Pub. L. 97–221, § 2(a)(2), July 23, 1982, 96 Stat. 231; amended Pub. L. 103–329, title VI, § 629(a)(2)(A), (b)(2), Sept. 30, 1994, 108 Stat. 2423.)

AMENDMENTS

1994—Pub. L. 103–329 substituted "6307(a) and (d)" for "6307(a) and (c)" and inserted "6327," after "6326,".

§ 6130. Application of programs in the case of collective bargaining agreements

(a)(1) In the case of employees in a unit represented by an exclusive representative, any flexible or compressed work schedule, and the establishment and termination of any such schedule, shall be subject to the provisions of this subchapter and the terms of a collective bargaining agreement between the agency and the exclusive representative.

(2) Employees within a unit represented by an exclusive representative shall not be included within any program under this subchapter except to the extent expressly provided under a collective bargaining agreement between the agency and the exclusive representative.

(b) An agency may not participate in a flexible or compressed schedule program under a collective bargaining agreement which contains premium pay provisions which are inconsistent with the provisions of section 6123 or 6128 of this title, as applicable.

(Added Pub. L. 97–221, § 2(a)(2), July 23, 1982, 96 Stat. 231.)

SECTION REFERRED TO IN OTHER SECTIONS

This section is referred to in section 6122 of this title.

§ 6131. Criteria and review

(a) Notwithstanding the preceding provisions of this subchapter or any collective bargaining agreement and subject to subsection (c) of this section, if the head of an agency finds that a particular flexible or compressed schedule under this subchapter has had or would have an adverse agency impact, the agency shall promptly determine not to—

(1) establish such schedule; or

(2) continue such schedule, if the schedule has already been established.

(b) For purposes of this section, "adverse agency impact" means—

(1) a reduction of the productivity of the agency;

(2) a diminished level of services furnished to the public by the agency; or

(3) an increase in the cost of agency operations (other than a reasonable administrative cost relating to the process of establishing a flexible or compressed schedule).

(c)(1) This subsection shall apply in the case of any schedule covering employees in a unit represented by an exclusive representative.

(2)(A) If an agency and an exclusive representative reach an impasse in collective bargaining with respect to an agency determination under subsection (a)(1) not to establish a flexible or compressed schedule, the impasse shall be presented to the Federal Service Impasses Panel (hereinafter in this section referred to as the "Panel").

(B) The Panel shall promptly consider any case presented under subparagraph (A), and shall take final action in favor of the agency's determination if the finding on which it is based is supported by evidence that the schedule is likely to cause an adverse agency impact.

(3)(A) If an agency and an exclusive representative have entered into a collective bargaining agreement providing for use of a flexible or compressed schedule under this subchapter and the head of the agency determines under subsection (a)(2) to terminate a flexible or compressed schedule, the agency may reopen the agreement to seek termination of the schedule involved.

(B) If the agency and exclusive representative reach an impasse in collective bargaining with respect to terminating such schedule, the impasse shall be presented to the Panel.

(C) The Panel shall promptly consider any case presented under subparagraph (B), and shall rule on such impasse not later than 60 days after the date the Panel is presented the impasse. The Panel shall take final action in favor of the agency's determination to terminate a schedule if the finding on which the determination is based is supported by evidence that the schedule has caused an adverse agency impact.

(D) Any such schedule may not be terminated until—

(i) the agreement covering such schedule is renegotiated or expires or terminates pursuant to the terms of that agreement; or

(ii) the date of the Panel's final decision, if an impasse arose in the reopening of the agreement under subparagraph (A) of this paragraph.

(d) This section shall not apply with respect to flexible schedules that may be established without regard to the authority provided under this subchapter.

(Added Pub. L. 97–221, § 2(a)(2), July 23, 1982, 96 Stat. 231.)

SECTION REFERRED TO IN OTHER SECTIONS

This section is referred to in section 6103 of this title.

§ 6132. Prohibition of coercion

(a) An employee may not directly or indirectly intimidate, threaten, or coerce, or attempt to intimidate, threaten, or coerce, any other employee for the purpose of interfering with—

(1) such employee's rights under sections 6122 through 6126 of this title to elect a time of arrival or departure, to work or not to work credit hours, or to request or not to request compensatory time off in lieu of payment for overtime hours; or

(2) such employee's right under section 6127(b)(1) of this title to vote whether or not to be included within a compressed schedule program or such employee's right to request an agency determination under section 6127(b)(2) of this title.

(b) For the purpose of subsection (a), the term "intimidate, threaten, or coerce" includes, but is not limited to, promising to confer or conferring any benefit (such as appointment, promotion, or compensation), or effecting or threatening to effect any reprisal (such as deprivation of appointment, promotion, or compensation).

(Added Pub. L. 97–221, § 2(a)(2), July 23, 1982, 96 Stat. 232.)

§ 6133. Regulations; technical assistance; program review

(a) The Office of Personnel Management shall prescribe regulations necessary for the administration of the programs established under this subchapter.

(b)(1) The Office shall provide educational material, and technical aids and assistance, for use by an agency in connection with establishing and maintaining programs under this subchapter.

(2) In order to provide the most effective materials, aids, and assistance under paragraph (1), the Office shall conduct periodic reviews of programs established by agencies under this subchapter particularly insofar as such programs may affect—

(A) the efficiency of Government operations;

(B) mass transit facilities and traffic;

(C) levels of energy consumption;

(D) service to the public;

(E) increased opportunities for full-time and part-time employment; and

(F) employees' job satisfaction and nonwork-life.

(c)(1) With respect to employees in the Library of Congress, the authority granted to the Office of Personnel Management under this subchapter shall be exercised by the Librarian of Congress.

(2) With respect to employees in the Government Printing Office, the authority granted to the Office of Personnel Management under this subchapter shall be exercised by the Public Printer.

(Added Pub. L. 97–221, § 2(a)(2), July 23, 1982, 96 Stat. 233; amended Pub. L. 101–163, title III, § 312, Nov. 21, 1989, 103 Stat. 1065.)

AMENDMENTS

1989—Subsec. (c). Pub. L. 101–163 designated existing provisions as par. (1) and added par. (2).

CHAPTER 63—LEAVE

SUBCHAPTER I—ANNUAL AND SICK LEAVE

AMENDMENTS

1999—Pub. L. 106–56, §1(c)(2), Sept. 24, 1999, 113 Stat. 407, added item 6328.

1997—Pub. L. 105–18, title II, §9004(b), June 12, 1997, 111 Stat. 197, added heading of subchapter VI and item 6391.

1994—Pub. L. 103–329, title VI, §629(a)(2)(B), Sept. 30, 1994, 108 Stat. 2423, added item 6327.

1993—Pub. L. 103–103, §5(a)(2), Oct. 8, 1993, 107 Stat. 1023, substituted "Authority to participate in both programs" for "Limitation on employee participation" in item 6373.

Pub. L. 103–3, title II, §201(a)(2), Feb. 5, 1993, 107 Stat. 23, added heading of subchapter V and items 6381 to 6387.

1990—Pub. L. 101–508, title VII, §7202(i)(2), Nov. 5, 1990, 104 Stat. 1388–337, inserted "and nonappropriated fund" after "office" in item 6312.

1988—Pub. L. 100–566, §2(d)(1)(B), Oct. 31, 1988, 102 Stat. 2844, which provided that the table of sections for subchapters III and IV were to be repealed effective 5 years after Oct. 31, 1988, was repealed by Pub. L. 103–103, §2, Oct. 8, 1993, 107 Stat. 1022, effective Oct. 30, 1993.

Pub. L. 100–566, §2(b), Oct. 31, 1988, 102 Stat. 2843, added heading of subchapter III and items 6331 to 6340 and heading of subchapter IV and items 6361 to 6373.

1975—Pub. L. 94–183, §2(27), Dec. 31, 1975, 89 Stat. 1058, struck out item 6309 "Leave of absence; rural carriers".

1970—Pub. L. 91–563, §1(b), Dec. 19, 1970, 84 Stat. 1476, included witness service and official duty status for certain witness service in item 6322.

1968—Pub. L. 90–588, §1(b), Oct. 17, 1968, 82 Stat. 1151, added item 6326.

Pub. L. 90–367, §2(b), June 29, 1968, 82 Stat. 277, added item 6312.

1967—Pub. L. 90–221, §3(b), Dec. 23, 1967, 81 Stat. 671, added item 6325.

1966—Pub. L. 89–747, §1(3), Nov. 2, 1966, 80 Stat. 1179, inserted reference to leave for crews of vessels in item 6305.

CHAPTER REFERRED TO IN OTHER SECTIONS

This chapter is referred to in section 4703 of this title; title 24 section 225e; title 25 section 2012.

SUBCHAPTER I—ANNUAL AND SICK LEAVE

SUBCHAPTER REFERRED TO IN OTHER SECTIONS

This subchapter is referred to in sections 5508, 5551, 6332, 6337, 6362, 6382, 8339 of this title; title 7 section 1766c; title 22 section 3942; title 28 sections 153, 156, 603, 631, 634, 712, 752, 794; title 42 section 242*l*.

§ 6301. Definitions

For the purpose of this subchapter—

(1) "United States", when used in a geographical sense means the several States and the District of Columbia; and

(2) "employee" means—

(A) an employee as defined by section 2105 of this title; and

(B) an individual first employed by the government of the District of Columbia before October 1, 1987;

but does not include—

(i) a teacher or librarian of the public schools of the District of Columbia;

(ii) a part-time employee who does not have an established regular tour of duty during the administrative workweek;

(iii) a temporary employee engaged in construction work at an hourly rate;

(iv) an employee of the Panama Canal Commission when employed on the Isthmus of Panama;

(v) a physician, dentist, or nurse in the Veterans Health Administration of the Department of Veterans Affairs;

(vi) an employee of either House of Congress or of the two Houses;

(vii) an employee of a corporation supervised by the Farm Credit Administration if private interests elect or appoint a member of the board of directors;

(viii) an alien employee who occupies a position outside the United States, except as provided by section 6310 of this title;

(ix) a "teacher" or an individual holding a "teaching position" as defined by section 901 of title 20;

(x) an officer in the executive branch or in the government of the District of Columbia who is appointed by the President and whose rate of basic pay exceeds the highest rate payable under section 5332 of this title;

(xi) an officer in the executive branch or in the government of the District of Columbia who is designated by the President, except a postmaster, United States attorney, or United States marshal;

(xii) a chief of mission (as defined in section 102(a)(3) of the Foreign Service Act of 1980); or

(xiii) an officer in the legislative or judicial branch who is appointed by the President.

Notwithstanding clauses (x)–(xii) of paragraph (2), the term "employee" includes any member of the Senior Foreign Service or any Foreign Service officer (other than a member or officer serving as chief of mission or in a position which requires appointment by and with the advice and consent of the Senate) and any member of the Foreign Service commissioned as a diplomatic or consular officer, or both, under section 312 of the Foreign Service Act of 1980.

(Pub. L. 89–554, Sept. 6, 1966, 80 Stat. 517; Pub. L. 91–375, § 6(c)(17), Aug. 12, 1970, 84 Stat. 776; Pub. L. 95–519, § 1, Oct. 25, 1978, 92 Stat. 1819; Pub. L. 96–70, title III, § 3302(e)(2), Sept. 27, 1979, 93 Stat. 498; Pub. L. 96–465, title II, §§ 2312(a), 2314(f)(1), Oct. 17, 1980, 94 Stat. 2166, 2168; Pub. L. 99–335, title II, § 207(c)(1), formerly § 207(c), June 6, 1986, 100 Stat. 595, renumbered § 207(c)(1), Pub. L. 99–556, title II, § 201(1), Oct. 27, 1986, 100 Stat. 3135; Pub. L. 102–54, § 13(b)(2), June 13, 1991, 105 Stat. 274.)

HISTORICAL AND REVISION NOTES

Derivation	U.S. Code	Revised Statutes and Statutes at Large
(1)	5 U.S.C. 2061(d).	Sept. 6, 1960, Pub. L. 86–707, § 402(c), 74 Stat. 800.
(2)	5 U.S.C. 2061(a), (b), (c)(1) (less last sentence).	Oct. 30, 1951, ch. 631, § 202, 65 Stat. 679.
		July 2, 1953, ch. 178, § 1 "(c)(1) (less last sentence)", 67 Stat. 136.
		Sept. 6, 1960, Pub. L. 86–707, § 402(a), 74 Stat. 800.
		Aug. 21, 1964, Pub. L. 88–471, § 6(a), 78 Stat. 583.
	5 U.S.C. 2067.	Aug. 21, 1964, Pub. L. 88–471, § 1, 78 Stat. 582.
	5 U.S.C. 2358(a) (less applicability to the Federal Employees Pay Act of 1945, as amended).	July 17, 1959, Pub. L. 86–91, § 10(a) (less applicability to the Federal Employees Pay Act of 1945, as amended), 73 Stat. 217.

In paragraph (1), the words "when used in a geographical sense" are added for clarity.

In paragraph (2), the words "an employee as defined by section 2105 of this title" are coextensive with and substituted for "civilian officers and employees of the United States . . . including officers and employees of corporations wholly owned or controlled by the United States". Specific reference to officers and members of the Metropolitan Police force of the District of Columbia, the Fire Department of the District of Columbia, the United States Park Police force, and the White House Police force, as set forth in former section 2067, is omitted as unnecessary in view of the provisions of paragraph (2)(A), (B). The exception for "commissioned officers of the Public Health Service" and "commissioned officers of the Coast and Geodetic Survey" in former section 2061(b)(1)(E), (F) is omitted as unnecessary since these officers are excluded by the definition of the word "employee" in section 2105.

In paragraph (2)(ix), the words "as defined by section 901 of title 20" are added on authority of former section 2351, which section is scheduled for transfer to section 901 of title 20.

Standard changes are made to conform with the definitions applicable and the style of this title as outlined in the preface to the report.

REFERENCES IN TEXT

Section 102(a)(3) of the Foreign Service Act of 1980, referred to in par. (2)(xii), was redesignated section 102(3) of that Act by Pub. L. 98–164, which struck out the designation "(a)" and struck out subsec. (b) of section 102. Section 102 is classified to section 3902 of Title 22, Foreign Relations and Intercourse.

Section 312 of the Foreign Service Act of 1980, referred to in text, is classified to section 3952 of Title 22.

AMENDMENTS

1991—Par. (2)(v). Pub. L. 102–54 substituted "Veterans Health Administration of the Department of Veterans Affairs" for "Department of Medicine and Surgery, Veterans' Administration".

1986—Par. (2)(B). Pub. L. 99–335 amended subpar. (B) generally, substituting "first employed" for "employed" and inserting "before October 1, 1987".

1980—Pub. L. 96–465, § 2312(a), inserted provision at end of par. (2) extending definition of "employee" notwithstanding cls. (x) to (xii) of par. (2).

Par. (2)(xii). Pub. L. 96–465, § 2314(f)(1), substituted "a chief of mission (as defined in section 102(a)(3) of the Foreign Service Act of 1980)" for "an officer who receives pay under section 866 of title 22".

1979—Par. (2)(iv). Pub. L. 96–70 substituted "Panama Canal Commission" for "Canal Zone Government or the Panama Canal Company".

1978—Par. (2)(xiii). Pub. L. 95–519 added cl. (xiii).

1970—Par. (2)(ii). Pub. L. 91–375 struck out ", except an hourly employee in the postal field service," after "part-time employee".

EFFECTIVE DATE OF 1986 AMENDMENT

Amendment by Pub. L. 99–335 effective Jan. 1, 1987, see section 702(a) of Pub. L. 99–335, set out as an Effective Date note under section 8401 of this title.

EFFECTIVE DATE OF 1980 AMENDMENT

Amendment by Pub. L. 96–465 effective Feb. 15, 1981, except as otherwise provided, see section 2403 of Pub. L. 96–465, set out as an Effective Date note under section 3901 of Title 22, Foreign Relations and Intercourse.

EFFECTIVE DATE OF 1979 AMENDMENT

Amendment by Pub. L. 96–70 effective Oct. 1, 1979, see section 3304 of Pub. L. 96–70, set out as an Effective Date note under section 3601 of Title 22, Foreign Relations and Intercourse.

EFFECTIVE DATE OF 1978 AMENDMENT

Amendment by Pub. L. 95–519 effective beginning on first day of first applicable pay period beginning on or after Oct. 25, 1978, see section 4(a) of Pub. L. 95–519, set out as a note under section 5551 of this title.

EFFECTIVE DATE OF 1970 AMENDMENT

Amendment by Pub. L. 91–375 effective within 1 year after Aug. 12, 1970, on date established therefor by Board of Governors of United States Postal Service and published by it in Federal Register, see section 15(a) of Pub. L. 91–375, set out as an Effective Date note preceding section 101 of Title 39, Postal Service.

SHORT TITLE OF 1999 AMENDMENT

Pub. L. 106–56, § 1(a), Sept. 24, 1999, 113 Stat. 407, provided that: "This Act [amending section 6327 of this title and renumbering another section 6327 of this title as section 6328] may be cited as the 'Organ Donor Leave Act'."

SHORT TITLE OF 1994 AMENDMENT

Pub. L. 103–388, § 1, Oct. 22, 1994, 108 Stat. 4079, provided that: "This Act [amending section 6307 of this title] may be cited as the 'Federal Employees Family Friendly Leave Act'."

SHORT TITLE OF 1993 AMENDMENT

Pub. L. 103–103, § 1, Oct. 8, 1993, 107 Stat. 1022, provided that: "This Act [amending sections 6331, 6337, 6361, 6362, and 6373 of this title, enacting provisions set out as notes under section 6331 of this title, and repealing provisions set out as a note under section 6331 of this title] may be cited as the 'Federal Employees Leave Sharing Amendments Act of 1993'."

SHORT TITLE OF 1988 AMENDMENT

Pub. L. 100–566, § 1, Oct. 31, 1988, 102 Stat. 2834, provided that: "This Act [enacting subchapters III and IV of this chapter, amending sections 5724 and 8112 of this title, and enacting provisions set out as notes under section 6331 of this title] may be cited as the 'Federal Employees Leave Sharing Act of 1988'."

EMPLOYEES OF THE DISTRICT OF COLUMBIA

Pub. L. 99–335, title II, § 207(c)(2), as added by Pub. L. 99–556, title II, § 201, Oct. 27, 1986, 100 Stat. 3135, provided that: "The amendment made by paragraph (1) [amending this section] shall not result in the coverage, under subchapter I of chapter 63 of title 5, United States Code, of any individual (or class of individuals) employed by the government of the District of Columbia who would not have been covered under such subchapter if such amendment had not been made."

EXECUTIVE ORDER NO. 10540

Ex. Ord. No. 10540, June 29, 1954, 19 F.R. 3983, which related to the designation of certain officers as exempt from the Annual and Sick Leave Act of 1951, was revoked by section 2–201 of Ex. Ord. No. 12107, Dec. 28, 1978, 44 F.R. 1055, set out as a note under section 1101 of this title.

SECTION REFERRED TO IN OTHER SECTIONS

This section is referred to in sections 5551, 6302, 6305, 6306, 6308, 6325, 6331, 6361, 6381, 8339 of this title.

§ 6302. General provisions

(a) The days of leave provided by this subchapter are days on which an employee would otherwise work and receive pay and are exclusive of holidays and nonworkdays established by Federal statute, Executive order, or administrative order.

(b) For the purpose of this subchapter an employee is deemed employed for a full biweekly pay period if he is employed during the days within that period, exclusive of holidays and nonworkdays established by Federal statute, Executive order, or administrative order, which fall within his basic administrative workweek.

(c) A part-time employee, unless otherwise excepted, is entitled to the benefits provided by subsection (d) of this section and sections 6303, 6304(a), (b), 6305(a), 6307, and 6310 of this title on a pro rata basis.

(d) The annual leave provided by this subchapter, including annual leave that will accrue to an employee during the year, may be granted at any time during the year as the head of the agency concerned may prescribe.

(e) If an officer excepted from this subchapter by section 6301(2)(x)–(xiii) of this title, without a break in service, again becomes subject to this subchapter on completion of his service as an excepted officer, the unused annual and sick leave standing to his credit when he was excepted from this subchapter is deemed to have remained to his credit.

(f) An employee who uses excess annual leave credited because of administrative error may elect to refund the amount received for the days of excess leave by lump-sum or installment payments or to have the excess leave carried forward as a charge against later-accruing annual leave, unless repayment is waived under section 5584 of this title.

(g) An employee who is being involuntarily separated from an agency due to a reduction in force or transfer of function under subchapter I of chapter 35 or section 3595 may elect to use annual leave to the employee's credit to remain on the agency's rolls after the date the employee would otherwise have been separated if, and only to the extent that, such additional time in a pay status will enable the employee to qualify for an immediate annuity under section 8336, 8412, 8414, or to qualify to carry health benefits coverage into retirement under section 8905(b).

(Pub. L. 89–554, Sept. 6, 1966, 80 Stat. 517; Pub. L. 93–181, § 4, Dec. 14, 1973, 87 Stat. 706; Pub. L. 95–519, § 2, Oct. 25, 1978, 92 Stat. 1819; Pub. L. 104–208, div. A, title I, § 101(f) [title VI, § 634], Sept. 30, 1996, 110 Stat. 3009–314, 3009–363; Pub. L. 105–277, div. A, § 101(h) [title VI, § 653], Oct. 21, 1998, 112 Stat. 2681–480, 2681–528.)

HISTORICAL AND REVISION NOTES

Derivation	U.S. Code	Revised Statutes and Statutes at Large
(a)–(c)	5 U.S.C. 2064 (less (d), (e)).	Oct. 30, 1951, ch. 631, § 205 (less (d)), 65 Stat. 681.
(d)	5 U.S.C. 2062(h).	Oct. 30, 1951, ch. 631, § 203(h), 65 Stat. 681.
(e)	5 U.S.C. 2061a(b).	July 2, 1953, ch. 178, § 2(b), 67 Stat. 137.

In subsection (d), the words "the head of the agency concerned" are substituted for "the heads of the various departments and independent establishments".

Standard changes are made to conform with the definitions applicable and the style of this title as outlined in the preface to the report.

AMENDMENTS

1998—Subsec. (g). Pub. L. 105–277 inserted "or section 3595" after "chapter 35".

1996—Subsec. (g). Pub. L. 104–208 added subsec. (g).

1978—Subsec. (e). Pub. L. 95–519 substituted "6301(2)(x)–(xiii)" for "6301(2)(x)–(xii)".

1973—Subsec. (f). Pub. L. 93–181 added subsec. (f).

EFFECTIVE DATE OF 1978 AMENDMENT

Amendment by Pub. L. 95–519 effective beginning on first day of first applicable pay period beginning on or after Oct. 25, 1978, see section 4(a) of Pub. L. 95–519, set out as a note under section 5551 of this title.

TEMPORARY AUTHORITY TO TRANSFER LEAVE

Pub. L. 101–237, title II, § 206(b)(2), Dec. 18, 1989, 103 Stat. 2068, provided that: "The authority of the Department of Veterans Affairs under section 618 of the Treasury, Postal Service and General Government Appropriations Act, 1989 [Pub. L. 100–440, set out below], to operate a leave-transfer program for employees subject to section 4108 of title 38, United States Code, is extended until the programs provided for in subsection (e) of such section 4108 (as added by subsection (a) of this section) are implemented, but not later than October 1, 1990."

Similar provisions were contained in the following acts:

Pub. L. 101–144, title V, § 518, Nov. 9, 1989, 103 Stat. 874.

Pub. L. 101–110, § 1(d), Oct. 6, 1989, 103 Stat. 682.

Pub. L. 100–440, title VI, § 618, Sept. 22, 1988, 102 Stat. 1755, provided that: "In order to ensure that the experimental use of voluntary leave transfers established under Public Laws 99–500, 99–591 [Pub. L. 99–500, § 101(m) [title VII], Oct. 18, 1986, 100 Stat. 1783–308, 1783–334, and Pub. L. 99–591, § 101(m) [title VII], Oct. 30, 1986, 100 Stat. 3341–308, 3341–334], and 100–202 [Pub. L. 100–202, § 101(m) [title VI, § 625], Dec. 22, 1987, 101 Stat. 1329–390, 1329–430] may continue and may cover additional employees in fiscal year 1989, the Office of Personnel Management may continue to operate by regulation, notwithstanding chapter 63 of title 5, United States Code, a program under which the unused accrued annual leave of officers or employees of the Federal Government may be transferred for use by other officers or employees who need such leave due to a personal emergency as defined in the regulations. The Office may provide by regulation for such exceptions from the provisions of section 7351 of title 5 as the Office may determine appropriate for the transfer of leave under this section. The Veterans' Administration may operate a similar program for employees subject to section 4108 of title 38, United States Code. The programs operated under this section shall expire at the end of fiscal year 1989, but any leave that has been transferred to an officer or employee under the programs shall remain available for use until the personal emergency has ended, and any remaining unused transferred leave shall, to the extent administratively feasible, be restored to the leave accounts of the officers or employees from whose accounts it was originally transferred.''

Similar provisions were contained in the following prior appropriations act:

Pub. L. 100–202, § 101(m) [title VI, § 625], Dec. 22, 1987, 101 Stat. 1329–390, 1329–430.

For provisions ratifying any actions of the Secretary of Veterans Affairs in carrying out section 618 of Pub. L. 100–440, set out above, during the period Dec. 1, 1989, to Dec. 18, 1989, see section 604 of Pub. L. 101–237, set out as a note under section 1720B of Title 38, Veterans' Benefits. Similar provisions for the period Oct. 1, 1989, to Oct. 6, 1989, were contained in section 3(b) of Pub. L. 101–110, set out as a note under section 1720B of Title 38.

§ 6303. Annual leave; accrual

(a) An employee is entitled to annual leave with pay which accrues as follows—

(1) one-half day for each full biweekly pay period for an employee with less than 3 years of service;

(2) three-fourths day for each full biweekly pay period, except that the accrual for the last full biweekly pay period in the year is one and one-fourth days, for an employee with 3 but less than 15 years of service; and

(3) one day for each full biweekly pay period for an employee with 15 or more years of service.

In determining years of service, an employee is entitled to credit for all service of a type that would be creditable under section 8332, regardless of whether or not the employee is covered by subchapter III of chapter 83. However, an employee who is a retired member of a uniformed service as defined by section 3501 of this title is entitled to credit for active military service only if—

(A) his retirement was based on disability—

(i) resulting from injury or disease received in line of duty as a direct result of armed conflict; or

(ii) caused by an instrumentality of war and incurred in line of duty during a period of war as defined by sections 101 and 1101 of title 38;

(B) that service was performed in the armed forces during a war, or in a campaign or expedition for which a campaign badge has been authorized; or

(C) on November 30, 1964, he was employed in a position to which this subchapter applies and thereafter he continued to be so employed without a break in service of more than 30 days.

The determination of years of service may be made on the basis of an affidavit of the employee. Leave provided by this subchapter accrues to an employee who is not paid on the basis of biweekly pay periods on the same basis as it would accrue if the employee were paid on the basis of biweekly pay periods.

(b) Notwithstanding subsection (a) of this section, an employee whose current employment is limited to less than 90 days is entitled to annual leave under this subchapter only after being currently employed for a continuous period of 90 days under successive appointments without a break in service. After completing the 90-day period, the employee is entitled to be credited with the leave that would have accrued to him under subsection (a) of this section except for this subsection.

(c) A change in the rate of accrual of annual leave by an employee under this section takes effect at the beginning of the pay period after the pay period, or corresponding period for an employee who is not paid on the basis of biweekly pay periods, in which the employee completed the prescribed period of service.

(d) Leave granted under this subchapter is exclusive of time actually and necessarily occupied in going to or from a post of duty and time necessarily occupied awaiting transportation, in the case of an employee—

(1) to whom section 6304(b) of this title applies;

(2) whose post of duty is outside the United States; and

(3) who returns on leave to the United States, or to his place of residence, which is outside the area of employment, in its territories or possessions including the Commonwealth of Puerto Rico.

This subsection does not apply to more than one period of leave in a prescribed tour of duty at a post outside the United States.

(Pub. L. 89–554, Sept. 6, 1966, 80 Stat. 518; Pub. L. 93–181, § 2, Dec. 14, 1973, 87 Stat. 705; Pub. L. 99–335, title II, § 207(d), June 6, 1986, 100 Stat. 595; Pub. L. 102–83, § 5(c)(2), Aug. 6, 1991, 105 Stat. 406; Pub. L. 102–378, § 2(52), Oct. 2, 1992, 106 Stat. 1353.)

HISTORICAL AND REVISION NOTES

Derivation	U.S. Code	Revised Statutes and Statutes at Large
....	5 U.S.C. 2062(a), (b), (e), (i).	Oct. 30, 1951, ch. 631, § 203(a), (b), (e), (i), 65 Stat. 679–681. Sept. 6, 1960, Pub. L. 86–707, § 401 "(e)", 74 Stat. 799. Aug. 19, 1964, Pub. L. 88–448, § 203, 78 Stat. 487.
....	5 U.S.C. 3101 (as applicable to 5 U.S.C. 2062(a)).	Aug. 19, 1964, Pub. L. 88–448, § 101 (as applicable to § 203), 78 Stat. 484.

In subsection (a), the words "Except as otherwise provided in this subsection" are omitted as unnecessary in view of the specific inclusion of the exception in the third sentence. The words "for the purposes of this subsection" are omitted as surplusage. The reference to "section 8332 of this title for the purpose of an annuity under subchapter III of chapter 83 of this title" is substituted for "section 3 of the Civil Service Retirement Act for the purposes of an annuity under such Act to reflect the codification of that Act in this title. In paragraph (B), the words "on November 30, 1964, he was employed in a position to which this subchapter applies and thereafter he continued to be so employed" are substituted for "immediately prior to the effective date of this sentence he was employed in a civilian office to which this Act applies and, on and after such date, he continued to be employed in any such office".

Standard changes are made to conform with the definitions applicable and the style of this title as outlined in the preface to the report.

AMENDMENTS

1992—Subsec. (a). Pub. L. 102–378 amended second sentence generally. Prior to amendment, second sentence read as follows: "In determining years of service, an employee is entitled to credit for all service creditable under section 8332 of this title for the purpose of an annuity under subchapter III of chapter 83 of this title and all service creditable under section 8411 of this title for the purpose of chapter 84 of this title."

1991—Subsec. (a)(A)(ii). Pub. L. 102–83 substituted reference to section 1101 of title 38 for reference to section 301 of title 38.

1986—Subsec. (a). Pub. L. 99–335 inserted "and all service creditable under section 8411 of this title for the purpose of chapter 84 of this title" at end of second sentence.

1973—Subsec. (b). Pub. L. 93–181 substituted "an employee whose current employment is limited to less than 90 days is entitled" and "under successive appointments" for "an employee is entitled" and "under one or more appointments" respectively.

EFFECTIVE DATE OF 1992 AMENDMENT

Section 9 of Pub. L. 102–378 provided that:

"(a) IN GENERAL.—Except as otherwise provided in this section, this Act and the amendments made by this Act [see Tables for classification] shall take effect as of the date of enactment of this Act [Oct. 2, 1992].

"(b) EXCEPTIONS.—(1) The amendment made by section 4(c) [amending provisions set out as a note under section 31–2 of Title 2, The Congress] shall be effective as of December 31, 1991.

"(2) The amendments made by section 5(d) [amending section 8440d of this title] shall be effective as of December 9, 1991.

"(3) The amendments made by sections 2(13) and 2(17) [amending section 4109 of this title and repealing section 3342 of this title] shall be effective as of October 1, 1991.

"(4) The amendments made by sections 2(11), 2(19), 2(29), and 2(38) [amending sections 3324, 4505a, 5332, and 5403 of this title] shall be effective as of May 4, 1991.

"(5) The amendments made by section 2(25) [amending section 5302 of this title] shall be effective as of February 3, 1991.

"(6) The provisions of section 8(a) and the amendments made by sections 2(57)(A), 2(60), 2(64), 2(67), 2(71), 2(75)(A), 3(1), 3(4), 3(6), and 5(a) [amending sections 5532, 8331, 8335, 8344, 8347, 8425, 8461, 8468, and 8901 of this title, repealing section 5380 of this title, enacting provisions set out as a note under section 5532 of this title, amending provisions set out as notes under sections 2105, 5304, 5305, 5378, and 8348 of this title, and repealing provisions set out as notes under sections 5380 and 5532 of this title] shall be effective as of November 5, 1990.

"(7) The amendment made by section 2(52) [amending this section] shall be effective as of January 1, 1989, except that no amount shall become payable, as a result of the enactment of such amendment, under—

"(A) subchapter VI of chapter 55 of title 5, United States Code, based on a separation that takes effect or an election that is made before the date of enactment of this Act [Oct. 2, 1992]; or

"(B) section 5551(b) of title 5, United States Code, which is attributable to an individual's being excepted from subchapter I of chapter 63 of such title before the date of enactment of this Act.

"(8) The amendment made by section 2(69) [amending section 8440 of this title] shall be effective as of November 10, 1988.

"(9) The amendments made by sections 2(40), 2(41), 2(42), 2(43), and 3(5) [amending sections 5541, 5542, 5544, and 5547 of this title and provisions set out as a note under section 5305 of this title] shall be effective as of the first day of the first applicable pay period beginning on or after the date of enactment of this Act [Oct. 2, 1992].

"(10) The amendments made by section 2(28) [amending section 5314 of this title] shall be effective as of the first day of the first applicable pay period beginning on or after November 5, 1990.

"(11) The amendment made by section 2(49) [amending section 5724 of this title] shall apply with respect to

a separation that takes effect on or after the date of enactment of this Act [Oct. 2, 1992].

"(12) The amendment made by section 5(e) [amending section 1441a of Title 12, Banks and Banking] shall apply with respect to any action (described in subclause (I) or (II) of the provisions struck by such amendment) occurring on or after the date of enactment of this Act [Oct. 2, 1992]."

EFFECTIVE DATE OF 1986 AMENDMENT

Amendment by Pub. L. 99–335 effective Jan. 1, 1987, see section 702(a) of Pub. L. 99–335, set out as an Effective Date note under section 8401 of this title.

SECTION REFERRED TO IN OTHER SECTIONS

This section is referred to in sections 6129, 6302, 6304, 6305, 6312, 6333, 6367 of this title; title 42 section 237.

§ 6304. Annual leave; accumulation

(a) Except as provided by subsections (b), (d), (e), (f), and (g) of this section, annual leave provided by section 6303 of this title, which is not used by an employee, accumulates for use in succeeding years until it totals not more than 30 days at the beginning of the first full biweekly pay period, or corresponding period for an employee who is not paid on the basis of biweekly pay periods, occurring in a year.

(b) Annual leave not used by an employee of the Government of the United States in one of the following classes of employees stationed outside the United States accumulates for use in succeeding years until it totals not more than 45 days at the beginning of the first full biweekly pay period, or corresponding period for an employee who is not paid on the basis of biweekly pay periods, occurring in a year:

(1) Individuals directly recruited or transferred by the Government of the United States from the United States or its territories or possessions including the Commonwealth of Puerto Rico for employment outside the area of recruitment or from which transferred.

(2) Individuals employed locally but—

(A)(i) who were originally recruited from the United States or its territories or possessions including the Commonwealth of Puerto Rico but outside the area of employment;

(ii) who have been in substantially continuous employment by other agencies of the United States, United States firms, interests, or organizations, international organizations in which the United States participates, or foreign governments; and

(iii) whose conditions of employment provide for their return transportation to the United States or its territories or possessions including the Commonwealth of Puerto Rico; or

(B)(i) who were at the time of employment temporarily absent, for the purpose of travel or formal study, from the United States, or from their respective places of residence in its territories or possessions including the Commonwealth of Puerto Rico; and

(ii) who, during the temporary absence, have maintained residence in the United States or its territories or possessions including the Commonwealth of Puerto Rico but outside the area of employment.

(3) Individuals who are not normally residents of the area concerned and who are dis-

charged from service in the armed forces to accept employment with an agency of the Government of the United States.

(c) Annual leave in excess of the amount allowable—

(1) under subsection (a) or (b) of this section which was accumulated under earlier statute; or

(2) under subsection (a) of this section which was accumulated under subsection (b) of this section by an employee who becomes subject to subsection (a) of this section;

remains to the credit of the employee until used. The excess annual leave is reduced at the beginning of the first full biweekly pay period, or corresponding period for an employee who is not paid on the basis of biweekly pay periods, occurring in a year, by the amount of annual leave the employee used during the preceding year in excess of the amount which accrued during that year, until the employee's accumulated leave does not exceed the amount allowed under subsection (a) or (b) of this section, as appropriate.

(d)(1) Annual leave which is lost by operation of this section because of—

(A) administrative error when the error causes a loss of annual leave otherwise accruable after June 30, 1960;

(B) exigencies of the public business when the annual leave was scheduled in advance; or

(C) sickness of the employee when the annual leave was scheduled in advance;

shall be restored to the employee.

(2) Annual leave restored under paragraph (1) of this subsection, or under clause (2) of section 5562(a) of this title, which is in excess of the maximum leave accumulation permitted by law shall be credited to a separate leave account for the employee and shall be available for use by the employee within the time limits prescribed by regulations of the Office of Personnel Management. Leave credited under this paragraph but unused and still available to the employee under the regulations prescribed by the Office shall be included in the lump-sum payment under section 5551 or 5552(1) of this title but may not be retained to the credit of the employee under section 5552(2) of this title.

(3)(A) For the purpose of this subsection, the closure of, and any realignment with respect to, an installation of the Department of Defense pursuant to the Defense Base Closure and Realignment Act of 1990 (part A of title XXIX of Public Law 101–510; 10 U.S.C. 2687 note) during any period, the closure of an installation of the Department of Defense in the Republic of Panama in accordance with the Panama Canal Treaty of 1977, and the closure of any other installation of the Department of Defense, during the period beginning on October 1, 1992, and ending on December 31, 1997, shall be deemed to create an exigency of the public business and any leave that is lost by an employee of such installation by operation of this section (regardless of whether such leave was scheduled) shall be restored and shall be credited and available in accordance with paragraph (2).

(B) For the purpose of subparagraph (A), the term "realignment" means a base realignment

(as defined in subsection (e)(3) of section 2687 of title 10) that meets the requirements of subsection (a)(2) of such section.

(4)(A) For the purpose of this subsection, service of a Department of Defense emergency essential employee in a combat zone is an exigency of the public business for that employee. Any leave that, by reason of such service, is lost by the employee by operation of this section (regardless of whether such leave was scheduled) shall be restored to the employee and shall be credited and available in accordance with paragraph (2).

(B) As used in subparagraph (A)—

(i) the term "Department of Defense emergency essential employee" means an employee of the Department of Defense who is designated under section 1580 of title 10 as an emergency essential employee; and

(ii) the term "combat zone" has the meaning given such term in section 112(c)(2) of the Internal Revenue Code of 1986.

(e) Annual leave otherwise accruable after June 30, 1960, which is lost by operation of this section because of administrative error and which is not credited under subsection (d)(2) of this section because the employee is separated before the error is discovered, is subject to credit and liquidation by lump-sum payment only if a claim therefor is filed within 3 years immediately following the date of discovery of the error. Payment shall be made by the agency of employment when the lump-sum payment provisions of section 5551 of this title last became applicable to the employee at the rate of basic pay in effect on the date the lump-sum provisions became applicable.

(f)(1) This subsection applies with respect to annual leave accrued by an individual while serving in a position in—

(A) the Senior Executive Service;

(B) the Senior Foreign Service;

(C) the Defense Intelligence Senior Executive Service;

(D) the Senior Cryptologic Executive Service; or

(E) the Federal Bureau of Investigation and Drug Enforcement Administration Senior Executive Service.

(2) For purposes of applying any limitation on accumulation under this section with respect to any annual leave described in paragraph (1)—

(A) "30 days" in subsection (a) shall be deemed to read "90 days"; and

(B) "45 days" in subsection (b) shall be deemed to read "90 days".

(Pub. L. 89–554, Sept. 6, 1966, 80 Stat. 519; Pub. L. 93–181, § 3, Dec. 14, 1973, 87 Stat. 705; Pub. L. 95–454, title IV, § 410, title IX, § 906(a)(2), (3), Oct. 13, 1978, 92 Stat. 1173, 1224; Pub. L. 96–54, § 2(a)(39), Aug. 14, 1979, 93 Stat. 383; Pub. L. 96–465, title II, § 2312(b), Oct. 17, 1980, 94 Stat. 2166; Pub. L. 97–89, title VIII, § 802, Dec. 4, 1981, 95 Stat. 1161; Pub. L. 100–325, § 2(k), May 30, 1988, 102 Stat. 582; Pub. L. 102–378, § 2(53), Oct. 2, 1992, 106 Stat. 1354; Pub. L. 102–484, div. D, title XLIV, § 4434, Oct. 23, 1992, 106 Stat. 2722; Pub. L. 103–337, div. A, title III, § 341(c), div. B, title XXVIII, § 2816(a), Oct. 5, 1994, 108 Stat. 2720, 3056; Pub. L. 103–356, title II, § 201(a), Oct. 13, 1994, 108 Stat.

3411; Pub. L. 105–261, div. A, title XI, § 1105, Oct. 17, 1998, 112 Stat. 2142; Pub. L. 106–65, div. A, title XI, § 1103(a), Oct. 5, 1999, 113 Stat. 776.)

HISTORICAL AND REVISION NOTES

Derivation	U.S. Code	Revised Statutes and Statutes at Large
(a)	5 U.S.C. 2062(c).	Oct. 30, 1951, ch. 631, § 203(c), 65 Stat. 680. July 2, 1953, ch. 178, § 3(a), 67 Stat. 137.
(b)	5 U.S.C. 2602(d).	Oct. 30, 1951, ch. 631, § 203(d), 65 Stat. 680. July 2, 1953, ch. 178, § 3(b), 67 Stat. 137. Sept. 6, 1960, Pub. L. 86–707, § 401 "(d)", 74 Stat. 799.
(c)	5 U.S.C. 2066(a).	Oct. 30, 1951, ch. 631, § 208(a), 65 Stat. 682. July 2, 1953, ch. 178, § 3(c), 67 Stat. 137.

The words "Except as provided by subsection (b) of this section" are added to subsection (a), and the words "Notwithstanding the provisions of subsection (c)" in former section 2062(d) are omitted as unnecessary because of the exception added to subsection (a).

The words "full biweekly pay period" are substituted for "complete biweekly pay period" to conform to section 6303.

Standard changes are made to conform with the definitions applicable and the style of this title as outlined in the preface to the report.

REFERENCES IN TEXT

The Defense Base Closure and Realignment Act of 1990, referred to in subsec. (d)(3)(A), is part A of title XXIX of div. B of Pub. L. 101–510, Nov. 5, 1990, 104 Stat. 1808, as amended, which is set out as a note under section 2687 of Title 10, Armed Forces. For complete classification of this Act to the Code, see Tables.

Section 112(c)(2) of the Internal Revenue Code of 1986, referred to in subsec. (d)(4)(B)(ii), is classified to section 112(c)(2) of Title 26, Internal Revenue Code.

AMENDMENTS

1999—Subsec. (d)(4). Pub. L. 106–65 added par. (4).

1998—Subsec. (d)(3)(A). Pub. L. 105–261 inserted "the closure of an installation of the Department of Defense in the Republic of Panama in accordance with the Panama Canal Treaty of 1977," after "2687 note) during any period,".

1994—Subsec. (d)(3). Pub. L. 103–337, § 2816(a), designated existing provisions as subpar. (A), substituted "closure of, and any realignment with respect to," for "closure of", and added subpar. (B).

Pub. L. 103–337, § 341(c), substituted "the closure of an installation of the Department of Defense pursuant to the Defense Base Closure and Realignment Act of 1990 (part A of title XXIX of Public Law 101–510; 10 U.S.C. 2687 note) during any period, and the closure of any other installation" for "the closure of an installation".

Subsec. (f). Pub. L. 103–356 amended subsec. (f) generally. Prior to amendment, subsec. (f) read as follows: "Annual leave accrued shall not be subject to the limitation on accumulation otherwise imposed by this section if such leave is accrued by an individual while serving in a position in—

"(1) the Senior Executive Service;

"(2) the Senior Foreign Service;

"(3) the Defense Intelligence Senior Executive Service;

"(4) the Senior Cryptologic Executive Service; or

"(5) the Federal Bureau of Investigation and Drug Enforcement Administration Senior Executive Service."

1992—Subsec. (d)(3). Pub. L. 102–484 added par. (3).

Subsec. (e). Pub. L. 102–378 substituted "date" for "date of" in last sentence.

1988—Subsec. (f)(5). Pub. L. 100–325 added par. (5).

1981—Subsec. (f). Pub. L. 97–89 amended subsec. (f) generally, transferring from former subsec. (g) provisions excepting from the limitation on accumulation otherwise imposed by this section any annual leave accrued by members of the Senior Foreign Service and inserting provisions relating to annual leave accrued by individuals while serving in positions in the Defense Intelligence Senior Executive Service or the Senior Cryptologic Executive Service.

Subsec. (g). Pub. L. 97–89 struck out subsec. (g). Provisions formerly set out in subsec. (g), relating to annual leave accrued by members of the Senior Foreign service, were incorporated in subsec. (f).

1980—Subsec. (a). Pub. L. 96–465, § 2312(b)(1), inserted reference to subsec. (g).

Subsec. (g). Pub. L. 96–465, § 2312(b)(2), added subsec. (g).

1979—Subsec. (e). Pub. L. 96–54 substituted "rate of basic pay" for "salary rate".

1978—Subsec. (a). Pub. L. 95–454, § 410(1), inserted reference to subsec. (f).

Subsec. (d)(2). Pub. L. 95–454, § 906(a)(2), (3), substituted "Office of Personnel Management" and "Office" for "Civil Service Commission" and "Commission", respectively.

Subsec. (f). Pub. L. 95–454, § 410(2), added subsec. (f).

1973—Subsec. (a). Pub. L. 93–181, § 3(1), substituted "subsections (b), (d), and (e) of this section" for "subsection (b) of this section".

Subsecs. (d), (e). Pub. L. 93–181, § 3(2), added subsecs. (d) and (e).

EFFECTIVE DATE OF 1994 AMENDMENTS

Section 201(a) of Pub. L. 103–356 provided that the amendment made by that section is effective on the first day of the first applicable pay period beginning after Oct. 13, 1994.

Section 2816(b) of Pub. L. 103–337 provided that: "The amendments made by subsection (a) [amending this section] shall apply only with respect to the restoration of annual leave of employees at military installations undergoing realignment if such leave is lost by operation of section 6304 of title 5, United States Code, on or after the date of the enactment of this Act [Oct. 5, 1994]."

EFFECTIVE DATE OF 1981 AMENDMENT

Amendment by Pub. L. 97–89 effective Oct. 1, 1981, see section 806 of Pub. L. 97–89, set out as an Effective Date note under section 1621 of Title 10, Armed Forces.

EFFECTIVE DATE OF 1980 AMENDMENT

Amendment by Pub. L. 96–465 effective Feb. 15, 1981, except as otherwise provided, see section 2403 of Pub. L. 96–465, set out as an Effective Date note under section 3901 of Title 22, Foreign Relations and Intercourse.

EFFECTIVE DATE OF 1979 AMENDMENT

Amendment by Pub. L. 96–54 effective July 12, 1979, see section 2(b) of Pub. L. 96–54, set out as a note under section 305 of this title.

EFFECTIVE DATE OF 1978 AMENDMENT

Amendment by section 410 of Pub. L. 95–454 effective 9 months after Oct. 13, 1978, and congressional review of provisions of sections 401 through 412 of Pub. L. 95–454, see section 415 of Pub. L. 95–454, set out as an Effective Date note under section 3131 of this title.

Amendment by section 906(a)(2), (3) of Pub. L. 95–454 effective 90 days after Oct. 13, 1978, see section 907 of Pub. L. 95–454, set out as an Effective Date of 1978 Amendment note under section 1101 of this title.

USE OF EXCESS LEAVE

Section 201(b) of Pub. L. 103–356 provided that: "Notwithstanding the amendment made by subsection (a) [amending this section], in the case of an employee who, on the effective date of subsection (a) [see Effective Date of 1994 Amendments note above], is subject to subsection (f) of section 6304 of title 5, United States Code, and who has to such employee's credit annual leave in excess of the maximum accumulation otherwise permitted by subsection (a) or (b) of section 6304 (determined applying the amendment made by subsection (a)), such excess annual leave shall remain to the credit of the employee and be subject to reduction, in the same manner as provided in subsection (c) of section 6304.''

LUMP-SUM PAYMENT FOR ACCRUED ANNUAL LEAVE TO FORMER EMPLOYEES

Section 5 of Pub. L. 93–181 provided that where former employees (other than former employees of Post Office Department or United States Postal Service) had accrued annual leave after June 30, 1960, but had not been on the rolls on Dec. 14, 1973, and where annual leave thus accrued had been lost because of administrative error, such accrued annual leave was subject to credit and liquidation by lump-sum payment but only if a claim therefor was filed within three years after Dec. 14, 1973, with agency by which the employees had been employed when lump-sum payment provision of section 5551 of this title had last become applicable to them.

Section 6 of Pub. L. 93–181 provided that where former employees of Post Office Department or United States Postal Service with prior civilian service with Post Office Department or other Federal agency had accrued annual leave after June 30, 1960, and before July 1, 1971, but had not on the rolls on Dec. 14, 1973, and where annual leave thus accrued had been lost because of administrative error, such accrued annual leave was subject to credit and liquidation by lump-sum payment, but only if a claim therefor was filed within three years after Dec. 14, 1973, with Postal Service, at salary rate in effect on date these employees had been employed when lump-sum payment provision of section 5551 of this title or comparable provisions of regulations of Postal Service had last become applicable to them. With respect to present employees of Postal Service who had prior Federal civilian service with Post Office Department or other Federal agency, annual leave which had accrued after June 30, 1960, and before July 1, 1971, but, because of administrative error had been lost, was subject to credit and liquidation by lump-sum payment only if a claim therefor was filed within three years of Dec. 14, 1973, with Postal Service, at salary rate in effect on Dec. 14, 1973.

SECTION REFERRED TO IN OTHER SECTIONS

This section is referred to in sections 5551, 5562, 6129, 6302, 6303, 6305, 6333, 6334, 6365, 6367 of this title; title 10 section 1606; title 40 section 174j–8.

§ 6305. Home leave; leave for Chiefs of Missions; leave for crews of vessels

(a) After 24 months of continuous service outside the United States (or after a shorter period of such service if the employee's assignment is terminated for the convenience of the Government), an employee may be granted leave of absence, under regulations of the President, at a rate not to exceed 1 week for each 4 months of that service without regard to other leave provided by this subchapter. Leave so granted—

(1) is for use in the United States, or if the employee's place of residence is outside the area of employment, in its territories or possessions including the Commonwealth of Puerto Rico;

(2) accumulates for future use without regard to the limitation in section 6304(b) of this title; and

(3) may not be made the basis for terminal leave or for a lump-sum payment.

(b) The President may authorize leave of absence to a chief of mission excepted from this subchapter by section 6301(2)(xii) of this title for use in the United States and its territories or possessions. Leave so authorized does not constitute a leave system and may not be made the basis for a lump-sum payment.

(c) An officer, crewmember, or other employee serving aboard an oceangoing vessel on an extended voyage may be granted leave of absence, under regulations of the Office of Personnel Management, at a rate not to exceed 2 days for each 30 calendar days of that service without regard to other leave provided by this subchapter. Leave so granted—

(1) accumulates for future use without regard to the limitation in section 6304(b) of this title;

(2) may not be made the basis for a lump-sum payment, except that civil service mariners of the Military Sealift Command on temporary promotion aboard ship may be paid the difference between their temporary and permanent rates of pay for leave accrued under this section and section 6303 and not otherwise used during the temporary promotion upon the expiration or termination of the temporary promotion; and

(3) may not be made the basis for terminal leave except under such special or emergency circumstances as may be prescribed under the regulations of the Office.

(Pub. L. 89–554, Sept. 6, 1966, 80 Stat. 520; Pub. L. 89–747, §1(1), (2), Nov. 2, 1966, 80 Stat. 1179; Pub. L. 90–623, §1(16), Oct. 22, 1968, 82 Stat. 1313; Pub. L. 95–454, title IX, §906(a)(2), Oct. 13, 1978, 92 Stat. 1224; Pub. L. 96–54, §2(a)(15), Aug. 14, 1979, 93 Stat. 382; Pub. L. 96–465, title II, §§2312(c), 2314(f)(2), Oct. 17, 1980, 94 Stat. 2167, 2168; Pub. L. 106–398, §1 [[div. A], title XI, §1133], Oct. 30, 2000, 114 Stat. 1654, 1654A–318.)

HISTORICAL AND REVISION NOTES

Derivation	U.S. Code	Revised Statutes and Statutes at Large
(a)	5 U.S.C. 2062(f).	Oct. 30, 1951, ch. 631, §203(f), 65 Stat. 680. Sept. 6, 1960, Pub. L. 86–707, §401 ''(f)'', 74 Stat. 799.
(b)	5 U.S.C. 2061(c)(2).	July 2, 1953, ch. 178, §1 ''(c)(2)'', 67 Stat. 136.

The words ''in his discretion'' are omitted as unnecessary in view of the permissive grant of authority.

Standard changes are made to conform with the definitions applicable and the style of this title as outlined in the preface to the report.

AMENDMENTS

2000—Subsec. (c)(2). Pub. L. 106–398 amended par. (2) generally. Prior to amendment, par. (2) read as follows: ''may not be made the basis for a lump-sum payment; and''.

1980—Subsec. (a). Pub. L. 96–465, §2312(c), inserted ''(or after a shorter period of such service if the employee's assignment is terminated for the convenience of the Government)'' after ''outside the United States''.

Subsec. (b). Pub. L. 96–465, §2314(f)(2), substituted ''a chief of mission'' for ''an officer'' after ''leave of absence to''.

1979—Subsec. (c)(3). Pub. L. 96–54 substituted ''Office'' for ''Commission''.

1978—Subsec. (c). Pub. L. 95–454 substituted ''Office of Personnel Management'' for ''Civil Service Commission''.

1968—Subsec. (c). Pub. L. 90–623 substituted "2" and "30" for "two" and "thirty", respectively.

1966—Pub. L. 89–747 added subsec. (c) and inserted reference to leave for crews of vessels in section catchline.

EFFECTIVE DATE OF 1980 AMENDMENT

Amendment by Pub. L. 96–465 effective Feb. 15, 1981, except as otherwise provided, see section 2403 of Pub. L. 96–465, set out as an Effective Date note under section 3901 of Title 22, Foreign Relations and Intercourse.

EFFECTIVE DATE OF 1979 AMENDMENT

Amendment by Pub. L. 96–54 effective July 12, 1979, see section 2(b) of Pub. L. 96–54, set out as a note under section 305 of this title.

EFFECTIVE DATE OF 1978 AMENDMENT

Amendment by Pub. L. 95–454 effective 90 days after Oct. 13, 1978, see section 907 of Pub. L. 95–454, set out as a note under section 1101 of this title.

EFFECTIVE DATE OF 1968 AMENDMENT

Amendment by Pub. L. 90–623 intended to restate without substantive change the law in effect on Oct. 22, 1968, see section 6 of Pub. L. 90–623, set out as a note under section 5334 of this title.

DELEGATION OF FUNCTIONS

Functions of President under subsec. (a) of this section delegated to Office of Personnel Management, see section 1(2) of Ex. Ord. No. 11228, June 14, 1965, 30 F.R. 7739, set out as a note under section 301 of Title 3, The President.

EX. ORD. NO. 10471. AUTHORIZATION TO GRANT LEAVES OF ABSENCE

Ex. Ord. No. 10471, July 17, 1953, 18 F.R. 4231, as amended by Ex. Ord. No. 12292, Feb. 23, 1981, 46 F.R. 13967, provided:

1. The heads of the several departments and agencies of the Government are hereby authorized and empowered, without the approval, ratification, or other action of the President, to exercise, with respect to personnel in their respective department or agency, the authority conferred upon the President by section 6305(b) of title 5 of the United States Code, to authorize leaves of absence in accordance with the said section 6305(b) to persons who receive compensation in accordance with section 401 of the Foreign Service Act of 1980 (22 U.S.C. 3961).

2. This order shall be effective as of July 5, 1953.

SECTION REFERRED TO IN OTHER SECTIONS

This section is referred to in section 6302 of this title; title 22 section 4083.

§ 6306. Annual leave; refund of lump-sum payment; recredit of annual leave

(a) When an individual who received a lump-sum payment for leave under section 5551 of this title is reemployed before the end of the period covered by the lump-sum payment in or under the Government of the United States or the government of the District of Columbia, except in a position excepted from this subchapter by section 6301(2)(ii), (iii), (vi), or (vii) of this title, he shall refund to the employing agency an amount equal to the pay covering the period between the date of reemployment and the expiration of the lump-sum period.

(b) An amount refunded under subsection (a) of this section shall be deposited in the Treasury of the United States to the credit of the employing agency. When an individual is reemployed under the same leave system, an amount of leave equal to the leave represented by the refund shall be recredited to him in the employing agency. When an individual is reemployed under a different leave system, an amount of leave equal to the leave represented by the refund shall be recredited to him in the employing agency on an adjusted basis under regulations prescribed by the Office of Personnel Management. When an individual is reemployed in a position excepted from this subchapter by section 6301(2)(x)–(xiii) of this title, an amount of leave equal to the leave represented by the refund is deemed, on separation from the service, death, or transfer to another position in the service, to have remained to his credit.

(Pub. L. 89–554, Sept. 6, 1966, 80 Stat. 520; Pub. L. 95–454, title IX, § 906(a)(2), Oct. 13, 1978, 92 Stat. 1224; Pub. L. 95–519, § 2, Oct. 25, 1978, 92 Stat. 1819.)

HISTORICAL AND REVISION NOTES

Derivation	U.S. Code	Revised Statutes and Statutes at Large
....	5 U.S.C. 61b (3d–5th sentences).	Dec. 21, 1944, ch. 632, § 1 (1st proviso and so much of last sentence as precedes 2d proviso), 58 Stat. 845. July 2, 1953, ch. 178, § 4(a) (2d–4th sentences), 67 Stat. 137. Aug. 18, 1959, Pub. L. 86–168, § 202(e), 73 Stat. 389.

Standard changes are made to conform with the definitions applicable and the style of this title as outlined in the preface to the report.

AMENDMENTS

1978—Subsec. (b). Pub. L. 95–519 substituted "6301(2)(x)–(xiii)" for "6301(2)(x)–(xii)".

Pub. L. 95–454 substituted "Office of Personnel Management" for "Civil Service Commission".

EFFECTIVE DATE OF 1978 AMENDMENTS

Amendment by Pub. L. 95–519 effective beginning on first day of first applicable pay period beginning on or after Oct. 25, 1978, see section 4(a) of Pub. L. 95–519, set out as a note under section 5551 of this title.

Amendment by Pub. L. 95–454 effective 90 days after Oct. 13, 1978, see section 907 of Pub. L. 95–454, set out as a note under section 1101 of this title.

SECTION REFERRED TO IN OTHER SECTIONS

This section is referred to in sections 6335, 6368 of this title; title 20 section 4416; title 25 section 2012.

§ 6307. Sick leave; accrual and accumulation

(a) An employee is entitled to sick leave with pay which accrues on the basis of one-half day for each full biweekly pay period, except that sick leave with pay accrues to a member of the Firefighting Division of the Fire Department of the District of Columbia on the basis of two-fifths of a day for each full biweekly pay period.

(b) Sick leave provided by this section, which is not used by an employee, accumulates for use in succeeding years.

(c) Sick leave provided by this section may be used for purposes relating to the adoption of a child.

(d) When required by the exigencies of the situation, a maximum of 30 days sick leave with pay may be advanced for serious disability or ailment, or for purposes relating to the adoption of a child, except that a maximum of 24 days sick leave with pay may be advanced to a member of the Firefighting Division of the Fire Department of the District of Columbia.

(d)(1)[1] For the purpose of this subsection, the term "family member" shall have such meaning as the Office of Personnel Management shall by regulation prescribe, except that such term shall include any individual who meets the definition given that term, for purposes of the leave transfer program under subchapter III, under regulations prescribed by the Office (as in effect on January 1, 1993).

(2) Subject to paragraph (3) and in addition to any other allowable purpose, sick leave may be used by an employee—

(A) to give care or otherwise attend to a family member having an illness, injury, or other condition which, if an employee had such condition, would justify the use of sick leave by such an employee; or

(B) for purposes relating to the death of a family member, including to make arrangements for or attend the funeral of such family member.

(3)(A) Sick leave may be used by an employee for the purposes provided under paragraph (2) only to the extent the amount used for such purposes does not exceed—

(i) 40 hours in any year, plus

(ii) up to an additional 64 hours in any year, but only to the extent the use of such additional hours does not cause the amount of sick leave to the employee's credit to fall below 80 hours.

(B) In the case of a part-time employee or an employee on an uncommon tour of duty, the Office of Personnel Management shall establish limitations that are proportional to those prescribed under subparagraph (A).

(4)(A) This subsection shall be effective during the 3-year period that begins upon the expiration of the 2-month period that begins on the date of the enactment of this subsection.

(B) Not later than 6 months before the date on which this subsection is scheduled to cease to be effective, the Office shall submit a report to Congress in which it shall evaluate the operation of this subsection and make recommendations as to whether or not this subsection should be continued beyond such date.

(Pub. L. 89–554, Sept. 6, 1966, 80 Stat. 520; Pub. L. 103–329, title VI, § 629(b)(1), Sept. 30, 1994, 108 Stat. 2423; Pub. L. 103–388, § 2, Oct. 22, 1994, 108 Stat. 4079.)

HISTORICAL AND REVISION NOTES

Derivation	U.S. Code	Revised Statutes and Statutes at Large
....	5 U.S.C. 2063.	Oct. 30, 1951, ch. 631, § 204, 65 Stat. 681. Aug. 21, 1964, Pub. L. 88–471, § 6(b), (c), 78 Stat. 583.

The word "officer", referring to an officer of the Firefighting Division, is omitted as covered by the words "a member of the Firefighting Division".

In subsection (c), the words "with pay" are added for clarity.

_____
[1] So in original. Probably should be "(e)(1)".

Standard changes are made to conform with the definitions applicable and style of this title as outlined in the preface to the report.

AMENDMENTS

1994—Subsec. (c). Pub. L. 103–329, § 629(b)(1)(B), added subsec. (c). Former subsec. (c) redesignated (d).

Subsec. (d). Pub. L. 103–388 added subsec. (d) relating to use of sick leave for purposes relating to family member.

Pub. L. 103–329, § 629(b)(1)(A), (C), redesignated subsec. (c) as (d) and inserted "or for purposes relating to the adoption of a child," after "ailment,".

REGULATIONS

Section 629(b)(3) of Pub. L. 103–329 provided that:

"(3)(A) The Office of Personnel Management shall prescribe regulations under which any employee who used or uses annual leave for an adoption-related purpose, after September 30, 1991, and before the date as of which sick leave first becomes available for such purpose as a result of the enactment of this subsection may, upon appropriate written application, elect to have such employee's leave accounts adjusted to reflect the amount of annual leave and sick leave, respectively, which would remain had sick leave been used instead of all or any portion of the annual leave actually used, as designated by the employee.

"(B) An application under this paragraph may not be approved unless it is submitted—

"(i) within 1 year after the date of the enactment of this Act [September 30, 1994] or such later date as the Office may prescribe;

"(ii) in such form and manner as the Office shall require; and

"(iii) by an individual who is an employee as of the time of application.

"(C) For the purpose of this paragraph, the term 'employee' has the meaning given such term by section 6301(2) of title 5, United States Code."

ADOPTIONS DURING FISCAL YEAR 1991

Pub. L. 101–509, title V, § 536, Nov. 5, 1990, 104 Stat. 1470, for fiscal year 1991, authorized sick leave provided by section 6307 of this title to be approved for purposes related to the adoption of a child.

SECTION REFERRED TO IN OTHER SECTIONS

This section is referred to in sections 6129, 6302 of this title.

§ 6308. Transfers between positions under different leave systems

(a) The annual and sick leave to the credit of an employee who transfers between positions under different leave systems without a break in service shall be transferred to his credit in the employing agency on an adjusted basis under regulations prescribed by the Office of Personnel Management, unless the individual is excepted from this subchapter by section 6301(2)(ii), (iii), (vi), or (vii) of this title. However, when a former member receiving a retirement annuity under sections 521–535 of title 4, District of Columbia Code, is reemployed in a position to which this subchapter applies, his sick leave balance may not be recredited to his account on the later reemployment.

(b) The annual leave, sick leave, and home leave to the credit of a nonappropriated fund employee of the Department of Defense or the Coast Guard described in section 2105(c) who moves without a break in service of more than 3 days to a position in the Department of Defense or the Coast Guard, respectively, that is subject to this subchapter shall be transferred to the employee's credit. The annual leave, sick leave, and home leave to the credit of an employee of the Department of Defense or the Coast Guard who is subject to this subchapter and who moves without a break in service of more than 3 days to a position under a nonappropriated fund instrumentality of the Department of Defense or the Coast Guard, respectively, described in section 2105(c), shall be transferred to the employee's credit under the nonappropriated fund instrumentality. The Secretary of Defense or the Secretary of Transportation, as appropriate, may provide for a transfer of funds in an amount equal to the value of the transferred annual leave to compensate the gaining entity for the cost of a transfer of annual leave under this subsection.

(Pub. L. 89–554, Sept. 6, 1966, 80 Stat. 521; Pub. L. 95–454, title IX, § 906(a)(2), Oct. 13, 1978, 92 Stat. 1224; Pub. L. 101–508, title VII, § 7202(h), Nov. 5, 1990, 104 Stat. 1388–336.)

HISTORICAL AND REVISION NOTES

Derivation	U.S. Code	Revised Statutes and Statutes at Large
....	5 U.S.C. 2064(e).	July 2, 1953, ch. 178, § 4(b), 67 Stat. 138. Aug. 18, 1959, Pub. L. 86–168, § 202(e), 73 Stat. 389. Aug. 21, 1964, Pub. L. 88–471, § 6(d), 78 Stat. 583.

In the last sentence, the word "officer" is omitted as covered by the word "member", and the words "sections 521–535 of title 4, District of Columbia Code" are substituted for "the Policemen and Firemen's Retirement and Disability Act, as amended".

Standard changes are made to conform with the definitions applicable and the style of this title as outlined in the preface to the report.

AMENDMENTS

1990—Pub. L. 101–508 designated existing provisions as subsec. (a) and added subsec. (b).

1978—Pub. L. 95–454 substituted "Office of Personnel Management" for "Civil Service Commission".

EFFECTIVE DATE OF 1990 AMENDMENT

Amendment by Pub. L. 101–508 applicable with respect to any individual who, on or after Jan. 1, 1987, moves from employment in nonappropriated fund instrumentality of Department of Defense or Coast Guard, that is described in section 2105(c) of this title, to employment in Department or Coast Guard, that is not described in section 2105(c), or who moves from employment in Department or Coast Guard, that is not described in section 2105(c), to employment in nonappropriated fund instrumentality of Department or Coast Guard, that is described in section 2105(c), see section 7202(m)(1) of Pub. L. 101–508, set out as a note under section 2105 of this title.

EFFECTIVE DATE OF 1978 AMENDMENT

Amendment by Pub. L. 95–454 effective 90 days after Oct. 13, 1978, see section 907 of Pub. L. 95–454, set out as a note under section 1101 of this title.

ELECTION OF LEAVE OR LUMP-SUM PAYMENT FOR CERTAIN EMPLOYEES

Pub. L. 102–484, div. A, title X, § 1077, Oct. 23, 1992, 106 Stat. 2512, authorized an employee referred to in section 6308(b) of this title, who made an employment move described in such subsection after Dec. 31, 1986, and before Apr. 16, 1991, to elect to repay the lump-sum payment received based on such employment move in lieu of annual leave and have the annual leave recredited to the employee's leave account, or to keep the lump-sum payment in lieu of that annual leave.

SECTION REFERRED TO IN OTHER SECTIONS

This section is referred to in sections 5551, 6312 of this title.

[§ 6309. Repealed. Pub. L. 94–183, § 2(26), Dec. 31, 1975, 89 Stat. 1058]

Section, Pub. L. 89–554, Sept. 6, 1966, 80 Stat. 521, related to authorized leave of absence of a rural postal carrier which occurred at beginning, during, or at end of a period of annual or sick leave.

§ 6310. Leave of absence; aliens

The head of the agency concerned may grant leave of absence with pay, not in excess of the amount of annual and sick leave allowable to citizen employees under this subchapter, to alien employees who occupy positions outside the United States.

(Pub. L. 89–554, Sept. 6, 1966, 80 Stat. 521.)

HISTORICAL AND REVISION NOTES

Derivation	U.S. Code	Revised Statutes and Statutes at Large
....	5 U.S.C. 2062(g).	Oct. 30, 1951, ch. 631, § 203 (g), 65 Stat. 681. Sept. 6, 1960, Pub. L. 86–707, § 402(b), 74 Stat. 800.

The words "head of the agency concerned" are substituted for "head of the department or agency concerned".

Standard changes are made to conform with the definitions applicable and the style of this title as outlined in the preface to the report.

SECTION REFERRED TO IN OTHER SECTIONS

This section is referred to in sections 6301, 6302, 6325 of this title; title 22 section 3968.

§ 6311. Regulations

The Office of Personnel Management may prescribe regulations necessary for the administration of this subchapter.

(Pub. L. 89–554, Sept. 6, 1966, 80 Stat. 521; Pub. L. 95–454, title IX, § 906(a)(2), Oct. 13, 1978, 92 Stat. 1224.)

HISTORICAL AND REVISION NOTES

Derivation	U.S. Code	Revised Statutes and Statutes at Large
....	5 U.S.C. 2065.	Oct. 30, 1951, ch. 631, § 206, 65 Stat. 681.

Standard changes are made to conform with the definitions applicable and the style of this title as outlined in the preface to the report.

AMENDMENTS

1978—Pub. L. 95–454 substituted "Office of Personnel Management" for "Civil Service Commission".

EFFECTIVE DATE OF 1978 AMENDMENT

Amendment by Pub. L. 95–454 effective 90 days after Oct. 13, 1978, see section 907 of Pub. L. 95–454, set out as a note under section 1101 of this title.

§ 6312. Accrual and accumulation for former ASCS county office and nonappropriated fund employees

(a) Credit shall be given in determining years of service for the purpose of section 6303(a) for—

(1) service as an employee of a county committee established pursuant to section 8(b) of the Soil Conservation and Allotment Act or of a committee or an association of producers described in section 10(b) of the Agricultural Adjustment Act; and

(2) service under a nonappropriated fund instrumentality of the Department of Defense or the Coast Guard described in section 2105(c) by an employee who has moved without a break in service of more than 3 days to a position subject to this subchapter in the Department of Defense or the Coast Guard, respectively.

(b) The provisions of subsections (a) and (b) of section 6308 for transfer of leave between leave systems shall apply to the leave systems established for such county office employees and employees of such Department of Defense and Coast Guard nonappropriated fund instrumentalities, respectively.

(Added Pub. L. 90–367, § 2(a), June 29, 1968, 82 Stat. 277; amended Pub. L. 90–623, § 1(25), Oct. 22, 1968, 82 Stat. 1314; Pub. L. 99–251, title III, § 306(c), Feb. 27, 1986, 100 Stat. 27; Pub. L. 101–508, title VII, § 7202(i)(1), Nov. 5, 1990, 104 Stat. 1388–337.)

REFERENCES IN TEXT

Section 8(b) of the Soil Conservation and Allotment Act, referred to in subsec. (a)(1), probably means section 8(b) of the Soil Conservation and Domestic Allotment Act, which is classified to section 590h(b) of Title 16, Conservation.

Section 10(b) of the Agricultural Adjustment Act, referred to in subsec. (a)(1), is classified to section 610(b) of Title 7, Agriculture.

AMENDMENTS

1990—Pub. L. 101–508 inserted "and nonappropriated fund" after "office" in section catchline and amended text generally. Prior to amendment, text read as follows: "Service rendered as an employee of a county committee established pursuant to section 590h(b) of title 16, or of a committee or an association of producers described in section 610(b) of title 7, shall be included in determining years of service for the purpose of section 6303(a) of this title. The provisions of section 6308 of this title for transfer of annual and sick leave between leave systems shall apply to the leave system established for such employees."

1986—Pub. L. 99–251 struck out "in the case of any officer or employee in or under the Department of Agriculture" at end of first sentence.

1968—Pub. L. 90–623 substituted "section 590h(b) of title 16" and "section 610(b) of title 7" for "section 8(b) of the Soil Conservation and Domestic Allotment Act (16 U.S.C. 590h(b))" and "section 10(b) of the Agricultural Adjustment Act of May 12, 1933 (48 Stat. 37)" respectively.

EFFECTIVE DATE OF 1990 AMENDMENT

Amendment by Pub. L. 101–508 applicable with respect to any individual who, on or after Jan. 1, 1987, moves from employment in nonappropriated fund instrumentality of Department of Defense or Coast Guard, that is described in section 2105(c) of this title, to employment in Department or Coast Guard, that is not described in section 2105(c), or who moves from employment in Department or Coast Guard, that is not described in section 2105(c), to employment in nonappropriated fund instrumentality of Department or Coast Guard, that is described in section 2105(c), see section 7202(m)(1) of Pub. L. 101–508, set out as a note under section 2105 of this title.

EFFECTIVE DATE OF 1968 AMENDMENT

Amendment by Pub. L. 90–623 intended to restate without substantive change the law in effect on Oct. 22, 1968, see section 6 of Pub. L. 90–623, set out as a note under section 5334 of this title.

SUBCHAPTER II—OTHER PAID LEAVE

§ 6321. Absence of veterans to attend funeral services

An employee in or under an Executive agency who is a veteran of a war, or of a campaign or expedition for which a campaign badge has been authorized, or a member of an honor or ceremonial group of an organization of those veterans, may be excused from duty without loss of pay or deduction from annual leave for the time necessary, not to exceed 4 hours in any one day, to enable him to participate as an active pallbearer or as a member of a firing squad or a guard of honor in a funeral ceremony for a member of the armed forces whose remains are returned from abroad for final interment in the United States.

(Pub. L. 89–554, Sept. 6, 1966, 80 Stat. 521.)

HISTORICAL AND REVISION NOTES

Derivation	U.S. Code	Revised Statutes and Statutes at Large
....	5 U.S.C. 30q.	Aug. 16, 1949, ch. 441, 63 Stat. 608. July 17, 1952, ch. 932, § 1, 66 Stat. 758.

The words "Executive agency" are coextensive with and substituted for "executive branch of the Government" in view of the definition of "Executive agency" in section 105. Applicability to the General Accounting Office is based on former section 933a.

Standard changes are made to conform with the definitions applicable and the style of this title as outlined in the preface to the report.

§ 6322. Leave for jury or witness service; official duty status for certain witness service

(a) An employee as defined by section 2105 of this title (except an individual whose pay is disbursed by the Secretary of the Senate or the Chief Administrative Officer of the House of Representatives) or an individual employed by the government of the District of Columbia is entitled to leave, without loss of, or reduction in, pay, leave to which he otherwise is entitled, credit for time or service, or performance of efficiency rating, during a period of absence with respect to which he is summoned, in connection with a judicial proceeding, by a court or authority responsible for the conduct of that proceeding, to serve—

(1) as a juror; or

(2) other than as provided in subsection (b) of this section, as a witness on behalf of any party in connection with any judicial proceeding to which the United States, the District of Columbia, or a State or local government is a party;

in the District of Columbia, a State, territory, or possession of the United States including the

Commonwealth of Puerto Rico or the Trust Territory of the Pacific Islands. For the purpose of this subsection, "judicial proceeding" means any action, suit, or other judicial proceeding, including any condemnation, preliminary, informational, or other proceeding of a judicial nature, but does not include an administrative proceeding.

(b) An employee as defined by section 2105 of this title (except an individual whose pay is disbursed by the Secretary of the Senate or the Chief Administrative Officer of the House of Representatives) or an individual employed by the government of the District of Columbia is performing official duty during the period with respect to which he is summoned, or assigned by his agency, to—

(1) testify or produce official records on behalf of the United States or the District of Columbia; or

(2) testify in his official capacity or produce official records on behalf of a party other than the United States or the District of Columbia.

(c) The Office of Personnel Management may prescribe regulations for the administration of this section.

(Pub. L. 89–554, Sept. 6, 1966, 80 Stat. 522; Pub. L. 91–563, §1(a), Dec. 19, 1970, 84 Stat. 1476; Pub. L. 94–310, §1, June 15, 1976, 90 Stat. 687; Pub. L. 95–454, title IX, §906(a)(2), Oct. 13, 1978, 92 Stat. 1224; Pub. L. 96–70, title I, §1251, Sept. 27, 1979, 93 Stat. 476; Pub. L. 104–186, title II, §215(10), Aug. 20, 1996, 110 Stat. 1746; Pub. L. 104–201, div. C, title XXXV, §3548(a)(8), Sept. 23, 1996, 110 Stat. 2869.)

HISTORICAL AND REVISION NOTES

Derivation	U.S. Code	Revised Statutes and Statutes at Large
....	5 U.S.C. 30n.	June 29, 1940, ch. 446, §1, 54 Stat. 689.

Standard changes are made to conform with the definitions applicable and the style of this title as outlined in the preface to the report.

AMENDMENTS

1996—Subsec. (a). Pub. L. 104–201, in concluding provisions, substituted "Puerto Rico or" for "Puerto Rico," and struck out ", or the Republic of Panama" after "Pacific Islands".

Pub. L. 104–186 substituted "Chief Administrative Officer" for "Clerk" in introductory provisions.

Subsec. (b). Pub. L. 104–186 substituted "Chief Administrative Officer" for "Clerk".

1979—Subsec. (a). Pub. L. 96–70 substituted "the Trust Territory of the Pacific Islands, or the Republic of Panama" for "the Canal Zone, or the Trust Territory of the Pacific Islands".

1978—Subsec. (c). Pub. L. 95–454 substituted "Office of Personnel Management" for "Civil Service Commission".

1976—Subsec. (a)(2). Pub. L. 94–310 substituted "other than as provided in subsection (b) of this section, as a witness on behalf of any party in connection with any judicial proceeding to which the United States, the District of Columbia, or a State or local government is a party" for "as a witness on behalf of a party other than the United States, the District of Columbia, or a private party".

1970—Pub. L. 91–563 included witness service and official duty status for certain witness service in section catchline.

Subsec. (a). Pub. L. 91–563 designated existing provisions as subsec. (a) and expanded such provisions to authorize leave for jury service in courts in the District of Columbia and in territories and possessions of the United States, to permit leave for persons summoned as witnesses in behalf of a party other than the United States, the District of Columbia, or a private party, defined "judicial proceeding", and excepted individuals whose pay is disbursed by the Secretary of the Senate or the Clerk of the House of Representatives.

Subsecs. (b), (c). Pub. L. 91–563 added subsecs. (b) and (c).

EFFECTIVE DATE OF 1979 AMENDMENT

Amendment by Pub. L. 96–70 effective Oct. 1, 1979, see section 3304 of Pub. L. 96–70, set out as an Effective Date note under section 3601 of Title 22, Foreign Relations and Intercourse.

EFFECTIVE DATE OF 1978 AMENDMENT

Amendment by Pub. L. 95–454 effective 90 days after Oct. 13, 1978, see section 907 of Pub. L. 95–454, set out as a note under section 1101 of this title.

EFFECTIVE DATE OF 1976 AMENDMENT

Amendment by Pub. L. 94–310 effective Oct. 1, 1976, see section 4 of Pub. L. 94–310, set out as a note under section 130b of Title 2, The Congress.

TERMINATION OF TRUST TERRITORY OF THE PACIFIC ISLANDS

For termination of Trust Territory of the Pacific Islands, see note set out preceding section 1681 of Title 48, Territories and Insular Possessions.

SECTION REFERRED TO IN OTHER SECTIONS

This section is referred to in section 5515 of this title.

§ 6323. Military leave; Reserves and National Guardsmen

(a)(1) Subject to paragraph (2) of this subsection, an employee as defined by section 2105 of this title or an individual employed by the government of the District of Columbia, permanent or temporary indefinite, is entitled to leave without loss in pay, time, or performance or efficiency rating for active duty, inactive-duty training (as defined in section 101 of title 37), or engaging in field or coast defense training under sections 502–505 of title 32 as a Reserve of the armed forces or member of the National Guard. Leave under this subsection accrues for an employee or individual at the rate of 15 days per fiscal year and, to the extent that it is not used in a fiscal year, accumulates for use in the succeeding fiscal year until it totals 15 days at the beginning of a fiscal year.

(2) In the case of an employee or individual employed on a part-time career employment basis (as defined in section 3401(2) of this title), the rate at which leave accrues under this subsection shall be a percentage of the rate prescribed under paragraph (1) which is determined by dividing 40 into the number of hours in the regularly scheduled workweek of that employee or individual during that fiscal year.

(3) The minimum charge for leave under this subsection is one hour, and additional charges are in multiples thereof.

(b) Except as provided by section 5519 of this title, an employee as defined by section 2105 of this title or an individual employed by the government of the District of Columbia, permanent or temporary indefinite, who—

(1) is a member of a Reserve component of the Armed Forces, as described in section 10101 of title 10, or the National Guard, as described in section 101 of title 32; and

(2) performs, for the purpose of providing military aid to enforce the law or for the purpose of providing assistance to civil authorities in the protection or saving of life or property or the prevention of injury—

(A) Federal service under section 331, 332, 333, or 12406 of title 10, or other provision of law, as applicable, or

(B) full-time military service for his State, the District of Columbia, the Commonwealth of Puerto Rico, or a territory of the United States;

is entitled, during and because of such service, to leave without loss of, or reduction in, pay, leave to which he otherwise is entitled, credit for time or service, or performance or efficiency rating. Leave granted by this subsection shall not exceed 22 work-days in a calendar year. Upon the request of an employee, the period for which an employee is absent to perform service described in paragraph (2) may be charged to the employee's accrued annual leave or to compensatory time available to the employee instead of being charged as leave to which the employee is entitled under this subsection. The period of absence may not be charged to sick leave.

(c) An employee as defined by section 2105 of this title or an individual employed by the government of the District of Columbia, who is a member of the National Guard of the District of Columbia, is entitled to leave without loss in pay or time for each day of a parade or encampment ordered or authorized under title 39, District of Columbia Code. This subsection covers each day of service the National Guard, or a portion thereof, is ordered to perform by the commanding general.

(d)(1) A military reserve technician described in section 8401(30)[1] is entitled at such person's request to leave without loss of, or reduction in, pay, leave to which such person is otherwise entitled, credit for time or service, or performance or efficiency rating for each day, not to exceed 44 workdays in a calendar year, in which such person is on active duty without pay, as authorized pursuant to section 12315 of title 10, under section 12301(b) or 12301(d) of title 10 (other than active duty during a war or national emergency declared by the President or Congress) for participation in operations outside the United States, its territories and possessions.

(2) An employee who requests annual leave or compensatory time to which the employee is otherwise entitled, for a period during which the employee would have been entitled upon request to leave under this subsection, may be granted such annual leave or compensatory time without regard to this section or section 5519.

(Pub. L. 89–554, Sept. 6, 1966, 80 Stat. 522; Pub. L. 90–588, § 2(a), Oct. 17, 1968, 82 Stat. 1151; Pub. L. 90–623, § 1(17), Oct. 22, 1968, 82 Stat. 1313; Pub. L. 91–375, § 6(c)(18), Aug. 12, 1970, 84 Stat. 776; Pub. L. 96–54, § 2(a)(40), Aug. 14, 1979, 93 Stat. 383; Pub. L. 96–70, title III, § 3302(e)(5), Sept. 27, 1979, 93

---

[1] See References in Text note below.

Stat. 498; Pub. L. 96–431, § 1, Oct. 10, 1980, 94 Stat. 1850; Pub. L. 102–190, div. A, title V, § 528, Dec. 5, 1991, 105 Stat. 1364; Pub. L. 103–337, div. A, title XVI, § 1677(a)(2), Oct. 5, 1994, 108 Stat. 3019; Pub. L. 104–106, div. A, title V, § 516(a), title X, § 1039, Feb. 10, 1996, 110 Stat. 309, 432; Pub. L. 106–65, div. A, title VI, § 672(b), title XI, §§ 1105(a), 1106(a), Oct. 5, 1999, 113 Stat. 674, 777; Pub. L. 106–554, § 1(a)(3) [title VI, § 642], Dec. 21, 2000, 114 Stat. 2763, 2763A–169.)

HISTORICAL AND REVISION NOTES

Derivation	U.S. Code	Revised Statutes and Statutes at Large
....	5 U.S.C. 30r(a).	Aug. 10, 1956, ch. 1041, § 29 (a), 70A Stat. 632. Sept. 2, 1958, Pub. L. 85–861, § 13, 72 Stat. 1557. June 30, 1960, Pub. L. 86–559, § 7, 74 Stat. 282. Oct. 4, 1961, Pub. L. 87–378, § 7(a), 75 Stat. 809.

In subsection (a), the words "without regard to classification or terminology peculiar to the Civil Service system" are omitted as unnecessary. The word "performance" is added on authority of the Performance Rating Act of 1950, which is carried into chapter 43 of this title.

Standard changes are made to conform with the definitions applicable and the style of this title as outlined in the preface to the report.

REFERENCES IN TEXT

Section 8401(30) of this title, referred to in subsec. (d)(1), was amended generally by Pub. L. 106–65, div. A, title V, § 522(c)(2), Oct. 5, 1999, 113 Stat. 597, and, as so amended, no longer describes military reserve technicians.

AMENDMENTS

2000—Subsec. (a)(3). Pub. L. 106–554 added par. (3).

1999—Subsec. (a)(1). Pub. L. 106–65, § 1106(a), inserted ", inactive-duty training (as defined in section 101 of title 37)," after "active duty" in first sentence.

Subsec. (d)(1). Pub. L. 106–65, §§ 672(b) and 1105(a), amended par. (1) identically, striking out "noncombat" after "for participation in".

1996—Subsec. (b). Pub. L. 104–106, § 516(a), inserted at end "Upon the request of an employee, the period for which an employee is absent to perform service described in paragraph (2) may be charged to the employee's accrued annual leave or to compensatory time available to the employee instead of being charged as leave to which the employee is entitled under this subsection. The period of absence may not be charged to sick leave."

Subsec. (d). Pub. L. 104–106, § 1039, added subsec. (d).

1994—Subsec. (b)(1). Pub. L. 103–337, § 1677(a)(2)(A), substituted "section 10101" for "section 261".

Subsec. (b)(2)(A). Pub. L. 103–337, § 1677(a)(2)(B), substituted "or 12406 of title 10" for "3500, or 8500 of title 10".

1991—Subsec. (b)(2). Pub. L. 102–190 substituted "law or for the purpose of providing assistance to civil authorities in the protection or saving of life or property or the prevention of injury—" for "law—" in introductory provisions.

1980—Subsec. (a). Pub. L. 96–431 designated existing provisions as par. (1), substituted "Subject to paragraph (2) of this subsection, an employee" for "An employee" and "for active duty or engaging in field or coast defense training" for "for each day, not in excess of 15 days in a calendar year, in which he is on active duty or is engaged in field or coast defense training", inserted provision relating to accrual and accumulation of leave, and added par. (2).

1979—Subsec. (b)(2)(B). Pub. L. 96–70 which directed the amendment of subsec. (c)(2)(B) by striking out "the

Canal Zone,'' was executed to subsec. (b)(2)(B) in view of the redesignation of subsec. (c) as (b) by Pub. L. 96–54. See 1979 Amendment note below.

Subsec. (b). Pub. L. 96–54 redesignated subsec. (c), as added by Pub. L. 90–588, as (b). Former subsec. (b), relating to military leave, was repealed by Pub. L. 91–375, § 6(c)(18)(B), Aug. 12, 1970, 84 Stat. 776.

Subsec. (c). Pub. L. 96–54 redesignated subsec. (c), as added by Pub. L. 90–588, as (b).

1970—Subsec. (a). Pub. L. 91–375, § 6(c)(18)(A), struck out "(except a substitute in the postal field service)" after "section 2105 of this title".

Subsec. (b). Pub. L. 91–375, § 6(c)(18)(B), struck out subsec. (b) relating to military leave, without loss in pay, time, or efficiency rating, of substitute employees of the postal service, not in excess of 80 hours in a calendar year, for National Guard training as Reserves of the Armed Forces or members of the National Guard, on basis of 1 hour for 26 hours of work, including minimum working period of 1,040 hours in the prior calendar year.

Subsec. (c). Pub. L. 91–375, § 6(c)(18)(A), struck out "(except a substitute in the postal field service)" after "section 2105 of this title".

Subsec. (d). Pub. L. 91–375, § 6(c)(18)(B), struck out subsec. (d) relating to military leave, without loss of or reduction in pay, leave, service credit, or efficiency rating, of substitute employees of the postal service, not in excess of 160 hours in a calendar year, for service as members of Reserve components of the Armed Forces or the National Guard, for Federal service under insurrection provisions of sections 331, 332, and 333 and in the Army National Guard and Air National Guard under sections 3500 and 8500 of Title 10 and non-Federal service (in the States, District of Columbia, Puerto Rico, Canal Zone, and the territories) for purpose of providing military aid to enforce the law, on basis of 1 hour for 13 hours of work, including minimum working period of 1,040 hours in the prior calendar year.

1968—Subsecs. (a), (b). Pub. L. 90–623, § 1(17)(A), substituted "loss in" for "loss of".

Subsec. (c). Pub. L. 90–623, § 1(17)(B), added subsec. (c), set out second.

Subsec. (c). Pub. L. 90–588 added subsec. (c), set out first.

Subsec. (d). Pub. L. 90–588 added subsec. (d).

EFFECTIVE DATE OF 1999 AMENDMENT

Pub. L. 106–65, div. A, title XI, § 1105(b), Oct. 5, 1999, 113 Stat. 777, provided that: "The amendment made by subsection (a) [amending this section] shall take effect on the date of the enactment of this Act [Oct. 5, 1999] and shall apply with respect to days of leave under section 6323(d)(1) of title 5, United States Code, on or after that date."

Pub. L. 106–65, div. A, title XI, § 1106(b), Oct. 5, 1999, 113 Stat. 777, provided that: "The amendment made by subsection (a) [amending this section] shall not apply with respect to any inactive-duty training (as defined in such amendment) occurring before the date of the enactment of this Act [Oct. 5, 1999]."

EFFECTIVE DATE OF 1994 AMENDMENT

Amendment by Pub. L. 103–337 effective Dec. 1, 1994, except as otherwise provided, see section 1691 of Pub. L. 103–337, set out as an Effective Date note under section 10001 of Title 10, Armed Forces.

EFFECTIVE DATE OF 1980 AMENDMENT

Section 2 of Pub. L. 96–431 provided that: "The amendments made by the first section of this Act [amending this section] shall take effect October 1, 1980."

EFFECTIVE DATE OF 1979 AMENDMENTS

Amendment by Pub. L. 96–70 effective Oct. 1, 1979, see section 3304 of Pub. L. 96–70, set out as an Effective Date note under section 3601 of Title 22, Foreign Relations and Intercourse.

Amendment by Pub. L. 96–54 effective July 12, 1979, see section 2(b) of Pub. L. 96–54, set out as a note under section 305 of this title.

EFFECTIVE DATE OF 1970 AMENDMENT

Amendment by Pub. L. 91–375 effective within 1 year after Aug. 12, 1970, on date established therefor by Board of Governors of United States Postal Service and Published by it in Federal Register, see section 15(a) of Pub. L. 91–375, set out as an Effective Date note preceding section 101 of Title 39, Postal Service.

EFFECTIVE DATE OF 1968 AMENDMENT

Amendment by Pub. L. 90–623 effective as of Sept. 6, 1966, for all purposes, see section 6 of Pub. L. 90–623, set out as a note under section 5334 of this title.

DEFINITION OF OFFICERS AND EMPLOYEES

Section 4 of act July 1, 1947, ch. 192, 61 Stat. 239, as amended by act June 22, 1956, ch. 428, 70 Stat. 331, provided that: "The words 'officers and employees of the United States or of the District of Columbia' as used in the third paragraph, subheading 'Ordinance Stores and Equipment for Reserve Officers Training Corps', of the Act of May 12, 1917 (40 Stat. 72; 10 U.S.C. Annotated 371) [covered by this section], as now or hereafter amended, as used in that part of section 80 of the Act of June 3, 1916 (39 Stat. 203; 32 U.S.C. 75) [covered by this section], as now or hereafter amended, which precedes the proviso, and as used in the first proviso of section 9 of the Naval Reserve Act of 1938 (52 Stat. 1177; 34 U.S.C. 853g) [covered by this section], as now or hereafter amended, shall be construed to mean all officers and employees of the United States or of the District of Columbia, permanent or temporary indefinite, without regard to classifications or terminology peculiar to the Federal Civil Service System. The words 'officers and employees of the United States or of the District of Columbia', as used in such provisions of law, as now or hereafter amended, also shall be construed to mean substitute employees in the postal field service; such substitute employees shall be entitled to military leave of absence on the basis of one hour of such leave for each period or periods aggregating twenty-six hours of work performed in the calendar year immediately preceding the year in which they are ordered to duty by proper authority: *Provided*, That the number of hours worked during the preceding calendar year shall not be less than one thousand forty hours before such substitute employee shall be entitled to military leave of absence, pay for such leave not to exceed eighty hours in each calendar year."

SECTION REFERRED TO IN OTHER SECTIONS

This section is referred to in sections 5519, 6129 of this title; title 22 section 3664; title 37 section 1002.

§ 6324. Absence of certain police and firemen

(a) Sick leave may not be charged to the account of a member of the Metropolitan Police force or the Fire Department of the District of Columbia, the United States Park Police force, or the Executive Protective Service force for an absence due to injury or illness resulting from the performance of duty.

(b) The determination of whether an injury or illness resulted from the performance of duty shall be made under regulations prescribed by—

(1) the District of Columbia Council for members of the Metropolitan Police force and the Fire Department of the District of Columbia;

(2) the Secretary of the Interior for the United States Park Police force; and

(3) The Secretary of the Treasury for the Executive Protective Service force.

(Pub. L. 89–554, Sept. 6, 1966, 80 Stat. 522; Pub. L. 90–623, §1(18), Oct. 22, 1968, 82 Stat. 1313; Pub. L. 94–183, §2(28), (29), Dec. 31, 1975, 89 Stat. 1058.)

HISTORICAL AND REVISION NOTES

Derivation	U.S. Code	Revised Statutes and Statutes at Large
....	5 U.S.C. 2071.	Aug. 21, 1964, Pub. L. 88–471, §5, 78 Stat. 583.

The word "officer" is omitted as covered by "member".

In subsection (b), the words "injury or illness" are substituted for "injury or disease" to conform to subsection (a).

Standard changes are made to conform with the definitions applicable and the style of this title as outlined in the preface to the report.

AMENDMENTS

1975—Subsecs. (a), (b)(3). Pub. L. 94–183 substituted "Executive Protective Service" for "White House Police".

1968—Subsec. (b)(1). Pub. L. 90–623 substituted "District of Columbia Council" for "Commissioners of the District of Columbia".

CHANGE OF NAME

Reference to Executive Protective Service held to refer to United States Secret Service Uniformed Division pursuant to Pub. L. 95–179, set out as a note under section 202 of Title 3, The President.

EFFECTIVE DATE OF 1968 AMENDMENT

Amendment by Pub. L. 90–623 intended to restate without substantive change the law in effect on Oct. 22, 1968, see section 6 of Pub. L. 90–623, set out as a note under section 5334 of this title.

TRANSFER OF FUNCTIONS

District of Columbia Council, as established by Reorg. Plan No. 3 of 1967, abolished as of noon Jan. 2, 1975, by Pub. L. 93–198, title VII, §711, Dec. 24, 1973, 87 Stat. 818, and replaced by Council of District of Columbia, as provided by section 401 of Pub. L. 93–198.

§ 6325. Absence resulting from hostile action abroad

Leave may not be charged to the account of an employee for absence, not to exceed one year, due to an injury—

(1) incurred while serving abroad and resulting from war, insurgency, mob violence, or similar hostile action; and

(2) not due to vicious habits, intemperance, or willful misconduct on the part of the employee.

The preceding provisions of this section shall apply in the case of an alien employee referred to in section 6301(2)(viii) of this title with respect to any leave granted to such alien employee under section 6310 of this title or section 408 of the Foreign Service Act of 1980.

(Added Pub. L. 90–221, §3(a), Dec. 23, 1967, 81 Stat. 671; amended Pub. L. 96–54, §2(a)(41), Aug. 14, 1979, 93 Stat. 383; Pub. L. 99–399, title VIII, §804, Aug. 27, 1986, 100 Stat. 883.)

REFERENCES IN TEXT

Section 408 of the Foreign Service Act of 1980, referred to in text, is classified to section 3968 of Title 22, Foreign Relations and Intercourse.

AMENDMENTS

1986—Pub. L. 99–399 inserted sentence at end relating to alien employees.

1979—Pub. L. 96–54 substituted provisions relating to leave charged to an account of an employee for absence, for provisions relating to leave charged to an account of any officer or employee for absence, and designated qualifying provisions as cls. (1) and (2).

EFFECTIVE DATE OF 1979 AMENDMENT

Amendment by Pub. L. 96–54 effective July 12, 1979, see section 2(b) of Pub. L. 96–54, set out as a note under section 305 of this title.

EFFECTIVE DATE

Section 3(c) of Pub. L. 90–221 provided that: "The amendment made by subsection (a) of this section [enacting this section] shall take effect as of the first day of the first pay period which began on or after January 1, 1965."

§ 6326. Absence in connection with funerals of immediate relatives in the Armed Forces

(a) An employee of an executive agency or an individual employed by the government of the District of Columbia is entitled to not more than three days of leave without loss of, or reduction in, pay, leave to which he is otherwise entitled, credit for time or service, or performance or efficiency rating, to make arrangements for, or attend the funeral of, or memorial service for, an immediate relative who died as a result of wounds, disease, or injury incurred while serving as a member of the Armed Forces in a combat zone (as determined by the President in accordance with section 112 of the Internal Revenue Code).

(b) The Office of Personnel Management is authorized to issue regulations for the administration of this section.

(c) This section shall not be considered as affecting the authority of an Executive agency, except to the extent and under the conditions covered under this section, to grant administrative leave excusing an employee from work when it is in the public interest.

(Added Pub. L. 90–588, §1(a), Oct. 17, 1968, 82 Stat. 1151; amended Pub. L. 95–454, title IX, §906(a)(2), Oct. 13, 1978, 92 Stat. 1224.)

REFERENCES IN TEXT

Section 112 of the Internal Revenue Code, referred to in subsec. (a), is classified to section 112 of Title 26, Internal Revenue Code.

AMENDMENTS

1978—Subsec. (b). Pub. L. 95–454 substituted "Office of Personnel Management" for "Civil Service Commission".

EFFECTIVE DATE OF 1978 AMENDMENT

Amendment by Pub. L. 95–454 effective 90 days after Oct. 13, 1978, see section 907 of Pub. L. 95–454, set out as a note under section 1101 of this title.

SECTION REFERRED TO IN OTHER SECTIONS

This section is referred to in section 6129 of this title.

§ 6327. Absence in connection with serving as a bone-marrow or organ donor

(a) An employee in or under an Executive agency is entitled to leave without loss of or reduction in pay, leave to which otherwise entitled, credit for time or service, or performance or efficiency rating, for the time necessary to permit such employee to serve as a bone-marrow or organ donor.

(b) An employee may, in any calendar year, use—

(1) not to exceed 7 days of leave under this section to serve as a bone-marrow donor; and

(2) not to exceed 30 days of leave under this section to serve as an organ donor.

(c) The Office of Personnel Management may prescribe regulations for the administration of this section.

(Added Pub. L. 103–329, title VI, § 629(a)(1), Sept. 30, 1994, 108 Stat. 2423; amended Pub. L. 106–56, § 1(b), Sept. 24, 1999, 113 Stat. 407.)

Another section 6327 was renumbered section 6328 of this title.

AMENDMENTS

1999—Subsec. (b). Pub. L. 106–56 amended subsec. (b) generally. Prior to amendment, subsec. (b) read as follows: "Not to exceed 7 days of leave may be used under this section by an employee in a calendar year."

SECTION REFERRED TO IN OTHER SECTIONS

This section is referred to in section 6129 of this title.

§ 6328. Absence in connection with funerals of fellow Federal law enforcement officers

A Federal law enforcement officer or a Federal firefighter may be excused from duty without loss of, or reduction in, pay or leave to which such officer is otherwise entitled, or credit for time or service, or performance or efficiency rating, to attend the funeral of a fellow Federal law enforcement officer or Federal firefighter, who was killed in the line of duty. When so excused from duty, attendance at such service shall for the purposes of section 1345(a) of title 31, be considered to be an official duty of the officer or firefighter.

(Added Pub. L. 103–329, title VI, § 642, Sept. 30, 1994, 108 Stat. 2432, § 6327; renumbered § 6328, Pub. L. 106–56, § 1(c)(1), Sept. 24, 1999, 113 Stat. 407.)

CODIFICATION

Section 642 of Pub. L. 103–329, which directed that this section be added "following the word 'Forces' in section 6326" was executed by adding the section after section 6327, as added by section 629(a)(1) of Pub. L. 103–329, to reflect the probable intent of Congress.

AMENDMENTS

1999—Pub. L. 106–56 renumbered section 6327 of this title as this section.

SUBCHAPTER III—VOLUNTARY TRANSFERS OF LEAVE

SUBCHAPTER REFERRED TO IN OTHER SECTIONS

This subchapter is referred to in sections 6307, 6373 of this title; title 20 section 904; title 22 section 3968; title 38 section 7423.

§ 6331. Definitions

For the purpose of this subchapter—

(1) the term "employee" means an employee as defined by section 6301(2), excluding an individual employed by the government of the District of Columbia;

(2) the term "leave recipient" means an employee whose application to receive donations of leave under this subchapter is approved;

(3) the term "leave donor" means an employee whose application to make 1 or more donations of leave under this subchapter is approved; and

(4) the term "medical emergency" means a medical condition of an employee or a family member of such employee that is likely to require the prolonged absence of such employee from duty and to result in a substantial loss of income to such employee because of the unavailability of paid leave (disregarding any advanced leave).

(Added Pub. L. 100–566, § 2(a), Oct. 31, 1988, 102 Stat. 2834; amended Pub. L. 103–103, § 3, Oct. 8, 1993, 107 Stat. 1022.)

AMENDMENTS

1993—Par. (4). Pub. L. 103–103 inserted "the term" after par. designation and inserted before period at end "(disregarding any advanced leave)".

EFFECTIVE DATE OF 1993 AMENDMENT

Section 6 of Pub. L. 103–103 provided that: "Except as provided in section 2 [enacting and repealing provisions set out as notes under this section], this Act [amending this section and sections 6337, 6361, 6362, and 6373 of this title and enacting provisions set out as a note under section 6301 of this title] and the amendments made by this Act shall take effect as of the 120th day after the date of the enactment of this Act [Oct. 8, 1993] or such earlier date as the Office of Personnel Management may by regulation prescribe."

REPEALS

Section 2(d) of Pub. L. 100–566, which provided for the repeal of subchapters III (§ 6331 et seq.) and IV (§ 6361 et seq.) of this chapter effective 5 years after Oct. 31, 1988, and which also contained savings provisions for continued availability of certain leave as if such program had not been terminated, was repealed by Pub. L. 103–103, § 2, Oct. 8, 1993, 107 Stat. 1022, effective Oct. 30, 1993.

[Section 2 of Pub. L. 103–103 provided that the repeal made by that section is effective Oct. 30, 1993.]

IMPLEMENTATION OF LEAVE TRANSFER AND LEAVE BANK PROGRAMS

Section 2(c) of Pub. L. 100–566 provided that:

"(1) No later than 3 months after the date of the enactment of this Act [Oct. 31, 1988], the Office of Personnel Management shall prescribe regulations to implement leave transfer programs pursuant to the amendments made by this Act [see Short Title of 1988 Amendment note set out under section 6301 of this title].

"(2) No later than 6 months after the date of the enactment of this Act—

"(A) the head of each agency involved under sections 6332 and 6339 of title 5, United States Code, shall establish and begin operating a leave transfer program in accordance with applicable provisions of subchapter III of chapter 63 of title 5, United States Code, and applicable regulations prescribed by the Office; and

"(B) the Office of Personnel Management shall prescribe regulations to implement leave bank programs pursuant to the amendments made by this Act.

"(3) No later than 9 months after the date of the enactment of this Act, the head of each agency involved under section 6362 of title 5, United States Code, shall establish and begin operating a leave bank in accordance with subchapter IV of chapter 63 of title 5, United States Code, and applicable regulations prescribed by the Office."

REPORT TO CONGRESS

Section 2(e) of Pub. L. 100–566 provided that:

"(1)(A) Within 2 years after the date of the enactment of this Act [Oct. 31, 1988] and again no later than 6 months before the scheduled termination date of any program under subchapter III or subchapter IV of chapter 63 of title 5, United States Code (excluding any program under sections 6339 and 6372 of such chapter) the Office of Personnel Management shall submit a written report to the Congress with respect to the operations of such programs.

"(B) The Office of Personnel Management may require agencies to maintain such records and to provide such information as the Office may need to carry out subparagraph (A).

"(2) The excepted agencies that establish programs under sections 6339 and 6372 of title 5, United States Code, shall report to the Congress on the operation of such programs within 2 years after the date of the enactment of this Act and again no later than 6 months before the scheduled termination of any such programs."

CONTINUATION OF TEMPORARY LEAVE TRANSFER PROGRAMS

Section 2(f) of Pub. L. 100–566 provided that: "Any temporary program allowing for transfers of leave among officers or employees of the Federal Government may, if such program is being implemented with respect to an agency (or any unit thereof) as of the date of the enactment of this Act [Oct. 31, 1988], continue to be implemented with respect to such agency (or unit), notwithstanding any provision of law which would otherwise terminate the authority for such program, pending the commencement of a leave transfer program with respect to such agency pursuant to amendments made by this Act [see Short Title of 1988 Amendment note set out under section 6301 of this title]. The Office of Personnel Management (or, in the case of a program established by another agency, such other agency) shall prescribe regulations to ensure that any leave which has been transferred to the credit of an officer or employee and which remains unused as of the date on which any such temporary program terminates (and a successor program commences pursuant to amendments made by this Act) shall not be lost by reason of that termination."

SECTION REFERRED TO IN OTHER SECTIONS

This section is referred to in section 6391 of this title.

§ 6332. General authority

Notwithstanding any provision of subchapter I, and subject to the provisions of this subchapter, the Office of Personnel Management shall establish a program under which annual leave accrued or accumulated by an employee may be transferred to the annual leave account of any other employee if such other employee requires additional leave because of a medical emergency.

(Added Pub. L. 100–566, § 2(a), Oct. 31, 1988, 102 Stat. 2834.)

SECTION REFERRED TO IN OTHER SECTIONS

This section is referred to in section 6334 of this title.

§ 6333. Receipt and use of transferred leave

(a)(1) An application to receive donations of leave under this subchapter, whether submitted by or on behalf of an employee—

(A) shall be submitted to the employing agency of the proposed leave recipient; and

(B) shall include—

(i) the name, position title, and grade or pay level of the proposed leave recipient;

(ii) the reasons why transferred leave is needed, including a brief description of the nature, severity, anticipated duration, and, if it is a recurring one, the approximate frequency of the medical emergency involved;

(iii) if the employing agency so requires, certification from 1 or more physicians, or other appropriate experts, with respect to any matter under clause (ii); and

(iv) any other information which the employing agency may reasonably require.

(2) If an agency requires that an employee obtain certification under paragraph (1)(B)(iii) from 2 or more sources, the agency shall ensure, either by direct payment to the expert involved or by reimbursement, that the employee is not required to pay for the expenses associated with obtaining certification from more than 1 of such sources.

(3) An employing agency shall approve or disapprove an application of a proposed leave recipient for leave under this subchapter, and, to the extent practicable, shall notify the proposed leave recipient (or other person acting on behalf of the proposed recipient, if appropriate) of the decision of the agency, in writing, within 10 days (excluding Saturdays, Sundays, and legal public holidays) after receiving such application.

(b) A leave recipient may use annual leave received under this subchapter in the same manner and for the same purposes as if such leave recipient had accrued that leave under section 6303, except that any annual leave, and any sick leave, accrued or accumulated by the leave recipient and available for the purpose involved must be exhausted before any transferred annual leave may be used.

(c) Transferred annual leave—

(1) may accumulate without regard to any limitation under section 6304; and

(2) may be substituted retroactively for any period of leave without pay, or used to liquidate an indebtedness for any period of advanced leave, which began on or after a date fixed by the employing agency of the employee as the beginning of the medical emergency involved.

(Added Pub. L. 100–566, § 2(a), Oct. 31, 1988, 102 Stat. 2834.)

§ 6334. Donations of leave

(a) An employee may, by written application to the employing agency of such employee, request that a specified number of hours be transferred from the annual leave account of such employee to the annual leave account of a leave recipient in accordance with section 6332.

(b)(1) In any one leave year, a leave donor may donate no more than a total of one-half of the amount of annual leave such donor would be entitled to accrue during the leave year in which the donation is made.

(2) A leave donor who is projected to have annual leave that otherwise would be subject to forfeiture at the end of the leave year under section 6304(a) may donate no more than the number of hours remaining in the leave year (as of the date of the transfer) for which the leave donor is scheduled to work and receive pay.

(3) The employing agency of a leave donor may waive the limitation under paragraphs (1) and (2). Any such waiver shall be made in writing.

(c) The Office of Personnel Management shall prescribe regulations to include procedures to carry out this subchapter when the leave donor and the leave recipient are employed by different agencies.

(Added Pub. L. 100–566, § 2(a), Oct. 31, 1988, 102 Stat. 2835.)

SECTION REFERRED TO IN OTHER SECTIONS

This section is referred to in section 6336 of this title.

§ 6335. Termination of medical emergency

(a) The medical emergency affecting a leave recipient shall, for purposes of this subchapter, be considered to have terminated on the date as of which—

(1) the leave recipient notifies the employing agency of such leave recipient, in writing, that the medical emergency no longer exists;

(2) the employing agency of such leave recipient determines, after written notice and opportunity for the leave recipient (or, if appropriate, another person acting on behalf of the leave recipient) to answer orally or in writing, that the medical emergency no longer exists; or

(3) the leave recipient is separated from service.

(b)(1) The employing agency of a leave recipient shall, consistent with guidelines prescribed by the Office of Personnel Management, establish procedures to ensure that a leave recipient is not permitted to use or receive any transferred leave under this subchapter after the medical emergency terminates.

(2) Nothing in section 5551, 5552, or 6306 shall apply with respect to any annual leave transferred to a leave recipient under this subchapter.

(Added Pub. L. 100–566, § 2(a), Oct. 31, 1988, 102 Stat. 2836.)

SECTION REFERRED TO IN OTHER SECTIONS

This section is referred to in section 6337 of this title.

§ 6336. Restoration of transferred leave

(a)(1) The Office of Personnel Management shall establish procedures under which, except as provided in paragraph (2), any transferred leave remaining to the credit of a leave recipient when the medical emergency affecting the leave recipient terminates shall be restored on a prorated basis by transfer to the appropriate accounts of the respective leave donors.

(2) Nothing in paragraph (1) shall require the restoration of leave to a leave donor—

(A) if the amount of leave which would be restored to such donor would be less than 1 hour or any other shorter period of time which the Office may by regulation prescribe;

(B) if such donor retires, dies, or is otherwise separated from service, before the date on which such restoration would otherwise be made; or

(C) if such restoration is not administratively feasible, as determined under regulations prescribed by the Office.

(b) At the election of the leave donor, transferred annual leave restored to such leave donor under subsection (a) may be restored by—

(1) crediting such leave to the leave donor's annual leave account in the then current leave year;

(2) crediting such leave to the leave donor's annual leave account, effective as of the first day of the first leave year beginning after the date of the election; or

(3) donating such leave in whole or part to another leave recipient; if a leave donor elects to donate only part of restored leave to another recipient, the donor may elect to have the remaining leave credited to the donor's annual leave account in accordance with paragraph (1) or (2).

(c) The Office shall prescribe regulations under which this section shall be applied in the case of an employee who is paid other than on the basis of biweekly pay periods.

(d) Restorations of leave under this section shall be carried out in a manner consistent with regulations prescribed to carry out section 6334(c), if applicable.

(Added Pub. L. 100–566, § 2(a), Oct. 31, 1988, 102 Stat. 2836.)

§ 6337. Accrual of leave

(a) For the purpose of this section—

(1) the term "paid leave status under subchapter I", as used with respect to an employee, means the administrative status of such employee while such employee is using sick leave, or annual leave, accrued or accumulated under subchapter I; and

(2) the term "transferred leave status", as used with respect to an employee, means the administrative status of such employee while such employee is using transferred leave under this subchapter.

(b)(1) Except as otherwise provided in this section, while an employee is in a transferred leave status, annual leave and sick leave shall accrue to the credit of such employee at the same rate as if such employee were then in a paid leave status under subchapter I, except that—

(A) the maximum amount of annual leave which may be accrued by an employee while in transferred leave status in connection with any particular medical emergency may not exceed 5 days; and

(B) the maximum amount of sick leave which may be accrued by an employee while in transferred leave status in connection with any particular medical emergency may not exceed 5 days.

(2) Any annual or sick leave accrued by an employee under this section—

(A) shall be credited to an annual leave or sick leave account, as appropriate, separate from any leave account of such employee under subchapter I; and

(B) shall not become available for use by such employee, and may not otherwise be taken into account under subchapter I, until, in accordance with subsection (c), it is transferred to the appropriate leave account of such employee under subchapter I.

(c)(1) Any annual or sick leave accrued by an employee under this section shall be transferred to the appropriate leave account of such employee under subchapter I, and shall be available for use—

(A) as of the beginning of the first applicable pay period beginning after the date on which the employee's medical emergency terminates as described in paragraph (1) or (2) of section 6335(a); or

(B) if the employee's medical emergency has not yet terminated, once the employee has exhausted all transferred leave made available to such employee under this subchapter.

(2) In the event that the employee's medical emergency terminates as described in section 6335(a)(3)—

(A) any leave accrued but not yet transferred under this section shall not be credited to such employee; or

(B) if there remains, as of the date the emergency so terminates, any leave which became available to such employee under paragraph (1)(B), such leave shall cease to be available for any purpose.

(d) Nothing in this section shall be considered to prevent, with respect to a continuing medical emergency, further transfers of leave for use after leave accrued under this section has been exhausted by the employee.

(Added Pub. L. 100–566, §2(a), Oct. 31, 1988, 102 Stat. 2837; amended Pub. L. 103–103, §4, Oct. 8, 1993, 107 Stat. 1022.)

AMENDMENTS

1993—Subsecs. (c), (d). Pub. L. 103–103 amended subsec. (c) generally and added subsec. (d). Prior to amendment, subsec. (c) read as follows:

"(1) Any annual or sick leave accrued by an employee under this section shall be transferred to the appropriate leave account of such employee under subchapter I, effective as of the beginning of the first applicable pay period beginning after the date on which the employee's medical emergency terminates as described in paragraph (1) or (2) of section 6335(a).

"(2) If the employee's medical emergency terminates as described in section 6335(a)(3), no leave shall be credited to such employee under this section."

EFFECTIVE DATE OF 1993 AMENDMENT

Amendment by Pub. L. 103–103 effective as of the 120th day after Oct. 8, 1993, or such earlier date as the Office of Personnel Management may by regulation prescribe, see section 6 of Pub. L. 103–103, set out as a note under section 6331 of this title.

SECTION REFERRED TO IN OTHER SECTIONS

This section is referred to in sections 6371, 6373 of this title.

§ 6338. Prohibition of coercion

(a) An employee may not directly or indirectly intimidate, threaten, or coerce, or attempt to intimidate, threaten, or coerce, any other employee for the purpose of interfering with any right which such employee may have with respect to contributing, receiving, or using annual leave under this subchapter.

(b) For the purpose of subsection (a), the term "intimidate, threaten, or coerce" includes promising to confer or conferring any benefit (such as an appointment, promotion, or compensation),

or effecting or threatening to effect any reprisal (such as deprivation of appointment, promotion, or compensation).

(Added Pub. L. 100–566, §2(a), Oct. 31, 1988, 102 Stat. 2837.)

§ 6339. Additional leave transfer programs

(a) For the purpose of this section—

(1) the term "excepted agency" means—

(A) the Central Intelligence Agency;
(B) the Defense Intelligence Agency;
(C) the National Security Agency;
(D) the Federal Bureau of Investigation;
(E) the National Imagery and Mapping Agency; and
(F) as determined by the President, any Executive agency or unit thereof, the principal function of which is the conduct of foreign intelligence or counterintelligence activities; and

(2) the term "head of an excepted agency" means—

(A) with respect to the Central Intelligence Agency, the Director of Central Intelligence;
(B) with respect to the Defense Intelligence Agency, the Director of the Defense Intelligence Agency;
(C) with respect to the National Security Agency, the Director of the National Security Agency;
(D) with respect to the Federal Bureau of Investigation, the Director of the Federal Bureau of Investigation;
(E) with respect to the National Imagery and Mapping Agency, the Director of the National Imagery and Mapping Agency; and
(F) with respect to an Executive agency designated under paragraph (1)(F), the head of such Executive agency, and with respect to a unit of an Executive agency designated under paragraph (1)(F), such individual as the President may determine.

(b) Notwithstanding any other provision of this subchapter, neither an excepted agency nor any individual employed in or under an excepted agency may be included in a leave transfer program established under any of the preceding provisions of this subchapter.

(c)(1) The head of an excepted agency shall, by regulation, establish a program under which annual leave accrued or accumulated by an employee of such agency may be transferred to the annual leave account of any other employee of such agency if such other employee requires additional leave because of a medical emergency.

(2) To the extent practicable, and consistent with the protection of intelligence sources and methods (if applicable), each program under this section shall be established—

(A) in a manner consistent with the provisions of this subchapter applicable to the program; and
(B) without regard to any provisions relating to transfers or restorations of leave between employees in different agencies.

(d) The Office of Personnel Management shall provide the head of an excepted agency with such advice and assistance as the head of such agency may request in order to carry out the purposes of this section.

(Added Pub. L. 100–566, § 2(a), Oct. 31, 1988, 102 Stat. 2838; amended Pub. L. 103–359, title V, § 501(i), Oct. 14, 1994, 108 Stat. 3429; Pub. L. 104–201, div. A, title XI, § 1122(a), Sept. 23, 1996, 110 Stat. 2687.)

AMENDMENTS

1996—Subsec. (a)(1)(E). Pub. L. 104–201, § 1122(a)(1), substituted "National Imagery and Mapping Agency" for "Central Imagery Office".

Subsec. (a)(2)(E). Pub. L. 104–201, § 1122(a)(2), substituted "National Imagery and Mapping Agency, the Director of the National Imagery and Mapping Agency" for "Central Imagery Office, the Director of the Central Imagery Office".

1994—Subsec. (a)(1)(E), (F). Pub. L. 103–359, § 501(i)(1), added subpar. (E) and redesignated former subpar. (E) as (F).

Subsec. (a)(2)(E), (F). Pub. L. 103–359, § 501(i)(2), added subpar. (E), redesignated former subpar. (E) as (F), and substituted "paragraph (1)(F)" for "paragraph (1)(E)" in two places in subpar. (F).

EFFECTIVE DATE OF 1996 AMENDMENT

Amendment by Pub. L. 104–201 effective Oct. 1, 1996, see section 1124 of Pub. L. 104–201, set out as a note under section 193 of Title 10, Armed Forces.

SECTION REFERRED TO IN OTHER SECTIONS

This section is referred to in section 6372 of this title.

§ 6340. Inapplicability of certain provisions

Except to the extent that the Office of Personnel Management may prescribe regulations, nothing in section 7351 shall apply with respect to a solicitation, donation, or acceptance of leave under this subchapter.

(Added Pub. L. 100–566, § 2(a), Oct. 31, 1988, 102 Stat. 2838.)

SUBCHAPTER IV—VOLUNTARY LEAVE BANK PROGRAM

SUBCHAPTER REFERRED TO IN OTHER SECTIONS

This subchapter is referred to in section 6391 of this title; title 20 section 904; title 22 section 3968; title 38 section 7423.

§ 6361. Definitions

For the purpose of this subchapter the term—

(1) "employee" means an employee as defined by section 6301(2), but shall exclude any individual employed by the government of the District of Columbia;

(2) "executive agency" means any executive agency or any administrative unit thereof;

(3) "leave bank" means a leave bank established under section 6363;

(4) "leave contributor" means an employee who contributes leave to an agency leave bank under section 6365;

(5) "leave recipient" means an employee whose application under section 6367 to receive contributions of leave from a leave bank is approved; and

(6) "medical emergency" means a medical condition of an employee or a family member of such employee that is likely to require the prolonged absence of such employee from duty and to result in a substantial loss of income to such employee because of the unavailability of paid leave (disregarding any advanced leave).

(Added Pub. L. 100–566, § 2(a), Oct. 31, 1988, 102 Stat. 2839; amended Pub. L. 103–103, § 3(a), Oct. 8, 1993, 107 Stat. 1022.)

AMENDMENTS

1993—Par. (6). Pub. L. 103–103 inserted before period at end "(disregarding any advanced leave)".

EFFECTIVE DATE OF 1993 AMENDMENT

Amendment by Pub. L. 103–103 effective as of the 120th day after Oct. 8, 1993, or such earlier date as the Office of Personnel Management may by regulation prescribe, see section 6 of Pub. L. 103–103, set out as a note under section 6331 of this title.

LEAVE BANK FOR JUDICIAL BRANCH EMPLOYEES OF FEDERAL GOVERNMENT IN RESERVES WHO WERE ACTIVATED DURING PERSIAN GULF WAR

Pub. L. 102–58, § 3, June 18, 1991, 105 Stat. 299, provided that:

"(a) JUDICIAL BRANCH EMPLOYEES.—The Director of the Administrative Office of the United States Courts shall establish a leave bank program under which—

"(1) an employee of the Judicial Branch may (during a period specified by the Director of the Administrative Office) donate any unused annual leave from the employee's annual leave account to a leave bank established by the Director;

"(2) the total amount of annual leave that has been donated under paragraph (1) shall be divided equally among the annual leave accounts of all employees who have been members of the Armed Forces serving on active duty during the Persian Gulf conflict pursuant to an order issued under section 672(a) [now 12301(a)], 672(g) [now 12301(g)], 673 [now 12302], 673b [now 12304], 674 [now 12306], 675 [now 12307], or 688 of title 10, United States Code, and who return to employment with the Judicial Branch; and

"(3) such Persian Gulf conflict participants who have returned to Judicial Branch employment may use such annual leave, after it is credited to their leave accounts, in the same manner as any other annual leave to their credit.

"(b) DEFINITIONS.—For purposes of subsection (a), the term 'employee' means an employee as defined in section 6301(2) of title 5, United States Code.

"(c) DEADLINE FOR REGULATIONS.—Within 30 days after the date of the enactment of this Act [June 18, 1991], the Director of the Administration [Administrative] Office shall prescribe regulations necessary for the administration of subsection (a)."

LEAVE BANK FOR FEDERAL CIVILIAN EMPLOYEES IN RESERVES WHO WERE ACTIVATED DURING PERSIAN GULF WAR

Pub. L. 102–25, title III, § 361, Apr. 6, 1991, 105 Stat. 92, as amended by Pub. L. 102–484, div. A, title X, § 1054(c)(1), Oct. 23, 1992, 106 Stat. 2502, provided that:

"(a) CIVIL SERVICE EMPLOYEES.—The Office of Personnel Management shall establish a leave bank program under which—

"(1) an employee in any executive agency may (during a period specified by the Office of Personnel Management) donate any unused annual leave from the employee's annual leave account to a leave bank established by the Office of Personnel Management;

"(2) the total annual leave that has been donated under paragraph (1) shall be divided equally among the annual leave accounts of all employees who have been members of the Armed Forces serving on active duty during the Persian Gulf conflict pursuant to an order issued under section 672(a) [now 12301(a)], 672(g) [now 12301(g)], 673 [now 12302], 673b [now 12304], 674 [now 12306], 675 [now 12307], or 688 of title 10, United States Code, and who return to civilian employment with their agencies; and

"(3) such Persian Gulf concflict [sic] participants who have returned to civilian employment may use such annual leave, after it is credited to their leave accounts, in the same manner as any other annual leave to their credit.

"(b) DEFINITIONS.—For purposes of subsection (a), the term 'employee' means an employee as defined in section 6361(1) of title 5, United States Code.

"(c) DEADLINE FOR REGULATIONS.—Within 30 days after the date of the enactment of this Act [Apr. 6, 1991], the Office of Personnel Management shall prescribe regulations necessary for the administration of subsection (a).

"(d) DEPARTMENT OF VETERANS AFFAIRS HEALTH-CARE PROFESSIONALS.—The Secretary of Veterans Affairs shall establish a program similar to that established under subsection (a) for the benefit of health-care professionals covered under section 7423(e) of title 38, United States Code. Such program shall be as similar and [as] practicable to the program established under subsection (a)."

§ 6362. General authority

Notwithstanding any provision of subchapter I, and subject to the provisions of this subchapter, the Office of Personnel Management shall establish a program under which—

(1) annual leave accrued or accumulated by an employee may be contributed to a leave bank established by the employing agency of such employee; and

(2) leave from such a leave bank may be made available to an employee who requires such leave because of a medical emergency.

(Added Pub. L. 100–566, § 2(a), Oct. 31, 1988, 102 Stat. 2839; amended Pub. L. 103–103, § 5(b), Oct. 8, 1993, 107 Stat. 1023.)

AMENDMENTS

1993—Pub. L. 103–103 struck out subsec. (a) designation and struck out subsec. (b) which read as follows: "To test voluntary leave bank programs under the provisions of this subchapter, the Office of Personnel Management shall establish a demonstration project in at least 3 Executive agencies, of which—

"(1) one such agency shall include approximately, but not less than, the equivalent of 100,000 full-time positions;

"(2) one such agency shall include approximately, but not less than, the equivalent of 25,000 full-time positions; and

"(3) one such agency shall include approximately, but not less than, the equivalent of 1,000 full-time positions."

EFFECTIVE DATE OF 1993 AMENDMENT

Amendment by Pub. L. 103–103 effective as of the 120th day after Oct. 8, 1993, or such earlier date as the Office of Personnel Management may by regulation prescribe, see section 6 of Pub. L. 103–103, set out as a note under section 6331 of this title.

SECTION REFERRED TO IN OTHER SECTIONS

This section is referred to in section 6363 of this title.

§ 6363. Establishment of leave banks

Each agency that establishes a leave bank program under section 6362 shall establish 1 or more leave banks in accordance with regulations prescribed by the Office of Personnel Management.

(Added Pub. L. 100–566, § 2(a), Oct. 31, 1988, 102 Stat. 2839.)

SECTION REFERRED TO IN OTHER SECTIONS

This section is referred to in section 6361 of this title.

§ 6364. Establishment of Leave Bank Boards

(a)(1) Each agency that establishes a leave bank shall establish a Leave Bank Board consisting of 3 members, at least one of whom shall represent a labor organization or employee group, to administer the leave bank under the provisions of this subchapter, in consultation with the Office of Personnel Management.

(2) An agency may establish more than 1 Leave Bank Board based upon the administrative units within the agency. No more than 1 board may be established for each leave bank.

(b) Each such Board shall—

(1) review and approve applications to the leave bank under section 6367;

(2) monitor each case of a leave recipient; and

(3) monitor the amount of leave in the leave bank and the number of applications for use of leave from the bank; and

(4) maintain an adequate amount of leave in the leave bank to the greatest extent practicable.

(Added Pub. L. 100–566, § 2(a), Oct. 31, 1988, 102 Stat. 2839.)

§ 6365. Contributions of annual leave

(a)(1) An employee may, by written application to the Leave Bank Board, request that a specified number of hours be transferred from the annual leave account of such employee to the leave bank established by such agency.

(2) An employee may state a concern and desire to aid a specified proposed leave recipient or a leave recipient in the application filed under paragraph (1).

(b)(1) Upon approving an application under subsection (a), the employing agency of the leave contributor may transfer all or any part of the number of hours requested for transfer, except that the number of hours so transferred may not exceed the limitations under paragraph (2).

(2)(A) In any one leave year, a leave contributor may contribute no more than a total of one-half of the amount of annual leave such contributor would be entitled to accrue during the leave year in which the contribution is made.

(B) A leave contributor who is projected to have annual leave that otherwise would be subject to forfeiture at the end of the leave year under section 6304(a) may contribute no more than the number of hours remaining in the leave year (as of the date of the contribution) for which the leave contributor is scheduled to work and receive pay.

(c) The Leave Bank Board of a leave contributor may waive the limitations under subsection (b)(2). Any such waiver shall be in writing.

(d) The Office of Personnel Management shall prescribe regulations establishing an open enrollment period during which an employee may contribute leave under subsection (a) for a leave year.

(Added Pub. L. 100–566, § 2(a), Oct. 31, 1988, 102 Stat. 2840.)

SECTION REFERRED TO IN OTHER SECTIONS

This section is referred to in sections 6361, 6366 of this title.

§ 6366. Eligibility for leave recipients

(a) An employee is eligible to be a leave recipient if such employee—

(1) experiences a medical emergency and submits an application pursuant to section 6367(a); and

(2)(A) contributes the minimum number of hours as required under subsection (b) of accrued or accumulated annual leave to the leave bank of the employing agency of such employee, in the leave year (beginning in and including any part of a leave year in which such leave bank is established) that such employee submits an application to be a leave recipient under section 6367(a); and

(B) such contribution is made before such employee submits an application under section 6367(a).

(b)(1) An employee shall contribute the minimum number of hours required under subsection (a)(2)(A), if such employee is an employee—

(A) for less than 3 years of service and contributes a minimum of 4 hours;

(B) for between 3 years and less than 15 years of service and contributes a minimum of 6 hours; or

(C) for 15 years or more of service and contributes a minimum of 8 hours.

(2) Notwithstanding the provisions of paragraph (1), the Leave Bank Board of an agency, after consultation with the Office of Personnel Management, may—

(A) reduce the minimum number of hours required under paragraph (1) for any leave year, if such Board determines there is a surplus of leave in the leave bank; and

(B) increase the number of minimum hours required under paragraph (1) for the succeeding leave year, in any leave year in which the Board determines there is a shortage of leave in the leave bank.

(c) An employee shall meet the requirements of subsection (a)(2)(A) if such employee contributes the minimum number of hours as required under subsection (b) of accrued or accumulated annual leave to the leave bank with which such employee submits an application to be a leave recipient under section 6367(a).

(d) The provisions of subsection (a) may not be construed to limit the amount of the voluntary contribution of annual leave to a leave bank, which does not exceed the limitations of section 6365(b).

(Added Pub. L. 100–566, § 2(a), Oct. 31, 1988, 102 Stat. 2840.)

SECTION REFERRED TO IN OTHER SECTIONS

This section is referred to in sections 6361, 6364, 6366 of this title.

§ 6367. Receipt and use of leave from a leave bank

(a) An application to receive contributions of leave from a leave bank, whether submitted by or on behalf of an employee—

(1) shall be submitted to the Leave Bank Board of the employing agency of the proposed leave recipient; and

(2) shall include—

(A) the name, position title, and grade or pay level of the proposed leave recipient;

(B) the reasons why leave is needed, including a brief description of the nature, severity, anticipated duration, and, if it is a recurring one, the approximate frequency of the medical emergency involved;

(C) if such Board so requires, certification from 1 or more physicians, or other appropriate experts, with respect to any matter under subparagraph (B); and

(D) any other information which such Board may reasonably require.

If a Board requires that an employee obtain certification under paragraph (2)(C) from 2 or more sources, the agency shall ensure, either by direct payment to the expert involved or by reimbursement, that the employee is not required to pay for the expenses associated with obtaining certification from more than 1 of such sources.

(b) The Leave Bank Board of an employing agency may approve an application submitted under subsection (a).

(c) A leave recipient may use annual leave received from the leave bank established by the employing agency of such employee under this subchapter in the same manner and for the same purposes as if such leave recipient had accrued such leave under section 6303, except that any annual leave and, if applicable, any sick leave accrued or accumulated to the leave recipient shall be used before any leave from the leave bank may be used.

(d) Transferred annual leave—

(1) may accumulate without regard to any limitation under section 6304; and

(2) may be substituted retroactively for any period of leave without pay, or used to liquidate an indebtedness for any period of advanced leave, which began on or after a date fixed by the employing agency of the employee as the beginning of the medical emergency involved.

(e) Except to the extent that the Office of Personnel Management may prescribe regulations, nothing in the provisions of section 7351 shall apply to any solicitation, contribution, or use of leave to or from a leave bank under this subchapter.

(Added Pub. L. 100–566, § 2(a), Oct. 31, 1988, 102 Stat. 2841.)

§ 6368. Termination of medical emergency

(a) The medical emergency affecting a leave recipient shall, for purposes of this subchapter, be considered to have terminated on the date as of which—

(1) the leave recipient notifies the Leave Bank Board in writing, that the medical emergency no longer exists;

(2) the Leave Bank Board of such leave recipient determines, after written notice and opportunity for the leave recipient (or, if appropriate, another person acting on behalf of the leave recipient) to answer orally or in writing, that the medical emergency no longer exists; or

(3) the leave recipient is separated from service.

(b)(1) The Leave Bank Board of a recipient shall, consistent with guidelines prescribed by the Office of Personnel Management, establish procedures to ensure that a leave recipient is not permitted to use or receive any transferred leave under this subchapter after the medical emergency terminates.

(2) Nothing in section 5551, 5552, or 6306 shall apply with respect to any annual leave transferred to a leave recipient under this subchapter.

(Added Pub. L. 100–566, §2(a), Oct. 31, 1988, 102 Stat. 2842.)

§ 6369. Restoration of transferred leave

The Office of Personnel Management shall establish procedures under which any transferred leave remaining to the credit of a leave recipient when the medical emergency affecting the leave recipient terminates, shall be restored to the leave bank.

(Added Pub. L. 100–566, §2(a), Oct. 31, 1988, 102 Stat. 2842.)

§ 6370. Prohibition of coercion

(a) An employee may not directly or indirectly intimidate, threaten, or coerce, or attempt to intimidate, threaten, or coerce, any other employee for the purpose of interfering with any right which such employee may have with respect to contributing, receiving, or using annual leave under this subchapter.

(b) For the purpose of subsection (a), the term "intimidate, threaten, or coerce" includes promising to confer or conferring any benefit (such as an appointment, promotion, or compensation), or effecting or threatening to effect any reprisal (such as deprivation of appointment, promotion, or compensation).

(Added Pub. L. 100–566, §2(a), Oct. 31, 1988, 102 Stat. 2842.)

§ 6371. Accrual of leave

While using leave made available to an employee from a leave bank, annual and sick leave shall accrue to the credit of such employee and shall become available for use by such employee in the same manner as provided for under section 6337.

(Added Pub. L. 100–566, §2(a), Oct. 31, 1988, 102 Stat. 2843.)

SECTION REFERRED TO IN OTHER SECTIONS

This section is referred to in section 6373 of this title.

§ 6372. Additional leave bank programs

(a) For the purpose of this section—

(1) the term "excepted agency" has the same meaning as such term is defined under section 6339(a)(1) of this title; and

(2) the term "head of an excepted agency" has the same meaning as such term is defined under section 6339(a)(2) of this title.

(b) Notwithstanding any other provision of this subchapter, neither an excepted agency nor any individual employed in or under an excepted agency may be included in a leave bank program established under any of the preceding provisions of this subchapter.

(c)(1) The head of an excepted agency may, by regulation, establish a voluntary leave bank program under which annual leave accrued or accumulated by an employee of such agency may be contributed to a leave bank, and any other employee of such agency may receive additional leave from such leave bank because of a medical emergency.

(2) To the extent practicable, and consistent with the protection of intelligence sources and methods (if applicable), each program under this section shall be established in a manner consistent with the provisions of this subchapter applicable to the program.

(d) The Office of Personnel Management shall provide the head of an excepted agency with such advice and assistance as the head of such agency may request in order to carry out the purposes of this section.

(Added Pub. L. 100–566, §2(a), Oct. 31, 1988, 102 Stat. 2843.)

§ 6373. Authority to participate in both programs

(a) The Office of Personnel Management shall prescribe regulations under which an employee participating in a leave bank program under this subchapter may, subject to such terms or conditions as the Office may establish, also make or receive donations of leave under subchapter III.

(b) Notwithstanding any provision of section 6337 or 6371, if an employee uses leave transferred to such employee under subchapter III and leave made available to such employee under this subchapter in connection with the same medical emergency, the maximum number of days of annual leave and sick leave, respectively, which may accrue to such employee in connection with such medical emergency shall be the same as if all of that leave had been made available to such employee under this subchapter.

(Added Pub. L. 100–566, §2(a), Oct. 31, 1988, 102 Stat. 2843; amended Pub. L. 103–103, §5(a)(1), Oct. 8, 1993, 107 Stat. 1023.)

AMENDMENTS

1993—Pub. L. 103–103 substituted "Authority to participate in both programs" for "Limitation on employee participation" in section catchline and amended text generally. Prior to amendment, text read as follows: "An employee in a unit of an agency that establishes a leave bank program under the provisions of this subchapter may not participate in a leave transfer program under the provisions of subchapter III."

EFFECTIVE DATE OF 1993 AMENDMENT

Amendment by Pub. L. 103–103 effective as of the 120th day after Oct. 8, 1993, or such earlier date as the Office of Personnel Management may by regulation prescribe, see section 6 of Pub. L. 103–103, set out as a note under section 6331 of this title.

SUBCHAPTER V—FAMILY AND MEDICAL LEAVE

SUBCHAPTER REFERRED TO IN OTHER SECTIONS

This subchapter is referred to in sections 2105, 9507 of this title; title 3 section 412; title 29 section 2611; title 42 section 12631.

§ 6381. Definitions

For the purpose of this subchapter—

(1) the term "employee" means any individual who—

(A) is an "employee", as defined by section 6301(2), including any individual employed in a position referred to in clause (v) or (ix) of section 6301(2), but excluding any individual employed by the government of the District of Columbia[1] any individual employed on a temporary or intermittent basis, and any employee of the General Accounting Office or the Library of Congress; and

(B) has completed at least 12 months of service as an employee (within the meaning of subparagraph (A));

(2) the term "health care provider" means—

(A) a doctor of medicine or osteopathy who is authorized to practice medicine or surgery (as appropriate) by the State in which the doctor practices; and

(B) any other person determined by the Director of the Office of Personnel Management to be capable of providing health care services;

(3) the term "parent" means the biological parent of an employee or an individual who stood in loco parentis to an employee when the employee was a son or daughter;

(4) the term "reduced leave schedule" means a leave schedule that reduces the usual number of hours per workweek, or hours per workday, of an employee;

(5) the term "serious health condition" means an illness, injury, impairment, or physical or mental condition that involves—

(A) inpatient care in a hospital, hospice, or residential medical care facility; or

(B) continuing treatment by a health care provider; and

(6) the term "son or daughter" means a biological, adopted, or foster child, a stepchild, a legal ward, or a child of a person standing in loco parentis, who is—

(A) under 18 years of age; or

(B) 18 years of age or older and incapable of self-care because of a mental or physical disability.

(Added Pub. L. 103–3, title II, § 201(a)(1), Feb. 5, 1993, 107 Stat. 19; amended Pub. L. 104–1, title II, § 202(c)(2), Jan. 23, 1995, 109 Stat. 9.)

AMENDMENTS

1995—Par. (1)(A). Pub. L. 104–1 struck out "and" after "District of Columbia" and inserted ", and any employee of the General Accounting Office or the Library of Congress" before semicolon.

EFFECTIVE DATE OF 1995 AMENDMENT

Amendment by Pub. L. 104–1 effective 1 year after transmission to Congress of the study under section 1371 of Title 2, The Congress, see section 1312(e)(2) of Title 2. The study required under section 1371 of Title 2, dated Dec. 31, 1996, was transmitted to Congress by the Board of Directors of the Office of Compliance on Dec. 30, 1996.

EFFECTIVE DATE

Subchapter effective 6 months after Feb. 5, 1993, see section 405(b)(1) of Pub. L. 103–3, set out as a note under section 2601 of Title 29, Labor.

---

[1] So in original. Probably should be followed by a comma.

SECTION REFERRED TO IN OTHER SECTIONS

This section is referred to in title 2 section 1371; title 42 section 12631.

§ 6382. Leave requirement

(a)(1) Subject to section 6383, an employee shall be entitled to a total of 12 administrative workweeks of leave during any 12-month period for one or more of the following:

(A) Because of the birth of a son or daughter of the employee and in order to care for such son or daughter.

(B) Because of the placement of a son or daughter with the employee for adoption or foster care.

(C) In order to care for the spouse, or a son, daughter, or parent, of the employee, if such spouse, son, daughter, or parent has a serious health condition.

(D) Because of a serious health condition that makes the employee unable to perform the functions of the employee's position.

(2) The entitlement to leave under subparagraph (A) or (B) of paragraph (1) based on the birth or placement of a son or daughter shall expire at the end of the 12-month period beginning on the date of such birth or placement.

(b)(1) Leave under subparagraph (A) or (B) of subsection (a)(1) shall not be taken by an employee intermittently or on a reduced leave schedule unless the employee and the employing agency of the employee agree otherwise. Subject to paragraph (2), subsection (e)(2), and section 6383(b)(5), leave under subparagraph (C) or (D) of subsection (a)(1) may be taken intermittently or on a reduced leave schedule when medically necessary. In the case of an employee who takes leave intermittently or on a reduced leave schedule pursuant to this paragraph, any hours of leave so taken by such employee shall be subtracted from the total amount of leave remaining available to such employee under subsection (a), for purposes of the 12-month period involved, on an hour-for-hour basis.

(2) If an employee requests intermittent leave, or leave on a reduced leave schedule, under subparagraph (C) or (D) of subsection (a)(1), that is foreseeable based on planned medical treatment, the employing agency may require such employee to transfer temporarily to an available alternative position offered by the employing agency for which the employee is qualified and that—

(A) has equivalent pay and benefits; and

(B) better accommodates recurring periods of leave than the regular employment position of the employee.

(c) Except as provided in subsection (d), leave granted under subsection (a) shall be leave without pay.

(d) An employee may elect to substitute for leave under subparagraph (A), (B), (C), or (D) of subsection (a)(1) any of the employee's accrued or accumulated annual or sick leave under subchapter I for any part of the 12-week period of leave under such subsection, except that nothing in this subchapter shall require an employing agency to provide paid sick leave in any situation in which such employing agency would not normally provide any such paid leave.

(e)(1) In any case in which the necessity for leave under subparagraph (A) or (B) of subsection (a)(1) is foreseeable based on an expected birth or placement, the employee shall provide the employing agency with not less than 30 days' notice, before the date the leave is to begin, of the employee's intention to take leave under such subparagraph, except that if the date of the birth or placement requires leave to begin in less than 30 days, the employee shall provide such notice as is practicable.

(2) In any case in which the necessity for leave under subparagraph (C) or (D) of subsection (a)(1) is foreseeable based on planned medical treatment, the employee—

(A) shall make a reasonable effort to schedule the treatment so as not to disrupt unduly the operations of the employing agency, subject to the approval of the health care provider of the employee or the health care provider of the son, daughter, spouse, or parent of the employee, as appropriate; and

(B) shall provide the employing agency with not less than 30 days' notice, before the date the leave is to begin, of the employee's intention to take leave under such subparagraph, except that if the date of the treatment requires leave to begin in less than 30 days, the employee shall provide such notice as is practicable.

(Added Pub. L. 103–3, title II, § 201(a)(1), Feb. 5, 1993, 107 Stat. 20.)

SECTION REFERRED TO IN OTHER SECTIONS

This section is referred to in sections 6383, 6384, 6386 of this title; title 2 section 1371.

§ 6383. Certification

(a) An employing agency may require that a request for leave under subparagraph (C) or (D) of section 6382(a)(1) be supported by certification issued by the health care provider of the employee or of the son, daughter, spouse, or parent of the employee, as appropriate. The employee shall provide, in a timely manner, a copy of such certification to the employing agency.

(b) A certification provided under subsection (a) shall be sufficient if it states—

(1) the date on which the serious health condition commenced;

(2) the probable duration of the condition;

(3) the appropriate medical facts within the knowledge of the health care provider regarding the condition;

(4)(A) for purposes of leave under section 6382(a)(1)(C), a statement that the employee is needed to care for the son, daughter, spouse, or parent, and an estimate of the amount of time that such employee is needed to care for such son, daughter, spouse, or parent; and

(B) for purposes of leave under section 6382(a)(1)(D), a statement that the employee is unable to perform the functions of the position of the employee; and

(5) in the case of certification for intermittent leave, or leave on a reduced leave schedule, for planned medical treatment, the dates on which such treatment is expected to be given and the duration of such treatment.

(c)(1) In any case in which the employing agency has reason to doubt the validity of the certification provided under subsection (a) for leave under subparagraph (C) or (D) of section 6382(a)(1), the employing agency may require, at the expense of the agency, that the employee obtain the opinion of a second health care provider designated or approved by the employing agency concerning any information certified under subsection (b) for such leave.

(2) Any health care provider designated or approved under paragraph (1) shall not be employed on a regular basis by the employing agency.

(d)(1) In any case in which the second opinion described in subsection (c) differs from the original certification provided under subsection (a), the employing agency may require, at the expense of the agency, that the employee obtain the opinion of a third health care provider designated or approved jointly by the employing agency and the employee concerning the information certified under subsection (b).

(2) The opinion of the third health care provider concerning the information certified under subsection (b) shall be considered to be final and shall be binding on the employing agency and the employee.

(e) The employing agency may require, at the expense of the agency, that the employee obtain subsequent recertifications on a reasonable basis.

(Added Pub. L. 103–3, title II, § 201(a)(1), Feb. 5, 1993, 107 Stat. 21.)

SECTION REFERRED TO IN OTHER SECTIONS

This section is referred to in section 6382 of this title; title 2 section 1371.

§ 6384. Employment and benefits protection

(a) Any employee who takes leave under section 6382 for the intended purpose of the leave shall be entitled, upon return from such leave—

(1) to be restored by the employing agency to the position held by the employee when the leave commenced; or

(2) to be restored to an equivalent position with equivalent benefits, pay, status, and other terms and conditions of employment.

(b) The taking of leave under section 6382 shall not result in the loss of any employment benefit accrued prior to the date on which the leave commenced.

(c) Except as otherwise provided by or under law, nothing in this section shall be construed to entitle any restored employee to—

(1) the accrual of any employment benefits during any period of leave; or

(2) any right, benefit, or position of employment other than any right, benefit, or position to which the employee would have been entitled had the employee not taken the leave.

(d) As a condition to restoration under subsection (a) for an employee who takes leave under section 6382(a)(1)(D), the employing agency may have a uniformly applied practice or policy that requires each such employee to receive certification from the health care provider of the employee that the employee is able to resume work.

(e) Nothing in this section shall be construed to prohibit an employing agency from requiring an employee on leave under section 6382 to report periodically to the employing agency on the status and intention of the employee to return to work.

(Added Pub. L. 103–3, title II, § 201(a)(1), Feb. 5, 1993, 107 Stat. 22.)

SECTION REFERRED TO IN OTHER SECTIONS

This section is referred to in title 2 section 1371.

§ 6385. Prohibition of coercion

(a) An employee shall not directly or indirectly intimidate, threaten, or coerce, or attempt to intimidate, threaten, or coerce, any other employee for the purpose of interfering with the exercise of any rights which such other employee may have under this subchapter.

(b) For the purpose of this section—
(1) the term "intimidate, threaten, or coerce" includes promising to confer or conferring any benefit (such as appointment, promotion, or compensation), or taking or threatening to take any reprisal (such as deprivation of appointment, promotion, or compensation); and
(2) the term "employee" means any "employee", as defined by section 2105.

(Added Pub. L. 103–3, title II, § 201(a)(1), Feb. 5, 1993, 107 Stat. 22.)

SECTION REFERRED TO IN OTHER SECTIONS

This section is referred to in title 2 section 1371.

§ 6386. Health insurance

An employee enrolled in a health benefits plan under chapter 89 who is placed in a leave status under section 6382 may elect to continue the health benefits enrollment of the employee while in such leave status and arrange to pay currently into the Employees Health Benefits Fund (described in section 8909), the appropriate employee contributions.

(Added Pub. L. 103–3, title II, § 201(a)(1), Feb. 5, 1993, 107 Stat. 23.)

SECTION REFERRED TO IN OTHER SECTIONS

This section is referred to in title 2 section 1371.

§ 6387. Regulations

The Office of Personnel Management shall prescribe regulations necessary for the administration of this subchapter. The regulations prescribed under this subchapter shall, to the extent appropriate, be consistent with the regulations prescribed by the Secretary of Labor to carry out title I of the Family and Medical Leave Act of 1993.

(Added Pub. L. 103–3, title II, § 201(a)(1), Feb. 5, 1993, 107 Stat. 23.)

REFERENCES IN TEXT

The Family and Medical Leave Act of 1993, referred to in text, is Pub. L. 103–3, Feb. 5, 1993, 107 Stat. 6. Title I of the Act is classified generally to subchapter I (§ 2611 et seq.) of chapter 28 of Title 29, Labor. For complete classification of this Act to the Code, see Short Title note set out under section 2601 of Title 29 and Tables.

SECTION REFERRED TO IN OTHER SECTIONS

This section is referred to in title 2 section 1371.

SUBCHAPTER VI—LEAVE TRANSFER IN DISASTERS AND EMERGENCIES

§ 6391. Authority for leave transfer program in disasters and emergencies

(a) For the purpose of this section—
(1) "employee" means an employee as defined in section 6331(1); and
(2) "agency" means an Executive agency.

(b) In the event of a major disaster or emergency, as declared by the President, that results in severe adverse effects for a substantial number of employees, the President may direct the Office of Personnel Management to establish an emergency leave transfer program under which any employee in any agency may donate unused annual leave for transfer to employees of the same or other agencies who are adversely affected by such disaster or emergency.

(c) The Office shall establish appropriate requirements for the operation of the emergency leave transfer program under subsection (b), including appropriate limitations on the donation and use of annual leave under the program. An employee may receive and use leave under the program without regard to any requirement that any annual leave and sick leave to a leave recipient's credit must be exhausted before any transferred annual leave may be used.

(d) A leave bank established under subchapter IV may, to the extent provided in regulations prescribed by the Office, donate annual leave to the emergency leave transfer program established under subsection (b).

(e) Except to the extent that the Office may prescribe by regulation, nothing in section 7351 shall apply to any solicitation, donation, or acceptance of leave under this section.

(f) The Office shall prescribe regulations necessary for the administration of this section.

(Added Pub. L. 105–18, title II, § 9004(a), June 12, 1997, 111 Stat. 196.)

Subpart F—Labor-Management and Employee Relations

CHAPTER 71—LABOR-MANAGEMENT RELATIONS

AMENDMENTS

1978—Pub. L. 95–454, title VII, §§ 701, 703(a)(2), Oct. 13, 1978, 92 Stat. 1191, 1217, in heading for Subpart F inserted "Labor-Management and" before "Employee", in heading for chapter 71 substituted "LABOR-MANAGEMENT RELATIONS" for "POLICIES", in heading for subchapter I substituted "GENERAL PROVISIONS" for "EMPLOYEE ORGANIZATIONS", in item 7101 substituted "Findings and purpose" for "Right to organize; postal employees", in item 7102 substituted "Employees' rights" for "Right to petition Congress; employees", added items 7103 to 7106, and added subchapter II and items 7111 to 7120, subchapter III and items 7121 to 7123, and subchapter IV and items 7131 to 7135. Former subchapter II heading "ANTIDISCRIMINATION IN EMPLOYMENT" and items 7151 to 7154, "Policy", "Marital status", "Physical handicap", and "Other prohibitions", respectively, were transferred to subchapter I of chapter 72 and renumbered and amended.

CHAPTER REFERRED TO IN OTHER SECTIONS

This chapter is referred to in sections 4505a, 4703, 5366, 5596, 6121, 8473, 9501 of this title; title 2 sections 1302, 1351, 1371, 1434; title 3 sections 402, 431; title 7 section 7011; title 10 section 461; title 18 section 205; title 20 section 4416; title 22 sections 3664, 3701, 4107, 4109; title 31 section 732; title 38 sections 7422, 7461, 7463; title 45 section 1203.

SUBCHAPTER I—GENERAL PROVISIONS

§ 7101. Findings and purpose

(a) The Congress finds that—

(1) experience in both private and public employment indicates that the statutory protection of the right of employees to organize, bargain collectively, and participate through labor organizations of their own choosing in decisions which affect them—

(A) safeguards the public interest,

(B) contributes to the effective conduct of public business, and

(C) facilitates and encourages the amicable settlements of disputes between employees and their employers involving conditions of employment; and

(2) the public interest demands the highest standards of employee performance and the continued development and implementation of modern and progressive work practices to facilitate and improve employee performance and the efficient accomplishment of the operations of the Government.

Therefore, labor organizations and collective bargaining in the civil service are in the public interest.

(b) It is the purpose of this chapter to prescribe certain rights and obligations of the employees of the Federal Government and to establish procedures which are designed to meet the special requirements and needs of the Government. The provisions of this chapter should be interpreted in a manner consistent with the requirement of an effective and efficient Government.

(Added Pub. L. 95–454, title VII, § 701, Oct. 13, 1978, 92 Stat. 1192.)

PRIOR PROVISIONS

A prior section 7101, Pub. L. 89–554, Sept. 6, 1966, 80 Stat. 523; Pub. L. 91–375, § 6(c)(19), Aug. 12, 1970, 84 Stat. 776, related to right of postal employees to organize, prior to the general amendment of this chapter by Pub. L. 94–454.

EFFECTIVE DATE

Chapter effective 90 days after Oct. 13, 1978, see section 907 of Pub. L. 95–454, set out as an Effective Date of 1978 Amendment note under section 1101 of this title.

EXECUTIVE ORDER NO. 10988

Ex. Ord. No. 10988, Jan. 17, 1962, 27 F.R. 551, which related to employee-management cooperation in the Federal service, was revoked by Ex. Ord. No. 11491, Oct. 29, 1969, 34 F.R. 17605, set out below.

EX. ORD. NO. 11491. LABOR-MANAGEMENT RELATIONS IN THE FEDERAL SERVICE

Ex. Ord. No. 11491, Oct. 29, 1969, 34 F.R. 17605, as amended by Ex. Ord. No. 11616, Aug. 26, 1971, 36 F.R. 17319; Ex. Ord. No. 11636, Dec. 17, 1971, 36 F.R. 24901; Ex. Ord. No. 11838, Feb. 6, 1975, 40 F.R. 5743; Ex. Ord. No. 11901, Jan. 30, 1976, 41 F.R. 4807; Ex. Ord. No. 12027, Dec. 5, 1977, 42 F.R. 61851; Ex. Ord. No. 12107, Dec. 28, 1978, 44 F.R. 1055, provided:

WHEREAS the public interest requires high standards of employee performance and the continual development and implementation of modern and progressive work practices to facilitate improved employee performance and efficiency; and

WHEREAS the well-being of employees and efficient administration of the Government are benefited by providing employees an opportunity to participate in the formulation and implementation of personnel policies and practices affecting the conditions of their employment; and

WHEREAS the participation of employees should be improved through the maintenance of constructive and cooperative relationships between labor organizations and management officials; and

WHEREAS subject to law and the paramount requirements of public service, effective labor-management relations within the Federal service require a clear statement of the respective rights and obligations of labor organizations and agency management:

NOW, THEREFORE, by virtue of the authority vested in me by the Constitution and statutes of the United States, including sections 3301 and 7301 of title 5 of the United States Code and as President of the United States, I hereby direct that the following policies shall govern officers and agencies of the executive branch of the Government in all dealings with Federal employees and organizations representing such employees.

GENERAL PROVISIONS

SECTION 1. *Policy.* (a) Each employee of the executive branch of the Federal Government has the right, freely and without fear of penalty or reprisal, to form, join, and assist a labor organization or to refrain from any such activity, and each employee shall be protected in the exercise of this right. Except as otherwise expressly provided in this Order, the right to assist a labor organization extends to participation in the management of the organization and acting for the organization in the capacity of an organization representative, including presentation of its views to officials of the executive branch, the Congress, or other appropriate authority. The head of each agency shall take the action required to assure that employees in the agency are apprised of their rights under this section and that no interference, restraint, coercion, or discrimination is practiced within his agency to encourage or discourage membership in a labor organization.

(b) Paragraph (a) of this section does not authorize participation in the management of a labor organization or acting as a representative of such an organization by a supervisor, except as provided in section 24 of this Order, or by an employee when the participation or activity would result in a conflict or apparent conflict of interest or otherwise be incompatible with law or with the official duties of the employee.

SEC. 2. *Definitions.* When used in this Order, the term—

(a) "Agency" means an executive department, a Government corporation, and an independent establishment as defined in section 104 of title 5, United States Code, except the General Accounting Office;

(b) "Employee" means an employee of an agency and an employee of a nonappropriated fund instrumentality of the United States but does not include, for the purpose of exclusive recognition or national consultation rights, a supervisor, except as provided in section 24 of this Order;

(c) "Supervisor" means an employee having authority, in the interest of an agency, to hire, transfer, suspend, lay off, recall, promote, discharge, assign, reward, or discipline other employees, or responsibly to direct them, or to adjust their grievances, or effectively to recommend such action, if in connection with the foregoing the exercise of authority is not of a merely routine or clerical nature, but requires the use of independent judgment;

(d) [Revoked by Ex. Ord. No. 11838, Feb. 6, 1975, 40 F.R. 5743.]

(e) "Labor organization" means a lawful organization of any kind in which employees participate and which exists for the purpose, in whole or in part, of dealing with agencies concerning grievances, personnel policies and practices, or other matters affecting the working conditions of their employees; but does not include an organization which—

(1) consists of management officials or supervisors, except as provided in section 24 of this Order;

(2) assists or participates in a strike against the Government of the United States or any agency thereof, or imposes a duty or obligation to conduct, assist, or participate in such a strike;

(3) advocates the overthrow of the constitutional form of government in the United States; or

(4) discriminates with regard to the terms or conditions of membership because of race, color, creed, sex, age, or national origin;

(f) "Agency management" means the agency head and all management officials, supervisors, and other representatives of management having authority to act for the agency on any matters relating to the implementation of the agency labor-management relations program established under this Order;

(g) "Authority" means the Federal Labor Relations Authority;

(h) "Panel" means the Federal Service Impasses Panel;

(i) "Assistant Secretary" means the Assistant Secretary of Labor for Labor Management Relations; and

(j) "General Counsel" means the General Counsel of the Authority.

SEC. 3. *Application.* (a) This Order applies to all employees and agencies in the executive branch, except as provided in paragraphs (b), (c) and (d) of this section.

(b) This Order (except section 22) does not apply to—

(1) the Federal Bureau of Investigation;

(2) the Central Intelligence Agency;

(3) any other agency, or office, bureau, or entity within an agency, which has as a primary function intelligence, investigative, or security work, when the head of the agency determines, in his sole judgment, that the Order cannot be applied in a manner consistent with national security requirements and considerations; or

(4) any office, bureau or entity, within an agency which has as a primary function investigation or audit of the conduct or work of officials or employees of the agency for the purpose of ensuring honesty and integrity in the discharge of their official duties, when the head of the agency determines, in his sole judgment, that the Order cannot be applied in a manner consistent with the internal security of the agency.

(5) The Foreign Service of the United States: Department of State, United States Information Agency and Agency for International Development and its successor agency or agencies.

(6) The Tennessee Valley Authority; or

(7) Personnel of the Federal Labor Relations Authority (including the Office of the General Counsel and the Federal Service Impasses Panel).

(c) The head of an agency may, in his sole judgment, suspend any provision of this Order (except section 22) with respect to any agency installation or activity located outside the United States, when he determines that this is necessary in the national interest, subject to the conditions he prescribes.

(d) Employees engaged in administering a labor-management relations law or this Order who are otherwise authorized by this Order to be represented by a labor organization shall not be represented by a labor organization which also represents other groups of employees under the law or this Order, or which is affiliated directly or indirectly with an organization which represents such a group of employees.

ADMINISTRATION

SEC. 4. *Powers and Duties of the Federal Labor Relations Authority.*

(a) [Revoked].

(b) The Authority shall administer and interpret this Order, decide major policy issues, and prescribe regulations.

(c) The Authority shall, subject to its regulations:

(1) decide questions as to the appropriate unit for the purpose of exclusive recognition and related issues submitted for its considerations;

(2) supervise elections to determine whether a labor organization is the choice of a majority of the employees in an appropriate unit as their exclusive representative, and certify the results;

(3) decide questions as to the eligibility of labor organizations for national consultation rights;

(4) decide unfair labor practice complaints; and

(5) decide questions as to whether a grievance is subject to a negotiated grievance procedure or subject to arbitration under an agreement as provided in Section 13(d) of this Order.

(d) The Authority may consider, subject to its regulations:

(1) appeals on negotiability issues as provided in Section 11(c) of this Order;

(2) exceptions to arbitration awards;

(3) appeals from decisions of the Assistant Secretary of Labor for Labor-Management Relations issued pursuant to Section 6(b) of this Order; and

(4) other matters it deems appropriate to assure the effectuation of the purposes of this Order.

(e) In any matters arising under subsection (c) and (d)(3) of this Section, the Authority may require an agency or a labor organization to cease and desist from violations of this Order and require it to take such affirmative action as the Authority considers appropriate to effectuate the policies of this Order.

(f) In performing the duties imposed on it by this Section, the Authority may request and use the services and assistance of employees of other agencies in accordance with Section 1 of the Act of March 4, 1915 (38 Stat. 1084, as amended; 31 U.S.C. 686) [31 U.S.C. 1535].

SEC. 5. *Powers and Duties of the Federal Service Impasses Panel.* (a) There is hereby established the Federal

Service Impasses Panel as a distinct organizational entity within the Authority. The Panel consists of at least three members appointed by the President, one of whom he designates as chairman. The Authority shall provide the services and staff assistance needed by the Panel.

(b) The Panel may consider negotiation impasses as provided in section 17 of this Order and may take any action it considers necessary to settle an impasse.

(c) The Panel shall prescribe regulations needed to administer its function under this Order.

SEC. 6. *Powers and Duties of the Office of the General Counsel and the Assistant Secretary of Labor for Labor-Management Relations.*

(a) The General Counsel is authorized, upon direction by the Authority, to:

(1) investigate complaints of violations of Section 19 of this Order;

(2) make final decisions as to whether to issue unfair labor practice complaints and prosecute such complaints before the Authority;

(3) direct and supervise all employees in the Office of General Counsel, including employees of the General Counsel in the regional office of the Authority;

(4) perform such other duties as the Authority may prescribe; and

(5) prescribe regulations needed to administer his functions under this Order.

(b) The Assistant Secretary shall:

(1) decide alleged violations of the standards of conduct for labor organizations, established in Section 18 of this Order; and

(2) prescribe regulations needed to administer his functions under this Order.

(c) In any matter arising under paragraph (b) of this Section, the Assistant Secretary may require a labor organization to cease and desist from violations of this Order and require it to take such affirmative action as he considers appropriate to effectuate the policies of this Order.

(d) In performing the duties imposed on them by this Section, the General Counsel and the Assistant Secretary may request and use the services and assistance of employees of other agencies in accordance with Section 1 of the Act of March 4, 1915 (38 Stat. 1084, as amended; 31 U.S.C. 686) [31 U.S.C. 1535].

RECOGNITION

SEC. 7. *Recognition in general.* (a) An agency shall accord exclusive recognition or national consultation rights at the request of a labor organization which meets the requirements for the recognition or consultation rights under this Order.

(b) A labor organization seeking recognition shall submit to the agency a roster of its officers and representatives, a copy of its constitution and by-laws, and a statement of its objectives.

(c) When recognition of a labor organization has been accorded, the recognition continues as long as the organization continues to meet the requirements of this Order applicable to that recognition, except that this section does not require an election to determine whether an organization should become, or continue to be recognized as, exclusive representative of the employees in any unit or subdivision thereof within 12 months after a prior valid election with respect to such unit.

(d) Recognition of a labor organization does not—

(1) preclude an employee, regardless of whether he is in a unit of exclusive recognition, from exercising grievance or appellate rights established by law or regulation, or from choosing his own representative in a grievance or appellate action, except when the grievance is covered under a negotiated procedure as provided in section 13;

(2) preclude or restrict consultations and dealings between an agency and a veterans organization with respect to matters of particular interest to employees with veterans preference; or

(3) preclude an agency from consulting or dealing with a religious, social, fraternal, professional or other

lawful association, not qualified as a labor organization, with respect to matters or policies which involve individual members of the association or are of particular applicability to it or its members. Consultations and dealings under subparagraph (3) of this paragraph shall be so limited that they do not assume the character of formal consultation on matters of general employee-management policy covering employees in that unit or extend to areas where recognition of the interests of one employee group may result in discrimination against or injury to the interests of other employees.

(e) [Revoked by Ex. Ord. No. 11838, Feb. 6, 1975, 40 F.R. 5743.]

(f) Informal recognition or formal recognition shall not be accorded.

SEC. 8. [Revoked by Ex. Ord. No. 11616, Aug. 26, 1971, 36 F.R. 17319.]

SEC. 9. *National consultation rights.* (a) An agency shall accord national consultation rights to a labor organization which qualifies under criteria established by the Federal Labor Relations Authority as the representative of a substantial number of employees of the agency. National consultation rights shall not be accorded for any unit where a labor organization already holds exclusive recognition at the national level for that unit. The granting of national consultation rights does not preclude an agency from appropriate dealings at the national level with other organizations on matters affecting their members. An agency shall terminate national consultation rights when the labor organization ceases to qualify under the established criteria.

(b) When a labor organization has been accorded national consultation rights, the agency, through appropriate officials, shall notify representatives of the organization of proposed substantive changes in personnel policies that affect employees it represents and provide an opportunity for the organization to comment on the proposed changes. The labor organization may suggest changes in the agency's personnel policies and have its views carefully considered. It may consult in person at reasonable times, on request, with appropriate officials on personnel policy matters, and at all times present its views thereon in writing. An agency is not required to consult with a labor organization on any matter on which it would not be required to meet and confer if the organization were entitled to exclusive recognition.

(c) Questions as to the eligibility of labor organizations for national consultation rights may be referred to the Authority for decision.

SEC. 10. *Exclusive recognition.* (a) An agency shall accord exclusive recognition to a labor organization when the organization has been selected, in a secret ballot election, by a majority of the employees in an appropriate unit as their representative; provided that this section shall not preclude an agency from according exclusive recognition to a labor organization, without an election, where the appropriate unit is established through the consolidation of existing exclusively recognized units represented by that organization.

(b) A unit may be established on a plant or installation, craft, functional, or other basis which will ensure a clear and identifiable community of interest among the employees concerned and will promote effective dealings and efficiency of agency operations. A unit shall not be established solely on the basis of the extent to which employees in the proposed unit have organized, nor shall a unit be established if it includes—

(1) any management official or supervisor, except as provided in section 24;

(2) an employee engaged in Federal personnel work in other than a purely clerical capacity; or

(3) [Revoked by Ex. Ord. No. 11838, Feb. 6, 1975, 40 F.R. 5743.]

(4) both professional and nonprofessional employees, unless a majority of the professional employees vote for inclusion in the unit. Questions as to the appropriate unit and related issues may be referred to the Authority for decision.

(c) [Revoked by Ex. Ord. No. 11838, Feb. 6, 1975, 40 F.R. 5743.]

(d) All elections shall be conducted under the supervision of the Authority, or persons designated by it, and shall be by secret ballot. Each employee eligible to vote shall be provided the opportunity to choose the labor organization he wishes to represent him, from among those on the ballot, or "no union", except as provided in subparagraph (4) of this paragraph. Elections may be held to determine whether—

(1) a labor organization should be recognized as the exclusive representative of employees in a unit;

(2) a labor organization should replace another labor organization as the exclusive representative;

(3) a labor organization should cease to be the exclusive representative; or

(4) a labor organization should be recognized as the exclusive representative of employees in a unit composed of employees in units currently represented by that labor organization or continue to be recognized in the existing separate units.

(e) When a labor organization has been accorded exclusive recognition, it is the exclusive representative of employees in the unit and is entitled to act for and to negotiate agreements covering all employees in the unit. It is responsible for representing the interests of all employees in the unit without discrimination and without regard to labor organization membership. The labor organization shall be given the opportunity to be represented at formal discussions between management and employees or employee representatives concerning grievances, personnel policies and practices, or other matters affecting general working conditions of employees in the unit.

AGREEMENTS

SEC. 11. *Negotiation of agreements.* (a) An agency and a labor organization that has been accorded exclusive recognition, through appropriate representatives, shall meet at reasonable times and confer in good faith with respect to personnel policies and practices and matters affecting working conditions, so far as may be appropriate under applicable laws and regulations, including policies set forth in the Federal Personnel Manual; published agency policies and regulations for which a compelling need exists under criteria established by the Federal Labor Relations Authority and which are issued at the agency headquarters level or at the level of a primary national subdivision; a national or other controlling agreement at a higher level in the agency; and this order. They may negotiate an agreement, or any question arising thereunder; determine appropriate techniques, consistent with section 17 of this order, to assist in such negotiation; and execute a written agreement or memorandum of understanding.

(b) In prescribing regulations relating to personnel policies and practices and working conditions, an agency shall have due regard for the obligation imposed by paragraph (a) of this section. However, the obligation to meet and confer does not include matters with respect to the mission of an agency; its budget; its organization; the number of employees; and the numbers, types, and grades of positions or employees assigned to an organizational unit, work project or tour of duty; the technology of performing its work; or its internal security practices. This does not preclude the parties from negotiating agreements providing appropriate arrangements for employees adversely affected by the impact of realignment of work forces or technological change.

(c) If, in connection with negotiations, an issue develops as to whether a proposal is contrary to law, regulation, controlling agreement, or this order and therefore not negotiable, it shall be resolved as follows:

(1) An issue which involves interpretation of a controlling agreement at a higher agency level is resolved under the procedures of the controlling agreement, or, if none, under agency regulations;

(2) An issue other than as described in subparagraph (1) of this paragraph which arises at a local level may be referred by either party to the head of the agency for determination;

(3) An agency head's determination as to the interpretation of the agency's regulations with respect to a proposal is final;

(4) A labor organization may appeal to the Authority for a decision when—

(i) it disagrees with an agency head's determination that a proposal would violate applicable law, regulation of appropriate authority outside the agency, or this order, or

(ii) it believes that an agency's regulations, as interpreted by the agency head, violate applicable law, regulation of appropriate authority outside the agency, or this order, or are not otherwise applicable to bar negotiations under paragraph (a) of this section.

(d) [Revoked by Ex. Ord. No. 12107, Dec. 28, 1978, 44 F.R. 1055.]

SEC. 12. *Basic provisions of agreements.* Each agreement between an agency and a labor organization is subject to the following requirements—

(a) in the administration of all matters covered by the agreement, officials and employees are governed by existing or future laws and the regulations of appropriate authorities, including policies set forth in the Federal Personnel Manual; by published agency policies and regulations in existence at the time the agreement was approved; and by subsequently published agency policies and regulations required by law or by the regulations of appropriate authorities, or authorized by the terms of a controlling agreement at a higher agency level;

(b) management officials of the agency retain the right, in accordance with applicable laws and regulations—

(1) to direct employees of the agency;

(2) to hire, promote, transfer, assign, and retain employees in positions within the agency, and to suspend, demote, discharge, or take other disciplinary action against employees;

(3) to relieve employees from duties because of lack of work or for other legitimate reasons;

(4) to maintain the efficiency of the Government operations entrusted to them;

(5) to determine the methods, means, and personnel by which such operations are to be conducted; and

(6) to take whatever actions may be necessary to carry out the mission of the agency in situations of emergency; and

(c) nothing in the agreement shall require an employee to become or to remain a member of a labor organization, or to pay money to the organization except pursuant to a voluntary written authorization by a member for the payment of dues through payroll deductions. The requirements of this section shall be expressly stated in the initial or basic agreement and apply to all supplemental, implementing, subsidiary, or informal agreements between the agency and the organization.

SEC. 13. *Grievance and arbitration procedures.* (a) An agreement between an agency and a labor organization shall provide a procedure, applicable only to the unit, for the consideration of grievances. The coverage and scope of the procedure shall be negotiated by the parties to the agreement with the exception that it may not cover matters for which a statutory appeal procedure exists and so long as it does not otherwise conflict with statute or this order. It shall be the exclusive procedure available to the parties and the employees in the unit for resolving grievances which fall within its coverage. However, any employee or group of employees in the unit may present such grievances to the agency and have them adjusted, without the intervention of the exclusive representative, as long as the adjustment is not inconsistent with the terms of the agreement and the exclusive representative has been given opportunity to be present at the adjustment.

(b) A negotiated procedure may provide for arbitration of grievances. Arbitration may be invoked only by the agency or the exclusive representative. Either party may file exceptions to an arbitrator's award with the Authority, under regulations prescribed by the Authority.

(c) [Revoked.]

(d) Questions that cannot be resolved by the parties as to whether or not a grievance is on a matter for which a statutory appeal procedure exists, shall be referred to the Authority for decision. Other questions as to whether or not a grievance is on a matter subject to the grievance procedure in an existing agreement, or is subject to arbitration under that agreement, may by agreement of the parties be submitted to arbitration or may be referred to the Authority for decision.

(e) [Revoked.]

SEC. 14. [Revoked by Ex. Ord. No. 11616, Aug. 26, 1971, 36 F.R. 17319.]

SEC. 15. *Approval of agreements.* An agreement with a labor organization as the exclusive representative of employees in a unit is subject to the approval of the head of the agency or an official designated by him. An agreement shall be approved within forty-five days from the date of its execution if it conforms to applicable laws, the order, existing published agency policies and regulations (unless the agency has granted an exception to a policy or regulation) and regulations of other appropriate authorities. An agreement which has not been approved or disapproved within forty-five days from the date of its execution shall go into effect without the required approval of the agency head and shall be binding on the parties subject to the provisions of law, the order and the regulations of appropriate authorities outside the agency. A local agreement subject to a national or other controlling agreement at a higher level shall be approved under the procedures of the controlling agreement, or, if none, under agency regulations.

NEGOTIATION DISPUTES AND IMPASSES

SEC. 16. *Negotiation disputes.* The Federal Mediation and Conciliation Service shall provide services and assistance to Federal agencies and labor organizations in the resolution of negotiation disputes. The Service shall determine under what circumstances and in what manner it shall proffer its services.

SEC. 17. *Negotiation impasses.* When voluntary arrangements, including the services of the Federal Mediation and Conciliation Service or other third-party mediation, fail to resolve a negotiation impasse, either party may request the Federal Service Impasses Panel to consider the matter. The Panel, in its discretion and under the regulations it prescribes, may consider the matter and may recommend procedures to the parties for the resolution of the impasse or may settle the impasse by appropriate action. Arbitration or third-party fact finding with recommendations to assist in the resolution of an impasse may be used by the parties only when authorized or directed by the Panel.

CONDUCT OF LABOR ORGANIZATIONS AND MANAGEMENT

SEC. 18. *Standards of conduct for labor organizations.*

(a) An agency shall accord recognition only to a labor organization that is free from corrupt influences and influences opposed to basic democratic principles. Except as provided in paragraph (b) of this section, an organization is not required to prove that it has the required freedom when it is subject to governing requirements adopted by the organization or by a national or international labor organization or federation of labor organizations with which it is affiliated or in which it participates, containing explicit and detailed provisions to which it subscribes calling for—

(1) the maintenance of democratic procedures and practices, including provisions for periodic elections to be conducted subject to recognized safeguards and provisions defining and securing the right of individual members to participation in the affairs of the organization, to fair and equal treatment under the governing rules of the organization, and to fair process in disciplinary proceedings;

(2) the exclusion from office in the organization of persons affiliated with Communist or other totalitarian movements and persons identified with corrupt influences;

(3) the prohibition of business or financial interests on the part of organization officers and agents which conflict with their duty to the organization and its members; and

(4) the maintenance of fiscal integrity in the conduct of the affairs of the organization, including provision for accounting and financial controls and regular financial reports or summaries to be made available to members.

(b) Notwithstanding the fact that a labor organization has adopted or subscribed to standards of conduct as provided in paragraph (a) of this section, the organization is required to furnish evidence of its freedom from corrupt influences or influences opposed to basic democratic principles when there is reasonable cause to believe that—

(1) the organization has been suspended or expelled from or is subject to other sanction by a parent labor organization or federation of organizations with which it had been affiliated because it has demonstrated an unwillingness or inability to comply with governing requirements comparable in purpose to those required by paragraph (a) of this section; or

(2) the organization is in fact subject to influences that would preclude recognition under this Order.

(c) A labor organization which has or seeks recognition as a representative of employees under this Order shall file financial and other reports, provide for bonding of officials and employees of the organization, and comply with trusteeship and election standards.

(d) The Assistant Secretary shall prescribe the regulations needed to effectuate this section. These regulations shall conform generally to the principles applied to unions in the private sector. Complaints of violations of this section shall be filed with the Assistant Secretary.

SEC. 19. *Unfair labor practices.* (a) Agency management shall not—

(1) interfere with, restrain, or coerce an employee in the exercise of the rights assured by this Order;

(2) encourage or discourage membership in a labor organization by discrimination in regard to hiring, tenure, promotion, or other conditions of employment;

(3) sponsor, control, or otherwise assist a labor organization, except that an agency may furnish customary and routine services and facilities under section 23 of this Order when consistent with the best interests of the agency, its employees, and the organization, and when the services and facilities are furnished, if requested, on an impartial basis to organizations having equivalent status;

(4) discipline or otherwise discriminate against an employee because he has filed a complaint or given testimony under this Order;

(5) refuse to accord appropriate recognition to a labor organization qualified for such recognition; or

(6) refuse to consult, confer, or negotiate with a labor organization as required by this Order.

(b) A labor organization shall not—

(1) interfere with, restrain, or coerce an employee in the exercise of his rights assured by this Order;

(2) attempt to induce agency management to coerce an employee in the exercise of his rights under this Order;

(3) coerce, attempt to coerce, or discipline, fine, or take other economic sanction against a member of the organization as punishment or reprisal for, or for the purpose of hindering or impeding his work performance, his productivity, or the discharge of his duties owed as an officer or employee of the United States;

(4) call or engage in a strike, work stoppage, or slowdown; picket an agency in a labor-management dispute; or condone any such activity by failing to take affirmative action to prevent or stop it;

(5) discriminate against an employee with regard to the terms or conditions of membership because of race, color, creed, sex, age, or national origin; or

(6) refuse to consult, confer, or negotiate with an agency as required by this Order.

(c) A labor organization which is accorded exclusive recognition shall not deny membership to any employee in the appropriate unit except for failure to meet reasonable occupational standards uniformly required for admission, or for failure to tender initiation fees and dues uniformly required as a condition of acquiring and retaining membership. This paragraph does not preclude a labor organization from enforcing discipline in accordance with procedures under its constitution or by-laws which conform to the requirements of this Order.

(d) Issues which can properly be raised under an appeals procedure may not be raised under this section. Issues which can be raised under a grievance procedure may, in the discretion of the aggrieved party, be raised under that procedure or the complaint procedure under this section, but not under both procedures. Appeals or grievance decisions shall not be construed as unfair labor practice decisions under this Order nor as precedent for such decisions. All complaints under this section that cannot be resolved by the parties shall be filed with the Authority.

MISCELLANEOUS PROVISIONS

SEC. 20. *Use of official time.* Solicitation of membership or dues, and other internal business of a labor organization, shall be conducted during the non-duty hours of the employees concerned. Employees who represent a recognized labor organization shall not be on official time when negotiating an agreement with agency management, except to the extent that the negotiating parties agree to other arrangements which may provide that the agency will either authorize official time for up to 40 hours or authorize up to one-half the time spent in negotiations during regular working hours, for a reasonable number of employees, which number normally shall not exceed the number of management representatives.

SEC. 21. *Allotment of dues.* (a) When a labor organization holds formal or exclusive recognition, and the agency and the organization agree in writing to this course of action, an agency may deduct the regular and periodic dues of the organization from the pay of members of the organization in the unit of recognition who make a voluntary allotment for that purpose, and shall recover the costs of making the deductions. Such an allotment is subject to the regulations of the Office of Personnel Management, which shall include provision for the employee to revoke his authorization at stated six-month intervals. Such an allotment terminates when—

(1) the dues withholding agreement between the agency and the labor organization is terminated or ceases to be applicable to the employee; or

(2) the employee has been suspended or expelled from the labor organization.

(b) [Revoked by Ex. Ord. No. 11838, Feb. 6, 1975, 40 F.R. 5743.]

SEC. 22. *Adverse action appeals.* The head of each agency, in accordance with the provisions of this Order and regulations prescribed by the Office of Personnel Management, shall extend to all employees in the competitive civil service rights identical in adverse action cases to those provided preference eligibles under sections 7511–7512 of title 5 of the United States Code. Each employee in the competitive service shall have the right to appeal to the Merit Systems Protection Board from an adverse decision of the administrative officer so acting, such appeal to be processed in an identical manner to that provided for appeals under section 7701 of title 5 of the United States Code. Any recommendation by the Merit Systems Protection Board submitted to the head of an agency on the basis of an appeal by an employee in the competitive service shall be complied with by the head of the agency.

SEC. 23. *Agency implementation.* No later than April 1, 1970, each agency shall issue appropriate policies and regulations consistent with this Order for its implementation. This includes but is not limited to a clear statement of the rights of its employees under this Order; procedures with respect to recognition of labor organizations, determination of appropriate units, con-

sultation and negotiation with labor organizations, approval of agreements, mediation, and impasse resolution; policies with respect to the use of agency facilities by labor organizations; and policies and practices regarding consultation with other organizations and associations and individual employees. Insofar as practicable, agencies shall consult with representatives of labor organizations in the formulation of these policies and regulations.

SEC. 24. *Savings clauses.* (a) This Order does not preclude—

(1) the renewal or continuation of a lawful agreement between an agency and a representative of its employees entered into before the effective date of Executive Order No. 10988 (January 17, 1962); or

(2) the renewal, continuation, or initial according of recognition for units of management officials or supervisors represented by labor organizations which historically or traditionally represent the management officials or supervisors in private industry and which hold exclusive recognition for units of such officials or supervisors in any agency on the date of this Order.

(b) All grants of informal recognition under Executive Order No. 10988 terminate on July 1, 1970.

(c) All grants of formal recognition under Executive Order No. 10988 terminate under regulations which the Federal Labor Relations Council shall issue before October 1, 1970.

(d) By not later than December 31, 1970, all supervisors shall be excluded from units of formal and exclusive recognition and from coverage by negotiated agreements, except as provided in paragraph (a) of this section.

SEC. 25. *Guidance, training, review and information.* (a) The Office of Personnel Management, in conjunction with the Director of the Office of Management and Budget, shall establish and maintain a program for the policy guidance of agencies on labor-management relations in the Federal service and shall periodically review the implementation of these policies. The Office of Personnel Management shall be responsible for the day-to-day policy guidance under that program. The Office of Personnel Management also shall continuously review the operation of the Federal labor-management relations program to assist in assuring adherence to its provisions and merit system requirements; implement technical advice and information programs for the agencies; assist in the development of programs for training agency personnel and management officials in labor-management relations; and, from time to time, report to the Authority on the state of the program with any recommendations for its improvement.

(b) The Office of Personnel Management shall develop programs for the collection and dissemination of information appropriate to the needs of agencies, organizations and the public.

SEC. 26. *Effective date.* This Order is effective on January 1, 1970, except sections 7(f) and 8 which are effective immediately. Effective January 1, 1970, Executive Order No. 10988 and the President's Memorandum of May 21, 1963, entitled Standards of Conduct for Employee Organizations and Code of Fair Labor Practices, are revoked.

[For abolition of United States Information Agency (other than Broadcasting Board of Governors and International Broadcasting Bureau), transfer of functions, and treatment of references thereto, see sections 6531, 6532, and 6551 of Title 22, Foreign Relations and Intercourse.]

EX. ORD. NO. 12871. LABOR-MANAGEMENT PARTNERSHIPS

Ex. Ord. No. 12871, Oct. 1, 1993, 58 F.R. 52201, as amended by Ex. Ord. No. 12983, Dec. 21, 1995, 60 F.R. 66855; Ex. Ord. No. 13156, § 1, May 17, 2000, 65 F.R. 31785, provided:

The involvement of Federal Government employees and their union representatives is essential to achieving the National Performance Review's Government reform objectives. Only by changing the nature of Federal labor-management relations so that managers, employees, and employees' elected union representatives serve as partners will it be possible to design and implement comprehensive changes necessary to reform Government. Labor-management partnerships will champion change in Federal Government agencies to transform them into organizations capable of delivering the highest quality services to the American people.

By the authority vested in me as President by the Constitution and the laws of the United States, including section 301 of title 3, United States Code, and in order to establish a new form of labor-management relations throughout the executive branch to promote the principles and recommendations adopted as a result of the National Performance Review, it is hereby ordered:

SECTION 1. THE NATIONAL PARTNERSHIP COUNCIL. (a) *Establishment and Membership.* There is established the National Partnership Council ("Council"). The Council shall comprise the following members appointed by the President:

(1) Director of the Office of Personnel Management ("OPM");

(2) Deputy Secretary of Labor;

(3) Deputy Director for Management, Office of Management and Budget;

(4) Chair, Federal Labor Relations Authority;

(5) Federal Mediation and Conciliation Director;

(6) President, American Federation of Government Employees, AFL–CIO;

(7) President, National Federation of Federal Employees;

(8) President, National Treasury Employees Union;

(9) Secretary-Treasurer of the Public Employees Department, AFL–CIO;

(10) A deputy Secretary or other officer with department- or agency-wide authority from three executive departments or agencies (hereafter collectively "agency"), not otherwise represented on the Council; and

(11) one elected office holder each from both the Senior Executives Association and the Federal Managers Association.

Members shall have 2-year terms on the Council, which may be extended by the President.

(b) *Responsibilities and Functions.* The Council shall advise the President on matters involving labor-management relations in the executive branch. Its activities shall include:

(1) supporting the creation of labor-management partnerships and promoting partnership efforts in the executive branch, to the extent permitted by law;

(2) proposing to the President by January 1994 statutory changes necessary to achieve the objectives of this order, including legislation consistent with the National Performance Review's recommendations for the creation of a flexible and responsive hiring system and the reform of the General Schedule classification system;

(3) collecting and disseminating information about, and providing guidance on, partnership efforts in the executive branch, including results achieved, to the extent permitted by law;

(4) utilizing the expertise of individuals both within and outside the Federal Government to foster partnership arrangements;

(5) working with the President's Management Council toward reform consistent with the National Performance Review's recommendations throughout the executive branch; and

(6) reporting to the President by October 1996 on the progress of and results achieved through labor-management partnership throughout the executive branch.

(c) *Administration.* (1) The President shall designate a member of the Council who is a full-time Federal employee to serve as Chairperson. The responsibilities of the Chairperson shall include scheduling meetings of the Council.

(2) The Council shall seek input from nonmember Federal agencies, particularly smaller agencies. It also may, from time to time, invite experts from the private and public sectors to submit information. The Council shall also seek input from Federal manager and professional associations, companies, nonprofit organizations, State and local governments, Federal employees, and customers of Federal services, as needed.

(3) To the extent permitted by law and subject to the availability of appropriations, OPM shall provide such facilities, support, and administrative services to the Council as the Director of OPM deems appropriate.

(4) Members of the Council shall serve without compensation for their work on the Council, but may be allowed travel expenses, including per diem in lieu of subsistence, as authorized by law, for persons serving intermittently in Government service.

(5) All agencies shall, to the extent permitted by law, provide to the Council such assistance, information, and advice as the Council may request.

(d) *General.* (1) I have determined that the Council shall be established in compliance with the Federal Advisory Committee Act, as amended (5 U.S.C. App.).

(2) Notwithstanding any other executive order, the functions of the President under the Federal Advisory Committee Act, as amended, except that of reporting to the Congress, that are applicable to the Council, shall be performed by the Director of OPM, in accordance with guidelines and procedures issued by the Administrator of General Services.

(3) The Council shall exist for a period of 2 years from the date of this order, unless extended.

(4) Members of the Council who are not otherwise officers or employees of the Federal Government shall serve in a representative capacity and shall not be considered special Government employees for any purpose.

SEC. 2. IMPLEMENTATION OF LABOR-MANAGEMENT PARTNERSHIPS THROUGHOUT THE EXECUTIVE BRANCH. The head of each agency subject to the provisions of chapter 71 of title 5, United States Code shall:

(a) create labor-management partnerships by forming labor-management committees or councils at appropriate levels, or adapting existing councils or committees if such groups exist, to help reform Government;

(b) involve employees and their union representatives as full partners with management representatives to identify problems and craft solutions to better serve the agency's customers and mission;

(c) provide systematic training of appropriate agency employees (including line managers, first line supervisors, and union representatives who are Federal employees) in consensual methods of dispute resolution, such as alternative dispute resolution techniques and interest-based bargaining approaches;

(d) negotiate over the subjects set forth in 5 U.S.C. 7106(b)(1), and instruct subordinate officials to do the same; and

(e) evaluate progress and improvements in organizational performance resulting from the labor-management partnerships.

SEC. 3. NO ADMINISTRATIVE OR JUDICIAL REVIEW. This order is intended only to improve the internal management of the executive branch and is not intended to, and does not, create any right to administrative or judicial review, or any other right, substantive or procedural, enforceable by a party against the United States, its agencies or instrumentalities, its officers or employees, or any other person.

WILLIAM J. CLINTON.

EXTENSION OF TERM OF NATIONAL PARTNERSHIP COUNCIL

Term of the National Partnership Council extended until Sept. 30, 1997, by Ex. Ord. No. 12974, Sept. 29, 1995, 60 F.R. 51875, formerly set out as a note under section 14 of the Federal Advisory Committee Act in the Appendix to this title.

Term of the National Partnership Council extended until Sept. 30, 1999, by Ex. Ord. No. 13062, §1(c), Sept. 29, 1997, 62 F.R. 51755, formerly set out as a note under section 14 of the Federal Advisory Committee Act in the Appendix to this title.

Term of the National Partnership Council extended until Sept. 30, 2001, by Ex. Ord. No. 13138, Sept. 30, 1999, 64 F.R. 53879, set out as a note under section 14 of the Federal Advisory Committee Act in the Appendix to this title.

§ 7102. Employees' rights

Each employee shall have the right to form, join, or assist any labor organization, or to refrain from any such activity, freely and without fear of penalty or reprisal, and each employee shall be protected in the exercise of such right. Except as otherwise provided under this chapter, such right includes the right—

(1) to act for a labor organization in the capacity of a representative and the right, in that capacity, to present the views of the labor organization to heads of agencies and other officials of the executive branch of the Government, the Congress, or other appropriate authorities, and

(2) to engage in collective bargaining with respect to conditions of employment through representatives chosen by employees under this chapter.

(Added Pub. L. 95–454, title VII, § 701, Oct. 13, 1978, 92 Stat. 1192.)

PRIOR PROVISIONS

A prior section 7102, Pub. L. 89–554, Sept. 6, 1966, 80 Stat. 523, related to right of employees to petition Congress, prior to the general amendment of this chapter by Pub. L. 95–454. See section 7211 of this title.

PARTIAL SUSPENSION OF FEDERAL SERVICE LABOR-MANAGEMENT RELATIONS

Par. (2) of this section suspended with respect to any matter proposed for bargaining which would substantially impair the implementation by the United States Forces of any treaty or agreement, including any minutes or understandings thereto, between the United States and the Government of the host nation, see section 1(b) of Ex. Ord. No. 12391, Nov. 4, 1982, 47 F.R. 50457, set out as a note under section 7103 of this title.

SECTION REFERRED TO IN OTHER SECTIONS

This section is referred to in title 2 section 1351.

§ 7103. Definitions; application

(a) For the purpose of this chapter—

(1) "person" means an individual, labor organization, or agency;

(2) "employee" means an individual—

(A) employed in an agency; or

(B) whose employment in an agency has ceased because of any unfair labor practice under section 7116 of this title and who has not obtained any other regular and substantially equivalent employment, as determined under regulations prescribed by the Federal Labor Relations Authority;

but does not include—

(i) an alien or noncitizen of the United States who occupies a position outside the United States;

(ii) a member of the uniformed services;

(iii) a supervisor or a management official;

(iv) an officer or employee in the Foreign Service of the United States employed in the Department of State, the International Communication Agency, the Agency for International Development, the Department

of Agriculture, or the Department of Commerce; or

(v) any person who participates in a strike in violation of section 7311 of this title;

(3) "agency" means an Executive agency (including a nonappropriated fund instrumentality described in section 2105(c) of this title and the Veterans' Canteen Service, Department of Veterans Affairs), the Library of Congress, the Government Printing Office, and the Smithsonian Institution[1] but does not include—

(A) the General Accounting Office;

(B) the Federal Bureau of Investigation;

(C) the Central Intelligence Agency;

(D) the National Security Agency;

(E) the Tennessee Valley Authority;

(F) the Federal Labor Relations Authority;

(G) the Federal Service Impasses Panel; or

(H) the United States Secret Service and the United States Secret Service Uniformed Division.

(4) "labor organization" means an organization composed in whole or in part of employees, in which employees participate and pay dues, and which has as a purpose the dealing with an agency concerning grievances and conditions of employment, but does not include—

(A) an organization which, by its constitution, bylaws, tacit agreement among its members, or otherwise, denies membership because of race, color, creed, national origin, sex, age, preferential or nonpreferential civil service status, political affiliation, marital status, or handicapping condition;

(B) an organization which advocates the overthrow of the constitutional form of government of the United States;

(C) an organization sponsored by an agency; or

(D) an organization which participates in the conduct of a strike against the Government or any agency thereof or imposes a duty or obligation to conduct, assist, or participate in such a strike;

(5) "dues" means dues, fees, and assessments;

(6) "Authority" means the Federal Labor Relations Authority described in section 7104(a) of this title;

(7) "Panel" means the Federal Service Impasses Panel described in section 7119(c) of this title;

(8) "collective bargaining agreement" means an agreement entered into as a result of collective bargaining pursuant to the provisions of this chapter;

(9) "grievance" means any complaint—

(A) by any employee concerning any matter relating to the employment of the employee;

(B) by any labor organization concerning any matter relating to the employment of any employee; or

(C) by any employee labor organization, or agency concerning—

(i) the effect or interpretation, or a claim of breach, of a collective bargaining agreement; or

_____

[1] So in original. Probably should be followed by a comma.

(ii) any claimed violation, misinterpretation, or misapplication of any law, rule, or regulation affecting conditions of employment;

(10) "supervisor" means an individual employed by an agency having authority in the interest of the agency to hire, direct, assign, promote, reward, transfer, furlough, layoff, recall, suspend, discipline, or remove employees, to adjust their grievances, or to effectively recommend such action, if the exercise of the authority is not merely routine or clerical in nature but requires the consistent exercise of independent judgment, except that, with respect to any unit which includes firefighters or nurses, the term "supervisor" includes only those individuals who devote a preponderance of their employment time to exercising such authority;

(11) "management official" means an individual employed by an agency in a position the duties and responsibilities of which require or authorize the individual to formulate, determine, or influence the policies of the agency;

(12) "collective bargaining" means the performance of the mutual obligation of the representative of an agency and the exclusive representative of employees in an appropriate unit in the agency to meet at reasonable times and to consult and bargain in a good-faith effort to reach agreement with respect to the conditions of employment affecting such employees and to execute, if requested by either party, a written document incorporating any collective bargaining agreement reached, but the obligation referred to in this paragraph does not compel either party to agree to a proposal or to make a concession;

(13) "confidential employee" means an employee who acts in a confidential capacity with respect to an individual who formulates or effectuates management policies in the field of labor-management relations;

(14) "conditions of employment" means personnel policies, practices, and matters, whether established by rule, regulation, or otherwise, affecting working conditions, except that such term does not include policies, practices, and matters—

(A) relating to political activities prohibited under subchapter III of chapter 73 of this title;

(B) relating to the classification of any position; or

(C) to the extent such matters are specifically provided for by Federal statute;

(15) "professional employee" means—

(A) an employee engaged in the performance of work—

(i) requiring knowledge of an advanced type in a field of science or learning customarily acquired by a prolonged course of specialized intellectual instruction and study in an institution of higher learning or a hospital (as distinguished from knowledge acquired by a general academic education, or from an apprenticeship, or from training in the performance of routine mental, manual, mechanical, or physical activities);

(ii) requiring the consistent exercise of discretion and judgment in its performance;

(iii) which is predominantly intellectual and varied in character (as distinguished from routine mental, manual, mechanical, or physical work); and

(iv) which is of such character that the output produced or the result accomplished by such work cannot be standardized in relation to a given period of time; or

(B) an employee who has completed the courses of specialized intellectual instruction and study described in subparagraph (A)(i) of this paragraph and is performing related work under appropriate direction or guidance to qualify the employee as a professional employee described in subparagraph (A) of this paragraph;

(16) "exclusive representative" means any labor organization which—

(A) is certified as the exclusive representative of employees in an appropriate unit pursuant to section 7111 of this title; or

(B) was recognized by an agency immediately before the effective date of this chapter as the exclusive representative of employees in an appropriate unit—

(i) on the basis of an election, or

(ii) on any basis other than an election,

and continues to be so recognized in accordance with the provisions of this chapter;

(17) "firefighter" means any employee engaged in the performance of work directly connected with the control and extinguishment of fires or the maintenance and use of firefighting apparatus and equipment; and

(18) "United States" means the 50 States, the District of Columbia, the Commonwealth of Puerto Rico, Guam, the Virgin Islands, the Trust Territory of the Pacific Islands, and any territory or possession of the United States.

(b)(1) The President may issue an order excluding any agency or subdivision thereof from coverage under this chapter if the President determines that—

(A) the agency or subdivision has as a primary function intelligence, counterintelligence, investigative, or national security work, and

(B) the provisions of this chapter cannot be applied to that agency or subdivision in a manner consistent with national security requirements and considerations.

(2) The President may issue an order suspending any provision of this chapter with respect to any agency, installation, or activity located outside the 50 States and the District of Columbia, if the President determines that the suspension is necessary in the interest of national security.

(Added Pub. L. 95–454, title VII, §701, Oct. 13, 1978, 92 Stat. 1192; amended Pub. L. 96–465, title II, §2314(g), Oct. 17, 1980, 94 Stat. 2168; Pub. L. 102–54, §13(b)(1), June 13, 1991, 105 Stat. 274; Pub. L. 103–359, title V, §501(j), Oct. 14, 1994, 108 Stat. 3430; Pub. L. 104–201, div. A, title XVI, §1634(a),

Sept. 23, 1996, 110 Stat. 2752; Pub. L. 105–220, title III, § 341(e), Aug. 7, 1998, 112 Stat. 1092; Pub. L. 105–277, div. G, subdiv. A, title XIV, § 1422(b)(1), Oct. 21, 1998, 112 Stat. 2681–792; Pub. L. 106–554, § 1(a)(4) [div. B, title I, § 139], Dec. 21, 2000, 114 Stat. 2763, 2763A–235.)

AMENDMENTS

2000—Subsec. (a)(3)(H). Pub. L. 106–554 added subpar. (H).

1998—Subsec. (a)(2)(B)(iv). Pub. L. 105–277 substituted "Agency for International Development" for "United States International Development Cooperation Agency".

Subsec. (a)(3). Pub. L. 105–220, in introductory provisions, struck out "and" after "Library of Congress," and inserted "and the Smithsonian Institution" after "Government Printing Office,".

1996—Subsec. (a)(3)(F) to (H). Pub. L. 104–201 inserted "or" at end of subpar. (F), substituted a period for "; or" at end of subpar. (G), and struck out subpar. (H) which read as follows: "the Central Imagery Office;".

1994—Subsec. (a)(3)(H). Pub. L. 103–359 added subpar. (H).

1991—Subsec. (a)(3). Pub. L. 102–54 substituted "Department of Veterans Affairs" for "Veterans' Administration".

1980—Subsec. (a)(2)(iv). Pub. L. 96–465 struck out "the Agency for International Development, or" after "Department of State," and inserted "the United States International Development Cooperation Agency, the Department of Agriculture, or the Department of Commerce" after "Communication Agency".

CHANGE OF NAME

International Communication Agency, referred to in subsec. (a)(2)(B)(iv), redesignated United States Information Agency and Director or any other official of International Communication Agency redesignated as Director or other official, as appropriate, of United States Information Agency by section 303 of Pub. L. 97–241, title III, Aug. 24, 1982, 96 Stat. 291, set out as a note under section 1461 of Title 22, Foreign Relations and Intercourse. United States Information Agency (other than Broadcasting Board of Governors and International Broadcasting Bureau) abolished and functions transferred to Secretary of State by sections 6531 and 6532 of Title 22.

EFFECTIVE DATE OF 1998 AMENDMENT

Amendment by Pub. L. 105–277 effective Apr. 1, 1999, see section 1401 of Pub. L. 105–277, set out as an Effective Date note under section 6561 of Title 22, Foreign Relations and Intercourse.

EFFECTIVE DATE OF 1996 AMENDMENT

Amendment by Pub. L. 104–201 effective Oct. 1, 1996, see section 1635 of Pub. L. 104–201, set out as a note under section 1593 of Title 10, Armed Forces.

EFFECTIVE DATE OF 1980 AMENDMENT

Amendment by Pub. L. 96–465 effective Feb. 15, 1981, except as otherwise provided, see section 2403 of Pub. L. 96–465, set out as an Effective Date note under section 3901 of Title 22, Foreign Relations and Intercourse.

TERMINATION OF TRUST TERRITORY OF THE PACIFIC ISLANDS

For termination of Trust Territory of the Pacific Islands, see note set out preceding section 1681 of Title 48, Territories and Insular Possessions.

EX. ORD. NO. 12171. EXCLUSIONS FROM COVERAGE OF PROGRAM

Ex. Ord. No. 12171, Nov. 19, 1979, 44 F.R. 66565, as amended by Ex. Ord. No. 12338, Jan. 11, 1982, 47 F.R. 1369; Ex. Ord. No. 12410, Mar. 28, 1983, 48 F.R. 13143; Ex.

Ord. No. 12559, May 20, 1986, 51 F.R. 18761; Ex. Ord. No. 12632, Mar. 23, 1988, 53 F.R. 9852; Ex. Ord. No. 12666, Jan. 12, 1989, 54 F.R. 1921; Ex. Ord. No. 12671, Mar. 14, 1989, 54 F.R. 11157; Ex. Ord. No. 12681, July 6, 1989, 54 F.R. 28997; Ex. Ord. No. 12693, Sept. 29, 1989, 54 F.R. 40629; Ex. Ord. No. 13039, Mar. 11, 1997, 62 F.R. 12529, provided:

By the authority vested in me as President by the Constitution and statutes of the United States of America, including Section 7103(b) of Title 5 of the United States Code, and in order to exempt certain agencies or subdivisions thereof from coverage of the Federal Labor-Management Relations Program, it is hereby ordered as follows:

1–1. DETERMINATIONS

1–101. The agencies or subdivisions thereof set forth in Section 1–2 of this Order are hereby determined to have as a primary function intelligence, counterintelligence, investigative, or national security work. It is also hereby determined that Chapter 71 of Title 5 of the United States Code cannot be applied to those agencies or subdivisions in a manner consistent with national security requirements and considerations. The agencies or subdivisions thereof set forth in Section 1–2 of this Order are hereby excluded from coverage under Chapter 71 of Title 5 of the United States Code.

1–102. Having determined that it is necessary in the interest of national security, the provisions of Chapter 71 of Title 5 of the United States Code are suspended with respect to any agency, installation, or activity listed in Section 1–3 of this Order. However, such suspension shall be applicable only to that portion of the agency, installation, or activity which is located outside the 50 States and the District of Columbia.

1–2. EXCLUSIONS

1–201. The Information Security Oversight Office, General Services Administration.

1–202. The Federal Research Division, Research Services, the Library of Congress.

1–203. Agencies or subdivisions of the Department of the Treasury:

(a) The U.S. Secret Service.

(b) The U.S. Secret Service Uniformed Division.

(c) The Office of Special Assistant to the Secretary (National Security).

(d) The Office of Intelligence Support (OIS).

(e) The Office of the Assistant Secretary (Enforcement and Operations) (OEO).

(f) The Office of Criminal Enforcement, Bureau of Alcohol, Tobacco, and Firearms.

(g) The Office of Enforcement (Headquarters and Regional Components), U.S. Customs Service.

(h) The Criminal Investigation Division, Internal Revenue Service.

1–204. Agencies or subdivisions of the Department of the Army, Department of Defense:

(a) Office of Assistant Chief of Staff for Intelligence.

(b) U.S. Army Intelligence and Security Command.

(c) U.S. Army Foreign Science and Technology Center.

(d) U.S. Army Intelligence Center and School.

(e) U.S. Army Missile Intelligence Agency.

(f) Foreign Intelligence Office, U.S. Army Missile Research and Development Command.

1–205. Agencies or subdivisions of the Department of the Navy, Department of Defense:

(a) Office of Naval Intelligence.

(b) Naval Intelligence Command Headquarters and Subordinate Commands.

(c) Headquarters, Naval Security Group Command.

(d) Naval Security Group Activities and Detachments.

(e) Fleet Intelligence Center, Europe and Atlantic (FICEURLANT).

(f) Fleet Intelligence Center, Pacific (FICPAC).

(g) Units composed primarily of employees engaged in the operation, repair, and/or maintenance of "off line" or "on line" cryptographic equipment.

(h) Units composed primarily of employees of naval telecommunications activities in positions which require a cryptographic authorization.

(i) Naval Special Warfare Development Group.

1–206. Agencies or subdivisions of the Department of the Air Force, Department of Defense:

(a) Office of Space Systems, Office of the Secretary of the Air Force.

(b) Office of Special Projects, Office of the Secretary of the Air Force.

(c) Engineering Office, Space and Missile Systems Organization (Air Force Systems Command).

(d) Program Control Office, Space and Missile Systems Organization (Air Force Systems Command).

(e) Detachment 3, Space and Missile Systems Organization (Air Force Systems Command).

(f) Defense Dissemination Systems Program Office, Space and Missile Systems Organization (Air Force Systems Command).

(g) Satellite Data System Program Office, Space and Missile Systems Organization (Air Force Systems Command).

(h) Project Office at El Segundo, California, Office of the Secretary of the Air Force.

(i) Project Office at Patrick Air Force Base, Florida, Office of the Secretary of the Air Force.

(j) Project Office at Fort Myer, Virginia, Office of the Secretary of the Air Force.

(k) Air Force Office of Special Investigations.

(l) U.S. Air Force Security Service.

(m) Foreign Technology Division, Air Force Systems Command, Wright-Patterson Air Force Base.

(n) 1035 Technical Operations Group (Air Force Technical Applications Center), Air Force Systems Command, and subordinate units.

(o) 3480 Technical Training Wing, Air Training Command, Goodfellow Air Force Base, Texas.

(p) Office of the Assistant Chief of Staff, Intelligence.

(q) Air Force Intelligence Service.

1–207. The Defense Intelligence Agency, Department of Defense.

1–208. The Defense Investigative Service, Department of Defense.

1–209. Agencies or subdivisions of the Department of Justice:

a. The Office of Enforcement and the Office of Intelligence, including all domestic field offices and intelligence units, of the Drug Enforcement Administration.

b. The Office of Special Operations, the Threat Analysis Group, the Enforcement Operations Division, the Witness Security Division and the Court Security Division in the Office of the Director and the Enforcement Division in Offices of the United States Marshals in the United States Marshals Service.

1–210. Agencies or subdivisions of the Department of Energy.

(a) The Albuquerque, Nevada and Savannah River operations offices under the Under Secretary of Energy.

(b) Offices of the Assistant Secretary for Defense Programs.

1–211. Offices within the Agency for International Development:

(a) The Immediate Office of the Auditor General.

(b) The Office of Inspections and Investigations.

(c) The Office of Security.

(d) The Office of the Area Auditor General/Washington.

1–212. Agencies or subdivisions under the operational jurisdiction of the Joint Chiefs of Staff (JCS).

(a) Intelligence Division (J–2), Headquarters Atlantic Command (LANTCOM).

(b) Atlantic Command Electronic Intelligence Center.

(c) Intelligence Directorate (J–2), Headquarters U.S. European Command (USEUCOM).

(d) Special Security Office (SSO), Headquarters U.S. European Command (USEUCOM).

(e) European Defense Analysis Center (EUDAC).

(f) Intelligence Directorate (J–2), Headquarters Pacific Command (PACOM).

(g) Intelligence Center Pacific (IPAC).

(h) Intelligence Directorate (J–2), Headquarters U.S. Southern Command (USSOUTHCOM).

(i) Intelligence Directorate (J–2), Headquarters U.S. Readiness Command (USREDCOM)/Joint Deployment Agency.

(j) Deputy Chief of Staff/Intelligence, Headquarters Strategic Air Command (SAC).

(k) 544th Strategic Intelligence Wing, Strategic Air Command (SAC).

(l) Deputy Chief of Staff/Intelligence, Headquarters 15th Air Force, Strategic Air Command (SAC).

(m) Deputy Chief of Staff/Intelligence, Headquarters 8th Air Force, Strategic Air Command (SAC).

(n) Strategic Reconnaissance Center, Headquarters Strategic Air Command (SAC).

(o) 6th Strategic Wing, Strategic Air Command (SAC).

(p) 9th Strategic Reconnaissance Wing, Strategic Air Command (SAC).

(q) 55th Strategic Reconnaissance Wing, Strategic Air Command (SAC).

(r) 306th Strategic Wing, Strategic Air Command (SAC).

(s) 376th Strategic Wing, Strategic Air Command (SAC).

(t) Deputy Chief of Staff/Operations Plans, Headquarters Strategic Air Command (SAC).

(u) The Joint Strategic Target Planning Staff (JSTPS).

(v) The Joint Special Operations Command (JSOC) and all elements under its operational control.

1–213. The subdivisions of the Federal Aviation Administration, Department of Transportation:

(a) Federal Air Marshal Branch, International Civil Aviation Security Division, Office of Civil Aviation Security.

(b) Units composed of Civil Aviation Security Inspectors in Civil Aviation Security divisions whose responsibilities require Federal air marshal functions.

1–214. Subdivisions of the National Preparedness Directorate of the Federal Emergency Management Agency.

(a) Office of Associate Director.

(b) Office of Analysis and Support.

(c) Office of Mobilization Preparedness.

(d) The following offices of the Office of Systems Engineering.

(1) Office of the Assistant Associate Director.

(2) NEMS–DCWS Program Office.

(3) Systems Design Division.

(4) Telecommunications Systems Development Division.

(5) Systems Support Division.

(e) The following offices of the Office of Operations.

(1) Office of the Assistant Associate Director.

(2) Planning Division.

(3) The following branches of the Readiness Division.

(A) Exercise Branch.

(B) Operations Branch.

(C) National Warning Center.

(D) Alternate National Warning Center.

(4) Mobile Emergency Response Support Operations Divisions.

(5) Federal Agency Support and Coordination Division.

(f) The following offices in the Office of Information Resource Management.

(1) Office of the Assistant Associate Director.

(2) Information Systems Policy, Planning and Evaluation Policy and Planning Branch.

(3) Information Systems Application Branch.

(4) EICC Support Center.

1–215. The Defense Mapping Agency Reston Center, Department of Defense.

1–3. UNITS OUTSIDE THE 50 STATES AND THE DISTRICT OF COLUMBIA

1–301. The Drug Enforcement Administration, Department of Justice.

EX. ORD. NO. 12391. PARTIAL SUSPENSION OF FEDERAL SERVICE LABOR-MANAGEMENT RELATIONS

Ex. Ord. No. 12391, Nov. 4, 1982, 47 F.R. 50457, provided:

By the authority vested in me as President by the Constitution and statutes of the United States of America, including Section 7103(b)(2) of Title 5 and Section 301 of Title 3 of the United States Code, and having determined that it is necessary in the interest of national security to suspend certain labor-management relations provisions with respect to overseas activities of the Department of Defense, it is hereby ordered as follows:

SECTION 1. *Suspensions*. With regard to United States citizen employees of the Department of Defense, including the Military Departments, who are employed outside the United States as defined in 5 U.S.C. 7103(a)(18), with the exception of those employed in the Republic of Panama:

(a) The provisions of 5 U.S.C. 7105(a)(2)(D), (E), (G), and (H) and of 5 U.S.C. 7123(b) are suspended with respect to any matter which substantially impairs the implementation by the United States Forces of any treaty or agreement, including any minutes or understandings thereto, between the United States and the Government of the host nation;

(b) The provisions of 5 U.S.C. 7102(2), 7114(a)(1), 7114(a)(4), 7116(a)(5), and 7117(c) are suspended with respect to any matter proposed for bargaining which would substantially impair the implementation by the United States Forces of any treaty or agreement, including any minutes or understandings thereto, between the United States and the Government of the host nation;

(c) The provisions of 5 U.S.C. 7116(a)(7) and 7117(b) are suspended with regard to any regulation governing the implementation by the United States Forces of any treaty or agreement, including any minutes or understandings thereto, between the United States and the Government of the host nations; and

(d) The provisions of 5 U.S.C. 7121(b)(3)(C) are suspended with respect to any grievance involving the implementation by the United States Forces of any treaty or agreement, including any minutes or understandings thereto, between the United States and the Government of the host nation.

SEC. 2. *Disputes*. Disputes between a labor organization and the United States Forces as to whether a particular matter is covered by one or more of the suspensions set forth in this Order shall be referred to the Secretary of Defense. The decision of the Secretary in such disputes shall be made after consultation with the Secretary of State and shall be final. The Secretary of Defense may delegate this authority, but only to the Deputy Secretary of Defense, an Under Secretary of Defense, or an Assistant Secretary of Defense. The functions assigned to the Secretary of State may not be delegated or assigned to anyone below the rank of an Assistant Secretary of State.

RONALD REAGAN.

EX. ORD. NO. 12632. EXCLUSIONS FROM FEDERAL LABOR-MANAGEMENT RELATIONS PROGRAM

Ex. Ord. No. 12632, Mar. 23, 1988, 53 F.R. 9852, provided:

By virtue of the authority vested in me as President by the Constitution and laws of the United States of America, including Section 7103(b) of Title 5 of the United States Code, and in order to exempt certain agencies or subdivisions thereof from coverage of the Federal Labor-Management Relations Program, it is hereby ordered as follows:

SECTION 1. *Determinations*. The agencies or subdivisions thereof set forth in Section 3 of this Order are hereby determined to have as a primary function intelligence, counterintelligence, investigative, or national security work. It is also hereby determined that Chapter 71 of Title 5 of the United States Code cannot be applied to these agencies or subdivisions in a manner consistent with national security requirements and considerations. These agencies or subdivisions thereof are hereby excluded from coverage under Chapter 71 of Title 5 of the United States Code.

SEC. 2. *Relationship to Executive Order No. 12559*. The determinations set forth in Section 1 of this Order are the same determinations that I made at the time of and as a predicate to my issuance on May 20, 1986, of Executive Order No. 12559 [amending Ex. Ord. No. 12171, set out as a note above], which was issued for the same purpose as this Order. On July 10, 1987, Executive Order No. 12559 was held by a United States District Court to be incomplete as a matter of form, and therefore invalid, because it did not expressly set forth these determinations. *AFGE v. Reagan*, Civil No. 86–1587 (D.D.C.). These determinations were not expressly set forth in the text of Executive Order No. 12559 because all that Order did was amend Executive Order No. 12171 [set out as a note above] by adding the agencies or subdivisions referred to in Section 1 of this Order to the list in Executive Order No. 12171 of entities excluded from coverage of the Federal Labor-Management Relations Program, and these determinations were already expressly set forth in the text of Executive Order No. 12171, which remains in effect (as amended). This Order is not intended to reflect any belief that the form of Executive Order No. 12559 was invalid, but is intended solely to accomplish the purpose of that Order.

SEC. 3. *Amendment of Executive Order No. 12171*. Executive Order No. 12171 is amended by deleting Section 1–209 and inserting in its place:

SEC. 1–209. *Agencies or subdivisions of the Department of Justice*. (a) The Office of Enforcement and the Office of Intelligence, including all domestic field offices and intelligence units, of the Drug Enforcement Administration.

(b) The Office of Special Operations, the Threat Analysis Group, the Enforcement Operations Division, the Witness Security Division and the Court Security Division in the Office of the Director and the Enforcement Division in Offices of the United States Marshals in the United States Marshals Service.

RONALD REAGAN.

SECTION REFERRED TO IN OTHER SECTIONS

This section is referred to in sections 4703, 5596, 6121, 7323, 8473 of this title; title 2 section 1351; title 7 section 7011; title 10 section 1614; title 22 sections 3701, 6613; title 38 section 711.

§ 7104. Federal Labor Relations Authority

(a) The Federal Labor Relations Authority is composed of three members, not more than 2 of whom may be adherents of the same political party. No member shall engage in any other business or employment or hold another office or position in the Government of the United States except as otherwise provided by law.

(b) Members of the Authority shall be appointed by the President by and with the advice and consent of the Senate, and may be removed by the President only upon notice and hearing and only for inefficiency, neglect of duty, or malfeasance in office. The President shall designate one member to serve as Chairman of the Authority. The Chairman is the chief executive and administrative officer of the Authority.

(c) A member of the Authority shall be appointed for a term of 5 years. An individual chosen to fill a vacancy shall be appointed for the unexpired term of the member replaced. The term of any member shall not expire before the earlier of—

(1) the date on which the member's successor takes office, or

(2) the last day of the Congress beginning after the date on which the member's term of office would (but for this paragraph) expire.

(d) A vacancy in the Authority shall not impair the right of the remaining members to exercise all of the powers of the Authority.

(e) The Authority shall make an annual report to the President for transmittal to the Congress which shall include information as to the cases it has heard and the decisions it has rendered.

(f)(1) The General Counsel of the Authority shall be appointed by the President, by and with the advice and consent of the Senate, for a term of 5 years. The General Counsel may be removed at any time by the President. The General Counsel shall hold no other office or position in the Government of the United States except as provided by law.

(2) The General Counsel may—

(A) investigate alleged unfair labor practices under this chapter,

(B) file and prosecute complaints under this chapter, and

(C) exercise such other powers of the Authority as the Authority may prescribe.

(3) The General Counsel shall have direct authority over, and responsibility for, all employees in the office of General Counsel, including employees of the General Counsel in the regional offices of the Authority.

(Added Pub. L. 95–454, title VII, §701, Oct. 13, 1978, 92 Stat. 1196; amended Pub. L. 98–224, §3, Mar. 2, 1984, 98 Stat. 47.)

AMENDMENTS

1984—Subsec. (b). Pub. L. 98–224, §3(a), inserted provision directing that Chairman be chief executive and administrative officer.

Subsec. (c). Pub. L. 98–224, §3(b), substituted provision that a member of Authority be appointed for a term of 5 years and an individual chosen to fill a vacancy be appointed for unexpired term of member replaced for provision that one original member of Authority be appointed for a term of 1 year, one for a term of 3 years, and Chairman for a term of 5 years, and thereafter each member be appointed for a term of 5 years.

TERMINATION OF REPORTING REQUIREMENTS

For termination, effective May 15, 2000, of provisions in subsection (e) of this section relating to transmittal to Congress of an annual report on cases heard and decisions rendered, see section 3003 of Pub. L. 104–66, as amended, set out as a note under section 1113 of Title 31, Money and Finance, and page 171 of House Document No. 103–7.

SECTION REFERRED TO IN OTHER SECTIONS

This section is referred to in section 7103 of this title; title 2 section 1351; title 22 section 4102.

§ 7105. Powers and duties of the Authority

(a)(1) The Authority shall provide leadership in establishing policies and guidance relating to matters under this chapter, and, except as otherwise provided, shall be responsible for carrying out the purpose of this chapter.

(2) The Authority shall, to the extent provided in this chapter and in accordance with regulations prescribed by the Authority—

(A) determine the appropriateness of units for labor organization representation under section 7112 of this title;

(B) supervise or conduct elections to determine whether a labor organization has been selected as an exclusive representative by a majority of the employees in an appropriate unit and otherwise administer the provisions of section 7111 of this title relating to the according of exclusive recognition to labor organizations;

(C) prescribe criteria and resolve issues relating to the granting of national consultation rights under section 7113 of this title;

(D) prescribe criteria and resolve issues relating to determining compelling need for agency rules or regulations under section 7117(b) of this title;

(E) resolves issues relating to the duty to bargain in good faith under section 7117(c) of this title;

(F) prescribe criteria relating to the granting of consultation rights with respect to conditions of employment under section 7117(d) of this title;

(G) conduct hearings and resolve complaints of unfair labor practices under section 7118 of this title;

(H) resolve exceptions to arbitrator's awards under section 7122 of this title; and

(I) take such other actions as are necessary and appropriate to effectively administer the provisions of this chapter.

(b) The Authority shall adopt an official seal which shall be judicially noticed.

(c) The principal office of the Authority shall be in or about the District of Columbia, but the Authority may meet and exercise any or all of its powers at any time or place. Except as otherwise expressly provided by law, the Authority may, by one or more of its members or by such agents as it may designate, make any appropriate inquiry necessary to carry out its duties wherever persons subject to this chapter are located. Any member who participates in the inquiry shall not be disqualified from later participating in a decision of the Authority in any case relating to the inquiry.

(d) The Authority shall appoint an Executive Director and such regional directors, administrative law judges under section 3105 of this title, and other individuals as it may from time to time find necessary for the proper performance of its functions. The Authority may delegate to officers and employees appointed under this subsection authority to perform such duties and make such expenditures as may be necessary.

(e)(1) The Authority may delegate to any regional director its authority under this chapter—

(A) to determine whether a group of employees is an appropriate unit;

(B) to conduct investigations and to provide for hearings;

(C) to determine whether a question of representation exists and to direct an election; and

(D) to supervise or conduct secret ballot elections and certify the results thereof.

(2) The Authority may delegate to any administrative law judge appointed under subsection (d) of this section its authority under section 7118 of this title to determine whether any person has engaged in or is engaging in an unfair labor practice.

(f) If the Authority delegates any authority to any regional director or administrative law judge to take any action pursuant to subsection (e) of this section, the Authority may, upon application by any interested person filed within 60 days after the date of the action, review such action, but the review shall not, unless specifically ordered by the Authority, operate as a stay of action. The Authority may affirm, modify, or reverse any action reviewed under this subsection. If the Authority does not undertake to grant review of the action under this subsection within 60 days after the later of—

(1) the date of the action; or

(2) the date of the filing of any application under this subsection for review of the action;

the action shall become the action of the Authority at the end of such 60-day period.

(g) In order to carry out its functions under this chapter, the Authority may—

(1) hold hearings;

(2) administer oaths, take the testimony or deposition of any person under oath, and issue subpenas as provided in section 7132 of this title; and

(3) may require an agency or a labor organization to cease and desist from violations of this chapter and require it to take any remedial action it considers appropriate to carry out the policies of this chapter.

(h) Except as provided in section 518 of title 28, relating to litigation before the Supreme Court, attorneys designated by the Authority may appear for the Authority and represent the Authority in any civil action brought in connection with any function carried out by the Authority pursuant to this title or as otherwise authorized by law.

(i) In the exercise of the functions of the Authority under this title, the Authority may request from the Director of the Office of Personnel Management an advisory opinion concerning the proper interpretation of rules, regulations, or policy directives issued by the Office of Personnel Management in connection with any matter before the Authority.

(Added Pub. L. 95–454, title VII, § 701, Oct. 13, 1978, 92 Stat. 1196.)

PARTIAL SUSPENSION OF FEDERAL SERVICE LABOR-MANAGEMENT RELATIONS

Subsec. (a)(2)(D), (E), (G), and (H) of this section suspended with respect to any matter which substantially impairs the implementation by the United States Forces of any treaty or agreement, including any minutes or understandings thereto, between the United States and the Government of the host nation, see section 1(a) of Ex. Ord. No. 12391, Nov. 4, 1982, 47 F.R. 50457, set out as a note under section 7103 of this title.

SECTION REFERRED TO IN OTHER SECTIONS

This section is referred to in section 7118 of this title; title 2 section 1351; title 7 section 7011.

§ 7106. Management rights

(a) Subject to subsection (b) of this section, nothing in this chapter shall affect the authority of any management official of any agency—

(1) to determine the mission, budget, organization, number of employees, and internal security practices of the agency; and

(2) in accordance with applicable laws—

(A) to hire, assign, direct, layoff, and retain employees in the agency, or to suspend, remove, reduce in grade or pay, or take other disciplinary action against such employees;

(B) to assign work, to make determinations with respect to contracting out, and to determine the personnel by which agency operations shall be conducted;

(C) with respect to filling positions, to make selections for appointments from—

(i) among properly ranked and certified candidates for promotion; or

(ii) any other appropriate source; and

(D) to take whatever actions may be necessary to carry out the agency mission during emergencies.

(b) Nothing in this section shall preclude any agency and any labor organization from negotiating—

(1) at the election of the agency, on the numbers, types, and grades of employees or positions assigned to any organizational subdivision, work project, or tour of duty, or on the technology, methods, and means of performing work;

(2) procedures which management officials of the agency will observe in exercising any authority under this section; or

(3) appropriate arrangements for employees adversely affected by the exercise of any authority under this section by such management officials.

(Added Pub. L. 95–454, title VII, § 701, Oct. 13, 1978, 92 Stat. 1198.)

SECTION REFERRED TO IN OTHER SECTIONS

This section is referred to in title 2 section 1351.

SUBCHAPTER II—RIGHTS AND DUTIES OF AGENCIES AND LABOR ORGANIZATIONS

§ 7111. Exclusive recognition of labor organizations

(a) An agency shall accord exclusive recognition to a labor organization if the organization has been selected as the representative, in a secret ballot election, by a majority of the employees in an appropriate unit who cast valid ballots in the election.

(b) If a petition is filed with the Authority—

(1) by any person alleging—

(A) in the case of an appropriate unit for which there is no exclusive representative, that 30 percent of the employees in the appropriate unit wish to be represented for the purpose of collective bargaining by an exclusive representative, or

(B) in the case of an appropriate unit for which there is an exclusive representative, that 30 percent of the employees in the unit allege that the exclusive representative is no longer the representative of the majority of the employees in the unit; or

(2) by any person seeking clarification of, or an amendment to, a certification then in effect or a matter relating to representation;

the Authority shall investigate the petition, and if it has reasonable cause to believe that a question of representation exists, it shall provide an opportunity for a hearing (for which a transcript shall be kept) after a reasonable notice. If the Authority finds on the record of the hearing that a question of representation exists, the Authority shall supervise or conduct an election on the question by secret ballot and shall certify the results thereof. An election under this subsection shall not be conducted in any appropriate unit or in any subdivision thereof within which, in the preceding 12 calendar months, a valid election under this subsection has been held.

(c) A labor organization which—

(1) has been designated by at least 10 percent of the employees in the unit specified in any petition filed pursuant to subsection (b) of this section;

(2) has submitted a valid copy of a current or recently expired collective bargaining agreement for the unit; or

(3) has submitted other evidence that it is the exclusive representative of the employees involved;

may intervene with respect to a petition filed pursuant to subsection (b) of this section and shall be placed on the ballot of any election under such subsection (b) with respect to the petition.

(d) The Authority shall determine who is eligible to vote in any election under this section and shall establish rules governing any such election, which shall include rules allowing employees eligible to vote the opportunity to choose—

(1) from labor organizations on the ballot, that labor organization which the employees wish to have represent them; or

(2) not to be represented by a labor organization.

In any election in which no choice on the ballot receives a majority of the votes cast, a runoff election shall be conducted between the two choices receiving the highest number of votes. A labor organization which receives the majority of the votes cast in an election shall be certified by the Authority as the exclusive representative.

(e) A labor organization seeking exclusive recognition shall submit to the Authority and the agency involved a roster of its officers and representatives, a copy of its constitution and by-laws, and a statement of its objectives.

(f) Exclusive recognition shall not be accorded to a labor organization—

(1) if the Authority determines that the labor organization is subject to corrupt influences or influences opposed to democratic principles;

(2) in the case of a petition filed pursuant to subsection (b)(1)(A) of this section, if there is not credible evidence that at least 30 percent of the employees in the unit specified in the petition wish to be represented for the purpose of collective bargaining by the labor organization seeking exclusive recognition;

(3) if there is then in effect a lawful written collective bargaining agreement between the agency involved and an exclusive representative (other than the labor organization seeking exclusive recognition) covering any employees included in the unit specified in the petition, unless—

(A) the collective bargaining agreement has been in effect for more than 3 years, or

(B) the petition for exclusive recognition is filed not more than 105 days and not less than 60 days before the expiration date of the collective bargaining agreement; or

(4) if the Authority has, within the previous 12 calendar months, conducted a secret ballot election for the unit described in any petition under this section and in such election a majority of the employees voting chose a labor organization for certification as the unit's exclusive representative.

(g) Nothing in this section shall be construed to prohibit the waiving of hearings by stipulation for the purpose of a consent election in conformity with regulations and rules or decisions of the Authority.

(Added Pub. L. 95–454, title VII, § 701, Oct. 13, 1978, 92 Stat. 1199.)

Section Referred to in Other Sections

This section is referred to in sections 7103, 7105 of this title; title 2 section 1351; title 7 section 7011; title 10 sections 461, 2467; title 49 section 40122.

§ 7112. Determination of appropriate units for labor organization representation

(a) The Authority shall determine the appropriateness of any unit. The Authority shall determine in each case whether, in order to ensure employees the fullest freedom in exercising the rights guaranteed under this chapter, the appropriate unit should be established on an agency, plant, installation, functional, or other basis and shall determine any unit to be an appropriate unit only if the determination will ensure a clear and identifiable community of interest among the employees in the unit and will promote effective dealings with, and efficiency of the operations of the agency involved.

(b) A unit shall not be determined to be appropriate under this section solely on the basis of the extent to which employees in the proposed unit have organized, nor shall a unit be determined to be appropriate if it includes—

(1) except as provided under section 7135(a)(2) of this title, any management official or supervisor;

(2) a confidential employee;

(3) an employee engaged in personnel work in other than a purely clerical capacity;

(4) an employee engaged in administering the provisions of this chapter;

(5) both professional employees and other employees, unless a majority of the professional employees vote for inclusion in the unit;

(6) any employee engaged in intelligence, counterintelligence, investigative, or security work which directly affects national security; or

(7) any employee primarily engaged in investigation or audit functions relating to the work of individuals employed by an agency whose duties directly affect the internal security of the agency, but only if the functions are undertaken to ensure that the duties are discharged honestly and with integrity.

(c) Any employee who is engaged in administering any provision of law relating to labor-management relations may not be represented by a labor organization—

　(1) which represents other individuals to whom such provision applies; or

　(2) which is affiliated directly or indirectly with an organization which represents other individuals to whom such provision applies.

(d) Two or more units which are in an agency and for which a labor organization is the exclusive representative may, upon petition by the agency or labor organization, be consolidated with or without an election into a single larger unit if the Authority considers the larger unit to be appropriate. The Authority shall certify the labor organization as the exclusive representative of the new larger unit.

(Added Pub. L. 95–454, title VII, § 701, Oct. 13, 1978, 92 Stat. 1200; amended Pub. L. 102–378, § 2(54), Oct. 2, 1992, 106 Stat. 1354.)

Amendments

1992—Subsec. (a). Pub. L. 102–378 struck out "(1)" after subsec. (a) designation.

Section Referred to in Other Sections

This section is referred to in sections 7105, 7123 of this title; title 2 section 1351; title 7 section 7011.

§ 7113. National consultation rights

(a) If, in connection with any agency, no labor organization has been accorded exclusive recognition on an agency basis, a labor organization which is the exclusive representative of a substantial number of the employees of the agency, as determined in accordance with criteria prescribed by the Authority, shall be granted national consultation rights by the agency. National consultation rights shall terminate when the labor organization no longer meets the criteria prescribed by the Authority. Any issue relating to any labor organization's eligibility for, or continuation of, national consultation rights shall be subject to determination by the Authority.

(b)(1) Any labor organization having national consultation rights in connection with any agency under subsection (a) of this section shall—

　(A) be informed of any substantive change in conditions of employment proposed by the agency, and

　(B) be permitted reasonable time to present its views and recommendations regarding the changes.

(2) If any views or recommendations are presented under paragraph (1) of this subsection to an agency by any labor organization—

　(A) the agency shall consider the views or recommendations before taking final action on any matter with respect to which the views or recommendations are presented; and

　(B) the agency shall provide the labor organization a written statement of the reasons for taking the final action.

(c) Nothing in this section shall be construed to limit the right of any agency or exclusive representative to engage in collective bargaining.

(Added Pub. L. 95–454, title VII, § 701, Oct. 13, 1978, 92 Stat. 1201; amended Pub. L. 102–378, § 2(55), Oct. 2, 1992, 106 Stat. 1354.)

Amendments

1992—Subsec. (a). Pub. L. 102–378 struck out "(1)" after subsec. (a) designation.

Section Referred to in Other Sections

This section is referred to in section 7105 of this title; title 2 section 1351.

§ 7114. Representation rights and duties

(a)(1) A labor organization which has been accorded exclusive recognition is the exclusive representative of the employees in the unit it represents and is entitled to act for, and negotiate collective bargaining agreements covering, all employees in the unit. An exclusive representative is responsible for representing the interests of all employees in the unit it represents without discrimination and without regard to labor organization membership.

(2) An exclusive representative of an appropriate unit in an agency shall be given the opportunity to be represented at—

　(A) any formal discussion between one or more representatives of the agency and one or more employees in the unit or their representatives concerning any grievance or any personnel policy or practices or other general condition of employment; or

　(B) any examination of an employee in the unit by a representative of the agency in connection with an investigation if—

　　(i) the employee reasonably believes that the examination may result in disciplinary action against the employee; and

　　(ii) the employee requests representation.

(3) Each agency shall annually inform its employees of their rights under paragraph (2)(B) of this subsection.

(4) Any agency and any exclusive representative in any appropriate unit in the agency, through appropriate representatives, shall meet and negotiate in good faith for the purposes of arriving at a collective bargaining agreement. In addition, the agency and the exclusive representative may determine appropriate techniques, consistent with the provisions of section 7119 of this title, to assist in any negotiation.

(5) The rights of an exclusive representative under the provisions of this subsection shall not be construed to preclude an employee from—

　(A) being represented by an attorney or other representative, other than the exclusive representative, of the employee's own choosing in any grievance or appeal action; or

　(B) exercising grievance or appellate rights established by law, rule, or regulation;

except in the case of grievance or appeal procedures negotiated under this chapter.

(b) The duty of an agency and an exclusive representative to negotiate in good faith under subsection (a) of this section shall include the obligation—

　(1) to approach the negotiations with a sincere resolve to reach a collective bargaining agreement;

　(2) to be represented at the negotiations by duly authorized representatives prepared to discuss and negotiate on any condition of employment;

　(3) to meet at reasonable times and convenient places as frequently as may be necessary, and to avoid unnecessary delays;

(4) in the case of an agency, to furnish to the exclusive representative involved, or its authorized representative, upon request and, to the extent not prohibited by law, data—

(A) which is normally maintained by the agency in the regular course of business;

(B) which is reasonably available and necessary for full and proper discussion, understanding, and negotiation of subjects within the scope of collective bargaining; and

(C) which does not constitute guidance, advice, counsel, or training provided for management officials or supervisors, relating to collective bargaining; and

(5) if agreement is reached, to execute on the request of any party to the negotiation a written document embodying the agreed terms, and to take such steps as are necessary to implement such agreement.

(c)(1) An agreement between any agency and an exclusive representative shall be subject to approval by the head of the agency.

(2) The head of the agency shall approve the agreement within 30 days from the date the agreement is executed if the agreement is in accordance with the provisions of this chapter and any other applicable law, rule, or regulation (unless the agency has granted an exception to the provision).

(3) If the head of the agency does not approve or disapprove the agreement within the 30-day period, the agreement shall take effect and shall be binding on the agency and the exclusive representative subject to the provisions of this chapter and any other applicable law, rule, or regulation.

(4) A local agreement subject to a national or other controlling agreement at a higher level shall be approved under the procedures of the controlling agreement or, if none, under regulations prescribed by the agency.

(Added Pub. L. 95–454, title VII, § 701, Oct. 13, 1978, 92 Stat. 1202.)

PARTIAL SUSPENSION OF FEDERAL SERVICE LABOR-MANAGEMENT RELATIONS

Subsec. (a)(1) and (4) of this section suspended with respect to any matter proposed for bargaining which would substantially impair the implementation by the United States Forces of any treaty or agreement, including any minutes or understandings thereto, between the United States and the Government of the host nation, see section 1(b) of Ex. Ord. No. 12391, Nov. 4, 1982, 47 F.R. 50457, set out as a note under section 7103 of this title.

SECTION REFERRED TO IN OTHER SECTIONS

This section is referred to in title 2 section 1351.

§ 7115. Allotments to representatives

(a) If an agency has received from an employee in an appropriate unit a written assignment which authorizes the agency to deduct from the pay of the employee amounts for the payment of regular and periodic dues of the exclusive representative of the unit, the agency shall honor the assignment and make an appropriate allotment pursuant to the assignment. Any such allotment shall be made at no cost to the exclusive representative or the employee. Except as provided under subsection (b) of this section, any such assignment may not be revoked for a period of 1 year.

(b) An allotment under subsection (a) of this section for the deduction of dues with respect to any employee shall terminate when—

(1) the agreement between the agency and the exclusive representative involved ceases to be applicable to the employee; or

(2) the employee is suspended or expelled from membership in the exclusive representative.

(c)(1) Subject to paragraph (2) of this subsection, if a petition has been filed with the Authority by a labor organization alleging that 10 percent of the employees in an appropriate unit in an agency have membership in the labor organization, the Authority shall investigate the petition to determine its validity. Upon certification by the Authority of the validity of the petition, the agency shall have a duty to negotiate with the labor organization solely concerning the deduction of dues of the labor organization from the pay of the members of the labor organization who are employees in the unit and who make a voluntary allotment for such purpose.

(2)(A) The provisions of paragraph (1) of this subsection shall not apply in the case of any appropriate unit for which there is an exclusive representative.

(B) Any agreement under paragraph (1) of this subsection between a labor organization and an agency with respect to an appropriate unit shall be null and void upon the certification of an exclusive representative of the unit.

(Added Pub. L. 95–454, title VII, § 701, Oct. 13, 1978, 92 Stat. 1203.)

SECTION REFERRED TO IN OTHER SECTIONS

This section is referred to in title 2 section 1351.

§ 7116. Unfair labor practices

(a) For the purpose of this chapter, it shall be an unfair labor practice for an agency—

(1) to interfere with, restrain, or coerce any employee in the exercise by the employee of any right under this chapter;

(2) to encourage or discourage membership in any labor organization by discrimination in connection with hiring, tenure, promotion, or other conditions of employment;

(3) to sponsor, control, or otherwise assist any labor organization, other than to furnish, upon request, customary and routine services and facilities if the services and facilities are also furnished on an impartial basis to other labor organizations having equivalent status;

(4) to discipline or otherwise discriminate against an employee because the employee has filed a complaint, affidavit, or petition, or has given any information or testimony under this chapter;

(5) to refuse to consult or negotiate in good faith with a labor organization as required by this chapter;

(6) to fail or refuse to cooperate in impasse procedures and impasse decisions as required by this chapter;

(7) to enforce any rule or regulation (other than a rule or regulation implementing sec-

tion 2302 of this title) which is in conflict with any applicable collective bargaining agreement if the agreement was in effect before the date the rule or regulation was prescribed; or

(8) to otherwise fail or refuse to comply with any provision of this chapter.

(b) For the purpose of this chapter, it shall be an unfair labor practice for a labor organization—

(1) to interfere with, restrain, or coerce any employee in the exercise by the employee of any right under this chapter;

(2) to cause or attempt to cause an agency to discriminate against any employee in the exercise by the employee of any right under this chapter;

(3) to coerce, discipline, fine, or attempt to coerce a member of the labor organization as punishment, reprisal, or for the purpose of hindering or impeding the member's work performance or productivity as an employee or the discharge of the member's duties as an employee;

(4) to discriminate against an employee with regard to the terms or conditions of membership in the labor organization on the basis of race, color, creed, national origin, sex, age, preferential or nonpreferential civil service status, political affiliation, marital status, or handicapping condition;

(5) to refuse to consult or negotiate in good faith with an agency as required by this chapter;

(6) to fail or refuse to cooperate in impasse procedures and impasse decisions as required by this chapter;

(7)(A) to call, or participate in, a strike, work stoppage, or slowdown, or picketing of an agency in a labor-management dispute if such picketing interferes with an agency's operations, or

(B) to condone any activity described in subparagraph (A) of this paragraph by failing to take action to prevent or stop such activity; or

(8) to otherwise fail or refuse to comply with any provision of this chapter.

Nothing in paragraph (7) of this subsection shall result in any informational picketing which does not interfere with an agency's operations being considered as an unfair labor practice.

(c) For the purpose of this chapter it shall be an unfair labor practice for an exclusive representative to deny membership to any employee in the appropriate unit represented by such exclusive representative except for failure—

(1) to meet reasonable occupational standards uniformly required for admission, or

(2) to tender dues uniformly required as a condition of acquiring and retaining membership.

This subsection does not preclude any labor organization from enforcing discipline in accordance with procedures under its constitution or bylaws to the extent consistent with the provisions of this chapter.

(d) Issues which can properly be raised under an appeals procedure may not be raised as unfair labor practices prohibited under this section.

Except for matters wherein, under section 7121(e) and (f) of this title, an employee has an option of using the negotiated grievance procedure or an appeals procedure, issues which can be raised under a grievance procedure may, in the discretion of the aggrieved party, be raised under the grievance procedure or as an unfair labor practice under this section, but not under both procedures.

(e) The expression of any personal view, argument, opinion or the making of any statement which—

(1) publicizes the fact of a representational election and encourages employees to exercise their right to vote in such election,

(2) corrects the record with respect to any false or misleading statement made by any person, or

(3) informs employees of the Government's policy relating to labor-management relations and representation,

shall not, if the expression contains no threat of reprisal or force or promise of benefit or was not made under coercive conditions, (A) constitute an unfair labor practice under any provision of this chapter, or (B) constitute grounds for the setting aside of any election conducted under any provisions of this chapter.

(Added Pub. L. 95–454, title VII, § 701, Oct. 13, 1978, 92 Stat. 1204.)

PARTIAL SUSPENSION OF FEDERAL SERVICE LABOR-MANAGEMENT RELATIONS

Subsec. (a)(5) of this section suspended with respect to any matter proposed for bargaining which would substantially impair the implementation by the United States Forces, and subsec. (a)(7) of this section suspended with regard to any regulation governing the implementation by the United States Forces, of any treaty or agreement, including any minutes or understandings thereto, between the United States and the Government of the host nation, see section 1(b), (c) of Ex. Ord. No. 12391, Nov. 4, 1982, 47 F.R. 50457, set out as a note under section 7103 of this title.

SECTION REFERRED TO IN OTHER SECTIONS

This section is referred to in sections 5596, 7103, 7120 of this title; title 2 section 1351.

§ 7117. Duty to bargain in good faith; compelling need; duty to consult

(a)(1) Subject to paragraph (2) of this subsection, the duty to bargain in good faith shall, to the extent not inconsistent with any Federal law or any Government-wide rule or regulation, extend to matters which are the subject of any rule or regulation only if the rule or regulation is not a Government-wide rule or regulation.

(2) The duty to bargain in good faith shall, to the extent not inconsistent with Federal law or any Government-wide rule or regulation, extend to matters which are the subject of any agency rule or regulation referred to in paragraph (3) of this subsection only if the Authority has determined under subsection (b) of this section that no compelling need (as determined under regulations prescribed by the Authority) exists for the rule or regulation.

(3) Paragraph (2) of the subsection applies to any rule or regulation issued by any agency or issued by any primary national subdivision of

such agency, unless an exclusive representative represents an appropriate unit including not less than a majority of the employees in the issuing agency or primary national subdivision, as the case may be, to whom the rule or regulation is applicable.

(b)(1) In any case of collective bargaining in which an exclusive representative alleges that no compelling need exists for any rule or regulation referred to in subsection (a)(3) of this section which is then in effect and which governs any matter at issue in such collective bargaining, the Authority shall determine under paragraph (2) of this subsection, in accordance with regulations prescribed by the Authority, whether such a compelling need exists.

(2) For the purpose of this section, a compelling need shall be determined not to exist for any rule or regulation only if—

(A) the agency, or primary national subdivision, as the case may be, which issued the rule or regulation informs the Authority in writing that a compelling need for the rule or regulation does not exist; or

(B) the Authority determines that a compelling need for a rule or regulation does not exist.

(3) A hearing may be held, in the discretion of the Authority, before a determination is made under this subsection. If a hearing is held, it shall be expedited to the extent practicable and shall not include the General Counsel as a party.

(4) The agency, or primary national subdivision, as the case may be, which issued the rule or regulation shall be a necessary party at any hearing under this subsection.

(c)(1) Except in any case to which subsection (b) of this section applies, if an agency involved in collective bargaining with an exclusive representative alleges that the duty to bargain in good faith does not extend to any matter, the exclusive representative may appeal the allegation to the Authority in accordance with the provisions of this subsection.

(2) The exclusive representative may, on or before the 15th day after the date on which the agency first makes the allegation referred to in paragraph (1) of this subsection, institute an appeal under this subsection by—

(A) filing a petition with the Authority; and

(B) furnishing a copy of the petition to the head of the agency.

(3) On or before the 30th day after the date of the receipt by the head of the agency of the copy of the petition under paragraph (2)(B) of this subsection, the agency shall—

(A) file with the Authority a statement—

(i) withdrawing the allegation; or

(ii) setting forth in full its reasons supporting the allegation; and

(B) furnish a copy of such statement to the exclusive representative.

(4) On or before the 15th day after the date of the receipt by the exclusive representative of a copy of a statement under paragraph (3)(B) of this subsection, the exclusive representative shall file with the Authority its response to the statement.

(5) A hearing may be held in the discretion of the Authority, before a determination is made

under this subsection. If a hearing is held, it shall not include the General Counsel as a party.

(6) The Authority shall expedite proceedings under this subsection to the extent practicable and shall issue to the exclusive representative and to the agency a written decision on the allegation and specific reasons therefore at the earliest practicable date.

(d)(1) A labor organization which is the exclusive representative of a substantial number of employees, determined in accordance with criteria prescribed by the Authority, shall be granted consultation rights by any agency with respect to any Government-wide rule or regulation issued by the agency effecting any substantive change in any condition of employment. Such consultation rights shall terminate when the labor organization no longer meets the criteria prescribed by the Authority. Any issue relating to a labor organization's eligibility for, or continuation of, such consultation rights shall be subject to determination by the Authority.

(2) A labor organization having consultation rights under paragraph (1) of this subsection shall—

(A) be informed of any substantive change in conditions of employment proposed by the agency, and

(B) shall be permitted reasonable time to present its views and recommendations regarding the changes.

(3) If any views or recommendations are presented under paragraph (2) of this subsection to an agency by any labor organization—

(A) the agency shall consider the views or recommendations before taking final action on any matter with respect to which the views or recommendations are presented; and

(B) the agency shall provide the labor organization a written statement of the reasons for taking the final action.

(Added Pub. L. 95–454, title VII, § 701, Oct. 13, 1978, 92 Stat. 1205.)

PARTIAL SUSPENSION OF FEDERAL SERVICE LABOR-MANAGEMENT RELATIONS

Subsec. (b) of this section suspended with regard to any regulation governing the implementation by the United States Forces, and subsec. (c) of this section suspended with respect to any matter proposed for bargaining which would substantially impair the implementation by the United States Forces, of any treaty or agreement, including any minutes or understandings thereto, between the United States and the Government of the host nation, see section 1(b), (c) of Ex. Ord. No. 12391, Nov. 4, 1982, 47 F.R. 50457, set out as a note under section 7103 of this title.

SECTION REFERRED TO IN OTHER SECTIONS

This section is referred to in sections 5514, 7105 of this title; title 2 section 1351.

§ 7118. Prevention of unfair labor practices

(a)(1) If any agency or labor organization is charged by any person with having engaged in or engaging in an unfair labor practice, the General Counsel shall investigate the charge and may issue and cause to be served upon the agency or labor organization a complaint. In any case in which the General Counsel does not issue a complaint because the charge fails to state an unfair labor practice, the General Counsel shall provide the person making the charge a written statement of the reasons for not issuing a complaint.

(2) Any complaint under paragraph (1) of this subsection shall contain a notice—

(A) of the charge;

(B) that a hearing will be held before the Authority (or any member thereof or before an individual employed by the authority and designated for such purpose); and

(C) of the time and place fixed for the hearing.

(3) The labor organization or agency involved shall have the right to file an answer to the original and any amended complaint and to appear in person or otherwise and give testimony at the time and place fixed in the complaint for the hearing.

(4)(A) Except as provided in subparagraph (B) of this paragraph, no complaint shall be issued based on any alleged unfair labor practice which occurred more than 6 months before the filing of the charge with the Authority.

(B) If the General Counsel determines that the person filing any charge was prevented from filing the charge during the 6-month period referred to in subparagraph (A) of this paragraph by reason of—

(i) any failure of the agency or labor organization against which the charge is made to perform a duty owed to the person, or

(ii) any concealment which prevented discovery of the alleged unfair labor practice during the 6-month period,

the General Counsel may issue a complaint based on the charge if the charge was filed during the 6-month period beginning on the day of the discovery by the person of the alleged unfair labor practice.

(5) The General Counsel may prescribe regulations providing for informal methods by which the alleged unfair labor practice may be resolved prior to the issuance of a complaint.

(6) The Authority (or any member thereof or any individual employed by the Authority and designated for such purpose) shall conduct a hearing on the complaint not earlier than 5 days after the date on which the complaint is served. In the discretion of the individual or individuals conducting the hearing, any person involved may be allowed to intervene in the hearing and to present testimony. Any such hearing shall, to the extent practicable, be conducted in accordance with the provisions of subchapter II of chapter 5 of this title, except that the parties shall not be bound by rules of evidence, whether statutory, common law, or adopted by a court. A transcript shall be kept of the hearing. After such a hearing the Authority, in its discretion, may upon notice receive further evidence or hear argument.

(7) If the Authority (or any member thereof or any individual employed by the Authority and designated for such purpose) determines after any hearing on a complaint under paragraph (5) of this subsection that the preponderance of the evidence received demonstrates that the agency or labor organization named in the complaint has engaged in or is engaging in an unfair labor practice, then the individual or individuals conducting the hearing shall state in writing their findings of fact and shall issue and cause to be served on the agency or labor organization an order—

(A) to cease and desist from any such unfair labor practice in which the agency or labor organization is engaged;

(B) requiring the parties to renegotiate a collective bargaining agreement in accordance with the order of the Authority and requiring that the agreement, as amended, be given retroactive effect;

(C) requiring reinstatement of an employee with backpay in accordance with section 5596 of this title; or

(D) including any combination of the actions described in subparagraphs (A) through (C) of this paragraph or such other action as will carry out the purpose of this chapter.

If any such order requires reinstatement of an employee with backpay, backpay may be required of the agency (as provided in section 5596 of this title) or of the labor organization, as the case may be, which is found to have engaged in the unfair labor practice involved.

(8) If the individual or individuals conducting the hearing determine that the preponderance of the evidence received fails to demonstrate that the agency or labor organization named in the complaint has engaged in or is engaging in an unfair labor practice, the individual or individuals shall state in writing their findings of fact and shall issue an order dismissing the complaint.

(b) In connection with any matter before the Authority in any proceeding under this section, the Authority may request, in accordance with the provisions of section 7105(i) of this title, from the Director of the Office of Personnel Management an advisory opinion concerning the proper interpretation of rules, regulations, or other policy directives issued by the Office of Personnel Management.

(Added Pub. L. 95–454, title VII, § 701, Oct. 13, 1978, 92 Stat. 1207.)

SECTION REFERRED TO IN OTHER SECTIONS

This section is referred to in sections 7105, 7123 of this title; title 2 section 1351; title 3 section 431.

§ 7119. Negotiation impasses; Federal Service Impasses Panel

(a) The Federal Mediation and Conciliation Service shall provide services and assistance to agencies and exclusive representatives in the resolution of negotiation impasses. The Service shall determine under what circumstances and in what manner it shall provide services and assistance.

(b) If voluntary arrangements, including the services of the Federal Mediation and Conciliation Service or any other third-party mediation, fail to resolve a negotiation impasse—

(1) either party may request the Federal Service Impasses Panel to consider the matter, or

(2) the parties may agree to adopt a procedure for binding arbitration of the negotiation

impasse, but only if the procedure is approved by the Panel.

(c)(1) The Federal Service Impasses Panel is an entity within the Authority, the function of which is to provide assistance in resolving negotiation impasses between agencies and exclusive representatives.

(2) The Panel shall be composed of a Chairman and at least six other members, who shall be appointed by the President, solely on the basis of fitness to perform the duties and functions involved, from among individuals who are familiar with Government operations and knowledgeable in labor-management relations.

(3) Of the original members of the Panel, 2 members shall be appointed for a term of 1 year, 2 members shall be appointed for a term of 3 years, and the Chairman and the remaining members shall be appointed for a term of 5 years. Thereafter each member shall be appointed for a term of 5 years, except that an individual chosen to fill a vacancy shall be appointed for the unexpired term of the member replaced. Any member of the Panel may be removed by the President.

(4) The Panel may appoint an Executive Director and any other individuals it may from time to time find necessary for the proper performance of its duties. Each member of the Panel who is not an employee (as defined in section 2105 of this title) is entitled to pay at a rate equal to the daily equivalent of the maximum annual rate of basic pay then currently paid under the General Schedule for each day he is engaged in the performance of official business of the Panel, including travel time, and is entitled to travel expenses as provided under section 5703 of this title.

(5)(A) The Panel or its designee shall promptly investigate any impasse presented to it under subsection (b) of this section. The Panel shall consider the impasse and shall either—

(i) recommend to the parties procedures for the resolution of the impasse; or

(ii) assist the parties in resolving the impasse through whatever methods and procedures, including factfinding and recommendations, it may consider appropriate to accomplish the purpose of this section.

(B) If the parties do not arrive at a settlement after assistance by the Panel under subparagraph (A) of this paragraph, the Panel may—

(i) hold hearings;

(ii) administer oaths, take the testimony or deposition of any person under oath, and issue subpenas as provided in section 7132 of this title; and

(iii) take whatever action is necessary and not inconsistent with this chapter to resolve the impasse.

(C) Notice of any final action of the Panel under this section shall be promptly served upon the parties, and the action shall be binding on such parties during the term of the agreement, unless the parties agree otherwise.

(Added Pub. L. 95–454, title VII, §701, Oct. 13, 1978, 92 Stat. 1208.)

REFERENCES IN TEXT

The General Schedule, referred to in subsec. (c)(4), is set out under section 5332 of this title.

SECTION REFERRED TO IN OTHER SECTIONS

This section is referred to in sections 7103, 7114, 7133, 9501 of this title; title 2 section 1351; title 22 section 4110.

§ 7120. Standards of conduct for labor organizations

(a) An agency shall only accord recognition to a labor organization that is free from corrupt influences and influences opposed to basic democratic principles. Except as provided in subsection (b) of this section, an organization is not required to prove that it is free from such influences if it is subject to governing requirements adopted by the organization or by a national or international labor organization or federation of labor organizations with which it is affiliated, or in which it participates, containing explicit and detailed provisions to which it subscribes calling for—

(1) the maintenance of democratic procedures and practices including provisions for periodic elections to be conducted subject to recognized safeguards and provisions defining and securing the right of individual members to participate in the affairs of the organization, to receive fair and equal treatment under the governing rules of the organization, and to receive fair process in disciplinary proceedings;

(2) the exclusion from office in the organization of persons affiliated with communist or other totalitarian movements and persons identified with corrupt influences;

(3) the prohibition of business or financial interests on the part of organization officers and agents which conflict with their duty to the organization and its members; and

(4) the maintenance of fiscal integrity in the conduct of the affairs of the organization, including provisions for accounting and financial controls and regular financial reports or summaries to be made available to members.

(b) Notwithstanding the fact that a labor organization has adopted or subscribed to standards of conduct as provided in subsection (a) of this section, the organization is required to furnish evidence of its freedom from corrupt influences or influences opposed to basic democratic principles if there is reasonable cause to believe that—

(1) the organization has been suspended or expelled from, or is subject to other sanction, by a parent labor organization, or federation of organizations with which it had been affiliated, because it has demonstrated an unwillingness or inability to comply with governing requirements comparable in purpose to those required by subsection (a) of this section; or

(2) the organization is in fact subject to influences that would preclude recognition under this chapter.

(c) A labor organization which has or seeks recognition as a representative of employees under this chapter shall file financial and other reports with the Assistant Secretary of Labor for Labor Management Relations, provide for bonding of officials and employees of the organization, and comply with trusteeship and election standards.

(d) The Assistant Secretary shall prescribe such regulations as are necessary to carry out the purposes of this section. Such regulations shall conform generally to the principles applied to labor organizations in the private sector. Complaints of violations of this section shall be filed with the Assistant Secretary. In any matter arising under this section, the Assistant Secretary may require a labor organization to cease and desist from violations of this section and require it to take such actions as he considers appropriate to carry out the policies of this section.

(e) This chapter does not authorize participation in the management of a labor organization or acting as a representative of a labor organization by a management official, a supervisor, or a confidential employee, except as specifically provided in this chapter, or by an employee if the participation or activity would result in a conflict or apparent conflict of interest or would otherwise be incompatible with law or with the official duties of the employee.

(f) In the case of any labor organization which by omission or commission has willfully and intentionally, with regard to any strike, work stoppage, or slowdown, violated section 7116(b)(7) of this title, the Authority shall, upon an appropriate finding by the Authority of such violation—

(1) revoke the exclusive recognition status of the labor organization, which shall then immediately cease to be legally entitled and obligated to represent employees in the unit; or

(2) take any other appropriate disciplinary action.

(Added Pub. L. 95–454, title VII, § 701, Oct. 13, 1978, 92 Stat. 1210.)

SECTION REFERRED TO IN OTHER SECTIONS

This section is referred to in title 2 section 1351; title 7 section 7011.

SUBCHAPTER III—GRIEVANCES, APPEALS, AND REVIEW

AMENDMENTS

1979—Pub. L. 96–54, § 2(a)(42), Aug. 14, 1979, 93 Stat. 383, inserted ", APPEALS, AND REVIEW" after "GRIEVANCES".

§ 7121. Grievance procedures

(a)(1) Except as provided in paragraph (2) of this subsection, any collective bargaining agreement shall provide procedures for the settlement of grievances, including questions of arbitrability. Except as provided in subsections (d), (e), and (g) of this section, the procedures shall be the exclusive administrative procedures for resolving grievances which fall within its coverage.

(2) Any collective bargaining agreement may exclude any matter from the application of the grievance procedures which are provided for in the agreement.

(b)(1) Any negotiated grievance procedure referred to in subsection (a) of this section shall—

(A) be fair and simple,

(B) provide for expeditious processing, and

(C) include procedures that—

(i) assure an exclusive representative the right, in its own behalf or on behalf of any employee in the unit represented by the exclusive representative, to present and process grievances;

(ii) assure such an employee the right to present a grievance on the employee's own behalf, and assure the exclusive representative the right to be present during the grievance proceeding; and

(iii) provide that any grievance not satisfactorily settled under the negotiated grievance procedure shall be subject to binding arbitration which may be invoked by either the exclusive representative or the agency.

(2)(A) The provisions of a negotiated grievance procedure providing for binding arbitration in accordance with paragraph (1)(C)(iii) shall, if or to the extent that an alleged prohibited personnel practice is involved, allow the arbitrator to order—

(i) a stay of any personnel action in a manner similar to the manner described in section 1221(c) with respect to the Merit Systems Protection Board; and

(ii) the taking, by an agency, of any disciplinary action identified under section 1215(a)(3) that is otherwise within the authority of such agency to take.

(B) Any employee who is the subject of any disciplinary action ordered under subparagraph (A)(ii) may appeal such action to the same extent and in the same manner as if the agency had taken the disciplinary action absent arbitration.

(c) The preceding subsections of this section shall not apply with respect to any grievance concerning—

(1) any claimed violation of subchapter III of chapter 73 of this title (relating to prohibited political activities);

(2) retirement, life insurance, or health insurance;

(3) a suspension or removal under section 7532 of this title;

(4) any examination, certification, or appointment; or

(5) the classification of any position which does not result in the reduction in grade or pay of an employee.

(d) An aggrieved employee affected by a prohibited personnel practice under section 2302(b)(1) of this title which also falls under the coverage of the negotiated grievance procedure may raise the matter under a statutory procedure or the negotiated procedure, but not both. An employee shall be deemed to have exercised his option under this subsection to raise the matter under either a statutory procedure or the negotiated procedure at such time as the employee timely initiates an action under the applicable statutory procedure or timely files a grievance in writing, in accordance with the provisions of the parties' negotiated procedure, whichever event occurs first. Selection of the negotiated procedure in no manner prejudices the right of an aggrieved employee to request the Merit Systems Protection Board to review the final decision pursuant to section 7702 of this title in the case of any personnel action that could have been appealed to the Board, or, where applicable, to request the Equal Employment

Opportunity Commission to review a final decision in any other matter involving a complaint of discrimination of the type prohibited by any law administered by the Equal Employment Opportunity Commission.

(e)(1) Matters covered under sections 4303 and 7512 of this title which also fall within the coverage of the negotiated grievance procedure may, in the discretion of the aggrieved employee, be raised either under the appellate procedures of section 7701 of this title or under the negotiated grievance procedure, but not both. Similar matters which arise under other personnel systems applicable to employees covered by this chapter may, in the discretion of the aggrieved employee, be raised either under the appellate procedures, if any, applicable to those matters, or under the negotiated grievance procedure, but not both. An employee shall be deemed to have exercised his option under this subsection to raise a matter either under the applicable appellate procedures or under the negotiated grievance procedure at such time as the employee timely files a notice of appeal under the applicable appellate procedures or timely files a grievance in writing in accordance with the provisions of the parties' negotiated grievance procedure, whichever event occurs first.

(2) In matters covered under sections 4303 and 7512 of this title which have been raised under the negotiated grievance procedure in accordance with this section, an arbitrator shall be governed by section 7701(c)(1) of this title, as applicable.

(f) In matters covered under sections 4303 and 7512 of this title which have been raised under the negotiated grievance procedure in accordance with this section, section 7703 of this title pertaining to judicial review shall apply to the award of an arbitrator in the same manner and under the same conditions as if the matter had been decided by the Board. In matters similar to those covered under sections 4303 and 7512 of this title which arise under other personnel systems and which an aggrieved employee has raised under the negotiated grievance procedure, judicial review of an arbitrator's award may be obtained in the same manner and on the same basis as could be obtained of a final decision in such matters raised under applicable appellate procedures.

(g)(1) This subsection applies with respect to a prohibited personnel practice other than a prohibited personnel practice to which subsection (d) applies.

(2) An aggrieved employee affected by a prohibited personnel practice described in paragraph (1) may elect not more than one of the remedies described in paragraph (3) with respect thereto. For purposes of the preceding sentence, a determination as to whether a particular remedy has been elected shall be made as set forth under paragraph (4).

(3) The remedies described in this paragraph are as follows:

(A) An appeal to the Merit Systems Protection Board under section 7701.

(B) A negotiated grievance procedure under this section.

(C) Procedures for seeking corrective action under subchapters II and III of chapter 12.

(4) For the purpose of this subsection, a person shall be considered to have elected—

(A) the remedy described in paragraph (3)(A) if such person has timely filed a notice of appeal under the applicable appellate procedures;

(B) the remedy described in paragraph (3)(B) if such person has timely filed a grievance in writing, in accordance with the provisions of the parties' negotiated procedure; or

(C) the remedy described in paragraph (3)(C) if such person has sought corrective action from the Office of Special Counsel by making an allegation under section 1214(a)(1).

(h) Settlements and awards under this chapter shall be subject to the limitations in section 5596(b)(4) of this title.

(Added Pub. L. 95–454, title VII, §701, Oct. 13, 1978, 92 Stat. 1211; amended Pub. L. 103–424, §9, Oct. 29, 1994, 108 Stat. 4365; Pub. L. 105–261, div. A, title XI, §1104(b), Oct. 17, 1998, 112 Stat. 2142.)

AMENDMENTS

1998—Subsec. (h). Pub. L. 105–261 added subsec. (h).

1994—Subsec. (a)(1). Pub. L. 103–424, §9(c), substituted "(d), (e), and (g)" for "(d) and (e)" and inserted "administrative" after "exclusive".

Subsec. (b). Pub. L. 103–424, §9(a), designated existing provisions as par. (1) and redesignated former pars. (1) to (3) as subpars. (A) to (C), respectively, and subpars. (A) to (C) of former par. (3) as cls. (i) to (iii) of subpar. (a)(1)(C), respectively, and added par. (2).

Subsec. (g). Pub. L. 103–424, §9(b), added subsec. (g).

PARTIAL SUSPENSION OF FEDERAL SERVICE LABOR-MANAGEMENT RELATIONS

Subsec. (b)(3)(C) of this section suspended with respect to any grievance involving the implementation by the United States Forces of any treaty or agreement, including any minutes or understandings thereto, between the United States and the Government of the host nation, see section 1(d) of Ex. Ord. No. 12391, Nov. 4, 1982, 47 F.R. 50457, set out as a note under section 7103 of this title.

SECTION REFERRED TO IN OTHER SECTIONS

This section is referred to in sections 7116, 7122 of this title; title 2 section 1351; title 22 section 3701.

§ 7122. Exceptions to arbitral awards

(a) Either party to arbitration under this chapter may file with the Authority an exception to any arbitrator's award pursuant to the arbitration (other than an award relating to a matter described in section 7121(f) of this title). If upon review the Authority finds that the award is deficient—

(1) because it is contrary to any law, rule, or regulation; or

(2) on other grounds similar to those applied by Federal courts in private sector labor-management relations;

the Authority may take such action and make such recommendations concerning the award as it considers necessary, consistent with applicable laws, rules, or regulations.

(b) If no exception to an arbitrator's award is filed under subsection (a) of this section during the 30-day period beginning on the date the award is served on the party, the award shall be final and binding. An agency shall take the actions required by an arbitrator's final award. The award may include the payment of backpay (as provided in section 5596 of this title).

(Added Pub. L. 95–454, title VII, § 701, Oct. 13, 1978, 92 Stat. 1212; amended Pub. L. 98–224, § 4, Mar. 2, 1984, 98 Stat. 48.)

AMENDMENTS

1984—Subsec. (b). Pub. L. 98–224 amended subsec. (b) generally, substituting "beginning on the date the award is served on the party" for "beginning on the date of such award".

SECTION REFERRED TO IN OTHER SECTIONS

This section is referred to in sections 7105, 7123 of this title; title 2 section 1351.

§ 7123. Judicial review; enforcement

(a) Any person aggrieved by any final order of the Authority other than an order under—

(1) section 7122 of this title (involving an award by an arbitrator), unless the order involves an unfair labor practice under section 7118 of this title, or

(2) section 7112 of this title (involving an appropriate unit determination),

may, during the 60-day period beginning on the date on which the order was issued, institute an action for judicial review of the Authority's order in the United States court of appeals in the circuit in which the person resides or transacts business or in the United States Court of Appeals for the District of Columbia.

(b) The Authority may petition any appropriate United States court of appeals for the enforcement of any order of the Authority and for appropriate temporary relief or restraining order.

(c) Upon the filing of a petition under subsection (a) of this section for judicial review or under subsection (b) of this section for enforcement, the Authority shall file in the court the record in the proceedings, as provided in section 2112 of title 28. Upon the filing of the petition, the court shall cause notice thereof to be served to the parties involved, and thereupon shall have jurisdiction of the proceeding and of the question determined therein and may grant any temporary relief (including a temporary restraining order) it considers just and proper, and may make and enter a decree affirming and enforcing, modifying and enforcing as so modified, or setting aside in whole or in part the order of the Authority. The filing of a petition under subsection (a) or (b) of this section shall not operate as a stay of the Authority's order unless the court specifically orders the stay. Review of the Authority's order shall be on the record in accordance with section 706 of this title. No objection that has not been urged before the Authority, or its designee, shall be considered by the court, unless the failure or neglect to urge the objection is excused because of extraordinary circumstances. The findings of the Authority with respect to questions of fact, if supported by substantial evidence on the record considered as a whole, shall be conclusive. If any person applies to the court for leave to adduce additional evidence and shows to the satisfaction of the court that the additional evidence is material and that there were reasonable grounds for the failure to adduce the evidence in the hearing before the Authority, or its designee, the court may order the additional evidence to be taken before the Authority, or its designee, and to be made a part of the record. The Authority may modify its findings as to the facts, or make new findings by reason of additional evidence so taken and filed. The Authority shall file its modified or new findings, which, with respect to questions of fact, if supported by substantial evidence on the record considered as a whole, shall be conclusive. The Authority shall file its recommendations, if any, for the modification or setting aside of its original order. Upon the filing of the record with the court, the jurisdiction of the court shall be exclusive and its judgment and decree shall be final, except that the judgment and decree shall be subject to review by the Supreme Court of the United States upon writ of certiorari or certification as provided in section 1254 of title 28.

(d) The Authority may, upon issuance of a complaint as provided in section 7118 of this title charging that any person has engaged in or is engaging in an unfair labor practice, petition any United States district court within any district in which the unfair labor practice in question is alleged to have occurred or in which such person resides or transacts business for appropriate temporary relief (including a restraining order). Upon the filing of the petition, the court shall cause notice thereof to be served upon the person, and thereupon shall have jurisdiction to grant any temporary relief (including a temporary restraining order) it considers just and proper. A court shall not grant any temporary relief under this section if it would interfere with the ability of the agency to carry out its essential functions or if the Authority fails to establish probable cause that an unfair labor practice is being committed.

(Added Pub. L. 95–454, title VII, § 701, Oct. 13, 1978, 92 Stat. 1213.)

PARTIAL SUSPENSION OF FEDERAL SERVICE LABOR-MANAGEMENT RELATIONS

Subsec. (b) of this section suspended with respect to any matter which substantially impairs the implementation by the United States Forces of any treaty or agreement, including any minutes or understandings thereto, between the United States and the Government of the host nation, see section 1(a) of Ex. Ord. No. 12391, Nov. 4, 1982, 47 F.R. 50457, set out as a note under section 7103 of this title.

SECTION REFERRED TO IN OTHER SECTIONS

This section is referred to in title 2 section 1351; title 3 section 431; title 22 section 4109; title 28 section 1296; title 38 section 7422.

SUBCHAPTER IV—ADMINISTRATIVE AND OTHER PROVISIONS

§ 7131. Official time

(a) Any employee representing an exclusive representative in the negotiation of a collective bargaining agreement under this chapter shall be authorized official time for such purposes, including attendance at impasse proceeding, during the time the employee otherwise would be in a duty status. The number of employees for whom official time is authorized under this subsection shall not exceed the number of individuals designated as representing the agency for such purposes.

(b) Any activities performed by any employee relating to the internal business of a labor organization (including the solicitation of membership, elections of labor organization officials, and collection of dues) shall be performed during the time the employee is in a non-duty status.

(c) Except as provided in subsection (a) of this section, the Authority shall determine whether any employee participating for, or on behalf of, a labor organization in any phase of proceedings before the Authority shall be authorized official time for such purpose during the time the employee otherwise would be in a duty status.

(d) Except as provided in the preceding subsections of this section—

(1) any employee representing an exclusive representative, or

(2) in connection with any other matter covered by this chapter, any employee in an appropriate unit represented by an exclusive representative,

shall be granted official time in any amount the agency and the exclusive representative involved agree to be reasonable, necessary, and in the public interest.

(Added Pub. L. 95–454, title VII, § 701, Oct. 13, 1978, 92 Stat. 1214.)

<small>SECTION REFERRED TO IN OTHER SECTIONS</small>

This section is referred to in title 2 section 1351.

§ 7132. Subpenas

(a) Any member of the Authority, the General Counsel, or the Panel, any administrative law judge appointed by the Authority under section 3105 of this title, and any employee of the Authority designated by the Authority may—

(1) issue subpenas requiring the attendance and testimony of witnesses and the production of documentary or other evidence from any place in the United States; and

(2) administer oaths, take or order the taking of depositions, order responses to written interrogatories, examine witnesses, and receive evidence.

No subpena shall be issued under this section which requires the disclosure of intra-management guidance, advice, counsel, or training within an agency or between an agency and the Office of Personnel Management.

(b) In the case of contumacy or failure to obey a subpena issued under subsection (a)(1) of this section, the United States district court for the judicial district in which the person to whom the subpena is addressed resides or is served may issue an order requiring such person to appear at any designated place to testify or to produce documentary or other evidence. Any failure to obey the order of the court may be punished by the court as a contempt thereof.

(c) Witnesses (whether appearing voluntarily or under subpena) shall be paid the same fee and mileage allowances which are paid subpenaed witnesses in the courts of the United States.

(Added Pub. L. 95–454, title VII, § 701, Oct. 13, 1978, 92 Stat. 1214.)

<small>SECTION REFERRED TO IN OTHER SECTIONS</small>

This section is referred to in sections 7105, 7119 of this title; title 22 section 4110.

§ 7133. Compilation and publication of data

(a) The Authority shall maintain a file of its proceedings and copies of all available agreements and arbitration decisions, and shall publish the texts of its decisions and the actions taken by the Panel under section 7119 of this title.

(b) All files maintained under subsection (a) of this section shall be open to inspection and reproduction in accordance with the provisions of sections 552 and 552a of this title.

(Added Pub. L. 95–454, title VII, § 701, Oct. 13, 1978, 92 Stat. 1215.)

§ 7134. Regulations

The Authority, the General Counsel, the Federal Mediation and Conciliation Service, the Assistant Secretary of Labor for Labor Management Relations, and the Panel shall each prescribe rules and regulations to carry out the provisions of this chapter applicable to each of them, respectively. Provisions of subchapter II of chapter 5 of this title shall be applicable to the issuance, revision, or repeal of any such rule or regulation.

(Added Pub. L. 95–454, title VII, § 701, Oct. 13, 1978, 92 Stat. 1215.)

§ 7135. Continuation of existing laws, recognitions, agreements, and procedures

(a) Nothing contained in this chapter shall preclude—

(1) the renewal or continuation of an exclusive recognition, certification of an exclusive representative, or a lawful agreement between an agency and an exclusive representative of its employees, which is entered into before the effective date of this chapter; or

(2) the renewal, continuation, or initial according of recognition for units of management officials or supervisors represented by labor organizations which historically or traditionally represent management officials or supervisors in private industry and which hold exclusive recognition for units of such officials or supervisors in any agency on the effective date of this chapter.

(b) Policies, regulations, and procedures established under and decisions issued under Executive Orders 11491, 11616, 11636, 11787, and 11838, or under any other Executive order, as in effect on the effective date of this chapter, shall remain in full force and effect until revised or revoked by the President, or unless superseded by specific provisions of this chapter or by regulations or decisions issued pursuant to this chapter.

(Added Pub. L. 95–454, title VII, § 701, Oct. 13, 1978, 92 Stat. 1215.)

<small>REFERENCES IN TEXT</small>

For the effective date of this chapter, referred to in text, as 90 days after the date of the enactment of Pub. L. 95–454, which was approved Oct. 13, 1978, see section 907 of Pub. L. 95–454, set out as an Effective Date of 1978 Amendment note under section 1101 of this title.

Executive Orders 11491, 11616, 11636, and 11838, referred to in subsec. (b), are set out as notes under section 7101 of this title.

Executive Order 11787, referred to in subsec. (b), which was set out as a note under section 7701 of this title, was revoked by Ex. Ord. No. 12553, Feb. 25, 1986, 51 F.R. 7237.

SECTION REFERRED TO IN OTHER SECTIONS

This section is referred to in section 7112 of this title.

[§§ 7151 to 7154. Transferred]

CODIFICATION

Section 7151, Pub. L. 89–554, Sept. 6, 1966, 80 Stat. 523, which related to antidiscrimination policy of United States with respect to employment, was renumbered section 7201 of this title by Pub. L. 95–454, title VII, § 703(a)(1), Oct. 13, 1978, 92 Stat. 1216.

Section 7152, Pub. L. 89–554, Sept. 6, 1966, 80 Stat. 523; Pub. L. 92–187, § 3, Dec. 15, 1971, 85 Stat. 644, which related to prohibition respecting employment discrimination because of marital status, was renumbered section 7202 of this title by Pub. L. 95–454, title VII, § 703(a)(1), Oct. 13, 1978, 92 Stat. 1216.

Section 7153, Pub. L. 89–554, Sept. 6, 1966, 80 Stat. 523, which related to prohibition respecting employment discrimination because of physical handicap, was renumbered section 7203 of this title by Pub. L. 95–454, title VII, 703(a)(1), Oct. 13, 1978, 92 Stat. 1216.

Section 7154, Pub. L. 89–554, Sept. 6, 1966, 80 Stat. 523; Pub. L. 90–83, § 1(44), Sept. 11, 1967, 81 Stat. 208; Pub. L. 92–392, § 8, Aug. 19, 1972, 86 Stat. 573, which related to prohibition respecting discrimination because of race, color, creed, sex, or marital status in administration of chapter 51, subchapter III and IV of chapter 53, and sections 305 and 3324 of this title, was renumbered section 7204 of this title by Pub. L. 95–454, title VII, § 703(a)(1), Oct. 13, 1978, 92 Stat. 1216.

CHAPTER 72—ANTIDISCRIMINATION; RIGHT TO PETITION CONGRESS

SUBCHAPTER I—ANTIDISCRIMINATION IN EMPLOYMENT

AMENDMENTS

1978—Pub. L. 95–454, title VII, § 703(a)(2), Oct. 13, 1978, 92 Stat. 1217, struck out heading "SUBCHAPTER II—ANTIDISCRIMINATION IN EMPLOYMENT" and substituted therefor a chapter heading "CHAPTER 72—ANTIDISCRIMINATION; RIGHT TO PETITION CONGRESS" together with the analysis of chapter 72 containing subchapters I, consisting of items 7201 to 7204, and subchapter II, consisting of item 7211.

CHAPTER REFERRED TO IN OTHER SECTIONS

This chapter is referred to in title 39 section 410.

SUBCHAPTER I—ANTIDISCRIMINATION IN EMPLOYMENT

AMENDMENTS

1979—Pub. L. 96–54, § 2(a)(43), Aug. 14, 1979, 93 Stat. 383, added heading for subchapter I.

§ 7201. Antidiscrimination policy; minority recruitment program

(a) For the purpose of this section—

(1) "underrepresentation" means a situation in which the number of members of a minority group designation (determined by the Equal Employment Opportunity Commission in consultation with the Office of Personnel Management, on the basis of the policy set forth in subsection (b) of this section) within a category of civil service employment constitutes a lower percentage of the total number of employees within the employment category than the percentage that the minority constituted within the labor force of the United States, as determined under the most recent decennial or mid-decade census, or current population survey, under title 13, and

(2) "category of civil service employment" means—

(A) each grade of the General Schedule described in section 5104 of this title;

(B) each position subject to subchapter IV of chapter 53 of this title;

(C) such occupational, professional, or other groupings (including occupational series) within the categories established under subparagraphs (A) and (B) of this paragraph as the Office determines appropriate.

(b) It is the policy of the United States to insure equal employment opportunities for employees without discrimination because of race, color, religion, sex, or national origin. The President shall use his existing authority to carry out this policy.

(c) Not later than 180 days after the date of the enactment of the Civil Service Reform Act of 1978, the Office of Personnel Management shall, by regulation, implement a minority recruitment program which shall provide, to the maximum extent practicable—

(1) that each Executive agency conduct a continuing program for the recruitment of members of minorities for positions in the agency to carry out the policy set forth in subsection (b) in a manner designed to eliminate underrepresentation of minorities in the various categories of civil service employment within the Federal service, with special efforts directed at recruiting in minority communities, in educational institutions, and from other sources from which minorities can be recruited; and

(2) that the Office conduct a continuing program of—

(A) assistance to agencies in carrying out programs under paragraph (1) of this subsection, and

(B) evaluation and oversight and such recruitment programs to determine their effectiveness in eliminating such minority underrepresentation.

(d) Not later than 60 days after the date of enactment of the Civil Service Reform Act of 1978, the Equal Employment Opportunity Commission shall—

(1) establish the guidelines proposed to be used in carrying out the program required under subsection (c) of this section; and

(2) make determinations of underrepresentation which are proposed to be used initially under such program; and

(3) transmit to the Executive agencies involved, to the Office of Personnel Management, and to the Congress the determinations made under paragraph (2) of this subsection.

(e) Not later than January 31 of each year, the Office shall prepare and transmit to each House of the Congress a report on the activities of the Office and of Executive agencies under subsection (c) of this section, including the affirmative action plans submitted under section 717 of the Civil Rights Act of 1964 (42 U.S.C. 2000e–16), the personnel data file maintained by the Office of Personnel Management, and any other data necessary to evaluate the effectiveness of the program for each category of civil service employment and for each minority group designation, for the preceding fiscal year, together with recommendations for administrative or legislative action the Office considers appropriate.

(Pub. L. 89–554, Sept. 6, 1966, 80 Stat. 523, §7151; renumbered §7201 and amended Pub. L. 95–454, title III, §310, title VII, §703(a)(1), Oct. 13, 1978, 92 Stat. 1152, 1216.)

HISTORICAL AND REVISION NOTES

Derivation	U.S. Code	Revised Statutes and Statutes at Large
....	42 U.S.C. 2000e(b) (2d proviso).	July 2, 1964, Pub. L. 88–352, §701(b) (2d proviso), 78 Stat. 254.

The word "Federal" is omitted as unnecessary in view of the definition of "employee" in section 2105.

Standard changes are made to conform with the definitions applicable and the style of this title as outlined in the preface to the report.

REFERENCES IN TEXT

The date of the enactment of the Civil Service Reform Act of 1978, referred to in subsecs. (c) and (d), is the date of the enactment of Pub. L. 95–454, which was approved Oct. 13, 1978.

AMENDMENTS

1978—Pub. L. 95–454, §703(a)(1), renumbered section 7151 of this title as this section.

Pub. L. 95–454, §310(1), substituted "Antidiscrimination policy; minority recruitment program" for "Policy" in section catchline.

Subsecs. (a) to (e). Pub. L. 95–454, §310(2)–(4), added subsec. (a), designated existing provisions as subsec. (b), and added subsecs. (c) to (e).

EFFECTIVE DATE OF 1978 AMENDMENT

Amendment by section 310 of Pub. L. 95–454 effective 90 days after Oct. 13, 1978, see section 907 of Pub. L. 95–454, set out as a note under section 1101 of this title.

TERMINATION OF REPORTING REQUIREMENTS

For termination, effective May 15, 2000, of reporting provisions in subsec. (e) of this section, see section 3003 of Pub. L. 104–66, as amended, set out as a note under section 1113 of Title 31, Money and Finance, and page 187 of House Document No. 103–7.

DISCRIMINATION PROHIBITED IN EMPLOYMENT OF CIVILIAN PERSONNEL AT FACILITIES OPERATED BY THE DEPARTMENT OF DEFENSE IN FOREIGN COUNTRIES

Pub. L. 92–129, title I, §106, Sept. 28, 1971, 85 Stat. 355, provided that: "Unless prohibited by treaty, no person shall be discriminated against by the Department of Defense or by any officer or employee thereof, in the employment of civilian personnel at any facility or installation operated by the Department of Defense in any foreign country because such person is a citizen of the United States or is a dependent of a member of the Armed Forces of the United States. As used in this section, the term 'facility or installation operated by the Department of Defense' shall include, but shall not be limited to, any officer's club, non-commissioned officers' club, post exchange, or commissary store."

SECTION REFERRED TO IN OTHER SECTIONS

This section is referred to in title 22 sections 3905, 3922a; title 31 section 732.

§ 7202. Marital status

(a) The President may prescribe rules which shall prohibit, as nearly as conditions of good administration warrant, discrimination because of marital status in an Executive agency or in the competitive service.

(b) Regulations prescribed under any provision of this title, or under any other provision of law, granting benefits to employees, shall provide the same benefits for a married female employee and her spouse and children as are provided for a married male employee and his spouse and children.

(c) Notwithstanding any other provision of law, any provision of law providing a benefit to a male Federal employee or to his spouse or family shall be deemed to provide the same benefit to a female Federal employee or to her spouse or family.

(Pub. L. 89–554, Sept. 6, 1966, 80 Stat. 523, §7152; Pub. L. 92–187, §3, Dec. 15, 1971, 85 Stat. 644; renumbered §7202, Pub. L. 95–454, title VII, §703(a)(1), Oct. 13, 1978, 92 Stat. 1216.)

HISTORICAL AND REVISION NOTES

Derivation	U.S. Code	Revised Statutes and Statutes at Large
....	5 U.S.C. 633(2)6 (less 1st sentence).	July 26, 1937, ch. 522, 50 Stat. 533.

The authority of the President to prescribe rules is added on authority of former section 633(1), which is carried into section 3302. The section is rewritten as a general prohibition instead of specifying each of the personnel actions to which the prohibition applies. The words "in an Executive agency or in the competitive service" are added for clarity. The sentence "All Acts or parts of Acts inconsistent herewith are repealed." is omitted as unnecessary.

Standard changes are made to conform with the definitions applicable and the style of this title as outlined in the preface to the report.

AMENDMENTS

1978—Pub. L. 95–454, renumbered section 7152 of this title as this section.

1971—Pub. L. 92–187 designated existing provisions as subsec. (a) and added subsecs. (b) and (c).

SECTION REFERRED TO IN OTHER SECTIONS

This section is referred to in section 3302 of this title.

§ 7203. Handicapping condition

The President may prescribe rules which shall prohibit, as nearly as conditions of good administration warrant, discrimination because of handicapping condition in an Executive agency or in the competitive service with respect to a position the duties of which, in the opinion of the Office of Personnel Management, can be performed efficiently by an individual with a handicapping condition, except that the employment may not endanger the health or safety of the individual or others.

(Pub. L. 89–544, Sept. 6, 1966, 80 Stat. 523, §7153; renumbered §7203 and amended Pub. L. 95–454, title I, § 101(b)(2), title VII, § 703(a)(1), title IX, § 906(a)(2), Oct. 13, 1978, 92 Stat. 1118, 1216, 1224.)

HISTORICAL AND REVISION NOTES

Derivation	U.S. Code	Revised Statutes and Statutes at Large
....	5 U.S.C. 633(2)9.	June 10, 1948, ch. 434, 62 Stat. 351.

The authority of the President to prescribe rules is added on authority of former section 633(1), which is carried into section 3302. The section is rewritten as a general prohibition instead of specifying the personnel actions included in former section 633(2)9. The words "in an Executive agency or in the competitive service" are added for clarity.

Standard changes are made to conform with the definitions applicable and the style of this title as outlined in the preface to the report.

AMENDMENTS

1978—Pub. L. 95–454, § 703(a)(1), renumbered section 7153 of this title as this section.

Pub. L. 95–454, §§ 101(b)(2), 906(a)(2), substituted "Handicapping condition" for "Physical handicap" in section catchline, "handicapping condition" for "physical handicap" wherever appearing in text, and "Office of Personnel Management" for "Civil Service Commission".

EFFECTIVE DATE OF 1978 AMENDMENT

Amendment by sections 101(b)(2) and 906(a)(2) of Pub. L. 95–454 effective 90 days after Oct. 13, 1978, see section 907 of Pub. L. 95–454, set out as a note under section 1101 of this title.

SECTION REFERRED TO IN OTHER SECTIONS

This section is referred to in section 3302 of this title.

§ 7204. Other prohibitions

[(a) Repealed. Pub. L. 90–83, § 1(44), Sept. 11, 1967, 81 Stat. 208.]

(b) In the administration of chapter 51, subchapters III and IV of chapter 53, and sections 305 and 3324 of this title, discriminations because of race, color, creed, sex, or marital status is prohibited with respect to an individual or a position held by an individual.

(c) The Office of Personnel Management may prescribe regulations necessary for the administration of subsection (b) of this section.

(Pub. L. 89–554, Sept. 6, 1966, 80 Stat. 523, § 7154; Pub. L. 90–83, § 1(44), Sept. 11, 1967, 81 Stat. 208; Pub. L. 92–392, § 8, Aug. 19, 1972, 86 Stat. 573; renumbered § 7204 and amended Pub. L. 95–454, title VII, § 703(a)(1), title IX, § 906(a)(2), Oct. 13, 1978, 92 Stat. 1216, 1224.)

HISTORICAL AND REVISION NOTES
1966 ACT

Derivation	U.S. Code	Revised Statutes and Statutes at Large
(a)	5 U.S.C. 33.	R.S. § 165.
(b)	5 U.S.C. 1074.	Oct. 28, 1949, ch. 782, § 1103, 63 Stat. 972.

In subsection (a), the words "Executive department" are substituted for "department" as the definition of "department" applicable to this section is coextensive with the definition of "Executive department" in section 101. The words "or military department" are inserted to preserve the application of the source law. Before enactment of the National Security Act Amendments of 1949 (63 Stat. 578), the Department of the Army, the Department of the Navy, and the Depart-

ment of the Air Force were Executive departments. The National Security Act Amendments of 1949 established the Department of Defense as an Executive department including the Department of the Army, the Department of the Navy, and the Department of the Air Force as military departments, not as Executive departments. However, the source law for this subsection, which was in effect in 1949, remained applicable to the Secretaries of the military departments by virtue of section 12(g) of the National Security Act Amendments of 1949 (63 Stat. 591), which is set out in the reviser's note for section 301. The words "in the discretion of" are omitted as unnecessary in view of the permissive grant of authority. The words "positions in the department" are substituted for "any of the clerkships therein authorized by law". The words "upon the same requisites and conditions" are omitted as unnecessary. The words "legal pay of the position to which appointed" are substituted for "same compensations, as are prescribed for men".

This subsection was part of title IV of the Revised Statutes. The Act of July 26, 1947, ch. 343, § 201(d), as added Aug. 10, 1949, ch. 412, § 4, 63 Stat. 579 (former 5 U.S.C. 171–1), which provides "Except to the extent inconsistent with the provisions of this Act [National Security Act of 1947], the provisions of title IV of the Revised Statutes as now or hereafter amended shall be applicable to the Department of Defense" is omitted from this title, but is not repealed.

Subsection (c) is added on authority of former sections 1072 and 1072a, which are codified in section 5115.

Standard changes are made to conform with the definitions applicable and the style of this title as outlined in the preface to the report.

1967 ACT

This section deletes subsection (a) of 5 U.S.C. 7154 to reflect the repeal of the source statute of that subsection by Public Law 89–261, 79 Stat. 987.

AMENDMENTS

1978—Pub. L. 95–454, § 703(a)(1), renumbered section 7154 of this title as this section.

Subsec. (c). Pub. L. 95–454, § 906(a)(2), substituted "Office of Personnel Management" for "Civil Service Commission".

1972—Subsec. (b). Pub. L. 92–392 inserted reference to subchapter IV of chapter 53 of this title.

EFFECTIVE DATE OF 1978 AMENDMENT

Amendment by section 906(a)(2) of Pub. L. 95–454 effective 90 days after Oct. 13, 1978, see section 907 of Pub. L. 95–454, set out as a note under section 1101 of this title.

EFFECTIVE DATE OF 1972 AMENDMENT

Amendment by Pub. L. 92–392 effective on first day of first applicable pay period beginning on or after 90th day after Aug. 19, 1972, see section 15(a) of Pub. L. 92–392, set out as an Effective Date note under section 5341 of this title.

SECTION REFERRED TO IN OTHER SECTIONS

This section is referred to in section 2105 of this title; title 10 sections 4540, 7212, 9540.

SUBCHAPTER II—EMPLOYEES' RIGHT TO PETITION CONGRESS

§ 7211. Employees' right to petition Congress

The right of employees, individually or collectively, to petition Congress or a Member of Congress, or to furnish information to either House of Congress, or to a committee or Member thereof, may not be interfered with or denied.

(Added Pub. L. 95–454, title VII, § 703(a)(3), Oct. 13, 1978, 92 Stat. 1217.)

PRIOR PROVISIONS

Provisions of this section were contained in section 7102 of this title prior to the general amendment of chapter 71 of this title by Pub. L. 95–454, title VII, § 701, Oct. 13, 1978, 92 Stat. 1191.

EFFECTIVE DATE

Section effective 90 days after Oct. 13, 1978, see section 907 of Pub. L. 95–454, set out as an Effective Date of 1978 Amendment note under section 1101 of this title.

SECTION REFERRED TO IN OTHER SECTIONS

This section is referred to in title 39 section 1002.

CHAPTER 73—SUITABILITY, SECURITY, AND CONDUCT

AMENDMENTS

2000—Pub. L. 106–554, § 1(a)(3) [title VI, § 639(b)], Dec. 21, 2000, 114 Stat. 2763, 2763A–168, added subchapter VII heading and item 7371.

1993—Pub. L. 103–94, § 2(b)(2), Oct. 6, 1993, 107 Stat. 1004, amended analysis for subchapter III generally, reenacting subchapter III heading without change, substituting "participation" for "contributions and services" in item 7321, "Definitions" for "Political use of authority or influence; prohibition" in item 7322, "activity authorized; prohibitions" for "contributions; prohibition" in item 7323, "Political activities on duty; prohibition" for "Influencing elections; taking part in political campaigns; prohibitions; exceptions" in item 7324, "Political activity permitted; employees residing in certain municipalities" for "Penalties" in item 7325, and "Penalties" for "Nonpartisan political activity permitted" in item 7326, and striking out item 7327 "Political activity permitted; employees residing in

certain municipalities" and item 7328 "General Accounting Office employees".

1989—Pub. L. 101–194, title III, § 303(b), Nov. 30, 1989, 103 Stat. 1747, added item 7353.

1986—Pub. L. 99–570, title VI, § 6002(a)(2), Oct. 27, 1986, 100 Stat. 3207–158, added subchapter VI heading and items 7361 to 7363.

1980—Pub. L. 96–191, § 8(e)(2), Feb. 15, 1980, 94 Stat. 33, added item 7328.

1968—Pub. L. 90–351, title V, § 1001(b), June 19, 1968, 82 Stat. 235, substituted "EMPLOYMENT LIMITATIONS" for "LOYALTY, SECURITY, AND STRIKING" in subchapter II heading and added item 7313.

1967—Pub. L. 90–83, § 1(46), Sept. 11, 1967, 81 Stat. 209, inserted "GIFTS AND" before "DECORATIONS" in subchapter IV heading, struck out item 7341 "Receipt and display of foreign decorations", and added item 7342.

CHAPTER REFERRED TO IN OTHER SECTIONS

This chapter is referred to in section 3374 of this title; title 39 section 410; title 42 sections 2991c, 3522.

SUBCHAPTER I—REGULATION OF CONDUCT

§ 7301. Presidential regulations

The President may prescribe regulations for the conduct of employees in the executive branch.

(Pub. L. 89–554, Sept. 6, 1966, 80 Stat. 524.)

HISTORICAL AND REVISION NOTES

Derivation	U.S. Code	Revised Statutes and Statutes at Large
....	5 U.S.C. 631 (last 16 words).	R.S. § 1753 (last 16 words).

The words "employees in the executive branch" are substituted for "persons who may receive appointments in the civil service".

Standard changes are made to conform with the definitions applicable and the style of this title as outlined in the preface to the report.

SHORT TITLE OF 1993 AMENDMENT

Pub. L. 103–94, § 1, Oct. 6, 1993, 107 Stat. 1001, provided: "That this Act [enacting sections 5520a and 7321 to 7326 of this title and section 610 of Title 18, Crimes and Criminal Procedure, amending sections 1216, 2302, 3302 and 3303 of this title, sections 602 and 603 of Title 18, section 410 of Title 39, Postal Service, and sections 1973d and 9904 of Title 42, The Public Health and Welfare, omitting former sections 7321 to 7328 of this title, and enacting provisions set out as notes under section 7321 of this title and section 410 of Title 39] may be cited as the 'Hatch Act Reform Amendments of 1993'."

SHORT TITLE OF 1986 AMENDMENT

Pub. L. 99–570, title VI, § 6001, Oct. 27, 1986, 100 Stat. 3207–157, provided that: "This title [enacting sections 7361 to 7363 and 7904 of this title, amending sections 290dd–1 and 290ee–1 of Title 42, The Public Health and Welfare, and enacting provisions set out as notes under section 7361 of this title and section 801 of Title 21, Food and Drugs] may be cited as the 'Federal Employee Substance Abuse Education and Treatment Act of 1986'."

EMERGENCY PREPAREDNESS FUNCTIONS

For assignment of certain emergency preparedness functions to the Director of the Office of Personnel Management, see Parts 1, 2, and 22 of Ex. Ord. No. 12656, Nov. 18, 1988, 53 F.R. 47491, set out as a note under section 5195 of Title 42, The Public Health and Welfare.

CONTINUATION OF RANDOM DRUG TESTING PROGRAM FOR CERTAIN DEPARTMENT OF DEFENSE EMPLOYEES

Pub. L. 105–261, div. A, title XI, § 1108, Oct. 17, 1998, 112 Stat. 2142, provided that:

"(a) CONTINUATION OF EXISTING PROGRAM.—The Secretary of Defense shall continue to actively carry out the drug testing program, originally required by section 3(a) of Executive Order No. 12564 (51 Fed. Reg. 32889; September 15, 1986) [set out below], involving civilian employees of the Department of Defense who are considered to be employees in sensitive positions. The Secretary shall comply with the drug testing procedures prescribed pursuant to section 4 of the Executive order.

"(b) TESTING UPON REASONABLE SUSPICION OF ILLEGAL DRUG USE.—The Secretary of Defense shall ensure that the drug testing program referred to in subsection (a) authorizes the testing of a civilian employee of the Department of Defense for illegal drug use when there is a reasonable suspicion that the employee uses illegal drugs.

"(c) NOTIFICATION TO APPLICANTS.—The Secretary of Defense shall notify persons who apply for employment with the Department of Defense that, as a condition of employment by the Department, the person may be required to submit to drug testing under the drug testing program required by Executive Order No. 12564 (51 Fed. Reg. 32889; September 15, 1986) pursuant to the terms of the Executive order.

"(d) DEFINITIONS.—In this section, the terms 'illegal drugs' and 'employee in a sensitive position' have the meanings given such terms in section 7 of Executive Order No. 12564 (51 Fed. Reg. 32889; September 15, 1986)."

ANNUAL CERTIFICATION OF DRUG-FREE WORKPLACE PLAN ADMINISTRATORS

Pub. L. 106–58, title VI, § 624, Sept. 29, 1999, 113 Stat. 471, provided that: "Notwithstanding any provision of law, the President, or his designee, must certify to Congress, annually, that no person or persons with direct or indirect responsibility for administering the Executive Office of the President's Drug-Free Workplace Plan are themselves subject to a program of individual random drug testing."

Similar provisions were contained in the following prior appropriations acts:

Pub. L. 105–277, div. A, § 101(h) [title VI, § 634], Oct. 21, 1998, 112 Stat. 2681–480, 2681–524.

Pub. L. 105–61, title VI, § 621, Oct. 10, 1997, 111 Stat. 1313.

Pub. L. 104–208, div. A, title I, § 101(f) [title VI, § 623], Sept. 30, 1996, 110 Stat. 3009–314, 3009–358.

Pub. L. 104–52, title VI, § 624, Nov. 19, 1995, 109 Stat. 502.

Pub. L. 103–329, title VI, § 638, Sept. 30, 1994, 108 Stat. 2432.

DESIGNATION OF DIRECTOR OF THE BUREAU OF THE BUDGET AS MEMBER OF FEDERAL LABOR RELATIONS COUNCIL

Presidential Order of December 8, 1969, provided that: Pursuant to the provisions of section 4 of Executive Order 11491 [set out as a note under this section], I hereby designate the Director of the Bureau of the Budget [now the Office of Management and Budget] as a member of the Federal Labor Relations Council. This order of designation shall be published in the Federal Register.

RICHARD NIXON.

DISPLAY IN FEDERAL BUILDINGS OF CODE OF ETHICS FOR GOVERNMENT SERVICE

Pub. L. 96–303, July 3, 1980, 94 Stat. 855, which provided that each agency, under regulations prescribed by Administrator of General Services Administration, display in appropriate areas of Federal buildings copies of the Code of Ethics for Government Service, authorized publication and distribution of such Code, and set forth text of the Code of Ethics for Government Service, was repealed by Pub. L. 104–179, § 4(a), Aug. 6, 1996, 110 Stat. 1566.

AGENCY ACCEPTANCE OF DONATIONS FOR FEDERAL EMPLOYEES

Pub. L. 102–368, title XI, § 901, Sept. 23, 1992, 106 Stat. 1156, effective through Sept. 30, 1993, authorized Federal agencies to accept gifts of property, money, or anything else of value from non-Federal sources for extraordinary and unanticipated expenses incurred by agency employees in their personal capacity within areas designated as disaster areas pursuant to President's declaration of a disaster resulting from Hurricane Andrew, Typhoon Omar, and Hurricane Iniki, directed agencies to establish written procedures to implement this program, and authorized agencies to accept gifts designated for individual employees.

RESTRICTION ON AVAILABILITY OF FUNDS TO ADMINISTER OR IMPLEMENT DRUG TESTING

Pub. L. 100–71, title V, § 503, July 11, 1987, 101 Stat. 468, as amended by Pub. L. 102–54, § 13(b)(6), June 13, 1991, 105 Stat. 274, provided:

"(a)(1) Except as provided in subsection (b) or (c), none of the funds appropriated or made available by this Act, or any other Act, with respect to any fiscal year, shall be available to administer or implement any drug testing pursuant to Executive Order Numbered 12564 (dated September 15, 1986) [set out as a note below], or any subsequent order, unless and until—

"(A) the Secretary of Health and Human Services certifies in writing to the Committees on Appropriations of the House of Representatives and the Senate, and other appropriate committees of the Congress, that—

"(i) each agency has developed a plan for achieving a drug-free workplace in accordance with Executive Order Numbered 12564 and applicable provisions of law (including applicable provisions of this section);

"(ii) the Department of Health and Human Services, in addition to the scientific and technical guidelines dated February 13, 1987, and any subsequent amendments thereto, has, in accordance with paragraph (3), published mandatory guidelines which—

"(I) establish comprehensive standards for all aspects of laboratory drug testing and laboratory procedures to be applied in carrying out Executive Order Numbered 12564, including standards which require the use of the best available technology for ensuring the full reliability and accuracy of drug tests and strict procedures governing the chain of custody of specimens collected for drug testing;

"(II) specify the drugs for which Federal employees may be tested; and

"(III) establish appropriate standards and procedures for periodic review of laboratories and criteria for certification and revocation of certification of laboratories to perform drug testing in carrying out Executive Order Numbered 12564; and

"(iii) all agency drug-testing programs and plans established pursuant to Executive Order Numbered 12564 comply with applicable provisions of law, including applicable provisions of the Rehabilitation Act of 1973 (29 U.S.C. 701 et seq.), title 5 of the United States Code, and the mandatory guidelines under clause (ii);

"(B) the Secretary of Health and Human Services has submitted to the Congress, in writing, a detailed, agency-by-agency analysis relating to—

"(i) the criteria and procedures to be applied in designating employees or positions for drug testing, including the justification for such criteria and procedures;

"(ii) the position titles designated for random drug testing; and

"(iii) the nature, frequency, and type of drug testing proposed to be instituted; and

"(C) the Director of the Office of Management and Budget has submitted in writing to the Committees on Appropriations of the House of Representatives and the Senate a detailed, agency-by-agency analysis (as of the time of certification under subparagraph (A)) of the anticipated annual costs associated with carrying out Executive Order Numbered 12564 and all other requirements under this section during the 5-year period beginning on the date of the enactment of this Act [July 11, 1987].

"(2) Notwithstanding subsection (g), for purposes of this subsection, the term "agency" means—

"(A) the Executive Office of the President;

"(B) an Executive department under section 101 of title 5, United States Code;

"(C) the Environmental Protection Agency;

"(D) the General Services Administration;

"(E) the National Aeronautics and Space Administration;

"(F) the Office of Personnel Management;

"(G) the Small Business Administration;

"(H) the United States Information Agency; and

"(I) the Department of Veterans Affairs;

except that such term does not include the Department of Transportation or any other entity (or component thereof) covered by subsection (b).

"(3) Notwithstanding any provision of chapter 5 of title 5, United States Code, the mandatory guidelines to be published pursuant to subsection (a)(1)(A)(ii) shall be published and made effective exclusively according to the provisions of this paragraph. Notice of the mandatory guidelines proposed by the Secretary of Health and Human Services shall be published in the Federal Register, and interested persons shall be given not less than 60 days to submit written comments on the proposed mandatory guidelines. Following review and consideration of written comments, final mandatory guidelines shall be published in the Federal Register and shall become effective upon publication.

"(b)(1) Nothing in subsection (a) shall limit or otherwise affect the availability of funds for drug testing by—

"(A) the Department of Transportation;

"(B) Department of Energy, for employees specifically involved in the handling of nuclear weapons or nuclear materials;

"(C) any agency with an agency-wide drug-testing program in existence as of September 15, 1986; or

"(D) any component of an agency if such component had a drug-testing program in existence as of September 15, 1986.

"(2) The Departments of Transportation and Energy and any agency or component thereof with a drug-testing program in existence as of September 15, 1986—

"(A) shall be brought into full compliance with Executive Order Numbered 12564 [set out as a note below] no later than the end of the 6-month period beginning on the date of the enactment of this Act [July 11, 1987]; and

"(B) shall take such actions as may be necessary to ensure that their respective drug-testing programs or plans are brought into full compliance with the mandatory guidelines published under subsection (a)(1)(A)(ii) no later than 90 days after such mandatory guidelines take effect, except that any judicial challenge that affects such guidelines should not affect drug-testing programs or plans subject to this paragraph.

"(c) In the case of an agency (or component thereof) other than an agency as defined by subsection (a)(2) or an agency (or component thereof) covered by subsection (b), none of the funds appropriated or made available by this Act, or any other Act, with respect to any fiscal year, shall be available to administer or implement any drug testing pursuant to Executive Order Numbered 12564 [set out as a note below], or any subsequent order, unless and until—

"(1) the Secretary of Health and Human Services provides written certification with respect to that agency (or component) in accordance with clauses (i) and (iii) of subsection (a)(1)(A);

"(2) the Secretary of Health and Human Services has submitted a written, detailed analysis with respect to that agency (or component) in accordance with subsection (a)(1)(B); and

"(3) the Director of the Office of Management and Budget has submitted a written, detailed analysis with respect to that agency (or component) in accordance with subsection (a)(1)(C).

"(d) Any Federal employee who is the subject of a drug test under any program or plan shall, upon written request, have access to—

"(1) any records relating to such employee's drug test; and

"(2) any records relating to the results of any relevant certification, review, or revocation-of-certification proceedings, as referred to in subsection (a)(1)(A)(ii)(III).

"(e) The results of a drug test of a Federal employee may not be disclosed without the prior written consent of such employee, unless the disclosure would be—

"(1) to the employee's medical review official (as defined in the scientific and technical guidelines referred to in subsection (a)(1)(A)(ii));

"(2) to the administrator of any Employee Assistance Program in which the employee is receiving counseling or treatment or is otherwise participating;

"(3) to any supervisory or management official within the employee's agency having authority to take the adverse personnel action against such employee; or

"(4) pursuant to the order of a court of competent jurisdiction where required by the United States Government to defend against any challenge against any adverse personnel action.

"(f) [Terminated, effective May 15, 2000, see section 3003 of Pub. L. 104–66, as amended, set out as a note under section 1113 of Title 31, Money and Finance, and page 151 of House Document No. 103–7.]

"(g) For purposes of this section, the terms 'agency' and 'Employee Assistance Program' each has the meaning given such term under section 7(b) of Executive Order Numbered 12564 [set out as a note below], as in effect on September 15, 1986."

[For abolition of United States Information Agency (other than Broadcasting Board of Governors and International Broadcasting Bureau), transfer of functions, and treatment of references thereto, see sections 6531, 6532, and 6551 of Title 22, Foreign Relations and Intercourse.]

LIMITATION ON GRATUITIES AT NAVAL SHIPBUILDING CEREMONIES

Pub. L. 99–145, title XIV, § 1461, Nov. 8, 1985, 99 Stat. 765, provided that:

"(a) GENERAL RULE.—A Federal officer, employee, or Member of Congress may not accept, directly or indirectly, any tangible thing of value as a gift or memento in connection with a ceremony to mark the completion of a naval shipbuilding milestone.

"(b) EXCLUSION.—Subsection (a) does not apply to a gift or memento that has a value of less than $100.

"(c) DEFINITIONS.—For purposes of this section, the terms 'officer', 'employee', and 'Member of Congress' have the meanings given those terms in sections 2104, 2105, and 2106, respectively, of title 5, United States Code."

EXECUTIVE ORDER NO. 9845

Ex. Ord. No. 9845, Apr. 28, 1947, 12 F.R. 2799, which permitted Bureau of Reclamation employees to accept appointments as constables or deputy sheriffs under state or territorial laws, was revoked by Ex. Ord. No. 11408, Apr. 25, 1968, 33 F.R. 6459.

EX. ORD. NO. 12564. DRUG-FREE FEDERAL WORKPLACE

Ex. Ord. No. 12564, Sept. 15, 1986, 51 F.R. 32889, provided:

I, RONALD REAGAN, President of the United States of America, find that:

Drug use is having serious adverse effects upon a significant proportion of the national work force and results in billions of dollars of lost productivity each year;

The Federal government, as an employer, is concerned with the well-being of its employees, the successful accomplishment of agency missions, and the need to maintain employee productivity;

The Federal government, as the largest employer in the Nation, can and should show the way towards achieving drug-free workplaces through a program designed to offer drug users a helping hand and, at the same time, demonstrating to drug users and potential drug users that drugs will not be tolerated in the Federal workplace;

The profits from illegal drugs provide the single greatest source of income for organized crime, fuel violent street crime, and otherwise contribute to the breakdown of our society;

The use of illegal drugs, on or off duty, by Federal employees is inconsistent not only with the law-abiding behavior expected of all citizens, but also with the special trust placed in such employees as servants of the public;

Federal employees who use illegal drugs, on or off duty, tend to be less productive, less reliable, and prone to greater absenteeism than their fellow employees who do not use illegal drugs;

The use of illegal drugs, on or off duty, by Federal employees impairs the efficiency of Federal departments and agencies, undermines public confidence in them, and makes it more difficult for other employees who do not use illegal drugs to perform their jobs effectively. The use of illegal drugs, on or off duty, by Federal employees also can pose a serious health and safety threat to members of the public and to other Federal employees;

The use of illegal drugs, on or off duty, by Federal employees in certain positions evidences less than the complete reliability, stability, and good judgment that is consistent with access to sensitive information and creates the possibility of coercion, influence, and irresponsible action under pressure that may pose a serious risk to national security, the public safety, and the effective enforcement of the law; and

Federal employees who use illegal drugs must themselves be primarily responsible for changing their behavior and, if necessary, begin the process of rehabilitating themselves.

By the authority vested in me as President by the Constitution and laws of the United States of America, including section 3301(2) of Title 5 of the United States Code, section 7301 of Title 5 of the United States Code, section 290ee–1 of Title 42 of the United States Code, deeming such action in the best interests of national security, public health and safety, law enforcement and the efficiency of the Federal service, and in order to establish standards and procedures to ensure fairness in achieving a drug-free Federal workplace and to protect the privacy of Federal employees, it is hereby ordered as follows:

SECTION 1. *Drug-Free Workplace.* (a) Federal employees are required to refrain from the use of illegal drugs.

(b) The use of illegal drugs by Federal employees, whether on duty or off duty, is contrary to the efficiency of the service.

(c) Persons who use illegal drugs are not suitable for Federal employment.

SEC. 2. *Agency Responsibilities.* (a) The head of each Executive agency shall develop a plan for achieving the objective of a drug-free workplace with due consideration of the rights of the government, the employee, and the general public.

(b) Each agency plan shall include:

(1) A statement of policy setting forth the agency's expectations regarding drug use and the action to be anticipated in response to identified drug use;

(2) Employee Assistance Programs emphasizing high level direction, education, counseling, referral to rehabilitation, and coordination with available community resources;

(3) Supervisory training to assist in identifying and addressing illegal drug use by agency employees;

(4) Provision for self-referrals as well as supervisory referrals to treatment with maximum respect for individual confidentiality consistent with safety and security issues; and

(5) Provision for identifying illegal drug users, including testing on a controlled and carefully monitored basis in accordance with this Order.

SEC. 3. *Drug Testing Programs.* (a) The head of each Executive agency shall establish a program to test for the use of illegal drugs by employees in sensitive positions. The extent to which such employees are tested and the criteria for such testing shall be determined by the head of each agency, based upon the nature of the agency's mission and its employees' duties, the efficient use of agency resources, and the danger to the public health and safety or national security that could result from the failure of an employee adequately to discharge his or her position.

(b) The head of each Executive agency shall establish a program for voluntary employee drug testing.

(c) In addition to the testing authorized in subsections (a) and (b) of this section, the head of each Executive agency is authorized to test an employee for illegal drug use under the following circumstances:

(1) When there is a reasonable suspicion that any employee uses illegal drugs;

(2) In an examination authorized by the agency regarding an accident or unsafe practice; or

(3) As part of or as a follow-up to counseling or rehabilitation for illegal drug use through an Employee Assistance Program.

(d) The head of each Executive agency is authorized to test any applicant for illegal drug use.

SEC. 4. *Drug Testing Procedures.* (a) Sixty days prior to the implementation of a drug testing program pursuant to this Order, agencies shall notify employees that testing for use of illegal drugs is to be conducted and that they may seek counseling and rehabilitation and inform them of the procedures for obtaining such assistance through the agency's Employee Assistance Program. Agency drug testing programs already ongoing are exempted from the 60-day notice requirement. Agencies may take action under section 3(c) of this Order without reference to the 60-day notice period.

(b) Before conducting a drug test, the agency shall inform the employee to be tested of the opportunity to submit medical documentation that may support a legitimate use for a specific drug.

(c) Drug testing programs shall contain procedures for timely submission of requests for retention of records and specimens; procedures for retesting; and procedures, consistent with applicable law, to protect the confidentiality of test results and related medical and rehabilitation records. Procedures for providing urine specimens must allow individual privacy, unless the agency has reason to believe that a particular individual may alter or substitute the specimen to be provided.

(d) The Secretary of Health and Human Services is authorized to promulgate scientific and technical guidelines for drug testing programs, and agencies shall conduct their drug testing programs in accordance with these guidelines once promulgated.

SEC. 5. *Personnel Actions.* (a) Agencies shall, in addition to any appropriate personnel actions, refer any employee who is found to use illegal drugs to an Employee Assistance Program for assessment, counseling, and referral for treatment or rehabilitation as appropriate.

(b) Agencies shall initiate action to discipline any employee who is found to use illegal drugs, *provided that* such action is not required for an employee who:

(1) Voluntarily identifies himself as a user of illegal drugs or who volunteers for drug testing pursuant to section 3(b) of this Order, prior to being identified through other means;

(2) Obtains counseling or rehabilitation through an Employee Assistance Program; and

(3) Thereafter refrains from using illegal drugs.

(c) Agencies shall not allow any employee to remain on duty in a sensitive position who is found to use illegal drugs, prior to successful completion of rehabilitation through an Employee Assistance Program. However, as part of a rehabilitation or counseling program, the head of an Executive agency may, in his or her discretion, allow an employee to return to duty in a sensitive position if it is determined that this action would not pose a danger to public health or safety or the national security.

(d) Agencies shall initiate action to remove from the service any employee who is found to use illegal drugs and:

(1) Refuses to obtain counseling or rehabilitation through an Employee Assistance Program; or

(2) Does not thereafter refrain from using illegal drugs.

(e) The results of a drug test and information developed by the agency in the course of the drug testing of the employee may be considered in processing any adverse action against the employee or for other administrative purposes. Preliminary test results may not be used in an administrative proceeding unless they are confirmed by a second analysis of the same sample or unless the employee confirms the accuracy of the initial test by admitting the use of illegal drugs.

(f) The determination of an agency that an employee uses illegal drugs can be made on the basis of any appropriate evidence, including direct observation, a criminal conviction, administrative inquiry, or the results of an authorized testing program. Positive drug test results may be rebutted by other evidence that an employee has not used illegal drugs.

(g) Any action to discipline an employee who is using illegal drugs (including removal from the service, if appropriate) shall be taken in compliance with otherwise applicable procedures, including the Civil Service Reform Act [Pub. L. 95–454, see Tables for classification].

(h) Drug testing shall not be conducted pursuant to this Order for the purpose of gathering evidence for use in criminal proceedings. Agencies are not required to report to the Attorney General for investigation or prosecution any information, allegation, or evidence relating to violations of Title 21 of the United States Code received as a result of the operation of drug testing programs established pursuant to this Order.

SEC. 6. *Coordination of Agency Programs.* (a) The Director of the Office of Personnel Management shall:

(1) Issue government-wide guidance to agencies on the implementation of the terms of this Order;

(2) Ensure that appropriate coverage for drug abuse is maintained for employees and their families under the Federal Employees Health Benefits Program;

(3) Develop a model Employee Assistance Program for Federal agencies and assist the agencies in putting programs in place;

(4) In consultation with the Secretary of Health and Human Services, develop and improve training programs for Federal supervisors and managers on illegal drug use; and

(5) In cooperation with the Secretary of Health and Human Services and heads of Executive agencies, mount an intensive drug awareness campaign throughout the Federal work force.

(b) The Attorney General shall render legal advice regarding the implementation of this Order and shall be consulted with regard to all guidelines, regulations, and policies proposed to be adopted pursuant to this Order.

(c) Nothing in this Order shall be deemed to limit the authorities of the Director of Central Intelligence under the National Security Act of 1947, as amended [50 U.S.C. 401 et seq.], or the statutory authorities of the National Security Agency or the Defense Intelligence Agency. Implementation of this Order within the Intelligence Community, as defined in Executive Order No. 12333 [50 U.S.C. 401 note], shall be subject to the approval of the head of the affected agency.

SEC. 7. *Definitions.* (a) This Order applies to all agencies of the Executive Branch.

(b) For purposes of this Order, the term "agency" means an Executive agency, as defined in 5 U.S.C. 105; the Uniformed Services, as defined in 5 U.S.C. 2101(3) (but excluding the armed forces as defined by 5 U.S.C. 2101(2)); or any other employing unit or authority of the Federal government, except the United States Postal Service, the Postal Rate Commission, and employing units or authorities in the Judicial and Legislative Branches.

(c) For purposes of this Order, the term "illegal drugs" means a controlled substance included in Schedule I or II, as defined by section 802(6) of Title 21 of the United States Code, the possession of which is unlawful under chapter 13 of that Title. The term "illegal drugs" does not mean the use of a controlled substance pursuant to a valid prescription or other uses authorized by law.

(d) For purposes of this Order, the term "employee in a sensitive position" refers to:

(1) An employee in a position that an agency head designates Special Sensitive, Critical-Sensitive, or Noncritical-Sensitive under Chapter 731 of the Federal Personnel Manual or an employee in a position that an agency head designates as sensitive in accordance with Executive Order No. 10450, as amended [5 U.S.C. 7311 note];

(2) An employee who has been granted access to classified information or may be granted access to classified information pursuant to a determination of trustworthiness by an agency head under Section 4 of Executive Order No. 12356 [50 U.S.C. 435 note];

(3) Individuals serving under Presidential appointments;

(4) Law enforcement officers as defined in 5 U.S.C. 8331(20); and

(5) Other positions that the agency head determines involve law enforcement, national security, the protection of life and property, public health or safety, or other functions requiring a high degree of trust and confidence.

(e) For purposes of this Order, the term "employee" means all persons appointed in the Civil Service as described in 5 U.S.C. 2105 (but excluding persons appointed in the armed services as defined in 5 U.S.C. 2102(2)).

(f) For purposes of this Order, the term "Employee Assistance Program" means agency-based counseling programs that offer assessment, short-term counseling, and referral services to employees for a wide range of drug, alcohol, and mental health programs that affect employee job performance. Employee Assistance Programs are responsible for referring drug-using employees for rehabilitation and for monitoring employees' progress while in treatment.

SEC. 8. *Effective Date.* This Order is effective immediately.

RONALD REAGAN.

EX. ORD. NO. 12674. PRINCIPLES OF ETHICAL CONDUCT FOR GOVERNMENT OFFICERS AND EMPLOYEES

Ex. Ord. No. 12674, Apr. 12, 1989, 54 F.R. 15159, as amended by Ex. Ord. No. 12731, Oct. 17, 1990, 55 F.R. 42547, provided:

By virtue of the authority vested in me as President by the Constitution and the laws of the United States of America, and in order to establish fair and exacting standards of ethical conduct for all executive branch employees, it is hereby ordered as follows:

PART I—PRINCIPLES OF ETHICAL CONDUCT

SECTION 101. *Principles of Ethical Conduct.* To ensure that every citizen can have complete confidence in the integrity of the Federal Government, each Federal employee shall respect and adhere to the fundamental principles of ethical service as implemented in regulations promulgated under sections 201 and 301 of this order:

(a) Public service is a public trust, requiring employees to place loyalty to the Constitution, the laws, and ethical principles above private gain.

(b) Employees shall not hold financial interests that conflict with the conscientious performance of duty.

(c) Employees shall not engage in financial transactions using nonpublic Government information or allow the improper use of such information to further any private interest.

(d) An employee shall not, except pursuant to such reasonable exceptions as are provided by regulation, solicit or accept any gift or other item of monetary value from any person or entity seeking official action from, doing business with, or conducting activities regulated by the employee's agency, or whose interests may be substantially affected by the performance or nonperformance of the employee's duties.

(e) Employees shall put forth honest effort in the performance of their duties.

(f) Employees shall make no unauthorized commitments or promises of any kind purporting to bind the Government.

(g) Employees shall not use public office for private gain.

(h) Employees shall act impartially and not give preferential treatment to any private organization or individual.

(i) Employees shall protect and conserve Federal property and shall not use it for other than authorized activities.

(j) Employees shall not engage in outside employment or activities, including seeking or negotiating for employment, that conflict with official Government duties and responsibilities.

(k) Employees shall disclose waste, fraud, abuse, and corruption to appropriate authorities.

(l) Employees shall satisfy in good faith their obligations as citizens, including all just financial obligations, especially those—such as Federal, State, or local taxes—that are imposed by law.

(m) Employees shall adhere to all laws and regulations that provide equal opportunity for all Americans regardless of race, color, religion, sex, national origin, age, or handicap.

(n) Employees shall endeavor to avoid any actions creating the appearance that they are violating the law or the ethical standards promulgated pursuant to this order.

SEC. 102. *Limitations on Outside Earned Income.*

(a) No employee who is appointed by the President to a full-time noncareer position in the executive branch (including full-time noncareer employees in the White House Office, the Office of Policy Development, and the Office of Cabinet Affairs), shall receive any earned income for any outside employment or activity performed during that Presidential appointment.

(b) The prohibition set forth in subsection (a) shall not apply to any full-time noncareer employees employed pursuant to 3 U.S.C. 105 and 3 U.S.C. 107(a) at salaries below the minimum rate of basic pay then paid for GS-9 of the General Schedule. Any outside employment must comply with relevant agency standards of conduct, including any requirements for approval of outside employment.

PART II—OFFICE OF GOVERNMENT ETHICS AUTHORITY

SEC. 201. *The Office of Government Ethics.* The Office of Government Ethics shall be responsible for administering this order by:

(a) Promulgating, in consultation with the Attorney General and the Office of Personnel Management, regulations that establish a single, comprehensive, and clear set of executive-branch standards of conduct that shall be objective, reasonable, and enforceable.

(b) Developing, disseminating, and periodically updating an ethics manual for employees of the executive branch describing the applicable statutes, rules, decisions, and policies.

(c) Promulgating, with the concurrence of the Attorney General, regulations interpreting the provisions of the post-employment statute, section 207 of title 18, United States Code; the general conflict-of-interest statute, section 208 of title 18, United States Code; and

the statute prohibiting supplementation of salaries, section 209 of title 18, United States Code.

(d) Promulgating, in consultation with the Attorney General and the Office of Personnel Management, regulations establishing a system of nonpublic (confidential) financial disclosure by executive branch employees to complement the system of public disclosure under the Ethics in Government Act of 1978 [Pub. L. 95-521, see Tables for classification]. Such regulations shall include criteria to guide agencies in determining which employees shall submit these reports.

(e) Ensuring that any implementing regulations issued by agencies under this order are consistent with and promulgated in accordance with this order.

SEC. 202. *Executive Office of the President.* In that the agencies within the Executive Office of the President (EOP) currently exercise functions that are not distinct and separate from each other within the meaning and for the purposes of section 207(e) of title 18, United States Code, those agencies shall be treated as one agency under section 207(c) of title 18, United States Code.

PART III—AGENCY RESPONSIBILITIES

SEC. 301. *Agency Responsibilities.* Each agency head is directed to:

(a) Supplement, as necessary and appropriate, the comprehensive executive branch-wide regulations of the Office of Government Ethics, with regulations of special applicability to the particular functions and activities of that agency. Any supplementary agency regulations shall be prepared as addenda to the branch-wide regulations and promulgated jointly with the Office of Government Ethics, at the agency's expense, for inclusion in Title 5 of the Code of Federal Regulations.

(b) Ensure the review by all employees of this order and regulations promulgated pursuant to the order.

(c) Coordinate with the Office of Government Ethics in developing annual agency ethics training plans. Such training shall include mandatory annual briefings on ethics and standards of conduct for all employees appointed by the President, all employees in the Executive Office of the President, all officials required to file public or nonpublic financial disclosure reports, all employees who are contracting officers and procurement officials, and any other employees designated by the agency head.

(d) Where practicable, consult formally or informally with the Office of Government Ethics prior to granting any exemption under section 208 of title 18, United States Code, and provide the Director of the Office of Government Ethics a copy of any exemption granted.

(e) Ensure that the rank, responsibilities, authority, staffing, and resources of the Designated Agency Ethics Official are sufficient to ensure the effectiveness of the agency ethics program. Support should include the provision of a separate budget line item for ethics activities, where practicable.

PART IV—DELEGATIONS OF AUTHORITY

SEC. 401. *Delegations to Agency Heads.* Except in the case of the head of an agency, the authority of the President under sections 203(d), 205(e), and 208(b) of title 18, United States Code, to grant exemptions or approvals to individuals, is delegated to the head of the agency in which an individual requiring an exemption or approval is employed or to which the individual (or the committee, commission, board, or similar group employing the individual) is attached for purposes of administration.

SEC. 402. *Delegations to the Counsel to the President.*

(a) Except as provided in section 401, the authority of the President under sections 203(d), 205(e), and 208(b) of title 18, United States Code, to grant exemptions or approvals for Presidential appointees to committees, commissions, boards, or similar groups established by the President is delegated to the Counsel to the President.

(b) The authority of the President under sections 203(d), 205(e), and 208(b) of title 18, United States Code, to grant exemptions or approvals for individuals appointed pursuant to 3 U.S.C. 105 and 3 U.S.C. 107(a), is delegated to the Counsel to the President.

SEC. 403. *Delegation Regarding Civil Service.* The Office of Personnel Management and the Office of Government Ethics, as appropriate, are delegated the authority vested in the President by 5 U.S.C. 7301 to establish general regulations for the implementation of this Executive order.

PART V—GENERAL PROVISIONS

SEC. 501. *Revocations.* The following Executive orders are hereby revoked:

(a) Executive Order No. 11222 of May 8, 1965.

(b) Executive Order No. 12565 of September 25, 1986.

SEC. 502. *Savings Provision.*

(a) All actions already taken by the President or by his delegates concerning matters affected by this order and in force when this order is issued, including any regulations issued under Executive Order 11222, Executive Order 12565, or statutory authority, shall, except as they are irreconcilable with the provisions of this order or terminate by operation of law or by Presidential action, remain in effect until properly amended, modified, or revoked pursuant to the authority conferred by this order or any regulations promulgated under this order. Notwithstanding anything in section 102 of this order, employees may carry out preexisting contractual obligations entered into before April 12, 1989.

(b) Financial reports filed in confidence (pursuant to the authority of Executive Order No. 11222, 5 C.F.R. Part 735, and individual agency regulations) shall continue to be held in confidence.

SEC. 503. *Definitions.* For purposes of this order, the term:

(a) "Contracting officers and procurement officials" means all such officers and officials as defined in the Office of Federal Procurement Policy Act Amendments of 1988 [see 41 U.S.C. 423].

(b) "Employee" means any officer or employee of an agency, including a special Government employee.

(c) "Agency" means any executive agency as defined in 5 U.S.C. 105, including any executive department as defined in 5 U.S.C. 101, Government corporation as defined in 5 U.S.C. 103, or an independent establishment in the executive branch as defined in 5 U.S.C. 104 (other than the General Accounting Office), and the United States Postal Service and Postal Rate Commission.

(d) "Head of an agency" means, in the case of an agency headed by more than one person, the chair or comparable member of such agency.

(e) "Special Government employee" means a special Government employee as defined in 18 U.S.C. 202(a).

SEC. 504. *Judicial Review.* This order is intended only to improve the internal management of the executive branch and is not intended to create any right or benefit, substantive or procedural, enforceable at law by a party against the United States, its agencies, its officers, or any person.

EX. ORD. NO. 12820. FACILITATING FEDERAL EMPLOYEES' PARTICIPATION IN COMMUNITY SERVICE ACTIVITIES

Ex. Ord. No. 12820, Nov. 5, 1992, 57 F.R. 53429, provided:

By the authority vested in me as President by the Constitution and the laws of the United States of America, including Public Law 101–610, as amended [42 U.S.C. 12501 et seq.], and in order to ensure that the Federal Government encourages its employees' participation in community service, it is hereby ordered as follows:

SECTION 1. *Charge to the Cabinet and Members of the Executive Branch Departments and Agencies.*

(a) The head of each Executive department and agency shall encourage agency employees to participate voluntarily in direct and consequential community service. Community service participation may include, among other things, participation in programs, activities and initiatives designed to address problems such as drug abuse, crime, homelessness, illiteracy, AIDS,

teenage pregnancy, and hunger, and problems associated with low-income housing, education, health care and the environment. The White House Office of National Service and the Commission on National and Community Service shall serve as a resource to provide information and support.

(b) The head of each Executive department and agency shall designate a senior official of his or her department or agency to provide leadership in and support for the Federal commitment to community service through employee awareness and participation within his or her department and agency. The senior official shall report to his or her department or agency head to ensure that community service activities receive a high level of visibility and promotion.

(c) The head of each Executive department and agency shall designate an existing office in his or her department or agency to perform the functions listed below. The office shall serve as the Office of Community Service and will be responsible for:

(1) Providing information to employees of the department or agency concerning community service opportunities;

(2) Working with the White House Office of National Service and the Office of Personnel Management to consider any appropriate changes in department or agency policies or practices that would encourage employee participation in community service activities; and

(3) Acting as a liaison with the White House Office of National Service and the Commission on National and Community Service.

SEC. 2. *Administrative Provisions.*

The White House Office of National Service and the Commission on National and Community Service shall provide such information with respect to community service programs and activities and such advice and assistance as may be required by the departments and agencies for the purpose of carrying out their functions under this order.

SEC. 3. *Reporting Provisions.*

The head of each Executive department or agency, or his or her designee, shall submit an annual report on the actions the department or agency has taken to encourage its employees to participate in community service to the White House Office of National Service not later than December 30 each year.

GEORGE BUSH.

EXECUTIVE ORDER NO. 12834

Ex. Ord. No. 12834, Jan. 20, 1993, 58 F.R. 5911, which provided for ethics commitments by executive branch appointees, was revoked by Ex. Ord. No. 13184, Dec. 28, 2000, 66 F.R. 697, eff. noon Jan. 20, 2001.

EX. ORD. NO. 13058. PROTECTING FEDERAL EMPLOYEES AND THE PUBLIC FROM EXPOSURE TO TOBACCO SMOKE IN THE FEDERAL WORKPLACE

Ex. Ord. No. 13058, Aug. 9, 1997, 62 F.R. 43451, provided:

By the authority vested in me as President by the Constitution and the laws of the United States of America and in order to protect Federal Government employees and members of the public from exposure to tobacco smoke in the Federal workplace, it is hereby ordered as follows:

SECTION 1. *Policy.* It is the policy of the executive branch to establish a smoke-free environment for Federal employees and members of the public visiting or using Federal facilities. The smoking of tobacco products is thus prohibited in all interior space owned, rented, or leased by the executive branch of the Federal Government, and in any outdoor areas under executive branch control in front of air intake ducts.

SEC. 2. *Exceptions.* The general policy established by this order is subject to the following exceptions: (a) The order does not apply in designated smoking areas that are enclosed and exhausted directly to the outside and away from air intake ducts, and are maintained under negative pressure (with respect to surrounding spaces) sufficient to contain tobacco smoke within the designated area. Agency officials shall not require workers to enter such areas during business hours while smoking is ongoing.

(b) The order does not extend to any residential accommodation for persons voluntarily or involuntarily residing, on a temporary or long-term basis, in a building owned, leased, or rented by the Federal Government.

(c) The order does not extend to those portions of federally owned buildings leased, rented, or otherwise provided in their entirety to nonfederal parties.

(d) The order does not extend to places of employment in the private sector or in other nonfederal governmental units that serve as the permanent or intermittent duty station of one or more Federal employees.

(e) The head of any agency may establish limited and narrow exceptions that are necessary to accomplish agency missions. Such exception shall be in writing, approved by the agency head, and to the fullest extent possible provide protection of nonsmokers from exposure to environmental tobacco smoke. Authority to establish such exceptions may not be delegated.

SEC. 3. *Other Locations.* The heads of agencies shall evaluate the need to restrict smoking at doorways and in courtyards under executive branch control in order to protect workers and visitors from environmental tobacco smoke, and may restrict smoking in these areas in light of this evaluation.

SEC. 4. *Smoking Cessation Programs.* The heads of agencies are encouraged to use existing authority to establish programs designed to help employees stop smoking.

SEC. 5. *Responsibility for Implementation.* The heads of agencies are responsible for implementing and ensuring compliance with the provisions of this order. "Agency" as used in this order means an Executive agency, as defined in 5 U.S.C. 105, and includes any employing unit or authority of the Federal Government, other than those of the legislative and judicial branches. Independent agencies are encouraged to comply with the provisions of this order.

SEC. 6. *Phase-In of Implementation.* Implementation of the policy set forth in this order shall be achieved no later than 1 year after the date of this order. This 1 year phase-in period is designed to establish a fixed but reasonable time for implementing this policy. Agency heads are directed during this period to inform all employees and visitors to executive branch facilities about the requirements of this order, inform their employees of the health risks of exposure to environmental tobacco smoke, and undertake related activities as necessary.

SEC. 7. *Consistency with Other Laws.* The provisions of this order shall be implemented consistent with applicable law, including the Federal Service Labor-Management Relations Act (5 U.S.C. 7101 et seq.) and the National Labor Relations Act (29 U.S.C. 151 et seq.)[.] Provisions of existing collective bargaining agreements shall be honored and agencies shall consult with employee labor representatives about the implementation of this order. Nothing herein shall be construed to impair or alter the powers and duties of Federal agencies established under law. Nothing herein shall be construed to replace any agency policy currently in effect, if such policy is legally established, in writing, and consistent with the terms of this order. Agencies shall review their current policy to confirm that agency policy comports with this order, and policy found not in compliance shall be revised to comply with the terms of this order.

SEC. 8. *Cause of Action.* This order does not create any right to administrative or judicial review, or any other right or benefit, substantive or procedural, enforceable by a party against the United States, its agencies or instrumentalities, its officers or employees, or any other person or affect in any way the liability of the executive branch under the Federal Tort Claims Act [28 U.S.C. 2671 et seq.].

SEC. 9. *Construction.* Nothing in this order shall limit an agency head from establishing more protective policies on smoking in the Federal workplace for employees and members of the public visiting or using Federal facilities.

WILLIAM J. CLINTON.

SUBCHAPTER II—EMPLOYMENT LIMITATIONS

AMENDMENTS

1968—Pub. L. 90–351, title V, § 1001(c), June 19, 1968, 82 Stat. 235, substituted "EMPLOYMENT LIMITATIONS" for "LOYALTY, SECURITY, AND STRIKING" in subchapter heading.

SUBCHAPTER REFERRED TO IN OTHER SECTIONS

This subchapter is referred to in title 22 section 3664.

§ 7311. Loyalty and striking

An individual may not accept or hold a position in the Government of the United States or the government of the District of Columbia if he—

(1) advocates the overthrow of our constitutional form of government;

(2) is a member of an organization that he knows advocates the overthrow of our constitutional form of government;

(3) participates in a strike, or asserts the right to strike, against the Government of the United States or the government of the District of Columbia; or

(4) is a member of an organization of employees of the Government of the United States or of individuals employed by the government of the District of Columbia that he knows asserts the right to strike against the Government of the United States or the government of the District of Columbia.

(Pub. L. 89–554, Sept. 6, 1966, 80 Stat. 524.)

HISTORICAL AND REVISION NOTES

Derivation	U.S. Code	Revised Statutes and Statutes at Large
....	5 U.S.C. 118p.	Aug. 9, 1955, ch. 690, § 1, 69 Stat. 624.
....	[Uncodified].	June 29, 1956, ch. 479, § 3, (as applicable to the Act of Aug. 9, 1955, ch. 690, § 1, 69 Stat. 624), 70 Stat. 453.

The word "position" is coextensive with and is substituted for "office or employment".

In paragraphs (1) and (2), the words "in the United States" in former section 118p(1), (2) are omitted as unnecessary in view of the reference to "our constitutional form of government".

In paragraphs (3) and (4), the reference to the "government of the District of Columbia" is added on authority of the Act of June 29, 1956, in order to make these paragraphs meaningful with respect to individuals employed by the government of the District of Columbia. The words "From and after July 1, 1956", appearing in the Act of June 29, 1956, are omitted as executed.

Standard changes are made to conform with the definitions applicable and the style of this title as outlined in the preface to the report.

EX. ORD. NO. 10450. SECURITY REQUIREMENTS FOR GOVERNMENT EMPLOYEES

Ex. Ord. No. 10450, Apr. 27, 1953, 18 F.R. 2489, as amended by Ex. Ord. No. 10491, Oct. 15, 1953, 18 F.R. 6583; Ex. Ord. No. 10531, May 27, 1954, 19 F.R. 3069; Ex. Ord. No. 10548, Aug. 3, 1954, 19 F.R. 4871; Ex. Ord. No. 10550, Aug. 6, 1954, 19 F.R. 4981; Ex. Ord. No. 11605, July 2, 1971,

36 F.R. 12831; Ex. Ord. No. 11785, June 4, 1974, 39 F.R. 20053; Ex. Ord. No. 12107, Dec. 28, 1978, 44 F.R. 1055, provided:

WHEREAS the interests of the national security require that all persons privileged to be employed in the departments and agencies of the Government shall be reliable, trustworthy, of good conduct and character, and of complete and unswerving loyalty to the United States; and

WHEREAS the American tradition that all persons should receive fair, impartial, and equitable treatment at the hands of the Government requires that all persons seeking the privilege of employment or privileged to be employed in the departments and agencies of the Government be adjudged by mutually consistent and no less than minimum standards and procedures among the departments and agencies governing the employment and retention in employment of persons in the Federal service:

NOW, THEREFORE, by virtue of the authority vested in me by the Constitution and statutes of the United States, including section 1753 of the Revised Statutes of the United States (5 U.S.C. 631) [sections 3301 and 7301 of this title]; the Civil Service Act of 1883 (22 Stat. 403; 5 U.S.C. 632, et seq.) [section 1101 et seq. of this title]; section 9A of the act of August 2, 1939, 53 Stat. 1148 (5 U.S.C. 118j) [sections 3333 and 7311 of this title]; and the act of August 26, 1950, 64 Stat. 476 (5 U.S.C. 22–1, et seq.) [section 7501 et seq. of this title], and as President of the United States, and deeming such action necessary in the best interests of the national security it is hereby ordered as follows:

SECTION 1. In addition to the departments and agencies specified in the said act of August 26, 1950, and Executive Order No. 10237 of April 26, 1951 the provisions of that act shall apply to all other departments and agencies of the Government.

SEC. 2. The head of each department and agency of the Government shall be responsible for establishing and maintaining within his department or agency an effective program to insure that the employment and retention in employment of any civilian officer or employee within the department or agency is clearly consistent with the interests of the national security.

SEC. 3. (a) The appointment of each civilian officer or employee in any department or agency of the Government shall be made subject to investigation. The scope of the investigation shall be determined in the first instance according to the degree of adverse effect the occupant of the position sought to be filled could bring about, by virtue of the nature of the position, on the national security, but in no event shall the investigation include less than a national agency check (including a check of the fingerprint files of the Federal Bureau of Investigation), and written inquiries to appropriate local law enforcement agencies, former employers and supervisors, references, and schools attended by the person under investigation: Provided, that upon request of the head of the department or agency concerned, the Office of Personnel Management may, in its discretion, authorize such less investigation as may meet the requirements of the national security with respect to per-diem, intermittent, temporary, or seasonal employees, or aliens employed outside the United States. Should there develop at any stage of investigation information indicating that the employment of any such person may not be clearly consistent with the interests of the national security, there shall be conducted with respect to such person a full field investigation, or such less investigation as shall be sufficient to enable the head of the department or agency concerned to determine whether retention of such person is clearly consistent with the interests of the national security.

(b) The head of any department or agency shall designate, or cause to be designated, any position within his department or agency the occupant of which could bring about, by virtue of the nature of the position, a material adverse effect on the national security as a sensitive position. Any position so designated shall be filled or occupied only by a person with respect to whom a full field investigation has been conducted: Provided, that a person occupying a sensitive position at the time it is designated as such may continue to occupy such position pending the completion of a full field investigation, subject to the other provisions of this order: And provided further, that in case of emergency a sensitive position may be filled for a limited period by a person with respect to whom a full field pre-appointment investigation has not been completed if the head of the department or agency concerned finds that such action is necessary in the national interest, which finding shall be made a part of the records of such department or agency.

SEC. 4. The head of each department and agency shall review, or cause to be reviewed, the cases of all civilian officers and employees with respect to whom there has been conducted a full field investigation under Executive Order No. 9835 of March 21, 1947, and, after such further investigation as may be appropriate, shall readjudicate, or cause to be re-adjudicated, in accordance with the said act of August 26, 1950, such of those cases as have not been adjudicated under a security standard commensurate with that established under this order.

SEC. 5. Whenever there is developed or received by any department or agency information indicating that the retention in employment of any officer or employee of the Government may not be clearly consistent with the interests of the national security, such information shall be forwarded to the head of the employing department or agency or his representative, who, after such investigation as may be appropriate, shall review, or cause to be reviewed, and, where necessary, re-adjudicate, or cause to be re-adjudicated, in accordance with the said act of August 26, 1950, the case of such officer or employee.

SEC. 6. Should there develop at any stage of investigation information indicating that the employment of any officer or employees of the Government may not be clearly consistent with the interests of the national security, the head of the department or agency concerned or his representative shall immediately suspend the employment of the person involved if he deems such suspension necessary in the interests of the national security and, following such investigation and review as he deems necessary the head of the department or agency concerned shall terminate the employment of such suspended officer in the interests of the national security, or employee whenever he shall determine such termination necessary or advisable in accordance with the said act of August 26, 1950.

SEC. 7. Any person whose employment is suspended or terminated under the authority granted to heads of departments and agencies by or in accordance with the said act of August 26, 1950, or pursuant to the said Executive Order No. 9835 or any other security or loyalty program relating to officers or employees of the Government, shall not be reinstated or restored to duty or reemployed in the same department or agency and shall not be reemployed in any other department or agency, unless the head of the department or agency concerned finds that such reinstatement, restoration, or reemployment is clearly consistent with the interests of the national security, which finding shall be made a part of the records of such department or agency: Provided, that no person whose employment has been terminated under such authority thereafter may be employed by any other department or agency except after a determination by the Office of Personnel Management that such person is eligible for such employment.

SEC. 8. (a) The investigations conducted pursuant to this order shall be designed to develop information as to whether the employment or retention in employment in the Federal service of the person being investigated is clearly consistent with the interests of the national security. Such information shall relate, but shall not be limited, to the following:

(1) Depending on the relation of the Government employment to the national security:

(i) Any behavior, activities, or associations which tend to show that the individual is not reliable or trustworthy.

(ii) Any deliberate misrepresentations, falsifications or omissions of material facts.

(iii) Any criminal, infamous, dishonest, immoral, or notoriously disgraceful conduct, habitual use of intoxicants to excess, drug addiction or sexual perversion.

(iv) Any illness, including any mental condition, of a nature which in the opinion of competent medical authority may cause significant defect in the judgment or reliability of the employee, with due regard to the transient or continuing effect of the illness and the medical findings in such case.

(v) Any facts which furnish reason to believe that the individual may be subjected to coercion, influence, or pressure which may cause him to act contrary to the best interests of the national security.

(2) Commission of any act of sabotage, espionage, treason, or sedition, or attempts thereat or preparation therefor, or conspiring with, or aiding or abetting another to commit or attempt to commit any act of sabotage, espionage, treason, or sedition.

(3) Establishing or continuing a sympathetic association with a saboteur, spy, traitor, seditionist, anarchist, or revolutionist, or with any espionage or other secret agent or representative of a foreign nation, or any representative of a foreign nation whose interests may be inimical to the interests of the United States, or with any person who advocates the use of force or violence to overthrow the government of the United States or the alteration of the form of government of the United States by unconstitutional means.

(4) Advocacy of use of force or violence to overthrow the government of the United States, or of the alteration of the form of government of the United States by unconstitutional means.

(5) Knowing membership with the specific intent of furthering the aims of, or adherence to and active participation in, any foreign or domestic organization, association, movement, group, or combination of persons (hereinafter referred to as organizations) which unlawfully advocates or practices the commission of acts of force or violence to prevent others from exercising their rights under the Constitution or laws of the United States or of any State, or which seeks to overthrow the Government of the United States or any State or subdivision thereof by unlawful means.

(6) Intentional unauthorized disclosure to any person of security information, or of other information disclosure of which is prohibited by law, or willful violation or disregard of security regulations.

(7) Performing or attempting to perform his duties, or otherwise acting, so as to serve the interests of another government in preference to the interests of the United States.

(8) Refusal by the individual, upon the ground of constitutional privilege against self-incrimination, to testify before a congressional committee regarding charges of his alleged disloyalty or other misconduct.

(b) The investigation of persons entering or employed in the competitive service shall primarily be the responsibility of the Office of Personnel Management, except in cases in which the head of a department or agency assumes that responsibility pursuant to law or by agreement with the Office. The Office shall furnish a full investigative report to the department or agency concerned.

(c) The investigation of persons (including consultants, however employed), entering employment of, or employed by, the Government other than in the competitive service shall primarily be the responsibility of the employing department or agency. Departments and agencies without investigative facilities may use the investigative facilities of the Office of Personnel Management, and other departments and agencies may use such facilities under agreement with the Office.

(d) There shall be referred promptly to the Federal Bureau of Investigation all investigations being conducted by any other agencies which develop informa-

tion indicating that an individual may have been subjected to coercion, influence, or pressure to act contrary to the interests of the national security, or information relating to any of the matters described in subdivisions (2) through (8) of subsection (a) of this section. In cases so referred to it, the Federal Bureau of Investigation shall make a full field investigation.

SEC. 9. (a) There shall be established and maintained in the Office of Personnel Management a security-investigations index covering all persons as to whom security investigations have been conducted by any department or agency of the Government under this order. The central index established and maintained by the Office under Executive Order No. 9835 of March 21, 1947, shall be made a part of the security-investigations index. The security-investigations index shall contain the name of each person investigated, adequate identifying information concerning each such person, and a reference to each department and agency which has conducted an investigation concerning the person involved or has suspended or terminated the employment of such person under the authority granted to heads of departments and agencies by or in accordance with the said act of August 26, 1950.

(b) The heads of all departments and agencies shall furnish promptly to the Office of Personnel Management information appropriate for the establishment and maintenance of the security-investigations index.

(c) The reports and other investigative material and information developed by investigations conducted pursuant to any statute, order, or program described in section 7 of this order shall remain the property of the investigative agencies conducting the investigations, but may, subject to considerations of the national security, be retained by the department or agency concerned. Such reports and other investigative material and information shall be maintained in confidence, and no access shall be given thereto except with the consent of the investigative agency concerned, to other departments and agencies conducting security programs under the authority granted by or in accordance with the said act of August 26, 1950, as may be required for the efficient conduct of Government business.

SEC. 10. Nothing in this order shall be construed as eliminating or modifying in any way the requirement for any investigation or any determination as to security which may be required by law.

SEC. 11. On and after the effective date of this order the Loyalty Review Board established by Executive Order No. 9835 of March 21, 1947, shall not accept agency findings for review, upon appeal or otherwise. Appeals pending before the Loyalty Review Board on such date shall be heard to final determination in accordance with the provisions of the said Executive Order No. 9835, as amended. Agency determinations favorable to the officer or employee concerned pending before the Loyalty Review Board on such date shall be acted upon by such Board, and whenever the Board is not in agreement with such favorable determination the case shall be remanded to the department or agency concerned for determination in accordance with the standards and procedures established pursuant to this order. Cases pending before the regional loyalty boards of the Office of Personnel Management on which hearings have not been initiated on such date shall be referred to the department or agency concerned. Cases being heard by regional loyalty boards on such date shall be heard to conclusion, and the determination of the board shall be forwarded to the head of the department or agency concerned: Provided, that if no specific department or agency is involved, the case shall be dismissed without prejudice to the applicant. Investigations pending in the Federal Bureau of Investigation or the Office of Personnel Management on such date shall be completed, and the reports thereon shall be made to the appropriate department or agency.

SEC. 12. Executive Order No. 9835 of March 21, 1947, as amended, is hereby revoked.

SEC. 13. The Attorney General is requested to render to the heads of departments and agencies such advice as may be requisite to enable them to establish and maintain an appropriate employee-security program.

SEC. 14. (a) The Office of Personnel Management, with the continuing advice and collaboration of representatives of such departments and agencies as the National Security Council may designate, shall make a continuing study of the manner in which this order is being implemented by the departments and agencies of the Government for the purpose of determining:

(1) Deficiencies in the department and agency security programs established under this order which are inconsistent with the interests of or directly or indirectly weaken, the national security.

(2) Tendencies in such programs to deny to individual employees fair, impartial and equitable treatment at the hands of the Government, or rights under the Constitution and laws of the United States or this order.

Information affecting any department or agency developed or received during the course of such continuing study shall be furnished immediately to the head of the department or agency concerned. The Office of Personnel Management shall report to the National Security Council, at least semiannually, on the results of such study, shall recommend means to correct any such deficiencies or tendencies, and shall inform the National Security Council immediately of any deficiency which is deemed to be of major importance.

(b) All departments and agencies of the Government are directed to cooperate with the Office of Personnel Management to facilitate the accomplishment of the responsibilities assigned to it by subsection (a) of this section.

(c) To assist the Office of Personnel Management in discharging its responsibilities under this order, the head of each department and agency shall, as soon as possible and in no event later than ninety days after receipt of the final investigative report on a civilian officer or employee subject to a full field investigation under the provisions of this order, advise the Office as to the action taken with respect to such officer or employee. The information furnished by the heads of departments and agencies pursuant to this section shall be included in the reports which the Office of Personnel Management is required to submit to the National Security Council in accordance with subsection (a) of this section. Such reports shall set forth any deficiencies on the part of the heads of departments and agencies in taking timely action under this order, and shall mention specifically any instances of noncompliance with this subsection.

SEC. 15. This order shall become effective thirty days after the date hereof.

EXECUTIVE ORDER NO. 11605

Ex. Ord. No. 11605. July 2, 1971, 36 F.R. 12831, which amended Ex. Ord. No. 10450, Apr. 27, 1953, 18 F.R. 2489, which related to security requirements for government employees, was revoked by Ex. Ord. No. 11785, June 4, 1974, 39 F.R. 20053, set out below.

EX. ORD. NO. 11785. SECURITY REQUIREMENTS FOR GOVERNMENTAL EMPLOYEES

Ex. Ord. No. 11785, June 4, 1974, 39 F.R. 20053, provided:

By virtue of the authority vested in me by the Constitution and statutes of the United States, including 5 U.S.C. 1101 et seq., 3301, 3571, 7301, 7313, 7501(c), 7512, 7532, and 7533; and as President of the United States, and finding such action necessary in the best interests of national security, it is hereby ordered as follows:

SECTION 1. Section 12 of Executive Order No. 10450 of April 27, 1953, as amended [set out as a note under this section], is revised to read in its entirety as follows:

"SEC. 12. Executive Order No. 9835 of March 21, 1947, as amended, is hereby revoked."

SEC. 2. Neither the Attorney General, nor the Subversive Activities Control Board, nor any other agency shall designate organizations pursuant to section 12 of Executive Order No. 10450, as amended, nor circulate nor publish a list of organizations previously so des-

ignated. The list of organizations previously designated is hereby abolished and shall not be used for any purpose.

SEC. 3. Subparagraph (5) of paragraph (a) of section 8 of Executive Order No. 10450, as amended, is revised to read as follows:

"Knowing membership with the specific intent of furthering the aims of, or adherence to and active participation in, any foreign or domestic organization, association, movement, group, or combination of persons (hereinafter referred to as organizations) which unlawfully advocates or practices the commission of acts of force or violence to prevent others from exercising their rights under the Constitution or laws of the United States or of any State, or which seeks to overthrow the Government of the United States or any State or subdivision thereof by unlawful means."

SEC. 4. Executive Order No. 11605 of July 2, 1971, is revoked.

RICHARD NIXON.

SECTION REFERRED TO IN OTHER SECTIONS

This section is referred to in sections 3333, 7103 of this title; title 18 section 1918; title 22 section 4102.

§ 7312. Employment and clearance; individuals removed for national security

Removal under section 7532 of this title does not affect the right of an individual so removed to seek or accept employment in an agency of the United States other than the agency from which removed. However, the appointment of an individual so removed may be made only after the head of the agency concerned has consulted with the Office of Personnel Management. The Office, on written request of the head of the agency or the individual so removed, may determine whether the individual is eligible for employment in an agency other than the agency from which removed.

(Pub. L. 89–554, Sept. 6, 1966, 80 Stat. 524; Pub. L. 95–454, title IX, § 906(a)(2), (3), Oct. 13, 1978, 92 Stat. 1224.)

HISTORICAL AND REVISION NOTES

Derivation	U.S. Code	Revised Statutes and Statutes at Large
....	5 U.S.C. 22–1 (4th and 5th provisos).	Aug. 26, 1950, ch. 803, § 1 (4th and 5th provisos), 64 Stat. 477.

The words "Removal under section 7532 of this title" and "so removed" are coextensive with and substituted for "termination of employment herein provided" and "whose employment has been terminated under the provisions of said sections", respectively.

Standard changes are made to conform with the definitions applicable and the style of this title as outlined in the preface to the report.

AMENDMENTS

1978—Pub. L. 95–454 substituted "Office of Personnel Management" and "Office" for "Civil Service Commission" and "Commission", respectively.

EFFECTIVE DATE OF 1978 AMENDMENT

Amendment by Pub. L. 95–454 effective 90 days after Oct. 13, 1978, see section 907 of Pub. L. 95–454, set out as a note under section 1101 of this title.

§ 7313. Riots and civil disorders

(a) An individual convicted by any Federal, State, or local court of competent jurisdiction of—

(1) inciting a riot or civil disorder;

(2) organizing, promoting, encouraging, or participating in a riot or civil disorder;

(3) aiding or abetting any person in committing any offense specified in clause (1) or (2); or

(4) any offense determined by the head of the employing agency to have been committed in furtherance of, or while participating in, a riot or civil disorder;

shall, if the offense for which he is convicted is a felony, be ineligible to accept or hold any position in the Government of the United States or in the government of the District of Columbia for the five years immediately following the date upon which his conviction becomes final. Any such individual holding a position in the Government of the United States or the government of the District of Columbia on the date his conviction becomes final shall be removed from such position.

(b) For the purposes of this section, "felony" means any offense for which imprisonment is authorized for a term exceeding one year.

(Added Pub. L. 90–351, title V, § 1001(a), June 19, 1968, 82 Stat. 235.)

EFFECTIVE DATE

Section 1002 of Pub. L. 90–351 provided that: "The provisions of section 1001(a) of this title [enacting this section] shall apply only with respect to acts referred to in section 7313(a)(1)–(4) of title 5, United States Code, as added by section 1001 of this title, which are committed after the date of enactment of this title [June 19, 1968]."

RECEIPT OF BENEFITS UNDER LAWS PROVIDING RELIEF FOR DISASTER VICTIMS

Section 1106(e) of Pub. L. 90–448, title XI, Aug. 1, 1968, 82 Stat. 567, provided that: "No person who has been convicted of committing a felony during and in connection with a riot or civil disorder shall be permitted, for a period of one year after the date of his conviction, to receive any benefit under any law of the United States providing relief for disaster victims."

SUBCHAPTER III—POLITICAL ACTIVITIES

AMENDMENTS

1993—Pub. L. 103–94, § 2(a), Oct. 6, 1993, 107 Stat. 1001, reenacted subchapter heading without change.

SUBCHAPTER REFERRED TO IN OTHER SECTIONS

This subchapter is referred to in sections 1212, 1216, 4703, 7103, 7121 of this title; title 22 sections 3664, 4102; title 31 section 732; title 42 sections 1973d, 5055.

§ 7321. Political participation

It is the policy of the Congress that employees should be encouraged to exercise fully, freely, and without fear of penalty or reprisal, and to the extent not expressly prohibited by law, their right to participate or to refrain from participating in the political processes of the Nation.

(Added Pub. L. 103–94, § 2(a), Oct. 6, 1993, 107 Stat. 1001.)

PRIOR PROVISIONS

A prior section 7321, Pub. L. 89–554, Sept. 6, 1966, 80 Stat. 525, related to political contributions and services of employees in Executive agencies or competitive service, prior to the general revision of this subchapter by Pub. L. 103–94.

EFFECTIVE DATE; SAVINGS PROVISION

Section 12 of Pub. L. 103–94 provided that:

"(a) The amendments made by this Act [enacting sections 5520a and 7321 to 7326 of this title and section 610 of Title 18, Crimes and Criminal Procedure, amending sections 1216, 2302, 3302 and 3303 of this title, sections 602 and 603 of Title 18, section 410 of Title 39, Postal Service, and sections 1973d and 9904 of Title 42, The Public Health and Welfare, and omitting former sections 7321 to 7328 of this title] shall take effect 120 days after the date of the enactment of this Act [Oct. 6, 1993], except that the authority to prescribe regulations granted under section 7325 of title 5, United States Code (as added by section 2 of this Act), shall take effect on the date of the enactment of this Act.

"(b) Any repeal or amendment made by this Act of any provision of law shall not release or extinguish any penalty, forfeiture, or liability incurred under that provision, and that provision shall be treated as remaining in force for the purpose of sustaining any proper proceeding or action for the enforcement of that penalty, forfeiture, or liability.

"(c) No provision of this Act shall affect any proceedings with respect to which the charges were filed on or before the effective date of the amendments made by this Act. Orders shall be issued in such proceedings and appeals shall be taken therefrom as if this Act had not been enacted."

DELEGATION OF AUTHORITY

Memorandum of President of the United States, Oct. 27, 1994, 59 F.R. 54515, provided:

Memorandum for the Secretary of Defense

Pursuant to authority vested in me as the Chief Executive Officer of the United States, and consistent with the provisions of the Hatch Act Reform Amendment regulations, 5 CFR 734.104, and section 301 of title 3, United States Code, I delegate to you the authority to limit the political activities of political appointees of the Department of Defense, including Presidential appointees, Presidential appointees with Senate confirmation, noncareer SES appointees, and Schedule C appointees.

You are authorized and directed to publish this memorandum in the Federal Register.

WILLIAM J. CLINTON.

Memorandum of President of the United States, Oct. 24, 1994, 59 F.R. 54121, provided:

Memorandum for the Secretary of State

Pursuant to authority vested in me as the Chief Executive Officer of the United States, and consistent with the provisions of the Hatch Act Reform Amendment regulations, 5 CFR 734.104, and section 301 of title 3, United States Code, I delegate to you the authority to limit the political activities of political appointees of the Department of State, including Presidential appointees, Presidential appointees with Senate confirmation, noncareer SES appointees, and Schedule C appointees.

You are authorized and directed to publish this memorandum in the Federal Register.

WILLIAM J. CLINTON.

Memorandum of President of the United States, Sept. 30, 1994, 59 F.R. 50809, provided:

Memorandum for the Attorney General

Pursuant to authority vested in me as the Chief Executive Officer of the United States, and consistent with the provisions of the Hatch Act Reform Amendment regulations, 5 CFR 734.104, and section 301 of title 3, United States Code, I delegate to you the authority to limit the political activities of political appointees of the Department of Justice, including Presidential appointees, Presidential appointees with Senate confirmation, noncareer SES appointees, and Schedule C appointees.

You are authorized and directed to publish this memorandum in the Federal Register.

WILLIAM J. CLINTON.

§ 7322. Definitions

For the purpose of this subchapter—

(1) "employee" means any individual, other than the President and the Vice President, employed or holding office in—

(A) an Executive agency other than the General Accounting Office;

(B) a position within the competitive service which is not in an Executive agency; or

(C) the government of the District of Columbia, other than the Mayor or a member of the City Council or the Recorder of Deeds;

but does not include a member of the uniformed services;

(2) "partisan political office" means any office for which any candidate is nominated or elected as representing a party any of whose candidates for Presidential elector received votes in the last preceding election at which Presidential electors were selected, but shall exclude any office or position within a political party or affiliated organization; and

(3) "political contribution"—

(A) means any gift, subscription, loan, advance, or deposit of money or anything of value, made for any political purpose;

(B) includes any contract, promise, or agreement, express or implied, whether or not legally enforceable, to make a contribution for any political purpose;

(C) includes any payment by any person, other than a candidate or a political party or affiliated organization, of compensation for the personal services of another person which are rendered to any candidate or political party or affiliated organization without charge for any political purpose; and

(D) includes the provision of personal services for any political purpose.

(Added Pub. L. 103–94, § 2(a), Oct. 6, 1993, 107 Stat. 1001.)

Prior Provisions

A prior section 7322, Pub. L. 89–554, Sept. 6, 1966, 80 Stat. 525, prohibited employees in Executive agencies or competitive service from using official authority or influence to coerce political actions of persons or bodies, prior to the general revision of this subchapter by Pub. L. 103–94.

Section Referred to in Other Sections

This section is referred to in title 18 sections 602, 603, 610.

§ 7323. Political activity authorized; prohibitions

(a) Subject to the provisions of subsection (b), an employee may take an active part in political management or in political campaigns, except an employee may not—

(1) use his official authority or influence for the purpose of interfering with or affecting the result of an election;

(2) knowingly solicit, accept, or receive a political contribution from any person, unless such person is—

(A) a member of the same Federal labor organization as defined under section 7103(4) of this title or a Federal employee organization which as of the date of enactment of the Hatch Act Reform Amendments of 1993 had a multicandidate political committee (as defined under section 315(a)(4) of the Federal Election Campaign Act of 1971 (2 U.S.C. 441a(a)(4)));

(B) not a subordinate employee; and

(C) the solicitation is for a contribution to the multicandidate political committee (as defined under section 315(a)(4) of the Federal Election Campaign Act of 1971 (2 U.S.C. 441a(a)(4))) of such Federal labor organization as defined under section 7103(4) of this title or a Federal employee organization which as of the date of the enactment of the Hatch Act Reform Amendments of 1993 had a multicandidate political committee (as defined under section 315(a)(4) of the Federal Election Campaign Act of 1971 (2 U.S.C. 441a(a)(4))); or

(3) run for the nomination or as a candidate for election to a partisan political office; or

(4) knowingly solicit or discourage the participation in any political activity of any person who—

(A) has an application for any compensation, grant, contract, ruling, license, permit, or certificate pending before the employing office of such employee; or

(B) is the subject of or a participant in an ongoing audit, investigation, or enforcement action being carried out by the employing office of such employee.

(b)(1) An employee of the Federal Election Commission (except one appointed by the President, by and with the advice and consent of the Senate), may not request or receive from, or give to, an employee, a Member of Congress, or an officer of a uniformed service a political contribution.

(2)(A) No employee described under subparagraph (B) (except one appointed by the President, by and with the advice and consent of the Senate), may take an active part in political management or political campaigns.

(B) The provisions of subparagraph (A) shall apply to—

(i) an employee of—

(I) the Federal Election Commission;

(II) the Federal Bureau of Investigation;

(III) the Secret Service;

(IV) the Central Intelligence Agency;

(V) the National Security Council;

(VI) the National Security Agency;

(VII) the Defense Intelligence Agency;

(VIII) the Merit Systems Protection Board;

(IX) the Office of Special Counsel;

(X) the Office of Criminal Investigation of the Internal Revenue Service;

(XI) the Office of Investigative Programs of the United States Customs Service;

(XII) the Office of Law Enforcement of the Bureau of Alcohol, Tobacco, and Firearms; or

(XIII) the National Imagery and Mapping Agency; or

(ii) a person employed in a position described under section 3132(a)(4), 5372, 5372a, or 5372b of title 5, United States Code.

(3) No employee of the Criminal Division of the Department of Justice (except one appointed

by the President, by and with the advice and consent of the Senate), may take an active part in political management or political campaigns.

(4) For purposes of this subsection, the term "active part in political management or in a political campaign" means those acts of political management or political campaigning which were prohibited for employees of the competitive service before July 19, 1940, by determinations of the Civil Service Commission under the rules prescribed by the President.

(c) An employee retains the right to vote as he chooses and to express his opinion on political subjects and candidates.

(Added Pub. L. 103–94, § 2(a), Oct. 6, 1993, 107 Stat. 1002; amended Pub. L. 103–359, title V, § 501(k), Oct. 14, 1994, 108 Stat. 3430; Pub. L. 104–201, div. A, title XI, § 1122(a)(1), Sept. 23, 1996, 110 Stat. 2687; Pub. L. 106–554, § 1(a)(3) [title VI, § 645(a)(2)], Dec. 21, 2000, 114 Stat. 2763, 2763A–170.)

REFERENCES IN TEXT

The date of enactment of the Hatch Act Reform Amendments of 1993, referred to in subsec. (a)(2)(A), (C), is the date of enactment of Pub. L. 103–94, which was approved Oct. 6, 1993.

PRIOR PROVISIONS

A prior section 7323, Pub. L. 89–554, Sept. 6, 1966, 80 Stat. 525, prohibited employee in Executive agency from requesting, receiving from, or giving to, an employee, a Member of Congress, or an officer of a uniformed service, a thing of value for political purposes and provided for removal from service of employee for violation, prior to the general revision of this subchapter by Pub. L. 103–94.

AMENDMENTS

2000—Subsec. (b)(2)(B)(ii). Pub. L. 106–554 substituted "5372a, or 5372b" for "or 5372a".

1996—Subsec. (b)(2)(B)(i)(XIII). Pub. L. 104–201 substituted "National Imagery and Mapping Agency" for "Central Imagery Office".

1994—Subsec. (b)(2)(B)(i)(XIII). Pub. L. 103–359 added subcl. (XIII).

EFFECTIVE DATE OF 1996 AMENDMENT

Amendment by Pub. L. 104–201 effective Oct. 1, 1996, see section 1124 of Pub. L. 104–201, set out as a note under section 193 of Title 10, Armed Forces.

SECTION REFERRED TO IN OTHER SECTIONS

This section is referred to in sections 7325, 7326 of this title; title 18 sections 602, 603.

§ 7324. Political activities on duty; prohibition

(a) An employee may not engage in political activity—

(1) while the employee is on duty;

(2) in any room or building occupied in the discharge of official duties by an individual employed or holding office in the Government of the United States or any agency or instrumentality thereof;

(3) while wearing a uniform or official insignia identifying the office or position of the employee; or

(4) using any vehicle owned or leased by the Government of the United States or any agency or instrumentality thereof.

(b)(1) An employee described in paragraph (2) of this subsection may engage in political activity otherwise prohibited by subsection (a) if the costs associated with that political activity are not paid for by money derived from the Treasury of the United States.

(2) Paragraph (1) applies to an employee—

(A) the duties and responsibilities of whose position continue outside normal duty hours and while away from the normal duty post; and

(B) who is—

(i) an employee paid from an appropriation for the Executive Office of the President; or

(ii) an employee appointed by the President, by and with the advice and consent of the Senate, whose position is located within the United States, who determines policies to be pursued by the United States in relations with foreign powers or in the nationwide administration of Federal laws.

(Added Pub. L. 103–94, § 2(a), Oct. 6, 1993, 107 Stat. 1003.)

PRIOR PROVISIONS

A prior section 7324, Pub. L. 89–554, Sept. 6, 1966, 80 Stat. 525; Pub. L. 93–268, § 4(a), Apr. 17, 1974, 88 Stat. 87, prohibited Executive agency employees and employees of the District of Columbia from influencing elections or taking part in political campaigns, prior to the general revision of this subchapter by Pub. L. 103–94.

SECTION REFERRED TO IN OTHER SECTIONS

This section is referred to in section 7326 of this title; title 18 sections 602, 603; title 42 section 2000e–4; title 50 App. section 463.

§ 7325. Political activity permitted; employees residing in certain municipalities

The Office of Personnel Management may prescribe regulations permitting employees, without regard to the prohibitions in paragraphs (2) and (3) of section 7323(a) and paragraph (2) of section 7323(b) of this title, to take an active part in political management and political campaigns involving the municipality or other political subdivision in which they reside, to the extent the Office considers it to be in their domestic interest, when—

(1) the municipality or political subdivision is in Maryland or Virginia and in the immediate vicinity of the District of Columbia, or is a municipality in which the majority of voters are employed by the Government of the United States; and

(2) the Office determines that because of special or unusual circumstances which exist in the municipality or political subdivision it is in the domestic interest of the employees and individuals to permit that political participation.

(Added Pub. L. 103–94, § 2(a), Oct. 6, 1993, 107 Stat. 1004; amended Pub. L. 104–93, title III, § 308, Jan. 6, 1996, 109 Stat. 966.)

PRIOR PROVISIONS

A prior section 7325, Pub. L. 89–554, Sept. 6, 1966, 80 Stat. 526; Pub. L. 96–54, § 2(a)(44), Aug. 14, 1979, 93 Stat. 384, related to penalties, prior to the general revision of this subchapter by Pub. L. 103–94.

AMENDMENTS

1996—Pub. L. 104–93 inserted "and paragraph (2) of section 7323(b)" after "section 7323(a)".

§ 7326. Penalties

An employee or individual who violates section 7323 or 7324 of this title shall be removed from his position, and funds appropriated for the position from which removed thereafter may not be used to pay the employee or individual. However, if the Merit System Protection Board finds by unanimous vote that the violation does not warrant removal, a penalty of not less than 30 days' suspension without pay shall be imposed by direction of the Board.

(Added Pub. L. 103–94, § 2(a), Oct. 6, 1993, 107 Stat. 1004.)

PRIOR PROVISIONS

A prior section 7326, Pub. L. 89–554, Sept. 6, 1966, 80 Stat. 526, authorized nonpartisan political activities, prior to the general revision of this subchapter by Pub. L. 103–94.

A prior section 7327, Pub. L. 89–554, Sept. 6, 1966, 80 Stat. 526; Pub. L. 96–54, § 2(a)(14), (15), Aug. 14, 1979, 93 Stat. 382; Pub. L. 97–468, title VI, § 615(b)(1)(E), Jan. 14, 1983, 96 Stat. 2578, related to permitted political activity in certain municipalities where employees reside, prior to the general revision of this subchapter by Pub. L. 103–94.

A prior section 7328, added Pub. L. 96–191, § 8(e)(1), Feb. 15, 1980, 94 Stat. 33, exempted employees of the General Accounting Office from provisions of this subchapter, prior to the general revision of this subchapter by Pub. L. 103–94.

SUBCHAPTER IV—FOREIGN GIFTS AND DECORATIONS

AMENDMENTS

1967—Pub. L. 90–83, § 1(45)(A), Sept. 11, 1967, 81 Stat. 208, substituted "FOREIGN GIFTS AND DECORATIONS" for "FOREIGN DECORATIONS" in subchapter heading.

[§ 7341. Repealed. Pub. L. 90–83, § 1(45)(B), Sept. 11, 1967, 81 Stat. 208]

Section, Pub. L. 89–554, Sept. 6, 1966, 80 Stat. 526, related to receipt and display of foreign decorations. See section 7342 of this title.

§ 7342. Receipt and disposition of foreign gifts and decorations

(a) For the purpose of this section—

(1) "employee" means—

(A) an employee as defined by section 2105 of this title and an officer or employee of the United States Postal Service or of the Postal Rate Commission;

(B) an expert or consultant who is under contract under section 3109 of this title with the United States or any agency, department, or establishment thereof, including, in the case of an organization performing services under such section, any individual involved in the performance of such services;

(C) an individual employed by, or occupying an office or position in, the government of a territory or possession of the United States or the government of the District of Columbia;

(D) a member of a uniformed service;

(E) the President and the Vice President;

(F) a Member of Congress as defined by section 2106 of this title (except the Vice President) and any Delegate to the Congress; and

(G) the spouse of an individual described in subparagraphs (A) through (F) (unless such individual and his or her spouse are separated) or a dependent (within the meaning of section 152 of the Internal Revenue Code of 1986) of such an individual, other than a spouse or dependent who is an employee under subparagraphs (A) through (F);

(2) "foreign government" means—

(A) any unit of foreign governmental authority, including any foreign national, State, local, and municipal government;

(B) any international or multinational organization whose membership is composed of any unit of foreign government described in subparagraph (A); and

(C) any agent or representative of any such unit or such organization, while acting as such;

(3) "gift" means a tangible or intangible present (other than a decoration) tendered by, or received from, a foreign government;

(4) "decoration" means an order, device, medal, badge, insignia, emblem, or award tendered by, or received from, a foreign government;

(5) "minimal value" means a retail value in the United States at the time of acceptance of $100 or less, except that—

(A) on January 1, 1981, and at 3 year intervals thereafter, "minimal value" shall be redefined in regulations prescribed by the Administrator of General Services, in consultation with the Secretary of State, to reflect changes in the consumer price index for the immediately preceding 3-year period; and

(B) regulations of an employing agency may define "minimal value" for its employees to be less than the value established under this paragraph; and

(6) "employing agency" means—

(A) the Committee on Standards of Official Conduct of the House of Representatives, for Members and employees of the House of Representatives, except that those responsibilities specified in subsections (c)(2)(A), (e)(1), and (g)(2)(B) shall be carried out by the Clerk of the House;

(B) the Select Committee on Ethics of the Senate, for Senators and employees of the Senate, except that those responsibilities (other than responsibilities involving approval of the employing agency) specified in subsections (c)(2), (d), and (g)(2)(B) shall be carried out by the Secretary of the Senate;

(C) the Administrative Office of the United States Courts, for judges and judicial branch employees; and

(D) the department, agency, office, or other entity in which an employee is employed, for other legislative branch employees and for all executive branch employees.

(b) An employee may not—

(1) request or otherwise encourage the tender of a gift or decoration; or

(2) accept a gift or decoration, other than in accordance with the provisions of subsections (c) and (d).

(c)(1) The Congress consents to—

(A) the accepting and retaining by an employee of a gift of minimal value tendered and received as a souvenir or mark of courtesy; and

(B) the accepting by an employee of a gift of more than minimal value when such gift is in the nature of an educational scholarship or medical treatment or when it appears that to refuse the gift would likely cause offense or embarrassment or otherwise adversely affect the foreign relations of the United States, except that—

(i) a tangible gift of more than minimal value is deemed to have been accepted on behalf of the United States and, upon acceptance, shall become the property of the United States; and

(ii) an employee may accept gifts of travel or expenses for travel taking place entirely outside the United States (such as transportation, food, and lodging) of more than minimal value if such acceptance is appropriate, consistent with the interests of the United States, and permitted by the employing agency and any regulations which may be prescribed by the employing agency.

(2) Within 60 days after accepting a tangible gift of more than minimal value (other than a gift described in paragraph (1)(B)(ii)), an employee shall—

(A) deposit the gift for disposal with his or her employing agency; or

(B) subject to the approval of the employing agency, deposit the gift with that agency for official use.

Within 30 days after terminating the official use of a gift under subparagraph (B), the employing agency shall forward the gift to the Administrator of General Services in accordance with subsection (e)(1) or provide for its disposal in accordance with subsection (e)(2).

(3) When an employee deposits a gift of more than minimal value for disposal or for official use pursuant to paragraph (2), or within 30 days after accepting travel or travel expenses as provided in paragraph (1)(B)(ii) unless such travel or travel expenses are accepted in accordance with specific instructions of his or her employing agency, the employee shall file a statement with his or her employing agency or its delegate containing the information prescribed in subsection (f) for that gift.

(d) The Congress consents to the accepting, retaining, and wearing by an employee of a decoration tendered in recognition of active field service in time of combat operations or awarded for other outstanding or unusually meritorious performance, subject to the approval of the employing agency of such employee. Without this approval, the decoration is deemed to have been accepted on behalf of the United States, shall become the property of the United States, and shall be deposited by the employee, within sixty days of acceptance, with the employing agency for official use, for forwarding to the Administrator of General Services for disposal in accordance with subsection (e)(1), or for disposal in accordance with subsection (e)(2).

(e)(1) Except as provided in paragraph (2), gifts and decorations that have been deposited with an employing agency for disposal shall be (A) returned to the donor, or (B) forwarded to the Administrator of General Services for transfer, donation, or other disposal in accordance with the provisions of the Federal Property and Administrative Services Act of 1949. However, no gift or decoration that has been deposited for disposal may be sold without the approval of the Secretary of State, upon a determination that the sale will not adversely affect the foreign relations of the United States. Gifts and decorations may be sold by negotiated sale.

(2) Gifts and decorations received by a Senator or an employee of the Senate that are deposited with the Secretary of the Senate for disposal, or are deposited for an official use which has terminated, shall be disposed of by the Commission on Arts and Antiquities of the United States Senate. Any such gift or decoration, may be returned by the Commission to the donor or may be transferred or donated by the Commission, subject to such terms and conditions as it may prescribe, (A) to an agency or instrumentality of (i) the United States, (ii) a State, territory, or possession of the United States, or a political subdivision of the foregoing, or (iii) the District of Columbia, or (B) to an organization described in section 501(c)(3) of the Internal Revenue Code of 1986 which is exempt from taxation under section 501(a) of such Code. Any such gift or decoration not disposed of as provided in the preceding sentence shall be forwarded to the Administrator of General Services for disposal in accordance with paragraph (1). If the Administrator does not dispose of such gift or decoration within one year, he shall, at the request of the Commission, return it to the Commission and the Commission may dispose of such gift or decoration in such manner as it considers proper, except that such gift or decoration may be sold only with the approval of the Secretary of State upon a determination that the sale will not adversely affect the foreign relations of the United States.

(f)(1) Not later than January 31 of each year, each employing agency or its delegate shall compile a listing of all statements filed during the preceding year by the employees of that agency pursuant to subsection (c)(3) and shall transmit such listing to the Secretary of State who shall publish a comprehensive listing of all such statements in the Federal Register.

(2) Such listings shall include for each tangible gift reported—

(A) the name and position of the employee;

(B) a brief description of the gift and the circumstances justifying acceptance;

(C) the identity, if known, of the foreign government and the name and position of the individual who presented the gift;

(D) the date of acceptance of the gift;

(E) the estimated value in the United States of the gift at the time of acceptance; and

(F) disposition or current location of the gift.

(3) Such listings shall include for each gift of travel or travel expenses—

(A) the name and position of the employee;

(B) a brief description of the gift and the circumstances justifying acceptance; and

(C) the identity, if known, of the foreign government and the name and position of the individual who presented the gift.

(4) In transmitting such listings for the Central Intelligence Agency, the Director of Central Intelligence may delete the information described in subparagraphs (A) and (C) of paragraphs (2) and (3) if the Director certifies in writing to the Secretary of State that the publication of such information could adversely affect United States intelligence sources.

(g)(1) Each employing agency shall prescribe such regulations as may be necessary to carry out the purpose of this section. For all employing agencies in the executive branch, such regulations shall be prescribed pursuant to guidance provided by the Secretary of State. These regulations shall be implemented by each employing agency for its employees.

(2) Each employing agency shall—

(A) report to the Attorney General cases in which there is reason to believe that an employee has violated this section;

(B) establish a procedure for obtaining an appraisal, when necessary, of the value of gifts; and

(C) take any other actions necessary to carry out the purpose of this section.

(h) The Attorney General may bring a civil action in any district court of the United States against any employee who knowingly solicits or accepts a gift from a foreign government not consented to by this section or who fails to deposit or report such gift as required by this section. The court in which such action is brought may assess a penalty against such employee in any amount not to exceed the retail value of the gift improperly solicited or received plus $5,000.

(i) The President shall direct all Chiefs of a United States Diplomatic Mission to inform their host governments that it is a general policy of the United States Government to prohibit United States Government employees from receiving gifts or decorations of more than minimal value.

(j) Nothing in this section shall be construed to derogate any regulation prescribed by any employing agency which provides for more stringent limitations on the receipt of gifts and decorations by its employees.

(k) The provisions of this section do not apply to grants and other forms of assistance to which section 108A of the Mutual Educational and Cultural Exchange Act of 1961 applies.

(Added Pub. L. 90–83, §1(45)(C), Sept. 11, 1967, 81 Stat. 208; amended Pub. L. 95–105, title V, §515(a)(1), Aug. 17, 1977, 91 Stat. 862; Pub. L. 95–426, title VII, §712(a)–(c), Oct. 7, 1978, 92 Stat. 994; Pub. L. 99–514, §2, Oct. 22, 1986, 100 Stat. 2095.)

HISTORICAL AND REVISION NOTES

Section of title 5	Source (U.S.Code)	Source (Statutes at Large)
7342(a)	22:2621.	Oct. 15, 1966, Pub. L. 89–673, §2, 80 Stat. 952.
7342(b)	22:2622.	Oct. 15, 1966, Pub. L. 89–673, §3, 80 Stat. 952.
7342(c)	22:2623.	Oct. 15, 1966, Pub. L. 89–673, §4, 80 Stat. 952.

HISTORICAL AND REVISION NOTES—CONTINUED

Section of title 5	Source (U.S.Code)	Source (Statutes at Large)
7342(d)	22:2624.	Oct. 15, 1966, Pub. L. 89–673, §5, 80 Stat. 952.
7342(e)	22:2626.	Oct. 15, 1966, Pub. L. 89–673, §7, 80 Stat. 952.

The definitions of "employee" and "uniformed services" in 5 U.S.C. 2105 and 2101 are broad enough to cover the persons included in 22 U.S.C. 2621(1) with the exception of (1) individuals employed by, or occupying an office or position in, the government of a territory or possession of the United States or of the District of Columbia, (2) the President, and (3) Members of Congress, who, accordingly, are covered in paragraphs (B), (D), and (E). As the Canal Zone Government is an independent agency of the United States, see section 31 of title 2, Canal Zone Code, an employee thereof is an "employee" as defined in 5 U.S.C. 2105.

In subsection (b), the words "An employee may not" are substituted for "No person shall" to conform to the definition applicable and style of title 5, United States Code.

In subsection (c), the words "under regulations prescribed under this section" are substituted for "in accordance with the rules and regulations issued pursuant to this Act".

In subsection (e), the words "The President may prescribe regulations to carry out the purpose of this section" are substituted for "Rules and regulations to carry out the purposes of this Act may be prescribed by or under the authority of the President". Under 3 U.S.C. 301, the President may delegate the authority vested in him by this subsection.

REFERENCES IN TEXT

Section 152 of the Internal Revenue Code of 1986, referred to in subsec. (a)(1)(G), is classified to section 152 of Title 26, Internal Revenue Code.

The Federal Property and Administrative Services Act of 1949, as amended, referred to in subsec. (e)(1), is act June 30, 1949, ch. 288, 63 Stat. 377, as amended. Provisions of that act relating to disposal of government property are classified to chapter 10 (§471 et seq.) of Title 40, Public Buildings, Property, and Works. For complete classification of this Act to the Code, see Short Title note set out under section 471 of Title 40 and Tables.

Section 501 of the Internal Revenue Code of 1986, referred to in subsec. (e)(2), is classified to section 501 of Title 26, Internal Revenue Code.

Section 108A of the Mutual Educational and Cultural Exchange Act of 1961, referred to in subsec. (k), is classified to section 2458a of Title 22, Foreign Relations and Intercourse.

AMENDMENTS

1986—Subsecs. (a)(1)(G), (e)(2). Pub. L. 99–514 substituted "Internal Revenue Code of 1986" for "Internal Revenue Code of 1954".

1978—Subsec. (a)(6)(A). Pub. L. 95–426, §712(a)(1), substituted "(e)(1)" for "(e)".

Subsec. (a)(6)(B). Pub. L. 95–426, §712(a)(2), inserted ", except that those responsibilities (other than responsibilities involving approval of the employing agency) specified in subsection (c)(2), (d), and (g)(2)(B) shall be carried out by the Secretary of the Senate".

Subsec. (c)(2). Pub. L. 95–426, §712(b)(1), substituted "subsection (e)(1) or provide for its disposal in accordance with subsection (e)(2)" for "subsection (e)".

Subsec. (d). Pub. L. 95–426, §712(b)(2), substituted "official use, for forwarding", for "official use, or forwarding", and "subsection (e)(1), or for disposal in accordance with subsection (e)(2)" for "subsection (e)".

Subsec. (e). Pub. L. 95–426, §712(c), designated existing provisions as par. (1), substituted "Except as provided in paragraph (2), gifts" for "Gifts", "(A)" and "(B)" for "(1)" and "(2)", respectively, and added par. (2).

1977—Subsec. (a). Pub. L. 95–105 in par. (1) inserted provisions expanding definition of "employee" to include an officer or employee of the United States Postal Service or Postal Rate Commission, certain experts and consultants, the Vice President, and any Delegate to Congress, in par. (2) incorporated existing provisions into subpars. (A) and (C) and added subpar. (B), in par. (3) substituted reference to tangible or intangible present for reference to present, in par. (4) inserted reference to award, and added pars. (5) and (6).

Subsec. (b). Pub. L. 95–105 designated existing provisions as par. (1) and added par. (2).

Subsec. (c). Pub. L. 95–105 incorporated existing provisions of pars. (1) and (2) into par. (1), inserted provisions giving congressional consent to acceptance of a gift in the nature of an educational scholarship, medical treatment, or travel or travel expenses, and added pars. (2) and (3).

Subsec. (d). Pub. L. 95–105 struck out provisions requiring the Secretary of State to concur with the approval of the employing agency and substituted provisions requiring the employee to deposit property within 60 days of acceptance with the employing agency for official use or forwarding to the Administrator of General Services for disposal for provisions requiring the employee to deposit the decoration for use and disposal as the property of the United States under regulations prescribed under this section.

Subsec. (e). Pub. L. 95–105 substituted provisions relating to the disposal of decorations for provisions authorizing the President to prescribe regulations to carry out the purposes of this section.

Subsecs. (f) to (k). Pub. L. 95–105 added subsecs. (f) to (k).

EFFECTIVE DATE OF 1977 AMENDMENT

Section 515(a)(2) of Pub. L. 95–105 provided that: "The amendment made by paragraph (1) of this subsection [amending this section] shall take effect on January 1, 1978."

TRANSFER OF FUNCTIONS

Certain functions of Clerk of House of Representatives transferred to Director of Non-legislative and Financial Services by section 7 of House Resolution No. 423, One Hundred Second Congress, Apr. 9, 1992. Director of Non-legislative and Financial Services replaced by Chief Administrative Officer of House of Representatives by House Resolution No. 6, One Hundred Fourth Congress, Jan. 4, 1995.

LEASING OF SPACE AND FACILITIES FOR STORING AND SAFEGUARDING PROPERTY

Section 712(d) of Pub. L. 95–426 provided that: "In the event that the space and facilities available to the Secretary of the Senate for carrying out his responsibilities in storing and safeguarding property in his custody under section 7342 of title 5, United States Code, are insufficient for such purpose, he may, with the approval of the Committee on Rules and Administration of the Senate, lease such space and facilities as may be necessary for such purpose. Rental payments under any such lease and expenses incurred in connection therewith shall be paid from the contingent fund of the Senate upon vouchers approved by the Secretary of the Senate."

WEARING OF CERTAIN DECORATIONS

Section 33A of act Aug. 10, 1956, ch. 1041, as added by Pub. L. 85–861, Sept. 2, 1958, §33(e), 72 Stat. 1567, provided: "A member or former member of an armed force of the United States holding any office of profit or trust under the United States may wear any decoration, order, medal, or emblem accepted (1) under the Act of July 20, 1942, chapter 508 (56 Stat. 662), or (2) before August 1, 1947, from the government of a cobelligerent or neutral nation or an American Republic."

EXECUTIVE ORDER NO. 11320

Ex. Ord. No. 11320, Dec. 12, 1966, 31 F.R. 15789, which delegated to the Secretary of State the authority of the President under 22 U.S.C. 2626 to prescribe rules and regulations to carry out the Foreign Gifts and Decorations Act of 1966, was revoked by Ex. Ord. No. 12553, Feb. 25, 1986, 51 F.R. 7237.

EX ORD. NO. 11446. ACCEPTANCE OF SERVICE MEDALS AND RIBBONS FROM MULTILATERAL ORGANIZATIONS OTHER THAN UNITED NATIONS

Ex. Ord. No. 11446, Jan. 16, 1969, 34 F.R. 803, provided:

By virtue of the authority vested in me as President of the United States and as Commander in Chief of the Armed Forces of the United States, I hereby authorize the Secretary of Defense, with respect to members of the Army, Navy, Air Force, and Marine Corps, and the Secretary of Transportation, with respect to members of the Coast Guard when it is not operating as a service in the Navy, to prescribe regulations for the acceptance of medals and ribbons which are offered by multilateral organizations, other than the United Nations, to members of the Armed Forces of the United States in recognition of service conducted under the auspices of those organizations. A determination that service for a multilateral organization in a particular geographical area or for a particular purpose constitutes a justifiable basis for authorizing acceptance of the medal or ribbon offered to eligible members of the Armed Forces of the United States shall be made with the concurrence of the Secretary of State.

LYNDON B. JOHNSON.

SECTION REFERRED TO IN OTHER SECTIONS

This section is referred to in title 2 section 31–2; title 15 section 278g; title 22 sections 2458a, 2694; title 31 section 1353.

SUBCHAPTER V—MISCONDUCT

§7351. Gifts to superiors

(a) An employee may not—
(1) solicit a contribution from another employee for a gift to an official superior;
(2) make a donation as a gift or give a gift to an official superior; or
(3) accept a gift from an employee receiving less pay than himself.

(b) An employee who violates this section shall be subject to appropriate disciplinary action by the employing agency or entity.

(c) Each supervising ethics office (as defined in section 7353(d)(1)) is authorized to issue regulations implementing this section, including regulations exempting voluntary gifts or contributions that are given or received for special occasions such as marriage or retirement or under other circumstances in which gifts are traditionally given or exchanged.

(Pub. L. 89–554, Sept. 6, 1966, 80 Stat. 527; Pub. L. 101–194, title III, §301, Nov. 30, 1989, 103 Stat. 1745; Pub. L. 101–280, §4(a), May 4, 1990, 104 Stat. 157.)

HISTORICAL AND REVISION NOTES

Derivation	U.S. Code	Revised Statutes and Statutes at Large
....	5 U.S.C. 113.	R.S. §1784.

The application of the section is confined to employees, since the President and Members of Congress, though officers, could not have been intended to be "summarily discharged", and members of uniformed services are not covered by this statute. In the last sentence, the word "removed" is substituted for "summarily discharged" because of the provisions of the Lloyd-LaFollette Act, 37 Stat. 555, as amended, and the Veterans' Preference Act of 1944, 58 Stat. 387, as amended, which are carried into this title.

Standard changes are made to conform with the definitions applicable and the style of this title as outlined in the preface to the report.

AMENDMENTS

1990—Subsec. (a)(2). Pub. L. 101–280, § 4(a)(1), inserted "or give a gift" after "donation as a gift".

Subsec. (c). Pub. L. 101–280, § 4(a)(2), substituted "Each supervising ethics office (as defined in section 7353(d)(1))" for "The Office of Government Ethics" and "circumstances in which gifts are traditionally given or exchanged" for "similar circumstances".

1989—Pub. L. 101–194 designated existing provisions as subsec. (a), struck out "An employee who violates this section shall be removed from the service." at end, and added subsecs. (b) and (c).

INAPPLICABILITY TO TRANSFERS OF UNUSED ACCRUED ANNUAL LEAVE BY FEDERAL EMPLOYEES; EXCEPTION

Pub. L. 100–284, Apr. 7, 1988, 102 Stat. 81, provided: "That, except as the Office of Personnel Management may by regulation prescribe, nothing in section 7351 of title 5, United States Code, shall apply with respect to a solicitation, donation, or acceptance of leave under any program under which, during the fiscal year ending on September 30, 1988, unused accrued annual leave of officers or employees of the Federal Government may be transferred for use by other officers or employees who need such leave due to a personal emergency."

SECTION REFERRED TO IN OTHER SECTIONS

This section is referred to in sections 6340, 6367, 6391 of this title.

§ 7352. Excessive and habitual use of intoxicants

An individual who habitually uses intoxicating beverages to excess may not be employed in the competitive service.

(Pub. L. 89–554, Sept. 6, 1966, 80 Stat. 527.)

HISTORICAL AND REVISION NOTES

Derivation	U.S. Code	Revised Statutes and Statutes at Large
....	5 U.S.C. 640.	Jan. 16, 1883, ch. 27, § 8, 22 Stat. 406.

The word "employed" is substituted for "appointed to, or retained in" because it includes both.

Standard changes are made to conform with the definitions applicable and the style of this title as outlined in the preface to the report.

SECTION REFERRED TO IN OTHER SECTIONS

This section is referred to in title 22 section 3622.

§ 7353. Gifts to Federal employees

(a) Except as permitted by subsection (b), no Member of Congress or officer or employee of the executive, legislative, or judicial branch shall solicit or accept anything of value from a person—

(1) seeking official action from, doing business with, or (in the case of executive branch officers and employees) conducting activities regulated by, the individual's employing entity; or

(2) whose interests may be substantially affected by the performance or nonperformance of the individual's official duties.

(b)(1) Each supervising ethics office is authorized to issue rules or regulations implementing the provisions of this section and providing for such reasonable exceptions as may be appropriate.

(2)(A) Subject to subparagraph (B), a Member, officer, or employee may accept a gift pursuant to rules or regulations established by such individual's supervising ethics office pursuant to paragraph (1).

(B) No gift may be accepted pursuant to subparagraph (A) in return for being influenced in the performance of any official act.

(3) Nothing in this section precludes a Member, officer, or employee from accepting gifts on behalf of the United States Government or any of its agencies in accordance with statutory authority.

(c) A Member of Congress or an officer or employee who violates this section shall be subject to appropriate disciplinary and other remedial action in accordance with any applicable laws, Executive orders, and rules or regulations.

(d) For purposes of this section—

(1) the term "supervising ethics office" means—

(A) the Committee on Standards of Official Conduct of the House of Representatives or the House of Representatives as a whole, for Members, officers, and employees of the House of Representatives;

(B) the Select Committee on Ethics of the Senate, or the Senate as a whole, for Senators, officers, and employees of the Senate;

(C) the Judicial Conference of the United States for judges and judicial branch officers and employees;

(D) the Office of Government Ethics for all executive branch officers and employees; and

(E) in the case of legislative branch officers and employees other than those specified in subparagraphs (A) and (B), the committee referred to in either such subparagraph to which reports filed by such officers and employees under title I of the Ethics in Government Act of 1978 are transmitted under such title, except that the authority of this section may be delegated by such committee with respect to such officers and employees; and

(2) the term "officer or employee" means an individual holding an appointive or elective position in the executive, legislative, or judicial branch of Government, other than a Member of Congress.

(Added Pub. L. 101–194, title III, § 303(a), Nov. 30, 1989, 103 Stat. 1746; amended Pub. L. 101–280, § 4(d), May 4, 1990, 104 Stat. 158.)

REFERENCES IN TEXT

The Ethics in Government Act of 1978, referred to in subsec. (d)(1)(E), is Pub. L. 95–521, Oct. 26, 1978, 92 Stat. 1824, as amended. Title I of the Act, which was classified principally to chapter 18 (§ 701 et seq.) of Title 2, The Congress, was amended generally by Pub. L. 101–194, title II, § 202, Nov. 30, 1989, 103 Stat. 1724, and as so amended, is set out in the Appendix to this title. For complete classification of this Act to the Code, see Short Title note set out under section 101 of Pub. L. 95–521 in the Appendix to this title and Tables.

AMENDMENTS

1990—Subsec. (a). Pub. L. 101–280, § 4(d)(1)(A), substituted "branch" for "branches" in introductory provisions.

Subsec. (a)(1). Pub. L. 101–280, § 4(d)(1)(B), substituted "by, the" for "by the" and "entity" for "agency".

Subsec. (c). Pub. L. 101–280, § 4(d)(2), substituted "A Member of Congress or an officer or employee" for "An employee".

Subsec. (d)(1)(B). Pub. L. 101–280, § 4(d)(3)(A)(i), substituted "officers," for "officers".

Subsec. (d)(1)(E). Pub. L. 101–280, § 4(d)(3)(A)(ii), amended subpar. (E) generally. Prior to amendment, subpar. (E) read as follows: "the ethics committee with which the officer or employee is required to file financial disclosure forms, for all legislative branch officers and employees other than those specified in subparagraphs (A) and (B), except that such authority may be delegated; and".

Subsec. (d)(2). Pub. L. 101–280, § 4(d)(3)(B), substituted "Government," for "Government".

SECTION REFERRED TO IN OTHER SECTIONS

This section is referred to in section 7351 of this title.

SUBCHAPTER VI—DRUG ABUSE, ALCOHOL ABUSE, AND ALCOHOLISM

§ 7361. Drug abuse

(a) The Office of Personnel Management shall be responsible for developing, in cooperation with the President, with the Secretary of Health and Human Services (acting through the National Institute on Drug Abuse), and with other agencies, and in accordance with applicable provisions of this subchapter, appropriate prevention, treatment, and rehabilitation programs and services for drug abuse among employees. Such agencies are encouraged to extend, to the extent feasible, such programs and services to the families of employees and to employees who have family members who are drug abusers. Such programs and services shall make optimal use of existing governmental facilities, services, and skills.

(b) Section 527[1] of the Public Health Service Act (42 U.S.C. 290ee–3), relating to confidentiality of records, and any regulations prescribed thereunder, shall apply with respect to records maintained for the purpose of carrying out this section.

(c) Each agency shall, with respect to any programs or services provided by such agency, submit such written reports as the Office may require in connection with any report required under section 7363 of this title.

(d) For the purpose of this section, the term "agency" means an Executive agency.

(Added Pub. L. 99–570, title VI, § 6002(a)(1), Oct. 27, 1986, 100 Stat. 3207–157.)

REFERENCES IN TEXT

Section 527 of the Public Health Service Act, referred to in subsec. (b) and formerly classified to section 290ee–3 of Title 42, The Public Health and Welfare, was renumbered section 548 of that Act by Pub. L. 100–77, title VI, § 611(2), July 22, 1987, 101 Stat. 516 and then omitted in the general revision of Part D of Subchapter III–A of Chapter 6A of Title 42 by Pub. L. 102–321, title I, § 131, July 10, 1992, 106 Stat. 366. Provisions relating to the confidentiality of patient records are now classified to section 290dd–2 of Title 42.

EDUCATIONAL PROGRAM FOR FEDERAL EMPLOYEES RELATING TO DRUG AND ALCOHOL ABUSE

Section 6003 of Pub. L. 99–570 provided that:

"(a) ESTABLISHMENT.—The Director of the Office of Personnel Management shall, in consultation with the Secretary of Health and Human Services, establish a Government-wide education program, using seminars and such other methods as the Director considers appropriate, to carry out the purposes prescribed in subsection (b).

"(b) PURPOSES.—The program established under this section shall be designed to provide information to Federal Government employees with respect to—

"(1) the short-term and long-term health hazards associated with alcohol abuse and drug abuse;

"(2) the symptoms of alcohol abuse and drug abuse;

"(3) the availability of any prevention, treatment, or rehabilitation programs or services relating to alcohol abuse or drug abuse, whether provided by the Federal Government or otherwise;

"(4) confidentiality protections afforded in connection with any prevention, treatment, or rehabilitation programs or services;

"(5) any penalties provided under law or regulation, and any administrative action (permissive or mandatory), relating to the use of alcohol or drugs by a Federal Government employee or the failure to seek or receive appropriate treatment or rehabilitation services; and

"(6) any other matter which the Director considers appropriate."

SECTION REFERRED TO IN OTHER SECTIONS

This section is referred to in section 7363 of this title.

§ 7362. Alcohol abuse and alcoholism

(a) The Office of Personnel Management shall be responsible for developing, in cooperation with the Secretary of Health and Human Services and with other agencies, and in accordance with applicable provisions of this subpart, appropriate prevention, treatment, and rehabilitation programs and services for alcohol abuse and alcoholism among employees. Such agencies are encouraged to extend, to the extent feasible, such programs and services to the families of alcoholic employees and to employees who have family members who are alcoholics. Such programs and services shall make optimal use of existing governmental facilities, services, and skills.

(b) Section 523[1] of the Public Health Service Act (42 U.S.C. 290dd–3), relating to confidentiality of records, and any regulations prescribed thereunder, shall apply with respect to records maintained for the purpose of carrying out this section.

(c) Each agency shall, with respect to any programs or services provided by such agency, submit such written reports as the Office may require in connection with any report required under section 7363 of this title.

(d) For the purpose of this section, the term "agency" means an Executive agency.

(Added Pub. L. 99–570, title VI, § 6002(a)(1), Oct. 27, 1986, 100 Stat. 3207–157.)

REFERENCES IN TEXT

Section 523 of the Public Health Service Act, referred to in subsec. (b) and formerly classified to section 290dd–3 of Title 42, The Public Health and Welfare, was renumbered section 544 of that Act by Pub. L. 100–77, title VI, § 611(2), July 22, 1987, 101 Stat. 516 and then omitted in the general revision of Part D of Subchapter III–A of Chapter 6A of Title 42 by Pub. L. 102–321, title I, § 131, July 10, 1992, 106 Stat. 366. Provisions relating to the confidentiality of patient records are now classified to section 290dd–2 of Title 42.

---

[1] See References in Text note below.

[1] See References in Text note below.

SECTION REFERRED TO IN OTHER SECTIONS

This section is referred to in section 7363 of this title.

§ 7363. Reports to Congress

(a) The Office of Personnel Management shall, within 6 months after the date of the enactment of the Federal Employee Substance Abuse Education and Treatment Act of 1986 and annually thereafter, submit to each House of Congress a report containing the matters described in subsection (b).

(b) Each report under this section shall include—

(1) a description of any programs or services provided under section 7361 or 7362 of this title, including the costs associated with each such program or service and the source and adequacy of any funding[1] such program or service;

(2) a description of the levels of participation in each program and service provided under section 7361 or 7362 of this title, and the effectiveness of such programs and services;

(3) a description of the training and qualifications required of the personnel providing any program or service under section 7361 or 7362 of this title;

(4) a description of the training given to supervisory personnel in connection with recognizing the symptoms of drug or alcohol abuse and the procedures (including those relating to confidentiality) under which individuals are referred for treatment, rehabilitation, or other assistance;

(5) any recommendations for legislation considered appropriate by the Office and any proposed administrative actions; and

(6) information describing any other related activities under section 7904 of this title, and any other matter which the Office considers appropriate.

(Added Pub. L. 99–570, title VI, § 6002(a)(1), Oct. 27, 1986, 100 Stat. 3207–158.)

REFERENCES IN TEXT

The date of the enactment of the Federal Employee Substance Abuse Education and Treatment Act of 1986, referred to in subsec. (a), is the date of enactment of title VI of Pub. L. 99–570 which was approved Oct. 27, 1986.

TERMINATION OF REPORTING REQUIREMENTS

For termination, effective May 15, 2000, of reporting provisions in this section, see section 3003 of Pub. L. 104–66, as amended, set out as a note under section 1113 of Title 31, Money and Finance, and page 187 of House Document No. 103–7.

SECTION REFERRED TO IN OTHER SECTIONS

This section is referred to in sections 7361, 7362 of this title.

SUBCHAPTER VII—MANDATORY REMOVAL FROM EMPLOYMENT OF CONVICTED LAW ENFORCEMENT OFFICERS

§ 7371. Mandatory removal from employment of law enforcement officers convicted of felonies

(a) In this section, the term—

(1) "conviction notice date" means the date on which an agency that employs a law enforcement officer has notice that the officer has been convicted of a felony that is entered by a Federal or State court, regardless of whether that conviction is appealed or is subject to appeal; and

(2) "law enforcement officer" has the meaning given that term under section 8331(20) or 8401(17).

(b) Any law enforcement officer who is convicted of a felony shall be removed from employment as a law enforcement officer on the last day of the first applicable pay period following the conviction notice date.

(c)(1) This section does not prohibit the removal of an individual from employment as a law enforcement officer before a conviction notice date if the removal is properly effected other than under this section.

(2) This section does not prohibit the employment of any individual in any position other than that of a law enforcement officer.

(d) If the conviction is overturned on appeal, the removal shall be set aside retroactively to the date on which the removal occurred, with back pay under section 5596 for the period during which the removal was in effect, unless the removal was properly effected other than under this section.

(e)(1) If removal is required under this section, the agency shall deliver written notice to the employee as soon as practicable, and not later than 5 calendar days after the conviction notice date. The notice shall include a description of the specific reasons for the removal, the date of removal, and the procedures made applicable under paragraph (2).

(2) The procedures under section 7513(b)(2), (3), and (4), (c), (d), and (e) shall apply to any removal under this section. The employee may use the procedures to contest or appeal a removal, but only with respect to whether—

(A) the employee is a law enforcement officer;

(B) the employee was convicted of a felony; or

(C) the conviction was overturned on appeal.

(3) A removal required under this section shall occur on the date specified in subsection (b) regardless of whether the notice required under paragraph (1) of this subsection and the procedures made applicable under paragraph (2) of this subsection have been provided or completed by that date.

(Added Pub. L. 106–554, § 1(a)(3) [title VI, § 639(a)], Dec. 21, 2000, 114 Stat. 2763, 2763A–168.)

EFFECTIVE DATE

Pub. L. 106–554, § 1(a)(3) [title VI, § 639(c)], Dec. 21, 2000, 114 Stat. 2763, 2763A–168, provided that: "The amendments made by this section [enacting this subchapter] shall take effect 30 days after the date of enactment of this Act [Dec. 21, 2000] and shall apply to any conviction of a felony entered by a Federal or State court on or after that date."

[1] So in original. Probably should be followed by "of".

CHAPTER 75—ADVERSE ACTIONS

AMENDMENTS

1978—Pub. L. 95–454, title II, § 204(b), title IV, § 411(1), Oct. 13, 1978, 92 Stat. 1137, 1173, substituted "SUSPENSION OF 14 DAYS OR LESS" for "COMPETITIVE SERVICE" in subchapter I heading, substituted "Definitions" for "Cause; procedure; exception" in item 7501, added items 7502 to 7504, substituted "REMOVAL, SUSPENSION FOR MORE THAN 14 DAYS, REDUCTION IN GRADE OR PAY, OR FURLOUGH FOR 30 DAYS OR LESS" for "PREFERENCE ELIGIBLES" in subchapter II heading, inserted "; application" in item 7511, substituted "Actions covered" for "Cause; procedure; exception" in item 7512, added items 7513 and 7514, substituted "ADMINISTRATIVE LAW JUDGES" for "HEARING EXAMINERS" in subchapter III heading, substituted "Actions against administrative law judges" for "Removal" in item 7521, and added subchapter V heading and items 7541 to 7543.

CHAPTER REFERRED TO IN OTHER SECTIONS

This chapter is referred to in sections 2108, 2302, 3382, 9508 of this title; title 10 section 1612; title 29 section 783; title 31 section 732; title 39 section 1005; title 41 section 423; title 42 section 237.

SUBCHAPTER I—SUSPENSION FOR 14 DAYS OR LESS

AMENDMENTS

1978—Pub. L. 95–454, title II, § 204(a), Oct. 13, 1978, 92 Stat. 1134, substituted "SUSPENSION FOR 14 DAYS OR LESS" for "COMPETITIVE SERVICE" in subchapter heading.

§ 7501. Definitions

For the purpose of this subchapter—
(1) "employee" means an individual in the competitive service who is not serving a probationary or trial period under an initial appointment or who has completed 1 year of current continuous employment in the same or similar positions under other than a temporary appointment limited to 1 year or less; and

---

[1] So in original. Does not conform to subchapter heading.

(2) "suspension" means the placing of an employee, for disciplinary reasons, in a temporary status without duties and pay.

(Added Pub. L. 95–454, title II, § 204(a), Oct. 13, 1978, 92 Stat. 1134.)

PRIOR PROVISIONS

A prior section 7501, Pub. L. 89–554, Sept. 6, 1966, 80 Stat. 527, related to removal or suspension without pay of an individual in the competitive service and procedures applicable to such removal or suspension, prior to repeal by Pub. L. 95–454, § 204(a).

EFFECTIVE DATE

Subchapter effective 90 days after Oct. 13, 1978, see section 907 of Pub. L. 95–454, set out as an Effective Date of 1978 Amendment note under section 1101 of this title.

SHORT TITLE OF 1990 AMENDMENT

Pub. L. 101–376, § 1, Aug. 17, 1990, 104 Stat. 461, provided that: "This Act [amending sections 4303, 7511, and 7701 of this title and enacting provisions set out as notes under section 4303 of this title] may be cited as the 'Civil Service Due Process Amendments'."

SECTION REFERRED TO IN OTHER SECTIONS

This section is referred to in sections 7511, 7541 of this title.

§ 7502. Actions covered

This subchapter applies to a suspension for 14 days or less, but does not apply to a suspension under section 7521 or 7532 of this title or any action initiated under section 1215 of this title.

(Added Pub. L. 95–454, title II, § 204(a), Oct. 13, 1978, 92 Stat. 1135; amended Pub. L. 101–12, § 9(a)(2), Apr. 10, 1989, 103 Stat. 35.)

AMENDMENTS

1989—Pub. L. 101–12 substituted "1215" for "1206".

EFFECTIVE DATE OF 1989 AMENDMENT

Amendment by Pub. L. 101–12 effective 90 days following Apr. 10, 1989, see section 11 of Pub. L. 101–12, set out as a note under section 1201 of this title.

§ 7503. Cause and procedure

(a) Under regulations prescribed by the Office of Personnel Management, an employee may be suspended for 14 days or less for such cause as will promote the efficiency of the service (including discourteous conduct to the public confirmed by an immediate supervisor's report of four such instances within any one-year period or any other pattern of discourteous conduct).

(b) An employee against whom a suspension for 14 days or less is proposed is entitled to—
(1) an advance written notice stating the specific reasons for the proposed action;
(2) a reasonable time to answer orally and in writing and to furnish affidavits and other documentary evidence in support of the answer;
(3) be represented by an attorney or other representative; and
(4) a written decision and the specific reasons therefor at the earliest practicable date.

(c) Copies of the notice of proposed action, the answer of the employee if written, a summary thereof if made orally, the notice of decision and

reasons therefor, and any order effecting[1] the suspension, together with any supporting material, shall be maintained by the agency and shall be furnished to the Merit Systems Protection Board upon its request and to the employee affected upon the employee's request.

(Added Pub. L. 95–454, title II, §204(a), Oct. 13, 1978, 92 Stat. 1135.)

§ 7504. Regulations

The Office of Personnel Management may prescribe regulations to carry out the purpose of this subchapter.

(Added Pub. L. 95–454, title II, §204(a), Oct. 13, 1978, 92 Stat. 1135.)

SUBCHAPTER II—REMOVAL, SUSPENSION FOR MORE THAN 14 DAYS, REDUCTION IN GRADE OR PAY, OR FURLOUGH FOR 30 DAYS OR LESS

AMENDMENTS

1978—Pub. L. 95–454, title II, §204(a), Oct. 13, 1978, 92 Stat. 1135, substituted "REMOVAL, SUSPENSION FOR MORE THAN 14 DAYS, REDUCTION IN GRADE OR PAY, OR FURLOUGH FOR 30 DAYS OR LESS" for "PREFERENCE ELIGIBLES" in subchapter heading.

SUBCHAPTER REFERRED TO IN OTHER SECTIONS

This subchapter is referred to in sections 2302, 4303, 7541, 7701, 9503 of this title; title 22 section 3701; title 39 section 1005.

§ 7511. Definitions; application

(a) For the purpose of this subchapter—
(1) "employee" means—
(A) an individual in the competitive service—
(i) who is not serving a probationary or trial period under an initial appointment; or
(ii) who has completed 1 year of current continuous service under other than a temporary appointment limited to 1 year or less;

(B) a preference eligible in the excepted service who has completed 1 year of current continuous service in the same or similar positions—
(i) in an Executive agency; or
(ii) in the United States Postal Service or Postal Rate Commission; and

(C) an individual in the excepted service (other than a preference eligible)—
(i) who is not serving a probationary or trial period under an initial appointment pending conversion to the competitive service; or
(ii) who has completed 2 years of current continuous service in the same or similar positions in an Executive agency under other than a temporary appointment limited to 2 years or less;

(2) "suspension" has the same meaning as set forth in section 7501(2) of this title;
(3) "grade" means a level of classification under a position classification system;

(4) "pay" means the rate of basic pay fixed by law or administrative action for the position held by an employee; and
(5) "furlough" means the placing of an employee in a temporary status without duties and pay because of lack of work or funds or other nondisciplinary reasons.

(b) This subchapter does not apply to an employee—
(1) whose appointment is made by and with the advice and consent of the Senate;
(2) whose position has been determined to be of a confidential, policy-determining, policy-making or policy-advocating character by—
(A) the President for a position that the President has excepted from the competitive service;
(B) the Office of Personnel Management for a position that the Office has excepted from the competitive service; or
(C) the President or the head of an agency for a position excepted from the competitive service by statute;

(3) whose appointment is made by the President;
(4) who is receiving an annuity from the Civil Service Retirement and Disability Fund, or the Foreign Service Retirement and Disability Fund, based on the service of such employee;
(5) who is described in section 8337(h)(1), relating to technicians in the National Guard;
(6) who is a member of the Foreign Service, as described in section 103 of the Foreign Service Act of 1980;
(7) whose position is within the Central Intelligence Agency or the General Accounting Office;
(8) whose position is within the United States Postal Service, the Postal Rate Commission, the Panama Canal Commission, the Tennessee Valley Authority, the Federal Bureau of Investigation, an intelligence component of the Department of Defense (as defined in section 1614 of title 10), or an intelligence activity of a military department covered under subchapter I of chapter 83 of title 10, unless subsection (a)(1)(B) of this section or section 1005(a) of title 39 is the basis for this subchapter's applicability;
(9) who is described in section 5102(c)(11) of this title; or
(10) who holds a position within the Veterans Health Administration which has been excluded from the competitive service by or under a provision of title 38, unless such employee was appointed to such position under section 7401(3) of such title.

(c) The Office may provide for the application of this subchapter to any position or group of positions excepted from the competitive service by regulation of the Office which is not otherwise covered by this subchapter.

(Added Pub. L. 95–454, title II, §204(a), Oct. 13, 1978, 92 Stat. 1135; amended Pub. L. 101–376, §2(a), Aug. 17, 1990, 104 Stat. 461; Pub. L. 102–378, §6(a), Oct. 2, 1992, 106 Stat. 1358; Pub. L. 103–359, title V, §501(l), Oct. 14, 1994, 108 Stat. 3430; Pub. L. 104–201, div. A, title XVI, §1634(b), Sept. 23, 1996, 110 Stat. 2752.)

---

[1] So in original. Probably should be "affecting".

REFERENCES IN TEXT

Section 103 of the Foreign Service Act of 1980, referred to in subsec. (b)(6), is classified to section 3903 of Title 22, Foreign Relations and Intercourse.

PRIOR PROVISIONS

A prior section 7511, Pub. L. 89–554, Sept. 6, 1966, 80 Stat. 528; Pub. L. 94–183, § 2(30), Dec. 31, 1975, 89 Stat. 1058, defined "preference eligible employee" and "adverse action" for purposes of this subchapter, prior to repeal by Pub. L. 95–454, § 204(a).

AMENDMENTS

1996—Subsec. (b)(8). Pub. L. 104–201 substituted "an intelligence component of the Department of Defense (as defined in section 1614 of title 10), or an intelligence activity of a military department covered under subchapter I of chapter 83 of title 10" for "the National Security Agency, the Defense Intelligence Agency, the Central Imagery Office, or an intelligence activity of a military department covered under section 1590 of title 10".

1994—Subsec. (b)(8). Pub. L. 103–359 inserted "the Central Imagery Office," after "Defense Intelligence Agency,".

1992—Subsec. (b)(7). Pub. L. 102–378, § 6(a)(1), amended par. (7) generally. Prior to amendment, par. (7) read as follows: "whose position is with the Central Intelligence Agency, the General Accounting Office, or the Veterans Health Services and Research Administration;".

Subsec. (b)(10). Pub. L. 102–378, § 6(a)(2)–(4), added par. (10).

1990—Pub. L. 101–376 amended section generally. Prior to amendment, section read as follows:

"(a) For the purpose of this subchapter—

"(1) 'employee' means—

"(A) an individual in the competitive service who is not serving a probationary or trial period under an initial appointment or who has completed 1 year of current continuous employment under other than a temporary appointment limited to 1 year or less; and

"(B) a preference eligible in an Executive agency in the excepted service, and a preference eligible in the United States Postal Service or the Postal Rate Commission, who has completed 1 year of current continuous service in the same or similar positions;

"(2) 'suspension' has the meaning as set forth in section 7501(2) of this title;

"(3) 'grade' means a level of classification under a position classification system;

"(4) 'pay' means the rate of basic pay fixed by law or administrative action for the position held by an employee; and

"(5) 'furlough' means the placing of an employee in a temporary status without duties and pay because of lack of work or funds or other nondisciplinary reasons.

"(b) This subchapter does not apply to an employee—

"(1) whose appointment is made by and with the advice and consent of the Senate;

"(2) whose position has been determined to be of a confidential, policy-determining, policy-making or policy-advocating character by—

"(A) the Office of Personnel Management for a position that it has excepted from the competitive service; or

"(B) the President or the head of an agency for a position which is excepted from the competitive service by statute.

"(c) The Office may provide for the application of this subchapter to any position or group of positions excepted from the competitive service by regulation of the Office."

EFFECTIVE DATE OF 1996 AMENDMENT

Amendment by Pub. L. 104–201 effective Oct. 1, 1996, see section 1635 of Pub. L. 104–201, set out as a note under section 1593 of Title 10, Armed Forces.

EFFECTIVE DATE OF 1992 AMENDMENT

Section 6(b) of Pub. L. 102–378 provided that:

"(1) The amendments made by subsection (a) [amending this section] shall apply with respect to any personnel action taking effect on or after the date of enactment of this Act [Oct. 2, 1992].

"(2) In the case of an employee or former employee of the Veterans Health Administration (or predecessor agency in name)—

"(A) against whom an adverse personnel action was taken before the date of enactment of this Act,

"(B) who, as a result of the enactment of the Civil Service Due Process Amendments (5 U.S.C. 7501 note) [Pub. L. 101–376], became ineligible to appeal such action to the Merit Systems Protection Board,

"(C) as to whom that appeal right is restored as a result of the enactment of subsection (a), or would have been restored but for the passage of time, and

"(D) who is not precluded, by section 7121(e)(1) of title 5, United States Code, from appealing to the Merit Systems Protection Board,

the deadline for bringing an appeal under section 7513(d) or section 4303(e) of such title with respect to such action shall be the latter of—

"(i) the 60th day after the date of enactment of this Act; or

"(ii) the deadline which would otherwise apply if this paragraph had not been enacted."

EFFECTIVE DATE OF 1990 AMENDMENT

Amendment by Pub. L. 101–376 applicable with respect to any personnel action taking effect on or after Aug. 17, 1990, see section 2(c) of Pub. L. 101–376, set out as a note under section 4303 of this title.

EFFECTIVE DATE

Subchapter effective 90 days after Oct. 13, 1978, see section 907 of Pub. L. 95–454, set out as an Effective Date of 1978 Amendment note under section 1101 of this title.

SECTION REFERRED TO IN OTHER SECTIONS

This section is referred to in section 2302 of this title; title 2 section 1602; title 10 section 1610; title 22 sections 1438, 3701; title 25 section 2012; title 32 section 709; title 39 section 1005; title 49 section 44506.

§ 7512. Actions covered

This subchapter applies to—

(1) a removal;

(2) a suspension for more than 14 days;

(3) a reduction in grade;

(4) a reduction in pay; and

(5) a furlough of 30 days or less;

but does not apply to—

(A) a suspension or removal under section 7532 of this title,

(B) a reduction-in-force action under section 3502 of this title,

(C) the reduction in grade of a supervisor or manager who has not completed the probationary period under section 3321(a)(2) of this title if such reduction is to the grade held immediately before becoming such a supervisor or manager,

(D) a reduction in grade or removal under section 4303 of this title, or

(E) an action initiated under section 1215 or 7521 of this title.

(Added Pub. L. 95–454, title II, § 204(a), Oct. 13, 1978, 92 Stat. 1136; amended Pub. L. 101–12, § 9(a)(2), Apr. 10, 1989, 103 Stat. 35.)

PRIOR PROVISIONS

A prior section 7512, Pub. L. 89–554, Sept. 6, 1966, 80 Stat. 528, related to adverse action against a preference eligible employee and procedures applicable to such adverse action, prior to repeal by Pub. L. 95–454, §204(a).

AMENDMENTS

1989—Par. (E). Pub. L. 101–12 substituted "1215" for "1206".

EFFECTIVE DATE OF 1989 AMENDMENT

Amendment by Pub. L. 101–12 effective 90 days following Apr. 10, 1989, see section 11 of Pub. L. 101–12, set out as a note under section 1201 of this title.

SECTION REFERRED TO IN OTHER SECTIONS

This section is referred to in sections 3315, 5545a, 7121 of this title; title 22 sections 1438, 3701; title 32 section 709; title 50 section 832.

§ 7513. Cause and procedure

(a) Under regulations prescribed by the Office of Personnel Management, an agency may take an action covered by this subchapter against an employee only for such cause as will promote the efficiency of the service.

(b) An employee against whom an action is proposed is entitled to—

(1) at least 30 days' advance written notice, unless there is reasonable cause to believe the employee has committed a crime for which a sentence of imprisonment may be imposed, stating the specific reasons for the proposed action;

(2) a reasonable time, but not less than 7 days, to answer orally and in writing and to furnish affidavits and other documentary evidence in support of the answer;

(3) be represented by an attorney or other representative; and

(4) a written decision and the specific reasons therefor at the earliest practicable date.

(c) An agency may provide, by regulation, for a hearing which may be in lieu of or in addition to the opportunity to answer provided under subsection (b)(2) of this section.

(d) An employee against whom an action is taken under this section is entitled to appeal to the Merit Systems Protection Board under section 7701 of this title.

(e) Copies of the notice of proposed action, the answer of the employee when written, a summary thereof when made orally, the notice of decision and reasons therefor, and any order effecting an action covered by this subchapter, together with any supporting material, shall be maintained by the agency and shall be furnished to the Board upon its request and to the employee affected upon the employee's request.

(Added Pub. L. 95–454, title II, §204(a), Oct. 13, 1978, 92 Stat. 1136.)

SECTION REFERRED TO IN OTHER SECTIONS

This section is referred to in sections 1221, 7371, 9508 of this title; title 38 section 7101A.

§ 7514. Regulations

The Office of Personnel Management may prescribe regulations to carry out the purpose of this subchapter, except as it concerns any matter with respect to which the Merit Systems Protection Board may prescribe regulations.

(Added Pub. L. 95–454, title II, §204(a), Oct. 13, 1978, 92 Stat. 1137.)

SUBCHAPTER III—ADMINISTRATIVE LAW JUDGES

AMENDMENTS

1978—Pub. L. 95–454, title II, §204(a), Oct. 13, 1978, 92 Stat. 1137, substituted "ADMINISTRATIVE LAW JUDGES" for "HEARING EXAMINERS" in subchapter heading.

§ 7521. Actions against administrative law judges

(a) An action may be taken against an administrative law judge appointed under section 3105 of this title by the agency in which the administrative law judge is employed only for good cause established and determined by the Merit Systems Protection Board on the record after opportunity for hearing before the Board.

(b) The actions covered by this section are—

(1) a removal;

(2) a suspension;

(3) a reduction in grade;

(4) a reduction in pay; and

(5) a furlough of 30 days or less;

but do not include—

(A) a suspension or removal under section 7532 of this title;

(B) a reduction-in-force action under section 3502 of this title; or

(C) any action initiated under section 1215 of this title.

(Added Pub. L. 95–454, title II, §204(a), Oct. 13, 1978, 92 Stat. 1137; amended Pub. L. 101–12, §9(a)(2), Apr. 10, 1989, 103 Stat. 35.)

PRIOR PROVISIONS

A prior section 7521, Pub. L. 89–554, Sept. 6, 1966, 80 Stat. 528; Pub. L. 95–251, §2(a)(1), Mar. 27, 1978, 92 Stat. 183, related to removal of an administrative law judge appointed under section 3105 of this title, prior to repeal by Pub. L. 95–454, §204(a).

AMENDMENTS

1989—Subsec. (b)(C). Pub. L. 101–12 substituted "1215" for "1206".

EFFECTIVE DATE OF 1989 AMENDMENT

Amendment by Pub. L. 101–12 effective 90 days following Apr. 10, 1989, see section 11 of Pub. L. 101–12, set out as a note under section 1201 of this title.

EFFECTIVE DATE

Section effective 90 days after Oct. 13, 1978, see section 907 of Pub. L. 95–454, set out as an Effective Date of 1978 Amendment note under section 1101 of this title.

SECTION REFERRED TO IN OTHER SECTIONS

This section is referred to in sections 559, 1305, 7502, 7512 of this title; title 15 section 1715; title 29 section 661; title 30 section 823; title 38 section 7101A; title 39 section 3601; title 42 sections 2000e–4, 3608.

SUBCHAPTER IV—NATIONAL SECURITY

§ 7531. Definitions

For the purpose of this subchapter, "agency" means—

(1) the Department of State;

(2) the Department of Commerce;

(3) the Department of Justice;

(4) the Department of Defense;

(5) a military department;

(6) the Coast Guard;

(7) the Atomic Energy Commission;

(8) the National Aeronautics and Space Administration; and

(9) such other agency of the Government of the United States as the President designates in the best interests of national security.

The President shall report any designation to the Committees on the Armed Services of the Congress.

(Pub. L. 89–554, Sept. 6, 1966, 80 Stat. 528.)

HISTORICAL AND REVISION NOTES

Derivation	U.S. Code	Revised Statutes and Statutes at Large
....	5 U.S.C. 22–3.	Aug. 26, 1950, ch. 823, § 3, 64 Stat. 477.

Paragraphs (1)–(8) are supplied on authority of former section 22–1, which is carried in part into section 7532. The references to "the Foreign Service of the United States" and "several field services" are omitted as unnecessary since they are within the agencies concerned. The words "military departments" are substituted for the enumeration of the military departments in view of the definition of "military department" in section 102.

The reference to the National Security Resources Board is omitted as the Board was abolished by 1953 Reorg. Plan No. 3, § 6, eff. June 12, 1953, 67 Stat. 636.

Paragraph (9) is restated to conform to the style of this title.

Standard changes are made to conform with the definitions applicable and the style of this title as outlined in the preface to the report.

ABOLITION OF ATOMIC ENERGY COMMISSION

Atomic Energy Commission abolished and functions transferred by sections 5814 and 5841 of Title 42, The Public Health and Welfare. See, also, Transfer of Functions notes set out under those sections.

PANAMA CANAL AND PANAMA RAILROAD COMPANY

Ex. Ord. No. 10237, Apr. 27, 1951, 16 F.R. 3627, made the provisions of former sections 22–1 and 22–3 of this title [see Disposition Table preceding section 101 of this title] applicable to the Panama Canal Government and to the Panama Canal Company.

DESIGNATION OF NATIONAL SECURITY AGENCY, DEFENSE INTELLIGENCE AGENCY, AND DEFENSE MAPPING AGENCY AS "AGENCIES"

Memorandum of the President of the United States, May 23, 1988, 53 F.R. 26023, provided:

Memorandum for the Secretary of Defense

I have reviewed the personnel security requirements of the National Security Agency, the Defense Intelligence Agency, and the Defense Mapping Agency and the termination provisions of 5 U.S.C. Section 7532. I have determined that these Agencies are sensitive agencies and that it is in the best interests of national security that they be designated "agencies" within the meaning of that section.

Therefore, pursuant to the authority set forth in 5 U.S.C. Section 7531(9), I hereby designate the National Security Agency, the Defense Intelligence Agency, and the Defense Mapping Agency as "agencies" within the meaning of 5 U.S.C. Section 7532.

You are hereby authorized and directed to report these designations to the Committees on Armed Services of the Congress and to publish this memorandum in the Federal Register.

RONALD REAGAN.

§ 7532. Suspension and removal

(a) Notwithstanding other statutes, the head of an agency may suspend without pay an employee of his agency when he considers that action necessary in the interests of national security. To the extent that the head of the agency determines that the interests of national security permit, the suspended employee shall be notified of the reasons for the suspension. Within 30 days after the notification, the suspended employee is entitled to submit to the official designated by the head of the agency statements or affidavits to show why he should be restored to duty.

(b) Subject to subsection (c) of this section, the head of an agency may remove an employee suspended under subsection (a) of this section when, after such investigation and review as he considers necessary, he determines that removal is necessary or advisable in the interests of national security. The determination of the head of the agency is final.

(c) An employee suspended under subsection (a) of this section who—

(1) has a permanent or indefinite appointment;

(2) has completed his probationary or trial period; and

(3) is a citizen of the United States;

is entitled, after suspension and before removal, to—

(A) a written statement of the charges against him within 30 days after suspension, which may be amended within 30 days thereafter and which shall be stated as specifically as security considerations permit;

(B) an opportunity within 30 days thereafter, plus an additional 30 days if the charges are amended, to answer the charges and submit affidavits;

(C) a hearing, at the request of the employee, by an agency authority duly constituted for this purpose;

(D) a review of his case by the head of the agency or his designee, before a decision adverse to the employee is made final; and

(E) a written statement of the decision of the head of the agency.

(Pub. L. 89–554, Sept. 6, 1966, 80 Stat. 529.)

HISTORICAL AND REVISION NOTES

Derivation	U.S. Code	Revised Statutes and Statutes at Large
....	5 U.S.C. 22–1 (less 3d–5th provisos).	Aug. 26, 1950, ch. 803, § 1 (less 3d–5th provisos), 64 Stat. 476. July 29, 1958, Pub. L. 85–568, § 301(c), 72 Stat. 432.

The application of this section is covered by the definition in section 7531.

In subsection (a), the words "Notwithstanding the provisions of section 652 of this title" are omitted but are carried into section 7501(c). The words "in his absolute discretion" are omitted as unnecessary in view of the permissive grant of authority. The word "reinstated" is omitted as it is commonly used in other statutes to denote action different from that referred to here.

In subsections (b) and (c), the words "remove" and "removal" are coextensive with and substituted for "terminate the employment", "termination", and "employment is terminated", as appropriate.

Standard changes are made to conform with the definitions applicable and the style of this title as outlined in the preface to the report.

SECTION REFERRED TO IN OTHER SECTIONS

This section is referred to in sections 3393, 3571, 7121, 7312, 7502, 7512, 7521, 7542 of this title; title 50 section 832.

§ 7533. Effect on other statutes

This subchapter does not impair the powers vested in the Atomic Energy Commission by chapter 23 of title 42, or the requirement in section 2201(d) of title 42 that adequate provision be made for administrative review of a determination to dismiss an employee of the Atomic Energy Commission.

(Pub. L. 89–554, Sept. 6, 1966, 80 Stat. 529.)

HISTORICAL AND REVISION NOTES

Derivation	U.S. Code	Revised Statutes and Statutes at Large
....	5 U.S.C. 22–2.	Aug. 26, 1950, ch. 803, § 2, 64 Stat. 477.

Standard changes are made to conform with the definitions applicable and the style of this title as outlined in the preface to the report.

TRANSFER OF FUNCTIONS

Atomic Energy Commission abolished and functions transferred by sections 5814 and 5841 of Title 42, The Public Health and Welfare. See, also, Transfer of Functions notes set out under those sections.

SUBCHAPTER V—SENIOR EXECUTIVE SERVICE

SUBCHAPTER REFERRED TO IN OTHER SECTIONS

This subchapter is referred to in section 7701 of this title; title 38 section 7425.

§ 7541. Definitions

For the purpose of this subchapter—
(1) "employee" means a career appointee in the Senior Executive Service who—
(A) has completed the probationary period prescribed under section 3393(d) of this title; or
(B) was covered by the provisions of subchapter II of this chapter immediately before appointment to the Senior Executive Service; and
(2) "suspension" has the meaning set forth in section 7501(2) of this title.

(Added Pub. L. 95–454, title IV, § 411(2), Oct. 13, 1978, 92 Stat. 1174.)

EFFECTIVE DATE

Subchapter effective 9 months after Oct. 13, 1978, and congressional review of provisions of sections 401 through 412 of Pub. L. 95–454, see section 415 of Pub. L. 95–454, set out as a note under section 3131 of this title.

§ 7542. Actions covered

This subchapter applies to a removal from the civil service or suspension for more than 14 days, but does not apply to an action initiated under section 1215 of this title, to a suspension or removal under section 7532 of this title, or to a removal under section 3592 or 3595 of this title.

(Added Pub. L. 95–454, title IV, § 411(2), Oct. 13, 1978, 92 Stat. 1174; amended Pub. L. 97–35, title XVII, § 1704(d)(1), Aug. 13, 1981, 95 Stat. 758; Pub. L. 101–12, § 9(a)(2), Apr. 10, 1989, 103 Stat. 35.)

AMENDMENTS

1989—Pub. L. 101–12 substituted "1215" for "1206".
1981—Pub. L. 97–35 inserted reference to section 3595 of this title.

EFFECTIVE DATE OF 1989 AMENDMENT

Amendment by Pub. L. 101–12 effective 90 days following Apr. 10, 1989, see section 11 of Pub. L. 101–12, set out as a note under section 1201 of this title.

EFFECTIVE DATE OF 1981 AMENDMENT

Amendment by Pub. L. 97–35 effective June 1, 1981, with certain exceptions and conditions, see section 1704(e) of Pub. L. 97–35, set out as an Effective Date note under section 3595 of this title.

§ 7543. Cause and procedure

(a) Under regulations prescribed by the Office of Personnel Management, an agency may take an action covered by this subchapter against an employee only for misconduct, neglect of duty, malfeasance, or failure to accept a directed reassignment or to accompany a position in a transfer of function.

(b) An employee against whom an action covered by this subchapter is proposed is entitled to—
(1) at least 30 days' advance written notice, unless there is reasonable cause to believe that the employee has committed a crime for which a sentence of imprisonment can be imposed, stating specific reasons for the proposed action;
(2) a reasonable time, but not less than 7 days, to answer orally and in writing and to furnish affidavits and other documentary evidence in support of the answer;
(3) be represented by an attorney or other representative; and
(4) a written decision and specific reasons therefor at the earliest practicable date.

(c) An agency may provide, by regulation, for a hearing which may be in lieu of or in addition to the opportunity to answer provided under subsection (b)(2) of this section.

(d) An employee against whom an action is taken under this section is entitled to appeal to the Merit Systems Protection Board under section 7701 of this title.

(e) Copies of the notice of proposed action, the answer of the employee when written, and a summary thereof when made orally, the notice of decision and reasons therefor, and any order effecting an action covered by this subchapter, together with any supporting material, shall be maintained by the agency and shall be furnished to the Merit Systems Protection Board upon its request and to the employee affected upon the employee's request.

(Added Pub. L. 95–454, title IV, § 411(2), Oct. 13, 1978, 92 Stat. 1174; amended Pub. L. 97–35, title XVII, § 1704(d)(2), Aug. 13, 1981, 95 Stat. 758; Pub. L. 98–615, title III, § 304(c), Nov. 8, 1984, 98 Stat. 3219.)

AMENDMENTS

1984—Subsec. (a). Pub. L. 98–615 inserted reference to failure to accept a directed reassignment or to accompany a position in a transfer of function.
1981—Subsec. (a). Pub. L. 97–35 substituted "misconduct, neglect of duty, or malfeasance" for "such cause as will promote the efficiency of the service".

EFFECTIVE DATE OF 1984 AMENDMENT

Amendment by Pub. L. 98–615 effective Nov. 8, 1984, see section 307 of Pub. L. 98–615, set out as a note under section 3393 of this title.

EFFECTIVE DATE OF 1981 AMENDMENT

Amendment by Pub. L. 97–35 effective June 1, 1981, with certain exceptions and conditions, see section 1704(e) of Pub. L. 97–35, set out as an Effective Date note under section 3595 of this title.

SECTION REFERRED TO IN OTHER SECTIONS

This section is referred to in sections 3151, 3393 of this title; title 10 section 1606; title 31 section 733.

CHAPTER 77—APPEALS

AMENDMENTS

1978—Pub. L. 95–454, title II, § 205, Oct. 13, 1978, 92 Stat. 1138, substituted "Appellate procedures" for "Appeals of preference eligibles" in item 7701, and added items 7702 and 7703.

CHAPTER REFERRED TO IN OTHER SECTIONS

This chapter is referred to in title 29 section 783.

§ 7701. Appellate procedures

(a) An employee, or applicant for employment, may submit an appeal to the Merit Systems Protection Board from any action which is appealable to the Board under any law, rule, or regulation. An appellant shall have the right—

(1) to a hearing for which a transcript will be kept; and

(2) to be represented by an attorney or other representative.

Appeals shall be processed in accordance with regulations prescribed by the Board.

(b)(1) The Board may hear any case appealed to it or may refer the case to an administrative law judge appointed under section 3105 of this title or other employee of the Board designated by the Board to hear such cases, except that in any case involving a removal from the service, the case shall be heard by the Board, an employee experienced in hearing appeals, or an administrative law judge. The Board, administrative law judge, or other employee (as the case may be) shall make a decision after receipt of the written representations of the parties to the appeal and after opportunity for a hearing under subsection (a)(1) of this section. A copy of the decision shall be furnished to each party to the appeal and to the Office of Personnel Management.

(2)(A) If an employee or applicant for employment is the prevailing party in an appeal under this subsection, the employee or applicant shall be granted the relief provided in the decision effective upon the making of the decision, and remaining in effect pending the outcome of any petition for review under subsection (e), unless—

(i) the deciding official determines that the granting of such relief is not appropriate; or

(ii)(I) the relief granted in the decision provides that such employee or applicant shall return or be present at the place of employment during the period pending the outcome of any petition for review under subsection (e); and

(II) the employing agency, subject to the provisions of subparagraph (B), determines that the return or presence of such employee or applicant is unduly disruptive to the work environment.

(B) If an agency makes a determination under subparagraph (A)(ii)(II) that prevents the return or presence of an employee at the place of employment, such employee shall receive pay, compensation, and all other benefits as terms and conditions of employment during the period pending the outcome of any petition for review under subsection (e).

(C) Nothing in the provisions of this paragraph may be construed to require any award of back pay or attorney fees be paid before the decision is final.

(3) With respect to an appeal from an adverse action covered by subchapter V of chapter 75, authority to mitigate the personnel action involved shall be available, subject to the same standards as would apply in an appeal involving an action covered by subchapter II of chapter 75 with respect to which mitigation authority under this section exists.

(c)(1) Subject to paragraph (2) of this subsection, the decision of the agency shall be sustained under subsection (b) only if the agency's decision—

(A) in the case of an action based on unacceptable performance described in section 4303 or a removal from the Senior Executive Service for failure to be recertified under section 3393a, is supported by substantial evidence; or

(B) in any other case, is supported by a preponderance of the evidence.

(2) Notwithstanding paragraph (1), the agency's decision may not be sustained under subsection (b) of this section if the employee or applicant for employment—

(A) shows harmful error in the application of the agency's procedures in arriving at such decision;

(B) shows that the decision was based on any prohibited personnel practice described in section 2302(b) of this title; or

(C) shows that the decision was not in accordance with law.

(d)(1) In any case in which—

(A) the interpretation or application of any civil service law, rule, or regulation, under the jurisdiction of the Office of Personnel Management is at issue in any proceeding under this section; and

(B) the Director of the Office of Personnel Management is of the opinion that an erroneous decision would have a substantial impact on any civil service law, rule, or regulation under the jurisdiction of the Office;

the Director may as a matter of right intervene or otherwise participate in that proceeding before the Board. If the Director exercises his right to participate in a proceeding before the Board, he shall do so as early in the proceeding as practicable. Nothing in this title shall be construed to permit the Office to interfere with the independent decisionmaking of the Merit Systems Protection Board.

(2) The Board shall promptly notify the Director whenever the interpretation of any civil service law, rule, or regulation under the jurisdiction of the Office is at issue in any proceeding under this section.

(e)(1) Except as provided in section 7702 of this title, any decision under subsection (b) of this section shall be final unless—

(A) a party to the appeal or the Director petitions the Board for review within 30 days after the receipt of the decision; or

(B) the Board reopens and reconsiders a case on its own motion.

The Board, for good cause shown, may extend the 30-day period referred to in subparagraph (A) of this paragraph. One member of the Board may grant a petition or otherwise direct that a decision be reviewed by the full Board. The preceding sentence shall not apply if, by law, a decision of an administrative law judge is required to be acted upon by the Board.

(2) The Director may petition the Board for a review under paragraph (1) of this subsection only if the Director is of the opinion that the decision is erroneous and will have a substantial impact on any civil service law, rule, or regulation under the jurisdiction of the Office.

(f) The Board, or an administrative law judge or other employee of the Board designated to hear a case, may—

(1) consolidate appeals filed by two or more appellants, or

(2) join two or more appeals filed by the same appellant and hear and decide them concurrently,

if the deciding official or officials hearing the cases are of the opinion that the action could result in the appeals' being processed more expeditiously and would not adversely affect any party.

(g)(1) Except as provided in paragraph (2) of this subsection, the Board, or an administrative law judge or other employee of the Board designated to hear a case, may require payment by the agency involved of reasonable attorney fees incurred by an employee or applicant for employment if the employee or applicant is the prevailing party and the Board, administrative law judge, or other employee (as the case may be) determines that payment by the agency is warranted in the interest of justice, including any case in which a prohibited personnel practice was engaged in by the agency or any case in which the agency's action was clearly without merit.

(2) If an employee or applicant for employment is the prevailing party and the decision is based on a finding of discrimination prohibited under section 2302(b)(1) of this title, the payment of attorney fees shall be in accordance with the standards prescribed under section 706(k) of the Civil Rights Act of 1964 (42 U.S.C. 2000e–5(k)).

(h) The Board may, by regulation, provide for one or more alternative methods for settling matters subject to the appellate jurisdiction of the Board which shall be applicable at the election of an applicant for employment or of an employee who is not in a unit for which a labor organization is accorded exclusive recognition, and shall be in lieu of other procedures provided for under this section. A decision under such a method shall be final, unless the Board reopens and reconsiders a case at the request of the Office of Personnel Management under subsection (e) of this section.

(i)(1) Upon the submission of any appeal to the Board under this section, the Board, through reference to such categories of cases, or other means, as it determines appropriate, shall establish and announce publicly the date by which it intends to complete action on the matter. Such date shall assure expeditious consideration of the appeal, consistent with the interests of fairness and other priorities of the Board. If the Board fails to complete action on the appeal by the announced date, and the expected delay will exceed 30 days, the Board shall publicly announce the new date by which it intends to complete action on the appeal.

(2) Not later than March 1 of each year, the Board shall submit to the Congress a report describing the number of appeals submitted to it during the preceding fiscal year, the number of appeals on which it completed action during that year, and the number of instances during that year in which it failed to conclude a proceeding by the date originally announced, together with an explanation of the reasons therefor.

(3) The Board shall by rule indicate any other category of significant Board action which the Board determines should be subject to the provisions of this subsection.

(4) It shall be the duty of the Board, an administrative law judge, or employee designated by the Board to hear any proceeding under this section to expedite to the extent practicable that proceeding.

(j) In determining the appealability under this section of any case involving a removal from the service (other than the removal of a reemployed annuitant), neither an individual's status under any retirement system established by or under Federal statute nor any election made by such individual under any such system may be taken into account.

(k) The Board may prescribe regulations to carry out the purpose of this section.

(Pub. L. 89–554, Sept. 6, 1966, 80 Stat. 530; Pub. L. 95–454, title II, § 205, Oct. 13, 1978, 92 Stat. 1138; Pub. L. 96–54, § 2(a)(45), Aug. 14, 1979, 93 Stat. 384; Pub. L. 99–386, title II, § 208, Aug. 22, 1986, 100 Stat. 824; Pub. L. 101–12, § 6, Apr. 10, 1989, 103 Stat. 33; Pub. L. 101–194, title V, § 506(b)(6), Nov. 30, 1989, 103 Stat. 1758; Pub. L. 101–280, § 6(d)(2), May 4, 1990, 104 Stat. 160; Pub. L. 101–376, § 3, Aug. 17, 1990, 104 Stat. 462; Pub. L. 102–175, § 5, Dec. 2, 1991, 105 Stat. 1223; Pub. L. 102–378, § 2(56), Oct. 2, 1992, 106 Stat. 1354.)

HISTORICAL AND REVISION NOTES

Derivation	U.S. Code	Revised Statutes and Statutes at Large
....	5 U.S.C. 863 (less 1st 168 words, and less 2d proviso).	June 27, 1944, ch. 287, § 14 (less 1st 168 words, and less 2d proviso), 58 Stat. 390. Aug. 4, 1947, ch. 447, 61 Stat. 723.
....	5 U.S.C. 868 (proviso).	June 22, 1948, ch. 604, 62 Stat. 575.

The application of the section is established by the words "A preference eligible employee as defined by section 7511 of this title". Specific mention of the actions appealable are covered by the reference to "an adverse decision under section 7512 of this title". The words "administrative authority" are substituted for "administrative officer" to avoid conflict with the definitions of "employee" and "officer" in chapter 21 of this title and to include an individual who is employed by the government of the District of Columbia or who is a member of a uniformed service as such an individual could have been an "administrative officer" under former section 863. The words "the date of" in the phrase "after the date of receipt of notice" are omitted as unnecessary. The words "reasonable rules and" in the phrase "reasonable rules and regulations" are omitted as unnecessary. The word "proper" in the phrase "proper administrative officer" is omitted as unnecessary. The word "designated" in the phrase "designated representative" is omitted as unnecessary.

Standard changes are made to conform with the definitions applicable and the style of this title outlined in preface to the report.

REFERENCES IN TEXT

The civil service law, referred to in subsecs. (d) and (e)(2), is set out in this title. See, particularly, section 3301 et seq. of this title.

AMENDMENTS

1992—Subsec. (c)(1)(A). Pub. L. 102–378 amended subpar. (A) generally. Prior to amendment, subpar. (A) read as follows: "in the case of an action based on unacceptable performance described in section 4303 or a removal from the Senior Executive Service for failure to be recertified under section 3393a of this title, is supported by substantial evidence, or".

1991—Subsec. (b)(3). Pub. L. 102–175 added par. (3).

1990—Subsec. (c)(1)(A). Pub. L. 101–280 amended Pub. L. 101–194, see 1989 Amendment note below.

Subsecs. (j), (k). Pub. L. 101–376 added subsec. (j) and redesignated former subsec. (j) as (k).

1989—Subsec. (b). Pub. L. 101–12 designated existing provisions as par. (1) and added par. (2).

Subsec. (c)(1)(A). Pub. L. 101–194, as amended by Pub. L. 101–280, which directed the substitution of "or a removal from the Senior Executive Service for failure to be recertified under section 3393a of" for "of", was executed by making the substitution for the second reference to "of" as the probable intent of Congress.

1986—Subsec. (i)(2). Pub. L. 99–386 substituted "fiscal" for "calendar".

1979—Subsec. (e)(1). Pub. L. 96–54, § 2(a)(45)(A), substituted "administrative" for "administration".

Subsec. (g)(1). Pub. L. 96–54, § 2(a)(45)(B), substituted "(as the case may be)" for ", as the case may be,".

Subsec. (h). Pub. L. 96–54, § 2(a)(45)(C), substituted "subsection (e)" for "subsection (d)".

1978—Pub. L. 95–454 substituted "Appellate procedures" for "Appeals of preference eligibles" in section catchline, and in text substituted provisions relating to procedures applicable with respect to the Merit Systems Protection Board for an employee or applicant for employment, for provisions relating to appeals of preference eligible employees.

EFFECTIVE DATE OF 1990 AMENDMENT

Amendment by Pub. L. 101–376 effective Aug. 17, 1990, and applicable with respect to any appeal or other proceeding brought on or after such date, see section 4 of Pub. L. 101–376, set out as a note under section 4303 of this title.

EFFECTIVE DATE OF 1989 AMENDMENTS

Amendment by Pub. L. 101–194 effective Jan. 1, 1991, see section 506(d) of Pub. L. 101–194, set out as a note under section 3151 of this title.

Amendment by Pub. L. 101–12 effective 90 days following Apr. 10, 1989, see section 11 of Pub. L. 101–12, set out as a note under section 1201 of this title.

EFFECTIVE DATE OF 1979 AMENDMENT

Amendment by Pub. L. 96–54 effective July 12, 1979, see section 2(b) of Pub. L. 96–54, set out as a note under section 305 of this title.

EFFECTIVE DATE OF 1978 AMENDMENT

Amendment by Pub. L. 95–454 effective 90 days after Oct. 13, 1978, see section 907 of Pub. L. 95–454, set out as a note under section 1101 of this title.

SAVINGS PROVISION

For effect of Pub. L. 101–12 on orders, rules, and regulations issued before effective date of Pub. L. 101–12, administrative proceedings pending at time provisions of Pub. L. 101–12 take effect, and suits and other proceedings as in effect immediately before effective date of Pub. L. 101–12, see section 7 of Pub. L. 101–12, set out as a note under section 1201 of this title.

TERMINATION OF REPORTING REQUIREMENTS

For termination, effective May 15, 2000, of reporting provisions in subsec. (i)(2) of this section, see section 3003 of Pub. L. 104–66, as amended, set out as a note under section 1113 of Title 31, Money and Finance, and page 177 of House Document No. 103–7.

EXECUTIVE ORDER NO. 11787

Ex. Ord. No. 11787, June 11, 1974, 39 F.R. 20675; Ex. Ord. No. 12107, Dec. 28, 1978, 44 F.R. 1055, which provided that the appeals system established by the Merit Systems Protection Board is the sole system of appeal for an employee covered by that appeal system, was revoked by Ex. Ord. No. 12553, Feb. 25, 1986, 51 F.R. 7237.

SECTION REFERRED TO IN OTHER SECTIONS

This section is referred to in sections 1212, 2105, 2302, 3395a, 3592, 3593, 3595, 4303, 5596, 7121, 7513, 7543, 7702, 7703, 8347, 8451, 8461 of this title; title 10 section 1610; title 22 sections 1438, 4137; title 28 section 569; title 31 section 753.

§ 7702. Actions involving discrimination

(a)(1) Notwithstanding any other provision of law, and except as provided in paragraph (2) of this subsection, in the case of any employee or applicant for employment who—

(A) has been affected by an action which the employee or applicant may appeal to the Merit Systems Protection Board, and

(B) alleges that a basis for the action was discrimination prohibited by—

(i) section 717 of the Civil Rights Act of 1964 (42 U.S.C. 2000e–16),

(ii) section 6(d) of the Fair Labor Standards Act of 1938 (29 U.S.C. 206(d)),

(iii) section 501 of the Rehabilitation Act of 1973 (29 U.S.C. 791),

(iv) sections 12 and 15 of the Age Discrimination in Employment Act of 1967 (29 U.S.C. 631, 633a), or

(v) any rule, regulation, or policy directive prescribed under any provision of law described in clauses (i) through (iv) of this subparagraph,

the Board shall, within 120 days of the filing of the appeal, decide both the issue of discrimination and the appealable action in accordance with the Board's appellate procedures under section 7701 of this title and this section.

(2) In any matter before an agency which involves—

(A) any action described in paragraph (1)(A) of this subsection; and

(B) any issue of discrimination prohibited under any provision of law described in paragraph (1)(B) of this subsection;

the agency shall resolve such matter within 120 days. The decision of the agency in any such matter shall be a judicially reviewable action unless the employee appeals the matter to the Board under paragraph (1) of this subsection.

(3) Any decision of the Board under paragraph (1) of this subsection shall be a judicially reviewable action as of—

(A) the date of issuance of the decision if the employee or applicant does not file a petition with the Equal Employment Opportunity Commission under subsection (b)(1) of this section, or

(B) the date the Commission determines not to consider the decision under subsection (b)(2) of this section.

(b)(1) An employee or applicant may, within 30 days after notice of the decision of the Board under subsection (a)(1) of this section, petition the Commission to consider the decision.

(2) The Commission shall, within 30 days after the date of the petition, determine whether to consider the decision. A determination of the Commission not to consider the decision may not be used as evidence with respect to any issue of discrimination in any judicial proceeding concerning that issue.

(3) If the Commission makes a determination to consider the decision, the Commission shall, within 60 days after the date of the determination, consider the entire record of the proceedings of the Board and, on the basis of the evidentiary record before the Board, as supplemented under paragraph (4) of this subsection, either—

(A) concur in the decision of the Board; or

(B) issue in writing another decision which differs from the decision of the Board to the extent that the Commission finds that, as a matter of law—

(i) the decision of the Board constitutes an incorrect interpretation of any provision of any law, rule, regulation, or policy directive referred to in subsection (a)(1)(B) of this section, or

(ii) the decision involving such provision is not supported by the evidence in the record as a whole.

(4) In considering any decision of the Board under this subsection, the Commission may refer the case to the Board, or provide on its own, for the taking (within such period as permits the Commission to make a decision within the 60-day period prescribed under this subsection) of additional evidence to the extent it considers necessary to supplement the record.

(5)(A) If the Commission concurs pursuant to paragraph (3)(A) of this subsection in the decision of the Board, the decision of the Board shall be a judicially reviewable action.

(B) If the Commission issues any decision under paragraph (3)(B) of this subsection, the Commission shall immediately refer the matter to the Board.

(c) Within 30 days after receipt by the Board of the decision of the Commission under subsection (b)(5)(B) of this section, the Board shall consider the decision and—

(1) concur and adopt in whole the decision of the Commission; or

(2) to the extent that the Board finds that, as a matter of law, (A) the Commission decision constitutes an incorrect interpretation of any provision of any civil service law, rule, regulation or policy directive, or (B) the Commission decision involving such provision is not supported by the evidence in the record as a whole—

(i) reaffirm the initial decision of the Board; or

(ii) reaffirm the initial decision of the Board with such revisions as it determines appropriate.

If the Board takes the action provided under paragraph (1), the decision of the Board shall be a judicially reviewable action.

(d)(1) If the Board takes any action under subsection (c)(2) of this section, the matter shall be immediately certified to a special panel described in paragraph (6) of this subsection. Upon certification, the Board shall, within 5 days (excluding Saturdays, Sundays, and holidays), transmit to the special panel the administrative record in the proceeding, including—

(A) the factual record compiled under this section,

(B) the decisions issued by the Board and the Commission under this section, and

(C) any transcript of oral arguments made, or legal briefs filed, before the Board or the Commission.

(2)(A) The special panel shall, within 45 days after a matter has been certified to it, review the administrative record transmitted to it and, on the basis of the record, decide the issues in dispute and issue a final decision which shall be a judicially reviewable action.

(B) The special panel shall give due deference to the respective expertise of the Board and Commission in making its decision.

(3) The special panel shall refer its decision under paragraph (2) of this subsection to the Board and the Board shall order any agency to take any action appropriate to carry out the decision.

(4) The special panel shall permit the employee or applicant who brought the complaint and the employing agency to appear before the panel to present oral arguments and to present written arguments with respect to the matter.

(5) Upon application by the employee or applicant, the Commission may issue such interim relief as it determines appropriate to mitigate any exceptional hardship the employee or applicant might otherwise incur as a result of the certification of any matter under this subsection, except that the Commission may not stay, or order any agency to review on an interim basis, the action referred to in subsection (a)(1) of this section.

(6)(A) Each time the Board takes any action under subsection (c)(2) of this section, a special panel shall be convened which shall consist of—

(i) an individual appointed by the President, by and with the advice and consent of the Senate, to serve for a term of 6 years as chairman of the special panel each time it is convened;

(ii) one member of the Board designated by the Chairman of the Board each time a panel is convened; and

(iii) one member of the Commission designated by the Chairman of the Commission each time a panel is convened.

The chairman of the special panel may be removed by the President only for inefficiency, neglect of duty, or malfeasance in office.

(B) The chairman is entitled to pay at a rate equal to the maximum annual rate of basic pay payable under the General Schedule for each day he is engaged in the performance of official business on the work of the special panel.

(C) The Board and the Commission shall provide such administrative assistance to the special panel as may be necessary and, to the extent practicable, shall equally divide the costs of providing the administrative assistance.

(e)(1) Notwithstanding any other provision of law, if at any time after—

(A) the 120th day following the filing of any matter described in subsection (a)(2) of this section with an agency, there is not judicially reviewable action under this section or an appeal under paragraph (2) of this subsection;

(B) the 120th day following the filing of an appeal with the Board under subsection (a)(1) of this section, there is no judicially reviewable action (unless such action is not as the result of the filing of a petition by the employee under subsection (b)(1) of this section); or

(C) the 180th day following the filing of a petition with the Equal Employment Opportunity Commission under subsection (b)(1) of this section, there is no final agency action under subsection (b), (c), or (d) of this section;

an employee shall be entitled to file a civil action to the same extent and in the same manner as provided in section 717(c) of the Civil Rights Act of 1964 (42 U.S.C. 2000e–16(c)), section 15(c) of the Age Discrimination in Employment Act of 1967 (29 U.S.C. 633a(c)), or section 16(b) of the Fair Labor Standards Act of 1938 (29 U.S.C. 216(b)).

(2) If, at any time after the 120th day following the filing of any matter described in subsection (a)(2) of this section with an agency, there is no judicially reviewable action, the employee may appeal the matter to the Board under subsection (a)(1) of this section.

(3) Nothing in this section shall be construed to affect the right to trial de novo under any provision of law described in subsection (a)(1) of this section after a judicially reviewable action, including the decision of an agency under subsection (a)(2) of this section.

(f) In any case in which an employee is required to file any action, appeal, or petition under this section and the employee timely files the action, appeal, or petition with an agency other than the agency with which the action, appeal, or petition is to be filed, the employee shall be treated as having timely filed the action, appeal, or petition as of the date it is filed with the proper agency.

(Added Pub. L. 95–454, title II, § 205, Oct. 13, 1978, 92 Stat. 1140; amended Pub. L. 96–54, § 2(a)(46), Aug. 14, 1979, 93 Stat. 384.)

REFERENCES IN TEXT

The civil service law, referred to in subsec. (c)(2), is set out in this title. See, particularly, section 3301 et seq. of this title. The General Schedule, referred to in subsec. (d)(6)(B), is set out under section 5332 of this title.

AMENDMENTS

1979—Subsec. (a)(1)(A). Pub. L. 96–54, § 2(a)(46)(A), substituted "affected" for "effected".

Subsec. (a)(1)(B)(i). Pub. L. 96–54, § 2(a)(46)(B), substituted "2000e–16" for "2000e–16c".

Subsec. (e)(1). Pub. L. 96–54, § 2(a)(46)(C), (D), substituted "of this section" for "of this title" in subpar. (C), and "216(b)" for "216(d)" in provision following subpar. (C).

EFFECTIVE DATE OF 1979 AMENDMENT

Amendment by Pub. L. 96–54 effective July 12, 1979, see section 2(b) of Pub. L. 96–54, set out as a note under section 305 of this title.

EFFECTIVE DATE

Section effective 90 days after Oct. 13, 1978, see section 907 of Pub. L. 95–454, set out as an Effective Date of 1978 Amendment note under section 1101 of this title.

SECTION REFERRED TO IN OTHER SECTIONS

This section is referred to in sections 7121, 7701, 7703 of this title; title 3 section 454; title 31 section 753.

§ 7703. Judicial review of decisions of the Merit Systems Protection Board

(a)(1) Any employee or applicant for employment adversely affected or aggrieved by a final order or decision of the Merit Systems Protection Board may obtain judicial review of the order or decision.

(2) The Board shall be named respondent in any proceeding brought pursuant to this subsection, unless the employee or applicant for employment seeks review of a final order or decision on the merits on the underlying personnel action or on a request for attorney fees, in which case the agency responsible for taking the personnel action shall be the respondent.

(b)(1) Except as provided in paragraph (2) of this subsection, a petition to review a final order or final decision of the Board shall be filed in the United States Court of Appeals for the Federal Circuit. Notwithstanding any other provision of law, any petition for review must be filed within 60 days after the date the petitioner received notice of the final order or decision of the Board.

(2) Cases of discrimination subject to the provisions of section 7702 of this title shall be filed under section 717(c) of the Civil Rights Act of 1964 (42 U.S.C. 2000e–16(c)), section 15(c) of the Age Discrimination in Employment Act of 1967 (29 U.S.C. 633a(c)), and section 16(b) of the Fair Labor Standards Act of 1938, as amended (29 U.S.C. 216(b)), as applicable. Notwithstanding any other provision of law, any such case filed under any such section must be filed within 30 days after the date the individual filing the case received notice of the judicially reviewable action under such section 7702.

(c) In any case filed in the United States Court of Appeals for the Federal Circuit, the court shall review the record and hold unlawful and set aside any agency action, findings, or conclusions found to be—

(1) arbitrary, capricious, an abuse of discretion, or otherwise not in accordance with law;

(2) obtained without procedures required by law, rule, or regulation having been followed; or

(3) unsupported by substantial evidence;

except that in the case of discrimination brought under any section referred to in subsection (b)(2) of this section, the employee or applicant shall have the right to have the facts subject to trial de novo by the reviewing court.

(d) The Director of the Office of Personnel Management may obtain review of any final order or decision of the Board by filing, within 60 days after the date the Director received notice of the final order or decision of the Board, a petition for judicial review in the United States Court of Appeals for the Federal Circuit if the Director determines, in his discretion, that the Board erred in interpreting a civil service law, rule, or regulation affecting personnel management and that the Board's decision will have a substantial impact on a civil service law, rule, regulation, or policy directive. If the Director did not intervene in a matter before the Board, the Director may not petition for review of a Board decision under this section unless the Director first petitions the Board for a reconsideration of its decision, and such petition is denied. In addition to the named respondent, the Board and all other parties to the proceedings before the Board shall have the right to appear in the proceeding before the Court of Appeals. The granting of the petition for judicial review shall be at the discretion of the Court of Appeals.

(Added Pub. L. 95–454, title II, § 205, Oct. 13, 1978, 92 Stat. 1143; amended Pub. L. 97–164, title I, § 144, Apr. 2, 1982, 96 Stat. 45; Pub. L. 101–12, § 10, Apr. 10, 1989, 103 Stat. 35; Pub. L. 105–311, § 10(a), Oct. 30, 1998, 112 Stat. 2954.)

REFERENCES IN TEXT

The civil service law, referred to in subsec. (d), is set out in this title. See, particularly, section 3301 et seq. of this title.

AMENDMENTS

1998—Subsec. (b)(1). Pub. L. 105–311, § 10(a)(1), substituted "within 60 days" for "within 30 days".

Subsec. (d). Pub. L. 105–311, § 10(a)(2), in first sentence, inserted ", within 60 days after the date the Director received notice of the final order or decision of the Board," after "filing".

1989—Subsec. (a)(2). Pub. L. 101–12 amended par. (2) generally. Prior to amendment, par. (2) read as follows: "The Board shall be the named respondent in any proceeding brought pursuant to this subsection, unless the employee or applicant for employment seeks review of a final order or decision issued by the Board under section 7701. In review of a final order or decision issued under section 7701, the agency responsible for taking the action appealed to the Board shall be the named respondent."

1982—Subsec. (b)(1). Pub. L. 97–164, § 144(1), substituted "United States Court of Appeals for the Federal Circuit" for "Court of Claims or a United States court of appeals as provided in chapters 91 and 158, respectively, of title 28".

Subsec. (c). Pub. L. 97–164, § 144(2), substituted "Court of Appeals for the Federal Circuit" for "Court of Claims or a United States court of appeals".

Subsec. (d). Pub. L. 97–164, § 144(3), substituted "United States Court of Appeals for the Federal Circuit" for "United States Court of Appeals for the District of Columbia".

EFFECTIVE DATE OF 1998 AMENDMENT

Pub. L. 105–311, § 10(b), Oct. 30, 1998, 112 Stat. 2954, provided that: "The amendments made by this section [amending this section] shall take effect on the date of enactment of this Act [Oct. 30, 1998], and apply to any suit, action, or other administrative or judicial proceeding pending on such date or commenced on or after such date."

EFFECTIVE DATE OF 1989 AMENDMENT

Amendment by Pub. L. 101–12 effective 90 days following Apr. 10, 1989, see section 11 of Pub. L. 101–12, set out as a note under section 1201 of this title.

EFFECTIVE DATE OF 1982 AMENDMENT

Amendment by Pub. L. 97–164 effective Oct. 1, 1982, see section 402 of Pub. L. 97–164, set out as a note under section 171 of Title 28, Judiciary and Judicial Procedure.

EFFECTIVE DATE

Section effective 90 days after Oct. 13, 1978, see section 907 of Pub. L. 95–454, set out as an Effective Date of 1978 Amendment note under section 1101 of this title.

SAVINGS PROVISION

For effect of Pub. L. 101–12 on orders, rules, and regulations issued before effective date of Pub. L. 101–12, administrative proceedings pending at time provisions of Pub. L. 101–12 take effect, and suits and other proceedings as in effect immediately before effective date of Pub. L. 101–12, see section 7 of Pub. L. 101–12 set out as a note under section 1201 of this title.

SECTION REFERRED TO IN OTHER SECTIONS

This section is referred to in sections 1214, 1215, 1221, 7121, 8347, 8461 of this title; title 28 section 1295; title 38 section 4324.

CHAPTER 79—SERVICES TO EMPLOYEES

AMENDMENTS

1993—Pub. L. 103–172, § 2(b), Dec. 2, 1993, 107 Stat. 1996, added item 7905.

1986—Pub. L. 99–570, title VI, § 6004(b), Oct. 27, 1986, 100 Stat. 3207–159, added item 7904.

STATE OR LOCAL GOVERNMENT PROGRAMS ENCOURAGING EMPLOYEE USE OF PUBLIC TRANSPORTATION; FEDERAL AGENCY PARTICIPATION

Pub. L. 102–241, § 44, Dec. 19, 1991, 105 Stat. 2226, provided that: "The Department of Transportation may include military personnel of the Coast Guard in any program in which the Department participates under section 629 of the Treasury, Postal Service and General Government Appropriations Act, 1991, Public Law 101–509 [set out below], notwithstanding section 629(c)(2) of that Act."

Pub. L. 101–509, title VI, § 629, Nov. 5, 1990, 104 Stat. 1478, authorized Federal agencies and employees to participate in State or local government programs encouraging employees to use public transportation, directed General Accounting Office, not later than June 30, 1993, to conduct a study and submit a report on the implementation of such programs, and provided that this section was repealed effective Dec. 31, 1993.

§ 7901. Health service programs

(a) The head of each agency of the Government of the United States may establish, within the limits of appropriations available, a health service program to promote and maintain the physical and mental fitness of employees under his jurisdiction.

(b) A health service program may be established by contract or otherwise, but only—

(1) after consultation with the Secretary of Health, Education, and Welfare and consideration of its recommendations; and

(2) in localities where there are a sufficient number of employees to warrant providing the service.

(c) A health service program is limited to—

(1) treatment of on-the-job illness and dental conditions requiring emergency attention;

(2) preemployment and other examinations;

(3) referral of employees to private physicians and dentists; and

(4) preventive programs relating to health.

(d) The Secretary of Health, Education, and Welfare, on request, shall review a health service program conducted under this section and shall submit comment and recommendations to the head of the agency concerned.

(e) When this section authorizes the use of the professional services of physicians, that authorization includes the use of the professional services of surgeons and osteopathic practitioners within the scope of their practice as defined by State law.

(f) The health programs conducted by the Tennessee Valley Authority are not affected by this section.

(Pub. L. 89–554, Sept. 6, 1966, 80 Stat. 530; Pub. L. 90–83, §1(47), Sept. 11, 1967, 81 Stat. 209; Pub. L. 104–201, div. C, title XXXV, §3548(a)(9), Sept. 23, 1996, 110 Stat. 2869.)

HISTORICAL AND REVISION NOTES
1966 ACT

Derivation	U.S. Code	Revised Statutes and Statutes at Large
....	5 U.S.C. 150.	Aug. 8, 1946, ch. 865, 60 Stat. 903. Sept. 23, 1950, ch. 1010, §8, 64 Stat. 986.

In subsection (a), the words "agency of the Government of the United States" are coextensive with and substituted for "departments and agencies including Government-owned and controlled corporations" to avoid confusion with the definitions in sections 101–105.

In subsection (d) the word "appropriate" in the phrase "appropriate comment and recommendations" is omitted as unnecessary. The words "to the head of the agency concerned" are added for clarity.

In subsection (e), the substance of the definition of "physician" in former section 790 is substituted for the reference to that section.

In subsection (f)(2) and (3), the words "Canal Zone Government" and "Panama Canal Company" are substituted for "Panama Canal" and "Panama Railroad", respectively, on the authority of the Act of Sept. 26, 1950, ch. 1049, §2(a), 64 Stat. 1038.

The last proviso of the first sentence of the Act of Aug. 8, 1946, is omitted as executed.

Standard changes are made to conform with the definitions applicable and the style of this title as outlined in the preface to the report.

1967 ACT

This section amends 5 U.S.C. 7901 to reflect 1966 Reorganization Plan No. 3, effective June 25, 1966, 80 Stat.

1610, section 1 of which transferred all functions of the Public Health Service to the Secretary of Health, Education, and Welfare.

AMENDMENTS

1996—Subsec. (f). Pub. L. 104–201 amended subsec. (f) generally. Prior to amendment, subsec. (f) read as follows: "The health programs conducted by the following agencies are not affected by this section—

"(1) the Tennessee Valley Authority;

"(2) the Canal Zone Government; and

"(3) the Panama Canal Company."

CHANGE OF NAME

Secretary of Health, Education, and Welfare redesignated Secretary of Health and Human Services by section 3508 of Title 20, Education.

SHORT TITLE OF 1993 AMENDMENT

Pub. L. 103–172, §1(a), Dec. 2, 1993, 107 Stat. 1995, provided that: "This Act [enacting section 7905 of this title and provisions set out as notes under section 7905 of this title] may be cited as the 'Federal Employees Clean Air Incentives Act'."

DEMONSTRATION PROJECT: HEALTH PROTECTION; HEALTH PROMOTION; DISEASE PREVENTION; AND SECONDARY PREVENTION

Pub. L. 99–251, title I, §110, Feb. 27, 1986, 100 Stat. 17, directed Director of Office of Personnel Management to conduct a demonstration project to determine most effective method of furnishing health protection, health promotion, disease prevention, and secondary prevention services to Federal Government employees, with Director to report to Congress no later than 60 days after termination of project on Feb. 27, 1988.

SECTION REFERRED TO IN OTHER SECTIONS

This section is referred to in title 50 section 403j.

§ 7902. Safety programs

(a) For the purpose of this section—

(1) "employee" means an employee as defined by section 8101 of this title; and

(2) "agency" means an agency in any branch of the Government of the United States (not including the United States Postal Service), including an instrumentality wholly owned by the United States, and the government of the District of Columbia.

(b) The Secretary of Labor shall carry out a safety program under section 941(b)(1) of title 33 covering the employment of each employee of an agency.

(c) The President may—

(1) establish by Executive order a safety council composed of representatives of the agencies and of labor organizations representing employees to serve as an advisory body to the Secretary in furtherance of the safety program carried out by the Secretary under subsection (b) of this section; and

(2) undertake such other measures as he considers proper to prevent injuries and accidents to employees of the agencies.

(d) The head of each agency shall develop and support organized safety promotion to reduce accidents and injuries among employees of his agency, encourage safe practices, and eliminate work hazards and health risks.

(e) Each agency shall—

(1) keep a record of injuries and accidents to its employees whether or not they result in

loss of time or in the payment or furnishing of benefits; and

(2) make such statistical or other reports on such forms as the Secretary may prescribe by regulation.

(Pub. L. 89–554, Sept. 6, 1966, 80 Stat. 530; Pub. L. 91–596, § 19(c), Dec. 29, 1970, 84 Stat. 1610; Pub. L. 105–241, § 2(b)(2), Sept. 28, 1998, 112 Stat. 1572.)

HISTORICAL AND REVISION NOTES

Derivation	U.S. Code	Revised Statutes and Statutes at Large
....	5 U.S.C. 784 (less (a)).	Sept. 16, 1916, ch. 458, § 33 (less (a)); added Dec. 22, 1944, ch. 664, 58 Stat. 887. Oct. 14, 1949, ch. 691, § 209, 63 Stat. 865.

Subsection (a) is added on authority of former sections 790(b) and 794 (1st sentence), which are carried into section 8101.

The words "Secretary of Labor" and "Secretary" are substituted for "Administrator" on authority of section 1 of 1950 Reorg. Plan No. 19, eff. May 24, 1950, 64 Stat. 1271.

Subsection (b) is restated for clarity. The words "under section 941(b)(1) of title 33" are substituted for "The provisions of section 941 of title 33 shall, insofar as not inapplicable, apply" on authority of section 941(g)(2) of title 33. The reference to "a safety program" is based in part on the words "in furtherance of the safety program carried out by the Secretary pursuant to this section" in former section 784(c).

In subsection (d), the word "foster" is omitted as included in "develop and support". The words "and reduce compensable injuries" are omitted as unnecessary.

Standard changes are made to conform with the definitions applicable and the style of this title as outlined in the preface to the report.

AMENDMENTS

1998—Subsec. (a)(2). Pub. L. 105–241 inserted "(not including the United States Postal Service)" after "Government of the United States".

1970—Subsec. (c)(1). Pub. L. 91–596 included representatives of labor organizations representing employees.

EXECUTIVE ORDER NO. 10990

Ex. Ord. No. 10990, Feb. 5, 1962, 27 F.R. 1065, which provided for the establishment of a Federal Safety Council, was superseded by Ex. Ord. No. 11612, July 26, 1971, 36 F.R. 13891, formerly set out below.

EXECUTIVE ORDER NO. 11612

Ex. Ord. No. 11612, July 26, 1971, 36 F.R. 13891, which related to occupational safety and health programs for federal employees, was superseded by Ex. Ord. 11807, Sept. 28, 1974, 39 F.R. 35559, formerly set out below.

EXECUTIVE ORDER NO. 11807

Ex. Ord. No. 11807, Sept. 28, 1974, 39 F.R. 35559, which related to occupational safety and health programs for federal employees and continued the Federal Advisory Council on Occupational Safety and Health, was revoked by Ex. Ord. No. 12196, Feb. 26, 1980, 45 F.R. 12769, set out below.

EX. ORD. NO. 12196. OCCUPATIONAL SAFETY AND HEALTH PROGRAMS FOR FEDERAL EMPLOYEES

Ex. Ord. No. 12196, Feb. 26, 1980, 45 F.R. 12769, as amended by Ex. Ord. No. 12223, June 30, 1980, 45 F.R. 45235; Ex. Ord. No. 12608, Sept. 9, 1987, 52 F.R. 34617, provided:

By the authority vested in me as President by the Constitution and statutes of the United States of America, including Section 7902(c) of Title 5 of the United States Code and in accord with Section 19 of the Occupational Safety and Health Act of 1970, as amended (29 U.S.C 668), it is ordered:

1–1. SCOPE OF THIS ORDER

1–101. This order applies to all agencies of the Executive Branch except military personnel and uniquely military equipment, systems, and operations.

1–102. For the purposes of this order, the term "agency" means an Executive department, as defined in 5 U.S.C. 101, or any employing unit or authority of the Federal government, other than those of the judicial and legislative branches. Since section 19 [29 U.S.C. 668] of the Occupational Safety and Health Act ("the Act") [29 U.S.C. 651 et seq.] covers all Federal employees, however, the Secretary of Labor ("the Secretary") shall cooperate and consult with the heads of agencies in the legislative and judicial branches of the government to help them adopt safety and health programs.

1–2. HEADS OF AGENCIES

1–201. The head of each agency shall:

(a) Furnish to employees places and conditions of employment that are free from recognized hazards that are causing or are likely to cause death or serious physical harm.

(b) Operate an occupational safety and health program in accordance with the requirements of this order and basic program elements promulgated by the Secretary.

(c) Designate an agency official with sufficient authority to represent the interest and support of the agency head to be responsible for the management and administration of the agency occupational safety and health program.

(d) Comply with all standards issued under section 6 of the Act [29 U.S.C. 655], except where the Secretary approves compliance with alternative standards. When an agency head determines it necessary to apply a different standard, that agency head shall, after consultation with appropriate occupational safety and health committees where established, notify the Secretary and provide justification that equivalent or greater protection will be assured by the alternate standard.

(e) Assure prompt abatement of unsafe or unhealthy working conditions. Whenever an agency cannot promptly abate such conditions, it shall develop an abatement plan setting forth a timetable for abatement and a summary of interim steps to protect employees. Employees exposed to the conditions shall be informed of the provisions of the plan. When a hazard cannot be abated without assistance of the General Services Administration or other Federal lessor agency, an agency shall act with the lessor agency to secure abatement.

(f) Establish procedures to assure that no employee is subject to restraint, interference, coercion, discrimination or reprisal for filing a report of an unsafe or unhealthy working condition, or other participation in agency occupational safety and health program activities.

(g) Assure that periodic inspections of all agency workplaces are performed by personnel with equipment and competence to recognize hazards.

(h) Assure response to employee reports of hazardous conditions and require inspections within twenty-four hours for imminent dangers, three working days for potential serious conditions, and twenty working days for other conditions. Assure the right to anonymity of those making the reports.

(i) Assure that employee representatives accompany inspections of agency workplaces.

(j) Operate an occupational safety and health management information system, which shall include the maintenance of such records as the Secretary may require.

(k) Provide safety and health training for supervisory employees, employees responsible for conducting occupational safety and health inspections, all members of occupational safety and health committees where established, and other employees.

(l) Submit to the Secretary an annual report on the agency occupational safety and health program that includes information the Secretary prescribes.

1-3. OCCUPATIONAL SAFETY AND HEALTH COMMITTEES

1-301. Agency heads may establish occupational safety and health committees. If committees are established, they shall be established at both the national level and, for agencies with field or regional offices, other appropriate levels. The committees shall be composed of representatives of management and an equal number of nonmanagement employees or their representatives. Where there are exclusive bargaining representatives for employees at the national or other level in an agency, such representatives shall select the appropriate nonmanagement members of the committee.

1-302. The committees shall, except where prohibited by law,

(a) Have access to agency information relevant to their duties, including information on the nature and hazardousness of substances in agency workplaces.

(b) Monitor performance, including agency inspections, of the agency safety and health programs at the level they are established.

(c) Consult and advise the agency on the operation of the program.

1-303. A Committee may request the Secretary of Labor to conduct an evaluation or inspection pursuant to this order if half of a Committee is not substantially satisfied with an agency's response to a report of hazardous working conditions.

1-4. DEPARTMENT OF LABOR

1-401. The Secretary of Labor shall:

(a) Provide leadership and guidance to the heads of agencies to assist them with their occupational safety and health responsibilities.

(b) Maintain liaison with the Office of Management and Budget in matters relating to this order and coordinate the activities of the Department with those of other agencies that have responsibilities or functions related to Federal employee safety and health, including the Office of Personnel Management, the Department of Health and Human Services, and the General Services Administration.

(c) Issue, subject to the approval of the Director of the Office of Management and Budget, and in consultation with the Federal Advisory Council on Occupational Safety and Health, a set of basic program elements. The program elements shall help agency heads establish occupational safety and health committees and operate effective occupational safety and health programs, and shall provide flexibility to each agency head to implement a program consistent with its mission, size and organization. Upon request of an agency head, and after consultation with the Federal Advisory Council on Occupational Safety and Health, the Secretary may approve alternate program elements.

(d) Prescribe recordkeeping and reporting requirements.

(e) Assist agencies by providing training materials, and by conducting training programs upon request and with reimbursement.

(f) Facilitate the exchange of ideas and information throughout the government about occupational safety and health.

(g) Provide technical services to agencies upon request, where the Secretary deems necessary, and with reimbursement. These services may include studies of accidents, causes of injury and illness, identification of unsafe and unhealthful working conditions, and means to abate hazards.

(h) Evaluate the occupational safety and health programs of agencies and promptly submit reports to the agency heads. The evaluations shall be conducted through such scheduled headquarters or field reviews, studies or inspections as the Secretary deems necessary, at least annually for the larger or more hazardous agencies or operations, and as the Secretary deems appropriate for the smaller or less hazardous agencies.

(i) Conduct unannounced inspections of agency workplaces when the Secretary determines necessary if an agency does not have occupational safety and health committees; or in response to reports of unsafe or unhealthful working conditions, upon request of occupational safety and health committees under Section 1-3; or, in the case of a report of an imminent danger, when such a committee has not responded to an employee who has alleged to it that the agency has not adequately responded to a report as required in 1-201(h). When the Secretary or his designee performs an inspection and discovers unsafe or unhealthy conditions, a violation of any provisions of this order, or any safety or health standards adopted by an agency pursuant to this order, or any program element approved by the Secretary, he shall promptly issue a report to the head of the agency and to the appropriate occupational safety and health committee, if any. The report shall describe the nature of the findings and may make recommendations for correcting the violation.

(j) Submit to the President each year a summary report of the status of the occupational safety and health of Federal employees, and, together with agency responses, evaluations of individual agency progress and problems in correcting unsafe and unhealthful working conditions, and recommendations for improving their performance.

(k) Submit to the President unresolved disagreements between the Secretary and agency heads, with recommendations.

(l) Enter into agreements or other arrangements as necessary or appropriate with the National Institute for Occupational Safety and Health and delegate to it the inspection and investigation authority provided under this section.

1-5. THE FEDERAL ADVISORY COUNCIL ON OCCUPATIONAL SAFETY AND HEALTH

1-501. The Federal Advisory Council on Occupational Safety and Health, established pursuant to Executive Order No. 11612, is continued. It shall advise the Secretary in carrying out responsibilities under this order. The Council shall consist of sixteen members appointed by the Secretary, of whom eight shall be representatives of Federal agencies and eight shall be representatives of labor organizations representing Federal employees. The members shall serve three-year terms with the terms of five or six members expiring each year, provided this Council is renewed every two years in accordance with the Federal Advisory Committee Act [5 U.S.C. App.]. The members currently serving on the Council shall be deemed to be its initial members under this order and their terms shall expire in accordance with the terms of their appointment.

1-502. The Secretary, or a designee, shall serve as the Chairman of the Council, and shall prescribe rules for the conduct of its business.

1-503. The Secretary shall make available necessary office space and furnish the Council necessary equipment, supplies, and staff services, and shall perform such functions with respect to the Council as may be required by the Federal Advisory Committee Act, as amended (5 U.S.C. App.).

1-6. GENERAL SERVICES ADMINISTRATION

1-601. Within six months of the effective date of this order the Secretary of Labor and the Administrator of the General Services Administration shall initiate a study of conflicts that may exist in their standards and other requirements affecting Federal employee safety and health, and shall establish a procedure for resolving conflicting standards for space leased by the General Services Administration.

1-602. In order to assist the agencies in carrying out their duties under Section 19 of the Act [29 U.S.C. 668] and this order the Administrator shall:

(a) Upon request, require personnel of the General Services Administration to accompany the Secretary or an agency head on any inspection or investigation conducted pursuant to this order of a facility subject to the authority of the General Services Administration.

(b) Assure prompt attention to reports from agencies of unsafe or unhealthy conditions of facilities subject to the authority of the General Services Administration; where abatement cannot be promptly effected, submit to the agency head a timetable for action to correct the conditions; and give priority in the allocation of resources available to the Administrator for prompt abatement of the conditions.

(c) Procure and provide safe supplies, devices, and equipment, and establish and maintain a product safety program for those supplies, devices, equipment and services furnished to agencies, including the issuance of Material Safety Data Sheets when hazardous substances are furnished them.

1–7. GENERAL PROVISIONS

1–701. Employees shall be authorized official time to participate in the activities provided for by this order.

1–702. Nothing in this order shall be construed to impair or alter the powers and duties of the Secretary or heads of other Federal agencies pursuant to Section 19 of the Occupational Safety and Health Act of 1970 [29 U.S.C. 668]. Chapter 71 of Title 5 of the United States Code, Sections 7901, 7902, and 7903 of Title 5 of the United States Code, nor shall it be construed to alter any other provisions of law or Executive Order providing for collective bargaining agreements and related procedures, or affect the responsibilities of the Director of Central Intelligence to protect intelligence sources and methods (50 U.S.C. 403(d)(3)).

1–703. Executive Order No. 11807 of September 28, 1974, is revoked.

1–704. This order is effective October 1, 1980.

EXECUTIVE ORDER NO. 12566

Ex. Ord. No. 12566, Sept. 26, 1986, 51 F.R. 34575, which related to safety belt use by Federal employees, was revoked by Ex. Ord. No. 13043, §6, Apr. 16, 1997, 62 F.R. 19218, set out as a note under section 402 of Title 23, Highways.

EXTENSION OF TERM OF FEDERAL ADVISORY COUNCIL ON OCCUPATIONAL SAFETY AND HEALTH

Term of the Federal Advisory Council on Occupational Safety and Health extended until Dec. 31, 1978, by Ex. Ord. No. 11948, Dec. 20, 1976, 41 F.R. 55705, formerly set out as a note under section 14 of the Federal Advisory Committee Act in the Appendix to this title.

Term of the Federal Advisory Council on Occupational Safety and Health extended until Dec. 31, 1980, by Ex. Ord. No. 12110, Dec. 28, 1978, 44 F.R. 1069, formerly set out as a note under section 14 of the Federal Advisory Committee Act in the Appendix to this title.

Term of the Federal Advisory Council on Occupational Safety and Health extended until Dec. 31, 1982, by Ex. Ord. No. 12258, Dec. 31, 1980, 46 F.R. 1251, formerly set out as a note under section 14 of the Federal Advisory Committee Act in the Appendix to this title.

Term of the Federal Advisory Council on Occupational Safety and Health extended until Sept. 30, 1984, by Ex. Ord. No. 12399, Dec. 31, 1982, 48 F.R. 379, formerly set out as a note under section 14 of the Federal Advisory Committee Act in the Appendix to this title.

Term of the Federal Advisory Council on Occupational Safety and Health extended until Sept. 30, 1985, by Ex. Ord. No. 12489, Sept. 28, 1984, 49 F.R. 38927, formerly set out as a note under section 14 of the Federal Advisory Committee Act in the Appendix to this title.

Term of the Federal Advisory Council on Occupational Safety and Health extended until Sept. 30, 1987, by Ex. Ord. No. 12534, Sept. 30, 1985, 50 F.R. 40319, formerly set out as a note under section 14 of the Federal Advisory Committee Act in the Appendix to this title.

Term of the Federal Advisory Council on Occupational Safety and Health extended until Sept. 30, 1989,

by Ex. Ord. No. 12610, Sept. 30, 1987, 52 F.R. 36901, formerly set out as a note under section 14 of the Federal Advisory Committee Act in the Appendix to this title.

Term of the Federal Advisory Council on Occupational Safety and Health extended until Sept. 30, 1991, by Ex. Ord. No. 12692, Sept. 29, 1989, 54 F.R. 40627, formerly set out as a note under section 14 of the Federal Advisory Committee Act in the Appendix to this title.

Term of the Federal Advisory Council on Occupational Safety and Health extended until Sept. 30, 1993, by Ex. Ord. No. 12774, Sept. 27, 1991, 56 F.R. 49835, formerly set out as a note under section 14 of the Federal Advisory Committee Act in the Appendix to this title.

Term of the Federal Advisory Council on Occupational Safety and Health extended until Sept. 30, 1995, by Ex. Ord. No. 12869, Sept. 30, 1993, 58 F.R. 51751, formerly set out as a note under section 14 of the Federal Advisory Committee Act in the Appendix to this title.

Term of the Federal Advisory Council on Occupational Safety and Health extended until Sept. 30, 1997, by Ex. Ord. No. 12974, Sept. 29, 1995, 60 F.R. 51875, formerly set out as a note under section 14 of the Federal Advisory Committee Act in the Appendix to this title.

Term of the Federal Advisory Council on Occupational Safety and Health extended until Sept. 30, 1999, by Ex. Ord. No. 13062, §1(b), Sept. 29, 1997, 62 F.R. 51755, formerly set out as a note under section 14 of the Federal Advisory Committee Act in the Appendix to this title.

Term of the Federal Advisory Council on Occupational Safety and Health extended until Sept. 30, 2001, by Ex. Ord. No. 13138, Sept. 30, 1999, 64 F.R. 53879, set out as a note under section 14 of the Federal Advisory Committee Act in the Appendix to this title.

SECTION REFERRED TO IN OTHER SECTIONS

This section is referred to in section 2105 of this title; title 2 section 1371; title 29 section 668.

§ 7903. Protective clothing and equipment

Appropriations available for the procurement of supplies and material or equipment are available for the purchase and maintenance of special clothing and equipment for the protection of personnel in the performance of their assigned tasks. For the purpose of this section, "appropriations" includes funds made available by statute under section 9104 of title 31.

(Pub. L. 89–554, Sept. 6, 1966, 80 Stat. 531; Pub. L. 97–258, §3(a)(16), Sept. 13, 1982, 96 Stat. 1063.)

HISTORICAL AND REVISION NOTES

Derivation	U.S. Code	Revised Statutes and Statutes at Large
....	5 U.S.C. 118g.	Aug. 2, 1946, ch. 744, §13, 60 Stat. 809.

The definition of the word "appropriations" is added on authority of section 18 of the Act of Aug. 2, 1946, ch. 744, 60 Stat. 811.

Standard changes are made to conform with the definitions applicable and the style of this title as outlined in the preface to the report.

AMENDMENTS

1982—Pub. L. 97–258 substituted "section 9104" for "section 849".

§ 7904. Employee assistance programs relating to drug abuse and alcohol abuse

(a) The head of each Executive agency shall, in a manner consistent with guidelines prescribed under subsection (b) of this section and applicable provisions of law, establish appropriate prevention, treatment, and rehabilitation programs and services for drug abuse and alcohol abuse for employees in or under such agency.

(b) The Office of Personnel Management shall, after such consultations as the Office considers appropriate, prescribe guidelines for programs and services under this section.

(c) The Secretary of Health and Human Services, on request of the head of an Executive agency, shall review any program or service provided under this section and shall submit comments and recommendations to the head of the agency concerned.

(Added Pub. L. 99–570, title VI, § 6004(a), Oct. 27, 1986, 100 Stat. 3207–159.)

SECTION REFERRED TO IN OTHER SECTIONS

This section is referred to in section 7363 of this title.

§ 7905. Programs to encourage commuting by means other than single-occupancy motor vehicles

(a) For the purpose of this section—

(1) the term "employee" means an employee as defined by section 2105 and a member of a uniformed service;

(2) the term "agency" means—

(A) an Executive agency;

(B) an entity of the legislative branch; and

(C) the judicial branch;

(3) the term "entity of the legislative branch" means the House of Representatives, the Senate, the Office of the Architect of the Capitol (including the Botanic Garden), the Capitol Police, the Congressional Budget Office, the Copyright Royalty Tribunal, the Government Printing Office, the Library of Congress, and the Office of Technology Assessment; and

(4) the term "transit pass" means a transit pass as defined by section 132(f)(5) of the Internal Revenue Code of 1986.

(b)(1) The head of each agency may establish a program to encourage employees of such agency to use means other than single-occupancy motor vehicles to commute to or from work.

(2) A program established under this section may involve such options as—

(A) transit passes (including cash reimbursements therefor, but only if a voucher or similar item which may be exchanged only for a transit pass is not readily available for direct distribution by the agency);

(B) furnishing space, facilities, or services to bicyclists; and

(C) any non-monetary incentive which the agency head may otherwise offer under any other provision of law or other authority.

(c) The functions of an agency head under this section shall—

(1) with respect to the judicial branch, be carried out by the Director of the Administrative Office of the United States Courts;

(2) with respect to the House of Representatives, be carried out by the Committee on House Administration of the House of Representatives; and

(3) with respect to the Senate, be carried out by the Committee on Rules and Administration of the Senate.

(d) The President shall designate 1 or more agencies which shall—

(1) prescribe guidelines for programs under this section;

(2) on request, furnish information or technical advice on the design or operation of any program under this section; and

(3) submit to the President and the Congress, before January 1, 1995, and at least every 2 years thereafter, a written report on the operation of this section, including, with respect to the period covered by the report—

(A) the number of agencies offering programs under this section;

(B) a brief description of each of the various programs;

(C) the extent of employee participation in, and the costs to the Government associated with, each of the various programs;

(D) an assessment of any environmental or other benefits realized as a result of programs established under this section; and

(E) any other matter which may be appropriate.

(Added Pub. L. 103–172, § 2(a), Dec. 2, 1993, 107 Stat. 1995.)

REFERENCES IN TEXT

Section 132(f)(5) of the Internal Revenue Code of 1986, referred to in subsec. (a)(4), is classified to section 132(f)(5) of Title 26, Internal Revenue Code.

EFFECTIVE DATE

Section 3 of Pub. L. 103–172 provided that: "This Act [enacting this section and provisions set out as notes under this section and section 7901 of this title] and the amendments made by this Act shall take effect on January 1, 1994."

TRANSIT SUBSIDIES; APPROPRIATIONS

Pub. L. 105–277, div. A, § 101(f) [title II, § 210], Oct. 21, 1998, 112 Stat. 2681–337, 2681–359, provided that: "Funds appropriated in this Act or subsequent Departments of Labor, Health and Human Services, and Education, and Related Agencies Appropriations Acts, for the National Institutes of Health may be used to provide transit subsidies in amounts consistent with the transportation subsidy programs authorized under section 629 of Public Law 101–509 [see note preceding section 7901 of this title] to non-FTE bearing positions including trainees, visiting fellows and volunteers."

Similar provisions were contained in the following prior appropriations act:

Pub. L. 105–78, title II, § 210, Nov. 13, 1997, 111 Stat. 1489.

PURPOSE OF PUB. L. 103–172

Section 1(b) of Pub. L. 103–172 provided that: "The purpose of this Act [enacting this section and provisions set out as notes under this section and section 7901 of this title] is to improve air quality and to reduce traffic congestion by providing for the establishment of programs to encourage Federal employees to commute by means other than single-occupancy motor vehicles."

EX. ORD. NO. 13150. FEDERAL WORKFORCE TRANSPORTATION

Ex. Ord. No. 13150, Apr. 21, 2000, 65 F.R. 24613, provided:

By the authority vested in me as President by the Constitution and the laws of the United States of America, including the Transportation Equity Act for the 21st Century (Public Law 105–178) [see Tables for classification], section 1911 of the Energy Policy Act of

1992 (Public Law 102–486) [amending section 132 of Title 26, Internal Revenue Code], section 531(a)(1) of the Deficit Reduction Act of 1984 (26 U.S.C. 132), and the Federal Employees Clean Air Incentives Act (Public Law 103–172) [enacting this section and provisions set out as notes above], and in order to reduce Federal employees' contribution to traffic congestion and air pollution and to expand their commuting alternatives, it is hereby ordered as follows:

SECTION 1. *Mass Transportation and Vanpool Transportation Fringe Benefit Program.* (a) By no later than October 1, 2000, Federal agencies shall implement a transportation fringe benefit program that offers qualified Federal employees the option to exclude from taxable wages and compensation, consistent with section 132 of title 26, United States Code, employee commuting costs incurred through the use of mass transportation and vanpools, not to exceed the maximum level allowed by law (26 U.S.C. 132 (f)(2)). These agency programs shall comply with the requirements of Internal Revenue Service regulations for qualified transportation fringe benefits under section 1.132–9 of title 26, Code of Federal Regulations, and other guidance.

(b) Federal agencies are encouraged to use any nonmonetary incentive that the agencies may otherwise offer under any other provision of law or other authority to encourage mass transportation and vanpool use, as provided for in section 7905(b)(2)(C) of title 5, United States Code.

SEC. 2. *Federal Agencies in the National Capital Region.* Federal agencies in the National Capital Region shall implement a "transit pass" transportation fringe benefit program for their qualified Federal employees by no later than October 1, 2000. Under this program, agencies shall provide their qualified Federal employees, in addition to current compensation, transit passes as defined in section 132(f)(5) of title 26, United States Code, in amounts approximately equal to employee commuting costs, not to exceed the maximum level allowed by law (26 U.S.C. 132(f)(2)). The National Capital Region is defined as the District of Columbia; Montgomery, Prince George's, and Frederick Counties in Maryland; Arlington, Fairfax, Loudon, and Prince William Counties in Virginia; and all cities now or hereafter existing in Maryland or Virginia within the geographic area bounded by the outer boundaries of the combined area of said counties.

SEC. 3. *Nationwide Pilot Program.* The Department of Transportation, the Environmental Protection Agency, and the Department of Energy shall implement a "transit pass" transportation fringe benefit program, as described in section 2 of this order, for all of their qualified Federal employees as a 3 year pilot program by no later than October 1, 2000. Before determining whether the program should be extended to other Federal employees nationwide, it shall be analyzed by an entity determined by the agencies identified in section 4 of this order to ascertain, among other things, if it is effective in reducing single occupancy vehicle travel and local area traffic congestion.

SEC. 4. *Guidance.* Federal agencies shall develop plans to implement this order in consultation with the Department of the Treasury, the Department of Transportation, the Environmental Protection Agency, the Office of Personnel Management, the General Services Administration, and the Office of Management and Budget. Federal agencies that currently have more generous programs or benefits in place may continue to offer those programs or benefits. Agencies shall absorb the costs of implementing this order within the sums received pursuant to the President's FY 2001 budget request to the Congress.

SEC. 5. *Judicial Review.* This order is not intended to and does not create any right or benefit, substantive or procedural, enforceable at law by any party against the United States, its agencies or instrumentalities, its officers or employees, or any other person.

WILLIAM J. CLINTON.

Subpart G—Insurance and Annuities

SUBPART REFERRED TO IN OTHER SECTIONS

This subpart is referred to in sections 4703, 9507 of this title.

CHAPTER 81—COMPENSATION FOR WORK INJURIES

SUBCHAPTER I—GENERALLY

[1] So in original. Does not conform to section catchline.

AMENDMENTS

1995—Pub. L. 104–66, title I, § 1102(b)(3)(B), Dec. 21, 1995, 109 Stat. 723, added item 8152.

1994—Pub. L. 103–333, title I, § 101(a)(2), Sept. 30, 1994, 108 Stat. 2547, added item 8148.

1979—Pub. L. 96–70, title III, § 3302(e)(12), Sept. 27, 1979, 93 Stat. 499, substituted "Panama Canal Commission" for "Canal Zone" in item 8146.

1974—Pub. L. 93–416, §§ 12(b), 23(a), Sept. 7, 1974, 88 Stat. 1146, 1150, substituted "Notice of injury or death" for "Notice of injury; failure to give" in item 8119, and added item 8151.

1968—Pub. L. 90–291, § 1(b), Apr. 19, 1968, 82 Stat. 100, added subchapter III consisting of items 8191, 8192, and 8193.

1967—Pub. L. 90–83, § 1(59), (66)(B), (67)(B), (70), Sept. 11, 1967, 81 Stat. 211, 212, 213, inserted "; hearings" in item 8124, added item 8143a relating to members of the National Teachers Corps and item 8146a relating to cost-of-living adjustment of compensation, and struck out item 8148 relating to reports.

CHAPTER REFERRED TO IN OTHER SECTIONS

This chapter is referred to in sections 3102, 3111, 3161, 5948 of this title; title 7 sections 2272, 2279c; title 8 section 1357; title 10 sections 1588, 2113, 2360, 2904, 7086; title 14 sections 93, 823a; title 15 section 4102; title 16 sections 565a–2, 831b–1, 1703, 3602, 3640, 5608, 5708; title 18 section 4126; title 20 sections 76l, 4416; title 22 sections 2124c, 2391, 3508, 3715a, 3715d, 3649, 3658, 3664; title 24 sections 225e, 422; title 25 sections 2020, 3115, 3733; title 28 sections 376, 995, 996; title 33 section 569c; title 36 section 2113; title 38 sections 3115, 3485, 7453, 7458; title 40 sections 216c, 851; title 42 sections 405, 3788, 9843a; title 43 sections 50d, 1475; title 49 sections 106, 49104; title 50 section 2081.

SUBCHAPTER I—GENERALLY

SUBCHAPTER REFERRED TO IN OTHER SECTIONS

This subchapter is referred to in sections 2105, 3373, 3374, 3582, 5595, 8191, 8192, 8332, 8337, 8347, 8411, 8464a, 8705, 8706, 8707, 8708, 8714a, 8714b, 8714c, 8901 of this title; title 2 sections 31b–5, 905; title 7 sections 1507, 2225; title 10 section 1588; title 15 section 637; title 16 sections 1a–6, 18i, 558c, 580j, 670c, 742f, 773a, 831b, 1881b, 4604; title 18 sections 292, 1920, 1922; title 22 sections 3620, 3970, 4048, 4606, 5422; title 24 sections 421, 422; title 25 section 450i; title 28 sections 677, 1877; title 29 section 2897; title 32 section 509; title 33 section 941; title 38 sections 106, 1316, 1317, 7802; title 39 section 1005; title 40 section 290; title 42 sections 251, 1654, 1701, 1702, 1706, 1856c, 2996d, 5055, 7142, 10704, 12620, 12651g, 12655n; title 43 section 1737; title 50 sections 2031, 2051; title 50 App. sections 1291, 1292, 2004.

§ 8101. Definitions

For the purpose of this subchapter—

(1) "employee" means—

(A) a civil officer or employee in any branch of the Government of the United States, including an officer or employee of an instrumentality wholly owned by the United States;

(B) an individual rendering personal service to the United States similar to the service of a civil officer or employee of the United States, without pay or for nominal pay, when a statute authorizes the acceptance or use of the service, or authorizes payment of travel or other expenses of the individual;

(C) an individual, other than an independent contractor or an individual employed by an independent contractor, employed on the Menominee Indian Reservation in Wisconsin in operations conducted under a statute relating to tribal timber and logging operations on that reservation;

(D) an individual employed by the government of the District of Columbia; and

(E) an individual appointed to a position on the office staff of a former President under section 1(b) of the Act of August 25, 1958 (72 Stat. 838);

but does not include—

(i) a commissioned officer of the Regular Corps of the Public Health Service;

(ii) a commissioned officer of the Reserve Corps of the Public Health Service on active duty;

(iii) a commissioned officer of the Environmental Science Services Administration; or

(iv) a member of the Metropolitan Police or the Fire Department of the District of Columbia who is pensioned or pensionable under sections 521–535 of title 4, District of Columbia Code; and

(F)[1] an individual selected pursuant to chapter 121 of title 28, United States Code, and serving as a petit or grand juror;

(2) "physician" includes surgeons, podiatrists, dentists, clinical psychologists, optometrists, chiropractors, and osteopathic practitioners within the scope of their practice as defined by State law. The term "physician" includes chiropractors only to the extent that their reimbursable services are limited to treatment consisting of manual manipulation of the spine to correct a subluxation as demonstrated by X-ray to exist, and subject to regulation by the Secretary;

(3) "medical, surgical, and hospital services and supplies" includes services and supplies by podiatrists, dentists, clinical psychologists, optometrists, chiropractors, osteopathic practitioners and hospitals within the scope of their practice as defined by State law. Reimbursable chiropractic services are limited to treatment consisting of manual manipulation of the spine to correct a subluxation as demonstrated by X-ray to exist, and subject to regulation by the Secretary;

(4) "monthly pay" means the monthly pay at the time of injury, or the monthly pay at the time disability begins, or the monthly pay at the time compensable disability recurs, if the recurrence begins more than 6 months

---

[1] So in original. Pub. L. 93–416 added par. (F) immediately after par. (iv), rather than after par. (E).

after the injured employee resumes regular full-time employment with the United States, whichever is greater, except when otherwise determined under section 8113 of this title with respect to any period;

(5) "injury" includes, in addition to injury by accident, a disease proximately caused by the employment, and damage to or destruction of medical braces, artificial limbs, and other prosthetic devices which shall be replaced or repaired, and such time lost while such device or appliance is being replaced or repaired; except that eyeglasses and hearing aids would not be replaced, repaired, or otherwise compensated for, unless the damages or destruction is incident to a personal injury requiring medical services;

(6) "widow" means the wife living with or dependent for support on the decedent at the time of his death, or living apart for reasonable cause or because of his desertion;

(7) "parent" includes stepparents and parents by adoption;

(8) "brother" and "sister" mean one who at the time of the death of the employee is under 18 years of age or over that age and incapable of self-support, and include stepbrothers and stepsisters, half brothers and half sisters, and brothers and sisters by adoption, but do not include married brothers or married sisters;

(9) "child" means one who at the time of the death of the employee is under 18 years of age or over that age and incapable of self-support, and includes stepchildren, adopted children, and posthumous children, but does not include married children;

(10) "grandchild" means one who at the time of the death of the employee is under 18 years of age or over that age and incapable of self-support;

(11) "widower" means the husband living with or dependent for support on the decedent at the time of her death, or living apart for reasonable cause or because of her desertion;

(12) "compensation" includes the money allowance payable to an employee or his dependents and any other benefits paid for from the Employees' Compensation Fund, but this does not in any way reduce the amount of the monthly compensation payable for disability or death;

(13) "war-risk hazard" means a hazard arising during a war in which the United States is engaged; during an armed conflict in which the United States is engaged, whether or not war has been declared; or during a war or armed conflict between military forces of any origin, occurring in the country in which an individual to whom this subchapter applies is serving; from—

(A) the discharge of a missile, including liquids and gas, or the use of a weapon, explosive, or other noxious thing by a hostile force or individual or in combating an attack or an imagined attack by a hostile force or individual;

(B) action of a hostile force or individual, including rebellion or insurrection against the United States or any of its allies;

(C) the discharge or explosion of munitions intended for use in connection with a war or armed conflict with a hostile force or individual;

(D) the collision of vessels on convoy or the operation of vessels or aircraft without running lights or without other customary peacetime aids to navigation; or

(E) the operation of vessels or aircraft in a zone of hostilities or engaged in war activities;

(14) "hostile force or individual" means a nation, a subject of a foreign nation, or an individual serving a foreign nation—

(A) engaged in a war against the United States or any of its allies;

(B) engaged in armed conflict, whether or not war has been declared, against the United States or any of its allies; or

(C) engaged in a war or armed conflict between military forces of any origin in a country in which an individual to whom this subchapter applies is serving;

(15) "allies" means any nation with which the United States is engaged in a common military effort or with which the United States has entered into a common defensive military alliance;

(16) "war activities" includes activities directly relating to military operations;

(17) "student" means an individual under 23 years of age who has not completed 4 years of education beyond the high school level and who is regularly pursuing a full-time course of study or training at an institution which is—

(A) a school or college or university operated or directly supported by the United States, or by a State or local government or political subdivision thereof;

(B) a school or college or university which has been accredited by a State or by a State-recognized or nationally recognized accrediting agency or body;

(C) a school or college or university not so accredited but whose credits are accepted, on transfer, by at least three institutions which are so accredited, for credit on the same basis as if transferred from an institution so accredited; or

(D) an additional type of educational or training institution as defined by the Secretary of Labor.

Such an individual is deemed not to have ceased to be a student during an interim between school years if the interim is not more than 4 months and if he shows to the satisfaction of the Secretary that he has a bona fide intention of continuing to pursue a full-time course of study or training during the semester or other enrollment period immediately after the interim or during periods of reasonable duration during which, in the judgment of the Secretary, he is prevented by factors beyond his control from pursuing his education. A student whose 23rd birthday occurs during a semester or other enrollment period is deemed a student until the end of the semester or other enrollment period;

(18) "price index" means the Consumer Price Index (all items—United States city average) published monthly by the Bureau of Labor Statistics; and

(19) "organ" means a part of the body that performs a special function, and for purposes of this subchapter excludes the brain, heart, and back; and

(20) "United States medical officers and hospitals" includes medical officers and hospitals of the Army, Navy, Air Force, Department of Veterans Affairs, and United States Public Health Service, and any other medical officer or hospital designated as a United States medical officer or hospital by the Secretary of Labor.

(Pub. L. 89–554, Sept. 6, 1966, 80 Stat. 532; Pub. L. 90–83, §1(4), (48), Sept. 11, 1967, 81 Stat. 196, 209; Pub. L. 93–416, §1, Sept. 7, 1974, 88 Stat. 1143; Pub. L. 96–499, title IV, §421(b), Dec. 5, 1980, 94 Stat. 2608; Pub. L. 97–463, §4, Jan. 12, 1983, 96 Stat. 2532; Pub. L. 102–54, §13(b)(1), June 13, 1991, 105 Stat. 274.)

HISTORICAL AND REVISION NOTES
1966 ACT

Derivation	U.S. Code	Revised Statutes and Statutes at Large
(1)–(5), (12)–(16).	5 U.S.C. 790.	Sept. 7, 1916, ch. 458, §40, 39 Stat. 750. June 5, 1924, ch. 261, §2, 43 Stat. 389. May 31, 1938, ch. 293, 52 Stat. 586. Apr. 11, 1940, ch. 79, §1, 54 Stat. 105. July 1, 1944, ch. 373, §605(b), 58 Stat. 712. Aug. 13, 1946, ch. 958, §5, 60 Stat. 1049. Oct. 14, 1949, ch. 691, §108, 63 Stat. 860. July 30, 1956, ch. 779, §3(b), 70 Stat. 721. Aug. 1, 1956, ch. 837, §501(e), 70 Stat. 883. Aug. 8, 1958, Pub. L. 85–608, §302, 72 Stat. 539. Sept. 13, 1960, Pub. L. 86–767, §208, 74 Stat. 908. Sept. 4, 1964, Pub. L. 88–581, §4(b), 78 Stat. 919.
	5 U.S.C. 794 (1st sentence). [Uncodified].	July 11, 1919, ch. 7, §11 (1st sentence), 41 Stat. 104. Aug. 25, 1958, Pub. L. 85–745, §1(b) (last sentence, as applicable to the Federal Employees' Compensation Act), 72 Stat. 838.
(6)–(10)	5 U.S.C. 760(H).	Sept. 7, 1916, ch. 458, §10(H), 39 Stat. 745. Feb. 12, 1927, ch. 110, §2, 44 Stat. 1087.
(11)	5 U.S.C. 760(B) (last 23 words of 1st sentence).	Sept. 7, 1916, ch. 458, §10(B) (last 15 words of 1st sentence), 39 Stat. 744. Oct. 14, 1949, ch. 691, §106(c) "(B) (last 23 words of 1st sentence)", 63 Stat. 859.

Former section 790(a) is omitted as unnecessary in view of section 1 of title 1, United States Code.

Former section 790(c) is omitted as unnecessary as the term "commission" is not used in this subchapter.

Former section 790(i) is omitted as unnecessary as the title "Secretary of Labor" (substituted for "Federal Security Administrator" by 1950 Reorg. Plan No. 19, §1, eff. May 24, 1950, 64 Stat. 1271) is fully set out the first time it is used in each section.

In paragraph (1)(B), the words "to the United States" are substituted for "to any department, independent establishment, or agency thereof (including instrumentalities of the United States wholly owned by it)".

In paragraph (1)(C), the words "subsequent to September 7, 1916" are omitted as obsolete.

In paragraph (1)(iv), the words "under sections 521–535 of title 4, District of Columbia Code" are substituted for "under the provisions of the District of Columbia Appropriation Act approved September 1, 1916".

Standard changes are made to conform with the definitions applicable and the style of this title as outlined in the preface to the report.

1967 ACT

Section of title 5	Source (U.S.Code)	Source (Statutes at Large)
8101(17)	5 App.: 760(M).	July 4, 1966, Pub. L. 89–488, §§7(c), 14 "Sec. 43(c)", 80 Stat. 254, 256.
8101(18)	5 App.: 793a(c)(1).	
8101(19)	5 App.: 793a(c)(2).	

Paragraph (17) is reorganized and restated for clarity and to conform to the style of title 5, United States Code. In clause (D), the words "Secretary of Labor" are substituted for "Secretary" on authority of section 40(i) of the Federal Employees' Compensation Act.

In paragraph (19), the words "July 1966 and each later month" are substituted for "the month this section becomes effective and each month thereafter". The words "section 8146a of this title" are substituted for "this section" to reflect the codification of section 43 in title 5.

REFERENCES IN TEXT

Act of August 25, 1958, 72 Stat. 838, referred to in par. (1)(E), is set out as a note under section 102 of Title 3, The President.

AMENDMENTS

1991—Par. (20). Pub. L. 102–54 substituted "Department of Veterans Affairs" for "Veterans' Administration".

1983—Par. (1)(F). Pub. L. 97–463 struck out "and who is otherwise an employee for the purposes of this subchapter as defined by paragraph (A), (B), (C), (D), and (E) of this subsection" after "petit or grand juror".

1980—Pars. (19) to (21). Pub. L. 96–499 struck out par. (19) which defined "base month" as the month of July 1966 and each later month which was used as a basis for calculating an increase under section 8146a of this title, and redesignated pars. (20) and (21) as (19) and (20), respectively.

1974—Par. (1)(D). Pub. L. 93–416, §1(g), struck out "and" after the semicolon.

Par. (1)(F). Pub. L. 93–416, §1(a), added par. (1)(F).

Par. (2). Pub. L. 93–416, §1(b), expanded definition of "physician" to include podiatrists, dentists, clinical psychologists, optometrists, and chiropractors and inserted provision limiting the extent to which chiropractors are included.

Par. (3). Pub. L. 93–416, §1(c), included within "medical, surgical, and hospital services and supplies" those supplied by podiatrists, dentists, clinical psychologists, optometrists, and chiropractors and limited the reimbursable services of chiropractors.

Par. (5). Pub. L. 93–416, §1(d), added to definition of "injury" damage to or destruction of medical braces, artificial limbs, and other prosthetic devices and excepted eyeglasses and hearing aids unless damage or destruction is incidental to a personal injury requiring medical services.

Par. (11). Pub. L. 93–416, §1(e), substituted "the husband living with or dependent for support on the decedent at the time of her death, or living apart for reasonable cause because of her desertion" for "one who, because of physical or mental disability, was wholly dependent for support on the employee at the time of her death" as definition of "widower".

Pars. (20), (21). Pub. L. 93–416, §1(f), added pars. (20) and (21).

1967—Par. (1)(iii). Pub. L. 90–83, §1(4), substituted "Environmental Science Services Administration" for "Coast and Geodetic Survey". See Historical and Revision Notes under section 2101 of this title.

EFFECTIVE DATE OF 1980 AMENDMENT

Section 422 of Pub. L. 96–499 provided that: "The amendments made by section 421 [amending this section and section 8146a of this title] shall take effect on the date of the enactment of this Act [Dec. 5, 1980] with respect to any adjustments which are to be made on or after that date; except that the period specified in such section as extending from December to December shall, with respect to the adjustment to be made on March 1, 1981, extend instead from the last month in which the price index resulted in an adjustment prior to enactment to December of 1980."

EFFECTIVE DATE OF 1974 AMENDMENT

Section 28(a) of Pub. L. 93–416 provided that: "Except as otherwise provided by this section this Act [enacting section 8151 of this title, amending this section and sections 8103, 8104, 8107, 8110, 8111, 8113, 8116, 8117, 8118, 8119, 8121, 8122, 8132, 8135, 8142, 8143, 8146a of this title, repealing section 3315a of this title, and enacting provisions set out as notes under this section and section 8116 of this title] shall take effect on the date of enactment [Sept. 7, 1974] and be applicable to any injury or death occurring on or after such effective date [Sept. 7, 1974]. The amendments made by sections 1(b) and (c) [amending this section], 2 [amending section 8103 of this title], 3 [amending section 8104 of this title], 7(a) and (b) [amending section 8111 of this title], 8(a) [amending section 8113 of this title], 8(b) [amending section 8143 of this title], 9 [amending section 8116 of this title], 16(a) [amending section 8133 of this title], 16(b) [amending section 8135 of this title], 17 [amending section 8133 of this title], 19 [amending section 8135 of this title], 20 [amending section 8135 of this title], 21 [amending section 8146a of this title], 22 [enacting section 8151 of this title], 24 [amending section 8146a of this title], and 25 [amending section 8147 of this title], shall be applicable to cases where the injury or death occurred prior to the date of enactment [Sept. 7, 1974] but the provisions of these sections shall be applicable only to a period beginning on or after the date of enactment [Sept. 7, 1974]."

SHORT TITLE OF 1990 AMENDMENT

Pub. L. 101–534, § 1, Nov. 7, 1990, 104 Stat. 2352, provided that: "This Act [amending section 8111 of this title and enacting provisions set out as a note under section 8111 of this title] may be cited as the 'Attendant Allowance Adjustment Act'."

TRANSFER OF FUNCTIONS

Environmental Science Services Administration in Department of Commerce, including offices of Administrator and Deputy Administrator thereof, abolished by Reorg. Plan No. 4 of 1970, eff. Oct. 3, 1970, 35 F.R. 15627, 84 Stat. 2090, set out in the Appendix to this title, which created National Oceanic and Atmospheric Administration in Department of Commerce and transferred personnel, property, records, and unexpended balances of funds of Environmental Science Services Administration to such newly created National Oceanic and Atmospheric Administration. Components of Environmental Science Services Administration thus transferred included Weather Bureau [now National Weather Service], Coast and Geodetic Survey [now National Ocean Survey], Environmental Data Services, National Environmental Satellite Center, and ESSA Research Laboratories.

Functions of Public Health Service, Surgeon General of Public Health Service, and all other officers and employees of Public Health Service, and functions of all agencies of or in Public Health Service, transferred to Secretary of Health, Education, and Welfare by 1966 Reorg. Plan No. 3, 31 F.R. 8855, 80 Stat. 1610, effective June 25, 1966, set out in the Appendix to this title. Secretary of Health, Education, and Welfare redesignated Secretary of Health and Human Services by section 3508 of Title 20, Education.

PROCESSING OF CLAIMS FILED BY DISTRICT OF COLUMBIA EMPLOYEES

Pub. L. 93–198, title II, § 204(e), Dec. 24, 1973, 87 Stat. 783, provided that: "All functions of the Secretary under chapter 81 of title 5 of the United States Code, with respect to the processing of claims filed by employees of the government of the District for compensation for work injuries, are transferred to and shall be exercised by the Commissioner, effective the day after the day on which the District establishes an independent personnel system or systems." An independent personnel system was established for the District by D.C. Law 2–139, Mar. 3, 1979, 25 DCR 5740.

STUDY AND REPORT TO CONGRESS BY SECRETARY OF LABOR OF PROVISIONS AND PROGRAMS UNDER SUBCHAPTER

Section 27 of Pub. L. 93–416 directed Secretary of Labor to conduct a study of the provisions of this subchapter and its programs which was to include: hearings, research, and other activities necessary to formulate recommendations; an examination of need for authority to increase allowances for services of attendants above the maximum fixed by section 8111 of this title in exceptional circumstances; an examination of the effectiveness of this subchapter; and recommendations as to survivor benefits; report results of the study together with his findings and recommendations not later than 12 months after Sept. 7, 1974.

SECTION REFERRED TO IN OTHER SECTIONS

This section is referred to in sections 3373, 3374, 7902, 8110, 8118, 8133, 8191, 8192 of this title; title 16 sections 1a–6, 18i, 558c, 670c, 742f, 773a, 4604; title 20 section 76l; title 22 section 3973; title 29 section 2897; title 30 section 902; title 42 sections 3796b, 5055, 12620, 12651g, 12655n.

§ 8102. Compensation for disability or death of employee

(a) The United States shall pay compensation as specified by this subchapter for the disability or death of an employee resulting from personal injury sustained while in the performance of his duty, unless the injury or death is—

(1) caused by willful misconduct of the employee;

(2) caused by the employee's intention to bring about the injury or death of himself or of another; or

(3) proximately caused by the intoxication of the injured employee.

(b) Disability or death from a war-risk hazard or during or as a result of capture, detention, or other restraint by a hostile force or individual, suffered by an employee who is employed outside the continental United States or in Alaska or in the areas and installations in the Republic of Panama made available to the United States pursuant to the Panama Canal Treaty of 1977 and related agreements (as described in section 3(a) of the Panama Canal Act of 1979), is deemed to have resulted from personal injury sustained while in the performance of his duty, whether or not the employee was engaged in the course of employment when the disability or disability resulting in death occurred or when he was taken by the hostile force or individual. This subsection does not apply to an individual—

(1) whose residence is at or in the vicinity of the place of his employment and who was not living there solely because of the exigencies of his employment, unless he was injured or taken while engaged in the course of his employment; or

(2) who is a prisoner of war or a protected individual under the Geneva Conventions of 1949 and is detained or utilized by the United States.

This subsection does not affect the payment of compensation under this subchapter derived otherwise than under this subsection, but compensation for disability or death does not accrue for a period for which pay, other benefit, or gratuity from the United States accrues to the disabled individual or his dependents on account of detention by the enemy or because of the same disability or death, unless that pay, benefit, or gratuity is refunded or renounced.

(Pub. L. 89–554, Sept. 6, 1966, 80 Stat. 534; Pub. L. 96–70, title I, § 1231(d), Sept. 27, 1979, 93 Stat. 470.)

HISTORICAL AND REVISION NOTES

Derivation	U.S. Code	Revised Statutes and Statutes at Large
....	5 U.S.C. 751.	Sept. 7, 1916, ch. 458, § 1, 39 Stat. 742. Aug. 8, 1958, Pub. L. 85–608, § 301, 72 Stat. 538.

Standard changes are made to conform with the definitions applicable and the style of this title as outlined in the preface to the report.

REFERENCES IN TEXT

Section 3(a) of the Panama Canal Act of 1979, referred to in subsec. (b), is classified to section 3602(a) of Title 22, Foreign Relations and Intercourse.

AMENDMENTS

1979—Subsec. (b). Pub. L. 96–70 substituted "areas and installations in the Republic of Panama made available to the United States pursuant to the Panama Canal Treaty of 1977 and related agreements (as described in section 3(a) of the Panama Canal Act of 1979)" for "Canal Zone".

EFFECTIVE DATE OF 1979 AMENDMENT

Amendment by Pub. L. 96–70 effective Oct. 1, 1979, see section 3304 of Pub. L. 96–70, set out as an Effective Date note under section 3601 of Title 22, Foreign Relations and Intercourse.

SECTION REFERRED TO IN OTHER SECTIONS

This section is referred to in title 22 section 3691.

§ 8103. Medical services and initial medical and other benefits

(a) The United States shall furnish to an employee who is injured while in the performance of duty, the services, appliances, and supplies prescribed or recommended by a qualified physician, which the Secretary of Labor considers likely to cure, give relief, reduce the degree or the period of disability, or aid in lessening the amount of the monthly compensation. These services, appliances, and supplies shall be furnished—

(1) whether or not disability has arisen;
(2) notwithstanding that the employee has accepted or is entitled to receive benefits under subchapter III of chapter 83 of this title or another retirement system for employees of the Government; and
(3) by or on the order of United States medical officers and hospitals, or, at the employee's option, by or on the order of physicians and hospitals designated or approved by the Secretary.

The employee may initially select a physician to provide medical services, appliances, and supplies, in accordance with such regulations and instructions as the Secretary considers necessary, and may be furnished necessary and reasonable transportation and expenses incident to the securing of such services, appliances, and supplies. These expenses, when authorized or approved by the Secretary, shall be paid from the Employees' Compensation Fund.

(b) The Secretary, under such limitations or conditions as he considers necessary, may authorize the employing agencies to provide for the initial furnishing of medical and other benefits under this section. The Secretary may certify vouchers for these expenses out of the Employees' Compensation Fund when the immediate superior of the employee certifies that the expense was incurred in respect to an injury which was accepted by the employing agency as probably compensable under this subchapter. The Secretary shall prescribe the form and content of the certificate.

(Pub. L. 89–554, Sept. 6, 1966, 80 Stat. 535; Pub. L. 90–83, § 1(49), Sept. 11, 1967, 81 Stat. 209; Pub. L. 93–416, § 2, Sept. 7, 1974, 88 Stat. 1144.)

HISTORICAL AND REVISION NOTES
1966 ACT

Derivation	U.S. Code	Revised Statutes and Statutes at Large
....	5 U.S.C. 759(a).	Sept. 7, 1916, ch. 458, § 9, 39 Stat. 743. June 26, 1926, ch. 695, § 1, 44 Stat. 772. Oct. 14, 1949, ch. 691, § 202(b), 63 Stat. 862. Sept. 13, 1960, Pub. L. 86–767, § 203, 74 Stat. 907.

In subsection (b), the words "when the immediate superior of the employee certifies" are substituted for "upon certification by the person required by section 774 of this title to make reports of injury".

The last sentence of former section 759(a) is omitted as executed.

Administration of this subchapter was transferred to the Secretary of Labor by section 1 of 1950 Reorg. Plan No. 19, 64 Stat. 1271 (see section 8145).

Standard changes are made to conform with the definitions applicable and the style of this title as outlined in the preface to the report.

1967 ACT

Section of title 5	Source (U.S. Code)	Source (Statutes at Large)
8103(a)(2) ...	5 App.: 759(a).	July 4, 1966, Pub. L. 89–488, § 5(b), 80 Stat. 253.

The words "another retirement system for employees of the Government" are substituted for "any other Federal Act or program providing retirement benefits for employees".

AMENDMENTS

1974—Subsec. (a). Pub. L. 93–416 substituted "at the employee's option" for "when this is not practicable", struck out "private" before "physicians and hospitals" in par. (3), and, in provision following par. (3), added authorization for the employee to initially select a physician in accordance with such regulations and instructions considered necessary by the Secretary.

Amendment by Pub. L. 93–416 applicable to cases where injury or death occurred prior to Sept. 7, 1974, but only to a period beginning on or after Sept. 7, 1974, see section 28(a) of Pub. L. 93–416, set out as a note under section 8101 of this title.

PERSONNEL NOT AFFECTED BY 1967 INCREASE

Section 7 of Pub. L. 90–83 provided that: "Nothing in this or any other Act makes the increases authorized by section 1(49)—(52) [amending this section and sections 8107, 8108, and 8109 of this title], 53(B) and (C) [amending section 8110 of this title], (54)—(58) [amending section 8111, 8112, 8116, 8122, and 8124 of this title], (60) [amending section 8131 of this title], (61) [amending section 8132 of this title], (62) (B) [amending section 8133(e) of this title], (63) [amending section 8135 of this title], (67) [adding section 8146a of this title], (68) [amending section 8147 of this title], and (71) [amending section 8149 of this title] of this Act applicable to—

"(1) an employee or individual not within the definition of 'employee' in section 8101(1)(A), (B), or (D) of title 5, United States Code;

"(2) a member of the Metropolitan Police or the Fire Department of the District of Columbia who is pensioned or pensionable under sections 521—535 of title 4, District of Columbia Code; or

"(3) a member of a uniformed service."

SECTION REFERRED TO IN OTHER SECTIONS

This section is referred to in sections 8104, 8117, 8146 of this title.

§ 8104. Vocational rehabilitation

(a) The Secretary of Labor may direct a permanently disabled individual whose disability is compensable under this subchapter to undergo vocational rehabilitation. The Secretary shall provide for furnishing the vocational rehabilitation services. In providing for these services, the Secretary, insofar as practicable, shall use the services or facilities of State agencies and corresponding agencies which cooperate with the Secretary of Health, Education, and Welfare in carrying out the purposes of chapter 4 of title 29, except to the extent that the Secretary of Labor provides for furnishing these services under section 8103 of this title. The cost of providing these services to individuals undergoing vocational rehabilitation under this section shall be paid from the Employees' Compensation Fund. However, in reimbursing a State or corresponding agency under an arrangement pursuant to this section the cost to the agency reimbursable in full under section 32(b)(1) of title 29 is excluded.

(b) Notwithstanding section 8106, individuals directed to undergo vocational rehabilitation by the Secretary shall, while undergoing such rehabilitation, receive compensation at the rate provided in sections 8105 and 8110 of this title, less the amount of any earnings received from remunerative employment, other than employment undertaken pursuant to such rehabilitation.

(Pub. L. 89–554, Sept. 6, 1966, 80 Stat. 535; Pub. L. 93–416, § 3, Sept. 7, 1974, 88 Stat. 1144.)

HISTORICAL AND REVISION NOTES

Derivation	U.S. Code	Revised Statutes and Statutes at Large
....	5 U.S.C. 759(b).	Oct. 14, 1949, ch. 691, § 202(a), 63 Stat. 862.

In the third sentence, the words "the Secretary of Health, Education, and Welfare" are substituted for "him", referring to the Administrator, on authority of section 1 (proviso) of 1950 Reorg. Plan No. 19, 64 Stat. 1271, and section 5 of 1953 Reorg. Plan No. 1, 67 Stat. 632.

The words "State agencies or corresponding agencies" are substituted for "State agencies (or corresponding agencies in Territories or possessions)" as the agencies available for cooperation are set out in the Vocational Rehabilitation Act (chapter 4 of title 29).

The words "section 32(b)(1) of title 29" are substituted for "section 33(a) (4) of title 29" on authority of the Act of Aug. 3, 1954, ch. 655, § 2, 68 Stat. 652. Reference is limited to section 32(b)(1) since section 32(b) (2), (3) is obsolete.

Administration of this subchapter was transferred to the Secretary of Labor by section 1 of 1950 Reorg. Plan No. 19, 64 Stat. 1271 (see section 8145).

Standard changes are made to conform with the definitions applicable and the style of this title as outlined in the preface to the report.

REFERENCES IN TEXT

Chapter 4 of title 29, referred to in subsec. (a), refers to the Vocational Rehabilitation Act, act June 2, 1920, ch. 219, 41 Stat. 735, as amended. Section 32(b)(1) of title 29, also referred to in subsec. (a) (enacted Sept. 6, 1966), did not reflect amendment of section 32(b) by Pub. L. 89–333 § 2(a), Nov. 8, 1965, 79 Stat. 1282, which eliminated obsolete pars. (2) and (3) and redesignated par. (1) provisions as subsec. (b) and amended such subsection. Section 32(b) of title 29, refers to section 2(b) of act June 2, 1920, as amended. Such provisions were repealed by former section 500(a) of Pub. L. 93–112, title V, Sept. 26, 1973, 87 Stat. 390, and pursuant to former section 500(a) of Pub. L. 93–112, which also provided that references to the Vocational Rehabilitation Act in other provisions of law were to be deemed a reference to the Rehabilitation Act of 1973, and were covered by sections 701 et seq. and 731(a), respectively, of Title 29, Labor.

AMENDMENTS

1974—Pub. L. 93–416 designated existing provisions as subsec. (a) and added subsec. (b).

EFFECTIVE DATE OF 1974 AMENDMENT

Amendment by Pub. L. 93–416 applicable to cases where injury or death occurred prior to Sept. 7, 1974, but only to a period beginning on or after Sept. 7, 1974, see section 28(a) of Pub. L. 93–416, set out as a note under section 8101 of this title.

TRANSFER OF FUNCTIONS

For transfer of functions and offices (relating to Rehabilitation Act of 1973) of Secretary and Department of Health, Education, and Welfare to Secretary and Department of Education, see section 3441 of Title 20, Education.

SECTION REFERRED TO IN OTHER SECTIONS

This section is referred to in sections 8111, 8113, 8117 of this title.

§ 8105. Total disability

(a) If the disability is total, the United States shall pay the employee during the disability monthly monetary compensation equal to 66⅔ percent of his monthly pay, which is known as his basic compensation for total disability.

(b) The loss of use of both hands, both arms, both feet, or both legs, or the loss of sight of both eyes, is prima facie permanent total disability.

(Pub. L. 89–554, Sept. 6, 1966, 80 Stat. 535.)

HISTORICAL AND REVISION NOTES

Derivation	U.S. Code	Revised Statutes and Statutes at Large
....	5 U.S.C. 753.	Sept. 7, 1916, ch. 458, §3, 39 Stat. 743. Oct. 14, 1949, ch. 691, §102, 63 Stat. 855.

In subsection (a), the words "Except as otherwise provided in sections 751–756, 757–781, 783–791, and 793 of this title" are omitted as surplusage.

In subsection (b), the words "Loss, or" are omitted as included in "loss of use of". The words "or the loss of sight of both eyes" are substituted for "or both eyes or the sight thereof".

Standard changes are made to conform with the definitions applicable and the style of this title as outlined in the preface to the report.

SECTION REFERRED TO IN OTHER SECTIONS

This section is referred to in sections 8104, 8107, 8110 of this title.

§ 8106. Partial disability

(a) If the disability is partial, the United States shall pay the employee during the disability monthly monetary compensation equal to 66⅔ percent of the difference between his monthly pay and his monthly wage-earning capacity after the beginning of the partial disability, which is known as his basic compensation for partial disability.

(b) The Secretary of Labor may require a partially disabled employee to report his earnings from employment or self-employment, by affidavit or otherwise, in the manner and at the times the Secretary specifies. The employee shall include in the affidavit or report the value of housing, board, lodging, and other advantages which are part of his earnings in employment or self-employment and which can be estimated in money. An employee who—

(1) fails to make an affidavit or report when required; or

(2) knowingly omit or understates any part of his earnings;

forfeits his right to compensation with respect to any period for which the affidavit or report was required. Compensation forfeited under this subsection, if already paid, shall be recovered by a deduction from the compensation payable to the employee or otherwise recovered under section 8129 of this title, unless recovery is waived under that section.

(c) A partially disabled employee who—

(1) refuses to seek suitable work; or

(2) refuses or neglects to work after suitable work is offered to, procured by, or secured for him;

is not entitled to compensation.

(Pub. L. 89–554, Sept. 6, 1966, 80 Stat. 536.)

HISTORICAL AND REVISION NOTES

Derivation	U.S. Code	Revised Statutes and Statutes at Large
....	5 U.S.C. 754.	Sept. 7, 1916, ch. 458, §4, 39 Stat. 743. Oct. 14, 1949, ch. 691, §103(a), 63 Stat. 855.

In subsection (a), the words "Except as otherwise provided in sections 751–756, 757–781, 783–791, and 793 of this title" are omitted as surplusage.

In subsection (b), the word "remuneration" is omitted as covered by the word "earnings".

Administration of this subchapter was transferred to the Secretary of Labor by section 1 of 1950 Reorg. Plan No. 19, 64 Stat. 1271 (see section 8145).

Standard changes are made to conform with the definitions applicable and the style of this title as outlined in the preface to the report.

SECTION REFERRED TO IN OTHER SECTIONS

This section is referred to in sections 8104, 8107, 8110, 8148 of this title.

§ 8107. Compensation schedule

(a) If there is permanent disability involving the loss, or loss of use, of a member or function of the body or involving disfigurement, the employee is entitled to basic compensation for the disability, as provided by the schedule in subsection (c) of this section, at the rate of 66⅔ percent of his monthly pay. The basic compensation is—

(1) payable regardless of whether the cause of the disability originates in a part of the body other than that member;

(2) payable regardless of whether the disability also involves another impairment of the body; and

(3) in addition to compensation for temporary total or temporary partial disability.

(b) With respect to any period after payments under subsection (a) of this section have ended, an employee is entitled to compensation as provided by—

(1) section 8105 of this title if the disability is total; or

(2) section 8106 of this title if the disability is partial.

(c) The compensation schedule is as follows:

(1) Arm lost, 312 weeks' compensation.

(2) Leg lost, 288 weeks' compensation.

(3) Hand lost, 244 weeks' compensation.

(4) Foot lost, 205 weeks' compensation.

(5) Eye lost, 160 weeks' compensation.

(6) Thumb lost, 75 weeks' compensation.

(7) First finger lost, 46 weeks' compensation.

(8) Great toe lost, 38 weeks' compensation.

(9) Second finger lost, 30 weeks' compensation.

(10) Third finger lost, 25 weeks' compensation.

(11) Toe other than great toe lost, 16 weeks' compensation.

(12) Fourth finger lost, 15 weeks' compensation.

(13) Loss of hearing—

(A) complete loss of hearing of one ear, 52 weeks' compensation; or

(B) complete loss of hearing of both ears, 200 weeks' compensation.

(14) Compensation for loss of binocular vision or for loss of 80 percent or more of the vision of an eye is the same as for loss of the eye.

(15) Compensation for loss of more than one phalanx of a digit is the same as for loss of the entire digit. Compensation for loss of the first phalanx is one-half of the compensation for loss of the entire digit.

(16) If, in the case of an arm or a leg, the member is amputated above the wrist or

ankle, compensation is the same as for loss of the arm or leg, respectively.

(17) Compensation for loss of use of two or more digits, or one or more phalanges of each of two or more digits, of a hand or foot, is proportioned to the loss of use of the hand or foot occasioned thereby.

(18) Compensation for permanent total loss of use of a member is the same as for loss of the member.

(19) Compensation for permanent partial loss of use of a member may be for proportionate loss of use of the member. The degree of loss of vision or hearing under this schedule is determined without regard to correction.

(20) In case of loss of use of more than one member or parts of more than one member as enumerated by this schedule, the compensation is for loss of use of each member or part thereof, and the awards run consecutively. However, when the injury affects only two or more digits of the same hand or foot, paragraph (17) of this subsection applies, and when partial bilateral loss of hearing is involved, compensation is computed on the loss as affecting both ears.

(21) For serious disfigurement of the face, head, or neck of a character likely to handicap an individual in securing or maintaining employment, proper and equitable compensation not to exceed $3,500 shall be awarded in addition to any other compensation payable under this schedule.

(22) For permanent loss or loss of use of any other important external or internal organ of the body as determined by the Secretary, proper and equitable compensation not to exceed 312 weeks' compensation for each organ so determined shall be paid in addition to any other compensation payable under this schedule.

(Pub. L. 89–554, Sept. 6, 1966, 80 Stat. 536; Pub. L. 90–83, § 1(50), Sept. 11, 1967, 81 Stat. 210; Pub. L. 93–416, §§ 4, 5, Sept. 7, 1974, 88 Stat. 1144, 1145.)

HISTORICAL AND REVISION NOTES
1966 ACT

Derivation	U.S. Code	Revised Statutes and Statutes at Large
....	5 U.S.C. 755(a), (b).	Sept. 7, 1916, ch. 458, § 5, 39 Stat. 743. Oct. 14, 1949, ch. 691, § 104 "Sec. 5(a), (b)", 63 Stat. 855. Sept. 13, 1960, Pub. L. 86–767, § 201, 74 Stat. 907.

The words "loss, or" are omitted throughout this section as included in "loss of use".

In subsection (a)(B), the words "under sections 751–754 of this title" are omitted as surplusage.

In subsection (b)(1), the words "(including paragraphs (16) and (20) thereof)" are omitted as surplusage.

Standard changes are made to conform with the definitions applicable and the style of this title as outlined in the preface to the report.

1967 ACT

Section of title 5	Source (U.S.Code)	Source (Statutes at Large)
8107(a), (b).	5 App.: 755(a), (b).	July 4, 1966, Pub. L. 89–488, § 2(a), (b), 80 Stat. 252.

In subsection (a), the words "If there is" are substituted for "In any case of". The words "loss, or" are omitted as included in "loss of use" and to conform to the remainder of the section. The words "the employee is entitled to basic compensation for the disability" are substituted for "basic compensation for such disability shall be payable to the disabled employee". The words "by the schedule in subsection (c) of this section" are substituted for "in the following schedule" to reflect the codification of the schedule in subsection (c). The words "The schedule referred to in the first sentence is as follows:" are omitted as unnecessary in view of the codification of that schedule in subsection (c).

In subsection (b), the words "an employee is entitled to compensation" are substituted for "compensation shall be paid" for consistency with subsection (a). In subsections (b) (1) and (2), the words "section 8105 of this title" and "section 8106 of this title" are substituted for "section 3" and "subsection (a) of section 4", respectively, to reflect the codification of title 5.

AMENDMENTS

1974—Subsec. (a). Pub. L. 93–416, § 4, substituted "involving the loss, or loss of use" for "involving the loss of use".

Subsec. (c)(22). Pub. L. 93–416, § 5, added par. (22).

EFFECTIVE DATE OF 1974 AMENDMENT

Amendment by Pub. L. 93–416 effective Sept. 7, 1974, and applicable to any injury or death occurring on or after such effective date, see section 28(a) of Pub. L. 93–416, set out as a note under section 8101 of this title.

PERSONNEL NOT AFFECTED BY 1967 INCREASE

Increases authorized under amendment by Pub. L. 90–83 not applicable to specified personnel, see section 7 of Pub. L. 90–83, set out as a note under section 8103 of this title.

SECTION REFERRED TO IN OTHER SECTIONS

This section is referred to in sections 8108, 8109, 8110, 8115, 8116, 8337, 8464a of this title; title 18 section 1921; title 22 section 4048; title 50 section 2051.

§ 8108. Reduction of compensation for subsequent injury to same member

The period of compensation payable under the schedule in section 8107(c) of this title is reduced by the period of compensation paid or payable under the schedule for an earlier injury if—

(1) compensation in both cases is for disability of the same member or function or different parts of the same member or function or for disfigurement; and

(2) the Secretary of Labor finds that compensation payable for the later disability in whole or in part would duplicate the compensation payable for the preexisting disability.

In such a case, compensation for disability continuing after the scheduled period starts on expiration of that period as reduced under this section.

(Pub. L. 89–554, Sept. 6, 1966, 80 Stat. 538; Pub. L. 90–83, § 1(51), Sept. 11, 1967, 81 Stat. 210.)

HISTORICAL AND REVISION NOTES
1966 ACT

Derivation	U.S. Code	Revised Statutes and Statutes at Large
....	5 U.S.C. 755(c).	Oct. 14, 1949, ch. 691, § 104 "Sec. 5(c)", 63 Stat. 857.

Standard changes are made to conform with the definitions applicable and the style of this title as outlined in the preface to the report.

1967 ACT

Section of title 5	Source (U.S.Code)	Source (Statutes at Large)
8108	5 App.: 755(c).	July 4, 1966, Pub. L. 89–488, § 2(c), 80 Stat. 252.

PERSONNEL NOT AFFECTED BY 1967 INCREASE

Increases authorized under amendment by Pub. L. 90–83 not applicable to specified personnel, see section 7 of Pub. L. 90–83, set out as a note under section 8103 of this title.

SECTION REFERRED TO IN OTHER SECTIONS

This section is referred to in section 8115 of this title; title 18 section 1921.

§ 8109. Beneficiaries of awards unpaid at death; order of precedence

(a) If an individual—

(1) has sustained disability compensable under section 8107(a) of this title;

(2) has filed a valid claim in his lifetime; and

(3) dies from a cause other than the injury before the end of the period specified by the schedule;

the compensation specified by the schedule that is unpaid at his death, whether or not accrued or due at his death, shall be paid—

(A) under an award made before or after the death;

(B) for the period specified by the schedule;

(C) to and for the benefit of the persons then in being within the classes and proportions and on the conditions specified by this section; and

(D) in the following order of precedence:

(i) If there is no child, to the widow or widower.

(ii) If there are both a widow or widower and a child or children, one-half to the widow or widower and one-half to the child or children.

(iii) If there is no widow or widower, to the child or children.

(iv) If there is no survivor in the above classes, to the parent or parents wholly or partly dependent for support on the decedent, or to other wholly dependent relatives listed by section 8133(a)(5) of this title, or to both in proportions provided by regulation.

(v) If there is no survivor in the above classes and no burial allowance is payable under section 8134 of this title, an amount not exceeding that which would be expendable under section 8134 of this title if applicable shall be paid to reimburse a person equitably entitled thereto to the extent and in the proportion that he has paid the burial expenses, but a compensated insurer or other person obligated by law or contract to pay the burial expenses or a State or political subdivision or entity is deemed not equitably entitled.

(b) Payments under subsection (a) of this section, except for an amount payable for a period preceding the death of the individual, are at the basic rate of compensation for permanent disability specified by section 8107(a) of this title even if at the time of death the individual was entitled to the augmented rate specified by section 8110 of this title.

(c) A surviving beneficiary under subsection (a) of this section, except one under subsection (a)(D)(v), does not have a vested right to payment and must be alive to receive payment.

(d) A beneficiary under subsection (a) of this section, except one under subsection (a)(D)(v), ceases to be entitled to payment on the happening of an event which would terminate his right to compensation for death under section 8133 of this title. When that entitlement ceases, compensation remaining unpaid under subsection (a) of this section is payable to the surviving beneficiary in accordance with subsection (a) of this section.

(Pub. L. 89–554, Sept. 6, 1966, 80 Stat. 538; Pub. L. 90–83, § 1(52), Sept. 11, 1967, 81 Stat. 210.)

HISTORICAL AND REVISION NOTES
1966 ACT

Derivation	U.S. Code	Revised Statutes and Statutes at Large
....	5 U.S.C. 755(d).	Oct. 14, 1949, ch. 691, § 104 "Sec. 5(d)", 63 Stat. 857.

The references in former section 755(d) to definitions in former section 760(B), (H) are omitted as unnecessary as the definitions are included in section 8101 for the entire subchapter.

Standard changes are made to conform with the definitions applicable and the style of this title as outlined in the preface to the report.

1967 ACT

Section of title 5	Source (U.S.Code)	Source (Statutes at Large)
8109(a)(1) ...	5 App.: 755(d)(1).	July 4, 1966, Pub. L. 89–488, § 2(d), 80 Stat. 252.

PERSONNEL NOT AFFECTED BY 1967 INCREASE

Increases authorized under amendment by Pub. L. 90–83 not applicable to specified personnel, see section 7 of Pub. L. 90–83, set out as a note under section 8103 of this title.

SECTION REFERRED TO IN OTHER SECTIONS

This section is referred to in section 8115 of this title; title 18 section 1921.

§ 8110. Augmented compensation for dependents

(a) For the purpose of this section, "dependent" means—

(1) a wife, if—

(A) she is member of the same household as the employee;

(B) she is receiving regular contributions from the employee for her support; or

(C) the employee has been ordered by a court to contribute to her support;

(2) a husband, if—

(A) he is a member of the same household as the employee; or

(B) he is receiving regular contributions from the employee for his support; or

(C) the employee has been ordered by a court to contribute to his support;

(3) an unmarried child, while living with the employee or receiving regular contributions

from the employee toward his support, and who is—

    (A) under 18 years of age; or

    (B) over 18 years of age and incapable of self-support because of physical or mental disability; and

    (4) a parent, while wholly dependent on and supported by the employee.

Notwithstanding paragraph (3) of this subsection, compensation payable for a child that would otherwise end because the child has reached 18 years of age shall continue if he is a student as defined by section 8101 of this title at the time he reaches 18 years of age for so long as he continues to be such a student or until he marries.

(b) A disabled employee with one or more dependents is entitled to have his basic compensation for disability augmented—

    (1) at the rate of 8⅓ percent of his monthly pay if that compensation is payable under section 8105 or 8107(a) of this title; and

    (2) at the rate of 8⅓ percent of the difference between his monthly pay and his monthly wage-earning capacity if that compensation is payable under section 8106(a) of this title.

(Pub. L. 89–554, Sept. 6, 1966, 80 Stat. 539; Pub. L. 90–83, § 1(53), Sept. 11, 1967, 81 Stat. 210; Pub. L. 93–416, § 6, Sept. 7, 1974, 88 Stat. 1145.)

HISTORICAL AND REVISION NOTES
1966 ACT

Derivation	U.S. Code	Revised Statutes and Statutes at Large
....	5 U.S.C. 756(a).	Sept. 7, 1916, ch. 458, § 6, 39 Stat. 743. Feb. 12, 1927, ch. 110, § 1, 44 Stat. 1086. May 13, 1936, ch. 382, 49 Stat. 1270. Oct. 14, 1949, ch. 691, § 105 "Sec. 6(a)", 63 Stat. 858.

The references in former section 756(a)(2) to definitions in former section 760(H) are omitted as unnecessary as the definitions are included in section 8101 for the entire subchapter.

Standard changes are made to conform with the definitions applicable and the style of this title as outlined in the preface to the report.

1967 ACT

Section of title 5	Source (U.S.Code)	Source (Statutes at Large)
8110(a)	5 App.: 756(a)(2) (C).	July 4, 1966, Pub. L. 89–488, § 7(b), 80 Stat. 254.
8110(b)	5 App.: 756(a)(1).	July 4, 1966, Pub. L. 89–488, §§ 2(e), 3(a), 80 Stat. 252.

In subsection (a), the words "Notwithstanding paragraph (3) of this subsection" are substituted for "Notwithstanding any other provision of this section" for clarity. The word "he" is substituted for "he or she" in two places on authority of 1 U.S.C. 1. The words "section 8101 of this title" are substituted for "section 10(M) of this Act" to reflect the codification of that section in title 5.

AMENDMENTS

1974—Subsec. (a)(2). Pub. L. 93–416 substituted provisions of subpars. (A), (B) and (C) for "wholly dependent on the employee for support because of his own physical or mental disability".

EFFECTIVE DATE OF 1974 AMENDMENT

Amendment by Pub. L. 93–416 effective Sept. 7, 1974, and applicable to any injury or death occurring on or after such effective date, see section 28(a) of Pub. L. 93–416, set out as a note under section 8101 of this title.

PERSONNEL NOT AFFECTED BY 1967 INCREASE

Increases authorized under amendment by section 1(53)(B), (C) of Pub. L. 90–83 not applicable to specified personnel, see section 7 of Pub. L. 90–83, set out as a note under section 8103 of this title.

SECTION REFERRED TO IN OTHER SECTIONS

This section is referred to in sections 8104, 8109, 8112, 8148 of this title; title 18 section 1921.

§ 8111. Additional compensation for services of attendants or vocational rehabilitation

(a) The Secretary of Labor may pay an employee who has been awarded compensation an additional sum of not more than $1,500 a month, as the Secretary considers necessary, when the Secretary finds that the service of an attendant is necessary constantly because the employee is totally blind, or has lost the use of both hands or both feet, or is paralyzed and unable to walk, or because of other disability resulting from the injury making him so helpless as to require constant attendance.

(b) The Secretary may pay an individual undergoing vocational rehabilitation under section 8104 of this title additional compensation necessary for his maintenance, but not to exceed $200 a month.

(Pub. L. 89–554, Sept. 6, 1966, 80 Stat. 539; Pub. L. 90–83, § 1(54), Sept. 11, 1967, 81 Stat. 210; Pub. L. 93–416, § 7, Sept. 7, 1974, 88 Stat. 1145; Pub. L. 101–534, § 2, Nov. 7, 1990, 104 Stat. 2352.)

HISTORICAL AND REVISION NOTES
1966 ACT

Derivation	U.S. Code	Revised Statutes and Statutes at Large
....	5 U.S.C. 756(b).	Oct. 14, 1949, ch. 691, § 105 "Sec. 6(b)", 63 Stat. 858. Sept. 13, 1960, Pub. L. 86–767, § 101 (less last 13 words), 74 Stat. 906.

In subsection (a), the words "In addition to the monthly compensation otherwise specified in sections 751–756, 757–871, 783–791, and 793 of this title" are omitted as surplusage.

In subsection (b), the words "pursuant to the Secretary's direction" are omitted as unnecessary.

Administration of this subchapter was transferred to the Secretary of Labor by section 1 of 1950 Reorg. Plan No. 19, 64 Stat. 1271 (see section 8145).

Standard changes are made to conform with the definitions applicable and the style of this title as outlined in the preface to the report.

1967 ACT

Section of title 5	Source (U.S.Code)	Source (Statutes at Large)
8111(a)	5 App.: 756(b)(1).	July 4, 1966, Pub. L. 89–488, § 4(a), 80 Stat. 253.

AMENDMENTS

1990—Subsec. (a). Pub. L. 101–534 substituted "$1,500" for "$500".

1974—Subsec. (a). Pub. L. 93–416, § 7(a), substituted "$500" for "$300".

Subsec. (b). Pub. L. 93–416, §7(b), substituted "$200" for "$100".

EFFECTIVE DATE OF 1990 AMENDMENT

Section 3 of Pub. L. 101–534 provided that: "The amendment made by section 2 [amending this section] shall take effect October 1, 1990."

EFFECTIVE DATE OF 1974 AMENDMENT

Amendment by Pub. L. 93–416 applicable to cases where injury or death occurred prior to Sept. 7, 1974, but only to a period beginning on or after Sept. 7, 1974, see section 28(a) of Pub. L. 93–416, set out as a note under section 8101 of this title.

PERSONNEL NOT AFFECTED BY 1967 INCREASE

Increases authorized under amendment by section 1(54) of Pub. L. 90–83 not applicable to specified personnel, see section 7 of Pub. L. 90–83, set out as a note under section 8103 of this title.

SECTION REFERRED TO IN OTHER SECTIONS

This section is referred to in section 8112 of this title; title 18 section 1921.

§ 8112. Maximum and minimum monthly payments

(a) Except as provided by section 8138 of this title, the monthly rate of compensation for disability, including augmented compensation under section 8110 of this title but not including additional compensation under section 8111 of this title, may not be more than 75 percent of the monthly pay of the maximum rate of basic pay for GS–15, and in case of total disability may not be less than 75 percent of the monthly pay of the minimum rate of basic pay for GS–2 or the amount of the monthly pay of the employee, whichever is less.

(b) The provisions of subsection (a) shall not apply to any employee whose disability is a result of an assault which occurs during an assassination or attempted assassination of a Federal official described under section 351(a) or 1751(a) of title 18, and was sustained in the performance of duty.

(Pub. L. 89–554, Sept. 6, 1966, 80 Stat. 540; Pub. L. 90–83, §1(55), Sept. 11, 1967, 81 Stat. 210; Pub. L. 100–566, §5, Oct. 31, 1988, 102 Stat. 2845.)

HISTORICAL AND REVISION NOTES
1966 ACT

Derivation	U.S. Code	Revised Statutes and Statutes at Large
....	5 U.S.C. 756(c).	Oct. 14, 1949, ch. 691, §105 "Sec. 6(c)", 63 Stat. 859. Sept. 13, 1960, Pub. L. 86–767, §101 (last 13 words), 74 Stat. 906.

Standard changes are made to conform with the definitions applicable and the style of this title as outlined in the preface to the report.

1967 ACT

Section of title 5	Source (U.S.Code)	Source (Statutes at Large)
8112	5 App.: 756(c).	July 4, 1966, Pub. L. 89–488, §3(b), 80 Stat. 252.

The words "maximum rate of basic pay for GS–15" and "minimum rate of basic pay for GS–2" are substituted for "highest rate of basic compensation provided for grade 15 of the General Schedule of the Classification Act of 1949" and "lowest rate of basic compensation provided for grade 2 by such General Schedule", respectively, for consistency of style within title 5 and to reflect the codification of the Classification Act of 1949 in title 5.

AMENDMENTS

1988—Pub. L. 100–566 designated existing provisions as subsec. (a) and added subsec. (b).

PERSONNEL NOT AFFECTED BY 1967 INCREASE

Increases authorized under amendment by section 1(55) of Pub. L. 90–83 not applicable to specified personnel, see section 7 of Pub. L. 90–83, set out as a note under section 8103 of this title.

SECTION REFERRED TO IN OTHER SECTIONS

This section is referred to in section 8138 of this title; title 18 section 1921.

§ 8113. Increase or decrease of basic compensation

(a) If an individual—
(1) was a minor or employed in a learner's capacity at the time of injury; and
(2) was not physically or mentally handicapped before the injury;

the Secretary of Labor, on review under section 8128 of this title after the time the wage-earning capacity of the individual would probably have increased but for the injury, shall recompute prospectively the monetary compensation payable for disability on the basis of an assumed monthly pay corresponding to the probable increased wage-earning capacity.

(b) If an individual without good cause fails to apply for and undergo vocational rehabilitation when so directed under section 8104 of this title, the Secretary, on review under section 8128 of this title and after finding that in the absence of the failure the wage-earning capacity of the individual would probably have substantially increased, may reduce prospectively the monetary compensation of the individual in accordance with what would probably have been his wage-earning capacity in the absence of the failure, until the individual in good faith complies with the direction of the Secretary.

(Pub. L. 89–554, Sept. 6, 1966, 80 Stat. 540; Pub. L. 90–83, §1(100), Sept. 11, 1967, 81 Stat. 220; Pub. L. 93–416, §8(a), Sept. 7, 1974, 88 Stat. 1145.)

HISTORICAL AND REVISION NOTES
1966 ACT

Derivation	U.S. Code	Revised Statutes and Statutes at Large
....	5 U.S.C. 756(d).	Oct. 14, 1949, ch. 691, §105 "Sec. 6(d)", 63 Stat. 859.

Administration of this subchapter was transferred to the Secretary of Labor by section 1 of 1950 Reorg. Plan No. 19, 64 Stat. 1271 (see section 8145).

Standard changes are made to conform with the definitions applicable and the style of this title as outlined in the preface to the report.

1967 ACT

This section amends section 8113(b) of title 5, United States Code, to conform to the source statute (sec. 6(d)(1) of the Federal Employees' Compensation Act, as amended (63 Stat. 859)).

AMENDMENTS

1974—Subsecs. (b), (c). Pub. L. 93–416 struck out subsec. (b) which authorized the Secretary to prospectively recompute compensation because of decreased wage earning power after age 70, aside from injury, and redesignated subsec. (c) as (b).

EFFECTIVE DATE OF 1974 AMENDMENT

Amendment by Pub. L. 93–416 applicable to case where injury or death occurred prior to Sept. 7, 1974, but only to a period beginning on or after Sept. 7, 1974, see section 28(a) of Pub. L. 93–416, set out as a note under section 8101 of this title.

EFFECTIVE DATE OF 1967 AMENDMENT

Amendment by Pub. L. 90–83 effective as of Sept. 6, 1966, for all purposes, see section 9(h) of Pub. L. 90–83, set out as a note under section 5102 of this title.

SECTION REFERRED TO IN OTHER SECTIONS

This section is referred to in sections 8101, 8143 of this title; title 18 section 1921; title 42 section 5055.

§ 8114. Computation of pay

(a) For the purpose of this section—

(1) "overtime pay" means pay for hours of service in excess of a statutory or other basic workweek or other basic unit of worktime, as observed by the employing establishment; and

(2) "year" means a period of 12 calendar months, or the equivalent thereof as specified by regulations prescribed by the Secretary of Labor.

(b) In computing monetary compensation for disability or death on the basis of monthly pay, that pay is determined under this section.

(c) The monthly pay at the time of injury is deemed one-twelfth of the average annual earnings of the employee at that time. When compensation is paid on a weekly basis, the weekly equivalent of the monthly pay is deemed one-fifty-second of the average annual earnings. However, for so much of a period of total disability as does not exceed 90 calendar days from the date of the beginning of compensable disability, the compensation, in the discretion of the Secretary of Labor, may be computed on the basis of the actual daily wage of the employee at the time of injury in which event he may be paid compensation for the days he would have worked but for the injury.

(d) Average annual earnings are determined as follows:

(1) If the employee worked in the employment in which he was employed at the time of his injury during substantially the whole year immediately preceding the injury and the employment was in a position for which an annual rate of pay—

(A) was fixed, the average annual earnings are the annual rate of pay; or

(B) was not fixed, the average annual earnings are the product obtained by multiplying his daily wage for the particular employment, or the average thereof if the daily wage has fluctuated, by 300 if he was employed on the basis of a 6-day workweek, 280 if employed on the basis of a 5½-day week, and 260 if employed on the basis of a 5-day week.

(2) If the employee did not work in employment in which he was employed at the time of his injury during substantially the whole year immediately preceding the injury, but the position was one which would have afforded employment for substantially a whole year, the average annual earnings are a sum equal to the average annual earnings of an employee of the same class working substantially the whole immediately preceding year in the same or similar employment by the United States in the same or neighboring place, as determined under paragraph (1) of this subsection.

(3) If either of the foregoing methods of determining the average annual earnings cannot be applied reasonably and fairly, the average annual earnings are a sum that reasonably represents the annual earning capacity of the injured employee in the employment in which he was working at the time of the injury having regard to the previous earnings of the employee in Federal employment, and of other employees of the United States in the same or most similar class working in the same or most similar employment in the same or neighboring location, other previous employment of the employee, or other relevant factors. However, the average annual earnings may not be less than 150 times the average daily wage the employee earned in the employment during the days employed within 1 year immediately preceding his injury.

(4) If the employee served without pay or at nominal pay, paragraphs (1), (2), and (3) of this subsection apply as far as practicable, but the average annual earnings of the employee may not exceed the minimum rate of basic pay for GS-15. If the average annual earnings cannot be determined reasonably and fairly in the manner otherwise provided by this section, the average annual earnings shall be determined at the reasonable value of the service performed but not in excess of $3,600 a year.

(e) The value of subsistence and quarters, and of any other form of remuneration in kind for services if its value can be estimated in money, and premium pay under section 5545(c)(1) of this title are included as part of the pay, but account is not taken of—

(1) overtime pay;

(2) additional pay or allowance authorized outside the United States because of differential in cost of living or other special circumstances; or

(3) bonus or premium pay for extraordinary service including bonus or pay for particularly hazardous service in time of war.

(Pub. L. 89–554, Sept. 6, 1966, 80 Stat. 540; Pub. L. 89–737, § 1(1), Nov. 2, 1966, 80 Stat. 1164.)

HISTORICAL AND REVISION NOTES

Derivation	U.S. Code	Revised Statutes and Statutes at Large
....	5 U.S.C. 762.	Sept. 7, 1916, ch. 458, § 12, 39 Stat. 746. Oct. 14, 1949, ch. 691, § 203, 63 Stat. 862.

In subsection (d)(4), the words "the minimum rate of basic pay for GS–15" are substituted for "the basic rate of annual compensation specified under the Classification Act of 1949, as amended, for positions in grade GS–15 at the bottom of such grade". In former section

762, the words "Classification Act of 1949" were substituted for "Classification Act of 1923" on authority of §1106(a) of the Act of Oct. 28, 1949, ch. 782, 63 Stat. 972.

Administration of this subchapter was transferred to the Secretary of Labor by section 1 of 1950 Reorg. Plan No. 19, 64 Stat. 1271 (see section 8145).

Standard changes are made to conform with the definitions applicable and the style of this title as outlined in the preface to the report.

AMENDMENTS

1966—Subsec. (e). Pub. L. 89–737 inserted reference to premium pay under section 5545(c)(1) of this title.

EFFECTIVE DATE OF 1966 AMENDMENT

Section 4 of Pub. L. 89–737, which provided that the amendments made by this Act [amending this section and sections 8331 and 8704 of this title] apply with respect to premium pay payable from and after the first day of the first pay period which begins after the date of enactment of this Act [Nov. 2, 1966], was repealed by Pub. L. 90–83, §10(b), Sept. 11, 1967, 81 Stat. 223.

SECTION REFERRED TO IN OTHER SECTIONS

This section is referred to in sections 5545a, 5545b, 8115, 8133 of this title; title 28 section 1877.

§ 8115. Determination of wage-earning capacity

(a) In determining compensation for partial disability, except permanent partial disability compensable under sections 8107–8109 of this title, the wage-earning capacity of an employee is determined by his actual earnings if his actual earnings fairly and reasonably represent his wage-earning capacity. If the actual earnings of the employee do not fairly and reasonably represent his wage-earning capacity or if the employee has no actual earnings, his wage-earning capacity as appears reasonable under the circumstances is determined with due regard to—

(1) the nature of his injury;
(2) the degree of physical impairment;
(3) his usual employment;
(4) his age;
(5) his qualifications for other employment;
(6) the availability of suitable employment; and
(7) other factors or circumstances which may affect his wage-earning capacity in his disabled condition.

(b) Section 8114(d) of this title is applicable in determining the wage-earning capacity of an employee after the beginning of partial disability.

(Pub. L. 89–554, Sept. 6, 1966, 80 Stat. 542.)

HISTORICAL AND REVISION NOTES

Derivation	U.S. Code	Revised Statutes and Statutes at Large
....	5 U.S.C. 763.	Sept. 7, 1916, ch. 458, §13, 39 Stat. 746. Oct. 14, 1949, ch. 691, §204, 63 Stat. 864. Sept. 13, 1960, Pub. L. 86–767, §204, 74 Stat. 908.

Standard changes are made to conform with the definitions applicable and the style of this title as outlined in the preface to the report.

§ 8116. Limitations on right to receive compensation

(a) While an employee is receiving compensation under this subchapter, or if he has been paid a lump sum in commutation of installment payments until the expiration of the period during which the installment payments would have continued, he may not receive salary, pay, or remuneration of any type from the United States, except—

(1) in return for service actually performed;
(2) pension for service in the Army, Navy, or Air Force;
(3) other benefits administered by the Department of Veterans Affairs unless such benefits are payable for the same injury or the same death; and
(4) retired pay, retirement pay, retainer pay, or equivalent pay for service in the Armed Forces or other uniformed services.

However, eligibility for or receipt of benefits under subchapter III of chapter 83 of this title, or another retirement system for employees of the Government, does not impair the right of the employee to compensation for scheduled disabilities specified by section 8107(c) of this title.

(b) An individual entitled to benefits under this subchapter because of his injury, or because of the death of an employee, who also is entitled to receive from the United States under a provision of statute other than this subchapter payments or benefits for that injury or death (except proceeds of an insurance policy), because of service by him (or in the case of death, by the deceased) as an employee or in the armed forces, shall elect which benefits he will receive. The individual shall make the election within 1 year after the injury or death or within a further time allowed for good cause by the Secretary of Labor. The election when made is irrevocable, except as otherwise provided by statute.

(c) The liability of the United States or an instrumentality thereof under this subchapter or any extension thereof with respect to the injury or death of an employee is exclusive and instead of all other liability of the United States or the instrumentality to the employee, his legal representative, spouse, dependents, next of kin, and any other person otherwise entitled to recover damages from the United States or the instrumentality because of the injury or death in a direct judicial proceeding, in a civil action, or in admiralty, or by an administrative or judicial proceeding under a workmen's compensation statute or under a Federal tort liability statute. However, this subsection does not apply to a master or a member of a crew of a vessel.

(d) Notwithstanding the other provisions of this section, an individual receiving benefits for disability or death under this subchapter who is also receiving benefits under subchapter III of chapter 84 of this title or benefits under title II of the Social Security Act shall be entitled to all such benefits, except that—

(1) benefits received under section 223 of the Social Security Act (on account of disability) shall be subject to reduction on account of benefits paid under this subchapter pursuant to the provisions of section 224 of the Social Security Act; and

(2) in the case of benefits received on account of age or death under title II of the Social Security Act, compensation payable under this subchapter based on the Federal service of an employee shall be reduced by the amount of

any such social security benefits payable that are attributable to Federal service of that employee covered by chapter 84 of this title. However, eligibility for or receipt of benefits under chapter 84 of this title, or benefits under title II of the Social Security Act by virtue of service covered by chapter 84 of this title, does not affect the right of the employee to compensation for scheduled disabilities specified by section 8107(c) of this title.

(Pub. L. 89–554, Sept. 6, 1966, 80 Stat. 542; Pub. L. 90–83, § 1(56), Sept. 11, 1967, 81 Stat. 210; Pub. L. 93–416, § 9(a), Sept. 7, 1974, 88 Stat. 1145; Pub. L. 99–335, title II, § 207(e), June 6, 1986, 100 Stat. 595; Pub. L. 102–54, § 13(b)(1), June 13, 1991, 105 Stat. 274; Pub. L. 106–398, § 1 [[div. A], title X, § 1087(f)(3)], Oct. 30, 2000, 114 Stat. 1654, 1654A–293.)

HISTORICAL AND REVISION NOTES
1966 ACT

Derivation	U.S. Code	Revised Statutes and Statutes at Large
....	5 U.S.C. 757.	Sept. 7, 1916, ch. 458, § 7, 39 Stat. 743. July 1, 1944, ch. 373, § 605(a), 58 Stat. 712. Aug. 13, 1946, ch. 958, § 5, 60 Stat. 1049. Oct. 14, 1949, ch. 691, § 201, 63 Stat. 861. July 30, 1956, ch. 779, § 3(b), 70 Stat. 721. Sept. 13, 1960, Pub. L. 86–767, § 202, 74 Stat. 907. Sept. 4, 1964, Pub. L. 88–581, § 4(b), 78 Stat. 919.

In subsection (a)(2), "Air Force" is added on authority of the Act of July 26, 1947, ch. 343, § 207(a), (f), 61 Stat. 502, and sections 8010—8013 of title 10, United States Code. This does not affect the operation of this subsection insofar as it concerns members of the Coast Guard whose pension is based in whole or in part on service with the Coast Guard when it operated as a part of the Navy.

In subsection (b), the reference to the definition of "employee" in former section 790 is omitted as unnecessary as the definition is included in section 8101 for the entire subchapter.

Administration of this subchapter was transferred to the Secretary of Labor by section 1 of 1950 Reorg. Plan No. 19, 64 Stat. 1271 (see section 8145).

Standard changes are made to conform with the definitions applicable and the style of this title as outlined in the preface to the report.

1967 ACT

Section of title 5	Source (U.S.Code)	Source (Statutes at Large)
8116(a)	5 App.: 757(a).	July 4, 1966, Pub. L. 89–488, § 5(a), 80 Stat. 253.

The words "another retirement system for employees of the Government" are substituted for "any other Federal Act or program providing retirement benefits for employees".

REFERENCES IN TEXT

The Social Security Act, referred to in subsec. (d), is act Aug. 14, 1935, ch. 531, 49 Stat. 620, as amended. Title II of the Social Security Act is classified generally to subchapter II (§ 401 et seq.) of chapter 7 of Title 42, The Public Health and Welfare. Sections 223 and 224 are classified to sections 423 and 424a, respectively, of Title 42. For complete classification of this Act to the Code, see section 1305 of Title 42 and Tables.

AMENDMENTS

2000—Subsec. (a)(4). Pub. L. 106–398 struck out ", subject to the reduction of such pay in accordance with section 5532(b) of title 5, United States Code" after "uniformed services".

1991—Subsec. (a)(3). Pub. L. 102–54 substituted "Department of Veterans Affairs" for "Veterans' Administration".

1986—Subsec. (d). Pub. L. 99–335 added subsec. (d).

1974—Subsec. (a). Pub. L. 93–416 struck out "and" in cl. (1), substituted a semicolon for a period in cl. (2), and added cls. (3) and (4).

EFFECTIVE DATE OF 1986 AMENDMENT

Amendment by Pub. L. 99–335 effective Jan. 1, 1987, see section 702(a) of Pub. L. 99–335, set out as an Effective Date note under section 8401 of this title.

EFFECTIVE DATE OF 1974 AMENDMENT

Section 9(b) of Pub. L. 93–416 provided that: "The amendment made by this section [amending this section] shall be effective with respect to disability or death occurring before or after the date of enactment of this Act [Sept. 7, 1974] and without regard to any election under section 8116(b) of the Act [subsec. (b) of this section]; but no payment shall be made by reason of such amendment for any period prior to the date of enactment of this Act."

PERSONNEL NOT AFFECTED BY 1967 INCREASE

Increases authorized under amendment by section 1(56) of Pub. L. 90–83 not applicable to specified personnel, see section 7 of Pub. L. 90–83, set out as a note under section 8103 of this title.

SECTION REFERRED TO IN OTHER SECTIONS

This section is referred to in title 22 section 3715d.

§ 8117. Time of accrual of right

An employee is not entitled to compensation for the first 3 days of temporary disability, except—

(1) when the disability exceeds 14 days;

(2) when the disability is followed by permanent disability; or

(3) as provided by sections 8103 and 8104 of this title.

(Pub. L. 89–554, Sept. 6, 1966, 80 Stat. 543; Pub. L. 93–416, § 10, Sept. 7, 1974, 88 Stat. 1145.)

HISTORICAL AND REVISION NOTES

Derivation	U.S. Code	Revised Statutes and Statutes at Large
....	5 U.S.C. 752.	Sept. 7, 1916, ch. 458, § 2, 39 Stat. 743. Oct. 14, 1949, ch. 691, § 101(a), 63 Stat. 854.

Standard changes are made to conform with the definitions applicable and the style of this title as outlined in the preface to the report.

AMENDMENTS

1974—Pub. L. 93–416 substituted "14 days" for "21 days".

EFFECTIVE DATE OF 1974 AMENDMENT

Amendment by Pub. L. 93–416 effective Sept. 7, 1974, and applicable to any injury or death occurring on or after Sept. 7, 1974, see section 28(a) of Pub. L. 93–416, set out as a note under section 8101 of this title.

SECTION REFERRED TO IN OTHER SECTIONS

This section is referred to in section 8118 of this title.

§ 8118. Continuation of pay; election to use annual or sick leave

(a) The United States shall authorize the continuation of pay of an employee, as defined in section 8101(1) of this title (other than those referred to in clause (B) or (E)), who has filed a claim for a period of wage loss due to a traumatic injury with his immediate superior on a form approved by the Secretary of Labor within the time specified in section 8122(a)(2) of this title.

(b) Continuation of pay under this subchapter shall be furnished—

(1) without a break in time unless controverted under regulations of the Secretary;

(2) for a period not to exceed 45 days; and

(3) under accounting procedures and such other regulations as the Secretary may require.

(c) An employee may use annual or sick leave to his credit at the time the disability begins, but his compensation for disability does not begin, and the time periods specified by section 8117 of this title do not begin to run, until termination of pay as set forth in subsections (a) and (b) or the use of annual or sick leave ends.

(d) If a claim under subsection (a) is denied by the Secretary, payments under this section shall, at the option of the employee, be charged to sick or annual leave or shall be deemed overpayments of pay within the meaning of section 5584 of title 5, United States Code.

(e) Payments under this section shall not be considered as compensation as defined by section 8101(12) of this title.

(Pub. L. 89–554, Sept. 6, 1966, 80 Stat. 543; Pub. L. 93–416, § 11, Sept. 7, 1974, 88 Stat. 1145.)

HISTORICAL AND REVISION NOTES

Derivation	U.S. Code	Revised Statutes and Statutes at Large
....	5 U.S.C. 758.	Sept. 7, 1916, ch. 458, § 8, 39 Stat. 743. Oct. 14, 1949, ch. 691, § 101(b), 63 Stat. 854.

Standard changes are made to conform with the definitions applicable and the style of this title as outlined in the preface to the report.

AMENDMENTS

1974—Pub. L. 93–416 inserted in section catchline the reference to continuation of pay, added subsecs. (a), (b), (d) and (e), designated existing provisions as subsec. (c), and in subsec. (c) as so designated, substituted "until termination of pay as set forth in subsections (a) and (b) or the use of annual or sick leave ends" for "until the use of the annual or sick leave ends".

EFFECTIVE DATE OF 1974 AMENDMENT

Section 28(b) of Pub. L. 93–416 provided that: "Section 11 of this Act [amending this section] shall become effective 60 days from enactment [Sept. 7, 1974] and be applicable to any injury occurring on or after such effective date."

SECTION REFERRED TO IN OTHER SECTIONS

This section is referred to in title 22 section 3715a.

§ 8119. Notice of injury or death

An employee injured in the performance of his duty, or someone on his behalf, shall give notice thereof. Notice of a death believed to be related to the employment shall be given by an eligible beneficiary specified in section 8133 of this title, or someone on his behalf. A notice of injury or death shall—

(a) be given within 30 days after the injury or death;

(b) be given to the immediate superior of the employee by personal delivery or by depositing it in the mail properly stamped and addressed;

(c) be in writing;

(d) state the name and address of the employee;

(e) state the year, month, day, and hour when and the particular locality where the injury or death occurred;

(f) state the cause and nature of the injury, or, in the case of death, the employment factors believed to be the cause; and

(g) be signed by and contain the address of the individual giving the notice.

(Pub. L. 89–554, Sept. 6, 1966, 80 Stat. 543; Pub. L. 93–416, § 12(a), Sept. 7, 1974, 88 Stat. 1146.)

HISTORICAL AND REVISION NOTES

Derivation	U.S. Code	Revised Statutes and Statutes at Large
(a)	5 U.S.C. 765.	Sept. 7, 1916, ch. 458, § 15, 39 Stat. 746.
	5 U.S.C. 766.	Sept. 7, 1916, ch. 458, § 16, 39 Stat. 746.
(b)	5 U.S.C. 767.	Sept. 7, 1916, ch. 458, § 17, 39 Stat. 746.

Subsection (b)(2) is added on authority of former section 770, which is carried into section 8122, to complete the coverage of this section.

Administration of this subchapter was transferred to the Secretary of Labor by section 1 of 1950 Reorg. Plan No. 19, 64 Stat. 1271 (see section 8145).

Standard changes are made to conform with the definitions applicable and the style of this title as outlined in the preface to the report.

AMENDMENTS

1974—Pub. L. 93–416 substituted "or death" for "; failure to give" in section catchline, struck out designation of subsec. (a), redesignated cls. (1) to (7) as (a) to (g), and, as so redesignated, inserted provisions relating to notice of death and substituted "30 days" for "48 hours" in cl. (a), and struck out subsec. (b) relating to allowance of compensation.

EFFECTIVE DATE OF 1974 AMENDMENT

Amendment by Pub. L. 93–416 effective Sept. 7, 1974, and applicable to any injury or death occurring on or after Sept. 7, 1974, see section 28(a) of Pub. L. 93–416, set out as a note under section 8101 of this title.

SECTION REFERRED TO IN OTHER SECTIONS

This section is referred to in section 8122 of this title.

§ 8120. Report of injury

Immediately after an injury to an employee which results in his death or probable disability, his immediate superior shall report to the Secretary of Labor. The Secretary may—

(1) prescribe the information that the report shall contain;

(2) require the immediate superior to make supplemental reports; and

(3) obtain such additional reports and information from employees as are agreed on by

the Secretary and the head of the employing agency.

(Pub. L. 89–554, Sept. 6, 1966, 80 Stat. 543.)

HISTORICAL AND REVISION NOTES

Derivation	U.S. Code	Revised Statutes and Statutes at Large
....	5 U.S.C. 774(a).	Sept. 7, 1916, ch. 458, § 24, 39 Stat. 747.
....	5 U.S.C. 779.	Sept. 7, 1916, ch. 458, § 28a, 39 Stat. 748. Oct. 14, 1949, ch. 691, § 205(b), 63 Stat. 864.

Administration of this subchapter was transferred to the Secretary of Labor by section 1 of 1950 Reorg. Plan No. 19, 64 Stat. 1271 (see section 8145).

Standard changes are made to conform with the definitions applicable and the style of this title as outlined in the preface to the report.

SECTION REFERRED TO IN OTHER SECTIONS

This section is referred to in section 8141 of this title; title 18 section 1922.

§ 8121. Claim

Compensation under this subchapter may be allowed only if an individual or someone on his behalf makes claim therefor. The claim shall—

(1) be made in writing within the time specified by section 8122 of this title;

(2) be delivered to the office of the Secretary of Labor or to an individual whom the Secretary may designate by regulation, or deposited in the mail properly stamped and addressed to the Secretary or his designee;

(3) be on a form approved by the Secretary;

(4) contain all information required by the Secretary;

(5) be sworn to by the individual entitled to compensation or someone on his behalf; and

(6) except in case of death, be accompanied by a certificate of the physician of the employee stating the nature of the injury and the nature and probable extent of the disability.

The Secretary may waive paragraphs (3)–(6) of this section for reasonable cause shown.

(Pub. L. 89–554, Sept. 6, 1966, 80 Stat. 543; Pub. L. 93–416, § 13, Sept. 7, 1974, 88 Stat. 1147.)

HISTORICAL AND REVISION NOTES

Derivation	U.S. Code	Revised Statutes and Statutes at Large
....	5 U.S.C. 768.	Sept. 7, 1916, ch. 458, § 18, 39 Stat. 746.
....	5 U.S.C. 769.	Sept. 7, 1916, ch. 458, § 19, 39 Stat. 746.

The words "except as provided in section 788" in former section 768 are omitted as unnecessary as former section 788 dealt with recovery of overpayments after claims were made.

Administration of this subchapter was transferred to the Secretary of Labor by section 1 of 1950 Reorg. Plan No. 19, 64 Stat. 1271 (see section 8145).

Standard changes are made to conform with the definitions applicable and the style of this title as outlined in the preface to the report.

AMENDMENTS

1974—Par. (3). Pub. L. 93–416 substituted "approved" for "furnished".

EFFECTIVE DATE OF 1974 AMENDMENT

Amendment by Pub. L. 93–416 effective Sept. 7, 1974, and applicable to any injury or death occurring on or after Sept. 7, 1974, see section 23(a) of Pub. L. 93–416, set out as a note under section 8101 of this title.

SECTION REFERRED TO IN OTHER SECTIONS

This section is referred to in section 8146 of this title.

§ 8122. Time for making claim

(a) An original claim for compensation for disability or death must be filed within 3 years after the injury or death. Compensation for disability or death, including medical care in disability cases, may not be allowed if claim is not filed within that time unless—

(1) the immediate superior had actual knowledge of the injury or death within 30 days. The knowledge must be such to put the immediate superior reasonably on notice of an on-the-job injury or death; or

(2) written notice of injury or death as specified in section 8119 of this title was given within 30 days.

(b) In a case of latent disability, the time for filing claim does not begin to run until the employee has a compensable disability and is aware, or by the exercise of reasonable diligence should have been aware, of the causal relationship of the compensable disability to his employment. In such a case, the time for giving notice of injury begins to run when the employee is aware, or by the exercise of reasonable diligence should have been aware, that his condition is causally related to his employment, whether or not there is a compensable disability.

(c) The timely filing of a disability claim because of injury will satisfy the time requirements for a death claim based on the same injury.

(d) The time limitations in subsections (a) and (b) of this section do not—

(1) begin to run against a minor until he reaches 21 years of age or has had a legal representative appointed; or

(2) run against an incompetent individual while he is incompetent and has no duly appointed legal representative; or

(3) run against any individual whose failure to comply is excused by the Secretary on the ground that such notice could not be given because of exceptional circumstances.

(Pub. L. 89–554, Sept. 6, 1966, 80 Stat. 544; Pub. L. 90–83, § 1(57), Sept. 11, 1967, 81 Stat. 210; Pub. L. 93–416, § 14, Sept. 7, 1974, 88 Stat. 1147.)

HISTORICAL AND REVISION NOTES
1966 ACT

Derivation	U.S. Code	Revised Statutes and Statutes at Large
....	5 U.S.C. 770.	Sept. 7, 1916, ch. 458, § 20, 39 Stat. 747. June 13, 1922, ch. 219, 42 Stat. 650. July 28, 1945, ch. 328, § 1, 59 Stat. 503. Sept. 13, 1960, Pub. L. 86–767, § 205, 74 Stat. 908.

The last sentence of the Act of June 13, 1922, 42 Stat. 650, is omitted as obsolete.

Administration of this subchapter was transferred to the Secretary of Labor by section 1 of 1950 Reorg. Plan No. 19, 64 Stat. 1271 (see section 8145).

Standard changes are made to conform with the definitions applicable and the style of this title as outlined in the preface to the report.

1967 ACT

Section of title 5	Source (U.S. Code)	Source (Statutes at Large)
8122(b), (d)	5 App.: 770.	July 4, 1966, Pub. L. 89–488, § 9, 80 Stat. 254.

AMENDMENTS

1974—Subsec. (a). Pub. L. 93–416, § 14(1), substituted provisions requiring filing of claims for compensation within three years after death or disability, and setting forth conditions for waiver of filing within required time periods, for provisions requiring claim for death to be made within one year after death and for disability to be made within 60 days after injury and authorizing extension of time for good cause.

Subsec. (c). Pub. L. 93–416, § 14(2), substituted provisions relating to timeliness of claim for death when claim for injury was timely filed and death was based on same injury, for provisions relating to waiver of compliance with requirements for giving notice of injury and filing claim for compensation.

Subsec. (d). Pub. L. 93–416, § 14(3), substituted "(a) and (b)" for "(a)–(c)", and added cl. (3).

EFFECTIVE DATE OF 1974 AMENDMENT

Amendment by Pub. L. 93–416 effective Sept. 7, 1974, and applicable to any injury or death occurring on or after Sept. 7, 1974, see section 23(a) of Pub. L. 93–416, set out as a note under section 8101 of this title.

PERSONNEL NOT AFFECTED BY 1967 INCREASE

Increases authorized under amendment by section 1(57) of Pub. L. 90–83 not applicable to specified personnel, see section 7 of Pub. L. 90–83, set out as a note under section 8103 of this title.

SECTION REFERRED TO IN OTHER SECTIONS

This section is referred to in sections 8118, 8121 of this title.

§ 8123. Physical examinations

(a) An employee shall submit to examination by a medical officer of the United States, or by a physician designated or approved by the Secretary of Labor, after the injury and as frequently and at the times and places as may be reasonably required. The employee may have a physician designated and paid by him present to participate in the examination. If there is disagreement between the physician making the examination for the United States and the physician of the employee, the Secretary shall appoint a third physician who shall make an examination.

(b) An employee is entitled to be paid expenses incident to an examination required by the Secretary which in the opinion of the Secretary are necessary and reasonable, including transportation and loss of wages incurred in order to be examined. The expenses, when authorized or approved by the Secretary, are paid from the Employees' Compensation Fund.

(c) The Secretary shall fix the fees for examinations held under this section by physicians not employed by or under contract to the United States to furnish medical services to employees. The fees, when authorized or approved by the

Secretary, are paid from the Employees' Compensation Fund.

(d) If an employee refuses to submit to or obstructs an examination, his right to compensation under this subchapter is suspended until the refusal or obstruction stops. Compensation is not payable while a refusal or obstruction continues, and the period of the refusal or obstruction is deducted from the period for which compensation is payable to the employee.

(Pub. L. 89–554, Sept. 6, 1966, 80 Stat. 544.)

HISTORICAL AND REVISION NOTES

Derivation	U.S. Code	Revised Statutes and Statutes at Large
....	5 U.S.C. 771.	Sept. 7, 1916, ch. 458, § 21, 39 Stat. 747. June 26, 1926, ch. 695, § 2, 44 Stat. 772.
....	5 U.S.C. 772.	Sept. 7, 1916, ch. 458, § 22, 39 Stat. 747.
....	5 U.S.C. 773(a).	Sept. 7, 1916, ch. 458, § 23, 39 Stat. 747. June 26, 1926, ch. 695, § 3, 44 Stat. 772. Oct. 14, 1949, ch. 691, § 208 "Sec. 23(a)", 63 Stat. 865.

In subsections (a) and (c), the words "duly qualified" in former sections 771 and 772 are omitted as unnecessary in view of the definition of "physician" in section 8101.

In subsection (c) the words "fees for examinations" in former section 773(a) are substituted for "fees or examinations" since the word "or" was erroneously in the 1949 amendment. The words "any sum payable to the employee under section 771 of this title" in former section 773(a) are omitted as unnecessary because the same provision appeared in former section 771, which is carried into subsection (b).

Administration of this subchapter was transferred to the Secretary of Labor by section 1 of 1950 Reorg. Plan No. 19, 64 Stat. 1271 (see section 8145).

Standard changes are made to conform with the definitions applicable and the style of this title as outlined in the preface to the report.

SECTION REFERRED TO IN OTHER SECTIONS

This section is referred to in section 8146 of this title.

§ 8124. Findings and award; hearings

(a) The Secretary of Labor shall determine and make a finding of facts and make an award for or against payment of compensation under this subchapter after—

(1) considering the claim presented by the beneficiary and the report furnished by the immediate superior; and

(2) completing such investigation as he considers necessary.

(b)(1) Before review under section 8128(a) of this title, a claimant for compensation not satisfied with a decision of the Secretary under subsection (a) of this section is entitled, on request made within 30 days after the date of the issuance of the decision, to a hearing on his claim before a representative of the Secretary. At the hearing, the claimant is entitled to present evidence in further support of his claim. Within 30 days after the hearing ends, the Secretary shall notify the claimant in writing of his further decision and any modifications of the award he may make and of the basis of his decision.

(2) In conducting the hearing, the representative of the Secretary is not bound by common law or statutory rules of evidence, by technical or formal rules of procedure, or by section 554 of this title except as provided by this subchapter, but may conduct the hearing in such manner as to best ascertain the rights of the claimant. For this purpose, he shall receive such relevant evidence as the claimant adduces and such other evidence as he determines necessary or useful in evaluating the claim.

(Pub. L. 89–554, Sept. 6, 1966, 80 Stat. 545; Pub. L. 90–83, § 1(58), Sept. 11, 1967, 81 Stat. 210.)

HISTORICAL AND REVISION NOTES
1966 ACT

Derivation	U.S. Code	Revised Statutes and Statutes at Large
....	5 U.S.C. 786.	Sept. 7, 1916, ch. 458, § 36, 39 Stat. 749.

The last sentence of former section 786 is omitted as surplusage because it is covered by section 8147.

Administration of this subchapter was transferred to the Secretary of Labor by section 1 of 1950 Reorg. Plan No. 19, 64 Stat. 1271 (see section 8145).

Standard changes are made to conform with the definitions applicable and the style of this title as outlined in the preface to the report.

1967 ACT

Section of title 5	Source (U.S. Code)	Source (Statutes at Large)
8124(b)	5 App.: 786(b).	July 4, 1966, Pub. L. 89–488, § 11(b), 80 Stat. 255.

In subsection (b)(1), the words "section 8128(a) of this title" are substituted for "section 37" to reflect the codification of section 37 in title 5, United States Code. The words "a claimant * * * is entitled * * * to a hearing" are substituted for "any claimant * * * shall * * * be afforded an opportunity for a hearing". The words "under subsection (a) of this section" are substituted for "under this section" for clarity. In the second sentence, the words "is entitled to present evidence" are substituted for "shall be afforded an opportunity to present evidence".

In subsection (b)(2), the words "section 554 of this title * * * this subchapter" are substituted for "section 5 of the Administrative Procedure Act * * * this Act" to reflect the codification of the cited section and act in title 5. In the second sentence, the words "shall, in addition, receive" are omitted as unnecessary.

PERSONNEL NOT AFFECTED BY 1967 INCREASE

Increases authorized under amendment by section 1(58) of Pub. L. 90–83 not applicable to specified personnel, see section 7 of Pub. L. 90–83, set out as a note under section 8103 of this title.

SECTION REFERRED TO IN OTHER SECTIONS

This section is referred to in section 8149 of this title.

§ 8125. Misbehavior at proceedings

If an individual—

(1) disobeys or resists a lawful order or process in proceedings under this subchapter before the Secretary of Labor or his representative; or

(2) misbehaves during a hearing or so near the place of hearing as to obstruct it;

the Secretary or his representative shall certify the facts to the district court having jurisdiction in the place where he is sitting. The court, in a summary manner, shall hear the evidence as to the acts complained of and if the evidence warrants, punish the individual in the same manner and to the same extent as for a contempt committed before the court, or commit the individual on the same conditions as if the forbidden act had occurred with reference to the process of or in the presence of the court.

(Pub. L. 89–554, Sept. 6, 1966, 80 Stat. 545.)

HISTORICAL AND REVISION NOTES

Derivation	U.S. Code	Revised Statutes and Statutes at Large
....	5 U.S.C. 773(c).	Oct. 14, 1949, ch. 691, § 208 "Sec. 23(c)", 63 Stat. 865.

The words "the district court of the United States for the District of Columbia" are omitted as included in "district court". The words "under this subchapter" are added for clarity since this section which was formerly a subsection referred to the subsection preceding it which identified the proceedings.

Administration of this subchapter was transferred to the Secretary of Labor by section 1 of 1950 Reorg. Plan No. 19, 64 Stat. 1271 (see section 8145).

Standard changes are made to conform with the definitions applicable and the style of this title as outlined in the preface to the report.

§ 8126. Subpenas; oaths; examination of witnesses

The Secretary of Labor, on any matter within his jurisdiction under this subchapter, may—

(1) issue subpenas for and compel the attendance of witnesses within a radius of 100 miles;

(2) administer oaths;

(3) examine witnesses; and

(4) require the production of books, papers, documents, and other evidence.

(Pub. L. 89–554, Sept. 6, 1966, 80 Stat. 545.)

HISTORICAL AND REVISION NOTES

Derivation	U.S. Code	Revised Statutes and Statutes at Large
....	5 U.S.C. 780.	Sept. 7, 1916, ch. 458, § 29, 39 Stat. 748. Oct. 14, 1949, ch. 691, § 205(c)(2), 63 Stat. 864.

The words "under this subchapter" are added to preserve the original grant of power in the Act of Sept. 7, 1916.

Administration of this subchapter was transferred to the Secretary of Labor by section 1 of 1950 Reorg. Plan No. 19, 64 Stat. 1271 (see section 8145).

Standard changes are made to conform with the definitions applicable and the style of this title as outlined in the preface to the report.

§ 8127. Representation; attorneys' fees

(a) A claimant may authorize an individual to represent him in any proceeding under this subchapter before the Secretary of Labor.

(b) A claim for legal or other services furnished in respect to a case, claim, or award for compensation under this subchapter is valid only if approved by the Secretary.

(Pub. L. 89–554, Sept. 6, 1966, 80 Stat. 545.)

HISTORICAL AND REVISION NOTES

Derivation	U.S. Code	Revised Statutes and Statutes at Large
....	5 U.S.C. 773(b) (less last sentence).	Oct. 14, 1949, ch. 691, §208 "Sec. 23(b) (less last sentence)", 63 Stat. 865.

Administration of this subchapter was transferred to the Secretary of Labor by section 1 of 1950 Reorg. Plan No. 19, 64 Stat. 1271 (see section 8145).

Standard changes are made to conform with the definitions applicable and the style of this title as outlined in the preface to the report.

§ 8128. Review of award

(a) The Secretary of Labor may review an award for or against payment of compensation at any time on his own motion or on application. The Secretary, in accordance with the facts found on review, may—

(1) end, decrease, or increase the compensation previously awarded; or

(2) award compensation previously refused or discontinued.

(b) The action of the Secretary or his designee in allowing or denying a payment under this subchapter is—

(1) final and conclusive for all purposes and with respect to all questions of law and fact; and

(2) not subject to review by another official of the United States or by a court by mandamus or otherwise.

Credit shall be allowed in the accounts of a certifying or disbursing official for payment in accordance with that action.

(Pub. L. 89–554, Sept. 6, 1966, 80 Stat. 545.)

HISTORICAL AND REVISION NOTES

Derivation	U.S. Code	Revised Statutes and Statutes at Large
(a)	5 U.S.C. 787.	Sept. 7, 1916, ch. 458, §37, 39 Stat. 749. June 5, 1924, ch. 261, §1, 43 Stat. 389.
(b)	5 U.S.C. 793 (penultimate sentence of 5th par.).	July 28, 1945, ch. 328, §4 (penultimate sentence), 59 Stat. 504.

In subsection (a), the words "If the original claim for compensation has been made within the time specified in section 770 of this title" are omitted as surplusage. The words "an award for or against payment of compensation" are coextensive with and, for clarity and consistency with section 8124, substituted for "the award". The second sentence of former section 787 is omitted as included in the penultimate sentence of former section 793, which is carried into subsection (b). The last sentence of former section 787 is omitted as executed.

In subsection (b), the word "official" is substituted for "officer" because of the definition of "officer" in section 2104 which excludes a member of a uniformed service.

Administration of this subchapter was transferred to the Secretary of Labor by section 1 of 1950 Reorg. Plan No. 19, 64 Stat. 1271 (see section 8145).

Standard changes are made to conform with the definitions applicable and the style of this title as outlined in the preface of the report.

SECTION REFERRED TO IN OTHER SECTIONS

This section is referred to in sections 8113, 8124, 8146 of this title.

§ 8129. Recovery of overpayments

(a) When an overpayment has been made to an individual under this subchapter because of an error of fact or law, adjustment shall be made under regulations prescribed by the Secretary of Labor by decreasing later payments to which the individual is entitled. If the individual dies before the adjustment is completed, adjustment shall be made by decreasing later benefits payable under this subchapter with respect to the individual's death.

(b) Adjustment or recovery by the United States may not be made when incorrect payment has been made to an individual who is without fault and when adjustment or recovery would defeat the purpose of this subchapter or would be against equity and good conscience.

(c) A certifying or disbursing official is not liable for an amount certified or paid by him when—

(1) adjustment or recovery of the amount is waived under subsection (b) of this section; or

(2) adjustment under subsection (a) of this section is not completed before the death of all individuals against whose benefits deductions are authorized.

(Pub. L. 89–554, Sept. 6, 1966, 80 Stat. 546.)

HISTORICAL AND REVISION NOTES

Derivation	U.S. Code	Revised Statutes and Statutes at Large
....	5 U.S.C. 788.	Sept. 7, 1916, ch. 458, §38, 39 Stat. 749. Oct. 14, 1949, ch. 691, §206, 63 Stat. 864.

In subsection (a), the words "Subject to the provisions of sections 786 and 787 of this title" and "if any" are omitted as surplusage.

In subsection (c), the word "official" is substituted for "officer" as the definition of "officer" in section 2104 excludes a member of a uniformed service.

Administration of this subchapter was transferred to the Secretary of Labor by section 1 of 1950 Reorg. Plan No. 19, 64 Stat. 1271 (see section 8145).

Standard changes are made to conform with the definitions applicable and the style of this title as outlined in the preface to the report.

SECTION REFERRED TO IN OTHER SECTIONS

This section is referred to in sections 8106, 8148 of this title.

§ 8130. Assignment of claim

An assignment of a claim for compensation under this subchapter is void. Compensation and claims for compensation are exempt from claims of creditors.

(Pub. L. 89–554, Sept. 6, 1966, 80 Stat. 546.)

HISTORICAL AND REVISION NOTES

Derivation	U.S. Code	Revised Statutes and Statutes at Large
....	5 U.S.C. 775.	Sept. 7, 1916, ch. 458, §25, 39 Stat. 747.

Standard changes are made to conform with the definitions applicable and the style of this title as outlined in the preface to the report.

§ 8131. Subrogation of the United States

(a) If an injury or death for which compensation is payable under this subchapter is caused under circumstances creating a legal liability on a person other than the United States to pay damages, the Secretary of Labor may require the beneficiary to—

(1) assign to the United States any right of action he may have to enforce the liability or any right he may have to share in money or other property received in satisfaction of that liability; or

(2) prosecute the action in his own name.

An employee required to appear as a party or witness in the prosecution of such an action is in an active duty status while so engaged.

(b) A beneficiary who refuses to assign or prosecute an action in his own name when required by the Secretary is not entitled to compensation under this subchapter.

(c) The Secretary may prosecute or compromise a cause of action assigned to the United States. When the Secretary realizes on the cause of action, he shall deduct therefrom and place to the credit of the Employees' Compensation Fund the amount of compensation already paid to the beneficiary and the expense of realization or collection. Any surplus shall be paid to the beneficiary and credited on future payments of compensation payable for the same injury. However, the beneficiary is entitled to not less than one-fifth of the net amount of a settlement or recovery remaining after the expenses thereof have been deducted.

(d) If an injury or death for which compensation is payable under this subchapter is caused under circumstances creating a legal liability in the Panama Canal Company to pay damages under the law of a State, a territory or possession of the United States, the District of Columbia, or a foreign country, compensation is not payable until the individual entitled to compensation—

(1) releases to the Panama Canal Company any right of action he may have to enforce the liability of the Panama Canal Company; or

(2) assigns to the United States any right he may have to share in money or other property received in satisfaction of the liability of the Panama Canal Company.

(Pub. L. 89–554, Sept. 6, 1966, 80 Stat. 546; Pub. L. 90–83, §1(60), Sept. 11, 1967, 81 Stat. 211.)

HISTORICAL AND REVISION NOTES
1966 ACT

Derivation	U.S. Code	Revised Statutes and Statutes at Large
(a)–(c)	5 U.S.C. 776.	Sept. 7, 1916, ch. 458, §26, 39 Stat. 747.
		Sept. 13, 1960, Pub. L. 86–767, §207, 74 Stat. 908.
(d)	5 U.S.C. 791.	Sept. 7, 1916, ch. 458, §41, 39 Stat. 750.

In subsection (d), the first 45 words of section 41 of the Act of Sept. 7, 1916, are omitted as executed. The words "Panama Canal Company" are substituted for "Panama Railroad Company" on authority of the Act of Sept. 26, 1950, ch. 1049, §2(a) (2), 64 Stat. 1038.

Administration of this subchapter was transferred to the Secretary of Labor by section 1 of 1950 Reorg. Plan. No. 19, 64 Stat. 1271 (see section 8145).

Standard changes are made to conform with the definitions applicable and the style of this title as outlined in the preface to the report.

1967 ACT

Section of title 5	Source (U.S. Code)	Source (Statutes at Large)
8131(c)	5 App.: 776 (proviso).	July 4, 1966, Pub. L. 89–488, §10(a), 80 Stat. 255.

REFERENCES IN TEXT

For definition of Panama Canal Company, referred to in text, see section 3602(b) of Title 22, Foreign Relations and Intercourse.

PERSONNEL NOT AFFECTED BY 1967 INCREASE

Increases authorized under amendment by Pub. L. 90–83 not applicable to specified personnel, see section 7 of Pub. L. 90–83, set out as a note under section 8103 of this title.

SECTION REFERRED TO IN OTHER SECTIONS

This section is referred to in section 8147 of this title.

§ 8132. Adjustment after recovery from a third person

If an injury or death for which compensation is payable under this subchapter is caused under circumstances creating a legal liability in a person other than the United States to pay damages, and a beneficiary entitled to compensation from the United States for that injury or death receives money or other property in satisfaction of that liability as the result of suit or settlement by him or in his behalf, the beneficiary, after deducting therefrom the costs of suit and a reasonable attorney's fee, shall refund to the United States the amount of compensation paid by the United States and credit any surplus on future payments of compensation payable to him for the same injury. No court, insurer, attorney, or other person shall pay or distribute to the beneficiary or his designee the proceeds of such suit or settlement without first satisfying or assuring satisfaction of the interest of the United States. The amount refunded to the United States shall be credited to the Employees' Compensation Fund. If compensation has not been paid to the beneficiary, he shall credit the money or property on compensation payable to him by the United States for the same injury. However, the beneficiary is entitled to retain, as a minimum, at least one-fifth of the net amount of the money or other property remaining after the expenses of a suit or settlement have been deducted; and in addition to this minimum and at the time of distribution, an amount equivalent to a reasonable attorney's fee proportionate to the refund to the United States.

(Pub. L. 89–554, Sept. 6, 1966, 80 Stat. 547; Pub. L. 90–83, §1(61), Sept. 11, 1967, 81 Stat. 211; Pub. L. 93–416, §15, Sept. 7, 1974, 88 Stat. 1147.)

HISTORICAL AND REVISION NOTES
1966 ACT

Derivation	U.S. Code	Revised Statutes and Statutes at Large
....	5 U.S.C. 777.	Sept. 7, 1916, ch. 458, §27, 39 Stat. 747.

Standard changes are made to conform with the definitions applicable and the style of this title as outlined in the preface to the report.

1967 ACT

Section of title 5	Source (U.S. Code)	Source (Statutes at Large)
8132	5 App.: 777(b) (proviso).	July 4, 1966, Pub. L. 89–488, § 10(b), 80 Stat. 255.

The words "However, * * * is entitled to retain * * * plus" are substituted for "*Provided,* That * * * shall have the right to retain * * * and, in addition, to retain".

AMENDMENTS

1974—Pub. L. 93–416 made minor changes in phraseology and inserted provision prohibiting a court, etc., from distributing proceeds of suit or settlement without satisfying or assuring satisfaction of the interests of the United States.

EFFECTIVE DATE OF 1974 AMENDMENT

Amendment by Pub. L. 93–416 effective Sept. 7, 1974, and applicable to any injury or death occurring on or after Sept. 7, 1974, see section 28(a) of Pub. L. 93–416, set out as a note under section 8101 of this title.

PERSONNEL NOT AFFECTED BY 1967 INCREASE

Increases authorized under amendment by Pub. L. 90–83 not applicable to specified personnel, see section 7 of Pub. L. 90–83, set out as a note under section 8103 of this title.

SECTION REFERRED TO IN OTHER SECTIONS

This section is referred to in section 8147 of this title.

§ 8133. Compensation in case of death

(a) If death results from an injury sustained in the performance of duty, the United States shall pay a monthly compensation equal to a percentage of the monthly pay of the deceased employee in accordance with the following schedule:

(1) To the widow or widower, if there is no child, 50 percent.

(2) To the widow or widower, if there is a child, 45 percent and in addition 15 percent for each child not to exceed a total of 75 percent for the widow or widower and children.

(3) To the children, if there is no widow or widower, 40 percent for one child and 15 percent additional for each additional child not to exceed a total of 75 percent, divided among the children share and share alike.

(4) To the parents, if there is no widow, widower, or child, as follows—

(A) 25 percent if one parent was wholly dependent on the employee at the time of death and the other was not dependent to any extent;

(B) 20 percent to each if both were wholly dependent; or

(C) a proportionate amount in the discretion of the Secretary of Labor if one or both were partly dependent.

If there is a widow, widower, or child, so much of the percentages are payable as, when added to the total percentages payable to the widow, widower, and children, will not exceed a total of 75 percent.

(5) To the brothers, sisters, grandparents, and grandchildren, if there is no widow, widower, child, or dependent parent, as follows—

(A) 20 percent if one was wholly dependent on the employee at the time of death;

(B) 30 percent if more than one was wholly dependent, divided among the dependents share and share alike; or

(C) 10 percent if no one is wholly dependent but one or more is partly dependent, divided among the dependents share and share alike.

If there is a widow, widower, child, or dependent parent, so much of the percentages are payable as, when added to the total percentages payable to the widow, widower, children, and dependent parents, will not exceed a total of 75 percent.

(b) The compensation payable under subsection (a) of this section is paid from the time of death until—

(1) a widow, or widower dies or remarries before reaching age 55;

(2) a child, a brother, a sister, or a grandchild dies, marries, or becomes 18 years of age, or if over age 18 and incapable of self-support becomes capable of self-support; or

(3) a parent or grandparent dies, marries, or ceases to be dependent.

Notwithstanding paragraph (2) of this subsection, compensation payable to or for a child, a brother or sister, or grandchild that would otherwise end because the child, brother or sister, or grandchild has reached 18 years of age shall continue if he is a student as defined by section 8101 of this title at the time he reaches 18 years of age for so long as he continues to be such a student or until he marries. A widow or widower who has entitlements to benefits under this title derived from more than one husband or wife shall elect one entitlement to be utilized.

(c) On the cessation of compensation under this section to or on account of an individual, the compensation of the remaining individuals entitled to compensation for the unexpired part of the period during which their compensation is payable, is that which they would have received if they had been the only individuals entitled to compensation at the time of the death of the employee.

(d) When there are two or more classes of individuals entitled to compensation under this section and the apportionment of compensation under this section would result in injustice, the Secretary may modify the apportionment to meet the requirements of the case.

(e) In computing compensation under this section, the monthly pay is deemed not less than the minimum rate of basic pay for GS–2. However, the total monthly compensation may not exceed—

(1) the monthly pay computed under section 8114 of this title, except for increases authorized by section 8146a of this title; or

(2) 75 percent of the monthly pay of the maximum rate of basic pay for GS–15.

(f) Notwithstanding any funeral and burial expenses paid under section 8134, there shall be paid a sum of $200 to the personal representative of a deceased employee within the meaning of section 8101(1) of this title for reimbursement of the costs of termination of the decedent's status as an employee of the United States.

(Pub. L. 89–554, Sept. 6, 1966, 80 Stat. 547; Pub. L. 90–83, § 1(62), Sept. 11, 1967, 81 Stat. 211; Pub. L. 93–416, §§ 16(a), 17, 18, Sept. 7, 1974, 88 Stat. 1147, 1149; Pub. L. 101–303, § 3(1), May 29, 1990, 104 Stat. 251.)

HISTORICAL AND REVISION NOTES
1966 ACT

Derivation	U.S. Code	Revised Statutes and Statutes at Large
....	5 U.S.C. 760 (less last 23 words of 1st sentence in (B); and less (H) and (L)).	Sept. 7, 1916, ch. 458, § 10 (less last 15 words of 1st sentence in (B); and less (H) and (L)), 39 Stat. 744. Feb. 12, 1927, ch. 110, § 3, 44 Stat. 1087. July 28, 1945, ch. 328, §§ 2 (less last 24 words), 3, 59 Stat. 503. Oct. 14, 1949, ch. 691, § 106 (less last 23 words of 1st sentence in "(B)" of (c); and less (e)), 63 Stat. 859. Sept. 13, 1960, Pub. L. 86–767, § 102, 74 Stat. 906.

In subsection (a), the words "an injury sustained in the performance of duty" are substituted for "the injury" to clearly identify the type of injury to which the section refers.

Administration of this subchapter was transferred to the Secretary of Labor by section 1 of 1950 Reorg. Plan. No. 19, 64 Stat. 1271 (see section 8145).

Standard changes are made to conform with the definitions applicable and the style of this title as outlined in the preface to the report.

1967 ACT

Section of title 5	Source (U.S. Code)	Source (Statutes at Large)
8133(b)	5 App.: 760(G) (last sentence).	July 4, 1966, Pub. L. 89–488, § 7(a), 80 Stat. 253.
8133(e)	5 App.: 760(K).	July 4, 1966, Pub. L. 89–488, § 3(c), 80 Stat. 252.

In subsection (b), the words "Notwithstanding paragraph (3) of this subsection" are substituted for "Notwithstanding any other provision of this section" for clarity. The words "section 8101 of this title" are substituted for "section 10(M) of this Act" to reflect the codification of that section in title 5.

In subsection (e), the words "is deemed" are substituted for "shall be considered to be". The words "minimum rate of basic pay for GS–2" and "maximum rate of basic pay for GS–15" are substituted for "lowest rate of basic compensation provided for grade 2 by the General Schedule of the Classification Act of 1949" and "highest rate of basic compensation provided for grade 15 of the General Schedule of the Classification Act of 1949," respectively, for consistency of style and to reflect the codification of the Classification Act of 1949 in title 5. The words "under section 8114 of this title" are substituted for "as provided in section 12" to reflect the codification of that section in title 5.

AMENDMENTS

1990—Subsec. (b)(1). Pub. L. 101–303 substituted "age 55" for "age 60".

1974—Subsec. (a)(1). Pub. L. 93–416, § 16(a), substituted "50" for "45".

Subsec. (a)(2). Pub. L. 93–416, § 16(a), substituted "45" for "40".

Subsec. (a)(3). Pub. L. 93–416, § 16(a), substituted "40" for "35".

Subsec. (b). Pub. L. 93–416, § 16(a), inserted "before reaching age 60" after "remarries" in par. (1), struck out par. (2) referring to widower who dies, remarries or becomes capable of self-support, redesignated pars. (3) and (4) as (2) and (3), respectively, changed the ref-

erence in closing paragraph from paragraph (3) of this subsection to paragraph (2) of this subsection, and inserted provision for election by widower or widow of benefits derived from more than one husband or wife.

Subsec. (e)(1). Pub. L. 93–416, § 17, inserted ", except for increases authorized by section 8146a of this title" before "; or".

Subsec. (f). Pub. L. 93–416, § 18, added subsec. (f).

EFFECTIVE DATE OF 1974 AMENDMENT

Amendment by sections 16(a) and 17 of Pub. L. 93–416 applicable to cases where injury or death occurred prior to Sept. 7, 1974 but only to a period beginning on or after Sept. 7, 1974, see section 28(a) of Pub. L. 93–416, set out as a note under section 8101 of this title.

Amendment by section 18 of Pub. L. 93–416 effective on Sept. 7, 1974, and applicable to any injury or death occurring on or after Sept. 7, 1974, see section 28(a) of Pub. L. 93–416, set out as a note under section 8101 of this title.

GRATUITY FOR DEATH OF CIVILIAN EMPLOYEE FROM INJURY SUSTAINED IN LINE OF DUTY

Pub. L. 104–208, div. A, title I, § 101(f) [title VI, § 651], Sept. 30, 1996, 110 Stat. 3009–314, 3009–368, provided that: "Notwithstanding section 8116 of title 5, United States Code, and in addition to any payment made under 5 U.S.C. 8101 et seq., beginning in fiscal year 1997 and thereafter, the head of any department or agency is authorized to pay from appropriations made available to the department or agency a death gratuity to the personal representative (as that term is defined by applicable law) of a civilian employee of that department or agency whose death resulted from an injury sustained in the line of duty on or after August 2, 1990: *Provided*, That payments made pursuant to this section, in combination with the payments made pursuant to sections 8133(f) and 8134(a) of such title 5 and section 312 of Public Law 103–332 (108 Stat. 2537) [5 U.S.C. 8134 note], may not exceed a total of $10,000 per employee."

PERSONNEL NOT AFFECTED BY 1967 INCREASE

Increases authorized under amendment by section 1(62)(B) of Pub. L. 90–83 not applicable to specified personnel, see section 7 of Pub. L. 90–83, set out as a note under section 8103 of this title.

SECTION REFERRED TO IN OTHER SECTIONS

This section is referred to in sections 8109, 8119, 8135, 8138, 8141, 8148 of this title; title 14 sections 707, 760; title 18 section 1921; title 22 section 3973.

§ 8134. Funeral expenses; transportation of body

(a) If death results from an injury sustained in the performance of duty, the United States shall pay, to the personal representative of the deceased or otherwise, funeral and burial expenses not to exceed $800, in the discretion of the Secretary of Labor.

(b) The body of an employee whose home is in the United States, in the discretion of the Secretary, may be embalmed and transported in a hermetically sealed casket to his home or last place of residence at the expense of the Employees' Compensation Fund if—

(1) the employee dies from—

(A) the injury while away from his home or official station or outside the United States; or

(B) from other causes while away from his home or official station for the purpose of receiving medical or other services, appliances, supplies, or examination under this subchapter; and

(2) the relatives of the employee request the return of his body.

If the relatives do not request the return of the body of the employee, the Secretary may provide for its disposition and incur and pay from the Employees' Compensation Fund the necessary and reasonable transportation, funeral, and burial expenses.

(Pub. L. 89–554, Sept. 6, 1966, 80 Stat. 548.)

HISTORICAL AND REVISION NOTES

Derivation	U.S. Code	Revised Statutes and Statutes at Large
....	5 U.S.C. 761.	Sept. 7, 1916, ch. 458, § 11, 39 Stat. 745. Feb. 12, 1927, ch. 110, § 4, 44 Stat. 1087. July 28, 1945, ch. 328, § 2 (last 24 words), 59 Stat. 503. Oct. 14, 1949, ch. 691, § 107, 63 Stat. 860. Sept. 13, 1960, Pub. L. 86–767, § 103, 74 Stat. 906.

In subsection (a), the words "an injury sustained in the performance of duty" are substituted for "the injury" to clearly identify the type of injury to which the section refers.

Administration of this subchapter was transferred to the Secretary of Labor by section 1 of 1950 Reorg. Plan. No. 19, 64 Stat. 1271 (see section 8145).

Standard changes are made to conform with the definitions applicable and the style of this title as outlined in the preface to the report.

AVAILABILITY OF DEPARTMENT OF THE INTERIOR AND RELATED AGENCIES APPROPRIATIONS TO REIMBURSE REPRESENTATIVES OF EMPLOYEES KILLED IN LINE OF DUTY

Pub. L. 103–332, title III, § 312, Sept. 30, 1994, 108 Stat. 2537, provided that: "Notwithstanding any other provision of law in fiscal year 1995 and thereafter, appropriations made available to any department or agency in a Department of the Interior and Related Agencies Appropriations Act shall be available to that department or agency to reimburse the representative (as that term is defined by applicable law) of employees killed in the line of duty after January 1, 1994, and in subsequent fiscal years, for burial costs and related out-of-pocket expenses: *Provided*, That the amount of such reimbursement may exceed the $800 limitation in 5 U.S.C. 8134(a): *Provided further*, That funds provided pursuant to this authority may not exceed $10,000 per employee."

SECTION REFERRED TO IN OTHER SECTIONS

This section is referred to in sections 8109, 8133, 8146 of this title; title 38 section 2307.

§ 8135. Lump-sum payment

(a) The liability of the United States for compensation to a beneficiary in the case of death or of permanent total or permanent partial disability may be discharged by a lump-sum payment equal to the present value of all future payments of compensation computed at 4 percent true discount compounded annually if—

(1) the monthly payment to the beneficiary is less than $50 a month;

(2) the beneficiary is or is about to become a nonresident of the United States; or

(3) the Secretary of Labor determines that it is for the best interest of the beneficiary.

The probability of the death of the beneficiary before the expiration of the period during which he is entitled to compensation shall be determined according to the most current United States Life Tables, as developed by the United States Department of Health, Education, and Welfare, which shall be updated from time to time, but the lump-sum payment to a widow or widower of the deceased employee may not exceed 60 months' compensation. The probability of the happening of any other contingency affecting the amount or duration of compensation shall be disregarded.

(b) On remarriage before reaching age 55 a widow or widower entitled to compensation under section 8133 of this title, shall be paid a lump sum equal to twenty-four times the monthly compensation payment (excluding compensation on account of another individual) to which he was entitled immediately before the remarriage.

(Pub. L. 89–554, Sept. 6, 1966, 80 Stat. 548; Pub. L. 90–83, § 1(63), Sept. 11, 1967, 81 Stat. 211; Pub. L. 93–416, §§ 16(b), 19, 20, Sept. 7, 1974, 88 Stat. 1149; Pub. L. 101–303, § 3(2), May 29, 1990, 104 Stat. 251.)

HISTORICAL AND REVISION NOTES
1966 ACT

Derivation	U.S. Code	Revised Statutes and Statutes at Large
....	5 U.S.C. 764.	Sept. 7, 1916, ch. 458, § 14, 39 Stat. 746.

Administration of this subchapter was transferred to the Secretary of Labor by section 1 of 1950 Reorg. Plan No. 19, 64 Stat. 1271 (see section 8145).

Standard changes are made to conform with the definitions applicable and the style of this title as outlined in the preface to the report.

1967 ACT

Section of title 5	Source (U.S. Code)	Source (Statutes at Large)
8135(b)	5 App.: 764(b).	July 4, 1966, Pub. L. 89–488, § 8, 80 Stat. 254.

The word "widower" is substituted for "dependent widower" to conform to the definition in 5 U.S.C. 8101(11). The words "section 8133 of title 5" are substituted for "section 10" to reflect the codification of that section in title 5, United States Code.

AMENDMENTS

1990—Subsec. (b). Pub. L. 101–303 substituted "age 55" for "age 60".

1974—Subsec. (a). Pub. L. 93–416, § 20, substituted provisions relating to use of the most current United States Life Tables, for provisions relating to determination by the American Experience Tables of Mortality.

Subsec. (a)(1). Pub. L. 93–416, § 19, substituted "$50" for "$5".

Subsec. (b). Pub. L. 93–416, § 16(b), inserted "before reaching age 60" after "On remarriage".

CHANGE OF NAME

United States Department of Health, Education, and Welfare redesignated the United States Department of Health and Human Services by section 3508 of Title 20, Education.

EFFECTIVE DATE OF 1974 AMENDMENT

Amendment by Pub. L. 93–416 applicable to cases where injury or death occurred prior to Sept. 7, 1974, but only to a period beginning on or after Sept. 7, 1974, see section 28(a) of Pub. L. 93–416, set out as a note under section 8101 of this title.

PERSONNEL NOT AFFECTED BY 1967 INCREASE

Increases authorized under amendment by section 1(63) of Pub. L. 90–83 not applicable to specified personnel, see section 7 of Pub. L. 90–83, set out as a note under section 8103 of this title.

SECTION REFERRED TO IN OTHER SECTIONS

This section is referred to in sections 8137, 8337, 8464a of this title; title 22 section 4048; title 50 section 2051.

§ 8136. Initial payments outside the United States

If an employee is injured outside the continental United States, the Secretary of Labor may arrange and provide for initial payment of compensation and initial furnishing of other benefits under this subchapter by an employee or agent of the United States designated by the Secretary for that purpose in the locality in which the employee was employed or the injury incurred.

(Pub. L. 89–554, Sept. 6, 1966, 80 Stat. 549.)

HISTORICAL AND REVISION NOTES

Derivation	U.S. Code	Revised Statutes and Statutes at Large
....	5 U.S.C. 793 (2d sentence of 4th par.)	July 29, 1942, ch. 533 (2d sentence), 56 Stat. 725.

The word "continental" is added on authority of the last sentence of the fifth paragraph of former section 793, which is carried into section 8137.

Administration of this subchapter was transferred to the Secretary of Labor by section 1 of 1950 Reorg. Plan. No. 19, 64 Stat. 1271 (see section 8145).

Standard changes are made to conform with the definitions applicable and the style of this title as outlined in the preface to the report.

§ 8137. Compensation for noncitizens and nonresidents

(a) When the Secretary of Labor finds that the amount of compensation payable to an employee who is neither a citizen nor resident of the United States or Canada, or payable to a dependent of such an employee, is substantially disproportionate to compensation for disability or death payable in similar cases under local statute, regulations, custom, or otherwise at the place outside the continental United States or Canada where the employee is working at the time of injury, he may provide for payment of compensation on a basis reasonably in accord with prevailing local payments in similar cases by—

(1) the adoption or adaption of the substantive features, by a schedule or otherwise, of local workmen's compensation provisions or other local statute, regulation, or custom applicable in cases of personal injury or death; or

(2) establishing special schedules of compensation for injury, death, and loss of use of members and functions of the body for specific classes of employees, areas, and places.

Irrespective of the basis adopted, the Secretary may at any time—

(A) modify or limit the maximum monthly and total aggregate payments for injury, death, and medical or other benefits;

(B) modify or limit the percentages of the wage of the employee payable as compensation for the injury or death; and

(C) modify, limit, or redesignate the class or classes of beneficiaries entitled to death benefits, including the designation of persons, representatives, or groups entitled to payment under local statute or custom whether or not included in the classes of beneficiaries otherwise specified by this subchapter.

(b) In a case under this section, the Secretary or his designee may—

(1) make a lump-sum award in the manner prescribed by section 8135 of this title when he or his designee considers it to be for the best interest of the United States; and

(2) compromise and pay a claim for benefits, including a claim in which there is a dispute as to jurisdiction or other fact or a question of law.

Compensation paid under this subsection is instead of all other compensation from the United States for the same injury or death, and a payment made under this subsection is deemed compensation under this subchapter and is satisfaction of all liability of the United States in respect to the particular injury or death.

(c) The Secretary may delegate to an employee or agency of the United States, with such limitations and right of review as he considers advisable, authority to process, adjudicate, commute by lump-sum award, compromise, and pay a claim or class of claims for compensation, and to provide other benefits, locally, under this section, in accordance with such regulations and instructions as the Secretary considers necessary. For this purpose, the Secretary may provide or transfer funds, including reimbursement of amounts paid under this subchapter.

(d) The Secretary may waive the application of this subchapter in whole or in part and for such period or periods as he may fix if he finds that—

(1) conditions prevent the establishment of facilities for processing and adjudicating claims under this section; or

(2) claimants under this section are alien enemies.

(e) The Secretary may apply this section retrospectively with adjustment of compensation and benefits as he considers necessary and proper.

(Pub. L. 89–554, Sept. 6, 1966, 80 Stat. 549.)

HISTORICAL AND REVISION NOTES

Derivation	U.S. Code	Revised Statutes and Statutes at Large
....	5 U.S.C. 793 (5th par., less penultimate sentence).	July 28, 1945, ch. 328, §4 (less penultimate sentence), 59 Stat. 503.

The last sentence of former section 793 is omitted as it consists of a definition which is fully spelled out when the words "United States" are used as a geographical reference.

Administration of this subchapter was transferred to the Secretary of Labor by section 1 of 1950 Reorg. Plan. No. 19, 64 Stat. 1271 (see section 8145).

Standard changes are made to conform with the definitions applicable and the style of this title as outlined in the preface to the report.

§ 8138. Minimum limit modification for noncitizens and aliens

(a) Except as provided by subsection (b) of this section, the minimum limit on monthly compensation for disability under section 8112 of this title and the minimum limit on monthly pay on which death compensation is computed under section 8133 of this title do not apply in the case of a noncitizen employee, or a class or classes of noncitizen employees, who sustain injury outside the continental United States. The Secretary of Labor may establish a minimum monthly pay on which death compensation is computed in the case of a class or classes of such noncitizen employees.

(b) The President may remove or modify the minimum limit on monthly compensation for disability under section 8112 of this title and the minimum limit on monthly pay on which death compensation is computed under section 8133 of this title in the case of an alien employee, or a class or classes of alien employees, of the Canal Zone Government or the Panama Canal Company.

(Pub. L. 89–554, Sept. 6, 1966, 80 Stat. 550.)

HISTORICAL AND REVISION NOTES

Derivation	U.S. Code	Revised Statutes and Statutes at Large
(a)	5 U.S.C. 793 (4th par., less 2d sentence).	July 29, 1942, ch. 533 (less 2d sentence), 56 Stat. 725. Sept. 13, 1960, Pub. L. 86–767, § 210, 74 Stat. 910.
(b)	5 U.S.C. 793 (2d sentence of 2d par.).	Sept. 7, 1916, ch. 458, § 42 (2d sentence of 2d par.), 39 Stat. 750. Apr. 6, 1938, ch. 79 "Sec. 42 (2d sentence of 2d par.)", 52 Stat. 201.

In subsection (a), the words "in his discretion" are omitted as unnecessary in view of the permissive nature of the authority. The word "continental" is added on authority of the last sentence of the fifth paragraph of former section 793, which is carried into section 8137.

In subsection (b), the words "Canal Zone Government" and "Panama Canal Company" are substituted for "Panama Canal" and "Panama Railroad Company", respectively, on authority of the Act of Sept. 26, 1950, ch. 1049, § 2(a), 64 Stat. 1038.

Administration of this subchapter was transferred to the Secretary of Labor by section 1 of 1950 Reorg. Plan No. 19, 64 Stat. 1271 (see section 8145).

Standard changes are made to conform with the definitions applicable and the style of this title as outlined in the preface to the report.

REFERENCES IN TEXT

For definition of Canal Zone Government and Panama Canal Company, referred to in text, see section 3602(b) of Title 22, Foreign Relations and Intercourse.

SECTION REFERRED TO IN OTHER SECTIONS

This section is referred to in section 8112 of this title.

§ 8139. Employees of the District of Columbia

Compensation awarded to an employee of the government of the District of Columbia shall be paid in the manner provided by statute for the payment of the general expenses of the government of the District of Columbia.

(Pub. L. 89–554, Sept. 6, 1966, 80 Stat. 550.)

HISTORICAL AND REVISION NOTES

Derivation	U.S. Code	Revised Statutes and Statutes at Large
....	5 U.S.C. 794 (less 1st sentence).	July 11, 1919, ch. 7, § 11 (less 1st sentence), 41 Stat. 104.

The words "Compensation awarded" are substituted for "Such compensation as the Secretary may award".

The last sentence of former section 794, requiring that the Commissioners of the District of Columbia submit to Congress through the Bureau of the Budget estimates of appropriations, is omitted as obsolete. The Budget and Accounting Act, 1921, as amended, 31 U.S.C. 2 et seq., prescribes the procedures for presenting all budget estimates for the government of the District of Columbia and provides that the budget submission to Congress be made by the President.

Standard changes are made to conform with the definitions applicable and the style of this title as outlined in the preface to the report.

PROCESSING OF CLAIMS FILED BY DISTRICT OF COLUMBIA EMPLOYEES

See Pub. L. 93–198, title II, § 204(e), Dec. 24, 1973, 87 Stat. 783, set out as a note under section 8101 of this title.

§ 8140. Members of the Reserve Officers' Training Corps

(a) Subject to the provisions of this section, this subchapter applies to a member of, or applicant for membership in, the Reserve Officers' Training Corps of the Army, Navy, or Air Force who suffers an injury, disability, or death incurred, or an illness contracted, in line of duty—

(1) while engaged in a flight or in flight instruction under chapter 103 of title 10; or

(2) during the period of the member's attendance at training or a practice cruise under chapter 103 of title 10, United States Code, beginning when the authorized travel to the training or practice cruise begins and ending when authorized travel from the training or practice cruise ends.

(b) For the purpose of this section, an injury, disability, death, or illness of a member referred to in subsection (a) may be considered as incurred or contracted in line of duty only if the injury, disability, or death is incurred, or the illness is contracted, by the member during a period described in that subsection. Subject to review by the Secretary of Labor, the Secretary of the military department concerned (under regulations prescribed by that Secretary), shall determine whether an injury, disability, or death was incurred, or an illness was contracted, by a member in line of duty.

(c) In computing the compensation payable under this section, the monthly pay received by the injured or deceased individual, in cash and kind, is deemed $150.

(d) The Secretary of the military department concerned shall cooperate fully with the Department of Labor in the prompt investigation and prosecution of a case involving the legal liability of a third party other than the United States.

(e) An individual may not receive disability benefits under this section while on active duty with the armed forces, but these benefits may be reinstated when the individual is released from that active duty.

(f) Expenses incurred by a military department in providing hospitalization, medical and surgical care, necessary transportation incident to that hospitalization or medical and surgical care, or in connection with a funeral and burial on behalf of an individual covered by subsection (a) of this section shall be reimbursed by the Secretary of Labor from the Employees' Compensation Fund in accordance with this subchapter. However, reimbursement may not be made for hospitalization or medical or surgical care provided an individual by a military department in a facility of a military department.

(g) For purposes of this section, the term "applicant for membership" includes a student enrolled, during a semester or other enrollment term, in a course which is part of Reserve Officers' Training Corps instruction at an educational institution.

(Pub. L. 89–554, Sept. 6, 1966, 80 Stat. 550; Pub. L. 100–456, div. A, title VI, § 633(b), Sept. 29, 1988, 102 Stat. 1986; Pub. L. 105–261, div. A, title VI, § 655(a)–(c), Oct. 17, 1998, 112 Stat. 2053.)

HISTORICAL AND REVISION NOTES

Derivation	U.S. Code	Revised Statutes and Statutes at Large
....	5 U.S.C. 802.	Aug. 1, 1956, ch. 830, § 4, 70 Stat. 805. Oct. 13, 1964, Pub. L. 88–647, § 302, 78 Stat. 1073.

In subsection (a), the words "Subject to the provisions of this section" are added for clarity.

In subsection (c), the last sentence of former section 802(b) is omitted as unnecessary.

In subsection (d), the words "Nothing in this section shall be construed to hinder the prompt action authorized by sections 776 and 777 of this title in any case involving the legal liability of a third party other than the United States" are omitted as unnecessary as there is nothing in the section that reasonably could be so construed.

Standard changes are made to conform with the definitions applicable and the style of this title as outlined in the preface to the report.

AMENDMENTS

1998—Subsec. (a). Pub. L. 105–261, § 655(c), inserted ", or an illness contracted," after "death incurred" in introductory provisions.

Subsec. (a)(2). Pub. L. 105–261, § 655(a), amended par. (2) generally. Prior to amendment, par. (2) read as follows: "while performing authorized travel to or from, or while attending, training or a practice cruise under chapter 103 of title 10."

Subsec. (b). Pub. L. 105–261, § 655(b), amended subsec. (b) generally. Prior to amendment, subsec. (b) read as follows: "For the purpose of this section, an injury is incurred in line of duty only if it is the proximate result of the performance of military training by the member concerned, or of his travel to or from that training, during the periods specified by subsection (a)(2) of this section. A member or applicant for membership who contracts a disease or illness which is the proximate result of the performance of training during the periods specified by subsection (a)(2) of this section is considered for the purpose of this section to have been injured in line of duty during that period. Subject to review by the Secretary of Labor, the Secretary of the military department concerned, under regulations prescribed by him, shall determine whether or not an injury, disease, or illness was incurred or contracted in line of duty and was the proximate result of the performance of military training by the member concerned or of his travel to or from that military training."

1988—Subsec. (a). Pub. L. 100–456, § 633(b)(1)(A), substituted "who suffers an injury, disability, or death" for "who suffers disability or death from an injury" in introductory provisions.

Subsec. (a)(2). Pub. L. 100–456, § 633(b)(1)(B), struck out "field" before "training".

Subsec. (f). Pub. L. 100–456, § 633(b)(2), substituted "by a military department in a facility of a military department" for "while attending field training or a practice cruise under chapter 103 of title 10".

Subsec. (g). Pub. L. 100–456, § 633(b)(3), added subsec. (g).

EFFECTIVE DATE OF 1998 AMENDMENT

Pub. L. 105–261, div. A, title VI, § 655(d), Oct. 17, 1998, 112 Stat. 2053, provided that: "The amendments made by subsections (a) and (b) [amending this section] shall take effect on the date of the enactment of this Act [Oct. 17, 1998] and apply with respect to injuries, illnesses, disabilities, and deaths incurred or contracted on or after that date."

EFFECTIVE DATE OF 1988 AMENDMENT

Amendment by Pub. L. 100–456 applicable only with respect to training performed after Sept. 30, 1988, see section 633(e) of Pub. L. 100–456, set out as a note under section 2109 of Title 10, Armed Forces.

DIFFERENT COVERAGE FOR RESERVE OFFICER TRAINING CORPS MEMBERS

Pub. L. 97–306, title I, § 113(c), Oct. 14, 1982, 96 Stat. 1432, provided that: "Notwithstanding section 8140 of title 5, United States Code, subchapter I of chapter 81 of such title does not apply in the case of a disability suffered by a member of the Reserve Officers' Training Corps of the Army, Navy, or Air Force that is compensable under chapter 11 of title 38, United States Code, or a death suffered by such a member for which dependency and indemnity compensation is payable under chapter 13 of such title [section 401 et seq. of Title 38]."

[Section 113(d) of Pub. L. 97–306 provided that these provisions shall apply only with respect to deaths and disabilities resulting from diseases or injuries incurred or aggravated after September 30, 1982.]

SECTION REFERRED TO IN OTHER SECTIONS

This section is referred to in title 38 section 101.

§ 8141. Civil Air Patrol volunteers

(a) Subject to the provisions of this section, this subchapter applies to a volunteer civilian member of the Civil Air Patrol, except a Civil Air Patrol Cadet under 18 years of age.

(b) In administering this subchapter for a member of the Civil Air Patrol covered by this section—

(1) the monthly pay of a member is deemed the rate of basic pay payable for step 1 of grade GS–9 in the General Schedule under section 5332 of this title for the purpose of computing compensation for disability or death;

(2) the percentages applicable to payments under section 8133 of this title are—

(A) 45 percent for section 8133(a)(2) of this title, if the member dies fully or currently insured under subchapter II of chapter 7 of title 42, with no additional payments for a child or children while the widow or widower remains eligible for payments under section 8133(a)(2) of this title;

(B) 20 percent for section 8133(a)(3) of this title for one child and 10 percent additional for each additional child, but not to exceed a total of 75 percent, if the member died fully or currently insured under subchapter II of chapter 7 of title 42; and

(C) 25 percent for section 8133(a)(4) of this title, if one parent was wholly dependent on the deceased member at the time of his death and the other was not dependent to any extent; 16 percent to each, if both were wholly dependent; and if one was or both were partly dependent, a proportionate amount in the discretion of the Secretary of Labor;

(3) a payment may not be made under section 8133(a)(5) of this title;

(4) "performance of duty" means only active service, and travel to and from that service, rendered in performance or support of operational missions of the Civil Air Patrol under direction of the Department of the Air Force and under written authorization by competent authority covering a specific assignment and prescribing a time limit for the assignment; and

(5) the Secretary of Labor or his designee shall inform the Commissioner of Social Security when a claim is filed and eligibility for compensation is established under section 8133(a)(2) or (3) of this title, and the Commissioner of Social Security shall certify to the Secretary of Labor as to whether or not the member concerned was fully or currently insured under subchapter II of chapter 7 of title 42 at the time of his death.

(c) The Secretary of Labor or his designee may inform the Secretary of the Air Force or his designee when a claim is filed. The Secretary of the Air Force, on request of the Secretary of Labor, shall advise him of the facts concerning the injury and whether or not the member was rendering service, or engaged in travel to or from service, in performance or support of an operational mission of the Civil Air Patrol at the time of injury. This subsection does not dispense with the report of the immediate superior of the member required by section 8120 of this title, or other reports agreed on under that section.

(Pub. L. 89–554, Sept. 6, 1966, 80 Stat. 551; Pub. L. 98–94, title XII, § 1258(a), Sept. 24, 1983, 97 Stat. 702; Pub. L. 103–296, title I, § 108(e)(4), Aug. 15, 1994, 108 Stat. 1486.)

HISTORICAL AND REVISION NOTES

Derivation	U.S. Code	Revised Statutes and Statutes at Large
....	5 U.S.C. 803 (less (d)).	Aug. 3, 1956, ch. 926, § 1 "Sec. 3 (less (d))", 70 Stat. 980.

Subsection (d) of former section 803, providing for retroactive applicability, is omitted as executed (see Table II).

Standard changes are made to conform with the definitions applicable and the style of this title as outlined in the preface to the report.

REFERENCES IN TEXT

Subchapter II of chapter 7 of title 42, referred to in text, is section 401 et seq. of Title 42, The Public Health and Welfare.

AMENDMENTS

1994—Subsec. (b)(5). Pub. L. 103–296 substituted "Commissioner of Social Security" for "Secretary of Health, Education, and Welfare" in two places.

1983—Subsec. (a). Pub. L. 98–94, § 1258(a)(1), inserted "under 18 years of age" after "Civil Air Patrol Cadet".

Subsec. (b)(1). Pub. L. 98–94, § 1258(a)(2), substituted "the rate of basic pay payable for step 1 of grade GS–9 in the General Schedule under section 5332 of this title" for "$300".

EFFECTIVE DATE OF 1994 AMENDMENT

Amendment by Pub. L. 103–296 effective Mar. 31, 1995, see section 110(a) of Pub. L. 103–296, set out as a note under section 401 of Title 42, The Public Health and Welfare.

EFFECTIVE DATE OF 1983 AMENDMENT

Section 1258(b) of Pub. L. 98–94 provided that:

"(1) The amendments made by subsection (a) [amending this section] shall take effect on the date of the enactment of this Act [Sept. 24, 1983].

"(2) The amendment made by subsection (a)(1) [amending this section] shall apply only to deaths or injuries occurring on or after the date of the enactment of this Act [Sept. 24, 1983].

"(3) The amendment made by subsection (a)(2) [amending this section] shall apply only to the computation of compensation payable for periods commencing on or after the date of the enactment of this Act [Sept. 24, 1983]."

SECTION REFERRED TO IN OTHER SECTIONS

This section is referred to in section 8150 of this title.

§ 8142. Peace Corps volunteers

(a) For the purpose of this section, "volunteer" means—

(1) a volunteer enrolled in the Peace Corps under section 2504 of title 22;

(2) a volunteer leader enrolled in the Peace Corps under section 2505 of title 22; and

(3) an applicant for enrollment as a volunteer or volunteer leader during a period of training under section 2507(a) of title 22 before enrollment.

(b) Subject to the provisions of this section, this subchapter applies to a volunteer, except that entitlement to disability compensation payments does not commence until the day after the date of termination of his service as a volunteer.

(c) For the purpose of this subchapter—

(1) a volunteer is deemed receiving monthly pay at the minimum rate for GS–7;

(2) a volunteer leader referred to by section 2505 of title 22, or a volunteer with one or more minor children as defined in section 2504 of title 22, is deemed receiving monthly pay at the minimum rate for GS–11;

(3) an injury suffered by a volunteer when he is outside the several States and the District of Columbia is deemed proximately caused by his employment, unless the injury or disease is—

(A) caused by willful misconduct of the volunteer;

(B) caused by the volunteer's intention to bring about the injury or death of himself or of another; or

(C) proximately caused by the intoxication of the injured volunteer; and

(4) the period of service of an individual as a volunteer includes—

(A) any period of training under section 2507(a) of title 22 before enrollment as a volunteer; and

(B) the period between enrollment as a volunteer and the termination of service as a volunteer by the President or by death or resignation.

(Pub. L. 89–554, Sept. 6, 1966, 80 Stat. 552; Pub. L. 90–83, § 1(64), Sept. 11, 1967, 81 Stat. 212; Pub. L. 93–416, § 23(b), Sept. 7, 1974, 88 Stat. 1150.)

HISTORICAL AND REVISION NOTES
1966 ACT

Derivation	U.S. Code	Revised Statutes and Statutes at Large
....	22 U.S.C. 2504(d).	Sept. 22, 1961, Pub. L. 87–293, § 5(d), 75 Stat. 613.

Subsection (a) is based on sections 2504(a), 2505, and 2507(a) of title 22.

In subsection (b), the words "Subject to the provisions of this section" are added for clarity and to conform to the style of sections 8140 and 8141. The words "of the United States Government" are omitted as unnecessary in view of the definition of "employee" in section 8101(1).

In subsection (c), the words "outside the several States, territories and possessions of the United States, and the District of Columbia" are substituted for "abroad" on authority of section 2522(a), (b) of title 22. References to "the general schedule established by the Classification Act of 1949, as amended" are omitted as unnecessary.

Subsection (c)(4) is added on authority of section 2522(e) of title 22.

Standard changes are made to conform with the definitions applicable and the style of this title as outlined in the preface to the report.

1967 ACT

Section 8142 of title 5 was derived from section 2504(d) of title 22. This amendment reflects changes, effected by the act of Sept. 13, 1966, Public Law 89–572, section 4, 80 Stat. 765, in the definitions applicable to section 2504(d) by virtue of section 2522(a), (b) of title 22.

AMENDMENTS

1974—Subsec. (c)(2). Pub. L. 93–416 inserted provision relating to a volunteer with one or more minor children.

EFFECTIVE DATE OF 1974 AMENDMENT

Amendment by Pub. L. 93–416 effective on Sept. 7, 1974, and applicable to any injury or death occurring on or after such effective date, see section 23(a) of Pub. L. 93–416, set out as a note under section 8101 of this title.

SECTION REFERRED TO IN OTHER SECTIONS

This section is referred to in section 5732 of this title.

§ 8143. Job Corps enrollees; volunteers in service to America

(a) Subject to the provisions of this subsection, this subchapter applies to an enrollee in the Job Corps, except that compensation for disability does not begin to accrue until the day after the date on which the injured enrollee is terminated. In administering this subchapter for an enrollee covered by this subsection—

(1) the monthly pay of an enrollee is deemed that received at the minimum rate for GS–2;

(2) section 8113(a) of this title applies to an enrollee; and

(3) "performance of duty" does not include an act of an enrollee while absent from his assigned post of duty, except while participating in an activity (including an activity while on pass or during travel to or from the post of duty) authorized by or under the direction and supervision of the Job Corps.

(b) This subchapter applies to a volunteer in service to America who receives either a living allowance or a stipend under part A of subchapter VIII of chapter 34 of title 42, with respect to that service and training, to the same extent as enrollees of the Job Corps under subsection (a) of this section. However, for the purpose of the computation described in subsection (a)(1) of this section, the monthly pay of a volunteer is deemed that received at the minimum rate for GS–5 of the General Schedule under section 5332 of title 5, United States Code.

(Pub. L. 89–554, Sept. 6, 1966, 80 Stat. 553; Pub. L. 90–83, § 1(65), Sept. 11, 1967, 81 Stat. 212; Pub. L. 90–623, § 1(19), Oct. 22, 1968, 82 Stat. 1313; Pub. L. 93–416, § 8(b), Sept. 7, 1974, 88 Stat. 1145; Pub. L. 103–82, title III, § 384, Sept. 21, 1993, 107 Stat. 915.)

HISTORICAL AND REVISION NOTES
1966 ACT

Derivation	U.S. Code	Revised Statutes and Statutes at Large
(a)	42 U.S.C. 2716(c).	Aug. 20, 1964, Pub. L. 88–452, § 106(c), 78 Stat. 510.
(b)	42 U.S.C. 2943(d) (words after 6th comma, as applicable to 42 U.S.C. 2716(c)).	Aug. 20, 1964, Pub. L. 88–452, § 603(d) (words after 6th comma, as applicable to § 106(c)), 78 Stat. 531.

In subsection (a)(1), reference to "the Classification Act of 1949 (5 U.S.C. 1071 et seq.)" is omitted as unnecessary. In subsection (a)(3)(B), the word "his" is substituted for "his or her" on authority of 1 U.S.C. 1.

In subsection (b), the words "in service to America" are inserted after "volunteer" for clarity.

Standard changes are made to conform with the definitions applicable and the style of this title as outlined in the preface to the report.

1967 ACT

Section of title 5	Source (U.S. Code)	Source (Statutes at Large)
8143(a)(1) ...	42: 2716(c)(2)(B).	Nov. 8, 1966, Pub. L. 89–794, § 109, 80 Stat. 1453.
8143(a)(3) ...	42: 2716(c)(2)(A).	Oct. 9, 1965, Pub. L. 89–253, § 6, 79 Stat. 973.
8143(b)	42: 2991c(b) (as applicable to 42: 2716(c)).	Nov. 8, 1966, Pub. L. 89–794, § 801 "Sec. 804(b) (as applicable to § 106(c) of the Economic Opportunity Act of 1964)", 80 Stat. 1474.

In subsection (a)(3), the words "in the Federal Employees' Compensation Act" are omitted as unnecessary since that act is codified in that subchapter of title 5, United States Code, in which section 8143 is a part. The word "his" is substituted for "his or hers" on authority of 1 U.S.C. 1. The words "Job Corps" are substituted for "Corps" on authority of 42 U.S.C. 2712.

In subsection (b), the words "in service to America" are inserted after "volunteer" in two places for clarity. The words "subsection (a)(2) of this section" are substituted for "paragraph (2)(B) of section 106(c)" to reflect the codification of that paragraph in title 5. The words "at the minimum rate for GS–7" are substituted for "under the entrance salary for GS–7 of the General Schedule for section 5332, title 5, United States Code" to conform to the style of title 5.

REFERENCES IN TEXT

Part A of subchapter VIII of chapter 34 of title 42, referred to in subsec. (b), is part A of title VIII of Pub.

L. 88–452, Aug. 20, 1964, 73 Stat. 508, as amended, known as the Economic Opportunity Act of 1964. Part A of title VIII of that Act, as added by Pub. L. 90–222, title I, § 110, Dec. 23, 1967, 81 Stat. 722, was classified generally to part A (§ 2992 et seq.) of subchapter VIII of chapter 34 of Title 42, The Public Health and Welfare, prior to its repeal by Pub. L. 93–113, title VI, § 603, Oct. 1, 1973, 87 Stat. 417. See sections 4951 et seq. and 5055 of Title 42.

AMENDMENTS

1993—Subsec. (b). Pub. L. 103–82 substituted "GS–5 of the General Schedule under section 5332 of title 5, United States Code" for "GS–7".

1974—Pub. L. 93–416 struck out ", (b)" after "section 8113(a)".

1968—Pub. L. 90–623 reenacted section in its entirety making minor changes in phraseology.

EFFECTIVE DATE OF 1993 AMENDMENT

Amendment by Pub. L. 103–82 effective Oct. 1, 1993, see section 392 of Pub. L. 103–82, set out as a note under section 4951 of Title 42, The Public Health and Welfare.

EFFECTIVE DATE OF 1974 AMENDMENT

Amendment by Pub. L. 93–416 applicable to case where injury or death occurred prior to Sept. 7, 1974, but only to a period beginning on or after Sept. 7, 1974, see section 28(a) of Pub. L. 93–416, set out as a note under section 8101 of this title.

EFFECTIVE DATE OF 1968 AMENDMENT

Amendment by Pub. L. 90–623 intended to restate without substantive change the law in effect on Oct. 22, 1968, see section 6 of Pub. L. 90–623, set out as a note under section 5334 of this title.

SECTION REFERRED TO IN OTHER SECTIONS

This section is referred to in title 29 section 2897.

§ 8143a. Members of the National Teacher Corps

Subject to the provisions of this section, this subchapter applies to a member of the National Teacher Corps. In administering this subchapter for a member covered by this section—

　(1) "performance of duty" does not include an act of a member while—

　　(A) on authorized leave; or

　　(B) absent from his assigned post of duty, except while participating in an activity authorized by or under the direction or supervision of the Commissioner of Education; and

　(2) In computing compensation for disability or death, the monthly pay of a member is deemed his actual pay or that received at the minimum rate for GS–6, whichever is greater.

(Added Pub. L. 90–83, § 1(66)(A), Sept. 11, 1967, 81 Stat. 212.)

HISTORICAL AND REVISION NOTES

Section of title 5	Source (U.S. Code)	Source (Statutes at Large)
8143a	20: 1105(b).	Nov. 8, 1965, Pub. L. 89–329, § 515(b), 79 Stat. 1257.

The words "a member of the National Teacher Corps" are substituted for "such members" on authority of 20 U.S.C. 1102, 1105(a). In paragraph (1)(B), the words "Commissioner of Education" are substituted for "Commissioner" on authority of 20 U.S.C. 1141(f). In paragraph (2), the words "at the minimum rate for GS–6" are substituted for "under the entrance salary for grade 6," and the reference to the General Schedule

of the Classification Act of 1949 is omitted as unnecessary.

TRANSFER OF FUNCTIONS

Functions of Commissioner of Education of Department of Health, Education, and Welfare transferred to Secretary of Education by section 3441(a)(1) of Title 20, Education.

§ 8144. Student-employees

A student-employee as defined by section 5351 of this title who suffers disability or death as a result of personal injury arising out of and in the course of training, or incurred in the performance of duties in connection with that training, is considered for the purpose of this subchapter an employee who incurred the injury in the performance of duty.

(Pub. L. 89–554, Sept. 6, 1966, 80 Stat. 553.)

HISTORICAL AND REVISION NOTES

Derivation	U.S. Code	Revised Statutes and Statutes at Large
....	5 U.S.C. 1053.	Aug. 4, 1947, ch. 452, § 4, 61 Stat. 727.

Standard changes are made to conform with the definitions applicable and the style of this title as outlined in the preface to the report.

§ 8145. Administration

The Secretary of Labor shall administer, and decide all questions arising under, this subchapter. He may—

　(1) appoint employees to administer this subchapter; and

　(2) delegate to any employee of the Department of Labor any of the powers conferred on him by this subchapter.

(Pub. L. 89–554, Sept. 6, 1966, 80 Stat. 553.)

HISTORICAL AND REVISION NOTES

Derivation	U.S. Code	Revised Statutes and Statutes at Large
....	5 U.S.C. 778.	Sept. 7, 1916, ch. 458, § 28, 39 Stat. 748.
		Oct. 14, 1949, ch. 691, § 205(a), (c)(1), 63 Stat. 864.
....	[Uncodified].	1946 Reorg. Plan No. 2, § 3 (less 2d sentence), eff. July 16, 1946, 60 Stat. 1095.
....	[Uncodified].	1950 Reorg. Plan No. 19, § 1, eff. May 24, 1950, 64 Stat. 1271.
....	5 U.S.C. 781.	Sept. 7, 1916, ch. 458, § 30, 39 Stat. 748.
....	5 U.S.C. 783 (last 9 words).	Sept. 7, 1916, ch. 458, § 32 (last 9 words), 39 Stat. 749.

The last 20 words of former section 781 are omitted as unnecessary in view of the definition of "competitive service" in section 2102 and the provisions of subchapter I of chapter 33 concerning examination and certification for and appointment in the competitive service.

Administration of this subchapter was transferred to the Secretary of Labor by section 1 of 1950 Reorg. Plan No. 19, 64 Stat. 1271.

Standard changes are made to conform with the definitions applicable and the style of this title as outlined in the preface to the report.

PROCESSING OF CLAIMS FILED BY DISTRICT OF COLUMBIA EMPLOYEES

See Pub. L. 93–198, title II, § 204(e), Dec. 24, 1973, 87 Stat. 783, set out as a note under section 8101 of this title.

§ 8146. Administration for the Panama Canal Commission and The Alaska Railroad

(a) The President, from time to time, may transfer the administration of this subchapter—

(1) so far as employees of the Panama Canal Commission are concerned to the Commission; and

(2) so far as employees of The Alaska Railroad are concerned to the general manager of The Alaska Railroad.

(b) When administration is transferred under subsection (a) of this section, the expenses incident to physical examinations which are payable under section 8123 of this title shall be paid from appropriations for the Panama Canal Commission or for The Alaska Railroad, as the case may be, instead of from the Employees' Compensation Fund. The President may authorize the Panama Canal Commission and the general manager of The Alaska Railroad to pay the compensation provided by this subchapter, including medical, surgical, and hospital services and supplies under section 8103 of this title and the transportation and burial expenses under sections 8103 and 8134 of this title, from appropriations for the Panama Canal Commission and for The Alaska Railroad, and these appropriations shall be reimbursed for the payments by transfer of funds from the Employees' Compensation Fund.

(c) The President may authorize the Panama Canal Commission to waive, at its discretion, the making of the claim required by section 8121 of this title in the case of compensation to an employee of the Panama Canal Commission for temporary disability, either total or partial.

(d) When administration is transferred under subsection (a) of this section to the general manager of The Alaska Railroad, the Secretary of Labor is not divested of jurisdiction and a claimant is entitled to appeal from the decision of the general manager of The Alaska Railroad to the Secretary of Labor. The Secretary on receipt of an appeal shall, or on his own motion may, review the decision of the general manager of The Alaska Railroad, and in accordance with the facts found on review may proceed under section 8128 of this title. The Secretary shall provide the form and manner of taking an appeal.

(e) The same right of appeal exists with respect to claims filed by employees of the Panama Canal Commission or their dependents in case of death, as is provided with respect to the claims of other employees to whom this subchapter applies, under section 8149 of this title. The Employees' Compensation Appeals Board referred to by section 8149 of this title has jurisdiction, under regulations prescribed by the Secretary, over appeals relating to claims of the employees or their dependents.

(Pub. L. 89–554, Sept. 6, 1966, 80 Stat. 553; Pub. L. 96–70, title III, § 3302(e)(9), Sept. 27, 1979, 93 Stat. 498.)

HISTORICAL AND REVISION NOTES

Derivation	U.S. Code	Revised Statutes and Statutes at Large
....	5 U.S.C. 793 (1st 3 pars., less 2d sentence of 2d par.).	Sept. 7, 1916, ch. 458, § 42 (less 2d sentence of 2d par.), 39 Stat. 750. Apr. 6, 1938, ch. 79 "Sec. 42 (less 2d sentence of 2d par.)", 52 Stat. 200. Aug. 30, 1964, Pub. L. 88–508, 78 Stat. 666.

In subsection (a), the words "in which cases the words 'Secretary' and 'his' wherever they appear in sections 751–756, 757–781, 783–791, and 793 of this title shall, so far as necessary to give effect to such transfer, be read, 'Governor of the Canal Zone' or 'the general manager of The Alaska Railroad', as the case may be, and 'his'" are omitted as surplusage.

In subsection (b), the words "the Employees' Compensation Fund" are substituted for "appropriation for the work of the Secretary" in view of former section 771, which is carried into section 8123, which provides that all such expenses shall be paid from the Fund.

In subsections (b) and (c), the words "Canal Zone Government", "Panama Canal Company", and "Governor of the Canal Zone" are substituted for "Panama Canal", "Panama Railroad Company", and "Governor of the Panama Canal", respectively, on authority of the Act of Sept. 26, 1950, ch. 1049, § 2, 64 Stat. 1038.

In subsection (e), the words "of other employees to whom this subchapter applies" are substituted for "of other employees of the Federal Government" for clarity and in view of the provisions of section 8149. The words "Employees' Compensation Appeals Board" are substituted for "Appeals Board" to reflect the full title of the Board

Administration of this subchapter was transferred to the Secretary of Labor by section 1 of 1950 Reorg. Plan No. 19, 64 Stat. 1271 (see section 8145).

Standard changes are made to conform with the definitions applicable and the style of this title as outlined in the preface to the report.

AMENDMENTS

1979—Pub. L. 96–70, § 3302(e)(9)(A), substituted "Panama Canal Commission" for "Canal Zone" in section catchline.

Subsec. (a)(1). Pub. L. 96–70, § 3302(e)(9)(B), substituted "Panama Canal Commission are concerned to the Commission" for "Canal Zone Government and of the Panama Canal Company are concerned to the Governor of the Canal Zone".

Subsec. (b). Pub. L. 96–70, § 3302(e)(9)(C)–(E), substituted "Panama Canal Commission" for "Canal Zone Government" in two places and "Panama Canal Commission" for "Governor of the Canal Zone" and struck out "or from funds from the Panama Canal Company" after "The Alaska Railroad".

Subsec. (c). Pub. L. 96–70, § 3302(e)(9)(F), substituted "Panama Canal Commission" for "Governor of the Canal Zone" and "employee of the Panama Canal Commission" for "employee of the Canal Zone Government or the Panama Canal Company".

Subsec. (e). Pub. L. 96–70, § 3302(e)(9)(G), substituted "Panama Canal Commission" for "Canal Zone Government and of the Panama Canal Company".

EFFECTIVE DATE OF 1979 AMENDMENT

Amendment by Pub. L. 96–70 effective Oct. 1, 1979, see section 3304 of Pub. L. 96–70, set out as an Effective Date note under section 3601 of Title 22, Foreign Relations and Intercourse.

SECTION REFERRED TO IN OTHER SECTIONS

This section is referred to in section 8149 of this title.

§ 8146a. Cost-of-living adjustment of compensation

(a) Compensation payable on account of disability or death which occurred more than one year before March 1 of each year shall be annually increased on that date by the amount determined by the Secretary of Labor to represent the percent change in the price index published for December of the preceding year over the price index published for the December of the year prior to the preceding year, adjusted to the nearest one-tenth of 1 percent.

(b) The regular periodic compensation payments after adjustment under this section shall be fixed at the nearest dollar. However, the regular periodic compensation after adjustment shall reflect an increase of at least $1.

(c) This section shall be applicable to persons excluded by section 15 of the Federal Employees' Compensation Act Amendments of 1966 (Public Law 89–488) under the following statutes: Act of February 15, 1934 (48 Stat. 351); Act of June 26, 1936 (49 Stat. 2035); Act of April 8, 1935 (49 Stat. 115); Act of July 25, 1942 (56 Stat. 710); Public Law 84–955 (August 3, 1956); Public Law 77–784 (December 2, 1942); Public Law 84–879 (August 1, 1956); Public Law 80–896 (July 3, 1948); Act of September 8, 1959 (73 Stat. 469). Benefit payments to these persons shall initially be increased by the total percentage of the increases in the price index from the base month of July 1966, to the next most recent base month following the effective date of this subsection.

(Added Pub. L. 90–83, § 1(67)(A), Sept. 11, 1967, 81 Stat. 212; amended Pub. L. 93–416, §§ 21, 24, Sept. 7, 1974, 88 Stat. 1149, 1150; Pub. L. 96–499, title IV, § 421(a), Dec. 5, 1980, 94 Stat. 2608.)

HISTORICAL AND REVISION NOTES

Section of title 5	Source (U.S. Code)	Source (Statutes at Large)
8146a(a)	5 App.: 793a(a).	July 4, 1966, Pub. L. 89–488,
8146a(b)	5 App.: 793a(b).	§ 14 "Sec. 43(a), (b)", 80 Stat. 256.

In subsection (a), the words "After the month during which this section becomes effective," following "Each month," are omitted as executed and unnecessary. The words "Secretary of Labor" are substituted for "Secretary" on authority of section 40(i) of the Federal Employees' Compensation Act. In the second sentence, the words "latest base month" are substituted for "most recent base month."

So much of section 14 of Public Law 89–488 as redesignated section 43 of the Federal Employees' Compensation Act as section 44 is omitted as unnecessary in view of the codification of that act in title 5, United States Code.

REFERENCES IN TEXT

"Persons excluded by section 15 of the Federal Employees' Compensation Act Amendments of 1966", referred to in subsec. (c), means persons excluded by section 15 of Pub. L. 89–488, July 4, 1966, 80 Stat. 256, which was set out as a note under section 756 of former Title 5, Executive Departments and Government Officers and Employees, prior to the 1966 revision of Title 5 by Pub. L. 89–554. Such section 15 of the Federal Employees' Compensation Act Amendments of 1966 directed that benefit increases mandated by the Federal Employees' Compensation Act Amendments of 1966 not apply to employees unless such employees fell within the definition of "employees" in section 40(b) (1) or (2) of the

Federal Employees' Compensation Act [section 790(b)(1) or (2) of former Title 5]. As a result section 15 of the Federal Employees' Compensation Act Amendments of 1966 served to prohibit increases to persons to whom the benefits of the Federal Employees' Compensation Act had been extended over the years by Acts described in subsec. (c) as follows:

Act of February 15, 1934 (48 Stat. 351) which extended coverage to employees of the Federal Civil Works Administration and was classified to section 796 of former Title 5.

Act of June 26, 1936 (49 Stat. 2035) probably means Act of June 29, 1936 which extended coverage to certain W.W. I veterans and was set out as a note under section 134 of former Title 38, Pensions, Bonuses, and Veterans' Relief.

Act of April 8, 1935 (49 Stat. 115) which extended coverage to certain emergency relief personnel, is act April 8, 1935, ch. 48, 49 Stat. 115, which was enacted as legislation supplementary to the Federal Emergency Relief Act of 1933, was classified to sections 721 and 728 of Title 15, Commerce and Trade, and was omitted from the Code as temporary.

Act of July 25, 1942 (56 Stat. 710) which extended coverage to certain personnel of the War Relocation Authority, was set out as a note under section 796 of former Title 5, Executive Departments and Government Officers and Employees.

Public Law 84–955 (Aug. 3, 1956) which extended coverage to certain Civil Air Patrol personnel was set out as a note under section 760 of former Title 5.

Public Law 77–784 (December 2, 1942), which extended coverage to war risk hazards of certain employees of federal contractors, is act Dec. 2, 1942, ch. 668, 56 Stat. 1028, as amended, titles I and II of which are popularly known as the War Hazards Compensation Act, and is classified principally to chapter 12 (§ 1701 et seq.) of Title 42, The Public Health and Welfare. For complete classification of this Act to the Code, see Tables.

Public Law 84–879 (August 1, 1956), which extended coverage to certain members of the Reserve Officers Training Corps of the Army, Navy, and Air Force, was classified to section 802 of former Title 5, Executive Departments and Government Officers and Employees.

Public Law 80–896 (July 3, 1948), which extended coverage to certain persons entitled to war claims, is act July 3, 1948, ch. 826, 62 Stat. 1240, as amended, popularly known as the War Claims Act of 1948, which is classified generally to section 2001 et seq. of Title 50, Appendix, War and National Defense. For complete classification of this Act to the Code, see Short Title note set out under section 2001 of Title 50, Appendix, and Tables.

Act of September 8, 1959 (73 Stat. 469) which transferred from the Department of Commerce to the Department of Labor certain functions in respect to insurance benefits and disability payments to seamen for W.W. II service-connected injuries, death, or disability, was not classified to the Code.

AMENDMENTS

1980—Subsec. (a). Pub. L. 96–499 substituted "Compensation" for "Each month the Secretary of Labor shall determine the percent change in the price index. Effective the first day of the month which begins after the price index change equals a rise of at least 3 percent for 3 consecutive months over the price index for the latest base month, compensation", "March 1 of each year shall be annually increased" for "that first day shall be increased" and "amount determined by the Secretary of Labor to represent the percent change in the price index published for December of the preceding year over the price index published for the December of the year prior to the preceding year," for "percent rise in the price index (calculated on the highest level of the price index during the 3 consecutive months)".

1974—Subsec. (a). Pub. L. 93–416, § 21, substituted "Effective the first day of the month" for "Effective the first day of the third month".

Subsec. (b). Pub. L. 93–416, § 21, substituted "regular periodic compensation payments" for "monthly compensation".

Subsec. (c). Pub. L. 93–416, § 24, added subsec. (c).

EFFECTIVE DATE OF 1980 AMENDMENT

For effective date of amendment by Pub. L. 96–499, see section 422 of Pub. L. 96–499, set out as a note under section 8101 of this title.

EFFECTIVE DATE OF 1974 AMENDMENT

Amendment by Pub. L. 93–416 applicable to cases where injury or death occurred prior to Sept. 7, 1974, but only to the period beginning on or after Sept. 7, 1974, see section 28(a) of Pub. L. 93–416, set out as a note under section 8101 of this title.

PERSONNEL NOT AFFECTED BY COST-OF-LIVING ADJUSTMENT

Increases authorized by this section not applicable to employees and individuals not within the definition of "employee" in section 8101(1)(A), (B), or (D) of this title, members of the Metropolitan Police or the Fire Department of the District of Columbia who are pensioned or pensionable under sections 521 to 535 of title 4, District of Columbia Code, or members of a uniformed service, see section 7 of Pub. L. 90–83, set out as a note under section 8103 of this title.

SECTION REFERRED TO IN OTHER SECTIONS

This section is referred to in section 8133 of this title; title 22 section 3715a.

§ 8147. Employees' Compensation Fund

(a) There is in the Treasury of the United States the Employees' Compensation Fund which consists of sums that Congress, from time to time, may appropriate for or transfer to it, and amounts that otherwise accrue to it under this subchapter or other statute. The Fund is available without time limit for the payment of compensation and other benefits and expenses, except administrative expenses, authorized by this subchapter or any extension or application thereof, except as otherwise provided by this subchapter or other statute. The Secretary of Labor shall submit annually to the Office of Management and Budget estimates of appropriations necessary for the maintenance of the Fund. For the purpose of this subsection, "administrative expenses" does not include expenses for legal services performed by or for the Secretary under sections 8131 and 8132 of this title.

(b) Before August 15 of each year, the Secretary shall furnish to each agency and instrumentality of the United States having an employee who is or may be entitled to compensation benefits under this subchapter or any extension or application thereof a statement showing the total cost of benefits and other payments made from the Employees' Compensation Fund during the preceding July 1 through June 30 expense period on account of the injury or death of employees or individuals under the jurisdiction of the agency or instrumentality. Each agency and instrumentality shall include in its annual budget estimates for the fiscal year beginning in the next calendar year a request for an appropriation in an amount equal to the costs. Sums appropriated pursuant to the request shall be deposited in the Treasury to the credit of the Fund within 30 days after they are

available. An agency or instrumentality not dependent on an annual appropriation shall make the deposit required by this subsection from funds under its control during the first fifteen days of October following the furnishing of the statement. If an agency or instrumentality (or part or function thereof) is transferred to another agency or instrumentality, the cost of compensation benefits and other expenses paid from the Fund on account of the injury or death of employees of the transferred agency or instrumentality (or part or function) shall be included in costs of the receiving agency or instrumentality.

(c) In addition to the contributions for the maintenance of the Employees' Compensation Fund required by this section, the United States Postal Service, or a mixed ownership corporation as defined by section 9101(2) of title 31, or any other corporation or agency or instrumentality (or activity thereof) which is required by statute to submit an annual budget pursuant to or as provided by chapter 91 of title 31, shall pay an additional amount for its fair share of the cost of administration of this subchapter as determined by the Secretary. With respect to these corporations, agencies, and instrumentalities, the charges billed by the Secretary under this section shall include an additional amount for these costs, which shall be paid into the Treasury as miscellaneous receipts from the sources authorized and in the manner otherwise provided by this section.

(Pub. L. 89–554, Sept. 6, 1966, 80 Stat. 554; Pub. L. 90–83, § 1(68), Sept. 11, 1967, 81 Stat. 213; Pub. L. 93–416, §§ 25, 26, Sept. 7, 1974, 88 Stat. 1150; Pub. L. 94–273, § 42, Apr. 21, 1976, 90 Stat. 381; Pub. L. 97–258, § 3(a)(17), Sept. 13, 1982, 96 Stat. 1063.)

HISTORICAL AND REVISION NOTES
1966 ACT

Derivation	U.S. Code	Revised Statutes and Statutes at Large
....	5 U.S.C. 785.	Sept. 7, 1916, ch. 458, § 35, 39 Stat. 749. Sept. 12, 1950, ch. 946, § 301(92), 64 Stat. 844. Sept. 13, 1960, Pub. L. 86–767, § 209, 74 Stat. 909.

In subsection (b), the words "each agency and instrumentality of the United States" are substituted for "each executive department and each agency or instrumentality of the United States or other establishment". The words "(hereinafter called 'agency')" are omitted as unnecessary because "agency or instrumentality" is substituted for "agency" in the remainder of this subsection and in subsection (c). The words "occurring after December 1, 1960" are omitted as executed.

Standard changes are made to conform with the definitions applicable and the style of this title as outlined in the preface to the report.

1967 ACT

Section of title 5	Source (U.S. Code)	Source (Statutes at Large)
8147(a)	5 App.: 785(d).	July 4, 1966, Pub. L. 89–488, § 10(c), 80 Stat. 255.

The word "performed" is substituted for "rendered" to conform to the style of title 5. The words "sections 8131 and 8132 of this title" are substituted for "sections 26 and 27" to reflect the codification of those sections in title 5.

AMENDMENTS

1982—Subsec. (c). Pub. L. 97–258 substituted "section 9101(2)" for "section 856", and "chapter 91" for "sections 841–869".

1976—Subsec. (b). Pub. L. 94–273 inserted "during the first fifteen days of October following the furnishing of the statement" after "its control" and substituted "July 1 through June 30 expense period" for "fiscal year" and "the fiscal year beginning in the next calendar year" for "the next fiscal year".

1974—Subsec. (a). Pub. L. 93–416, § 26, substituted "Office of Management and Budget" for "Bureau of the Budget".

Subsec. (c). Pub. L. 93–416, § 25, inserted reference to the United States Postal Service.

EFFECTIVE DATE OF 1974 AMENDMENT

Amendment by section 25 of Pub. L. 93–416 applicable to cases where injury or death occurred prior to Sept. 7, 1974, but only to a period beginning on or after Sept. 7, 1974, see section 28(a) of Pub. L. 93–416, set out as a note under section 8101 of this title.

Amendment by section 26 of Pub. L. 93–416 effective Sept. 7, 1974, and applicable to any death or injury occurring on or after Sept. 7, 1974, see section 28(a) of Pub. L. 93–416, set out as a note under section 8101 of this title.

GOVERNMENT PRINTING OFFICE PAYMENT OF COST OF ADMINISTRATION

Pub. L. 105–275, title III, § 313, Oct. 21, 1998, 112 Stat. 2460, provided that: "For purposes of section 8147 of title 5, United States Code, the Government Printing Office is not considered an agency which is required by statute to submit an annual budget pursuant to or as provided by chapter 91 of title 31, United States Code, and is not required to pay an additional amount for the cost of administration."

FISCAL YEAR 1994 PROHIBITION ON PAYMENTS TO INDIVIDUALS CONVICTED OF ISSUING FALSE STATEMENTS OR FRAUD

Pub. L. 103–112, title I, § 102, Oct. 21, 1993, 107 Stat. 1089, Department of Labor Appropriation Act, 1994, provided that: "None of the funds in the Employees' Compensation Fund under 5 U.S.C. 8147 shall be expended for payment of compensation, benefits, and expenses to any individual convicted of a violation of 18 U.S.C. 1920, or of any felony fraud related to the application for or receipt of benefits under subchapters I or III of chapter 81 of title 5, United States Code."

DEPOSIT INTO FUND BETWEEN JULY 1, AND JULY 15, 1976, OF SPECIFIED PART OF AUGUST 15, 1975, STATEMENT

Pub. L. 94–274, title I, § 120, Apr. 21, 1976, 90 Stat. 389, provided that for the purposes of 5 U.S.C. 8147(b), each agency and instrumentality of the United States dependent upon an annual appropriation and having an employee who is or may be entitled to compensation benefits under this subchapter or any extension or application thereof shall deposit in the Treasury to the credit of the Employees' Compensation Fund, no later than July 15, 1976, but no earlier than July 1, 1976, 25 per centum of the amount stated in the August 15, 1975, statement.

PERSONNEL NOT AFFECTED BY 1967 INCREASE

Increases authorized under amendment by section 1(71) of Pub. L. 90–83 not applicable to specified personnel, see section 7 of Pub. L. 90–83, set out as a note under section 8103 of this title.

SECTION REFERRED TO IN OTHER SECTIONS

This section is referred to in title 2 section 95d; title 39 section 2003; title 42 sections 1701, 1704, 1705; title 49 section 49104.

§ 8148. Forfeiture of benefits by convicted felons

(a) Any individual convicted of a violation of section 1920 of title 18, or any other Federal or State criminal statute relating to fraud in the application for or receipt of any benefit under this subchapter or subchapter III of this chapter, shall forfeit (as of the date of such conviction) any entitlement to any benefit such individual would otherwise be entitled to under this subchapter or subchapter III for any injury occurring on or before the date of such conviction. Such forfeiture shall be in addition to any action the Secretary may take under section 8106 or 8129.

(b)(1) Notwithstanding any other provision of this chapter (except as provided under paragraph (3)), no benefits under this subchapter or subchapter III of this chapter shall be paid or provided to any individual during any period during which such individual is confined in a jail, prison, or other penal institution or correctional facility, pursuant to that individual's conviction of an offense that constituted a felony under applicable law.

(2) Such individual shall not be entitled to receive the benefits forfeited during the period of incarceration under paragraph (1), after such period of incarceration ends.

(3) If an individual has one or more dependents as defined under section 8110(a), the Secretary of Labor may, during the period of incarceration, pay to such dependents a percentage of the benefits that would have been payable to such individual computed according to the percentages set forth in section 8133(a)(1) through (5).

(c) Notwithstanding the provision of section 552a of this title, or any other provision of Federal or State law, any agency of the United States Government or of any State (or political subdivision thereof) shall make available to the Secretary of Labor, upon written request, the names and Social Security account numbers of individuals who are confined in a jail, prison, or other penal institution or correctional facility under the jurisdiction of such agency, pursuant to such individuals' conviction of an offense that constituted a felony under applicable law, which the Secretary of Labor may require to carry out the provisions of this section.

(Added Pub. L. 103–333, title I, § 101(a)(1), Sept. 30, 1994, 108 Stat. 2546; amended Pub. L. 105–247, § 1, Oct. 9, 1998, 112 Stat. 1863.)

PRIOR PROVISIONS

A prior section 8148, Pub. L. 89–554, Sept. 6, 1966, 80 Stat. 555, provided for a report to Congress by Secretary of Labor at beginning of each regular session covering work for preceding fiscal year under this subchapter, prior to repeal by Pub. L. 90–83, § 1(69), Sept. 11, 1967, 81 Stat. 213.

AMENDMENTS

1998—Subsec. (a). Pub. L. 105–247 substituted "or receipt" for "a receipt".

EFFECTIVE DATE

Section 101(c) of Pub. L. 103–333 provided that: "The amendments made by this section [enacting this section and amending section 1920 of Title 18, Crimes and Criminal Procedure] shall take effect on the date of the enactment of this Act [Sept. 30, 1994]. The amendments made by subsection (a) [enacting this section] shall apply to claims filed before, on, or after the date of enactment of this Act, and shall apply only to individuals convicted after such date of enactment.''

§ 8149. Regulations

The Secretary of Labor may prescribe rules and regulations necessary for the administration and enforcement of this subchapter including rules and regulations for the conduct of hearings under section 8124 of this title. The rules and regulations shall provide for an Employee's Compensation Appeals Board of three individuals designated or appointed by the Secretary with authority to hear and, subject to applicable law and the rules and regulations of the Secretary, make final decisions on appeals taken from determinations and awards with respect to claims of employees. In adjudicating claims under section 8146 of this title, the Secretary may determine the nature and extent of the proof and evidence required to establish the right to benefits under this subchapter without regard to the date of injury or death for which claim is made.

(Pub. L. 89–554, Sept. 6, 1966, 80 Stat. 555; Pub. L. 90–83, § 1(71), Sept. 11, 1967, 81 Stat. 213.)

HISTORICAL AND REVISION NOTES
1966 ACT

Derivation	U.S. Code	Revised Statutes and Statutes at Large
....	5 U.S.C. 783 (less last 9 words).	Sept. 7, 1916, ch. 458, § 32 (less last 9 words), 39 Stat. 749.
....	[Uncodified].	1946 Reorg. Plan No. 2, § 3 (2d sentence), eff. July 16, 1946, 60 Stat. 1095.
....	[Uncodified].	1950 Reorg. Plan No. 19, § 2, eff. May 24, 1950, 64 Stat. 1272.

The words "administration and" are added for clarity.

Administration of this subchapter was transferred to the Secretary of Labor by section 1 of 1950 Reorg. Plan No. 19, 64 Stat. 1271 (see section 8145).

The first sentence of section 2 of 1950 Reorg. Plan No. 19 is omitted as executed. The word "employees" is coextensive with and substituted for "employees of the Federal Government or of the District of Columbia" in view of the definition of "employee" in section 8101.

Standard changes are made to conform with the definitions applicable and the style of this title as outlined in the preface to the report.

1967 ACT

Section of title 5	Source (U.S. Code)	Source (Statutes at Large)
8149	5 App.: 783.	July 4, 1966, Pub. L. 89–488, §§ 11(a), 12, 80 Stat. 255.

In the first sentence, the words "section 8124 of this title" are substituted for "section 36" to reflect the codification of that section in title 5, United States Code.

In the second sentence, the word "adjudicating" is substituted for "in the adjudication of". The words "section 8146 of this title" and "this subchapter" are substituted for "section 42 of this Act" and "this Act", respectively, to reflect the codification of the Federal Employees' Compensation Act in title 5, United States Code.

PERSONNEL NOT AFFECTED BY 1967 INCREASE

Increases authorized under amendment by section 1(71) of Pub. L. 90–83 not applicable to specified personnel, see section 7 of Pub. L. 90–83, set out as a note under section 8103 of this title.

SECTION REFERRED TO IN OTHER SECTIONS

This section is referred to in section 8146 of this title.

§ 8150. Effect on other statutes

(a) This subchapter does not affect the maritime rights and remedies of a master or member of the crew of a vessel.

(b) Section 8141 of this title and section 9441 of title 10 do not confer military or veteran status on any individual.

(Pub. L. 89–554, Sept. 6, 1966, 80 Stat. 555.)

HISTORICAL AND REVISION NOTES

Derivation	U.S. Code	Revised Statutes and Statutes at Large
(a)	5 U.S.C. 791–4(b).	Oct. 14, 1949, ch. 691, § 305(b), 63 Stat. 868.
(b)	5 U.S.C. 803a.	Aug. 3, 1956, ch. 926, § 1 "Sec. 4", 70 Stat. 981.

Standard changes are made to conform with the definitions applicable and the style of this title as outlined in the preface to the report.

§ 8151. Civil service retention rights

(a) In the event the individual resumes employment with the Federal Government, the entire time during which the employee was receiving compensation under this chapter shall be credited to the employee for the purposes of within-grade step increases, retention purposes, and other rights and benefits based upon length of service.

(b) Under regulations issued by the Office of Personnel Management—

(1) the department or agency which was the last employer shall immediately and unconditionally accord the employee, if the injury or disability has been overcome within one year after the date of commencement of compensation or from the time compensable disability recurs if the recurrence begins after the injured employee resumes regular full-time employment with the United States, the right to resume his former or an equivalent position, as well as all other attendant rights which the employee would have had, or acquired, in his former position had he not been injured or disabled, including the rights to tenure, promotion, and safeguards in reductions-in-force procedures, and

(2) the department or agency which was the last employer shall, if the injury or disability is overcome within a period of more than one year after the date of commencement of compensation, make all reasonable efforts to place, and accord priority to placing, the employee in his former or equivalent position within such department or agency, or within any other department or agency.

(Added Pub. L. 93–416, § 22, Sept. 7, 1974, 88 Stat. 1149; amended Pub. L. 95–454, title IX, § 906(a)(2), Oct. 13, 1978, 92 Stat. 1224.)

AMENDMENTS

1978—Subsec. (b). Pub. L. 95–454 substituted "Office of Personnel Management" for "Civil Service Commission".

EFFECTIVE DATE OF 1978 AMENDMENT

Amendment by Pub. L. 95–454 effective 90 days after Oct. 13, 1978, see section 907 of Pub. L. 95–454, set out as a note under section 1101 of this title.

EFFECTIVE DATE

Section applicable to cases where injury or death occurred prior to Sept. 7, 1974, but only to a period beginning on or after Sept. 7, 1974, see section 28(a) of Pub. L. 93–416, set out as an Effective Date of 1974 Amendment note under section 8101 of this title.

§ 8152. Annual report

The Secretary of Labor shall, at the end of each fiscal year, prepare a report with respect to the administration of this chapter. Such report shall be submitted to Congress in accordance with the requirement with respect to submission under section 42 of the Longshore[1] Harbor Workers' Compensation Act (33 U.S.C. 942).

(Added Pub. L. 104–66, title I, § 1102(b)(3)(A), Dec. 21, 1995, 109 Stat. 723.)

SUBCHAPTER II—EMPLOYEES OF NONAPPROPRIATED FUND INSTRUMENTALITIES

SUBCHAPTER REFERRED TO IN OTHER SECTIONS

This subchapter is referred to in title 10 section 1588.

§ 8171. Compensation for work injuries; generally

(a) The Longshore and Harbor Workers' Compensation Act (33 U.S.C. 901 et seq.) applies with respect to disability or death resulting from injury, as defined by section 2(2) of such Act (33 U.S.C. 902(2)), occurring to an employee of a nonappropriated fund instrumentality described by section 2105(c) of this title, or to a volunteer providing such an instrumentality with services accepted under section 1588 of title 10, who is—

　(1) a United States citizen or a permanent resident of the United States or a territory or possession of the United States employed outside the continental United States; or

　(2) employed inside the continental United States.

However, that part of section 3(a) of such Act (33 U.S.C. 903(a)) which follows the second comma does not apply to such an employee.

(b) For the purpose of this subchapter, the term "employer" in section 2(4) of the Longshore and Harbor Workers' Compensation Act (33 U.S.C. 902(4)) includes the nonappropriated fund instrumentalities described by section 2105(c) of this title.

(c) The Secretary of Labor may—

　(1) extend compensation districts established under section 39(b) of the Longshore and Harbor Workers' Compensation Act (33 U.S.C. 939(b)), or establish new districts to include the areas outside the continental United States; and

　(2) assign to each district one or more deputy commissioners as the Secretary considers advisable.

---

[1] So in original. Probably should be "Longshore and".

(d) Judicial proceedings under sections 18 and 21 of the Longshore and Harbor Workers' Compensation Act (33 U.S.C. 918 and 921) with respect to an injury or death occurring outside the continental United States shall be instituted in the district court within the territorial jurisdiction of which is located the office of the deputy commissioner having jurisdiction with respect to the injury or death.

(Pub. L. 89–554, Sept. 6, 1966, 80 Stat. 555; Pub. L. 103–337, div. A, title X, §§ 1061(c), 1070(d)(8)(A), Oct. 5, 1994, 108 Stat. 2847, 2858; Pub. L. 104–106, div. A, title XV, § 1505(b)(1), Feb. 10, 1996, 110 Stat. 514.)

HISTORICAL AND REVISION NOTES

Derivation	U.S. Code	Revised Statutes and Statutes at Large
....	5 U.S.C. 150k–1(a).	June 19, 1952, ch. 444, § 2, 66 Stat. 139. July 18, 1958, Pub. L. 85–538, § 1 "Sec. 2(a)", 72 Stat. 397.

In subsection (a), the word "civilian" is omitted as unnecessary as the definition of "employee" in section 2105 includes only civilians.

In subsection (d), the reference to "the United States District Court for the District of Columbia" is omitted as included in the words "district court".

Standard changes are made to conform with the definitions applicable and the style of this title as outlined in the preface to the report.

REFERENCES IN TEXT

The Longshore and Harbor Workers' Compensation Act, referred to in subsec. (a), is act Mar. 4, 1927, ch. 509, 44 Stat. 1424, as amended, which is classified generally to chapter 18 (§ 901 et seq.) of Title 33, Navigation and Navigable Waters. For complete classification of this Act to the Code, see section 901 of Title 33 and Tables.

AMENDMENTS

1996—Subsec. (a). Pub. L. 104–106, § 1505(b)(1)(A), substituted "903(a))" for "903(3))" in concluding provisions.

Subsec. (c)(1). Pub. L. 104–106, § 1505(b)(1)(B), inserted "section" before "39(b)".

Subsec. (d). Pub. L. 104–106, § 1505(b)(1)(C), substituted "(33 U.S.C. 918 and 921)" for "(33 U.S.C. 18 and 21, respectively)".

1994—Subsec. (a). Pub. L. 103–337, § 1070(d)(8)(A)(i)(III), substituted "section 3(a) of such Act (33 U.S.C. 903(3)) which follows the second comma" for "section 903(a) of title 33 which follows the first comma" in second sentence.

Pub. L. 103–337, § 1070(d)(8)(A)(i)(I), (II), substituted "The Longshore and Harbor Workers' Compensation Act (33 U.S.C. 901 et seq.)" for "Chapter 18 of title 33" and "section 2(2) of such Act (33 U.S.C. 902(2))" for "section 902(2) of title 33", in introductory provisions.

Pub. L. 103–337, § 1061(c), inserted ", or to a volunteer providing such an instrumentality with services accepted under section 1588 of title 10," after "described by section 2105(c) of this title" in introductory provisions.

Subsec. (b). Pub. L. 103–337, § 1070(d)(8)(A)(ii), substituted "section 2(4) of the Longshore and Harbor Workers' Compensation Act (33 U.S.C. 902(4))" for "section 902(4) of title 33".

Subsec. (c)(1). Pub. L. 103–337, § 1070(d)(8)(A)(iii), substituted "39(b) of the Longshore and Harbor Workers' Compensation Act (33 U.S.C. 939(b))" for "section 939(b) of title 33".

Subsec. (d). Pub. L. 103–337, § 1070(d)(8)(A)(iv), substituted "sections 18 and 21 of the Longshore and Harbor Workers' Compensation Act (33 U.S.C. 18 and 21, respectively)" for "sections 918 and 921 of title 33".

SECTION REFERRED TO IN OTHER SECTIONS

This section is referred to in section 8173 of this title.

§ 8172. Employees not citizens or residents of the United States

In case of disability or death, resulting from injury, as defined by section 2(2) of the Longshore and Harbor Workers' Compensation Act (33 U.S.C. 902(2)), occurring to an employee of a nonappropriated fund instrumentality described by section 2105(c) of this title who is—

(1) not a citizen or permanent resident of the United States or a territory or possession of the United States; and

(2) employed outside the continental United States;

compensation shall be provided in accordance with regulations prescribed by the Secretary of the military department concerned and approved by the Secretary of Defense or regulations prescribed by the Secretary of Transportation, as the case may be.

(Pub. L. 89–554, Sept. 6, 1966, 80 Stat. 556; Pub. L. 103–272, § 4(b)(3), July 5, 1994, 108 Stat. 1361; Pub. L. 103–337, div. A, title X, § 1070(d)(8)(B), Oct. 5, 1994, 108 Stat. 2859; Pub. L. 104–106, div. A, title XV, § 1505(b)(2), Feb. 10, 1996, 110 Stat. 514.)

HISTORICAL AND REVISION NOTES

Derivation	U.S. Code	Revised Statutes and Statutes at Large
....	5 U.S.C. 150k–1(b).	July 18, 1958, Pub. L. 85–538, § 1 "Sec. 2(b)", 72 Stat. 397.

Standard changes are made to conform with the definitions applicable and the style of this title as outlined in the preface to the report.

AMENDMENTS

1996—Pub. L. 104–106 substituted "(33 U.S.C. 902(2))" for "(33 U.S.C. 2(2))" in introductory provisions.

1994—Pub. L. 103–337 substituted "section 2(2) of the Longshore and Harbor Workers' Compensation Act (33 U.S.C. 2(2))" for "section 902(2) of title 33" in introductory provisions.

Pub. L. 103–272 substituted "Secretary of Transportation" for "Secretary of the Treasury" in concluding provisions.

SECTION REFERRED TO IN OTHER SECTIONS

This section is referred to in section 8173 of this title.

§ 8173. Liability under this subchapter exclusive

The liability of the United States or of a nonappropriated fund instrumentality described by section 2105(c) of this title, with respect to the disability or death resulting from injury, as defined by section 2(2) of the Longshore and Harbor Workers' Compensation Act (33 U.S.C. 902(2)), of an employee referred to by sections 8171 and 8172 of this title, shall be determined as provided by this subchapter. This liability is exclusive and instead of all other liability of the United States or the instrumentality to the employee, his legal representative, spouse, dependents, next of kin, and any other person otherwise entitled to recover damages from the United States or the instrumentality because of the disability or death in a direct judicial proceeding, in a civil action, or in admiralty, or by an administrative or judicial proceeding under a workmen's compensation statute or under a Federal tort liability statute.

(Pub. L. 89–554, Sept. 6, 1966, 80 Stat. 556; Pub. L. 103–337, div. A, title X, § 1070(d)(8)(B), Oct. 5, 1994, 108 Stat. 2859; Pub. L. 104–106, div. A, title XV, § 1505(b)(2), Feb. 10, 1996, 110 Stat. 514.)

HISTORICAL AND REVISION NOTES

Derivation	U.S. Code	Revised Statutes and Statutes at Large
....	5 U.S.C. 150k–1(c).	July 18, 1958, Pub. L. 85–538, § 1 "Sec. 2(c)", 72 Stat. 397.

Standard changes are made to conform with the definitions applicable and the style of this title as outlined in the preface to the report.

AMENDMENTS

1996—Pub. L. 104–106 substituted "(33 U.S.C. 902(2))" for "(33 U.S.C. 2(2))".

1994—Pub. L. 103–337 substituted "section 2(2) of the Longshore and Harbor Workers' Compensation Act (33 U.S.C. 2(2))" for "section 902(2) of title 33".

SUBCHAPTER III—LAW ENFORCEMENT OFFICERS NOT EMPLOYED BY THE UNITED STATES

SUBCHAPTER REFERRED TO IN OTHER SECTIONS

This subchapter is referred to in section 8148 of this title; title 16 section 742l; title 18 section 1920; title 25 section 2804.

§ 8191. Determination of eligibility

The benefits of this subchapter are available as provided in this subchapter to eligible law enforcement officers (referred to in this subchapter as "eligible officers") and their survivors. For the purposes of this subchapter, an eligible officer is any person who is determined by the Secretary of Labor in his discretion to have been on any given occasion—

(1) a law enforcement officer and to have been engaged on that occasion in the apprehension or attempted apprehension of any person—

(A) for the commission of a crime against the United States, or

(B) who at that time was sought by a law enforcement authority of the United States for the commission of a crime against the United States, or

(C) who at that time was sought as a material witness in a criminal proceeding instituted by the United States; or

(2) a law enforcement officer and to have been engaged on that occasion in protecting or guarding a person held for the commission of a crime against the United States or as a material witness in connection with such a crime; or

(3) a law enforcement officer and to have been engaged on that occasion in the lawful prevention of, or lawful attempt to prevent, the commission of a crime against the United States;

and to have been on that occasion not an employee as defined in section 8101(1), and to have sustained on that occasion a personal injury for which the United States would be required under subchapter I of this chapter to pay compensation if he had been on that occasion such an employee engaged in the performance of his duty. No person otherwise eligible to receive a benefit under this subchapter because of the disability or death of an eligible officer shall be barred from the receipt of such benefit because the person apprehended or attempted to be apprehended by such officer was then sought for the commission of a crime against a sovereignty other than the United States.

(Added Pub. L. 90–291, § 1(a), Apr. 19, 1968, 82 Stat. 98; amended Pub. L. 90–623, § 1(20), Oct. 22, 1968, 82 Stat. 1313.)

AMENDMENTS

1968—Pub. L. 90–623 substituted "For the purposes of this subchapter" for "For the purposes of this Act".

EFFECTIVE DATE OF 1968 AMENDMENT

Amendment by Pub. L. 90–623 intended to restate without substantive change the law in effect on Oct. 22, 1968, see section 6 of Pub. L. 90–623, set out as a note under section 5334 of this title.

EFFECTIVE DATE

Section 2 of Pub. L. 90–291 provided that: "The amendments made by section 1 of this Act [enacting this section and sections 8192 and 8193 of this title] are effective only with respect to personal injuries sustained on or after the date of enactment of this Act [Apr. 19, 1968]."

SECTION REFERRED TO IN OTHER SECTIONS

This section is referred to in section 8193 of this title; title 42 section 3796.

§ 8192. Benefits

(a) BENEFITS IN EVENT OF INJURY.—The Secretary of Labor shall furnish to any eligible officer the benefits to which he would have been entitled under subchapter I of this chapter if, on the occasion giving rise to his eligibility, he had been an employee as defined in section 8101(1) engaged in the performance of his duty, reduced or adjusted as the Secretary of Labor in his discretion may deem appropriate to reflect comparable benefits, if any, received by the officer (or which he would have been entitled to receive but for this subchapter) by virtue of his actual employment on that occasion. When an enforcement officer has contributed to a disability compensation fund, the reduction of Federal benefits provided for in this subsection is to be limited to the amount of the State or local government benefits which bears the same proportion to the full amount of such benefits as the cost or contribution paid by the State or local government bears to the cost of disability coverage for the individual officer.

(b) BENEFITS IN EVENT OF DEATH.—The Secretary of Labor shall pay to any survivor of an eligible officer the difference, as determined by the Secretary in his discretion, between the benefits to which that survivor would be entitled if the officer had been an employee as defined in section 8101(1) engaged in the performance of his duty on the occasion giving rise to his eligibility, and the comparable benefits, if any, received by the survivor (or which that survivor would have been entitled to receive but for this

subchapter) by virtue of the officer's actual employment on that occasion. When an enforcement officer has contributed to a survivor's benefit fund, the reduction of Federal benefits provided for in this subsection is to be limited to the amount of the State or local government benefits which bears the same proportion to the full amount of such benefits as the cost or contribution paid by the State or local government bears to the cost of survivor's benefits coverage for the individual officer.

(Added Pub. L. 90–291, § 1(a), Apr. 19, 1968, 82 Stat. 99.)

EFFECTIVE DATE

Section effective only with respect to personal injuries sustained on or after Apr. 19, 1968, see section 2 of Pub. L. 90–291, set out as a note under section 8191 of this title.

§ 8193. Administration

(a) DEFINITIONS AND RULES OF CONSTRUCTION.— For the purpose of this subchapter—

(1) The term "Attorney General" includes any person to whom the Attorney General has delegated any function pursuant to subsection (b) of this section.

(2) The term "Secretary of Labor" includes any person to whom the Secretary of Labor has delegated any function pursuant to subsection (b) of this section.

(b) DELEGATION.—

(1) The Attorney General may delegate to any division, officer, or employee of the Department of Justice any function conferred upon the Attorney General by this subchapter.

(2) The Secretary of Labor may delegate to any bureau, officer, or employee of the Department of Labor any function conferred upon the Secretary of Labor by this subchapter.

(c) APPLICATIONS.—An application for any benefit under this subchapter may be made only—

(1) to the Secretary of Labor

(2) by

(A) any eligible officer or survivor of an eligible officer,

(B) any guardian, personal representative, or other person legally authorized to act on behalf of an eligible officer, his estate, or any of his survivors, or

(C) any association of law enforcement officers which is acting on behalf of an eligible officer or any of his survivors;

(3) within five years after the injury or death; and

(4) in such form as the Secretary of Labor may require.

(d) CONSULTATION WITH ATTORNEY GENERAL AND OTHER AGENCIES.—The Secretary of Labor may refer any application received by him pursuant to this subchapter to the Attorney General for his assistance, comments and advice as to any determination required to be made pursuant to paragraph (1), (2), or (3) of section 8191. To insure that all Federal assistance under this subchapter is carried out in a coordinated manner, the Secretary of Labor is authorized to request any Federal department or agency to supply any statistics, data, or any other materials he deems necessary to carry out his functions under this subchapter. Each such department or agency is authorized to cooperate with the Secretary of Labor and, to the extent permitted by law, to furnish such materials to him.

(e) COOPERATION WITH STATE AGENCIES.—The Secretary of Labor shall cooperate fully with the appropriate State and local officials, and shall take all other practicable measures, to assure that the benefits of this subchapter are made available to eligible officers and their survivors with a minimum of delay and difficulty.

(f) APPROPRIATIONS.—There are authorized to be appropriated such sums as may be necessary to carry out this subchapter.

(Added Pub. L. 90–291, § 1(a), Apr. 19, 1968, 82 Stat. 99; amended Pub. L. 94–183, § 2(31), Dec. 31, 1975, 89 Stat. 1058.)

AMENDMENTS

1975—Subsec. (f). Pub. L. 94–183 redesignated subsec. (e), relating to appropriations, as subsec. (f).

EFFECTIVE DATE

Section effective only with respect to personal injuries sustained on or after Apr. 19, 1968, see section 2 of Pub. L. 90–291, set out as a note under section 8191 of this title.

CHAPTER 83—RETIREMENT

SUBCHAPTER I—GENERAL PROVISIONS

AMENDMENTS

1986—Pub. L. 99–335, title II, §§ 201(b)(2), 204(b)(1), 205(b), 206(a)(2), June 6, 1986, 100 Stat. 591–594, added items 8343a, 8349, 8350, and 8351.

CHAPTER REFERRED TO IN OTHER SECTIONS

This chapter is referred to in sections 3374, 5304, 5362, 8432c, 8468, 8473 of this title; title 15 section 4105; title 22 sections 2391, 3649, 3664, 3681, 3951, 4064, 4071c, 4606; title 24 section 225e; title 25 section 450i; title 26 section 6103; title 28 sections 178, 375, 611, 627, 996; title 31 section 732a; title 37 section 211; title 38 sections 7257, 7438, 7453, 7458; title 39 section 1005; title 42 sections 426, 2996d, 3035r, 10704; title 50 sections 403r, 403s, 2442.

SUBCHAPTER I—GENERAL PROVISIONS

§ 8301. Uniform retirement date

(a) Except as otherwise specifically provided by this title or other statute, retirement authorized by statute is effective on the first day of the month following the month in which retirement would otherwise be effective.

(b) Notwithstanding subsection (a) of this section, the rate of active or retired pay or allowance is computed as of the date retirement would have occurred but for subsection (a) of this section.

(Pub. L. 89–554, Sept. 6, 1966, 80 Stat. 557.)

HISTORICAL AND REVISION NOTES

Derivation	U.S. Code	Revised Statutes and Statutes at Large
....	5 U.S.C. 47a.	Apr. 23, 1930, ch. 209, § 1, 46 Stat. 253.

In subsection (a), the words "Except as otherwise specifically provided by this title or other statute" are added because of the statutes carried into subchapter III of chapter 83. The words "of Federal personnel of whatever class, civil, military, naval, judicial, legislative, or otherwise, and for whatever cause retired" are omitted as unnecessary. The words "and said first day of the month for retirements made after July 1, 1930, shall be for all purposes in lieu of such date for retirement as was on April 23, 1930, authorized" are omitted as executed.

Standard changes are made to conform with the definitions applicable and the style of this title as outlined in the preface to the report.

SECTION REFERRED TO IN OTHER SECTIONS

This section is referred to in title 10 sections 580, 1164, 1210, 1221, 1263, 1305, 1404, 12731.

SUBCHAPTER II—FORFEITURE OF ANNUITIES AND RETIRED PAY

SUBCHAPTER REFERRED TO IN OTHER SECTIONS

This subchapter is referred to in section 8432 of this title.

§ 8311. Definitions

For the purpose of this subchapter—
(1) "employee" means—
(A) an employee as defined by section 2105 of this title:

(B) a Member of Congress as defined by section 2106 of this title and a Delegate to Congress;

(C) a member or former member of a uniformed service; and

(D) an individual employed by the government of the District of Columbia;

(2) "annuity" means a retirement benefit, including a disability insurance benefit and a dependent's or survivor's benefit under subchapter II of chapter 7 of title 42, and a monthly annuity under section 228b or 228e of title 45, payable by an agency of the Government of the United States or the government of the District of Columbia on the basis of service as a civilian employee and other service which is creditable to an employee toward the benefit under the statute, regulation, or agreement which provides the benefit, but does not include—

(A) a benefit provided under statutes administered by the Department of Veterans Affairs;

(B) pay or compensation which may not be diminished under section 1 of Article III of the Constitution of the United States;

(C) that portion of a benefit payable under subchapter II of chapter 7 of title 42 which would be payable without taking into account, for any of the purposes of that subchapter, including determinations of periods of disability under section 416(i) of title 42, pay for services as an employee;

(D) monthly annuity awarded under section 228b or 228e of title 45 before September 26, 1961, whether or not computed under section 228c(e) of title 45;

(E) that portion of an annuity awarded under section 228b or 228e of title 45 after September 25, 1961, which would be payable without taking into account military service creditable under section 228c–1 of title 45;

(F) a retirement benefit, including a disability insurance benefit and a dependent's or survivor's benefit under subchapter II of chapter 7 of title 42, awarded before September 1, 1954, to an individual or his survivor or beneficiary, insofar as the individual, before September 1, 1954—

(i) was convicted of an offense named by subsection (b) of section 8312 of this title, to the extent provided by that subsection; or

(ii) violated section 8314 or 8315(a)(1) of this title; or

(G) a retirement benefit, including a disability insurance benefit and a dependent's or survivor's benefit under subchapter II of chapter 7 of title 42, awarded before September 26, 1961, to an individual or his survivor or beneficiary, insofar as the individual, before September 26, 1961—

(i) was convicted of an offense named by subsection (c) of section 8312 of this title, to the extent provided by that subsection; or

(ii) violated section 8315(a)(2) of this title; and

(3) "retired pay" means retired pay, retirement pay, retainer pay, or equivalent pay,

payable under a statute to a member or former member of a uniformed service, and an annuity payable to an eligible beneficiary of the member or former member under chapter 73 of title 10 or section 5 of the Uniformed Services Contingency Option Act of 1953 (67 Stat. 504), but does not include—

(A) a benefit provided under statutes administered by the Department of Veterans Affairs;

(B) retired pay, retirement pay, retainer pay, or equivalent pay, awarded before September 1, 1954, to an individual, insofar as the individual, before September 1, 1954—

(i) was convicted of an offense named by subsection (b) of section 8312 of this title, to the extent provided by that subsection; or

(ii) violated section 8314 or 8315(a)(1) of this title;

(C) retired pay, retirement pay, retainer pay, or equivalent pay, awarded before September 26, 1961, to an individual, insofar as the individual, before September 26, 1961—

(i) was convicted of an offense named by subsection (c) of section 8312 of this title, to the extent provided by that subsection; or

(ii) violated section 8315(a)(2) of this title; or

(D) an annuity payable to an eligible beneficiary of an individual under chapter 73 of title 10 or section 5 of the Uniformed Services Contingency Option Act of 1953 (67 Stat. 504), if the annuity was awarded to the beneficiary, or if retired pay was awarded to the individual, before September 26, 1961, insofar as the individual, on the basis of whose service the annuity was awarded, before September 26, 1961—

(i) was convicted of an offense named by section 8312 of this title, to the extent provided by that section; or

(ii) violated section 8314 or 8315 of this title.

(Pub. L. 89–554, Sept. 6, 1966, 80 Stat. 557; Pub. L. 102–54, § 13(b)(1), June 13, 1991, 105 Stat. 274.)

HISTORICAL AND REVISION NOTES

Derivation	U.S. Code	Revised Statutes and Statutes at Large
....	5 U.S.C. 2281.	Sept. 26, 1961, Pub. L. 87–299, § 1 "Sec. 10", 75 Stat. 646.

The words "and section 3282 of Title 18" are omitted as unnecessary.

In paragraph (1)(A), the words "an employee as defined by section 2105 of this title" are coextensive with and substituted for "an officer or employee in or under the legislative, executive, or judicial branch of the Government of the United States".

In paragraph (1)(B), the reference to "Resident Commissioner" is omitted as included in "Member of Congress" in view of the definition of "Member of Congress" in section 2106.

In paragraph (1)(C), the words "uniformed service" are coextensive with and substituted for "armed forces, the Coast and Geodetic Survey, or the Public Health Service" in view of the definition of "uniformed services" in section 2101.

In paragraph (3), the words "uniformed service" are coextensive with and substituted for "armed forces, the

Coast and Geodetic Survey, and the Public Health Service" in view of the definition of "uniformed services" in section 2101.

The definition of "armed forces" in former section 2281(4) is omitted as unnecessary in view of the definition of "armed forces" in section 2101.

Standard changes are made to conform with the definitions applicable and the style of this title as outlined in the preface to the report.

REFERENCES IN TEXT

Subchapter II of chapter 7 of title 42, referred to in par. (2), is classified to section 401 et seq. of Title 42, The Public Health and Welfare.

Sections 228b, 228c(e), 228c–1, and 228e of title 45, referred to in par. (2), are references to sections 2, 3(e), 4, and 5 of the Railroad Retirement Act of 1937. That Act was amended in its entirety and completely revised by Pub. L. 93–445, Oct. 16, 1974, 88 Stat. 1305. The Act, as thus amended and revised, was redesignated the Railroad Retirement Act of 1974, and is classified to subchapter IV (section 231 et. seq.) of chapter 9 of Title 45, Railroads.

Section 5 of the Uniformed Services Contingency Option Act of 1953 (67 Stat. 504), referred to in text, is covered by section 1438 of Title 10, Armed Forces.

AMENDMENTS

1991—Pars. (2)(A), (3)(A). Pub. L. 102–54 substituted "Department of Veterans Affairs" for "Veterans' Administration".

SECTION REFERRED TO IN OTHER SECTIONS

This section is referred to in sections 5531, 8312, 8313, 8314, 8315 of this title.

§ 8312. Conviction of certain offenses

(a) An individual, or his survivor or beneficiary, may not be paid annuity or retired pay on the basis of the service of the individual which is creditable toward the annuity or retired pay, subject to the exceptions in section 8311(2) and (3) of this title, if the individual—

(1) was convicted, before, on, or after September 1, 1954, of an offense named by subsection (b) of this section, to the extent provided by that subsection; or

(2) was convicted, before, on, or after September 26, 1961, of an offense named by subsection (c) of this section, to the extent provided by that subsection.

The prohibition on payment of annuity or retired pay applies—

(A) with respect to the offenses named by subsection (b) of this section, to the period after the date of the conviction or after September 1, 1954, whichever is later; and

(B) with respect to the offenses named by subsection (c) of this section, to the period after the date of conviction or after September 26, 1961, whichever is later.

(b) The following are the offenses to which subsection (a) of this section applies if the individual was convicted before, on, or after September 1, 1954:

(1) An offense within the purview of—

(A) section 792 (harboring or concealing persons), 793 (gathering, transmitting, or losing defense information), 794 (gathering or delivering defense information to aid foreign government), or 798 (disclosure of classified information), of chapter 37 (relating to espionage and censorship) of title 18;

(B) chapter 105 (relating to sabotage) of title 18;

(C) section 2381 (treason), 2382 (misprision of treason), 2383 (rebellion or insurrection), 2384 (seditious conspiracy), 2385 (advocating overthrow of government), 2387 (activities affecting armed forces generally), 2388 (activities affecting armed forces during war), 2389 (recruiting for service against United States), or 2390 (enlistment to serve against United States), of chapter 115 (relating to treason, sedition, and subversive activities) of title 18;

(D) section 10(b)(2), (3), or (4) of the Atomic Energy Act of 1946 (60 Stat. 766, 767), as in effect August 30, 1954;

(E) section 16(a) or (b) of the Atomic Energy Act of 1946 (60 Stat. 773), as in effect before August 30, 1954, insofar as the offense is committed with intent to injure the United States or with intent to secure an advantage to a foreign nation; or

(F) an earlier statute on which a statute named by subparagraph (A), (B), or (C) of this paragraph (1) is based.

(2) An offense within the purview of—

(A) article 104 (aiding the enemy), article 106 (spies), or article 106a (espionage) of the Uniform Code of Military Justice (chapter 47 of title 10) or an earlier article on which article 104 or article 106, as the case may be, is based; or

(B) a current article of the Uniform Code of Military Justice (or an earlier article on which the current article is based) not named by subparagraph (A) of this paragraph (2) on the basis of charges and specifications describing a violation of a statute named by paragraph (1), (3), or (4) of this subsection, if the executed sentence includes death, dishonorable discharge, or dismissal from the service, or if the defendant dies before execution of that sentence as finally approved.

(3) Perjury committed under the statutes of the United States or the District of Columbia—

(A) in falsely denying the commission of an act which constitutes an offense within the purview of—

(i) a statute named by paragraph (1) of this subsection; or

(ii) an article or statute named by paragraph (2) of this subsection insofar as the offense is within the purview of an article or statute named by paragraph (1) or (2) (A) of this subsection;

(B) in falsely testifying before a Federal grand jury, court of the United States, or court-martial with respect to his service as an employee in connection with a matter involving or relating to an interference with or endangerment of, or involving or relating to a plan or attempt to interfere with or endanger, the national security or defense of the United States; or

(C) in falsely testifying before a congressional committee in connection with a matter under inquiry before the congressional committee involving or relating to an interference with or endangerment of, or involving or relating to a plan or attempt to interfere with or endanger, the national security or defense of the United States.

(4) Subornation of perjury committed in connection with the false denial or false testimony of another individual as specified by paragraph (3) of this subsection.

(c) The following are the offenses to which subsection (a) of this section applies if the individual was convicted before, on, or after September 26, 1961:

(1) An offense within the purview of—

(A) section 2272 (violation of specific sections) or 2273 (violation of sections generally of chapter 23 of title 42) of title 42 insofar as the offense is committed with intent to injure the United States or with intent to secure an advantage to a foreign nation;

(B) section 2274 (communication of restricted data), 2275 (receipt of restricted data), or 2276 (tampering with restricted data) of title 42; or

(C) section 783 (conspiracy and communication or receipt of classified information) of title 50 or section 601 of the National Security Act of 1947 (50 U.S.C. 421) (relating to intelligence identities).

(2) An offense within the purview of a current article of the Uniform Code of Military Justice (chapter 47 of title 10) or an earlier article on which the current article is based, as the case may be, on the basis of charges and specifications describing a violation of a statute named by paragraph (1), (3), or (4) of this subsection, if the executed sentence includes death, dishonorable discharge, or dismissal from the service, or if the defendant dies before execution of that sentence as finally approved.

(3) Perjury committed under the statutes of the United States or the District of Columbia in falsely denying the commission of an act which constitutes an offense within the purview of a statute named by paragraph (1) of this subsection.

(4) Subornation of perjury committed in connection with the false denial of another individual as specified by paragraph (3) of this subsection.

(d)(1) For purposes of subsections (b)(1) and (c)(1), an offense within the meaning of such subsections is established if the Attorney General of the United States certifies to the agency administering the annuity or retired pay concerned—

(A) that an individual subject to this chapter has been convicted by an impartial court of appropriate jurisdiction within a foreign country in circumstances in which the conduct violates the provisions of law enumerated in subsections (b)(1) and (c)(1), or would violate such provisions had such conduct taken place within the United States, and that such conviction is not being appealed or that final action has been taken on such appeal;

(B) that such conviction was obtained in accordance with procedures that provided the defendant due process rights comparable to

such rights provided by the United States Constitution, and such conviction was based upon evidence which would have been admissible in the courts of the United States; and

(C) that such conviction occurred after the date of enactment of this subsection.

(2) Any certification made pursuant to this subsection shall be subject to review by the United States Court of Claims based upon application of the individual concerned, or his or her attorney, alleging that any of the conditions set forth in subparagraphs[1] (A), (B), or (C) of paragraph (1), as certified by the Attorney General, have not been satisfied in his or her particular circumstances. Should the court determine that any of these conditions has not been satisfied in such case, the court shall order any annuity or retirement benefit to which the person concerned is entitled to be restored and shall order that any payments which may have been previously denied or withheld to be paid by the department or agency concerned.

(Pub. L. 89–554, Sept. 6, 1966, 80 Stat. 559; Pub. L. 92–128, § 2(b), Sept. 25, 1971, 85 Stat. 348; Pub. L. 99–569, title VI, § 603, Oct. 27, 1986, 100 Stat. 3204; Pub. L. 103–337, div. A, title VI, § 639(a), Oct. 5, 1994, 108 Stat. 2791; Pub. L. 103–359, title VIII, § 805, Oct. 14, 1994, 108 Stat. 3441.)

HISTORICAL AND REVISION NOTES

Derivation	U.S. Code	Revised Statutes and Statutes at Large
....	5 U.S.C. 2282.	Sept. 26, 1961, Pub. L. 87–299, § 1 "Sec. 1", 75 Stat. 640.

Standard changes are made to conform with the definitions applicable and the style of this title as outlined in the preface to the report.

REFERENCES IN TEXT

Pars. (2), (3) and (4) of subsec. (b) of section 10 of the Atomic Energy Act of 1946 (60 Stat. 766, 767), as in effect before August 30, 1954, referred to in subsec. (b)(1)(D), are covered by sections 2274, 2275 and 2276, respectively, of Title 42, The Public Health and Welfare.

Subsecs. (a) and (b) of section 16 of the Atomic Energy Act of 1946 (60 Stat. 773), as in effect before August 30, 1954, referred to in subsec. (b)(1)(E), are covered by sections 2272 and 2273, respectively, of Title 42.

Articles 104, 106, and 106a of the Uniform Code of Military Justice, referred to in subsec. (b)(2)(A), are sections 904, 906, and 906a, respectively, of Title 10, Armed Forces. The Uniform Code of Military Justice, in its entirety, is set out in section 801 et seq. of Title 10.

The date of enactment of this subsection, referred to in subsec. (d)(1)(C), is the date of enactment of Pub. L. 103–359, which was approved Oct. 14, 1994.

AMENDMENTS

1994—Subsec. (b)(2)(A). Pub. L. 103–337 substituted ", article 106 (spies), or article 106a (espionage)" for "or article 106 (spies)".

Subsec. (d). Pub. L. 103–359 added subsec. (d).

1986—Subsec. (c)(1)(C). Pub. L. 99–569 inserted provisions relating to section 601 of the National Security Act of 1947.

1971—Subsec. (c)(1)(C). Pub. L. 92–128 struck out ", 822 (conspiracy or evasion of apprehension during internal security emergency), or 823 (aiding evasion or apprehension during internal security emergency)" after "classified information)".

_____

[1] So in original. Probably should be "subparagraph".

EFFECTIVE DATE OF 1994 AMENDMENT

Section 639(b) of Pub. L. 103–337 provided that: "The amendment made by subsection (a) [amending this section] shall take effect on the date of the enactment of this Act [Oct. 5, 1994] and shall apply to persons convicted of espionage under section 906a of title 10, United States Code (article 106a of the Uniform Code of Military Justice), on or after the date of the enactment of this Act."

SECTION REFERRED TO IN OTHER SECTIONS

This section is referred to in sections 5569, 8311, 8313, 8315, 8316, 8318, 8320 of this title; title 37 section 559.

§ 8313. Absence from the United States to avoid prosecution

(a) An individual, or his survivor or beneficiary, may not be paid annuity or retired pay on the basis of the service of the individual which is creditable toward the annuity or retired pay, subject to the exceptions in section 8311(2) and (3) of this title, if the individual—

(1) is under indictment, or has outstanding against him charges preferred under the Uniform Code of Military Justice—

(A) after July 31, 1956, for an offense named by section 8312(b) of this title; or

(B) after September 26, 1961, for an offense named by section 8312(c) of this title; and

(2) willfully remains outside the United States, or its territories and possessions including the Commonwealth of Puerto Rico, for more than 1 year with knowledge of the indictment or charges, as the case may be.

(b) The prohibition on payment of annuity or retired pay under subsection (a) of this section applies to the period after the end of the 1-year period and continues until—

(1) a nolle prosequi to the entire indictment is entered on the record or the charges are dismissed by competent authority;

(2) the individual returns and thereafter the indictment or charges is or are dismissed; or

(3) after trial by court or court-martial, the accused is found not guilty of the offense or offenses.

(Pub. L. 89–554, Sept. 6, 1966, 80 Stat. 561.)

HISTORICAL AND REVISION NOTES

Derivation	U.S. Code	Revised Statutes and Statutes at Large
....	5 U.S.C. 2283a.	Sept. 26, 1961, Pub. L. 87–299, § 1, "Sec. 3", 75 Stat. 643.

Standard changes are made to conform with the definitions applicable and the style of this title as outlined in the preface to the report.

REFERENCES IN TEXT

The Uniform Code of Military Justice, referred to in text, is classified to chapter 47 (§ 801 et seq.) of Title 10, Armed Forces.

SUSPENSION OF PAYMENT OF RETIRED PAY OF MEMBERS WHO ARE ABSENT FROM UNITED STATES TO AVOID PROSECUTION

Pub. L. 104–201, div. A, title VI, § 633, Sept. 23, 1996, 110 Stat. 2550, provided that:

"(a) DEVELOPMENT OF PROCEDURES FOR SUSPENSION.— The Secretary of Defense shall develop uniform procedures under which the Secretary of a military department may suspend the payment of the retired pay of a member or former member of the Armed Forces during periods in which the member willfully remains outside the United States to avoid criminal prosecution or civil liability. The procedures shall address the types of criminal offenses and civil proceedings for which the procedures may be used, including the offenses specified in section 8312 of title 5, United States Code, and the manner by which a member, upon the return of the member to the United States, may obtain retired pay withheld during the member's absence.

"(b) REPORT TO CONGRESS.—The Secretary of Defense shall submit to Congress a report describing the procedures developed under subsection (a). The report shall include recommendations regarding changes to existing provisions of law (including section 8313 of title 5, United States Code) that the Secretary determines are necessary to fully implement the procedures.

"(c) RETIRED PAY DEFINED.—For purposes of this section, the term 'retired pay' means retired pay, retirement pay, retainer pay, or equivalent pay, payable under a statute to a member or former member of a uniformed service.

"(d) EFFECTIVE DATE.—The uniform procedures required by subsection (a) shall be developed not later than 30 days after the date of the enactment of this Act [Sept. 23, 1996]."

SECTION REFERRED TO IN OTHER SECTIONS

This section is referred to in section 8318 of this title.

§ 8314. Refusal to testify

(a) An individual, or his survivor or beneficiary, may not be paid annuity or retired pay on the basis of the service of the individual which is creditable toward the annuity or retired pay, subject to the exceptions in section 8311(2) and (3) of this title, if the individual, before, on, or after September 1, 1954, refused or refuses, or knowingly and willfully failed or fails, to appear, testify, or produce a book, paper, record, or other document, relating to his service as an employee, before a Federal grand jury, court of the United States, court-martial, or congressional committee, in a proceeding concerning—

(1) his past or present relationship with a foreign government; or

(2) a matter involving or relating to an interference with or endangerment of, or involving or relating to a plan or attempt to interfere with or endanger, the national security or defense of the United States.

(b) The prohibition on payment of annuity or retired pay under subsection (a) of this section applies to the period after the date of the failure or refusal of the individual, or after September 1, 1954, whichever is later.

(Pub. L. 89–554, Sept. 6, 1966, 80 Stat. 561.)

HISTORICAL AND REVISION NOTES

Derivation	U.S. Code	Revised Statutes and Statutes at Large
....	5 U.S.C. 2283(a).	Sept. 26, 1961, Pub. L. 87–299, § 1 "Sec. 2(a)", 75 Stat. 642.

Standard changes are made to conform with the definitions applicable and the style of this title as outlined in the preface to the report.

SECTION REFERRED TO IN OTHER SECTIONS

This section is referred to in sections 8311, 8315, 8316, 8318, 8320 of this title.

§ 8315. Falsifying employment applications

(a) An individual, or his survivor or beneficiary, may not be paid annuity or retired pay on the basis of the service of the individual which is creditable toward the annuity or retired pay, subject to the exceptions in section 8311(2) and (3) of this title, if the individual knowingly and willfully made or makes a false, fictitious, or fraudulent statement or representation, or knowingly and willfully concealed or conceals a material fact—

(1) before, on, or after September 1, 1954, concerning his—

(A) past or present membership in, affiliation or association with, or support of the Communist Party, or a chapter, branch, or subdivision thereof, in or outside the United States, or other organization, party, or group advocating—

(i) the overthrow, by force, violence, or other unconstitutional means, of the Government of the United States;

(ii) the establishment, by force, violence, or other unconstitutional means, of a Communist totalitarian dictatorship in the United States; or

(iii) the right to strike against the United States;

(B) conviction of an offense named by subsection (b) of section 8312 of this title, to the extent provided by that subsection; or

(C) failure or refusal to appear, testify, or produce a book, paper, record, or other document, as specified by section 8314 of this title; or

(2) before, on, or after September 26, 1961, concerning his conviction of an offense named by subsection (c) of section 8312 of this title, to the extent provided by that subsection;

in a document executed by the individual in connection with his employment in, or application for, a civilian or military office or position in or under the legislative, executive, or judicial branch of the Government of the United States or the government of the District of Columbia.

(b) The prohibition on the payment of annuity or retired pay applies—

(1) with respect to matters specified by subsection (a)(1) of this section, to the period after the statement, representation, or concealment of fact is made or occurs, or after September 1, 1954, whichever is later; and

(2) with respect to matters specified by subsection (a)(2) of this section, to the period after the statement, representation, or concealment of fact is made or occurs, or after September 26, 1961, whichever is later.

(Pub. L. 89–554, Sept. 6, 1966, 80 Stat. 562.)

HISTORICAL AND REVISION NOTES

Derivation	U.S. Code	Revised Statutes and Statutes at Large
....	5 U.S.C. 2283(b), (c).	Sept. 26, 1961, Pub. L. 87–299, §1 "Sec. 2(b), (c)", 75 Stat. 642.

Standard changes are made to conform with the definitions applicable and the style of this title as outlined in the preface to the report.

SECTION REFERRED TO IN OTHER SECTIONS

This section is referred to in sections 8311, 8316, 8318, 8320 of this title.

§ 8316. Refund of contributions and deposits

(a) When payment of annuity or retired pay is denied under this subchapter because an individual was convicted of an offense named by section 8312 of this title, to the extent provided by that section, or violated section 8314 or 8315 of this title—

(1) the amount, except employment taxes, contributed by the individual toward the annuity, less the amount previously refunded or paid as annuity benefits; and

(2) deposits made under section 1438 of title 10 or section 5 of the Uniformed Services Contingency Option Act of 1953 (67 Stat. 504) to provide the eligible beneficiary with annuity for any period, less the amount previously paid as retired pay benefits;

shall be refunded, on appropriate application therefor—

(A) to the individual;

(B) if the individual is dead, to the beneficiary designated to receive refunds by or under the statute, regulation, or agreement under which the annuity, the benefits of which are denied under this subchapter, would have been payable; or

(C) if a beneficiary is not designated, in the order of precedence prescribed by section 8342(c) of this title or section 2771 of title 10, as the case may be.

(b) A refund under subsection (a) of this section shall be made with interest at the rate and for the period provided under the statute, regulation, or agreement under which the annuity would have been payable. However, interest may not be computed—

(1) if the individual was convicted of an offense named by section 8312(b) of this title, or violated section 8314 or 8315(a)(1) of this title, for the period after the conviction or commission of the violation, or after September 1, 1954, whichever is later; or

(2) if the individual was convicted of an offense named by section 8312(c) of this title, or violated section 8315(a)(2) of this title, for the period after the conviction or commission of the violation, or after September 26, 1961, whichever is later.

(Pub. L. 89–554, Sept. 6, 1966, 80 Stat. 563.)

HISTORICAL AND REVISION NOTES

Derivation	U.S. Code	Revised Statutes and Statutes at Large
....	5 U.S.C. 2284(a), (b).	Sept. 26, 1961, Pub. L. 87–299, §1 "Sec. 4(a), (b)", 75 Stat. 644.
....	5 U.S.C. 2284a(b).	Sept. 26, 1961, Pub. L. 87–299, §1 "Sec. 5(b)", 75 Stat. 645.

This section is reorganized for clarity and conciseness.

The words "and section 3282 of Title 18" in former section 2284(a) are omitted as unnecessary.

Standard changes are made to conform with the definitions applicable and the style of this title as outlined in the preface to the report.

REFERENCES IN TEXT

Section 5 of the Uniform Services Contingency Option Act of 1953 (67 Stat. 504), referred to in text, is covered by section 1438 of Title 10, Armed Forces.

SECTION REFERRED TO IN OTHER SECTIONS

This section is referred to in section 8318 of this title.

§ 8317. Repayment of annuity or retired pay properly paid; waiver

(a) An individual, or his survivor or beneficiary, to whom payment of annuity is denied under this subchapter is not thereafter required to repay that part of the annuity otherwise properly paid to the individual, or to his survivor or beneficiary on the basis of the service of the individual, which is in excess of the aggregate amount of the contributions of the individual toward the annuity, with applicable interest.

(b) An individual, including an eligible beneficiary under chapter 73 of title 10 or section 5 of the Uniformed Services Contingency Option Act of 1953 (67 Stat. 504), to whom payment of retired pay is denied under this subchapter is not thereafter required to repay retired pay otherwise properly paid to the individual or beneficiary which is paid in violation of this subchapter.

(Pub. L. 89–554, Sept. 6, 1966, 80 Stat. 563.)

HISTORICAL AND REVISION NOTES

Derivation	U.S. Code	Revised Statutes and Statutes at Large
(a)	5 U.S.C. 2284(c), (d).	Sept. 26, 1961, Pub. L. 87–299, §1 "Sec. 4(c), (d)", 75 Stat. 644.
(b)	5 U.S.C. 2284a(a).	Sept. 26, 1961, Pub. L. 87–299, §1 "Sec. 5(a)", 75 Stat. 645.

The words "and section 3282 of Title 18" are omitted as unnecessary.

Standard changes are made to conform with the definitions applicable and the style of this title as outlined in the preface to the report.

REFERENCES IN TEXT

Section 5 of the Uniformed Services Contingency Option Act of 1953 (67 Stat. 504), referred to in text, is covered by section 1438 of Table 10, Armed Forces.

§ 8318. Restoration of annuity or retired pay

(a) If an individual who was convicted, before, on, or after September 1, 1954, of—

(1) an offense named by section 8312 of this title; or

(2) an offense constituting a violation of section 8314 or 8315 of this title;

is pardoned by the President, the right of the individual and his survivor or beneficiary to receive annuity or retired pay previously denied under this subchapter is restored as of the date of the pardon.

(b) The President may restore, effective as of the date he prescribes, the right to receive annuity or retired pay which is denied, before, on, or after September 1, 1954, under section 8314 or 8315 of this title, to the individual and to his survivor or beneficiary.

(c) Payment of annuity or retired pay which results from pardon or restoration by the President under subsection (a) or (b) of this section may not be made for a period before—

(1) the date of pardon referred to by subsection (a) of this section; or

(2) the effective date of restoration referred to by subsection (b) of this section.

(d) Credit for a period of service covered by a refund under section 8316 of this title is allowed only after the amount refunded has been redeposited.

(e) The spouse of an individual whose annuity or retired pay is forfeited under section 8312 or 8313 after the date of enactment of this subsection shall be eligible for spousal pension benefits if the Attorney General of the United States determines that the spouse fully cooperated with Federal authorities in the conduct of a criminal investigation and subsequent prosecution of the individual which resulted in such forfeiture.

(Pub. L. 89–554, Sept. 6, 1966, 80 Stat. 563; Pub. L. 104–93, title III, § 305, Jan. 6, 1996, 109 Stat. 965.)

HISTORICAL AND REVISION NOTES

Derivation	U.S. Code	Revised Statutes and Statutes at Large
....	5 U.S.C. 2285(a), (b).	Sept. 26, 1961, Pub. L. 87–299, §1 "Sec. 6(a), (b)", 75 Stat. 645.

The section is reorganized for clarity and conciseness.

The words "and section 3282 of Title 18" are omitted as unnecessary.

Standard changes are made to conform with the definitions applicable and the style of this title as outlined in the preface to the report.

REFERENCES IN TEXT

The date of enactment of this subsection, referred to in subsec. (e), is the date of enactment of Pub. L. 104–93, which was approved Jan. 6, 1996.

AMENDMENTS

1996—Subsec. (e). Pub. L. 104–93 added subsec. (e).

§ 8319. Removal of members of the uniformed services from rolls; restoration; reappointment

(a) The President may drop from the rolls a member of a uniformed service who is deprived of retired pay under this subchapter.

(b) The President may restore—

(1) military status to an individual dropped from the rolls to whom retired pay is restored under this subchapter or under section 2 of the Act of September 26, 1961 (75 Stat. 648); and

(2) all rights and privileges to the individual and his beneficiaries of which he or they were deprived because his name was dropped from the rolls.

(c) If the individual restored was a commissioned officer, the President alone may reappoint him to the grade and position on the retired list held when his name was dropped from the rolls.

(Pub. L. 89–554, Sept. 6, 1966, 80 Stat. 564.)

HISTORICAL AND REVISION NOTES

Derivation	U.S. Code	Revised Statutes and Statutes at Large
....	5 U.S.C. 2287.	Sept. 26, 1961, Pub. L. 87–299, §1 "Sec. 8", 75 Stat. 646.

The words "and section 3282 of Title 18" are omitted as unnecessary.

Standard changes are made to conform with the definitions applicable and the style of this title as outlined in the preface to the report.

REFERENCES IN TEXT

Section 2 of the Act of September 26, 1961 (75 Stat. 648), referred to in subsec. (b)(1), is set out as a note under section 8318 of this title.

§ 8320. Offense or violation committed in compliance with orders

When it is established by satisfactory evidence that an individual—

(1) was convicted of an offense named by section 8312 of this title; or

(2) violated section 8314 or 8315 of this title;

as a result of proper compliance with orders issued, in a confidential relationship, by an agency or other authority of the Government of the United States or the government of the District of Columbia, the right to receive annuity or retired pay may not be denied.

(Pub. L. 89–554, Sept. 6, 1966, 80 Stat. 564.)

HISTORICAL AND REVISION NOTES

Derivation	U.S. Code	Revised Statutes and Statutes at Large
....	5 U.S.C. 2285(c).	Sept. 26, 1961, Pub. L. 87–299, §1 "Sec. 6(c)", 75 Stat. 645.

The reference to conviction of an offense which constitutes a violation of former section 2283 (which is carried into this title as sections 8314 and 8315) is omitted as being covered by the words "violated section 8314 or 8315 of this title" which are added on authority of the words "conviction or violation" in former section 2285(c).

Standard changes are made to conform with the definitions applicable and the style of this title as outlined in the preface to the report.

§ 8321. Liability of accountable employees

An accountable employee may not be held responsible for a payment made in violation of this subchapter when the payment made is in due course and without fraud, collusion, or gross negligence.

(Pub. L. 89–554, Sept. 6, 1966, 80 Stat. 564.)

HISTORICAL AND REVISION NOTES

Derivation	U.S. Code	Revised Statutes and Statutes at Large
....	5 U.S.C. 2286.	Sept. 26, 1961, Pub. L. 87–299, §1 "Sec. 7", 75 Stat. 645.

The words "and section 3282 of Title 18" are omitted as unnecessary.

Standard changes are made to conform with the definitions applicable and the style of this title as outlined in the preface to the report.

§ 8322. Effect on other statutes

This subchapter does not restrict authority under a statute, other than this subchapter, to deny or withhold benefits authorized by statute.

(Pub. L. 89–554, Sept. 6, 1966, 80 Stat. 564.)

HISTORICAL AND REVISION NOTES

Derivation	U.S. Code	Revised Statutes and Statutes at Large
....	5 U.S.C. 2288.	Sept. 26, 1961, Pub. L. 87–299, §1 "Sec. 9", 75 Stat. 646.

The words "and section 3282 of Title 18" are omitted as unnecessary.

Standard changes are made to conform with the definitions applicable and the style of this title as outlined in the preface to the report.

RETROACTIVE RESTORATION OF ANNUITY AND RETIRED PAY; REDEPOSITS OF CONTRIBUTIONS AND OFFSETS

Section 2 of Pub. L. 87–299, Sept. 26, 1961, 75 Stat. 648, provided that:

"(a) Subject to subsection (b) of this section, any person, including his survivor or beneficiary, to whom annuity or retired pay is not payable under the Act of September 1, 1954 [this subchapter], as in effect at any time prior to the date of enactment of this Act [Sept. 26, 1961], by reason of any conviction of an offense, any commission of a violation, any refusal to answer, or any absence under indictment, or under charges, for any offense, shall be restored the right to receive such annuity or retired pay for any and all periods for which he would have had the right to receive such annuity or retired pay if the Act of September 1, 1954 [this subchapter], had not been enacted, unless, under the amendment made by the first section of this Act [amending former chapter 31 of this title, now this subchapter, and section 3282 of Title 18, Crimes and Criminal Procedure], such annuity or retired pay remains nonpayable to such person, including his survivor or beneficiary.

"(b) No annuity accrued or accruing, prior to, on, or after the date of enactment of this Act [Sept. 26, 1961], on account of the restoration, by reason of the amendment made by the first section of this Act [amending former chapter 31 of this title, now this subchapter, and section 3282 of Title 18] and by reason of subsection (a) of this section, of the right to receive such annuity, shall be paid until any sum refunded under section 3 of the Act of September 1, 1954 [former section 2284 of this title, now section 8316 of this title, prior to amendment Sept. 26, 1961], as in effect prior to the date of enactment of such amendment [Sept. 26, 1961], is deposited or is collected by offset against the annuity."

SUBCHAPTER III—CIVIL SERVICE RETIREMENT

SUBCHAPTER REFERRED TO IN OTHER SECTIONS

This subchapter is referred to in sections 3329, 3373, 3374, 5541, 5581, 5595, 5597, 5724, 6303, 8103, 8116, 8402, 8411, 8431, 8442, 8443, 8462, 8501, 8901 of this title; title 2 sections 31b–5, 60e–3, 72a, 130a; title 7 section 331; title 10 sections 942, 945, 1450, 1452, 2467; title 12 section 1723a; title 16 section 1168; title 20 sections 125, 4416; title 22 sections 2025, 3658, 3673, 3682, 3968, 3970, 4045, 4067, 4069, 4071b, 4071c, 4071d, 4071i; title 26 section 3121; title 28 sections 155, 178, 332, 376, 377, 611, 625, 627, 634, 636, 753, 797; title 31 section 772; title 38 sections 7426, 7802; title 40 section 13b; title 42 sections 212, 410, 415, 417, 1395s, 4276, 7297; title 45 section 1206; title 49 section 49107; title 50 sections 403r, 403s, 2082, 2141, 2151, 2154, 2442; title 50 App. section 1291.

§ 8331. Definitions

For the purpose of this subchapter—

(1) "employee" means—

(A) an employee as defined by section 2105 of this title;

(B) the Architect of the Capitol, an employee of the Architect of the Capitol, and an employee of the Botanic Garden;

(C) a Congressional employee as defined by section 2107 of this title (other than the Architect of the Capitol, an employee of the Architect of the Capitol, and an employee of the Botanic Garden), after he gives notice in writing to the official by whom he is paid of his desire to become subject to this subchapter;

(D) a temporary Congressional employee appointed at an annual rate of pay, after he gives notice in writing to the official by whom he is paid of his desire to become subject to this subchapter;

(E) a United States Commissioner whose total pay for services performed as Commissioner is not less than $3,000 in each of the last 3 consecutive calendar years ending after December 31, 1954;

(F) an individual employed by a county committee established under section 590h(b) of title 16;

(G) an individual first employed by the government of the District of Columbia before October 1, 1987;

(H) an individual employed by Gallaudet College;

(I) an individual appointed to a position on the office staff of a former President under section 1(b) of the Act of August 25, 1958 (72 Stat. 838);

(J) an alien (i) who was previously employed by the Government, (ii) who is employed full time by a foreign government for the purpose of protecting or furthering the interests of the United States during an interruption of diplomatic or consular relations, and (iii) for whose services reimbursement is made to the foreign government by the United States;

(K) an individual appointed to a position on the office staff of a former President, or a former Vice President under section 4 of the Presidential Transition Act of 1963, as amended (78 Stat. 153), who immediately before the date of such appointment was an employee as defined under any other subparagraph of this paragraph; and

(L) an employee described in section 2105(c) who has made an election under section 8347(q)(1) to remain covered under this subchapter;

but does not include—

(i) a justice or judge of the United States as defined by section 451 of title 28;

(ii) an employee subject to another retirement system for Government employees (besides any employee excluded by clause (x), but including any employee who has made an election under section 8347(q)(2) to remain covered by a retirement system established for employees described in section 2105(c));

(iii) an employee or group of employees in or under an Executive agency excluded by the Office of Personnel Management under section 8347(g) of this title;

(iv) an individual or group of individuals employed by the government of the District of Columbia excluded by the Office under section 8347(h) of this title;

(v) an employee of the Administrative Office of the United States Courts, the Federal Judicial Center, or a court named by section 610 of title 28, excluded by the Director of the Administrative Office under section 8347(o) of this title;

(vi) a construction employee or other temporary, part-time, or intermittent employee of the Tennessee Valley Authority;

(vii) an employee under the Office of the Architect of the Capitol excluded by the Architect of the Capitol under section 8347(i) of this title;

(viii) an employee under the Library of Congress excluded by the Librarian of Congress under section 8347(j) of this title;

(ix) a student-employee as defined by section 5351 of this title;

(x) an employee subject to the Federal Employees' Retirement System;

(xi) an employee under the Botanic Garden excluded by the Director or Acting Director of the Botanic Garden under section 8347(l) of this title; or

(xii) a member of the Foreign Service (as described in section 103(6) of the Foreign Service Act of 1980), appointed after December 31, 1987.

Notwithstanding this paragraph, the employment of a teacher in the recess period between two school years in a position other than a teaching position in which he served immediately before the recess period does not qualify the individual as an employee for the purpose of this subchapter. For the purpose of the preceding sentence, "teacher" and "teaching position" have the meanings given them by section 901 of title 20;

(2) "Member" means a Member of Congress as defined by section 2106 of this title, after he gives notice in writing to the official by whom he is paid of his desire to become subject to this subchapter, but does not include any such Member of Congress who is subject to the Federal Employees' Retirement System or who makes an election under section 8401(20) of this title not to be subject to such System;

(3) "basic pay" includes—

(A) the amount a Member received from April 1, 1954, to February 28, 1955, as expense allowance under section 601(b) of the Legislative Reorganization Act of 1946 (60 Stat. 850), as amended; and that amount from January 3, 1953, to March 31, 1954, if deposit is made therefor as provided by section 8334 of this title;

(B) additional pay provided by—

(i) subsection (a) of section 60e–7 of title 2 and the provisions of law referred to by that subsection; and

(ii) sections 60e–8, 60e–9, 60e–10, 60e–11, 60e–12, 60e–13, and 60e–14 of title 2;

(C) premium pay under section 5545(c)(1) of this title;

(D) with respect to a law enforcement officer, premium pay under section 5545(c)(2) of this title;

(E) with respect to a criminal investigator, availability pay under section 5545a of this title;

(F) pay as provided in section 5545b(b)(2) and (c)(2);

(G) with respect to a customs officer (referred to in subsection (e)(1) of section 5 of the Act of February 13, 1911), compensation for overtime inspectional services provided for under subsection (a) of such section 5, but not to exceed 50 percent of any statutory maximum in overtime pay for customs officers which is in effect for the year involved; and

(H) any amount received under section 5948 (relating to physicians comparability allowances);

but does not include bonuses, allowances, overtime pay, military pay, pay given in addition to the base pay of the position as fixed by law or regulation except as provided by subparagraphs (B) through (H) of this paragraph[1] retroactive pay under section 5344 of this title in the case of a retired or deceased employee, uniform allowances under section 5901 of this title, or lump-sum leave payments under subchapter VI of chapter 55 of this title. For an employee paid on a fee basis, the maximum amount of basic pay which may be used is $10,000;

(4) "average pay" means the largest annual rate resulting from averaging an employee's or Member's rates of basic pay in effect over any 3 consecutive years of creditable service or, in the case of an annuity under subsection (d) or (e)(1) of section 8341 of this title based on service of less than 3 years, over the total service, with each rate weighted by the time it was in effect;

(5) "Fund" means the Civil Service Retirement and Disability Fund;

[(6) Repealed. Pub. L. 96–499, title IV, § 403(b), Dec. 5, 1980, 94 Stat. 2606]

(7) "Government" means the Government of the United States, the government of the District of Columbia, Gallaudet University, and, in the case of an employee described in paragraph (1)(L), a nonappropriated fund instrumentality of the Department of Defense or the Coast Guard described in section 2105(c);

(8) "lump-sum credit" means the unrefunded amount consisting of—

(A) retirement deductions made from the basic pay of an employee or Member;

(B) amounts deposited by an employee or Member covering earlier service, including any amounts deposited under section 8334(j) of this title; and

(C) interest on the deductions and deposits at 4 percent a year to December 31, 1947, and 3 percent a year thereafter compounded annually to December 31, 1956, or, in the case of an employee or Member separated or transferred to a position in which he does not continue subject to this subchapter before he has completed 5 years of civilian service, to the date of the separation or transfer;

but does not include interest—

(i) if the service covered thereby aggregates 1 year or less; or

(ii) for the fractional part of a month in the total service;

(9) "annuitant" means a former employee or Member who, on the basis of his service, meets all requirements of this subchapter for title to annuity and files claim therefor;

(10) "survivor" means an individual entitled to annuity under this subchapter based on the service of a deceased employee, Member, or annuitant;

(11) "survivor annuitant" means a survivor who files claim for annuity;

(12) "service" means employment creditable under section 8332 of this title;

(13) "military service" means honorable active service—

(A) in the armed forces;

(B) in the Regular or Reserve Corps of the Public Health Service after June 30, 1960; or

(C) as a commissioned officer of the Environmental Science Services Administration after June 30, 1961;

but does not include service in the National Guard except when ordered to active duty in the service of the United States or full-time National Guard duty (as such term is defined in section 101(d) of title 10) if such service interrupts creditable civilian service under this subchapter and is followed by reemployment in accordance with chapter 43 of title 38 that occurs on or after August 1, 1990;

(14) "Member service" means service as a Member and includes the period from the date of the beginning of the term for which elected or appointed to the date on which he takes office as a Member;

(15) "price index" means the Consumer Price Index (all items—United States city average) published monthly by the Bureau of Labor Statistics;

(16) "base month" means the month for which the price index showed a percent rise forming the basis for a cost-of-living annuity increase;

(17) "normal cost" means the entry-age normal cost computed by the Office of Personnel Management in accordance with generally accepted actuarial practice and expressed as a level percentage of aggregate basic pay;

(18) "Fund balance" means the sum of—

(A) the investments of the Fund calculated at par value; and

(B) the cash balance of the Fund on the books of the Treasury;

but does not include any amount attributable to—

(i) the Federal Employees' Retirement System; or

(ii) contributions made under the Federal Employees' Retirement Contribution Temporary Adjustment Act of 1983 by or on behalf of any individual who became subject to the Federal Employees' Retirement System;

(19) "unfunded liability" means the estimated excess of the present value of all benefits payable from the Fund to employees and Members, and former employees and Members,

---

[1] So in original. Probably should be followed by a comma.

subject to this subchapter, and to their survivors, over the sum of—

(A) the present value of deductions to be withheld from the future basic pay of employees and Members currently subject to this subchapter and of future agency contributions to be made in their behalf; plus

(B) the present value of Government payments to the Fund under section 8348(f) of this title; plus

(C) the Fund balance as of the date the unfunded liability is determined;

(20) "law enforcement officer" means an employee, the duties of whose position are primarily the investigation, apprehension, or detention of individuals suspected or convicted of offenses against the criminal laws of the United States, including an employee engaged in this activity who is transferred to a supervisory or administrative position. For the purpose of this paragraph, "detention" includes the duties of—

(A) employees of the Bureau of Prisons and Federal Prison Industries, Incorporated;

(B) employees of the Public Health Service assigned to the field service of the Bureau of Prisons or of the Federal Prison Industries, Incorporated;

(C) employees in the field service at Army or Navy disciplinary barracks or at confinement and rehabilitation facilities operated by any of the armed forces; and

(D) employees of the Department of Corrections of the District of Columbia, its industries and utilities;

whose duties in connection with individuals in detention suspected or convicted of offenses against the criminal laws of the United States or of the District of Columbia or offenses against the punitive articles of the Uniformed Code of Military Justice (chapter 47 of title 10) require frequent (as determined by the appropriate administrative authority with the concurrence of the Office) direct contact with these individuals in their detention, direction, supervision, inspection, training, employment, care, transportation, or rehabilitation;

(21) "firefighter" means an employee, the duties of whose position are primarily to perform work directly connected with the control and extinguishment of fires or the maintenance and use of firefighting apparatus and equipment, including an employee engaged in this activity who is transferred to a supervisory or administrative position;

(22) "bankruptcy judge" means an individual—

(A) who is appointed under section 34 of the Bankruptcy Act (11 U.S.C. 62) or under section 404(d) of the Act of November 6, 1978 (Public Law 95–598; 92 Stat. 2549), and—

(i) who is serving as a United States bankruptcy judge on March 31, 1984; or

(ii) whose service as a United States bankruptcy judge at any time in the period beginning on October 1, 1979, and ending on July 10, 1984, is terminated by reason of death or disability; or

(B) who is appointed as a bankruptcy judge under section 152 of title 28;

(23) "former spouse" means a former spouse of an individual—

(A) if such individual performed at least 18 months of civilian service covered under this subchapter as an employee or Member, and

(B) if the former spouse was married to such individual for at least 9 months;

(24) "Indian court" means an Indian court as defined by section 201(3) of the Act entitled "An Act to prescribe penalties for certain acts of violence or intimidation, and for other purposes", approved April 11, 1968 (25 U.S.C. 1301(3); 82 Stat. 77);

(25) "magistrate judge" or "United States magistrate judge" means an individual appointed under section 631 of title 28;

(26) "Court of Federal Claims judge" means a judge of the United States Court of Federal Claims who is appointed under chapter 7 of title 28 or who has served under section 167 of the Federal Courts Improvement Act of 1982;

(27) "Nuclear materials courier"—

(A) means an employee of the Department of Energy, the duties of whose position are primarily to transport, and provide armed escort and protection during transit of, nuclear weapons, nuclear weapon components, strategic quantities of special nuclear materials or other materials related to national security; and

(B) includes an employee who is transferred directly to a supervisory or administrative position within the same Department of Energy organization, after performing duties referred to in subparagraph (A) for at least 3 years; and

(28) "Government physician" has the meaning given that term under section 5948.

(Pub. L. 89–554, Sept. 6, 1966, 80 Stat. 564; Pub. L. 89–737, §1(2), Nov. 2, 1966, 80 Stat. 1164; Pub. L. 90–83, §1(72), Sept. 11, 1967, 81 Stat. 213; Pub. L. 90–623, §1(21), Oct. 22, 1968, 82 Stat. 1313; Pub. L. 91–93, title I, §101, title II, §201(a), Oct. 20, 1969, 83 Stat. 136, 138; Pub. L. 92–352, title I, §105(a), July 13, 1972, 86 Stat. 490; Pub. L. 93–350, §2, July 12, 1974, 88 Stat. 355; Pub. L. 94–183, §2(38), Dec. 31, 1975, 89 Stat. 1058; Pub. L. 95–454, title IX, §906(a)(2), (3), Oct. 13, 1978, 92 Stat. 1224; Pub. L. 95–598, title III, §338(e), Nov. 6, 1978, 92 Stat. 2681; Pub. L. 96–54, §2(a)(47), Aug. 14, 1979, 93 Stat. 384; Pub. L. 96–499, title IV, §403(b), Dec. 5, 1980, 94 Stat. 2606; Pub. L. 97–253, title III, §306(a), Sept. 8, 1982, 96 Stat. 795; Pub. L. 98–249, §3(b), Mar. 31, 1984, 98 Stat. 117; Pub. L. 98–271, §3(b), Apr. 30, 1984, 98 Stat. 163; Pub. L. 98–299, §3(b), May 25, 1984, 98 Stat. 214; Pub. L. 98–325, §3(b), June 20, 1984, 98 Stat. 268; Pub. L. 98–353, title I, §§116(a), 121(g), July 10, 1984, 98 Stat. 343, 346; Pub. L. 98–531, §2(a), Oct. 19, 1984, 98 Stat. 2704; Pub. L. 98–615, §2(1), Nov. 8, 1984, 98 Stat. 3195; Pub. L. 99–335, title II, §§202, 207(f), June 6, 1986, 100 Stat. 591, 595; Pub. L. 100–53, §2(a), June 18, 1987, 101 Stat. 367; Pub. L. 100–238, title I, §§112, 123, Jan. 8, 1988, 101 Stat. 1750, 1754; Pub. L. 100–679, §13(a)(1), Nov. 17, 1988, 102 Stat. 4071; Pub. L. 101–474, §5(m), Oct. 30, 1990, 104 Stat. 1100; Pub. L. 101–508, title VII, §7202(j)(1), Nov. 5, 1990, 104 Stat. 1388–337; Pub. L. 101–650, title III, §§306(c)(1), 321, Dec. 1, 1990, 104 Stat. 5110, 5117; Pub. L. 102–378, §2(57), Oct. 2, 1992, 106 Stat. 1354;

Pub. L. 102–572, title IX, §902(b), Oct. 29, 1992, 106
Stat. 4516; Pub. L. 103–66, title XIII, §13812(a),
Aug. 10, 1993, 107 Stat. 670; Pub. L. 103–353, §5(a),
Oct. 13, 1994, 108 Stat. 3173; Pub. L. 105–261, div.
C, title XXXI, §3154(b), Oct. 17, 1998, 112 Stat.
2254; Pub. L. 105–277, div. A, §101(h) [title VI,
§628(d)], Oct. 21, 1998, 112 Stat. 2681–480, 2681–521;
Pub. L. 106–571, §3(a), (b)(2), Dec. 28, 2000, 114
Stat. 3054, 3055.)

HISTORICAL AND REVISION NOTES
1966 ACT

Derivation	U.S. Code	Revised Statutes and Statutes at Large
....	5 U.S.C. 2251 (less (h)–(j)).	July 31, 1956, ch. 804, §401 "Sec. 1 (less (h)–(j))", 70 Stat. 743. Apr. 8, 1960, Pub. L. 86–415, §6(c), 74 Stat. 35. July 7, 1960, Pub. L. 86–604, §1(a), 74 Stat. 358. Sept. 14, 1961, Pub. L. 87–233, §2, 75 Stat. 507. Oct. 11, 1962, Pub. L. 87–793, §1102(a), 76 Stat. 869. Feb. 7, 1964, Pub. L. 88–267, §1(a), 78 Stat. 8.
....	5 U.S.C. 2252 (less (e), (f) (words after semicolon), (g) (2d sentence), (h) (words after colon)).	July 31, 1956, ch. 804, §401 "Sec. 2 (less (e), (f) (words after semicolon), (g) (2d sentence))", 70 Stat. 745. July 1, 1960, Pub. L. 86–568, §115(b)(1) "(h) (less words after colon)", 74 Stat. 302. Feb. 7, 1964, Pub. L. 88–267, §1(b), (c), 78 Stat. 9.
....	5 U.S.C. 1054 (1st 27 words).	Aug. 4, 1947, ch. 452, §5 (1st 27 words), 61 Stat. 728.
....	[Uncodified].	Aug. 25, 1958, Pub. L. 85–745, §1(b) (last sentence, as applicable to the Civil Service Retirement Act), 72 Stat. 838.
....	5 U.S.C. 2358(c) (as applicable to the Civil Service Retirement Act).	July 17, 1959, Pub. L. 86–91, §10(c) (as applicable to the Civil Service Retirement Act), 73 Stat. 217.
....	5 U.S.C. 932c(d).	June 28, 1955, ch. 189, §4(i), 69 Stat. 178.
....	5 U.S.C. 932d(d).	June 20, 1958, Pub. L. 85–462, §4(g), 72 Stat. 208.
....	5 U.S.C. 932e(f).	July 1, 1960, Pub. L. 86–568, §117(i), 74 Stat. 304.
....	5 U.S.C. 932f(e).	Oct. 11, 1962, Pub. L. 87–793, §1005(h), 76 Stat. 867.
....	5 U.S.C. 932g(d).	Aug. 14, 1964, Pub. L. 88–426, §202(d), 78 Stat. 413.
....	5 U.S.C. 1182(b).	Sept. 2, 1958, Pub. L. 85–872, §2(b), 72 Stat. 1696.
....	5 U.S.C. 2132 (as applicable to the Civil Service Retirement Act, as amended).	Sept. 1, 1954, ch. 1208, §403 (as applicable to the Civil Service Retirement Act, as amended), 68 Stat. 1115.

In paragraph (1), the specific exception of the President, appearing in former section 2252(b), is omitted as unnecessary because he is not included in the definition of "employee".

In paragraph (1)(B), the definition of "Congressional employee" in former section 2251(c) is omitted as unnecessary in view of the definition of the term in section 2107.

In paragraph (1)(E), the words "Notwithstanding any other provision of law or any Executive order" are omitted as unnecessary.

In paragraph (1)(i), the words "justice or" are added on authority of section 371 and 372 of title 28.

Paragraph (1)(iii) and (iv) is based on former section 2252(e), which is carried into section 8347(g) and (h).

Paragraph (1)(vii) and (viii) is based on former section 2252(f), which is carried in part into section 8347(i) and (j).

In paragraph (1), the last sentence is added on authority of former section 2351, which is scheduled for transfer to section 901 of title 20.

In paragraph (3), the words "or lump-sum leave payments under subchapter VI of chapter 55 of this title" are added on authority of former section 61b (6th sentence), which is carried into section 5551.

In paragraph (4)(B), references to sections 60e–7, 60e–8, 60e–9, 60e–10, and 60e–11 of title 2 are substituted for the words "this section", appearing in former sections 932c(d), 932d(d), 932e(f), 932f(e), and 932g(d), to reflect the scheduled transfer of those sections to title 2.

In paragraph (5), the words "the Civil Service Retirement and Disability Fund" are substituted for "the civil service retirement and disability fund created by the Act of May 22, 1920".

In paragraph (7), the words "Government of the United States" are coextensive with and substituted for "the executive, judicial, and legislative branches of the United States Government, including Government-owned or controlled corporation".

In paragraph (13), the words "armed forces" are coextensive with and substituted for "Army, Navy, Air Force, Marine Corps, or Coast Guard of the United States" in view of the definition of "armed forces" in section 2101.

The definition of "Commission" in former section 2251(m) is omitted as unnecessary as the title "Civil Service Commission" is fully set out the first time it is used in each section.

Standard changes are made to conform with the definitions applicable and the style of this title as outlined in the preface to the report.

1967 ACT

Section of title 5	Source (U.S. Code)	Source (Statutes at Large)
8331(1)(B), (C).	5 App.: 2252(c).	Sept. 26, 1966, Pub. L. 89–604, §1(b), 80 Stat. 846.
8331(3)(B) (ii).	5 App.: 932h(c).	Oct. 29, 1965, Pub. L. 89–301, §11(d), 79 Stat. 1120.
	5 App.: 932i(c).	July 18, 1966, Pub. L. 89–504, §302(b), 80 Stat. 295.
8331(13)	[No source].	[No source].
8331(15), (16)	5 App.: 2251(t).	Sept. 27, 1965, Pub. L. 89–205, §1(a), 79 Stat. 840.

In paragraphs (1)(C), (D) and (2), the words "become subject to" are substituted for "come within the purview of" for consistency within the subchapter.

In paragraph (3)(B)(ii), references to sections 60e–12 and 60e–13 of title 2 are substituted for the words "this section" appearing in 5 U.S.C. App. 932h(c) and 932i(c), to reflect the scheduled transfer of those sections to title 2 (See table IV).

In paragraph (8)(C), the words "in which he does not continue subject to" are substituted for "not within the purview of" for consistency within the subchapter and to reflect that it is the individual, rather than the position, that is subject to this subchapter.

The amendment to paragraph (13) reflects Reorganization Plan No. 2 of 1965 (79 Stat. 1318), effective July 13, 1965, which consolidated the Coast and Geodetic Survey and the Weather Bureau to form a new agency in the Department of Commerce to be known as the Environmental Science Services Administration.

REFERENCES IN TEXT

Section 1(b) of the act of August 25, 1958 (72 Stat. 838), referred to in par. (1)(I), is set out as a note under section 102 of Title 3, The President.

Section 4 of the Presidential Transition Act of 1963, referred to in par. (1)(K), is section 4 of Pub. L. 88–277, which is set out as a note under section 102 of Title 3.

Section 103(6) of the Foreign Service Act of 1980, referred to in par. (1)(xii), is classified to section 3903(6) of Title 22, Foreign Relations and Intercourse.

Section 601(b) of the Legislative Reorganization Act of 1946 (60 Stat. 850), as amended, referred to in par. (3)(A), was classified to section 31a of Title 2, The Congress, which was repealed by act Mar. 2, 1955, ch. 9, § 4(b), 69 Stat. 11.

Sections 60e–7, 60e–8, 60e–9, 60e–10, 60e–11, 60e–12, 60e–13, and 60e–14 of title 2, referred to in par. (3)(B), were omitted from the Code.

Section 5 of the Act of February 13, 1911, referred to in par. (3)(G), is classified to section 267 of Title 19, Customs Duties.

The Federal Employees' Retirement Contribution Temporary Adjustment Act of 1983, referred to in par. (18)(ii), is Pub. L. 98–168, title II, Nov. 29, 1983, 97 Stat. 1106, as amended, which is set out as a note below.

The Bankruptcy Act, referred to in par. (22)(A), is act July 1, 1898, ch. 541, 30 Stat. 544, as amended, which was classified generally to former Title 11, Bankruptcy. The Act was repealed effective Oct. 1, 1979, by Pub. L. 95–598, §§ 401(a), 402(a), Nov. 6, 1978, 92 Stat. 2682, section 101 of which enacted revised Title 11.

Section 404(d) of the Act of November 6, 1978, referred to in par. (22)(A), is section 404(d) of Pub. L. 95–598, title IV, Nov. 6, 1978, 92 Stat. 2684, which was set out in a note preceding section 151 of Title 28, Judiciary and Judicial Procedure, and was repealed by Pub. L. 98–353, title I, § 114, July 10, 1984, 98 Stat. 343.

Section 167 of the Federal Courts Improvement Act of 1982, referred to in par. (26), is section 167 of Pub. L. 97–164, which is set out as a note under section 171 of Title 28.

AMENDMENTS

2000—Par. (3). Pub. L. 106–571, § 3(a)(4), substituted "through (H)" for "through (G)" in concluding provisions.

Par. (3)(H). Pub. L. 106–571, § 3(a)(1)–(3), added subpar. (H).

Par. (28). Pub. L. 106–571, § 3(b)(2), added par. (28).

1998—Par. (3). Pub. L. 105–277 struck out "and" at end of subpar. (D), added subpars. (E) and (F), redesignated former subpar. (E) as (G), and, in concluding provisions, substituted "subparagraphs (B) through (G)" for "subparagraphs (B), (C), (D), and (E)".

Par. (27). Pub. L. 105–261 added par. (27).

1994—Par. (13). Pub. L. 103–353 inserted before semicolon at end "or full-time National Guard duty (as such term is defined in section 101(d) of title 10) if such service interrupts creditable civilian service under this subchapter and is followed by reemployment in accordance with chapter 43 of title 38 that occurs on or after August 1, 1990".

1993—Par. (3). Pub. L. 103–66 added subpar. (E), and in closing provisions substituted "subparagraphs (B), (C), (D), and (E) of this paragraph" for "subparagraphs (B), (C), and (D) of this paragraph,".

1992—Par. (1)(L). Pub. L. 102–378, § 2(57)(A)(i), substituted "section 8347(q)(1)" for "section 8347(p)(1)".

Par. (1)(ii). Pub. L. 102–378, § 2(57)(A)(ii), substituted "section 8347(q)(2)" for "section 8347(p)(2)".

Par. (7). Pub. L. 102–378, § 2(57)(B), substituted "University" for "College".

Par. (26). Pub. L. 102–572 substituted "Court of Federal Claims" for "Claims Court" and "United States Court of Federal Claims" for "United States Claims Court".

1990—Par. (1)(L). Pub. L. 101–508, § 7202(j)(1)(A)–(C), added subpar. (L).

Par. (1)(ii). Pub. L. 101–508, § 7202(j)(1)(D), substituted "(besides any employee excluded by clause (x), but including any employee who has made an election under section 8347(p)(2) to remain covered by a retirement system established for employees described in section 2105(c))" for "(other than an employee described in clause (x)".

Par. (1)(v). Pub. L. 101–474 amended cl. (v) generally. Prior to amendment, cl. (v) read as follows: "a temporary employee of the Administrative Office of the United States Courts or of a court named by section 610 of title 28;".

Par. (7). Pub. L. 101–508, § 7202(j)(1)(E), substituted "Gallaudet College, and, in the case of an employee described in paragraph (1)(L), a nonappropriated fund in-

strumentality of the Department of Defense or the Coast Guard described in section 2105(c)" for "and Gallaudet College".

Par. (26). Pub. L. 101–650 added par. (26).

1988—Par. (1)(K). Pub. L. 100–679 added subpar. (K).

Par. (1)(xii). Pub. L. 100–238, § 112, added cl. (xii).

Par. (18). Pub. L. 100–238, § 123, inserted "but does not include any amount attributable to—

"(i) the Federal Employees' Retirement System; or

"(ii) contributions made under the Federal Employees' Retirement Contribution Temporary Adjustment Act of 1983 by or on behalf of any individual who became subject to the Federal Employees' Retirement System;".

1987—Par. (22). Pub. L. 100–53, § 2(a)(1), amended par. (22) generally. Prior to amendment, par. (22) read as follows: "'bankruptcy judge' means an individual appointed under section 34 of the Bankruptcy Act (11 U.S.C. 62) or under section 404(d) of the Act of November 6, 1978 (Public Law 95–598; 92 Stat. 2549)—

"(A) who is serving as a United States bankruptcy judge on March 31, 1984;

"(B) whose service as United States bankruptcy judge at any time in the period beginning on October 1, 1979, and ending on July 10, 1984, is terminated by reason of death or disability; or

"(C) who is appointed as a bankruptcy judge under section 152 of title 28;".

Par. (25). Pub. L. 100–53, § 2(a)(2)–(4), added par. (25).

1986—Par. (1)(G). Pub. L. 99–335, § 207(f)(1), amended subpar. (G) generally, substituting "first employed" for "employed" and inserting "before October 1, 1987".

Par. (1)(ii). Pub. L. 99–335, § 202(a)(1), amended cl. (ii) generally, inserting "(other than an employee described in clause (x)".

Par. (1)(x). Pub. L. 99–335, § 202(a)(2)–(4), added cl. (x).

Par. (1)(xi). Pub. L. 99–335, § 207(f)(2), added cl. (xi).

Par. (2). Pub. L. 99–335, § 202(b), inserted ", but does not include any such Member of Congress who is subject to the Federal Employees' Retirement System or who makes an election under section 8401(20) of this title not to be subject to such System".

1984—Par. (22). Pub. L. 98–353, § 116(a)(1), substituted "of November 6, 1978 (Public Law 95–598; 92 Stat. 2549)" for "adding this paragraph" in provision preceding subpar. (A).

Par. (22)(A). Pub. L. 98–531 substituted "who is serving as a United States bankruptcy judge on March 31, 1984;" for "who is serving as a United States bankruptcy judge on the date of enactment of the Bankruptcy Amendments and Federal Judgeship Act of 1984, and continues to serve as a bankruptcy judge after such date until either the date on which a successor for such judge is appointed, or October 1, 1986, whichever date is earlier;".

Pub. L. 98–353, § 121(g), substituted "the day before the date of enactment of the Bankruptcy Amendments and Federal Judgeship Act of 1984" for "June 27, 1984".

Pub. L. 98–353, § 116(a)(2), substituted "who is serving as a United States bankruptcy judge on the date of enactment of the Bankruptcy Amendments and Federal Judgeship Act of 1984, and continues to serve as a bankruptcy judge after such date until either the date on which a successor for such judge is appointed, or October 1, 1986, whichever date is earlier;" for "who is serving as a United States bankruptcy judge on June 27, 1984, and that has agreed by filing a notice of such agreement with the President, the Senate, and the Director of the Administrative Office of the United States Courts, to accept an appointment as a judge of a United States bankruptcy court established under section 201 of this Act but that is not appointed by the President as a judge of such court; or".

Pub. L. 98–325 substituted "June 27, 1984" for "June 20, 1984".

Pub. L. 98–299 substituted "June 20, 1984" for "May 25, 1984".

Pub. L. 98–271 substituted "May 25, 1984" for "April 30, 1984".

Pub. L. 98–249 substituted "April 30, 1984" for "March 31, 1984".

Par. (22)(B). Pub. L. 98–531 substituted "whose service as United States bankruptcy judge at any time in the period beginning on October 1, 1979, and ending on July 10, 1984, is terminated by reason of death or disability" for "whose service as a United States bankruptcy judge during the period beginning on October 1, 1979, and ending on the date of enactment of the Bankruptcy Amendments and Federal Judgeship Act of 1984 is terminated by reason of death or disability".

Pub. L. 98–353, § 116(a)(3)(A), substituted "period beginning on October 1, 1979, and ending on the date of enactment of the Bankruptcy Amendments and Federal Judgeship Act of 1984" for "transition period".

Par. (22)(C). Pub. L. 98–353, § 116(a)(4), added subpar. (C).

Pars. (23), (24). Pub. L. 98–615 added pars. (23) and (24).

1982—Par. (8)(B). Pub. L. 97–253, § 306(a), inserted ", including any amounts deposited under section 8334(j) of this title".

1980—Par. (6). Pub. L. 96–499 struck out par. (6) which defined "disabled" and "disability" as meaning totally disabled or total disability for useful and efficient service in the grade or class of position last occupied by the employee or Member because of disease or injury not due to vicious habits, intemperance, or wilful misconduct on his part within 5 years of becoming disabled.

1979—Par. (2). Pub. L. 96–54, § 2(a)(47)(A), struck out "and a Delegate to Congress," after "title,".

Par. (19)(C). Pub. L. 96–54, § 2(a)(47)(B), struck out "and" after "determined;".

1978—Pars. (1), (17), (20). Pub. L. 95–454 substituted "Office of Personnel Management" and "Office" for "Civil Service Commission" and "Commission", respectively, wherever appearing.

Par. (22). Pub. L. 95–598 added par. (22).

1975—Par. (4). Pub. L. 94–183 struck out provision relating to member's option of having average pay computed from averaging rates of basic pay in effect over all periods of member's service after August 2, 1946.

1974—Par. (3). Pub. L. 93–350, § 2(a), added subpar. (D) and inserted reference to subpar. (D) in closing provisions of par. (3).

Pars. (20), (21). Pub. L. 93–350, § 2(b), added pars. (20) and (21).

1972—Par. (1)(J). Pub. L. 92–352 added par. (1)(J).

1969—Par. (4)(A). Pub. L. 91–93, § 201(a), reduced the number of years of creditable service from 5 to 3 consecutive years and provided for averaging rate of basic pay over the total service in the case of an annuity under subsec. (d) or (e)(1) of section 8341 of this title based on service of less than three years.

Pars. (17) to (19). Pub. L. 91–93, § 101, added pars. (17) to (19).

1968—Par. (3)(B)(ii). Pub. L. 90–623 inserted reference to section 60e–14 of title 2.

1966—Par. (3). Pub. L. 89–737 added subpar. (C) and, in the exception set out in provisions following subpar. (C), substituted reference to subpars. (B) and (C) for reference to subpar. (B).

Change of Name

Words "magistrate judge" and "United States magistrate judge" substituted for "magistrate" and "United States magistrate", respectively, in par. (25) pursuant to section 321 of Pub. L. 101–650, set out as a note under section 631 of Title 28, Judiciary and Judicial Procedure.

Gallaudet College, referred to in par. (1)(H), redesignated Gallaudet University by section 101(a) of Pub. L. 99–371, which is classified to section 4301(a) of Title 20, Education.

Commissioned Officer Corps of Environmental Science Services Administration, referred to in par. (13)(C), changed to Commissioned Officer Corps of National Oceanic and Atmospheric Administration, see 1970 Reorg. Plan No. 4, § 4(d), eff. Oct. 3, 1970, 35 F.R. 15627, 84 Stat. 2090, set out in the Appendix to this title.

Effective Date of 1998 Amendments

Amendment by Pub. L. 105–277 effective on first day of first applicable pay period which begins on or after Oct. 1, 1998, see section 101(h) [title VI, § 628(e)] of Pub. L. 105–277, set out as a note under section 4109 of this title.

Pub. L. 105–261, div. C, title XXXI, § 3154(m), (n), Oct. 17, 1998, 112 Stat. 2256, provided that:

"(m) APPLICABILITY.—Subsections (b) through (l) [amending this section and sections 8334 to 8336, 8401, 8412, 8415, 8422, 8423, and 8425 of this title and enacting provisions set out as notes under sections 8334, 8348, and 8422 of this title] shall apply only to an individual who is employed as a nuclear materials courier, as defined by section 8331(27) or 8401(33) of title 5, United States Code (as amended by this section), after the later of—

"(1) September 30, 1998; or

"(2) the date of the enactment of this Act [Oct. 17, 1998].

"(n) EFFECTIVE DATES.—(1) Except as provided in paragraph (2), the amendments made by this section [amending this section and sections 3307, 8334 to 8336, 8401, 8412, 8415, 8422, 8423, and 8425 of this title] shall take effect at the beginning of the first pay period that begins after the later of—

"(A) October 1, 1998; or

"(B) the date of the enactment of this Act.

"(2)(A) The amendments made by subsection (a) [amending section 3307 of this title] shall take effect on the date of the enactment of this Act.

"(B) The amendments made by subsections (d) and (k) [amending sections 8335 and 8425 of this title] shall take effect 1 year after the date of the enactment of this Act."

Effective Date of 1994 Amendment

Amendment by Pub. L. 103–353 effective with respect to reemployments initiated on or after the first day after the 60-day period beginning Oct. 13, 1994, with transition rules, see section 8 of Pub. L. 103–353, set out as an Effective Date note under section 4301 of Title 38, Veterans' Benefits.

Effective Date of 1993 Amendment

Section 13812(c)(1) of Pub. L. 103–66 provided that: "The amendments made by subsection (a) [amending this section] take effect on January 1, 1994, and apply only with respect to service performed on or after such date."

Effective Date of 1992 Amendments

Amendment by Pub. L. 102–572 effective Oct. 29, 1992, see section 911 of Pub. L. 102–572, set out as a note under section 171 of Title 28, Judiciary and Judicial Procedure.

Amendment by section 2(57)(A) of Pub. L. 102–378 effective Nov. 5, 1990, and amendment by section 2(57)(B) of Pub. L. 102–378 effective Oct. 2, 1992, see section 9(a), (b)(6) of Pub. L. 102–378, set out as a note under section 6303 of this title.

Effective Date of 1990 Amendments

Section 306(f) of Pub. L. 101–650, as amended by Pub. L. 102–572, title IX, § 902(b)(1), Oct. 29, 1992, 106 Stat. 4516, provided that: "This section and the amendments made by this section [enacting section 8440b [now 8440c] of this title and section 178 of Title 28, Judiciary and Judicial Procedure and amending this section, sections 8334, 8336, 8339, and 8402 of this title, and sections 376 and 604 of Title 28] shall apply to judges of, and senior judges in active service with, the United States Court of Federal Claims on or after the date of the enactment of this Act [Dec. 1, 1990]."

Amendment by Pub. L. 101–508 applicable with respect to any individual who, on or after Jan. 1, 1987, moves from employment in nonappropriated fund instrumentality of Department of Defense or Coast Guard, that is described in section 2105(c) of this title, to employment in Department or Coast Guard, that is not described in section 2105(c), or who moves from employment in Department or Coast Guard, that is not described in section 2105(c), to employment in nonappropriated fund instrumentality of Department or Coast Guard, that is described in section 2105(c), see section 7202(m)(1) of Pub. L. 101–508, set out as a note under section 2105 of this title.

EFFECTIVE DATE OF 1987 AMENDMENT

Section 3 of Pub. L. 100–53, as amended by Pub. L. 101–650, title III, § 321, Dec. 1, 1990, 104 Stat. 5117, provided that: "This Act [amending this section and sections 8334, 8336, and 8339 of this title and enacting provisions set out as a note under this section] shall take effect on October 1, 1987, and shall apply to bankruptcy judges and United States magistrate judges in office on that date and to individuals subsequently appointed to such positions to whom chapter 83 of title 5, United States Code, otherwise applies."

EFFECTIVE DATE OF 1986 AMENDMENT

Amendment by Pub. L. 99–335 effective Jan. 1, 1987, see section 702(a) of Pub. L. 99–335, set out as an Effective Date note under section 8401 of this title.

EFFECTIVE DATE OF 1984 AMENDMENTS

Amendment by Pub. L. 98–615 effective May 7, 1985, with enumerated exceptions and specific applicability provisions, see section 4(a)(1) of Pub. L. 98–615 as amended, set out as a note under section 8341 of this title.

Section 3 of Pub. L. 98–531 provided that:

"(a) Except as provided in subsection (b), this Act and the amendments made by this Act [renumbering a provision set out as a note under section 101 of Title 11, Bankruptcy] shall take effect on July 10, 1984.

"(b) The amendments made by section 2 [amending this section and sections 8336 and 8339 of this title] shall take effect on March 31, 1984."

Amendment by Pub. L. 98–353 effective July 10, 1984, see section 122(a) of Pub. L. 98–353, set out as an Effective Date note under section 151 of Title 28, Judiciary and Judicial Procedure.

Section 116(e) of Pub. L. 98–353 provided that: "The amendments made by this section [amending this section and sections 8334, 8336, and 8339 of this title] shall take effect on the date of enactment [July 10, 1984] and shall apply to bankruptcy judges who retire on or after such date."

EFFECTIVE DATE OF 1982 AMENDMENT

Section 306(g) of Pub. L. 97–253, as amended by Pub. L. 97–346, § 3(e)(2), Oct. 15, 1982, 96 Stat. 1648; Pub. L. 98–369, div. B, title II, § 2205, July 18, 1984, 98 Stat. 1059, provided that: "The amendments made by this section [amending this section and sections 8332, 8334, and 8348 of this title] shall take effect October 1, 1982; except that any employee or Member who retired after the date of the enactment of this Act [Sept. 8, 1982] and before October 1, 1985, or is entitled to an annuity under chapter 83 of title 5, United States Code, based on a separation from service occurring during such period, or a survivor of such individual, may make a payment under section 8334(j)(1) of title 5, United States Code. Regulations required to be issued under section 8334(j)(1) of title 5, United States Code, shall be issued by the Office of Personnel Management within 90 days after such effective date."

EFFECTIVE DATE OF 1980 AMENDMENT

Section 403(c) of Pub. L. 96–499 provided that: "The amendments made by this section [amending this section and section 8337 of this title] shall take effect on the 90th day after the date of the enactment of this Act [Dec. 5, 1980]."

EFFECTIVE DATE OF 1979 AMENDMENT

Amendment by Pub. L. 96–54 effective July 12, 1979, see section 2(b) of Pub. L. 96–54, set out as a note under section 305 of this title.

EFFECTIVE DATE OF 1978 AMENDMENTS

Amendment by Pub. L. 95–598 effective Nov. 6, 1978, see section 402(d) of Pub. L. 95–598, set out as an Effec-

tive Date note preceding section 101 of Title 11, Bankruptcy.

Amendment by Pub. L. 95–454 effective 90 days after Oct. 13, 1978, see section 907 of Pub. L. 95–454, set out as a note under section 1101 of this title.

EFFECTIVE DATE OF 1974 AMENDMENT

Amendment by section 2(a) of Pub. L. 93–350 effective at beginning of first applicable pay period which begins after Dec. 31, 1974, and amendment by section 2(b) of Pub. L. 93–350 effective July 12, 1974, see section 7 of Pub. L. 93–350, set out as a note under section 3307 of this title.

EFFECTIVE DATE OF 1972 AMENDMENT

Section 105(b) of Pub. L. 92–352 provided that: "Subsection (a) of this section [amending this section] shall become effective on the first day of the second month which begins after its enactment [July 13, 1972]."

EFFECTIVE DATE OF 1969 AMENDMENT

Section 207(a) of Pub. L. 91–93 provided that: "The amendments made by sections 201, 202, 203, and 206(a) of this Act [amending this section and sections 8333, 8334, 8339, and 8341 of this title] shall not apply in the case of persons retired or otherwise separated prior to the date of enactment of this Act [Oct. 20, 1969], and the rights of such persons and their survivors shall continue in the same manner and to the same extent as if such sections had not been enacted."

EFFECTIVE DATE OF 1968 AMENDMENT

Amendment by Pub. L. 90–623 intended to restate without substantive change the law in effect on Oct. 22, 1968, see section 6 of Pub. L. 90–623, set out as a note under section 5334 of this title.

EFFECTIVE DATE OF 1966 AMENDMENT

Amendment by Pub. L. 89–737 applicable with respect to premium pay payable from and after first day of first pay period which begins after Nov. 2, 1966, see section 4 of Pub. L. 89–737, set out in the note under section 8114 of this title.

SHORT TITLE OF 1994 AMENDMENT

Pub. L. 103–358, § 1, Oct. 14, 1994, 108 Stat. 3420, provided that: "This Act [amending sections 8345, 8437, and 8467 of this title and enacting provisions set out as a note under section 8345 of this title] may be cited as the 'Child Abuse Accountability Act'."

SHORT TITLE OF 1990 AMENDMENT

Pub. L. 101–428, § 1(a), Oct. 15, 1990, 104 Stat. 928, provided that: "This Act [amending sections 8335 to 8337, 8339, 8341, 8344, 8412, and 8425 of this title and enacting provisions set out as notes under sections 8335, 8339, and 8425 of this title] may be cited as the 'Capitol Police Retirement Act'."

SHORT TITLE OF 1987 AMENDMENT

Section 1 of Pub. L. 100–53 provided that: "This Act [amending this section and sections 8334, 8336, and 8339 of this title and enacting provisions set out as a note under this section] may be cited as the 'Magistrates' Retirement Parity Act of 1987'."

SHORT TITLE OF 1986 AMENDMENT

Pub. L. 99–638, § 2(a), Nov. 10, 1986, 100 Stat. 3535, provided that: "This section [amending sections 2105 and 8332 of this title and enacting provisions set out as a note under section 8332 of this title] may be cited as the 'Nonappropriated Fund Instrumentalities Employees' Retirement Credit Act of 1986'."

SHORT TITLE OF 1984 AMENDMENT

Section 1 of Pub. L. 98–615 provided: "That this Act [enacting sections 3595a, 4302a and 5406–5410 of this title, amending this section and sections 3135, 3393, 3395, 3593–3595, 4312, 4501, 5332, 5334–5336, 5361, 5362, 5383, 5384, 5401–5405, 5948, 7543, 8334, 8336, 8339, 8341, 8342, 8345, 8348, 8901–8903, 8905, 8907, 8909, and 8913 of this title, section 1602 of Title 10, Armed Forces, and section 731 of Title 31, Money and Finance, and enacting provisions set out as notes under sections 3131, 3135, 5401, and 8341 of this title] may be cited as the 'Civil Service Retirement Spouse Equity Act of 1984'."

SHORT TITLE OF 1969 AMENDMENT

Section 1 of Pub. L. 91–93 provided: "That this Act [amending this section and sections 1308, 8333, 8334, 8339, 8340, 8341, and 8348 of this title, enacting provisions set out as notes under sections 8334, 8340, 8341, and 8348 of this title, and repealing provisions set out as a note under section 8339 of this title] may be cited as the 'Civil Service Retirement Amendments of 1969'."

SAVINGS PROVISION

Section 105(c) of Pub. L. 92–352 provided that: "The amendments made by such subsection (a) [amending this section] shall not apply in the cases of persons retired or otherwise separated prior to the effective date established under subsection (b) of this section [see Effective Date of 1972 Amendment note above], and the rights of such persons and their survivors shall continue in the same manner and to the same extent as if such amendments had not been enacted."

SUPREME COURT POLICE RETIREMENT

Pub. L. 106–553, § 1(a)(2) [title III, § 308], Dec. 21, 2000, 114 Stat. 2762, 2762A–86, provided that:

"(a) SUPREME COURT POLICE RETIREMENT.—

"(1) SERVICE DEEMED TO BE SERVICE AS LAW ENFORCEMENT OFFICER.—Any period of service performed before the effective date of this section by an individual as a member of the Supreme Court Police, who is such a member on such date, shall be deemed to be service performed as a law enforcement officer for purposes of chapters 83 and 84 of title 5, United States Code. Notwithstanding any amendment made by this section, any period of service performed before the effective date of this section by an individual as a member of the Supreme Court Police, who is not such a member on such date, shall be employee service for purposes of chapters 83 and 84 of title 5, United States Code.

"(2) CONTRIBUTIONS.—The Marshal of the Supreme Court of the United States shall pay an amount determined by the Office of Personnel Management equal to—

"(A)(i) the difference between—

"(I) the amount that was deducted and withheld from basic pay under chapters 83 and 84 of title 5, United States Code, for the period of service described in the first sentence of paragraph (1); and

"(II) the amount that should have been deducted and withheld for such period of service, if it had instead been performed as a law enforcement officer; and

"(ii) interest as prescribed under section 8334(e) of title 5, United States Code, based on the amount determined under clause (i); and

"(B) with respect to the period of service described in subparagraph (A), the difference between the Government contributions that were in fact made to the Civil Service Retirement and Disability Fund for such service, and the amount that would have been required if such service had instead been performed as a law enforcement officer, subject to subsection (f).

"(3) DEPOSIT OF PAYMENTS.—Payments under paragraph (2) shall be paid from the salaries and expenses account from appropriations to the Supreme Court of the United States, including any prior year unobligated balances, and deposited in the Civil Service Retirement and Disability Fund.

"(b) AMENDMENTS TO CHAPTER 83.—[Amended sections 8334 to 8336 and 8339 of this title.]

"(c) AMENDMENTS TO CHAPTER 84.—[Amended sections 8412, 8415, 8422, 8423, and 8425 of this title.]

"(d) PAYMENTS FOR OTHER LIABILITY.—

"(1) IN GENERAL.—The Marshal of the Supreme Court of the United States shall pay into the Civil Service Retirement and Disability Fund an amount determined by the Director of the Office of Personnel Management to be necessary to reimburse the Fund for any estimated increase in the unfunded liability of the Fund resulting from the amendments related to the Civil Service Retirement System under this section, and for any estimated increase in the supplemental liability of the Fund resulting from the amendments related to the Federal Employees' Retirement System under this section.

"(2) INSTALLMENTS.—The amount determined under paragraph (1) shall be paid in 5 equal annual installments with interest computed at the rates used in the most recent valuation of the Federal Employees' Retirement System.

"(3) SOURCE OF FUNDS.—Payments under this subsection shall be made from amounts available from the salaries and expenses account from appropriations to the Supreme Court of the United States, including any prior year unobligated balances.

"(e) NO MANDATORY SEPARATION FOR A 2-Year Period.—Nothing in section 8335(e) or 8425(d) of title 5, United States Code, as added by this section, shall require the automatic separation of any member of the Supreme Court Police before the end of the 2-year period beginning on the effective date of this section.

"(f) NONREDUCTION IN GOVERNMENT CONTRIBUTIONS.—Notwithstanding any other provision of this section, Government contributions to the Civil Service Retirement and Disability Fund on behalf of a member of the Supreme Court Police shall, with respect to any service performed during the period beginning on January 1, 1999, and ending on December 31, 2002, while subject to the Federal Employees' Retirement System, be determined in the same way as if this section had never been enacted.

"(g) SAVINGS PROVISION.—Nothing in this section or in any amendment made by this section shall, with respect to any service performed before the effective date of such amendment, have the effect of reducing the percentage applicable in computing any portion of an annuity based on service as a member of the Supreme Court Police below the percentage which would otherwise apply if this section had not been enacted.

"(h) TECHNICAL AND CONFORMING AMENDMENTS.—[Amended sections 8337, 8339, 8341, 8343a, and 8344 of this title.]

"(i) APPLICABILITY.—This section and the amendments made by this section shall apply only to an individual who is employed as a member of the Supreme Court Police after the later of October 1, 2000, or the date of enactment of this Act [Dec. 21, 2000].

"(j) EFFECTIVE DATE.—Except as otherwise provided in this section, this section and the amendments made by this section shall take effect on the first day of the first applicable pay period that begins on the later of October 1, 2000, or the date of enactment of this Act."

FEDERAL RETIREMENT COVERAGE ERRORS CORRECTION

Pub. L. 106–265, title II, Sept. 19, 2000, 114 Stat. 770, provided that:

"SEC. 2001. SHORT TITLE; TABLE OF CONTENTS.

"(a) SHORT TITLE.—This title may be cited as the 'Federal Erroneous Retirement Coverage Corrections Act'.

"(b) TABLE OF CONTENTS.—[Omitted.]

"SEC. 2002. DEFINITIONS.

"For purposes of this title:

"(1) ANNUITANT.—The term 'annuitant' has the meaning given such term under section 8331(9) or 8401(2) of title 5, United States Code.

"(2) CSRS.—The term 'CSRS' means the Civil Service Retirement System.

"(3) CSRDF.—The term 'CSRDF' means the Civil Service Retirement and Disability Fund.

"(4) CSRS COVERED.—The term 'CSRS covered', with respect to any service, means service that is subject to the provisions of subchapter III of chapter 83 of title 5, United States Code, other than service subject to section 8334(k) of such title.

"(5) CSRS-OFFSET COVERED.—The term 'CSRS-Offset covered', with respect to any service, means service that is subject to the provisions of subchapter III of chapter 83 of title 5, United States Code, and to section 8334(k) of such title.

"(6) EMPLOYEE.—The term 'employee' has the meaning given such term under section 8331(1) or 8401(11) of title 5, United States Code.

"(7) EXECUTIVE DIRECTOR.—The term 'Executive Director of the Federal Retirement Thrift Investment Board' or 'Executive Director' means the Executive Director appointed under section 8474 of title 5, United States Code.

"(8) FERS.—The term 'FERS' means the Federal Employees' Retirement System.

"(9) FERS COVERED.—The term 'FERS covered', with respect to any service, means service that is subject to chapter 84 of title 5, United States Code.

"(10) FORMER EMPLOYEE.—The term 'former employee' means an individual who was an employee, but who is not an annuitant.

"(11) OASDI TAXES.—The term 'OASDI taxes' means the OASDI employee tax and the OASDI employer tax.

"(12) OASDI EMPLOYEE TAX.—The term 'OASDI employee tax' means the tax imposed under section 3101(a) of the Internal Revenue Code of 1986 [26 U.S.C. 3101(a)] (relating to Old-Age, Survivors and Disability Insurance).

"(13) OASDI EMPLOYER TAX.—The term 'OASDI employer tax' means the tax imposed under section 3111(a) of the Internal Revenue Code of 1986 [26 U.S.C. 3111(a)] (relating to Old-Age, Survivors and Disability Insurance).

"(14) OASDI TRUST FUNDS.—The term 'OASDI trust funds' means the Federal Old-Age and Survivors Insurance Trust Fund and the Federal Disability Insurance Trust Fund.

"(15) OFFICE.—The term 'Office' means the Office of Personnel Management.

"(16) RETIREMENT COVERAGE DETERMINATION.—The term 'retirement coverage determination' means a determination by an employee or agent of the Government as to whether a particular type of Government service is CSRS covered, CSRS-Offset covered, FERS covered, or Social Security-Only covered.

"(17) RETIREMENT COVERAGE ERROR.—The term 're-tirement coverage error' means an erroneous retirement coverage determination that was in effect for a minimum period of 3 years of service after December 31, 1986.

"(18) SOCIAL SECURITY-ONLY COVERED.—The term 'Social Security-Only covered', with respect to any service, means Government service that—

"(A) constitutes employment under section 210 of the Social Security Act (42 U.S.C. 410); and

"(B)(i) is subject to OASDI taxes; but

"(ii) is not subject to CSRS or FERS.

"(19) SURVIVOR.—The term 'survivor' has the meaning given such term under section 8331(10) or 8401(28) of title 5, United States Code.

"(20) THRIFT SAVINGS FUND.—The term 'Thrift Savings Fund' means the Thrift Savings Fund established under section 8437 of title 5, United States Code.

"SEC. 2003. APPLICABILITY.

"(a) IN GENERAL.—This title shall apply with respect to retirement coverage errors that occur before, on, or after the date of the enactment of this Act [Sept. 19, 2000].

"(b) LIMITATION.—Except as otherwise provided in this title, this title shall not apply to any erroneous re-tirement coverage determination that was in effect for a period of less than 3 years of service after December 31, 1986.

"SEC. 2004. IRREVOCABILITY OF ELECTIONS.

"Any election made (or deemed to have been made) by an employee or any other individual under this title shall be irrevocable.

"SUBTITLE A—DESCRIPTION OF RETIREMENT COVERAGE ERRORS TO WHICH THIS TITLE APPLIES AND MEAS-URES FOR THEIR RECTIFICATION

"CHAPTER 1—EMPLOYEES AND ANNUITANTS WHO SHOULD HAVE BEEN FERS COVERED, BUT WHO WERE ERRO-NEOUSLY CSRS COVERED OR CSRS-OFFSET COVERED IN-STEAD, AND SURVIVORS OF SUCH EMPLOYEES AND AN-NUITANTS

"SEC. 2101. EMPLOYEES.

"(a) APPLICABILITY.—This section shall apply in the case of any employee or former employee who should be (or should have been) FERS covered but, as a result of a retirement coverage error, is (or was) CSRS cov-ered or CSRS-Offset covered instead.

"(b) UNCORRECTED ERROR.—

"(1) APPLICABILITY.—This subsection applies if the retirement coverage error has not been corrected be-fore the effective date of the regulations described under paragraph (3). As soon as practicable after dis-covery of the error, and subject to the right of an election under paragraph (2), if CSRS covered or CSRS-Offset covered, such individual shall be treated as CSRS-Offset covered, retroactive to the date of the retirement coverage error.

"(2) COVERAGE.—

"(A) ELECTION.—Upon written notice of a retire-ment coverage error, an individual may elect to be CSRS-Offset covered or FERS covered, effective as of the date of the retirement coverage error. Such election shall be made not later than 180 days after the date of receipt of such notice.

"(B) NONELECTION.—If the individual does not make an election by the date provided under sub-paragraph (A), a CSRS-Offset covered individual shall remain CSRS-Offset covered and a CSRS cov-ered individual shall be treated as CSRS-Offset cov-ered.

"(3) REGULATIONS.—The Office shall prescribe regu-lations to carry out this subsection.

"(c) CORRECTED ERROR.—

"(1) APPLICABILITY.—This subsection applies if the retirement coverage error was corrected before the effective date of the regulations described under sub-section (b).

"(2) COVERAGE.—

"(A) ELECTION.—

"(i) CSRS-OFFSET COVERED.—Not later than 180 days after the date of the enactment of this Act [Sept. 19, 2000], the Office shall prescribe regula-tions authorizing individuals to elect, during the 18-month period immediately following the effec-tive date of such regulations, to be CSRS-Offset covered, effective as of the date of the retirement coverage error.

"(ii) THRIFT SAVINGS FUND CONTRIBUTIONS.—If under this section an individual elects to be CSRS-Offset covered, all employee contributions to the Thrift Savings Fund made during the pe-riod of FERS coverage (and earnings on such con-tributions) may remain in the Thrift Savings Fund in accordance with regulations prescribed by the Executive Director, notwithstanding any limit under title 5, United States Code, that would otherwise be applicable.

"(B) PREVIOUS SETTLEMENT PAYMENT.—An individ-ual who previously received a payment ordered by a court or provided as a settlement of claim for losses resulting from a retirement coverage error shall not be entitled to make an election under this subsection unless that amount is waived in whole or in part under section 2208, and any amount not waived is repaid.

"(C) INELIGIBILITY FOR ELECTION.—An individual who, subsequent to correction of the retirement coverage error, received a refund of retirement deductions under section 8424 of title 5, United States Code, or a distribution under section 8433(b), (c), or (h)(1)(A) of title 5, United States Code, may not make an election under this subsection.

"(3) CORRECTIVE ACTION TO REMAIN IN EFFECT.—If an individual is ineligible to make an election or does not make an election under paragraph (2) before the end of any time limitation under this subsection, the corrective action taken before such time limitation shall remain in effect.

"SEC. 2102. ANNUITANTS AND SURVIVORS.

"(a) IN GENERAL.—This section shall apply in the case of an individual who is—

"(1) an annuitant who should have been FERS covered but, as a result of a retirement coverage error, was CSRS covered or CSRS-Offset covered instead; or

"(2) a survivor of an employee who should have been FERS covered but, as a result of a retirement coverage error, was CSRS covered or CSRS-Offset covered instead.

"(b) COVERAGE.—

"(1) ELECTION.—Not later than 180 days after the date of the enactment of this Act [Sept. 19, 2000], the Office shall prescribe regulations authorizing an individual described under subsection (a) to elect CSRS-Offset coverage or FERS coverage, effective as of the date of the retirement coverage error.

"(2) TIME LIMITATION.—An election under this subsection shall be made not later than 18 months after the effective date of the regulations prescribed under paragraph (1).

"(3) REDUCED ANNUITY.—

"(A) AMOUNT IN ACCOUNT.—If the individual elects CSRS-Offset coverage, the amount in the employee's Thrift Savings Fund account under subchapter III of chapter 84 of title 5, United States Code, on the date of retirement that represents the Government's contributions and earnings on those contributions (whether or not such amount was subsequently distributed from the Thrift Savings Fund) will form the basis for a reduction in the individual's annuity, under regulations prescribed by the Office.

"(B) REDUCTION.—The reduced annuity to which the individual is entitled shall be equal to an amount which, when taken together with the amount referred to in subparagraph (A), would result in the present value of the total being actuarially equivalent to the present value of an unreduced CSRS-Offset annuity that would have been provided the individual.

"(4) REDUCED BENEFIT.—If—

"(A) a surviving spouse elects CSRS-Offset benefits; and

"(B) a FERS basic employee death benefit under section 8442(b) of title 5, United States Code, was previously paid,

then the survivor's CSRS-Offset benefit shall be subject to a reduction, under regulations prescribed by the Office. The reduced annuity to which the individual is entitled shall be equal to an amount which, when taken together with the amount of the payment referred to under subparagraph (B) would result in the present value of the total being actuarially equivalent to the present value of an unreduced CSRS-Offset annuity that would have been provided the individual.

"(5) PREVIOUS SETTLEMENT PAYMENT.—An individual who previously received a payment ordered by a court or provided as a settlement of claim for losses resulting from a retirement coverage error may not make an election under this subsection unless repayment of that amount is waived in whole or in part under section 2208, and any amount not waived is repaid.

"(c) NONELECTION.—If the individual does not make an election under subsection (b) before any time limitation under this section, the retirement coverage shall be subject to the following rules:

"(1) CORRECTIVE ACTION PREVIOUSLY TAKEN.—If corrective action was taken before the end of any time limitation under this section, that corrective action shall remain in effect.

"(2) CORRECTIVE ACTION NOT PREVIOUSLY TAKEN.—If corrective action was not taken before such time limitation, the employee shall be CSRS-Offset covered, retroactive to the date of the retirement coverage error.

"CHAPTER 2—EMPLOYEE WHO SHOULD HAVE BEEN FERS COVERED, CSRS-OFFSET COVERED, OR CSRS COVERED, BUT WHO WAS ERRONEOUSLY SOCIAL SECURITY-ONLY COVERED INSTEAD

"SEC. 2111. APPLICABILITY.

"This chapter shall apply in the case of any employee who—

"(1) should be (or should have been) FERS covered but, as a result of a retirement coverage error, is (or was) Social Security-Only covered instead;

"(2) should be (or should have been) CSRS-Offset covered but, as a result of a retirement coverage error, is (or was) Social Security-Only covered instead; or

"(3) should be (or should have been) CSRS covered but, as a result of a retirement coverage error, is (or was) Social Security-Only covered instead.

"SEC. 2112. CORRECTION MANDATORY.

"(a) UNCORRECTED ERROR.—If the retirement coverage error has not been corrected, as soon as practicable after discovery of the error, such individual shall be covered under the correct retirement coverage, effective as of the date of the retirement coverage error.

"(b) CORRECTED ERROR.—If the retirement coverage error has been corrected, the corrective action previously taken shall remain in effect.

"CHAPTER 3—EMPLOYEE WHO SHOULD OR COULD HAVE BEEN SOCIAL SECURITY-ONLY COVERED BUT WHO WAS ERRONEOUSLY CSRS-OFFSET COVERED OR CSRS COVERED INSTEAD

"SEC. 2121. EMPLOYEE WHO SHOULD BE SOCIAL SECURITY-ONLY COVERED, BUT WHO IS ERRONEOUSLY CSRS OR CSRS-OFFSET COVERED INSTEAD.

"(a) APPLICABILITY.—This section applies in the case of a retirement coverage error in which a Social Security-Only covered employee was erroneously CSRS covered or CSRS-Offset covered.

"(b) UNCORRECTED ERROR.—

"(1) APPLICABILITY.—This subsection applies if the retirement coverage error has not been corrected before the effective date of the regulations described in paragraph (3).

"(2) COVERAGE.—In the case of an individual who is erroneously CSRS covered, as soon as practicable after discovery of the error, and subject to the right of an election under paragraph (3), such individual shall be CSRS-Offset covered, effective as of the date of the retirement coverage error.

"(3) ELECTION.—

"(A) IN GENERAL.—Upon written notice of a retirement coverage error, an individual may elect to be CSRS-Offset covered or Social Security-Only covered, effective as of the date of the retirement coverage error. Such election shall be made not later than 180 days after the date of receipt of such notice.

"(B) NONELECTION.—If the individual does not make an election before the date provided under subparagraph (A), the individual shall remain CSRS-Offset covered.

"(C) REGULATIONS.—The Office shall prescribe regulations to carry out this paragraph.

"(c) CORRECTED ERROR.—

"(1) APPLICABILITY.—This subsection applies if the retirement coverage error was corrected before the effective date of the regulations described under subsection (b)(3).

"(2) ELECTION.—Not later than 180 days after the date of the enactment of this Act [Sept. 19, 2000], the Office shall prescribe regulations authorizing individuals to elect, during the 18-month period immediately following the effective date of such regulations, to be CSRS-Offset covered or Social Security-Only covered, effective as of the date of the retirement coverage error.

"(3) NONELECTION.—If an eligible individual does not make an election under paragraph (2) before the end of any time limitation under this subsection, the corrective action taken before such time limitation shall remain in effect.

"CHAPTER 4—EMPLOYEE WHO WAS ERRONEOUSLY FERS COVERED

"SEC. 2131. EMPLOYEE WHO SHOULD BE SOCIAL SECURITY-ONLY COVERED, CSRS COVERED, OR CSRS-OFFSET COVERED AND IS NOT FERS-ELIGIBLE, BUT WHO IS ERRONEOUSLY FERS COVERED INSTEAD.

"(a) APPLICABILITY.—This section applies in the case of a retirement coverage error in which a Social Security-Only covered, CSRS covered, or CSRS-Offset covered employee not eligible to elect FERS coverage under authority of section 8402(c) of title 5, United States Code, was erroneously FERS covered.

"(b) UNCORRECTED ERROR.—

"(1) APPLICABILITY.—This subsection applies if the retirement coverage error has not been corrected before the effective date of the regulations described in paragraph (2).

"(2) COVERAGE.—

"(A) ELECTION.—

"(i) IN GENERAL.—Upon written notice of a retirement coverage error, an individual may elect to remain FERS covered or to be Social Security-Only covered, CSRS covered, or CSRS-Offset covered, as would have applied in the absence of the erroneous retirement coverage determination, effective as of the date of the retirement coverage error. Such election shall be made not later than 180 days after the date of receipt of such notice.

"(ii) TREATMENT OF FERS ELECTION.—An election of FERS coverage under this subsection is deemed to be an election under section 301 of the Federal Employees Retirement System Act of 1986 (5 U.S.C. 8331 note; Public Law 99–335; 100 Stat. 599).

"(B) NONELECTION.—If the individual does not make an election before the date provided under subparagraph (A), the individual shall remain FERS covered, effective as of the date of the retirement coverage error.

"(3) EMPLOYEE CONTRIBUTIONS IN THRIFT SAVINGS FUND.—If under this section, an individual elects to be Social Security-Only covered, CSRS covered, or CSRS-Offset covered, all employee contributions to the Thrift Savings Fund made during the period of erroneous FERS coverage (and all earnings on such contributions) may remain in the Thrift Savings Fund in accordance with regulations prescribed by the Executive Director, notwithstanding any limit under section 8351 or 8432 of title 5, United States Code.

"(4) REGULATIONS.—Except as provided under paragraph (3), the Office shall prescribe regulations to carry out this subsection.

"(c) CORRECTED ERROR.—

"(1) APPLICABILITY.—This subsection applies if the retirement coverage error was corrected before the effective date of the regulations described under paragraph (2).

"(2) ELECTION.—Not later than 180 days after the date of the enactment of this Act [Sept. 19, 2000], the

Office shall prescribe regulations authorizing individuals to elect, during the 18-month period immediately following the effective date of such regulations to remain Social Security-Only covered, CSRS covered, or CSRS-Offset covered, or to be FERS covered, effective as of the date of the retirement coverage error.

"(3) NONELECTION.—If an eligible individual does not make an election under paragraph (2), the corrective action taken before the end of any time limitation under this subsection shall remain in effect.

"(4) TREATMENT OF FERS ELECTION.—An election of FERS coverage under this subsection is deemed to be an election under section 301 of the Federal Employees Retirement System Act of 1986 (5 U.S.C. 8331 note; Public Law 99–335; 100 Stat. 599).

"SEC. 2132. FERS-ELIGIBLE EMPLOYEE WHO SHOULD HAVE BEEN CSRS COVERED, CSRS-OFFSET COVERED, OR SOCIAL SECURITY-ONLY COVERED, BUT WHO WAS ERRONEOUSLY FERS COVERED INSTEAD WITHOUT AN ELECTION.

"(a) IN GENERAL.—

"(1) FERS ELECTION PREVENTED.—If an individual was prevented from electing FERS coverage because the individual was erroneously FERS covered during the period when the individual was eligible to elect FERS under title III of the Federal Employees Retirement System Act [Pub. L. 99–335] or the Federal Employees' Retirement System Open Enrollment Act of 1997 (Public Law 105–61; 111 Stat. 1318 et seq.) [5 U.S.C. 8331 notes], the individual—

"(A) is deemed to have elected FERS coverage; and

"(B) shall remain covered by FERS, unless the individual declines, under regulations prescribed by the Office, to be FERS covered.

"(2) DECLINING FERS COVERAGE.—If an individual described under paragraph (1)(B) declines to be FERS covered, such individual shall be CSRS covered, CSRS-Offset covered, or Social Security-Only covered, as would apply in the absence of a FERS election, effective as of the date of the erroneous retirement coverage determination.

"(b) EMPLOYEE CONTRIBUTIONS IN THRIFT SAVINGS FUND.—If under this section, an individual declines to be FERS covered and instead is Social Security-Only covered, CSRS covered, or CSRS-Offset covered, as would apply in the absence of a FERS election, all employee contributions to the Thrift Savings Fund made during the period of erroneous FERS coverage (and all earnings on such contributions) may remain in the Thrift Savings Fund in accordance with regulations prescribed by the Executive Director, notwithstanding any limit under title 5, United States Code, that would otherwise be applicable.

"(c) INAPPLICABILITY OF DURATION OF ERRONEOUS COVERAGE.—This section shall apply regardless of the length of time the erroneous coverage determination remained in effect.

"SEC. 2133. RETROACTIVE EFFECT.

"This chapter shall be effective as of January 1, 1987, except that section 2132 shall not apply to individuals who made or were deemed to have made elections similar to those provided in this section under regulations prescribed by the Office before the effective date of this title.

"CHAPTER 5—EMPLOYEE WHO SHOULD HAVE BEEN CSRS-OFFSET COVERED, BUT WHO WAS ERRONEOUSLY CSRS COVERED INSTEAD

"SEC. 2141. APPLICABILITY.

"This chapter shall apply in the case of any employee who should be (or should have been) CSRS-Offset covered but, as a result of a retirement coverage error, is (or was) CSRS covered instead.

"SEC. 2142. CORRECTION MANDATORY.

"(a) UNCORRECTED ERROR.—If the retirement coverage error has not been corrected, as soon as practicable after discovery of the error, such individual shall be covered under the correct retirement coverage, effective as of the date of the retirement coverage error.

"(b) CORRECTED ERROR.—If the retirement coverage error has been corrected before the effective date of this title, the corrective action taken before such date shall remain in effect.

"CHAPTER 6—EMPLOYEE WHO SHOULD HAVE BEEN CSRS COVERED, BUT WHO WAS ERRONEOUSLY CSRS-OFFSET COVERED INSTEAD

"SEC. 2151. APPLICABILITY.

"This chapter shall apply in the case of any employee who should be (or should have been) CSRS covered but, as a result of a retirement coverage error, is (or was) CSRS-Offset covered instead.

"SEC. 2152. CORRECTION MANDATORY.

"(a) UNCORRECTED ERROR.—If the retirement coverage error has not been corrected, as soon as practicable after discovery of the error, such individual shall be covered under the correct retirement coverage, effective as of the date of the retirement coverage error.

"(b) CORRECTED ERROR.—If the retirement coverage error has been corrected before the effective date of this title, the corrective action taken before such date shall remain in effect.

"SUBTITLE B—GENERAL PROVISIONS

"SEC. 2201. IDENTIFICATION AND NOTIFICATION REQUIREMENTS.

"Government agencies shall take all such measures as may be reasonable and appropriate to promptly identify and notify individuals who are (or have been) affected by a retirement coverage error of their rights under this title.

"SEC. 2202. INFORMATION TO BE FURNISHED TO AND BY AUTHORITIES ADMINISTERING THIS TITLE.

"(a) APPLICABILITY.—The authorities identified in this subsection are—

"(1) the Director of the Office of Personnel Management;

"(2) the Commissioner of Social Security; and

"(3) the Executive Director of the Federal Retirement Thrift Investment Board.

"(b) AUTHORITY TO OBTAIN INFORMATION.—Each authority identified in subsection (a) may secure directly from any department or agency of the United States information necessary to enable such authority to carry out its responsibilities under this title. Upon request of the authority involved, the head of the department or agency involved shall furnish that information to the requesting authority.

"(c) AUTHORITY TO PROVIDE INFORMATION.—Each authority identified in subsection (a) may provide directly to any department or agency of the United States all information such authority believes necessary to enable the department or agency to carry out its responsibilities under this title.

"(d) LIMITATION; SAFEGUARDS.—Each of the respective authorities under subsection (a) shall—

"(1) request or provide only such information as that authority considers necessary; and

"(2) establish, by regulation or otherwise, appropriate safeguards to ensure that any information obtained under this section shall be used only for the purpose authorized.

"SEC. 2203. SERVICE CREDIT DEPOSITS.

"(a) CSRS DEPOSIT.—In the case of a retirement coverage error in which—

"(1) a FERS covered employee was erroneously CSRS covered or CSRS-Offset covered;

"(2) the employee made a service credit deposit under the CSRS rules; and

"(3) there is a subsequent retroactive change to FERS coverage,

the excess of the amount of the CSRS civilian or military service credit deposit over the FERS civilian or military service credit deposit, together with interest computed in accordance with paragraphs (2) and (3) of section 8334(e) of title 5, United States Code, and regulations prescribed by the Office, shall be paid to the employee, the annuitant or, in the case of a deceased employee, to the individual entitled to lump-sum benefits under section 8424(d) of title 5, United States Code.

"(b) FERS DEPOSIT.—

"(1) APPLICABILITY.—This subsection applies in the case of an erroneous retirement coverage determination in which—

"(A) the employee owed a service credit deposit under section 8411(f) of title 5, United States Code; and

"(B)(i) there is a subsequent retroactive change to CSRS or CSRS-Offset coverage; or

"(ii) the service becomes creditable under chapter 83 of title 5, United States Code.

"(2) REDUCED ANNUITY.—

"(A) IN GENERAL.—If at the time of commencement of an annuity there is remaining unpaid CSRS civilian or military service credit deposit for service described under paragraph (1), the annuity shall be reduced based upon the amount unpaid together with interest computed in accordance with section 8334(e)(2) and (3) of title 5, United States Code, and regulations prescribed by the Office.

"(B) AMOUNT.—The reduced annuity to which the individual is entitled shall be equal to an amount that, when taken together with the amount referred to under subparagraph (A), would result in the present value of the total being actuarially equivalent to the present value of the unreduced annuity benefit that would have been provided the individual.

"(3) SURVIVOR ANNUITY.—

"(A) IN GENERAL.—If at the time of commencement of a survivor annuity, there is remaining unpaid any CSRS service credit deposit described under paragraph (1), and there has been no actuarial reduction in an annuity under paragraph (2), the survivor annuity shall be reduced based upon the amount unpaid together with interest computed in accordance with section 8334(e)(2) and (3) of title 5, United States Code, and regulations prescribed by the Office.

"(B) AMOUNT.—The reduced survivor annuity to which the individual is entitled shall be equal to an amount that, when taken together with the amount referred to under subparagraph (A), would result in the present value of the total being actuarially equivalent to the present value of an unreduced survivor annuity benefit that would have been provided the individual.

"SEC. 2204. PROVISIONS RELATED TO SOCIAL SECURITY COVERAGE OF MISCLASSIFIED EMPLOYEES.

"(a) DEFINITIONS.—In this section, the term—

"(1) 'covered individual' means any employee, former employee, or annuitant who—

"(A) is or was employed erroneously subject to CSRS coverage as a result of a retirement coverage error; and

"(B) is or was retroactively converted to CSRS-offset coverage, FERS coverage, or Social Security-Only coverage; and

"(2) 'excess CSRS deduction amount' means an amount equal to the difference between the CSRS deductions withheld and the CSRS-Offset or FERS deductions, if any, due with respect to a covered individual during the entire period the individual was erroneously subject to CSRS coverage as a result of a retirement coverage error.

"(b) REPORTS TO COMMISSIONER OF SOCIAL SECURITY.—

"(1) IN GENERAL.—In order to carry out the Commissioner of Social Security's responsibilities under title II of the Social Security Act [42 U.S.C. 401 et seq.], the Commissioner may request the head of each agency that employs or employed a covered individual to report (in coordination with the Office of Personnel Management) in such form and within such timeframe as the Commissioner may specify, any or all of—

"(A) the total wages (as defined in section 3121(a) of the Internal Revenue Code of 1986 [26 U.S.C. 3121(a)]) paid to such individual during each year of the entire period of the erroneous CSRS coverage; and

"(B) such additional information as the Commissioner may require for the purpose of carrying out the Commissioner's responsibilities under title II of the Social Security Act (42 U.S.C. 401 et seq.).

"(2) COMPLIANCE.—The head of an agency or the Office shall comply with a request from the Commissioner under paragraph (1).

"(3) WAGES.—For purposes of section 201 of the Social Security Act (42 U.S.C. 401), wages reported under this subsection shall be deemed to be wages reported to the Secretary of the Treasury or the Secretary's delegates pursuant to subtitle F of the Internal Revenue Code of 1986 [26 U.S.C. 6001 et seq.].

"(c) PAYMENT RELATING TO OASDI EMPLOYEE TAXES.—The Office shall transfer from the Civil Service Retirement and Disability Fund to the General Fund of the Treasury an amount equal to the lesser of the excess CSRS deduction amount or the OASDI taxes due for covered individuals (as adjusted by amounts transferred relating to applicable OASDI employee taxes as a result of corrections made, including corrections made before the date of the enactment of this Act [Sept. 19, 2000]. If the excess CSRS deductions exceed the OASDI taxes, any difference shall be paid to the covered individual or survivors, as appropriate.

"(d) PAYMENT OF OASDI EMPLOYER TAXES.—

"(1) IN GENERAL.—Each employing agency shall pay an amount equal to the OASDI employer taxes owed with respect to covered individuals during the applicable period of erroneous coverage (as adjusted by amounts transferred for the payment of such taxes as a result of corrections made, including corrections made before the date of the enactment of this Act [Sept. 19, 2000]).

"(2) PAYMENT.—Amounts paid under this subsection shall be determined subject to any limitation under section 6501 of the Internal Revenue Code of 1986 [26 U.S.C. 6501].

"SEC. 2205. THRIFT SAVINGS PLAN TREATMENT FOR CERTAIN INDIVIDUALS.

"(a) APPLICABILITY.—This section applies to an individual who—

"(1) is eligible to make an election of coverage under section 2101 or 2102, and only if FERS coverage is elected (or remains in effect) for the employee involved; or

"(2) is described in section 2111, and makes or has made retroactive employee contributions to the Thrift Savings Fund under regulations prescribed by the Executive Director.

"(b) PAYMENT INTO THRIFT SAVINGS FUND.—

"(1) IN GENERAL.—

"(A) PAYMENT.—With respect to an individual to whom this section applies, the employing agency shall pay to the Thrift Savings Fund under subchapter III of chapter 84 of title 5, United States Code, for credit to the account of the employee involved, an amount equal to the earnings which are disallowed under section 8432a(a)(2) of such title on the employee's retroactive contributions to such Fund.

"(B) AMOUNT.—Earnings under subparagraph (A) shall be computed in accordance with the procedures for computing lost earnings under section 8432a of title 5, United States Code. The amount paid by the employing agency shall be treated for all purposes as if that amount had actually been earned on the basis of the employee's contributions.

"(C) EXCEPTIONS.—If an individual made retroactive contributions before the effective date of the regulations under section 2101(c), the Director may provide for an alternative calculation of lost earnings to the extent that a calculation under subparagraph (B) is not administratively feasible. The alternative calculation shall yield an amount that is as close as practicable to the amount computed under subparagraph (B), taking into account earnings previously paid.

"(2) ADDITIONAL EMPLOYEE CONTRIBUTION.—In cases in which the retirement coverage error was corrected before the effective date of the regulations under section 2101(c), the employee involved shall have an additional opportunity to make retroactive contributions for the period of the retirement coverage error (subject to applicable limits), and such contributions (including any contributions made after the date of the correction) shall be treated in accordance with paragraph (1).

"(c) REGULATIONS.—

"(1) EXECUTIVE DIRECTOR.—The Executive Director shall prescribe regulations appropriate to carry out this section relating to retroactive employee contributions and payments made on or after the effective date of the regulations under section 2101(c).

"(2) OFFICE.—The Office, in consultation with the Federal Retirement Thrift Investment Board, shall prescribe regulations appropriate to carry out this section relating to the calculation of lost earnings on retroactive employee contributions made before the effective date of the regulations under section 2101(c).

"SEC. 2206. CERTAIN AGENCY AMOUNTS TO BE PAID INTO OR REMAIN IN THE CSRDF.

"(a) CERTAIN EXCESS AGENCY CONTRIBUTIONS TO REMAIN IN THE CSRDF.—

"(1) IN GENERAL.—Any amount described under paragraph (2) shall—

"(A) remain in the CSRDF; and

"(B) may not be paid or credited to an agency.

"(2) AMOUNTS.—Paragraph (1) refers to any amount of contributions made by an agency under section 8423 of title 5, United States Code, on behalf of any employee, former employee, or annuitant (or survivor of such employee, former employee, or annuitant) who makes an election to correct a retirement coverage error under this title, that the Office determines to be excess as a result of such election.

"(b) ADDITIONAL EMPLOYEE RETIREMENT DEDUCTIONS TO BE PAID BY AGENCY.—If a correction in a retirement coverage error results in an increase in employee deductions under section 8334 or 8422 of title 5, United States Code, that cannot be fully paid by a reallocation of otherwise available amounts previously deducted from the employee's pay as employment taxes or retirement deductions, the employing agency—

"(1) shall pay the required additional amount into the CSRDF; and

"(2) shall not seek repayment of that amount from the employee, former employee, annuitant, or survivor.

"SEC. 2207. CSRS COVERAGE DETERMINATIONS TO BE APPROVED BY OPM.

"No agency shall place an individual under CSRS coverage unless—

"(1) the individual has been employed with CSRS coverage within the preceding 365 days; or

"(2) the Office has agreed in writing that the agency's coverage determination is correct.

"SEC. 2208. DISCRETIONARY ACTIONS BY DIRECTOR.

"(a) IN GENERAL.—The Director of the Office of Personnel Management may—

"(1) extend the deadlines for making elections under this title in circumstances involving an individual's inability to make a timely election due to a cause beyond the individual's control;

"(2) provide for the reimbursement of necessary and reasonable expenses incurred by an individual with respect to settlement of a claim for losses resulting from a retirement coverage error, including attorney's fees, court costs, and other actual expenses;

"(3) compensate an individual for monetary losses that are a direct and proximate result of a retirement coverage error, excluding claimed losses relating to forgone contributions and earnings under the Thrift Savings Plan under subchapter III of chapter 84 of title 5, United States Code, and all other investment opportunities; and

"(4) waive payments required due to correction of a retirement coverage error under this title.

"(b) SIMILAR ACTIONS.—In exercising the authority under this section, the Director shall, to the extent practicable, provide for similar actions in situations involving similar circumstances.

"(c) JUDICIAL REVIEW.—Actions taken under this section are final and conclusive, and are not subject to administrative or judicial review.

"(d) REGULATIONS.—The Office of Personnel Management shall prescribe regulations regarding the process and criteria used in exercising the authority under this section.

"(e) REPORT.—The Office of Personnel Management shall, not later than 180 days after the date of the enactment of this Act [Sept. 19, 2000], and annually thereafter for each year in which the authority provided in this section is used, submit a report to each House of Congress on the operation of this section.

"SEC. 2209. REGULATIONS.

"(a) IN GENERAL.—In addition to the regulations specifically authorized in this title, the Office may prescribe such other regulations as are necessary for the administration of this title.

"(b) FORMER SPOUSE.—The regulations prescribed under this title shall provide for protection of the rights of a former spouse with entitlement to an apportionment of benefits or to survivor benefits based on the service of the employee.

"SUBTITLE C—OTHER PROVISIONS

"SEC. 2301. PROVISIONS TO AUTHORIZE CONTINUED CONFORMITY OF OTHER FEDERAL RETIREMENT SYSTEMS.

"(a) FOREIGN SERVICE.—Sections 827 and 851 of the Foreign Service Act of 1980 (22 U.S.C. 4067 and 4071) shall apply with respect to this title in the same manner as if this title were part of—

"(1) the Civil Service Retirement System, to the extent this title relates to the Civil Service Retirement System; and

"(2) the Federal Employees' Retirement System, to the extent this title relates to the Federal Employees' Retirement System.

"(b) CENTRAL INTELLIGENCE AGENCY.—Sections 292 and 301 of the Central Intelligence Agency Retirement Act (50 U.S.C. 2141 and 2151) shall apply with respect to this title in the same manner as if this title were part of—

"(1) the Civil Service Retirement System, to the extent this title relates to the Civil Service Retirement System; and

"(2) the Federal Employees' Retirement System, to the extent this title relates to the Federal Employees' Retirement System.

"SEC. 2302. AUTHORIZATION OF PAYMENTS.

"All payments authorized or required by this title to be paid from the Civil Service Retirement and Disability Fund, together with administrative expenses incurred by the Office in administering this title, shall be deemed to have been authorized to be paid from that Fund, which is appropriated for the payment thereof.

"SEC. 2303. INDIVIDUAL RIGHT OF ACTION PRESERVED FOR AMOUNTS NOT OTHERWISE PROVIDED FOR UNDER THIS TITLE.

"Nothing in this title shall preclude an individual from bringing a claim against the Government of the United States which such individual may have under section 1346(b) or chapter 171 of title 28, United States Code, or any other provision of law (except to the extent the claim is for any amounts otherwise provided for under this title).

"SUBTITLE D—EFFECTIVE DATE

"SEC. 2401. EFFECTIVE DATE.

"Except as otherwise provided in this title, this title shall take effect on the date of the enactment of this Act [Sept. 19, 2000]."

FEDERAL EMPLOYEES' RETIREMENT SYSTEM OPEN ENROLLMENT ACT OF 1997

Pub. L. 105–61, title VI, § 642(a)–(c), Oct. 10, 1997, 111 Stat. 1318, as amended by Pub. L. 105–66, title III, § 348, Oct. 27, 1997, 111 Stat. 1451, known as the "Federal Employees' Retirement System Open Enrollment Act of 1997", provided that any individual who, as of Jan. 1, 1998, was employed by the Federal Government, and on such date was subject to subchapter III of chapter 83 of this title, other than a Member of Congress, could elect to become subject to chapter 84 of this title, and directed Office of Personnel Management to promulgate regulations which would provide for an election to be made not before July 1, 1998, or after Dec. 31, 1998.

PILOT PROGRAMS FOR DEFENSE EMPLOYEES CONVERTED TO CONTRACTOR EMPLOYEES DUE TO PRIVATIZATION AT CLOSED MILITARY INSTALLATIONS

Pub. L. 104–201, div. A, title XVI, § 1616, Sept. 23, 1996, 110 Stat. 2741, provided that:

"(a) PILOT PROGRAMS AUTHORIZED.—(1) The Secretary of Defense, after consultation with the Director of the Office of Personnel Management, may establish one or more pilot programs under which Federal retirement benefits are provided in accordance with this section to persons who convert from Federal employment to employment by a Department of Defense contractor in connection with the privatization of the performance of functions at selected military installations being closed under the base closure and realignment process.

"(2) The Secretary of Defense shall select the military installations to be covered by a pilot program under this section.

"(b) ELIGIBLE CONVERTED EMPLOYEES.—(1) A person is a converted employee eligible for Federal retirement benefits under this section if the person is a former employee of the Department of Defense (other than a temporary employee) who—

"(A) while employed by the Department of Defense at a military installation selected to participate in a pilot program, performed a function that was recommended, in a report of the Defense Base Closure and Realignment Commission submitted to the President under the Defense Base Closure and Realignment Act of 1990 ([part A of] title XXIX of Public Law 101–510; 10 U.S.C. 2687 note), to be privatized for performance by a defense contractor at the same installation or in the vicinity of the installation;

"(B) while so employed, separated from Federal service after being notified that the employee would be separated in a reduction in force resulting from such privatization;

"(C) at the time separated from Federal service, was covered under the Civil Service Retirement System, but was not eligible for an immediate annuity under the Civil Service Retirement System;

"(D) does not withdraw retirement contributions under section 8342 of title 5, United States Code;

"(E) within 60 days following such separation, is employed by the defense contractor selected to privatize the function to perform substantially the same function performed by the person before the separation; and

"(F) remains employed by the defense contractor (or a successor defense contractor) or subcontractor of the defense contractor (or successor defense contractor) until attaining early deferred retirement age (unless the employment is sooner involuntarily terminated for reasons other than performance or conduct of the employee).

"(2) A person who, under paragraph (1), would otherwise be eligible for an early deferred annuity under this section shall not be eligible for such benefits if the person received separation pay or severance pay due to a separation described in subparagraph (B) of that paragraph unless the person repays the full amount of such pay with interest (computed at a rate determined appropriate by the Director of the Office of Personnel Management) to the Department of Defense before attaining early deferred retirement age.

"(c) RETIREMENT BENEFITS OF CONVERTED EMPLOYEES.—In the case of a converted employee covered by a pilot program, payment of a deferred annuity for which the converted employee is eligible under section 8338(a) of title 5, United States Code, shall commence on the first day of the first month that begins after the date on which the converted employee attains early deferred retirement age, notwithstanding the age requirement under that section. If the employment of a converted employee is involuntarily terminated by the defense contractor or subcontractor as described in subsection (b)(1)(F) and the converted employee resumes Federal service before the converted employee attains early deferred retirement age, the converted employee shall once again be covered under the Civil Service Retirement System instead of the pilot program.

"(d) COMPUTATION OF AVERAGE PAY.—(1)(A) This paragraph applies to a converted employee who was employed in a position classified under the General Schedule immediately before the employee's covered separation from Federal service.

"(B) Subject to subparagraph (C), for purposes of computing the deferred annuity for a converted employee referred to in subparagraph (A), the average pay of the converted employee, computed under section 8331(4) of title 5, United States Code, as of the date of the employee's covered separation from Federal service, shall be adjusted at the same time and by the same percentage that rates of basic pay are increased under section 5303 of such title during the period beginning on that date and ending on the date on which the converted employee attains early deferred retirement age.

"(C) The average pay of a converted employee, as adjusted under subparagraph (B), may not exceed the amount to which an annuity of the converted employee could be increased under section 8340 of title 5, United States Code, in accordance with the limitation in subsection (g)(1) of such section (relating to maximum pay, final pay, or average pay).

"(2)(A) This paragraph applies to a converted employee who was a prevailing rate employee (as defined under section 5342(2) [5342(a)(2)] of title 5, United States Code) immediately before the employee's covered separation from Federal service.

"(B) For purposes of computing the deferred annuity for a converted employee referred to in subparagraph (A), the average pay of the converted employee, computed under section 8331(4) of title 5, United States Code, as of the date of the employee's covered separation from Federal service, shall be adjusted at the same time and by the same percentage that pay rates for positions that are in the same area as, and are comparable to, the last position the converted employee held as a prevailing rate employee, are increased under section 5343(a) of such title during the period beginning on that date and ending on the date on which the converted employee attains early deferred retirement age.

"(e) PAYMENT OF UNFUNDED LIABILITY.—(1) The military department concerned shall be liable for that portion of any estimated increase in the unfunded liability of the Civil Service Retirement and Disability Fund established under section 8348 of title 5, United States Code, which is attributable to any benefits payable from such Fund to a converted employee, and any survivor of a converted employee, when the increase results from—

"(A) an increase in the average pay of the converted employee under subsection (d) upon which such benefits are computed; and

"(B) the commencement of an early deferred annuity in accordance with this section before the attainment of 62 years of age by the converted employee.

"(2) The estimated increase in the unfunded liability for each department referred to in paragraph (1) shall be determined by the Director of the Office of Personnel Management. In making the determination, the Director shall consider any savings to the Fund as a result of a pilot program established under this section. The Secretary of the military department concerned shall pay the amount so determined to the Director in 10 equal annual installments with interest computed at the rate used in the most recent valuation of the Civil Service Retirement System, with the first payment thereof due at the end of the fiscal year in which an increase in average pay under subsection (d) becomes effective.

"(f) CONTRACTOR SERVICE NOT CREDITABLE.—Service performed by a converted employee for a defense contractor after the employee's covered separation from Federal service is not creditable service for purposes of subchapter III of chapter 83 of title 5, United States Code.

"(g) RECEIPT OF BENEFITS WHILE EMPLOYED BY A DEFENSE CONTRACTOR.—A converted employee may commence receipt of an early deferred annuity in accordance with this section while continuing to work for a defense contractor.

"(h) LUMP-SUM CREDIT PAYMENT.—If a converted employee dies before attaining early deferred retirement age, such employee shall be treated as a former employee who dies not retired for purposes of payment of the lump-sum credit under section 8342(d) of title 5, United States Code.

"(i) CONTINUED FEDERAL HEALTH BENEFITS COVERAGE.—Notwithstanding section 8905a(e)(1)(A) of title 5, United States Code, the continued coverage of a converted employee for health benefits under chapter 89 of such title by reason of the application of section 8905a of such title to such employee shall terminate 90 days after the date of the employee's covered separation from Federal employment. For the purposes of the preceding sentence, a person who, except for subsection (b)(2), would be a converted employee shall be considered a converted employee.

"(j) REPORT BY GENERAL ACCOUNTING OFFICE.—The Comptroller General shall conduct a study of each pilot program, if any, established under this section and submit a report on the pilot program to Congress not later than two years after the date on which the program is established. The report shall contain the following:

"(1) A review and evaluation of the program, including—

"(A) an evaluation of the success of the privatization outcomes of the program;

"(B) a comparison and evaluation of such privatization outcomes with the privatization outcomes with respect to facilities at other military installations closed or realigned under the base closure laws;

"(C) an evaluation of the impact of the program on the Federal workforce and whether the program results in the maintenance of a skilled workforce for defense contractors at an acceptable cost to the military department concerned; and

"(D) an assessment of the extent to which the program is a cost-effective means of facilitating privatization of the performance of Federal activities.

"(2) Recommendations relating to the expansion of the program to other installations and employees.

"(3) Any other recommendation relating to the program.

"(k) IMPLEMENTING REGULATIONS.—Not later than 30 days after the Secretary of Defense notifies the Director of the Office of Personnel Management of a decision to establish a pilot program under this section, the Director shall prescribe regulations to carry out the provisions of this section with respect to that pilot program. Before prescribing the regulations, the Director shall consult with the Secretary.

"(*l*) DEFINITIONS.—In this section:

"(1) The term 'converted employee' means a person who, pursuant to subsection (b), is eligible for benefits under this section.

"(2) The term 'covered separation from Federal service' means a separation from Federal service as described under subsection (b)(1)(B).

"(3) The term 'Civil Service Retirement System' means the retirement system under subchapter III of chapter 83 of title 5, United States Code.

"(4) The term 'defense contractor' means any entity that—

"(A) contracts with the Department of Defense to perform a function previously performed by Department of Defense employees;

"(B) performs that function at the same installation at which such function was previously performed by Department of Defense employees or in the vicinity of that installation; and

"(C) is the employer of one or more converted employees.

"(5) The term 'early deferred retirement age' means the first age at which a converted employee would have been eligible for immediate retirement under subsection (a) or (b) of section 8336 of title 5, United States Code, if such converted employee had remained an employee within the meaning of section 8331(1) of such title continuously until attaining such age.

"(6) The term 'severance pay' means severance pay payable under section 5595 of title 5, United States Code.

"(7) The term 'separation pay' means separation pay payable under section 5597 of title 5, United States Code.

"(m) APPLICATION OF PILOT PROGRAM.—In the event that a pilot program is established for a military installation, the pilot program shall apply to a covered separation from Federal service by an employee of the Department of Defense at the installation occurring on or after August 1, 1996."

ADDITIONAL AGENCY CONTRIBUTIONS TO RETIREMENT FUND

Pub. L. 103–226, § 4, Mar. 30, 1994, 108 Stat. 114, as amended by Pub. L. 104–52, title IV, § 3, Nov. 19, 1995, 109 Stat. 490, provided that:

"(a) RELATING TO VOLUNTARY SEPARATION INCENTIVE PAYMENTS.—

"(1) IN GENERAL.—In addition to any other payments which it is required to make under subchapter III of chapter 83 of title 5, United States Code, an agency shall remit to the Office of Personnel Management for deposit in the Treasury of the United States to the credit of the Civil Service Retirement and Disability Fund an amount equal to 9 percent of the final basic pay of each employee of the agency—

"(A) who, on or after the date of the enactment of this Act [Mar. 30, 1994] retires under section 8336(d)(2) of such title; and

"(B) to whom a voluntary separation incentive payment has been or is to be paid by such agency based on that retirement.

"(2) DEFINITIONS.—For the purpose of this subsection—

"(A) the term 'final basic pay', with respect to an employee, means the total amount of basic pay which would be payable for a year of service by such employee, computed using the employee's final rate of basic pay, and, if last serving on other than a full-time basis, with appropriate adjustment therefor; and

"(B) the term 'voluntary separation incentive payment' means—

"(i) a voluntary separation incentive payment under section 3 [5 U.S.C. 5597 note] (including under any program established under section 3(f)); and

"(ii) any separation pay under section 5597 of title 5, United States Code, or section 2 of the

Central Intelligence Agency Voluntary Separation Pay Act (Public Law 103–36; 107 Stat. 104 [50 U.S.C. 403–4 note]).

"(b) RELATING TO FISCAL YEARS 1995 THROUGH 1998.—

"(1) IN GENERAL.—In addition to any other payments which it is required to make under subchapter III of chapter 83 or chapter 84 of title 5, United States Code, in fiscal years 1995, 1996, 1997, and 1998 (and in addition to any amounts required under subsection (a)), each agency shall, before the end of each such fiscal year, remit to the Office of Personnel Management for deposit in the Treasury of the United States to the credit of the Civil Service Retirement and Disability Fund an amount equal to the product of—

"(A) the number of employees of such agency who, as of March 31st of such fiscal year, are subject to subchapter III of chapter 83 or chapter 84 of such title; multiplied by

"(B) $80.

"(2) DEFINITION.—For the purpose of this subsection, the term 'agency' means an Executive agency (as defined by section 105 of title 5, United States Code), but does not include the General Accounting Office.

"(c) REGULATIONS.—The Director of the Office of Personnel Management may prescribe any regulations necessary to carry out this section."

COORDINATION WITH PAY PERIODS

Pub. L. 99–556, title V, § 505, Oct. 27, 1986, 100 Stat. 3141, provided that: "Under regulations prescribed by the Office of Personnel Management, any reference to a specific date in section 302, 303, 305 [5 U.S.C. 8331 notes], or 702(a) [5 U.S.C. 8401 note] of the Federal Employees' Retirement System Act of 1986 (Public Law 99–335; 100 Stat. 514) shall, for purposes of individual contributions (including deductions from basic pay), Government contributions, and refunds, be deemed to be a reference to the first day of the first applicable pay period beginning on or after such date, or to the day before such first day, as appropriate."

CONTINUED COVERAGE UNDER CERTAIN FEDERAL EMPLOYEE BENEFIT PROGRAMS FOR CERTAIN EMPLOYEES OF SAINT ELIZABETHS HOSPITAL

Pub. L. 99–335, title II, § 207(*o*), as added by Pub. L. 100–238, title I, § 109(a), Jan. 8, 1988, 101 Stat. 1748, provided that: "An employee of Saint Elizabeths Hospital who is appointed to a position in the government of the District of Columbia on October 1, 1987, pursuant to the Saint Elizabeths Hospital and District of Columbia Mental Health Services Act (Public Law 98–621; 98 Stat. 3369 and following) [see Short Title note set out under section 225 of Title 24, Hospitals and Asylums] shall, for purposes of chapters 83, 87, and 89 of title 5, United States Code, be treated in the same way as an individual first employed by the government of the District of Columbia before October 1, 1987."

[Section 109(b) of Pub. L. 100–238 provided that: "The amendment made by this section [enacting note above] shall be effective as of October 1, 1987."]

ELECTION OF COVERAGE UNDER CHAPTER 84

Sections 301–303 of Pub. L. 99–335, as amended by Pub. L. 99–556, title III, §§ 301, 302, Oct. 27, 1986, 100 Stat. 3135, 3136; Pub. L. 100–20, § 1(a), Apr. 7, 1987, 101 Stat. 265; Pub. L. 100–238, title I, §§ 106, 107, 113(a)(1), 118, 119, 134(b), (c), Jan. 8, 1988, 101 Stat. 1746, 1747, 1750, 1752, 1764, 1765, provided that:

"SEC. 301. ELECTIONS.

"(a) ELECTIONS FOR INDIVIDUALS SUBJECT TO THE CIVIL SERVICE RETIREMENT SYSTEM.—(1)(A) Any individual (other than an individual under subsection (b)) who, as of June 30, 1987, is employed by the Federal Government, and who is then subject to subchapter III of chapter 83 of title 5, United States Code, may elect to become subject to chapter 84 of such title.

"(B) An election under this paragraph may not be made before July 1, 1987, or after December 31, 1987.

"(2)(A) Any individual who, after June 30, 1987, becomes reemployed by the Federal Government, and who is then subject to subchapter III of chapter 83 of title 5, United States Code, may elect to become subject to chapter 84 of such title.

"(B) An election under this paragraph shall not be effective unless it is made during the six-month period beginning on the date on which reemployment commences.

"(3)(A) Except as provided in subparagraph (B), any individual—

"(i) who is excluded from the operation of subchapter III of chapter 83 of title 5, United States Code, under subsection (g), (i), (j), or (*l*) of section 8347 of such title, and

"(ii) with respect to whom chapter 84 of title 5, United States Code, does not apply because of section 8402(b)(2) of such title,

shall, for purposes of an election under paragraph (1) or (2), be treated as if such individual were subject to subchapter III of chapter 83 of title 5, United States Code.

"(B) An election under this paragraph may not be made by any individual who would be excluded from the operation of chapter 84 of title 5, United States Code, under section 8402(c) of such title (relating to exclusions based on the temporary or intermittent nature of one's employment).

"(4) A member of the Foreign Service described in section 103(6) of the Foreign Service Act of 1980 [22 U.S.C. 3903(6)] shall be ineligible to make any election under this subsection.

"(b) ELECTIONS FOR CERTAIN INDIVIDUALS SERVING CONTINUOUSLY SINCE DECEMBER 31, 1983.—The following rules shall apply in the case of any individual described in section 8402(b)(1) of title 5, United States Code:

"(1) If, as of December 31, 1986, the individual is subject to subchapter III of chapter 83 of title 5, United States Code, but is not subject to section 204 of the Federal Employees' Retirement Contribution Temporary Adjustment Act of 1983 [section 204 of Pub. L. 98–168, set out below], the individual shall remain so subject to such subchapter unless the individual elects, after June 30, 1987, and before January 1, 1988—

"(A) to become subject to such subchapter under the same terms and conditions as apply in the case of an individual described in section 8402(b)(2) of such title who is subject to such subchapter; or

"(B) to become subject to chapter 84 of such title. An individual eligible to make an election under this paragraph may make the election described in subparagraph (A) or (B), but not both.

"(2) If, as of December 31, 1986, the individual is subject to subchapter III of chapter 83 of title 5, United States Code, and is also subject to section 204 of the Federal Employees' Retirement Contribution Temporary Adjustment Act of 1983 [set out below], the individual—

"(A) shall, as of January 1, 1987, become subject to such subchapter under the same terms and conditions as apply in the case of an individual described in section 8402(b)(2) of such title who is subject to such subchapter; and

"(B) may (during the six-month period described in subsection (a)(1)(B)) elect to become subject to chapter 84 of such title.

"(3)(A) If, as of December 31, 1986, the individual is not subject to subchapter III of chapter 83 of title 5, United States Code, such individual may, during the 6-month period described in subsection (a)(1)(B)—

"(i) elect to become subject to chapter 84 of such title; or

"(ii) if such individual has not since made an election described in subparagraph (B), elect to become subject to subchapter III of chapter 83 of such title under the same terms and conditions as apply in the case of an individual described in section 8402(b)(2) of such title who is subject to such subchapter.

"(B) Nothing in this paragraph shall be considered to preclude the individual from electing to become subject to subchapter III of chapter 83 of such title pursuant to notification under section 8331(2) of such title—

"(i) during the period after December 31, 1986, and before July 1, 1987; or

"(ii) after December 31, 1987, if such individual has not since become subject to subchapter III of chapter 83, or chapter 84, of such title.

"(C) Any individual who becomes subject to subchapter III of chapter 83 of such title pursuant to notification under section 8331(2) of such title after December 31, 1986, shall become subject to such subchapter under the same terms and conditions as apply in the case of an individual described in section 8402(b)(2) of such title who is subject to such subchapter.

"(c) EFFECTIVE DATE; IRREVOCABILITY.—An election made under this section—

"(1) shall take effect beginning with the first pay period beginning after the date of the election; and

"(2) shall be irrevocable.

"(d) CONDITION FOR MAKING AN ELECTION; EXTENSION TO SATISFY CONDITION.—(1) An election under this section to become subject to chapter 84 of title 5, United States Code, shall not be considered effective in the case of an individual having one or more former spouses, unless the election is made with the written consent of such former spouse (or each such former spouse, if there is more than one).

"(2)(A) This subsection applies with respect to a former spouse who (based on the service of the individual involved) is entitled to benefits under section 8341(h) or 8345(j) of title 5, United States Code, under the terms of a decree of divorce or annulment, or a court order or court-approved property settlement incident to any such decree, with respect to which the Office of Personnel Management has been duly notified.

"(B) This subsection does not apply with respect to a former spouse who has ceased to be so entitled as a result of remarrying before age 55.

"(3) The requirement under paragraph (1) shall be considered satisfied with respect to a former spouse if the individual seeking to make the election establishes to the satisfaction of the Office (in accordance with regulations prescribed by the Office)—

"(A) that the former spouse's whereabouts cannot be determined; or

"(B) that, due to exceptional circumstances, requiring the individual to seek the former spouse's consent would otherwise be inappropriate.

"(4)(A) The Office shall, upon application of an individual, grant an extension for such individual to make an election referred to in paragraph (1) if such individual—

"(i) files application for extension before the end of the period during which such individual would otherwise be eligible to make such election; and

"(ii) demonstrates to the satisfaction of the Office that the extension is needed to secure the modification of a decree of divorce or annulment (or a court order or court-approved property settlement incident to any such decree) in order to satisfy the consent requirement under paragraph (1).

"(B) An extension under this paragraph shall be for 6 months or for such longer period as the Office considers appropriate.

"(e) EXCLUSIONS.—This section does not apply to an individual under section 8331(1)(G) of title 5, United States Code.

"SEC. 302. EFFECT OF AN ELECTION UNDER SECTION 301 TO BECOME SUBJECT TO THE FEDERAL EMPLOYEES' RETIREMENT SYSTEM.

"(a) GENERAL AND SPECIAL RULES.—All provisions of chapter 84 of title 5, United States Code (including those relating to disability benefits, survivor benefits, and any reductions to provide for survivor benefits) shall apply with respect to any individual who becomes subject to such chapter pursuant to an election under section 301, except if, or to the extent that, such provisions are inconsistent with the following:

"(1)(A) Any civilian service which is performed before the effective date of the election under section 301 shall not be creditable under chapter 84 of title 5, United States Code, except as otherwise provided in this subsection.

"(B) Any service described in subparagraph (A) which is covered service within the meaning of section 203(a)(3) of the Federal Employees' Retirement Contribution Temporary Adjustment Act of 1983 (97 Stat. 1107; 5 U.S.C. 8331 note) (hereinafter in this section referred to as 'covered service') shall be creditable under chapter 84 of title 5, United States Code, if—

"(i) with respect to any such service performed before January 1, 1987, 1.3 percent of basic pay for such service was withheld in accordance with such Act or, if either such withholding was not made or was made, but the amount so withheld was subsequently refunded, 1.3 percent of basic pay for such period is deposited to the credit of the Civil Service Retirement and Disability Fund (hereinafter in this section referred to as the 'Fund'), with interest (computed under section 8334(e) of such title); and

"(ii) with respect to any such service performed after December 31, 1986, and before the effective date of the election, an amount equal to the percentage of basic pay for such service which would be required to be withheld under section 8422(a) of title 5, United States Code, has been contributed to the Fund by the individual involved, whether by withholdings from pay or, if either no withholding was made or was made, but the amount withheld was subsequently refunded, the aforementioned percentage of basic pay for such period is deposited to the credit of the Fund, with interest (computed under section 8334(e) of such title).

"(C) Any service described in subparagraph (A)—
"(i) which is not covered service;
"(ii) which constitutes service of a type described in section 8411(b)(3) of title 5, United States Code (determined without regard to whether such service was performed before, on, or after January 1, 1989, and without regard to the provisions of section 8411(f) of such title); and
"(iii) which, in the aggregate, is equal to less than 5 years;
shall be creditable under chapter 84 of such title, subject to section 8411(f) of such title.

"(D) Any service described in subparagraph (A)—
"(i) which is not covered service;
"(ii) which constitutes service of a type described in section 8411(b)(3) of title 5, United States Code (determined without regard to whether such service was performed before, on, or after January 1, 1989, and without regard to the provisions of section 8411(f) of such title); and
"(iii) which, in the aggregate, is equal to 5 years or more;
shall be creditable for purposes of—
"(I) section 8410 of such title, relating to the minimum period of civilian service required to be eligible for an annuity;
"(II) any provision of section 8412 (other than subsection (d) or (e) thereof), 8413, 8414, 8442(b)(1), 8443(a)(1), or 8451 of such title which relates to a minimum period of service for entitlement to an annuity;
"(III) the provisions of paragraphs (4) and (6);
"(IV) any provision of section 8412(d) of such title which relates to a minimum period of service for entitlement to an annuity, but only if and to the extent that the service described in subparagraph (A) was as a law enforcement officer or firefighter;
"(V) any provision of section 8412(e) of such title which relates to a minimum period of service for entitlement to an annuity, but only if and to the extent that the service described in subparagraph (A) was as an air traffic controller; and
"(VI) the provision of subsection (g) of section 8415 which relates to the minimum period of service

required to qualify for the higher accrual rate under such subsection.

"(2)(A) Except as provided in subparagraph (B), the creditability under chapter 84 of title 5, United States Code, of any military service which is performed before the effective date of the election under section 301 shall be determined in accordance with applicable provisions of such chapter.

"(B) If the electing individual has performed service described in clauses (i) through (iii) of paragraph (1)(D), service described in subparagraph (A) which, but for the provisions of subsection (b), would be creditable under subchapter III of chapter 83 of title 5, United States Code, as in effect on December 31, 1986, shall be creditable for purposes of—
"(i) any provision of section 8412 (other than subsection (d) or (e) thereof), 8413, or 8414 of such title which relates to a minimum period of service for entitlement to an annuity; and
"(ii) the provisions of paragraph (4).

"(3)(A)(i) If the electing individual becomes entitled to an annuity under subchapter II of chapter 84 of title 5, United States Code, or dies leaving a survivor or survivors entitled to benefits under subchapter IV of such chapter, the annuity for such individual shall be equal to the sum of the individual's accrued benefits under the Civil Service Retirement System (as determined under paragraph (4)) and the individual's accrued benefits under the Federal Employees' Retirement System (as determined under paragraph (5)).

"(ii) An annuity computed under this subparagraph shall be deemed to be the individual's annuity computed under section 8415 of title 5, United States Code.

"(B) If the electing individual becomes entitled to an annuity under subchapter V of chapter 84 of title 5, United States Code, and if it becomes necessary to compute an annuity under section 8415 of such title with respect to such individual as a result of such individual's having become so entitled, the methodology set forth in subparagraph (A) shall be used in computing any such annuity under section 8415.

"(4) Accrued benefits under this paragraph shall be computed in accordance with applicable provisions of subchapter III of chapter 83 of title 5, United States Code (but without regard to subsection (j) or (k), or the second sentence of subsection (e), of section 8339 of such title) using only any civilian service under paragraph (1)(D), and any military service under paragraph (2)(B), which would be creditable for purposes of computing an annuity under such subchapter. Notwithstanding the preceding sentence, in computing accrued benefits under this paragraph for an individual retiring under section 8412(g) or 8413(b) of title 5, United States Code, section 8339(h) of such title (relating to reductions based on age at date of separation) shall not apply.

"(5) Accrued benefits under this paragraph shall be computed under section 8415 of title 5, United States Code, using—
"(A) total service creditable under chapter 84 of such title which is performed on or after the effective date of the election under section 301; and
"(B) with respect to service performed before such effective date—
"(i) creditable civilian service (as determined under applicable provisions of this subsection) other than any service described in paragraph (1)(D); and
"(ii) creditable military service (as determined under applicable provisions of this subsection) other than any service described in paragraph (2)(B).

"(6)(A) For purposes of any computation under paragraph (4) or (5), the average pay to be used shall be the largest annual rate resulting from averaging the individual's rates of basic pay in effect over any 3 consecutive years of creditable service or, in the case of an annuity based on service of less than 3 years, over the total period of service so creditable, with each rate weighted by the period it was in effect.

"(B) For purposes of subparagraph (A), service shall be considered creditable if it would be considered creditable for purposes of determining average pay under chapter 83 or 84 of title 5, United States Code.

"(7) The cost-of-living adjustments for the annuity of the electing individual shall be made as follows:

"(A) The portion of the annuity attributable to paragraph (4) shall be adjusted at the time and in the amount provided for under section 8340 of title 5, United States Code.

"(B) The portion of the annuity attributable to paragraph (5) shall be adjusted at the time and in the amount provided for under section 8462 of title 5, United States Code.

"(8) For purposes of any computation under paragraph (4) in the case of an individual who retires under section 8412 or 8414 of title 5, United States Code, or who dies leaving a survivor or survivors entitled to benefits under subchapter IV of such chapter, sick leave creditable under section 8339(m) of such title shall be equal to the number of days of unused sick leave to the individual's credit as of the date of retirement or as of the effective date of the individual's election under section 301, whichever is less.

"(9) In computing the annuity under paragraph (3) for an individual retiring under section 8412(g) or 8413(b) of title 5, United States Code, the reduction under section 8415(f) of such title shall apply with respect to the sum computed under such paragraph.

"(10) An annuity supplement under section 8421 of title 5, United States Code, shall be computed using the same service as is used for the computation under paragraph (5).

"(11) Effective from its commencing date, an annuity payable to an annuitant's survivor (other than a child under section 8443 of title 5, United States Code) shall be increased by the total percent by which the deceased annuitant's annuity was increased under paragraph (7).

"(12)(A)(i) If the electing individual is a reemployed annuitant under section 8344 of title 5, United States Code, under conditions allowing the annuity to continue during reemployment, payment of the annuitant's annuity shall continue after the effective date of the election, and an amount equal to the annuity allocable to the period of actual employment shall continue to be deducted from the annuitant's pay and deposited as provided in subsection (a) of such section. Deductions from pay under section 8422(a) of such title and contributions under section 8423 of such title shall begin effective on the effective date of the election.

"(ii) Notwithstanding any provision of section 301, an election under such section shall not be available to any reemployed annuitant who would be excluded from the operation of chapter 84 of title 5, United States Code, under section 8402(c) of such title (relating to exclusions based on the temporary or intermittent nature of one's employment).

"(B) If the annuitant serves on a full-time basis for at least 1 year, or on a part-time basis for periods equivalent to at least 1 year of full-time service, such annuitant's annuity, on termination of reemployment, shall be increased by an annuity computed—

"(i) with respect to reemployment service before the effective date of the election, under section 8339(a), (b), (d), (e), (h), (i), and (n) of title 5, United States Code, as may apply based on the reemployment in which such annuitant was engaged before such effective date; and

"(ii) with respect to reemployment service on or after the effective date of the election, under section 8415(a) through (f) of such title, as may apply based on the reemployment in which such annuitant was engaged on or after such effective date;

with the 'average pay' used in any computation under clause (i) or (ii) being determined (based on rates of pay in effect during the period of reemployment,

whether before, on, or after the effective date of the election) in the same way as provided for in paragraph (6). If the annuitant is receiving a reduced annuity as provided in section 8339(j) or section 8339(k)(2) of title 5, United States Code, the increase in annuity payable under this subparagraph is reduced by 10 percent and the survivor annuity payable under section 8341(b) of such title is increased by 55 percent of the increase in annuity payable under this subparagraph, unless, at the time of claiming the increase payable under this subparagraph, the annuitant notifies the Office of Personnel Management in writing that such annuitant does not desire the survivor annuity to be increased. If the annuitant dies while still reemployed, after having been reemployed for at least 1 full year (or the equivalent thereof, in the case of part-time employment), any survivor annuity payable under section 8341(b) of such title based on the service of such annuitant is increased as though the reemployment had otherwise terminated. In applying paragraph (7) to an amount under this subparagraph, any portion of such amount attributable to clause (i) shall be adjusted under subparagraph (A) of such paragraph, and any portion of such amount attributable to clause (ii) shall be adjusted under subparagraph (B) of such paragraph.

"(C)(i) If the annuitant serves on a full-time basis for at least 5 years, or on a part-time basis for periods equivalent to at least 5 years of full-time service, such annuitant may elect, instead of the benefit provided by subparagraph (B), to have such annuitant's rights redetermined, effective upon separation from employment. If the annuitant so elects, the redetermined annuity will become payable as if such annuitant were retiring for the first time based on the separation from reemployment service, and the provisions of this section concerning computation of annuity (other than any provision of this paragraph) shall apply.

"(ii) If the annuitant dies while still reemployed, after having been reemployed for at least 5 full years (or the equivalent thereof, in the case of part-time employment), any person entitled to a survivor annuity under section 8341(b) of title 5, United States Code, based on the service of such annuitant shall be permitted to elect to have such person's rights redetermined in accordance with regulations which the Office shall prescribe. Redetermined benefits elected under this clause shall be in lieu of any increased benefits which would otherwise be payable in accordance with the next to last sentence of subparagraph (B).

"(D) If the annuitant serves on a full-time basis for less than 1 year (or the equivalent thereof, in the case of part-time employment), any amounts withheld under section 8422(a) of title 5, United States Code, from such annuitant's pay for the period (or periods) involved shall, upon written application to the Office, be payable to such annuitant (or the appropriate survivor or survivors, determined in the order set forth in section 8342(c) of such title).

"(E) For purposes of determining the period of an annuitant's reemployment service under this paragraph, a period of reemployment service shall not be taken into account unless—

"(i) with respect to service performed before the effective date of the election under section 301, it is service which, if performed for at least 1 full year, would have allowed such annuitant to elect under section 8344(a) of title 5, United States Code, to have deductions withheld from pay; or

"(ii) with respect to service performed on or after the effective date of the election under section 301, it is service with respect to which deductions from pay would be required to be withheld under the second sentence of section 8468(a) of title 5, United States Code.

"(b) CHAPTER 83 GENERALLY INAPPLICABLE.—(1) Except as provided in subsection (a) or paragraph (2), subchapter III of chapter 83 of title 5, United States Code, shall not apply with respect to any individual who becomes subject to chapter 84 of title 5, United States Code, pursuant to an election under section 301.

"(2)(A) Nothing in paragraph (1), or in subchapter III of chapter 83 of title 5, United States Code, shall preclude the making of a deposit under such subchapter with respect to any civilian service under subsection (a)(1)(D) or military service under subsection (a)(2)(B) either by the electing individual or, for purposes of survivor annuities, by a survivor of such individual.

"(B) Nothing in paragraph (1) shall preclude the payment of any lump-sum credit in accordance with section 8342 of title 5, United States Code.

"(c) Refunds Relating to Certain Civilian Service.—(1) Any individual who makes an election under section 301 to become subject to chapter 84 and who, with respect to any period before the effective date of the election, has made a contribution to the Civil Service Retirement System (whether by deductions from pay or by a deposit or redeposit) and has not taken a refund of the contribution (as so made), shall be entitled to a refund equal to—

"(A) for a period of service under clause (i) of subsection (a)(1)(B), the amount by which—

"(i) the amount contributed with respect to such period, exceeds

"(ii) the amount required under such clause (i) with respect to such period;

"(B) for a period of service under clause (ii) of subsection (a)(1)(B), the amount by which—

"(i) the amount so contributed with respect to such period, exceeds

"(ii) the amount required under such clause (ii) with respect to such period; and

"(C) for a period of service under subparagraph (C) of subsection (a)(1), the amount by which—

"(i) the amount so contributed with respect to such period, exceeds

"(ii) the amount required under such subparagraph with respect to such period.

"(2) In accordance with regulations prescribed by the Office of Personnel Management, a refund under this subsection shall be payable upon written application therefor filed with the Office and shall include interest at the rate provided in section 8334(e)(3) of title 5, United States Code. Interest on the refund shall accrue monthly and shall be compounded annually.

"SEC. 303. PROVISIONS RELATING TO AN ELECTION TO BECOME SUBJECT TO CHAPTER 83 SUBJECT TO CERTAIN OFFSETS RELATING TO SOCIAL SECURITY.

"(a) Refund.—Any individual who makes an election under section 301(b)(1)(A) shall, upon written application to the Office of Personnel Management, be entitled to a refund equal to—

"(1) for the period beginning on January 1, 1984, and ending on December 31, 1986, the amount by which—

"(A) the total amount deducted from such individual's basic pay under section 8334(a)(1) of title 5, United States Code, for such period, exceeds

"(B) 1.3 percent of such individual's total basic pay for such period; and

"(2) for the period beginning on January 1, 1987, and ending on the day before the effective date of the election, the amount by which—

"(A) the total amount deducted from such individual's basic pay under such section 8334(a)(1) for such period, exceeds

"(B) the total amount which would have been deducted if such individual's basic pay had instead been subject to section 8334(k) of such title during such period.

A refund under this subsection shall be computed with interest in accordance with section 302(c)(2) and regulations prescribed by the Office of Personnel Management.

"(b) Deposit Requirements.—(1) In the case of an individual who becomes subject to subchapter III of chapter 83 of title 5, United States Code, pursuant to notifi-

cation as described in the second sentence of section 301(b)(3)(B), service performed by such individual before the effective date of the notification shall not be considered creditable under such subchapter unless—

"(A) for any service during the period beginning on January 1, 1987, and ending on the day before such effective date, there is deposited to the credit of the Fund a percentage of basic pay for such period equal to the percentage which would have applied under section 8334(k) of such title if such individual's pay had been subject to such section during such period;

"(B) for any period of service beginning on January 1, 1984, and ending on December 31, 1986, there is deposited to the credit of the Fund an amount equal to 1.3 percent of basic pay for such period; and

"(C) for any period of service before January 1, 1984, there is deposited to the credit of the Fund any amount required with respect to such period under such subchapter.

"(2) A deposit under this subsection may be made by the individual or, for purposes of survivor annuities, a survivor of such individual."

[Section 113(a)(2) of Pub. L. 100–238 provided that: "The amendment made by paragraph (1) [amending section 301(a) of Pub. L. 99–335 set out above] shall be effective as of June 30, 1987. Any refund which becomes payable as a result of the preceding sentence shall, to the extent that such refund involves an individual's contributions to the Thrift Savings Fund (established under section 8437 of title 5, United States Code), be adjusted to reflect any earnings attributable thereto."]

[Amendment by section 134(b) of Pub. L. 100–238 to section 302(a) of Pub. L. 99–335 applicable with respect to any election made by a reemployed annuitant on or after Jan. 8, 1988, see section 134(d) of Pub. L. 100–238, set out as an Effective Date of 1988 Amendment note under section 8468 of this title.]

Construction of Adjustments in Retirement Provisions Made by Pub. L. 98–353

Section 117 of Pub. L. 98–353 provided that: "The adjustments in the retirement provisions made by this Act shall not be construed to be a 'new government retirement system' for purposes of the Federal Employees Retirement Contribution Temporary Adjustment Act of 1983 (Public Law 98–168) [set out below]".

Election of Retirement Plan Under Federal Employees' Retirement Contribution Temporary Adjustment Act of 1983

Pub. L. 98–369, div. B, title II, § 2206, July 18, 1984, 98 Stat. 1059, provided that:

"(a) For the purposes of this section, the term 'covered retirement system' shall have the same meaning as provided in section 203(a)(2) of the Federal Employees' Retirement Contribution Temporary Adjustment Act of 1983 (Public Law 98–168; 97 Stat. 1107) [set out below].

"(b)(1) Any individual who was entitled to make an election under section 208(a) of the Federal Employees' Retirement Contribution Temporary Adjustment Act of 1983 (97 Stat. 1111) [set out below], but who did not make such an election, may make an election under such section not later than September 15, 1984.

"(2)(A) Not later than September 15, 1984, any such individual who made an election under paragraph (1) of section 208(a) of the Federal Employees' Retirement Contribution Temporary Adjustment Act of 1983 [set out below] may—

"(i) make any other election which such individual was entitled to make under such section before January 1, 1984; or

"(ii) elect to become a participant in a covered retirement system (if such individual is otherwise eligible to participate in such system), subject to sections 201 through 207 of such Act [set out below].

"(B) Not later than September 15, 1984, any such individual who made an election under paragraph (2) of section 208(a) of the Federal Employees' Retirement Contribution Temporary Adjustment Act of 1983 may—

"(i) make any other election which such individual was entitled to make under such section before January 1, 1984; or

"(ii) elect to terminate participation in the covered retirement system with respect to which such individual made the election under such paragraph (2).

"(3) An election under this subsection shall be made by a written application submitted to the official by whom the electing individual is paid.

"(4) An election made as provided in this subsection shall take effect with respect to service performed on or after the first day of the first applicable pay period commencing after September 15, 1984.

"(c)(1) Section 8342(a)(4) of title 5, United States Code, does not apply for the purpose of determining an entitlement to a refund under section 208(c) of the Federal Employees' Retirement Contribution Temporary Adjustment Act of 1983 (97 Stat. 1111) [set out below].

"(2) Paragraph (1) shall take effect with respect to any election made under section 208(a) of such Act or this Act before, on, or after January 1, 1984.

"(d) Nothing in this section or the Federal Employees' Retirement Contribution Temporary Adjustment Act of 1983 [set out below] affects any entitlement to benefits accrued under a covered retirement system before January 1, 1984, except to the extent that any amount refunded under section 208(c) of such Act is not redeposited in the applicable retirement fund."

FEDERAL EMPLOYEES' RETIREMENT CONTRIBUTION TEMPORARY ADJUSTMENT

Pub. L. 98–168, title II, Nov. 29, 1983, 97 Stat. 1106, as amended by Pub. L. 99–190, § 147, Dec. 19, 1985, 99 Stat. 1324; Pub. L. 99–335, title III, §§ 305(a), 309, June 6, 1986, 100 Stat. 606, 607; Pub. L. 99–514, § 2, Oct. 22, 1986, 100 Stat. 2095, provided that:

"SHORT TITLE

"SEC. 201. This title may be cited as the 'Federal Employees' Retirement Contribution Temporary Adjustment Act of 1983'.

"STATEMENT OF POLICY

"SEC. 202. It is the policy of the Government—

"(1) that the amount required to be contributed to certain public retirement systems by employees and officers of the Government who are also required to pay employment taxes relating to benefits under title II of the Social Security Act [42 U.S.C. 401 et seq.] for service performed after December 31, 1983, be modified until the date on which such employees and officers are covered by a new Government retirement system (the design, structure, and provisions of which have not been determined on the date of enactment of this Act [Nov. 29, 1983]) or January 1, 1987, whichever is earlier;

"(2) that the Treasury be required to pay into such retirement systems the remainder of the amount such employees and officers would have contributed during such period but for the temporary modification;

"(3) that the employing agencies make contributions to the retirement systems with respect to such service in amounts required by law in effect before January 1, 1984, without reduction in such amounts;

"(4) that such employees and officers accrue credit for service for the purposes of the public retirement systems in effect on the date of enactment of this Act [Nov. 29, 1983] until a new Government retirement system covering such employees and officers is established;

"(5) that, where appropriate, deposits to the credit of such a retirement system be required with respect to service performed by an employee or officer of the Government during the period described in clause (1), and, where appropriate, annuities be offset by the amount of certain social security benefits attributable to such service; and

"(6) that such employees and officers who are first employed in civilian service by the Government or first take office in civilian service in the Government on or after January 1, 1984, become subject to such new Government retirement system as may be established for employees and officers of the Government on or after January 1, 1984, and before January 1, 1987, with credit for service performed after December 31, 1983, by such employees and officers transferred to such new Government retirement system.

"DEFINITIONS

"SEC. 203. (a) For the purposes of this title—

"(1) the term 'covered employee' means any individual whose service is covered service;

"(2) the term 'covered retirement system' means—

"(A) the Civil Service Retirement and Disability System under subchapter III of chapter 83 of title 5, United States Code;

"(B) the Foreign Service Retirement and Disability System under chapter 8 of the Foreign Service Act of 1980 (22 U.S.C. 4041 et seq.);

"(C) the Central Intelligence Agency Retirement and Disability System under the Central Intelligence Agency Retirement Act of 1964 for Certain Employees (50 U.S.C. 403 note); and

"(D) any other retirement system (other than a new Government retirement system) under which a covered employee who is a participant in the system is required to make contributions to the system in an amount equal to a portion of the participant's basic pay for covered service, as determined by the President;

"(3) the term 'covered service' means service which is employment for the purposes of title II of the Social Security Act [42 U.S.C. 401 et seq.] and chapter 21 of the Internal Revenue Code of 1986 [26 U.S.C. 3101 et seq.] by reason of the amendments made by section 101 of the Social Security Amendments of 1983 (97 Stat. 67) [amending section 3121 of Title 26, Internal Revenue Code, and sections 409 and 410 of Title 42, The Public Health and Welfare, and enacting provisions set out as notes under section 3121 of Title 26 and section 410 of Title 42]; and

"(4) the term 'new Government retirement system' means any retirement system which (A) is established for officers or employees of the Government by or pursuant to a law enacted after December 31, 1983, and before January 1, 1987, and (B) takes effect on or before January 1, 1987.

"(b) The President shall publish the determinations made for the purpose of subsection (a)(2)(D) in an Executive order.

"CONTRIBUTION ADJUSTMENTS

"SEC. 204. (a) In the case of a covered employee who is participating in a covered retirement system, an employing agency shall deduct and withhold only 1.3 percent of the basic pay of such employee under—

"(1) section 8334 of title 5, United States Code;

"(2) section 805 of the Foreign Service Act of 1980 (22 U.S.C. 4045);

"(3) section 211 of the Central Intelligence Agency Retirement Act of 1964 for Certain Employees (50 U.S.C. 403 note); or

"(4) any other provision of any other covered retirement system which requires a participant in the system to make contributions of a portion of the basic pay of the participant;

for covered service which is performed after December 31, 1983, and before the earlier of the effective date of a new Government retirement system or January 1, 1987. Deductions shall be made and withheld as provided by such provisions in the case of covered service which is performed on or after such effective date or January 1, 1987, as the case may be, and is not subject to a new Government retirement system.

"(b) Employing agencies of the Government shall make contributions with respect to service to which subsection (a) of this section applies under the second sentence of section 8334(a)(1) of title 5, United States

Code, the second sentence of section 805(a) of the Foreign Service Act of 1980 (22 U.S.C. 4045(a)), the second sentence of section 211(a) of the Central Intelligence Agency Retirement Act of 1964 for Certain Employees (50 U.S.C. 403 note), and any provision of any other covered retirement system requiring a contribution by the employing agency, as if subsection (a) of this section had not been enacted.

"REIMBURSEMENT FOR CONTRIBUTION DEFICIENCY

"SEC. 205. (a) For purposes of this section—

"(1) the term 'contribution deficiency', when used with respect to a covered retirement system, means the excess of—

"(A) the total amount which, but for section 204(a) of this Act, would have been deducted and withheld under a provision referred to in such section from the pay of covered employees participating in such retirement system for service to which such section applies, over

"(B) the total amount which was deducted and withheld from the pay of covered employees for such service as provided in section 204(a) of this Act; and

"(2) the term 'appropriate agency head' means—

"(A) the Director of the Office of Personnel Management, with respect to the Civil Service Retirement and Disability System under subchapter III of chapter 83 of title 5, United States Code;

"(B) the Secretary of State, with respect to the Foreign Service Retirement and Disability System under chapter 8 of the Foreign Service Retirement Act of 1980 (22 U.S.C. 404 et seq.) [22 U.S.C. 4041 et seq.];

"(C) the Director of Central Intelligence, with respect to the Central Intelligence Agency Retirement and Disability System under the Central Intelligence Agency Retirement Act of 1964 for Certain Employees (50 U.S.C. 403 note); and

"(D) the officer designated by the President for that purpose in the case of any retirement system described in section 203(a)(2)(D) of this Act.

"(b) At the end of each of fiscal years 1984, 1985, 1986, and 1987, the appropriate agency head—

"(1) shall determine the amount of the contribution deficiency for such fiscal year in the case of each covered retirement system, including the interest that those contributions would have earned had they been credited to the fund established for the payment of benefits under such retirement system in the same manner and at the same time as deductions under the applicable provision of law referred to in section 204(a) of this Act; and

"(2) shall notify the Secretary of the Treasury of the amount of the contribution deficiency in each such case.

"(c) Before closing the accounts for each of fiscal years 1984, 1985, 1986, and 1987, the Secretary of the Treasury shall credit to the fund established for the payment of benefits under each covered retirement system, as a Government contribution, out of any money in the Treasury not otherwise appropriated, an amount equal to the amount determined under subsection (b) with respect to that covered retirement system for the fiscal year involved.

"(d) Amounts credited to a fund under subsection (c) shall be accounted for separately than amounts credited to such fund under any other provision of law.

"SPECIAL DEPOSIT AND OFFSET RULES RELATING TO RETIREMENT BENEFITS FOR INTERIM COVERED SERVICE

"SEC. 206. (a) For the purposes of this section, the term 'interim covered service' means covered service to which section 204(a) applies.

"(b)(1) Paragraphs (2) and (3) apply according to the provisions thereof only with respect to a covered employee who is employed by the Government on December 31, 1983.

"(2)(A) Notwithstanding any other provision of law, the interim covered service of such covered employee shall be considered—

"(i) in determining entitlement to and computing the amount of an annuity (other than a disability or survivor annuity) commencing under a covered retirement system during the period beginning January 1, 1984, and ending on the earlier of the date a new Government retirement system takes effect or January 1, 1987, by reason of the retirement of such covered employee during such period only if such covered employee makes a deposit to the credit of such covered retirement system for such covered service in an amount computed as provided in subsection (f); and

"(ii) in computing a disability or survivor annuity which commences under a covered retirement system during such period and is based in any part on such interim covered service.

"(B) Notwithstanding any other provision of law, an annuity to which subparagraph (A)(ii) applies shall be reduced by the portion of the amount of any benefits which is payable under title II of the Social Security Act [42 U.S.C. 401 et seq.] and is attributable to the interim covered service considered in computing the amount of such annuity, as determined under subsection (g), unless, in the case of a survivor annuity, a covered employee has made a deposit with respect to such covered service for the purposes of subparagraph (A)(i) before the date on which payment of such annuity commences.

"(3) Notwithstanding any other provision of law, if a new Government retirement system is not established or is inapplicable to such a covered employee who retires or dies subject to a covered retirement system after the date on which such new Government retirement system takes effect, the interim covered service of such covered employee shall be considered in determining entitlement to and computing the amount of an annuity under a covered retirement system based on the service of such covered employee only if such covered employee makes a deposit to the credit of such covered retirement system for such covered service in an amount computed as provided in subsection (f).

"(c)(1) Paragraphs (2) and (3) apply according to the provisions thereof only with respect to a covered employee who was not employed by the Government on December 31, 1983.

"(2) Notwithstanding any other provision of law, any annuity which commences under a covered retirement system during the period described in subsection (b)(2)(A)(i) and is based, in any part, on interim covered service shall be reduced by the portion of the amount of any benefits which is payable under title II of the Social Security Act [42 U.S.C. 401 et seq.] to the annuitant and is attributable to such service, as determined under subsection (g).

"(3) Notwithstanding any other provision of law, if a new Government retirement system is not established, the interim covered service of such a covered employee who retires or dies after January 1, 1987, shall be considered in determining entitlement to and computing the amount of an annuity under a covered retirement system based on the service of such covered employee only if such covered employee makes a deposit to the credit of such covered retirement system for such covered service in an amount computed as provided in subsection (f).

"(d) If a covered employee with respect to whom subsection (b)(3) or (c)(3) applies dies without having made a deposit pursuant to such subsection, any individual who is entitled to an annuity under a covered retirement system based on the service of such covered employee or who would be entitled to such an annuity if such deposit had been made by the covered employee before death may make such deposit after the date of death of such covered employee. Service covered by a deposit made pursuant to the first sentence shall be considered in determining, in the case of each individual to whom the first sentence applies, the entitlement to and the amount of an annuity under a covered retirement system based on the service of such covered employee.

"(e) A reduction in annuity under subsection (b)(2)(B) or (c)(2) shall commence on the first day of the first month after the date on which payment of benefits under title II of the Social Security Act [42 U.S.C. 401 et seq.] commence and shall be redetermined each time an increase in such benefits takes effect pursuant to section 215(i) of the Social Security Act [42 U.S.C. 415(i)]. In the case of an annuity of a participant or former participant in a covered retirement system, of a surviving spouse or child of such participant or former participant, or of any other person designated by such participant or former participant to receive an annuity, under a covered retirement system (other than a former spouse) the reduction in annuity under subsection (b)(2)(B) or (c)(2) shall be calculated before any reduction in such annuity provided under such system for the purpose of paying an annuity under such system to any former spouse of such participant or former participant based on the service of such participant or former participant.

"(f) For the purposes of subsection (b) or (c), the amount of a deposit to the credit of the applicable covered retirement system shall be equal to the excess of—

"(1) the total amount which would have been deducted and withheld from the basic pay of the covered employee for the interim covered service under such covered retirement system but for the application of section 204(a), over

"(2) the amount which was deducted and withheld from such basic pay for such interim covered service pursuant to section 204(a) and was not refunded to such covered employee.

"(g) For the purpose of subsections (b)(2)(B) and (c)(2), the portion of the amount of the benefits which is payable under title II of the Social Security Act [42 U.S.C. 401 et seq.] to an individual and is attributable to interim covered service shall be determined by—

"(1) computing the amount of such benefits including credit for such service;

"(2) computing the amount of such benefits, if any, without including credit for such service; and

"(3) subtracting the amount computed under clause (2) from the amount computed under clause (1).

"(h) The Secretary of Health and Human Services shall furnish to the appropriate agency head (as defined in section 205(a)(2)) such information as such agency head considers necessary to carry out this section.

"TRANSFER OF CREDIT TO NEW RETIREMENT SYSTEM

"SEC. 207. [Repealed. Pub. L. 99–335, title III, § 309, June 6, 1986, 100 Stat. 607]

"SEC. 208. (a) Any individual performing service of a type referred to in clause (i), (ii), (iii), or (iv) of section 210(a)(5) of the Social Security Act [42 U.S.C. 410(a)(5)(i)–(iv)] beginning on or before December 31, 1983, may—

"(1) if such individual is then currently a participant in a covered retirement system, elect by written application submitted before January 1, 1984—

"(A) to terminate participation in such system, effective after December 31, 1983; or

"(B) to remain under such system, as if the preceding sections of this Act [probably means this 'title'] and the amendments made by this Act had not been enacted; or

"(2) if such individual is then currently not a participant in a covered retirement system, elect by written application—

"(A) to become a participant under such system (if such individual is otherwise eligible to participate in the system), subject to the preceding sections of this Act [probably means this 'title'] and the amendments made by this Act; or

"(B) to become a participant under such system (if such individual is otherwise eligible to participate in the system), as if the preceding sections of this Act and the amendments made by this Act had not been enacted.

"(b) An application by an individual under subsection (a) shall be submitted to the official by whom such covered employee is paid.

"(c) Any individual who elects to terminate participation in a covered retirement system under subsection (a)(1)(A) is entitled to have such individual's contributions to the retirement system refunded, in accordance with applicable provisions of law, as if such individual had separated from service as of the effective date of the election.

"(d) Any individual who is eligible to make an election under subparagraph (A) or (B) of subsection (a)(1), but who does not make an election under either such subparagraph, shall be subject to the preceding sections of this Act [probably means this 'title'] and the amendments made by this Act."

[Amendment to section 206(c)(3) of Pub. L. 98–168 by section 305(a)(1) of Pub. L. 99–335 directing the substitution of "January 1, 1987" for "January 1, 1986" has been executed by substituting "January 1, 1987" for "April 30, 1986" to reflect the probable intent of Congress.]

[Section 305(b) of Pub. L. 99–335 provided that:

"(1) The amendments made by subsection (a) [amending Pub. L. 98–168 set out above] shall be effective as of May 1, 1986.

"(2) Any refund payable to an individual as a result of paragraph (1) shall be paid out of funds of the appropriate retirement system.

"(3) For purposes of this subsection, the term 'retirement system' means a covered retirement system as defined by section 203(a)(2) of the Federal Employees' Retirement Contribution Temporary Adjustment Act of 1983 (97 Stat. 1107; 5 U.S.C. 8331 note)."]

[The Central Intelligence Agency Retirement Act of 1964 for Certain Employees, referred to in Pub. L. 98–168, set out above, is Pub. L. 88–643, Oct. 13, 1964, 78 Stat. 1043, which was revised generally by Pub. L. 102–496, title VIII, § 802, Oct. 24, 1992, 106 Stat. 3196, is known as the Central Intelligence Agency Retirement Act and is classified generally to chapter 38 (§ 2001 et seq.) of Title 50, War and National Defense.]

CANAL ZONE GOVERNMENT AND PANAMA CANAL COMPANY EMPLOYEES

Section 13 of Pub. L. 85–550, July 25, 1958, 72 Stat. 410, as amended by Pub. L. 87–845, § 2, Oct. 18, 1962, 76A Stat. 697, provided that:

"(a) Effective on and after the first day of the first pay period which begins in the third calendar month following the calendar month in which this Act is enacted [July 1958]—

"The Act of July 8, 1937 (50 Stat. 478; 68 Stat. 17; Public Numbered 191, Seventy-fifth Congress; Public Law 299, Eighty-third Congress), shall apply only with respect to those individuals within the classes of individuals subject to such Act of July 8, 1937, whose employment shall have been terminated, prior to such first day of such first pay period, in the manner provided by the first section of such Act; and

"(b) On or before the first day of the first pay period which begins in the third calendar month following the calendar month in which this Act is enacted [July 1958], the Panama Canal Company shall pay, as an agency contribution, into the civil service retirement and disability fund created by the Act of May 22, 1920, for each individual—

"(1) who is employed, on such first day of such first pay period, by the Canal Zone Government or by the Panama Canal Company, and

"(2) who, by reason of the enactment of this section and the operation of the Civil Service Retirement Act (5 U.S.C. 2251–2267) [this subchapter], is subject to such Act on and after such first day of such first pay period,

for service performed by such individual in the employment of—

"(A) the Panama Railroad Company during the period which began on June 29, 1948, and ended on June 30, 1951, or

"(B) the Panama Canal (former independent agency), the Canal Zone Government, or the Panama Canal Company during the period which began on

July 1, 1951, and which ends immediately prior to such first day of such first pay period,
an amount equal to the aggregate amount which such individual would have been required to contribute for retirement purposes if he had been subject to the Civil Service Retirement Act during such periods of service.

"(c) Nothing contained in this section shall affect—

"(1) the rights of any individual existing immediately prior to such first day of such first pay period above specified, or

"(2) the continuing obligations of the Canal Zone Government and the Panama Canal Company under section 4(a) of the Civil Service Retirement Act (5 U.S.C. 2254(a)) [section 8334(a) of this title], to reimburse the civil service retirement and disability fund for Government contributions to such fund covering service performed, on or after such first day of such first pay period above specified, by the employees concerned."

MEMBERS OF CIVILIAN FACULTIES OF UNITED STATES NAVAL ACADEMY AND UNITED STATES NAVAL POSTGRADUATE SCHOOL

Section 402 of act July 31, 1956, ch. 804, title IV, 70 Stat. 760, provided that:

"(a) On and after the effective date of this title [on the first day of the first month beginning more than sixty days after July 31, 1956] persons employed as members of the civilian faculties of the United States Naval Academy and the United States Naval Postgraduate School shall be included within the terms of the Civil Service Retirement Act [this subchapter], and on and after that date the Act of January 16, 1936 (49 Stat. 1092), as amended [covered by section 7081 et seq. of Title 10, Armed Forces] shall not apply to such persons.

"(b) In lieu of the deposit prescribed by section 4(c) of the Civil Service Retirement Act [section 8334(c) of this title] an employee who by virtue of subsection (a) is included within the terms of such Act [this subchapter] shall deposit, for service rendered prior to the effective date of this title as a member of the civilian faculty of the United States Naval Academy or of the United States Naval Postgraduate School, a sum equal to so much of the repurchase price of his annuity policy carried as required by the Act of January 16, 1936, as amended [covered by section 7081 et seq. of Title 10, Armed Forces], as is based on the monthly allotments which were registered with the Navy Allotment Office toward the purchase of that annuity, the deposit to be made within six months after the effective date of this title. Should the deposit not be made within that period no credit shall be allowed under the Civil Service Retirement Act [this subchapter] for service rendered as a member of the civilian faculty of the United States Naval Academy or of the United States Naval Postgraduate School subsequent to July 31, 1920, and prior to the effective date of this title. If the deposit is made, such service shall be held and considered to be service during which the employee was subject to the Civil Service Retirement Act [this subchapter]."

EX. ORD. NO. 12461. DESIGNATION AS A FEDERAL RETIREMENT SYSTEM

Ex. Ord. No. 12461, Feb. 17, 1984, 49 F.R. 6471, provided:

By the authority vested in me as President by the Federal Employees' Retirement Contribution Temporary Adjustment Act of 1983 (title II of Public Law 98–168) ("the Act") [set out as a note above], it is hereby ordered as follows:

SECTION 1. The District of Columbia Police and Firefighters' Retirement and Disability System, insofar as it applies to Federal employees who are covered under section 203(a)(1) of the Act [set out as a note above], is designated a covered retirement system under section 203(a)(2)(D) of the Act. The Secretary of the Treasury is designated the appropriate agency head with respect to such system, under section 205(a)(2)(D) of the Act [set out as a note above]. In discharging the responsibilities

delegated by this Order, the Secretary shall be guided by the information and recommendations provided by the Mayor of the District of Columbia.

SEC. 2. This Order shall be effective as of January 1, 1984.

RONALD REAGAN.

SECTION REFERRED TO IN OTHER SECTIONS

This section is referred to in sections 3307, 3323, 5541, 5545a, 5545b, 7371, 8332, 8339, 8342, 8344, 8347, 8401, 8411, 8415, 8467, 8704 of this title; title 10 section 945; title 12 section 1723a; title 19 section 58c; title 22 sections 3671, 3681, 3968, 4046; title 26 sections 402, 7447; title 28 section 376; title 38 sections 7296, 7426, 7438; title 45 section 1206; title 50 section 2036.

§ 8332. Creditable service

(a) The total service of an employee or Member is the full years and twelfth parts thereof, excluding from the aggregate the fractional part of a month, if any.

(b) The service of an employee shall be credited from the date of original employment to the date of separation on which title to annuity is based in the civilian service of the Government. Except as provided in paragraph (13)[1] of this subsection, credit may not be allowed for a period of separation from the service in excess of 3 calendar days. The service includes—

(1) employment as a substitute in the postal field service;

(2) service in the Pan American Sanitary Bureau;

(3) subject to section 8334(c) and 8339(i) of this title, service performed before July 10, 1960, as an employee of a county committee established under section 590h(b) of title 16 or of a committee or an association of producers described by section 610(b) of title 7;

(4) service as a student-employee as defined by section 5351 of this title only if he later becomes subject to this subchapter;

(5) a period of satisfactory service of a volunteer or volunteer leader under chapter 34 of title 22 only if he later becomes subject to this subchapter;

(6) employment under section 709 of title 32 or any prior corresponding provision of law;

(7) a period of service of a volunteer under part A of title VIII of the Economic Opportunity Act of 1964, or a period of service of a full-time volunteer enrolled in a program of at least one year's duration under part A, B, or C of title I of the Domestic Volunteer Service Act of 1973 only if he later becomes subject to this subchapter;

(8) subject to section 8334(c) and 8339(i) of this title, service performed after February 18, 1929, and before noon on January 3, 1971, as a United States Capitol Guide;

(9) subject to sections 8334(c) and 8339(i) of this title, service as a substitute teacher for the government of the District of Columbia after July 1, 1955, if such service is not credited for benefits under any other retirement system established by a law of the United States;

(10) periods of imprisonment of a foreign national for which compensation is provided under section 410 of the Foreign Service Act of

---

[1] So in original. Probably should be paragraph "(14)".

1980, if the individual (A) was subject to this subchapter during employment with the Government last preceding imprisonment, or (B) is qualified for an annuity under this subchapter on the basis of other service of the individual;

(11) subject to sections 8334(c) and 8339(i) of this title, service in any capacity of at least 130 days (or its equivalent) per calendar year performed after July 1, 1946, for the National Committee for a Free Europe; Free Europe Committee, Incorporated; Free Europe, Incorporated; Radio Liberation Committee; Radio Liberty Committee; subdivisions of any of those organizations; Radio Free Europe/Radio Liberty, Incorporated, Radio Free Asia; the Asia Foundation; or the Armed Forces Network, Europe (AFN–E), but only if such service is not credited for benefits under any other retirement system which is established for such entities and funded in whole or in part by the Government and only if the individual later becomes subject to this subchapter;

(12) service as a justice or judge of the United States, as defined by section 451 of title 28, and service as a judge of a court created by Act of Congress in a territory which is invested with any jurisdiction of a district court of the United States, but no credit shall be allowed for such service if the employee is entitled to a salary or an annuity under section 371, 372, or 373 of title 28;

(13) subject to sections 8334(c) and 8339(i) of this title, service performed on or after December 6, 1967, and before the effective date of this paragraph as an employee of the House Beauty Shop, only if he serves as such an employee for a period of at least five years after such effective date;

(14) one year of service to be credited for each year in which a Native of the Pribilof Islands performs service in the taking and curing of fur seal skins and other activities in connection with the administration of the Pribilof Islands, notwithstanding any period of separation from the service, and regardless of whether the Native who performs the service retires before, on, or after the effective date of this paragraph;

(15) subject to sections 8334(c) and 8339(i) of this title, service performed on or after January 3, 1969, and before January 4, 1973, as the Washington Representative for Guam or the Washington Representative for the Virgin Islands, only if the individual serves as a Member for a period of at least five years after January 2, 1973; and

(16) service performed by any individual as an employee described in section 2105(c) of this title after June 18, 1952, and before January 1, 1966, if (A) such service involved conducting an arts and crafts, drama, music, library, service club, youth activities, sports, or recreation program (including any outdoor recreation program) for personnel of the armed forces, and (B) such individual is an employee subject to this subchapter on the day before the date of the enactment of the Nonappropriated Fund Instrumentalities Employees' Retirement Credit Act of 1986.

The Office of Personnel Management shall accept the certification of the Secretary of Agriculture or his designee concerning service for the purpose of this subchapter of the type performed by an employee named by paragraph (3) of this subsection. The Office of Personnel Management shall accept the certification of the Secretary of Commerce or his designee concerning service for the purpose of this subchapter of the type performed by an employee named by paragraph (14) of this subsection. The Office of Personnel Management shall accept the certification of the Capitol Guide Board concerning service for the purpose of this subchapter of the type described in paragraph (8) of this subsection and performed by an employee. The Office of Personnel Management shall accept the certification of the Chief Administrative Officer of the House of Representatives concerning service for the purpose of this subchapter of the type described in paragraph (13) of this subsection. For the purpose of paragraph (5) of this subsection—

(A) a volunteer and a volunteer leader are deemed receiving pay during their service at the respective rates of readjustment allowances payable under sections 2504(c) and 2505(1) of title 22; and

(B) the period of an individual's service as a volunteer or volunteer leader under chapter 34 of title 22 is the period between enrollment as a volunteer or volunteer leader and the termination of that service by the President or by death or resignation.

The Office of Personnel Management shall accept the certification of the Executive Director of the Board for International Broadcasting, and the Secretary of State with respect to the Asia Foundation and the Secretary of Defense with respect to the Armed Forces Network, Europe (AFN–E), concerning services for the purposes of this subchapter of the type described in paragraph (11) of this subsection. For the purpose of this subchapter, service of the type described in paragraph (15) of this subsection shall be considered Member service. The Office of Personnel Management shall accept, for the purposes of this subchapter, the certification of the head of a nonappropriated fund instrumentality of the United States concerning service of the type described in paragraph (16) of this subsection which was performed for such appropriated fund instrumentality.

(c)(1) Except as provided in paragraphs (2) and (4) of this subsection and subsection (d) of this section—

(A) the service of an individual who first becomes an employee or Member before October 1, 1982, shall include credit for each period of military service performed before the date of the separation on which the entitlement to an annuity under this subchapter is based, subject to section 8332(j) of this title; and

(B) the service of an individual who first becomes an employee or Member on or after October 1, 1982, shall include credit for—

(i) each period of military service performed before January 1, 1957, and

(ii) each period of military service performed after December 31, 1956, and before the separation on which the entitlement to annuity under this subchapter is based, only if a deposit (with interest, if any) is made with respect to that period, as provided in section 8334(j) of this title.

(2) If an employee or Member is awarded retired pay based on any period of military service, the service of the employee or Member may not include credit for such period of military service unless the retired pay is awarded—

(A) based on a service-connected disability—

(i) incurred in combat with an enemy of the United States; or

(ii) caused by an instrumentality of war and incurred in line of duty during a period of war as defined by section 1101 of title 38; or

(B) under chapter 1223 of title 10 (or under chapter 67 of that title as in effect before the effective date of the Reserve Officer Personnel Management Act).

(3)(A) Notwithstanding paragraph (2) of this subsection, for purposes of computing a survivor annuity for a survivor of an employee or Member—

(i) who was awarded retired pay based on any period of military service, and

(ii) whose death occurs before separation from the service,

creditable service of the deceased employee or Member shall include each period of military service includable under subparagraph (A) or (B) of paragraph (1) of this subsection, as applicable. In carrying out this subparagraph, any amount deposited under section 8334(h) of this title shall be taken into account.

(B) A survivor annuity computed based on an amount which, under authority of subparagraph (A), takes into consideration any period of military service shall be reduced by the amount of any survivor's benefits—

(i) payable to a survivor (other than a child) under a retirement system for members of the uniformed services;

(ii) if, or to the extent that, such benefits are based on such period of military service.

(C) The Office of Personnel Management shall prescribe regulations to carry out this paragraph, including regulations under which—

(i) a survivor may elect not to be covered by this paragraph; and

(ii) this paragraph shall be carried out in any case which involves a former spouse.

(4) If, after January 1, 1997, an employee or Member waives retired pay that is subject to a court order for which there has been effective service on the Secretary concerned for purposes of section 1408 of title 10, the military service on which the retired pay is based may be credited as service for purposes of this subchapter only if the employee or Member authorizes the Director to deduct and withhold from the annuity payable to the employee or Member under this subchapter an amount equal to the amount that, if the annuity payment was instead a payment of the employee's or Member's retired pay, would have been deducted and withheld and paid to the former spouse covered by the court order under such section 1408. The amount deducted and withheld under this paragraph shall be paid to that former spouse. The period of civil service employment by the employee or Member shall not be taken into consideration in determining the amount of the deductions and withholding or the amount of the payment to the former spouse. The Director of the Office of Personnel Management shall prescribe regulations to carry out this paragraph.

(d) For the purpose of section 8339(c)(1) of this title, a Member—

(1) shall be allowed credit only for periods of military service not exceeding 5 years, plus military service performed by the Member on leaving his office, for the purpose of performing military service, during a war or national emergency proclaimed by the President or declared by Congress and before his final separation from service as Member; and

(2) may not receive credit for military service for which credit is allowed for purpose of retired pay under other statute.

(e) This subchapter does not affect the right of an employee or Member to retired pay, pension, or compensation in addition to an annuity payable under this subchapter.

(f) Credit shall be allowed for leaves of absence without pay granted an employee while performing military service or while receiving benefits under subchapter I of chapter 81 of this title. An employee or former employee who returns to duty after a period of separation is deemed, for the purpose of this subsection, to have been in a leave of absence without pay for that part of the period in which he was receiving benefits under subchapter I of chapter 81 of this title or any earlier statute on which such subchapter is based. Except for a substitute in the postal field service and service described in paragraph (14) of subsection (b) of this section,[2] credit may not be allowed for so much of other leaves of absence without pay as exceeds 6 months in the aggregate in a calendar year.

(g) An employee who during the period of a war, or of a national emergency as proclaimed by the President or declared by Congress, leaves his position to enter the military service is deemed, for the purpose of this subchapter, as not separated from his civilian position because of that military service, unless he applies for and receives a lump-sum credit under this subchapter. However, the employee is deemed as not retaining his civilian position after December 31, 1956, or after the expiration of 5 years of that military service, whichever, is later.

(h) An employee who—

(1) has at least 5 years' Member service; and

(2) serves as a Member at any time after August 2, 1946;

may not be allowed credit for service which is used in the computation of an annuity under section 8339(c) of this title.

(i) An individual who qualifies as an employee under section 8331(1)(E) of this title is entitled to credit for his service as a United States Commissioner, which is not credited for the purpose of this subchapter for service performed by him in a capacity other than Commissioner, on the basis of—

---

[2] So in original.

(1) 1/313 of a year for each day on which he performed service as a Commissioner before July 1, 1945; and

(2) 1/260 of a year for each day on which he performed service as a Commissioner after June 30, 1945.

Credit for service performed as Commissioner may not exceed 313 days in a year before July 1, 1945, or 260 days in a year after June 30, 1945. For the purpose of this subchapter, the employment and pay of a Commissioner is deemed on a daily basis when actually employed.

(j)(1) Notwithstanding any other provision of this section, military service, except military service covered by military leave with pay from a civilian position, performed by an individual after December 1956, the period of an individual's services as a volunteer under part A of title VIII of the Economic Opportunity Act of 1964, the period of an individual's service as a full-time volunteer enrolled in a program of at least 1 year's duration under part A, B, or C of title I of the Domestic Volunteer Service Act of 1973, and the period of an individual's service as a volunteer or volunteer leader under chapter 34 of title 22, shall be excluded in determining the aggregate period of service on which an annuity payable under this subchapter to the individual or to his spouse, former spouse or child is based, if the individual, spouse, former spouse, or child is entitled, or would on proper application be entitled, at the time of that determination, to monthly old-age or survivors benefits under section 402 of title 42 based on the individual's wages and self-employment income. If the military service or service as a volunteer under part A of title VIII of the Economic Opportunity Act of 1964, as a full-time volunteer enrolled in a program of at least 1 year's duration under part A, B, or C of title I of the Domestic Volunteer Service Act of 1973, or as a volunteer or volunteer leader under chapter 34 of title 22 is not excluded by the preceding sentence, but on becoming 62 years of age, the individual or spouse, former spouse[3] becomes entitled, or would on proper application be entitled, to the described benefits, the Office of Personnel Management shall redetermine the aggregate period of service on which the annuity is based, effective as of the first day of the month in which he or she becomes 62 years of age, so as to exclude that service. The Secretary of Health, Education, and Welfare, on request of the Office, shall inform the Office whether or not the individual, spouse, former spouse, or child is entitled at any named time to the described benefits. For the purpose of this subsection, the period of an individual's service as a volunteer or volunteer leader under chapter 34 of title 22 is the period between enrollment as a volunteer or volunteer leader and termination of that service by the President or by death or resignation and the period of an individual's service as a volunteer under part A of title VIII of the Economic Opportunity Act of 1964 or under part A, B, or C of title I of the Domestic Volunteer Service Act of 1973 is the period between enrollment as a volunteer and termination of that service by the Director of the Office of Economic Opportunity or the Chief Executive Officer of the Corporation for National and Community Service, as appropriate, or by death or resignation.

(2) The provisions of paragraph (1) of this subsection relating to credit for military service shall not apply to—

(A) any period of military service of an employee or Member with respect to which the employee or Member has made a deposit with interest, if any, under section 8334(j) of this title; or

(B) the service of any employee or Member described in section 8332(c)(1)(B) of this title.

(3) The provisions of paragraph (1) relating to credit for service as a volunteer or volunteer leader under the Economic Opportunity Act of 1964, part A, B, or C of title I of the Domestic Volunteer Service Act of 1973, or the Peace Corps Act shall not apply to any period of service as a volunteer or volunteer leader of an employee or Member with respect to which the employee or Member has made the deposit with interest, if any, required by section 8334(l).

(k)(1) An employee who enters on approved leave without pay to serve as a full-time officer or employee of an organization composed primarily of employees as defined by section 8331(1) of this title, within 60 days after entering on that leave without pay, may file with his employing agency an election to receive full retirement credit for his periods of that leave without pay and arrange to pay currently into the Fund, through his employing agency, amounts equal to the retirement deductions and agency contributions that would be applicable if he were in pay status. If the election and all payments provided by this paragraph are not made, the employee may not receive credit for the periods of leave without pay occurring after July 17, 1966, notwithstanding the third[4] sentence of subsection (f) of this section. For the purpose of the preceding sentence, "employee" includes an employee who was on approved leave without pay and serving as a full-time officer or employee of such an organization on July 18, 1966, and who filed a similar election before September 17, 1966.

(2) An employee may deposit with interest an amount equal to retirement deductions representing any period or periods of approved leave without pay while serving, before July 18, 1966, as a full-time officer or employee of an organization composed primarily of employees as defined by section 8331(1) of this title. An employee who makes the deposit shall be allowed full retirement credit for the period or periods of leave without pay. If the employee dies, a survivor as defined by section 8331(10) of this title may make the deposit. If the deposit is not made in full, retirement credit shall be allowed in accordance with the third[4] sentence of subsection (f) of this section.

(l)(1) Any employee or Member who—

(A) is of Japanese ancestry; and

(B) while a citizen of the United States or an alien lawfully admitted to the United States for permanent residence, was interned or

---

otherwise detained at any time during World War II in any camp, installation, or other facility in the United States, or in any territory or possession of the United States, under any policy or program of the United States respecting individuals of Japanese ancestry which was established during World War II in the interests of national security pursuant to—

(i) Executive Order Numbered 9066, dated February 19, 1942;

(ii) section 67 of the Act entitled "An Act to provide a government for the Territory of Hawaii", approved April 30, 1900 (chapter 339, Fifty-sixth Congress; 31 Stat. 153);

(iii) Executive Order Numbered 9489, dated October 18, 1944;

(iv) sections 4067 through 4070 of the Revised Statutes of the United States; or

(v) any other statute, rules, regulation, or order; or

(C) is of Aleut ancestry and while a citizen of the United States was interned or otherwise detained in, or relocated to any camp, installation, or other facility in the Territory of Alaska which was established during World War II for the purpose of the internment, detention, or relocation of Aleuts pursuant to any statute, rule, regulation, or order;

shall be allowed credit (as civilian service) for any period during which such employee or Member was so interned or otherwise detained after such employee became 18 years of age.

(2) For the purpose of this subsection, "World War II" means the period beginning on December 7, 1941, and ending on December 31, 1946.

(m)(1) Upon application to the Office of Personnel Management, any individual who is an employee on the date of the enactment of this subsection, and who has on such date or thereafter acquires 5 years or more of creditable civilian service under this section (exclusive of service for which credit is allowed under this subsection) shall be allowed credit (as service as a Congressional employee) for service before the date of the enactment of this subsection while employed by the Democratic Senatorial Campaign Committee, the Republican Senatorial Campaign Committee, the Democratic National Congressional Committee, or the Republican National Congressional Committee, if—

(A) such employee has at least 4 years and 6 months of service on such committees as of December 12, 1980; and

(B) such employee makes a deposit to the Fund in an amount equal to the amount which would be required under section 8834(c) of this title if such service were service as a Congressional employee.

(2) Upon application to the Office of Personnel Management, any individual who was an employee on the date of enactment of this paragraph, and who has on such date or thereafter acquires 5 years or more of creditable civilian service under this section (exclusive of service for which credit is allowed under this subsection) shall be allowed credit (as service as a congressional employee) for service before December 31, 1990, while employed by the Democratic Senatorial Campaign Committee, the Re-

publican Senatorial Campaign Committee, the Democratic National Congressional Committee, or the Republican National Congressional Committee, if—

(A) such employee has at least 4 years and 6 months of service on such committees as of December 31, 1990; and

(B) such employee makes a deposit to the Fund in an amount equal to the amount which would be required under section 8334(c) if such service were service as a congressional employee.

(3) The Office shall accept the certification of the President of the Senate (or his designee) or the Speaker of the House (or his designee), as the case may be, concerning the service of, and the amount of compensation received by, an employee with respect to which credit is to be sought under this subsection.

(4) An individual receiving credit for service for any period under this subsection shall not be granted credit for such service under the provisions of the Social Security Act.

(n) Any employee who—

(1) served in a position in which the employee was excluded from coverage under this subchapter because the employee was covered under a retirement system established under section 10 of the Federal Reserve Act; and

(2) transferred without a break in service to a position to which the employee was appointed by the President, with the advice and consent of the Senate, and in which position the employee is subject to this subchapter,

shall be treated for all purposes of this subchapter as if any service that would have been creditable under the retirement system established under section 10 of the Federal Reserve Act was service performed while subject to this subchapter if any employee and employer deductions, contributions or rights with respect to the employee's service are transferred from such retirement system to the Fund.

(Pub. L. 89–554, Sept. 6, 1966, 80 Stat. 567; Pub. L. 90–83, §1(73), Sept. 11, 1967, 81 Stat. 214; Pub. L. 90–486, §5(a), Aug. 13, 1968, 82 Stat. 757; Pub. L. 91–177, title I, §112(a), Dec. 30, 1969, 83 Stat. 831; Pub. L. 91–510, title IV, §442(b), Oct. 26, 1970, 84 Stat. 1191; Pub. L. 91–658, §1, Jan. 8, 1971, 84 Stat. 1961; Pub. L. 92–297, §7(1), May 16, 1972, 86 Stat. 144; Pub. L. 92–454, §1, Oct. 2, 1972, 86 Stat. 760; Pub. L. 93–113, title VI, §602, Oct. 1, 1973, 87 Stat. 417; Pub. L. 94–183, §2(32), (33), (39), Dec. 31, 1975, 89 Stat. 1058, 1059; Pub. L. 95–382, §1(a), Sept. 22, 1978, 92 Stat. 727; Pub. L. 95–454, title IX, §906(a)(2), (3), Oct. 13, 1978, 92 Stat. 1224; Pub. L. 96–54, §2(a)(48), Aug. 14, 1979, 93 Stat. 384; Pub. L. 96–465, title II, §2313, Oct. 17, 1980, 94 Stat. 2167; Pub. L. 96–523, §4(a), Dec. 12, 1980, 94 Stat. 3040; Pub. L. 97–164, title II, §207(a), Apr. 2, 1982, 96 Stat. 54; Pub. L. 97–253, title III, §306(b), (c), Sept. 8, 1982, 96 Stat. 795, 796; Pub. L. 97–346, §3(a), (b), Oct. 15, 1982, 96 Stat. 1647; Pub. L. 98–51, title I, §111(2), July 14, 1983, 97 Stat. 269; Pub. L. 89–702, title II, §209(a)–(e), as added Pub. L. 98–129, §2, Oct. 14, 1983, 97 Stat. 843; Pub. L. 98–369, div. B, title II, §2208(a), July 18, 1984, 98 Stat. 1060; Pub. L. 99–251, title II, §202, Feb. 27, 1986, 100 Stat. 23; Pub. L. 99–335, title II, §207(g), June 6, 1986, 100 Stat. 595; Pub. L. 99–556, title V, §502(a), Oct. 27, 1986, 100 Stat. 3140; Pub. L.

99–638, § 2(b)(2), Nov. 10, 1986, 100 Stat. 3536; Pub. L. 100–204, title V, § 503, Dec. 22, 1987, 101 Stat. 1383; Pub. L. 101–530, § 1, Nov. 6, 1990, 104 Stat. 2338; Pub. L. 102–83, § 5(c)(2), Aug. 6, 1991, 105 Stat. 406; Pub. L. 102–242, title IV, § 466(a), Dec. 19, 1991, 105 Stat. 2384; Pub. L. 102–378, § 2(58), Oct. 2, 1992, 106 Stat. 1354; Pub. L. 103–82, title III, § 371(a)(1), title IV, § 405(b), Sept. 21, 1993, 107 Stat. 909, 921; Pub. L. 103–337, div. A, title XVI, § 1677(a)(3), Oct. 5, 1994, 108 Stat. 3019; Pub. L. 104–186, title II, § 215(11), Aug. 20, 1996, 110 Stat. 1746; Pub. L. 104–201, div. A, title VI, § 637(a), Sept. 23, 1996, 110 Stat. 2580; Pub. L. 106–57, title III, § 312, Sept. 29, 1999, 113 Stat. 428; Pub. L. 106–554, § 1(a)(4) [div. A, § 901(a)(1)], Dec. 21, 2000, 114 Stat. 2763, 2763A–195.)

HISTORICAL AND REVISION NOTES
1966 ACT

Derivation	U.S. Code	Revised Statutes and Statutes at Large
....	5 U.S.C. 2253 (less (f) and (g)).	July 31, 1956, ch. 804, § 401 "Sec. 3 (less (f) and (g))", 70 Stat. 745. Aug. 1, 1956, ch. 837, § 409, 70 Stat. 877. June 17, 1957, Pub. L. 85–56, § 2201(2), 71 Stat. 157. Sept. 2, 1958, Pub. L. 85–857, § 13(c), 72 Stat. 1264. Sept. 21, 1959, Pub. L. 86–306, § 1, 73 Stat. 583. Sept. 22, 1961, Pub. L. 87–293, § 21, 75 Stat. 623.
....	5 U.S.C. 2252(g) (2d sentence).	July 31, 1956, ch. 804, § 401 "Sec. 2(g) (2d sentence)", 70 Stat. 745.
....	5 U.S.C. 2252(h)(2), (3).	July 1, 1960, Pub. L. 86–568, § 115(b)(1) "(h)(2), (3)", 74 Stat. 302. Oct. 4, 1961, Pub. L. 87–350, § 2(a), 75 Stat. 770.
....	5 U.S.C. 1054 (less 1st 27 words).	Aug. 4, 1947, ch. 452, § 5 (less 1st 27 words), 61 Stat. 728.
....	22 U.S.C. 2504(f) (as applicable to the Civil Service Retirement Act, as amended).	Sept. 22, 1961, Pub. L. 87–293, § 5(f) (as applicable to the Civil Service Retirement Act, as amended), 75 Stat. 614. Dec. 13, 1963, Pub. L. 88–200, § 2(c) (as applicable to the Civil Service Retirement Act, as amended), 77 Stat. 359.

The section is reorganized for clarity.

Subsection (b)(B) is added on authority of section 2522(e) of title 22.

In subsection (c)(1)(B), the words "as that term is defined by section 301 of title 38" are coextensive with and substituted for "as that term is used in chapter 11 of Title 38".

In subsection (c)(2), the words "under chapter 67 of title 10" are substituted for "title III of Public Law 810, Eightieth Congress" on authority of the Act of Aug. 10, 1956, ch. 104, § 49(b), 70A Stat. 640.

In subsection (f), the words "without pay" are added after "leaves of absence" in the first sentence for clarity and to align it with the use of the term in the second sentence. The words "postal field service" are coextensive with and substituted for "postal service".

In subsection (g), the words "has left" are omitted as executed.

In subsection (i), the words "but nothing contained in this chapter [chapter 30 of title 5] shall affect, otherwise than for the purposes of this chapter, the basis, under applicable law other than this chapter, on which such United States Commissioner is employed or on which his compensation is determined and paid" are omitted from the last sentence as surplusage as there is nothing in the chapter that can reasonably be con-

strued to affect that basis other than for the purposes of the chapter.

In subsection (j), the words "or section 2504(f) of Title 22" are omitted as unnecessary since the provisions of that section applicable to this subchapter are carried into subsection (b). The last sentence is added on authority of section 2522(e) of title 22.

Standard changes are made to conform with the definitions applicable and the style of this title as outlined in the preface to the report.

1967 ACT

Section of title 5	Source (U.S. Code)	Source (Statutes at Large)
8332(k)(1) ... 8332(k)(2) ...	5 App.: 2253(k)(1). 5 App.: 2253(k)(2).	July 18, 1966, Pub. L. 89–504, § 503, 80 Stat. 300.

In subsection (k)(1), the words "as defined by section 8331(1) of this title" are substituted for "as defined in section 1(a) of this Act". The words "occurring after July 17, 1966" are substituted for "occurring on or after date of enactment of this subsection". The words "notwithstanding the second sentence of subsection (f) of this section" are substituted for "notwithstanding the provisions of the second sentence of section 3(c) of this Act". The last sentence is substituted for the second sentence of former subsection (k)(1) to reflect the current effect of the subsection with regard to those employees who were on leave without pay on July 18, 1966, and who filed a similar election within the time prescribed by that sentence.

In subsection (k)(2), the words "before July 18, 1966" are substituted for "prior to the date of enactment of this subsection". The words "as defined by section 8331(1) of this title" are substituted for "as defined in section 1(a) of this Act". The second sentence is substituted for "and may receive full retirement credit for such period or periods of leave without pay". The words "If the employee dies" are substituted for "In the event of his death". The words "as defined by section 8331(10) of this title" are substituted for "as defined in section 1(o) of this Act". In the last sentence, the words "described in this paragraph" following "If the deposit" are omitted as unnecessary. The words "the second sentence of subsection (f) of this section" are substituted for "the second sentence of section 3(c) of this Act".

REFERENCES IN TEXT

The Economic Opportunity Act of 1964, referred to in subsecs. (b)(7) and (j)(1), (3), is Pub. L. 88–452, Aug. 20, 1964, 78 Stat. 508, as amended, which was classified generally to chapter 34 (§ 2701 et seq.) of Title 42, The Public Health and Welfare, prior to repeal, except for titles VIII and X, by Pub. L. 97–35, title VI, § 683(a), Aug. 13, 1981, 95 Stat. 519. Titles VIII and X of the Act are classified generally to subchapters VIII (§ 2991 et seq.) and X (§ 2996 et seq.) of chapter 34 of Title 42. Part A of title VIII of that Act is part A of title VIII of Pub. L. 88–452 as added by Pub. L. 90–222, title I, § 110, Dec. 23, 1967, 81 Stat. 722, which was classified generally to part A (§ 2992 et seq.) of subchapter VIII of chapter 34 of Title 42, prior to its repeal by Pub. L. 93–113, title VI, § 603, Oct. 1, 1973, 87 Stat. 417. See sections 4951 et seq. and 5055 of Title 42. For complete classification of this Act to the Code, see Tables.

Parts A, B, and C of title I of the Domestic Volunteer Service Act of 1973, referred to in subsecs. (b)(7) and (j)(1), (3), are classified to part A (§ 4951 et seq.), part B (§ 4971 et seq.), and part C (§ 4991 et seq.), respectively, of subchapter I of chapter 66 of Title 42.

Section 410 of the Foreign Service Act of 1980, referred to in subsec. (b)(10), is classified to section 3970 of Title 22, Foreign Relations and Intercourse.

The effective date of this paragraph, referred to in subsec. (b)(13), is Jan. 3, 1978, the effective date of section 111(2) of Pub. L. 98–51. See Effective Date of 1983 Amendment note below.

The effective date of this paragraph, referred to in subsec. (b)(14), is Oct. 14, 1983, the date of enactment of Pub. L. 98–129.

The date of the enactment of the Nonappropriated Fund Instrumentalities Employees' Retirement Credit Act of 1986, referred to in subsec. (b)(16), is the date of enactment of section 2 of Pub. L. 99–638, which was approved Nov. 10, 1986.

Chapter 67 of that title as in effect before the effective date of the Reserve Officer Personnel Management Act, referred to in subsec. (c)(2)(B), means chapter 67 (§ 1331 et seq.) of Title 10, Armed Forces, prior to its transfer to part II of subtitle E of Title 10, its renumbering as chapter 1223, and its general revision by section 1662(j)(1) of Pub. L. 103–337. A new chapter 67 (§ 1331) of Title 10 was added by section 1662(j)(7) of Pub. L. 103–337. For effective date of the Reserve Officer Personnel Management Act (Pub. L. 103–337, title XVI), see section 1691 of Pub. L. 103–337, set out as an Effective Date note under section 10001 of Title 10.

The Peace Corps Act, referred to in subsec. (j)(3), is Pub. L. 87–293, Sept. 22, 1961, 75 Stat. 612, as amended, which is classified principally to chapter 34 (§ 2501 et seq.) of Title 22, Foreign Relations and Intercourse. For complete classification of this Act to the Code, see Short Title note set out under section 2501 of Title 22 and Tables.

Section 67 of the Act entitled "An Act to provide a government for the Territory of Hawaii", approved April 30, 1900 (chapter 339, Fifty-sixth Congress; 31 Stat. 153), referred to in subsec. (l)(1)(B)(ii), formerly classified to section 532 of Title 48, Territories and Insular Possessions, was omitted from such Title following the statehood of Hawaii.

Sections 4067 through 4070 of the Revised Statutes, referred to in subsec. (l)(1)(B)(iv), are classified to sections 21 through 24 of Title 50, War and National Defense.

The date of enactment of this subsection, referred to in subsec. (m)(1), means the date of enactment of Pub. L. 96–523 which was approved Dec. 12, 1980.

The date of enactment of this paragraph, referred to in subsec. (m)(2), is the date of enactment of Pub. L. 106–554, which was approved Dec. 21, 2000.

The Social Security Act, referred to in subsec. (m)(4), is act Aug. 14, 1935, ch. 531, 49 Stat. 620, as amended, which is classified generally to chapter 7 (§ 301 et seq.) of Title 42, The Public Health and Welfare. For complete classification of this Act to the Code, see section 1305 of Title 42 and Tables.

Section 10 of the Federal Reserve Act, referred to in subsec. (n), is section 10 of act Dec. 23, 1913, ch. 6, 38 Stat. 260, as amended. For classification of section 10 to the Code, see Codification note set out under section 241 of Title 12, Banks and Banking, and Tables.

AMENDMENTS

2000—Subsec. (m)(2) to (4). Pub. L. 106–554 added par. (2) and redesignated former pars. (2) and (3) as (3) and (4), respectively.

1999—Subsec. (m)(1)(A). Pub. L. 106–57 amended subpar. (A) generally. Prior to amendment, subpar. (A) read as follows: "such employee has at least 5 years service on such committees as of the effective date of this section, and".

1996—Subsec. (b). Pub. L. 104–186 substituted "Chief Administrative Officer" for "Clerk" in fourth sentence of concluding provisions.

Subsec. (c)(1). Pub. L. 104–201, § 637(a)(2), in introductory provisions, substituted "Except as provided in paragraphs (2) and (4)" for "Except as provided in paragraph (2)".

Subsec. (c)(4). Pub. L. 104–201, § 637(a)(1), added par. (4).

1994—Subsec. (c)(2)(B). Pub. L. 103–337 substituted "chapter 1223 of title 10 (or under chapter 67 of that title as in effect before the effective date of the Reserve Officer Personnel Management Act)" for "chapter 67 of title 10".

1993—Subsec. (j)(1). Pub. L. 103–82, § 405(b), which directed that "the Chief Executive Officer of the Corporation for National and Community Service" be substituted for "the Director of ACTION", could not be executed because "the Director of ACTION" does not appear in text.

Pub. L. 103–82, § 371(a)(1)(A)(i), in first sentence inserted "the period of an individual's service as a full-time volunteer enrolled in a program of at least 1 year's duration under part A, B, or C of title I of the Domestic Volunteer Service Act of 1973," after "Economic Opportunity Act of 1964,".

Pub. L. 103–82, § 371(a)(1)(A)(ii), in second sentence inserted ", as a full-time volunteer enrolled in a program of at least 1 year's duration under part A, B, or C of title I of the Domestic Volunteer Service Act of 1973," after "Economic Opportunity Act of 1964".

Pub. L. 103–82, § 371(a)(1)(A)(iii), in last sentence inserted "or under part A, B, or C of title I of the Domestic Volunteer Service Act of 1973" after "Economic Opportunity Act of 1964", and inserted "or the Chief Executive Officer of the Corporation for National and Community Service, as appropriate," after "Director of the Office of Economic Opportunity".

Subsec. (j)(3). Pub. L. 103–82, § 371(a)(1)(B), added par. (3).

1992—Subsec. (b). Pub. L. 102–378 substituted "paragraph (16)" for "paragrpah (16)".

1991—Subsec. (c)(2)(A)(ii). Pub. L. 102–83 substituted "section 1101 of title 38" for "section 301 of title 38".

Subsec. (n). Pub. L. 102–242 added subsec. (n).

1990—Subsec. (b). Pub. L. 101–530 struck out at beginning of last paragraph "service referred to in paragraph (6) is allowable only in the case of persons performing service under section 709 of title 32 after December 31, 1968."

1987—Subsec. (b). Pub. L. 100–204 inserted ", and the Secretary of State with respect to the Asia Foundation and the Secretary of Defense with respect to the Armed Forces Network, Europe (AFN–E)," after "Board for International Broadcasting" in last paragraph.

1986—Subsec. (b). Pub. L. 99–638 which directed the amendment of subchapter (b) of section 8332 by adding par. (16) and closing provision relating to acceptance by the Office of Personnel Management of the certification of a nonappropriated fund instrumentality concerning service of the type described in par. (16) was executed to subsec. (b) of this section, as the probable intent of Congress.

Pub. L. 99–335, § 207(g)(1)(C), (D), substituted "paragraph (14)" for "paragraph (13)" in second sentence following par. (15), and inserted last sentence providing that for purposes of this subchapter, service of the type described in par. (15) of this subsection shall be considered Member service.

Subsec. (b)(13) to (15). Pub. L. 99–335, § 207(g)(1)(A), (B), redesignated the par. (13), relating to service credits for Pribilof Island Natives for taking and curing of fur seal skins and other activities, as par. (14), and added par. (15).

Subsec. (c)(3). Pub. L. 99–556 added par. (3).

Subsec. (f). Pub. L. 99–335, § 207(g)(2), substituted "paragraph (14)" for "paragraph (13)".

Subsec. (j)(1). Pub. L. 99–251 substituted "spouse, former spouse" for "widow" wherever appearing.

Subsec. (k). Pub. L. 99–335, § 207(g)(3), which directed the substitution of "third" for "second" in last sentence of par. (1), was executed by substituting "third" for "second" in penultimate sentence of par. (1) and last sentence of par. (2) as the probable intent of Congress.

1984—Subsec. (b)(13). Pub. L. 98–369 inserted in the par. (13) added by Pub. L. 98–129 ", and regardless of whether the Native who performs the service retires before, on, or after the effective date of this paragraph".

1983—Subsec. (b). Pub. L. 98–129 substituted "Except as provided in paragraph (13) of this subsection, credit" for "Credit" in provisions preceding par. (1), and inserted in provisions immediately following par. (13) the sentence providing that the Office of Personnel Management shall accept the certification of the Secretary of Commerce or his designee concerning service for the purpose of this subchapter of the type performed by an employee named by par. (13) of this subsection.

Pub. L. 98–51, § 111(2)(D), inserted in provisions immediately following par. (13) the sentence providing that the Office of Personnel Management shall accept the certification of the Clerk of the House of Representatives concerning service for the purpose of this subchapter of the type described in par. (13) of this subsection.

Subsec. (b)(13). Pub. L. 98–129 added a par. (13) relating to service performed by Pribilof Island Natives.

Pub. L. 98–51, § 111(2)(A)–(C), added a par. (13) relating to service by a person as an employee of the House Beauty Shop.

Subsec. (f). Pub. L. 98–129 inserted "and service described in paragraph (13) of subsection (b) of this section," after "postal field service".

Subsec. (l)(1)(C). Pub. L. 98–129 added subpar. (C).

1982—Subsec. (b)(12). Pub. L. 97–164 added par. (12).

Subsec. (c). Pub. L. 97–253, § 306(b), designated existing first sentence as par. (1), inserted provision differentiating between individuals who become employees or Members before Oct. 1, 1982, and those who become so on or after Oct. 1, 1982, and designated existing second sentence as par. (2) with accommodating redesignations of paragraphs and subparagraphs as subparagraphs and clauses accordingly.

Subsec. (c)(1)(A). Pub. L. 97–346, § 3(a), substituted "period" for "month".

Subsec. (c)(1)(B). Pub. L. 97–346, § 3(b), redesignated provisions following "shall include credit for" as cl. (i), substituted "each period of military service performed before January 1, 1957, and" for "each month of military service (performed before the date of the separation on which the entitlement to an annuity under this subchapter is based) only if a deposit with interest, if any, is made with respect to that month, as provided in section 8334(j) of this title", and added cl. (2).

Subsec. (j). Pub. L. 97–253, § 306(c), redesignated existing provisions as par. (1) and added par. (2).

Subsec. (j)(2)(A). Pub. L. 97–346, § 3(a), substituted "period" for "month".

1980—Subsec. (b)(10), (11). Pub. L. 96–465 added pars. (10) and (11) and last sentence relating to acceptance by the Office of Personnel Management of the certification of the Executive Director of the Board for International Broadcasting.

Subsec. (m). Pub. L. 96–523 added subsec. (m).

1979—Subsec. (b). Pub. L. 96–54, § 2(a)(48)(B), substituted "after December 31, 1968" for "United States Code, on or after the effective date of the National Guard Technicians Act of 1968" in last sentence.

Subsec. (b)(6). Pub. L. 96–54, § 2(a)(48)(A), struck out ", United States Code" after "32".

1978—Subsecs. (b), (j). Pub. L. 95–454 substituted "Office of Personnel Management" and "Office" for "Civil Service Commission" and "Commission", respectively, wherever appearing.

Subsec. (l). Pub. L. 95–382 added subsec. (l).

1975—Subsec. (b)(7). Pub. L. 94–183, § 2(39), struck out "(—U.S.C.—)" after "Domestic Volunteer Service Act of 1973".

Subsec. (b)(8). Pub. L. 94–183, § 2(32), substituted "after February 18, 1929, and before noon on January 3, 1971" for "on and after February 19, 1929, and prior to the effective date of section 442 of the Legislative Reorganization Act of 1970".

Subsec. (b)(9). Pub. L. 94–183, § 2(33), substituted "8339(i)" for "8339(h)".

1973—Subsec. (b)(7). Pub. L. 93–113 included period of service of a full-time volunteer enrolled in a program of at least one year's duration under part A, B, or C of title I of the Domestic Volunteer Service Act of 1973.

1972—Subsec. (b). Pub. L. 92–454 added par. (9).

Pub. L. 92–297 substituted "8339(i)" for "8339(h)" in pars. (3) and (8).

1971—Subsec. (f). Pub. L. 91–658 provided for leave-without-pay status for retirement purposes of employees or former employees who return to duty after a period of separation during which compensation benefits were received.

1970—Subsec. (b). Pub. L. 91–510 added par. (8) and provision for Civil Service Commission acceptance of cer-

tification of Capitol Guide Board concerning service for purpose of this subchapter, respectively.

1969—Subsec. (b)(7). Pub. L. 91–177, § 112(a)(1), added par. (7).

Subsec. (j). Pub. L. 91–177, § 112(a)(2), excluded period of an individual's services as a VISTA volunteer under part A of subchapter VIII of title 42, from aggregate period of service determining annuity payments.

Pub. L. 91–177, § 112(a)(3), inserted provision for computation of period of service of a VISTA volunteer under part A of subchapter VIII of title 42.

1968—Subsec. (b). Pub. L. 90–486 added par. (6), and provisions that service referred to in par. (6) is allowable only in the case of persons performing service under section 709 of title 32, on or after the specified effective date.

CHANGE OF NAME

Secretary of Health, Education, and Welfare redesignated Secretary of Health and Human Services by section 3508 of Title 20, Education.

EFFECTIVE DATE OF 1996 AMENDMENT

Section 637(c) of Pub. L. 104–201 provided that: "The amendments made by subsections (a) and (b) [amending this section and section 8411 of this title] shall take effect on January 1, 1997."

EFFECTIVE DATE OF 1994 AMENDMENT

Amendment by Pub. L. 103–337 effective Dec. 1, 1994, except as otherwise provided, see section 1691 of Pub. L. 103–337, set out as an Effective Date note under section 10001 of Title 10, Armed Forces.

EFFECTIVE DATE OF 1993 AMENDMENT

Section 371(c) of Pub. L. 103–82 provided that:

"(1) APPLICABILITY.—

"(A) AMENDMENTS RELATING TO CSRS.—

"(i) IN GENERAL.—The amendments made by subsection (a) [amending this section and section 8334 of this title] shall apply with respect to any individual entitled to an annuity on the basis of a separation from service occurring on or after the effective date of this subtitle [Oct. 1, 1993].

"(ii) RULES RELATING TO ANNUITIES BASED ON EARLIER SEPARATIONS.—An annuity under subchapter III of chapter 83 of title 5, United States Code, payable to an individual based on a separation from service occurring before the effective date of this subtitle shall be subject to the provisions of paragraph (2).

"(B) AMENDMENTS RELATING TO FERS.—

"(i) IN GENERAL.—The amendments made by subsection (b) [amending sections 8411 and 8422 of this title] shall apply with respect to any individual entitled to an annuity on the basis of a separation from service occurring before, on, or after the effective date of this subtitle [Oct. 1, 1993], subject to clause (ii).

"(ii) RULE RELATING TO ANNUITIES BASED ON EARLIER SEPARATIONS.—In the case of any individual whose entitlement to an annuity is based on a separation from service occurring before the effective date of this subtitle, any increase in such individual's annuity on the basis of a deposit made under section 8442(f) of title 5, United States Code, as amended by subsection (b)(2), shall be effective beginning with the annuity payment payable for the first calendar month beginning after the effective date of this subtitle.

"(2) SPECIAL RULES.—

"(A) OLD-AGE OR SURVIVORS INSURANCE BENEFITS.—Subject to subparagraph (B), in any case in which an individual described in paragraph (1)(A)(ii) is also entitled to old-age or survivors insurance benefits under section 202 of the Social Security Act [42 U.S.C. 402] (or would be entitled to such benefits upon filing an application therefor), the amount of the annuity to which such individual is entitled under subchapter III of chapter 83 of title 5, United States Code (after taking into account any creditable service as a volunteer or volunteer leader under the Economic Opportunity Act of 1964 [42 U.S.C. 2701 et seq.], the Domestic Volunteer Service Act of 1973 [42 U.S.C. 4950 et seq.], or the Peace Corps Act [22 U.S.C. 2501 et seq.]) which is payable for any month shall be reduced by an amount determined by multiplying the amount of such old-age or survivors insurance benefit for the determination month by a fraction—

"(i) the numerator of which is the total of the wages (within the meaning of section 209 of the Social Security Act [42 U.S.C. 409]) for service as a volunteer or volunteer leader under the Economic Opportunity Act of 1964, the Domestic Volunteer Service Act of 1973, or the Peace Corps Act of such individual credited for years before the calendar year in which the determination month occurs, up to the contribution and benefit base determined under section 230 of the Social Security Act [42 U.S.C. 430] (or other applicable maximum annual amount referred to in section 215(e)(1) of such Act [42 U.S.C. 415(e)(1)] for each such year); and

"(ii) the denominator of which is the total of all wages described in clause (i), plus all other wages (within the meaning of section 209 of such Act [42 U.S.C. 409]) and all self-employment income (within the meaning of section 211(b) of such Act [42 U.S.C. 411(b)]) of such individual credited for years after 1936 and before the calendar year in which the determination month occurs, up to the contribution and benefit base (or such other amount referred to in section 215(e)(1) of such Act [42 U.S.C. 415(e)(1)] for each such year.

"(B) LIMITATIONS.—

"(i) REDUCTION IN ANNUITY.—Subparagraph (A) shall not reduce the annuity of an individual below the amount of the annuity which would be payable to the individual for the determination month if the provisions of section 8332(j) of title 5, United States Code, relating to service as a volunteer or volunteer leader, applied to the individual for such month.

"(ii) APPLICATION.—Subparagraph (A) shall not apply in the case of an individual who, prior to the date of enactment of this Act [Sept. 21, 1993], made a deposit under section 8334(c) of title 5, United States Code, with respect to service as a volunteer or volunteer leader (as described in subparagraph (A)).

"(iii) DETERMINATION MONTH.—For purposes of this paragraph, the term 'determination month' means—

"(I) the first month the individual described in paragraph (1)(A)(ii) is entitled to old-age or survivors benefits under section 202 of the Social Security Act [42 U.S.C. 402] (or would be entitled to such benefits upon filing an application therefor); or

"(II) the first calendar month beginning after the date of enactment of this Act [Sept. 21, 1993], in the case of any individual entitled to such benefits for such month.

"(iv) RULE RELATING TO ANNUITIES BASED ON EARLIER SEPARATIONS.—Any increase in an annuity which occurs by virtue of the enactment of this paragraph shall be effective beginning with the annuity payment payable for the first calendar month beginning after the effective date of this subtitle [Oct. 1, 1993].

"(3) FURNISHING OF INFORMATION.—The Secretary of Health and Human Services shall furnish such information to the Office of Personnel Management as may be necessary to carry out this subsection.

"(4) ACTION TO INFORM INDIVIDUALS.—The Director of the Office of Personnel Management shall take such action as may be necessary and appropriate to inform individuals entitled to credit under this section for service as a volunteer or volunteer leader, or to have any annuity recomputed, or to make a deposit under this section, of such entitlement."

Amendment by section 371(a)(1) of Pub. L. 103–82 effective Oct. 1, 1993, see section 392 of Pub. L. 103–82, set out as a note under section 4951 of Title 42, The Public Health and Welfare.

Section 406(b) of Pub. L. 103–82 provided that: "The amendments made by sections 404 and 405 [amending this section, section 558a of Title 16, Conservation, section 2501–1 of Title 22, Foreign Relations and Intercourse, section 1542 of Title 25, Indians, and sections 3012, 3013, 3035a, 4950, 4953, 4995, 5025, 5043, 5048, 5056, 5061, 5065, 5590, 5616, 6863, 11312, 11851, 12312, 12638, and 12653 of Title 42, and amending provisions set out as notes under section 1701z–6 of Title 12, Banks and Banking, and sections 4954 and 5001 of Title 42] shall take effect on the effective date of section 203(c)(2)." [Section 203(c)(2) of Pub. L. 103–82 is effective Apr. 4, 1994, see section 203(d) of Pub. L. 103–82 and Proc. No. 6662, set out as notes under section 12651 of Title 42.]

EFFECTIVE DATE OF 1991 AMENDMENT

Section 466(c) of Pub. L. 102–242 provided that: "The amendment made by this section [amending this section and section 8411 of this title] shall apply with respect to any individual who transfers to a position in which he or she is subject to subchapter III of chapter 83 or chapter 84 of title 5, United States Code, on or after October 1, 1991."

EFFECTIVE DATE OF 1990 AMENDMENT

Section 3(a) of Pub. L. 101–530 provided that:

"(1) GENERAL RULE.—

"(A) ELIGIBILITY.—Except as provided in paragraph (2), the amendment made by section 1 [amending this section] applies only with respect to individuals who—

"(i) separate from employment with the Government on or after the date of enactment of this Act [Nov. 6, 1990]; and

"(ii) make an appropriate deposit, in accordance with section 8334(c) or 8411(f) of title 5, United States Code (as appropriate), for additional service that is creditable under such amendment.

"(B) DEPOSIT.—Any such deposit—

"(i) shall include interest, which shall be computed under section 8334(e) of such title (except that the rate of interest shall be 3 percent a year) from the midpoint of the period of additional service to the date deposit is made; and

"(ii) shall be made before date of retirement.

"(2) EXCEPTION.—

"(A) RULE FOR INDIVIDUALS SEPARATING AFTER DECEMBER 31, 1968, AND BEFORE THE ENACTMENT OF THIS ACT.—In the case of any individual who—

"(i) was employed under section 709 of title 32, United States Code, relating to National Guard technicians, or any prior corresponding provision of law, before January 1, 1969, and

"(ii) was separated from employment with the Government on or after January 1, 1969, and before the date of enactment of this Act [Nov. 6, 1990], any annuity under subchapter III of chapter 83 or chapter 84 of title 5, United States Code, based on such individual's service (as defined in section 8331(12) or 8401(26) of such title, as applicable) shall be determined or redetermined to take into account the amendment made by section 1 [amending this section], if application therefor is received by the Office of Personnel Management within 1 year after the date of enactment of this Act, and an appropriate deposit is made for any additional service that is creditable under such amendment. Any such deposit shall be computed, and must be paid either in a lump sum at the time of application or in installments over the 2-year period which begins on the date of application, or such shorter period as the Office may by regulation prescribe.

"(B) EARLIER PAYMENTS NOT AFFECTED BY RECOMPUTATION.—Any change in an annuity resulting from a redetermination under subparagraph (A) shall apply only with respect to monthly payments accruing after the date the deposit required under subparagraph (A) is made (or, if payments are to be made in installments, after an agreement has been entered into regarding the manner in which such payments will be made).

"(3) PAYMENT BY SURVIVORS.—For the purpose of survivor annuities, any deposit or installment payment required by paragraph (1) or (2) relating to service of an individual may also be made by a survivor of such individual."

EFFECTIVE DATE OF 1986 AMENDMENTS

Section 2(c) of Pub. L. 99–638 provided that: "Notwithstanding any other provision of this Act [amending this section and section 2105 of this title and enacting provisions set out as notes under this section and section 8331 of this title] which specifies an effective date for amendments made by this Act, the amendments made by this section [amending this section and section 2105 of this title] shall take effect on the date of the enactment of this Act [Nov. 10, 1986]."

Section 502(c) of Pub. L. 99–556 provided that:
"(1) The amendments made by this section [amending this section and section 8411 of this title] shall apply to a survivor of an employee or Member who dies on or after the 180th day after the date of the enactment of this Act [Oct. 27, 1986].

"(2) Upon application to the Office of Personnel Management, such amendments shall also apply to a survivor of an employee or Member whose date of death precedes such 180th day, except that any resulting recomputation shall not be effective for any period beginning before the 60th day after the date on which the application is received."

Amendment by Pub. L. 99–335 effective Jan. 1, 1987, see section 702(a) of Pub. L. 99–335, set out as an Effective Date note under section 8401 of this title.

EFFECTIVE DATE OF 1984 AMENDMENT

Amendment by Pub. L. 98–369 effective Oct. 14, 1983, see section 2208(c) of Pub. L. 98–369, set out as a note under section 1169a of Title 16, Conservation.

EFFECTIVE DATE OF 1983 AMENDMENT

Section 111(2) of Pub. L. 98–51 provided that the amendment made by that section is effective Jan. 3, 1978.

EFFECTIVE DATE OF 1982 AMENDMENTS

Section 3(n) of Pub. L. 97–346 provided that: "The amendments made by this section [amending this section and sections 8334, 8342, 8344, and 8348 of this title and provisions set out as notes under this section and sections 5504, 5532, 5728, 8331, 8334, and 8337 of this title] shall take effect as of the date of the enactment of the Omnibus Budget Reconciliation Act of 1982 [Sept. 8, 1982]."

Amendment by Pub. L. 97–253 effective Oct. 1, 1982, except that any employee or Member who retired after Sept. 8, 1982, and before Oct. 1, 1985, or is entitled to an annuity under chapter 83 of this title based on a separation from service occurring during such period, or a survivor of such individual, may make a payment under section 8334(j)(1) of this title, and regulations required to be issued under section 8334(j)(1) of this title, to be issued by the Office of Personnel Management within 90 days after such effective date, see section 306(g) of Pub. L. 97–253, as amended, set out as a note under section 8331 of this title.

Amendment by Pub. L. 97–164 effective Oct. 1, 1982, see section 402 of Pub. L. 97–164, set out as a note under section 171 of Title 28, Judiciary and Judicial Procedure.

EFFECTIVE DATE OF 1980 AMENDMENTS

Section 4(b) of Pub. L. 96–523 provided that: "The amendments made by this section [amending this section] shall take effect on the date of the enactment of this Act [Dec. 12, 1980]."

Amendment by Pub. L. 96–465 effective Feb. 15, 1981, except as otherwise provided, see section 2403 of Pub. L. 96–465, set out as an Effective Date note under section 3901 of Title 22, Foreign Relations and Intercourse.

EFFECTIVE DATE OF 1979 AMENDMENT

Amendment by Pub. L. 96–54 effective July 12, 1979, see section 2(b) of Pub. L. 96–54, set out as a note under section 305 of this title.

EFFECTIVE DATE OF 1978 AMENDMENT

Amendment by Pub. L. 95–454 effective 90 days after Oct. 13, 1978, see section 907 of Pub. L. 95–454, set out as a note under section 1101 of this title.

EFFECTIVE DATE OF 1978 AMENDMENT; APPLICABILITY TO ANNUITIES; RECOMPUTATION

Section 2 of Pub. L. 95–382 provided that:
"(a) The amendments made by this Act [amending this section and section 8334 of this title] shall take effect on the later of—
"(1) the date of the enactment of this Act [Sept. 22, 1978], or
"(2) October 1, 1978.

"(b) Subject to subsection (c) of this section, the amendments made by the first section of this Act [amending this section and section 8334 of this title], shall apply with respect to annuities which commence before, on, or after the effective date of this Act, but no monetary benefit by reason of such amendments shall accrue for any period before such effective date.

"(c)(1) An annuity or survivor annuity based on the service of an employee or Member who performed service described in section 8332(l) of title 5, United States Code, as added by the first section of this Act, shall, upon application to the Civil Service Commission, be recomputed in accordance with such section 8332(l).

"(2) Any recomputation of an annuity under paragraph (1) shall apply with respect to months beginning more than 30 days after the date on which application for such recomputation is received in the Commission.

"(d)(1) The Civil Service Commission shall take such action as may be necessary and and appropriate to inform individuals entitled to have any service credited under section 8332(l) of title 5, United States Code, as added by the first section of this Act, or to have any annuity recomputed under subsection (c), of their entitlement to such credit or recomputation.

"(2) The Civil Service Commission shall, on request, assist any individual referred to in paragraph (1) in obtaining from any department, agency, or other instrumentality of the United States such information possessed by such instrumentality as may be necessary to verify the entitlement of such individual to have any service credited under such section 8332(l) or to have any annuity recomputed under subsection (c).

"(3) Any department, agency, or other instrumentality of the United States which possesses any information with respect to the internment or other detention of any employee or Member as described in such section 8332(l) shall, at the request of the Commission, furnish such information to the Commission."

EFFECTIVE DATE OF 1972 AMENDMENT

Amendment by Pub. L. 92–297 effective on 90th day after May 16, 1972, see section 10 of Pub. L. 92–297, set out as an Effective Date note under section 3381 of this title.

EFFECTIVE DATE OF 1971 AMENDMENT

Section 5(a) of Pub. L. 91–658 provided that: "The amendment made by the first section of this Act [amending this section] is effective only with respect to annuity accruing for full months beginning after the date of enactment of this Act [Jan. 8, 1971]; but any part of a period of separation referred to in such amendment in which the employee or former employee was receiving benefits under subchapter I of chapter 81 of title 5, United States Code, or any earlier statute on which such subchapter is based shall be counted whether the employee returns to duty before, on, or after such date of enactment. With respect to any person retired before such date of enactment any such part of a period of separation shall be counted only upon application of the former employee."

EFFECTIVE DATE OF 1970 AMENDMENT

Amendment by Pub. L. 91–510 effective immediately prior to noon on Jan. 3, 1971, see section 601(1) of Pub. L. 91–510, set out as a note under section 72a of Title 2, The Congress.

EFFECTIVE DATE OF 1969 AMENDMENT

Amendment by Pub. L. 91–177 effective as to all former volunteers employed by the United States Government on or after the effective date of Pub. L. 91–177 which was approved on Dec. 30, 1969, see section 112(c) of Pub. L. 91–177.

EFFECTIVE DATE OF 1968 AMENDMENT

Amendment by Pub. L. 90–486 effective Jan. 1, 1969, except that no deductions or withholding from salary which result shall commence before first day of first pay period that begins on or after Jan. 1, 1968, see section 11 of Pub. L. 90–486, set out as a note under section 709 of Title 32, National Guard.

REGULATIONS

Section 4 of Pub. L. 101–530 provided that: "The Office of Personnel Management shall prescribe any regulations necessary for the implementation of this Act [amending this section, enacting provisions set out as a note above, and enacting and amending provisions set out as notes under section 709 of Title 32, National Guard]."

FORMER EMPLOYEES OF LEGISLATIVE SERVICE ORGANIZATIONS

Pub. L. 106–554, §1(a)(4) [div. A, §901(b)], Dec. 21, 2000, 114 Stat. 2763, 2763A–196, provided that:

"(1) SERVICE OF EMPLOYEES OF LEGISLATIVE SERVICE ORGANIZATIONS.—

"(A) IN GENERAL.—Subject to succeeding provisions of this paragraph, upon application to the Office of Personnel Management in such form and manner as the Office shall prescribe, any individual who performed service as an employee of a legislative service organization of the House of Representatives (as defined and authorized in the One Hundred Third Congress) and whose pay was paid in whole or in part by a source other than the Clerk Hire account of a Member of the House of Representatives (other than an individual described in paragraph (6)) shall be entitled—

"(i) to receive credit under the provisions of subchapter III of chapter 83 or chapter 84 of title 5, United States Code (whichever would be appropriate), as congressional employee service, for all such service; and

"(ii) to have all pay for such service which was so paid by a source other than the Clerk Hire account of a Member included (in addition to any amounts otherwise included in basic pay) for purposes of computing an annuity payable out of the Civil Service Retirement and Disability Fund.

"(B) DEPOSIT REQUIREMENT.—In order to be eligible for the benefits described in subparagraph (A), an individual shall be required to pay into the Civil Service Retirement and Disability Fund an amount equal to the difference between—

"(i) the employee contributions that were actually made to such Fund under applicable provisions of law with respect to the service described in subparagraph (A); and

"(ii) the employee contributions that would have been required with respect to such service if the amounts described in subparagraph (A)(ii) had also been treated as basic pay.

The amount required under this subparagraph shall include interest, which shall be computed under section 8334(e) of title 5, United States Code.

"(C) CERTAIN OFFSETS REQUIRED IN ORDER TO PREVENT DOUBLE CONTRIBUTIONS AND BENEFITS.—In the case of any period of service as an employee of a legislative service organization which constituted employment for purposes of title II of the Social Security Act [42 U.S.C. 401 et seq.]—

"(i) any pay for such service (as described in subparagraph (A)(ii)) with respect to which the deposit under subparagraph (B) would otherwise be computed by applying the first sentence of section 8334(a)(1) of title 5, United States Code, shall instead be computed in a manner based on section 8334(k) of such title; and

"(ii) any retirement benefits under subchapter III of chapter 83 of title 5, United States Code, shall be subject to offset (to reflect that portion of benefits under title II of the Social Security Act [42 U.S.C. 401 et seq.] attributable to pay referred to in subparagraph (A)) similar to that provided for under section 8349 of such title.

"(2) SURVIVOR ANNUITANTS.—For purposes of survivor annuities, an application authorized by this section may, in the case of an individual under paragraph (1) who has died, be made by a survivor of such individual.

"(3) RECOMPUTATION OF ANNUITIES.—Any annuity or survivor annuity payable as of when an individual makes the deposit required under paragraph (1) shall be recomputed to take into account the crediting of service under such paragraph for purposes of amounts accruing for any period beginning on or after the date on which the individual makes the deposit.

"(4) CERTIFICATION OF SPEAKER.—The Office of Personnel Management shall accept the certification of the Speaker of the House of Representatives (or the Speaker's designee) concerning the service of, and the amount of compensation received by, an employee with respect to whom credit is to be sought under this subsection.

"(5) NOTIFICATION AND OTHER DUTIES OF THE OFFICE OF PERSONNEL MANAGEMENT.—

"(A) NOTICE.—The Office of Personnel Management shall take such action as may be necessary and appropriate to inform individuals of any rights they might have as a result of enactment of this subsection.

"(B) ASSISTANCE.—The Office shall, on request, assist any individual in obtaining from any department, agency, or other instrumentality of the United States any information in the possession of such instrumentality which may be necessary to verify the entitlement of such individual to have any service credited under this subsection or to have an annuity recomputed under paragraph (3).

"(C) INFORMATION.—Any department, agency, or other instrumentality of the United States which possesses any information with respect to an individual's performance of any service described in paragraph (1) shall, at the request of the office, furnish such information to the Office.

"(6) EXCLUSION OF CERTAIN EMPLOYEES.—An individual is not eligible for credit under this subsection if the individual served as an employee of the House of Representatives for an aggregate period of 5 years or longer after the individual's final period of service as an employee of a legislative service organization of the House of Representatives.

"(7) MEMBER DEFINED.—In this subsection, the term 'Member of the House of Representatives' includes a Delegate or Resident Commissioner to Congress."

CREDITABILITY OF ICC EMPLOYEE'S ANNUAL LEAVE FOR PURPOSES OF MEETING MINIMUM ELIGIBILITY REQUIREMENTS FOR IMMEDIATE ANNUITY

Pub. L. 104–88, title I, §105, Dec. 29, 1995, 109 Stat. 920, provided that:

"(a) IN GENERAL.—An employee of the Interstate Commerce Commission who is separated from Government service pursuant to the abolition of that agency under section 101 [49 U.S.C. 701 note] shall, upon appropriate written application, be given credit, for purposes of determining eligibility for and computing the amount of any annuity under subchapter III of chapter 83 or chapter 84 of title 5, United States Code, for accrued annual leave standing to such employee's credit at the time of separation.

"(b) LIMITATION AND OTHER CONDITIONS.—Any regulations necessary to carry out this section shall be prescribed by the Office of Personnel Management. Such regulations shall include provisions—

"(1) defining the types of leave for which credit may be given under this section (such definition to be similar to the corresponding provisions of the regulations under section 351.608(c)(2) of title 5 of the Code of Federal Regulations, as in effect on the date of the enactment of this Act [Dec. 29, 1995]);

"(2) limiting the amount of accrued annual leave which may be used for the purposes specified in subsection (a) to the minimum period of time necessary in order to permit such employee to attain first eligibility for an immediate annuity under section 8336, 8412, or 8414 of title 5, United States Code (in a manner similar to the corresponding provisions of the regulations referred to in paragraph (1));

"(3) under which contributions (or arrangements for the making of contributions) shall be made so that—

"(A) employee contributions for any period of leave for which retirement credit may be obtained under this section shall be made by the employee; and

"(B) Government contributions with respect to such period shall similarly be made by the Interstate Commerce Commission or other appropriate officer or entity (out of appropriations otherwise available for such contributions); and

"(4) under which subsection (a) shall not apply with respect to an employee who declines a reasonable offer of employment in another position in the Department of Transportation made under this Act [see Tables for classification] or any amendment made by this Act.

"(c) EXTINGUISHMENT OF ELIGIBILITY FOR LUMP-SUM PAYMENT.—A lump-sum payment under section 5551 of title 5, United States Code, shall not be payable with respect to any leave for which retirement credit is obtained under this section."

[Interstate Commerce Commission abolished and functions of Commission transferred, except as otherwise provided in Pub. L. 104–88, to Surface Transportation Board effective Jan. 1, 1996, by section 702 of Title 49, Transportation, and section 101 of Pub. L. 104–88, set out as a note under section 701 of Title 49.]

CREDITABILITY UNDER CSRS OF CERTAIN SERVICE PERFORMED UNDER PERSONAL SERVICE CONTRACT WITH UNITED STATES

Pub. L. 100–238, title I, §110, Jan. 8, 1988, 101 Stat. 1749, provided that:

"(a) IN GENERAL.—

"(1) CONDITIONS FOR RECEIVING CREDIT.—Subject to the making of a deposit under section 8334(c) of title 5, United States Code, upon application to the Office of Personnel Management within 2 years after the date of the enactment of this Act [Jan. 8, 1988], any individual who is an employee (as defined by section 8331(1) or 8401(11) of such title) on such date shall be allowed credit under subchapter III of chapter 83 of such title for any service if such service was performed—

"(A) before November 5, 1985; and

"(B) under a personal service contract with the United States, except as provided in paragraph (3).

"(2) CERTIFICATION.—

"(A) IN GENERAL.—The Office shall, with respect to any service for which credit is sought under this subsection, accept the certification of the head of the agency which was party to the contract re-

ferred to in paragraph (1)(B), but only if such certification—

"(i) states that the agency had intended, through such contract, that the individual involved (or that persons like the individual involved) be considered as having been appointed to a position in which such individual would be subject to subchapter III of chapter 83 of title 5, United States Code; and

"(ii) indicates the period of service which was performed under the contract by the individual involved, and includes copies of appropriate records or other documentation to support the determination as to the length of such period.

"(B) FINALITY.—A decision by an agency head concerning whether or not to make a certification under this paragraph in any particular instance shall be at the sole discretion of the agency head, and shall not be subject to administrative or judicial review.

"(3) EXCEPTION.—Nothing in this subsection shall apply with respect to any service performed under—

"(A) a contract for which any appropriations, allocations, or funds were used under section 636(a)(3) of the Foreign Assistance Act of 1961 [22 U.S.C. 2396(a)(3)];

"(B) a contract entered into under section 10(a)(5) of the Peace Corps Act [22 U.S.C. 2509(a)(5)];

"(C) a contract under which the services of an individual may be terminated by a person other than the individual or the Government; or

"(D) a contract for a single transaction or a contract under which services are paid for in a single payment.

"(b) APPLICABILITY TO ANNUITANTS.—

"(1) IN GENERAL.—In the case of any individual who—

"(A) performed service for which credit is allowable under subsection (a), and

"(B) retired on an annuity payable under subchapter III of chapter 83 of title 5, United States Code, after January 23, 1980, and before the date of the enactment of this Act [Jan. 8, 1988],

any annuity under such subchapter based on the service of such individual shall be redetermined to take into account the amendment made by subsection (a) if application therefor is made, and the deposit requirement under such subsection is met, within 2 years after the date of the enactment of this Act.

"(2) AMOUNTS TO WHICH APPLICABLE.—Any change in an annuity resulting from a redetermination under paragraph (1) shall be effective with respect to payments accruing for months beginning after the date of the enactment of this Act."

CLARIFICATION RELATING TO CONSIDERATION OF PRE-1987 SERVICE AS AIR TRAFFIC CONTROLLER FOR RETIREMENT PURPOSES

Pub. L. 100–92, §2, Aug. 18, 1987, 101 Stat. 679, provided that:

"(a) For purposes of subchapter III of chapter 83 of title 5, United States Code, and chapter 84 of such title—

"(1) service as an air traffic controller shall, with respect to any annuity which is based on a separation from service, or death, occurring on or after January 1, 1987, include any service as an air traffic controller whether performed before, on, or after January 1, 1987; and

"(2) the Office of Personnel Management shall accept the certification of the Secretary, or the designee of the Secretary, in determining the amount of any service performed by an individual as an air traffic controller.

"(b) For purposes of this section—

"(1) the term 'air traffic controller' has the meaning given such term by section 2109(1) of title 5, United States Code, as amended by section 207(b) of the Federal Employees' Retirement System Act of 1986 (Public Law 99–335; 100 Stat. 594); and

"(2) the term 'Secretary' has the meaning given such term by section 2109(2) of title 5, United States Code."

CADET NURSE CORPS

Section 1 of Pub. L. 99–638 provided: "That (a) service described in subsection (b) shall be considered creditable civilian service for purposes of subchapter III of chapter 83, or chapter 84, of title 5, United States Code, as applicable, in the case of any individual who meets the requirements of subsection (c).

"(b) This section relates to any period of training as a student or graduate nurse under a plan approved under section 2 of the Act of June 15, 1943 (57 Stat. 153) [former 50 App. U.S.C. 1452], if the total period of training under such plan was at least 2 years.

"(c)(1) An individual may not receive credit for service pursuant to this Act [amending sections 2105 and 8332 of this title and enacting provisions set out as notes under sections 8331 and 8332 of this title] unless—

"(A) within 14 months after the date of the enactment of this Act [Nov. 10, 1986], and in accordance with regulations under subsection (d), the individual files appropriate written application with the Office of Personnel Management;

"(B) at the time of filing the application under subparagraph (A), the individual is employed by the Government and subject to subchapter III of chapter 83 of title 5, United States Code (other than section 8344 of such title), or chapter 84 of such title (other than section 8468 of such title);

"(C) before the date of the separation on which is based the individual's entitlement to an annuity under subchapter III of chapter 83 of title 5, United States Code, or chapter 84 of such title, as applicable, such individual deposits into the Civil Service Retirement and Disability Fund the amount required under paragraph (2) with respect to the period of training involved.

"(2) The amount to be deposited shall be determined by the Office of Personnel Management in a manner consistent with applicable provisions of subchapter III of chapter 83 of title 5, United States Code, chapter 84 of such title or title III of the Federal Employees' Retirement System Act of 1986 [Pub. L. 99–335, title III, see Tables for classification], as the case may be, relating to deposits for earlier periods of civilian service for which deductions from basic pay have not been made.

"(d) The Office of Personnel Management shall, not later than 2 months after the date of the enactment of this Act [Nov. 10, 1986], prescribe regulations to carry out this Act [amending sections 2105 and 8332 of this title and enacting provisions set out as notes under sections 8331 and 8332 of this title]."

RECOMPUTATION AT AGE 62 OF CREDIT FOR MILITARY SERVICE OF CURRENT ANNUITANTS

Section 307 of Pub. L. 97–253, as amended by Pub. L. 97–346, § 3(k), Oct. 15, 1982, 96 Stat. 1649, provided that:

"(a) The provisions of section 8332(j) of title 5, United States Code, relating to credit for military service, shall not apply with respect to any individual who is entitled to an annuity under subchapter III of chapter 83 of title 5, United States Code, on or before the date of enactment of this Act [Sept. 8, 1982] or who is entitled to an annuity based on a separation from service occurring on or before such date of enactment.

"(b) Subject to subsection (b), in any case in which an individual described in subsection (a) is also entitled to old-age or survivors' insurance benefits under section 202 of the Social Security Act [42 U.S.C. 402] (or would be entitled to such benefits upon filing application therefor), the amount of the annuity to which such individual is entitled under subchapter III of chapter 83 of title 5, United States Code, (after taking into account subsection (a)) which is payable for any month shall be reduced by an amount determined by multiplying the amount of such old-age or survivors' insurance benefit for the determination month by a fraction—

"(1) the numerator of which is the total of the wages (within the meaning of section 209 of the Social Security Act [42 U.S.C. 409]) for service referred to in section 210(l) of such Act [42 U.S.C. 410(l)] (relating to service in the uniformed services) and deemed additional wages (within the meaning of section 229 of such Act [42 U.S.C. 429]) of such individual credited for years after 1956 and before the calendar year in which the determination month occurs, up to the contribution and benefit base determined under section 230 of the Social Security Act [42 U.S.C. 430] (or other applicable maximum annual amount referred to in section 215(e)(1) of such Act [42 U.S.C. 415(e)(1)]) for each such year, and

"(2) the denominator of which is the total of all wages and deemed additional wages described in paragraph (1) of this subsection plus all other wages (within the meaning of section 209 of such Act [42 U.S.C. 409]) and all self-employment income (within the meaning of section 211(b) of such Act [42 U.S.C. 411(b)]) of such individual credited for years after 1936 and before the calendar year in which the determination month occurs, up to the contribution and benefit base (or such other amount referred to in such section 215(e)(1) [42 U.S.C. 415(e)(1)]) for each such year.

"(c) Subsection (b) shall not reduce the annuity of any individual below the amount of the annuity which would be payable under this subchapter to the individual for the determination month if section 8332(j) of title 5, United States Code, applied to the individual for such month.

"(d) For purposes of this section, the term 'determination month' means—

"(1) the first month the individual described in subsection (a) is entitled to old-age or survivors' insurance benefits under section 202 of the Social Security Act [42 U.S.C. 402] (or would be entitled to such benefits upon filing application therefor); or

"(2) October 1982, in the case of any individual so entitled to such benefits for such month.

"(e) The preceding provisions of this section shall take effect with respect to any annuity payment payable under subchapter III of chapter 83 of title 5, United States Code, for calendar months beginning after September 30, 1982.

"(f) The Secretary of Health and Human Services shall furnish such information to the Office of Personnel Management as may be necessary to carry out the preceding provisions of this section."

DISTRICT OF COLUMBIA SUBSTITUTE TEACHERS

Section 2 of Pub. L. 92–454 provided that: "An annuity or survivor annuity based on the service of an employee or annuitant who performed service described in section 1 of this Act [amending this section] shall, upon application to the Civil Service Commission, be recomputed, effective on the first day of the first month following the date of enactment of this Act [Oct. 2, 1972], in accordance with section 1 of this Act."

NATIONAL GUARD TECHNICIANS

Amendment by section 5(a)(4) of Pub. L. 90–486 not applicable to persons employed prior to Jan. 1, 1969 whose employment was covered by the civil service retirement provisions of section 8331 et seq. of this title, see section 5(d) of Pub. L. 90–486, set out as a note under section 709 of Title 32, National Guard.

CREDITABLE SERVICE OF CERTAIN COMMISSIONED OFFICERS OF THE REGULAR OR RESERVE CORPS OF THE PUBLIC HEALTH SERVICE

Section 6(a), (b) of Pub. L. 86–415, Apr. 8, 1960, 74 Stat. 35, provided that:

"(a) Except as provided in subsection (b), service as a commissioned officer in the Regular Corps of the Public Health Service prior to July 1, 1960, shall be considered, for purposes of credit under the Civil Service Retirement Act [this subchapter], other than section 3(f) thereof [section 8333(a) of this title], as civilian service performed by an employee (as defined in such Act [this subchapter]) and commissioned officers of the Reserve Corps of the Public Health Service, subject to the Civil Service Retirement Act [this subchapter] on June 30, 1960, shall be considered as voluntarily separated on that date, with respect to service as such officers, from civilian positions subject to such Act [this subchapter].

"(b) If a commissioned officer of the Regular or Reserve Corps of the Public Health Service is retired after June 30, 1960, and becomes entitled to retired pay from the Public Health Service, all service in the Regular or Reserve Corps of the Public Health Service prior to July 1, 1960, together with any other service which is performed at any time with the Public Health Service, other than as a commissioned officer, and which is credited to the officer for purposes of such retirement, shall be considered as military service for purposes of section 3(b) of the Civil Service Retirement Act [subsecs. (c)–(e) of this section]; except that, in the case of any such officer who is retired pursuant to subsection (a) of section 211 of the Public Health Service Act [section 212(a) of Title 42], any such service which was performed prior to July 1, 1960, which was subject to the Civil Service Retirement Act [this subchapter], and with respect to which he has not, prior to his retirement, received a refund of deductions under the Civil Service Retirement Act [this subchapter], shall not be considered as military service for purposes of such section 3(b) [subsecs. (c)–(e) of this section], but only if he waives his right to have such service included for purposes of computing the amount of his retired pay from the Service."

SECTION REFERRED TO IN OTHER SECTIONS

This section is referred to in sections 6303, 8331, 8334, 8339, 8345, 8411 of this title; title 16 section 1169a; title 22 sections 3671, 3681, 4048, 4056; title 25 section 450i; title 26 sections 3121, 7448; title 38 sections 7297, 7406, 7426; title 42 section 410; title 50 section 2082.

§ 8333. Eligibility for annuity

(a) An employee must complete at least 5 years of civilian service before he is eligible for an annuity under this subchapter.

(b) An employee or Member must complete, within the last 2 years before any separation from service, except a separation because of death or disability, at least 1 year of creditable civilian service during which he is subject to this subchapter before he or his survivors are eligible for annuity under this subchapter based on the separation. If an employee or Member, except an employee or Member separated from the service because of death or disability, fails to meet the service requirement of the preceding sentence, the amounts deducted from his pay during the service for which no eligibility for annuity is established based on the separation shall be returned to him on the separation. Failure to meet this service requirement does not deprive the individual or his survivors of annuity rights which attached on a previous separation.

(c) A Member or his survivor is eligible for an annuity under this subchapter only if the amounts named by section 8334 of this title have been deducted or deposited with respect to his last 5 years of civilian service, or, in the case of a survivor annuity under section 8341(d) or (e)(1) of this title, with respect to his total service.

(Pub. L. 89–554, Sept. 6, 1966, 80 Stat. 569; Pub. L. 91–93, title II, § 201(b), Oct. 20, 1969, 83 Stat. 138; Pub. L. 94–183, § 2(34), Dec. 31, 1975, 89 Stat. 1058.)

HISTORICAL AND REVISION NOTES

Derivation	U.S. Code	Revised Statutes and Statutes at Large
(a), (b)	5 U.S.C. 2253(f), (g).	July 31, 1956, ch. 804, § 401 "Sec. 3(f), (g)", 70 Stat. 746.
(c)	5 U.S.C. 2256(f) (last sentence).	July 31, 1956, ch. 804, § 401 "Sec. 6(f) (last sentence)", 70 Stat. 750. Aug. 27, 1958, Pub. L. 85–772, § 1(a), 72 Stat. 930.

In subsection (c), the words "eligible for" are substituted for "entitled to".

Standard changes are made to conform with the definitions applicable and the style of this title as outlined in the preface to the report.

AMENDMENTS

1975—Subsec. (c). Pub. L. 94–183 substituted "of this title" for "of title 5" and "of this title" for "of this chapter".

1969—Subsec. (c). Pub. L. 91–93 provided for eligibility for a survivor annuity under section 8341(d) or (e)(1) of this title only if the requisite amounts are deducted or deposited with respect to total service period.

EFFECTIVE DATE OF 1969 AMENDMENT

Amendment by Pub. L. 91–93 inapplicable in cases of persons retired or otherwise separated prior to Oct. 20, 1969, their rights and of their survivors continued as if such amendment had not been enacted, see section 207(a) of Pub. L. 91–93, set out as a note under section 8331 of this title.

SECTION REFERRED TO IN OTHER SECTIONS

This section is referred to in title 22 section 4051.

§ 8334. Deductions, contributions, and deposits

(a)(1) The employing agency shall deduct and withhold from the basic pay of an employee, Member, Congressional employee, law enforcement officer, firefighter, bankruptcy judge, judge of the United States Court of Appeals for the Armed Forces, United States magistrate,[1] Court of Federal Claims judge, member of the Capitol Police, member of the Supreme Court Police, or nuclear materials courier, as the case may be, the percentage of basic pay applicable under subsection (c). An equal amount shall be contributed from the appropriation or fund used to pay the employee or, in the case of an elected official, from an appropriation or fund available for payment of other salaries of the same office or establishment. When an employee in the legislative branch is paid by the Chief Administrative Officer of the House of Representatives, the Chief Administrative Officer may pay from the applicable accounts of the House of Representatives the contribution that otherwise would be contributed from the appropriation or fund used to pay the employee.

(2) The amounts so deducted and withheld, together with the amounts so contributed, shall be deposited in the Treasury of the United States to the credit of the Fund under such procedures as the Secretary of the Treasury may prescribe. Deposits made by an employee or Member also shall be credited to the Fund.

(b) Each employee or Member is deemed to consent and agree to these deductions from

---

[1] So in original. Probably should be "United States magistrate judge,".

basic pay. Notwithstanding any law or regulation affecting the pay of an employee or Member, payment less these deductions is a full and complete discharge and acquittance of all claims and demands for regular services during the period covered by the payment, except the right to the benefits to which the employee or Member is entitled under this subchapter.

(c) Each employee or Member credited with civilian service after July 31, 1920, for which retirement deductions or deposits have not been made, may deposit with interest an amount equal to the following percentages of his basic pay received for that service:

	Percentage of basic pay	Service period
Employee	2½	August 1, 1920, to June 30, 1926.
	3½	July 1, 1926, to June 30, 1942.
	5	July 1, 1942, to June 30, 1948.
	6	July 1, 1948, to October 31, 1956.
	6½	November 1, 1956, to December 31, 1969.
	7	January 1, 1970, to December 31, 1998.
	7.25	January 1, 1999, to December 31, 1999.
	7.4	January 1, 2000, to December 31, 2000.
	7	After December 31, 2000.
Member or employee for Congressional employee service.	2½	August 1, 1920, to June 30, 1926.
	3½	July 1, 1926, to June 30, 1942.
	5	July 1, 1942, to June 30, 1948.
	6	July 1, 1948, to October 31, 1956.
	6½	November 1, 1956, to December 31, 1969.
	7.5	January 1, 1970, to December 31, 1998.
	7.75	January 1, 1999, to December 31, 1999.
	7.9	January 1, 2000, to December 31, 2000.
	7.5	After December 31, 2000.
Member for Member service.	2½	August 1, 1920, to June 30, 1926.
	3½	July 1, 1926, to June 30, 1942.
	5	July 1, 1942, to August 1, 1946.
	6	August 2, 1946, to October 31, 1956.
	7½	November 1, 1956, to December 31, 1969.
	8	January 1, 1970, to December 31, 1998.
	8.25	January 1, 1999, to December 31, 1999.
	8.4	January 1, 2000, to December 31, 2000.
	8.5	January 1, 2001, to December 31, 2002.
	8	After December 31, 2002.
Law enforcement officer for law enforcement service, member of the Supreme Court Police for Supreme Court Police service, and firefighter for firefighter service.	2½	August 1, 1920, to June 30, 1926.
	3½	July 1, 1926, to June 30, 1942.
	5	July 1, 1942, to June 30, 1948.
	6	July 1, 1948, to October 31, 1956.
	6½	November 1, 1956, to December 31, 1969.
	7	January 1, 1970, to December 31, 1974.
	7.5	January 1, 1975, to December 31, 1998.
	7.75	January 1, 1999, to December 31, 1999.
	7.9	January 1, 2000, to December 31, 2000.
	7.5	After December 31, 2000.
Bankruptcy judge.	2½	August 1, 1920, to June 30, 1926.
	3½	July 3, 1926, to June 30, 1942.
	5	July 1, 1942, to June 30, 1948.
	6	July 1, 1948, to October 31, 1956.
	6½	November 1, 1956, to December 31, 1969.
	7	January 1, 1970, to December 31, 1983.
	8	January 1, 1984, to December 31, 1998.
	8.25	January 1, 1999, to December 31, 1999.
	8.4	January 1, 2000, to December 31, 2000.
	8	After December 31, 2000.

	Percentage of basic pay	Service period
Judge of the United States Court of Appeals for the Armed Forces for service as a judge of that court.	6	May 5, 1950, to October 31, 1956.
	6½	November 1, 1956, to December 31, 1969.
	7	January 1, 1970, to (but not including) the date of the enactment of the Department of Defense Authorization Act, 1984.
	8	The date of enactment of the Department of Defense Authorization Act, 1984, to December 31, 1998.
	8.25	January 1, 1999, to December 31, 1999.
	8.4	January 1, 2000, to December 31, 2000.
	8	After December 31, 2000.
United States magistrate judge.	2½	August 1, 1920, to June 30, 1926.
	3½	July 1, 1926, to June 30, 1942.
	5	July 1, 1942, to June 30, 1948.
	6	July 1, 1948, to October 31, 1956.
	6½	November 1, 1956, to December 31, 1969.
	7	January 1, 1970, to September 30, 1987.
	8	October 1, 1987, to December 31, 1998.
	8.25	January 1, 1999, to December 31, 1999.
	8.4	January 1, 2000, to December 31, 2000.
	8	After December 31, 2000.
Court of Federal Claims Judge.	2½	August 1, 1920, to June 30, 1926.
	3½	July 1, 1926, to June 30, 1942.
	5	July 1, 1942, to June 30, 1948.
	6	July 1, 1948, to October 31, 1956.
	6½	November 1, 1956, to December 31, 1969.
	7	January 1, 1970, to September 30, 1988.
	8	October 1, 1988, to December 31, 1998.
	8.25	January 1, 1999, to December 31, 1999.
	8.4	January 1, 2000, to December 31, 2000.
	8	After December 31, 2000.
Member of the Capitol Police.	2.5	August 1, 1920, to June 30, 1926.
	3.5	July 1, 1926, to June 30, 1942.
	5	July 1, 1942, to June 30, 1948.
	6	July 1, 1948, to October 31, 1956.
	6.5	November 1, 1956, to December 31, 1969.
	7.5	January 1, 1970, to December 31, 1998.
	7.75	January 1, 1999, to December 31, 1999.
	7.9	January 1, 2000, to December 31, 2000.
	7.5	After December 31, 2000.
Nuclear materials courier.	7	October 1, 1977 to October 16, 1998.
	7.5	October 17, 1998 to December 31, 1998.
	7.75	January 1, 1999 to December 31, 1999.
	7.9	January 1, 2000 to December 31, 2000.
	7.5	After December 31, 2000.

Notwithstanding the preceding provisions of this subsection and any provision of section 206(b)(3) of the Federal Employees' Retirement Contribution Temporary Adjustment Act of 1983, the percentage of basic pay required under this subsection in the case of an individual described in section 8402(b)(2) shall, with respect to any covered service (as defined by section 203(a)(3) of such Act) performed by such individual after December 31, 1983, and before January 1, 1987, be equal to 1.3 percent, and, with respect to any such service performed after December 31, 1986, be equal to the amount that would have been deducted from the employee's basic pay under subsection (k) of this section if the employee's pay had been subject to that subsection during such period.

(d)(1) Each employee or Member who has received a refund of retirement deductions under this or any other retirement system established for employees of the Government covering service for which he may be allowed credit under this subchapter may deposit the amount received, with interest. Credit may not be allowed for the service covered by the refund until the deposit is made.

(2)(A) This paragraph applies with respect to any employee or Member who—

(i) separates before October 1, 1990, and receives (or elects, in accordance with applicable provisions of this subchapter, to receive) a refund (described in paragraph (1)) which relates to a period of service ending before October 1, 1990;

(ii) is entitled to an annuity under this subchapter (other than a disability annuity) which is based on service of such employee or Member, and which commences on or after December 2, 1990; and

(iii) does not make the deposit (described in paragraph (1)) required in order to receive credit for the period of service with respect to which the refund relates.

(B) Notwithstanding the second sentence of paragraph (1), the annuity to which an employee or Member under this paragraph is entitled shall (subject to adjustment under section 8340) be equal to an amount which, when taken together with the unpaid amount referred to in subparagraph (A)(iii), would result in the present value of the total being actuarially equivalent to the present value of the annuity which would otherwise be provided the employee or Member under this subchapter, as computed under subsections (a)–(i) and (n) of section 8339 (treating, for purposes of so computing the annuity which would otherwise be provided under this subchapter, the deposit referred to in subparagraph (A)(iii) as if it had been timely made).

(C) The Office of Personnel Management shall prescribe such regulations as may be necessary to carry out this paragraph.

(e)(1) Interest under subsection (c), (d)(1), (j), (k), or (l) of this section is computed in accordance with paragraphs (2) and (3) of this subsection and regulations prescribed by the Office of Personnel Management.

(2) Interest accrues annually on the outstanding portion of any amount that may be deposited under subsection (c), (d)(1), (j), (k), or (l) of this section, and is compounded annually, until the portion is deposited. Such interest is computed from the mid-point of each service period included in the computation, or from the date refund was paid. The deposit may be made in one or more installments. Interest may not be charged for a period of separation from the service which began before October 1, 1956.

(3) The rate of interest is 4 percent a year through December 31, 1947, and 3 percent a year beginning January 1, 1948, through December 31, 1984. Thereafter, the rate of interest for any calendar year shall be equal to the overall average yield to the Fund during the preceding fiscal year from all obligations purchased by the Secretary of the Treasury during such fiscal year under section 8348(c), (d), and (e) of this title, as determined by the Secretary.

(f) Under such regulations as the Office of Personnel Management may prescribe, amounts deducted under subsection (a) or (k) of this section and deposited under subsections (c) and (d)(1) of

this section shall be entered on individual retirement records.

(g) Deposit may not be required for—

(1) service before August 1, 1920;

(2) military service, except to the extent provided under section 8332(c) or 8334(j) of this title;

(3) service for the Panama Railroad Company before January 1, 1924;

(4) service performed before October 29, 1983,[2] by natives of the Pribilof Islands in the taking and curing of fur seal skins and other activities in connection with the administration of the Pribilof Islands except where deductions, contributions, and deposits were made before October 29, 1983;

(5) days of unused sick leave credited under section 8339(m) of this title; or

(6) any period for which credit is allowed under section 8332(l) of this title.

(h) For the purpose of survivor annuities, deposits authorized by subsections (c), (d)(1), (j), and (k) of this section may also be made by a survivor of an employee or Member.

(i)(1) The Director of the Administrative Office of the United States Courts shall pay to the Fund the amount which an employee may deposit under subsection (c) of this section for service creditable under section 8332(b)(12) of this title if such creditable service immediately precedes service as an employee subject to this subchapter with a break in service of no more than ninety working days. The Director shall pay such amount from any appropriation available to him as a necessary expense of the appropriation concerned.

(2) The amount the Director pays in accordance with paragraph (1) of this subsection shall be reduced by the amount of any refund to the employee under section 376 of title 28. Except to the extent of such reduction, the amount the Director pays to the Fund shall satisfy the deposit requirement of subsection (c) of this section.

(3) Notwithstanding any other provision of law, the amount the Director pays under this subsection shall constitute an employer contribution to the Fund, excludable under section 402 of the Internal Revenue Code of 1986 from the employee's gross income until such time as the contribution is distributed or made available to the employee, and shall not be subject to refund or to lump-sum payment to the employee.

(4) Notwithstanding any other provision of law, a bankruptcy judge or magistrate judge who is covered by section 377 of title 28 or section 2(c) of the Retirement and Survivors' Annuities for Bankruptcy Judges and Magistrates Act of 1988 shall not be subject to deductions and contributions to the Fund, if the judge or magistrate judge notifies the Director of the Administrative Office of the United States Courts of an election of a retirement annuity under those provisions. Upon such an election, the judge or magistrate judge shall be entitled to a lump-sum credit under section 8342(a) of this title.

(5) Notwithstanding any other provision of law, a judge who is covered by section 7296 of title 38 shall not be subject to deductions and

---

[2] So in original.

contributions to the Fund, if the judge notifies the Director of the Office of Personnel Management of an election of a retirement annuity under that section. Upon such an election, the judge shall be entitled to a lump-sum credit under section 8342(a) of this title.

(6) Notwithstanding any other provision of law, a judge of the United States Court of Federal Claims who is covered by section 178 of title 28 shall not be subject to deductions and contributions to the Fund if the judge notifies the Director of the Administrative Office of the United States Courts of an election of a retirement annuity under those provisions. Upon such an election, the judge shall be entitled to a lump-sum credit under section 8342(a) of this title.

(j)(1)(A) Except as provided in subparagraph (B), and subject to paragraph (5), each employee or Member who has performed military service before the date of the separation on which the entitlement to any annuity under this subchapter is based may pay, in accordance with such regulations as the Office shall issue, to the agency by which the employee is employed, or, in the case of a Member or a Congressional employee, to the Secretary of the Senate or the Chief Administrative Officer of the House of Representatives, as appropriate, an amount equal to 7 percent of the amount of the basic pay paid under section 204 of title 37 to the employee or Member for each period of military service after December 1956. The amount of such payments shall be based on such evidence of basic pay for military service as the employee or Member may provide, or if the Office determines sufficient evidence has not been so provided to adequately determine basic pay for military service, such payment shall be based upon estimates of such basic pay provided to the Office under paragraph (4).

(B) In any case where military service interrupts creditable civilian service under this subchapter and reemployment pursuant to chapter 43 of title 38 occurs on or after August 1, 1990, the deposit payable under this paragraph may not exceed the amount that would have been deducted and withheld under subsection (a)(1) from basic pay during civilian service if the employee had not performed the period of military service.

(2) Any deposit made under paragraph (1) of this subsection more than two years after the later of—

(A) October 1, 1983; or

(B) the date on which the employee or Member making the deposit first becomes an employee or Member following the period of military service for which such deposit is due,

shall include interest on such amount computed and compounded annually beginning on the date of the expiration of the two-year period. The interest rate that is applicable in computing interest in any year under this paragraph shall be equal to the interest rate that is applicable for such year under subsection (e) of this section.

(3) Any payment received by an agency, the Secretary of the Senate, or the Chief Administrative Officer of the House of Representatives under this subsection shall be immediately remitted to the Office for deposit in the Treasury of the United States to the credit of the Fund.

(4) The Secretary of Defense, the Secretary of Transportation, the Secretary of Commerce, or the Secretary of Health and Human Services, as appropriate, shall furnish such information to the Office as the Office may determine to be necessary for the administration of this subsection.

(5) Effective with respect to any period of military service after December 31, 1998, the percentage of basic pay under section 204 of title 37 payable under paragraph (1) shall be equal to the same percentage as would be applicable under subsection (c) of this section for that same period for service as an employee, subject to paragraph (1)(B).

(k)(1) Effective with respect to pay periods beginning after December 31, 1986, in administering this section in the case of an individual described in section 8402(b)(2) of this title—

(A) the amount to be deducted and withheld by the employing agency shall be determined in accordance with paragraph (2) of this subsection instead of the first sentence of subsection (a)(1) of this section; and

(B) the amount of the contribution under the second sentence of subsection (a)(1) of this section shall be the amount which would have been contributed under such sentence if this subsection had not been enacted.

(2)(A) With respect to Federal wages of an employee or Member (or that portion thereof) not exceeding the contribution and benefit base during the calendar year involved, the appropriate amount to be deducted and withheld under this subsection is the amount by which—

(i) the total deduction for those wages (or for that portion) exceeds;

(ii) the OASDI contribution with respect to those wages (or that portion).

(B) With respect to any portion of Federal wages of an employee or Member which exceed the contribution and benefit base during the calendar year involved, the appropriate amount to be deducted and withheld under this subsection is an amount equal to the total deduction for that portion.

(C) For purposes of this paragraph—

(i) the term "Federal wages" means basic pay for service as an employee or Member, as the case may be;

(ii) the term "contribution and benefit base" means the contribution and benefit base in effect with respect to the period involved, as determined under section 230 of the Social Security Act;

(iii) the term "total deduction", as used with respect to any Federal wages (or portion thereof), means an amount equal to the amount of those wages (or of that portion), multiplied by the percentage which (but for this subsection) would apply under the first sentence of subsection (a)(1) with respect to the individual involved; and

(iv) the term "OASDI contribution", with respect to any income, means the amount of tax which may be imposed under section 3101(a) of the Internal Revenue Code of 1986 with respect to such income (determined without regard to any income which is not a part of Federal wages).

(3) The amount of a deposit under subsection (c) of this section for any service with respect to which paragraph (1) of this subsection applies shall be equal to an amount determined based on the preceding provisions of this subsection, and shall include interest.

(4) In administering paragraphs (1) through (3)—

(A) the term "an individual described in section 8402(b)(2) of this title" shall be considered to include any individual—

(i) who is subject to this subchapter as a result of a provision of law described in section 8347(o), and

(ii) whose employment (as described in section 8347(o)) is also employment for purposes of title II of the Social Security Act and chapter 21 of the Internal Revenue Code of 1986; and

(B) the term "Federal wages", as applied with respect to any individual to whom this subsection applies as a result of subparagraph (A), means basic pay for any employment referred to in subparagraph (A)(ii).

(l)(1) Each employee or Member who has performed service as a volunteer or volunteer leader under part A of title VIII of the Economic Opportunity Act of 1964, as a full-time volunteer enrolled in a program of at least 1 year's duration under part A, B, or C of title I of the Domestic Volunteer Service Act of 1973, or as a volunteer or volunteer leader under the Peace Corps Act before the date of the separation on which the entitlement to any annuity under this subchapter is based may pay, in accordance with such regulations as the Office of Personnel Management shall issue, an amount equal to 7 percent of the readjustment allowance paid to the employee or Member under title VIII of the Economic Opportunity Act of 1964 or section 5(c) or 6(1) of the Peace Corps Act or the stipend paid to the employee or Member under part A, B, or C of title I of the Domestic Volunteer Service Act of 1973, for each period of service as such a volunteer or volunteer leader. This paragraph shall be subject to paragraph (4).

(2) Any deposit made under paragraph (1) more than 2 years after the later of—

(A) October 1, 1993; or

(B) the date on which the employee or Member making the deposit first becomes an employee or Member,

shall include interest on such amount computed and compounded annually beginning on the date of the expiration of the 2-year period. The interest rate that is applicable in computing interest in any year under this paragraph shall be equal to the interest rate that is applicable for such year under subsection (e).

(3) The Director of the Peace Corps and the Chief Executive Officer of the Corporation for National and Community Service shall furnish such information to the Office of Personnel Management as the Office may determine to be necessary for the administration of this subsection.

(4) Effective with respect to any period of service after December 31, 1998, the percentage of the readjustment allowance or stipend (as the case may be) payable under paragraph (1) shall be equal to the same percentage as would be applicable under subsection (c) of this section for the same period for service as an employee.

(m) A Member who has served in a position in the executive branch for which the rate of basic pay was reduced for the duration of the service of the Member to remove the impediment to the appointment of the Member imposed by article I, section 6, clause 2 of the Constitution, or the survivor of such a Member, may deposit to the credit of the Fund an amount equal to the difference between the amount deducted from the basic pay of the Member during that period of service and the amount that would have been deducted if the rate of basic pay which would otherwise have been in effect during that period had been in effect, plus interest computed under subsection (e).

(Pub. L. 89–554, Sept. 6, 1966, 80 Stat. 569; Pub. L. 90–83, § 1(74), Sept. 11, 1967, 81 Stat. 214; Pub. L. 90–486, § 5(b), Aug. 13, 1968, 82 Stat. 757; Pub. L. 91–93, title I, § 102(a), title II, § 202, Oct. 20, 1969, 83 Stat. 136, 138; Pub. L. 92–297, § 7(2), May 16, 1972, 86 Stat. 144; Pub. L. 93–350, § 3, July 12, 1974, 88 Stat. 356; Pub. L. 94–126, §§ 1(a), 2(a), Nov. 12, 1975, 89 Stat. 679; Pub. L. 95–382, § 1(b), Sept. 22, 1978, 92 Stat. 727; Pub. L. 95–454, title IX, § 906(a)(2), Oct. 13, 1978, 92 Stat. 1224; Pub. L. 95–598, title III, § 338(b), Nov. 6, 1978, 92 Stat. 2681; Pub. L. 97–164, title II, § 207(b), Apr. 2, 1982, 96 Stat. 54; Pub. L. 97–253, title III, §§ 303(a)(1), 306(d), (e), Sept. 8, 1982, 96 Stat. 793, 796, 797; Pub. L. 97–346, § 3(a), (c)–(e)(1), Oct. 15, 1982, 96 Stat. 1647, 1648; Pub. L. 98–94, title XII, §§ 1256(a), 1257, Sept. 24, 1983, 97 Stat. 701, 702; Pub. L. 89–702, title II, § 209(f), as added Pub. L. 98–129, § 2, Oct. 14, 1983, 97 Stat. 843; Pub. L. 98–353, title I, § 116(b), July 10, 1984, 98 Stat. 344; Pub. L. 98–615, § 2(2), Nov. 8, 1984, 98 Stat. 3195; Pub. L. 99–335, title II, § 201(a), (c), June 6, 1986, 100 Stat. 588, 591; Pub. L. 99–514, § 2, Oct. 22, 1986, 100 Stat. 2095; Pub. L. 100–53, § 2(b), June 18, 1987, 101 Stat. 367; Pub. L. 100–238, title I, §§ 102, 108(b)(1), Jan. 8, 1988, 101 Stat. 1744, 1748; Pub. L. 100–659, § 6(b), Nov. 15, 1988, 102 Stat. 3919; Pub. L. 101–94, title I, § 102(a), Aug. 16, 1989, 103 Stat. 626; Pub. L. 101–508, title VII, § 7001(b)(1), (2)(A), (B), Nov. 5, 1990, 104 Stat. 1388–328, 1388–329; Pub. L. 101–650, title III, §§ 306(c)(2), (e)(2), 321, Dec. 1, 1990, 104 Stat. 5110, 5112, 5117; Pub. L. 102–40, title IV, § 402(d)(2), May 7, 1991, 105 Stat. 239; Pub. L. 102–378, § 2(59), Oct. 2, 1992, 106 Stat. 1354; Pub. L. 102–572, title IX, § 902(b), Oct. 29, 1992, 106 Stat. 4516; Pub. L. 103–66, title XI, § 11004(a)(3), Aug. 10, 1993, 107 Stat. 412; Pub. L. 103–82, title III, § 371(a)(2), Sept. 21, 1993, 107 Stat. 910; Pub. L. 103–337, div. A, title IX, § 924(d)(1)(A), Oct. 5, 1994, 108 Stat. 2832; Pub. L. 103–353, § 5(b), Oct. 13, 1994, 108 Stat. 3173; Pub. L. 104–186, title II, § 215(12), Aug. 20, 1996, 110 Stat. 1746; Pub. L. 104–316, title I, § 103(g), Oct. 19, 1996, 110 Stat. 3829; Pub. L. 105–33, title VII, § 7001(a)(3), (4), Aug. 5, 1997, 111 Stat. 653, 657; Pub. L. 105–61, title V, § 516(a)(1), Oct. 10, 1997, 111 Stat. 1306; Pub. L. 105–261, div. C, title XXXI, § 3154(c)(1), (2), Oct. 17, 1998, 112 Stat. 2254; Pub. L. 106–65, div. A, title X, § 1066(d)(3), Oct. 5, 1999, 113 Stat. 773; Pub. L. 106–346, § 101(a) [title V, § 505(a)], Oct. 23, 2000, 114 Stat. 1356, 1356A–50; Pub. L. 106–553, § 1(a)(2) [title III, § 308(b)(1)], Dec. 21, 2000, 114 Stat. 2762, 2762A–86.)

Derivation	U.S. Code	Revised Statutes and Statutes at Large
....	2 U.S.C. 129.	July 1, 1957, Pub. L. 85–75, §101 (proviso on p. 248), 71 Stat. 248.
....	5 U.S.C. 2254.	July 31, 1956, ch. 804, §401 "Sec. 4", 70 Stat. 747. June 29, 1957, Pub. L. 85–65, §1, 71 Stat. 209. May 27, 1958, Pub. L. 85–426, §214(b) (words before comma), 72 Stat. 143. Aug. 27, 1958, Pub. L. 85–772, §1(d), 72 Stat. 930.

In subsection (a), the words "From and after the first day of the first pay period which begins on or after the effective date of the Civil Service Retirement Act Amendments of 1956" and "From and after the first day of the first pay period which begins after June 30, 1957" in former section 2254 are omitted as executed. The words "on and after July 1, 1957" in former section 129 of title 2 are omitted as executed.

In subsection (b), the word "rule" is omitted as unnecessary.

Standard changes are made to conform with the definitions applicable and the style of this title as outlined in the preface to the report.

Section of title 5	Source (U.S. Code)	Source (Statutes at Large)
8334(g)(4) ...	5 App.: 2254(g).	Nov. 2, 1966, Pub. L. 89–702, §208(c), 80 Stat. 1096.

REFERENCES IN TEXT

The date of the enactment of the Department of Defense Authorization Act, 1984, referred to in the table in subsec. (c), is the date of enactment of Pub. L. 98–94 which was approved Sept. 24, 1983.

Sections 203 and 206 of the Federal Employees' Retirement Contribution Temporary Adjustment Act of 1983 [Pub. L. 98–168], referred to in subsec. (c), are set out as a note under section 8331 of this title.

Sections 402 and 3101(a) and chapter 21 of the Internal Revenue Code of 1986, referred to in subsecs. (i)(3) and (k)(2)(C)(iv), (4)(A)(ii), are classified to sections 402 and 3101(a) and chapter 21 (§3101 et seq.), respectively, of Title 26, Internal Revenue Code.

Section 2(c) of the Retirement and Survivors' Annuities for Bankruptcy Judges and Magistrates Act of 1988, referred to in subsec. (i)(4), is section 2(c) of Pub. L. 100–659, which is set out as a note under section 377 of Title 28, Judiciary and Judicial Procedure.

The Social Security Act, referred to in subsec. (k)(2)(C)(ii), (4)(A)(ii), is act Aug. 14, 1935, ch. 531, 49 Stat. 620, as amended. Title II of the Social Security Act is classified generally to subchapter II (§ 401 et seq.) of chapter 7 of Title 42, The Public Health and Welfare. Section 230 of the Social Security Act is classified to section 430 of Title 42. For complete classification of this Act to the Code, see section 1305 of Title 42 and Tables.

The Economic Opportunity Act of 1964, referred to in subsec. (l)(1), is Pub. L. 88–452, Aug. 20, 1964, 78 Stat. 508, as amended. Title VIII of the Act probably means title VIII of Pub. L. 88–452 as added by Pub. L. 89–794, title VIII, §801, Nov. 8, 1966, 80 Stat. 1472, and generally revised and amended by Pub. L. 90–222, title I, §110, Dec. 23, 1967, 81 Stat. 722, which was classified generally to subchapter VIII (§ 2991 et seq.) of chapter 34 of Title 42, prior to its repeal by Pub. L. 93–113, title VI, §603, Oct. 1, 1973, 87 Stat. 417. Part A of title VIII of the Act is part A of title VIII of Pub. L. 88–452 as added by Pub. L. 90–222, §110, which was classified generally to part A (§2992 et seq.) of subchapter VIII of chapter 34 of Title

42, prior to its repeal by Pub. L. 93–113, §603. See sections 4951 et seq. and 5055 of Title 42. For complete classification of this Act to the Code, see Tables.

Parts A, B, and C of title I of the Domestic Volunteer Service Act of 1973, referred to in subsec. (l)(1), are classified to part A (§4951 et seq.), part B (§4971 et seq.), and part C (§4991 et seq.), respectively, of subchapter I of chapter 66 of Title 42.

The Peace Corps Act, referred to in subsec. (l)(1), is Pub. L. 87–293, Sept. 22, 1961, 75 Stat. 612, as amended, which is classified principally to chapter 34 (§2501 et seq.) of Title 22, Foreign Relations and Intercourse. Sections 5(c) and 6(1) of the Act are classified to sections 2504(c) and 2505(1), respectively, of Title 22. For complete classification of this Act to the Code, see Short Title note set out under section 2501 of Title 22 and Tables.

AMENDMENTS

2000—Subsec. (a)(1). Pub. L. 106–553, §1(a)(2) [title III, §308(b)(1)(A)], inserted "member of the Supreme Court Police," after "member of the Capitol Police,".

Subsec. (c). Pub. L. 106–553, §1(a)(2) [title III, §308(b)(1)(B)], in table relating to law enforcement officer for law enforcement service and firefighter for firefighter service, inserted ", member of the Supreme Court Police for Supreme Court Police service," after "law enforcement service".

Pub. L. 106–346, in tables relating to an employee, a Member or employee for Congressional employee service, a law enforcement officer for law enforcement service and firefighter for firefighter service, a bankruptcy judge, a judge of the United States Court of Appeals for the Armed Forces for service as a judge of that court, a United States magistrate judge, a Court of Federal Claims judge, a member of the Capitol Police, and a nuclear materials courier, substituted item relating to service period after December 31, 2000, for former items relating to service periods January 1, 2001, to December 31, 2002, and after December 31, 2002.

1999—Subsec. (c). Pub. L. 106–65, in table relating to nuclear materials courier, substituted "October 16, 1998" for "the day before the date of the enactment of the Strom Thurmond National Defense Authorization Act for Fiscal Year 1999" and "October 17, 1998" for "The date of the enactment of the Strom Thurmond National Defense Authorization Act for Fiscal Year 1999".

1998—Subsec. (a)(1). Pub. L. 105–261, §3154(c)(1), substituted "member of the Capitol Police, or nuclear materials courier," for "or member of the Capitol Police,".

Subsec. (c). Pub. L. 105–261, §3154(c)(2), inserted table relating to nuclear materials courier.

1997—Subsec. (a)(1). Pub. L. 105–33, §7001(a)(3)(A), amended first sentence generally. Prior to amendment, first sentence read as follows: "The employing agency shall deduct and withhold 7 percent of the basic pay of an employee, 7½ percent of the basic pay of a Congressional employee, a law enforcement officer, and a firefighter, and 8 percent of the basic pay of a Member, a Court of Federal Claims judge, a United States magistrate, a judge of the United States Court of Appeals for the Armed Forces, and a bankruptcy judge."

Subsec. (c). Pub. L. 105–33, §7001(a)(3)(B)(ix), inserted table relating to member of the Capitol Police.

Pub. L. 105–33, §7001(a)(3)(B)(viii), in table relating to a Court of Federal Claims Judge, substituted items relating to service periods October 1, 1988, to after December 31, 2002, for former item relating to service period after September 30, 1988.

Pub. L. 105–33, §7001(a)(3)(B)(vii), in table relating to a United States magistrate, substituted items relating to service periods October 1, 1987, to after December 31, 2002, for former item relating to service period after September 30, 1987.

Pub. L. 105–33, §7001(a)(3)(B)(vi), in table relating to a judge of the United States Court of Appeals for the Armed Forces for service as a judge of that court, substituted items relating to service periods on and after the date of enactment of the Department of Defense Authorization Act, 1984, to after December 31, 2002, for former item relating to service period on and after the date of the enactment of the Department of Defense Authorization Act, 1984.

Pub. L. 105–33, § 7001(a)(3)(B)(v), in table relating to a bankruptcy judge, substituted items relating to service periods January 1, 1984, to after December 31, 2002, for former item relating to service period after December 31, 1983.

Pub. L. 105–33, § 7001(a)(3)(B)(iv), in table relating to a law enforcement officer for law enforcement service and firefighter for firefighter service, substituted items relating to service periods January 1, 1975, to after December 31, 2002, for former item relating to service period after December 31, 1974.

Pub. L. 105–33, § 7001(a)(3)(B)(i)–(iii), in tables relating to an employee, a Member or employee for Congressional employee service, and a Member for Member service, substituted items relating to service periods January 1, 1970, to after December 31, 2002, for former item relating to service period after December 31, 1969.

Subsec. (j)(1)(A). Pub. L. 105–33, § 7001(a)(4)(A)(i), inserted "and subject to paragraph (5)," after "Except as provided in subparagraph (B),".

Subsec. (j)(5). Pub. L. 105–33, § 7001(a)(4)(A)(ii), added par. (5).

Subsec. (l)(1). Pub. L. 105–33, § 7001(a)(4)(B)(i), inserted at end "This paragraph shall be subject to paragraph (4)."

Subsec. (l)(4). Pub. L. 105–33, § 7001(a)(4)(B)(ii), added par. (4).

Subsec. (m). Pub. L. 105–61 added subsec. (m).

1996—Subsec. (a)(1). Pub. L. 104–186, § 215(12)(A), substituted "Chief Administrative Officer of the House of Representatives, the Chief Administrative Officer may pay from the applicable accounts of the House of Representatives" for "Clerk of the House of Representatives, the Clerk may pay from the contingent fund of the House".

Subsec. (a)(2). Pub. L. 104–316 substituted "Secretary of the Treasury" for "Comptroller General of the United States".

Subsec. (j)(1)(A), (3). Pub. L. 104–186, § 215(12)(B), substituted "Chief Administrative Officer" for "Clerk".

1994—Subsec. (a)(1). Pub. L. 103–337 substituted "Court of Appeals for the Armed Forces" for "Court of Military Appeals".

Subsec. (c). Pub. L. 103–337 substituted "Court of Appeals for the Armed Forces" for "Court of Military Appeals" in table.

Subsec. (j)(1). Pub. L. 103–353, § 5(b)(1), designated existing provisions as subpar. (A) and substituted "Except as provided in subparagraph (B), each employee" for "Each employee" and added subpar. (B).

Subsec. (j)(2)(B). Pub. L. 103–353, § 5(b)(2), inserted before comma at end "following the period of military service for which such deposit is due".

1993—Subsec. (e)(1), (2). Pub. L. 103–82, § 371(a)(2)(B), substituted "(k), or (l)" for "or (k)".

Subsec. (h). Pub. L. 103–66 struck out "and by section 8339(j)(5)(C) and the last sentence of section 8339(k)(2) of this title" before "may also be made".

Subsec. (l). Pub. L. 103–82, § 371(a)(2)(A), added subsec. (l).

1992—Subsec. (a)(1). Pub. L. 102–572, § 902(b)(2), substituted "Court of Federal Claims" for "Claims Court".

Subsec. (c). Pub. L. 102–572, § 902(b)(2), substituted "Court of Federal Claims" for "Claims Court" in table.

Subsec. (i)(5). Pub. L. 102–378 redesignated par. (5), relating to United States Claims Court judges, as (6).

Subsec. (i)(6). Pub. L. 102–572, § 902(b)(1), substituted "United States Court of Federal Claims" for "United States Claims Court".

Pub. L. 102–378 redesignated par. (5), relating to United States Claims Court judges, as (6).

1991—Subsec. (i)(5). Pub. L. 102–40 substituted "section 7296 of title 38" for "section 4096 of title 38".

1990—Subsec. (a)(1). Pub. L. 101–650, § 306(c)(2)(A), inserted "a Claims Court Judge," after "Member,".

Subsec. (c). Pub. L. 101–650, § 306(c)(2)(B), inserted table covering percentages of pay and service periods for a Claims Court Judge.

Subsec. (d). Pub. L. 101–508, § 7001(b)(1), designated existing provisions as par. (1) and added par. (2).

Subsec. (e)(1), (2). Pub. L. 101–508, § 7001(b)(2)(A), substituted "(d)(1)," for "(d),".

Subsec. (f). Pub. L. 101–508, § 7001(b)(2)(B), substituted "(d)(1)" for "(d)".

Subsec. (h). Pub. L. 101–508, § 7001(b)(2)(A), substituted "(d)(1)," for "(d),".

Subsec. (i)(5). Pub. L. 101–650, § 3069(e)(2), added par. (5) relating to judges covered by a section of title 28.

1989—Subsec. (i)(5). Pub. L. 101–94 added par. (5) relating to judges covered by a section of title 38.

1988—Subsec. (c). Pub. L. 100–238, § 102, struck out period at end and inserted ", and, with respect to any such service performed after December 31, 1986, be equal to the amount that would have been deducted from the employee's basic pay under subsection (k) of this section if the employee's pay had been subject to that subsection during such period."

Subsec. (i)(4). Pub. L. 100–659 added par. (4).

Subsec. (k)(4). Pub. L. 100–238, § 108(b)(1), added par. (4).

1987—Subsec. (a)(1). Pub. L. 100–53, § 2(b)(1), substituted "Member, a United States magistrate, a judge" for "Member and a judge" and "Appeals," for "Appeals".

Subsec. (c). Pub. L. 100–53, § 2(b)(2), inserted table covering percentages of basic pay and service periods for United States magistrates.

1986—Subsec. (c). Pub. L. 99–335, § 201(c), inserted provision that notwithstanding preceding provisions of this subsection and any provision of section 206(b)(3) of Federal Employees' Retirement Contribution Temporary Adjustment Act of 1983, the percentage of basic pay required under this subsection in case of an individual described in section 8402(b)(2) of this title shall, with respect to any covered service performed after Dec. 31, 1983, and before Jan. 1, 1987, be equal to 1.3 percent.

Subsec. (e)(1), (2). Pub. L. 99–335, § 201(a)(2)(A), substituted "(j), or (k)" for "or (j)".

Subsec. (f). Pub. L. 99–335, § 201(a)(2)(B), inserted "or (k)" after "subsection (a)".

Subsec. (h). Pub. L. 99–335, § 201(a)(2)(C), substituted "(j), and (k)" for "and (j)".

Subsec. (i)(3). Pub. L. 99–514 substituted "Internal Revenue Code of 1986" for "Internal Revenue Code of 1954".

Subsec. (k). Pub. L. 99–335, § 201(a)(1), added subsec. (k).

Subsec. (k)(2)(C)(iv). Pub. L. 99–514 substituted "Internal Revenue Code of 1986" for "Internal Revenue Code of 1954".

1984—Subsec. (a)(1). Pub. L. 98–353, § 116(b)(1), inserted "and a bankruptcy judge".

Subsec. (c). Pub. L. 98–353, § 116(b)(2), substituted in the table relating to bankruptcy judges the items relating to 7 percent for the period Jan. 1, 1970 to Dec. 31, 1983, and 8 percent for the period after Dec. 31, 1983, for the prior item relating to 7 percent for the period after Jan. 1, 1970.

Subsec. (h). Pub. L. 98–615 substituted "annuities, deposits authorized by subsections (c), (d), and (j) of this section and by section 8339(j)(5)(C) and the last sentence of section 8339(k)(2) of this title may also be made by a survivor" for "annuity, deposits authorized by subsections (c), (d), and (j) of this section may also be made by the survivor".

1983—Subsec. (a)(1). Pub. L. 98–94, § 1256(a)(1), inserted "and a judge of the United States Court of Military Appeals" after "and 8 percent of the basic pay of a Member".

Subsec. (c). Pub. L. 98–94, § 1256(a)(2), added to the table items covering a judge of the United States Court of Military Appeals for service as a judge of that court.

Subsec. (g)(4). Pub. L. 98–129 substituted "October 29, 1983," for "January 1, 1950", and directed that the phrase "except where deductions, contributions, and deposits were made before October 29, 1983" be inserted after "the Pribilof Islands" which amendment was executed by inserting that phrase after "the Pribilof Islands" the second time those words appear, as the probable intent of Congress.

Subsec. (j)(2)(A). Pub. L. 98–94, § 1257, substituted "October 1, 1983" for "October 1, 1982".

1982—Subsec. (e). Pub. L. 97–253, § 303(a)(1), redesignated existing provisions as par. (2), inserted provision that interest accrues annually on the outstanding portion of any amount that may be deposited under subsec. (c), (d), or (j) of this section, and is compounded annually until the portion is deposited, substituted "Such interest" for "Interest under subsection (c) or (d) of this section", struck out ", to the date of deposit or commencing date of annuity, whichever is earlier" after "date refund was paid", and struck out provision that the interest was computed at the rate of four percent a year to Dec. 31, 1947, and 3 percent thereafter compounded annually, and added pars. (1) and (3).

Subsec. (e)(3). Pub. L. 97–346, § 3(c), substituted "the preceding fiscal year" for "the preceding calendar year" and "during such fiscal year" for "during such calendar year".

Subsec. (g)(2). Pub. L. 97–253, § 306(e), inserted ", except to the extent provided under section 8332(c) or section 8334(j) of this title".

Subsec. (h). Pub. L. 97–346, § 3(d), inserted reference to subsec. (j).

Subsec. (i). Pub. L. 97–164 added subsec. (i).

Subsec. (j). Pub. L. 97–253, § 306(d), added subsec. (j).

Subsec. (j)(1). Pub. L. 97–346, § 3(a), substituted "period" for "month".

Pub. L. 97–346, § 3(e)(1), struck out "within 90 days after the effective date of this subsection" after "regulations as the Office shall issue", and substituted "The amount of such payments shall be based on such evidence of basic pay for military service as the employee or Member may provide, or if the Office determines sufficient evidence has not been so provided to adequately determine basic pay for military service, such payment shall be based upon estimates of such basic pay provided to the Office under paragraph (4)" for "as certified to the agency, the Secretary of the Senate, or the Clerk of the House of Representatives, as appropriate, by the Secretary of Defense, the Secretary of Transportation, the Secretary of Commerce, or the Secretary of Health and Human Services, as appropriate, upon the employee's or Member's request".

1978—Subsec. (c). Pub. L. 95–598 inserted bankruptcy judge schedule of deposits.

Subsec. (f). Pub. L. 95–454 substituted "Office of Personnel Management" for "Civil Service Commission".

Subsec. (g)(6). Pub. L. 95–382 added par. (6).

1975—Subsec. (c), Pub. L. 94–126, § 1(a), struck out last sentence requiring that deposit, with respect to a period of service referred to in section 8332(b)(6) of this title performed before Jan. 1, 1969, shall be an amount equal to 55 percent of a deposit computed in accordance with such provisions.

Subsec. (g)(5). Pub. L. 94–126, § 2(a), substituted reference to "section 8339(m) of this title" for "section 8339(n) of this title".

1974—Subsec. (a)(1). Pub. L. 93–350, § 3(a), inserted "a law enforcement officer, and a firefighter," after "Congressional employee,".

Subsec. (c). Pub. L. 93–350, § 3(b), inserted schedule for law enforcement officer for law enforcement service and firefighter for firefighter service.

1972—Subsec. (g)(5). Pub. L. 92–297 substituted "section 8339(n)" for "section 8339(m)".

1969—Subsec. (a)(1). Pub. L. 91–93, § 102(a)(1), designated first and second sentences of subsec. (a) as subsec. (a)(1), increasing by one-half percent the deduction from the basic pay of an employee and a Member to 7 and 8 percent, respectively, and providing for a 7½ percent deduction from basic pay of a Congressional employee.

Subsec. (a)(2). Pub. L. 91–93, § 102(a)(1), designated third and fourth sentences of subsec. (a) as subsec. (a)(2), deleting "under this section" after "Member".

Subsec. (c). Pub. L. 91–93, § 102(a)(2), substituted service period Nov. 1, 1956, to Dec. 31, 1969, for prior service period after Oct. 31, 1956, for deductions of 6½ percent of basic pay of an employee, inserted provision for 7 percent deduction from basic pay of an employee for service period after Dec. 31, 1969, inserted percentage of basic pay and service period provisions for Member or employee for Congressional employee service, substituted service period Nov. 1, 1956; to Dec. 31, 1969, for prior service period after Oct. 31, 1956, for deduction of 7½ percent of basic pay of Member for Member service, inserted provision for 8 percent deduction from basic pay of Member for Member service after Dec. 31, 1969, and inserted provision for amount of deposit for period of service performed before Jan. 1, 1969.

Subsec. (g)(5). Pub. L. 91–93, § 202, added par. (5).

1968—Subsec. (c). Pub. L. 90–486 inserted provisions that the deposit with respect to a period of service referred to in section 8332(b)(6) of this title which was performed prior to the specified effective date shall be an amount equal to 55 percent of a deposit computed in accordance with such provisions.

CHANGE OF NAME

"United States magistrate judge" and "magistrate judge" substituted for "United States magistrate" and "magistrate", respectively, wherever appearing in subsecs. (c) and (i)(4) pursuant to section 321 of Pub. L. 101–650, set out as a note under section 631 of Title 28, Judiciary and Judicial Procedure.

EFFECTIVE DATE OF 2000 AMENDMENTS

Amendment by Pub. L. 106–553 effective on the first day of the first applicable pay period that begins on Dec. 21, 2000, and applicable only to an individual who is employed as a member of the Supreme Court Police after Dec. 21, 2000, see section 1(a)(2) [title III, § 308(i), (j)] of Pub. L. 106–553, set out in a Supreme Court Police Retirement note under section 8331 of this title.

Pub. L. 106–346, § 101(a) [title V, § 505(i)], Oct. 23, 2000, 114 Stat. 1356, 1356A–54, provided that: "The amendments made by this section [amending this section, section 8422 of this title, sections 4045, 4071c, and 4071e of Title 22, Foreign Relations and Intercourse, and section 2082 of Title 50, War and National Defense, enacting provisions set out as notes under this section, section 4045 of Title 22, and section 2021 of Title 50, and amending provisions set out as notes under section 4045 of Title 22 and section 2021 of Title 50] shall take effect upon the close of calendar year 2000, and shall apply thereafter."

EFFECTIVE DATE OF 1998 AMENDMENT

Amendment by Pub. L. 105–261 effective at the beginning of the first pay period that begins after Oct. 17, 1998, and applicable only to an individual who is employed as a nuclear materials courier, as defined by section 8331(27) or 8401(33) of this title, after Oct. 17, 1998, see section 3154(m), (n) of Pub. L. 105–261, set out as a note under section 8331 of this title.

EFFECTIVE DATE OF 1997 AMENDMENTS

Section 516(b) of Pub. L. 105–61 provided that: "The amendments made by subsection (a) [amending this section and sections 8337, 8339, 8341, 8343a, 8344, 8415, 8422, and 8468 of this title] shall be applicable to any annuity commencing before, on, or after the date of enactment of this Act [Oct. 10, 1997], and shall be effective with regard to any payment made after the first month following the date of enactment."

Section 7001(f) of Pub. L. 105–33 provided that:

"(1) IN GENERAL.—This section [amending this section, section 8422 of this title, sections 4045, 4071c, and 4071e of Title 22, Foreign Relations and Intercourse, and section 2082 of Title 50, War and National Defense, and enacting provisions set out as notes under this section, section 8422 of this title, sections 4045 and 4071c of Title 22, and section 2021 of Title 50] shall take effect on—

''(A) October 1, 1997; or

''(B) if later, the date of enactment of this Act [Aug. 5, 1997].

''(2) SPECIAL RULE.—If the date of enactment of this Act is later than October 1, 1997, then any reference to October 1, 1997, in subsection (a)(1), (c)(1), or (d)(1) shall be treated as a reference to the date of enactment of this Act.''

EFFECTIVE DATE OF 1994 AMENDMENT

Amendment by Pub. L. 103–353 effective with respect to reemployments initiated on or after the first day after the 60-day period beginning Oct. 13, 1994, with transition rules, see section 8 of Pub. L. 103–353, set out as an Effective Date note under section 4301 of Title 38, Veterans' Benefits.

EFFECTIVE DATE OF 1993 AMENDMENTS

Amendment by Pub. L. 103–82 effective Oct. 1, 1993, and applicable with respect to any individual entitled to an annuity on the basis of a separation from service occurring on or after Oct. 1, 1993, see sections 371(c) and 392 of Pub. L. 103 82, set out as notes under section 8332 of this title and section 4951 of Title 42, The Public Health and Welfare, respectively.

Amendment by Pub. L. 103–66 effective on first day of first month beginning at least 30 days after Aug. 10, 1993, and applicable to all deposits required under section 8339(j)(3) or (5), 8339(k)(2), or 8418 of this title, on which no payment has been made prior to such effective date, see section 11004(c) of Pub. L. 103–66, set out as a note under section 8339 of this title.

EFFECTIVE DATE OF 1992 AMENDMENT

Amendment by Pub. L. 102–572 effective Oct. 29, 1992, see section 911 of Pub. L. 102–572, set out as a note under section 171 of Title 28, Judiciary and Judicial Procedure.

EFFECTIVE DATE OF 1990 AMENDMENTS

Amendment by Pub. L. 101–650 applicable to judges of, and senior judges in active service with, the United States Court of Federal Claims on or after Dec. 1, 1990, see section 306(f) of Pub. L. 101–650, set out as a note under section 8331 of this title.

Section 7001(b)(3) of Pub. L. 101–508 provided that: ''The amendments made by this subsection [amending this section and sections 8339 and 8342 of this title] shall be effective with respect to any annuity having a commencement date later than December 1, 1990.''

EFFECTIVE DATE OF 1988 AMENDMENTS

Amendment by Pub. L. 100–659 effective Nov. 15, 1988, and applicable to bankruptcy judges and magistrate judges who retire on or after Nov. 15, 1988, with exception for judges and magistrate judges retiring on or after July 31, 1987, see section 9 of Pub. L. 100–659, as amended, set out as an Effective Date note under section 377 of Title 28, Judiciary and Judicial Procedure.

Section 108(b)(3) of Pub. L. 100–238 provided that: ''The amendments made by this subsection [amending this section and section 8349 of this title] shall be effective as of January 1, 1987.''

EFFECTIVE DATE OF 1987 AMENDMENT

Amendment by Pub. L. 100–53 effective Oct. 1, 1987, and applicable to bankruptcy judges and United States magistrate judges in office on that date and to individuals subsequently appointed to such positions to whom this chapter otherwise applies, see section 3 of Pub. L. 100–53, as amended, set out as a note under section 8331 of this title.

EFFECTIVE DATE OF 1986 AMENDMENT

Amendment by Pub. L. 99–335 effective Jan. 1, 1987, see section 702(a) of Pub. L. 99–335, set out as an Effective Date note under section 8401 of this title.

EFFECTIVE DATE OF 1984 AMENDMENTS

Amendment by Pub. L. 98–615 effective May 7, 1985, with enumerated exceptions and specific applicability provisions, see section 4(a)(1) of Pub. L. 98–615, as amended, set out as a note under section 8341 of this title.

Amendment by Pub. L. 98–353 effective July 10, 1984, and applicable to bankruptcy judges who retire on or after such date, see section 116(e) of Pub. L. 98–353, set out as a note under section 8331 of this title. See, also, section 122(a) of Pub. L. 98–353, set out as an Effective Date note under section 151 of Title 28, Judiciary and Judicial Procedure.

EFFECTIVE DATE OF 1983 AMENDMENT

Section 1256(f) of Pub. L. 98–94 provided that: ''The increase in deductions from the pay of a judge of the United States Court of Military Appeals [now United States Court of Appeals for the Armed Forces] required by section 8334(a) of title 5, United States Code, as amended by subsection (a), shall take effect with respect to the first pay period that begins after the date of the enactment of this Act [Sept. 24, 1983].''

EFFECTIVE DATE OF 1982 AMENDMENTS

Section 303(d)(1) of Pub. L. 97–253, as amended by Pub. L. 97–346, § 3(j)(1), Oct. 15, 1982, 96 Stat. 1649, provided that:

''The amendments made by subsections (a) and (b) [amending this section and sections 8339 and 8343 of this title] shall apply with respect to deposits for service performed on or after October 1, 1982, and with respect to refunds for which application is received by either the employing agency or the Office of Personnel Management on or after such date. The provisions of section 8334 and section 8339(i) of title 5, United States Code, as in effect the day before the date of the enactment of this Act [Sept. 7, 1982], shall continue to apply with respect to periods of service and refunds occurring on or before September 30, 1982. Notwithstanding the preceding two sentences, the amendments made by subsection (a) shall apply in the case of any deposit for military service under section 8334(j) of title 5, United States Code (as added by section 306(d) of this Act), regardless of whether such military service was performed before or after October 1, 1982.''

Amendment by section 306(d), (e) of Pub. L. 97–253 effective Oct. 1, 1982, except that any employee or Member who retired after Sept. 8, 1982, and before Oct. 1, 1985, or is entitled to an annuity under chapter 83 of this title based on a separation from service occurring during such period, or a survivor of such individual, may make a payment under section 8334(j)(1) of this title, and regulations required to be issued under section 8334(j)(1) of this title, to be issued by the Office of Personnel Management within 90 days after such effective date, see section 306(g) of Pub. L. 97–253, as amended, set out as a note under section 8331 of this title.

Amendment by Pub. L. 97–164 effective Oct. 1, 1982, see section 402 of Pub. L. 97–164, set out as a note under section 171 of Title 28, Judiciary and Judicial Procedure.

EFFECTIVE DATE OF 1978 AMENDMENTS

Amendment by Pub. L. 95–598 effective Nov. 6, 1978, see section 402(d) of Pub. L. 95–598, set out as an Effective Date note preceding section 101 of Title 11, Bankruptcy.

Amendment by Pub. L. 95–454 effective 90 days after Oct. 13, 1978, see section 907 of Pub. L. 95–454, set out as a note under section 1101 of this title.

Amendment by Pub. L. 95–382 effective Oct 1, 1978, and applicable to specified annuities, see section 2 of Pub. L. 95–382, set out as a note under section 8332 of this title.

EFFECTIVE DATE OF 1975 AMENDMENT

Section 3 of Pub. L. 94–126 provided that: ''The amendments made by the first section of this Act [amending this section and sections 8339 and 8345 of this title] shall become effective as of January 1, 1969, except that such amendments shall not apply to a person who, on the date of enactment of this Act [Nov. 12, 1975], is receiving or is entitled to receive benefits under any retirement system established by the United States or any instrumentality thereof, unless such person requests, in writing, the office which administers his retirement system to apply such amendments to him. Any additional benefits payable pursuant to such a written request shall commence on the first day of the month [December] following the date of the enactment of this Act.''

EFFECTIVE DATE OF 1974 AMENDMENT

Amendment by Pub. L. 93–350 effective at beginning of first applicable pay period which begins after Dec. 31, 1974, see section 7 of Pub. L. 93–350, set out as a note under section 3307 of this title.

EFFECTIVE DATE OF 1972 AMENDMENT

Amendment by Pub. L. 92–297 effective on 90th day after May 16, 1972, see section 10 of Pub. L. 92–297, set out as an Effective Date note under section 3381 of this title.

EFFECTIVE DATE OF 1969 AMENDMENT

Section 102(b) of Pub. L. 91–93 provided that: ''The amendment made by subsection (a)(1) of this section [amending this section] shall become effective at the beginning of the first applicable pay period beginning after December 31, 1969.''

Amendment by Pub. L. 91–93 inapplicable in cases of persons retired or otherwise separated prior to Oct. 20, 1969, their rights and of their survivors continued as if such amendment had not been enacted, see section 207(a) of Pub. L. 91–93, set out as a note under section 8331 of this title.

EFFECTIVE DATE OF 1968 AMENDMENT

Amendment by Pub. L. 90–486 effective Jan. 1, 1969, except that no deductions or withholding from salary which result therefrom shall commence before first day of first pay period that begins on or after Jan. 1, 1968, see section 11 of Pub. L. 90–486, set out as a note under section 709 of Title 32, National Guard.

CONTRIBUTIONS TO FEDERAL CIVIL SERVICE RETIREMENT SYSTEM

Pub. L. 106–346, § 101(a) [title V, § 505(f)], Oct. 23, 2000, 114 Stat. 1356, 1356A–54, provided that: ''Notwithstanding section 8334(a)(1) or (k)(1) of title 5, United States Code, during the period beginning on October 1, 2002, through December 31, 2002, each employing agency (other than the United States Postal Service or the Metropolitan Washington Airports Authority) shall contribute—

''(1) 7.5 percent of the basic pay of an employee;

''(2) 8 percent of the basic pay of a congressional employee, a law enforcement officer, a member of the Capitol Police, a firefighter, or a nuclear materials courier; and

''(3) 8.5 percent of the basic pay of a Member of Congress, a Court of Federal Claims judge, a United States magistrate [now United States magistrate judge], a judge of the United States Court of Appeals for the Armed Forces, or a bankruptcy judge, in lieu of the agency contributions otherwise required under section 8334(a)(1) of such title 5.''

Pub. L. 105–261, div. C, title XXXI, § 3154(c)(3), Oct. 17, 1998, 112 Stat. 2255, provided that: ''Notwithstanding subsection (a)(1) or (k)(1) of section 8334 of title 5, United States Code, or section 7001(a) of Public Law 105–33 [set out as a note below], during the period beginning on the effective date provided for under subsection (n)(1) [set out as an Effective Date of 1998 Amendment note under section 8331 of this title] and ending on September 30, 2002, the Department of Energy shall deposit in the Treasury of the United States to the credit of the Civil Service Retirement and Disability Fund on behalf of each nuclear materials courier from whose basic pay a deduction is made under

such subsection (a)(1) during that period an amount equal to 9.01 percent of such basic pay, in lieu of the agency contributions otherwise required under such subsection (a)(1) during that period.''

Section 7001(a)(1), (2) of Pub. L. 105–33 provided that:

''(1) AGENCY CONTRIBUTIONS.—

''(A) IN GENERAL.—Notwithstanding section 8334(a)(1) or (k)(1) of title 5, United States Code, during the period beginning on October 1, 1997, through September 30, 2002, each employing agency (other than the United States Postal Service or the Metropolitan Washington Airports Authority) shall contribute—

''(i) 8.51 percent of the basic pay of an employee;

''(ii) 9.01 percent of the basic pay of a congressional employee, a law enforcement officer, a member of the Capitol police, or a firefighter; and

''(iii) 9.51 percent of the basic pay of a Member of Congress, a Court of Federal Claims judge, a United States magistrate [now United States magistrate judge], a judge of the United States Court of Appeals for the Armed Forces, or a bankruptcy judge; in lieu of the agency contributions otherwise required under section 8334(a)(1) of title 5, United States Code.

''(B) APPLICATION.—For purposes of subparagraph (A) and notwithstanding the amendments made by paragraph (3) [amending this section], during the period beginning on January 1, 1999 through December 31, 2002, with respect to the United States Postal Service and the Metropolitan Washington Airports Authority, the agency contribution shall be determined as though those amendments had not been made.

''(2) NO REDUCTION IN AGENCY CONTRIBUTIONS BY THE POSTAL SERVICE.—Contributions by the Treasury of the United States or the United States Postal Service under section 8348(g), (h), or (m) of title 5, United States Code—

''(A) shall not be reduced as a result of the amendments made under paragraph (3) of this subsection; and

''(B) shall be computed as though such amendments had not been enacted.''

OFFSETS TO PREVENT FULL DOUBLE COVERAGE FOR EMPLOYEES OF PARK POLICE AND SECRET SERVICE

Section 103(e) of Pub. L. 100–238 provided that: ''Notwithstanding any other provision of law, in the case of an employee of the United States Secret Service or the United States Park Police whose pay is simultaneously subject to a deposit requirement under the District of Columbia Police and Firefighters' Retirement and Disability System and the contribution requirement under section 3101(a) of the Internal Revenue Code of 1986 [26 U.S.C. 3101(a)]—

''(1) any deposits under the District of Columbia Police and Firefighters' Retirement and Disability System shall be adjusted in a manner consistent with section 8334(k) of title 5, United States Code (relating to offsets in deductions from pay to reflect OASDI contributions); and

''(2) any benefits payable under the District of Columbia Police and Firefighters' Retirement and Disability System based on the service of any such employee shall be adjusted in a manner consistent with section 8349 of title 5, United States Code (relating to offsets to reflect benefits under title II of the Social Security Act [42 U.S.C. 401 et seq.]).''

REFUNDS OF CERTAIN EXCESS DEDUCTIONS TAKEN AFTER 1983 TO OFFSET EMPLOYEES UNDER CSRS

Section 128 of Pub. L. 100–238 provided that:

''(a) REFUND ELIGIBILITY.—An individual shall upon written application to the Office of Personnel Management, receive a refund under subsection (b), if such individual—

''(1) was subject to section 8334(a)(1) of title 5, United States Code, for any period of service after December 31, 1983, because of an election under section 208(a)(1)(B) of the Federal Employees' Retirement Contribution Temporary Adjustment Act of 1983 (97 Stat. 1107; 5 U.S.C. 8331 note);

"(2) is not eligible to make an election under section 301(b) of the Federal Employees' Retirement System Act of 1986 (Public Law 99–335; 100 Stat. 599) [5 U.S.C. 8331 note]; and

"(3) becomes subject to section 8334(k) of title 5, United States Code.

"(b) REFUND COMPUTATION.—An individual eligible for a refund under subsection (a) shall receive a refund—

"(1) for the period beginning on January 1, 1984, and ending on December 31, 1986, for the amount by which—

"(A) the total amount deducted from such individual's basic pay under section 8334(a)(1) of title 5, United States Code, for service described in subsection (a)(1) of this section, exceeds

"(B) 1.3 percent of such individual's total basic pay for such period; and

"(2) for the period beginning on January 1, 1987, and ending on the day before such individual becomes subject to section 8334(k) of title 5, United States Code, for the amount by which—

"(A) the total amount deducted from such individual's basic pay under section 8334(a)(1) of title 5, United States Code, for service described in subsection (a)(1) of this section, exceeds

"(B) the total amount which would have been deducted if such individual's basic pay had instead been subject to section 8334(k) of title 5, United States Code, during such period.

"(c) INTEREST COMPUTATION.—A refund under this section shall be computed with interest in accordance with section 8334(e) of title 5, United States Code, and regulations prescribed by the Office of Personnel Management."

NATIONAL GUARD TECHNICIANS

Amendment by Pub. L. 90–486 not applicable to persons employed prior to Jan. 1, 1969, whose employment was covered by the civil service retirement provisions of section 8331 et seq. of this title, see section 5(d) of Pub. L. 90–486, set out as a note under section 709 of Title 32, National Guard.

SECTION REFERRED TO IN OTHER SECTIONS

This section is referred to in sections 8331, 8332, 8333, 8339, 8342, 8344, 8348, 8411, 8422, 8432 of this title; title 10 sections 942, 945; title 12 section 1723a; title 22 sections 3671, 3681, 3968, 4045; title 26 section 3121; title 28 sections 611, 627; title 40 section 881; title 42 sections 410, 2297h–8; title 45 section 1206; title 50 sections 2021, 2031, 2082, 2121.

§ 8335. Mandatory separation

(a) An air traffic controller shall be separated from the service on the last day of the month in which he becomes 56 years of age. The Secretary, under such regulations as he may prescribe, may exempt a controller having exceptional skills and experience as a controller from the automatic separation provisions of this subsection until that controller becomes 61 years of age. The Secretary shall notify the controller in writing of the date of separation at least 60 days before that date. Action to separate the controller is not effective, without the consent of the controller, until the last day of the month in which the 60-day notice expires.

(b) A firefighter who is otherwise eligible for immediate retirement under section 8336(c) shall be separated from the service on the last day of the month in which such firefighter becomes 55 years of age or completes 20 years of service if then over that age. A law enforcement officer or

nuclear materials courier who is otherwise eligible for immediate retirement under section 8336(c) shall be separated from the service on the last day of the month in which that officer or courier, as the case may be, becomes 57 years of age or completes 20 years of service if then over that age. The head of the agency, when in his judgment the public interest so requires, may exempt such an employee from automatic separation under this subsection until that employee becomes 60 years of age. The employing office shall notify the employee in writing of the date of separation at least 60 days in advance thereof. Action to separate the employee is not effective, without the consent of the employee, until the last day of the month in which the 60-day notice expires.

(c) A member of the Capitol Police who is otherwise eligible for immediate retirement under section 8336(m) shall be separated from the service on the last day of the month in which such member becomes 57 years of age or completes 20 years of service if then over that age. The Capitol Police Board, when in its judgment the public interest so requires, may exempt such a member from automatic separation under this subsection until that member becomes 60 years of age. The Board shall notify the member in writing of the date of separation at least 60 days in advance thereof. Action to separate the member is not effective, without the consent of the member, until the last day of the month in which the 60-day notice expires.

(d) A member of the Supreme Court Police who is otherwise eligible for immediate retirement under section 8336(n) shall be separated from the service on the last day of the month in which such member becomes 57 years of age or completes 20 years of service if then over that age. The Marshal of the Supreme Court of the United States, when in his judgment the public interest so requires, may exempt such a member from automatic separation under this subsection until that member becomes 60 years of age. The Marshal shall notify the member in writing of the date of separation at least 60 days in advance thereof. Action to separate the member is not effective, without the consent of the member, until the last day of the month in which the 60-day notice expires.

(f)[1] The President, by Executive order, may exempt an employee (other than a member of the Capitol Police or the Supreme Court Police) from automatic separation under this section when he determines the public interest so requires.

(Pub. L. 89–554, Sept. 6, 1966, 80 Stat. 571; Pub. L. 92–297, §4, May 16, 1972, 86 Stat. 144; Pub. L. 93–350, §4, July 12, 1974, 88 Stat. 356; Pub. L. 95–256, §5(c), Apr. 6, 1978, 92 Stat. 191; Pub. L. 96–70, title III, §3302(e)(3), Sept. 27, 1979, 93 Stat. 498; Pub. L. 96–347, §1(b), Sept. 12, 1980, 94 Stat. 1150; Pub. L. 101–428, §2(b)(1)(A), (2), Oct. 15, 1990, 104 Stat. 928; Pub. L. 101–509, title V, §529 [title IV, §409(a)], Nov. 5, 1990, 104 Stat. 1427, 1468; Pub. L. 102–378, §2(60), Oct. 2, 1992, 106 Stat. 1354; Pub. L. 103–283, title III, §307(a), July 22, 1994, 108 Stat. 1441; Pub. L. 105–261, div. C, title XXXI,

---

[1] So in original. Probably should be "(e)".

§ 3154(d), Oct. 17, 1998, 112 Stat. 2255; Pub. L. 106–553, § 1(a)(2) [title III, § 308(b)(2)], Dec. 21, 2000, 114 Stat. 2762, 2762A–87; Pub. L. 106–554, § 1(a)(4) [div. B, title I, § 141(a)], Dec. 21, 2000, 114 Stat. 2763, 2763A–235.)

HISTORICAL AND REVISION NOTES

Derivation	U.S. Code	Revised Statutes and Statutes at Large
....	5 U.S.C. 2255.	July 31, 1956, ch. 804, § 401 "Sec. 5", 70 Stat. 748. Feb. 7, 1964, Pub. L. 88–267, § 1 (less (a)–(c)), 78 Stat. 9.

Standard changes are made to conform with the definitions applicable and style of this title as outlined in the preface to the report.

REFERENCES IN TEXT

For definition of Secretary, referred to in subsec. (a), see section 2109 of this title.

AMENDMENTS

2000—Subsec. (c). Pub. L. 106–554 redesignated subsec. (d) as (c) and struck out former subsec. (c) which read as follows: "An employee of the Alaska Railroad in Alaska and an employee who is a citizen of the United States employed on the Isthmus of Panama by the Panama Canal Commission, who becomes 62 years of age and completes 15 years of service in Alaska or on the Isthmus of Panama shall be automatically separated from the service. The separation is effective on the last day of the month in which the employee becomes age 62 or completes 15 years of service in Alaska or on the Isthmus of Panama if then over that age. The employing office shall notify the employee in writing of the date of separation at least 60 days in advance thereof. Action to separate the employee is not effective, without the consent of the employee, until the last day of the month in which the 60-day notice expires."

Subsec. (d). Pub. L. 106–554, § 1(a)(4) [div. B, title I, § 141(a)(2)], redesignated subsec. (e) as (d). Former subsec. (d) redesignated (c).

Subsec. (e). Pub. L. 106–554, § 1(a)(4) [div. B, title I, § 141(a)(2)], redesignated subsec. (e) as (d).

Pub. L. 106–553, § 1(a)(2) [title III, § 308(b)(2)(A)], added subsec. (e). Former subsec. (e) redesignated (f).

Subsec. (f). Pub. L. 106–553 redesignated subsec. (e) as (f) and substituted "Police or the Supreme Court Police" for "Police".

1998—Subsec. (b). Pub. L. 105–261, in second sentence, inserted "or nuclear materials courier" after "law enforcement officer" and "or courier, as the case may be," after "that officer".

1994—Subsec. (d). Pub. L. 103–283 substituted "57" for "55" in first sentence.

1992—Subsec. (b). Pub. L. 102–378 amended first sentence generally. Prior to amendment, first sentence read as follows: "A firefighter who is otherwise eligible for immediate retirement under section 8336(c) of this title shall be separated from the service on the last day of the month in which he becomes 55 years of age or completes 20 years of service if then over that age."

1990—Subsec. (b). Pub. L. 101–509, § 529 [title IV, § 409(a)(1)], which directed that "law enforcement officer of a" be struck out before "firefighter who is", was executed by striking out "law enforcement officer or a" as the probable intent of Congress.

Pub. L. 101–509, § 529 [title IV, § 409(a)(2)], inserted after first sentence "A law enforcement officer who is otherwise eligible for immediate retirement under section 8336(c) shall be separated from the service on the last day of the month in which that officer becomes 57 years of age or completes 20 years of service if then over that age."

Subsec. (d). Pub. L. 101–428, § 2(b)(1)(A), added subsec. (d). Former subsec. (d) redesignated (e).

Subsec. (e). Pub. L. 101–428, § 2(b)(2), inserted "(other than a member of the Capitol Police)" after "employee".

Pub. L. 101–428, § 2(b)(1)(A), redesignated subsec. (d) as (e).

1980—Subsec. (a). Pub. L. 96–347 substituted "Secretary" for "Secretary of Transportation" in two places.

1979—Subsec. (c). Pub. L. 96–70, which directed substitution of "Panama Canal Commission" for "Panama Canal Company or the Canal Zone Government" in subsec. (e), was executed to subsec. (c) to reflect the probable intent of Congress and Pub. L. 95–256 which struck out subsec. (e) and restated provisions thereof in subsec. (c).

1978—Subsec. (a). Pub. L. 95–256, § 5(c)(1), (2), redesignated subsec. (f) as (a). Former subsec. (a), relating to mandatory separation when an employee became 70 years of age and completed 15 years of service, was struck out.

Subsec. (b). Pub. L. 95–256, § 5(c)(1), (2), redesignated subsec. (g) as (b). Former subsec. (b), relating to notice by employing office of date of separation, was struck out.

Subsec. (c). Pub. L. 95–256, § 5(c)(1), (3), added subsec. (c) relating to provisions covered by former subsec. (e). Former subsec. (c), relating to exemption of an employee from automatic separation by President, was struck out. See subsec. (d).

Subsec. (d). Pub. L. 95–256, § 5(c)(1), (3), added subsec. (d). Former subsec. (d), relating to inapplicability of automatic separation provisions of this section, was struck out.

Subsec. (e). Pub. L. 95–256, § 5(c)(1), struck out subsec. (e) which related to applicability of provisions to employees of Alaskan Railroad, Panama Canal Company, and Canal Zone Government. See subsec. (c).

Subsecs. (f), (g). Pub. L. 95–256, § 5(c)(2), redesignated subsecs. (f) and (g) as (a) and (b), respectively.

1974—Subsec. (g). Pub. L. 93–350 added subsec. (g).

1972—Subsec. (f). Pub. L. 92–297 added subsec. (f).

EFFECTIVE DATE OF 2000 AMENDMENT

Amendment by Pub. L. 106–553 effective on the first day of the first applicable pay period that begins on Dec. 21, 2000, and applicable only to an individual who is employed as a member of the Supreme Court Police after Dec. 21, 2000, see section 1(a)(2) [title III, § 308(i), (j)] of Pub. L. 106–553, set out in a Supreme Court Police Retirement note under section 8331 of this title.

EFFECTIVE DATE OF 1998 AMENDMENT

Amendment by Pub. L. 105–261 effective 1 year after Oct. 17, 1998, and applicable only to an individual who is employed as a nuclear materials courier, as defined by section 8331(27) or 8401(33) of this title, after Oct. 17, 1998, see section 3154(m), (n) of Pub. L. 105–261, set out as a note under section 8331 of this title.

EFFECTIVE DATE OF 1992 AMENDMENT

Amendment by section 2(60) of Pub. L. 102–378 effective Nov. 5, 1990, see section 9(b)(6) of Pub. L. 102–378, set out as a note under section 6303 of this title.

EFFECTIVE DATE OF 1990 AMENDMENTS

Section 529 [title IV, § 409(c)] of Pub. L. 101–509 provided that: "For the purposes of this section [amending this section and section 8425 of this title], the effective date shall be the date of enactment of this Act [Nov. 5, 1990]."

Section 2(b)(1)(B) of Pub. L. 101–428 provided that: "The amendment made by subparagraph (A) [amending this section] shall take effect 2 years after the date of enactment of this Act [Oct. 15, 1990]."

EFFECTIVE DATE OF 1980 AMENDMENT

Amendment by Pub. L. 96–347 effective on 90th day after Sept. 12, 1980, see section 3 of Pub. L. 96–347, set out as a note under section 2109 of this title.

EFFECTIVE DATE OF 1979 AMENDMENT

Amendment by Pub. L. 96–70 effective Oct. 1, 1979, see section 3304 of Pub. L. 96–70, set out as an Effective

Date note under section 3601 of Title 22, Foreign Relations and Intercourse.

EFFECTIVE DATE OF 1978 AMENDMENT

Amendment by Pub. L. 95–256 effective Sept. 30, 1978, see section 5(f) of Pub. L. 95–256, set out as a note under section 633a of Title 29, Labor.

EFFECTIVE DATE OF 1974 AMENDMENT

Amendment by Pub. L. 93–350 effective Jan. 1, 1978, see section 7 of Pub. L. 93–350, set out as a note under section 3307 of this title.

EFFECTIVE DATE OF 1972 AMENDMENT

Amendment by Pub. L. 92–297 effective on 90th day after May 16, 1972, see section 10 of Pub. L. 92–297, set out as an Effective Date note under section 3381 of this title.

NONAPPLICABILITY OF SUBSECTION (a) TO AIR TRAFFIC CONTROLLERS APPOINTED BEFORE JANUARY 1, 1987

Pub. L. 99–556, title V, § 504, Oct. 27, 1986, 100 Stat. 3141, provided that:

"(a) IN GENERAL.—Section 8335(a) of title 5, United States Code, shall not apply to any air traffic controller appointed before January 1, 1987.

"(b) DEFINITION.—For purposes of this section, the term 'air traffic controller' means any individual who—

"(1) is an air traffic controller within the meaning of section 2109(1) of title 5, United States Code, as in effect on January 1, 1987; but

"(2) is not an air traffic controller within the meaning of section 2109(1) of title 5, United States Code, as in effect on December 31, 1986."

NONAPPLICABILITY OF SUBSECTION (a) TO DEPARTMENT OF DEFENSE AIR TRAFFIC CONTROLLERS APPOINTED BEFORE SEPTEMBER 12, 1980

Section 2 of Pub. L. 96–347 provided that: "Section 8335(a) of title 5, United States Code shall not apply to an individual appointed as an air traffic controller in the Department of Defense before the date of the enactment of this Act [Sept. 12, 1980]."

NONAPPLICABILITY OF SUBSECTION (f) TO AIR TRAFFIC CONTROLLERS APPOINTED BEFORE MAY 16, 1972

Section 8 of Pub. L. 92–297 provided that: "Section 8335(f) of title 5, United States Code, as added by this Act, does not apply to a person appointed as an air traffic controller by the Department of Transportation before the date of enactment of this Act [May 16, 1972]."

SECTION REFERRED TO IN OTHER SECTIONS

This section is referred to in section 8339 of this title; title 26 section 7447.

§ 8336. Immediate retirement

(a) An employee who is separated from the service after becoming 55 years of age and completing 30 years of service is entitled to an annuity.

(b) An employee who is separated from the service after becoming 60 years of age and completing 20 years of service is entitled to an annuity.

(c)(1) An employee who is separated from the service after becoming 50 years of age and completing 20 years of service as a law enforcement officer, firefighter, or nuclear materials courier, or any combination of such service totaling at least 20 years, is entitled to an annuity.

(2) An employee is entitled to an annuity if the employee—

(A) was a law enforcement officer or firefighter employed by the Panama Canal Company or the Canal Zone Government at any time during the period beginning March 31, 1979, and ending September 30, 1979; and

(B) is separated from the service before January 1, 2000, after becoming 48 years of age and completing 18 years of service as a law enforcement officer or firefighter, or any combination of such service totaling at least 18 years.

(d) An employee who—

(1) is separated from the service involuntarily, except by removal for cause on charges of misconduct or delinquency; or

(2) except in the case of an employee who is separated from the service under a program carried out under subsection (o),[1] while serving in a geographic area designated by the Office of Personnel Management, is separated from the service voluntarily during a period in which the Office determines that—

(A) the agency in which the employee is serving is undergoing a major reorganization, a major reduction in force, or a major transfer of function; and

(B) a significant percent of the employees serving in such agency will be separated or subject to an immediate reduction in the rate of basic pay (without regard to subchapter VI of chapter 53 of this title or comparable provisions);

after completing 25 years of service or after becoming 50 years of age and completing 20 years of service is entitled to an annuity. For purposes of paragraph (1) of this subsection, separation for failure to accept a directed reassignment to a position outside the commuting area of the employee concerned or to accompany a position outside of such area pursuant to a transfer of function shall not be considered to be a removal for cause on charges of misconduct or delinquency. Notwithstanding the first sentence of this subsection, an employee described in paragraph (1) of this subsection is not entitled to an annuity under this subsection if the employee has declined a reasonable offer of another position in the employee's agency for which the employee is qualified, which is not lower than 2 grades (or pay levels) below the employee's grade (or pay level), and which is within the employee's commuting area.

(e) An employee who is voluntarily or involuntarily separated from the service, except by removal for cause on charges of misconduct or delinquency, after completing 25 years of service as an air traffic controller or after becoming 50 years of age and completing 20 years of service as an air traffic controller, is entitled to an annuity.

(f) An employee who is separated from the service after becoming 62 years of age and completing 5 years of service is entitled to an annuity.

(g) A Member who is separated from the service after becoming 62 years of age and completing 5 years of civilian service or after becoming 60 years of age and completing 10 years of Member service is entitled to an annuity. A Member

---

[1] Probably means the subsec. (o) relating to Department of Defense employees.

who is separated from the service after becoming 55 years of age (but before becoming 60 years of age) and completing 30 years of service is entitled to a reduced annuity. A Member who is separated from the service, except by resignation or expulsion, after completing 25 years of service or after becoming 50 years of age and (1) completing 20 years of service or (2) serving in 9 Congresses is entitled to an annuity.

(h)(1) A member of the Senior Executive Service who is removed from the Senior Executive Service for failure to be recertified as a senior executive under section 3393a or for less than fully successful executive performance (as determined under subchapter II of chapter 43 of this title) after completing 25 years of service or after becoming 50 years of age and completing 20 years of service is entitled to an annuity.

(2) A member of the Defense Intelligence Senior Executive Service or the Senior Cryptologic Executive Service who is removed from such service for failure to be recertified as a senior executive or for less than fully successful executive performance after completing 25 years of service or after becoming 50 years of age and completing 20 years of service is entitled to an annuity.

(3) A member of the Federal Bureau of Investigation and Drug Enforcement Administration Senior Executive Service who is removed from such service for failure to be recertified as a senior executive or for less than fully successful executive performance after completing 25 years of service or after becoming 50 years of age and completing 20 years of service is entitled to an annuity.

(i)(1) An employee of the Panama Canal Commission or of an Executive agency conducting operations in the Canal Zone or Republic of Panama who is separated from the service before January 1, 2000, who was employed by the Canal Zone Government or the Panama Canal Company at any time during the period beginning March 31, 1979, and ending September 30, 1979, and who has had continuous Panama Canal service, without a break in service of more than 3 days, from that time until separation, is entitled to an annuity if the employee is separated—

(A) involuntarily, after completing 20 years of service or after becoming 48 years of age and completing 18 years of service, if the separation is a result of the implementation of any provision of the Panama Canal Treaty of 1977 and related agreements; or

(B) voluntarily, after completing 23 years of service or after becoming 48 years of age and completing 18 years of service.

(2) An employee of the Panama Canal Commission or of an Executive agency conducting operations in the Canal Zone or Republic of Panama who is separated from the service before January 1, 2000, who was employed, at a permanent duty station in the Canal Zone, by any Executive agency other than the Canal Zone Government or the Panama Canal Company at any time during the period beginning March 31, 1979, and ending September 30, 1979, and who has had continuous Panama Canal service, without a break in service of more than 3 days, from that time until separation, is entitled to an annuity if—

(A) the employee is separated involuntarily, after completing 20 years of service or after becoming 48 years of age and completing 18 years of service; and

(B) the separation is the result of the implementation of any provision of the Panama Canal Treaty of 1977 and related agreements.

(3) An employee of the Panama Canal Commission employed by that body after September 30, 1979, who is separated from the Panama Canal Commission before January 1, 2000, and who at the time of separation has a minimum of 11 years of continuous employment with the Commission (disregarding any break in service of 3 days or less) is entitled to an annuity if the employee is separated—

(A) involuntarily, after completing 20 years of service or after becoming 48 years of age and completing 18 years of service, if the separation is a result of the implementation of any provision of the Panama Canal Treaty of 1977 and related agreements; or

(B) voluntarily, after completing 23 years of service or after becoming 48 years of age and completing 18 years of service.

(4) For the purpose of this subsection—
(A) "Panama Canal service" means—
(i) service as an employee of the Canal Zone Government, the Panama Canal Company, or the Panama Canal Commission; or
(ii) service at a permanent duty station in the Canal Zone or Republic of Panama as an employee of an Executive agency conducting operations in the Canal Zone or the Republic of Panama; and

(B) "Executive agency" includes the United States District Court for the District of the Canal Zone and the Smithsonian Institution.

(j)(1) Except as provided in paragraph (3), an employee is entitled to an annuity if he—
(A)(i) is separated from the service after completing 25 years of service or after becoming 50 years of age and completing 20 years of service, or
(ii) is involuntarily separated, except by removal for cause on charges of misconduct or delinquency, during the 2-year period before the date on which he would meet the years of service and age requirements under clause (i),
(B) was employed in the Bureau of Indian Affairs, the Indian Health Service, a tribal organization (to the extent provided in paragraph (2)), or any combination thereof, continuously from December 21, 1972, to the date of his separation, and
(C) is not entitled to preference under the Indian preference laws.

(2) Employment in a tribal organization may be considered for purposes of paragraph (1)(B) of this subsection only if—
(A) the employee was employed by the tribal organization after January 4, 1975, and immediately before such employment he was an employee of the Bureau of Indian Affairs or the Indian Health Service, and
(B) at the time of such employment such employee and the tribal organization were eligible to elect, and elected, to have the employee retain the coverage, rights, and bene-

fits of this chapter under section 105(e)(2) of the Indian Self-Determination Act (25 U.S.C. 450i(a)(2);[2] 88 Stat. 2209).

(3)(A) The provisions of paragraph (1) of this subsection shall not apply with respect to any separation of any employee which occurs after the date 10 years after—

(i) the date the employee first meets the years of service and age requirements of paragraph (1)(A)(i), or

(ii) the date of the enactment of this paragraph, if the employee met those requirements before that date.

(B) For purposes of applying this paragraph with respect to any employee of the Bureau of Indian Affairs in the Department of the Interior or of the Indian Health Service in the Department of Health, Education, and Welfare, the Secretary of the department involved may postpone the date otherwise applicable under subparagraph (A) if—

(i) such employee consents to such postponement, and

(ii) the Secretary finds that such postponement is necessary for the continued effective operation of the agency.

The period of any postponement under this subparagraph shall not exceed 12 months and the total period of all postponements with respect to any employee shall not exceed 5 years.

(4) For the purpose of this subsection—

(A) "Bureau of Indian Affairs" means (i) the Bureau of Indian Affairs and (ii) all other organizational units in the Department of the Interior directly and primarily related to providing services to Indians and in which positions are filled in accordance with the Indian preference laws.

(B) "Indian preference laws" means section 12 of the Act of June 18, 1934 (25 U.S.C. 472; 48 Stat. 986), or any other provision of law granting a preference to Indians in promotions or other Federal personnel actions.

(k) A bankruptcy judge, United States magistrate judge, or Court of Federal Claims judge who is separated from service, except by removal, after becoming 62 years of age and completing 5 years of civilian service, or after becoming 60 years of age and completing 10 years of service as a bankruptcy judge, United States magistrate judge, or Court of Federal Claims judge, is entitled to an annuity.

(l) A judge of the United States Court of Appeals for the Armed Forces who is separated from the service after becoming 62 years of age and completing 5 years of civilian service or after completing the term of service for which he was appointed as a judge of such court is entitled to an annuity. A judge who is separated from the service before becoming 60 years of age is entitled to a reduced annuity.

(m) A member of the Capitol Police who is separated from the service after becoming 50 years of age and completing 20 years of service as a member of the Capitol Police or as a law enforcement officer, or any combination of such service totaling at least 20 years, is entitled to an annuity.

(n) A member of the Supreme Court Police who is separated from the service after becoming 50 years of age and completing 20 years of service as a member of the Supreme Court Police or as a law enforcement officer, or any combination of such service totaling at least 20 years, is entitled to an annuity.

(o)[3] An annuity or reduced annuity authorized by this section is computed under section 8339 of this title.

(o)(1)[3] The Secretary of Defense may, during fiscal years 2002 and 2003, carry out a program under which an employee of the Department of Defense may be separated from the service entitled to an immediate annuity under this subchapter if the employee—

(A) has—

(i) completed 25 years of service; or

(ii) become 50 years of age and completed 20 years of service; and

(B) is eligible for the annuity under paragraph (2) or (3).

(2)(A) For the purposes of paragraph (1), an employee referred to in that paragraph is eligible for an immediate annuity under this paragraph if the employee—

(i) is separated from the service involuntarily other than for cause; and

(ii) has not declined a reasonable offer of another position in the Department of Defense for which the employee is qualified, which is not lower than 2 grades (or pay levels) below the employee's grade (or pay level), and which is within the employee's commuting area.

(B) For the purposes of paragraph (2)(A)(i), a separation for failure to accept a directed reassignment to a position outside the commuting area of the employee concerned or to accompany a position outside of such area pursuant to a transfer of function may not be considered to be a removal for cause.

(3) For the purposes of paragraph (1), an employee referred to in that paragraph is eligible for an immediate annuity under this paragraph if the employee satisfies all of the following conditions:

(A) The employee is separated from the service voluntarily during a period in which the organization within the Department of Defense in which the employee is serving is undergoing a major organizational adjustment.

(B) The employee has been employed continuously by the Department of Defense for more than 30 days before the date on which the head of the employee's organization requests the determinations required under subparagraph (A).

(C) The employee is serving under an appointment that is not limited by time.

(D) The employee is not in receipt of a decision notice of involuntary separation for misconduct or unacceptable performance.

(E) The employee is within the scope of an offer of voluntary early retirement, as defined on the basis of one or more of the following objective criteria:

(i) One or more organizational units.

(ii) One or more occupational groups, series, or levels.

---

[2] See References in Text note below.

[3] So in original. Two subsecs. (o) have been enacted.

(iii) One or more geographical locations.

(iv) Any other similar objective and nonpersonal criteria that the Office of Personnel Management determines appropriate.

(4) Under regulations prescribed by the Office of Personnel Management, the determinations of whether an employee meets—

(A) the requirements of subparagraph (A) of paragraph (3) shall be made by the Office, upon the request of the Secretary of Defense; and

(B) the requirements of subparagraph (E) of such paragraph shall be made by the Secretary of Defense.

(5) A determination of which employees are within the scope of an offer of early retirement shall be made only on the basis of consistent and well-documented application of the relevant criteria.

(6) In this subsection, the term "major organizational adjustment" means any of the following:

(A) A major reorganization.

(B) A major reduction in force.

(C) A major transfer of function.

(D) A workforce restructuring—

(i) to meet mission needs;

(ii) to achieve one or more reductions in strength;

(iii) to correct skill imbalances; or

(iv) to reduce the number of high-grade, managerial, supervisory, or similar positions.

(Pub. L. 89–554, Sept. 6, 1966, 80 Stat. 571; Pub. L. 90–83, §1(75), Sept. 11, 1967, 81 Stat. 214; Pub. L. 92–297, §5, May 16, 1972, 86 Stat. 144; Pub. L. 92–382, Aug. 14, 1972, 86 Stat. 539; Pub. L. 93–39, June 12, 1973, 87 Stat. 73; Pub. L. 93–350, §5, July 12, 1974, 88 Stat. 356; Pub. L. 94–183, §2(40), (41), Dec. 31, 1975, 89 Stat. 1059; Pub. L. 95–454, title III, §306, title IV, §412(a), Oct. 13, 1978, 92 Stat. 1147, 1175; Pub. L. 96–70, title I, §1241(a), Sept. 27, 1979, 93 Stat. 471; Pub. L. 96–135, §1(a), Dec. 5, 1979, 93 Stat. 1056; Pub. L. 97–89, title VIII, §803, Dec. 4, 1981, 95 Stat. 1161; Pub. L. 97–253, title III, §308(a), Sept. 8, 1982, 96 Stat. 798; Pub. L. 98–94, title XII, §1256(b), Sept. 24, 1983, 97 Stat. 701; Pub. L. 98–353, title I, §116(c), July 10, 1984, 98 Stat. 344; Pub. L. 98–531, §2(b), Oct. 19, 1984, 98 Stat. 2704; Pub. L. 98–615, title III, §304(d), Nov. 8, 1984, 98 Stat. 3219; Pub. L. 99–190, §101(d) [title III, §315], Dec. 19, 1985, 99 Stat. 1224, 1266; Pub. L. 100–53, §2(c), June 18, 1987, 101 Stat. 368; Pub. L. 100–325, §2(*l*), May 30, 1988, 102 Stat. 582; Pub. L. 101–194, title V, §506(b)(7), Nov. 30, 1989, 103 Stat. 1758; Pub. L. 101–428, §2(a), Oct. 15, 1990, 104 Stat. 928; Pub. L. 101–510, div. C, title XXXV, §3506(a), Nov. 5, 1990, 104 Stat. 1846; Pub. L. 101–650, title III, §§306(c)(3), 321, Dec. 1, 1990, 104 Stat. 5110, 5117; Pub. L. 102–572, title IX, §902(b)(2), Oct. 29, 1992, 106 Stat. 4516; Pub. L. 103–337, div. A, title IX, §924(d)(1)(A), Oct. 5, 1994, 108 Stat. 2832; Pub. L. 105–261, div. A, title XI, §1109(a), div. C, title XXXI, §3154(e), Oct. 17, 1998, 112 Stat. 2143, 2255; Pub. L. 106–58, title VI, §651(b), Sept. 29, 1999, 113 Stat. 480; Pub. L. 106–398, §1 [[div. A], title XI, §1152(a)], Oct. 30, 2000, 114 Stat. 1654, 1654A–320; Pub. L. 106–553, §1(a)(2) [title III, §308(b)(3)], Dec. 21, 2000, 114 Stat. 2762, 2762A–87.)

APPLICATION OF SUBSECTION (d)(2)

Pub. L. 105–174, title III, §7001(a), May 1, 1998, 112 Stat. 91, as amended by Pub. L. 106–58, title VI, §651(a), Sept. 29, 1999, 113 Stat. 480, provided that, effective May 1, 1998, subsection (d)(2) of this section shall be applied as if it had been amended to read as follows:

(2)(A) has been employed continuously, by the agency in which the employee is serving, for at least the 31-day period ending on the date on which such agency requests the determination referred to in subparagraph (D);

(B) is serving under an appointment that is not time limited;

(C) has not been duly notified that such employee is to be involuntarily separated for misconduct or unacceptable performance;

(D) is separated from the service voluntarily during a period in which, as determined by the Office of Personnel Management (upon request of the agency) under regulations prescribed by the Office—

(i) such agency (or, if applicable, the component in which the employee is serving) is undergoing a major reorganization, a major reduction in force, or a major transfer of function; and

(ii) a significant percentage of the employees serving in such agency (or component) will be separated or subject to an immediate reduction in the rate of basic pay (without regard to subchapter VI of chapter 53, or comparable provisions); and

(E) as determined by the agency under regulations prescribed by the Office, is within the scope of the offer of voluntary early retirement, which may be made on the basis of—

(i) one or more organizational units;

(ii) one or more occupational series or levels;

(iii) one or more geographical locations;

(iv) other similar nonpersonal factors the Office determines appropriate; or

(v) any appropriate combination of such factors;

HISTORICAL AND REVISION NOTES
1966 ACT

Derivation	U.S. Code	Revised Statutes and Statutes at Large
....	5 U.S.C. 2256 (less last sentence in (f)).	July 31, 1956, ch. 804, §401 "Sec. 6 (less last sentence in (f))", 70 Stat. 749. July 7, 1960, Pub. L. 86–604, §1(b), 74 Stat. 358. July 12, 1960, Pub. L. 86–622, §3(b), 74 Stat. 410.

Standard changes are made to conform with the definition applicable and the style of this title as outlined in the preface to the report.

1967 ACT

Section of title 5	Source (U.S. Code)	Source (Statutes at Large)
8336(a)	5 App.: 2256(a).	July 18, 1966, Pub. L. 89–504, §504, 80 Stat. 301.
8336(b)	5 App.: 2256(b).	

In subsections (a) and (b), the words "is entitled to" are substituted for "shall * * * be paid". The words "computed as provided in section 9" are omitted as unnecessary in view of 5 U.S.C. 8339.

REFERENCES IN TEXT

Section 105(e)(2) of the Indian Self-Determination Act (25 U.S.C. 450i(a)(2); 88 Stat. 2209), referred to in subsec. (j)(2)(B), was renumbered section 104(e)(2) of that Act by Pub. L. 100–472, title II, §203(a), Oct. 5, 1988, 102 Stat.

2290, without corresponding amendment to this section. Section 104(e)(2) of the Indian Self-Determination Act is classified to section 450i(e)(2) of Title 25, Indians. Section 105 of that Act is classified to section 450j of Title 25.

The date of the enactment of this paragraph, referred to in subsec. (j)(3)(A)(ii), is Dec. 5, 1979, the date of the enactment of Pub. L. 96–135, which was approved Dec. 5, 1979.

AMENDMENTS

2000—Subsec. (d)(2). Pub. L. 106–398, §1 [[div. A], title XI, §1152(a)(1)], inserted "except in the case of an employee who is separated from the service under a program carried out under subsection (o)," before "while serving" in introductory provisions.

Subsec. (n). Pub. L. 106–553 added subsec. (n). Former subsec. (n), relating to computation of annuity under section 8339 of this title, redesignated (o).

Subsec. (o). Pub. L. 106–553 redesignated subsec. (n), relating to computation of annuity under section 8339 of this title, as (o).

Pub. L. 106–398, §1 [[div. A], title XI, §1152(a)(2)], added subsec. (o) relating to Department of Defense employees.

1999—Subsecs. (d)(2), (o). Pub. L. 106–58 repealed Pub. L. 105–261, §1109(a). See 1998 Amendment notes below.

1998—Subsec. (c)(1). Pub. L. 105–261, §3154(e), substituted ", firefighter, or nuclear materials courier" for "or firefighter".

Subsec. (d)(2). Pub. L. 105–261, §1109(a)(1), which directed insertion of "except in the case of an employee described in subsection (o)(1)," after "(2)", was repealed by Pub. L. 106–58.

Subsec. (o). Pub. L. 105–261, §1109(a)(2), which directed addition of subsec. (o), relating to authority of Department of Defense to offer employees voluntary early retirement, was repealed by Pub. L. 106–58.

1994—Subsec. (l). Pub. L. 103–337 substituted "Court of Appeals for the Armed Forces" for "Court of Military Appeals".

1992—Subsec. (k). Pub. L. 102–572 substituted "Court of Federal Claims" for "Claims Court" in two places.

1990—Subsec. (i)(3), (4). Pub. L. 101–510 added par. (3) and redesignated former par. (3) as (4).

Subsec. (k). Pub. L. 101–650 amended subsec. (k) generally. Prior to amendment, subsec. (k) read as follows: "A bankruptcy judge or United States magistrate who is separated from service, except by removal, after becoming 62 years of age and completing 5 years of civilian service, or after becoming 60 years of age and completing 10 years of service as a bankruptcy judge or United States magistrate, is entitled to an annuity."

Subsecs. (m), (n). Pub. L. 101–428 added subsec. (m) and redesignated former subsec. (m) as (n).

1989—Subsec. (h)(1). Pub. L. 101–194, §506(b)(7)(A), substituted "for failure to be recertified as a senior executive under section 3393a or for" for "for".

Subsec. (h)(2), (3). Pub. L. 101–194, §506(b)(7)(B), (C), substituted "for failure to be recertified as a senior executive or for" for "for".

1988—Subsec. (h)(3). Pub. L. 100–325 added par. (3).

1987—Subsec. (k). Pub. L. 100–53 amended subsec. (k) generally. Prior to amendment, subsec. (k) read as follows: "A bankruptcy judge who is separated from service, except by removal, after becoming sixty-two years of age and completing ten years of service as a bankruptcy judge is entitled to an annuity."

1985—Subsec. (j)(3)(A). Pub. L. 99–190 substituted "10 years" for "5 years".

1984—Subsec. (d). Pub. L. 98–615 inserted provision that for purposes of par. (1), separation for failure to accept a directed reassignment to a position outside the commuting area of the employee concerned or to accompany a position outside of such area pursuant to a transfer of function shall not be considered to be a removal for cause on charges of misconduct or delinquency.

Subsec. (k). Pub. L. 98–353, §116(c), added subsec. (k). Former subsec. (k) redesignated (l).

Subsec. (l). Pub. L. 98–531 redesignated the subsec. (l), which was redesignated by Pub. L. 98–94, as (m).

Pub. L. 98–353, §116(c)(1), redesignated subsec. (k) as (l).

Subsec. (m). Pub. L. 98–531 redesignated the subsec. (l), which was redesignated by Pub. L. 98–94, as (m).

1983—Subsecs. (k), (l). Pub. L. 98–94 added subsec. (k) and redesignated former subsec. (k) as (l).

1982—Subsec. (d). Pub. L. 97–253, §308(a), inserted provision that the agency which is undergoing a major reorganization, a major reduction in force, or a major transfer of function must have a significant percent of its employees who will be separated or subject to an immediate reduction in the rate of basic pay and inserted provision that notwithstanding the first sentence of this subsection, an employee described in paragraph (1) of this subsection is not entitled to an annuity under this subsection if the employee has declined a reasonable offer of another position in the employee's agency for which the employee is qualified, which is not lower than 2 grades (or pay levels) below the employee's grade (or pay level), and which is within the employee's commuting area.

1981—Subsec. (h). Pub. L. 97–89 designated existing provisions as par. (1) and added par. (2).

1979—Subsec. (c). Pub. L. 96–70 §1241(a)(1), designated existing provisions as par. (1) and added par. (2).

Subsec. (i). Pub. L. 96–70, §1241(a)(2), added subsec. (i). Former subsec. (i) redesignated (j).

Subsec. (j). Pub. L. 96–135 added subsec. (j). Former subsec. (j) redesignated (k).

Pub. L. 96–70, §1241(a)(2), redesignated former subsec. (i) as (j).

Subsec. (k). Pub. L. 96–135 redesignated former subsec. (j) as (k).

1978—Subsec. (d)(2). Pub. L. 95–454, §306, substituted provisions relating to the employee's agency undergoing a major reorganization, reduction in force, or transfer of function, as determined by the Office of Personnel Management, for provisions relating to the employee's agency undergoing a major reduction in force, as determined by the Commission.

Subsecs. (h), (i). Pub. L. 95–454, §412(a), added subsec. (h) and redesignated former subsec. (h) as (i).

1975—Subsecs. (d), (g). Pub. L. 94–183 substituted "an" for "a reduced" after "is entitled to".

1974—Subsec. (c). Pub. L. 93–350 substituted provisions granting annuity entitlement to employees separated from the service after becoming 50 years of age and completing 20 years of service as a law enforcement officer or firefighter or any combination of such service totaling at least 20 years for provisions requiring the head of the employing agency to recommend, and the Civil Service Commission to approve, the retirement of an otherwise eligible employee requiring the agency and the Commission to consider the degree of hazard the employee was subjected to in the performance of his duties, and defining "detention" to include the duties of specified employees.

1973—Subsec. (d). Pub. L. 93–39 reenacted existing provisions, designated part of such provisions as item (1) and added item (2).

1972—Subsec. (c). Pub. L. 92–382 inserted reference to employees performing work directly connected with the control and extinguishment of fires or the maintenance and use of firefighting apparatus and equipment for the purpose of retirement benefits.

Subsecs. (e) to (h). Pub. L. 92–297 added subsec. (e) and redesignated former subsecs. (e) to (g) as (f) to (h), respectively.

CHANGE OF NAME

"United States magistrate judge" substituted for "United States magistrate" wherever appearing in subsec. (k) pursuant to section 321 of Pub. L. 101–650, set out as a note under section 631 of Title 28, Judiciary and Judicial Procedure.

Secretary and Department of Health, Education, and Welfare redesignated Secretary and Department of Health and Human Services by section 3508 of Title 20, Education.

EFFECTIVE DATE OF 2000 AMENDMENT

Amendment by Pub. L. 106–553 effective on the first day of the first applicable pay period that begins on Dec. 21, 2000, and applicable only to an individual who is employed as a member of the Supreme Court Police after Dec. 21, 2000, see section 1(a)(2) [title III, § 308(i), (j)] of Pub. L. 106–553, set out in a Supreme Court Police Retirement note under section 8331 of this title.

EFFECTIVE DATE OF 1998 AMENDMENT

Pub. L. 105–261, div. A, title XI, § 1109(d), Oct. 17, 1998, 112 Stat. 2145, as amended by Pub. L. 106–65, div. A, title XI, § 1101, Oct. 5, 1999, 113 Stat. 775, which provided that the amendments made by section 1109 of Pub. L. 105–261 (amending this section and sections 8339, 8414, and 8464 of this title) were to be effective Oct. 1, 2000, and applicable with respect to an approval for voluntary early retirement made on or after that date, was repealed by Pub. L. 106–58, title VI, § 651(b), Sept. 29, 1999, 113 Stat. 480.

Amendment by section 3154(e) of Pub. L. 105–261 effective at the beginning of the first pay period that begins after Oct. 17, 1998, and applicable only to an individual who is employed as a nuclear materials courier, as defined by section 8331(27) or 8401(33) of this title, after Oct. 17, 1998, see section 3154(m), (n) of Pub. L. 105–261, set out as a note under section 8331 of this title.

EFFECTIVE DATE OF 1992 AMENDMENT

Amendment by Pub. L. 102–572 effective Oct. 29, 1992, see section 911 of Pub. L. 102–572, set out as a note under section 171 of Title 28, Judiciary and Judicial Procedure.

EFFECTIVE DATE OF 1990 AMENDMENT

Amendment by Pub. L. 101–650 applicable to judges of, and senior judges in active service with, the United States Court of Federal Claims on or after Dec. 1, 1990, see section 306(f) of Pub. L. 101–650, set out as a note under section 8331 of this title.

EFFECTIVE DATE OF 1989 AMENDMENT

Amendment by Pub. L. 101–194 effective Jan. 1, 1991, see section 506(d) of Pub. L. 101–194, set out as a note under section 3151 of this title.

EFFECTIVE DATE OF 1987 AMENDMENT

Amendment by Pub. L. 100–53 effective Oct. 1, 1987, and applicable to bankruptcy judges and United States magistrate judges in office on that date and to individuals subsequently appointed to such positions to whom this chapter otherwise applies, see section 3 of Pub. L. 100–53, as amended, set out as a note under section 8331 of this title.

EFFECTIVE DATE OF 1984 AMENDMENTS

Amendment by Pub. L. 98–615 effective Nov. 8, 1984, see section 307 of Pub. L. 98–615, set out as a note under section 3393 of this title.

Amendment by Pub. L. 98–531 effective Mar. 31, 1984, see section 3(b) of Pub. L. 98–531, set out as a note under section 8331 of this title.

Amendment by Pub. L. 98–353 effective July 10, 1984, and applicable to bankruptcy judges who retire on or after such date, see section 116(e) of Pub. L. 98–353, set out as a note under section 8331 of this title. See, also, section 122(a) of Pub. L. 98–353, set out as an Effective Date note under section 151 of Title 28, Judiciary and Judicial Procedure.

EFFECTIVE DATE OF 1982 AMENDMENT

Section 308(b) of Pub. L. 97–253 provided that: "The amendment made by subsection (a) [amending this section] shall take effect October 1, 1982."

EFFECTIVE DATE OF 1981 AMENDMENT

Amendment by Pub. L. 97–89 effective Oct. 1, 1981, see section 806 of Pub. L. 97–89, set out as an Effective Date note under section 1621 of Title 10, Armed Forces.

EFFECTIVE DATE OF 1979 AMENDMENTS

Section 1(d) of Pub. L. 96–135 provided that: "The amendments made by this section [amending this section and section 8339 of this title] shall take effect on the date of the enactment of this Act [Dec. 5, 1979]."

Section 1241(b)(1) of Pub. L. 96–70 provided that: "The amendments made by this section [amending this section] shall take effect on the date of the enactment of this Act [Sept. 27, 1979], but no amount of annuity under chapter 83 of title 5, United States Code, accruing by reason of those amendments shall be payable for any period before October 1, 1979."

EFFECTIVE DATE OF 1978 AMENDMENT

Amendment by section 306 of Pub. L. 95–454 effective 90 days after Oct. 13, 1978, see section 907 of Pub. L. 95–454, set out as a note under section 1101 of this title.

Amendment by section 412 of Pub. L. 95–454 effective 9 months after Oct. 13, 1978, and congressional review of provisions of sections 401 through 412 of Pub. L. 95–454, see section 415 of Pub. L. 95–454, set out as an Effective Date note under section 3131 of this title.

EFFECTIVE DATE OF 1974 AMENDMENT

Amendment by Pub. L. 93–350 effective July 12, 1974, see section 7 of Pub. L. 93–350, set out as a note under section 3307 of this title.

EFFECTIVE DATE OF 1972 AMENDMENT

Amendment by Pub. L. 92–297 effective on 90th day after May 16, 1972, see section 10 of Pub. L. 92–297, set out as an Effective Date note under section 3381 of this title.

TERMINATION OF UNITED STATES DISTRICT COURT FOR THE DISTRICT OF THE CANAL ZONE

For termination of the United States District Court for the District of the Canal Zone at end of the "transition period", being the 30-month period beginning Oct. 1, 1979, and ending midnight Mar. 31, 1982, see Paragraph 5 of Article XI of the Panama Canal Treaty of 1977 and sections 2101 and 2201 to 2203(a) of Pub. L. 96–70, title II, Sept. 27, 1979, 93 Stat. 493, formerly classified to sections 3831 and 3841 to 3843, respectively, of Title 22, Foreign Relations and Intercourse.

GENERAL ACCOUNTING OFFICE: VOLUNTARY EARLY RETIREMENT

Pub. L. 106–303, § 1, Oct. 13, 2000, 114 Stat. 1063, provided that:

"(a) CIVIL SERVICE RETIREMENT SYSTEM.—Effective for purposes of the period beginning on the date of the enactment of this Act [Oct. 13, 2000] and ending on December 31, 2003, paragraph (2) of section 8336(d) of title 5, United States Code, shall, with respect to officers and employees of the General Accounting Office, be applied as if it had been amended to read as follows:

"(2)(A) has been employed continuously by the General Accounting Office for at least the 31-day period immediately preceding the start of the period referred to in subparagraph (D);

"(B) is serving under an appointment that is not time limited;

"(C) has not received a notice of involuntary separation, for misconduct or unacceptable performance, with respect to which final action remains pending; and

"(D) is separated from the service voluntarily during a period with respect to which the Comptroller General determines that the application of this subsection is necessary and appropriate for the purpose of—

"(i) realigning the General Accounting Office's workforce in order to meet budgetary constraints or mission needs;

"(ii) correcting skill imbalances; or

"(iii) reducing high-grade, managerial, or supervisory positions;

"(b) FEDERAL EMPLOYEES' RETIREMENT SYSTEM.—Effective for purposes of the period beginning on the date of the enactment of this Act [Oct. 13, 2000] and ending on December 31, 2003, subparagraph (B) of section 8414(b)(1) of title 5, United States Code, shall, with respect to officers and employees of the General Accounting Office, be applied as if it had been amended to read as follows:

"(B)(i) has been employed continuously by the General Accounting Office for at least the 31-day period immediately preceding the start of the period referred to in clause (iv);

"(ii) is serving under an appointment that is not time limited;

"(iii) has not received a notice of involuntary separation, for misconduct or unacceptable performance, with respect to which final action remains pending; and

"(iv) is separated from the service voluntarily during a period with respect to which the Comptroller General determines that the application of this subsection is necessary and appropriate for the purpose of—

"(I) realigning the General Accounting Office's workforce in order to meet budgetary constraints or mission needs;

"(II) correcting skill imbalances; or

"(III) reducing high-grade, managerial, or supervisory positions;

"(c) NUMERICAL LIMITATION.—Not to exceed 10 percent of the General Accounting Office's workforce (as of the start of a fiscal year) shall be permitted to take voluntary early retirement in such fiscal year pursuant to this section.

"(d) REGULATIONS.—The Comptroller General shall prescribe any regulations necessary to carry out this section, including regulations under which an early retirement offer may be made to any employee or group of employees based on—

"(1) geographic area, organizational unit, or occupational series or level;

"(2) skills, knowledge, or performance; or

"(3) such other similar factors (or combination of factors described in this or any other paragraph of this subsection) as the Comptroller General considers necessary and appropriate in order to achieve the purpose involved."

INDIAN PREFERENCE LAWS APPLICABLE TO BUREAU OF INDIAN AFFAIRS AND INDIAN HEALTH SERVICE POSITIONS

Nonapplicability of annuity provisions of subsec. (j) of this section to individuals accepting waiver of Indian preference laws with respect to personnel actions, see section 472a(c)(2) of Title 25, Indians.

INDIVIDUALS ENTITLED TO ANNUITY PAYMENTS FOR PERIOD PRIOR TO OCTOBER 1, 1979

Section 1241(b)(2) of Pub. L. 96–70 provided that: "Effective October 1, 1979, any individual who, but for paragraph (1) of this subsection [set out as an Effective Date of 1979 Amendment note above], would have been entitled to one or more annuity payments pursuant to the amendments made by this section [amending this section] for periods before October 1, 1979, shall be entitled, to such extent or in such amounts as are provided in advance in appropriation Acts, to a lump sum payment equal to the total amount of all such annuity payments."

SECTION REFERRED TO IN OTHER SECTIONS

This section is referred to in sections 3381, 3382, 3396, 5597, 6302, 8335, 8339, 8348 of this title; title 10 section 10218; title 22 sections 3671, 3691, 4045, 4046, 4051, 4052; title 24 section 225d; title 25 section 472a; title 45 section 1206; title 50 sections 2053, 2442.

§ 8337. Disability retirement

(a) An employee who completes 5 years of civilian service and has become disabled shall be retired on the employee's own application or on application by the employee's agency. Any employee shall be considered to be disabled only if the employee is found by the Office of Personnel Management to be unable, because of disease or injury, to render useful and efficient service in the employee's position and is not qualified for reassignment, under procedures prescribed by the Office, to a vacant position which is in the agency at the same grade or level and in which the employee would be able to render useful and efficient service. For the purpose of the preceding sentence, an employee of the United States Postal Service shall be considered not qualified for a reassignment described in that sentence if the reassignment is to a position in a different craft or is inconsistent with the terms of a collective bargaining agreement covering the employee. A judge of the United States Court of Appeals for the Armed Forces who completes 5 years of civilian service and who is found by the Office to be disabled for useful and efficient service as a judge of such court or who is removed for mental or physical disability under section 942(c) of title 10 shall be retired on the judge's own application or upon such removal. A Member who completes 5 years of Member service and is found by the Office to be disabled for useful and efficient service as a Member because of disease or injury shall be retired on the Member's own application. An annuity authorized by this section is computed under section 8339(g) of this title, unless the employee or Member is eligible for a higher annuity computed under section 8339(a) through (e), (n), (q), (r), or (s).

(b) A claim may be allowed under this section only if the application is filed with the Office before the employee or Member is separated from the service or within 1 year thereafter. This time limitation may be waived by the Office for an employee or Member who at the date of separation from service or within 1 year thereafter is mentally incompetent, if the application is filed with the Office within 1 year from the date of restoration of the employee or Member to competency or the appointment of a fiduciary, whichever is earlier.

(c) An annuitant receiving disability retirement annuity from the Fund shall be examined under the direction of the Office—

(1) at the end of 1 year from the date of the disability retirement; and

(2) annually thereafter until he becomes 60 years of age;

unless his disability is permanent in character. If the annuitant fails to submit to examination as required by this section, payment of the annuity shall be suspended until continuance of the disability is satisfactorily established.

(d) If an annuitant receiving disability retirement annuity from the Fund, before becoming 60 years of age, recovers from his disability, payment of the annuity terminates on reemployment by the Government or 1 year after the date of the medical examination showing the recovery, whichever is earlier. If an annuitant receiving disability retirement annuity from the Fund, before becoming 60 years of age, is restored to an earning capacity fairly comparable to the current rate of pay of the position occupied at the time of retirement, payment of the annuity terminates on reemployment by the Government or 180 days after the end of the calendar year in which earning capacity is so restored, whichever is earlier. Earning capacity is deemed restored if in any calendar year the income of the annuitant from wages or self-employment or both equals at least 80 percent of the current rate of pay of the position occupied immediately before retirement.

(e) If an annuitant whose annuity is terminated under subsection (d) of this section is not reemployed in a position in which he is subject to this subchapter, he is deemed, except for service credit, to have been involuntarily separated from the service for the purpose of this subchapter as of the date of termination of the disability annuity, and after that termination is entitled to annuity under the applicable provisions of this subchapter. If an annuitant whose annuity is heretofore or hereafter terminated because of an earning capacity provision of this subchapter or an earlier statute—

(1) is not reemployed in a position in which he is subject to this subchapter; and

(2) has not recovered from the disability for which he was retired;

his annuity shall be restored at the same rate effective the first of the year following any calendar year in which his income from wages or self-employment or both is less than 80 percent of the current rate of pay of the position occupied immediately before retirement. If an annuitant whose annuity is heretofore or hereafter terminated because of a medical finding that he has recovered from disability is not reemployed in a position in which he is subject to this subchapter, his annuity shall be restored at the same rate effective from the date of medical examination showing a recurrence of the disability. The second and third sentences of this subsection do not apply to an individual who has become 62 years of age and is receiving or is eligible to receive annuity under the first sentence of this subsection.

(f)(1) An individual is not entitled to receive—

(A) an annuity under this subchapter, and

(B) compensation for injury to, or disability of, such individual under subchapter I of chapter 81, other than compensation payable under section 8107,

covering the same period of time.

(2) An individual is not entitled to receive an annuity under this subchapter and a concurrent benefit under subchapter I of chapter 81 on account of the death of the same person.

(3) Paragraphs (1) and (2) do not bar the right of a claimant to the greater benefit conferred by either this subchapter or subchapter I of chapter 81.

(g) If an individual is entitled to an annuity under this subchapter, and the individual receives a lump-sum payment for compensation under section 8135 based on the disability or death of the same person, so much of the compensation as has been paid for a period extended beyond the date payment of the annuity commences, as determined by the Department of Labor, shall be refunded to that Department for credit to the Employees' Compensation Fund. Before the individual may receive the annuity, the individual shall—

(1) refund to the Department of Labor the amount representing the commuted compensation payments for the extended period; or

(2) authorize the deduction of the amount from the annuity.

Deductions from the annuity may be made from accrued or accruing payments. The amounts deducted and withheld from the annuity shall be transmitted to the Department of Labor for reimbursement to the Employees' Compensation Fund. When the Department of Labor finds that the financial circumstances of an individual entitled to an annuity under this subchapter warrant deferred refunding, deductions from the annuity may be prorated against and paid from accruing payments in such manner as the Department determines appropriate.

(h)(1) As used in this subsection, the term "technician" means an individual employed under section 709(a) of title 32 or section 10216 of title 10 who, as a condition of the employment, is required under section 709(b) of title 32 or section 10216 of title 10, respectively, to be a member of the Selected Reserve.

(2)(A) Except as provided in subparagraph (B) of this paragraph, an individual shall be retired under this section if the individual—

(i) is separated from employment as a technician under section 709(e)(1) of title 32 or section 10216 of title 10 by reason of a disability that disqualifies the individual from membership in the Selected Reserve;

(ii) is not considered to be disabled under the second sentence of subsection (a) of this section;

(iii) is not appointed to a position in the Government (whether under paragraph (3) of this subsection or otherwise); and

(iv) has not declined an offer of an appointment to a position in the Government under paragraph (3) of this subsection.

(B) Payment of any annuity for an individual pursuant to this subsection terminates—

(i) on the date the individual is appointed to a position in the Government (whether pursuant to paragraph (3) of this subsection or otherwise);

(ii) on the date the individual declines an offer of appointment to a position in the Government under paragraph (3); or

(iii) as provided under subsection (d).

(3) Any individual applying for or receiving any annuity pursuant to this subsection shall, in accordance with regulations prescribed by the Office, be considered by any agency of the Government before any vacant position in the agency is filled if—

(A) the position is located within the commuting area of the individual's former position;

(B) the individual is qualified to serve in such position, as determined by the head of the agency; and

(C) the position is at the same grade or equivalent level as the position from which the individual was separated under section 709(e)(1) of title 32 or section 10216 of title 10.

(Pub. L. 89–554, Sept. 6, 1966, 80 Stat. 572; Pub. L. 90–83, §1(76), Sept. 11, 1967, 81 Stat. 214; Pub. L.

95–454, title IX, § 906(a)(2), (3), Oct. 13, 1978, 92 Stat. 1224; Pub. L. 96–499, title IV, § 403(a), Dec. 5, 1980, 94 Stat. 2605; Pub. L. 97–253, title III, § 302(a), Sept. 8, 1982, 96 Stat. 792; Pub. L. 98–94, title XII, § 1256(c), Sept. 24, 1983, 97 Stat. 701; Pub. L. 100–238, title I, § 124(a)(1)(A), Jan. 8, 1988, 101 Stat. 1755; Pub. L. 101–189, div. A, title XIII, § 1304(b)(2), Nov. 29, 1989, 103 Stat. 1577; Pub. L. 101–428, § 2(d)(1), Oct. 15, 1990, 104 Stat. 929; Pub. L. 102–378, § 2(61), Oct. 2, 1992, 106 Stat. 1354; Pub. L. 103–337, div. A, title IX, § 924(d)(1)(A), Oct. 5, 1994, 108 Stat. 2832; Pub. L. 105–61, title V, § 516(a)(2), Oct. 10, 1997, 111 Stat. 1306; Pub. L. 106–65, div. A, title V, § 522(d), Oct. 5, 1999, 113 Stat. 597; Pub. L. 106–553, § 1(a)(2) [title III, § 308(h)(1)], Dec. 21, 2000, 114 Stat. 2762, 2762A–88.)

HISTORICAL AND REVISION NOTES
1966 ACT

Derivation	U.S. Code	Revised Statutes and Statutes at Large
....	5 U.S.C. 2257.	July 31, 1956, ch. 804, § 401 "Sec. 7", 70 Stat. 750. Oct. 4, 1961, Pub. L. 87–350, § 4(a), 75 Stat. 771.

In subsection (c), the words "receiving disability retirement annuity from the Fund" are coextensive with and substituted for "retired under this section or under section 6 of the Act of May 29, 1930, as amended".

In subsection (g), the words "Notwithstanding any provision of law to the contrary" are omitted as unnecessary. The words "Employees' Compensation Fund" are substituted for "Federal Employees' Compensation Fund" to conform with the title of that Fund as set forth in section 8147.

Standard changes are made to conform with the definitions applicable and the style of this title as outlined in the preface to the report.

1967 ACT

This section amends 5 U.S.C. 8337(e) for consistency within the subchapter and to reflect that it is the individual, rather than the position, that is subject to the subchapter.

AMENDMENTS

2000—Subsec. (a). Pub. L. 106–553 substituted "8339(a) through (e), (n), (q), (r), or (s)" for "8339(a)–(e), (n), (q), or (r)" in last sentence.

1999—Subsec. (h)(1). Pub. L. 106–65, § 522(d)(1), inserted "or section 10216 of title 10" after "title 32" and substituted "title 32 or section 10216 of title 10, respectively, to be a member of the Selected Reserve." for "such title to be a member of the National Guard and to hold a specified military grade."

Subsec. (h)(2)(A)(i). Pub. L. 106–65, § 522(d)(2), inserted "or section 10216 of title 10" after "title 32" and substituted "Selected Reserve" for "National Guard or from holding the military grade required for such employment".

Subsec. (h)(3)(C). Pub. L. 106–65, § 522(d)(3), inserted "or section 10216 of title 10" after "title 32".

1997—Subsec. (a). Pub. L. 105–61 substituted "(q), or (r)" for "or (q)".

1994—Subsec. (a). Pub. L. 103–337 substituted "Court of Appeals for the Armed Forces" for "Court of Military Appeals".

1992—Subsec. (a). Pub. L. 102–378 substituted "if" for "is" after "employee" in second sentence.

1990—Subsec. (a). Pub. L. 101–428 substituted "8339(a)–(e), (n), or (q)" for "8339(a)–(e) or (n)".

1989—Subsec. (a). Pub. L. 101–189 substituted "section 942(c) of title 10" for "section 867(a)(2) of title 10".

1988—Subsec. (f). Pub. L. 100–238 added subsec. (f) and struck out former subsec. (f) which read as follows: "An individual is not entitled to receive an annuity under this subchapter and compensation for injury or disability to himself under subchapter I of chapter 81 of this title covering the same period of time. This provision does not bar the right of a claimant to the greater benefit conferred by either subchapter for any part of the same period of time. Neither this provision nor any provision of subchapter I of chapter 81 of this title denies to an individual an annuity accruing to him under this subchapter on account of service performed by him, or denies any concurrent benefit to him under subchapter I of chapter 81 of this title on account of the death of another individual."

Subsec. (g). Pub. L. 100–238 added subsec. (g) and struck out former subsec. (g) which read as follows: "The right of an individual entitled to an annuity under this subchapter is not affected because he has received a lump-sum payment for compensation under section 8135 of this title. However, if the annuity is payable on account of the same disability for which compensation under section 8135 of this title has been paid, so much of the compensation as has been paid for a period extended beyond the date the annuity becomes effective, as determined by the Department of Labor, shall be refunded to that Department to be covered into the Employees' Compensation Fund. Before the individual may receive the annuity he shall—

"(1) refund to the Department of Labor the amount representing the commuted compensation payments for the extended period; or

"(2) authorize the deduction of that amount from the annuity payable to him under this subchapter, which amount shall be transmitted to the Department of Labor for reimbursement to the Employees' Compensation Fund.

Deductions from the annuity may be made from accrued and accruing payments. When the Department of Labor finds that the financial circumstances of the annuitant warrant deferred refunding, deductions from the annuity may be prorated against and paid from accruing payments in such manner as that Department determines."

1983—Subsec. (a). Pub. L. 98–94 inserted provision that a judge of the United States Court of Military Appeals who completes 5 years of civilian service and who is found by the Office to be disabled for useful and efficient service as a judge of such court or who is removed for mental or physical disability under section 867(a)(2) of title 10 shall be retired on the judge's own application or upon such removal.

1982—Subsec. (d). Pub. L. 97–253, § 302(a)(1), (2), substituted "180 days" for "1 year" in provision relating to restoration of an annuitant to an earning capacity fairly comparable to the current rate of pay of the position occupied at the time of retirement, and "any calendar year" for "each of 2 succeeding calendar years".

Subsec. (h). Pub. L. 97–253, § 302(a)(3), added subsec. (h).

1980—Subsec. (a). Pub. L. 96–499 provided that an employee was to be considered disabled only if the employee were found by the Office of Personnel Management to be unable to render useful and efficient service in the employee's position and was not qualified for reassignment to a vacant position in the agency at the same grade or level and provided that an employee in the Postal Service was to be considered not qualified for such reassignment if such reassignment were to a position in a different craft or were inconsistent with the terms of the appropriate collective bargaining agreement.

1978—Subsecs. (a) to (c). Pub. L. 95–454 substituted "Office of Personnel Management" and "Office" for "Civil Service Commission" and "Commission", respectively, wherever appearing.

EFFECTIVE DATE OF 2000 AMENDMENT

Amendment by Pub. L. 106–553 effective on the first day of the first applicable pay period that begins on Dec. 21, 2000, and applicable only to an individual who is employed as a member of the Supreme Court Police after Dec. 21, 2000, see section 1(a)(2) [title III, § 308(i), (j)] of Pub. L. 106–553, set out in a Supreme Court Police Retirement note under section 8331 of this title.

EFFECTIVE DATE OF 1997 AMENDMENT

Amendment by Pub. L. 105–61 applicable to any annuity commencing before, on, or after Oct. 10, 1997, and effective with regard to any payment made after the first month following Oct. 10, 1997, see section 516(b) of Pub. L. 105–61, set out as a note under section 8334 of this title.

EFFECTIVE DATE OF 1988 AMENDMENT

Section 124(c) of Pub. L. 100–238 provided that:
"(1) IN GENERAL.—Except as provided in paragraph (2), the amendments made by this section [enacting section 8464a of this title, amending this section, renumbering section 8457 of this title as section 8456, and repealing former section 8456 of this title] shall be effective as of January 1, 1987, and shall apply with respect to benefits payable based on a death or disability occurring on or after that date.
"(2) EXCEPTION.—The amendment made by subsection (a)(1)(A) [amending this section] shall take effect on the date of the enactment of this Act [Jan. 8, 1988] and shall apply with respect to benefits payable based on a death or disability occurring on or after that date."

EFFECTIVE DATE OF 1982 AMENDMENT

Section 302(c) of Pub. L. 97–253, as amended by Pub. L. 97–346, § 3(i), Oct. 15, 1982, 96 Stat. 1649, provided that:
"(1) Except as provided in paragraphs (2) and (3), the amendments made by subsections (a) and (b) [amending this section and section 8347 of this title] shall take effective October 1, 1982.
"(2) The amendments made by paragraphs (1) and (2) of subsection (a) [amending this section] shall take effect with respect to income earned after December 31, 1982.
"(3) Subsection (h) of section 8337 of title 5, United States Code (as added by subsection (a)) shall apply to any technician (as defined in paragraph (1) of such subsection (h)) who is separated from employment as a technician on or after October 1, 1982. Such subsection (h) shall also apply to any technician separated from employment as a technician on or after December 31, 1979, and before October 1, 1982, if application therefor is made to the Office of Personnel Management within 12 months after the date of the enactment of this Act [Sept. 8, 1982]. Any annuity resulting from such application shall commence as of the day after the date such application is received by the Office."

EFFECTIVE DATE OF 1980 AMENDMENT

Amendment by Pub. L. 96–499 effective on 90th day after Dec. 5, 1980, see section 403(c) of Pub. L. 96–499, set out as a note under section 8331 of this title.

EFFECTIVE DATE OF 1978 AMENDMENT

Amendment by Pub. L. 95–454 effective 90 days after Oct. 13, 1978, see section 907 of Pub. L. 95–454, set out as a note under section 1101 of this title.

SECTION REFERRED TO IN OTHER SECTIONS

This section is referred to in sections 3304, 7511, 8339, 8343a, 8345, 8347, 8349, 8706, 8908 of this title; title 38 sections 7426, 7438; title 50 section 403s.

§ 8338. Deferred retirement

(a) An employee who is separated from the service or transferred to a position in which he does not continue subject to this subchapter after completing 5 years of civilian service is entitled to an annuity beginning at the age of 62 years.

(b) A Member who, after December 31, 1955, is separated from the service as a Member after completing 5 years of civilian service is entitled to an annuity beginning at the age of 62 years. A Member who is separated from the service after completing 10 or more years of Member service is entitled to an annuity beginning at the age of 60 years. A Member who is separated from the service after completing 20 or more years of service, including 10 or more years of Member service, is entitled to a reduced annuity beginning at the age of 50 years.

(c) A judge of the United States Court of Appeals for the Armed Forces who is separated from the service after completing 5 years of civilian service is entitled to an annuity beginning at the age of 62 years. A judge of such court who is separated from the service after completing the term of service for which he was appointed is entitled to an annuity. If an annuity is elected before the judge becomes 60 years of age, it shall be a reduced annuity.

(d) An annuity or reduced annuity authorized by this section is computed under section 8339 of this title.

(Pub. L. 89–554, Sept. 6, 1966, 80 Stat. 574; Pub. L. 90–83, § 1(77), Sept. 11, 1967, 81 Stat. 214; Pub. L. 98–94, title XII, § 1256(d), Sept. 24, 1983, 97 Stat. 702; Pub. L. 103–337, div. A, title IX, § 924(d)(1)(A), Oct. 5, 1994, 108 Stat. 2832.)

HISTORICAL AND REVISION NOTES
1966 ACT

Derivation	U.S. Code	Revised Statutes and Statutes at Large
....	5 U.S.C. 2258.	July 31, 1956, ch. 804, § 401 "Sec. 8", 70 Stat. 751. July 7, 1960, Pub. L. 86–604, § 1(c), 74 Stat. 358. July 12, 1960, Pub. L. 86–622, § 2(a), 74 Stat. 410.

In subsection (b), the words "after December 31, 1955" are substituted for "on or after January 1, 1956". The word "hereafter" is omitted as unnecessary.

Standard changes are made to conform with the definitions applicable and the style of this title as outlined in the preface to the report.

1967 ACT

This section amends 5 U.S.C. 8338(a) for consistency within the subchapter and to reflect that it is the individual, rather than the position, that is subject to the subchapter.

AMENDMENTS

1994—Subsec. (c). Pub. L. 103–337 substituted "Court of Appeals for the Armed Forces" for "Court of Military Appeals".
1983—Subsecs. (c), (d). Pub. L. 98–94 added subsec. (c), and redesignated former subsec. (c) as (d).

SAVINGS PROVISIONS DEFERRED ANNUITIES UNDER
LAWS REPEALED BY PUB. L. 90–83

Pub. L. 90–83, § 10(a), Sept. 11, 1967, 81 Stat. 222, provided that: "The right to a deferred annuity on satisfaction of the conditions attached thereto is continued notwithstanding the repeal by this Act of the law conferring the right."

SECTION REFERRED TO IN OTHER SECTIONS

This section is referred to in sections 8339, 8341 of this title; title 22 section 4051.

§ 8339. Computation of annuity

(a) Except as otherwise provided by this section, the annuity of an employee retiring under this subchapter is—

(1) 1½ percent of his average pay multiplied by so much of his total service as does not exceed 5 years; plus

(2) 1¾ percent of his average pay multiplied by so much of his total service as exceeds 5 years but does not exceed 10 years; plus

(3) 2 percent of his average pay multiplied by so much of his total service as exceeds 10 years.

However, when it results in a larger annuity, 1 percent of his average pay plus $25 is substituted for the percentage specified by paragraph (1), (2), or (3) of this subsection, or any combination thereof.

(b) The annuity of a Congressional employee, or former Congressional employee, retiring under this subchapter is computed under subsection (a) of this section, except, if he has had—

(1) at least 5 years' service as a Congressional employee or Member or any combination thereof; and

(2) deductions withheld from his pay or has made deposit covering his last 5 years of civilian service;

his annuity is computed with respect to his service as a Congressional employee, his military service not exceeding 5 years, and any Member service, by multiplying 2½ percent of his average pay by the years of that service.

(c) The annuity of a Member, or former Member with title to Member annuity, retiring under this subchapter is computed under subsection (a) of this section, except, if he has had at least 5 years' service as a Member or Congressional employee or any combination thereof, his annuity is computed with respect to—

(1) his service as a Member and so much of his military service as is creditable for the purpose of this paragraph; and

(2) his Congressional employee service;

by multiplying 2½ percent of his average pay by the years of that service.

(d)(1) The annuity of an employee retiring under section 8335(b) or 8336(c) of this title is—

(A) 2½ percent of his average pay multiplied by so much of his total service as does not exceed 20 years; plus

(B) 2 percent of his average pay multiplied by so much of his total service as exceeds 20 years.

(2) The annuity of an employee retiring under this subchapter who was employed by the Panama Canal Company or Canal Zone Government on September 30, 1979, is computed with respect to the period of continuous Panama Canal service from that date, disregarding any break in service of not more than 3 days, by adding—

(A) 2½ percent of the employee's average pay multiplied by so much of that service as does not exceed 20 years; plus

(B) 2 percent of the employee's average pay multiplied by so much of that service as exceeds 20 years.

(3) The annuity of an employee retiring under this subchapter who is employed by the Panama Canal Commission at any time during the period beginning October 1, 1990, and ending December 31, 1999, is computed, with respect to any period of service with the Panama Canal Commission, by adding—

(A) 2½ percent of the employee's average pay multiplied by so much of that service as does not exceed 20 years; plus

(B) 2 percent of the employee's average pay multiplied by so much of that service as exceeds 20 years.

(4)(A) In the case of an employee who has service as a law enforcement officer or firefighter to which paragraph (2) of this subsection applies, the annuity of that employee is increased by $8 for each full month of that service which is performed in the Republic of Panama.

(B) In the case of an employee retiring under this subchapter who—

(i) was employed as a law enforcement officer or firefighter by the Panama Canal Company or Canal Zone Government at any time during the period beginning March 31, 1979, and ending September 30, 1979; and

(ii) does not meet the age and service requirements of section 8336(c) of this title;

the annuity of that employee is increased by $12 for each full month of that service which occurred before October 1, 1979.

(C) An annuity increase under this paragraph does not apply with respect to service performed after completion of 20 years of service (or any combination of service) as a law enforcement officer or firefighter.

(5) For the purpose of this subsection—

(A) "Panama Canal service" means—

(i) service as an employee of the Panama Canal Commission; or

(ii) service at a permanent duty station in the Canal Zone or Republic of Panama as an employee of an Executive agency conducting operations in the Canal Zone or Republic of Panama; and

(B) "Executive agency" includes the Smithsonian Institution.

(6) The annuity of an employee retiring under section 8336(j) of this title is computed under subsection (a) of this section, except that with respect to service on or after December 21, 1972, the employee's annuity is—

(A) 2½ percent of the employee's average pay multiplied by so much of the employee's service on or after that date as does not exceed 20 years; plus

(B) 2 percent of the employee's average pay multiplied by so much of the employee's service on or after that date as exceeds 20 years.

(7) The annuity of an employee who is a judge of the United States Court of Appeals for the Armed Forces, or a former judge of such court, retiring under this subchapter is computed under subsection (a) of this section, except, with respect to his service as a judge of such court, his service as a Member, his congressional employee service, and his military service (not exceeding 5 years) creditable under section 8332 of this title, his annuity is computed by multiplying 2½ percent of his average pay by the years of that service.

(e) The annuity of an employee retiring under section 8336(e) of this title is computed under subsection (a) of this section. That annuity may not be less than 50 percent of the average pay of the employee unless such employee has received, pursuant to section 8342 of this title, payment of the lump-sum credit attributable to deductions under section 8334(a) of this title during any period of employment as an air traffic controller and such employee has not deposited in the Fund the amount received, with interest, pursuant to section 8334(d)(1) of this title.

(f) The annuity computed under subsections (a) through (e), (n), (q), (r), and (s) may not exceed 80 percent of—

(1) the average pay of the employee; or

(2) the greatest of—

(A) the final basic pay of the Member;

(B) the average pay of the Member; or

(C) the final basic pay of the appointive position of a former Member who elects to have his annuity computed or recomputed under section 8344(d)(1) of this title.

(g) The annuity of an employee or Member retiring under section 8337 of this title is at least the smaller of—

(1) 40 percent of his average pay; or

(2) the sum obtained under subsections (a) through (c), (n), (q), (r), or (s) after increasing his service of the type last performed by the period elapsing between the date of separation and the date he becomes 60 years of age.

However, if an employee or Member retiring under section 8337 of this title is receiving retired pay or retainer pay for military service (except that specified in section 8332(c)(1) or (2) of this title) or pension or compensation from the Department of Veterans Affairs in lieu of such retired or retainer pay, the annuity of that employee or Member shall be computed under subsection (a), (b), (c), (n), (q), (r), or (s), as appropriate, excluding credit for military service from that computation. If the amount of the annuity so computed, plus the retired or retainer pay which is received, or which would be received but for the pension or compensation from the Department of Veterans Affairs in lieu of such retired or retainer pay, is less than the smaller of the annuity otherwise payable under paragraph (1) or (2) of this subsection, an amount equal to the difference shall be added to the annuity payable under subsection (a), (b), (c), (n), (q), (r), or (s), as appropriate.

(h) The annuity computed under subsections (a), (b), (d)(5), and (f) of this section for an employee retiring under section 8336(d), (h), (j), or (o) of this title is reduced by 1/6 of 1 percent for each full month the employee is under 55 years of age at the date of separation, except that such reduction shall not apply in the case of an employee retiring under section 8336(h) for failure to be recertified as a senior executive. The annuity computed under subsections (c) and (f) of this section for a Member retiring under the second or third sentence of section 8336(g) of this title or the third sentence of section 8338(b) of this title is reduced by 1/12 of 1 percent for each full month not in excess of 60 months, and 1/6 of 1 percent for each full month in excess of 60 months the Member is under 60 years of age at the date of separation. The annuity computed under subsections (a), (d)(6), and (f) of this section for a judge of the United States Court of Appeals for the Armed Forces retiring under the second sentence of section 8336(k) of this title or the third sentence of section 8338(c) of this title is reduced by 1/12 of 1 percent for each full month not in excess of 60 months, and 1/6 of 1 percent for each full month in excess of 60 months, the judge is under 60 years of age at the date of separation.

(i) For the purposes of subsections (a)–(h), (n), (q), (r), or (s), the total service of any employee or Member shall not include any period of civilian service after July 31, 1920, for which retirement deductions or deposits have not been made under section 8334(a) of this title unless—

(1) the employee or Member makes a deposit for such period as provided in section 8334(c) or (d)(1) of this title; or

(2) no deposit is required for such service, as provided under section 8334(g) of this title or under any statute.

(j)(1) The annuity computed under subsections (a)–(i), (n), (q), (r), and (s) (or a portion of the annuity, if jointly designated for this purpose by the employee or Member and the spouse of the employee or Member under procedures prescribed by the Office of Personnel Management) for an employee or Member who is married at the time of retiring under this subchapter is reduced as provided in paragraph (4) of this subsection in order to provide a survivor annuity for the spouse under section 8341(b) of this title, unless the employee or Member and the spouse jointly waive the spouse's right to a survivor annuity in a written election filed with the Office at the time that the employee or Member retires. Each such election shall be made in accordance with such requirements as the Office shall, by regulation, prescribe, and shall be irrevocable. The Office shall provide, by regulation, that an employee or Member may waive the survivor annuity without the spouse's consent if the employee or Member establishes to the satisfaction of the Office—

(A) that the spouse's whereabouts cannot be determined, or

(B) that, due to exceptional circumstances, requiring the employee or Member to seek the spouse's consent would otherwise be inappropriate.

(2) If an employee or Member has a former spouse who is entitled to a survivor annuity as provided in section 8341(h) of this title, the annuity of the employee or Member computed under subsections (a)–(i), (n), (q), (r), and (s) (or any designated portion of the annuity, in the event that the former spouse is entitled to less than 55 percent of the employee or Member's annuity) is reduced as provided in paragraph (4) of this subsection.

(3) An employee or Member who has a former spouse may elect, under procedures prescribed by the Office, to have the annuity computed under subsections (a)–(i), (n), (q), (r), and (s) or a portion thereof reduced as provided in paragraph (4) of this subsection in order to provide a survivor annuity for such former spouse under section 8341(h) of this title, unless all rights to survivor benefits for such former spouse under this subchapter based on marriage to such employee or Member were waived under paragraph (1) of this subsection. An election under this paragraph shall be made at the time of retire-

ment or, if later, within 2 years after the date on which the marriage of the former spouse to the employee or Member is dissolved, subject to a deposit in the Fund by the retired employee or Member of an amount determined by the Office, as nearly as may be administratively feasible, to reflect the amount by which the annuity of such employee or Member would have been reduced if the election had been continuously in effect since the date the annuity commenced, plus interest. For the purposes of the preceding sentence, the annual rate of interest for each year during which the annuity would have been reduced if the election had been in effect since the date the annuity commenced shall be 6 percent. The Office shall, by regulation, provide for payment of the deposit required under this paragraph by a reduction in the annuity of the employee or Member. The reduction shall, to the extent practicable, be designed so that the present value of the future reduction is actuarially equivalent to the deposit required under this paragraph, except that the total reductions in the annuity of an employee or Member to pay deposits required by the provisions of this paragraph, paragraph (5), or subsection (k)(2) shall not exceed 25 percent of the annuity computed under subsections (a) through (i), (n), (q), and (r), including adjustments under section 8340. The reduction, which shall be effective on the same date as the election under this paragraph, shall be permanent and unaffected by any future termination of the entitlement of the former spouse. Such reduction shall be independent of and in addition to the reduction required under the first sentence of this paragraph. An election under this paragraph—

(A) shall not be effective to the extent that it—

(i) conflicts with—

(I) any court order or decree referred to in subsection (h)(1) of section 8341 of this title, which was issued before the date of such election; or

(II) any agreement referred to in such subsection which was entered into before such date; or

(ii) would cause the total of survivor annuities payable under subsections (b), (d), (f), and (h) of section 8341 of this title based on the service of the employee or Member to exceed 55 percent of the annuity to which the employee or Member is entitled under subsections (a)–(i), (n), (q), (r), and (s); and

(B) shall not be effective, in the case of an employee or Member who is then married, unless it is made with the spouse's written consent.

The Office shall provide by regulation that subparagraph (B) of this paragraph may be waived for either of the reasons set forth in the last sentence of paragraph (1) of this subsection. In the case of a retired employee or Member whose annuity is being reduced in order to provide a survivor annuity for a former spouse, an election to provide or increase a survivor annuity for any other former spouse (and to continue an appropriate reduction) may be made within the same period that, and subject to the same conditions under which, an election could be made under paragraph (5)(B) of this subsection for a current spouse (subject to the provisions of this paragraph relating to consent of a current spouse, if the retired employee or Member is then married). The opportunity to make an election under the preceding sentence is in addition to any opportunity otherwise afforded under this paragraph.

(4) In order to provide a survivor annuity or combination of survivor annuities under subsections (b), (d), (f), and (h) of section 8341 of this title, the annuity of an employee or Member (or any designated portion or portions thereof) is reduced by 2½ percent of the first $3,600 thereof plus 10 percent of so much thereof as exceeds $3,600.

(5)(A) Any reduction in an annuity for the purpose of providing a survivor annuity for the current spouse of a retired employee or Member shall be terminated for each full month—

(i) after the death of the spouse, or

(ii) after the dissolution of the spouse's marriage to the employee or Member, except that an appropriate reduction shall be made thereafter if the spouse is entitled, as a former spouse, to a survivor annuity under section 8341(h) of this title.

(B) Any reduction in an annuity for the purpose of providing a survivor annuity for a former spouse of a retired employee or Member shall be terminated for each full month after the former spouse remarries before reaching age 55 or dies. This reduction shall be replaced by an appropriate reduction or reductions under paragraph (4) of this subsection if the retired employee or Member has (i) another former spouse who is entitled to a survivor annuity under section 8341(h) of this title, (ii) a current spouse to whom the employee or Member was married at the time of retirement and with respect to whom a survivor annuity was not jointly waived under paragraph (1) of this subsection, or (iii) a current spouse whom the employee or Member married after retirement and with respect to whom an election has been made under subparagraph (C) of this paragraph or subsection (k)(2) of this section.

(C)(i) Upon remarriage, a retired employee or Member who was married at the time of retirement (including an employee or Member whose annuity was not reduced to provide a survivor annuity for the employee or Member's spouse or former spouse as of the time of retirement) may irrevocably elect during such marriage, in a signed writing received by the Office within 2 years after such remarriage or, if later, within 2 years after the death or remarriage of any former spouse of such employee or Member who was entitled to a survivor annuity under section 8341(h) of this title (or of the last such surviving former spouse, if there was more than one), a reduction in the employee or Member's annuity under paragraph (4) of this subsection for the purpose of providing an annuity for such employee or Member's spouse in the event such spouse survives the employee or Member.

(ii) Such election and reduction shall be effective the first day of the second month after the election is received by the Office, but not less than 9 months after the date of the remarriage, and the retired employee or Member shall deposit in the Fund an amount determined by the Office of Personnel Management, as nearly as may be administratively feasible, to reflect the amount by which the annuity of such retired employee or Member would have been reduced if the election had been in effect since the date of retirement or, if later, the date the previous reduction in such retired employee or Member's annuity was terminated under subparagraph (A) or (B) of this paragraph, plus interest. For the purposes of the preceding sentence, the annual rate of interest for each year during which an annuity would have been reduced if the election had been in effect on and after the applicable date referred to in such sentence shall be 6 percent.

(iii) The Office shall, by regulation, provide for payment of the deposit required under clause (ii) by a reduction in the annuity of the employee or Member. The reduction shall, to the extent practicable, be designed so that the present value of the future reduction is actuarially equivalent to the deposit required under clause (ii), except that total reductions in the annuity of an employee or Member to pay deposits required by the provisions of this paragraph or paragraph (3) shall not exceed 25 percent of the annuity computed under subsections (a) through (i), (n), (q), and (r), including adjustments under section 8340. The reduction required by this clause, which shall be effective on the same date as the election under clause (i), shall be permanent and unaffected by any future termination of the marriage. Such reduction shall be independent of and in addition to the reduction required under clause (i).

(iv) Notwithstanding any other provision of this subparagraph, an election under this subparagraph may not be made for the purpose of providing an annuity in the case of a spouse by remarriage if such spouse was married to the employee or Member at the time of such employee or Member's retirement, and all rights to survivor benefits for such spouse under this subchapter based on marriage to such employee or Member were then waived under paragraph (1) of this subsection or a similar prior provision of law.

(v) An election to provide a survivor annuity to a person under this subparagraph—

(I) shall prospectively void any election made by the employee or Member under subsection (k)(1) of this section with respect to such person; or

(II) shall, if an election was made by the employee or Member under such subsection (k)(1) with respect to a different person, prospectively void such election if appropriate written application is made by such employee or Member at the time of making the election under this subparagraph.

(vi) The deposit provisions of clauses (ii) and (iii) of this subparagraph shall not apply if—

(I) the employee or Member makes an election under this subparagraph after having made an election under subsection (k)(1) of this section; and

(II) the election under such subsection (k)(1) becomes void under clause (v) of this subparagraph.

(k)(1) At the time of retiring under section 8336 or 8338 of this title, an employee or Member who is found to be in good health by the Office may elect a reduced annuity instead of an annuity computed under subsections (a)–(i), (n), (q), (r), and (s) and name in writing an individual having an insurable interest in the employee or Member to receive an annuity under section 8341(c) of this title after the death of the retired employee or Member. The annuity of the employee or Member making the election is reduced by 10 percent, and by 5 percent for each full 5 years the individual named is younger than the retiring employee or Member. However, the total reduction may not exceed 40 percent. An annuity which is reduced under this paragraph or any similar prior provision of law shall, effective the first day of the month following the death of the individual named under this paragraph, be recomputed and paid as if the annuity had not been so reduced. In the case of a married employee or Member, an election under this paragraph on behalf of the spouse may be made only if any right of such spouse to a survivor annuity based on the service of such employee or Member is waived in accordance with subsection (j)(1) of this section.

(2)(A) An employee or Member, who is unmarried at the time of retiring under a provision of law which permits election of a reduced annuity with a survivor annuity payable to such employee or Member's spouse and who later marries, may irrevocably elect, in a signed writing received in the Office within 2 years after such employee or Member marries or, if later, within 2 years after the death or remarriage of any former spouse of such employee or Member who was entitled to a survivor annuity under section 8341(h) of this title (or of the last such surviving former spouse, if there was more than one), a reduction in the retired employee or Member's current annuity as provided in subsection (j) of this section.

(B)(i) The election and reduction shall take effect on the first day of the first month beginning after the expiration of the 9-month period beginning on the date of marriage. Any such election to provide a survivor annuity for a person—

(I) shall prospectively void any election made by the employee or Member under paragraph (1) of this subsection with respect to such person; or

(II) shall, if an election was made by the employee or Member under such paragraph with respect to a different person, prospectively void such election if appropriate written application is made by such employee or Member at the time of making the election under this paragraph.

(ii) The retired employee or Member shall deposit in the Fund an amount determined by the Office of Personnel Management, as nearly as may be administratively feasible, to reflect the amount by which the retired employee or Member's annuity would have been reduced under subsection (j)(4) of this section since the commencing date of the annuity, if the employee or Member had been married at the time of retirement and had elected to provide a survivor annuity at that time, plus interest. For the purposes of the preceding sentence, the annual rate of interest for each year during which the annuity would have been reduced if the election had been in effect since the date of the annuity commenced shall be 6 percent.

(C) The Office shall, by regulation, provide for payment of the deposit required under subparagraph (B)(ii) by a reduction in the annuity of the employee or Member. The reduction shall, to the extent practicable, be designed so that the present value of the future reduction is actuarially equivalent to the deposit required under subparagraph (B)(ii), except that total reductions in the annuity of an employee or Member to pay deposits required by this subsection or subsection (j)(3) shall not exceed 25 percent of the annuity computed under subsections (a) through (i), (n), (q), and (r), including adjustments under section 8340. The reduction required by this subparagraph, which shall be effective on the same date as the election under subparagraph (A), shall be permanent and unaffected by any future termination of the marriage. Such reduction shall be independent of and in addition to the reduction required under subparagraph (A).

(D) Subparagraphs (B)(ii) and (C) of this paragraph shall not apply if—

(i) the employee or Member makes an election under this paragraph after having made an election under paragraph (1) of this subsection; and

(ii) the election under such paragraph (1) becomes void under subparagraph (B)(i) of this paragraph.

(*l*) The annuity computed under subsections (a)–(k), (n), (q), (r), and (s) for an employee who is a citizen of the United States is increased by $36 for each year of service in the employ of—

(1) the Alaska Engineering Commission, or The Alaska Railroad, in Alaska between March 12, 1914, and July 1, 1923; or

(2) the Isthmian Canal Commission, or the Panama Railroad Company, on the Isthmus of Panama between May 4, 1904, and April 1, 1914.

(m) In computing any annuity under subsections (a) through (e), (n), (q), (r), and (s), the total service of an employee who retires on an immediate annuity or dies leaving a survivor or survivors entitled to annuity includes, without regard to the limitations imposed by subsection (f) of this section, the days of unused sick leave to his credit under a formal leave system, except that these days will not be counted in determining average pay or annuity eligible under this subchapter. For the purpose of this subsection, in the case of any such employee who is excepted from subchapter I of chapter 63 of this title under section 6301(2)(x)–(xiii) of this title, the days of unused sick leave to his credit include any unused sick leave standing to his credit when he was excepted from such subchapter.

(n) The annuity of an employee who is a Court of Federal Claims judge, bankruptcy judge, or United States magistrate judge is computed, with respect to service as a Court of Federal Claims judge, as a commissioner of the Court of Claims, as a referee in bankruptcy, as a bankruptcy judge, as a United States magistrate judge, and as a United States commissioner, and

with respect to the military service of any such individual (not exceeding 5 years) creditable under section 8332 of this title, by multiplying 2½ percent of the individual's average pay by the years of that service.

(*o*)(1)(A) An employee or Member—

(i) who, at the time of retirement, is married, and

(ii) who notifies the Office at such time (in accordance with subsection (j)) that a survivor annuity under section 8341(b) of this title is not desired,

may, during the 18-month period beginning on the date of the retirement of such employee or Member, elect to have a reduction under subsection (j) made in the annuity of the employee or Member (or in such portion thereof as the employee or Member may designate) in order to provide a survivor annuity for the spouse of such employee or Member.

(B) An employee or Member—

(i) who, at the time of retirement, is married, and

(ii) who at such time designates (in accordance with subsection (j)) that a limited portion of the annuity of such employee or Member is to be used as the base for a survivor annuity under section 8341(b) of this title,

may, during the 18-month period beginning on the date of the retirement of such employee or Member, elect to have a greater portion of the annuity of such employee or Member so used.

(2)(A) An election under subparagraph (A) or (B) of paragraph (1) of this subsection shall not be considered effective unless the amount specified in subparagraph (B) of this paragraph is deposited into the Fund before the expiration of the applicable 18-month period under paragraph (1).

(B) The amount to be deposited with respect to an election under this subsection is an amount equal to the sum of—

(i) the additional cost to the System which is associated with providing a survivor annuity under subsection (b)(2) of this section and results from such election taking into account (I) the difference (for the period between the date on which the annuity of the participant or former participant commences and the date of the election) between the amount paid to such participant or former participant under this subchapter and the amount which would have been paid if such election had been made at the time the participant or former participant applied for the annuity, and (II) the costs associated with providing for the later election; and

(ii) interest on the additional cost determined under clause (i) of this subparagraph computed using the interest rate specified or determined under section 8334(e) of this title for the calendar year in which the amount to be deposited is determined.

(3) An election by an employee or Member under this subsection voids prospectively any election previously made in the case of such employee or Member under subsection (j).

(4) An annuity which is reduced in connection with an election under this subsection shall be reduced by the same percentage reductions as

were in effect at the time of the retirement of the employee or Member whose annuity is so reduced.

(5) Rights and obligations resulting from the election of a reduced annuity under this subsection shall be the same as the rights and obligations which would have resulted had the employee or Member involved elected such annuity at the time of retiring.

(6) The Office shall, on an annual basis, inform each employee or Member who is eligible to make an election under this subsection of the right to make such election and the procedures and deadlines applicable to such election.

(p)(1) In computing an annuity under this subchapter for an employee whose service includes service that was performed on a part-time basis—

(A) the average pay of the employee, to the extent that it includes pay for service performed in any position on a part-time basis, shall be determined by using the annual rate of basic pay that would be payable for full-time service in the position; and

(B) the benefit so computed shall then be multiplied by a fraction equal to the ratio which the employee's actual service, as determined by prorating an employee's total service to reflect the service that was performed on a part-time basis, bears to the total service that would be creditable for the employee if all of the service had been performed on a full-time basis.

(2) For the purpose of this subsection, employment on a part-time basis shall not be considered to include employment on a temporary or intermittent basis.

(q) The annuity of a member of the Capitol Police, or former member of the Capitol Police, retiring under this subchapter is computed in accordance with subsection (b), except that, in the case of a member who retires under section 8335(c) or 8336(m), and who meets the requirements of subsection (b)(2), the annuity of such member is—

(1) 2½ percent of the member's average pay multiplied by so much of such member's total service as does not exceed 20 years; plus

(2) 2 percent of the member's average pay multiplied by so much of such member's total service as exceeds 20 years.

(r) The annuity of a member of the Supreme Court Police, or former member of the Supreme Court Police, retiring under this subchapter is computed in accordance with subsection (d).

(s)[1] The annuity of a Member who has served in a position in the executive branch for which the rate of basic pay was reduced for the duration of the service of the Member in that position to remove the impediment to the appointment of the Member imposed by article I, section 6, clause 2 of the Constitution, shall, subject to a deposit in the Fund as provided under section 8334(m), be computed as though the rate of basic pay which would otherwise have been in effect during that period of service had been in effect.

(s)(1)[1] For purposes of this subsection, the term "physicians comparability allowance" refers to an amount described in section 8331(3)(H).

(2) Except as otherwise provided in this subsection, no part of a physicians comparability allowance shall be treated as basic pay for purposes of any computation under this section unless, before the date of the separation on which entitlement to annuity is based, the separating individual has completed at least 15 years of service as a Government physician (whether performed before, on, or after the date of the enactment of this subsection).

(3) If the condition under paragraph (2) is met, then, any amounts received by the individual in the form of a physicians comparability allowance shall (for the purposes referred to in paragraph (2)) be treated as basic pay, but only to the extent that such amounts are attributable to service performed on or after the date of the enactment of this subsection, and only to the extent of the percentage allowable, which shall be determined as follows:

If the total amount of service performed, on or after the date of the enactment of this subsection, as a Government physician is:	Then, the percentage allowable is:
Less than 2 years	0
At least 2 but less than 4 years	25
At least 4 but less than 6 years	50
At least 6 but less than 8 years	75
At least 8 years	100.

(4) Notwithstanding any other provision of this subsection, 100 percent of all amounts received as a physicians comparability allowance shall, to the extent attributable to service performed on or after the date of the enactment of this subsection, be treated as basic pay (without regard to any of the preceding provisions of this subsection) for purposes of computing—

(A) an annuity under subsection (g); and

(B) a survivor annuity under section 8341, if based on the service of an individual who dies before separating from service.

(Pub. L. 89–554, Sept. 6, 1966, 80 Stat. 574; Pub. L. 90–83, §1(78), Sept. 11, 1967, 81 Stat. 214; Pub. L. 90–206, title II, §224(b), Dec. 16, 1967, 81 Stat. 642; Pub. L. 90–486, §5(c), Aug. 13, 1968, 82 Stat. 757; Pub. L. 91–93, title II, §203, Oct. 20, 1969, 83 Stat. 139; Pub. L. 91–658, §2, Jan. 8, 1971, 84 Stat. 1961; Pub. L. 92–297, §§6, 7(3), May 16, 1972, 86 Stat. 144; Pub. L. 93–260, §2(a), Apr. 9, 1974, 88 Stat. 76; Pub. L. 93–350, §6, July 12, 1974, 88 Stat. 356; Pub. L. 93–474, §1, Oct. 26, 1974, 88 Stat. 1438; Pub. L. 94–126, §1(b), Nov. 12, 1975, 89 Stat. 679; Pub. L. 94–397, §1(d), Sept. 3, 1976, 90 Stat. 1203; Pub. L. 95–256, §5(d), Apr. 6, 1978, 92 Stat. 191; Pub. L. 95–317, §§1(a), (c), 2, July 10, 1978, 92 Stat. 382; Pub. L. 95–454, title IV, §412(b), title IX, §906(a)(2), (3), Oct. 13, 1978, 92 Stat. 1175, 1224; Pub. L. 95–519, §3, Oct. 25, 1978, 92 Stat. 1819; Pub. L. 95–598, title III, §338(a), Nov. 6, 1978, 92 Stat. 2681; Pub. L. 96–54, §2(a)(49), Aug. 14, 1979, 93 Stat. 384; Pub. L. 96–70, title I, §1242(a), Sept. 27, 1979, 93 Stat. 472; Pub. L. 96–135, §1(b), (c), Dec. 5, 1979, 93 Stat. 1057; Pub. L. 96–391, §1, Oct. 7, 1980, 94 Stat. 1557; Pub. L. 96–499, title IV, §404(a), Dec. 5, 1980, 94 Stat. 2606; Pub. L. 97–253, title III, §303(b), Sept. 8, 1982, 96 Stat. 794; Pub. L. 97–276, §151(f), Oct. 2, 1982, 96 Stat. 1202; Pub.

---

[1] So in original. Two subsecs. (s) have been enacted.

L. 98–94, title XII, §1256(e), Sept. 24, 1983, 97 Stat. 702; Pub. L. 98–249, §3(a), Mar. 31, 1984, 98 Stat. 117; Pub. L. 98–271, §3(a), Apr. 30, 1984, 98 Stat. 163; Pub. L. 98–299, §3(a), May 25, 1984, 98 Stat. 214; Pub. L. 98–325, §3(a), June 20, 1984, 98 Stat. 268; Pub. L. 98–353, title I, §§112, 116(d), 121(f), July 10, 1984, 98 Stat. 343, 344, 346; Pub. L. 98–531, §2(c), Oct. 19, 1984, 98 Stat. 2704; Pub. L. 98–615, §2(3), Nov. 8, 1984, 98 Stat. 3195; Pub. L. 99–251, title II, §203(a)–(c), title III, §307(a), Feb. 27, 1986, 100 Stat. 23, 24, 28; Pub. L. 99–272, title XV, §15204(a)(1), Apr. 7, 1986, 100 Stat. 334; Pub. L. 100–53, §2(d), June 18, 1987, 101 Stat. 368; Pub. L. 101–194, title V, §506(b)(8), Nov. 30, 1989, 103 Stat. 1759; Pub. L. 101–428, §2(c)(1), (d)(2)–(6), Oct. 15, 1990, 104 Stat. 928, 929; Pub. L. 101–508, title VII, §7001(b)(2)(B), (C), Nov. 5, 1990, 104 Stat. 1388–329; Pub. L. 101–510, div. C, title XXXV, §3506(b), Nov. 5, 1990, 104 Stat. 1847; Pub. L. 101–650, title III, §§306(c)(4), 321, Dec. 1, 1990, 104 Stat. 5110, 5117; Pub. L. 102–54, §13(b)(4), June 13, 1991, 105 Stat. 274; Pub. L. 102–198, §7(b), Dec. 9, 1991, 105 Stat. 1624; Pub. L. 102–378, §2(62), Oct. 2, 1992, 106 Stat. 1354; Pub. L. 102–572, title IX, §902(b)(2), Oct. 29, 1992, 106 Stat. 4516; Pub. L. 103–66, title XI, §11004(a)(1), (2), Aug. 10, 1993, 107 Stat. 410, 411; Pub. L. 103–337, div. A, title IX, §924(d)(1)(A), Oct. 5, 1994, 108 Stat. 2832; Pub. L. 104–106, div. A, title XV, §1505(b)(3), Feb. 10, 1996, 110 Stat. 514; Pub. L. 105–61, title V, §516(a)(3), Oct. 10, 1997, 111 Stat. 1306; Pub. L. 105–261, div. A, title XI, §1109(c)(1), Oct. 17, 1998, 112 Stat. 2145; Pub. L. 106–58, title VI, §651(b), Sept. 29, 1999, 113 Stat. 480; Pub. L. 106–398, §1 [[div. A], title X, §1087(f)(4), title XI, §1152(c)(1)], Oct. 30, 2000, 114 Stat. 1654, 1654A–293, 1654A–322; Pub. L. 106–553, §1(a)(2) [title III, §308(b)(4), (h)(2)–(6)], Dec. 21, 2000, 114 Stat. 2762, 2762A–87 to 2762A–89; Pub. L. 106–554, §1(a)(4) [div. B, title I, §141(b)], Dec. 21, 2000, 114 Stat. 2763, 2763A–235; Pub. L. 106–571, §3(b)(1), Dec. 28, 2000, 114 Stat. 3055.)

HISTORICAL AND REVISION NOTES
1966 ACT

Derivation	U.S. Code	Revised Statutes and Statutes at Large
....	5 U.S.C. 2259.	July 31, 1956, ch. 804, §401 "Sec. 9", 70 Stat. 752. July 7, 1960, Pub. L. 86–604, §1(d), (e), 74 Stat. 358. July 12, 1960, Pub. L. 86–622, §2(b), 74 Stat. 410. Oct. 4, 1961, Pub. L. 87–350, §6, 75 Stat. 772. Oct. 11, 1962, Pub. L. 87–793, §1103(a), 76 Stat. 870.

The section is reorganized to eliminate repetition.

In subsection (f)(2), the words "service of the type last performed" are substituted for "total service" in former section 2259(a), "service as a Congressional employee" in former section 2259(b), and "Member service" in former section 2259(c).

In subsection (i), the words "by the employee or Member at the time of retirement" are added on authority of former section 2260(a)(1), which is carried into section 8341(b).

In subsection (j), the words "an annuity computed as provided in section 2259 of this title" and "an annuity so computed" are omitted as unnecessary as former sections 2256 and 2258, which are carried into this title as sections 8336 and 8338, respectively, expressly require that the annuities authorized thereby must be computed under former section 2259, which is carried into this section.

Standard changes are made to conform with the definitions applicable and the style of this title as outlined in the preface to the report.

1967 ACT

Section of title 5	Source (U.S. Code)	Source (Statutes at Large)
8339(g)	5 App.: 2259(d).	July 18, 1966, Pub. L. 89–504, §505, 80 Stat. 301.

REFERENCES IN TEXT

The date of the enactment of this subsection, referred to in subsec. (s), is the date of enactment of Pub. L. 106–571, which was approved Dec. 28, 2000.

AMENDMENTS

2000—Subsec. (f). Pub. L. 106–553, §1(a)(2) [title III, §308(h)(2)], substituted "subsections (a) through (e), (n), (q), (r), and (s)" for "subsections (a)–(e), (n), (q), and (r)" in introductory provisions.

Subsec. (g). Pub. L. 106–553, §1(a)(2) [title III, §308(h)(3)(B)], substituted "(q), (r), or (s)" for "(q), or (r)" in two places in concluding provisions.

Pub. L. 106–398, §1 [[div. A], title X, §1087(f)(4)], struck out "the application of the limitation in section 5532 of this title, or" after "received but for" in concluding provisions.

Subsec. (g)(2). Pub. L. 106–553, §1(a)(2) [title III, §308(h)(3)(A)], substituted "subsections (a) through (c), (n), (q), (r), or (s)" for "subsections (a)–(c), (n), (q), or (r)".

Subsec. (h). Pub. L. 106–398, §1 [[div. A], title XI, §1152(c)(1)], substituted "(j), or (o)" for "or (j)" in first sentence.

Subsec. (i). Pub. L. 106–553, §1(a)(2) [title III, §308(h)(4)], substituted "(a)–(h), (n), (q), (r), or (s)" for "(a)–(h), (n), (q), and (r)" in introductory provisions.

Subsecs. (j), (k)(1). Pub. L. 106–553, §1(a)(2) [title III, §308(h)(5)], substituted "(a)–(i), (n), (q), (r), and (s)" for "(a)–(i), (n), (q), and (r)" wherever appearing.

Subsec. (l). Pub. L. 106–553, §1(a)(2) [title III, §308(h)(6)], substituted "(a)–(k), (n), (q), (r), and (s)" for "(a)–(k), (n), (q), and (r)" in introductory provisions.

Subsec. (m). Pub. L. 106–553, §1(a)(2) [title III, §308(h)(2)], substituted "subsections (a) through (e), (n), (q), (r), and (s)" for 'subsections (a)–(e), (n), (q), and (r)".

Subsec. (q). Pub. L. 106–554 substituted "8335(c)" for "8335(d)".

Subsec. (r). Pub. L. 106–553, §1(a)(2) [title III, §308(b)(4)], added subsec. (r). Former subsec. (r), relating to the annuity of a Member who has served in a position in the executive branch, redesignated (s).

Subsec. (s). Pub. L. 106–571 added subsec. (s), relating to physicians comparability allowance.

Pub. L. 106–553, §1(a)(2) [title III, §308(b)(4)], redesignated subsec. (r), relating to computation of annuity of a Member who has served in a position in the executive branch, as (s).

1999—Subsec. (h). Pub. L. 106–58 repealed Pub. L. 105–261, §1109(c)(1). See 1998 Amendment note below.

1998—Subsec. (h). Pub. L. 105–261, §1109(c)(1), which directed substitution of "(j), or (o)" for "or (j)" in the first sentence, was repealed by Pub. L. 106–58.

1997—Subsec. (f). Pub. L. 105–61, §516(a)(3)(A), substituted "(q), and (r)" for "and (q) of this section".

Subsec. (g). Pub. L. 105–61, §516(a)(3)(B), substituted "(q), or (r)" for "or (q) of this section" in par. (2) and in two places in concluding provisions.

Subsecs. (i) to (m). Pub. L. 105–61, §516(a)(3)(A), substituted "(q), and (r)" for "and (q)" and "and (q) of this section" wherever appearing.

Subsec. (r). Pub. L. 105–61, §516(a)(3)(C), added subsec. (r).

1996—Subsec. (d)(7). Pub. L. 104–106 substituted "Court of Appeals for the Armed Forces" for "Court of Military Appeals".

1994—Subsec. (d)(6). Pub. L. 103–337, which directed amendment of par. (6) by substituting "Court of Appeals for the Armed Forces'' for ''Court of Military Appeals'', could not be executed because the words ''Court of Military Appeals'' did not appear in par. (6).

Subsec. (h). Pub. L. 103–337 substituted ''Court of Appeals for the Armed Forces'' for ''Court of Military Appeals''.

1993—Subsec. (j)(3). Pub. L. 103–66, §11004(a)(1)(A)(i), struck out '', within such 2-year period,'' after ''retired employee or Member'' in second sentence.

Pub. L. 103–66, §11004(a)(1)(A)(ii), substituted fourth through seventh sentences for former fourth sentence which read as follows: ''If the employee or Member does not make such a deposit, the Office shall collect the amount of the deposit by offset against the employee or Member's annuity, up to a maximum of 25 percent of the net annuity otherwise payable to the employee or Member, and the employee or Member is deemed to consent to such offset.''

Subsec. (j)(5)(C)(ii). Pub. L. 103–66, §11004(a)(1)(B)(i), struck out '', within 2 years after the date of the remarriage or, if later, the death or remarriage of the former spouse (or of the last such surviving former spouse),'' after ''employee or Member shall''.

Subsec. (j)(5)(C)(iii). Pub. L. 103–66, §11004(a)(1)(B)(ii), amended cl. (iii) generally. Prior to amendment, cl. (iii) read as follows: ''If the employee or Member does not make such deposit, the Office shall collect such amount by offset against the employee or Member's annuity, up to a maximum of 25 percent of the net annuity otherwise payable to the employee or Member, and the employee or Member is deemed to consent to such offset.''

Subsec. (k)(2)(B)(ii). Pub. L. 103–66, §11004(a)(2)(A), which directed amendment of cl. (ii) by substituting in first sentence ''The retired employee'' for ''Within 2 years after the date of the marriage, the retired employee'', was executed by making the substitution for ''Within 2 years after the date of marriage, the retired employee'' to reflect the probable intent of Congress.

Subsec. (k)(2)(C). Pub. L. 103–66, §11004(a)(2)(B), amended subpar. (C) generally. Prior to amendment, subpar. (C) read as follows: ''If the employee or Member does not make such deposit, the Office shall collect such amount by offset against the employee or Member's annuity, up to a maximum of 25 percent of the net annuity otherwise payable to the employee or Member, and the employee or Member is deemed to consent to such offset.''

1992—Subsec. (n). Pub. L. 102–572 substituted ''Court of Federal Claims'' for ''Claims Court'' in two places.

Subsecs. (o), (p). Pub. L. 102–378, §2(62), redesignated subsec. (o), relating to employee whose service includes service performed on part-time basis, as (p).

1991—Subsec. (g). Pub. L. 102–54 substituted ''pension or compensation from the Department of Veterans Affairs'' for ''Veterans' Administration pension or compensation'' in second and third sentences.

Subsec. (n). Pub. L. 102–198 inserted a comma after ''United States commissioner''.

1990—Subsec. (d)(3) to (7). Pub. L. 101–510 added par. (3) and redesignated former pars. (3) to (6) as (4) to (7), respectively.

Subsec. (e). Pub. L. 101–508, §7001(b)(2)(C), substituted ''8334(d)(1)'' for ''8334(d)''.

Subsec. (f). Pub. L. 101–428, §2(d)(2), substituted ''(a)–(e), (n), and (q)'' for ''(a)–(e) and (n)''.

Subsec. (g). Pub. L. 101–428, §2(d)(3)(B), substituted ''(c), (n), or (q)'' for ''(c), or (n)'' wherever appearing in closing provisions.

Subsec. (g)(2). Pub. L. 101–428, §2(d)(3)(A), substituted ''(a)–(c), (n), or (q)'' for ''(a)–(c) or (n)''.

Subsec. (i). Pub. L. 101–428, §2(d)(4), substituted ''(a)–(h), (n), and (q)'' for ''(a)–(h) and (n)''.

Subsec. (i)(1). Pub. L. 101–508, §7001(b)(2)(B), substituted ''(d)(1)'' for ''(d)''.

Subsec. (j). Pub. L. 101–428, §2(d)(5), substituted ''(a)–(i), (n), and (q)'' for ''(a)–(i) and (n)'' in pars. (1) and (2), and in introductory provisions and subpar. (A)(ii) of par. (3).

Subsec. (k)(1). Pub. L. 101–428, §2(d)(5), substituted ''(a)–(i), (n), and (q)'' for ''(a)–(i) and (n)''.

Subsec. (l). Pub. L. 101–428, §2(d)(6), substituted ''(a)–(k), (n), and (q)'' for ''(a)–(k) and (n)''.

Subsec. (m). Pub. L. 101–428, §2(d)(2), substituted ''(a)–(e), (n), and (q)'' for ''(a)–(e) and (n)''.

Subsec. (n). Pub. L. 101–650 amended subsec. (n) generally. Prior to amendment, subsec. (n) read as follows: ''The annuity of an employee who is a bankruptcy judge or United States magistrate is computed, with respect to service as a referee in bankruptcy, as a bankruptcy judge, as a United States magistrate, and as a United States commissioner and with respect to the military service of any such individual (not exceeding 5 years) creditable under section 8332 of this title, by multiplying 2½ percent of the individual's average pay by the years of that service.''

Subsec. (q). Pub. L. 101–428, §2(c)(1), added subsec. (q).

1989—Subsec. (h). Pub. L. 101–194 inserted '', except that such reduction shall not apply in the case of an employee retiring under section 8336(h) for failure to be recertified as a senior executive'' before period at end of first sentence.

1987—Subsec. (n). Pub. L. 100–53 amended subsec. (n) generally. Prior to amendment, subsec. (n) read as follows: ''The annuity of an employee who is a bankruptcy judge is computed with respect to service after as a referee in bankruptcy and as a bankruptcy judge and his military service (not exceeding five years) creditable under section 8332 of this title by multiplying 2½ percent of his average annual pay by the years of that service.''

1986—Subsec. (j)(3). Pub. L. 99–251, §203(a), inserted '', unless all rights to survivor benefits for such former spouse under this subchapter based on marriage to such employee or Member were waived under paragraph (1) of this subsection'' at end of first sentence.

Subsec. (j)(5)(B). Pub. L. 99–251, §203(b), amended subpar. (B) generally. Prior to amendment, subpar. (B) read as follows:

''(B)(i) Any reduction in an annuity for the purpose of providing a survivor annuity for a former spouse of a retired employee or Member shall be terminated for each full month after the former spouse remarries before reaching age 55 or dies, unless the employee or Member elects, within 2 years after the former spouse's death or remarriage, to continue the reduction in order to provide a survivor annuity or increase the survivor annuity for the current spouse of the retired employee or Member.

''(ii) Notwithstanding clause (i) of this subparagraph—

''(I) a reduction in an annuity shall not be terminated under such clause, and

''(II) an election made under such clause with respect to a current spouse after a remarriage before age 55 or the death of a former spouse shall not be effective,

if, and to the extent that, continuation of the reduction is necessary in order to provide for any survivor annuity, or any increase in a survivor annuity, which becomes payable under section 8341(h)(2) of this title to any other former spouse as a result of such remarriage or death.''

Subsec. (j)(5)(C)(v), (vi). Pub. L. 99–251, §203(c)(1), added cls. (v) and (vi).

Subsec. (k)(1). Pub. L. 99–251, §203(c)(2), inserted at end ''In the case of a married employee or Member, an election under this paragraph on behalf of the spouse may be made only if any right of such spouse to a survivor annuity based on the service of such employee or Member is waived in accordance with subsection (j)(1) of this section.''

Subsec. (k)(2)(B)(i). Pub. L. 99–251, §203(c)(3)(A), substituted provisions directing that the election and reduction shall take effect on the first day of the first month beginning after the expiration of the 9-month period beginning on the date of marriage and that any such election to provide a survivor annuity for a person shall prospectively void any election made by the employee or Member under paragraph (1) of this subsection with respect to such person, or shall, if an election was made by the employee or Member under such paragraph with respect to a different person, prospectively void such election if appropriate written application is made by such employee or Member at the time of making the election under this paragraph, for provisions which directed that the election and reduction had to take effect the first day of the first month beginning 9 months after the date of marriage and would prospectively void any election previously made under paragraph (1) of this subsection.

Subsec. (k)(2)(B)(ii). Pub. L. 99–251, §203(c)(3)(B), struck out "(other than an employee or Member who made a previous election under paragraph (1) of this subsection)" after "retired employee or Member".

Subsec. (k)(2)(D). Pub. L. 99–251, §203(c)(3)(C), added subpar. (D).

Subsec. (o). Pub. L. 99–272 added subsec. (o), set out second, relating to computation of annuities for part-time service.

Pub. L. 99–251, §307(a), added subsec. (o), set out first, relating to 18-month period for election of survivor annuities.

1984—Subsec. (f). Pub. L. 98–353, §112, substituted "and (n)" for "and (o)".

Subsec. (g). Pub. L. 98–353, §116(d)(1), (2), inserted "or (n)" after "(c)" in par. (2), and substituted "(c), or (n)" for "or (c)" in two places in provisions following par. (2).

Subsec. (j)(1). Pub. L. 98–615, §2(3)(A), substituted provisions that at the time of retirement an employee's pension will be reduced to provide survivor benefits to the spouse unless the employee or Member and the spouse jointly waive the spouse's right to the survivor annuity in a written statement filed with the Office of Personnel Management which shall be made in accordance with such requirements as prescribed by the Office by regulation and which shall be irrevocable and that the Office, by regulation, must provide that an employee may waive the survivor annuity without the spouse's consent only when the spouse's whereabouts are unknown to the employee or, due to exceptional circumstances it would be inappropriate to require the employee to seek the spouse's consent for provisions that at the time of retirement an employee's pension would be reduced by 2½ percent of so much thereof as did not exceed $3,600 and by 10 percent of so much thereof as exceeded that amount, unless the employee or member notified the Office of Personnel Management in writing at the time of retirement that he did not desire any surviving spouse to receive an annuity under section 8341(b) of this title, and struck out provisions for the restoration to the employee or Member of his full pension, as if such reduction had not taken place, for each full month in which such employee or Member was not married, and providing the employee or Member a right of irrevocable election of reduction for the benefit of a subsequent spouse, in the event of remarriage, in an amount equal to the prior reduction, to take effect 1 year after remarriage.

Pub. L. 98–353, §112, substituted "and (n)" for "and (o)".

Subsec. (j)(2). Pub. L. 98–615, §2(3)(A), substituted provision that if an employee or Member has a former spouse who is entitled to a survivor annuity as provided in section 8341(h) of this title, the annuity of the employee or Member computed under subsecs. (a)–(i) and (n) (or any designated portion of the annuity, in the event that the former spouse is entitled to less than 55 percent of the employee or Member's annuity) is reduced as provided in par. (4) for provision that any written notification (or designation) by any employee or Member under the first sentence of par. (1) would not be considered valid unless the employee or Member established to the satisfaction of the Office that the spouse had been notified of the loss of or reduction in survivor benefits or that the employee or Member had complied with such notification requirements as the Office would, by regulation, prescribe.

Subsec. (j)(3) to (5). Pub. L. 98–615, §2(3)(A), added pars. (3) to (5).

Subsec. (k)(1). Pub. L. 98–615, §2(3)(B), substituted "an employee or Member" for "an unmarried employee or Member".

Pub. L. 98–353, §112, substituted "and (n)" for "and (o)".

Subsec. (k)(2). Pub. L. 98–615, §2(3)(C), designated existing provisions as subpar. (A), substituted "such employee or Member's spouse" for "his spouse" and "within 2 years after such employee or Member marries or, if later, within 2 years after the death or remarriage of any former spouse of such employee or Member who was entitled to a survivor annuity under section 8341(h) of this title (or of the last such surviving former spouse, if there was more than one), a reduction in the retired employee or Member's current annuity as provided in subsection (j) of this section" for "within 1 year after he marries, a reduction in his current annuity as provided in subsection (j) of this section. The reduced annuity shall be effective the first day of the first month beginning 1 year after the date of marriage. The election voids prospectively any election previously made under paragraph (1) of this subsection", and added subpars. (B) and (C).

Subsec. (l). Pub. L. 98–353, §112, substituted "and (n)" for "and (o)" in provisions preceding par. (1).

Subsec. (m). Pub. L. 98–353, §112, substituted "and (n)" for "and (o)".

Subsec. (n). Pub. L. 98–531 substituted "as a referee in bankruptcy and" for "March 31, 1979, and before the date of the enactment of the Bankruptcy Amendments and Federal Judgeship Act of 1984".

Pub. L. 98–353, §121(f), substituted "the date of enactment of the Bankruptcy Amendments and Federal Judgeship Act of 1984" for "June 28, 1984".

Pub. L. 98–353, §116(d)(3), substituted "as a referee in bankruptcy and" for "March 31, 1979, and before June 27, 1984,".

Pub. L. 98–325 substituted "June 28, 1984" for "June 21, 1984".

Pub. L. 98–299 substituted "June 21, 1984" for "May 26, 1984".

Pub. L. 98–271 substituted "May 26, 1984" for "April 1, 1984".

Pub. L. 98–249 which purported to amend subsec. (o) by substituting "May 1, 1984" for "April 1, 1984" was probably intended as an amendment of subsec. (n). See amendment of subsec. (n) by Pub. L. 98–271.

1983—Subsec. (d)(6). Pub. L. 98–94, §1256(e)(1), added par. (6).

Subsec. (h). Pub. L. 98–94, §1256(e)(2), inserted provision that the annuity computed under subsections (a), (d)(6), and (f) of this section for a judge of the United States Court of Military Appeals retiring under the second sentence of section 8336(k) of this title or the third sentence of section 8338(c) of this title is reduced by ½2 of 1 percent for each full month not in excess of 60 months, and ⅙ of 1 percent for each full month in excess of 60 months, the judge is under 60 years of age at the date of separation.

1982—Subsec. (e). Pub. L. 97–276 inserted "unless such employee has received, pursuant to section 8342 of this title, payment of the lump-sum credit attributable to deductions under section 8334(a) of this title during any period of employment as an air traffic controller and such employee has not deposited in the Fund the amount received, with interest, pursuant to section 8334(d) of this title".

Subsec. (i). Pub. L. 97–253 redesignated former unnumbered subsection into provisions preceding par. (1) and par. (1) and (2) and completely revised such provisions as so redesignated. Prior to amendment subsec. (i) read as follows: "The annuity computed under subsections (a)–(h) and (o) of this section is reduced by 10 percent of a deposit described by section 8334(c) of this title remaining unpaid, unless the employee or Member elects to eliminate the service involved for the purpose of annuity computation."

1980—Subsec. (g). Pub. L. 96–499 provided for a minimum disability retirement annuity where an employee or Member retiring under section 8337 of this title was receiving retired or retainer pay for military service or a Veterans' Administration pension or compensation.

Subsec. (j). Pub. L. 96–391 redesignated existing provisions as par. (1) and added par. (2).

1979—Subsec. (d). Pub. L. 96–70 designated existing provisions as par. (1) and added pars. (2) to (4).

Subsec. (d)(5). Pub. L. 96–135, §1(b), added par. (5).

Subsec. (h). Pub. L. 96–135, §1(c), inserted references to subsections (d)(5) and (j) of this section.

Subsecs. (n), (o). Pub. L. 96–54 redesignated subsec. (o) as (n). Former subsec. (n) redesignated (m) by Pub. L. 94–126.

1978—Subsec. (d). Pub. L. 95–256 substituted "(b)" for "(g)".

Subsec. (f). Pub. L. 95–598, §338(a)(1), inserted reference to subsec. (o) of this section.

Subsec. (h). Pub. L. 95–454, §412(b), substituted "section 8336(d) or (h)" for "section 8336(d)".

Subsec. (i). Pub. L. 95–598, §338(a)(2), inserted reference to subsec. (o) of this section.

Subsec. (j). Pub. L. 95–598, §338(a)(3), inserted reference to subsec. (o) of this section.

Pub. L. 95–454, §906(a)(2), (3), substituted "Office of Personnel Management" and "Office" for "Civil Service Commission" and "Commission", respectively.

Pub. L. 95–317, §1(a), inserted "(or is remarried if there is no election in effect under the following sentence)" after "or Member is not married", and substituted provisions authorizing, upon remarriage, an irrevocable election in a signed writing received by the Commission within 1 year after remarriage for a reduction and computation of such reduction, for provisions authorizing the annuity, upon remarriage, to be reduced by the same percentage reductions in effect at the time of retirement.

Subsec. (k). Pub. L. 95–454, §906(a)(3), substituted "Office" for "Commission" wherever appearing.

Subsec. (k)(1). Pub. L. 95–598, §338(a)(3), inserted reference to subsec. (o) of this section.

Pub. L. 95–317, §2, inserted provisions relating to recomputation and payment of an annuity reduced under this par. or any similar prior provision of law.

Subsec. (k)(2). Pub. L. 95–317, §1(c), substituted "The reduced annuity shall be effective the first day of the first month beginning 1 year after the date of marriage" for "His reduced annuity is effective the first day of the month after his election is received in the Commission".

Subsec. (l). Pub. L. 95–598, §338(a)(4), inserted reference to subsec. (o) of this section.

Subsec. (m). Pub. L. 95–598, §338(a)(5), inserted reference to subsec. (o) of this section.

Pub. L. 95–519 inserted provision relating to computation of days of unused sick leave for employees excepted from subchapter I of chapter 63 of this title.

Subsec. (o). Pub. L. 95–598, §338(a)(6), added subsec. (o).

1976—Subsec. (f)(2)(C). Pub. L. 94–397 substituted "8344(d)(1)" for "8344(b)(1)".

1975—Subsecs. (m), (n). Pub. L. 94–126 struck out subsec. (m) which required that 45 per centum of each year, or fraction thereof, of service referred to in section 8332(b)(6) which was performed prior to the effective date of the National Guard Technicians Act of 1968, be disregarded in determining service for the purpose of computing an annuity under each paragraph of this section, and redesignated subsec. (n) as (m).

1974—Subsec. (d). Pub. L. 93–350 inserted reference to employees retiring under section 8335(g) of this title and substituted a schedule of 2½ percent of his average pay multiplied by so much of his total service as does not exceed 20 years plus 2 percent of his average pay multiplied by so much of his total service as exceeds 20 years for a schedule of 2 percent of his average pay multiplied by his total service.

Subsec. (f)(2). Pub. L. 93–260 substituted "greatest" for "greater", redesignated cl. (B) as cl. (C), and added cl. (B).

Subsec. (j). Pub. L. 93–474 inserted provision that an annuity reduced under this subsection or any similar provision of law shall be recomputed and paid as if the annuity had not been so reduced for each full month during which a retired employee or member is not married and that upon marriage the annuity shall be reduced by the same percentage reductions which were in effect at the time of retirement.

1972—Subsec. (e). Pub. L. 92–297, §6(1), (2), added subsec. (e) and redesignated former subsec. (e) as (f).

Subsec. (f). Pub. L. 92–297, §§6(1), 7(3)(A), redesignated former subsec. (e) as (f) and substituted references to subsecs. (a) to (e) for references to subsecs. (a) to (d). Former subsec. (f) redesignated (g).

Subsec. (g). Pub. L. 92–297, §6(1), redesignated former subsec. (f) as (g). Former subsec. (g) redesignated (h).

Subsec. (h). Pub. L. 92–297, §§6(1), 7(3)(B), redesignated former subsec. (g) as (h) and substituted "subsections (a), (b), and (f)", "subsections (c) and (f)", and "section 8336(g)" for "subsections (a), (b), and (e)", "subsections (c) and (e)", and "section 8336(f)" respectively. Former subsec. (h) redesignated (i).

Subsec. (i). Pub. L. 92–297, §§6(1), 7(3)(C), redesignated former subsec. (h) as (i) and substituted reference to subsections (a)–(h) for reference to subsections (a)–(g). Former subsec. (i) redesignated (j).

Subsec. (j). Pub. L. 92–297, §§6(1), 7(3)(D), redesignated former subsec. (i) as (j) and substituted reference to subsections (a) to (i) for reference to subsections (a) to (h). Former subsec. (j) redesignated (k).

Subsec. (k). Pub. L. 92–297, §§6(1), 7(3)(E), redesignated former subsec. (j) as (k) and substituted "subsections (a)–(i)" and "subsection (j)" for "subsections (a)–(h)" and "subsection (i)", respectively. Former subsec. (k) redesignated (l).

Subsec. (l). Pub. L. 92–297, §§6(1), 7(3)(F), redesignated former subsec. (k) as (l) and substituted "subsections (a)–(e)" for "subsections (a)–(j)". Former subsec. (l) redesignated (m).

Subsec. (m). Pub. L. 92–297, §6(1) redesignated former subsec. (l) as (m). Former subsec. (m) redesignated (n).

Subsec. (n). Pub. L. 92–297, §§6(1), 7(3)(G), redesignated former subsec. (m) as (n) and substituted "subsections (a)–(e)" and "subsection (f)" for "subsections (a)–(d)" and "subsection (e)", respectively.

1971—Subsec. (i). Pub. L. 91–658, §2(a), substituted "any spouse surviving him" for "his spouse".

Subsec. (j). Pub. L. 91–658, §2(b), designated existing provisions as par. (1) and added par. (2).

1969—Subsec. (b). Pub. L. 91–93, §203(1), substituted "his service as a Congressional employee, his military service not exceeding 5 years," for "so much of his service as a Congressional employee and his military service as does not exceed a total of 15 years".

Subsec. (c)(2). Pub. L. 91–93, §203(2), struck out "so much of" and "as does not exceed 15 years" before and after "his Congressional employee service".

Subsec. (f). Pub. L. 91–93, §203(3), struck out last sentence providing "However, this subsection does not increase the annuity of a survivor."

Subsec. (i). Pub. L. 91–93, §203(4), struck out "(excluding any increase because of retirement under section 8337 of this title)" after "subsections (a)–(h) of this section".

Subsec. (m). Pub. L. 91–93, §203(5), added subsec. (m).

1968—Subsec. (l). Pub. L. 90–486 added subsec. (l).

1967—Subsec. (e)(2). Pub. L. 90–206 inserted provision for the use of the final basic pay of the appointive position of a former Member who elects to have his annuity computed or recomputed under section 8344(b)(1) of this title in making the determination of the maximum allowable annuity.

CHANGE OF NAME

"United States magistrate judge" substituted for "United States magistrate" wherever appearing in subsec. (n) pursuant to section 321 of Pub. L. 101–650, set out as a note under section 631 of Title 28, Judiciary and Judicial Procedure.

EFFECTIVE DATE OF 2000 AMENDMENT

Amendment by Pub. L. 106–553 effective on the first day of the first applicable pay period that begins on

Dec. 21, 2000, and applicable only to an individual who is employed as a member of the Supreme Court Police after Dec. 21, 2000, see section 1(a)(2) [title III, § 308(i), (j)] of Pub. L. 106–553, set out in a Supreme Court Police Retirement note under section 8331 of this title.

EFFECTIVE DATE OF 1997 AMENDMENT

Amendment by Pub. L. 105–61 applicable to any annuity commencing before, on, or after Oct. 10, 1997, and effective with regard to any payment made after the first month following Oct. 10, 1997, see section 516(b) of Pub. L. 105–61, set out as a note under section 8334 of this title.

EFFECTIVE DATE OF 1993 AMENDMENT

Section 11004(c) of Pub. L. 103–66 provided that:

"(1) IN GENERAL.—The amendments made by this section [amending this section and sections 8334 and 8418 of this title] shall take effect on the first day of the first month beginning at least 30 days after the date of the enactment of this Act [Aug. 10, 1993] and shall apply to all deposits required under section 8339(j)(3) or (5), 8339(k)(2), or 8418 of title 5, United States Code, on which no payment has been made prior to such effective date.

"(2) PARTIAL DEPOSIT.—For any deposit required under section 8339(j)(3) or (5), 8339(k)(2), or 8418 of title 5, United States Code, or section 4(b) or (c) of the Civil Service Retirement Spouse Equity Act of 1984 [Pub. L. 98–615] (5 U.S.C. 8341 note) that has been partially, but not fully, paid before the effective date of this Act [probably should be "the effective date of the amendments made by this section"], the Office shall by regulation provide for determining the remaining portion of the deposit and for payment of the remaining portion of the deposit by a prospective reduction in the annuity of the employee or Member. The reduction shall be similar to the reductions provided pursuant to the amendments made under this section."

EFFECTIVE DATE OF 1992 AMENDMENT

Amendment by Pub. L. 102–572 effective Oct. 29, 1992, see section 911 of Pub. L. 102–572, set out as a note under section 171 of Title 28, Judiciary and Judicial Procedure.

EFFECTIVE DATE OF 1990 AMENDMENTS

Amendment by Pub. L. 101–650 applicable to judges of, and senior judges in active service with, the United States Court of Federal Claims on or after Dec. 1, 1990, see section 306(f) of Pub. L. 101–650, set out as a note under section 8331 of this title.

Amendment by Pub. L. 101–508 effective with respect to any annuity having a commencement date later than Dec. 1, 1990, see section 7001(b)(3) of Pub. L. 101–508, set out as a note under section 8334 of this title.

Section 2(c)(2) of Pub. L. 101–428 provided that:

"(A) The amendment made by paragraph (1) [amending this section] shall take effect 4 years after the date of enactment of this Act [Oct. 15, 1990], and shall apply with respect to any annuity, entitlement to which is based on a separation occurring on or after that effective date, subject to subparagraph (B).

"(B) Nothing in this subsection or in the amendment made by this subsection [amending this section] shall, with respect to any service performed before the effective date of such amendment, have the effect of reducing the percentage applicable in computing any portion of an annuity based on such service below the percentage which would otherwise apply if this Act had not been enacted."

EFFECTIVE DATE OF 1989 AMENDMENT

Amendment by Pub. L. 101–194 effective Jan. 1, 1991, see section 506(d) of Pub. L. 101–194, set out as a note under section 3151 of this title.

EFFECTIVE DATE OF 1987 AMENDMENT

Amendment by Pub. L. 100–53 effective Oct. 1, 1987, and applicable to bankruptcy judges and United States magistrate judges in office on that date and to individuals subsequently appointed to such positions to whom this chapter otherwise applies, see section 3 of Pub. L. 100–53, as amended, set out as a note under section 8331 of this title.

EFFECTIVE DATE OF 1986 AMENDMENTS

Section 15204(b), formerly 15204(c), of Pub. L. 99–272, as redesignated by Pub. L. 99–509, title VII, § 7003(b), Oct. 21, 1986, 100 Stat. 1949, provided that: "The amendments made by this section [amending this section, section 8341 of this title, and former section 4109 of Title 38, Veterans' Benefits] shall be effective with respect to service performed on or after the date of the enactment of this Act [Apr. 7, 1986]."

Section 203(d) of Pub. L. 99–251 provided that: "The amendments made by this section [amending this section] shall take effect May 7, 1985."

Section 307(b) of Pub. L. 99–251 provided that:

"(1) The amendment made by subsection (a) [amending this section] shall take effect 3 months after the date of the enactment of this Act [Feb. 27, 1986].

"(2)(A) Subject to subparagraph (B), the amendment made by subsection (a) shall apply with respect to employees and Members who retire before, on, or after such amendment first takes effect.

"(B) For the purpose of applying the provisions of paragraph (1) of section 8339(o) of title 5, United States Code (as added by subsection (a) of this section) to employees and Members who retire before the date on which the amendment made by subsection (a) first takes effect—

"(i) the period referred to in subparagraph (A) or (B) of such paragraph (as the case may be) shall be considered to begin on the date on which such amendment first becomes effective; and

"(ii) the amount referred to in paragraph (2) of such section 8339(o) shall be computed without regard to the provisions of subparagraph (B)(ii) of such paragraph (relating to interest).

"(3) For purposes of this subsection, the terms 'employee' and 'Member' each has the meaning given that term in sections 8331(1) and 8331(2) of title 5, United States Code, respectively."

EFFECTIVE DATE OF 1984 AMENDMENTS

Amendment by Pub. L. 98–615 effective May 7, 1985, with enumerated exceptions and specific applicability provisions, see section 4(a)(1), (4) of Pub. L. 98–615, as amended, set out as a note under section 8341 of this title.

Amendment by Pub. L. 98–531 effective Mar. 31, 1984, see section 3(b) of Pub. L. 98–531, set out as a note under section 8331 of this title.

Amendment by Pub. L. 98–353 effective July 10, 1984, and applicable to bankruptcy judges who retire on or after such date, see section 116(e) of Pub. L. 98–353, set out as a note under section 8331 of this title. See, also, section 122(a) of Pub. L. 98–353, set out as an Effective Date note under section 151 of Title 28, Judiciary and Judicial Procedure.

EFFECTIVE DATE OF 1982 AMENDMENTS

Section 151(h)(3) of Pub. L. 97–276 provided that: "The amendment made by subsection 152(f) [151(f)] of this joint resolution [amending this section] shall take effect on the date of the enactment of this joint resolution [Oct. 2, 1982]."

Amendment by Pub. L. 97–253 effective with respect to deposits for service performed, on or after Oct. 1, 1982, and with respect to refunds for which application is received by Office of Personnel Management on or after Oct. 1, 1982, and provisions of section 8339(i) of title 5, as in effect the day before Sept. 7, 1982, to continue to apply with respect to periods of service and refunds occurring on or before Sept. 30, 1982, see section 303(d)(1) of Pub. L. 97–253, as amended by Pub. L. 97–346, § 3(j)(1), Oct. 15, 1982, 96 Stat. 1649, set out as a note under section 8334 of this title.

EFFECTIVE DATE OF 1980 AMENDMENTS

Section 404(c) of Pub. L. 96–499 provided that: "The amendments made by this section [amending this section and section 8347 of this title] shall take effect on the date of the enactment of this Act [Dec. 5, 1980]."

Section 3 of Pub. L. 96–391 provided that: "The amendments made by the first section of this Act [amending this section] shall take effect with respect to notifications and designations made under the first sentence of section 8339(j) of title 5, United States Code, on or after the ninetieth day after the date of the enactment of this Act [Oct. 7, 1980]."

EFFECTIVE DATE OF 1979 AMENDMENTS

Amendment by Pub. L. 96–135 effective Dec. 5, 1979, see section 1(d) of Pub. L. 96–135, set out as a note under section 8336 of this title.

Section 1242(b)(1) of Pub. L. 96–70 provided that: "The amendments made by this section [amending this section] shall take effect on the date of the enactment of this Act [Sept. 27, 1979], but no amount of annuity under chapter 83 of title 5, United States Code, accruing by reason of those amendments shall be payable for any period before October 1, 1979."

Amendment by Pub. L. 96–54 effective July 12, 1979, see section 2(b) of Pub. L. 96–54, set out as a note under section 305 of this title.

EFFECTIVE DATE OF 1978 AMENDMENTS

Amendment by Pub. L. 95–598 effective Nov. 6, 1978, see section 402(d) of Pub. L. 95–598, set out as an Effective Date note preceding section 101 of Title 11, Bankruptcy.

Amendment by Pub. L. 95–519 applicable only with respect to employees who retire or die on or after Oct. 25, 1978, see section 4(b) of Pub. L. 95–519, set out as a note under section 5551 of this title.

Amendment by section 412(b) of Pub. L. 95–454 effective 9 months after Oct. 13, 1978, and congressional review of provisions of sections 401 through 412 of Pub. L. 95–454, see section 415 of Pub. L. 95–454, set out as an Effective Date note under section 3131 of this title.

Amendment by section 906(a)(2), (3) of Pub. L. 95–454 effective 90 days after Oct. 13, 1978, see section 907 of Pub. L. 95–454, set out as a note under section 1101 of this title.

Amendment by Pub. L. 95–256 effective Sept. 30, 1978, see section 5(f) of Pub. L. 95–256, set out as a note under section 633a of Title 29, Labor.

EFFECTIVE DATE OF 1978 AMENDMENTS; SURVIVOR ANNUITIES SUBJECT TO REDUCTION, ETC.

Section 4 of Pub. L. 95–317 provided that:

"(a) This act [amending this section and section 8341 of this title and enacting provisions set out as notes under this section] shall take effect—

"(1) the first day of the first month which begins on or after the date of the enactment of this Act [July 10, 1978], or

"(2) October 1, 1978,

whichever is later.

"(b) Except as provided under subsection (c) of this section, the amendments made by the first section and section 2 of this Act [amending this section and section 8341 of this title] shall apply with respect to annuities which commence before, on, or after the effective date of this Act, but no monetary benefit by reason of such amendments shall accrue for any period before such effective date.

"(c) The amendments made by the first section of this Act [amending this section and section 8341 of this title] shall not affect the eligibility of any individual to a survivor annuity under section 8341(b) of title 5, United States Code, or the reduction therefor under section 8339(j) of such title, in the case of an annuitant who remarried before the effective date of this Act, unless the annuitant notifies the Civil Service Commission in a signed writing received in the Commission within one year after the effective date of this Act that

such annuitant does not desire the spouse of the annuitant to receive a survivor annuity in the event of the annuitant's death. Such notification shall take effect the first day of the first month after it is received in the Commission."

EFFECTIVE DATE OF 1976 AMENDMENT

Amendment by Pub. L. 94–397 effective Oct. 1, 1976, and applicable to annuitants serving in appointive or elective positions on and after such date, see section 2 of Pub. L. 94–397, set out as a note under section 8344 of this title.

EFFECTIVE DATE OF 1975 AMENDMENT

Amendment by Pub. L. 94–126 effective Jan. 1, 1969, applicable to a person who, on Nov. 12, 1975, is receiving or is entitled to receive benefits under any Federal retirement system and requests in writing the application of the amendment to him by the office administering his retirement system, and additional benefits to commence Dec. 1, 1975, see section 3 of Pub. L. 94–126, set out as a note under section 8334 of this title.

EFFECTIVE DATE OF 1974 AMENDMENTS

Section 2 of Pub. L. 93–474 provided that: "The amendment made by this Act [amending this section] shall apply to annuities which commence before, on, or after the date of enactment of this Act [Oct. 26, 1974], but no increase in annuity shall be paid for any period prior to the first day of the first month which begins on or after the date of enactment of this Act."

Amendment by Pub. L. 93–350 effective on July 12, 1974, see section 7 of Pub. L. 93–350, set out as a note under section 3307 of this title.

Section 2(b) of Pub. L. 93–260 provided that: "The amendments made by subsection (a) of this section [amending this section] shall apply to annuities paid for months beginning after the date of enactment of this Act [Apr. 9, 1974]."

EFFECTIVE DATE OF 1972 AMENDMENT

Amendment by Pub. L. 92–297 effective on 90th day after May 16, 1972, see section 10 of Pub. L. 92–297, set out as an Effective Date note under section 3381 of this title.

EFFECTIVE DATE OF 1971 AMENDMENT

Section 5(b) of Pub. L. 91–658 provided that: "The amendments made by section 2(a) and 3 of this Act [amending this section and section 8341 of this title] shall not apply in the cases of employees, Members, or annuitants who died before the date of enactment of this Act [Jan. 8, 1971]. The rights of such persons and their survivors shall continue in the same manner and to the same extent as if such amendments had not been enacted."

Section 5(c) of Pub. L. 91–658 provided that: "The amendments made by section 2(b) of this Act [amending this section] shall apply to an annuitant who was unmarried at the time of retiring, but who later married, only if the election is made within 1 year after the date of enactment of this Act [Jan. 8, 1971]."

EFFECTIVE DATE OF 1969 AMENDMENT

Amendment by Pub. L. 91–93 inapplicable in cases of persons retired or otherwise separated prior to Oct. 20, 1969, their rights and of their survivors continued as if such amendment had not been enacted, see section 207(a) of Pub. L. 91–93, set out as a note under section 8331 of this title.

EFFECTIVE DATE OF 1968 AMENDMENT

Amendment by Pub. L. 90–486 effective Jan. 1, 1969, except that no deductions or withholding from salary which result therefrom shall commence before first day of first pay period that begins on or after Jan. 1, 1968, see section 11 of Pub. L. 90–486, set out as a note under section 709 of Title 32, National Guard.

EFFECTIVE DATE OF 1967 AMENDMENT

Amendment by Pub. L. 90–206 effective Dec. 16, 1967, see section 220(a)(1) of Pub. L. 90–206, set out as an Effective Date note under section 3110 of this title.

INDIVIDUALS ENTITLED TO ANNUITY PAYMENTS FOR PERIOD PRIOR TO OCTOBER 1, 1979

Section 1242(b)(2) of Pub. L. 96–70 provided that: "Effective October 1, 1979, any individual who, but for paragraph (1) of this subsection [set out as an Effective Date of 1979 Amendment note above], would have been entitled to one or more annuity payments pursuant to the amendments made by this section [amending this section] for periods before October 1, 1979, shall be entitled, to such extent or in such amounts as are provided in advance in appropriation Acts, to a lump sum payment equal to the total amount of all such annuity payments."

ANNUAL NOTICE TO ANNUITANT OF RIGHTS OF ELECTION UNDER SUBSECS. (j) AND (k)(2) OF THIS SECTION

Section 3 of Pub. L. 95–317, as amended by 1978 Reorg. Plan No. 2, § 102, 43 F.R. 36037, 92 Stat. 3783, provided that: "The Director of the Office of Personnel Management shall, on an annual basis, inform each annuitant of such annuitant's rights of election under sections 8339(j) and 8339(k)(2) of title 5, United States Code."

INCREASE IN ANNUITY FOR EMPLOYEES OR MEMBERS SEPARATED FROM CIVIL SERVICE PRIOR TO OCT. 20, 1969

Section 2(a) of Pub. L. 93–273, Apr. 26, 1974, 88 Stat. 93, provided that: "An annuity payable from the Civil Service Retirement and Disability Fund to a former employee or Member, which is based on a separation occurring prior to October 20, 1969, is increased by $240."

Section 3 of Pub. L. 93–273 provided in part that annuity increases under this provision shall apply to annuities which commence before, on, or after Apr. 26, 1974, but that no increase in annuity shall be paid for any period prior to the first day of the first month which begins on or after the ninetieth day after Apr. 26, 1974, or the date on which the annuity commences, whichever is later. See section 3 of Pub. L. 93–273, set out as a note under section 8345 of this title.

1970 INCREASE IN PAY RATES OF CERTAIN EMPLOYEES OF THE LEGISLATIVE BRANCH

Adjustment by the President pro tempore of the Senate with respect to the United States Senate, by the Finance Clerk of the House of Representatives with respect to the United States House of Representatives, and by the Architect of the Capitol with respect to the Office of the Architect of the Capitol, effective on the first day of the first pay period which begins on or after Dec. 27, 1969, of the rates of pay of employees of the legislative branch subject to section 214 of Pub. L. 90–206 with certain exceptions, by the amounts of the adjustment for corresponding rates for employees subject to the General Schedule, set out in section 5332 of this title, which had been made by section 2 of Pub. L. 91–231 raising such rates by 6 percent, see Pub. L. 91–231, set out as a note under section 5332 of this title.

1967 INCREASE IN COMPENSATION AS PART OF BASIC PAY RATE

Section 214(d) of Pub. L. 90–206, title II, Dec. 16, 1967, 81 Stat. 636, providing for the inclusion of the additional compensation pursuant to section 214 of Pub. L. 90–206 as part of basic pay for purposes of civil service retirement, was repealed by section 7(a)(4) of Pub. L. 90–623, Oct. 22, 1968, 82 Stat. 1315, except with respect to rights and duties which matured, penalties that were incurred, and proceedings that were begun before Oct. 22, 1968.

1962 INCREASE IN ANNUITIES

Section 1101 of Pub. L. 87–793, Oct. 11, 1962, 76 Stat. 868, provided that:

"(a) The annuity of each person who, on the effective date of this section [Jan. 1, 1963], is receiving or entitled to receive an annuity from the civil service retirement and disability fund shall be increased by 5 per centum of the amount of such annuity.

"(b) The annuity of each person who receives or is entitled to receive an annuity from the civil service retirement and disability fund commencing during the period which begins on the day following the effective date of this section [Jan. 1, 1963] and ends five years after such date, shall be increased in accordance with the following table:

"If the annuity commences between—	The annuity shall be increased by—
"January 2, 1963, and December 31, 1963	4 per centum
"January 1, 1964, and December 31, 1964	3 per centum
"January 1, 1965, and December 31, 1965	2 per centum
"January 1, 1966, and December 31, 1966	1 per centum

"(c) In lieu of any other increase provided by this section, the annuity of a survivor of a retired employee or Member of Congress who received an increase under this section shall be increased by a percentage equal to the percentage by which the annuity of such employee or Member was so increased.

"(d) No increase provided by this section shall be computed on any additional annuity purchased at retirement by voluntary contributions.

"(e) The limitation reading 'or (3) the sum necessary to increase such annuity, exclusive of annuity purchased by voluntary contributions under the second paragraph of section 10 of this Act, to $2,160' contained in section 8(c)(1) of the Civil Service Retirement Act of May 29, 1930, as amended by the Acts of July 16, 1952 (66 Stat. 722; Public Law 555, Eighty-second Congress), and August 31, 1954 (68 Stat. 1043; Public Law 747, Eighty-third Congress), shall not be effective on or after the effective date of this section [Jan. 1, 1963].

"(f) The limitation contained in the next to the last sentence of section 8(d)(1) of the Civil Service Retirement Act of May 29, 1930, as amended, as enacted by the Act of August 11, 1955 (69 Stat. 692; Public Law 369, Eighty-fourth Congress) shall not be effective on and after the effective date of this section [Jan. 1, 1963].

"(g) The increases provided by this section shall take effect on the effective date of this section [Jan. 1, 1963], except that any increase under subsection (b) or (c) shall take effect on the beginning date of the annuity.

"(h) The monthly installment of annuity after adjustment under this section shall be fixed at the nearest dollar".

Section 1104 of Pub. L. 87–793 provided in part that section 1101 of Pub. L. 87–793 shall take effect on January 1, 1963.

1958 INCREASE IN ANNUITIES

Pub. L. 85–465, June 25, 1958, 72 Stat. 218, as amended by Pub. L. 86–604, § 3(a), July 7, 1960, 74 Stat. 359; Pub. L. 87–114, July 31, 1961, 75 Stat. 241, provided:

"That (a) the annuity of each retired employee or Member of Congress who, on August 1, 1958, is receiving or entitled to receive an annuity from the civil service retirement and disability fund based on service which terminated prior to October 1, 1956, shall be increased by 10 per centum, but no such increase shall exceed $500 per annum.

"(b) The annuity otherwise payable from the civil service retirement and disability fund to—

"(1) each survivor who on August 1, 1958, is receiving or entitled to receive an annuity based on service which terminated prior to October 1, 1956, and

"(2) each survivor of a retired employee or Member of Congress described in subsection (a) of this section, shall be increased by 10 per centum. No increase provided by this subsection shall exceed $250 per annum.

"(c) No increase provided by this section shall be computed on any additional annuity purchased at retirement by voluntary contributions.

"SEC. 2. The unmarried widow or widower of an employee—

"(1) who had completed at least ten years of service creditable for civil service retirement purposes.

"(2) who (A) died February 29, 1948, or (B), if retired under the Alaska Railroad Retirement Act of June 29, 1936, as amended, or under sections 91 to 107, inclusive, of title 2 of the Canal Zone Code, approved June 19, 1934, as amended, died before April 1, 1948; and

"(3) who was at the time of his death

(A) subject to an Act under which annuities granted before February 20, 1948, were or are now payable from the civil service retirement and disability fund or (B) retired under such an Act,

(B) etc.

shall be entitled to receive an annuity. In order to qualify for such annuity, the widow or widower shall have been married to the employee for at least five years immediately prior to his death and must be not entitled to any other annuity from the civil service retirement and disability fund based on the service of such employee. Such annuity shall be equal to one-half of the annuity which the employee was receiving on the date of his death if retired, or would have been receiving if he had been retired for disability on the date of his death, but shall not exceed $750 per annum and shall not be increased by the provisions of this or any other prior law. Any annuity granted under this section shall cease upon the death or remarriage of the widow or widower.

"SEC. 3. (a) An increase in annuity provided by subsection (a), or clause (1) of subsection (b), of the first section of this Act shall take effect on August 1, 1958. An increase in annuity provided by clause (2) of such subsection (b) shall take effect on the commencing date of the survivor annuity.

"(b) An annuity provided by section 2 of this Act shall commence on August 1, 1958, or on the first day of the month in which application for such annuity is received in the Civil Service Commission, whichever occurs later.

"SEC. 4. Notwithstanding any other provision of law, the annuities and increases in annuities provided by the preceding sections of this Act shall be paid from the civil service retirement and disability fund.

"(c) The monthly installment of each annuity increased or provided by this Act shall be fixed at the nearest dollar.

"SEC. 5. (a) The amendments made by section 401 of the Civil Service Retirement Act Amendments of 1956 (70 Stat. 743–760; 5 U.S.C. 2251–2267) [amending provisions covered by this subchapter] may apply at the option of any employee who, prior to July 31, 1956, was separated from the service under the automatic separation provisions of the Civil Service Retirement Act [this subchapter] but whose separation would not have taken effect until after July 30, 1965, if he had been permitted to remain in the service until the expiration of any accumulated or current accrued annual leave to his credit at the time of his separation from the service. Such option shall be exercised by a writing received in the Civil Service Commission before January 1, 1959.

"(b) No increase in annuity provided by this Act or any prior provision of law shall apply in the case of any retired employee who exercises the option permitted by subsection (a) of this section."

1962 AND 1958 INCREASES IN ANNUITIES; CLARIFICATION

Pub. L. 89–17, May 1, 1965, 79 Stat. 109, provided: "That for the purposes of section 1(a) of the Act of June 25, 1958 (Public Law 85–465) [1958 Increase in Annuities note set out above], and section 1101(a) of the Act of October 11, 1962 (Public Law 87–793) [1962 Increase in Annuities note set out under this section], the words 'entitled to receive an annuity' shall, from and after the respective effective dates (August 1, 1958, and January 1, 1963) of the annuity increases provided by such Acts, not include any person whose annuity commencing date occurs after the effective date of the annuity increase involved."

PAYMENT OF ANNUITIES TO CERTAIN UNREMARRIED WIDOWS OR WIDOWERS OF EMPLOYEES RETIRED UNDER RAILROAD RETIREMENT ACT OR CANAL ZONE CODE

Section 3(b), (c) of Pub. L. 86–604, July 7, 1960, 74 Stat. 359, made section 4 of act June 25, 1958, set out in the 1958 Increase in Annuities note under this section, applicable to annuities authorized by section 2(2)(B) of act June 25, 1958, and provided that such annuities should commence Aug. 1, 1958, or on the first day of the month in which application therefor was received in the Civil Service Commission, whichever occurred later.

ESTIMATES OF APPROPRIATIONS FOR REIMBURSING FUND FOR AMOUNTS PAID UNDER 1958 INCREASE IN ANNUITIES

Pub. L. 91–93, title I, §105, Oct. 20, 1969, 83 Stat. 138, repealed part of Pub. L. 87–141, title I, §101, Aug. 17, 1961, 75 Stat. 345, which required the Civil Service Commission to include annually in its estimates to the Bureau of the Budget, estimates of appropriations necessary to reimburse the civil service retirement and disability fund for amounts paid out of the fund by reason of enactment of Pub. L. 85–465, set out in the 1958 Increase in Annuities note under this section, and the Bureau of the Budget to submit such estimates annually to the Congress.

ANNUITY OF DIRECTOR OF FBI

Pub. L. 86–734, §5, Sept. 8, 1960, 74 Stat. 868, provided that: "Any person who shall retire for age after serving at least thirty years as Director of the Federal Bureau of Investigation shall receive an annuity during the remainder of his life equal to the salary payable to him at the time of his retirement."

NATIONAL GUARD TECHNICIANS

Amendment by Pub. L. 90–486 not applicable to persons employed prior to Jan. 1, 1969, whose employment was covered by the civil service retirement provisions of section 8331 et seq. of this title, see section 5(d) of Pub. L. 90–486, set out as a note under section 709 of Title 32, National Guard.

SECTION REFERRED TO IN OTHER SECTIONS

This section is referred to in sections 6129, 8332, 8334, 8336, 8337, 8338, 8341, 8342, 8343a, 8344, 8348, 8901, 8905 of this title; title 10 sections 1450, 1452; title 22 sections 3671, 3691, 4045, 4046, 4069–1; title 38 section 7426; title 50 section 403r.

§ 8340. Cost-of-living adjustment of annuities

(a) For the purpose of this section—

(1) the term "base quarter", as used with respect to a year, means the calendar quarter ending on September 30, of such year; and

(2) the price index for a base quarter is the arithmetical mean of such index for the 3 months comprising such quarter.

(b) Except as provided in subsection (c) of this section, effective December 1 of each year, each annuity payable from the Fund having a commencing date not later than such December 1 shall be increased by the percent change in the price index for the base quarter of such year over the price index for the base quarter of the preceding year in which an adjustment under this subsection was made, adjusted to the nearest 1/10 of 1 percent.

(c) Eligibility for an annuity increase under this section is governed by the commencing date of each annuity payable from the Fund as of the effective date of an increase, except as follows:

(1) The first increase (if any) made under subsection (b) of this section to an annuity

which is payable from the Fund to an employee or Member who retires, to the widow, widower, or former spouse,[1] of a deceased employee or Member, or to the widow, widower, former spouse, or insurable interest designee of a deceased annuitant whose annuity has not been increased under this subsection or subsection (b) of this section, shall be equal to the product (adjusted to the nearest 1/10 of 1 percent) of—

(A) 1/12 of the applicable percent change computed under subsection (b) of this section, multiplied by

(B) the number of months (not to exceed 12 months, counting any portion of a month as a month)—

(i) for which the annuity was payable from the Fund before the effective date of the increase, or

(ii) in the case of a widow, widower, former spouse, or insurable interest designee of a deceased annuitant whose annuity has not been so increased, since the annuity was first payable to the deceased annuitant.

(2) Effective from its commencing date, an annuity payable from the Fund to an annuitant's survivor (except a child entitled under section 8341(e) of this title), which annuity commences the day after the death of the annuitant and after the effective date of the first increase under this section, shall be increased by the total percent increase the annuitant was receiving under this section at death. However, the increase in a survivor annuity authorized by section 8 of the Act of May 29, 1930, as amended to July 6, 1950, shall be computed as if the annuity commencing date had been the effective date of the first increase under this section.

(3) For the purpose of computing the annuity of a child under section 8341(e) of this title that commences after October 31, 1969, the items $900, $1,080, $2,700, and $3,240 appearing in section 8341(e) of this title shall be increased by the total percent increases allowed and in force under this section on or after such day and, in case of a deceased annuitant, the items 60 percent and 75 percent appearing in section 8341(e) of this title shall be increased by the total percent allowed and in force to the annuitant under this section on or after such day.

(d) This section does not authorize an increase in an additional annuity purchased at retirement by voluntary contributions.

(e) The monthly installment of annuity after adjustment under this section shall be rounded to the next lowest dollar. However, the monthly installment shall after adjustment reflect an increase of at least $1.

(f) Effective September 1, 1966, or on the commencing date of annuity, whichever is later, the annuity of each surviving spouse whose entitlement to annuity payable from the Fund resulted from the death of—

(1) an employee or Member before October 11, 1962; or

(2) a retired employee or Member whose retirement was based on a separation from service before October 11, 1962;

is increased by 10 percent.

(g)(1) An annuity shall not be increased by reason of any adjustment under this section to an amount which exceeds the greater of—

(A) the maximum pay payable for GS–15 30 days before the effective date of the adjustment under this section; or

(B) the final pay (or average pay, if higher) of the employee or Member with respect to whom the annuity is paid, increased by the overall annual average percentage adjustments (compounded) in rates of pay of the General Schedule under subchapter I of chapter 53 of this title during the period—

(i) beginning on the date the annuity commenced (or, in the case of a survivor of the retired employee or Member, the date the employee's or Member's annuity commenced), and

(ii) ending on the effective date of the adjustment under this section.

(2) For the purposes of paragraph (1) of this subsection, "pay" means the rate of salary or basic pay as payable under any provision of law, including any provision of law limiting the expenditure of appropriated funds.

(Pub. L. 89–554, Sept. 6, 1966, 80 Stat. 576; Pub. L. 90–83, §1(79), Sept. 11, 1967, 81 Stat. 215; Pub. L. 91–93, title II, §204, Oct. 20, 1969, 83 Stat. 139; Pub. L. 93–136, §1, Oct. 24, 1973, 87 Stat. 490; Pub. L. 94–126, §2(b), Nov. 12, 1975, 89 Stat. 679; Pub. L. 94–183, §2(35), Dec. 31, 1975, 89 Stat. 1058; Pub. L. 94–440, title XIII, §1306(a), (c)(1), Oct. 1, 1976, 90 Stat. 1462; Pub. L. 95–454, title IX, §906(a)(2), (3), Oct. 13, 1978, 92 Stat. 1224; Pub. L. 96–499, title IV, §401(a), Dec. 5, 1980, 94 Stat. 2605; Pub. L. 97–35, title XVII, §1702(a), (b), Aug. 13, 1981, 95 Stat. 754; Pub. L. 97–253, title III, §§304(a), 309(a), Sept. 8, 1982, 96 Stat. 795, 798; Pub. L. 98–270, title II, §201(a), Apr. 18, 1984, 98 Stat. 157; Pub. L. 98–369, div. B, title II, §2201(b), July 18, 1984, 98 Stat. 1058; Pub. L. 99–251, title II, §204, Feb. 27, 1986, 100 Stat. 25.)

HISTORICAL AND REVISION NOTES
1966 ACT

Derivation	U.S. Code	Revised Statutes and Statutes at Large
....	5 U.S.C. 2268.	July 31, 1956, ch. 804, §401 "Sec. 18"; added Oct. 11, 1962, Pub. L. 87–793, §1102(b) (less so much as redesignated §18 as 19), 76 Stat. 869.

In subsection (a), the words "After January 1, 1964" and "other than 1964" and subsection (a)(1) of former section 2268, are omitted as executed.

In subsection (b), the words "subsection (a) of this section" are substituted for "subsection (a)(1) or (a)(2) of this section" since subsection (a)(1) has been omitted as executed.

Standard changes are made to conform with the definitions applicable and the style of this title as outlined in the preface to the report.

---

[1] So in original. The comma probably should not appear.

1967 ACT

Section of title 5	Source (U.S. Code)	Source (Statutes at Large)
8340(a)	5 App.: 2268(a), (f).	Sept. 27, 1965, Pub. L. 89–205,
8340(b)	5 App.: 2268(b).	§ 1(c), 79 Stat. 840.
8340(c)	5 App.: 2268(c).	Nov. 1, 1965, Pub. L. 89–314,
8340(d)	5 App.: 2268(d).	§ 1, 79 Stat. 1162.
8340(e)	5 App.: 2268(e).	July 18, 1966, Pub. L. 89–504,
8340(f)	5 App.: 2268(g).	§ 507, 80 Stat. 302.

In subsection (a), the words "Effective December 1, 1965 * * * before December 2, 1965," are substituted for "Effective the first day of the third month which begins after the date of enactment of this amendment * * * not later than such effective date." In clause (1), the words "month of July 1965" are substituted for "month latest published on date of enactment of this amendment" for clarity and since the July 1965 price index was the price index for the month latest published on September 27, 1965, the date of enactment of the amendment. The word "base" is inserted before "month of July 1965" for clarity and on authority of the second sentence of 5 U.S.C. App. 2268(a) which provided: "The month used in determining the increase based on the per centum rise in the price index under this subsection shall be the base month for determining the per centum change in the price index until the next succeeding increase occurs." In view of the foregoing and of the definition of "base month" in 5 U.S.C. 8331(16), the quoted sentence is omitted as executed and unnecessary. In clause (2), the words "before October 2, 1956," are substituted for "on or before October 1, 1956." In the second sentence, which is based on 5 App. U.S.C. 2268(f), the words "before January 1, 1966," are substituted for "not later than December 31, 1965." In clause (B), the words "Act of June 25, 1958 (72 Stat. 219)" are substituted for "Public Law 85–465" to conform to the style of title 5, United States Code.

In the first sentence of subsection (b), the words "after the first increase under this section," following "Each month," are omitted as executed and unnecessary.

In subsection (f), the words "September 1, 1966," are substituted for "the first day of the second month after the enactment of this subsection."

REFERENCES IN TEXT

Section 8 of the Act of May 29, 1930, as amended to July 6, 1950, referred to in subsec. (c)(2), is the predecessor of section 8338 of this title.

AMENDMENTS

1986—Subsec. (c)(1). Pub. L. 99–251 substituted ", widower, or former spouse," for first reference to "or widower", and ", widower, former spouse, or insurable interest designee" for second and third references to "or widower".

1984—Subsec. (a). Pub. L. 98–270 substituted provisions defining term "base quarter" as meaning the calendar quarter ending Sept. 30 of a year and providing that the price index for a base quarter is the arithmetical mean of such index for the three months comprising such quarter for former provisions which had directed that, effective Dec. 1, 1965, each annuity payable from the Fund having a commencing date before Dec. 2, 1965, was increased by (1) the percent rise in the price index, adjusted to the nearest ¹⁄₁₀ of 1 percent, determined by the Office of Personnel Management on the basis of the annual average price index for calendar year 1962 and the price index for the base month of July 1965; plus (2) 6½ percent if the commencing date (or in the case of the survivor of a deceased annuitant the commencing date of the annuity of the retired employee) occurred before Oct. 2, 1956, or 1½ percent if the commencing date (or in the case of the survivor of a deceased annuitant the commencing date of the annuity of the retired employee) occurred after Oct. 1, 1956, that each annuity payable from the Fund (other than the immediate annuity of an annuitant's survivor or of a child entitled under section 8341(e) of this title) having a commencing date after Dec. 1, 1965, but before Jan. 1, 1966, was increased from its commencing date as if the annuity commencing date were Dec. 1, 1965, and that each survivor annuity authorized by (A) section 8 of the Act of May 29, 1930, as amended to July 6, 1950, or (B) section 2 of the Act of June 25, 1958 (72 Stat. 219), was increased by any additional amount required to make the total increase under this subsection equal to the smaller of 15 percent or $10 a month.

Subsec. (b). Pub. L. 98–270 substituted "Except as provided in subsection (c) of this section, effective December 1 of each year, each annuity payable from the Fund having a commencing date not later than such December 1 shall be increased by the percent change in the price index for the base quarter of such year over the price index for the base quarter of the preceding year in which an adjustment under this subsection was made, adjusted to the nearest ¹⁄₁₀ of 1 percent" for "Except as provided in subsection (c) of this section, effective March 1 of each year each annuity payable from the Fund having a commencing date not later than such March 1 shall be increased by the percent change in the price index published for December of the preceding year over the price index published for December of the year prior to the preceding year, adjusted to the nearest ¹⁄₁₀ of 1 percent".

Subsec. (c)(1)(A). Pub. L. 98–369, § 2201(b)(1), substituted "computed" for "computer".

Subsec. (c)(2)(B). Pub. L. 98–369, § 2201(b)(2), substituted "not to exceed 12 months, counting" for "counting".

1982—Subsec. (e). Pub. L. 97–253, § 304(a), substituted "rounded to the next lowest" for "fixed at the nearest".

Subsec. (g). Pub. L. 97–253, § 309(a), added subsec. (g).

1981—Subsec. (b). Pub. L. 97–35, § 1702(a), substituted provisions that except as provided in subsec. (c), the annuities payable from the Fund having a commencing date not later than March 1 of each year shall be increased by the percent change in the price index published for December of the preceding year over the price index published for December of the year prior to the preceding year, adjusted to the nearest ¹⁄₁₀ of 1 percent, for provisions requiring the Office to determine on Jan. 1 and July 1 of each year the percent change in the price index based on the data for a six month period and to adjust the annuities in March and September of each year according to specified formula when there is a rise in the price index.

Subsec. (c)(1). Pub. L. 97–35, § 1702(b), in opening provision inserted reference to the widow or widower of a deceased annuitant whose annuity has not been increased under this subsection or subsection (b) of this section, in par. (A) substituted "¹⁄₁₂" for "¹⁄₈", and in subpar. (B) designated existing provisions as item (i) and added item (ii).

1980—Subsec. (c)(1). Pub. L. 96–499, substituted formula for computing the first increase to be made under subsec. (b) of this section to an annuity which is payable from the Fund to an employee or Member who retires, to the widow or widower of a deceased employee or Member for provisions that an annuity, except a deferred annuity under section 8338 of this title or any other provision of law, payable from the Fund to an employee or Member who retires, or to the widow or widower of a deceased employee or Member and having a commencing date after the effective date of the then last preceding annuity increase under subsec. (b) of this section shall not be less than the annuity which would have been payable if the commencing date of such annuity had been the effective date of the then last preceding annuity increase under subsec. (b) of this section and that employees or deceased employees were to be deemed, for purposes of section 8339(m) of this title to have to their credit, on the effective date of the last preceding increase under subsec. (b), unused sick leave equal to that unused sick leave to his credit on the date of separation from service.

1978—Subsecs. (a)(1), (b)(1). Pub. L. 95–454 substituted "Office of Personnel Management" for "Civil Service Commission" and "Office" for "Commission".

1976—Subsec. (b). Pub. L. 94–440, § 1306(a), struck out "1 percent plus" after "shall be increased by".

Pub. L. 94–440, § 1306(c)(1), substituted provisions requiring that Commission shall determine percent change in price index on Jan. 1 and July 1 of each year and effective Mar. 1 or Sept. 1, each annuity payable from Fund shall be increased by the computed percent change in the price index adjusted to the nearest ¹⁄₁₀ of 1 percent, for provisions requiring that Commission shall determine percent change in price index on a monthly basis and effective the first day of the third month that begins after the price index change equals a rise of 3 percent for 3 consecutive months over the prior price index, each annuity payable from Fund shall be increased by the highest rise in the price index over those months adjusted to the nearest ¹⁄₁₀ of 1 percent.

1975—Subsec. (c)(1). Pub. L. 94–126 substituted reference to "section 8339(m) of this title" for "section 8339(n) of this title".

Subsec. (c)(3). Pub. L. 94–183 substituted "after October 31, 1969" for "on or after the first day of the first month that begins on or after the date of enactment of the Civil Service Retirement Amendments of 1969".

1973—Subsec. (c). Pub. L. 93–136 redesignated existing pars. (1) and (2) as pars. (2) and (3) and added par. (1).

1969—Subsec. (b). Pub. L. 91–93, § 204(a), increased the annuity payable from the Fund by 1 percent.

Subsec. (c)(2). Pub. L. 91–93, § 204(b), increased the minimum survivor annuity for children of a deceased Federal employee, substituting dollar and percentage references to $900, $1,080, $2,700, $3,240, and 60 and 75 percent for prior references to $600, $720, $1,800, $2,160 and 40 and 50 percent respectively, such new increases to commence on or after the first day of the first month that begins on or after Oct. 20, 1969, the date of enactment of the Civil Service Retirement Amendments of 1969, whereas prior provisions were for computation of a child's annuity commencing after effective date of first increase under this section based on employee annuity that commenced after Oct. 1, 1956, or was payable at death.

Effective Date of 1984 Amendment

Section 201(b) of Pub. L. 98–270 provided that:

"(1) The amendments made by subsection (a) [amending this section] shall take effect on the date of the enactment of this Act [Apr. 18, 1984], except that no adjustment under section 8340(b) of title 5, United States Code (as amended by such subsection), shall be made during the period beginning on the date of the enactment of this Act and ending November 30, 1984.

"(2)(A) For purposes of the first adjustment under section 8340(b) of title 5, United States Code (as amended by subsection (a)), the base quarter ending September 30, 1983, shall be considered to have been a base quarter in which an adjustment under such section (as so amended) was made.

"(B) As used in subparagraph (A), the term 'base quarter' has the meaning given such term by section 8340(a)(1) of title 5, United States Code (as amended by subsection (a))."

Effective Date of 1982 Amendment

Section 304(c) of Pub. L. 97–253 provided that: "The amendments made by subsections (a) and (b) [amending this section and section 8345 of this title] shall apply with respect to any annuity commencing on or after October 1, 1982, and with respect to any adjustment or redetermination of any annuity made on or after such date".

Section 309(b) of Pub. L. 97–253 provided that: "The amendment made by subsection (a) of this section [amending this section] shall not cause any annuity to be reduced below the rate that is payable on the date of the enactment of this Act [Sept. 8, 1982], but shall apply to any adjustment occurring on or after such date of enactment under section 8340 of title 5, United States Code, to any annuity payable from the Civil Service Retirement and Disability Fund, whether such

annuity has a commencing date before, on, or after the date of enactment of this Act."

Effective Date of 1981 Amendment

Section 1702(c) of Pub. L. 97–35 provided that: "The amendments made by this section [amending this section] shall take effect on the date of the enactment of this Act [Aug. 13, 1981] and shall apply to annuities which commence before, on, or after such date."

Effective Date of 1980 Amendment

Section 401(b) of Pub. L. 96–499 provided that:

"(1) The amendment made by subsection (a)(1) [amending this section] shall apply with respect to annuities commencing after the 45th day after the date of the enactment of this Act [Dec. 5, 1980].

"(2) The amendment made by subsection (a)(2) [amending this section] shall take effect with respect to any annuity increase which takes effect after the date of the enactment of this Act [Dec. 5, 1980]."

Effective Date of 1978 Amendment

Amendment by Pub. L. 95–454 effective 90 days after Oct. 13, 1978, see section 907 of Pub. L. 95–454, set out as a note under section 1101 of this title.

Effective Date of 1976 Amendment

Section 1306(b) of Pub. L. 94–440 provided that: "The amendment made by subsection (a) [amending this section] shall apply to any increase in annuities after the date of enactment of this Act [Oct. 1, 1976]."

Section 1306(c)(2) of Pub. L. 94–440 provided that: "The amendment made by subsection (1) [amending this section] shall apply to any increase in annuities after the date of enactment of this Act [Oct. 1, 1976], except that with respect to the first date after the date of enactment of this Act on which the Commission is to determine a percent change, such percent change shall be determined by computing the change in the price index published for the month immediately preceding such first date over the price index for the last month prior to the date of enactment of this Act for which the price index showed a percent rise forming the basis for a cost-of-living annuity increase under section 8340(b) of title 5, United States Code [subsec. (b) of this section], as in effect immediately prior to the date of the enactment of this Act [Oct. 1, 1976]."

Effective Date of 1973 Amendment

Section 2 of Pub. L. 93–136 provided that: "The amendments made by this Act [amending this section] shall apply only with respect to annuities which commence on or after July 2, 1973."

Effective Date of 1969 Amendment

Section 207(b) of Pub. L. 91–93 provided that: "The amendments made by section 204(a) of this Act to section 8340 of title 5, United States Code, shall apply only to annuity increases which become effective under such section 8340 after the date of enactment of this Act [Oct. 20, 1969]."

Delay in Cost-of-Living Adjustments During Fiscal Years 1994, 1995, and 1996

Pub. L. 103–66, title XI, § 11001, Aug. 10, 1993, 107 Stat. 408, provided that:

"(a) Applicability.—This section shall apply with respect to any cost-of-living increase scheduled to take effect, during fiscal year 1994, 1995, or 1996, under—

"(1) section 8340(b) or 8462(b) of title 5, United States Code;

"(2) section 826 or 858 of the Foreign Service Act of 1980 [22 U.S.C. 4066, 4071g]; or

"(3) section 291 of the Central Intelligence Agency Retirement Act (50 U.S.C. 2131), as set forth in section 802 of the CIARDS Technical Corrections Act of 1992 (Public Law 102–496; 106 Stat. 3196).

"(b) Delay in Effective Date of Adjustments.—A cost-of-living increase described in subsection (a) shall not take effect until the first day of the third calendar month after the date such increase would otherwise take effect.

"(c) RULE OF CONSTRUCTION.—Nothing in this section shall be considered to affect any determination relating to eligibility for an annuity increase or the amount of the first increase in an annuity under section 8340(b) or (c) or section 8462(b) or (c) of title 5, United States Code, or comparable provisions of law."

TIME OF PAYMENT OF ANNUITY OR RETIRED OR RETIREMENT PAY WHICH PRESIDENT ADJUSTS

Section 2201(a) of Pub. L. 98–369 provided that: "Notwithstanding any other provision of law, beginning with the monthly rate payable for December 1984, any annuity or retired or retirement pay payable under any retirement system for Government officers or employees which the President adjusts pursuant to section 8340(b) of title 5, United States Code, shall be paid no earlier than the first business day of the succeeding month."

COST-OF-LIVING ADJUSTMENTS DURING FISCAL YEARS 1983, 1984, AND 1985

Section 301(a)–(c) of Pub. L. 97–253, as amended by Pub. L. 98–270, title I, § 201(c), Apr. 18, 1984, 98 Stat. 158; Pub. L. 98–396, title I, Aug. 22, 1984, 98 Stat. 1403, provided that:

"(a)(1) Except as provided in paragraph (3), the cost-of-living increase under any Government retirement system in annuity or retired or retainer pay of any early retiree taking effect in each of fiscal years 1983, 1984, and 1985, shall be equal to one-half of the assumed increase in the price index for that year.

"(2) For purposes of this subsection, an individual shall be considered to be an early retiree if—

"(A) the individual is under the age of 62 years as of the effective date of the cost-of-living increase involved (determined without regard to subsection (b));

"(B) the annuity or retired or retainer pay of the individual is not computed in whole or in part based on any disability of the individual; and

"(C) the annuity or retired or retainer pay of the individual is based upon the Government service of the individual.

"(3) If the percentage increase in the price index for fiscal year 1983, 1984, or 1985 (as determined by the Office of Personnel Management under section 8340(b) of title 5, United States Code) exceeds the assumed increase in the price index for that year, then the increase in the annuity or retired or retainer pay of an early retiree under paragraph (1) taking effect in that fiscal year shall be equal to—

"(A) one-half of the assumed increase in the price index for that year, plus

"(B) the amount by which the percentage increase in the price index exceeds the assumed price index increase.

If the percentage increase in the price index for fiscal year 1985 (as determined by the Office of Personnel Management under section 8340(b) of title 5, United States Code) is less than the assumed increase in the price index for that year, then the increase in the annuity or retired or retainer pay of an early retiree under paragraph (1) taking effect in that fiscal year shall be equal to the percentage increase in the price index for that year (as so determined).

"(4) As used in this subsection—

"(A) the term 'price index' has the meaning given such term in section 8331(15) of title 5, United States Code; and

"(B) the term 'assumed increase in the price index' means—

"(i) 6.6 percent, in the case of fiscal year 1983,

"(ii) 7.2 percent, in the case of fiscal year 1984, and

"(iii) 6.6 percent, in the case of fiscal year 1985.

"(5) The amount of any survivor annuity which is based on the service of any early retiree subject to this subsection shall be computed as if this subsection had not been enacted.

"(b) [Repealed. Pub. L. 98–270, title II, § 201(c)(2), Apr. 18, 1984, 98 Stat. 158.]

"(c) For purposes of this section, the term 'cost-of-living increase under a Government retirement system' means any increase under—

"(1) section 8340(b) of title 5, United States Code;

"(2) section 826 of the Foreign Service Act of 1980 [22 U.S.C. 4066];

"(3) the Central Intelligence Agency Act of 1964 for Certain Employees (50 U.S.C. 403 note);

"(4) section 1401a(b) of title 10, United States Code; or

"(5) any other adjustment of any annuity under a retirement system for Government officers or employees which the President determines, by Executive order, is based on adjustments under any of the provisions referred to in the preceding paragraph."

COST-OF-LIVING ADJUSTMENT OF RETIRED PAY OR RETAINER PAY OF MEMBERS AND FORMER MEMBERS OF ARMED FORCES AND COMMISSIONED OFFICERS OF NATIONAL OCEANIC AND ATMOSPHERIC ADMINISTRATION AND PUBLIC HEALTH SERVICE; EFFECTIVE DATE OF AMENDMENT

See provisions of section 801(c) of Pub. L. 94–361, title VIII, July 14, 1976, 90 Stat. 929, set out as a note under section 1401a of Title 10, Armed Forces.

SECTION REFERRED TO IN OTHER SECTIONS

This section is referred to in sections 8334, 8339, 8341, 8344, 8348, 8349, 8443, 8462 of this title; title 22 sections 3682, 4066; title 28 sections 373, 376, 377, 611, 627; title 31 section 777; title 50 section 2131.

§ 8341. Survivor annuities

(a) For the purpose of this section—

(1) "widow" means the surviving wife of an employee or Member who—

(A) was married to him for at least 9 months immediately before his death; or

(B) is the mother of issue by that marriage;

(2) "widower" means the surviving husband of an employee or Member who—

(A) was married to her for at least 9 months immediately before her death; or

(B) is the father of issue by that marriage;

(3) "dependent", in the case of any child, means that the employee or Member involved was, at the time of the employee or Member's death, either living with or contributing to the support of such child, as determined in accordance with such regulations as the Office of Personnel Management shall prescribe; and

(4) "child" means—

(A) an unmarried dependent child under 18 years of age, including (i) an adopted child, and (ii) a stepchild but only if the stepchild lived with the employee or Member in a regular parent-child relationship, and (iii) a recognized natural child, and (iv) a child who lived with and for whom a petition of adoption was filed by an employee or Member, and who is adopted by the surviving spouse of the employee or Member after his death;

(B) such unmarried dependent child regardless of age who is incapable of self-support because of mental or physical disability incurred before age 18; or

(C) such unmarried dependent child between 18 and 22 years of age who is a student regularly pursuing a full-time course of study or training in residence in a high school, trade school, technical or vocational institute, junior college, college, university, or comparable recognized educational institution.

For the purpose of this paragraph and subsection (e) of this section, a child whose 22nd birthday occurs before July 1 or after August 31 of a calendar year, and while he is regularly pursuing such a course of study or training, is deemed to have become 22 years of age on the first day of July after that birthday. A child who is a student is deemed not to have ceased to be a student during an interim between school years if the interim is not more than 5 months and if he shows to the satisfaction of the Office of Personnel Management that he has a bona fide intention of continuing to pursue a course of study or training in the same or different school during the school semester (or other period into which the school year is divided) immediately after the interim.

(b)(1) Except as provided in paragraph (2) of this subsection, if an employee or Member dies after having retired under this subchapter and is survived by a widow or widower, the widow or widower is entitled to an annuity equal to 55 percent (or 50 percent if retired before October 11, 1962) of an annuity computed under section 8339(a)–(i), (n), (p), (q), (r), and (s) as may apply with respect to the annuitant, or of such portion thereof as may have been designated for this purpose under section 8339(j)(1) of this title, unless the right to a survivor annuity was waived under such section 8339(j)(1) or, in the case of remarriage, the employee or Member did not file an election under section 8339(j)(5)(C) or section 8339(k)(2) of this title, as the case may be.

(2) If an annuitant—

(A) who retired before April 1, 1948; or

(B) who elected a reduced annuity provided in paragraph (2) of section 8339(k) of this title;

dies and is survived by a widow or widower, the widow or widower is entitled to an annuity in an amount which would have been paid had the annuitant been married to the widow or widower at the time of retirement.

(3) A spouse acquired after retirement is entitled to a survivor annuity under this subsection only upon electing this annuity instead of any other survivor benefit to which he may be entitled under this subchapter or another retirement system for Government employees. The annuity of the widow or widower under this subsection commences on the day after the annuitant dies. This annuity and the right thereto terminate on the last day of the month before the widow or widower—

(A) dies; or

(B) except as provided in subsection (k), remarries before becoming 55 years of age.

(4) Notwithstanding the preceding provisions of this subsection, the annuity payable under this subsection to the widow or widower of a retired employee or Member may not exceed the difference between—

(A) the amount which would otherwise be payable to such widow or widower under this subsection (determined without regard to any waiver or designation under section 8339(j)(1) of this title or a prior similar provision of law), and

(B) the amount of the survivor annuity payable to any former spouse of such employee or Member under subsection (h) of this section.

(c) The annuity of a survivor named under section 8339(k)(1) of this title is 55 percent of the reduced annuity of the retired employee or Member. The annuity of the survivor commences on the day after the retired employee or Member dies. This annuity and the right thereto terminate on the last day of the month before the survivor dies.

(d) If an employee or Member dies after completing at least 18 months of civilian service, his widow or widower is entitled to an annuity equal to 55 percent of an annuity computed under section 8339(a)–(f), (i), (n), (p), (q), (r), and (s) as may apply with respect to the employee or Member, except that, in the computation of the annuity under such section, the annuity of the employee or Member shall be at least the smaller of—

(1) 40 percent of his average pay; or

(2) the sum obtained under such section after increasing his service of the type last performed by the period elapsing between the date of death and the date he would have become 60 years of age.

Notwithstanding the preceding sentence, the annuity payable under this subsection to the widow or widower of an employee or Member may not exceed the difference between—

(A) the amount which would otherwise be payable to such widow or widower under this subsection, and

(B) the amount of the survivor annuity payable to any former spouse of such employee or Member under subsection (h) of this section.

The annuity of the widow or widower commences on the day after the employee or Member dies. This annuity and the right thereto terminate on the last day of the month before the widow or widower—

(i) dies; or

(ii) except as provided in subsection (k), remarries before becoming 55 years of age.

(e)(1) For the purposes of this subsection, "former spouse" includes a former spouse who was married to an employee or Member for less than 9 months and a former spouse of an employee or Member who completed less than 18 months of service covered by this subchapter.

(2) If an employee or Member dies after completing at least 18 months of civilian service, or an employee or Member dies after retiring under this subchapter, and is survived by a spouse or a former spouse who is the natural or adoptive parent of a surviving child of the employee or Member, that surviving child is entitled to an annuity equal to the smallest of—

(A) 60 percent of the average pay of the employee or Member divided by the number of children;

(B) $900; or

(C) $2,700 divided by the number of children;

subject to section 8340 of this title. If the employee or Member is not survived by a spouse or a former spouse who is the natural or adoptive parent of a surviving child of the employee or Member, that surviving child is entitled to an annuity equal to the smallest of—

(i) 75 percent of the average pay of the employee or Member divided by the number of children;

(ii) $1,080; or

(iii) $3,240 divided by the number of children;

subject to section 8340 of this title.

(3) The annuity of a child under this subchapter or under the Act of May 29, 1930, as amended from and after February 28, 1948, commences on the day after the employee or Member dies, or commences or resumes on the first day of the month in which the child later becomes or again becomes a student as described by subsection (a)(3) of this section, if any lump sum paid is returned to the Fund. This annuity and the right thereto terminate on the last day of the month before the child—

(A) becomes 18 years of age unless he is then a student as described or incapable of self-support;

(B) becomes capable of self-support after becoming 18 years of age unless he is then such a student;

(C) becomes 22 years of age if he is then such a student and capable of self-support;

(D) ceases to be such a student after becoming 18 years of age unless he is then incapable of self-support; or

(E) dies or marries;

whichever first occurs. On the death of the surviving spouse or former spouse or termination of the annuity of a child, the annuity of any other child or children shall be recomputed and paid as though the spouse, former spouse, or child had not survived the employee or Member.

(4) If the annuity of a child under this subchapter terminates under paragraph (3)(E) because of marriage, then, if such marriage ends, such annuity shall resume on the first day of the month in which it ends, but only if—

(A) any lump sum paid is returned to the Fund; and

(B) that individual is not otherwise ineligible for such annuity.

(f) If a Member heretofore or hereafter separated from the service with title to deferred annuity from the Fund hereafter dies before having established a valid claim for annuity and is survived by a spouse to whom married at the date of separation, the surviving spouse—

(1) is entitled to an annuity equal to 55 percent of the deferred annuity of the Member commencing on the day after the Member dies and terminating on the last day of the month before the surviving spouse dies or remarries; or

(2) may elect to receive the lump-sum credit instead of annuity if the spouse is the individual who would be entitled to the lump-sum credit and files application therefor with the Office before the award of the annuity.

Notwithstanding the preceding sentence, an annuity payable under this subsection to the surviving spouse of a Member may not exceed the difference between—

(A) the annuity which would otherwise be payable to such surviving spouse under this subsection, and

(B) the amount of the survivor annuity payable to any former spouse of such Member under subsection (h) of this section.

(g) In the case of a surviving spouse whose annuity under this section is terminated because of remarriage before becoming 55 years of age, annuity at the same rate shall be restored commencing on the day the remarriage is dissolved by death, annulment, or divorce, if—

(1) the surviving spouse elects to receive this annuity instead of a survivor benefit to which he may be entitled, under this subchapter or another retirement system for Government employees, by reason of the remarriage; and

(2) any lump sum paid on termination of the annuity is returned to the Fund.

(h)(1) Subject to paragraphs (2) through (5) of this subsection, a former spouse of a deceased employee, Member, annuitant, or former Member who was separated from the service with title to a deferred annuity under section 8338(b) of this title is entitled to a survivor annuity under this subsection, if and to the extent expressly provided for in an election under section 8339(j)(3) of this title, or in the terms of any decree of divorce or annulment or any court order or court-approved property settlement agreement incident to such decree.

(2)(A) The annuity payable to a former spouse under this subsection may not exceed the difference between—

(i) the amount applicable in the case of such former spouse, as determined under subparagraph (B) of this paragraph, and

(ii) the amount of any annuity payable under this subsection to any other former spouse of the employee, Member, or annuitant, based on an election previously made under section 8339(j)(3) of this title, or a court order previously issued.

(B) The applicable amount, for purposes of subparagraph (A)(i) of this paragraph in the case of a former spouse, is the amount which would be applicable—

(i) under subsection (b)(4)(A) of this section in the case of a widow or widower, if the deceased was an employee or Member who died after retirement;

(ii) under subparagraph (A) of subsection (d) of this section in the case of a widow or widower, if the deceased was an employee or Member described in the first sentence of such subsection; or

(iii) under subparagraph (A) of subsection (f) of this section in the case of a surviving spouse, if the deceased was a Member described in the first sentence of such subsection.

(3) The commencement and termination of an annuity payable under this subsection shall be governed by the terms of the applicable order, decree, agreement, or election, as the case may be, except that any such annuity—

(A) shall not commence before—

(i) the day after the employee, Member, or annuitant dies, or

(ii) the first day of the second month beginning after the date on which the Office receives written notice of the order, decree, agreement, or election, as the case may be, together with such additional information or documentation as the Office may prescribe,

whichever is later, and

(B) shall terminate—

(i) except as provided in subsection (k), in the case of an annuity computed by reference to clause (i) or (ii) of paragraph (2)(B) of this subsection, no later than the last day of the month before the former spouse remarries before becoming 55 years of age or dies; or

(ii) in the case of an annuity computed by reference to clause (iii) of such paragraph, no later than the last day of the month before the former spouse remarries or dies.

(4) For purposes of this subchapter, a modification in a decree, order, agreement, or election referred to in paragraph (1) of this subsection shall not be effective—

(A) if such modification is made after the retirement or death of the employee or Member concerned, and

(B) to the extent that such modification involves an annuity under this subsection.

(5) For purposes of this subchapter, a decree, order, agreement, or election referred to in paragraph (1) of this subsection shall not be effective, in the case of a former spouse, to the extent that it is inconsistent with any joint designation or waiver previously executed with respect to such former spouse under section 8339(j)(1) of this title or a similar prior provision of law.

(6) Any payment under this subsection to a person bars recovery by any other person.

(7) As used in this subsection, "court" means any court of any State, the District of Columbia, the Commonwealth of Puerto Rico, Guam, the Northern Mariana Islands, or the Virgin Islands, and any Indian court.

(i) The requirement in subsections (a)(1)(A) and (a)(2)(A) of this section that the surviving spouse of an employee or Member have been married to such employee or Member for at least 9 months immediately before the employee or Member's death in order to qualify as the widow or widower of such employee or Member shall be deemed satisfied in any case in which the employee or Member dies within the applicable 9-month period, if—

(1) the death of the employee or Member was accidental; or

(2) the surviving spouse of such individual had been previously married to the individual and subsequently divorced, and the aggregate time married is at least 9 months.

(k)(1)[1] Subsections (b)(3)(B), (d)(ii), and (h)(3)(B)(i) (to the extent that they provide for termination of a survivor annuity because of a remarriage before age 55) shall not apply if the widow, widower, or former spouse was married

for at least 30 years to the individual on whose service the survivor annuity is based.

(2) A remarriage described in paragraph (1) shall not be taken into account for purposes of section 8339(j)(5)(B) or (C) or any other provision of this chapter which the Office may by regulation identify in order to carry out the purposes of this subsection.

(Pub. L. 89–554, Sept. 6, 1966, 80 Stat. 577; Pub. L. 90–83, §1(80), Sept. 11, 1967, 81 Stat. 216; Pub. L. 91–93, title II, §206, Oct. 20, 1969, 83 Stat. 140; Pub. L. 91–658, §3, Jan. 8, 1971, 84 Stat. 1961; Pub. L. 92–243, §1, Mar. 9, 1972, 86 Stat. 56; Pub. L. 92–297, §7(4), May 16, 1972, 86 Stat. 145; Pub. L. 93–260, §1(a), Apr. 9, 1974, 88 Stat. 76; Pub. L. 94–183, §2(36), Dec. 31, 1975, 89 Stat. 1058; Pub. L. 95–317, §1(b), July 10, 1978, 92 Stat. 382; Pub. L. 95–318, §2, July 10, 1978, 92 Stat. 384; Pub. L. 95–454, title IX, §906(a)(2), (3), Oct. 13, 1978, 92 Stat. 1224; Pub. L. 95–598, title III, §338(c), Nov. 6, 1978, 92 Stat. 2681; Pub. L. 96–179, §1, Jan. 2, 1980, 93 Stat. 1299; Pub. L. 98–353, title I, §112, July 10, 1984, 98 Stat. 343; Pub. L. 98–615, §2(4), Nov. 8, 1984, 98 Stat. 3199; Pub. L. 99–251, title II, §§205–207, Feb. 27, 1986, 100 Stat. 25; Pub. L. 99–272, title XV, §15204(a)(2), Apr. 7, 1986, 100 Stat. 335; Pub. L. 101–428, §2(d)(7), Oct. 15, 1990, 104 Stat. 929; Pub. L. 102–378, §2(63), Oct. 2, 1992, 106 Stat. 1354; Pub. L. 104–208, div. A, title I, §101(f) [title VI, §633(a)(1)], Sept. 30, 1996, 110 Stat. 3009–314, 3009–362; Pub. L. 105–61, title V, §§516(a)(4), 518(a), Oct. 10, 1997, 111 Stat. 1306, 1307; Pub. L. 106–553, §1(a)(2) [title III, §308(h)(7)], Dec. 21, 2000, 114 Stat. 2762, 2762A–89.)

HISTORICAL AND REVISION NOTES
1966 ACT

Derivation	U.S. Code	Revised Statutes and Statutes at Large
(a)	5 U.S.C. 2251(h)–(j).	July 31, 1956, ch. 804, §401 "Sec. 1(h)–(j)", 70 Stat. 744. Oct. 11, 1962, Pub. L. 87–793, §1103(f)(A), 76 Stat. 871.
(b)–(f)	5 U.S.C. 2260.	July 31, 1956, ch. 804, §401 "Sec. 10", 70 Stat. 754. Aug. 27, 1958, Pub. L. 85–772, §1(b), (c), 72 Stat. 930. Sept. 6, 1960, Pub. L. 86–713, §1(a), 74 Stat. 813. Oct. 11, 1962, Pub. L. 87–793, §1103 (less (a) and (f)(A)), 76 Stat. 870, 871.

In subsection (b), the words "designated for this purpose under section 8339(i) of this title" are substituted for "designated in writing for such purpose by the employee or Member at the time of retirement" in view of the provisions of section 8339(i).

In subsection (f), the words "heretofore or hereafter" are substituted "either prior to, on, or after the effective date of the Civil Service Retirement Act Amendments of 1956".

Standard changes are made to conform with the definitions applicable and the style of this title as outlined in the preface to the report.

1967 ACT

Section of title 5	Source (U.S. Code)	Source (Statutes at Large)
8341(a)(4) ...	5 App.: 2251(j) (less last sentence).	Apr. 25, 1966, Pub. L. 89–407, §1 (words before 1st comma), 80 Stat. 131. July 18, 1966, Pub. L. 89–504, §502, 80 Stat. 300.

[1] So in original. No subsec. (j) has been enacted.

1967 ACT—CONTINUED

Section of title 5	Source (U.S. Code)	Source (Statutes at Large)
8341(b) (last sentence).	5 App.: 2260(a)(2).	July 18, 1966, Pub. L. 89–504, §506(a), 80 Stat. 301.
8341(d) (last sentence).	5 App.: 2260(c) (last sentence).	July 18, 1966, Pub. L. 89–504, §506(b), 80 Stat. 301.
8341(e)	5 App.: 2260(d).	July 18, 1966, Pub. L. 89–504, §506(c), 80 Stat. 301.
8341(g)	5 App.: 2260(f).	July 18, 1966, Pub. L. 89–504, §506(d), 80 Stat. 302.

In subsection (a)(4), the words "for the purposes of section 10(d)" are omitted as covered by the words "For the purpose of this section."

In clause (2) of the last sentence of subsection (b), the word "retired" is inserted before "Member" for clarity and to conform to the penultimate sentence and clause (1) of the last sentence.

In subsection (e), the words "any lump sum paid" are substituted for "the lump-sum credit, if paid" for clarity and consistency with subsection (g)(2).

In subsection (e)(2)(C), the words "capable of self-support" are substituted for "not incapable of self-support."

In subsection (g), the words "after July 18, 1966" are substituted for "hereafter." In clause (1), the word "he" is substituted for "he or she" on authority of 1 U.S.C. 1. The words "another retirement system for Government employees" are substituted for "any other retirement system established for employees of the Government" for consistency with section 8101(1)(ii).

REFERENCES IN TEXT

The Act of May 29, 1930, as amended from and after February 28, 1948, referred to in subsec. (e)(3), is the predecessor of section 8338 of this title.

AMENDMENTS

2000—Subsecs. (b)(1), (d). Pub. L. 106–553 substituted "(q), (r), and (s)" for "(q), and (r)".

1997—Subsec. (b)(1). Pub. L. 105–61, §516(a)(4), substituted "(q), and (r)" for "and (q) of this title".

Subsec. (b)(3)(B). Pub. L. 105–61, §518(a)(2)(A), substituted "except as provided in subsection (k), remarries" for "remarries".

Subsec. (d). Pub. L. 105–61, §§516(a)(4), 518(a)(2)(A), substituted "(q), and (r)" for "and (q) of this title" in introductory provisions and "except as provided in subsection (k), remarries" for "remarries" in cl. (ii).

Subsec. (h)(3)(B)(i). Pub. L. 105–61, §518(a)(2)(B), substituted "except as provided in subsection (k), in" for "in".

Subsec. (k). Pub. L. 105–61, §518(a)(1), added subsec. (k).

1996—Subsec. (e)(4). Pub. L. 104–208 added par. (4).

1992—Subsecs. (b)(1), (d). Pub. L. 102–378 substituted "(p)," for "(o),".

1990—Subsecs. (b)(1), (d). Pub. L. 101–428 substituted "(n), (o), and (q)" for "(n), and (o)".

1986—Subsecs. (b)(1), (d). Pub. L. 99–272 substituted ", (n) and (o)" for "and (n)" in subsec. (b)(1), and "(n), and (o)" for "and (n)" in subsec. (d).

Subsec. (e). Pub. L. 99–251, §205, added par. (1), redesignated existing pars. (1) and (2) as (2) and (3), respectively, and in par. (2) as redesignated substituted "that surviving child" for "each surviving child" in two places.

Subsec. (h)(1). Pub. L. 99–251, §206, substituted "annuitant, or former Member who was separated from the service with title to a deferred annuity under section 8338(b) of this title" for "or annuitant".

Subsec. (h)(4)(A). Pub. L. 99–251, §207, inserted "or death" after "retirement".

1984—Subsec. (a)(1)(A), (2)(A). Pub. L. 98–615, §2(4)(A), substituted "9 months" for "1 year".

Subsec. (b)(1). Pub. L. 98–615, §2(4)(B)(i), substituted "by a widow or widower, the widow or widower is entitled to an annuity equal to 55 percent (or 50 percent if retired before October 11, 1962)" for "by a spouse to whom he was married at the time of retirement, or by a widow or widower whom he married after retirement, the spouse, widow, or widower is entitled to an annuity equal to 55 percent, or 50 percent if retired before October 11, 1962" and "section 8339(j)(1) of this title, unless the right to a survivor annuity was waived under such section 8339(j)(1) or, in the case of remarriage, the employee or Member did not file an election under section 8339(j)(5)(C) or section 8339(k)(2) of this title, as the case may be" for "section 8339(j) of this title, unless the employee or Member has notified the Office in writing at the time of retirement that he does not desire any spouse surviving him to receive his annuity, or in the case of remarriage, he did not file an election under the third sentence of section 8339(j) of this title".

Pub. L. 98–353 substituted "and (n)" for "and (o)".

Subsec. (b)(3). Pub. L. 98–615, §2(4)(B)(ii), substituted "widow or widower" for "spouse, widow, or widower" wherever appearing in provisions preceding subpar. (A).

Subsec. (b)(3)(B). Pub. L. 98–615, §2(4)(B)(iii), substituted "55 years of age" for "60 years of age".

Subsec. (b)(4). Pub. L. 98–615, §2(4)(B)(iv), added par. (4).

Subsec. (d). Pub. L. 98–615, §2(4)(C)(i), inserted provision that the annuity payable under this subsection to the widow or widower of an employee or Member may not exceed the difference between the amount which would otherwise be payable to such widow or widower under this subsection and the amount of the survivor annuity payable to any former spouse of such employee or Member under subsec. (h).

Pub. L. 98–353 substituted "and (n)" for "and (o)".

Subsec. (d)(i). Pub. L. 98–615, §2(4)(C)(ii), redesignated subpar. (A) as cl. (i).

Subsec. (d)(ii). Pub. L. 98–615, §2(4)(C)(ii), redesignated subpar. (B) as cl. (ii) and substituted "55 years of age" for "60 years of age".

Subsec. (e)(1). Pub. L. 98–615, §2(4)(D)(i), inserted "or a former spouse who is the natural or adoptive parent of a surviving child of the employee or Member" in provisions preceding subpar. (A) and following subpar. (C).

Subsec. (e)(2). Pub. L. 98–615, §2(4)(D)(ii), substituted "surviving spouse or former spouse" for "surviving spouse" and "spouse, former spouse, or child" for "spouse or child" in provisions following subpar. (E).

Subsec. (f). Pub. L. 98–615, §2(4)(E), inserted provision that an annuity payable under this subsection to the surviving spouse of a Member may not exceed the difference between the annuity which would otherwise be payable to such surviving spouse under this subsection and the amount of the survivor annuity payable to any former spouse of such Member under subsec. (h) of this section in provisions following par. (2).

Subsec. (g). Pub. L. 98–615, §2(4)(F), substituted "55 years of age" for "60 years of age" in provisions preceding par. (1).

Subsecs. (h), (i). Pub. L. 98–615, §2(4)(G), added subsecs. (h) and (i).

1980—Subsec. (a)(2)(B). Pub. L. 96–179, §1(1), struck out "and" after "marriage;".

Subsec. (a)(3). Pub. L. 96–179, §1(2), added par. (3). Former par. (3) redesignated (4).

Subsec. (a)(4). Pub. L. 96–179, §1(3), redesignated former par. (3) as (4), substituted "unmarried dependent child" for "unmarried child" wherever appearing in subpars. (A), (B), and (C), substituted "but only if the stepchild" for "or recognized natural child who" in subpar. (A)(ii), and inserted "a recognized natural child, and (iv)" after "(iii)".

1978—Subsec. (a)(3). Pub. L. 95–454, §906(a)(2), substituted "Office of Personnel Management" for "Civil Service Commission".

Subsec. (b)(1). Pub. L. 95–598, §338(c)(1), inserted reference to subsec. (o) of section 8339 of this title.

Pub. L. 95–454, §906(a)(3), substituted "Office" for "Commission".

Pub. L. 95–317 inserted provisions relating to failure to file an election under section 8339(j) of this title in the case of remarriage.

Subsec. (d). Pub. L. 95–598, §338(c)(2), inserted reference to subsec. (*o*) of section 8339 of this title.

Subsec. (f)(2). Pub. L. 95–454, §906(a)(3), substituted "Office" for "Commission".

Subsec. (g). Pub. L. 95–318 struck out "after July 18, 1966," after "terminated".

1975—Subsec. (c). Pub. L. 94–183 substituted "8339(k)(1)" for "8339(k)".

1974—Subsec. (a)(1)(A), (2)(A). Pub. L. 93–260 substituted "1 year" for "2 years".

1972—Subsec. (a)(3)(A). Pub. L. 92–243 added cl. (iii).

Subsec. (c). Pub. L. 92–297, §7(4)(i), substituted "section 8339(a)–(i)", "section 8339(j)", and "section 8339(k)" for "section 8339(a)–(h)", "section 8339(i)", and "section 8339(j)", respectively.

Pub. L. 92–297, §7(4)(ii), substituted "section 8339(k)" for "section 8339(j)".

Subsec. (d). Pub. L. 92–297, §7(4)(iii), substituted "section 8339(a)–(f) and (i)" for "section 8339(a)–(e) and (h)".

1971—Subsec. (a)(3), (4). Pub. L. 91–658, §3(a), struck out par. (3) which defined "dependent widower", and redesignated par. (4) as (3).

Subsec. (b). Pub. L. 91–658, §3(b), designated existing first sentence as par. (1), and inserted exception phrase, provision for survival by widow or widower whom employee or Member marries after retirement, entitlement of widow or widower to 55 percent annuity (limited to 50 percent where retirement before Oct. 11, 1962), and substituted "any spouse surviving him" for "his spouse"; added par. (2); and added par. (3), first sentence, respecting entitlement to survivor annuity by a spouse acquired after retirement upon election from available survivor benefits, and designated as second and third sentences former second and third sentences, providing for widows and widowers and substituting "annuitant" for "retired employee or member".

Subsec. (d). Pub. L. 91–658, §3(c), substituted "his widow or widower" for "the widow or dependent widower of the employee or Member" in first sentence, struck out "or dependent" before "widower" in second sentence, and substituted in third sentence provision for termination of annuity where widow or widower dies or remarries before becoming 60 years of age for prior termination of annuity before widow or dependent widower dies, the dependent widower becomes capable of self-support, the widow or dependent widower of an employee remarries before becoming 60 years of age, or the widow or dependent widower of a member remarries.

Subsec. (e)(2). Pub. L. 91–658, §3(d), substituted reference to "subsection (a)(3)" for "subsection (a)(4)".

1969—Subsec. (d). Pub. L. 91–93, §206(a), provided for entitlement to a survivor annuity after an 18 month rather than a 5 year period of civilian service and prescribed as the annuity the smaller of two computations when computing the annuity under section 8399 (a) to (e) and (h) of this title.

Subsec. (e)(1). Pub. L. 91–93, §206(b), increased annuity of a surviving child, substituting "eighteen months" for "five years" of civilian service in par. (1), "60 percent", "$900", and "$2,700" for "40 percent", "$600", and "$1,800" in cls. (A), (B), and (C), respectively, and "75 percent", "$1,080", and "$3,240", for "50 percent", "$720", and "$2,160" in cls. (i), (ii), and (iii), respectively.

EFFECTIVE DATE OF 2000 AMENDMENT

Amendment by Pub. L. 106–553 effective on the first day of the first applicable pay period that begins on Dec. 21, 2000, and applicable only to an individual who is employed as a member of the Supreme Court Police after Dec. 21, 2000, see section 1(a)(2) [title III, §308(i), (j)] of Pub. L. 106–553, set out in a Supreme Court Police Retirement note under section 8331 of this title.

EFFECTIVE DATE OF 1997 AMENDMENT

Amendment by section 516(a) of Pub. L. 105–61 applicable to any annuity commencing before, on, or after Oct. 10, 1997, and effective with regard to any payment made after the first month following Oct. 10, 1997, see section 516(b) of Pub. L. 105–61, set out as a note under section 8334 of this title.

Section 518(c) of Pub. L. 105–61 provided that: "The amendments made by this section [amending this section and sections 8442 and 8445 of this title] shall apply with respect to remarriages occurring on or after January 1, 1995."

EFFECTIVE DATE OF 1996 AMENDMENT

Section 101(f) [title VI, §633(b)] of Pub. L. 104–208 provided that: "The amendments made by subsection (a) [amending this section and sections 8443 and 8908 of this title] shall apply with respect to any termination of marriage taking effect before, on, or after the date of enactment of this Act [Sept. 30, 1996], except that benefits shall be payable only with respect to amounts accruing for periods beginning on the first day of the month beginning after the later of such termination of marriage or such date of enactment."

EFFECTIVE DATE OF 1986 AMENDMENT

Amendment by Pub. L. 99–272 effective with respect to service performed on or after Apr. 7, 1986, see section 15204(b) of Pub. L. 99–272, as amended, set out as a note under section 8339 of this title.

EFFECTIVE DATE OF 1984 AMENDMENTS

Section 4 of Pub. L. 98–615, as amended by Pub. L. 99–251, title II, §201(a)–(c), Feb. 27, 1986, 100 Stat. 20, 22; Pub. L. 99–549, §9(a), Oct. 27, 1986, 100 Stat. 3065; Pub. L. 99–556, title V, §501(a), Oct. 27, 1986, 100 Stat. 3139; Pub. L. 100–238, title I, §127, Jan. 8, 1988, 101 Stat. 1758, provided that:

"(a)(1) Except as provided in paragraphs (3), (4), (5), and (6) and subsections (b) and (c), the amendments made by section 2 of this Act [amending this section and sections 8331, 8334, 8339, 8342, 8345, and 8348 of this title] shall take effect May 7, 1985, and shall apply—

"(A) to any individual who, on or after such date, is married to an employee or Member who, on or after such date, retires, dies, or applies for a refund of contributions under subchapter III of chapter 83 of title 5, United States Code, and

"(B) to any individual who, as of such date, is married to a retired employee or Member,

unless (i) such employee or Member has waived, under the first sentence of section 8339(j)(1) of such title (or a similar prior provision of law), the right of that individual's spouse to receive a survivor annuity, or (ii) in the case of a post-retirement marriage or remarriage, an election has not been made before such date by such employee or Member with respect to such individual under the applicable provisions of section 8339(j)(1) or 8339(k)(2) of such title, as the case may be (or a similar prior provision of law).

"(2) Except as provided in subsection (f), the amendments made by section 3 of this Act [amending sections 8901 to 8903, 8905, 8907, 8909, and 8913 of this title] shall take effect May 7, 1985, and shall apply to any individual who, on or after such date, is married to an employee or annuitant.

"(3) The amendments made by subparagraphs (B)(iii) and (C)(ii) of section 2(4) of this Act [amending section 8341 of this title] (relating to the termination of survivor benefits for a widow or widower who remarries before age 55) and the amendments made by subparagraph (F) of such section 2(4) [amending section 8341 of this title] (relating to the restoration of a survivor annuity upon the dissolution of such a remarriage) shall apply—

"(A) in the case of a remarriage occurring on or after the date of the enactment of this Act [Nov. 8, 1984]; and

"(B) with respect to periods beginning on or after such date.

"(4)(A) Except as provided in subparagraph (B), the amendment made by section 2(3)(A) of this Act [amending section 8339 of this title] (but only to the extent that it amends title 5, United States Code, by adding a new section 8339(j)(5)(C)) and the amendment made by section 2(3)(C) of this Act [amending section 8339 of this title] (which relate to the election of a survivor annuity for a spouse in the case of a post-retirement marriage or remarriage) shall apply—

"(i) to an employee or Member who retires before, on, or after May 7, 1985; and

"(ii) in the case of a marriage occurring on or after May 7, 1985.

"(B) The amendments referred to in subparagraph (A) shall not apply in the case of a marriage of an employee or Member retiring before May 7, 1985, if the marriage occurred after May 6, 1985, and before the date of the enactment of the Federal Employees Benefits Improvement Act of 1986 [Feb. 27, 1986].

"(C) Any election by an employee or Member described in subparagraph (B) to provide a survivor annuity for that individual's spouse by a marriage described in such subparagraph shall be effective if made in accordance with the applicable provisions of section 8339(j)(1) or 8339(k)(2) of title 5, United States Code, as the case may be, as in effect on May 6, 1985.

"(5)(A) Paragraphs (3), (4), and (5)(B) of section 8339(j) of title 5, United States Code (as added by section 2(3)(A) of this Act), shall apply in the case of a former spouse of an employee or Member whose marriage to such employee or Member terminated before May 7, 1985, if such employee or Member retires on or after such date. The paragraphs referred to in the preceding sentence shall so apply only insofar as they relate to an election to provide a survivor annuity for a former spouse.

"(B)(i) The requirement described in clause (ii) shall not apply to an election made by an employee or Member under section 8339(j)(3) of title 5, United States Code (as amended by section 2(3)(A) of this Act), in order to provide a survivor annuity under section 8341(h) of such title (as amended by section 2(4)(G) of this Act) in the case of a former spouse referred to in subparagraph (A) if the election meets the requirements of clause (iii).

"(ii) The requirement referred to in clause (i) is the requirement prescribed in section 8339(j)(3) of title 5, United States Code, for an employee or Member to make an election in the case of a former spouse under such section 8339(j)(3) at the time of retirement or, if later, within 2 years after the date on which the marriage of the former spouse to the employee or Member is dissolved.

"(iii) Clause (i) applies to an election which is made by an employee or Member who retires on or after May 7, 1985, and before the date of the enactment of the Federal Employees Benefits Improvement Act of 1986 [Feb. 27, 1986], and is received by the Office of Personnel Management within the 2-year period beginning on the date of the enactment of such Act.

"(C) A survivor annuity shall be paid a former spouse as provided in section 8341(h) of title 5, United States Code (as amended by section 2(4)(G) of this Act), pursuant to an election made in the case of such former spouse under this paragraph.

"(D) The amendments made by paragraphs (6) and (7) of section 2 of this Act [amending sections 8345 and 8348 of this title] shall apply in the case of survivor annuities and elections authorized by this paragraph.

"(6) The amendment made by section 2(4)(A) of this Act [amending section 8341 of this title] (relating to the definition of a widow or widower) and the amendment made by section 2(4)(G) of this Act (but only to the extent that it amends title 5, United States Code, by adding a new section 8341(i)) shall apply with respect to any marriage occurring on or after the date of the enactment of this Act [Nov. 8, 1984].

"(b)(1) Notwithstanding subsection (a)(1) of this section, a former spouse of an employee or Member who retired before May 7, 1985, or who died after becoming eligible to retire and before such date, is entitled to a survivor annuity under section 8341(b) of title 5, United States Code, as amended by this Act, if—

"(A) the retired employee or Member elects, in writing, within eighteen months after the date of enactment of this Act, according to procedures prescribed by the Office of Personnel Management, to have the annuity or Member reduced under section 8339(j) of title 5, United States Code, as amended by this Act, and, except as provided in paragraph (3) of this subsection, to deposit in the Civil Service Retirement and Disability Fund an amount determined by the Office, as nearly as may be administratively feasible, to reflect the amount by which such employee or Member's annuity would have been reduced had the reduction been in effect since such employee or Member's annuity commenced, plus interest computed at the annual rate of six percent for each year during which the annuity would have been reduced if the election had been in effect on and after the date the annuity commenced; or

"(B) where the employee or Member dies or died on or before the one hundred and eightieth day after the date of enactment of this Act or does not make the election described in subparagraph (A)—

"(i) the former spouse's marriage to the employee or Member was dissolved after September 14, 1978, and before May 8, 1987;

"(ii) the former spouse was married to the employee or Member for at least ten years during periods of creditable service under section 8332 of title 5, United States Code;

"(iii) the former spouse has not remarried before age fifty-five after September 14, 1978;

"(iv) the former spouse files an application for the survivor annuity with the Office on or before May 7, 1989; and

"(v) the former spouse is at least fifty years of age on May 7, 1987.

A survivor annuity under subparagraph (B) shall commence on the day after the employee or Member dies or the first day of the second month after the former spouse's application is received by the Office, whichever occurs later.

"(2) Except as provided in paragraph (3), if a retired employee or Member who makes an election under subparagraph (A) of paragraph (1) does not make the deposit required by such subparagraph, the Office shall collect the amount of the deposit by offset against the employee or Member's annuity, up to a maximum of 25 per centum of the net annuity otherwise payable to the employee or Member, and the employee or Member is deemed to consent to such offset.

"(3) An election made by an individual under subparagraph (A) of paragraph (1) of this subsection to provide a survivor annuity for any person prospectively voids any election previously made by such individual with respect to such person under section 8339(k)(1) of title 5, United States Code, as amended by this Act, or any similar prior provision of law. Notwithstanding the provisions of such subparagraph (A), an individual who made such an election under such section 8339(k)(1) (or prior provision) shall not be required to make the deposit described in such subparagraph.

"(4)(A) A former spouse of an employee or Member referred to in the matter before subparagraph (A) in paragraph (1) of this section shall be entitled to a survivor annuity under subparagraph (B) of such paragraph if—

"(i) the former spouse satisfies the requirements of clauses (ii) through (v) of such subparagraph (B); and

"(ii) there is no surviving spouse of the employee or Member and no other former spouse of such employee or Member who is entitled to receive a survivor annuity under subchapter III of chapter 83 of title 5, United States Code, based on the service of such employee or Member which is creditable under such subchapter and there is no other person who has been designated to receive a survivor annuity under such subchapter by reason of an insurable interest in such employee or Member.

"(B) For the purposes of this paragraph, the term 'surviving spouse' means a widow or a widower as defined in paragraphs (1) and (2), respectively, of section 8341(a) of title 5, United States Code.

"(5) A survivor annuity provided under this subsection shall be 55 per centum of the annuity of the retired employee or Member (or of that portion of the annuity which such employee or Member may have designated for this purpose under paragraph (1)(A) of this subsection), as determined under section 8339(a)–(i) and (n) of title 5, United States Code, increased by—

"(A) the total percent increase the retired employee or Member was receiving under section 8340 of such title at death, or

"(B) in the case of a retired employee or Member whose date of death precedes the one hundred and eightieth day after the date of enactment of this Act [Nov. 8, 1984], the total percent increase the retired employee or Member would have received under such section 8340 had such individual died on the one hundred and eightieth day after such date of enactment, and shall not be subject to reduction under section 8341(h)(2) of such title, as amended by this Act.

"(c) Notwithstanding subsection (a)(1) of this section, an employee or Member who retired before the one hundred and eightieth day after the date of enactment of this Act [Nov. 8, 1984] and who is married to a spouse acquired after retirement for whom such employee or Member was unable to provide a survivor annuity because—

"(1) the employee or Member was married at the time of retirement and elected not to provide a survivor annuity for the employee or Member's spouse at the time of retirement, or

"(2) the employee or Member failed to notify the Office of the employee or Member's post-retirement marriage within one year after the marriage,

may elect in writing, within one year after the date of enactment of this Act, in accordance with procedures prescribed by the Office, to provide for a survivor annuity for such spouse under section 8341(b) of title 5, United States Code, as amended by this Act, to have the retired employee or Member's annuity reduced under section 8339(j) of such title, as so amended, and to deposit in the Civil Service Retirement and Disability Fund an amount determined by the Office, as nearly as may be administratively feasible, to reflect the amount by which such employee or Member's annuity would have been reduced had the election been continuously in effect since the annuity commenced, plus interest. For the purposes of the preceding sentence, the annual rate of interest for each year during which the annuity would have been reduced if the election had been in effect on and after the date the annuity commenced shall be 6 percent. If the retired employee or Member does not make such deposit, the Office shall collect such amount by offset against such employee or Member's annuity, up to a maximum of 25 percent of the net annuity otherwise payable to such employee or Member, and such employee or Member is deemed to consent to such offset. The Office shall provide for general public notice of the right to make an election under this subsection. In cases to which paragraph (2) of this subsection applies, the retired employee or Member shall provide the Office with such documentation as the Office shall decide is appropriate, that such employee or Member attempted to elect a reduced annuity with survivor benefit for such employee or Member's current spouse and that such employee or Member's election was rejected by the Office because it was untimely filed.

"(d) A deposit required by subsection (b)(1)(A) or (c) of this section may be made by the surviving former spouse or spouse, as applicable, of the retired employee or Member.

"(e) The Office shall determine at the end of each fiscal year—

"(1) the cost of survivor annuities provided under subsections (b) and (c) of this section, less an amount determined appropriate by the Office to reflect the value of any deposits made under subsection (b)(1)(A), (c), or (d), and

"(2) the cost of administering subsections (b) and (c).

The Office shall notify the Secretary of the Treasury of the amounts so determined. The Secretary of the Treasury, before closing the account for the fiscal year in question, shall credit to the Civil Service Retirement and Disability Fund, out of any money in the Treasury not otherwise appropriated, such amounts, which shall be available in the same manner as provided under subparagraphs (A) and (B) of section 8348(a)(1) of title 5, United States Code, as amended by this Act.

"(f) Any individual—

"(1) who is entitled to a survivor annuity under subsection (b) of this section or pursuant to an election authorized by reason of the application of subsection (a)(5) of this section,

"(2) as to whom a court order or decree referred to in section 8345(j) of title 5, United States Code (or similar provision of law under a retirement system for Government employees other than the Civil Service Retirement System) has been issued before May 7, 1985, or

"(3) who is entitled (other than as described in paragraph (2)) to an annuity or any portion of an annuity as a former spouse under a retirement system for Government employees as of May 7, 1985,

shall be considered to have satisfied section 8901(10)(C) of title 5, United States Code, as amended by this Act. Notwithstanding subsection (a)(2) of this section, any such individual who otherwise meets the definition of a former spouse under section 8901 of title 5, United States Code, as so amended, may, within 12 months after the date of the enactment of the Federal Employees Benefits Improvement Act of 1986 [Feb. 27, 1986], enroll in an approved health benefits plan described by section 8903 of such title, under the conditions set forth in section 8905(c) of such title, as so amended (other than the conditions prescribed in subparagraphs (A) and (B) of paragraph (1) of such section 8905(c)).

"(g)(1) For purposes of subsections (a)(1), (b), (c), (d), and (e), 'employee', 'Member', and 'former spouse' each has the meaning given that term under section 8331 of title 5, United States Code, as amended by this Act.

"(2) For purposes of subsection (a)(2), 'employee' and 'annuitant' each has the meaning given that term under section 8901 of title 5, United States Code.

"(h) Section 827 of the Foreign Service Act of 1980 [22 U.S.C. 4067] and section 292 of the Central Intelligence Agency Retirement Act of 1964 for Certain Employees [50 U.S.C. 403 note] shall not apply with respect to either the amendments made by section 2 [amending sections 8331, 8334, 8339, 8341, 8342, 8345, and 8348 of this title] or the preceding provisions of this section."

[Section 501(b) of Pub. L. 99–556 provided that: "The amendments made by this section [amending note above] shall be effective as of May 7, 1985."]

[Section 9(b) of Pub. L. 99–549 provided that: "The amendments made by this section [amending note above] shall be effective as of May 7, 1985."]

[The Central Intelligence Agency Retirement Act of 1964 for Certain Employees, referred to in Pub. L. 98–615, set out above, is Pub. L. 88–643, Oct. 13, 1964, 78 Stat. 1043, which was revised generally by Pub. L. 102–496, title VIII, § 802, Oct. 24, 1992, 106 Stat. 3196, is known as the Central Intelligence Agency Retirement Act and is classified generally to chapter 38 (§ 2001 et seq.) of Title 50, War and National Defense.]

Amendment by Pub. L. 98–353 effective July 10, 1984, see section 122(a) of Pub. L. 98–353, set out as an Effective Date note under section 151 of Title 28, Judiciary and Judicial Procedure.

EFFECTIVE DATE OF 1980 AMENDMENT

Section 5(a) of Pub. L. 96–179 provided that: "The amendments made by the first section [amending this section] and section 2 of this Act [amending section 8901 of this title] shall take effect on the date of the enactment of this Act [Jan. 2, 1980], except that no benefits under chapter 89 of title 5, United States Code, made available by reason of such amendments shall be payable for any period before October 1, 1979.''

EFFECTIVE DATE OF 1978 AMENDMENTS

Amendment by Pub. L. 95–598 effective Nov. 6, 1978, see section 402(d) of Pub. L. 95–598, set out as an Effective Date note preceding section 101 of Title 11, Bankruptcy.

Amendment by Pub. L. 95–454 effective 90 days after Oct. 13, 1978, see section 907 of Pub. L. 95–454, set out as a note under section 1101 of this title.

Section 3 of Pub. L. 95–318 provided that: "The foregoing provisions of this Act [amending this section and enacting provisions set out as notes under this section] shall take effect on—

"(1) the first day of the month following the date of the enactment of this Act [July 10, 1978], or

"(2) October 1, 1978,

whichever date is later.''

EFFECTIVE DATE OF 1978 AMENDMENT; SURVIVOR ANNUITIES SUBJECT TO REDUCTION, ETC.

For effective date of amendment by Pub. L. 95–317 as first day of first month which begins on or after date of enactment of Pub. L. 95–317, which was approved July 10, 1978, or Oct. 1, 1978, whichever is later, and provisions respecting eligibility of an individual to a survivor annuity, or the reduction therefor, see section 4 of Pub. L. 95–317, set out as a note under section 8339 of this title.

EFFECTIVE DATE OF 1974 AMENDMENT

Section 1(b) of Pub. L. 93–260 provided that: "The amendments made by subsection (a) of this section [amending this section] shall not apply in the cases of employees, Members, or annuitants who died before the date of enactment of this Act [Apr. 9, 1974]. The rights of such individuals and their survivors shall continue in the same manner and to the same extent as if such amendments had not been enacted.''

EFFECTIVE DATE OF 1972 AMENDMENTS

Amendment by Pub. L. 92–297 effective on 90th day after May 16, 1972, see section 10 of Pub. L. 92–297, set out as an Effective Date note under section 3381 of this title.

Section 2 of Pub. L. 92–243 provided that: "The amendment made by the first section of this Act [amending this section] is effective upon enactment [Mar. 9, 1972]. Upon application to the Civil Service Commission, it also applies to a child of an employee or Member who died or retired before such date of enactment [Mar. 9, 1972] but no annuity shall be paid by reason of the amendment for any period prior to the date of enactment.''

EFFECTIVE DATE OF 1969 AMENDMENTS

Section 2 of Pub. L. 91–189 provided that: "The provisions of section 8341(e) of title 5, United States Code, as amended by section 206(b) of Public Law 91–93 (83 Stat. 140), shall be effective as of October 20, 1969.''

Amendment by Pub. L. 91–93 inapplicable in cases of persons retired or otherwise separated prior to Oct. 20, 1969, their rights and of their survivors continued as if such amendment had not been enacted, see section 207(a) of Pub. L. 91–93 set out as a note under section 8331 of this title.

EFFECTIVE DATE OF 1969 AMENDMENT; RECOMPUTATION AND REDUCTION OF SURVIVOR ANNUITIES

Section 207(c) of Pub. L. 91–93 provided that:

"(1) The amendment made by section 206(b) of this Act [amending this section] shall become effective on the first day of the first month which begins on or after the date of enactment of this Act [Oct. 20, 1969].

"(2) The annuity of each surviving child who, immediately prior to the effective date of such amendment [amending this section] is receiving an annuity

under section 8341(e) of title 5, United States Code, or under a comparable provision of any prior law, or who hereafter becomes entitled to receive annuity under the Act of May 29, 1930, as amended from and after February 28, 1948, shall be recomputed effective on such date, or computed from commencing date if later, in accordance with such amendment. No increase allowed and in force prior to such date shall be included in the computation or recomputation of any such annuity. This paragraph shall not operate to reduce any annuity.''

ADDITIONAL ELECTIONS UNDER CIVIL SERVICE RETIREMENT SPOUSE EQUITY ACT OF 1984

Section 201(d) of Pub. L. 99–251 provided that:

"(1) Notwithstanding the time limitation prescribed in subparagraph (A) of section 4(b)(1) of the Civil Service Retirement Spouse Equity Act of 1984 [Pub. L. 98–615, §4(b)(1)(A), set out as a note above], an election may be made under such subparagraph before the expiration of the 12-month period beginning on the date on which the regulations under paragraph (3) of this subsection first take effect.

"(2) Any retired employee or Member who has made an election under section 4(b)(1)(A) of the Civil Service Retirement Spouse Equity Act of 1984 [set out as a note above] (as in effect at the time of such election) before the regulations under paragraph (3) of this subsection become effective may modify such election by designating, in writing, that only a portion of such employee or Member's annuity is to be used as the base for the survivor annuity for the former spouse for whom the election was made. A modification under this subparagraph shall be subject to the deadline under paragraph (1) of this subsection.

"(3) The Office of Personnel Management shall prescribe regulations to carry out this subsection, including regulations under which an appropriate refund shall be made in the case of a modification under paragraph (2) of this subsection.''

RESTORATION OF SURVIVOR ANNUITIES FOR CERTAIN WIDOWS AND WIDOWERS REMARRYING BEFORE JULY 18, 1966, AND WHERE MEMBER DIED BEFORE JANUARY 8, 1971

Section 1 of Pub. L. 95–318, eff. Oct. 1, 1978, provided that:

"(a) Upon application to the Civil Service Commission, the annuity of—

"(1) a surviving spouse of an employee which was terminated under the provisions of section 8341 (b) or (d) of title 5, United States Code, or of any prior applicable law, because of the remarriage of such spouse before July 18, 1966, and

"(2) a surviving spouse of a Member who died before January 8, 1971, which was terminated under any such provision, because of the remarriage of such spouse,

shall be restored in accordance with the provisions of subsection (b) of this section.

"(b)(1) In the case of a remarriage occurring after the surviving spouse became sixty years of age, the annuity shall be restored to such spouse under subsection (a) of this section only if any lump sum paid on termination of the annuity is returned to the Civil Service Retirement and Disability Fund. If such amount is paid, the annuity shall be so restored commencing on the effective date of this section at the rate which would have been in effect if the annuity had not been terminated.

"(2) In the case of a remarriage occurring before the surviving spouse became sixty years of age, the annuity shall be restored to such spouse under subsection (a) of this section only if—

"(A) such spouse elects to receive this annuity instead of a survivor benefit to which the spouse may be entitled under subchapter III of chapter 83 of such title 5 or under another retirement system for Government employees by reason of the marriage; and

"(B) any lump sum paid on termination of the annuity is returned to such fund.

If the requirements of the preceding sentence are satisfied, such annuity shall be so restored commencing on the effective date of this section or on the first day of the month following the date the remarriage is dissolved by death, annulment, or divorce, whichever date is later, at the rate which was in effect when the annuity was terminated."

INCREASE IN ANNUITY PAYABLE TO SURVIVING SPOUSES OF MEMBERS, EMPLOYEES, OF ANNUITIES BASED ON SEPARATION OCCURRING PRIOR TO OCT. 20, 1969

Section 2(b) of Pub. L. 93–273, Apr. 26, 1974, 88 Stat. 93, provided that: "In lieu of any increase based on an increase under subsection (a) of this section, an annuity payable from the Civil Service Retirement and Disability Fund to the surviving spouse of an employee, Member, or annuitant, which is based on a separation occurring prior to October 20, 1969 shall be increased by $132."

Section 3 of Pub. L. 93–273, Apr. 26, 1974, 88 Stat. 93 provided in part that annuity increases under this pension shall apply to annuities which commence before, on, or after Apr. 26, 1974, but that no increase in annuity shall be paid for any period prior to the first day of the first month which begins on or after the ninetieth day after Apr. 26, 1974, or the date on which the annuity commences, whichever is later. See section 3 of Pub. L. 93–273, set out as a note under section 8345 of this title.

REMARRIAGE PROVISIONS

Section 205 of Pub. L. 91–93 provided that: "The provisions of subsection (b)(1), (d)(3), and (g) of section 8341 of title 5, United States Code, also shall apply in the case of any widow or widower—
"(1) of an employee who died, retired, or was otherwise finally separated before July 18, 1966;
"(2) who shall have remarried on or after such date; and
"(3) who, immediately before such remarriage, was receiving annuity from the Civil Service Retirement and Disability Fund;
except that no annuity shall be paid by reason of this section for any period prior to the enactment of this section. No annuity shall be terminated solely by reason of the enactment of this section. Notwithstanding the prohibition contained in the first sentence of this section on the payment of annuity for any period prior to the enactment of this section, in any case in which the Civil Service Commission determines that—
"(1) the remarriage of any widow or widower described in such sentence was entered into by the widow or widower in good faith and in reliance on erroneous information provided by Government authority prior to that remarriage that the then existing survivor annuity of the widow or widower would not be terminated because of the remarriage; and
"(2) such annuity was terminated by law because of that remarriage;
then payment of annuity may be made by reason of this section in such case, beginning as of the effective date of the termination because of the remarriage."

SECTION REFERRED TO IN OTHER SECTIONS

This section is referred to in sections 8331, 8333, 8339, 8340, 8342, 8343a, 8344, 8348, 8901, 8905, 8908 of this title; title 10 sections 1450, 1452; title 22 section 4069–1; title 38 sections 7426, 7438; title 50 section 403s.

§ 8342. Lump-sum benefits; designation of beneficiary; order of precedence

(a) Subject to subsection (j) of this section, an employee or Member who—

(1)(A) is separated from the service for at least thirty-one consecutive days; or

(B) is transferred to a position in which he is not subject to this subchapter, or chapter 84 of this title, and remains in such a position for at least thirty-one consecutive days;

(2) files an application with the Office of Personnel Management for payment of the lump-sum credit;

(3) is not reemployed in a position in which he is subject to this subchapter, or chapter 84 of this title, at the time he files the application; and

(4) will not become eligible to receive an annuity within thirty-one days after filing the application,

is entitled to be paid the lump-sum credit. Except as provided in section 8343a or 8334(d)(2) of this title, the receipt of the payment of the lump-sum credit by the employee or Member voids all annuity rights under this subchapter based on the service on which the lump-sum credit is based, until the employee or Member is reemployed in the service subject to this subchapter. In applying this subsection to an employee or Member who becomes subject to chapter 84 (other than by an election under title III of the Federal Employees' Retirement System Act of 1986) and who, while subject to such chapter, files an application with the Office for a payment under this subsection—

(i) entitlement to payment of the lump-sum credit shall be determined without regard to paragraph (1) or (3) if, or to the extent that, such lump-sum credit relates to service of a type described in clauses (i) through (iii) of section 302(a)(1)(C) of the Federal Employees' Retirement System Act of 1986; and

(ii) if, or to the extent that, the lump-sum credit so relates to service of a type referred to in clause (i), it shall (notwithstanding section 8331(8)) consist of—

(I) the amount by which any unrefunded amount described in section 8331(8)(A) or (B) relating to such service, exceeds 1.3 percent of basic pay for such service; and

(II) interest on the amount payable under subclause (I), computed in a manner consistent with applicable provisions of section 8331(8).

(b) Under regulations prescribed by the Office, a present or former employee or Member may designate a beneficiary or beneficiaries for the purpose of this subchapter.

(c) Lump-sum benefits authorized by subsections (d)–(f) of this section shall be paid to the person or persons surviving the employee or Member and alive at the date title to the payment arises in the following order of precedence, and the payment bars recovery by any other person:

First, to the beneficiary or beneficiaries designated by the employee or Member in a signed and witnessed writing received in the Office before his death. For this purpose, a designation, change, or cancellation of beneficiary in a will or other document not so executed and filed has no force or effect.

Second, if there is no designated beneficiary, to the widow or widower of the employee or Member.

Third, if none of the above, to the child or children of the employee or Member and descendants of deceased children by representation.

Fourth, if none of the above, to the parents of the employee or Member or the survivor of them.

Fifth, if none of the above, to the duly appointed executor or administrator of the estate of the employee or Member.

Sixth, if none of the above, to such other next of kin of the employee or Member as the Office determines to be entitled under the laws of the domicile of the employee or Member at the date of his death.

For the purpose of this subsection, "child" includes a natural child and an adopted child, but does not include a stepchild.

(d) If an employee or Member dies—

(1) without a survivor; or

(2) with a survivor or survivors and the right of all survivors terminates before a claim for survivor annuity is filed;

or if a former employee or Member not retired dies, the lump-sum credit shall be paid.

(e) If all annuity rights under this subchapter based on the service of a deceased employee or Member terminate before the total annuity paid equals the lump-sum credit, the difference shall be paid.

(f) If an annuitant dies, annuity accrued and unpaid shall be paid.

(g) Annuity accrued and unpaid on the termination, except by death, of the annuity of an annuitant or survivor annuitant shall be paid to that individual. Annuity accrued and unpaid on the death of a survivor annuitant shall be paid in the following order of precedence, and the payment bars recovery by any other person:

First, to the duly appointed executor or administrator of the estate of the survivor annuitant.

Second, if there is no executor or administrator, payment may be made, after 30 days from the date of death of the survivor annuitant, to such next of kin of the survivor annuitant as the Office determines to be entitled under the laws of the domicile of the survivor annuitant at the date of his death.

(h) Amounts deducted and withheld from the basic pay of an employee or Member from the first day of the first month which begins after he has performed sufficient service (excluding service which the employee or Member elects to eliminate for the purpose of annuity computation under section 8339 of this title) to entitle him to the maximum annuity provided by section 8339 of this title, together with interest on the amounts at the rate of 3 percent a year compounded annually from the date of the deductions to the date of retirement or death, shall be applied toward any deposit due under section 8334 of this title, and any balance not so required is deemed a voluntary contribution for the purpose of section 8343 of this title.

(i) An employee who—

(1) is separated from the service before July 12, 1960; and

(2) continues in the service after July 12, 1960, without break in service of 1 workday or more;

is entitled to the benefits of subsection (h) of this section.

(j)(1)(A) Payment of the lump-sum credit under subsection (a) may be made only if the spouse, if any, and any former spouse of the employee or Member are notified of the employee or Member's application.

(B) The Office shall prescribe regulations under which the lump-sum credit shall not be paid without the consent of a spouse or former spouse of the employee or Member where the Office has received such additional information and documentation as the Office may require that—

(i) a court order bars payment of the lump-sum credit in order to preserve the court's ability to award an annuity under section 8341(h) or section 8345(j); or

(ii) payment of the lump-sum credit would extinguish the entitlement of the spouse or former spouse, under a court order on file with the Office, to a survivor annuity under section 8341(h) or to any portion of an annuity under section 8345(j).

(2)(A) Notification of a spouse or former spouse under this subsection shall be made in accordance with such requirements as the Office shall by regulation prescribe.

(B) Under the regulations, the Office may provide that paragraph (1)(A) of this subsection may be waived with respect to a spouse or former spouse if the employee or Member establishes to the satisfaction of the Office that the whereabouts of such spouse or former spouse cannot be determined.

(3) The Office shall prescribe regulations under which this subsection shall be applied in any case in which the Office receives two or more such orders or decrees.

(Pub. L. 89–554, Sept. 6, 1966, 80 Stat. 579; Pub. L. 90–83, §1(81), Sept. 11, 1967, 81 Stat. 217; Pub. L. 95–454, title IX, §906(a)(2), (3), Oct. 13, 1978, 92 Stat. 1224; Pub. L. 97–253, title III, §303(c), Sept. 8, 1982, 96 Stat. 794; Pub. L. 97–346, §3(f), Oct. 15, 1982, 96 Stat. 1648; Pub. L. 98–615, §2(5), Nov. 8, 1984, 98 Stat. 3201; Pub. L. 99–251, title II, §208, Feb. 27, 1986, 100 Stat. 25; Pub. L. 99–335, title II, §§204(b)(2), 207(h), June 6, 1986, 100 Stat. 592, 596; Pub. L. 100–238, title I, §105(b), Jan. 8, 1988, 101 Stat. 1746; Pub. L. 101–508, title VII, §7001(b)(2)(D), Nov. 5, 1990, 104 Stat. 1388–329; Pub. L. 106–361, §3(a), Oct. 27, 2000, 114 Stat. 1402.)

HISTORICAL AND REVISION NOTES
1966 ACT

Derivation	U.S. Code	Revised Statutes and Statutes at Large
....	5 U.S.C. 2261.	July 31, 1956, ch. 804, §401 "Sec. 11" 70 Stat. 755. July 12, 1960, Pub. L. 86–622, §1(a), 74 Stat. 409. Oct. 4, 1961, Pub. L. 87–350, §3, 75 Stat. 771.

In subsection (a), the words "before October 1, 1956" are substituted for "prior to the effective date of the Civil Service Retirement Act Amendments of 1956" on authority of §406 of the Act of July 31, 1956, ch. 804, 70 Stat. 761.

In subsection (g), the words "the expiration of" are omitted as surplusage.

Standard changes are made to conform with the definitions applicable and the style of this title as outlined in the preface to the report.

1967 ACT

Section of title 5	Source (U.S. Code)	Source (Statutes at Large)
8342(a)	[No source].	[No source.]
8342(c)	5 App.: 2261(c).	Mar. 23, 1966, Pub. L. 89–373, § 2, 80 Stat. 78.
	5 App.: 2251(j) (last sentence).	Apr. 25, 1966, Pub. L. 89–407, § 1 (less words before 1st comma), 80 Stat. 131.

In subsection (a), the amendment is made for consistency within the subchapter and to reflect that it is the individual, rather than the position, that is subject to the subchapter.

In the last sentence of subsection (c), the words "this subsection" are substituted for "section 11" to reflect the codification of title 5, United States Code.

REFERENCES IN TEXT

The Federal Employees' Retirement System Act of 1986, referred to in subsec. (a), is Pub. L. 99–335, June 6, 1986, 100 Stat. 514, as amended. Title III of the Federal Employees' Retirement System Act of 1986 amended sections 3121 and 6103 of Title 26, Internal Revenue Code, section 1005 of Title 39, Postal Service, and section 410 of Title 42, The Public Health and Welfare, enacted provisions set out as notes under sections 8331, 8401, 8432, and 8472 of this title and section 6103 of Title 26, and amended provisions set out as a note under section 8331 of this title. Section 302 of that Act is set out as a note under section 8331 of this title. For complete classification of this Act to the Code, see Short Title note set out under section 8401 of this title and Tables.

AMENDMENTS

2000—Subsec. (j)(1). Pub. L. 106–361 amended par. (1) generally. Prior to amendment, par. (1) read as follows: "Payment of the lump-sum credit under subsection (a) of this section—

"(A) may be made only if any current spouse and any former spouse of the employee or Member are notified of the employee or Member's application; and

"(B) shall be subject to the terms of a court decree of divorce, annulment, or legal separation or any court order or court approved property settlement agreement incident to such decree if—

"(i) the decree, order, or agreement expressly relates to any portion of the lump-sum credit involved; and

"(ii) payment of the lump-sum credit would extinguish entitlement of the employee's or Member's spouse or former spouse to a survivor annuity under section 8341(h) of this title or to any portion of an annuity under section 8345(j) of this title."

1990—Subsec. (a). Pub. L. 101–508 inserted "or 8334(d)(2)" after "8343a" in second sentence.

1988—Subsec. (a). Pub. L. 100–238 amended last sentence of subsec. (a) generally. Prior to amendment, last sentence read as follows: "In applying this subsection with respect to an employee or Member who becomes subject to chapter 84 of this title, entitlement to payment of the lump-sum credit shall be determined without regard to paragraph (1) or (3) if, and to the extent that, such lump-sum credit relates to service of a type described in clauses (i) through (iii) of section 302(a)(1)(C) of the Federal Employees' Retirement System Act of 1986."

1986—Subsec. (a). Pub. L. 99–335 inserted ", or chapter 84 of this title," in pars. (1)(B) and (3), substituted "Except as provided in section 8343a of this title, the" for "The" in second sentence, and inserted provisions regarding entitlement by an employee or Member who becomes subject to chapter 84 of this title to payment of a lump-sum credit.

Subsec. (j)(1)(B). Pub. L. 99–251 amended subpar. (B) generally. Prior to amendment, subpar. (B) read as follows: "in any case in which there is a former spouse, shall be subject to the terms of a court order or decree issued with respect to such former spouse if—

"(i) the order or decree expressly relates to any portion of the lump-sum credit involved, and

"(ii) payment of the lump-sum credit would extinguish entitlement of the former spouse to a survivor annuity under section 8341(h) of this title or to any portion of an annuity under section 8345(j) of this title."

1984—Subsec. (a). Pub. L. 98–615, § 2(5)(A), substituted "Subject to subsection (j) of this section, an" for "An" in provisions preceding par. (1).

Subsec. (j). Pub. L. 98–615, § 2(5)(B), added subsec. (j).

1982—Subsec. (a). Pub. L. 97–346 substituted "such a position" for "such position" in par. (1)(B).

Pub. L. 97–253, § 303(c), substituted provisions that an employee or Member who is separated from the service for at least 31 consecutive days or is transferred to a position in which he is not subject to this subchapter for 31 days, and who files an application with the Office of Personnel Management for payment of a lump-sum credit, is not reemployed in a position subject to this subchapter at the time of filing, and will not be eligible for an annuity within 31 days of filing, is entitled to be paid the lump-sum credit and upon receipt of such payment, all annuity rights based on the service upon which the credit is based are voided until reemployment under this subchapter occurs for provisions that such employee or Member who was separated from the service, or was transferred to a position in which he did not continue subject to this subchapter, was entitled to be paid the lump-sum credit if his separation or transfer occurred and application for payment was filed with the Office of Personnel Management at least 31 days before the earliest commencing date of any annuity for which he was eligible, that the receipt of payment of the lump-sum credit by the individual voided all annuity rights under this subchapter until he was reemployed in the service subject to this subchapter, and that this subsection also applied to an employee or Member separated before October 1, 1956, after completing at least 20 years of civilian service.

1978—Subsecs. (a) to (c), (g). Pub. L. 95–454 substituted "Office of Personnel Management" for "Civil Service Commission" and "Office" for "Commission".

EFFECTIVE DATE OF 1990 AMENDMENT

Amendment by Pub. L. 101–508 effective with respect to any annuity having a commencement date later than Dec. 1, 1990, see section 7001(b)(3) of Pub. L. 101–508, set out as a note under section 8334 of this title.

EFFECTIVE DATE OF 1986 AMENDMENT

Amendment by Pub. L. 99–335 effective Jan. 1, 1987, see section 702(a) of Pub. L. 99–335, set out as an Effective Date note under section 8401 of this title.

EFFECTIVE DATE OF 1984 AMENDMENT

Amendment by Pub. L. 98–615 effective May 7, 1985, with enumerated exceptions and specific applicability provisions, see section 4(a)(1) of Pub. L. 98–615, as amended, set out as a note under section 8341 of this title.

EFFECTIVE DATE OF 1982 AMENDMENT

Section 303(d)(2) of Pub. L. 97–253 provided that: "The amendment made by subsection (c) [amending this section] shall take effect October 1, 1982."

EFFECTIVE DATE OF 1978 AMENDMENT

Amendment by Pub. L. 95–454 effective 90 days after Oct. 13, 1978, see section 907 of Pub. L. 95–454, set out as a note under section 1101 of this title.

REESTABLISHMENT OF RIGHT TO RECEIVE ANNUITY BY JUDGES WHO RECEIVED LUMP-SUM CREDIT

Pub. L. 96–504, § 2, Dec. 5, 1980, 94 Stat. 2741, provided that: "A present or former justice or judge of the United States, as defined by section 451 of title 28, United States Code, who, prior to the effective date of this section [Dec. 5, 1980], voided his right to receive an annuity under subchapter III of chapter 83 of title 5, United States Code, by applying for and receiving a refund of his lump-sum credit while serving as such a justice or judge may, upon application filed with the Office of Personnel Management within one year following the effective date of this section, redeposit such refund with interest computed under section 8334(e) of such title 5 and thereby reestablish his right to receive an annuity under such subchapter effective on the date he otherwise was eligible to receive an annuity. The surviving spouse of any such justice or judge who dies before the effective date of this section may apply to make such redeposit within one year following the effective date of this section and receive both (1) the amount of the annuity which the justice or judge would have been entitled to receive before his death had application been made by him for the annuity and (2) any survivor annuity the justice or judge could have provided under the provisions of law in effect at the time of separation from the service on which title to the annuity is based.''

SECTION REFERRED TO IN OTHER SECTIONS

This section is referred to in sections 8316, 8334, 8339, 8343, 8344 of this title; title 16 section 1168; title 26 section 3121; title 42 section 410.

§ 8343. Additional annuities; voluntary contributions

(a) Under regulations prescribed by the Office of Personnel Management, an employee or Member may voluntarily contribute additional sums in multiples of $25, but the total may not exceed 10 percent of his basic pay for creditable service after July 31, 1920. The voluntary contribution account in each case is the sum of unrefunded contributions, plus interest at 3 percent a year through December 31, 1984, and thereafter at the rate computed under section 8334(e) of this title, compounded annually to—

(1) the date of payment under subsection (d) of this section, separation, or transfer to a position in which he does not continue subject to this subchapter, whichever is earliest; or

(2) the commencing date fixed for a deferred annuity or date of death, whichever is earlier, in the case of an individual who is separated with title to deferred annuity and does not claim the voluntary contribution account.

(b) The voluntary contribution account is used to purchase at retirement an annuity in addition to the annuity otherwise provided. For each $100 in the voluntary contribution account, the additional annuity consists of $7, increased by 20 cents for each full year, if any, the employee or Member is over 55 years of age at the date of retirement.

(c) A retiring employee or Member may elect a reduced additional annuity instead of the additional annuity described by subsection (b) of this section and designate in writing an individual to receive after his death an annuity of 50 percent of his reduced additional annuity. The additional annuity of the employee or Member making the election is reduced by 10 percent, and by 5 percent for each full 5 years the individual designated is younger than the retiring employee or Member. However, the total reduction may not exceed 40 percent.

(d) A present or former employee or Member is entitled to be paid the voluntary contribution account if he files application for payment with the Office before receiving an additional annuity. An individual who has been paid the voluntary contribution account may not again deposit additional sums under this section until, after a separation from the service of more than 3 calendar days, he again becomes subject to this subchapter.

(e) If a present or former employee or Member not retired dies, the voluntary contribution account is paid under section 8342(c) of this title. If all additional annuities or any right thereto based on the voluntary contribution account of a deceased employee or Member terminate before the total additional annuity paid equals the account, the difference is paid under section 8342(c) of this title.

(Pub. L. 89–554, Sept. 6, 1966, 80 Stat. 580; Pub. L. 90–83, §1(82), Sept. 11, 1967, 81 Stat. 217; Pub. L. 95–454, title IX, §906(a)(2), (3), Oct. 13, 1978, 92 Stat. 1224; Pub. L. 97–253, title III, §303(a)(2), Sept. 8, 1982, 96 Stat. 794.)

HISTORICAL AND REVISION NOTES
1966 ACT

Derivation	U.S. Code	Revised Statutes and Statutes at Large
....	5 U.S.C. 2262.	July 31, 1956, ch. 804, §401 "Sec. 12", 70 Stat. 756. Aug. 14, 1958, Pub. L. 85–661, §1, 72 Stat. 614.

In subsection (a), the words "after July 31, 1920" are substituted for "on or after August 1, 1920". In paragraph (1), the words "payment under subsection (d) of this section" are based on "but such account shall not in any case include interest beyond date of payment" in former section 2262(d); the latter, accordingly, are omitted from subsection (d).

Standard changes are made to conform with the definitions applicable and the style of this title as outlined in the preface to the report.

1967 ACT

This section amends 5 U.S.C. 8343(a)(1) for consistency within the subchapter and to reflect that it is the individual, rather than the position, that is subject to the subchapter.

AMENDMENTS

1982—Subsec. (a). Pub. L. 97–253 inserted "through December 31, 1984, and thereafter at the rate computed under section 8334(e) of this title,".

1978—Subsecs. (a), (d). Pub. L. 95–454 substituted "Office of Personnel Management" for "Civil Service Commission" and "Office" for "Commission".

EFFECTIVE DATE OF 1982 AMENDMENT

Amendment by Pub. L. 97–253 effective with respect to deposits for service performed, on or after Oct. 1, 1982, and with respect to refunds for which application is received by Office of Personnel Management on or after Oct. 1, 1982, see section 303(d)(1) of Pub. L. 97–253, as amended by Pub. L. 97–346, §3(j)(1), Oct. 15, 1982, 96 Stat. 1649, set out as a note under section 8334 of this title.

EFFECTIVE DATE OF 1978 AMENDMENT

Amendment by Pub. L. 95–454 effective 90 days after Oct. 13, 1978, see section 907 of Pub. L. 95–454, set out as a note under section 1101 of this title.

SECTION REFERRED TO IN OTHER SECTIONS

This section is referred to in section 8342 of this title; title 10 section 942.

§ 8343a. Alternative forms of annuities

(a) The Office of Personnel Management shall prescribe regulations under which any employee or Member who has a life-threatening affliction or other critical medical condition may, at the time of retiring under this subchapter (other than under section 8337 of this title), elect annuity benefits under this section instead of any other benefits under this subchapter (including any benefits under section 8341 of this title) based on the service of the employee or Member.

(b) Subject to subsection (c), the Office shall by regulation provide for such alternative forms of annuities as the Office considers appropriate, except that among the alternatives offered shall be—

(1) an alternative which provides for—

(A) payment of the lump-sum credit to the employee or Member; and

(B) payment of an annuity to the employee or Member for life; and

(2) in the case of an employee or Member who is married at the time of retirement, an alternative which provides for—

(A) payment of the lump-sum credit to the employee or Member; and

(B) payment of an annuity to the employee or Member for life, with a survivor annuity payable for the life of a surviving spouse.

(c) Each alternative provided for under subsection (b) shall, to the extent practicable, be designed such that the present value of the benefits provided under such alternative (including any lump-sum credit) is actuarially equivalent to the present value of the annuity which would otherwise be provided the employee or Member under this subchapter, as computed under subsections (a)–(i), (n), (q), (r), and (s) of section 8339.

(d) An employee or Member who, at the time of retiring under this subchapter—

(1) is married, shall be ineligible to make an election under this section unless a waiver is made under section 8339(j)(1) of this title; or

(2) has a former spouse, shall be ineligible to make an election under this section if the former spouse is entitled to benefits under section 8341(h) or 8345(j) of this title (based on the service of the employee or Member) under the terms of a decree of divorce or annulment, or a court order or court-approved property settlement incident to any such decree, with respect to which the Office has been duly notified.

(e) An employee or Member who is married at the time of retiring under this subchapter and who makes an election under this section may, during the 18-month period beginning on the date of retirement, make the election provided for under section 8339(o) of this title, subject to the deposit requirement thereunder.

(Added Pub. L. 99–335, title II, §204(a), June 6, 1986, 100 Stat. 591; amended Pub. L. 101–428, §2(d)(5), Oct. 15, 1990, 104 Stat. 929; Pub. L. 101–508, title VII, §7001(a)(1), Nov. 5, 1990, 104 Stat. 1388–327; Pub. L. 103–66, title XI, §11002(a), Aug. 10, 1993, 107 Stat. 409; Pub. L. 105–61, title V, §516(a)(5), Oct. 10, 1997, 111 Stat. 1306; Pub. L. 106–553, §1(a)(2) [title III, §308(h)(5)], Dec. 21, 2000, 114 Stat. 2762, 2762A–89.)

AMENDMENTS

2000—Subsec. (c). Pub. L. 106–553 substituted "(a)–(i), (n), (q), (r), and (s)" for "(a)–(i), (n), (q), and (r)".

1997—Subsec. (c). Pub. L. 105–61, which directed the substitution of "(q), and (r) of section 8339" for "and (q) of section 8339 of this title" in section 8334a(c), was executed by making the substitution in subsec. (c) of this section to reflect the probable intent of Congress, because there is no section 8334a in this title.

1993—Subsec. (a). Pub. L. 103–66, §11002(a)(1), substituted "any employee or Member who has a life-threatening affliction or other critical medical condition" for "an employee or Member".

Subsec. (f). Pub. L. 103–66, §11002(a)(2), struck out subsec. (f) which prohibited election of alternative form of annuity where commencement date would be after Dec. 1, 1990, with certain exceptions.

1990—Subsec. (c). Pub. L. 101–428 substituted "(a)–(i), (n), and (q)" for "(a)–(i) and (n)".

Subsec. (f). Pub. L. 101–508 added subsec. (f).

EFFECTIVE DATE OF 2000 AMENDMENT

Amendment by Pub. L. 106–553 effective on the first day of the first applicable pay period that begins on Dec. 21, 2000, and applicable only to an individual who is employed as a member of the Supreme Court Police after Dec. 21, 2000, see section 1(a)(2) [title III, §308(i), (j)] of Pub. L. 106–553, set out in a Supreme Court Police Retirement note under section 8331 of this title.

EFFECTIVE DATE OF 1997 AMENDMENT

Amendment by Pub. L. 105–61 applicable to any annuity commencing before, on, or after Oct. 10, 1997, and effective with regard to any payment made after the first month following Oct. 10, 1997, see section 516(b) of Pub. L. 105–61, set out as a note under section 8334 of this title.

EFFECTIVE DATE OF 1993 AMENDMENT

Section 11002(d) of Pub. L. 103–66 provided that: "The amendments made by this section [amending this section and section 8420a of this title, section 4047 of Title 22, Foreign Relations and Intercourse, and section 2143 of Title 50, War and National Defense] shall become effective on October 1, 1994, and shall apply with respect to any annuity commencing on or after that date."

EFFECTIVE DATE

Section effective June 6, 1986, see section 702(b)(3) of Pub. L. 99–335, set out as a note under section 8401 of this title.

APPLICABILITY OF SECTIONS 8343a(f) AND 8420a(f) TO INDIVIDUALS CALLED TO OR PERFORMING DUTY IN CONNECTION WITH OPERATION DESERT SHIELD

Section 7001(a)(4) of Pub. L. 101–508 provided that:

"(A) In applying the provisions of section 8343a(f) or 8420a(f) of title 5, United States Code (as amended by paragraph (1)) to any individual described in subparagraph (B), the reference in such provisions to 'December 1, 1990' shall be deemed to read 'December 1, 1991'.

"(B) This paragraph applies with respect to any individual who—

"(i)(I) is a member of the Armed Forces of the United States who, before December 1, 1990, was called or ordered to active duty (other than for training) pursuant to section 672 [now 12301], 673 [now 12302], 673b [now 12304], 674 [now 12306], 675 [now 12307], or 688 of title 10, United States Code, in connection with Operation Desert Shield; or

"(II) is an employee of the Department of Defense who is certified by the Secretary of Defense to have performed, after November 30, 1990, duties essential for the support of Operation Desert Shield; and

"(ii) would have been eligible to make an election under section 8343a or 8420a of title 5, United States Code (as amended by paragraph (1)) as of November 30, 1990.

"(C) The Office of Personnel Management may prescribe such regulations as may be necessary to carry out this paragraph."

PARTIAL DEFERRED PAYMENT OF LUMP-SUM CREDIT FOR CERTAIN INDIVIDUALS ELECTING ALTERNATIVE FORMS OF ANNUITIES

Pub. L. 101–239, title IV, § 4005, Dec. 19, 1989, 103 Stat. 2135, as amended by Pub. L. 101–508, title VII, § 7001(a)(2)(A)–(C)(i), Nov. 5, 1990, 104 Stat. 1388–328, provided that:

"(a) IN GENERAL.—Notwithstanding any other provision of law, and except as provided in subsection (c), any lump-sum credit payable to an employee or Member pursuant to the election of an alternative form of annuity by such employee or Member under section 8343a or section 8420a of title 5, United States Code, shall be paid in accordance with the schedule under subsection (b) (instead of the schedule which would otherwise apply), if the commencement date of the annuity payable to such employee or Member occurs after December 2, 1989, and before December 2, 1990.

"(b) SCHEDULE OF PAYMENTS.—The schedule of payment of any lump-sum credit subject to this section is as follows:

"(1) 50 percent of the lump-sum credit shall be payable on the date on which, but for the enactment of this section, the full amount of the lump-sum credit would otherwise be payable.

"(2) The remainder of the lump-sum credit shall be payable on the date which occurs 12 months after the date on which the payment described in paragraph (1) is paid.

An amount payable in accordance with paragraph (2) shall be payable with interest, computed using the rate under section 8334(e)(3) of title 5, United States Code.

"(c) EXCEPTIONS.—The Office of Personnel Management shall prescribe regulations to provide that, unless the individual involved indicates otherwise by written notice to the Office (submitted at such time and in such manner as the regulations may require), this section shall not apply—

"(1) in the case of any individual who is separated from Government service involuntarily, other than for cause on charges of misconduct or delinquency; and

"(2) in the case of any individual as to whom the application of this section would be against equity and good conscience, due to a life-threatening affliction or other critical medical condition affecting such individual.

"(d) ANNUITY BENEFITS NOT AFFECTED.—Nothing in this section shall affect the commencement date, the amount, or any other aspect of any annuity benefits payable under section 8343a or section 8420a of title 5, United States Code.

"(e) DEFINITIONS.—For purposes of this section, the terms 'lump-sum credit', 'employee', and 'Member' each has the meaning given such term by section 8331 or section 8401 of title 5, United States Code, as appropriate.

"(f) CONTINUED APPLICABILITY.—The preceding provisions of this section (disregarding the provision in subsection (a) limiting this section's applicability to annuities commencing before the date specified in such provision) shall also apply in the case of any employee or Member whose election of an alternative form of annuity would not have been allowable under section 8343a(f) or 8420a(f) of title 5, United States Code (as the case may be), but for—

"(1) paragraph (2)(A) thereof; or

"(2) section 7001(a)(4) of the Omnibus Budget Reconciliation Act of 1990 [Pub. L. 101–508, set out as a note above]."

[Section 7001(a)(2)(C)(ii) of Pub. L. 101–508 provided that: "The amendments made by clause (i) [amending section 4005 of Pub. L. 101–239 and section 6001 of Pub. L. 100–203, set out as notes above and below] shall not apply in any case in which the first half of the lump-sum payment involved was paid before the beginning of the 11-month period which ends on the date of the enactment of this Act [Nov. 5, 1990]."]

Similar provisions were contained in the following acts:

Pub. L. 101–227, § 2, Dec. 12, 1989, 103 Stat. 1943, which was repealed by Pub. L. 101–508, title VII, § 7001(a)(2)(D), Nov. 5, 1990, 104 Stat. 1388–328.

Pub. L. 100–203, title VI, § 6001, Dec. 22, 1987, 101 Stat. 1330–275, as amended by Pub. L. 101–103, § 6, Sept. 30, 1989, 103 Stat. 672; Pub. L. 101–508, title VII, § 7001(a)(2)(C)(i), Nov. 5, 1990, 104 Stat. 1388–328.

SECTION REFERRED TO IN OTHER SECTIONS

This section is referred to in sections 8342, 8348 of this title; title 50 section 2143.

§ 8344. Annuities and pay on reemployment

(a) If an annuitant receiving annuity from the Fund, except—

(1) a disability annuitant whose annuity is terminated because of his recovery or restoration of earning capacity;

(2) an annuitant whose annuity, based on an involuntary separation (other than an automatic separation or an involuntary separation for cause on charges of misconduct or delinquency), is terminated under subsection (b) of this section;

(3) an annuitant whose annuity is terminated under subsection (c) of this section; or

(4) a Member receiving annuity from the Fund;

becomes employed in an appointive or elective position, his service on and after the date he is so employed is covered by this subchapter. Deductions for the Fund may not be withheld from his pay unless the individual elects to have such deductions withheld under subparagraph (A). An amount equal to the annuity allocable to the period of actual employment shall be deducted from his pay, except for lump-sum leave payment purposes under section 5551 of this title. The amounts so deducted shall be deposited in the Treasury of the United States to the credit of the Fund. If the annuitant serves on a full-time basis, except as President, for at least 1 year, on a part-time basis for periods equivalent to at least 1 year of full-time service, in employment not excluding him from coverage under section 8331(1)(i) or (ii) of this title—

(A) deductions for the Fund may be withheld from his pay (if the employee so elects), and his annuity on termination of employment is increased by an annuity computed under section 8339(a), (b), (d), (e), (h), (i), (n), (q), (r), and (s) as may apply based on the period of employment and the basic pay, before deduction, averaged during that employment; and

(B) his lump-sum credit may not be reduced by annuity paid during that employment.

If the annuitant is receiving a reduced annuity as provided in section 8339(j) or section 8339(k)(2) of this title, the increase in annuity payable under subparagraph (A) of this subsection is reduced by 10 percent and the survivor annuity payable under section 8341(b) of this title is increased by 55 percent of the increase in annuity payable under such subparagraph (A), unless, at the time of claiming the increase payable under such subparagraph (A), the annuitant notifies the Office of Personnel Management in writing that he does not desire the survivor annuity to be increased. If the annuitant dies while still reemployed, the survivor annuity payable is increased as though the reemployment had otherwise terminated. If the described employment of the annuitant continues for at least 5 years, or the equivalent of 5 years in the case of part-time employment, he may elect, instead of the benefit provided by subparagraph (A) of this subsection, to deposit in the Fund (to the extent deposits or deductions have not otherwise been made) an amount computed under section 8334(c) of this title covering that employment and have his rights redetermined under this subchapter. If the annuitant dies while still reemployed and the described employment had continued for at least 5 years, or the equivalent of 5 years in the case of part-time employment, the person entitled to survivor annuity under section 8341(b) of this title may elect to deposit in the Fund and have his rights redetermined under this subchapter.

(b) If an annuitant, other than a Member receiving an annuity from the Fund, whose annuity is based on an involuntary separation (other than an automatic separation or an involuntary separation for cause or charges on misconduct or delinquency) is reemployed in a position in which he is subject to this subchapter, payment of the annuity terminates on reemployment.

(c) If an annuitant, other than a Member receiving an annuity from the Fund, is appointed by the President to a position in which he is subject to this subchapter, or is elected as a Member, payment of the annuity terminates on reemployment. Upon separation from such position, an individual whose annuity is so terminated is entitled to have his rights redetermined under this subchapter, except that the amount of the annuity resulting from such redetermination shall be at least equal to the amount of the terminated annuity plus any increases under section 8340 of this title occurring after the termination and before the commencement of the redetermined annuity.

(d) If a Member receiving annuity from the Fund becomes employed in an appointive or elective position, annuity payments are discontinued during the employment and resumed on termination of the employment in the amount equal to the sum of the amount of the annuity the member was receiving immediately before the commencement of the employment and the amount of the increases which would have been made in the amount of the annuity under section 8340 of this title during the period of the employment if the annuity had been payable during that period, except that—

(1) the retired Member or Member separated with title to immediate or deferred annuity, who serves at any time after separation as a Member in an appointive position in which he is subject to this subchapter, is entitled, if he so elects, to have his Member annuity computed or recomputed as if the service had been performed before his separation as a Member and the annuity as so computed or recomputed is effective—

(A) the day Member annuity commences; or

(B) the day after the date of separation from the appointive position;

whichever is later;

(2) if the retired Member becomes employed after December 31, 1958, in an appointive position on an intermittent-service basis—

(A) his annuity continues during the employment and is not increased as a result of service performed during that employment;

(B) retirement deductions may not be withheld from his pay;

(C) an amount equal to the annuity allocable to the period of actual employment shall be deducted from his pay, except for lump-sum leave payment purposes under section 5551 of this title; and

(D) the amounts so deducted shall be deposited in the Treasury of the United States to the credit of the Fund;

(3) if the retired Member becomes employed after December 31, 1958, in an appointive position without pay on a full-time or substantially full-time basis, his annuity continues during the employment and is not increased as a result of service performed during the employment; and

(4) if the retired Member takes office as Member and gives notice as provided by section 8331(2) of this title, his service as Member during that period shall be credited in determining his right to and the amount of later annuity.

(e) This section does not apply to an individual appointed to serve as a Governor of the Board of Governors of the United States Postal Service.

(f) Notwithstanding the provisions of subsection (a) of this section, if an annuitant receiving annuity from the Fund, except a Member receiving annuity from the Fund, becomes employed as a justice or judge of the United States, as defined by section 451 of title 28, annuity payments are discontinued during such employment and are resumed in the same amount upon resignation or retirement from regular active service as such a justice or judge.

(g) A former employee or a former Member who becomes employed as a justice or judge of the United States, as defined by section 451 of title 28, may, at any time prior to resignation or retirement from regular active service as such a justice or judge, apply for and be paid, in accordance with section 8342(a) of this title, the amount (if any) by which the lump-sum credit exceeds the total annuity paid, notwithstanding the time limitation contained in such section for filing an application for payment.

(h)(1) Subject to paragraph (2) of this subsection, subsections (a), (b), (c), and (d) of this section shall not apply to any annuitant receiving an annuity from the Fund while such annuitant is employed, during any period described in section 5532(f) of this title (as in effect before the repeal of that section by section 651(a) of Public Law 106–65) or any portion thereof, under the administrative authority of the Administrator, Federal Aviation Administration, or the Secretary of Defense to perform duties in the operation of the air traffic control system or to train other individuals to perform such duties: *Provided, however,* That the amount such an annuitant may receive in pay, excluding premium pay, in any pay period when aggregated with the annuity payable during that same period shall not exceed the rate payable for level V of the Executive Schedule.

(2) Paragraph (1) of this subsection shall apply only in the case of any annuitant receiving an annuity from the Fund who, before December 31, 1987, applied for retirement or separated from the service while being entitled to an annuity under this chapter.

(i)(1) The Director of the Office of Personnel Management may, at the request of the head of an Executive agency—

(A) waive the application of the preceding provisions of this section on a case-by-case basis for employees in positions for which there is exceptional difficulty in recruiting or retaining a qualified employee; or

(B) grant authority to the head of such agency to waive the application of the preceding provisions of this section, on a case-by-case basis, for an employee serving on a temporary basis, but only if, and for so long as, the authority is necessary due to an emergency involving a direct threat to life or property or other unusual circumstances.

(2) The Office shall prescribe regulations for the exercise of any authority under this subsection, including criteria for any exercise of authority and procedures for terminating a delegation of authority under paragraph (1)(B).

(j)(1) If warranted by circumstances described in subsection (i)(1)(A) or (B) (as applicable), the Director of the Administrative Office of the United States Courts shall, with respect to an employee in the judicial branch, have the same waiver authority as would be available to the Director of the Office of Personnel Management, or a duly authorized agency head, under subsection (i) with respect to an employee of an Executive agency.

(2) Authority under this subsection may not be exercised with respect to a justice or judge of the United States, as defined in section 451 of title 28.

(k)(1) If warranted by circumstances described in subsection (i)(1)(A) or (B) (as applicable), an official or committee designated in paragraph (2) shall, with respect to the employees specified in the applicable subparagraph of such paragraph, have the same waiver authority as would be available to the Director of the Office of Personnel Management, or a duly authorized agency head, under subsection (i) with respect to an employee of an Executive agency.

(2) Authority under this subsection may be exercised—

(A) with respect to an employee of an agency in the legislative branch, by the head of such agency;

(B) with respect to an employee of the House of Representatives, by the Committee on House Oversight of the House of Representatives; and

(C) with respect to an employee of the Senate, by the Committee on Rules and Administration of the Senate.

(3) Any exercise of authority under this subsection shall be in conformance with such written policies and procedures as the agency head, the Committee on House Oversight of the House of Representatives, or the Committee on Rules and Administration of the Senate (as applicable) shall prescribe, consistent with the provisions of this subsection.

(4) For the purpose of this subsection, "agency in the legislative branch", "employee of the House of Representatives", "employee of the Senate", and "congressional employee" each has the meaning given to it in section 5531 of this title.

(*l*)(1) For the purpose of subsections (i) through (k), "Executive agency" shall not include the General Accounting Office.

(2) An employee as to whom a waiver under subsection (i), (j), or (k) is in effect shall not be considered an employee for purposes of this chapter or chapter 84 of this title.

(Pub. L. 89–554, Sept. 6, 1966, 80 Stat. 581; Pub. L. 90–83, §1(83), Sept. 11, 1967, 81 Stat. 217; Pub. L. 91–375, §6(c)(20), Aug. 12, 1970, 84 Stat. 776; Pub. L. 91–658, §4, Jan. 8, 1971, 84 Stat. 1962; Pub. L. 92–297, §7(5), May 16, 1972, 86 Stat. 145; Pub. L. 94–397, §1(a)–(c), Sept. 3, 1976, 90 Stat. 1202, 1303; Pub. L. 95–454, title IX, §906(a)(14), Oct. 13, 1978, 92 Stat. 1226; Pub. L. 95–598, title III, §338(d), Nov. 6, 1978, 92 Stat. 2681; Pub. L. 96–179, §4, Jan. 2, 1980, 93 Stat. 1299; Pub. L. 96–504, §1, Dec. 5, 1980, 94 Stat. 2741; Pub. L. 97–141, §5(a), Dec. 29, 1981, 95 Stat. 1719; Pub. L. 97–276, §151(g), Oct. 2, 1982, 96 Stat. 1202; Pub. L. 97–346, §3(j)(2), Oct. 15, 1982, 96 Stat. 1649; Pub. L. 98–353, title I, §112, July 10, 1984, 98 Stat. 343; Pub. L. 98–396, title I, Aug. 22, 1984, 98 Stat. 1403; Pub. L. 98–525, title XV, §1537(e), Oct. 19, 1984, 98 Stat. 2636; Pub. L. 99–88, title I, §100, Aug. 15, 1985, 99 Stat. 351; Pub. L. 99–500, §101(*l*), Oct. 18, 1986, 100 Stat. 1783–308, and Pub. L. 99–591, §101(*l*), Oct. 30, 1986, 100 Stat. 3341–308; Pub. L. 100–202, §§101(*l*) [title I], 106, Dec. 22, 1987, 101 Stat. 1329–358, 1329–362, 1329–433; Pub. L. 100–457, title I, Sept. 30, 1988, 102 Stat. 2129; Pub. L. 101–428, §2(d)(8), Oct. 15, 1990, 104 Stat. 929; Pub. L. 101–509, title V, §529 [title I, §108(b)], Nov. 5, 1990, 104 Stat. 1427, 1450; Pub. L. 101–510, div. A, title XII, §1206(j)(2), Nov. 5, 1990, 104 Stat. 1664; Pub. L. 102–190, div. A, title VI, §655(b), Dec. 5, 1991, 105 Stat. 1391; Pub. L. 102–378, §8(a), Oct. 2, 1992, 106 Stat. 1359; Pub. L. 105–55, title I, §107, Oct. 7, 1997, 111 Stat. 1184; Pub. L. 105–61, title V, §516(a)(6), Oct. 10, 1997, 111 Stat. 1306; Pub. L. 106–398, §1 [[div. A], title X, §1087(f)(5)], Oct. 30, 2000, 114 Stat. 1654, 1654A–293; Pub. L. 106–553, §1(a)(2) [title III, §308(h)(8)], Dec. 21, 2000, 114 Stat. 2762, 2762A–89.)

HISTORICAL AND REVISION NOTES
1966 ACT

Derivation	U.S. Code	Revised Statutes and Statutes at Large
....	5 U.S.C. 2263 (less (a)).	July 31, 1956, ch. 804, §401 "Sec. 13 (less (a))", 70 Stat. 757. July 7, 1960, Pub. L. 86–604, §1(f), 74 Stat. 358. July 12, 1960, Pub. L. 86–622, §3(a), 74 Stat. 410. Oct. 4, 1961, Pub. L. 87–350, §5, 75 Stat. 771.

In subsections (a) and (b), the words "except for lump-sum leave payment purposes under section 61b of this title" are omitted as unnecessary as section 5551(a) provides that a "lump-sum leave payment is considered pay for taxation purposes only".

In subsection (a), the words "after September 30, 1956" are substituted for "hereafter" on authority of § 406 of the Act of July 31, 1956, ch. 804, 70 Stat. 761. In paragraph (2), the words "other than an automatic separation" are substituted for "excluding a separation under the automatic separation provisions of this chapter". In the third sentence, the words "and this provision concerning the lump-sum leave payments shall also be effective in the case of each retired employee separated from reemployment after December 15, 1953, and before the effective date of the Civil Service Retirement Act Amendments of 1956" are omitted as executed, and any existing rights are preserved by technical section 8. In the fourth sentence, the words "except as President" are added to preserve the exception stated in former section 2252(b). In the penultimate sentence, the words "after October 3, 1961" are substituted for "on or after October 4, 1961". In the last sentence, the words "in any manner" are omitted as unnecessary.

In subsection (b), the words "receiving annuity from the Fund" are substituted for "heretofore or hereafter retired under this chapter". The word "hereafter" is omitted as unnecessary. In paragraph (1)(B), the words "the day after" are substituted for "the first day of the month following" on authority of former section 2264(b), which is carried into section 8345(b). In paragraph (1), former clause (C) is omitted as obsolete. In paragraph (2)(D), the words "of the United States" are omitted as unnecessary.

Standard changes are made to conform with the definitions applicable and the style of this title as outlined in the preface to the report.

1967 ACT

Section of title 5	Source (U.S. Code)	Source (Statutes at Large)
8344(a)	5 App.: 2263(b) (last sentence).	Mar. 30, 1966, Pub. L. 89–378, § 1, 80 Stat. 93.

In subsection (a), the words "after July 11, 1960" are substituted for "on or after July 12, 1960." In subsection (b)(1), the amendment is made for consistency within the subchapter.

In the codification of 5 U.S.C. 8344 by Public Law 89–554, the words "except for lump-sum leave payment purposes under section 61b of this title" were omitted from the third sentence of subsection (a) and from subsection (b)(2)(C) on the basis that they were unnecessary since former 5 U.S.C. 61b [now codified as 5 U.S.C. 5551(a)] provided that a lump-sum leave payment was considered pay for taxation purposes only. This amendment restores to 5 U.S.C. 8344 the language that was so omitted to conform to the source statute (section 13 of the Civil Service Retirement Act, as amended) and in recognition that the language was expressly placed in the source statute to overcome certain decisions of the Comptroller General of the United States (see 28 Comp. Gen. 294; 33 id. 591, and 36 id. 209).

REFERENCES IN TEXT

Level V of the Executive Schedule, referred to in subsec. (h)(1), is set out in section 5316 of this title.

CODIFICATION

Amendment of subsec. (h)(2) by Pub. L. 99–500 and 99–591 is based on provisions under the subheading "Federal Aviation Administration, Operations", in title I of H.R. 5205 (Department of Transportation and Related Agencies Appropriations Act, 1987), as incorporated by reference by section 101(l) of Pub. L. 99–500 and 99–591, and enacted into law by section 106 of Pub. L. 100–202.

Pub. L. 99–591 is a corrected version of Pub. L. 99–500.

AMENDMENTS

2000—Subsec. (a)(A). Pub. L. 106–553 substituted "(q), (r), and (s)" for "(q), and (r)".

Subsec. (h)(1). Pub. L. 106–398 inserted "(as in effect before the repeal of that section by section 651(a) of Public Law 106–65)" after "section 5532(f)(2) of this title".

1997—Subsec. (a)(A). Pub. L. 105–61 substituted "(q), and (r)" for "and (q) of this title".

Subsec. (k)(2)(B), (3). Pub. L. 105–55 substituted "the Committee on House Oversight of the House of Representatives" for "the Speaker of the House of Representatives".

1992—Subsec. (i). Pub. L. 102–378 repealed Pub. L. 101–510, § 1206(j)(2). See 1990 Amendment note below.

1991—Subsec. (i)(3). Pub. L. 102–190, § 655(b)(2), struck out par. (3) which read as follows: "An employee to whom a waiver under subparagraph (A) or (B) of paragraph (1) applies shall not be deemed an employee for the purposes of this chapter or chapter 84 while such waiver is in effect."

Subsecs. (j) to (l). Pub. L. 102–190, § 655(b)(1), added subsecs. (j) to (l).

1990—Subsec. (a)(A). Pub. L. 101–428 substituted "(i), (n), and (q)" for "(i), and (n)".

Subsec. (i). Pub. L. 101–510, § 1206(j)(2), added a subsec. (i) identical to that added by Pub. L. 101–509, see below. Pub. L. 102–378, § 8(a), repealed Pub. L. 101–510, § 1206(j)(2), and provided that this title shall read as if such section 1206(j)(2) had not been enacted.

Pub. L. 101–509 added subsec. (i).

1988—Subsec. (h)(2). Pub. L. 100–457 substituted "1987" for "1986".

1987—Subsec. (h)(2). Pub. L. 100–202, § 101(l) [title I], substituted "December 31, 1986" for "April 1, 1986".

For amendment by section 106 of Pub. L. 100–202, see 1986 Amendment note below.

1986—Subsec. (h)(2). Pub. L. 99–500 and Pub. L. 99–591, § 101(l), as enacted by Pub. L. 100–202, § 106, substituted "April 1, 1986" for "April 1, 1985". See Codification note above.

1985—Subsec. (h)(1). Pub. L. 99–88 inserted proviso directing that the amount an annuitant may receive in pay, excluding premium pay, in any pay period when aggregated with the annuity payable during that same period shall not exceed the rate payable for level V of the Executive Schedule.

Subsec. (h)(2). Pub. L. 99–88 substituted "April 1, 1985" for "August 3, 1981".

1984—Subsec. (a)(A). Pub. L. 98–353 substituted "and (n)" for "and (o)".

Subsec. (d). Pub. L. 98–396 substituted "on termination of the employment in the amount equal to the sum of the amount of the annuity the member was receiving immediately before the commencement of the employment and the amount of the increases which would have been made in the amount of the annuity under section 8340 of this title during the period of the employment if the annuity had been payable during that period" for "in the same amount on termination of the employment".

Subsec. (h)(1). Pub. L. 98–525 inserted "or the Secretary of Defense".

1982—Subsec. (a). Pub. L. 97–346 inserted "unless the individual elects to have such deductions withheld under subparagraph (A)" and "(to the extent deposits or deductions have not otherwise been made)".

Subsec. (a)(4)(A). Pub. L. 97–346 inserted "deductions for the Fund may be withheld from his pay (if the employee so elects)".

Subsec. (h). Pub. L. 97–276 added subsec. (h).

1981—Subsec. (c). Pub. L. 97–141 inserted provision that upon separation from such position, an individual whose annuity is so terminated is entitled to have his rights redetermined under this subchapter, except that the amount of the annuity resulting from such redetermination shall be at least equal to the amount of the terminated annuity plus any increases under section 8340 of this title occurring after the termination and before the commencement of the redetermined annuity.

1980—Subsec. (c). Pub. L. 96–179 inserted "or is elected as a Member," after "subject to this subchapter,".

Subsecs. (f), (g). Pub. L. 96–504 added subsecs. (f) and (g).

1978—Subsec. (a). Pub. L. 95–598 inserted reference to subsec. (*o*) of section 8339 of this title in par. (A).

Pub. L. 95–454 substituted "Office of Personnel Management" for "Commission" in provisions following par. (B).

1976—Subsec. (a). Pub. L. 94–397, § 1(a), inserted provisions requiring applicability to annuitants whose annuity is terminated under subsecs. (b) and (c) of this section, authorizing deducted amounts to be deposited in the Treasury to the credit of the Fund, and covering described employment continuing for the equivalent of five years in the case of part-time employment, and struck out provisions requiring employment after Sept. 30, 1956, or service on July 31, 1956, for application of coverage, and redetermination rights for an annuitant whose annuity is based on involuntary separation from the service and who is separated after July 11, 1960 for full-time employment began before Oct. 1, 1956.

Subsecs. (b), (c). Pub. L. 94–397, § 1(b), added subsecs. (b) and (c). Former subsecs. (b) and (c) redesignated (d) and (e), respectively.

Subsec. (d). Pub. L. 94–397, § 1(b), (c), redesignated former subsec. (b) as (d) and struck out prohibition of application of subsec. to a Member appointed by the President to a position not requiring confirmation by the Senate.

Subsec. (e). Pub. L. 94–397, § 1(b), redesignated former subsec. (c) as (e).

1972—Subsec. (a). Pub. L. 92–297 substituted "section 8339(a), (b), (d), (e), (h), and (i)" for "section 8339(a), (b), (d), (g), and (h)", in subpar. (A), and "section 8339(j) or section 8339(k)(2)" for "section 8339(i) or section 8339(j)(2)", in sentence following cl. (ii).

1971—Subsec. (a). Pub. L. 91–658 substituted provisions respecting reemployed annuitants and reduction in their annuity and increase in survivor annuity, notice to Commission of a desire not to increase the survivor annuity, increase in survivor annuity where annuitant dies while still reemployed, and redetermination of rights to survivor annuity where reemployment continued for five or more years upon election to deposit in the Fund, for prior provision that employment of an annuitant did not create an annuity for or affect the annuity of a survivor.

1970—Subsec. (c). Pub. L. 91–375 added subsec. (c).

CHANGE OF NAME

Committee on House Oversight of House of Representatives changed to Committee on House Administration of House of Representatives by House Resolution No. 5, One Hundred Sixth Congress, Jan. 6, 1999.

EFFECTIVE DATE OF 2000 AMENDMENT

Amendment by Pub. L. 106–553 effective on the first day of the first applicable pay period that begins on Dec. 21, 2000, and applicable only to an individual who is employed as a member of the Supreme Court Police after Dec. 21, 2000, see section 1(a)(2) [title III, § 308(i), (j)] of Pub. L. 106–553, set out in a Supreme Court Police Retirement note under section 8331 of this title.

EFFECTIVE DATE OF 1997 AMENDMENT

Amendment by Pub. L. 105–61 applicable to any annuity commencing before, on, or after Oct. 10, 1997, and effective with regard to any payment made after the first month following Oct. 10, 1997, see section 516(b) of Pub. L. 105–61, set out as a note under section 8334 of this title.

EFFECTIVE DATE OF 1992 AMENDMENT

Amendment by Pub. L. 102–378 effective Nov. 5, 1990, see section 9(b)(6) of Pub. L. 102–378, set out as a note under section 6303 of this title.

EFFECTIVE DATE OF 1990 AMENDMENT

Amendment by Pub. L. 101–509 effective on such date as the President shall determine, but not earlier than 90 days, and not later than 180 days, after Nov. 5, 1990, see section 529 [title III, § 305] of Pub. L. 101–509, set out

as an Effective Date of 1990 Amendment note under section 5301 of this title.

EFFECTIVE DATE OF 1986 AMENDMENT

Section 106 of Pub. L. 100–202 provided that the amendment by Pub. L. 99–500 and 99–591 is effective on date of enactment [Oct. 18, 1986] of the "pertinent joint resolution" making continuing appropriations for fiscal year 1987 [Pub. L. 99–500 and 99–591].

EFFECTIVE DATE OF 1984 AMENDMENTS

Amendment by Pub. L. 98–525 effective Oct. 1, 1984, see section 1537(f) of Pub. L. 98–525, set out as a note under section 4109 of this title.

Amendment by Pub. L. 98–353 effective July 10, 1984, see section 122(a) of Pub. L. 98–353, set out as an Effective Date note under section 151 of Title 28, Judiciary and Judicial Procedure.

EFFECTIVE DATE OF 1982 AMENDMENT

Amendment by Pub. L. 97–276 effective at 5 o'clock ante meridian eastern daylight time, Aug. 3, 1981, see section 151(h)(1) of Pub. L. 97–276, set out as an Effective Date note under section 5546a of this title.

EFFECTIVE DATE OF 1981 AMENDMENT

Section 5(b) of Pub. L. 97–141 provided that:

"(1) Subject to paragraph (2), the amendment made by subsection (a) [amending this section] shall apply to individuals whose annuities terminate under section 8344(c) of title 5, United States Code, on or after October 1, 1976.

"(2) In the case of an individual whose reemployment ended before the date of the enactment of this Act [Dec. 29, 1981], the amendment shall apply only upon application by the individual to the Office of Personnel Management within one year after the date of enactment. Upon receipt of such application, the Office shall recompute the annuity, effective as of the day following the day reemployment ended."

EFFECTIVE DATE OF 1980 AMENDMENT

Section 6 of Pub. L. 96–504 provided that:

"(a) The provisions of this Act [amending this section, repealing section 375 of Title 28, Judiciary and Judicial Procedure, and enacting provisions set out as notes under sections 8342 of this title and section 376 of Title 28] shall take effect on—

"(1) the date of the enactment of this Act [Dec. 5, 1980], or

"(2) October 1, 1980,

whichever date is later.

"(b) The provisions of subsection (f) of section 8344 of title 5, United States Code, as added by the first section of this Act, shall apply only to an individual who becomes employed as a justice or judge of the United States on or after the effective date of this Act. The provisions of subsection (g) of such section, as added by the first section of this Act, shall apply to an individual employed as a justice or judge of the United States on the effective date of this Act and to an individual appointed as such a justice or judge on or after such effective date."

EFFECTIVE DATE OF 1978 AMENDMENTS

Amendment by Pub. L. 95–598 effective Nov. 6, 1978, see section 402(d) of Pub. L. 95–598, set out as an Effective Date note preceding section 101 of Title 11, Bankruptcy.

Amendment by Pub. L. 95–454 effective 90 days after Oct. 13, 1978, see section 907 of Pub. L. 95–454, set out as a note under section 1101 of this title.

EFFECTIVE DATE OF 1976 AMENDMENT

Section 2 of Pub. L. 94–397 provided that:

"(a) Except as provided under subsection (b) of this section, the amendments made by this Act [amending this section and section 8339 of this title] shall become effective on the date of the enactment of this Act [Sept. 3, 1976] or October 1, 1976, whichever is later, and shall apply to annuitants serving in appointive or elective positions on and after such date.

"(b) The amendment made by subsection (c) of the first section of this Act [amending this section] shall become effective on the date of the enactment of this Act [Sept. 3, 1976] or October 1, 1976, whichever is later, but shall not apply to any annuitant reemployed before such date."

EFFECTIVE DATE OF 1972 AMENDMENT

Amendment by Pub. L. 92–297 effective on 90th day after May 16, 1972, see section 10 of Pub. L. 92–297, set out as an Effective Date note under section 3381 of this title.

EFFECTIVE DATE OF 1971 AMENDMENT

Section 5(d) of Pub. L. 91–658 provided that: "The amendment made by section 4 of this Act [amending this section] shall apply only with respect to a reemployed annuitant whose employment terminates on or after the date of enactment of this Act [Jan. 8, 1971]."

EFFECTIVE DATE OF 1970 AMENDMENT

Amendment by Pub. L. 91–375 effective within 1 year after Aug. 12, 1970, on date established therefor by Board of Governors of United States Postal Service and published by it in Federal Register, see section 15(a) of Pub. L. 91–375, set out as an Effective Date note preceding section 101 of Title 39, Postal Service.

EFFECTIVE DATE OF 1967 AMENDMENT

Amendment by section 1(83)(A), (D) of Pub. L. 90–83 effective as of Sept. 6, 1966, for all purposes, see section 9(h) of Pub. L. 90–83, set out as a note under section 5102 of this title.

ELIMINATION OF DUPLICATIVE AMENDMENTS

Pub. L. 102–378, § 8(a), Oct. 2, 1992, 106 Stat. 1359, provided that: "Subsections (i) and (j) of section 1206 of the Defense Acquisition Workforce Improvement Act, as contained in the National Defense Authorization Act for Fiscal Year 1991 (Public Law 101–510; 104 Stat. 1662, 1663) [enacting section 5380 of this title, amending this section and sections 5532 and 8468 of this title, and enacting provisions set out as notes under sections 5532 and 5380 of this title], are repealed, and title 5, United States Code, shall read as if such subsections had not been enacted."

ANNUAL REPORT TO CONGRESS

Pub. L. 102–190, div. A, title VI, § 655(d), Dec. 5, 1991, 105 Stat. 1393, provided that:

"(1) For the purpose of this subsection, the term 'agency in the legislative branch' has the meaning given such term by section 5531(4) of title 5, United States Code, as amended by subsection (a).

"(2) Each agency in the legislative branch shall submit to the Speaker of the House of Representatives and the Committee on Rules and Administration of the Senate, for each calendar year, a written report on how any authority made available as a result of the enactment of this section [amending this section and sections 5531, 5532, and 8468 of this title] was used by such agency during the period covered by such report.

"(3) A report under this subsection—

"(A) shall include the number of instances in which each type of authority was exercised, the circumstances justifying the exercise of authority, and, unless previously submitted, a description of the policies and procedures governing each type of authority exercised; and

"(B) shall be submitted not later than 30 days after the end of the calendar year to which it relates."

COMMISSION ON THE OPERATION OF THE SENATE

Pub. L. 94–252, Mar. 30, 1976, 90 Stat. 294, provided that: "On and after the date of the enactment of the joint resolution [Mar. 30, 1976], the provisions of section 8344 of title 5, United States Code, shall not apply to any individual serving as a member of the Commission on the Operation of the Senate."

SECTION REFERRED TO IN OTHER SECTIONS

This section is referred to in section 8339 of this title; title 16 sections 463, 5958; title 20 section 4512; title 22 section 2512; title 28 sections 625, 634; title 39 section 1005.

§ 8345. Payment of benefits; commencement, termination, and waiver of annuity

(a) Each annuity is stated as an annual amount, one-twelfth of which, rounded to the next lowest dollar, constitutes the monthly rate payable on the first business day of the month after the month or other period for which it has accrued.

(b)(1) Except as otherwise provided—

(A) an annuity of an employee or Member commences on the first day of the month after—

(i) separation from the service; or

(ii) pay ceases and the service and age requirements for title to annuity are met; and

(B) any other annuity payable from the Fund commences on the first day of the month after the occurrence of the event on which payment thereof is based.

(2) The annuity of—

(A) an employee involuntarily separated from service, except by removal for cause on charges of misconduct or delinquency; and

(B) an employee or Member retiring under section 8337 of this title due to a disability;

shall commence on the day after separation from the service or the day after pay ceases and the service and age or disability requirements for title to annuity are met.

(c) The annuity of a retired employee or Member terminates on the day death or other terminating event provided by this subchapter occurs. The annuity of a survivor terminates on the last day of the month before death or other terminating event occurs.

(d) An individual entitled to annuity from the Fund may decline to accept all or any part of the annuity by a waiver signed and filed with the Office of Personnel Management. The waiver may be revoked in writing at any time. Payment of the annuity waived may not be made for the period during which the waiver was in effect.

(e) Payment due a minor, or an individual mentally incompetent or under other legal disability, may be made to the person who is constituted guardian or other fiduciary by the law of the State of residence of the claimant or is otherwise legally vested with the care of the claimant or his estate. If a guardian or other fiduciary of the individual under legal disability has not been appointed under the law of the State of residence of the claimant, payment may be made to any person who, in the judgment of the Office, is responsible for the care of the claimant, and the payment bars recovery by any other person.

[(f) Repealed. Pub. L. 99–251, title III, § 305(a), Feb. 27, 1986, 100 Stat. 26.]

(g) The Office shall prescribe regulations to provide that the amount of any monthly annuity payable under this section accruing for any month and which is computed with regard to service that includes any service referred to in section 8332(b)(6) performed by an individual prior to January 1, 1969, shall be reduced by the portion of any benefits under any State retirement system to which such individual is entitled (or on proper application would be entitled) for such month which is attributable to such service performed by such individual before such date.

(h) An individual entitled to an annuity from the Fund may make allotments or assignments of amounts from his annuity for such purposes as the Office of Personnel Management in its sole discretion considers appropriate.

(i)(1) No payment shall be made from the Fund unless an application for benefits based on the service of an employee or Member is received in the Office of Personnel Management before the one hundred and fifteenth anniversary of his birth.

(2) Notwithstanding paragraph (1) of this subsection, after the death of an employee, Member, or annuitant, no benefit based on his service shall be paid from the Fund unless an application therefor is received in the Office of Personnel Management within 30 years after the death or other event which gives rise to title to the benefit.

(j)(1) Payments under this subchapter which would otherwise be made to an employee, Member, or annuitant based on service of that individual shall be paid (in whole or in part) by the Office to another person if and to the extent expressly provided for in the terms of—

(A) any court decree of divorce, annulment, or legal separation, or the terms of any court order or court-approved property settlement agreement incident to any court decree of divorce, annulment, or legal separation; or

(B) any court order or other similar process in the nature of garnishment for the enforcement of a judgment rendered against such employee, Member, or annuitant, for physically, sexually, or emotionally abusing a child.

In the event that the Office is served with more than 1 decree, order, or other legal process with respect to the same moneys due or payable to any individual, such moneys shall be available to satisfy such processes on a first-come, first-served basis, with any such process being satisfied out of such moneys as remain after the satisfaction of all such processes which have been previously served.

(2) Paragraph (1) shall only apply to payments made by the Office under this subchapter after the date of receipt in the Office of written notice of such decree, order, other legal process, or agreement, and such additional information and documentation as the Office may prescribe.

(3) For the purpose of this subsection—

(A) the term "court" means any court of any State, the District of Columbia, the Commonwealth of Puerto Rico, Guam, the Northern Mariana Islands, or the Virgin Islands, and any Indian court;

(B) the term "judgment rendered for physically, sexually, or emotionally abusing a child" means any legal claim perfected through a final enforceable judgment, which

claim is based in whole or in part upon the physical, sexual, or emotional abuse of a child, whether or not that abuse is accompanied by other actionable wrongdoing, such as sexual exploitation or gross negligence; and

(C) the term "child" means an individual under 18 years of age.

(k)(1) The Office shall, in accordance with this subsection, enter into an agreement with any State within 120 days of a request for agreement from the proper State official. The agreement shall provide that the Office shall withhold State income tax in the case of the monthly annuity of any annuitant who voluntarily requests, in writing, such withholding. The amounts withheld during any calendar quarter shall be held in the Fund and disbursed to the States during the month following that calendar quarter.

(2) An annuitant may have in effect at any time only one request for withholding under this subsection, and an annuitant may not have more than two such requests in effect during any one calendar year.

(3) Subject to paragraph (2) of this subsection, an annuitant may change the State designated by that annuitant for purposes of having withholdings made, and may request that the withholdings be remitted in accordance with such change. An annuitant also may revoke any request of that annuitant for withholding. Any change in the State designated or revocation is effective on the first day of the month after the month in which the request or the revocation is processed by the Office, but in no event later than on the first day of the second month beginning after the day on which such request or revocation is received by the Office.

(4) This subsection does not give the consent of the United States to the application of a statute which imposes more burdensome requirements on the United States than on employers generally, or which subjects the United States or any annuitant to a penalty or liability because of this subsection. The Office may not accept pay from a State for services performed in withholding State income taxes from annuities. Any amount erroneously withheld from an annuity and paid to a State by the Office shall be repaid by the State in accordance with regulations issued by the Office.

(5) For the purpose of this subsection, "State" means a State, the District of Columbia, or any territory or possession of the United States.

(l) Transfers of contributions and deposits authorized by section 408(a)(3) of the Foreign Service Act of 1980 shall be deemed to be a complete and final payment of benefits under this chapter.

(Pub. L. 89–544, Sept. 6, 1966, 80 Stat. 582; Pub. L. 93–273, §1, Apr. 26, 1974, 88 Stat. 93; Pub. L. 94–126, §1(c), Nov. 12, 1975, 89 Stat. 679; Pub. L. 94–166, §1, Dec. 23, 1975, 89 Stat. 1002; Pub. L. 94–183, §1, Dec. 31, 1975, 89 Stat. 1057; Pub. L. 95–366, §1(a), Sept. 15, 1978, 92 Stat. 600; Pub. L. 95–454, title IX, §906(a)(2), (3), Oct. 13, 1978, 92 Stat. 1224; Pub. L. 97–35, title XVII, §1705(a), Aug. 13, 1981, 95 Stat. 758; Pub. L. 97–253, title III, §§304(b), 305(a), Sept. 8, 1982, 96 Stat. 795; Pub. L. 98–615, §2(6), Nov. 8, 1984, 98 Stat. 3202; Pub. L. 99–251, title III,

§ 305(a), Feb. 27, 1986, 100 Stat. 26; Pub. L. 101–246, title I, § 141(b), Feb. 16, 1990, 104 Stat. 35; Pub. L. 103–358, § 2(a), Oct. 14, 1994, 108 Stat. 3420.)

HISTORICAL AND REVISION NOTES

Derivation	U.S. Code	Revised Statutes and Statutes at Large
....	5 U.S.C. 2264.	July 31, 1956, ch. 804, § 401 "Sec. 14", 70 Stat. 757. Sept. 6, 1960, Pub. L. 86–713, § 1(b), 74 Stat. 814.

In subsection (b), the second sentence of former section 2264(b) is omitted as included in the second sentence of the revised subsection. The words "after September 5, 1960" are substituted for "on or after September 6, 1960".

In subsection (c), the first sentence of former section 2264(c) is omitted as covered by the remainder of the subsection. The words "on or after September 6, 1960" are omitted as obsolete.

Standard changes are made to conform with the definitions applicable and the style of this title as outlined in the preface to the report.

REFERENCES IN TEXT

Section 408(a)(3) of the Foreign Service Act of 1980, referred to in subsec. (*l*), is classified to section 3968(a)(3) of Title 22, Foreign Relations and Intercourse.

AMENDMENTS

1994—Subsec. (j)(1). Pub. L. 103–358, § 2(a)(1), amended par. (1) generally. Prior to amendment, par. (1) read as follows: "Payments under this subchapter which would otherwise be made to an employee, Member, or annuitant based upon his service shall be paid (in whole or in part) by the Office to another person if and to the extent expressly provided for in the terms of any court decree of divorce, annulment, or legal separation, or the terms of any court order or court-approved property settlement agreement incident to any court decree of divorce, annulment, or legal separation. Any payment under this paragraph to a person bars recovery by any other person."

Subsec. (j)(2). Pub. L. 103–358, § 2(a)(2), inserted "other legal process," after "order,".

Subsec. (j)(3). Pub. L. 103–358, § 2(a)(3), amended par. (3) generally. Prior to amendment, par. (3) read as follows: "As used in this subsection, 'court' means any court of any State, the District of Columbia, the Commonwealth of Puerto Rico, Guam, the Northern Mariana Islands, or the Virgin Islands, and any Indian court."

1990—Subsec. (*l*). Pub. L. 101–246 added subsec. (*l*).

1986—Subsec. (f). Pub. L. 99–251 struck out subsec. (f) which provided minimum monthly rates of annuity payable under subsec. (a) with certain exceptions.

1984—Subsec. (f)(4). Pub. L. 98–615, § 2(6)(A), added par. (4).

Subsec. (j)(3). Pub. L. 98–615, § 2(6)(B), inserted reference to the Commonwealth of Puerto Rico, Guam, the Northern Mariana Islands, the Virgin Islands, and any Indian court.

1982—Subsec. (a). Pub. L. 97–253, § 304(b), substituted "rounded to the next lowest" for "fixed at the nearest".

Subsec. (b). Pub. L. 97–253, § 305(a), substituted provisions that an annuity of an employee or Member commences on the first day of the month after separation from service or pay ceases and the service and age requirements for title to annuity are met, that any other annuity payable from the Fund commences on the first day of the month after the occurrence of the event on which the payment thereof is based, and that the annuity of an employee involuntarily separated from service or of an employee or Member retiring due to a disability shall commence on the day after separation from the service or the day after pay ceases and the service

and age or disability requirements for title to annuity are met for provisions that the annuity of an employee or Member would commence on the day after he was separated from the service, or on the day after his pay ceased and he met the service and the age or disability requirements for title to annuity and that an annuity payable from the Fund allowed after September 5, 1960, would commence on the day after the occurrence of the event on which payment thereof was based.

1981—Subsec. (k). Pub. L. 97–35 added subsec. (k).

1978—Subsecs. (d), (e). Pub. L. 95–454, § 906(a)(2), (3), substituted "Office of Personnel Management" for "Civil Service Commission" and "Office" for "Commission".

Subsec. (g). Pub. L. 95–454, § 906(a)(3), substituted "Office" for "Commission" in the subsec. (g) added by Pub. L. 94–126.

Pub. L. 95–366 redesignated as subsec. (h) the subsec. (g) added by Pub. L. 94–166.

Subsec. (h). Pub. L. 95–454, § 906(a)(2), substituted "Office of Personnel Management" for "Civil Service Commission".

Pub. L. 95–366 redesignated former subsec. (g), added by Pub. L. 94–166, as (h). Former subsec. (h) redesignated (i).

Subsec. (i). Pub. L. 95–454, § 906(a)(2), substituted "Office of Personnel Management" for "Civil Service Commission" wherever appearing.

Pub. L. 95–366 redesignated former subsec. (h) as (i).

Subsec. (j). Pub. L. 95–454, § 906(a)(3), substituted "Office" for "Commission" wherever appearing.

Pub. L. 95–366 added subsec. (j).

1975—Subsec. (g). Pub. L. 94–166 added subsec. (g) authorizing allotment or assignment of amounts from annuities.

Pub. L. 94–126 added subsec. (g) relating to the crediting of National Guard technician service in connection with civil service retirement.

Subsec. (h). Pub. L. 94–183 added subsec. (h).

1974—Subsec. (f). Pub. L. 93–273 added subsec. (f).

EFFECTIVE DATE OF 1994 AMENDMENT

Section 3 of Pub. L. 103–358 provided that: "The amendments made by this Act [amending this section and sections 8437 and 8467 of this title] take effect on the date of enactment of this Act [Oct. 14, 1994], and shall apply with respect to any decree, order, or other legal process, or notice of agreement received by the Office of Personnel Management or the Executive Director of the Federal Retirement Thrift Investment Board on or after such date of enactment."

EFFECTIVE DATE OF 1984 AMENDMENT

Amendment by Pub. L. 98–615 effective May 7, 1985, with enumerated exceptions and specific applicability provisions, see section 4(a)(1), (5)(D) of Pub. L. 98–615, as amended, set out as a note under section 8341 of this title.

EFFECTIVE DATE OF 1982 AMENDMENT

Amendment by section 304(b) of Pub. L. 97–253 applicable with respect to any annuity commencing on or after Oct. 1, 1982, and with respect to any adjustment or redetermination of any annuity made on or after such date, see section 304(c) of Pub. L. 97–253, set out as a note under section 8340 of this title.

Section 305(b) of Pub. L. 97–253, as amended by Pub. L. 97–377, title I, § 124, Dec. 21, 1982, 96 Stat. 1913, provided that: "The amendment made by subsection (a) [amending this section] shall apply to annuities which commence on or after October 1, 1982, except for those individuals who serve three days or less in the month of retirement."

EFFECTIVE DATE OF 1981 AMENDMENT

Section 1705(b) of Pub. L. 97–35 provided that: "The amendment made by subsection (a) [amending this section] shall take effect October 1, 1981."

EFFECTIVE DATE OF 1978 AMENDMENTS

Amendment by Pub. L. 95–454 effective 90 days after Oct. 13, 1978, see section 907 of Pub. L. 95–454, set out as a note under section 1101 of this title.

Section 2 of Pub. L. 95–366 provided that: "The amendments made by the first section of this Act [amending this section and section 8346 of this title] shall only apply to payments made from the Civil Service Retirement and Disability Fund after the date of the enactment of this Act [Sept. 15, 1978]."

EFFECTIVE DATE OF 1975 AMENDMENT

Amendment by Pub. L. 94–126 effective as of Jan. 1, 1969, applicable to a person who, on Nov. 12, 1975, is receiving or is entitled to receive benefits under any Federal retirement system and requests in writing the application of the amendment to him by the office administering his retirement system, and additional benefits to commence Dec. 1, 1975, see section 3 of Pub. L. 94–126, set out as a note under section 8334 of this title.

EFFECTIVE DATE OF 1974 AMENDMENT

Section 3 of Pub. L. 93–273 provided that: "This Act [amending this section and enacting provisions set out as notes under this section and sections 8339 and 8341 of this title] shall become effective on the date of enactment [Apr. 26, 1974]. Annuity increases under this Act shall apply to annuities which commence before, on, or after the date of enactment of this Act, but no increase in annuity shall be paid for any period prior to the first day of the first month which begins on or after the ninetieth day after the date of enactment of this Act, or the date on which the annuity commences, whichever is later."

MINIMUM ANNUITY UNDER CIVIL SERVICE RETIREMENT AND DISABILITY SYSTEM

Section 305(b)–(d) of Pub. L. 99–251 provided that:

"(b) SAVINGS PROVISION.—An annuity payable from the Civil Service Retirement and Disability Fund as of the day before the date of enactment of this Act [Feb. 27, 1986] shall not be reduced—

"(1) by reason of the repeal of section 8345(f) of title 5, United States Code; or

"(2) if or to the extent that the reduction is to be made for the purpose of eliminating an overpayment resulting from the manner in which such section 8345(f) has been administered by the Office of Personnel Management.

"(c) RATIFICATION OF ERRONEOUS PAYMENTS.—Any individual to whom an overpayment of an annuity has been made from the Civil Service Retirement and Disability Fund before the date of enactment of this Act [Feb. 27, 1986] shall be deemed to have been entitled to that overpayment if and to the extent that such overpayment resulted from the manner in which the Office of Personnel Management has administered section 8345(f) of title 5, United States Code.

"(d) ADJUSTMENTS OF CERTAIN REDUCTIONS.—(1) Effective for any month after the date of enactment of this Act [Feb. 27, 1986], the amount of any annuity which—

"(A) is payable from the Civil Service Retirement and Disability Fund; and

"(B) was reduced after June 30, 1985, and before the date of enactment of this Act, to eliminate any overpayment resulting from the manner in which the Office of Personnel Management administered section 8345(f) of title 5, United States Code,

shall not be less than the amount which would have been payable as of such date of enactment if the reduction described in clause (B) had not been made.

"(2)(A) The Office shall make a lump-sum payment to each individual receiving an annuity to which paragraph (1) applies.

"(B) The lump-sum payment made to any individual under this paragraph shall be equal to the excess of—

"(i) the total amount of the annuity payments which would have been made to the individual for the period beginning with the first month in which the reduction described in paragraph (1)(B) was made and ending on the last day of the month in which this Act is enacted if the reduction had not been made, over

"(ii) the total amount of the annuity payments which have been paid to such individual for that period."

AVAILABILITY OF THE CIVIL SERVICE RETIREMENT AND DISABILITY FUND FOR EXPENSES INCURRED BY THE OFFICE OF PERSONNEL MANAGEMENT

Section 1705(c) of Pub. L. 97–35 provided that: "The Civil Service Retirement and Disability Fund is available for expenses incurred by the Office of Personnel Management in the initial implementation of the amendments made by this section [amending this section]."

MONTHLY RATE OF MINIMUM ANNUITY

Section 2(c) of Pub. L. 93–273 provided that: "The monthly rate of an annuity resulting from an increase under this section [enacting provisions set out as notes under sections 8339 and 8341 of this title] shall be considered as the monthly rate of annuity payable under section 8345(a) of title 5, United States Code [subsec. (a) of this section], for purposes of computing the minimum annuity under section 8345(f) of title 5 [subsec. (f) of this section], as added by the first section of this Act."

SECTION REFERRED TO IN OTHER SECTIONS

This section is referred to in sections 8342, 8343a, 8346, 8348, 8349, 8901, 8905 of this title.

§ 8346. Exemption from legal process; recovery of payments

(a) The money mentioned by this subchapter is not assignable, either in law or equity, except under the provisions of subsections (h) and (j) of section 8345 of this title, or subject to execution, levy, attachment, garnishment, or other legal process, except as otherwise may be provided by Federal laws.

(b) Recovery of payments under this subchapter may not be made from an individual when, in the judgment of the Office of Personnel Management, the individual is without fault and recovery would be against equity and good conscience. Withholding or recovery of money mentioned by this subchapter on account of a certification or payment made by a former employee of the United States in the discharge of his official duties may be made only if the head of the agency on behalf of which the certification or payment was made certifies to the Office that the certification or payment involved fraud on the part of the former employee.

(Pub. L. 89–554, Sept. 6, 1966, 80 Stat. 583; Pub. L. 94–166, § 2, Dec. 23, 1975, 89 Stat. 1002; Pub. L. 95–366, § 1(b), Sept. 15, 1978, 92 Stat. 600; Pub. L. 95–454, title IX, § 906(a)(2), (3), Oct. 13, 1978, 92 Stat. 1224.)

HISTORICAL AND REVISION NOTES

Derivation	U.S. Code	Revised Statutes and Statutes at Large
....	5 U.S.C. 2265.	July 31, 1956, ch. 804, § 401 "Sec. 15", 70 Stat. 758.

In subsection (b), the words "Notwithstanding any other provision of law" are omitted as unnecessary. The second word of the second sentence "or" is substituted for "of" to correct a printing error.

Standard changes are made to conform with the definitions applicable and the style of this title as outlined in the preface to the report.

AMENDMENTS

1978—Subsec. (a). Pub. L. 95–366 substituted references to subsecs. (h) and (j) of section 8345 for reference to subsec. (g) of section 8345.

Subsec. (b). Pub. L. 95–454 substituted "Office of Personnel Management" and "Office" for "Civil Service Commission" and "Commission", respectively.

1975—Subsec. (a). Pub. L. 94–166 inserted "except under the provisions of section 8345(g) of this title," after "equity", and ", except as otherwise may be provided by Federal laws" after "process".

EFFECTIVE DATE OF 1978 AMENDMENTS

Amendment by Pub. L. 95–454 effective 90 days after Oct. 13, 1978, see section 907 of Pub. L. 95–454, set out as a note under section 1101 of this title.

Amendment by Pub. L. 95–366 applicable to payments made from Civil Service Retirement and Disability Fund after Sept. 15, 1978, see section 2 of Pub. L. 95–366, set out as a note under section 8345 of this title.

§ 8347. Administration; regulations

(a) The Office of Personnel Management shall administer this subchapter. Except as otherwise specifically provided herein, the Office shall perform, or cause to be performed, such acts and prescribe such regulations as are necessary and proper to carry out this subchapter.

(b) Applications under this subchapter shall be in such form as the Office prescribes. Agencies shall support the applications by such certificates as the Office considers necessary to the determination of the rights of applicants. The Office shall adjudicate all claims under this subchapter.

(c) The Office shall determine questions of disability and dependency arising under this subchapter. Except to the extent provided under subsection (d) of this section, the decisions of the Office concerning these matters are final and conclusive and are not subject to review. The Office may direct at any time such medical or other examinations as it considers necessary to determine the facts concerning disability or dependency of an individual receiving or applying for annuity under this subchapter. The Office may suspend or deny annuity for failure to submit to examination.

(d)(1) Subject to paragraph (2) of this subsection, an administrative action or order affecting the rights or interests of an individual or of the United States under this subchapter may be appealed to the Merit Systems Protection Board under procedures prescribed by the Board.

(2) In the case of any individual found by the Office to be disabled in whole or in part on the basis of the individual's mental condition, and that finding was made pursuant to an application by an agency for purposes of disability retirement under section 8337(a) of this title, the procedures under section 7701 of this title shall apply and the decision of the Board shall be subject to judicial review under section 7703 of this title.

(e) The Office shall fix the fees for examinations made under this subchapter by physicians or surgeons who are not medical officers of the United States. The fees and reasonable traveling and other expenses incurred in connection with the examinations are paid from appropriations for the cost of administering this subchapter.

(f) The Office shall select three actuaries, to be known as the Board of Actuaries of the Civil Service Retirement System. The Office shall fix the pay of the members of the Board, except members otherwise in the employ of the United States. The Board shall report annually on the actuarial status of the System and furnish its advice and opinion on matters referred to it by the Office. The Board may recommend to the Office and to Congress such changes as in the Board's judgment are necessary to protect the public interest and maintain the System on a sound financial basis. The Office shall keep, or cause to be kept, such records as it considers necessary for making periodic actuarial valuations of the System. The Board shall make actuarial valuations every 5 years, or oftener if considered necessary by the Office.

(g) The Office may exclude from the operation of this subchapter an employee or group of employees in or under an Executive agency whose employment is temporary or intermittent. However, the Office may not exclude any employee who occupies a position on a part-time career employment basis (as defined in section 3401(2) of this title).

(h) The Office, on recommendation by the Mayor of the District of Columbia, may exclude from the operation of this subchapter an individual or group of individuals employed by the government of the District of Columbia whose employment is temporary or intermittent.

(i) The Architect of the Capitol may exclude from the operation of this subchapter an employee under the Office of the Architect of the Capitol whose employment is temporary or of uncertain duration.

(j) The Librarian of Congress may exclude from the operation of this subchapter an employee under the Library of Congress whose employment is temporary or of uncertain duration.

(k) The Secretary of Agriculture shall prescribe regulations to effect the application and operation of this subchapter to an individual named by section 8331(1)(F) of this title.

(l) The Director or Acting Director of the Botanic Garden may exclude from the operation of this subchapter an employee under the Botanic Garden whose employment is temporary or of uncertain duration.

(m) Notwithstanding any other provision of law, for the purpose of ensuring the accuracy of information used in the administration of this chapter, at the request of the Director of the Office of Personnel Management—

(1) the Secretary of Defense or the Secretary's designee shall provide information on retired or retainer pay provided under title 10;

(2) the Secretary of Veterans Affairs shall provide information on pensions or compensation provided under title 38;

(3) the Commissioner of Social Security or the Secretary's[1] designee shall provide information contained in the records of the Social Security Administration; and

(4) the Secretary of Labor or the Secretary's designee shall provide information on benefits paid under subchapter I of chapter 81 of this title.

The Director shall request only such information as the Director determines is necessary.

---

[1] So in original. Probably should be "Commissioner's".

The Director, in consultation with the officials from whom information is requested, shall establish, by regulation and otherwise, such safeguards as are necessary to ensure that information made available under this subsection is used only for the purpose authorized.

(n)(1) Notwithstanding any other provision of this subchapter, the Director of Central Intelligence shall, in a manner consistent with the administration of this subchapter by the Office, and to the extent considered appropriate by the Director of Central Intelligence—

(A) determine entitlement to benefits under this subchapter based on the service of employees of the Central Intelligence Agency;

(B) maintain records relating to the service of such employees;

(C) compute benefits under this subchapter based on the service of such employees;

(D) collect deposits to the Fund made by such employees, their spouses, and their former spouses;

(E) authorize and direct disbursements from the Fund to the extent based on service of such employees; and

(F) perform such other functions under this subchapter as the Director of Central Intelligence, in consultation with the Director of the Office of Personnel Management, determines to be appropriate.

(2) The Director of the Office of Personnel Management shall furnish such information and, on a reimbursable basis, such services to the Director of Central Intelligence as the Director of Central Intelligence requests to carry out paragraph (1) of this subsection.

(3)(A) The Director of Central Intelligence, in consultation with the Director of the Office of Personnel Management, shall by regulation prescribe appropriate procedures to carry out this subsection.

(B) The regulations shall provide procedures for the Director of the Office of Personnel Management to inspect and audit disbursements from the Civil Service Retirement and Disability Fund under this subchapter.

(C) The Director of Central Intelligence shall submit the regulations prescribed under subparagraph (A) to the Select Committee on Intelligence of the Senate and the Permanent Select Committee on Intelligence of the House of Representatives before the regulations take effect.

(4)(A) Section 201(c) of the Central Intelligence Agency Retirement Act shall apply in the administration of this subchapter to the extent that the provisions of this subchapter are administered under this subsection.

(B) Notwithstanding subparagraph (A) of this paragraph, section 8347(d) of this title shall apply with respect to employees of the Central Intelligence Agency who are subject to the Civil Service Retirement System.

(o) Any provision of law outside of this subchapter which provides coverage, service credit, or any other benefit under this subchapter to any individuals who (based on their being employed by an entity other than the Government) would not otherwise be eligible for any such coverage, credit, or benefit, shall not apply with respect to any individual appointed, transferred, or otherwise commencing that type of employment on or after October 1, 1988.

(p) The Director of the Administrative Office of the United States Courts may exclude from the operation of this subchapter an employee of the Administrative Office of the United States Courts, the Federal Judicial Center, or a court named by section 610 of title 28, whose employment is temporary or of uncertain duration.

(q)(1) Under regulations prescribed by the Office of Personnel Management, an employee who—

(A) has not previously made an election under this subsection or had an opportunity to make an election under this paragraph;

(B) has 5 or more years of civilian service creditable under this subchapter; and

(C) moves, without a break in service of more than 1 year, to employment in a nonappropriated fund instrumentality of the Department of Defense or the Coast Guard, respectively, described in section 2105(c),

shall be given the opportunity to elect irrevocably, within 30 days after such move, to remain covered as an employee under this subchapter during any employment described in section 2105(c) after such move.

(2) Under regulations prescribed by the Office of Personnel Management, an employee of a nonappropriated fund instrumentality of the Department of Defense or the Coast Guard, described in section 2105(c), who—

(A) has not previously made an election under this subsection or had an opportunity to make an election under this paragraph;

(B) is a vested participant in a retirement system established for employees described in section 2105(c), as the term "vested participant" is defined by such system;

(C) moves, without a break in service of more than 1 year, to a position that is not described in section 2105(c); and

(D) is excluded from coverage under chapter 84 by section 8402(b),

shall be given the opportunity to elect irrevocably, within 30 days after such move, to remain covered, during any subsequent employment as an employee as defined in section 2105(a) or section 2105(c), by the retirement system applicable to such employee's current or most recent employment described in section 2105(c) rather than be subject to this subchapter.

(Pub. L. 89–554, Sept. 6, 1966, 80 Stat. 583; Pub. L. 90–83, §1(84), Sept. 11, 1967, 81 Stat. 218; Pub. L. 90–623, §1(22), Oct. 22, 1968, 82 Stat. 1313; Pub. L. 95–437, §4(a), Oct. 10, 1978, 92 Stat. 1058; Pub. L. 95–454, title IX, §906(a)(2), (3), (9), (c)(2)(F), Oct. 13, 1978, 92 Stat. 1224, 1225, 1227; Pub. L. 96–54, §2(a)(50), Aug. 14, 1979, 93 Stat. 384; Pub. L. 96–499, title IV, §404(b), Dec. 5, 1980, 94 Stat. 2606; Pub. L. 96–500, §1, Dec. 5, 1980, 94 Stat. 2696; Pub. L. 97–253, title III, §302(b), Sept. 8, 1982, 96 Stat. 793; Pub. L. 99–335, title II, §207(i), June 6, 1986, 100 Stat. 596; Pub. L. 100–238, title I, §108(a)(1), Jan. 8, 1988, 101 Stat. 1747; Pub. L. 101–474, §5(n), Oct. 30, 1990, 104 Stat. 1100; Pub. L. 101–508, title VII, §7202(j)(2), Nov. 5, 1990, 104 Stat. 1388–337; Pub. L. 102–54, §13(b)(5), June 13, 1991, 105 Stat. 274; Pub. L. 102–378, §2(64), Oct. 2, 1992, 106 Stat. 1354; Pub. L. 102–496, title VIII, §803(c), Oct. 24, 1992, 106 Stat. 3253; Pub. L. 103–296, title I, §108(e)(5), Aug. 15, 1994, 108 Stat. 1486; Pub. L.

104–106, div. A, title X, § 1043(a)(1), Feb. 10, 1996, 110 Stat. 434.)

HISTORICAL AND REVISION NOTES
1966 ACT

Derivation	U.S. Code	Revised Statutes and Statutes at Large
(a)–(f)	5 U.S.C. 2266 (less (f)).	July 31, 1956, ch. 804, § 401 "Sec. 16 (less (f))", 70 Stat. 758.
(g)–(k)	5 U.S.C. 2252(e), (f) (words after semicolon), (h) (1).	July 31, 1956, ch. 804, § 401 "Sec. 2(e), (f) (words after semicolon)", 70 Stat. 745. July 1, 1960, Pub. L. 86–568, § 115(b)(1) "(h) (1)", 74 Stat. 302.

In subsection (a), the words "to carry out this subchapter" are substituted for "for the purpose of carrying the provisions of this chapter into full force and effect".

Standard changes are made to conform with the definitions applicable and the style of this title as outlined in the preface to the report.

1967 ACT

Section of title 5	Source (U.S. Code)	Source (Statutes at Large)
8347(l)	5 App.: 2252(f).	Sept. 26, 1966, Pub. L. 89–604, § 1(c), 80 Stat. 847.

REFERENCES IN TEXT

Section 201(c) of the Central Intelligence Agency Retirement Act, referred to in subsec. (n)(4)(A), is classified to section 2011(c) of Title 50, War and National Defense.

AMENDMENTS

1996—Subsec. (q)(1). Pub. L. 104–106, § 1043(a)(1)(A), struck out "of the Department of Defense or the Coast Guard" after "an employee" in introductory provisions and substituted "1 year" for "3 days" in subpar. (C).

Subsec. (q)(2)(C). Pub. L. 104–106, § 1043(a)(1)(B), substituted "1 year" for "3 days" and struck out "in the Department of Defense or the Coast Guard, respectively," after "to a position".

1994—Subsec. (m)(3). Pub. L. 103–296 substituted "Commissioner of Social Security" for "Secretary of Health and Human Services".

1992—Subsec. (n)(4)(A). Pub. L. 102–496 substituted "the Central Intelligence Agency Retirement Act" for "the Central Intelligence Agency Retirement Act of 1964 for Certain Employees".

Subsec. (p). Pub. L. 102–378, § 2(64)(A), redesignated subsec. (p), relating to employees of Department of Defense and Coast Guard, as (q).

Subsec. (q). Pub. L. 102–378, § 2(64)(A), redesignated subsec. (p), relating to employees of Department of Defense and Coast Guard, as (q).

Subsec. (q)(1)(A), (2)(A). Pub. L. 102–378, § 2(64)(B), amended subpars. (A) generally. Prior to amendment, subpars. (A) read as follows: "has not previously made or had an opportunity to make an election under this subsection;".

1991—Subsec. (m)(2). Pub. L. 102 54 substituted "Secretary" for "Administrator".

1990—Subsec. (p). Pub. L. 101–508 added subsec. (p) relating to elections by employees of Department of Defense, Coast Guard, or a nonappropriated fund instrumentality of Department of Defense or Coast Guard.

Pub. L. 101–474 added subsec. (p) relating to Director of Administrative Office of United States Courts.

1988—Subsec. (o). Pub. L. 100–238 added subsec. (o).

1986—Subsec. (n). Pub. L. 99–335 added subsec. (n).

1982—Subsec. (m)(3), (4). Pub. L. 97–253 added pars. (3) and (4).

1980—Subsec. (c). Pub. L. 96–500, § 1(a), substituted "Except to the extent provided under subsection (d) of

this section, the decisions of the Office concerning" for "The decisions of the Office concerning".

Subsec. (d). Pub. L. 96–500, § 1(b), designated existing provisions as par. (1), made such par. (1) subject to the provisions of par. (2), and added par. (2).

Subsec. (m). Pub. L. 96–499 added subsec. (m).

1979—Subsec. (h). Pub. L. 96–54 substituted "Mayor" for "Commissioner".

1978—Subsecs. (a) to (c). Pub. L. 95–454, § 906(a)(2), (3), substituted "Office of Personnel Management" and "Office" for "Civil Service Commission" and "Commission", respectively.

Subsec. (d). Pub. L. 95–454, § 906(a)(9), substituted "Merit Systems Protection Board" for "Commission", and "Board" for "Commission".

Subsecs. (e), (f). Pub. L. 95–454, § 906(a)(3) substituted "Office" for "Commission" wherever appearing.

Subsec. (g). Pub. L. 95–454, § 906(a)(3), (c)(2)(F), substituted "Office" for "Commission" wherever appearing, and "3401" for "3391".

Pub. L. 95–437 inserted provision prohibiting the Commission from excluding any employee who occupies a position on a part-time career employment basis, as defined in section 3391(2) of this title.

Subsec. (h). Pub. L. 95–454, § 906(a)(3), substituted "Office" for "Commission".

1968—Subsec. (h). Pub. L. 90–623 substituted "Commissioner" for "Commissioners".

EFFECTIVE DATE OF 1996 AMENDMENT

For effective date of amendments by Pub. L. 104–106, see Regulations; Effective Date of 1996 Amendment note below.

EFFECTIVE DATE OF 1994 AMENDMENT

Amendment by Pub. L. 103–296 effective Mar. 31, 1995, see section 110(a) of Pub. L. 103–296, set out as a note under section 401 of Title 42, The Public Health and Welfare.

EFFECTIVE DATE OF 1992 AMENDMENTS

Amendment by Pub. L. 102–496 effective on first day of fourth month beginning after Oct. 24, 1992, see section 805 of Pub. L. 102–496, set out as an Effective Date note under section 2001 of Title 50, War and National Defense.

Amendment by section 2(64) of Pub. L. 102–378 effective Nov. 5, 1990, see section 9(b)(6) of Pub. L. 102–378, set out as a note under section 6303 of this title.

EFFECTIVE DATE OF 1990 AMENDMENT

Amendment by Pub. L. 101–508 applicable with respect to any individual who, on or after Jan. 1, 1987, moves from employment in nonappropriated fund instrumentality of Department of Defense or Coast Guard, that is described in section 2105(c) of this title, to employment in Department or Coast Guard, that is not described in section 2105(c), or who moves from employment in Department or Coast Guard, that is not described in section 2105(c), to employment in nonappropriated fund instrumentality of Department or Coast Guard, that is described in section 2105(c), see section 7202(m)(1) of Pub. L. 101–508, set out as a note under section 2105 of this title.

EFFECTIVE DATE OF 1986 AMENDMENT

Amendment by Pub. L. 99–335 effective Jan. 1, 1987, see section 702(a) of Pub. L. 99–335, set out as an Effective Date note under section 8401 of this title.

EFFECTIVE DATE OF 1982 AMENDMENT

Amendment by Pub. L. 97–253 effective Oct. 1, 1982, see section 302(c)(1) of Pub. L. 97–253, as amended by section 3(i) of Pub. L. 97–346, set out as a note under section 8337 of this title.

EFFECTIVE DATE OF 1980 AMENDMENTS

Section 2 of Pub. L. 96–500 provided that: "The amendments made by the first section of this Act [amending this section] shall apply with respect to determinations made by the Office of Personnel Management on or after the first day of the first month beginning after the date of the enactment of this Act [Dec. 5, 1980]."

Amendment by Pub. L. 96–499 effective Dec. 5, 1980, see section 404(c) of Pub. L. 96–499, set out as a note under section 8339 of this title.

EFFECTIVE DATE OF 1979 AMENDMENT

Amendment by Pub. L. 96–54 effective July 12, 1979, see section 2(b) of Pub. L. 96–54, set out as a note under section 305 of this title.

EFFECTIVE DATE OF 1978 AMENDMENT

Amendment by Pub. L. 95–454 effective 90 days after Oct. 13, 1978, see section 907 of Pub. L. 95–454, set out as a note under section 1101 of this title.

EFFECTIVE DATE OF 1968 AMENDMENT

Amendment by Pub. L. 90–623 intended to restate without substantive change the law in effect on Oct. 22, 1968, see section 6 of Pub. L. 90–623, set out as a note under section 5334 of this title.

REGULATIONS; EFFECTIVE DATE OF 1996 AMENDMENT

Section 1043(b), (c) of Pub. L. 104–106 provided that:

"(b) REGULATIONS.—Not later than 6 months after the date of the enactment of this Act [Feb. 10, 1996], the Office of Personnel Management (and each of the other administrative authorities, within the meaning of subsection (c)(2)(C)(iii)) shall prescribe any regulations (or make any modifications in existing regulations) necessary to carry out this section [amending this section and sections 3502 and 8461 of this title and enacting provisions set out as a note under section 3502 of this title] and the amendments made by this section, including regulations to provide for the notification of individuals who may be affected by the enactment of this section. All regulations (and modifications to regulations) under the preceding sentence shall take effect on the same date.

"(c) APPLICABILITY; RELATED PROVISIONS.—

"(1) PROSPECTIVE RULES.—Except as otherwise provided in this subsection, the amendments made by this section [amending this section and sections 3502 and 8461 of this title] shall apply with respect to moves occurring on or after the effective date of the regulations under subsection (b). Moves occurring on or after the date of the enactment of this Act [Feb. 10, 1996] and before the effective date of such regulations shall be subject to applicable provisions of title 5, United States Code, disregarding the amendments made by this section, except that any individual making an election pursuant to this sentence shall be ineligible to make an election otherwise allowable under paragraph (2).

"(2) RETROACTIVE RULES.—

"(A) IN GENERAL.—The regulations under subsection (b) shall include provisions for the application of sections 8347(q) and 8461(n) of title 5, United States Code, as amended by this section, with respect to any individual who, at any time after December 31, 1965, and before the effective date of such regulations, moved between positions in circumstances that would have qualified such individual to make an election under the provisions of such section 8347(q) or 8461(n), as so amended, if such provisions had then been in effect.

"(B) DEADLINE; RELATED PROVISIONS.—An election pursuant to this paragraph—

"(i) shall be made within 1 year after the effective date of the regulations under subsection (b), and

"(ii) shall have the same force and effect as if it had been timely made at the time of the move,

except that no such election may be made by any individual—

"(I) who has previously made, or had an opportunity to make, an election under section 8347(q)

or 8461(n) of title 5, United States Code (as in effect before being amended by this section); however, this subclause shall not be considered to render an individual ineligible, based on an opportunity arising out of a move occurring during the period described in the second sentence of paragraph (1), if no election has in fact been made by such individual based on such move;

"(II) who has not, since the move on which eligibility for the election is based, remained continuously subject (disregarding any break in service of less than 3 days) to CSRS or FERS or both seriatim (if the move was from a NAFI position) or any retirement system (or 2 or more such systems seriatim) established for employees described in section 2105(c) of such title (if the move was to a NAFI position); or

"(III) if such election would be based on a move to the Civil Service Retirement System from a retirement system established for employees described in section 2105(c) of such title.

"(C) TRANSFERS OF CONTRIBUTIONS.—

"(i) IN GENERAL.—If an individual makes an election under this paragraph to be transferred back to a retirement system in which such individual previously participated (in this section referred to as the 'previous system'), all individual contributions (including interest) and Government contributions to the retirement system in which such individual is then currently participating (in this section referred to as the 'current system'), excluding those made to the Thrift Savings Plan or any other defined contribution plan, which are attributable to periods of service performed since the move on which the election is based, shall be paid to the fund, account, or other repository for contributions made under the previous system. For purposes of this section, the term 'current system' shall be considered also to include any retirement system (besides the one in which the individual is participating at the time of making the election) in which such individual previously participated since the move on which the election is based.

"(ii) CONDITION SUBSEQUENT RELATING TO REPAYMENT OF LUMP-SUM CREDIT.—In the case of an individual who has received such individual's lump-sum credit (within the meaning of section 8401(19) of title 5, United States Code, or a similar payment) from such individual's previous system, the payment described in clause (i) shall not be made (and the election to which it relates shall be ineffective) unless such lump-sum credit is redeposited or otherwise paid at such time and in such manner as shall be required under applicable regulations. Regulations to carry out this clause shall include provisions for the computation of interest (consistent with section 8334(e)(2) and (3) of title 5, United States Code), if no provisions for such computation otherwise exist.

"(iii) CONDITION SUBSEQUENT RELATING TO DEFICIENCY IN PAYMENTS RELATIVE TO AMOUNTS NEEDED TO ENSURE THAT BENEFITS ARE FULLY FUNDED.—

"(I) IN GENERAL.—Except as provided in subclause (II), the payment described in clause (i) shall not be made (and the election to which it relates shall be ineffective) if the actuarial present value of the future benefits that would be payable under the previous system with respect to service performed by such individual after the move on which the election under this paragraph is based and before the effective date of the election, exceeds the total amounts required to be transferred to the previous system under the preceding provisions of this subparagraph with respect to such service, as determined by the authority administering such previous system (in this section referred to as the 'administrative authority').

"(II) PAYMENT OF DEFICIENCY.—A determination of a deficiency under this clause shall not render an election ineffective if the individual pays or arranges to pay, at a time and in a manner satisfactory to such administrative authority, the full amount of the deficiency described in subclause (I).

"(D) ALTERNATIVE ELECTION FOR AN INDIVIDUAL THEN PARTICIPATING IN FERS.—

"(i) APPLICABILITY.—This subparagraph applies with respect to any individual who—

"(I) is then currently participating in FERS; and

"(II) would then otherwise be eligible to make an election under subparagraphs (A) through (C) of this paragraph, determined disregarding the matter in subclause (I) of subparagraph (B) before the first semicolon therein.

"(ii) ELECTION.—An individual described in clause (i) may, instead of making an election for which such individual is otherwise eligible under this paragraph, elect to have all prior qualifying NAFI service of such individual treated as creditable service for purposes of any annuity under FERS payable out of the Civil Service Retirement and Disability Fund.

"(iii) QUALIFYING NAFI SERVICE.—For purposes of this subparagraph, the term 'qualifying NAFI service' means any service which, but for this subparagraph, would be creditable for purposes of any retirement system established for employees described in section 2105(c) of title 5, United States Code.

"(iv) SERVICE CEASES TO BE CREDITABLE FOR NAFI RETIREMENT SYSTEM PURPOSES.—Any qualifying NAFI service that becomes creditable for FERS purposes by virtue of an election made under this subparagraph shall not be creditable for purposes of any retirement system referred to in clause (iii).

"(v) CONDITIONS.—An election under this subparagraph shall be subject to requirements, similar to those set forth in subparagraph (C), to ensure that—

"(I) appropriate transfers of individual and Government contributions are made to the Civil Service Retirement and Disability Fund; and

"(II) the actuarial present value of future benefits under FERS attributable to service made creditable by such election is fully funded.

"(E) ALTERNATIVE ELECTION FOR AN INDIVIDUAL THEN PARTICIPATING IN A NAFI RETIREMENT SYSTEM.—

"(i) APPLICABILITY.—This subparagraph applies with respect to any individual who—

"(I) is then currently participating in any retirement system established for employees described in section 2105(c) of title 5, United States Code (in this subparagraph referred to as a 'NAFI retirement system'); and

"(II) would then otherwise be eligible to make an election under subparagraphs (A) through (C) of this paragraph (determined disregarding the matter in subclause (I) of subparagraph (B) before the first semicolon therein) based on a move from FERS.

"(ii) ELECTION.—An individual described in clause (i) may, instead of making an election for which such individual is otherwise eligible under this paragraph, elect to have all prior qualifying FERS service of such individual treated as creditable service for purposes of determining eligibility for benefits under a NAFI retirement system, but not for purposes of computing the amount of any such benefits except as provided in clause (v)(II).

"(iii) QUALIFYING FERS SERVICE.—For purposes of this subparagraph, the term 'qualifying FERS service' means any service which, but for this subparagraph, would be creditable for purposes of the Federal Employees' Retirement System.

"(iv) SERVICE CEASES TO BE CREDITABLE FOR PURPOSES OF FERS.—Any qualifying FERS service that becomes creditable for NAFI purposes by virtue of an election made under this subparagraph shall not be creditable for purposes of the Federal Employees' Retirement System.

"(v) FUNDING REQUIREMENTS.—

"(I) IN GENERAL.—Except as provided in subclause (II), nothing in this section or in any other provision of law or any other authority shall be considered to require any payment or transfer of monies in order for an election under this subparagraph to be effective.

"(II) CONTRIBUTION REQUIRED ONLY IF INDIVIDUAL ELECTS TO HAVE SERVICE MADE CREDITABLE FOR COMPUTATION PURPOSES AS WELL.—Under regulations prescribed by the appropriate administrative authority, an individual making an election under this subparagraph may further elect to have the qualifying FERS service made creditable for computation purposes under a NAFI retirement system, but only if the individual pays or arranges to pay, at a time and in a manner satisfactory to such administrative authority, the amount necessary to fully fund the actuarial present value of future benefits under the NAFI retirement system attributable to the qualifying FERS service.

"(3) INFORMATION.—The regulations under subsection (b) shall include provisions under which any individual—

"(A) shall, upon request, be provided information or assistance in determining whether such individual is eligible to make an election under paragraph (2) and, if so, the exact amount of any payment which would be required of such individual in connection with any such election; and

"(B) may seek any other information or assistance relating to any such election."

TERMINATION OF REPORTING REQUIREMENTS

For termination, effective May 15, 2000, of provisions of law requiring submittal to Congress of any annual, semiannual, or other regular periodic report listed in House Document No. 103–7 (in which the report required by subsec. (f) of this section is listed on page 187), see section 3003 of Pub. L. 104–66, as amended, set out as a note under section 1113 of Title 31, Money and Finance.

TREATMENT OF INDIVIDUALS ELECTING TO REMAIN SUBJECT TO THEIR FORMER RETIREMENT SYSTEM

For provisions relating to the deductions and contributions required with respect to individuals electing under section 8347(q) or 8461(n) of this title to remain covered under subchapter III of chapter 83 of this title, chapter 84 of this title, or a retirement system for employees described in section 2105(c) of this title, see section 7202(n) of Pub. L. 101–508, set out as a note under section 2105 of this title.

SECTION REFERRED TO IN OTHER SECTIONS

This section is referred to in sections 8331, 8334, 8348, 8349, 8423, 8461 of this title; title 22 section 6103; title 25 section 450i.

§ 8348. Civil Service Retirement and Disability Fund

(a) There is a Civil Service Retirement and Disability Fund. The Fund—

(1) is appropriated for the payment of—

(A) benefits as provided by this subchapter or by the provisions of chapter 84 of this title which relate to benefits payable out of the Fund; and

(B) administrative expenses incurred by the Office of Personnel Management in placing in effect each annuity adjustment granted under section 8340 or 8462 of this title, in administering survivor annuities and elections providing therefor under sections 8339 and 8341 of this title or subchapters II and IV of chapter 84 of this title, in administering alternative forms of annuities under sections 8343a and 8420a (and related provisions of law), in making an allotment or assignment made by an individual under section 8345(h) or 8465(b) of this title, and in withholding taxes pursuant to section 3405 of title 26 or section 8345(k) or 8469 of this title;

(2) is made available, subject to such annual limitation as the Congress may prescribe, for any expenses incurred by the Office in connection with the administration of this chapter, chapter 84 of this title, and other retirement and annuity statutes; and

(3) is made available, subject to such annual limitation as the Congress may prescribe, for any expenses incurred by the Merit Systems Protection Board in the administration of appeals authorized under sections 8347(d) and 8461(e) of this title.

(b) The Secretary of the Treasury may accept and credit to the Fund money received in the form of a donation, gift, legacy, or bequest, or otherwise contributed for the benefit of civilservice employees generally.

(c) The Secretary shall immediately invest, in interest-bearing securities of the United States such currently available portions of the Fund as are not immediately required for payments from the Fund. The income derived from these investments constitutes a part of the Fund.

(d) The purposes for which obligations of the United States may be issued under chapter 31 of title 31 are extended to authorize the issuance at par of public-debt obligations for purchase by the Fund. The obligations issued for purchase by the Fund shall have maturities fixed with due regard for the needs of the Fund and bear interest at a rate equal to the average market yield computed as of the end of the calendar month next preceding the date of the issue, borne by all marketable interest-bearing obligations of the United States then forming a part of the public debt which are not due or callable until after the expiration of 4 years from the end of that calendar month. If the average market yield is not a multiple of 1/8 of 1 percent, the rate of interest on the obligations shall be the multiple of 1/8 of 1 percent nearest the average market yield.

(e) The Secretary may purchase other interest-bearing obligations of the United States, or obligations guaranteed as to both principal and interest by the United States, on original issue or at the market price only if he determines that the purchases are in the public interest.

(f) Any statute which authorizes—

(1) new or liberalized benefits payable from the Fund, including annuity increases other than under section 8340 of this title;

(2) extension of the coverage of this subchapter to new groups of employees; or

(3) increases in pay on which benefits are computed;

is deemed to authorize appropriations to the Fund to finance the unfunded liability created by that statute, in 30 equal annual installments with interest computed at the rate used in the then most recent valuation of the Civil Service Retirement System and with the first payment thereof due as of the end of the fiscal year in which each new or liberalized benefit, extension of coverage, or increase in pay is effective.

(g) At the end of each fiscal year, the Office shall notify the Secretary of the Treasury of the amount equivalent to (1) interest on the unfunded liability computed for that year at the interest rate used in the then most recent valuation of the System, and (2) that portion of disbursement for annuities for that year which the Office estimates is attributable to credit allowed for military service, less an amount determined by the Office to be appropriate to reflect the value of the deposits made to the credit of the Fund under section 8334(j) of this title. Before closing the accounts for each fiscal year, the Secretary shall credit to the Fund, as a Government contribution, out of any money in the Treasury of the United States not otherwise appropriated, the following percentages of such amounts; 10 percent for 1971; 20 percent for 1972; 30 percent for 1973; 40 percent for 1974; 50 percent for 1975; 60 percent for 1976; 70 percent for 1977; 80 percent for 1978; 90 percent for 1979; and 100 percent for 1980 and for each fiscal year thereafter.

(h)(1) Notwithstanding any other statute, the United States Postal Service shall be liable for that portion of any estimated increase in the unfunded liability of the Fund which is attributable to any benefits payable from the Fund to active and retired Postal Service officers and employees, and to their survivors, when the increase results from an employee-management agreement under title 39, or any administrative action by the Postal Service taken pursuant to law, which authorizes increases in pay on which benefits are computed.

(2) The estimated increase in the unfunded liability, referred to in paragraph (1) of this subsection, shall be determined by the Office of Personnel Management. The United States Postal Service shall pay the amount so determined to the Office in 30 equal annual installments with interest computed at the rate used in the most recent valuation of the Civil Service Retirement System, with the first payment thereof due at the end of the fiscal year in which an increase in pay becomes effective.

(i)(1) Notwithstanding any other provision of law, the Panama Canal Commission shall be liable for that portion of any estimated increase in the unfunded liability of the fund which is attributable to any benefits payable from the Fund to or on behalf of employees and their survivors to the extent attributable to the amendments made by sections 1241 and 1242, and the provisions of sections 1231(b) and 1243(a)(1), of the Panama Canal Act of 1979, and the amendments made by section 3506 of the Panama Canal Commission Authorization Act for Fiscal Year 1991.

(2) The estimated increase in the unfunded liability referred to in paragraph (1) of this subsection shall be determined by the Office of Personnel Management. The Panama Canal Commission shall pay to the Fund from funds available to it for that purpose the amount so determined in annual installments with interest computed at the rate used in the most recent valuation of the Civil Service Retirement System.

(j)(1) Notwithstanding subsection (c) of this section, the Secretary of the Treasury may suspend additional investment of amounts in the Fund if such additional investment could not be made without causing the public debt of the United States to exceed the public debt limit.

(2) Any amounts in the Fund which, solely by reason of the public debt limit, are not invested shall be invested by the Secretary of the Treasury as soon as such investments can be made without exceeding the public debt limit.

(3) Upon expiration of the debt issuance suspension period, the Secretary of the Treasury shall immediately issue to the Fund obligations under chapter 31 of title 31 that (notwithstanding subsection (d) of this section) bear such interest rates and maturity dates as are necessary to ensure that, after such obligations are issued, the holdings of the Fund will replicate to the maximum extent practicable the obligations that would then be held by the Fund if the suspension of investment under paragraph (1) of this subsection, and any redemption or disinvestment under subsection (k) of this section for the purpose described in such paragraph, during such period had not occurred.

(4) On the first normal interest payment date after the expiration of any debt issuance suspension period, the Secretary of the Treasury shall pay to the Fund, from amounts in the general fund of the Treasury of the United States not otherwise appropriated, an amount determined by the Secretary to be equal to the excess of—

(A) the net amount of interest that would have been earned by the Fund during such debt issuance suspension period if—

(i) amounts in the Fund that were not invested during such debt issuance suspension period solely by reason of the public debt limit had been invested, and

(ii) redemptions and disinvestments with respect to the Fund which occurred during such debt issuance suspension period solely by reason of the public debt limit had not occurred, over

(B) the net amount of interest actually earned by the Fund during such debt issuance suspension period.

(5) For purposes of this subsection and subsections (k) and (l) of this section—

(A) the term "public debt limit" means the limitation imposed by section 3101(b) of title 31; and

(B) the term "debt issuance suspension period" means any period for which the Secretary of the Treasury determines for purposes of this subsection that the issuance of obligations of the United States may not be made without exceeding the public debt limit.

(k)(1) Subject to paragraph (2) of this subsection, the Secretary of the Treasury may sell or redeem securities, obligations, or other invested assets of the Fund before maturity in order to prevent the public debt of the United States from exceeding the public debt limit.

(2) The Secretary may sell or redeem securities, obligations, or other invested assets of the Fund under paragraph (1) of this subsection only during a debt issuance suspension period, and only to the extent necessary to obtain any

amount of funds not exceeding the amount equal to the total amount of the payments authorized to be made from the Fund under the provisions of this subchapter or chapter 84 of this title or related provisions of law during such period. A sale or redemption may be made under this subsection even if, before the sale or redemption, there is a sufficient amount in the Fund to ensure that such payments are made in a timely manner.

(l)(1) The Secretary of the Treasury shall report to Congress on the operation and status of the Fund during each debt issuance suspension period for which the Secretary is required to take action under paragraph (3) or (4) of subsection (j) of this section. The report shall be submitted as soon as possible after the expiration of such period, but not later than the date that is 30 days after the first normal interest payment date occurring after the expiration of such period.

(2) Whenever the Secretary of the Treasury determines that, by reason of the public debt limit, the Secretary will be unable to fully comply with the requirements of subsection (c) of this section, the Secretary shall immediately notify Congress of the determination. The notification shall be made in writing.

(m)(1) Notwithstanding any other provision of law, the United States Postal Service shall be liable for that portion of any estimated increase in the unfunded liability of the Fund which is attributable to any benefits payable from the Fund to former employees of the Postal Service who first become annuitants by reason of separation from the Postal Service on or after July 1, 1971, or to their survivors, or to the survivors of individuals who die on or after July 1, 1971, while employed by the Postal Service, when the increase results from a cost-of-living adjustment under section 8340 of this title.

(2) The estimated increase in the unfunded liability referred to in paragraph (1) of this subsection shall be determined by the Office after consultation with the Postal Service. The Postal Service shall pay the amount so determined to the Office in 15 equal annual installments with interest computed at the rate used in the most recent valuation of the Civil Service Retirement System, and with the first payment thereof due at the end of the fiscal year in which the cost-of-living adjustment with respect to which the payment relates becomes effective.

(3) In determining any amount for which the Postal Service is liable under this subsection, the amount of the liability shall be prorated to reflect only that portion of total service (used in computing the benefits involved) which is attributable to civilian service performed after June 30, 1971, as estimated by the Office.

(Pub. L. 89–554, Sept. 6, 1966, 80 Stat. 584; Pub. L. 90–83, § 1(85), Sept. 11, 1967, 81 Stat. 218; Pub. L. 91–93, title I, § 103(a), Oct. 20, 1969, 83 Stat. 137; Pub. L. 93–349, § 1, July 12, 1974, 88 Stat. 354; Pub. L. 94–183, § 2(37), Dec. 31, 1975, 89 Stat. 1058; Pub. L. 95–454, title IX, § 906(a)(2), (3), Oct. 13, 1978, 92 Stat. 1224; Pub. L. 96–70, title I, § 1244, Sept. 27, 1979, 93 Stat. 474; Pub. L. 97–253, title III, § 306(f), Sept. 8, 1982, 96 Stat. 797; Pub. L. 97–346, § 3(g), Oct. 15, 1982, 96 Stat. 1648; Pub. L. 98–216, § 3(a)(5), Feb. 14, 1984, 98 Stat. 6; Pub. L. 98–615, § 2(7), Nov.

8, 1984, 98 Stat. 3202; Pub. L. 99–335, title II, § 207(j), June 6, 1986, 100 Stat. 597; Pub. L. 99–509, title VI, § 6002, Oct. 21, 1986, 100 Stat. 1931; Pub. L. 100–203, title V, § 5428(d), Dec. 22, 1987, 101 Stat. 1330–274; Pub. L. 101–239, title IV, § 4002(a), Dec. 19, 1989, 103 Stat. 2133; Pub. L. 101–508, title VII, §§ 7001(a)(3), 7101(a), Nov. 5, 1990, 104 Stat. 1388–328, 1388–331; Pub. L. 101–510, div. C, title XXXV, § 3506(c), Nov. 5, 1990, 104 Stat. 1847; Pub. L. 103–424, § 10, Oct. 29, 1994, 108 Stat. 4366; Pub. L. 104–52, title IV, § 2, Nov. 19, 1995, 109 Stat. 490; Pub. L. 104–316, title I, § 103(h), Oct. 19, 1996, 110 Stat. 3829; Pub. L. 105–362, title XIII, § 1302(c), Nov. 10, 1998, 112 Stat. 3293.)

HISTORICAL AND REVISION NOTES
1966 ACT

Derivation	U.S. Code	Revised Statutes and Statutes at Large
(a)–(f)	5 U.S.C. 2267.	July 31, 1956, ch. 804, § 401 "Sec. 17", 70 Stat. 759. Oct. 4, 1961, Pub. L. 87–350, § 1(a), 75 Stat. 770.
(g)	[Uncodified].	Aug. 28, 1958, Pub. L. 85–844, § 101 (par. under "Civil Service Retirement and Disability Fund"), 72 Stat. 1064.

In subsection (a), the first sentence is based on former section 2251(f), which is carried into section 8331.

In subsection (f), the words "to carry out this subchapter" are substituted for "to continue this chapter in full force and effect".

In subsection (g), the words "after the enactment of this Act" are omitted as executed.

Standard changes are made to conform with the definitions applicable and the style of this title as outlined in the preface to the report.

1967 ACT

Section of title 5	Source (U.S. Code)	Source (Statutes at Large)
8348(a)	5 App.: 2267(a).	Sept. 27, 1965, Pub. L. 89–205, § 1(b), 79 Stat. 840.

The change in subsection (f) is made for uniformity in style and because the full title of the Commission appears in subsection (a).

REFERENCES IN TEXT

Sections 1241 and 1242 of the Panama Canal Act of 1979 [Pub. L. 96–70], referred to in subsec. (i)(1), amended sections 8336 and 8339 of this title, respectively.

Sections 1231(b) and 1243(a)(1) of the Panama Canal Act of 1979 [Pub. L. 96–70], referred to in subsec. (i)(1), are classified to sections 3671(b) and 3681(a)(1) of Title 22, Foreign Relations and Intercourse, respectively.

Section 3506 of the Panama Canal Commission Authorization Act for Fiscal Year 1991 [Pub. L. 101–510, div. C, title XXXV], referred to in subsec. (i)(1), amended sections 8336, 8339, and 8348 of this title.

AMENDMENTS

1998—Subsec. (g). Pub. L. 105–362 struck out at end "The Office shall report to the President and to the Congress the sums credited to the Fund under this subsection."

1996—Subsec. (l)(1). Pub. L. 104–316 struck out at end "The Secretary shall concurrently transmit a copy of such report to the Comptroller General of the United States."

1995—Subsec. (a)(1)(B). Pub. L. 104–52 inserted "in making an allotment or assignment made by an individual under section 8345(h) or 8465(b) of this title," after "of law)," and "or section 8345(k) or 8469 of this title" before semicolon at end.

1994—Subsec. (a)(3). Pub. L. 103–424 added par. (3).

1990—Subsec. (a)(1)(B). Pub. L. 101–508, § 7001(a)(3), inserted "in administering alternative forms of annuities under sections 8343a and 8420a (and related provisions of law)," before "and in withholding".

Subsec. (i)(1). Pub. L. 101–510 substituted "1979, and the amendments made by section 3506 of the Panama Canal Commission Authorization Act for Fiscal Year 1991" for "1979".

Subsec. (m)(1). Pub. L. 101–508, § 7101(a), substituted "July 1, 1971" for "October 1, 1986" in two places.

1989—Subsec. (m). Pub. L. 101–239 added subsec. (m).

1987—Subsec. (i)(2). Pub. L. 100–203 substituted "The Panama Canal Commission shall pay to the Fund from funds available to it" for "The Secretary of the Treasury shall pay to the Fund from appropriations".

1986—Subsec. (a). Pub. L. 99–335 inserted reference to provisions of chapter 84 of this title which relate to benefits payable out of the Fund in par. (1)(A), inserted "or 8462" and reference to subchapters II and IV of chapter 84 of this title in par. (1)(B), and inserted reference to chapter 84 of this title in par. (2).

Subsecs. (j) to (l). Pub. L. 99–509 added subsecs. (j) to (l).

1984—Subsec. (a)(1)(B). Pub. L. 98–615 inserted ", in administering survivor annuities and elections providing therefor under sections 8339 and 8341 of this title,".

Subsec. (d). Pub. L. 98–216 substituted "chapter 31 of title 31" for "the Second Liberty Bond Act, as amended,".

1982—Subsec. (a)(1)(B). Pub. L. 97–346 inserted "and in withholding taxes pursuant to section 3405 of title 26".

Subsec. (g). Pub. L. 97–253, § 306(f), inserted ", less an amount determined by the Office to be appropriate to reflect the value of the deposits made to the credit of the Fund under section 8334(j) of this title" after "allowed for military service".

1979—Subsec. (i). Pub. L. 96–70 added subsec. (i).

1978—Subsecs. (a), (g), (h)(2). Pub. L. 95–454 substituted "Office of Personnel Management" and "Office" for "Civil Service Commission" and "Commission", respectively, wherever appearing.

1975—Subsec. (h)(2). Pub. L. 94–183 substituted "30" for "thirty".

1974—Subsec. (h). Pub. L. 93–349 added subsec. (h).

1969—Subsec. (a). Pub. L. 91–93, § 103(a)(1), designated existing provisions as par. (1)(A) and (B) and added par. (2).

Subsec. (f). Pub. L. 91–93, § 103(a)(2), added subsec. (f) and struck out former subsec. (f) which required the Commission to submit estimates of appropriations necessary to finance the Fund on a normal cost plus interest basis and to carry out this subchapter.

Subsec. (g). Pub. L. 91–93, § 103(a)(2), added subsec. (g) and struck out former subsec. (g) which contained restriction against use of Fund money to pay an increase in annuity benefits or a new annuity benefit under this subchapter or an earlier statute without an appropriation being made to the Fund in a sufficient amount to prevent an immediate increase in the unfunded accrued liability of the Fund.

EFFECTIVE DATE OF 1990 AMENDMENT

Section 7101(d) of Pub. L. 101–508 provided that: "This section and the amendments made by this section [amending this section, enacting provisions set out as a note under this section, and repealing provisions set out as notes under this section] shall take effect on October 1, 1990."

EFFECTIVE DATE OF 1989 AMENDMENT

Section 4002(b)(1) of Pub. L. 101–239, which provided that section 4002 of Pub. L. 101–239 (amending this section and enacting provisions set out as notes under this section) be effective as of Oct. 1, 1986, was repealed by Pub. L. 101–508, title VII, § 7101(b), Nov. 5, 1990, 104 Stat. 1388–331.

EFFECTIVE DATE OF 1987 AMENDMENT

Amendment by Pub. L. 100–203 effective Jan. 1, 1988, see section 5429 of Pub. L. 100–203, set out as a note under section 3712 of Title 22, Foreign Relations and Intercourse.

EFFECTIVE DATE OF 1986 AMENDMENT

Amendment by Pub. L. 99–335 effective Jan. 1, 1987, see section 702(a) of Pub. L. 99–335, set out as an Effective Date note under section 8401 of this title.

EFFECTIVE DATE OF 1984 AMENDMENT

Amendment by Pub. L. 98–615 effective May 7, 1985, with enumerated exceptions and specific applicability provisions, see section 4(a)(1), (5)(D) of Pub. L. 98–615, as amended, set out as a note under section 8341 of this title.

EFFECTIVE DATE OF 1982 AMENDMENTS

Amendment by Pub. L. 97–346 effective Sept. 8, 1982, see section 3(n) of Pub. L. 97–346, set out as a note under section 8332 of this title.

Amendment by Pub. L. 97–253 effective Oct. 1, 1982, except that any employee or Member who retired after Sept. 8, 1982, and before Oct. 1, 1985, or is entitled to an annuity under chapter 83 of this title based on a separation from service occurring during such period, or a survivor of such individual, may make a payment under section 8334(j)(1) of this title, and regulations required to be issued under section 8334(j)(1) of this title, to be issued by the Office of Personnel Management within 90 days after such effective date, see section 306(g) of Pub. L. 97–253, as amended, set out as a note under section 8331 of this title.

EFFECTIVE DATE OF 1979 AMENDMENT

Amendment by Pub. L. 96–70 effective Oct. 1, 1979, see section 3304 of Pub. L. 96–70, set out as an Effective Date note under section 3601 of Title 22, Foreign Relations and Intercourse.

EFFECTIVE DATE OF 1978 AMENDMENT

Amendment by Pub. L. 95–454 effective 90 days after Oct. 13, 1978, see section 907 of Pub. L. 95–454, set out as a note under section 1101 of this title.

EFFECTIVE DATE OF 1974 AMENDMENT

Amendment by Pub. L. 93–349 effective July 1, 1971, except that the Postal Service shall not be required to make (1) the payments due June 30, 1972, June 30, 1973, and June 30, 1974, attributable to pay increases granted by the Postal Service prior to July 1, 1973, until such time as funds are appropriated to the Postal Service for that purpose, and (2) the transfer to the Civil Service Retirement and Disability Fund required by title II of the Treasury, Postal Service, and General Government Appropriation Act, 1974, Public Law 93–143, see section 3 of Pub. L. 93–349, set out as a note under section 1005 of Title 39, Postal Service.

EFFECTIVE DATE OF 1969 AMENDMENT

Section 103(b)(1) of Pub. L. 91–93 provided that: "The provisions of subsection (g) of section 8348 of title 5, United States Code, as contained in the amendment made by subsection (a)(2) of this section, shall become effective at the beginning of the fiscal year which ends on June 30, 1971."

PAYMENTS TO REIMBURSE FUND FOR INCREASE IN UNFUNDED LIABILITY

Pub. L. 105–261, div. C, title XXXI, § 3154(l), Oct. 17, 1998, 112 Stat. 2256, provided that:

"(1) The Department of Energy shall pay into the Civil Service Retirement and Disability Fund an amount determined by the Director of the Office of Personnel Management to be necessary to reimburse the Fund for any estimated increase in the unfunded liability of the Fund resulting from the amendments related to the Civil Service Retirement System under this section [amending sections 3307, 8331, 8334 to 8336, 8401, 8412, 8415, 8422, 8423, and 8425 of this title], and for any estimated increase in the supplemental liability of the Fund resulting from the amendments related to the Federal Employees Retirement System under this section.

"(2) The Department shall pay the amount so determined in five equal annual installments with interest computed at the rate used in the most recent valuation of the Federal Employees Retirement System.

"(3) The Department shall make payments under this subsection from amounts available for weapons activities of the Department."

PAYMENTS BY POSTAL SERVICE RELATING TO COR-RECTED CALCULATIONS FOR PAST RETIREMENT COLAS

Pub. L. 103–66, title XI, § 11101(a), Aug. 10, 1993, 107 Stat. 413, provided that: "In addition to any other payments required under section 8348(m) of title 5, United States Code, or any other provision of law, the United States Postal Service shall pay into the Civil Service Retirement and Disability Fund a total of $693,000,000, of which—

"(1) at least one-third shall be paid not later than September 30, 1996;

"(2) at least two-thirds shall be paid not later than September 30, 1997; and

"(3) any remaining balance shall be paid not later than September 30, 1998."

TIMELY PROCESSING OF RETIREMENT BENEFITS

Pub. L. 102–484, div. D, title XLIV, § 4436(d), Oct. 23, 1992, 106 Stat. 2724, as amended by Pub. L. 103–337, div. A, title III, § 341(b)(2), Oct. 5, 1994, 108 Stat. 2720; Pub. L. 105–85, div. A, title XI, § 1106(b)(2), Nov. 18, 1997, 111 Stat. 1924, provided that:

"(1) In order to ensure the timely processing of applications for retirement benefits, under the Civil Service Retirement System or the Federal Employees' Retirement System, for civilian employees of the Department of Defense and other employees who retire when their agency is undergoing a major reorganization, a major reduction in force, or a major transfer of function, the costs incurred by the Office of Personnel Management in processing any such application shall be deemed to be an administrative expense described in section 8348(a)(1)(B) of title 5, United States Code.

"(2) This subsection shall apply with respect to applications for retirement benefits based on separations occurring before January 1, 2002."

PRE-1991 COST-OF-LIVING ADJUSTMENTS

Section 7101(c) of Pub. L. 101–508, as amended by Pub. L. 102–378, § 5(a)(1), Oct. 2, 1992, 106 Stat. 1358, provided that:

"(1) For the purpose of this subsection—

"(A) the term 'pre-1991 COLA' means a cost-of-living adjustment which took effect in any of the fiscal years specified in subparagraphs (A)–(N) of paragraph (3);

"(B) the term 'post-1990 fiscal year' means a fiscal year after fiscal year 1990; and

"(C) the term 'pre-1991 fiscal year' means a fiscal year before fiscal year 1991.

"(2) Notwithstanding any other provision of law, an installment (equal to an amount determined by reference to paragraph (3)) shall be payable by the United States Postal Service in a post-1990 fiscal year, with respect to a pre-1991 COLA, if such fiscal year occurs within the 15-fiscal-year period which begins with the first fiscal year in which that COLA took effect.

"(3) Notwithstanding any provision of section 8348(m) of title 5, United States Code, or any determination thereunder (including any made under such provision, as in effect before October 1, 1990), the estimated increase in the unfunded liability referred to in paragraph (1) of such section 8348(m) shall be payable, in accordance with this subsection, based on annual installments equal to—

"(A) $6,500,000 each, with respect to the cost-of-living adjustment which took effect in fiscal year 1977;

"(B) $7,000,000 each, with respect to the cost-of-living adjustment which took effect in fiscal year 1978;

"(C) $10,400,000 each, with respect to the cost-of-living adjustment which took effect in fiscal year 1979;

"(D) $20,500,000 each, with respect to the cost-of-living adjustment which took effect in fiscal year 1980;

"(E) $26,100,000 each, with respect to the cost-of-living adjustment which took effect in fiscal year 1981;

"(F) $28,100,000 each, with respect to the cost-of-living adjustment which took effect in fiscal year 1982;

"(G) $30,600,000 each, with respect to the cost-of-living adjustment which took effect in fiscal year 1983;

"(H) $5,700,000 each, with respect to the cost-of-living adjustment which took effect in fiscal year 1984;

"(I) $19,400,000 each, with respect to the cost-of-living adjustment which took effect in fiscal year 1985;

"(J) $7,400,000 each, with respect to the cost-of-living adjustment which took effect in fiscal year 1986;

"(K) $8,500,000 each, with respect to the cost-of-living adjustment which took effect in fiscal year 1987;

"(L) $36,800,000 each, with respect to the cost-of-living adjustment which took effect in fiscal year 1988;

"(M) $51,600,000 each, with respect to the cost-of-living adjustment which took effect in fiscal year 1989; and

"(N) $63,500,000 each, with respect to the cost-of-living adjustment which took effect in fiscal year 1990.

"(4) Any installment payable under this subsection shall be paid by the Postal Service at the same time as when it pays any installments due in that same fiscal year under section 8348(m) of title 5, United States Code.

"(5) An installment payable under this subsection in a fiscal year, with respect to a pre-1991 COLA, shall be in lieu of any other installment for which the Postal Service might otherwise be liable in such fiscal year, with respect to such COLA, under section 8348(m) of title 5, United States Code."

[Amendment by Pub. L. 102–378 to section 7101(c) of Pub. L. 101–508, set out above, effective Nov. 5, 1990, see section 9(b)(6) of Pub. L. 102–378, set out as an Effective Date of 1992 Amendment note under section 6303 of this title.]

PAYMENTS RELATING TO AMOUNTS WHICH WOULD HAVE BEEN DUE BEFORE FISCAL YEAR 1987

Section 7103 of Pub. L. 101–508 provided that:

"(a) DEFINITION.—For the purpose of this section, the term 'pre-1987 fiscal year' means a fiscal year before fiscal year 1987.

"(b) FOR PAST RETIREMENT COLAs.—As payment for any amounts which would have been due in any pre-1987 fiscal year under the provisions of section 8348(m) of title 5, United States Code (as amended by section 7101) if such provisions had been in effect as of July 1, 1971, the United States Postal Service shall pay into the Civil Service Retirement and Disability Fund—

"(1) $216,000,000, not later than September 30, 1991;

"(2) $266,000,000, not later than September 30, 1992;

"(3) $316,000,000, not later than September 30, 1993;

"(4) $416,000,000, not later than September 30, 1994; and

"(5) $471,000,000, not later than September 30, 1995.

"(c) FOR PAST HEALTH BENEFITS.—As payment for any amounts which would, for any period ending before the start of fiscal year 1987, have been payable under the provisions of section 8906(g)(2) of title 5, United States Code (as amended by section 7102) if such provisions had been in effect as of July 1, 1971, the United States Postal Service shall pay into the Employees Health Benefits Fund—

"(1) $56,000,000, not later than September 30, 1991;

"(2) $47,000,000, not later than September 30, 1992;

"(3) $62,000,000, not later than September 30, 1993;

"(4) $56,000,000, not later than September 30, 1994; and

"(5) $234,000,000, not later than September 30, 1995."

CERTAIN POSTAL SERVICE ANNUITANTS; SIZE OF ANNUAL INSTALLMENTS TO FUND PREVIOUS YEARS' COLAS

Section 4002(b)(2) of Pub. L. 101–239, which provided that notwithstanding any provision of section 8348(m)

of this title the estimated increase in the unfunded liability referred to in section 8348(m)(1) was to be payable based on annual installments equal to specified amounts for fiscal years 1987 to 1989, was repealed by Pub. L. 101–508, title VII, § 7101(b), Nov. 5, 1990, 104 Stat. 1388–331.

CERTAIN POSTAL SERVICE ANNUITANTS; ADDITIONAL AMOUNT PAYABLE

Section 4002(b)(3) of Pub. L. 101–239, which provided that first payment made under provisions of section 8348(m) of this title was to include, in addition to the amount which would otherwise have been payable at that time, an amount equal to the sum of any amounts which would have been due under those provisions in any prior year if this section had been enacted before Oct. 1, 1986, and which provided the method of computation, was repealed by Pub. L. 101–508, title VII, § 7101(b), Nov. 5, 1990, 104 Stat. 1388–331.

STATUS OF ORIGINAL SUBSEC. (g) PROVISIONS DURING PERIOD FROM OCT. 20, 1969 TO JUNE 30, 1970

Section 103(b)(2) of Pub. L. 91–93 provided that: "Paragraph (1) of this subsection [set out as Effective Date of 1969 Amendment note above], shall not be held or considered to continue in effect after the enactment of this Act [Oct. 20, 1969], the provisions of section 8348(g) of title 5, United States Code, as in effect immediately prior to such enactment."

INAPPLICABILITY TO BENEFITS UNDER PUB. L. 89–737 OF PROHIBITION AGAINST PAYMENT OF INCREASED ANNUITY BENEFIT WITHOUT COMPENSATING APPROPRIATION

Section 3 of Pub. L. 89–737, Nov. 2, 1966, 80 Stat. 1164, which provided that section 8348(g) of title 5, United States Code, does not apply with respect to annuity benefits resulting from the enactment of this Act [amending sections 8114, 8331, and 8704 of this title and section 1117 of former Title 5, Executive Departments and Government Officers and Employees], was repealed by Pub. L. 90–83, § 10(b), Sept. 11, 1967, 81 Stat. 223.

REDEMPTION OF OBLIGATIONS HELD PRIOR TO OCT. 4, 1961; REINVESTMENT OF PROCEEDS

Pub. L. 87–350, § 1(b) Oct. 4, 1961, 75 Stat. 770, provided that: "All special issues in which the civil service retirement and disability fund is invested in accordance with section 17(d) of the Civil Service Retirement Act [subsecs. (d) and (e) of this section] as in effect prior to the enactment of this Act [Oct. 4, 1961] shall be redeemed and the moneys reinvested by the Secretary of the Treasury, as nearly as may be practicable, in equal annual amounts over the period of ten calendar years beginning with the calendar year 1962, in accordance with such section 17(d), as amended by subsection (a) of this section."

SECTION REFERRED TO IN OTHER SECTIONS

This section is referred to in sections 8331, 8401 of this title; title 20 section 125; title 25 section 450i; title 42 section 2297h–8.

§ 8349. Offset relating to certain benefits under the Social Security Act

(a)(1) Notwithstanding any other provision of this subchapter, if an individual under section 8402(b)(2) is entitled, or would on proper application be entitled, to old-age insurance benefits under title II of the Social Security Act, the annuity otherwise payable to such individual shall be reduced under this subsection.

(2) A reduction under this subsection commences beginning with the first month for which the individual both—

(A) is entitled to an annuity under this subchapter; and

(B) is entitled, or would on proper application be entitled, to old-age insurance benefits under title II of the Social Security Act.

(3)(A)(i) Subject to clause (ii) and subparagraphs (B) and (C), the amount of a reduction under this subsection shall be equal to the difference between—

(I) the old-age insurance benefit which would be payable to the individual for the month referred to in paragraph (2); and

(II) the old-age insurance benefit which would be so payable, excluding all wages derived from Federal service of the individual, and assuming the individual were fully insured (as defined by section 214(a) of the Social Security Act).

(ii) For purposes of this subsection, the amount of a benefit referred to in subclause (I) or (II) of clause (i) shall be determined without regard to subsections (b) through (l) of section 203 of the Social Security Act, and without regard to the requirement that an application for such benefit be filed.

(B) A reduction under this subsection—

(i) may not exceed an amount equal to the product of—

(I) the old-age insurance benefit to which the individual is entitled (or would on proper application be entitled) for the month referred to in paragraph (2), determined without regard to subsections (b) through (l) of section 203 of the Social Security Act; and

(II) a fraction, as determined under section 8421(b)(3) with respect to the individual, except that the reference to "service" in subparagraph (A) of such section shall be considered to mean Federal service; and

(ii) may not cause the annuity payment for an individual to be reduced below zero.

(C) An amount computed under subclause (I) or (II) of subparagraph (A)(i), or under subparagraph (B)(i)(I), for purposes of determining the amount of a reduction under this subsection shall be adjusted under section 8340 of this title.

(4) A reduction under this subsection applies with respect to the annuity otherwise payable to such individual under this subchapter (other than under section 8337) for the month involved—

(A) based on service of such individual; and

(B) without regard to section 8345(j), if otherwise applicable.

(5) The operation of the preceding paragraphs of this subsection shall not be considered for purposes of applying the provisions of the second sentence of section 215(a)(7)(B)(i) or the provisions of section 215(d)(5)(ii) of the Social Security Act in determining any amount under subclause (I) or (II) of paragraph (3)(A)(i) or paragraph (3)(B)(i)(I) for purposes of this subsection.

(b)(1) Notwithstanding any other provision of this subchapter—

(A) a disability annuity to which an individual described in section 8402(b)(2) is entitled under this subchapter, and

(B) a survivor annuity to which a person is entitled under this subchapter based on the service of an individual described in section 8402(b)(2),

shall be subject to reduction under this subsection if that individual or person is also entitled (or would on proper application also be entitled) to any similar benefits under title II of the Social Security Act based on the wages and self-employment income of such individual described in section 8402(b)(2).

(2)(A) Subject to subparagraph (B), reductions under this subsection shall be made in a manner consistent with the manner in which reductions under subsection (a) are computed and otherwise made.

(B) Reductions under this subsection shall be discontinued if, or for so long as, entitlement to the similar benefits under title II of the Social Security Act (as referred to in paragraph (1)) is terminated (or, in the case of an individual who has not made proper application therefor, would be terminated).

(3) For the purpose of applying section 224 of the Social Security Act to the disability insurance benefit used to compute the reduction under this subsection, the amount of the CSRS annuity considered shall be the amount of the CSRS annuity before application of this section.

(4) The Office shall prescribe regulations to carry out this subsection.

(c) For the purpose of this section, the term "Federal service" means service which is employment for the purposes of title II of the Social Security Act and chapter 21 of the Internal Revenue Code of 1986 by reason of the amendments made by section 101 of the Social Security Amendments of 1983.

(d) In administering subsections (a) through (c)—

(1) the terms "an individual under section 8402(b)(2)" and "an individual described in section 8402(b)(2)" shall each be considered to include any individual—

(A) who is subject to this subchapter as a result of any provision of law described in section 8347(o), and

(B) whose employment (as described in section 8347(o)) is also employment for purposes of title II of the Social Security Act and chapter 21 of the Internal Revenue Code of 1986; and

(2) the term "Federal service", as applied with respect to any individual to whom this section applies as a result of paragraph (1), means any employment referred to in paragraph (1)(B) performed after December 31, 1983.

(Added Pub. L. 99–335, title II, § 201(b)(1), June 6, 1986, 100 Stat. 589; amended Pub. L. 99–514, § 2, Oct. 22, 1986, 100 Stat. 2095; Pub. L. 100–238, title I, § 108(b)(2), Jan. 8, 1988, 101 Stat. 1748.)

REFERENCES IN TEXT

The Social Security Act, referred to in text, is act Aug. 14, 1935, ch. 531, 49 Stat. 620, as amended. Title II of the Social Security Act is classified generally to subchapter II (§ 401 et seq.) of chapter 7 of Title 42, The Public Health and Welfare. Sections 203, 214, 215, and 224 of the Social Security Act are classified to sections 403, 414, 415, and 424a, respectively, of Title 42. For complete classification of this Act to the Code, see section 1305 of Title 42 and Tables.

Chapter 21 of the Internal Revenue Code of 1986, referred to in subsecs. (c) and (d)(1)(B), is classified to chapter 21 (§ 3101 et seq.) of Title 26, Internal Revenue Code.

Section 101 of the Social Security Amendments of 1983 [Pub. L. 98–21], referred to in subsec. (c), amended section 3121 of Title 26 and sections 409 and 410 of Title 42, The Public Health and Welfare, and enacted provisions set out as notes under section 3121 of Title 26 and section 410 of Title 42.

AMENDMENTS

1988—Subsec. (d). Pub. L. 100–238 added subsec. (d).

1986—Subsec. (c). Pub. L. 99–514 substituted "Internal Revenue Code of 1986" for "Internal Revenue Code of 1954".

EFFECTIVE DATE OF 1988 AMENDMENT

Amendment by Pub. L. 100–238 effective Jan. 1, 1987, see section 108(b)(3) of Pub. L. 100–238, set out as a note under section 8334 of this title.

EFFECTIVE DATE

Section effective Jan. 1, 1987, see section 702(a) of Pub. L. 99–335, set out as a note under section 8401 of this title.

OFFSETS TO PREVENT FULL DOUBLE COVERAGE FOR EMPLOYEES OF PARK POLICE AND SECRET SERVICE

For provisions relating to offsets for prevention of full double coverage for employees of Park Police and Secret Service, see section 103(e) of Pub. L. 100–238, set out as a note under section 8334 of this title.

SECTION REFERRED TO IN OTHER SECTIONS

This section is referred to in title 22 section 4046; title 50 section 2031.

§ 8350. Retirement counseling

(a) For the purposes of this section, the term "retirement counselor", when used with respect to an agency, means an employee of the agency who is designated by the head of the agency to furnish information on benefits under this subchapter and chapter 84 of this title and counseling services relating to such benefits to other employees of the agency.

(b) The Director of the Office of Personnel Management shall establish a training program for all retirement counselors of agencies of the Federal Government.

(c)(1) The training program established under subsection (b) of this section shall provide for comprehensive training in the provisions and administration of this subchapter and chapter 84 of this title, shall be designed to promote fully informed retirement decisions by employees and Members under this subchapter and individuals subject to chapter 84 of this title, and shall be revised as necessary to assure that the information furnished to retirement counselors of agencies under the program is current.

(2) The Director shall conduct a training session under the training program at least once every 3 months.

(3) Once each year, each retirement counselor of an agency shall successfully complete a training session conducted under the training program.

(Added Pub. L. 99–335, title II, § 205(a), June 6, 1986, 100 Stat. 592; amended Pub. L. 99–556, title II, § 202, Oct. 27, 1986, 100 Stat. 3135.)

AMENDMENTS

1986—Subsec. (c)(1). Pub. L. 99–556 substituted "subsection (b)" for "subsection (b)(1)".

EFFECTIVE DATE

Section effective June 6, 1986, see section 702(b)(3) of Pub. L. 99–335, set out as a note under section 8401 of this title.

§ 8351. Participation in the Thrift Savings Plan

(a)(1) An employee or Member may elect to contribute to the Thrift Savings Fund established by section 8437 of this title.

(2) An election may be made under paragraph (1) only during a period provided under section 8432(b) for individuals who are subject to chapter 84 of this title.

(b)(1) Except as otherwise provided in this subsection, the provisions of subchapters III and VII of chapter 84 of this title shall apply with respect to employees and Members making contributions to the Thrift Savings Fund under subsection (a) of this section.

(2)(A) An employee or Member may contribute to the Thrift Savings Fund in any pay period any amount not exceeding the maximum percentage of such employee's or Member's basic pay for such pay period allowable under subparagraph (B).

(B) The maximum percentage allowable under this subparagraph shall be determined in accordance with the following table:

In the case of a pay period beginning in fiscal year:	The maximum percentage allowable is:
2001	6
2002	7
2003	8
2004	9
2005	10
2006 or thereafter	100.

(3) No contributions may be made by an employing agency for the benefit of an employee or Member under section 8432(c) of this title.

(4) Section 8433(b) of this title applies to any employee or Member who elects to make contributions to the Thrift Savings Fund under subsection (a) of this section and separates from Government employment.

(5)(A) The provisions of section 8435 of this title that require a waiver or consent by the spouse of an employee or Member (or former employee or Member) shall not apply with respect to sums in the Thrift Savings Fund contributed by the employee or Member (or former employee or Member) and earnings in the fund attributable to such sums.

(B) An election or change of election authorized by subchapter III of chapter 84 of this title shall be effective in the case of a married employee or Member, and a loan or withdrawal may be approved under section 8433(g) and (h) of this title in such case, only after the Executive Director notifies the employee's or Member's spouse that the election or change of election has been made or that the Executive Director has received an application for such loan or withdrawal, as the case may be.

(C) Subparagraph (B) may be waived with respect to a spouse if the employee or Member establishes to the satisfaction of the Executive Director of the Federal Retirement Thrift Investment Board that the whereabouts of such spouse cannot be determined.

(D) Except with respect to the making of loans or withdrawals under section 8433(g) or (h), none of the provisions of this paragraph requiring notification to a spouse or former spouse of an employee, Member, former employee, or former Member shall apply in any case in which the nonforfeitable account balance of the employee, Member, former employee, or former Member is $3,500 or less.

(6) Notwithstanding paragraph (4), if an employee or Member separates from Government employment and such employee's or Member's nonforfeitable account balance is less than an amount that the Executive Director prescribes by regulation, the Executive Director shall pay the nonforfeitable account balance to the participant in a single payment.

(7) For the purpose of this section, the term "nonforfeitable account balance" has the same meaning as under section 8401(32).

(8) In applying section 8432b to an employee contributing to the Thrift Savings Fund after being restored to or reemployed in a position subject to this subchapter, pursuant to chapter 43 of title 38—

(A) any reference in such section to contributions under section 8432(a) shall be considered a reference to employee contributions under this section;

(B) the contribution rate under section 8432b(b)(2)(A) shall be the maximum percentage allowable under subsection (b)(2) of this section; and

(C) subsections (c) and (d) of section 8432b shall be disregarded.

(9) For the purpose of this section, separation from Government employment includes a transfer described in section 8431.

(c) A member of the Foreign Service described in section 103(6) of the Foreign Service Act of 1980 shall be ineligible to make any election under this section.

(d) A foreign national employee of the Central Intelligence Agency whose services are performed outside the United States shall be ineligible to make an election under this section.

(e) The Executive Director of the Federal Retirement Thrift Investment Board may prescribe regulations to carry out this section.

(Added Pub. L. 99–335, title II, § 206(a)(1), June 6, 1986, 100 Stat. 593; amended Pub. L. 100–238, title I, § 111(a), Jan. 8, 1988, 101 Stat. 1750; Pub. L. 101–335, §§ 3(b)(1), 6(b)(1), July 17, 1990, 104 Stat. 320, 323; Pub. L. 102–183, title III, § 308(a), Dec. 4, 1991, 105 Stat. 1265; Pub. L. 102–484, div. D, title XLIV, § 4437(c), Oct. 23, 1992, 106 Stat. 2724; Pub. L. 103–226, § 9(a), (i)(1), (2), Mar. 30, 1994, 108 Stat. 118, 121; Pub. L. 103–353, § 4(d), Oct. 13, 1994, 108 Stat. 3172; Pub. L. 104–208, div. A, title I, § 101(f) [title VI, § 659 [title II, § 202]], Sept. 30, 1996, 110 Stat. 3009–314, 3009–372, 3009–374; Pub. L. 106–65, div. A, title VI, § 661(a)(3)(B), Oct. 5, 1999, 113 Stat. 671; Pub. L. 106–168, title II, § 203(b), Dec. 12, 1999, 113 Stat. 1820; Pub. L. 106–554, § 1(a)(4) [div. B, title I, § 138(b)], Dec. 21, 2000, 114 Stat. 2763, 2763A–234.)

AMENDMENT OF SUBSECTION (b)(8)(A)

Pub. L. 106–65, div. A, title VI, §§ 661(a)(3)(B)(ii), 663, Oct. 5, 1999, 113 Stat. 671, 673, as amended by Pub. L. 106–398, § 1 [[div. A], title VI, § 661(a)], Oct. 30, 2000, 114 Stat. 1654,

1654A–167, provided that effective 180 days after Oct. 30, 2000, unless postponed, subsection (b)(8)(A) of this section is amended by striking the semicolon and inserting the following: ", except that the reference in section 8432b(b)(2)(B) to employee contributions under section 8432(a) shall be considered a reference to employee contributions under this subchapter and section 8440e;".

REFERENCES IN TEXT

Section 103(6) of the Foreign Service Act of 1980, referred to in subsec. (c), is classified to section 3903(6) of Title 22, Foreign Relations and Intercourse.

AMENDMENTS

2000—Subsec. (b)(2). Pub. L. 106–554 designated existing provisions as subpar. (A), substituted "the maximum percentage of such employee's or Member's basic pay for such pay period allowable under subparagraph (B)." for "5 percent of the amount of the employee's or Member's basic pay for such period.", and added subpar. (B).

1999—Subsec. (b)(8). Pub. L. 106–65, § 661(a)(3)(B)(i), and Pub. L. 106–168, amended subsec. (b) identically, redesignating par. (11) as (8).

Subsec. (b)(9). Pub. L. 106–168 added par. (9).

Subsec. (b)(11). Pub. L. 106–65, § 661(a)(3)(B)(i), and Pub. L. 106–168, amended subsec. (b) identically, redesignating par. (11) as (8).

1996—Subsec. (b)(5)(B). Pub. L. 104–208, § 101(f) [title VI, § 659 [title II, § 202(1)(A)]], substituted "An election or change of election" for "An election, change of election, or modification (relating to the commencement date of a deferred annuity)", inserted "or withdrawal" after "and a loan" and "and (h)" after "8433(g)", substituted "the election or change of election" for "the election, change of election, or modification", and inserted "or withdrawal" after "for such loan".

Subsec. (b)(5)(D). Pub. L. 104–208, § 101(f) [title VI, § 659 [title II, § 202(1)(B)]], inserted "or withdrawals" after "of loans" and "or (h)" after "8433(g)".

Subsec. (b)(6). Pub. L. 104–208, § 101(f) [title VI, § 659 [title II, § 202(2)]], substituted "less than an amount that the Executive Director prescribes by regulation" for "$3,500 or less" and struck out "unless the employee or Member elects, at such time and otherwise in such manner as the Executive Director prescribes, one of the options available under subsection (b)" before period at end.

1994—Subsec. (b)(4). Pub. L. 103–226, § 9(a)(1), amended par. (4) generally. Prior to amendment, par. (4) read as follows: "Section 8433(b) of this title applies to any employee or Member who elects to make contributions to the Thrift Savings Fund under subsection (a) of this section and separates from Government employment entitled to an immediate annuity under this subchapter (including a disability retirement annuity under section 8337 of this title), separates from Government employment pursuant to regulations under section 3502(a) of this title or procedures under section 3595(a) of this title in a reduction in force, or separates from Government employment entitled to benefits under subchapter I of chapter 81 of this title."

Subsec. (b)(5). Pub. L. 103–226, § 9(a)(2), (3), redesignated par. (7) as (5) and struck out former par. (5) which read as follows: "Section 8433(c) of this title applies to any employee or Member who elects to make contributions to the Thrift Savings Fund under subsection (a) of this section and separates entitled to a deferred annuity under this subchapter."

Subsec. (b)(5)(B) to (D). Pub. L. 103–226, § 9(a)(4), (i)(1), (2), substituted "section 8433(g)" for "section 8433(i)" in subpars. (B) and (D) and struck out "or former spouse" after "spouse" in two places in subpar. (C).

Subsec. (b)(6). Pub. L. 103–226, § 9(a)(5), amended par. (6) generally. Prior to amendment, par. (6) read as follows: "Notwithstanding paragraphs (4) and (5), if an employee or Member separates from Government employment under circumstances making such employee or Member eligible to make an election under subsection (b) or (c) of section 8433, and such employee's or Member's nonforfeitable account balance is $3,500 or less, the Executive Director shall pay the nonforfeitable account balance to the participant in a single payment unless the employee or Member elects, at such time and otherwise in such manner as the Executive Director prescribes, one of the options available under such subsection (b) or (c), as applicable.''

Pub. L. 103–226, § 9(a)(2), (3), redesignated par. (9) as (6) and struck out former par. (6) which read as follows: "Section 8433(d) of this title applies to any employee or Member who elects to make contributions to the Thrift Savings Fund under subsection (a) of this section and separates from the service before becoming entitled to an immediate or deferred annuity under this subchapter.''

Subsec. (b)(7). Pub. L. 103–226, § 9(a)(6), which directed substitution of "nonforfeitable" for "nonforfeiture", could not be executed because the term "nonforfeiture" does not appear in text.

Pub. L. 103–226, § 9(a)(3), redesignated par. (10) as (7). Former par. (7) redesignated (5).

Subsec. (b)(8). Pub. L. 103–226, § 9(a)(2), struck out par. (8) which read as follows: "Notwithstanding paragraph (6), if an employee or Member who elects to make contributions to the Thrift Savings Fund under subsection (a) separates from Government employment before becoming entitled to a deferred or immediate annuity under this subchapter, and such employee's or Member's nonforfeitable account balance is $3,500 or less, the Executive Director shall pay the nonforfeitable account balance to the participant in a single payment unless the employee or Member elects, at such time and otherwise in such manner as the Executive Director prescribes, to have the nonforfeitable account balance transferred to an eligible retirement plan as provided in section 8433(e).''

Subsec. (b)(9), (10). Pub. L. 103–226, § 9(a)(3), redesignated pars. (9) and (10) as (6) and (7), respectively.

Subsec. (b)(11). Pub. L. 103–353 added par. (11).

1992—Subsec. (b)(4). Pub. L. 102–484 inserted ", separates from Government employment pursuant to regulations under section 3502(a) of this title or procedures under section 3595(a) of this title in a reduction in force,'' after "section 8337 of this title)''.

1991—Subsecs. (d), (e). Pub. L. 102–183 added subsec. (d) and redesignated former subsec. (d) as (e).

1990—Subsec. (b)(7)(D). Pub. L. 101–335, § 6(b)(1)(B), added subpar. (D).

Subsec. (b)(8). Pub. L. 101–335, § 6(b)(1)(A), added par. (8).

Pub. L. 101–335, § 3(b)(1), struck out par. (8) which read as follows: "Sums contributed under this section and earnings attributable to such sums may be invested and reinvested only in the Government Securities Investment Fund established under section 8438(b)(1)(A) of this title.''

Subsec. (b)(9), (10). Pub. L. 101–335, § 6(b)(1)(A), added pars. (9) and (10).

1988—Subsecs. (c), (d). Pub. L. 100–238 added subsec. (c) and redesignated former subsec. (c) as (d).

EFFECTIVE DATE OF 2000 AMENDMENT

Pub. L. 106–554, § 1(a)(4) [div. B, title I, § 138(c)], Dec. 21, 2000, 114 Stat. 2763, 2763A–234, provided that:

"(1) IN GENERAL.—The amendments made by this section [enacting section 8440f of this title and amending this section and sections 8432 and 8440a to 8440e of this title] shall take effect on the date of enactment of this Act [Dec. 21, 2000].

"(2) COORDINATION WITH ELECTION PERIODS.—The Executive Director shall by regulation determine the first election period in which elections may be made consistent with the amendments made by this section.

"(3) DEFINITIONS.—For purposes of this section—

"(A) the term 'election period' means a period afforded under section 8432(b) of title 5, United States Code; and

"(B) the term 'Executive Director' has the meaning given such term by section 8401(13) of title 5, United States Code.''

EFFECTIVE DATE OF 1999 AMENDMENTS

Amendment by Pub. L. 106–168 applicable with respect to transfers occurring before, on, or after Dec. 12, 1999, with special rule for applying amendment with respect to transfers occurring before Dec. 12, 1999, see section 203(c) of Pub. L. 106–168, set out as an Effective Date note under section 8431 of this title.

Amendment by section 661(a)(3)(B)(ii) of Pub. L. 106–65 effective 180 days after Oct. 30, 2000, unless postponed, see section 663 of Pub. L. 106–65, as amended, set out as an Effective Date note under section 8440e of this title.

EFFECTIVE DATE OF 1996 AMENDMENT

Amendment by Pub. L. 104–208 effective Sept. 30, 1996, and withdrawals and elections as provided under such amendment to be made at earliest practicable date as determined by Executive Director in regulations, see section 101(f) [title VI, § 659 [title II, § 207]] of Pub. L. 104–208, set out as a note under section 5545a of this title.

EFFECTIVE DATE OF 1994 AMENDMENTS

Amendment by Pub. L. 103–353 effective Oct. 13, 1994, and applicable to any employee whose release from military service, discharge from hospitalization, or other similar event making the individual eligible to seek restoration or reemployment under chapter 43 of Title 38, Veterans' Benefits, occurs on or after Aug. 2, 1990, with special rules for applying amendment to employees restored or reemployed before effective date, see section 4(e), (f) of Pub. L. 103–353, set out as an Effective Date note under section 8432b of this title.

Section 9(j) of Pub. L. 103–226 provided that: "This section [amending this section and sections 8433 to 8435, 8437, and 8440a to 8440d of this title] shall take effect 1 year after the date of the enactment of this Act [Mar. 30, 1994] or on such earlier date as the Executive Director of the Federal Retirement Thrift Investment Board shall provide in regulation.'' [Implementing regulations were published in the Federal Register Feb. 21, 1995, 60 F.R. 9595, effective Mar. 10, 1995.]

EFFECTIVE DATE OF 1992 AMENDMENT

Section 4437(d) of Pub. L. 102–484 provided that: "The amendments made by this section [amending this section and sections 8433 and 8435 of this title] shall apply with respect to separations occurring after December 31, 1993, or such earlier date as the Executive Director (appointed under section 8474 of title 5, United States Code) may by regulation prescribe.''

EFFECTIVE DATE OF 1991 AMENDMENT

Section 308(b) of Pub. L. 102–183 provided that:

"(1) The amendment made by subsection (a) [amending this section] shall take effect as of January 1, 1987.

"(2) Any refund which becomes payable as a result of the effective date specified in paragraph (1) shall, to the extent that that refund involves an individual's contributions to the Thrift Savings Fund (established under section 8437 of title 5, United States Code), be adjusted to reflect any earnings attributable thereto.''

EFFECTIVE DATE OF 1990 AMENDMENT

Section 3(c) of Pub. L. 101–335 provided that: "Subsections (a) and (b), and the amendments made by such subsections [amending this section and sections 8438, 8440a, and 8440b of this title and enacting provisions set out as a note under section 8438 of this title], shall be effective as of the second election period described in section 8432(b) of title 5, United States Code, beginning after the date of enactment of this Act [July 17, 1990], or as of such earlier date as the Executive Director may by regulation prescribe.''

Section 6(c) of Pub. L. 101–335 provided that: "This section, and the amendments made by this section [amending this section and sections 8401, 8433, 8435, 8440a, and 8440b of this title and enacting provisions set out as a note under section 8433 of this title], shall be effective as of the second election period described in section 8432(b) of title 5, United States Code, beginning after the date of enactment of this Act [July 17, 1990] (or as of such earlier date as the Executive Director may by regulation prescribe), and shall apply with respect to separations occurring before, on, or after that effective date."

EFFECTIVE DATE OF 1988 AMENDMENT

Section 111(b) of Pub. L. 100–238 provided that: "The amendments made by subsection (a) [amending this section] shall be effective as of March 31, 1987. Any refund which becomes payable as a result of the preceding sentence shall, to the extent that such refund involves an individual's contributions to the Thrift Savings Fund (established under section 8437 of title 5, United States Code), be adjusted to reflect any earnings attributable thereto."

EFFECTIVE DATE

Section effective Jan. 1, 1987, see section 702(a) of Pub. L. 99–335, set out as a note under section 8401 of this title.

PERIOD WHEN ELECTION MAY FIRST BE MADE

Section 206(b) of Pub. L. 99–335, as amended by Pub. L. 99–509, title VI, § 6001(b), Oct. 21, 1986, 100 Stat. 1930, provided that an election could first be made by a Federal employee or a Member of Congress under 5 U.S.C. 8351 (a)(2) during an election period prescribed by Executive Director of Federal Retirement Thrift Investment Board to begin on Apr. 1, 1987, with such election to take effect on first day of employee's or Member's first pay period which began on or after the date of the election. The maximum amount that an employee or Member could elect to contribute during any pay period which began on or after Apr. 1, 1987, and before Oct. 1, 1987, was an amount equal to 7.5 percent of the individual's basic pay for that period.

SECTION REFERRED TO IN OTHER SECTIONS

This section is referred to in sections 8432, 8432c, 8439, 8440, 8440a, 8440d of this title; title 10 section 945; title 22 section 4069; title 42 section 2297h–8; title 50 section 2142.

CHAPTER 84—FEDERAL EMPLOYEES' RETIREMENT SYSTEM

SUBCHAPTER I—GENERAL PROVISIONS

Sec.	
8478.	Bonding.
8478a.	Investigative authority.
8479.	Exculpatory provisions; insurance.

CHANGE OF NAME

Words "magistrate judges" substituted for "magistrates" in item 8440b pursuant to section 321 of Pub. L. 101–650, set out as a note under section 631 of Title 28, Judiciary and Judicial Procedure.

CHAPTER REFERRED TO IN OTHER SECTIONS

This chapter is referred to in sections 2105, 3329, 5304, 5362, 5541, 5597, 5724, 8116, 8342, 8344, 8347, 8348, 8350, 8351, 8432c, 8901 of this title; title 2 sections 92, 162b; title 10 section 942; title 20 section 4416; title 22 sections 3649, 3658, 3664, 3673, 3951, 4009, 4064, 4067, 4069, 4071, 4071c, 4071d, 4071h; title 25 section 450i; title 26 sections 3121, 6103; title 28 sections 155, 178, 375, 376, 377, 611, 627, 636, 753, 797; title 31 sections 732a, 772; title 37 section 211; title 38 sections 7257, 7297, 7438, 7453, 7458; title 39 section 1005; title 40 section 214d; title 42 sections 402, 410, 3035r, 7237, 10704; title 49 section 49107; title 50 sections 2021, 2151, 2152, 2153, 2154, 2155, 2157, 2442.

SUBCHAPTER I—GENERAL PROVISIONS

§ 8401. Definitions

For the purpose of this chapter—

(1) the term "account" means an account established and maintained under section 8439(a) of this title;

(2) the term "annuitant" means a former employee or Member who, on the basis of that individual's service, meets all requirements for title to an annuity under subchapter II or V of this chapter and files claim therefor;

(3) the term "average pay" means the largest annual rate resulting from averaging an employee's or Member's rates of basic pay in effect over any 3 consecutive years of service or, in the case of an annuity under this chapter based on service of less than 3 years, over the total service, with each rate weighted by the period it was in effect;

(4) the term "basic pay" has the meaning given such term by section 8331(3);

(5) the term "Board" means the Federal Retirement Thrift Investment Board established by section 8472(a) of this title;

(6) the term "Civil Service Retirement and Disability Fund" or "Fund" means the Civil Service Retirement and Disability Fund under section 8348;

(7) the term "court" means any court of any State, the District of Columbia, the Commonwealth of Puerto Rico, Guam, the Northern Mariana Islands, or the Virgin Islands, and any Indian court;

(8) the term "Director" means the Director of the Office of Personnel Management;

(9) the term "dynamic assumptions" means economic assumptions that are used in determining actuarial costs and liabilities of a retirement system and in anticipating the effects of long-term future—

(A) investment yields;

(B) increases in rates of basic pay; and

(C) rates of price inflation;

(10) the term "earnings", when used with respect to the Thrift Savings Fund, means the amount of the gain realized or yield received from the investment of sums in such Fund;

(11) the term "employee" means—

(A) an individual referred to in subparagraph (A), (E), (F), (H), (I), (J), or (K) of section 8331(1) of this title;

(B) a Congressional employee as defined in section 2107 of this title, including a temporary Congressional employee and an employee of the Congressional Budget Office; and

(C) an employee described in section 2105(c) who has made an election under section 8461(n)(1) to remain covered under this chapter;

whose civilian service after December 31, 1983, is employment for the purposes of title II of the Social Security Act and chapter 21 of the Internal Revenue Code of 1986, except that such term does not include—

(i) any individual referred to in—

(I) clause (i), (vi), or (ix) of paragraph (1) of section 8331;

(II) clause (ii) of such paragraph; or

(III) the undesignated material after the last clause of such paragraph;

(ii) any individual excluded under section 8402(c) of this title;

(iii) a member of the Foreign Service described in section 103(6) of the Foreign Service Act of 1980; or

(iv) an employee who has made an election under section 8461(n)(2) to remain covered by a retirement system established for employees described in section 2105(c);

(12) the term "former spouse" means a former spouse of an individual—

(A) if such individual performed at least 18 months of civilian service creditable under section 8411 as an employee or Member; and

(B) if the former spouse was married to such individual for at least 9 months;

(13) the term "Executive Director" means the Executive Director appointed under section 8474(a);

(14) the term "firefighter" means—

(A) an employee, the duties of whose position—

(i) are primarily to perform work directly connected with the control and extinguishment of fires; and

(ii) are sufficiently rigorous that employment opportunities should be limited to young and physically vigorous individuals, as determined by the Director considering the recommendations of the employing agency; and

(B) an employee who is transferred directly to a supervisory or administrative position after performing duties described in subparagraph (A) for at least 3 years;

(15) the term "Government" means the Federal Government, Gallaudet College, and, in the case of an employee described in paragraph (11)(C), a nonappropriated fund instrumentality of the Department of Defense or the Coast Guard described in section 2105(c);

(16) the term "Indian court" has the meaning given such term by section 8331(24);

(17) the term "law enforcement officer" means—

(A) an employee, the duties of whose position—

(i) are primarily—

(I) the investigation, apprehension, or detention of individuals suspected or convicted of offenses against the criminal laws of the United States, or

(II) the protection of officials of the United States against threats to personal safety; and

(ii) are sufficiently rigorous that employment opportunities should be limited to young and physically vigorous individuals, as determined by the Director consid-

ering the recommendations of the employing agency;

(B) an employee of the Department of the Interior or the Department of the Treasury (excluding any employee under subparagraph (A)) who occupies a position that, but for the enactment of the Federal Employees' Retirement System Act of 1986, would be subject to the District of Columbia Police and Firefighters' Retirement System, as determined by the Secretary of the Interior or the Secretary of the Treasury, as appropriate;

(C) an employee who is transferred directly to a supervisory or administrative position after performing duties described in subparagraph (A) and (B) for at least 3 years; and

(D) an employee—

(i) of the Bureau of Prisons or Federal Prison Industries, Incorporated;

(ii) of the Public Health Service assigned to the field service of the Bureau of Prisons or of the Federal Prison Industries, Incorporated; or

(iii) in the field service at Army or Navy disciplinary barracks or at any other confinement and rehabilitation facility operated by any of the armed forces;

whose duties in connection with individuals in detention suspected or convicted of offenses against the criminal laws of the United States or of the District of Columbia or offenses against the punitive articles of the Uniform Code of Military Justice (chapter 47 of title 10) require frequent direct contact with these individuals in their detention and are sufficiently rigorous that employment opportunities should be limited to young and physically vigorous individuals, as determined by the head of the employing agency;

(18) the term "loss", as used with respect to the Thrift Savings Fund, includes the amount of any loss resulting from the investment of sums in such Fund, or from the breach of any responsibility, duty, or obligation under section 8477.[1]

(19) the term "lump-sum credit" means the unrefunded amount consisting of—

(A) retirement deductions made from the basic pay of an employee or Member under section 8422(a) of this title (or under section 204 of the Federal Employees' Retirement Contribution Temporary Adjustment Act of 1983);

(B) amounts deposited by an employee or Member under section 8422(e);

(C) amounts deposited by an employee, Member, or survivor under section 8411(f); and

(D) interest on the deductions and deposits which, for any calendar year, shall be equal to the overall average yield to the Fund during the preceding fiscal year from all obligations purchased by the Secretary of the Treasury during such fiscal year under section 8348(c), (d), and (e), as determined by the Secretary (compounded annually);

---

[1] So in original. The period probably should be a semicolon.

but does not include interest—

(i) if the service covered thereby aggregates 1 year or less; or

(ii) for a fractional part of a month in the total service;

(20) the term "Member" has the same meaning as provided in section 2106, except that such term does not include an individual who irrevocably elects, by written notice to the official by whom such individual is paid, not to participate in the Federal Employees' Retirement System;

(21) the term "net earnings" means the excess of earnings over losses;

(22) the term "net losses" means the excess of losses over earnings;

(23) the term "normal-cost percentage" means the entry-age normal cost of the provisions of the System which relate to the Fund, computed by the Office in accordance with generally accepted actuarial practice and standards (using dynamic assumptions) and expressed as a level percentage of aggregate basic pay;

(24) the term "Office" means the Office of Personnel Management;

(25) the term "price index" has the same meaning as provided in section 8331(15);

(26) the term "service" means service which is creditable under section 8411;

(27) the term "supplemental liability" means the estimated excess of—

(A) the actuarial present value of all future benefits payable from the Fund under this chapter based on the service of current or former employees or Members, over

(B) the sum of—

(i) the actuarial present value of deductions to be withheld from the future basic pay of employees and Members currently subject to this chapter pursuant to section 8422;

(ii) the actuarial present value of the future contributions to be made pursuant to section 8423(a) with respect to employees and Members currently subject to this chapter;

(iii) the Fund balance as of the date the supplemental liability is determined, to the extent that such balance is attributable—

(I) to the System, or

(II) to contributions made under the Federal Employees' Retirement Contribution Temporary Adjustment Act of 1983 by or on behalf of an individual who became subject to the System; and

(iv) any other appropriate amount, as determined by the Office in accordance with generally accepted actuarial practices and principles;

(28) the term "survivor" means an individual entitled to an annuity under subchapter IV of this chapter;

(29) the term "System" means the Federal Employees' Retirement System described in section 8402(a);

(30) the term "military technician (dual status)" means an employee described in section 10216 of title 10;

(31) the term "military service" means honorable active service—

(A) in the armed forces;

(B) in the commissioned corps of the Public Health Service after June 30, 1960; or

(C) in the commissioned corps of the National Oceanic and Atmospheric Administration, or a predecessor entity in function, after June 30, 1961;

but does not include service in the National Guard except when ordered to active duty in the service of the United States or full-time National Guard duty (as such term is defined in section 101(d) of title 10) if such service interrupts creditable civilian service under this subchapter and is followed by reemployment in accordance with chapter 43 of title 38 that occurs on or after August 1, 1990;

(32) the term "nonforfeitable account balance" means any amounts in an account, established and maintained under subchapter III, which are nonforfeitable (as determined under section 8432(g));

(33) "Nuclear materials courier" has the meaning given that term in section 8331(27); and

(34) the term "Government physician" has the meaning given such term under section 5948.

(Added Pub. L. 99–335, title I, § 101(a), June 6, 1986, 100 Stat. 517; amended Pub. L. 99–556, title I, §§ 107, 109, 119, Oct. 27, 1986, 100 Stat. 3132, 3134; Pub. L. 100–238, title I, §§ 103(a)(2), (c), (d)(2), 113(b)(1), Jan. 8, 1988, 101 Stat. 1744, 1745, 1750; Pub. L. 100–679, § 13(a)(2), Nov. 17, 1988, 102 Stat. 4071; Pub. L. 101–335, § 6(a)(1), July 17, 1990, 104 Stat. 322; Pub. L. 101–474, § 5(o), Oct. 30, 1990, 104 Stat. 1100; Pub. L. 101–508, title VII, § 7202(k)(1), Nov. 5, 1990, 104 Stat. 1388–338; Pub. L. 103–337, div. A, title XVI, § 1677(a)(4), Oct. 5, 1994, 108 Stat. 3019; Pub. L. 103–353, § 5(c), (e)(1), Oct. 13, 1994, 108 Stat. 3174; Pub. L. 104–208, div. A, title I, § 101(f) [title VI, § 659 [title II, § 206(a)(1)]], Sept. 30, 1996, 110 Stat. 3009–314, 3009–372, 3009–378; Pub. L. 105–261, div. C, title XXXI, § 3154(f), Oct. 17, 1998, 112 Stat. 2255; Pub. L. 106–65, div. A, title V, § 522(c)(2), Oct. 5, 1999, 113 Stat. 597; Pub. L. 106–571, § 3(c)(2), Dec. 28, 2000, 114 Stat. 3056.)

REFERENCES IN TEXT

The Social Security Act, referred to in par. (11), is act Aug. 14, 1935, ch. 531, 49 Stat. 620, as amended. Title II of the Social Security Act is classified generally to subchapter II (§ 401 et seq.) of chapter 7 of Title 42, The Public Health and Welfare. For complete classification of this Act to the Code, see section 1305 of Title 42 and Tables.

Chapter 21 of the Internal Revenue Code of 1986, referred to in par. (11), is classified to chapter 21 (§ 3101 et seq.) of Title 26, Internal Revenue Code.

Section 103(6) of the Foreign Service Act of 1980, referred to in par. (11)(iii), is classified to section 3903(6) of Title 22, Foreign Relations and Intercourse.

The Federal Employees' Retirement System Act of 1986, referred to in par. (17)(B), is Pub. L. 99–335, June 6, 1986, 100 Stat. 514, as amended. For complete classification of this Act to the Code, see Short Title note set out under section 8401 of this title and Tables.

The Federal Employees' Retirement Contribution Temporary Adjustment Act of 1983, referred to in pars. (19)(A) and (27)(B)(iii)(II), is Pub. L. 98–168, title II, Nov. 29, 1983, 97 Stat. 1106, as amended, which is set out as a note under section 8331 of this title.

2000—Par. (34). Pub. L. 106–571 added par. (34).

1999—Par. (30). Pub. L. 106–65 amended par. (30) generally. Prior to amendment, par. (30) read as follows: "the term 'military reserve technician' means a member of one of the reserve components of the armed forces specified in section 10101 of title 10 who—

"(A) is assigned to a civilian position as a technician in the administration and training of such reserve components or in the maintenance and repair of supplies issued to such reserve components; and

"(B) as a condition of employment in such position, is required to be a member of one of such reserve components serving in a specified military grade;".

1998—Par. (33). Pub. L. 105–261 added par. (33).

1996—Par. (4). Pub. L. 104–208 struck out "except as provided in subchapter III of this chapter," before "the term".

1994—Par. (11). Pub. L. 103–353, § 5(e)(1), in flush provisions before cl. (i), substituted "Internal Revenue Code of 1986" for "Internal Revenue Code of 1954".

Par. (30). Pub. L. 103–337 substituted "section 10101" for "section 261(a)" in introductory provisions.

Par. (31). Pub. L. 103–353, § 5(c), in closing provisions, inserted before semicolon "or full-time National Guard duty (as such term is defined in section 101(d) of title 10) if such service interrupts creditable civilian service under this subchapter and is followed by reemployment in accordance with chapter 43 of title 38 that occurs on or after August 1, 1990".

1990—Par. (11)(C). Pub. L. 101–508, § 7202(k)(1)(A)(i)–(iii), added subpar. (C).

Par. (11)(i)(I). Pub. L. 101–474 struck out "(v)," after "(i),".

Par. (11)(iv). Pub. L. 101–508, § 7202(k)(1)(A)(iv)–(vi), added cl. (iv).

Par. (15). Pub. L. 101–508, § 7202(k)(1)(B), substituted ", Gallaudet College, and, in the case of an employee described in paragraph (11)(C), a nonappropriated fund instrumentality of the Department of Defense or the Coast Guard described in section 2105(c);" for "and Gallaudet College;".

Par. (32). Pub. L. 101–335 added par. (32).

1988—Par. (11)(A). Pub. L. 100–679 substituted "(J), or (K)" for "or (J)".

Par. (11)(i)(II). Pub. L. 100–238, § 103(d)(2), struck out "(other than an employee of the United States Park Police, or the United States Secret Service, whose civilian service after December 31, 1983, is such employment)".

Par. (11)(iii). Pub. L. 100–238, § 113(b)(1), added cl. (iii).

Par. (14)(A)(ii). Pub. L. 100–238, § 103(a)(2), substituted "should be" for "are required to be".

Par. (14)(B). Pub. L. 100–238, § 103(c)(2), substituted "for at least 3 years" for "for at least 10 years".

Par. (17). Pub. L. 100–238, § 103(a)(2), (c)(1), in subpar. (A)(ii), substituted "should be" for "are required to be", added subpar. (B), redesignated former subpar. (B) as (C) and amended it generally, substituting "subparagraph (A) and (B) for at least 3 years" for "subparagraph (A) for at least 10 years", redesignated former subpar. (C) as (D), and in concluding provisions, substituted "should be" for "are required to be".

1986—Par. (11). Pub. L. 99–556, § 119, struck out "any of" before "whose civilian service" in two places.

Par. (18). Pub. L. 99–556, § 100, amended par. (18) generally. Prior to amendment, par. (18) read as follows: "the term 'loss', when used with respect to the Thrift Savings Fund, means the amount of the loss resulting from the investment of sums in such Fund;".

Par. (19)(C), (D). Pub. L. 99–556, § 107, added subpar. (C) and redesignated former subpar. (C) as (D).

EFFECTIVE DATE OF 1998 AMENDMENT

Amendment by Pub. L. 105–261 effective at the beginning of the first pay period that begins after Oct. 17, 1998, and applicable only to an individual who is employed as a nuclear materials courier, as defined by section 8331(27) or 8401(33) of this title, after Oct. 17, 1998, see section 3154(m), (n) of Pub. L. 105–261, set out as a note under section 8331 of this title.

EFFECTIVE DATE OF 1996 AMENDMENT

Amendment by Pub. L. 104–208 effective Sept. 30, 1996, and withdrawals and elections as provided under such amendment to be made at earliest practicable date as determined by Executive Director in regulations, see section 101(f) [title VI, § 659 [title II, § 207]] of Pub. L. 104–208, set out as a note under section 5545a of this title.

EFFECTIVE DATE OF 1994 AMENDMENTS

Amendment by Pub. L. 103–353 effective with respect to reemployments initiated on or after the first day after the 60-day period beginning Oct. 13, 1994, with transition rules, see section 8 of Pub. L. 103–353, set out as an Effective Date note under section 4301 of Title 38, Veterans' Benefits.

Amendment by Pub. L. 103–337 effective Dec. 1, 1994, except as otherwise provided, see section 1691 of Pub. L. 103–337, set out as an Effective Date note under section 10001 of Title 10, Armed Forces.

EFFECTIVE DATE OF 1990 AMENDMENTS

Amendment by Pub. L. 101–508 applicable with respect to any individual who, on or after Jan. 1, 1987, moves from employment in nonappropriated fund instrumentality of Department of Defense or Coast Guard, that is described in section 2105(c) of this title, to employment in Department or Coast Guard, that is not described in section 2105(c), or who moves from employment in Department or Coast Guard, that is not described in section 2105(c), to employment in nonappropriated fund instrumentality of Department or Coast Guard, that is described in section 2105(c), see section 7202(m)(1) of Pub. L. 101–508, set out as a note under section 2105 of this title.

Amendment by Pub. L. 101–335 effective as of second election period described in section 8432(b) of this title beginning after July 17, 1990, or such earlier date as Executive Director may by regulation prescribe, and applicable with respect to separations occurring before, on, or after that effective date, see section 6(c) of Pub. L. 101–335, set out as a note under section 8351 of this title.

EFFECTIVE DATE OF 1988 AMENDMENT

Amendment by section 103(a)(2), (c), and (d)(2) of Pub. L. 100–238, effective Jan. 1, 1987, see section 103(f) of Pub. L. 100–238, set out as a note under section 3307 of this title.

Section 113(b)(2) of Pub. L. 100–238 provided that: "The amendments made by paragraph (1) [amending this section] shall be effective as of January 1, 1987. Any refund which becomes payable as a result of the preceding sentence shall, to the extent that such refund involves an individual's contributions to the Thrift Savings Fund (established under section 8437 of title 5, United States Code), be adjusted to reflect any earnings attributable thereto."

EFFECTIVE DATE

Section 702(a), (b) of Pub. L. 99–335 provided that:

"(a) IN GENERAL.—Except as provided in subsection (b), this Act and the amendments made by this Act [see Short Title note below] shall take effect on January 1, 1987.

"(b) EXCEPTIONS.—(1) Subchapter VII of chapter 84 of title 5, United States Code, as added by section 101 of this Act, shall take effect on the date of the enactment of this Act [June 6, 1986].

"(2) Except as provided in section 305 of this Act [enacting and amending provisions set out as notes under section 8331 of this title], title III of this Act, and the amendments made by such title [amending sections 3121 and 6103 of Title 26, Internal Revenue Code, section 1005 of Title 39, Postal Service, and section 410 of Title 42, The Public Health and Welfare, enacting provisions set out as notes under this section and sections 8331, 8432, and 8472 of this title and section 6103 of Title 26, and amending provisions set out as a note under section 8331 of this title], shall take effect on the date of the enactment of this Act.

"(3) The amendments made by sections 204 and 205 of this Act [enacting sections 8343a and 8350 of this title and amending section 8342 of this title] shall take effect on the date of the enactment of this Act.

"(4) Section 701 of this Act [enacting provisions set out as a note under section 8472 of this title] shall take effect on the date of the enactment of this Act.

"(5) Sections 505 [amending provisions formerly set out as a note under section 403 of Title 50, War and National Defense] and 601 of this Act and the amendments made by such section 601 [not classified to the Code] shall take effect on the date of the enactment of this Act."

Reference to a specific date in section 702(a) of Pub. L. 99–335, set out above, for certain purposes, deemed to be a reference to the first day of the first pay period beginning after such date, or to the day before such day, as appropriate, see section 505 of Pub. L. 99–556, set out as a Coordination With Pay Periods note under section 8331 of this title.

Short Title of 1999 Amendment

Pub. L. 106–168, title II, § 201, Dec. 12, 1999, 113 Stat. 1817, provided that: "This title [enacting section 8431 of this title, amending sections 8351, 8402, and 8411 of this title, and enacting provisions set out as notes under sections 8402 and 8431 of this title] may be cited as the 'Federal Reserve Board Retirement Portability Act'."

Short Title of 1998 Amendment

Pub. L. 105–274, § 1, Oct. 20, 1998, 112 Stat. 2419, provided that: "This Act [amending section 8402 of this title and enacting provisions set out as a note under section 8402 of this title] may be cited as the 'District of Columbia Courts and Justice Technical Corrections Act of 1998'."

Short Title of 1996 Amendment

Section 101(f) [title VI, § 659 [title I, § 101]] of Pub. L. 104–208 provided that: "This title [title I (§§ 101–104) of section 659 of section 101(f) of Pub. L. 104–208, amending sections 8438 and 8439 of this title and enacting provisions set out as a note under section 8438 of this title] may be cited as the 'Thrift Savings Investment Funds Act of 1996'."

Section 101(f) [title VI, § 659 [title II, § 201]] of Pub. L. 104–208 provided that: "This title [title II (§§ 201–207) of section 659 of section 101(f) of Pub. L. 104–208, amending this section and sections 5545a, 8351, 8433, 8435, and 8440a to 8440c of this title, repealing section 8431 of this title, enacting provisions set out as notes under sections 5545a and 8433 of this title, and amending provisions set out as a note under section 5343 of this title] may be cited as the 'Thrift Savings Plan Act of 1996'."

Short Title of 1990 Amendment

Section 1 of Pub. L. 101–335 provided that: "This Act [enacting section 8432a of this title, amending this section and sections 3392, 8351, 8433 to 8435, 8438, 8440a, 8440b, and 8477 of this title, renumbering former section 8440a of this title as section 8440b, enacting provisions set out as notes under sections 3392, 8351, 8432a, 8433, 8434, and 8438 of this title, and amending provisions set out as a note under section 8477 of this title] may be cited as the 'Thrift Savings Plan Technical Amendments Act of 1990'."

Short Title of 1987 Amendment

Pub. L. 100–43, § 1, May 22, 1987, 101 Stat. 315, provided: "That this Act [amending section 8438 of this title] may be cited as the 'Thrift Savings Fund Investment Act of 1987'."

Short Title of 1986 Amendment

Section 1 of Pub. L. 99–556 provided that: "This Act [enacting section 8478a of this title and section 4069 of

Title 22, Foreign Relations and Intercourse, amending this section and sections 6301, 8332, 8350, 8402, 8411 to 8413, 8415, 8421a, 8442, 8443, 8452, 8457, 8461, 8462, 8477, 8478, and 8901 of this title and sections 4046, 4064, 4071c, 4071d, and 4071j of Title 22, enacting provisions set out as notes under sections 6301, 8331, 8332, 8335, 8341, 8477, and 8478 of this title and section 4046 of Title 22, and amending provisions set out as notes under sections 8331 and 8341 of this title] may be cited as the 'Federal Employees' Retirement System Technical Corrections Act of 1986'."

Short Title

Section 100(a) of Pub. L. 99–335 provided that: "This Act [enacting this chapter, sections 8343a, 8349, 8350, and 8351 of this title, and sections 4068 and 4071 to 4071k of Title 22, Foreign Relations and Intercourse, amending sections 2105, 2109, 5102, 5314, 6301, 6303, 8116, 8331, 8332, 8334, 8342, 8347, 8348, 8701, 8706, 8714, 8714b, 8714c, 8901, and 8905 of this title, section 1605 of Title 10, Armed Forces, sections 4041 to 4049, 4054 to 4056, 4058, 4060, 4061, 4063, 4064, 4066, and 4067 of Title 22, sections 3121 and 6103 of Title 26, Internal Revenue Code, section 1005 of Title 39, Postal Service, and section 410 of Title 42, The Public Health and Welfare, enacting provisions set out as notes under this section and sections 8331, 8351, 8432, and 8472 of this title, sections 3901 and 4046 of Title 22, and section 6103 of Title 26, and amending provisions set out as notes under section 8331 of this title and sections 402 and 403 of Title 50, War and National Defense] may be cited as the 'Federal Employees' Retirement System Act of 1986'."

Service as Law Enforcement Officer

Pub. L. 104–52, title VI, § 640, Nov. 19, 1995, 109 Stat. 513, as amended by Pub. L. 104–208, div. A, title I, § 101(f) [title VI, § 629(a)], Sept. 30, 1996, 110 Stat. 3009–314, 3009–362, provided that: "Hereafter, service performed during the period January 1, 1984, through December 31, 1986, which would, if performed after that period, be considered service as a law enforcement officer, as defined in section 8401(17)(A)(i)(II) and (B) of title 5, United States Code, shall be deemed service as a law enforcement officer for the purposes of chapter 84 of such title."

[Pub. L. 104–208, div. A, title I, § 101(f) [title VI, § 629(b)], Sept. 30, 1996, 110 Stat. 3009–314, 3009–362, provided that: "The amendment made by subsection (a) [amending section 640 of Pub. L. 104–52, set out above] shall take effect as if included in Public Law 104–52 on the date of its enactment [Nov. 19, 1995]."]

Congressional Declaration of Purpose

Section 100A of Pub. L. 99–335 provided that: "The purposes of this Act [see Short Title note above] are—

"(1) to establish a Federal employees' retirement plan which is coordinated with title II of the Social Security Act [42 U.S.C. 401 et seq.];

"(2) to ensure a fully funded and financially sound retirement benefits plan for Federal employees;

"(3) to enhance portability of retirement assets earned as an employee of the Federal Government;

"(4) to provide options for Federal employees with respect to retirement planning;

"(5) to assist in building a quality career work force in the Federal Government;

"(6) to encourage Federal employees to increase personal savings for retirement; and

"(7) to extend financial protection from disability to additional Federal employees and to increase such protection for eligible Federal employees."

Use of Normal-Cost Percentage

Section 307 of Pub. L. 99–335, as amended by Pub. L. 100–366, § 1, July 13, 1988, 102 Stat. 826, provided that: "Notwithstanding any other provision of law, the normal-cost percentage (as defined by section 8401(23) of title 5, United States Code, as added by this Act) of the Federal Employees' Retirement System shall be used to value the cost of such System to the Civil Service Retirement and Disability Fund for all purposes in which the cost of the System is required to be determined by the Federal Government. For any comparisons between the cost of performing commercial activities under the contract with commercial sources and the cost of performing such activities using Government facilities and personnel, the cost of the System shall include the cost of such System to the Civil Service Retirement and Disability Fund as specified in the preceding sentence, the cost of the thrift savings plan under subchapter III of chapter 84 of title 5, United States Code, and the cost of social security.''

FIRST COST-OF-LIVING ADJUSTMENT

Section 702(c) of Pub. L. 99–335 provided that:

''(1) For purposes of the first adjustment under subsection (b) of section 8462 of title 5, United States Code (as added by section 101 of this Act), the base quarter ending on September 30, 1986, shall be considered to have been the base quarter for a year in which an adjustment under such subsection was made.

''(2) As used in paragraph (1), the term 'base quarter' has the meaning provided by section 8462(a)(1) of title 5, United States Code (as added by section 101 of this Act).''

SECTION REFERRED TO IN OTHER SECTIONS

This section is referred to in sections 3307, 3323, 3329, 5541, 6323, 7371, 8331, 8351, 8411, 8440e, 8477, 8704 of this title; title 10 sections 2467, 10217; title 22 section 4046; title 38 sections 7296, 7426, 7438; title 50 sections 2152, 2154.

§ 8402. Federal Employees' Retirement System; exclusions

(a) The provisions of this chapter comprise the Federal Employees' Retirement System.

(b) The provisions of this chapter shall not apply with respect to—

(1) any individual who has performed service of a type described in subparagraph (C), (D), (E), or (F) of section 210(a)(5) of the Social Security Act continuously since December 31, 1983 (determined in accordance with the provisions of section 210(a)(5)(B) of the Social Security Act, relating to continuity of employment); or

(2)(A) any employee or Member who has separated from the service after—

(i) having been subject to—

(I) subchapter III of chapter 83 of this title;

(II) subchapter I of chapter 8 of title I of the Foreign Service Act of 1980; or

(III) the benefit structure for employees of the Board of Governors of the Federal Reserve System appointed before January 1, 1984, that is a component of the Retirement Plan for Employees of the Federal Reserve System, established under section 10 of the Federal Reserve Act; and

(ii) having completed—

(I) at least 5 years of civilian service creditable under subchapter III of chapter 83 of this title;

(II) at least 5 years of civilian service creditable under subchapter I of chapter 8 of title I of the Foreign Service Act of 1980; or

(III) at least 5 years of civilian service (other than any service performed in the employ of a Federal Reserve Bank) cred-

itable under the benefit structure for employees of the Board of Governors of the Federal Reserve System appointed before January 1, 1984, that is a component of the Retirement Plan for Employees of the Federal Reserve System, established under section 10 of the Federal Reserve Act,

determined without regard to any deposit or redeposit requirement under either such subchapter or under such benefit structure, or any requirement that the individual become subject to either such subchapter or to such benefit structure after performing the service involved; or

(B) any employee having at least 5 years of civilian service performed before January 1, 1987, creditable under subchapter III of chapter 83 of this title (determined without regard to any deposit or redeposit requirement under such subchapter, any requirement that the individual become subject to such subchapter after performing the service involved, or any requirement that the individual give notice in writing to the official by whom such individual is paid of such individual's desire to become subject to such subchapter);

except to the extent provided for under subsection (d) of this section or title III of the Federal Employees' Retirement System Act of 1986 pursuant to an election under such title to become subject to this chapter.

(c)(1) The Office may exclude from the operation of this chapter an employee or group of employees in or under an Executive agency, the United States Postal Service, or the Postal Rate Commission, whose employment is temporary or intermittent, except an employee whose employment is part-time career employment (as defined in section 3401(2)).

(2) The Architect of the Capitol may exclude from the operation of this chapter an employee under the Office of the Architect of the Capitol whose employment is temporary or of uncertain duration.

(3) The Librarian of Congress may exclude from the operation of this chapter an employee under the Library of Congress whose employment is temporary or of uncertain duration.

(4) The Director or Acting Director of the Botanic Garden may exclude from the operation of this chapter an employee under the Botanic Garden whose employment is temporary or of uncertain duration.

(5) The Chief Administrative Officer of the House of Representatives and the Secretary of the Senate each may exclude from the operation of this chapter a Congressional employee—

(A) whose employment is temporary or intermittent; and

(B) who is paid by such Chief Administrative Officer or Secretary, as the case may be.

(6) The Director of the Office of Technology Assessment may exclude from the operation of this chapter an employee under the Office of Technology Assessment whose employment is temporary or intermittent.

(7) The Director of the Congressional Budget Office may exclude from the operation of this chapter an employee under the Congressional

Budget Office whose employment is temporary or intermittent.

(8) The Director of the Administrative Office of the United States Courts may exclude from the operation of this chapter an employee of the Administrative Office of the United States Courts, the Federal Judicial Center, or a court named by section 610 of title 28, whose employment is temporary or of uncertain duration.

(9) The Joint Committee on Judicial Administration in the District of Columbia may exclude from the operation of this chapter an employee of the District of Columbia Courts whose employment is temporary or of uncertain duration.

(d) Paragraph (2) of subsection (b) shall not apply to an individual who—

(1) becomes subject to—

(A) subchapter II of chapter 8 of title I of the Foreign Service Act of 1980 (relating to the Foreign Service Pension System) pursuant to an election; or

(B) the benefit structure in which employees of the Board of Governors of the Federal Reserve System appointed on or after January 1, 1984, participate, which benefit structure is a component of the Retirement Plan for Employees of the Federal Reserve System, established under section 10 of the Federal Reserve Act (and any redesignated or successor version of such benefit structure, if so identified in writing by the Board of Governors of the Federal Reserve System for purposes of this chapter); and

(2) subsequently enters a position in which, but for paragraph (2) of subsection (b), such individual would be subject to this chapter.

(e) A bankruptcy judge or magistrate judge who is covered by section 377 of title 28 or section 2(c) of the Retirement and Survivors' Annuities for Bankruptcy Judges and Magistrates Act of 1988 shall be excluded from the operation of this chapter, other than subchapters III and VII of such chapter, if the judge or magistrate judge notifies the Director of the Administrative Office of the United States Courts of an election of a retirement annuity under those provisions. Upon such election, the judge or magistrate judge shall be entitled to a lump-sum credit under section 8424 of this title.

(f) A judge who is covered by section 7296 of title 38 shall be excluded from the operation of this chapter if the judge notifies the Director of the Office of Personnel Management of an election of a retirement annuity under that section. Upon such election, the judge shall be entitled to a lump-sum credit under section 8424 of this title.

(g) A judge of the United States Court of Federal Claims who is covered by section 178 of title 28 shall be excluded from the operation of this chapter, other than subchapters III and VII of such chapter, if the judge notifies the Director of the Administrative Office of the United States Courts of an election of a retirement annuity under those provisions. Upon such election, the judge shall be entitled to a lump-sum credit under section 8424 of this title.

(Added Pub. L. 99–335, title I, § 101(a), June 6, 1986, 100 Stat. 521; amended Pub. L. 99–556, title I, § 116, Oct. 27, 1986, 100 Stat. 3134; Pub. L.

100–238, title I, § 130, Jan. 8, 1988, 101 Stat. 1759; Pub. L. 100–659, § 6(c), Nov. 15, 1988, 102 Stat. 3919; Pub. L. 101–94, title I, § 102(b), Aug. 16, 1989, 103 Stat. 626; Pub. L. 101–474, § 5(p), Oct. 30, 1990, 104 Stat. 1100; Pub. L. 101–650, title III, §§ 306(e)(3), 321, Dec. 1, 1990, 104 Stat. 5112, 5117; Pub. L. 102–40, title IV, § 402(d)(2), May 7, 1991, 105 Stat. 239; Pub. L. 102–198, § 7(d), Dec. 9, 1991, 105 Stat. 1625; Pub. L. 102–572, title IX, § 902(b)(1), Oct. 29, 1992, 106 Stat. 4516; Pub. L. 104–53, title I, § 115, Nov. 19, 1995, 109 Stat. 527; Pub. L. 104–186, title II, § 215(13), Aug. 20, 1996, 110 Stat. 1746; Pub. L. 105–274, § 6(a), Oct. 20, 1998, 112 Stat. 2424; Pub. L. 106–168, title II, § 202(b), Dec. 12, 1999, 113 Stat. 1818.)

REFERENCES IN TEXT

Section 210(a)(5) of the Social Security Act, referred to in subsec. (b)(1), is classified to section 410(a)(5) of Title 42, The Public Health and Welfare.

The Federal Employees' Retirement System Act of 1986, referred to in subsec. (b), is Pub. L. 99–335, June 6, 1986, 100 Stat. 514. Title III of the Federal Employees' Retirement System Act of 1986 amended sections 3121 and 6103 of Title 26, Internal Revenue Code, section 1005 of Title 39, Postal Service, and section 410 of Title 42, enacted provisions set out as notes under sections 8331, 8401, 8432, and 8472 of this title and section 6103 of Title 26, and amended provisions set out as a note under section 8331 of this title. For complete classification of this Act to the Code, see Short Title note set out under section 8401 of this title and Tables.

The Foreign Service Act of 1980, referred to in subsecs. (b)(2)(A)(i)(II), (ii)(II) and (d)(1)(A), is Pub. L. 96–465, Oct. 17, 1980, 94 Stat. 2071. Subchapters I and II of chapter 8 of title I of the Act are classified generally to parts I (§ 4041 et seq.) and II (§ 4071 et seq.), respectively, of subchapter VIII of chapter 52 of Title 22, Foreign Relations and Intercourse. For complete classification of this Act to the Code, see Short Title note set out under section 3901 of Title 22 and Tables.

Section 10 of the Federal Reserve Act, referred to in subsecs. (b)(2)(A)(i)(III), (ii)(III) and (d)(1)(B), is section 10 of act Dec. 23, 1913, ch. 6, 38 Stat. 260, as amended. For classification of section 10 to the Code, see Codification note set out under section 241 of Title 12, Banks and Banking, and Tables.

Section 2(c) of the Retirement and Survivors' Annuities for Bankruptcy Judges and Magistrates Act of 1988, referred to in subsec. (e), is section 2(c) of Pub. L. 100–659, which is set out as a note under section 377 of Title 28, Judiciary and Judicial Procedure.

AMENDMENTS

1999—Subsec. (b)(2)(A). Pub. L. 106–168, § 202(b)(1), added subpar. (A) and struck out former subpar. (A) which read as follows: "any employee or Member who has separated from the service after—

"(i) having been subject to subchapter III of chapter 83 of this title, or subchapter I of chapter 8 of the Foreign Service Act of 1980; and

"(ii) having completed at least 5 years of civilian service creditable under subchapter III of chapter 83 of this title, or at least 5 years of civilian service creditable under subchapter I of the Foreign Service Act of 1980 (determined without regard to any deposit or redeposit requirement under either such subchapter, or any requirement that the individual become subject to either such subchapter after performing the service involved); or".

Subsec. (d). Pub. L. 106–168, § 202(b)(2), amended subsec. (d) generally. Prior to amendment, text read as follows: "Paragraph (2) of subsection (b) shall not apply to an individual who becomes subject to subchapter II of chapter 8 of title I of the Foreign Service Act of 1980 (relating to the Foreign Service Pension System) pursuant to an election and who subsequently enters a position in which, but for such paragraph (2), he would be subject to this chapter."

1998—Subsec. (c)(9). Pub. L. 105–274 added par. (9).

1996—Subsec. (c)(5). Pub. L. 104–186 substituted "Chief Administrative Officer" for "Clerk" in introductory provisions and subpar. (B).

1995—Subsec. (c)(7), (8). Pub. L. 104–53 added par. (7) and redesignated former par. (7) as (8).

1992—Subsec. (g). Pub. L. 102–572 substituted "United States Court of Federal Claims" for "United States Claims Court".

1991—Subsec. (f). Pub. L. 102–40 substituted "section 7296 of title 38" for "section 4096 of title 38".

Subsec. (g). Pub. L. 102–198 inserted a comma after "such chapter".

1990—Subsec. (c)(7). Pub. L. 101–474 added par. (7).

Subsec. (g). Pub. L. 101–650 added subsec. (g).

1989—Subsec. (f). Pub. L. 101–94 added subsec. (f).

1988—Subsec. (b)(2). Pub. L. 100–238, § 130(1), inserted "subsection (d) of this section or" before "title III" in concluding provisions.

Subsec. (d). Pub. L. 100–238, § 130(2), added subsec. (d).

Subsec. (e). Pub. L. 100–659 added subsec. (e).

1986—Subsec. (c)(5), (6). Pub. L. 99–556 added pars. (5) and (6).

CHANGE OF NAME

Words "magistrate judge" substituted for "magistrate" wherever appearing in subsec. (e) pursuant to section 321 of Pub. L. 101–650, set out as a note under section 631 of Title 28, Judiciary and Judicial Procedure.

EFFECTIVE DATE OF 1999 AMENDMENT

Pub. L. 106–168, title II, § 202(d), Dec. 12, 1999, 113 Stat. 1819, provided that:

"(1) IN GENERAL.—Subject to succeeding provisions of this subsection, this section [amending this section and section 8411 of this title and enacting provisions set out as a note under this section] and the amendments made by this section shall take effect on the date of the enactment of this Act [Dec. 12, 1999].

"(2) PROVISIONS RELATING TO CREDITABILITY AND CERTAIN FORMER EMPLOYEES.—The amendments made by subsection (a) [amending section 8411 of this title] and the provisions of subsection (c) [set out as a note below] shall apply only to individuals who separate from service subject to chapter 84 of title 5, United States Code, on or after the date of the enactment of this Act [Dec. 12, 1999].

"(3) PROVISIONS RELATING TO EXCLUSION FROM CHAPTER.—The amendments made by subsection (b) [amending this section] shall not apply to any former employee of the Board of Governors of the Federal Reserve System who, subsequent to his or her last period of service as an employee of the Board of Governors of the Federal Reserve System and prior to the date of the enactment of this Act [Dec. 12, 1999], became subject to subchapter III of chapter 83 or chapter 84 of title 5, United States Code, under the law in effect at the time of the individual's appointment."

EFFECTIVE DATE OF 1998 AMENDMENT

Pub. L. 105–274, § 10, Oct. 20, 1998, 112 Stat. 2429, provided that: "Except as otherwise specifically provided, this Act [amending this section and enacting provisions set out as a note under section 8401 of this title] and the amendments made by this Act shall take effect as if included in the enactment of title XI of the Balanced Budget Act of 1997 [Pub. L. 105–33]."

EFFECTIVE DATE OF 1992 AMENDMENT

Amendment by Pub. L. 102–572 effective Oct. 29, 1992, see section 911 of Pub. L. 102–572, set out as a note under section 171 of Title 28, Judiciary and Judicial Procedure.

EFFECTIVE DATE OF 1990 AMENDMENT

Amendment by Pub. L. 101–650 applicable to judges of, and senior judges in active service with, the United States Court of Federal Claims on or after Dec. 1, 1990, see section 306(f) of Pub. L. 101–650, set out as a note under section 8331 of this title.

EFFECTIVE DATE OF 1988 AMENDMENT

Amendment by Pub. L. 100–659 effective Nov. 15, 1988, and applicable to bankruptcy judges and magistrate judges who retire on or after Nov. 15, 1988, with exception for judges and magistrate judges retiring on or after July 31, 1987, see section 9 of Pub. L. 100–659, as amended, set out as an Effective Date note under section 377 of Title 28, Judiciary and Judicial Procedure.

PROVISIONS RELATING TO CERTAIN FORMER EMPLOYEES

Pub. L. 106–168, title II, § 202(c), Dec. 12, 1999, 113 Stat. 1819, provided that: "A former employee of the Board of Governors of the Federal Reserve System who—

"(1) has at least 5 years of civilian service (other than any service performed in the employ of a Federal Reserve Bank) creditable under the benefit structure for employees of the Board of Governors of the Federal Reserve System appointed before January 1, 1984, that is a component of the Retirement Plan for Employees of the Federal Reserve System, established under section 10 of the Federal Reserve Act [Act Dec. 23, 1913, ch. 6, see Codification note set out under 12 U.S.C. 241];

"(2) was subsequently employed subject to the benefit structure in which employees of the Board of Governors of the Federal Reserve System appointed on or after January 1, 1984, participate, which benefit structure is a component of the Retirement Plan for Employees of the Federal Reserve System, established under section 10 of the Federal Reserve Act (and any redesignated or successor version of such benefit structure, if so identified in writing by the Board of Governors of the Federal Reserve System for purposes of chapter 84 of title 5, United States Code); and

"(3) after service described in paragraph (2), becomes subject to and thereafter entitled to benefits under chapter 84 of title 5, United States Code,

shall, for purposes of section 302 of the Federal Employees' Retirement System Act of 1986 [Pub. L. 99–335] (100 Stat. 601; 5 U.S.C. 8331 note) be considered to have become subject to chapter 84 of title 5, United States Code, pursuant to an election under section 301 of such Act [5 U.S.C. 8331 note]."

SECTION REFERRED TO IN OTHER SECTIONS

This section is referred to in sections 8334, 8347, 8349, 8401 of this title; title 50 section 2151.

§ 8403. Relationship to the Social Security Act

Except as otherwise provided in this chapter, the benefits payable under the System are in addition to the benefits payable under the Social Security Act.

(Added Pub. L. 99–335, title I, § 101(a), June 6, 1986, 100 Stat. 522.)

REFERENCES IN TEXT

The Social Security Act, referred to in text, is act Aug. 14, 1935, ch. 531, 49 Stat. 620, as amended, which is classified generally to chapter 7 (§ 301 et seq.) of Title 42, The Public Health and Welfare. For complete classification of this Act to the Code, see section 1305 of Title 42 and Tables.

SUBCHAPTER II—BASIC ANNUITY

SUBCHAPTER REFERRED TO IN OTHER SECTIONS

This subchapter is referred to in sections 5595, 8348, 8401, 8435, 8455, 8461, 8464, 8464a, 8466, 8470 of this title; title 10 sections 942, 945; title 22 section 4071j; title 38 section 7426; title 39 section 1005; title 50 sections 2153, 2154.

§ 8410. Eligibility for annuity

Notwithstanding any other provision of this chapter, an employee or Member must complete at least 5 years of civilian service creditable under section 8411 in order to be eligible for an annuity under this subchapter.

(Added Pub. L. 99–335, title I, § 101(a), June 6, 1986, 100 Stat. 522.)

§ 8411. Creditable service

(a)(1) The total service of an employee or Member is the full years and twelfth parts thereof, excluding from the aggregate the fractional part of a month, if any.

(2) Credit may not be allowed for a period of separation from the service in excess of 3 calendar days.

(b) For the purpose of this chapter, creditable service of an employee or Member includes—

(1) employment as an employee, and any service as a Member (including the period from the date of the beginning of the term for which elected or appointed to the date of taking office as a Member), after December 31, 1986;

(2) except as provided in subsection (f), service with respect to which deductions and withholdings under section 204(a)(1) of the Federal Employees' Retirement Contribution Temporary Adjustment Act of 1983 have been made;

(3) except as provided in subsection (f) or (h), any civilian service (performed before January 1, 1989, other than any service under paragraph (1) or (2)) which, but for the amendments made by subsections (a)(4) and (b) of section 202 of the Federal Employees' Retirement System Act of 1986, would be creditable under subchapter III of chapter 83 of this title (determined without regard to any deposit or redeposit requirement under such subchapter, any requirement that the individual become subject to such subchapter after performing the service involved, or any requirement that the individual give notice in writing to the official by whom such individual is paid of such individual's desire to become subject to such subchapter);

(4) a period of service (other than any service under any other paragraph of this subsection and other than any military service) that was creditable under the Foreign Service Pension System described in subchapter II of chapter 8[1] of the Foreign Service Act of 1980, if the employee or Member waives credit for such service under the Foreign Service Pension System and makes a payment to the Fund equal to the amount that would have been deducted from pay under section 8422(a) had the employee been subject to this chapter during such period of service (together with interest on such amount computed under paragraphs (2) and (3) of section 8334(e)); and

(5) a period of service (other than any service under any other paragraph of this subsection, any military service, and any service performed in the employ of a Federal Reserve Bank) that was creditable under the Bank Plan (as defined in subsection (i)), if the employee waives credit for such service under the Bank Plan and makes a payment to the Fund equal to the amount that would have been deducted from pay under section 8422(a) had the employee been subject to this chapter during such period of service (together with interest on such amount computed under paragraphs (2) and (3) of section 8334(e)).

Paragraph (5) shall not apply in the case of any employee as to whom subsection (g) (or, to the extent subchapter III of chapter 83 is involved, section 8332(n)) otherwise applies.

(c)(1) Except as provided in paragraphs (2), (3), and (5), an employee or Member shall be allowed credit for—

(A) each period of military service performed before January 1, 1957; and

(B) each period of military service performed after December 31, 1956, and before the separation on which title to annuity is based, if a deposit (including interest, if any) is made with respect to such period in accordance with section 8422(e).

(2) If an employee or Member is awarded retired pay based on any period of military service, the service of the employee or Member may not include credit for such period of military service unless the retired pay is awarded—

(A) based on a service-connected disability—

(i) incurred in combat with an enemy of the United States; or

(ii) caused by an instrumentality of war and incurred in line of duty during a period of war as defined by section 1101 of title 38; or

(B) under chapter 1223 of title 10 (or under chapter 67 of that title as in effect before the effective date of the Reserve Officer Personnel Management Act).

(3) An employee or Member who has made a deposit under section 8334(j) (or a similar prior provision of law) with respect to a period of military service, and who has not taken a refund of such deposit—

(A) shall be allowed credit for such service without regard to the deposit requirement under paragraph (1)(B); and

(B) shall be entitled, upon filing appropriate application therefor with the Office, to a refund equal to the difference between—

(i) the amount deposited with respect to such period under such section 8334(j) (or prior provision), excluding interest; and

(ii) the amount which would otherwise have been required with respect to such period under paragraph (1)(B).

(4)(A) Notwithstanding paragraph (2), for purposes of computing a survivor annuity for a survivor of an employee or Member—

(i) who was awarded retired pay based on any period of military service, and

(ii) whose death occurs before separation from the service,

creditable service of the deceased employee or Member shall include each period of military service includable under subparagraph (A) or (B) of paragraph (1) or under paragraph (3). In carry-

---

[1] See References in Text note below.

ing out this subparagraph, any amount deposited under section 8422(e)(5) shall be taken into account.

(B) A survivor annuity computed based on an amount which, under authority of subparagraph (A), takes into consideration any period of military service shall be reduced by the amount of any survivor's benefits—

(i) payable to a survivor (other than a child) under a retirement system for members of the uniformed services;

(ii) if, or to the extent that, such benefits are based on such period of military service.

(C) The Office of Personnel Management shall prescribe regulations to carry out this paragraph, including regulations under which—

(i) a survivor may elect not to be covered by this paragraph; and

(ii) this paragraph shall be carried out in any case which involves a former spouse.

(5) If, after January 1, 1997, an employee or Member waives retired pay that is subject to a court order for which there has been effective service on the Secretary concerned for purposes of section 1408 of title 10, the military service on which the retired pay is based may be credited as service for purposes of this chapter only if the employee or Member authorizes the Director to deduct and withhold from the annuity payable to the employee or Member under this subchapter an amount equal to the amount that, if the annuity payment was instead a payment of the employee's or Member's retired pay, would have been deducted and withheld and paid to the former spouse covered by the court order under such section 1408. The amount deducted and withheld under this paragraph shall be paid to that former spouse. The period of civil service employment by the employee or Member shall not be taken into consideration in determining the amount of the deductions and withholding or the amount of the payment to the former spouse. The Director of the Office of Personnel Management shall prescribe regulations to carry out this paragraph.

(d) Credit under this chapter shall be allowed for leaves of absence without pay granted an employee while performing military service, or while receiving benefits under subchapter I of chapter 81. An employee or former employee who returns to duty after a period of separation is deemed, for the purpose of this subsection, to have been on leave of absence without pay for that part of the period in which that individual was receiving benefits under subchapter I of chapter 81. Credit may not be allowed for so much of other leaves of absence without pay as exceeds 6 months in the aggregate in a calendar year.

(e) Credit shall be allowed for periods of approved leave without pay granted an employee to serve as a full-time officer or employee of an organization composed primarily of employees (as defined by section 8331(1) or 8401(11)), subject to the employee arranging to pay, through the employee's employing agency, within 60 days after commencement of such leave without pay, amounts equal to the retirement deductions and agency contributions which would be applicable under sections 8422(a) and 8423(a), respectively, if the employee were in pay status. If the election and all payments provided by this subsection are not made, the employee may not receive credit for the periods of leave without pay, notwithstanding the third sentence of subsection (d).

(f)(1) An employee or Member who has received a refund of retirement deductions under subchapter III of chapter 83 with respect to any service described in subsection (b)(2) or (b)(3) may not be allowed credit for such service under this chapter unless such employee or Member deposits an amount equal to 1.3 percent of basic pay for such service, with interest. A deposit under this paragraph may be made only with respect to a refund received pursuant to an application filed with the Office before the date on which the employee or Member first becomes subject to this chapter.

(2) An employee or Member may not be allowed credit under this chapter for any service described in subsection (b)(3) for which retirement deductions under subchapter III of chapter 83 have not been made, unless such employee or Member deposits an amount equal to 1.3 percent of basic pay for such service, with interest.

(3) Interest under paragraph (1) or (2) shall be computed in accordance with paragraphs (2) and (3) of section 8334(e) and regulations prescribed by the Office.

(4) For the purpose of survivor annuities, deposits authorized by the preceding provisions of this subsection may also be made by a survivor of an employee or Member.

(g) Any employee who—

(1) served in a position in which the employee was excluded from coverage under this subchapter because the employee was covered under a retirement system established under section 10 of the Federal Reserve Act; and

(2) transferred without a break in service to a position to which the employee was appointed by the President, with the advice and consent of the Senate, and in which position the employee is subject to this subchapter,

shall be treated for all purposes of this subchapter as if any service that would have been creditable under the retirement system established under section 10 of the Federal Reserve Act was service performed while subject to this subchapter if any employee and employer deductions, contributions or rights with respect to the employee's service are transferred from such retirement system to the Fund.

(h) An employee or Member shall be allowed credit for service as a volunteer or volunteer leader under part A of title VIII of the Economic Opportunity Act of 1964, as a full-time volunteer enrolled in a program of at least 1 year's duration under part A, B, or C of title I of the Domestic Volunteer Service Act of 1973, or as a volunteer or volunteer leader under the Peace Corps Act performed at any time prior to the separation on which the entitlement to any annuity under this subchapter is based if the employee or Member has made a deposit with interest, if any, with respect to such service under section 8422(f).

(i)[2] For purposes of subsection (b)(5), the term "Bank Plan" means the benefit structure in

---

[2] So in original. Two subsecs. (i) have been enacted.

which employees of the Board of Governors of the Federal Reserve System appointed on or after January 1, 1984, participate, which benefit structure is a component of the Retirement Plan for Employees of the Federal Reserve System, established under section 10 of the Federal Reserve Act (and any redesignated or successor version of such benefit structure, if so identified in writing by the Board of Governors of the Federal Reserve System for purposes of this chapter).

(i)(1) [2] Upon application to the Office of Personnel Management, any individual who was an employee on the date of enactment of this paragraph, and who has on such date or thereafter acquired 5 years or more of creditable civilian service under this section (exclusive of service for which credit is allowed under this subsection) shall be allowed credit (as service as a congressional employee) for service before December 31, 1990, while employed by the Democratic Senatorial Campaign Committee, the Republican Senatorial Campaign Committee, the Democratic National Congressional Committee, or the Republican National Congressional Committee, if—

(A) such employee has at least 4 years and 6 months of service on such committees as of December 31, 1990; and

(B) such employee deposits to the Fund an amount equal to 1.3 percent of the base pay for such service, with interest.

(2) The Office shall accept the certification of the President of the Senate (or the President's designee) or the Speaker of the House of Representatives (or the Speaker's designee), as the case may be, concerning the service of, and the amount of compensation received by, an employee with respect to whom credit is to be sought under this subsection.

(3) An individual shall not be granted credit for such service under this subsection if eligible for credit under section 8332(m) for such service.

(Added Pub. L. 99–335, title I, § 101(a), June 6, 1986, 100 Stat. 522; amended Pub. L. 99–556, title I, § 103, title V, § 502(b), Oct. 27, 1986, 100 Stat. 3131, 3140; Pub. L. 100–238, title I, §§ 104(b), 105(a), Jan. 8, 1988, 101 Stat. 1746; Pub. L. 102–83, § 5(c)(2), Aug. 6, 1991, 105 Stat. 406; Pub. L. 102–242, title IV, § 466(b), Dec. 19, 1991, 105 Stat. 2385; Pub. L. 103–82, title III, § 371(b)(1), Sept. 21, 1993, 107 Stat. 910; Pub. L. 103–337, div. A, title XVI, § 1677(a)(3), Oct. 5, 1994, 108 Stat. 3019; Pub. L. 104–201, div. A, title VI, § 637(b), Sept. 23, 1996, 110 Stat. 2580; Pub. L. 106–168, title II, § 202(a), Dec. 12, 1999, 113 Stat. 1817; Pub. L. 106–554, § 1(a)(4) [div. A, § 901(a)(2)], Dec. 21, 2000, 114 Stat. 2763, 2763A–196.)

REFERENCES IN TEXT

Section 204(a)(1) of the Federal Employees' Retirement Contribution Temporary Adjustment Act of 1983 [Pub. L. 98–168], referred to in subsec. (b)(2), is set out as a note under section 8331 of this title.

Subsections (a)(4) and (b) of section 202 of the Federal Employees' Retirement System Act of 1986 [Pub. L. 99–335], referred to in subsec. (b)(3), amended section 8331(1) and (2) of this title.

The Foreign Service Act of 1980, referred to in subsec. (b)(4), is Pub. L. 96–465, Oct. 17, 1980, 94 Stat. 2071, as amended. Subchapter II of chapter 8 of the Act probably means subchapter II of chapter 8 of title I of the

Act which is classified generally to part II (§ 4071 et seq.) of subchapter VIII of chapter 52 of Title 22, Foreign Relations and Intercourse. For complete classification of this Act to the Code, see Short Title note set out under section 3901 of Title 22 and Tables.

Chapter 67 of that title as in effect before the effective date of the Reserve Officer Personnel Management Act, referred to in subsec. (c)(2)(B), means chapter 67 (§ 1331 et seq.) of Title 10, Armed Forces, prior to its transfer to part II of subtitle E of Title 10, its renumbering as chapter 1223, and its general revision by section 1662(j)(1) of Pub. L. 103–337. A new chapter 67 (§ 1331) of Title 10 was added by section 1662(j)(7) of Pub. L. 103–337. For effective date of the Reserve Officer Personnel Management Act (Pub. L. 103–337, title XVI), see section 1691 of Pub. L. 103–337, set out as an Effective Date note under section 10001 of Title 10.

Section 10 of the Federal Reserve Act, referred to in subsecs. (g) and (i), is section 10 of act Dec. 23, 1913, ch. 6, 38 Stat. 260, as amended. For classification of section 10 to the Code, see Codification note set out under section 241 of Title 12, Banks and Banking, and Tables.

The Economic Opportunity Act of 1964, referred to in subsec. (h), is Pub. L. 88–452, Aug. 20, 1964, 73 Stat. 508, as amended. Part A of title VIII of that Act is part A of title VIII of Pub. L. 88–452 as added by Pub. L. 90–222, title I, § 110, Dec. 23, 1967, 81 Stat. 722, which was classified generally to part A (§ 2992 et seq.) of subchapter VIII of chapter 34 of Title 42, The Public Health and Welfare, prior to its repeal by Pub. L. 93–113, title VI, § 603, Oct. 1, 1973, 87 Stat. 417. See sections 4951 et seq. and 5055 of Title 42.

Parts A, B, and C of title I of the Domestic Volunteer Service Act of 1973, referred to in subsec. (h), are classified to part A (§ 4951 et seq.), part B (§ 4971 et seq.), and part C (§ 4991 et seq.), respectively, of subchapter I of chapter 66 of Title 42.

The Peace Corps Act, referred to in subsec. (h), is Pub. L. 87–293, Sept. 22, 1961, 75 Stat. 612, as amended, which is classified principally to chapter 34 (§ 2501 et seq.) of Title 22, Foreign Relations and Intercourse. For complete classification of this Act to the Code, see Short Title note set out under section 2501 of Title 22 and Tables.

The date of enactment of this paragraph, referred to in subsec. (i)(1), is the date of enactment of Pub. L. 106–554, which was approved Dec. 21, 2000.

AMENDMENTS

2000—Subsec. (i). Pub. L. 106–554 added subsec. (i) relating to credit for service as congressional employee for certain service before Dec. 31, 1990.

1999—Subsec. (b). Pub. L. 106–168, § 202(a)(1), in par. (3), struck out "and" at end, in par. (4), substituted "other paragraph" for "of the preceding provisions" and "; and" for period at end, and added par. (5) and concluding provisions.

Subsec. (i). Pub. L. 106–168, § 202(a)(2), added subsec. (i) defining "Bank Plan" for purposes of subsec. (b)(5).

1996—Subsec. (c)(1). Pub. L. 104–201, § 637(b)(2), in introductory provisions, substituted "Except as provided in paragraphs (2), (3), and (5)" for "Except as provided in paragraph (2) or (3)".

Subsec. (c)(5). Pub. L. 104–201, § 637(b)(1), added par. (5).

1994—Subsec. (c)(2)(B). Pub. L. 103–337 substituted "chapter 1223 of title 10 (or under chapter 67 of that title as in effect before the effective date of the Reserve Officer Personnel Management Act)" for "chapter 67 of title 10".

1993—Subsec. (b)(3). Pub. L. 103–82, § 371(b)(1)(A), substituted "subsection (f) or (h)" for "subsection (f)".

Subsec. (h). Pub. L. 103–82, § 371(b)(1)(B), added subsec. (h).

1991—Subsec. (c)(2)(A)(ii). Pub. L. 102–83 substituted "section 1101 of title 38" for "section 301 of title 38".

Subsec. (g). Pub. L. 102–242 added subsec. (g).

1988—Subsec. (c)(4)(A). Pub. L. 100–238, § 104(b), substituted "section 8422(e)(5)" for "subsection (f)(4)" in concluding provisions.

Subsec. (f)(1). Pub. L. 100–238, §105(a), inserted at end "A deposit under this paragraph may be made only with respect to a refund received pursuant to an application filed with the Office before the date on which the employee or Member first becomes subject to this chapter."

1986—Subsec. (b)(2). Pub. L. 99–556, §103(1), inserted "except as provided in subsection (f),".

Subsec. (c)(4). Pub. L. 99–556, §502(b), added par. (4).

Subsec. (f)(1). Pub. L. 99–556, §103(2), inserted "(b)(2) or".

EFFECTIVE DATE OF 1999 AMENDMENT

Amendment by Pub. L. 106–168 effective Dec. 12, 1999, and applicable only to individuals who separate from service subject to chapter 84 of this title on or after Dec. 12, 1999, see section 202(d) of Pub. L. 106–168, set out as a note under section 8402 of this title.

EFFECTIVE DATE OF 1996 AMENDMENT

Amendment by Pub. L. 104–201 effective Jan. 1, 1997, see section 637(c) of Pub. L. 104–201, set out as a note under section 8332 of this title.

EFFECTIVE DATE OF 1994 AMENDMENT

Amendment by Pub. L. 103–337 effective Dec. 1, 1994, except as otherwise provided, see section 1691 of Pub. L. 103–337, set out as an Effective Date note under section 10001 of Title 10, Armed Forces.

EFFECTIVE DATE OF 1993 AMENDMENT

Amendment by Pub. L. 103–82 effective Oct. 1, 1993, and applicable with respect to any individual entitled to an annuity on the basis of a separation from service occurring before, on, or after Oct. 1, 1993, subject to rule relating to annuities based on earlier separations, see sections 371(c) and 392 of Pub. L. 103–82, set out as notes under section 8332 of this title and section 4951 of Title 42, The Public Health and Welfare, respectively.

EFFECTIVE DATE OF 1991 AMENDMENT

Amendment by Pub. L. 102–242 applicable with respect to any individual who transfers to a position in which he or she is subject to subchapter III of chapter 83 of this title or chapter 84 of this title, on or after Oct. 1, 1991, see section 466(c) of Pub. L. 102–242, set out as a note under section 8332 of this title.

EFFECTIVE DATE OF 1986 AMENDMENT

Amendment by section 502(b) of Pub. L. 99–556 applicable to a survivor of an employee or member who dies on or after the 180th day after Oct. 27, 1986, and to other survivors upon application, see section 502(c) of Pub. L. 99–556, set out as a note under section 8332 of this title.

SECTION REFERRED TO IN OTHER SECTIONS

This section is referred to in sections 8401, 8410, 8432, 8442, 8443, 8451 of this title; title 2 sections 121b, 162b; title 16 section 460lll–47; title 38 section 7426; title 40 section 214d; title 50 section 2154.

§ 8412. Immediate retirement

(a) An employee or Member who is separated from the service after attaining the applicable minimum retirement age under subsection (h) and completing 30 years of service is entitled to an annuity.

(b) An employee or Member who is separated from the service after becoming 60 years of age and completing 20 years of service is entitled to an annuity.

(c) An employee or Member who is separated from the service after becoming 62 years of age and completing 5 years of service is entitled to an annuity.

(d) An employee who is separated from the service, except by removal for cause on charges of misconduct or delinquency—

(1) after completing 25 years of service as a law enforcement officer, member of the Capitol Police or Supreme Court Police, firefighter, or nuclear materials courier, or any combination of such service totaling at least 25 years, or

(2) after becoming 50 years of age and completing 20 years of service as a law enforcement officer, member of the Capitol Police or Supreme Court Police, firefighter, or nuclear materials courier, or any combination of such service totaling at least 20 years,

is entitled to an annuity.

(e) An employee who is separated from the service, except by removal for cause on charges of misconduct or delinquency—

(1) after completing 25 years of service as an air traffic controller, or

(2) after becoming 50 years of age and completing 20 years of service as an air traffic controller,

is entitled to an annuity.

(f) A Member who is separated from the service, except by resignation or expulsion—

(1) after completing 25 years of service, or

(2) after becoming 50 years of age and completing 20 years of service,

is entitled to an annuity.

(g)(1) An employee or Member who is separated from the service after attaining the applicable minimum retirement age under subsection (h) and completing 10 years of service is entitled to an annuity. This subsection shall not apply to an employee or Member who is entitled to an annuity under any other provision of this section.

(2) An employee or Member entitled to an annuity under this subsection may defer the commencement of such annuity by written election. The date to which the commencement of the annuity is deferred may not precede the 31st day after the date of filing the election, and must precede the date on which the employee or Member becomes 62 years of age.

(3) The Office shall prescribe regulations under which an election under paragraph (2) shall be made.

(h)(1) The applicable minimum retirement age under this subsection is—

(A) for an individual whose date of birth is before January 1, 1948, 55 years of age;

(B) for an individual whose date of birth is after December 31, 1947, and before January 1, 1953, 55 years of age plus the number of months in the age increase factor determined under paragraph (2)(A);

(C) for an individual whose date of birth is after December 31, 1952, and before January 1, 1965, 56 years of age;

(D) for an individual whose date of birth is after December 31, 1964, and before January 1, 1970, 56 years of age plus the number of months in the age increase factor determined under paragraph (2)(B); and

(E) for an individual whose date of birth is after December 31, 1969, 57 years of age.

(2)(A) For an individual whose date of birth occurs during the 5-year period consisting of calendar years 1948 through 1952, the age increase factor shall be equal to two-twelfths times the number of months in the period beginning with January 1948 and ending with December of the year in which the date of birth occurs.

(B) For an individual whose date of birth occurs during the 5-year period consisting of calendar years 1965 through 1969, the age increase factor shall be equal to two-twelfths times the number of months in the period beginning with January 1965 and ending with December of the year in which the date of birth occurs.

(Added Pub. L. 99–335, title I, §101(a), June 6, 1986, 100 Stat. 524; amended Pub. L. 99–556, title I, §105(a), Oct. 27, 1986, 100 Stat. 3131; Pub. L. 101–428, §3(a), Oct. 15, 1990, 104 Stat. 929; Pub. L. 105–261, div. C, title XXXI, §3154(g), Oct. 17, 1998, 112 Stat. 2255; Pub. L. 106–553, §1(a)(2) [title III, §308(c)(1)], Dec. 21, 2000, 114 Stat. 2762, 2762A–87.)

AMENDMENTS

2000—Subsec. (d). Pub. L. 106–553 inserted "or Supreme Court Police" after "Capitol Police" in pars. (1) and (2).

1998—Subsec. (d)(1), (2). Pub. L. 105–261 substituted "firefighter, or nuclear materials courier" for "or firefighter".

1990—Subsec. (d)(1), (2). Pub. L. 101–428 substituted "officer, member of the Capitol Police," for "officer".

1986—Subsec. (g). Pub. L. 99–556 designated existing provisions as par. (1) and added par. (2).

EFFECTIVE DATE OF 2000 AMENDMENT

Amendment by Pub. L. 106–553 effective on the first day of the first applicable pay period that begins on Dec. 21, 2000, and applicable only to an individual who is employed as a member of the Supreme Court Police after Dec. 21, 2000, see section 1(a)(2) [title III, §308(i), (j)] of Pub. L. 106–553, set out in a Supreme Court Police Retirement note under section 8331 of this title.

EFFECTIVE DATE OF 1998 AMENDMENT

Amendment by Pub. L. 105–261 effective at the beginning of the first pay period that begins after Oct. 17, 1998, and applicable only to an individual who is employed as a nuclear materials courier, as defined by section 8331(27) or 8401(33) of this title, after Oct. 17, 1998, see section 3154(m), (n) of Pub. L. 105–261, set out as a note under section 8331 of this title.

SECTION REFERRED TO IN OTHER SECTIONS

This section is referred to in sections 5597, 6302, 8413, 8414, 8415, 8420, 8421, 8421a, 8425, 8442, 8452, 8462, 8464, 8901 of this title; title 10 section 10218; title 22 sections 4045, 4046, 4052, 4071d.

§ 8413. Deferred retirement

(a) An employee or Member who is separated from the service, or transferred to a position in which the employee or Member does not continue subject to this chapter, after completing 5 years of service is entitled to an annuity beginning at the age of 62 years.

(b)(1) An employee or Member who is separated from the service, or transferred to a position in which the employee or Member does not continue subject to this chapter, after completing 10 years of service but before attaining the applicable minimum retirement age under section 8412(h) is entitled to an annuity beginning on the date designated by the employee or Member in a written election under this subsection. The date designated under this subsection may not precede the date on which the employee or

Member attains such minimum retirement age and must precede the date on which the employee or Member becomes 62 years of age.

(2) The election of an annuity under this subsection shall not be effective unless—

(A) it is made at such time and in such manner as the Office shall by regulation prescribe; and

(B) the employee or Member will not otherwise be eligible to receive an annuity within 31 days after filing the election.

(3) The election of an annuity under this subsection extinguishes the right of the employee or Member to receive any other annuity based on the service on which the annuity under this subsection is based.

(Added Pub. L. 99–335, title I, §101(a), June 6, 1986, 100 Stat. 525; amended Pub. L. 99–556, title I, §105(b)(1), Oct. 27, 1986, 100 Stat. 3132.)

AMENDMENTS

1986—Subsec. (b)(1). Pub. L. 99–556 inserted "but before attaining the applicable minimum retirement age under section 8412(h)" in first sentence and substituted "such minimum retirement age" for "the applicable minimum retirement age under section 8412(h)" in second sentence.

SECTION REFERRED TO IN OTHER SECTIONS

This section is referred to in sections 8415, 8420, 8442, 8445, 8462, 8464 of this title; title 22 section 4071d.

§ 8414. Early retirement

(a)(1) A member of the Senior Executive Service who is removed from the Senior Executive Service for failure to be recertified as a senior executive under section 3393a or for less than fully successful executive performance (as determined under subchapter II of chapter 43 of this title) after completing 25 years of service, or after becoming 50 years of age and completing 20 years of service, is entitled to an annuity.

(2) A member of the Defense Intelligence Senior Executive Service or the Senior Cryptologic Executive Service who is removed from such service for failure to be recertified as a senior executive or for less than fully successful executive performance after completing 25 years of service, or after becoming 50 years of age and completing 20 years of service, is entitled to an annuity.

(3) A member of the Federal Bureau of Investigation and Drug Enforcement Administration Senior Executive Service who is removed from such service for failure to be recertified as a senior executive or for less than fully successful executive performance after completing 25 years of service or after becoming 50 years of age and completing 20 years of service is entitled to an annuity.

(b)(1) Except as provided in paragraphs (2) and (3), an employee who—

(A) is separated from the service involuntarily, except by removal for cause on charges of misconduct or delinquency; or

(B) except in the case of an employee who is separated from the service under a program carried out under subsection (d), while serving in a geographic area designated by the Director, is separated from the service voluntarily during a period in which (as determined by the Director)—

(i) the agency in which the employee is serving is undergoing a major reorganization, a major reduction in force, or a major transfer of function; and

(ii) a significant percentage of the total number of employees serving in such agency will be separated or subject to an immediate reduction in the rate of basic pay (without regard to subchapter VI of chapter 53 of this title or comparable provisions);

after completing 25 years of service, or after becoming 50 years of age and completing 20 years of service, is entitled to an annuity.

(2) An employee under paragraph (1) who is separated as described in subparagraph (A) of such paragraph is not entitled to an annuity under this subsection if the employee has declined a reasonable offer of another position in the employee's agency for which the employee is qualified, and the offered position is not lower than 2 grades (or pay levels) below the employee's grade (or pay level) and is within the employee's commuting area.

(3) Paragraph (1) shall not apply to an employee entitled to an annuity under subsection (d) or (e) of section 8412.

(c)(1) An employee who was hired as a military reserve technician on or before February 10, 1996 (under the provisions of this title in effect before that date), and who is separated from technician service, after becoming 50 years of age and completing 25 years of service, by reason of being separated from the Selected Reserve of the employee's reserve component or ceasing to hold the military grade specified by the Secretary concerned for the position held by the employee is entitled to an annuity.

(2) An employee who is initially hired as a military technician (dual status) after February 10, 1996, and who is separated from the Selected Reserve or ceases to hold the military grade specified by the Secretary concerned for the position held by the technician—

(A) after completing 25 years of service as a military technician (dual status), or

(B) after becoming 50 years of age and completing 20 years of service as a military technician (dual status),

is entitled to an annuity.

(d)(1) The Secretary of Defense may, during fiscal years 2002 and 2003, carry out a program under which an employee of the Department of Defense may be separated from the service entitled to an immediate annuity under this subchapter if the employee—

(A) has—

(i) completed 25 years of service; or

(ii) become 50 years of age and completed 20 years of service; and

(B) is eligible for the annuity under paragraph (2) or (3).

(2)(A) For the purposes of paragraph (1), an employee referred to in that paragraph is eligible for an immediate annuity under this paragraph if the employee—

(i) is separated from the service involuntarily other than for cause; and

(ii) has not declined a reasonable offer of another position in the Department of Defense for which the employee is qualified, which is not lower than 2 grades (or pay levels) below the employee's grade (or pay level), and which is within the employee's commuting area.

(B) For the purposes of paragraph (2)(A)(i), a separation for failure to accept a directed reassignment to a position outside the commuting area of the employee concerned or to accompany a position outside of such area pursuant to a transfer of function may not be considered to be a removal for cause.

(3) For the purposes of paragraph (1), an employee referred to in that paragraph is eligible for an immediate annuity under this paragraph if the employee satisfies all of the following conditions:

(A) The employee is separated from the service voluntarily during a period in which the organization within the Department of Defense in which the employee is serving is undergoing a major organizational adjustment.

(B) The employee has been employed continuously by the Department of Defense for more than 30 days before the date on which the head of the employee's organization requests the determinations required under subparagraph (A).

(C) The employee is serving under an appointment that is not limited by time.

(D) The employee is not in receipt of a decision notice of involuntary separation for misconduct or unacceptable performance.

(E) The employee is within the scope of an offer of voluntary early retirement, as defined on the basis of one or more of the following objective criteria:

(i) One or more organizational units.

(ii) One or more occupational groups, series, or levels.

(iii) One or more geographical locations.

(iv) Any other similar objective and nonpersonal criteria that the Office of Personnel Management determines appropriate.

(4) Under regulations prescribed by the Office of Personnel Management, the determinations of whether an employee meets—

(A) the requirements of subparagraph (A) of paragraph (3) shall be made by the Office upon the request of the Secretary of Defense; and

(B) the requirements of subparagraph (E) of such paragraph shall be made by the Secretary of Defense.

(5) A determination of which employees are within the scope of an offer of early retirement shall be made only on the basis of consistent and well-documented application of the relevant criteria.

(6) In this subsection, the term "major organizational adjustment" means any of the following:

(A) A major reorganization.

(B) A major reduction in force.

(C) A major transfer of function.

(D) A workforce restructuring—

(i) to meet mission needs;

(ii) to achieve one or more reductions in strength;

(iii) to correct skill imbalances; or

(iv) to reduce the number of high-grade, managerial, supervisory, or similar positions.

(Added Pub. L. 99–335, title I, §101(a), June 6, 1986, 100 Stat. 526; amended Pub. L. 100–325, §2(m), May 30, 1988, 102 Stat. 583; Pub. L. 101–194, title V, §506(b)(9), Nov. 30, 1989, 103 Stat. 1759; Pub. L. 105–261, div. A, title XI, §1109(b), Oct. 17, 1998, 112 Stat. 2144; Pub. L. 106–58, title VI, §651(b), Sept. 29, 1999, 113 Stat. 480; Pub. L. 106–65, div. A, title V, §522(b), Oct. 5, 1999, 113 Stat. 597; Pub. L. 106–398, §1 [[div. A], title XI, §1152(b)]], Oct. 30, 2000, 114 Stat. 1654, 1654A–321.)

APPLICATION OF SUBSECTION (b)(1)(B)

Pub. L. 105–174, title III, §7001(b), May 1, 1998, 112 Stat. 91, as amended by Pub. L. 106–58, title VI, §651(a), Sept. 29, 1999, 113 Stat. 480, provided that, effective May 1, 1998, subsection (b)(1)(B) of this section shall be applied as if it had been amended to read as follows:

(B)(i) has been employed continuously, by the agency in which the employee is serving, for at least the 31-day period ending on the date on which such agency requests the determination referred to in clause (iv);

(ii) is serving under an appointment that is not time limited;

(iii) has not been duly notified that such employee is to be involuntarily separated for misconduct or unacceptable performance;

(iv) is separated from the service voluntarily during a period in which, as determined by the Office of Personnel Management (upon request by the agency) under regulations prescribed by the Office—

(I) such agency (or, if applicable, the component in which the employee is serving) is undergoing a major reorganization, a major reduction in force, or a major transfer of function; and

(II) a significant percentage of the employees serving in such agency (or component) will be separated or subject to an immediate reduction in the rate of basic pay (without regard to subchapter VI of chapter 53, or comparable provisions); and

(v) as determined by the agency under regulations prescribed by the Office, is within the scope of the offer of voluntary early retirement, which may be made on the basis of—

(I) one or more organizational units;

(II) one or more occupational series or levels;

(III) one or more geographical locations;

(IV) other similar nonpersonal factors the Office determines appropriate; or

(V) any appropriate combination of such factors;

AMENDMENTS

2000—Subsec. (b)(1)(B). Pub. L. 106–398, §1 [[div. A], title XI, §1152(b)(1)], inserted "except in the case of an employee who is separated from the service under a program carried out under subsection (d)," before "while serving" in introductory provisions.

Subsec. (d). Pub. L. 106–398, §1 [[div. A], title XI, §1152(b)(2)], added subsec. (d).

1999—Subsec. (b)(1)(B). Pub. L. 106–58 repealed Pub. L. 105–261, §1109(b)(1). See 1998 Amendment note below.

Subsec. (c). Pub. L. 106–65 amended subsec. (c) generally. Prior to amendment, subsec. (c) read as follows: "A military reserve technician who is separated from technician service, after becoming 50 years of age and completing 25 years of service, by reason of ceasing to satisfy the condition described in section 8401(30)(B) is entitled to an annuity."

Subsec. (d). Pub. L. 106–58 repealed Pub. L. 105–261, §1109(b)(2). See 1998 Amendment note below.

1998—Subsec. (b)(1)(B). Pub. L. 105–261, §1109(b)(1), which directed insertion of "except in the case of an employee described in subsection (d)(1)," after "(B)", was repealed by Pub. L. 106–58.

Subsec. (d). Pub. L. 105–261, §1109(b)(2), which directed addition of subsec. (d), relating to authority of Department of Defense to offer employees voluntary early retirement, was repealed by Pub. L. 106–58.

1989—Subsec. (a)(1). Pub. L. 101–194, §506(b)(9)(A), substituted "for failure to be recertified as a senior executive under section 3393a or for" for "for".

Subsec. (a)(2), (3). Pub. L. 101–194, §506(b)(9)(B), (C), substituted "for failure to be recertified as a senior executive or for" for "for".

1988—Subsec. (a)(3). Pub. L. 100–325 added par. (3).

EFFECTIVE DATE OF 1989 AMENDMENT

Amendment by Pub. L. 101–194 effective Jan. 1, 1991, see section 506(d) of Pub. L. 101–194, set out as a note under section 3151 of this title.

GENERAL ACCOUNTING OFFICE: VOLUNTARY EARLY RETIREMENT

For provisions relating to the application of subsection (b)(1)(B) of this section to officers and employees of the General Accounting Office during the period beginning on Oct. 13, 2000 and ending on Dec. 31, 2003, see section 1 of Pub. L. 106–303, set out as a note under section 8336 of this title.

SECTION REFERRED TO IN OTHER SECTIONS

This section is referred to in sections 5597, 6302, 8420, 8421, 8421a, 8456, 8462, 8464, 8901 of this title; title 10 section 10218; title 50 sections 2053, 2442.

§ 8415. Computation of basic annuity

(a) Except as otherwise provided in this section, the annuity of an employee retiring under this subchapter is 1 percent of that individual's average pay multiplied by such individual's total service.

(b) The annuity of a Member, or former Member with title to a Member annuity, retiring under this subchapter is computed under subsection (a), except that if the individual has had at least 5 years of service as a Member or Congressional employee, or any combination thereof, so much of the annuity as is computed with respect to either such type of service (or a combination thereof), not exceeding a total of 20 years, shall be computed by multiplying 1^{7}/10 percent of the individual's average pay by the years of such service.

(c) The annuity of a Congressional employee, or former Congressional employee, retiring under this subchapter is computed under subsection (a), except that if the individual has had at least 5 years of service as a Congressional employee or Member, or any combination thereof, so much of the annuity as is computed with respect to either such type of service (or a combination thereof), not exceeding a total of 20 years, shall be computed by multiplying 1^{7}/10 percent of the individual's average pay by the years of such service.

(d) The annuity of an employee retiring under subsection (d) or (e) of section 8412 or under subsection (a), (b), or (c) of section 8425 is—

(1) 1^{7}/10 percent of that individual's average pay multiplied by so much of such individual's total service as does not exceed 20 years; plus

(2) 1 percent of that individual's average pay multiplied by so much of such individual's total service as exceeds 20 years.

(e)(1) In computing an annuity under this subchapter for an employee whose service includes service performed on a part-time basis—

(A) the average pay of the employee, to the extent that it includes pay for service performed in any position on a part-time basis, shall be determined by using the annual rate of basic pay that would be payable for full-time service in the position; and

(B) the benefit so computed shall then be multiplied by a fraction equal to the ratio which the employee's actual service, as determined by prorating the employee's total service to reflect the service that was performed on a part-time basis, bears to the total service that would be creditable for the employee if all of the service had been performed on a full-time basis.

(2) For the purpose of this subsection, employment on a part-time basis shall not be considered to include employment on a temporary or intermittent basis.

(f)(1) The annuity of an employee or Member retiring under section 8412(g) or 8413(b) is computed in accordance with applicable provisions of this section, except that the annuity shall be reduced by five-twelfths of 1 percent for each full month by which the commencement date of the annuity precedes the sixty-second anniversary of the birth of the employee or Member.

(2)(A) Paragraph (1) does not apply in the case of an employee or Member retiring under section 8412(g) or 8413(b) if the employee or Member would satisfy the age and service requirements for title to an annuity under section 8412(a), (b), (d)(2), (e)(2), or (f)(2), determined as if the employee or Member had, as of the date of separation, attained the age specified in subparagraph (B).

(B) A determination under subparagraph (A) shall be based on how old the employee or Member will be as of the date on which the annuity under section 8412(g) or 8413(b) is to commence.

(g)(1) In applying subsection (a) with respect to an employee under paragraph (2), the percentage applied under such subsection shall be 1.1 percent, rather than 1 percent.

(2) This subsection applies in the case of an employee who—

(A) retires entitled to an annuity under section 8412; and

(B) at the time of the separation on which entitlement to the annuity is based, is at least 62 years of age and has completed at least 20 years of service;

but does not apply in the case of a Congressional employee, military technician (dual status), law enforcement officer, member of the Supreme Court Police, firefighter, nuclear materials courier, or air traffic controller.

(h) The annuity of a Member who has served in a position in the executive branch for which the rate of basic pay was reduced for the duration of the service of the Member in that position to remove the impediment to the appointment of the Member imposed by article I, section 6, clause 2 of the Constitution, shall, subject to a deposit in the Fund as provided under section 8422(g), be computed as though the rate of basic pay which would otherwise have been in effect during that period of service had been in effect.

(i)(1) For purposes of this subsection, the term "physicians comparability allowance" refers to an amount described in section 8331(3)(H).

(2) Except as otherwise provided in this subsection, no part of a physicians comparability allowance shall be treated as basic pay for purposes of any computation under this section unless, before the date of the separation on which entitlement to annuity is based, the separating individual has completed at least 15 years of service as a Government physician (whether performed before, on, or after the date of the enactment of this subsection).

(3) If the condition under paragraph (2) is met, then, any amounts received by the individual in the form of a physicians comparability allowance shall (for the purposes referred to in paragraph (2)) be treated as basic pay, but only to the extent that such amounts are attributable to service performed on or after the date of the enactment of this subsection, and only to the extent of the percentage allowable, which shall be determined as follows:

If the total amount of service performed, on or after the date of the enactment of this subsection, as a Government physician is:	Then, the percentage allowable is:
Less than 2 years	0
At least 2 but less than 4 years	25
At least 4 but less than 6 years	50
At least 6 but less than 8 years	75
At least 8 years	100.

(4) Notwithstanding any other provision of this subsection, 100 percent of all amounts received as a physicians comparability allowance shall, to the extent attributable to service performed on or after the date of the enactment of this subsection, be treated as basic pay (without regard to any of the preceding provisions of this subsection) for purposes of computing—

(A) an annuity under section 8452; and

(B) a survivor annuity under subchapter IV, if based on the service of an individual who dies before separating from service.

(Added Pub. L. 99–335, title I, §101(a), June 6, 1986, 100 Stat. 527; amended Pub. L. 99–556, title I, §105(b)(2), Oct. 27, 1986, 100 Stat. 3132; Pub. L. 103–283, title III, §307(b)(2), July 22, 1994, 108 Stat. 1442; Pub. L. 105–61, title V, §516(a)(7), Oct. 10, 1997, 111 Stat. 1306; Pub. L. 105–261, div. C, title XXXI, §3154(h), Oct. 17, 1998, 112 Stat. 2255; Pub. L. 106–65, div. A, title V, §522(c)(1), Oct. 5, 1999, 113 Stat. 597; Pub. L. 106–553, §1(a)(2) [title III, §308(c)(2)], Dec. 21, 2000, 114 Stat. 2762, 2762A–87; Pub. L. 106–571, §3(c)(1), Dec. 28, 2000, 114 Stat. 3055.)

REFERENCES IN TEXT

The date of the enactment of this subsection, referred to in subsec. (i), is the date of enactment of Pub. L. 106–571, which was approved Dec. 28, 2000.

AMENDMENTS

2000—Subsec. (g). Pub. L. 106–553 inserted "member of the Supreme Court Police," after "law enforcement officer," in concluding provisions.

Subsec. (i). Pub. L. 106–571 added subsec. (i).

1999—Subsec. (g)(2). Pub. L. 106–65 substituted "military technician (dual status)" for "military reserve technician" in concluding provisions.

1998—Subsec. (g)(2). Pub. L. 105–261 inserted "nuclear materials courier," after "firefighter," in concluding provisions.

1997—Subsec. (h). Pub. L. 105–61 added subsec. (h).

1994—Subsec. (d). Pub. L. 103–283 substituted "(a), (b), or (c)" for "(a) or (b)".

1986—Subsec. (f)(2). Pub. L. 99–556 inserted "8412(g) or" in subpars. (A) and (B).

EFFECTIVE DATE OF 2000 AMENDMENT

Amendment by Pub. L. 106–553 effective on the first day of the first applicable pay period that begins on Dec. 21, 2000, and applicable only to an individual who is employed as a member of the Supreme Court Police after Dec. 21, 2000, see section 1(a)(2) [title III, §308(i), (j)] of Pub. L. 106–553, set out in a Supreme Court Police Retirement note under section 8331 of this title.

EFFECTIVE DATE OF 1998 AMENDMENT

Amendment by Pub. L. 105–261 effective at the beginning of the first pay period that begins after Oct. 17, 1998, and applicable only to an individual who is employed as a nuclear materials courier, as defined by section 8331(27) or 8401(33) of this title, after Oct. 17, 1998, see section 3154(m), (n) of Pub. L. 105–261, set out as a note under section 8331 of this title.

EFFECTIVE DATE OF 1997 AMENDMENT

Amendment by Pub. L. 105–61 applicable to any annuity commencing before, on, or after Oct. 10, 1997, and effective with regard to any payment made after the first month following Oct. 10, 1997, see section 516(b) of Pub. L. 105–61, set out as a note under section 8334 of this title.

CLARIFICATION RELATING TO CONSIDERATION OF PRE-1987 SERVICE AS AN AIR TRAFFIC CONTROLLER FOR RETIREMENT PURPOSES

See section 2 of Pub. L. 100–92, set out as a note under section 8332 of this title.

SECTION REFERRED TO IN OTHER SECTIONS

This section is referred to in sections 8418, 8419, 8420, 8420a, 8421, 8442, 8452, 8468 of this title; title 22 sections 4045, 4046, 4071d; title 38 section 7426; title 50 section 2153.

§ 8416. Survivor reduction for a current spouse

(a)(1) If an employee or Member is married at the time of retiring under this chapter, the reduction described in section 8419(a) shall be made unless the employee or Member and the spouse jointly waive, by written election, any right which the spouse may have to a survivor annuity under section 8442 based on the service of such employee or Member. A waiver under this paragraph shall be filed with the Office under procedures prescribed by the Office.

(2) Notwithstanding paragraph (1), an employee or Member who is married at the time of retiring under this chapter may waive the annuity for a surviving spouse without the spouse's consent if the employee or Member establishes to the satisfaction of the Office (in accordance with regulations prescribed by the Office)—

(A) that the spouse's whereabouts cannot be determined; or

(B) that, due to exceptional circumstances, requiring the employee or Member to seek the spouse's consent would otherwise be inappropriate.

(3) Except as provided in subsection (d), a waiver made under this subsection shall be irrevocable.

(b)(1) Upon remarriage, a retired employee or Member who was married at the time of retirement (including an employee or Member whose annuity was not reduced to provide a survivor annuity for the employee's or Member's spouse or former spouse as of the time of retirement) may irrevocably elect during such marriage, in a signed writing received by the Office within 2 years after such remarriage or, if later, within 2 years after the death or remarriage of any former spouse of such employee or Member who was entitled to a survivor annuity under section 8445 (or of the last such surviving former spouse, if there was more than one), a reduction in the employee's or Member's annuity under section 8419(a) for the purpose of providing an annuity for such employee's or Member's spouse in the event such spouse survives the employee or Member.

(2) The election and reduction shall be effective the first day of the second month after the election is received by the Office, but not less than 9 months after the date of the remarriage.

(3) An election to provide a survivor annuity to an individual under this subsection—

(A) shall prospectively void any election made by the employee or Member under section 8420 with respect to such individual; or

(B) shall, if an election was made by the employee or Member under section 8420 with respect to a different individual, prospectively void such election if appropriate written application is made by such employee or Member at the time of making the election under this subsection.

(4) Any election under this subsection made by an employee or Member on behalf of an individual after the retirement of such employee or Member shall not be effective if—

(A) the employee or Member was married to such individual at the time of retirement; and

(B) the annuity rights of such individual based on the service of such employee or Member were then waived under subsection (a).

(c)(1) An employee or Member who is unmarried at the time of retiring under this chapter and who later marries may irrevocably elect, in a signed writing received by the Office within 2 years after such employee or Member marries or, if later, within 2 years after the death or remarriage of any former spouse of such employee or Member who was entitled to a survivor annuity under section 8445 (or of the last such surviving former spouse, if there was more than one), a reduction in the current annuity of the retired employee or Member, in accordance with section 8419(a).

(2) The election and reduction shall take effect the first day of the first month beginning 9 months after the date of marriage. Any such election to provide a survivor annuity for an individual—

(A) shall prospectively void any election made by the employee or Member under section 8420 with respect to such individual; or

(B) shall, if an election was made by the employee or Member under section 8420 with respect to a different individual, prospectively void such election if appropriate written application is made by such employee or Member at the time of making the election under this subsection.

(d)(1) An employee or Member—

(A) who is married on the date of retiring under this chapter, and

(B) with respect to whose spouse a waiver under subsection (a) has been made,

may, during the 18-month period beginning on such date, elect to have a reduction made under section 8419 in order to provide a survivor annuity under section 8442 for such spouse.

(2)(A) An election under this subsection shall not be effective unless the amount described in subparagraph (B) is deposited into the Fund before the expiration of the 18-month period referred to in paragraph (1).

(B) The amount to be deposited under this subparagraph is equal to the sum of—

(i) the difference (for the period between the date on which the annuity of the former employee or Member commences and the date on which reductions pursuant to the election under this subsection commence) between the amount paid to the former employee or Member from the Fund under this chapter and the amount which would have been paid if such election had been made at the time of retirement; and

(ii) the costs associated with providing for the election under this subsection.

The amount to be deposited under clause (i) shall include interest, computed at the rate of 6 percent a year.

(3) An annuity which is reduced pursuant to an election by a former employee or Member under this subsection shall be reduced by the same percentage as was in effect under section 8419 as of the date of the employee's or Member's retirement.

(4) Rights and obligations under this chapter resulting from an election under this subsection shall be the same as the rights and obligations which would have resulted had the election been made at the time of retirement.

(5) The Office shall inform each employee and Member who is eligible to make an election under this subsection of the right to make such election and the procedures and deadlines applicable in making any such election.

(Added Pub. L. 99–335, title I, §101(a), June 6, 1986, 100 Stat. 528.)

SECTION REFERRED TO IN OTHER SECTIONS

This section is referred to in sections 8417, 8418, 8419, 8420, 8420a, 8442, 8445 of this title; title 50 section 2154.

§ 8417. Survivor reduction for a former spouse

(a) If an employee or Member has a former spouse who is entitled to a survivor annuity as provided in section 8445, the reduction described in section 8419(a) shall be made.

(b)(1) An employee or Member who has a former spouse may elect, under procedures prescribed by the Office, a reduction in the annuity of the employee or Member under section 8419(a) in order to provide a survivor annuity for such former spouse under section 8445.

(2) An election under this subsection shall be made at the time of retirement or, if the marriage is dissolved after the date of retirement, within 2 years after the date on which the marriage of the former spouse to the employee or Member is so dissolved.

(3) An election under this subsection—

(A) shall not be effective to the extent that it—

(i) conflicts with—

(I) any court order or decree referred to in section 8445(a) which was issued before the date of such election; or

(II) any agreement referred to in such section 8445(a) which was entered into before such date; or

(ii) would cause the total of survivor annuities payable under sections 8442 and 8445, respectively, based on the service of the employee or Member to exceed the amount which would be payable to a widow or widower of such employee or Member under such section 8442 (determined without regard to any reduction to provide for an annuity under such section 8445); and

(B) shall not be effective, in the case of an employee or Member who is then married, unless it is made with the spouse's written consent.

The Office shall by regulation provide that subparagraph (B) may be waived for either of the reasons set forth in section 8416(a)(2).

(Added Pub. L. 99–335, title I, §101(a), June 6, 1986, 100 Stat. 530.)

SECTION REFERRED TO IN OTHER SECTIONS

This section is referred to in sections 8418, 8442, 8445, 8901, 8905 of this title; title 22 section 4071j; title 50 section 2154.

§ 8418. Survivor elections; deposit; offsets

(a)(1) An individual who makes an election under subsection (b) or (c) of section 8416 or section 8417(b) which is required to be made within 2 years after the date of a prescribed event shall deposit into the Fund an amount determined by the Office (as nearly as may be administratively feasible) to reflect the amount by which the annuity of such individual would have been reduced if the election had been in effect since the date of retirement (or, if later, and in the case of an election under such section 8416(b), since the date the previous reduction in the annuity of such individual was terminated under paragraph (1) or (2) of section 8419(b)), plus interest.

(2) Interest under paragraph (1) shall be computed at the rate of 6 percent a year.

(b) The Office shall, by regulation, provide for payment of the deposit required under subsection (a) by a reduction in the annuity of the employee or Member. The reduction shall, to the extent practicable, be designed so that the present value of the future reduction is actuarially equivalent to the deposit required under subsection (a), except that the total reductions in the annuity of an employee or Member to pay deposits required by this section shall not exceed 25 percent of the annuity computed under section 8415 or section 8452, including adjustments under section 8462. The reduction required by this subsection, which shall be effective at the same time as the election under section 8416(b) and (c) or section 8417(b), shall be permanent and unaffected by any future termination of the marriage or the entitlement of the former spouse. Such reduction shall be independent of and in addition to the reduction required under section 8416(b) and (c) or section 8417(b).

(c) Subsections (a) and (b) shall not apply if—

(1) the employee or Member makes an election under section 8416(b) or (c) after having made an election under section 8420; and

(2) the election under such section 8420 becomes void under subsection (b)(3) or (c)(2) of such section 8416.

(d) The Office shall prescribe regulations under which the survivor of an employee or Member may make a deposit under this section.

(Added Pub. L. 99–335, title I, §101(a), June 6, 1986, 100 Stat. 530; amended Pub. L. 103–66, title XI, §11004(b), Aug. 10, 1993, 107 Stat. 412.)

AMENDMENTS

1993—Subsec. (a)(1). Pub. L. 103–66, §11004(b)(1), struck out ", before the expiration of the 2-year period involved," after "into the Fund".

Subsec. (b). Pub. L. 102–66, §11004(b)(2), amended subsec. (b) generally. Prior to amendment, subsec. (b) read as follows: "If the electing individual does not make the deposit required under subsection (a), the Office shall collect such amount by offset against such individual's annuity, up to a maximum of 25 percent of the net annuity otherwise payable, and the individual is deemed to consent to such offset."

EFFECTIVE DATE OF 1993 AMENDMENT

Amendment by Pub. L. 103–66 effective on first day of first month beginning at least 30 days after Aug. 10, 1993, and applicable to all deposits required under section 8339(j)(3) or (5), 8339(k)(2), or 8418 of this title, on which no payment has been made prior to such effective date, with provision for partial deposit, see section 11004(c) of Pub. L. 103–66, set out as a note under section 8339 of this title.

SECTION REFERRED TO IN OTHER SECTIONS

This section is referred to in title 22 section 4071j; title 50 section 2154.

§ 8419. Survivor reductions; computation

(a)(1) Except as provided in paragraph (2), the annuity of an annuitant computed under section 8415, or under section 8452 (including subsection (a)(2) of such section, if applicable) or one-half of the annuity, if jointly designated for this purpose by the employee or Member and the spouse of the employee or Member under procedures prescribed by the Office of Personnel Management, shall be reduced by 10 percent if a survivor annuity, or a combination of survivor annuities, under section 8442 or 8445 (or both) are to be provided for.

(2)(A) If no survivor annuity under section 8442 is to be provided for, but one or more survivor annuities under section 8445 involving a total of less than the entirety of the amount referred to in subsection (b)(2) of such section are to be provided for, the annuity of the annuitant involved (as computed under section 8415, or under section 8452 (including subsection (a)(2) of such section, if applicable)) or one-half of the annuity, if jointly designated for this purpose by the employee or Member and the spouse of the employee or Member under procedures prescribed by the Office of Personnel Management, shall be reduced by an appropriate percentage determined under subparagraph (B).

(B) The Office shall prescribe regulations under which an appropriate reduction under this paragraph, not to exceed a total of 10 percent, shall be made.

(b)(1) Any reduction in an annuity for the purpose of providing a survivor annuity for the current spouse of a retired employee or Member shall be terminated for each full month—

(A) after the death of the spouse; or

(B) after the dissolution of the spouse's marriage to the employee or Member, except that an appropriate reduction shall be made thereafter if the spouse is entitled, as a former spouse, to a survivor annuity under section 8445.

(2) Any reduction in an annuity for the purpose of providing a survivor annuity for a former spouse of a retired employee or Member shall be terminated for each full month after the former spouse remarries before reaching age 55 or dies. This reduction shall be replaced by appropriate reductions under subsection (a) if the retired employee or Member has one or more of the following:

(A) another former spouse who is entitled to a survivor annuity under section 8445;

(B) a current spouse to whom the employee or Member was married at the time of retirement and with respect to whom a survivor annuity was not waived under section 8416(a) (or, if waived, with respect to whom an election under section 8416(d) has been made); or

(C) a current spouse whom the employee or Member married after retirement and with respect to whom an election has been made under subsection (b) or (c) of section 8416.

(Added Pub. L. 99–335, title I, §101(a), June 6, 1986, 100 Stat. 531; amended Pub. L. 100–238, title I, §131(a), Jan. 8, 1988, 101 Stat. 1759.)

AMENDMENTS

1988—Subsec. (a)(1), (2)(A). Pub. L. 100–238 inserted "or one-half of the annuity, if jointly designated for this purpose by the employee or Member and the spouse of the employee or Member under procedures prescribed by the Office of Personnel Management" before ", shall be reduced".

SECTION REFERRED TO IN OTHER SECTIONS

This section is referred to in sections 8416, 8417, 8418, 8442, 8445, 8468 of this title.

§ 8420. Insurable interest reductions

(a)(1) At the time of retiring under section 8412, 8413, or 8414, an employee or Member who is found to be in good health by the Office may elect to have such employee's or Member's annuity (as computed under section 8415) reduced under paragraph (2) in order to provide an annuity under section 8444 for an individual having an insurable interest in the employee or Member. Such individual shall be designated by the employee or Member in writing.

(2) The annuity of the employee or Member making the election is reduced by 10 percent, and by 5 percent for each full 5 years the individual named is younger than the retiring employee or Member, except that the total reduction may not exceed 40 percent.

(3) An annuity which is reduced under this subsection shall, effective the first day of the

month following the death of the individual named under this subsection, be recomputed and paid as if the annuity had not been so reduced.

(b)(1) In the case of a married employee or Member, an election under this section on behalf of the spouse may be made only if any right of such spouse to a survivor annuity based on the service of such employee or Member is waived in accordance with section 8416(a).

(2) Paragraph (1) does not apply in the case of an employee or Member if such employee or Member has a former spouse who would become entitled to an annuity under section 8445 as a survivor of such employee or Member.

(Added Pub. L. 99–335, title I, § 101(a), June 6, 1986, 100 Stat. 532.)

This section is referred to in sections 8416, 8418, 8444 of this title.

§ 8420a. Alternative forms of annuities

(a) The Office shall prescribe regulations under which any employee or Member who has a life-threatening affliction or other critical medical condition may, at the time of retiring under this subchapter, elect annuity benefits under this section instead of any other benefits under this subchapter, and any benefits under subchapter IV of this chapter, based on the service of the employee or Member.

(b) Subject to subsection (c), the Office shall by regulation provide for such alternative forms of annuities as the Office considers appropriate, except that among the alternatives offered shall be—

(1) an alternative which provides for—

(A) payment of the lump-sum credit (excluding interest) to the employee or Member; and

(B) payment of an annuity to the employee or Member for life; and

(2) in the case of an employee or Member who is married at the time of retirement, an alternative which provides for—

(A) payment of the lump-sum credit (excluding interest) to the employee or Member; and

(B) payment of an annuity to the employee or Member for life, with a survivor annuity payable for the life of a surviving spouse.

(c) Each alternative provided for under subsection (b) shall, to the extent practicable, be designed such that the present value of the benefits provided under such alternative (including any lump-sum credit) is actuarially equivalent to the sum of—

(1) the present value of the annuity which would otherwise be provided under this subchapter, as computed under section 8415; and

(2) the present value of the annuity supplement which would otherwise be provided (if any) under section 8421.

(d) An employee or Member who, at the time of retiring under this subchapter—

(1) is married, shall be ineligible to make an election under this section unless a waiver is made under section 8416(a); or

(2) has a former spouse, shall be ineligible to make an election under this section if the

former spouse is entitled to benefits under section 8445 or 8467 (based on the service of the employee or Member) under the terms of a decree of divorce or annulment, or a court order or court-approved property settlement incident to any such decree, with respect to which the Office has been duly notified.

(e) An employee or Member who is married at the time of retiring under this subchapter and who makes an election under this section may, during the 18-month period beginning on the date of retirement, make the election provided for under section 8416(d), subject to the deposit requirement thereunder.

(Added Pub. L. 99–335, title I, § 101(a), June 6, 1986, 100 Stat. 532; amended Pub. L. 101–508, title VII, § 7001(a)(1), Nov. 5, 1990, 104 Stat. 1388–327; Pub. L. 103–66, title XI, § 11002(a), Aug. 10, 1993, 107 Stat. 409.)

1993—Subsec. (a). Pub. L. 103–66, § 11002(a)(1), substituted "any employee or Member who has a life-threatening affliction or other critical medical condition" for "an employee or Member".

Subsec. (f). Pub. L. 103–66, § 11002(a)(2), struck out subsec. (f) which prohibited election of alternative form of annuity where commencement date would be after Dec. 1, 1990, with certain exceptions.

1990—Subsec. (f). Pub. L. 101–508 added subsec. (f).

Amendment by Pub. L. 103–66 effective Oct. 1, 1994, and applicable with respect to any annuity commencing on or after that date, see section 11002(d) of Pub. L. 103–66, set out as a note under section 8343a of this title.

For provisions relating to application of subsec. (f) of this section to certain members of Armed Forces who were called or ordered to active duty in connection with Operation Desert Shield and to certain employees of Department of Defense who are certified to have performed duties essential for support of Operation Desert Shield, see section 7001(a)(4) of Pub. L. 101–508, set out as a note under section 8343a of this title.

For provisions relating to deferred payment of lump-sum credit for certain individuals electing alternative forms of annuities, see notes set out under section 8343a of this title.

This section is referred to in sections 8348, 8424 of this title.

§ 8421. Annuity supplement

(a)(1) Subject to paragraph (3), an individual shall, if and while entitled to an annuity under subsection (a), (b), (d), or (e) of section 8412, or under section 8414(c), also be entitled to an annuity supplement under this section.

(2) Subject to paragraph (3), an individual shall, if and while entitled to an annuity under section 8412(f), or under subsection (a) or (b) of section 8414, also be entitled to an annuity supplement under this section if such individual is at least the applicable minimum retirement age

under section 8412(h), except that an individual entitled to an annuity under section 8414(a) for failure to be recertified as a senior executive shall be entitled to an annuity supplement without regard to such applicable minimum retirement age.

(3)(A) An individual whose entitlement to an annuity under section 8412 or 8414 does not commence before age 62 is not entitled to an annuity supplement under this section.

(B) An individual entitled to an annuity supplement under this section ceases to be so entitled after the last day of the month preceding the first month for which such individual would, on proper application, be entitled to old-age insurance benefits under title II of the Social Security Act, but not later than the last day of the month in which such individual attains age 62.

(b)(1) The amount of the annuity supplement of an annuitant under this section for any month shall be equal to the product of—

(A) an amount determined under paragraph (2), multiplied by

(B) a fraction, as described in paragraph (3).

(2) The amount under this paragraph for an annuitant is an amount equal to the old-age insurance benefit which would be payable to such annuitant under title II of the Social Security Act (without regard to sections 203, 215(a)(7), and 215(d)(5) of such Act) upon attaining age 62 and filing application therefor, determined as if the annuitant had attained such age and filed application therefor, and were a fully insured individual (as defined in section 214(a) of such Act), on January 1 of the year in which such annuitant's entitlement to any payment under this section commences, except that the reduction of such old-age insurance benefit under section 202(q) of such Act shall be the maximum applicable for an individual born in the same year as the annuitant. In computing the primary insurance amount under section 215 of such Act for purposes of this paragraph, the number of elapsed years (referred to in section 215(b)(2)(B)(iii) of such Act and used to compute the number of benefit computation years) shall not include years beginning with the year in which such annuitant's entitlement to any payment under this section commences, and—

(A) only basic pay for service performed (if any) shall be taken into account in computing the total wages and self-employment income of the annuitant for a benefit computation year;

(B) for a benefit computation year which commences after the date of the separation with respect to which entitlement to the annuitant's annuity under this subchapter is based and before the date as of which such annuitant is treated, under the preceding sentence, to have attained age 62, the total wages and self-employment income of such annuitant for such year shall be deemed to be zero; and

(C) for a benefit computation year after age 21 which precedes the separation referred to in subparagraph (B), and during which the individual did not perform a full year of service, the total wages and self-employment income of such annuitant for such year shall be deemed to have been an amount equal to the product of—

(i) the average total wages of all workers for that year, multiplied by

(ii) a fraction—

(I) the numerator of which is the total basic pay of the individual for service performed in the first year thereafter in which such individual performed a full year of service; and

(II) the denominator of which is the average total wages of all workers for the year referred to in subclause (I).

(3) The fraction under this paragraph for any annuitant is a fraction—

(A) the numerator of which is the annuitant's total years of service (rounding a fraction to the nearest whole number, with ½ being rounded to the next higher number), not to exceed the number under subparagraph (B); and

(B) the denominator of which is 40.

(4) For the purpose of this subsection—

(A) the term "benefit computation year" has the meaning provided in section 215(b)(2)(B)(i) of the Social Security Act;

(B) the term "average total wages of all workers", for a year, means the average of the total wages, as defined and computed under section 215(b)(3)(A)(ii)(I) of the Social Security Act for such year; and

(C) the term "service" does not include military service.

(c) An amount under this section shall, for purposes of section 8467, be treated in the same way as an amount computed under section 8415.

(Added Pub. L. 99–335, title I, § 101(a), June 6, 1986, 100 Stat. 533; amended Pub. L. 101–194, title V, § 506(b)(10), Nov. 30, 1989, 103 Stat. 1759; Pub. L. 102–378, § 2(65), Oct. 2, 1992, 106 Stat. 1354.)

REFERENCES IN TEXT

The Social Security Act, referred to in subsecs. (a)(3)(B) and (b)(2), (4)(A), (B), is act Aug. 14, 1935, ch. 531, 49 Stat. 620, as amended. Title II of the Social Security Act is classified generally to subchapter II (§ 401 et seq.) of chapter 7 of Title 42, The Public Health and Welfare. Sections 202, 203, 214, and 215 of the Social Security Act are classified to sections 402, 403, 414, and 415, respectively, of Title 42. For complete classification of this Act to the Code, see section 1305 of Title 42 and Tables.

AMENDMENTS

1992—Subsec. (a)(2). Pub. L. 102–378 inserted period at end.

1989—Subsec. (a)(2). Pub. L. 101–194 substituted ", except that an individual entitled to an annuity under section 8414(a) for failure to be recertified as a senior executive shall be entitled to an annuity supplement without regard to such applicable minimum retirement age" for period at end.

EFFECTIVE DATE OF 1989 AMENDMENT

Amendment by Pub. L. 101–194 effective Jan. 1, 1991, see section 506(d) of Pub. L. 101–194, set out as a note under section 3151 of this title.

SECTION REFERRED TO IN OTHER SECTIONS

This section is referred to in sections 8349, 8420a, 8421a, 8442 of this title; title 22 section 4071d; title 50 section 2154.

§ 8421a. Reductions on account of earnings from work performed while entitled to an annuity supplement

(a) The amount of the annuity supplement to which an individual is entitled under section 8421 for any month (determined without regard to subsection (c) of such section) shall be reduced by the amount of any excess earnings of such individual which are required to be charged to such supplement for such month, as determined under subsection (b).

(b) The amount of an individual's excess earnings shall be charged to months as follows:

(1)(A) There shall be charged to each month of a year under subsection (a) an amount equal to the individual's excess earnings (as determined under paragraph (2) with respect to such year), divided by the number of the individual's supplement entitlement months for such year (as determined under paragraph (3)).

(B) Notwithstanding subparagraph (A), the amount charged to a month under subsection (a) may not exceed the amount of the annuity supplement to which the individual is entitled under section 8421 for such month (determined without regard to subsection (c) of such section).

(2) The excess earnings based on which reductions under subsection (a) shall be made with respect to an individual in a year—

(A) shall be equal to 50 percent of so much of such individual's earnings for the immediately preceding year as exceeds the applicable exempt amount for such preceding year; but

(B) may not exceed the total amount of the annuity supplement payments to which such individual was entitled for such preceding year under section 8421 (determined without regard to subsection (c) of such section, and without regard to this section).

(3)(A) Subject to subparagraph (B), the number of an individual's supplement entitlement months for a year shall be 12.

(B) The number determined under subparagraph (A) shall be reduced so as not to include any month after which such individual ceases to be entitled to an annuity supplement by reason of section 8421(a)(3)(B), relating to cessation of entitlement upon attaining age 62.

(4)(A) For purposes of this section, and except as provided in subparagraph (B), the "earnings" and the "applicable exempt amount" of an individual shall be determined in a manner consistent with applicable provisions of section 203 of the Social Security Act.

(B) For purposes of this section—

(i) in determining the excess earnings of any individual, only earnings attributable to periods during which such individual was entitled to an annuity supplement under section 8421 shall be considered; and

(ii) any earnings attributable to a period before attaining the applicable retirement age under section 8412(h) shall not be considered in determining the excess earnings of an individual who retires under section 8412(d) or (e), or section 8414(c).

(5) Notwithstanding paragraphs (1) through (4), the reduction required by subsection (a)

shall be effective with respect to the annuity supplement payable for each month in the 12-month period beginning on the first day of the seventh month after the end of the calendar year in which the excess earnings were earned.

(c) The Office shall prescribe regulations under which this section shall be applied in the case of a reemployed annuitant.

(Added Pub. L. 99–335, title I, § 101(a), June 6, 1986, 100 Stat. 535; amended Pub. L. 99–556, title I, § 121, Oct. 27, 1986, 100 Stat. 3134; Pub. L. 106–394, § 3(a), Oct. 30, 2000, 114 Stat. 1630.)

REFERENCES IN TEXT

Section 203 of the Social Security Act, referred to in subsec. (b)(4)(A), is classified to section 403 of Title 42, The Public Health and Welfare.

AMENDMENTS

2000—Subsec. (b)(5). Pub. L. 106–394 added par. (5).

1986—Subsecs. (c), (d). Pub. L. 99–556 redesignated subsec. (d) as (c) and struck out former subsec. (c) which read as follows: "If, after an individual ceases to be entitled to an annuity supplement under section 8421 by reason of subsection (a)(3)(B) of such section, any portion of the individual's excess earnings remains outstanding, an amount not to exceed 25 percent of the amount otherwise payable to such individual under this chapter for each month shall be deducted from such monthly payment until the full amount of that outstanding portion has been accounted for. To the extent practicable, reductions under this subsection shall be made by a level percentage."

EFFECTIVE DATE OF 2000 AMENDMENT

Pub. L. 106–394, § 3(b), Oct. 30, 2000, 114 Stat. 1630, provided that: "The amendment made by subsection (a) [amending this section] shall apply with respect to reductions required to be made in calendar years beginning after the date of the enactment of this Act [Oct. 30, 2000]."

SECTION REFERRED TO IN OTHER SECTIONS

This section is referred to in title 22 section 4071d; title 50 section 2154.

§ 8422. Deductions from pay; contributions for military service

(a)(1) The employing agency shall deduct and withhold from basic pay of each employee and Member a percentage of basic pay determined in accordance with paragraph (2).

(2) The percentage to be deducted and withheld from basic pay for any pay period shall be equal to—

(A) the applicable percentage under paragraph (3), minus

(B) the percentage then in effect under section 3101(a) of the Internal Revenue Code of 1986 (relating to rate of tax for old-age, survivors, and disability insurance).

(3) The applicable percentage under this paragraph for civilian service shall be as follows:

Employee	7	January 1, 1987, to December 31, 1998.
	7.25	January 1, 1999, to December 31, 1999.
	7.4	January 1, 2000, to December 31, 2000.
	7	After December 31, 2000.
Congressional employee.	7.5	January 1, 1987, to December 31, 1998.
	7.75	January 1, 1999, to December 31, 1999.

	7.9	January 1, 2000, to December 31, 2000.
	7.5	After December 31, 2000.
Member	7.5	January 1, 1987, to December 31, 1998.
	7.75	January 1, 1999, to December 31, 1999.
	7.9	January 1, 2000, to December 31, 2000.
	8	January 1, 2001, to December 31, 2002.
	7.5	After December 31, 2002.
Law enforcement officer, firefighter, member of the Capitol Police, member of the Supreme Court Police, or air traffic controller.	7.5	January 1, 1987, to December 31, 1998.
	7.75	January 1, 1999, to December 31, 1999.
	7.9	January 1, 2000, to December 31, 2000.
	7.5	After December 31, 2000.
Nuclear materials courier.	7	January 1, 1987, to October 16, 1998.
	7.5	October 17, 1998, to December 31, 1998.
	7.75	January 1, 1999, to December 31, 1999.
	7.9	January 1, 2000, to December 31, 2000.
	7.5	After December 31, 2000.

(b) Each employee or Member is deemed to consent and agree to the deductions under subsection (a). Notwithstanding any law or regulation affecting the pay of an employee or Member, payment less such deductions is a full and complete discharge and acquittance of all claims and demands for regular services during the period covered by the payment, except the right to any benefits under this subchapter, or under subchapter IV or V of this chapter, based on the service of the employee or Member.

(c) The amounts deducted and withheld under this section shall be deposited in the Treasury of the United States to the credit of the Fund under such procedures as the Secretary of the Treasury may prescribe.

(d) Under such regulations as the Office may prescribe, amounts deducted under subsection (a) shall be entered on individual retirement records.

(e)(1)(A) Except as provided in subparagraph (B), and subject to paragraph (6), each employee or Member who has performed military service before the date of the separation on which the entitlement to any annuity under this subchapter, or subchapter V of this chapter, is based may pay, in accordance with such regulations as the Office shall issue, to the agency by which the employee is employed, or, in the case of a Member or a Congressional employee, to the Secretary of the Senate or the Chief Administrative Officer of the House of Representatives, as appropriate, an amount equal to 3 percent of the amount of the basic pay paid under section 204 of title 37 to the employee or Member for each period of military service after December 1956. The amount of such payments shall be based on such evidence of basic pay for military service as the employee or Member may provide, or if the Office determines sufficient evidence has not been so provided to adequately determine basic pay for military service, such payment shall be based on estimates of such basic pay provided to the Office under paragraph (4).

(B) In any case where military service interrupts creditable civilian service under this subchapter and reemployment pursuant to chapter 43 of title 38 occurs on or after August 1, 1990, the deposit payable under this paragraph may not exceed the amount that would have been deducted and withheld under subsection (a)(1) from basic pay during civilian service if the employee had not performed the period of military service.

(2) Any deposit made under paragraph (1) more than two years after the later of—

(A) January 1, 1987; or

(B) the date on which the employee or Member making the deposit first becomes an employee or Member following the period of military service for which such deposit is due,

shall include interest on such amount computed and compounded annually beginning on the date of the expiration of the two-year period. The interest rate that is applicable in computing interest in any year under this paragraph shall be equal to the interest rate that is applicable for such year under section 8334(e).

(3) Any payment received by an agency, the Secretary of the Senate, or the Chief Administrative Officer of the House of Representatives under this subsection shall be immediately remitted to the Office for deposit in the Treasury of the United States to the credit of the Fund.

(4) The Secretary of Defense, the Secretary of Transportation, the Secretary of Commerce, or the Secretary of Health and Human Services, as appropriate, shall furnish such information to the Office as the Office may determine to be necessary for the administration of this subsection.

(5) For the purpose of survivor annuities, deposits authorized by this subsection may also be made by a survivor of an employee or Member.

(6) The percentage of basic pay under section 204 of title 37 payable under paragraph (1), with respect to any period of military service performed during—

(A) January 1, 1999, through December 31, 1999, shall be 3.25 percent; and

(B) January 1, 2000, through December 31, 2000, shall be 3.4 percent.

(f)(1) Each employee or Member who has performed service as a volunteer or volunteer leader under part A of title VIII of the Economic Opportunity Act of 1964, as a full-time volunteer enrolled in a program of at least 1 year's duration under part A, B, or C of title I of the Domestic Volunteer Service Act of 1973, or as a volunteer or volunteer leader under the Peace Corps Act before the date of the separation on which the entitlement to any annuity under this subchapter, or subchapter V of this chapter, is based may pay, in accordance with such regulations as the Office of Personnel Management shall issue, an amount equal to 3 percent of the readjustment allowance paid to the employee or Member under title VIII of the Economic Opportunity Service Act of 1964 or section 5(c) or 6(1) of the Peace Corps Act or the stipend paid to the employee or Member under part A, B, or C of title I of the Domestic Volunteer Service Act of 1973, for each period of service as such a volunteer or volunteer leader. This paragraph shall be subject to paragraph (4).

(2) Any deposit made under paragraph (1) more than 2 years after the later of—

(A) October 1, 1993, or

(B) the date on which the employee or Member making the deposit first becomes an employee or Member,

shall include interest on such amount computed and compounded annually beginning on the date of the expiration of the 2-year period. The interest rate that is applicable in computing interest in any year under this paragraph shall be equal to the interest rate that is applicable for such year under section 8334(e).

(3) The Director of the Peace Corps and the Chief Executive Officer of the Corporation for National and Community Service shall furnish such information to the Office of Personnel Management as the Office may determine to be necessary for the administration of this subsection.

(4) The percentage of the readjustment allowance or stipend (as the case may be) payable under paragraph (1), with respect to any period of volunteer service performed during—

(A) January 1, 1999, through December 31, 1999, shall be 3.25 percent; and

(B) January 1, 2000, through December 31, 2000, shall be 3.4 percent.

(g) A Member who has served in a position in the executive branch for which the rate of basic pay was reduced for the duration of the service of the Member to remove the impediment to the appointment of the Member imposed by article I, section 6, clause 2 of the Constitution, or the survivor of such a Member, may deposit to the credit of the Fund an amount equal to the difference between the amount deducted from the basic pay of the Member during that period of service and the amount that would have been deducted if the rate of basic pay which would otherwise have been in effect during that period had been in effect, plus interest computed under section 8334(e).

(Added Pub. L. 99–335, title I, §101(a), June 6, 1986, 100 Stat. 536; amended Pub. L. 100–238, title I, §104(a), Jan. 8, 1988, 101 Stat. 1746; Pub. L. 103–82, title III, §371(b)(2), Sept. 21, 1993, 107 Stat. 911; Pub. L. 103–353, §5(d), (e)(2), Oct. 13, 1994, 108 Stat. 3174; Pub. L. 104–186, title II, §215(14), Aug. 20, 1996, 110 Stat. 1746; Pub. L. 104–316, title I, §103(g), Oct. 19, 1996, 110 Stat. 3829; Pub. L. 105–33, title VII, §7001(b)(1), Aug. 5, 1997, 111 Stat. 657; Pub. L. 105–61, title V, §516(a)(8), Oct. 10, 1997, 111 Stat. 1307; Pub. L. 105–261, div. C, title XXXI, §3154(i)(1), Oct. 17, 1998, 112 Stat. 2255; Pub. L. 106–65, div. A, title X, §1066(d)(3), Oct. 5, 1999, 113 Stat. 773; Pub. L. 106–346, §101(a) [title V, §505(b)], Oct. 23, 2000, 114 Stat. 1356, 1356A–52; Pub. L. 106–553, §1(a)(2) [title III, §308(c)(3)], Dec. 21, 2000, 114 Stat. 2762, 2762A–87.)

REFERENCES IN TEXT

Section 3101(a) of the Internal Revenue Code of 1986, referred to in subsec. (a)(2)(B), is classified to section 3101(a) of Title 26, Internal Revenue Code.

The Economic Opportunity Act of 1964, referred to in subsec. (f)(1), is Pub. L. 88–452, Aug. 20, 1964, 78 Stat. 508, as amended. Title VIII of the Act probably means title VIII of Pub. L. 88–452 as added by Pub. L. 89–794, title VIII, §801, Nov. 8, 1966, 80 Stat. 1472, and generally revised and amended by Pub. L. 90–222, title I, §110, Dec. 23, 1967, 81 Stat. 722, which was classified generally to subchapter VIII (§2991 et seq.) of chapter 34 of Title 42,

The Public Health and Welfare, prior to its repeal by Pub. L. 93–113, title VI, §603, Oct. 1, 1973, 87 Stat. 417. Part A of title VIII of the Act is part A of title VIII of Pub. L. 88–452 as added by Pub. L. 90–222, §110, which was classified generally to part A (§2992 et seq.) of subchapter VIII of chapter 34 of Title 42, prior to its repeal by Pub. L. 93–113, §603. See sections 4951 et seq. and 5055 of Title 42. For complete classification of this Act to the Code, see Tables.

Parts A, B, and C of title I of the Domestic Volunteer Service Act of 1973, referred to in subsec. (f)(1), are classified to part A (§4951 et seq.), part B (§4971 et seq.), and part C (§4991 et seq.), respectively, of subchapter I of chapter 66 of Title 42.

The Peace Corps Act, referred to in subsec. (f)(1), is Pub. L. 87–293, Sept. 22, 1961, 75 Stat. 612, as amended, which is classified principally to chapter 34 (§2501 et seq.) of Title 22, Foreign Relations and Intercourse. Sections 5(c) and 6(1) of the Act are classified to sections 2504(c) and 2505(1), respectively, of Title 22. For complete classification of this Act to the Code, see Short Title note set out under section 2501 of Title 22 and Tables.

AMENDMENTS

2000—Subsec. (a)(3). Pub. L. 106–553 inserted "member of the Supreme Court Police," after "member of the Capitol Police," in table for law enforcement officer, firefighter, member of the Capitol Police, or air traffic controller.

Pub. L. 106–346, §101(a) [title V, §505(b)(1)], added par. (3) and struck out former par. (3), which set out tables of applicable percentages for employee, Congressional employee, Member, law enforcement officer, firefighter, member of the Capitol Police, air traffic controller, and nuclear materials courier.

Subsec. (e)(6). Pub. L. 106–346, §101(a) [title V, §505(b)(2)], inserted "and" at end of subpar. (A), substituted a period for "; and" at end of subpar. (B), and struck out subpar. (C) which read as follows: "January 1, 2001, through December 31, 2002, shall be 3.5 percent."

Subsec. (f)(4). Pub. L. 106–346, §101(a) [title V, §505(b)(3)], inserted "and" at end of subpar. (A), substituted a period for "; and" at end of subpar. (B), and struck out subpar. (C) which read as follows: "January 1, 2001, through December 31, 2002, shall be 3.5 percent."

1999—Subsec. (a)(3). Pub. L. 106–65, in table for nuclear materials courier, substituted "October 16, 1998" for "the day before the date of the enactment of the Strom Thurmond National Defense Authorization Act for Fiscal Year 1999" and "October 17, 1998" for "The date of the enactment of the Strom Thurmond National Defense Authorization Act for Fiscal Year 1999".

1998—Subsec. (a)(3). Pub. L. 105–261 inserted table for nuclear materials courier.

1997—Subsec. (a)(2), (3). Pub. L. 105–33, §7001(b)(1)(A), added pars. (2) and (3) and struck out former par. (2) which read as follows: "The applicable percentage under this subsection for any pay period shall be—

"(A) in the case of an employee (other than a law enforcement officer, firefighter, air traffic controller, or Congressional employee) a percentage equal to—

"(i) 7 percent, minus

"(ii) the percentage then in effect under section 3101(a) of the Internal Revenue Code of 1986 (relating to rate of tax for old-age, survivors, and disability insurance); and

"(B) in the case of a Member, law enforcement officer, firefighter, air traffic controller, or Congressional employee, a percentage equal to—

"(i) 7½ percent, minus

"(ii) the same percentage as would apply in the case of an employee under subparagraph (A)(ii)."

Subsec. (e)(1)(A). Pub. L. 105–33, §7001(b)(1)(B)(i), inserted "and subject to paragraph (6)," after "Except as provided in subparagraph (B),".

Subsec. (e)(6). Pub. L. 105–33, §7001(b)(1)(B)(ii), added par. (6).

Subsec. (f)(1). Pub. L. 105–33, §7001(b)(1)(C)(i), inserted at end "This paragraph shall be subject to paragraph (4)."

Subsec. (f)(4). Pub. L. 105–33, §7001(b)(1)(C)(ii), added par. (4).

Subsec. (g). Pub. L. 105–61 added subsec. (g).

1996—Subsec. (c). Pub. L. 104–316 substituted "Secretary of the Treasury" for "Comptroller General of the United States".

Subsec. (e)(1)(A), (3). Pub. L. 104–186 substituted "Chief Administrative Officer" for "Clerk".

1994—Subsec. (a)(2)(A)(ii). Pub. L. 103–353, §5(e)(2), substituted "Internal Revenue Code of 1986" for "Internal Revenue Code of 1954".

Subsec. (e)(1). Pub. L. 103–353, §5(d)(1), designated existing provisions as subpar. (A) and substituted "Except as provided in subparagraph (B), each employee" for "Each employee" and added subpar. (B).

Subsec. (e)(2)(B). Pub. L. 103–353, §5(d)(2), inserted before comma at end "following the period of military service for which such deposit is due".

1993—Subsec. (f). Pub. L. 103–82 added subsec. (f).

1988—Subsec. (e)(5). Pub. L. 100–238 added par. (5).

EFFECTIVE DATE OF 2000 AMENDMENTS

Amendment by Pub. L. 106–553 effective on the first day of the first applicable pay period that begins on Dec. 21, 2000, and applicable only to an individual who is employed as a member of the Supreme Court Police after Dec. 21, 2000, see section 1(a)(2) [title III, §308(i), (j)] of Pub. L. 106–553, set out in a Supreme Court Police Retirement note under section 8331 of this title.

Amendment by Pub. L. 106–346 effective upon the close of calendar year 2000 and applicable thereafter, see section 101(a) [title V, §505(i)] of Pub. L. 106–346, set out as a note under section 8334 of this title.

EFFECTIVE DATE OF 1998 AMENDMENT

Amendment by Pub. L. 105–261 effective at the beginning of the first pay period that begins after Oct. 17, 1998, and applicable only to an individual who is employed as a nuclear materials courier, as defined by section 8331(27) or 8401(33) of this title, after Oct. 17, 1998, see section 3154(m), (n) of Pub. L. 105–261, set out as a note under section 8331 of this title.

EFFECTIVE DATE OF 1997 AMENDMENTS

Amendment by Pub. L. 105–61 applicable to any annuity commencing before, on, or after Oct. 10, 1997, and effective with regard to any payment made after the first month following Oct. 10, 1997, see section 516(b) of Pub. L. 105–61, set out as a note under section 8334 of this title.

Amendment by Pub. L. 105–33 effective Oct. 1, 1997, see section 7001(f) of Pub. L. 105–33, set out as a note under section 8334 of this title.

EFFECTIVE DATE OF 1994 AMENDMENT

Amendment by Pub. L. 103–353 effective with respect to reemployments initiated on or after the first day after the 60-day period beginning Oct. 13, 1994, with transition rules, see section 8 of Pub. L. 103–353, set out as an Effective Date note under section 4301 of Title 38, Veterans' Benefits.

EFFECTIVE DATE OF 1993 AMENDMENT

Amendment by Pub. L. 103–82 effective Oct. 1, 1993, and applicable with respect to any individual entitled to an annuity on the basis of a separation from service occurring before, on, or after Oct. 1, 1993, subject to rule relating to annuities based on earlier separations, see sections 371(c) and 392 of Pub. L. 103–82, set out as notes under section 8332 of this title and section 4951 of Title 42, The Public Health and Welfare, respectively.

NO REDUCTION IN AGENCY CONTRIBUTIONS

Pub. L. 105–261, div. C, title XXXI, §3154(i)(2), Oct. 17, 1998, 112 Stat. 2256, provided that: "Contributions under subsections (a) and (b) of section 8423 of title 5, United States Code, shall not be reduced as a result of that portion of the amendment made by paragraph (1)

[amending this section] requiring employee deductions at a rate in excess of 7.5 percent for the period beginning on January 1, 1999, and ending on December 31, 2002."

Section 7001(b)(2) of Pub. L. 105–33 provided that: "Contributions under section 8423(a) and (b) of title 5, United States Code, shall not be reduced as a result of the amendments made under paragraph (1) [amending this section] of this subsection."

SECTION REFERRED TO IN OTHER SECTIONS

This section is referred to in sections 8401, 8411, 8415, 8423, 8468 of this title; title 2 sections 121b, 162b; title 10 section 942; title 22 section 4045; title 28 sections 611, 627; title 40 section 214d; title 42 section 2297h–8; title 50 section 2152.

§ 8423. Government contributions

(a)(1) Each employing agency having any employees or Members subject to section 8422(a) shall contribute to the Fund an amount equal to the sum of—

(A) the product of—

(i) the normal-cost percentage, as determined for employees (other than employees covered by subparagraph (B)), multiplied by

(ii) the aggregate amount of basic pay payable by the agency, for the period involved, to employees (under clause (i)) who are within such agency; and

(B) the product of—

(i) the normal-cost percentage, as determined for Members, Congressional employees, law enforcement officers, members of the Supreme Court Police, firefighters, nuclear materials couriers, air traffic controllers, military reserve technicians, and employees under sections 302 and 303 of the Central Intelligence Agency Retirement Act, multiplied by

(ii) the aggregate amount of basic pay payable by the agency, for the period involved, to employees and Members (under clause (i)) who are within such agency.

(2) In determining any normal-cost percentage to be applied under this subsection, amounts provided for under section 8422 shall be taken into account.

(3) Contributions under this subsection shall be paid—

(A) in the case of law enforcement officers, members of the Supreme Court Police, firefighters, nuclear materials couriers, air traffic controllers, military reserve technicians, and other employees, from the appropriation or fund used to pay such law enforcement officers, members of the Supreme Court Police, firefighters, nuclear materials couriers, air traffic controllers, military reserve technicians, or other employees, respectively;

(B) in the case of elected officials, from an appropriation or fund available for payment of other salaries of the same office or establishment; and

(C) in the case of employees of the legislative branch paid by the Chief Administrative Officer of the House of Representatives, from the applicable accounts of the House of Representatives.

(4) A contribution to the Fund under this subsection shall be deposited under such procedures

as the Comptroller General of the United States may prescribe.

(b)(1) The Office shall compute—

(A) the amount of the supplemental liability of the Fund with respect to individuals other than those to whom subparagraph (B) relates, and

(B) the amount of the supplemental liability of the Fund with respect to current or former employees of the United States Postal Service (and the Postal Rate Commission) and their survivors;

as of the close of each fiscal year beginning after September 30, 1987.

(2) The amount of any supplemental liability computed under paragraph (1)(A) or (1)(B) shall be amortized in 30 equal annual installments, with interest computed at the rate used in the most recent valuation of the System.

(3) At the end of each fiscal year, the Office shall notify—

(A) the Secretary of the Treasury of the amount of the installment computed under this subsection for such year with respect to individuals under paragraph (1)(A); and

(B) the Postmaster General of the United States of the amount of the installment computed under this subsection for such year with respect to individuals under paragraph (1)(B).

(4)(A) Before closing the accounts for a fiscal year, the Secretary of the Treasury shall credit to the Fund, as a Government contribution, out of any money in the Treasury of the United States not otherwise appropriated, the amount under paragraph (3)(A) for such year.

(B) Upon receiving notification under paragraph (3)(B), the United States Postal Service shall pay the amount specified in such notification to the Fund.

(5) For the purpose of carrying out paragraph (1) with respect to any fiscal year, the Office may—

(A) require the Board of Actuaries of the Civil Service Retirement System to make actuarial determinations and valuations, make recommendations, and maintain records in the same manner as provided in section 8347(f); and

(B) use the latest actuarial determinations and valuations made by such Board of Actuaries.

(c) Under regulations prescribed by the Office, the head of an agency may request reconsideration of any amount determined to be payable with respect to such agency under subsection (a) or (b). Any such request shall be referred to the Board of Actuaries of the Civil Service Retirement System. The Board of Actuaries shall review the computations of the Office and may make any adjustment with respect to any such amount which the Board determines appropriate. A determination by the Board of Actuaries under this subsection shall be final.

(Added Pub. L. 99–335, title I, §101(a), June 6, 1986, 100 Stat. 537; amended Pub. L. 102–378, §2(66), Oct. 2, 1992, 106 Stat. 1354; Pub. L. 102–496, title VIII, §803(c), Oct. 24, 1992, 106 Stat. 3253; Pub. L. 104–186, title II, §215(15), Aug. 20, 1996, 110 Stat. 1746; Pub. L. 105–261, div. C, title XXXI,

§3154(j), Oct. 17, 1998, 112 Stat. 2256; Pub. L. 106–553, §1(a)(2) [title III, §308(c)(4)], Dec. 21, 2000, 114 Stat. 2762, 2762A–87.)

References in Text

Sections 302 and 303 of the Central Intelligence Agency Retirement Act, referred to in subsec. (a)(1)(B)(i), are classified to sections 2152 and 2153, respectively, of Title 50, War and National Defense.

Amendments

2000—Subsec. (a). Pub. L. 106–553 inserted "members of the Supreme Court Police," after "law enforcement officers," wherever appearing.

1998—Subsec. (a)(1)(B)(i), (3)(A). Pub. L. 105–261 inserted "nuclear materials couriers," after "firefighters," wherever appearing.

1996—Subsec. (a)(3)(C). Pub. L. 104–186 substituted "Chief Administrative Officer of the House of Representatives, from the applicable accounts of the House of Representatives" for "Clerk of the House of Representatives, from the contingent fund of the House".

1992—Subsec. (a)(1)(B)(i). Pub. L. 102–496 substituted "the Central Intelligence Agency Retirement Act" for "the Central Intelligence Agency Retirement Act of 1964 for Certain Employees".

Pub. L. 102–378 substituted "multiplied" for "multipled".

Effective Date of 2000 Amendment

Amendment by Pub. L. 106–553 effective on the first day of the first applicable pay period that begins on Dec. 21, 2000, and applicable only to an individual who is employed as a member of the Supreme Court Police after Dec. 21, 2000, see section 1(a)(2) [title III, §308(i), (j)] of Pub. L. 106–553, set out in a Supreme Court Police Retirement note under section 8331 of this title.

Effective Date of 1998 Amendment

Amendment by Pub. L. 105–261 effective at the beginning of the first pay period that begins after Oct. 17, 1998, and applicable only to an individual who is employed as a nuclear materials courier, as defined by section 8331(27) or 8401(33) of this title, after Oct. 17, 1998, see section 3154(m), (n) of Pub. L. 105–261, set out as a note under section 8331 of this title.

Effective Date of 1992 Amendment

Amendment by Pub. L. 102–496 effective first day of fourth month beginning after Oct. 24, 1992, see section 805 of Pub. L. 102–496, set out as an Effective Date note under section 2001 of Title 50, War and National Defense.

Section Referred to in Other Sections

This section is referred to in sections 8401, 8411, 8468 of this title; title 2 section 162b; title 22 section 4071f; title 40 section 214d; title 42 section 2297h–8.

§ 8424. Lump-sum benefits; designation of beneficiary; order of precedence

(a) Subject to subsection (b), an employee or Member who—

(1)(A) is separated from the service for at least 31 consecutive days; or

(B) is transferred to a position in which the individual is not subject to this chapter and remains in such a position for at least 31 consecutive days;

(2) files an application with the Office for payment of the lump-sum credit;

(3) is not reemployed in a position in which the individual is subject to this chapter at the time of filing the application; and

(4) will not become eligible to receive an annuity within 31 days after filing the application;

is entitled to be paid the lump-sum credit. Except as provided in section 8420a, payment of the lump-sum credit to an employee or Member voids all annuity rights under this subchapter, and subchapters IV and V of this chapter, based on the service on which the lump-sum credit is based.

(b)(1)(A) Payment of the lump-sum credit under subsection (a) may be made only if the spouse, if any, and any former spouse of the employee or Member are notified of the employee or Member's application.

(B) The Office shall prescribe regulations under which the lump-sum credit shall not be paid without the consent of a spouse or former spouse of the employee or Member where the Office has received such additional information or documentation as the Office may require that—

(i) a court order bars payment of the lump-sum credit in order to preserve the court's ability to award an annuity under section 8445 or 8467; or

(ii) payment of the lump-sum credit would extinguish the entitlement of the spouse or former spouse, under a court order on file with the Office, to a survivor annuity under section 8445 or to any portion of an annuity under section 8467.

(2)(A) Notification of a spouse or former spouse under this subsection shall be made in accordance with such requirements as the Office shall by regulation prescribe.

(B) Under the regulations, the Office may provide that paragraph (1)(A) may be waived with respect to a spouse or former spouse if the employee or Member establishes to the satisfaction of the Office that the whereabouts of such spouse or former spouse cannot be determined.

(3) The Office shall prescribe regulations under which this subsection shall be applied in any case in which the Office receives two or more orders or decrees referred to in paragraph (1)(B)(i).

(c) Under regulations prescribed by the Office, an employee or Member, or a former employee or Member, may designate one or more beneficiaries under this section.

(d) Lump-sum benefits authorized by subsections (e) through (g) shall be paid to the individual or individuals surviving the employee or Member and alive at the date title to the payment arises in the following order of precedence, and the payment bars recovery by any other individual:

First, to the beneficiary or beneficiaries designated by the employee or Member in a signed and witnessed writing received in the Office before the death of such employee or Member. For this purpose, a designation, change, or cancellation of beneficiary in a will or other document not so executed and filed has no force or effect.

Second, if there is no designated beneficiary, to the widow or widower of the employee or Member.

Third, if none of the above, to the child or children of the employee or Member and descendants of deceased children by representation.

Fourth, if none of the above, to the parents of the employee or Member or the survivor of them.

Fifth, if none of the above, to the duly appointed executor or administrator of the estate of the employee or Member.

Sixth, if none of the above, to such other next of kin of the employee or Member as the Office determines to be entitled under the laws of the domicile of the employee or Member at the date of death of the employee or Member.

For the purpose of this subsection, "child" includes a natural child and an adopted child, but does not include a stepchild.

(e) If an employee or Member, or former employee or Member, dies—

(1) without a survivor, or

(2) with a survivor or survivors and the right of all survivors under subchapter IV terminates before a claim for survivor annuity under such subchapter is filed,

the lump-sum credit shall be paid.

(f) If all annuity rights under this chapter (other than under subchapter III of this chapter) based on the service of a deceased employee or Member terminate before the total annuity paid equals the lump-sum credit, the difference shall be paid.

(g) If an annuitant dies, annuity accrued and unpaid shall be paid.

(h) Annuity accrued and unpaid on the termination, except by death, of the annuity of an annuitant or survivor shall be paid to that individual. Annuity accrued and unpaid on the death of a survivor shall be paid in the following order of precedence, and the payment bars recovery by any other person:

First, to the duly appointed executor or administrator of the estate of the survivor.

Second, if there is no executor or administrator, payment may be made, after 30 days from the date of death of the survivor, to such next of kin of the survivor as the Office determines to be entitled under the laws of the domicile of the survivor at the date of death.

(Added Pub. L. 99–335, title I, §101(a), June 6, 1986, 100 Stat. 539; amended Pub. L. 106–361, §3(b), Oct. 27, 2000, 114 Stat. 1402.)

AMENDMENTS

2000—Subsec. (b)(1). Pub. L. 106–361 amended par. (1) generally. Prior to amendment, par. (1) read as follows: "Payment of the lump-sum credit under subsection (a)—

"(A) may be made only if any current spouse and any former spouse of the employee or Member are notified of the application by the employee or Member; and

"(B) in any case in which there is a former spouse, shall be subject to the terms of a court decree of divorce, annulment, or legal separation issued with respect to such former spouse if—

"(i) the decree expressly relates to any portion of the lump-sum credit involved; and

"(ii) payment of the lump-sum credit would affect any right or interest of the former spouse with respect to a survivor annuity under section 8445, or to any portion of an annuity under section 8467."

SECTION REFERRED TO IN OTHER SECTIONS

This section is referred to in sections 8402, 8433, 8442, 8468 of this title; title 50 section 2154.

§ 8425. Mandatory separation

(a) An air traffic controller who is otherwise eligible for immediate retirement under section

8412(e) shall be separated from the service on the last day of the month in which that air traffic controller becomes 56 years of age or completes 20 years of service if then over that age. The Secretary, under such regulations as the Secretary may prescribe, may exempt a controller having exceptional skills and experience as a controller from the automatic separation provisions of this subsection until that controller becomes 61 years of age. The Secretary shall notify the controller in writing of the date of separation at least 60 days before that date. Action to separate the controller is not effective, without the consent of the controller, until the last day of the month in which the 60-day notice expires.

(b) A firefighter who is otherwise eligible for immediate retirement under section 8412(d) shall be separated from the service on the last day of the month in which such firefighter becomes 55 years of age or completes 20 years of service if then over that age. A law enforcement officer or nuclear materials courier who is otherwise eligible for immediate retirement under section 8412(d) shall be separated from the service on the last day of the month in which that law enforcement officer or nuclear materials courier becomes 57 years of age or completes 20 years of service if then over that age. If the head of the agency judges that the public interest so requires, that agency head may exempt such an employee from automatic separation under this subsection until that employee becomes 60 years of age. The employing office shall notify the employee in writing of the date of separation at least 60 days before that date. Action to separate the employee is not effective, without the consent of the employee, until the last day of the month in which the 60-day notice expires.

(c) A member of the Capitol Police who is otherwise eligible for immediate retirement under section 8412(d) shall be separated from the service on the last day of the month in which such member becomes 57 years of age or completes 20 years of service if then over that age. The Capitol Police Board, when in its judgment the public interest so requires, may exempt such a member from automatic separation under this subsection until that member becomes 60 years of age. The Board shall notify the member in writing of the date of separation at least 60 days before that date. Action to separate the member is not effective, without the consent of the member, until the last day of the month in which the 60-day notice expires.

(d) A member of the Supreme Court Police who is otherwise eligible for immediate retirement under section 8412(d) shall be separated from the service on the last day of the month in which such member becomes 57 years of age or completes 20 years of service if then over that age. The Marshal of the Supreme Court of the United States, when in his judgment the public interest so requires, may exempt such a member from automatic separation under this subsection until that member becomes 60 years of age. The Marshal shall notify the member in writing of the date of separation at least 60 days before the date. Action to separate the member is not effective, without the consent of the member, until the last day of the month in which the 60-day notice expires.

(e) The President, by Executive order, may exempt an employee (other than a member of the Capitol Police or Supreme Court Police) from automatic separation under this section if the President determines the public interest so requires.

(Added Pub. L. 99–335, title I, §101(a), June 6, 1986, 100 Stat. 540; amended Pub. L. 101–428, §3(b)(1)(A), (2), Oct. 15, 1990, 104 Stat. 929, 930; Pub. L. 101–509, title V, §529 [title IV, §409(b)], Nov. 5, 1990, 104 Stat. 1427, 1468; Pub. L. 102–378, §2(67), Oct. 2, 1992, 106 Stat. 1354; Pub. L. 103–283, title III, §307(b)(1), July 22, 1994, 108 Stat. 1441; Pub. L. 105–261, div. C, title XXXI, §3154(k), Oct. 17, 1998, 112 Stat. 2256; Pub. L. 106–553, §1(a)(2) [title III, §308(c)(5)], Dec. 21, 2000, 114 Stat. 2762, 2762A–87.)

AMENDMENTS

2000—Subsec. (d). Pub. L. 106–553, §1(a)(2) [title III, §308(c)(5)(A)], added subsec. (d). Former subsec. (d) redesignated (e).

Subsec. (e). Pub. L. 106–553, §1(a)(2) [title III, §308(c)(5)], redesignated subsec. (d) as (e) and substituted "Police or Supreme Court Police)" for "Police)".

1998—Subsec. (b). Pub. L. 105–261, in second sentence, inserted "or nuclear materials courier" after "law enforcement officer" in two places.

1994—Subsec. (b). Pub. L. 103–283, §307(b)(1)(A), struck out "member of the Capitol Police or" before "firefighter who is" and "member or" before "firefighter becomes" in first sentence.

Subsecs. (c), (d). Pub. L. 103–283, §307(b)(1)(B), (C), added subsec. (c) and redesignated former subsec. (c) as (d).

1992—Subsec. (b). Pub. L. 102–378 amended first sentence generally and, in second sentence, substituted "becomes" for "become". Prior to amendment, first sentence read as follows: "A law enforcement officer, member of the Capitol Police, or firefighter who is otherwise eligible for immediate retirement under section 8412(d) shall be separated from the service on the last day of the month in which that law enforcement officer, member of the Capitol Police, or firefighter becomes 55 years of age or completes 20 years of service if then over that age."

1990—Subsec. (b). Pub. L. 101–509, §529 [title IV, §409(b)(1)], which directed the amendment of subsec. (b) by striking out "law enforcement officer or" wherever appearing in first sentence, could not be executed because of a prior amendment by Pub. L. 101–428, §3(b)(1)(A), see below.

Pub. L. 101–509, §529 [title IV, §409(b)(2)], inserted after first sentence "A law enforcement officer who is otherwise eligible for immediate retirement under section 8412(d) shall be separated from the service on the last day of the month in which that law enforcement officer become 57 years of age or completes 20 years of service if then over that age."

Pub. L. 101–428, §3(b)(1)(A), substituted "officer, member of the Capitol Police, or" for "officer or" in two places.

Subsec. (c). Pub. L. 101–428, §3(b)(2), inserted "(other than a member of the Capitol Police)" after "employee".

EFFECTIVE DATE OF 2000 AMENDMENT

Amendment by Pub. L. 106–553 effective on the first day of the first applicable pay period that begins on Dec. 21, 2000, and applicable only to an individual who is employed as a member of the Supreme Court Police after Dec. 21, 2000, see section 1(a)(2) [title III, §308(i), (j)] of Pub. L. 106–553, set out in a Supreme Court Police Retirement note under section 8331 of this title.

EFFECTIVE DATE OF 1998 AMENDMENT

Amendment by Pub. L. 105–261 effective 1 year after Oct. 17, 1998, and applicable only to an individual who is employed as a nuclear materials courier, as defined by section 8331(27) or 8401(33) of this title, after Oct. 17, 1998, see section 3154(m), (n) of Pub. L. 105–261, set out as a note under section 8331 of this title.

EFFECTIVE DATE OF 1992 AMENDMENT

Amendment by Pub. L. 102–378 effective Nov. 5, 1990, see section 9(b)(6) of Pub. L. 102–378, set out as a note under section 6303 of this title.

EXCEPTION TO AUTOMATIC SEPARATION OF MEMBERS OF CAPITOL POLICE

Section 3(b)(1)(B) of Pub. L. 101–428 provided that: "Nothing in section 8425(b) of title 5, United States Code, as amended by subparagraph (A), shall require the automatic separation of any member of the Capitol Police before the end of the 2-year period beginning on the date of enactment of this Act [Oct. 15, 1990]."

SECTION REFERRED TO IN OTHER SECTIONS

This section is referred to in section 8415 of this title.

SUBCHAPTER III—THRIFT SAVINGS PLAN

SUBCHAPTER REFERRED TO IN OTHER SECTIONS

This subchapter is referred to in sections 8116, 8351, 8402, 8424, 8461, 8471, 8472, 8473, 8474, 8477 of this title; title 2 section 162b; title 10 sections 945, 2467; title 22 sections 4069, 4071h; title 26 sections 3121, 7701; title 28 sections 178, 377, 611, 627; title 31 section 9503; title 37 section 211; title 39 section 1005; title 40 section 214d; title 50 section 2154.

§ 8431. Certain transfers to be treated as a separation

(a) For purposes of this subchapter, separation from Government employment includes a transfer from a position that is subject to one of the retirement systems described in subsection (b) to a position that is not subject to any of them.

(b) The retirement systems described in this subsection are—

(1) the retirement system under this chapter;

(2) the retirement system under subchapter III of chapter 83; and

(3) any other retirement system under which individuals may contribute to the Thrift Savings Fund through withholdings from pay.

(Added Pub. L. 106–168, title II, § 203(a)(1), Dec. 12, 1999, 113 Stat. 1820.)

PRIOR PROVISIONS

A prior section 8431, added Pub. L. 99–335, title I, § 101(a), June 6, 1986, 100 Stat. 541; amended Pub. L. 101–509, title V, § 529 [title I, § 101(b)(6)(B)], Nov. 5, 1990, 104 Stat. 1427, 1440, provided a definition of "basic pay" for this subchapter, prior to repeal by Pub. L. 104–208, div. A, title I, § 101(f) [title VI, § 659 [title II, §§ 206(a)(2), 207]], Sept. 30, 1996, 110 Stat. 3009–314, 3009–372, 3009–378, effective Sept. 30, 1996.

EFFECTIVE DATE

Pub. L. 106–168, title II, § 203(c), Dec. 12, 1999, 113 Stat. 1820, provided that: "The amendments made by this section [enacting this section and amending section 8351 of this title] shall apply with respect to transfers occurring before, on, or after the date of the enactment of this Act [Dec. 12, 1999], except that, for purposes of applying such amendments with respect to any transfer occurring before such date of enactment, the date of such transfer shall be considered to be the date of the enactment of this Act. The Executive Director (within the meaning of section 8401(13) of title 5, United States Code) may prescribe any regulations necessary to carry out this subsection."

SECTION REFERRED TO IN OTHER SECTIONS

This section is referred to in section 8351 of this title.

§ 8432. Contributions

(a)(1) An employee or Member may contribute to the Thrift Savings Fund in any pay period, pursuant to an election under subsection (b), an amount not to exceed the maximum percentage of such employee's or Member's basic pay for such pay period allowable under paragraph (2). Contributions under this subsection pursuant to such an election shall, with respect to each pay period for which such election remains in effect, be made in accordance with a program of regular contributions provided in regulations prescribed by the Executive Director.

(2) The maximum percentage allowable under this paragraph shall be determined in accordance with the following table:

In the case of a pay period beginning in fiscal year:	The maximum percentage allowable is:
2001	11
2002	12
2003	13
2004	14
2005	15
2006 or thereafter	100.

(b)(1)(A) The Executive Director shall prescribe regulations under which employees and Members shall be afforded a reasonable period every 6 months to elect to make contributions under subsection (a), to modify the amount to be contributed under such subsection, or to terminate such contributions. An election to make such contributions shall remain in effect until modified or terminated.

(B) The amount to be contributed pursuant to an election under subparagraph (A) (or any election allowable by virtue of paragraph (4)) shall be the percentage of basic pay or amount designated by the employee or Member.

(2) Under the regulations—

(A) an employee or Member who has not previously been eligible to make an election under this subsection shall not become so eligible until the second period (described in paragraph (1)) beginning after the date of commencing service as an employee or Member;

(B) an employee or Member whose appointment or election to a position or office in the Federal Government follows a previous period of service during which that individual met the requirements of subparagraph (A) shall be eligible to make an election under this subsection notwithstanding any period of separation;

(C) an employee or Member who elects under subparagraph (D) to terminate contributions shall not again become eligible to make an election under this subsection until the second period (described in paragraph (1)) commencing after the election to terminate; and

(D) an election to terminate may be made under this subparagraph at any time other than during a period afforded under paragraph (1).

(3) An employee or Member who elects to become subject to this chapter under section 301 of the Federal Employees' Retirement System Act

of 1986 may make the first election for the purpose of subsection (a) during the period prescribed for such purpose by the Executive Director. The period prescribed by the Executive Director shall commence on the date on which the employee or Member makes the election to become subject to this chapter.

(4) The Executive Director shall prescribe such regulations as may be necessary to carry out the following:

(A) Notwithstanding subparagraph (A) of paragraph (2), an employee or Member described in such subparagraph shall be afforded a reasonable opportunity to first make an election under this subsection beginning on the date of commencing service or, if that is not administratively feasible, beginning on the earliest date thereafter that such an election becomes administratively feasible, as determined by the Executive Director.

(B) An employee or Member described in subparagraph (B) of paragraph (2) shall be afforded a reasonable opportunity to first make an election under this subsection (based on the appointment or election described in such subparagraph) beginning on the date of commencing service pursuant to such appointment or election or, if that is not administratively feasible, beginning on the earliest date thereafter that such an election becomes administratively feasible, as determined by the Executive Director.

(C) Notwithstanding the preceding provisions of this paragraph, contributions under paragraphs (1) and (2) of subsection (c) shall not be payable with respect to any pay period before the earliest pay period for which such contributions would otherwise be allowable under this subsection if this paragraph had not been enacted.

(D) Sections 8351(a)(2), 8440a(a)(2), 8440b(a)(2), 8440c(a)(2), and 8440d(a)(2) shall be applied in a manner consistent with the purposes of subparagraphs (A) and (B), to the extent those subparagraphs can be applied with respect thereto.

(E) Nothing in this paragraph shall affect paragraph (3).

(c)(1)(A) At the time prescribed by the Executive Director, but no later than 12 days after the end of the pay period that includes the first date on which an employee or Member may make contributions under subsection (a) (without regard to whether the employee or Member has elected to make such contributions during such pay period), and within such time as the Executive Director may prescribe with respect to succeeding pay periods (but no later than 12 days after the end of each such pay period), the employing agency shall contribute to the Thrift Savings Fund for the benefit of such employee or Member the amount equal to 1 percent of the basic pay of such employee or Member for such pay period.

(B) In the case of each employee or Member who is an employee or Member on January 1, 1987, and continues as an employee or Member without a break in service through April 1, 1987, the employing agency shall contribute to the Thrift Savings Fund for the benefit of such employee or Member the amount equal to 1 percent of the total basic pay paid to such employee or Member for that period of service.

(C) If an employee or Member—
(i) is an employee or Member on January 1, 1987;
(ii) separates from Government employment before April 1, 1987; and
(iii) before separation, completes the number of years of civilian service applicable to such employee or Member under subparagraph (A) or (B) of subsection (g)(2),

the employing agency shall contribute to the Thrift Savings Fund for the benefit of such employee or Member the amount equal to 1 percent of the total basic pay paid to such employee or Member for service performed on or after January 1, 1987, and before the date of the separation.

(2)(A) In addition to contributions made under paragraph (1), the employing agency of an employee or Member who contributes to the Thrift Savings Fund under subsection (a) for any pay period shall make a contribution to the Thrift Savings Fund for the benefit of such employee or Member. The employing agency's contribution shall be made within such time as the Executive Director may prescribe, but no later than 12 days after the end of each such pay period.

(B) The amount contributed under subparagraph (A) by an employing agency with respect to a contribution of an employee or Member during any pay period shall be the amount equal to the sum of—

(i) such portion of the total amount of the employee's or Member's contribution as does not exceed 3 percent of such employee's or Member's basic pay for such period; and

(ii) one-half of such portion of the amount of the employee's or Member's contribution as exceeds 3 percent, but does not exceed 5 percent, of such employee's or Member's basic pay for such pay period.

(C) Notwithstanding subparagraph (B), the amount contributed under subparagraph (A) by an employing agency with respect to any contribution made by an employee or Member during any pay period which begins after the date on which such employee or Member makes an election under subsection (b)(4) and before July 1, 1987, shall be the amount equal to the sum of—

(i) two times such portion of the total amount of the employee's or Member's contribution as does not exceed 3 percent of such employee's or Member's basic pay for such pay period; and

(ii) such portion of the total amount of the employee's or Member's contributions as exceeds 3 percent, but does not exceed 5 percent, of such employee's or Member's basic pay for such pay period.

(3)(A) There shall be contributed to the Thrift Savings Fund on behalf of each employee or Member described in subparagraph (B) the amount determined under subparagraph (C).

(B) An employee or Member referred to in subparagraph (A) is an employee or Member who—
(i) is an employee or Member on January 1, 1987;
(ii) has creditable service described in section 8411(b)(2) of this title; and

(iii) has not received a refund of the amount of the retirement deductions made with respect to such service under section 204 of the Federal Employees' Retirement Contribution Temporary Adjustment Act of 1983.

(C) The amount referred to in subparagraph (A) in the case of an employee or Member is equal to the sum of—

(i) 1 percent of the total basic pay paid to such employee or Member for service described in section 8411(b)(2) of this title; and

(ii) interest on such amount computed with respect to such service in the manner provided in paragraphs (2) and (3) of section 8334(e) of this title.

(D) The Secretary of the Treasury shall credit to the Thrift Savings Fund, out of any sums in the Treasury not otherwise appropriated, the amounts determined by the Director to be necessary to carry out this paragraph.

(d) Notwithstanding any other provision of this section, no contribution may be made under this section for any year to the extent that such contribution, when added to prior contributions for such year, exceeds any limitation under section 415 of the Internal Revenue Code of 1986. However, no contribution made under subsection (c)(3) shall be subject to, or taken into account, for purposes of the preceding sentence.

(e) The sums required to be contributed to the Thrift Savings Fund by an employing agency under subsection (c) for the benefit of an employee or Member shall be paid from the appropriation or fund available to such agency for payment of salaries of the employee's or Member's office or establishment. When an employee or Member in the legislative branch is paid by the Chief Administrative Officer of the House of Representatives, the Chief Administrative Officer may pay from the applicable accounts of the House of Representatives the contribution that otherwise would be contributed from the appropriation or fund used to pay the employee or Member.

(f) Amounts contributed by an employee or Member under subsection (a) and amounts contributed with respect to such employee or Member under subsection (c) shall be deposited in the Thrift Savings Fund to the credit of that employee's or Member's account in accordance with such procedures as the Secretary of the Treasury may, in consultation with the Executive Director, prescribe in regulations.

(g)(1) Except as otherwise provided in this subsection, all contributions made under this section shall be fully nonforfeitable when made.

(2) Contributions made for the benefit of an employee under subsection (c)(1) and all earnings attributable to such contributions shall be forfeited if the employee separates from Government employment before completing—

(A) 2 years of civilian service in the case of an employee who, at the time of separation, is serving in—

(i) a position in the Senior Executive Service as a noncareer appointee (as defined in section 3132(a)(7) of this title);

(ii) a position listed in section 5312, 5313, 5314, 5315, or 5316 of this title or a position placed in level IV or V of the Executive Schedule under section 5317 of this title; or

(iii) a position in the Executive branch which is excepted from the competitive service by the Office by reason of the confidential and policy-determining character of the position; or

(B) 3 years of civilian service in the case of an employee who is not serving in a position described in subparagraph (A) at the time of separation.

(3) Contributions made for the benefit of a Member or Congressional employee under subsection (c)(1) and all earnings attributable to such contributions shall be forfeited if the Member or Congressional employee separates from Government employment before completing 2 years of civilian service.

(4) Nothing in paragraph (2) or (3) shall cause the forfeiture of any contributions made for the benefit of an employee, Member, or Congressional employee under subsection (c)(1), or any earnings attributable thereto, if such employee, Member, or Congressional employee is not separated from Government employment as of date of death.

(5) Notwithstanding any other provision of law, contributions made by the Government for the benefit of an employee or Member under subsection (c), and all earnings attributable to such contributions, shall be forfeited if the annuity of the employee or Member, or that of a survivor or beneficiary, is forfeited under subchapter II of chapter 83.

(h) No transfers or contributions may be made to the Thrift Savings Fund except as provided in this chapter or section 8351 of this title.

(i)(1) This subsection applies to any employee—

(A) to whom section 8432b applies; and

(B) who, during the period of such employee's absence from civilian service (as referred to in section 8432b(b)(2)(B))—

(i) is eligible to make an election described in subsection (b)(1); or

(ii) would be so eligible but for having either elected to terminate individual contributions to the Thrift Savings Fund within 2 months before commencing military service or separated in order to perform military service.

(2) The Executive Director shall prescribe regulations to ensure that any employee to whom this subsection applies shall, within a reasonable time after being restored or reemployed (in the manner described in section 8432b(a)(2)), be afforded the opportunity to make, for purposes of this section, any election which would be allowable during a period described in subsection (b)(1)(A).

(j)(1) For the purpose of this subsection—

(A) the term "eligible rollover distribution" has the meaning given such term by section 402(c)(4) of the Internal Revenue Code of 1986; and

(B) the term "qualified trust" has the meaning given such term by section 402(c)(8) of the Internal Revenue Code of 1986.

(2) An employee or Member may contribute to the Thrift Savings Fund an eligible rollover that a qualified trust could accept under the Internal

Revenue Code of 1986. A contribution made under this subsection shall be made in the form described in section 401(a)(31) of the Internal Revenue Code of 1986. In the case of an eligible rollover distribution, the maximum amount transferred to the Thrift Savings Fund shall not exceed the amount which would otherwise have been included in the employee's or Member's gross income for Federal income tax purposes.

(3) The Executive Director shall prescribe regulations to carry out this subsection.

(Added Pub. L. 99–335, title I, § 101(a), June 6, 1986, 100 Stat. 541; amended Pub. L. 99–509, title VI, § 6001(a)(1), (2), Oct. 21, 1986, 100 Stat. 1929, 1930; Pub. L. 100–20, § 1(b), Apr. 7, 1987, 101 Stat. 265; Pub. L. 100–238, title I, §§ 114, 115, 121, Jan. 8, 1988, 101 Stat. 1751, 1752; Pub. L. 103–353, §§ 4(c), 5(e)(3), Oct. 13, 1994, 108 Stat. 3172, 3174; Pub. L. 104–93, title III, § 304(a), Jan. 6, 1996, 109 Stat. 965; Pub. L. 104–186, title II, § 215(16), Aug. 20, 1996, 110 Stat. 1746; Pub. L. 104–316, title I, § 103(g), Oct. 19, 1996, 110 Stat. 3829; Pub. L. 106–361, §§ 1(a), 2(a), (b)(1)–(3), Oct. 27, 2000, 114 Stat. 1400, 1401; Pub. L. 106–554, § 1(a)(4) [div. B, title I, § 138(a)(1)], Dec. 21, 2000, 114 Stat. 2763, 2763A–233.)

REFERENCES IN TEXT

Section 301 of the Federal Employees' Retirement System Act of 1986 [Pub. L. 99–335], referred to in subsec. (b)(3), is set out as a note under section 8331 of this title.

Section 204 of the Federal Employees' Retirement Contribution Temporary Adjustment Act of 1983 [Pub. L. 98–168], referred to in subsec. (c)(3)(B)(iii), is set out as a note under section 8331 of this title.

The Internal Revenue Code of 1986, referred to in subsecs. (d) and (j), is classified generally to Title 26, Internal Revenue Code.

AMENDMENTS

2000—Subsec. (a). Pub. L. 106–554 designated existing provisions as par. (1), substituted "the maximum percentage of such employee's or Member's basic pay for such pay period allowable under paragraph (2)." for "10 percent of such individual's basic pay for such period.", and added par. (2).

Pub. L. 106–361, § 2(b)(1), substituted "(b)" for "(b)(1)" and "Contributions under this subsection pursuant to such an election shall, with respect to each pay period for which such election remains in effect, be made in accordance with a program of regular contributions provided in regulations prescribed by the Executive Director" for "Contributions made under this subsection during any 6-month period for which an election period is provided under subsection (b)(1) shall be made each pay period during such 6-month period pursuant to a program of regular contributions provided in regulations prescribed by the Executive Director".

Subsec. (b)(1)(B). Pub. L. 106–361, § 2(b)(2), inserted "(or any election allowable by virtue of paragraph (4))" after "subparagraph (A)".

Subsec. (b)(3). Pub. L. 106–361, § 2(b)(3), substituted "An" for "Notwithstanding paragraph (2)(A), an".

Subsec. (b)(4). Pub. L. 106–361, § 2(a), amended par. (4) generally. Prior to amendment, par. (4) read as follows:

"(A) Notwithstanding paragraph (2)(A), an employee or Member who is an employee or Member on January 1, 1987, and continues as an employee or Member without a break in service through April 1, 1987, may make the first election for the purpose of subsection (a) during the election period prescribed for such purpose by the Executive Director. The Executive Director shall prescribe an election period for such purpose which shall commence on April 1, 1987. An election by such an employee or Member during that election period shall be effective on the first day of the employee's or Mem-

ber's first pay period which begins after the date on which the employee or Member makes that election.

"(B) Notwithstanding subsection (a), the maximum amount that an employee or Member may contribute during any pay period which begins on or after April 1, 1987, and before October 1, 1987, pursuant to an election made during the election period provided under subparagraph (A) is the amount equal to 15 percent of such individual's basic pay for such pay period."

Subsec. (j). Pub. L. 106–361, § 1(a), added subsec. (j).

1996—Subsec. (e). Pub. L. 104–186 substituted "Chief Administrative Officer of the House of Representatives, the Chief Administrative Officer may pay from the applicable accounts" for "Clerk of the House of Representatives, the Clerk may pay from the contingent fund".

Subsec. (f). Pub. L. 104–316 substituted "Secretary of the Treasury" for "Comptroller General of the United States".

Subsec. (g)(5). Pub. L. 104–93 added par. (5).

1994—Subsec. (d). Pub. L. 103–353, § 5(e)(3), substituted "Internal Revenue Code of 1986" for "Internal Revenue Code of 1954".

Subsec. (i). Pub. L. 103–353, § 4(c), added subsec. (i).

1988—Subsec. (c)(1)(A). Pub. L. 100–238, § 121(a), substituted "At the time prescribed by the Executive Director, but no later than 12 days after the end of" for "At the end of" and "within such time as the Executive Director may prescribe with respect to succeeding pay periods (but no later than 12 days after the end of each such pay period)" for "at the end of each succeeding pay period".

Subsec. (c)(2)(A). Pub. L. 100–238, § 121(b), substituted "within such time as the Executive Director may prescribe, but no later than 12 days after the end of each such pay period" for "at the end of such pay period".

Subsec. (d). Pub. L. 100–238, § 114, inserted at end "However, no contribution made under subsection (c)(3) shall be subject to, or taken into account, for purposes of the preceding sentence."

Subsec. (g)(1). Pub. L. 100–238, § 115(1), substituted "Except as otherwise provided in this subsection" for "Except as provided in paragraphs (2) and (3)".

Subsec. (g)(4). Pub. L. 100–238, § 115(2), added par. (4).

1987—Subsec. (b)(4)(A). Pub. L. 100–20 substituted "Notwithstanding paragraph (2)(A), an employee or Member who is an employee or Member on January 1, 1987, and continues as an employee or Member without a break in service through April 1, 1987, may make the first election for the purpose of subsection (a) during the election period prescribed for such purpose by the Executive Director" for "Notwithstanding paragraph (2)(A), an employee or Member who is an employee or Member on January 1, 1987, continues as an employee or Member without a break in service through April 1, 1987, and has creditable service described in section 8411(b)(2) of this title may make the first election for the purpose of subsection (a) during the election period prescribed for such purpose by the Executive Director".

1986—Subsec. (b)(4). Pub. L. 99–509, § 6001(a)(1), designated existing provisions as subpar. (A), inserted "continues as an employee or Member without a break in service through April 1, 1987," substituted "April 1, 1987" for "January 1, 1987", substituted "the date on which the employee or Member makes that election" for "the last day of that election period", and added subpar. (B).

Subsec. (c)(1). Pub. L. 99–509, § 6001(a)(2)(A), designated existing provisions as subpar. (A) and added subpars. (B) and (C).

Subsec. (c)(2)(C). Pub. L. 99–509, § 6001(a)(2)(B), added subpar. (C).

EFFECTIVE DATE OF 2000 AMENDMENT

Pub. L. 106–361, § 1(b), Oct. 27, 2000, 114 Stat. 1400, provided that: "The amendment made by this section [amending this section] shall take effect at the earliest practicable date after September 30, 2000, as determined by the Executive Director in regulations."

Pub. L. 106–361, § 2(c)(1), Oct. 27, 2000, 114 Stat. 1401, provided that: "The amendments made by this section [amending this section and sections 8439, 8440a, and 8440d of this title] shall take effect at the earliest practicable date after September 30, 2000, as determined by the Executive Director in regulations."

EFFECTIVE DATE OF 1996 AMENDMENT

Section 304(b) of Pub. L. 104–93 provided that: "The amendment made by subsection (a) [amending this section] shall apply to offenses upon which the requisite annuity forfeitures are based occurring on or after the date of the enactment of this Act [Jan. 6, 1996]."

EFFECTIVE DATE OF 1994 AMENDMENT

Amendment by section 4(c) of Pub. L. 103–353 effective Oct. 13, 1994, and applicable to any employee whose release from military service, discharge from hospitalization, or other similar event making the individual eligible to seek restoration or reemployment under chapter 43 of Title 38, Veterans' Benefits, occurs on or after Aug. 2, 1990, with special rules for applying amendment to employees restored or reemployed before effective date, see section 4(e), (f) of Pub. L. 103–353, set out as an Effective Date note under section 8432b of this title.

Amendment by section 5(e)(3) of Pub. L. 103–353 effective with respect to reemployments initiated on or after the first day after the 60-day period beginning Oct. 13, 1994, with transition rules, see section 8 of Pub. L. 103–353, set out as an Effective Date note under section 4301 of Title 38.

EFFECTIVE DATE OF 1986 AMENDMENT

Section 6001(f) of Pub. L. 99–509 provided that: "This section [amending this section and section 8472 of this title, enacting provisions set out as notes under this section, and amending provisions set out as a note under section 8351 of this title], other than subsection (d) [set out below], and the amendments made by this section shall take effect on January 1, 1987."

REGULATIONS

Section 6001(d) of Pub. L. 99–509 provided that: "The Executive Director of the Federal Retirement Thrift Investment Board may prescribe regulations to carry out subsections (a), (b), and (c) [amending this section, enacting provisions set out as notes under this section, and amending provisions set out as a note under section 8351 of this title] and the amendments made by subsections (a) and (b)."

SAVINGS PROVISIONS

Pub. L. 106–361, §2(c)(2), Oct. 27, 2000, 114 Stat. 1401, provided that: "Notwithstanding any other provision of this section [amending this section and sections 8439, 8440a, and 8440d of this title and enacting provisions set out as a note under this section], until the amendments made by this section take effect [see Effective Date of 2000 Amendment note above], title 5, United States Code, shall be applied as if this section had not been enacted."

ELIGIBILITY OF CERTAIN INDIVIDUALS TO PARTICIPATE IN THRIFT SAVINGS PLAN

Section 125 of Pub. L. 100–238 provided that:

"(a) DEFINITIONS.—For purposes of this section—

"(1) the term 'Executive Director' means the Executive Director under section 8474 of title 5, United States Code; and

"(2) the term 'Thrift Savings Plan' refers to the program under subchapter III of chapter 84 of title 5, United States Code.

"(b) REGULATIONS.—

"(1) IN GENERAL.—The Executive Director shall prescribe regulations relating to participation in the Thrift Savings Plan by an individual described in subsection (c).

"(2) SPECIFIC MATTERS TO BE INCLUDED.—Under the regulations—

"(A) in computing a percentage of basic pay to determine an amount to be contributed to the Thrift Savings Fund, the rate of basic pay to be used shall be the same as that used in computing any amount which the individual involved is otherwise required, as a condition for participating in the Civil Service Retirement System or the Federal Employees' Retirement System (as the case may be), to contribute to the Civil Service Retirement and Disability Fund; and

"(B) an employing authority which would not otherwise make contributions to the Thrift Savings Fund shall be allowed, with respect to any individual under subsection (c) who is serving under such authority, and at the sole discretion of such authority, to make any contributions on behalf of such individual which would be permitted or required under the provisions of section 8432(c) of title 5, United States Code, if such authority were the individual's employing agency under such provisions.

"(c) APPLICABILITY.—This section applies with respect to—

"(1) any individual participating in the Civil Service Retirement System or the Federal Employees' Retirement System as—

"(A) an individual who has entered on approved leave without pay to serve as a full-time officer or employee of an organization composed primarily of employees (as defined by section 8331(1) or 8401(11) of title 5, United States Code);

"(B) an individual assigned from a Federal agency to a State or local government under subchapter VI of chapter 33 of title 5, United States Code; or

"(C) an individual appointed or otherwise assigned to one of the cooperative extension services, as defined by section 1404(5) of the National Agricultural Research, Extension, and Teaching Policy Act of 1977 (7 U.S.C. 3103(5)); and

"(2) any individual who is participating in the Civil Service Retirement System as a result of a provision of law described in section 8347(o).

"(d) EFFECTIVE DATE.—

"(1) IN GENERAL.—Except as provided in paragraph (2), the regulations prescribed under this section shall become effective in accordance with the provisions of such regulations.

"(2) EXCEPTION.—The regulations prescribed under this section shall, with respect to individuals under subsection (c)(1)(C), be effective as of January 1, 1987."

CONTRIBUTIONS TO THRIFT SAVINGS FUND

Section 6001(a)(3) of Pub. L. 99–509 directed that contributions made to Thrift Savings Fund under 5 U.S.C. 8432(c)(1)(B), (C) and (3) be made as soon as practicable during the 15-day period which began on Apr. 1, 1987.

INAPPLICABILITY OF LIMITATION ON NUMBER OF ELECTIONS WITHIN A SIX-MONTH PERIOD

Section 6001(c) of Pub. L. 99–509 provided that the requirement that contributions be made for a 6-month period after an election, as provided in 5 U.S.C. 8432(a), did not apply to contributions made pursuant to an election made during the period provided in 5 U.S.C. 8432(b)(4) or 206(b) of the Federal Employees' Retirement System Act of 1986; that the first election period prescribed under 5 U.S.C. 8432(b)(1) commence on July 1, 1987; and that each employee or Member who made such an election could make an election under 5 U.S.C. 8432(b)(1) during the election period that began on July 1, 1987.

PLAN FOR DELAYED CONTRIBUTIONS TO THRIFT SAVINGS FUND

Section 312 of Pub. L. 99–335 directed Executive Director of Federal Retirement Thrift Investment Board to transmit to Congress, not later than Jan. 1, 1988, a plan to afford Federal employees and Members of Congress who make less than maximum amount of authorized contributions to Thrift Savings Fund in any period an opportunity to contribute to such Fund, in a later period, the excess of such amount over the amount contributed during such period, with plan to include such recommendations for legislation as Executive Director considered appropriate.

SECTION REFERRED TO IN OTHER SECTIONS

This section is referred to in sections 8351, 8401, 8432a, 8432b, 8432c, 8433, 8437, 8439, 8440a, 8440b, 8440c, 8440d, 8440e, 8479 of this title; title 2 section 162b; title 10 section 942; title 37 section 211; title 40 section 214d; title 42 section 2297h–8.

§ 8432a. Payment of lost earnings

(a)(1) The Executive Director shall prescribe regulations under which an employing agency shall be required to pay to the Thrift Savings Fund amounts representing lost earnings resulting from errors (including errors of omission) made by such agency in carrying out this subchapter, subject to paragraph (2).

(2) If the error involves an employing agency's failure to deduct from basic pay contributions (in whole or in part) on behalf of an individual in accordance with section 8432(a), the regulations shall not provide for the payment of any lost earnings which would be attributable to—

(A) the contributions that the agency failed to deduct from basic pay in accordance with section 8432(a); or

(B) any related contributions under section 8432(c)(2) that the employing agency is not required (by statute or otherwise) to make up.

(b) The regulations—

(1) shall include—

(A) procedures for computing lost earnings; and

(B) procedures under which amounts paid to the Thrift Savings Fund under this section shall be credited to appropriate accounts;

(2) may provide for exceptions from the requirements of this section to the extent that correction of an error is not administratively feasible;

(3) may require an employing agency to reimburse the Thrift Savings Fund for costs incurred by the Thrift Savings Fund in implementing corrections of employing agency errors under this section; and

(4) may include such other provisions as the Executive Director determines appropriate to carry out this section.

(c) Any amounts required to be paid by an employing agency under this section shall be paid from the appropriation or fund available to the employing agency for payment of salaries of the participant's office or establishment. If a participant in the legislative branch is paid by the Chief Administrative Officer of the House of Representatives, the Chief Administrative Officer may pay from the applicable accounts of the House of Representatives the amount required to be paid to correct errors relating to the Thrift Savings Fund that otherwise would be paid from the appropriation or fund used to pay the participant.

(Added Pub. L. 101–335, § 2(a)(1), July 17, 1990, 104 Stat. 319; amended Pub. L. 104–186, title II, § 215(17), Aug. 20, 1996, 110 Stat. 1746.)

AMENDMENTS

1996—Subsec. (c). Pub. L. 104–186 substituted "Chief Administrative Officer of the House of Representatives, the Chief Administrative Officer may pay from the applicable accounts" for "Clerk of the House of Representatives, the Clerk may pay from the contingent fund".

EFFECTIVE DATE

Section 2(b) of Pub. L. 101–335 provided that: "The amendments made by this section [enacting this section] shall apply with respect to lost earnings attributable to errors made before, on, or after the date of enactment of this Act [July 17, 1990]."

§ 8432b. Contributions of persons who perform military service

(a) This section applies to any employee who—

(1) separates or enters leave-without-pay status in order to perform military service; and

(2) is subsequently restored to or reemployed in a position which is subject to this chapter, pursuant to chapter 43 of title 38.

(b)(1) Each employee to whom this section applies may contribute to the Thrift Savings Fund, in accordance with this subsection, an amount not to exceed the amount described in paragraph (2).

(2) The maximum amount which an employee may contribute under this subsection is equal to—

(A) the contributions under section 8432(a) which would have been made, over the period beginning on date of separation or commencement of leave-without-pay status (as applicable) and ending on the day before the date of restoration or reemployment (as applicable); reduced by

(B) any contributions under section 8432(a) actually made by such employee over the period described in subparagraph (A).

(3) Contributions under this subsection—

(A) shall be made at the same time and in the same manner as would any contributions under section 8432(a);

(B) shall be made over the period of time specified by the employee under paragraph (4)(B); and

(C) shall be in addition to any contributions then actually being made under section 8432(a).

(4) The Executive Director shall prescribe the time, form, and manner in which an employee may specify—

(A) the total amount such employee wishes to contribute under this subsection with respect to any particular period referred to in paragraph (2)(B); and

(B) the period of time over which the employee wishes to make contributions under this subsection.

The employing agency may place a maximum limit on the period of time referred to in subparagraph (B), which cannot be shorter than two times the period referred to in paragraph (2)(B) and not longer than four times such period.

(c) If an employee makes contributions under subsection (b), the employing agency shall make contributions to the Thrift Savings Fund on such employee's behalf—

(1) in the same manner as would be required under section 8432(c)(2) if the employee contributions were being made under section 8432(a); and

(2) disregarding any contributions then actually being made under section 8432(a) and any agency contributions relating thereto.

(d) An employee to whom this section applies is entitled to have contributed to the Thrift Savings Fund on such employee's behalf an amount equal to—

(1) 1 percent of such employee's basic pay (as determined under subsection (e)) for the period referred to in subsection (b)(2)(B); reduced by

(2) any contributions actually made on such employee's behalf under section 8432(c)(1) with respect to the period referred to in subsection (b)(2)(B).

(e) For purposes of any computation under this section, an employee shall, with respect to the period referred to in subsection (b)(2)(B), be considered to have been paid at the rate which would have been payable over such period had such employee remained continuously employed in the position which such employee last held before separating or entering leave-without-pay status to perform military service.

(f)(1) The employing agency may be required to pay lost earnings on contributions made pursuant to subsections (c) and (d). Such earnings, if required, shall be calculated retroactively to the date the contribution would have been made had the employee not separated or entered leave without pay status to perform military service.

(2) Procedures for calculating and crediting the earnings payable pursuant to paragraph (1) shall be prescribed by the Executive Director.

(g) Amounts paid under subsection (c), (d), or (f) shall be paid—

(1) by the agency to which the employee is restored or in which such employee is reemployed;

(2) from the same source as would be the case under section 8432(e) with respect to sums required under section 8432(c); and

(3) within the time prescribed by the Executive Director.

(h)(1) For purposes of section 8432(g), in the case of an employee to whom this section applies—

(A) a separation from civilian service in order to perform the military service on which the employee's restoration or reemployment rights are based shall be disregarded; and

(B) such employee shall be credited with a period of civilian service equal to the period referred to in subsection (b)(2)(B).

(2)(A) An employee to whom this section applies may elect, for purposes of section 8433(d), or paragraph (1) or (2) of section 8433(h),[1] as the case may be, to have such employee's separation (described in subsection (a)(1)) treated as if it had never occurred.

(B) An election under this paragraph shall be made within such period of time after restoration or reemployment (as the case may be) and otherwise in such manner as the Executive Director prescribes.

---
[1] See References in Text note below.

(i) The Executive Director shall prescribe regulations to carry out this section.

(Added Pub. L. 103–353, §4(a)(1), Oct. 13, 1994, 108 Stat. 3170; amended Pub. L. 106–65, div. A, title VI, §661(a)(3)(A), (C), Oct. 5, 1999, 113 Stat. 671.)

AMENDMENT OF SUBSECTIONS (b)(2)(B) AND (c)

Pub. L. 106–65, div. A, title VI, §§661(a)(3)(A), (C), 663, Oct. 5, 1999, 113 Stat. 671, 673, as amended by Pub. L. 106–398, §1 [[div. A], title VI, §661(a)], Oct. 30, 2000, 114 Stat. 1654, 1654A–167, provided that effective 180 days after Oct. 30, 2000, unless postponed, this section is amended as follows:

(1) in subsection (b)(2)(B) by inserting "or 8440e" after "section 8432(a); and

(2) in subsection (c) by redesignating paragraphs (1) and (2) as subparagraphs (A) and (B), respectively, by striking "(c)" and inserting "(c)(1)", and by adding at the end the following:

(2) An employee to whom this section applies is entitled to have contributed to the Thrift Savings Fund on such employee's behalf an amount equal to—

(A) the total contributions to which that individual would have been entitled under section 8432(c)(2), based on the amounts contributed by such individual under section 8440e (other than under subsection (d)(2) thereof) with respect to the period referred to in subsection (b)(2)(B), if those amounts had been contributed by such individual under section 8432(a); reduced by

(B) any contributions actually made on such employee's behalf under section 8432(c)(2) (including pursuant to an agreement under section 211(d) of title 37) with respect to the period referred to in subsection (b)(2)(B).

REFERENCES IN TEXT

Section 8433(h), referred to in subsec. (h)(2)(A), was redesignated section 8433(f) by Pub. L. 103–226, §9(b)(2), Mar. 30, 1994, 108 Stat. 119.

EFFECTIVE DATE OF 1999 AMENDMENT

Amendment by Pub. L. 106–65 effective 180 days after Oct. 30, 2000, unless postponed, see section 663 of Pub. L. 106–65, as amended, set out as an Effective Date note under section 8440e of this title.

EFFECTIVE DATE

Section 4(e), (f) of Pub. L. 103–353 provided that:

"(e) EFFECTIVE DATE; APPLICABILITY.—This section [enacting this section and amending sections 8351, 8432, and 8433 of this title] and the amendments made by this section—

"(1) shall take effect on the date of enactment of this Act [Oct. 13, 1994]; and

"(2) shall apply to any employee whose release from military service, discharge from hospitalization, or other similar event making the individual eligible to seek restoration or reemployment under chapter 43 of title 38, United States Code, occurs on or after August 2, 1990.

"(f) RULES FOR APPLYING AMENDMENTS TO EMPLOYEES RESTORED OR REEMPLOYED BEFORE EFFECTIVE DATE.—In the case of any employee (described in subsection (e)(2)) who is reemployed or restored (in the circumstances described in section 8432b(a) of title 5, United States Code, as amended by this section) before the date of enactment of this Act [Oct. 13, 1994], the amendments made by this section [enacting this section and amending sections 8351, 8432, and 8433 of this title] shall apply to such employee, in accordance with their terms, subject to the following:

"(1) The employee shall be deemed not to have been reemployed or restored until—

"(A) the date of enactment of this Act, or

"(B) the first day following such employee's reemployment or restoration on which such employee is or was eligible to make an election relating to contributions to the Thrift Savings Fund,

whichever occurs or occurred first.

"(2) If the employee changed agencies during the period between the date of actual reemployment or restoration and the date of enactment of this Act, the employing agency as of such date of enactment shall be considered the reemploying or restoring agency.

"(3)(A) For purposes of any computation under section 8432b of such title, pay shall be determined in accordance with subsection (e) of such section, except that, with respect to the period described in subparagraph (B), actual pay attributable to such period shall be used.

"(B) The period described in this subparagraph is the period beginning on the first day of the first applicable pay period beginning on or after the date of the employee's actual reemployment or restoration and ending on the day before the date determined under paragraph (1).

"(4) Deem section 8432b(b)(2)(A) of such title to be amended by striking 'ending on the day before the date of restoration or reemployment (as applicable)' and inserting 'ending on the date determined under section 4(f)(1) of the Uniformed Services Employment and Reemployment Rights Act of 1994'."

SECTION REFERRED TO IN OTHER SECTIONS

This section is referred to in sections 8351, 8432, 8432c, 8433 of this title; title 38 section 4318.

§ 8432c. Contributions of certain persons reemployed after service with international organizations

(a) In this section, the term "covered person" means any person who—

(1) transfers from a position of employment covered by chapter 83 or 84 or subchapter I or II of chapter 8[1] of the Foreign Service Act of 1980 to a position of employment with an international organization pursuant to section 3582;

(2) pursuant to section 3582 elects to retain coverage, rights, and benefits under any system established by law for the retirement of persons during the period of employment with the international organization and currently deposits the necessary deductions in payment for such coverage, rights, and benefits in the system's fund; and

(3) is reemployed pursuant to section 3582(b) to a position covered by chapter 83 or 84 or subchapter I or II of chapter 8[1] of the Foreign Service Act of 1980 after separation from the international organization.

(b)(1) Each covered person may contribute to the Thrift Savings Fund, in accordance with this subsection, an amount not to exceed the amount described in paragraph (2).

(2) The maximum amount which a covered person may contribute under paragraph (1) is equal to—

(A) the total amount of all contributions under section 8351(b)(2) or 8432(a), as applicable, which the person would have made over

the period beginning on the date of transfer of the person (as described in subsection (a)(1)) and ending on the day before the date of reemployment of the person (as described in subsection (a)(3)), minus

(B) the total amount of all contributions, if any, under section 8351(b)(2) or 8432(a), as applicable, actually made by the person over the period described in subparagraph (A).

(3) Contributions under paragraph (1)—

(A) shall be made at the same time and in the same manner as would any contributions under section 8351(b)(2) or 8432(a), as applicable;

(B) shall be made over the period of time specified by the person under paragraph (4)(B); and

(C) shall be in addition to any contributions actually being made by the person during that period under section 8351(b)(2) or 8432(a), as applicable.

(4) The Executive Director shall prescribe the time, form, and manner in which a covered person may specify—

(A) the total amount the person wishes to contribute with respect to any period described in paragraph (2)(A); and

(B) the period of time over which the covered person wishes to make contributions under this subsection.

(c) If a covered person who makes contributions under section 8432(a) makes contributions under subsection (b), the agency employing the person shall make those contributions to the Thrift Savings Fund on the person's behalf in the same manner as contributions are made for an employee described in section 8432b(a) under sections 8432b(c), 8432b(d), and 8432b(f). Amounts paid under this subsection shall be paid in the same manner as amounts are paid under section 8432b(g).

(d) For purposes of any computation under this section, a covered person shall, with respect to the period described in subsection (b)(2)(A), be considered to have been paid at the rate which would have been payable over such period had the person remained continuously employed in the position that the person last held before transferring to the international organization.

(e) For purposes of section 8432(g), a covered person shall be credited with a period of civilian service equal to the period beginning on the date of transfer of the person (as described in subsection (a)(1)) and ending on the day before the date of reemployment of the person (as described in subsection (a)(3)).

(f) The Executive Director shall prescribe regulations to carry out this section.

(Added Pub. L. 106–113, div. B, § 1000(a)(7) [div. A, title III, § 334(a)], Nov. 29, 1999, 113 Stat. 1536, 1501A–440.)

REFERENCES IN TEXT

The Foreign Service Act of 1980, referred to in subsec. (a)(1), (3), is Pub. L. 96–465, Oct. 17, 1980, 94 Stat. 2071, as amended. Subchapters I and II of chapter 8 of the Act probably mean subchapters I and II of chapter 8 of title I of the Act which are classified generally to parts I (§ 4041 et seq.) and II (§ 4071 et seq.), respectively, of subchapter VIII of chapter 52 of Title 22, Foreign Rela-

[1] See References in Text note below.

tions and Intercourse. For complete classification of this Act to the Code, see Short Title note set out under section 3901 of Title 22 and Tables.

EFFECTIVE DATE

Pub. L. 106–113, div. B, § 1000(a)(7) [div. A, title III, § 334(c)], Nov. 29, 1999, 113 Stat. 1536, 1501A–441, provided that: "The amendment made by subsection (a) [enacting this section] shall apply to persons reemployed on or after the date of enactment of this Act [Nov. 29, 1999]."

§ 8433. Benefits and election of benefits

(a) An employee or Member who separates from Government employment is entitled to the amount of the balance in the employee's or Member's account (except for the portion of such amount forfeited under section 8432(g) of this title, if any) as provided in this section.

(b) Subject to section 8435 of this title, any employee or Member who separates from Government employment is entitled and may elect to withdraw from the Thrift Savings Fund the balance of the employee's or Member's account as—

(1) an annuity;

(2) a single payment;

(3) 2 or more substantially equal payments to be made not less frequently than annually; or

(4) any combination of payments as provided under paragraphs (1) through (3) as the Executive Director may prescribe by regulation.

(c)(1) In addition to the right provided under subsection (b) to withdraw the balance of the account, an employee or Member who separates from Government service and who has not made a withdrawal under subsection (h)(1)(A) may make one withdrawal of any amount as a single payment in accordance with subsection (b)(2) from the employee's or Member's account.

(2) An employee or Member may request that the amount withdrawn from the Thrift Savings Fund in accordance with subsection (b)(2) be transferred to an eligible retirement plan.

(3) The Executive Director shall make each transfer elected under paragraph (2) directly to an eligible retirement plan or plans (as defined in section 402(c)(8) of the Internal Revenue Code of 1986) identified by the employee, Member, former employee, or former Member for whom the transfer is made.

(4) A transfer may not be made for an employee, Member, former employee, or former Member under paragraph (2) until the Executive Director receives from that individual the information required by the Executive Director specifically to identify the eligible retirement plan or plans to which the transfer is to be made.

(d)(1) Subject to paragraph (3)[1] and subsections (a) and (c) of section 8435 of this title, an employee or Member may change an election previously made under this subchapter.

(2) A former employee or Member may not change an election under this section on or after the date on which a payment is made in accordance with such election or, in the case of an election to receive an annuity, the date on which an annuity contract is purchased to pro-

vide for the annuity elected by the former employee or Member.

(e) If an employee or Member (or former employee or Member) dies without having made an election under this section or after having elected an annuity under this section but before making an election under section 8434 of this title, an amount equal to the value of that individual's account (as of death) shall, subject to any decree, order, or agreement referred to in section 8435(c)(2) of this title be paid in a manner consistent with section 8424(d) of this title.

(f)(1) Notwithstanding subsection (b), if an employee or Member separates from Government employment, and such employee's or Member's nonforfeitable account balance is less than an amount that the Executive Director prescribes by regulation, the Executive Director shall pay the nonforfeitable account balance to the participant in a single payment, unless an election under section 8432b(h)(2) is made to treat such separation for purposes of this paragraph as if it had never occurred.

(2) Unless otherwise elected under this section, and subject to paragraph (1), benefits under this subchapter shall be paid as an annuity commencing for an employee, Member, former employee, or former Member on April 1 of the year following the latest of the year in which—

(A) the employee, Member, former employee, or former Member becomes 70½ years of age; or

(B) the employee, Member, former employee, or former Member separates from Government employment.

(g)(1) At any time before separation, an employee or Member may apply to the Board for permission to borrow from the employee's or Member's account an amount not exceeding the value of that portion of such account which is attributable to contributions made by the employee or Member under section 8432(a) of this title. Before a loan is issued, the Executive Director shall provide in writing the employee or Member with appropriate information concerning the cost of the loan relative to other sources of financing, as well as the lifetime cost of the loan, including the difference in interest rates between the funds offered by the Thrift Savings Fund, and any other effect of such loan on the employee's or Member's final account balance.

(2) Loans under this subsection shall be available to all employees and Members on a reasonably equivalent basis, and shall be subject to such other conditions as the Board may by regulation prescribe. The restrictions of section 8477(c)(1) of this title shall not apply to loans made under this subsection.

(3) A loan may not be made under this subsection to the extent that the loan would be treated as a taxable distribution under section 72(p) of the Internal Revenue Code of 1986.

(4) A loan may not be made under this subsection unless the requirements of section 8435(e) of this title are satisfied.

(h)(1) An employee or Member may apply, before separation, to the Board for permission to withdraw an amount from the employee's or Member's account based upon—

---

[1] So in original. Probably should be paragraph "(2)".

(A) the employee or Member having attained age 59½; or

(B) financial hardship.

(2) A withdrawal under paragraph (1)(A) shall be available to each eligible participant one time only.

(3) A withdrawal under paragraph (1)(B) shall be available only for an amount not exceeding the value of that portion of such account which is attributable to contributions made by the employee or Member under section 8432(a) of this title.

(4) Withdrawals under paragraph (1) shall be subject to such other conditions as the Executive Director may prescribe by regulation.

(5) A withdrawal may not be made under this subsection unless the requirements of section 8435(e) of this title are satisfied.

(Added Pub. L. 99–335, title I, § 101(a), June 6, 1986, 100 Stat. 544; amended Pub. L. 100–238, title I, § 132, Jan. 8, 1988, 101 Stat. 1760; Pub. L. 101–335, §§ 5(a), 6(a)(2), July 17, 1990, 104 Stat. 321, 322; Pub. L. 102–484, div. D, title XLIV, § 4437(a), Oct. 23, 1992, 106 Stat. 2724; Pub. L. 103–226, § 9(b), (i)(3)–(7), Mar. 30, 1994, 108 Stat. 119, 121, 122; Pub. L. 103–353, §§ 4(b), 5(e)(4), Oct. 13, 1994, 108 Stat. 3172, 3174; Pub. L. 104–208, div. A, title I, § 101(f) [title VI, § 659 [title II, § 203(a)]], Sept. 30, 1996, 110 Stat. 3009–314, 3009–372, 3009–374; Pub. L. 106–65, div. A, title VI, § 661(a)(4), Oct. 5, 1999, 113 Stat. 672.)

AMENDMENT OF SUBSECTIONS (g)(1) AND (h)(3)

Pub. L. 106–65, div. A, title VI, §§ 661(a)(4), 663, Oct. 5, 1999, 113 Stat. 672, 673, as amended by Pub. L. 106–398, § 1 [[div. A], title VI, § 661(a)], Oct. 30, 2000, 114 Stat. 1654, 1654A–167, provided that effective 180 days after Oct. 30, 2000, unless postponed, subsections (g)(1) and (h)(3) of this section are amended by striking "under section 8432(a) of this title".

REFERENCES IN TEXT

Sections 72(p) and 402(c)(8) of the Internal Revenue Code of 1986, referred to in subsecs. (c)(3) and (g)(3), are classified to sections 72(p) and 402(c)(8), respectively, of Title 26, Internal Revenue Code.

AMENDMENTS

1996—Subsec. (b). Pub. L. 104–208, § 101(f) [title VI, § 659 [title II, § 203(a)(1)]], added subsec. (b) and struck out former subsec. (b) which read as follows: "Subject to section 8435 of this title, any employee or Member who separates from Government employment is entitled and may elect—

"(1) to receive an immediate annuity from the Thrift Savings Fund;

"(2) to defer the commencement of the payment of an annuity from the Thrift Savings Fund until such date as the employee or Member specifies, but not later than April 1 of the year following the year in which the employee or Member becomes 70½ years of age;

"(3) to withdraw the amount of the balance in the employee's or Member's account in the Thrift Savings Fund in one or more substantially equal payments to be made not less frequently than annually and to commence before April 1 of the year following the year in which the employee or Member becomes 70½ years of age; or

"(4) to transfer the amount of the balance in the employee's or Member's account to an eligible retirement plan as provided in subsection (c)."

Subsec. (c). Pub. L. 104–208, § 101(f) [title VI, § 659 [title II, § 203(a)(1)]], added subsec. (c) and struck out former subsec. (c) which read as follows:

"(1) The Executive Director shall make each transfer elected under subsection (b)(4) directly to an eligible retirement plan or plans (as defined in section 402(c)(8) of the Internal Revenue Code of 1986) identified by the employee, Member, former employee, or former Member for whom the transfer is made.

"(2) A transfer may not be made for an employee, Member, former employee, or former Member under paragraph (1) until the Executive Director receives from that individual the information required by the Executive Director specifically to identify the eligible retirement plan or plans to which the transfer is to be made."

Subsec. (d)(1). Pub. L. 104–208, § 101(f) [title VI, § 659 [title II, § 203(a)(2)(A)]], substituted "(3)" for "(3)(A)" after "Subject to paragraph".

Subsec. (d)(2). Pub. L. 104–208, § 101(f) [title VI, § 659 [title II, § 203(a)(2)(C)]], struck out subpar. (A) designation before "A former employee" and struck out subpar. (B) which read as follows: "A modification of a date may not be made under paragraph (2) on or after the date on which an annuity contract is purchased to provide for the annuity involved, and may not specify a date for the commencement of an annuity earlier than 90 days after the date on which the modification is submitted to the Executive Director (or such period shorter than 90 days as the Executive Director may by regulation prescribe)."

Pub. L. 104–208, § 101(f) [title VI, § 659 [title II, § 203(a)(2)(B)]], redesignated par. (3) as (2) and struck out former par. (2) which read as follows: "Subject to paragraph (3)(B) and section 8435(c) of this title, a former employee or Member who has made an election pursuant to subsection (b)(2) may modify the date specified in such election or in a previous modification under this paragraph."

Subsec. (d)(3). Pub. L. 104–208, § 101(f) [title VI, § 659 [title II, § 203(a)(2)(B)]], redesignated par. (3) as (2).

Subsec. (f)(1). Pub. L. 104–208, § 101(f) [title VI, § 659 [title II, § 203(a)(3)]], substituted "less than an amount that the Executive Director prescribes by regulation" for "$3,500 or less" and substituted a comma for "unless the employee or Member elects, at such time and otherwise in such manner as the Executive Director prescribes, one of the options available under subsection (b), or".

Subsec. (f)(2). Pub. L. 104–208, § 101(f) [title VI, § 659 [title II, § 203(a)(4)]], in introductory provisions substituted "April 1" for "February 1", in subpar. (A) substituted "70½" for "65" and inserted "or" after semicolon, redesignated subpar. (C) as (B), and struck out former subpar. (B) which read as follows: "occurs the tenth anniversary of the year in which the employee, Member, former employee, or former Member became subject to this subchapter; or".

Subsec. (g)(1). Pub. L. 104–208, § 101(f) [title VI, § 659 [title II, § 203(a)(5)(A)]], struck out "after December 31, 1987, and" after "At any time", and inserted at end "Before a loan is issued, the Executive Director shall provide in writing the employee or Member with appropriate information concerning the cost of the loan relative to other sources of financing, as well as the lifetime cost of the loan, including the difference in interest rates between the funds offered by the Thrift Savings Fund, and any other effect of such loan on the employee's or Member's final account balance."

Subsec. (g)(2) to (5). Pub. L. 104–208, § 101(f) [title VI, § 659 [title II, § 203(a)(5)(B)]], redesignated pars. (3) to (5) as (2) to (4), respectively, and struck out former par. (2) which read as follows: "An application under this subsection may be approved only for—

"(A) the purchase of a primary residence;

"(B) educational expenses;

"(C) medical expenses; or

"(D) financial hardship."

Subsec. (h). Pub. L. 104–208, § 101(f) [title VI, § 659 [title II, § 203(a)(6)]], added subsec. (h).

1994—Subsec. (b). Pub. L. 103–226, § 9(b)(1), amended introductory provisions generally, substituting "Subject to section 8435 of this title, any employee or Member who separates from Government employment is entitled and may elect—" for "Subject to section 8435 of this title, any employee or Member who separates from Government employment entitled to an immediate annuity under subchapter II of this chapter, any employee or Member who separates from Government employment entitled to benefits under subchapter I of chapter 81 of this title, any employee who separates from Government employment pursuant to regulations under section 3502(a) of this title or procedures under section 3595(a) of this title in a reduction in force, and any employee or Member who is entitled to receive disability benefits under subchapter V of this chapter is entitled and may elect—".

Subsec. (b)(4). Pub. L. 103–226, § 9(i)(3), substituted "subsection (c)" for "subsection (e)".

Subsec. (c). Pub. L. 103–226, § 9(b)(2), redesignated subsec. (e) as (c) and struck out former subsec. (c) which related to permissible elections by employees separating from Government who are entitled to a deferred annuity.

Subsec. (c)(1). Pub. L. 103–226, § 9(b)(3), substituted "directly to an eligible retirement plan or plans (as defined in section 402(c)(8) of the Internal Revenue Code of 1986)" for "or (c)(4) or required under subsection (d) directly to an eligible retirement plan or plans (as defined in section 402(a)(5)(E) of the Internal Revenue Code of 1954)".

Subsec. (d). Pub. L. 103–353, § 4(b)(1), inserted before period at end ", unless an election under section 8432b(h)(2) is made to treat such separation for purposes of this subsection as if it had never occurred".

Pub. L. 103–226, § 9(b)(2), redesignated subsec. (f) as (d) and struck out former subsec. (d) which read as follows: "Subject to section 8435 of this title, any employee or Member who separates from Government employment before becoming entitled to a deferred annuity under subchapter II of this chapter shall transfer the amount of the balance in the employee's or Member's account to an eligible retirement plan as provided in subsection (e), unless an election under section 8432b(h)(2) is made to treat such separation for purposes of this subsection as if it had never occurred."

Subsec. (d)(1). Pub. L. 103–226, § 9(i)(4), substituted "(c) of section 8435" for "(d) of section 8435".

Subsec. (d)(2). Pub. L. 103–226, § 9(b)(4), (i)(5), substituted "section 8435(c)" for "section 8435(d)" and struck out "or (c)(2)" after "subsection (b)(2)".

Subsec. (e). Pub. L. 103–226, § 9(b)(2), (i)(6), redesignated subsec. (g) as (e) and substituted "section 8435(c)(2)" for "section 8435(d)(2)". Former subsec. (e) redesignated (c).

Subsec. (f). Pub. L. 103–226, § 9(b)(2), redesignated subsec. (h) as (f). Former subsec. (f) redesignated (d).

Subsec. (f)(1). Pub. L. 103–226, § 9(b)(5)(A), (B), redesignated par. (2) as (1), substituted "Notwithstanding subsection (b), if an employee or Member separates from Government employment, and such employee's or Member's" for "Notwithstanding subsections (b) and (c), if an employee or Member separates from Government employment under circumstances making such employee or Member eligible to make an election under either of those subsections, and such employee's or Member's", struck out "or (c), as applicable" before period at end, and struck out former par. (1) which read as follows: "Notwithstanding subsection (d), if an employee or Member separates from Government employment before becoming entitled to a deferred annuity under subchapter II, and such employee's or Member's nonforfeitable account balance is $3,500 or less, the Executive Director shall pay the nonforfeitable account balance to the participant in a single payment unless the employee or Member elects, at such time and otherwise in such manner as the Executive Director prescribes, to have the nonforfeitable account balance transferred to an eligible retirement plan as provided in subsection (e), or unless an election under section

8432b(h)(2) is made to treat such separation for purposes of this paragraph as if it had never occurred."

Subsec. (f)(2). Pub. L. 103–226, § 9(b)(5)(A), (C), redesignated par. (3) as (2) and substituted "paragraph (1)" for "paragraphs (1) and (2)" before ", benefits under this chapter". Former par. (2) redesignated (1).

Subsec. (f)(3). Pub. L. 103–226, § 9(b)(5)(A), redesignated par. (3) as (2).

Subsec. (g). Pub. L. 103–226, § 9(b)(2), redesignated subsec. (i) as (g). Former subsec. (g) redesignated (e).

Subsec. (g)(5). Pub. L. 103–226, § 9(i)(7), substituted "section 8435(e)" for "section 8435(f)".

Subsec. (h). Pub. L. 103–226, § 9(b)(2), redesignated subsec. (h) as (f).

Subsec. (h)(1), (2). Pub. L. 103–353, § 4(b)(2), inserted before period at end ", or unless an election under section 8432b(h)(2) is made to treat such separation for purposes of this paragraph as if it had never occurred".

Subsec. (i). Pub. L. 103–226, § 9(b)(2), redesignated subsec. (i) as (g).

Subsec. (i)(4). Pub. L. 103–353, § 5(e)(4), substituted "Internal Revenue Code of 1986" for "Internal Revenue Code of 1954".

1992—Subsec. (b). Pub. L. 102–484 inserted "any employee who separates from Government employment pursuant to regulations under section 3502(a) of this title or procedures under section 3595(a) of this title in a reduction in force," after "chapter 81 of this title,".

1990—Subsec. (f)(3)(A). Pub. L. 101–335, § 5(a)(1), substituted "an annuity contract is purchased to provide for the annuity elected by the former employee or Member" for "an annuity elected by the former employee or Member commences".

Subsec. (f)(3)(B). Pub. L. 101–335, § 5(a)(2), amended subpar. (B) generally. Prior to amendment, subpar. (B) read as follows: "A modification of a date may not be made under paragraph (2) on or after such date and may not specify a date for the commencement of an annuity earlier than 1 month after the date on which the modification is submitted to the Executive Director."

Subsec. (h). Pub. L. 101–335, § 6(a)(2), amended subsec. (h) generally. Prior to amendment, subsec. (h) read as follows: "Unless otherwise elected under this section, benefits under this subchapter shall be paid as an annuity commencing for an employee, Member, former employee, or former Member on February 1 of the year following the latest of the year in which—

"(1) the employee, Member, former employee, or former Member becomes 65 years of age;

"(2) occurs the tenth anniversary of the year in which the employee, Member, former employee, or former Member became subject to this subchapter; or

"(3) the employee, Member, former employee, or former Member separates from Government employment."

1988—Subsec. (i)(3). Pub. L. 100–238 amended par. (3) generally. Prior to amendment, par. (3) read as follows: "Loans under this subsection shall be subject to such conditions as the Board may prescribe consistent with section 408(b)(1) of the Employee Retirement Income Security Act of 1974 (29 U.S.C. 1108(b)(1)). The conditions shall be included in regulations issued by the Executive Director."

EFFECTIVE DATE OF 1999 AMENDMENT

Amendment by Pub. L. 106–65 effective 180 days after Oct. 30, 2000, unless postponed, see section 663 of Pub. L. 106–65, as amended, set out as an Effective Date note under section 8440e of this title.

EFFECTIVE DATE OF 1996 AMENDMENT

Amendment by Pub. L. 104–208 effective Sept. 30, 1996, and withdrawals and elections as provided under such amendment to be made at earliest practicable date as determined by Executive Director in regulations, see section 101(f) [title VI, § 659 [title II, § 207]] of Pub. L. 104–208, set out as a note under section 5545a of this title.

EFFECTIVE DATE OF 1994 AMENDMENTS

Amendment by section 4(b) of Pub. L. 103–353 effective Oct. 13, 1994, and applicable to any employee whose release from military service, discharge from hospitalization, or other similar event making the individual eligible to seek restoration or reemployment under chapter 43 of Title 38, Veterans' Benefits, occurs on or after Aug. 2, 1990, with special rules for applying amendment to employees restored or reemployed before effective date, see section 4(e), (f) of Pub. L. 103–353, set out as an Effective Date note under section 8432b of this title.

Amendment by section 5(e)(4) of Pub. L. 103–353 effective with respect to reemployments initiated on or after the first day after the 60-day period beginning Oct. 13, 1994, with transition rules, see section 8 of Pub. L. 103–353, set out as an Effective Date note under section 4301 of Title 38.

Amendment by Pub. L. 103–226 effective Mar. 10, 1995, see section 9(j) of Pub. L. 103–226, set out as a note under section 8351 of this title.

EFFECTIVE DATE OF 1992 AMENDMENT

Amendment by Pub. L. 102–484 applicable with respect to separations occurring after Dec. 31, 1993, or such earlier date as Executive Director (appointed under section 8474 of this title) may by regulation prescribe, see section 4437(d) of Pub. L. 102–484, set out as a note under section 8351 of this title.

EFFECTIVE DATE OF 1990 AMENDMENT

Section 5(d) of Pub. L. 101–335 provided that: "The amendments made by this section [amending this section and sections 8434, and 8435 of this title] shall be effective as of April 1, 1987."

Amendment by section 6(a)(2) of Pub. L. 101–335 effective as of second election period described in section 8432(b) of this title beginning after July 17, 1990, or such earlier date as Executive Director may by regulation prescribe, and applicable with respect to separations occurring before, on, or after that effective date, see section 6(c) of Pub. L. 101–335, set out as a note under section 8351 of this title.

REGULATIONS

Section 6(b)(4) of Pub. L. 101–335 provided that: "The Executive Director (as appointed under section 8474(a) of title 5, United States Code) shall prescribe regulations under which the purposes of the amendments made by this section [amending this section and sections 8351, 8401, 8435, 8440a, and 8440b of this title] shall be carried out with respect to any individuals participating in the Thrift Savings Plan who would not otherwise be affected by this section."

INVALIDITY OF CERTAIN PRIOR ELECTIONS

Section 101(f) [title VI, § 659 [title II, § 203(b)]] of Pub. L. 104–208 provided that: "Any election made under section 8433(b)(2) of title 5, United States Code (as in effect before the effective date of this title [Sept. 30, 1996]), with respect to an annuity which has not commenced before the implementation date of this title as provided by regulation by the Executive Director in accordance with section 207 of this title [5 U.S.C. 5545a note], shall be invalid."

SECTION REFERRED TO IN OTHER SECTIONS

This section is referred to in sections 8351, 8434, 8432b, 8435, 8436, 8437, 8440a, 8440b, 8440c, 8440d of this title; title 22 section 4071j; title 50 section 2154.

§ 8434. Annuities: methods of payment; election; purchase

(a)(1) The Board shall prescribe methods of payment of annuities under this subchapter.

(2) The methods of payment prescribed under paragraph (1) shall include, but not be limited to—

(A) a method which provides for the payment of a monthly annuity only to an annuitant during the life of the annuitant;

(B) a method which provides for the payment of a monthly annuity to an annuitant for the joint lives of the annuitant and the spouse of the annuitant and an appropriate monthly annuity to the one of them who survives the other of them for the life of the survivor;

(C) a method described in subparagraph (A) which provides for automatic adjustments in the amount of the annuity payable so long as the amount of the annuity payable in any one year shall not be less than the amount payable in the previous year;

(D) a method described in subparagraph (B) which provides for automatic adjustments in the amount of the annuity payable so long as the amount of the annuity payable in any one year shall not be less than the amount payable in the previous year; and

(E) a method which provides for the payment of a monthly annuity—

(i) to the annuitant for the joint lives of the annuitant and an individual who is designated by the annuitant under regulations prescribed by the Executive Director and (I) is a former spouse of the annuitant, or (II) has an insurable interest in the annuitant; and

(ii) to the one of them who survives the other of them for the life of the survivor.

(b) Subject to section 8435(b) of this title, under such regulations as the Executive Director shall prescribe, an employee, Member, former employee, or former Member who elects under section 8433 of this title to receive an annuity under this subchapter shall elect, on or before the date on which an annuity contract is purchased to provide for that annuity, one of the methods of payment prescribed under subsection (a).

(c) Notwithstanding the elimination of a method of payment by the Board, an employee, Member, former employee, or former Member may elect the eliminated method if the elimination of such method becomes effective less than 5 years before the date on which that individual's annuity commences.

(d)(1) Not earlier than 90 days (or such shorter period as the Executive Director may by regulation prescribe) before an annuity is to commence under this subchapter, the Executive Director shall expend the balance in the annuitant's account to purchase an annuity contract from any entity which, in the normal course of its business, sells and provides annuities.

(2) The Executive Director shall assure, by contract entered into with each entity from which an annuity contract is purchased under paragraph (1), that the annuity shall be provided in accordance with the provisions of this subchapter and subchapter VII of this chapter.

(3) An annuity contract purchased under paragraph (1) shall include such terms and conditions as the Executive Director requires for the protection of the annuitant.

(4) The Executive Director shall require, from each entity from which an annuity contract is purchased under paragraph (1), a bond or proof of financial responsibility sufficient to protect the annuitant.

(e)(1) No tax, fee, or other monetary payment may be imposed or collected by any State, the

District of Columbia, or the Commonwealth of Puerto Rico, or by any political subdivision or other governmental authority thereof, on, or with respect to, any amount paid to purchase an annuity contract under this section.

(2) Paragraph (1) shall not be construed to exempt any company or other entity issuing an annuity contract under this section from the imposition, payment, or collection of a tax, fee, or other monetary payment on the net income or profit accruing to or realized by that entity from the sale of an annuity contract under this section if that tax, fee, or payment is applicable to a broad range of business activity.

(Added Pub. L. 99–335, title I, §101(a), June 6, 1986, 100 Stat. 546; amended Pub. L. 100–238, title I, §129, Jan. 8, 1988, 101 Stat. 1759; Pub. L. 101–335, §§4(a), 5(b), July 17, 1990, 104 Stat. 321; Pub. L. 103–226, §9(c), (i)(8), Mar. 30, 1994, 108 Stat. 120, 122.)

AMENDMENTS

1994—Subsec. (b). Pub. L. 103–226, §9(i)(8), substituted "section 8435(b)" for "section 8435(c)".

Subsec. (c). Pub. L. 103–226, §9(c), amended subsec. (c) generally. Prior to amendment, subsec. (c) read as follows: "Notwithstanding an elimination of a method of payment by the Board—

"(1) an employee, Member, former employee, or former Member who is entitled under section 8412 of this title to an immediate annuity not reduced under section 8415(f) of this title may elect the eliminated method if the elimination of such method became effective less than 5 years before the date on which the annuity commences; and

"(2) any other employee, Member, former employee, or former Member may elect such method of payment for amounts contributed by or on behalf of the employee, Member, former employee, or former Member under section 8432 of this title before such effective date and for earnings attributable to such amounts."

1990—Subsec. (b). Pub. L. 101–335, §5(b)(1), substituted "an annuity contract is purchased to provide for that annuity," for "the annuity commences,".

Subsec. (d)(1). Pub. L. 101–335, §5(b)(2), substituted "Not earlier than 90 days (or such shorter period as the Executive Director may by regulation prescribe) before an annuity" for "At the time an annuity".

Subsec. (e). Pub. L. 101–335, §4(a), added subsec. (e).

1988—Subsec. (a)(2)(C), (D). Pub. L. 100–238 amended subpars. (C) and (D) generally. Prior to amendment, subpars. (C) and (D) read as follows:

"(C) a method described in subparagraph (A) which provides annual increases in the amount of the annuity payable;

"(D) a method described in subparagraph (B) which provides annual increases in the amount of the annuity payable; and".

EFFECTIVE DATE OF 1994 AMENDMENT

Amendment by Pub. L. 103–226 effective Mar. 10, 1995, see section 9(j) of Pub. L. 103–226, set out as a note under section 8351 of this title.

EFFECTIVE DATE OF 1990 AMENDMENT

Section 4(b) of Pub. L. 101–335 provided that: "The amendment made by subsection (a) [amending this section] shall take effect 30 days after the date of enactment of this Act [July 17, 1990]."

Amendment by section 5(b) of Pub. L. 101–335 effective Apr. 1, 1987, see section 5(d) of Pub. L. 101–335, set out as a note under section 8433 of this title.

SECTION REFERRED TO IN OTHER SECTIONS

This section is referred to in sections 8433, 8435, 8436 of this title.

§ 8435. Protections for spouses and former spouses

(a)(1)(A) A married employee or Member (or former employee or Member) may withdraw all or part of a Thrift Savings Fund account under subsection (b)(2), (3), or (4) of section 8433 of this title or change a withdrawal election only if the employee or Member (or former employee or Member) satisfies the requirements of subparagraph (B). A married employee or Member (or former employee or Member) may make a withdrawal from a Thrift Savings Fund account under subsection (c)(1) of section 8433 of this title only if the employee or Member (or former employee or Member) satisfies the requirements of subparagraph (B).

(B) An employee or Member (or former employee or Member) may make an election or change referred to in subparagraph (A) if the employee or Member and the employee's or Member's spouse (or the former employee or Member and the former employee's or Member's spouse) jointly waive, by written election, any right which the spouse may have to a survivor annuity with respect to such employee or Member (or former employee or Member) under section 8434 of this title or subsection (b).

(2) Paragraph (1) shall not apply to an election or change of election by an employee or Member (or former employee or Member) who establishes to the satisfaction of the Executive Director (at the time of the election or change and in accordance with regulations prescribed by the Executive Director)—

(A) that the spouse's whereabouts cannot be determined; or

(B) that, due to exceptional circumstances, requiring the spouse's waiver would otherwise be inappropriate.

(b)(1) Notwithstanding any election under subsection (b) of section 8434 of this title, the method described in subsection (a)(2)(B) of such section (or, if more than one form of such method is available, the form which the Board determines to be the one which provides for a surviving spouse a survivor annuity most closely approximating the annuity of a surviving spouse under section 8442 of this title) shall be deemed the applicable method under such subsection (b) in the case of an employee, Member, former employee, or former Member who is married on the date on which an annuity contract is purchased to provide for the employee's, Member's, former employee's, or former Member's annuity under this subchapter.

(2) Paragraph (1) shall not apply if—

(A) a joint waiver of such method is made, in writing, by the employee or Member and the spouse; or

(B) the employee or Member waives such method, in writing, after establishing to the satisfaction of the Executive Director that circumstances described under subsection (a)(2)(A) or (B) make the requirement of a joint waiver inappropriate.

(c)(1) An election or change of election shall not be effective under this subchapter to the extent that the election, change, or transfer conflicts with any court decree, order, or agreement described in paragraph (2).

(2) A court decree, order, or agreement referred to in paragraph (1) is, with respect to an employee or Member (or former employee or Member), a court decree of divorce, annulment, or legal separation issued in the case of such employee or Member (or former employee or Member) and any former spouse of the employee or Member (or former employee or Member) or any court order or court-approved property settlement agreement incident to such decree if—

(A) the decree, order, or agreement expressly relates to any portion of the balance in the employee's or Member's (or former employee's or Member's) account; and

(B) notice of the decree, order, or agreement was received by the Executive Director before—

(i) the date on which payment is made, or

(ii) in the case of an annuity, the date on which an annuity contract is purchased to provide for the annuity,

in accordance with the election, change, or contribution referred to in paragraph (1).

(3) The Executive Director shall prescribe regulations under which this subsection shall be applied in any case in which the Executive Director receives two or more decrees, orders, or agreements referred to in paragraph (1).

(d)(1) Subject to paragraphs (2) through (7), a former spouse of a deceased employee or Member (or a deceased former employee or Member) who died after performing 18 or more months of service and a former spouse of a deceased former employee or Member who died entitled to an immediate or deferred annuity under subchapter II of this chapter is entitled to a survivor annuity under this subsection if and to the extent that—

(A) an election under section 8434(a)(2)(E) of this title, or

(B) any court decree, order, or agreement (described in subsection (c)(2), without regard to subparagraph (B) of such subsection) which relates to such deceased individual and such former spouse,

expressly provides for such survivor annuity.

(2) Paragraph (1) shall apply only to payments made by the Executive Director after the date on which the Executive Director receives written notice of the election, decree, order, or agreement, and such additional information and documentation as the Executive Director may require.

(3) The amount of the survivor annuity payable from the Thrift Savings Fund to a former spouse of a deceased employee, Member, former employee, or former Member under this section may not exceed the excess, if any, of—

(A) the amount of the survivor annuity determined for a surviving spouse of the deceased employee, Member, former employee, or former Member under the method described in subsection (b)(1), over

(B) the total amount of all other survivor annuities payable under this subchapter to other former spouses of such deceased employee, Member, former employee, or former Member based on the order of precedence provided in paragraph (4).

(4) If more than one former spouse of a deceased employee, Member, former employee, or

former Member is entitled to a survivor annuity pursuant to this subsection, the amount of each such survivor annuity shall be limited appropriately to carry out paragraph (3) in the order of precedence established for the entitlements by the chronological order of the dates on which elections are properly made pursuant to section 8434(a)(2)(E) of this title and the dates on which the court decrees, orders, or agreements applicable to the entitlement were issued, as the case may be.

(5) Subsections (c) and (d) of section 8445 of this title shall apply to an entitlement of a former spouse to a survivor annuity under this subsection.

(6) For the purposes of this section, a court decree, order, or agreement or an election referred to in subsection (a) of this section shall not be effective, in the case of a former spouse, to the extent that the election is inconsistent with any joint waiver previously executed with respect to such former spouse under subsection (a)(2) or (b)(2).

(7) Any payment under this subsection to any individual bars recovery by any other individual.

(e)(1)(A) A loan or withdrawal may be made to a married employee or Member under section 8433(g) and (h) of this title only if the employee's or Member's spouse consents to such loan or withdrawal in writing.

(B) A consent under subparagraph (A) shall be irrevocable with respect to the loan or withdrawal to which the consent relates.

(C) Subparagraph (A) shall not apply to a loan or withdrawal to an employee or Member who establishes to the satisfaction of the Executive Director (at the time the employee or Member applies for such loan or withdrawal and in accordance with regulations prescribed by the Executive Director)—

(i) that the spouse's whereabouts cannot be determined; or

(ii) that, due to exceptional circumstances, requiring the employee or Member to seek the spouse's consent would otherwise be inappropriate.

(2) An application for a loan or withdrawal under section 8433(g) and (h) of this title shall not be approved if approval would have the result described under subsection (c)(1).

(f) Waivers and notifications required by this section and waivers of the requirements for such waivers and notifications (as authorized by this section) may be made only in accordance with procedures prescribed by the Executive Director.

(g) Except with respect to the making of loans or withdrawals under section 8433(g) and (h), none of the provisions of this section requiring notification to, or the consent or waiver of, a spouse or former spouse of an employee, Member, former employee, or former Member shall apply in any case in which the nonforfeitable account balance of the employee, Member, former employee, or former Member is $3,500 or less.

(h) The protections provided by this section are in addition to the protections provided by section 8467 of this title.

(Added Pub. L. 99–335, title I, §101(a), June 6, 1986, 100 Stat. 547; amended Pub. L. 101–335,

§§ 5(c), 6(a)(3), July 17, 1990, 104 Stat. 322, 323; Pub. L. 102–484, div. D, title XLIV, § 4437(b), Oct. 23, 1992, 106 Stat. 2724; Pub. L. 103–226, § 9(d), (i)(9)–(15), Mar. 30, 1994, 108 Stat. 120, 122; Pub. L. 104–208, div. A, title I, § 101(f) [title VI, § 659 [title II, § 204]], Sept. 30, 1996, 110 Stat. 3009–314, 3009–372, 3009–376.)

AMENDMENTS

1996—Subsec. (a)(1)(A). Pub. L. 104–208, § 101(f) [title VI, § 659 [title II, § 204(1)]], substituted "may withdraw all or part of a Thrift Savings Fund account under subsection (b)(2), (3), or (4) of section 8433 of this title or change a withdrawal election" for "may make an election under subsection (b)(3) or (b)(4) of section 8433 of this title or change an election previously made under subsection (b)(1) or (b)(2) of such section" and inserted at end "A married employee or Member (or former employee or Member) may make a withdrawal from a Thrift Savings Fund account under subsection (c)(1) of section 8433 of this title only if the employee or Member (or former employee or Member) satisfies the requirements of subparagraph (B)."

Subsec. (c)(1). Pub. L. 104–208, § 101(f) [title VI, § 659 [title II, § 204(2)(A)]], substituted "An election or change of election" for "An election, change of election, or modification of the commencement date of a deferred annuity" and "or transfer" for "modification, or transfer".

Subsec. (c)(2)(B). Pub. L. 104–208, § 101(f) [title VI, § 659 [title II, § 204(2)(B)]], struck out "modification," after "change," in closing provisions.

Subsec. (e)(1). Pub. L. 104–208, § 101(f) [title VI, § 659 [title II, § 204(3)(A)]], in subpar. (A) inserted "or withdrawal" after "A loan", "and (h)" after "8433(g)", and "or withdrawal" after "such loan", in subpar. (B) inserted "or withdrawal" after "loan", and in subpar. (C) inserted "or withdrawal" after "to a loan" and after "for such loan".

Subsec. (e)(2). Pub. L. 104–208, § 101(f) [title VI, § 659 [title II, § 204(3)(B)(i)]], inserted "or withdrawal" after "loan".

Pub. L. 104–208, § 101(f) [title VI, § 659 [title II, § 204(3)(B)(ii)]], which directed insertion of "and (h)" after "8344(g)", was executed by making the insertion after "8433(g)" to reflect the probable intent of Congress.

Subsec. (g). Pub. L. 104–208, § 101(f) [title VI, § 659 [title II, § 204(4)(A)]], inserted "or withdrawals" after "loans".

Pub. L. 104–208, § 101(f) [title VI, § 659 [title II, § 204(4)(B)]], which directed insertion of "and (h)" after "8344(g)" was executed by making the insertion after "8433(g)" to reflect the probable intent of Congress.

1994—Subsec. (a)(1)(A). Pub. L. 103–226, § 9(d)(1), substituted "subsection (b)(3) or (b)(4) of section 8433 of this title or change an election previously made under subsection (b)(1) or (b)(2)" for "subsection (b)(3), (b)(4), (c)(3), or (c)(4) of section 8433 of this title or change an election previously made under subsection (b)(1), (b)(2), (c)(1), or (c)(2)".

Subsec. (a)(1)(B). Pub. L. 103–226, § 9(i)(9), substituted "subsection (b)" for "subsection (c)".

Subsec. (b). Pub. L. 103–226, § 9(d)(4), amended par. (2) generally. Prior to amendment, par. (2) read as follows: "Paragraph (1) shall not apply—

"(A) in the case of an employee or Member retiring under section 8412, 8413, 8414, or 8451 of this title, or who separates from Government employment pursuant to regulations under section 3502(a) of this title or procedures under section 3595(a) of this title in a reduction in force, if—

"(i) a joint waiver of such method is made, in writing, by the employee or Member and the spouse; or

"(ii) the employee or Member waives such method, in writing, after establishing to the satisfaction of the Executive Director that circumstances described in subsection (a)(2)(A) or (a)(2)(B) make the requirement of a joint waiver inappropriate; or

"(B) in the case of an employee or Member not covered by subparagraph (A), if the employee or Member waives such method after—

"(i) having provided notification to the spouse of intent to waive; or

"(ii) establishing to the satisfaction of the Executive Director that the whereabouts of such spouse cannot be determined."

Pub. L. 103–226, § 9(d)(2), redesignated subsec. (c) as (b) and struck out former subsec. (b) which read as follows:

"(b)(1) Except as provided in paragraph (2), a transfer may be made by an employee or Member (or former employee or Member) under section 8433(d) of this title only after the Executive Director notifies any current spouse and each former spouse of the employee or Member (or former employee or Member), if any, that the transfer is to be made.

"(2) Paragraph (1) may be waived with respect to a spouse or former spouse if the employee or Member (or former employee or Member) establishes to the satisfaction of the Executive Director that the whereabouts of such spouse or former spouse cannot be determined."

Subsec. (c). Pub. L. 103–226, § 9(d)(3), (5), redesignated subsec. (d) as (c) and, in par. (1), struck out "and a transfer may not be made under section 8433(d) of this title" after "effective under this subchapter". Former subsec. (c) redesignated (b).

Subsec. (d). Pub. L. 103–226, § 9(d)(3), redesignated subsec. (e) as (d). Former subsec. (d) redesignated (c).

Subsec. (d)(1)(B). Pub. L. 103–226, § 9(i)(10), substituted "subsection (c)(2)" for "subsection (d)(2)".

Subsec. (d)(3)(A). Pub. L. 103–226, § 9(i)(11), substituted "subsection (b)(1)" for "subsection (c)(1)".

Subsec. (d)(6). Pub. L. 103–226, § 9(i)(12), substituted "or (b)(2)" for "or (c)(2)".

Subsec. (e). Pub. L. 103–226, § 9(d)(3), redesignated subsec. (f) as (e). Former subsec. (e) redesignated (d).

Subsec. (e)(1)(A). Pub. L. 103–226, § 9(i)(13), substituted "section 8433(g)" for "section 8433(i)".

Subsec. (e)(2). Pub. L. 103–226, § 9(i)(14), substituted "section 8433(g) of this title shall not be approved if approval would have the result described under subsection (c)(1)" for "section 8433(i) of this title shall not be approved if approval would have the result described in subsection (d)(1)".

Subsec. (f). Pub. L. 103–226, § 9(d)(3), redesignated subsec. (g) as (f). Former subsec. (f) redesignated (e).

Subsec. (g). Pub. L. 103–226, § 9(d)(3), (i)(15), redesignated subsec. (h) as (g) and substituted "section 8433(g)" for "section 8433(i)". Former subsec. (g) redesignated (f).

Subsecs. (h), (i). Pub. L. 103–226, § 9(d)(3), redesignated subsec. (i) as (h). Former subsec. (h) redesignated (g).

1992—Subsec. (c)(2)(A). Pub. L. 102–484 inserted ", or who separates from Government employment pursuant to regulations under section 3502(a) of this title or procedures under section 3595(a) of this title in a reduction in force," after "8451 of this title".

1990—Subsec. (c)(1). Pub. L. 101–335, § 5(c)(1), inserted "an annuity contract is purchased to provide for" after "the date on which" and struck out "commences" after "former Member's annuity".

Subsec. (d)(2)(B)(ii). Pub. L. 101–335, § 5(c)(2), substituted "an annuity contract is purchased to provide for the annuity" for "the annuity commences".

Subsecs. (h), (i). Pub. L. 101–335, § 6(a)(3), added subsec. (h) and redesignated former subsec. (h) as (i).

EFFECTIVE DATE OF 1996 AMENDMENT

Amendment by Pub. L. 104–208 effective Sept. 30, 1996, and withdrawals and elections as provided under such amendment to be made at earliest practicable date as determined by Executive Director in regulations, see section 101(f) [title VI, § 659 [title II, § 207]] of Pub. L. 104–208, set out as a note under section 5545a of this title.

EFFECTIVE DATE OF 1994 AMENDMENT

Amendment by Pub. L. 103–226 effective Mar. 10, 1995, see section 9(j) of Pub. L. 103–226, set out as a note under section 8351 of this title.

EFFECTIVE DATE OF 1992 AMENDMENT

Amendment by Pub. L. 102–484 applicable with respect to separations occurring after Dec. 31, 1993, or such earlier date as Executive Director (appointed under section 8474 of this title) may by regulation prescribe, see section 4437(d) of Pub. L. 102–484, set out as a note under section 8351 of this title.

EFFECTIVE DATE OF 1990 AMENDMENT

Amendment by section 5(c) of Pub. L. 101–335 effective Apr. 1, 1987, see section 5(d) of Pub. L. 101–335, set out as a note under section 8433 of this title.

Amendment by section 6(a)(3) of Pub. L. 101–335 effective as of second election period described in section 8432(b) of this title beginning after July 17, 1990, or such earlier date as Executive Director may by regulation prescribe, and applicable with respect to separations occurring before, on, or after that effective date, see section 6(c) of Pub. L. 101–335, set out as a note under section 8351 of this title.

SECTION REFERRED TO IN OTHER SECTIONS

This section is referred to in sections 8351, 8433, 8434, 8436 of this title.

§ 8436. Administrative provisions

(a) The Executive Director shall make or provide for payments and transfers in accordance with an election of an employee or Member under section 8433 or 8434(b) of this title or, if applicable, in accordance with section 8435 of this title.

(b) Any election, change of election, or modification of a deferred annuity commencement date made under this subchapter shall be in writing and shall be filed with the Executive Director in accordance with regulations prescribed by the Executive Director.

(Added Pub. L. 99–335, title I, § 101(a), June 6, 1986, 100 Stat. 550.)

§ 8437. Thrift Savings Fund

(a) There is established in the Treasury of the United States a Thrift Savings Fund.

(b) The Thrift Savings Fund consists of the sum of all amounts contributed under section 8432 of this title and all amounts deposited under section 8479(b) of this title, increased by the total net earnings from investments of sums in the Thrift Savings Fund or reduced by the total net losses from investments of the Thrift Savings Fund, and reduced by the total amount of payments made from the Thrift Savings Fund (including payments for administrative expenses).

(c) The sums in the Thrift Savings Fund are appropriated and shall remain available without fiscal year limitation—

(1) to invest under section 8438 of this title;

(2) to pay benefits or purchase annuity contracts under this subchapter;

(3) to pay the administrative expenses of the Federal Retirement Thrift Investment Management System prescribed in subchapter VII of this chapter;

(4) to make distributions for the purposes of section 8440(b) of this title;

(5) to make loans to employees and Members as authorized under section 8433(g) of this title; and

(6) to purchase insurance as provided in section 8479(b)(2) of this title.

(d) Administrative expenses incurred to carry out this subchapter and subchapter VII of this chapter shall be paid first out of any sums in the Thrift Savings Fund forfeited under section 8432(g) of this title and then out of net earnings in such Fund.

(e)(1) Subject to subsection (d) and paragraphs (2) and (3), sums in the Thrift Savings Fund credited to the account of an employee, Member, former employee, or former Member may not be used for, or diverted to, purposes other than for the exclusive benefit of the employee, Member, former employee, or former Member or his beneficiaries under this subchapter.

(2) Except as provided in paragraph (3), sums in the Thrift Savings Fund may not be assigned or alienated and are not subject to execution, levy, attachment, garnishment, or other legal process. For the purposes of this paragraph, a loan made from such Fund to an employee or Member shall not be considered to be an assignment or alienation.

(3) Moneys due or payable from the Thrift Savings Fund to any individual and, in the case of an individual who is an employee or Member (or former employee or Member), the balance in the account of the employee or Member (or former employee or Member) shall be subject to legal process for the enforcement of the individual's legal obligations to provide child support or make alimony payments as provided in section 459 of the Social Security Act (42 U.S.C. 659) or relating to the enforcement of a judgment for physically, sexually, or emotionally abusing a child as provided under section 8467(a). For the purposes of this paragraph, an amount contributed for the benefit of an individual under section 8432(c)(1) (including any earnings attributable thereto) shall not be considered part of the balance in such individual's account unless such amount is nonforfeitable, as determined under applicable provisions of section 8432(g).

(f) The sums in the Thrift Savings Fund shall not be appropriated for any purpose other than the purposes specified in this section and may not be used for any other purpose.

(g) All sums contributed to the Thrift Savings Fund by an employee or Member or by an employing agency for the benefit of such employee or Member and all net earnings in such Fund attributable to investment of such sums are held in such Fund in trust for such employee or Member.

(Added Pub. L. 99–335, title I, § 101(a), June 6, 1986, 100 Stat. 550; amended Pub. L. 100–238, title I, §§ 116, 117(a), Jan. 8, 1988, 101 Stat. 1751; Pub. L. 103–226, § 9(i)(16), Mar. 30, 1994, 108 Stat. 122; Pub. L. 103–358, § 2(b)(4), Oct. 14, 1994, 108 Stat. 3421.)

AMENDMENTS

1994—Subsec. (c)(5). Pub. L. 103–226 substituted "section 8433(g)" for "section 8433(i)".

Subsec. (e)(3). Pub. L. 103–358 substituted "or relating to the enforcement of a judgment for physically, sexually, or emotionally abusing a child as provided under section 8467(a)." for period at end of first sentence.

1988—Subsec. (d). Pub. L. 100–238, § 117(a)(1), struck out "attributable to sums contributed to such Fund under section 8432(c) of this title" after "such Fund".

Subsec. (e)(1). Pub. L. 100–238, § 117(a)(2), inserted "subsection (d) and" after "Subject to".

Subsec. (e)(3). Pub. L. 100–238, § 116, inserted at end "For the purposes of this paragraph, an amount contributed for the benefit of an individual under section 8432(c)(1) (including any earnings attributable thereto) shall not be considered part of the balance in such individual's account unless such amount is nonforfeitable, as determined under applicable provisions of section 8432(g)."

Amendment by Pub. L. 103–358 effective Oct. 14, 1994, and applicable with respect to any decree, order, or other legal process, or notice of agreement received by Office of Personnel Management or Executive Director of Federal Retirement Thrift Investment Board on or after Oct. 14, 1994, see section 3 of Pub. L. 103–358, set out as a note under section 8345 of this title.

Amendment by Pub. L. 103–226 effective Mar. 10, 1995, see section 9(j) of Pub. L. 103–226, set out as a note under section 8351 of this title.

EFFECTIVE DATE OF 1988 AMENDMENT

Section 117(b) of Pub. L. 100–238 provided that: "The amendments made by subsection (a) [amending this section] shall take effect on the first day of the first month beginning on or after the date of the enactment of this Act [Jan. 8, 1988]."

SECTION REFERRED TO IN OTHER SECTIONS

This section is referred to in sections 8351, 8439, 8471 of this title.

§ 8438. Investment of Thrift Savings Fund

(a) For the purposes of this section—

(1) the term "Common Stock Index Investment Fund" means the Common Stock Index Investment Fund established under subsection (b)(1)(C);

(2) the term "equity capital" means common and preferred stock, surplus, undivided profits, contingency reserves, and other capital reserves;

(3) the term "Fixed Income Investment Fund" means the Fixed Income Investment Fund established under subsection (b)(1)(B);

(4) the term "Government Securities Investment Fund" means the Government Securities Investment Fund established under subsection (b)(1)(A);

(5) the term "International Stock Index Investment Fund" means the International Stock Index Investment Fund established under subsection (b)(1)(E);

(6) the term "net worth" means capital, paid-in and contributed surplus, unassigned surplus, contingency reserves, group contingency reserves, and special reserves;

(7) the term "plan" means an employee benefit plan, as defined in section 3(3) of the Employee Retirement Income Security Act of 1974 (29 U.S.C. 1002(3));

(8) the term "qualified professional asset manager" means—

(A) a bank, as defined in section 202(a)(2) of the Investment Advisers Act of 1940 (15 U.S.C. 80b–2(a)(2)) which—

(i) has the power to manage, acquire, or dispose of assets of a plan; and

(ii) has, as of the last day of its latest fiscal year ending before the date of a determination for the purpose of this clause, equity capital in excess of $1,000,000;

(B) a savings and loan association, the accounts of which are insured by the Federal Deposit Insurance Corporation, which—

(i) has applied for and been granted trust powers to manage, acquire, or dispose of assets of a plan by a State or Government authority having supervision over savings and loan associations; and

(ii) has, as of the last day of its latest fiscal year ending before the date of a determination for the purpose of this clause, equity capital or net worth in excess of $1,000,000;

(C) an insurance company which—

(i) is qualified under the laws of more than one State to manage, acquire, or dispose of any assets of a plan;

(ii) has, as of the last day of its latest fiscal year ending before the date of a determination for the purpose of this clause, net worth in excess of $1,000,000; and

(iii) is subject to supervision and examination by a State authority having supervision over insurance companies; or

(D) an investment adviser registered under section 203 of the Investment Advisers Act of 1940 (15 U.S.C. 80b–3) if the investment adviser has, on the last day of its latest fiscal year ending before the date of a determination for the purpose of this subparagraph, total client assets under its management and control in excess of $50,000,000, and—

(i) the investment adviser has, on such day, shareholder's or partner's equity in excess of $750,000; or

(ii) payment of all of the investment adviser's liabilities, including any liabilities which may arise by reason of a breach or violation of a duty described in section 8477 of this title, is unconditionally guaranteed by—

(I) a person (as defined in section 8471(4) of this title) who directly or indirectly, through one or more intermediaries, controls, is controlled by, or is under common control with the investment adviser and who has, on the last day of the person's latest fiscal year ending before the date of a determination for the purpose of this clause, shareholder's or partner's equity in an amount which, when added to the amount of the shareholder's or partner's equity of the investment adviser on such day, exceeds $750,000;

(II) a qualified professional asset manager described in subparagraph (A), (B), or (C); or

(III) a broker or dealer registered under section 15 of the Securities Exchange Act of 1934 (15 U.S.C. 78o) that has, on the last day of the broker's or dealer's latest fiscal year ending before the date of a determination for the purpose of this clause, net worth in excess of $750,000;

(9) the term "shareholder's or partner's equity", as used in paragraph (8)(D) with respect to an investment adviser or a person (as defined in section 8471(4) of this title) who is affiliated with the investment adviser in a manner described in clause (ii)(I) of such paragraph (8)(D), means the equity shown in the

most recent balance sheet prepared for such investment adviser or affiliated person, in accordance with generally accepted accounting principles, within 2 years before the date on which the investment adviser's status as a qualified professional asset manager is determined for the purposes of this section; and

(10) the term "Small Capitalization Stock Index Investment Fund" means the Small Capitalization Stock Index Investment Fund established under subsection (b)(1)(D).

(b)(1) The Board shall establish—

(A) a Government Securities Investment Fund under which sums in the Thrift Savings Fund are invested in securities of the United States Government issued as provided in subsection (e);

(B) a Fixed Income Investment Fund under which sums in the Thrift Savings Fund are invested in—

   (i) insurance contracts;

   (ii) certificates of deposits; or

   (iii) other instruments or obligations selected by qualified professional asset managers,

which return the amount invested and pay interest, at a specified rate or rates, on that amount during a specified period of time;

(C) a Common Stock Index Investment Fund as provided in paragraph (2);

(D) a Small Capitalization Stock Index Investment Fund as provided in paragraph (3); and

(E) an International Stock Index Investment Fund as provided in paragraph (4).

(2)(A) The Board shall select an index which is a commonly recognized index comprised of common stock the aggregate market value of which is a reasonably complete representation of the United States equity markets.

(B) The Common Stock Index Investment Fund shall be invested in a portfolio designed to replicate the performance of the index selected under subparagraph (A). The portfolio shall be designed such that, to the extent practicable, the percentage of the Common Stock Index Investment Fund that is invested in each stock is the same as the percentage determined by dividing the aggregate market value of all shares of that stock by the aggregate market value of all shares of all stocks included in such index.

(3)(A) The Board shall select an index which is a commonly recognized index comprised of common stock the aggregate market value of which represents the United States equity markets excluding the common stocks included in the Common Stock Index Investment Fund.

(B) The Small Capitalization Stock Index Investment Fund shall be invested in a portfolio designed to replicate the performance of the index in subparagraph (A). The portfolio shall be designed such that, to the extent practicable, the percentage of the Small Capitalization Stock Index Investment Fund that is invested in each stock is the same as the percentage determined by dividing the aggregate market value of all shares of that stock by the aggregate market value of all shares of all stocks included in such index.

(4)(A) The Board shall select an index which is a commonly recognized index comprised of

stock the aggregate market value of which is a reasonably complete representation of the international equity markets excluding the United States equity markets.

(B) The International Stock Index Investment Fund shall be invested in a portfolio designed to replicate the performance of the index in subparagraph (A). The portfolio shall be designed such that, to the extent practicable, the percentage of the International Stock Index Investment Fund that is invested in each stock is the same as the percentage determined by dividing the aggregate market value of all shares of that stock by the aggregate market value of all shares of all stocks included in such index.

(c)(1) The Executive Director shall invest the sums available in the Thrift Savings Fund for investment as provided in elections made under subsection (d).

(2) If an election has not been made with respect to any sums in the Thrift Savings Fund available for investment, the Executive Director shall invest such sums in the Government Securities Investment Fund.

(d)(1) At least twice each year, an employee or Member (or former employee or Member) may elect the investment funds referred to in subsection (b) into which the sums in the Thrift Savings Fund credited to such individual's account are to be invested or reinvested.

(2) An election may be made under paragraph (1) only in accordance with regulations prescribed by the Executive Director and within such period as the Executive Director shall provide in such regulations.

(e)(1) The Secretary of the Treasury is authorized to issue special interest-bearing obligations of the United States for purchase by the Thrift Savings Fund for the Government Securities Investment Fund.

(2)(A) Obligations issued for the purpose of this subsection shall have maturities fixed with due regard to the needs of such Fund as determined by the Executive Director, and shall bear interest at a rate equal to the average market yield (computed by the Secretary of the Treasury on the basis of market quotations as of the end of the calendar month next preceding the date of issue of such obligations) on all marketable interest-bearing obligations of the United States then forming a part of the public debt which are not due or callable earlier than 4 years after the end of such calendar month.

(B) Any average market yield computed under subparagraph (A) which is not a multiple of one-eighth of 1 percent, shall be rounded to the nearest multiple of one-eighth of 1 percent.

(f) The Board, other Government agencies, the Executive Director, an employee, a Member, a former employee, and a former Member may not exercise voting rights associated with the ownership of securities by the Thrift Savings Fund.

(g)(1) Notwithstanding subsection (e) of this section, the Secretary of the Treasury may suspend the issuance of additional amounts of obligations of the United States, if such issuances could not be made without causing the public debt of the United States to exceed the public debt limit, as determined by the Secretary of the Treasury.

(2) Any issuances of obligations to the Government Securities Investment Fund which, solely

by reason of the public debt limit are not issued, shall be issued under subsection (e) by the Secretary of the Treasury as soon as such issuances can be issued without exceeding the public debt limit.

(3) Upon expiration of the debt issuance suspension period, the Secretary of the Treasury shall immediately issue to the Government Securities Investment Fund obligations under chapter 31 of title 31 that (notwithstanding subsection (e)(2) of this section) bear such interest rates and maturity dates as are necessary to ensure that, after such obligations are issued, the holdings of obligations of the United States by the Government Securities Investment Fund will replicate the obligations that would then be held by the Government Securities Investment Fund under the procedure set forth in paragraph (5), if the suspension of issuances under paragraph (1) of this subsection had not occurred.

(4) On the first business day after the expiration of any debt issuance suspension period, the Secretary of the Treasury shall pay to the Government Securities Investment Fund, from amounts in the general fund of the Treasury of the United States not otherwise appropriated, an amount equal to the excess of the net amount of interest that would have been earned by the Government Securities Investment Fund from obligations of the United States during such debt issuance suspension period if—

(A) amounts in the Government Securities Investment Fund that were available for investment in obligations of the United States and were not invested during such debt issuance suspension period solely by reason of the public debt limit had been invested under the procedure set forth in paragraph (5), over

(B) the net amount of interest actually earned by the Government Securities Investment Fund from obligations of the United States during such debt issuance suspension period.

(5) On each business day during the debt limit suspension period, the Executive Director shall notify the Secretary of the Treasury of the amounts, by maturity, that would have been invested or redeemed each day had the debt issuance suspension period not occurred.

(6) For purposes of this subsection and subsection (h) of this section—

(A) the term "public debt limit" means the limitation imposed by section 3101(b) of title 31; and

(B) the term "debt issuance suspension period" means any period for which the Secretary of the Treasury determines for purposes of this subsection that the issuance of obligations of the United States may not be made without exceeding the public debt limit.

(h)(1) The Secretary of the Treasury shall report to Congress on the operation and status of the Thrift Savings Fund during each debt issuance suspension period for which the Secretary is required to take action under paragraph (3) or (4) of subsection (g) of this section. The report shall be submitted as soon as possible after the expiration of such period, but not later than 30 days after the first business day after the expiration of such period. The Secretary shall con-

currently transmit a copy of such report to the Executive Director.

(2) Whenever the Secretary of the Treasury determines that, by reason of the public debt limit, the Secretary will be unable to fully comply with the requirements of subsection (e) of this section, the Secretary shall immediately notify Congress and the Executive Director of the determination. The notification shall be made in writing.

(Added Pub. L. 99–335, title I, § 101(a), June 6, 1986, 100 Stat. 551; amended Pub. L. 100–43, § 2, May 22, 1987, 101 Stat. 315; Pub. L. 100–366, § 2(a), July 13, 1988, 102 Stat. 826; Pub. L. 101–335, § 3(a), July 17, 1990, 104 Stat. 320; Pub. L. 102–378, § 2(68), Oct. 2, 1992, 106 Stat. 1355; Pub. L. 104–208, div. A, title I, § 101(f) [title VI, § 659 [title I, § 102]], Sept. 30, 1996, 110 Stat. 3009–314, 3009–372; Pub. L. 104–316, title I, § 103(i), Oct. 19, 1996, 110 Stat. 3829.)

AMENDMENTS

1996—Subsec. (a). Pub. L. 104–208, § 101(f) [title VI, § 659 [title I, § 102(1)]], added par. (5), redesignated former pars. (5) to (8) as (6) to (9), respectively, in par. (9) substituted "paragraph (8)(D)" for "paragraph (7)(D)" in two places, and added par. (10).

Subsec. (b). Pub. L. 104–208, § 101(f) [title VI, § 659 [title I, § 102(2)]], in par. (1) added subpars. (D) and (E) and added pars. (3) and (4).

Subsec. (h)(1). Pub. L. 104–316 struck out "and the Comptroller General of the United States" before period at end.

1992—Subsec. (a)(7)(B). Pub. L. 102–378 substituted "Deposit" for "Savings and Loan".

1990—Subsec. (b)(1)(A). Pub. L. 101–335, § 3(a)(2), substituted "subsection (e)" for "subsection (f)".

Subsec. (c)(1). Pub. L. 101–335, § 3(a)(3), substituted "The" for "Subject to subsection (e), the".

Subsec. (d)(1). Pub. L. 101–335, § 3(a)(4), struck out "and not subject to subsection (e)" after "individual's account".

Subsec. (e). Pub. L. 101–335, § 3(a)(1), redesignated subsec. (f) as (e) and struck out former subsec. (e) which related to minimum percentages to be invested in Government Securities Investment Fund and limitations on reinvestment of sums invested in Government Securities Investment Fund prior to years 1992 and 1997.

Subsec. (f). Pub. L. 101–335, § 3(a)(1), redesignated subsec. (g) as (f). Former subsec. (f) redesignated (e).

Subsec. (g). Pub. L. 101–335, § 3(a)(1), (5), (6), redesignated subsec. (h) as (g) and substituted "subsection (e)" for "subsection (f)" in pars. (1) and (2), "subsection (e)(2)" for "subsection (f)(2)" in par. (3), and "subsection (h)" for "subsection (i)" in par. (6). Former subsec. (g) redesignated (f).

Subsecs. (h), (i). Pub. L. 101–335, § 3(a)(1), (7), redesignated subsec. (i) as (h) and substituted "subsection (g)" for "subsection (h)" in par. (1) and "subsection (e)" for "subsection (f)" in par. (2). Former subsec. (h) redesignated (g).

1988—Subsec. (e)(3)(A). Pub. L. 100–366 struck out "and the earnings attributable to the investment of such sums" after "paragraph (1)".

1987—Subsecs. (h), (i). Pub. L. 100–43 added subsecs. (h) and (i).

EFFECTIVE DATE OF 1996 AMENDMENT

Section 101(f) [title VI, § 659 [title I, § 104]] provided that: "This title [title I (§§ 101–104) of section 659 of section 101(f) of Pub. L. 104–208, amending this section and section 8439 of this title and enacting provisions set out as a note under section 8401 of this title] shall take effect on the date of enactment of this Act [Sept. 30, 1996], and the Funds established under this title shall be offered for investment at the earliest practicable election period (described in section 8432(b) of title 5, United States Code) as determined by the Executive Director in regulations."

EFFECTIVE DATE OF 1990 AMENDMENT

Amendment by Pub. L. 101–335 effective as of second election period described in section 8432(b) of this title beginning after July 17, 1990, or as of such earlier date as Executive Director may by regulation prescribe, see section 3(c) of Pub. L. 101–335, set out as a note under section 8351 of this title.

EFFECTIVE DATE OF 1988 AMENDMENT

Section 2(b) of Pub. L. 100–366 provided that: "The amendment made by subsection (a) [amending this section] shall apply with respect to earnings attributable to contributions made to the Thrift Savings Fund on or after April 1, 1987."

REMOVAL OF INVESTMENT RESTRICTIONS

Section 3(b)(4) of Pub. L. 101–335 provided that: "Any other provision of law, in effect on the date of enactment of this Act [July 17, 1990], which provides that any amounts contributed to the Thrift Savings Fund, or earnings thereon, may be invested or reinvested only in the Government Securities Investment Fund established under section 8438(b)(1)(A) of title 5, United States Code, shall cease to be effective."

SECTION REFERRED TO IN OTHER SECTIONS

This section is referred to in sections 8437, 8439, 8472, 8477 of this title.

§ 8439. Accounting and information

(a)(1) The Executive Director shall establish and maintain an account for each individual who makes contributions or for whom contributions are made under section 8432 of this title or who makes contributions to the Thrift Savings Fund under section 8351 of this title.

(2) The balance in an individual's account at any time is the excess of—

(A) the sum of—

(i) all contributions made to the Thrift Savings Fund by the individual under section 8432(a) or 8351 of this title;

(ii) all contributions made to such Fund for the benefit of the individual under section 8432(c) of this title; and

(iii) the total amount of the allocations made to and reductions made in the account pursuant to paragraph (3), over

(B) the amounts paid out of the Thrift Savings Fund with respect to such individual under this subchapter.

(3) Pursuant to regulations prescribed by the Executive Director, the Executive Director shall allocate to each account an amount equal to a pro rata share of the net earnings and net losses from each investment of sums in the Thrift Savings Fund attributable to sums credited to such account, reduced by an appropriate share of the administrative expenses paid out of the net earnings under section 8437(d) of this title, as determined by the Executive Director.

(b)(1) For the purposes of this subsection, the term "qualified public accountant" shall have the same meaning as provided in section 103(a)(3)(D) of the Employee Retirement Income Security Act of 1974 (29 U.S.C. 1023(a)(3)(D)).

(2) The Executive Director shall annually engage, on behalf of all individuals for whom an account is maintained, an independent qualified public accountant, who shall conduct an examination of all accounts and other books and records maintained in the administration of this subchapter and subchapter VII as the public accountant considers necessary to enable the public accountant to make the determination required by paragraph (3). The examination shall be conducted in accordance with generally accepted auditing standards and shall involve such tests of the accounts, books, and records as the public accountant considers necessary.

(3) The public accountant conducting an examination under paragraph (2) shall determine whether the accounts, books, and records referred to in such paragraph have been maintained in conformity with generally accepted accounting principles applied on a basis consistent with the manner in which such principles were applied during the examination conducted under such paragraph during the preceding year. The public accountant shall transmit to the Board a report on his examination, including his determination under this paragraph.

(4) In making a determination under paragraph (3), a public accountant may rely on the correctness of any actuarial matter certified by an enrolled actuary if the public accountant states his reliance in the report transmitted to the Board under such paragraph.

(c)(1) The Board shall prescribe regulations under which each individual for whom an account is maintained shall be furnished with—

(A) a periodic statement relating to the individual's account; and

(B) a summary description of the investment options under section 8438 of this title covering, and an evaluation of, each such option the 5-year period preceding the date as of which such evaluation is made.

(2) Information under this subsection shall be provided at least 30 calendar days before the beginning of each election period under section 8432(b)(1)(A) of this title, and in a manner designed to facilitate informed decisionmaking with respect to elections under sections 8432 and 8438 of this title. Nothing in this paragraph shall be considered to limit the dissemination of information only to the times required under the preceding sentence.

(d) Each employee, Member, former employee, or former Member who elects to invest in the Common Stock Index Investment Fund, the Fixed Income Investment Fund, the International Stock Index Investment Fund, or the Small Capitalization Stock Index Investment Fund, defined in paragraphs (1), (3), (5), and (10), respectively, of section 8438(a) of this title shall sign an acknowledgement prescribed by the Executive Director which states that the employee, Member, former employee, or former Member understands that an investment in either such Fund is made at the employee's, Member's, former employee's, or former Member's risk, that the employee, Member, former employee, or former Member is not protected by the Government against any loss on such investment, and that a return on such investment is not guaranteed by the Government.

(Added Pub. L. 99–335, title I, § 101(a), June 6, 1986, 100 Stat. 555; amended Pub. L. 104–208, div.

A, title I, §101(f) [title VI, §659 [title I, §103]], Sept. 30, 1996, 110 Stat. 3009–314, 3009–372, 3009–373; Pub. L. 104–316, title I, §103(j), Oct. 19, 1996, 110 Stat. 3829; Pub. L. 106–65, div. A, title VI, §661(a)(5), Oct. 5, 1999, 113 Stat. 672; Pub. L. 106–361, §2(b)(4), (5), Oct. 27, 2000, 114 Stat. 1401.)

AMENDMENT OF SUBSECTION (a)(1), (2)

Pub. L. 106–65, div. A, title VI, §§ 661(a)(5), 663, Oct. 5, 1999, 113 Stat. 672, 673, as amended by Pub. L. 106–398, § 1 [[div. A], title VI, § 661(a)], Oct. 30, 2000, 114 Stat. 1654, 1654A–167, provided that effective 180 days after Oct. 30, 2000, unless postponed, subsection (a) of this section is amended as follows:

(1) in paragraph (1), by striking "under section 8432(c)(1) of this title" and "under section 8351 of this title";

(2) in paragraph (2)(A)(i), by striking all after "individual" and inserting a semicolon; and

(3) in paragraph (2)(A)(ii), by striking all after "individual" and inserting "; and".

AMENDMENTS

2000—Subsec. (a)(1). Pub. L. 106–361, §2(b)(4), inserted "who makes contributions or" after "for each individual" and substituted "section 8432" for "section 8432(c)(1)".

Subsec. (c)(2). Pub. L. 106–361, §2(b)(5), inserted at end "Nothing in this paragraph shall be considered to limit the dissemination of information only to the times required under the preceding sentence."

1996—Subsec. (b)(3). Pub. L. 104–316 struck out "and the Comptroller General of the United States" after "to the Board".

Subsec. (d). Pub. L. 104–208 substituted "Each employee, Member, former employee, or former Member who elects to invest in the Common Stock Index Investment Fund, the Fixed Income Investment Fund, the International Stock Index Investment Fund, or the Small Capitalization Stock Index Investment Fund, defined in paragraphs (1), (3), (5), and (10)," for "Each employee, Member, former employee, or former Member who elects to invest in the Common Stock Index Investment Fund or the Fixed Income Investment Fund described in paragraphs (1) and (3),".

EFFECTIVE DATE OF 2000 AMENDMENT

Amendment by Pub. L. 106–361 effective at the earliest practicable date after Sept. 30, 2000, as determined by the Executive Director in regulations, see section 2(c)(1) of Pub. L. 106–361, set out as a note under section 8432 of this title.

EFFECTIVE DATE OF 1999 AMENDMENT

Amendment by Pub. L. 106–65 effective 180 days after Oct. 30, 2000, unless postponed, see section 663 of Pub. L. 106–65, as amended, set out as an Effective Date note under section 8440e of this title.

EFFECTIVE DATE OF 1996 AMENDMENT

Amendment by Pub. L. 104–208 effective Sept. 30, 1996, with provisions for certain funds to be offered for investment at earliest practicable election period, see section 101(f) [title VI, §659 [title I, §104]] of Pub. L. 104–208, set out as a note under section 8438 of this title.

SECTION REFERRED TO IN OTHER SECTIONS

This section is referred to in sections 8401, 8461, 8471 of this title; title 31 section 9503.

§ 8440. Tax treatment of the Thrift Savings Fund

(a) For purposes of the Internal Revenue Code of 1986—

(1) the Thrift Savings Fund shall be treated as a trust described in section 401(a) of such Code which is exempt from taxation under section 501(a) of such Code;

(2) any contribution to, or distribution from, the Thrift Savings Fund shall be treated in the same manner as contributions to or distributions from such a trust; and

(3) subject to section 401(k)(4)(B) of such Code and any dollar limitation on the application of section 402(a)(8) of such Code, contributions to the Thrift Savings Fund shall not be treated as distributed or made available to an employee or Member nor as a contribution made to the Fund by an employee or Member merely because the employee or Member has, under the provisions of this subchapter and section 8351 of this title, an election whether the contribution will be made to the Thrift Savings Fund or received by the employee or Member in cash.

(b) NONDISCRIMINATION REQUIREMENTS.—Notwithstanding any other provision of law, the Thrift Savings Fund is not subject to the nondiscrimination requirements applicable to arrangements described in section 401(k) of title 26, United States Code, or to matching contributions (as described in section 401(m) of title 26, United States Code), so long as it meets the requirements of this section.

(c) Subsection (a) shall not be construed to provide that any amount of the employee's or Member's basic pay which is contributed to the Thrift Savings Fund shall not be included in the term "wages" for the purposes of section 209 of the Social Security Act or section 3121(a) of the Internal Revenue Code of 1986.

(Added Pub. L. 99–335, title I, §101(a), June 6, 1986, 100 Stat. 557; amended Pub. L. 100–202, §101(m) [title VI, §624(b)], Dec. 22, 1987, 101 Stat. 1329–390, 1329–430; Pub. L. 100–647, title I, §1011A(m)(2), Nov. 10, 1988, 102 Stat. 3483; by Pub. L. 102–378, §2(69), Oct. 2, 1992, 106 Stat. 1355; Pub. L. 103–353, §5(e)(5), Oct. 13, 1994, 108 Stat. 3174.)

REFERENCES IN TEXT

The Internal Revenue Code of 1986, referred to in subsecs. (a) and (c), is classified generally to Title 26, Internal Revenue Code.

Section 209 of the Social Security Act, referred to in subsec. (c), is classified to section 409 of Title 42, The Public Health and Welfare.

AMENDMENTS

1994—Subsecs. (a), (c). Pub. L. 103–353 substituted "Internal Revenue Code of 1986" for "Internal Revenue Code of 1954".

1992—Subsec. (a)(3). Pub. L. 102–378 inserted "section 401(k)(4)(B) of such Code and" after "subject to".

1988—Subsec. (a)(3). Pub. L. 100–647, which directed the insertion of ", 401(k)(4)(B) of such Code," after "subsection (b)", could not be executed because of previous amendment by Pub. L. 100–202, §101(m) [title VI, §624(b)(1)] which struck out "subsection (b)". See 1987 Amendment note below.

1987—Subsec. (a)(3). Pub. L. 100–202, §101(m) [title VI, §624(b)(1)], struck out "the provisions of subsection (b) and" after "subject to".

Subsec. (b). Pub. L. 100–202, §101(m) [title VI, §624(b)(2)], added subsec. (b) and struck out former subsec. (b) which consisted of pars. (1) and (2) providing that subsec. (a)(3) not apply to the Thrift Savings Fund unless the Fund meets the antidiscrimination requirements applicable to arrangements described in section 401(k) of title 26 and to matching contributions.

Amendment by Pub. L. 103–353 effective with respect to reemployments initiated on or after the first day after the 60-day period beginning Oct. 13, 1994, with transition rules, see section 8 of Pub. L. 103–353, set out as an Effective Date note under section 4301 of Title 38, Veterans' Benefits.

EFFECTIVE DATE OF 1992 AMENDMENT

Amendment by Pub. L. 102–378 effective Nov. 10, 1988, see section 9(b)(8) of Pub. L. 102–378, set out as a note under section 6303 of this title.

EFFECTIVE DATE OF 1988 AMENDMENT

Amendment by Pub. L. 100–647 effective as if included in the provision of the Tax Reform Act of 1986, Pub. L. 99–514, to which such amendment relates, see section 1019(a) of Pub. L. 100–647, set out as a note under section 1 of Title 26, Internal Revenue Code.

SECTION REFERRED TO IN OTHER SECTIONS

This section is referred to in section 8437 of this title.

§ 8440a. Justices and judges

(a)(1) A justice or judge of the United States as defined by section 451 of title 28 may elect to contribute an amount of such individual's basic pay to the Thrift Savings Fund. Basic pay does not include an annuity or salary received by a justice or judge who has retired under section 371(a) or (b) or section 372(a) of title 28, United States Code.

(2) An election may be made under paragraph (1) only during a period provided under section 8432(b) for individuals subject to this chapter.

(b)(1) Except as otherwise provided in this subsection, the provisions of this subchapter and subchapter VII shall apply with respect to justices and judges making contributions to the Thrift Savings Fund.

(2) The amount contributed by a justice or judge for any pay period shall not exceed the maximum percentage of such justice's or judge's basic pay for such pay period allowable under section 8440f.

(3) No contributions shall be made for the benefit of a justice or judge under section 8432(c) of this title.

(4) Section 8433(b) of this title applies with respect to elections available to any justice or judge who retires under section 371(a) or (b) or section 372(a) of title 28. Retirement under section 371(a) or (b) or section 372(a) of title 28 is a separation from service for the purposes of subchapters III and VII of chapter 84 of this title.

(5) Section 8433(b) of this title applies to any justice or judge who resigns without having met the age and service requirements set forth in section 371(c) of title 28.

(6) The provisions of section 8351(b)(5) of this title shall govern the rights of spouses of justices or judges contributing to the Thrift Savings Fund under this section.

(7) Notwithstanding paragraphs (4) and (5), if any justice or judge retires under subsection (a) or (b) of section 371 or section 372(a) of title 28, or resigns without having met the age and service requirements set forth under section 371(c) of title 28, and such justice's or judge's nonforfeitable account balance is less than an amount that the Executive Director prescribes by regulation, the Executive Director shall pay the non-forfeitable account balance to the participant in a single payment.

(Added Pub. L. 100–654, title IV, § 401(a), Nov. 14, 1988, 102 Stat. 3847; amended Pub. L. 101–335, §§ 3(b)(2), 6(b)(2), July 17, 1990, 104 Stat. 320, 323; Pub. L. 102–378, § 2(70), Oct. 2, 1992, 106 Stat. 1355; Pub. L. 103–226, § 9(e), (i)(17), Mar. 30, 1994, 108 Stat. 120, 122; Pub. L. 104–208, div. A, title I, § 101(f) [title VI, § 659 [title II, § 205(a)]], Sept. 30, 1996, 110 Stat. 3009–314, 3009–372, 3009–377; Pub. L. 106–361, § 2(b)(6), Oct. 27, 2000, 114 Stat. 1401; Pub. L. 106–554, § 1(a)(4) [div. B, title I, § 138(a)(2)], Dec. 21, 2000, 114 Stat. 2763, 2763A–233.)

CODIFICATION

Another section 8440a was renumbered section 8440b of this title.

AMENDMENTS

2000—Subsec. (a)(2). Pub. L. 106–361 substituted "this chapter" for "chapter 84 of this title: *Provided, however*, That a justice or judge may make the first such election within 60 days of the effective date of this section".

Subsec. (b)(2). Pub. L. 106–554 amended par. (2) generally. Prior to amendment, par. (2) read as follows: "The amount contributed by a justice or judge shall not exceed 5 percent of basic pay."

1996—Subsec. (b)(7). Pub. L. 104–208 substituted "less than an amount that the Executive Director prescribes by regulation" for "$3,500 or less" and struck out "unless the justice or judge elects, at such time and otherwise in such manner as the Executive Director prescribes, one of the options available under section 8433(b)" before period at end.

1994—Subsec. (b)(5). Pub. L. 103–226, § 9(e)(1), substituted "Section 8433(b)" for "Section 8433(d)".

Subsec. (b)(6). Pub. L. 103–226, § 9(i)(17), substituted "section 8351(b)(5)" for "section 8351(b)(7)".

Subsec. (b)(7), (8). Pub. L. 103–226, § 9(e)(2), added par. (7) and struck out former pars. (7) and (8) which read as follows:

"(7) Notwithstanding paragraph (5), if any justice or judge who elects to make contributions to the Thrift Savings Fund under subsection (a) resigns without having met the age and service requirements set forth in section 371(c) of title 28, and such justice's or judge's nonforfeitable account balance is $3,500 or less, the Executive Director shall pay the nonforfeitable account balance to the participant in a single payment unless the justice or judge elects, at such time and otherwise in such manner as the Executive Director prescribes, to have the nonforfeitable account balance transferred to an eligible retirement plan as provided in section 8433(e).

"(8) Notwithstanding paragraph (4), if any justice or judge retires under subsection (a) or (b) of section 371 or section 372(a) of title 28, and such justice's or judge's nonforfeitable account balance is $3,500 or less, the Executive Director shall pay the nonforfeitable account balance to the participant in a single payment unless the justice or judge elects, at such time and otherwise in such manner as the Executive Director prescribes, one of the options available under section 8433(b)."

1992—Subsec. (b)(1). Pub. L. 102–378 substituted "this subchapter and subchapter VII" for "subchapters III and VII of chapter 84 of this title".

1990—Subsec. (b)(6). Pub. L. 101–335, § 3(b)(2), redesignated par. (7) as (6) and struck out former par. (6) which read as follows: "Sums contributed under this section and earnings attributable to such sums may be invested and reinvested only in the Government Securities Investment Fund established under section 8438(b)(1)(A) of this title."

Subsec. (b)(7), (8). Pub. L. 101–335, § 6(b)(2), added pars. (7) and (8). Former par. (7) redesignated (6).

Amendment by Pub. L. 106–361 effective at the earliest practicable date after Sept. 30, 2000, as determined by the Executive Director in regulations, see section 2(c)(1) of Pub. L. 106–361, set out as a note under section 8432 of this title.

EFFECTIVE DATE OF 1996 AMENDMENT

Amendment by Pub. L. 104–208 effective Sept. 30, 1996, and withdrawals and elections as provided under such amendment to be made at earliest practicable date as determined by Executive Director in regulations, see section 101(f) [title VI, § 659 [title II, § 207]] of Pub. L. 104–208, set out as a note under section 5545a of this title.

EFFECTIVE DATE OF 1994 AMENDMENT

Amendment by Pub. L. 103–226 effective Mar. 10, 1995, see section 9(j) of Pub. L. 103–226, set out as a note under section 8351 of this title.

EFFECTIVE DATE OF 1990 AMENDMENT

Amendment by section 3(b)(2) of Pub. L. 101–335 effective as of second election period described in section 8432(b) of this title beginning after July 17, 1990, or as of such earlier date as Executive Director may by regulation prescribe, see section 3(c) of Pub. L. 101–335, set out as a note under section 8351 of this title.

Amendment by section 6(b)(2) of Pub. L. 101–335 effective as of second election period described in section 8432(b) of this title beginning after July 17, 1990, or such earlier date as Executive Director may by regulation prescribe, and applicable with respect to separations occurring before, on, or after that effective date, see section 6(c) of Pub. L. 101–335, set out as a note under section 8351 of this title.

SECTION REFERRED TO IN OTHER SECTIONS

This section is referred to in section 8432 of this title.

§ 8440b. Bankruptcy judges and magistrate judges

(a)(1) A bankruptcy judge or magistrate judge who is covered by section 377 of title 28 or section 2(c) of the Retirement and Survivors' Annuities for Bankruptcy Judges and Magistrates Act of 1988 may elect to contribute an amount of such individual's basic pay to the Thrift Savings Fund.

(2) An election may be made under paragraph (1) only during a period provided under section 8432(b) for individuals subject to this chapter.

(b)(1) Except as otherwise provided in this subsection, the provisions of this subchapter and subchapter VII shall apply with respect to bankruptcy judges and magistrate judges who make contributions to the Thrift Savings Fund under subsection (a) of this section.

(2) The amount contributed by a bankruptcy judge or magistrate judge for any pay period shall not exceed the maximum percentage of such bankruptcy judge's or magistrate's[1] basic pay for such pay period allowable under section 8440f.

(3) No contributions shall be made under section 8432(c) of this title for the benefit of a bankruptcy judge or magistrate judge making contributions under subsection (a) of this section.

(4)(A) Section 8433(b) of this title applies to a bankruptcy judge or magistrate judge who elects to make contributions to the Thrift Savings Fund under subsection (a) of this section

and who retires entitled to an immediate annuity under section 377 of title 28 (including a disability annuity under subsection (d) of such section) or section 2(c) of the Retirement and Survivors' Annuities for Bankruptcy Judges and Magistrates Act of 1988.

(B) Section 8433(b) of this title applies to any bankruptcy judge or magistrate[2] who elects to make contributions to the Thrift Savings Fund under subsection (a) of this section and who retires before attaining age 65 but is entitled, upon attaining age 65, to an annuity under section 377 of title 28 or section 2(c) of the Retirement and Survivors Annuities for Bankruptcy Judges and Magistrates Act of 1988.

(C) Section 8433(b) of this title applies to any bankruptcy judge or magistrate judge who elects to make contributions to the Thrift Savings Fund under subsection (a) of this section and who retires before becoming entitled to an immediate annuity, or an annuity upon attaining age 65, under section 377 of title 28 or section 2(c) of the Retirement and Survivors' Annuities for Bankruptcy Judges and Magistrates Act of 1988.

(5) With respect to bankruptcy judges and magistrate judges to whom this section applies, any of the actions described under paragraph (4)(A), (B), or (C) shall be considered a separation from service for purposes of this subchapter and subchapter VII.

(6) For purposes of this section, the terms "retirement" and "retire" include removal from office under section 377(d) of title 28 on the sole ground of mental or physical disability.

(7) In the case of a bankruptcy judge or magistrate judge who receives a distribution from the Thrift Savings Plan and who later receives an annuity under section 377 of title 28, that annuity shall be offset by an amount equal to the amount of the distribution which represents the Government's contribution to that person's Thrift Savings Account, without regard to earnings attributable to that amount. Where such an offset would exceed 50 percent of the annuity to be received in the first year, the offset may be divided equally over the first 2 years in which that person receives the annuity.

(8) Notwithstanding paragraph (4), if any bankruptcy judge or magistrate[2] retires under circumstances making such bankruptcy judge or magistrate[2] eligible to make an election under subsection (b) of section 8433, and such bankruptcy judge's or magistrate judge's nonforfeitable account balance is less than an amount that the Executive Director prescribes by regulation, the Executive Director shall pay the nonforfeitable account balance to the participant in a single payment.

(Added Pub. L. 100–659, § 7(a), Nov. 15, 1988, 102 Stat. 3919, § 8440a; renumbered § 8440b and amended Pub. L. 101–335, §§ 3(b)(3), 6(b)(3), 9(a), July 17, 1990, 104 Stat. 320, 324, 326; Pub. L. 101–650, title III, § 321, Dec. 1, 1990, 104 Stat. 5117; Pub. L. 103–226, § 9(f), Mar. 30, 1994, 108 Stat. 120; Pub. L. 104–208, div. A, title I, § 101(f) [title VI, § 659 [title II, § 205(b)]], Sept. 30, 1996, 110 Stat. 3009–314, 3009–372, 3009–377; Pub. L. 106–554, § 1(a)(4) [div. B,

---

[1] So in original. Probably should be "magistrate judge's".

[2] So in original. Probably should be "magistrate judge".

title I, § 138(a)(3)], Dec. 21, 2000, 114 Stat. 2763, 2763A–233.)

Section 2(c) of the Retirement and Survivors' Annuities for Bankruptcy Judges and Magistrates Act of 1988, referred to in subsecs. (a)(1) and (b)(4), is section 2(c) of Pub. L. 100–659, which is set out as a note under section 377 of Title 28, Judiciary and Judicial Procedure.

CODIFICATION

Another section 8440b was renumbered section 8440c of this title.

AMENDMENTS

2000—Subsec. (b)(2). Pub. L. 106–554 substituted "the maximum percentage of such bankruptcy judge's or magistrate's basic pay for such pay period allowable under section 8440f." for "5 percent of basic pay for such pay period."

1996—Subsec. (b)(7). Pub. L. 104–208, § 101(f) [title VI, § 659 [title II, § 205(b)(1)]], inserted "of the distribution" after "equal to the amount" in first sentence.

Subsec. (b)(8). Pub. L. 104–208, § 101(f) [title VI, § 659 [title II, § 205(b)(2)(A)]], substituted "less than an amount that the Executive Director prescribes by regulation" for "$3,500 or less".

Pub. L. 104–208, § 101(f) [title VI, § 659 [title II, § 205(b)(2)(B)]], which directed that par. (8) be amended by striking out "unless the bankruptcy judge or magistrate elects, at such time and otherwise in such manner as the Executive Director prescribes, one of the options available under subsection (b)", was executed by striking out "unless the bankruptcy judge or magistrate elects, at such time and otherwise in such manner as the Executive Director prescribes, one of the options available under such subsection (b)" before period at end, to reflect the probable intent of Congress.

1994—Subsec. (b)(4)(B). Pub. L. 103–226, § 9(f)(1), amended subpar. (B) generally. Prior to amendment, subpar. (B) read as follows: "Section 8433(c) of this title applies to any bankruptcy judge or magistrate who elects to make contributions to the Thrift Savings Fund under subsection (a) of this section and who retires before attaining age 65 but is entitled, upon attaining age 65, to an annuity under section 377 of title 28 or section 2(c) of the Retirement and Survivors' Annuities for Bankruptcy Judges and Magistrates Act of 1988; except that the period described in paragraph (3) of section 8433(c) commences on or after the date on which payment of the bankruptcy judge's or magistrate's annuity under section 377 of title 28 commences."

Subsec. (b)(4)(C). Pub. L. 103–226, § 9(f)(2), substituted "Section 8433(b)" for "Section 8433(d)".

Subsec. (b)(5). Pub. L. 103–226, § 9(f)(3), substituted "any of the actions described under paragraph (4)(A), (B), or (C) shall be considered" for "retirement under section 377 of title 28 is".

Subsec. (b)(8). Pub. L. 103–226, § 9(f)(5)(B), which directed striking out "and (c), as applicable", was executed by striking out "or (c), as applicable" before period at end to reflect the probable intent of Congress.

Pub. L. 103–226, § 9(f)(5)(A), substituted "Notwithstanding paragraph (4), if any bankruptcy judge or magistrate retires under circumstances making such bankruptcy judge or magistrate eligible to make an election under subsection (b)" for "Notwithstanding subparagraphs (A) and (B) of paragraph (4), if any bankruptcy judge or magistrate retires under circumstances making such bankruptcy judge or magistrate eligible to make an election under subsection (b) or (c)".

Pub. L. 103–226, § 9(f)(4), redesignated par. (9) as (8) and struck out former par. (8) which read as follows: "Notwithstanding paragraph (4)(C), if any bankruptcy judge or magistrate who elects to make contributions to the Thrift Savings Fund under subsection (a) retires before becoming entitled to an immediate annuity, or

an annuity upon attaining age 65, under section 377 of title 28 or section 2(c) of the Retirement and Survivors' Annuities for Bankruptcy Judges and Magistrates Act of 1988, and such bankruptcy judge's or magistrate's nonforfeitable account balance is $3,500 or less, the Executive Director shall pay the nonforfeitable account balance to the participant in a single payment unless the bankruptcy judge or magistrate elects, at such time and otherwise in such manner as the Executive Director prescribes, to have the nonforfeitable account balance transferred to an eligible retirement plan as provided in section 8433(e)."

Subsec. (b)(9). Pub. L. 103–226, § 9(f)(4), redesignated par. (9) as (8).

1990—Pub. L. 101–335, § 9(a), renumbered section 8440a of this title as this section.

Subsec. (b)(7). Pub. L. 101–335, § 3(b)(3), redesignated par. (8) as (7) and struck out former par. (7) which read as follows: "Sums contributed pursuant to this section by bankruptcy judges or magistrates, as well as all previous contributions to the Thrift Savings Fund by those bankruptcy judges and magistrates, and earnings attributable to such sums and contributions, may be invested and reinvested only in the Government Securities Investment Fund established under section 8438(b)(1)(A) of this title."

Subsec. (b)(8), (9). Pub. L. 101–335, § 6(b)(3), added pars. (8) and (9). Former par. (8) redesignated (7).

CHANGE OF NAME

Words "magistrate judge", "magistrate judges", and "magistrate judge's" substituted for "magistrate", "magistrates", and "magistrate's", respectively, in section catchline and in subsecs. (a)(1) and (b)(1)–(3), (4)(A), (C), (5), (7), and (8), pursuant to section 321 of Pub. L. 101–650, set out as a note under section 631 of Title 28, Judiciary and Judicial Procedure.

EFFECTIVE DATE OF 1996 AMENDMENT

Amendment by Pub. L. 104–208 effective Sept. 30, 1996, and withdrawals and elections as provided under such amendment to be made at earliest practicable date as determined by Executive Director in regulations, see section 101(f) [title VI, § 659 [title II, § 207]] of Pub. L. 104–208, set out as a note under section 5545a of this title.

EFFECTIVE DATE OF 1994 AMENDMENT

Amendment by Pub. L. 103–226 effective Mar. 10, 1995, see section 9(j) of Pub. L. 103–226, set out as a note under section 8351 of this title.

EFFECTIVE DATE OF 1990 AMENDMENT

Amendment by section 3(b)(3) of Pub. L. 101–335 effective as of second election period described in section 8432(b) of this title beginning after July 17, 1990, or as of such earlier date as Executive Director may by regulation prescribe, see section 3(c) of Pub. L. 101–335, set out as a note under section 8351 of this title.

Amendment by section 6(b)(3) of Pub. L. 101–335 effective as of second election period described in section 8432(b) of this title beginning after July 17, 1990, or such earlier date as Executive Director may by regulation prescribe, and applicable with respect to separations occurring before, on, or after that effective date, see section 6(c) of Pub. L. 101–335, set out as a note under section 8351 of this title.

EFFECTIVE DATE

Section effective Nov. 15, 1988, and applicable to bankruptcy judges and magistrate judges who retire on or after Nov. 15, 1988, with exception for judges and magistrate judges retiring on or after July 31, 1987, see section 9 of Pub. L. 100–659, as amended, set out as a note under section 377 of Title 28, Judiciary and Judicial Procedure.

SECTION REFERRED TO IN OTHER SECTIONS

This section is referred to in section 8432 of this title.

§ 8440c. Court of Federal Claims judges

(a)(1) A judge of the United States Court of Federal Claims who is covered by section 178 of title 28 may elect to contribute an amount of such individual's basic pay to the Thrift Savings Fund.

(2) An election may be made under paragraph (1) only during a period provided under section 8432(b) for individuals subject to this chapter.

(b)(1) Except as otherwise provided in this subsection, the provisions of this subchapter and subchapter VII shall apply with respect to Court of Federal Claims judges who make contributions to the Thrift Savings Fund under subsection (a) of this section.

(2) The amount contributed by a Court of Federal Claims judge for any pay period shall not exceed the maximum percentage of such judge's basic pay for such pay period allowable under section 8440f.

(3) No contributions shall be made under section 8432(c) of this title for the benefit of a Court of Federal Claims judge making contributions under subsection (a) of this section.

(4)(A) Section 8433(b) of this title applies to a Court of Federal Claims judge who elects to make contributions to the Thrift Savings Fund under subsection (a) of this section and who retires entitled to an annuity under section 178 of title 28 (including a disability annuity under subsection (c) of such section).

(B) Section 8433(b) of this title applies to any Court of Federal Claims judge who elects to make contributions to the Thrift Savings Fund under subsection (a) of this section and who retires before becoming entitled to an annuity under section 178 of title 28.

(5) With respect to Court of Federal Claims judges to whom this section applies, any of the actions described in paragraph (4)(A) or (B) shall be considered a separation from service for purposes of this subchapter and subchapter VII.

(6) For purposes of this section, the terms "retirement" and "retire" include removal from office under section 178(c) of title 28 on the sole ground of mental or physical disability.

(7) In the case of a Court of Federal Claims judge who receives a distribution from the Thrift Savings Plan and who later receives an annuity under section 178 of title 28, such annuity shall be offset by an amount equal to the amount of the distribution which represents the Government's contribution to that person's Thrift Savings Account, without regard to earnings attributable to that amount. Where such an offset would exceed 50 percent of the annuity to be received in the first year, the offset may be divided equally over the first 2 years in which that person receives the annuity.

(8) Notwithstanding paragraph (4), if any Court of Federal Claims judge retires under circumstances making such judge eligible to make an election under section 8433(b), and such judge's nonforfeitable account balance is less than an amount that the Executive Director prescribes by regulation, the Executive Director shall pay the nonforfeitable account balance to the participant in a single payment.

(Added Pub. L. 101–650, title III, § 306(d)(1), Dec. 1, 1990, 104 Stat. 5110, § 8440b; renumbered § 8440c

and amended Pub. L. 102–198, § 7(c)(1), Dec. 9, 1991, 105 Stat. 1624; Pub. L. 102–572, title IX, § 902(b), Oct. 29, 1992, 106 Stat. 4516; Pub. L. 103–226, § 9(g), Mar. 30, 1994, 108 Stat. 121; Pub. L. 104–208, div. A, title I, § 101(f) [title VI, § 659 [title II, § 205(c)]], Sept. 30, 1996, 110 Stat. 3009–314, 3009–372, 3009–378; Pub. L. 106–554, § 1(a)(4) [div. B, title I, § 138(a)(4)], Dec. 21, 2000, 114 Stat. 2763, 2763A–233.)

CODIFICATION

Another section 8440c was renumbered section 8440d of this title.

AMENDMENTS

2000—Subsec. (b)(2). Pub. L. 106–554 substituted "the maximum percentage of such judge's basic pay for such pay period allowable under section 8440f." for "5 percent of basic pay for such pay period."

1996—Subsec. (b)(7). Pub. L. 104–208, § 101(f) [title VI, § 659 [title II, § 205(c)(1)]], inserted "of the distribution" after "equal to the amount".

Subsec. (b)(8). Pub. L. 104–208, § 101(f) [title VI, § 659 [title II, § 205(c)(2)]], substituted "less than an amount that the Executive Director prescribes by regulation" for "$3,500 or less" and struck out "unless the judge elects, at such time and otherwise in such manner as the Executive Director prescribes, one of the options available under section 8433(b)" before period at end.

1994—Subsec. (b)(4)(B). Pub. L. 103–226, § 9(g)(1), substituted "Section 8433(b)" for "Section 8433(d)".

Subsec. (b)(5). Pub. L. 103–226, § 9(g)(2), substituted "any of the actions described in paragraph (4)(A) or (B) shall be considered" for "retirement under section 178 of title 28 is".

Subsec. (b)(8), (9). Pub. L. 103–226, § 9(g)(3), (4), redesignated par. (9) as (8), substituted "Notwithstanding paragraph (4)" for "Notwithstanding paragraph (4)(A)", and struck out former par. (8) which read as follows: "Notwithstanding paragraph (4)(B), if any Court of Federal Claims judge who elects to make contributions to the Thrift Savings Fund under subsection (a) retires before becoming entitled to an annuity under section 178 of title 28, and such judge's nonforfeitable account balance is $3,500 or less, the Executive Director shall pay the nonforfeitable account balance to the participant in a single payment unless the judge elects, at such time and otherwise in such manner as the Executive Director prescribes, to have the nonforfeitable account balance transferred to an eligible retirement plan as provided in section 8433(e)."

1992—Pub. L. 102–572, § 902(b)(2), substituted "Court of Federal Claims" for "Claims Court" in section catchline.

Subsec. (a)(1). Pub. L. 102–572, § 902(b)(1), substituted "United States Court of Federal Claims" for "United States Claims Court".

Subsec. (b)(1) to (5), (7) to (9). Pub. L. 102–572, § 902(b)(2), substituted "Court of Federal Claims" for "Claims Court" wherever appearing.

1991—Pub. L. 102–198, § 7(c)(1)(A), renumbered section 8440b of this title as this section.

Subsec. (b)(4)(A). Pub. L. 102–198, § 7(c)(1)(B)(i), substituted "subsection (c)" for "subsection (d)".

Subsec. (b)(7). Pub. L. 102–198, § 7(c)(1)(B)(ii), redesignated par. (8) as (7) and struck out former par. (7) which read as follows: "Sums contributed pursuant to this section by Claims Court judges, as well as all previous contributions to the Thrift Savings Fund by those judges, and earnings attributable to such sums and contributions, may be invested and reinvested only in the Government Securities Investment Fund established under section 8438(b)(1)(A) of this title."

Subsec. (b)(8). Pub. L. 102–198, § 7(c)(1)(B)(ii), (iii) added par. (8) and redesignated former par. (8) as (7).

Subsec. (b)(9). Pub. L. 102–198, § 7(c)(1)(B)(iii), added par. (9).

EFFECTIVE DATE OF 1996 AMENDMENT

Amendment by Pub. L. 104–208 effective Sept. 30, 1996, and withdrawals and elections as provided under such amendment to be made at earliest practicable date as determined by Executive Director in regulations, see section 101(f) [title VI, § 659 [title II, § 207]] of Pub. L. 104–208, set out as a note under section 5545a of this title.

EFFECTIVE DATE OF 1994 AMENDMENT

Amendment by Pub. L. 103–226 effective Mar. 10, 1995, see section 9(j) of Pub. L. 103–226, set out as a note under section 8351 of this title.

EFFECTIVE DATE OF 1992 AMENDMENT

Amendment by Pub. L. 102–572 effective Oct. 29, 1992, see section 911 of Pub. L. 102–572, set out as a note under section 171 of Title 28, Judiciary and Judicial Procedure.

EFFECTIVE DATE OF 1991 AMENDMENT

Section 7(c)(3) of Pub. L. 102–198, as amended by Pub. L. 102–572, title IX, § 902(b)(2), Oct. 29, 1992, 106 Stat. 4516, provided that: "Paragraphs (8) and (9) of section 8440c(b) of title 5, United States Code (as added by paragraph (1)) shall be effective as of January 1, 1991, and shall apply to any Court of Federal Claims judge retiring on or after such date."

EFFECTIVE DATE

Section applicable to judges of, and senior judges in active service with, the United States Court of Federal Claims on or after Dec. 1, 1990, see section 306(f) of Pub. L. 101–650, set out as an Effective Date of 1990 Amendment note under section 8331 of this title.

SECTION REFERRED TO IN OTHER SECTIONS

This section is referred to in section 8432 of this title.

§ 8440d. Judges of the United States Court of Appeals for Veterans Claims

(a)(1) A judge of the United States Court of Appeals for Veterans Claims may elect to contribute to the Thrift Savings Fund.

(2) An election may be made under paragraph (1) only during a period provided under section 8432(b) of this title for individuals subject to this chapter.

(b)(1) Except as otherwise provided in this subsection, the provisions of this subchapter and subchapter VII of this chapter shall apply with respect to a judge making contributions to the Thrift Savings Fund.

(2) The amount contributed by a judge of the United States Court of Appeals for Veterans Claims for any pay period may not exceed the maximum percentage of such judge's basic pay for such pay period allowable under section 8440f. Basic pay does not include any retired pay paid pursuant to section 7296 of title 38.

(3) No contributions may be made for the benefit of a judge under section 8432(c) of this title.

(4) Section 8433(b) of this title applies with respect to a judge who elects to make contributions to the Thrift Savings Fund and retires under section 7296(b) of title 38.

(5) Section 8433(b) of this title applies in the case of a judge who elects to make contributions to the Thrift Savings Fund and thereafter ceases to serve as a judge of the United States Court of Appeals for Veterans Claims but does not retire under section 7296(b) of title 38.

(6) The provisions of section 8351(b)(7)[1] of this title shall apply with respect to a judge who has

elected to contribute to the Thrift Savings Fund under this section.

(Added Pub. L. 102–82, § 5(a)(1), Aug. 6, 1991, 105 Stat. 376, § 8440c; renumbered § 8440d, Pub. L. 102–198, § 7(c)(4)(A), Dec. 9, 1991, 105 Stat. 1625, as amended by Pub. L. 102–378, § 5(d)(1), Oct. 2, 1992, 106 Stat. 1358; amended Pub. L. 103–226, § 9(h), Mar. 30, 1994, 108 Stat. 121; Pub. L. 105–368, title V, § 512(b)(1)(A), (2)(A), Nov. 11, 1998, 112 Stat. 3342; Pub. L. 106–361, § 2(b)(6), Oct. 27, 2000, 114 Stat. 1401; Pub. L. 106–554, § 1(a)(4) [div. B, title I, § 138(a)(5)], Dec. 21, 2000, 114 Stat. 2763, 2763A–233.)

REFERENCES IN TEXT

Section 8351(b)(7) of this title, referred to in subsec. (b)(6), was redesignated section 8351(b)(5) of this title by Pub. L. 103–226, § 9(a)(3), Mar. 30, 1994, 108 Stat. 119.

AMENDMENTS

2000—Subsec. (a)(2). Pub. L. 106–361 substituted "this chapter" for "chapter 84 of this title".

Subsec. (b)(2). Pub. L. 106–554 amended first sentence generally. Prior to amendment, first sentence read as follows: "The amount contributed by a judge may not exceed 5 percent of the amount of the judge's basic pay."

1998—Pub. L. 105–368, § 512(b)(2)(A), substituted "Judges of the United States Court of Appeals for Veterans Claims" for "Judges of the United States Court of Veterans Appeals" in section catchline.

Subsecs. (a)(1), (b)(5). Pub. L. 105–368, § 512(b)(1)(A), substituted "Court of Appeals for Veterans Claims" for "Court of Veterans Appeals".

1994—Subsec. (b)(5). Pub. L. 103–226 substituted "Section 8433(b) of this title applies" for "A transfer shall be made as provided in section 8433(d) of this title".

1992—Pub. L. 102–378 amended Pub. L. 102–198. See 1991 Amendment note below.

1991—Pub. L. 102–198, as amended by Pub. L. 102–378, renumbered section 8440c of this title as this section.

EFFECTIVE DATE OF 2000 AMENDMENT

Amendment by Pub. L. 106–361 effective at the earliest practicable date after Sept. 30, 2000, as determined by the Executive Director in regulations, see section 2(c)(1) of Pub. L. 106–361, set out as a note under section 8432 of this title.

EFFECTIVE DATE OF 1998 AMENDMENT

Amendment by Pub. L. 105–368 effective on first day of first month beginning more than 90 days after Nov. 11, 1998, see section 513 of Pub. L. 105–368, set out as a note under section 7251 of Title 38, Veterans' Benefits.

EFFECTIVE DATE OF 1994 AMENDMENT

Amendment by Pub. L. 103–226 effective Mar. 10, 1995, see section 9(j) of Pub. L. 103–226, set out as a note under section 8351 of this title.

EFFECTIVE DATE OF 1992 AMENDMENT

Amendment by Pub. L. 102–378 effective Dec. 9, 1991, see section 9(b)(2) of Pub. L. 102–378, set out as a note under section 6303 of this title.

FIRST ELECTION

Section 5(b) of Pub. L. 102–82, as amended by Pub. L. 102–198, § 7(c)(4)(C), Dec. 9, 1991, 105 Stat. 1625, provided that: "A judge of the United States Court of Veterans Appeals on the date of the enactment of this Act [Aug. 6, 1991] may make an election under section 8440d(a) of title 5, United States Code, within 60 days after the date of the enactment of this Act."

SECTION REFERRED TO IN OTHER SECTIONS

This section is referred to in section 8432 of this title; title 38 sections 7296, 7297.

---

[1] See References in Text note below.

§ 8440e. Members of the uniformed services

(a) For purposes of this section—

(1) the term "member" has the meaning given such term by section 211 of title 37; and

(2) the term "basic pay" means basic pay payable under section 204 of title 37.

(b)(1) Any member eligible to participate in the Thrift Savings Plan by virtue of section 211(b) of title 37 may contribute to the Thrift Savings Fund.

(2)(A) Except as provided in subparagraph (B), an election to contribute to the Thrift Savings Fund under this section may be made only during a period provided under section 8432(b), subject to the same conditions as prescribed under paragraph (2) (A)–(D) thereof.

(B)(i) Notwithstanding subparagraph (A), any individual who is a member as of the effective date that applies with respect to such individual under section 663 of the National Defense Authorization Act for Fiscal Year 2000 may make the first such election during the 60-day period beginning on such effective date.

(ii) An election made under this subparagraph shall take effect on the first day of the first applicable pay period beginning after the close of the 60-day period referred to in clause (i).

(c) Except as otherwise provided in this section, the provisions of this subchapter and subchapter VII shall apply with respect to members making contributions to the Thrift Savings Fund, and such members shall, for purposes of this subchapter and subchapter VII, be considered employees within the meaning of section 8401(11).

(d)(1)(A) The amount contributed by a member described in section 211(a)(1) of title 37 for any pay period out of basic pay may not exceed the maximum percentage of such member's basic pay for such pay period allowable under section 8440f.

(B) The amount contributed by a member described in section 211(a)(2) of title 37 for any pay period out of any compensation received under section 206 of title 37 may not exceed the maximum percentage of such member's compensation for such pay period (received under such section 206) allowable under section 8440f.

(2) A member making contributions to the Thrift Savings Fund out of basic pay, or out of compensation under section 206 of title 37, may also contribute (by direct transfer to the Fund) any part of any special or incentive pay that such member receives under chapter 5 of title 37.

(3) Nothing in this section or section 211 of title 37 shall be considered to waive any dollar limitation under the Internal Revenue Code of 1986 which otherwise applies with respect to the Thrift Savings Fund.

(e) Except as provided in section 211(d) of title 37, no contribution under section 8432(c) of this title may be made for the benefit of a member making contributions to the Thrift Savings Fund under this section.

(Added Pub. L. 106–65, div. A, title VI, § 661(a)(2)(A), Oct. 5, 1999, 113 Stat. 670; amended Pub. L. 106–398, § 1 [[div. A], title VI, § 661(c)], Oct. 30, 2000, 114 Stat. 1654, 1654A–167; Pub. L. 106–554, § 1(a)(4) [div. B, title I, § 138(a)(6)], Dec. 21, 2000, 114 Stat. 2763, 2763A–233.)

References in Text

Section 663 of the National Defense Authorization Act for Fiscal Year 2000, referred to in subsec. (b)(2)(B)(i), is section 663 of Pub. L. 106–65, as amended, which is set out as an Effective Date note below.

The Internal Revenue Code of 1986, referred to in subsec. (d)(3), is classified generally to Title 26, Internal Revenue Code.

Amendments

2000—Subsec. (b)(2)(B)(i). Pub. L. 106–398 substituted "as of the effective date that applies with respect to such individual under section 663 of the National Defense Authorization Act for Fiscal Year 2000" for "as of the effective date described in paragraph (1) of section 663(a) of the National Defense Authorization Act for Fiscal Year 2000 (or, if applicable, paragraph (2) thereof)".

Subsec. (d)(1)(A). Pub. L. 106–554, § 138(a)(6)(A)], substituted "the maximum percentage of such member's basic pay for such pay period allowable under section 8440f." for "5 percent of such member's basic pay for such pay period."

Subsec. (d)(1)(B). Pub. L. 106–554, § 138(a)(6)(B)], substituted "the maximum percentage of such member's compensation for such pay period (received under such section 206) allowable under section 8440f." for "5 percent of such compensation, payable to such member for such pay period."

Effective Date

Pub. L. 106–65, div. A, title VI, § 663, Oct. 5, 1999, 113 Stat. 673, as amended by Pub. L. 106–398, § 1 [[div. A], title VI, § 661(a)], Oct. 30, 2000, 114 Stat. 1654, 1654A–167, provided that:

"(a) In General.—Except as provided in subsection (b), the amendments made by this subtitle [subtitle F (§§ 661–663) of title VI of div. A of Pub. L. 106–65, enacting this section and section 211 of Title 37, Pay and Allowances of the Uniformed Services, and amending sections 8351, 8432b, 8433, 8439, and 8473 of this title and section 211 of Title 37] shall take effect 180 days after the date of the enactment of the Floyd D. Spence National Defense Authorization Act for Fiscal Year 2001 [Oct. 30, 2000].

"(b) Postponement Authority.—(1) The Secretary of Defense may postpone by up to 180 days after the date that would otherwise apply under subsection (a)—

"(A) the date as of which the amendments made by this subtitle shall take effect; or

"(B) the date as of which section 211(a)(2) of title 37, United States Code (as added by this subtitle) shall take effect.

"(2) Postponement authority under this subsection may be exercised only to the extent that the failure to do so would prevent the Federal Retirement Thrift Investment Board from being able to provide timely and accurate services to investors or would place an excessive burden on the administrative capacity of the Board to accommodate participants in the Thrift Savings Plan, as determined by the Secretary of Defense after consultation with the Executive Director (appointed by the Board).

"(3) Paragraph (1) includes the authority to postpone the effective date of the amendments made by this subtitle (apart from section 211(a)(2) of title 37, United States Code), and the effective date of such section 211(a)(2), by different lengths of time.

"(4) The Secretary shall notify the congressional defense committees [Committees on Armed Services and Appropriations of the Senate and the House of Representatives], the Committee on Government Reform of the House of Representatives, and the Committee on Governmental Affairs of the Senate of any determination made under this subsection."

Regulations

Pub. L. 106–65, div. A, title VI, § 661(b), Oct. 5, 1999, 113 Stat. 672, as amended by Pub. L. 106–398, § 1 [[div. A], title VI, § 661(b)], Oct. 30, 2000, 114 Stat. 1654, 1654A–167, provided that: "Not later than the 180th day after the date of the enactment of the Floyd D. Spence National Defense Authorization Act for Fiscal Year 2001 [Oct. 30, 2000], the Executive Director (appointed by the Federal Retirement Thrift Investment Board) shall issue regulations to implement the amendments made by this subtitle [subtitle F (§§ 661–663) of title VI of div. A of Pub. L. 106–65, enacting this section and section 211 of Title 37, Pay and Allowances of the Uniformed Services, and amending sections 8351, 8432b, 8433, 8439, and 8473 of this title and section 211 of Title 37]."

SECTION REFERRED TO IN OTHER SECTIONS

This section is referred to in sections 8351, 8432b, 8473 of this title; title 37 section 211.

§ 8440f. Maximum percentage allowable for certain participants

The maximum percentage allowable under this section shall be determined in accordance with the following table:

In the case of a pay period beginning in fiscal year:	The maximum percentage allowable is:
2001	6
2002	7
2003	8
2004	9
2005	10
2006 or thereafter	100.

(Added Pub. L. 106–554, § 1(a)(4) [div. B, title I, § 138(a)(7)(A)], Dec. 21, 2000, 114 Stat. 2763, 2763A–234.)

SECTION REFERRED TO IN OTHER SECTIONS

This section is referred to in sections 8440a to 8440e of this title.

SUBCHAPTER IV—SURVIVOR ANNUITIES

SUBCHAPTER REFERRED TO IN OTHER SECTIONS

This subchapter is referred to in sections 8348, 8401, 8415, 8420a, 8422, 8424, 8461, 8464a, 8466, 8468, 8470 of this title; title 2 sections 121b, 162b; title 22 section 4071j; title 38 section 7426; title 40 section 214d; title 50 section 2154.

§ 8441. Definitions

For the purpose of this subchapter—

(1) the term "widow" means the surviving wife of an employee, Member, or annuitant, or of a former employee or Member, who—

(A) was married to him for at least 9 months immediately before his death; or

(B) is the mother of issue by that marriage;

(2) the term "widower" means the surviving husband of an employee, Member, or annuitant, or of a former employee or Member, who—

(A) was married to her for at least 9 months immediately before her death; or

(B) is the father of issue by that marriage;

(3) the term "dependent", in the case of any child, means that the employee, Member, or annuitant involved was, at the time of death of the employee, Member, or annuitant either living with or contributing to the support of such child, as determined in accordance with such regulations as the Office shall prescribe; and

(4) the term "child" means—

(A) an unmarried dependent child under 18 years of age, including (i) an adopted child, (ii) a stepchild but only if the stepchild lived with the employee, Member, or annuitant in a regular parent-child relationship, (iii) a recognized natural child, and (iv) a child who lived with and for whom a petition of adoption was filed by an employee, Member, or annuitant and who is adopted by the widow or widower of the employee, Member, or annuitant after the death of such employee, Member, or annuitant;

(B) such unmarried dependent child regardless of age who is incapable of self-support because of mental or physical disability incurred before age 18; or

(C) such unmarried dependent child between 18 and 22 years of age who is a student regularly pursuing a full-time course of study or training in residence in a high school, trade school, technical or vocational institute, junior college, college, university, or comparable recognized educational institution.

For the purpose of this paragraph and section 8443, a child whose 22nd birthday occurs before July 1 or after August 31 of a calendar year, and while regularly pursuing such a course of study or training, is deemed to have become 22 years of age on the first day of July after that birthday. A child who is a student is deemed not to have ceased to be a student during an interim between school years if the interim is not more than 5 months and if such child shows to the satisfaction of the Office that such child has a bona fide intention of continuing to pursue a course of study or training in the same or different school during the school semester (or other period into which the school year is divided) immediately after the interim.

(Added Pub. L. 99–335, title I, § 101(a), June 6, 1986, 100 Stat. 558.)

SECTION REFERRED TO IN OTHER SECTIONS

This section is referred to in sections 8442, 8443 of this title.

§ 8442. Rights of a widow or widower

(a)(1) Except as provided in subsection (g), if an annuitant dies and is survived by a widow or widower, the widow or widower is entitled to an annuity equal to 50 percent of an annuity computed under section 8415 with respect to the annuitant, (or one-half thereof, if designated for this purpose under section 8419 of this title), unless—

(A) the right to an annuity was waived under section 8416(a) (and no election was subsequently made under section 8416(d) nullifying the waiver); or

(B) in the case of a marriage after retirement, the annuitant did not file an election under section 8416(b) or (c), as the case may be.

(2) A spouse acquired after retirement is entitled to an annuity under this subsection (as provided in paragraph (1)) only upon electing this annuity instead of any other survivor benefit to which such spouse may be entitled under this

subchapter or section 8424 or under another retirement system for Government employees.

(b)(1) If an employee or Member dies after completing at least 18 months of civilian service creditable under section 8411 and is survived by a widow or widower, the widow or widower is entitled to—

(A) an amount equal to the sum of—

(i) 50 percent of the final annual rate of basic pay (or of the average pay, if higher) of the employee or Member; and

(ii) $15,000 as adjusted under section 8462(e); and

(B) if the employee or Member completed at least 10 years of service, an annuity equal to 50 percent of an annuity computed under section 8415 with respect to the employee or Member, but without regard to subsection (f) of such section.

(2) The Office shall prescribe regulations under which the total amount payable to a widow or widower under paragraph (1)(A) may, at the election of the widow or widower, be paid—

(A) in a lump sum; or

(B) on a monthly basis—

(i) over a period of 3 years beginning on the day after the employee's or Member's death; or

(ii) over any other period established under the regulations.

Any method of payment provided for under subparagraph (B) shall be designed such that the present value of the benefits provided under such method is actuarially equivalent to the present value of a lump-sum payment under subparagraph (A).

(3) An amount payable under paragraph (1)(A) shall not be considered to be part of an annuity for purposes of this chapter.

(c)(1) If a former employee or Member dies after having separated from the service with title to a deferred annuity under section 8413 but before having established a valid claim for an annuity, and is survived by a widow or widower to whom married on the date of separation, the widow or widower may elect to receive—

(A) an annuity under paragraph (2); or

(B) the lump-sum credit, if the widow or widower is the individual who would be entitled to the lump-sum credit and if such widow or widower files application therefor with the Office.

(2)(A)(i) Subject to clause (ii) and subparagraph (B)(ii), the annuity of the widow or widower is equal to 50 percent of an annuity computed under section 8415 for the former employee or Member.

(ii)(I) In computing an amount under section 8415 for a former employee or Member (described in subclause (II)) in order to compute the annuity for a widow or widower under this subsection, the computation under section 8415 shall be made as if the former employee or Member had attained the applicable minimum retirement age under section 8412(h).

(II) This clause applies with respect to a former employee or Member who dies before having attained the applicable minimum retirement age under section 8412(h).

(B)(i) Notwithstanding the first sentence of subsection (d)(1), the annuity of the widow or widower of a former employee or Member under subparagraph (A)(ii) commences—

(I) on the day after the date on which the former employee or Member would have attained age 62 (or, if applicable, either age 60 if the former employee or Member completed at least 20 years of service, or the applicable minimum retirement age (under section 8412(h)) if the former employee or Member completed at least 30 years of service); or

(II) if the widow or widower so designates in the election, as of the day after the death of the former employee or Member.

(ii) The present value of the annuity of a widow or widower who chooses the earlier commencement date under clause (i)(II) shall be actuarially equivalent to the present value of an annuity computed for the widow or widower, determined as if the commencement date under clause (i)(I) were applicable.

(3)(A) Paragraphs (1) and (2) shall apply only in the case of an employee or Member who completes at least 10 years of service.

(B) Nothing in this subsection shall be considered to affect the provisions of this chapter relating to a lump-sum credit in the case of the widow or widower of a former employee or Member who dies after completing less than 10 years of service.

(d)(1) The annuity of a widow or widower under this section commences on the day after the death of the individual on whose service such annuity is based. This annuity and the right thereto terminate on the last day of the month before the widow or widower—

(A) dies; or

(B) except as provided in paragraph (3), remarries before becoming 55 years of age.

(2) In the case of a widow or widower whose annuity under this section is terminated because of remarriage before becoming 55 years of age, the annuity shall be restored at the same rate commencing on the day the remarriage is dissolved by death, divorce, or annulment, if—

(A) the widow or widower elects to receive this annuity instead of any other survivor benefit to which such widow or widower may be entitled (under this subchapter or section 8424 or under another retirement system for Government employees) by reason of the remarriage; and

(B) any lump sum paid on termination of the annuity is returned to the Fund.

(3) Paragraph (1)(B) (relating to termination of a survivor annuity because of a remarriage before age 55) shall not apply if the widow or widower was married for at least 30 years to the individual on whose service the survivor annuity is based.

(e) The requirement in paragraphs (1)(A) and (2)(A) of section 8441 that the widow or widower of an annuitant, employee, or Member, or of a former employee or Member, have been married to such individual for at least 9 months immediately before the death of the individual in order to qualify as the widow or widower of such individual shall be deemed satisfied in any case in which the individual dies within the applicable 9-month period, if—

(1) the death of the individual was accidental; or

(2) the surviving spouse of the individual had been previously married to such individual and subsequently divorced, and the aggregate time married is at least 9 months.

(f)(1) Subject to paragraph (4), a survivor who is entitled to an annuity under subsection (a) shall also be entitled to a supplementary annuity under this subsection.

(2) A supplementary annuity under this subsection shall be equal to the lesser of—

(A) the amount by which the survivor's assumed CSRS annuity exceeds the annuity payable to such survivor under subsection (a); or

(B) the amount determined under paragraph (3).

(3)(A) Except as provided in subparagraph (B), the amount under this paragraph for a survivor is the amount of widow's or widower's insurance benefits which would be payable to such survivor under title II of the Social Security Act (without regard to sections 202(e)(7), 202(f)(2), and 203 of such Act) based on the wages and self-employment income of the deceased annuitant, and determined—

(i) as of the date on which the annuitant died; and

(ii) as if the survivor had attained age 60 and made application for those benefits under subsection (e) or (f) of section 202 of such Act, as the case may be.

(B) Any computation or determination under this paragraph shall be made in accordance with the applicable provisions of the Social Security Act, except that in computing any primary insurance amount under section 215 of such Act for purposes of determining an amount under this subsection, subparagraphs (A) and (C) of section 8421(b)(2) shall apply.

(4) A supplementary annuity under this subsection—

(A) shall be payable to a survivor only for calendar months ending before the calendar month in which such survivor first satisfies the minimum age requirement under section 202(e)(1)(B)(i) or 202(f)(1)(B)(i) of the Social Security Act, as the case may be;

(B) shall not be payable to a survivor who would not be entitled to benefits under subsection (e) or (f) of section 202 of the Social Security Act based on the wages and self-employment income of the deceased annuitant (determined, as of the date of the annuitant's death, as if the survivor had attained age 60 and made appropriate application for benefits, but without regard to any restriction under either such subsection relating to remarriage); and

(C) shall not be payable to a survivor for any calendar month in which such survivor is entitled (or would, on proper application, be entitled) to benefits under section 202(g) of the Social Security Act (relating to mother's and father's insurance benefits), or under section 202(e) or (f) of such Act by reason of having become disabled, based on the wages and self-employment income of the deceased annuitant.

(5) For the purpose of this subsection, the term "assumed CSRS annuity", as used in the case of a survivor, means the amount of the annuity to which such survivor would be entitled under subchapter III of chapter 83 of this title based on the service of the deceased annuitant, determined—

(A) as of the day after the date of the annuitant's death;

(B) as if the survivor had made appropriate application therefor; and

(C) as if the service of the deceased annuitant were creditable under such subchapter.

(6) An amount payable under this subsection shall be adjusted under section 8462 and shall otherwise be treated under this chapter in the same way as an amount payable under subsection (a).

(g)(1) If the widow or widower of an annuitant under section 8452 (hereinafter in this subsection referred to as a "disability annuitant") is determined under subsection (a) to be entitled to an annuity based on the service of such disability annuitant, the annuity of the widow or widower shall be equal to 50 percent of the amount determined under paragraph (2) (or one-half thereof if designated for this purpose under section 8419 of this title), rather than of the amount referred to in subsection (a).

(2)(A) Except as provided in subparagraph (B), the amount on which the annuity of the widow or widower of a disability annuitant is based shall be the amount of the annuity to which such disability annuitant was entitled, as computed under section 8452 (including appropriate reduction under subsection (a)(2) of such section and any adjustments under section 8462 allowed under section 8452), as of the day before the date of the disability annuitant's death.

(B)(i) In the case of a widow or widower entitled to an annuity based on the service of a disability annuitant who dies before age 62, the amount under clause (ii) shall apply instead of the amount which would otherwise apply under subparagraph (A).

(ii)(I) Subject to subclause (II), the amount of the annuity to which the disability annuitant was entitled as of the day before the date of death shall be considered to be the amount which would be computed with respect to such disability annuitant under section 8452(b) if the disability annuitant had attained age 62 on the day before date of death.

(II) For purposes of any such computation under section 8452(b)(2) pursuant to this clause, creditable service shall (in addition to the service which would otherwise be used under subparagraph (B)(i) of such section) include the period of time between date of death and the date of the sixty-second anniversary of the birth of the annuitant, and average pay shall be adjusted in accordance with subparagraph (B)(ii) of such section only through date of death.

(h) The following rules shall apply notwithstanding any other provision of this section:

(1) The annuity payable under this section to a widow or widower may not exceed the difference between—

(A) the amount of the annuity which would otherwise be payable to such widow or widower under this section; and

(B) the amount of the annuity payable to any former spouse of the deceased employee,

Member, or annuitant, or former employee or Member, based on an election made under section 8417(b) or a court order previously issued or agreement previously entered into as described in section 8445(a).

(2) The amount payable under subsection (b)(1)(A) to a widow or widower may not exceed the difference between—

(A) the amount which would otherwise be payable to such widow or widower under such subsection; and

(B) the portion of such amount payable to any former spouse of the deceased employee, Member, or annuitant, or former employee or Member, based on a court order previously issued or agreement previously entered into.

(3) A lump-sum credit under subsection (c)(2) shall be subject to the same terms and conditions as apply with respect to a lump-sum credit under section 8424(b).

(Added Pub. L. 99–335, title I, § 101(a), June 6, 1986, 100 Stat. 559; amended Pub. L. 99–556, title I, § 120, Oct. 27, 1986, 100 Stat. 3134; Pub. L. 100–238, title I, § 131(b), Jan. 8, 1988, 101 Stat. 1760; Pub. L. 105–61, title V, § 518(b)(1), Oct. 10, 1997, 111 Stat. 1307.)

REFERENCES IN TEXT

The Social Security Act, referred to in subsec. (f)(3), (4), is act Aug. 14, 1935, ch. 531, 49 Stat. 620, as amended, which is classified generally to chapter 7 (§ 301 et seq.) of Title 42, The Public Health and Welfare. Title II of the Social Security Act is classified generally to subchapter II (§ 401 et seq.) of chapter 7 of Title 42. Sections 202, 203, and 215 are classified to sections 402, 403, and 415, respectively, of Title 42. For complete classification of this Act to the Code, see section 1305 of Title 42 and Tables.

AMENDMENTS

1997—Subsec. (d)(1)(B). Pub. L. 105–61, § 518(b)(1)(B), substituted "except as provided in paragraph (3), remarries" for "remarries".

Subsec. (d)(3). Pub. L. 105–61, § 518(b)(1)(A), added par. (3).

1988—Subsec. (a)(1). Pub. L. 100–238, § 131(b)(1), inserted "(or one-half thereof, if designated for this purpose under section 8419 of this title)," after "with respect to the annuitant,".

Subsec. (g)(1). Pub. L. 100–238, § 131(b)(2), inserted "(or one-half thereof if designated for this purpose under section 8419 of this title)" after "paragraph (2)".

1986—Subsec. (c)(2)(B)(i)(I). Pub. L. 99–556 which directed that subsec. (c)(2)(B)(i)(I) of this section be amended generally was executed to subsec. (c)(2)(B)(i)(I) of this section, as the probable intent of Congress. Prior to the amendment, subcl. (I) read as follows: "on the day after the date on which the former employee or Member would have attained age 62; or".

EFFECTIVE DATE OF 1997 AMENDMENT

Amendment by Pub. L. 105–61 applicable with respect to remarriages occurring on or after Jan. 1, 1995, see section 518(c) of Pub. L. 105–61, set out as a note under section 8341 of this title.

SECTION REFERRED TO IN OTHER SECTIONS

This section is referred to in sections 8416, 8417, 8419, 8435, 8445, 8462, 8468, 8901 of this title; title 22 section 4071d; title 38 section 7438; title 50 section 2154.

§ 8443. Rights of a child

(a)(1) If an employee or Member dies after completing at least 18 months of civilian service

which is creditable under section 8411, or an annuitant dies, each surviving child is, for any month, entitled to an annuity equal to—

(A) the amount by which the applicable amount under paragraph (2) for such month exceeds the applicable amount under paragraph (3) for such month, divided by

(B) the number of children entitled to a payment under this section for such month.

(2) The applicable amount under this paragraph for any month is the total amount to which the surviving child or children (as the case may be) of the annuitant, employee, or Member would be entitled for such month under subchapter III of chapter 83 (including any adjustment based on section 8340) based on the service of such annuitant, employee, or Member, if the service of such annuitant, employee, or Member were creditable under such subchapter.

(3) The applicable amount under this paragraph for any month is the total amount of child's insurance benefits which are payable (or would, on proper application, be payable) under title II of the Social Security Act for such month based on the wages and self-employment income of such annuitant, employee, or Member.

(b) The annuity of a child under this subchapter—

(1) commences on the day after the annuitant, employee, or Member dies;

(2) commences or resumes on the first day of the month in which the child later becomes or again becomes a student as described by section 8441(4), if any lump sum paid is returned to the Fund; or

(3) commences or resumes on the first day of the month in which the child later becomes or again becomes incapable of self-support because of a mental or physical disability incurred before age 18 (or a later recurrence of such disability), if any lump sum paid is returned to the Fund.

This annuity and the right thereto terminate on the last day of the month before the child—

(A) becomes 18 years of age unless then a student as described or incapable of self-support;

(B) becomes capable of self-support after becoming 18 years of age unless then such a student;

(C) becomes 22 years of age if then such a student and capable of self-support;

(D) ceases to be such a student after becoming 18 years of age unless then incapable of self-support; or

(E) dies or marries;

whichever occurs first. On the death of the surviving wife or husband, or former wife or husband, or termination of the annuity of a child, the annuity of any other child or children shall be recomputed and paid as though the wife or husband, former wife or husband, or child had not survived the annuitant, employee, or Member. If the annuity of a child under this subchapter terminates under subparagraph (E) because of marriage, then, if such marriage ends, such annuity shall resume on the first day of the month in which it ends, but only if any lump sum paid is returned to the Fund, and that individual is not otherwise ineligible for such annuity.

(Added Pub. L. 99–335, title I, §101(a), June 6, 1986, 100 Stat. 563; amended Pub. L. 99–556, title I, §117(a), Oct. 27, 1986, 100 Stat. 3134; Pub. L. 104–208, div. A, title I, §101(f) [title VI, §633(a)(2)], Sept. 30, 1996, 110 Stat. 3009–314, 3009–363.)

REFERENCES IN TEXT

The Social Security Act, referred to in subsec. (a)(3), is act Aug. 14, 1935, ch. 531, 49 Stat. 620, as amended. Title II of the Social Security Act is classified generally to subchapter II (§401 et seq.) of chapter 7 of Title 42, The Public Health and Welfare. For complete classification of this Act to the Code, see section 1305 of Title 42 and Tables.

AMENDMENTS

1996—Subsec. (b). Pub. L. 104–208 inserted at end "If the annuity of a child under this subchapter terminates under subparagraph (E) because of marriage, then, if such marriage ends, such annuity shall resume on the first day of the month in which it ends, but only if any lump sum paid is returned to the Fund, and that individual is not otherwise ineligible for such annuity."

1986—Subsec. (a)(2). Pub. L. 99–556 inserted "(including any adjustment based on section 8340)".

EFFECTIVE DATE OF 1996 AMENDMENT

Amendment by Pub. L. 104–208 applicable with respect to termination of marriage taking effect before, on, or after Sept. 30, 1996, except that benefits are payable only with respect to amounts accruing for periods beginning on first day of month beginning after the later of termination of marriage or Sept. 30, 1996, see section 101(f) [title VI, §633(b)] of Pub. L. 104–208, set out as a note under section 8341 of this title.

SECTION REFERRED TO IN OTHER SECTIONS

This section is referred to in sections 8441, 8462, 8908 of this title; title 38 section 7438.

§ 8444. Rights of a named individual with an insurable interest

The annuity of a survivor named under section 8420(a) is 55 percent of the reduced annuity of the retired employee or Member determined under paragraph (2) of such section 8420(a). The annuity of the survivor commences on the day after the retired employee or Member dies. This annuity and the right thereto terminate on the last day of the month before the survivor dies.

(Added Pub. L. 99–335, title I, §101(a), June 6, 1986, 100 Stat. 563.)

SECTION REFERRED TO IN OTHER SECTIONS

This section is referred to in section 8420 of this title.

§ 8445. Rights of a former spouse

(a) Subject to subsections (b) through (e), a former spouse of a deceased employee, Member, or annuitant (or of a former employee or Member who dies after having separated from the service with title to a deferred annuity under section 8413 but before having established a valid claim for annuity) is entitled to an annuity under this section, if and to the extent expressly provided for in an election under section 8417(b), or in the terms of any decree of divorce or annulment or any court order or court-approved property settlement agreement incident to such decree.

(b)(1) The annuity payable to a former spouse under this section may not exceed the difference between—

(A) the amount applicable in the case of such former spouse, as determined under paragraph (2); and

(B) the amount of any annuity payable under this section to any other former spouse of the employee, Member, or annuitant, or former employee or Member, based on an election previously made under section 8417(b), or a court order previously issued or agreement previously entered into as described in subsection (a).

(2) The applicable amount, for purposes of paragraph (1)(A) in the case of a former spouse, is the amount of the annuity which would be payable under the provisions of section 8442 (including subsection (f) of such section, but without regard to subsection (h) of such section) if such former spouse were a widow or widower entitled to an annuity under such provisions based on the service of the deceased employee, Member, or annuitant, or former employee or Member.

(c) The commencement and termination of an annuity payable under this section shall be governed by the terms of the applicable order, decree, agreement, or election, as the case may be, except that any such annuity—

(1) shall not commence before—

(A) the day after the employee, Member, or annuitant, or former employee or Member, dies; or

(B) the first day of the second month beginning after the date on which the Office receives written notice of the order, decree, agreement, or election, as the case may be, together with such additional information or documentation as the Office may prescribe;

whichever is later; and

(2) except as provided in subsection (h), shall terminate no later than the last day of the month before the former spouse remarries before becoming 55 years of age or dies.

(d) For purposes of this chapter, a modification in a decree, order, agreement, or election referred to in subsection (a) shall not be effective—

(1) if such modification is made after the retirement or death of the employee, Member, or annuitant, or former employee or Member, concerned; and

(2) to the extent that such modification involves an annuity under this section.

(e) For purposes of this chapter, a decree, order, agreement, or election referred to in subsection (a) shall not be effective, in the case of a former spouse, to the extent that it is inconsistent with any joint waiver previously executed with respect to such former spouse under section 8416(a).

(f)(1) Any amount under section 8442(b)(1)(A) which would otherwise be payable to a widow or widower based on the service of another individual shall be paid (in whole or in part) by the Office to a former spouse of such individual if and to the extent expressly provided for in the terms of a court decree of divorce, annulment, or legal separation, or the terms of a court order or court-approved property settlement incident to any decree of divorce, annulment, or legal separation.

(2) Paragraph (1) shall apply only to payments made by the Office after the date of receipt in the Office of written notice of such decree, order, or agreement, and such additional information and documentation as the Office may prescribe.

(g) Any payment under this section to a person bars recovery by any other person.

(h)(1) Subsection (c)(2) (to the extent that it provides for termination of a survivor annuity because of a remarriage before age 55) shall not apply if the former spouse was married for at least 30 years to the individual on whose service the survivor annuity is based.

(2) A remarriage described in paragraph (1) shall not be taken into account for purposes of section 8419(b)(1)(B) or any other provision of this chapter which the Office may by regulation identify in order to carry out the purposes of this subsection.

(Added Pub. L. 99–335, title I, §101(a), June 6, 1986, 100 Stat. 564; amended Pub. L. 105–61, title V, §518(b)(2), Oct. 10, 1997, 111 Stat. 1308.)

AMENDMENTS

1997—Subsec. (c)(2). Pub. L. 105–61, §518(b)(2)(B), substituted "except as provided in subsection (h), shall" for "shall".
Subsec. (h). Pub. L. 105–61, §518(b)(2)(A), added subsec. (h).

EFFECTIVE DATE OF 1997 AMENDMENT

Amendment by Pub. L. 105–61 applicable with respect to remarriages occurring on or after Jan. 1, 1995, see section 518(c) of Pub. L. 105–61, set out as a note under section 8341 of this title.

SECTION REFERRED TO IN OTHER SECTIONS

This section is referred to in sections 8416, 8417, 8419, 8420, 8420a, 8424, 8435, 8442, 8468, 8901, 8905 of this title; title 50 section 2154.

SUBCHAPTER V—DISABILITY BENEFITS

SUBCHAPTER REFERRED TO IN OTHER SECTIONS

This subchapter is referred to in sections 8401, 8422, 8424, 8461, 8464, 8464a, 8470 of this title; title 2 sections 121b, 162b; title 40 section 214d; title 50 section 2154.

§ 8451. Disability retirement

(a)(1)(A) An employee who completes at least 18 months of civilian service creditable under section 8411 and has become disabled shall be retired on the employee's own application or on application by the employee's agency.

(B) For purposes of this subsection, an employee shall be considered disabled only if the employee is found by the Office to be unable, because of disease or injury, to render useful and efficient service in the employee's position.

(2)(A) Notwithstanding paragraph (1), an employee shall not be eligible for disability retirement under this section if the employee has declined a reasonable offer of reassignment to a vacant position in the employee's agency for which the employee is qualified if the position—

(i) is at the same grade (or pay level) as the employee's most recent grade (or pay level) or higher;

(ii) is within the employee's commuting area; and

(iii) is one in which the employee would be able to render useful and efficient service.

(B) An employee who is applying for disability retirement under this subchapter shall be considered for reassignment by the employee's agency to a vacant position described in subparagraph (A) in accordance with such procedures as the Office shall by regulation prescribe.

(C) An employee is entitled to appeal to the Merit Systems Protection Board under section 7701 any determination that the employee is not unable, because of disease or injury, to render useful and efficient service in a position to which the employee has declined reassignment under this section.

(D) For purposes of subparagraph (A), an employee of the United States Postal Service shall not be considered qualified for a position if such position is in a different craft or if reassignment to such position would be inconsistent with the terms of a collective-bargaining agreement covering the employee.

(b) A Member who completes at least 18 months of service as a Member and is found by the Office to be disabled for useful and efficient service as a Member because of disease or injury shall be retired on the Member's own application.

(c) An employee or Member retiring under this section is entitled to an annuity computed under section 8452.

(Added Pub. L. 99–335, title I, §101(a), June 6, 1986, 100 Stat. 565.)

SECTION REFERRED TO IN OTHER SECTIONS

This section is referred to in sections 8456, 8461, 8464 of this title; title 38 sections 7426, 7438.

§ 8452. Computation of disability annuity

(a)(1)(A) Except as provided in paragraph (2), or subsection (b), (c), or (d), the annuity of an annuitant under this subchapter—

(i) for the period beginning on the date on which such annuity commences, or is restored (as described in section 8455(b)(2) or (3)), and ending at the end of the twelfth month beginning on or after such date, shall be equal to 60 percent of the annuitant's average pay; and

(ii) after the end of the period referred to in clause (i), shall be equal to 40 percent of the annuitant's average pay.

(B) An annuity computed under this paragraph—

(i) shall not, during any period referred to in subparagraph (A)(i), be adjusted under section 8462; but

(ii) shall, after the end of any period referred to in subparagraph (A)(i), be adjusted to reflect all adjustments made under section 8462(b) after the end of the period referred to in subparagraph (A)(i), whether the amount actually payable to the annuitant under this section in any month is determined under this subsection or otherwise.

(2)(A) For any month in which an annuitant is entitled both to an annuity under this subchapter as computed under paragraph (1) and to a disability insurance benefit under section 223 of the Social Security Act, the annuitant's annuity for such month (as so computed) shall—

(i) if such month occurs during a period referred to in paragraph (1)(A)(i), be reduced by 100 percent of the annuitant's assumed disability insurance benefit for such month; or

(ii) if such month occurs other than during a period referred to in paragraph (1)(A)(i), be reduced by 60 percent of the annuitant's assumed disability insurance benefit for such month;

except that an annuity may not be reduced below zero by reason of this paragraph.

(B)(i) For purposes of this paragraph, the assumed disability insurance benefit of an annuitant for any month shall be equal to—

(I) the amount of the disability insurance benefit to which the annuitant is entitled under section 223 of the Social Security Act for the month in which the annuity under this subchapter commences, or is restored, or, if no entitlement to such disability insurance benefits exists for such month, the first month thereafter for which the annuitant is entitled both to an annuity under this subchapter and disability insurance benefits under section 223 of the Social Security Act, adjusted by

(II) all adjustments made under section 8462(b) after the end of the period referred to in paragraph (1)(A)(i) (or, if later, after the end of the month preceding the first month for which the annuitant is entitled both to an annuity under this subchapter and disability insurance benefits under section 223 of the Social Security Act) and before the start of the month involved (without regard to whether the annuitant's annuity was affected by any of those adjustments).

(ii) For purposes of applying section 224 of the Social Security Act to the assumed disability insurance benefit used to compute the reduction under this paragraph, the amount of the annuity under this subchapter which is considered shall be the amount of the annuity as determined before the application of this paragraph.

(3) Section 8462 shall apply with respect to amounts under this subsection only as provided in paragraphs (1) and (2).

(b)(1) Except as provided in subsection (d), if an annuitant is entitled to an annuity under this subchapter as of the day before the date of the sixty-second anniversary of the annuitant's birth (hereinafter in this section referred to as the annuitant's "redetermination date"), such annuity shall be redetermined by the Office in accordance with paragraph (2). Effective as of the annuitant's redetermination date, the annuity (as so redetermined) shall be in lieu of any annuity to which such annuitant would otherwise be entitled under this subchapter.

(2)(A) An annuity redetermined under this subsection shall be equal to the amount of the annuity to which the annuitant would be entitled under section 8415, taking into account the provisions of subparagraph (B).

(B) In performing a computation under this paragraph—

(i) creditable service of an annuitant shall be increased by including any period (or periods) before the annuitant's redetermination date during which the annuitant was entitled to an annuity under this subchapter; and

(ii) the average pay which would otherwise be used shall be adjusted to reflect all adjustments made under section 8462(b) with respect to any period (or periods) referred to in clause (i) (without regard to whether the annuitant's annuity was affected by any of those adjustments).

(c) Except as provided in subsection (d), the annuity of an annuitant under this subchapter shall be computed under section 8415 if—

(1) such annuity commences, or is restored, beginning on or after the redetermination date of the annuitant; or

(2) as of the day on which such annuity commences, or is restored, the annuitant satisfies the age and service requirements for entitlement to an annuity under section 8412 (other than subsection (g) of such section).

(d)(1) The annuity to which an annuitant is entitled under this section (after the reduction under subsection (a)(2), if applicable, has been made) shall not be less than the amount of an annuity computed under section 8415 (excluding subsection (f) of such section).

(2) In applying this subsection with respect to any annuitant, the amount of an annuity so computed under section 8415 shall be adjusted under section 8462 (including subsection (c) thereof)—

(A) to the same extent, and otherwise in the same manner, as if it were an annuity—

(i) subject to adjustment under such section; and

(ii) with a commencement date coinciding with the date the annuitant's annuity commenced or was restored under this subchapter, as the case may be; and

(B) whether the amount actually payable to the annuitant under this section in any month is determined under this subsection or otherwise.

(Added Pub. L. 99–335, title I, § 101(a), June 6, 1986, 100 Stat. 566; amended Pub. L. 99–556, title I, §§ 104, 106, Oct. 27, 1986, 100 Stat. 3131, 3132; Pub. L. 100–238, title I, § 122(a)–(c), Jan. 8, 1988, 101 Stat. 1753, 1754.)

REFERENCES IN TEXT

Sections 223 and 224 of the Social Security Act, referred to in subsec. (a)(2), are classified to sections 423 and 424a, respectively, of Title 42, The Public Health and Welfare.

AMENDMENTS

1988—Subsec. (a)(1)(B). Pub. L. 100–238, § 122(c)(2)(A), amended subpar. (B) generally. Prior to amendment, subpar. (B) read as follows: "An annuity computed under this paragraph shall not, for purposes of any adjustment under section 8462 (including any adjustment under subsection (c)(1) of such section), be considered to have commenced until after such annuity ceases to be determined under subparagraph (A)(i)."

Subsec. (a)(2)(B)(i). Pub. L. 100–238, § 122(a), amended cl. (i) generally. Prior to amendment, cl. (i) read as follows: "For purposes of this paragraph, the assumed disability insurance benefit of an annuitant for any month shall be equal to—

"(I) the amount of the disability insurance benefit to which the annuitant would have been entitled under section 223 of the Social Security Act for the month in which the annuity under this subchapter commenced, or was restored, determined as if such annuitant had then satisfied all requirements for entitlement to a benefit under such section, adjusted by "(II) all adjustments made under section 8462(b) between the date on which the annuity commenced, or was restored, and the start of the month involved (without regard to whether the annuitant's annuity was affected by any of those adjustments).

For purposes of computing the assumed disability insurance benefit, the month in which the annuitant's disability began (as determined under section 216(i)(2)(C) of the Social Security Act) shall be the month in which the annuity commenced or, if earlier (and if a determination was actually made) the month determined under such section."

Subsec. (a)(3). Pub. L. 100–238, § 122(c)(2)(B), added par. (3).

Subsec. (b). Pub. L. 100–238, § 122(b), amended subsec. (b) generally, substituting pars. (1) and (2) for former pars. (1) to (4).

Subsec. (d). Pub. L. 100–238, § 122(c)(1), designated existing provisions as par. (1) and added par. (2).

1986—Subsec. (b)(3). Pub. L. 99–556, § 106, substituted "(a)(1)(A)(i)" for "(a)(1)(A)" in second sentence.

Subsec. (d). Pub. L. 99–556, § 104, inserted "(after the reduction under subsection (a)(2), if applicable, has been made)".

EFFECTIVE DATE OF 1988 AMENDMENT

Section 122(d) of Pub. L. 100–238 provided that: "The amendments made by this section [amending this section] shall be effective as of January 1, 1987, as if they had been enacted as part of the Federal Employees' Retirement System Act of 1986 (Public Law 99–335; 100 Stat. 514 and following)."

SECTION REFERRED TO IN OTHER SECTIONS

This section is referred to in sections 8415, 8418, 8419, 8442, 8451, 8455, 8462 of this title; title 22 section 4071d.

§ 8453. Application

A claim may be allowed under this subchapter only if application is filed with the Office before the employee or Member is separated from the service or within 1 year thereafter. This time limitation may be waived by the Office for an employee or Member who, at the date of separation from service or within 1 year thereafter, is mentally incompetent if the application is filed with the Office within 1 year from the date of restoration of the employee or Member to competency or the appointment of a fiduciary, whichever is earlier.

(Added Pub. L. 99–335, title I, § 101(a), June 6, 1986, 100 Stat. 568.)

§ 8454. Medical examination

An annuitant receiving a disability retirement annuity from the Fund shall be examined under the direction of the Office—

(1) at the end of 1 year from the date of the disability retirement; and

(2) annually thereafter until becoming 60 years of age;

unless the disability is permanent in character. If the annuitant fails to submit to examination as required by this section, payment of the annuity shall be suspended until continuance of the disability is satisfactorily established.

(Added Pub. L. 99–335, title I, § 101(a), June 6, 1986, 100 Stat. 568.)

§ 8455. Recovery; restoration of earning capacity

(a)(1) If an annuitant receiving a disability retirement annuity from the Fund recovers from

the disability before becoming 60 years of age, payment of the annuity terminates on reemployment by the Government or 1 year after the date on which the Office determines that the annuitant has recovered, whichever is earlier.

(2) If an annuitant receiving a disability annuity from the Fund, before becoming 60 years of age, is restored to an earning capacity fairly comparable to the current rate of pay of the position occupied at the time of retirement, payment of the annuity terminates 180 days after the end of the calendar year in which earning capacity is so restored. Earning capacity is deemed restored if in any calendar year the income of the annuitant from wages or self-employment or both equals at least 80 percent of the current rate of pay of the position occupied immediately before retirement.

(b)(1) If an annuitant whose annuity is terminated under subsection (a) is not reemployed in a position in which that individual is subject to this chapter, such individual is deemed, except for service credit, to have been involuntarily separated from the service for the purpose of subchapter II of this chapter as of the date of termination of the disability annuity, and after that termination is entitled to annuity under the applicable provisions of such subchapter.

(2) If an annuitant whose annuity is terminated under subsection (a)(2)—

(A) is not reemployed in a position subject to this chapter; and

(B) has not recovered from the disability for which that individual was retired;

the annuity of such individual shall be restored at the applicable rate under section 8452 effective the first of the year following any calendar year in which such individual's income from wages or self-employment or both is less than 80 percent of the current rate of pay of the position occupied immediately before retirement.

(3) If an annuitant whose annuity is terminated because of a medical finding that the individual has recovered from disability is not reemployed in a position in which such individual is subject to this chapter, the annuity of such individual shall be restored at the applicable rate under section 8452 effective from the date on which the Office determines that there has been a recurrence of the disability.

(4) Paragraphs (2) and (3) shall not apply in the case of an annuitant receiving an annuity from the Fund under subchapter II of this chapter.

(Added Pub. L. 99–335, title I, § 101(a), June 6, 1986, 100 Stat. 568.)

SECTION REFERRED TO IN OTHER SECTIONS

This section is referred to in sections 8452, 8456 of this title.

§ 8456. Military reserve technicians

(a)(1) Except as provided in paragraph (2) or (3), an individual shall be retired under this subchapter if the individual—

(A) is separated from employment as a military reserve technician by reason of a disability that disqualifies the individual from membership in a reserve component of the Armed Forces specified in section 10101 of title 10 or from holding the military grade required for such employment;

(B) is not considered to be disabled under section 8451(a)(1)(B);

(C) is not appointed to a position in the Government (whether under subsection (b) or otherwise); and

(D) has not declined an offer of an appointment to a position in the Government under subsection (b).

(2) Payment of any annuity for an individual pursuant to this section terminates—

(A) on the date the individual is appointed to a position in the Government (whether pursuant to subsection (b) or otherwise);

(B) on the date the individual declines an offer of appointment to a position in the Government under subsection (b); or

(C) as provided under section 8455(a).

(3) An individual eligible to retire under section 8414(c) shall not be eligible to retire under this section.

(b) Any individual applying for or receiving any annuity pursuant to this section shall, in accordance with regulations prescribed by the Office, be considered by any agency of the Government before any vacant position in the agency is filled if—

(1) the position is located within the commuting area of the individual's former position;

(2) the individual is qualified to serve in such position, as determined by the head of the agency; and

(3) the position is at the same grade or equivalent level as the position from which the individual was separated.

(Added Pub. L. 99–335, title I, § 101(a), June 6, 1986, 100 Stat. 570, § 8457; amended Pub. L. 99–556, title I, § 118, Oct. 27, 1986, 100 Stat. 3134; renumbered § 8456, Pub. L. 100–238, title I, § 124(b)(1)(B), Jan. 8, 1988, 101 Stat. 1756; Pub. L. 103–337, div. A, title XVI, § 1677(a)(4), Oct. 5, 1994, 108 Stat. 3019.)

PRIOR PROVISIONS

A prior section 8456, added Pub. L. 99–355, title I, § 101(a), June 6, 1986, 100 Stat. 569, related to relationship between annuity and workers' compensation, prior to repeal by Pub. L. 100–238, title I, § 124(b)(1)(A), Jan. 8, 1988, 101 Stat. 1756. See section 8464a of this title.

AMENDMENTS

1994—Subsec. (a)(1)(A). Pub. L. 103–337 substituted "section 10101" for "section 261(a)".

1988—Pub. L. 100–238 renumbered section 8457 of this title as this section.

1986—Subsec. (a)(1)(C), (D), (2)(A), (B). Pub. L. 99–556 substituted "subsection (b)" for "subsection (c)".

EFFECTIVE DATE OF 1994 AMENDMENT

Amendment by Pub. L. 103–337 effective Dec. 1, 1994, except as otherwise provided, see section 1691 of Pub. L. 103–337, set out as an Effective Date note under section 10001 of Title 10, Armed Forces.

[§ 8457. Renumbered § 8456]

SUBCHAPTER VI—GENERAL AND ADMINISTRATIVE PROVISIONS

SUBCHAPTER REFERRED TO IN OTHER SECTIONS

This subchapter is referred to in section 8461 of this title.

§ 8461. Authority of the Office of Personnel Management

(a) The Office shall pay all benefits that are payable under subchapter II, IV, V, or VI of this chapter from the Fund.

(b) The Office shall administer all provisions of this chapter not specifically required to be administered by the Board, the Executive Director, the Secretary of Labor, or any other officer or agency.

(c) The Office shall adjudicate all claims under the provisions of this chapter administered by the Office.

(d) The Office shall determine questions of disability and dependency arising under the provisions of this chapter administered by the Office. Except to the extent provided under subsection (e), the decisions of the Office concerning these matters are final and conclusive and are not subject to review. The Office may direct at any time such medical or other examinations as it considers necessary to determine the facts concerning disability or dependency of an individual receiving or applying for annuity under the provisions of this chapter administered by the Office. The Office may suspend or deny annuity for failure to submit to examination.

(e)(1) Subject to paragraph (2), an administrative action or order affecting the rights or interests of an individual or of the United States under the provisions of this chapter administered by the Office may be appealed to the Merit Systems Protection Board under procedures prescribed by the Board.

(2) In the case of any individual found by the Office to be disabled in whole or in part on the basis of the individual's mental condition, and that finding was made pursuant to an application by an agency for purposes of disability retirement under section 8451, the procedures under section 7701 shall apply and the decision of the Board shall be subject to judicial review under section 7703.

(f) The Office shall fix the fees for examinations made under subchapter V of this chapter by physicians or surgeons who are not medical officers of the United States. The fees and reasonable traveling and other expenses incurred in connection with the examinations are paid from appropriations for the cost of administering the provisions of this chapter administered by the Office.

(g) The Office may prescribe regulations to carry out the provisions of this chapter administered by the Office.

(h)(1) Each Government agency shall furnish the Director with such information as the Director determines necessary in order to administer this chapter.

(2) The Director, in consultation with the officials from whom such information is requested, shall establish (by regulation or otherwise) such safeguards as are necessary to ensure that information made available under this subsection is used only for the purpose authorized.

(i) In making a determination of "actuarial equivalence" under this chapter, the economic assumptions used shall be the same as the economic assumptions most recently used by the Office (before the determination of actuarial equivalence involved) in determining the normal-cost percentage of the System.

(j)(1) Notwithstanding any other provision of this chapter, the Director of Central Intelligence shall, in a manner consistent with the administration of this chapter by the Office, and to the extent considered appropriate by the Director of Central Intelligence—

(A) determine entitlement to benefits under this chapter based on the service of employees of the Central Intelligence Agency;

(B) maintain records relating to the service of such employees;

(C) compute benefits under this chapter based on the service of such employees;

(D) collect deposits to the Fund made by such employees, their spouses, their former spouses, and their survivors;

(E) authorize and direct disbursements from the Fund to the extent based on service of such employees; and

(F) perform such other functions under this chapter (other than under subchapters III and VII of this chapter) with respect to employees of the Central Intelligence Agency as the Director of Central Intelligence, in consultation with the Director of the Office of Personnel Management, determines to be appropriate.

(2) The Director of the Office of Personnel Management shall furnish such information and, on a reimbursable basis, such services to the Director of Central Intelligence as the Director of Central Intelligence requests to carry out paragraph (1).

(k)(1) The Director of Central Intelligence, in consultation with the Executive Director of the Federal Retirement Thrift Investment Board, may—

(A) maintain exclusive records relating to elections, contributions, and accounts under the Thrift Savings Plan provided in subchapter III of this chapter in the case of employees of the Central Intelligence Agency;

(B) provide that contributions by, or on behalf of, such employees to the Thrift Savings Plan be accounted for by such Executive Director in aggregate amounts;

(C) make the necessary disbursements from, and the necessary allocations of earnings, losses, and charges to, individual accounts of such employees under the Thrift Savings Plan; and

(D) perform such other functions under subchapters III and VII of this chapter (but not including investing sums in the Thrift Savings Fund) with respect to employees of the Central Intelligence Agency as the Director of Central Intelligence, in consultation with the Executive Director of the Federal Retirement Thrift Investment Board, determines to be appropriate.

(2) The Executive Director of the Federal Retirement Thrift Investment Board may not exercise authority under this chapter in the case of employees of the Central Intelligence Agency to the extent that the Director of Central Intelligence exercises authority provided in paragraph (1).

(3) The Executive Director of the Federal Retirement Thrift Investment Board shall furnish such information and, on a reimbursable basis, such services to the Director of Central Intelligence as the Director of Central Intelligence determines necessary to carry out this subsection.

(l) Subsection (h)(1), and sections 8439(b) and 8474(c)(4), shall be applied with respect to information relating to employees of the Central Intelligence Agency in a manner that protects intelligence sources, methods, and activities.

(m)(1) The Director of Central Intelligence, in consultation with the Director of the Office of Personnel Management and the Executive Director of the Federal Retirement Thrift Investment Board, shall by regulation prescribe appropriate procedures to carry out subsections (j), (k), and (l).

(2) The regulations shall provide procedures for the Director of the Office of Personnel Management to inspect and audit disbursements from the Fund under this chapter.

(3) The Director of Central Intelligence shall submit the regulations prescribed under paragraph (1) to the Select Committee on Intelligence of the Senate and the Permanent Select Committee on Intelligence of the House of Representatives before the regulations take effect.

(n)(1) Under regulations prescribed by the Office, an employee who—

(A) has not previously made an election under this subsection or had an opportunity to make an election under this paragraph;

(B) has 5 or more years of civilian service creditable under this chapter; and

(C) moves, without a break in service of more than 1 year, to employment in a nonappropriated fund instrumentality of the Department of Defense or the Coast Guard, respectively, described in section 2105(c),

shall be given the opportunity to elect irrevocably, within 30 days after such move, to remain covered as an employee under this chapter during any employment described in section 2105(c) after such move.

(2) Under regulations prescribed by the Office, an employee of a nonappropriated fund instrumentality of the Department of Defense or the Coast Guard described in section 2105(c), who—

(A) has not previously made an election under this subsection or had an opportunity to make an election under this paragraph;

(B) is a vested participant in a retirement system established for employees described in section 2105(c), as the term "vested participant" is defined by such system;

(C) moves, without a break in service of more than 1 year, to a position that is not described by section 2105(c); and

(D) is not eligible to make an election under section 8347(q),

shall be given the opportunity to elect irrevocably, within 30 days after such move, to remain covered, during any subsequent employment as an employee as defined by section 2105(a) or section 2105(c), by the retirement system applicable to such employee's current or most recent employment described by section 2105(c) rather than be subject to this chapter.

(Added Pub. L. 99–335, title I, §101(a), June 6, 1986, 100 Stat. 570; amended Pub. L. 99–556, title

I, § 102, Oct. 27, 1986, 100 Stat. 3131; Pub. L. 101–508, title VII, § 7202(k)(2), Nov. 5, 1990, 104 Stat. 1388–339; Pub. L. 102–378, § 2(71), Oct. 2, 1992, 106 Stat. 1355; Pub. L. 104–106, div. A, title X, § 1043(a)(2), Feb. 10, 1996, 110 Stat. 434.)

Amendments

1996—Subsec. (n)(1). Pub. L. 104–106, § 1043(a)(2)(A), struck out "of the Department of Defense or the Coast Guard" after "an employee" in introductory provisions and substituted "1 year" for "3 days" in subpar. (C).

Subsec. (n)(2)(C). Pub. L. 104–106, § 1043(a)(2)(B), substituted "1 year" for "3 days" and struck out "in the Department of Defense or the Coast Guard, respectively," after "to a position".

1992—Subsec. (n)(1)(A), (2)(A). Pub. L. 102–378, § 2(71)(A), amended subpars. (A) generally. Prior to amendment, subpars. (A) read as follows: "has not previously made or had an opportunity to make an election under this subsection;".

Subsec. (n)(2)(D). Pub. L. 102–378, § 2(71)(B), substituted "8347(q)" for "8347(p)".

1990—Subsec. (n). Pub. L. 101–500 added subsec. (n).

1986—Subsec. (m)(2). Pub. L. 99–556 struck out ", and from the Thrift Savings Fund," after "from the Fund".

Effective Date of 1996 Amendment

For effective date of amendments by Pub. L. 104–106, see Regulations; Effective Date of 1996 Amendment note below.

Effective Date of 1992 Amendment

Amendment by Pub. L. 102–378 effective Nov. 5, 1990, see section 9(b)(6) of Pub. L. 102–378, set out as a note under section 6303 of this title.

Effective Date of 1990 Amendment

Amendment by Pub. L. 101–508 applicable with respect to any individual who, on or after Jan. 1, 1987, moves from employment in nonappropriated fund instrumentality of Department of Defense or Coast Guard, that is described in section 2105(c) of this title, to employment in Department or Coast Guard, that is not described in section 2105(c), or who moves from employment in Department or Coast Guard, that is not described in section 2105(c), to employment in nonappropriated fund instrumentality of Department or Coast Guard, that is described in section 2105(c), see section 7202(m)(1) of Pub. L. 101–508, set out as a note under section 2105 of this title.

Regulations; Effective Date of 1996 Amendment

For provisions relating to promulgation of regulations necessary to carry out amendment by Pub. L. 104–106, and effective date of such amendment in connection with those regulations, see section 1043(b), (c) of Pub. L. 104–106, set out as a note under section 8347 of this title.

Treatment of Individuals Electing To Remain Subject to Their Former Retirement System

For provisions relating to the deductions and contributions required with respect to individuals electing under section 8347(q) or 8461(n) of this title to remain covered under subchapter III of chapter 83 of this title, chapter 84 of this title, or a retirement system for employees described in section 2105(c) of this title, see section 7202(n) of Pub. L. 101–508, set out as a note under section 2105 of this title.

Section Referred To in Other Sections

This section is referred to in sections 8348, 8401, 8901 of this title; title 50 sections 2142, 2155.

§ 8462. Cost-of-living adjustments

(a) For the purpose of this section—

(1) the term "base quarter", as used with respect to a year, means the calendar quarter ending on September 30 of such year;

(2) the price index for a base quarter is the arithmetical mean of such index for the 3 months comprising such quarter; and

(3) the term "percent change in the price index", as used with respect to a year, means the percentage derived by—

(A) reducing—

(i) the price index for the base quarter of such year, by

(ii) the price index for the base quarter of the preceding year in which an adjustment under this subsection was made;

(B) dividing the difference under subparagraph (A) by the price index referred to in subparagraph (A)(ii); and

(C) multiplying the quotient under subparagraph (B) by 100.

(b)(1) Except as provided in subsection (c), effective December 1 of any year in which an adjustment under this subsection is to be made, as determined under paragraph (2), each annuity payable from the Fund under this chapter (other than an annuity under section 8443) having a commencing date not later than such December 1 shall be adjusted as follows:

(A) If the percent change in the price index for the year does not exceed 3 percent, each annuity subject to adjustment under this subsection shall be increased by the lesser of—

(i) the percent change in the price index (rounded to the nearest one-tenth of 1 percent); or

(ii) 2 percent.

(B) If the percent change in the price index for the year exceeds 3 percent, each annuity subject to adjustment under this subsection shall be increased by the excess of—

(i) the percent change in the price index (rounded to the nearest one-tenth of 1 percent), over

(ii) 1 percent.

(2) An adjustment under this subsection shall be made in a year only if the price index for the base quarter of such year exceeds the price index for the base quarter of the preceding year in which an adjustment under this subsection was made.

(3) An annuity under this chapter shall not be subject to adjustment under section 8340. Nothing in the preceding sentence shall affect the computation of any amount under section 8443(a)(2).

(c) Eligibility for an annuity increase under this section is governed by the commencing date of each annuity payable from the Fund as of the effective date of an increase, except as follows:

(1) The first increase (if any) made under subsection (b) to an annuity which is payable from the Fund to an annuitant or survivor (other than a child under section 8443) whose annuity has not been increased under this subsection or subsection (b) shall be equal to the product (adjusted to the nearest one-tenth of 1 percent) of—

(A) one-twelfth of the applicable percent change computed under subsection (b), multiplied by

(B) the number of months (not to exceed 12 months, counting any portion of a month as a month)—

(i) for which the annuity was payable from the Fund before the effective date of the increase; or

(ii) in the case of a survivor of a deceased annuitant whose annuity has not been so increased, since the annuity was first payable to the deceased annuitant.

(2) Effective from its commencing date, an annuity payable from the Fund to an annuitant's survivor (other than a widow or widower whose annuity is computed under section 8442(g) or a child under section 8443) shall be increased by the total percentage by which the deceased annuitant's annuity had been increased under this section during the period beginning on the date the deceased annuitant's annuity commenced and ending on the date of the deceased annuitant's death.

(3)(A) An adjustment under subsection (b) for any year shall not be effective with respect to the annuity of an annuitant who is under 62 years of age as of the date on which such adjustment would otherwise first take effect.

(B)(i) Except as provided in clause (ii), this paragraph applies only with respect to an annuitant under section 8412, 8413, or 8414.

(ii) This paragraph does not apply with respect to an annuitant under subsection (d) or (e) of section 8412 or (in the case of an annuitant separated from service as a military reserve technician as a result of disability) under section 8414(c).

(4) The first increase (if any) made under subsection (b) to an annuity which is payable from the Fund to a widow or widower whose annuity is computed under section 8442(g) shall be equal to the product (adjusted to the nearest one-tenth of 1 percent) of—

(A) one-twelfth of the applicable percent change computed under subsection (b), multiplied by

(B) the number of months (not to exceed 12 months, counting any portion of a month as a month) since—

(i) the effective date of the adjustment last made under this section in the annuity of the annuitant on whose service on the widow's or widower's annuity is based; or

(ii) if the annuity of the annuitant (referred to in clause (i)) has not been increased under this section, the commencement date of such annuitant's annuity (determined subject to section 8452(a)(1)(B)).

(d) The monthly installment of an annuity after adjustment under this section shall be rounded to the next lowest dollar. However, the monthly installment shall, after adjustment, reflect an increase of at least $1.

(e) The $15,000 amount referred to in section 8442(b)(1)(A)(ii) shall be increased at the same time that, and by the same percent as the percentage by which, annuities under subchapter III of chapter 83 are increased.

(Added Pub. L. 99–335, title I, §101(a), June 6, 1986, 100 Stat. 572; amended Pub. L. 99–556, title I, §117(b), Oct. 27, 1986, 100 Stat. 3134.)

1986—Subsec. (b)(3). Pub. L. 99–556 inserted provision relating to the computation of any amount under section 8443(a)(2).

DELAY IN COST-OF-LIVING ADJUSTMENTS DURING FISCAL YEARS 1994, 1995, AND 1996

Any cost-of-living increase scheduled to take effect during fiscal year 1994, 1995, or 1996 under subsec. (b) of this section delayed until first day of third calendar month after date such increase would otherwise take effect, see section 11001 of Pub. L. 103–66, set out as a note under section 8340 of this title.

SECTION REFERRED TO IN OTHER SECTIONS

This section is referred to in sections 8348, 8418, 8442, 8452 of this title; title 22 section 4071g.

§ 8463. Rate of benefits

Each annuity payable from the Fund is stated as an annual amount, one-twelfth of which, rounded to the next lower dollar, constitutes the monthly rate payable on the first business day of the first month beginning after the month for which it has accrued.

(Added Pub. L. 99–335, title I, §101(a), June 6, 1986, 100 Stat. 574.)

§ 8464. Commencement and termination of annuities of employees and Members

(a)(1) Except as otherwise provided in this chapter—

(A) an annuity payable from the Fund commences on the first day of the month after—

(i) separation from the service, in the case of an employee or Member retiring under section 8412, or subsection (a), (b)(1)(B), or (d) of section 8414; or

(ii) pay ceases, and the applicable age and service requirements are met, in the case of an employee or Member retiring under section 8413;

(B) an annuity payable from the Fund commences on the day after separation from the service in the case of an employee retiring under subsection (b)(1)(A) or (c) of section 8414; and

(C) an annuity payable from the Fund commences on the day after separation from the service or the day after pay ceases and the requirements for title to an annuity are met in the case of an employee or Member retiring under section 8451.

(2) Notwithstanding paragraph (1)(A)(i), an annuity payable from the Fund commences on the day after separation from the service in the case of an employee or Member—

(A) who retires under section 8412; and

(B) whose separation occurs upon the expiration of a term (or other period) for which the individual was appointed or elected.

(b) Except as otherwise provided in this chapter, the annuity of an annuitant under subchapter II or V of this chapter terminates on the date death or other terminating event occurs.

(Added Pub. L. 99–335, title I, §101(a), June 6, 1986, 100 Stat. 574; amended Pub. L. 105–261, div. A, title XI, §1109(c)(2), Oct. 17, 1998, 112 Stat. 2145; Pub. L. 106–58, title VI, §651(b), Sept. 29, 1999, 113 Stat. 480; Pub. L. 106–398, §1 [[div. A], title XI, §1152(c)(2)], Oct. 30, 2000, 114 Stat. 1654, 1654A–323.)

2000—Subsec. (a)(1)(A)(i). Pub. L. 106–398, which directed amendment of cl. (i) by "striking out 'or (b)(1)(B)' and ', (b)(1)(B), or (d)'", was executed by striking out "or (b)(1)(B)" and inserting in lieu thereof ", (b)(1)(B), or (d)" to reflect the probable intent of Congress.

1999—Subsec. (a)(1)(A)(i). Pub. L. 106–58 repealed Pub. L. 105–261, § 1109(c)(2). See 1998 Amendment note below.

1998—Subsec. (a)(1)(A)(i). Pub. L. 105–261, § 1109(c)(2), which directed substitution of ", (b)(1)(B), or (d)" for "or (b)(1)(B)", was repealed by Pub. L. 106–58.

§ 8464a. Relationship between annuity and workers' compensation

(a)(1) An individual is not entitled to receive—

(A) an annuity under subchapter II or V, and

(B) compensation for injury to, or disability of, such individual under subchapter I of chapter 81, other than compensation payable under section 8107,

covering the same period of time.

(2) An individual is not entitled to receive an annuity under subchapter IV and a concurrent benefit under subchapter I of chapter 81 on account of the death of the same person.

(3) Paragraphs (1) and (2) do not bar the right of a claimant to the greater benefit conferred by either this chapter or subchapter I of chapter 81.

(b) If an individual is entitled to an annuity under subchapter II, IV, or V, and the individual receives a lump-sum payment for compensation under section 8135 based on the disability or death of the same person, so much of the compensation as has been paid for a period extended beyond the date payment of the annuity commences, as determined by the Department of Labor, shall be refunded to that Department for credit to the Employees' Compensation Fund. Before the individual may receive the annuity, the individual shall—

(1) refund to the Department of Labor the amount representing the commuted compensation payments for the extended period; or

(2) authorize the deduction of the amount from the annuity.

Deductions from the annuity may be made from accrued or accruing payments. The amounts deducted and withheld from the annuity shall be transmitted to the Department of Labor for reimbursement to the Employees' Compensation Fund. When the Department of Labor finds that the financial circumstances of an individual entitled to an annuity under subchapter II, IV, or V warrant deferred refunding, deductions from the annuity may be prorated against and paid from accruing payments in such manner as the Department determines appropriate.

(Added Pub. L. 100–238, title I, § 124(a)(1)(B), Jan. 8, 1988, 101 Stat. 1755.)

PRIOR PROVISIONS

Provisions similar to this section were contained in section 8456 of this title prior to repeal by Pub. L. 100–238.

EFFECTIVE DATE

Section effective Jan. 1, 1987, and applicable with respect to benefits payable based on a death or disability occurring on or after that date, see section 124(c) of Pub. L. 100–238 set out as an Effective Date of 1988 Amendment note under section 8337 of this title.

§ 8465. Waiver, allotment, and assignment of benefits

(a) An individual entitled to an annuity payable from the Fund may decline to accept all or any part of the amount of the annuity by a waiver signed and filed with the Office. The waiver may be revoked in writing at any time. Payment of the annuity waived may not be made for the period during which the waiver is in effect.

(b) An individual entitled to an annuity payable from the Fund may make allotments or assignments of amounts from the annuity for such purposes as the Office considers appropriate.

(Added Pub. L. 99–335, title I, § 101(a), June 6, 1986, 100 Stat. 575.)

SECTION REFERRED TO IN OTHER SECTIONS

This section is referred to in sections 8348, 8470 of this title.

§ 8466. Application for benefits

(a) No payment of benefits based on the service of an employee or Member shall be made from the Fund unless an application for payment of the benefits is received by the Office before the one hundred and fifteenth anniversary of the birth of the employee or Member.

(b) Notwithstanding subsection (a), after the death of an employee, Member, or annuitant, or former employee or Member, a benefit based on the service of such employee, Member, or annuitant, or former employee or Member, shall not be paid under subchapter II or IV of this chapter unless an application therefor is received by the Office within 30 years after the death or other event which establishes the entitlement to the benefit.

(c) Payment due a minor, or an individual mentally incompetent or under other legal disability, may be made to the person who is constituted guardian or other fiduciary by the law of the State of residence of the claimant or is otherwise legally vested with the care of the claimant or his estate. If a guardian or other fiduciary of the individual under legal disability has not been appointed under the law of the State of residence of the claimant, payment may be made to any person who, in the judgment of the Office, is responsible for the care of the claimant, and the payment bars recovery by any other person.

(Added Pub. L. 99–335, title I, § 101(a), June 6, 1986, 100 Stat. 575.)

§ 8467. Court orders

(a) Payments under this chapter which would otherwise be made to an employee, Member, or annuitant (including an employee, Member, or annuitant as defined in section 8331) based on service of that individual shall be paid (in whole or in part) by the Office or the Executive Director, as the case may be, to another person if and to the extent expressly provided for in the terms of—

(1) any court decree of divorce, annulment, or legal separation, or the terms of any court order or court-approved property settlement agreement incident to any court decree of divorce, annulment, or legal separation; or

(2) any court order or other similar process in the nature of garnishment for the enforcement of a judgment rendered against such employee, Member, or annuitant, for physically, sexually, or emotionally abusing a child.

In the event that the Office or the Executive Director, as the case may be, is served with more than 1 decree, order, or other legal process with respect to the same moneys due or payable to any individual, such moneys shall be available to satisfy such processes on a first-come, first-served basis, with any such process being satisfied out of such moneys as remain after the satisfaction of all such processes which have been previously served.

(b) Subsection (a) shall apply only to payments made by the Office or the Executive Director under this chapter after the date on which the Office or the Executive Director (as the case may be) receives written notice of such decree, order, other legal process, or agreement, and such additional information and documentation as the Office or the Executive Director may require.

(c) For the purpose of this section—

(1) the term "judgment rendered for physically, sexually, or emotionally abusing a child" means any legal claim perfected through a final enforceable judgment, which claim is based in whole or in part upon the physical, sexual, or emotional abuse of a child, whether or not that abuse is accompanied by other actionable wrongdoing, such as sexual exploitation or gross negligence; and

(2) the term "child" means an individual under 18 years of age.

(Added Pub. L. 99–335, title I, § 101(a), June 6, 1986, 100 Stat. 575; amended Pub. L. 103–358, § 2(b)(1)–(3), Oct. 14, 1994, 108 Stat. 3421.)

AMENDMENTS

1994—Subsec. (a). Pub. L. 103–358, § 2(b)(1), amended subsec. (a) generally. Prior to amendment, subsec. (a) read as follows: "Payments under this chapter which would otherwise be made to an employee, Member, or annuitant (including an employee, Member, or annuitant as defined under section 8331) based on the service of that individual shall be paid (in whole or in part) by the Office or the Executive Director (as the case may be), to another person if and to the extent that the terms of any court decree of divorce, annulment, or legal separation, or the terms of any court order or court-approved property settlement agreement incident to any court decree of divorce, annulment, or legal separation expressly provide. Any payment under this subsection to a person bars recovery by any other person."

Subsec. (b). Pub. L. 103–358, § 2(b)(2), inserted "other legal process," after "order,".

Subsec. (c). Pub. L. 103–358, § 2(b)(3), added subsec. (c).

EFFECTIVE DATE OF 1994 AMENDMENT

Amendment by Pub. L. 103–358 effective Oct. 14, 1994, and applicable with respect to any decree, order, or other legal process, or notice of agreement received by Office of Personnel Management or Executive Director of Federal Retirement Thrift Investment Board on or after Oct. 14, 1994, see section 3 of Pub. L. 103–358, set out as a note under section 8345 of this title.

SECTION REFERRED TO IN OTHER SECTIONS

This section is referred to in sections 8420a, 8421, 8424, 8435, 8437, 8470, 8901, 8905 of this title.

§ 8468. Annuities and pay on reemployment

(a) If an annuitant, except a disability annuitant whose annuity is terminated because of the annuitant's recovery or restoration of earning capacity, becomes employed in an appointive or elective position, an amount equal to the annuity allocable to the period of actual employment shall be deducted from the annuitant's pay, except for lump-sum leave payment purposes under section 5551. Unless the annuitant's appointment is on an intermittent basis or is to a position as a justice or judge (as defined by section 451 of title 28) or as an employee subject to another retirement system for Government employees, or unless the annuitant is serving as President, deductions for the Fund shall be withheld from the annuitant's pay under section 8422(a) and contributions under section 8423 shall be made. The deductions and contributions referred to in the preceding provisions of this subsection shall be deposited in the Treasury of the United States to the credit of the Fund. The annuitant's lump-sum credit may not be reduced by annuity paid during the reemployment.

(b)(1)(A) If an annuitant subject to deductions under the second sentence of subsection (a) serves on a full-time basis for at least 1 year, or on a part-time basis for periods equivalent to at least 1 year of full-time service, the annuitant's annuity on termination of reemployment shall be increased by an annuity computed under section 8415(a) through (g) as may apply based on the period of reemployment and the basic pay, before deduction, averaged during the reemployment.

(B)(i) If the annuitant is receiving a reduced annuity as provided in section 8419, the increase in annuity payable under subparagraph (A) is reduced by 10 percent and the survivor annuity or combination of survivor annuities payable under section 8442 or 8445 (or both) is increased by 50 percent of the increase in annuity payable under subparagraph (A), unless, at the time of claiming the increase payable under subparagraph (A), the annuitant notifies the Office in writing that the annuitant does not desire the survivor annuity to be increased.

(ii) If an annuitant who is subject to the deductions referred to in subparagraph (A) dies while still reemployed, after having been reemployed for not less than 1 year of full-time service (or the equivalent thereof, in the case of full-time[1] employment), the survivor annuity payable is increased as though the reemployment had otherwise terminated.

(2)(A) If an annuitant subject to deductions under the second sentence of subsection (a) serves on a full-time basis for at least 5 years, or on a part-time basis for periods equivalent to at least 5 years of full-time service, the annuitant may elect, instead of the benefit provided by paragraph (1), to have such annuitant's rights redetermined under this chapter.

(B) If an annuitant who is subject to the deductions referred to in subparagraph (A) dies while still reemployed, after having been reemployed for at least 5 years of full-time service (or the equivalent thereof in the case of part-

---

[1] So in original. Probably should be "part-time".

time employment), any person entitled to a survivor annuity under section 8442 or 8445 based on the service of such annuitant shall be permitted to elect, in accordance with regulations prescribed by the Office of Personnel Management, to have such person's rights under subchapter IV redetermined. A redetermined survivor annuity elected under this subparagraph shall be in lieu of an increased annuity which would otherwise be payable in accordance with paragraph (1)(B)(ii).

(3) If an annuitant subject to deductions under the second sentence of subsection (a) serves on a full-time basis for a period of less than 1 year, or on a part-time basis for periods equivalent to less than 1 year of full-time service, the total amount withheld under section 8422(a) from the annuitant's basic pay for the period or periods involved shall, upon written application to the Office, be payable to the annuitant (or the appropriate survivor or survivors, determined in the order set forth in section 8424(d)).

(c) This section does not apply to an individual appointed to serve as a Governor of the Board of Governors of the United States Postal Service.

(d) If an annuitant becomes employed as a justice or judge of the United States, as defined by section 451 of title 28, the annuitant may, at any time prior to resignation or retirement from regular active service as such a justice or judge, apply for and be paid, in accordance with section 8424(a), the amount (if any) by which the lump-sum credit exceeds the total annuity paid, notwithstanding the time limitation contained in such section for filing an application for payment.

(e) A reference in this section to an "annuity" shall not be considered to include any amount payable from a source other than the Fund.

(f)(1) The Director of the Office of Personnel Management may, at the request of the head of an Executive agency—

(A) waive the application of the preceding provisions of this section on a case-by-case basis for employees in positions for which there is exceptional difficulty in recruiting or retaining a qualified employee; or

(B) grant authority to the head of such agency to waive the application of the preceding provisions of this section, on a case-by-case basis, for an employee serving on a temporary basis, but only if, and for so long as, the authority is necessary due to an emergency involving a direct threat to life or property or other unusual circumstances.

(2) The Office shall prescribe regulations for the exercise of any authority under this subsection, including criteria for any exercise of authority and procedures for terminating a delegation of authority under paragraph (1)(B).

(g)(1) If warranted by circumstances described in subsection (f)(1)(A) or (B) (as applicable), the Director of the Administrative Office of the United States Courts shall, with respect to an employee in the judicial branch, have the same waiver authority as would be available to the Director of the Office of Personnel Management, or a duly authorized agency head, under subsection (f) with respect to an employee of an Executive agency.

(2) Authority under this subsection may not be exercised with respect to a justice or judge of the United States, as defined in section 451 of title 28.

(h)(1) If warranted by circumstances described in subsection (f)(1)(A) or (B) (as applicable), an official or committee designated in paragraph (2) shall, with respect to the employees specified in the applicable subparagraph of such paragraph, have the same waiver authority as would be available to the Director of the Office of Personnel Management, or a duly authorized agency head, under subsection (f) with respect to an employee of an Executive agency.

(2) Authority under this subsection may be exercised—

(A) with respect to an employee of an agency in the legislative branch, by the head of such agency;

(B) with respect to an employee of the House of Representatives, by the Committee on House Oversight of the House of Representatives; and

(C) with respect to an employee of the Senate, by the Committee on Rules and Administration of the Senate.

(3) Any exercise of authority under this subsection shall be in conformance with such written policies and procedures as the agency head, the Committee on House Oversight of the House of Representatives, or the Committee on Rules and Administration of the Senate (as applicable) shall prescribe, consistent with the provisions of this subsection.

(4) For the purpose of this subsection, "agency in the legislative branch", "employee of the House of Representatives", "employee of the Senate", and "congressional employee" each has the meaning given to it in section 5531 of this title.

(i)(1) For the purpose of subsections (f) through (h), "Executive agency" shall not include the General Accounting Office.

(2) An employee as to whom a waiver under subsection (f), (g), or (h) is in effect shall not be considered an employee for purposes of this chapter or chapter 83 of this title.

(Added Pub. L. 99–335, title I, §101(a), June 6, 1986, 100 Stat. 576; amended Pub. L. 100–238, title I, §134(a), Jan. 8, 1988, 101 Stat. 1762; Pub. L. 101–509, title V, §529 [title I, §108(c)], Nov. 5, 1990, 104 Stat. 1427, 1450; Pub. L. 101–510, div. A, title XII, §1206(j)(3), Nov. 5, 1990, 104 Stat. 1664; Pub. L. 102–190, div. A, title VI, §655(c), Dec. 5, 1991, 105 Stat. 1392; Pub. L. 102–378, §8(a), Oct. 2, 1992, 106 Stat. 1359; Pub. L. 105–55, title I, §107, Oct. 7, 1997, 111 Stat. 1184; Pub. L. 105–61, title V, §516(a)(9), Oct. 10, 1997, 111 Stat. 1307.)

AMENDMENTS

1997—Subsec. (b)(1)(A). Pub. L. 105–61 substituted "through (g)" for "through (f)".

Subsec. (h)(2)(B), (3). Pub. L. 105–55 substituted "the Committee on House Oversight of the House of Representatives" for "the Speaker of the House of Representatives".

1992—Subsec. (f). Pub. L. 102–378 repealed Pub. L. 101–510, §1206(j)(3). See 1990 Amendment note below.

1991—Subsec. (f)(3). Pub. L. 102–190, §655(c)(2), struck out par. (3) which read as follows: "An employee to whom a waiver under subparagraph (A) or (B) of paragraph (1) applies shall not be deemed an employee for the purposes of chapter 83 or this chapter while such waiver is in effect.''

Subsecs. (g) to (i). Pub. L. 102–190, § 655(c)(1), added subsecs. (g) to (i).

1990—Subsec. (f). Pub. L. 101–510, § 1206(j)(3), added a subsec. (f) identical to that added by Pub. L. 101–509, see below. Pub. L. 102–378, § 8(a), repealed Pub. L. 101–510, § 1206(j)(3), and provided that this title shall read as if section 1206(j)(3) had not been enacted.

Pub. L. 101–509 added subsec. (f).

1988—Pub. L. 100–238 amended section generally, substituting subsecs. (a) to (e) for former subsecs. (a) to (c).

Committee on House Oversight of House of Representatives changed to Committee on House Administration of House of Representatives by House Resolution No. 5, One Hundred Sixth Congress, Jan. 6, 1999.

EFFECTIVE DATE OF 1997 AMENDMENT

Amendment by Pub. L. 105–61 applicable to any annuity commencing before, on, or after Oct. 10, 1997, and effective with regard to any payment made after the first month following Oct. 10, 1997, see section 516(b) of Pub. L. 105–61, set out as a note under section 8334 of this title.

EFFECTIVE DATE OF 1992 AMENDMENT

Amendment by Pub. L. 102–378 effective Nov. 5, 1990, see section 9(b)(6) of Pub. L. 102–378, set out as a note under section 6303 of this title.

EFFECTIVE DATE OF 1990 AMENDMENT

Amendment by Pub. L. 101–509 effective on such date as the President shall determine, but not earlier than 90 days, and not later than 180 days, after Nov. 5, 1990, see section 529 [title III, § 305] of Pub. L. 101–509, set out as an Effective Date of 1990 Amendment note under section 5301 of this title.

EFFECTIVE DATE OF 1988 AMENDMENT

Section 134(d) of Pub. L. 100–238 provided that:

''(1) GENERALLY.—The amendments made by this section [amending this section and provisions set out as notes under section 8331 of this title] shall take effect on the date of the enactment of this Act [Jan. 8, 1988], and as provided in paragraph (2), shall apply with respect to any individual who becomes a reemployed annuitant on or after such date.

''(2) EXCEPTION.—The amendment made by subsection (b) [amending provisions set out as a note under section 8331 of this title] shall apply with respect to any election made by a reemployed annuitant on or after the date of the enactment of this Act [Jan. 8, 1988].''

ANNUAL REPORT TO CONGRESS

Each agency in legislative branch to submit to Speaker of House of Representatives and Committee on Rules and Administration of Senate, for each calendar year, a written report on how authority made available as result of amendment by Pub. L. 102–190 was used by such agency during the period covered by such report, see section 655(d) of Pub. L. 102–190, set out as a note under section 8344 of this title.

SECTION REFERRED TO IN OTHER SECTIONS

This section is referred to in title 2 section 61h–6; title 20 section 4512; title 22 section 4064; title 39 section 1005.

§ 8469. Withholding of State income taxes

(a) The Office shall, in accordance with this section, enter into an agreement with any State within 120 days of a request for agreement from the proper State official. The agreement shall provide that the Office shall withhold State income tax in the case of the monthly annuity of any annuitant who voluntarily requests, in writing, such withholding. The amounts withheld during any calendar quarter shall be held in the Fund and disbursed to the States during the month following that calendar quarter.

(b) An annuitant may have in effect at any time only one request for withholding under this section, and an annuitant may not have more than two such requests in effect during any one calendar year.

(c) Subject to subsection (b), an annuitant may change the State designated by that annuitant for purposes of having withholdings made, and may request that the withholdings be remitted in accordance with such change. An annuitant also may revoke any request of that annuitant for withholding. Any change in the State designated or revocation is effective on the first day of the month after the month in which the request or the revocation is processed by the Office, but in no event later than on the first day of the second month beginning after the day on which such request or revocation is received by the Office.

(d) This section does not give the consent of the United States to the application of a statute which imposes more burdensome requirements on the United States than on employers generally, or which subjects the United States or any annuitant to a penalty or liability because of this section. The Office may not accept pay from a State for services performed in withholding State income taxes from annuities. Any amount erroneously withheld from an annuity and paid to a State by the Office shall be repaid by the State in accordance with regulations issued by the Office.

(e) For the purpose of this section—

(1) the term ''State'' means a State, the District of Columbia, or any territory or possession of the United States; and

(2) the term ''annuitant'' includes a survivor who is receiving an annuity from the Fund.

(Added Pub. L. 99–335, title I, § 101(a), June 6, 1986, 100 Stat. 576.)

SECTION REFERRED TO IN OTHER SECTIONS

This section is referred to in section 8348 of this title.

§ 8470. Exemption from legal process; recovery of payments

(a) An amount payable under subchapter II, IV, or V of this chapter is not assignable, either in law or equity, except under the provisions of section 8465 or 8467, or subject to execution, levy, attachment, garnishment or other legal process, except as otherwise may be provided by Federal laws.

(b) Recovery of payments under subchapter II, IV, or V of this chapter may not be made from an individual when, in the judgment of the Office, the individual is without fault and recovery would be against equity and good conscience. Withholding or recovery of money paid under subchapter II, IV, or V of this chapter on account of a certification or payment made by a former employee of the United States in the discharge of his official duties may be made only if the head of the agency on behalf of which the certification or payment was made certifies to the Office that the certification or payment involved fraud on the part of the former employee.

(Added Pub. L. 99–335, title I, § 101(a), June 6, 1986, 100 Stat. 577.)

SUBCHAPTER VII—FEDERAL RETIREMENT THRIFT INVESTMENT MANAGEMENT SYSTEM

SUBCHAPTER REFERRED TO IN OTHER SECTIONS

This subchapter is referred to in sections 8351, 8402, 8434, 8437, 8439, 8440a, 8440b, 8440c, 8440d, 8440e, 8461 of this title; title 22 section 4071h; title 28 sections 178, 377; title 37 section 211.

§ 8471. Definitions

For the purposes of this subchapter—

(1) the term "beneficiary" means an individual (other than a participant) entitled to payment from the Thrift Savings Fund under subchapter III of this chapter;

(2) the term "Council" means the Employee Thrift Advisory Council established under section 8473 of this title;

(3) the term "participant" means an individual for whom an account has been established under section 8439 of this title;

(4) the term "person" means an individual, partnership, joint venture, corporation, mutual company, joint-stock company, trust, estate, unincorporated organization, association, or labor organization; and

(5) the term "Thrift Savings Fund" means the Thrift Savings Fund established under section 8437 of this title.

(Added Pub. L. 99–335, title I, § 101(a), June 6, 1986, 100 Stat. 577.)

EFFECTIVE DATE

Subchapter VII effective June 6, 1986, see section 702(b)(1) of Pub. L. 99–335, set out as a note under section 8401 of this title.

SECTION REFERRED TO IN OTHER SECTIONS

This section is referred to in section 8438 of this title; title 39 section 1005.

§ 8472. Federal Retirement Thrift Investment Board

(a) There is established in the Executive branch of the Government a Federal Retirement Thrift Investment Board.

(b) The Board shall be composed of—

(1) 3 members appointed by the President, of whom 1 shall be designated by the President as Chairman; and

(2) 2 members appointed by the President, of whom—

(A) 1 shall be appointed by the President after taking into consideration the recommendation made by the Speaker of the House of Representatives in consultation with the minority leader of the House of Representatives; and

(B) 1 shall be appointed by the President after taking into consideration the recommendation made by the majority leader of the Senate in consultation with the minority leader of the Senate.

(c) Except as provided in section 311 of the Federal Employees' Retirement System Act of 1986, appointments under subsection (a) shall be made by and with the advice and consent of the Senate.

(d) Members of the Board shall have substantial experience, training, and expertise in the management of financial investments and pension benefit plans.

(e)(1) Except as provided in section 311 of the Federal Employees' Retirement System Act of 1986, a member of the Board shall be appointed for a term of 4 years, except that of the members first appointed (other than the members appointed under such section)—

(A) the Chairman shall be appointed for a term of 4 years;

(B) the members appointed under subsection (b)(2) shall be appointed for terms of 3 years; and

(C) the remaining members shall be appointed for terms of 2 years.

(2)(A) A vacancy on the Board shall be filled in the manner in which the original appointment was made and shall be subject to any conditions which applied with respect to the original appointment.

(B) An individual chosen to fill a vacancy shall be appointed for the unexpired term of the member replaced.

(3) The term of any member shall not expire before the date on which the member's successor takes office.

(f) The Board shall—

(1) establish policies for—

(A) the investment and management of the Thrift Savings Fund; and

(B) the administration of subchapter III of this chapter;

(2) review the performance of investments made for the Thrift Savings Fund; and

(3) review and approve the budget of the Board.

(g)(1) The Board may—

(A) adopt, alter, and use a seal;

(B) except as provided in paragraph (2), direct the Executive Director to take such action as the Board considers appropriate to carry out the provisions of this subchapter and subchapter III of this chapter and the policies of the Board;

(C) upon the concurring votes of four members, remove the Executive Director from office for good cause shown; and

(D) take such other actions as may be necessary to carry out the functions of the Board.

(2) Except in the case of investments required by section 8438 of this title to be invested in securities of the Government, the Board may not direct the Executive Director to invest or to cause to be invested any sums in the Thrift Savings Fund in a specific asset or to dispose of or cause to be disposed of any specific asset of such Fund.

(h) The members of the Board shall discharge their responsibilities solely in the interest of participants and beneficiaries under this subchapter and subchapter III of this chapter.

(i) The Board shall prepare and submit to the President, and, at the same time, to the appropriate committees of Congress, an annual budget of the expenses and other items relating to the Board which shall be included as a separate item in the budget required to be transmitted to the Congress under section 1105 of title 31.

(j) The Board may submit to the President, and, at the same time, shall submit to each House of the Congress, any legislative recommendations of the Board relating to any of its functions under this title or any other provision of law.

(Added Pub. L. 99–335, title I, § 101(a), June 6, 1986, 100 Stat. 578; amended Pub. L. 99–509, title VI, § 6001(e), Oct. 21, 1986, 100 Stat. 1931.)

REFERENCES IN TEXT

Section 311 of the Federal Employees' Retirement System Act of 1986 [Pub. L. 99–335], referred to in subsecs. (c) and (e)(1), is set out as a note below.

AMENDMENTS

1986—Subsecs. (i), (j). Pub. L. 99–509 added subsecs. (i) and (j).

EFFECTIVE DATE OF 1986 AMENDMENT

Amendment by Pub. L. 99–509 effective Jan. 1, 1987, see section 6001(f) of Pub. L. 99–509, set out as a note under section 8432 of this title.

INITIAL APPOINTMENTS TO FEDERAL RETIREMENT THRIFT INVESTMENT BOARD

Section 311 of Pub. L. 99–335 provided that:

"(a) INITIAL APPOINTMENT OF MEMBERS.—Section 8472(c) of title 5, United States Code (as added by section 101(a) of this Act) shall not apply to the members of the Federal Retirement Thrift Investment Board first appointed to such Board.

"(b) TERMS OF SERVICE.—Notwithstanding subsection (e)(1) of section 8472 of title 5, United States Code (as added by section 101(a) of this Act), the term of service of each member of the Federal Retirement Thrift Investment Board appointed pursuant to subsection (a) shall be 1 year, except that such member shall continue to serve until his successor is appointed under subsection (b) of such section 8472 and confirmed under subsection (c) of such section."

AUTHORIZATION OF APPROPRIATIONS FOR CERTAIN EXPENSES OF FEDERAL RETIREMENT THRIFT INVESTMENT MANAGEMENT SYSTEM

Section 701 of Pub. L. 99–335, as amended by Pub. L. 99–500, § 101(m) [title IV, § 401], Oct. 18, 1986, 100 Stat. 1783–308, 1783–322, and Pub. L. 99–591, § 101(m) [title IV, § 401], Oct. 30, 1986, 100 Stat. 3341–308, 3341–322, provided that:

"(a) TEMPORARY ALTERNATIVE FUNDING.—Notwithstanding section 8434(c)(3) [probably should be "section 8437(c)(3)"] of title 5, United States Code (as added by section 101 of this Act), the expenses incurred in the administration of the Federal Retirement Thrift Investment Management System under subchapter VII of chapter 84 of such title (as so added) during fiscal years 1986 and 1987 may be paid from sums appropriated pursuant to subsection (b).

"(b) AUTHORIZATION OF APPROPRIATIONS.—There are authorized to be appropriated to the Federal Retirement Thrift Investment Board, for fiscal years 1986 and 1987, such sums as may be necessary to pay the expenses incurred in the administration of the Federal Retirement Thrift Investment Management System during such fiscal years."

SECTION REFERRED TO IN OTHER SECTIONS

This section is referred to in sections 8401, 8475, 8476, 8477 of this title.

§ 8473. Employee Thrift Advisory Council

(a) The Board shall establish an Employee Thrift Advisory Council. The Council shall be composed of 14 members appointed by the Chairman of the Board in accordance with subsection (b).

(b) The Chairman shall appoint 14 members of the Council, of whom—

(1) 4 shall be appointed to represent the respective labor organizations representing (as exclusive representatives) the first, second, third, and fourth largest numbers of individuals subject to chapter 71 of this title;

(2) 2 shall be appointed to represent the respective labor organizations which have been accorded exclusive recognition under section 1203(a) of title 39 representing the largest and second largest numbers of individuals employed by the United States Postal Service;

(3) 1 shall be appointed to represent the labor organization which has been accorded exclusive recognition under section 1203(a) of title 39 representing the largest number of individuals employed by the United States Postal Service as rural letter carriers;

(4) 2 shall be appointed to represent the respective managerial organizations (other than an organization described in paragraph (5)) which consult with the United States Postal Service under section 1004(b) of title 39 and which represent the largest and second largest numbers of individuals employed by the United States Postal Service as managerial personnel;

(5) 1 shall be appointed to represent the supervisors' organization as defined in section 1004(h) of title 39;

(6) 1 shall be appointed to represent employee organizations having as a purpose promoting the interests of women in Government service;

(7) 1 shall be appointed to represent the organization representing the largest number of individuals receiving annuities under this chapter or chapter 83 of this title;

(8) 1 shall be appointed to represent the organization representing the largest number of supervisors and management officials (as defined by section 7103(a)); and

(9) 1 shall be appointed to represent the organization representing the largest number of members of the Senior Executive Service.

(c)(1) The Chairman of the Board shall designate 1 member of the Council to serve as head of the Council.

(2) A member of the Council shall be appointed for a term of 4 years.

(3)(A) A vacancy in the Council shall be filled in the manner in which the original appointment was made and shall be subject to any conditions which applied with respect to the original appointment.

(B) An individual chosen to fill a vacancy shall be appointed for the unexpired term of the member replaced.

(C) The term of any member shall not expire before the date on which the member's successor takes office.

(d) The Council shall act by resolution of a majority of the members.

(e) The Council shall—

(1) advise the Board and the Executive Director on matters relating to—

(A) investment policies for the Thrift Savings Fund; and

(B) the administration of this subchapter and subchapter III of this chapter; and

(2) perform such other duties as the Board may direct with respect to investment funds established in accordance with subchapter III of this chapter.

(f) Section 14(a)(2) of the Federal Advisory Committee Act shall not apply to the Council.

(Added Pub. L. 99–335, title I, §101(a), June 6, 1986, 100 Stat. 579; amended Pub. L. 103–89, §3(b)(1)(N), Sept. 30, 1993, 107 Stat. 982; Pub. L. 106–65, div. A, title VI, §661(a)(6), Oct. 5, 1999, 113 Stat. 672.)

AMENDMENT OF SECTION

Pub. L. 106–65, div. A, title VI, §§661(a)(6), 663, Oct. 5, 1999, 113 Stat. 672, 673, as amended by Pub. L. 106–398, §1 [[div. A], title VI, §661(a)], Oct. 30, 2000, 114 Stat. 1654, 1654A–167, provided that effective 180 days after Oct. 30, 2000, unless postponed, this section is amended—

(1) in subsection (a), by striking "14 members" and inserting "15 members"; and

(2) in subsection (b)—

(A) by striking "14 members" and inserting "15 members";

(B) by striking "and" at the end of paragraph (8);

(C) by striking the period at the end of paragraph (9) and inserting "; and"; and

(D) by adding at the end the following:

(10) 1 shall be appointed to represent participants (under section 8440e) who are members of the uniformed services.

REFERENCES IN TEXT

Section 14(a)(2) of the Federal Advisory Committee Act [Pub. L. 92–463], referred to in subsec. (f), is section 14(a)(2) of Pub. L. 92–463, which is set out in the Appendix to this title.

AMENDMENTS

1993—Subsec. (b)(8). Pub. L. 103–89 substituted "supervisors and management officials (as defined by section 7103(a))" for "individuals subject to the Performance Management and Recognition System under chapter 54 of this title".

EFFECTIVE DATE OF 1999 AMENDMENT

Amendment by Pub. L. 106–65 effective 180 days after Oct. 30, 2000, unless postponed, see section 663 of Pub. L. 106–65, as amended, set out as an Effective Date note under section 8440e of this title.

EFFECTIVE DATE OF 1993 AMENDMENT

Amendment by Pub. L. 103–89 effective Nov. 1, 1993, see section 3(c) of Pub. L. 103–89, set out as a note under section 3372 of this title.

SECTION REFERRED TO IN OTHER SECTIONS

This section is referred to in section 8471 of this title.

§ 8474. Executive Director

(a)(1) The Board shall appoint, without regard to the provisions of law governing appointments in the competitive service, an Executive Director by action agreed to by a majority of the members of the Board.

(2) The Executive Director shall have substantial experience, training, and expertise in the management of financial investments and pension benefit plans.

(b) The Executive Director shall—

(1) carry out the policies established by the Board;

(2) invest and manage the Thrift Savings Fund in accordance with the investment policies and other policies established by the Board;

(3) purchase annuity contracts and provide for the payment of other benefits under subchapter III of this chapter;

(4) administer the provisions of this subchapter and subchapter III of this chapter;

(5) prescribe such regulations (other than regulations relating to fiduciary responsibilities) as may be necessary for the administration of this subchapter and subchapter III of this chapter; and

(6) meet from time to time with the Council upon request of the Council.

(c) The Executive Director may—

(1) prescribe such regulations as may be necessary to carry out the responsibilities of the Executive Director under this section, other than regulations relating to fiduciary responsibilities;

(2) appoint such personnel as may be necessary to carry out the provisions of this subchapter and subchapter III of this chapter;

(3) subject to approval by the Board, procure the services of experts and consultants under section 3109 of this title;

(4) secure directly from an Executive agency, the United States Postal Service, or the Postal Rate Commission any information necessary to carry out the provisions of this subchapter or subchapter III of this chapter and policies of the Board;

(5) make such payments out of sums in the Thrift Savings Fund as the Executive Director determines are necessary to carry out the provisions of this subchapter and subchapter III of this chapter and the policies of the Board;

(6) pay the compensation, per diem, and travel expenses of individuals appointed under paragraphs (2), (3), and (7) of this subsection from the Thrift Savings Fund;

(7) accept and use the services of individuals employed intermittently in the Government service and reimburse such individuals for travel expenses, as authorized by section 5703 of this title, including per diem as authorized by section 5702 of this title;

(8) except as otherwise expressly prohibited by law or the policies of the Board, delegate any of the Executive Director's functions to such employees under the Board as the Executive Director may designate and authorize such successive redelegations of such functions to such employees under the Board as the Executive Director may consider to be necessary or appropriate; and

(9) take such other actions as are appropriate to carry out the functions of the Executive Director.

(Added Pub. L. 99–335, title I, §101(a), June 6, 1986, 100 Stat. 580.)

REFERENCES IN TEXT

The provisions of law governing appointments in the competitive service, referred to in subsec. (a)(1), are classified generally to section 3301 et seq. of this title.

SECTION REFERRED TO IN OTHER SECTIONS

This section is referred to in sections 5102, 8401, 8461, 8476 of this title.

§ 8475. Investment policies

The Board shall develop investment policies under section 8472(f)(1) of this title which provide for—

(1) prudent investments suitable for accumulating funds for payment of retirement income; and

(2) low administrative costs.

(Added Pub. L. 99–335, title I, §101(a), June 6, 1986, 100 Stat. 581.)

§ 8476. Administrative provisions

(a) The Board shall meet—

(1) not less than once during each month; and

(2) at additional times at the call of the Chairman.

(b)(1) Except as provided in sections 8472(g)(1)(C) and 8474(a)(1) of this title, the Board shall perform the functions and exercise the powers of the Board on a majority vote of a quorum of the Board.

(2) A vacancy on the Board shall not impair the authority of a quorum of the Board to perform the functions and exercise the powers of the Board.

(c) Three members of the Board shall constitute a quorum for the transaction of business.

(d)(1) Each member of the Board who is not an officer or employee of the Federal Government shall be compensated at the daily rate of basic pay for level IV of the Executive Schedule for each day during which such member is engaged in performing a function of the Board.

(2) A member of the Board shall be paid travel, per diem, and other necessary expenses under subchapter I of chapter 57 of this title while traveling away from such member's home or regular place of business in the performance of the duties of the Board.

(3) Payments authorized under this subsection shall be paid from the Thrift Savings Fund.

(e) The accrued annual leave of any employee who is a member of the Board or the Council shall not be charged for any time used in performing services for the Board or the Council.

(Added Pub. L. 99–335, title I, §101(a), June 6, 1986, 100 Stat. 581; amended Pub. L. 101–509, title V, §529 [title I, §101(b)(9)(K)], Nov. 5, 1990, 104 Stat. 1427, 1442.)

REFERENCES IN TEXT

Level IV of the Executive Schedule, referred to in subsec. (d)(1), is set out in section 5315 of this title.

AMENDMENTS

1990—Subsec. (d)(1). Pub. L. 101–509 substituted "level IV of the Executive Schedule" for "grade GS–18 of the General Schedule".

EFFECTIVE DATE OF 1990 AMENDMENT

Amendment by Pub. L. 101–509 effective on such date as the President shall determine, but not earlier than 90 days, and not later than 180 days, after Nov. 5, 1990, see section 529 [title III, §305] of Pub. L. 101–509, set out as a note under section 5301 of this title.

§ 8477. Fiduciary responsibilities; liability and penalties

(a) For the purposes of this section—

(1) the term "account" is not limited by the definition provided in section 8401(1);

(2) the term "adequate consideration" means—

(A) in the case of a security for which there is a generally recognized market—

(i) the price of the security prevailing on a national securities exchange which is registered under section 6 of the Securities Exchange Act of 1934; or

(ii) if the security is not traded on such a national securities exchange, a price not less favorable to the Thrift Savings Fund than the offering price for the security as established by the current bid and asked prices quoted by persons independent of the issuer and of any party in interest; and

(B) in the case of an asset other than a security for which there is a generally recognized market, the fair market value of the asset as determined in good faith by a fiduciary or fiduciaries in accordance with regulations prescribed by the Secretary of Labor;

(3) the term "fiduciary" means—

(A) a member of the Board;

(B) the Executive Director;

(C) any person who has or exercises discretionary authority or discretionary control over the management or disposition of the assets of the Thrift Savings Fund; and

(D) any person who, with respect to the Thrift Savings Fund, is described in section 3(21)(A) of the Employee Retirement Income Security Act of 1974 (29 U.S.C. 1002(21)(A)); and

(4) the term "party in interest" includes—

(A) any fiduciary;

(B) any counsel to a person who is a fiduciary, with respect to the actions of such person as a fiduciary;

(C) any participant;

(D) any person providing services to the Board and, with respect to the actions of the Executive Director as a fiduciary any person providing services to the Executive Director;

(E) a labor organization, the members of which are participants;

(F) a spouse, sibling, ancestor, lineal descendant, or spouse of a lineal descendant of a person described in subparagraph (A), (B), or (D);

(G) a corporation, partnership, or trust or estate of which, or in which, at least 50 percent of—

(i) the combined voting power of all classes of stock entitled to vote or the total value of shares of all classes of stock of such corporation;

(ii) the capital interest or profits interest of such partnership; or

(iii) the beneficial interest of such trust or estate,

is owned directly or indirectly, or held by a person described in subparagraph (A), (B), (D), or (E);

(H) an official (including a director) of, or an individual employed by, a person described in subparagraph (A), (B), (D), (E), or (G), or an individual having powers or responsibilities similar to those of such an official;

(I) a holder (directly or indirectly) of at least 10 percent of the shares in a person described in any subparagraph referred to in subparagraph (H); and

(J) a person who, directly or indirectly, is at least a 10 percent partner or joint venturer (measured in capital or profits) in a person described in any subparagraph referred to in subparagraph (H).

(b)(1) To the extent not inconsistent with the provisions of this chapter and the policies prescribed by the Board, a fiduciary shall discharge his responsibilities with respect to the Thrift Savings Fund or applicable portion thereof solely in the interest of the participants and beneficiaries and—

(A) for the exclusive purpose of—

(i) providing benefits to participants and their beneficiaries; and

(ii) defraying reasonable expenses of administering the Thrift Savings Fund or applicable portions thereof;

(B) with the care, skill, prudence, and diligence under the circumstances then prevailing that a prudent individual acting in a like capacity and familiar with such matters would use in the conduct of an enterprise of a like character and with like objectives; and

(C) to the extent permitted by section 8438 of this title, by diversifying the investments of the Thrift Savings Fund or applicable portions thereof so as to minimize the risk of large losses, unless under the circumstances it is clearly prudent not to do so.

(2) No fiduciary may maintain the indicia of ownership of any assets of the Thrift Savings Fund outside the jurisdiction of the district courts of the United States.

(c)(1) A fiduciary shall not permit the Thrift Savings Fund to engage in any of the following transactions, except in exchange for adequate consideration:

(A) A transfer of any assets of the Thrift Savings Fund to any person the fiduciary knows or should know to be a party in interest or the use of such assets by any such person.

(B) An acquisition of any property from or sale of any property to the Thrift Savings Fund by any person the fiduciary knows or should know to be a party in interest.

(C) A transfer or exchange of services between the Thrift Savings Fund and any person the fiduciary knows or should know to be a party in interest.

(2) Notwithstanding paragraph (1), a fiduciary with respect to the Thrift Savings Fund shall not—

(A) deal with any assets of the Thrift Savings Fund in his own interest or for his own account;

(B) act, in an individual capacity or any other capacity, in any transaction involving the Thrift Savings Fund on behalf of a party, or representing a party, whose interests are adverse to the interests of the Thrift Savings Fund or the interests of its participants or beneficiaries; or

(C) receive any consideration for his own personal account from any party dealing with sums credited to the Thrift Savings Fund in connection with a transaction involving assets of the Thrift Savings Fund.

(3)(A) The Secretary of Labor may, in accordance with procedures which the Secretary shall by regulation prescribe, grant a conditional or unconditional exemption of any fiduciary or transaction, or class of fiduciaries or transactions, from all or part of the restrictions imposed by paragraph (2).

(B) An exemption granted under this paragraph shall not relieve a fiduciary from any other applicable provision of this chapter.

(C) The Secretary of Labor may not grant an exemption under this paragraph unless he finds that such exemption is—

(i) administratively feasible;

(ii) in the interests of the Thrift Savings Fund and of its participants and beneficiaries; and

(iii) protective of the rights of participants and beneficiaries of such Fund.

(D) An exemption under this paragraph may not be granted unless—

(i) notice of the proposed exemption is published in the Federal Register;

(ii) interested persons are given an opportunity to present views; and

(iii) the Secretary of Labor affords an opportunity for a hearing and makes a determination on the record with respect to the respective requirements of clauses (i), (ii), and (iii) of subparagraph (C).

(E) Notwithstanding subparagraph (D), the Secretary of Labor may determine that an exemption granted for any class of fiduciaries or transactions under section 408(a) of the Employee Retirement Income Security Act of 1974 shall, upon publication of notice in the Federal Register under this subparagraph, constitute an exemption for purposes of the provisions of paragraph (2).

(d) This section does not prohibit any fiduciary from—

(1) receiving any benefit which the fiduciary is entitled to receive under this subchapter or subchapter III of this chapter as a participant or beneficiary;

(2) receiving any reasonable compensation authorized by this subchapter for services rendered, or for reimbursement of expenses properly and actually incurred, in the performance of the fiduciary's duties under this chapter; or

(3) serving as a fiduciary in addition to being an officer, employee, agent, or other representative of a party in interest.

(e)(1)(A) Any fiduciary that breaches the responsibilities, duties, and obligations set out in subsection (b) or violates subsection (c) shall be personally liable to the Thrift Savings Fund for any losses to such Fund resulting from each such breach or violation and to restore to such Fund any profits made by the fiduciary through use of assets of such Fund by the fiduciary, and shall be subject to such other equitable or remedial relief as a court considers appropriate, except as provided in paragraphs (3) and (4) of this subsection. A fiduciary may be removed for a breach referred to in the preceding sentence.

(B) The Secretary of Labor may assess a civil penalty against a party in interest with respect to each transaction which is engaged in by the party in interest and is prohibited by subsection (c). The amount of such penalty shall be equal to 5 percent of the amount involved in each such transaction (as defined in section 4975(f)(4) of the Internal Revenue Code of 1986) for each year or part thereof during which the prohibited transaction continues, except that, if the transaction is not corrected (in such manner as the Secretary of Labor shall prescribe by regulation consistent with section 4975(f)(5) of such Code) within 90 days after the date the Secretary of Labor transmits notice to the party in interest (or such longer period as the Secretary of Labor may permit), such penalty may be in an amount not more than 100 percent of the amount involved.

(C) A fiduciary shall not be liable under subparagraph (A) with respect to a breach of fiduciary duty under subsection (b) committed before becoming a fiduciary or after ceasing to be a fiduciary.

(D) A fiduciary shall be jointly and severally liable under subparagraph (A) for a breach of fiduciary duty under subsection (b) by another fiduciary only if—

(i) the fiduciary participates knowingly in, or knowingly undertakes to conceal, an act or omission of such other fiduciary, knowing such act or omission is such a breach;

(ii) by the fiduciary's failure to comply with subsection (b) in the administration of the fiduciary's specific responsibilities which give rise to the fiduciary status, the fiduciary has enabled such other fiduciary to commit such a breach; or

(iii) the fiduciary has knowledge of a breach by such other fiduciary, unless the fiduciary makes reasonable efforts under the circumstances to remedy the breach.

(E) The Secretary of Labor shall prescribe, in regulations, procedures for allocating fiduciary responsibilities among fiduciaries, including investment managers. Any fiduciary who, pursuant to such procedures, allocates to a person or persons any fiduciary responsibility shall not be liable for an act or omission of such person or persons unless—

(i) such fiduciary violated subsection (b) with respect to the allocation, with respect to the implementation of the procedures prescribed by the Secretary of Labor (or the Board under section 114 of the Federal Employees' Retirement System Technical Corrections Act of 1986), or in continuing such allocation; or

(ii) such fiduciary would otherwise be liable in accordance with subparagraph (D).

(2) No civil action may be maintained against any fiduciary with respect to the responsibilities, liabilities, and penalties authorized or provided for in this section except in accordance with paragraphs (3) and (4).

(3) A civil action may be brought in the district courts of the United States—

(A) by the Secretary of Labor against any fiduciary other than a Member of the Board or the Executive Director of the Board—

(i) to determine and enforce a liability under paragraph (1)(A);

(ii) to collect any civil penalty under paragraph (1)(B);

(iii) to enjoin any act or practice which violates any provision of subsection (b) or (c);

(iv) to obtain any other appropriate equitable relief to redress a violation of any such provision; or

(v) to enjoin any act or practice which violates subsection (g)(2) or (h) of section 8472 of this title;

(B) by any participant, beneficiary, or fiduciary against any fiduciary—

(i) to enjoin any act or practice which violates any provision of subsection (b) or (c);

(ii) to obtain any other appropriate equitable relief to redress a violation of any such provision;

(iii) to enjoin any act or practice which violates subsection (g)(2) or (h) of section 8472 of this title; or

(C) by any participant or beneficiary—

(i) to recover benefits of such participant or beneficiary under the provisions of subchapter III of this chapter, to enforce any right of such participant or beneficiary under such provisions, or to clarify any such right to future benefits under such provisions; or

(ii) to enforce any claim otherwise cognizable under sections 1346(b) and 2671 through 2680 of title 28, provided that the remedy against the United States provided by sections 1346(b) and 2672 of title 28 for damages for injury or loss of property caused by the negligent or wrongful act or omission of any fiduciary while acting within the scope of his duties or employment shall be exclusive of any other civil action or proceeding by the participant or beneficiary for recovery of money by reason of the same subject matter against the fiduciary (or the estate of such fiduciary) whose act or omission gave rise to such action or proceeding, whether or not such action or proceeding is based on an alleged violation of subsection (b) or (c).

(4)(A) In all civil actions under paragraph (3)(A), attorneys appointed by the Secretary may represent the Secretary (except as provided in section 518(a) of title 28), however all such litigation shall be subject to the direction and control of the Attorney General.

(B) The Attorney General shall defend any civil action or proceeding brought in any court against any fiduciary referred to in paragraph (3)(C)(ii) (or the estate of such fiduciary) for any such injury. Any fiduciary against whom such a civil action or proceeding is brought shall deliver, within such time after date of service or knowledge of service as determined by the Attorney General, all process served upon such fiduciary (or an attested copy thereof) to the Executive Director of the Board, who shall promptly furnish copies of the pleading and process to the Attorney General and the United States Attorney for the district wherein the action or proceeding is brought.

(C) Upon certification by the Attorney General that a fiduciary described in paragraph (3)(C)(ii) was acting in the scope of such fiduciary's duties or employment as a fiduciary at the time of the occurrence or omission out of which the action arose, any such civil action or proceeding commenced in a State court shall be—

　　(i) removed without bond at any time before trial by the Attorney General to the district court of the United States for the district and division in which it is pending; and

　　(ii) deemed a tort action brought against the United States under the provisions of title 28 and all references thereto.

(D) The Attorney General may compromise or settle any claim asserted in such civil action or proceeding in the manner provided in section 2677 of title 28, and with the same effect. To the extent section 2672 of title 28 provides that persons other than the Attorney General or his designee may compromise and settle claims, and that payment of such claims may be made from agency appropriations, such provisions shall not apply to claims based upon an alleged violation of subsection (b) or (c).

(E) For the purposes of paragraph (3)(C)(ii) the provisions of sections 2680(h) of title 28 shall not apply to any claim based upon an alleged violation of subsection (b) or (c).

(F) Notwithstanding sections 1346(b) and 2671 through 2680 of title 28, whenever an award, compromise, or settlement is made under such sections upon any claim based upon an alleged violation of subsection (b) or (c), payment of such award, compromise, or settlement shall be made to the appropriate account within the Thrift Savings Fund, or where there is no such appropriate account, to the participant or beneficiary bringing the claim.

(G) For purposes of paragraph (3)(C)(ii), fiduciary includes only the Members of the Board and the Board's Executive Director.

(5) Any relief awarded against a Member of the Board or the Executive Director of the Board in a civil action authorized by paragraph (3) may not include any monetary damages or any other recovery of money.

(6) An action may not be commenced under paragraph (3)(A) or (B) with respect to a fiduciary's breach of any responsibility, duty, or obligation under subsection (b) or a violation of subsection (c) after the earlier of—

　　(A) 6 years after (i) the date of the last action which constituted a part of the breach or violation, or (ii) in the case of an omission, the latest date on which the fiduciary could have cured the breach or violation; or

　　(B) 3 years after the earliest date on which the plaintiff had actual knowledge of the breach or violation, except that, in the case of fraud or concealment, such action may be commenced not later than 6 years after the date of discovery of such breach or violation.

(7)(A) The district courts of the United States shall have exclusive jurisdiction of civil actions under this subsection.

(B) An action under this subsection may be brought in the District Court of the United States for the District of Columbia or a district court of the United States in the district where the breach alleged in the complaint or petition filed in the action took place or in the district where a defendant resides or may be found. Process may be served in any other district where a defendant resides or may be found.

(8)(A) A copy of the complaint or petition filed in any action brought under this subsection (other than by the Secretary of Labor) shall be served on the Executive Director, the Secretary of Labor, and the Secretary of the Treasury by certified mail.

(B) Any officer referred to in subparagraph (A) of this paragraph shall have the right in his discretion to intervene in any action. If the Secretary of Labor brings an action under paragraph (2) of this subsection on behalf of a participant or beneficiary, he shall notify the Executive Director and the Secretary of the Treasury.

(f) The Secretary of Labor may prescribe regulations to carry out this section.

(g)(1) The Secretary of Labor shall establish a program to carry out audits to determine the level of compliance with the requirements of this section relating to fiduciary responsibilities and prohibited activities of fiduciaries.

(2) An audit under this subsection may be conducted by the Secretary of Labor, by contract with a qualified non-governmental organization, or in cooperation with the Comptroller General of the United States, as the Secretary considers appropriate.

(Added Pub. L. 99–335, title I, § 101(a), June 6, 1986, 100 Stat. 582; amended Pub. L. 99–514, § 2, Oct. 22, 1986, 100 Stat. 2095; Pub. L. 99–556, title I, §§ 112, 114(b), Oct. 27, 1986, 100 Stat. 3133; Pub. L. 100–238, title I, § 133(a), (c), Jan. 8, 1988, 101 Stat. 1760, 1762; Pub. L. 100–366, § 3(a), July 13, 1988, 102 Stat. 826; Pub. L. 101–335, § 8, July 17, 1990, 104 Stat. 325.)

REFERENCES IN TEXT

Section 6 of the Securities Exchange Act of 1934, referred to in subsec. (a)(2)(A)(i), is classified to section 78f of Title 15, Commerce and Trade.

Section 408(a) of the Employee Retirement Income Security Act of 1974, referred to in subsec. (c)(3)(E), is classified to section 1108(a) of Title 29, Labor.

Section 4975(f)(4) and (5) of the Internal Revenue Code of 1986, referred to in subsec. (e)(1)(B), is classified to section 4975(f)(4) and (5) of Title 26, Internal Revenue Code.

Section 114 of the Federal Employees' Retirement System Technical Corrections Act of 1986, referred to in subsec. (e)(1)(E)(i), is section 114 of Pub. L. 99–556 which amended this section and enacted provisions set out as a note under this section.

AMENDMENTS

1990—Pub. L. 101–335 repealed section 133(c) of Pub. L. 100–238. See Effective Date of 1988 Amendment note below.

1988—Subsec. (e)(1)(A). Pub. L. 100–238, § 133(a)(1), inserted ", except as provided in paragraphs (3) and (4) of this subsection".

Subsec. (e)(1)(B). Pub. L. 100–238, § 133(a)(2), substituted "Internal Revenue Code of 1986" for "Internal Revenue Code of 1954".

Subsec. (e)(1)(D). Pub. L. 100–238, § 133(a)(3), inserted "only" in introductory provisions.

Subsec. (e)(2), (3). Pub. L. 100–238, § 133(a)(5), added pars. (2) and (3) and struck out former pars. (2) and (3) which read as follows:

"(2) A civil action may be brought in the district courts of the United States—

"(A) by the Secretary of Labor—

"(i) to determine and enforce a liability under paragraph (1)(A);

"(ii) to collect any civil penalty under paragraph (1)(B); or

"(iii) to enjoin any act or practice which violates subsection (g)(2) or (h) of section 8472 of this title;

"(B) by the Secretary of Labor, any participant, beneficiary, or fiduciary—

"(i) to enjoin any act or practice which violates any provision of subsection (b) or (c); or

"(ii) to obtain any other appropriate equitable relief to redress a violation of any such provision; or

"(C) by any participant or beneficiary to recover benefits due to him or her under the provisions of subchapter III of this chapter, to enforce his or her rights under such provisions, or to clarify his or her rights to future benefits under such provisions.

"(3) An action may not be commenced under paragraph (2) with respect to a fiduciary's breach of any responsibility, duty, or obligation under subsection (b) or a violation of subsection (c) after the earlier of—

"(A) 6 years after (i) the date of the last action which constituted a part of the breach or violation, or (ii) in the case of an omission, the latest date on which the fiduciary could have cured the breach or violation; or

"(B) 3 years after the earliest date on which the plaintiff had actual knowledge of the breach or violation, except that, in the case of fraud or concealment, such action may be commenced not later than 6 years after the date of discovery of such breach or violation."

Subsec. (e)(3)(C)(ii). Pub. L. 100–366, § 3(a)(1), substituted "28, provided that" for "28, if" and "shall be exclusive of" for "is exclusive of".

Subsec. (e)(4) to (8). Pub. L. 100–238, § 133(a)(4), (5), added pars. (4) to (6) and redesignated former pars. (4) and (5) as (7) and (8), respectively.

Subsec. (e)(5). Pub. L. 100–366, § 3(a)(2), substituted "paragraph (3)" for "paragraphs (3) and (4)".

1986—Subsec. (c)(3)(E). Pub. L. 99–556, § 112, added subpar. (E).

Subsec. (e)(1)(B). Pub. L. 99–514 substituted "Internal Revenue Code of 1986" for "Internal Revenue Code of 1954".

Subsec. (e)(1)(E)(i). Pub. L. 99–556, § 114(b), substituted "Secretary of Labor (or the Board under section 114 of the Federal Employees' Retirement System Technical Corrections Act of 1986)" for "Board".

EFFECTIVE DATE OF 1988 AMENDMENTS

Section 3(b) of Pub. L. 100–366 provided that: "Section 8477(e) of title 5, United States Code, as amended by subsection (a), shall apply to any civil action or proceeding arising from any act or omission occurring on or after October 1, 1986."

Section 133(b) of Pub. L. 100–238 provided that: "The provisions of section 8477(e)(1), (2), (3), (4), (5), and (6) of title 5, United States Code (as amended by subsection (a) of this section), shall apply to any civil action or proceeding arising from any act or omission occurring on or after October 1, 1986."

Section 133(c) of Pub. L. 100–238, which provided that the provisions of subsection (a) (and the amendments to section 8477(e) of title 5 contained therein) and subsection (b) of this section were to be repealed effective on Dec. 31, 1990, and that on and after Dec. 31, 1990, the provisions of section 8477(e) of title 5 were to be in effect as such provisions were in effect on Jan. 7, 1988, was repealed by Pub. L. 101–335, § 8, July 17, 1990, 104 Stat. 325.

INTERIM EXEMPTION PROCEDURES

Section 111 of Pub. L. 99–556 provided that:

"(a) IN GENERAL.—Subject to subsection (b), until such time as final regulations under subparagraph (A) of section 8477(c)(3) of title 5, United States Code, become effective, the Secretary of Labor may, in accordance with procedures under section 408(a) of the Employee Retirement Income Security Act of 1974 [29 U.S.C. 1108(a)], grant any exemption allowable under such section 8477(c)(3).

"(b) TERMINATION OF INTERIM AUTHORITY.—The authority to grant an exemption under section 8477(c)(3) of title 5, United States Code, using the procedures under section 408(a) of the Employee Retirement Income Security Act of 1974 shall expire not later than December 31, 1988."

ALLOCATION OF FIDUCIARY RESPONSIBILITIES

Section 114(a) of Pub. L. 99–556 provided that:

"(1) Subject to paragraph (2), until such time as final regulations under subparagraph (E) of section 8477(e)(1) of title 5, United States Code, become effective, a fiduciary (as defined by section 8477(a)(3) of title 5, United States Code) may, in accordance with procedures established by the Federal Retirement Thrift Investment Board, make any allocation of fiduciary responsibilities.

"(2) The authority to make any allocation under section 8477(e)(1)(E) using the procedures referred to in paragraph (1), and any allocation so made using such procedures, shall expire not later than December 31, 1988."

SECTION REFERRED TO IN OTHER SECTIONS

This section is referred to in sections 8401, 8433, 8438, 8478a of this title.

§ 8478. Bonding

(a)(1) Except as provided in paragraph (2), each fiduciary and each person who handles funds or property of the Thrift Savings Fund shall be bonded as provided in this section.

(2)(A) Bond shall not be required of a fiduciary (or of any officer or employee of such fiduciary) if such fiduciary—

(i) is a corporation organized and doing business under the laws of the United States or of any State;

(ii) is authorized under such laws to exercise trust powers or to conduct an insurance business;

(iii) is subject to supervision or examination by Federal or State authority; and

(iv) has at all times a combined capital and surplus in excess of such minimum amount (not less than $1,000,000) as the Secretary of Labor prescribes in regulations.

(B) If—

(i) a bank or other financial institution would, but for this subparagraph, not be required to be bonded under this section by reason of the application of the exception provided in subparagraph (A),

(ii) the bank or financial institution is authorized to exercise trust powers, and

(iii) the deposits of the bank or financial institution are not insured by the Federal Deposit Insurance Corporation,

such exception shall apply to such bank or financial institution only if the bank or institution meets bonding requirements under State law which the Secretary of Labor determines are at least equivalent to those imposed on banks by Federal law.

(b)(1) The Secretary of Labor shall prescribe the amount of a bond under this section at the beginning of each fiscal year. Except as otherwise provided in this paragraph, such amount shall not be less than 10 percent of the amount of funds handled. In no case shall such bond be less than $1,000 nor more than $500,000, except that the Secretary of Labor, after due notice and opportunity for hearing to all interested parties, and other consideration of the record, may prescribe an amount in excess of $500,000.

(2) For the purpose of prescribing the amount of a bond under paragraph (1), the amount of funds handled shall be determined by reference to the amount of the funds handled by the person, group, or class to be covered by such bond or by their predecessor or predecessors, if any, during the preceding fiscal year, or to the amount of funds to be handled during the current fiscal year by such person, group, or class, estimated as provided in regulations prescribed by the Secretary of Labor.

(c) A bond required by subsection (a)—

(1) shall include such terms and conditions as the Secretary of Labor considers necessary to protect the Thrift Savings Fund against loss by reason of acts of fraud or dishonesty on the part of the bonded person directly or through connivance with others;

(2) shall have as surety thereon a corporate surety company which is an acceptable surety on Federal bonds under authority granted by the Secretary of the Treasury pursuant to sections 9304 through 9308 of title 31; and

(3) shall be in a form or of a type approved by the Secretary of Labor, including individual bonds or schedule or blanket forms of bonds which cover a group or class.

(d)(1) It shall be unlawful for any person to whom subsection (a) applies, to receive, handle, disburse, or otherwise exercise custody or control of any of the funds or other property of the Thrift Savings Fund without being bonded as required by this section.

(2) It shall be unlawful for any fiduciary, or any other person having authority to direct the performance of functions described in paragraph (1), to permit any such function to be performed by any person to whom subsection (a) applies unless such person has met the requirements of such subsection.

(e) Notwithstanding any other provision of law, any person who is required to be bonded as provided in subsection (a) shall be exempt from any other provision of law which would, but for this subsection, require such person to be bonded for the handling of the funds or other property of the Thrift Savings Fund.

(f) The Secretary of Labor shall prescribe such regulations as may be necessary to carry out the provisions of this section, including exempting a person or class of persons from the requirements of this section.

(Added Pub. L. 99–335, title I, §101(a), June 6, 1986, 100 Stat. 586; amended Pub. L. 99–556, title I, §§108, 115, Oct. 27, 1986, 100 Stat. 3132, 3134; Pub. L. 102–378, §2(72), Oct. 2, 1992, 106 Stat. 1355.)

AMENDMENTS

1992—Subsec. (a)(2)(B)(iii). Pub. L. 102–378 struck out "Corporation or the Federal Savings and Loan Insurance" before "Corporation".

1986—Subsec. (a)(1). Pub. L. 99–556, §108, struck out "(other than a member of the Employee Thrift Advisory Council with respect to his duties as a member)" after "each fiduciary".

Subsec. (c)(2). Pub. L. 99–556, §115, substituted "sections 9304 through 9308 of title 31" for "sections 6 through 13 of title 6".

INTERIM BONDING REGULATIONS

Section 113 of Pub. L. 99–556 provided that:

"(a) IN GENERAL.—Subject to subsection (b), until such time as the Secretary of Labor promulgates final regulations under section 8478 of title 5, United States Code, the Secretary of Labor may, with respect to the Thrift Savings Fund, apply the temporary regulations under section 412 of the Employee Retirement Income Security Act of 1974 [29 U.S.C. 1112] that are set forth in section 2550.412–1, and subchapter I of chapter XXV, of title 29 of the Code of Federal Regulations, as in effect on September 23, 1986.

"(b) TERMINATION OF INTERIM AUTHORITY.—The authority to apply the temporary regulations referred to in subsection (a) with respect to the Thrift Savings Fund shall expire not later than December 31, 1989."

SECTION REFERRED TO IN OTHER SECTIONS

This section is referred to in section 8478a of this title.

§ 8478a. Investigative authority

Any authority available to the Secretary of Labor under section 504 of the Employee Retirement Income Security Act of 1974 is hereby made available to the Secretary of Labor, and any officer designated by the Secretary of Labor, to determine whether any person has violated, or is about to violate, any provision of section 8477 or 8478.

(Added Pub. L. 99–556, title I, §110(a), Oct. 27, 1986, 100 Stat. 3132.)

REFERENCES IN TEXT

Section 504 of the Employee Retirement Income Security Act of 1974, referred to in text, is classified to section 1134 of Title 29, Labor.

§ 8479. Exculpatory provisions; insurance

(a) Any provision in an agreement or instrument which purports to relieve a fiduciary from responsibility or liability for any responsibility, obligation, or duty under this subchapter shall be void.

(b)(1) The Executive Director may require employing agencies to contribute an amount not to exceed 1 percent of the amount such agencies are required to contribute in accordance with section 8432(c) of this title to the Thrift Savings Fund.

(2) The sums credited to the Thrift Savings Fund under paragraph (1) shall be available and may be used at the discretion of the Executive Director to purchase insurance to cover potential liability of persons who serve in a fiduciary capacity with respect to the Thrift Savings Fund, without regard to whether a policy of insurance permits recourse by the insurer against the fiduciary in the case of a breach of a fiduciary obligation.

(Added Pub. L. 99–335, title I, §101(a), June 6, 1986, 100 Stat. 588.)

SECTION REFERRED TO IN OTHER SECTIONS

This section is referred to in section 8437 of this title.

CHAPTER 85—UNEMPLOYMENT COMPENSATION

SUBCHAPTER I—EMPLOYEES GENERALLY

AMENDMENTS

1992—Pub. L. 102–378, §2(73), Oct. 2, 1992, 106 Stat. 1355, added item 8509.

1975—Pub. L. 94–183, §2(42), Dec. 31, 1975, 89 Stat. 1059, substituted "Repealed" for "Accrued leave" in item 8524.

CHAPTER REFERRED TO IN OTHER SECTIONS

This chapter is referred to in title 2 section 906; title 18 section 1919; title 19 section 2319; title 22 section 3664; title 28 section 996.

SUBCHAPTER I—EMPLOYEES GENERALLY

SUBCHAPTER REFERRED TO IN OTHER SECTIONS

This subchapter is referred to in sections 3373, 8521 of this title; title 39 section 1005.

§ 8501. Definitions

For the purpose of this subchapter—

(1) "Federal service" means service performed after 1952 in the employ of the United States or an instrumentality of the United States which is wholly or partially owned by the United States, but does not include service (except service to which subchapter II of this chapter applies) performed—

(A) by an elective official in the executive or legislative branch;

(B) as a member of the armed forces or the Commissioned Corps of the National Oceanic and Atmospheric Administration;

(C) by members of the Foreign Service for whom payments are provided under section 609(b)(1) of the Foreign Service Act of 1980;

(D) outside the United States, the Commonwealth of Puerto Rico, and the Virgin Islands by an individual who is not a citizen of the United States;

(E) by an individual excluded by regulations of the Office of Personnel Management from the operation of subchapter III of chapter 83 of this title because he is paid on a contract or fee basis;

(F) by an individual receiving nominal pay and allowances of $12 or less a year;

(G) in a hospital, home, or other institution of the United States by a patient or inmate thereof;

(H) by a student-employee as defined by section 5351 of this title;

(I) by an individual serving on a temporary basis in case of fire, storm, earthquake, flood, or other similar emergency;

(J) by an individual employed under a Federal relief program to relieve him from unemployment;

(K) as a member of a State, county, or community committee under the Agricultural Stabilization and Conservation Service or of any other board, council, committee, or other similar body, unless the board, council, committee, or other body is composed exclusively of individuals otherwise in the full-time employ of the United States; or

(L) by an officer or a member of the crew on or in connection with an American vessel—

(i) owned by or bareboat chartered to the United States; and

(ii) whose business is conducted by a general agent of the Secretary of Commerce;

if contributions on account of the service are required to be made to an unemployment fund under a State unemployment compensation law under section 3305(g) of title 26;

(2) "Federal wages" means all pay and allowances, in cash and in kind, for Federal service;

(3) "Federal employee" means an individual who has performed Federal service;

(4) "compensation" means cash benefits payable to an individual with respect to his unemployment including any portion thereof payable with respect to dependents;

(5) "benefit year" means the benefit year as defined by the applicable State unemployment compensation law, and if not so defined the term means the period prescribed in the agreement under this subchapter with a State or, in the absence of such an agreement, the period prescribed by the Secretary of Labor;

(6) "State" means the several States, the District of Columbia, the Commonwealth of Puerto Rico, and the Virgin Islands;

(7) "United States", when used in a geographical sense, means the States; and

(8) "base period" means the base period as defined by the applicable State unemployment compensation law for the benefit year.

(Pub. L. 89–554, Sept. 6, 1966, 80 Stat. 585; Pub. L. 94–566, title I, §116(e)(1), title II, §214(b), Oct. 20, 1976, 90 Stat. 2672, 2678; Pub. L. 95–454, title IX, §906(a)(2), Oct. 13, 1978, 92 Stat. 1224; Pub. L. 96–215, §4(a), Mar. 25, 1980, 94 Stat. 124; Pub. L. 96–465, title II, §2314(h), Oct. 17, 1980, 94 Stat. 2168.)

HISTORICAL AND REVISION NOTES

Derivation	U.S. Code	Revised Statutes and Statutes at Large
....	42 U.S.C. 1361.	Sept. 1, 1954, ch. 1212, §4(a) "Sec. 1501", 68 Stat. 1130. Aug. 28, 1958, Pub. L. 85–848, §2, 72 Stat. 1087. July 12, 1960, Pub. L. 86–624, §30(g), 74 Stat. 420. Sept. 13, 1960, Pub. L. 86–778, §§531(e), 542(d), 74 Stat. 984, 986.

Clause (4) of former section 1361(a) is omitted as obsolete.

In paragraph (1)(A), the word "official" is substituted for "officer" because of the definition of "officer" in section 2104. The words "of the Government of the United States" are omitted as unnecessary.

In paragraph (1)(E), the words "by regulations of the Civil Service Commission from the operation of subchapter III of chapter 83 of this title" are substituted for "by Executive order from the operation of the Civil Service Retirement Act of 1930" on authority of the Civil Service Retirement Act Amendments of 1956, which are carried into subchapter III of chapter 83.

In paragraph (1)(K), the words "Agricultural Stabilization and Conservation Service" are substituted for "Production and Marketing Administration" on authority of Secretary's memorandum 1320, supp. 4 of November 2, 1953.

In paragraph (1)(L), the words "section 1606(g) of Title 26, Internal Revenue Code of 1939" in former section 1361(a)(13) are omitted as obsolete.

The last sentence of former section 1361 is omitted as its substance is included in paragraph (1)(D).

Former section 1361(f) is omitted as unnecessary as the full title of the Secretary of Labor is set out the first time it is used in each section.

Paragraphs (6) and (7) are added on authority of section 1101(a)(1), (2) of the Act of Aug. 14, 1935, ch. 531, 49 Stat. 647, as amended; 42 U.S.C. 1301(a)(1), (2).

Standard changes are made to conform with the definitions applicable and the style of this title as outlined in the preface to the report.

REFERENCES IN TEXT

Section 609(b)(1) of the Foreign Service Act of 1980, referred to in par. (1)(C), is classified to section 4009(b)(1) of Title 22, Foreign Relations and Intercourse.

AMENDMENTS

1980—Par. (1)(B). Pub. L. 96–215 inserted "or the Commissioned Corps of the National Oceanic and Atmospheric Administration" after "armed forces".

Par. (1)(C). Pub. L. 96–465 substituted "members of the Foreign Service for whom payments are provided under section 609(b)(1) of the Foreign Service Act of 1980" for "Foreign Service personnel for whom special separation allowances are provided under chapter 14 of title 22".

1978—Par. (1)(E). Pub. L. 95–454 substituted "Office of Personnel Management" for "Civil Service Commission".

1976—Par. (6). Pub. L. 94–566, § 116(e)(1), added the Virgin Islands in definition of "State".

Par. (8). Pub. L. 94–566, § 214(b), added par. (8).

EFFECTIVE DATE OF 1980 AMENDMENTS

Amendment by Pub. L. 96–465 effective Feb. 15, 1981, except as otherwise provided, see section 2403 of Pub. L. 96–465, set out as an Effective Date note under section 3901 of Title 22, Foreign Relations and Intercourse.

Section 4(c) of Pub. L. 96–215 provided that: "The amendments made by this section [amending this section and section 8521 of this title] shall apply with respect to assignments of services and wages pursuant to any first claim (for a benefit year) which is filed after the date of the enactment of this Act [Mar. 25, 1980]."

EFFECTIVE DATE OF 1978 AMENDMENT

Amendment by Pub. L. 95–454 effective 90 days after Oct. 13, 1978, see section 907 of Pub. L. 95–454, set out as a note under section 1101 of this title.

EFFECTIVE DATE OF 1976 AMENDMENT

Amendment by section 116(e)(1) of Pub. L. 94–566 applicable with respect to benefit years beginning on or after the later of Oct. 1, 1976, or the first day of the first week for which compensation becomes payable under an unemployment compensation law of the Virgin Islands which is approved by the Secretary of Labor under section 3304(a) of Title 26, Internal Revenue Code, see section 116(f)(3) of Pub. L. 94–566, set out as a note under section 3304 of Title 26.

Section 214(c) of Pub. L. 94–566 provided that: "The amendments made by this section [amending this sec-

tion and section 8505 of this title] shall apply with regard to compensation paid on the basis of claims for compensation filed on or after July 1, 1977".

TEMPORARY 1990 CENSUS SERVICES CONSTITUTING FEDERAL SERVICE

Determination respecting temporary 1990 census services as Federal service for purposes of this subchapter, see section 141 of Pub. L. 101–382, set out as a note under section 23 of Title 13, Census.

§ 8502. Compensation under State agreement

(a) The Secretary of Labor, on behalf of the United States, may enter into an agreement with a State, or with an agency administering the unemployment compensation law of a State, under which the State agency shall—

(1) pay, as agent of the United States, compensation under this subchapter to Federal employees; and

(2) otherwise cooperate with the Secretary and with other State agencies in paying compensation under this subchapter.

(b) The agreement shall provide that compensation will be paid by the State to a Federal employee in the same amount, on the same terms, and subject to the same conditions as the compensation which would be payable to him under the unemployment compensation law of the State if his Federal service and Federal wages assigned under section 8504 of this title to the State had been included as employment and wages under that State law.

[(c) Repealed. Pub. L. 90–83, § 1(86)(B), Sept. 11, 1967, 81 Stat. 218.]

(d) A determination by a State agency with respect to entitlement to compensation under an agreement is subject to review in the same manner and to the same extent as determinations under the State unemployment compensation law, and only in that manner and to that extent.

(e) Each agreement shall provide the terms and conditions on which it may be amended or terminated.

(Pub. L. 89–554, Sept. 6, 1966, 80 Stat. 586; Pub. L. 90–83, § 1(86), Sept. 11, 1967, 81 Stat. 218.)

HISTORICAL AND REVISION NOTES
1966 ACT

Derivation	U.S. Code	Revised Statutes and Statutes at Large
....	42 U.S.C. 1362.	Sept. 1, 1954, ch. 1212, § 4(a) "Sec. 1502", 68 Stat. 1131. Sept. 13, 1960, Pub. L. 86–778, § 542(b)(1)(A), 74 Stat. 985.

In subsection (a), the words "under this subchapter" are substituted for "on the basis provided in subsection (b) of this section".

In subsection (b), the words "with respect to unemployment after December 31, 1954" are omitted as obsolete.

In subsection (c), the words "with respect to unemployment after December 31, 1960" are omitted as obsolete. In the last sentence, the application to section 8503(b) is omitted and carried into that section.

Standard changes are made to conform with the definitions applicable and the style of this title as outlined in the preface to the report.

1967 ACT

This section amends 5 U.S.C. 8502 to eliminate certain provisions that are now obsolete. The obsolete provisions were based on section 542(b)(1)(A) of the act of September 13, 1960, 74 Stat. 985, that amended section 1502(b) of the Social Security Act effective January 1, 1961, but only in the case of weeks of unemployment beginning before January 1, 1966. Any existing rights are preserved by section 7 of this bill.

SECTION REFERRED TO IN OTHER SECTIONS

This section is referred to in sections 8507, 8523 of this title.

§ 8503. Compensation absent State agreement

(a) In the case of a Federal employee whose Federal service and Federal wages are assigned under section 8504 of this title to a State which does not have an agreement with the Secretary of Labor, the Secretary, under regulations prescribed by him, shall, on the filing by the Federal employee of a claim for compensation under this subsection, pay compensation to him in the same amount, on the same terms, and subject to the same conditions as would be paid to him under the unemployment compensation law of the State if his Federal service and Federal wages had been included as employment and wages under that State law. However, if the Federal employee, without regard to his Federal service and Federal wages, has employment or wages sufficient to qualify for compensation during the benefit year under that State law, then payments of compensation under this subsection may be made only on the basis of his Federal service and Federal wages.

(b) A Federal employee whose claim for compensation under subsection (a) of this section is denied is entitled to a fair hearing under regulations prescribed by the Secretary. A final determination by the Secretary with respect to entitlement to compensation under this section is subject to review by the courts in the same manner and to the same extent as is provided by section 405(g) of title 42.

(Pub. L. 89–554, Sept. 6, 1966, 80 Stat. 587; Pub. L. 90–83, § 1(87), Sept. 11, 1967, 81 Stat. 218; Pub. L. 94–566, title I, § 116(e)(2), Oct. 20, 1976, 90 Stat. 2673.)

HISTORICAL AND REVISION NOTES
1966 ACT

Derivation	U.S. Code	Revised Statutes and Statutes at Large
....	42 U.S.C. 1363.	Sept. 1, 1954, ch. 1212, § 4(a) "Sec. 1503", 68 Stat. 1132. Sept. 13, 1960, Pub. L. 86–778, § 542(b)(1)(B), (C), (c)(1), 74 Stat. 986.

In subsections (a) and (b), the words "with respect to unemployment after December 31, 1954" are omitted as obsolete.

In subsection (b), the last sentence is added on authority of the last sentence of former section 1362(b), which section is carried into section 8502.

In subsection (c), the words "with respect to final decisions of the Secretary of Health, Education, and Welfare under subchapter II of this chapter" are omitted as unnecessary.

Standard changes are made to conform with the definitions applicable and the style of this title as outlined in the preface to the report.

1967 ACT

Section of title 5	Source (U.S. Code)	Source (Statutes at Large)
8503(b)	[Uncodified].	Sept. 13, 1960, Pub. L. 86–778, § 542(a)(1), 74 Stat. 985.

This section also amends 5 U.S.C. 8503 to eliminate certain provisions that are now obsolete. The obsolete provisions were based on section 542(b)(1)(B) and (C) of the act of September 13, 1960, 74 Stat. 986, that amended section 1503 (a) and (b) of the Social Security Act effective January 1, 1961, but only in the case of weeks of unemployment beginning before January 1, 1966. Any existing rights are preserved by section 7 of this bill.

AMENDMENTS

1976—Subsecs. (b), (c). Pub. L. 94–566, § 116(e)(2), redesignated subsec. (c) as (b) and substituted "subsection (a)" for "subsection (a) or (b)". Former subsec. (b), which made special provision for Federal employees whose Federal service and Federal wages were assigned to the Virgin Islands, was struck out.

Subsec. (d). Pub. L. 94–566, § 116(e)(2)(A), struck out subsec. (d) which authorized the Secretary to use the personnel and facilities of the agency in the Virgin Islands cooperating with the United States Employment Service.

EFFECTIVE DATE OF 1976 AMENDMENT

Amendment by Pub. L. 94–566 applicable with respect to benefit years beginning on or after later of Oct. 1, 1976, or first day of first week for which compensation becomes payable under an unemployment compensation law of Virgin Islands which is approved by Secretary of Labor under section 3304(a) of Title 26, Internal Revenue Code, see section 116(f)(3) of Pub. L. 94–566, set out as a note under section 3304 of Title 26.

SECTION REFERRED TO IN OTHER SECTIONS

This section is referred to in sections 8507, 8523 of this title.

§ 8504. Assignment of Federal service and wages

Under regulations prescribed by the Secretary of Labor, the Federal service and Federal wages of a Federal employee shall be assigned to the State in which he had his last official station in Federal service before the filing of his first claim for compensation for the benefit year. However—

(1) if, at the time of filing his first claim, he resides in another State in which he performed, after the termination of his Federal service, service covered under the unemployment compensation law of the other State, his Federal service and Federal wages shall be assigned to the other State; and

(2) if his last official station in Federal service, before filing his first claim, was outside the United States, his Federal service and Federal wages shall be assigned to the State where he resides at the time he files his first claim.

(Pub. L. 89–554, Sept. 6, 1966, 80 Stat. 588; Pub. L. 90–83, § 1(88), Sept. 11, 1967, 81 Stat. 218; Pub. L. 94–566, title I, § 116(e)(3), Oct. 20, 1976, 90 Stat. 2673.)

HISTORICAL AND REVISION NOTES
1966 ACT

Derivation	U.S. Code	Revised Statutes and Statutes at Large
....	42 U.S.C. 1364.	Sept. 1, 1954, ch. 1212, § 4(a) "Sec. 1504", 68 Stat. 1133.

HISTORICAL AND REVISION NOTES—CONTINUED
1966 ACT

Derivation	U.S. Code	Revised Statutes and Statutes at Large
		Sept. 13, 1960, Pub. L. 86–778, § 542(b)(2), 74 Stat. 986.

Standard changes are made to conform with the definitions applicable and the style of this title as outlined in the preface to the report.

1967 ACT

Section of title 5	Source (U.S. Code)	Source (Statutes at Large)
8504(3)	[Uncodified].	Sept. 13, 1960, Pub. L. 86–778, § 542(a)(2), 74 Stat. 985.

This section also amends 5 U.S.C. 8504 to eliminate certain provisions that are now obsolete. The obsolete provisions were based on section 542(b)(2) of the act of September 13, 1960, 74 Stat. 986, that amended section 1504 of the Social Security Act effective January 1, 1961, but only in the case of first claims filed before January 1, 1966. Any existing rights are preserved by section 7 of this bill.

AMENDMENTS

1976—Par. (3). Pub. L. 94–566 struck out par. (3) which covered the assignment to the Virgin Islands of the Federal service and Federal wages of Federal employees whose first claims were filed while residing in the Virgin Islands.

EFFECTIVE DATE OF 1976 AMENDMENT

Amendment by Pub. L. 94–566 applicable with respect to benefit years beginning on or after later of Oct. 1, 1976, or first day of first week for which compensation becomes payable under an unemployment compensation law of Virgin Islands which is approved by Secretary of Labor under section 3304(a) of Title 26, Internal Revenue Code, see section 116(f)(3), set out as a note under section 3304 of Title 26.

SECTION REFERRED TO IN OTHER SECTIONS

This section is referred to in sections 8502, 8503, 8522 of this title.

§ 8505. Payments to States

(a) Each State is entitled to be paid by the United States with respect to each individual whose base period wages included Federal wages an amount which shall bear the same ratio to the total amount of compensation paid to such individual as the amount of his Federal wages in his base period bears to the total amount of his base period wages.

(b) Each State shall be paid, either in advance or by way of reimbursement, as may be determined by the Secretary of Labor, the sum that the Secretary estimates the State is entitled to receive under this subchapter for each calendar month. The sum shall be reduced or increased by the amount which the Secretary finds that his estimate for an earlier calendar month was greater or less than the sum which should have been paid to the State. An estimate may be made on the basis of a statistical, sampling, or other method agreed on by the Secretary and the State agency.

(c) The Secretary, from time to time, shall certify to the Secretary of the Treasury the sum payable to each State under this section. The Secretary of the Treasury, before audit or settlement by the General Accounting Office, shall pay the State in accordance with the certification from the funds for carrying out the purposes of this subchapter.

(d) Money paid a State under this subchapter may be used solely for the purposes for which it is paid. Money so paid which is not used for these purposes shall be returned, at the time specified by the agreement, to the Treasury of the United States and credited to current applicable appropriations, funds, or accounts from which payments to States under this subchapter may be made.

(e) An agreement may—

(1) require each State officer or employee who certifies payments or disburses funds under the agreement, or who otherwise participates in its performance, to give a surety bond to the United States in the amount the Secretary considers necessary; and

(2) provide for payment of the cost of the bond from funds for carrying out the purposes of this subchapter.

(f) In the absence of gross negligence or intent to defraud the United States, an individual designated by the Secretary, or designated under an agreement, as a certifying official is not liable for the payment of compensation certified by him under this subchapter.

(g) In the absence of gross negligence or intent to defraud the United States, a disbursing official is not liable for a payment by him under this subchapter if it was based on a voucher signed by a certifying official designated as provided by subsection (f) of this section.

(h) For the purpose of payments made to a State under subchapter III of chapter 7 of title 42, administration by a State agency under an agreement is deemed a part of the administration of the State unemployment compensation law.

(Pub. L. 89–554, Sept. 6, 1966, 80 Stat. 588; Pub. L. 94–566, title II, § 214(a), Oct. 20, 1976, 90 Stat. 2678.)

HISTORICAL AND REVISION NOTES

Derivation	U.S. Code	Revised Statutes and Statutes at Large
....	42 U.S.C. 1366.	Sept. 1, 1954, ch. 1212, § 4(a) "Sec. 1506", 68 Stat. 1133.

In the first sentence of subsection (d), the word "may" is substituted for "shall" since the sentence does not direct the use of the money, rather it limits the purposes for which the money may be used.

In subsections (f) and (g), the word "official" is substituted for "officer" because of the definition of "officer" in section 2104.

Standard changes are made to conform with the definitions applicable and the style of this title as outlined in the preface to the report.

AMENDMENTS

1976—Subsec. (a). Pub. L. 94–566 substituted provisions that each State is entitled to be paid by the United States with respect to each individual whose base period wages included Federal wages an amount which shall bear the same ratio to the total amount of compensation paid to such individual as the amount of his Federal wages in his base period bears to the total amount of his base period wages for provisions that each State is entitled to be paid by the United States an amount equal to the additional cost to the State of payments of compensation in accordance with an agreement under this subchapter which would not have been made by the State but for the agreement.

EFFECTIVE DATE OF 1976 AMENDMENT

Amendment by Pub. L. 94–566 applicable with regard to compensation paid on the basis of claims for compensation filed on or after July 1, 1977, see section 214(c) of Pub. L. 94–566, set out as a note under section 8501 of this title.

§ 8506. Dissemination of information

(a) Each agency of the United States and each wholly or partially owned instrumentality of the United States shall make available to State agencies which have agreements under this subchapter, or to the Secretary of Labor, as the case may be, such information concerning the Federal service and Federal wages of a Federal employee as the Secretary considers practicable and necessary for the determination of the entitlement of the Federal employee to compensation under this subchapter. The information shall include the findings of the employing agency concerning—

(1) whether or not the Federal employee has performed Federal service;

(2) the periods of Federal service;

(3) the amount of Federal wages; and

(4) the reasons for termination of Federal service.

The employing agency shall make the findings in the form and manner prescribed by regulations of the Secretary. The regulations shall include provision for correction by the employing agency of errors and omissions. This subsection does not apply with respect to Federal service and Federal wages covered by subchapter II of this chapter.

(b) The agency administering the unemployment compensation law of a State shall furnish the Secretary such information as he considers necessary or appropriate in carrying out this subchapter. The information is deemed the report required by the Secretary for the purpose of section 503(a)(6) of title 42.

(Pub. L. 89–554, Sept. 6, 1966, 80 Stat. 589; Pub. L. 94–566, title III, § 313(a), Oct. 20, 1976, 90 Stat. 2680.)

HISTORICAL AND REVISION NOTES

Derivation	U.S. Code	Revised Statutes and Statutes at Large
....	42 U.S.C. 1367.	Sept. 1, 1954, ch. 1212, § 4(a) "Sec. 1507", 68 Stat. 1134. Aug. 28, 1958, Pub. L. 85–848, § 4, 72 Stat. 1089. Sept. 13, 1960, Pub. L. 86–778, § 531(f), 74 Stat. 984.

Standard changes are made to conform with the definitions applicable and the style of this title as outlined in the preface to the report.

AMENDMENTS

1976—Subsec. (a). Pub. L. 94–566 struck out provision that findings made in accordance with the Secretary's regulations were final and conclusive for the purpose of sections 8502(d) and 8503(c) of this title.

EFFECTIVE DATE OF 1976 AMENDMENT

Section 313(b) of Pub. L. 94–566 provided that: "The amendment made by subsection (a) [amending this sec-

tion] shall apply with respect to findings made after the date of the enactment of this Act [Oct. 20, 1976]."

§ 8507. False statements and misrepresentations

(a) If a State agency, the Secretary of Labor, or a court of competent jurisdiction finds that an individual—

(1) knowingly has made, or caused to be made by another, a false statement or representation of a material fact, or knowingly has failed, or caused another to fail, to disclose a material fact; and

(2) as a result of that action has received an amount as compensation under this subchapter to which he was not entitled;

the individual shall repay the amount to the State agency or the Secretary. Instead of requiring repayment under this subsection, the State agency or the Secretary may recover the amount by deductions from compensation payable to the individual under this subchapter during the 2-year period after the date of the finding. A finding by a State agency or the Secretary may be made only after an opportunity for a fair hearing, subject to such further review as may be appropriate under sections 8502(d) and 8503(c) of this title.

(b) An amount repaid under subsection (a) of this section shall be—

(1) deposited in the fund from which payment was made, if the repayment was to a State agency; or

(2) returned to the Treasury of the United States and credited to the current applicable appropriation, fund, or account from which payment was made, if the repayment was to the Secretary.

(Pub. L. 89–554, Sept. 6, 1966, 80 Stat. 590.)

HISTORICAL AND REVISION NOTES

Derivation	U.S. Code	Revised Statutes and Statutes at Large
....	42 U.S.C. 1368(b).	Sept. 1, 1954, ch. 1212, § 4(a), "Sec. 1508(b)", 68 Stat. 1135.

In subsection (a), the words "as the case may be", "be liable to", and "of any amount" are omitted as unnecessary.

Standard changes are made to conform with the definitions applicable and the style of this title as outlined in the preface to the report.

§ 8508. Regulations

The Secretary of Labor may prescribe rules and regulations necessary to carry out this subchapter and subchapter II of this chapter. The Secretary, insofar as practicable, shall consult with representatives of the State unemployment compensation agencies before prescribing rules or regulations which may affect the performance by the State agencies of functions under agreements under this subchapter.

(Pub. L. 89–554, Sept. 6, 1966, 80 Stat. 590.)

HISTORICAL AND REVISION NOTES

Derivation	U.S. Code	Revised Statutes and Statutes at Large
....	42 U.S.C. 1369.	Sept. 1, 1954, ch. 1212, § 4(a) "Sec. 1509", 68 Stat. 1135.

Standard changes are made to conform with the definitions applicable and the style of this title as outlined in the preface to the report.

§ 8509. Federal Employees Compensation Account

(a) The Federal Employees Compensation Account (as established by section 909 of the Social Security Act, and hereafter in this section referred to as the "Account") in the Unemployment Trust Fund (as established by section 904 of such Act) shall consist of—

(1) funds appropriated to or transferred thereto, and

(2) amounts deposited therein pursuant to subsection (c).

(b) Moneys in the Account shall be available only for the purpose of making payments to States pursuant to agreements entered into under this chapter and making payments of compensation under this chapter in States which do not have in effect such an agreement.

(c)(1) Each employing agency shall deposit into the Account amounts equal to the expenditures incurred under this chapter on account of Federal service performed by employees and former employees of that agency.

(2) Deposits required by paragraph (1) shall be made during each calendar quarter and the amount of the deposit to be made by any employing agency during any quarter shall be based on a determination by the Secretary of Labor as to the amounts of payments, made prior to such quarter from the Account based on Federal service performed by employees of such agency after December 31, 1980, with respect to which deposit has not previously been made. The amount to be deposited by any employing agency during any calendar quarter shall be adjusted to take account of any overpayment or underpayment of deposit during any previous quarter for which adjustment has not already been made.

(3) If any Federal agency does not deposit in the Federal Employees Compensation Account any amount before the date 30 days after the date on which the Secretary of Labor has notified such agency that it is required to so deposit such amount, the Secretary of Labor shall notify the Secretary of the Treasury of the failure to make such deposit and the Secretary of the Treasury shall transfer such amount to the Federal Employees Compensation Account from amounts otherwise appropriated to such Federal agency.

(d) The Secretary of Labor shall certify to the Secretary of the Treasury the amount of the deposit which each employing agency is required to make to the Account during any calendar quarter, and the Secretary of the Treasury shall notify the Secretary of Labor as to the date and amount of any deposit made to such Account by any such agency.

(e) Prior to the beginning of each fiscal year (commencing with the fiscal year which begins October 1, 1981) the Secretary of Labor shall estimate—

(1) the amount of expenditures which will be made from the Account during such year, and

(2) the amount of funds which will be available during such year for the making of such expenditures,

and if, on the basis of such estimate, he determines that the amount described in paragraph (2) is in excess of the amount necessary—

(3) to meet the expenditures described in paragraph (1), and

(4) to provide a reasonable contingency fund so as to assure that there will, during all times in such year, be sufficient sums available in the Account to meet the expenditures described in paragraph (1),

he shall certify the amount of such excess to the Secretary of the Treasury and the Secretary of the Treasury shall transfer, from the Account to the general fund of the Treasury, an amount equal to such excess.

(f) The Secretary of Labor is authorized to establish such rules and regulations as may be necessary or appropriate to carry out the provisions of this section.

(g) Any funds appropriated after the establishment of the Account, for the making of payments for which expenditures are authorized to be made from moneys in the Account, shall be made to the Account; and there are hereby authorized to be appropriated to the Account, from time to time, such sums as may be necessary to assure that there will, at all times, be sufficient sums available in the Account to meet the expenditures authorized to be made from moneys therein.

(h) For purposes of this section, the term "Federal service" includes Federal service as defined in section 8521(a).

(Added Pub. L. 96–499, title X, § 1023(b), Dec. 5, 1980, 94 Stat. 2657; amended Pub. L. 97–362, title II, § 202(a), Oct. 25, 1982, 96 Stat. 1732; Pub. L. 102–318, title V, § 532(a), July 3, 1992, 106 Stat. 317.)

REFERENCES IN TEXT

Sections 909 and 904 of the Social Security Act, referred to in subsec. (a), are classified to sections 1109 and 1104, respectively, of Title 42, The Public Health and Welfare.

AMENDMENTS

1992—Subsec. (c)(3). Pub. L. 102–318 added par. (3).

1982—Subsecs. (b), (c)(1). Pub. L. 97–362, § 202(a)(1), substituted "chapter" for "subchapter" wherever appearing.

Subsec. (h). Pub. L. 97–362, § 202(a)(2), added subsec. (h).

EFFECTIVE DATE OF 1992 AMENDMENT

Section 532(b) of Pub. L. 102–318 provided that: "The amendment made by subsection (a) [amending this section] shall apply to failures outstanding on the date of the enactment of this Act [July 3, 1992] or at any time thereafter."

EFFECTIVE DATE OF 1982 AMENDMENT

Section 202(b)(1) of Pub. L. 97–362 provided that: "The amendments made by subsection (a) [amending this section] shall take effect on October 1, 1983."

TRANSFER OF APPROPRIATED UNEMPLOYMENT COMPENSATION FUNDS

Pub. L. 97–362, title II, § 202(b)(2), Oct. 25, 1982, 96 Stat. 1733, provided that: "All funds appropriated which are available (on October 1, 1983) for the making of payments to States under chapter 85 of title 5, United States Code, on the basis of Federal service (as defined in section 8521(a) of such title 5) or for the making of payments under such chapter on the basis of such service in States which do not have in effect an agreement under such chapter, shall be transferred on such date to the Federal Employees Compensation Account established by section 909 of the Social Security Act [42 U.S.C. 1109]. On and after such date, all payments described in the preceding sentence shall be made from such account as provided by section 8509 of such title 5.''

Section 1023(c) of Pub. L. 96–499 provided that: "All funds appropriated which are available for the making of payments to States after December 31, 1980, pursuant to agreements entered into under subchapter I of chapter 85 of title 5, United States Code, or for the making of payments after such date of compensation under such subchapter in States which do not have in effect such an agreement, shall be transferred on January 1, 1981, to the Federal Employees Compensation Account established by section 909 of the Social Security Act [42 U.S.C. 1109]. On and after such date, all payments described in the preceding sentence shall be made from such Account as provided by section 8509 of title 5, United States Code.''

SECTION REFERRED TO IN OTHER SECTIONS

This section is referred to in title 42 section 1109.

SUBCHAPTER II—EX-SERVICEMEN

SUBCHAPTER REFERRED TO IN OTHER SECTIONS

This subchapter is referred to in sections 8501, 8506, 8508 of this title.

§ 8521. Definitions; application

(a) For the purpose of this subchapter—

(1) "Federal service" means active service (not including active duty in a reserve status unless for a continuous period of 90 days or more) in the armed forces or the Commissioned Corps of the National Oceanic and Atmospheric Administration if with respect to that service—

(A) the individual was discharged or released under honorable conditions (and, if an officer, did not resign for the good of the service); and

(B)(i) the individual was discharged or released after completing his first full term of active service which the individual initially agreed to serve, or

(ii) the individual was discharged or released before completing such term of active service—

(I) for the convenience of the Government under an early release program,

(II) because of medical disqualification, pregnancy, parenthood, or any service-incurred injury or disability,

(III) because of hardship, or

(IV) because of personality disorders or inaptitude but only if the service was continuous for 365 days or more;

(2) "Federal wages" means all pay and allowances, in cash and in kind, for Federal service, computed on the basis of the pay and allowances for the pay grade of the individual at the time of his latest discharge or release from Federal service as specified in the schedule applicable at the time he files his first claim for compensation for the benefit year. The Secretary of Labor shall issue, from time to time, after consultation with the Secretary of Defense, schedules specifying the pay and allowances for each pay grade of servicemen covered by this subchapter, which reflect representative amounts for appropriate elements of the pay and allowances whether in cash or in kind; and

(3) "State" means the several States, the District of Columbia, the Commonwealth of Puerto Rico, and the Virgin Islands.

(b) The provisions of subchapter I of this chapter, subject to the modifications made by this subchapter, apply to individuals who have had Federal service as defined by subsection (a) of this section.

(Pub. L. 89–554, Sept. 6, 1966, 80 Stat. 590; Pub. L. 90–83, § 1(89), Sept. 11, 1967, 81 Stat. 218; Pub. L. 94–566, title I, § 116(e)(4), Oct. 20, 1976, 90 Stat. 2673; Pub. L. 96–215, § 4(b), Mar. 25, 1980, 94 Stat. 124; Pub. L. 96–364, title IV, § 415(a), Sept. 26, 1980, 94 Stat. 1310; Pub. L. 97–35, title XXIV, § 2405(a), Aug. 13, 1981, 95 Stat. 876; Pub. L. 97–362, title II, § 201(a), (b), Oct. 25, 1982, 96 Stat. 1732; Pub. L. 102–164, title III, § 301(a), (b), Nov. 15, 1991, 105 Stat. 1059.)

HISTORICAL AND REVISION NOTES
1966 ACT

Derivation	U.S. Code	Revised Statutes and Statutes at Large
....	42 U.S.C. 1371 (a)–(c).	Aug. 28, 1958, Pub. L. 85–848, § 3 "Sec. 1511(a)–(c)", 72 Stat. 1088.

In subsection (a)(1), the words "armed forces" are co-extensive with and substituted for "Army, Navy, Air Force, Marine Corps, or Coast Guard of the United States" in view of the definition of "armed forces" in section 2101. The words "after October 27, 1958" are substituted for "after the sixtieth day after August 28, 1958".

In subsection (b), the words "with respect to weeks of unemployment ending after the sixtieth day after August 28, 1958" are omitted as obsolete because the law is here stated with prospective effect.

Standard changes are made to conform with the definitions applicable and the style of this title as outlined in the preface to the report.

1967 ACT

This incorporates into 5 U.S.C. 8521 the definition of "State" which is applicable to the source statute of that section by virtue of section 1301(a)(1) of title 42.

CODIFICATION

Section 8 of Pub. L. 102–107, Aug. 17, 1991, 105 Stat. 546, which contained provisions substantially identical to those of section 301 of Pub. L. 102–164, amending this section and enacting provisions set out below, did not become effective pursuant to section 10(b) of Pub. L. 102–107, because the President did not take the action required by that section by Aug. 17, 1991.

AMENDMENTS

1991—Subsec. (a)(1). Pub. L. 102–164, § 301(b), substituted "90 days" for "180 days".

Subsec. (c). Pub. L. 102–164, § 301(a), struck out subsec. (c) which read as follows:

"(1) An individual shall not be entitled to compensation under this subchapter for any week before the fifth week beginning after the week in which the individual was discharged or released.

"(2) The aggregate amount of compensation payable on the basis of Federal service (as defined in subsection (a)) to any individual with respect to any benefit year shall not exceed 13 times the individual's weekly benefit amount for total unemployment."

1982—Subsec. (a)(1). Pub. L. 97–362, § 201(a), substituted provision that "Federal service" means active service (not including active duty in a reserve status unless for a continuous period of 180 days or more) in the armed forces or the Commissioned Corps of the National Oceanic and Atmospheric Administration if with respect to that service the individual was discharged or released under honorable conditions (and, if an officer, did not resign for the good of the service), and the individual was discharged or released after completing his first full term of active service which the individual initially agreed to serve, or the individual was discharged or released before completing such term of active service for the convenience of the Government under an early release program, because of medical disqualification, pregnancy, parenthood, or any service-incurred injury or disability, because of hardship, or because of personality disorders or inaptitude but only if the service was continuous for 365 days or more, for provision that "Federal service" meant active service, including active duty for training purposes, in the armed forces or the Commissioned Corps of the National Oceanic and Atmospheric Administration which either began after January 31, 1955, or terminated after October 27, 1958, if that service was continuous for 365 days or more, or was terminated earlier because of an actual service-incurred injury or disability, and with respect to that service, the individual was discharged or released under honorable conditions, did not resign or voluntarily leave the service, and was not released or discharged for cause as defined by the Department of Defense.

Subsec. (c). Pub. L. 97–362, § 201(b), added subsec. (c).

1981—Subsec. (a)(1)(B). Pub. L. 97–35 substituted "honorable conditions;" for "conditions other than dishonorable; and" in cl. (i), and "did not resign or voluntarily leave the service; and" for "was not given a bad conduct discharge, or, if an officer, did not resign for the good of the service;" in cl. (ii), and added cl. (iii).

1980—Subsec. (a)(1). Pub. L. 96–215 inserted "or the Commissioned Corps of the National Oceanic and Atmospheric Administration" after "armed forces" in provisions preceding subpar. (A).

Subsec. (a)(1)(A). Pub. L. 96–364 substituted "365" for "90".

1976—Subsec. (a)(3). Pub. L. 94–566 added the Virgin Islands to definition of "State".

EFFECTIVE DATE OF 1991 AMENDMENT

Section 301(c) of Pub. L. 102–164 provided that: "The amendments made by this section [amending this section] shall apply to weeks of unemployment beginning on or after the date of the enactment of this Act [Nov. 15, 1991]."

EFFECTIVE DATE OF 1982 AMENDMENT; TRANSITIONAL RULE

Section 201(c) of Pub. L. 97–362 provided that:

"(1) IN GENERAL.—Except as provided in paragraph (2), the amendments made by this section [amending this section], shall apply with respect to terminations of service on or after July 1, 1981, but only for purposes of determining eligibility for benefits for weeks of unemployment beginning after the date of the enactment of this Act [Oct. 25, 1982].

"(2) TRANSITIONAL RULE.—The amendments made by this section shall not apply to the extent that such amendments would (but for this paragraph) reduce the amount of compensation payable in the case of benefit years established before the date of the enactment of this Act [Oct. 25, 1982]."

EFFECTIVE DATE OF 1981 AMENDMENT

Section 2405(b) of Pub. L. 97–35 provided that: "The amendment made by subsection (a) [amending this section] shall apply with respect to terminations of service on or after July 1, 1981, but only in the case of weeks of unemployment beginning after the date of the enactment of this Act [Aug. 13, 1981]."

EFFECTIVE DATE OF 1980 AMENDMENTS

Section 415(b) of Pub. L. 96–364 provided that: "The amendment made by subsection (a) [amending this section] shall apply with respect to determinations of Federal service in the case of individuals filing claims for unemployment compensation on or after October 1, 1980."

Amendment by Pub. L. 96–215 applicable with respect to assignments of services and wages pursuant to any first claim (for a benefit year) which is filed after Mar. 25, 1980, see section 4(c) of Pub. L. 96–215, set out as a note under section 8501 of this title.

EFFECTIVE DATE OF 1976 AMENDMENT

Amendment by Pub. L. 94–566 applicable with respect to benefit years beginning on or after later of Oct. 1, 1976, or first day of first week for which compensation becomes payable under an unemployment compensation law of Virgin Islands which is approved by Secretary of Labor under section 3304(a) of Title 26, Internal Revenue Code, see section 116(f)(3) of Pub. L. 94–566, set out as a note under section 3304 of Title 26.

EFFECTIVE DATE OF 1967 AMENDMENT

Amendment by Pub. L. 90–83 effective as of Sept. 6, 1966, for all purposes, see section 9(h) of Pub. L. 90–83, set out as a note under section 5102 of this title.

SECTION REFERRED TO IN OTHER SECTIONS

This section is referred to in sections 8509, 8523 of this title; title 19 section 2291.

§ 8522. Assignment of Federal service and wages

Notwithstanding section 8504 of this title, Federal service and Federal wages not previously assigned shall be assigned to the State in which the claimant first files claim for unemployment compensation after his latest discharge or release from Federal service. This assignment is deemed as assignment under section 8504 of this title for the purpose of this subchapter.

(Pub. L. 89–554, Sept. 6, 1966, 80 Stat. 591; Pub. L. 94–566, title I, § 116(e)(5), Oct. 20, 1976, 90 Stat. 2673.)

HISTORICAL AND REVISION NOTES

Derivation	U.S. Code	Revised Statutes and Statutes at Large
....	42 U.S.C. 1371(e).	Aug. 28, 1958, Pub. L. 85–848, § 3 "Sec. 1511(e)", 72 Stat. 1088. Sept. 13, 1960, Pub. L. 86–778, § 542(c)(2), 74 Stat. 986.

Standard changes are made to conform with the definitions applicable and the style of this title as outlined in the preface to the report.

AMENDMENTS

1976—Pub. L. 94–566 struck out "or to the Virgin Islands, as the case may be," after "shall be assigned to the State".

EFFECTIVE DATE OF 1976 AMENDMENT

Amendment by Pub. L. 94–566 applicable with respect to benefit years beginning on or after later of Oct. 1, 1976, or first day of first week for which compensation becomes payable under an unemployment compensation law of Virgin Islands which is approved by Secretary of Labor under section 3304(a) of Title 26, Internal Revenue Code, see section 116(f)(3) of Pub. L. 94–566, set out as a note under section 3304 of Title 26.

§ 8523. Dissemination of information

(a) When designated by the Secretary of Labor, an agency of the United States shall make available to the appropriate State agency or to the Secretary, as the case may be, such information, including findings in the form and manner prescribed by regulations of the Secretary, as the Secretary considers practicable and necessary for the determination of the entitlement of an individual to compensation under this subchapter.

(b) Subject to correction of errors and omissions as prescribed by regulations of the Secretary, the following are final and conclusive for the purpose of sections 8502(d) and 8503(c) of this title:

(1) Findings by an agency of the United States made in accordance with subsection (a) of this section with respect to—

(A) whether or not an individual has met any condition specified by section 8521(a)(1) of this title;

(B) the periods of Federal service; and

(C) the pay grade of the individual at the time of his latest discharge or release from Federal service.

(2) The schedules of pay and allowances prescribed by the Secretary under section 8521(a)(2) of this title.

(Pub. L. 89–554, Sept. 6, 1966, 80 Stat. 591.)

HISTORICAL AND REVISION NOTES

Derivation	U.S. Code	Revised Statutes and Statutes at Large
....	42 U.S.C. 1371(d).	Aug. 28, 1958, Pub. L. 85–848, §3 "Sec. 1511(d)", 72 Stat. 1088.

Standard changes are made to conform with the definitions applicable and the style of this title as outlined in the preface to the report.

[§ 8524. Repealed. Pub. L. 91–373, title I, § 107, Aug. 10, 1970, 84 Stat. 701]

Section, Pub. L. 89–554, Sept. 6, 1966, 80 Stat. 591, provided that a payment to ex-servicemen for unused accrued leave was to be deemed to continue Federal service during period after termination with respect to which the serviceman received payment and that such payment was to be deemed Federal wages subject to regulations concerning allocation over the period after termination.

EFFECTIVE DATE OF REPEAL

Section 107 of Pub. L. 91–373 provided that the repeal is effective with respect to benefit years which begin more than 30 days after the date of enactment of Pub. L. 91–373, which was approved on Aug. 10, 1970.

§ 8525. Effect on other statutes

[(a) Repealed. Pub. L. 90–83, § 1(90), Sept. 11, 1967, 81 Stat. 219.]

(b) An individual is not entitled to compensation under this subchapter for any period with respect to which he receives—

(1) a subsistence allowance under chapter 31 of title 38 or under part VIII of Veterans Regulation Numbered 1(a); or

(2) an educational assistance allowance under chapter 35 of title 38.

(Pub. L. 89–554, Sept. 6, 1966, 80 Stat. 591; Pub. L. 90–83, § 1(90), Sept. 11, 1967, 81 Stat. 219.)

HISTORICAL AND REVISION NOTES
1966 ACT

Derivation	U.S. Code	Revised Statutes and Statutes at Large
....	42 U.S.C. 1371(g)–(i).	Aug. 28, 1958, Pub. L. 85–848, §3 "Sec. 1511 (g)–(i)", 72 Stat. 1089. Sept. 2, 1958, Pub. L. 85–857, §13(i)(3), 72 Stat. 1265.

In subsection (b), the words "an education and training allowance under subsection (a), (b), (c), or (d) of section 1632 of title 38" are omitted as obsolete. The authority to pay an education and training allowance under section 1632 of title 38 terminated on January 31, 1965, pursuant to section 1613(a) of title 38.

Section 1371(i) of title 42, providing that certain individuals are not entitled to unemployment compensation under the provisions of subchapter I of chapter 41 of title 38, is omitted as obsolete. Subchapter I of chapter 41 of title 38, which related to unemployment compensation for Korean conflict veterans, was repealed by the Act of Sept. 19, 1962, Pub. L. 87–675, 76 Stat. 558.

Standard changes are made to conform with the definitions applicable and the style of this title as outlined in the preface to the report.

1967 ACT

This section deletes subsection (a) of 5 U.S.C. 8525. That subsection is now obsolete in view of the repeal, effective July 1, 1966, of chapter 43 of title 38, U.S.C., by Public Law 89–50, section 1(a) (79 Stat. 173).

CHAPTER 87—LIFE INSURANCE

Sec.	
8701.	Definitions.
8702.	Automatic coverage.
8703.	Benefit certificate.
8704.	Group insurance; amounts.
8705.	Death claims; order of precedence; escheat.
8706.	Termination of insurance; assignment of ownership.
8707.	Employee deductions; withholding.
8708.	Government contributions.
8709.	Insurance policies.
8710.	Reinsurance.
8711.	Basic tables of premium rates.
8712.	Annual accounting; special contingency reserve.
8713.	Effect of other statutes.
8714.	Employees' Life Insurance Fund.
8714a.	Optional insurance.
8714b.	Additional optional life insurance.
8714c.	Optional life insurance on family members.
8714d.	Option to receive "living benefits".
8715.	Jurisdiction of courts.
8716.	Regulations.

AMENDMENTS

1994—Pub. L. 103–409, § 2(b), Oct. 25, 1994, 108 Stat. 4232, added item 8714d.

1988—Pub. L. 100–238, title I, § 108(a)(2)(B), Jan. 8, 1988, 101 Stat. 1747, added item 8713.

1984—Pub. L. 98–353, title II, § 208(b), July 10, 1984, 98 Stat. 351, inserted "; assignment of ownership" in item 8706.

1980—Pub. L. 96–427, §§ 2(e), 7(b), 8(c), and 9(b), Oct. 10, 1980, 94 Stat. 1832, 1836, 1837, added items 8714b and 8714c, substituted "Definitions" for "Definition" in item 8701, and struck out item 8713 "Advisory committee".

1967—Pub. L. 90–206, title IV, § 404(2), Dec. 16, 1967, 81 Stat. 648, added item 8714a.

Pub. L. 90–83, § 1(94), Sept. 11, 1967, 81 Stat. 219, substituted "Advisory committee" for "Advisors" in item 8713.

CHAPTER REFERRED TO IN OTHER SECTIONS

This chapter is referred to in sections 1103, 3373, 3374, 3582, 5304, 5362, 5948 of this title; title 2 sections 31b–5,

72a, 92, 130a, 162b; title 20 section 125; title 22 sections 2025, 2391, 3649, 3658, 3664, 4606; title 25 section 450i; title 28 sections 332, 627, 634, 996; title 38 sections 7438, 7453, 7458; title 39 section 1005; title 40 section 214d; title 42 sections 2996d, 4276, 10704; title 45 section 1206.

§ 8701. Definitions

(a) For the purpose of this chapter, "employee" means—

(1) an employee as defined by section 2105 of this title;

(2) a Member of Congress as defined by section 2106 of this title;

(3) a Congressional employee as defined by section 2107 of this title;

(4) the President;

(5) a justice or judge of the United States appointed to hold office during good behavior (i) who is in regular active judicial service, or (ii) who is retired from regular active service under section 371(b) or 372(a) of title 28, United States Code, or (iii) who has resigned the judicial office under section 371(a) of title 28 with the continued right during the remainder of his lifetime to receive the salary of the office at the time of his resignation;

(6) an individual first employed by the government of the District of Columbia before October 1, 1987;

(7) an individual employed by Gallaudet College; [1]

(8) an individual employed by a county committee established under section 590h(b) of title 16;

(9) an individual appointed to a position on the office staff of a former President under section 1(b) of the Act of August 25, 1958 (72 Stat. 838); and

(10) an individual appointed to a position on the office staff of a former President, or a former Vice President under section 4 of the Presidential Transition Act of 1963, as amended (78 Stat. 153), who immediately before the date of such appointment was an employee as defined under any other paragraph of this subsection;

but does not include—

(A) an employee of a corporation supervised by the Farm Credit Administration if private interests elect or appoint a member of the board of directors;

(B) an individual who is not a citizen or national of the United States and whose permanent duty station is outside the United States, unless the individual was an employee for the purpose of this chapter on September 30, 1979, by reason of service in an Executive agency, the United States Postal Service, or the Smithsonian Institution in the area which was then known as the Canal Zone; or

(C) an employee excluded by regulation of the Office of Personnel Management under section 8716(b) of this title.

(b) Notwithstanding subsection (a) of this section, the employment of a teacher in the recess period between two school years in a position other than a teaching position in which he served immediately before the recess period does not qualify the individual as an employee for the purpose of this chapter. For the purpose of this subsection, "teacher" and "teaching position" have the meanings given them by section 901 of title 20.

(c) For the purpose of this chapter, "basic insurance amount" means, in the case of any employee under this chapter, an amount equal to the greater of—

(1) the annual rate of basic pay payable to the employee, rounded to the next higher multiple of $1,000, plus $2,000, or

(2) $10,000.

In the case of any former employee entitled to coverage under this chapter, the term means the basic insurance amount applicable for the employee at the time the insurance to which the employee is entitled as an employee under this chapter stops pursuant to section 8706(a) of this title.

(d)(1) For the purpose of this chapter, "family member", when used with respect to any individual, means—

(A) the spouse of the individual; and

(B) an unmarried dependent child of the individual (other than a stillborn child), including an adopted child, stepchild or foster child (but only if the stepchild or foster child lived with the individual in a regular parent-child relationship), or recognized natural child—

(i) who is less than 22 years of age, or

(ii) who is 22 years of age or older and is incapable of self-support because of a mental or physical disability which existed before the child became 22 years of age.

(2) For the purpose of this subsection, "dependent", in the case of any child, means that the individual involved was, at the time of the child's death, either living with or contributing to the support of the child, as determined in accordance with the regulations the Office shall prescribe.

(Pub. L. 89–554, Sept. 6, 1966, 80 Stat. 592; Pub. L. 91–418, § 3(a), Sept. 25, 1970, 84 Stat. 869; Pub. L. 93–160, § 1(a), Nov. 27, 1973, 87 Stat. 635; Pub. L. 95–454, title IX, § 906(a)(2), Oct. 13, 1978, 92 Stat. 1224; Pub. L. 96–54, § 2(a)(51), Aug. 14, 1979, 93 Stat. 384; Pub. L. 96–70, title I, § 1209(b), Sept. 27, 1979, 93 Stat. 463; Pub. L. 96–427, §§ 2(a), 8(b), Oct. 10, 1980, 94 Stat. 1831, 1837; Pub. L. 98–353, title II, § 205, July 10, 1984, 98 Stat. 350; Pub. L. 99–335, title II, § 207(k)(1), June 6, 1986, 100 Stat. 597; Pub. L. 100–679, § 13(b), Nov. 17, 1988, 102 Stat. 4071; Pub. L. 105–311, §§ 3(1), 4, Oct. 30, 1998, 112 Stat. 2950.)

HISTORICAL AND REVISION NOTES

Derivation	U.S. Code	Revised Statutes and Statutes at Large
(a)	2 U.S.C. 126.	Sept. 1, 1954, ch. 1208, § 603, 68 Stat. 1116.

[1] See Change of Name note below.

HISTORICAL AND REVISION NOTES—CONTINUED

Derivation	U.S. Code	Revised Statutes and Statutes at Large
	5 U.S.C. 2091(a) (1st sentence, less words between 6th and 7th commas), (b), (d) (1st sentence, less words between 1st and 2d commas).	Aug. 17, 1954, ch. 752, §2(a) (1st sentence, less words between 6th and 7th commas), (b), 68 Stat. 736. Aug. 1, 1956, ch. 837, §501(c)(1) (as applicable to §2 (b)), 70 Stat. 882. Aug. 2, 1956, ch. 901, §1, 70 Stat. 955. July 1, 1960, Pub. L. 86–568, §115(c) "(d) (1st sentence, less words between 1st and 2d commas)". 74 Stat. 302. Aug. 31, 1964, Pub. L. 88–531 §2, 78 Stat. 737.
	[Uncodified].	Aug. 25, 1958, Pub. L. 85–745, §1(b) (last sentence, as applicable to the Federal Employees' Group Life Insurance Act of 1954), 72 Stat. 838.
(b)	5 U.S.C. 2358(c) (less applicability to the Civil Service Retirement Act).	July 17, 1959, Pub. L. 86–91, §10(c) (less applicability to the Civil Service Retirement Act), 73 Stat. 217.

The definition of "Congressional employee" in section 2107 of this title includes an Official Reporter of Debates of the Senate and an individual employed by an Official Reporter of Debates of the Senate so that the inclusion of "a Congressional employee" in subsection (a)(3) provides the coverage for those individuals which was given by former section 126 of title 2.

The definition of "employee" in section 2105 of this title is broad enough to cover the officers and employees set out in former section 2091(a) with the exception of Members of Congress, the President, individuals employed either by the government of the District of Columbia or by Gallaudet College, and United States commissioners. Accordingly, these have been added specifically in paragraphs (2), (4), (5), (6), and (7).

In subsection (a) (B), the words "United States" are substituted for "a State of the United States or the District of Columbia".

Subsection (a)(C) is added for clarity.

In subsection (b), the last sentence is added on authority of former section 2351, which section is scheduled for transfer to section 901 of title 20.

Standard changes are made to conform with the definitions applicable and the style of this title as outlined in the preface to the report.

REFERENCES IN TEXT

Act of August 25, 1958 (72 Stat. 838), referred to in subsec. (a)(9), is Pub. L. 85–745 and is set out as a note under section 102 of Title 3, The President.

Section 4 of the Presidential Transition Act of 1963, referred to in subsec. (a)(10), is section 4 of Pub. L. 88–277, which is set out as a note under section 102 of Title 3.

AMENDMENTS

1998—Subsec. (c). Pub. L. 105–311, §3(1), substituted a period for comma after "$10,000" in par. (2) and struck out "except that the amount of insurance may not exceed the annual rate of basic pay payable for positions at level II of the Executive Schedule under section 5313 of this title, rounded to the next higher multiple of $1,000, plus $2,000." before last sentence.

Subsec. (d)(1)(B). Pub. L. 105–311, §4, inserted "or foster child" after "stepchild" in two places in introductory provisions.

1988—Subsec. (a)(10). Pub. L. 100–679 added par. (10).

1986—Subsec. (a)(6). Pub. L. 99–335 amended par. (6) generally, substituting "first employed" for "employed" and inserting "before October 1, 1987".

1984—Subsec. (a)(5) to (9). Pub. L. 98–353 added par. (5) and redesignated former pars. (5) to (8) as (6) to (9), respectively.

1980—Pub. L. 96–427, §2(a)(1), substituted "Definitions" for "Definition" in section catchline.

Subsec. (c). Pub. L. 96–427, §2(a)(2), added subsec. (c).

Subsec. (d). Pub. L. 96–427, §8(b), added subsec. (d).

1979—Subsec. (a)(7) to (9). Pub. L. 96–54 struck out cl. (7) which related to coverage within term "employee" of a United States Commissioner, and redesignated cls. (8) and (9) as (7) and (8), respectively.

Subsec. (a)(B). Pub. L. 96–70 inserted provisions relating to an individual who was an employee for the purpose of this chapter on Sept. 30, 1979, by reason of service in an Executive agency, the United States Postal Service, or the Smithsonian Institution in the area which was then known as the Canal Zone.

1978—Subsec. (a)(C). Pub. L. 95–454 substituted "Office of Personnel Management" for "Civil Service Commission".

1973—Subsec. (a)(B). Pub. L. 93–160 excluded from definition of "employee" persons who are not nationals of the United States and whose permanent duty station is outside the United States and the Panama Canal Zone.

1970—Subsec. (a)(B). Pub. L. 91–418 excluded from definition of "employee" a noncitizen employee whose permanent duty station is outside the Panama Canal Zone.

CHANGE OF NAME

Gallaudet College, referred to in subsec. (a)(7), redesignated Gallaudet University by section 101(a) of Pub. L. 99–371, which is classified to section 4301(a) of Title 20, Education.

EFFECTIVE DATE OF 1998 AMENDMENT

Pub. L. 105–311, §11, Oct. 30, 1998, 112 Stat. 2954, provided that:

"(a) IN GENERAL.—Except as otherwise provided in this Act [see Short Title of 1998 Amendment note below], the amendments made by this Act shall take effect on the date of enactment of this Act [Oct. 30, 1998].

"(b) MAXIMUM LIMITATION ON EMPLOYEE INSURANCE.—Section 3 [amending this section and section 8714b of this title] shall take effect on the first day of the first applicable pay period beginning on or after the date of enactment of this Act.

"(c) ERRONEOUS COVERAGE.—Section 5 [amending section 8706 of this title] shall be effective in any case in which a finding of erroneous insurance coverage is made on or after the date of enactment of this Act.

"(d) DIRECT PAYMENT OF INSURANCE CONTRIBUTIONS.—Section 6 [amending sections 8707 and 8714a to 8714c of this title] shall take effect on the first day of the first applicable pay period beginning on or after the date of enactment of this Act.

"(e) ADDITIONAL OPTIONAL LIFE INSURANCE.—

"(1) IN GENERAL.—Section 7 [amending section 8714b of this title and enacting provisions set out as a note under section 8714b of this title] shall take effect on the first day of the first pay period that begins on or after the 180th day following the date of enactment of this Act, or on any earlier date that the Office of Personnel Management may prescribe that is at least 60 days after the date of enactment of this Act.

"(2) REGULATIONS.—The Office shall prescribe regulations under which an employee may elect to continue additional optional insurance that remains in force on such effective date without subsequent reduction and with the full cost withheld from annuity or compensation on and after such effective date if that employee—

"(A) separated from service before such effective date due to retirement or entitlement to compensation under subchapter I of chapter 81 of title 5, United States Code; and

"(B) continued additional optional insurance pursuant to section 8714b(c)(2) as in effect immediately before such effective date.

"(f) IMPROVED OPTIONAL LIFE INSURANCE ON FAMILY MEMBERS.—The amendments made by section 8 [amending section 8714c of this title] shall take effect on the first day of the first pay period which begins on or after the 180th day following the date of enactment of this Act or on any earlier date that the Office of Personnel Management may prescribe.

"(g) OPEN SEASON.—Any election made by an employee under section 9 [set out as a note below], and applicable withholdings, shall be effective on the first day of the first applicable pay period that—

"(1) begins on or after the date occurring 365 days after the first day of the election period authorized under section 9; and

"(2) follows a pay period in which the employee was in a pay and duty status."

EFFECTIVE DATE OF 1986 AMENDMENT

Amendment by Pub. L. 99–335 effective Jan. 1, 1987, see section 702(a) of Pub. L. 99–335, set out as an Effective Date note under section 8401 of this title.

EFFECTIVE DATE OF 1980 AMENDMENT

Section 10 of Pub. L. 96–427 provided that:

"(a) Unless otherwise specified, this Act [see Short Title note below] shall take effect on the date of the enactment of this Act [Oct. 10, 1980] and shall have no effect in the case of an employee who died, was separated, or retired before the date of enactment.

"(b) The amendment made by subsection (d) of section 2 of this Act [amending section 8704 of this title] shall apply with respect to premium pay payable under section 5545(c)(2) of title 5, United States Code, from and after the first day of the first pay period which begins on or after the date of the enactment of this Act [Oct. 10, 1980].

"(c) The amendment made by section 3 of this Act [amending section 8706 of this title] shall apply only in the case of an employee who retires or become entitled to receive compensation for work injury on or after the 180th day following the date of the enactment of this Act [Oct. 10, 1980], or any earlier date that the Office of Personnel Management may prescribe which is at least 60 days after the date of enactment.

"(d) The amendments made by sections 7 and 8 of this Act [enacting sections 8714b and 8714c of this title and amending this section] shall take effect on the first day of the first pay period which begins on or after the 180th day following the date of the enactment of this Act [Oct. 10, 1980], or on any earlier date that the Office may prescribe which is at least 60 days after the date of enactment, and shall have no effect in the case of an employee who died, was finally separated, or retired before the effective date."

EFFECTIVE DATE OF 1979 AMENDMENTS

Amendment by Pub. L. 96–70 effective Oct. 1, 1979, see section 3304 of Pub. L. 96–70, set out as an Effective Date note under section 3601 of Title 22, Foreign Relations and Intercourse.

Amendment by Pub. L. 96–54 effective July 12, 1979, see section 2(b) of Pub. L. 96–54, set out as a note under section 305 of this title.

EFFECTIVE DATE OF 1978 AMENDMENT

Amendment by Pub. L. 95–454 effective 90 days after Oct. 13, 1978, see section 907 of Pub. L. 95–454, set out as a note under section 1101 of this title.

SHORT TITLE OF 1998 AMENDMENT

Pub. L. 105–311, § 1, Oct. 30, 1998, 112 Stat. 2950, provided that: "This Act [amending this section and sections 7703, 8706, 8707, and 8714a to 8714c of this title and enacting provisions set out as notes under this section and sections 7703 and 8714b of this title] may be cited as the 'Federal Employees Life Insurance Improvement Act'."

SHORT TITLE OF 1994 AMENDMENT

Pub. L. 103–409, § 1, Oct. 25, 1994, 108 Stat. 4230, provided that: "This Act [enacting section 8714d of this title and provisions set out as notes under this section and sections 8704, 8714, and 8901 of this title] may be cited as the 'FEGLI Living Benefits Act'."

SHORT TITLE OF 1980 AMENDMENT

Section 1 of Pub. L. 96–427 provided that: "This Act [enacting sections 8714b and 8714c of this title, amending this section and sections 8704, 8706, 8707, 8709, and 8714a of this title, repealing section 8713 of this title and enacting provisions set out as notes under this section and sections 8704 and 8714a of this title] may be cited as the 'Federal Employees' Group Life Insurance Act of 1980'."

OPEN SEASON

Pub. L. 105–311, § 9, Oct. 30, 1998, 112 Stat. 2954, provided that: "Beginning not later than 180 days after the date of enactment of this Act [Oct. 30, 1998], the Office of Personnel Management shall conduct an open enrollment opportunity for purposes of chapter 87 of title 5, United States Code, over a period of not less than 8 weeks. During this period, an employee (as defined under section 8701(a) of such title)—

"(1) may, if the employee previously declined or voluntarily terminated any coverage under chapter 87 of such title, elect to begin, resume, or increase group life insurance (and acquire applicable accidental death and dismemberment insurance) under all sections of such chapter without submitting evidence of insurability; and

"(2) may, if currently insured for optional life insurance on family members, elect an amount above the minimum insurance on a spouse."

Pub. L. 103–409, § 3(b), Oct. 25, 1994, 108 Stat. 4232, provided that:

"(1) The Office of Personnel Management shall prescribe regulations under which, beginning not later than 9 months after the date of the enactment of this Act [Oct. 25, 1994], and over a period of not less than 8 weeks—

"(A) an employee (as defined by section 8701(a) of title 5, United States Code) who declined or voluntarily terminated coverage under chapter 87 of such title—

"(i) may elect to begin, or to resume, group life insurance and group accidental death and dismemberment insurance; and

"(ii) may make such other elections under such chapter as the Office may allow; and

"(B) such other elections as the Office allows may be made.

"(2) The Office shall take such action as may be necessary to ensure that employees and any other individuals who would be eligible to make an election under this subsection are afforded advance notification to that effect."

CONTINUED COVERAGE UNDER CERTAIN FEDERAL EMPLOYEE BENEFIT PROGRAMS FOR CERTAIN EMPLOYEES OF SAINT ELIZABETHS HOSPITAL

For provisions relating to treatment of certain Federal employees of Saint Elizabeths Hospital under certain Federal employee benefit programs, see section 207(o) of Pub. L. 99–335, set out as a note under section 8331 of this title.

SECTION REFERRED TO IN OTHER SECTIONS

This section is referred to in sections 8706, 8714a, 8714b, 8714c, 8716 of this title; title 2 section 162b; title 40 section 214d.

§ 8702. Automatic coverage

(a) An employee is automatically insured on the date he becomes eligible for insurance and each policy of insurance purchased by the Office of Personnel Management under this chapter shall provide for that automatic coverage.

(b) An employee desiring not to be insured shall give written notice to his employing office on a form prescribed by the Office. If the notice is received before he has become insured, he shall not be insured. If the notice is received after he has become insured, his insurance stops at the end of the pay period in which the notice is received.

(c) Notwithstanding a notice previously given under subsection (b), an employee of the Department of Defense who is designated as an emergency essential employee under section 1580 of title 10 shall be insured if the employee, within 60 days after the date of the designation, elects to be insured under a policy of insurance under this chapter. An election under the preceding sentence shall be effective when provided to the Office in writing, in the form prescribed by the Office, within such 60-day period.

(Pub. L. 89–554, Sept. 6, 1966, 80 Stat. 593; Pub. L. 95–454, title IX, § 906(a)(2), (3), Oct. 13, 1978, 92 Stat. 1224; Pub. L. 106–398, § 1 [[div. A], title XI, § 1134(a)], Oct. 30, 2000, 114 Stat. 1654, 1654A–318.)

HISTORICAL AND REVISION NOTES

Derivation	U.S. Code	Revised Statutes and Statutes at Large
....	5 U.S.C. 2094(a) (less 1st par.).	Aug. 17, 1954, ch. 752, § 5(a) (less 1st par.), 68 Stat. 738.

In subsection (a), the words "eligible for insurance" are coextensive with and substituted for "eligible under the terms of this chapter".

Standard changes are made to conform with the definitions applicable and the style of this title as outlined in the preface to the report.

AMENDMENTS

2000—Subsec. (c). Pub. L. 106–398 added subsec. (c).
1978—Subsecs. (a), (b). Pub. L. 95–454 substituted "Office of Personnel Management" for "Civil Service Commission" and "Office" for "Commission".

EFFECTIVE DATE OF 1978 AMENDMENT

Amendment by Pub. L. 95–454 effective 90 days after Oct. 13, 1978, see section 907 of Pub. L. 95–454, set out as a note under section 1101 of this title.

APPLICABILITY

Pub. L. 106–398, § 1 [[div. A], title XI, § 1134(b)], Oct. 30, 2000, 114 Stat. 1654, 1654A–318, provided that: "For purposes of section 8702(c) of title 5, United States Code (as added by subsection (a)), an employee of the Department of Defense who is designated as an emergency essential employee under section 1580 of title 10, United States Code, before the date of the enactment of this Act [Oct. 30, 2000] shall be deemed to be so designated on the date of the enactment of this Act."

SECTION REFERRED TO IN OTHER SECTIONS

This section is referred to in sections 8714b, 8714c of this title.

§ 8703. Benefit certificate

The Office of Personnel Management shall arrange to have each insured employee receive a certificate setting forth the benefits to which he is entitled, to whom the benefits are payable, to whom the claims shall be submitted, and summarizing the provisions of the policy principally affecting him. The certificate is issued instead of the certificate which the insurance company would otherwise be required to issue.

(Pub. L. 89–554, Sept. 6, 1966, 80 Stat. 593; Pub. L. 95–454, title IX, § 906(a)(2), Oct. 13, 1978, 92 Stat. 1224.)

HISTORICAL AND REVISION NOTES

Derivation	U.S. Code	Revised Statutes and Statutes at Large
....	5 U.S.C. 2098.	Aug. 17, 1954, ch. 752, § 9, 68 Stat. 742.

The words "each insured employee" are coextensive with and substituted for "each employee insured under such policy".

Standard changes are made to conform with the definitions applicable and the style of this title as outlined in the preface to the report.

AMENDMENTS

1978—Pub. L. 95–454 substituted "Office of Personnel Management" for "Civil Service Commission".

EFFECTIVE DATE OF 1978 AMENDMENT

Amendment by Pub. L. 95–454 effective 90 days after Oct. 13, 1978, see section 907 of Pub. L. 95–454, set out as a note under section 1101 of this title.

§ 8704. Group insurance; amounts

(a) An employee eligible for insurance is entitled to be insured for an amount of group life insurance equal to—

(1) the employee's basic insurance amount, multiplied by

(2) the appropriate factor determined on the basis of the employee's age in accordance with the following schedule:

If the age of the employee is	The appropriate factor is:
35 or under	2.0
36	1.9
37	1.8
38	1.7
39	1.6
40	1.5
41	1.4
42	1.3
43	1.2
44	1.1
45 or over	1.0.

(b) An employee eligible for insurance is entitled to be insured for group accidental death and dismemberment insurance in accordance with this subsection. Subject to the conditions and limitations approved by the Office of Personnel Management which are contained in the policy purchased by the Office, the group accidental death and dismemberment insurance provides payment as follows:

Loss	Amount payable
For loss of life	Full amount of the employee's basic insurance amount.
Loss of one hand or of one foot or loss of sight of one eye.	One-half the amount of the employee's basic insurance amount.
Loss of two or more such members.	Full amount of the employee's basic insurance amount.

For any one accident the aggregate amount of group accidental death and dismemberment insurance that may be paid may not exceed an amount equal to the employee's basic insurance amount.

(c) The Office shall prescribe regulations providing for the conversion of other than annual rates of pay to annual rates of pay and shall specify the types of pay included in annual pay. For the purpose of this chapter, "annual pay" includes—

(1) premium pay under section 5545(c)(1) of this title; and

(2) with respect to a law enforcement officer as defined in section 8331(20) or 8401(17) of this title, premium pay under section 5545(c)(2) of this title.

(d) In determining the amount of insurance to which an employee is entitled—

(1) a change in rate of pay under subchapter VI of chapter 53 of this title is deemed effective as of the first day of the pay period after the pay period in which the payroll change is approved; and

(2) a change in rate of pay under section 5344 or 5349 of this title is deemed effective as of the date of issuance of the order granting the increase or the effective date of the increase, whichever is later, except, that in the case of an employee who dies or retires during the period beginning on the effective date of the increase and ending on the date of the issuance of the order granting the increase, a change in rate of pay under either of such sections shall be deemed as having been in effect for such employee during that period.

(Pub. L. 89–554, Sept. 6, 1966, 80 Stat. 593; Pub. L. 89–737, §1(3), Nov. 2, 1966, 80 Stat. 1164; Pub. L. 90–206, title IV, §401, Dec. 16, 1967, 81 Stat. 646; Pub. L. 92–392, §11, Aug. 19, 1972, 86 Stat. 575; Pub. L. 95–454, title VIII, §801(a)(3)(E), title IX, §906(a)(2), (3), Oct. 13, 1978, 92 Stat. 1222, 1224; Pub. L. 96–427, §2(b)–(d), Oct. 10, 1980, 94 Stat. 1831, 1832; Pub. L. 100–238, title I, §103(b), Jan. 8, 1988, 101 Stat. 1744.)

HISTORICAL AND REVISION NOTES

Derivation	U.S. Code	Revised Statutes and Statutes at Large
(a)–(c)	5 U.S.C. 2092 (less (d))	Aug. 17, 1954, ch. 752, §3 (less (d)), 68 Stat. 737.
(d)(1)	[Uncodified].	Aug. 23, 1958, Pub. L. 85–737, §3, 72 Stat. 831.
(d)(2)	5 U.S.C. 1183.	Sept. 2, 1958, Pub. L. 85–872, §3, 72 Stat. 1697.

In subsection (a), the words "An employee eligible for insurance is entitled" are coextensive with and substituted for "Each employee to whom this chapter applies shall be eligible".

Standard changes are made to conform with the definitions applicable and the style of this title as outlined in the preface to the report.

AMENDMENTS

1988—Subsec. (c)(2). Pub. L. 100–238 inserted "or 8401(17)" after "8331(20)".

1980—Subsec. (a). Pub. L. 96–427, §2(b), substituted new formula for group life insurance to be computed by multiplying the basic insurance with a factor to be obtained from the table based on age for provisions calling for group life insurance and an equal amount of death and dismemberment insurance in accordance with a schedule based on the basic pay with special provision for extension by the amount of increase in the annual rates of basic pay for positions at level II of the Executive Schedule under section 5313 of this title. Prior to this amendment, the table was as follows:

If annual pay is—		The amount of group life insurance is—	The amount of group accidental death and dismemberment insurance is—
Greater than—	But not greater than—		
0	$8,000	$10,000	$10,000
$8,000	9,000	11,000	11,000
9,000	10,000	12,000	12,000
10,000	11,000	13,000	13,000
11,000	12,000	14,000	14,000
12,000	13,000	15,000	15,000
13,000	14,000	16,000	16,000
14,000	15,000	17,000	17,000
15,000	16,000	18,000	18,000
16,000	17,000	19,000	19,000
17,000	18,000	20,000	20,000
18,000	19,000	21,000	21,000
19,000	20,000	22,000	22,000
20,000	21,000	23,000	23,000
21,000	22,000	24,000	24,000
22,000	23,000	25,000	25,000
23,000	24,000	26,000	26,000
24,000	25,000	27,000	27,000
25,000	26,000	28,000	28,000
26,000	27,000	29,000	29,000
27,000	28,000	30,000	30,000
28,000	29,000	31,000	31,000
29,000		32,000	32,000

Subsec. (b). Pub. L. 96–427, §2(c), inserted provision that an employee eligible for insurance is entitled to be insured for group accidental death and dismemberment insurance in accordance with this subsection and substituted reference to employee's basic insurance amount for reference to the amount shown in the schedule in subsec. (a) of this section in four places.

Subsec. (c). Pub. L. 96–427, §2(d), expanded definition of "annual pay" to include premium pay under section 5545(c)(2) of this title with respect to a law enforcement officer as defined in section 8331(20) of this title.

1978—Subsecs. (b), (c). Pub. L. 95–454, §906(a)(2), (3), substituted "Office of Personnel Management" and "Office" for "Civil Service Commission" and "Commission", respectively, wherever appearing.

Subsec. (d)(1). Pub. L. 95–454, §801(a)(3)(E), substituted "subchapter VI of chapter 53" for "section 5337".

1972—Subsec. (d)(2). Pub. L. 92–392 substituted "section 5344 or 5349 of this title" for "section 5343 of this title" and added the exception.

1967—Subsec. (a). Pub. L. 90–206, in material preceding the table, struck out reference to an approximate relationship between the amount of group life insurance and the eligible employee's annual pay and inserted reference to an automatic extension of the schedule correspondingly by the amounts of increases in the annual rate of basic pay for positions at level II of the Executive Schedule under section 5313 of this title, and raised the insurance coverages for both life and accidental death and dismemberment.

1966—Subsec. (c). Pub. L. 89–737 inserted provision that, for the purpose of this chapter, "annual pay" includes premium pay under section 5545(c)(1) of this title.

EFFECTIVE DATE OF 1988 AMENDMENT

Amendment by Pub. L. 100–238 effective Jan. 1, 1987, see section 103(f) of Pub. L. 100–238 set out as a note under section 3307 of this title.

EFFECTIVE DATE OF 1980 AMENDMENT

Amendment by section 2(d) of Pub. L. 96–427 applicable with respect to premium pay payable under section 5545(c)(2) of this title from and after the first day of the first pay period which begins on or after Oct. 10, 1980, see section 10(b) of Pub. L. 96–427, set out as a note under section 8701 of this title.

Section 2(f) of Pub. L. 96–427 provided that: "Subsections (b) and (c) of this section [amending this section] shall take effect beginning with the first pay period beginning on or after October 1, 1981."

EFFECTIVE DATE OF 1978 AMENDMENT

Amendment by section 801(a)(3)(E) of Pub. L. 95–454 effective on first day of first applicable pay period beginning on or after 90th day after Oct. 13, 1978, see section 801(a)(4) of Pub. L. 95–454, set out as an Effective Date note under section 5361 of this title.

Amendment by section 906(a)(2), (3) of Pub. L. 95–454 effective 90 days after Oct. 13, 1978, see section 907 of Pub. L. 95–454, set out as a note under section 1101 of this title.

EFFECTIVE DATE OF 1972 AMENDMENT

Amendment by Pub. L. 92–392 effective on first day of first applicable pay period beginning on or after 90th day after Aug. 19, 1972, see section 15(a) of Pub. L. 92–392, set out as an Effective Date note under section 5341 of this title.

EFFECTIVE DATE OF 1967 AMENDMENT

Section 405(a) of Pub. L. 90–206 provided that: "The amendments made by sections 401 to 403, inclusive, of this Act [amending this section and sections 8707 and 8708 of this title] shall take effect on the first day of the first pay period which begins on or after the sixtieth day following the date of enactment [Dec. 16, 1967]. In the case of an employee who dies or retires during the period beginning on the date of enactment of this Act and prior to the effective date prescribed by this subsection, the amount of insurance shall be determined as if the amendments made by section 401 [amending this section] were in effect for such employee during such period."

EFFECTIVE DATE OF 1966 AMENDMENT

Amendment by Pub. L. 89–737 applicable with respect to premium pay payable from and after first day of first pay period which begins after date of enactment of Pub. L. 89–737, which was approved Nov. 2, 1966, see section 4 of Pub. L. 89–737, set out in the note under section 8114 of this title.

RETROACTIVE EFFECT OF 1967 AMENDMENT

Section 405(c) of Pub. L. 90–206 provided that: "The amendments made by sections 401 to 404, inclusive, of this Act [enacting section 8714a of this title and amending this section and sections 8707 and 8708 of this title] shall have no effect in the case of an employee who died, was finally separated, or retired prior to the date of enactment [Dec. 16, 1967]."

1967 ADJUSTMENT IN AMOUNT OF INSURANCE

Section 220(b) of Pub. L. 90–206 provided that: "For the purposes of determining the amount of insurance for which an individual is eligible chapter 87 of title 5, United States Code, relating to group life insurance for Federal employees—

"(1) all changes in rates of pay which result from the enactment of this title [see Short Title Note under section 5332 of this title] except Postal Field Service Schedule II, Rural Carrier Schedule II, and sections 207, 212, 213(d) and (e), 215, 219, and 225] shall be held and considered to become effective as of the date of such enactment [Dec. 16, 1967]; and

"(2) all changes in rates of pay which result from the enactment of section 212 of this title [enacting provisions set out as a note under section 5303 of this title] and which take effect retroactively from the date on which the adjustments thereof are actually ordered under such section, shall be held and considered to become effective on the date on which such adjustments are actually ordered."

[Section 220(b) of Pub. L. 90–206 effective Dec. 16, 1967, see section 220(a) (1) of Pub. L. 90–206, set out as an Effective Date note under section 3110 of this title.]

SECTION REFERRED TO IN OTHER SECTIONS

This section is referred to in sections 5545a, 5545b, 8714a, 8714d of this title.

§ 8705. Death claims; order of precedence; escheat

(a) Except as provided in subsection (e), the amount of group life insurance and group accidental death insurance in force on an employee at the date of his death shall be paid, on the establishment of a valid claim, to the person or persons surviving at the date of his death, in the following order of precedence:

First, to the beneficiary or beneficiaries designated by the employee in a signed and witnessed writing received before death in the employing office or, if insured because of receipt of annuity or of benefits under subchapter I of chapter 81 of this title as provided by section 8706(b) of this title, in the Office of Personnel Management. For this purpose, a designation, change, or cancellation of beneficiary in a will or other document not so executed and filed has no force or effect.

Second, if there is no designated beneficiary, to the widow or widower of the employee.

Third, if none of the above, to the child or children of the employee and descendants of deceased children by representation.

Fourth, if none of the above, to the parents of the employee or the survivor of them.

Fifth, if none of the above, to the duly appointed executor or administrator of the estate of the employee.

Sixth, if none of the above, to other next of kin of the employee entitled under the laws of the domicile of the employee at the date of his death.

(b) If, within 1 year after the death of the employee, no claim for payment has been filed by a person entitled under the order of precedence named by subsection (a) of this section, or if payment to the person within that period is prohibited by Federal statute or regulation, payment may be made in the order of precedence as if the person had predeceased the employee, and the payment bars recovery by any other person.

(c) If, within 2 years after the death of the employee, no claim for payment has been filed by a person entitled under the order of precedence named by subsection (a) of this section, and neither the Office nor the administrative office established by the company concerned pursuant to section 8709(b) of this title has received notice that such a claim will be made, payment may be made to the claimant who in the judgment of the Office is equitably entitled thereto, and the payment bars recovery by any other person.

(d) If, within 4 years after the death of the employee, payment has not been made under this section and no claim for payment by a person entitled under this section is pending, the amount payable escheats to the credit of the Employees' Life Insurance Fund.

(e)(1) Any amount which would otherwise be paid to a person determined under the order of precedence named by subsection (a) shall be paid (in whole or in part) by the Office to another person if and to the extent expressly provided for in the terms of any court decree of divorce, annulment, or legal separation, or the terms of any court order or court-approved property settlement agreement incident to any court decree of divorce, annulment, or legal separation.

(2) For purposes of this subsection, a decree, order, or agreement referred to in paragraph (1) shall not be effective unless it is received, before the date of the covered employee's death, by the employing agency or, if the employee has separated from service, by the Office.

(3) A designation under this subsection with respect to any person may not be changed except—

(A) with the written consent of such person, if received as described in paragraph (2); or

(B) by modification of the decree, order, or agreement, as the case may be, if received as described in paragraph (2).

(4) The Office shall prescribe any regulations necessary to carry out this subsection, including regulations for the application of this subsection in the event that two or more decrees, orders, or agreements, are received with respect to the same amount.

(Pub. L. 89–554, Sept. 6, 1966, 80 Stat. 594; Pub. L. 90–83, §1(91), Sept. 11, 1967, 81 Stat. 219; Pub. L. 95–454, title IX, §906(a)(2), (3), Oct. 13, 1978, 92 Stat. 1224; Pub. L. 95–583, §1(b), Nov. 2, 1978, 92 Stat. 2481; Pub. L. 105–205, §1, July 22, 1998, 112 Stat. 683.)

HISTORICAL AND REVISION NOTES
1966 ACT

Derivation	U.S. Code	Revised Statutes and Statutes at Large
....	5 U.S.C. 2093.	Aug. 17, 1954, ch. 752, §4, 68 Stat. 738. Aug. 28, 1962, Pub. L. 87–611, §1, 76 Stat. 406.

In subsection (c), the words "Employees' Life Insurance Fund" are substituted for "fund created pursuant to section 2094(c) of this title".

Standard changes are made to conform with the definitions applicable and the style of this title as outlined in the preface to the report.

1967 ACT

Section of title 5	Source (U.S. Code)	Source (Statutes at Large)
8705(a)	5 App.: 2093.	Mar. 23, 1966, Pub. L. 89–373, §1, 80 Stat. 78.

In subsection (a), "Civil Service Commission" is substituted for "Commission" on authority of former 5 U.S.C. 2091(a).

In subsection (c), "Commission" is substituted for "Civil Service Commission" for consistency of style. The full title of the Commission is set forth the first time it is used in a section.

AMENDMENTS

1998—Subsec. (a). Pub. L. 105–205, §1(1), substituted "Except as provided in subsection (e), the" for "The".

Subsec. (e). Pub. L. 105–205, §1(2), added subsec. (e).

1978—Subsec. (a). Pub. L. 95–583 struck out "or (c)" after "section 8706(b)".

Pub. L. 95–454 substituted "Office of Personnel Management" for "Civil Service Commission".

Subsec. (c). Pub. L. 95–454 substituted "Office" for "Commission" wherever appearing.

EFFECTIVE DATE OF 1978 AMENDMENTS

Amendment by Pub. L. 95–583 effective Nov. 2, 1978, see section 3 of Pub. L. 95–583, set out as a note under section 8706 of this title.

Amendment by Pub. L. 95–454 effective 90 days after Oct. 13, 1978, see section 907 of Pub. L. 95–454, set out as a note under section 1101 of this title.

SECTION REFERRED TO IN OTHER SECTIONS

This section is referred to in sections 8714a, 8714b, 8714c of this title.

§ 8706. Termination of insurance; assignment of ownership

(a) A policy purchased under this chapter shall contain a provision, approved by the Office of Personnel Management, to the effect that insurance of an employee stops on his separation from the service or 12 months after discontinuance of his pay, whichever is earlier, subject to a provision for temporary extension of life insurance coverage and for conversion to an individual policy of life insurance under conditions approved by the Office. Justices and judges of the United States described in section 8701(a)(5)(ii) and (iii) of this chapter are deemed to continue in active employment for purposes of this chapter.

(b)(1) In the case of any employee who retires on an immediate annuity and has been insured under this chapter throughout—

(A) the 5 years of service immediately preceding the date of the employee's retirement, or

(B) the full period or periods of service during which the employee was entitled to be insured, if fewer than 5 years,

life insurance, without accidental death and dismemberment insurance, may be continued, under conditions determined by the Office.

(2) In the case of any employee who becomes entitled to receive compensation under subchapter I of chapter 81 of this title because of disease or injury to the employee and has been insured under this chapter throughout—

(A) the 5 years of service immediately preceding the date the employee becomes entitled to compensation, or

(B) the full period or periods of service during which the employee was entitled to be insured, if fewer than 5 years,

life insurance, without accidental death and dismemberment insurance, may be continued, under conditions determined by the Office, during the period the employee is receiving compensation and is held by the Secretary of Labor or the Secretary's delegate to be unable to return to duty.

(3) The amount of life insurance continued under paragraph (1) or (2) of this subsection shall be continued, with or without reduction, at the end of each full calendar month after the date the employee becomes 65 years of age and is retired or is receiving compensation for disease or injury, in accordance with the employee's written election at the time eligibility to continue insurance during retirement or receipt of compensation arises, as follows:

(A) the employee may elect to have the deductions required by section 8707 of this title withheld from annuity or compensation, and the employee's life insurance shall be reduced each month by 2 percent of the face value until 25 percent of the amount of life insurance in force before the first reduction remains; or

(B) in addition to any deductions which would be required if the insurance were continued as provided under subparagraph (A) of this paragraph, the employee may elect continuous withholdings from annuity or compensation in amounts determined by the Office, and the employee's life insurance coverage shall be either continued without reduction or reduced each month by no more than 1 percent of its face value until no less than 50 percent of the amount of insurance in force before the first reduction remains.

(4) If an employee elects to continue insurance under subparagraph (B) of paragraph (3) of this subsection at the time eligibility to continue insurance during retirement or receipt of compensation for disease or injury arises, the individual may later cancel that election and life insurance coverage shall continue as if the individual had originally elected coverage under subparagraph (A) of paragraph (3) of this subsection.

(c) Notwithstanding subsections (a) and (b) of this section, an employee who enters on approved leave without pay to serve as a full-time officer or employee of an organization composed primarily of employees as defined by section 8701(a) of this title, within 60 days after entering on that leave without pay, may elect to continue his insurance and arrange to pay currently into the Employees' Life Insurance Fund, through his employing agency, both employee and agency contributions from the beginning of leave without pay. The employing agency shall forward the premium payments to the Fund. If the employee does not so elect, his insurance will continue during nonpay status and stop as provided by subsection (a) of this section.

(d) If the insurance of an employee stops because of separation from the service or suspension without pay, and the separation or suspension is thereafter officially found to have been erroneous, the employee is deemed to have been insured during the period of erroneous separation or suspension. Deductions otherwise required by section 8707 of this chapter shall not be withheld from any backpay awarded for the period of separation or suspension unless death or accidental dismemberment of the employee occurs during such period.

(e)(1) Under regulations prescribed by the Office, each policy purchased under this chapter shall provide that an insured employee or former employee may make an irrevocable assignment of the employee's or former employee's incidents of ownership in the policy.

(2) A court decree of divorce, annulment, or legal separation, or the terms of a court-approved property settlement agreement incident to any court decree of divorce, annulment, or legal separation, may direct that an insured employee or former employee make an irrevocable assignment of the employee's or former employee's incidents of ownership in insurance under this chapter (if there is no previous assignment) to the person specified in the court order or court-approved property settlement agreement.

(f) If the insurance of a former employee receiving a disability annuity under section 8337 of this title stops because of the termination of such annuity, and such annuity is thereafter restored under the second or third sentence of subsection (e) of such section, such former employee may, under regulations prescribed by the Office, elect to resume the insurance coverage which was so stopped.

(g) The insurance of an employee under a policy purchased under section 8709 shall not be invalidated based on a finding that the employee erroneously became insured, or erroneously continued insurance upon retirement or entitlement to compensation under subchapter I of chapter 81 of this title, if such finding occurs after the erroneous insurance and applicable withholdings have been in force for 2 years during the employee's lifetime.

(Pub. L. 89–554, Sept. 6, 1966, 80 Stat. 595; Pub. L. 90–83, §1(92), Sept. 11, 1967, 81 Stat. 219; Pub. L. 92–529, Oct. 21, 1972, 86 Stat. 1050; Pub. L. 95–454, title IX, §906(a)(2), (3), Oct. 13, 1978, 92 Stat. 1224; Pub. L. 95–583, §1(a), Nov. 2, 1978, 92 Stat. 2481; Pub. L. 96–427, §3(a), Oct. 10, 1980, 94 Stat. 1832; Pub. L. 98–353, title II, §§206, 208, July 10, 1984, 98 Stat. 351, as amended by Pub. L. 99–336, §7(1), June 19, 1986, 100 Stat. 639; Pub. L. 99–53, §3(b), June 17, 1985, 99 Stat. 95; Pub. L. 99–335, title II, §207(k)(2), June 6, 1986, 100 Stat. 597; Pub. L. 99–336, §7(1), June 19, 1986, 100 Stat. 639; Pub. L. 102–378, §2(74), Oct. 2, 1992, 106 Stat. 1355; Pub. L. 103–336, §4, Oct. 3, 1994, 108 Stat. 2662; Pub. L. 105–205, §2, July 22, 1998, 112 Stat. 683; Pub. L. 105–311, §5, Oct. 30, 1998, 112 Stat. 2951.)

HISTORICAL AND REVISION NOTES
1966 ACT

Derivation	U.S. Code	Revised Statutes and Statutes at Large
(a)–(c)	5 U.S.C. 2095.	Aug. 17, 1954, ch. 752, §6, 68 Stat. 739. Aug. 11, 1955, ch. 794, §2(a), 69 Stat. 677. May 28, 1956, ch. 328, §1, 70 Stat. 213. Sept. 23, 1959, Pub. L. 86–377, §4(c), 73 Stat. 701.
(d)	5 U.S.C. 2091(c).	Aug. 1, 1956, ch. 837, §501(c)(1) (less applicability to §2(b)), 70 Stat. 882.

In subsection (b), the words "armed forces" are coextensive with and substituted for "Army, Navy, Air Force, and Marine Corps, or Coast Guard of the United States" in view of the definition of "armed forces" in section 2101.

In subsection (c), the word "only" is supplied for clarity and for consistency with subsection (b). The words "under conditions determined by the Commission, without cost to him" are coextensive with and substituted for "as provided in subsection (b) of this section".

In subsection (d), the first sentence of former section 2091(c) is omitted as unnecessary as the definition of "employee" in section 8701 precludes acquisition of coverage by a member of a uniformed service. The words "section 101 of title 38" are substituted for "section 1101 of title 38" on authority of section 5(a) of the Act of Sept. 2, 1958, Pub. L. 85–857, 72 Stat. 1262.

Standard changes are made to conform with the definitions applicable and the style of this title as outlined in the preface to the report.

1967 ACT

Section of title 5	Source (U.S. Code)	Source (Statutes at Large)
8706(e)	5 App.: 2095(d).	July 18, 1966, Pub. L. 89–504, §406(a), 80 Stat. 298.

The words "subsections (a)–(c) of this section" are substituted for "the foregoing" to reflect the codification of former 5 U.S.C. 2095. The word "officer" is omitted as included in "employee." The words "as defined by section 8701(a) of this title" are substituted for "as defined in section 2 of the Act" to reflect the codification of that section in 5 U.S.C. 8701(a). The words "Employees' Life Insurance Fund'' and "Fund" are substituted for "fund" and "fund established by section 5 of this Act", respectively.

AMENDMENTS

1998—Subsec. (e). Pub. L. 105–205 designated existing provisions as par. (1) and added par. (2).

Subsec. (g). Pub. L. 105–311 added subsec. (g).

1994—Subsec. (e). Pub. L. 103–336 substituted "employee or former employee" for "Federal judge", "employee's or former employee's" for "judge's", and "purchased" for "purchase".

1992—Subsecs. (f), (g). Pub. L. 102–378 redesignated subsec. (g) as (f).

1986—Subsec. (a). Pub. L. 98–353, §206, as amended generally by Pub. L. 99–336, §7(1), inserted sentence which deemed justices and judges described in section 8701(a)(5)(ii) and (iii) of this chapter to continue in active employment for purposes of this chapter.

Subsecs. (c) to (f). Pub. L. 99–335 struck out subsec. (c) and redesignated subsecs. (d) to (f) as (c) to (e), respectively. Former subsec. (c) provided that insurance granted an employee stops, except for a 31-day extension of life insurance coverage, on the day immediately before his entry on active duty or active duty for training unless the period is covered by military leave with pay but does not stop during a period of inactive duty training and defined "active duty", "active duty for training", and "inactive duty training" as having the meanings given them by section 101 of title 38.

1985—Subsec. (g). Pub. L. 99–53 added subsec. (g).

1984—Pub. L. 98–353, §208(b), inserted "; assignment of ownership" in section catchline.

Subsec. (f). Pub. L. 98–353, §208(a), added subsec. (f).

1980—Subsec. (b). Pub. L. 96–427 added subsec. (b) and struck out former subsec. (b) which read as follows:

"(1) If on the date the insurance would otherwise stop the employee retires on an immediate annuity and has been insured under this chapter throughout—

"(A) the 5 years of service immediately preceding such date, or

"(B) the full period or periods of service during which the employee was entitled to be insured, if less than 5 years,

life insurance only may be continued, without cost to the employee, under conditions determined by the Office.

"(2) If on the date the insurance would otherwise stop the employee is receiving compensation under subchapter I of chapter 81 of this title because of disease or injury to the employee and has been insured under this chapter throughout—

"(A) the 5 years of service immediately preceding such date, or

"(B) the full period or periods of service during which the employee was entitled to be insured, if less than 5 years,

life insurance only may be continued, without cost to the employee, under conditions determined by the Office, during the period the employee is receiving compensation for work injuries and is held by the Secretary of Labor or his delegate to be unable to return to duty.

"(3) The amount of life insurance continued under paragraph (1) or paragraph (2) of this subsection shall be reduced by 2 percent at the end of each full calendar month after the date the employee becomes 65 years of age and is retired or is receiving such compensation for disease or injury. The Office shall prescribe minimum amounts, not less than 25 percent of the amount of life insurance in force before the first reduction, to which the insurance may be reduced."

1978—Subsec. (a). Pub. L. 95–454 substituted "Office of Personnel Management" and "Office" for "Civil Service Commission" and "Commission", respectively.

Subsec. (b). Pub. L. 95–583, §1(a)(1), added subsec. (b) and struck out former subsec. (b) which read as follows: "If on the date the insurance would otherwise stop the employee retires on an immediate annuity and—

"(1) his retirement is for disability; or

"(2) he has completed 12 years of creditable service as determined by the Commission;

his life insurance only may be continued, without cost to him, under conditions determined by the Commission. Periods of honorable, active service in the armed forces shall be credited toward the required 12 years if the employee has completed at least 5 years of civilian service. The amount of life insurance continued under this subsection shall be reduced by 2 percent at the end of each full calendar month after the date the employee becomes 65 years of age or retires, whichever is later. The Commission may prescribe minimum amounts, not less than 25 percent of the amount of life insurance in force before the first reduction, to which the insurance may be reduced."

Pub. L. 95–454, which substituted "Office" for "Commission", was executed to text of subsec. (b) as amended by Pub. L. 95–583. See Effective Date of 1978 Amendments note below.

Subsec. (c). Pub. L. 95–583, §1(a)(1), (2), struck out "If on the date the insurance would otherwise stop the employee is receiving benefits under subchapter I of chapter 81 of this title because of disease or injury to himself, his life insurance only may be continued, without cost to him, under conditions determined by the Commission while he is receiving the benefits and is held by the Department of Labor to be unable to return to duty." and redesignated subsec. (d) as (c).

Subsec. (d). Pub. L. 95–583, §1(a)(2), (3), redesignated subsec. (e) as (d) and substituted reference to "subsections (a) and (b) of this section" for "subsections (a)–(c) of this section". Former subsec. (d) redesignated (c).

Subsecs. (e), (f). Pub. L. 95–583, §1(a)(2), redesignated subsecs. (e) and (f) as (d) and (e), respectively.

1972—Subsec. (f). Pub. L. 92–529 added subsec. (f).

EFFECTIVE DATE OF 1998 AMENDMENT

Amendment by Pub. L. 105–311 effective in any case in which a finding of erroneous insurance coverage is made on or after Oct. 30, 1998, see section 11(c) of Pub. L. 105–311, set out as a note under section 8701 of this title.

EFFECTIVE DATE OF 1986 AMENDMENTS

Section 207 of Pub. L. 98–353, as amended generally by Pub. L. 99–336, §7(2), provided that: "The amendments to chapter 87 of title 5, United States Code, made by section 206 of this Act [which, as amended generally by Pub. L. 99–336, §7(1), amended this section and sections 8714a to 8714c of this title] shall apply in the case of any justice or judge who is retired under section 371(a) or 371(b) or 372(a) of title 28, United States Code. The amendments apply to those who retire on or after January 1, 1982."

Amendment by Pub. L. 99–335 effective Jan. 1, 1987, see section 702(a) of Pub. L. 99–335, set out as an Effective Date note under section 8401 of this title.

EFFECTIVE DATE OF 1984 AMENDMENT

Section 209 of Pub. L. 98–353 provided that:

"(a) Except as provided in subsection (b), the amendments made by this Act to section 8706 of title 5, United States Code, shall apply to policies purchased by judges after the date of enactment of this Act [July 10, 1984].

"(b) If a company which issued a policy which is in effect on the date of the enactment of this Act agrees, the amendments made by this Act [probably should be 'made by this Act to section 8706 of title 5'] shall apply to such policy."

EFFECTIVE DATE OF 1980 AMENDMENT

Amendment by Pub. L. 96–427 applicable only in case of an employee who retires or becomes entitled to receive compensation for work injury on or after 180th day following Oct. 10, 1980, or any earlier date that Office of Personnel Management may prescribe which is at least 60 days after Oct. 10, 1980, see section 10(c) of Pub. L. 96–427, set out as a note under section 8701 of this title.

EFFECTIVE DATE OF 1978 AMENDMENTS

Section 3 of Pub. L. 95–583 provided that: "The amendments made by this Act [amending this section and sections 8705, 8714a, and 8901 of this title] shall take effect on the date of the enactment of this Act [Nov. 2, 1978]."

Amendment by Pub. L. 95–454 effective 90 days after Oct. 13, 1978, see section 907 of Pub. L. 95–454, set out as a note under section 1101 of this title.

INSURANCE COVERAGE FOR RESTORED DISABILITY ANNUITANTS

Section 3(c) of Pub. L. 99–53 provided that:

"(1) The amendments made by this section [amending this section and section 8908 of this title] shall apply with respect to any individual whose disability annuity is or was restored under section 8337(e) of title 5, United States Code, after December 31, 1983.

"(2)(A) The Office of Personnel Management shall notify each individual under subparagraph (B) of any rights which such individual may have under section 8706(g) or section 8908(c) of title 5, United States Code, as amended by this section, including any procedures or deadlines which may apply with respect to the exercise of those rights.

"(B) Notification under this paragraph shall be provided to any individual who, as of the 90th day after the date of enactment of this Act [June 17, 1985], is receiving a disability annuity which was restored to such individual under section 8337(e) of title 5, United States Code, after December 31, 1983.

"(3)(A) Nothing in this section shall be construed to authorize—

"(i) coverage under chapter 87 of title 5, United States Code, in the case of any individual who makes an election under section 8706(g) of such title (as amended by this Act), for any period before the date of such election; or

"(ii) coverage under chapter 89 of title 5, United States Code, in the case of any individual who becomes enrolled in a health benefits plan under section 8908(c) of such title (as amended by this Act), for any period before the date as of which such individual becomes so enrolled.

"(B) This paragraph applies with respect to any individual receiving a disability annuity which is or was restored under section 8337(e) of title 5, United States Code, after December 31, 1983, and before the expiration of the 90-day period beginning on the date of enactment of this Act [June 17, 1985]."

ELECTION OF LIFE INSURANCE OR HEALTH BENEFITS DURING PERIOD OF SERVICE AS OFFICER OR EMPLOYEE OF AN EMPLOYEE ORGANIZATION; CONTRIBUTIONS INTO EMPLOYEES LIFE INSURANCE FUND OR EMPLOYEES HEALTH BENEFITS FUND, NON-ELECTION; REGULATIONS

Pub. L. 89–504, title IV, § 406(c), July 18, 1966, 80 Stat. 298, provided that: "An officer or employee who is on approved leave without pay and serving as a full-time officer or employee of an organization composed primarily of employees, as defined in section 2 of the Federal Employees' Group Life Insurance Act of 1954, as amended (5 U.S.C. 2091) [section 8701 of this title] or section 2 of the Federal Employees Health Benefits Act of 1959, as amended (5 U.S.C. 3001) [section 8901 of this title] as the case may be, may, within sixty days after the date of enactment of this Act [July 18, 1966], file with his employing agency an election (1) to continue any insurance status or health benefits enrollment, or both, that he has on the date of enactment of this Act [July 18, 1966], (2) to reacquire any insurance status or health benefits enrollment, or both, which he may have lost while on leave without pay, or (3) to acquire as insured status or enroll in a health benefits plan, or both, if he was never previously eligible to do so, by arranging to pay currently and continuously into the employees' life insurance fund and the employees' health benefits fund, as appropriate, through his employing agency, both employee and agency contributions. The employing agency shall forward such payments to the employees' life insurance fund and the employees' health benefits fund, as appropriate. If he does not so elect, his insurance status or health benefits enrollment will continue and terminate as for other employees in nonpay status, or he will remain ineligible for insurance and health benefits, as the case may be, as though this paragraph had not been enacted. The United States Civil Service Commission is authorized to issue regulations to carry out the purposes of this paragraph."

[Provision effective July 18, 1966, see section 410(1) of Pub. L. 89–504.]

SECTION REFERRED TO IN OTHER SECTIONS

This section is referred to in sections 8705, 8707, 8708, 8714a, 8714b, 8714d of this title.

§ 8707. Employee deductions; withholding

(a) Subject to subsection (c)(2), during each period in which an employee is insured under a policy purchased by the Office of Personnel Management under section 8709 of this title, there shall be withheld from the employee's pay a share of the cost of the group life insurance and accidental death and dismemberment insurance.

(b)(1) Subject to subsection (c)(2), whenever life insurance continues after an employee retires on an immediate annuity or while the employee is receiving compensation under subchapter I of chapter 81 of this title because of disease or injury to the employee, as provided in section 8706(b) of this title, deductions for insurance shall be withheld from the employee's annuity or compensation, except that, in any case in which the insurance is continued as provided in section 8706(b)(3)(A) of this title, the deductions shall not be made for months after the calendar month in which the employee becomes 65 years of age.

(2) Notwithstanding paragraph (1) of this subsection, insurance shall be so continued without cost (other than as provided under section 8706(b)(3)(B)) to each employee who so retires, or commences receiving compensation, on or before December 31, 1989.

(c)(1) The amount withheld from the pay, annuity, or compensation of each employee subject to insurance deductions shall be at the rate, adjusted to the nearest half-cent, of 66⅔ percent of the level cost as determined by the Office for each $1,000 of the employee's basic insurance amount.

(2) An employee who is subject to withholdings under this section and whose pay, annuity, or compensation is insufficient to cover such withholdings may nevertheless continue insurance if the employee arranges to pay currently into the Employees' Life Insurance Fund, through the agency or retirement system that administers pay, annuity, or compensation, an amount equal to the withholdings that would otherwise be required under this section.

(d) If an agency fails to withhold the proper amount of life insurance deductions from an individual's salary, compensation, or retirement annuity, the collection of unpaid deductions may be waived by the agency if, in the judgment of the agency, the individual is without fault and recovery would be against equity and good conscience. However, if the agency so waives the collection of unpaid deductions, the agency shall submit an amount equal to the sum of the uncollected deductions and related agency contributions required under section 8708 of this title to the Office for deposit to the Employees' Life Insurance Fund.

(Pub. L. 89–554, Sept. 6, 1966, 80 Stat. 595; Pub. L. 90–206, title IV, §402, Dec. 16, 1967, 81 Stat. 647; Pub. L. 95–454, title IX, §906(a)(2), (3), Oct. 13, 1978, 92 Stat. 1224; Pub. L. 96–427, §4(a), Oct. 10, 1980, 94 Stat. 1833; Pub. L. 105–311, §6(1), Oct. 30, 1998, 112 Stat. 2951.)

HISTORICAL AND REVISION NOTES

Derivation	U.S. Code	Revised Statutes and Statutes at Large
....	5 U.S.C. 2094(a) (1st par.).	Aug. 17, 1954, ch. 752, §5(a) (1st par.), 68 Stat. 738. Sept. 23, 1959, Pub. L. 86–377, §4(b), 73 Stat. 701.

Standard changes are made to conform with the definitions applicable and the style of this title as outlined in the preface to the report.

AMENDMENTS

1998—Subsec. (a). Pub. L. 105–311, §6(1)(A), substituted "Subject to subsection (c)(2), during" for "During".

Subsec. (b)(1). Pub. L. 105–311, §6(1)(B), substituted "Subject to subsection (c)(2), whenever" for "Whenever".

Subsec. (c). Pub. L. 105–311, §6(1)(C), designated existing provisions as par. (1) and added par. (2).

1980—Subsec. (a). Pub. L. 96–427 designated first sentence of existing section as subsec. (a) and substituted "a policy purchased" for "a policy of insurance purchased" and "the employee's pay a share of the cost" for "the pay of the employee his share of the cost".

Subsec. (b). Pub. L. 96–427 added subsec. (b).

Subsec. (c). Pub. L. 96–427 designated second sentence of existing section as subsec. (c) and inserted reference to pay, annuity, or compensation of each employee.

Subsec. (d). Pub. L. 96–427 added subsec. (d).

1978—Pub. L. 95–454 substituted "Office of Personnel Management" and "Office" for "Civil Service Commission" and "Commission", respectively.

1967—Pub. L. 90–206 struck out reference to the Civil Service Commission's function of determining the amount to be withheld for group insurance and substituted provisions setting a rate of 66⅔ percent of the level cost of each $1,000 of insurance as determined by the Commission for provisions setting a limit of 25 cents biweekly for each $1,000 of group life insurance and directing the withholding of the amount from employees paid on other than a biweekly basis at a proportional rate adjusted to the nearest cent.

EFFECTIVE DATE OF 1998 AMENDMENT

Amendment by Pub. L. 105–311 effective on the first day of the first applicable pay period beginning on or after Oct. 30, 1998, see section 11(d) of Pub. L. 105–311, set out as a note under section 8701 of this title.

EFFECTIVE DATE OF 1980 AMENDMENT

Amendment by Pub. L. 96–427 effective Oct. 10, 1980, with the amendment to have no effect in case of an employee who died, was separated, or retired before Oct. 10, 1980, see section 10(a) of Pub. L. 96–427, set out as a note under section 8701 of this title.

EFFECTIVE DATE OF 1978 AMENDMENT

Amendment by Pub. L. 95–454 effective 90 days after Oct. 13, 1978, see section 907 of Pub. L. 95–454, set out as a note under section 1101 of this title.

EFFECTIVE DATE OF 1967 AMENDMENT

Amendment by Pub. L. 90–206 effective on first day of first pay period which begins on or after sixtieth day following Dec. 16, 1967, see section 405(a) of Pub. L. 90–206, set out as a note under section 8704 of this title.

RETROACTIVE EFFECT OF 1967 AMENDMENT

Amendment by Pub. L. 90–206 to have no effect in case of an employee who died, was finally separated, or retired prior to Dec. 16, 1967, see section 405(c) of Pub. L. 90–206, set out as a note under section 8704 of this title.

SECTION REFERRED TO IN OTHER SECTIONS

This section is referred to in sections 8706, 8708, 8714, 8714a, 8714d of this title; title 2 section 162b; title 40 section 214d.

§ 8708. Government contributions

(a) For each period in which an employee is insured under a policy of insurance purchased by the Office of Personnel Management under section 8709 of this title, a sum equal to one-half the amount which is withheld from the pay of the employee under section 8707 of this title shall be contributed from the appropriation or fund which is used to pay him.

(b) When an employee is paid by the Chief Administrative Officer of the House of Representatives, the Chief Administrative Officer may contribute the sum required by subsection (a) of this section from the applicable accounts of the House of Representatives.

(c) When the employee is an elected official, the sum required by subsection (a) of this section is contributed from an appropriation or fund available for payment of other salaries of the same office or establishment.

(d)(1) Except as otherwise provided in this subsection, for each period in which an employee continues life insurance after retirement or while in receipt of compensation under subchapter I of chapter 81 of this title because of disease or injury to the employee, as provided under section 8706(b) of this title, a sum equal to one-half of the amount which is withheld from the employee's annuity or compensation under section 8707 of this title shall be contributed by the Office from annual appropriations which are authorized to be made for that purpose and which may be made available until expended.

(2) Contributions under this subsection—

(A) shall not be made other than with respect to individuals who retire, or commence receiving compensation, after December 31, 1989;

(B) shall not be made with respect to any individual for months after the calendar month in which such individual becomes 65 years of age; and

(C) shall, in the case of any individual who elects coverage under subparagraph (B) of section 8706(b)(3) of this title, be equal to the amount which would apply under this subsection if such individual had instead elected coverage under subparagraph (A) of such section.

(3) The United States Postal Service shall pay the contributions required under this subsection with respect to any individual who—

(A) first becomes an annuitant by reason of retirement from employment with the United

States Postal Service after December 31, 1989; or

(B) commences receiving compensation under subchapter I of chapter 81 of this title (because of disease or injury to the individual) after December 31, 1989, if the position last held by the individual before commencing to receive such compensation was within the United States Postal Service.

(Pub. L. 89–554, Sept. 6, 1966, 80 Stat. 595; Pub. L. 90–206, title IV, § 403, Dec. 16, 1967, 81 Stat. 647; Pub. L. 95–454, title IX, § 906(a)(2), Oct. 13, 1978, 92 Stat. 1224; Pub. L. 101–303, § 2, May 29, 1990, 104 Stat. 250; Pub. L. 104–186, title II, § 215(18), Aug. 20, 1996, 110 Stat. 1746.)

HISTORICAL AND REVISION NOTES

Derivation	U.S. Code	Revised Statutes and Statutes at Large
(a), (c)	5 U.S.C. 2094(b).	Aug. 17, 1954, ch. 752, § 5(b), 68 Stat. 738.
(b)	2 U.S.C. 128.	Aug. 5, 1955, ch. 568, § 101 (4th par. under "Administrative Provisions"), 69 Stat. 513.

Standard changes are made to conform with the definitions applicable and the style of this title as outlined in the preface to the report.

AMENDMENTS

1996—Subsec. (b). Pub. L. 104–186 substituted "Chief Administrative Officer of the House of Representatives, the Chief Administrative Officer may contribute the sum required by subsection (a) of this section from the applicable accounts of the House of Representatives." for "Clerk of the House of Representatives, the Clerk may contribute the sum required by subsection (a) of this section from the contingent fund of the House."

1990—Subsec. (d). Pub. L. 101–303 added subsec. (d).

1978—Subsec. (a). Pub. L. 95–454 substituted "Office of Personnel Management" for "Civil Service Commission".

1967—Subsec. (a). Pub. L. 90–206 substituted provisions setting the sum to be withheld at one-half the amount withheld from the pay of the employee under section 8707 of this title for provisions setting the sum to be withheld at a rate to be determined by the Commission not to exceed one-half of the amount withheld under section 8707 of this title.

EFFECTIVE DATE OF 1978 AMENDMENT

Amendment by Pub. L. 95–454 effective 90 days after Oct. 13, 1978, see section 907 of Pub. L. 95–454, set out as a note under section 1101 of this title.

EFFECTIVE DATE OF 1967 AMENDMENT

Amendment by Pub. L. 90–206 effective on first day of first pay period which begins on or after sixtieth day following December 16, 1967, see section 405(a) of Pub. L. 90–206, set out as a note under section 8704 of this title.

RETROACTIVE EFFECT OF 1967 AMENDMENT

Amendment by Pub. L. 90–206 to have no effect in case of an employee who died, was finally separated, or retired prior to Dec. 16, 1967, see section 405(c) of Pub. L. 90–206, set out as a note under section 8704 of this title.

SECTION REFERRED TO IN OTHER SECTIONS

This section is referred to in sections 8707, 8714, 8714a, 8714d of this title; title 2 section 162b; title 40 section 214d.

§ 8709. Insurance policies

(a) The Office of Personnel Management, without regard to section 5 of title 41, may purchase from one or more life insurance companies a policy or policies of group life and accidental death and dismemberment insurance to provide the benefits specified by this chapter. A company must meet the following requirements:

(1) It must be licensed to transact life and accidental death and dismemberment insurance under the laws of 48 of the States and the District of Columbia.

(2) It must have in effect, on the most recent December 31 for which information is available to the Office, an amount of employee group life insurance equal to at least 1 percent of the total amount of employee group life insurance in the United States in all life insurance companies.

(b) A company issuing a policy under subsection (a) of this section shall establish an administrative office under a name approved by the Office.

(c) The Office at any time may discontinue a policy purchased from a company under subsection (a) of this section.

(d)(1) The provisions of any contract under this chapter which relate to the nature or extent of coverage or benefits (including payments with respect to benefits) shall supersede and preempt any law of any State or political subdivision thereof, or any regulation issued thereunder, which relates to group life insurance to the extent that the law or regulation is inconsistent with the contractual provisions.

(2) For the purpose of this section, "State" means a State of the United States, the District of Columbia, the Commonwealth of Puerto Rico, and a territory or possession of the United States.

(Pub. L. 89–554, Sept. 6, 1966, 80 Stat. 596; Pub. L. 95–454, title IX, § 906(a)(2), (3), Oct. 13, 1978, 92 Stat. 1224; Pub. L. 96–427, § 5(a), Oct. 10, 1980, 94 Stat. 1834.)

HISTORICAL AND REVISION NOTES

Derivation	U.S. Code	Revised Statutes and Statutes at Large
....	5 U.S.C. 2096 (less (c)–(e)).	Aug. 17, 1954, ch. 752, § 7 (less (c)–(e)), 68 Stat. 739.

In subsection (a), the words "as determined by it" are omitted as unnecessary.

Standard changes are made to conform with the definitions applicable and the style of this title as outlined in the preface to the report.

AMENDMENTS

1980—Subsec. (d). Pub. L. 96–427 added subsec. (d).

1978—Subsecs. (a) to (c). Pub. L. 95–454 substituted "Office of Personnel Management" and "Office" for "Civil Service Commission" and "Commission", respectively, wherever appearing.

EFFECTIVE DATE OF 1980 AMENDMENT

Amendment by Pub. L. 96–427 effective Oct. 10, 1980, with the amendment to have no effect in case of an employee who died, was separated, or retired before Oct. 10, 1980, see section 10(a) of Pub. L. 96–427, set out as a note under section 8701 of this title.

EFFECTIVE DATE OF 1978 AMENDMENT

Amendment by Pub. L. 95–454 effective 90 days after Oct. 13, 1978, see section 907 of Pub. L. 95–454, set out as a note under section 1101 of this title.

SECTION REFERRED TO IN OTHER SECTIONS

This section is referred to in sections 8705, 8706, 8707, 8708, 8714a, 8714b, 8714c of this title.

§ 8710. Reinsurance

(a) The Office of Personnel Management shall arrange with a company issuing a policy under this chapter for the reinsurance, under conditions approved by the Office, of portions of the total amount of insurance under the policy, determined under this section, with other life insurance companies which elect to participate in the reinsurance.

(b) The Office shall determine for and in advance of a policy year which companies are eligible to participate as reinsurers and the amount of insurance under a policy which is to be allocated to the issuing company and to reinsurers. The Office shall make this determination at least every 3 years and when a participating company withdraws.

(c) The Office shall establish a formula under which the amount of insurance retained by an issuing company after ceding reinsurance, and the amount of reinsurance ceded to each reinsurer, is in proportion to the total amount of each company's group life insurance, excluding insurance purchased under this chapter, in force in the United States on the determination date, which is the most recent December 31 for which information is available to the Office. In determining the proportions, the portion of a company's group life insurance in force on the determination date in excess of $100,000,000 shall be reduced by—

(1) 25 percent of the first $100,000,000 of the excess;

(2) 50 percent of the second $100,000,000 of the excess;

(3) 75 percent of the third $100,000,000 of the excess; and

(4) 95 percent of the remaining excess.

However, the amount retained by or ceded to a company may not exceed 25 percent of the amount of the company's total life insurance in force in the United States on the determination date.

(d) A fraternal benefit association which is—

(1) licensed to transact life insurance under the laws of a State or the District of Columbia; and

(2) engaged in issuing insurance certificates on the lives of employees of the United States exclusively;

is eligible to act as a reinsuring company and may be allocated an amount of reinsurance equal to 25 percent of its total life insurance in force on employees of the United States on the determination date named by subsection (c) of this section.

(e) An issuing company or reinsurer is entitled, as a minimum, to be allocated an amount of insurance under the policy equal to any reduction from December 31, 1953, to the determination date, in the amount of the company's group life insurance under policies issued to associations of employees of the United States. However, any increase under this subsection in the amount allocated is reduced by the amount in force on the determination date of any policy

covering life insurance agreements assumed by the Office.

(f) The Office may modify the computations under this section as necessary to carry out the intent of this section.

(Pub. L. 89–554, Sept. 6, 1966, 80 Stat. 596; Pub. L. 95–454, title IX, § 906(a)(2), (3), Oct. 13, 1978, 92 Stat. 1224.)

HISTORICAL AND REVISION NOTES

Derivation	U.S. Code	Revised Statutes and Statutes at Large
....	5 U.S.C. 2096(c)–(e).	Aug. 17, 1954, ch. 752, § 7(c)–(e), 68 Stat. 739. Aug. 11, 1955, ch. 794, § 3, 69 Stat. 677.

The section is reorganized to clarify the steps in the computation of the insurance allocable to issuing and reinsuring companies.

In subsections (c) and (d), references to the first determination date, December 31, 1953, are omitted as executed.

Standard changes are made to conform with the definitions applicable and the style of this title as outlined in the preface to the report.

AMENDMENTS

1978—Subsecs. (a) to (c), (e), (f). Pub. L. 95–454 substituted "Office of Personnel Management" and "Office" for "Civil Service Commission" and "Commission", respectively, wherever appearing.

EFFECTIVE DATE OF 1978 AMENDMENT

Amendment by Pub. L. 95–454 effective 90 days after Oct. 13, 1978, see section 907 of Pub. L. 95–454, set out as a note under section 1101 of this title.

SECTION REFERRED TO IN OTHER SECTIONS

This section is referred to in sections 8714a, 8714b, 8714c of this title.

§ 8711. Basic tables of premium rates

(a) A policy purchased under this chapter shall include, for the first policy year, basic tables of premium rates as follows:

(1) For group life insurance, a schedule of basic premium rates by age which the Office of Personnel Management determines to be consistent with the lowest schedule of basic premium rates generally charged for new group life insurance policies issued to large employers.

(2) For group accidental death and dismemberment insurance, a basic premium rate which the Office determines is consistent with the lowest rate generally charged for new group accidental death and dismemberment policies issued to large employers.

The schedule for group life insurance, except as otherwise provided by this section, shall be applied to the distribution by age of the amounts of group life insurance under the policy at its date of issuance to determine an average basic premium rate per $1,000 of life insurance.

(b) The policy shall provide that the basic premium rates determined for the first policy year continue for later policy years except as readjusted for a later year based on experience under the policy. The company issuing the policy may make the readjustment on a basis that the Office determines in advance of the policy year is consistent with the general practice of life insurance companies under policies of group life and group accidental death and dismemberment insurance issued to large employers.

(c) The policy shall provide that if the Office determines that ascertaining the actual age distribution of the amounts of group life insurance in force at the date of issue of the policy or at the end of the first or any later year of insurance thereunder would not be possible except at a disproportionately high expense, the Office may approve the determination of a tentative average group life premium rate, for the first or any later policy year, instead of using the actual age distribution. The Office, on request by the company issuing the policy, shall redetermine the tentative average premium rate during any policy year, if experience indicates that the assumptions made in determining that rate were incorrect for that year.

(d) The policy shall stipulate the maximum expense and risk charges for the first policy year. The Office shall determine these charges on a basis consistent with the general level of charges made by life insurance companies under policies of group life and accidental death and dismemberment insurance issued to large employers. The maximum charges continue from year to year, except that the Office may redetermine them for any year either by agreement with the company issuing the policy or on written notice given to the company at least 1 year before the beginning of the year for which the redetermined maximum charges will be effective.

(Pub. L. 89–554, Sept. 6, 1966, 80 Stat. 597; Pub. L. 95–454, title IX, § 906(a)(2), (3), Oct. 13, 1978, 92 Stat. 1224.)

HISTORICAL AND REVISION NOTES

Derivation	U.S. Code	Revised Statutes and Statutes at Large
....	5 U.S.C. 2097 (less (d)).	Aug. 17, 1954, ch. 752, § 8 (less (d)), 68 Stat. 740.

In subsection (a), the word "policy" is substituted for "policy or policies" on authority of 1 U.S.C. 1. In subsections (b) and (c), the words "The policy" are substituted for "Each policy so purchased". In subsections (b), (c), and (d), the word "insurance", preceding the word "company", is omitted as unnecessary; and the word "company" is substituted for "company or companies" on authority of 1 U.S.C. 1.

Standard changes are made to conform with the definitions applicable and the style of this title as outlined in the preface to the report.

AMENDMENTS

1978—Subsecs. (a) to (d). Pub. L. 95–454 substituted "Office of Personnel Management" and "Office" for "Civil Service Commission" and "Commission", respectively, wherever appearing.

EFFECTIVE DATE OF 1978 AMENDMENT

Amendment by Pub. L. 95–454 effective 90 days after Oct. 13, 1978, see section 907 of Pub. L. 95–454, set out as a note under section 1101 of this title.

SECTION REFERRED TO IN OTHER SECTIONS

This section is referred to in sections 8714a, 8714b, 8714c of this title.

§ 8712. Annual accounting; special contingency reserve

A policy purchased under this chapter shall provide for an accounting to the Office of Personnel Management not later than 90 days after the end of each policy year. The accounting shall set forth, in a form approved by the Office—

(1) the amounts of premiums actually accrued under the policy from its date of issue to the end of the policy year;

(2) the total of all mortality and other claim charges incurred for that period; and

(3) the amounts of the insurers' expense and risk charges for that period.

An excess of the total of paragraph (1) of this section over the sum of paragraphs (2) and (3) of this section shall be held by the company issuing the policy as a special contingency reserve to be used by the company only for charges under the policy. The reserve shall bear interest at a rate determined in advance of each policy year by the company and approved by the Office as being consistent with the rate generally used by the company for similar funds held under other group life insurance policies. When the Office determines that the special contingency reserve has attained an amount estimated by it to make satisfactory provision for adverse fluctuations in future charges under the policy, any further excess shall be deposited in the Treasury of the United States to the credit of the Employees' Life Insurance Fund. When a policy is discontinued, any balance remaining in the special contingency reserve after all charges have been made shall be deposited in the Treasury to the credit of the Fund. The company may make the deposit in equal monthly installments over a period of not more than 2 years.

(Pub. L. 89–554, Sept. 6, 1966, 80 Stat. 598; Pub. L. 95–454, title IX, § 906(a)(2), (3), Oct. 13, 1978, 92 Stat. 1224.)

HISTORICAL AND REVISION NOTES

Derivation	U.S. Code	Revised Statutes and Statutes at Large
....	5 U.S.C. 2097(d).	Aug. 17, 1954, ch. 752, §8(d), 68 Stat. 741.

The words "A policy purchased under this chapter" are substituted for "Each such policy" for clarity. The word "insurance", preceding the word "company", is omitted as unnecessary; and the word "company" is substituted for "company or companies" on authority of 1 U.S.C. 1.

The words "Employees' Life Insurance Fund" are substituted for "fund".

Standard changes are made to conform with the definitions applicable and the style of this title as outlined in the preface to the report.

AMENDMENTS

1978—Pub. L. 95–454 substituted "Office of Personnel Management" and "Office" for "Civil Service Commission" and "Commission", respectively.

EFFECTIVE DATE OF 1978 AMENDMENT

Amendment by Pub. L. 95–454 effective 90 days after Oct. 13, 1978, see section 907 of Pub. L. 95–454, set out as a note under section 1101 of this title.

SECTION REFERRED TO IN OTHER SECTIONS

This section is referred to in sections 8714a, 8714b, 8714c of this title.

§ 8713. Effect of other statutes

Any provision of law outside of this chapter provides coverage or any other benefit under this chapter to any individuals who (based on their being employed by an entity other than the Government) would not otherwise be eligible for any such coverage or benefit shall not apply with respect to any individual appointed, transferred, or otherwise commencing that type of employment on or after October 1, 1988.

(Added Pub. L. 100–238, title I, § 108(a)(2)(A), Jan. 8, 1988, 101 Stat. 1747.)

PRIOR PROVISIONS

A prior section 8713, Pub. L. 89–554, Sept. 6, 1966, 80 Stat. 598; Pub. L. 90–83, § 1(93), Sept. 11, 1967, 81 Stat. 219; Pub. L. 95–454, title IX, § 906(a)(1), (4), Oct. 13, 1978, 92 Stat. 1224, 1225, provided for an advisory committee to be appointed by the Director of the Office of Personnel Management to be composed of five employees insured under this chapter, to serve without additional pay, to advise the Office regarding matters of concern to employees under this chapter, prior to repeal by Pub. L. 96–427, § 9(a), Oct. 10, 1980, 94 Stat. 1837, effective Oct. 10, 1980, with the repeal to have no effect in the case of an employee who died, was separated, or retired before Oct. 10, 1980.

SECTION REFERRED TO IN OTHER SECTIONS

This section is referred to in title 22 section 6103; title 25 section 450i.

§ 8714. Employees' Life Insurance Fund

(a) The amounts withheld from employees under section 8707 of this title and the sums contributed from appropriations and funds under section 8708 of this title shall be deposited in the Treasury of the United States to the credit of the Employees' Life Insurance Fund. The Fund is available without fiscal year limitation for—

(1) premium payments under an insurance policy purchased under this chapter; and

(2) expenses incurred by the Office of Personnel Management in the administration of this chapter within the limitations that may be specified annually by appropriation acts.

(b) The Secretary of the Treasury may invest and reinvest any of the money in the Fund in interest-bearing obligations of the United States, and may sell these obligations for the purposes of the Fund. The interest on and the proceeds from the sale of these obligations, and the income derived from dividend or premium rate adjustments from insurers, become a part of the Fund.

(c)(1) No tax, fee, or other monetary payment may be imposed or collected by any State, the District of Columbia, or the Commonwealth of Puerto Rico, or by any political subdivision or other governmental authority thereof, on, or with respect to, any premium paid under an insurance policy purchased under this chapter.

(2) Paragraph (1) of this subsection shall not be construed to exempt any company issuing a policy of insurance under this chapter from the imposition, payment, or collection of a tax, fee, or other monetary payment on the net income

or profit accruing to or realized by that company from business conducted under this chapter, if that tax, fee, or payment is applicable to a broad range of business activity.

(Pub. L. 89–554, Sept. 6, 1966, 80 Stat. 598; Pub. L. 95–454, title IX, § 906(a)(2), Oct. 13, 1978, 92 Stat. 1224; Pub. L. 96–499, title IV, § 405(a), Dec. 5, 1980, 94 Stat. 2606.)

HISTORICAL AND REVISION NOTES

Derivation	U.S. Code	Revised Statutes and Statutes at Large
....	5 U.S.C. 2094(c) (less applicability to 5 U.S.C. 2099), (d).	Aug. 17, 1954, ch. 752, § 5(c) (less applicability to § 10), 68 Stat. 739. Aug. 11, 1955, ch. 794, § 1(a) "(c) (less applicability to § 10)", (b), 69 Stat. 676. Apr. 11, 1958, Pub. L. 85–377, § 1 (less applicability to § 10), 72 Stat. 87.

In subsection (a), the words "of the Employees' Life Insurance Fund" are substituted for "of a fund which is hereby created". The proviso which made appropriations available to the Commission for salaries and expenses for the fiscal year 1955 available on a reimbursable basis for necessary administrative expenses for carrying out the purposes of this chapter is omitted as executed.

Standard changes are made to conform with the definitions applicable and the style of this title as outlined in the preface to the report.

AMENDMENTS

1980—Subsec. (c). Pub. L. 96–499 added subsec. (c).

1978—Subsec. (a)(2). Pub. L. 95–454 substituted "Office of Personnel Management" for "Civil Service Commission".

EFFECTIVE DATE OF 1980 AMENDMENT

Section 405(b) of Pub. L. 96–499 provided that: "The amendment made by subsection (a) [amending this section] shall take effect on the date of the enactment of this Act [Dec. 5, 1980], and shall apply with respect to premiums paid on or after such date."

EFFECTIVE DATE OF 1978 AMENDMENT

Amendment by Pub. L. 95–454 effective 90 days after Oct. 13, 1978, see section 907 of Pub. L. 95–454, set out as a note under section 1101 of this title.

FUNDING

Pub. L. 103–409, § 4, Oct. 25, 1994, 108 Stat. 4232, provided that: "Notwithstanding section 8714(a)(1) of title 5, United States Code, the Office of Personnel Management shall retain in the Employees' Life Insurance Fund such portion of premium payments otherwise due as will, no later than September 30, 1995, permanently reduce the contingency reserve established under the third sentence of section 8712 of such title 5 by an amount equal to the amount by which payments from the Employees' Life Insurance Fund during the fiscal year ending September 30, 1995, exceed the payments that would have been paid had the amendments made by this Act [enacting section 8714d of this title] not been enacted."

SECTION REFERRED TO IN OTHER SECTIONS

This section is referred to in sections 8714a, 8714b, 8714c of this title; title 20 section 125; title 25 section 450i.

§ 8714a. Optional insurance

(a) Under the conditions, directives, and terms specified in sections 8709–8712 of this title, the

Office of Personnel Management, without regard to section 5 of title 41, may purchase a policy which shall make available to each insured employee equal amounts of optional life insurance and accidental death and dismemberment insurance in addition to the amounts provided in section 8704(a) of this title.

(b) The optional life insurance and accidental death and dismemberment insurance shall be made available to each insured employee under such conditions as the Office shall prescribe and in amounts approved by the Office but not more than the greater of $10,000 or an amount which, when added to the amount provided in section 8704(a) of this title, makes the sum of his insurance equal to his annual pay.

(c)(1) Except as otherwise provided in this subsection, the optional insurance on an employee stops on his separation from service or 12 months after discontinuance of his pay, whichever is earlier, subject to a provision for temporary extension of life insurance coverage and for conversion to an individual policy of life insurance under conditions approved by the Office.

(2)(A) In the case of any employee who retires on an immediate annuity and has been insured under this section throughout—

(i) the 5 years of service immediately preceding the date of such retirement, or

(ii) the full period or periods of service during which the employee was entitled to be insured, if less than 5 years,

the amount of optional life insurance only which has been in force throughout such period may be continued, under conditions determined by the Office.

(B) In the case of any employee who becomes entitled to receive compensation under subchapter I of chapter 81 of this title because of disease or injury to the employee and has been insured under this section throughout—

(i) the 5 years of service immediately preceding the date such employee becomes entitled to such compensation, or

(ii) the full period or periods of service during which the employee was entitled to be insured, if less than 5 years,

the amount of optional life insurance only which has been in force throughout such period may be continued, under conditions determined by the Office, during the period the employee is receiving such compensation for disease or injury and is held by the Secretary of Labor or his delegate to be unable to return to duty.

(C) The amount of optional life insurance continued under subparagraph (A) or subparagraph (B) of this paragraph shall be reduced by 2 percent at the end of each full calendar month after the date the employee becomes 65 years of age and is retired or is receiving compensation for disease or injury. The Office shall prescribe minimum amounts, not less than 25 percent of the amount of life insurance in force before the first reduction, to which the insurance may be reduced.

(3) Notwithstanding paragraph (c)(1) of this section,[1] a justice or judge of the United States

as defined by section 8701(a)(5) of this title who resigns his office without meeting the requirements of section 371(a) of title 28, United States Code, for continuation of the judicial salary shall have the right to convert regular optional life insurance coverage issued under this section during his judicial service to an individual policy of life insurance under the same conditions approved by the Office governing conversion of basic life insurance coverage for employees eligible as provided in section 8706(a) of this title.

(d)(1) During each period in which an employee has the optional insurance the full cost thereof shall be withheld from his pay. During each period in which an employee continues optional life insurance after retirement or while in receipt of compensation for work injuries, as provided in section 8706(b) of this title, the full cost thereof shall be withheld from his annuity or compensation, except that, at the end of the calendar month in which he becomes 65 years of age, the optional life insurance shall be without cost to him. Amounts so withheld shall be deposited, used, and invested as provided in section 8714 of this title and shall be reported and accounted for separately from amounts withheld and contributed under sections 8707 and 8708 of this title.

(2) If an agency fails to withhold the proper cost of optional insurance from an individual's salary, compensation, or retirement annuity, the collection of amounts properly due may be waived by the agency if, in the judgment of the agency, the individual is without fault and recovery would be against equity and good conscience. However, if the agency so waives the collection of any unpaid amount, the agency shall submit an amount equal to the uncollected amount to the Office for deposit in the Employees' Life Insurance Fund.

(3) Notwithstanding paragraph (1), an employee who is subject to withholdings under this subsection and whose pay, annuity, or compensation is insufficient to cover such withholdings may nevertheless continue optional insurance if the employee arranges to pay currently into the Employees' Life Insurance Fund, through the agency or retirement system which administers pay, annuity, or compensation, an amount equal to the withholdings that would otherwise be required under this subsection.

(e) The cost of the optional insurance shall be determined from time to time by the Office on the basis of such age groups as it considers appropriate.

(f) The amount of optional life, or life and accidental death, insurance in force on an employee at the date of his death shall be paid as provided in section 8705 of this title.

(Added Pub. L. 90–206, title IV, § 404(1), Dec. 16, 1967, 81 Stat. 647; amended Pub. L. 95–454, title IX, § 906(a)(2), (3), Oct. 13, 1978, 92 Stat. 1224; Pub. L. 95–583, § 1(c), Nov. 2, 1978, 92 Stat. 2481; Pub. L. 96–427, § 6, Oct. 10, 1980, 94 Stat. 1834; Pub. L. 98–353, title II, § 206, July 10, 1984, 98 Stat. 351, as amended by Pub. L. 99–336, § 7(1), June 19, 1986, 100 Stat. 639; Pub. L. 99–335, title II, § 207(k)(3), June 6, 1986, 100 Stat. 597; Pub. L. 99–336, § 7(1), June 19, 1986, 100 Stat. 639; Pub. L. 105–311, § 6(2), Oct. 30, 1998, 112 Stat. 2951.)

---

[1] So in original. Probably should be "paragraph (1) of this subsection,".

AMENDMENTS

1998—Subsec. (d)(3). Pub. L. 105–311 added par. (3).

1986—Subsec. (c)(1). Pub. L. 99–336 amended Pub. L. 98–353, § 206, generally. See 1984 Amendment note below.

Pub. L. 99–335 amended par. (1) generally, effective Jan. 1, 1987. Prior to such effective date, par. (1) read as follows: "The optional insurance on an employee stops on his separation from service, 12 months after discontinuance of his pay, or on his entry on active duty or active duty for training, as provided in sections 8706(a) and 8706(c) of this title. Justices and judges of the United States described in section 8701(a)(5)(ii) and (iii) of this chapter are deemed to continue in active employment for purposes of this chapter."

1984—Subsec. (c)(1). Pub. L. 98–353, § 206, as amended generally by Pub. L. 99–336, inserted sentence which deemed justices and judges described in section 8701(a)(5)(ii) and (iii) of this chapter to continue in active employment for purposes of this chapter.

Subsec. (c)(3). Pub. L. 98–353, § 206, added par. (3).

1980—Subsec. (c)(2)(C). Pub. L. 96–427, § 6(a), substituted provisions that the amount of optional life insurance shall be reduced by 2% at the end of each calendar month after the date the employee becomes 65 years of age and is retired or is receiving compensation for disease or injury and that the Office shall prescribe minimum amount of life insurance in force before the first reduction to which the insurance may be reduced for provisions that such optional insurance be subject to the same monthly reductions as required for regular life insurance under section 8706(b)(3) of this title.

Subsec. (d). Pub. L. 96–427, § 6(b), designated existing provisions as par. (1) and added par. (2).

1978—Subsecs. (a), (b). Pub. L. 95–454 substituted "Office of Personnel Management" for "Civil Service Commission" and "Office" for "Commission" wherever appearing.

Subsec. (c)(1). Pub. L. 95–583, § 1(c)(1), substituted reference to section "8706(c)" for "8706(d)".

Subsec. (c)(2). Pub. L. 95–583, § 1(c)(2), added par. (2) and struck out former par. (2) which read as follows: "So much of the optional life insurance in force on an employee on the date he retires on an immediate annuity or becomes entitled to receive compensation for work injuries which has been in force for not less than—

"(A) the full period or periods of service during which the optional insurance was available to him; or

"(B) the 12 years of service immediately preceding his retirement or beginning date of entitlement to compensation for work injuries and during which the optional insurance was available to him;

whichever is shorter, may be continued—

"(A) after retirement, under the same conditions (except with respect to cost but including reduction of the amount continued) as provided in section 8706(b) of this title; or

"(B) while in receipt of compensation for work injuries under the same conditions (except with respect to cost) as provided in section 8706(c) of this title."

Pub. L. 95–454, which substituted "Office" for "Commission", was executed to text of subsec. (c)(2) as amended by Pub. L. 95–583. See Effective Date of 1978 Amendments note below.

Subsec. (d). Pub. L. 95–583, § 1(c)(3), struck out "or 8706(c)" after "section 8706(b)".

Subsec. (e). Pub. L. 95–454 substituted "Office" for "Commission".

EFFECTIVE DATE OF 1998 AMENDMENT

Amendment by Pub. L. 105–311 effective on the first day of the first applicable pay period beginning on or after Oct. 30, 1998, see section 11(d) of Pub. L. 105–311, set out as a note under section 8701 of this title.

EFFECTIVE DATE OF 1986 AMENDMENT

Amendment by Pub. L. 99–335 effective Jan. 1, 1987, see section 702(a) of Pub. L. 99–335, set out as an Effective Date note under section 8401 of this title.

EFFECTIVE DATE OF 1984 AMENDMENT

Amendment by Pub. L. 98–353, § 206, as amended generally by Pub. L. 99–336, § 7(1), applicable to any justice or judge who retires under 28 U.S.C. 371(a) or (b) or 372(a) on or after January 1, 1982, see section 207 of Pub. L. 98–353, as amended generally by Pub. L. 99–336, § 7(2), set out as a note under section 8706 of this title.

EFFECTIVE DATE OF 1980 AMENDMENT

Amendment by Pub. L. 96–427 effective Oct. 10, 1980, with amendment to have no effect in case of an employee who died, was separated, or retired before Oct. 10, 1980, see section 10(a) of Pub. L. 96–427, set out as a note under section 8701 of this title.

EFFECTIVE DATE OF 1978 AMENDMENTS

Amendment by Pub. L. 95–583 effective Nov. 2, 1978, see section 3 of Pub. L. 95–583, set out as a note under section 8706 of this title.

Amendment by Pub. L. 95–454 effective 90 days after Oct. 13, 1978, see section 907 of Pub. L. 95–454, set out as a note under section 1101 of this title.

EFFECTIVE DATE

Section 405(b) of Pub. L. 90–206 provided that:

"(1) The amendments made by section 404 of this Act [enacting this section and amending analysis preceding section 8701 of this title] shall take effect on the first day of the first pay period which begins on or after the one hundred and eightieth day following the date of enactment [Dec. 16, 1967], or on any earlier date that the Civil Service Commission may prescribe, which is at least sixty days after the date of enactment [Dec. 16, 1967]. In the case of an employee who dies during the period beginning on the date of enactment [Dec. 16, 1967] and ending on the effective date prescribed by or pursuant to this subsection, or during the sixty days immediately following such period if the Commission determines that he did not have a reasonable opportunity to elect the optional insurance made available by section 404, the insurance of such employee shall be determined as if the amendments made by section 404 had been in effect on the date of such death, and the employee had elected to receive the maximum amount of optional insurance available to him under such amendments. An employee who retires during the period beginning on the date of enactment and ending on the effective date prescribed by or pursuant to this subsection shall have an opportunity to elect the optional insurance made available by section 404.

"(2) In the case of an employee in the service on the effective date prescribed by or pursuant to this subsection, (i) the period during which such employee may elect to receive optional insurance under the amendment made by section 404 shall not expire prior to the sixtieth day after such effective date, and (ii) for the purpose of determining the amount of insurance to be continued after retirement, the period during which such optional insurance was available to such employee shall not be considered to have commenced prior to the expiration of sixty days following such effective date."

RETROACTIVE EFFECT

Enactment of this section by Pub. L. 90–206 to have no effect in the case of an employee who died, was finally separated, or retired prior to Dec. 16, 1967, see section 405(c) of Pub. L. 90–206, set out as an Retroactive Effect of 1967 Amendment note under section 8704 of this title.

AVAILABILITY OF CERTAIN FUNDS IN EMPLOYEES' LIFE INSURANCE FUND

Section 11 of Pub. L. 96–427 provided that: "Amounts credited to the Employees' Life Insurance Fund under section 8714a(d) of title 5, United States Code shall be available for expenses incurred by the Office of Personnel Management in implementing the amendments made by sections 7 and 8 of this Act [enacting sections 8714b, 8714c, and 8701(d) of this title]."

SECTION REFERRED TO IN OTHER SECTIONS

This section is referred to in sections 8714b, 8714c, 8714d of this title.

§ 8714b. Additional optional life insurance

(a) Under the conditions, directives, and terms specified in sections 8709 through 8712 of this title, the Office of Personnel Management, without regard to section 5 of title 41, may purchase a policy which shall make available to each employee insured under section 8702 of this title amounts of additional optional life insurance (without accidental death and dismemberment insurance). An employee may elect coverage under this section without regard to whether the employee has elected coverage under optional insurance available under section 8714a of this title.

(b) The additional optional insurance provided under this section shall be made available to each eligible employee who has elected coverage under this section, under conditions the Office shall prescribe, in multiples, at the employee's election, of 1, 2, 3, 4, or 5 times the annual rate of basic pay payable to the employee (rounded to the next higher multiple of $1,000). An employee may reduce or stop coverage elected pursuant to this section at any time.

(c)(1) Except as otherwise provided in this subsection, the additional optional insurance elected by an employee pursuant to this section shall stop on separation from service or 12 months after discontinuance of his pay, whichever is earlier, subject to a provision for temporary extension of life insurance coverage and for conversion to an individual policy of life insurance under conditions approved by the Office. Justices and judges of the United States described in section 8701(a)(5)(ii) and (iii) of this chapter are deemed to continue in active employment for purposes of this chapter. A justice or judge of the United States as defined by section 8701(a)(5) of this title who resigns his office without meeting the requirements of section 371(a) of title 28, United States Code, for continuation of the judicial salary shall have the right to convert additional optional life insurance coverage issued under this section during his judicial service to an individual policy of life insurance under the same conditions approved by the Office governing conversion of basic life insurance coverage for employees eligible as provided in section 8706(a) of this title.

(2) In the case of any employee who retires on an immediate annuity or who becomes entitled to receive compensation under subchapter I of chapter 81 of this title because of disease or injury to the employee, so much of the additional optional insurance as has been in force for not less than—

(A) the 5 years of service immediately preceding the date of retirement or entitlement to compensation, or

(B) the full period or periods of service during which the insurance was available to the employee, if fewer than 5 years,

may be continued under conditions determined by the Office after retirement or while the employee is receiving compensation under subchapter I of chapter 81 of this title and is held by the Secretary of Labor (or the Secretary's delegate) to be unable to return to duty.

(3) The amount of additional optional insurance continued under paragraph (2) shall be continued, with or without reduction, in accordance with the employee's written election at the time eligibility to continue insurance during retirement or receipt of compensation arises, as follows:

(A) The employee may elect to have withholdings cease in accordance with subsection (d), in which case—

(i) the amount of additional optional insurance continued under paragraph (2) shall be reduced each month by 2 percent effective at the beginning of the second calendar month after the date the employee becomes 65 years of age and is retired or is in receipt of compensation; and

(ii) the reduction under clause (i) shall continue for 50 months at which time the insurance shall stop.

(B) The employee may, instead of the option under subparagraph (A), elect to have the full cost of additional optional insurance continue to be withheld from such employee's annuity or compensation on and after the date such withholdings would otherwise cease pursuant to an election under subparagraph (A), in which case the amount of additional optional insurance continued under paragraph (2) shall not be reduced, subject to paragraph (4).

(C) An employee who does not make any election under the preceding provisions of this paragraph shall be treated as if such employee had made an election under subparagraph (A).

(4) If an employee makes an election under paragraph (3)(B), that individual may subsequently cancel such election, in which case additional optional insurance shall be determined as if the individual had originally made an election under paragraph (3)(A).

(5)(A) An employee whose additional optional insurance under this section would otherwise stop in accordance with paragraph (1) and who is not eligible to continue insurance under paragraph (2) may elect, under conditions prescribed by the Office of Personnel Management, to continue all or a portion of so much of the additional optional insurance as has been in force for not less than—

(i) the 5 years of service immediately preceding the date of the event which would cause insurance to stop under paragraph (1); or

(ii) the full period or periods of service during which the insurance was available to the employee, if fewer than 5 years,

at group rates established for purposes of this section, in lieu of conversion to an individual policy. The amount of insurance continued under this paragraph shall be reduced by 50 percent effective at the beginning of the second calendar month after the date the employee or former employee attains age 70 and shall stop at the beginning of the second calendar month after attainment of age 80, subject to a provision for temporary extension of life insurance coverage and for conversion to an individual policy of life insurance under conditions approved by the Office. Alternatively, insurance continued under this paragraph may be reduced or stopped at any time the employee or former employee elects.

(B) When an employee or former employee elects to continue additional optional insurance under this paragraph following separation from service or 12 months without pay, the insured individual shall submit timely payment of the full cost thereof, plus any amount the Office determines necessary to cover associated administrative expenses, in such manner as the Office shall prescribe by regulation. Amounts required under this subparagraph shall be deposited, used, and invested as provided under section 8714 and shall be reported and accounted for together with amounts withheld under section 8714a(d).

(C)(i) Subject to clause (ii), no election to continue additional optional insurance may be made under this paragraph 3 years after the effective date of this paragraph.

(ii) On and after the date on which an election may not be made under clause (i), all additional optional insurance under this paragraph for former employees shall terminate, subject to a provision for temporary extension of life insurance coverage and for conversion to an individual policy of life insurance under conditions approved by the Office.

(d)(1) During each period in which the additional optional insurance is in force on an employee the full cost thereof shall be withheld from the employee's pay. During each period in which an employee continues additional optional insurance after retirement or while in receipt of compensation under subchapter I of chapter 81 of this title because of disease or injury to the employee, as provided in subsection (c) of this section, the full cost thereof shall be withheld from the former employee's annuity or compensation, except that, if insurance is continued as provided under subsection (c)(3)(A), beginning at the end of the calendar month in which the former employee becomes 65 years of age, the additional optional life insurance shall be without cost to the former employee. Amounts so withheld (and any amounts withheld as provided in subsection (c)(3)(B)) shall be deposited, used, and invested as provided in section 8714 of this title and shall be reported and accounted for together with amounts withheld under section 8714a(d) of this title.

(2) If an agency fails to withhold the proper cost of additional optional insurance from an individual's salary, compensation, or retirement annuity, the collection of amounts properly due may be waived by the agency if, in the judgment of the agency, the individual is without fault and recovery would be against equity and good conscience. However, if the agency so waives the collection of any unpaid amount, the agency shall submit an amount equal to the uncollected amount to the Office for deposit to the Employees' Life Insurance Fund.

(3) Notwithstanding paragraph (1), an employee who is subject to withholdings under this subsection and whose pay, annuity, or compensation is insufficient to cover such withholdings may nevertheless continue additional optional insurance if the employee arranges to pay currently into the Employees' Life Insurance Fund, through the agency or retirement system which administers pay, annuity, or compensation, an amount equal to the withholdings that would otherwise be required under this subsection.

(e) The cost of the additional optional insurance shall be determined from time to time by the Office on the basis of the employee's age relative to such age groups as the Office establishes under section 8714a(e) of this title.

(f) The amount of additional optional life insurance in force on an employee at the date of his death shall be paid as provided in section 8705 of this title.

(Added Pub. L. 96–427, § 7(a), Oct. 10, 1980, 94 Stat. 1834; amended Pub. L. 98–353, title II, §§ 206, 207, July 10, 1984, 98 Stat. 351, as amended by Pub. L. 99–336, § 7(1), June 19, 1986, 100 Stat. 639; Pub. L. 99–335, title II, § 207(k)(4), June 6, 1986, 100 Stat. 597; Pub. L. 99–336, § 7(1), June 19, 1986, 100 Stat. 639; Pub. L. 105–311, §§ 3(2), 6(3), 7(a), (c), Oct. 30, 1998, 112 Stat. 2950–2953.)

AMENDMENTS

1998—Subsec. (b). Pub. L. 105–311, § 3(2), in first sentence, struck out "except that coverage may not exceed an amount equal to 5 times the annual rate of basic pay payable for positions at level II of the Executive Schedule under section 5313 of this title (rounded to the next higher multiple of $1,000)" after "$1,000)".

Subsec. (c)(2). Pub. L. 105–311, § 7(a)(1)(A), struck out at end "The amount of insurance continued under this paragraph shall be reduced each month by 2 percent effective at the beginning of the second calendar month after the date the employee becomes 65 years of age and is retired or is in receipt of compensation. The reduction shall continue for 50 months at which time the insurance stops."

Subsec. (c)(3) to (5). Pub. L. 105–311, § 7(a)(1)(B), added pars. (3) to (5).

Subsec. (d)(1). Pub. L. 105–311, § 7(a)(2), (c), inserted "if insurance is continued as provided under subsection (c)(3)(A)," after "except that," and "(and any amounts withheld as provided in subsection (c)(3)(B))" after "Amounts so withheld".

Subsec. (d)(3). Pub. L. 105–311, § 6(3), added par. (3).

1986—Subsec. (c)(1). Pub. L. 98–353, § 206, as amended generally by Pub. L. 99–336, § 7(1), inserted sentence which deemed justices and judges described in section 8701(a)(5)(ii) and (iii) of this chapter to continue in active employment for purposes of this chapter.

Pub. L. 99–335 substituted "Except as otherwise provided in this subsection, the additional optional insurance elected by an employee pursuant to this section shall stop on separation from service or 12 months after discontinuance of his pay, whichever is earlier, subject to a provision for temporary extension of life insurance coverage and for conversion to an individual policy of life insurance under conditions approved by the Office" for "The additional optional insurance elected by an employee pursuant to this section shall stop on separation from service, 12 months after discontinuance of pay, or on entry on active military duty or active duty for training, subject to provision for a 31-day temporary extension of insurance coverage and for conversion to an individual policy, as provided in sections 8706(a) and 8706(c) of this title".

1984—Subsec. (c)(1). Pub. L. 98–353 inserted "A justice or judge of the United States as defined by section 8701(a)(5) of this title who resigns his office without meeting the requirements of section 371(a) of title 28, United States Code, for continuation of the judicial salary shall have the right to convert additional optional life insurance coverage issued under this section during his judicial service to an individual policy of life insurance under the same conditions approved by the Office governing conversion of basic life insurance coverage for employees eligible as provided in section 8706(a) of this title."

§ 8714c. Optional life insurance on family members

(a) Under the conditions, directives, and terms specified in sections 8709 through 8712 of this title, the Office of Personnel Management, without regard to section 5 of title 41, may purchase a policy which shall make available to each employee insured under section 8702 of this title amounts of optional life insurance (without accidental death and dismemberment insurance) on the employee's family members.

(b)(1) The optional life insurance on family members provided under this section shall be made available to each eligible employee who has elected coverage under this section, under conditions the Office shall prescribe, in multiples, at the employee's election, of 1, 2, 3, 4, or 5 times—

(A) $5,000 for a spouse; and

(B) $2,500 for each child described under section 8701(d).

(2) An employee may reduce or stop coverage elected pursuant to this section at any time.

(c)(1) Except as otherwise provided in this subsection, the optional life insurance on family members shall stop at the earlier of the employee's death, the employee's separation from the service, or 12 months after discontinuance of pay, subject to a provision for temporary extension of life insurance coverage and for conversion to individual policies of life insurance under conditions approved by the Office.

(2) In the case of any employee who retires on an immediate annuity or who becomes entitled to receive compensation under subchapter I of chapter 81 of this title because of disease or injury to the employee and who has had in force insurance under this section for no less than—

(A) the 5 years of service immediately preceding the date of retirement or entitlement to compensation, or

(B) the full period or periods of service during which the insurance was available to the employee, if fewer than 5 years,

optional life insurance on family members may be continued under the same conditions as provided in section 8714b(c)(2) through (4).

(d)(1) During each period in which the optional life insurance on family members is in force the full cost thereof shall be withheld from the employee's pay. During each period in which an employee continues optional life insurance on family members after retirement or while in receipt of compensation under subchapter I of chapter 81 of this title because of disease or injury to the employee, as provided in subsection (c) of this section, the full cost shall be withheld from the annuity or compensation, except that, beginning at the end of the calendar month in which the former employee becomes 65 years of age, the optional life insurance on family members shall be without cost to the employee. Notwithstanding the preceding sentence, the full cost shall be continued after the calendar month in which the former employee becomes 65 years of age if, and for so long as, an election under this section corresponding to that described in section 8714b(c)(3)(B) remains in effect with respect to such former employee. Amounts so withheld shall be deposited, used, and invested as provided in section 8714 of this title and shall be reported and accounted for together with amounts withheld under section 8714a(d) of this title.

(2) If an agency fails to withhold the proper cost of optional life insurance on family members from an individual's salary, compensation, or retirement annuity, the collection of amounts properly due may be waived by the agency if, in the judgment of the agency, the individual is without fault and recovery would be against equity and good conscience. However, if the agency so waives the collection of any unpaid amount, the agency shall submit an amount equal to the uncollected amount to the Office for deposit to the Employees' Life Insurance Fund.

(3) Notwithstanding paragraph (1), an employee who is subject to withholdings under this subsection and whose pay, annuity, or compensation is insufficient to cover such withholdings may nevertheless continue optional life

insurance on family members if the employee arranges to pay currently into the Employees' Life Insurance Fund, through the agency or retirement system that administers pay, annuity, or compensation, an amount equal to the withholdings that would otherwise be required under this subsection.

(e) The cost of the optional life insurance on family members shall be determined from time to time by the Office on the basis of the employee's age relative to such age groups as the Office establishes under section 8714a(e) of this title.

(f) The amount of optional life insurance which is in force under this section on a family member of an employee or former employee on the date of the death of the family member shall be paid, on the establishment of a valid claim by the employee, to such employee or, in the event of the death of the employee before payment can be made, to the person or persons entitled to the group life insurance in force on the employee under section 8705 of this title.

(Added Pub. L. 96–427, § 8(a), Oct. 10, 1980, 94 Stat. 1836; amended Pub. L. 98–353, title II, § 206, as amended by Pub. L. 99–336, § 7(1), June 19, 1986, 100 Stat. 639; Pub. L. 99–335, title II, § 207(k)(5), June 6, 1986, 100 Stat. 598; Pub. L. 99–336, § 7(1), June 19, 1986, 100 Stat. 639; Pub. L. 105–311, §§ 6(4), 8, Oct. 30, 1998, 112 Stat. 2951, 2953.)

AMENDMENTS

1998—Subsec. (b). Pub. L. 105–311, § 8(a), amended subsec. (b) generally. Prior to amendment, subsec. (b) read as follows: "The optional life insurance on family members provided under this section shall be made available to each eligible employee who elects coverage under this section, under conditions the Office shall prescribe, in the amount of $5,000 for a spouse and $2,500 for each child described in section 8701(d). The employee may stop coverage elected under this section at any time."

Subsec. (c)(2). Pub. L. 105–311, § 8(b)(1), substituted "section 8714b(c)(2) through (4)" for "section 8714b(c)(2) of this title".

Subsec. (d)(1). Pub. L. 105–311, § 8(b)(2), inserted before last sentence "Notwithstanding the preceding sentence, the full cost shall be continued after the calendar month in which the former employee becomes 65 years of age if, and for so long as, an election under this section corresponding to that described in section 8714b(c)(3)(B) remains in effect with respect to such former employee."

Subsec. (d)(3). Pub. L. 105–311, § 6(4), added par. (3).

1986—Subsec. (c)(1). Pub. L. 99–336 amended Pub. L. 98–353, § 206, generally. See 1984 Amendment note below.

Pub. L. 99–335 amended par. (1) generally, effective Jan. 1, 1977. Prior to such effective date, par. (1) read as follows: "Optional life insurance on family members shall stop at the earlier of the employee's death, the employee's separation from the service, 12 months after discontinuance of pay, or the employee's entry on active duty or active duty for training, as provided in sections 8706(a) and 8706(c) of this title, subject to provision for a 31-day temporary extension of insurance coverage and for conversion to individual policies under conditions approved by the Office. Justices and judges of the United States described in section 8701(a)(5)(ii) and (iii) of this chapter are deemed to continue in active employment for purposes of this chapter."

1984—Subsec. (c)(1). Pub. L. 98–353, § 206, as amended generally by Pub. L. 99–336, inserted sentence which deemed justices and judges described in section 8701(a)(5)(ii) and (iii) of this chapter to continue in active employment for purposes of this chapter.

EFFECTIVE DATE OF 1998 AMENDMENT

Amendment by section 6(4) of Pub. L. 105–311 effective on the first day of the first applicable pay period beginning on or after Oct. 30, 1998, and amendment by section 8 of Pub. L. 105–311 effective on the first day of the first pay period which begins on or after the 180th day following Oct. 30, 1998, or on any earlier date that the Office of Personnel Management may prescribe, see section 11(d), (f) of Pub. L. 105–311, set out as a note under section 8701 of this title.

EFFECTIVE DATE OF 1986 AMENDMENT

Amendment by Pub. L. 99–335 effective Jan. 1, 1987, see section 702(a) of Pub. L. 99–335, set out as an Effective Date note under section 8401 of this title.

EFFECTIVE DATE OF 1984 AMENDMENT

Amendment by Pub. L. 98–353, § 206, as amended generally by Pub. L. 99–336, § 7(1), applicable to any justice or judge who retires under 28 U.S.C. 371(a) or (b) or 372(a) on or after January 1, 1982, see section 207 of Pub. L. 98–353, as amended generally by Pub. L. 99–336, § 7(2), set out as a note under section 8706 of this title.

EFFECTIVE DATE

Section effective on first day of first pay period which begins on or after 180th day following Oct. 10, 1980, or on any earlier date that Office may prescribe which is at least 60 days after Oct. 10, 1980, and shall have no effect in case of an employee who died, was finally separated, or retired before effective date, see section 10(d) of Pub. L. 96–427 set out as an Effective Date of 1980 Amendment note under section 8701 of this title.

SECTION REFERRED TO IN OTHER SECTIONS

This section is referred to in section 8714d of this title.

§ 8714d. Option to receive "living benefits"

(a) For the purpose of this section, an individual shall be considered to be "terminally ill" if such individual has a medical prognosis that such individual's life expectancy is 9 months or less.

(b) The Office of Personnel Management shall prescribe regulations under which any individual covered by group life insurance under section 8704(a) may, if such individual is terminally ill, elect to receive a lump-sum payment equal to—

(1) the full amount of insurance under section 8704(a) (or portion thereof designated for this purpose under subsection (d)(4)) which would otherwise be payable under this chapter (on the establishment of a valid claim)—

(A) computed based on a date determined under regulations of the Office (but not later than 30 days after the date on which the individual's application for benefits under this section is approved or deemed approved under subsection (d)(3)); and

(B) assuming continued coverage under this chapter at that time;

reduced by

(2) an amount necessary to assure that there is no increase in the actuarial value of the benefit paid (as determined under regulations of the Office).

(c)(1) If a lump-sum payment is taken under this section—

(A) no insurance under the provisions of section 8704(a) or (b) shall be payable based on the death or any loss of the individual involved, unless the lump-sum payment represents only a portion of the total benefits which could have been taken, in which case benefits under those provisions shall remain in effect, except that the basic insurance amount on which they are based—

(i) shall be reduced by the percentage which the designated portion comprised relative to the total benefits which could have been taken (rounding the result to the nearest multiple of $1,000 or, if midway between multiples of $1,000, to the next higher multiple of $1,000); and

(ii) shall not be subject to further adjustment; and

(B) deductions and withholdings under section 8707, and contributions under section 8708, shall be terminated with respect to such individual (or reduced in a manner consistent with the percentage reduction in the individual's basic insurance amount, if applicable), effective with respect to any amounts which would otherwise become due on or after the date of payment under this section.

(2) An individual who takes a lump-sum payment under this section (whether full or partial) remains eligible for optional benefits under sections 8714a–8714c (subject to payment of the full cost of those benefits in accordance with applicable provisions of the section or sections involved, to the same extent as if no election under this section had been made).

(d)(1) The Office's regulations shall include provisions regarding the form and manner in which an application under this section shall be made and the procedures in accordance with which any such application shall be considered.

(2) An application shall not be considered to be complete unless it includes such information and supporting evidence as the regulations require, including certification by an appropriate medical authority as to the nature of the individual's illness and that the individual is not expected to live more than 9 months because of that illness.

(3)(A) In order to ascertain the reliability of any medical opinion or finding submitted as part of an application under this section, the covered individual may be required to submit to a medical examination under the direction of the agency or entity considering the application. The individual shall not be liable for the costs associated with any examination required under this subparagraph.

(B) Any decision by the reviewing agency or entity with respect to an application for benefits under this section (including one relating to an individual's medical prognosis) shall not be subject to administrative review.

(4)(A) An individual making an election under this section may designate that only a limited portion (expressed as a multiple of $1,000) of the total amount otherwise allowable under this section be paid pursuant to such election.

(B) A designation under this paragraph may not be made by an individual described in paragraph (1) or (2) of section 8706(b).

(5) An election to receive benefits under this section shall be irrevocable, and not more than

one such election may be made by any individual.

(6) The regulations shall include provisions to address the question of how to apply section 8706(b)(3)(B) in the case of an electing individual who has attained 65 years of age.

(Added Pub. L. 103–409, §2(a), Oct. 25, 1994, 108 Stat. 4230.)

EFFECTIVE DATE OF 1994 AMENDMENT

Pub. L. 103–409, §3(a), Oct. 25, 1994, 108 Stat. 4232, provided that: "The amendments made by section 2 [enacting this section] shall take effect 9 months after the date of the enactment of this Act [Oct. 25, 1994]."

§ 8715. Jurisdiction of courts

The district courts of the United States have original jurisdiction, concurrent with the United States Court of Federal Claims, of a civil action or claim against the United States founded on this chapter.

(Pub. L. 89–554, Sept. 6, 1966, 80 Stat. 599; Pub. L. 97–164, title I, §160(a)(2), Apr. 2, 1982, 96 Stat. 48; Pub. L. 102–572, title IX, §902(b)(1), Oct. 29, 1992, 106 Stat. 4516.)

HISTORICAL AND REVISION NOTES

Derivation	U.S. Code	Revised Statutes and Statutes at Large
....	5 U.S.C. 2103 (less applicability to 5 U.S.C. 2099).	Aug. 17, 1954, ch. 752, §14 (less applicability to §10), 68 Stat. 743.

Standard changes are made to conform with the definitions applicable and the style of this title as outlined in the preface to the report.

AMENDMENTS

1992—Pub. L. 102–572 substituted "United States Court of Federal Claims" for "United States Claims Court".

1982—Pub. L. 97–164 substituted "United States Claims Court" for "Court of Claims".

EFFECTIVE DATE OF 1992 AMENDMENT

Amendment by Pub. L. 102–572 effective Oct. 29, 1992, see section 911 of Pub. L. 102–572, set out as a note under section 171 of Title 28, Judiciary and Judicial Procedure.

EFFECTIVE DATE OF 1982 AMENDMENT

Amendment by Pub. L. 97–164 effective Oct. 1, 1982, see section 402 of Pub. L. 97–164, set out as a note under section 171 of Title 28, Judiciary and Judicial Procedure.

§ 8716. Regulations

(a) The Office of Personnel Management may prescribe regulations necessary to carry out the purposes of this chapter.

(b) The regulations of the Office may prescribe the time at which and the conditions under which an employee is eligible for coverage under this chapter. The Office, after consulting the head of the agency or other employing authority concerned, may exclude an employee on the basis of the nature and type of his employment or conditions pertaining to it, such as short-term appointment, seasonal, intermittent employment, and employment of like nature. The Office may not exclude—

(1) an employee or group of employees solely on the basis of the hazardous nature of employment;

(2) a teacher in the employ of the Board of Education of the District of Columbia, whose pay is fixed by section 1501 of title 31, District of Columbia Code, on the basis of the fact that the teacher is serving under a temporary appointment if the teacher has been so employed by the Board for a period or periods totaling not less than two school years; or

(3) an employee who is occupying a position on a part-time career employment basis (as defined in section 3401(2) of this title).

(c) The Secretary of Agriculture shall prescribe regulations to effect the application and operation of this chapter to an individual named by section 8701(a)(8) of this title.

(Pub. L. 89–554, Sept. 6, 1966, 80 Stat. 599; Pub. L. 95–437, § 4(b), Oct. 10, 1978, 92 Stat. 1058; Pub. L. 95–454, title IX, § 906(a)(2), (3), (c)(2)(F), (G), Oct. 13, 1978, 92 Stat. 1224, 1227.)

HISTORICAL AND REVISION NOTES

Derivation	U.S. Code	Revised Statutes and Statutes at Large
(a)	5 U.S.C. 2100 (less applicability to 5 U.S.C. 2099).	Aug. 17, 1954, ch. 752, § 11 (less applicability to § 10), 68 Stat. 742.
(b), (c)	5 U.S.C. 2091(a) (words between 6th and 7th commas of 1st sentence and 2d sentence), (d) (words between 1st and 2d commas of 1st sentence, and 2d sentence).	Aug. 17, 1954, ch. 752, § 2(a) (words between 6th and 7th commas of 1st sentence and 2d sentence), 68 Stat. 736. July 1, 1960, Pub. L. 86–568, § 115(c) "(d) (words between 1st and 2d commas of 1st sentence, and 2d sentence)", 74 Stat. 302. Oct. 6, 1964, Pub. L. 88–631, § 2, 78 Stat. 1007.

In subsection (a), the words "Except as otherwise provided herein" are omitted as unnecessary since the authority to prescribe regulations is carried into this section.

In subsection (b), the words "section 1501 of title 31, District of Columbia Code" are substituted for "section 1 of the District of Columbia Teachers' Salary Act of 1955 (69 Stat. 521), as amended (Sec. 31–1501, D.C. Code, 1961 edition)".

Standard changes are made to conform with the definitions applicable and the style of this title as outlined in the preface to the report.

AMENDMENTS

1978—Subsec. (a). Pub. L. 95–454, § 906(a)(2), substituted "Office of Personnel Management" for "Civil Service Commission".

Subsec. (b). Pub. L. 95–454, § 906(a)(3), substituted "Office" for "Commission" wherever appearing.

Pub. L. 95–437 substituted "intermittent employment" for "intermittent or part-time employment" in provision preceding par. (1), and added par. (3).

Pub. L. 95–454, § 906(c)(2)(F), (G), substituted "3401" for "3391" in par. (3).

EFFECTIVE DATE OF 1978 AMENDMENT

Amendment by Pub. L. 95–454 effective 90 days after Oct. 13, 1978, see section 907 of Pub. L. 95–454, set out as a note under section 1101 of this title.

SECTION REFERRED TO IN OTHER SECTIONS

This section is referred to in section 8701 of this title.

CHAPTER 89—HEALTH INSURANCE

AMENDMENTS

1998—Pub. L. 105–266, § 6(a)(2), Oct. 19, 1998, 112 Stat. 2369, added item 8903b.

1988—Pub. L. 100–654, title I, § 101(b), title II, § 201(a)(2), title III, § 301(b), Nov. 14, 1988, 102 Stat. 3841, 3845, 3846, added items 8902a, 8905a, and 8906a.

Pub. L. 100–238, title I, § 108(a)(3)(B), Jan. 8, 1988, 101 Stat. 1748, added item 8914.

1985—Pub. L. 99–53, §§ 1(b)(2), 3(a)(2)(B), June 17, 1985, 99 Stat. 94, 95, added item 8903a and inserted "or disability" after "and survivor" in item 8908.

1984—Pub. L. 98–615, § 3(8), Nov. 8, 1984, 98 Stat. 3204, substituted "Information to individuals eligible to enroll" for "Information to employees" in item 8907.

1976—Pub. L. 94–342, § 1(b), July 6, 1976, 90 Stat. 808, substituted "employees and survivor annuitants" for "employee" in item 8908.

CHAPTER REFERRED TO IN OTHER SECTIONS

This chapter is referred to in sections 3373, 3374, 3582, 6386 of this title; title 2 sections 31b–5, 72a, 92, 130a, 162b; title 10 section 1108; title 22 sections 2391, 3649, 3664, 4069c, 4069c–1, 4606; title 25 section 450i; title 26 section 9801; title 28 sections 332, 627, 634, 996; title 29 section 1181; title 39 section 1005; title 40 section 214c; title 42 sections 300e–1, 300e–6, 300gg, 426a, 1320a–7b, 1320d, 1395w–21, 1395y, 2996d, 10704, 14402; title 45 section 1206; title 50 section 403p.

§ 8901. Definitions

For the purpose of this chapter—

(1) "employee" means—

(A) an employee as defined by section 2105 of this title;

(B) a Member of Congress as defined by section 2106 of this title;

(C) a Congressional employee as defined by section 2107 of this title;

(D) the President;

(E) an individual first employed by the government of the District of Columbia before October 1, 1987;

(F) an individual employed by Gallaudet College;[1]

(G) an individual employed by a county committee established under section 590h(b) of title 16;

(H) an individual appointed to a position on the office staff of a former President under section 1(b) of the Act of August 25, 1958 (72 Stat. 838); and

(I) an individual appointed to a position on the office staff of a former President, or a

---

[1] See Change of Name note below.

former Vice President under section 4 of the Presidential Transition Act of 1963, as amended (78 Stat. 153), who immediately before the date of such appointment was an employee as defined under any other subparagraph of this paragraph;

but does not include—

(i) an employee of a corporation supervised by the Farm Credit Administration if private interests elect or appoint a member of the board of directors;

(ii) an individual who is not a citizen or national of the United States and whose permanent duty station is outside the United States, unless the individual was an employee for the purpose of this chapter on September 30, 1979, by reason of service in an Executive agency, the United States Postal Service, or the Smithsonian Institution in the area which was then known as the Canal Zone;

(iii) an employee of the Tennessee Valley Authority; or

(iv) an employee excluded by regulation of the Office of Personnel Management under section 8913(b) of this title;

(2) "Government" means the Government of the United States and the government of the District of Columbia;

(3) "annuitant" means—

(A) an employee who retires—

(i) on an immediate annuity under subchapter III of chapter 83 of this title, or another retirement system for employees of the Government, after 5 or more years of service;

(ii) under section 8412 or 8414 of this title;

(iii) for disability under subchapter III of chapter 83 of this title, chapter 84 of this title, or another retirement system for employees of the Government; or

(iv) on an immediate annuity under a retirement system established for employees described in section 2105(c), in the case of an individual who elected under section 8347(q)(2) or 8461(n)(2) to remain subject to such a system;

(B) a member of a family who receives an immediate annuity as the survivor of an employee (including a family member entitled to an amount under section 8442(b)(1)(A), whether or not such family member is entitled to an annuity under section 8442(b)(1)(B)) or of a retired employee described by subparagraph (A) of this paragraph;

(C) an employee who receives monthly compensation under subchapter I of chapter 81 of this title and who is determined by the Secretary of Labor to be unable to return to duty; and

(D) a member of a family who receives monthly compensation under subchapter I of chapter 81 of this title as the surviving beneficiary of—

(i) an employee who dies as a result of injury or illness compensable under that subchapter; or

(ii) a former employee who is separated after having completed 5 or more years of service and who dies while receiving monthly compensation under that subchapter and who has been held by the Secretary to have been unable to return to duty;

(4) "service", as used by paragraph (3) of this section, means service which is creditable under subchapter III of chapter 83 or chapter 84 of this title;

(5) "member of family" means the spouse of an employee or annuitant and an unmarried dependent child under 22 years of age, including—

(A) an adopted child or recognized natural child; and

(B) a stepchild or foster child but only if the child lives with the employee or annuitant in a regular parent-child relationship;

or such an unmarried dependent child regardless of age who is incapable of self-support because of mental or physical disability which existed before age 22;

(6) "health benefits plan" means a group insurance policy or contract, medical or hospital service agreement, membership or subscription contract, or similar group arrangements provided by a carrier for the purpose of providing, paying for, or reimbursing expenses for health services;

(7) "carrier" means a voluntary association, corporation, partnership, or other nongovernmental organization which is lawfully engaged in providing, paying for, or reimbursing the cost of, health services under group insurance policies or contracts, medical or hospital service agreements, membership or subscription contracts, or similar group arrangements, in consideration of premiums or other periodic charges payable to the carrier, including a health benefits plan duly sponsored or underwritten by an employee organization and an association of organizations or other entities described in this paragraph sponsoring a health benefits plan;

(8) "employee organization" means—

(A) an association or other organization of employees which is national in scope, or in which membership is open to all employees of a Government agency who are eligible to enroll in a health benefits plan under this chapter and which, after December 31, 1978, and before January 1, 1980, applied to the Office for approval of a plan provided under section 8903(3) of this title; and

(B) an association or other organization which is national in scope, in which membership is open only to employees, annuitants, or former spouses, or any combination thereof, and which, during the 90-day period beginning on the date of enactment of section 8903a of this title, applied to the Office for approval of a plan provided under such section;

(9) "dependent", in the case of any child, means that the employee or annuitant involved is either living with or contributing to the support of such child, as determined in accordance with such regulations as the Office shall prescribe;

(10) "former spouse" means a former spouse of an employee, former employee, or annuitant—

(A) who has not remarried before age 55 after the marriage to the employee, former employee, or annuitant was dissolved,

(B) who was enrolled in an approved health benefits plan under this chapter as a family member at any time during the 18-month period before the date of the dissolution of the marriage to the employee, former employee, or annuitant, and

(C)(i) who is receiving any portion of an annuity under section 8345(j) or 8467 of this title or a survivor annuity under section 8341(h) or 8445 of this title (or benefits similar to either of the aforementioned annuity benefits under a retirement system for Government employees other than the Civil Service Retirement System or the Federal Employees' Retirement System),

(ii) as to whom a court order or decree referred to in section 8341(h), 8345(j), 8445, or 8467 of this title (or similar provision of law under any such retirement system other than the Civil Service Retirement System or the Federal Employees' Retirement System) has been issued, or for whom an election has been made under section 8339(j)(3) or 8417(b) of this title (or similar provision of law), or

(iii) who is otherwise entitled to an annuity or any portion of an annuity as a former spouse under a retirement system for Government employees,

except that such term shall not include any such unremarried former spouse of a former employee whose marriage was dissolved after the former employee's separation from the service (other than by retirement); and

(11) "qualified clinical social worker" means an individual—

(A) who is licensed or certified as a clinical social worker by the State in which such individual practices; or

(B) who, if such State does not provide for the licensing or certification of clinical social workers—

(i) is certified by a national professional organization offering certification of clinical social workers; or

(ii) meets equivalent requirements (as prescribed by the Office).

(Pub. L. 89–554, Sept. 6, 1966, 80 Stat. 600; Pub. L. 90–83, §1(95), Sept. 11, 1967, 81 Stat. 219; Pub. L. 91–418, §§2, 3(b), Sept. 25, 1970, 84 Stat. 869; Pub. L. 93–160, §1(b), Nov. 27, 1973, 87 Stat. 635; Pub. L. 95–368, §2, Sept. 17, 1978, 92 Stat. 606; Pub. L. 95–454, title IX, §906(a)(2), (3), Oct. 13, 1978, 92 Stat. 1224; Pub. L. 95–583, §2, Nov. 2, 1978, 92 Stat. 2482; Pub. L. 96–54, §2(a)(52), Aug. 14, 1979, 93 Stat. 384; Pub. L. 96–70, title I, §1209(c), Sept. 27, 1979, 93 Stat. 463; Pub. L. 96–179, §2, Jan. 2, 1980, 93 Stat. 1299; Pub. L. 98–615, §3(1), Nov. 8, 1984, 98 Stat. 3202; Pub. L. 99–53, §1(a), June 17, 1985, 99 Stat. 93; Pub. L. 99–251, title I, §105(a), Feb. 27, 1986, 100 Stat. 15; Pub. L. 99–335, title II, §207(*l*), June 6, 1986, 100 Stat. 598; Pub. L. 99–556, title V, §503, Oct. 27, 1986, 100 Stat. 3141; Pub. L. 100–679, §13(c), Nov. 17, 1988, 102 Stat. 4071; Pub. L. 101–508, title VII, §7202(*l*), Nov. 5, 1990, 104 Stat. 1388–339; Pub. L. 102–378, §2(75), Oct. 2, 1992, 106 Stat. 1355; Pub. L. 105–266, §3(a), Oct. 19, 1998, 112 Stat. 2366.)

HISTORICAL AND REVISION NOTES
1966 ACT

Derivation	U.S. Code	Revised Statutes and Statutes at Large
....	5 U.S.C. 3001.	Sept. 28, 1959, Pub. L. 86–382, §2, 73 Stat. 709. July 8, 1963, Pub. L. 88–59, §1, 77 Stat. 76. Mar. 17, 1964, Pub. L. 88–284, §1(1)–(4), 78 Stat. 164. Aug. 31, 1964, Pub. L. 88–531, §1, 78 Stat. 737.
....	5 U.S.C. 3002(f) (1st sentence, less words between 1st and 2d commas).	July 1, 1960, Pub. L. 86–568, §115(d) "(f) (1st sentence, less words between 1st and 2d commas)", 74 Stat. 303.

The definition of "employee" in section 2105 of this title is broad enough to cover the officers and employees covered by former section 3001 with the exception of a Member of Congress, the President, an individual employed by the government of the District of Columbia, an individual employed by Gallaudet College, a United States commissioner, and an Official Reporter of Debates of the Senate and an individual employed by him. The first five have been added in paragraphs (1)(B), (D), (E), (F), and (G). The latter are covered by the definition of "Congressional employee" in section 2107 of this title and are included by the addition of a Congressional employee in paragraph (1)(C).

In paragraph (1)(ii), the words "the United States" are substituted for "a State of the United States or the District of Columbia".

Paragraph (1)(iv) is added for clarity.

In paragraph (8), the words "before January 1, 1964" are substituted for "on or before December 31, 1963".

The definition of "Commission" in former section 3001(h) is omitted as unnecessary as the full title "Civil Service Commission" is set forth the first time it is used in a section.

Standard changes are made to conform with the definitions applicable and the style of this title as outlined in the preface to the report.

1967 ACT

Section of title 5	Source (U.S. Code)	Source (Statutes at Large)
8901(5)	5 App.: 3001(d).	July 18, 1966, Pub. L. 89–504, §601, 80 Stat. 303.

REFERENCES IN TEXT

Section 1(b) of the Act of August 25, 1958 (72 Stat. 838), referred to in par. (1)(H), is section 1(b) of Pub. L. 85–745 which is set out as a note under section 102 of Title 3, The President.

Section 4 of the Presidential Transition Act of 1963, referred to in par. (1)(I), is section 4 of Pub. L. 88–277, which is set out as a note under section 102 of Title 3.

The date of enactment of section 8903a of this title, referred to in par. (8)(B), means the date of enactment of Pub. L. 99–53, which enacted section 8903a and which was approved June 17, 1985.

AMENDMENTS

1998—Par. (7). Pub. L. 105–266 substituted "organization and an association of organizations or other entities described in this paragraph sponsoring a health benefits plan;" for "organization;".

1992—Par. (3)(A)(iv). Pub. L. 102–378, §2(75)(A), substituted "8347(q)(2)" for "8347(p)(2)".

Par. (10)(C)(ii). Pub. L. 102–378, §2(75)(B), inserted comma after "8341(h)".

1990—Par. (3)(A)(iv). Pub. L. 101–508 added cl. (iv).

1988—Par. (1)(H), (I). Pub. L. 100–679 added subpars. (H) and (I).

1986—Par. (1)(E). Pub. L. 99–335, § 207(*l*)(1), amended subpar. (E) generally, substituting "first employed" for "employed" and inserting "before October 1, 1987".

Par. (3)(A). Pub. L. 99–335, § 207(*l*)(2), amended subpar. (A) generally. Prior to amendment, subpar. (A) read as follows: "an employee who retires on an immediate annuity under subchapter III of chapter 83 of this title or another retirement system for employees of the Government, after 5 or more years of service or for disability".

Par. (3)(B). Pub. L. 99–556 inserted "(including a family member entitled to an amount under section 8442(b)(1)(A), whether or not such family member is entitled to an annuity under section 8442(b)(1)(B))".

Par. (4). Pub. L. 99–335, § 207(*l*)(3), inserted "or chapter 84".

Par. (10)(C)(i). Pub. L. 99–335, § 207(*l*)(4), inserted "or 8467", "or 8445", and "or the Federal Employees' Retirement System".

Par. (10)(C)(ii). Pub. L. 99–335, § 207(*l*)(5), substituted "8345(j), 8445, or 8467" for "or 8345(j)" and inserted "or the Federal Employees' Retirement System" and "or 8417(b)".

Par. (11). Pub. L. 99–251 added par. (11).

1985—Par. (8). Pub. L. 99–53 amended par. (8) generally, designating existing provisions as subpar. (A) and adding subpar. (B).

1984—Par. (10). Pub. L. 98–615 added par. (10).

1980—Par. (5). Pub. L. 96–179, § 2(1), inserted "dependent" after "unmarried" in provisions preceding subpar. (A) and in provisions following subpar. (B), inserted "or recognized natural child" after "child" in subpar. (A), and substituted "or foster child but only if the child;" for ", foster child, or recognized natural child who" in subpar. (B).

Par. (9). Pub. L. 96–179, § 2(2)–(4), added par. (9).

1979—Par. (1). Pub. L. 96–70 in cl. (ii) substituted provisions relating to an individual who was an employee for the purpose of this chapter on Sept. 30, 1979, by reason of service in an Executive agency, United States Postal Service, or Smithsonian Institution in area which was then known as Canal Zone for provisions relating to Panama Canal Zone.

Pub. L. 96–54 struck out cl. (G) which related to coverage of a United States Commissioner as an "employee", and redesignated cl. (H) as (G).

1978—Par. (1)(iv). Pub. L. 95–454 substituted "Office of Personnel Management" for "Civil Service Commission".

Par. (3)(A). Pub. L. 95–583 reduced period of service to 5 from 12 years.

Par. (8). Pub. L. 95–454 substituted "Office" for "Commission".

Pub. L. 95–368 substituted "after December 31, 1978, and before January 1, 1980" for "before January 1, 1964".

1973—Par. (1)(ii). Pub. L. 93–160 excluded from definition of "employee" persons who are not nationals of United States and whose permanent duty station is outside United States and Panama Canal Zone.

1970—Par. (1)(ii). Pub. L. 91–418, § 3(b), excluded from definition of "employee" a noncitizen employee whose permanent duty station is outside Panama Canal Zone.

Par. (3)(B). Pub. L. 91–418, § 2(a), redefined "annuitant" to be a member of a family who receives an immediate annuity as the survivor of an employee who dies after completing 5 or more years of service rather than as the survivor of an employee who dies after completing 5 or more years of service.

Par. (3)(D)(i). Pub. L. 91–418, § 2(b), redefined "annuitant" to be a member of a family who receives monthly compensation as the surviving beneficiary of an employee who dies as a result of a compensable injury or illness rather than as the survivor of an employee who, having completed 5 or more years of service, so dies.

CHANGE OF NAME

Gallaudet College, referred to in par. (1)(F), was redesignated Gallaudet University by section 101(a) of Pub. L. 99–371, which is classified to section 4301(a) of Title 20, Education.

EFFECTIVE DATE OF 1992 AMENDMENT

Amendment by section 2(75)(A) of Pub. L. 102–378 effective Nov. 5, 1990, and amendment by section 2(75)(B) of Pub. L. 102–378 effective Oct. 2, 1992, see section 9(a), (b)(6) of Pub. L. 102–378, set out as a note under section 6303 of this title.

EFFECTIVE DATE OF 1990 AMENDMENT

Amendment by Pub. L. 101–508 applicable with respect to any individual who, on or after Jan. 1, 1987, moves from employment in nonappropriated fund instrumentality of Department of Defense or Coast Guard, that is described in section 2105(c) of this title, to employment in Department or Coast Guard, that is not described in section 2105(c), or who moves from employment in Department or Coast Guard, that is not described in section 2105(c), to employment in nonappropriated fund instrumentality of Department or Coast Guard, that is described in section 2105(c), see section 7202(m)(1) of Pub. L. 101–508, set out as a note under section 2105 of this title.

EFFECTIVE DATE OF 1986 AMENDMENTS

Amendment by Pub. L. 99–335 effective Jan. 1, 1987, see section 702(a) of Pub. L. 99–335, set out as an Effective Date note under section 8401 of this title.

Section 105(c) of Pub. L. 99–251 provided that: "The amendments made by subsections (a) and (b) [amending this section and section 8902 of this title] shall be effective with respect to contracts entered into or renewed for calendar years beginning after December 31, 1986."

EFFECTIVE DATE OF 1984 AMENDMENT

Amendment by Pub. L. 98–615 effective May 7, 1985, with enumerated exceptions, and applicable to any individual who is married to an employee or annuitant on or after that date, see section 4(a)(2) of Pub. L. 98–615, as amended, set out as a note under section 8341 of this title.

EFFECTIVE DATE OF 1980 AMENDMENT

Amendment by Pub. L. 96–179 effective Jan. 2, 1980, except that no benefits under this chapter that are made available by reason of amendment of this section and section 8341 of this title by Pub. L. 96–179 shall be payable for any period before Oct. 1, 1979, see section 5(a) of Pub. L. 96–179, set out as a note under section 8341 of this title.

EFFECTIVE DATE OF 1979 AMENDMENTS

Amendment by Pub. L. 96–70 effective Oct. 1, 1979, see section 3304 of Pub. L. 96–70, set out as an Effective Date note under section 3601 of Title 22, Foreign Relations and Intercourse.

Amendment by Pub. L. 96–54 effective July 12, 1979, see section 2(b) of Pub. L. 96–54, set out as a note under section 305 of this title.

EFFECTIVE DATE OF 1978 AMENDMENTS

Amendment by Pub. L. 95–583 effective Nov. 2, 1978, see section 3 of Pub. L. 95–583, set out as a note under section 8706 of this title.

Amendment by Pub. L. 95–454 effective 90 days after Oct. 13, 1978, see section 907 of Pub. L. 95–454, set out as a note under section 1101 of this title.

SHORT TITLE OF 2000 AMENDMENT

Pub. L. 106–394, § 1, Oct. 30, 2000, 114 Stat. 1629, provided that: "This Act [amending sections 8421a and 8905 of this title and enacting provisions set out as a note under section 8421a of this title] may be cited as the 'Federal Employees Health Benefits Children's Equity Act of 2000'."

SHORT TITLE OF 1998 AMENDMENT

Pub. L. 105–266, § 1, Oct. 19, 1998, 112 Stat. 2363, provided that: "This Act [enacting section 8903b of this title, amending this section and sections 5948, 8902 to 8903, and 8909 of this title, and enacting provisions set out as notes under this section and sections 5948, 8902, 8902a, 8903b, and 8909 of this title] may be cited as the 'Federal Employees Health Care Protection Act of 1998'.''

SHORT TITLE OF 1988 AMENDMENT

Pub. L. 100–654, §1, Nov. 14, 1988, 102 Stat. 3837, provided that: ''This Act [enacting sections 8440a, 8902a, 8905a, and 8906a of this title, amending sections 8902, 8903, 8905, 8909, and 8913 of this title, and enacting provisions set out as notes under sections 8902, 8902a, and 8906a of this title] may be cited as the 'Federal Employees Health Benefits Amendments Act of 1988'.''

SHORT TITLE OF 1986 AMENDMENT

Section 1 of Pub. L. 99–251 provided that: ''This Act [amending this section, sections 1103, 3502, 5334, 5924, 6312, 8332, 8339 to 8342, 8345, 8902, 8903, 8905, and 8909 of this title, and section 35 of Title 24, Hospitals and Asylums, enacting provisions set out as notes under this section and sections 7901, 8339, 8341, 8345, 8902, 8904, 8905, and 8909 of this title, and amending provisions set out as notes under sections 8341 and 8902 of this title] may be cited as the 'Federal Employees Benefits Improvement Act of 1986'.''

CONTINUED COVERAGE FOR INDIVIDUALS ENROLLED IN PLAN ADMINISTERED BY FEDERAL DEPOSIT INSURANCE CORPORATION OR FOR EMPLOYEES OF BOARD OF GOVERNORS OF FEDERAL RESERVE SYSTEM

Pub. L. 105–266, §4, Oct. 19, 1998, 112 Stat. 2367, provided that:

''(a) ENROLLMENT IN CHAPTER 89 PLAN.—For purposes of chapter 89 of title 5, United States Code, any period of enrollment—

''(1) in a health benefits plan administered by the Federal Deposit Insurance Corporation before the termination of such plan on or before January 2, 1999; or

''(2) subject to subsection (c), in a health benefits plan (not under chapter 89 of such title) with respect to which the eligibility of any employees or retired employees of the Board of Governors of the Federal Reserve System terminates on or before January 2, 1999,

shall be deemed to be a period of enrollment in a health benefits plan under chapter 89 of such title.

''(b) CONTINUED COVERAGE.—(1) Subject to subsection (c), any individual who, on or before January 2, 1999, is enrolled in a health benefits plan described in subsection (a)(1) or (2) may enroll in an approved health benefits plan under chapter 89 of title 5, United States Code, either as an individual or for self and family, if, after taking into account the provisions of subsection (a), such individual—

''(A) meets the requirements of such chapter for eligibility to become so enrolled as an employee, annuitant, or former spouse (within the meaning of such chapter); or

''(B) would meet those requirements if, to the extent such requirements involve either retirement system under such title 5, such individual satisfies similar requirements or provisions of the Retirement Plan for Employees of the Federal Reserve System.

Any determination under subparagraph (B) shall be made under guidelines which the Office of Personnel Management shall establish in consultation with the Board of Governors of the Federal Reserve System.

''(2) Subject to subsection (c), any individual who, on or before January 2, 1999, is entitled to continued coverage under a health benefits plan described in subsection (a)(1) or (2) shall be deemed to be entitled to continued coverage under section 8905a of title 5, United States Code, but only for the same remaining period as would have been allowable under the health benefits plan in which such individual was enrolled on or before January 2, 1999, if—

''(A) such individual had remained enrolled in such plan; and

''(B) such plan did not terminate, or the eligibility of such individual with respect to such plan did not terminate, as described in subsection (a).

''(3) Subject to subsection (c), any individual (other than an individual under paragraph (2)) who, on or before January 2, 1999, is covered under a health benefits plan described in subsection (a)(1) or (2) as an unmarried dependent child, but who does not then qualify for coverage under chapter 89 of title 5, United States Code, as a family member (within the meaning of such chapter) shall be deemed to be entitled to continued coverage under section 8905a of such title, to the same extent and in the same manner as if such individual had, on or before January 2, 1999, ceased to meet the requirements for being considered an unmarried dependent child of an enrollee under such chapter.

''(4) Coverage under chapter 89 of title 5, United States Code, pursuant to an enrollment under this section shall become effective on January 3, 1999 or such earlier date as established by the Office of Personnel Management after consultation with the Federal Deposit Insurance Corporation or the Board of Governors of the Federal Reserve System, as appropriate.

''(c) ELIGIBILITY FOR FEHBP LIMITED TO INDIVIDUALS LOSING ELIGIBILITY UNDER FORMER HEALTH PLAN.—Nothing in subsection (a)(2) or any paragraph of subsection (b) (to the extent such paragraph relates to the plan described in subsection (a)(2)) shall be considered to apply with respect to any individual whose eligibility for coverage under such plan does not involuntarily terminate on or before January 2, 1999.

''(d) TRANSFERS TO THE EMPLOYEES HEALTH BENEFITS FUND.—The Federal Deposit Insurance Corporation and the Board of Governors of the Federal Reserve System shall transfer to the Employees Health Benefits Fund under section 8909 of title 5, United States Code, amounts determined by the Director of the Office of Personnel Management, after consultation with the Federal Deposit Insurance Corporation and the Board of Governors of the Federal Reserve System, to be necessary to reimburse the Fund for the cost of providing benefits under this section not otherwise paid for by the individuals covered by this section. The amounts so transferred shall be held in the Fund and used by the Office of Personnel Management in addition to amounts available under section 8906(g)(1) of such title.

''(e) ADMINISTRATION AND REGULATIONS.—The Office of Personnel Management—

''(1) shall administer the provisions of this section to provide for—

''(A) a period of notice and open enrollment for individuals affected by this section; and

''(B) no lapse of health coverage for individuals who enroll in a health benefits plan under chapter 89 of title 5, United States Code, in accordance with this section; and

''(2) may prescribe regulations to implement this section.''

CONTINUED COVERAGE FOR INDIVIDUALS ENROLLED IN PLAN ADMINISTERED BY FARM CREDIT ADMINISTRATION

Pub. L. 104–37, title VI, §601, Oct. 21, 1995, 109 Stat. 328, provided that:

''(a) For purposes of the administration of chapter 89 of title 5, United States Code, any period of enrollment under a health benefits plan administered by the Farm Credit Administration prior to the effective date of this Act [Oct. 21, 1995] shall be deemed to be a period of enrollment in a health benefits plan under chapter 89 of such title.

''(b)(1) An individual who, on September 30, 1995, is covered by a health benefits plan administered by the Farm Credit Administration may enroll in an approved health benefits plan described under section 8903 or 8903a of title 5, United States Code—

''(A) either as an individual or for self and family, if such individual is an employee, annuitant, or former spouse as defined under section 8901 of such title; and

''(B) for coverage effective on and after September 30, 1995.

"(2) An individual who, on September 30, 1995, is entitled to continued coverage under a health benefits plan administered by the Farm Credit Administration—

"(A) shall be deemed to be entitled to continued coverage under section 8905a of title 5, United States Code, for the same period that would have been permitted under the plan administered by the Farm Credit Administration; and

"(B) may enroll in an approved health benefits plan described under sections 8903 or 8903a of such title in accordance with section 8905A of such title for coverage effective on and after September 30, 1995.

"(3) An individual who, on September 30, 1995, is covered as an unmarried dependent child under a health benefits plan administered by the Farm Credit Administration and who is not a member of family as defined under section 8901(5) of title 5, United States Code—

"(A) shall be deemed to be entitled to continued coverage under section 8905a of such title as though the individual had, on September 30, 1995, ceased to meet the requirements for being considered an unmarried dependent child under chapter 89 of such title; and

"(B) may enroll in an approved health benefits plan described under section 8903 or 8903a of such title in accordance with section 8905a for continued coverage on and after September 30, 1995.

"(c) The Farm Credit Administration shall transfer to the Federal Employees Health Benefits Fund established under section 8909 of title 5, United States Code, amounts determined by the Director of the Office of Personnel Management, after consultation with the Farm Credit Administration, to be necessary to reimburse the Fund for the cost of providing benefits under this section not otherwise paid for by the individuals covered by this section. The amount so transferred shall be held in the Fund and used by the Office in addition to the amounts available under section 8906(g)(1) of such title.

"(d) The Office of Personnel Management—

"(1) shall administer the provisions of this section to provide for—

"(A) a period of notice and open enrollment for individuals affected by this section; and

"(B) no lapse of health coverage for individuals who enroll in a health benefits plan under chapter 89 of title 5, United States Code, in accordance with this section; and

"(2) may prescribe regulations to implement this section."

CONTINUED COVERAGE FOR INDIVIDUALS ENROLLED IN PLAN ADMINISTERED BY OFFICE OF THE COMPTROLLER OF THE CURRENCY OR OFFICE OF THRIFT SUPERVISION

Pub. L. 103–409, § 5, Oct. 25, 1994, 108 Stat. 4232, provided that:

"(a) ENROLLMENT IN CHAPTER 89 PLAN.—For purposes of the administration of chapter 89 of title 5, United States Code, any period of enrollment under a health benefits plan administered by the Office of the Comptroller of the Currency or the Office of Thrift Supervision before the termination of such plans on January 7, 1995, shall be deemed to be a period of enrollment in a health benefits plan under chapter 89 of such title.

"(b) CONTINUED COVERAGE.—(1) Any individual who, on January 7, 1995, is covered by a health benefits plan administered by the Office of the Comptroller of the Currency or the Office of Thrift Supervision may enroll in an approved health benefits plan described under section 8903 or 8903a of title 5, United States Code—

"(A) either as an individual or for self and family, if such individual is an employee, annuitant, or former spouse as defined under section 8901 of such title; and

"(B) for coverage effective on and after January 8, 1995.

"(2) An individual who, on January 7, 1995, is entitled to continued coverage under a health benefits plan administered by the Office of the Comptroller of the Currency or the Office of Thrift Supervision—

"(A) shall be deemed to be entitled to continued coverage under section 8905a of title 5, United States Code, for the same period that would have been permitted under the plan administered by the Office of the Comptroller of the Currency or the Office of Thrift Supervision; and

"(B) may enroll in an approved health benefits plan described under section 8903 or 8903a of such title in accordance with section 8905a of such title for coverage effective on and after January 8, 1995.

"(3) An individual who, on January 7, 1995, is covered as an unmarried dependent child under a health benefits plan administered by the Office of the Comptroller of the Currency or the Office of Thrift Supervision and who is not a member of family as defined under section 8901(5) of title 5, United States Code—

"(A) shall be deemed to be entitled to continued coverage under section 8905a of such title as though the individual had, on January 7, 1995, ceased to meet the requirements for being considered an unmarried dependent child under chapter 89 of such title; and

"(B) may enroll in an approved health benefits plan described under section 8903 or 8903a of such title in accordance with section 8905a for continued coverage effective on and after January 8, 1995.

"(c) TRANSFERS TO THE EMPLOYEES HEALTH BENEFITS FUND.—The Office of the Comptroller of the Currency and the Office of Thrift Supervision shall transfer to the Employees Health Benefits Fund established under section 8909 of title 5, United States Code, amounts determined by the Director of the Office of Personnel Management, after consultation with the Office of the Comptroller of the Currency and the Office of Thrift Supervision, to be necessary to reimburse the Fund for the cost of providing benefits under this section not otherwise paid for by the individuals covered by this section. The amounts so transferred shall be held in the Fund and used by the Office in addition to amounts available under section 8906(g)(1) of such title.

"(d) ADMINISTRATION AND REGULATIONS.—The Office of Personnel Management—

"(1) shall administer the provisions of this section to provide for—

"(A) a period of notice and open enrollment for individuals affected by this section; and

"(B) no lapse of health coverage for individuals who enroll in a health benefits plan under chapter 89 of title 5, United States Code, in accordance with this section; and

"(2) may prescribe regulations to implement this section."

CONTINUED COVERAGE UNDER CERTAIN FEDERAL EMPLOYEE BENEFIT PROGRAMS FOR CERTAIN EMPLOYEES OF SAINT ELIZABETHS HOSPITAL

For provisions relating to treatment of certain Federal employees of Saint Elizabeths Hospital under certain Federal employee benefit programs, see section 207(o) of Pub. L. 99–335, set out as a note under section 8331 of this title.

SECTION REFERRED TO IN OTHER SECTIONS

This section is referred to in sections 8902, 8903, 8903a, 8905, 8905a, 8906, 8909, 8913, 9001 of this title; title 2 section 162b; title 10 section 1108; title 40 section 214c; title 42 section 251.

§ 8902. Contracting authority

(a) The Office of Personnel Management may contract with qualified carriers offering plans described by section 8903 or 8903a of this title, without regard to section 5 of title 41 or other statute requiring competitive bidding. Each contract shall be for a uniform term of at least 1 year, but may be made automatically renewable from term to term in the absence of notice of termination by either party.

(b) To be eligible as a carrier for the plan described by section 8903(2) of this title, a company must be licensed to issue group health insurance in all the States and the District of Columbia.

(c) A contract for a plan described by section 8903(1) or (2) of this title shall require the carrier—

(1) to reinsure with other companies which elect to participate, under an equitable formula based on the total amount of their group health insurance benefit payments in the United States during the latest year for which the information is available, to be determined by the carrier and approved by the Office; or

(2) to allocate its rights and obligations under the contract among its affiliates which elect to participate, under an equitable formula to be determined by the carrier and the affiliates and approved by the Office.

(d) Each contract under this chapter shall contain a detailed statement of benefits offered and shall include such maximums, limitations, exclusions, and other definitions of benefits as the Office considers necessary or desirable.

(e) The Office may prescribe reasonable minimum standards for health benefits plans described by section 8903 or 8903a of this title and for carriers offering the plans. Approval of a plan may be withdrawn only after notice and opportunity for hearing to the carrier concerned without regard to subchapter II of chapter 5 and chapter 7 of this title. The Office may terminate the contract of a carrier effective at the end of the contract term, if the Office finds that at no time during the preceding two contract terms did the carrier have 300 or more employees and annuitants, exclusive of family members, enrolled in the plan.

(f) A contract may not be made or a plan approved which excludes an individual because of race, sex, health status, or, at the time of the first opportunity to enroll, because of age.

(g) A contract may not be made or a plan approved which does not offer to each employee, annuitant, family member, former spouse, or person having continued coverage under section 8905a of this title whose enrollment in the plan is ended, except by a cancellation of enrollment, a temporary extension of coverage during which he may exercise the option to convert, without evidence of good health, to a nongroup contract providing health benefits. An employee, annuitant, family member, former spouse, or person having continued coverage under section 8905a of this title who exercises this option shall pay the full periodic charges of the nongroup contract.

(h) The benefits and coverage made available under subsection (g) of this section are noncancelable by the carrier except for fraud, over-insurance, or nonpayment of periodic charges.

(i) Rates charged under health benefits plans described by section 8903 or 8903a of this title shall reasonably and equitably reflect the cost of the benefits provided. Rates under health benefits plans described by section 8903(1) and (2) of this title shall be determined on a basis which, in the judgment of the Office, is consistent with the lowest schedule of basic rates generally charged for new group health benefit plans issued to large employers. The rates determined for the first contract term shall be continued for

later contract terms, except that they may be readjusted for any later term, based on past experience and benefit adjustments under the later contract. Any readjustment in rates shall be made in advance of the contract term in which they will apply and on a basis which, in the judgment of the Office, is consistent with the general practice of carriers which issue group health benefit plans to large employers.

(j) Each contract under this chapter shall require the carrier to agree to pay for or provide a health service or supply in an individual case if the Office finds that the employee, annuitant, family member, former spouse, or person having continued coverage under section 8905a of this title is entitled thereto under the terms of the contract.

(k)(1) When a contract under this chapter requires payment or reimbursement for services which may be performed by a clinical psychologist, optometrist, nurse midwife, nursing school administered clinic, or nurse practitioner/clinical specialist, licensed or certified as such under Federal or State law, as applicable, or by a qualified clinical social worker as defined in section 8901(11), an employee, annuitant, family member, former spouse, or person having continued coverage under section 8905a of this title covered by the contract shall be free to select, and shall have direct access to, such a clinical psychologist, qualified clinical social worker, optometrist, nurse midwife, nursing school administered clinic, or nurse practitioner/nurse clinical specialist without supervision or referral by another health practitioner and shall be entitled under the contract to have payment or reimbursement made to him or on his behalf for the services performed.

(2) Nothing in this subsection shall be considered to preclude a health benefits plan from providing direct access or direct payment or reimbursement to a provider in a health care practice or profession other than a practice or profession listed in paragraph (1), if such provider is licensed or certified as such under Federal or State law.

(3) The provisions of this subsection shall not apply to comprehensive medical plans as described in section 8903(4) of this title.

(l) The Office shall contract under this chapter for a plan described in section 8903(4) of this title with any qualified health maintenance carrier which offers such a plan. For the purpose of this subsection, "qualified health maintenance carrier" means any qualified carrier which is a qualified health maintenance organization within the meaning of section 1310(d)(1)[1] of title XIII of the Public Health Service Act (42 U.S.C. 300c-9(d)).

(m)(1) The terms of any contract under this chapter which relate to the nature, provision, or extent of coverage or benefits (including payments with respect to benefits) shall supersede and preempt any State or local law, or any regulation issued thereunder, which relates to health insurance or plans.

(2)(A) Notwithstanding the provisions of paragraph (1) of this subsection, if a contract under this chapter provides for the provision of, the payment for, or the reimbursement of the cost of health services for the care and treatment of any particular health condition, the carrier shall provide, pay, or reimburse up to the limits of its contract for any such health service properly provided by any person licensed under State law to provide such service if such service is provided to an individual covered by such contract in a State where 25 percent or more of the population is located in primary medical care manpower shortage areas designated pursuant to section 332 of the Public Health Service Act (42 U.S.C. 254e).

(B) The provisions of subparagraph (A) shall not apply to contracts entered into providing prepayment plans described in section 8903(4) of this title.

(n) A contract for a plan described by section 8903(1), (2), or (3), or section 8903a, shall require the carrier—

(1) to implement hospitalization-cost-containment measures, such as measures—

(A) for verifying the medical necessity of any proposed treatment or surgery;

(B) for determining the feasibility or appropriateness of providing services on an outpatient rather than on an inpatient basis;

(C) for determining the appropriate length of stay (through concurrent review or otherwise) in cases involving inpatient care; and

(D) involving case management, if the circumstances so warrant; and

(2) to establish incentives to encourage compliance with measures under paragraph (1).

(o) A contract may not be made or a plan approved which includes coverage for any benefit, item, or service for which funds may not be used under the Assisted Suicide Funding Restriction Act of 1997.

(Pub. L. 89–554, Sept. 6, 1966, 80 Stat. 601; Pub. L. 93–246, §3, Jan. 31, 1974, 88 Stat. 4; Pub. L. 93–363, §1, July 30, 1974, 88 Stat. 398; Pub. L. 94–183, §2(43), Dec. 31, 1975, 89 Stat. 1059; Pub. L. 94–460, title I, §110(b), Oct. 8, 1976, 90 Stat. 1952; Pub. L. 95–368, §1, Sept. 17, 1978, 92 Stat. 606; Pub. L. 95–454, title IX, §906(a)(2), (3), Oct. 13, 1978, 92 Stat. 1224; Pub. L. 96–179, §3, Jan. 2, 1980, 93 Stat. 1299; Pub. L. 98–615, §3(2), Nov. 8, 1984, 98 Stat. 3203; Pub. L. 99–53, §2(a), June 17, 1985, 99 Stat. 94; Pub. L. 99–251, title I, §§105(b), 106(a)(3), Feb. 27, 1986, 100 Stat. 15, 16; Pub. L. 100–202, §101(m) [title VI, §626], Dec. 22, 1987, 101 Stat. 1329–390, 1329–430; Pub. L. 100–654, title II, §§201(b), 202(a), Nov. 14, 1988, 102 Stat. 3845; Pub. L. 101–508, title VII, §7002(a), Nov. 5, 1990, 104 Stat. 1388–329; Pub. L. 101–509, title IV, §1, Nov. 5, 1990, 104 Stat. 1421; Pub. L. 102–393, title V, §537(a), (b), Oct. 6, 1992, 106 Stat. 1765; Pub. L. 105–12, §9(g), Apr. 30, 1997, 111 Stat. 27; Pub. L. 105–266, §§3(c), 8, Oct. 19, 1998, 112 Stat. 2366, 2370.)

HISTORICAL AND REVISION NOTES

Derivation	U.S. Code	Revised Statutes and Statutes at Large
....	5 U.S.C. 3005.	Sept. 28, 1959, Pub. L. 86–382, §6, 73 Stat. 712. Mar. 17, 1964, Pub. L. 88–284, §1(7)–(9), 78 Stat. 165.

Standard changes are made to conform with the definitions applicable and the style of this title as outlined in the preface to the report.

REFERENCES IN TEXT

Section 1310(d)(1) of title XIII of the Public Health Service Act (42 U.S.C. 300c–9(d)), referred to in subsec. (l), probably is intended as a reference to section 300e–9(d) of Title 42, The Public Health and Welfare. Section 300e–9(d) of Title 42 was redesignated section 300e–9(c) of Title 42 by Pub. L. 100–517, §7(b), Oct. 24, 1988, 102 Stat. 2580.

The Assisted Suicide Funding Restriction Act of 1997, referred to in subsec. (o), is Pub. L. 105–12, Apr. 30, 1997, 111 Stat. 23, which is classified principally to chapter 138 (§14401 et seq.) of Title 42, The Public Health and Welfare. For complete classification of this Act to the Code, see Short Title note set out under section 14401 of Title 42 and Tables.

CODIFICATION

Another section 1 of title IV of Pub. L. 101–509, 104 Stat. 1416, enacted sections 2701 to 2706 of Title 44, Public Printing and Documents, and provisions set out as a note under section 2102 of Title 44.

AMENDMENTS

1998—Subsec. (k)(2), (3). Pub. L. 105–266, §8, added par. (2) and redesignated former par. (2) as (3).

Subsec. (m)(1). Pub. L. 105–266, §3(c), added par. (1) and struck out former par. (1) which read as follows: "The provisions of any contract under this chapter which relate to the nature or extent of coverage or benefits (including payments with respect to benefits) shall supersede and preempt any State or local law, or any regulation issued thereunder, which relates to health insurance or plans to the extent that such law or regulation is inconsistent with such contractual provisions."

1997—Subsec. (o). Pub. L. 105–12 added subsec. (o).

1992—Pub. L. 102–393 amended subsec. (k) generally. Prior to amendment, subsec. (k) read as follows:

"(1) When a contract under this chapter requires payment or reimbursement for services which may be performed by a clinical psychologist, optometrist, nurse midwife, or nurse practitioner/clinical specialist, licensed or certified as such under Federal or State law, as applicable, or by a qualified clinical social worker as defined in section 8901(11), an employee, annuitant, family member, former spouse, or person having continued coverage under section 8905a of this title covered by the contract shall be free to select, and shall have direct access to, such a clinical psychologist, qualified clinical social worker, optometrist, nurse midwife, or nurse practitioner/nurse clinical specialist without supervision or referral by another health practitioner and shall be entitled under the contract to have payment or reimbursement made to him or on his behalf for the services performed.

"(2) The provisions of this subsection shall not apply to group practice prepayment plans."

1990—Subsec. (k)(1). Pub. L. 101–509 substituted "performed by a clinical psychologist, optometrist, nurse midwife, or nurse practitioner/clinical specialist" for "performed by a clinical psychologist or optometrist" and "qualified clinical social worker, optometrist, nurse midwife, or nurse practitioner/nurse clinical specialist" for "qualified clinical social worker or optometrist".

Subsec. (n). Pub. L. 101–508 added subsec. (n).

1988—Subsecs. (g), (j), (k)(1). Pub. L. 100–654 substituted "former spouse, or person having continued coverage under section 8905a of this title" for "or former spouse" wherever appearing.

1987—Subsec. (k)(1). Pub. L. 100–202, §101(m) [title VI, §626(1), (2)], inserted "or by a qualified clinical social worker as defined in section 8901(11)," after "as applicable," and ", qualified clinical social worker" after "such a clinical psychologist".

Subsec. (k)(2), (3). Pub. L. 100–202, §101(m) [title VI, §626(3)], redesignated par. (3) as (2) and struck out former par. (2) which read as follows: "When a contract under this chapter requires payment or reimbursement for services which may be performed by a qualified clinical social worker, an employee, annuitant, family member, or former spouse covered by the contract shall be entitled under the contract to have payment or reimbursement made to him or on his behalf for the services performed. As a condition for the payment or reimbursement, the contract—

"(A) may require that the services be performed pursuant to a referral by a psychiatrist; but

"(B) may not require that the services be performed under the supervision of a psychiatrist or other health practitioner."

Subsec. (m)(2)(A). Pub. L. 100–202, § 101(m) [title VI, § 626(4)], struck out "This paragraph shall apply with respect to a qualified clinical social worker covered by subsection (k)(2) of this section without regard to whether such contract contains the requirement authorized by clause (i) of the second sentence of subparagraph (A) of such subsection (k)(2)."

1986—Subsec. (k). Pub. L. 99–251, § 105(b), designated existing provisions as par. (1), struck out last sentence providing that the provisions of this subsection shall not apply to group practice prepayment plans, and added pars. (2) and (3).

Subsec. (m)(2)(A). Pub. L. 99–251, § 106(a)(3), inserted last sentence relating to applicability of this paragraph with respect to a qualified clinical social worker covered by subsection (k)(2) of this section.

1985—Subsecs. (a), (e), (i). Pub. L. 99–53 inserted reference to section 8903a of this title.

1984—Subsec. (g). Pub. L. 98–615, § 3(2)(A), substituted "employee, annuitant, family member, or former spouse" for "employee or annuitant" in two places.

Subsecs. (j), (k). Pub. L. 98–615, § 3(2)(B), substituted "family member, or former spouse" for "or family member".

1980—Subsec. (m)(2)(A). Pub. L. 96–179 substituted "in a State where 25 percent or more of the population is located in primary medical care manpower shortage areas designated pursuant to section 332 of the Public Health Service Act (42 U.S.C. 254e)" for "who is a member of a medically underserved population (within the meaning of section 1302(7) of the Public Health Service Act (42 U.S.C. 300e–17))".

1978—Subsecs. (a), (c) to (e), (i), (j), (l). Pub. L. 95–454 substituted "Office of Personnel Management" for "Civil Service Commission" and "Office" for "Commission" wherever appearing.

Subsec. (m). Pub. L. 95–368 added subsec. (m).

1976—Subsec. (l). Pub. L. 94–460 added subsec. (l).

1975—Subsecs. (j), (k). Pub. L. 94–183 redesignated subsec. (j), added by Pub. L. 93–363 and relating to services performed by a clinical psychologist or optometrist, as (k).

1974—Subsec. (j). Pub. L. 93–363 added subsec. (j) covering services performed by a clinical psychologist or optometrist.

Pub. L. 93–246 added subsec. (j) requiring the carrier to pay for or provide a health service or supply in specified cases.

EFFECTIVE DATE OF 1997 AMENDMENT

Amendment by Pub. L. 105–12 effective Apr. 30, 1997, and applicable to Federal payments made pursuant to obligations incurred after Apr. 30, 1997, for items and services provided on or after such date, subject to also being applicable with respect to contracts entered into, renewed, or extended after Apr. 30, 1997, as well as contracts entered into before Apr. 30, 1997, to the extent permitted under such contracts, see section 11 of Pub. L. 105–12, set out as an Effective Date note under section 14401 of Title 42, The Public Health and Welfare.

EFFECTIVE DATE OF 1992 AMENDMENT

Section 537(c) of Pub. L. 102–393 provided that: "The amendments made by this section [amending this section] shall be effective with respect to contract years beginning after the date of enactment of this Act [Oct. 6, 1992]."

EFFECTIVE DATE OF 1990 AMENDMENT

Section 7002(g) of Pub. L. 101–508 provided that: "Except as provided in subsection (f) [set out as a note under section 8904 of this title], the amendments made by this section [amending this section, sections 8904, 8909, and 8910 of this title, and provisions set out as a note under section 8906 of this title] shall apply with respect to contract years beginning on or after January 1, 1991."

EFFECTIVE DATE OF 1988 AMENDMENT

Section 203 of title II of Pub. L. 100–654 provided that: "(a) IN GENERAL.—The amendments made by this title [enacting section 8905a of this title and amending this section and sections 8903, 8905, and 8909 of this title] shall apply with respect to—

"(1) any calendar year beginning, and contracts entered into or renewed for any calendar year beginning, after the end of the 9-month period beginning on the date of the enactment of this Act [Nov. 14, 1988]; and

"(2) any qualifying event occurring on or after the first day of the first calendar year beginning after the end of the 9-month period referred to in paragraph (1).

"(b) DEFINITION.—For the purpose of this section, the term 'qualifying event' means any of the following events:

"(1) A separation from Government service.

"(2) A divorce, annulment, or legal separation.

"(3) Any change in circumstances which causes an individual to become ineligible to be considered an unmarried dependent child under chapter 89 of such title [section 8901 et seq. of this title]."

EFFECTIVE DATE OF 1986 AMENDMENT

Amendment by section 105(b) of Pub. L. 99–251 effective with respect to contracts entered into or renewed for calendar years beginning after Dec. 31, 1986, see section 105(c) of Pub. L. 99–251, set out as a note under section 8901 of this title.

Section 106(b) of Pub. L. 99–251 provided that: "The amendments made by subsection (a) [amending this section and provisions set out as notes under this section] shall take effect with respect to services provided after December 31, 1984."

EFFECTIVE DATE OF 1984 AMENDMENT

Amendment by Pub. L. 98–615 effective May 7, 1985, with enumerated exceptions, and applicable to any individual who is married to an employee or annuitant on or after that date, see section 4(a)(2) of Pub. L. 98–615, as amended, set out as a note under section 8341 of this title.

EFFECTIVE DATE OF 1980 AMENDMENT

Section 5(b) of Pub. L. 96–179, as amended by Pub. L. 99–251, title I, § 106(a)(2), Feb. 27, 1986, 100 Stat. 16, provided that: "The amendments made by section 3 [amending this section] shall apply to services provided after December 31, 1979, under any contract entered into or renewed after December 31, 1979."

EFFECTIVE DATE OF 1978 AMENDMENTS

Amendment by Pub. L. 95–454 effective 90 days after Oct. 13, 1978, see section 907 of Pub. L. 95–454, set out as a note under section 1101 of this title.

Section 3 of Pub. L. 95–368, as amended by Pub. L. 99–251, title I, § 106(a)(1), Feb. 27, 1986, 100 Stat. 16, provided that: "The provisions of section 8902(m)(2) of title 5, United States Code, as added by the first section of this Act, shall apply to services provided under any contract entered into or renewed after December 31, 1979."

EFFECTIVE DATE OF 1976 AMENDMENT

Amendment by Pub. L. 94–460 effective Oct. 8, 1976, see section 118 of Pub. L. 94–460, set out as a note under section 300e of Title 42, The Public Health and Welfare.

Section 2 of Pub. L. 93–363 provided that: "The amendment made by this Act [amending this section] shall become effective with respect to any contract entered into or renewed on or after the date of enactment of this Act [July 30, 1974]."

Section 4(c) of Pub. L. 93–246 provided that: "Section 3 [amending this section] shall become effective with respect to any contract entered into or renewed on or after the date of enactment of this Act [Jan. 31, 1974]."

FULL DISCLOSURE IN HEALTH PLAN CONTRACTS

Pub. L. 105–266, § 5, Oct. 19, 1998, 112 Stat. 2368, provided that: "The Office of Personnel Management shall encourage carriers offering health benefits plans described by section 8903 or section 8903a of title 5, United States Code, with respect to contractual arrangements made by such carriers with any person for purposes of obtaining discounts from providers for health care services or supplies furnished to individuals enrolled in such plan, to seek assurance that the conditions for such discounts are fully disclosed to the providers who grant them."

RATE REDUCTION FOR MEDICARE ELIGIBLE FEDERAL ANNUITANTS

Pub. L. 100–360, title IV, § 422, July 1, 1988, 102 Stat. 810, which directed the Office of Personnel Management to reduce the rates charged medicare eligible individuals participating in health benefit plans by a prorated amount, was repealed by Pub. L. 101–234, title III, § 301(a), Dec. 13, 1989, 103 Stat. 1985.

AUTHORITY OF CARRIER TO CONTRACT FOR COMPREHENSIVE MEDICAL SERVICES FROM A GROUP PRACTICE UNIT OR ORGANIZATION

Pub. L. 91–515, title IV, § 401, Oct. 30, 1970, 84 Stat. 1309, authorized Secretary of Health, Education, and Welfare to permit any carrier which is a party to a contract entered into under this chapter or under the Retired Federal Employees Health Benefits Act, or which participates in carrying out of any such contract, to issue in any State contracts entitling any person as a beneficiary to receive comprehensive medical services from a group practice unit or organization with which such carrier has contracted or otherwise arranged for the provision of such services.

SECTION REFERRED TO IN OTHER SECTIONS

This section is referred to in sections 8902a, 8910, 8913 of this title.

§ 8902a. Debarment and other sanctions

(a)(1) For the purpose of this section—

(A) the term "provider of health care services or supplies" or "provider" means a physician, hospital, or other individual or entity which furnishes health care services or supplies;

(B) the term "individual covered under this chapter" or "covered individual" means an employee, annuitant, family member, or former spouse covered by a health benefits plan described by section 8903 or 8903a;

(C) an individual or entity shall be considered to have been "convicted" of a criminal offense if—

(i) a judgment of conviction for such offense has been entered against the individual or entity by a Federal, State, or local court;

(ii) there has been a finding of guilt against the individual or entity by a Federal, State, or local court with respect to such offense;

(iii) a plea of guilty or nolo contendere by the individual or entity has been accepted by a Federal, State, or local court with respect to such offense; or

(iv) in the case of an individual, the individual has entered a first offender or other program pursuant to which a judgment of conviction for such offense has been withheld;

without regard to the pendency or outcome of any appeal (other than a judgment of acquittal based on innocence) or request for relief on behalf of the individual or entity; and

(D) the term "should know" means that a person, with respect to information, acts in deliberate ignorance of, or in reckless disregard of, the truth or falsity of the information, and no proof of specific intent to defraud is required;[1]

(2)(A) Notwithstanding section 8902(j) or any other provision of this chapter, if, under subsection (b), (c), or (d) a provider is barred from participating in the program under this chapter, no payment may be made by a carrier pursuant to any contract under this chapter (either to such provider or by reimbursement) for any service or supply furnished by such provider during the period of the debarment.

(B) Each contract under this chapter shall contain such provisions as may be necessary to carry out subparagraph (A) and the other provisions of this section.

(b) The Office of Personnel Management shall bar the following providers of health care services or supplies from participating in the program under this chapter:

(1) Any provider that has been convicted, under Federal or State law, of a criminal offense relating to fraud, corruption, breach of fiduciary responsibility, or other financial misconduct in connection with the delivery of a health care service or supply.

(2) Any provider that has been convicted, under Federal or State law, of a criminal offense relating to neglect or abuse of patients in connection with the delivery of a health care service or supply.

(3) Any provider that has been convicted, under Federal or State law, in connection with the interference with or obstruction of an investigation or prosecution of a criminal offense described in paragraph (1) or (2).

(4) Any provider that has been convicted, under Federal or State law, of a criminal offense relating to the unlawful manufacture, distribution, prescription, or dispensing of a controlled substance.

(5) Any provider that is currently debarred, suspended, or otherwise excluded from any procurement or nonprocurement activity (within the meaning of section 2455 of the Federal Acquisition Streamlining Act of 1994).

(c) The Office may bar the following providers of health care services from participating in the program under this chapter:

(1) Any provider—

(A) whose license to provide health care services or supplies has been revoked, suspended, restricted, or not renewed, by a State licensing authority for reasons relat-

---

[1] So in original. The semicolon probably should be a period.

ing to the provider's professional competence, professional performance, or financial integrity; or

(B) that surrendered such a license while a formal disciplinary proceeding was pending before such an authority, if the proceeding concerned the provider's professional competence, professional performance, or financial integrity.

(2) Any provider that is an entity directly or indirectly owned, or with a control interest of 5 percent or more held, by an individual who has been convicted of any offense described in subsection (b), against whom a civil monetary penalty has been assessed under subsection (d), or who has been debarred from participation under this chapter.

(3) Any individual who directly or indirectly owns or has a control interest in a sanctioned entity and who knows or should know of the action constituting the basis for the entity's conviction of any offense described in subsection (b), assessment with a civil monetary penalty under subsection (d), or debarment from participation under this chapter.

(4) Any provider that the Office determines, in connection with claims presented under this chapter, has charged for health care services or supplies in an amount substantially in excess of such provider's customary charge for such services or supplies (unless the Office finds there is good cause for such charge), or charged for health care services or supplies which are substantially in excess of the needs of the covered individual or which are of a quality that fails to meet professionally recognized standards for such services or supplies.

(5) Any provider that the Office determines has committed acts described in subsection (d).

Any determination under paragraph (4) relating to whether a charge for health care services or supplies is substantially in excess of the needs of the covered individual shall be made by trained reviewers based on written medical protocols developed by physicians. In the event such a determination cannot be made based on such protocols, a physician in an appropriate specialty shall be consulted.

(d) Whenever the Office determines—

(1) in connection with claims presented under this chapter, that a provider has charged for a health care service or supply which the provider knows or should have known involves—

(A) an item or service not provided as claimed;

(B) charges in violation of applicable charge limitations under section 8904(b); or

(C) an item or service furnished during a period in which the provider was debarred from participation under this chapter pursuant to a determination by the Office under this section, other than as permitted under subsection (g)(2)(B);

(2) that a provider of health care services or supplies has knowingly made, or caused to be made, any false statement or misrepresentation of a material fact which is reflected in a claim presented under this chapter; or

(3) that a provider of health care services or supplies has knowingly failed to provide any information required by a carrier or by the Office to determine whether a payment or reimbursement is payable under this chapter or the amount of any such payment or reimbursement;

the Office may, in addition to any other penalties that may be prescribed by law, and after consultation with the Attorney General, impose a civil monetary penalty of not more than $10,000 for any item or service involved. In addition, such a provider shall be subject to an assessment of not more than twice the amount claimed for each such item or service. In addition, the Office may make a determination in the same proceeding to bar such provider from participating in the program under this chapter.

(e) The Office—

(1) may not initiate any debarment proceeding against a provider, based on such provider's having been convicted of a criminal offense, later than 6 years after the date on which such provider is so convicted; and

(2) may not initiate any action relating to a civil penalty, assessment, or debarment under this section, in connection with any claim, later than 6 years after the date the claim is presented, as determined under regulations prescribed by the Office.

(f) In making a determination relating to the appropriateness of imposing or the period of any debarment under this section (where such debarment is not mandatory), or the appropriateness of imposing or the amount of any civil penalty or assessment under this section, the Office shall take into account—

(1) the nature of any claims involved and the circumstances under which they were presented;

(2) the degree of culpability, history of prior offenses or improper conduct of the provider involved; and

(3) such other matters as justice may require.

(g)(1)(A) Except as provided in subparagraph (B), debarment of a provider under subsection (b) or (c) shall be effective at such time and upon such reasonable notice to such provider, and to carriers and covered individuals, as shall be specified in regulations prescribed by the Office. Any such provider that is debarred from participation may request a hearing in accordance with subsection (h)(1).

(B) Unless the Office determines that the health or safety of individuals receiving health care services warrants an earlier effective date, the Office shall not make a determination adverse to a provider under subsection (c)(5) or (d) until such provider has been given reasonable notice and an opportunity for the determination to be made after a hearing as provided in accordance with subsection (h)(1).

(2)(A) Except as provided in subparagraph (B), a debarment shall be effective with respect to any health care services or supplies furnished by a provider on or after the effective date of such provider's debarment.

(B) A debarment shall not apply with respect to inpatient institutional services furnished to an individual who was admitted to the institution before the date the debarment would otherwise become effective until the passage of 30 days after such date, unless the Office determines that the health or safety of the individual receiving those services warrants that a shorter period, or that no such period, be afforded.

(3) Any notice of debarment referred to in paragraph (1) shall specify the date as of which debarment becomes effective and the minimum period of time for which such debarment is to remain effective. In the case of a debarment under paragraph (1), (2), (3), or (4) of subsection (b), the minimum period of debarment shall not be less than 3 years, except as provided in paragraph (4)(B)(ii).

(4)(A) A provider barred from participating in the program under this chapter may, after the expiration of the minimum period of debarment referred to in paragraph (3), apply to the Office, in such manner as the Office may by regulation prescribe, for termination of the debarment.

(B) The Office may—

(i) terminate the debarment of a provider, pursuant to an application filed by such provider after the end of the minimum debarment period, if the Office determines, based on the conduct of the applicant, that—

(I) there is no basis under subsection (b), (c), or (d) for continuing the debarment; and

(II) there are reasonable assurances that the types of actions which formed the basis for the original debarment have not recurred and will not recur; or

(ii) notwithstanding any provision of subparagraph (A), terminate the debarment of a provider, pursuant to an application filed by such provider before the end of the minimum debarment period, if the Office determines that—

(I) based on the conduct of the applicant, the requirements of subclauses (I) and (II) of clause (i) have been met; and

(II) early termination under this clause is warranted based on the fact that the provider is the sole community provider or the sole source of essential specialized services in a community, or other similar circumstances.

(5) The Office shall—

(A) promptly notify the appropriate State or local agency or authority having responsibility for the licensing or certification of a provider barred from participation in the program under this chapter of the fact of the debarment, as well as the reasons for such debarment;

(B) request that appropriate investigations be made and sanctions invoked in accordance with applicable law and policy; and

(C) request that the State or local agency or authority keep the Office fully and currently informed with respect to any actions taken in response to the request.

(h)(1) Any provider of health care services or supplies that is the subject of an adverse determination by the Office under this section shall be entitled to reasonable notice and an opportunity to request a hearing of record, and to judicial review as provided in this subsection after the Office renders a final decision. The Office shall grant a request for a hearing upon a showing that due process rights have not previously been afforded with respect to any finding of fact which is relied upon as a cause for an adverse determination under this section. Such hearing shall be conducted without regard to subchapter II of chapter 5 and chapter 7 of this title by a hearing officer who shall be designated by the Director of the Office and who shall not otherwise have been involved in the adverse determination being appealed. A request for a hearing under this subsection shall be filed within such period and in accordance with such procedures as the Office shall prescribe by regulation.

(2) Any provider adversely affected by a final decision under paragraph (1) made after a hearing to which such provider was a party may seek review of such decision in the United States District Court for the District of Columbia or for the district in which the plaintiff resides or has his or her principal place of business by filing a notice of appeal in such court within 60 days after the date the decision is issued, and by simultaneously sending copies of such notice by certified mail to the Director of the Office and to the Attorney General. In answer to the appeal, the Director of the Office shall promptly file in such court a certified copy of the transcript of the record, if the Office conducted a hearing, and other evidence upon which the findings and decision complained of are based. The court shall have power to enter, upon the pleadings and evidence of record, a judgment affirming, modifying, or setting aside, in whole or in part, the decision of the Office, with or without remanding the case for a rehearing. The district court shall not set aside or remand the decision of the Office unless there is not substantial evidence on the record, taken as whole, to support the findings by the Office of a cause for action under this section or unless action taken by the Office constitutes an abuse of discretion.

(3) Matters that were raised or that could have been raised in a hearing under paragraph (1) or an appeal under paragraph (2) may not be raised as a defense to a civil action by the United States to collect a penalty or assessment imposed under this section.

(i) A civil action to recover civil monetary penalties or assessments under subsection (d) shall be brought by the Attorney General in the name of the United States, and may be brought in the United States district court for the district where the claim involved was presented or where the person subject to the penalty resides. Amounts recovered under this section shall be paid to the Office for deposit into the Employees Health Benefits Fund. The amount of a penalty or assessment as finally determined by the Office, or other amount the Office may agree to in compromise, may be deducted from any sum then or later owing by the United States to the party against whom the penalty or assessment has been levied.

(j) The Office shall prescribe regulations under which, with respect to services or supplies furnished by a debarred provider to a covered individual during the period of such provider's debarment, payment or reimbursement under this chapter may be made, notwithstanding the fact of such debarment, if such individual did not know or could not reasonably be expected to have known of the debarment. In any such instance, the carrier involved shall take appropriate measures to ensure that the individual is informed of the debarment and the minimum period of time remaining under the terms of the debarment.

(Added Pub. L. 100–654, title I, § 101(a), Nov. 14, 1988, 102 Stat. 3837; amended Pub. L. 105–266, § 2(a), Oct. 19, 1998, 112 Stat. 2363.)

REFERENCES IN TEXT

Section 2455 of the Federal Acquisition Streamlining Act of 1994, referred to in subsec. (b)(5), is section 2455 of Pub. L. 103–355, which is set out as a note under section 6101 of Title 31, Money and Finance.

AMENDMENTS

1998—Subsec. (a)(1)(D). Pub. L. 105–266, § 2(a)(1)(A), added subpar. (D).

Subsec. (a)(2)(A). Pub. L. 105–266, § 2(a)(1)(B), substituted "subsection (b), (c), or (d)" for "subsection (b) or (c)".

Subsec. (b). Pub. L. 105–266, § 2(a)(2)(A), substituted "shall" for "may" in introductory provisions.

Subsec. (b)(5). Pub. L. 105–266, § 2(a)(2)(B), amended par. (5) generally. Prior to amendment, par. (5) read as follows: "Any provider—

"(A) whose license to provide health care services or supplies has been revoked, suspended, restricted, or not renewed, by a State licensing authority for reasons relating to the provider's professional competence, professional performance, or financial integrity; or

"(B) that surrendered such a license while a formal disciplinary proceeding was pending before such an authority, if the proceeding concerned the provider's professional competence, professional performance, or financial integrity."

Subsec. (c). Pub. L. 105–266, § 2(a)(3), added subsec. (c). Former subsec. (c) redesignated (d).

Subsec. (d). Pub. L. 105–266, § 2(a)(3), redesignated subsec. (c) as (d). Former subsec. (d) redesignated (e).

Subsec. (d)(1). Pub. L. 105–266, § 2(a)(4), amended par. (1) generally. Prior to amendment, par. (1) read as follows: "in connection with a claim presented under this chapter, that a provider of health care services or supplies—

"(A) has charged for health care services or supplies that the provider knows or should have known were not provided as claimed; or

"(B) has charged for health care services or supplies in an amount substantially in excess of such provider's customary charges for such services or supplies, or charged for health care services or supplies which are substantially in excess of the needs of the covered individual or which are of a quality that fails to meet professionally recognized standards for such services or supplies;".

Subsec. (e). Pub. L. 105–266, § 2(a)(3), redesignated subsec. (d) as (e). Former subsec. (e) redesignated (f).

Subsec. (f). Pub. L. 105–266, § 2(a)(3), (5), redesignated subsec. (e) as (f) and inserted "(where such debarment is not mandatory)" after "debarment under this section". Former subsec. (f) redesignated (g).

Subsec. (g). Pub. L. 105–266, § 2(a)(3), redesignated subsec. (f) as (g). Former subsec. (g) redesignated (h).

Subsec. (g)(1). Pub. L. 105–266, § 2(a)(6)(A), added par. (1) and struck out former par. (1) which read as follows: "The debarment of a provider under subsection (b) or (c) shall be effective at such time and upon such reasonable notice to such provider, and to carriers and covered individuals, as may be specified in regulations prescribed by the Office."

Subsec. (g)(3). Pub. L. 105–266, § 2(a)(6)(B), inserted "of debarment" after "notice" and inserted at end "In the case of a debarment under paragraph (1), (2), (3), or (4) of subsection (b), the minimum period of debarment shall not be less than 3 years, except as provided in paragraph (4)(B)(ii)."

Subsec. (g)(4)(B)(i)(I). Pub. L. 105–266, § 2(a)(6)(C), substituted "subsection (b), (c), or (d)" for "subsection (b) or (c)".

Subsec. (g)(6). Pub. L. 105–266, § 2(a)(6)(D), struck out par. (6) which read as follows: "The Office shall, upon written request and payment of a reasonable charge to defray the cost of complying with such request, furnish a current list of any providers barred from participating in the program under this chapter, including the minimum period of time remaining under the terms of each provider's debarment."

Subsec. (h). Pub. L. 105–266, § 2(a)(3), redesignated subsec. (g) as (h). Former subsec. (h) redesignated (i).

Subsec. (h)(1), (2). Pub. L. 105–266, § 2(a)(7), added pars. (1) and (2) and struck out former pars. (1) and (2) which read as follows:

"(1) The Office may not make a determination under subsection (b) or (c) adverse to a provider of health care services or supplies until such provider has been given written notice and an opportunity for a hearing on the record. A provider is entitled to be represented by counsel, to present witnesses, and to cross-examine witnesses against the provider in any such hearing.

"(2) Notwithstanding section 8912, any person adversely affected by a final decision under paragraph (1) may obtain review of such decision in the United States Court of Appeals for the Federal Circuit. A written petition requesting that the decision be modified or set aside must be filed within 60 days after the date on which such person is notified of such decision."

Subsec. (i). Pub. L. 105–266, § 2(a)(3), (8), redesignated subsec. (h) as (i), substituted "subsection (d)" for "subsection (c)", and inserted at end "The amount of a penalty or assessment as finally determined by the Office, or other amount the Office may agree to in compromise, may be deducted from any sum then or later owing by the United States to the party against whom the penalty or assessment has been levied." Former subsec. (i) redesignated (j).

Subsec. (j). Pub. L. 105–266, § 2(a)(3), redesignated subsec. (i) as (j).

EFFECTIVE DATE OF 1998 AMENDMENT

Pub. L. 105–266, § 2(b), Oct. 19, 1998, 112 Stat. 2366, provided that:

"(1) IN GENERAL.—Except as provided in paragraph (2), the amendments made by this section [amending this section] shall take effect on the date of the enactment of this Act [Oct. 19, 1998].

"(2) EXCEPTIONS.—(A) Paragraphs (2), (3), and (5) of section 8902a(c) of title 5, United States Code, as amended by subsection (a)(3), shall apply only to the extent that the misconduct which is the basis for debarment under paragraph (2), (3), or (5), as applicable, occurs after the date of the enactment of this Act.

"(B) Paragraph (1)(B) of section 8902a(d) of title 5, United States Code, as amended by subsection (a)(4), shall apply only with respect to charges which violate section 8904(b) of such title for items or services furnished after the date of the enactment of this Act.

"(C) Paragraph (3) of section 8902a(g) of title 5, United States Code, as amended by subsection (a)(6)(B), shall apply only with respect to debarments based on convictions occurring after the date of the enactment of this Act."

EFFECTIVE DATE; PRIOR CONDUCT

Section 102 of title I of Pub. L. 100–654 provided that:

"(a) APPLICABILITY.—The amendments made by this title [enacting this section] shall be effective with respect to any calendar year beginning, and contracts entered into or renewed for any calendar year beginning, after the date of the enactment of this Act [Nov. 14, 1988].

"(b) PRIOR CONDUCT NOT TO BE CONSIDERED.—In carrying out section 8902a of title 5, United States Code, as added by this title, no debarment, civil monetary penalty, or assessment may be imposed under such section based on any criminal or other conduct occurring before the beginning of the first calendar year which begins after the date of the enactment of this Act [Nov. 14, 1988].''

§ 8903. Health benefits plans

The Office of Personnel Management may contract for or approve the following health benefits plans:

(1) SERVICE BENEFIT PLAN.—One Government-wide plan, which may be underwritten by participating affiliates licensed in any number of States, offering two levels of benefits, under which payment is made by a carrier under contracts with physicians, hospitals, or other providers of health services for benefits of the types described by section 8904(1) of this title given to employees, annuitants, members of their families, former spouses, or persons having continued coverage under section 8905a of this title, or, under certain conditions, payment is made by a carrier to the employee, annuitant, family member, former spouse, or person having continued coverage under section 8905a of this title.

(2) INDEMNITY BENEFIT PLAN.—One Government-wide plan, offering two levels of benefits, under which a carrier agrees to pay certain sums of money, not in excess of the actual expenses incurred, for benefits of the types described by section 8904(2) of this title.

(3) EMPLOYEE ORGANIZATION PLANS.—Employee organization plans which offer benefits of the types referred to by section 8904(3) of this title, which are sponsored or underwritten, and are administered, in whole or substantial part, by employee organizations described in section 8901(8)(A) of this title, which are available only to individuals, and members of their families, who at the time of enrollment are members of the organization.

(4) COMPREHENSIVE MEDICAL PLANS.—

(A) GROUP-PRACTICE PREPAYMENT PLANS.— Group-practice prepayment plans which offer health benefits of the types referred to by section 8904(4) of this title, in whole or in substantial part on a prepaid basis, with professional services thereunder provided by physicians practicing as a group in a common center or centers. The group shall include at least 3 physicians who receive all or a substantial part of their professional income from the prepaid funds and who represent 1 or more medical specialties appropriate and necessary for the population proposed to be served by the plan.

(B) INDIVIDUAL-PRACTICE PREPAYMENT PLANS.—Individual-practice prepayment plans which offer health services in whole or substantial part on a prepaid basis, with professional services thereunder provided by individual physicians who agree, under certain conditions approved by the Office, to accept the payments provided by the plans as full payment for covered services given by them including, in addition to in-hospital services, general care given in their offices and the patients' homes, out-of-hospital diagnostic procedures, and preventive care, and which

plans are offered by organizations which have successfully operated similar plans before approval by the Office of the plan in which employees may enroll.

(C) MIXED MODEL PREPAYMENT PLANS.— Mixed model prepayment plans which are a combination of the type of plans described in subparagraph (A) and the type of plans described in subparagraph (B).

(Pub. L. 89–554, Sept. 6, 1966, 80 Stat. 602; Pub. L. 95–454, title IX, § 906(a)(2), (3), Oct. 13, 1978, 92 Stat. 1224; Pub. L. 98–615, § 3(3), Nov. 8, 1984, 98 Stat. 3203; Pub. L. 99–53, § 2(b), June 17, 1985, 99 Stat. 94; Pub. L. 99–251, title I, §§ 102, 111, Feb. 27, 1986, 100 Stat. 14, 19; Pub. L. 100–654, title II, § 202(b), Nov. 14, 1988, 102 Stat. 3845; Pub. L. 105–266, § 3(b), Oct. 19, 1998, 112 Stat. 2366.)

HISTORICAL AND REVISION NOTES

Derivation	U.S. Code	Revised Statutes and Statutes at Large
....	5 U.S.C. 3003.	Sept. 28, 1959, Pub. L. 86–382, § 4, 73 Stat. 711. July 8, 1963, Pub. L. 88–59, § 1(b), 77 Stat. 77.

Standard changes are made to conform with the definitions applicable and the style of this title as outlined in the preface to the report.

AMENDMENTS

1998—Par. (1). Pub. L. 105–266 substituted "plan, which may be underwritten by participating affiliates licensed in any number of States," for "plan,".

1988—Par. (1). Pub. L. 100–654 substituted "former spouses, or persons having continued coverage under section 8905a of this title," for "or former spouses," and "former spouse, or person having continued coverage under section 8905a of this title." for "or former spouse."

1986—Par. (4)(A). Pub. L. 99–251, § 102, amended second sentence generally, substituting "at least 3 physicians" for "physicians representing at least three major medical specialties" and inserted "and who represent 1 or more medical specialties appropriate and necessary for the population proposed to be served by the plan".

Par. (4)(C). Pub. L. 99–251, § 111, added subpar. (C).

1985—Par. (3). Pub. L. 99–53 inserted "described in section 8901(8)(A) of this title" after "employee organizations".

1984—Par. (1). Pub. L. 98–615, § 3(3), substituted "employees, annuitants, members of their families, or former spouses" for "employees or annuitants, or members of their families" and "employee, annuitant, family member, or former spouse" for "employee or annuitant or member of his family".

1978—Pub. L. 95–454 substituted "Office of Personnel Management" and "Office" for "Civil Service Commission" and "Commission", respectively, wherever appearing.

EFFECTIVE DATE OF 1988 AMENDMENT

Amendment by Pub. L. 100–654 applicable with respect to any calendar year beginning, and contracts entered into or renewed for any calendar year beginning, after end of 9-month period beginning Nov. 14, 1988, and with respect to any qualifying event occurring on or after first day of first calendar year beginning after end of such 9-month period, see section 203 of Pub. L. 100–654, set out as a note under section 8902 of this title.

EFFECTIVE DATE OF 1984 AMENDMENT

Amendment by Pub. L. 98–615 effective May 7, 1985, with enumerated exceptions, and applicable to any individual who is married to an employee or annuitant on or after that date, see section 4(a)(2) of Pub. L. 98–615, as amended, set out as a note under section 8341 of this title.

EFFECTIVE DATE OF 1978 AMENDMENT

Amendment by Pub. L. 95–454 effective 90 days after Oct. 13, 1978, see section 907 of Pub. L. 95–454, set out as a note under section 1101 of this title.

SECTION REFERRED TO IN OTHER SECTIONS

This section is referred to in sections 8901, 8902, 8902a, 8903a, 8903b, 8904, 8905, 8907, 8908, 8909, 8910, 8913 of this title; title 42 sections 1395s, 1397cc.

§ 8903a. Additional health benefits plans

(a) In addition to any plan under section 8903 of this title, the Office of Personnel Management may contract for or approve one or more health benefits plans under this section.

(b) A plan under this section may not be contracted for or approved unless it—

(1) is sponsored or underwritten, and administered, in whole or substantial part, by an employee organization described in section 8901(8)(B) of this title;

(2) offers benefits of the types named by paragraph (1) or (2) of section 8904 of this title or both;

(3) provides for benefits only by paying for, or providing reimbursement for, the cost of such benefits (as provided for under paragraph (1) or (2) of section 8903 of this title) or a combination thereof; and

(4) is available only to individuals who, at the time of enrollment, are full members of the organization and to members of their families.

(c) A contract for a plan approved under this section shall require the carrier—

(1) to enter into an agreement approved by the Office with an underwriting subcontractor licensed to issue group health insurance in all the States and the District of Columbia; or

(2) to demonstrate ability to meet reasonable minimum financial standards prescribed by the Office.

(d) For the purpose of this section, an individual shall be considered a full member of an organization if such individual is eligible to exercise all rights and privileges incident to full membership in such organization (determined without regard to the right to hold elected office).

(Added Pub. L. 99–53, § 1(b)(1), June 17, 1985, 99 Stat. 93.)

SECTION REFERRED TO IN OTHER SECTIONS

This section is referred to in sections 8901, 8902, 8902a, 8903b, 8905, 8907, 8908, 8909, 8910, 8913 of this title; title 42 section 1395s.

§ 8903b. Authority to readmit an employee organization plan

(a) In the event that a plan described by section 8903(3) or 8903a is discontinued under this chapter (other than in the circumstance described in section 8909(d)), that discontinuation shall be disregarded, for purposes of any determination as to that plan's eligibility to be considered an approved plan under this chapter, but only for purposes of any contract year later than the third contract year beginning after such plan is so discontinued.

(b) A contract for a plan approved under this section shall require the carrier—

(1) to demonstrate experience in service delivery within a managed care system (including provider networks) throughout the United States; and

(2) if the carrier involved would not otherwise be subject to the requirement set forth in section 8903a(c)(1), to satisfy such requirement.

(Added Pub. L. 105–266, § 6(a)(1), Oct. 19, 1998, 112 Stat. 2368.)

EFFECTIVE DATE

Pub. L. 105–266, § 6(a)(3), Oct. 19, 1998, 112 Stat. 2369, provided that:

"(A) IN GENERAL.—The amendments made by this subsection [enacting this section] shall apply as of the date of the enactment of this Act [Oct. 19, 1998], including with respect to any plan which has been discontinued as of such date.

"(B) TRANSITION RULE.—For purposes of applying section 8903b(a) of title 5, United States Code (as amended by this subsection) with respect to any plan seeking to be readmitted for purposes of any contract year beginning before January 1, 2000, such section shall be applied by substituting 'second contract year' for 'third contract year'."

§ 8904. Types of benefits

(a) The benefits to be provided under plans described by section 8903 of this title may be of the following types:

(1) SERVICE BENEFIT PLAN.—

(A) Hospital benefits.

(B) Surgical benefits.

(C) In-hospital medical benefits.

(D) Ambulatory patient benefits.

(E) Supplemental benefits.

(F) Obstetrical benefits.

(2) INDEMNITY BENEFIT PLAN.—

(A) Hospital care.

(B) Surgical care and treatment.

(C) Medical care and treatment.

(D) Obstetrical benefits.

(E) Prescribed drugs, medicines, and prosthetic devices.

(F) Other medical supplies and services.

(3) EMPLOYEE ORGANIZATION PLANS.—Benefits of the types named under paragraph (1) or (2) of this subsection or both.

(4) COMPREHENSIVE MEDICAL PLANS.—Benefits of the types named under paragraph (1) or (2) of this subsection or both.

All plans contracted for under paragraphs (1) and (2) of this subsection shall include benefits both for costs associated with care in a general hospital and for other health services of a catastrophic nature.

(b)(1)(A) A plan, other than a prepayment plan described in section 8903(4) of this title, may not provide benefits, in the case of any retired enrolled individual who is age 65 or older and is not covered to receive Medicare hospital and insurance benefits under part A of title XVIII of the Social Security Act (42 U.S.C. 1395c et seq.), to pay a charge imposed by any health care provider, for inpatient hospital services which are covered for purposes of benefit payments under this chapter and part A of title XVIII of the Social Security Act, to the extent that such charge exceeds applicable limitations on hospital charges established for Medicare purposes under section 1886 of the Social Security Act (42 U.S.C. 1395ww). Hospital providers who have in force participation agreements with the Secretary of Health and Human Services consistent with sections 1814(a) and 1866 of the Social Security Act (42 U.S.C. 1395f(a) and 1395cc), whereby the participating provider accepts Medicare benefits as full payment for covered items and services after applicable patient copayments under section 1813 of such Act (42 U.S.C. 1395e) have been satisfied, shall accept equivalent benefit payments and enrollee copayments under this chapter as full payment for services described in the preceding sentence. The Office of Personnel Management shall notify the Secretary of Health and Human Services if a hospital is found to knowingly and willfully violate this subsection on a repeated basis and the Secretary may invoke appropriate sanctions in accordance with section 1866(b)(2) of the Social Security Act (42 U.S.C. 1395cc(b)(2)) and applicable regulations.

(B)(i) A plan, other than a prepayment plan described in section 8903(4), may not provide benefits, in the case of any retired enrolled individual who is age 65 or older and is not entitled to Medicare supplementary medical insurance benefits under part B of title XVIII of the Social Security Act (42 U.S.C. 1395j et seq.), to pay a charge imposed for physicians' services (as defined in section 1848(j) of such Act, 42 U.S.C. 1395w–4(j)) which are covered for purposes of benefit payments under this chapter and under such part, to the extent that such charge exceeds the fee schedule amount under section 1848(a) of such Act (42 U.S.C. 1395w–4(a)).

(ii) Physicians and suppliers who have in force participation agreements with the Secretary of Health and Human Services consistent with section 1842(h)(1) of such Act (42 U.S.C. 1395u(h)(1)), whereby the participating provider accepts Medicare benefits (including allowable deductible and coinsurance amounts) as full payment for covered items and services shall accept equivalent benefit and enrollee cost-sharing under this chapter as full payment for services described in clause (i). Physicians and suppliers who are nonparticipating physicians and suppliers for purposes of part B of title XVIII of such Act shall not impose charges that exceed the limiting charge under section 1848(g) of such Act (42 U.S.C. 1395w–4(g)) with respect to services described in clause (i) provided to enrollees described in such clause. The Office of Personnel Management shall notify a physician or supplier who is found to have violated this clause and inform them of the requirements of this clause and sanctions for such a violation. The Office of Personnel Management shall notify the Secretary of Health and Human Services if a physician or supplier is found to knowingly and willfully violate this clause on a repeated basis and the Secretary of Health and Human Services may invoke appropriate sanctions in accordance with sections 1128A(a) and 1848(g)(1) of such Act (42 U.S.C. 1320a–7a(a), 1395w–4(g)(1)) and applicable regulations.

(C) If the Secretary of Health and Human Services determines that a violation of this sub-

section warrants excluding a provider from participation for a specified period under title XVIII of the Social Security Act, the Office shall enforce a corresponding exclusion of such provider for purposes of this chapter.

(2) Notwithstanding any other provision of law, the Secretary of Health and Human Services and the Director of the Office of Personnel Management, and their agents, shall exchange any information necessary to implement this subsection.

(3)(A) Not later than December 1, 1991, and periodically thereafter, the Secretary of Health and Human Services (in consultation with the Director of the Office of Personnel Management) shall supply to carriers of plans described in paragraphs (1) through (3) of section 8903 the Medicare program information necessary for them to comply with paragraph (1).

(B) For purposes of this paragraph, the term "Medicare program information" includes (i) the limitations on hospital charges established for Medicare purposes under section 1886 of the Social Security Act (42 U.S.C. 1395ww) and the identity of hospitals which have in force agreements with the Secretary of Health and Human Services consistent with section 1814(a) and 1866 of the Social Security Act (42 U.S.C. 1395f(a) and 1395cc), and (ii) the fee schedule amounts and limiting charges for physicians' services established under section 1848 of such Act (42 U.S.C. 1395w–4) and the identity of participating physicians and suppliers who have in force agreements with such Secretary under section 1842(h) of such Act (42 U.S.C. 1395u(h)).

(4) The Director of the Office of Personnel Management shall enter into an arrangement with the Secretary of Health and Human Services, to be effective before the first day of the fifth month that begins before each contract year, under which—

(A) physicians and suppliers (whether or not participating) under the Medicare program will be notified of the requirements of paragraph (1)(B);

(B) enforcement procedures will be in place to carry out such paragraph (including enforcement of protections against overcharging of beneficiaries); and

(C) Medicare program information described in paragraph (3)(B)(ii) will be supplied to carriers under paragraph (3)(A).

(Pub. L. 89–554, Sept. 6, 1966, 80 Stat. 603; Pub. L. 101–508, title VII, § 7002(f)(1), Nov. 5, 1990, 104 Stat. 1388–330; Pub. L. 102–378, § 2(76), Oct. 2, 1992, 106 Stat. 1355; Pub. L. 103–66, title XI, § 11003(a), Aug. 10, 1993, 107 Stat. 409.)

HISTORICAL AND REVISION NOTES

Derivation	U.S. Code	Revised Statutes and Statutes at Large
....	5 U.S.C. 3004.	Sept. 28, 1959, Pub. L. 86–382, § 5, 73 Stat. 712.

Standard changes are made to conform with the definitions applicable and the style of this title as outlined in the preface to the report.

REFERENCES IN TEXT

The Social Security Act, referred to in subsec. (b)(1), is act Aug. 14, 1935, ch. 531, 49 Stat. 620, as amended.

Title XVIII of the Act is classified generally to subchapter XVIII (§1395 et seq.) of chapter 7 of Title 42, The Public Health and Welfare. Parts A and B of title XVIII of the Act are classified generally to part A (§1395c et seq.) and part B (§1395j et seq.), respectively, of subchapter XVIII of chapter 7 of Title 42. For complete classification of this Act to the Code, see section 1305 of Title 42 and Tables.

AMENDMENTS

1993—Subsec. (b)(1). Pub. L. 103–66, §11003(a)(1), designated existing provisions as subpar. (A) and added subpars. (B) and (C).

Subsec. (b)(3)(B). Pub. L. 103–66, §11003(a)(2), inserted cl. (i) designation and added cl. (ii).

Subsec. (b)(4). Pub. L. 103–66, §11003(a)(3), added par. (4).

1992—Subsec. (a). Pub. L. 102–378 substituted "this subsection" for "this section" in pars. (3) and (4) and in last sentence.

1990—Pub. L. 101–508 designated existing provisions as subsec. (a) and added subsec. (b).

EFFECTIVE DATE OF 1993 AMENDMENT

Section 11003(b) of Pub. L. 103–66 provided that: "The amendments made by subsection (a) [amending this section] shall apply with respect to contract years beginning on or after January 1, 1995."

EFFECTIVE DATE OF 1990 AMENDMENT

Section 7002(f)(2) of Pub. L. 101–508 provided that: "The amendments made by this subsection [amending this section] shall apply with respect to contract years beginning on or after January 1, 1992."

MENTAL HEALTH, ALCOHOLISM, AND DRUG ADDICTION BENEFITS; CONGRESSIONAL FINDINGS; SENSE OF CONGRESS

Pub. L. 99–251, title I, §107, Feb. 27, 1986, 100 Stat. 16, provided that:

"(a) FINDINGS.—The Congress finds that—

"(1) the treatment of mental illness, alcoholism, and drug addiction are basic health care services which are needed by approximately 40,000,000 Americans each year;

"(2) treatment of mental illness, alcoholism, and drug addiction is increasingly successful;

"(3) timely and appropriate treatment of mental illness, alcoholism, and drug addiction is cost effective in terms of restored productivity, reduced utilization of other health services, and reduced social dependence; and

"(4) mental illness is a problem of grave concern to the people of the United States and is widely but unnecessarily feared and misunderstood.

"(b) SENSE OF THE CONGRESS.—It is the sense of the Congress—

"(1) that participants in the Federal employees health benefits program should receive adequate benefits coverage for treatment of mental illness, alcoholism, and drug addiction; and

"(2) that the Office of Personnel Management should encourage participating health benefits plans to provide adequate benefits relating to treatment of mental illness, alcoholism, and drug addiction (including benefits relating to coverage for inpatient and outpatient treatment and catastrophic protection benefits)."

SECTION REFERRED TO IN OTHER SECTIONS

This section is referred to in sections 8902a, 8903, 8903a of this title.

§ 8905. Election of coverage

(a) An employee may enroll in an approved health benefits plan described by section 8903 or 8903a of this title either as an individual or for self and family.

(b) An annuitant who at the time he becomes an annuitant was enrolled in a health benefits plan under this chapter—

(1) as an employee for a period of not less than—

(A) the 5 years of service immediately before retirement;

(B) the full period or periods of service between the last day of the first period, as prescribed by regulations of the Office of Personnel Management, in which he is eligible to enroll in the plan and the date on which he becomes an annuitant; or

(C) the full period or periods of service beginning with the enrollment which became effective before January 1, 1965, and ending with the date on which he becomes an annuitant;

whichever is shortest; or

(2) as a member of the family of an employee or annuitant;

may continue his enrollment under the conditions of eligibility prescribed by regulations of the Office. The Office may, in its sole discretion, waive the requirements of this subsection in the case of an individual who fails to satisfy such requirements if the Office determines that, due to exceptional circumstances, it would be against equity and good conscience not to allow such individual to be enrolled as an annuitant in a health benefits plan under this chapter[1]

(c)(1) A former spouse may—

(A) within 60 days after the dissolution of the marriage, or

(B) in the case of a former spouse of a former employee whose marriage was dissolved after the employee's retirement, within 60 days after the dissolution of the marriage or, if later, within 60 days after an election is made under section 8339(j)(3) or 8417(b) of this title for such former spouse by the retired employee,

enroll in an approved health benefits plan described by section 8903 or 8903a of this title as an individual or for self and family as provided in paragraph (2) of this subsection, subject to agreement to pay the full subscription charge of the enrollment, including the amounts determined by the Office to be necessary for administration and reserves pursuant to section 8909(b) of this title. The former spouse shall submit an enrollment application and make premium payments to the agency which, at the time of divorce or annulment, employed the employee to whom the former spouse was married or, in the case of a former spouse who is receiving annuity payments under section 8341(h), 8345(j), 8445, or 8467 of this title, to the Office of Personnel Management.

(2) Coverage for self and family under this subsection shall be limited to—

(A) the former spouse; and

(B) unmarried dependent natural or adopted children of the former spouse and the employee who are—

(i) under 22 years of age; or

(ii) incapable of self-support because of mental or physical disability which existed before age 22.

---

[1] So in original. Probably should be followed by a period.

(d) An individual whom the Secretary of Defense determines is an eligible beneficiary under subsection (b) of section 1108 of title 10 may enroll, as part of the demonstration project under such section, in a health benefits plan under this chapter in accordance with the agreement under subsection (a) of such section between the Secretary and the Office and applicable regulations under this chapter.

(e) If an employee, annuitant, or other individual eligible to enroll in a health benefits plan under this chapter has a spouse who is also eligible to enroll, either spouse, but not both, may enroll for self and family, or each spouse may enroll as an individual. However, an individual may not be enrolled both as an employee, annuitant, or other individual eligible to enroll and as a member of the family.

(f) An employee, annuitant, former spouse, or person having continued coverage under section 8905a of this title enrolled in a health benefits plan under this chapter may change his coverage or that of himself and members of his family by an application filed within 60 days after a change in family status or at other times and under conditions prescribed by regulations of the Office.

(g)(1) Under regulations prescribed by the Office, the Office shall, before the start of any contract term in which—

(A) an adjustment is made in any of the rates charged or benefits provided under a health benefits plan described by section 8903 or 8903a of this title,

(B) a newly approved health benefits plan is offered, or

(C) an existing plan is terminated,

provide a period of not less than 3 weeks during which any employee, annuitant, former spouse, or person having continued coverage under section 8905a of this title enrolled in a health benefits plan described by such section shall be permitted to transfer that individual's enrollment to another such plan or to cancel such enrollment.

(2) In addition to any opportunity afforded under paragraph (1) of this subsection, an employee, annuitant, former spouse, or person having continued coverage under section 8905a of this title enrolled in a health benefits plan under this chapter shall be permitted to transfer that individual's enrollment to another such plan, or to cancel such enrollment, at such other times and subject to such conditions as the Office may prescribe in regulations.

(3)(A) In addition to any informational requirements otherwise applicable under this chapter, the regulations shall include provisions to ensure that each employee eligible to enroll in a health benefits plan under this chapter (whether actually enrolled or not) is notified in writing as to the rights afforded under section 8905a of this title.

(B) Notification under this paragraph shall be provided by employing agencies at an appropriate point in time before each period under paragraph (1) so that employees may be aware of their rights under section 8905a of this title when making enrollment decisions during such period.

(h)(1) An unenrolled employee who is required by a court or administrative order to provide health insurance coverage for a child who meets the requirements of section 8901(5) may enroll for self and family coverage in a health benefits plan under this chapter. If such employee fails to enroll for self and family coverage in a health benefits plan that provides full benefits and services in the location in which the child resides, and the employee does not provide documentation showing that such coverage has been provided through other health insurance, the employing agency shall enroll the employee in a self and family enrollment in the option which provides the lower level of coverage under the Service Benefit Plan.

(2) An employee who is enrolled as an individual in a health benefits plan under this chapter and who is required by a court or administrative order to provide health insurance coverage for a child who meets the requirements of section 8901(5) may change to a self and family enrollment in the same or another health benefits plan under this chapter. If such employee fails to change to a self and family enrollment and the employee does not provide documentation showing that such coverage has been provided through other health insurance, the employing agency shall change the enrollment of the employee to a self and family enrollment in the plan in which the employee is enrolled if that plan provides full benefits and services in the location where the child resides. If the plan in which the employee is enrolled does not provide full benefits and services in the location in which the child resides, or, if the employee fails to change to a self and family enrollment in a plan that provides full benefits and services in the location where the child resides, the employing agency shall change the coverage of the employee to a self and family enrollment in the option which provides the lower level of coverage under the Service Benefits Plan.

(3) The employee may not discontinue the self and family enrollment in a plan that provides full benefits and services in the location in which the child resides for so long as the court or administrative order remains in effect and the child continues to meet the requirements of section 8901(5), unless the employee provides documentation showing that such coverage has been provided through other health insurance.

(Pub. L. 89–554, Sept. 6, 1966, 80 Stat. 603; Pub. L. 95–454, title IX, § 906(a)(2), (3), Oct. 13, 1978, 92 Stat. 1224; Pub. L. 98–615, § 3(4), Nov. 8, 1984, 98 Stat. 3203; Pub. L. 99–53, § 2(a), (c), June 17, 1985, 99 Stat. 94; Pub. L. 99–251, title I, §§ 103, 104(a), Feb. 27, 1986, 100 Stat. 14; Pub. L. 99–335, title II, § 207(m), June 6, 1986, 100 Stat. 598; Pub. L. 100–654, title II, §§ 201(c), (d), 202(c), Nov. 14, 1988, 102 Stat. 3845; Pub. L. 102–378, § 2(77), Oct. 2, 1992, 106 Stat. 1355; Pub. L. 105–261, div. A, title VII, § 721(b)(1), Oct. 17, 1998, 112 Stat. 2065; Pub. L. 106–394, § 2, Oct. 30, 2000, 114 Stat. 1629.)

HISTORICAL AND REVISION NOTES

Derivation	U.S. Code	Revised Statutes and Statutes at Large
....	5 U.S.C. 3002(a) (1st sentence, less words between 1st and 4th commas), (b)–(e).	Sept. 28, 1959, Pub. L. 86–382, § 3(a) (1st sentence, less words between 1st and 4th commas), (b)–(e), 73 Stat. 710.

HISTORICAL AND REVISION NOTES—CONTINUED

Derivation	U.S. Code	Revised Statutes and Statutes at Large
		Mar. 17, 1964, Pub. L. 88–284, §1(5), 78 Stat. 164.

In subsection (b)(1), the words "as an employee" are inserted for clarity.

In subsection (b)(1)(C), the words "before January 1, 1965" are substituted for "not later than December 31, 1964".

Standard changes are made to conform with the definitions applicable and the style of this title as outlined in the preface to the report.

AMENDMENTS

2000—Subsec. (h). Pub. L. 106–394 added subsec. (h).

1998—Subsecs. (d) to (g). Pub. L. 105–261 added subsec. (d) and redesignated former subsecs. (d) to (f) as (e) to (g), respectively.

1992—Subsec. (b). Pub. L. 102–378, §2(77)(A), substituted "this chapter" for "this subchapter." at end.

Subsec. (c)(1). Pub. L. 102–378, §2(77)(B), inserted comma after "8341(h)" in last sentence.

1988—Subsec. (d). Pub. L. 100–654, §202(c), amended subsec. (d) generally. Prior to amendment, subsec. (d) read as follows: "If an employee has a spouse who is an employee, either spouse, but not both, may enroll for self and family, or each spouse may enroll as an individual. However, an individual may not be enrolled both as an employee or annuitant and as a member of the family."

Subsecs. (e), (f)(1), (2). Pub. L. 100–654, §201(c), (d)(1), substituted "former spouse, or person having continued coverage under section 8905a of this title" for "or former spouse".

Subsec. (f)(3). Pub. L. 100–654, §201(d)(2), added par. (3).

1986—Subsec. (b). Pub. L. 99–251, §103, inserted last sentence relating to waiver of the requirements of this subsection if it would be against equity to prohibit enrollment.

Subsec. (c)(1). Pub. L. 99–335 inserted in subpar. (B) "or 8417(b)" and substituted in provision following subpar. (B) "8345(j), 8445, or 8467" for "or 8345(j)".

Subsec. (f). Pub. L. 99–251, §104(a), amended subsec. (f) generally. Prior to amendment, subsec. (f) read as follows: "An employee, annuitant, or former spouse enrolled in a health benefits plan under this chapter may change his coverage or that of himself and members of his family by an application filed within 60 days after a change in family status or at other times and under conditions prescribed by regulations of the Office."

1985—Subsecs. (a), (c)(1). Pub. L. 99–53, §2(a), inserted reference to section 8903a of this title.

Subsec. (f). Pub. L. 99–53, §2(a), (c), inserted reference to section 8903a of this title and substituted "such plan" for "plan described by that section".

1984—Subsec. (c). Pub. L. 98–615, §3(4)(A), added subsec. (c). Former subsec. (c) redesignated (d).

Subsec. (d). Pub. L. 98–615, §3(4)(A), redesignated former subsec. (c) as (d). Former subsec. (d) redesignated (e).

Subsec. (e). Pub. L. 98–615, §3(4), redesignated former subsec. (d) as (e) and substituted "An employee, annuitant, or former spouse" for "An employee or annuitant". Former subsec. (e) redesignated (f).

Subsec. (f). Pub. L. 98–615, §3(4), redesignated former subsec. (e) as (f) and substituted "An employee, annuitant, or former spouse" for "An employee or annuitant".

1978—Subsecs. (b), (d), (e). Pub. L. 95–454 substituted "Office of Personnel Management" and "Office" for "Civil Service Commission" and "Commission", respectively, wherever appearing.

EFFECTIVE DATE OF 1988 AMENDMENT

Amendment by Pub. L. 100–654 applicable with respect to any calendar year beginning, and contracts entered into or renewed for any calendar year beginning, after end of 9-month period beginning Nov. 14, 1988, and with respect to any qualifying event occurring on or after first day of first calendar year beginning after end of such 9-month period, see section 203 of Pub. L. 100–654, set out as a note under section 8902 of this title.

EFFECTIVE DATE OF 1986 AMENDMENTS

Amendment by Pub. L. 99–335 effective Jan. 1, 1987, see section 702(a) of Pub. L. 99–335, set out as an Effective Date note under section 8401 of this title.

Section 104(b) of Pub. L. 99–251 provided that: "The amendment made by subsection (a) [amending this section] shall be effective with respect to contracts entered into or renewed for calendar years beginning after December 31, 1986."

EFFECTIVE DATE OF 1984 AMENDMENT

Amendment by Pub. L. 98–615 effective May 7, 1985, with enumerated exceptions, and applicable to any individual who is married to an employee or annuitant on or after that date, see section 4(a)(2) of Pub. L. 98–615, as amended, set out as a note under section 8341 of this title.

EFFECTIVE DATE OF 1978 AMENDMENT

Amendment by Pub. L. 95–454 effective 90 days after Oct. 13, 1978, see section 907 of Pub. L. 95–454, set out as a note under section 1101 of this title.

ELECTION OF HEALTH BENEFITS COVERAGE AND ENTITLEMENT TO HEALTH BENEFITS UNDER THIS CHAPTER RATHER THAN UNDER RETIRED FEDERAL EMPLOYEES HEALTH BENEFITS ACT

Pub. L. 93–246, §§2, 4(b), Jan. 31, 1974, 88 Stat. 4, provided that:

"SEC. 2. (a) Notwithstanding any other provision of law, an annuitant, as defined under section 8901(3) of title 5, United States Code, who is participating or who is eligible to participate in the health benefits program offered under the Retired Federal Employees Health Benefits Act (74 Stat. 849; Public Law 86–724), may elect, in accordance with regulations prescribed by the United States Civil Service Commission, to be covered under the provisions of chapter 89 of title 5, United States Code [this chapter], in lieu of coverage under such Act.

"(b) An annuitant who elects to be covered under the provisions of chapter 89 of title 5, United States Code [this chapter], in accordance with subsection (a) of this section, shall be entitled to the benefits under such chapter 89.

"[Sec. 4] (b) Section 2 [set out above] shall take effect on the one hundred and eightieth day following the date of enactment [Jan. 1, 1974] or on such earlier date as the United States Civil Service Commission may prescribe."

SECTION REFERRED TO IN OTHER SECTIONS

This section is referred to in section 6302 of this title; title 2 section 162b.

§ 8905a. Continued coverage

(a) Any individual described in paragraph (1) or (2) of subsection (b) may elect to continue coverage under this chapter in accordance with the provisions of this section.

(b) This section applies with respect to—

(1) any employee who—

(A) is separated from service, whether voluntarily or involuntarily, except that if the separation is involuntary, this section shall not apply if the separation is for gross misconduct (as defined under regulations which the Office of Personnel Management shall prescribe); and

(B) would not otherwise be eligible for any benefits under this chapter (determined without regard to any temporary extension of coverage and without regard to any benefits available under a nongroup contract); and

(2) any individual who—

(A) ceases to meet the requirements for being considered an unmarried dependent child under this chapter;

(B) on the day before so ceasing to meet the requirements referred to in subparagraph (A), was covered under a health benefits plan under this chapter as a member of the family of an employee or annuitant; and

(C) would not otherwise be eligible for any benefits under this chapter (determined without regard to any temporary extension of coverage and without regard to any benefits available under a nongroup contract).

(c)(1) The Office shall prescribe regulations and provide for the inclusion of appropriate terms in contracts with carriers to provide that—

(A) with respect to an employee who becomes (or will become) eligible for continued coverage under this section as a result of separation from service, the separating agency shall, before the end of the 30-day period beginning on the date as of which coverage (including any temporary extensions of coverage) would otherwise end, notify the individual of such individual's rights under this section; and

(B) with respect to a child of an employee or annuitant who becomes eligible for continued coverage under this section as a result of ceasing to meet the requirements for being considered a member of the employee's or annuitant's family—

(i) the employee or annuitant may provide written notice of the child's change in status (complete with the child's name, address, and such other information as the Office may by regulation require)—

(I) to the employee's employing agency; or

(II) in the case of an annuitant, to the Office; and

(ii) if the notice referred to in clause (i) is received within 60 days after the date as of which the child involved first ceases to meet the requirements involved, the employing agency or the Office (as the case may be) must, within 14 days after receiving such notice, notify the child of such child's rights under this section.

(2) In order to obtain continued coverage under this section, an appropriate written election (submitted in such manner as the Office by regulation prescribes) must be made—

(A) in the case of an individual seeking continued coverage based on a separation from service, before the end of the 60-day period beginning on the later of—

(i) the effective date of the separation; or

(ii) the date the separated individual receives the notice required under paragraph (1)(A); or

(B) in the case of an individual seeking continued coverage based on a change in circumstances making such individual ineligible for coverage as an unmarried dependent child, before the end of the 60-day period beginning on the later of—

(i) the date as of which such individual first ceases to meet the requirements for being considered an unmarried dependent child; or

(ii) the date such individual receives notice under paragraph (1)(B)(ii);

except that if a parent fails to provide the notice required under paragraph (1)(B)(i) in timely fashion, the 60-day period under this subparagraph shall be based on the date under clause (i), irrespective of whether or not any notice under paragraph (1)(B)(ii) is provided.

(d)(1)(A) Except as provided in paragraphs (4) and (5), an individual receiving continued coverage under this section shall be required to pay currently into the Employees Health Benefits Fund, under arrangements satisfactory to the Office, an amount equal to the sum of—

(i) the employee and agency contributions which would be required in the case of an employee enrolled in the same health benefits plan and level of benefits; and

(ii) an amount, determined under regulations prescribed by the Office, necessary for administrative expenses, but not to exceed 2 percent of the total amount under clause (i).

(B) Payments under this section to the Fund shall—

(i) in the case of an individual whose continued coverage is based on such individual's separation, be made through the agency which last employed such individual; or

(ii) in the case of an individual whose continued coverage is based on a change in circumstances referred to in subsection (c)(2)(B), be made through—

(I) the Office, if, at the time coverage would (but for this section) otherwise have been discontinued, the individual was covered as the child of an annuitant; or

(II) if, at the time referred to in subclause (I), the individual was covered as the child of an employee, the employee's employing agency as of such time.

(2) If an individual elects to continue coverage under this section before the end of the applicable period under subsection (c)(2), but after such individual's coverage under this chapter (including any temporary extensions of coverage) expires, coverage shall be restored retroactively, with appropriate contributions (determined in accordance with paragraph (1), (4), or (5), as the case may be) and claims (if any), to the same extent and effect as though no break in coverage had occurred.

(3)(A) An individual making an election under subsection (c)(2)(B) may, at such individual's option, elect coverage either as an individual or, if appropriate, for self and family.

(B) For the purpose of this paragraph, members of an individual's family shall be determined in the same way as would apply under this chapter in the case of an enrolled employee.

(C) Nothing in this paragraph shall be considered to limit an individual making an election under subsection (c)(2)(A) to coverage for self alone.

(4)(A) If the basis for continued coverage under this section is an involuntary separation from a position, or a voluntary separation from a surplus position, in or under the Department of Defense due to a reduction in force, or the Department of Energy due to a reduction in force resulting from the establishment of the National Nuclear Security Administration—

  (i) the individual shall be liable for not more than the employee contributions referred to in paragraph (1)(A)(i); and

  (ii) the agency which last employed the individual shall pay the remaining portion of the amount required under paragraph (1)(A).

(B) This paragraph shall apply with respect to any individual whose continued coverage is based on a separation occurring on or after the date of enactment of this paragraph and before—

  (i) October 1, 2003; or

  (ii) February 1, 2004, if specific notice of such separation was given to such individual before October 1, 2003.

(C) For the purpose of this paragraph, "surplus position" means a position which is identified in pre-reduction-in-force planning as no longer required, and which is expected to be eliminated under formal reduction-in-force procedures.

(5)(A) If the basis for continued coverage under this section is an involuntary separation from a position in or under the Department of Veterans Affairs due to a reduction in force or a title 38 staffing readjustment, or a voluntary or involuntary separation from a Department of Energy position at a Department of Energy facility at which the Secretary is carrying out a closure project selected under section 3143 of the National Defense Authorization Act for Fiscal Year 1997 (42 U.S.C. 7274n)—

  (i) the individual shall be liable for not more than the employee contributions referred to in paragraph (1)(A)(i); and

  (ii) the agency which last employed the individual shall pay the remaining portion of the amount required under paragraph (1)(A).

(B) This paragraph shall only apply with respect to individuals whose continued coverage is based on a separation occurring on or after the date of the enactment of this paragraph.

(e)(1) Continued coverage under this section may not extend beyond—

  (A) in the case of an individual whose continued coverage is based on separation from service, the date which is 18 months after the effective date of the separation; or

  (B) in the case of an individual whose continued coverage is based on ceasing to meet the requirements for being considered an unmarried dependent child, the date which is 36 months after the date on which the individual first ceases to meet those requirements, subject to paragraph (2).

(2) In the case of an individual who—

  (A) ceases to meet the requirements for being considered an unmarried dependent child;

  (B) as of the day before so ceasing to meet the requirements referred to in subparagraph

(A), was covered as the child of a former employee receiving continued coverage under this section based on the former employee's separation from service; and

  (C) so ceases to meet the requirements referred to in subparagraph (A) before the end of the 18-month period beginning on the date of the former employee's separation from service,

extended coverage under this section may not extend beyond the date which is 36 months after the separation date referred to in subparagraph (C).

(f)(1) The Office shall prescribe regulations under which, in addition to any individual otherwise eligible for continued coverage under this section, and to the extent practicable, continued coverage may also, upon appropriate written application, be afforded under this section—

  (A) to any individual who—

    (i) if subparagraphs (A) and (C) of paragraph (10) of section 8901 were disregarded, would be eligible to be considered a former spouse within the meaning of such paragraph; but

    (ii) would not, but for this subsection, be eligible to be so considered; and

  (B) to any individual whose coverage as a family member would otherwise terminate as a result of a legal separation.

(2) The terms and conditions for coverage under the regulations shall include—

  (A) consistent with subsection (c), any necessary notification provisions, and provisions under which an election period of at least 60 days' duration is afforded;

  (B) terms and conditions identical to those under subsection (d), except that contributions to the Employees Health Benefits Fund shall be made through such agency as the Office by regulation prescribes;

  (C) provisions relating to the termination of continued coverage, except that continued coverage under this section may not (subject to paragraph (3)) extend beyond the date which is 36 months after the date on which the qualifying event under this subsection (the date of divorce, annulment, or legal separation, as the case may be) occurs; and

  (D) provisions designed to ensure that any coverage pursuant to this subsection does not adversely affect any eligibility for coverage which the individual involved might otherwise have under this chapter (including as a result of any change in personal circumstances) if this subsection had not been enacted.

(3) In the case of an individual—

  (A) who becomes eligible for continued coverage under this subsection based on a divorce, annulment, or legal separation from a person who, as of the day before the date of the divorce, annulment, or legal separation (as the case may be) was receiving continued coverage under this section for self and family based on such person's separation from service; and

  (B) whose divorce, annulment, or legal separation (as the case may be) occurs before the end of the 18-month period beginning on the date of the separation from service referred to in subparagraph (A),

extended coverage under this section may not extend beyond the date which is 36 months after the date of the separation from service, as referred to in subparagraph (A).

(Added Pub. L. 100–654, title II, § 201(a)(1), Nov. 14, 1988, 102 Stat. 3841; amended Pub. L. 102–484, div. D, title XLIV, § 4438(a), Oct. 23, 1992, 106 Stat. 2725; Pub. L. 103–337, div. A, title III, § 341(d), Oct. 5, 1994, 108 Stat. 2720; Pub. L. 104–106, div. A, title X, § 1036, Feb. 10, 1996, 110 Stat. 431; Pub. L. 106–65, div. A, title XI, § 1104(c), div. C, title XXXII, § 3244, Oct. 5, 1999, 113 Stat. 777, 965; Pub. L. 106–117, title XI, § 1106, Nov. 30, 1999, 113 Stat. 1598; Pub. L. 106–398, § 1 [div. C, title XXXI, § 3136(h)], Oct. 30, 2000, 114 Stat. 1654, 1654A–459.)

REFERENCES IN TEXT

The date of enactment of this paragraph, referred to in subsec. (d)(4)(B), is the date of enactment of Pub. L. 102–484, which was approved Oct. 23, 1992.

The date of the enactment of this paragraph, referred to in subsec. (d)(5)(B), is the date of enactment of Pub. L. 106–117, which was approved Nov. 30, 1999.

AMENDMENTS

2000—Subsec. (d)(5)(A). Pub. L. 106–398, in introductory provisions, inserted ", or a voluntary or involuntary separation from a Department of Energy position at a Department of Energy facility at which the Secretary is carrying out a closure project selected under section 3143 of the National Defense Authorization Act for Fiscal Year 1997 (42 U.S.C. 7274n)" after "readjustment".

1999—Subsec. (d)(1)(A). Pub. L. 106–117, § 1106(1), substituted "paragraphs (4) and (5)" for "paragraph (4)" in introductory provisions.

Subsec. (d)(2). Pub. L. 106–117, § 1106(2), substituted "(1), (4), or (5)" for "(1) or (4)".

Subsec. (d)(4)(A). Pub. L. 106–65, § 3244, inserted ", or the Department of Energy due to a reduction in force resulting from the establishment of the National Nuclear Security Administration" after "reduction in force" in introductory provisions.

Subsec. (d)(4)(B). Pub. L. 106–65, § 1104(c), added cls. (i) and (ii) and struck out former cls. (i) and (ii) which read as follows:

"(i) October 1, 1999; or

"(ii) February 1, 2000, if specific notice of such separation was given to such individual before October 1, 1999."

Subsec. (d)(5). Pub. L. 106–117, § 1106(3), added par. (5).

1996—Subsec. (d)(4)(A). Pub. L. 104–106, § 1036(1), inserted ", or a voluntary separation from a surplus position," after "an involuntary separation from a position" in introductory provisions.

Subsec. (d)(4)(C). Pub. L. 104–106, § 1036(2), added subpar. (C).

1994—Subsec. (d)(4)(B). Pub. L. 103–337 substituted "October 1, 1999" for "October 1, 1997" in cls. (i) and (ii) and "February 1, 2000" for "February 1, 1998" in cl. (ii).

1992—Subsec. (d)(1)(A). Pub. L. 102–484, § 4438(a)(1), substituted "Except as provided in paragraph (4), an individual" for "An individual".

Subsec. (d)(2). Pub. L. 102–484, § 4438(a)(2), substituted "in accordance with paragraph (1) or (4), as the case may be)" for "in accordance with paragraph (1))".

Subsec. (d)(4). Pub. L. 102–484, § 4438(a)(3), added par. (4).

EFFECTIVE DATE OF 1999 AMENDMENT

Amendment by section 3244 of Pub. L. 106–65 effective Mar. 1, 2000, see section 3299 of Pub. L. 106–65, set out as an Effective Date note under section 2401 of Title 50, War and National Defense.

EFFECTIVE DATE

Section applicable with respect to any calendar year beginning, and contracts entered into or renewed for any calendar year beginning, after the end of the 9-month period beginning Nov. 14, 1988, and with respect to any qualifying event occurring on or after the first day of the first calendar year beginning after the end of such 9-month period, see section 203 of Pub. L. 100–654, set out as an Effective Date of 1988 Amendment note under section 8902 of this title.

SOURCE OF PAYMENTS

Section 4438(b)(1) of Pub. L. 102–484 provided that: "Any amount which becomes payable by an agency as a result of the enactment of subsection (a) [amending this section] shall be paid out of funds or appropriations available for salaries and expenses of such agency."

SECTION REFERRED TO IN OTHER SECTIONS

This section is referred to in sections 8902, 8903, 8905, 8909 of this title; title 10 sections 1078a, 1086a, 1145.

§ 8906. Contributions

(a)(1) Not later than October 1 of each year, the Office of Personnel Management shall determine the weighted average of the subscription charges that will be in effect during the following contract year with respect to—

(A) enrollments under this chapter for self alone; and

(B) enrollments under this chapter for self and family.

(2) In determining each weighted average under paragraph (1), the weight to be given to a particular subscription charge shall, with respect to each plan (and option) to which it is to apply, be commensurate with the number of enrollees enrolled in such plan (and option) as of March 31 of the year in which the determination is being made.

(3) For purposes of paragraph (2), the term "enrollee" means any individual who, during the contract year for which the weighted average is to be used under this section, will be eligible for a Government contribution for health benefits.

(b)(1) Except as provided in paragraphs (2), (3), and (4), the biweekly Government contribution for health benefits for an employee or annuitant enrolled in a health benefits plan under this chapter is adjusted to an amount equal to 72 percent of the weighted average under subsection (a)(1)(A) or (B), as applicable. For an employee, the adjustment begins on the first day of the employee's first pay period of each year. For an annuitant, the adjustment begins on the first day of the first period of each year for which an annuity payment is made.

(2) The biweekly Government contribution for an employee or annuitant enrolled in a plan under this chapter shall not exceed 75 percent of the subscription charge.

(3) In the case of an employee who is occupying a position on a part-time career employment basis (as defined in section 3401(2) of this title), the biweekly Government contribution shall be equal to the percentage which bears the same ratio to the percentage determined under this subsection (without regard to this paragraph) as the average number of hours of such employee's regularly scheduled workweek bears to the aver-

age number of hours in the regularly scheduled workweek of an employee serving in a comparable position on a full-time career basis (as determined under regulations prescribed by the Office).

(4) In the case of persons who are enrolled in a health benefits plan as part of the demonstration project under section 1108 of title 10, the Government contribution shall be subject to the limitation set forth in subsection (i) of that section.

(c) There shall be withheld from the pay of each enrolled employee and (except as provided in subsection (i) of this section) the annuity of each enrolled annuitant and there shall be contributed by the Government, amounts, in the same ratio as the contributions of the employee or annuitant and the Government under subsection (b) of this section, which are necessary for the administrative costs and the reserves provided for by section 8909(b) of this title.

(d) The amount necessary to pay the total charge for enrollment, after the Government contribution is deducted, shall be withheld from the pay of each enrolled employee and (except as provided in subsection (i) of this section) from the annuity of each enrolled annuitant. The withholding for an annuitant shall be the same as that for an employee enrolled in the same health benefits plan and level of benefits.

(e)(1)(A) An employee enrolled in a health benefits plan under this chapter who is placed in a leave without pay status may have his coverage and the coverage of members of his family continued under the plan for not to exceed 1 year under regulations prescribed by the Office.

(B) During each pay period in which an enrollment continues under subparagraph (A)—

(i) employee and Government contributions required by this section shall be paid on a current basis; and

(ii) if necessary, the head of the employing agency shall approve advance payment, recoverable in the same manner as under section 5524a(c), of a portion of basic pay sufficient to pay current employee contributions.

(C) Each agency shall establish procedures for accepting direct payments of employee contributions for the purposes of this paragraph.

(2) An employee who enters on approved leave without pay to serve as a full-time officer or employee of an organization composed primarily of employees as defined by section 8901 of this title, within 60 days after entering on that leave without pay, may file with his employing agency an election to continue his health benefits enrollment and arrange to pay currently into the Employees Health Benefits Fund, through his employing agency, both employee and agency contributions from the beginning of leave without pay. The employing agency shall forward the enrollment charges so paid to the Fund. If the employee does not so elect, his enrollment will continue during nonpay status and end as provided by paragraph (1) of this subsection and implementing regulations.

(f) The Government contributions for health benefits for an employee shall be paid—

(1) in the case of employees generally, from the appropriation or fund which is used to pay the employee;

(2) in the case of an elected official, from an appropriation or fund available for payment of other salaries of the same office or establishment;

(3) in the case of an employee of the legislative branch who is paid by the Chief Administrative Officer of the House of Representatives, from the applicable accounts of the House of Representatives; and

(4) in the case of an employee in a leave without pay status, from the appropriation or fund which would be used to pay the employee if he were in a pay status.

(g)(1) Except as provided in paragraphs (2) and (3), the Government contributions authorized by this section for health benefits for an annuitant shall be paid from annual appropriations which are authorized to be made for that purpose and which may be made available until expended.

(2)(A) The Government contributions authorized by this section for health benefits for an individual who first becomes an annuitant by reason of retirement from employment with the United States Postal Service on or after July 1, 1971, or for a survivor of such an individual or of an individual who died on or after July 1, 1971, while employed by the United States Postal Service, shall be paid by the United States Postal Service.

(B) In determining any amount for which the Postal Service is liable under this paragraph, the amount of the liability shall be prorated to reflect only that portion of total service which is attributable to civilian service performed (by the former postal employee or by the deceased individual referred to in subparagraph (A), as the case may be) after June 30, 1971, as estimated by the Office of Personnel Management.

(3) The Government contribution for persons enrolled in a health benefits plan as part of the demonstration project under section 1108 of title 10 shall be paid as provided in subsection (i) of that section.

(h) The Office shall provide for conversion of biweekly rates of contribution specified by this section to rates for employees and annuitants paid on other than a biweekly basis, and for this purpose may provide for the adjustment of the converted rate to the nearest cent.

(i) An annuitant whose annuity is insufficient to cover the withholdings required for enrollment in a particular health benefits plan may enroll (or remain enrolled) in such plan, notwithstanding any other provision of this section, if the annuitant elects, under conditions prescribed by regulations of the Office, to pay currently into the Employees Health Benefits Fund, through the retirement system that administers the annuitant's health benefits enrollment, an amount equal to the withholdings that would otherwise be required under this section.

(Pub. L. 89–554, Sept. 6, 1966, 80 Stat. 604; Pub. L. 90–83, §1(96), Sept. 11, 1967, 81 Stat. 219; Pub. L. 91–418, §1(a), Sept. 25, 1970, 84 Stat. 869; Pub. L. 93–246, §1, Jan. 31, 1974, 88 Stat. 3; Pub. L. 94–310, §3(a), June 15, 1976, 90 Stat. 687; Pub. L. 95–437, §4(c)(2)(A), Oct. 10, 1978, 92 Stat. 1059; Pub. L. 95–454, title IX, §906(a)(15), (c)(2)(F), Oct. 13, 1978, 92 Stat. 1226, 1227; Pub. L. 96–54, §2(a)(53), Aug. 14, 1979, 93 Stat. 384; Pub. L. 99–272, title XV,

§ 15202(b), Apr. 7, 1986, 100 Stat. 334; Pub. L. 101–239, title IV, § 4003(a), Dec. 19, 1989, 103 Stat. 2135; Pub. L. 101–303, § 1(a), (b), May 29, 1990, 104 Stat. 250; Pub. L. 101–508, title VII, § 7102(a), (b), Nov. 5, 1990, 104 Stat. 1388–333; Pub. L. 102–378, § 2(78), Oct. 2, 1992, 106 Stat. 1355; Pub. L. 104–186, title II, § 215(19), Aug. 20, 1996, 110 Stat. 1747; Pub. L. 104–208, div. A, title I, § 101(f) [title IV, § 422], Sept. 30, 1996, 110 Stat. 3009–314, 3009–343; Pub. L. 105–33, title VII, § 7002(a), Aug. 5, 1997, 111 Stat. 662; Pub. L. 105–261, div. A, title VII, § 721(b)(2), (3), Oct. 17, 1998, 112 Stat. 2065.)

HISTORICAL AND REVISION NOTES
1966 ACT

Derivation	U.S. Code	Revised Statutes and Statutes at Large
....	5 U.S.C. 3006.	Sept. 28, 1959, Pub. L. 86–382, § 7, 73 Stat. 713. Mar. 17, 1964, Pub. L. 88–284, § 1(10), (11), 78 Stat. 165.

In subsection (f)(1), the words "in the case of employees generally" are inserted for clarity.

In subsection (h), the word "biweekly" is inserted for clarity.

Standard changes are made to conform with the definitions applicable and the style of this title as outlined in the preface to the report.

1967 ACT

Section of title 5	Source (U.S. Code)	Source (Statutes at Large)
8906(a)	5 App.: 3006(a)(1).	July 18, 1966, Pub. L. 89–504, §§ 406(b), 602, 80 Stat. 298, 303.
8906(b)	5 App.: 3006(a)(2).	
8906(e)(2) ...	5 App.: 3006(b)(2).	

In subsection (a), the words "subsection (b) of this section", "this chapter", and "subsection (c) of this section" are substituted for "paragraph (2) of this subsection", "this Act", and "paragraph (3)", respectively, to reflect the codification of title 5, United States Code.

In subsection (e)(2), the words "as defined by section 8901 of this title" are substituted for "as defined in section 2 of this Act" to reflect the codification of that section in 5 U.S.C. 8901. The words "Employees Health Benefits Fund" and "Fund" are substituted for "fund" and "fund", respectively. In the penultimate sentence, the words "will continue during nonpay status and end" are substituted for "will terminate" for clarity and on authority of 5 U.S.C. 8906(e)(1).

AMENDMENTS

1998—Subsec. (b)(1). Pub. L. 105–261, § 721(b)(2)(A), substituted "paragraphs (2), (3), and (4)" for "paragraphs (2) and (3)".

Subsec. (b)(4). Pub. L. 105–261, § 721(b)(2)(B), added par. (4).

Subsec. (g)(1). Pub. L. 105–261, § 721(b)(3)(A), substituted "paragraphs (2) and (3)" for "paragraph (2)".

Subsec. (g)(3). Pub. L. 105–261, § 721(b)(3)(B), added par. (3).

1997—Subsec. (a). Pub. L. 105–33 added subsec. (a) and struck out former subsec. (a) which read as follows: "The Office of Personnel Management shall determine the average of the subscription charges in effect on the beginning date of each contract year with respect to self alone or self and family enrollments under this chapter, as applicable, for the highest level of benefits offered by—

"(1) the service benefit plan;

"(2) the indemnity benefit plan;

"(3) the two employee organization plans with the largest number of enrollments, as determined by the Office; and

"(4) the two comprehensive medical plans with the largest number of enrollments, as determined by the Office."

Subsec. (b)(1). Pub. L. 105–33 added par. (1) and struck out former par. (1) which read as follows: "Except as provided by paragraphs (2) and (3) of this subsection, the biweekly Government contribution for health benefits for an employee or annuitant enrolled in a health benefits plan under this chapter is adjusted to an amount equal to 60 percent of the average subscription charge determined under subsection (a) of this section. For an employee, the adjustment begins on the first day of the employee's first pay period of each year. For an annuitant, the adjustment begins on the first day of the first period of each year for which an annuity payment is made."

1996—Subsec. (e)(1). Pub. L. 104–208 struck out at end "The regulations may provide for the waiving of contributions by the employee and the Government.", inserted subpar. (A) designation, and added subpars. (B) and (C).

Subsec. (f)(3). Pub. L. 104–186 substituted "Chief Administrative Officer of the House of Representatives, from the applicable accounts of the House of Representatives" for "Clerk of the House of Representatives, from the contingent fund of the House".

1992—Subsec. (b)(3). Pub. L. 102–378, § 2(78)(A), inserted period after "Office)".

Subsec. (c). Pub. L. 102–378, § 2(78)(B), substituted "and (except" for "and except".

1990—Subsec. (c). Pub. L. 101–303, § 1(b)(1), inserted "except as provided in subsection (i) of this section)" after "enrolled employee and".

Subsec. (d). Pub. L. 101–303, § 1(b)(2), inserted "(except as provided in subsection (i) of this section)" after "enrolled employee and".

Subsec. (g)(2). Pub. L. 101–508 designated existing provisions as subpar. (A), substituted "July 1, 1971," for "October 1, 1986," in two places, and added subpar. (B).

Subsec. (i). Pub. L. 101–303, § 1(a), added subsec. (i).

1989—Subsec. (g)(2). Pub. L. 101–239 inserted "or for a survivor of such an individual or of an individual who died on or after October 1, 1986, while employed by the United States Postal Service," after "1986,".

1986—Subsec. (g). Pub. L. 99–272 designated existing provisions as par. (1) and added par. (2).

1979—Subsec. (b)(1). Pub. L. 96–54 substituted provisions setting forth adjustment amount of the Government contribution of equal to 60 percent of the average subscription charge under subsec. (a) and determinations respecting the commencement date of the adjustment, for provisions setting forth adjustment amounts of the Government contribution of equal to 50 percent of the average subscription charge under subsec. (a) for applicable pay periods beginning in 1974, and equal to 60 percent for pay periods beginning in 1975 and after, and determinations respecting the commencement date of the adjustment.

1978—Subsec. (a). Pub. L. 95–454, § 906(a)(15), substituted "Office of Personnel Management" for "Commission" in introductory material, and "Office" for "Commission" in cls. (3) and (4).

Subsec. (b)(1). Pub. L. 95–437, § 4(c)(2)(A)(i), substituted "paragraphs (2) and (3)" for "paragraph (2)".

Subsec. (b)(3). Pub. L. 95–454, § 906(a)(15), (c)(2)(F), substituted "Office" for "Commission", and "3401" for "3391".

Pub. L. 95–437, § 4(c)(2)(A)(ii), added par. (3).

Subsecs. (e)(1), (h). Pub. L. 95–454, § 906(a)(15), substituted "Office" for "Commission".

1976—Subsec. (g). Pub. L. 94–310 provided for payment of Government contributions from annual appropriations which may be made available until expended.

1974—Subsec. (a). Pub. L. 93–246, § 1(a), struck out introductory text "Except as provided by subsection (b) of this section, the biweekly Government contribution for health benefits for employees or annuitants enrolled in health benefits plans under this chapter shall be adjusted", now incorporated in subsec. (b)(1) of this section, required Commission determination of average of subscription charges, and reenacted remainder of existing provisions, substituting "beginning date of each contract year" for "beginning date of the adjustment".

Subsec. (b)(1). Pub. L. 93–246, §1(a), incorporated introductory text of former subsec. (a) reading "Except as provided by subsection (b) of this section, the biweekly Government contribution for health benefits for employees or annuitants enrolled in health benefits plans under this chapter shall be adjusted", as initial text of provisions designated as subsec. (b)(1), substituted provision for amount of biweekly Government contribution equal to 50 percent of average subscription charge for applicable pay periods commencing in 1974 and 60 percent for applicable pay periods commencing in 1975, and annually thereafter, for former subsec. (a) provision for an amount equal to 40 percent of average of subscription charges and former subsec. (b) provision for 50 percent of subscription charge where the biweekly subscription charge was less than twice the Government contribution.

Subsec. (b)(2). Pub. L. 93–246, §1(a), added par. (2).

Subsec. (c). Pub. L. 93–246, §1(b), struck out reference to subsec. (a).

Subsec. (g). Pub. L. 93–246, §1(c), substituted "by this section" for "by subsection (a) of this section".

1970—Subsec. (a). Pub. L. 91–418, in increasing the Government contribution to the cost of health benefits insurance, substituted provision for adjustment of such contribution, beginning on the first day of the first pay period of each year, to an amount equal to 40 percent of the adjustment, with respect to self alone or self and family enrollments, as applicable, for the highest level of benefits offered by the service benefit plan, the indemnity benefit plan, the two employee organization plans, and the two comprehensive medical plans, for prior provision for a contribution, in addition to requirement of subsec. (c) of this section, of $1.62 if the enrollment is for self or $3.94 if the enrollment is for self and family.

Effective Date of 1997 Amendment

Section 7002(b) of Pub. L. 105–33 provided that: "This section [amending this section] shall take effect on the first day of the contract year that begins in 1999. Nothing in this subsection shall prevent the Office of Personnel Management from taking any action, before such first day, which it considers necessary in order to ensure the timely implementation of this section."

Effective Date of 1990 Amendments

Section 7102(c) of Pub. L. 101–508 provided that: "The amendments made by this section [amending this section] shall take effect on October 1, 1990, and shall apply with respect to amounts payable for periods beginning on or after that date."

Section 1(c) of Pub. L. 101–303 provided that: "The amendments made by this section [amending this section] shall take effect on the date of enactment of this Act [May 29, 1990]. Any annuitant whose enrollment was terminated at any time before such date on account of such annuitant's annuity being insufficient to cover the amount of the required withholdings may, under regulations prescribed by the Office of Personnel Management, be prospectively reinstated in any available health benefits plan upon application of the annuitant."

Effective Date of 1989 Amendment

Section 4003(b) of Pub. L. 101–239 provided that: "The amendment made by subsection (a) [amending this section] shall take effect on October 1, 1989, and shall apply with respect to amounts payable for periods beginning on or after that date."

Effective Date of 1979 Amendment

Amendment by Pub. L. 96–54 effective July 12, 1979, see section 2(b) of Pub. L. 96–54, set out as a note under section 305 of this title.

Effective Date of 1978 Amendment

Amendment by Pub. L. 95–454 effective 90 days after Oct. 13, 1978, see section 907 of Pub. L. 95–454, set out as a note under section 1101 of this title.

Effective Date of 1976 Amendment

Amendment by Pub. L. 94–310 effective Oct. 1, 1976, see section 4 of Pub. L. 94–310, set out as a note under section 130b of Title 2, The Congress.

Effective Date of 1974 Amendment

Section 4(a) of Pub. L. 93–246 provided that: "The first section of this Act [amending this section] shall take effect on the first day of the first applicable pay period which begins on or after January 1, 1974."

Section 4(d) of Pub. L. 93–246 provided that: "The determination of the average of subscription charges and the adjustment of the Government contributions for 1973, under section 8906 of title 5, United States Code, as amended by the first section of this Act [amending this section], shall take effect on the first day of the first applicable pay period which begins on or after the thirtieth day following the date of enactment of this Act [Jan. 31, 1974]."

Effective Date of 1970 Amendment

Section 1(b) of Pub. L. 91–418 provided that: "The amendment made by subsection (a) of this section [amending this section] shall become effective at the beginning of the first applicable pay period which commences after December 31, 1970."

Payments by Postal Service Relating to Corrected Calculations for Past Health Benefits

Pub. L. 103–66, title XI, §11101(b), Aug. 10, 1993, 107 Stat. 413, provided that: "In addition to any other payments required under section 8906(g)(2) of title 5, United States Code, or any other provision of law, the United States Postal Service shall pay into the Employees Health Benefits Fund a total of $348,000,000, of which—

"(1) at least one-third shall be paid not later than September 30, 1996;

"(2) at least two-thirds shall be paid not later than September 30, 1997; and

"(3) any remaining balance shall be paid not later than September 30, 1998."

Computation of Government Contributions to Federal Employees Health Benefits Program for 1990 Through 1993

Pub. L. 101–76, Aug. 11, 1989, 103 Stat. 556, as amended by Pub. L. 101–508, title VII, §7002(e), Nov. 5, 1990, 104 Stat. 1388–330; Pub. L. 103–66, title XI, §11005, Aug. 10, 1993, 107 Stat. 412, provided: "That (a)(1) in the administration of chapter 89 of title 5, United States Code, for each of contract years 1990 through 1998 (inclusive), in order to compute the average subscription charges under section 8906(a) of such title for such contract years, the subscription charges in effect for the indemnity benefit plan on the beginning date of each such contract year—

"(A) shall be deemed to be the subscription charges which were in effect for such plan on the beginning date of the preceding contract year as adjusted under paragraph (2); or

"(B) if subparagraph (A) does not apply, shall be deemed to be—

"(i) the subscription charges which were deemed under this Act to have been in effect for such plan with respect to the preceding contract year as adjusted under paragraph (2), except as provided in clause (ii); or

"(ii) for each of contract years 1997 and 1998, the subscription charges which would be derived by applying the terms of clause (i), reduced by 1 percent.

"(2) The subscription charges under paragraph (1) shall be increased or decreased (as appropriate) by the average percentage by which the respective subscription charges taken into account under paragraphs (1), (3), and (4) of such section 8906(a) for that contract year increased or decreased from the subscription charges taken into account under such paragraphs (1), (3), and (4) for the preceding contract year.

"(b) Separate percentages shall be computed under subsection (a)(2) with respect to enrollments for self alone and enrollments for self and family, respectively.

"(c) The provisions of this Act shall not apply to a contract year (or any period thereafter), if comprehensive reform legislation is enacted to amend section 8906 of title 5, United States Code, and such amendment is required to be implemented by the commencement of negotiations pertaining to rates and benefits for such contract year.

"(d) Any reference in this Act to a 'contract year' shall be considered to be a reference to a contract year under chapter 89 of title 5, United States Code.

"(e) No later than 180 days after the date of the enactment of this Act [Aug. 11, 1989], the Director of the Office of Personnel Management shall transmit recommendations to the Congress for comprehensive reform of the Federal Employee Health Benefits Program."

CONTRIBUTIONS BY UNITED STATES POSTAL SERVICE TO EMPLOYEES HEALTH BENEFITS FUND

Pub. L. 100–203, title VI, § 6003, Dec. 22, 1987, 101 Stat. 1330–277, directed Postal Service to pay $160,000,000 in fiscal year 1988 and $270,000,000 in fiscal year 1989 into Employee Health Benefits Fund in addition to any amount deposited into Fund pursuant to this section in each such fiscal year.

EMPLOYEES SERVING ON PART-TIME CAREER EMPLOYMENT BASIS ON OCTOBER 10, 1978

Section 4(c)(2)(B) of Pub. L. 95–437 provided that: "The amendments made by subparagraph (A) [amending subsec. (b)(1) and (3) of this section] shall not apply with respect to any employee serving in a position on a part-time career employment basis on the date of the enactment of this Act [Oct. 10, 1978] for such period as the employee continues to serve without a break in service in that or any other position on such part-time basis."

CALCULATION AND PAYMENT BY GOVERNMENT OF CONTRIBUTIONS TO CONTINGENCY RESERVES OF ALL HEALTH BENEFIT PLANS

Pub. L. 97–346, § 4, Oct. 15, 1982, 96 Stat. 1650, directed Office of Personnel Management to determine amount by which Government contribution under 5 U.S.C. 8906(b) for the 1983 contract year was less than the Government contribution which would have been determined under such section for such contract year if Government contribution had been calculated by using the two employee organization plans which in 1981 satisfied the standard set forth in 5 U.S.C. 8906(a)(3) directed Government to pay amount of difference thus determined to contingency reserves of all health benefits plans for contract year 1983 in proportion to estimated number of individuals enrolled in such plans during 1983, and directed such payments be paid by appropriate agencies (including Postal Service and Postal Rate Commission) from appropriations referred to in 5 U.S.C. 8906(f) and (g) in same manner as if such payments were Government contributions, and in amounts determined appropriate by Office of Personnel Management.

ELECTION OF HEALTH BENEFITS DURING PERIOD OF SERVICE AS OFFICER OR EMPLOYEE OF AN EMPLOYEE ORGANIZATION; CONTRIBUTIONS INTO EMPLOYEES HEALTH BENEFITS FUND; NON-ELECTION; REGULATIONS

Election of health benefits within sixty days after July 18, 1966, by certain employees on leave without pay for service as officer or employee of an employee organization, contributions into Fund, effect of nonelection of benefits, and regulations, see note set out under section 8706 of this title.

SECTION REFERRED TO IN OTHER SECTIONS

This section is referred to in sections 8906a, 8909 of this title; title 2 section 162b; title 10 section 1108; title 40 section 214c; title 42 sections 1395s, 2297h–8; title 45 section 1212.

§ 8906a. Temporary employees

(a)(1) The Office of Personnel Management shall prescribe regulations to provide for offering health benefits plans to temporary employees (who meet the requirements of paragraph (2)) under the provisions of this chapter.

(2) To be eligible to participate in a health benefits plan offered under this section a temporary employee shall have completed 1 year of current continuous employment, excluding any break in service of 5 days or less.

(b) Notwithstanding the provisions of section 8906—

(1) any temporary employee enrolled in a health benefits plan under this section shall have an amount withheld from the pay of such employee, as determined by the Office of Personnel Management, equal to—

(A) the amount withheld from the pay of an employee under the provisions of section 8906; and

(B) the amount of the Government contribution for an employee under section 8906; and

(2) the employing agency of any such temporary employee shall not pay the Government contribution under the provisions of section 8906.

(Added Pub. L. 100–654, title III, § 301(a), Nov. 14, 1988, 102 Stat. 3846.)

EFFECTIVE DATE

Section 301(d) of Pub. L. 100–654 provided that: "The amendments made by this section [enacting this section and amending section 8913 of this title] shall be effective 120 days after the date of enactment of this section [Nov. 14, 1988]."

SECTION REFERRED TO IN OTHER SECTIONS

This section is referred to in section 8913 of this title.

§ 8907. Information to individuals eligible to enroll

(a) The Office of Personnel Management shall make available to each individual eligible to enroll in a health benefits plan under this chapter such information, in a form acceptable to the Office after consultation with the carrier, as may be necessary to enable the individual to exercise an informed choice among the types of plans described by sections 8903 and 8903a of this title.

(b) Each individual enrollee in a health benefits plan shall be issued an appropriate document setting forth or summarizing the—

(1) services or benefits, including maximums, limitations, and exclusions, to which the enrollee or the enrollee and any eligible family members are entitled thereunder;

(2) procedure for obtaining benefits; and

(3) principal provisions of the plan affecting the enrollee and any eligible family members.

(Pub. L. 89–554, Sept. 6, 1966, 80 Stat. 605; Pub. L. 95–454, title IX, § 906(a)(2), (3), Oct. 13, 1978, 92

Stat. 1224; Pub. L. 98–615, §3(5), Nov. 8, 1984, 98 Stat. 3204; Pub. L. 99–53, §2(d), June 17, 1985, 99 Stat. 94.)

HISTORICAL AND REVISION NOTES

Derivation	U.S. Code	Revised Statutes and Statutes at Large
....	5 U.S.C. 3009(d).	Sept. 28, 1959, Pub. L. 86–382, §10(d), 73 Stat. 715.

Standard changes are made to conform with the definitions applicable and the style of this title as outlined in the preface to the report.

AMENDMENTS

1985—Subsec. (a). Pub. L. 99–53 inserted reference to section 8903a of this title.

1984—Pub. L. 98–615, §3(5)(C), substituted "individuals eligible to enroll" for "employees" in section catchline.

Subsec. (a). Pub. L. 98–615, §3(5)(A), substituted "individual" for "employee" in two places.

Subsec. (b). Pub. L. 98–615, §3(5)(B)(i), substituted "enrollee" for "employee enrolled" in provisions preceding par. (1).

Subsec. (b)(1). Pub. L. 98–615, §3(5)(B)(ii), substituted "enrollee or the enrollee and any eligible family members" for "employee or the employee and members of his family".

Subsec. (b)(3). Pub. L. 98–615, §3(5)(B)(iii), substituted "the enrollee and any eligible family members" for "the employee or members of his family".

1978—Subsec. (a). Pub. L. 95–454 substituted "Office of Personnel Management" and "Office" for "Civil Service Commission" and "Commission", respectively.

EFFECTIVE DATE OF 1984 AMENDMENT

Amendment by Pub. L. 98–615 effective May 7, 1985, with enumerated exceptions, and applicable to any individual who is married to an employee or annuitant on or after that date, see section 4(a)(2) of Pub. L. 98–615, as amended, set out as a note under section 8341 of this title.

EFFECTIVE DATE OF 1978 AMENDMENT

Amendment by Pub. L. 95–454 effective 90 days after Oct. 13, 1978, see section 907 of Pub. L. 95–454, set out as a note under section 1101 of this title.

§ 8908. Coverage of restored employees and survivor or disability annuitants

(a) An employee enrolled in a health benefits plan under this chapter who is removed or suspended without pay and later reinstated or restored to duty on the ground that the removal or suspension was unjustified or unwarranted may, at his option, enroll as a new employee or have his coverage restored, with appropriate adjustments made in contributions and claims, to the same extent and effect as though the removal or suspension had not taken place.

(b) A surviving spouse whose survivor annuity under this title was terminated because of remarriage and is later restored may, under such regulations as the Office of Personnel Management may prescribe, enroll in a health benefits plan described by section 8903 or 8903a of this title if such spouse was covered by any such plan immediately before such annuity was terminated.

(c) A disability annuitant whose disability annuity under section 8337 of this title was terminated and is later restored under the second or third sentence of subsection (e) of such section

may, under regulations prescribed by the Office, enroll in a health benefits plan described by section 8903 or 8903a of this title if such annuitant was covered by any such plan immediately before such annuity was terminated.

(d) A surviving child whose survivor annuity under section 8341(e) or 8443(b) was terminated and is later restored under paragraph (4) of section 8341(e) or the last sentence of section 8443(b) may, under regulations prescribed by the Office, enroll in a health benefits plan described by section 8903 or 8903a if such surviving child was covered by any such plan immediately before such annuity was terminated.

(Pub. L. 89–554, Sept. 6, 1966, 80 Stat. 605; Pub. L. 94–342, §1(a), July 6, 1976, 90 Stat. 808; Pub. L. 95–454, title IX, §906(a)(2), Oct. 13, 1978, 92 Stat. 1224; Pub. L. 99–53, §§2(a), 3(a)(1), (2)(A), June 17, 1985, 99 Stat. 94, 95; Pub. L. 104–208, div. A, title I, §101(f) [title VI, §633(a)(3)], Sept. 30, 1996, 110 Stat. 3009–314, 3009–363.)

HISTORICAL AND REVISION NOTES

Derivation	U.S. Code	Revised Statutes and Statutes at Large
....	5 U.S.C. 3009(c).	Sept. 28, 1959, Pub. L. 86–382, §10(c), 73 Stat. 715. Mar. 17, 1964, Pub. L. 88–284, §1 (less (1)–(13)), 78 Stat. 165.

Standard changes are made to conform with the definitions applicable and the style of this title as outlined in the preface to the report.

AMENDMENTS

1996—Subsec. (d). Pub. L. 104–208 added subsec. (d).

1985—Pub. L. 99–53, §3(a)(2)(A), inserted "or disability" after "and survivor" in section catchline.

Subsec. (b). Pub. L. 99–53, §2(a), inserted reference to section 8903a of this title.

Subsec. (c). Pub. L. 99–53, §3(a)(1), added subsec. (c).

1978—Subsec. (b). Pub. L. 95–454 substituted "Office of Personnel Management" for "Civil Service Commission".

1976—Pub. L. 94–342 designated existing provisions as subsec. (a), added subsec. (b), and substituted "employees and survivor annuitants" for "employee" in section catchline.

EFFECTIVE DATE OF 1996 AMENDMENT

Amendment by Pub. L. 104–208 applicable with respect to termination of marriage taking effect before, on, or after Sept. 30, 1996, except that benefits are payable only with respect to amounts accruing for periods beginning on first day of month beginning after the later of termination of marriage or Sept. 30, 1996, see section 101(f) [title VI, §633(b)] of Pub. L. 104–208, set out as a note under section 8341 of this title.

EFFECTIVE DATE OF 1978 AMENDMENT

Amendment by Pub. L. 95–454 effective 90 days after Oct. 13, 1978, see section 907 of Pub. L. 95–454, set out as a note under section 1101 of this title.

EFFECTIVE DATE OF 1976 AMENDMENT

Section 2 of Pub. L. 94–342 provided that: "The amendments made by the first section of this Act [amending this section] shall take effect on October 1, 1976, or on the date of the enactment of this Act [July 6, 1976], whichever date is later. Such amendments shall apply with respect to individuals whose survivor annuities are restored before, on, or after such date."

INSURANCE COVERAGE FOR RESTORED DISABILITY ANNUITANTS

For provisions directing that subsec. (c) of this section shall apply with respect to any individual whose disability annuity is or was restored under section 8337(e) of this title after December 31, 1983, directing that the Office of Personnel Management notify each individual of any rights which such individual may have under subsec. (c) of this section, including any procedures or deadlines which might apply with respect to the exercise of those rights, directing that such notification be provided to any individual who, as of the 90th day after June 17, 1985, is receiving a disability annuity which was restored to such individual under section 8337(e) of this title after December 31, 1983, directing that nothing in subsec. (c) of this section be construed to authorize coverage under this chapter in the case of any individual who becomes enrolled in a health benefits plan under subsec. (c) of this section for any period before the date as of which such individual becomes so enrolled, and directing that such rule of construction apply with respect to any individual receiving a disability annuity which is or was restored under section 8337(e) of this title after December 31, 1983, and before the expiration of the 90-day period beginning on June 17, 1985, see section 3(c) of Pub. L. 99–53, set out as a note under section 8706 of this title.

§ 8909. Employees Health Benefits Fund

(a) There is in the Treasury of the United States an Employees Health Benefits Fund which is administered by the Office of Personnel Management. The contributions of enrollees and the Government described by section 8906 of this title shall be paid into the Fund. The Fund is available—

(1) without fiscal year limitation for all payments to approved health benefits plans; and

(2) to pay expenses for administering this chapter within the limitations that may be specified annually by Congress.

Payments from the Fund to a plan participating in a letter-of-credit arrangement under this chapter shall, in connection with any payment or reimbursement to be made by such plan for a health service or supply, be made, to the maximum extent practicable, on a checks-presented basis (as defined under regulations of the Department of the Treasury).

(b) Portions of the contributions made by enrollees and the Government shall be regularly set aside in the Fund as follows:

(1) A percentage, not to exceed 1 percent of all contributions, determined by the Office to be reasonably adequate to pay the administrative expenses made available by subsection (a) of this section.

(2) For each health benefits plan, a percentage, not to exceed 3 percent of the contributions toward the plan, determined by the Office to be reasonably adequate to provide a contingency reserve.

The Office, from time to time and in amounts it considers appropriate, may transfer unused funds for administrative expenses to the contingency reserves of the plans then under contract with the Office. When funds are so transferred, each contingency reserve shall be credited in proportion to the total amount of the subscription charges paid and accrued to the plan for the contract term immediately before the contract term in which the transfer is made. The income

derived from dividends, rate adjustments, or other refunds made by a plan shall be credited to its contingency reserve. The contingency reserves may be used to defray increases in future rates, or may be applied to reduce the contributions of enrollees and the Government to, or to increase the benefits provided by, the plan from which the reserves are derived, as the Office from time to time shall determine.

(c) The Secretary of the Treasury may invest and reinvest any of the money in the Fund in interest-bearing obligations of the United States, and may sell these obligations for the purposes of the Fund. The interest on and the proceeds from the sale of these obligations become a part of the Fund.

(d) When the assets, liabilities, and membership of employee organizations sponsoring or underwriting plans approved under section 8903(3) or 8903a of this title are merged, the assets (including contingency reserves) and liabilities of the plans sponsored or underwritten by the merged organizations shall be transferred at the beginning of the contract term next following the date of the merger to the plan sponsored or underwritten by the successor organization. Each employee, annuitant, former spouse, or person having continued coverage under section 8905a of this title affected by a merger shall be transferred to the plan sponsored or underwritten by the successor organization unless he enrolls in another plan under this chapter. If the successor organization is an organization described in section 8901(8)(B) of this title, any employee, annuitant, former spouse, or person having continued coverage under section 8905a of this title so transferred may not remain enrolled in the plan after the end of the contract term in which the merger occurs unless that individual is a full member of such organization (as determined under section 8903a(d) of this title).

(e)(1) Except as provided by subsection (d) of this section, when a plan described by section 8903(3) or (4) or 8903a of this title is discontinued under this chapter, the contingency reserve of that plan shall be credited to the contingency reserves of the plans continuing under this chapter for the contract term following that in which termination occurs, each reserve to be credited in proportion to the amount of the subscription charges paid and accrued to the plan for the year of termination.

(2) Any crediting required under paragraph (1) pursuant to the discontinuation of any plan under this chapter shall be completed by the end of the second contract year beginning after such plan is so discontinued.

(3) The Office shall prescribe regulations in accordance with which this subsection shall be applied in the case of any plan which is discontinued before being credited with the full amount to which it would otherwise be entitled based on the discontinuation of any other plan.

(f)(1) No tax, fee, or other monetary payment may be imposed, directly or indirectly, on a carrier or an underwriting or plan administration subcontractor of an approved health benefits plan by any State, the District of Columbia, or the Commonwealth of Puerto Rico, or by any political subdivision or other governmental authority thereof, with respect to any payment made from the Fund.

(2) Paragraph (1) shall not be construed to exempt any carrier or underwriting or plan administration subcontractor of an approved health benefits plan from the imposition, payment, or collection of a tax, fee, or other monetary payment on the net income or profit accruing to or realized by such carrier or underwriting or plan administration subcontractor from business conducted under this chapter, if that tax, fee, or payment is applicable to a broad range of business activity.

(g) The fund described in subsection (a) is available to pay costs that the Office incurs for activities associated with implementation of the demonstration project under section 1108 of title 10.

(Pub. L. 89–554, Sept. 6, 1966, 80 Stat. 605; Pub. L. 95–454, title IX, § 906(a)(2), (3), Oct. 13, 1978, 92 Stat. 1224; Pub. L. 98–615, § 3(6), Nov. 8, 1984, 98 Stat. 3204; Pub. L. 99–53, § 2(e), (f), June 17, 1985, 99 Stat. 94; Pub. L. 99–251, title I, § 101, Feb. 27, 1986, 100 Stat. 14; Pub. L. 100–654, title II, § 202(a), Nov. 14, 1988, 102 Stat. 3845; Pub. L. 101–508, title VII, § 7002(b), (c), Nov. 5, 1990, 104 Stat. 1388–330; Pub. L. 105–261, div. A, title VII, § 721(b)(4), Oct. 17, 1998, 112 Stat. 2065; Pub. L. 105–266, § 6(b)(1), Oct. 19, 1998, 112 Stat. 2369.)

HISTORICAL AND REVISION NOTES

Derivation	U.S. Code	Revised Statutes and Statutes at Large
....	5 U.S.C. 3007.	Sept. 28, 1959, Pub. L. 86–382, § 8, 73 Stat. 714. Mar. 17, 1964, Pub. L. 88–284, § 1(12), (13), 78 Stat. 165.
....	5 U.S.C. 3008(b).	Sept. 23, 1959, Pub. L. 86–382, § 9(b), 73 Stat. 715.

In subsection (a), the words "hereby created" are omitted as executed. The words "hereinafter referred to as the 'Fund'" are omitted as unnecessary. The words "to reimburse the Employees Health Benefits Fund for sums expended by the Commission in administering the provisions of this chapter for the fiscal years 1960 and 1961" in former section 3008(b) are omitted as executed.

In subsection (d), the requirement that the assets and liabilities of plans of organizations that have been merged be transferred at the beginning of the contract term next following the date of the merger or enactment of this subsection is omitted as executed. The next beginning contract term referred to was November 1, 1964, and the transfers have been made. In the last sentence, the word "hereafter" is omitted as unnecessary.

In subsection (e), the word "is" is substituted for "is or has been" as this title is stated prospectively, and any existing rights and duties are preserved by technical section 8.

Standard changes are made to conform with the definitions applicable and the style of this title as outlined in the preface of the report.

AMENDMENTS

1998—Subsec. (e). Pub. L. 105–266 designated existing provisions as par. (1) and added pars. (2) and (3).

Subsec. (g). Pub. L. 105–261 added subsec. (g).

1990—Subsec. (a). Pub. L. 101–508, § 7002(b), inserted at end "Payments from the Fund to a plan participating in a letter-of-credit arrangement under this chapter shall, in connection with any payment or reimbursement to be made by such plan for a health service or supply, be made, to the maximum extent practicable, on a checks-presented basis (as defined under regulations of the Department of the Treasury)."

Subsec. (f). Pub. L. 101–508, § 7002(c), added subsec. (f).

1988—Subsec. (d). Pub. L. 100–654 substituted "former spouse, or person having continued coverage under section 8905a of this title" for "or former spouse" in two places.

1986—Subsec. (b). Pub. L. 99–251 substituted "enrollees" for "employees" in last sentence.

1985—Subsec. (d). Pub. L. 99–53, § 2(e), substituted "section 8903(3) or 8903a" for "section 8903(3)" and inserted provision directing that if the successor organization is an organization described in section 8901(8)(B) of this title, any transferred employee, annuitant, or former spouse may not remain enrolled in the plan after the end of the contract term in which the merger occurs unless the individual is a full member of such organization (as determined under section 8903a(d) of this title).

Subsec. (e). Pub. L. 99–53, § 2(f), inserted "or 8903a" before "of this title".

1984—Subsecs. (a), (b). Pub. L. 98–615, § 3(6)(A), substituted "enrollees" for "employees, annuitants," in provisions preceding par. (1).

Subsec. (d). Pub. L. 98–615, § 3(6)(B), substituted "Each employee, annuitant, or former spouse" for "Each employee or annuitant".

1978—Subsecs. (a), (b). Pub. L. 95–454 substituted "Office of Personnel Management" for "Civil Service Commission" and "Office" for "Commission" wherever appearing.

EFFECTIVE DATE OF 1990 AMENDMENT

Amendment by Pub. L. 101–508 applicable with respect to contract years beginning on or after Jan. 1, 1991, see section 7002(g) of Pub. L. 101–508, set out as a note under section 8902 of this title.

EFFECTIVE DATE OF 1988 AMENDMENT

Amendment by Pub. L. 100–654 applicable with respect to any calendar year beginning, and contracts entered into or renewed for any calendar year beginning, after end of 9-month period beginning Nov. 14, 1988, and with respect to any qualifying event occurring on or after first day of first calendar year beginning after end of such 9-month period, see section 203 of Pub. L. 100–654, set out as a note under section 8902 of this title.

EFFECTIVE DATE OF 1984 AMENDMENT

Amendment by Pub. L. 98–615 effective May 7, 1985, with enumerated exceptions, and applicable to any individual who is married to an employee or annuitant on or after that date, see section 4(a)(2) of Pub. L. 98–615, as amended, set out as a note under section 8341 of this title.

EFFECTIVE DATE OF 1978 AMENDMENT

Amendment by Pub. L. 95–454 effective 90 days after Oct. 13, 1978, see section 907 of Pub. L. 95–454, set out as a note under section 1101 of this title.

DISPOSAL OF AMOUNTS REMAINING AS OF OCTOBER 19, 1998, IN CONTINGENCY RESERVE OF DISCONTINUED PLAN

Pub. L. 105–266, § 6(b)(2), Oct. 19, 1998, 112 Stat. 2369, provided that: "In the case of any amounts remaining as of the date of the enactment of this Act [Oct. 19, 1998] in the contingency reserve of a discontinued plan, such amounts shall be disposed of in accordance with section 8909(e) of title 5, United States Code, as amended by this subsection, by—

"(A) the deadline set forth in section 8909(e) of such title (as so amended); or

"(B) if later, the end of the 6-month period beginning on such date of enactment."

AMOUNTS TO BE REFUNDED FROM CARRIERS' SPECIAL RESERVES

Pub. L. 99–272, title XV, § 15202(a), Apr. 7, 1986, 100 Stat. 333, provided that:

"(1) The Office of Personnel Management—

"(A) shall determine the minimum level of financial reserves necessary to be held by a carrier for each health benefits plan under chapter 89 of such title for the purpose of ensuring the stable and efficient operation of such plan; and

"(B) shall require the carrier to refund to the Employees Health Benefits Fund (described in section 8909(a) of title 5, United States Code) any such reserves in excess of such minimum level in such amounts and at such times during fiscal years 1986 and 1987 as the Office determines appropriate.

"(2) In carrying out its responsibilities under this subsection, the Office shall ensure that the aggregate amount to be refunded to the Employees Health Benefits Fund under this subsection—

"(A) during fiscal year 1986 shall be not less than $800,000,000; and

"(B) during fiscal year 1987 shall be not less than $300,000,000.

"(3) No amount in the Employees Health Benefits Fund may be transferred to the general fund of the Treasury of the United States as a result of a refund made under this subsection.

"(4)(A) Subject to subparagraphs (B) and (C), any amounts refunded to the Employees Health Benefits Fund under this subsection may be used solely for the purpose of paying the Government contribution under chapter 89 of title 5, United States Code, for health benefits for annuitants, as defined by section 8901(3) of title 5, United States Code, (including the Government contribution for former employees of the United States Postal Service) enrolled in health benefits plans under such chapter.

"(B) This paragraph applies to a refund to the extent that such refund represents amounts attributable to Government contributions which were made under section 8906(b) of title 5, United States Code, (including contributions made by the United States Postal Service) as determined under regulations which the Office of Personnel Management shall prescribe.

"(C) Any part of the amount in the Employees Health Benefits Fund as a result of a refund made under this subsection may be transferred—

"(i) to the government of the District of Columbia, except that the amount of any such part so transferred shall not exceed the amount attributable to the contributions made by the government of the District of Columbia to subscription charges under this chapter (as determined by the Office of Personnel Management); and

"(ii) to the United States Postal Service, except that the amount of any such part so transferred shall not exceed the amount attributable to the contributions made by the United States Postal Service to subscription charges under this chapter (as determined by the Office).

"(5) The provisions of this subsection shall apply notwithstanding any provision of the Federal Employees Benefits Improvement Act of 1985 [probably means the Federal Employees Benefits Improvement Act of 1986, Pub. L. 99–251, see Short Title of 1986 Amendment note set out under section 8901 of this title for classification]."

RESTRICTIONS RELATING TO AMOUNTS REFUNDED TO EMPLOYEES HEALTH BENEFITS FUND FROM CARRIERS' SPECIAL RESERVES

Section 112 of Pub. L. 99–251 provided that:

"(a) PROHIBITED TRANSFERS.—(1) No amount in the Employees Health Benefits Fund may be transferred to the general fund of the Treasury of the United States or the United States Postal Service as a result of a refund described in paragraph (2).

"(2) This subsection applies with respect to any refund made by a carrier during fiscal year 1986 or 1987 to the Employees Health Benefits Fund to the extent that such refund represents amounts in excess of the minimum level of financial reserves necessary to be held by such carrier to ensure the stable and efficient operation of its health benefits plan.

"(b) RESTRICTION RELATING TO USE OF CERTAIN AMOUNTS IN THE FUND.—(1) Any amount which is in the Employees Health Benefits Fund, and which is described in paragraph (2), may be used solely for the purpose of paying the Government contribution under chapter 89 of title 5, United States Code, for health benefits for annuitants enrolled in health benefits plans (without regard to the health benefits plan or plans from which the refunds were received).

"(2) This subsection applies with respect to any amounts—

"(A) which are referred to in subsection (a)(2); and

"(B) which are attributable to Government contributions (other than contributions by the government of the District of Columbia, which shall be returned to such government) that were made under section 8906(b) of title 5, United States Code, as determined under regulations which the Office of Personnel Management shall prescribe.

"(c) DEFINITIONS.—For the purpose of this section—

"(1) the term 'Employees Health Benefits Fund' refers to the fund described in section 8909(a) of title 5, United States Code;

"(2) the term 'carrier' has the meaning given such term by section 8901(7) of such title; and

"(3) the term 'health benefits plan' has the meaning given such term by section 8901(6) of such title."

SECTION REFERRED TO IN OTHER SECTIONS

This section is referred to in sections 6386, 8903b, 8905, 8906 of this title; title 22 sections 4069c, 4069c–1; title 25 section 450i; title 50 section 403p.

§ 8910. Studies, reports, and audits

(a) The Office of Personnel Management shall make a continuing study of the operation and administration of this chapter, including surveys and reports on health benefits plans available to employees and on the experience of the plans.

(b) Each contract entered into under section 8902 of this title shall contain provisions requiring carriers to—

(1) furnish such reasonable reports as the Office determines to be necessary to enable it to carry out its functions under this chapter; and

(2) permit the Office and representatives of the General Accounting Office to examine records of the carriers as may be necessary to carry out the purposes of this chapter.

(c) Each Government agency shall keep such records, make such certifications, and furnish the Office with such information and reports as may be necessary to enable the Office to carry out its functions under this chapter.

(d) The Office, in consultation with the Department of Health and Human Services, shall develop and implement a system through which the carrier for an approved health benefits plan described by section 8903 or 8903a will be able to identify those annuitants or other individuals covered by such plan who are entitled to benefits under part A or B of title XVIII of the Social Security Act in order to ensure that payments under coordination of benefits with Medicare do not exceed the statutory maximums which physicians may charge Medicare enrollees.

(Pub. L. 89–554, Sept. 6, 1966, 80 Stat. 606; Pub. L. 95–454, title IX, § 906(a)(2), (3), Oct. 13, 1978, 92 Stat. 1224; Pub. L. 101–508, title VII, § 7002(d), Nov. 5, 1990, 104 Stat. 1388–330.)

HISTORICAL AND REVISION NOTES

Derivation	U.S. Code	Revised Statutes and Statutes at Large
....	5 U.S.C. 3010.	Sept. 28, 1959, Pub. L. 86–382, § 11, 73 Stat. 716.

In subsection (b), the word "agency" is substituted for "department, agency, and independent establishment".

Standard changes are made to conform with the definitions applicable and the style of this title as outlined in the preface to the report.

REFERENCES IN TEXT

The Social Security Act, referred to in subsec. (d), is act Aug. 14, 1935, ch. 531, 49 Stat. 620, as amended. Parts A and B of title XVIII of the Social Security Act are classified generally to parts A (§ 1395c et seq.) and B (§ 1395j et seq.), respectively, of subchapter XVIII of chapter 7 of Title 42, The Public Health and Welfare. For complete classification of this Act to the Code, see section 1305 of Title 42 and Tables.

AMENDMENTS

1990—Subsec. (d). Pub. L. 101–508 added subsec. (d).
1978—Subsecs. (a) to (c). Pub. L. 95–454 substituted "Office of Personnel Management" for "Civil Service Commission" and "Office" for "Commission" wherever appearing.

EFFECTIVE DATE OF 1990 AMENDMENT

Amendment by Pub. L. 101–508 applicable with respect to contract years beginning on or after Jan. 1, 1991, see section 7002(g) of Pub. L. 101–508, set out as a note under section 8902 of this title.

EFFECTIVE DATE OF 1978 AMENDMENT

Amendment by Pub. L. 95–454 effective 90 days after Oct. 13, 1978, see section 907 of Pub. L. 95–454, set out as a note under section 1101 of this title.

§ 8911. Advisory committee

The Director of the Office of Personnel Management shall appoint a committee composed of five members, who serve without pay, to advise the Office regarding matters of concern to employees under this chapter. Each member of the committee shall be an employee enrolled under this chapter or an elected official of an employee organization.

(Pub. L. 89–554, Sept. 6, 1966, 80 Stat. 607; Pub. L. 95–454, title IX, § 906(a)(1), (4), Oct. 13, 1978, 92 Stat. 1224, 1225.)

HISTORICAL AND REVISION NOTES

Derivation	U.S. Code	Revised Statutes and Statutes at Large
....	5 U.S.C. 3012.	Sept. 28, 1959, Pub. L. 86–382, § 13, 73 Stat. 716.

Standard changes are made to conform with the definitions applicable and the style of this title as outlined in the preface to the report.

AMENDMENTS

1978—Pub. L. 95–454 substituted "Director of the Office of Personnel Management" for "Chairman of the Civil Service Commission" and "Office" for "Commission".

EFFECTIVE DATE OF 1978 AMENDMENT

Amendment by Pub. L. 95–454 effective 90 days after Oct. 13, 1978, see section 907 of Pub. L. 95–454, set out as a note under section 1101 of this title.

TERMINATION OF ADVISORY COMMITTEES

Advisory committees in existence on Jan. 5, 1973, to terminate not later than the expiration of the 2-year period following Jan. 5, 1973, unless, in the case of a committee established by the President or an officer of the Federal Government, such committee is renewed by appropriate action prior to the expiration of such 2-year period, or in the case of a committee established by the Congress, its duration is otherwise provided by law. See section 14 of Pub. L. 92–463, Oct. 6, 1972, 86 Stat. 776, set out in the Appendix to this title.

§ 8912. Jurisdiction of courts

The district courts of the United States have original jurisdiction, concurrent with the United States Court of Federal Claims, of a civil action or claim against the United States founded on this chapter.

(Pub. L. 89–554, Sept. 6, 1966, 80 Stat. 607; Pub. L. 97–164, title I, § 160(a)(3), Apr. 2, 1982, 96 Stat. 48; Pub. L. 102–572, title IX, § 902(b)(1), Oct. 29, 1992, 106 Stat. 4516.)

HISTORICAL AND REVISION NOTES

Derivation	U.S. Code	Revised Statutes and Statutes at Large
....	5 U.S.C. 3014.	Sept. 28, 1959, Pub. L. 86–382, § 15, 73 Stat. 716.

Standard changes are made to conform with the definitions applicable and the style of this title as outlined in the preface to the report.

AMENDMENTS

1992—Pub. L. 102–572 substituted "United States Court of Federal Claims" for "United States Claims Court".
1982—Pub. L. 97–164 substituted "United States Claims Court" for "Court of Claims".

EFFECTIVE DATE OF 1992 AMENDMENT

Amendment by Pub. L. 102–572 effective Oct. 29, 1992, see section 911 of Pub. L. 102–572, set out as a note under section 171 of Title 28, Judiciary and Judicial Procedure.

EFFECTIVE DATE OF 1982 AMENDMENT

Amendment by Pub. L. 97–164 effective Oct. 1, 1982, see section 402 of Pub. L. 97–164, set out as a note under section 171 of Title 28, Judiciary and Judicial Procedure.

§ 8913. Regulations

(a) The Office of Personnel Management may prescribe regulations necessary to carry out this chapter.

(b) The regulations of the Office may prescribe the time at which and the manner and conditions under which an employee is eligible to enroll in an approved health benefits plan described in section 8903 or 8903a of this title. The regulations may exclude an employee on the basis of the nature and type of his employment or conditions pertaining to it, such as short-term appointment, seasonal or intermittent employment, and employment of like nature. The Office may not exclude—

(1) an employee or group of employees solely on the basis of the hazardous nature of employment;

(2) a teacher in the employ of the Board of Education of the District of Columbia, whose

pay is fixed by section 1501 of title 31, District of Columbia Code, on the basis of the fact that the teacher is serving under a temporary appointment if the teacher has been so employed by the Board for a period or periods totaling not less than two school years;

    (3) an employee who is occupying a position on a part-time career employment basis (as defined in section 3401(2) of this title); or

    (4) an employee who is employed on a temporary basis and is eligible under section 8906a(a).

(c) The regulations of the Office shall provide for the beginning and ending dates of coverage of employees, annuitants, members of their families, and former spouses under health benefit plans. The regulations may permit the coverage to continue, exclusive of the temporary extension of coverage described by section 8902(g) of this title, until the end of the pay period in which an employee is separated from the service, or until the end of the month in which an annuitant or former spouse ceases to be entitled to annuity, and in case of the death of an employee or annuitant, may permit a temporary extension of the coverage of members of his family for not to exceed 90 days.

(d) The Secretary of Agriculture shall prescribe regulations to effect the application and operation of this chapter to an individual named by section 8901(1)(H) of this title.

(Pub. L. 89–554, Sept. 6, 1966, 80 Stat. 607; Pub. L. 95–437, §4(c)(1), Oct. 10, 1978, 92 Stat. 1058; Pub. L. 95–454, title IX, §906(a)(2), (3), (c)(2)(F), (H), Oct. 13, 1978, 92 Stat. 1224, 1227; Pub. L. 98–615, §3(7), Nov. 8, 1984, 98 Stat. 3204; Pub. L. 99–53, §2(a), June 17, 1985, 99 Stat. 94; Pub. L. 100–654, title III, §301(c), Nov. 14, 1988, 102 Stat. 3846.)

HISTORICAL AND REVISION NOTES

Derivation	U.S. Code	Revised Statutes and Statutes at Large
(a)	5 U.S.C. 3009(a).	Sept. 28, 1959, Pub. L. 86–382, §10(a), 73 Stat. 715.
(b)	5 U.S.C. 3002(a) (words between 1st and 4th commas of 1st sentence, and 2d sentence), (f) (words between 1st and 2d commas of 1st sentence).	Sept. 28, 1959, Pub. L. 86–382, §3(a) (words between 1st and 4th commas of 1st sentence, and 2d sentence), 73 Stat. 710. July 1, 1960, Pub. L. 86–568, §115(d) "(f) (words between 1st and 2d commas of 1st sentence)", 74 Stat. 303. Oct. 6, 1964, Pub. L. 88–631, §1, 78 Stat. 1007.
(c)	5 U.S.C. 3009(b).	Sept. 28, 1959, Pub. L. 86–382, §10(b), 73 Stat. 715.
(d)	5 U.S.C. 3002(f) (2d sentence).	July 1, 1960, Pub. L. 86–568, §115(d) "(f) (2d sentence)", 74 Stat. 303.

In subsection (b)(2), the words "section 1501 of title 31, District of Columbia Code" are substituted for "section 1 of the District of Columbia Teachers' Salary Act of 1955 (69 Stat. 521), as amended (sec. 31–1501, D.C. Code, 1961 edition)".

Standard changes are made to conform with the definitions applicable and the style of this title as outlined in the preface to the report.

AMENDMENTS

1988—Subsec. (b)(4). Pub. L. 100–654 added par. (4).

1985—Subsec. (b). Pub. L. 99–53 inserted reference to section 8903a of this title.

1984—Subsec. (c). Pub. L. 98–615, §3(7), substituted "employees, annuitants, members of their families, and former spouses" for "employees and annuitants and members of their families", and "in which an annuitant or former spouse" for "in which an annuitant".

1978—Subsecs. (a), (b). Pub. L. 95–454, §906(a)(2), (3), substituted "Office of Personnel Management" for "Civil Service Commission" and "Office" for "Commission" wherever appearing.

Subsec. (b)(3). Pub. L. 95–454, §906(c)(2)(F), (H), substituted "3401" for "3391".

Pub. L. 95–437 added par. (3).

Subsec. (c). Pub. L. 95–454, §906(a)(3), substituted "Office" for "Commission".

EFFECTIVE DATE OF 1988 AMENDMENT

Amendment by Pub. L. 100–654 effective 120 days after Nov. 14, 1988, see section 301(d) of Pub. L. 100–654, set out as an Effective Date note under section 8906a of this title.

EFFECTIVE DATE OF 1984 AMENDMENT

Amendment by Pub. L. 98–615 effective May 7, 1985, with enumerated exceptions, and applicable to any individual who is married to an employee or annuitant on or after that date, see section 4(a)(2) of Pub. L. 98–615, as amended, set out as a note under section 8341 of this title.

EFFECTIVE DATE OF 1978 AMENDMENT

Amendment by Pub. L. 95–454 effective 90 days after Oct. 13, 1978, see section 907 of Pub. L. 95–454, set out as a note under section 1101 of this title.

SECTION REFERRED TO IN OTHER SECTIONS

This section is referred to in section 8901 of this title.

§ 8914. Effect of other statutes

Any provision of law outside of this chapter which provides coverage or any other benefit under this chapter to any individuals who (based on their being employed by an entity other than the Government) would not otherwise be eligible for any such coverage or benefit shall not apply with respect to any individual appointed, transferred, or otherwise commencing that type of employment on or after October 1, 1988.

(Added Pub. L. 100–238, title I, §108(a)(3)(A), Jan. 8, 1988, 101 Stat. 1747.)

SECTION REFERRED TO IN OTHER SECTIONS

This section is referred to in title 22 section 6103; title 25 section 450i.

CHAPTER 90—LONG-TERM CARE INSURANCE

§ 9001. Definitions

For purposes of this chapter:

    (1) EMPLOYEE.—The term "employee" means—

        (A) an employee as defined by section 8901(1);

        (B) an individual described in section 2105(e); and

(C) an individual employed by the Tennessee Valley Authority,

but does not include an individual employed by the government of the District of Columbia.

(2) ANNUITANT.—The term "annuitant" has the meaning such term would have under paragraph (3) of section 8901 if, for purposes of such paragraph, the term "employee" were considered to have the meaning given to it under paragraph (1) of this subsection.

(3) MEMBER OF THE UNIFORMED SERVICES.— The term "member of the uniformed services" means a member of the uniformed services, other than a retired member of the uniformed services, who is—

(A) on active duty or full-time National Guard duty for a period of more than 30 days; and

(B) a member of the Selected Reserve.

(4) RETIRED MEMBER OF THE UNIFORMED SERVICES.—The term "retired member of the uniformed services" means a member or former member of the uniformed services entitled to retired or retainer pay, including a member or former member retired under chapter 1223 of title 10 who has attained the age of 60 and who satisfies such eligibility requirements as the Office of Personnel Management prescribes under section 9008.

(5) QUALIFIED RELATIVE.—The term "qualified relative" means each of the following:

(A) The spouse of an individual described in paragraph (1), (2), (3), or (4).

(B) A parent, stepparent, or parent-in-law of an individual described in paragraph (1) or (3).

(C) A child (including an adopted child, a stepchild, or, to the extent the Office of Personnel Management by regulation provides, a foster child) of an individual described in paragraph (1), (2), (3), or (4), if such child is at least 18 years of age.

(D) An individual having such other relationship to an individual described in paragraph (1), (2), (3), or (4) as the Office may by regulation prescribe.

(6) ELIGIBLE INDIVIDUAL.—The term "eligible individual" refers to an individual described in paragraph (1), (2), (3), (4), or (5).

(7) QUALIFIED CARRIER.—The term "qualified carrier" means an insurance company (or consortium of insurance companies) that is licensed to issue long-term care insurance in all States, taking any subsidiaries of such a company into account (and, in the case of a consortium, considering the member companies and any subsidiaries thereof, collectively).

(8) STATE.—The term "State" includes the District of Columbia.

(9) QUALIFIED LONG-TERM CARE INSURANCE CONTRACT.—The term "qualified long-term care insurance contract" has the meaning given such term by section 7702B of the Internal Revenue Code of 1986.

(10) APPROPRIATE SECRETARY.—The term "appropriate Secretary" means—

(A) except as otherwise provided in this paragraph, the Secretary of Defense;

(B) with respect to the Coast Guard when it is not operating as a service of the Navy, the Secretary of Transportation;

(C) with respect to the commissioned corps of the National Oceanic and Atmospheric Administration, the Secretary of Commerce; and

(D) with respect to the commissioned corps of the Public Health Service, the Secretary of Health and Human Services.

(Added Pub. L. 106–265, title I, §1002(a), Sept. 19, 2000, 114 Stat. 762.)

REFERENCES IN TEXT

Section 7702B of the Internal Revenue Code of 1986, referred to in par. (9), is classified to section 7702B of Title 26, Internal Revenue Code.

EFFECTIVE DATE

Pub. L. 106–265, title I, §1003, Sept. 19, 2000, 114 Stat. 770, provided that: "The Office of Personnel Management shall take such measures as may be necessary to ensure that long-term care insurance coverage under title 5, United States Code, as amended by this title [enacting this chapter], may be obtained in time to take effect not later than the first day of the first applicable pay period of the first fiscal year which begins after the end of the 18-month period beginning on the date of the enactment of this Act [Sept. 19, 2000]."

SHORT TITLE

Pub. L. 106–265, title I, §1001, Sept. 19, 2000, 114 Stat. 762, provided that: "This title [enacting this chapter] may be cited as the 'Long-Term Care Security Act'."

SECTION REFERRED TO IN OTHER SECTIONS

This section is referred to in sections 9002, 9004, 9008 of this title.

§ 9002. Availability of insurance

(a) IN GENERAL.—The Office of Personnel Management shall establish and, in consultation with the appropriate Secretaries, administer a program through which an individual described in paragraph (1), (2), (3), (4), or (5) of section 9001 may obtain long-term care insurance coverage under this chapter for such individual.

(b) GENERAL REQUIREMENTS.—Long-term care insurance may not be offered under this chapter unless—

(1) the only coverage provided is under qualified long-term care insurance contracts; and

(2) each insurance contract under which any such coverage is provided is issued by a qualified carrier.

(c) DOCUMENTATION REQUIREMENT.—As a condition for obtaining long-term care insurance coverage under this chapter based on one's status as a qualified relative, an applicant shall provide documentation to demonstrate the relationship, as prescribed by the Office.

(d) UNDERWRITING STANDARDS.—

(1) DISQUALIFYING CONDITION.—Nothing in this chapter shall be considered to require that long-term care insurance coverage be made available in the case of any individual who would be eligible for benefits immediately.

(2) SPOUSAL PARITY.—For the purpose of underwriting standards, a spouse of an individual described in paragraph (1), (2), (3), or (4) of section 9001 shall, as nearly as practicable, be treated like that individual.

(3) GUARANTEED ISSUE.—Nothing in this chapter shall be considered to require that

long-term care insurance coverage be guaranteed to an eligible individual.

(4) REQUIREMENT THAT CONTRACT BE FULLY INSURED.—In addition to the requirements otherwise applicable under section 9001(9), in order to be considered a qualified long-term care insurance contract for purposes of this chapter, a contract must be fully insured, whether through reinsurance with other companies or otherwise.

(5) HIGHER STANDARDS ALLOWABLE.—Nothing in this chapter shall, in the case of an individual applying for long-term care insurance coverage under this chapter after the expiration of such individual's first opportunity to enroll, preclude the application of underwriting standards more stringent than those that would have applied if that opportunity had not yet expired.

(e) GUARANTEED RENEWABILITY.—The benefits and coverage made available to eligible individuals under any insurance contract under this chapter shall be guaranteed renewable (as defined by section 7A(2) of the model regulations described in section 7702B(g)(2) of the Internal Revenue Code of 1986), including the right to have insurance remain in effect so long as premiums continue to be timely made. However, the authority to revise premiums under this chapter shall be available only on a class basis and only to the extent otherwise allowable under section 9003(b).

(Added Pub. L. 106–265, title I, §1002(a), Sept. 19, 2000, 114 Stat. 764.)

REFERENCES IN TEXT

Section 7702B(g)(2) of the Internal Revenue Code of 1986, referred to in subsec. (e), is classified to section 7702B(g)(2) of Title 26, Internal Revenue Code.

§9003. Contracting authority

(a) IN GENERAL.—The Office of Personnel Management shall, without regard to section 5 of title 41 or any other statute requiring competitive bidding, contract with one or more qualified carriers for a policy or policies of long-term care insurance. The Office shall ensure that each resulting contract (hereafter in this chapter referred to as a "master contract") is awarded on the basis of contractor qualifications, price, and reasonable competition.

(b) TERMS AND CONDITIONS.—

(1) IN GENERAL.—Each master contract under this chapter shall contain—

(A) a detailed statement of the benefits offered (including any maximums, limitations, exclusions, and other definitions of benefits);

(B) the premiums charged (including any limitations or other conditions on their subsequent adjustment);

(C) the terms of the enrollment period; and

(D) such other terms and conditions as may be mutually agreed to by the Office and the carrier involved, consistent with the requirements of this chapter.

(2) PREMIUMS.—Premiums charged under each master contract entered into under this section shall reasonably and equitably reflect the cost of the benefits provided, as determined by the Office. The premiums shall not

be adjusted during the term of the contract unless mutually agreed to by the Office and the carrier.

(3) NONRENEWABILITY.—Master contracts under this chapter may not be made automatically renewable.

(c) PAYMENT OF REQUIRED BENEFITS; DISPUTE RESOLUTION.—

(1) IN GENERAL.—Each master contract under this chapter shall require the carrier to agree—

(A) to provide payments or benefits to an eligible individual if such individual is entitled thereto under the terms of the contract; and

(B) with respect to disputes regarding claims for payments or benefits under the terms of the contract—

(i) to establish internal procedures designed to expeditiously resolve such disputes; and

(ii) to establish, for disputes not resolved through procedures under clause (i), procedures for one or more alternative means of dispute resolution involving independent third-party review under appropriate circumstances by entities mutually acceptable to the Office and the carrier.

(2) ELIGIBILITY.—A carrier's determination as to whether or not a particular individual is eligible to obtain long-term care insurance coverage under this chapter shall be subject to review only to the extent and in the manner provided in the applicable master contract.

(3) OTHER CLAIMS.—For purposes of applying the Contract Disputes Act of 1978 to disputes arising under this chapter between a carrier and the Office—

(A) the agency board having jurisdiction to decide an appeal relative to such a dispute shall be such board of contract appeals as the Director of the Office of Personnel Management shall specify in writing (after appropriate arrangements, as described in section 8(c) of such Act); and

(B) the district courts of the United States shall have original jurisdiction, concurrent with the United States Court of Federal Claims, of any action described in section 10(a)(1) of such Act relative to such a dispute.

(4) RULE OF CONSTRUCTION.—Nothing in this chapter shall be considered to grant authority for the Office or a third-party reviewer to change the terms of any contract under this chapter.

(d) DURATION.—

(1) IN GENERAL.—Each master contract under this chapter shall be for a term of 7 years, unless terminated earlier by the Office in accordance with the terms of such contract. However, the rights and responsibilities of the enrolled individual, the insurer, and the Office (or duly designated third-party administrator) under such contract shall continue with respect to such individual until the termination of coverage of the enrolled individual or the effective date of a successor contract thereto.

(2) EXCEPTION.—

(A) SHORTER DURATION.—In the case of a master contract entered into before the end of the period described in subparagraph (B), paragraph (1) shall be applied by substituting "ending on the last day of the 7-year period described in paragraph (2)(B)" for "of 7 years".

(B) DEFINITION.—The period described in this subparagraph is the 7-year period beginning on the earliest date as of which any long-term care insurance coverage under this chapter becomes effective.

(3) CONGRESSIONAL NOTIFICATION.—No later than 180 days after receiving the second report required under section 9006(c), the President (or his designee) shall submit to the Committees on Government Reform and on Armed Services of the House of Representatives and the Committees on Governmental Affairs and on Armed Services of the Senate, a written recommendation as to whether the program under this chapter should be continued without modification, terminated, or restructured. During the 180-day period following the date on which the President (or his designee) submits the recommendation required under the preceding sentence, the Office of Personnel Management may not take any steps to rebid or otherwise contract for any coverage to be available at any time following the expiration of the 7-year period described in paragraph (2)(B).

(4) FULL PORTABILITY.—Each master contract under this chapter shall include such provisions as may be necessary to ensure that, once an individual becomes duly enrolled, long-term care insurance coverage obtained by such individual pursuant to that enrollment shall not be terminated due to any change in status (such as separation from Government service or the uniformed services) or ceasing to meet the requirements for being considered a qualified relative (whether as a result of dissolution of marriage or otherwise).

(Added Pub. L. 106–265, title I, § 1002(a), Sept. 19, 2000, 114 Stat. 764.)

REFERENCES IN TEXT

The Contract Disputes Act of 1978, referred to in subsec. (c)(3), is Pub. L. 95–563, Nov. 1, 1978, 92 Stat. 2383, as amended, which is classified principally to chapter 9 (§ 601 et seq.) of Title 41, Public Contracts. Sections 8(c) and 10(a)(1) of the Act are classified to sections 607(c) and 609(a)(1), respectively, of Title 41. For complete classification of this Act to the Code, see Short Title note set out under section 601 of Title 41 and Tables.

SECTION REFERRED TO IN OTHER SECTIONS

This section is referred to in sections 9002, 9004, 9007 of this title.

§ 9004. Financing

(a) IN GENERAL.—Each eligible individual obtaining long-term care insurance coverage under this chapter shall be responsible for 100 percent of the premiums for such coverage.

(b) WITHHOLDINGS.—

(1) IN GENERAL.—The amount necessary to pay the premiums for enrollment may—

(A) in the case of an employee, be withheld from the pay of such employee;

(B) in the case of an annuitant, be withheld from the annuity of such annuitant;

(C) in the case of a member of the uniformed services described in section 9001(3), be withheld from the pay of such member; and

(D) in the case of a retired member of the uniformed services described in section 9001(4), be withheld from the retired pay or retainer pay payable to such member.

(2) VOLUNTARY WITHHOLDINGS FOR QUALIFIED RELATIVES.—Withholdings to pay the premiums for enrollment of a qualified relative may, upon election of the appropriate eligible individual (described in section 9001(1)–(4)), be withheld under paragraph (1) to the same extent and in the same manner as if enrollment were for such individual.

(c) DIRECT PAYMENTS.—All amounts withheld under this section shall be paid directly to the carrier.

(d) OTHER FORMS OF PAYMENT.—Any enrollee who does not elect to have premiums withheld under subsection (b) or whose pay, annuity, or retired or retainer pay (as referred to in subsection (b)(1)) is insufficient to cover the withholding required for enrollment (or who is not receiving any regular amounts from the Government, as referred to in subsection (b)(1), from which any such withholdings may be made, and whose premiums are not otherwise being provided for under subsection (b)(2)) shall pay an amount equal to the full amount of those charges directly to the carrier.

(e) SEPARATE ACCOUNTING REQUIREMENT.—Each carrier participating under this chapter shall maintain records that permit it to account for all amounts received under this chapter (including investment earnings on those amounts) separate and apart from all other funds.

(f) REIMBURSEMENTS.—

(1) REASONABLE INITIAL COSTS.—

(A) IN GENERAL.—The Employees' Life Insurance Fund is available, without fiscal year limitation, for reasonable expenses incurred by the Office of Personnel Management in administering this chapter before the start of the 7-year period described in section 9003(d)(2)(B), including reasonable implementation costs.

(B) REIMBURSEMENT REQUIREMENT.—Such Fund shall be reimbursed, before the end of the first year of that 7-year period, for all amounts obligated or expended under subparagraph (A) (including lost investment income). Such reimbursement shall be made by carriers, on a pro rata basis, in accordance with appropriate provisions which shall be included in master contracts under this chapter.

(2) SUBSEQUENT COSTS.—

(A) IN GENERAL.—There is hereby established in the Employees' Life Insurance Fund a Long-Term Care Administrative Account, which shall be available to the Office, without fiscal year limitation, to defray reasonable expenses incurred by the Office in administering this chapter after the start of the 7-year period described in section 9003(d)(2)(B).

(B) REIMBURSEMENT REQUIREMENT.—Each master contract under this chapter shall include appropriate provisions under which the carrier involved shall, during each year, make such periodic contributions to the Long-Term Care Administrative Account as necessary to ensure that the reasonable anticipated expenses of the Office in administering this chapter during such year (adjusted to reconcile for any earlier overestimates or underestimates under this subparagraph) are defrayed.

(Added Pub. L. 106–265, title I, § 1002(a), Sept. 19, 2000, 114 Stat. 766.)

§ 9005. Preemption

The terms of any contract under this chapter which relate to the nature, provision, or extent of coverage or benefits (including payments with respect to benefits) shall supersede and preempt any State or local law, or any regulation issued thereunder, which relates to long-term care insurance or contracts.

(Added Pub. L. 106–265, title I, § 1002(a), Sept. 19, 2000, 114 Stat. 768.)

§ 9006. Studies, reports, and audits

(a) PROVISIONS RELATING TO CARRIERS.—Each master contract under this chapter shall contain provisions requiring the carrier—

(1) to furnish such reasonable reports as the Office of Personnel Management determines to be necessary to enable it to carry out its functions under this chapter; and

(2) to permit the Office and representatives of the General Accounting Office to examine such records of the carrier as may be necessary to carry out the purposes of this chapter.

(b) PROVISIONS RELATING TO FEDERAL AGENCIES.—Each Federal agency shall keep such records, make such certifications, and furnish the Office, the carrier, or both, with such information and reports as the Office may require.

(c) REPORTS BY THE GENERAL ACCOUNTING OFFICE.—The General Accounting Office shall prepare and submit to the President, the Office of Personnel Management, and each House of Congress, before the end of the third and fifth years during which the program under this chapter is in effect, a written report evaluating such program. Each such report shall include an analysis of the competitiveness of the program, as compared to both group and individual coverage generally available to individuals in the private insurance market. The Office shall cooperate with the General Accounting Office to provide periodic evaluations of the program.

(Added Pub. L. 106–265, title I, § 1002(a), Sept. 19, 2000, 114 Stat. 768.)

SECTION REFERRED TO IN OTHER SECTIONS

This section is referred to in section 9003 of this title.

§ 9007. Jurisdiction of courts

The district courts of the United States have original jurisdiction of a civil action or claim described in paragraph (1) or (2) of section 9003(c), after such administrative remedies as required under such paragraph (1) or (2) (as applicable) have been exhausted, but only to the extent judicial review is not precluded by any dispute resolution or other remedy under this chapter.

(Added Pub. L. 106–265, title I, § 1002(a), Sept. 19, 2000, 114 Stat. 768.)

§ 9008. Administrative functions

(a) IN GENERAL.—The Office of Personnel Management shall prescribe regulations necessary to carry out this chapter.

(b) ENROLLMENT PERIODS.—The Office shall provide for periodic coordinated enrollment, promotion, and education efforts in consultation with the carriers.

(c) CONSULTATION.—Any regulations necessary to effect the application and operation of this chapter with respect to an eligible individual described in paragraph (3) or (4) of section 9001, or a qualified relative thereof, shall be prescribed by the Office in consultation with the appropriate Secretary.

(d) INFORMED DECISIONMAKING.—The Office shall ensure that each eligible individual applying for long-term care insurance under this chapter is furnished the information necessary to enable that individual to evaluate the advantages and disadvantages of obtaining long-term care insurance under this chapter, including the following:

(1) The principal long-term care benefits and coverage available under this chapter, and how those benefits and coverage compare to the range of long-term care benefits and coverage otherwise generally available.

(2) Representative examples of the cost of long-term care, and the sufficiency of the benefits available under this chapter relative to those costs. The information under this paragraph shall also include—

(A) the projected effect of inflation on the value of those benefits; and

(B) a comparison of the inflation-adjusted value of those benefits to the projected future costs of long-term care.

(3) Any rights individuals under this chapter may have to cancel coverage, and to receive a total or partial refund of premiums. The information under this paragraph shall also include—

(A) the projected number or percentage of individuals likely to fail to maintain their coverage (determined based on lapse rates experienced under similar group long-term care insurance programs and, when available, this chapter); and

(B)(i) a summary description of how and when premiums for long-term care insurance under this chapter may be raised;

(ii) the premium history during the last 10 years for each qualified carrier offering long-term care insurance under this chapter; and

(iii) if cost increases are anticipated, the projected premiums for a typical insured individual at various ages.

(4) The advantages and disadvantages of long-term care insurance generally, relative to

other means of accumulating or otherwise acquiring the assets that may be needed to meet the costs of long-term care, such as through tax-qualified retirement programs or other investment vehicles.

(Added Pub. L. 106–265, title I, § 1002(a), Sept. 19, 2000, 114 Stat. 768.)

SECTION REFERRED TO IN OTHER SECTIONS

This section is referred to in section 9001 of this title.

§ 9009. Cost accounting standards

The cost accounting standards issued pursuant to section 26(f) of the Office of Federal Procurement Policy Act (41 U.S.C. 422(f)) shall not apply with respect to a long-term care insurance contract under this chapter.

(Added Pub. L. 106–265, title I, § 1002(a), Sept. 19, 2000, 114 Stat. 769.)

Subpart H—Access to Criminal History Record Information

CHAPTER 91—ACCESS TO CRIMINAL HISTORY RECORDS FOR NATIONAL SECURITY AND OTHER PURPOSES

AMENDMENTS

2000—Pub. L. 106–398, § 1 [[div. A], title X, § 1076(f)(1)(A), (2)(B)], Oct. 30, 2000, 114 Stat. 1654, 1654A–282, substituted "AND OTHER PURPOSES" for "PURPOSES" in chapter heading and "Access to criminal history records for national security and other purposes" for "Criminal history record information for national security purposes" in item 9101.

§ 9101. Access to criminal history records for national security and other purposes

(a) As used in this section:

(1) The term "criminal justice agency" means (A) any Federal, State, or local court, and (B) any Federal, State, or local agency, or any subunit thereof, which performs the administration of criminal justice pursuant to a statute or Executive order, and which allocates a substantial part of its annual budget to the administration of criminal justice.

(2) The term "criminal history record information" means information collected by criminal justice agencies on individuals consisting of identifiable descriptions and notations of arrests, indictments, informations, or other formal criminal charges, and any disposition arising therefrom, sentencing, correction supervision, and release. The term does not include identification information such as fingerprint records to the extent that such information does not indicate involvement of the individual in the criminal justice system. The term does not include those records of a State or locality sealed pursuant to law from access by State and local criminal justice agencies of that State or locality.

(3) The term "classified information" means information or material designated pursuant to the provisions of a statute or Executive order as requiring protection against unauthorized disclosure for reasons of national security.

(4) The term "State" means any of the several States, the District of Columbia, the Commonwealth of Puerto Rico, the Commonwealth of the Northern Mariana Islands, Guam, the Virgin Islands, American Samoa, and any other territory or possession of the United States.

(5) The term "local" and "locality" means any local government authority or agency or component thereof within a State having jurisdiction over matters at a county, municipal, or other local government level.

(6) The term "covered agency" means any of the following:

(A) The Department of Defense.

(B) The Department of State.

(C) The Department of Transportation.

(D) The Office of Personnel Management.

(E) The Central Intelligence Agency.

(F) The Federal Bureau of Investigation.

(b)(1) Upon request by the head of a covered agency, criminal justice agencies shall make available criminal history record information regarding individuals under investigation by that covered agency for the purpose of determining eligibility for any of the following:

(A) Access to classified information.

(B) Assignment to or retention in sensitive national security duties.

(C) Acceptance or retention in the armed forces.

(D) Appointment, retention, or assignment to a position of public trust or a critical or sensitive position while either employed by the Government or performing a Government contract.

(2) Such a request to a State central criminal history record repository shall be accompanied by the fingerprints of the individual who is the subject of the request if required by State law and if the repository uses the fingerprints in an automated fingerprint identification system.

(3) Fees, if any, charged for providing criminal history record information pursuant to this subsection shall not exceed the reasonable cost of providing such information.

(4) This subsection shall apply notwithstanding any other provision of law or regulation of any State or of any locality within a State, or any other law of the United States.

(c) A covered agency shall not obtain criminal history record information pursuant to this section unless it has received written consent from the individual under investigation for the release of such information for the purposes set forth in paragraph (b)(1).

(d) Criminal history record information received under this section shall be disclosed or used only for the purposes set forth in paragraph (b)(1) or for national security or criminal justice purposes authorized by law, and such information shall be made available to the individual who is the subject of such information upon request.

(e)(1) Automated information delivery systems shall be used to provide criminal history record information to a covered agency under subsection (b) whenever available.

(2) Fees, if any, charged for automated access through such systems may not exceed the reasonable cost of providing such access.

(3) The criminal justice agency providing the criminal history record information through such systems may not limit disclosure on the basis that the repository is accessed from outside the State.

(4) Information provided through such systems shall be the full and complete criminal history record.

(5) Criminal justice agencies shall accept and respond to requests for criminal history record information through such systems with printed or photocopied records when requested.

(f) The authority provided under this section with respect to the Department of State may be exercised only so long as the Department of State continues to extend to its employees and applicants for employment, at a minimum, those procedural safeguards provided for as part of the security clearance process that were made available, as of May 1, 1987, pursuant to section 163.4 of volume 3 of the Foreign Affairs Manual.

(Added Pub. L. 99–169, title VIII, § 801(a), Dec. 4, 1985, 99 Stat. 1009; amended Pub. L. 99–569, title IV, § 402(a), Oct. 27, 1986, 100 Stat. 3196; Pub. L. 101–246, title I, § 114, Feb. 16, 1990, 104 Stat. 22; Pub. L. 106–398, § 1 [[div. A], title X, § 1076(a)–(e), (f)(2)(A)], Oct. 30, 2000, 114 Stat. 1654, 1654A–280 to 1654A–282.)

AMENDMENTS

2000—Pub. L. 106–398, § 1 [[div. A], title X, § 1076(f)(2)(A)], substituted "Access to criminal history records for national security and other purposes" for "Criminal history record information for national security purposes" in section catchline.

Subsec. (a)(1). Pub. L. 106–398, § 1 [[div. A], title X, § 1076(e)(1)], substituted "means (A) any Federal, State, or local court, and (B) any Federal, State, or local agency, or any subunit thereof, which" for "includes Federal, State, and local agencies and means: (A) courts, or (B) a Government agency or any subunit thereof which".

Subsec. (a)(4). Pub. L. 106–398, § 1 [[div. A], title X, § 1076(e)(2)], inserted "the Commonwealth of" before "the Northern Mariana Islands" and struck out "the Trust Territory of the Pacific Islands," after "American Samoa,".

Subsec. (a)(6). Pub. L. 106–398, § 1 [[div. A], title X, § 1076(a)(1)], added par. (6).

Subsec. (b). Pub. L. 106–398, § 1 [[div. A], title X, § 1076(c)], in first sentence of par. (1), inserted "any of the following:" after "eligibility for" and substituted subpars. (A) to (D) for "(A) access to classified information or (B) assignment to or retention in sensitive national security duties.", designated second sentence of par. (1) as par. (2), designated third sentence of par. (1) as par. (3) and substituted a period for ", nor shall they in any event exceed those charged to State or local agencies other than criminal justice agencies for such information.", and redesignated former par. (2) as (4).

Subsec. (b)(1). Pub. L. 106–398, § 1 [[div. A], title X, § 1076(a)(2)], substituted "by the head of a covered agency" for "by the Department of Defense, the Department of State, the Office of Personnel Management, the Central Intelligence Agency, or the Federal Bureau of Investigation" and "that covered agency" for "such department, office, agency, or bureau".

Subsec. (b)(3). Pub. L. 106–398, § 1 [[div. A], title X, § 1076(b)], struck out par. (3) which related to agreements between Federal departments and agencies and States and localities to indemnify and hold harmless the States and localities from claims arising from the disclosure or use of criminal history record information.

Subsec. (c). Pub. L. 106–398, § 1 [[div. A], title X, § 1076(a)(3)], substituted "A covered agency" for "The Department of Defense, the Department of State, the Office of Personnel Management, the Central Intelligence Agency, or the Federal Bureau of Investigation".

Subsecs. (e), (f). Pub. L. 106–398, § 1 [[div. A], title X, § 1076(d)], added subsec. (e) and redesignated former subsec. (e) as (f).

1990—Subsecs. (b)(1), (3)(A), (B), (c). Pub. L. 101–246, § 114(1), inserted "the Department of State," after "Defense," wherever appearing.

Subsec. (e). Pub. L. 101–246, § 114(2), added subsec. (e).

1986—Subsecs. (b)(1), (3), (c). Pub. L. 99–569 inserted references to the Federal Bureau of Investigation and such bureau.

EFFECTIVE DATE OF 1986 AMENDMENT

Section 402(c) of Pub. L. 99–569 provided that: "The amendments made by this section [amending this section and provisions set out as a note under this section] shall become effective with respect to any inquiry which begins after the date of enactment of this Act [Oct. 27, 1986] conducted by the Federal Bureau of Investigation for purposes specified in paragraph (b)(1) of section 9101 of title 5, United States Code."

EFFECTIVE DATE

Section 802 of Pub. L. 99–169 provided that: "The amendments made by section 801(a) of this Act [enacting this section] shall become effective with respect to any inquiry which begins after the date of enactment of this Act [Dec. 4, 1985] conducted by the Department of Defense, the Office of Personnel Management, or the Central Intelligence Agency, for the purposes specified in paragraph (b)(1) of section 9101 of title 5, United States Code, as added by this Act."

TERMINATION DATE OF SUBSECTION (b)(3) OF THIS SECTION

Pub. L. 100–453, title I, § 101(d), Sept. 29, 1988, 102 Stat. 1904, extended the expiration date provided in section 803(b) of Pub. L. 99–169, formerly set out below, until Dec. 31, 1989.

Section 803(b) of Pub. L. 99–169 provided that subsec. (b)(3) of this section expired three years after Dec. 4, 1985.

REPORT TO CONGRESSIONAL COMMITTEES ON EFFECT OF PROVISIONS FOR INDEMNIFICATION AGREEMENTS

Section 803(a) of Pub. L. 99–169, as amended by Pub. L. 99–569, title IV, § 402(b), Oct. 27, 1986, 100 Stat. 3196, directed Department of Justice, within two years after Dec. 4, 1985, and after consultation with Department of Defense, Office of Personnel Management, Central Intelligence Agency, and Federal Bureau of Investigation, to report to appropriate committees of Congress concerning the effect of 5 U.S.C. 9101(b)(3), as added by this Act, including the effect of the absence of indemnification agreements upon States and localities not eligible under 5 U.S.C. 9101(b)(3) for such agreements.

SECTION REFERRED TO IN OTHER SECTIONS

This section is referred to in title 42 section 14614.

Subpart I—Miscellaneous

CHAPTER 95—PERSONNEL FLEXIBILITIES RELATING TO THE INTERNAL REVENUE SERVICE

Sec.	
9501.	Internal Revenue Service personnel flexibilities.
9502.	Pay authority for critical positions.
9503.	Streamlined critical pay authority.

Sec.
9504.   Recruitment, retention, relocation incentives, and relocation expenses.
9505.   Performance awards for senior executives.
9506.   Limited appointments to career reserved Senior Executive Service positions.
9507.   Streamlined demonstration project authority.
9508.   General workforce performance management system.
9509.   General workforce classification and pay.
9510.   General workforce staffing.

§ 9501. Internal Revenue Service personnel flexibilities

(a) Any flexibilities provided by sections 9502 through 9510 of this chapter shall be exercised in a manner consistent with—

(1) chapter 23 (relating to merit system principles and prohibited personnel practices);

(2) provisions relating to preference eligibles;

(3) except as otherwise specifically provided, section 5307 (relating to the aggregate limitation on pay);

(4) except as otherwise specifically provided, chapter 71 (relating to labor-management relations); and

(5) subject to subsections (b) and (c) of section 1104, as though such authorities were delegated to the Secretary of the Treasury under section 1104(a)(2).

(b) The Secretary of the Treasury shall provide the Office of Personnel Management with any information that Office requires in carrying out its responsibilities under this section.

(c) Employees within a unit to which a labor organization is accorded exclusive recognition under chapter 71 shall not be subject to any flexibility provided by sections 9507 through 9510 of this chapter unless the exclusive representative and the Internal Revenue Service have entered into a written agreement which specifically provides for the exercise of that flexibility. Such written agreement may be imposed by the Federal Services Impasses Panel under section 7119.

(Added Pub. L. 105–206, title I, § 1201(a), July 22, 1998, 112 Stat. 712.)

§ 9502. Pay authority for critical positions

(a) When the Secretary of the Treasury seeks a grant of authority under section 5377 for critical pay for 1 or more positions at the Internal Revenue Service, the Office of Management and Budget may fix the rate of basic pay, notwithstanding sections 5377(d)(2) and 5307, at any rate up to the salary set in accordance with section 104 of title 3.

(b) Notwithstanding section 5307, no allowance, differential, bonus, award, or similar cash payment may be paid to any employee receiving critical pay at a rate fixed under subsection (a), in any calendar year if, or to the extent that, the employee's total annual compensation will exceed the maximum amount of total annual compensation payable at the salary set in accordance with section 104 of title 3.

(Added Pub. L. 105–206, title I, § 1201(a), July 22, 1998, 112 Stat. 712.)

Section Referred to in Other Sections

This section is referred to in sections 9501, 9503, 9504, 9507 of this title.

§ 9503. Streamlined critical pay authority

(a) Notwithstanding section 9502, and without regard to the provisions of this title governing appointments in the competitive service or the Senior Executive Service and chapters 51 and 53 (relating to classification and pay rates), the Secretary of the Treasury may, for a period of 10 years after the date of enactment of this section, establish, fix the compensation of, and appoint individuals to, designated critical administrative, technical, and professional positions needed to carry out the functions of the Internal Revenue Service, if—

(1) the positions—

(A) require expertise of an extremely high level in an administrative, technical, or professional field; and

(B) are critical to the Internal Revenue Service's successful accomplishment of an important mission;

(2) exercise of the authority is necessary to recruit or retain an individual exceptionally well qualified for the position;

(3) the number of such positions does not exceed 40 at any one time;

(4) designation of such positions are approved by the Secretary of the Treasury;

(5) the terms of such appointments are limited to no more than 4 years;

(6) appointees to such positions were not Internal Revenue Service employees prior to June 1, 1998;

(7) total annual compensation for any appointee to such positions does not exceed the highest total annual compensation payable at the rate determined under section 104 of title 3; and

(8) all such positions are excluded from the collective bargaining unit.

(b) Individuals appointed under this section shall not be considered to be employees for purposes of subchapter II of chapter 75.

(Added Pub. L. 105–206, title I, § 1201(a), July 22, 1998, 112 Stat. 712.)

References in Text

The provisions of this title governing appointments in the competitive service, referred to in subsec. (a), are classified generally to section 3301 et seq. of this title.

The date of enactment of this section, referred to in subsec. (a), is the date of enactment of Pub. L. 105–206, which was approved July 22, 1998.

Section Referred to in Other Sections

This section is referred to in sections 9501, 9504, 9507 of this title; title 26 section 7803.

§ 9504. Recruitment, retention, relocation incentives, and relocation expenses

(a) For a period of 10 years after the date of enactment of this section and subject to approval by the Office of Personnel Management, the Secretary of the Treasury may provide for variations from sections 5753 and 5754 governing payment of recruitment, relocation, and retention incentives.

(b) For a period of 10 years after the date of enactment of this section, the Secretary of the Treasury may pay from appropriations made to the Internal Revenue Service allowable relocation expenses under section 5724a for employees transferred or reemployed and allowable travel and transportation expenses under section 5723 for new appointees, for any new appointee appointed to a position for which pay is fixed under section 9502 or 9503 after June 1, 1998.

(Added Pub. L. 105–206, title I, § 1201(a), July 22, 1998, 112 Stat. 713.)

REFERENCES IN TEXT

The date of enactment of this section, referred to in text, is the date of enactment of Pub. L. 105–206, which was approved July 22, 1998.

SECTION REFERRED TO IN OTHER SECTIONS

This section is referred to in sections 9501, 9507 of this title.

§ 9505. Performance awards for senior executives

(a) For a period of 10 years after the date of enactment of this section, Internal Revenue Service senior executives who have program management responsibility over significant functions of the Internal Revenue Service may be paid a performance bonus without regard to the limitation in section 5384(b)(2) if the Secretary of the Treasury finds such award warranted based on the executive's performance.

(b) In evaluating an executive's performance for purposes of an award under this section, the Secretary of the Treasury shall take into account the executive's contributions toward the successful accomplishment of goals and objectives established under the Government Performance and Results Act of 1993, division E of the Clinger-Cohen Act of 1996 (Public Law 104–106; 110 Stat. 679), Revenue Procedure 64–22 (as in effect on July 30, 1997), taxpayer service surveys, and other performance metrics or plans established in consultation with the Internal Revenue Service Oversight Board.

(c) Any award in excess of 20 percent of an executive's rate of basic pay shall be approved by the Secretary of the Treasury.

(d) Notwithstanding section 5384(b)(3), the Secretary of the Treasury shall determine the aggregate amount of performance awards available to be paid during any fiscal year under this section and section 5384 to career senior executives in the Internal Revenue Service. Such amount may not exceed an amount equal to 5 percent of the aggregate amount of basic pay paid to career senior executives in the Internal Revenue Service during the preceding fiscal year. The Internal Revenue Service shall not be included in the determination under section 5384(b)(3) of the aggregate amount of performance awards payable to career senior executives in the Department of the Treasury other than the Internal Revenue Service.

(e) Notwithstanding section 5307, a performance bonus award may not be paid to an executive in a calendar year if, or to the extent that, the executive's total annual compensation will exceed the maximum amount of total annual compensation payable at the rate determined under section 104 of title 3.

(Added Pub. L. 105–206, title I, § 1201(a), July 22, 1998, 112 Stat. 713.)

REFERENCES IN TEXT

The date of enactment of this section, referred to in subsec. (a), is the date of enactment of Pub. L. 105–206, which was approved July 22, 1998.

The Government Performance and Results Act of 1993, referred to in subsec. (b), is Pub. L. 103–62, Aug. 3, 1993, 107 Stat. 285, which enacted section 306 of this title, sections 1115 to 1119, 9703, and 9704 of Title 31, Money and Finance, and sections 2801 to 2805 of Title 39, Postal Service, amended section 1105 of Title 31, and enacted provisions set out as notes under sections 1101 and 1115 of Title 31. For complete classification of this Act to the Code, see Short Title of 1993 Amendment note set out under section 1101 of Title 31 and Tables.

The Clinger-Cohen Act of 1996, referred to in subsec. (b), is div. D (§§ 4001–4402) and div. E (§§ 5001–5703) of Pub. L. 104–106, Feb. 10, 1996, 110 Stat. 642, 679. Div. E of Pub. L. 104–106 is classified principally to chapter 25 (§ 1401 et seq.) of Title 40, Public Buildings, Property, and Works. For complete classification of this Act to the Code, see Short Title note set out under section 1401 of Title 40, Short Title of 1996 Amendment note set out under section 251 of Title 41, Public Contracts, and Tables.

SECTION REFERRED TO IN OTHER SECTIONS

This section is referred to in sections 9501, 9507 of this title.

§ 9506. Limited appointments to career reserved Senior Executive Service positions

(a) In the application of section 3132, a "career reserved position" in the Internal Revenue Service means a position designated under section 3132(b) which may be filled only by—

(1) a career appointee; or

(2) a limited emergency appointee or a limited term appointee—

(A) who, immediately upon entering the career reserved position, was serving under a career or career-conditional appointment outside the Senior Executive Service; or

(B) whose limited emergency or limited term appointment is approved in advance by the Office of Personnel Management.

(b)(1) The number of positions described under subsection (a) which are filled by an appointee as described under paragraph (2) of such subsection may not exceed 10 percent of the total number of Senior Executive Service positions in the Internal Revenue Service.

(2) Notwithstanding section 3132—

(A) the term of an appointee described under subsection (a)(2) may be for any period not to exceed 3 years; and

(B) such an appointee may serve—

(i) two such terms; or

(ii) two such terms in addition to any unexpired term applicable at the time of appointment.

(Added Pub. L. 105–206, title I, § 1201(a), July 22, 1998, 112 Stat. 714.)

SECTION REFERRED TO IN OTHER SECTIONS

This section is referred to in sections 9501, 9507 of this title.

§ 9507. Streamlined demonstration project authority

(a) The exercise of any of the flexibilities under sections 9502 through 9510 shall not affect the authority of the Secretary of the Treasury to implement for the Internal Revenue Service a demonstration project subject to chapter 47, as provided in subsection (b).

(b) In applying section 4703 to a demonstration project described in section 4701(a)(4) which involves the Internal Revenue Service—

(1) section 4703(b)(1) shall be deemed to read as follows:

"(1) develop a plan for such project which describes its purpose, the employees to be covered, the project itself, its anticipated outcomes, and the method of evaluating the project;";

(2) section 4703(b)(3) shall not apply;

(3) the 180-day notification period in section 4703(b)(4) shall be deemed to be a notification period of 30 days;

(4) section 4703(b)(6) shall be deemed to read as follows:

"(6) provides each House of Congress with the final version of the plan.";

(5) section 4703(c)(1) shall be deemed to read as follows:

"(1) subchapter V of chapter 63 or subpart G of part III of this title;";

(6) the requirements of paragraphs (1)(A) and (2) of section 4703(d) shall not apply; and

(7) notwithstanding section 4703(d)(1)(B), based on an evaluation as provided in section 4703(h), the Office of Personnel Management and the Secretary of the Treasury, except as otherwise provided by this subsection, may waive the termination date of a demonstration project under section 4703(d).

(c) At least 90 days before waiving the termination date under subsection (b)(7), the Office of Personnel Management shall publish in the Federal Register a notice of its intention to waive the termination date and shall inform in writing both Houses of Congress of its intention.

(Added Pub. L. 105–206, title I, § 1201(a), July 22, 1998, 112 Stat. 715.)

Section Referred to in Other Sections

This section is referred to in section 9501 of this title.

§ 9508. General workforce performance management system

(a) In lieu of a performance appraisal system established under section 4302, the Secretary of the Treasury shall, within 1 year after the date of enactment of this section, establish for the Internal Revenue Service a performance management system that—

(1) maintains individual accountability by—

(A) establishing one or more retention standards for each employee related to the work of the employee and expressed in terms of individual performance, and communicating such retention standards to employees;

(B) making periodic determinations of whether each employee meets or does not meet the employee's established retention standards; and

(C) taking actions, in accordance with applicable laws and regulations, with respect to any employee whose performance does not meet established retention standards, including denying any increases in basic pay, promotions, and credit for performance under section 3502, and taking one or more of the following actions:

(i) Reassignment.

(ii) An action under chapter 43 or chapter 75 of this title.

(iii) Any other appropriate action to resolve the performance problem; and

(2) except as provided under section 1204 of the Internal Revenue Service Restructuring and Reform Act of 1998, strengthens the system's effectiveness by—

(A) establishing goals or objectives for individual, group, or organizational performance (or any combination thereof), consistent with the Internal Revenue Service's performance planning procedures, including those established under the Government Performance and Results Act of 1993, division E of the Clinger-Cohen Act of 1996 (Public Law 104–106; 110 Stat. 679), Revenue Procedure 64–22 (as in effect on July 30, 1997), and taxpayer service surveys, and communicating such goals or objectives to employees;

(B) using such goals and objectives to make performance distinctions among employees or groups of employees; and

(C) using performance assessments as a basis for granting employee awards, adjusting an employee's rate of basic pay, and other appropriate personnel actions, in accordance with applicable laws and regulations.

(b)(1) For purposes of subsection (a)(2), the term "performance assessment" means a determination of whether or not retention standards established under subsection (a)(1)(A) are met, and any additional performance determination made on the basis of performance goals and objectives established under subsection (a)(2)(A).

(2) For purposes of this title, the term "unacceptable performance" with respect to an employee of the Internal Revenue Service covered by a performance management system established under this section means performance of the employee which fails to meet a retention standard established under this section.

(c)(1) The Secretary of the Treasury may establish an awards program designed to provide incentives for and recognition of organizational, group, and individual achievements by providing for granting awards to employees who, as individuals or members of a group, contribute to meeting the performance goals and objectives established under this chapter by such means as a superior individual or group accomplishment, a documented productivity gain, or sustained superior performance.

(2) A cash award under subchapter I of chapter 45 may be granted to an employee of the Internal Revenue Service without the need for any approval under section 4502(b).

(d)(1) In applying sections 4303(b)(1)(A) and 7513(b)(1) to employees of the Internal Revenue Service, "30 days" may be deemed to be "15 days".

(2) Notwithstanding the second sentence of section 5335(c), an employee of the Internal Revenue Service shall not have a right to appeal the

denial of a periodic step increase under section 5335 to the Merit Systems Protection Board.

(Added Pub. L. 105–206, title I, § 1201(a), July 22, 1998, 112 Stat. 715.)

REFERENCES IN TEXT

The date of enactment of this section, referred to in subsec. (a), is the date of enactment of Pub. L. 105–206, which was approved July 22, 1998.

Section 1204 of the Internal Revenue Service Restructuring and Reform Act of 1998, referred to in subsec. (a)(2), is section 1204 of Pub. L. 105–206, which is set out as a note under section 7804 of Title 26, Internal Revenue Code.

The Government Performance and Results Act of 1993, referred to in subsec. (a)(2)(A), is Pub. L. 103–62, Aug. 3, 1993, 107 Stat. 285, which enacted section 306 of this title, sections 1115 to 1119, 9703, and 9704 of Title 31, Money and Finance, and sections 2801 to 2805 of Title 39, Postal Service, amended section 1105 of Title 31, and enacted provisions set out as notes under sections 1101 and 1115 of Title 31. For complete classification of this Act to the Code, see Short Title of 1993 Amendment note set out under section 1101 of Title 31 and Tables.

The Clinger-Cohen Act of 1996, referred to in subsec. (a)(2)(A), is div. D (§§ 4001–4402) and div. E (§§ 5001–5703) of Pub. L. 104–106, Feb. 10, 1996, 110 Stat. 642, 679. Div. E of Pub. L. 104–106 is classified principally to chapter 25 (§ 1401 et seq.) of Title 40, Public Buildings, Property, and Works. For complete classification of this Act to the Code, see Short Title note set out under section 1401 of Title 40, Short Title of 1996 Amendment note set out under section 251 of Title 41, Public Contracts, and Tables.

SECTION REFERRED TO IN OTHER SECTIONS

This section is referred to in sections 9501, 9507, 9510 of this title.

§ 9509. General workforce classification and pay

(a) For purposes of this section, the term "broad-banded system" means a system for grouping positions for pay, job evaluation, and other purposes that is different from the system established under chapter 51 and subchapter III of chapter 53 as a result of combining grades and related ranges of rates of pay in one or more occupational series.

(b)(1)(A) The Secretary of the Treasury may, subject to criteria to be prescribed by the Office of Personnel Management, establish one or more broad-banded systems covering all or any portion of the Internal Revenue Service workforce.

(B) With the approval of the Office of Personnel Management, a broad-banded system established under this section may either include or consist of positions that otherwise would be subject to subchapter IV of chapter 53 or section 5376.

(2) The Office of Personnel Management may require the Secretary of the Treasury to submit information relating to broad-banded systems at the Internal Revenue Service.

(3) Except as otherwise provided under this section, employees under a broad-banded system shall continue to be subject to the laws and regulations covering employees under the pay system that otherwise would apply to such employees.

(4) The criteria to be prescribed by the Office of Personnel Management shall, at a minimum—

(A) ensure that the structure of any broad-banded system maintains the principle of equal pay for substantially equal work;

(B) establish the minimum and maximum number of grades that may be combined into pay bands;

(C) establish requirements for setting minimum and maximum rates of pay in a pay band;

(D) establish requirements for adjusting the pay of an employee within a pay band;

(E) establish requirements for setting the pay of a supervisory employee whose position is in a pay band or who supervises employees whose positions are in pay bands; and

(F) establish requirements and methodologies for setting the pay of an employee upon conversion to a broad-banded system, initial appointment, change of position or type of appointment (including promotion, demotion, transfer, reassignment, reinstatement, placement in another pay band, or movement to a different geographic location), and movement between a broad-banded system and another pay system.

(c) With the approval of the Office of Personnel Management and in accordance with a plan for implementation submitted by the Secretary of the Treasury, the Secretary may, with respect to Internal Revenue Service employees who are covered by a broad-banded system established under this section, provide for variations from the provisions of subchapter VI of chapter 53.

(Added Pub. L. 105–206, title I, § 1201(a), July 22, 1998, 112 Stat. 716.)

SECTION REFERRED TO IN OTHER SECTIONS

This section is referred to in sections 9501, 9507 of this title.

§ 9510. General workforce staffing

(a)(1) Except as otherwise provided by this section, an employee of the Internal Revenue Service may be selected for a permanent appointment in the competitive service in the Internal Revenue Service through internal competitive promotion procedures if—

(A) the employee has completed, in the competitive service, 2 years of current continuous service under a term appointment or any combination of term appointments;

(B) such term appointment or appointments were made under competitive procedures prescribed for permanent appointments;

(C) the employee's performance under such term appointment or appointments met established retention standards, or, if not covered by a performance management system established under section 9508, was rated at the fully successful level or higher (or equivalent thereof); and

(D) the vacancy announcement for the term appointment from which the conversion is made stated that there was a potential for subsequent conversion to a permanent appointment.

(2) An appointment under this section may be made only to a position in the same line of work as a position to which the employee received a term appointment under competitive procedures.

(b)(1) Notwithstanding subchapter I of chapter 33, the Secretary of the Treasury may establish category rating systems for evaluating applicants for Internal Revenue Service positions in the competitive service under which qualified candidates are divided into two or more quality categories on the basis of relative degrees of merit, rather than assigned individual numerical ratings.

(2) Each applicant who meets the minimum qualification requirements for the position to be filled shall be assigned to an appropriate category based on an evaluation of the applicant's knowledge, skills, and abilities relative to those needed for successful performance in the position to be filled.

(3) Within each quality category established under paragraph (1), preference eligibles shall be listed ahead of individuals who are not preference eligibles. For other than scientific and professional positions at or higher than GS–9 (or equivalent), preference eligibles who have a compensable service-connected disability of 10 percent or more, and who meet the minimum qualification standards, shall be listed in the highest quality category.

(4) An appointing authority may select any applicant from the highest quality category or, if fewer than three candidates have been assigned to the highest quality category, from a merged category consisting of the highest and second highest quality categories.

(5) Notwithstanding paragraph (4), the appointing authority may not pass over a preference eligible in the same or higher category from which selection is made unless the requirements of section 3317(b) or 3318(b), as applicable, are satisfied.

(c) The Secretary of the Treasury may detail employees among the offices of the Internal Revenue Service without regard to the 120-day limitation in section 3341(b).

(d) Notwithstanding any other provision of law, the Secretary of the Treasury may establish a probationary period under section 3321 of up to 3 years for Internal Revenue Service positions if the Secretary of the Treasury determines that the nature of the work is such that a shorter period is insufficient to demonstrate complete proficiency in the position.

(e) Nothing in this section exempts the Secretary of the Treasury from—

(1) any employment priority established under direction of the President for the placement of surplus or displaced employees; or

(2) any obligation under a court order or decree relating to the employment practices of the Internal Revenue Service or the Department of the Treasury.

(Added Pub. L. 105–206, title I, § 1201(a), July 22, 1998, 112 Stat. 717.)

REFERENCES IN TEXT

GS–9, referred to in subsec. (b)(3), is contained in the General Schedule which is set out under section 5332 of this title.

SECTION REFERRED TO IN OTHER SECTIONS

This section is referred to in sections 9501, 9507 of this title.